Gale's publications in the acronyms and abbreviations field include:

Acronyms, Initialisms & Abbreviations Dictionary series:

Acronyms, Initialisms & Abbreviations Dictionary (Volume 1). A guide to acronyms, initialisms, abbreviations, and similar contractions, arranged alphabetically by abbreviation.

New Acronyms, Initialisms & Abbreviations (Volume 2). An interedition supplement in which terms are arranged both by abbreviation and by meaning.

Reverse Acronyms, Initialisms & Abbreviations Dictionary (Volume 3). A companion to Volume 1 in which terms are arranged alphabetically by meaning of the acronym, initialism, or abbreviation.

Acronyms, Initialisms & Abbreviations Dictionary Subject Guide series:

Computer & Telecommunications Acronyms (Volume 1). A guide to acronyms, initialisms, abbreviations, and similar contractions used in the field of computers and telecommunications in which terms are arranged alphabetically both by abbreviation and by meaning.

Business Acronyms (Volume 2). A guide to business-oriented acronyms, initialisms, abbreviations, and similar contractions in which terms are arranged alphabetically both by abbreviation and by meaning.

International Acronyms, Initialisms & Abbreviations Dictionary series:

International Acronyms, Initialisms & Abbreviations Dictionary (Volume 1). A guide to foreign and international acronyms, initialisms, abbreviations, and similar contractions, arranged alphabetically by abbreviation.

New International Acronyms, Initialisms & Abbreviations (Volume 2). An interedition supplement in which terms are arranged alphabetically both by abbreviation and by meaning.

Reverse International Acronyms, Initialisms & Abbreviations Dictionary (Volume 3). A companion to Volume 1, in which terms are arranged alphabetically by meaning of the acronym, initialism, or abbreviation.

Periodical Title Abbreviations series:

Periodical Title Abbreviations: By Abbreviation (Volume 1). A guide to abbreviations commonly used for periodical titles, arranged alphabetically by abbreviation.

Periodical Title Abbreviations: By Title (Volume 2). A guide to abbreviations commonly used for periodical titles, arranged alphabetically by title.

New Periodical Title Abbreviations (Volume 3). An interedition supplement in which terms are arranged alphabetically both by abbreviation and by title.

Acronyms, Initialisms &
Abbreviations Dictionary

ISSN 0270-4404

Acronyms, Initialisms & Abbreviations Dictionary

A Guide to More Than 520,000 Acronyms, Initialisms, Abbreviations, Contractions, Alphabetic Symbols, and Similar Condensed Appellations

Covering: Aerospace, Associations, Banking, Biochemistry, Business, Data Processing, Domestic and International Affairs, Economics, Education, Electronics, Genetics, Government, Information Technology, Investment, Labor, Law, Medicine, Military Affairs, Periodicals, Pharmacy, Physiology, Politics, Religion, Science, Societies, Sports, Technical Drawings and Specifications, Telecommunications, Trade, Transportation, and Other Fields

Sixteenth Edition
1992

Volume 1

Part 3
P-Z

Jennifer Mossman,
Editor

Pamela Dear
Prindle LaBarge
Ellen Paré,
Associate Editors

 **Gale Research Inc.** • DETROIT • LONDON

Senior Editor:	Donna Wood
Editor:	Jennifer Mossman
Associate Editors:	Pamela Dear, Prindle LaBarge, Ellen Paré
Assistant Editors:	Yvonne Y. Lee, Alice M. Walsh
Contributing Editors:	Leland G. Alkire, Jr., Mildred Hunt, Edwin B. Steen, Miriam M. Steinert
Data Entry Supervisor:	Benita L. Spight
Data Entry Associate:	Merrie Ann Carpenter
Production Manager:	Mary Beth Trimper
Production Assistant:	Mary Winterhalter
Art Director:	Arthur Chartow
Keyliners:	C.J. Jonik, Yolanda Y. Latham
Supervisor of Systems and Programming:	Theresa A. Rocklin
Programmers:	Charles Beaumont, David Trotter

The paper used in this publication meets the minimum requirements of American National Standard for Information Sciences—Permanence Paper for Printed Library Materials, ANSI Z39.48-1984. ∞™

Copyright © 1991
Gale Research Inc.
835 Penobscot Building
Detroit, MI 48226-4094

Library of Congress Catalog Card Number 84-643188
ISBN 0-8103-5077-7 (Volume 1 Complete)
ISBN 0-8103-5099-8 (Part 1: A-F only)
ISBN 0-8103-5352-0 (Part 2: G-O only)
ISBN 0-8103-5353-9 (Part 3: P-Z only)
ISSN 0270-4404

Printed in the United States of America

Published simultaneously in the United Kingdom
by Gale Research International Limited
(An affiliated company of Gale Research Inc.)

Contents

User's Guide

The following examples illustrate the possible elements of entries in *AIAD*:

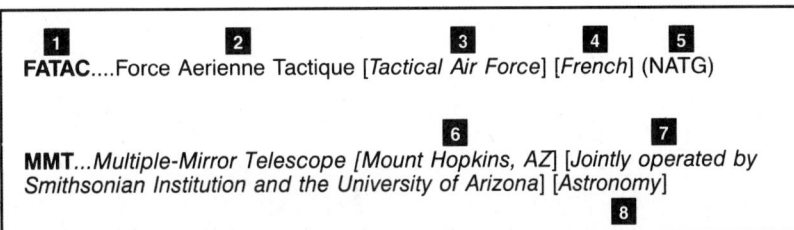

1 Acronym, Initialism, or Abbreviation

2 Meaning or Phrase

3 English translation

4 Language (for non-English entries)

5 Source code (Allows you to verify entries or find additional information. Decoded in the List of Selected Sources)

6 Location or Country of origin (Provides geographic identifiers for airports, colleges and universities, libraries, military bases, political parties, radio and television stations, and others)

7 Sponsoring organization

8 Subject category (Clarifies entries by providing appropriate context)

The completeness of a listing is dependent upon both the nature of the term and the amount of information provided by the source. If additional information becomes available during future research, an entry is revised.

Arrangement of Entries

Acronyms, initialisms, and abbreviations are arranged alphabetically in letter-by-letter sequence. Spacing, punctuation, and capitalization are not considered. If the same term has more than one meaning, the various meanings are subarranged in word-by-word sequence.

Should you wish to eliminate the guesswork from acronym formation and usage, a companion volume could help. *Reverse Acronyms, Initialisms and Abbreviations Dictionary* contains essentially the same entries as *AIAD*, but arranges them alphabetically by meaning, rather than by acronym or initialism.

List of Selected Sources

Each of the print sources included in the following list contributed at least 50 terms. It would be impossible to cite a source for every entry in *Acronyms, Initialisms, and Abbreviations Dictionary (AIAD)* becuase the majority of terms are sent by outside contributors, are uncovered through independent research by the editorial staff, or surface as miscellaneous broadcast or print media references.

For sources used on an ongoing basis, only the latest edition is listed. For most of the remaining sources, the edition that was used is cited. The editors will provide further information about these sources upon request.

Unless further described in an annotation, the publications listed here contain no additional information about the acronym, initialism, or abbreviation cited in *AIAD*.

(AABC) *Catalog of Abbreviations and Brevity Codes.* Washington, DC: U.S. Department of the Army, 1981. [Use of source began in 1969]

(AAG) *Aerospace Abbreviations Glossary.* Report Number AG60-0014. Prepared by General Dynamics/Astronautics. San Diego: 1962.

(ADA) *The Australian Dictionary of Acronyms and Abbreviations.* 2nd ed. Compiled by David J. Jones. Leura, NSW, Australia: Second Back Row Press Pty. Ltd., 1981.

(AFIT) *Compendium of Authenticated Systems and Logistics.* Washington, DC: Air Force Institute of Technology. [Use of source began in 1984]

(AFM) *Air Force Manual of Abbreviations.* Washington, DC: U.S. Department of the Air Force, 1975. [Use of source began in 1969]

(AIA) *Aviation Insurance Abbreviations, Organisations and Institutions.* By M.J. Spurway. London: Witherby & Co. Ltd., 1983.

(APTA) *Australian Periodical Title Abbreviations.* Compiled by David J. Jones. Leura, NSW, Australia: Second Back Row Press Pty. Ltd., 1985.

(ARC) *Agricultural Research Centres: A World Directory of Organizations and Programmes.* 2 vols. Edited by Nigel Harvey. Harlow, Essex, England: Longman Group, 1983; distributed in the U.S. by Gale Research Inc., Detroit.
    A world guide to official, educational, industrial, and independent research centers which support research in the fields of agriculture, veterinary medicine, horticulture, aquaculture, food science, forestry, zoology, and botany.

(ASF) *Guide to Names and Acronyms of Organizations, Activities, and Projects.* Food and Agriculture Organization of the United Nations. Fishery Information, Data, and Statistics Service and U.S. National Oceanic and Atmospheric Administration. Aquatic Sciences and Fisheries Information System Reference Series, Number 10, 1982. n.p.

(BIB) *Bibliotech.* Ottawa, Canada: National Library of Canada, 1988-89.

(BJA) *Biblical and Judaic Acronyms.* By Lawrence Marwick. New York: Ktav Publishing House, Inc., 1979.

(BUR)   *Computer Acronyms and Abbreviations Handbook.* Tokyo: Burroughs Co. Ltd., 1978.

(BYTE)   *Byte: The Small Systems Journal.* Peterborough, NH: McGraw- Hill Information Systems, Inc., 1987-89.

(CAAL)   *CAAL COMOPTEVFOR Acronym and Abbreviation List.* Norfolk, VA: (CAAL-U) Operational Test and Evaluation Force, 1981.

(CB)   *Centres & Bureaux: A Directory of Concentrations of Effort, Information and Expertise.* Edited by Lindsay Sellar. Beckenham, Kent, England: CBD Research Ltd., 1987.
           A guide to British organizations which include the words "centre" or "bureau" in their names. Entries include name and address; telephone and telex numbers; chief official; and a description of the purposes, activities, and services of the organization.

(CED)   *Current European Directories.* 2nd ed. Edited by G.P. Henderson, Beckenham, Kent, England: CBD Research, 1981; distributed in U.S. by Gale Research Inc., Detroit.

(CET)   *Communications-Electronics Terminology.* AFM 11-1. Vol. 3 U.S. Department of the Air Force, 1973.

(CINC)   *A CINCPAC Glossary of Commonly Used Abbreviations and Short Titles.* By Ltc. J.R. Johnson. Washington, DC: 1968.

(CMD)   *Complete Multilingual Dictionary of Computer Terminology.* Compiled by Georges Nania. Chicago: National Textbook Co., 1984.
           Computer-related terms in Spanish, French, Italian, Portuguese, and English. Indexes in French, Italian, Spanish, and Portuguese are also provided.

(CNC)   *American National Standard Codes for the Representation of Names of Countries, Dependencies, and Areas of Special Sovereignty for Information Interchange.* U.S. National Bureau of Standards. Washington, DC: Government Printing Office, 1986. [Use of source began in 1977]
           These standard codes, approved by the International Organization for Standardization and the American National Standards Institute, are used in the international interchange of data in many fields.

(CRD)   *Computer-Readable Databases: A Directory and Data Sourcebook.* 6th ed. Edited by Kathleen Young Marcaccio. Detroit: Gale Research Inc., 1990.
           A guide to online databases, offline files available in various magnetic formats, and CD-ROM files. Entries include producer name, address, telephone number, description of coverage, vendors, and contact person.

(CSR)   *Computer Science Resources: A Guide to Professional Literature.* Edited by Darlene Myers. White Plains, NY: Knowledge Industry Publications, Inc., 1981.
           Covers several types of computer-related literature including journals, technical reports, directories, dictionaries, handbooks, and university computer center newsletters. Five appendices cover career and salary trends in the computer industry, user group acronyms, university computer libraries, and trade fairs and shows.

(CTT)   *Corporate TrendTrac.* Edited by A. Dale Timpe. Detroit: Gale Research Inc., 1988-89.
           Covers mergers and acquisitions, stock exchange listings and suspensions, company name changes, bankruptcies, liquidations, and reorganizations.

(DAS)   *Dictionary of Abbreviations and Symbols.* By Edward Frank Allen. London: Cassell and Co. Ltd.

(DBQ)   *A Dictionary of British Qualifications.* London: Kogan Page Ltd., 1985.

(DCTA)   *Dictionary of Commercial Terms and Abbreviations.* By Alan E. Branch. London: Witherby & Co. Ltd., 1984.

(DEN)   *Dictionary of Electronics and Nucleonics.* By L.E.C. Hughes, R.W.B. Stephens, and L.D. Brown. New York: Barnes & Noble, 1969.

(DHSM)   *Dictionary of Health Services Management.* 2nd ed. By Thomas C. Timmreck. Owings Mills, MD: Rynd Communications, 1987.

(DIT)   *Dictionary of Informatics Terms in Russian and English.* By G.S. Zhdanov, E.S. Kolobrodov, V.A. Polushkin, and A.I. Cherny. Moscow: Nauka, 1971.

(DLA)   *Bieber's Dictionary of Legal Abbreviations.* 3rd ed. By Mary Miles Prince. Buffalo, NY: William S. Hein & Co., 1988.

(DMA)   *Dictionary of Military Abbreviations: British, Empire, Commonwealth.* By. B.K.C. Scott. Hastings, East Sussex, England: Tamarisk Books, 1982.

(DS)   *Dictionary of Shipping International Trade Terms and Abbreviations.* 3rd ed. By Alan E. Branch. London: Witherby & Co. Ltd., 1986.

(DSA)   *Dictionary of Sigla and Abbreviations to and in Law Books before 1607.* By William Hamilton Bryson. Charlottesville, VA: University Press of Virginia, 1975.

(DSUE)   *A Dictionary of Slang and Unconventional English.* 8th ed. By Eric Partridge. New York: Macmillan Publishing Co., 1984.

(EA)   *Encyclopedia of Associations.* 25th ed. Vol. 1, National Organizations of the U.S. Edited by Deborah M. Burek. Detroit: Gale Research Inc., 1990. (and supplement, 1991) [Use of source began in 1960]
A guide to trade, professional, and other nonprofit associations that are national and international in scope and membership and that are headquartered in the United States. Entries include name and address; telephone and telex number; chief official; and a description of the purpose, activities, and structure of the organization.

(EAAP)   *Encyclopedia of Associations: Association Periodicals.* 3 vols. Edited by Denise M. Allard and Robert C. Thomas. Detroit: Gale Research Inc., 1987.
A directory of publications issued by all types of national nonprofit organizations in the United States. Entries include title and organization name, address, telephone number; description of periodical, frequency of publication, and price.

(EAIO)   *Encyclopedia of Associations: International Organizations.* 24th ed. Edited by Kenneth Estell. Detroit: Gale Research Inc., 1990. [Use of source began in 1985]
A guide to trade, professional, and other nonprofit associations that are national or international in scope and membership and that are headquartered outside the United States. Entries include name and address; principal foreign language name; telephone and telex number; chief official; and a description of the purpose, activities, and structure of the organization.

(ECON)   *The Economist.* London: The Economist Newspaper Ltd., 1991. [Use of source began in 1988]

(EGAO)   *Encyclopedia of Government Advisory Organizations.* 6th ed. Edited by Denise M. Allard and Donna Batten. Detroit: Gale Research Inc., 1988 [Use of source began in 1975]
> A reference guide to permanent, continuing, and ad hoc U.S. presidential advisory committees, interagency committees, and other government-related boards, panels, task forces, commissions, conferences, and other similar bodies serving in a consultative, coordinating, advisory, research, or investigative capacity. Entries include name and address, telephone number, designated federal employee, history, recommendation and findings of the committee, staff size, publications, and subsidiaries. Also includes indexes to personnel, reports, federal agencies, presidential administration, and an alphabetical and keyword index.

(EY)   *The Europa Year Book 1987: A World Survey.* London: Europa Publications Ltd., 1987. distributed in U.S. by Gale Research Inc., Detroit.
> An annual survey containing detailed information about the political, economic, statistical, and commercial situation of the regions and countries covered.

(FAAC)   *Contractions Handbook.* Changes. U.S. Department of Transportation. Federal Aviation Administration, 1985. [Use of source began in 1969]

(FAAL)   *Location Identifiers.* U.S. Department of Transportation. Federal Aviation Administration. Air Traffic Service, 1982.

(FEA)   *The Far East and Australasia 1987.* 18th ed. London: Europa Publications Ltd., 1986; distributed in U.S. by Gale Research Inc., Detroit.
> Annual survey containing detailed information about the political, economic, statistical, and commercial situation of the regions and countries covered.

(GEA)   *Government Economic Agencies of the World: An International Directory of Governmental Organisations Concerned with Economic Development and Planning.* A Keesing's Reference Publication. Edited by Alan J. Day. Harlow, Essex, England: Longman Group Ltd., 1985; distributed in U.S. by Gale Research Inc., Detroit.
> Covers over 170 countries and territories. Two introductory sections for each area cover economic data and prevailing economic and political conditions. Individual entries provide title, address, and names of chief officials of each agency. Current activities and financial structure of each agency are also detailed. An index of agency officials is provided.

(GPO)   *Style Manual.* Washington, DC: Government Printing Office, 1984. Terms are included in Chapter 24, Foreign Languages.

(GRD)   *Government Research Directory.* 5th ed. Edited by Kay Gill and Susan E. Tufts. Detroit: Gale Research Inc., 1989. (and supplement, 1989)
> A descriptive guide to U.S. government research and development centers, institutes, laboratories, bureaus, test facilities, experiment stations, data collection and analysis centers, and grants management and research coordinating offices in agriculture, business, education, energy, engineering, environment, the humanities, medicine, military science, and basic applied sciences.

(IBMDP)   *IBM Data Processing Glossary.* 6th ed. White Plains, NY: IBM Corp., 1977.

(ICAO)   *Aircraft Type Designators.* 13th ed. International Civil Aviation Organization, August, 1981.

(ICDA)   *Designators for Aircraft Operating Agencies, Aeronautical Authorities and Services.* 49th ed. International Civil Aviation Organization, June 1982.
> Document also includes telephony designators and postal and telegraphic addresses of government civil aviation authorities.

(ICLI)   *Location Indicators.* 51st ed. International Civil Aviation Organization, February 1987.
> Document also contains addresses of flight information centers.

(IEEE)   *IEEE Standard Dictionary of Electrical and Electronics Terms.* Edited by Frank Jay. New York: The Institute of Electrical and Electronics Engineers, Inc., 1977, 1984.
           Includes definitions for thousands of electrical and electronics terms.
           Each entry includes a numeric source code.

(IID)   *Information Industry Directory.* 11th ed. Edited by Bradley J. Morgan. Detroit: Gale Research Inc., 1991 (and supplement, 1991).
           An international guide to computer-readable databases, database producers, and publishers, online vendors and time-sharing companies, telecommunications networks, and many other information systems and services. Entries include name and address, telephone number, chief official, and a detailed description of the purpose and function of the system or service.

(ILCA)   *Index to Legal Citations and Abbreviations.* By Donald Raistrick. Abingdon, Oxfordshire, England: Professional Books Ltd., 1981.

(IMH)   *International Marketing Handbook.* 2nd ed. Edited by Frank Bair. Detroit: Gale Research Inc., 1985.
           An in-depth guide to commercial and trade data on 142 countries of the world. Features include a list of European trade fairs and a report on growth markets in Western Europe.

(INF)   *Infantry.* Fort Benning, GA: U.S. Army Infantry Training School, 1989. [Use of source began in 1983]

(IRC)   *International Research Centers Directory 1988-89.* 4th ed. Edited by Darren L. Smith. Detroit: Gale Research Inc., 1988.
           A world guide to government, university, independent, nonprofit, and commercial research and development centers, institutes, laboratories, bureaus, test facilities, experiment stations, and data collection and analysis centers, as well as foundations, councils, and other organizations which support research.

(IRUK)   *Industrial Research in the United Kingdom.* 12th ed. Harlow, Essex, England: Longman Group UK Ltd., 1987.
           A guide to all groups conducting or funding research relevant to British industrial development. Entries include name, address, telephone and telex numbers; chief officials; and scope of activities.

(IT)   *Information Today: The Newspaper for Users and Producers of Electronic Information Services.* Medford, NJ: Learned Information Inc., 1988-89.

(ITD)   *International Tradeshow Directory.* 5th ed. Frankfurt am Main: M + A Publishers for Fairs, Exhibitions and Conventions Ltd., 1989.
           A guide to trade fairs and exhibitions throughout the world. Entries include event name, dates, frequency, location,description of purpose, profile of exhibitors and attendees.

(IYR)   *The 1989-92 International Yacht Racing Rules.* London: International Yacht Racing Union, 1989.

(KSC)   *A Selective List of Acronyms and Abbreviations.* Compiled by the Documents Department, Kennedy Space Center Library, 1971, 1973.

(LCCP)   *MARC Formats for Bibliographic Data.* Appendix II. Washington, DC: Library of Congress, 1982.

(LCLS)   *Symbols of American Libraries.* 13th ed. Washington, DC: Catalog Management and Publication Division, Library of Congress, 1985. [Use of source began in 1980]

(MCD)   *Acronyms, Abbreviations, and Initialisms.* Compiled by Carl Lauer. St. Louis: McDonnell Douglas Corp., 1989 [Use of source began in 1969]

(MDG)   *Microcomputer Dictionary and Guide.* By Charles J. Sippl. Champaign, IL: Matrix Publishers, Inc., 1975.
        A listing of definitions for over 5,000 microelectronics terms. Seven appendices.

(MENA)   *The Middle East and North Africa 1987.* 33rd ed. London: Europa Publications Ltd., 1986; distributed in U.S. by Gale Research Inc., Detroit.
        An annual survey containing detailed information about the political, economic, statistical, and commercial situation of the regions and countries covered.

(MSA)   *Military Standard Abbreviations for Use on Drawings, and in Specifications, Standards, and Technical Documents.* MIL-STD-12D. U.S. Department of Defense, 1981. [Use of source began in 1975]

(MSC)   *Annotated Acronyms and Abbreviations of Marine Science Related Activities.* 3rd ed. Revised by Charlotte M. Ashby and Alan R. Flesh. Washington, DC: U.S. Department of Commerce. National Oceanographic and Atmospheric Administration. Environmental Data Service. National Oceanographic Data Center, 1976, 1981.

(MUGU)   *The Mugu Book of Acronyms and Abbreviations.* Management Engineering Office, Pacific Missile Range, California, 1963, 1964.

(NASA)   *Space Transportation System and Associated Payloads: Glossary, Acronyms, and Abbreviations.* Washington, DC: U.S. National Aeronautics and Space Administration, 1985.

(NATG)   *Glossary of Abbreviations Used in NATO Documents.* AAP 15, n.p., 1979. [Use of source began in 1976]

(NG)   *NAVAIR Glossary of Unclassified Common-Use Abbreviated Titles and Phrases.* NAVAIRNOTE 5216 AIR-6031, n.p., July 1969.

(NLC)   *Symbols of Canadian Libraries.* 12th ed. National Library of Canada. Minister of Supply and Services Canada, 1987.

(NOAA)   *NOAA Directives Manual.* 66-13 Acronyms. 1977.

(NQ)   *NASDAQ Company Directory.* New York: National Association of Securities Dealers Inc., 1990. [Use of source began in 1983]
        Entries include company name, SIC code, contact person's name, title, address, and telephone number.

(NRCH)   *A Handbook of Acronyms and Initialisms.* Washington, DC: U.S. Nuclear Regulatory Commission. Division of Technical Information and Document Control, 1985.

(NVT)   *Naval Terminology.* NWP3. Rev. B. U.S. Department of the Navy. Office of the Chief of Naval Operations, 1980 [Use of source began in 1974]
        Includes a section on definitions of naval terminology.

(OAG)   *Official Airline Guide Worldwide Edition.* Oak Brook, IL: Official Airlines Guide, Inc., 1984. [Use of source began in 1975]

(OCD)   *Oxford Classical Dictionary.* 2nd ed. Edited by N.G. Hammond and H.H. Scullard. London: Oxford University Press, 1970.

(OCLC)   *OCLC Participating Institutions Arranged by OCLC Symbol.* Dublin, OH: OCLC, 1981.

(OICC)   *Abbreviations and Acronyms.* Des Moines, IA: Iowa State Occupational Information Coordinating Committee, 1986.

(OLDSS) *Online Database Search Services Directory*. 2nd ed. Edited by Doris Morris Maxfield. Detroit: Gale Research Inc., 1988.
> Provides detailed descriptions of the online information retrieval services offered by libraries, private information firms, and other organizations in the United States and Canada. Entries include name and address, telephone number, and key contact, as well as online systems accessed, frequently searched databases, and access hardware.

(PCM) *PC Magazine*. New York: Ziff-Davis Publishing Co., 1989. [Use of source began in 1987]

(PD) *Political Dissent: An International Guide to Dissident, Extra-Parliamentary, Guerrilla and Illegal Political Movements*. A Keesing's Reference Publication. Compiled by Henry W. Degenhardt. Edited by Alan J. Day. Harlow, Essex, England: Longman Group, 1983; distributed in U.S. by Gale Research Inc., Detroit.
> Includes the history and aims of approximately 1,000 organizations, with details of their leaderships.

(PPE) *Political Parties of Europe*. 2 vols. Edited by Vincent E. McHale. The Greenwood Historical Encyclopedia of the World's Political Parties. Westport, CT: Greenwood Press, 1983.
> One of a series of reference guides to the world's significant political parties. Each guide provides concise histories of the political parties of a region and attempts to detail the evolution of ideology, changes in organization, membership, leadership, and each party's impact upon society.

(PPW) *Political Parties of the World*. 2nd ed. A Keesing's Reference Publication. Compiled and edited by Alan J. Day and Henry W. Degenhardt. Harlow, Essex, England: Longman Group, 1980, 1984; distributed in U.S. by Gale Research Inc., Detroit.
> Covers historical development, structure, leadership, membership, policy, publications, and international affiliations. For each country, an overview of the current political situation and constitutional structure is provided.

(RCD) *Research Centers Directory*. 14th ed. Edited by Peter D. Dresser and Karen Hill. Detroit: Gale Research Inc., 1989 (and supplement, 1990). [Use of source began in 1986]
> A guide to university-related and other nonprofit research organizations carrying on research in agriculture, astronomy and space sciences, behavioral and social sciences, computers and mathematics, engineering and technology, physical and earth sciences and regional and area studies.

(RDA) *Army RD and A Magazine*. Alexandria, VA: Development, Engineering, and Acquisition Directorate, Army Materiel Command, 1989. [Use of source began in 1979]

(ROG) *Dictionary of Abbreviations*. By Walter T. Rogers. London: George Allen & Co. Ltd., 1913; reprinted by Gale Research Inc., 1969.

(SDI) *Report to the Congress on the Strategic Defense Initiative*. U.S. Department of Defense. Strategic Defense Initiative Organization, April 1987.

(SEIS) *Seismograph Station Codes and Characteristics*. Geological Survey. Circular 791. By Barbara B. Poppe, Debbi A. Naab, and John S. Derr. Washington, DC: U.S. Department of the Interior, 1978.

(SPSG) *Security Owner's Stock Guide*. New York: Standard & Poor's Corp., 1991. [Use of source began in 1988]

(TEL) *Telephony's Dictionary*. 2nd ed. By Graham Langley. Chicago: Telephony Publishing Corp., 1986.
> Includes definitions for U.S. and international telecommunications terms. Ten appendices.

(TSPED)   *Trade Shows and Professional Exhibits Directory.* 2nd ed. Edited by Robert J. Elster. Detroit: Gale Research Inc., 1987. [Use of source began in 1986]
A guide to scheduled events providing commercial display facilities including conferences, conventions, meetings, fairs and festivals, etc. Entries include name of trade show; sponsor name, address, and telephone number; attendance figures; principal exhibits; special features; publications; and date and location of shows.

(TSSD)   *Telecommunications Systems and Services Directory.* 4th ed. (and supplement) Edited by John Krol. Detroit: Gale Research Inc., 1989. [Use of source began in 1985]
An international descriptive guide to telecommunications organizations, systems, and services. Entries include name and address, telephone number, chief official, and a description of the purposes, technical structure, and background of the service or system.

Acronyms, Initialisms & Abbreviations Dictionary

P-Z

P

P .... Aircraft [*Wind triangle problems*]
P .... All India Reporter, Patna [*A publication*]   (DLA)
P .... Armour Pharmaceutical Co. [*Research code symbol*]
P .... Assistant in Private Practice [*Chiropody*] [*British*]
P .... Asta Werke AG [*Germany*] [*Research code symbol*]
P .... Bristol Laboratories [*Research code symbol*]
P .... cis-Platinum [*Cisplatin*] [*Also, cis-DDP, CDDP, CPDD, CPT, DDP*] [*Antineoplastic drug*]
P .... Dainippon Pharmaceutical Co. [*Japan*] [*Research code symbol*]
p .... Density [*Heat transmission symbol*]
P .... Departure
p .... Difficulty [*Of a test item*] [*Psychology*]
P .... Farbenfabriken Bayer [*Germany*] [*Research code symbol*]
P .... Farmitalia [*Italy*] [*Research code symbol*]
P .... Faulty Punctuation [*Used in correcting manuscripts, etc.*]
P .... Force of Concentrated Load
P .... Games [*or Matches*] Played [*Sports statistics*]
P .... Hole P-Type Semiconductor Material
P .... Indian Law Reports, Patna Series [*A publication*]   (DLA)
P .... Law Reports, Probate, Divorce, and Admiralty [*Since 1890*] [*England*] [*A publication*]   (DLA)
P .... Lepetit [*Italy*] [*Research code symbol*]
p .... Momentum [*Symbol*] [*IUPAC*]
P .... Office of Personnel [*Coast Guard*]
p .... On Probation [*Navy*] [*British*]
P .... Orbital Period [*of a comet*] [*In years*]
p .... P-Doped Semiconductor [*Photovoltaic energy systems*]
P .... P-Register [*Data processing*]
P .... Pacer
P .... Pacht [*A publication*]
P .... Pacific Coast Stock Exchange [*Later, PSE*]
p---------- .... Pacific Ocean [*MARC geographic area code*] [*Library of Congress*]   (LCCP)
P .... Pacific Reporter [*A publication*]   (DLA)
P .... Pacific Standard Time   (FAAC)
P .... Pack [*JETDS*]
P .... Packed Lunches [*School meals*] [*British*]
P .... Paddington Railway Station   (ROG)
P .... Paddle   (DS)
P .... Page
P .... Paid This Year [*In stock listings of newspapers*]
P .... Pain [*Medicine*]
P .... Paired [*for or against*] [*Votes in Congress*]
P .... Paise [*Monetary unit*] [*India*]
P .... Palace   (ROG)
P .... Palacio [*A publication*]
P .... Palaestra [*A publication*]
P .... Pale   (ADA)
P .... Palimpsest [*A publication*]
P .... Pallet [*Spacelab*] [*NASA*]   (NASA)
P .... Pamphlet
P .... Pancuronium [*A muscle relaxant*]
P .... Pandects [*A publication*] [*Authority cited in pre-1607 legal work*]   (DSA)
P .... Papa [*Phonetic alphabet*] [*International*]   (DSUE)
P .... Papa [*Pope*] [*Latin*]
P .... Paper
P .... Papilla [*Optic*] [*Medicine*]
P .... Papillate [*A type of seed*] [*Botany*]
P .... Para [*Chemistry*]
p .... Para [*Monetary unit*] [*Yugoslavia*]
P .... Parachutist [*Army skill qualification identifier*]   (INF)
P .... Paragraph   (ADA)
P .... Paralegal Program [*Association of Independent Colleges and Schools specialization code*]
P .... Parallax
P .... Parallel
P .... Paramecin [*A protozoan toxin*]
P .... Parashah   (BJA)
P .... Pardon   (ADA)
P .... Parenchyma [*Botany*]

P .... Parental
P .... Parish   (ROG)
P .... Parity [*Atomic physics*]
P .... Park
P .... Parking Place [*Traffic sign*] [*British*]
P .... Parlophone [*Record label*] [*Great Britain, Italy, Australia, etc.*]
P .... Parson
P .... Part
P .... Parthian [*Language, etc.*]
P .... Partial [*Astronomy*]
P .... Participle [*Grammar*]
P .... Partim [*In Part*]
P .... Partnership
P .... Party
P .... Parve [*or Pareve*] [*In food labeling, indicates food is kosher and can be used with either meat or dairy products*]
P .... Passed [*Examination*]
P .... Passing Showers [*Meteorology*]
P .... Past
P .... Paste
P .... Pasteurella [*Genus of bacteria*]
P .... Pastor
P .... Patchy [*Decelerometer readings*] [*Aviation*]   (FAAC)
P .... Patent
P .... Pater [*Father*] [*Latin*]
P .... Patient
P .... Patrol [*Designation for all US military aircraft*]
P .... Patrol Service Gunnery Instructor [*Officer's rating*] [*British Royal Navy*]
P .... Patron
P .... Pattern
P .... Paulus de Liazaris [*Deceased, 1356*] [*Authority cited in pre-1607 legal work*]   (DSA)
P .... Paused Program [*Data processing*]
P .... Pavilion   (ROG)
P .... Pawn [*Chess*]
P .... Pax [*Peace*] [*Latin*]
P .... Pay
P .... Payee
P .... Paymaster [*Military*]   (ROG)
P .... Pazmaveb [*A publication*]
P .... Peak
P .... Peat   (ROG)
P .... Pebbles [*Quality of the bottom*] [*Nautical charts*]
P .... Pectoral [*Anatomy*]   (ROG)
p .... Peculiar [*Astronomy*]
P .... Pelagius [*Deceased, 1232*] [*Authority cited in pre-1607 legal work*]   (DSA)
P .... Pen [*Sports*]
p .... Pence [*Monetary unit*] [*Great Britain*]
P .... Pencil Tube   (MDG)
P .... Pengo [*Monetary unit in Hungary until 1946*]
P .... Penicillin
p .... Penni(a) [*Penny or Pence*] [*Monetary unit*] [*Finland*]   (GPO)
P .... Pennsylvania   (DLA)
P .... Pennsylvania State Library, Harrisburg, PA [*Library symbol*] [*Library of Congress*]   (LCLS)
P .... Penny
P .... Pensamiento [*A publication*]
P .... Pentachlorophenol [*Also, PCP*] [*Wood preservative*] [*Organic chemistry*]   (TEL)
P .... Peony [*Horticulture*]
P .... People
P .... Per
P .... Percentile
P .... Perceptual
P .... Perceptual Speed [*A factor ability*] [*Psychology*]
P .... Perch
P .... Perchloroethylene [*Also, TCE*] [*Dry cleaning*]
P .... Percussion
P .... Pere [*Father*] [*French*]

P................ Perforation
P................ Performance [Army]   (INF)
P................ Performer
P................ Perianth
P................ Pericardium [Medicine]
P................ Perimeter
P................ Period
P................ Perishable
P................ Permanent Stay [in hospital] [British]
P................ Perpetuus [Uninterrupted] [Latin]
p................ Perseverate [Psychology]
P................ Persian   (DLA)
P................ Persimmon
P................ Persistence [Medicine]
P................ Person
P................ Person to Person [Telecommunications]   (TEL)
P................ Personality Organization and Stability [Eysenck] [Psychology]
P................ Personnel
P................ Perspectives [A publication]
P................ Perstetur [Continue] [Pharmacy]   (ROG)
P................ Persuasion [Novel by Jane Austen]
P................ Perth [Mint mark] [Australia]
P................ Peseta [Monetary unit] [Spain and Latin America]
P................ Pesewa [Monetary unit] [Ghana]
P................ Pesher   (BJA)
P................ Peshitta   (BJA)
P................ Peso [Monetary unit] [Spain and Latin America]
P................ Peta [A prefix meaning multiplied by 10^15 SI symbol]
P................ Peter [New Testament book]
P................ Peter [Phonetic alphabet] [World War II]   (DSUE)
P................ Peters' United States Supreme Court Reports [26-41 United
                      States] [A publication]   (DLA)
P................ Petiole [Botany]
P................ Petrol [British Waterways Board sign]
P................ Petrus Hispanus [Authority cited in pre-1607 legal
                      work]   (DSA)
P................ Peyote
P................ Pfizer, Inc. [Research code symbol]
P................ Pharmacopoeia
P................ Phencyclidine [An anesthetic]
P................ Phenolphthalein [Chemical indicator]
P................ Philadelphia [Pennsylvania] [Mint mark, when appearing on
                      US coins]
P................ Phillips Petroleum Co. [NYSE symbol]   (SPSG)
P................ Philologus. Zeitschrift fuer Klassische Altertum [A publication]
P................ Philosophy [A publication]
P................ Phoenician   (BJA)
P................ Phon [Unit of loudness level]
p................ Phosphate [One-letter symbol] [Biochemistry]
p................ Phosphoric Residue [As substituent on nucleoside]
                      [Biochemistry]
P................ Phosphorus [Chemical element]
P................ Photographic Reconnaissance Capability [When suffix to Navy
                      aircraft designation]
P................ Phototropism [Botany]
P................ Phrase Structure Rule [Linguistics]
P................ Physics [Secondary school course] [British]
P................ Physiology [Medical Officer designation] [British]
P................ Phytophthora [A fungus]
P................ Piaggio Rinaldo [Industria Aeronautiche & Meccaniche SpA]
                      [Italy] [ICAO aircraft manufacturer identifier]   (ICAO)
P................ Pianissimo [Very Softly] [Music]
P................ Piano [Musical instrument]
P................ Piano [Softly] [Music]
P................ Piaster [Monetary unit] [Spain, Republic of Vietnam, and some
                      Middle Eastern countries]
P................ Pica [Typography]   (ADA)
P................ Pickering's Massachusetts Reports [18-41 Massachusetts] [A
                      publication]   (DLA)
p................ Pico [A prefix meaning divided by one trillion] [SI symbol]
P................ Picot [Crochet]   (ROG)
P................ Pie
P................ Pied [Foot] [French]
P................ Pierced [Quilting]
P................ Pigs   (ROG)
P................ Pilaster [Technical drawings]
P................ Pillar [Buoy]
P................ Pilot
P................ [Marc] Pincherle [When used in identifying Vivaldi's
                      compositions, refers to cataloging of his works by
                      musicologist Pincherle]
P................ Pink
P................ Pinnule
P................ Pint
P................ Pip [Phonetic alphabet] [Pre-World War II]   (DSUE)
P................ Pipe
P................ Pipe Rolls [British]
P................ Pique; Inclusions [Diamond clarity grade]
P................ Pitch [or Pitcher] [Baseball]
P................ Pitch [Technical drawings]
P................ Pith [Botany]

P................ Pitman Examination Institute [British]
P................ Pitman-Moore Co. [Research code symbol]
P................ Pius [Dutiful] [Latin]
P................ Placebo [Medicine]
P................ Placentinus [Deceased, 1192] [Authority cited in pre-1607 legal
                      work]   (DSA)
P................ Placitum [or Placita] [Agreeable, Agreed Upon] [Latin] [Legal
                      term]   (DLA)
P................ Planed
P................ Planning
P................ Plasma
P................ Plastid [Botany]
P................ Plate [Electron tube] [Technical drawings]
P................ Platform   (DCTA)
P................ Players League [Major league in baseball, 1890]
P................ Pleasant
P................ Pleinsbachian [Geology]
P................ Plotter [British military]   (DMA)
P................ Plug
P................ Plus [More]
P................ Poco [Somewhat] [Music]
P................ Poetry [A publication]
P................ Poids [Feet] [French]
P................ Point
P................ Point [Lacrosse position]
P................ Point-to-Point Radio [FAA designator]   (CET)
P................ Poise [Unit of dynamic viscosity]
P................ Poison
P................ Polar [Air mass]   (FAAC)
P................ Polar Distance [Navigation]
P................ Polarization
P................ Pole
P................ Political Division [Geography]
P................ Polka [Music]
P................ Pollen [Botany]
P................ Polonystyka [A publication]
P................ Polymorphic [Biology]
P................ Polyneuropathy [Medicine]
P................ Polyphagous [Biology]
P................ Pond [Maps and charts]
P................ Pondere [By Weight] [Latin]
P................ Ponendum [To Be Placed] [Latin]
P................ Ponte [A publication]
P................ Pontifex [Bishop] [Latin]
P................ Pool
P................ Poop [Portion of a ship]
P................ Poor Skiing Conditions
P-............... Poorly Organized, Unstable Personality [Eysenck] [Psychology]
P................ Pope
P................ Popular Response [Rorschach] [Psychology]
P................ Population
P................ Populus [People] [Latin]
P%.............. Por Ciento [Per Cent] [Spanish]
P................ Porcelain
P................ Port [Maps and charts]
P................ Portable   (MDG)
P................ Portable [JETDS nomenclature]
P................ Portion
P................ Portugal [IYRU nationality code]
P................ Position
p................ Positive [Crystal]
P................ Post [After] [Latin]
P................ Post
P................ Postage
P................ Posten [Sentry] [German military]
P................ Posterior
P................ Postpartum [Medicine]
P................ Pouce [Inch] [French]
P................ Pounds [As measurement of total stress] [Aerospace]   (AAG)
P................ Pour [For] [French]
P................ Power [Symbol] [IUPAC]
P................ Poynting Vector [Electromagnetism]   (DEN)
P................ Practical
P................ Practical Intelligence
P................ Pre-1920 [Deltiology]
P................ Preceding
P................ Precipitation Ceiling [Aviation weather reports]   (FAAC)
P................ Precipitation Static
P................ Predators Present [Ecology]
P................ Predicate
P................ Predictor [British military]   (DMA)
P................ Prednisolone [Endocrinology]
P................ Prednisone [Also, PDN, Pr, Pred, Pro] [Antineoplastic drug]
                      [Endocrinology]
P................ Preferred
P................ Prefix [Indicating a private radiotelegram]
P................ Preliminary
P................ Premolar [Dentistry]
P................ Presbyopia [Ophthalmology]
P................ Presbyterian
P................ Prescribing

P.............. Present
P.............. Present BIT [*Binary Digit*] [*Data processing*]
P.............. Preset
P.............. President
P.............. Press [*Publishing*]
P.............. Pressure [*or p*] [*Symbol*] [*IUPAC*]
P.............. Pressurized Tank [*Liquid gas carriers*]
P.............. Preview
P.............. Prey [*Zoology*]
P.............. Price [*Economics*]
P.............. Pridie [*The Day Before*] [*Latin*]
P.............. Priest
P.............. Priestly Source [*Biblical scholarship*]
P.............. Prilled
P.............. Primary
P.............. Primary [*or Push*] Wave [*Earthquakes*]
P.............. Primitive
P.............. Primus [*First*] [*Latin*]
P.............. Prince
P.............. Princeps [*First Edition*] [*French*]
P.............. Princess   (ROG)
P.............. Principal
P.............. Print
P.............. Priority [*Telecommunications*]   (TEL)
P.............. Priory
P.............. Prisoner [*Military*]
P.............. Private
P.............. Private Trust [*Includes testamentary, investment, life insurance, holding title, etc.*] [*Legal term*]   (DLA)
P.............. Private Venture
P.............. Privy   (ROG)
P.............. Pro [*For*] [*Latin*]
P.............. Probability [*or Probability Ratio*] [*Statistics*]
P.............. Probate
P.............. Probe   (MSA)
P.............. Probucol [*Anticholesteremic*]
P.............. Procarbazine [*Also, PC, PCB, Pr*] [*Antineoplastic drug*]
P.............. Procedure
P.............. Processor [*Data processing*]
P.............. Proconsul
P.............. Producer [*Films, television, etc.*]
P.............. Product
P.............. Production [*of Energy*]
P.............. Profession
P.............. Professional [*Civil Service employees designation*]
P.............. Proficiency
P.............. Profit
P.............. Progesterone [*A hormone*]
P.............. Program   (KSC)
P.............. Programmable
P.............. Progressive
P.............. Prohibited Area [*Followed by identification*]
P.............. Proliferation [*Biology*]
P.............. Proline [*One-letter symbol; see Pro*]
P.............. Promoter [*Genetics*]
P.............. Prompt [*i.e., the right side*] [*A stage direction*]
P.............. Proof [*Philately*]
P.............. Prop   (DS)
P.............. Propagation Distribution [*Broadcasting*]
P.............. Proportion in a Specific Class
P.............. Proposed Departure [*Aviation*]   (FAAC)
P.............. Propulsion   (AAG)
P.............. Protein
P.............. Proteinuria [*Clinical chemistry*]
P.............. Protestant
P.............. Protet [*Protest*] [*French*]
P.............. Proto [*Linguistics*]
p.............. Proton [*A nuclear particle*]
P.............. Protoplasmic [*Freeze etching in microscopy*]
P.............. Prototroch
P.............. Prototype   (AAG)
P.............. Provisional
P.............. Psychiatry
P.............. Psychometrist [*Psychology*]
P.............. Public Houses [*Public-performance tariff class*] [*British*]
P.............. Publications
P.............. Pudding [*Phonetic alphabet*] [*Royal Navy*] [*World War I*]   (DSUE)
P.............. Pugillum [*Medicine*]   (ROG)
P.............. Pugillus [*A Pinch*] [*Pharmacy*]   (ROG)
P.............. Pulled Up [*Horse racing*]
P.............. Pulse
P.............. Pump   (AAG)
P.............. Punch
P.............. Punic   (BJA)
P.............. Punkt [*Point*] [*German military*]
P.............. Punter [*Football*]
P.............. Pupil
P.............. Purchased   (AAG)
P.............. Purified [*Animal breeding*]

P.............. Purinethol [*Mercaptopurine*] [*Also, M, MP*] [*Antineoplastic drug*]
P.............. Purkinje Cell [*Neuroanatomy*]
P.............. Purl [*Knitting*]
P.............. Purple
P.............. Purpure [*Purple*] [*Heraldry*]
P.............. Pursuit [*Airplane designation*]
P.............. Put [*In options listings of newspapers*]
P.............. Pya [*Monetary unit*] [*Burma*]
p.............. Pyranose [*One-letter symbol*] [*Biochemistry*]
P.............. Pyroxene Subgroup [*Acmite, sodium metasilicate, potassium metasilicate, diopside, wollastonite, hypersthene*] [*CIPW classification*] [*Geology*]
P.............. RADAR [*JETDS nomenclature*]
P.............. Reproducing [*JETDS nomenclature*]
P.............. Single Paper [*Wire insulation*]   (AAG)
P.............. Soft Pad [*Missile launch environment symbol*]
P.............. Warner-Lambert Pharmaceutical Co. [*Research code symbol*]
P-2............ Propaganda Due [*Secret Italian Masonic organization, allegedly tied to the Roman Catholic church*]
P₂............ Pulmonic Second Sound [*Medicine*]
P2............ Second Pilot [*Aviation*]   (AIA)
P3............ Industry Composites and Polymer Processing Program [*Massachusetts Institute of Technology*] [*Research center*]   (RCD)
P3............ Portable Plotting Package [*Nuclear energy*]   (NRCH)
3P............ Three-Pole [*or Triple Pole*] [*Switch*]
4P............ Four-Pole [*Switch*]
7P............ Lesotho [*Aircraft nationality and registration mark*]   (FAAC)
8P............ Barbados [*Aircraft nationality and registration mark*]   (FAAC)
P 14.......... Pattern 14 Rifle [*Made in the US for Great Britain, beginning in 1914*]
P₅₀ .... Partial pressure of oxygen at 50% hemoglobin saturation [*Medicine*]
5P's .... Poet, Printer, Publisher, Publican, and Player [*Nickname given to William Oxberry (fl. 1784-1824)*]
P (Card) ..... Personal Card [*Containing person's name, address, age, description, job, habits, haunts, movements*] [*Used in Belfast, Northern Ireland*]
P (Day)...... Production Day [*Army*]   (AABC)
PA .... B. F. Jones Memorial Library, Aliquippa, PA [*Library symbol*] [*Library of Congress*]   (LCLS)
PA .... [*The*] Item Requested Is a Controlled Item That May Be Released Only By Written Authority of the Proponent. Please See DA Pamphlet 310-1 for Identification of and Address of Proponent [*Supply action error code*] [*Army*]
PA .... Office of Public Affairs [*DoD*]
PA .... Onze Pius-Almanak [*A publication*]
PA .... Pacific Affairs [*A publication*]
PA .... Pad Abort [*NASA*]   (KSC)
P & A........ Page and Adams' Code [*1912*] [*A publication*]   (DLA)
PA .... Paging and Area Warning   (MCD)
Pa .... Paideia [*A publication*]
Pa .... Paine's United States Circuit Court Reports [*A publication*]   (DLA)
PA .... Paired Associates [*Psychometrics*]
PA .... Pakistan Army
PA .... Paleopathology Association
PA .... Palestine Affairs [*New York*] [*A publication*]   (BJA)
PA .... Palladium [*Chemical element*]   (ROG)
PA .... Pamatky Archeologicke [*A publication*]
PA .... Pan American World Airways, Inc. [*See also PAA, PAN-AM, PN*] [*ICAO designator*]   (MCD)
PA .... Panama [*ANSI two-letter standard code*]   (CNC)
PA .... Panatlas Energy, Inc. [*Toronto Stock Exchange symbol*]
PA .... Paper Advance   (BUR)
PA .... Par Amitie [*By Favor*] [*French*]
PA .... Par Autorite [*By Authority*] [*French*]
PA .... Para-Amps   (EA)
Pa .... Parachutist [*British military*]   (DMA)
P in A .... Parallax in Altitude [*Navigation*]
PA .... Paralysis Agitans
PA .... Parametric Amplifier
Pa .... Paranoia [*Psychology*]
PA .... Parapsychological Association   (EA)
PA .... Parents Anonymous   (EA)
PA .... Parents' Association
PA .... Parish
Pa .... Parkett [*A publication*]
PA .... Parliamentary Affairs [*A publication*]
PA .... Parti de l'Action [*Party of Action*] [*Morocco*] [*Political party*]   (PPW)
PA .... Parti Affectae [*To the Affected Part*] [*Pharmacy*]
PA .... Partial Application [*Military*]   (AFIT)
PA .... Participating Activity [*Responsible for standardization efforts*] [*DoD*]
PA .... Participial Adjective [*Grammar*]
PA .... Particular Average
PA .... Partners of the Americas   (EA)
Pa .... Paru [*A publication*]
Pa .... Pascal [*Symbol*] [*SI unit of pressure*]

PA	Passenger Agent
PA	Passenger Ship
PA	Pastoral Music [*A publication*]
PA	Pathfinder Association (EAIO)
PA	Patient
PA	Patrol Aircraft (NATG)
PA	Pattern Analysis [*Test*]
P & A	Pay and Allowances
PA	Paying Agent [*Legal term*] (DLA)
P/A	Payment Authority [*Business term*]
PA	Pending Availability
PA	Pendulous Axis [*Accelerometer*] (IEEE)
PA	Pennsylvania [*Postal code*]
PA	Pennsylvania Supreme Court Reports [*1845-date*] [*A publication*] (DLA)
PA	People's Alliance [*Althydubandalag*] [*Iceland*] [*Political party*] (PPW)
PA	Peoples Association [*Singapore*] (DS)
PA	Peptide Absorption
PA	Per Abdomen
PA	Per Adresse [*Care Of*] [*German*]
PA	Per Annum [*By the Year*] [*Latin*]
PA	Per Auguri [*Used on visiting cards to express congratulations, birthday wishes, etc.*] [*Italian*]
P & A	Percussion and Auscultation [*Medicine*]
PA	Performance Analysis
PA	Performance Appraisal Required [*Civil Service*]
PA	Performing Arts [*US Copyright Office class*]
PA	Periodic Acid [*Inorganic chemistry*]
pA	Periplanone A [*Biochemistry*]
PA	Permanent Address (ROG)
PA	Permanent Appointment
PA	Permanently Associated [*Telecommunications*] (TEL)
PA	Pernicious Anemia [*Hematology*]
PA	Personal Accident [*Insurance*] (AIA)
PA	Personal Affairs (AFM)
PA	Personal Appearance
PA	Personal Assistant [*British*]
PA	Personal Audit [*Psychological testing*]
P & A	Personnel and Administration [*Army*] (AABC)
PA	Personnel Administrator [*American Society for Personnel Administration*] [*A publication*] [*Information service or system*]
PA	Personnel Area (NRCH)
PA	Petroleum Abstracts [*Also, an information service or system*] [*A publication*]
PA	Pfizer, Inc. [*Research code symbol*]
PA	Pharmacology, Clinical [*Medical specialty*] (DHSM)
PA	Phentolamine [*Antiadrenergic*]
PA	Philippine Army
PA	Philippine Association (EA)
PA	Philosophische Abhandlungen [*A publication*]
PA	Phonocardiogram Amplifier [*Cardiology*]
PA	Phosphatidic Acid [*Biochemistry*]
PA	Phosphoarginine [*Biochemistry*]
PA	Photoallergenic [*Response*] [*Medicine*]
PA	Photodiode Amplifier
PA	Phthalic Anhydride [*Organic chemistry*]
PA	Physical Activity (MCD)
PA	Physician's Assistant
PA	Physics Abstracts [*Institution of Electrical Engineers*] [*Information service or system*] [*A publication*] (CRD)
PA	Phytoalexin [*Plant pathology*]
PA	Picatinny Arsenal [*New Jersey*] [*Later, Armament Development Center*] [*Army*]
pA	Picoampere
PA	Pierre Allain [*Lightweight rock-climbing boot named after its designer*]
PA	Pierre Arpels [*Jewelry designer*]
PA	Pills Anonymous [*Later, DA*] [*An association*] (EA)
P/A	Pilotless Aircraft
P & A	Pioneer and Ammunition
PA	Piper Aircraft Corp. [*ICAO aircraft manufacturer identifier*] (ICAO)
PA	Pirke Avot (BJA)
PA	[*Pension*] Plan Administrator
PA	Planning Assistance (EA)
P & A	Plans and Analysis
PA	Plasma Aldosterone [*Endocrinology*]
PA	Plasminogen Activator [*Biochemistry*]
PA	Platelet Adhesiveness [*Hematology*]
PA	Platform Assembly (MCD)
PA	Point of Aim [*Military*]
PA	Points Against [*Football*]
P/A	Polar to Analog (KSC)
PA	Polar Atlantic [*American air mass*]
PA	Polarization Approximation [*Physical chemistry*]
PA	Polarographic Analyzer
PA	Police Academy
PA	Pollution Abstracts [*A publication*]
Pa	Polonystyka [*A publication*]
PA	Polyacetal [*Organic chemistry*]
PA	Polyacrylic [*Organic chemistry*]
PA	Polyanhydride [*Organic chemistry*]
PA	Polyarteritis [*Medicine*]
PA	Polymer Adhesive
PA	Port Agency [*Army*]
PA	Position Angle [*Astronomy*]
PA	Position Approximate [*Nautical charts*]
PA	Positive Addiction [*Self-improvement method developed by William Glasser, MD*]
PA	Positive Attitude
PA	Post Adjutant
PA	Post Amplifier
PA	Postal Assistant (DCTA)
PA	Posterior Anterior [*Medicine*]
PA	Posterior Aorta
PA	Postmortem Aging [*of meat*]
PA	Potato Agar [*Microbiology*]
PA	Potsmokers Anonymous (EA)
PA	Power Amplifier
PA	Power Approach [*Aerospace*]
PA	Power of Attorney
P/A	Power of Authority
PA	Practice Amendment (AAG)
PA	Prealbumin [*Biochemistry*]
PA	Preamplifier
PA	Preapproved
PA	Prearm
PA	Preavailability
PA	Precision Approach (FAAC)
PA	Precomputed Altitude
P & A	Prediction and Allocation
PA	Predictive Analyzer [*Data processing*] (DIT)
PA	Prefect-Apostolic [*Roman Catholic*]
PA	Preliminary Acceptance (KSC)
PA	Preparing Activity [*Responsible for Federal document and study projects*]
P/A	Presence or Absence
PA	Presence Africaine [*A publication*]
PA	Present Again (ADA)
PA	Preservation Action (EA)
PA	Presidents Association [*New York, NY*] (EA)
PA	Press Agent
PA	Press Association Ltd. (IID)
PA	Pressure Actuated [*Switch*]
PA	Pressure Alarm [*Nuclear energy*] (NRCH)
PA	Pressure Altitude [*Aviation*]
PA	Pressure Angle (MSA)
PA	Pressure Area [*Medicine*]
PA	Price Analyst
P & A	Price and Availability
Pa	Prima [*First Class*] [*Business term*] [*German*]
PA	Primary Aerospace Vehicle [*or Aircraft*]
PA	Primary Anemia [*Medicine*]
PA	Primerica Corp. [*NYSE symbol*] (SPSG)
PA	Prince Albert Coat [*Slang*]
PA	Principal Assistant (NOAA)
PA	Principal Axes
PA	Principle of Adding [*New math*]
PA	Prior to Admission [*Medicine*]
P & A	Priorities and Allocations (MUGU)
PA	Priority Aggregate
PA	Privacy Act
PA	Private Account [*Banking*]
PA	Private Architect [*British*]
PA	Pro Anno [*For the Year*] [*Latin*]
PA	Pro Applicatione [*To Be Applied*] [*Pharmacy*] (ROG)
PA	Pro Arte [*A publication*]
PA	Proactivator [*Medicine*]
PA	Proanthocyanidin (Assay) [*Analytical chemistry*]
PA	Probability of Acceptance (KSC)
PA	Probability of Acquisition [*Military*]
P/A	Problem Analysis (NASA)
PA	Probleme der Agyptologie [*A publication*] (BJA)
PA	Procainamide [*Cardiac depressant*]
P & A	Procedures and Analysis
PA	Process Allocator [*Telecommunications*] (TEL)
PA	Process Automation (CMD)
PA	Procurement Agency (MCD)
PA	Procurement Appropriations [*Army*] (AABC)
PA	Procurement, Army
P & A	Procurement and Assignment
PA	Procurement Authorization
PA	Procuring Activity [*Military*]
PA	Product Analysis (IEEE)
PA	Product Assurance (NASA)
PA	Production Adjustment
PA	Production Assistant
PA	Professional Administration [*A publication*]
P & A	Professional and Administrative (AAG)
PA	Professional Administrator [*Australia*] [*A publication*]

PA .... Professional Agent [*Professional Insurance Agents*] [*A publication*]
PA .... Professional Association [*Telecommunications*]
PA .... Profile Angle   (MSA)
PA .... Program Access
PA .... Program Account   (NG)
PA .... Program Address
PA .... Program Administrator   (MCD)
PA .... Program Agent   (OICC)
PA .... Program for the Aging   (OICC)
PA .... Program Aid [*A publication*]
PA .... Program Analysis [*Data processing*]
PA .... Program Application Instructions [*Telecommunications*]   (TEL)
PA .... Program Assessment   (MCD)
PA .... Program Attention Key [*Data processing*]
PA .... Program Authorization   (AFM)
PA .... Programmable Automation
PA .... Progressive Alliance [*Defunct*]   (EA)
PA .... Project Administration   (MCD)
PA .... Project Authorization
PA .... Proliferating Angioendotheliomatosis
PA .... Prolonged-Action [*Pharmacy*]
PA .... Prolotherapy Association   (EA)
PA .... Property Administrator [*DoD*]
PA .... Prophylactic Antibiotic
PA .... Proponent Agency [*Army*]
PA .... Proportional Action   (AAG)
PA .... Proposal Authorization
PA .... [*The*] Proprietary Association [*Later, NDMA*]   (EA)
PA .... Propulsion Assistance   (DS)
PA .... Prosecuting Attorney
Pa .... Protactinium [*or Protoactinium*] [*Chemical element*]
PA .... Protected Area [*Nuclear energy*]   (NRCH)
P & A .... Protection and Advocacy [*System*] [*To protect the rights of developmentally disabled persons*]
PA .... Protective Antigen
PA .... Prothonotary Apostolic
PA .... Proton Affinity [*Surface ionization*]
PA .... Provisional Allowance
PA .... Pseudo-Astronomy
PA .... Pseudoaneurysm [*Medicine*]
PA .... Pseudomonas aeruginosa [*Bacterium*]
PA .... Psychoanalyst
PA .... Psychogenic Aspermia [*Medicine*]
PA .... Psychological Abstracts [*A publication*]
PA .... Psychological Age
PA .... Public Accountant
PA .... Public Act
PA .... Public Address [*Amplification equipment*] [*Communications*]
PA .... Public Administration
PA .... Public Administration [*A publication*]   (APTA)
PA .... Public Advocate   (EA)
PA .... Public Affairs
PA .... Public Archives [*of Canada*]
PA .... Public Assistance
PA .... Publication Announcement
PA .... Publishers' Alliance   (EA)
PA .... Publishers' Association [*London, England*]   (DIT)
PA .... Pull and Adjust [*Brace*] [*Medicine*]
PA .... Pulmonary Angiography [*Medicine*]
PA .... Pulmonary Artery [*Medicine*]
PA .... Pulmonary Atresia [*Medicine*]
PA .... Pulpoaxial [*Dentistry*]
PA .... Pulse Amplifier
PA .... Puppeteers of America   (EA)
PA .... Purchasing Agent
PA .... Purge Alarm [*Nuclear energy*]   (NRCH)
PA .... Put Away [*Papers*] [*British*]
PA .... Puumala [*Vole virus*]
PA .... Pyro Ammonia   (ROG)
PA .... Pyrrolizidine Alkaloid [*Toxicology*]
PA .... Pythium aphanidermatum [*A fungus*]
PAA .... Pa-An [*Burma*] [*Airport symbol*]   (OAG)
PAA .... Pacific Arts Association   (EA)
PAA .... Pan American Minerals Corp. [*Toronto Stock Exchange symbol*] [*Vancouver Stock Exchange symbol*]
PAA .... Pan American World Airways, Inc. [*See also PA, PAN-AM, PN*]
PAA .... Pancretan Association of America   (EA)
PAA .... Pancyprian Association of America [*Defunct*]   (EA)
PAA .... Panguna [*Solomon Islands*] [*Seismograph station code, US Geological Survey*]   (SEIS)
paa .... Papuan-Australian [*MARC language code*] [*Library of Congress*]   (LCCP)
PAA .... Para-Azoxyanisole [*Organic chemistry*]
PAA .... Parke, Davis & Co. [*Research code symbol*]
PAA .... Parti Affectae Applicandus [*Apply to the Affected Part*] [*Pharmacy*]
PAA .... Pay Adjustment Authorization
PAA .... Peracetic Acid [*Organic chemistry*]
PAA .... Peruvian American Association   (EA)

PAA .... Petroleum Administration Act [*Canada*]
PAA .... Phased Array Antenna
PAA .... Phenanthrene Amino Alcohol [*Organic chemistry*]
PAA .... Phenanthrylacetamide [*Organic chemistry*]
PAA .... Phenylacetic Acid [*Organic chemistry*]
PAA .... Philippine Automotive Association   (DS)
PAA .... Phosphonoacetic Acid [*Antiviral compound*]
PAA .... Photographers Association of America [*Later, Professional Photographers of America*]
PAA .... Photon Activation Analysis
PAA .... Pi Alpha Alpha   (EA)
PAA .... Planar Array Antenna
PAA .... Plasminogen Activator Activity [*Biochemistry*]
PAA .... Platelet Associated Activity [*Pharmacology*]
PAA .... Polish Association of America [*Later, NFLI*]   (EA)
PAA .... Polyacrylamide [*Also, PAAM, PAM*] [*Organic chemistry*]
PAA .... Polyacrylic Acid [*Organic chemistry*]
PAA .... Polyaspartic Acid [*Biochemistry*]
PAA .... Polycyclic Aromatic Amine [*Organic chemistry*]
PAA .... Population Association of America   (EA)
PAA .... Post Award Action
PAA .... Potato Association of America   (EA)
PAA .... Power Amplifier Assembly
PAA .... Pragmateiai tes Akademias Athenon [*A publication*]
PAA .... Praktika tes Akademias Athenon [*A publication*]
PAA .... Pre-Apprenticeship Allowance
PAA .... Primary Aircraft Authorized [*Air Force*]
PAA .... Primary Auxiliary Area [*Nuclear energy*]   (NRCH)
PAA .... Print Advertising Association [*Defunct*]   (EA)
PAA .... Procurement of Ammunition, Army   (AABC)
PAA .... Procurement Appropriation, Army   (MCD)
PAA .... Professional Archers Association   (EA)
PAA .... Programme d'Aide aux Athletes [*Athlete Assistance Program*] [*Canada*]
PAA .... Pyridineacetic Acid [*Organic chemistry*]
P/AA3 .... Probationary Aircraft Artificer 3rd Class [*British military*]   (DMA)
PAAA .... Premium Advertising Association of America [*Later, PMAA*]   (EA)
P/AAA2 ..... Probationary Aircraft Artificer, Acting, 2nd Class [*British military*]   (DMA)
PAAAS ...... Proceedings. American Academy of Arts and Sciences [*A publication*]
PAAAS ...... Publication. American Association for the Advancement of Science [*A publication*]
PAABA ...... Para-Acetamidobenzoic Acid [*Biochemistry*]
PAABS ...... PanAmerican Association of Biochemical Societies   (EA)
PAABS Rev ... PAABS [*Pan-American Association of Biochemical Societies*] Revista [*United States*] [*A publication*]
PAABS Symp ... PAABS [*Pan-American Association of Biochemical Societies*] Symposium [*A publication*]
PAAC .... Pacific and Asian Affairs Council
PAAC .... Program Analysis Adaptable Control [*Data processing*]
PA Acad Sci Proc ... Pennsylvania Academy of Science. Proceedings [*A publication*]
PAACE ...... Precision Aircraft Armament Control Experiment   (RDA)
PAACS ...... Prior Active Army Commissioned Service
PAADAR... Passive Airborne Detection and Ranging   (MSA)
PAADC...... Principal Air Aide-de-Camp [*RAF*] [*British*]
PA Admin Bull ... Pennsylvania Bulletin [*A publication*]   (DLA)
PA Admin Code ... Pennsylvania Administrative Code [*A publication*]   (DLA)
PAAECI .... Pan American Association of Educational Credit Institutions [*See also APICE*]   (EAIO)
PAAES ...... Prior Active Army Enlisted Service
PAAES ...... Publications. American Archaeological Expedition to Syria [*A publication*]   (BJA)
PAAFCS.... Prior Active Air Force Commissioned Service
PAAFES.... Prior Active Air Force Enlisted Service
PAAGE...... Panel on Alternate Approaches to Graduate Education   (EA)
PA Ag Exp ... Pennsylvania. Agricultural Experiment Station. Publications [*A publication*]
PA Agric Exp Stn Bull ... Pennsylvania. Agricultural Experiment Station. Bulletin [*A publication*]
PA Agric Exp Stn Prog Rep ... Pennsylvania. Agricultural Experiment Station. Progress Report [*A publication*]
PAAH .... Polyacrylamide-Hydrazide [*Organic chemistry*]
PAAH .... Praktika tes en Athenais Archaiologikes Hetaireias [*A publication*]
PAAHA ..... Para-Acetamidohippuric Acid [*Biochemistry*]
PAAJR ...... Proceedings. American Academy for Jewish Research [*A publication*]
PAAM .... Polyacrylamide [*Also, PAA, PAM*] [*Organic chemistry*]
PAAM .... Projective Assessment of Aging Method [*Personality development test*] [*Psychology*]
P/AAMHRC ... Pacific/Asian American Mental Health Research Center [*University of Illinois at Chicago*] [*Research center*]   (RCD)
PAAN .... Product Assurance Alert Notice   (MCD)
PAANA ..... Proceedings. Australian Society of Animal Production [*A publication*]
PAANS...... Pan African Association of Neurological Sciences   (EAIO)

PAAO .... Pan-American Association of Ophthalmology (EA)
PAAOD8 ... Proceedings. American Association for Cancer Research and American Society of Clinical Oncology [A publication]
PAAORLBE ... Pan-American Association of Oto-Rhino-Laryngology and Broncho-Esophagology [Mexico City, Mexico] (EAIO)
PAAP .... Panjabi Adabi Academy. Publication [A publication]
PAAP .... Peaceful Alternatives to the Atlantic Pact
PAAP .... Provisional Algal Assay Procedure [Test measuring impact of chemicals on algal growth]
PAAQ .... Palmer [Alaska] [ICAO location identifier] (ICLI)
PAAR .... American Academy in Rome. Papers and Monographs [A publication]
PA Arch ..... Pennsylvania Archaeologist [A publication]
PA Archaeol ... Pennsylvania Archaeologist [A publication]
PAAS......... Pan American Allergy Society (EA)
PAAS......... Performance Assessment and Appraisal System
PAAS......... Phased Array Analysis System
PAAS......... Phased Array Antenna System
PAAS......... Proceedings. American Antiquarian Society [A publication]
PAAT........ Parent as a Teacher Inventory [Psychology]
PAAT........ Personnel and Administrative Assistance Team [Navy] (NVT)
PAAT........ Personnel Assistance and Audit Team [Military]
PAAT........ Programmer Analyst Aptitude Test
PAAT........ Public Affairs Assist Team [Hazardous substance emergency response]
PAATA...... Praktika tes Akademias Athenon [A publication]
PAATI...... Phased Array Antenna Technology Investigation
PAAWWW ... Pacific Asian American Women Writers West (EA)
PAAXOP... Pan-Dodecanesian Association of America "Xanthos O Philikos" (EA)
PAAZA...... Progressive Agriculture in Arizona [A publication]
PAb .... Abington Free Library, Abington, PA [Library symbol] [Library of Congress] (LCLS)
PAB .... Cabrini College, Library, Radnor, PA [OCLC symbol] (OCLC)
PAB .... Panair do Brasil, SA
PAB .... Para-Aminobenzoic Acid [Also, PABA] [Biochemistry]
PAB .... Paramaribo [Suriname] [Geomagnetic observatory code]
PAB .... Parti des Paysans, Artisans, et Bourgeois [Farmers', Artisans', and Burghers' Party] [Switzerland] [Political party] (PPE)
PAB .... Patent Abstracts Bibliography [NASA]
PAB .... Patrick Air Force Base [Florida]
PAB .... Peanut Advisory Board (EA)
PAB .... Pension Appeals Board [Canada]
PAB .... Petroleum Administrative Board [Terminated, 1936]
PAB .... Planning Appeals Board [Australia]
PAB .... Plastic Assault Boat [Navy]
PAB .... Police Administration Building
PAB .... Prealbumin [Biochemistry]
PAB .... Preliminary As-Built [Nuclear energy] (NRCH)
PAB .... Price Adjustment Board
PAB .... Price Agreement Bulletin
PAB .... Primary Auxiliary Building [Nuclear energy] (NRCH)
PAB .... Priorities Allotment Board
PAB .... Priority Assignment Base (MCD)
PAB .... Product Application Bulletins [A publication] (EAAP)
PAB .... Program Advisory Board (MCD)
PAB .... Psychiatric Attitudes Battery [Psychology]
PAB .... Psychology of Addictive Behaviors [An association] (EA)
PAB .... Pulmonary Artery Banding [Cardiology]
PAB .... Pulsed Adsorption Bed [Process]
PAB .... Purple Agar Base [Media] [Microbiology]
PABA........ Barter Island [Alaska] [ICAO location identifier] (ICLI)
PABA........ Para-Aminobenzoic Acid [Also, PAB] [Biochemistry]
PA BA .... Pennsylvania Bar Association. Reports [A publication] (DLA)
PABA........ Progressive Angus Breeders Association
PABAQ...... Pennsylvania Bar Association. Quarterly [A publication]
PA Bar Asso Q ... Pennsylvania Bar Association. Quarterly [A publication]
PA B Ass'n Q ... Pennsylvania Bar Association. Quarterly [A publication]
PA B Brief ... Pennsylvania Bar Brief [A publication] (DLA)
PABC........ Pacific Bancorporation [NASDAQ symbol] (NQ)
PABC........ Pan American Basketball Confederation [See also CPB] (EAIO)
PABCA8... Annual Biology Colloquium [A publication]
PABD .... Precise Access Block Diagram
PABE........ Bethel [Alaska] [ICAO location identifier] (ICLI)
PABE........ Program and Budget Estimate (MCD)
PABFSA... Pediatric Association of Black French-Speaking Africa (EAIO)
PABG........ Big Delta [Alaska] [ICAO location identifier] (ICLI)
P Abh .... Philosophische Abhandlungen [A publication]
PABI......... Delta Junction/Allen Army Air Field [Alaska] [ICAO location identifier] (ICLI)
PABIA ...... Pathologie et Biologie [A publication]
PA Bk Cas ... Pennsylvania Bank Cases [A publication] (DLA)
PABLA...... Problem Analysis by Logical Approach
PABLE...... Payable (ROG)
PABLI ...... Pages Bleues Informatisees [Commission of the European Communities] [Information service or system] (CRD)
PABM....... Big Mountain Air Force Station [Alaska] [ICAO location identifier] (ICLI)
PABMA... Philippine Association of Battery Manufacturers, Inc. (DS)
PABMI ..... Performing Arts Biography Master Index [A publication]
PABP......... Poly(A)-Binding Protein

PABR........ Barrow [Alaska] [ICAO location identifier] (ICLI)
PABR........ Planning Appeals Board. Reports [A publication]
P Abr.......... Pulton's Abridgment of the Statutes [A publication] (DLA)
PA Browne (PA) ... Browne's Reports (Pennsylvania) [A publication] (DLA)
PA Browne R ... Browne's Reports [Pennsylvania] [A publication] (DLA)
PABS .... Pan-American Biodeterioration Society (EA)
PABS .... Para-Aminobenzensulfonamide [Antibiotic]
PA Bsns Survey ... Pennsylvania Business Survey [A publication]
PABST .... Primary Adhesively Bonded Structural Technology [Aviation]
PABT........ Bettles [Alaska] [ICAO location identifier] (ICLI)
PABT........ Pabst Brewing Co. [NASDAQ symbol] (NQ)
PA Bur Topogr Geol Surv Miner Resour Rep ... Pennsylvania. Bureau of Topographic and Geologic Survey. Mineral Resource Report [A publication]
PABV .... Pyroactuated Ball Valve
PABVA...... Pesquisa Agropecuaria Brasileira. Serie Veterinaria [A publication]
P(A)BX...... Private (Automatic) Branch Exchange [Telecommunications] (DEN)
PAC .... Canada. Fisheries and Marine Service. Northern Operations Branch. Pacific Region. Data Report Series [A publication]
PAC .... cis-Platinum [Cisplatin], Adriamycin, Cyclophosphamide [Antineoplastic drug regimen]
PAC .... Pacific (AFM)
Pac .... Pacific [Record label] [France]
PAC .... Pacific Air Command [Air Force]
PAC .... Pacific Ocean
Pac .... Pacific Reporter [A publication] (DLA)
PAC .... Pacific Telesis Group [NYSE symbol] (SPSG)
Pac .... Pacifica: Australian Theological Studies [A publication] (APTA)
PAC .... Package Attitude Control [NASA]
PAC .... Packaged Assembly Circuit
Pac .... Packaging [A publication]
PAC .... Packard Automobile Classics (EA)
PAC .... Pak-Man Resources, Inc. [Vancouver Stock Exchange symbol]
PAC .... Palo Alto - Branner [California] [Seismograph station code, US Geological Survey] [Closed] (SEIS)
PAC .... Pan-Africanist Congress [South Africa]
PAC .... Pan American College [Texas]
PAC .... Pan-American Congress
PAC .... Panama City [Panama] Paitilla Airport [Airport symbol] (OAG)
PAC .... Papular Acrodermatitis of Childhood
PAC .... Para-Aminoclonidine [Biochemistry]
PAC .... Para-Aminosalicylic Acid Calcium Salt [Pharmacology]
PAC .... Parachute and Cable Defence [British military]
PAC .... Parametric Amplifier Converter
P-A-C........ Parent-Adult-Child [Transactional analysis]
PAC .... Parker Aircraft Corporation (MCD)
PAC .... Partido Autentico Constitucional [Authentic Constitutional Party] [El Salvador] [Political party]
PAC .... Parts Allocation Chart (MCD)
PAC .... Pascagoula, MS [Location identifier] [FAA] (FAAL)
PAC .... Passed the Final Examination of the Advanced Class [Military College of Science] [British]
PAC .... Passive Acoustic Classification (NVT)
PAC .... Patents Advisory Committee [British]
PAC .... Patient Airlift Center [Aeromedical evacuation]
PAC .... Payment after Closing [Insurance]
PAC .... Peace Action Center [Defunct] (EA)
PAC .... Pearson Aircraft, Inc. [Port Angeles, WA] [FAA designator] (FAAC)
PAC .... Pedagogic Automatic Computer (IEEE)
PAC .... Pediatric AIDS [Acquired Immune Deficiency Syndrome] Coalition (EA)
PA C .... Pennsylvania Commonwealth Court Reports [A publication] (DLA)
PAC .... People's Army Congress (CINC)
PAC .... Peptide Acid [Organic chemistry]
PAC .... Performance Analysis and Control
PAC .... Performance Assured Certification
PAC .... Personal Analog Computer
PAC .... Personnel Action Center [Army] (INF)
PAC .... Personnel Action Code
PAC .... Personnel and Administration Center [Army] (AABC)
PAC .... Perturbed Angular Correlation
PAC .... Petroleum Advisory Committee [of Organization for Economic Cooperation and Development] [Terminated, 1976] (EGAO)
PAC .... Pharmaceutical Advertising Council [New York, NY] (EA)
PAC .... Phenacetin [Acetophenetidin], Aspirin, Caffeine [Pharmacology]
PAC .... Photoacoustic [Spectroscopy]
PAC .... Piper Aircraft Corporation
PAC .... Planned-Amortization-Class Bond [Investment term]
PAC .... Planning Advisory Committee (OICC)
PAC .... Plasma Arc Chamber
PAC .... Plasma Arc Cutting [Welding]
PAC .... Platinol [Cisplatin], Adriamycin, Cyclophosphamide [Antineoplastic drug regimen]

PAC .... Plowshare Advisory Committee [*AEC*]
PAC .... Pneumatic Analog Computer
PAC .... Pneumatic Auxiliary Console　(AAG)
PAC .... Pod Air Conditioner　(AAG)
PAC .... Policy Advisory Center
PAC .... Policy Advisory Committee [*of Office of Economic Opportunity local program*]
PAC .... Polish American Congress　(EA)
PAC .... Political Action Caucus [*Superseded by LPAC*]　(EA)
PAC .... Political Action Committee [*Generic term*]
PAC .... Polled Access Circuit
PAC .... Pollution Abatement and Control
PAC .... Polyanionic Cellulose [*Organic chemistry*]
PAC .... Polycyclic Aromatic Compound [*Organic chemistry*]
PAC .... Population Action Council　(EA)
PAC .... Porterfield Airplane Club　(EA)
PAC .... Post-Adoption Centre [*British*]　(CB)
PAC .... Post Award Conference　(MCD)
PAC .... Powdered Activated Carbon [*Adsorbent*]
PAC .... Pre-Action Calibration [*Gunnery*]　(NVT)
PAC .... Preauthorized Check Plan [*Insurance*]
PAC .... Premature Atrial Contraction [*Medicine*]
PAC .... Pressure Alpha Center　(MCD)
PAC .... Primary Address Code　(AFM)
PAC .... Prime [*or Principal*] Associate Contractor　(MCD)
PAC .... Printing Accountants Club　(EA)
PAC .... Probe Aerodynamic Center [*NASA*]
PAC .... Problem Action Center [*NASA*]　(NASA)
PAC .... Process Analytical Chemistry
PAC .... Production Acceleration Capacity [*Manufacturing*]
PAC .... Professional Activities Survey [*Medicine*]
PAC .... Program Acquisition Cost　(MCD)
PAC .... Program Adjustment Committee
PAC .... Program Advisory Committee
PAC .... Program Allocation Checker
PAC .... Program Authorized Credentials [*Data processing*]
PAC .... Programmable Automatic Comparator
PAC .... Progress Assessment Chart [*Psychology*]
PAC .... Project Advisory Committee　(EGAO)
PAC .... Promoting Achievement through Communications [*Education*]
PAC .... Protect America's Children [*An association*]　(EA)
PAC .... Protection Auxiliary Cabinet [*Nuclear energy*]　(NRCH)
PAC .... Public Access Catalogue　(ADA)
PAC .... Public Access Control
PAC .... Public Accounts Committee [*British government*]
PAC .... Public Affairs Committee [*Defunct*]　(EA)
PAC .... Public Affairs Coordinator [*Nuclear energy*]　(NRCH)
PAC .... Public Affairs Council　(EA)
PAC .... Public Archives of Canada
PAC .... Publishers' Ad Club [*New York, NY*]　(EA)
PAC .... Pulmonary Artery Catheter [*Medicine*]
PAC .... Pure and Applied Chemistry [*IUPAC*]
PAC .... Pursuant to Authority Contained In [*Army*]
PAC .... Put and Call [*Stock exchange term*]
PAC-10 ...... Pacific 10 Conference　(EA)
Pac A .... Pacific Affairs [*A publication*]
PACA.......... Packard Automobile Club of Australia
PACA........ Perishable Agricultural Commodities Act, 1930
PACA........ Picture Agency Council of America　(EA)
PACA........ Principal Assistant County Architect [*British*]
PACA........ Proceedings. African Classical Association [*A publication*]
PACAB .... Pacific Affairs. Current Awareness Bulletin [*A publication*]　(APTA)
PACADV... Pacific Fleet Advance Headquarters [*Guam*]
PACAF ...... Pacific Air Forces
PACAFBASECOM ... Pacific Air Forces Base Command
Pac Aff .... Pacific Affairs [*A publication*]
Pac Affairs ... Pacific Affairs [*A publication*]
PACAF-OA ... Pacific Air Forces Operations Analysis
Pac Arts Newsl ... Pacific Arts Newsletter [*A publication*]
PACAS...... Patient Care System [*Army*]　(AABC)
PA Cas....... Pennsylvania Supreme Court Cases (Sadler) [*A publication*]　(DLA)
PACAS...... Personnel Access Control Accountability System [*NASA*]　(MCD)
PACAS...... Psychological Abstracts Current Awareness Service　(IID)
PACAust..... Packard Automobile Club of Australia
PACB......... Pan-American Coffee Bureau [*Defunct*]　(EA)
Pac Bird Obs ... Pacific Bird Observer [*A publication*]
Pac Builder Eng ... Pacific Builder and Engineer [*A publication*]
PA CC .... Pennsylvania County Court Reports [*A publication*]　(DLA)
PACC......... Portable Arm Control Console　(KSC)
P(ACC)...... Probability of Acceptance
PACC......... Problem Action Control Center [*NASA*]　(NASA)
PACC........ Products Administration Contract Control
PACC......... Protected Air-Cooled Condenser [*Nuclear energy*]　(NRCH)
PACC......... Provident Life & Accident Insurance Co. of America [*NASDAQ symbol*]　(NQ)
PACCA...... Policy Alternatives for the Caribbean and Central America　(EA)
PACCALL ... Pacific Fleet Calls [*Radio call signs*]

PACCAR... Pacific Car and Foundry
Pac Chem Eng Cong Proc ... Pacific Chemical Engineering Congress. Proceedings [*United States*] [*A publication*]
Pac Chem Eng Congr ... Pacific Chemical Engineering Congress [*A publication*]
Pac Chem Metall Ind ... Pacific Chemical and Metallurgical Industries [*A publication*]
PACCIOS ... Pan American Council of International Committee of Scientific Management
PACCO...... Cisplatin, Adriamycin, Cyclophosphamide, CCNU [*Lomustine*], Oncovin [*Vincristine*] [*Antineoplastic drug regimen*]
Pac Coast Gas Assoc Proc ... Pacific Coast Gas Association. Proceedings [*A publication*]
Pac Coast Int ... Pacific Coast International [*A publication*]　(ILCA)
Pac Coast LJ ... Pacific Coast Law Journal [*A publication*]　(DLA)
Pac Coast Med ... Pacific Coast Medicine [*A publication*]
PACCOM ... Pacific Command [*Military*]
Pac Com..... Pacific Community [*Tokyo*] [*A publication*]
PACCOM ... Pacific Fleet Communications Instructions
Pac Commun ... Pacific Community [*A publication*]
PA CCR..... Pennsylvania County Court Reports [*A publication*]　(DLA)
PA CC Reps ... Pennsylvania County Court Reports [*A publication*]　(DLA)
PACCS ..... Pan American Cancer Cytology Society [*Defunct*]　(EA)
PACCS ..... Post-Attack Command and Control System [*Military*]
PACCS/ADA ... Post-Attack Command and Control System/Airborne Data Automation [*Military*]
PACCSq .... Post-Attack Command Control Squadron [*Air Force*]
PACCT...... PERT [*Program Evaluation and Review Technique*] and Cost Correlation Technique
PACD .... Cold Bay [*Alaska*] [*ICAO location identifier*]　(ICLI)
PACD .... Pacific Division [*Military*]
PACD .... Parachute and Cable Defence [*British military*]　(DMA)
Pac 2d .... Pacific Reporter, Second Series [*A publication*]　(DLA)
PACDA..... Personnel and Administration, Combat Development Activity [*Army*]　(AABC)
PA C Dec WCC ... Pennsylvania Courts, Decisions in Workmen's Compensation Cases [*A publication*]　(DLA)
Pac Discov ... Pacific Discovery [*A publication*]
Pac Discovery ... Pacific Discovery [*A publication*]
PACDIV.... Pacific Division [*Military*]
Pac D Rep .. Pacific Defence Reporter [*A publication*]
PACE........ Committee for Promotion and Action in Community Education [*Australia*]
PACE........ PACE. Pacing and Clinical Electrophysiology [*A publication*]
PACE........ PACE. Process and Chemical Engineering [*A publication*]　(APTA)
PACE........ Pacesetter Homes, Inc. [*NASDAQ symbol*]　(NQ)
PACE........ Pacific Agricultural Cooperative for Export [*Corte Madera, CA*]　(EA)
PACE........ Pacific Alternate Command Element　(CINC)
PACE........ Packaged CRAM [*Card Random-Access Memory*] Executive [*NCR Corp.*] [*Data processing*]
PACE.......... Packet of Accelerated Christian Education [*Educational material marketed by fundamentalist company, Accelerated Christian Education*]
PACE........ Passive Attitude Control Experimental [*Satellite*]
PACE........ Patrol Airship Concept Evaluation
PACE........ Performance Advantage with Cummins Electronics [*Automotive engineering*]
PACE........ Performance and Cost Evaluation
PACE........ Performing Arts, Culture, and Entertainment [*Proposed cable television system*]
PACE........ Peripheral Automatic Channel Emulator [*Data processing*]
PACE........ Personalized Aerobics for Cardiovascular Enhancement
PACE........ Petroleum Association for Conservation of the Canadian Environment
PACE........ Phased Array Control Electronics
PACE........ Physics and Chemistry Experiment
PACE........ Plan for Action by Citizens in Education
PACE........ Planetary Association for Clean Energy　(EA)
PACE........ Planned Action with Constant Evaluation [*Data processing*]
PACE........ Plant Acquisition and Construction Equipment [*Nuclear energy*]　(NRCH)
PACE........ Plant and Capital Equipment　(MCD)
PACE........ Plasma-Assisted Chemical Etching [*Metallurgy*]
PACE........ Police and Criminal Evidence Act [*1964*] [*British*]
PACE........ Policy Analysis for California Education [*Research center*]　(RCD)
PACE........ Portable Acoustic Collection Equipment　(MCD)
PACE........ Precision Analog Computing Equipment
PACE........ Preflight Acceptance Checkout Equipment
PACE........ Prelaunch Automatic Checkout Equipment [*NASA*]
PACE........ Priority Activities in Cancer Education
PACE........ Prisoners Accelerated Creative Exposure [*An association*]
PACE........ Procedural Approach to the Composition of Essays [*In book title*]
PACE........ Professional Activities for Continuing Education [*AEC*]
PACE........ Professional and Administrative Career Examination [*Formerly, FSEE*] [*Civil Service*]
PACE........ Professional Association of Consulting Engineers

PACE......... Program for Afloat College Education [*Navy*] (NVT)
PACE......... Programmable Autonomously-Controlled Electrode [*Instrumentation*]
PACE......... Programmed Automatic Communications Equipment
PACE......... Programming Analysis Consulting Education (IEEE)
PACE......... Project for the Advancement of Church Education
PACE......... Projects to Advance Creativity in Education [*HEW*]
PACE......... Providing Avenues for Continuing Encouragement [*Scholarship awarded by Fraternity of Recording Executives*]
PACE......... Provisioning Action Control Evaluation [*Military*] (AFIT)
PACE......... Pulse-Synthesized Advanced Conversion Equipment
P/ACEA2 .. Probationary Control Electrical Artificer, Acting, 2nd Class [*British military*] (DMA)
PACED..... Program for Advanced Concepts in Electronic Design
Pace LR..... Pace Law Review [*A publication*]
Pace L Rev ... Pace Law Review [*A publication*]
PACE/LV ... Preflight Acceptance Checkout Equipment-Launch Vehicle
PACEMAKER ... Public Agency Career Employment Maker [*OEO project*]
PACENS ... Patient Census
PACE Process Chem Eng ... PACE. Process and Chemical Engineering [*A publication*]
PACER...... Part and Component Evaluation Report [*NASA*]
PACER...... Planning Automation and Control for Evaluating Requirements
PACER...... Portable Aircraft Condition Evaluator Recorder
PACER...... Postadoption Center for Education and Research
PACER...... Postoperational Analysis Critique and Exercise Report [*Military*] (CAAL)
PACER...... Prescriptive Analysis for Curriculum Evaluation [*Vocational guidance*]
PACER...... Priority for Allocation/Application of COMSEC Equipment Resources (MCD)
PACER...... Process Assembly Case Evaluator Routine [*Data processing*]
PACER...... Program of Active Cooling Effects and Requirements
PACER...... Program-Assisted Console Evaluation and Review [*Air Force*]
PACER...... Programmed Automatic Circuit Evaluator and Recorder
PACERS...... Pacing and Cardiac Electrophysiology Retrieval System [*Intermedics, Inc.*] [*Information service or system*] (IID)
PACES ...... Political Action Committee for Engineers and Scientists
PACE-S/C ... Preflight Acceptance Checkout Equipment for Spacecraft
PAC-EX..... Canadian National Packaging Exposition [*Packaging Association of Canada*] (TSPED)
PACEX...... Pacific Exchange [*System*] [*Military*] (AFM)
PACF........ Pacific
PACFDP ... Proceedings. Annual Conference on Restoration of Coastal Vegetation in Florida [*A publication*]
Pac Fisherman ... Pacific Fisherman [*A publication*]
PACFLAP ... Pacific Fleet Augmentation Plan [*Navy*] (NVT)
PACFLT.... Pacific Fleet
PACFLTCOM ... Pacific Fleet Command
PACFLTMOPHOTOU ... Pacific Fleet Mobile Photographic Unit (MUGU)
PACFORNET ... Pacific Coast Forest Research Information Network [*Later, WESTFORNET*] [*Forest Service*] (IID)
PACFW..... President's Advisory Committee for Women [*Terminated, 1980*] (EGAO)
PACGCS ... Prior Active Coast Guard Commissioned Service
PACGEEIA ... Pacific Area Ground Environment Electronic Installation Agency (CINC)
Pac Geol..... Pacific Geology [*A publication*]
PACGES ... Prior Active Coast Guard Enlisted Service
PACGO ..... President's Advisory Committee on Government Organization [*Abolished, 1961*]
PACGSR ... Pan American Center for Geographical Studies and Research [*See also CEPEIGE*] (EAIO)
PacH .... Pacific Historian [*A publication*]
PACH .... Performing Arts Center for Health [*New York University/ Bellevue Hospital, New York, NY*] [*Superseded by Center for Dance Medicine -CDM*]
PACH .... Public Administration Clearing House [*1931-1956*]
PACHACH ... Partizanim-Chayalim-Chalutzim (BJA)
PACHEDPEARL ... Pacific Headquarters, Pearl Harbor, Hawaii [*Navy*]
Pac Hist R ... Pacific Historical Review [*A publication*]
Pac Hist Rev ... Pacific Historical Review [*A publication*]
Pac Hist Rev ... Pacific History Review [*A publication*] (APTA)
Pac Hortic ... Pacific Horticulture [*A publication*]
PacHR ...... Pacific Historical Review [*A publication*] ·
PACIA .... Particle Counting Immunoassay
PACIF .... Pacific
Pacif Aff..... Pacific Affairs [*A publication*]
Pacif Bs N ... Pacific Business News [*A publication*]
Pacif Coa J Nurs ... Pacific Coast Journal of Nursing [*A publication*]
Pacif Defence Reporter ... Pacific Defence Reporter [*A publication*]
Pacif Hist R ... Pacific Historical Review [*A publication*]
Pacific Bus ... Pacific Business [*A publication*]
Pacific CLJ ... Pacific Coast Law Journal [*San Francisco*] [*A publication*] (DLA)
Pacific His R ... Pacific Historical Review [*A publication*]
Pacific Islands M ... Pacific Islands Monthly [*A publication*] (APTA)
Pacific Islands Yrbk ... Pacific Islands Year Book [*A publication*] (APTA)
Pacific J Math ... Pacific Journal of Mathematics [*A publication*]
Pacific Law Mag ... Pacific Law Magazine [*A publication*] (DLA)
Pacific L J ... Pacific Law Journal [*A publication*]

Pacific Med Surg ... Pacific Medicine and Surgery [*A publication*]
Pacific Northw Q ... Pacific Northwest Quarterly [*A publication*]
Pacific Perspect ... Pacific Perspective [*A publication*]
Pacific Rep ... Pacific Reporter [*A publication*] (DLA)
Pacific Sci.. Pacific Science [*A publication*]
Pacific Sociol R ... Pacific Sociological Review [*A publication*]
Pacif Imp ... Pacific Imperialism Notebook [*A publication*]
Pacif Insects ... Pacific Insects [*A publication*]
Pacif Is Mon ... Pacific Islands Monthly [*A publication*]
Pacif J Math ... Pacific Journal of Mathematics [*A publication*]
Pacif Rep.... Pacific Reporter [*A publication*] (DLA)
Pacif Sci..... Pacific Science [*A publication*]
Pacif Soc Rev ... Pacific Sociological Review [*A publication*]
PACIFY..... Parents and Alumni Committee Involved for Youth [*Brown University*]
PACIMS.... Passive Chemical Ionization Mass Spectrometry
Pac Insects ... Pacific Insects [*A publication*]
Pac Insects Mongr ... Pacific Insects Monograph [*A publication*]
Pac Insects Monogr ... Pacific Insects Monograph [*A publication*]
PACIR...... Practical Approach to Chemical Information Retrieval
PACIT...... Passive and Active Interface Test [*Electronic warfare*]
Pac J Math ... Pacific Journal of Mathematics [*A publication*]
Pack .... Packaging [*A publication*]
Packag Abstr ... Packaging Abstracts [*A publication*]
PACKAGE ... Planned Aids for Cross-Culture Knowledge, Action and Growth in Effectiveness
Package Dev ... Package Development [*A publication*]
Package Dev Syst ... Package Development and Systems [*A publication*]
Package Eng ... Package Engineering [*A publication*]
Package Engng ... Package Engineering [*A publication*]
Packag (India) ... Packaging (India) [*A publication*]
Packag Inst Spec Rep ... Packaging Institute. Special Report [*A publication*]
Packag Rev ... Packaging Review [*A publication*]
Packag Rev (S Afr) ... Packaging Review (South Africa) [*A publication*]
Packa Rev... Packaging Review [*A publication*]
Pack Encyc ... Packaging Encyclopedia [*A publication*]
Packer Process ... Packer, Processor [*A publication*]
Pack Print and Dyecutting ... Package Printing and Dyecutting [*A publication*]
PACL......... Clear [*Alaska*] [*ICAO location identifier*] (ICLI)
Pac Law Mag ... Pacific Law Magazine [*A publication*] (DLA)
Pac Law Reptr ... Pacific Law Reporter [*San Francisco*] [*A publication*] (DLA)
Pac Leg N .. Pacific Legal News [*A publication*] (DLA)
Pac LJ........ Pacific Law Journal [*A publication*]
PACM .... Passive Countermeasures (MSA)
PACM .... Pulse Amplitude Code Modulation [*Electronics*]
Pac Mar Fish Comm Annu Rep ... Pacific Marine Fisheries Commission. Annual Report [*A publication*]
Pac Mar Fish Comm Bull ... Pacific Marine Fisheries Commission. Bulletin [*A publication*]
Pac Mar Sci Rep ... Pacific Marine Science Report [*A publication*]
Pac Med Surg ... Pacific Medicine and Surgery [*A publication*]
PACMETNET ... Pacific Meteorological Network (AAG)
PACMI...... President's Advisory Committee on Management Improvement [*Terminated, 1973*]
Pac Miner Rev ... Pacific Minerals Review [*A publication*]
PACMISRAN ... Pacific Missile Range [*Later, WTR*] (MUGU)
PACMISRANFAC ... Pacific Missile Range Facility [*Obsolete*]
PACMISTESTCEN ... Pacific Missile Test Center [*Navy*]
Pac Mo....... Pacific Monthly [*Portland, Oregon*] [*A publication*]
PA Cmwlth ... Pennsylvania Commonwealth Court Reports [*A publication*] (DLA)
PACN .... Pacific Nuclear Systems, Inc. [*Federal Way, WA*] [*NASDAQ symbol*] (NQ)
P Ac Nat S ... Proceedings. Academy of Natural Sciences of Philadelphia [*A publication*]
PACNAVFACENGCOM ... Pacific Division Naval Facilities Engineering Command
PACNCO .. Personnel Assistance Center Noncommissioned Officer (INF)
PACNDF... AAZPA [*American Association of Zoological Parks and Aquariums*] Annual Proceedings [*A publication*]
Pac Neighbours ... Pacific Neighbours [*A publication*] (APTA)
PACNET ... OCLC Pacific Network [*Claremont, CA*] [*Information service or system*] (IID)
PACNET... Plymouth Audioconferencing Network [*Plymouth Polytechnic*] [*Plymouth, England*] [*Telecommunications*] (TSSD)
Pac Northw ... Pacific Northwest Quarterly [*A publication*]
Pac Northwest ... Pacific Northwesterner [*A publication*]
Pac Northwesterner ... Pacific Northwesterner [*A publication*]
Pac Northwest For Range Exp Stn Res Note PNW ... Research Note PNW [*A publication*]
Pac Northwest For Range Exp Stn Res Pap PNW ... Pacific Northwest Forest and Range Experiment Station. Research Paper PNW [*A publication*]
Pac Northwest Q ... Pacific Northwest Quarterly [*A publication*]
Pac Northwest Sea ... Pacific Northwest Sea [*A publication*]
PacNQ .... Pacific Northwest Quarterly [*A publication*]
Pac NWQ .. Pacific Northwest Quarterly [*A publication*]
PACNY...... Pawnbrokers' Association of the City of New York (EA)
PacO .... Pacific Ocean

PACO .... Pivot Ambulating Crutchless Orthosis [*Medicine*]
PACO .... Polaris Accelerated Change Operation [*Missiles*]
PACO .... Primary Administrative Contracting Officer [*Military*] (AFIT)
PACOB ...... Propulsion Auxiliary Control Box (AAG)
PA Co Ct .... Pennsylvania County Court Reports [*A publication*] (DLA)
PA Co Ct R ... Pennsylvania County Court Reports [*A publication*] (DLA)
PACOM .... Pacific Command [*Military*]
PACOMEP ... Pacific Command Emergency Procedures (CINC)
PACOMEW ... Pacific Command Electronic Warfare (CINC)
PACOMINTS ... Pacific Command Intelligence School (CINC)
PA Commw ... Pennsylvania Commonwealth Court Reports [*A publication*] (DLA)
PA Commw Ct ... Pennsylvania Commonwealth Court Reports [*A publication*] (DLA)
PA Com Pl ... Pennsylvania Common Pleas Reporter [*A publication*] (DLA)
PA Cons Stat ... Pennsylvania Consolidated Statutes [*A publication*] (DLA)
PA Cons Stat Ann ... Pennsylvania Consolidated Statutes, Annotated [*A publication*] (DLA)
PA Cons Stat Ann (Purdon) ... Pennsylvania Consolidated Statutes, Annotated (Purdon) [*A publication*] (DLA)
PACOPS ... Pacific Air Force Operations (MCD)
PACOR ...... Passive Correlation and Ranging
PACORE... Parabolic Corner Reflector
PACORNALOG ... Pacific Coast Coordinator of Naval Logistics
PA Corp .... Pennsylvania Corporation Reporter [*A publication*] (DLA)
PA Corp R ... Pennsylvania Corporation Reporter [*A publication*] (DLA)
PA Corp Rep ... Pennsylvania Corporation Reporter [*A publication*] (DLA)
PA County Ct ... Pennsylvania County Court Reports [*A publication*] (DLA)
PA CP ... Pennsylvania Common Pleas Reporter [*A publication*] (DLA)
PACP........ Propulsion Auxiliary Control Panel [*NASA*] (KSC)
PACPhA .... Proceedings. American Catholic Philosophical Association [*A publication*]
Pac Pharm ... Pacific Pharmacist [*A publication*]
Pac Philos Q ... Pacific Philosophical Quarterly [*A publication*]
Pac Phil Q ... Pacific Philosophical Quarterly [*A publication*]
Pac Phil Quart ... Pacific Philosophical Quarterly [*A publication*]
Pac Plast .... Pacific Plastics [*A publication*]
P Ac Poli S ... Proceedings. Academy of Political Science [*A publication*]
Pac Pulp Pap Ind ... Pacific Pulp and Paper Industry [*A publication*]
Pac Q .... Pacific Quarterly [*A publication*]
PACQI...... Probability of Acquisition [*Military*]
PACR........ Pacer Corp. [*Bothell, WA*] [*NASDAQ symbol*] (NQ)
Pac R........ Pacific Reporter [*Commonly cited as P*] [*A publication*] (DLA)
PA CR .... Pennsylvania County Court Reports [*A publication*] (DLA)
PACR........ Performance and Compatibility Requirements
PACR........ Perimeter Acquisition RADAR (MSA)
PACRAO... Pacific Association of Collegiate Registrars and Admission Officers
Pac Rep ...... Pacific Reporter [*Commonly cited as P*] [*A publication*] (DLA)
PACREP.... Port Activities Report [*Navy*]
Pac Repr .... Pacific Reporter [*A publication*] (DLA)
Pac Res ...... Pacific Research [*Formerly, Pacific Research and World Empire Telegram*] [*A publication*]
PACRESFLT ... Pacific Reserve Fleet
Pac Rockets ... Pacific Rockets [*A publication*]
Pac Rocket Soc Bull ... Pacific Rocket Society. Bulletin [*A publication*]
PACS........ Cape Sarichef Air Force Station [*Alaska*] [*ICAO location identifier*] (ICLI)
PACS........ Pacific Area Communications System (MCD)
PACS........ Particle Analysis Cameras for the Shuttle [*NASA*]
PACS....... Patient Accounting, Census, and Statistics
PACS....... Peace and Common Security (EA)
PACS........ Physics and Astronomy Classification Scheme
PACS........ Picture Archival and Communication System
PACS........ Plant Automation Communication System [*IBM Corp.*]
PACS........ Pointing and Attitude Control System [*Aerospace*] (NASA)
PACS........ Post-Attack Communication System
PACS........ Principal Appreciation Conversion Security [*Finance*]
PACS........ Process Automation & Computer Systems
PACS........ Program Authorization Control System (MCD)
Pa CSA ...... Pennsylvania Consolidated Statutes, Annotated [*A publication*] (DLA)
PACSAT.... Passive Communications Satellite
PACSCAT ... Pacific Ionospheric Scatter (CINC)
Pac Sci .... Pacific Science [*A publication*]
Pac Sci Congr Proc ... Pacific Science Congress. Proceedings [*A publication*]
Pac Sci Congr Rec Proc ... Pacific Science Congress. Record of Proceedings [*A publication*]
Pac Search ... Pacific Search [*United States*] [*A publication*]
Pac Sociol R ... Pacific Sociological Review [*A publication*]
Pac Soc R ... Pacific Sociological Review [*A publication*]
Pac Soc Rev ... Pacific Sociological Review [*A publication*]
PacSp........ Pacific Spectator [*A publication*]
PACT........ Pacific Area Co-Operative Telecommunications [*Australia*]
PACT........ Pan American Commission of Tampa (EA)
PACT........ Parents Assist Children and Teachers [*Australia*]
PACT........ Participating and Assertive Consumer Training [*Health education*]
PACT........ Paved Concrete Track [*Railways*]
PACT........ Pay Actual Computer Time
PACT........ Performing Arts Council for the Transvaal

PACT......... Performing Arts for Crisis Training [*In association name, PACT Training*] (EA)
PACT......... Perturbed-Anisotropic-Chain Theory [*Chemistry*]
PACT......... Philco Automatic Circuit Tester
PACT......... Plan of Action for Challenging Times (EA)
PACT......... Portable Aircraft Calibration Tracker [*NASA*]
PACT......... Powdered Activated Carbon Treatment [*For wastewater*] [*E. I. Du Pont De Nemours & Co., Inc.*]
PACT......... Precision Aircraft Control Technology (MCD)
PACT......... Prevention des Accidents, Controles Techniques, Hygiene, et Maladies Professionnelles [*A publication*]
PACT......... Private Agencies Collaborating Together (EA)
PACT......... Processing and Communications Terminal (MCD)
PACT......... Production Analysis Control Technique [*Navy*]
PACT......... Professional Association of Canadian Theatres
PACT......... Professional Association of Classroom Teachers of the Australian Capital Territory
PACT......... Program for Automatic Coding Techniques [*Data processing*]
PACT......... Programmable Asynchronous Clustered Teleprocessing
PACT......... Programmed Analysis Computer Transfer (KSC)
PACT......... Programmed Automatic Circuit Tester
PACT......... Project for the Advancement of Coding Techniques
PACT......... Provide Addict Care Today [*Later, NADAP*]
PACT......... Public Action Coalition on Toys [*Opposes sexist toys*]
PACT......... Publicly Accountable Classroom Teaching [*Australia*]
PACTA...... Packed Tape Assembly
PACTEL..... PA Computers & Telecommunications [*Information service or system*] (IID)
PacTel .... Pacific Telesis Group [*San Francisco, CA*] (TSSD)
PACTEX..... Pacific-Texas [*Pipeline*]
PACTIV .... Principos Activos [*Ministerio de Sanidad y Consumo*] [*Spain*] [*Information service or system*] (CRD)
PACTS ...... Parents, Administrators, Community, Teachers, and Students [*School-community groups*]
PACTS ...... Programmer Aptitude Competence Test System
PACUSA ... Pacific Air Command, United States Army
PACV........ Cordova [*Alaska*] [*ICAO location identifier*] (ICLI)
PACV......... Patrol Air-Cushion Vehicle [*Also called Hovercraft*] [*Navy*]
PACV......... Personnel Air-Cushion Vehicle
PACV......... Post-Accident Containment Venting [*Nuclear energy*] (NRCH)
PACVD...... Plasma-Assisted Chemical Vapor Deposition [*Coating technology*]
Pac View .... Pacific Viewpoint [*New Zealand*] [*A publication*]
Pac Viewp .. Pacific Viewpoint [*A publication*]
PACWID... Presidential Action Committee on Wood Industry Development [*Philippines*] (DS)
Pac Wine Spirit Rev ... Pacific Wine Spirit Review [*A publication*]
PACX........ Private Automatic Computer Exchange
PACZ......... Cape Romanzof Air Force Station [*Alaska*] [*ICAO location identifier*] (ICLI)
PAD .... Anthropology of Development Programme [*McGill University*] [*Canada*] [*Research center*] (RCD)
PAD .... Packet Assembler/Disassembler [*Switching technique*] [*Data processing*]
PAD .... Padder [*Capacitor*] [*Electronics*]
PAD .... Paderborn [*West Germany*] [*Airport symbol*] (OAG)
PAD .... Padova [*Italy*] [*Seismograph station code, US Geological Survey*] (SEIS)
PAD .... Padstow [*Town in England*]
PAD .... Palestine Arab Delegation (EA)
PAD .... Partido de Accion Democrata [*Democratic Action Party*] [*Spain*] [*Political party*] (PPW)
PAD .... Partido Accion Democratica [*Democratic Action Party*] [*El Salvador*] [*Political party*] (PPW)
PAD .... Passive Acoustic Detection [*Military*] (CAAL)
PAD .... Passive Air Defense [*British*]
PAD .... Payable after Death [*Insurance*] (ADA)
PAD .... Pedagogischer Austauschdienst [*Pedagogical Exchange Service*] [*German*]
PAD .... Performance Analysis and Design [*Nuclear energy*] (NRCH)
PAD .... Performing Arts Directory [*A publication*]
PAD .... Peripheral Arterial Disease [*Medicine*]
PAD .... Permissible Accumulated Dose
PAD .... Personal Articulation Device [*Facetious term for pre-word-processing equipment*]
PAD .... Personnel Administrator [*A publication*]
PAD .... Peters' United States District Court Reports, Admiralty Decisions [*A publication*] (DLA)
PAD .... Petroleum Administration for Defense [*Abolished, 1954*]
PAD .... Phenacetin [*Acetophenetidin*], Aspirin, Deoxyephedrine [*Pharmacology*]
PAD .... Pilotless Aircraft Division [*Navy*]
PAD .... Pitch Axis Definition
PAD .... Pitless Adapter Division of Water Systems Council (EA)
PAD .... Planning Action Directive [*Military*] (AFIT)
PAD .... Polar and Auroral Dynamics [*Meteorology*]
PAD .... Polyaperture Device [*NASA*] (KSC)
PAD .... Pontoon Assembly Depot (NVT)
PAD .... Pontoon Assembly Detachment
PAD .... Poor Acquisition Data (AAG)
PAD .... Port of Aerial Debarkation [*Air Force*]

PAD .... Positioning Arm Disk
PAD .... Post-Activation Diffusion (IEEE)
PAD .... Potential Area of Danger [Navigation]
PAD .... Power Amplifier Device [or Driver]
PAD .... Preadvisory Data (KSC)
PAD .... Precise Access Diagram
PAD .... Preferred Arrival Date (AFM)
PAD .... Preliminary Advisory Data (MCD)
PAD .... Presence and Amplitude Detector
PAD .... Preventive Aggressive Device [Restraint] [Medicine]
PAD .... Primary Afferent Depolarization [Electrophysiology]
PAD .... Product Assurance Directorate [Armament, Munitions, and
       Chemical Command] [Army]
PAD .... Professional Administrative Development [Medicine]
PAD .... Program Action Directive (AFM)
PAD .... Program Analysis for Documentation [Data processing]
PAD .... Program Approval Document [NASA] (KSC)
PAD .... Project Approval Document [NASA]
PAD .... Propellant Acquistion Device (NASA)
PAD .... Propellant-Actuated Device
PAD .... Provisional Acceptance Date (NATG)
PAD .... Public Affairs Division [Military] (AABC)
PAD .... Public Assistance Director [Federal disaster planning]
PAD .... Pueblo Army Depot [Colorado]
PAD .... Pulmonary Artery Diastolic [Pressure] [Cardiology]
PAD .... Pulsatile Assist Device [Cardiology]
PAD .... Pulse Averaging Discriminator
PAD .... Pulsed Amperometric Detection [Electroanalytical chemistry]
PADA .... Payroll Automation for Department of Agriculture
PADA .... Pharmacists Against Drug Abuse (EA)
PADA .... Prespin Automatic Dynamic Alignment
PADA .... Public Address Assembly [Ground Communications Facility,
       NASA]
PADA .... (Pyridylazo)dimethylaniline [Organic chemistry]
PADAC...... Professional Art Dealers Association of Canada
PADAF...... Pacific Command Air Defense Analysis Facility (CINC)
PADAL...... Pattern for Analysis, Decision, Action, and Learning
PADAR...... Passive Airborne Detection and Ranging
PADAR...... Program Approval Disposal and Redistribution
       [Army] (AABC)
PADAT...... Psychological Abstracts Direct Access Terminal
PADC .... Pennsylvania Avenue Development Corporation [Washington,
       DC] [Federal corporation]
PA D & C... Pennsylvania District and County Reports [A
       publication] (DLA)
PADC .... Philippine Aerospace Development Corporation (DS)
PADC .... Piccole Apostole della Carita [Ponte Lambro, Italy] (EAIO)
PA D & C 2d ... Pennsylvania District and County Reports, Second Series [A
       publication] (DLA)
PA D & C 3d ... Pennsylvania District and County Reports, Third Series [A
       publication] (DLA)
PA D & C Rep ... Pennsylvania District and County Reports [A
       publication] (DLA)
PADD .... Petroleum Administration for Defense District [Department of
       Energy]
PADD .... Planned Active Duty Date [Military]
PADD .... Portable Acoustic Doppler Detector
PADDS...... Procurement Automated Data Document System
       [Military] (RDA)
PADEL...... Pattern Description Language
PA Dent J .. Pennsylvania Dental Journal [A publication]
PA Dep Environ Resour Water Resour Bull ... Pennsylvania. Department of
       Environmental Resources. Water Resources Bulletin [A
       publication]
PA Dep For Waters Water Resour Bull ... Pennsylvania. Department of
       Forests and Waters. Water Resources Bulletin [A
       publication]
PA Dep L & I Dec ... Pennsylvania Department of Labor and Industry
       Decisions [A publication] (DLA)
PA Dep Rep ... Pennsylvania Department Reports [A publication] (DLA)
PA Dept Int Affairs Monthly Bull ... Pennsylvania. Department of Internal
       Affairs. Monthly Bulletin [A publication]
PADESM .. Parti des Desherites de Madagascar [Party of the Deprived of
       Madagascar]
PADF......... Driftwood Bay Air Force Station [Alaska] [ICAO location
       identifier] (ICLI)
PADF......... Pan American Development Foundation (EA)
PADGERC ... PACOM [Pacific Command] Air Defense Ground
       Environment Requirements Committee (CINC)
PADGT...... Past Assistant Deputy Grand Treasurer [Freemasonry]
PADI......... Parti pour l'Avancement de la Democratie en Ituri [Party for
       Democratic Advancement in Ituri] [Political party]
PADI......... Professional Association of Diving Instructors (EA)
Padiatr Pad ... Paediatrie und Paedologie [A publication]
Padin.......... Partido de Integracion Nacional [National Integration Party]
       [Peru] [Political party] (PPW)
PADIS .... Pan-African Documentation and Information System
       [Economic Commission for Africa] [United
       Nations] (IID)
PA Dist ...... Pennsylvania District Reporter [A publication] (DLA)

PA Dist & Co R ... Pennsylvania District and County Reports [A
       publication] (DLA)
PA Dist & Co Repts ... Pennsylvania District and County Reports [A
       publication] (DLA)
PA Dist & C Rep ... Pennsylvania District and County Reports [A
       publication] (DLA)
PA Dist R... Pennsylvania District Reporter [A publication] (DLA)
PA Dist Rep ... Pennsylvania District Reports [A publication] (DLA)
PADK .... Adak/Davis [Alaska] [ICAO location identifier] (ICLI)
PADL........ Dillingham [Alaska] [ICAO location identifier] (ICLI)
PADL........ Part and Assembly Description Language [Data processing]
PADL........ Pilotless Aircraft Development Laboratory [Navy]
PADLA ...... Programmable Asynchronous Dual Line Adapter
PADLOC... Passive Active Detection and Location (IEEE)
PADLOC... Passive Detection and Location of Countermeasures [Air Force]
PADMIS ... Patient Administration Information System [Army] (AABC)
PADO .... Proposed Advanced Development Objective [Army] (AABC)
PADOC ..... Pay Adjustment Document [Army]
PADP........ Physicians Against the Death Penalty (EA)
PADP........ Program of Aids for Disabled People [Australia]
PADP........ Proposal for Advanced Development Program
PA Dp Agr An Rp ... Pennsylvania. Department of Agriculture. Annual
       Report [A publication]
PADQ .... Kodiak [Alaska] [ICAO location identifier] (ICLI)
PADR .... Parts and Data Record System (MCD)
PA DR....... Pennsylvania District Reports [A publication] (DLA)
PADR .... Preferential Arrival/Departure Route [Aviation] (FAAC)
PADR .... Production Administration Deficiency Report [DoD]
PADRA..... Pass to Air Defense RADAR (FAAC)
PADRE..... Patient Automatic Data Recording Equipment (IEEE)
PADRE..... Portable Automatic Data Recording Equipment
PADRES ... Padres Asociados para Derechos, Religiosos, Educativos, y
       Sociales [Organization of Mexican-American priests]
PADS........ Passive-Active Data Simulation
PADS........ Passive Advanced Sonobuoy
PADS........ Performance Analysis and Design Synthesis [Computer
       program] [NASA]
PADS........ Peroxylaminedisulfonate [Organic chemistry]
PADS........ Personnel Automated Data System [TIMMS] [Navy]
PADS........ Plant Alarm and Display System [Nuclear energy] (NRCH)
PADS........ Position and Azimuth Determining System [Aviation]
PADS........ Precision Aerial Display System
PADS........ Professional Application Development System [Slate] [Data
       processing]
PADS........ Programmer Advanced Debugging System [Data processing]
PADS........ Publications. American Dialect Society [A publication]
PADS........ Sports Marketing, Inc. [Minneapolis, MN] [NASDAQ
       symbol] (NQ)
PADSD...... Proceedings. Analytical Division. Chemical Society [A
       publication]
PADT .... Postalloy Diffusion Transistor
PADU .... Dutch Harbour [Alaska] [ICAO location identifier] (ICLI)
PADUD ..... Program of Advanced Professional Development, University of
       Denver College of Law (DLA)
PAE .... Everett, WA [Location identifier] [FAA] (FAAL)
PAE .... Executive Air Charter [San Jose, CA] [FAA
       designator] (FAAC)
PAE .... Paea [Society Islands] [Seismograph station code, US
       Geological Survey] (SEIS)
Pae .... Paedagogik [A publication]
P AE........... Partes Aequales [Equal Parts] [Pharmacy]
PAE........... Passed Assistant Engineer [British]
PAE........... Peoria & Eastern Railway [Absorbed into Consolidated Rail
       Corp.] [AAR code]
PAE .... Phase Angle Error
PAE .... Phthalic Acid Esters [Organic chemistry]
PAE .... Physical Aptitude Examination (AFM)
PAE .... Pioneer Systems, Inc. [AMEX symbol] (SPSG)
PAE .... Port of Aerial Embarkation [Air Force]
PAE .... Post-Accident Environment [Nuclear energy] (IEEE)
PAE .... Preliminary Airworthiness Evaluations
PAE .... Preliminary Army Evaluation (MCD)
PAE .... Preventive Action Engineer (NASA)
PAE .... Problem Assessment Engineering (NASA)
PA & E....... Program Analysis and Evaluation
PAE .... Projets pour une Agriculture Ecologique [Ecological Agriculture
       Projects - EAP] [Sainte Anne De Bellevue, PQ] (EAIO)
PAE .... Public Affairs Event (NVT)
PAEAC...... Parliamentary Association for Euro-Arab Cooperation (EA)
PAEC........ Pakistan Army Education Corps [British military] (DMA)
PAEC........ Philippines Atomic Energy Commission
PAECI ...... Pan American Association of Educational Credit Institutions
       [Bogota, Colombia] (EAIO)
PAECT...... Pollution Abatement and Environmental Control Technology
       [Army] (AABC)
PAED .... Anchorage/Elmendorf Air Force Base [Alaska] [ICAO location
       identifier] (ICLI)
PAED .... Paediatric [or Paediatrics]
PAED .... Plans, Analysis, and Evaluation Division [Army] (MCD)
Paedag Hist ... Paedagogica Historica [A publication]
Paedagog Hist ... Paedagogica Historica [A publication]

Paedagogica Hist ... Paedagogica Historica [*A publication*]
Paedagog Run ... Paedagogische Rundschau [*A publication*]
Paediatr Fortbildungskurse Prax ... Paediatrische Fortbildungskurse fuer die Praxis [*A publication*]
Paediatr Grenzgeb ... Paediatrie und Grenzgebiete [*A publication*]
Paediatr Indones ... Paediatrica Indonesiana [*A publication*]
Paediatr Paedol ... Paediatrie und Paedologie [*A publication*]
Paediatr Paedol (Suppl) ... Paediatrie und Paedologie (Supplementum) [*A publication*]
Paediatr Univ Tokyo ... Paediatria Universitatis Tokyo [*A publication*]
PAEDP...... Pulmonary Artery End-Diastolic Pressure [*Cardiology*]
PAEH .... Cape Newenham Air Force Station [*Alaska*] [*ICAO location identifier*] (ICLI)
PAEI.......... Fairbanks/Eielson Air Force Base [*Alaska*] [*ICAO location identifier*] (ICLI)
PAEI.......... Periscope Azimuth Error Indicator
PAEI.......... Purchasing Agents of the Electronic Industry [*Rosedale, NY*] (EA)
PAEL........ Preliminary Allowance Equipage List [*Military*] (CAAL)
PA Elec Ass Eng Sect Transm Distrib ... Pennsylvania Electric Association. Engineering Section. Transmission and Distribution Committee. Minutes [*A publication*]
PA Electr Assoc Annu Rep ... Pennsylvania Electric Association. Annual Report [*A publication*]
PA Electr Assoc Eng Sect Minutes Meet ... Pennsylvania Electric Association. Engineering Section. Minutes of the Meeting [*A publication*]
PAEM........ Program Analysis and Evaluation Model (IEEE)
PAEN .... Kenai [*Alaska*] [*ICAO location identifier*] (ICLI)
PA Energy Ext Serv News ... Pennsylvania Energy Extension Service. News [*A publication*]
PAEP......... Preliminary Annual Engineering Plan [*Military*] (AFIT)
P AEQ........ Partes Aequales [*Equal Parts*] [*Pharmacy*]
PAES......... Phenyl(aminoethyl)sulfide [*Biochemistry*]
PAES......... Publications. Princeton University Archaeological Expeditions to Syria [*A publication*]
PAET......... Planetary Atmosphere Experimental [*or Experiments*] Test [*NASA*]
PAEWCC .. Peace Activists East and West Coordinating Committee (EA)
PAF........... Pacific Affairs [*A publication*]
PAF........... Pacific Air Forces
PAF........... Pacific American Airlines, Inc. [*Burbank, CA*] [*FAA designator*] (FAAC)
PAF........... Pacific Aqua Foods Ltd. [*Toronto Stock Exchange symbol*]
PAF........... Page Address Field
PAF........... Pan American Foundation [*Defunct*] (EA)
PAF........... Payload Attachment Fitting [*NASA*]
PAF........... Peak Annual Funding (NASA)
PA F........... Pennsylvania Folklife [*A publication*]
PA & F....... Percussion, Auscultation, and Fremitus [*Medicine*]
PAF........... Performing Arts Foundation (EA)
PAF........... Peripheral Address Field
PAF........... Personal Article Floater [*Air baggage insurance*]
PAF........... Philippine Air Force
PAF........... Platelet-Activating Factor [*Hematology*]
PAF........... Platelet Aggregation Factor [*Hematology*]
PAF........... Polaris Accelerated Flight [*Chamber*] [*Missiles*]
PAF........... Port-Aux-Francais [*Kerguelen Islands*] [*Seismograph station code, US Geological Survey*] [*Closed*] (SEIS)
PAF........... Portable Arc Furnace
PAF........... Portuguese Air Force
PAF........... Posterior Auditory Field
PAF........... Preadmission Assessment Form [*Health Care Financing Administration*]
PAF........... Prearranged Fire
PAF........... Preatomized Fuel [*Trademark*] [*Petroferm product*]
PAF........... Premature Anti-Fascist [*World War II designation used by Army Counterintelligence Department*]
PAF........... Price Analysis File (AFIT)
PAF........... Printed and Fired Circuit
PAF........... Pro-American Forum (EA)
PAF........... Production Assembly Facility [*Manufacturing*]
PAF........... Pseudo-Archaic Forgery
PAF........... Pseudoamniotic Fluid [*Gynecology*]
PAF........... Psychoanalytic Assistance Fund (EA)
PAF........... Public Agenda Foundation (EA)
PAF........... Public Art Fund (EA)
PAF........... Publication Authority Form (AAG)
PAF........... Pulmonary Arteriovenous Fistula [*Medicine*]
PAFA........ Fairbanks/International [*Alaska*] [*ICAO location identifier*] (ICLI)
PAFA........ Pan-American Festival Association (EA)
PAFA........ Pennsylvania Academy of the Fine Arts
PAFA........ Philippine Australian Friendship Association
PAFAM..... Performance and Failure Assessment Monitor (MCD)
PAFAMS... Pan American Federation of Associations of Medical Schools [*See also FEPAFEM*] [*Caracas, Venezuela*] (EAIO)
PA Farm Econ ... Pennsylvania Farm Economics [*A publication*]
PAFATU ... Pan-African Federation of Agricultural Trade Unions (EA)
PAFB......... Fairbanks/Wainwright Army Air Field [*Alaska*] [*ICAO location identifier*] (ICLI)

PAFB......... Patrick Air Force Base [*Florida*]
PAFC......... Paul Anka Fan Club (EA)
PAFC......... Phase-Locked Automatic Frequency Control [*Telecommunications*]
PAFC......... Phosphoric Acid Fuel Cell [*Energy source*]
PAFCS....... Prior Active Foreign Commissioned Service
PAFE......... Place Accepted for Enlistment
PAFEA....... Patologicheskaya Fiziologiya i Eksperimental'naya Terapiya [*A publication*]
PAFES....... Pan American Federation of Engineering Societies
PAFFWA... Parents and Friends Federation of Western Australia
PA Fid........ Pennsylvania Fiduciary Reporter [*A publication*] (DLA)
PA Fiduc..... Pennsylvania Fiduciary Reporter [*A publication*] (DLA)
PAFMECSA ... Pan African Freedom Movement for East, Central, and Southern Africa [*Superseded in 1963 by the liberation committee of the Organization of African Unity*] (PD)
PAFMI....... Philippine Association of Feed [*or Flour*] Millers, Inc. (DS)
PA Folklife ... Pennsylvania Folklife [*A publication*]
PA For ...... Pennsylvania Forests [*A publication*]
PAFP......... Photochemical Aerosol-Forming Potential of Polluted Air [*Environmental chemistry*]
PAFR......... Fort Richardson/Bryant Army Air Field [*Alaska*] [*ICAO location identifier*] (ICLI)
PA Fruit News ... Pennsylvania Fruit News [*A publication*]
PAFS......... Primary Air Force Specialty
PAFS .... Publications. American Folklore Society [*A publication*]
PAFSC....... Primary Air Force Specialty Code
PAFT......... Polish American Folk Theatre
PAFT......... Programme for Alternative Fluorocarbon Toxicity Testing [*British*]
PAFTT....... Program for Alternative Fluorocarbon Toxicity Testing [*Environmental science*]
PAFVA...... Polish Air Force Veterans Association (EA)
PAFW....... Farewell [*Alaska*] [*ICAO location identifier*] (ICLI)
PAFZDW .. Fundacao Zoobotanica do Rio Grande Do Sul. Publicacoes Avulsas [*A publication*]
PAG .... I Pagliacci [*Opera*] (DSUE)
PAG .... Packaging [*A publication*]
PAG .... Pagadian [*Philippines*] [*Airport symbol*] (OAG)
Pag .... Page's Three Early Assize Rolls, County of Northumberland [*Surtees Society Publications, Vol. 88*] [*A publication*] (ILCA)
PAG .... Paget Resources Ltd. [*Vancouver Stock Exchange symbol*]
Pag .... Pagoda
PAG .... Panagjuriste [*Bulgaria*] [*Geomagnetic observatory code*]
PAG .... Parts Acquisition Group
PAG .... Party for the Autonomy of Gibraltar [*Political party*] (PPW)
PAG .... Pentaacetylglucose [*Laundry bleach activator*]
PAG .... Periaqueductal Gray Matter [*Brain anatomy*]
PAG .... Polyacrylamide Gel [*Analytical chemistry*]
PAG .... Polyalkylene Glycol [*Organic chemistry*]
PAg .... Poultry-Related Antigens [*Immunology*]
PAG .... Poverty Advisory Group
PAG .... Precision Alignment Gyrocompass
PAG .... Precursor Active Galaxies
PAG .... Pregnancy-Associated alpha-Glycoprotein [*Gynecology*]
PAG .... Preliminary Analysis Group (NATG)
PAG .... Prince Albert's Guard [*British military*] (DMA)
PAG .... Professional Activities Group
PAG .... Professional Auto Group, Inc.
PAG .... Program Assessment Guide [*Department of Labor*] (OICC)
PAG .... Progress Analysis Group [*Navy*] (MCD)
PAG .... Project Advisory Group [*Army*]
PAG .... Property Advisory Group [*British*] (DCTA)
PAG .... Protective Action Guide [*Nuclear energy*]
PAG .... Protein Advisory Group [*United Nations*]
PAG .... Protein-Calorie Advisory Group [*United Nations*]
PAG .... Spring Garden College, Philadelphia, PA [*OCLC symbol*] (OCLC)
PAGA .... Galena [*Alaska*] [*ICAO location identifier*] (ICLI)
PAGA .... Pan American Grace Airways, Inc. [*Also, PANAGRA*]
PaGa .... Printing and Graphic Arts [*A publication*]
PAGAA ..... Pesquisa Agropecuaria Brasileira. Serie Agronomia [*A publication*]
PAGAN ..... Pattern Generation Language [*Data processing*]
PAGDC ..... Past Assistant Grand Director of Ceremonies [*Freemasonry*] (ROG)
pagdo.......... Pagadero [*Payable*] [*Business term*] [*Spanish*]
Page .... Page's Three Early Assize Rolls, County of Northumberland [*Surtees Society Publications, Vol. 88*] [*A publication*] (DLA)
PAGE........ PERT [*Program Evaluation and Review Technique*] Automated Graphical Extension (KSC)
PAGE........ Philatelic Association of Government Employees
PAGE........ Piston Arrestment Gas Entrapment System [*SPRINT launch cell*] [*Army*] (AABC)
PAGE........ Polyacrylamide Gel Electrophoresis [*Analytical chemistry*]
PAGE........ Preliminary Automated Ground Environment
Page Contr ... Page on Contracts [*A publication*] (DLA)
Page Div..... Page on Divorce [*A publication*] (DLA)
PAGEL...... Priced Aerospace Ground Equipment List

PA Gen As ... Pennsylvania General Assembly [*A publication*]
PA Geol...... Pennsylvania Geology [*A publication*]
PA Geol Surv Atlas ... Pennsylvania. Geological Survey. Atlas [*A publication*]
PA Geol Surv Gen Geol Rep ... Pennsylvania. Geological Survey. General
     Geology Report [*A publication*]
PA Geol Surv Inf Circ ... Pennsylvania. Geological Survey. Information
     Circular [*A publication*]
PA Geol Surv Miner Resour Rep ... Pennsylvania. Geological Survey. Mineral
     Resource Report [*A publication*]
PA Geol Surv Prog Rep ... Pennsylvania. Geological Survey. Progress Report
     [*A publication*]
PA Geol Surv Water Resour Rep ... Pennsylvania. Geological Survey. Water
     Resource Report [*A publication*]
PAGEOS... Passive Geodetic Earth-Orbiting Satellite [*NASA*]
PA-Ger...... Pennsylvania-German [*A publication*]
PA Ger Folk Soc Yr Bk ... Pennsylvania German Folklore Society. Year Book
     [*A publication*]
PAGES...... Program Affinity Grouping and Evaluation System
PAGH........ Pacific Agricultural Holdings, Inc. [*NASDAQ symbol*]   (NQ)
PAGI........ Photographic and Gelatin Industries [*Japan*]
PAGICEP ... Petroleum and Gas Industry Communications Emergency Plan
     [*FCC*]
Pag Jud Puz ... Paget's Judicial Puzzles [*A publication*]   (DLA)
PAGK .... Gulkana [*Alaska*] [*ICAO location identifier*]   (ICLI)
PAGL........ Pulsed Argon Gas LASER
PAGMK .... Primary African Green Monkey Kidney [*Cells*]
PAGN........ Pagnall [*England*]
PAGO........ Pacific Gold Corp. [*NASDAQ symbol*]   (NQ)
PAGR .... Professional Agricultural Management, Inc. [*Firebaugh, CA*]
     [*NASDAQ symbol*]   (NQ)
PAGS........ Parti de l'Avant-Garde Socialiste [*Socialist Vanguard Party*]
     [*Algeria*] [*Political party*]   (PD)
PA G S ...... Pennsylvania. Geological Survey [*A publication*]
PAGS........ Polish-American Guardian Society   (EA)
PAGS........ Proceedings. Australian Goethe Society [*A publication*]
PAGTU .... Pan-American Ground Training Unit
PAGVA...... Progres Agricole et Viticole [*A publication*]
PAGYB...... Pennsylvania Geology [*A publication*]
PAGYDY... Pediatric and Adolescent Gynecology [*A publication*]
PAH .... Paducah [*Kentucky*] [*Airport symbol*]   (OAG)
PAH.......... Pahoa [*Hawaii*] [*Seismograph station code, US Geological
     Survey*] [*Closed*]   (SEIS)
PAH.......... Panorama Air Tour, Inc. [*Honolulu, HI*] [*FAA
     designator*]   (FAAC)
PAH.......... Para-Aminohippuric [*Biochemistry*]
PAH.......... Parts Application Handbook
PAH.......... Pathtechnics Ltd. [*Vancouver Stock Exchange symbol*]
PAH.......... Payload Accommodations Handbook [*NASA*]   (NASA)
PAH.......... Phase Adjusting Hub
PAH.......... Phenylalanine Hydroxylase [*An enzyme*]
PAH.......... Polycyclic [*or Polynuclear*] Aromatic Hydrocarbon [*Organic
     chemistry*]
PAH.......... Princess Alexandra Hospital [*Australia*]
PAH.......... Pulmonary Artery Hypertension [*Medicine*]
PAH.......... Push and Hold [*Push button*]
PAHA........ Para-Aminohippuric Acid
PAHA........ Polish American Historical Association   (EA)
Pahasapa Q ... Pahasapa Quarterly [*A publication*]
PAHBAH .. Para-Hydroxybenzoic Acid Hydrazide [*Organic chemistry*]
PAHC........ Pan American Highway Congresses   (EA)
PAHC........ Pioneer American Holding Corporation [*Carbondale, PA*]
     [*NASDAQ symbol*]   (NQ)
PAHC........ Pontifical Association of the Holy Childhood   (EA)
PAHEA...... Pharmaceutica Acta Helvetiae [*A publication*]
PAHEF...... Pan American Health and Education Foundation   (EA)
PAHEL...... Pay Records and Health Records
PAHEO .... Particle Accelerators in High Earth Orbit [*Proposed*]
PAHF .... Pan American Hockey Federation [*Winnipeg, MB*]   (EAIO)
PA His .... Pennsylvania History [*A publication*]
PA Hist...... Pennsylvania History [*A publication*]
PAHL .... Pressure Alarm, High-Limit [*Nuclear energy*]   (NRCH)
Pahlavi Med J ... Pahlavi Medical Journal [*A publication*]
PAHO........ Homer [*Alaska*] [*ICAO location identifier*]   (ICLI)
PAHO........ Pan American Health Organization   (EA)
PAHO........ Paraho Development Corp. [*NASDAQ symbol*]   (NQ)
PAHO/B .... Bulletin. Pan American Health Organization [*A publication*]
PAHR .... Post-Accident Heat Removal [*Nuclear energy*]
PAHS .... Passive Annual Heat Storage [*Housing technology*]
PAI........... Pacific Aerospace Index [*A publication*]
PAI........... Pacific American Income Shares, Inc. [*NYSE symbol*]   (SPSG)
PAI........... Pacific American Institute   (EA)
PAI........... Pacoima, CA [*Location identifier*] [*FAA*]   (FAAL)
Pai............. Paige's New York Chancery Reports [*A publication*]   (DLA)
Pai............. Paine's United States Circuit Court Reports [*A
     publication*]   (DLA)
PAI........... Pair Attraction Inventory [*Premarital, marital, and family
     counseling test*] [*Psychology*]
PAI........... Parti Africain de l'Independance [*African Independence Party*]
     [*Senegal*] [*Political party*]   (PPW)
PAI........... Parts Application Information [*Manufacturing*]
PAI........... Passive-Aggressive Index [*Psychology*]

PAI........... Percent Adherence Index
PAI........... Personal Accident Insurance
PAI........... Personal Adjustment Inventory [*Psychology*]
PAI........... Personnel Accreditation Institute   (EA)
PAI........... Phosphate Adsorption Index [*Analytical chemistry*]
PAI........... Photographic Administrators, Incorporated   (EA)
PAI........... Piedmont Aviation, Incorporated [*Air carrier designation
     symbol*]
PAI........... Pirchei Agudath Israel   (EA)
PA & I .... Planning, Analysis, and Integration
PAI........... Plasminogen-Activator Inhibitor [*Biochemistry*]
PAI........... Plunger Actuated Indexer
PAI........... Poale Agudath Israel of America   (EA)
PAI........... Polish Assistance, Incorporated   (EA)
PAI........... Polyamide-Imide [*Organic chemistry*]
PAI........... Prearrival Inspection
PAI........... Precise Angle Indicator
PAI........... Primary Aerospace Vehicle [*or Aircraft*] Inventory
PAI........... Processed Apples Institute   (EA)
PAI........... Production Adjustment Index [*Word processing*]
PAI........... Professional Athletes International [*Later, NFLPA*]   (EA)
PAI........... Programmer Appraisal Instrument [*Data processing*]   (IEEE)
PAI........... Property Agents International
PAI........... Public Affairs Information, Inc. [*Sacramento, CA*] [*Database
     producer*] [*Information service or system*]
PAI........... Public Affairs Institute [*Defunct*]   (EA)
PAI........... Public Assistance Information [*A publication*]
PAIA........ Pan American Implant Association   (EA)
PAIAA ...... Proceedings. National Academy of Sciences (India). Section A
     [*A publication*]
PAIB .... Polish-American Information Bureau [*Later, PATIB*]   (EA)
PAIC .... Persia and Iraq Command [*World War II*]
PAIC .... Public Address Intercom System   (NRCH)
PAICC ...... Professional Association of the Interstate Commerce
     Commission
Pai Ch .... Paige's New York Chancery Reports [*A publication*]   (DLA)
PAID......... Pan African Institute for Development   (EAIO)
PAID......... Personnel and Accounting Integrated Data [*System*] [*Veterans
     Administration*]
PAID......... Price and Item Display [*British*]
Paid Dues... Paid My Dues [*A publication*]
Paideia Studies in Nature of Modern Math ... Paideia Studies in the Nature of
     Modern Mathematics [*A publication*]
PAIDOL.... Paidologist [*A publication*]
PAIDS .... Pediatric Acquired Immune Deficiency Syndrome [*Medicine*]
PAIF .... Persia and Iraq Force [*World War II*]
PAIFORCE ... Persia and Iraq Force [*World War II*]   (DMA)
PAIg.......... Platelet-Associated Immunoglobulin [*Hematology*]
PAIGC....... Partido Africano da Independencia da Guine e do Cabo Verde
     [*African Party for the Independence of Guinea and Cape
     Verde*] [*Political party*]   (PPW)
Paige .... Paige's New York Chancery Reports [*A publication*]   (DLA)
Paige Ch..... Paige's New York Chancery Reports [*1828-45*] [*A
     publication*]   (DLA)
Paige Ch Rep ... Paige's New York Chancery Reports [*A publication*]   (DLA)
Paige's Ch ... Paige's New York Chancery Reports [*A publication*]   (DLA)
PAIgG........ Platelet-Associated Immunoglobulin G [*Hematology*]
PAIGH ...... Pan American Institute of Geography and History [*Mexico*]
     [*Research center*]   (IRC)
PAIGH/H ... Revista de Historia de America. Instituto Panamericano de
     Geografia e Historia. Comision de Historia [*A publication*]
PAIGS....... Performing Arts Information Guide Series [*A publication*]
PAIL......... Iliamna [*Alaska*] [*ICAO location identifier*]   (ICLI)
PAIL......... Post-Attack Intercontinental Link
PAILS....... Projectile Airburst and Impact Location System
PAILS....... Publication Automated Information Locator System [*Army*]
PAIM........ Indian Mountain Air Force Station [*Alaska*] [*ICAO location
     identifier*]   (ICLI)
PAIM........ Parti Africain pour l'Independance des Masses [*African Party
     for the Independence of the Masses*] [*Senegal*] [*Political
     party*]   (PPW)
PAIM........ Primary Air Inlet Muffler   (MCD)
PAIMEG ... Pan American Institute of Mining, Engineering, and Geology
     [*Defunct*]
PAIN .... Pain Suppression Labs, Inc. [*Elmwood Park, NJ*] [*NASDAQ
     symbol*]   (NQ)
Paine .... Paine's United States Circuit Court Reports [*A
     publication*]   (DLA)
Paine CC.... Paine's United States Circuit Court Reports [*A
     publication*]   (DLA)
Paine CCR ... Paine's United States Circuit Court Reports [*A
     publication*]   (DLA)
Paine Cir Ct R ... Paine's United States Circuit Court Reports [*A
     publication*]   (DLA)
Paine & D Pr ... Paine and Duer's Practice [*A publication*]   (DLA)
Paine Elect ... Paine on Elections [*A publication*]   (DLA)
Paine Webb ... Paine, Webber, Jackson & Curtis, Inc. Research Notes [*A
     publication*]
Pain Fr .... Pain Francais [*A publication*]
Pain Suppl ... Pain. Supplement [*A publication*]
Paint.......... Paintbrush [*A publication*]

PAINT...... Painting (ROG)

PAINT...... Post-Attack Intelligence

PAINT...... Primera Asociacion Internacional de Noticieros y Television [*First International Newsreel and TV Association*]

Paint Colour J Master Painter Aust ... Paint Colour; Journal of the Master Painter of Australia [*A publication*]

Paint Colour Rec ... Paint and Colour Record [*A publication*]

Paint Decor ... Painting and Decorating [*A publication*]

Painters J... Painters and Allied Trades Journal [*A publication*]

Paint Ind .... Paint Industry [*A publication*]

Paint Ind Mag ... Paint Industry Magazine [*A publication*]

Painting Technol (Tokyo) ... Painting Technology (Tokyo) [*A publication*]

Paint J........ Paint Journal [*A publication*]

Paint J........ Paint Journal of Australia and New Zealand [*A publication*] (APTA)

Paint J Aust NZ ... Paint Journal of Australia and New Zealand [*A publication*]

Paint Manuf ... Paint Manufacture [*England*] [*A publication*]

Paint Oil Chem Rev ... Paint Oil and Chemical Review [*A publication*]

Paint Oil Colour J ... Paint Oil and Colour Journal [*A publication*]

Paint Res.... Paint and Resin [*A publication*]

Paints Pak ... Paints in Pakistan [*A publication*]

Paint Technol ... Paint Technology [*A publication*]

Paint Varn Prod ... Paint and Varnish Production [*A publication*]

Paint Varn Prod Manager ... Paint and Varnish Production Manager [*A publication*]

PAIP......... Preverbal Assessment-Intervention Profile [*Test*]

PAIP......... Production Acceleration Insurance Program

PAIP......... Public Affairs and Information Program [*Atomic Industrial Forum*] (NRCH)

PAIR......... Performance Assessment in Reading [*Educational test*]

PAIR......... Performance and Improved Reliability

PAIR......... Performance and Integration Retrofit

PAIR......... Precision Approach Interferometer RADAR (MCD)

PAIR......... Preliminary Assessment Information Rule [*Environmental Protection Agency*]

PAIR......... Presidential Airways, Inc. [*Herndon, VA*] [*NASDAQ symbol*] (NQ)

PAIR......... Procurement Automated Integrated Requirements (MCD)

PAIR......... Psychological Audit for Interpersonal Relations [*Psychology*]

PAIRC...... Polish American Immigration and Relief Committee (EA)

PAIRS...... Product Assurance Information Retrieval System [*Boeing*]

PAIRS...... Program for the Analysis of Infrared Spectra [*Computer program*] [*Analytical chemistry*]

PAIS......... Padre Island National Seashore [*National Park Service designation*]

PAIS......... Partido Autentico Institucional Salvadoreno [*Salvadoran Authentic Institutional Party*] [*Political party*] (PPW)

PAIS......... Personnel Authentication Identification System (MCD)

PAIS......... Petroleum Abstracts Information Services [*University of Tulsa*] [*Oklahoma*] [*Information service or system*] (IID)

PAIS......... Project Analysis Information System [*Agency for International Development*]

PAIS......... Prototype Advanced Indicator System (MCD)

PAIS......... Psychological Abstracts Information Services [*American Psychological Association*]

PAIS......... Psychosocial Adjustment to Illness Scale [*Personality development test*] [*Psychology*]

PAIS......... Public Affairs Information Service [*Bibliographic database*] [*A publication*]

PAISER..... Proceedings. Annual Conference and International Symposium of the North American Lake Management Society [*A publication*]

PAIT......... Program for Advancement of Industrial Technology [*Canada*]

PAIX........ Pacific Alaska Airlines [*Air carrier designation symbol*]

PA J.......... American Academy of Physicians' Assistants. Journal [*A publication*]

PAJ........... Kansas City, MO [*Location identifier*] [*FAA*] (FAAL)

PA J......... PA Journal [*Formerly, Physician's Associate*] [*A publication*]

PAJ........... Pan-African Journal [*A publication*]

PAJ......... Performing Arts Journal [*A publication*]

PAJA........ Parachute Jumping Activity (FAAC)

PAJAR...... Parti Rakyat Jati Sarawak [*Sarawak Native People's Party*] [*Malaysia*] [*Political party*] (PPW)

PAJHS...... Publication. American Jewish Historical Society [*A publication*]

PAJN........ Juneau [*Alaska*] [*ICAO location identifier*] (ICLI)

PAK......... Hanapepe, HI [*Location identifier*] [*FAA*] (FAAL)

PAK .... Pacific Alaska Airlines [*Fairbanks, AK*] [*FAA designator*] (FAAC)

PAK .... Pakistan [*ANSI three-letter standard code*] (CNC)

PAK .... Panzer Abwehr Kanone [*Cannon Against Armor*] [*German antitank gun*]

PAK .... Performance Advantage Kit [*Personal computers*]

PAK .... Polycyclic Aromatic Ketone [*Organic chemistry*]

PAK .... Power Amplifier Klystron

PAK .... Program Attention Key [*Data processing*] (BUR)

Pak Agric ... Pakistan Agriculture [*A publication*]

Pak Assoc Adv Sci Annu Rep ... Pakistan Association for the Advancement of Science. Annual Report [*A publication*]

PAKBA...... Promyshlennost Armenii [*A publication*]

Pak Bar J ... Pakistan Bar Journal [*A publication*] (DLA)

Pak Cottons ... Pakistan Cottons [*A publication*]

Pak Crim LJ ... Pakistan Criminal Law Journal [*A publication*] (DLA)

Pak CSIR Bull Monogr ... Pakistan Council of Scientific and Industrial Research. Bulletin. Monograph [*A publication*]

Pak Dent Rev ... Pakistan Dental Review [*A publication*]

Pak Dev R ... Pakistan Development Review [*A publication*]

Pak Dev Rev ... Pakistan Development Review [*A publication*]

Pak DR ...... Pakistan Development Review [*A publication*]

Pak Eng ...... Pakistan Engineer [*A publication*]

PAKEX...... International Packaging Exhibition [*Great Britain*] (ITD)

Pak Geogr R ... Pakistan Geographical Review [*A publication*]

Pak Geogr Rev ... Pakistan Geographical Review [*A publication*]

Pak Geol Surv Inf Release ... Pakistan Geological Survey. Information Release [*A publication*]

Pak Geol Surv Rec ... Pakistan Geological Survey. Records [*A publication*]

PAKISTAN ... Nation in Asia, the name of which is said to be coined from Punjab (P), Afghan border states (A), Kashmir (K), Sind (S), and Baluchistan (TAN). Name also means "land of the pure" in Hindustani.

Pakistan Develop R ... Pakistan Development Review [*A publication*]

Pakistan Econ and Social R ... Pakistan Economic and Social Review [*A publication*]

Pakistan Eng ... Pakistan Engineer [*A publication*]

Pakistan J Biol Agr Sci ... Pakistan Journal of Biological and Agricultural Sciences [*A publication*]

Pakistan J For ... Pakistan Journal of Forestry [*A publication*]

Pakistan J Med Res ... Pakistan Journal of Medical Research [*A publication*]

Pakistan J Sci ... Pakistan Journal of Science [*A publication*]

Pakistan J Sci Ind Res ... Pakistan Journal of Scientific and Industrial Research [*A publication*]

Pakistan J Sci Res ... Pakistan Journal of Scientific Research [*A publication*]

Pakistan J Soil Sci ... Pakistan Journal of Soil Sciences [*A publication*]

Pakistan Lib Bull ... Pakistan Library Bulletin [*A publication*]

Pakistan Lib R ... Pakistan Library Review [*A publication*]

Pakistan Phil J ... Pakistan Philosophical Journal [*A publication*]

Pakist J Agric Sci ... Pakistan Journal of Agricultural Sciences [*A publication*]

Pakist J Bot ... Pakistan Journal of Botany [*A publication*]

Pakist J Scient Res ... Pakistan Journal of Scientific Research [*A publication*]

Pakist J Zool ... Pakistan Journal of Zoology [*A publication*]

Pakistn Pl .. Sixth Five-Year Plan, 1983-88 (Pakistan) [*A publication*]

Pak J Agric Sci ... Pakistan Journal of Agricultural Sciences [*A publication*]

Pak J Agri Res ... Pakistan Journal of Agricultural Research [*A publication*]

Pak J Biochem ... Pakistan Journal of Biochemistry [*A publication*]

Pak J Biol Agric Sci ... Pakistan Journal of Biological and Agricultural Sciences [*A publication*]

Pak J Bot ... Pakistan Journal of Botany [*A publication*]

Pak J Fam Plann ... Pakistan Journal of Family Planning [*A publication*]

Pak J For ... Pakistan Journal of Forestry [*A publication*]

Pak J Geriatr ... Pakistan Journal of Geriatrics [*A publication*]

Pak J Health ... Pakistan Journal of Health [*A publication*]

Pak J Med Res ... Pakistan Journal of Medical Research [*A publication*]

Pak J Nematol ... Pakistan Journal of Nematology [*A publication*]

Pak J Pharm ... Pakistan Journal of Pharmacy [*A publication*]

Pak J Pharmacol ... Pakistan Journal of Pharmacology [*A publication*]

Pak J Pharm Sci ... Pakistan Journal of Pharmaceutical Sciences [*A publication*]

Pak J Sci.... Pakistan Journal of Science [*A publication*]

Pak J Sci Ind Res ... Pakistan Journal of Scientific and Industrial Research [*A publication*]

Pak J Sci and Ind Res ... Pakistan Journal of Scientific and Industrial Research [*A publication*]

Pak J Sci Res ... Pakistan Journal of Scientific Research [*A publication*]

Pak J Surg Gynaecol Obstet ... Pakistan Journal of Surgery, Gynaecology, and Obstetrics [*A publication*]

Pak J Surg Gyn Obst ... Pakistan Journal of Surgery, Gynaecology, and Obstetrics [*A publication*]

Pak J Zool ... Pakistan Journal of Zoology [*A publication*]

Pak Libr Ass Q J ... Pakistan Library Association. Quarterly Journal [*A publication*]

Pak Libr Rev ... Pakistan Library Review [*A publication*]

Pak LR...... Pakistan Law Reports [*India*] [*A publication*] (DLA)

Pak L Rev .. Pakistan Law Review [*A publication*] (DLA)

Pak Med For ... Pakistan Medical Forum [*A publication*]

Pak Med Forum ... Pakistan Medical Forum [*A publication*]

Pak Med J ... Pakistan Medical Journal [*A publication*]

Pak Med Rev ... Pakistan Medical Review [*A publication*]

PAKN .... King Salmon [*Alaska*] [*ICAO location identifier*] (ICLI)

Pak Nurs Health Rev ... Pakistan Nursing and Health Review [*A publication*]

Pak Philos Congr Proc ... Pakistan Philosophical Congress. Proceedings [*A publication*]

PakQ......... Pakistan Quarterly [*A publication*]

PakR......... Pakistan Review [*A publication*]

Pak Rev Agric ... Pakistan Review of Agriculture [*A publication*]

PAKS........ Packaging Systems Corp. [*NASDAQ symbol*] (NQ)

Pak Sci Conf Proc ... Pakistan Science Conference. Proceedings [*A publication*]

Pak Sup Ct Q ... Pakistan Supreme Court Law Quarterly [*Lahore, Pakistan*] [*A publication*] (DLA)

PAKT........ Ketchikan [*Alaska*] [*ICAO location identifier*] (ICLI)

PAKT........ Petroleum Acreage Corp. of Texas [*NASDAQ symbol*] (NQ)

Pak Text J ... Pakistan Textile Journal [*A publication*]

Pak Vet J ... Pakistan Veterinary Journal [*A publication*]
PAL............ Allegheny County Law Library, Pittsburgh, PA [*OCLC symbol*] (OCLC)
PAL............ Pacific Aeronautical Library
PAL............ Pacific Air Lines
pal .... Pahlavi [*MARC language code*] [*Library of Congress*] (LCCP)
PAL............ Paired-Associates Learning [*Task*] [*Psychology*]
PAL............ Palace
Pal............. Palamedes [*of Gorgias*] [*Classical studies*] (OCD)
PAL............ Palatine [*or Palatinate*] [*Genealogy*]
PAL............ Paleography (ROG)
PAL............ Paleontology
PAL............ Paleozoic [*Period, era, or system*] [*Geology*]
PAL............ Palestine
PAL............ Palisades [*New York*] [*Seismograph station code, US Geological Survey*] (SEIS)
PAL............ Pallor (KSC)
Pal............. Palmer's Assizes at Cambridge [*England*] [*A publication*] (DLA)
Pal............. Palmer's English King's Bench Reports [*1619-29*] [*A publication*] (DLA)
Pal............. Palmer's Reports [*53-60 Vermont*] [*A publication*] (DLA)
PAL............ Paloma Petroleum Ltd. [*Toronto Stock Exchange symbol*]
PAL............ Paradox Application Language [*ANSA*] [*Data processing*]
PAL............ Parcel Air Lift [*US Postal Service*]
PAL............ Parser Assembly Language [*Data processing*]
PAL............ Parts and Assemblies Locator [*ADP/CES*]
PAL............ Parts Authorization List (KSC)
PAL............ Patent Associated Literature
PAL............ Pathology Laboratory [*Test*]
PAL............ Pectin Acid Lyase [*An enzyme*]
PAL............ Pedagogic Algorithmic Language [*Data processing*]
PAL............ People Against Chlordane (EA)
PAL............ People-Animals-Love (EA)
PAL............ Perceptual Alternatives Laboratory [*University of Louisville*] [*Research center*] (RCD)
PAL............ Performance Assessment Logic
PAL............ Peripheral Access Lattices
PAL............ Permanent Artificial Lighting (IEEE)
PAL............ Permissive Action Link [*Army*]
PAL............ Permissive Arming Line [*or Link*]
PAL............ Peroxide Assisted Leach [*Ore processing*]
PAL............ Personal Assets Line
PAL............ Personnel Accounting Level [*Air Force*] (AFM)
PAL............ Personnel Airlock [*Nuclear energy*] (NRCH)
PAL............ Personnel Augmentation List [*Military*]
PAL............ Phase Alternation Line [*West German color television system*]
PAL............ Phenylalanine Ammonia-Lyase [*An enzyme*]
PAL............ Philippine Air Lines
PAL............ Pipe Analysis Log [*Gas well*]
PAL............ Police Athletic League
PAL............ Poly-DL-alanine Poly-L-lysine [*Biochemical analysis*]
PAL............ Portable Ambush Light [*Military*] [*Australia*] (RDA)
PAL............ Posterior Axillary Line [*Medicine*]
PAL............ Power Assist Lathe
PAL......... Pre-Academic Learning Inventory [*Child development test*]
PAL......... Preapproved Loan [*Business term*]
PAL............ Precision Artwork Language [*Data processing*]
PAL............ Prescribed Action Link [*DoD*]
PAL............ Present Atmospheric Level
PAL............ Price and Availability List (CINC)
PAL............ Princeton Accelerator Laboratory
PAL............ Princeton Air Link
PAL............ Prisoner-at-Large
PAL............ Pro Alesia [*A publication*]
PAL............ Problem Action Log (AAG)
PAL............ Process Assembler Language
PALY......... Process Audit List (MCD)
PAL............ Production and Application of Light (MCD)
PAL............ Profile Automobile League (EA)
PAL............ Programmable Algorithm Machine Assembly Language [*Data processing*]
PAL............ Programmable Array Logic [*Data processing*] (IEEE)
PAL............ Programmed Application Library [*IBM Corp.*]
PAL............ Programmed Audit Library
PAL............ Programmer Assistance and Liaison [*Data processing*] (NRCH)
PAL............ Progressive Alliance of Liberia [*Political party*] (PPW)
PAL............ Prototype Application Loop [*Nuclear energy*] (NRCH)
PAL............ Psycho-Acoustic Laboratory [*Harvard University*] (MCD)
PAL............ Public Archives of Canada Library [*UTLAS symbol*]
PAL............ Publications Allowance List [*Military*] (CAAL)
PAL............ Pulsed Argon LASER
PAL............ Push and Latch [*Push button*]
PA L......... University of Pennsylvania. Law Review [*A publication*]
PALA......... N-(Phosphoacetyl)-L-aspartate [*Biochemistry*]
Pala............ Partido Laborista [*Labor Party*] [*Panama*] [*Political party*] (PPW)
PALA......... Partition Affinity Ligand Assay [*Analytical microbiology*]
PALA......... Passenger Acceptance and Load Accumulation [*Aviation*]
PALA......... Phosphonoacetyl-L-Aspartate [*Biochemistry*]
PALA......... Polish American Librarians Association (EA)

PALA......... Prison Atheist League of America (EA)
Palabra Hom ... Palabra y el Hombre [*A publication*]
PALAEOB ... Palaeobotany
Palaeoecol Afr Surround Isl ... Palaeoecology of Africa and the Surrounding Islands [*A publication*]
PALAEOG ... Palaeography
Palaeogeogr Palaeoclimatol Palaeoecol ... Palaeogeography, Palaeoclimatology, Palaeoecology [*A publication*]
Palaeogeo P ... Palaeogeography, Palaeoclimatology, Palaeoecology [*A publication*]
Palaeont ..... Palaeontographica [*A publication*]
PALAEONT ... Palaeontology
Palaeont Abh (Dames u Kayser) ... Palaeontologische Abhandlungen (Dames und Kayser) [*A publication*]
Palaeontogr Abt A ... Palaeontographica. Abteilung A. Palaeozoologie-Stratigraphie [*A publication*]
Palaeontogr Abt A Palaeozool-Stratigr ... Palaeontographica. Abteilung A. Palaeozoologie-Stratigraphie [*A publication*]
Palaeontogr Abt B ... Palaeontographica. Abteilung B. Palaeophytologie [*A publication*]
Palaeontogr Abt B Palaeophytol ... Palaeontographica. Abteilung B. Palaeophytologie [*A publication*]
Palaeontogr Am ... Palaeontographica Americana [*A publication*]
Palaeontogr Can ... Palaeontographica Canadiana [*A publication*]
Palaeontogr Ital ... Palaeontographia Italia [*A publication*]
Palaeontogr Soc Monogr ... Palaeontographical Society. Monographs [*A publication*]
Palaeontogr Soc Monogr (Lond) ... Palaeontographical Society. Monographs (London) [*A publication*]
Palaeontol Afr ... Palaeontologia Africana [*A publication*]
Palaeontol Jugosl ... Palaeontologia Jugoslavica [*A publication*]
Palaeontol Jugoslav ... Palaeontologia Jugoslavica [*A publication*]
Palaeontol Mex Inst Geol (Mex) ... Palaeontologia Mexicana. Instituto de Geologia (Mexico) [*A publication*]
Palaeontol Pap Publ Geol Surv Queensl ... Palaeontology Papers. Geological Survey of Queensland [*A publication*] (APTA)
Palaeontol Pol ... Palaeontologia Polonica [*A publication*]
Palaeontol Sin Ser B ... Palaeontologia Sinica. Series B [*A publication*]
Palaeontol Sin Ser C ... Palaeontologia Sinica. Series C [*A publication*]
Palaeontol Sin Ser D ... Palaeontologia Sinica. Series D [*A publication*]
Palaeontol Soc Japan Trans Proc NS ... Palaeontological Society of Japan. Transactions and Proceedings. New Series [*A publication*]
Palaeontol Soc Jpn Spec Pap ... Palaeontological Society of Japan. Special Papers [*A publication*]
Palaeontol Stratigr Lithol ... Palaeontology, Stratigraphy, and Lithology [*A publication*]
Palaeontol Z ... Palaeontologische Zeitschrift [*A publication*]
Palaeont Soc Japan Trans and Proc ... Palaeontological Society of Japan. Transactions and Proceedings [*A publication*]
Palaeont Soc Mon ... Palaeontographical Society. Monographs [*A publication*]
Palaeont Zeitschr ... Palaeontologische Zeitschrift [*A publication*]
Palaeont Zs ... Palaeontologische Zeitschrift [*A publication*]
Palaeovertebrata. Mem Extraordinaire ... Palaeovertebrata. Memoire Extraordinaire [*A publication*]
Palaeovertebr (Montp) ... Palaeovertebrata (Montpellier) [*A publication*]
Pal Ag .... Paley on Principal and Agent [*3rd ed.*] [*1833*] [*A publication*] (DLA)
Pa Lang & Lit ... Papers on Language and Literature [*A publication*]
PALAPA ... Indonesian satellite
PALASM .. Programmable Array Logic Assembler [*Data processing*] (IEEE)
PA Law J ... Pennsylvania Law Journal [*A publication*] (DLA)
PA Law Jour ... Pennsylvania Law Journal [*Philadelphia*] [*A publication*] (DLA)
PA Laws..... Laws of the General Assembly of the Commonwealth of Pennsylvania [*A publication*] (DLA)
PA Law Ser ... Pennsylvania Law Series [*A publication*] (DLA)
PALAY...... Palabora Mining Cl A ADR [*NASDAQ symbol*] (NQ)
Pal B .... Paleontological Bulletins [*A publication*]
PALC........ Passenger Acceptance and Load Control [*Aviation*]
PALC........ Point Arguello Launch Complex
PALC........ Precastable Autoclaved Lightweight Concrete [*Residential construction*]
PAL-C........ Profile of Adaptation to Life - Clinical [*Personality development test*] [*Psychology*]
PALCDR ... Annual Lightwood Research Conference. Proceedings [*A publication*]
PalCl.......... Palestra del Clero [*Rovigo, Italy*] [*A publication*]
PALCO...... Pan American Liaison Committee of Women's Organizations (EA)
PALCON... Pallet-Size Container (MCD)
Pal Conv..... Paley on Summary Convictions [*10th ed.*] [*1953*] [*A publication*] (DLA)
PALCOR... Palestine Correspondence [*A publication*]
PALCRU... Pay and Allowances Accrue From [*Air Force*]
PALCS....... Permissive Action Link Cypher System (MCD)
PAL-D....... Phase Alternation Line Delay (IEEE)
PALE........ Pelvis and Legs Elevating [*Pilot seat*]
PA Leg Gaz ... Legal Gazette (Pennsylvania) [*A publication*] (DLA)
PA Leg Gaz ... Legal Gazette Reports (Campbell) [*Pennsylvania*] [*A publication*] (DLA)

PA Legis Serv ... Pennsylvania Legislative Service (Purdon) [*A publication*] (DLA)
Paleobiol Cont ... Paleobiologie Continentale [*A publication*]
PALEOECOL ... Paleoecologic
paleog .... Paleography
PALEOGEOG ... Paleogeographic
paleon .... Paleontology
PALEONT ... Paleontologic
Paleontol Evol-Barc Inst Prov Paleontol ... Paleontologia y Evolucion-Barcelona. Instituto Provincial de Paleontologia [*A publication*]
Paleontol J ... Paleontological Journal [*A publication*]
Paleontol J (Engl Transl Paleontol Zh) ... Paleontological Journal (English Translation of Paleontologicheskii Zhurnal) [*A publication*]
Paleontol Mex ... Paleontologia Mexicana [*A publication*]
Paleontol Sb ... Paleontologicheskiy Sbornik [*A publication*]
Paleontol Soc Mem ... Paleontological Society. Memoir [*A publication*]
Paleontol Stratigr Litol ... Paleontologiya Stratigrafiya i Litologiya [*A publication*]
Paleontol Zh ... Paleontologicheskii Zhurnal [*A publication*]
Paleont Pap Publs Geol Suv QD ... Paleontology Papers. Publications. Geological Survey of Queensland [*A publication*] (APTA)
Paleont Research Lab Special Inv Rept ... Paleontological Research Laboratories. Special Investigation. Report [*A publication*]
Paleopathol Newsl ... Paleopathological Newsletter [*A publication*]
PalEQ .... Palestine Exploration Quarterly [*A publication*]
Palest Board Sci Ind Res Rep ... Palestine Board for Scientific and Industrial Research. Reports [*A publication*]
Palest Citrogr ... Palestine Citrograph [*A publication*]
Palest Econ ... Palestine Economist [*A publication*]
Palestine Explor Q ... Palestine Exploration Quarterly [*A publication*]
Palestine Explor Quart ... Palestine Exploration Quarterly [*A publication*]
Palest J Bot Hortic Sci ... Palestine Journal of Botany and Horticultural Science [*A publication*]
Palest J Bot Jerusalem Ser ... Palestine Journal of Botany. Jerusalem Series [*A publication*]
Palest J Bot Jerus Ser ... Palestine Journal of Botany. Jerusalem Series [*A publication*]
Palest J Bot Rehovot Ser ... Palestine Journal of Botany. Rehovot Series [*A publication*]
Palest Trib ... Palestine Tribune [*A publication*]
PALEX ...... Pacific Armies Look Exercise
Pal Ex Q .... Palestine Exploration Quarterly [*A publication*]
Paley Ag ..... Paley on Principal and Agent [*A publication*] (DLA)
Paley Mor Ph ... [*William*] Paley's Moral Philosophy [*England*] [*A publication*] (DLA)
Paley Princ & Ag ... Paley on Principal and Agent [*3rd ed.*] [*1833*] [*A publication*] (DLA)
PA LG .... Legal Gazette (Pennsylvania) [*A publication*] (DLA)
PA LG .... Legal Gazette Reports (Campbell) [*Pennsylvania*] [*A publication*] (DLA)
Palg Ch ...... Palgrave's Proceedings in Chancery [*A publication*] (DLA)
Palgrave ..... Palgrave's Proceedings in Chancery [*A publication*] (DLA)
Palgrave ..... Palgrave's Rise and Progress of the English Commonwealth [*A publication*] (DLA)
Palg Rise Etc ... Palgrave's Rise and Progress of the English Commonwealth [*A publication*] (DLA)
Palg Rise & Prog ... Palgrave's Rise and Progress of the English Commonwealth [*1832*] [*A publication*] (DLA)
PAL-H .... Profile of Adaptation to Life - Holistic [*Personality development test*] [*Psychology*]
PALI .... Pacific and Asian Linguistics Institute [*University of Hawaii*]
PALI .... Prince Albert's Light Infantry [*Military unit*] [*British*]
PA Lib Assn Bull ... Pennsylvania Library Association. Bulletin [*A publication*]
PALINET ... Pennsylvania Area Library Network
PALINET/ULC ... PALINET and Union Library Catalogue of Pennsylvania [*Philadelphia, PA*] [*Library network*]
PALIS .... Property and Liability Information System
PalJ .... Palaestina-Jahrbuch [*A publication*]
PA LJ .... Pennsylvania Law Journal [*A publication*] (DLA)
PA LJ .... Pennsylvania Law Journal Reports [*1842-52*] [*A publication*] (DLA)
PalJb .... Palaestina-Jahrbuch [*A publication*]
PA LJR ...... Clark's Pennsylvania Law Journal Reports [*A publication*] (DLA)
PA LJ Rep ... Pennsylvania Law Journal-Reporter [*A publication*]
PALL .... Pallet [*Freight*]
Palladio ...... Palladio. Rivista di Storia dell'Architettura [*A publication*]
Pall Mall M ... Pall Mall Magazine [*A publication*]
PALM .... PALFED, Inc. [*NASDAQ symbol*] (NQ)
Palm .... Palmer's Assizes at Cambridge [*England*] [*A publication*] (DLA)
Palm .... Palmer's English King's Bench Reports [*1619-29*] [*A publication*] (DLA)
Palm .... Palmer's Reports [*53-60 Vermont*] [*A publication*] (DLA)
PALM .... Palmistry (ADA)
Palm .... Palmyrene (BJA)
PALM .... Precision Altitude and Landing Monitor [*Aircraft location*]
Palm Comp L ... Palmer's Company Law [*22nd ed.*] [*1976*] [*A publication*] (DLA)

Palm Comp Prec ... Palmer's Company Precedents [*17th ed.*] [*1956-60*] [*A publication*] (DLA)
Palmer .... Palmer's Assizes at Cambridge [*England*] [*A publication*] (DLA)
Palmer .... Palmer's English King's Bench Reports [*A publication*] (DLA)
Palmer .... Palmer's Reports [*53-60 Vermont*] [*A publication*] (DLA)
Palmer Co Prec ... Palmer's Company Precedents [*16 eds.*] [*1877-1952*] [*A publication*] (DLA)
Palmer Pr Comp ... Palmer's Private Companies [*41st ed.*] [*1950*] [*A publication*] (DLA)
Palm Pr Lords ... Palmer's Practice in the House of Lords [*1830*] [*A publication*] (DLA)
Palms .... Paulian Association Lay Missionary Secretariat [*Australia*]
PALMS ..... Provisioning Automated Logistics Material System (MCD)
Palm Sh ..... Palmer's Shareholders [*34th ed.*] [*1936*] [*A publication*] (DLA)
Palm Wr ..... Palmer's Law of Wreck [*1843*] [*A publication*] (DLA)
PALO .... Phosphonoacetyl-L-Ornithine [*Biochemistry*]
PALO .... Port Amenities Liaison Officer [*British*] (DSUE)
PALOS ...... Pacific Logistic Operations - Streamline [*Army*]
PALP .... Palpable [*Medicine*]
PALP .... Pyridoxal Phosphate [*Also, PLP*] [*Biochemistry*]
PALPI .... Palpitation [*Medicine*]
palpit .... Palpitation [*Medicine*]
PALR .... Permissive Action Link Report [*Army*] (AABC)
PA L Rec .... Pennsylvania Law Record [*A publication*] (DLA)
PA L Rev .... University of Pennsylvania. Law Review [*A publication*]
PALS .... Patient Advocacy Legal Service [*An association*] [*Defunct*] (EA)
PA LS .... Pennsylvania Law Series [*A publication*] (DLA)
PALS .... Permissive Action Link System [*Army*]
PALS .... Phase Alternation Line Simple [*TV decoding system*]
PALS .... Photo Area and Location System (NASA)
PALS .... Point Arguello Launch Site (AAG)
PALS .... Precision Approach and Landing System (NASA)
PALS .... Prestaged Ammunition Loading System [*Army*] (RDA)
PALS .... Principle of the Alphabet Literacy System [*Software*] [*IBM Corp.*]
PalSb .... Palestinskii Sbornik [*Moscow/Leningrad*] [*A publication*]
Pal Sbor ..... Palestinskii Sbornik [*A publication*]
PALSD ...... Program: Automated Library and Information Systems [*A publication*]
PA L Ser .... Pennsylvania Law Series [*A publication*] (DLA)
PALS-G ..... Passive Artillery Locating System - Ground Based (MCD)
PALSG ...... Personnel and Logistics Systems Group [*Army*] (AABC)
PALSGR .... Palsgrave Dictionary [*A publication*]
PALST .... Picture Articulation and Screening Test
PAlt .... Altoona Area Public Library, Altoona, PA [*Library symbol*] [*Library of Congress*] (LCLS)
PALT .... Present Altitude [*Aviation*] (FAAC)
PALT .... Procurement Administrative Lead Time
PALTREU ... Palaestina Treuhandstelle zur Beratung Deutscher Juden [*A publication*]
PALU .... Cape Lisburne Air Force Station [*Alaska*] [*ICAO location identifier*] (ICLI)
PALU .... Progressive Arbeiders- en Landbouwersunie [*Progressive Workers' and Farm Laborers' Union*] [*Surinam*] [*Political party*] (PPW)
Palud .... Paludonus [*Pierre de la Palu*] [*Deceased, 1342*] [*Authority cited in pre-1607 legal work*] (DSA)
Palyaval Tanacs ... Palyavalasztasi Tanacsadas [*A publication*]
Palynol Bull ... Palynological Bulletin [*A publication*]
PAM .... Palermo [*California*] [*Seismograph station code, US Geological Survey*] (SEIS)
PAM .... Palestine Archaeological Museum [*Jerusalem*] (BJA)
PAM .... Pamida Holdings Corp. [*AMEX symbol*] (SPSG)
PAM .... Pamour, Inc. [*Toronto Stock Exchange symbol*]
Pam .... Pampa [*Record label*] [*Brazil*]
PAM .... Pamphlet (AFM)
PAM .... Panama City, FL [*Location identifier*] [*FAA*] (FAAL)
PAM .... Panoramic
PAM .... Parameter Adjusting Mechanism
PAM .... Parametric Amplifier (NATG)
PAM .... Parents Against Molesters (EA)
PAM .... Partitioned Access Method [*Data processing*]
PAM .... Payload Assist Module [*NASA*] (MCD)
PA M .... Pennsylvania Magazine of History and Biography [*A publication*]
PAM .... People's Action Movement [*Nevis*] [*Political party*] (PPW)
PAM .... People's Anti-War Mobilization (EA)
PAM .... Performance Analysis Model (MCD)
PAM .... Performing Arts Medicine
PAM .... Peripheral Adapter Module
PAM .... Personal Accounting Management
PAM .... Personal Applications Manager [*Hewlett-Packard Co.*]
PAM .... Personnel Action Memorandum [*Military*]
PAM .... Phase-Amplitude Modulation
PAM .... Phased Array Module
PAM .... Philosophies, Ancient and Modern [*A publication*]
PAM .... Phoenix Airborne Missile
PAM .... Pittsburgh, Allegheny & McKees Rocks Railroad Co. [*AAR code*]

PAM .... Planning, Activation, Modification [*Army reorganization*]
PAM .... Plasma-Arc Machining [*Manufacturing term*]
PAM .... Pledged Account Mortgage
PAM .... Pole Amplitude Modulation　(IEEE)
PAM .... Polyacrylamide [*Also, PAA, PAAM*] [*Organic chemistry*]
PAM .... Portable Alpha Monitor
PAM .... Portable Automated Mesonet [*Meteorology*]
PAM .... Position and Altitude Monitor　(MCD)
PAM .... Post-Accident Monitoring [*Nuclear energy*]　(NRCH)
PAM .... Postacceptance Modification
PAM .... Potential Acuity Meter [*Instrumentation*]
PAM .... Power Assist Module [*NASA*]
PAM .... Pralidoxime Methiodide [*Biochemistry*]
PAM .... Presbyterian Association of Musicians　(EA)
PAM .... Primary Access Method [*Sperry UNIVAC*]
PAM .... Primary Acquired Melanosis [*Oncology*]
PAM .... Primary Amoebic Meningitis [*or Meningoencephalitis*]
　　　　　　[*Medicine*]
PAM .... Primary Auxiliary Memory [*Unit*] [*Data processing*]　(MCD)
PAM .... Priorities and Allocations Manual [*Army*]　(AABC)
PAM .... Process Automation Monitor [*Texas Instruments, Inc.*]
PAM .... Processor and Memory [*Data processing*]
PAM .... Procurement Aids Man [*Marine Corps*]
PAM .... Procurement of Aircraft and Missiles
PAM-M ...... Program Analysis Memorandum　(MCD)
PA-M .... Program Authorization - Map [*Military*]　(AFIT)
PAM .... Program Automated Method [*Data processing*]
PAM .... Programmable Algorithm Machine [*Data processing*]
PAM .... Programme Alimentaire Mondial [*World Food Program*]
PAM .... Pulmonary Alveolar Macrophage [*Attacks inhaled particles*]
PAM .... Pulse-Address MODEM
PAM .... Pulse Amplitude Modulation [*Electronics*]
PAM .... Pyridine Aldoxime Methiodide [*Biochemistry*]
PAM .... Pyridine Aldoxime Methyl [*Pharmacology*]
PAM .... University of Pennsylvania, School of Medicine, Philadelphia,
　　　　　　PA [*OCLC symbol*]　(OCLC)
PAm .... Wissahickon Valley Public Library, Ambler, PA [*Library
　　　　　　symbol*] [*Library of Congress*]　(LCLS)
PAM-A ...... PAM [*Payload Assist Module*] Atlas-Centaur Class
　　　　　　Spacecraft　(NASA)
Pam A .... Pamatky Archeologicke [*A publication*]
PAMA .... Pan American Medical Association [*Also known as Association
　　　　　　Medica Pan Americana*]　(EA)
PAMA .... Para-Dimethylaminophenylazopyridine [*An indicator*]
　　　　　　[*Chemistry*]
PAM-A ...... Payload Assist Module - Atlas Class Spacecraft　(MCD)
PAMA .... Polish Alma Mater of America　(EA)
PAMA .... Professional Aviation Maintenance Association　(EA)
PAMA .... Pulse-Address Multiple Access [*Satellite communications*]
PAMAC ..... Parts and Materials Accountability Control
P Am Ac Ins ... Proceedings. American Academy and Institute of Arts and
　　　　　　Letters [*A publication*]
PA Mag Hist ... Pennsylvania Magazine of History and Biography [*A
　　　　　　publication*]
PA Mag Hist Biogr ... Pennsylvania Magazine of History and Biography [*A
　　　　　　publication*]
PAMAI ...... Program of Action for Mediation, Arbitration, and Inquiry
　　　　　　[*American Library Association*]
PAMAM ... Polyamidoamine [*Organic chemistry*]
P Am Antiq ... Proceedings. American Antiquarian Society [*A publication*]
P Am Ass Ca ... Proceedings. American Association for Cancer Research [*A
　　　　　　publication*]
Pamatky Prir ... Pamatky a Priroda [*A publication*]
PAMB .... Pressure Ambient　(NASA)
PAMC .... McGrath [*Alaska*] [*ICAO location identifier*]　(ICLI)
PAMC .... Pakistan Army Medical Corps
PAMC .... Provident American Corporation [*Norristown, PA*] [*NASDAQ
　　　　　　symbol*]　(NQ)
PAMC .... Provisional Acceptable Means of Compliance　(MCD)
PAmC .... Temple University, Ambler Campus, Ambler, PA [*Library
　　　　　　symbol*] [*Library of Congress*]　(LCLS)
P Am Cath P ... Proceedings. American Catholic Philosophical Association [*A
　　　　　　publication*]
PAMCCS .. Prior Active Marine Corps Commissioned Service
PAMCES .. Prior Active Marine Corps Enlisted Service
PAMCS ..... Phoenix Airborne Missile Control System
PAM-D ...... PAM [*Payload Assist Module*] Delta Class Spacecraft　(NASA)
PAM-D ...... Payload Assist Module - Delta Class Spacecraft　(MCD)
PAMD .... Price and Management Data
PAMD .... Process Automation Monitor/Disk Version [*Texas Instruments,
　　　　　　Inc.*]
PAMDA .... Progress in Atomic Medicine [*A publication*]
Pam Div Wood Technol For Comm NSW ... Pamphlet. Division of Wood
　　　　　　Technology. Forestry Commission. New South Wales [*A
　　　　　　publication*]　(APTA)
PAMDS..... Price and Management Data Section [*of a stock list*] [*Navy*]
PAME........ Pandemokratiki Agrotikon Metapon Ellados [*Pan-Democratic
　　　　　　Agrarian Front of Greece*] [*Political party*]　(PPE)
PAME........ Primary Amoebic Meningoencephalitis [*Medicine*]
P/AMEA2 ... Probationary Marine Engineering Artificer, Acting, 2nd Class
　　　　　　[*British military*]　(DMA)

PA Med..... Pennsylvania Medicine [*A publication*]
PA Med J .. Pennsylvania Medical Journal [*A publication*]
PAMETON ... Paracetamol and Methionine [*Pain-relief drug*]
PAMF....... Portable Arc Melting Furnace
PAM-FM .. Pulse Amplitude Modulation - Frequency Modulation
　　　　　　[*Electronics*]
PAmh......... Amherst Papyri [*A publication*]　(OCD)
PAMI........ Personnel Accounting Machine Installation
PAMI........ Prairie Agricultural Machinery Institute [*Canada*]
PAMI........ Professional Arts Management Institute　(EA)
Pamiet Konf Nauk Otolaryngol Dzieciecej Zakopane ... Pamietnik Konferencji
　　　　　　Naukowej Otolaryngologii Dzieciecej Zakopane [*A
　　　　　　publication*]
Pamietnik L ... Pamietnik Literacki [*A publication*]
Pamiet Pulawski ... Pamietnik Pulawski [*A publication*]
Pamiet Zjazdu Otolaryngol Pol Katowicach ... Pamietnik Zjazdu
　　　　　　Otolaryngologow Polskich w Katowicach [*A publication*]
Pam Iowa State Univ Sci Tech Coop Ext Serv ... Pamphlet. Iowa State
　　　　　　University of Science and Technology. Cooperative
　　　　　　Extension Service [*A publication*]
PAMIS ...... Processing and Manufacturing in Space [*European Space
　　　　　　Agency*]
PAMIS ...... Psychological Operations Automated Management Information
　　　　　　System　(MCD)
PA Misc..... Pennsylvania Miscellaneous Reports [*A publication*]　(DLA)
PamL .... Pamietnik Literacki [*A publication*]
PAMLPU .. Pianoforte Action Makers' Labour Protection Union [*British*]
P Am Math S ... Proceedings. American Mathematical Society [*A publication*]
PAMN .... Procurement Aircraft and Missiles, Navy [*An appropriation*]
PAMO .... Pacific Airlift Management Office [*Military*]
PAMO .... Port Air Materiel Office
PAMP........ Pampero [*River Plate gale*] [*Nautical term*]　(DSUE)
PAMPA..... Pacific Area Movement Priority Agency [*Military*]
PamPAC .... Pamela's Political Action Committee [*Nickname of "Democrats
　　　　　　for the '80's," a committee founded by Pamela Harriman*]
PAMPER .. Practical Application of Mid-Points for Exponential Regression
PAMPH .... Pamphlet [*Freight*]
Pamph........ Pamphleteer [*A publication*]
Pamph Amat Ent Soc ... Pamphlet. Amateur Entomologists' Society [*A
　　　　　　publication*]
Pamph Dep Agric (Qd) ... Pamphlet. Department of Agriculture (Queensland)
　　　　　　[*A publication*]
Pamph Dep Agric (Tanganyika) ... Pamphlet. Department of Agriculture
　　　　　　(Tanganyika Territory) [*A publication*]
Pamph Dep Agric Un S Afr ... Pamphlet. Department of Agriculture. Union of
　　　　　　South Africa [*A publication*]
Pamph Div Sci Publs Volcani Cent Agric Res Orgn ... Pamphlet. Division of
　　　　　　Scientific Publications. Volcani Center. Agricultural
　　　　　　Research Organisation [*A publication*]
Pamph Div Wood Technol For Comm NSW ... Pamphlet. Division of Wood
　　　　　　Technology. Forestry Commission. New South Wales [*A
　　　　　　publication*]　(APTA)
Pamph Idaho Bur Mines Geol ... Pamphlet. Idaho Bureau of Mines and
　　　　　　Geology [*A publication*]
P Am Phil S ... Proceedings. American Philosophical Society [*A publication*]
Pamph Laws ... Pamphlet Laws, Acts [*A publication*]　(DLA)
Pamphlet Archre ... Pamphlet Architecture [*A publication*]
Pamphl For Res Educ Proj For Dep (Sudan) ... Pamphlet. Forestry Research
　　　　　　and Education Project. Forests Department (Khartoum,
　　　　　　Sudan) [*A publication*]
Pamphl Laws ... Pamphlet Laws, Acts [*A publication*]　(DLA)
Pamph Volcani Inst Agric Res ... Pamphlet. Volcani Institute of Agricultural
　　　　　　Research [*A publication*]
Pam Pulaw ... Pamietnik Pulawski [*A publication*]
Pam Pulawski ... Pamietnik Pulawski [*A publication*]
PAMPUS .. Photons for Atomic and Molecular Processes and Universal
　　　　　　Studies [*Physics*]
PAMR .... Anchorage/Merrill Field [*Alaska*] [*ICAO location
　　　　　　identifier*]　(ICLI)
PAMREA ... Proceedings. American Association for Cancer Research. Annual
　　　　　　Meeting [*A publication*]
PAMRF..... Palo Alto Medical Research Foundation [*Research
　　　　　　center*]　(RCD)
PAMRS..... Parameter Adaptive Model Reference System
PAMS....... North-Holland Series in Probability and Applied Mathematics
　　　　　　[*Elsevier Book Series*] [*A publication*]
PAMS....... Pacific Armies Management Seminar
PAMS....... Pad Abort Measuring System [*NASA*]　(KSC)
PAMS........ Papers. American Musicological Society [*A publication*]
PAMS....... Portable Acoustic Monitoring System
PAMS....... Post-Accident Monitoring System [*Nuclear energy*]　(NRCH)
PAMS....... Predictive Aircraft Maintenance System
PAMS....... Preselected Alternate Master-Slave
　　　　　　[*Telecommunications*]　(TEL)
PAMS....... Proceedings. American Mathematical Society [*A publication*]
PAMS....... Procurement Action Management System　(MCD)
PAMS....... Public Access Message System
PAMSB..... Pharos of Alpha Omega Alpha Honor Medical Society [*A
　　　　　　publication*]
P Am S Info ... Proceedings. American Society for Information Science [*A
　　　　　　publication*]

PamSL .... Pamietnik Slowianski Czasopismo Naukowe Posiecone Slowianoznawstwu [*A publication*]

PAMTGG ... Pan Am Makes the Going Great [*Title of ballet choreographed by George Balanchine, taken from Pan American World Airways' slogan*] [*Pronounced "pam-ti-guh-guh"*]

PAMUSA ... Post-Attack Mobilization of the United States Army

PAMWA ... Pan American Medical Women's Alliance (EA)

PAMWS .... Proceedings. Annual Meeting. Western Society for French History [*A publication*]

PAMX ...... Pancho's Mexican Buffet, Inc. [*NASDAQ symbol*] (NQ)

PAMYA ..... Proceedings. American Mathematical Society [*A publication*]

PAN .... National Action Party [*Mexico*] [*Political party*] (PD)

PAN .... Packaging News [*A publication*]

PAN .... Paladin Fuel Technology [*Vancouver Stock Exchange symbol*]

Pan .... Panache [*A publication*]

PAN .... Panama [*ANSI three-letter standard code*] (CNC)

PAN .... Panchromatic (DEN)

Pan .... Panegyricus [*of Pliny the Younger*] [*Classical studies*] (OCD)

PAN .... Panimavida [*Chile*] [*Seismograph station code, US Geological Survey*] [*Closed*] (SEIS)

PAN .... Panis [*Bread*] [*Pharmacy*] (ROG)

pan .... Panjabi [*MARC language code*] [*Library of Congress*] (LCCP)

Pan .... Panorama [*A publication*]

PAN .... Panoramic (MSA)

Pan .... Panormitanus [*Nicholas de Tudeschis*] [*Deceased, 1445*] [*Authority cited in pre-1607 legal work*] (DSA)

Pan .... Pantheon [*Record label*] [*France, etc.*]

PAN .... Pantry (MSA)

PAN .... Pastoral Music Notebook [*A publication*]

PAN .... Pattani [*Thailand*] [*Airport symbol*] (OAG)

PAN .... Peace Action Network (EA)

PAN .... Pennsylvania Animal Network [*Coalition operated by Trans-Species Unlimited*]

PAN .... Pennsylvania Association of Notaries (EA)

PAN .... Performing Artists Network [*Electronic network*]

PAN .... Periarteritis Nodosa [*Also, PN*] [*Medicine*]

PAN .... Periodic Alternating Nystagmus [*Ophthalmology*]

PAN .... Peroxyacetyl Nitrate [*Lacrimator*]

PAN .... Pesticides Action Network (EA)

PAN .... Polled Access Network

PAN .... Polska Akademia Nauk [*Polish Academy of Sciences*] [*Also, an information service or system*] (IID)

PAN .... Polyacrylonitrile [*Organic chemistry*]

PAN .... Polyarteritis Nodosa [*Medicine*]

PAN .... Porte-Avion Nucleaire [*French*]

PAN .... Positional Alcohol Nystagmus [*Physiology*]

PAN .... Primary Account Number [*Business term*]

PAN .... Project Authorization Notice (MCD)

PAN .... Propodial Anlage [*Zoology*]

PAN .... Publications Account Number [*DoD*]

PAN .... Pyridylazonaphthol [*An indicator*] [*Chemistry*]

PAN .... Switchboard Panel [*Telecommunications*] (TEL)

PanA .... Pan-Africanist [*A publication*]

PANA .... Pan-Asia News Agency Ltd. [*Also, PANASIA*] [*Hong Kong*]

PANA .... PanAfrican News Agency (EAIO)

PANA .... Polish-American Numismatic Association (EA)

PANAGRA ... Pan American Grace Airways, Inc. [*Also, PAGA*]

PANAIR ... Panama Air Lines

PANAL ...... Papuan National Alliance [*Political party*] (PPW)

PANALU ... Parti National Lumumba [*Lumumba National Party*] [*Political party*]

PAN-AM ... Pan American World Airways, Inc. [*See also PA, PAA, PN*]

Panama Admin Recursos Minerales Mapa ... Republica de Panama. Administracion de Recursos Minerales. Mapa [*A publication*]

PANAMAC ... Pan American World Airways Communications System

Panama Univ Dept Geografia Pub ... Panama Universidad. Departamento de Geografia. Publicacion [*A publication*]

Pan Am Fisherman ... Pan American Fisherman [*A publication*]

Pan Am Health Organ Off Doc ... Pan American Health Organization. Official Document [*A publication*]

Pan Am Health Organ Res Prog ... Pan American Health Organization. Research in Progress [*A publication*]

Pan Am Health Organ Sci Publ ... Pan American Health Organization. Scientific Publication [*A publication*]

Pan-Am Inst Geography and History Pub ... Pan-American Institute of Geography and History. Publication [*A publication*]

Pan Am Inst Min Eng Geol US Sect Tech Pap ... Pan American Institute of Mining Engineering and Geology. United States Section. Technical Paper [*A publication*]

Pan Am M ... Pan American Magazine [*A publication*]

PanAmSat ... Pan American Satellite [*Greenwich, CT*] [*Telecommunications service*] (TSSD)

Pan-Am TS ... Pan-American Treaty Series [*A publication*] (DLA)

Pan Am Union Bol Ciencia y Tecnologia ... Pan American Union. Boletin de Ciencia y Tecnologia [*A publication*]

Pan Am Union Bul ... Pan American Union. Bulletin [*A publication*]

PanAR .... Pan American Review [*A publication*]

PANAR ..... Panoramic RADAR

PANASIA ... Organization of Pan Asian American Women (EA)

PANASIA ... Pan-Asia News Agency Ltd. [*Also, PANA*] [*Hong Kong*]

PANB .... Panic Bolt

PANC .... Anchorage/International [*Alaska*] [*ICAO location identifier*] (ICLI)

PANC .... Pasta & Cheese, Inc. [*Long Island City, NY*] [*NASDAQ symbol*] (NQ)

PANC .... Power Amplifier Neutralizing Capacitor (DEN)

PANCAN .. [*The*] Panama Canal

PANCANCO ... Panama Canal Company [*Superseded by Panama Canal Commission*]

PANCAP ... Practical Annual Capacity [*FAA*]

P de Ancha ... Petrus de Ancharano [*Deceased, 1416*] [*Authority cited in pre-1607 legal work*] (DSA)

Pancir .... [*Guido*] Pancirolus [*Deceased, 1599*] [*Authority cited in pre-1607 legal work*] (DSA)

Pancirol ..... [*Guido*] Pancirolus [*Deceased, 1599*] [*Authority cited in pre-1607 legal work*] (DSA)

PANCO ...... Procurement Aids Noncommissioned Officer [*Marine Corps*]

Pand .... [*The*] Pandects [*A publication*] (DLA)

PAND .... Pandering [*FBI standardized term*]

PAND .... Passive Air Navigation Device

PAND .... Performing Artists for Nuclear Disarmament (EA)

PANDA ..... Prestel Advanced Network Design Architecture

Pand B .... Pandectes Belges [*A publication*]

Pandect Flor ... Pandectae Florentinae [*A publication*] (DSA)

PANDEX ... Name of an all-inclusive index covering fields of science, technology and medicine; composed of Greek prefix Pan meaning all and -Dex from word index

Pand Flo ..... Pandectae Florentinae [*A publication*] (DSA)

PANDLCHAR ... Pay and Allowances Chargeable

PANDORA ... Passive and Active Signal Digital Correlator Analyzer (MCD)

PANDS ..... Pay and Supply [*Coast Guard*]

PANDS ..... Print and Search Processor [*Data processing*]

PANE .... Park News [*A publication*]

PANE .... Performance Analysis of Networks, Electrical

Paneg .... Panegyricus [*of Isocrates*] [*Classical studies*] (OCD)

panendo ..... Panendoscopy [*Medicine*]

PAN/ES .... Estudios Latinoamericanos. Polska Akademia Nauk [*A publication*]

PANES ...... Prior Active Navy Enlisted Service

PANES ...... Program for Analysis of Nonlinear Equilibrium and Stability [*NASA*]

PANF .... Plan Account Number File [*IRS*]

PANFI .... Precision Automatic Noise Figure Indicator

PANGCS ... Prior Active National Guard Commissioned Service

PANGES ... Prior Active National Guard Enlisted Service

PANH .... Panhandling [*FBI standardized term*]

PANH .... Picolinaldehyde Nicotinoylhydrazone [*Reagent*]

Panhandle Geol Soc Strat Cross Sec ... Panhandle Geological Society. Stratigraphic Cross Section [*A publication*]

PANHONLIB ... Panama, Honduras, and Liberia [*Acronym used to refer to merchant ships operating under "flags of convenience"*]

PANI .... Patriarch Athenagoras National Institute (EA)

PANIC .... Planned Attack on Nine Inner Cities [*to build education parks*]

Pan Indian Ocean Sci Congr Proc Sect D Agr Sci ... Pan Indian Ocean Science Congress. Proceedings. Section D. Agricultural Sciences [*A publication*]

Panjab Univ (Chandigarh) Cent Adv Stu Geol Publ ... Panjab University (Chandigarh). Centre of Advanced Study in Geology. Publication [*A publication*]

Panj C .... Panjab Code [*India*] [*A publication*] (DLA)

Pank Jur .... Pankhurst's Jurisprudence [*A publication*] (DLA)

PAnL .... Lebanon Valley College, Annville, PA [*Library symbol*] [*Library of Congress*] (LCLS)

PANL .... PanelGraphic Corp. [*NASDAQ symbol*] (CTT)

PANLAR ... PanAmerican League Against Rheumatism (EA)

PANLIBHON ... Panama, Liberia, and Honduras [*Acronym used to refer to merchant ships operating under "flags of convenience"*]

PANLIBHONCO ... Panama-Liberia-Honduras-Costa Rica

Panminerva Med ... Panminerva Medica [*A publication*]

PANNAP ... Panavia New Aircraft Project (MCD)

PANNDA .. Precedent Analysis by Nearest Neighbor Discriminant Analysis

PANNR ..... Previous Applicants Need Not Reapply [*Civil Service*]

Panor .... Panormitanus [*Nicholas de Tudeschis*] [*Deceased, 1445*] [*Authority cited in pre-1607 legal work*] (DSA)

Panorama Democr Chr ... Panorama Democrate Chretien [*A publication*]

Panorama Econ (Chile) 2a Epoca ... Panorama Economico (Chile). Segunda Epoca [*A publication*]

Panorama Econ (Mexico) ... Panorama Economico (Mexico) [*A publication*]

Panorama M Instruments ... Panorama de la Musique et des Instruments [*A publication*]

PA NP .... Brightly's Pennsylvania Nisi Prius Reports [*A publication*] (DLA)

PANP .... Pan Petroleum Master LP [*NASDAQ symbol*] (NQ)

PANPA ...... Pacific Area Newspaper Publishers Association (EAIO)

Pan-Pac Ent ... Pan-Pacific Entomologist [*A publication*]

Pan-Pac Entomol ... Pan-Pacific Entomologist [*A publication*]

Pan-Pacif Ent ... Pan-Pacific Entomologist [*A publication*]

Pan Pipes ... Pan Pipes of Sigma Alpha Iota [*A publication*]

PANPJ ...... Polska Akademia Nauk. Komitet Jezykoznawstwa. Prace Jezykoznawcze [*A publication*]

PANPKHL ... Polska Akademia Nauk. Oddzial w Krakowie. Prace Komisji Historycznoliterackiej [*A publication*]
PANPKS ... Polska Akademia Nauk. Oddzial w Krakowie. Prace Komisji Slowianoznawstwa [*A publication*]
Pan i Prawo ... Panstwo i Prawo [*A publication*]
PANPUB... Panel Publishers (DLA)
P An Rel M ... Proceedings. Annual Reliability and Maintainability Symposium [*A publication*]
PANS........ Pest Articles News Summaries [*Commonwealth Mycological Institute*] [*Kew, England*] [*A publication*]
PANS........ Positioning and Navigation System
PANS........ Procedures for Air Navigation Services [*ICAO*]
PANS........ Programmable Augmented Noise Source [*Military*] (CAAL)
PANS........ Puromycin Aminonucleoside [*Biochemistry*]
PANSDOC ... Pakistan National Scientific and Documentation Center [*Later, PASTIC*]
PANSEAFRON ... Panama Sea Frontier
PANSMET ... Procedures for Air Navigation Services - Meteorology (IEEE)
PANS Pest Artic News Summ ... PANS. Pest Articles and News Summaries [*A publication*]
Panstw Sluzba Geol Panstw Inst Geol Biul ... Panstwowa Sluzba Geologiczna. Pantswowy Instytut. Geologiczny Biuletyn [*A publication*]
PANT .... Annette Island [*Alaska*] [*ICAO location identifier*] (ICLI)
PANT .... Pantera's Corp. [*NASDAQ symbol*] (NQ)
PANT .... Pantograph (KSC)
pant .... Pantomine
Panta J Med ... Panta Journal of Medicine [*A publication*]
PANTDK... Progress in Anatomy [*A publication*]
PAntin........ [*The*] Antinoe Papyrus of Theocritus [*Classical studies*] (OCD)
PAntinoop ... Antinoopolis Papyri [*A publication*] (OCD)
PantiP........ Peroxidase-Antiperoxidase [*Immunochemistry*]
Pantnagar J Res ... Pantnagar Journal of Research [*A publication*]
PANTO ..... Pantomime
pantrop....... Pantropical [*Botany*]
PANTS........ Pantaloons (DSUE)
PA Nurse... Pennsylvania Nurse [*A publication*]
PANW .... Pan-Western Corp. [*NASDAQ symbol*] (NQ)
PANX .... Panex Industries [*NASDAQ symbol*] (NQ)
PANY .... Platinumsmiths Association of New York (EA)
PANY .... Port Authority of New York [*Later, PANYNJ*]
PANYNJ ... Port Authority of New York and New Jersey [*Formerly, PANY*]
Panz Ann ... Panzer Annales [*A publication*]
PAO .... Palo Alto, CA [*Location identifier*] [*FAA*] (FAAL)
PAO .... Paotow [*Republic of China*] [*Seismograph station code, US Geological Survey*] (SEIS)
PAO .... Paramount Resources, Inc. [*Vancouver Stock Exchange symbol*]
PaO .... Paranoia Obvious [*Psychology*]
PAO .... Peacetime Acquisition Objective [*DoD*] (AFIT)
PAO .... Peak Acid Output [*Physiology*]
PAO .... Penalty Appeals Officer [*IRS*]
PA/O .... Performing Arts/Omaha [*Nebraska*]
PAO .... Phenylarsine Oxide
PAO .... Pinellas Area Office [*Energy Research and Development Administration*]
PAO .... Polyalkyleneoxide [*Organic chemistry*]
PAO .... Polyalphaolefin [*Organic chemistry*]
PAO .... Preisanordnung [*Price Order*] [*German*]
PAO .... Primary Action Office [*or Officer*] [*Army*]
PAO .... Prince Albert's Own [*Military unit*] [*British*]
PAO .... Principal Administrative Officer
PAO .... Pro Athletes Outreach (EA)
PAO .... Product Activity/Operational Code (MCD)
PAO .... Product Assurance Operations [*Army*]
PAO .... Program Action Officer [*Navy*] (CAAL)
PAO .... Project Action Officer [*Air Force*] (AFIT)
PAO .... Project Administration Officer [*Military*] (AFIT)
PAO .... Property Action Order
PAO .... Public Affairs Office [*NASA*]
PAO .... Public Affairs Officer [*Embassies*]
PAO .... Pulsed Avalanche Diode Oscillator [*Telecommunications*] (IEEE)
PAOA .... Pan American Odontological Association (EA)
PAOC .... Pakistan Army Ordnance Corps [*British military*] (DMA)
PAOC .... Pan-African Ornithological Congress
PAOC .... Pentacostal Assemblies of Canada
PAOC .... Pollution Abatement Operations Center (MCD)
PAOC .... Principal Administrative Officers Committee [*Chiefs of Staff*] [*World War II*]
P/AOEA2 ... Probationary Ordnance Electrical Artificer, Acting, 2nd Class [*British military*] (DMA)
PAOL .... Poly-alpha-olefin [*Organic chemistry*]
PAOM .... Nome [*Alaska*] [*ICAO location identifier*] (ICLI)
PAOP .... Pulmonary Artery Occlusion Pressure [*Cardiology*]
PAOR .... Northway [*Alaska*] [*ICAO location identifier*] (ICLI)
PAORB....... Problemes Actuels d'Oto-Rhino-Laryngologie [*A publication*]
PAOS........ Proceedings. American Oriental Society [*A publication*]
PAOT .... Kotzebue [*Alaska*] [*ICAO location identifier*] (ICLI)
PAOT .... Persons at One Time
PAOTA ..... Problemes Actuels d'Ophtalmologie [*A publication*]
P/AP......... Painter/Apprentice Painter (AAG)

PAP........... Papain [*An enzyme*]
PAP........... Papanicolaou [*Diagnosis, smear, stain, or test*] [*Medicine*]
PAP........... Paper (DSUE)
PAP........... Paper Bound [*Books*] (ROG)
pap .... Papilla [*Medicine*]
Pap........... [*Aemilius*] Papinianus [*Deceased, 212*] [*Authority cited in pre-1607 legal work*] (DSA)
PAP........... Papyrologica [*A publication*]
Pap........... Papyrus (BJA)
PAP........... Para-Aminophenol [*Organic chemistry*]
PAP........... Parti d'Action Paysanne [*Farmers Actions Party*] [*Upper Volta*] [*Political party*]
PAP........... Participatory Anthropic Principle [*Term coined by authors John Barrow and Frank Tipler in their book, "The Anthropic Cosmological Principle"*]
PAP........... Partido Accion Popular [*Popular Action Party*] [*Peru*] [*Political party*]
PAP........... Partido Accion Popular [*Popular Action Party*] [*Ecuador*] [*Political party*]
PAP........... Partido Aprista Peruano [*Peruvian Aprista Party*] [*Peru*] [*Political party*] (EAIO)
PaP........... Past and Present [*A publication*]
PAP........... Patrol Amphibian Plane
PaP........... Patterns of Prejudice [*A publication*]
PAP........... Paulin [*H.*] & Co. Ltd. [*Toronto Stock Exchange symbol*]
PAP........... Payload Activity Planner [*NASA*]
PAP........... Peak Airway Pressure [*Physiology*]
PAP........... Pension Administration Plan [*Insurance*]
PAP........... People's Action Party [*Malaya*] [*Political party*]
PAP........... People's Action Party [*Singapore*] [*Political party*] (PPW)
PAP........... People's Alliance Party [*Solomon Islands*] [*Political party*] (PPW)
PAP........... Peroxidase-Antiperoxidase [*Immunochemistry*]
PAP........... Personal Auto Policy [*Insurance*]
PAP........... Personnel Allocation Plan [*Navy*]
PAP........... Personnel Assistance Point [*Army*] (AABC)
PAP........... Phase Advance Pulse
PAP........... Phenolphthalein in Paraffin [*Emulsion*]
PAP........... Phenyl Acid Phosphate [*Organic chemistry*]
PAP........... Phosphoadenosine Phosphate [*Biochemistry*]
PAP........... Photodiode Array Processing (MCD)
PAP........... Photonic Array Processor [*Device for manipulating light beams in an optical computer*]
PAP........... Physics and Astronomy Programs [*NASA*]
PAP........... Pierced Aluminum Plank [*Technical drawings*]
PAP........... Pilotless Aircraft Program (NG)
PAP........... Platelet Aggregation Profiler [*Hematology*]
PAP........... Platelet Alkaline Phosphatase [*An enzyme*]
PAP........... Pokeweed Antiviral Protein [*Immunochemistry*]
PAP........... Political Asylum Project (EA)
PAP........... Politiki Aneksartitos Parataksis [*Independent Political Front*] [*Greek*] [*Political party*] (PPE)
PAP........... Polska Agencja Prasowa [*Polish Press Agency*]
PAP........... Poly(acryloylpyrrolidine) [*Organic chemistry*]
PAP........... Port-Au-Prince [*Haiti*] [*Airport symbol*] (OAG)
PAP........... Prearranged Payments [*Business term*]
PAP........... Primary Atypical Pneumonia [*Medicine*]
PAP........... Printer Access Protocol (BYTE)
PAP........... Prison-Ashram Project (EA)
PAP........... Procurement and Production (AFIT)
PAP........... Product Assurance Plan [*Army*] (AABC)
PAP........... Production Allocation Program
PAP........... Project Aerospace Plane (AAG)
PAP........... Projected Average Progress (NG)
PAP........... Prostatic Acid Phosphatase [*An enzyme*]
PAP........... Proton Attenuation Procedure
PAP........... Psychobiology and Psychopathology [*Elsevier Book Series*] [*A publication*]
PAP........... Public Affairs Program [*of the American Friends Service Committee*] (EA)
PAP........... Public Assistance Program
PAP........... Pulmonary Alveolar Proteinosis [*Medicine*]
PAP........... Pulmonary Arterial [*or Artery*] Pressure [*Medicine*]
PAPA........ Probabilistic Automatic Pattern Analyzer [*Data processing*]
PAPA........ Proceedings. American Philological Association [*A publication*]
PAPA........ Programmer and Probability Analyzer [*Data processing*] (IEEE)
PAPA........ Publications. Arkansas Philological Association [*A publication*]
PAPAA4.... American Psychopathological Association. Proceedings [*A publication*]
Pap Am Chem Soc Div Paint Plast Print Ink ... Papers. American Chemical Society. Division of Paint, Plastics, and Printing Ink [*A publication*]
Pap Amer Soc Agr Eng ... Paper. American Society of Agricultural Engineers [*A publication*]
Pap Am Soc Ch Hist ... Papers. American Society of Church History [*A publication*]
Pap Annu Conv West Can Water Sewage Conf ... Papers Presented at the Annual Convention. Western Canada Water and Sewage Conference [*A publication*]
Pap Anthro ... Papers in Anthropology [*Oklahoma*] [*A publication*]

Pap Archit Sci Unit Univ Queensl ... Paper. Architectural Science Unit. University of Queensland [*A publication*] (APTA)
PAPAS ...... Pin and Pellet Assay System [*Nuclear energy*] (NRCH)
Pap ASAE ... Paper. American Society of Agricultural Engineers [*A publication*]
PAPAV ...... Papaver Poppy [*Botany*] (ROG)
Pap Avulsos Dep Zool (Sao Paulo) ... Papeis Avulsos. Departmento de Zoologia (Sao Paulo) [*A publication*]
Pap Avulsos Dep Zool Secr Agric Ind Comer (Sao Paulo) ... Papeis Avulsos. Departmento de Zoologia. Secretaria de Agricultura Industria e Comercio (Sao Paulo) [*A publication*]
Pap Avul Zool ... Papeis Avulsos de Zoologia [*A publication*]
PAPB .... Point Barrow [*Alaska*] [*ICAO location identifier*] (ICLI)
Pap Bibliog ... Papers. Bibliographical Society of America [*A publication*]
Pap Bibliogr Soc Am ... Papers. Bibliographical Society of America [*A publication*]
Pap Bibliog Soc Am ... Papers. Bibliographical Society of America [*A publication*]
Pap Bibl Soc Am ... Papers. Bibliographical Society of America [*A publication*]
Papbrd Pkg ... Paperboard Packaging [*A publication*]
Pap Brit Sch Rome ... Papers. British School at Rome [*A publication*]
PAPC .... Philological Association of the Pacific Coast [*A publication*]
PAPCA ...... Pan-American Progressive Consumers Alliance [*Later, NPCA*] (EA)
Pap Carton Cellul ... Papier. Carton et Cellulose [*A publication*]
Pap Celul ... Papir a Celuloza [*A publication*]
PAPCNY ... Portuguese American Progressive Club of New York (EA)
Pap Coal Util Symp Focus SO₂ Emiss Control ... Papers. Coal Utilization Symposium. Focus on SO_2 Emission Control [*A publication*]
Pap Commonw For Conf ... Paper. Commonwealth Forestry Conference [*A publication*]
Pap Congr Aust NZ Assoc Adv Sci ... Australian and New Zealand Association for the Advancement of Science. Congress. Papers [*A publication*] (APTA)
Pap Congr Fed Int Precontrainte ... Papers. Congress of the Federation Internationale de la Precontrainte [*A publication*]
Pap Conv Am Nurs Assoc ... Papers from the Convention. American Nurses' Association [*A publication*]
Pap Converting ... Paper Converting [*A publication*]
Pap Czech Soil Sci Conf ... Papers. Czechoslovak Soil Science Conference [*A publication*]
Pap Dep Agric QD Univ ... Papers. Department of Agriculture. University of Queensland [*A publication*] (APTA)
Pap Dep Geol QD Univ ... Papers. Department of Geology. University of Queensland [*A publication*] (APTA)
Pap Dep Geol Queensl Univ ... Papers. Department of Geology. University of Queensland [*A publication*] (APTA)
Pap Dep Geol Univ QD ... Papers. Department of Geology. University of Queensland [*A publication*] (APTA)
Pap Dep Zool QD Univ ... Papers. Department of Zoology. University of Queensland [*A publication*] (APTA)
PAPE .... Parkside Petroleum, Inc. [*NASDAQ symbol*] (NQ)
PAPE .... Photoactive Pigment Electrophotography (IEEE)
PAPEDJ .... Pesquisa Agropecuaria Pernambucana [*A publication*]
PAPER ...... Prairie Association of Publishers Education Representatives [*Canada*]
Paper & Board Abs ... Paper and Board Abstracts [*A publication*]
Paperboard Packag ... Paperboard Packaging [*A publication*]
Paperboard Pkg ... Paperboard Packaging [*A publication*]
Paper Bul ... Paper and Packaging Bulletin [*A publication*]
PAPERCHEM ... Paper Chemistry [*Institute of Paper Chemistry*] [*Appleton, WI*] [*Bibliographic database*]
Paper Film Foil Conv ... Paper, Film, and Foil Converter [*A publication*]
Paper Jour ... Paper Trade Journal [*A publication*]
Paper Makers Merch Dir ... Paper Makers and Merchants. Directory of All Nations [*A publication*]
PAPERMAN ... Payroll and Accounting, Personnel Management, Manpower Utilization [*Air Force*]
Paper Mkr ... Paper Maker [*A publication*]
Paper Pulp Mill Catalogue ... Paper and Pulp Mill Catalogue/Engineering Handbook [*A publication*]
Papers Biblio Soc Am ... Papers. Bibliographical Society of America [*A publication*]
Papers in Ed (Anstey Coll) ... Papers in Education (Anstey College of Physical Education) [*A publication*]
Papers Far East Hist ... Papers on Far Eastern History [*A publication*]
Papers & Proc Roy Soc Tas ... Papers and Proceedings. Royal Society of Tasmania [*A publication*] (APTA)
Papers and Proc Roy Soc Tasmania ... Papers and Proceedings. Royal Society of Tasmania [*A publication*]
Papers Proc Roy Soc Tasmania ... Papers and Proceedings. Royal Society of Tasmania [*A publication*]
Papers & Proc Tas Hist Res Assn ... Papers and Proceedings. Tasmanian Historical Research Association [*A publication*] (APTA)
Paper Technol ... Paper Technology [*A publication*]
Paper Technol Ind ... Paper Technology and Industry [*A publication*]
Paper Tr J ... Paper Trade Journal [*A publication*]
Paper Twine J ... Paper and Twine Journal [*A publication*]
Paper Yrb... Paper Year Book [*A publication*]

Papeterie Numero Spec ... Papeterie. Numero Special [*A publication*]
Pap FAO/IUFRO World Consult For Tree Breed ... Paper. FAO [*Food and Agriculture Organization of the United Nations*]/IUFRO [*International Union of Forestry Research Organization*] World Consultation on Forest Tree Breeding [*A publication*]
Pap Far Eas ... Papers on Far Eastern History [*A publication*]
Pap Far East Hist ... Papers on Far Eastern History [*Australia*] [*A publication*]
Pap Film Foil Converter ... Paper, Film, and Foil Converter [*A publication*]
Pap Geol Surv Can ... Papers. Geological Survey of Canada [*A publication*]
Pap Gifu Univ Sch Med ... Papers. Gifu University. School of Medicine [*Japan*] [*A publication*]
Pap Grt Barrier Reef Comm ... Papers. Great Barrier Reef Committee [*A publication*] (APTA)
PAPH .... (Pyridinealdehyde)pyridylhydrazone [*Organic chemistry*]
PAPhilosS ... Proceedings. American Philosophical Society [*A publication*]
PAPhS .... Proceedings. American Philosophical Society [*A publication*]
Papi .... Papi [*Aemilius*] Papinianus [*Deceased, 212*] [*Authority cited in pre-1607 legal work*] (DSA)
Papi .... Papirius Justus [*Flourished, 2nd century*] [*Authority cited in pre-1607 legal work*] (DSA)
PAPI .... Precision Approach Path Indicator [*Aviation*] (FAAC)
PAPI .... Professional Association of Pet Industries (EA)
Pap IAALD World Congr ... Papers. International Association of Agricultural Librarians and Documentalists. World Congress [*A publication*]
Papier (Darmstadt) Beil ... Papier (Darmstadt). Beilage [*A publication*]
Papierfabr Wochenbl Papierfabr ... Papierfabrikant - Wochenblatt fuer Papierfabrikation [*A publication*]
Papiergesch ... Papier Geschichte [*A publication*]
Papierverarb ... Papier- und Kunststoffverarbeiter [*A publication*]
Pap Ind ...... Paper Industry [*A publication*]
Pap Ind Pap World ... Paper Industry and Paper World [*A publication*]
Pap Inst Def Anal ... Paper. Institute for Defense Analyses [*A publication*]
Pap Inst Post Off Electr Eng ... Printed Papers. Institution of Post Office Electrical Engineers [*A publication*]
Pap Inst Therm Spring Res Okayama Univ ... Papers. Institute for Thermal Spring Research. Okayama University [*A publication*]
Pap Int Conf Fluid Sealing ... Paper. International Conference on Fluid Sealing [*A publication*]
Papirip Magy Grafika ... Papiripar es Magyar Grafika [*A publication*]
Pap Is Afr .. Papers in International Studies. Africa Series. Ohio University [*A publication*]
Pap Is Se A ... Papers in International Studies. Southeast Asia Series. Ohio University [*A publication*]
Pap J .... Papir-Journalen [*A publication*]
PAPL .... Preliminary Allowance Parts List [*Military*] (CAAL)
Pap Lab Tree-Ring Res Univ Ariz ... Papers. Laboratory of Tree-Ring Research. University of Arizona [*A publication*]
Pap Lanc Co Hist Soc ... Historical Papers. Lancaster County Historical Society [*Pennsylvania*] [*A publication*]
Pap Lang L ... Papers on Language and Literature [*A publication*]
Pap Lang Lit ... Papers on Language and Literature [*A publication*]
Pap Ling .... Papers in Linguistics [*A publication*]
PAPM .... Passed Assistant Paymaster [*British*]
PAPM .... Philippine Association of Paint Manufacturers, Inc. (DS)
PAPM .... Port Moller Air Force Station [*Alaska*] [*ICAO location identifier*] (ICLI)
Pap Maker (London) ... Paper Maker and British Paper Trade Journal (London) [*A publication*]
Pap Makers Assoc (GB Irel) Proc Tech Sect ... Paper Makers' Association (Great Britain and Ireland). Proceedings of the Technical Section [*A publication*]
Pap Makers Mon J ... Paper Makers' Monthly Journal [*A publication*]
Pap Maker (Wilmington Del) ... Paper Maker (Wilmington, Delaware) [*A publication*]
Pap Meteorol Geophys (Tokyo) ... Papers in Meteorology and Geophysics (Tokyo) [*A publication*]
Pap Met Geo ... Papers in Meteorology and Geophysics [*A publication*]
Pap Mich Acad ... Papers. Michigan Academy of Science, Arts, and Letters [*A publication*]
Pap Mich Acad Sci ... Papers. Michigan Academy of Science, Arts, and Letters [*A publication*]
Pap Mich Acad Sci Arts Lett ... Papers. Michigan Academy of Science, Arts, and Letters [*A publication*]
Pap Mill News ... Paper Mill News [*A publication*]
Pap Mill Wood Pulp News ... Paper Mill and Wood Pulp News [*A publication*]
Pap Miner Explor Res Inst McGill Univ ... Paper. Mineral Exploration Research Institute. McGill University [*A publication*]
Pap Minist Energy Mines Pet Resour (Br Columbia) ... Paper. Ministry of Energy, Mines, and Petroleum Resources (Province of British Columbia) [*A publication*]
PAPMOP ... Product Assurance Program Management Operations Plan (MCD)
Pap Natl Conf Prof Nurses Physicians ... Papers. National Conference for Professional Nurses and Physicians [*US*] [*A publication*]
Pap N Haven Col Hist Soc ... Papers. New Haven Colony Historical Society [*A publication*]

Pap Norw State Game Res Inst ... Papers. Norwegian State Game Research Institute [*A publication*]
Pap Nova Scotia Dep Mines ... Paper. Nova Scotia Department of Mines [*A publication*]
Pap Nyomdatech ... Papir es Nyomdatechnika [*A publication*]
Papo .... Partido de Accion Popular [*Popular Action Party*] [*Panama*] [*Political party*] (PPW)
PAPOC ..... Parents' Alliance to Protect Our Children (EA)
PAPOILA ... Pacis Amico, Persecutionis Osore, Joanne Lockio Anglo [*Pseudonym used by John Locke*]
PAPOVA ... Papilloma Virus, Polyoma Virus, Vacuolating Virus
PapOxy ...... Oxyrhynchus Papyri [*A publication*]
PAPP .... Para-Aminopropiophenone [*Pharmacology*]
PAPP .... Parametric Aircraft Performance Program (MCD)
PAPP .... Pregnancy-Associated Plasma Protein
PAPPA .... Pulp and Paper Prepackaging Association [*Later, SSI*] (EA)
Pap Peabody Mus Archaeol Ethnol Harv Univ ... Papers. Peabody Museum of Archaeology and Ethnology. Harvard University [*A publication*]
PAPPGM .. Preliminary Army Planning and Program Guidance Memorandum (MCD)
Pap Phil Ling ... Papers in Philippine Linguistics. Pacific Linguistics. Series A [*Canberra*] [*A publication*]
Pap Presentations Proc Digital Equip Comput Users Soc ... Papers and Presentations-Proceedings. Digital Equipment Computer Users Society [*A publication*]
Pap Print Dig ... Paper and Printing Digest [*A publication*]
Pap Proc R Soc Tas ... Papers and Proceedings. Royal Society of Tasmania [*A publication*] (APTA)
Pap Proc R Soc Tasm ... Papers and Proceedings. Royal Society of Tasmania [*A publication*] (APTA)
Pap Proc R Soc Tasmania ... Papers and Proceedings. Royal Society of Tasmania [*A publication*]
Pap Proc Tas Hist Res Assoc ... Tasmanian Historical Research Association. Papers and Proceedings [*A publication*] (APTA)
Pap ja Puu ... Paperi ja Puu [*A publication*]
Pap Puu ...... Paperi ja Puu - Papper och Tra [*A publication*]
Pap Puu B Painos ... Paperi ja Puu. B Painos [*A publication*]
Pap Puu Painos ... Paperi ja Puu. A Painos [*A publication*]
PAPR .... Paper Corporation of America [*Valley Forge, PA*] [*NASDAQ symbol*] (NQ)
PA Prac .... Standard Pennsylvania Practice [*A publication*] (DLA)
PAPRICAN ... Pulp and Paper Research Institute of Canada [*McGill University*] [*Research center*] (RCD)
Pap Roy Soc Tasm ... Royal Society of Tasmania. Papers and Proceedings [*A publication*] (APTA)
Pap R Sociol ... Papers. Revista de Sociologia [*A publication*]
PAPS .... Periodic Acid-Schiff with Phenylhydrazine Interposition [*A stain*]
PAPS .... Periodic Armaments Planning System (MCD)
PAPS .... Permissive Arming and Protection System [*AEC*]
PAPS .... Phosphoadenosine Phosphosulfate [*Also, APPS*] [*Biochemistry*]
PAPS .... Phosphoadenylyl Sulfate [*Biochemistry*]
PAPS .... Proceedings. American Philosophical Society [*A publication*]
PAPS .... Procurement and Production Status System
PAPS .... Public Assistance Processing System
PA PSC ...... Pennsylvania Public Service Commission Annual Report [*A publication*] (DLA)
PA PSC Dec ... Pennsylvania Public Service Commission Decisions [*A publication*] (DLA)
Pap Sci Ser ... Papers in Science Series [*A publication*]
Pap SE As Ling ... Papers in South East Asian Linguistics. Pacific Linguistics. Series A [*Canberra*] [*A publication*]
Pap SESA ... Paper. SESA [*Society for Experimental Stress Analysis*] [*A publication*]
Pap Ship Res Inst (Tokyo) ... Papers. Ship Research Institute (Tokyo) [*A publication*]
PAPSI .... Pregnancy-Associated Prostaglandin Synthetase Inhibitor [*Endocrinology*]
Pap S Shields Archaeol Hist Soc ... Papers. South Shields Archaeological and Historical Society [*A publication*]
P Ap St Dalho ... Applied Statistics. Proceedings of Conference at Dalhousie University [*A publication*]
Pap Sthn Afr ... Paper Southern Africa [*A publication*]
PA Psychiatr Q ... Pennsylvania Psychiatric Quarterly [*A publication*]
Pap Symp Coal Manage Tech ... Papers Presented before the Symposium on Coal Management Techniques [*A publication*]
Pap Symp Coal Mine Drainage Res ... Papers Presented before the Symposium on Coal Mine Drainage Research [*A publication*]
Pap Symp Coal Prep Util ... Papers Presented before the Symposium on Coal Preparation and Utilization [*A publication*]
Pap Symp Coal Prep (Washington DC) ... Papers Presented before the Symposium on Coal Preparation (Washington, DC) [*A publication*]
Pap Symp Coal Util ... Papers Presented before the Symposium on Coal Utilization [*A publication*]
Pap Symp Manage ... Papers Presented before the Symposium on Management [*A publication*]

Pap Symp Surf Min Reclam ... Papers Presented before the Symposium on Surface Mining and Reclamation [*A publication*]
Pap Symp Underground Min ... Papers Presented before the Symposium on Underground Mining [*A publication*]
Pap Synth Conf Proc ... Paper Synthetics Conference. Proceedings [*United States*] [*A publication*]
PAPTC ...... Pakistan Army Physical Training Corps [*British military*] (DMA)
PAPTC ...... Practical Approach to Patents, Trademarks, and Copyrights [*A publication*]
PAPTE ...... President's Advisory Panel on Timber and the Environment
Pap Tech Mtg Int Union Conserv Nature ... Paper. Technical Meeting. International Union for the Conservation of Nature and Natural Resources [*A publication*]
Pap Technol ... Paper Technology [*England*] [*A publication*]
Pap Technol ... Paper Technology and Industry [*A publication*]
Pap Technol Ind ... Paper Technology and Industry [*A publication*]
Pap Trade J ... Paper Trade Journal [*A publication*]
Papua New Guin Agric J ... Papua and New Guinea Agricultural Journal [*A publication*]
Papua New Guinea Agric J ... Papua and New Guinea Agricultural Journal [*A publication*]
Papua New Guinea Agr J ... Papua and New Guinea Agricultural Journal [*A publication*]
Papua New Guinea Dep Agric Stock Fish Annu Rep ... Papua New Guinea. Department of Agriculture, Stock, and Fisheries. Annual Report [*A publication*]
Papua New Guinea Dep Agric Stock Fish Res Bull ... Papua New Guinea. Department of Agriculture, Stock, and Fisheries. Research Bulletin [*A publication*]
Papua New Guinea Geol Surv Mem ... Papua New Guinea. Geological Survey. Memoir [*A publication*]
Papua New Guinea Inst Med Res Monogr Ser ... Papua New Guinea. Institute of Medical Research. Monograph Series [*A publication*]
Papua New Guinea J Agric For Fish ... Papua New Guinea Journal of Agriculture, Forestry, and Fisheries [*A publication*]
Papua New Guinea Med J ... Papua New Guinea Medical Journal [*A publication*]
Papua & NG ... Papua and New Guinea Law Reports [*A publication*]
PAPUFA ... Physiologically Active Polyunsaturated Fatty Acid [*Nutrition*]
Pap Univ Maine Technol Exp Stn ... Paper. University of Maine. Technology Experiment Station [*A publication*]
Pap Univ MO-Columbia Dep Agric Econ ... Paper. University of Missouri-Columbia. Department of Agricultural Economics [*A publication*]
Pap US Geol Surv Wat Supply ... Paper. United States Geological Survey. Water Supply [*A publication*]
PAPVR ...... Partial Anomalous Pulmonary Venous Return
PAPW .... Papworth [*England*]
Papy .... Papy's Reports [*5-8 Florida*] [*A publication*] (DLA)
Pap Ztg .... Papier-Zeitung [*A publication*]
PAQ .... Palmer, AK [*Location identifier*] [*FAA*] (FAAL)
PAQ .... Partially Allocated Quotas [*Ocean fishery management*]
PAQ .... Personal Attributes Questionnaire
PAQ .... Position Analysis Questionnaire
PAQ .... Preliminary Allowance Quantity [*Military*] (CAAL)
PAQ .... Process Average Quality
PAQ .... Public Administration Quarterly [*A publication*]
PAQR .... Polyacenequinone Radical [*Organic chemistry*]
Par .... Guiraudus Pargues [*Authority cited in pre-1607 legal work*] (DSA)
PAR .... Kosmetiek [*A publication*]
PAR .... Page Address Register
PAR .... Parabolic Aluminized Reflector [*Lamp*]
PAR .... Paracel Islands [*ANSI three-letter standard code*] (CNC)
PAR .... Parachute
PAR .... Paragon Resources Ltd. [*Vancouver Stock Exchange symbol*]
Par .... Paragone [*A publication*]
PAR .... Paragraph (AAG)
Par .... Parah (BJA)
PAR .... Paralipomenon [*Old Testament book*] [*Douay version*]
PAR .... Parallax
PAR .... Parallel (KSC)
PAR .... Parallelogram [*Geometry*] (ADA)
PAR .... Parameter
PAR .... Parametric Amplifier
PAR .... Paraphrase (ADA)
PAR .... Parcel
PAR .... Parenthesis
Par .... Parents' Magazine and Better Family Living [*Later, Parents' Magazine*] [*A publication*]
PAR .... Paris [*France*] [*Airport symbol*] (OAG)
PAR .... Paris - Parc St. Maur [*France*] [*Seismograph station code, US Geological Survey*] (SEIS)
PAR .... Parish
PAR .... Parity (ADA)
Par .... Parker's English Exchequer Reports [*A publication*] (DLA)
Par .... Parker's New York Criminal Reports [*A publication*] (DLA)
PAR .... Parochial
Par .... Parsons' Reports [*65-66 New Hampshire*] [*A publication*] (DLA)

PAR .... Partheite [*A zeolite*]
PAR .... Partido Accion Renovadora [*El Salvador*] [*Political party*]
PAR .... Partido Aragones Regionalista [*Aragonese Regional Party*] [*Spain*] [*Political party*] (PPW)
PAR .... Partito Anti-Reformista [*Anti-Reform Party*] [*Malta*] [*Political party*] (PPE)
PAR .... Parts Approval Request (MCD)
PAR .... Payload Adapter Ring
PAR .... [*The*] Payment Analysis Report [*Dun & Bradstreet Credit Services*] [*Information service or system*] (CRD)
PAR .... Peacetime Airborne Reconnaissance (AFM)
PAR .... Peak Accelerometer Recorder (IEEE)
PAR .... Peak-to-Average Ratio [*Telecommunications*]
PAR .... Pennsylvania Advanced Reactor
PAR .... People Against Racism [*Civil rights organization*]
PAR .... People Against Rape (EA)
PAR .... Perennial Allergic Rhinitis [*Medicine*]
PAR .... Performance Analysis and Review
PAR .... Performance Analysis Routine [*Data processing*]
PAR .... Performance Appraisal Report [*Nuclear energy*] (NRCH)
PAR .... Performing Arts Resources [*A publication*]
PAR .... Performing Arts Review [*A publication*]
PAR .... Perimeter Acquisition RADAR [*Army*]
PAR .... Perimeter Array RADAR (MCD)
PAR .... Personnel Activity Report [*Office of Management and Budget*]
PAR .... Personnel Activity Request
PAR .... Personnel Advancement Requirement [*Navy*] (NVT)
PAR .... PERT [*Program Evaluation and Review Technique*] Analysis Report (KSC)
PAR .... Phased Array RADAR
PAR .... Phosphoric Acid-Resistant
PAR .... Photosynthetically Active Radiation
PAR .... Physiological Aging Rate
PAR .... Planning Action Request [*NASA*] (MCD)
PAR .... Planning Activity Report
PAR .... Platelet Aggregate Ratio [*Hematology*]
PAR .... Pollen Accumulation Rate [*Botany*]
PAR .... Polyarylate [*Resin*]
PAR .... Positive Attitudinal Reinforcement [*In George Lee Walker novel "The Chronicles of Doodah"*]
PAR .... Post Adjudicative Review [*Social Security Administration*] (OICC)
PAR .... Post Attach Requirements (AAG)
PAR .... Postanesthesia [*or Postanesthetic*] Room [*Medicine*]
PAR .... Postanesthetic Recovery [*Medicine*]
PAR .... Potassium-Adsorption-Ratio
PAR .... Power Analysis Report [*Automobile testing*]
PAR .... Precedent, Action, and Result
PAR .... Precision Aerotech [*AMEX symbol*] (SPSG)
PAR .... Precision Aircraft Reference
PAR .... Precision Approach RADAR [*Aviation*]
PAR .... Prime Assets Ratio
PAR .... Princeton Applied Research Corp. [*Princeton University*]
PAR .... Priority Action Report (AAG)
PAR .... Priority Action Request (AAG)
PAR .... Probabilistic Analysis of Risk (KSC)
PAR .... Problem Accountability Record (NASA)
PAR .... Problem Action Record (KSC)
PAR .... Problem Action Request (NASA)
PAR .... Problem Analysis Report (MCD)
PAR .... Problem Analysis and Resolution
PAR .... Process Action Request
PAR .... Product Acceptance Review (NASA)
PAR .... Product of Antigenic Recognition [*Immunochemistry*]
PAR .... Production Action Request (MCD)
PAR .... Production Analysis Report
PAR .... Production, Augmentation, and Reliability (NG)
PAR .... Production Automated Riveting
PAR .... Professional Abstracts Registries [*Database Innovations, Inc.*]
PAR .... Profile of Average Reflectivity
PAR .... Program Address Register
PAR .... Program Adjustment Request [*Navy*]
PAR .... Program Administrator's [*Progress*] Report [*DoD*]
PAR .... Program-Aid Routine [*Data processing*]
PAR .... Program for Alcohol Recovery
PAR .... Program Allocation and Reimbursements (AFIT)
PAR .... Program Analysis and Review
PAR .... Program Appraisal Report
PAR .... Program Appraisal and Review (IEEE)
PAR .... Program Assessment Report [*or Review*] (MCD)
PAR .... Program Audience Rating
PAR .... Progressive Aircraft Repair [*or Rework*]
PAR .... Project Audit Report
PAR .... Projected Automation Requirement
PAR .... Promotion Appraisal Report (FAAC)
PAR .... Public Administration Review [*A publication*]
PAR .... Public Affairs Research Council [*Research center*] (RCD)
PAR .... Pulse Acquisition RADAR [*Military*] (NG)
PAR .... Purchasing Approval Request (NRCH)
PAR .... Push and Release [*Push button*]
PAR .... (Pyridylazo)resorcinol [*Organic chemistry*]

PARA .... Parachute
PARA .... Paragon Resources Ltd. [*NASDAQ symbol*] (NQ)
PARA .... Paragraph (AFM)
PARA .... Paraguay
para .... Paraplegic
PARA .... Particle Aiding Replication of Adenovirus [*Virology*]
PARA .... Policy Analysis and Resource Allocation [*Department of State*]
PARA .... Professional Audiovideo Retailers Association (EA)
P-88/ARA ... Project '88: Americans for the Reagan Agenda (EA)
PARABAT ... Parachute Battalion [*Army*]
paracent ..... Paracentesis [*Medicine*]
PARACOMPT ... Parameter Analysis of Respiration Agents Considering Operations Motivation Protection and Time Model (MCD)
PARACS ..... Perimeter Acquisition RADAR Attack Characterization System (MCD)
PARADE ..... Passive-Active Range Determination
Par Adm..... Parsons on the Law of Shipping and Admiralty [*A publication*] (DLA)
PARADROP ... Airdrop by Parachute
PAR AFF... Pars Affecta [*The Part Affected*] [*Pharmacy*]
PARAFRAG ... Parachute Fragmentation Bomb [*Air Force*]
PARAKU... Pasokan Rakyat Kalimantan Utara [*North Kalimantan People's Forces*] [*Malaya*]
PARAM..... Parameter (KSC)
Paramagn Rezon ... Paramagnitnyj Rezonans [*A publication*]
Paramaribo-Suriname Agric Exp Stn Bull ... Paramaribo-Suriname. Agricultural Experiment Station. Bulletin [*A publication*]
Para-Med... Para-Medico [*A publication*]
PARAMEDIC ... [*A*] Medical Service Person Qualified to Participate in Parachute Activities [*Air Force*] [*In a nonmilitary context, may refer to one who serves as a physician's assistant*]
Paramed Int ... Paramedics International [*A publication*]
PARAMI ... Parsons Active Ring-Around Miss Indicator
Par Am Law ... Parsons' Commentaries on American Law [*A publication*] (DLA)
Par Am Law Comm ... Parsons' Commentaries on American Law [*A publication*] (DLA)
PARAMP.. Parametric Amplifier
Par Ant ...... Parochial Antiquities [*A publication*] (DLA)
PARAPSYCH ... Parapsychology
PARARESCUE ... Rescue by Individuals Parachuted to Distressed Persons [*Air Force*]
Par Arter.... Paroi Arterielle-Arterial Wall [*A publication*]
PARASEV ... Paraglider Research Vehicle [*NASA*]
Parasit....... Parasitica [*A publication*]
Parasite Immunol ... Parasite Immunology [*A publication*]
Parasite Immunol (Oxf) ... Parasite Immunology (Oxford) [*A publication*]
Parasit Hung ... Parasitologia Hungarica [*A publication*]
Parasitol..... Parasitology [*A publication*]
PARASITOL ... Parasitology
Parasitol Hung ... Parasitologia Hungarica [*A publication*]
Parasitol Schriftenr ... Parasitologische Schriftenreihe [*A publication*]
Parasitol Today ... Parasitology Today [*A publication*]
Parasit Res ... Parasitology Research [*A publication*]
PARASYN ... Parametric Synthesis [*Data processing*]
PARATHORMONE ... Parathyroid Hormone [*Endocrinology*]
PARATROOPS ... Parachute Infantry [*Military*]
Parazitol Sb ... Parazitologicheskii Sbornik [*A publication*]
Parazit Sb .. Parazitologiceskii Sbornik [*A publication*]
Parazity Zhivotn Rast ... Parazity Zhivotnykh i Rastenii [*A publication*]
PARB........ Perimeter Acquisition RADAR Building [*Army*] (AABC)
Parbhani Agric Coll Mag ... Parbhani Agricultural College. Magazine [*A publication*]
PARBICA ... Pacific Regional Branch of the International Council on Archives (EAIO)
Par Bills & N ... Parsons on Bills and Notes [*A publication*] (DLA)
PARC........ Pacific Air Rescue Center [*or Command*] (CINC)
PARC........ Palo Alto Research Center [*Xerox Corp.*]
PARC........ Pan-African Resource Center (EA)
PARC........ Pan-African Rinderpest Campaign [*Organization of African Unity*]
PARC........ Park Communications, Inc. [*NASDAQ symbol*] (NQ)
PARC........ Plains Aquatic Research Conference. Proceedings [*A publication*]
PARC........ President's Appalachian Regional Commission
PARC........ Princeton Applied Research Corp.
PARC........ Principal Assistant Responsible for Contracting [*Army*]
PARC........ Progressive Aircraft Reconditioning [*or Repair*] Cycle
PARCA ...... Pan American Railway Congress Association
PARCH ..... Parchment (ADA)
PARCHM ... Parchment (ROG)
PARCHT ... Parchment
PaRCL....... Parsec Research Control Language [*Pronounced "parkul"*] [*Parsec Reseach*] [*Robotics*]
PARCOM ... Paris Commission [*See also CP*] (EAIO)
Par Cont..... Parsons on Contracts [*A publication*] (DLA)
Par Costs ... Parsons on Costs [*A publication*] (DLA)
PARCP...... PEMARS [*Procurement of Equipment and Missiles, Army Management and Accounting Reporting System*] Accounting and Reporting Control Point [*Army*]

PARCS ...... Perimeter Acquisition RADAR Attack Characterization System
             [*Army*]
PARD .... Parts Application Reliability Data   (IEEE)
PARD .... Periodic and Random Deviation
PARD .... Personnel Actions and Records Directorate [*Military Personnel
             Center*]   (AABC)
PARD .... Pilot Airborne Recovery Device [*A balloon-parachute*]
PARD .... Pilotless Aircraft Research Division [*Later, Applied Materials
             and Physics Division*] [*Langley Research Center*]
PARD .... Post-Accident Radioactivity Depletion [*Nuclear
             energy*]   (NRCH)
PARD .... Precision Annotated Retrieval Display [*System*] [*Data
             processing*]
PARDAC... Parallel Digital-to-Analog Converter
Par Dec ...... Parsons' Decisions [*2-7 Massachusetts*] [*A publication*]   (DLA)
PARDENTL ... Paradental
Pard Lois Mar ... Pardessus' Lois Maritimes [*A publication*]   (DLA)
PARDON .. Pastors' Anonymous Recovery-Directed Order for Newness
             [*Rehabilitation program for troubled clergymen*]
             [*Defunct*]
PARDOP... Passive Ranging Doppler
PARDP...... Perimeter Acquisition RADAR Data Processor
             [*Army*]   (AABC)
Pard Serv ... Pardessus' Traites des Servitudes [*A publication*]   (DLA)
PARE......... People Against Racism in Education
PAREA...... Pharmacological Reviews [*A publication*]
P/AREA .... Probationary Acting Radio Electrical Artificer [*British
             military*]   (DMA)
PAREC...... Pay Record
PA Rec .... Pennsylvania Record [*A publication*]   (DLA)
PAREN...... Parenthesis [*or Parentheses*]   (AFM)
PAREN...... Progressive Aircraft Engine Repair
PARENT... Parenteral
Parent Aust ... Parent Australia [*A publication*]   (APTA)
Parent & Cit ... Parent and Citizen [*A publication*]   (APTA)
Parents....... Parents' Magazine [*A publication*]
PARENTS ... People of America Responding to Educational Needs of
             Today's Society   (EA)
Parents Cit Guide ... Parents and Citizens Guide [*A publication*]
Parents' Mag ... Parents' Magazine and Better Family Living [*Later, Parents'
             Magazine*] [*A publication*]
PARENTSQ ... Parent Squadron Base [*Military*]   (NVT)
PA Rep....... Pennsylvania Reports [*A publication*]   (DLA)
Par Eq Cas ... Parsons' Select Equity Cases [*1842-51*] [*Pennsylvania*] [*A
             publication*]   (DLA)
Par Eq Cases ... Parsons' Select Equity Cases [*Pennsylvania*] [*A
             publication*]   (DLA)
Par Ess....... Parsons' Essays on Legal Topics [*A publication*]   (DLA)
PARET...... Parallel Architecture Research and Evaluation Tool [*Data
             processing*]
PAREX...... Programmed Accounts Receivable Extra Service [*Data
             processing*]
PARF......... Paradise Fruit Company, Inc. [*NASDAQ symbol*]   (NQ)
PARF......... Practical Allergy Research Foundation   (EA)
PARFAS... Passive Radio Frequency Acquisition System
Par & Fonb Med Jur ... Paris and Fonblanque's Medical Jurisprudence [*A
             publication*]   (DLA)
PARFOX... [*Front*] Parapet Foxhole   (MCD)
PARFR ...... Program for Applied Research on Fertility Regulation
             [*Northwestern University*] [*Research center*]
Parfuem Kosmet ... Parfuemerie und Kosmetik [*West Germany*] [*A
             publication*]
Parfum Cosmet Savons ... Parfums, Cosmetiques, Savons [*A publication*]
Parfum Mod ... Parfumerie Moderne [*A publication*]
Parfums Cos ... Parfums, Cosmetiques, Aromes [*A publication*]
Parfums Cosmet Savons ... Parfums, Cosmetiques, Savons [*A publication*]
Parfums Cosmet Savons Fr ... Parfums, Cosmetiques, Savons de France [*A
             publication*]
Parfums Fr ... Parfums de France [*A publication*]
Pargs.......... Guiraudus Pargues [*Authority cited in pre-1607 legal
             work*]   (DSA)
PARGS...... Parks and Recreation Girls Service
PARI......... Parent Attitude Research Instrument [*A questionnaire*]
PARIS .... Pictorial and Artifact Retrieval and Information System
             [*Canadian Heritage Information Network*] [*Information
             service or system*]
PARIS .... Planning Aid for Retail Information System [*IBM Corp.*]
PARIS .... Pour l'Amenagement et le Renouveau Institutionel et Social
             [*France*] [*Political party*]
PARIS .... Pulse Analysis-Recording Information System
Parisi.......... [*Petrus Paulus*] Parisius [*Flourished, 16th century*] [*Authority
             cited in pre-1607 legal work*]   (DSA)
Paris Med .. Paris Medical [*A publication*]
ParisR........ Paris Review [*A publication*]
Paris Rev.... Paris Review [*A publication*]
Paris Univ Lab Micropaleontol Trav ... Paris. Universite. Laboratoire de
             Micropaleontologie. Travaux [*A publication*]
Paris Univ Lab Paleontol Trav ... Paris. Universite. Laboratoire de
             Paleontologie. Travaux [*A publication*]
PARK......... Parkerized [*Metallurgy*] [*Tradename*]

Park .... Parker's English Exchequer Reports [*1743-67*] [*A
             publication*]   (DLA)
Park .... Parker's New Hampshire Reports [*A publication*]   (DLA)
Park .... Parker's New York Criminal Cases [*1823-68*] [*A
             publication*]   (DLA)
PARK........ Parks. International Journal for Managers of National Parks,
             Historic Sites, and Other Protected Areas [*A publication*]
PARKA...... Pacific Acoustic Research Kaneohe-Alaska [*Navy*]
Park Adm... Park Administration [*A publication*]
Park Arb .... Parker on Arbitration [*1820*] [*A publication*]   (DLA)
Park Ch...... Parker's Practice in Chancery [*A publication*]   (DLA)
Park CR..... Parker's New York Criminal Reports [*A publication*]   (DLA)
Park Cr Cas ... Parker's New York Criminal Cases [*A publication*]   (DLA)
Park Crim L ... Parker's New York Criminal Reports [*A publication*]   (DLA)
Park Crim (NY) ... Parker's New York Criminal Cases [*A publication*]   (DLA)
Park Crim R ... Parker's New York Criminal Reports [*A publication*]   (DLA)
Park Crim Rep ... Parker's New York Criminal Reports [*A
             publication*]   (DLA)
Park Cr Rep ... Parker's New York Criminal Reports [*A publication*]   (DLA)
Park Dig .... Parker's California Digest [*A publication*]   (DLA)
Park Dow ... Park. Dower [*1819*] [*A publication*]   (DLA)
Parker........ Parker on the Laws of Shipping and Insurance [*England*] [*A
             publication*]   (DLA)
Parker .... Parker's English Exchequer Reports [*A publication*]   (DLA)
Parker .... Parker's New Hampshire Reports [*A publication*]   (DLA)
Parker .... Parker's New York Criminal Reports [*6 vols.*] [*A
             publication*]   (DLA)
Parker Cr Cas ... Parker's New York Criminal Reports [*A
             publication*]   (ILCA)
Parker Cr Cas (NY) ... Parker's New York Criminal Reports [*A
             publication*]   (ILCA)
Parker Cr R ... Parker's New York Criminal Reports [*A publication*]   (ILCA)
Parker Cr R (NY) ... Parker's New York Criminal Reports [*A
             publication*]   (ILCA)
Parker's Crim R ... Parker's New York Criminal Reports [*A
             publication*]   (DLA)
Parker's Crim Rep (NY) ... Parker's New York Criminal Reports [*A
             publication*]   (DLA)
Parker's Cr R ... Parker's New York Criminal Reports [*A publication*]   (DLA)
Park Exch ... Parker's English Exchequer Reports [*1743-67*] [*A
             publication*]   (DLA)
Park Hist Ch ... Parkes' History of Court of Chancery [*1828*] [*A
             publication*]   (DLA)
Park Ins ..... Parker's Insurance [*8 eds.*] [*1787-1842*] [*England*] [*A
             publication*]   (DLA)
Park NH .... Parker's New Hampshire Reports [*A publication*]   (DLA)
Park Pr Ch ... Parker's Practice in Chancery [*A publication*]   (DLA)
Park Rev Cas ... Parker's English Exchequer Reports (Revenue Cases) [*A
             publication*]   (DLA)
Parks and R ... Parks and Recreation [*A publication*]
Parks & Rec ... Parks and Recreation [*A publication*]
Parks & Wild ... Parks and Wildlife [*A publication*]
Parks Wildl ... Parks and Wildlife [*A publication*]   (APTA)
PARL........ Parallel
Parl .... Parlament [*A publication*]
PARL........ Parliament
Parl .... Parliamentarian [*United Kingdom*] [*A publication*]
PARL........ Parlux Fragrances, Inc. [*NASDAQ symbol*]   (NQ)
Par L .... Parsons' Law by Hughes [*A publication*]   (DLA)
PARL........ Prince Albert RADAR Laboratory
Parl Aff ...... Parliamentary Affairs [*A publication*]
Parlam Beil Polit Zeitgesch ... Parlament Beilage aus Politik und
             Zeitgeschichte [*A publication*]
PARLARS ... Particulars
Par Laws Bus ... Parsons' Laws of Business [*A publication*]   (DLA)
PARLB ...... Parliamentary Borough
Parl Cas ..... Parliamentary Cases [*House of Lords Reports*] [*A
             publication*]   (DLA)
Parl Deb..... Parliamentary Debates [*A publication*]   (APTA)
Parl Deb HC ... Parliamentary Debates. House of Commons [*United
             Kingdom*] [*A publication*]
Parl Deb HL ... Parliamentary Debates. House of Lords [*United Kingdom*] [*A
             publication*]
PAR Legis Bul ... PAR [*Public Affairs Research*] Legislative Bulletin [*A
             publication*]
Parl Eur Doc ... Parlement Europeen. Documents de Seance [*A
             publication*]   (DLA)
Parl Hist Eng ... Parliamentary History of England [*Pre-1803*] [*A
             publication*]   (DLA)
Parliam Aff ... Parliamentary Affairs [*A publication*]
Parliamentary Aff ... Parliamentary Affairs [*A publication*]
Parliament Pap (Commonw Aust) ... Parliamentary Paper (Commonwealth of
             Australia) [*A publication*]
Parliam Liaison Group Altern Energy Strategies Bull ... Parliamentary Liaison
             Group for Alternative Energy Strategies. Bulletin [*A
             publication*]
PARLIKDER ... Partiya Litsom k Derevne [*The Party Face to Face with the
             Countryside*] [*Given name popular in Russia after the
             Bolshevik Revolution*]
Parlim Aff ... Parliamentary Affairs [*A publication*]
PARLO...... Parlando [*Music*]   (ROG)

Parl Reg ..... Parliamentary Register [*England*] [*A publication*]   (DLA)
PARLT ...... Parliament
PARLTY ... Parliamentary
PARLY ...... Parliamentary
PARM ...... Parallelogram [*Geometry*]   (ROG)
PARM ...... Parameter [*Data processing*]
Par M .... Parents' Magazine [*A publication*]
PARM ...... Participating Manager
PARM ...... Partido Autentico de la Revolucion Mexicana [*Authentic Party of the Mexican Revolution*] [*Political party*]   (PPW)
PARM ...... Persistent Antiradiation Missile   (MCD)
PARM ...... Program Analysis for Resource Management
PARMA ..... Program for Analysis, Reporting, and Maintenance [*Data processing*]
PARMA ..... Public Agency Risk Managers Association [*San Jose, CA*]   (EA)
Par Mar Ins ... Parsons on Marine Insurance and General Average [*A publication*]   (DLA)
Par Mar L ... Parsons on Maritime Law [*A publication*]   (DLA)
Par Med ..... Paris Medical [*A publication*]
PARMEDL ... Paramedical
Par Merc Law ... Parsons on Mercantile Law [*A publication*]   (DLA)
Par N & B .. Parsons' Notes and Bills [*A publication*]   (DLA)
Par Nucl ..... Particles and Nuclei [*A publication*]
PARO .... Partners Oil Co. [*NASDAQ symbol*]   (NQ)
PAROCH .. Parochial   (ROG)
Paroch Ant ... Kennett's Parochial Antiquities [*A publication*]   (DLA)
Parod Epic Gr Rel ... Parodorum Epicorum Graecorum Reliquiae [*A publication*]   (OCD)
Parodontol Stomatol Nuova ... Parodontologia e Stomatologia Nuova [*A publication*]
Parola Passato ... Parola del Passato. Rivista di Studi Antichi [*Naples*] [*A publication*]
Parole et Soc ... Parole et Societe [*A publication*]
Par Or .... Parole de l'Orient [*A publication*]
PAROS ..... Passive Ranging on Submarines [*Navy*]
PAROSS ... Passive/Active Reporting Ocean Surveillance System [*Navy*]   (NVT)
PAROX ..... Paroxysmal [*Medicine*]
PARP .... Production Assistance Report to Pricing [*DoD*]
Parpal .... [*Thomas*] Parpalea [*Flourished, 16th century*] [*Authority cited in pre-1607 legal work*]   (DSA)
Par Part ..... Parsons on Partnership [*1889*] [*A publication*]   (DLA)
Par Pass .... Parola del Passato [*A publication*]
PARPRO .... Peacetime Aerial Reconnaissance Program [*Military*]   (NVT)
PAR Pseudo-Allerg React ... PAR. Pseudo-Allergic Reactions [*A publication*]
PAR Pseudo-Allerg React Involvement Drugs Chem ... PAR. Pseudo-Allergic Reactions. Involvement of Drugs and Chemicals [*A publication*]
PARQ .... Parental Acceptance-Rejection Questionnaire [*Psychology*]
Parques Jard ... Parques y Jardines [*A publication*]
PARR .... Pakistan Atomic Research Reactor
ParR .... Paris Review [*A publication*]
Par R .... Parsons' Select Equity Cases [*Pennsylvania*] [*A publication*]   (DLA)
ParR .... Partisan Review [*A publication*]
PARR .... Post-Accident Radioactivity Removal [*Nuclear energy*]   (NRCH)
PARR .... Procurement Authorization and Receiving Report [*NASA*]   (KSC)
PARR .... Program Analysis and Resources Review
PARRA .... Parramatta [*Prison in New South Wales*] [*Australia*]   (DSUE)
PARRC ...... Pacific Aerospace Rescue and Recovery Center [*Air Force*]
Par Rights Cit ... Parsons on the Rights of a Citizen of the United States [*A publication*]   (DLA)
PARRS ...... Postal Analysis Response and Reporting System [*Computer system designed to track mail through the US Postal Service*] [*R. R. Donnelley & Sons Co.*]
PARRS ...... Psychological Abstracts Reference Retrieval System [*Syracuse University*]
PARS .... Parachute Altitude Recognition System   (MCD)
Pars .... Parsons' Select Equity Cases [*1842-51*] [*Pennsylvania*] [*A publication*]   (DLA)
PARS .... Passenger Airlines Reservation System
PARS .... Patrol Analysis Recording System [*British*]
PARS .... Perimeter Acquisition RADAR [*Characterization*] System   (MCD)
PARS .... Photoacoustic Raman Spectroscopy
PARS .... Pilotless Aircraft Research Station [*NASA*]
PARS .... Procurement Accounting and Reporting System [*Navy*]   (NVT)
PARS .... Programmed Airline Reservation System
PARS .... Property Accountability Record System   (NASA)
PARS .... Provincial Archives and Records Service [*Canada*]
PARSA ...... Parasitological Society of Southern Africa   (EAIO)
Pars Ans .... Parsons' Answer to the Fifth Part of Coke's Reports [*A publication*]   (DLA)
Pars Bills & N ... Parsons on Bills and Notes [*A publication*]   (DLA)
Pars Cont ... Parsons on Contracts [*A publication*]   (DLA)
Pars Dec ..... Parsons' Decisions [*2-7 Massachusetts*] [*A publication*]   (DLA)
PARSEC .... Parallax Second [*Unit of interstellar-space measure*]
PARSEC .... Parser and Extensible Compiler [*Programming language*]   (CSR)

PARSECS ... Program for Astronomical Research and Scientific Experiments Concerning Space
Pars Eq Cas ... Parsons' Select Equity Cases [*1842-51*] [*Pennsylvania*] [*A publication*]   (DLA)
PARSET .... Precision Askania Range System of Electronic Timing   (MUGU)
PARSEV .... Paraglider Research Vehicle [*NASA*]   (KSC)
Par Sh & Adm ... Parsons on the Law of Shipping and Admiralty [*A publication*]   (DLA)
PARSIM ... Perimeter Acquisition RADAR Simulation [*Missile system evaluation*]   (RDA)
PARSIP ..... Point Arguello Range Safety Impact Predictor   (MUGU)
Pars Mar Ins ... Parsons on Marine Insurance [*A publication*]   (DLA)
Pars Mar Law ... Parsons on Maritime Law [*A publication*]   (DLA)
Pars Merc Law ... Parsons on Mercantile Law [*A publication*]   (DLA)
Parsons' .... Parsons' Select Equity Cases [*Pennsylvania*] [*A publication*]   (DLA)
Parsons J ... Parsons Journal [*A publication*]
PARSQ ..... Pararescue
Pars Sel Eq Cas (PA) ... Parsons' Select Equity Cases [*Pennsylvania*] [*A publication*]   (DLA)
Pars S Eq Cas ... Parsons' Select Equity Cases [*Pennsylvania*] [*A publication*]   (DLA)
Pars Shipp & Adm ... Parsons on Shipping and Admiralty [*A publication*]   (DLA)
PARSYM .. Partial Symmetry
PARSYN ... Parametric Synthesis [*Data processing*]
PART .... Pan American Round Tables in the USA [*Defunct*]   (EA)
PART .... Partial   (MSA)
PART .... Participate   (AABC)
PART .... Participle [*Grammar*]
PART .... Particular
PART .... Partis [*A Part*] [*Pharmacy*]
PART .... Partition [*Ballistics*]
PART .... Partner   (ADA)
PART .... Parts Allocation Requirements Technique
PART .... Performing Arts Repertory Theater
PARTAC ... Precision Askania Range Target Acquisition and Control   (MUGU)
Part Accel .. Particle Accelerators [*A publication*]
PART AEQ ... Partes Aequales [*Equal Parts*] [*Pharmacy*]
PART AEQUAL ... Partes Aequales [*Equal Parts*] [*Pharmacy*]   (ROG)
Part An ...... De Partibus Animalium [*of Aristotle*] [*Classical studies*]   (OCD)
Part Charact ... Particle Characterization [*A publication*]
PART DOLENT ... Partes Dolentes [*Painful Parts*] [*Pharmacy*]
Parth .... Parthenius [*First century BC*] [*Classical studies*]   (OCD)
Partic .... Participating [*or Participation*]   (DLA)
PARTIC .... Participial [*Grammar*]
PARTIC .... Particle
PARTIC .... Particular
Particle B ... Particleboard and Medium Density Fibreboard. Annual Publication and Shipments [*A publication*]
Particleboard/Compos Mater Ser ... Particleboard/Composite Materials Series [*A publication*]
PARTICO ... Parti d'Interets Congolais [*Party for Congolese Interests*] [*Political party*]
Partidas ...... Moreau-Lislet and Carleton's Laws of Las Siete Partidas in Force in Louisiana [*A publication*]   (DLA)
Partisan R ... Partisan Review [*A publication*]
Partisan Rev ... Partisan Review [*A publication*]
PARTN ...... Partnership   (ADA)
PARTNER ... Proof of Analog Results through a Numerical Equivalent Routine [*Data processing*]
Part Nucl ... Particles and Nuclei [*A publication*]
Part and Nucl ... Particles and Nuclei [*A publication*]
Part Or .... Partitiones Oratoriae [*of Cicero*] [*Classical studies*]   (OCD)
PARTR ...... Particular   (ROG)
Part R .... Partisan Review [*A publication*]
PARTS ...... Precision Approach RADAR Training System   (MCD)
PARTS ...... Price Analysis and Review Technique for Spares
PART VIC ... Partitis Vicibus [*In Divided Parts*] [*Pharmacy*]
Party .... Party Newspapers [*A publication*]
Part Z .... Partiinaya Zhizn [*A publication*]
PARU .... Personnel Applied Research Unit [*Canadian military*]
PARU .... Photographic and Reproduction Unit
PARU .... Police Aerial Reinforcement [*or Resupply*] Unit [*Thailand*]   (CINC)
PARU .... Postanesthetic Recovery Unit [*Medicine*]
PARV .... Paravane [*Anti-moored-mine device*]   (KSC)
PARV .... Parvus [*Small*] [*Pharmacy*]
ParVec ...... Purdue Center for Parallel and Vector Computing [*Purdue University*] [*Research center*]   (RCD)
PARVSTRCRA ... Paravane and Stores Crane [*Engineering*]
PARWAC ... Archivum Veterinarium Polonicum [*A publication*]
Par WC ...... Parish Will Case [*A publication*]   (DLA)
Par Wills .... Parsons on Wills [*1854*] [*A publication*]   (DLA)
PARZEP .... Pochvoznanie Agrokhimiya i Rastitelna Zashtita [*A publication*]
PAS .... National Postsecondary Agriculture Student Organization   (EA)
PAS .... Palestine Aid Society of America   (EA)

PaS............ Pamietnik Slowianski [*A publication*]
PAS........... Papers. American School of Classical Studies [*Athens*] [*A publication*]
PAS........... Para-Aminosalicylic [*Acid*] [*Organic chemistry*]
PAS........... Parametric Amplifier System
PaS........... Paranoia Subtle [*Psychology*]
PAS........... Parent Attitude Scale
PAS........... Paros [*Greece*] [*Airport symbol*]   (OAG)
PAS........... Parti Islam se Malaysia [*Islamic Party of Malaysia*] [*Political party*]   (PPW)
PAS........... Partido de Accion Socialista [*Socialist Action Party*] [*Costa Rica*] [*Political party*]   (PPW)
PAS........... Partito di Azione de Sardegna [*Sardinian Action Party*] [*Italy*] [*Political party*]   (PPW)
PAS........... Pasadena [*California*] [*Seismograph station code, US Geological Survey*]   (SEIS)
PA S.......... Pascal Second
PAS........... Pascal Source File [*Data processing*]
PAS........... Passage   (AABC)
PAS........... Passed to the Adjacent Sector
Pas .... Passipoverus [*Flourished, 13th century*] [*Authority cited in pre-1607 legal work*]   (DSA)
PAS........... Patient Administration System [*British*]
PAS........... Patients' Aid Society
PAS........... Payload Accommodations Studies [*NASA*]   (NASA)
PA S.......... Pennsylvania Superior Court Reports [*A publication*]   (DLA)
PASA.......... Percussive Arts Society   (EA)
PAS........... Peredneaziatskij Sbornik [*A publication*]
PAS........... Perigee-Apogee Satellite [*Aerospace*]
PAS........... Perigee-Apogee Stage [*Aerospace*]
PAS........... Perigee-Apogee System [*Aerospace*]
PA/S.......... Periodic Acid/Schiff [*A stain*]
PAS........... Peripheral Anterior Synechia [*Ophthalmology*]
PAS........... Personal Acquaintance Service
PAS........... Personnel Accounting Symbol [*Air Force*]   (AFM)
PAS........... Personnel Accounting System [*Marine Corps*]
PAS........... Personnel Activity Sequence   (AAG)
PAS........... Personnel Administration Section [*Library Administration Division of ALA*]
PAS........... Personnel Assignment Survey   (MCD)
PAS........... Phase Address System
PAS........... Phase Array System
PAS........... Philanthropic Advisory Service
PAS........... Phosphoric Acid-Sensitive
PAS........... Photoacoustic Spectrometry [*Also, OAS*]
PAS........... Physicians for Automotive Safety [*Defunct*]   (EA)
PAS........... Pierce-Arrow Society   (EA)
PAS........... Pilots Advisory Service
PAS........... Pilot's Attack Sight [*British*]
PAS........... Pioneer America Society   (EA)
PAS........... Plasma Arc System
PAS........... Pneumatic Air Saw
PAS........... Polish Academy of Sciences
PAS........... Polish Astronautical Society [*See also PTA*]
PAS........... Poly(alkyl Sulfone) [*Organic chemistry*]
PAS........... Polyaminosiloxane [*Organic chemistry*]
PAS........... Polyarylsulfone [*Organic chemistry*]
PAS........... Postacoustic Spectroscopy
PAS........... Posterior Area of [*Loose*] Skin
PAST......... Postponed Accounting System [*Banking*]
PAS........... Power Apparatus and Systems   (MCD)
PAS........... Preaward Survey [*To determine a contractor's capability*] [*DoD*]
PAS........... Precise Acquisition System
PAS........... Pregnancy Advisory Service [*British*]
PAS........... Presidential Appointee Subject
PAS........... President's Advisor for Science
PAS........... Pressure-Assisted Sintering [*Forging*] [*Automotive engineering*]
PAS........... Pressurized Air Subsystem
PAS........... Primary Alerting System
Pas........... Primary Ascent System [*Aerospace*]   (NASA)
PAS........... Principal Assistant Secretary
PAS........... Privacy Act Statement   (NRCH)
PAS........... Problem Appraisal Scales [*Personality development test*] [*Psychology*]
PAS........... Proceedings. Aristotelian Society [*A publication*]
PAS........... Processed Array Signal
PAS........... Procurement Action System   (MCD)
PAS........... Procurement Appropriation, Secondary   (MCD)
PAS........... Product Assurance Survey
PAS........... Product Availability Search   (MCD)
PAS........... Professional Activity Study [*Later, CPHA*]
PAS........... Professor of Aerospace Studies [*Air Force*]   (AFIT)
PAS........... Professor of Air Science [*Air Force*]
PAS........... Program Activity Structure
PAS........... Program Address Storage   (IEEE)
PAS........... Program of Advanced Studies
PAS........... Progressive Accumulated Stress [*Psychiatry*]
PAS........... Propulsion and Auxiliary Systems Department [*David W. Taylor Naval Ship Research and Development Center*]
PAS........... Public Address System

PAS........... Public Administration Service   (EA)
PAS........... Pulmonary Artery Stenosis [*Medicine*]
PAS........... Pump Actuator Set
PAS........... Pyrotechnics Arming Switch
Pas .... Terminus Paschae [*Easter Term*] [*Latin*] [*Legal term*]   (DLA)
PASA........ Pacific American Steamship Association [*Later, AIMS*]
PASA........ Para-Aminosalicylic Acid [*Organic chemistry*]
PASA........ Personnel Administrative Services Agency [*Army*]
PASA........ Primary Acquired Sideroblastic Anemia [*Medicine*]
PASAR ...... Psychological Abstracts Search and Retrieval
PASAT ...... Poppleton-Allen Sales Aptitude Test
PASB .... Pan American Sanitary Bureau [*Executive organ of PAHO*]
PASb.......... Predneaziatskii Sbornik Voprosy Khattologii i Khurritologii [*A publication*]   (BJA)
PASBI....... Palo Alto Social Background Inventory [*Psychology*]
PASC .... Deadhorse [*Alaska*] [*ICAO location identifier*]   (ICLI)
PASC .... Pacific Area Standards Congress [*American National Standards Institute*]
PASC .... Palestine Armed Struggle Command   (PD)
PASC .... Pan American Sanitary Conference
PASC .... Pan American Standards Commission [*See also COPANT*]   (EAIO)
PASC .... Parkscan. Parks Canada [*A publication*]
Pasc........... Paschal [*Easter Term*] [*Legal term*]   (DLA)
Pasc........... Paschal's Reports [*25, 28-31 Texas*] [*A publication*]   (DLA)
PASC .... Primitive Art Society of Chicago   (EA)
PASCA ...... Positron Annihilation Spectroscopy for Chemical Analysis
PASCAL.... [*A*] programming language [*1968*] [*Named after French mathematician Blaise Pascal, 1623-62*]
PASCAL.... Philips Automatic Sequence Calculator
PASCAL.... Program Applique a la Selection et a la Compilation Automatique de la Litterature [*Centre National de la Recherche Scientifique-Informascience*] [*Bibliographic database*]
PASCH...... Pascha [*Easter*] [*Church calendars*]   (ROG)
Pasch......... Paschal [*Easter Term*] [*Legal term*]   (DLA)
Paschal ...... Paschal's Reports [*28-31 Texas*] [*Supplement to Vol. 25*] [*A publication*]   (DLA)
Paschal's Ann Const ... Paschal's United States Constitution, Annotated [*A publication*]   (DLA)
Pasch Dig... Paschal's Texas Digest of Decisions [*A publication*]   (DLA)
PA Sch J.... Pennsylvania School Journal [*A publication*]
PAS Cl St... Papers. American School of Classical Studies at Athens [*A publication*]
PASCT ...... Pan American Society for Chemotherapy of Tuberculosis [*See also SAQT*] [*Buenos Aires, Argentina*]   (EAIO)
PASE .... Post-Apollo Space Electrophoresis [*European Space Agency*]
PASE .... Power-Assisted Storage Equipment   (IEEE)
PASED ...... Proceedings. Annual Symposium. Society of Flight Test Engineers [*A publication*]
PASEP....... Passed Separately [*Military*]
PASES....... Performance Assessment of Syntax: Elicited and Spontaneous [*Educational test*]
PASF .... Photographic Art and Science Foundation   (EA)
PASG........ Patent Abstracts Section, Official Gazette [*Federal government*] [*A publication*]
PASG........ Pneumatic Antishock Garment [*Roentgenology*]
PASG........ Pulse Amplifier/Symbol Generator
PASG........ Pulse Analyzer Signal Generator
PASGT ...... Personnel Armor System for Ground Troops   (RDA)
PASI .... Pacific Silver Corp. [*NASDAQ symbol*]   (NQ)
PASI .... Pikunas Adult Stress Inventory [*Psychology*]
PASI .... Professional Associate, Chartered Surveyors' Institution [*Later, ARICS*]
PASI .... Sitka [*Alaska*] [*ICAO location identifier*]   (ICLI)
PASIC .... Percussive Arts Society International Convention [*Percussive Arts Society*]   (TSPED)
PASITAM ... Program of Advanced Studies of Institution Building and Technical Assistance Methodologies [*MUCIA*]
PASJD....... Passive Solar Journal [*A publication*]
Pas L......... Pasicrisie Luxembourgeoise [*A publication*]
PASL .... Polish Americans for the Statue of Liberty   (EA)
PASLA ...... Programmable Asynchronous Line Adapter
Pa Slow ..... Pamietnik Slowianski [*A publication*]
Pas Lux ..... Pasicrisie Luxembourgeoise [*Luxembourg Law Reports*] [*A publication*]   (ILCA)
PASM....... Periodic Acid - Silver Methenamine [*Biological stain*]
PASM....... Preaward Survey Monitor [*DoD*]
PASMB .... Proceedings. Australian Society for Medical Research [*A publication*]
Pas Mus..... Pastoral Music [*A publication*]
PASN........ Parisian, Inc. [*NASDAQ symbol*]   (NQ)
PASN........ St. Paul Island [*Alaska*] [*ICAO location identifier*]   (ICLI)
PASO........ Pan American Sanitary Organization
PASO........ Pan American Sports Organization [*See also ODEPA*] [*Mexico City, Mexico*]   (EAIO)
PA/SO....... Port Antisubmarine Officer [*Navy*]
PASO........ Principal Armament Supply Officer [*British military*]   (DMA)
PASOC...... Partido de Accion Socialista [*Party of Socialist Action*] [*Spain*] [*Political party*]   (PPW)

PASOK...... Panellinion Sosialistikon Kinema [*Pan-Hellenic Socialist Movement*] [*Greek*] [*Political party*] (PPE)
PASOLS.... Pacific Area Senior Officer Logistics Seminar (MCD)
PA/SP....... Positioner Antenna and Solar Panel [*NASA*]
PAS(PR).... Principal Assistant Secretary (Priority)
PASQ......... Pasquale Food Co., Inc. [*NASDAQ symbol*] (NQ)
PASRB ...... Preaward Survey Review Board [*DoD*]
PASS .... Panic Attack Sufferers' Support Groups (EA)
PASS .... Parents Against Subliminal Seduction (EA)
PASS .... Parts Analysis Summary Sheet
PASS .... Passage [*Maps and charts*] (KSC)
PASS .... Passenger (KSC)
PASS .... Passenger Automated Selection System (ADA)
PASS .... Passim [*Everywhere*] [*Latin*]
PASS .... Passive
PASS .... Passive-Active Surveillance System (MCD)
PASS .... Patrol Advanced Surveillance System (MCD)
PASS .... Pay/Personnel Administrative Support System (NVT)
PASS .... Penetration Aids/Strike System (NG)
PASS .... Performance Analysis Subsystem [*Military*] (CAAL)
PASS .... Personalized Automotive Security System [*In product name, PASS-Key*] [*Delco Electronics*] [*Automotive engineering*]
PASS .... Petroleum Abstracts Search Service [*Online information service*]
PASS .... Phased Array Sector Scanner [*Instrument for measuring ultrasound*] [*Trademark of General Electric Co.*]
PASS .... Phoenix Ability Survey System [*Test*]
PASS .... Planning and Scheduling Session
PASS .... Planning and Scheduling System (NASA)
PASS .... Policyowner Attitude Survey Service [*LIMRA*]
PASS .... Post-Accident Sampling Systems [*Nuclear energy*]
PASS .... Precision Autocollimating Solar Sensor
PASS .... Primary Academic Sentiment Scale [*Child development test*]
PASS .... Primary Avionics Software System (NASA)
PASS .... Private Alarm Signalling System
PASS .... Private Automatic Switching System [*Telecommunications*]
PASS .... Procurement Aging and Staging System [*Army*] (AABC)
PASS .... Procurement Automated Source System [*Small Business Administration*] [*Washington, DC*] [*Information service or system*] (IID)
PASS .... Production Automated Scheduling System (IEEE)
PASS .... Professional Airways Systems Specialists (EA)
PASS .... Professional Amateur Sports Systems [*Cable-television network*]
PASS .... Professional Association of Secretarial Services [*Later, NASS*] (EA)
PASS .... Program Aid Software Systems [*Data processing*] (IEEE)
PASS .... Program Alternative Simulation System (KSC)
PASS .... Program Analysis of Service Systems [*Procedure to evaluate human service programs*]
PASS .... Programmed Access/Security System [*Card Key Systems*]
PASSA....... Pacific American Steamship Association [*Later, AIMS*] (EA)
Passenger Transp ... Passenger Transport [*A publication*]
Passeng Transp J ... Passenger Transport Journal [*England*] [*A publication*]
PASSIM.... President's Advisory Staff on Scientific Information Management
PASS-IN-REVIEW ... Priority Aircraft Subsystem Suitability Intensive Review (MCD)
PASSION ... Program for Algebraic Sequences Specifically of Input-Output Nature [*Data processing*]
PASSR...... Passenger (DCTA)
PASSWD .. Password [*Data processing*]
PAST .... Pasteurella [*Genus of bacteria*]
PAST .... Pastillus [*A Lozenge, Troch, Pastil*] [*Pharmacy*] (ROG)
Past........... Pastoral Epistles (BJA)
PAST......... Pastorate
PA St.......... Pennsylvania State Reports [*A publication*] (DLA)
PAST .... Portable Arming System Trainer (MCD)
PAST .... Process Accessible Segment Table
PAST .... Professor of Air Science and Tactics
PAST .... Propulsion and Associated Systems Test (MCD)
PA Stat Ann ... Pennsylvania Statutes, Annotated [*A publication*] (DLA)
PA Stat Ann (Purdon) ... Pennsylvania Statutes, Annotated (Purdon) [*A publication*] (DLA)
PA State..... Pennsylvania State Reports [*A publication*] (DLA)
PA State Coll Miner Ind Exp Stn Bull ... Pennsylvania State College. Mineral Industries Experiment Station. Bulletin [*A publication*]
PA State Coll Miner Ind Exp Stn Circ ... Pennsylvania State College. Mineral Industries Experiment Station. Circular [*A publication*]
PA State Coll Stud ... Pennsylvania State College. Studies [*A publication*]
PA State R ... Pennsylvania State Reports [*A publication*] (DLA)
PA State Univ Coll Agric Agric Exp Stn Prog Rep ... Pennsylvania State University. College of Agriculture. Agricultural Experiment Station. Progress Report [*A publication*]
PA State Univ Coll Agric Ext Serv Spec Circ ... Pennsylvania State University. College of Agriculture. Agricultural Extension Service. Special Circular [*A publication*]
PA State Univ Coll Earth Miner Sci Exp Stn Circ ... Pennsylvania State University. College of Earth and Mineral Sciences. Experiment Station. Circular [*A publication*]

PA State Univ Coll Earth Miner Sci Spec Publ ... Pennsylvania State University. College of Earth and Mineral Sciences. Special Publication [*A publication*]
PA State Univ Coll Eng Eng Proc ... Pennsylvania State University. College of Engineering. Engineering Proceedings [*A publication*]
PA State Univ Coll Eng Eng Res Bull ... Pennsylvania State University. College of Engineering. Engineering Research Bulletin [*A publication*]
PA State Univ Earth Miner Sci Exp Stn Circ ... Pennsylvania State University. Earth and Mineral Sciences Experiment Station. Circular [*A publication*]
PA State Univ Miner Ind Exp Stn Bull ... Pennsylvania State University. Mineral Industries Experiment Station. Bulletin [*A publication*]
PA State Univ Miner Ind Exp Stn Circ ... Pennsylvania State University. Mineral Industries Experiment Station. Circular [*A publication*]
PA State Univ Sch For Resour Res Briefs ... Pennsylvania State University. School of Forest Resources. Research Briefs [*A publication*]
PA State Univ Stud ... Pennsylvania State University. Studies [*A publication*]
PastBl .... Pastoralblaetter [*Stuttgart*] [*A publication*]
Pastbl........ Pastoralblatt [*A publication*]
Past Care & Couns Abstr ... Pastoral Care and Counseling Abstracts [*A publication*]
PA St Coll An Rp ... Pennsylvania State College. Annual Report [*A publication*]
Pasteur Inst South India (Coonoor) Annu Rep Dir Sci Rep ... Pasteur Institute of Southern India (Coonoor). Annual Report of the Director and Scientific Report [*A publication*]
Past Forum ... Pastorales Forum fuer die Seelsorger im Erzbistum Muenchen-Freising [*A publication*]
PASTIC..... Pakistan Scientific and Technological Information Center [*Formerly, PANSDOC*] [*Quaid-I-Azan University Campus*] [*Islamabad, Pakistan*]
Past Mus.... Pastoral Music [*A publication*]
PAstO .... Our Lady of Angels College, Aston, PA [*Library symbol*] [*Library of Congress*] (LCLS)
Pastoralist ... Pastoralist and Grazier [*A publication*] (APTA)
Pastoral Rev ... Pastoral Review [*A publication*]
Pastoral Rev Graz Rec ... Pastoral Review and Graziers' Record [*A publication*] (APTA)
Pastor Care Educ ... Pastoral Care in Education [*A publication*]
Past & Pres ... Past and Present [*A publication*]
Past Pres.... Past and Present. Studies in the History of Civilization [*A publication*]
Past Presen ... Past and Present [*A publication*]
Past Psych ... Pastoral Psychology [*A publication*]
Past R........ Pastoral Review and Graziers' Record [*A publication*] (APTA)
PA St R .... Pennsylvania State Reports [*A publication*] (DLA)
PASTRAM ... Passenger Traffic Management System [*Army*]
Past Rev..... Pastoral Review and Graziers' Record [*A publication*] (APTA)
PA St Tr..... Pennsylvania State Trials (Hogan) [*A publication*] (DLA)
PASU......... Pan-African Socialist Union [*Southern Rhodesia*]
PASU......... Patrol Aircraft Service Unit
PASU......... Performing Arts Study Unit (EA)
PASU......... Preliminary Approval for Service Use [*Military*]
PASU......... Provisional Approval for Service Use [*Navy*] (NVT)
PA Summary ... Summary of Pennsylvania Jurisprudence [*A publication*] (DLA)
PA Super.... Pennsylvania Superior Court Reports [*A publication*] (DLA)
PA Super Ct ... Pennsylvania Superior Court Reports [*A publication*] (DLA)
PA Superior Ct ... Pennsylvania Superior Court Reports [*A publication*] (DLA)
PASUS ...... Pan American Society of the United States (EA)
PASV .... Sparrevohn Air Force Station [*Alaska*] [*ICAO location identifier*] (ICLI)
PASWEPS ... Passive Antisubmarine Warfare Environmental Protection System [*Navy*] (NATG)
PASY .... Shemya Air Force Base [*Alaska*] [*ICAO location identifier*] (ICLI)
PASYD...... Policy Analysis and Information Systems [*A publication*]
Pat............. All India Reporter, Patna Series [*A publication*] (ILCA)
PAt............. Allentown Public Library, Allentown, PA [*Library symbol*] [*Library of Congress*] (LCLS)
PAT .... Athenaeum of Philadelphia (EA)
PAT .... Athenaeum of Philadelphia, Philadelphia, PA [*OCLC symbol*] (OCLC)
Pat............. Indian Law Reports, Patna Series [*A publication*] (DLA)
Pat............. Indian Rulings, Patna Series [*A publication*] (DLA)
PAT .... International Brotherhood of Painters and Allied Trades
PAT .... National Patents Appeal Tribunal [*England*] (DLA)
PAT .... Paper Trade Journal [*A publication*]
PAT .... Papuan Air Transport
PAT .... Parametric Artificial Talker
PAT .... Paroxysmal Atrial [*or Auricular*] Tachycardia [*Medicine*]
PAT .... Parts Accountability Technique (MCD)
PAT .... Passive Acoustic Target [*Military*]
PAT .... Passive Acoustic Torpedo [*Military*]
PAT .... Passive Angle Track (NVT)
PAT .... Patent (KSC)
PAT .... Patent Rolls [*British*]

Pat............. Paterson's Scotch Appeals, House of Lords [*A publication*] (DLA)
Pat............. Pathe [*Record label*] [*France*]
PAT .... Patient
PAT .... Patna [*India*] [*Airport symbol*] (OAG)
Pat............. Paton's Scotch Appeal Cases, House of Lords [*A publication*] (DLA)
PAT .... Patras [*Greece*] [*Seismograph station code, US Geological Survey*] (SEIS)
PAT .... Patriarch [*Greek Church*] (ROG)
PAT .... Patrick Air Force Base [*Florida*] (KSC)
PAT .... Patrol
PAT .... Patten Corp. [*NYSE symbol*] (SPSG)
PAT .... Pattern
PAT .... Pattern Analysis Test [*Army*]
PAT .... Peninsula Air Transport Co. [*Michigan*] (FAAC)
PAT .... People's Action Team [*South Vietnam*]
PAT .... Performance Appraisal Team [*Nuclear energy*] (NRCH)
PAT .... Peripheral Assignment Table (CMD)
PAT .... Personalized Array Translator (IEEE)
PAT .... Personnel Assistance Team [*Military*]
PAT .... Personnel Authorization Table [*Air Force*]
PAT .... Petroleum Air Transport, Inc. [*Lafayette, IN*] [*FAA designator*] (FAAC)
PAT .... Phenylaminotetrazole [*Psychology*]
PAT .... Photo Articulation Test
PAT .... Physics Achievement Test
PAT .... Picric Acid Turbidity Test
PAT .... Picture Arrangement Test
PAT .... Plasma Arc Tunnel
PAT .... Plastic Apply Template (MCD)
PAT .... Plenum Air Tread [*Army amphibian vehicle*]
PAT .... Plutonium Air Transportable [*Nuclear energy*] (NRCH)
PAT .... Point after Touchdown [*Football*]
PAT .... Polar Auxin Transport [*Botany*]
PAT .... Political Action Teams
PAT .... Polyaminotriazole [*Organic chemistry*]
PAT .... Position Adjusting Type
PAT .... Postavailability Trials
PAT .... Power Ascension Testing (IEEE)
PAT .... Preadmission Testing
PAT .... Prearranged Transfers
PAT .... Precision Aim Technique [*for helicopters*] [*Army*] (RDA)
PAT .... Prediction Analysis Techniques
PAT .... Pregnancy at Term [*Gynecology*]
PAT .... Preliminary Acceptance Trials [*Navy*]
PAT .... Prescription Athletic Turf [*Trademark for an artificial turf*]
PAT .... Pressure Assembled Thyristor
PAT .... Priority Air Travel [*Army*]
PAT .... Prism Adaptation Test [*Ophthalmology*]
PAT .... Problem Action Team [*NASA*] (NASA)
PAT .... Procedures Authorized Task (MCD)
PAT .... Process-Activation Table [*Data processing*]
PAT .... Process Analysis Team
PAT .... Production Acceptance Test [*NASA*] (KSC)
PAT .... Production Assessment Test
PAT .... Professional, Administrative, and Technical (OICC)
PAT .... Professional Association of Teachers [*British*]
PAT .... Proficiency Analytical Testing [*National Institute on Occupational Safety and Health*]
PAT .... Program Analysis Team (KSC)
PAT .... Program Attitude Test (IEEE)
PAT .... Programmable Actuator-Transducer [*Automotive engineering*]
PAT .... Programmed Activity Transmission (MCD)
PAT .... Programmer Aptitude Test
PAT .... Property and Accounting Technician [*Navy*]
PAT .... Pseudoadder Tree [*Data processing*]
PAT .... Psychoacoustic Testing
PAT .... Public Administration and Development [*A publication*]
PAT .... Public Administration Times [*A publication*] (EAAP)
PAT .... Pulsed Amplifier Tube
PaT .... Purge-and-Trap [*Technique*] [*Environmental Protection Agency*]
PAtA.......... Air Products & Chemicals, Inc., Allentown, PA [*Library symbol*] [*Library of Congress*] (LCLS)
PATA......... Pacific American Tankship Association [*Defunct*] (EA)
PATA......... Pacific Area Travel Association [*San Francisco, CA*]
PATA......... Pacific Asia Travel Association (EA)
PATA......... Patagonia [*Region of South America*] (ROG)
PATA......... Plenum Air Tread, Amphibious [*Army vehicle*]
PATA......... Pneumatic All-Terrain Amphibian (IEEE)
PATA......... Professional Aeromedical Transport Association (EA)
PATA......... Tanana [*Alaska*] [*ICAO location identifier*] (ICLI)
Pat Abr....... Paterson's Abridgment of Poor Law Cases [*1857-63*] [*A publication*] (DLA)
PATADMIN ... Patent Administration System [*Australia*]
PATAIR .... Papuan Air Transport
Pat App...... Craigie, Stewart, and Paton's House of Lords Appeals from Scotland [*1726-1857*] [*A publication*] (DLA)
Pat App Cas ... Paterson's Scotch Appeal Cases [*A publication*] (DLA)

Pat App Cas ... Paton's Scotch Appeal Cases [*Craigie, Stewart, and Paton*] [*A publication*] (DLA)
PATASWDEVGRU ... Patrol Antisubmarine Warfare Development Group
PATB........ Patriot Bancorp [*NASDAQ symbol*] (NQ)
Pat Bl....... Patentblatt [*A publication*]
PATBOMRON ... Patrol-Bombing Squadron
PAtC.......... Cedar Crest College, Allentown, PA [*Library symbol*] [*Library of Congress*] (LCLS)
PATC......... Paroxysmal Atrial [*or Auricular*] Tachycardia [*Medicine*]
PATC........ PATCLASS [*Pergamon ORBIT InfoLine, Inc.*] [*Information service or system*] [*No longer available online*] (CRD)
PATC........ Pioneer Automobile Touring Club (EA)
PAT-C....... Position, Attitude, Trajectory-Control [*Aerospace*] (AAG)
PATC........ Potomac Appalachian Trail Club (EA)
PATC........ Professional, Administrative, Technical, and Clerical [*Bureau of Labor Statistics survey*]
PATC........ Tin City Air Force Station [*Alaska*] [*ICAO location identifier*] (ICLI)
PATCA...... Panama Air Traffic Control Area
PATCA...... Phase Lock Automatic Tuned Circuit Adjustment [*Telecommunications*]
PATCA...... Professional and Technical Consultants Association (EA)
Pat Cas....... Reports of Patent, Design, and Trade Mark Cases [*England, Scotland, Ireland*] [*A publication*] (DLA)
PATCENT ... Patching Central [*Army*] (AABC)
PA-TCH-SP ... Periodic Acid-Thiocarbohydrazide-Silver Proteinate [*Test*] [*Cytology*]
PATCO...... Prednisone, ara-C [*Cytarabine*], Thioguanine, Cyclophosphamide, Oncovin [*Vincristine*] [*Antineoplastic drug regimen*]
PATCO..... Professional Air Traffic Controllers Organization [*Defunct*] (EA)
PATCOM ... Patriot Communications Model (MCD)
Pat Comp ... Paterson's Compendium of English and Scotch Law [*A publication*] (DLA)
PATD .... Patented
Pat Dec....... Decisions of the Commissioner of Patents [*A publication*] (DLA)
Pat Des & TM Rev ... Patent, Design, and Trade Mark Review [*India*] [*A publication*] (DLA)
Pat Dig....... Pattison's Missouri Digest [*A publication*] (DLA)
PATDPA ... Deutsche Patent Datenbank [*German Patent Database*] [*German Patent Office*] [*Information service or system*] (IID)
PAT & E .... Product Acceptance Testing and Evaluation [*Marketing*] (MCD)
PATE........ Programmed Automatic Telemetry Evaluator
PATE........ Programmed Automatic Test Equipment
PATE........ Psychodynamics and Therapeutic Education
PATEFA News ... Printing and Allied Trades Employers' Federation. News [*A publication*]
PATELL.... Psychological Abstracts Tape Edition Lease or Licensing
Patentbl..... Patentblatt [*A publication*]
Patentbl Ausg A ... Patentblatt. Ausgabe A [*A publication*]
Patentbl Ausg B ... Patentblatt. Ausgabe B [*A publication*]
Patentjoernaal (S Afr) ... Patentjoernaal (South Africa) [*A publication*]
Patent Off Soc Jour ... Patent Office Society. Journal [*A publication*]
Pater.......... Paterson's New South Wales Reports [*A publication*] (DLA)
Pater.......... Paterson's Scotch Appeal Cases [*A publication*] (DLA)
Pater Ap Cas ... Paterson's Scotch Appeal Cases [*A publication*] (DLA)
Pater App... Paterson's Scotch Appeal Cases [*A publication*] (DLA)
Paters App ... Paterson's Appeal Cases [*A publication*] (ILCA)
Paters Comp ... Paterson's Compendium of English and Scotch Law [*A publication*] (DLA)
Paterson..... Paterson on the Game Laws [*A publication*] (DLA)
Paterson..... Paterson on the Liberty of the Subject [*A publication*] (DLA)
Paterson..... Paterson's Compendium of English and Scotch Law [*A publication*] (DLA)
Paterson..... Paterson's Law and Usages of the Stock Exchange [*A publication*] (DLA)
Paterson..... Paterson's Scotch Appeal Cases [*A publication*] (DLA)
Paterson..... Paterson's Supreme Court Reports [*New South Wales, Australia*] [*A publication*] (DLA)
Paterson Sc App Cas ... Paterson's Scotch Appeal Cases [*A publication*] (DLA)
PATF........ Pathfinder Petroleum [*NASDAQ symbol*] (NQ)
PATF........ Program Activation Task Force [*Military*] (AFIT)
PATF........ Property Accountability Task Force [*Army*] (MCD)
Pat Fiz Eksp Ter ... Patologiceskaya Fiziologiya i Eksperimental'naya Terapija [*A publication*]
PATFOR ... Patrol Force
Pat Game L ... Paterson on the Game Laws [*1861*] [*A publication*] (DLA)
PATGC...... Purge-and-Trap Gas Chromatography [*Environmental Protection Agency*]
PATH .... Pathology (AABC)
Pat & H...... Patton, Jr., and Heath's Reports [*Virginia Special Court of Appeals*] [*A publication*] (DLA)
PATH .... Performance Analysis and Test Histories (KSC)
PATH .... Pituitary Adrenotrophic Hormone [*Endocrinology*]
PATH .... Port Authority Trans-Hudson [*New York*]
PATH .... Preserve American Patriotic Holidays Committee (EA)

PATH .... Program for Appropriate Technology in Health (EA)
PATH .... Prospectors and Treasure Hunters Guild (EA)
PATHAT... Precision Aim-Technique Heliborne Antitank [*Gun system concept*] [*Ballistic Research Laboratory*] (RDA)
Path Biol.... Pathologie et Biologie [*Paris*] [*A publication*]
Path Europ ... Pathologia Europaea [*A publication*]
Pat HL Sc .. Paterson's Scotch Appeal Cases [*A publication*] (DLA)
Pat HL Sc .. Paton's Scotch Appeal Cases [*A publication*] (DLA)
Path Microb ... Pathologia et Microbiologia [*A publication*]
Pathobiol Annu ... Pathobiology Annual [*A publication*]
PATHOL... Pathological (MSA)
Pathol......... Pathology [*A publication*] (APTA)
Pathol Annu ... Pathology Annual [*A publication*]
Pathol Biol ... Pathologie et Biologie [*Paris*] [*A publication*]
Pathol Biol (Paris) ... Pathologie et Biologie (Paris) [*A publication*]
Pathol Biol Sem Hop ... Pathologie et Biologie. La Semaine des Hopitaux [*A publication*]
Pathol Clin Med (Tokyo) ... Pathology and Clinical Medicine (Tokyo) [*A publication*]
Pathol Eur ... Pathologia Europaea [*A publication*]
Pathol Eur Suppl ... Pathologia Europaea. Supplement [*A publication*]
Pathol Gen ... Pathologie Generale [*A publication*]
Pathol Immunopathol Res ... Pathology and Immunopathology Research [*A publication*]
Pathol Microbiol ... Pathologia et Microbiologia [*A publication*]
Pathol Microbiol Suppl ... Pathologia et Microbiologia. Supplementum [*Switzerland*] [*A publication*]
Pathol Res Pract ... Pathology. Research and Practice [*A publication*]
Pathol Vet ... Pathologia Veterinaria [*A publication*]
Path Res Pract ... Pathology. Research and Practice [*A publication*]
PATHS...... Peer Attitudes Toward the Handicapped Scale [*Educational testing*]
PATHS...... Precursor above the Horizon Sensor [*Strategic Defense Initiative*]
PATI......... Passive Airborne Time-Difference Intercept [*Navy*]
PATI.......... Phoenix Advanced Technology, Inc. [*NASDAQ symbol*] (NQ)
PATIA....... Pacific Area Trading and Investment Area
Patiala....... Indian Law Reports, Patiala Series [*A publication*] (DLA)
PATIB....... Polish-American Travel Information Bureau (EA)
Patient Acc ... Patient Accounts [*A publication*]
Patient Couns Health Educ ... Patient Counselling and Health Education [*A publication*]
Patient Educ Couns ... Patient Education and Counseling [*A publication*]
Patient Educ Newsl ... Patient Education Newsletter [*A publication*]
PATINA.... Potomac Antique Tools and Industries Association (EA)
Pat Ins....... Paton on Insurance [*1962*] [*A publication*] (DLA)
Pat J.......... Patent Journal, Including Trademarks and Models [*South Africa*] [*A publication*] (DLA)
Pat J Incl Trade Marks Des ... Patent Journal, Including Trade Marks and Designs [*A publication*]
Pat J Incl Trade Marks Des Copyright Cinematogr Films ... Patent Journal, Including Trade Marks, Designs, and Copyright in Cinematograph Films [*A publication*]
PATK........ Patrick Industries, Inc. [*NASDAQ symbol*] (NQ)
PATK........ Talkeetna [*Alaska*] [*ICAO location identifier*] (ICLI)
PAtL .... Lehigh County Historical Society, Allentown, PA [*Library symbol*] [*Library of Congress*] (LCLS)
PATL........ Pan Atlantic, Inc. [*NASDAQ symbol*] (NQ)
PATL........ Tatalina Air Force Station [*Alaska*] [*ICAO location identifier*] (ICLI)
Pat L Ann... Patent Law Annual [*A publication*]
Pat Law Rev ... Patent Law Review [*A publication*] (DLA)
Pat Licens... Paterson's Licensing Acts Annual [*A publication*] (DLA)
Pat LJ....... Patna Law Journal [*India*] [*A publication*] (DLA)
Pat LR....... Patent Law Review [*A publication*] (DLA)
Pat LR....... Patna Law Reports [*India*] [*A publication*] (DLA)
Pat L Reptr ... Patna Law Reporter [*India*] [*A publication*] (DLA)
Pat L Rev ... Patent Law Review [*A publication*] (DLA)
Pat LT....... Patna Law Times [*India*] [*A publication*] (DLA)
Pat LW ...... Patna Law Weekly [*A publication*] (DLA)
PAtM........ Muhlenberg College, Allentown, PA [*Library symbol*] [*Library of Congress*] (LCLS)
Patma-Banasirakan Handes Ist-Filol Zh ... Patma-Banasirakan Handes. Istoriko-Filologicheskii Zhurnal [*A publication*]
PATMI...... Powder Actuated Tool Manufacturers' Institute (EA)
Pat Mort .... Patch on Mortgages [*1821*] [*A publication*] (DLA)
Pat & Mr.... Paterson and Murray's Reports [*1870-71*] [*New South Wales*] [*A publication*] (DLA)
PATMRG ... PACOM [*Pacific Command*] Air Target Materials Review Group (CINC)
Pat & Mur ... Paterson and Murray's Supreme Court Reports [*New South Wales, Australia*] [*A publication*] (DLA)
PATN .... Pattern (MDG)
Patna J Med ... Patna Journal of Medicine [*A publication*]
PATO .... Partial Acceptance and Takeover Date [*Telecommunications*] (TEL)
PATO .... Pattetico [*Pathetically*] [*Music*] (ROG)
PATO .... Principal Ammunition Technical Officer [*British military*] (DMA)
Pat Off .... Patent Office (DLA)
Pat Off Gaz ... Official Gazette. United States Patent Office [*A publication*]

Pat Off J .... Patent Office Journal [*India*] [*A publication*] (DLA)
Pat Off Rep ... Patent Office Reports [*A publication*] (DLA)
Pat Off Soc J ... Patent Office Society. Journal [*A publication*]
Patog Ter Dermatozov ... Patogenez i Terapiya Dermatozov [*A publication*]
Patol Clin Ostet Ginecol ... Patologia e Clinica Ostetrica e Ginecologica [*A publication*]
Patol Fiziol Eksp Ter ... Patologicheskaya Fiziologiya i Eksperimental'naya Terapiya [*A publication*]
PATOLIS ... Patent Online Information System [*Database*] [*Japan*]
Patol-Mex ... Patologia-Mexico City [*A publication*]
Patol Pol .... Patologia Polska [*A publication*]
Patol Sper .. Patologia Sperimentale [*A publication*]
Paton......... Craigie, Stewart, and Paton's Scotch Appeal Cases [*1726-1821*] [*A publication*] (DLA)
Paton App Cas .. Paton's Scotch Appeal Cases [*A publication*] (DLA)
Paton Sc App Cas ... Paton's Scotch Appeal Cases [*A publication*] (DLA)
PATOOMB ... Phage and the Origins of Molecular Biology
PA Top G S Com ... Pennsylvania Topographic and Geologic Survey Commission [*A publication*]
PA Topogr Geol Surv Bull A ... Pennsylvania Topographic and Geologic Survey. Bulletin A. Atlas Series [*A publication*]
PA Topogr Geol Surv Bull C ... Pennsylvania. Bureau of Topographic and Geologic Survey. Bulletin C [*County Report*] [*A publication*]
PA Topogr Geol Surv Bull G ... Pennsylvania. Bureau of Topographic and Geologic Survey. Bulletin G [*General Geology Report*] [*A publication*]
PA Topogr Geol Surv Bull M ... Pennsylvania Topographic and Geologic Survey. Bulletin M [*A publication*]
PA Topogr Geol Surv Bull W ... Pennsylvania Topographic and Geologic Survey. Bulletin W [*A publication*]
PA Topogr Geol Surv Geol Atlas PA ... Pennsylvania. Bureau of Topographic and Geologic Survey. Geologic Atlas of Pennsylvania [*A publication*]
PA Topogr Geol Surv Inform Circ ... Pennsylvania. Bureau of Topographic and Geologic Survey. Information Circular [*A publication*]
PA Topogr Geol Surv Miner Resour Rep ... Pennsylvania Topographic and Geologic Survey. Mineral Resources Report [*A publication*]
PA Topogr Geol Surv Progr Rep ... Pennsylvania. Bureau of Topographic and Geologic Survey. Progress Report [*A publication*]
PA Topogr Geol Surv Spec Bull ... Pennsylvania. Bureau of Topographic and Geologic Survey. Special Bulletin [*A publication*]
PATOS...... Patent-Online-System [*Bertelsmann Datenbankdienste GmbH*] [*Database*]
PATP........ Preliminary Authority to Proceed (NASA)
PATP........ Production Acceptance Test Procedure (MCD)
PATP........ (Pyridylcarbonylamino)tetrahydropyridine [*Biochemistry*]
PATPEND ... Patent Pending
Pat Pol .... Patologia Polska [*A publication*]
PAT-PTR .. US Patent Data Base - Patent Technology Reports [*Patent and Trademark Office*] [*Database*]
PATR........ Patriarch
PATR........ Patriotic (ROG)
PATR........ Patron
PATR........ Production Acceptance Test Requirement (MCD)
PATRA...... Printing, Packaging, and Allied Trades Research Association
PATRA...... Professional and Technical Role Analyses [*Occupational therapy*]
Pa Trade J ... Paper Trade Journal [*A publication*]
PATRDL... Pan American Tung Research and Development League [*Defunct*] (EA)
Patr Elect Cas ... Patrick's Election Cases [*1824-49*] [*Upper Canada*] [*A publication*] (DLA)
PATREU... Palaestina Treuhandstelle zur Beratung Deutscher Juden [*A publication*]
PATRIC ... Pattern Recognition and Information Correlations [*Police crime-detection computer*]
PATRIC .... Pattern Recognition Interpretation and Correlation (CET)
PATRIC .... Position and Time-Resolved Ion Counting [*Detector*]
PATRICIA ... Practical Algorithm to Receive Information Coded in Alphanumeric [*Information retrieval*]
Patrick El Cas ... Patrick's Election Cases [*Canada*] [*A publication*] (DLA)
PATRIOT ... Phased Array Tracking to Intercept of Target [*Air defense system unit*] [*Army*] (RDA)
Patrist Sorb ... Patristica Sorbonensia [*A publication*]
Pa Tr J .... Paper Trade Journal [*A publication*]
PATROL... Program for Administrative Traffic Reports On-Line [*Computer program*] [*Bell System*]
PatrolGr..... Patrologia Graeca (BJA)
PatrolLat.... Patrologia Latina (BJA)
PATRON .. Patrol Squadron
Patronato Biol Anim Rev ... Patronato de Biologia Animal. Revista [*A publication*]
Patronato Invest Cient Tec "Juan De La Cierva" Mem ... Patronato de Investigacion Cientifica y Tecnica "Juan De La Cierva." Memoria [*A publication*]
Patronato Invest Cient Tec "Juan De La Cierva" Publ Tec ... Patronato de Investigacion Cientifica y Tecnica "Juan De La Cierva." Publicaciones Tecnicas [*A publication*]

PATS.........	Payment and Telecommunication Services Corp. [*New York, NY*] [*Telecommunications*] [*Defunct*] (TSSD)
PATS.........	People Against Tobacco Smoke (EA)
PATS.........	Personnel Assistance Teams [*Military*]
PATS.........	Personnel in an Awaiting Training Status [*Air Force*] (AFM)
PATS.........	Portable Acoustic Tracking System for Divers (MCD)
PATS.........	Preacademic Training Student [*Military*]
PATS.........	Preauthorized Automatic Transfer Scheme [*Banking*]
PATS.........	Precision Altimeter Techniques Study
PATS.........	Predicasts Abstract Terminal System [*Data processing*]
PATS.........	Program for Analysis of Time Series (NASA)
PATS.........	Programmatic and Technical Support [*Army*]
PATS.........	Propulsion Analysis Trajectory Simulation [*Computer program*] [*NASA*]
PATSEARCH ...	Patent Search [*Data processing*]
Pat Ser	Indian Law Reports, Patna Series [*A publication*] (DLA)
Pat St Tr ...	Paton on Stoppage in Transitu [*1859*] [*A publication*] (DLA)
PATSU......	Patrol Aircraft Service Unit
PATSY	Parametric Test Synthesis [*Data processing*]
PATSY	Picture Animal Top Star of the Year [*or Performing Animal Television Star of the Year*] [*American Humane Association award*]
PATSY	Programmer's Automatic Testing System
PATT........	Partial Automatic Translation Technique
PATT........	Patent (ROG)
PATT........	Pattern (AAG)
PATT.........	Patton Oil Co. [*NASDAQ symbol*] (NQ)
PATT.........	Project for the Analysis of Technology Transfer [*NASA*]
PATTERN ...	Planning Assistance Through Technical Evaluation of Relevance Numbers [*RAND Corp.*]
Pattern Recogn ...	Pattern Recognition [*A publication*]
Pattern Recognition ...	Journal. Pattern Recognition Society [*A publication*]
Pattern Recognition Lett ...	Pattern Recognition Letters [*A publication*]
Patt & H.....	Patton, Jr., and Heath's Reports [*Virginia*] [*A publication*] (DLA)
Patt & Heath R ...	Patton, Jr., and Heath's Reports [*Virginia*] [*A publication*] (DLA)
Patt & H (VA) ...	Patton, Jr., and Heath's Reports [*Virginia*] [*A publication*] (DLA)
Pat TM & Copy J ...	Patent, Trademark, and Copyright Journal [*A publication*]
Pat TM & Copyr J of R & Educ ...	Patent, Trademark, and Copyright Journal of Research and Education [*A publication*] (DLA)
Pat and TM Rev ...	Patent and Trade Mark Review [*A publication*]
Patton & H ...	Patton, Jr., and Heath's Reports [*Virginia Special Court of Appeals*] [*A publication*] (DLA)
Patton & Heath ...	Patton, Jr., and Heath's Reports [*Virginia*] [*A publication*] (DLA)
Patton & H (VA) ...	Patton, Jr., and Heath's Reports [*Virginia Special Court of Appeals*] [*A publication*] (DLA)
Pat Trademark & Copyright J (BNA) ...	Patent, Trademark, and Copyright Journal (Bureau of National Affairs) [*A publication*] (DLA)
Pat Trademark & Copyright J BNA ...	Patents, Trademark, and Copyright Journal. Bureau of National Affairs [*A publication*]
Patt Recog ...	Pattern Recognition [*A publication*]
Pat & Tr Mk Rev ...	Patent and Trade Mark Review [*A publication*]
PATU	Pan American Taekwondo Union (EA)
PATU	PanAfrican Telecommunications Union (EAIO)
PATUA......	Proceedings. Research Institute of Atmospherics. Nagoya University [*A publication*]
PATWAS ..	Pilots Automatic Telephone Weather Answering Service
PATWING ...	Patrol Wing [*Later, Fleet Air Wing*]
PATWINGLANTFLT ...	Patrol Wing [*later, Fleet Air Wing*] Atlantic Fleet
PATWINGSCOFOR ...	Patrol Wing [*later, Fleet Air Wing*] Scouting Force
PAU	Pacific Command Frequency Allocation and Uses (CINC)
PAU	Pamietnik Akademii Umiejetnosci Krakowie [*A publication*]
PAU	Pan American Union [*Central organ and permanent secretariat of the OAS*]
PAU	Pattern Articulation Unit [*Data processing*]
PAU	Pauk [*Burma*] [*Airport symbol*] (OAG)
PAU	Paulingite [*A zeolite*]
Pau	[*Julius*] Paulus [*Flourished, 3rd century*] [*Authority cited in pre-1607 legal work*] (DSA)
Pau	Paulus de Liazaris [*Deceased, 1356*] [*Authority cited in pre-1607 legal work*] (DSA)
PAU	Pauzhetka [*USSR*] [*Seismograph station code, US Geological Survey*] (SEIS)
pau	Pennsylvania [*MARC country of publication code*] [*Library of Congress*] (LCCP)
PAU	Pilotless Aircraft Unit
PAU	Polska Akademia Umiejetnosci [*A publication*]
PAU	Portable Annotation Unit [*Military*] (CAAL)
PAU	Position Analog Unit [*Manufacturing term*]
PAU	Precision Approach - UNICOM [*Aviation*]
PAU	Present Address Unknown
PAU	Probe Aerodynamic Upper [*NASA*] (MCD)
PAU	Production Assurance Unit (MCD)
PAU	Programmes Analysis Unit [*British*] (MCD)
PAU	University of Pennsylvania, Philadelphia, PA [*OCLC symbol*] (OCLC)
PAU-AN....	Polska Akademia Umiejetnosci. Archivum Neophilologicum [*A publication*]
PAUBM	Pan American Union of Baptist Men [*Defunct*] (EA)
PAUCA	Proceedings. Royal Australian Chemical Institute [*A publication*]
PAUCA	Providence Association of Ukrainian Catholics in America (EA)
Pau de Cast ...	Paulus de Castro [*Deceased, 1441*] [*Authority cited in pre-1607 legal work*] (DSA)
PAUDGET ...	Photometer, Automated Universal Distribution Gonielectric Type
Pau Hunga ...	Paulus Hungarus [*Deceased, 1242*] [*Authority cited in pre-1607 legal work*] (DSA)
Pau Hungar ...	Paulus Hungarus [*Deceased, 1242*] [*Authority cited in pre-1607 legal work*] (DSA)
PAUKO	Pan-American Union of Karatedo Organizations [*Later, PUKO*] (EA)
PAUL........	Paullum [*A Little*] [*Pharmacy*]
Pau de La ..	Paulus de Liazaris [*Deceased, 1356*] [*Authority cited in pre-1607 legal work*] (DSA)
Paul de Cast ...	Paulus de Castro [*Deceased, 1441*] [*Authority cited in pre-1607 legal work*] (DSA)
Paul de Castr ...	Paulus de Castro [*Deceased, 1441*] [*Authority cited in pre-1607 legal work*] (DSA)
Pau Leon....	Paulus Leonius [*Flourished, 16th century*] [*Authority cited in pre-1607 legal work*] (DSA)
Paul Liaz....	Paulus de Liazaris [*Deceased, 1356*] [*Authority cited in pre-1607 legal work*] (DSA)
PAULS	Pennsylvania Union List of Serials
Paulus	Julius Paulus. Sententiae Receptae [*A publication*] (DLA)
Pau de Montep ..	Paulus Ruinus de Montepico [*Flourished, 15th century*] [*Authority cited in pre-1607 legal work*] (DSA)
PAUN........	Unalakleet [*Alaska*] [*ICAO location identifier*] (ICLI)
PA Univ Lab Contr ...	Pennsylvania University. Laboratory Contributions [*A publication*]
PA Univ Mus Bul ...	Pennsylvania University. University Museum. Bulletin [*A publication*]
PA Univ Schoolmen's Week Proc ...	Pennsylvania University. Schoolmen's Week. Proceedings [*A publication*]
PAUP........	Phylogenic Analysis Using Parsimony [*Biology*]
Paus	Pausanias [*Second century AD*] [*Classical studies*] (OCD)
PAUS	Piedmontese Association of the United States (EA)
PAus	Poetry Australia [*A publication*]
PAUSE......	People Against Unconstitutional Sex Education
PAusL........	Papers in Australian Linguistics [*A publication*]
P Aust Bioc ...	Proceedings. Australian Biochemical Society [*A publication*]
PAUT	Pennsylvania & Atlantic Railroad Co. [*Absorbed into Consolidated Rail Corp.*] [*AAR code*]
PAUTDL...	Proceedings. Australian Society of Sugar Cane Technologists [*A publication*]
P Automtn ...	Process Automation [*A publication*]
PAUX	Pauxillum [*A Little*] [*Pharmacy*]
PAV	Packaging Review [*A publication*]
P/AV..........	Particular Average
PaV	Pathe-Vox [*Record label*] [*France*]
PAV	Paulo Afonso [*Brazil*] [*Airport symbol*] (OAG)
PAV	Pavia [*Italy*] [*Seismograph station code, US Geological Survey*] (SEIS)
PAV	Pavilion
Pav	Pavo [*Constellation*]
PAV	Pay Adjustment Voucher [*Military*]
PAV	Personnel Allotment Voucher [*Army*]
PAV	Phase Angle Voltmeter
PAV	Position and Velocity
PAV	Poste-Avion [*Airmail*] [*French*]
PAV	Potential Acquisition Valuation Method [*Management*]
PAV	Pressure-Actuated Valve (NASA)
PAV	Pressure Altitude Variation [*Aviation*]
PAV	Propellant-Actuated Valve
PAV	Public Access Videotex
PAV	Public Against Violence [*Czechoslovakia*] [*Political party*]
PAV	Puella Americana Vallensis [*Valley Girl*] [*Teenaged girl who follows the fads, fashions, and slang originated among teenagers in California's San Fernando Valley*]
PAVA	Polish Army Veterans Association of America (EA)
PAVAS.....	Performing and Visual Arts Society (EA)
PAVCSS...	Principals' Association of Victorian Catholic Secondary Schools [*Australia*]
PAVD	Valdez [*Alaska*] [*ICAO location identifier*] (ICLI)
PAVE........	Position and Velocity Extraction
PAVE........	Primary Auditory Visual Experience [*National Visitor Center*]
PAVE........	Principles and Applications of Value Engineering
PAVe........	Procarbazine, Alanine Nitrogen Mustard [*L-Phenylanine mustard, L-PAM*], Velban [*Vinblastine*] [*Antineoplastic drug regimen*]
PAVE........	Professional Audiovisual Education Study
PAVE........	Programmed Analysis for Value Engineers
PAVE PAWS ...	Precision Acquisition of Vehicle Entry Phased Array Warning System
PAVF........	Pulmonary Arteriovenous Fistula [*Medicine*]
PAVFC	Princeton Azimuthally-Varying-Field Cyclotron

PAVG .... Prince Albert's Volunteer Guards [*British military*]   (DMA)
Pavia Univ Ist Geol Atti ... Pavia Universita. Istituto Geologico. Atti [*A publication*]
Pav J Biol... Pavlovian Journal of Biological Science [*A publication*]
PAVLA ...... Papal Volunteers for Latin America [*Defunct*]
Pavlovian J Biol Sci ... Pavlovian Journal of Biological Science [*A publication*]
Pavlov J Biol Sci ... Pavlovian Journal of Biological Science [*A publication*]
Pavlov J Higher Nerv Act ... Pavlov Journal of Higher Nervous Activity [*A publication*]
PAVM .... Patrons of the Arts in the Vatican Museum   (EA)
PAVM .... Phase Angle Voltmeter
PAVMT ...... Pavement
PAVN .... People's Army of Vietnam
PAVO .... Prince Albert Victor's Own [*British military*]   (DMA)
PAVOC ...... Prince Albert Victor's Own Cavalry [*British military*]   (DMA)
PA/VR .... Public Assistance/Vocational Rehabilitation
PAVS .... Pulmonary Arterial Vasconstrictor Substance [*Medicine*]
PAVT .... Position and Velocity Tracking
P & AW ...... Paging and Area Warning
PAW .... Pambwa [*Papua New Guinea*] [*Airport symbol*]   (OAG)
PAW .... Panel of American Women   (EA)
PA of W ..... Pentecostal Assemblies of the World   (EA)
PAW .... People for the American Way   (EA)
PAW .... Percussive Arc Welder
PAW .... Performance Analysis Workstation [*Data processing*]
PAW .... Petroleum Administration for War [*World War II*]
PAW .... Plasma Arc Welding
PAW .... Powered All the Way
PAW .... Public Administered Whipping [*Slang*]
PAW .... Pulmonary Artery Wedge Pressure [*Cardiology*]
PAWA .... Pan American Women's Association   (EA)
PAWAF ..... Polish American Workmen's Aid Fund   (EA)
PAWC .... Pan-American Weightlifting Confederation   (EA)
PA WC Bd Dec ... Pennsylvania Workmen's Compensation Board Decisions [*A publication*]   (DLA)
PA WC Bd Dec Dig ... Digest of Decisions, Pennsylvania Workmen's Compensation Board [*A publication*]   (DLA)
PA WC Bd (Dep Rep Sup) ... Workmen's Compensation Supplement to Department Reports of Pennsylvania [*A publication*]   (DLA)
PAWD .... Kodiak/Municipal [*Alaska*] [*ICAO location identifier*]   (ICLI)
PAWE .... Program for Analysis of the World Ecosystem
PAWI .... Parks and Wilderness [*A publication*]
PAWLC ..... Pan-American Weightlifting Confederation   (EA)
Pawl Zs Hoeh Nerv Taet ... Pawlow-Zeitschrift fuer Hoehere Nerventaetigkeit [*A publication*]
PAWN .... Poole, Aberley, Worthington, and Nolen [*Four early residents of Pawn, Oregon. The city derives its name from the initial letters of their surnames*]
PAWOS ..... Portable Automatic Weather Observing Station   (MCD)
PAWP .... Pulmonary Artery Wedge Pressure [*Medicine*]
PAWS .... Parachute Altitude Wind Sensor
PAWS .... Pets Are Worth Safeguarding [*An association*]
PAWS .... Phased Array Warning System
PAWS .... Polar Automatic Weather Station   (NG)
PAWS .... Portable Automatic Weather Station   (MUGU)
PAWS .... Programmed Automatic Welding System
PAWT .... Wainwright [*Alaska*] [*ICAO location identifier*]   (ICLI)
PAWW ...... Wildwood [*Alaska*] [*ICAO location identifier*]   (ICLI)
PAX .... OPTEVFOR [*Operational Test and Evaluation Force*] Detachment, Patuxent River, MD [*Navy*]   (CAAL)
PAX .... Pan Central Explorations Ltd. [*Toronto Stock Exchange symbol*]
PAX .... Parallel Architecture Extended [*Data processing*]
PAX .... Passenger   (AFM)
PAX .... Patuxent River [*Maryland*]   (MCD)
PAX .... Paxson [*Alaska*] [*Seismograph station code, US Geological Survey*]   (SEIS)
Pax .... Paxton [*Record label*] [*Great Britain*]
PAX .... Person-to-Person Accelerated Xerography [*Office technology*] [*British*]
PAX .... Physical Address Extension
PAX .... Private Automatic Exchange [*Telecommunications*]
PAXCON .. Passenger Airlift Contract [*Military*]
PAXT .... Paxton [*Frank*] Co. [*NASDAQ symbol*]   (NQ)
PAY .... Pamol [*Malaysia*] [*Airport symbol*]   (OAG)
PAYA .... Yakutat [*Alaska*] [*ICAO location identifier*]   (ICLI)
PAYC .... Payco American Corp. [*NASDAQ symbol*]   (NQ)
PAYCOM ... Payload Command [*NASA*]   (MCD)
PAYDAT .... Payload Data [*NASA*]   (MCD)
PAYE .... Pay As You Earn
PAYE .... Pay As You Enter
PAYERS .... Program Accomplishment Year to Date Evaluation Reviews
PAYES ...... Program for Assessing Youth Employment Skills [*Vocational guidance test*]
Pay & Iv Carr ... Payne and Ivamy's Carriage by Sea [*10th ed.*] [*1976*] [*A publication*]   (DLA)
PAYLD ...... Payload
PAYM .... Paymaster [*Military*] [*British*]   (ROG)
PAYMARCORPS ... Paymaster, Marine Corps

PAYMR ..... Paymaster
PAYMT ..... Payment
PAYMTR .. Paymaster [*Military*] [*British*]   (ROG)
PAYN .... Pay'n Save, Inc. [*NASDAQ symbol*]   (NQ)
PAYS .... Patriotic American Youth Society
Pays .... Paysans [*A publication*]
Pays Gaumais ... Pays Gaumais. La Terre et les Hommes. Revue Regionale [*A publication*]
PAYSOP ... Payroll/Stock Ownership Plan
PAYSU ...... P'Eylim-American Yeshiva Student Union   (EA)
PAYT .... Payment
PAYX .... Paychex, Inc. [*NASDAQ symbol*]   (NQ)
PAZ .... Palaeozoic Axial Zone [*Geophysics*]
PAZ .... Paper and Packaging Bulletin [*A publication*]
PAZ .... Poza Rica [*Mexico*] [*Airport symbol*]   (OAG)
PAZA .... Anchorage [*Alaska*] [*ICAO location identifier*]   (ICLI)
PAZA .... Pan American Zebu Association [*Later, IZBA*]   (EA)
PAZF .... Fairbanks [*Alaska*] [*ICAO location identifier*]   (ICLI)
PB .... Air Burundi [*ICAO designator*]   (FAAC)
PB .... Bethlehem Public Library, Bethlehem, PA [*Library symbol*] [*Library of Congress*]   (LCLS)
PB .... Dr. Karl Thomae GmbH [*Germany*] [*Research code symbol*]
PB .... Document PB. National Technical Information Service [*A publication*]
P/B .... Pad and Boom [*Refueling*] [*Aerospace*]   (MSA)
PB .... Paedagogische Blaetter [*A publication*]
PB .... Painted Base   (AAG)
PB .... Panama Basin
PB .... Panic Bar [*Technical drawings*]
PB .... Pantheon Babylonicum: Nomina Deorum [*A publication*]
PB .... Paper Base   (MSA)
PB .... Paperboard Industries Corp. [*Toronto Stock Exchange symbol*]
PB .... Papua Besena [*Political party*] [*Papua New Guinea*]   (FEA)
PB .... Paraffin Bath [*Medicine*]
PB .... Paris Bourse [*The French stock exchange*]
PB .... Parke-Bernet [*Later, SPB*] [*Manhattan art auction house*]
PB .... Parliamentary Bill [*British*]   (ROG)
PB .... Parliamentary Broadcast Network [*Australia*]
PB .... Particle-Beam Weapon
PB .... Parts Breakdown
PB .... Passbook [*Banking*]
PB .... Passed Ball
PB .... Pastor Bonus [*A publication*]
PB .... Patrol Boat [*Navy symbol*]
PB .... Patrol Bomber
PB .... Pawnbroker
PB .... Pay Board
PB .... Peaceful Beginnings   (EA)
PB .... Peanut Butter [*Brand name of the Red Wing Co.*]
PB .... Pennsylvania Ballet
PB .... Pentaborane [*Rocket fuel*]
PB .... Pentobarbital [*Organic chemistry*]
PB .... Peribrachialis [*Anatomy*]
PB .... Peripheral Buffer
PB .... Permanent Ballast   (DS)
PB .... Permanent Bunkers
PB .... Permanently Blind
P de B .... Petrus de Bellapertica [*Deceased, 1308*] [*Authority cited in pre-1607 legal work*]   (DSA)
PB .... Petrus Brito [*Flourished, 13th century*] [*Authority cited in pre-1607 legal work*]   (DSA)
PB .... Phalangeal Bracket [*i.e., cup handle*] [*Slang*]
PB .... Pharmaceutical Benefits Scheme [*Australia*]
PB .... Pharmacopoeia Britannica [*British Pharmacopoeia*]
PB .... Phenobarbital [*A drug*]
P & B .... Phenobarbital and Belladonna [*A drug regimen*]
PB .... Philosophiae Baccalaureus [*Bachelor of Philosophy*]
PB .... Phonetically Balanced [*With reference to word lists*]
PB .... Phosphate Buffer
PB .... Phosphoribosyl
PB .... Photon Barrier [*Astrophysics*]
PB .... Physics Briefs [*Physikalische Berichte*] [*American Institute of Physics*] [*Database*] [*Information service or system*]   (IID)
PB .... Picket Boat [*Navy*]
PB .... Piebald
PB .... Pilotless Bomber [*Air Force*]
PB .... Pinchbeck [*Jewelry*]   (ROG)
PB .... Pine Bark
PB .... Pink Bollworm [*Cotton pest*]
PB .... Pipe Break [*Nuclear energy*]   (NRCH)
PB .... Piperonyl Butoxide [*Organic chemistry*]
PB .... Pit Border [*Paleobotany*]
PB .... Pitney-Bowes, Inc.
PB .... Planen und Bauen [*A publication*]
PB .... Planning Board
P & B .... Planning and Budgeting [*Military*]   (AFIT)
PB .... Plasminogen Binding [*Hematology*]
PB .... Plate Block [*Philately*]
PB .... Playback   (KSC)
Pb .... Playboy [*A publication*]

PB .... Plot Board (KSC)
PB .... Plugboard
Pb .... Plumbum [*Lead*] [*Chemical element*]
PB .... Plymouth Brethren (ROG)
PB .... Pocket Book
PB .... Poetry Bag [*A publication*]
PB .... Police Burgh
PB .... Policy Board (OICC)
PB .... Pollen Body [*Botany*]
PB .... Polybenzene [*Organic chemistry*]
PB .... Polybutylene [*Organic chemistry*]
PB .... Polymyxin B [*An antibiotic*]
PB .... Pony Baseball (EA)
PB .... Poop and Bridge [*of a ship*] (DS)
PB .... Population Biology
PB .... Ports and Beaches (NATG)
PB .... Power Boiler
PB .... Power Brakes [*Automotive engineering*]
PB .... Prabuddha Bharata [*Calcutta*] [*A publication*]
P and B ...... Pragmatics and Beyond [*A publication*]
PB .... Praktische Betriebswirt [*A publication*]
PB .... Pravoslav'nija Bukovyna [*A publication*]
PB .... Prayer Book
PB .... Preburner [*NASA*] (NASA)
PB .... Preliminary Breakdown
Pb .... Presbyopia [*Ophthalmology*]
PB .... Presentation Brothers [*See also FPM*] (EAIO)
PB .... Presiding Bishop [*Episcopal Church*]
PB .... Pressure Breathing
P & B .... Price and Budgeting (MCD)
PB .... Primary Buffer [*Chemistry*]
PB .... Primary Bus [*Data processing*] (CAAL)
PB .... Primitive Baptist
P & B .... Printing and Binding [*Publishing*]
PB .... Prisoners' Barracks (ADA)
PB .... Privatbetrieb [*Private Enterprise*] [*German*]
PB .... Private Business [*Slang*] [*British*]
PB .... Privately Bonded
Pb .... Probability (PCM)
PB .... Process Bulletin
PB .... Production Base (MCD)
PB .... Professional Books Ltd. (ILCA)
PB .... Profile Block (MCD)
PB .... Program Breakdown
P-as-B .... Program as Broadcast [*Radio*] (DEN)
PB .... Program Budgeting (ADA)
PB .... Property Book [*Army*] (AABC)
PB .... Proportional Band
PB .... Provisional Battalion [*Military*] [*A publication*] (ROG)
PB .... Przeglad Biblioteczny [*A publication*]
PB .... Pseudoterminal Bud [*Botany*]
PB .... Psychological Bulletin [*A publication*]
PB .... Ptychodiscus brevis [*An alga, the cause of the red tide*]
PB .... Public (DSUE)
Pb .... Publicatieblad van de Europese Gemeenschappen [*A publication*]
PB .... Publications Board [*Later, CFSTI, NTIS*]
PB .... Publications Bulletin
PB .... Publisher's Name [*Online database field identifier*]
P & B .... Pugsley and Burbridge's New Brunswick Reports [*A publication*] (DLA)
PB .... Pull Box (AAG)
PB .... Pulse Beacon (KSC)
PB .... Purplish Blue
PB .... Push from the Bush [*A publication*] (APTA)
PB .... Push Button
PB4 .... Plate Block of Four [*Philately*]
PBa .... Academy of the New Church, Bryn Athyn, PA [*Library symbol*] [*Library of Congress*] (LCLS)
PBA .... Academy of the New Church, Bryn Athyn, PA [*OCLC symbol*] (OCLC)
PBA .... Pacific Broadcasting Association (EAIO)
PBA .... Paid by Agent [*Business term*] (DCTA)
PBA .... Partido Barrientista Autentico [*Bolivia*] [*Political party*] (PPW)
PBA .... Patrol Boat, Air Cushion (MCD)
PBA .... Patrolmen's Benevolent Association
PBA .... Pencil Beam Antenna
PBA .... Permanent Budget Account
PBA .... Phenylboronic Acid [*Organic chemistry*]
PBA .... Physical Blowing Agent [*Plastics technology*]
PBA .... Pill Box Antenna
PBA .... Pine Bluff Arsenal [*Army*] (AABC)
PBA .... Plant Breeding Abstracts [*A publication*]
PbA .... Plasmodium Berghei Anka [*Bacteriology*]
PBA .... Plastic Bag Association (EA)
PBA .... Polar Bear Association (EA)
PBA .... Polish Beneficial Association (EA)
PBA .... Polska Bibliografia Analityczna [*A publication*]
PBA .... Polybenzamide [*Organic chemistry*]
PBA .... Polyclonal B Cell Activator [*Hematology*]

PBA .... Port Blair [*Andaman Islands*] [*Seismograph station code, US Geological Survey*] (SEIS)
PBA .... Port of Bristol Authority [*Great Britain*]
PBA .... Poultry Breeders of America (EA)
PBA .... Prescott Builders Association (EA)
PBA .... President of the British Academy
PBA .... Pressure Breathing Assistor [*Medicine*]
PBA .... Printing Brokerage Association (EA)
PBA .... Proceedings. British Academy [*A publication*]
PBA .... Professional Bookmen of America [*Later, Pi Beta Alpha*] (EA)
PBA .... Professional Bowlers Association of America (EA)
PBA .... Provincetown-Boston Airlines, Inc.
PBA .... Public Buildings Administration [*Functions transferred to PBS, 1949*]
PBA .... Pulpobuccoaxial [*Dentistry*]
PBA .... Pyrenebutyric Acid [*Organic chemistry*]
PBA .... Schoenvisie. Maandblad voor de Schoenhandel en Schoenindustrie [*A publication*]
PBAA ...... Periodical and Book Association of America (EA)
PBAA ...... Poly(butadiene-acrylic Acid) [*Organic chemistry*]
PBAC .... Pacific Bantam Austin Club (EA)
PBAC .... Pharmaceutical Benefits Advisory Committee [*Australia*]
PBAC .... ProBac International Corporation [*NASDAQ symbol*] (NQ)
PBACD ...... Program Budget Advisory Committee [*Army*]
PBAE .... Publications. Bureau of American Ethnology [*A publication*]
PB-AESRS ... Property Book - Army Equipment Status Reporting System (AABC)
PBAL .... Provincetown-Boston Airlines, Inc. [*NASDAQ symbol*] (NQ)
PBAN .... Pheromone Biosynthesis-Activating Neuropeptide [*Biochemistry*]
PBAN .... Poly(butadiene-acrylonitrile) [*Organic chemistry*]
PBAN .... Popular Bancshares Corp. [*NASDAQ symbol*] (NQ)
PBANB ...... Pathobiology Annual [*A publication*]
PBAPRS .... Program/Budget Accounting and Progress Reporting System [*Proposed*] [*Navy*]
PBAPS ...... Peach Bottom Atomic Power Station (NRCH)
PBAPS ...... Pipe Break Air Piping System (IEEE)
PBAPS ...... Pipe Break Automatic Protective System (IEEE)
PBAR .... Baker Island Army Air Field [*Baker Island*] [*ICAO location identifier*] (ICLI)
PBASA ...... Proceedings. Bihar Academy of Agricultural Sciences [*A publication*]
PBAT .... Pyro Battery (KSC)
P Bat Conf ... Proceedings. Battle Conference on Anglo-Norman Studies [*A publication*]
PBB .... Bloomsburg State College, Bloomsburg, PA [*OCLC symbol*] (OCLC)
PBB .... Parallel by Bit
PBB .... Paranaiba [*Brazil*] [*Airport symbol*] (OAG)
PBB .... Parti Pesaka Bumiputera Bersatu Sarawak [*United Bumiputra Party*] [*Political party*] [*Malaysia*] (FEA)
PBB .... Polybrominated Biphenyl [*Flame retardant, toxic chemical*]
PBB .... Posterior Basal Body [*Botany*]
PBB .... Private Boxes and Bags
PBB .... Project Blue Book [*An association*] (EA)
PBBCAS .... Program-Based Budget Classification and Analysis System [*Pronounced "pib-kaz"*] [*Office of Management and Budget*]
PBBCD ...... Promoclim B. Bulletin du Genie Climatique [*A publication*]
PBbCHi ..... Columbia County Historical Society, Bloomsburg, PA [*Library symbol*] [*Library of Congress*] (LCLS)
PBBFI .... Pearl S. Buck Birthplace Foundation, Incorporated (EA)
PBBH .... Peter Bent Brigham Hospital [*Boston*]
PBBHA ...... Pharmacology, Biochemistry, and Behavior [*A publication*]
PBbS .... Bloomsburg State College, Bloomsburg, PA [*Library symbol*] [*Library of Congress*] (LCLS)
PBBS .... Pertubuhan Bumiputera Bersatu Sarawak [*United Sarawak National Association*] [*Political party*] [*Malaysia*] (FEA)
PBC .... Columbia/Mt. Pleasant, TN [*Location identifier*] [*FAA*] (FAAL)
PBC .... Pacific Bible College [*California*]
PBC .... Packed by Carrier
PBC .... Pakistan Broadcasting Corporation (IMH)
PBC .... Panamerican Badminton Confederation (EAIO)
PBC .... Parallel by Character
PBC .... Pedal Branch of Columellar [*Muscle*]
PBC .... Pen and Brush Club (EA)
PBC .... People's Bicentennial [*later, Business*] Commission
PBC .... Peripheral Blood Cells [*Medicine*]
PBC .... Peripheral Bus Computer [*Bell System*]
PBC .... Personnel/Burden Carrier Manufacturers Association (EA)
PBC .... Plain Bond Copier [*Pitney Bowes*]
PBC .... Planning and the Black Community (EA)
PBC .... Point of Basal Convergence
PBC .... Practice Bomb Contained (NG)
PBC .... Presbyterians for Biblical Concerns (EA)
PBC .... Primary Biliary Cirrhosis [*Medicine*]
PBC .... Program Booking Center [*Telecommunications*] (TEL)
PBC .... Program Budget Committee [*Military*]
PBC .... Psychometric Behavior Checklist [*Psychology*]

PBC............ Public Buildings Commission [*Functions transferred to PBA, 1939*]
PBCA......... Pacific Bible College of Azusa [*California*]
PBCA......... Paperboard Butter Chip Association
PBCB........ Pierce-Blank Die (Class B)   (MCD)
PBCC........ Pitney Bowes Credit Corporation
PBCCH...... Pentabromochlorocyclohexane [*Flame retardant*] [*Organic chemistry*]
PBCE........ Pine Bluff Cotton Exchange   (EA)
PBCF......... Prudential-Bache Capital Funding
PBCI......... Pamrapo Bancorp, Inc. [*NASDAQ symbol*]   (NQ)
PBCMO...... Poly(bis(chloromethyl)oxetane) [*Organic chemistry*]
PB/COC..... Plymouth Barracuda/Cuda Owners Club   (EA)
PBCS........ Persian Bicolor and Calico Society   (EA)
PBCS........ Post Boost Control System [*Aerospace*]
PBCT........ People's Bank [*NASDAQ symbol*]   (NQ)
PBCT........ Proposed Boundary Crossing Time [*Aviation*]
PBC-USA.. Polar Bear Club - USA   (EA)
PBC-WS.... Polar Bear Club - Winter Swimmers [*Later, PBC-USA*]   (EA)
PBD........... Pacific Basin Development Corp. [*Vancouver Stock Exchange symbol*]
PBD .... Paperboard   (MSA)
PBD .... Particle Board [*Technical drawings*]
PBD .... Paul-Bunnell-Davidsohn [*Test*] [*Immunology*]
PBD .... Payload Bay Door [*NASA*]   (NASA)
PBD .... Phenylbiphenyloxadiazole [*Analytical biochemistry*]
PBD .... Pierce-Blank Die   (MCD)
PBD .... Plasterboard
PBD .... Plenum Bleed Duct [*Hovercraft*]
PBD .... Polybutadiene [*Organic chemistry*]
PBD .... Porbandar [*India*] [*Airport symbol*]   (OAG)
PBD .... Power Building   (NATG)
PBD .... Precise Block Diagram
PBD .... Pressboard   (MSA)
PBD .... Program Budget Decision [*DoD*]
PBD .... Program Budget Directive   (MCD)
PBD .... Program Budget Document   (MCD)
PBD .... Proliferative Breast Disease [*Medicine*]
Pbd Abstr.. Paper and Board Abstracts [*A publication*]
PBDC........ Pacific Basin Development Council   (EA)
PBDF......... Payload Bay Door Forward [*NASA*]   (MCD)
PBDG........ Push-Button Data Generator   (IEEE)
PBDI......... Position Bearing and Distance Indicator   (MCD)
PBDM ...... Payload Bay Door Mechanism [*NASA*]   (NASA)
PBDMA.... Poly(butadiene-malic Acid) [*A polymer*]
Pbd Pkg ... Paperboard Packaging [*A publication*]
PBDS........ Parti Bansa Dayak Sarawak [*Political party*] [*Malaysia*]   (FEA)
PBDU .... Pancreaticobiliary Ductal Union [*Anatomy*]
PBe........... Beaver Memorial Library, Beaver, PA [*Library symbol*] [*Library of Congress*]   (LCLS)
PBE........... Paint, Body, and Equipment [*Automotive engineering*]
PBE........... Paschen-Back Effect [*Spectroscopy*]
PBE........... Pemberton Exploration [*Vancouver Stock Exchange symbol*]
PBE........... Perlsucht Bacillary Emulsion [*Medicine*]
PBE........... Piggyback Experiment
PBE........... Present-Barrel-Equivalent
PBE........... Problemes Economiques. Selection de Textes Francais et Etrangers [*A publication*]
PBE........... Prompt Burst Experiments [*Nuclear energy*]   (NRCH)
PBE........... Prompt-by-Example [*Data processing*]
PBE........... Proton Balance Equation
PBE........... Proton Binding Energy
PBE........... Puerto Berrio [*Colombia*] [*Airport symbol*]   (OAG)
PBEA......... Paint, Body, and Equipment Association   (EA)
PBEA Newsletter ... Pennsylvania Business Education Association. Newsletter [*A publication*]
PBEB .... Pentabromoethylbenzene [*Flame retardant*] [*Organic chemistry*]
PBeC......... Beaver County Court House, Beaver, PA [*Library symbol*] [*Library of Congress*]   (LCLS)
PBEC......... Pacific Basin Economic Council   (FEA)
PBEC......... Public Broadcasting Environment Center [*Corporation for Public Broadcasting*]
P Bef G...... Personenbefoerderungsgesetz [*A publication*]
PBEIST ..... Planning Board European Inland Surface Transport [*Army*]   (AABC)
PBel .... Centre County Library, Bellefonte, PA [*Library symbol*] [*Library of Congress*]   (LCLS)
PBELB....... Promyshlennost Belorussii [*A publication*]
PBelC......... Centre County Court House, Bellefonte, PA [*Library symbol*] [*Library of Congress*]   (LCLS)
PBEN........ Puritan-Bennett Corp. [*NASDAQ symbol*]   (NQ)
PBER........ Program Budget Execution Review [*Army*]
PBerol .... Berlin Papyri [*A publication*]   (OCD)
PBf............ Carnegie Free Library, Beaver Falls, PA [*Library symbol*] [*Library of Congress*]   (LCLS)
PBF........... Fast Patrol Boat [*Ship symbol*] [*NATO*]   (NATG)
PBF........... Patriotic Burmese Forces [*World War II*]
PBF........... Patrol Boat, Fast [*British military*]   (DMA)
PBF........... Peribronchial Fibrosis [*Medicine*]
PBF........... Pine Bluff [*Arkansas*] [*Airport symbol*] [*Obsolete*]   (OAG)

PBF........... Plastic Bottle Feeder
PBF........... Plates for Beam Forming   (DEN)
PBF........... Poop, Bridge, and Forecastle [*of a ship*]   (DS)
PBF........... Portal Blood Flow [*Physiology*]
PBF........... Power Burst Facility [*Nuclear energy*]
PBF........... Praehistorische Bronzefunde [*A publication*]
PBF........... Public Budgeting and Finance [*A publication*]
PBF........... Pulmonary Blood Flow [*Medicine*]
PBFA .... Particle Beam Fusion Accelerator
PBFC .... Peter Breck Fan Club   (EA)
PBFC .... Pierce Brosnan Fan Club   (EA)
PBFD .... Pierce Bland and Form Die   (MSA)
PBfG .... Geneva College, Beaver Falls, PA [*Library symbol*] [*Library of Congress*]   (LCLS)
PBFG .... Guided Missile Fast Patrol Boat [*Ship symbol*]   (NATG)
PBFG .... Patrol Boat, Fast, Guided Weapon [*British military*]   (DMA)
PBFI .... Paris Business Forms, Incorporated [*Burlington, NJ*] [*NASDAQ symbol*]   (NQ)
PBFL .... Planning for Better Family Living [*UN Food and Agriculture Organization*]
PBFP .... Provisioning Budget Forecast Procedure   (MCD)
PBFPA...... Protides of the Biological Fluids. Proceedings of the Colloquium [*A publication*]
PBF/WR.... Presiding Bishop's Fund for World Relief   (EA)
PBG .... Phenylbiguanide [*Biochemistry*]
PBG .... Plattsburg, NY [*Location identifier*] [*FAA*]   (FAAL)
PBG .... Porphobilinogen [*Clinical chemistry*]
PBG .... Program and Budget Guidance [*Army*]
PBGC........ Pension Benefit Guaranty Corporation [*Government agency*]
PBGC Manual of Opinion Letters ... Pension Benefit Guaranty Corporation. Manual of Opinion Letters [*A publication*]
PBGI........ Piedmont BankGroup, Incorporated [*NASDAQ symbol*]   (NQ)
PBH .... Partial Bulkhead   (DS)
PBH .... Patma-Banasirakan Handes. Istoriko-Filologicheskii Zhurnal [*A publication*]
PBH .... Patrol Boat, Hydrofoil   (MCD)
PBH .... Phillips, WI [*Location identifier*] [*FAA*]   (FAAL)
PBH .... Post Biblical Hebrew [*Language, etc.*]   (BJA)
PBHF .... President Benjamin Harrison Foundation   (EA)
PBHP........ Pounds per Brake Horsepower
PB-HTGR ... Peach Bottom High-Temperature Gas-Cooled Reactor
PBI........... Paper Bag Institute   (EA)
PBI........... Parental Bonding Instrument
PBI........... Partial Background Investigation [*Army*]
PBI........... Paving Brick Institute
PBI........... Peace Brigades International   (EA)
PBI........... Pen and Brush, Incorporated   (EA)
PBI........... Philadelphia Bible Institute [*Pennsylvania*]
PBI........... Pitch Boundary Indicator   (MCD)
PBI........... Pitney-Bowes, Incorporated [*NYSE symbol*]   (SPSG)
PBI........... Plant Biological Institute [*University of Saskatchewan*] [*Canada*]
PBI........... Plant Biotechnology Institute [*National Research Council of Canada*] [*Research center*]   (RCD)
PBI........... Plant Breeding Institute [*British*]
PBI........... Plastic Bottle Institute   (EA)
PBI........... Plumbing Brass Institute [*Later, PMI*]   (EA)
PBI........... Polybenzimidazole [*Organic chemistry*]   (NATG)
PBI........... Poly(phenylenebibenzimidazole) [*Organic chemistry*]
PBI........... Poor Bloody Infantry [*British military slang*]
PBI........... Process Branch Indicator
PBI........... Programme Biologique Internationale [*International Biological Program - IBP*]   (MSC)
PBI........... Projected Books, Incorporated [*Defunct*]   (EA)
PBI........... Prophylactic Brain Irradiation [*Oncology*]
PBI........... Protein-Bound Iodine [*Clinical chemistry*]
PBI........... Pupil Behavior Inventory [*Psychology*]
PBI........... Push-Button Indicator
PBI........... Puzzle Buffs International   (EA)
PBI........... West Palm Beach [*Florida*] [*Airport symbol*]
PBIBA ...... Pochvy Bashkirii i Puti Ratsional'nogo Ikh Ispol'zovaniya [*A publication*]
PBIC .... Poly(butyl Isocyanate) [*Organic chemistry*]
PBIC .... Programmable Buffer Interface Card [*Data processing*]   (NASA)
PBICAG .... Publicaciones Biologicas. Instituto de Investigaciones Cientificas UANL [*Universidad Autonoma de Nuevo Leon*] [*A publication*]
PBICSGH ... Permanent Bureau of International Congresses for the Sciences of Genealogy and Heraldry   (EA)
PBIF .... Pacific Bible Institute of Fresno [*California*]
PBIL .... Polybenzimidazolone [*Organic chemistry*]
PBIM .... Programmable Buffer Interface Module   (MCD)
PBIOEM.... Plant Biology [*New York*] [*A publication*]
PBIP .... Paperbound Books in Print [*A publication*]
PBIP .... Pulse Beacon Impact Predictor   (AAG)
PBIS .... Prospezioni. Bollettino di Informazioni Scientifiche [*A publication*]
PBISTP .... Peter Burwash International Special Tennis Programs   (EA)
PBIT .... Parity BIT [*Binary Digit*] [*Data communications*]
PB/IWT..... Ports and Beaches and Inland Waterways Transports [*Military*]   (NATG)

PB and J .... Peanut Butter and Jelly
PBJ .... Presa Benito Juarez [*Mexico*] [*Seismograph station code, US Geological Survey*]   (SEIS)
PBJC .... Palm Beach Junior College [*Lakeworth, FL*]
PBJOD ...... Plant Biochemical Journal [*A publication*]
PBK .... Pamietnik Biblioteki Kornickiej [*A publication*]
PBK .... Paperback
PBK .... Payload Bay Kit [*NASA*]   (NASA)
PBK .... Peoples Bancorporation [*AMEX symbol*]   (SPSG)
PBK .... Phi Beta Kappa [*Honorary society*]
PBKB .... People's Savings Bank of Brockton [*Brockton, MA*] [*NASDAQ symbol*]   (NQ)
PBKC .... Premier Bankshares Corp. [*NASDAQ symbol*]   (NQ)
PBKS .... Provident Bankshares Corp. [*NASDAQ symbol*]   (NQ)
PBL .... Bethlehem Public Library, Bethlehem, PA [*OCLC symbol*]   (OCLC)
PBl .... Blairsville Public Library, Blairsville, PA [*Library symbol*] [*Library of Congress*]   (LCLS)
PBL .... Lehigh University, Bethlehem, PA [*Library symbol*] [*Library of Congress*]   (LCLS)
PBL .... Papers in Borneo Linguistics [*A publication*]
PBL .... Pastoralblaetter [*A publication*]
P Bl .... Patentblatt [*A publication*]
PBL .... Payload Bay Liner [*NASA*]   (MCD)
PBL .... Peripheral Blood Leukocyte [*or Lymphocyte*] [*Hematology*]
PBL .... [*The*] Philadelphia Belt Line Railroad Co. [*AAR code*]
PBL .... Photo Butt Line   (MSA)
PBL .... Planetary Boundary Layer [*Aerospace*]
PBL .... Potential Binding Level [*Of natural waters for metal ions*]
PBL .... Probable   (FAAC)
PBL .... Product Baseline   (MCD)
PBL .... Prune Brownline [*Plant pathology*]
PBL .... Public Broadcast Laboratory
Pbl .... Publicatieblad van de Europese Gemeenschappen [*A publication*]
pbl .... Publisher [*MARC relator code*] [*Library of Congress*]   (LCCP)
PBL .... Puerto Cabello [*Venezuela*] [*Airport symbol*]   (OAG)
PBlbM .... Montgomery County Community College, Blue Bell, PA [*Library symbol*] [*Library of Congress*]   (LCLS)
pble .... Payable [*Payable*] [*Business term*] [*French*]
pble .... Posible [*Possible*] [*Business term*] [*Spanish*]
PBLG .... Polybenzyl-L-glutamate [*Biochemistry*]
PBLS .... Production Baseline Set   (MCD)
PBLSA ...... Publius [*A publication*]
PBm .... Bryn Mawr College, Bryn Mawr, PA [*Library symbol*] [*Library of Congress*]   (LCLS)
PBM .... Paramaribo [*Surinam*] [*Airport symbol*]   (OAG)
PBM .... Patrol Search Plane [*Navy designation for Mariner aircraft*]
PBM .... Peripheral Blood Mononuclear [*Cells*] [*Hematology*]
PBM .... Permanent Bench Mark
PBM .... PIXEL Block Mode [*Data processing*]   (BYTE)
PBM .... Poetry Book Magazine [*A publication*]
PBM .... Pressure Bias Modulation   (MCD)
PBM .... Principal Beach Master [*RAF*] [*British*]
PBM .... Probability Based-Matched [*Database search techniques*]
PBM .... Production Base Modernization   (MCD)
PBM .... Program Budget Manager   (MCD)
PBM .... Program Business Management   (NASA)
PBmA .... American College of Life Underwriters, Bryn Mawr, PA [*Library symbol*] [*Library of Congress*]   (LCLS)
PBMA .... Peanut Butter Manufacturers Association [*Later, PBNPA*]   (EA)
PBMAA ..... Publications. Research Institute for Mathematical Sciences. Series A [*Japan*] [*A publication*]
PBMC .... Moravian College and Theological Seminary, Bethlehem, PA [*Library symbol*] [*Library of Congress*]   (LCLS)
PBMC .... Peripheral Blood Mononuclear Cells [*Hematology*]
PBMCA ..... Archives of the Moravian Church, Bethlehem, PA [*Library symbol*] [*Library of Congress*]   (LCLS)
PBMEA ..... Perspectives in Biology and Medicine [*A publication*]
PBmL .... Ludington Public Library, Bryn Mawr, PA [*Library symbol*] [*Library of Congress*]   (LCLS)
PBML .... Prague Bulletin of Mathematical Linguistics [*A publication*]
PBMOE8... Progress in Behavior Modification [*A publication*]
PBMR .... Pennsylvania Bureau of Municipal Research   (MCD)
PBMR .... Provisional Basic Military Requirements   (NATG)
PBM/STIRS ... Probability Based Matching and Self-Trained Interpretive and Retrieval Systems [*Database*] [*John Wiley & Sons, Inc.*] [*Information service or system*]   (CRD)
PBMW ...... Moravian College, Bethlehem, PA [*Library symbol*] [*Library of Congress*]   (LCLS)
PBN .... Northampton County Area Community College, Bethlehem, PA [*Library symbol*] [*Library of Congress*]   (LCLS)
PBN .... PE Ben Oilfield Services Ltd. [*Toronto Stock Exchange symbol*]
PBN .... Peribrachialis Nuclei [*Neurology*]
PBN .... Phenyl(butyl)nitrone [*Organic chemistry*]
PBN .... Physical Block Number
PBN .... Porto Amboin [*Angola*] [*Airport symbol*]   (OAG)
PBN .... Primary Block Number [*Data processing*]
PBN .... Pyrolytic Boron Nitride [*Inorganic chemistry*]
PBNA .... Partial Body Neutron Activation [*Radiology*]

PBNA .... Phenyl-beta-naphthylamine [*Organic chemistry*]
PBNB .... People's Savings Financial Corp. [*Formerly, People's Savings Bank New Britain*] [*NASDAQ symbol*]   (NQ)
PBNC .... Peoples Bancorporation [*NASDAQ symbol*]   (NQ)
PBNE .... Philadelphia, Bethlehem & New England Railroad Co. [*AAR code*]
PBNM .... Parallel Bar Noise Maker [*Antiacoustic torpedo device*]
PBNP .... Phipps Bend Nuclear Plant   (NRCH)
PBNP .... Point Beach Nuclear Plant   (NRCH)
PBNP .... Porcine Brain Natriuretic Peptide [*Biochemistry*]
PBNPA ...... Peanut Butter and Nut Processors Association   (EA)
PBNS .... Prospects Business News Survey [*A publication*]
PBO .... Packed by Owner
PBO .... Paleobioclimatic Operator
PBO .... Paraburdoo [*Australia*] [*Airport symbol*]   (OAG)
PBO .... Pauling Bond Order [*Physical chemistry*]
P Bo .... Petrus Boaterius [*Flourished, 1285-1321*] [*Authority cited in pre-1607 legal work*]   (DSA)
pbo .... Placebo [*Medicine*]
PBO .... Plotting Board Operator   (MUGU)
PBO .... Polski Biuletyn Orientalistyczny [*A publication*]
PBO .... Poor Bloody Observer [*British World War I military slang*]   (DSUE)
PBO .... Print Business Opportunities [*A publication*]   (EAAP)
PBO .... Property Book Officer [*Army*]   (AABC)
PBO .... Push-Button Operation
PBOD .... Phytoplankton Biochemical Oxygen Demand [*Oceanography*]
PBOI .... Public Board of Inquiry
PBOIP .... Preliminary Basis of Issue Plan [*Military*]   (MCD)
PBOS .... Planning Board for Ocean Shipping [*Army*] [*NATO*]   (AABC)
PBP .... [*The*] Paper Bag Players   (EA)
PBP .... Paperbound Books in Print [*A publication*]
PB/P .... Particleboard/Plywood
PBP .... Pay-Back Period [*Finance*]
PBP .... Pay by Phone [*Business term*]
PBP .... Pellin-Broca Prism [*Physics*]
PBP .... Penicillin-Binding Protein [*Biochemistry*]
P de Bp...... Petrus de Bellapertica [*Deceased, 1308*] [*Authority cited in pre-1607 legal work*]   (DSA)
PBP .... Pinkas Bractwa Pogrzebowego [*A publication*]
PBP .... Plotting Board Plot   (MUGU)
PBP .... Point by Point
PBP .... Power Bias Panel
PBP .... Pregnenolone Binding Protein [*Endocrinology*]
PBP .... Private Brand Proneness [*Marketing*]
PBP .... Production Base Plan   (MCD)
PBP .... Program Board Panel
PBP .... Program and Budget Planning
PBP .... Push-Button Panel
PBPB .... Para-bromophenacyl Bromide [*Organic chemistry*]
PBPB .... Pyridinium Bromide Perbromide [*Inorganic chemistry*]
PBPC .... Passenger and Baggage Processing Committee [*IATA*]   (DS)
PBPE .... Population Biology/Physiological Ecology [*Program*] [*National Science Foundation*]
PBPITMT ... Production Base Productivity Improvement through Manufacturing Technology   (MCD)
PBPK .... Physiologically Based Pharmacokinetics [*Biochemistry*]
PBPM .... Poultry Byproduct Meal
PBPS .... Painting Brushmakers' Provident Society [*A union*] [*British*]
PBPS .... Paulist Bible Pamphlet Series [*Glen Rock, NJ*] [*A publication*]   (BJA)
PBPS .... Post-Boost Propulsion System [*Aerospace*]
PBPTC ...... Palm Beach Psychotherapy Training Center   (EA)
PBQ .... Poste De La Baleine [*Quebec*] [*Seismograph station code, US Geological Survey*]   (SEIS)
PBQ .... Preschool Behavior Questionnaire
PBr .... Carnegie Public Library, Bradford, PA [*Library symbol*] [*Library of Congress*]   (LCLS)
PBR .... Pabst Blue Ribbon [*Beer*]
PBR .... Packed Bed Reactor
PBR .... Patapsco & Back Rivers Railroad Co. [*AAR code*]
P and BR .... Patristic and Byzantine Review [*A publication*]
PBR .... Patrol Boat, River [*Navy symbol*]
PBR .... Payment by Results [*Payment system*]
PBR .... Pebble-Bed Reactor [*Nuclear energy*]
PBR .... Pembroke, NH [*Location identifier*] [*FAA*]   (FAAL)
PBR .... Pencil Beam RADAR
PBR .... Pigment-Binder Ratio [*Weight*]
PBR .... Plant Breeders' Rights
PBR .... Plum Brook Reactor [*Nuclear energy*]
PBR .... Pole Broken [*Telecommunications*]   (TEL)
PBR .... Power Breeder Reactor   (AAG)
PBR .... Precision Bombing Range [*Army*]
PBR .... Pressurized Ballistic Range [*NASA*]
PBR .... Progress in Brain Research [*Elsevier Book Series*] [*A publication*]
PBR .... Pyridine-Butadiene Rubber
PBra .... Carnegie Free Library, Braddock, PA [*Library symbol*] [*Library of Congress*]   (LCLS)
PBRA .... Polska Bibliografja Biblijna Adnotowana [*A publication*]
PBRA .... Practical Bomb Rack Adapter   (NG)

PBRA......... Professional Bicycle Racers Association [*Defunct*]　(EA)
PBracAL.... Allegheny International, Inc., Brackenridge, PA [*Library symbol*] [*Library of Congress*]　(LCLS)
PBRCA...... Proceedings. British Ceramic Society [*A publication*]
PBRE......... Pebble-Bed Reactor Experiment [*Nuclear energy*]
PBREE3..... Plant Breeding Reviews [*A publication*]
PBRERP.... Permanent Board for Review of the Enlisted Retention Program
PBRERS..... Permanent Board for Review of the Enlisted Rating Structure
PBRESD.... Polar Branch, Research Environmental Science Division [*Army*]
PBRF .... Plant Breeding Research Forum　(EA)
PBRF .... Plum Brook Reactor Facility [*Lewis Research Center*]
PBriR .... Rohm & Haas Co., Bristol, PA [*Library symbol*] [*Library of Congress*]　(LCLS)
P/BRK .... Power Brake [*Automotive engineering*]
PBroGS...... Church of Jesus Christ of Latter-Day Saints, Genealogical Society Library, Philadelphia Branch, Broomall, PA [*Library symbol*] [*Library of Congress*]　(LCLS)
PBRS .... Pupil Behavior Rating Scale [*Psychology*]
PBRS .... Push-Button Rotary Switch
PBS............ Bethlehem Steel Corp., Charles H. Herty, Jr., Memorial Library, Bethlehem, PA [*Library symbol*] [*Library of Congress*]　(LCLS)
PBS............ Pacific Biological Station [*Department of Fisheries and Oceans*] [*Canada*] [*Research center*]　(RCD)
PBS............ Palestine Broadcasting Service　(BJA)
PBS............ Parenchymatous Bundle Sheath [*Botany*]
PBS............ Parimutuel Betting System
PBS............ Particulate Biogenic Silica [*Environmental science*]
PBS............ Parts Breakdown Structure
PBS............ Peninsular Base Section [*Military*]
PBS............ Periscope Bombsight Stabilizer
PBS............ Personal Bibliographic Software, Inc. [*Information service or system*]　(IID)
PBS............ Peterborough Board of Education [*UTLAS symbol*]
PBS............ Phosphate-Buffered Saline
PBS............ Pigeon Bay [*South Carolina*] [*Seismograph station code, US Geological Survey*]　(SEIS)
PBS............ Pilgrim Regional Bank Shares, Inc. [*NYSE symbol*]　(SPSG)
PBS............ Podiatry Bibliographical Society [*Defunct*]　(EA)
PBS............ Polarization Beam Splitter
PBS............ Polysteel Building Systems Ltd. [*Toronto Stock Exchange symbol*]
PBS............ Potere Battericida del Sangue [*Bactericidal Property of the Blood*] [*Medicine*]
PBS............ Power Breakfast Syndrome [*Suffered by late-risers forced to attend breakfast meetings*]
PBS............ Prefabricated Bituminous Surfacing
PBS............ Pressedienst fuer das Bauspar [*A publication*]
PBS............ Pressure Boundary Subsystem [*Nuclear energy*]　(NRCH)
PBS............ Primer Binding Site [*Genetics*]
PBS............ Production Base Support [*Army*]　(AABC)
PBS............ Professional Bibliographic System [*Database manager package*] [*Personal Bibliographic Software, Inc.*] [*Ann Arbor, MI*]
PBS............ Professional Bowhunters Society　(EA)
PBS............ Program Board Stowage
PBS............ Program Breakdown Structure [*Nuclear energy*]
PBS............ Program and Budgeting System　(OICC)
PBS............ Project Breakdown Structure [*Nuclear energy*]　(NRCH)
PBS............ Protestant Big Sisters
PBS............ Public Broadcasting Service　(EA)
PBS............ Public Buildings Service [*of General Services Administration*]
PBS............ Publications. Babylonian Section. University Museum. University of Pennsylvania [*Philadelphia*] [*A publication*]
PBS............ Push-Button Switch
PBSA .... Papers. Bibliographical Society of America [*A publication*]
PBSA .... Phosphate-Buffered Saline Azide [*Culture medium*]
PBSA .... Publications. Bibliographical Society of America [*A publication*]
PBSB .... Prudential Bancorporation [*NASDAQ symbol*]　(NQ)
PBSC .... Panelized Building Systems Council　(EA)
PBSC .... Papers. Bibliographical Society of Canada [*A publication*]
PBSCMA .. Peanut Butter Sandwich and Cookie Manufacturers Association [*Later, PBNPA*]　(EA)
PBSE .... Philadelphia-Baltimore Stock Exchange [*Later, Philadelphia-Baltimore-Washington Stock Exchange*]
PBSED ...... Proceedings. Bioenergy R and D Seminar [*A publication*]
PBSM .... Plastic Bonded Starter Mix
PBSR .... Papers. British School at Rome [*A publication*]
PBSteel ...... Bethlehem Steel Corp., Charles M. Schwab Memorial Library, Bethlehem, PA [*Library symbol*] [*Library of Congress*]　(LCLS)
PBSUV ...... Papers. Bibliographical Society. University of Virginia [*A publication*]
PBSW .... Push-Button Switch
PBSWA ..... Proceedings. Biological Society of Washington [*A publication*]
PBT........... Pacific Ballet Theatre
PBT........... Para-Bandit Target
PBT........... Parity BIT [*Binary Digit*] Test
PBT........... Passband Tuning
PBT........... Peoria Board of Trade　(EA)

PBT............ Permian Basin Royalty Trust [*NYSE symbol*]　(SPSG)
PBT............ Philippine Ballet Theater　(ECON)
PBT............ Piggyback Tape [*or Twistor*] [*Data processing*]
PBT............ Pittsburgh Ballet Theatre
PBT............ Polybay Tier
PBT............ Polybenzothiazole [*Organic chemistry*]
PBT............ Polybutylene Terephthalate [*Organic chemistry*]
PBT............ Preferred Body Temperature [*Physiology*]
PBT............ Preliminary-Breath-Test [*Device used by police to determine whether or not a driver is legally intoxicated*]
PBT............ Push-Button Telephone
PBT............ Red Bluff, CA [*Location identifier*] [*FAA*]　(FAAL)
PBTC .... Postal Business Training Centre [*British*]
PBTE .... Performance-Based Teacher Evaluation　(OICC)
PBTF .... Pump Bearing Test Facility [*Nuclear energy*]
P/BTN ...... Push Button [*Automotive engineering*]
PBTP .... Polybutylene Terephthalate [*Organic chemistry*]
PBTS .... Proton Beam Transport System
PBTX .... Ptychodiscus brevis Toxin [*Florida red-tide toxin*]
PBU .... Bucknell University, Lewisburg, PA [*OCLC symbol*]　(OCLC)
PBU .... Palm Beach County Utility Corp. [*Toronto Stock Exchange symbol*]
PBU .... Perry Basin [*Utah*] [*Seismograph station code, US Geological Survey*]　(SEIS)
PBU .... Putao [*Burma*] [*Airport symbol*]　(OAG)
PBUP........ Perforated Backup Plate
PBut .... Butler Public Library, Butler, PA [*Library symbol*] [*Library of Congress*]　(LCLS)
PButV .... United States Veterans Administration Hospital, Butler, PA [*Library symbol*] [*Library of Congress*]　(LCLS)
PBUZDC... Publicaciones de Biologia. Universidad de Navarra. Serie Zoologica [*A publication*]
PBV........... English Prayer Book Version　(BJA)
PBV........... Pedal Blood Vessel
PBV........... Platinol [*Cisplatin*], Bleomycin, Vinblastine [*Antineoplastic drug regimen*]
PBV........... Post Boost Vehicle [*Missiles*]　(AFM)
PBV........... Predicted Blood Volume [*Medicine*]
PBV........... Pulmonary Blood Volume [*Medicine*]
PBVM........ Presentation of the Blessed Virgin Mary [*Roman Catholic women's religious order*]
PBVR........ [*The*] Port Bienville Railroad [*AAR code*]
PBvu.......... Andrew Bayne Memorial Library, Bellevue, PA [*Library symbol*] [*Library of Congress*]　(LCLS)
PBW .... Particle-Beam Weapon
PBW .... Parts by Weight　(IEEE)
PBW .... Percussive Butt Welder
PBW .... Pink Bollworm [*Cotton pest*]
PBW .... Posterior Bite Wing [*Dentistry*]
PBW .... Power by Wire [*Flight control*]
PBW .... Proportional Bandwidth　(MCD)
PBW .... Pulse Burst Wave
PBWA .... Plasma Beta-Wave Accelerator [*Plasma physics*]
PBWAA..... Professional Basketball Writers' Association of America　(EA)
PBWEE..... Pilot Boll Weevil Eradication Experiment [*Department of Agriculture*]
PBWF .... Pulse Burst Waveform
PBWSE ..... Philadelphia-Baltimore-Washington Stock Exchange [*Later, Philadelphia Stock Exchange*]
PBX........... PBX Resources [*Vancouver Stock Exchange symbol*]
PBX........... Plastic Bonded Explosive
PBX........... Private Branch Exchange [*Telecommunications*]
PBY........... Kayenta, AZ [*Location identifier*] [*FAA*]　(FAAL)
PBY........... Patrol Bomber [*Navy designation for Catalina aircraft*]
PBY........... Pep Boys - Manny, Moe & Jack [*NYSE symbol*]　(SPSG)
PBZ........... Phenoxybenzamine [*Also, POB*] [*Adrenergic blocking agent*]
PBZ........... Phenylbutazone [*Anti-inflammatory compound*]
PBZ........... Plettenberg [*South Africa*] [*Airport symbol*]　(OAG)
PBZ........... Pyribenzamine [*Antihistamine*] [*Trademark*]
PBzN......... Peroxybenzoyl Nitrate [*Lacrimator*]
PC .... All India Reporter, Privy Council [*1914-50*] [*A publication*]　(DLA)
PC .... British and Colonial Prize Cases [*A publication*]　(DLA)
PC .... Civilian Personnel Division [*Coast Guard*]
PC .... Coastal Escort [*Ship symbol*]　(NATG)
PC .... Communist Party [*Peru*] [*Political party*]　(PD)
PC .... Indian Rulings, Privy Council [*1929-47*] [*A publication*]　(DLA)
PC .... J. Lewis Crozer [*Chester Public*] Library, Chester, PA [*Library symbol*] [*Library of Congress*]　(LCLS)
PC .... Judicial Committee of the Privy Council　(DLA)
PC .... Pacific Coast Railroad [*AAR code*] [*Terminated*]
PC .... Package Control [*or Controller*]
PC .... Pad Coordinator [*NASA*]
PC .... Palmitoyl Carnitine [*Biochemistry*]
PC .... Pan Malaysian Air Transport [*Malaysia*] [*ICAO designator*]　(FAAC)
PC .... [*The*] Panama Canal
Pc .... Pancuronium [*A muscle relaxant*]
PC .... Panoramic Camera
PC .... Paper Chromatography

PC	Paper or Cloth [*Freight*]
PC	Paper Copy
PC	Paracortical Hyperplasia [*Oncology*]
PC	Paraula Cristiana [*A publication*]
PC	Parent Care (EA)
PC	Parent Cells
PC	Parental Control [*Channel lockout*] [*Video technology*]
P & C	Parge and Core [*Construction*]
PC	Parish Church [*British*] (ROG)
PC	Parish Council
PC	Parliamentary Cases [*A publication*] (DLA)
PC	PARSEC [*Parallax Second*] [*See PARSEC*]
PC	Parti Communiste [*Communist Party*] [*Luxembourg*] [*Political party*] (PPW)
PC	Participation Certificate
PC	Partido Colorado [*Colorado Party*] [*Uruguay*] [*Political party*] (PPW)
PC	Partido Conservador [*Conservative Party*] [*Ecuador*] [*Political party*] (PPW)
PC	Parts Catalog (KSC)
PC	Passenger Certificate [*Shipping*] (DS)
PC	Past Commander
PC	Patent Cases [*A publication*] (DLA)
PC	Patent Committee (MCD)
PC	Path Control [*Data processing*] (IBMDP)
PC	Patres Conscripti [*Senators*] [*Latin*]
PC	Patrol Car [*British military*] (DMA)
PC	Patrol Craft
PC	Patrol Vessel, Submarine Chaser [*Navy symbol*]
PC	Pay Clerk
pc	Paye au Comptant [*Paid in Cash*] [*Business term*] [*French*]
PC	Paymaster-Captain [*Navy*] [*British*]
PC	Paymaster-Commander [*Navy*] [*British*]
PC	Peace Commissioner [*Ireland*]
PC	Peace Corps (EA)
PC	Peak Capacity
PC	Peake's Commentary on the Bible [*A publication*]
PC	Peg Count [*Telecommunications*] (TEL)
PC	Penal Code [*A publication*] (DLA)
PC	Penetrating Cell
PC	[*The*] Penn Central Corp. [*NYSE symbol*] (SPSG)
PC	Penn Central Transportation Co. [*Subsidiary of Penn Central Corp.*] [*Absorbed into Consolidated Rail Corp.*] [*AAR code*]
PC	Penny Cyclopoedia [*British*] [*A publication*] (ROG)
PC	Pensiero Critico [*A publication*]
PC	People for a Change [*An association*] (EA)
PC	People's China [*A publication*]
PC	People's Conference [*India*] [*Political party*] (PPW)
PC	Per Centum [*By the Hundred*] [*Latin*]
PC	Per Condoglianza [*Used on visiting cards to express condolence*] [*Italian*]
PC	Perciconia circinata [*A toxin-producing fungus*]
PC	Perfectae Caritatis [*Decree on the Appropriate Renewal of the Religious Life*] [*Vatican II document*]
PC	Perfins Club (EA)
PC	Performance Code
PC	Performance Contract (OICC)
PC	Pericarditis [*Avian pathology*]
PC	Pericentral
PC	Pericynthion [*Perilune, or low point, in lunar orbit*]
PC	Peripheral Cell
PC	Peripheral Control (BUR)
PC	Perpetual Curate
PC	Personal Computer
PC	Personal Copier [*In product name, PC-10*] [*Canon Inc.*]
PC	Personal Correction
PC	Personnel Carrier [*A vehicle*]
PC	Petro-Canada
PC	Petty Cash
PC	Pharmacy Corps [*Army*]
PC	Phase Coherent (CET)
PC	Pheochromocytoma [*Oncology*]
PC	Philippine Constabulary
PC	Philosophical Classics [*A publication*]
PC	Phobia Clinic (EA)
PC	Phosphatidylcholine [*Lecithin*] [*Biochemistry*]
PC	Phosphocholine [*Biochemistry*]
PC	Phosphocreatine [*Also, PCr*] [*Creatine phosphate; see CP*] [*Biochemistry*]
PC	Phosphorylcholine [*Biochemistry*]
PC	Photocell
PC	Photoconductor
PC	Photocounting
Pc	Phthalocyanine [*Organic chemistry*]
P & C	Physical and Chemical (AAG)
PC	Physocyanin [*Biochemistry*]
PC	Phytophthora Cinnamoni [*A fungus*]
PC	Pick Up Cargo (AFM)
pC	Picocoulomb
pC	Picocurie [*Also, pCi*]

PC	Picture (MDG)
PC	Piece (AAG)
pc	Pied Carre [*Square Foot*] [*French*]
pc	Pied Cube [*Cubic Foot*] [*French*]
PC	Pierre Cardin [*Fashion designer*]
PC	Pilotage Charts [*Air Force*]
PC	Pioneer Clubs (EA)
PC	Pioneer Corps [*British military*] (DMA)
pc	Pitcairn [*MARC country of publication code*] [*Library of Congress*] (LCCP)
PC	Pitch Channel
PC	Pitch Circle [*Technical drawings*]
PC	Pitch Control (KSC)
PC	Pittsburgh Commerce Institute
PC	Plaid Cymru [*Welsh national liberation party*] [*Political party*]
P/C	Plane Captain (MUGU)
PC	Plane Change (MCD)
PC	Plane Commander
PC	Planetary Citizens (EA)
PC	Planning Card (AAG)
PC	Planning Concept (MCD)
PC	Plant Computer (NRCH)
PC	Planting Council (EA)
PC	Plasma Cell [*Oncology*]
PC	Plasma Chromatography
PC	Plasmacytoma [*Medicine*]
PC	Plastic Core
Pc	Plastocyanin
PC	Plate Circuit (DEN)
PC	Platelet Concentrate [*Hematology*]
PC	Platelet Count [*Hematology*]
PC	Platform/Crane (DCTA)
PC	Pleas of the Crown [*A publication*] (DLA)
PC	Plenum Chamber
PC	Plug Cock (AAG)
PC	Plug Compatible [*Data processing*] (BUR)
PC	Pocket Computer
PC	Poesia e Critica [*A publication*]
P & C	Poet and Critic [*A publication*]
PC	Poetry Criticism [*A publication*]
PC	Point of Curve [*Technical drawings*]
P-C	Polar to Cartesian
PC	Polar Continental [*American air mass*]
PC	Polar Crane [*Nuclear energy*] (NRCH)
PC	Pole Cell [*Insect embryology*]
P/C	Police Car
PC	Police-Constable [*Scotland Yard*]
PC	Police Court [*British*] (ROG)
PC	Policy Control (ADA)
PC	Political Code [*A publication*] (ILCA)
P/C	Polizza di Carico [*Bill of Lading*] [*Italian*] [*Shipping*]
PC	Polycarbonate [*Organic chemistry*]
PC	Polycarbosilane [*Organic chemistry*]
PC	Polymer-Concrete (KSC)
PC	Pondus Civile [*Civil (Avoirdupois) Weight*] [*Pharmacy*] (ROG)
PC	Poni Curavit [*Caused to Be Placed*] [*Latin*]
PC	Poor Clares [*Roman Catholic women's religious order*]
PC	Poor Classes [*British*] (DSUE)
pc	Pop Corn [*Crochet*]
PC	Popular Cult
PC	Population Census
PC	Population Communication (EA)
PC	Population Council (EA)
PC	Port Call [*Army*]
PC	Port Committee (NATG)
PC	Port Control [*Telecommunications*] (TEL)
PC	Portable Computer
PC	Portacaval [*Medicine*]
PC	Portion Control [*Food service*]
PC	Portland Cement
PC	Positive Control
Pc	Positive Wave in Children [*Neurophysiology*]
PC	Post Card (ROG)
PC	Post Cibum [*After Meals*] [*Pharmacy*]
PC	Post Commander [*Military*]
PC	Post Consulatum [*After the Consulate*] [*Latin*]
PC	Postal Clerk [*Navy rating*]
PC	Postcard
PC	Postcode (ADA)
PC	Postcoital [*Medicine*]
PC	Posterior Chamber [*Ophthalmology*]
PC	Posterior Commissure [*Neuroanatomy*]
PC	Postinflammatory Corticoid [*Medicine*]
pc	Pottery Cache (BJA)
pc	Pour Cent [*Per Cent*] [*French*]
p/c	Pour Compte [*By Cash*] [*Business term*] [*French*]
PC	Pour Condoler [*To Offer Sympathy*] [*French*]
PC	Power Contactor
PC	Power Control [*System*] (NG)
P-C	Power Conversion (CET)

PC	Practice Cases [*A publication*] (DLA)
PC	Precarrier
PC	Precast
PC	Precaution Category [*For clinical laboratories*]
PC	Precedents in Chancery [*A publication*] (DLA)
PC	Precision Control [*Computer programming*] (BYTE)
PC	Precordia [*Anatomy*]
PC	Preliminary Commitment (IMH)
PC	Preparatory Commission
PC	Preparatory Committee
PC	Presence Chretienne [*A publication*]
PC	Present Complaint [*Medicine*]
PC	Presidents Club [*Commercial firm*] (EA)
PC	Press Council [*British*]
PC	Pressure Chamber
PC	Pressure Controller [*Nuclear energy*]
PC	Price Commission [*Cost of Living Council*]
PC	Price Control Cases [*A publication*] (DLA)
PC	Price per Copy [*of books*]
P/C	Price/Cost
PC	Prices Current
P & C	Prideaux and Cole's English Reports [*4 New Sessions Cases*] [*A publication*] (DLA)
P-in-C	Priest-in-Charge [*Church of England*]
PC	Priest Confessor
PC	Primary Center
PC	Primary Circuit (MCD)
PC	Primary Code
PC	Primary Contributor
PC	Primary Control (MCD)
PC	Prime Contractor
PC	Prime Cost
PC	Prince Edward Island Provincial Library, Charlottetown, Prince Edward Island [*Library symbol*] [*National Library of Canada*] (NLC)
PC	Principal Chaplain (ADA)
PC	Principal Component
PC	Print Club (EA)
PC	Printed Circuit
PC	Printer Control
P & C	Prism and Cover (Test) [*Ophthalmology*]
PC	Prisoner of Conscience (BJA)
PC	Private Concerns [*An association*] [*Defunct*] (EA)
PC	Private Contract [*Tea trade*] (ROG)
PC	Private Corporation
PC	Privatization Council [*New York, NY*] (EA)
PC	Privilege Car [*on a train*] [*Theatre slang*]
PC	Privileged Character [*A favored student*] [*Teen slang*]
PC	Privy Council [*or Councillor*] [*British*]
PC	Prize Court (DLA)
PC	Probable Cause [*Legal term*]
PC	Probate Court [*British*] (ROG)
PC	Problems of Communism [*A publication*]
PC	Procaer SpA [*Italy*] [*ICAO aircraft manufacturer identifier*] (ICAO)
PC	Procarbazine [*Also, P, PCB, Pr*] [*Antineoplastic drug*]
PC	Procedure Civile [*Civil Procedure*] [*A publication*] (DLA)
PC	Process Chemistry
PC	Process Computer (NRCH)
PC	Process Control (DEN)
PC	Processing Center [*Telecommunications*] (TEL)
PC	Processor Controller [*Data processing*] (MDG)
PC	Procurement Command [*Army*]
PC	Procurement Communication [*Military*]
P & C	Procurement and Contracting (AFM)
PC	Producers' Council [*Later, CPMC*] (EA)
PC	Production Certificate (MCD)
PC	Production Company [*Films, television, etc.*]
PC	Production Control (MCD)
PC	Production Costs
PC	Professional Communication (MCD)
PC	Professional Corporation
PC	Professors of Curriculum (EA)
PC	Program Change
PC	Program Committee [*UN Food and Agriculture Organization*]
P/C	Program Communications [*Military*] (AFIT)
PC	Program Control
PC	Program Coordination (IEEE)
PC	Program Counter
PC	Programmable Computer
PC	Programmed Check (AAG)
PC	Progressive Conservative [*Canada*] [*Political party*]
PC	Project Censored (EA)
PC	Project Children (EA)
PC	Project Control (NASA)
PC	Project Coordinator (NG)
PC	Projector Charge
PC	Proof Coins [*Numismatics*]
P/C	Property/Casualty [*Insurance*]
PC	Proportional Counter [*Instrumentation*]
PC	Proposed Change
PC	Propositional Calculus [*Logic*]
PC	Propulsive Coefficient
PC	Propylene Carbonate [*Organic chemistry*]
PC	Prospectors Club [*Later, PCI*]
PC	Prosthetics Center [*Veterans Administration*]
PC	Protective Climate [*Solar heating*]
PC	Protective Cover (MCD)
PC	Proto-Canaanite (BJA)
PC	Protocol Converter (MCD)
PC	Provincial Commissioner [*British government*]
PC	Provisional Costs
PC	Provocative Concentration [*Immunology*]
PC	Pseudocode (AAG)
PC	Pseudoconditioning Control [*Neurophysiology*]
PC	Public Citizen (EA)
PC	Public Contract
PC	Publications in Climatology (MCD)
PC	[*The*] Publishers' Circular [*A publication*] (ROG)
PC	Pubococcygeus [*Muscle*] [*Anatomy*]
PC	Pulmonary Capillary [*Medicine*]
PC	Pulsating Current
PC	Pulse Cleaned [*Dust filtration*]
PC	Pulse Comparator (AAG)
PC	Pulse Compression
PC	Pulse Controller
PC	Pulse Counter [*Data processing*] (MDG)
PC	Pulverized Coal [*Fuel technology*]
PC	Punched Card [*Data processing*]
PC	Punjab Cavalry [*British military*] (DMA)
PC	Puns Corps (EA)
PC	Purchase Card
PC	Purchasing and Contracting [*Army*]
P & C	Purchasing and Contracting
PC	Pure Clairvoyance [*Psychical research*]
PC	Purified Concentrate
PC	Purkinje Cell [*Neuroanatomy*]
P & C	Put and Call [*Stock exchange term*]
PC	Pyrrolinecarboxylic Acid [*Biochemistry*]
PC	Single Paper Single Cotton [*Wire insulation*] (AAG)
PC	Submarine Chaser [*173 foot*] [*Navy symbol*] [*Obsolete*]
PC	Sumitomo Chemical Co. [*Japan*] [*Research code symbol*]
PC	Veterans of the US Posse Comitatus (EA)
PC1	Postal Clerk, First Class [*Navy rating*]
PC1	Power Control One [*Hydraulic*] (MCD)
PC2	Postal Clerk, Second Class [*Navy rating*]
PC2	Power Control Two [*Hydraulic*] (MCD)
PC3	Postal Clerk, Third Class [*Navy rating*]
PCA	Acts of the Privy Council [*England*] [*A publication*] (DLA)
PCA	Calgon Corp., Pittsburgh, PA [*OCLC symbol*] (OCLC)
PCA	Pacific Communications Area [*Air Force*] (MCD)
PCA	Panama Canal Authority
PCA	Paper Converters Association [*Defunct*] (EA)
PCA	Paperweight Collectors' Association (EA)
PCA	Papillon Club of America (EA)
PCA	Para-Chloroaniline [*Organic chemistry*]
PCA	Para-Coumaric Acid [*Organic chemistry*]
PCA	Parachute Club of America [*Later, USPA*] (EA)
PCA	Parietal Cell Antibodies [*Immunology*]
PCA	Parliamentary Commissioner for Administration [*British*]
PCA	Parti Communiste Algerien [*Algerian Communist Party*] [*Political party*]
PCA	Partido Comunista de Argentina [*Communist Party of Argentina*] [*Political party*] (PD)
PCA	Parts Control Area [*NASA*] (KSC)
PCA	Passive Cutaneous Anaphylaxis [*Immunochemistry*]
PCA	Patient-Controlled Analgesia
PCA	Patriotic Catholic Association [*Name given to nationalized Catholic Church in China*]
P & CA	Paying and Collecting Area (AFM)
PCA	Peak Clipping Amplifier
PCA	Pekingese Club of America (EA)
PCA	Pennsylvania Commuter Airlines [*New Cumberland, PA*] [*FAA designator*] (FAAC)
PCA	Pentachloraniline [*Organic chemistry*]
PCA	Pentachloroanisole [*Organic chemistry*]
PCA	Percent Cortical Area [*Neurology*]
PCA	Perchloric Acid [*Inorganic chemistry*]
PCA	Pericruciate Association [*Cortex, of cat*]
PCA	Peripheral Circulatory Assist [*Medicine*]
PCA	Peritoneal Carcinomatosis [*Oncology*]
PCA	Permanent Change of Assignment [*Army*]
PCA	Permanent Court of Arbitration [*See also CPA*] [*Hague, Netherlands*] (EAIO)
PCA	Personal Care Aide [*or Assistant or Attendant*]
PCA	Personal Cash Allowance
PCA	Pest Control Association [*Australia*]
PCA	Philippine Contractors Association (DS)
PCA	Photon Counting Array [*Instrumentation*]
PCA	Physical Configuration Audit [*Military, NASA*]
PCA	Pinnacle [*Alaska*] [*Seismograph station code, US Geological Survey*] (SEIS)

PCA .... Pitcairn Cierva Autogiro [*Aeronautics*]
PCA .... Pitch Control Assembly   (MCD)
PCA .... Plane Circular Aperture
PCA .... Plasma Catecholamine [*Biochemistry*]
PCA .... Plasma-Covered Antenna
PCA .... Plate Count Agar [*Microbiology*]
PCA .... Pneumatic Control Assembly   (NASA)
PCA .... Point of Closest Approach
PCAO .... Polar Cap Absorption
PCA .... Police Complaint Authority [*British*]
PCA .... Polycrystalline Alumina
PCA .... Poodle Club of America   (EA)
PCA .... Pool Critical Assembly [*Nuclear reactor*]
PCA .... Popular Culture Association   (EA)
PCA .... Porous-Coated Anatomical [*Prosthesis*]
PCA .... Porsche Club of America   (EA)
PCA .... Port Communications Area [*Telecommunications*]   (TEL)
PCA .... Portacaval Anastomosis [*Animal model of chronic liver disease*]
PCA .... Portage Creek [*Alaska*] [*Airport symbol*]   (OAG)
PCA .... Portland Cement Association   (EA)
PCA .... Ports Canada
PCA .... Positive Control Area
PCA .... Positive Controlled Airspace
PCA .... Postconstruction Availability   (NVT)
PCA .... Posterior Cerebral Artery [*Brain anatomy*]
PCA .... Posterior Communicating Artery [*Anatomy*]
PCA .... Posterior Cricoarytenoid [*A muscle of the larynx*]
PCA .... Potash Company of America, Inc. [*Toronto Stock Exchange symbol*]
PCA .... Poultrymen's Cooperative Association   (EA)
PCA .... Power Conditioning Assembly
PCA .... Power Control Assembly   (NASA)
PCA .... Precontractual Authorization
PCA .... Prescribed Concentration of Alcohol   (ADA)
PCA .... President's Council on Aging [*Inactive*]
PCA .... Primary Carbon Assimilation [*Botany*]
PCA .... Primary Control Assembly [*Nuclear energy*]   (NRCH)
PCA .... Primary Coolant Activity [*Nuclear energy*]   (NRCH)
PCA .... Prime Candidate Alloy   (MCD)
PCA .... Prime Condition Aircraft
PCA .... Principal Component Analysis
PCA .... Principal Control Authority   (NATG)
PCA .... Prindle Class Association   (FA)
PCA .... Print Council of America   (EA)
PCA .... Printed Circuit Assembly [*Telecommunications*]   (TEL)
PCA .... Printer Communications Adapter
PCA .... Printing Corporation of America
PCA .... Private Communications Association [*Later, NCA*]
PCA .... Proceedings. Classical Association [*A publication*]
PCA .... Process Control Analyzer
PCA .... Procoagulant Activity
PCA .... Procrastinators' Club of America   (EA)
PCA .... Producers Commission Association   (EA)
PCA .... Professional Chess Association   (EA)
PCA .... Professional Comedians' Association   (EA)
PCA .... Program Change Analysis [*DoD*]
PCA .... Program Coupler Assembly   (KSC)
PCA .... Programmable Communications Adapter [*Data processing*]
PCA .... Progress Change Authority
PCA .... Progressive Citizens of America
PC & A ...... Project Control and Administration [*NASA*]
PCA .... Protective Clothing Arrangement [*Telecommunications*]   (TEL)
PCA .... Protective Connecting Arrangement [*Telecommunications*]   (TEL)
PCA .... Public Archives, Charlottetown, Prince Edward Island [*Library symbol*] [*National Library of Canada*]   (NLC)
PCA .... Puli Club of America   (EA)
PCA .... Pulp Chemicals Association   (EA)
PCA .... Pulse Counter Adapter
PCA .... Pyrotechnic Control Assembly [*NASA*]
PCA .... Pyrrolidonecarboxylic Acid [*Organic chemistry*]
PCAA .... Pancretan Association of America   (EA)
PCaab .... Parietal Cell Autoantibody [*Immunology*]
PCAABC ... Centre for Agricultural Publications and Documentation [*Wageningen*]. Annual Report [*A publication*]
PCAAS ...... Proceedings. Connecticut Academy of Arts and Sciences [*A publication*]
PCAC .... Partially Conserved Axial-Vector Current
PCAC .... Private College Admissions Center [*Later, NAAPHE*]
PC Act ...... Probate Court Act [*A publication*]   (DLA)
PCAE .... Polar Cap Absorption Event
PCAG .... Pentobarbital-Chlorpromazine-Alcohol Group [*Medicine*]
PCAG .... Research Station, Agriculture Canada [*Station de Recherches, Agriculture Canada*] Charlottetown, Prince Edward Island [*Library symbol*] [*National Library of Canada*]   (NLC)
PCAI .... PCA International, Inc. [*NASDAQ symbol*]   (NQ)
P Cal .... Petrus Calvelli [*Flourished, 14th century*] [*Authority cited in pre-1607 legal work*]   (DSA)

PCalS .... California State College, California, PA [*Library symbol*] [*Library of Congress*]   (LCLS)
PCAM .... Partitioned Content Addressable Memory
PCAM .... Punched Card Accounting Machine [*Data processing*]
PCamA ...... Alliance College, Cambridge Springs, PA [*Library symbol*] [*Library of Congress*]   (LCLS)
P Camb Ph S ... Proceedings. Cambridge Philological Society [*A publication*]
PCAMIC ... People Concerned about MIC [*Methyl Isocyanate*]   (EA)
PCAO .... President's Commission on Americans Outdoors
PCAP .... Physical Correlation Analysis Program [*Military*]
P-CAP........ Physically-Challenged Assistance Program [*Chrysler Motors Corp.*] [*Detroit, MI*] [*Information service or system*]   (IID)
PCAP .... Post Commercial Action Plan [*International Trade Administration*]
PCAP .... Programmer Capacity
PC App ...... Law Reports, Privy Council, Appeal Cases [*England*] [*A publication*]   (DLA)
PCAPS ...... Production Control and Planning System   (MCD)
PCAR .... PACCAR, Inc. [*NASDAQ symbol*]   (NQ)
PCARD ..... Philippine Council for Agriculture Resources, Research, and Development   (DS)
PCarl .... Bosler Free Library, Carlisle, PA [*Library symbol*] [*Library of Congress*]   (LCLS)
PCarlA ...... United States Army War College, Carlisle Barracks, PA [*Library symbol*] [*Library of Congress*]   (LCLS)
PCarlD ...... Dickinson College, Carlisle, PA [*Library symbol*] [*Library of Congress*]   (LCLS)
PCarlD-L... Dickinson School of Law, Sheeley-Lee Law Library, Carlisle, PA [*Library symbol*] [*Library of Congress*]   (LCLS)
PCarlH ...... Cumberland County Historical Society and Hamilton Library Association, Carlisle, PA [*Library symbol*] [*Library of Congress*]   (LCLS)
PCarlMH .. United States Army, Military History Research Collection, Carlisle Barracks, PA [*Library symbol*] [*Library of Congress*]   (LCLS)
PCarlPL..... United States Army, Carlisle Barracks Post Library, Carlisle Barracks, PA [*Library symbol*] [*Library of Congress*]   (LCLS)
PCARS ...... Point Credit Accounting and Reporting System   (AFM)
PCAS .... Persistent Chemical Agent Stimulant
PCAS .... Possible Carotid Artery System [*Medicine*]
PCAS .... Primary Central Alarm Station [*Nuclear energy*]   (NRCH)
P Cas .... Prize Cases [*1914-22*] [*England*] [*A publication*]   (DLA)
P Cas......... Prize Cases (Trehearn and Grant) [*England*] [*A publication*]   (DLA)
PCAS .... Proceedings. Cambridge Antiquarian Society [*A publication*]
PCAS .... Proceedings. Classical Association of Scotland [*A publication*]
PCAS .... Punch Card Accounting System [*Data processing*]
PCAS/CADS ... Persistent Chemical Agent Stimulant/Chemical Agent Disclosure Solution [*Army*]
PCASS ...... Parts Control Automated Support System [*Database*]
PCAST ...... President's Council of Advisers on Science and Technology [*1989*]
PCAT........ Pharmacy College Admission Test
pCAT .... Plasmid Chloramphenicol Acetyltransferase [*An enzyme*]
P Cath .... Pensee Catholique [*A publication*]
PCAU .... Parachute Course Administrative Unit [*Military*] [*British*]   (INF)
PCAU .... Philippine Civil Affairs Unit [*Army unit which supplied emergency subsistence after end of Japanese dominance*] [*World War II*]
PCAV........ Principal Component Analysis with Varimax Rotation
PCB............ Central Pennsylvania District Library Center, Bellefonte, PA [*OCLC symbol*]   (OCLC)
PcB............ Near Point of Convergence [*Ophthalmology*]
PCB............ Page Control Block [*Data processing*]   (IBMDP)
PCB............ Paracervical Block [*Anesthesiology*]
PCB............ Parti Communiste de Belgique [*Communist Party of Belgium*] [*See also KPB*] [*Political party*]   (PPE)
PCB............ Partido Comunista de Bolivia [*Communist Party of Bolivia*] [*Political party*]   (PPW)
PCB............ Partido Comunista do Brasil [*Communist Party of Brazil*] [*Pro-Albanian*] [*Political party*]   (PPW)
PCB............ Parts Control Board
PCB............ Patent Compensation Board [*Energy Research and Development Administration*]
PCB............ Petty Cash Book [*Business term*]
PCB............ Planning Change Board   (AAG)
PCB............ Plenum Chamber Burning
PCB............ Poetry Chapbook [*A publication*]
PCB............ Pollution. Environmental News Bulletin [*A publication*]
PCB............ Polychlorinated Biphenyl [*Organic chemistry*]
PCB............ Polychlorobenzene
PCB............ Port Check BIT [*Binary Digit*] [*Telecommunications*]   (TEL)
PCB............ Power Circuit Breaker   (MSA)
PCB............ Power Control Box   (NASA)
PCB............ Precambrian Shield Resources Ltd. [*Toronto Stock Exchange symbol*]
PCB............ Primary Carpet Backing
PCB............ Printed Circuit Board   (MCD)

PCB.......... Prix de Cession de Base [*Basic Wholesale Price*] [*French*]
PCB.......... Procarbazine [*Also, P, PC, Pr*] [*Antineoplastic drug*]
PCB.......... Process Control Block
PCB.......... Product Configuration Baseline (NASA)
PCB.......... Program Communication Block
PCB.......... Program Control Block [*Data processing*] (BUR)
PCB.......... Project Change Board (AAG)
PCB.......... Project Control Branch [*Social Security Administration*]
PCB.......... Property Control Branch [*of Allied Military Government*] [*Post-World War II*]
PCB.......... Proprietor of Copyright on a Work by a Corporate Body
PCB.......... Propulsion [*Ground*] Control Box (AAG)
PCB.......... Public Coin Box [*Telecommunications*] (TEL)
PCB.......... Publisher's Central Bureau
PCBA........ Pepsi-Cola Bottlers Association (EA)
PCBA........ Polyclonal B Cell Activation [*Hematology*]
PCBA........ Printed Circuit Board Assembly (MCD)
PCBB........ Power Conditioning Brass Board (MCD)
PCBB........ Primary Commercial Blanket Bond [*Insurance*]
PCBC........ Partially Conserved Baryon Current (IEEE)
PCBC........ Polk County Biomedical Consortium [*Library network*]
PCBC........ Progressive Conservative Broadcasting Corporation [*Fictional version of the Canadian Broadcasting Corp.*]
PCBCL...... Printed Circuit Board Configuration List (MCD)
PCBD........ Polychlorinated Benzodioxin [*Organic chemistry*]
PCBDA...... Put and Call Brokers and Dealers Association [*Inactive*] (EA)
PCBG........ Primary Care Block Grant
PCBMEM ... Progress in Clinical Biochemistry and Medicine [*A publication*]
PCB-ML.... Partido Comunista Marxista-Leninista de Bolivia [*Marxist-Leninist Communist Party of Bolivia*] [*Political party*] (PPW)
PCBN........ Polycrystalline Cubic Boron Nitrite
PCBPB...... Pesticide Biochemistry and Physiology [*A publication*]
PCBR........ Printed Circuit Board Repair (MCD)
PCBR........ Progress in Clinical and Biological Research [*Elsevier Book Series*] [*A publication*]
PC/BRD .... Printed Circuit Board [*Automotive engineering*]
PCBRD...... Progress in Clinical and Biological Research [*A publication*]
PCBS .... Plastic Connector Backing Shell
PCBS .... Positive Control Bombardment System [*Air Force*]
PCBS .... Printed Circuit Board Socket
PCBS .... Pupil Classroom Behavior Scale
PCBSA2 .... Canadian Federation of Biological Societies. Proceedings [*A publication*]
PCBTS....... Portable Cesium Beam Time Standard
PCC.......... Acts of the Privy Council, Colonial Series [*A publication*] (DLA)
PCC.......... Chief Postal Clerk [*Navy rating*]
PCC.......... Pacific Cal Air [*Oakland, CA*] [*FAA designator*] (FAAC)
PCC.......... Pacific Cruise Conference [*Formerly, TPPC*] [*Defunct*] (EA)
PCC.......... Package Carrier Committee (EA)
PCC.......... Pad Control Center [*NASA*] (NASA)
PCC.......... Paid Circulation Council [*Later, ASCMP*]
PCC.......... Palestinian Ceramic Chronology [*200BC-70AD*] [*A publication*] (BJA)
PCC.......... Panama Canal Commission [*Independent government agency*]
PCC.......... Panama Canal Company [*Superseded by Panama Canal Commission*]
PCC.......... Panamerican Cultural Circle (EA)
PCC.......... Parent and Child Center [*Project Head Start*]
PCC.......... Parochial Church Council [*Church of England*]
PCC.......... Partial Crystal Control (IEEE)
PCC.......... Partido Comunista Chileno [*Communist Party of Chile*] [*Political party*] (PD)
PCC.......... Partido Comunista Cubano [*Communist Party of Cuba*] [*Political party*] (PPW)
PCC.......... Partido Conservador Colombiano [*Conservative Party of Colombia*] [*Political party*] (PPW)
PCC.......... Party of Catalan Communists [*Political party*] (PPW)
PCC.......... Pasadena City College [*California*]
PCC.......... Pathe Communications Corp. [*NYSE symbol*] (SPSG)
PCC.......... Patient Care Coordinator [*Medicine*]
PCC.......... Payload Control and Checkout [*NASA*] (NASA)
PCC.......... Peak Cathode Current
PCC.......... People's Caretakers' Council [*Rhodesian*]
PCC.......... People's Christian Coalition [*Later, Sojourners*] (EA)
PCC.......... Pepper Community [*Later, IPC*]
PCC.......... Per-Command Course (MCD)
PCC.......... Per Copia Conforme [*True Copy*] [*Italian*]
PCC.......... Performance Certification Component [*SQT*] (MCD)
PCC.......... Performance Criteria Categories (MCD)
PCC.......... Peripheral Control Computer
PCc.......... Periscopic Concave [*Ophthalmology*]
PCC.......... Personal Computer Coprocessor
PCC.......... Personnel Control Center [*Air Force*] (AFM)
PCC.......... Personnel Coordination Center [*Army*]
PCC.......... Peters' United States Circuit Court Reports [*A publication*] (DLA)
PCC.......... Phenylchlorocarbene [*Organic chemistry*]
PCC.......... Pheochromocytoma [*Oncology*]
PCC.......... Phosphate Carrier Compound

PCC.......... Physical Coal Cleaning [*Fuel technology*]
PCC.......... Pilarcitos Creek [*California*] [*Seismograph station code, US Geological Survey*] (SEIS)
PCC.......... Pilot Control Console
PCC.......... Piperidinocyclohexanecarbonitrile [*Organic chemistry*]
PCC.......... Planning Consultative Council [*Victoria, Australia*]
PCC.......... Planning Coordination Conference [*NATO*] (NATG)
PCC.......... Plastics in Construction Council [*Later, CCS*]
PCC.......... Plug Compatible Computer (ADA)
PCC.......... Plutonium Concentrator Concentrate [*Nuclear energy*] (NRCH)
PCC.......... Point of Compound Curve (KSC)
PCC.......... Pointe Claire Public Library [*UTLAS symbol*]
PCC.......... Poison Control Center
PCC.......... Polarity Coincidence Correlator
PCC.......... Political Consultative Committee [*Warsaw Pact*]
PCC.......... Political Consultative Council (CINC)
PCC.......... Polycore Composite Construction [*Automotive engineering*]
PCC.......... Polymer-Cement Concrete (KSC)
PCC.......... Polynesian Cultural Center (EA)
PCC.......... Poor Clares of St. Colette [*Roman Catholic women's religious order*]
PCC.......... Population Crisis Committee (EA)
PCC.......... Portable Cable Checker
PCC.......... Portland Cement Concrete
PCC.......... Positive Control Communication
PCC.......... Postal Concentration Center [*Army*]
PCC.......... Postal and Courier Communications [*British*]
PCC.......... Pour Copie Conforme [*Certified True Copy*] [*French*]
PCC.......... Power Control Console [*Diving apparatus*]
PCC.......... Pre-Command Course [*Military*]
PCC.......... Precast Concrete [*Technical drawings*]
PCC.......... Precipitated Calcium Carbonate [*Inorganic chemistry*]
PCC.......... Precompressor Cooling (MCD)
PCC.......... Premature Chromosome Condensation [*Genetics*]
PCC.......... Prerogative Court of Canterbury [*English court previously having jurisdiction over wills*]
PCC.......... Presbyterian Charismatic Communion [*Later, PRR*] [*An association*] (EA)
PCC.......... President of the Canteen Committee [*Military*] [*British*]
PCC.......... President's Conference Committee
PCC.......... Printed Circuit Conference
PCC.......... Private Carrier Conference [*of ATA*] (EA)
PCC.......... Privy Council Cases [*British*]
PC(C)........ Privy Councillor (Canada)
PCC.......... Problem Control and Contact Unit [*IRS*]
PCC.......... Process Chemistry Cell (NRCH)
PCC.......... Process Control Computer
PCC.......... Processor Control Console [*Telecommunications*] (TEL)
PCC.......... Product Control Center [*DoD*]
PCC.......... Production Compression Capability
PCC.......... Productivity Communication Center (EA)
PCC.......... Program Control Counter
PCC.......... Program-Controlled Computer (DIT)
PCC.......... Progress Control Clerk [*DoD*]
PCC.......... Project Control Center
PCC.......... Propionyl CoA Carboxylase [*An enzyme*]
PCC.......... Prothrombin Complex Concentrates [*Hematology*]
PCC.......... Provincial Congress Committee
PCC.......... Provisioning Control Code [*Military*] (AFIT)
PCC.......... Psychometric Colorimeter Chamber (MCD)
PCC.......... Pulse Counter Chain
PCC.......... Pulverized Coal Combustion [*or Combustor*]
PCC.......... Pure Car Carrier [*Shipping*] (DS)
PCC.......... Pyridinium Chlorochromate [*Organic chemistry*]
PCC.......... Pyroconvective Cooling
PC(C)........ Submarine Chaser (Control) [*173 foot*] [*Navy symbol*] [*Obsolete*]
PCCA........ Confederation Art Gallery and Museum, Charlottetown, Prince Edward Island [*Library symbol*] [*National Library of Canada*] (NLC)
PCCA........ Pacific Class Catamaran Association (EA)
PCCA........ Pattern-Contingent Chromatic Aftereffects
PCCA........ Pewter Collectors Club of America (EA)
PCCA........ Pipe Collectors Club of America (EA)
PCCA........ Playing Card Collectors' Association (EA)
PCCA........ Police Car Collectors Association (EA)
PCCA........ Postcard Collector's Club of America [*Defunct*] (EA)
PCCA........ Power and Communication Contractors Association (EA)
PCCAF ...... Procedure Change Control Action Form (AAG)
PCCAF ...... Procedure Committee Change Authorization Form (AAG)
PCCB........ Payload Configuration Control Board [*NASA*] (MCD)
PCCB........ Program Configuration Control Board [*NASA*] (NASA)
PCCB........ Project Configuration Control Board [*Army*] (AABC)
PCCC........ Participating College Correspondence Course (MUGU)
PCCCD...... Proceedings. Annual Allerton Conference on Communication, Control, and Computing [*A publication*]
PCCD........ Peristaltic Charge-Coupled Device (IEEE)
PCCE........ Pacific Coast Coin Exchange
PCCE........ Payload Common Communication Equipment [*NASA*] (NASA)

PCCEI .... Permanent Charities Committee of the Entertainment Industries (EA)
PCCEMRSP ... Permanent Commission for the Conservation and Exploitation of the Maritime Resources of the South Pacific
PCCES....... Planning and Coordinating Committee for Environmental Studies [*National Research Council*]
PCCF .... Plan Case Control File [*IRS*]
PCCG......... Protestant Cinema Critics Guild [*Later, PCG*] (EA)
PCCH .... Pentachlorocyclohexene [*Organic chemistry*]
PCCI .... Paper Cup and Container Institute [*Later, SSI*] (EA)
PCCI .... Philippine Chamber of Commerce and Industry (DS)
PCCI .... President's Committee on Consumer Interests [*Terminated, 1971*]
PCCL .... People's Community Civic League (EA)
PCCL .... Precontract Cost Letter [*Navy*] (NG)
PCCLAS/P ... Proceedings. Pacific Coast Council on Latin American Studies [*A publication*]
PCCM........ Master Chief Postal Clerk [*Navy rating*]
PCCM........ Private Circuit Control Module [*Telecommunications*] (TEL)
PCCM........ Program Change Control Management (NASA)
PCCM........ Program Control Contract Manager (MCD)
PCC (M-L) ... Parti Communiste Canadien (Marxiste-Leniniste) [*Marxist-Leninist Communist Party of Canada*] [*Political party*]
PCCN .... Part Card Change Notice (KSC)
PCCN .... Port Call Control Number [*Army*] (AABC)
PCCN .... Preliminary Configuration Control Number (AAG)
PCCN .... Provisioning Contract Control Number (NASA)
PCCNL....... Pacific Coast Coordinator of Naval Logistics
PCCO .... Plant Clearance Contracting Officer [*DoD*]
PCCOA...... Coles Associates Ltd., Charlottetown, Prince Edward Island [*Library symbol*] [*National Library of Canada*] (NLC)
PCCOA...... Professional Contributions. Colorado School of Mines [*A publication*]
PCCP .... Canadian Pension Commission [*Commission Canadienne des Pensions*], Charlottetown, Prince Edward Island [*Library symbol*] [*National Library of Canada*] (BIB)
PCCP .... Preliminary Contract Change Proposal [*NASA*] (KSC)
PCCPS....... Pacific Coast Canned Pear Service (EA)
PCCR .... Publishing Center for Cultural Resources (EA)
PCCRD7.... Proceedings. Serono Clinical Colloquia on Reproduction [*A publication*]
PCCS .... Parti Conservateur Chretien-Social [*Conservative Christian-Social Party*] [*Switzerland*] [*Political party*] (PPE)
PCCS .... Photographic Camera Control System (KSC)
PCCS .... Positive Control Communications System
PCCS .... Processor Common Communications System
PCCS .... Program Change Control System (NG)
PCCS .... Program and Cost Control System [*Army*] (RDA)
PCCS .... Project Cost Control System
PCCS .... Publications Contract Coverage Schedule (MCD)
PCCS .... Senior Chief Postal Clerk [*Navy rating*]
PCCSD ...... Proceedings. International Conference on Cybernetics and Society [*A publication*]
PCCT .... Percept and Concept Cognition Test [*Psychology*]
P-CCU ...... Post Coronary Care Unit
PCCU .... President's Commission on Campus Unrest (EA)
PCCU .... Punched Card Control Unit [*Data processing*] (AABC)
PCD .... Democratic Conservative Party [*Nicaragua*] [*Political party*] (PD)
PCD .... Pacific Car Demurrage Bureau, San Francisco CA [*STAC*]
PCD .... Pacific Communications Division [*Military*]
PCD .... Panama Canal Department
PCD .... Parti Communiste du Dahomey [*Communist Party of Dahomey*] [*Political party*] [*Benin*]
PCD .... Partido Comunista Dominicano [*Dominican Communist Party*] [*Dominican Republic*] [*Political party*] (PPW)
PCD .... Patriotic Coalition for Democracy [*Political group*] [*Guyana*]
PCD .... Phenylchlorodiazirine [*Organic chemistry*]
PCD .... Photoconductive Decay [*Semiconductor material*]
PCD .... Pine Channel Gold [*Vancouver Stock Exchange symbol*]
PCD .... Planned Completion Date (TEL)
PCD .... Plasma Cell Dyscrasia [*Medicine*]
PCD .... Plutonium Concentrator Distillate [*Nuclear energy*] (NRCH)
PCD .... Pneumatic Control Distributors (KSC)
PCD .... Polycrystalline Diamond (ECON)
PCD .... Polycystic Disease [*of kidneys*] [*Medicine*]
PCD .... Port Control Diagnostic [*Telecommunications*] (TEL)
PCD .... Positive Control Document (MCD)
PCd .... Post Card [*Philately*]
Pcd .... Postcard (BJA)
PCD .... Pounds per Capita per Day (AAG)
PCD .... Power Control Device [*Nuclear energy*] (NRCH)
PCD .... Power Control and Distribution
PCD .... Precision Course Direction [*Aerospace*] (MCD)
PCD .... Pressure Control Distributor (KSC)
PC & D....... Priest, Confessor, and Doctor (ROG)
PCD .... Primary Ciliary Dyskinesia [*Medicine*]
PCD .... Primary Current Distribution [*Electroplating*]
PCD .... Problem Control and Display
PCD .... Procedural Change Directive (KSC)
PCD .... Procurement and Contracts Division [*NASA*]

PCD .... Procurement Control Document [*NASA*] (MCD)
PCD .... Production Common Digitizer
PCD .... Program Change Decision [*Army*]
PCD .... Program Control Display System [*NATO Air Defense Ground Environment*] (NATG)
PCD .... Program Control Document (KSC)
PCD .... Project Control Drawing (AAG)
PCD .... Protocatechuatedioxygenase [*An enzyme*]
PCD .... Pulmonary Clearance Delay [*Medicine*]
PCDA .... Post Card Distributors Association
PCDA .... Professional Currency Dealers Association (EA)
PCDB........ Poison Control Data Base [*Database*]
PCDC........ Diagnostic Chemicals Ltd., Charlottetown, Prince Edward Island [*Library symbol*] [*National Library of Canada*] (NLC)
PCDC........ Plutonium Canister Decontamination Cell [*Nuclear energy*] (NRCH)
PCDD .... Pentachlorodioxin [*Organic chemistry*]
PCDD .... Polychlorinated Dibenzodioxin [*Organic chemistry*]
PCDDS..... Private Circuit Digital Data Service [*Telecommunications*] (TEL)
PCDF........ Polychlorinated Dibenzofuran [*Organic chemistry*]
PCDHi....... Delaware County Historical Society, Chester, PA [*Library symbol*] [*Library of Congress*] (LCLS)
PCDI......... Per Capita Disposable Income [*Economics*]
PCDI......... Pierce Die
PCDJ .... Pakistan Committee for Democracy and Justice (EA)
PCDL........ Pro-Choice Defense League (EA)
PCdoB....... Partido Comunista do Brasil [*Communist Party of Brazil*] [*Political party*] (PPW)
PC-DOS .... Personal Computer Disk Operating System [*IBM's version of Microsoft program*]
PCDP........ Pilot Control and Display Panel
PCDP........ Punched Card Data Processing
PCD-PRP .. Pueblo, Cambio, y Democracia - Partido Roldosista Popular [*People, Change, and Democracy - Popular Roldosista Party*] [*Ecuador*] [*Political party*] (PPW)
PCDR........ Procedure (AAG)
PCDRR...... PC Digest Ratings Report [*A publication*]
PCDS .... Payload Command Decoder Subunit [*NASA*] (KSC)
PCDS .... Power Conversion and Distribution System
PCDS .... Procurement Congressional Descriptive Summary [*Army*] (RDA)
PCDS .... Project Control Drawing System (AAG)
PCDU .... Payload Command Decoder Unit [*NASA*] (NASA)
PCDUS..... Plasma Cell Dyscrasias of Unknown Significance [*Medicine*]
PCE........... Pacific East Air, Inc. [*Los Angeles, CA*] [*FAA designator*] (FAAC)
PCE........... Page Communications Engineers, Inc. [*Canada*] (MCD)
PCE........... Painter Creek, AK [*Location identifier*] [*FAA*] (FAAL)
PCE........... Partido Comunista Ecuatoriano [*Communist Party of Ecuador*] [*Political party*] (PPW)
PCE........... Partido Comunista de Espana [*Communist Party of Spain*] [*Political party*] (PPE)
PCE........... Patrol Escort [*Patrol Craft Escort*] [*Navy symbol*]
PCE........... Pedco Energy Ltd. [*Vancouver Stock Exchange symbol*]
PCE........... Perchloroethylene [*Organic chemistry*]
PCE........... Peripheral Control Element
PCE........... Personal Consumption Expenditure
PCE........... Physical Capacities Evaluation [*Test of hand skills*]
PCE........... Piece [*Numismatics*]
PCE........... Plasma Chamber Evacuation Subsystem (MCD)
PCE........... Plug Compatible Ethernet
PCE........... Polyarthrite Chronique Evolutive [*Chronic Evolutive Polyarthritis*] [*Medicine*] [*French*]
PCE........... Positive Continuous Engagement [*Automotive engineering*]
PCE........... Power Conditioning Equipment
PC of E...... Presbyterian Church of England
PCE........... Pressure to Clutch Engage [*Aerospace*] (AAG)
PCE........... Prince Edward Island Department of Education, Charlottetown, Prince Edward Island [*Library symbol*] [*National Library of Canada*] (NLC)
PCE........... Privy Councillor, England (ROG)
PCE........... Production Check Equipment (MCD)
PCE........... Professional Care, Inc. [*AMEX symbol*] (SPSG)
PCE........... Program Cost Estimate (AFM)
PCE........... Prohormone-Converting Endopeptidase
PCE........... Pseudocholinesterase [*Same as ACAH*] [*An enzyme*]
PCE........... Pulmocutaneous Exchange
PCE........... Punch Card Equipment [*Data processing*] (AFM)
PCE........... Pyrometric Cone Equivalent [*Refractory industry*]
PCE.......... Submarine Chaser Escort
PCEA....... Pacific Coast Electrical Association
PCEA....... Phosphate Chemicals Export Association (EA)
P/CEA3 ..... Probationary Control Electrical Artificer 3rd Class [*British military*] (DMA)
PCEAA...... Professional Construction Estimators Association of America (EA)
PCEA Bol Trimest Exp Agropecu ... PCEA [*Programa Cooperativo de Experimentacion Agropecuaria*] Boletin Trimestral de Experimentacion Agropecuaria [*A publication*]

PCE(C) ...... Patrol Vessel, Escort (Control) [*180 feet*] [*Navy symbol*] [*Obsolete*]
PCEDURE ... Procedure (ROG)
PCEEDGS ... Proceedings (ROG)
PCEEO...... President's Committee on Equal Employment Opportunity [*Later, OFCCP*] [*Department of Labor*]
PCEH .... President's Committee on Employment of the Handicapped [*Washington, DC*]
PCEI.......... Prime Contract End Item (MCD)
PCEM...... Parliamentary Council of the European Movement
PCEM....... Process Chain Evaluation Model (IEEE)
PCEM....... Program Committee on Education for Mission (EA)
PCEM....... Propulsion Contamination Effects Module (NASA)
PCEP .... Perception Technology Corp. [*Canton, MA*] [*NASDAQ symbol*] (NQ)
PCE-R....... Partido Comunista de Espana - Reconstituido [*Reconstituted Spanish Communist Party*] [*Political party*] (PD)
PCER........ Patrol Rescue Escort [*Patrol Craft Escort Rescue*] [*Navy symbol*]
P Cert Ed ... Professional Certificate in Education
PCET .... Personal Computer Extended Technology [*Computer bus*]
PCETF....... Power Conversion Equipment Test Facility [*Nuclear energy*]
PCEU........ Partido Comunista de Espana Unificado [*Unified Communist Party of Spain*] [*Political party*] (PPW)
PCEU........ Pulse Compression/Expansion Unit
PCEZ........ PC Etcetera, Inc. [*NASDAQ symbol*] (NQ)
PCF.......... Pacific Air Express [*Honolulu, HI*] [*FAA designator*] (FAAC)
PCF.......... Pacific Ridge Resources [*Vancouver Stock Exchange symbol*]
PCF.......... Pacificulture Foundation (EA)
PCF.......... Parents' Choice Foundation (EA)
PCF.......... Parti Communiste Francais [*French Communist Party*] [*Political party*] (PPW)
PCF.......... Patrol Craft (Fast) [*Navy symbol*]
PCF.......... Payload Control Facility [*NASA*] (MCD)
PCF........... Peace Centers Foundation [*Later, UDC*] (EA)
PCF........... Pentagon Counterintelligence Force
PCF........... Personal Card File
PCF........... Personnel Control Facility [*Army*] (AABC)
PCF........... Pharyngoconjunctival Fever [*Medicine*]
PCF........... Plan Characteristics File [*IRS*]
PCF........... Postcard Club Federation (EA)
PCF........... Potential Conflict Forecasts [*Army*]
PCF........... Potentially Critical Failures
PCF........... Pounds per Cubic Foot
PCF........... Power Cathode Follower
PCF........... Power per Cubic Foot
PCF........... Prairie Chicken Foundation (EA)
PCF........... Primary Checkpoint File
PCF........... Probability of Consequence Factor
PCF........... Processed Citation File
PCF........... Program Change Factor
PCF........... Program Checkout Facility
PCF........... Program Control Facility
PCF........... Programmed Cryptographic Facility [*Data processing*]
PCF........... Prothrombin Conversion Factor [*Hematology*]
PCF........... Public Concern Foundation (EA)
PCF........... Pulse Compression Filter
PCF........... Pulse-to-Cycle Fraction
PCF........... Pulverized Coal-Fired Plant
PCF........... Putnam High Income Convertible & Bond Fund [*NYSE symbol*] (SPSG)
PCFA .... Pin, Clip, and Fastener Association [*Later, PCFS*] (EA)
PCFC .... Phil Collins Fan Club (EA)
PCFC .... Polytechnics and Colleges Funding Council [*British*]
PCFE .... Polytrifluorochloroethylene [*Organic chemistry*]
PCFE .... Prime Contractor Furnished Equipment (MCD)
PCFFA...... Pacific Coast Federation of Fishermen's Associations (EA)
PCFIA .... Particle Concentration Fluorescence Immunoassay
PCFO .... Position Classification Field Office
PCFP .... Predicted Comparative Failure Probability
PCFR .... Programmatic Center for Fire Research [*National Institute of Standards and Technology*]
PCFS .... Pin, Clip, and Fastener Services (EA)
PCFT .... Information Centre, Prince Edward Island Food Technology Centre, Charlottetown [*Library symbol*] [*National Library of Canada*] (BIB)
PCG .... Guided Missile Coastal Escort [*Ship symbol*] (NATG)
PCG .... Pacific Gas & Electric Co. [*NYSE symbol*] (SPSG)
PCG .... Package Engineering [*A publication*]
PCG .... Paracervical Ganglion [*Anatomy*]
PCG .... Parti Communiste de Guadeloupe [*Communist Party of Guadeloupe*] [*Political party*] (PPW)
PCG .... PezCorona Gold Corp. [*Vancouver Stock Exchange symbol*]
PCG .... Phonocardiogram [*Cardiology*]
PCG .... Plain Clothes Gratuity [*British military*] (DMA)
PCG .... Plains Cotton Growers (EA)
PCG .... Planning Career Goals [*Vocational guidance test*]
PCG .... Planning and Control Guide
PCG .... Power Conditioning Group (MCD)
PCG .... Printed Circuit Generator
PCG .... Programmable Character Generator

PCG .... Protestant Cinema Guild [*Formerly, PCCG*] [*Defunct*]
PCG .... Pulsed Coaxial Gun
PCGD .... Pollution Control Guidance Document
PCGG .... Presidential Commission on Good Government [*Philippines*] (ECON)
PCGLA ...... Physics and Chemistry of Glasses [*A publication*]
PCGM .... Pacific Coast Garment Manufacturers [*Later, AAMA*] (EA)
PCGN .... Permanent Committee of Geographical Names [*Later, BGN*]
PCGS .... Protein Crystal Growth System
PCGVB ...... Pairwise Correlated Generalized Valence Bond [*Physics*]
PCH .... Cheyney State College, Cheyney, PA [*OCLC symbol*] (OCLC)
PC & H ...... Packing, Crating, and Handling [*Shipping*] (AFM)
PCH .... Parent Compound Handbook [*Later, Ring Systems Handbook*] [*American Chemical Society*]
PCH .... Paroxysmal Cold Hemoglobinuria [*Medicine*]
PCH .... Partido Comunista de Honduras [*Communist Party of Honduras*] [*Political party*] (PD)
PCH .... Patrol Craft (Hydrofoil) [*Navy symbol*]
PCH .... PCH Post Career [*Vancouver Stock Exchange symbol*]
PCh .... Phosphocholine [*Biochemistry*]
PCH .... Physicochemical Hydrodynamics [*A publication*]
PCH .... Pitch
P Ch .... Planovoe Chozjajstvo [*A publication*]
PCH .... Potlatch Corp. [*Formerly, PFI*] [*NYSE symbol*] (SPSG)
PCH .... Prepare Chassis
Pch .... Principal Chaplain [*Navy*] [*British*]
PCH .... Punch (KSC)
PCH .... Purchase (DCTA)
PCHAR .... Printing Character [*Data processing*]
PCHBD .... Patchboard (MSA)
PCHC .... Holland College, Charlottetown, Prince Edward Island [*Library symbol*] [*National Library of Canada*] (NLC)
PCHC .... People's Center for Housing Change (EA)
PChCo .... Conococheague District Library, Chambersburg, PA [*Library symbol*] [*Library of Congress*] (LCLS)
PCHCY ...... Parents Campaign for Handicapped Children and Youth (EA)
PCHD .... Purchased (ROG)
PCHE .... Poor Clare Nuns of the Holy Eucharist [*Roman Catholic religious order*]
PCHE .... Purchase (ROG)
PCHEA .... Petro/Chem Engineer [*A publication*]
Pchela Sof ... Pchela Sofiya [*A publication*]
Pchel Mir... Pchelovodnyi Mir [*A publication*]
Pchel Zhizn ... Pchelovodnaya Zhizn' [*A publication*]
PCheS........ Cheyney State College, Cheyney, PA [*Library symbol*] [*Library of Congress*] (LCLS)
PCHG .... Punching
PCHK .... Parity Check [*Data communications*] (TEL)
PCHL .... Pacific Coast Hockey League [*Later, Western Hockey League*] (EA)
PCHN....... Peerless Chain [*NASDAQ symbol*] (NQ)
PCHN....... Programmed Course, Home Nursing [*Red Cross*]
PCH PhysicoChem Hydrodyn ... PCH: PhysicoChemical Hydrodynamics [*Later, Physicochemical Hydrodynamics*] [*England*] [*A publication*]
PCHR .... Panamanian Committee for Human Rights (EA)
PCHR .... Pentecostal Coalition for Human Rights (EA)
PCHR .... Purchaser (ROG)
PCHRG .... Public Citizen Health Research Group (EA)
P Ch S .... Proceedings. Chemical Society [*A publication*]
PCHSR..... Purchaser
PCH & T .... Packaging, Crating, Handling, and Transportation [*Shipping*] (CINC)
PCHT .... Packaging, Crating, Handling, and Transportation [*Shipping*] (AABC)
PCHT .... Parchment (MSA)
PChW .... Wilson College, Chambersburg, PA [*Library symbol*] [*Library of Congress*] (LCLS)
PCI............ Pacific Viewpoint [*A publication*]
PCI............ Packet Communications, Incorporated
PCI............ Panel Call Indicator
PCI............ Pantone Color Institute (EA)
PCI............ Paramount Communications, Inc. [*NYSE symbol*] (SPSG)
PCI............ Parti Communiste Internationaliste [*Internationalist Communist Party*] [*France*] [*Political party*] (PPE)
PCI............ Partito Comunista Italiano [*Italian Communist Party*] [*Political party*]
PCI............ Paterson Candy International [*British*]
PCI............ Pattern of Cockpit Indication
PCI............ Pattern Correspondence Index
PCI............ Pax Christi International (EAIO)
PCI............ PCL Industries Ltd. [*Toronto Stock Exchange symbol*]
PCI............ Pellet Clad Interaction [*Nuclear energy*] (NRCH)
PCI............ Per Column Inch [*Publishing*]
PCI............ Periodic Conformance Inspection (MCD)
PCI............ Peripheral Command Indicator
PCI............ Peripheral Controller Interface
PCI............ Personal Computer Interface [*Varitronics Systems, Inc.*]
PCI............ Photographic Credit Institute (EA)
PCI............ Physical Configuration Inspection (AFIT)
PCI............ Physical Configuration Item [*Military*]

Pci .... Phytophthora Citricola [*A fungus*]
pCi............. Picocurie [*Also, pC*]
PCI............. Pilot Club International   (EA)
PCI............. Pilot Controller Integration   (IEEE)
PCI............. Pilots for Christ International   (EA)
PCI............. Pipe Collectors International [*Later, PCCA*]   (EA)
PCI............. Planning Card Index   (AAG)
PCI............. Plant Control Interface
PCI............. Pneumatic Circuit Indicator
PCI............. Political Campaign Institute [*Commercial firm*]   (EA)
PCI............. Population Communications International [*An association*]   (EA)
PCI............. Portable Cesium Irradiator
PCI............. Portable Compass Indicator
PCI............. Possible Criminal Informant
PCI............. Potato Chip Institute, International [*Later, PC/SFA*]   (EA)
PCI............. Powder Coating Institute   (EA)
PCI............. Pre-Counseling Inventory [*Psychology*]
PCI............. Precision Components, Incorporated [*Addison, IL*] [*Telecommunications service*]   (TSSD)
PCI............. Prestressed Concrete Institute   (EA)
PCI............. Private Citizen, Inc. [*An association*]   (EA)
PCI............. Privy Council Decisions [*India*] [*A publication*]   (DLA)
PCI............. Privy Councillor, Ireland   (ROG)
PCI............. Proceedings. Canadian Institute [*A publication*]
PCI............. Process Control Interface
PCI............. Product Configuration Identification   (KSC)
PCI............. Product Cost Index
PCI............. Program Check Interruption [*Data processing*]   (MDG)
PCI............. Program Control Input   (NASA)
PCI............. Program-Controlled Interruption [*Data processing*]   (IBMDP)
PCI............. Program in Correctional Institutions   (OICC)
PCI............. Programmable Communications Interface
PCI............. Project Concern International   (EA)
PCI............. Prophylactic Cranial Irradiation [*Oncology*]
PCI............. Proportional Change Index [*Occupational therapy*]
PCI............. Prospectors Club International   (EA)
PCI............. Protein C Inhibitor [*Organic chemistry*]
PCIAC....... Petro-Canada International Assistance Corporation
PCIAOH ... Permanent Commission and International Association on Occupational Health   (EAIO)
PCIC.......... Poison Control Information Center
PC & IC .... Polaris Control and Information Center [*Missiles*]
PCICP .... Primary Control Inventory Control Point [*Navy*]
PCICS........ Permanent Council of the International Convention of Stresa on Cheeses   (EAIO)
PCIEC .... Permanent Committee for International Eucharistic Congresses   (EA)
PCIFC........ Patsy Cline International Fan Club   (EA)
PCIFC........ Permanent Commission of the International Fisheries Convention
PCII .... Protocol Computers [*NASDAQ symbol*]   (NQ)
PCIJ.......... Permanent Court of International Justice Cases [*A publication*]   (DLA)
PCIJ Ann R ... Permanent Court of International Justice Annual Reports [*A publication*]   (DLA)
pCi/L........ Picocuries per Liter [*Measure of radioactivity*]
PCIL .... Pilot-Controlled Instrument Landing [*Aviation*]   (NASA)
PCILO .... Perturbative Configuration Interaction [*Based on*] Localized Orbitals [*Quantum mechanics*]
PCIM......... Packet Channel Interface Module [*Telecommunications*]
PCIM......... Parti du Congres de l'Independance de Madagascar [*Party of the Congress for Malagasy Independence*]
PCIMP ...... President's Commission on Income Maintenance Programs   (EA)
PCIMR ...... Centre for Information and Technical Assistance, Institute of Man and Resources, Charlottetown, Prince Edward Island [*Library symbol*] [*National Library of Canada*]   (NLC)
PCIN......... Program Change Identification Number   (NASA)
PCIN......... Program Change Integration   (NASA)
PC-INP..... Philippine Constabulary - Integrated National Police   (DS)
PCI/O........ Program-Controlled Input-Output
PC-IOC..... Posterior Chamber - Intraocular Lens [*Ophthalmology*]
PCIOMR... Preconditioning Interim Operating Management Recommendation [*Nuclear energy*]   (NRCH)
PCIOS .... Processor Common Input/Output System [*Data processing*]
PCIP .... Personal Computer, Instrument Product
PCIP .... Poseidon [*Missile*] Communication Improvement Program [*Navy*]
PCIPI......... Permanent Committee on Industrial Property [*World Intellectual Property Organization*] [*Switzerland*] [*Information service or system*]   (IID)
PCIRO....... Preparatory Commission for International Refugee Organization
PCIS .... Canton Island [*Phoenix Islands*] [*ICAO location identifier*]   (ICLI)
PCIS .... Patient Care Information System   (IID)
PCIS .... Primary Containment Isolation System [*Nuclear energy*]   (NRCH)
PCIS .... Production Control Information System   (NVT)
PCIS .... Professional Career Information Service [*Department of Labor*]

PCIYA ...... Progress in Clinical Immunology [*A publication*]
PCIYRA .... Pacific Coast Intercollegiate Yacht Racing Association
PCJ .... Bangladesh Development Studies [*A publication*]
PCJ .... Peoples Jewellers Ltd. [*Toronto Stock Exchange symbol*]
PCJ .... Pontifical College Josephinum [*Worthington, OH*]
PCJ .... Pontifical College Josephinum, Worthington, OH [*OCLC symbol*]   (OCLC)
PCJ .... Sisters of the Poor Child Jesus [*Roman Catholic religious order*]
PCJOAU ... Pharmaceutical Chemistry Journal [*A publication*]
PC Judg .... Privy Council Judgments [*India*] [*A publication*]   (DLA)
pck............. Peacock [*Philately*]
PCK .... Phase Control Keyboard
PCK .... Pilot Check   (FAAC)
PCK .... Porcupine Creek, AK [*Location identifier*] [*FAA*]   (FAAL)
PCK .... Premarital Counseling Kit [*Psychology*]
PCK .... Primary Chicken Kidney [*Cell line*]
PCK .... Printed Circuit Keyboard
PCK .... Processor Controlled Keying [*Data processing*]   (DCTA)
PCKB........ Printed Circuit Keyboard
PCKD........ Polycystic Kidney Disease [*Medicine*]
Pckg Eng En ... Package Engineering Encyclopedia, Including Modern Packaging Encyclopedia [*A publication*]
Pckgng Eng ... Packaging Engineering [*A publication*]
Pckgng Rev ... Packaging Review [*A publication*]
Pckgng Wek ... Packaging Week [*A publication*]
PCL............ Alberta Attorney General, Provincial Court Libraries [*UTLAS symbol*]
PCl............. Clarion Free Library, Clarion, PA [*Library symbol*] [*Library of Congress*]   (LCLS)
PCL............ Confederation Centre Library, Charlottetown, Prince Edward Island [*Library symbol*] [*National Library of Canada*]   (NLC)
PCL............ Pachaco Lake [*California*] [*Seismograph station code, US Geological Survey*]   (SEIS)
PCL............ Pacific Coast League [*Baseball*]
PCL............ Pallet Coolant Loop   (NASA)
PCL............ Parallel Communications Link
PCL............ Parcel
PCL............ Parti Communiste Libanais [*Lebanese Communist Party*] [*Political party*]   (PPW)
PCL............ Parti Communiste de Luxembourg [*Communist Party of Luxembourg*] [*Political party*]   (PPE)
PCL............ Pencil   (MSA)
PCL............ Permissible Contamination Limits [*Nuclear energy*]   (NRCH)
PCL............ Persistent Corpus Luteum [*Medicine*]
PCL............ Perspectives on Contemporary Literature [*A publication*]
P Cl .... Petrus Calvelli [*Flourished, 14th century*] [*Authority cited in pre-1607 legal work*]   (DSA)
PCL............ Phillips Cables Limited [*Toronto Stock Exchange symbol*]
PCL............ Pilot-Controlled Lighting [*Aviation*]   (FAAC)
PCL............ Planning Configuration List
PCL............ Planning and Conservation League   (EA)
PCL............ Plasma Cell Leukemia [*Oncology*]
PCL............ Playboy Club of London
PCL............ Plum Creek Timber Co., Inc. [*NYSE symbol*]   (SPSG)
PCL............ Polycaprolactone [*Organic chemistry*]
PCL............ [*The*] Polytechnic of Central London
PCL............ Positive Control Line
PCL............ Posterior Cruciate Ligament [*Anatomy*]
PCL............ PostScript and LASERJet-Type [*LASER printer*]
PCL............ Power Control List   (MCD)
PCL............ Preliminary Change Letter [*Navy*]   (NG)
PCL............ Premier Cruise Lines
PCL............ Primary Coolant Line   (NASA)
PCL............ Primary Coolant Loop   (NASA)
PCL............ Printed Circuit Lamp
PCL............ Printer Control Language
PCL............ Procedural Control Language [*1971*] [*Data processing*]   (CSR)
PCL............ Process Capability Laboratory
PCL............ Programming Checklist   (MCD)
PCL............ Programming Control Language [*Data processing*]   (PCM)
PCL............ Project Control Ledgers [*Navy*]   (NG)
PCL............ Pseudocleistogamous [*Botany*]
PCL............ Pucallpa [*Peru*] [*Airport symbol*]   (OAG)
PCL............ Pulse Compression Loop
PCLA........ Polish Canadian Librarians Association
PCLA........ Power Control Linkage Assembly
P Cl A....... Proceedings. Classical Association [*A publication*]
PCLA........ Process Control Language [*Texas Instruments, Inc.*]
PCLA........ Project Coordination and Liaison Administration   (OICC)
PCLAC ..... Proceedings. California Linguistics Association Conference [*A publication*]
PCLB .... [*The*] Price Company [*NASDAQ symbol*]   (NQ)
PCLD........ Dependent Political Entity [*Board on Geographic Names*]
PCLDI ...... Prototype Closed-Loop Development Installation [*Nuclear energy*]   (NRCH)
PCLG........ Public Citizen Litigation Group   (EA)
PCLI .... Independent Political Entity [*Board on Geographic Names*]
P Clin North America ... Pediatric Clinics of North America [*A publication*]
PCLJ......... Pacific Coast Law Journal [*A publication*]   (DLA)
PCLK .... Pay Clerk

PCLLG ...... Ollennu's Principles of Customary Land Law in Ghana [*A publication*] (DLA)

PCLMP ..... President's Advisory Committee on Labor-Management Policy [*Abolished, 1973*]

PCLN......... Personalcomputer Literaturnachweis [*Datendienst Weiss*] [*Database*]

PC-LNIM ... Personal Computer Local Network Interface Module (TSSD)

PCLO........ Passenger Control Liaison Office [*or Officer*] [*Army*] (AABC)

PCLQA....... Physics and Chemistry of Liquids [*A publication*]

P Cl R........ Parker's New York Criminal Reports [*A publication*] (DLA)

PCLR......... PR [*Public Relations*] Committee for Licensing and Registration (EA)

P Cl R........ Privy Council Reports [*A publication*] (DLA)

PClS........... Clarion State College, Clarion, PA [*Library symbol*] [*Library of Congress*] (LCLS)

PCLS .... Law Society of Prince Edward Island, Charlottetown, Prince Edward Island [*Library symbol*] [*National Library of Canada*] (NLC)

PCLS .... People's Committee for Libyan Students (EA)

PCLS .... Proceedings. Comparative Literature Symposium [*A publication*]

PCLS .... Prototype Closed-Loop System [*Nuclear energy*] (NRCH)

PCLT .... Portable Coded LASER Target

PCLT .... Prototype Closed-Loop Test [*Nuclear energy*] (NRCH)

PCLU......... Pioneer Civil Labour Unit [*British*]

PClvU .... Ursinus College, Collegeville, PA [*Library symbol*] [*Library of Congress*] (LCLS)

PCLX......... Section of Independent Political Entity [*Board on Geographic Names*]

PCM .... Coastal Escort Medium [*200-500 tons*] [*Ship symbol*] (NATG)

PCM .... Pacific Comox Resources [*Vancouver Stock Exchange symbol*]

PCM .... Parabolic Collimator Mirror

PCM .... Parallel Cutter Mechanism

PCM .... Parity Check Matrix (MCD)

PCM .... Parti des Classes Moyennes [*Middle Class Party*] [*Luxembourg*] [*Political party*] (PPE)

PCM .... Parti Communiste Marocain [*Moroccan Communist Party*] [*Political party*]

PCM .... Parti Communiste Martiniquais [*Communist Party of Martinique*] [*Political party*] (PPW)

PCM .... Partido Comunista Mexicano [*Mexican Communist Party*] [*Political party*] (PPW)

PCM .... Passive Countermeasure

PCM .... Penalty Cost Model

PCM .... Pending Contractual Matters (NRCH)

PCM .... Per Calendar Month [*Business term*] (ADA)

PCM .... Percent Milli (NRCH)

PCM .... Phase Change Materials [*Solar energy*]

PCM .... Phase Conjugate Mirror

PCM .... Phase Contrast Microscopy

PCM .... Philippine Campaign Medal

PCM .... Photochemical Machining [*Desktop manufacturing*]

PCM .... Photoformed Ceramic Modules [*Du Pont process for making microconductors*]

PCM .... PIPES Buffer with Calcium and Magnesium

PCM .... Pitch Control Motor

PCM .... Planning and Control Memorandum [*Army*]

PCM .... Plug Compatible Mainframe [*Data processing*]

PCM .... Plug Compatible Manufacturer [*Data processing*]

PCM .... Plug Compatible Memory

PCM .... Police Court Mission [*British*] (ROG)

PCM .... Polyimide Composite Material

PCM .... Port Command Area [*Telecommunications*] (TEL)

PCM .... Post Column Method [*Chromatography*]

PCM .... Postmammillary Caudal Magnocellular Nuclei [*Neuroanatomy*]

PCM .... Power Control Mission (NASA)

PCM .... Power-Cooling Mismatch [*Nuclear energy*]

PCM .... Precision Condenser Microphone

PCM .... President's Certificate of Merit [*Military decoration*] (AFM)

PCM .... Process Control Module [*Telecommunications*] (TEL)

PCM .... Productive Cost Management (ADA)

PCM .... Profiling Current Meter [*Oceanography*] (MSC)

PCM .... Program Configuration Manager

PCM .... Program Continuity Memorandum [*Military*]

PCM .... Program Cost Management (MCD)

PCM .... Protein-Calorie Malnutrition [*Medicine*]

PCM .... Pulse Code Modulation [*Telecommunications*]

PCM .... Pulse-Count Modulation [*Data processing*]

PCM .... Punch Card Machine [*Data processing*]

PCM .... Pyrotechnic Countermeasure [*Military*] (SDI)

PCMA .... Pennsylvania Coal Mining Association (EA)

PCMA .... Personal Computer Management Association [*Commercial firm*] [*Orange, CA*] [*Information service or system*] (EA)

PCMA .... Phenylcyclopropanemethylamine [*Organic chemistry*]

PCMA .... Post Card Manufacturers Association [*Inactive*] (EA)

PCMA .... Prince Edward Island Department of Municipal Affairs, Charlottetown, Prince Edward Island [*Library symbol*] [*National Library of Canada*] (NLC)

PCMA .... Professional Convention Management Association [*Birmingham, AL*] (EA)

PCMA .... Provincial Carters' and Motormen's Association [*A union*] [*British*]

PCMB....... Para-Chloromercuribenzoate [*Organic chemistry*]

PCMB....... Parents and Children after Marriage Breakdown [*Study*] [*Australia*]

PCMC....... Para-Chloro-meta-cresol [*Organic chemistry*]

PCMC....... Provided Chief of Mission Concurs [*Army*]

PCMC....... Psychemedics Corp. [*NASDAQ symbol*] (NQ)

PCMD ...... Particle Count Monitoring Device (KSC)

PCMD ...... Passive Count Monitoring Device (KSC)

PCMD ...... Pulse Code Modulation, Digital

PCME........ Pulse Code Modulation Event

PCMF .... Phi Chi Medical Fraternity (EA)

PCM-FM... Pulse Code Modulation - Frequency Modulation

PCMGS .... Pulse Code Modulated Ground Station

PCMH....... Postgraduate Center for Mental Health (EA)

PCMI........ Photo-Chemical Machining Institute (EA)

PCMI........ Photochromic Microimage [*Microfiche*]

PCMI........ Plastic Container Manufacturers Institute (EA)

PCMIA...... Pittsburgh Coal Mining Institute of America (EA)

PCMIP ..... Pontifical Commission for Migrants and Itinerant Peoples [*See also PCMT*] [*Vatican City, Vatican City State*] (EAIO)

PCMK....... Piece Mark

PC-ML ..... Marxist-Leninist Communist Party [*Bolivia*] [*Political party*] (PPW)

PCML....... Parti Communiste Marxiste-Leniniste [*Marxist-Leninist Communist Party*] [*France*] [*Political party*] (PPW)

PCML....... Partito Comunista Marxista-Leninista [*Marxist-Leninist Communist Party*] [*San Marino*] [*Political party*] (PPE)

PCML....... President's Committee on Migratory Labor [*Terminated, 1964*]

PCMLF ..... Parti Communiste Marxiste-Leniniste Francais [*French Marxist-Leninist Communist Party*] [*Dissolved, 1978*] [*Political party*] (PPW)

PC(ML)I.... Partito Comunista (Marxista-Leninista) de Italia [*Communist Party of Italy (Marxist-Leninist)*] [*Political party*] (PPE)

PCMMU ... Pulse Code Modulation Master Unit [*Electronics*] (NASA)

PCM/NRZ ... Pulse Code Modulation/Nonreturn to Zero (KSC)

PCMO ...... Principal Clinical Medical Officer [*British*]

PCMO ...... Principal Colonial Medical Officer [*British*]

PCMOD .... Personal Computer Modification Program

PCMP....... (Phenylcyclohexyl)methylpiperidine [*Organic chemistry*]

PCMP....... Preliminary Configuration Management Plan (MCD)

PCMPS ..... Para-Chloromercuriphenylsulfonic Acid [*Organic chemistry*]

PCM-PS .... Pulse Code Modulation - Phase-Shift

P Cmp Sc St ... Proceedings. Computer Science and Statistics [*A publication*]

PCMR....... Patient Computer Medical Record

PCMR....... Photochromic Microreproduction (DIT)

PCMR....... President's Committee on Mental Retardation [*Washington, DC*]

PCMS....... Para-Chloromercuriphenyl Sulfonate [*or Sulfonic Acid*] [*Organic chemistry*]

PCMS....... Photographic Cabinet Makers' Society [*A union*] [*British*]

PCMS....... Plasma Chromatography Mass Spectroscopy

PCMS....... Production Control Monitoring System (NVT)

PCMS....... Pulse Code Modulation Shared (MCD)

PCMS....... Punch Card Machine System [*Data processing*]

PCMT....... Pontificia Commissione Migrazioni e Turismo [*Pontifical Commission for Migrants and Itinerant Peoples - PCMIP*] [*Vatican City, Vatican City State*] (EAIO)

PCMTE .... Pulse Code Modulation and Timing Equipment (KSC)

PCMTEA .. Pulse Code Modulation and Timing Electronics Assembly

PCMTS .... Pulse Code Modulation Telemetry System (AAG)

PCMU ...... Physico-Chemical Measurements Unit [*British*]

PCMU ...... Propellant Calibration Measuring Unit (KSC)

PCMX ...... Para-Chloro-meta-xylenol [*Organic chemistry*]

PCN .... Package Control Number

PCN .... Page Change Notice (MCD)

PCN .... PanCana Minerals [*Toronto Stock Exchange symbol*]

PCN .... Part Control Number (AAG)

PCN .... Partido Comunista de Nicaragua [*Communist Party of Nicaragua*] [*Political party*] (PD)

PCN .... Partido de Conciliacion Nacional [*National Reconciliation Party*] [*El Salvador*] [*Political party*] (PPW)

PCN .... Partido Conservador Nicaraguense [*Nicaraguan Conservative Party*] [*Political party*] (PPW)

PCN .... Parts Change Notice (MCD)

PCN .... Penicillin [*Antibiotic*]

PCN .... Permanent Control Number (MCD)

PCN .... Personal Communications Network [*British*]

PCN .... Personal Computer Network [*Telecommunications*]

PCN .... Piacenza [*Italy*] [*Seismograph station code, US Geological Survey*] [*Closed*] (SEIS)

PCN .... Pitcairn Islands [*ANSI three-letter standard code*] (CNC)

PCN .... Planning Change Notice

PCN .... Players Chess News [*A publication*]

PCN .... Point Comfort & Northern Railway Co. [*AAR code*]

PCN .... Polychlorinated Naphthalene [*Organic chemistry*]

PCN .... Position Control Number (AFM)

PCN .... Post Christum Natum [*After the Birth of Christ*] [*Latin*] (ROG)

PCN .... Potato Cyst Nematode [*Plant pathology*]

PCN	Primary Care Network [*Medical insurance*]
PCN	Primary Care Nursing
PCN	Princeton Aviation Corp. [*Princeton, NJ*] [*FAA designator*] (FAAC)
PCN	Print Collector's Newsletter [*A publication*]
PCN	Procedure Change Notice
PCN	Processing Control Number
PCN	Procurement Control Number (AFM)
PCN	Product Control Number (AFM)
PCN	Production Change Number (KSC)
PCN	Program Change Notice (MCD)
PCN	Program Control Number (AFM)
PCN	Project Control Number (AAG)
PCN	Proposal Control Number (AAG)
PCN	Public Convenience and Necessity [*Department of Transportation*]
PCN	Publication Change Notice (MCD)
PCN	Pulse Compression Network
PCNA	Palestine Congress of North America [*Defunct*] (EA)
PCNA	Porsche Cars North America, Inc.
PCNA	Proliferating Cell Nuclear Antigen [*Cytology, immunology*]
PCNAC.....	Professionals Coalition for Nuclear Arms Control (EA)
PCNB........	Pentachloronitrobenzene [*Agricultural fungicide*]
PCNB........	Permanent Control Narcotics Board
PCNCDH..	Publications. Centre National pour l'Exploitation des Oceans. Actes de Colloques [*A publication*]
PCNDP......	Publication. Centre National de Documentation Pedagogique [*A publication*]
PCNF........	Pacific Central NOTAM [*Notice to Airmen*] Facility [*Military*]
PCNFDQ...	Publications. Centre National pour l'Exploitation des Oceans. Rapports Scientifiques et Techniques [*A publication*]
PCNMDD ...	Publications. Centre National pour l'Exploitation des Oceans. Resultats des Campagnes a la Mer [*A publication*]
PCNR	Part Control Number Request (AAG)
PCNR	Planning Change Notice Request
PCNS	Polar Coordinates Navigation System
PCNY	Proofreaders Club of New York (EA)
PCO	Conococheague District Library, Chambersburg, PA [*OCLC symbol*] (OCLC)
PCO	Parcel Concentration Office [*British*]
PCO	Passport Control Officer [*British*]
PCO	Patient Complains Of [*Medicine*]
PCO	Pest Control Operator
PCO	Philadelphia College of Osteopathy [*Pennsylvania*]
PCO	Phoenix Canada Oil Co. Ltd. [*Toronto Stock Exchange symbol*]
PCO	Photosynthetic Carbon Oxidation [*Plant metabolism*]
PCO	[*The*] Pittston Company [*NYSE symbol*] (SPSG)
PCO	Placement Contracting Officer [*Army*] (AABC)
P & CO......	Plans and Combat Operations
PCO	Plant Clearance Officer [*DoD*]
PCO	Plant Clearance Order
PCO	Police Commissioner's Office
PCO	Polycystic Ovary [*Gynecology*]
PCO	Ponca City [*Oklahoma*] [*Seismograph station code, US Geological Survey*] (SEIS)
PCO	Postcheckout (NASA)
PCO	Postcheckout Operations
PCO	Prince Consort's Own [*Military unit*] [*British*]
PCO	Principal Coast Officer [*Customs*] [*British*] (ROG)
PCO	Principal Contracting Officer [*Air Force*]
PCO	Printing Control Officer [*Air Force*] (AFM)
PCO	Privy Council Office [*British*]
PCO	Proceedings. Congress of Orientalists [*A publication*]
PCO	Procurement Change Order (MCD)
PCO	Procuring Contracting Office [*or Officer*] [*Military*]
PCO	Procuring Contrast Offer
PCO	Professional Conference Organizer
PCO	Program Comparator
PCO	Program-Controlled Output (NASA)
PCO	Program Coordination Office (AAG)
PCO	Project Control Office (MCD)
PCO	Property Control Office [*of Allied Military Government*] [*Post-World War II*]
PCO	Proposed Change Order (AFIT)
PCO	Prospective Commanding Officer [*Navy*]
PCO	Provisioning Contracting Officer [*Military*] (AFIT)
PCO	Public Call Office (DAS)
PCO	Publications Control Officer [*DoD*]
PCO	Purchase Change Order (MCD)
PCOA	Pharmacy Corporation of America [*NASDAQ symbol*] (NQ)
PCoA........	Principal Co-Ordinates Analysis
PCOAD	Powder Coatings [*A publication*]
P Coast LJ ...	Pacific Coast Law Journal [*A publication*] (DLA)
PCOB(UN) ...	Permanent Central Opium Board (United Nations)
PCOC	Partit Comunista Obrero de Catalunya [*Communist Workers' Party of Catalonia*] [*Political party*] (PPW)
PCOD	Polycystic Ovarian Disease [*Medicine*]
PCOE	Partido Comunista Obrero de Espana [*Communist Workers' Party of Spain*] [*Political party*] (PPW)
PCOG	Press Clippings of Greenland [*A publication*]
PCOGA	Pacific Coast Oyster Growers Association (EA)
PCOI.........	Purcell Company, Incorporated [*NASDAQ symbol*] (NQ)
PCOM	Philadelphia College of Osteopathic Medicine
PCOM	Photocomm, Inc. [*NASDAQ symbol*] (NQ)
PCOMB....	Physics of Condensed Matter [*A publication*]
P Comp Lit ...	Proceedings. Comparative Literature Symposium [*A publication*]
PCON	Para-Chloro-ortho-nitroaniline [*Also, PCONA*] [*Organic chemistry*]
PCON	Personnel Continuity
PCONA	Para-Chloro-ortho-nitroaniline [*Also, PCON*] [*Organic chemistry*]
PCONA	Pest Control [*A publication*]
PCOPF	President's Council on Physical Fitness [*Later, PCPFS*] (KSC)
PC & OR ...	Procurement, Commitment, and Obligation Record [*Navy*]
PCOR	Profit Commission on Renewal [*Insurance*] (AIA)
PCOR	PSICOR, Inc. [*NASDAQ symbol*] (NQ)
PCoR.........	Robert Morris College, Coraopolis, PA [*Library symbol*] [*Library of Congress*] (LCLS)
PCOS........	Polycystic Ovarian Syndrome [*Also, POS*] [*Gynecology*]
PCOS........	Primary Communications-Oriented System (IEEE)
PCOS........	Process Control Operating System
PCOS........	Project Concern's Options Service (EA)
PCOSD2 ...	Psychoanalysis and Contemporary Science [*A publication*]
P-COSWA ...	Pugwash Conferences on Science and World Affairs
PCOT	Payload Center Operations Team [*NASA*] (MCD)
PCOTES ...	Prototype Carrier Operational Test and Evaluation Site [*Military*] (CAAL)
PCOUNT ..	Parameter Count [*Data processing*]
PCOV	Precombustor Oxidizer Valve (KSC)
P(COV).....	Probability of No Covariate Effect [*Statistics*]
PCOYO	President's Council on Youth Opportunity [*Defunct*] (EA)
PCP...........	Centre for Personal Construct Psychology [*British*] (CB)
PCP...........	Pacific Coast Philology [*A publication*]
PCP...........	Paired Cone Pigments [*Vision physiology*]
PCP...........	Palestinian Communist Party [*Political party*] (PD)
PCP...........	PanCanadian Petroleum Ltd. [*Toronto Stock Exchange symbol*] [*Vancouver Stock Exchange symbol*]
PCP...........	Para-Chlorophenol [*Organic chemistry*]
PCP...........	Paraguayan Communist Party
PCP...........	Parallel Cascade Processor (IEEE)
PCP...........	Parallel Circular Plate (IEEE)
PCP...........	Partido Comunista Paraguayano [*Paraguayan Communist Party*] [*Political party*] (PD)
PCP...........	Partido Comunista Peruano [*Peruvian Communist Party*] [*Political party*] (PPW)
PCP...........	Partido Comunista Portugues [*Portuguese Communist Party*] [*Political party*] (PPE)
PCP...........	Partido Comunista Puertorriqueno [*Puerto Rican Communist Party*] [*Political party*] (PPW)
PCP...........	Passenger Control Point [*Army*] (AABC)
PCP...........	Past Chief Patriarch [*Freemasonry*]
PCP...........	Patient Care Publications
PCP...........	Payload Control Processor [*NASA*]
PCP...........	Peace Corps Physician
PCP...........	Pentachlorophenol [*Wood preservative*] [*Organic chemistry*]
PCP...........	Peripheral Control Program
PCP...........	Peripheral Control Pulse [*Data processing*]
PCP...........	Peter Collins Publishing [*British*]
PCP...........	(Phenylcyclohexyl)piperidine [*or Phencyclidine*] [*Anesthetic*] [*A street drug*]
PCP...........	Philadelphia College of Pharmacy and Science, Philadelphia, PA [*OCLC symbol*] (OCLC)
PCP...........	Phosphor Coated Paper
PCP...........	Photon-Coupled Pair (IEEE)
PCP...........	Pilot Control Panel
PCP...........	Planar Combat Problem
PCP...........	Platoon Command Post [*Military*] (RDA)
PCP...........	Pneumatics Control Panel (AAG)
PCP...........	Pneumocystis Carinii Pneumonia [*Microbiology*]
PCP...........	Polaroid Color Pack Camera
PCP...........	Polychloroprene [*Organic chemistry*]
PCP...........	Poorly Characterized Phase [*Mineralogy*]
PCP...........	Portable Code Processor
PCP...........	Portuguese Communist Party
PCP...........	Post-Construction Permit [*Nuclear energy*] (NRCH)
PCP...........	Posted County Price [*Agriculture*]
PCP...........	Postgraduate Center for Psychotherapy [*Later, Postgraduate Center for Mental Health*] (EA)
PCP...........	Potential Contractor Program (MCD)
PCP...........	Power Control Panel [*Aerospace*] (AAG)
PCP...........	Preassembled Cable in Pipe
PCP...........	Precision Castparts Corp. [*NYSE symbol*] (SPSG)
PCP...........	Preliminary Cost Proposal (MCD)
PCP...........	Pressurization Control Panel [*NASA*] (KSC)
PCP...........	Primary Care Physician
PCP...........	Primary Command Point [*Military*] (CAAL)
PCP...........	Primary Control Program [*Data processing*]
PCP...........	Primary Coolant Pump [*Nuclear energy*] (NRCH)
PCP...........	Printed Circuit Patchboard
PCP...........	Process Control Processor (IEEE)
PCP...........	Process Control Program [*Nuclear energy*] (NRCH)

PCP............	Processor Control Program
PCP............	Product Change Proposal (MCD)
PCP............	Production Change Point
PCP............	Program Change Procedure
PCP............	Program [*or Project*] Change Proposal
PCP............	Program Control Plan (AAG)
PCP............	Program Control Procedure [*Nuclear energy*] (NRCH)
PCP............	Programmable Communication Processor
PCP............	Progressive Conservative Party [*Australia*] [*Political party*]
PCP............	Progressive Conservative Party [*Canada*] [*Political party*] (PPW)
PCP............	Progressive Constitutionalist Party [*Malta*] [*Political party*] (PPE)
PCP............	Project Control Plan (IEEE)
PCP............	Project Cost Plan (NASA)
PCP............	Prototype Communications Processor
PCP............	Pulse Comparator
PCP............	Pulse Cytophotometry [*Hematology*]
PCP............	Punched Card Punch [*Data processing*] (IEEE)
PcP............	Reflected P Wave [*Earthquakes*]
PCPA........	Pacific Conservatory of the Performing Arts
PCPA........	Panel of Consultants for the Performing Arts [*of CFC*]
PCPA........	Para-Chlorophenoxyacetic Acid [*Organic chemistry*]
PCPA........	Para-Chlorophenylalanine [*Biochemistry*]
PCPA........	Poor Clares of Perpetual Adoration [*Roman Catholic women's religious order*]
PCPA........	Protestant Church-Owned Publishers Association (EA)
PCPAC.....	Parker-Coltrane Political Action Committee (EA)
PCPBMA ..	Pacific Coast Paper Box Manufacturers' Association (EA)
PCPC	Power Conversion Products Council [*Later, PCPCI*] (EA)
PCPCA	Pairpoint Cup Plate Collectors of America (EA)
PCPCI	Power Conversion Products Council International (EA)
PCPCN.....	Part Card Procurement Change Notice (KSC)
PCPE........	Partido Comunista de los Pueblos de Espana [*Communist Party of the Peoples of Spain*] [*Political party*] (EY)
PCPF........	President's Council on Physical Fitness [*Later, PCPFS*]
PCPFS.......	President's Council on Physical Fitness and Sports (EGAO)
PCPG........	Primary Clock Pulse Generator
PCPHA......	Plant and Cell Physiology [*A publication*]
PCPhS	Proceedings. Cambridge Philological Society [*A publication*]
PCPI	Parent Cooperative Pre-Schools International (EA)
PCPI	Permanent Committee on Patent Information [*World Intellectual Property Organization*] [*Information service or system*] (IID)
PCPI	Personal Computer Products, Incorporated [*San Diego, CA*] [*NASDAQ symbol*] (NQ)
PCPI	President's Commission on Personnel Interchange [*Later, President's Commission on Executive Exchange*]
PCPJ........	Peoples Coalition for Peace and Justice [*Defunct*]
PCPL........	Government Services Library, Charlottetown, Prince Edward Island [*Library symbol*] [*National Library of Canada*] (NLC)
PCPL........	Planning Library, Charlottetown, Prince Edward Island [*Library symbol*] [*National Library of Canada*] (NLC)
PCPL........	Production Control Priority List (MCD)
PCPL........	Proposed Change Point Line [*NASA*] (KSC)
PCPM........	PERT [*Program Evaluation and Review Technique*] Cost Performance Measurement
PCPMDN ...	Annual Research Reviews. Proteins of Animal Cell Plasma Membranes [*A publication*]
PCP M-L ...	Partido Comunista de Portugal, Marxista-Leninista [*Marxist-Leninist Communist Party of Portugal*] [*Political party*] (PPE)
PCPN........	Precipitation (FAAC)
PCPP	(Para-Chlorophenoxy)propionic Acid [*Organic chemistry*]
PCPP	Peace Corps Partnership Program (EA)
PCPP	Plasma Chemistry and Plasma Processing [*A publication*]
PCPPD	Plasma Chemistry and Plasma Processing [*A publication*]
PCPS	Philadelphia College of Pharmacy and Science [*Pennsylvania*]
PCPS	Pool Cooling and Purification System [*Nuclear energy*] (NRCH)
PCPS	Proceedings of the Cambridge Philological Society [*A publication*] (OCD)
PCPS	Pulse-Coded Processing System
PCPSA.......	Proceedings. Cambridge Philosophical Society [*England*] [*A publication*]
PCPSD	Progress in Colloid and Polymer Science [*A publication*]
PCPT	Para-Chlorophenylthio [*Organic chemistry*]
PCPT	Perception
PCPT	Perception. Canadian Magazine of Social Comment [*A publication*]
PCPT	Physical Combat Proficiency Test [*Army*]
PCPT	Post Conference Provisioning Tape (MCD)
PCPV	Prestressed Concrete Pressure Vessel
PCQ	Production Control Quantometer
PCQ	Productivity Criteria Quotient
PCQ	Professional Capabilities Questionnaire [*Jet Propulsion Laboratory, NASA*]
PCQ	Yuma, AZ [*Location identifier*] [*FAA*] (FAAL)
PCQEH......	Queen Elizabeth Hospital, Charlottetown, Prince Edward Island [*Library symbol*] [*National Library of Canada*] (NLC)

PCQT.........	PC Quote, Incorporated [*Chicago, IL*] [*NASDAQ symbol*] (NQ)
PCR...........	Island Pacific Air [*Maui, HI*] [*FAA designator*] (FAAC)
PCR...........	Page Control Register
PCR...........	Parker's Criminal Reports [*New York*] [*A publication*] (DLA)
PCR...........	Parti Communiste Reunionnais [*Communist Party of Reunion*] [*Political party*] (PPW)
PCR...........	Partido Comunista Revolucionario [*Revolutionary Communist Party*] [*Peru*] [*Political party*] (PPW)
PCR...........	Partidul Comunist Roman [*Romanian Communist Party*] [*Political party*] (PPE)
PCR...........	Pass Card Reader [*Telecommunications*] (TEL)
PCR...........	Patient Charge Ratio
PCR...........	Payload Changeout Room [*NASA*] (NASA)
PCR...........	Payload Checkout Room [*NASA*] (NASA)
P Cr...........	Paymaster-Commander [*Navy*] [*British*] (DMA)
PCR...........	PC Resource [*A publication*]
PCR...........	Peninsular Chemresearch [*Calgon Corp.*]
PCR...........	Pennsylvania Corporation Reporter [*A publication*] (DLA)
PCR...........	Pennsylvania County Court Reports [*A publication*] (DLA)
P & CR	Performance and Compatibility Requirements
PCR...........	Perini Corporation [*AMEX symbol*] (SPSG)
PCR...........	Periodic Current Reversal [*Electrochemistry*]
PCR...........	Peripheral Control Routine (CMD)
PCR...........	Personal Communications Report [*FutureComm Publications, Inc.*] [*Information service or system*] [*Defunct*] (CRD)
PCr...........	Phosphocreatine [*Also, CP, PC*] [*Biochemistry*]
PCR...........	Photoconductive Relay (IEEE)
PCR...........	Photoconductive Resonance [*Physics*]
PCR...........	Photosynthetic Carbon Reduction [*Plant metabolism*]
PCR...........	Planned Component Replacement [*Predictive maintenance schedule*]
PCR...........	Planning Change [*or Check*] Request (AAG)
P & CR	Planning and Compensation Reports [*British*]
PCR...........	Pneumatic Checkout Rack (KSC)
PCR...........	Pneumatic Control Regulator (KSC)
PCR...........	Pollution Control Report [*Navy*]
PCR...........	Polychromatic Color Removal [*Printing technology*]
PCR...........	Polymerase Chain Reaction [*Genetics*]
PCR...........	Population Census Report (OICC)
PCR...........	Powell Cycle Registry (EA)
PCR...........	Power Change Request [*NASA*] (NASA)
PCR...........	Power Conversion Room
PCR...........	Pressure Check Range
PCR...........	Prestressed Ceramic RADOME
PCR...........	Preventative Cyclic Retransmission [*Telecommunications*] (TEL)
PCR...........	Primary Chemotherapy-Radiotherapy [*Oncology*]
PCR...........	Primary Cosmic Radiation
PCR...........	Principal Components Regression
PCR...........	Print Command Register
PCR...........	Procedure Change Request [*NASA*]
PCR...........	Procurement Center Representative [*Small Business Administration*]
PCR...........	Production Capability Review [*Army*]
PCR...........	Production Change Request (MCD)
PCR...........	Production Control Record [*NASA*] (KSC)
PCR...........	Professional Casting Report [*A publication*]
PCR...........	Program Change Request [*DoD*]
PCR...........	Program Control Register
PCR...........	Program Control Report
PCR...........	Progress Curve Report
PCR...........	Project Control Room [*NASA*] (NASA)
PCR...........	Project on Corporate Responsibility (EA)
PCR...........	Project Cost Record [*or Report*] [*NASA*] (KSC)
P & CR	Property and Compensation Reports [*A publication*] (DLA)
PCR...........	Publication Change Request (MCD)
PCR...........	Publication Contract Requirements
PCR...........	Puerto Carreno [*Colombia*] [*Airport symbol*] (OAG)
PCR...........	Pulse Compression RADAR
PCR...........	Punched Card Reader [*Data processing*] (BUR)
PCR...........	Punched Card Requisition [*Data processing*] (MCD)
PCRA.........	Phantom Class Racing Association (EA)
PCR & A	Picked Cold, Rolled, and Annealed [*Metallurgy*] (ROG)
PCRA.........	Poland China Record Association (EA)
PCRAP	Personal Computer Response Analysis Program
PCRB.........	Parks Canada. Research Bulletin [*A publication*]
PCRB.........	Personnel and Control Room Building [*Nuclear energy*] (NRCH)
PCRB.........	Pollution Control Revenue Bond [*Environmental Protection Agency*]
PCRB.........	Program Change Review Board [*NASA*]
PCRC.........	Pacific Concerns Resource Center (EA)
PCRC.........	Paraffined Carton Research Council [*Later, Paperboard Packaging Council*]
PCRC.........	Perinatal Clinical Research Center [*Case Western Reserve University*] [*Research center*] (RCD)
PCRC.........	Primary Communications Research Centre [*University of Leicester*] [*Canada*]
PCRCA	Pickled, Cold-Rolled, and Close-Annealed [*Metal*]
PCRD.........	Primary Control Rod Driveline [*Nuclear energy*] (NRCH)

PCRDM..... Primary Control Rod Drive Mechanism [*Nuclear energy*] (NRCH)
PCRE......... ProCare Industries, Inc. [*Englewood, CO*] [*NASDAQ symbol*] (NQ)
PC Rep....... English Privy Council Reports [*A publication*] (DLA)
PCRF........ Paralysis Cure Research Foundation (EA)
PCRF .... Parker Chiropractic Resource Foundation (EA)
PCRI.......... Papanicolaou Cancer Research Institute [*University of Miami*] [*Research center*]
PCRM....... Physicians Committee for Responsible Medicine (EA)
PCRM........ Primary Certified Reference Material [*Nuclear energy*] (NRCH)
PCRMGPS ... Poor Clerks Regular of the Mother of God of the Pious Schools [*Rome, Italy*] (EAIO)
PCRML..... Parti Communiste Revolutionnaire - Marxiste-Leniniste [*Revolutionary Marxist-Leninist Communist Party*] [*France*] [*Political party*] (PPW)
PCRPD8.... Plant Cell Reports [*A publication*]
Pcr/Pi .... Phosphocreatine to Inorganic Phosphate Ratio
PCRPS....... Program for Collaborative Research in the Pharmaceutical Sciences [*University of Illinois at Chicago*] [*Information service or system*] (IID)
PCRR........ Pennsylvania Central Railroad (ROG)
PCRS........ Poor Clergy Relief Society [*British*]
PCRS........ Precision Chiropractic Research Society [*Also known as Spinal Stress Research Society*] (EA)
PCRS .... Primary Control Rod System [*Nuclear energy*] (NRCH)
PCRS .... Primary CRITICOMM [*Critical Intelligence Communications System*] Relay Station (CET)
PCRSAE.... Colston Research Society. Proceedings of the Symposium [*A publication*]
PCRSB....... Proceedings. Canadian Rock Mechanics Symposium [*A publication*]
PCRV........ Pressurized Concrete Reactor Vessel [*Nuclear energy*]
PCRV........ Prestressed Concrete Reactor Vessel [*Nuclear energy*]
PCS........... IEEE Professional Communication Society (EA)
PCS........... Pace Car Society (EA)
PCS........... Pacific Command Ship
PCS........... Palliative Care Service
PCS............ Paracas [*Peru*] [*Seismograph station code, US Geological Survey*] [*Closed*] (SEIS)
PCS............ Parents' Confidential Statement [*Education*]
PCS............ Parti Chretien-Social [*Christian Social Party*] [*Luxembourg*] [*Political party*] (PPW)
PCS............ Parti Communiste Suisse [*Communist Party of Switzerland*] [*Political party*] (PPE)
PCS........... Particle Counting System
PCS........... Particulates, Condensables, and Solubles [*In gases*]
PCS........... Partido Comunista Salvadoreno [*Salvadoran Communist Party*] [*Political party*] (PPW)
PCS........... Partito Comunista Sammarinese [*Communist Party of San Marino*] [*Political party*] (PPE)
PCS........... Parts, Components, Subassemblies
PCS........... Parts Control System [*DoD*]
PCS........... Passive Containment System [*Nuclear energy*] (NRCH)
PCS.......... Patrol Vessel, Submarine Chaser (Control) [*136 feet*] [*Navy symbol*] [*Obsolete*]
PCS........... Patterns of Care Study [*Roentgenography*]
PCS........... Paul Claudel Society (EA)
PCS........... Payload Checkout System [*NASA*] (NASA)
PCS........... Payload Control Supervisor [*NASA*] (MCD)
PCS........... Pergamon Compact Solution [*CD-ROM publisher*] (IT)
PCS........... Periodical Control System [*Libraries*]
PCS........... Permanent Change of Station [*Army*]
PCS........... Permanent Cruiser Service [*British military*] (DMA)
PCS........... Personal Communications Service [*Provided by Personal Communications Network*]
PCS........... Personal Computing System
PCS........... Personnel Capabilities System [*Jet Propulsion Laboratory, NASA*]
PCS........... Personnel Change of Station
PCS........... Personnel Consultancy Services Ltd. [*British*]
PCS........... Pharmaceutical Card System (MCD)
PCS........... Phase Combining System [*Trademark*] [*A solubilizer in scintillation counting*]
PCS........... Phase Compensator System
PCS........... Philippine Collectors Society (EA)
PCS........... PhonoCardioScan [*Cardiology*]
PCS........... Photoformed Ceramic Substrates [*Du Pont process for making microconductors*]
PCS........... Photon Correlation Spectroscopy
PCS........... Physical Control System
PCS........... Pictorial Cancellation Society (EA)
PCS........... Pieces
PCS........... Pilot Control System (MCD)
PCS........... Pitch Control System (MCD)
PCS........... Planning Control Sheet
PCS........... Plant Computer System (NRCH)
PCS........... Plant Control System [*Nuclear energy*] (NRCH)
PCS........... Plastic Connector Shell
PCS......... Platoon Combat Skills [*Army*] (INF)

PCS........... Plausible Conflict Situations [*Army*]
PCS........... Pneumatic Control System [*Gas chromatography*]
PCS........... Pointing-Control System [*Aerospace*]
PCS........... Port Command Store [*Telecommunications*] (TEL)
PCS........... Port Control Store [*Telecommunications*] (TEL)
PCS........... Port Control System [*Telecommunications*] (TEL)
PCS........... Portable Communications System
PCS........... Portacaval Shunt [*Medicine*]
PCS........... Position Classification Standard [*Civil Service*]
PCS........... Position Control System
PCS........... Position, Course, and Speed
PCS........... Positive Concatenation Structures [*Mathematics*]
PCS........... Postal Church Service
PCS........... Postal Commemorative Society (EA)
PCS........... Postcardiotomy Syndrome [*Medicine*]
PCS........... Postcaval [*or Portacaval*] Shunt [*Medicine*]
PCS........... Posterior Concave Side
PCS........... Posts, Camps, and Stations [*Military*]
PC & S .... Posts, Camps, and Stations [*Military*]
PCS........... Potash Corporation of Saskatchewan [*Canada*]
PCS........... Power Conditioning System
PCS........... Power Conversion System
PCS........... Powered Causeway Section [*Military*] (CAAL)
PCS........... Precision Casting Standard (MCD)
PCS........... Preconscious
PCS........... Preferred Capital Stock [*Investment term*]
PC & S .... Preliminary Command and Sequencing [*Viking lander mission*] [*NASA*]
PCS........... Preliminary Component Specification
PCS........... Pressure Control System
PCS........... Primary Calibration System
PCS........... Primary Cancer Site [*Oncology*]
PCS........... Primary Conditioning Solution
PCS........... Primary Control Ship [*Navy*]
PCS........... Primary Coolant System (MSA)
PCS........... Principal Clerk of Session
PCS........... Principal Coordinating Scientist [*NASA*] (KSC)
PCS........... Print Contrast Scale (IEEE)
PCS........... Print Contrast Signal [*Data processing*]
PCS........... Print Contrast System (BUR)
PCS........... Probability of Correct Selection [*Statistics*]
PCS........... Probability of Crew Survival (AAG)
PCS........... Procedure Completion Sheet [*NASA*] (MCD)
PCS.......... Process Computer System (NRCH)
PCS........... Process Control Sheet [*Nuclear energy*] (NRCH)
PCS........... Process Control System
PCS........... Production Control Section
PCS........... Production Control System (BUR)
PCS........... Professional Car Society (EA)
PCS........... Professional Careers Sourcebook [*A publication*]
PCS........... Program Cost Status [*Report*] (MCD)
PCS........... Program Counter Store
PCS........... Programmable Communications Subsystem
PCS........... Project Control Sheet [*Data processing*]
PCS........... Project Control System [*Data processing*]
PCS........... Project Coordination Staff [*NASA*] (KSC)
PCS........... Property Control System
PCS........... Proprietary Computer Systems, Inc. [*Information service or system*] (IID)
PCS........... Provision Coordinate Schedule (MCD)
PCS........... Public Choice Society (EA)
PCS........... Publication Control Sheet (MCD)
PCS........... Pump Control Sensor
PCS........... Punched Card System [*Data processing*]
PCS........... Pyrotechnics Circuit Simulator
PCS........... Sabah Chinese Party [*Political party*] [*Malaysia*] (FEA)
PCS........... Submarine Chaser
PCS........... Sun Shipbuilding & Dry Dock Co., Chester, PA [*Library symbol*] [*Library of Congress*] (LCLS)
PCSA .... Patrol Craft Sailors Association (EA)
PCSA .... Personal Computing Systems Architecture
PCSA .... Power Crane and Shovel Association (EA)
PCSA .... Seaman Apprentice, Postal Clerk, Striker [*Navy rating*]
PCS(A) ...... Submarine Chaser (Air Cushion) (MCD)
PCsB......... Baptist Bible College of Pennsylvania, Clarks Summit, PA [*Library symbol*] [*Library of Congress*] (LCLS)
PCSC .... Control Submarine Chaser [*136 feet*] [*Navy symbol*] [*Obsolete*]
PCSC .... Plant Cell Suspension Cultures [*Biotechnology*]
PCSC .... Power Conditioning, Switching, and Control
PCSC .... Principal Commonwealth Supply Committee [*World War II*]
PCSD........ Partido Cristao Social Democratico [*Christian Social Democratic Party*] [*Portugal*] [*Political party*] (PPE)
PCSD........ Polychloro(chloromethylsulfonamido)diphenyl Ether [*Insectproofing agent for wool*]
PCSE .... Pacific Coast Stock Exchange [*Later, PSE*] (EA)
PCSE .... President's Committee on Scientists and Engineers [*Expired, 1958*]
PCSE .... Printed Circuit Soldering Equipment
PC/SFA..... Potato Chip/Snack Food Association [*Formerly, NPCI, PCI*] [*Later, SFA*]
PCSFSK ... Phase Comparison Sinusoidal Frequency Shift Keying

PCSG......... Public Cryptography Study Group [Defunct]   (EA)
PCSH........ Pierce Shell
PCS(H)...... Submarine Chaser (Hydrofoil)   (MCD)
PCSI .... PCS, Inc. [NASDAQ symbol]   (NQ)
PCSIB....... Protection Civile et Securite Industrielle [A publication]
PCSIG ...... Personal Computer-Software Interest Group   (EA)
PCSJ......... All-Party Parliamentary Committee for the Release of Soviet Jewry   (EAIO)
PCSM....... Percutaneous Stone Manipulation [Medicine]
PCSN....... PC Satellite Network
PCSN....... Precision Standard, Inc. [NASDAQ symbol]   (NQ)
PCSN....... Seaman, Postal Clerk, Striker [Navy rating]
PCSNA...... Processing [England] [A publication]
PCSP .... Programmed Communications Support Program [Air Force]   (AFM)
PCSPS....... Principal Civil Service Pension Scheme [British]
PCSS........ Platform Check Subsystem
PCSS........ Princess   (ROG)
PCST .... President's Committee on Science and Technology
PCSW....... Police Chiefs Spouses - Worldwide [An association]   (EA)
PCSW....... President's Commission on the Status of Women
PCT........... Pacific Coast Tariff Bureau, San Francisco CA [STAC]
PCT........... Pacific Crest Trail
PCT........... Paper Crepe Tape
PCT........... Para-Chlorotoluene [Organic chemistry]
PCT........... Parti Communiste Tunisien [Tunisian Communist Party] [Political party]   (PD)
PCT........... Parti Congolais du Travail [Congolese Labor Party] [Political party]   (PPW)
PCT........... Partido Conservador Tradicional [Traditionalist Conservative Party] [Nicaragua] [Political party]
PCT........... Patent Cooperation Treaty [1978]
PCT........... Peak Centerline Temperature [Nuclear energy]   (NRCH)
PCT........... Peak Cladding Temperature [Nuclear energy]   (NRCH)
PCT........... Percent [or Percentage]
PCT........... Percentage [Used instead of "average"] [Baseball]
PCT........... Performance Correlation Technique
PCT........... Periodic Confidence Test
PCT........... Peripheral Control Terminal
PCT........... Personality Completion Test [Psychology]
PCT........... Pharmacy and Chemistry Technician [Navy]
PCT........... Philadelphia College of Textiles and Science, Philadelphia, PA [OCLC symbol]   (OCLC)
PCT........... Photoinduced Charge Transfer [Electrochemistry]
PCT........... Photon-Coupled Transistor   (IEEE)
PCT........... Physical Correlate Theory [Psychophysics]
PCT........... Picture
PCT........... Planning and Control Techniques
PCT........... Plasmacrit Test [Medicine]
PCT........... Plasmacytoma [Medicine]
PCT........... Platelet Count [Hematology]
PCT........... Police Complaints Tribunal [Australia]
PCT........... Polychemotherapy [Oncology]
PCT........... Polychlorinated Terphenyl [Pesticide]
PCT........... Polychloroterphenyl [Organic chemistry]
PCT........... Porphyria Cutanea Tarda [Disease] [Medicine]
PCT........... Portable Camera-Transmitter
PCT........... Portable Conference Telephone [Bell Laboratories]
PCT........... Positron Computed Tomography
PCT........... Potato Curly Top Disease [Plant pathology]
PCT........... Potential Current Transformer
PCT........... Precinct
PCT........... Preliminary Change Transmittal   (AAG)
PCT........... Pressure Concentration Temperature
PCT........... Prime Contract Termination   (AAG)
PCT........... Princeton [New Jersey] [Airport symbol] [Obsolete]   (OAG)
P Ct........... Probate Court   (DLA)
PCT........... Production Confirmatory Test   (MCD)
PCT........... Program Control Table [Data processing]
PCT........... Programa de Cooperacion Tecnica [Program of Technical Cooperation - PTC] [Organization of American States] [Washington, DC]
PCT........... Project Control Tool   (BUR)
PCT........... Property Capital Trust [AMEX symbol]   (SPSG)
PCT........... Proximal Convoluted Tubule [of a nephron]
PCT........... Puangchon Chao Thai [Thai Mass Party] [Thailand] [Political party]
PCT........... Pulse Compression Tube
PCT........... Pulse Count [Telecommunications]   (TEL)
PCT........... Wesman Personnel Classification Test
PCTA........ Pentachlorothioanisole [Organic chemistry]
p/cta........... Por Cuenta [On Account] [Spanish]
PCTB........ Pacific Coast Tariff Bureau
PCTC........ Penn Central Transportation Company
PCTC........ Pure Car Truck Carrier [Shipping]   (DS)
PCTC........ Pyrotechnic Circuit Test Console   (KSC)
PCTCA....... Protection [London] [A publication].
PCTDS...... Problem and Change Tracking Directory System
PCTE......... Portable Commercial Test Equipment   (NASA)
PCTEB ...... Pennsylvania Council of Teachers of English. Bulletin [A publication]

PCTE Bull ... Pennsylvania Council of Teachers of English. Bulletin [A publication]
PCTE Bulletin ... Pennsylvania Council of Teachers of English. Bulletin [A publication]
PCTF......... Plant Component Test Facility [Nuclear energy]
PCTFE....... Polychlorotrifluoroethylene [Organic chemistry]
PCT-GF .... Plasmacytoma Growth Factor [Oncology]
PCTHDS.... Psychoanalysis and Contemporary Thought [A publication]
PCTL........ PictureTel Corp. [NASDAQ symbol]   (NQ)
PCTM....... PC Telemart, Inc. [NASDAQ symbol]   (NQ)
PC/TM...... Performance Criteria and Test Methods Task
PCTM....... Pulse-Count Modulation   (MSA)
PCTNB...... Perception [A publication]
PCTO........ Payload Cost Tradeoff Optimization [NASA]   (NASA)
PCTP .... Partido Comunista dos Trabalhadores Portugueses [Portuguese Workers' Communist Party] [Political party]   (PPW)
PCTP .... Pierce Template
PCTR........ Physical Constant Test Reactor [Nuclear energy]
PCTR........ Program Counter
PCTR........ Property Control Transaction Report
PCTR........ Pulsed Column Test Rig [Chemical engineering]
PCTS .... Pentagon Consolidated Telecommunications System   (MCD)
PCTS .... Portable Cesium Time Standard
PCTS .... President's Committee for Traffic Safety   (EA)
PCTUULAW ... Permanent Congress of Trade Union Unity of Latin American Workers [See also CPUSTAL] [Mexico City, Mexico]   (EAIO)
PCTV......... Private Channel Television
PCtvL........ Lukens Steel Co., Coatesville, PA [Library symbol] [Library of Congress] [Obsolete]   (LCLS)
PCtvVA...... United States Veterans Administration Hospital, Medical Library, Coatesville, PA [Library symbol] [Library of Congress]   (LCLS)
PCU .... Packet Communications Unit
PCU .... Paging Control Unit [Telecommunications]   (TEL)
PCU .... Pain Control Unit
PCU .... Partido Conservador Unido [Chilean Catholic political party]
PCU .... Passenger Control Unit   (MCD)
PCU .... Payload Checkout Unit [NASA]   (MCD)
PCU .... Peripheral Control Unit   (CMD)
PCU .... Picayune, MS [Location identifier] [FAA]   (FAAL)
PCU .... Pneumatic Checkout Unit   (AAG)
PCU .... Pod Cooling Unit   (AAG)
PCU .... Policy Co-Ordination Unit [Australia]
PCU .... Portable Checkout Unit
PCU .... Portuguese Continental Union of the United States of America   (EA)
PCU .... Pound Centigrade Unit
PCU .... Power Conditioning Unit
PCU .... Power Control Unit
PCU .... Power Conversion Unit   (IEEE)
PCU .... Pressure Control Unit   (MCD)
PCU .... Price [Utah] [Seismograph station code, US Geological Survey]   (SEIS)
PCU .... Processor Control Unit
PCU .... Product Co-Ordination Unit [British Overseas Trade Board]   (DS)
PCU .... Program Control Unit [Data processing]
PCU .... Progress Control Unit   (KSC)
PCU .... Progressive Care Unit [Medicine]
PCU .... Protective Care Unit [Medicine]
PCU .... Protein-Calorie Undernutrition [Medicine]
PCU .... Punched Card Utility [Data processing]
PCU .... University of Prince Edward Island, Charlottetown, Prince Edward Island [Library symbol] [National Library of Canada]   (NLC)
PCUA .... Power Controller Unit Assembly   (IEEE)
PCUA .... PROFIT Control Users Association   (EA)
PCUC .... Positive Continuous Ullage Control
PCU/HDR ... Primary Control Unit, Hydraulics   (AAG)
PCUI........ Partito Comunista Unificado di Italia [Unified Communist Party of Italy] [Political party]   (PPE)
PCUR .... Pulsating Current
PCUS........ Propeller Club of the United States   (EA)
PC-USA..... Pax Christi - USA   (EA)
PCUSAW .. Pen Center USA West   (EA)
PCUSEQ ... Pressure Control Unit Sequencer   (AAG)
PCUUS...... Polish Council of Unity in the United States   (EA)
PCV .... Pacific Concord Resources Corp. [Vancouver Stock Exchange symbol]
PCV .... Packed Cell Volume [Hematocrit value]
PCV .... Partido Comunista Venezolana [Venezuelan Communist Party] [Political party]   (PPW)
PCV .... Peace Corps Volunteer
PCV .... Petty Cash Voucher   (MCD)
PCV .... Phenetic Coefficient of Variation
PCV .... Pneumatic Control Valve
PCV .... Pollution Control Valve   (IEEE)
PCV .... Polycythemia Vera [Also, PV] [Hematology]
PCV .... Porcine Cirovirus

PCV .... Positive Crankcase Ventilation [*For automotive antipollution systems*]
PCV .... Precheck Verification [*NASA*]   (NASA)
PCV .... Pressure [*or Pressurizer*] Control Valve   (AAG)
PCV .... Primate Calicivirus
PCV .... Purge Control Valve   (NASA)
PCV .... Pyrocatechol Violet [*Also, PV*] [*An indicator*] [*Chemistry*]
PCV .... Veterans Affairs, Canada [*Affaires des Anciens Combattants Canada*] Charlottetown, Prince Edward Island [*Library symbol*] [*National Library of Canada*]   (NLC)
PCvA .... Allentown College of Saint Francis De Sales, Center Valley, PA [*Library symbol*] [*Library of Congress*]   (LCLS)
PCVB .... Pyro Continuity Verification Box [*NASA*]   (NASA)
PCVC .... Public Citizens Visitors Center [*An association*] [*Defunct*]   (EA)
PCVD .... Plasma Chemical Vapor Deposition
PCVDA ..... Progress in Cardiovascular Diseases [*A publication*]
PCVL .... Pilot-Controlled Visual Landing [*Aviation*]   (NASA)
PCW .... Personal Computer World Show [*Montbuild Ltd.*]   (TSPED)
PCW .... Plate Control Wedge [*Printing technology*]
PCW .... Port Clinton, OH [*Location identifier*] [*FAA*]   (FAAL)
PCW .... Previously Complied With
PCW .... Primary Cooling Water [*Reactor*]
PCW .... Princess Charlotte of Wales [*Military unit*] [*British*]
PCW .... Principal Conductor of the Works [*Freemasonry*]
PCW .... Program Control Word
PCW .... Proprietor of Copyright on a Composite Work
PCW .... Pulmonary Capillary Wedge [*Medicine*]
PCW .... Pulsed Continuous Wave   (IEEE)
PCW .... Widener College, Chester, PA [*Library symbol*] [*Library of Congress*]   (LCLS)
PCWBS .... Preliminary Contract Work Breakdown Structure   (MCD)
PCWCA ..... Poured Concrete Wall Contractors Association   (EA)
PC-WNIM ... Personal Computer Wide Area Network Interface Module   (TSSD)
PCWO ...... Production Control Work Order   (MCD)
PCWP .... Pulmonary Capillary Wedge Pressure [*Medicine*]
PCWU ...... Port Commissioners Workers' Union [*Indian*]
PCX .... Pacific Express [*Chico, CA*] [*FAA designator*]   (FAAC)
PCx .... Periscopic Convex [*Ophthalmology*]
PCX .... Plasma Confinement Experiment [*Physics*]
PCY .... Pacific Cypress Minerals Ltd. [*Vancouver Stock Exchange symbol*]
PCY .... Pittsburgh, Chartiers & Youghiogheny Railway Co. [*AAR code*]
PCY .... Plastocyanin
PCY .... Prerogative Court of York [*English court previously having jurisdiction over wills*]
PCYF .... President's Council on Youth Fitness   (EA)
PCYF .... Progressive Conservative Youth Federation of Canada
PCYMF ..... Pacific Cypress Minerals Ltd. [*NASDAQ symbol*]   (NQ)
PCZ .... Canal Zone [*ANSI three-letter standard code*] [*Obsolete*]   (CNC)
PCZ .... Paracomp Technology, Inc. [*Vancouver Stock Exchange symbol*]
PCZ .... Physical Control Zone   (NASA)
PCZ .... Waupaca, WI [*Location identifier*] [*FAA*]   (FAAL)
PD .... Democratic Party [*Ecuador*] [*Political party*]   (PD)
PD .... Doctor of Pedagogy
PD .... Doctor of Pharmacy
Pd .... Dorsal Pressure Neuron [*of a leech*]
PD .... Dublin Pharmacopoeia
PD .... Interpupillary Distance
PD .... Ipec Aviation Pty. Ltd. [*Australia*] [*ICAO designator*]   (FAAC)
P & D .... Law Reports, Probate and Divorce [*England*] [*A publication*]   (DLA)
PD .... Law Reports, Probate, Divorce, and Admiralty Division [*1875-90*] [*England*] [*A publication*]   (DLA)
p/d .... Packs per Day [*Cigarettes*] [*Medicine*]
PD .... Pad   (MCD)
PD .... Paget's Disease [*Medicine*]
PD .... Paid
PD .... Paix et Droit [*Paris*] [*A publication*]
PD .... Palisade Diabase [*Geology*]
Pd .... Palladium [*Chemical element*]
PD .... Pancreatic Divisum [*Medicine*]
PD .... Pancreatic Duct [*Anatomy*]
PD .... Pants Down [*At a disadvantage*] [*Slang*]   (DSUE)
PD .... Papier und Druck [*A publication*]
pd .... Papilla Diameter [*Medicine*]
PD .... Papillary Distance
PD .... Parkinsonism Dementia [*Medicine*]
PD .... Parkinson's Disease [*Medicine*]
PD .... Parliamentary Debates [*A publication*]
PD .... Pars Distalis [*Medicine*]
PD .... Part Damaged   (ROG)
PD .... Parti Democratique [*Democratic Party*] [*Luxembourg*] [*Political party*]   (PPE)
PD .... Partial Discharge [*High-voltage testing*]   (IEEE)
PD .... Particle-Density [*Forensic science*]
PD .... Partido Democrata [*Democratic Party*] [*Costa Rica*] [*Political party*]   (PPW)

PD .... Partido Democrata [*Democratic Party*] [*Chile*] [*Political party*]
PD .... Partner Air Services A/S [*Norway*] [*ICAO designator*]   (FAAC)
PD .... Passed
PD .... Passive Detection [*Electronics*]
PD .... Past Due
PD .... Paste-Down [*Album*] [*Photography*]   (ROG)
PD .... Pay Department [*Army*] [*British*]   (ROG)
PD .... Pay Dirt
PD .... Peak Detector
PD .... Pediatric [*or Pediatrics*]
PD .... Pennsylvania Dutchman [*A publication*]
PD .... People's Democracy [*Ireland*] [*Political party*]
PD .... Pepper Dust [*An adulterating element*]
PD .... Per Diem [*By the Day*] [*Latin*]
PD .... Per Diliquium [*By Deliquescence*] [*Pharmacy*]   (ROG)
PD .... Performance Demonstration   (MCD)
PD .... Periderm [*Botany*]
PD .... Period   (AABC)
PD .... Peripheral Device   (BUR)
PD .... Peritoneal Dialysis [*Medicine*]
PD .... Permanent Deactivation
P & D .... Perry and Davison's English Queen's Bench Reports [*1834-44*] [*A publication*]   (DLA)
PD .... Personnel Department
PD .... Personnel Distribution [*Army*]
PD .... Pharmacy Dispenser [*British military*]   (DMA)
PD .... Phase Discriminator
PD .... Phelps Dodge Corp. [*NYSE symbol*]   (SPSG)
PD .... Phenyldichlorarsine [*A war gas*]
PD .... Philosophiae Doctor [*Doctor of Philosophy*]
PD .... Phosphate Dehydrogenase
PD .... Phosphodiester [*Organic chemistry*]
PD .... Photodiode
PD .... Phyllis Dorothy James White [*In name P. D. James*] [*Author*]
PD .... Physical Damage [*Insurance*]
PD .... Physical Disabilities
PD .... Physical Distribution   (ADA)
PD .... Physics Department
P & D .... Pick Up and Delivery [*Business term*]
PD .... Picknick Dam [*TVA*]
P/D .... Pickup and Deposit
PD .... Pictorial Display   (MCD)
PD .... Pierce's Disease [*Plant pathology*]
PD .... Pilot Dogs   (EA)
P & D .... Pioneer and Demolition Section [*Army*]
PD .... Piskei Din Shel Bet ha-Mishpat ha-'Elyon le-Yisrael   (BJA)
PD .... Pitch Diameter
PD .... Pitch Down   (MCD)
PD .... Pivoted Door   (AAG)
PD .... Plane Disagreement [*Telecommunications*]   (TEL)
PD .... Planned Derating [*Electronics*]   (IEEE)
PD .... Planning Directive   (NG)
PD .... Planning Document
PD .... Plans Division [*Military*]
PD .... Plasma Desorption [*of ions for analysis*]
PD .... Plasma Display
PD .... Plate Dissipation
PD .... Platelet Deaggregation [*Hematology*]
PD .... Plausible Deniability
PD .... Poetic Drama [*A publication*]
PD .... Point Defense
PD .... Point Detonating [*Projectile*]
PD .... Polar Distance [*Navigation*]
PD .... Police Department
pd .... Pond [*Pound*] [*Monetary unit*] [*Afrikaans*]
PD .... Pontoon Dock
PD .... Pool Density [*Pisciculture*]
PD .... Poorly Differentiated [*Medicine*]
PD .... Population Density   (NRCH)
PD .... Population Distribution   (NRCH)
PD .... Population Doubling
PD .... Pore Diameter
PD .... Port of Debarkation [*Navy*]
PD .... Port Director
PD .... Port Du [*Carriage Forward*] [*French*]
PD .... Port Dues
PD .... Position Description
PD .... Position Document
PD .... Position Doubtful [*Nautical charts*]
PD .... Positive Displacement
PD .... Post Diluvium [*After the Flood*] [*Latin*]   (ROG)
PD .... Postage Due
PD .... Postal District
PD .... Postdated
PD .... Postdoctorate
PD .... Posterior Deltoid [*Myology*]
PD .... Posterior Digestive [*Gland*]
PD .... Postnasal Drainage [*Medicine*]
PD .... Potential Difference [*Electricity*]
PD .... Pound   (ROG)
PD .... Power Distribution

PD............	Precision Device [*British military*] (DMA)
PD............	Precision Drilling (1987) Ltd. [*Toronto Stock Exchange symbol*]
PD............	Predeployment
P/D..........	Predicted [*NASA*] (KSC)
PD............	Predilute
PD............	Preference for Duty
PD............	Pregnanediol [*Biochemistry*]
PD............	Preliminary Design
PD............	Prescription Drug
PD............	Presidential Determination
PD............	Presidential Directive
PD............	Presidential Documents [*A publication*]
PD............	Pressor Dose [*Medicine*]
Pd............	Pressure, Diastolic [*Cardiology*]
PD............	Pressure Drop (KSC)
PD............	Presumptive Disability [*Title XVI*] [*Social Security Administration*] (OICC)
PD............	Prevention Detention [*Scotland Yard*]
PD............	Prime Driver
PD............	Printer Driver
PD............	Printer's Devil (ROG)
PD............	Priority Designator [*Army*]
PD............	Priority Directive
PD............	Prism Diopter
PD............	Prisoner's Dilemma [*Psychology*]
PD............	Privatdozent [*Tutor*] [*German*]
PD............	Private Detective
pd	Pro Defendente [*On Behalf of Defendant*] [*Latin*] [*Legal term*] (DLA)
PD............	Probability of Damage (MCD)
PD............	Probability of Death [*Biology*]
PD............	Probability of Detection
P & D	Probate and Divorce [*Legal*] [*British*]
PD............	Problem Definition [*Army*]
PD............	Probleme der Dichtung [*A publication*]
PD............	Process Diagnostic [*Interpersonal skills and attitudes test*]
PD............	Procurement Data
PD............	Procurement Directive [*Army*]
P & D	Procurement and Distribution [*Military*]
PD............	Procurement District [*Air Force*] (AFIT)
PD............	Procurement Division
PD............	Procurement Document (NASA)
PD............	Procurement Drawing
PD............	Product Design [*Phase*]
P/D..........	Product Development
PD............	Production Department
PD............	Production and Deployment Phase [*Military*] (MCD)
PD............	Professional Development (ADA)
PD............	Program Deceleration (KSC)
PD............	Program Decoder
PD............	Program Directive (NG)
PD............	Program Director [*Television*]
PD............	Programa Democratico [*Democratic Program*] [*Spain*] [*Political party*] (PPE)
PD............	Progression of Disease [*Medicine*]
PD............	Project Directive (NASA)
PD............	Project Document
PD............	Projected Decision Date (NRCH)
PD............	Projected Display
PD............	Promotion Director
PD............	Propellant Dispersion (KSC)
PD............	Property Damage
PD............	Proposal Development (AAG)
PD............	Protective Device (BUR)
PD............	Provisional District [*Church of England in Australia*]
PD............	Provisioning Document
PD............	Proximity Detector
PD............	Prussian Dollar [*Monetary unit*] (ROG)
PD............	Przemysl Drzewny [*A publication*]
PD............	Pseudohomogeneous Axial Dispersion Model [*Fluid dynamics*]
PD............	Psychodynamic
Pd............	Psychopathic Deviate [*Psychology*]
PD............	Psychotic Depression [*Medicine*]
PD............	Public Domain
PD............	Publication Date [*Online database field identifier*]
PD............	Publisher's Directory [*Formerly, BPD*] [*A publication*]
PD............	Pulmonary Disease [*Medicine*]
PD............	Pulpodistal [*Dentistry*]
PD............	Pulse Detector [*Spectroscopy*]
PD............	Pulse Doppler
PD............	Pulse Driver
PD............	Pulse Duration
P-D...........	Punch-Die (MSA)
PD............	Punch Driver
pd	Pupillary Distance [*Medicine*]
PD............	Purchase Description
PD............	Pyloric Dilator [*Neuron*]
PD............	Pyramidal Decussation [*Neuroanatomy*]
PD1...........	Portable Dictionary 1 [*English/Japanese electronic dictionary*] [*Sanyo Electric*]
P 2d	Pacific Reporter, Second Series [*A publication*] (DLA)

PDA	Pacific Dance Association (EA)
PDA	Pacific Dermatologic Association (EA)
PDA	Parallel Data Adapter
PDA	Parametric Design Analysis (RDA)
PDA	Parenteral Drug Association (EA)
PdA	Partei der Arbeit [*Labor Party*] [*Switzerland*] [*Political party*] (PPE)
PDA	Parti Democratico da Angola [*Democratic Party of Angola*] [*Political party*]
PDA	Parti Dolonti Applicandum [*Apply to Painful Part*] [*Pharmacy*] (ROG)
PDA	Partit Democrata d'Andorra [*Andorran Democratic Party*] [*Political party*] (PPW)
Pd'A	Partito d'Azione [*Action Party*] [*Italy*] [*Political party*] (PPE)
PDA	Parts Disposal Area (MCD)
PDA	Pasadena Energy [*Vancouver Stock Exchange symbol*]
PDA	Patent Ductus Arteriosus [*Cardiology*]
PDA	Patient Data Automation
PDA	Payroll Deduction Authorization (MCD)
PDA	Peak Distribution Analyzer
PDA	Pediatric Allergy
PDA	Permanent Duty Assignment [*Air Force*] (AFM)
PDA	Personal Deposit Account [*Banking*]
PDA	Petrol Dealers' Association [*British*]
PDA	Phenylenediamine [*Chemistry*]
PDA	Philadelphia Dance Alliance
PDA	Phorbol Diacetate [*Organic chemistry*]
PDA	Photodiode Array [*Instrumentation*]
PDA	Photon Detector Assembly (MCD)
PDA	Physical Device Address [*Data processing*] (IBMDP)
PDA	Piperidinedicarboxylic Acid [*Organic chemistry*]
PDA	Pisatin Demethylase [*An enzyme*]
PDA	Planning and Development in the Netherlands (Assen) [*A publication*]
PDA	Point Density Analysis [*Mathematics*]
PDA	Point Director Array
PDA	Pointing Device Adapter [*Data processing*]
PDA	Poise Distribution Amplifier (AFM)
PDA	Polarization Diversity Array
PDA	Polydiacetylene [*Organic chemistry*]
PDA	Poly(dimethylacrylamide) [*Organic chemistry*]
PDA	Ponta Delgada [*Azores*] [*Seismograph station code, US Geological Survey*] (SEIS)
PDA	Population Drainage Area [*Civil Defense*]
PDA	Post-Deflection Accelerator (DEN)
PDA	Post-Delivery Availability [*Military*] (NVT)
PDA	Post-Design Analysis
PDA	Potato Dextrose Agar [*Culture media*]
PDA	Pour Dire Adieu [*To Say Farewell*] [*On visiting cards*] [*French*]
PDA	Power Distribution Assembly (KSC)
PDA	Precision Drive Axis (KSC)
PDA	Predelivery Acceptance Test [*NASA*]
PDA	Predicted Drift Angle [*Navigation*]
PDA	Predocketed Application (NRCH)
PDA	Preliminary Design Acceptance (NRCH)
PDA	Preliminary Design Approval [*or Authorization*] (NRCH)
PDA	Preliminary Design Assessment [*Nuclear energy*] (NRCH)
PDA	Present Duty Assignment Option [*Military*]
PDA	Princeton Diagnostic Laboratories [*AMEX symbol*] (SPSG)
PDA	Principal Development Activity [*Navy*]
PDA	Principal Development Authority (MCD)
PDA	Private Doctors of America (EA)
PDA	Probabilistic Decision Algorithm [*Artificial intelligence job performance aid*] [*Army*]
PDA	Probability Discrete Automata (IEEE)
PDA	Probability Distribution Analyzer [*Statistics*]
PDA	Probate, Divorce, and Admiralty [*British*] [*Legal term*] (DLA)
PDA	Processor and Distribution Assembly [*Viking lander analysis equipment*] [*NASA*]
PdA	Procurement Defense Agencies [*DoD*]
PDA	Product Departure Authorization
PDA	Produktions- und Dienstleistungsabgabe [*Production and Services Tax (A type of turnover tax)*] [*German*]
PDA	Professional Drivers Association
PDA	Program Developing Agency [*Military*] (CAAL)
PDA	Prolonged Depolarizing Afterpotential [*Neurophysiology*]
PDA	Propanediamine [*Organic chemistry*]
PDA	Propellant Drain Area (NASA)
PDA	Property Disposal Account [*Military*] (NG)
PDA	Property Disposal Agent [*Military*] (NG)
PDA	Property Disposition Authorization
PDA	Proposed Development Approach [*Navy*]
PDA	Propylenediamine [*Organic chemistry*]
PDA	Prospectors' and Developers' Association [*Canada*]
PDA	Public Display of Affection [*Slang*]
PDA	Puerto Inirida [*Colombia*] [*Airport symbol*] (OAG)
PDA	Pulse Demodulation Analysis
PDA	Pulse Distribution Amplifier
PDA	Pump Drive Assembly
PDAB	Para-(Dimethylamino)benzaldehyde [*Organic chemistry*]
PDAB	Physical Disability Appeals Board [*Military*] (AFM)

PDAC .... Professional Development Advisory Committee [*American Occupational Therapy Association*]
PDAD .... Photodiode Array Detector [*Spectrophotometry*]
PDAD .... Probate, Divorce, and Admiralty Division [*Legal*] [*British*]   (ROG)
PDAFSC.... Projected Duty Air Force Specialty Code   (AFM)
PDAGA ..... Pediatriia, Akusherstvo, i Ginekologiia [*A publication*]
PDAID....... Problem Determination Aid [*Data processing*]   (MDG)
PDalCM .... College Misericordia, Dallas, PA [*Library symbol*] [*Library of Congress*]   (LCLS)
PDAM .... Periodontal Disease-Associated Microbiotae [*Dentistry*]
PDANB ..... Pediatric Annals [*A publication*]
PDanMHi ... Montour County Historical Society, Danville, PA [*Library symbol*] [*Library of Congress*]   (LCLS)
PDanSH .... Danville State Hospital, Danville, PA [*Library symbol*] [*Library of Congress*]   (LCLS)
PDAP........ Programmable Digital Autopilot   (MCD)
PDAP........ Provincial Development Assistance Program [*Agency for International Development*]
PDAR .... Parts Drawing Approval Request   (MCD)
PDAR .... Producibility Design Analysis Report   (AAG)
PDAR .... Program Description and Requirements [*NASA*]   (NASA)
PDARR...... Production Drawing and Assembly Release Record   (AAG)
PDAS........ PDA Engineering [*NASDAQ symbol*]   (NQ)
PDAS........ Photo Data Analysis System [*Navy*]
PDAS........ Plant Data Acquisition System   (NRCH)
PDAS........ [*A*] Popular Dictionary of Australian Slang [*A publication*]
PDASD..... Principal Deputy Assistant Secretary of Defense
PDate........ Pay Date
PDATE...... Production Date [*Data processing*]
Pd B .... Bachelor of Pedagogy
PDB .... Packard Data Bank   (EA)
PDB .... Pakistan Development Review [*A publication*]
PDB .... Para-Dichlorobenzene [*Insecticide for moths, etc.*]
PDB .... Partei der Deutschsprachigen Belgier [*Party of German-Speaking Belgians*] [*Political party*]   (PPW)
PDB .... Pedro Bay [*Alaska*] [*Airport symbol*]   (OAG)
PDB .... Pee Dee Belemnite [*An isotopic standard for oxygen and carbon*]
PDB .... Pentadecylbenzene [*Organic chemistry*]
PDB .... Performance Data Book   (NASA)
PDB .... Periodical Directories and Bibliographies [*A publication*]
PDB .... Personality Data Base
PDB .... Phorbol Dibutyrate [*Also, PDBu*] [*Organic chemistry*]
PDB .... Phosphorus-Dissolving Bacteria [*Microbiology*]
PDB .... Pierce's Disease Bacterium [*Plant pathology*]
PDB .... Plasma Diagnostic Base
PDB .... Positive Displacement Blower
PDB .... Potato Dextrose Broth [*Microbiology*]
PDB .... Power Distribution Box   (NASA)
PDB .... President's Daily Brief
PDB .... Price Decontrol Board [*Post-World War II*]
PDB .... Primary Data Bus [*Data processing*]
PDB .... Process Descriptor Base [*Telecommunications*]   (TEL)
PDB .... Project Development Brochure [*Military*]
PDB .... Protein Data Bank [*Brookhaven National Laboratory*] [*Information service or system*]   (CRD)
PDB .... Psychic Detective Bureau   (EA)
PDBA .... Personnel Database Application   (MCD)
PDBH .... Production Broach   (AAG)
PDBIA....... Periodicum Biologorum [*A publication*]
PDBM ...... Pulse Delay Binary Modulation   (MCD)
PDBMI...... Periodical Directories and Bibliographies Master Index [*A publication*]
PDBP........ Powered Disposal Bomb Pod   (AAG)
PDBR........ Page-Directory Base Register [*Data processing*]   (BYTE)
PDBS........ Parliamentary Database System [*Australia*]
PDBU .... Pesticides Documentation Bulletin
PDBu .... Phorbol Dibutyrate [*Also, PDB*] [*Organic chemistry*]
PDBz........ Phorbol Dibenzoate [*Organic chemistry*]
PDC .... Community College of Philadelphia, Philadelphia, PA [*OCLC symbol*]   (OCLC)
PDC .... Mueo [*New Caledonia*] [*Airport symbol*]   (OAG)
PDC .... Pacific Defense College   (CINC)
PDC .... Package Design Council [*New York, NY*]   (EA)
PDC .... Pacte Democratica per Catalunya [*Democratic Pact for Catalonia*] [*Spain*] [*Political party*]   (PPE)
PDC .... Paper Distribution Centers
PDC .... Paper Distribution Council   (EA)
PDC .... Parallel Data Communicator   (AAG)
PDC .... Parallel Data Controller
PDC .... Parametric Defense Coverage
PDC .... Parti Democrate Chretien [*Christian Democratic Party*] [*Burundi*] [*Political party*]
PDC .... Parti Democrate-Chretien Suisse [*Christian Democratic Party of Switzerland*] [*Political party*]   (PPE)
PDC .... Partido da Democracia Cristao [*Christian Democratic Party*] [*Portugal*] [*Political party*]   (PPW)
PDC .... Partido Democracia Cristiana [*Christian Democratic Party*] [*Guatemala*] [*Political party*]   (PPW)

PDC .... Partido Democrata Cristiano [*Christian Democratic Party*] [*El Salvador*] [*Political party*]
PDC .... Partido Democrata Cristiano [*Christian Democratic Party*] [*Costa Rica*] [*Political party*]   (PPW)
PDC .... Partido Democrata Cristiano [*Christian Democratic Party*] [*Panama*] [*Political party*]   (PPW)
PDC .... Partido Democrata Cristiano [*Christian Democratic Party*] [*Paraguay*] [*Political party*]   (PPW)
PDC .... Partido Democrata Cristiano [*Christian Democratic Party*] [*Bolivia*] [*Political party*]   (PPW)
PDC .... Partido Democrata Cristiano [*Christian Democratic Party*] [*Peru*] [*Political party*]   (PPW)
PDC .... Partido Democrata Cristiano [*Christian Democratic Party*] [*Honduras*] [*Political party*]   (PPW)
PDC .... Partido Democratico Cristao [*Christian Democratic Party*] [*Brazil*] [*Political party*]
PDC .... Partido Democratico Cristiano [*Christian Democratic Party*] [*Argentina*] [*Political party*]   (PPW)
PDC .... Partido Democratico Cristiano [*Christian Democratic Party*] [*Chile*] [*Political party*]   (PPW)
PDC .... Partito della Democrazia Cristiana [*Christian Democratic Party*] [*Italy*] [*Political party*]
PDC .... Pediatric Cardiology [*Medical specialty*]   (DHSM)
PDC .... Pentadecylcatechol [*An allergen*]
PDC .... People's Defence Committee [*Ghana*]   (PD)
PDC .... Per Diem, Travel and Transportation Allowance Committee for Departments of the Army, Navy, and Air Force
PDC .... Performance Data Computer
PDC .... Personnel Data Card
PDC .... Personnel Distribution Command
PDC .... Philosophy Documentation Center   (EA)
PDC .... Photo-Data Card [*Trademark*] [*Data processing*]
PDC .... Photonuclear Data Center [*National Institute of Standards and Technology*]
PDC .... Pieve Di Cadore [*Italy*] [*Seismograph station code, US Geological Survey*] [*Closed*]   (SEIS)
PDC .... Plastic Dielectric Capacitor
PDC .... Polaris Documentation Control [*Missiles*]
PDC .... Policy Determination Committee   (AAG)
PDC .... Polycrystalline Diamond Compact Drill Bit
PDC .... Polystyrene Dielectric Capacitor
PDC .... Population Documentation Center [*Food and Agriculture Organization*] [*United Nations*] [*Information service or system*]   (IID)
PDC .... Portable Data Carrier
PDC .... Portable Data Communications [*British*]
PDC .... Position Depth Charge
PDC .... Power Distribution and Control
PDC .... Power Distribution Cubiale   (NATG)
PDC .... Practice Depth Charge
PDC .... Prairie Du Chien, WI [*Location identifier*] [*FAA*]   (FAAL)
PDC .... Predefined Command   (MCD)
PDC .... Predeparture Check [*Aviation*]   (AIA)
PDC .... Predocketed Construction   (NRCH)
PDC .... Preliminary Diagnostic Clinic
PDC .... Premission Documentation Change [*NASA*]   (KSC)
PDC .... Premium and Dispersion Credits [*Insurance*]
PDC .... Prescott Development Corp. [*Vancouver Stock Exchange symbol*]
PDC .... Pressure Die Casting [*Commercial firm*] [*British*]
PDC .... Prevention of Deterioration Center [*Defunct*]   (EA)
PDC .... Price Decontrol Board [*Post-World War II*] [*A publication*]   (DLA)
PDC .... Private Diagnostic Clinic
PDC .... Probability of Detection and Conversion [*Military*]
PDC .... Procurement Document Change   (NASA)
PDC .... Production Decision Criteria
PDC .... Proficiency Data Card [*Army*]
PDC .... Program Data Cards   (OICC)
PDC .... Program Data Coordinator   (MCD)
PDC .... Project Data Card
PDC .... Project Data Control   (MCD)
PDC .... Prosthetic Distribution Center [*Veterans Administration*]
PDC .... Public Documents Commission [*Government agency*]
PDC .... Publications Distribution Center [*Military*]   (AFM)
PDC .... Publishers' Data Center, Inc.
PDC .... Pulse-Duration Commutator
PDC .... Pyridinium Dichromate [*Organic chemistry*]
PDC .... Pyrotechnic Devices Checker
PDC .... Single Paper Double Cotton [*Wire insulation*]   (AAG)
PDCA .... Painting and Decorating Contractors of America   (EA)
PDCA .... Pioneer Dairymen's Club of America   (EA)
PDCA .... Pug Dog Club of America   (EA)
PDCA .... Purebred Dairy Cattle Association   (EA)
PDCA .... United States Professional Diving Coaches Association   (EA)
PDCAU .... Pete Duel - Clube da Amizade do Universo [*Pete Duel Universal Friendship Club - PDUFC*]   (EAIO)
PDCG .... Partido Democracia Cristiana Guatemalteca [*Guatemalan Christian Democratic Party*] [*Political party*]   (PPW)
PDCI.......... Parti Democratique de la Cote-D'Ivoire [*Democratic Party of the Ivory Coast*] [*Political party*]   (PPW)

Pdck .... Probability of Detection Conversion and Kill [*for an interceptor system*] [*Military*]
PDCL .... Provisioning Data Check List [*NASA*]   (KSC)
PDCN .... Public Data Communications Network [*Library science*]
PDCO .... Perennial Development Corp. [*NASDAQ symbol*]   (NQ)
PDCO .... Property Disposal Contracting Officer [*Military*]
PDCP .... Pilot's Display Control Panel
PDCP .... Private Development Corporation of the Philippines
PDCR .... Project Data Compliance Report   (MCD)
PDCR .... Proprietary Data Control Record   (NASA)
PDCRC .... Periodontal Disease Clinical Research Center [*State University of New York at Buffalo*] [*Research center*]   (RCD)
PDCS .... Parallel Digital Computing System
PDCS .... Partito Democratico Cristiano Sammarinese [*Christian Democratic Party of San Marino*] [*Political party*]   (PPE)
PDCS .... Performance Data Computer System   (MCD)
PDCS .... Power Distribution and Control System [*or Subsystem*] [*NASA*]   (NASA)
PDCS .... Processing Distribution and Control System
PDCS .... Programmable Data Collection System [*Military*]   (CAAL)
PDCS .... Prototype Die Casting Service
PDCU .... Plotting Display Control Unit
Pd D .... Doctor of Pedagogy
PDD .... Pancreatic Dorsal Duct [*Anatomy*]
PDD .... Past Due Date
PDD .... Pervasive Developmental Disorder [*Medicine*]
PDD .... Phenyldodecane [*Organic chemistry*]
PDD .... Phorbol Didecanoate [*Organic chemistry*]
PDD .... Physical Damage Division [*Navy*]
PDD .... Physical Defense Division [*Army*]
PDD .... Plotting Data Distributor   (MCD)
P & DD .... Plumbing and Deck Drain   (MSA)
PDD .... Post Dialing Delay [*Telecommunications*]   (TEL)
PDD .... Precision Depth Digitizer [*Oceanography*]
PDD .... Preferred Delivery Date   (AFM)
PDD .... Preliminary Design and Development   (MCD)
PDD .... Premodulation Processor - Deep Space - Data
PDD .... Primary Degenerative Dementia [*Medicine*]
PDD .... Principal Distribution Depot [*DoD*]
PDD .... Priority Delivery Date   (AFM)
PDD .... Probability Density Distribution [*Statistics*]
PdD .... Probleme der Dichtung [*A publication*]
PDD .... Procurement Description Data [*DoD*]
PD & D ...... Product Design & Development [*Radnor, PA*] [*A publication*]
PDD .... Professional Development Division [*American Occupational Therapy Association*]
PDD .... Program Description Document [*Military*]   (CAAL)
PDD .... Program Design Data
PDD .... Program Dimension Drawing   (MCD)
PDD .... Program Directive Document   (RDA)
PDD .... Projected Data Display
PDD .... Projected Decision Date   (NRCH)
PDD .... Prospective Decision Date   (NRCH)
PDD .... Provisioning Description Data
PDD .... Public Documents Department [*Government Printing Office*]
PDD .... Pulse Delay Device
PDD .... Puy-De-Dome [*France*] [*Seismograph station code, US Geological Survey*] [*Closed*]   (SEIS)
PDDA .... Power Driver Decontamination Apparatus   (NATG)
PDDAIO ... Parts for Direct Discrete Analog Input/Output   (MCD)
PDDB .... Phenododecinium [*or Phenoxyethyldimethyl-dodecylammonium*] Bromide [*Antiseptic*]
PDDB .... Product Definition Database   (MCD)
PDDD .... Program Demonstration and Development Division [*ACTION*]
PDDF .... Propargyl(dideaza)folic Acid [*Biochemistry*]
PDDGM .... Past District Deputy Grand Master [*Freemasonry*]
PD Div'l Ct ... Probate, Divorce, and Admiralty Divisional Court [*England*]   (DLA)
PDDLS ...... Post D-Day Logistic Support [*Army*]   (AABC)
PDDM .... Disciples of the Divine Master [*Roman Catholic women's religious order*]
PDD/RDD ... Priority Delivery Date/Required Delivery Date   (AFM)
PDDS .... Program Definition Data Sheet
PDE .... Page-Directory Entry [*Data processing*]   (BYTE)
PDE .... Pandie Pandie [*Australia*] [*Airport symbol*] [*Obsolete*]   (OAG)
Pde .... Parade [*Record label*]
PDE .... Parade
PDE .... Paroxysmal Dyspnea on Exertion [*Medicine*]
PDE .... Partei fuer Deutschland und Europa [*Party for Germany and Europe*] [*Federal Republic of Germany*] [*Political party*]   (PPW)
PDE .... Partial Differential Equation
PDE .... Pediatric Endocrinology [*Medical specialty*]   (DHSM)
PDE .... Pee Dee Air Express, Inc. [*Florence, SC*] [*FAA designator*]   (FAAC)
PDE .... Personnel Development and Education   (MCD)
PDE .... Phosphatidyl(dimethyl)ethanolamine [*Biochemistry*]
PDE .... Phosphodiesterase [*An enzyme*]
PDE .... Pilot's Discrete Encoder
PDE .... Position-Determining Equipment

PDE .... Preliminary Determination of Epicenters [*A publication*] [*National Oceanic and Atmospheric Administration*]
PDE .... Pride Resources Ltd. [*Vancouver Stock Exchange symbol*]
PDE .... Production Design Engineers
PDE .... Projectile Development Establishment [*British*]
PDE .... Propellant Disposition Effects
PDE .... Prospective Data Element [*Army*]   (AABC)
PD & E .... Provisioning Documentation and Effort [*Military*]   (AFIT)
PDECS ...... Portable Detector and Cueing System
PDED .... Partial Double Error Detection
PDEI .... Phosphodiesterase Inhibitor [*Biochemistry*]
PDEL .... Partial Differential Equation Language [*Data processing*]
PDELAN .. Partial Differential Equation Language [*Data processing*]   (CSR)
PDENA ..... Production Engineer [*London*] [*A publication*]
PDEP .... Preliminary Draft Equipment Publication   (MCD)
PDEQ .... Profile of DARCOM Environmental Quality   (MCD)
PDES .... Preliminary Draft Environmental Statement   (NRCH)
PDES .... Product Definition Exchange Specification [*Army*]
P Det .... Port Detachment [*British military*]   (DMA)
PDET .... Post-Diapause Eclosion Time [*Entomology*]
PDET .... Probability of Detection, Evaluation, and Transfer   (MCD)
PDEX .... Pro-Dex, Inc. [*NASDAQ symbol*]   (NQ)
PDF .... Packaging Technology [*A publication*]
PDF .... Paget's Disease Foundation   (EA)
PDF .... Pair Distribution Function [*Physical chemistry*]
PDF .... Pakistan Democratic Front
PDF .... Panama Defense Forces [*Later, Public Forces*]
PDF .... Parkinson's Disease Foundation   (EA)
PDF .... Parti Democrate Francais [*French Democratic Party*] [*Political party*]   (PPW)
PDF .... Particle Distribution Function
PDF .... Passive Direction Finding
PDF .... Pavement Depth Factor   (ADA)
PDF .... Peace Development Fund   (EA)
PDF .... Planet Drum Foundation   (EA)
PDF .... Plant Design Factor [*Nuclear energy*]   (NRCH)
PDF .... Point Detonating Fuze [*Army*]
PDF .... Popular Democratic Front [*Jordan*] [*Political party*]
PDF .... Post Defense Force
PDF .... Post Detection Filter [*Telecommunications*]   (TEL)
PDF .... Principal Direction of Fire [*Military*]
PDF .... Probability Density Function [*Statistics*]
PDF .... Probability Distribution Function [*Statistics*]
PDF .... Processor Defined Function
PDF .... Production and Distribution of Foodstuffs [*British*]
PDF .... Program Data File
PDF .... Program Data Form [*Army*]
PDF .... Project Design Flood   (NRCH)
PDFCS ...... Pennsylvania Dutch Folk Culture Society   (EA)
PDFD .... Predemonstration Fusion Device
PDFD .... Pulsed Doppler Frequency Diversity   (NG)
PDFLP ...... Popular Democratic Front for the Liberation of Palestine
PDFM .... Phillips and Drew Fund Management [*England*] [*British*]
PDFRR ...... Program Directors Flight Readiness Review [*NASA*]   (KSC)
PDFWPR .. Physical Disabilities Fieldwork Performance Report [*Occupational therapy*]
PDG .... Padang [*Indonesia*] [*Airport symbol*]   (OAG)
PDG .... Parachute Drop Glider
PDG .... Parti Democratique Gabonais [*Gabonese Democratic Party*] [*Political party*]   (PPW)
PDG .... Parti Democratique de Guinee [*Democratic Party of Guinea*] [*Political party*]   (PPW)
PDG .... Passive Defense Group   (MUGU)
PDG .... Patent Documentation Group   (DIT)
PDG .... Personalistic Discussion Group - Eastern Division   (EA)
PDG .... Placer Dome, Inc. [*NYSE symbol*] [*Toronto Stock Exchange symbol*] [*Vancouver Stock Exchange symbol*]   (SPSG)
PDG .... Precision Drop Glider [*Army*]
PDG .... Pregnanediol Glucuronide [*Endocrinology*]
PDG .... President Directeur General [*President Director General*] [*French*]
PDG .... Pretty Damn Good
PDG .... Professional Dyers Guild [*Defunct*]
PDG .... Programs Development Group   (MUGU)
PDG .... Proposal Development Group [*Aerospace*]   (AAG)
PDGA .... Pteroyldiglutamic Acid [*Pharmacology*]
PDGDL ..... Plasma Dynamics and Gaseous Discharge Laboratory [*MIT*]   (MCD)
PDGF .... Platelet-Derived Growth Factor [*Genetics*]
PDGFR ...... Platelet-Derived Growth Factor Receptor [*Genetics*]
PDGMS ..... Peabody Developmental Gross Motor Scale
PDGS .... Precision Delivery Glider System
P-DGs .... Presidents-Directeurs Generaux
PDGS .... Probe Drill Guidance System
PDGY .... Prodigy Systems, Inc. [*NASDAQ symbol*]   (NQ)
PDH .... Packaged Disaster Hospital [*Public Health Service*]
PDH .... Passive Defense Handbook [*Navy*]   (MCD)
PDH .... Past Dental History
PDH .... Planned Derated Hours [*Electronics*]   (IEEE)
PDH .... Pocket Dosimeter-High   (MCD)

PDH............ Pyruvate Dehydrogenase [*An enzyme*]
PDHC........ Pyruvate Dehydrogenase Complex [*Biochemistry*]
PDH & DS ... Plant Data Handling and Display System [*Nuclear energy*] (NRCH)
PDHF .... Postdilution Hemofiltration [*Medicine*]
PDHMUA ... Publication. Department of History. Muslim University (Aligarh) [*A publication*]
PDHV-RDA ... Parti Democratique de la Haute Volta-Rassemblement Democratique Africain [*Democratic Party of Upper Volta-African Democratic Rally*]
PDI .... Palmer Drought Index
PDI .... Partai Demokrasi Indonesia [*Indonesian Democratic Party*] [*Political party*] (PPW)
PDI .... Parti Democratique de l'Independance [*Democratic Independence Party*] [*Morocco*] [*Political party*]
PDI .... Partito Democratica Italiana [*Italian Democratic Party*] [*Political party*] (PPE)
PDI .... Payload Data Interleaver [*NASA*] (NASA)
PDI .... Personal Disposable Income [*Economics*]
PDI .... Pictorial Deviation Indicator (AAG)
PDI .... Picture Description Instruction [*Telecommunications*]
PDI .... Pilot Direction Indicator [*Electronic communications*]
PDI .... Planned Innovation [*A publication*]
PDI .... Plumbing and Drainage Institute (EA)
PDI .... Porto D'Ischia [*Italy*] [*Seismograph station code, US Geological Survey*] [*Closed*] (SEIS)
PDI .... Post Detection Integration (MCD)
PDI .... Potential Determining Ions
PDI .... Powered Descent Initiation [*Aerospace*]
PDI .... Pre-Delivery Inspection (DCTA)
PDI .... Predeployment Inspection [*Navy*] (NVT)
PDI .... Premdor, Inc. [*Toronto Stock Exchange symbol*]
PDI .... Professional Development Institute [*Canada*]
PDI .... Program Design, Incorporated [*Commercial firm*]
PDI .... Program with Developing Institutions (EA)
PDI .... Project Data Index [*Jet Propulsion Laboratory, NASA*]
PDI .... Protein Dispersibility Index [*Analytical chemistry*]
PDI .... Protein Disulfide-Isomerase [*An enzyme*]
PDI .... Psychiatric Diagnostic Interview [*Personality development test*] [*Psychology*]
PDI .... Psychological Distress Inventory [*Student personality test*]
PDI .... Psychomotor Development Index [*Bayley Scales of Infant Development*]`
PDI .... Public Debt Interest (ADA)
PDI .... Public Demographics, Incorporated (IID)
PDI .... Putnam Dividend Income [*NYSE symbol*] (SPSG)
Pdi .... Transdiaphragmatic [*Pressure*]
PDial......... Poetry Dial [*A publication*]
PDIC........ Periodic (AFM)
PDIC......... Professional Driver Improvement Course
PDIC......... Public Demands Implementation Convention [*India*] (PPW)
PDII.......... Pusat Dokumentasi dan Informasi Ilmiah [*Indonesian Center for Scientific Documentation and Information*] [*Information service or system*] (IID)
PDIIS .... Priority Defense Items Information System
PDIL......... Power-Dependent Insertion Limit [*Nuclear energy*] (NRCH)
PDIL......... Prueba del Desarrollo Inicial del Lenguaje [*Standardized test of Spanish language-speaking ability in children from three to seven years old*]
PDIO .... Parallel Digital Input/Output
PDIO .... Photodiode
P-DIOL ..... Pregnanediol [*Biochemistry*]
PDIP......... Preflight Data Insertion Program (NVT)
PDIP......... Program Development Increment Package [*Military*]
PDIQ .... Protein Databases, Inc. [*NASDAQ symbol*] (NQ)
PDIR......... Priority Disassembly and Inspection Report
PDIS......... Parts Dissection Information System
PDIS......... Payload Data Interleaver System [*NASA*] (MCD)
PDIS......... Proceedings. National Symposia [*A publication*]
PDIS......... Product Description Information Standards [*or System*]
PDISCH.... Pump Discharge
PDISPL..... Positive Displacement [*Engineering*]
PDIUM ..... Partito Democratico Italiano di Unita Monarchica [*Italian Democratic Party of Monarchical Unity*] [*Political party*] (PPE)
P Div .... Law Reports, Probate Division [*England*] [*A publication*] (DLA)
PDJ........... Plaine Des Jarres [*South Vietnam*]
PDJ........... Precision Drill Jig
PDJB......... Precision Drill Jig Bushing
PD/JV .... Project Definition/Joint Validation (MCD)
PDK .... Atlanta [*Georgia*] De Kalb/Peachtree Airport [*Airport symbol*] [*Obsolete*] (OAG)
PDK .... Phi Delta Kappa [*Fraternity*]
PDK .... Phileleftheron Demokratikon Kendron [*Liberal Democratic Union*] [*Greek*] (PPE)
PDK .... Phileleftheron Demokratikon Komma [*Liberal Democratic Party*] [*Greek*] [*Political party*] (PPE)
PDK .... Promenade Deck [*of a ship*] (DS)
PDL .... Page Description Language [*Computer graphics*]

PDL .... Partido Democrata Liberal [*Liberal Democratic Party*] [*Spain*] [*Political party*] (EY)
PDL .... Parts Deletion List (MSA)
PDL .... Parts Difference List (MCD)
PDL .... Parts Documentation List (MCD)
PDL .... Pass Down the Line [*Book*] [*Navy*] (MUGU)
PDL .... Patent Depository Library [*Designated by the Patent and Trademark Office*]
PDL .... Periodontal Ligament [*Dentistry*]
PDL .... Permanent Duty Location
PDL .... Photodissociation Dye LASER
PDL .... Placer Development Limited [*Toronto Stock Exchange symbol*] [*Vancouver Stock Exchange symbol*]
PDL .... Pocket Dosimeter-Low (MCD)
PDL .... Ponta Delgada [*Portugal*] [*Airport symbol*] (OAG)
PDL .... Poorly Differentiated Lymphocytic [*Oncology*]
PDL .... Population Doubling Level [*Cytology*]
pdl .... Poundal [*Unit of force*]
PDL .... Poverty Datum Line
PDL .... Precision Delay Line
PDL .... Presidential Realty Corp. [*AMEX symbol*] (SPSG)
PDL .... Procedure Definition Language [*Data processing*] (BUR)
PDL .... Procedure Distribution List (MCD)
PDL .... Procurement Data List
PDL .... Product Disaster Loans [*Small Business Administration*]
PDL .... Professional Development League (EA)
PDL .... Program Description Language (MCD)
PDL .... Program Design Language (NASA)
PDL .... Programmed Digital Logic
PDL .... Project Document List
PdL .... Provincia di Lucca [*A publication*]
PDL .... Publishers' Databases Limited [*Publishing consortium*] [*British*]
PDL .... Pulsed Dye LASER
PDL .... Pumped Dye LASER
PDLC........ Partido Liberal de Cataluna [*Liberal Democratic Party of Catalonia*] [*Political party*] (PPW)
PDLC........ Polymer Dispersed Liquid Crystal [*Physical chemistry*]
PDL/FT² ... Poundals per Square Foot
PDLL........ Poorly Differentiated Lymphatic [*or Lymphocytic*] Lymphoma [*Oncology*]
PDLM .... Periodic Depot Level Maintenance
PDLM .... Programmed Depot Level Maintenance [*Air Force*]
PDLP......... Pacific Dunlop Ltd. [*NASDAQ symbol*] (NQ)
PDL S/FT² ... Poundal Seconds per Square Foot
PDLT........ P-Channel Depletion-Load Triode Inverter
Pd M .... Master of Pedagogy
PDM .... Parti Democratique Malgache [*Malagasy Democratic Party*]
PDM .... Partial Descriptive Method
PDM .... Partido de los Democratas Melillenses [*Political party*] [*Spanish North Africa*] (MENA)
PDM .... Patient Data Management
PDM .... Pendant Drop Method
PDM .... People's Democratic Movement [*Papua New Guinea*] [*Political party*] (FEA)
PDM .... People's Democratic Movement [*Turks and Caicos Islands*] [*Political party*] (PPW)
PDM .... Percent Deviation from the Median
PDM .... Physical Distribution Management
PDM .... Physicians Drug Manual [*A publication*]
PDM .... Physiological Data Monitor
PDM .... Pittsburgh - Des Moines, Inc. [*AMEX symbol*] (SPSG)
PDM .... Poetry and Drama Magazine [*A publication*]
PDM .... Portable Differential Magnetometer
PDM .... Power Density Meter
PDM .... Practical Data Manager [*Hitachi Ltd.*] [*Japan*]
PDM .... Precedence Diagraming Method (MCD)
PDM .... Preliminary Development Model
PDM .... Preliminary Draft Manuscript
PDM .... Presidential Decision Memorandum [*Jimmy Carter Administration*]
PDM .... Print Down Module
PDM .... Processor Data Monitor (NASA)
PDM .... Production Decision Criteria Matrix
PDM .... Program Data Manager (MCD)
PDM .... Program Decision Memorandum [*Military*]
PDM .... Programmed Depot Maintenance (MCD)
PDM .... Progres et Democratie Moderne [*Progress and Modern Democracy*] [*France*] [*Political party*] (PPE)
PDM .... Project Design Memo
PDM .... Publications Distribution Manager [*Military*] (AFM)
PDM .... Pulse Delay Mechanism [*British military*] (DMA)
PDM .... Pulse Delta Modulation (IEEE)
PDM .... Pulse-Duration Modulation [*Data transmission*]
PDM .... Push Down Memory [*Data processing*]
PDMA .... Peninsula Drafting Management Association
PDMA .... Product Development and Management Association [*Indianapolis, IN*] (EA)
PDMAC .... Prescription Drug Maximum Allowable Cost
PDME .... Pendant-Drop Melt Extraction [*Metal fiber technology*]
PDM-FM .. Pulse-Duration Modulation - Frequency Modulation (CET)

PDMLA..... PDM. Physicians' Drug Manual [*A publication*]
PDMLR..... Post-Development Maintainability Logistics Review   (MCD)
PDMM...... Push Down Memory MODEM [*Data processing*]
PDMO...... Production Mold   (AAG)
PDMP ...... Positive Displacement Mechanical [*or Metering*] Pump
PDMR....... Provisioning Data Master Record   (MCD)
PDMS....... Particle Desorption Mass Spectrometry
PDMS........ Physiological Data Monitoring System
PDMS........ Plasma Desorption Mass Spectroscopy
PDMS........ Point Defense Missile System [*NATO*]   (NATG)
PDMS........ Polydimethylsiloxane [*Organic chemistry*]
PDMS........ Power-Plant and Process Design Management System [*Data processing*]
PDMS........ Program Definition and Management System   (MCD)
PDMT .... Predominate   (FAAC)
PDMU...... Passive Data Memory Unit
PDMU....... Production Mock-Up   (AAG)
PDN.......... Partido Democratico Nacional [*National Democratic Party*] [*Chile*] [*Political party*]
PDN.......... Partido Democratico Nacional [*National Democratic Party*] [*Venezuela*] [*Political party*]
PDN.......... Partito Democratico Nazionalista [*Democratic Nationalist Party (1921-1926)*] [*Malta*] [*Political party*]   (PPE)
PDN.......... Partnerships Data Net   (EA)
PDN.......... Petition Denied
PDN.......... Port Heiden, AK [*Location identifier*] [*FAA*]   (FAAL)
PDN.......... Prednisone [*Also, P, Pr, Pred, Pro*] [*Antineoplastic drug*] [*Endocrinology*]
PDN.......... Problem Documentation Number   (AAG)
PDN.......... Production   (AFM)
PDN.......... Properly Driven Net
PDN.......... Public Data Network [*Packet-switching network*] [*British Telecommunications PLC*] [*London*]
PDN.......... Putnam Diversified Premium [*NYSE symbol*]   (SPSG)
PDNC........ Presidents' Day National Committee   (EA)
PDNPD...... Physica D. Nonlinear Phenomena [*A publication*]
PD/NSC.... Presidential Directives/National Security Council
PDO.......... Philips & Du Pont Optical Co. [*Wilmington, DE*]
PDO.......... Postman's Delivery Office   (DCTA)
PDO.......... Printer Direction Optimizer   (BUR)
PD-O......... Program Directive - Operations   (KSC)
PDO.......... Property Disposal Officer [*Army*]
PdO........... Psychopathic Deviate Obvious [*Psychology*]
PDO.......... Publications Distribution Officer [*Military*]
PDoB .... Bucks County Free Library, Doylestown, PA [*Library symbol*] [*Library of Congress*]   (LCLS)
PDoBHi..... Bucks County Historical Society, Doylestown, PA [*Library symbol*] [*Library of Congress*]   (LCLS)
PDOC........ Particulate and/or Dissolved Organic Carbon [*Chemistry*]
PDOC........ Proceed Directly on Course [*Aviation*]   (FAAC)
PDOD....... Phytoplankton Dissolved Oxygen Deficit [*Oceanography*]
PDOIS....... People's Democratic Organisation for Independence and Socialism [*Senegambia*] [*Political party*]
PDOL .... Publishers Discount Option List
PDoN........ Delaware Valley College of Science and Agriculture, Doylestown, PA [*Library symbol*] [*Library of Congress*]   (LCLS)
PDOP .... Position Dilution of Precision
PDOS .... Parent Diabetes Opinion Survey [*Test*]
PDowN ..... Newcomen Society in North America, Downingtown, PA [*Library symbol*] [*Library of Congress*]   (LCLS)
PDP .... Packaging Development Plan
PDP .... Pakistan Democratic Party [*Political party*]   (PD)
PDP .... Parallel Distributed Processing [*A simulation of mental processes*]
PDP .... Parker/Parsley Development LP [*AMEX symbol*]   (SPSG)
PDP .... Parliamentary Democratic Party [*Burma*] [*Political party*]
PdP .... Parola del Popolo [*A publication*]
PDP .... Parti Democrate Populaire [*Popular Democratic Party*] [*France*] [*Political party*]   (PPE)
PDP .... Partido Democrata Popular [*Popular Democratic Party*] [*Spain*] [*Political party*]   (PPW)
PDP .... Partido Democrata Popular [*Popular Democratic Party*] [*Dominican Republic*] [*Political party*]   (PPW)
PDP .... Partido da Direita Portuguesa [*Party of the Portuguese Right*] [*Political party*]   (PPE)
PDP .... Partito Democratico Populare [*Popular Democratic Party*] [*San Marino*] [*Political party*]   (PPE)
PDP .... Payload Distribution Panel [*NASA*]   (MCD)
PDP .... Pentadecylphenol [*Organic chemistry*]
PDP .... People's Democratic Party [*Sudanese*]
PDP .... Personal Development Program   (MCD)
PDP .... Philadelphia, PA [*Location identifier*] [*FAA*]   (FAAL)
PDP .... Philippine Democratic Party [*Pilipino Lakas Ng Bayan*] [*Political party*]   (PPW)
PDP .... Pilot District Project [*Office of Economic Opportunity*] [*Defunct*]   (EA)
PDP .... Pitch-Depitch   (AAG)
PDP .... Planning Development Program   (OICC)
PDP .... Plasma Diagnostics Package [*NASA*]
PDP .... Plasma Display Panel [*Data processing*]

PDP .... Plasma Display Processor [*Data processing*]
PDP .... Popular Democratic Party [*Puerto Rico*] [*Political party*]
PDP .... Positive Displacement Pump
PDP .... Post Detection Processor [*Military*]   (CAAL)
PDP .... Post-Drug Potentiation
PDP .... Post-Insertion Deorbit Preparation [*NASA*]   (MCD)
PDP .... Power Distribution Panel
PDP .... Preliminary Definition Plan   (NASA)
PDP .... Preliminary Design Phase
PDP .... Preliminary Design Proposal   (MCD)
PDP .... Present-Day Primers [*A publication*]
PDP .... Pressure Distribution Panel   (AAG)
PDP .... Principal Display Panel [*Packaging*]
PDP .... Procedure Definition Processor [*Data processing*]
PDP .... Process Development Pile NE
PDP .... Procurement Data Package [*Military*]   (AABC)
PDP .... Production Data Package   (MCD)
PDP .... Professional Development Program [*Military*]
PDP .... Program Decision Package [*Military*]
PDP .... Program Definition Phase [*Army*]
PDP .... Program Development Paper   (MCD)
PDP .... Program Development Plan [*NASA*]
PDP .... Programmed Data Processor
PDP .... Programmed Digital Processor
PDP .... Progressive Democratic Party [*St. Vincent*] [*Political party*]   (PPW)
PDP .... Progressive Democratic Party [*Montserrat*] [*Political party*]   (PPW)
PDP .... Project Definition Phase   (NRCH)
PDP .... Project Development Plan
PDP .... Punta Del Este [*Uruguay*] [*Airport symbol*]   (OAG)
PDPA......... People's Democratic Party of Afghanistan [*Political party*]   (PPW)
PDPA........ Production Pattern   (AAG)
PDPC........ Plant Diversity Protection Committee [*Total Environmental Centre, Sydney*] [*Australia*]
PDPC........ Position Display Parallax Corrected
PDPC........ Post Detection Pulse Compression [*Military*]   (CAAL)
PDPF........ Packet Data Processing Facility   (MCD)
PDPGM...... Past Deputy Provincial Grand Master [*Freemasonry*]
PDPM .... Preliminary Draft Presidential Memo
PDPOA ...... Proposal Directive Plan of Action   (MCD)
PDPR........ Pandick Press [*NASDAQ symbol*]   (NQ)
PDPR........ Present-Day Preachers [*A publication*]
PDPRA ..... Plastics Design and Processing [*A publication*]
PDPS......... Parts Data Processing System [*Bell Telephone*]
PDPS .... Program Data Processing Section   (AAG)
PDPS .... Program Definition Phase Studies [*Navy*]
PDPS .... Project Data Processing System
PDPT........ Parti Democratique des Populations Togolaises [*Togolese Democratic People's Party*] [*Political party*]
PDPUB...... Pedicel Pubescence [*Botany*]
PDPVF ...... Presidential and Democratic Party Victory Fund   (EA)
PDQ.......... Packages Delivered Quick [*Allegheny Airlines service*]
PDQ.......... Parental Diagnostic Questionnaire [*Speech evaluation test*]
PDQ........... Parodies Done Quirkily [*Humorous translation of Peter Schickele's PDQ Bach*]
PDQ.......... PDQ Air Charter, Inc. [*Pontiac, MI*] [*FAA designator*]   (FAAC)
PDQ.......... [*Javier*] Perez De Cuellar [*Peruvian diplomat*] [*Initialism is derived from the pronunciation of his last name*]
PDQ.......... Permanent Durable Quality [*Paper*]
PDQ.......... Personal Description Questionnaire
PDQ.......... Pertinent Data Quest   (MCD)
PDQ.......... Photo Data Quantizer
PDQ.......... Physician's Data Query [*NIH*]
PDQ.......... Please Draw Quickly [*Initialism used as title of TV series*]
PDQ.......... Point, Digital, Qualifier [*In automobile name Opel PDQ*]
PDQ.......... Prescreening Developmental Questionnaire [*Child development test*]
PDQ.......... Pretty Damn Quick
PDQ.......... Price and Delivery Quotations
PDQ.......... Prime Motor Inns [*NYSE symbol*]   (SPSG)
PDQ.......... Programmed Data Quantizer
PDQ.......... Protocol Data Query [*Database*] [*National Institutes of Health*]
PDQC........ Physicians Data Query: Cancer Information File [*Database*]
PDQD........ Physicians Data Query: Directory File [*Database*]
PDQP........ Physicians Data Query: Protocol File [*Database*]
PDR .... Page Data Register
PDR .... Pakistan Development Review [*A publication*]
PDR .... Peak Dose Rate [*Radiation*]   (AAG)
PDR .... Pediatric Radiology [*Medical specialty*]   (DHSM)
PDR .... Periscope Depth Range [*SONAR*]
PDR .... Periscope Detection RADAR   (NG)
PDR .... Peter De Ridder Press Publications [*A publication*]
PDR .... Pharma-Dokumentationsring [*Pharma Documentation Ring*] [*Information service or system*]   (IID)
PDR .... Phase Data Recorder   (KSC)
PDR .... Phase Delay Rectifier
PDR .... Philippine Defense Ribbon [*Military decoration*]
PDR .... Physicians' Desk Reference [*Also, an information service or system*] [*A publication*]

PDR............	Pilot's Display Recorder
PDR............	Piskei Din Shel Batei ha-Din ha-Rabaniyim be-Yisrael (BJA)
PDR............	Plant Disease Reporter [A publication]
PDR............	Plasma-Developed Resist Processing [Lithography]
PD & R......	Policy Development and Research
PDR............	Position Distribution Report [DoD]
PDR............	Pounder (MSA)
PDR............	Powder
PDR............	Power Directional Relay
PDR............	Precision Depth Recorder
PDR............	Predetection Recording
PDR............	Predetermined Demand Rate
PDR............	Preferential Departure Route [Aviation] (FAAC)
PDR............	Preliminary Data Report
PDR............	Preliminary Data Requirements (NASA)
PDR............	Preliminary Design Report (NRCH)
PDR............	Preliminary Design Review (NASA)
PDR............	Pressurized Deuterium Reactor [Nuclear energy]
P & DR......	Price and Delivery Request
PDR2...........	Price Description Record [Data processing] (IBMDP)
PDR............	Priority Data Reduction
PDR............	Process Dynamics Recorder
PDR............	Processed Data Recorder
PDR............	Processing Data Rate (IEEE)
PDR............	Procurement Data Reference
PDR............	Product Design Review [Army]
PDR............	Program Design Review (MCD)
PDR............	Program Director's Review [NASA] (NASA)
PDR............	Program Discrepancy Report (IEEE)
PDR............	Program Document Requirement (BUR)
PDR............	Program Drum Recording
PDR............	Proliferative Diabetic Retinopathy [Ophthalmology]
PDR............	Public Document Room (NRCH)
PDR............	Publications Data Request
PDR............	Pulse Doppler RADAR
PDR............	Pulse Duty Ratio
PDRA	Professional Drag Racing Association (EA)
PDRC.........	Clinical Research Center for Periodontal Disease [University of Florida] [Research center] (RCD)
PDRC.........	Personnel Despatch and Reception Centre [British military] (DMA)
PDRC.........	Peter Duel Remembrance Club (EA)
PDRC.........	Poultry Disease Research Center [University of Georgia] [Research center] (RCD)
PDRC.........	Preliminary Design Review Commercial (MCD)
PDRC.........	Pressure Difference Recording Controller
PDRC.........	Professional Development and Recruitment Career Program [Military]
PDRC.........	Program Development Review Committee [Navy] (CAAL)
PDRD	Procurement Data Requirements Document (NASA)
PDRE.........	People's Democratic Republic of Ethiopia
PDRF.........	Passive Defense Recovery Force (MUGU)
PDRF.........	Presbyterians for Democracy and Religious Freedom (EA)
PDRH........	Partido Democratico Revolucionario Hondureno [Revolutionary Democratic Party of Honduras] [Political party]
PDRI..........	Publications. Diaspora Research Institute [A publication]
PdRK	Pesikta de-Rav Kahana (BJA)
PDRL........	Permanent Disability Retired List
PDRL........	Procurement Data Requirements List (NASA)
PDRM	Payload Deployment and Retrieval Mechanism [NASA]
PDRM	Post-Depositional Remanent Magnetization [Geophysics]
PDRM	Postdetrital Remanent Magnetization [Geophysics]
PDRMA	Portable Drilling Rig Manufacturers Association [Defunct] (EA)
PDRP........	Program Data Requirement Plan [Nuclear Regulatory Commission] (NRCH)
PD & RS	Payload Deployment and Retrieval Subsystem [NASA] (NASA)
PDRSTA ...	Payload Deployment and Retrieval System Test Article [NASA] (NASA)
PDRY	People's Democratic Republic of Yemen [Political party]
PDS............	Auburn/Lewiston, ME [Location identifier] [FAA] (FAAL)
PDS............	Package Data System (NASA)
PDS............	Packet Data Satellites [Telecommunications] (TSSD)
PDS............	Paid-during-Service [Billing]
PDS............	Parkinson's Disease Society [British]
PDS............	Paroxysmal Depolarizing Shift [Physiology]
PDS............	Parti Democratique Senegalais [Senegalese Democratic Party] [Political party] (PPW)
PDS............	Partido Democrata Socialista [Socialist Democratic Party] [Panama] [Political party] (PPW)
PDS............	Partitioned Data Set [or System] [Data processing] (NASA)
PDS............	Partito di Democrazia Socialista [Socialist Democracy Party] [San Marino] [Political party] (PPW)
PDS............	Party of Democratic Socialism [German Democratic Republic] [Political party]
PDS............	Passive Detection System (NVT)
PDS............	Pediatric Surgery [Medical specialty] (DHSM)
PDS............	Penultimate Digit Storage [Telecommunications] (TEL)
PDS............	Performer Design Sheet

PDS............	Perimeter Defense System (MCD)
PDS............	Permanent Duty Station [Air Force] (AFM)
PDS............	Perry Drug Stores, Inc. [NYSE symbol] (SPSG)
PDS............	Personal Development Study [Psychology]
PDS............	Personnel Daily Summary [Army] (AABC)
PDS............	Personnel Data Summary (FAAC)
PDS............	Personnel Data System [Air Force]
PDS............	Personnel Decontamination Station (MCD)
PDS............	Personnel Delivery System
PDS............	Petroleum Data System [University of Oklahoma] [Databank] (IID)
PDS............	Petroleum Data System [Petroleum Information Corp.] [Information service or system] (IID)
PDS............	Pharma-Dokumentations-Service [Pharma Documentation Service] [Information service or system] (IID)
PDS............	Phased Development Shuttle [NASA] (KSC)
PDS............	Photo-Digital Store
PDS............	Photodischarge Spectroscopy (MCD)
PDS............	Photothermal Deflection Spectroscopy
PDS............	Planning Data Sheet (KSC)
PDS............	Planning Data Systems [Information service or system] (IID)
PDS............	Plant Data System [Nuclear energy] (NRCH)
PDS............	Plasma-Derived Serum
PDS............	Plasma Display (MCD)
PDS............	Pneumatic Distribution System
PDS............	Polydimethylsiloxane [Organic chemistry]
PDS............	Polydioxanone [Organic chemistry]
PDS............	Portable Data System (MCD)
PDS............	Portable Duress Sensor (MCD)
PDS............	Position-Determining System
PDS............	Post Design Services [British] (RDA)
PDS............	Power Density Spectra (IEEE)
PDS............	Power Distribution System [or Subsystem]
PDS-.........	Power Drive System
PDS............	Preadsorb-Dilute-Shake [Phage growth method]
PDS............	Predocketed Special Project (NRCH)
PDS............	Preliminary Draft Standards [for special libraries in Australia]
PDS............	Priority Distribution System [Military] (AFM)
PDS............	Prisoner Detention System
PDS............	Private Database Service [Australia]
PDS............	Probability Distribution Subprogram [Data processing] (BUR)
PDS............	Problem Data System (MCD)
PD/S..........	Problem Definition/Solution
PDS............	Problem Descriptor System
PDS............	Procedures Development Simulator (KSC)
PDS............	Processor Direct Slot [Data processing]
PDS............	Procurement Data Sheet
PDS............	Product Design Standard
PDS............	Production Data Sheet (MCD)
PDS............	Program Data Sheets [Army] (AABC)
PDS............	Program Data Source (BUR)
PDS............	Program Design Specification (CAAL)
PDS............	Program Development Specialist
PDS............	Program Development System [Data processing]
PDS............	Program Distribution System
PDS............	Programmable Data Station [or System]
PDS............	Propellant Dispersion System (MCD)
PdS............	Psychopathic Deviate Subtle [Psychology]
PDS............	Pulse Doppler Seeker
PDS............	Punch Driver Selectric
PDS............	Purchasing Department Specification (MSA)
PDSA.........	People's Dispensary for Sick Animals [British]
PDS-A	Personnel Data System - Airmen [Air Force]
PDSA.........	Predesign and Systems Analysis [NASA] (KSC)
PDS-A(I)...	Personnel Data System - Airmen (Interim) [Air Force] (AFM)
PDS-C.......	Personnel Data System - Civilian [Air Force] (AFM)
PDSC.........	Pressure Differential Scanning Calorimetry [Analytical technique]
PDSC.........	Publishers Data Service Corporation [Monterey, CA]
PDSD........	Point Detonating Self-Destroying [Projectile]
PDSDD......	Plotting Display Subchannel Data Distributor (MCD)
PDSE.........	Production Sample (AAG)
P & DSEC ...	Pioneer and Demolition Section [Army]
PDSI	Palmer Drought Severity Index [Meteorology]
PDSI	Performance Data Services, Incorporated [Falls Church, VA] [Software manufacturer]
PDSI	Portable Digital Strain Indicator
PDSK........	Petroleum Distribution System - Korea [Army] (MCD)
PDSM........	Powder Diffraction Search-Match System [International Data Center]
PDS/MAGEN ...	Problem Descriptor System/Matrix Generation [Programming language] [1965] (CSR)
PDSMS	Point Defense Surface Missile System
PDS-O	Personnel Data System - Officers [Air Force] (AFM)
PDSOF	Public Domain Software on File [Facts on File, Inc.] [Information service or system] (IID)
PDSP.........	Personnel Data System - Planning [Air Force] (AFM)
PDSPI.......	Polyurethane Division, Society of the Plastics Industry (EA)
PDSQ........	Point Detonating Super-Quick Fuze (NATG)
PDS-R.......	Parti Democratique Senegalais - Renovation [Senegalese Democratic Party - Reform] [Political party]

PDSS .... Physical Disabilities Special Interest Section [*American Occupational Therapy Association*]
PDSS .... Post-Deployment Software System (MCD)
PDST .... Pacific Daylight Saving Time (KSC)
PDSTT ...... Pulse Doppler Single Target Track [*Military*] (CAAL)
PDT .... Pacific Daylight Time
PDT .... Panoramic Design Technique
PDT .... Parallel Data Transmission
PdT .... Parti du Travail [*Labor Party*] [*Switzerland*] [*Political party*] (PPE)
PDT .... Partido Democratico Trabalhista [*Democratic Labour Party*] [*Political party*] (EAIO)
PDT .... Patriot Premium Dividend, Inc. II [*NYSE symbol*] (SPSG)
Pd T .... Pedagogisk Tidskrift [*A publication*]
PDT .... Pendleton [*Oregon*] [*Airport symbol*] (OAG)
PDT .... Performance Demonstration Test
PDT .... Personal Data Transmitter [*From the movie "Aliens"*]
PDT .... Photodynamic Therapy [*Oncology*]
PDT .... Planned Data to Transportation [*DoD*]
PDT .... Plasma Display Terminal [*Data processing*]
PDT .... Pollable Data Terminal [*Bell System*]
PDT .... Population Doubling Time [*Cytology*]
PDT .... Posting Data Transfer [*Air Force*] (AFM)
PDT .... Power Distribution Trailer (NATG)
PDT .... Predelivery Test (MCD)
PDT .... Predictor Display Technique
PDT .... President Mines [*Vancouver Stock Exchange symbol*]
PDT .... Proceedings. European Society of Drug Toxicity [*Elsevier Book Series*] [*A publication*]
PDT .... Processed Directional Transmission [*Military*] (NVT)
PDT .... Programmable Data Terminal [*Digital Equipment Corp.*] (IEEE)
PDT .... Pulse Delay Time
PDT .... (Pyridyl)diphenyltriazine [*Analytical chemistry*]
PDT-1 .... Picatinny Arsenal Detonation Trap Number 1 [*Army*] (AABC)
3PDT .... Triple-Pole, Double-Throw [*Switch*] (MUGU)
4PDT .... Four-Pole, Double-Throw [*Switch*]
PDTA .... Production Tape (AAG)
PDTA .... Professional Dance Teachers Association (EA)
PDTA .... Propylenediaminetetraacetic Acid [*Organic chemistry*]
PDTC........ Philadelphia Depository Trust Company
PDTF......... Program Development and Test Facility [*Social Security Administration*]
PDTMR..... Phalloidin Tetramethylrhodamine [*Biochemistry*]
PDTNBH .. Paediatrician [*A publication*]
PDTP........ Plasma Display Touch Panel [*Data processing*]
PDTRDV.... Pediatria [*Buenos Aires*] [*A publication*]
PDTS........ Program Development Tracking System [*Data processing*]
PDTS........ Programmable Data Terminal Set [*Military*] (CAAL)
PDT & T... Post-Delivery Test and Trials [*Military*] (CAAL)
PDTTT...... Post-Delivery Test and Trial Team (MCD)
PDU........ Pacific Democrat Union (EAIO)
PDU.......... Parti Dahomeen de l'Unite [*Dahomean Unity Party*] [*Benin*] [*Political party*]
PDU.......... Parti Democrate Unifie [*Unified Democratic Party*] [*Name replaced by Section Voltaique de Rassemblement*] [*Upper Volta*] [*Political party*]
PDU.......... Paysandu [*Uruguay*] [*Airport symbol*] (OAG)
PDU.......... Phase Demodulation Unit
PDU.......... Photomultiplier Detector Unit (KSC)
PDU.......... Pilot's Display Unit (MCD)
PDU.......... Power Distribution Unit (AAG)
PDU.......... Power Drive Unit (MCD)
PDU.......... Pressure Distribution Unit
PDU.......... Process Demonstration Unit [*Chemical engineering*]
PDU.......... Process Development Unit [*Chemical engineering*]
PDU.......... Production Distribution Unit (AAG)
PDU.......... Programmable Delay Unit
PDU.......... Programmable Diagnostic Unit [*TACOM*] [*Army*] (RDA)
PDU.......... Project Development Unit [*Chemical engineering*]
PDU.......... Projection Display Unit
PDU.......... Protocol Data Unit
PDU.......... Pulse Detection Unit (NASA)
PDUFC...... Pete Duel Universal Friendship Club (EAIO)
PdUP .... Partito di Unita Proletaria per il Comunismo [*Democratic Party of Proletarian Unity for Communism*] [*Italy*] [*Political party*] (PPE)
PDur .... Papyri Durani (BJA)
PDUR .... Predischarge Utilization Review [*Medicine*]
PDV .... Parcel Delivery Van
PDV .... Phocine Distemper Virus
PDV .... Polyhedra Derived Virus
PDV .... Ponderosa Ventures, Inc. [*Vancouver Stock Exchange symbol*]
PDV .... Premodulation Processor - Deep Space - Voice
PDV .... Pressure Disconnect Valve (MCD)
PDV .... Probability of Detection and Verification [*Military*] (CAAL)
PDV .... Prune Dwarf Virus
PDVN .... Power-Driven
PDW .... Evansville, IN [*Location identifier*] [*FAA*] (FAAL)
PDW .... Personal Defense Weapon [*Army*] (INF)
PDW .... Platelet Distribution Width [*Hematology*]

PDW .... Priority Delayed Weather [*Aviation*] (FAAC)
PDWHF .... Platelet-Derived Wound-Healing Factor [*Biochemistry*]
PDX .... Passive Dosimeter Experiment (KSC)
PDX .... Place Decrement in Index
PDX .... Poloidal Divertor Experiment [*Princeton University*]
PDX .... Portland [*Oregon*] [*Airport symbol*] (OAG)
PDX .... Prado Explorations Ltd. [*Toronto Stock Exchange symbol*]
PDX .... Private Digital Exchange
PDY .... Piccadilly Resources Ltd. [*Vancouver Stock Exchange symbol*]
PDY .... Principal Duty [*Military*]
PDZ .... Ontario, CA [*Location identifier*] [*FAA*] (FAAL)
PDZ .... Pedernales [*Venezuela*] [*Airport symbol*] (OAG)
PdZ .... Perspektiven der Zukunft [*A publication*]
PDZBDD... Publicaciones. Departamento de Zoologia [*Barcelona*] [*A publication*]
PDZI........ Przeglad Zachodni [*A publication*]
PDZRA..... Prace Dzialu Zywenia Roslin i Nawozenia [*A publication*]
PE .... British Aircraft Corp. Ltd. [*ICAO aircraft manufacturer identifier*] (ICAO)
PE .... Easton Area Public Library, Easton, PA [*Library symbol*] [*Library of Congress*] (LCLS)
PE .... Ice Pellets [*Meteorology*]
PE .... Pacific Electric Railway [*AAR code*]
PE .... Packaging Engineering [*A publication*]
PE .... Page-End Character [*Data processing*]
PE .... Parabolic Equation
PE .... Parity Error
PE .... Partes Aequales [*Equal Parts*] [*Pharmacy*]
PE .... Patrol Vessel, Eagle [*Eagle boat*] [*Navy symbol*] [*Obsolete*]
PE .... Peacetime Establishment [*Military*] (NATG)
Pe .... Peclet Number [*IUPAC*]
PE .... Pectinesterase [*Also, PME*] [*An enzyme*]
Pe .... Pelagius [*Deceased, 1232*] [*Authority cited in pre-1607 legal work*] (DSA)
PE .... Pennsylvania English [*A publication*]
Pe .... Pentyl [*Biochemistry*]
PE .... Percussionist [*A publication*]
PE .... Period Ending
PE .... Periodic (AAG)
PE .... Peripheral Equipment (AAG)
PE .... Periscope
PE .... Peritoneal Exudate [*Medicine*]
PE .... Perkin Elmer Corp.
PE .... Permanent Echo [*RADAR*]
PE .... Permissible Error (ADA)
PE .... Perry Ellis [*Fashion designer, 1940-86*]
PE .... Persistent Estrus [*Endocrinology*]
PE .... Personal Effects
PE .... Personnel, Enlisted [*or Enlisted Personnel Division*] [*Coast Guard*]
PE .... Personnel Equipment [*Air Force*] (AFM)
PE .... Personnel Equivalent [*DoD*]
PE .... Personnel Executive [*A publication*]
pe............ Peru [*MARC country of publication code*] [*Library of Congress*] (LCCP)
PE .... Peru [*ANSI two-letter standard code*] (CNC)
PE .... Petroleum Economist [*London*] [*A publication*] (BJA)
PE .... Petroleum Engineer
Pe .... Petrus de Bellapertica [*Deceased, 1308*] [*Authority cited in pre-1607 legal work*] (DSA)
Pe .... Petrus Hispanus [*Authority cited in pre-1607 legal work*] (DSA)
PE .... Pharmacopaeia Edinensis [*Edinburgh Pharmacopoeia*] [*A publication*] (ROG)
PE .... Pharyngoesophageal [*Medicine*]
PE .... Phase Encoding [*Magnetic tape recording*] [*Data processing*] (MDG)
PE .... Phenylephrine
PE .... Philadelphia Electric Co. [*NYSE symbol*] (SPSG)
PE .... Philippine Educator [*A publication*]
PE .... Phoenix Air Service GmbH, Munchen [*West Germany*] [*ICAO designator*] (FAAC)
PE .... Phosphatidylethanolamine [*Biochemistry*]
PE .... Photoelectric
PE .... Photoemission [*Physics*]
PE .... Photon Echo [*Spectroscopy*]
PE .... Phycoerythrin [*Biochemistry*]
PE .... Physical Education
PE .... Physical Examination
PE .... Physiological Ecology
PE .... Pictorial Eleven [*Later, PES*] [*An association*] (EA)
PE .... Pigment Epithelium [*of the retina*]
P & E.......... Pike and Eel [*A pub at Cambridge University*] [*British*] (DSUE)
PE .... Pilot Error
PE .... Pinion End
PE .... Pistol Expert
PE .... Planetary Explorer [*NASA*]
PE .... Planification de l'Emploi [*Canadian Jobs Strategy - CJS*]
P/E............ Planning Economics Group, Boston [*Information service or system*] (IID)

PE	Planning Estimate
P & E	Planning and Estimating (AAG)
PE	Plant Engineering (AAG)
PE	Plant Equipment (MCD)
PE	Plasma Emission [*Spectrophotometry*]
PE	Plasma Exchange [*Medicine*]
PE	Plastic Explosive (NATG)
PE	Pleural Effusion [*Medicine*]
PE	Poesia Espanola [*A publication*]
PE	Politique Etrangere [*A publication*]
PE	Pollen Equivalent [*Immunology*]
PE	Polyelectrolyte [*Organic chemistry*]
PE	Polyethylene [*Organic chemistry*]
PE	Porcelain Enamel [*Technical drawings*]
PE	Port of Embarkation [*Military*]
P of E	Port of Embarkation [*Military*]
P of E	Portal of Entry [*Bacteriology*]
PE	Position Effect [*Parapsychology*]
PE	Position Error
PE	Post Engineer [*Army*] (AABC)
PE	Post Exchange [*Marine Corps*]
PE	Postexposure [*Medicine*]
PE	Potato Eaters (EA)
PE	Potential Energy
PE	Potential Excess [*of stock*] [*DoD*]
PE	Powdered Extract [*Pharmacy*]
PE	Practical Exercise
PE	Pre-Eclampsia [*Medicine*]
PE	Pre-Emption [*Telecommunications*] (TEL)
P-E	Precipitation-Evaporation
PE	Preliminary Evaluation
PE	Preliminary Exploitation (MCD)
PE	Presiding Elder
PE	Pressure Enclosure (MCD)
Pe	Pressure on Expiration [*Medicine*]
P/E.............	Price [*or Profit*]/Earnings Ratio [*Relation between price of a company's stock and its annual net income*]
PE	Priced Exhibit (MCD)
PE	Primary Electricity
PE	Prime Equipment
PE	Primitive Endoderm [*Cytology*]
PE	Primitive Equation
PE	Prince Edward Island [*Canadian province*] [*Postal code*]
PE	Principal Engineer (AAG)
PE	Printer's Error
P & E	Privileges and Elections Subcommittee [*US Senate*]
PE	Probable Error [*Statistics*]
PE	Problems of Economics [*A publication*]
PE	Procedures Evaluation [*DoD*]
PE	Processing Element [*of central processing unit*]
PE	Procurement Executive [*British*]
P & E	Procurement and Expedition
PE	Production Engineering
PE	Production Executive [*British*]
PE	Professional Education (AFM)
PE	Professional Engineer
P/E.............	Professional and Executive [*Employment register*] [*British*]
PE	Program Element (AFM)
PE	Program Evaluation (OICC)
PE	Programmed Exciter
PE	Project Engineer
PE	Project Equality (EA)
PE	Prometheus-Europe [*Paris, France*] (EAIO)
P & E	Proof and Experimental [*Australian Army*]
P & E	Propellants and Explosives [*Military*] (AABC)
PE	Proponent Evaluation (MCD)
PE	Protect Enable [*Data processing*] (PCM)
PE	Protected Environment
PE	Protestant Episcopal
PE	Proteus Engine [*Hovercraft*]
PE	Proton Event
PE	Pulley End
PE	Pulmonary Edema [*Medicine*]
PE	Pulmonary Effusion [*Medicine*]
PE	Pulmonary Embolism [*Medicine*]
PE	Pulse Echo [*Materials research*]
PE	Pulse Encoding [*Data processing*]
PE	Punta Europa [*A publication*]
PE	Purchased Equipment
PE	Pyroelectric
P & E	Pyrotechnical and Explosive [*NASA*] (KSC)
Pe	Warner-Lambert Pharmaceutical Co. [*Research code symbol*]
2PE	Two-Pulse Photon Echo [*Spectroscopy*]
PEA	Papillary Eccrine Adenoma [*Oncology*]
PEA	Pattern Error Analysis
PEA	Patterson Experimental Array (MCD)
PEA	Payload Enclosure Assembly (MCD)
Pea	Peake's English Nisi Prius Reports [*1790-1812*] [*A publication*] (DLA)
PEA	Pella, IA [*Location identifier*] [*FAA*] (FAAL)
PEA	Penneshaw [*Australia*] [*Airport symbol*] (OAG)

PEA	Phenethyl Alcohol [*Organic chemistry*]
PEA	Phenylethylamine [*Biochemistry*]
PEA	Phosphoethanolamine [*Organic chemistry*]
PE(A)........	Physical Education (Association) [*British*]
PEA	Pilot's Employment Agency
PEA	Pitch Error Amplifier
PEA	Plant Engineering Agency
PEA	Plastics Engineers Association [*Defunct*] (EA)
PEA	Platform Electronics Assembly (KSC)
PEA	Poly(ethyl Acrylate) [*Organic chemistry*]
PEA	Portuguese East Africa [*Mozambique*]
PEA	Potash Export Association (EA)
PEA	Primary Expense Account
PEA	Private Employment Agency (OICC)
PEA	Process Environmental Analysis
PEA	Process Equipment Accessory (MCD)
PEA	Program Element Administrator [*Navy*] (NG)
PEA	Progressive Education Association [*Defunct*]
PEA	Provincial Electricity Authority [*Thailand*] (DS)
PEA	Public Education Association
PEA	Push-Effective Address [*Data processing*] (IEEE)
PEA	Pyridylethylamine [*Organic chemistry*]
Pea (2)........	Peake's Additional Cases Nisi Prius [*170 English Reprint*] [*1795-1812*] [*A publication*] (DLA)
PEAA........	Program Elements Activity Accounts (MCD)
P/EA(A)3 ..	Probationary Electrical Artificer (Air) 3rd Class [*British military*] (DMA)
Pea Add Cas ...	Peake's English Nisi Prius Reports [*Vol. 2*] [*A publication*] (DLA)
PEABA......	Petroleum Abstracts [*A publication*]
Peab L Rev ...	Peabody Law Review [*A publication*] (DLA)
Peabody J E ...	Peabody Journal of Education [*A publication*]
Peabody J Ed ...	Peabody Journal of Education [*A publication*]
Peabody J Educ ...	Peabody Journal of Education [*A publication*]
Peabody Mus Nat Hist Yale Univ Bull ...	Peabody Museum of Natural History. Yale University. Bulletin [*A publication*]
PEAC........	Photoelectric Auto Collimator
PEAC........	Photoelectroanalytical Chemistry
PEACA......	Progress in Nuclear Energy. Series 9 [*A publication*]
Peace..........	Peace Newsletter [*A publication*]
Peace..........	Peace/Non-Violence [*A publication*]
PEACE	People Emerging Against Corrupt Establishments [*Underground military newspaper*]
PEACE	Project Evaluation and Assistance, Civil Engineering [*Air Force*]
Peacemak...	Peacemaker [*A publication*]
Peace Nws ...	Peace News [*A publication*]
PeaceResAb ..	Peace Research Abstracts [*A publication*]
Peace Res Ja ...	Peace Research in Japan [*A publication*]
Peace Res Rev ...	Peace Research Reviews [*A publication*]
PEACESAT ...	Pan-Pacific Education and Communication Experiments by Satellites [*University of Hawaii*] [*NASA*]
Peace and Sci ...	Peace and the Sciences [*A publication*]
Peace Science Soc Internat Pas ...	Peace Science Society. International Papers [*A publication*]
PEACU......	Plastic Energy Absorption in Compression Unit (IEEE)
PEAD	Presidential Emergency Action Document
PEADS	Presidential Emergency Action Direction System (MCD)
Peake	Peake's Cases [*1790-1812*] [*A publication*] (DLA)
Peake Add Cas ...	Peake's Additional Cases Nisi Prius [*1795-1812*] [*A publication*] (DLA)
Peake Ev	Peake on the Law of Evidence [*A publication*] (DLA)
Peake NP...	Peake's English Nisi Prius Cases [*170 English Reprint*] [*A publication*] (DLA)
Peake NP Add Cas ...	Peake's Additional Cases Nisi Prius [*170 English Reprint*] [*England*] [*A publication*] (DLA)
Peake NP Add Cas (Eng) ...	Peake's Additional Cases Nisi Prius [*170 English Reprint*] [*England*] [*A publication*] (DLA)
Peake NP Cas ...	Peake's English Nisi Prius Cases [*170 English Reprint*] [*1790-1812*] [*A publication*] (DLA)
Peake NP Cas (Eng) ...	Peake's English Nisi Prius Cases [*170 English Reprint*] [*A publication*] (DLA)
PEAL........	Petro-Global, Inc. [*NASDAQ symbol*] (NQ)
PEAL........	Publishing, Entertainment, Advertising, and Allied Fields Law Quarterly [*A publication*]
PEALQ......	Publishing, Entertainment, Advertising, and Allied Fields Law Quarterly [*A publication*]
PEAM........	Personal Electronic Aid for Maintenance [*Military*]
Pea MS	Peachey on Marriage Settlements [*1860*] [*A publication*] (DLA)
PEAMUSE ...	Peabody Museum of Archaeology and Ethnology [*Harvard University*] [*Research center*] (RCD)
PEANA......	Proceedings. Easter School in Agricultural Science. University of Nottingham [*A publication*]
Pe de Ancar ...	Petrus de Ancharano [*Deceased, 1416*] [*Authority cited in pre-1607 legal work*] (DSA)
Pe de Anch ...	Petrus de Ancharano [*Deceased, 1416*] [*Authority cited in pre-1607 legal work*] (DSA)
Pe de Ancha ...	Petrus de Ancharano [*Deceased, 1416*] [*Authority cited in pre-1607 legal work*] (DSA)
Peanut J Nut World ...	Peanut Journal and Nut World [*A publication*]

Peanut Sci ... Peanut Science [*A publication*]
PEAP......... Pad Emergency Air Pack [*NASA*]　(KSC)
PEAP......... Parent Education and Assistance Project [*Australia*]
PEAP......... Pesticide Education and Action Project　(EA)
PEAP......... Principal Error Axis for Position
PEAP......... Program Evaluation Analysis Plan　(MCD)
PeAR......... Die Provinzeinteilung des Assyrischen Reiches [*A publication*]　(BJA)
Pearce CC .. Pearce's Reports in Dearsley's English Crown Cases [*A publication*]　(DLA)
Pearce-Sellards Ser Tex Mem Mus ... Pearce-Sellards Series. Texas Memorial Museum [*A publication*]
PEARL...... Committee for Public Education and Religious Liberty　(EA)
PEARL...... Performance Evaluation of Amplifiers from a Remote Location
PEARL...... Periodicals Automation, Rand Library
PEARL...... Personal Equipment and Rescue/Survivable Lowdown　(MCD)
PEARL...... Process and Experiment Automation Real-Time Language [*Data processing*]
PEARL...... Program for EPS [*Electrical Power System*] Analysis and Rapid Look-Ahead [*NASA computer program*]
PEARL...... Programmed Editor and Automated Resources for Learning
PEARLA ... Pupils Equal and React to Light and Accomodation [*Medicine*]
Pears......... Pearson's Reports [*1850-80*] [*Pennsylvania*] [*A publication*]　(DLA)
Pearson..... Pearson's Common Pleas [*Pennsylvania*] [*A publication*]　(DLA)
Pears (PA) ... Pearson's Reports [*1850-80*] [*Pennsylvania*] [*A publication*]　(DLA)
PEART...... Passive Electronic Advanced Receiver　(MCD)
PEAS........ Physical Estimation and Attraction Scales
PEAS........ Presbyterian Educational Association of the South [*Defunct*]　(EA)
Peasant Stud Newsl ... Peasant Studies Newsletter [*A publication*]
PEAT........ Phenylethanolaminotetralin [*Organic chemistry*]
PEAT........ Pricing Evaluation for Audit Technique [*Finance*]
PEAT........ Programme Elargi d'Assistance Technique [*Expanded Program of Technical Assistance*] [*United Nations*]
PEAT........ Programmer Exercised Autopilot Test　(AAG)
Peat Abstr ... Peat Abstracts [*A publication*]
Peat Plant Yearb ... Peat and Plant Yearbook [*A publication*]
PEAV......... Principal Error Axis for Velocity
PE B.......... Bachelor of Pedagogy　(ROG)
Pe B........... Bachelor of Pediatrics
PEB........... Parametric Empirical Bayes [*Statistics*]
PEB........... Pebble [*Jewelry*]　(ROG)
Peb .... Pebble [*A publication*]
PEB........... Pebble Gold Resources [*Vancouver Stock Exchange symbol*]
PEB........... Pensioners' Employment Bureau [*British*]
PEB........... Performance Evaluation Board [*NASA*]　(MCD)
PEB........... Philippine Economy Bulletin [*A publication*]
PEB........... Phycoerythrobilin [*Biochemistry*]
PEB........... Physical Evaluation Board [*Military*]
PEB........... Population-Environment Balance　(EA)
PEB........... Porcelain Enamel Bath [*Classified advertising*]　(ADA)
PEB........... Positive Expulsion Bladder
PEB........... Production Efficiency Board [*British*] [*World War II*]
PEB........... Propulsion Examining Board [*Navy*]　(NVT)
PEB........... Prototype Environmental Buoy [*Marine science*]　(MSC)
PEB........... Psycho-Educational Battery [*Educational test*]
PEB........... Pulmonary Ectopic Beat [*Cardiology*]
PEB........... Pulsed Electron Beam　(IEEE)
PEBA........ Polyether Block Amide [*Plastics technology*]
PEBA........ Pulsed Electron Beam Annealer [*Photovoltaic energy systems*]
PEBA........ Purified Extract of Brucella abortus
PEBAB ..... Para-(Ethoxybenzylidene)aminobenzonitrile [*Also, EBCA*] [*Organic chemistry*]
PEB & B ... Porcelain Enamel Bath and Basin [*Classified advertising*]　(ADA)
PEBB........ Public Employees Blanket Bond
PEBCO...... Port Elizabeth Black Civic Organization [*South Africa*]　(PD)
PEBCO...... Program Evaluation and Budget Committee [*American Library Association*]
PEBD........ Pay Entry Base Date
Pe de Bel ... Petrus de Bellapertica [*Deceased, 1308*] [*Authority cited in pre-1607 legal work*]　(DSA)
Pe de Belper ... Petrus de Bellapertica [*Deceased, 1308*] [*Authority cited in pre-1607 legal work*]　(DSA)
Pe de Bepe ... Petrus de Bellapertica [*Deceased, 1308*] [*Authority cited in pre-1607 legal work*]　(DSA)
PEBES....... Personal Earning and Benefit Estimate Statement [*Social Security Administration*]
PEBG........ Phenethylbiguanide [*Same as PEDG*] [*Antidiabetic compound*]
PEBH........ Physical Evaluation Board Hospital [*Military*]
PEBIDN.... Perspectives in Biometrics [*A publication*]
PEBK........ Peoples Bank [*Newton, NC*] [*NASDAQ symbol*]　(NQ)
PEBL........ Port Everglades Belt Line Railway [*AAR code*] [*Obsolete*]
PEBLO...... Physical Evaluation Board Liaison Officer [*Air Force*]　(AFM)
Pe de Blpti ... Petrus de Bellapertica [*Deceased, 1308*] [*Authority cited in pre-1607 legal work*]　(DSA)
PEBS .... Pulsed Electron Beam Source　(MCD)
PEBW........ People's Bancorp of Worcester, Inc. [*NASDAQ symbol*]　(NQ)

PEC........... Aero Sport [*Vancouver, WA*] [*FAA designator*]　(FAAC)
PEC........... American Irish Political Education Committee　(EA)
PEc............ Ellwood City Area Public Library, Ellwood City, PA [*Library symbol*] [*Library of Congress*]　(LCLS)
PEC........... IEEE Power Electronics Council　(EA)
PEC........... Pacific Command Electronic Intelligence Center　(MCD)
PEC........... Pacific Economic Community　(FEA)
PEC........... Palestine Economic Commission
PEC........... Panasonic Energy Corporation [*Vancouver Stock Exchange symbol*]
PEC........... Passive Equipment Cabinet [*Military*]　(CAAL)
PEC........... Peak Electrode Current
PEC........... Pectoral [*Lungs and Chest*] [*Medicine*]　(ROG)
PEC........... Pedal Excretory Cell
PEC........... Pelican [*Alaska*] [*Airport symbol*]　(OAG)
PEC........... Pennsylvania Engineering Corporation [*AMEX symbol*]　(SPSG)
PEC........... Perfil de Evaluacion del Comportamiento [*Standardized test of elementary through high school students' behavior at school, at home, and with peers*]
PEC........... Peritoneal Exudate Cells [*Hematology*]
PEC........... Perkin-Elmer Corporation　(MCD)
PEC........... Perris [*California*] [*Seismograph station code, US Geological Survey*]　(SEIS)
PEC........... Persistent Early Curvature
PEC........... Personal Effects Coverage [*Insurance*]
PEC........... Petro-Canada
PEC........... Phenylene Ether Copolymer [*Organic chemistry*]
PEC........... Photoelectric Cell
PEC........... Photoelectrochemical Cell [*Energy conversion device*]
PEC........... Physics, Engineering, and Chemistry　(AAG)
PEC........... Pigmented Emulsified Creosote
PEC........... Planetary Entry Capsule [*Aerospace*]
PEC........... Plant Equipment Codes [*DoD*]
PeC............ Poesia e Critica [*A publication*]
PEC........... Polish Economic News [*A publication*]
PEC........... Positive Engagement Clutch
PEC........... Potasse et Engrais Chimiques
PEC........... Potential Enviromental Concentration [*Pollution technology*]
PEC........... Predicted Environmental Concentration　(DCTA)
PEC........... Presbyterian Evangelical Coalition　(EA)
PEC........... Previous Element Coding
PEC........... Production Equipment Code [*Military*]
PEC........... Production Executive Committee
PEC........... Program Element Code　(AFM)
PEC........... Program Environment Control
PEC........... Program Evaluation Center [*Navy*]　(AFIT)
PEC........... Propulsion Environmental Chamber
PEC........... Prova Elementi Combustibili [*An Italian fast reactor*]
PEC........... Pugwash Etudiant du Canada
PEC........... Pyridylethylcysteine [*Biochemistry*]
PEC........... Pyrogenic Exotoxin C [*Medicine*]
PECA........ Petroleum Equipment Contractors Association　(EA)
Peca........... Petrus de Bellapertica [*Deceased, 1308*] [*Authority cited in pre-1607 legal work*]　(DSA)
PECAD4.... Pediatric Cardiology [*A publication*]
PECAM...... Platelet-Endothelial Cell Adhesion Molecule [*Cytology*]
PECAN...... Pulse Envelop Correlation Air Navigation
Pecan Q...... Pecan Quarterly [*A publication*]
PE CARD .. Production Estimate Card　(MSA)
PECBI....... Professional Engineers Conference Board for Industry　(EA)
PECC......... Pacific Economic Cooperation Conference [*Australia*]
PECC......... Panel of Experts on Climatic Change [*WMO*]　(MSC)
PECC......... Precanceled Envelope Collectors Club　(EA)
PECC......... Product Engineering Control Center [*Telecommunications*]　(TEL)
PECDS ...... Professional Engineering Career Development Series [*Book series*]
PECE......... Proposed Engineering Change Estimate
PECF .... Pseudoextracellular Fluid [*for biocompatibility testing*]
PECFA ..... Presidential Election Campaign Fund Act of 1966
PECHA ..... Petroleum Chemistry USSR [*English Translation*] [*A publication*]
Peche Mar ... Peche Maritime [*A publication*]
Peche Marit ... Peche Maritime [*A publication*]
PECI .... Preliminary Equipment Component Index [*or Inventory*]
PECI .... Productivity Enhancing Capital Investment [*DoD*]
PECIP....... Productivity Enhancing Capital Investment Program　(MCD)
Peck .... Peck's Reports [*7 Tennessee*] [*1921-24*] [*A publication*]　(DLA)
Peck .... Peck's Reports [*24-30 Illinois*] [*A publication*]　(DLA)
Peck .... Peckwell's English Election Cases [*1802-06*] [*A publication*]　(DLA)
Peck El Cas ... Peckwell's English Election Cases [*A publication*]　(DLA)
Peck Elec Cas ... Peckwell's English Election Cases [*1802-06*] [*A publication*]　(DLA)
Peck (Ill) .... Peck's Reports, Illinois Supreme Court Reports [*11-22, 24-30*] [*A publication*]　(DLA)
Peck (Tenn) ... Peck's Reports [*7 Tennessee*] [*A publication*]　(DLA)
Peck Tr ...... Peck's Trial (Impeachment) [*A publication*]　(DLA)
Peckw........ Peckwell's English Election Cases [*A publication*]　(DLA)
PECL .... Preliminary Engineering Configuration List

PECM........ Passive Electronics Countermeasures [*Military*] (NG)
PECM........ Preliminary Engineering Change Memorandum [*Air Force*] (CET)
PECN........ Publishers Equipment Corporation [*NASDAQ symbol*] (NQ)
PECO .... Peace Country [*Grande Prairie, Alberta*] [*A publication*]
PECO .... Pecos National Monument
PECO .... Premier Energy Corporation [*NASDAQ symbol*] (NQ)
PECOS...... Program Environment Checkout System
PECOS...... Project Evaluation and Control System (MCD)
PECP........ Preliminary Engineering Change Proposal
PECR........ Program Error Correction Report
Pe Cri........ Petrus Crispanus [*Authority cited in pre-1607 legal work*] (DSA)
PECS .... Plant Engineering Check Sheet (AAG)
PECS .... Portable Environmental Control System [*NASA*]
PECS .... Princeton Encyclopedia of Classical Sites [*A publication*]
Pecsi Muesz Sz ... Pecsi Mueszaki Szemle [*Hungary*] [*A publication*]
PECT........ Pectori [*To the Chest*] [*Pharmacy*]
PECTFE.... Polyethylene-Chlorotrifluoroethylene [*Organic chemistry*]
PECUL...... Peculiar (ROG)
PECUS ...... Personal Engineering Computer User's Society (EA)
PECUY...... Pecuniary (ROG)
PECVD...... Plasma-Enhanced Chemical Vapor Deposition [*Coating technology*]
PECWBS... Proposed Extended Contract Work Breakdown Structure [*Military*]
PECWG..... Piaster Expenditure Control Working Group [*Military*]
Ped .... Pedagogia [*A publication*]
PED .... Pedagogue
PED .... Pedal
PED .... Peddler [*or Peddling*] [*FBI standardized term*]
PED .... Pedestal (AAG)
PED .... Pedestrian
PED .... Pediatrics (AABC)
PED.......... Pedlary (ROG)
PED .... Pedro Aguirre Cerda [*Antarctica*] [*Seismograph station code, US Geological Survey*] [*Closed*] (SEIS)
PED .... Period End Date (MCD)
PED .... Personnel Equipment Data [*Army*]
PED .... Photoemission Diode
PEd .... Physical Education
PED .... Positive Expulsion Device
PED .... Production Eligibility Date (MUGU)
PED .... Production Engineering Division [*University of Wisconsin Madison*] [*Research center*] (RCD)
PED .... Program Element Description
PED .... Program Element Directive
PED .... Program Execution Directive (AAG)
PED .... Promotion Eligibility Date [*Military*]
PED .... Proton-Enhanced Diffusion
PED .... Public Employee Department (of AFL-CIO) (EA)
PEd .... Pulmonary Edema [*Medicine*]
PED .... Pure Edge Dislocation
PED .... Pyramid Element Designator
PED .... Springfield, TN [*Location identifier*] [*FAA*] (FAAL)
PEDA .... Pedal Artery
PEDA .... Personnel Equipment Data Analysis
Pedag Meddel ... Pedagogiska Meddelanden fran Skoloeverstyrelsen [*A publication*]
Pedagog Fak Plzni Sb Ser Chem ... Pedagogicka Fakulta v Plzni. Sbornik. Serie Chemie [*A publication*]
Pedagog Sem ... Pedagogical Seminary [*A publication*]
Pedag i Psihol ... Pedagogika i Psihologija [*A publication*]
Pedag Szle ... Pedagogiai Szemle [*A publication*]
Pedag Tidskr ... Pedagogisk Tidskrift [*A publication*]
Ped Akus Ginek ... Pediatriia, Akusherstvo, i Ginekologiia [*A publication*]
Ped B.......... Bachelor of Pedagogy
PEDB........ Process Engineering Database
PEDBA9.... Pediatria [*Bucharest*] [*A publication*]
PEDC........ Personal Effects Distribution Center
Ped Cal...... Pediatria in Calabria [*A publication*]
Ped Clin NA ... Pediatric Clinics of North America [*A publication*]
PEDCUG... Planning Engineers Desktop Computer Users Group (EA)
Ped D .... Doctor of Pedagogy
PEDD .... Program Element Descriptive Data (CAAL)
PEddyB...... Baldwin Locomotive Works, Eddystone, PA [*Library symbol*] [*Library of Congress*] [*Obsolete*] (LCLS)
PEDET...... Pedetemptim [*Gradually*] [*Pharmacy*]
PEDF........ Potential-Energy Distribution Function [*Physical chemistry*]
PEDG........ Phenethyldiguanide [*Same as PEBG*] [*Antidiabetic compound*]
PEDI........ Pediatrics [*Medicine*] (DHSM)
Pedia .... Pediatrics [*A publication*]
Pediat Akush Ginek ... Pediatriia, Akusherstvo, i Ginekologiia [*A publication*]
Pediat Clins N Am ... Pediatric Clinics of North America [*A publication*]
Pediat Inf ... Pediatric Infectious Disease [*A publication*]
Pediat Nurs ... Pediatric Nursing [*A publication*]
Pediatr Adolesc Endocrinol ... Pediatric and Adolescent Endocrinology [*A publication*]
Pediatr Adolesc Gynecol ... Pediatric and Adolescent Gynecology [*A publication*]

Pediatr Akush Ginekol ... Pediatriia, Akusherstvo, i Ginekologiia [*A publication*]
Pediatr Ann ... Pediatric Annals [*A publication*]
Pediatr Cardiol ... Pediatric Cardiology [*A publication*]
Pediatr Clin N Am ... Pediatric Clinics of North America [*A publication*]
Pediatr Clin North Am ... Pediatric Clinics of North America [*A publication*]
Pediatr Contin Educ Courses Pract ... Pediatric Continuing Education Courses for the Practitioner [*A publication*]
Pediatr Dent ... Pediatric Dentistry [*A publication*]
Pediatr Dermatol ... Pediatric Dermatology [*A publication*]
Pediatr Emerg Care ... Pediatric Emergency Care [*A publication*]
Pediat Res ... Pediatric Research [*A publication*]
Pediatr Esp ... Pediatria Espanola [*A publication*]
Pediatria Arch ... Pediatria. Archivio di Patologia e Clinica Pediatrica [*A publication*]
Pediatrics Suppl ... Pediatrics Supplement [*A publication*]
Pediatr Infect Dis ... Pediatric Infectious Disease [*A publication*]
Pediatr Int ... Pediatria Internazionale [*A publication*]
Pediatr Listy ... Pediatricke Listy [*A publication*]
Pediatr Med Chir ... Pediatria Medica e Chirurgica [*A publication*]
Pediatr Mod ... Pediatria Moderna [*A publication*]
Pediatr Nephrol ... Pediatric Nephrology [*A publication*]
Pediatr Neurosci ... Pediatric Neuroscience [*A publication*]
Pediatr News ... Pediatric News [*A publication*]
Pediatr Nurs ... Pediatric Nursing [*A publication*]
Pediatr Nurse Pract ... Pediatric Nurse Practitioner [*A publication*]
Pediatr Pathol ... Pediatric Pathology [*A publication*]
Pediatr Pharmacol ... Pediatric Pharmacology [*A publication*]
Pediatr Pol ... Pediatria Polska [*A publication*]
Pediatr Prat ... Pediatria Pratica [*A publication*]
Pediatr Pulmonol ... Pediatric Pulmonology [*A publication*]
Pediatr Radiol ... Pediatric Radiology [*A publication*]
Pediatr Res ... Pediatric Research [*A publication*]
PEDIEY .... Pedoatrocoam [*A publication*]
PEDIN....... Peapod Dinghy
P Edin Math ... Proceedings. Edinburgh Mathematical Society [*A publication*]
Ped Int .... Pediatria Internazionale [*A publication*]
PE Dir........ Physical Education Director
PEdiS......... Edinboro State College, Edinboro, PA [*Library symbol*] [*Library of Congress*] (LCLS)
PEDL........ Pedicel Length [*Botany*]
Ped M .... Master of Pedagogy
PEDMAN ... PACFLT [*Pacific Fleet*] Enlisted Personnel Distribution Manual (CINC)
PEDN .... Planned Event Discrepancy Notification [*NASA*] (KSC)
Pedobiolog ... Pedobiologia [*A publication*]
Pedod Fr ... Pedodontie Francaise [*A publication*]
PEDOL...... Pedology
Pedology (Leningr) ... Pedology (Leningrad) [*A publication*]
Ped Panam ... Pediatria Panamericana [*A publication*]
PEDRO ...... Pneumatic Energy Detector with Remote Optics
PEDRTC ... Pediatric
PEDS........ Packaging Engineering Data System (AFM)
PEDS........ Pediatrics
PEDS........ Peltier Effect Diffusion Separation [*Physical chemistry*]
PEDS........ Program Element Descriptive Summary (CAAL)
PEDS........ Protective Equipment Decontamination Section [*Nuclear energy*] (NRCH)
Ped Sem ..... Pedagogical Seminary [*A publication*]
PEDSTL.... Pedestal [*Freight*]
PEDT........ Pendant [*Jewelry*] (ROG)
PEDT........ Peridot [*Jewelry*] (ROG)
PEDTAT ... Pediatriya [*Moscow*] [*A publication*]
PEDUC...... Professeurs d'Economie Domestique des Universites Canadiennes [*Canadian University Teachers of Home Economics - CUTHE*]
P Educator ... Physical Educator [*A publication*]
PEE........... Photoelectron Emission [*Also, OSEE*]
PEE........... Photoemission Effect
PEE........... Pressure Environmental Equipment (NVT)
PEE........... Program Estimating Equation
P & EE .... Proof and Experimental Establishments (RDA)
PEE........... Talkeetna, AK [*Location identifier*] [*FAA*] (FAAL)
PEEAD...... Promoclim E. Etudes Thermiques et Aerauliques [*A publication*]
PEEC........ Personnel Emergency Estimator Capability
PEEC........ Programmable Electronic Engine Control [*Automotive engineering*]
PEEC........ Project for an Energy-Enriched Curriculum [*Department of Energy*]
PEECD...... Petroleum Economist [*A publication*]
PEEIC .... Programme des Economies d'Energie dans l'Industrie Canadienne
PEEID .... Petroleum Engineer International [*A publication*]
PEEK........ Peek 'n' Peak Recreation, Inc. [*Clymer, NY*] [*NASDAQ symbol*] (NQ)
PEEK........ People for the Enjoyment of Eyeballing Knees [*Group opposing below-the-knee fashions introduced in 1970*]
PEEK........ Periodically Elevated Electronic Kibitzer
PEEK........ Polyetherketone [*Organic chemistry*]

Peel Valley Hist Soc J ... Peel Valley Historical Society. Journal [*A publication*] (APTA)
PEEM........ Photoemission Electron Microscope
PEEP......... Panel of Experts on Environmental Pollution [*WMO*] (MSC)
PEEP......... Pilot's Electronic Eyelevel Presentation [*British*]
PEEP......... Porous Electrode Electrostatic Precipitation
PEEP......... Positive End Expiratory Pressure [*Medicine*]
PEEP......... Production Electronic Equipment Procurement Status Report
Peeples & Stevens ... Peeples and Stevens' Reports [*80-97 Georgia*] [*A publication*] (DLA)
PEER........ Pediatric Examination of Educational Readiness [*Child development test*]
Peer........... Peerless [*Record label*] [*USA, Mexico*]
PEER......... Planned Experience for Effective Relating
PEER......... Price Escalation Estimated Rates
PEER......... Program of Equal Employment Opportunity Evaluation Reports
PEER........ Project on Equal Education Rights (EA)
PEERAMID ... Pediatric Examination of Educational Readiness at Middle Childhood [*Child development test*] [*Psychology*]
PEERC...... Production Engineering Education and Research Center
Peere Wms ... Peere-Williams' English Chancery and King's Bench Cases [*1695-1736*] [*A publication*] (DLA)
PEET........ Printing Equipment Education Trust [*British*]
PEEX......... Pediatric Early Elementary Examination [*Child development test*] [*Psychology*]
PEF........... Pacific-European Growth Fund [*AMEX symbol*] (SPSG)
PEF........... Packaging Education Foundation (EA)
PEF........... Palestine Endowment Funds [*Later, PEF Israel Endowment Funds*] (EA)
PEF........... Palestine Exploration Fund
PEF........... Peak Expiratory Flow [*Pulmonary function*]
PEF........... Performance Efficiency Factor (AFIT)
PEF........... Personal Effects Floater [*Insurance*]
PEF........... Personality Evaluation Form [*Psychology*]
PEF........... Phil Esposito Foundation (EA)
PEF........... Physical Electronics Facility (MCD)
PEF........... Plastics Education Foundation (EA)
PEF........... Polyethylene Foam
PEF........... Prediction Error Filter [*Wave frequency and phase modifier*]
PEF........... Presbyterian Evangelistic Fellowship (EA)
PEF........... Pro Ecclesia Foundation (EA)
PEF........... Program Estimating Factor (AFM)
PEF........... Proposal Evaluation Form (AAG)
PEF........... Psychiatric Evaluation Form [*Psychology*]
PEFA........ Palestine Exploration Fund. Annual [*A publication*]
PEFC......... Private Export Funding Corporation (IMH)
PEFCO...... Private Export Funding Corporation
Pe Fi......... Petrus Filipi [*Authority cited in pre-1607 legal work*] (DSA)
Pe Fili....... Petrus Filipi [*Authority cited in pre-1607 legal work*] (DSA)
PEFM........ Palestine Exploration Fund. Memoirs [*A publication*]
PEF/NET ... Public Education Fund Network (EA)
PEFO......... Payload Effects Follow-On Study [*NASA*] (NASA)
PEFO......... Petrified Forest National Park
PEFQ......... Palestine Exploration Fund. Quarterly Statement [*A publication*]
PEFQS...... Palestine Exploration Fund. Quarterly Statement [*London*] [*A publication*] (BJA)
PEFQST.... Palestine Exploration Fund. Quarterly Statement [*London*] [*A publication*] (BJA)
PEFR......... Peak Expiratory Flow Rate
PEFT......... Peripheral Equipment Functional Test (CAAL)
PEFT......... Preschool Embedded Figures Test [*Child development test*]
PEFTOK .. Philippine Expeditionary Force to Korea [*United Nations*]
PEFU......... Panel of Experts on Fish Utilization [*FAO*] (ASF)
PEFV......... Partial Expiratory Flow-Volume [*Physiology*]
PEG.......... General Analine & Film Co., General Research Laboratory, Easton, PA [*Library symbol*] [*Library of Congress*] [*Obsolete*] (LCLS)
PEG.......... Pac Engo Materials [*Vancouver Stock Exchange symbol*]
PEG.......... Pacific Environmental Group [*Marine science*] (MSC)
Peg............ Pegaso [*A publication*]
Peg............ Pegasus [*Constellation*]
PEG.......... Performance Evaluation Group (CINC)
PEG.......... Petrochemical Energy Group (EA)
PEG.......... Pneumatic Explosion Generator
PEG.......... Pneumoencephalogram [*Medicine*]
PEG.......... Polyethylene Glycol [*Organic chemistry*]
PEG.......... Previous Endorsement(s) Guaranteed [*Banking*]
PEG.......... Principle of the Equivalent Generator
PEG.......... Priorities for ELINT Guidance (MCD)
PEG.......... Process Evaluation Guide [*Graphic Communications Association*]
PEG.......... Production Engineering [*A publication*]
PEG.......... Production Entitlement Guarantee [*International Agricultural Trade Research Consortium*] (ECON)
PEG.......... Program Evaluation Group [*Air Force*]
PEG.......... Project Engineering Guide (MCD)
PEG.......... Protected Employee Group [*Program*]
PEG.......... Protection Engineers Group [*United States Telephone Association*] [*Telecommunications*]

PEG.......... Public Service Enterprise Group, Inc. [*NYSE symbol*] (SPSG)
PEGA........ Polyethylene Glycol Adipate [*Organic chemistry*]
PEGDE...... Pentaethylene Glycol Dodecyl Ether [*Organic chemistry*]
PEGE........ Program for Evaluation of Ground Environment
PEGEA...... Petroleum Geology [*English Translation*] [*A publication*]
PEGLN...... Petiole Gland Pairs, Number Of [*Botany*]
Pegmatitovye Redkomet Mestorozhd ... Pegmatitovye Redkometal'nye Mestorozhdeniya [*A publication*]
PEGR......... Press Extracts on Greenland [*A publication*]
PEGR......... Proportional Exhaust Gas Recirculation [*Engines*]
Pegs........... Pegasus [*Constellation*]
PEGS......... Polyethylene Glycol Succinate [*Organic chemistry*]
PEGS......... Publications. English Goethe Society [*A publication*]
PEGTA...... Problemy Endokrinologii i Gormonoterapii [*A publication*]
PEH.......... Pehpei [*Republic of China*] [*Seismograph station code, US Geological Survey*] (SEIS)
PEH.......... Pehuajo [*Argentina*] [*Airport symbol*] (OAG)
PEH.......... Periods of European History [*A publication*]
PEH.......... Plus Each Hour [*Aviation*] (FAAC)
PEHA........ Pentaethylenehexamine [*Organic chemistry*]
PEHA........ Pony Express Historical Association (EA)
PEHi......... Northampton County Historical and Genealogical Society, Mary Illick Memorial Library, Easton, PA [*Library symbol*] [*Library of Congress*] (LCLS)
Pe His........ Petrus Hispanus [*Authority cited in pre-1607 legal work*] (DSA)
PEHPA...... Progress in Nuclear Energy. Series 12 [*A publication*]
PEHYA..... Petroleum and Hydrocarbons [*A publication*]
PEI............ Haszard and Warburton's Reports. Prince Edward Island [*Canada*] [*A publication*]
PeI............. Parole e le Idee [*A publication*]
PEI............ Patriotic Education, Inc. (EA)
PEI............ Peine [*Chile*] [*Seismograph station code, US Geological Survey*] [*Closed*] (SEIS)
PEI............ Pennsylvania Real Estate Investments Trust SBI [*AMEX symbol*] (SPSG)
PEI............ Pereira [*Colombia*] [*Airport symbol*] (OAG)
PEI............ Petrocel Industries, Inc. [*Vancouver Stock Exchange symbol*]
PEI............ Petroleum Equipment Institute (EA)
PEI............ Physical Education Index [*A publication*]
PEI............ Planning Executives Institute [*Later, PF*]
PEI............ Plant Engineering Inspection (AAG)
PEI............ Playboy Enterprises, Incorporated
PEI............ Polyethylenimine [*Organic chemistry*]
PEI............ Porcelain Enamel Institute (EA)
PEI............ Postejaculatory Interval [*Physiology*]
PEI............ Precipitation-Efficiency Index
PEI............ Preliminary Engineering Inspection [*NASA*] (KSC)
PEI............ Prince Edward Island [*Canadian province*]
PEI............ Prince Edward Island Provincial Library [*UTLAS symbol*]
PEI............ Prince Edward Island Reports (Haviland's) [*A publication*] (DLA)
PEI............ Professional Engineers in Industry
PEIA......... Poultry and Egg Institute of America (EA)
PEI Acts .... Acts of Prince Edward Island [*Canada*] [*A publication*]
PEIC......... Periodic Error Integrating Controller
PEID......... Program Element Identifier [*Military*] (AFIT)
PEIDD9.... Personality and Individual Differences [*A publication*]
PEILS....... PACOM [*Pacific Command*] Executive Intelligence Summary (MCD)
PEIN.......... PEI, Inc. [*NASDAQ symbol*] (NQ)
Peine Salzgitter Ber ... Peine und Salzgitter Berichte [*A publication*]
Peint Pigm Vernis ... Peintures, Pigments, Vernis [*A publication*]
PEIP......... Presidential Executive Interchange Program [*Federal government*]
PEIR......... Problem Equipment Indicator Reports (MCD)
PEIR......... Project Equipment Inspection Record [*NASA*] (KSC)
PEI Rep ..... Prince Edward Island Reports (Haviland's) [*1850-1914*] [*A publication*] (DLA)
PEI Rev Regs ... Revised Regulations of Prince Edward Island [*Canada*] [*A publication*]
PEI Rev Stat ... Prince Edward Island Revised Statutes [*Canada*] [*A publication*] (DLA)
PEIS.......... Programmatic Environmental Impact Statement (NRCH)
PEI Stat ..... Prince Edward Island Statutes [*Canada*] [*A publication*] (DLA)
PEITA...... Professional Equestrian Instructors and Trainers Association (EA)
PEITV...... Preliminary Encapsulated Inert Test Vehicle (MCD)
PEJ........... Pakistan Economic Journal [*A publication*]
PEJ........... Personnel Journal [*A publication*]
PEJ........... Premolded Expansion Joint [*Technical drawings*]
Pe Ja.......... Petrus Jacobi [*Flourished, 14th century*] [*Authority cited in pre-1607 legal work*] (DSA)
PEJO......... Plant Engineering Job Order (AAG)
PEJOA...... Personnel Journal [*A publication*]
PEK........... Beijing [*China*] [*Airport symbol*] (OAG)
PEK........... Jacksonville, FL [*Location identifier*] [*FAA*] (FAAL)
PEK........... Peking [*Chiufeng*] [*Republic of China*] [*Seismograph station code, US Geological Survey*] (SEIS)
PEK........... Peking [*Republic of China*] [*Geomagnetic observatory code*]
PEK........... Pekoe [*Tea trade*] (ROG)

PEK............ Perkiomen Airways Ltd. [*Reading, PA*] [*FAA designator*] (FAAC)
PEK............ Phase-Exchange Keying [*Data processing*] (IEEE)
PEK............ Phi Epsilon Kappa [*Fraternity*]
Peking Nat Hist Bull ... Peking Natural History Bulletin [*A publication*]
Peking R .... Peking Review [*A publication*]
PEL............ Lafayette College, Easton, PA [*Library symbol*] [*Library of Congress*] (LCLS)
PEL............ Panhandle Eastern Pipe Line Co. [*NYSE symbol*] (SPSG)
Pel............. Pelagius [*Deceased, 1232*] [*Authority cited in pre-1607 legal work*] (DSA)
PEL............ Pelaneng [*Lesotho*] [*Airport symbol*] (OAG)
PEL............ Peldehue [*Chile*] [*Seismograph station code, US Geological Survey*] (SEIS)
Pel............. Pelopidas [*of Plutarch*] [*Classical studies*] (OCD)
PEL............ Penguin English Library [*A publication*]
PEL............ Peritoneal Exudate Lymphocytes [*Hematology*]
PEL............ Permissible Exposure Limit [*OSHA*]
PEL............ Personal Exposure Level [*or Limit*]
PEL............ Personnel Licensing and Training [*ICAO*] (AIA)
PEL............ Philatelic Esperanto League [*See also ELF*] [*Solna, Sweden*] (EAIO)
PEL............ Photoelectron Layer
PEL............ Picture Element [*Single element of resolution in image processing*] (IBMDP)
PEL............ Precision Elastic Limit
PEL............ Priests Eucharistic League (EA)
PEL............ Professional Education Libraries [*UTLAS symbol*]
PEL............ Proportional Elastic Limit
PELAA ..... Progress in Nuclear Energy. Series 10 [*A publication*]
PElC .... Elizabethtown College, Elizabethtown, PA [*Library symbol*] [*Library of Congress*] (LCLS)
PELC .... Professional Engineers' Legislative Committee
PELEC ..... Photoelectric (MSA)
PEleph ...... Elephantine Papyri [*A publication*] (OCD)
PELG .... Poly(ethyl L-Glutamate) [*Organic chemistry*]
Pelham...... Pelham's South Australia Reports [*1865-66*] [*A publication*] (DLA)
PELL .... Papers on English Language and Literature [*A publication*]
PELR .... Peeler
PELR .... Pelsart Resources NL [*NASDAQ symbol*] (NQ)
PELS .... Precision Emitter Location System [*Air Force*] (MCD)
PELS .... Propionyl Erythromycin Lauryl Sulfate [*Antimicrobial agent*]
PELSS ...... Precision Emitter Location Strike System [*Air Force*]
Pelt.......... Peltier's Orleans Appeals [*1917-23*] [*A publication*] (DLA)
PELT .... Princeton Electronic Products, Inc. [*NASDAQ symbol*] (NQ)
PEM .... Parametric Earth Model [*Geodynamics*]
PEM .... Parasitic Encephalitis Meningitis [*Medicine*]
PeM .... Parole e Metodi [*A publication*]
PEM .... Payload Ejection Mechanism
PEM .... Pem Air Ltd. [*Pembroke, ON*] [*FAA designator*] (FAAC)
PEM .... Pembrokeshire [*County in Wales*] (ROG)
PEM .... Perrot Memorial Library, Old Greenwich, CT [*OCLC symbol*] (OCLC)
PEM .... Personal Exposure Monitor [*Environmental chemistry*]
PEM .... Perspectivas de la Economia Mundial [*A publication*]
PEM .... Perspectives de l'Economie Mondiale [*A publication*]
PEM .... Petrox Energy & Mineral Corp. [*Toronto Stock Exchange symbol*]
PEM .... Phased Equipment Modernization [*Army*] (AABC)
PEM .... Philco Electronic Module
PEM .... Photoelastic Modulator [*Instrumentation*]
PEM .... Photoelectromagnetic
PEM .... Photoelectron Microscopy
PEM .... Photoemission Microscope
PEM .... Photographic Equipment and Materials (NATG)
PEM .... Plant Engineer Mechanical (AAG)
PE & M...... Plant Engineering and Maintenance (MCD)
PEM .... Plant Engineering and Maintenance (NASA)
PEM .... Polaris Evaluation Missile
PEM .... Position Encoding Module (CAAL)
PEM .... Prescription-Event Monitoring
PEM .... Primary Enrichment Medium [*Microbiology*]
PEM .... Probable Error of Measurement
PEM .... Processing Element Memory [*Data processing*]
PEM .... Product Effectiveness Manual
PEM .... Production Engineering Measure [*Army*] (MCD)
PEM .... Production Evaluation Missile [*Military*] (CAAL)
PEM .... Program Element Monitor (AFM)
PEM .... Project Engineering Memorandum
PEM .... Proposal Evaluation Manager
PEM .... Protein Energy Malnutrition [*Medicine*]
PEM .... Puerto Maldonado [*Peru*] [*Airport symbol*] (OAG)
PEMA....... Process Equipment Manufacturers Association (EA)
PEMA....... Procurement Equipment Maintenance, Army (MCD)
PEMA....... Procurement, Equipment, Missiles, Army
PEMA....... Procurement of Equipment and Munition Appropriations [*Military*] (AABC)
PEMA....... Production-Equipment-Missile Agency [*Army*]
PEMAP..... President's Environmental Merit Award Program [*Environmental Protection Agency*]

PEMARS .. Procurement of Equipment and Missiles, Army Management and Accounting Reporting System (AABC)
PEMB....... Pembroke College [*Oxford and Cambridge Universities*] (ROG)
PEMB....... Pembrokeshire [*County in Wales*]
Pemb Eq... Pemberton's Practice in Equity by Way of Revivor and Supplement [*1867*] [*A publication*] (ILCA)
Pemb Judg ... Pemberton's Judgments and Orders [*A publication*] (DLA)
Pembroke Mag ... Pembroke Magazine [*A publication*]
PEMBS ..... Pembrokeshire [*County in Wales*]
PEMC........ Pele Medical Corporation [*NASDAQ symbol*] (NQ)
PEMCONS ... Photographic Equipment Management Control System
PEMD ...... Program for Export Market Development [*Canada*]
PEMF....... Pulsating Electromagnetic Field
PEMJ .... Pemmican Journal [*A publication*]
PEMJA ..... Pesticides Monitoring Journal [*A publication*]
P & EML ... Personnel and Equipment Modification List [*Air Force*]
Pe Mo........ Petrus Morini [*Authority cited in pre-1607 legal work*] (DSA)
PEMO ...... Plant Engineering Maintenance Order
PEMO .... Production Engineering and Manufacturing Organization (AAG)
Pe Mori...... Petrus Morini [*Authority cited in pre-1607 legal work*] (DSA)
PEM Process Eng Mag ... PEM Process Engineering Magazine [*A publication*]
PEMS .... Physical, Emotional, Mental, Safety [*Model for charting procedure*] [*Medicine*]
PEMS .... Portable Environmental Measuring System
PEMS .... Professional Education of the Media Specialist
PEMS .... Propulsion Energy Management Study (MCD)
PEMT .... Phosphatidylethanolamine Methyltransferase [*An enzyme*]
PeMV .... Pepper Mottle Virus
Pem Yeo.... Pembroke Yeomanry [*British military*] (DMA)
PEN .... Astoria, OR [*Location identifier*] [*FAA*] (FAAL)
PEN .... International PEN [*Official name; PEN, never spelled out in use, is said to stand for poets, playwrights, editors, essayists, novelists*] (EAIO)
PEN .... Peace Education Network (EA)
PEN .... PEN American Center (EA)
PEN .... Penang [*Malaysia*] [*Airport symbol*] (OAG)
PEN .... Pendeli [*Greece*] [*Geomagnetic observatory code*]
PEN .... Penetration (AFM)
PEN .... Penicillin [*Antibiotic*]
PEN .... Peninsula [*Maps and charts*]
PEN .... Penitent
Pen .... Pennewill's Delaware Reports [*A publication*] (DLA)
Pen .... Pennington's New Jersey Reports [*2, 3 New Jersey*] [*A publication*] (DLA)
PEN .... Pensacola [*Florida*] [*Seismograph station code, US Geological Survey*] [*Closed*] (SEIS)
Pen .... Pensamiento [*Madrid*] [*A publication*]
PEN .... Pentazocine [*An analgesic*]
PEN .... Pentobarbital [*Sedative*]
PEN .... Pentode (DEN)
PEN .... Pentron Industries, Inc. [*Later, KOA*] [*AMEX symbol*] (SPSG)
PEN .... Permanent Entry Number [*Data processing*]
PEN .... Petroleum News. Asia's Energy Journal [*A publication*]
PEN .... Pharmacology Equivalent Name
PEN .... Physicians Education Network (EA)
PEN .... Polyethylene Naphthalate [*Organic chemistry*]
PEN .... Professional Enrichment News [*Portuguese*] (BJA)
PEN .... Program Element Number [*Data processing*] (KSC)
PEN ...... Program Error Note [*Data processing*]
PENA .... Primary Emission Neuron Activation (IEEE)
PENAID.... Penetration Aid [*Weaponry*]
PENB........ Poultry and Egg National Board [*Later, AEB*] (EA)
PENBASE ... Peninsular Base Section [*Military*]
Pen C........ Penal Code [*A publication*] (DLA)
PENCIL .... Pictorial Encoding Language [*Data processing*] (IEEE)
PENCIL .... Portable Encoder/Illustrator [*Facetious term for pre-word-processing equipment*]
Pend .... Pendant (ROG)
PEND .... Pendens [*Weighing*] [*Pharmacy*]
PEND .... Pending
PENDA ..... Polish Endocrinology [*A publication*]
Pen Dec...... Pension Decisions [*Department of the Interior*] [*A publication*] (DLA)
PENDORF ... Penetrate Dorfman [*FBI investigation of Teamster leader Allen Dorfman*]
PENEE4.... Pediatric Neuroscience [*A publication*]
Penelitian Indones ... Penelitian Laut di Indonesia [*Marine Research in Indonesia*] [*A publication*]
Penelitian Laut Indones (Mar Res Indones) ... Penelitian Laut di Indonesia (Marine Research in Indonesia) [*A publication*]
P/E NEWS ... Petroleum/Energy Business News Index [*American Petroleum Institute*] [*New York, NY*] [*Bibliographic database*]
PenG .... Penicillin G [*Antibacterial agent*]
PEng .... Pennsylvania English [*A publication*]
PENG .... Photo-Electro-Nystagmography [*Medicine*]
PENG .... Prima Energy Corp. [*NASDAQ symbol*] (NQ)
PEng .... Professional Engineer

PENGEM ... Penetrate Gray Electronics Markets [*FBI "sting" operation, 1982, in which employees of Japanese computer firms were caught attempting to obtain proprietary information illegally from IBM Corp.*]

Pengum Lemb Penelit Kehutanan ... Pengumuman. Lembaga Penelitian Kehutanan [*A publication*]

PENIC ...... Penicillin

Penic Cam ... Penicillum Camelinum [*A Camel's-Hair Brush*] [*Pharmacy*]

penin ...... Peninsula

PENIT ...... Penitentiary

Penjelidikan Indones ... Penjelidikan Laut di Indonesia [*A publication*]

PENJERDEL ... Pennsylvania, New Jersey, Delaware

Penn .... Pennewill's Delaware Reports [*A publication*] (DLA)

Penn .... Pennington's New Jersey Reports [*A publication*] (DLA)

PENN .... Pennsylvania

Penn .... Pennsylvania State Reports [*A publication*] (DLA)

PENN .... Pennsylvanian [*Period, era, or system*] [*Geology*]

Penn .... Pennypacker's Unreported Pennsylvania Cases [*A publication*] (DLA)

PENNA ..... Pennsylvania

Penna Law Journal ... Pennsylvania Law Journal [*A publication*] (DLA)

Penna LJ .... Pennsylvania Law Journal [*A publication*] (DLA)

Penna R .... Pennsylvania State Reports [*A publication*] (DLA)

Penna SR ... Pennsylvania State Reports [*A publication*] (DLA)

Penna St ..... Pennsylvania State Reports [*A publication*] (DLA)

Penna State Rep ... Pennsylvania State Reports [*A publication*] (DLA)

Penn Ba Q ... Pennsylvania Bar Association. Quarterly [*A publication*]

Penn BAR ... Pennsylvania Bar Association. Report [*A publication*]

Penn Bar Assc Q ... Pennsylvania Bar Association. Quarterly [*A publication*]

Penn Beekpr ... Pennsylvania Beekeeper [*A publication*]

Penn Co Ct Rep ... Pennsylvania County Court Reports [*A publication*] (DLA)

Penn Corp Rep ... Pennsylvania Corporation Reporter [*A publication*] (DLA)

Penn Del ... Pennewill's Delaware Reports [*A publication*] (DLA)

Penn Dent J ... Penn Dental Journal [*A publication*]

Penn Dist & Co Rep ... Pennsylvania District and County Reports [*A publication*] (DLA)

Penn Dist Rep ... Pennsylvania District Reports [*A publication*] (DLA)

Penne .... Pennewill's Delaware Reports [*17-23 Delaware*] [*1897-1909*] [*A publication*] (DLA)

Pennew .... Pennewill's Delaware Reports [*A publication*] (DLA)

Pennewill ... Pennewill's Delaware Supreme Court Reports [*1897-1909*] [*A publication*] (DLA)

Penn Geol Surv Atlas ... Pennsylvania. Geological Survey. Atlas [*A publication*]

Penn Geol Surv Bull ... Pennsylvania. Geological Survey. Bulletin [*A publication*]

Penn Geol Surv Gen Geol Rep ... Pennsylvania. Geological Survey. General Geology Report [*A publication*]

Penn Geol Surv Ground Water Rep ... Pennsylvania. Geological Survey. Ground Water Report [*A publication*]

Penn Geol Surv Inform Circ ... Pennsylvania. Geological Survey. Information Circular [*A publication*]

Penn Geol Surv Progr Rep ... Pennsylvania. Geological Survey. Progress Report [*A publication*]

Penn German Soc Proc ... Pennsylvania German Society. Proceedings [*A publication*]

Penn Hist ... Pennsylvania History [*A publication*]

Penn Hosp Rep ... Pennsylvania Hospital Reports [*A publication*]

Penning ...... Pennington's New Jersey Reports [*2, 3 New Jersey*] [*A publication*] (DLA)

Pen NJ .... Pennington's New Jersey Reports [*2, 3 New Jersey*] [*A publication*] (DLA)

Penn Law ... Pennsylvania Lawyer [*A publication*]

Penn Law Jour ... Pennsylvania Law Journal [*A publication*] (DLA)

Penn LG ..... Pennsylvania Legal Gazette [*A publication*] (DLA)

Penn LG ..... Pennsylvania Legal Gazette Reports (Campbell) [*A publication*] (DLA)

Penn Lib Assn Bull ... Pennsylvania Library Association. Bulletin [*A publication*]

Penn LJ ...... Pennsylvania Law Journal [*A publication*] (DLA)

Penn LJR ... Pennsylvania Law Journal Reports, Edited by Clark [*1842-52*] [*A publication*] (DLA)

Penn L Rec ... Pennsylvania Law Record [*Philadelphia*] [*A publication*] (DLA)

Penn L Rev ... Pennsylvania Law Review [*A publication*] (DLA)

Penn Mag H ... Pennsylvania Magazine of History and Biography [*A publication*]

Penn Mag Hist Biog ... Pennsylvania Magazine of History and Biography [*A publication*]

Penn Mo .... Penn Monthly [*A publication*]

Penn Nurse ... Pennsylvania Nurse [*A publication*]

PENNORTH ... Pennyworth [*British*] (ROG)

Penn R .... Pennsylvania State Reports [*A publication*] (DLA)

Penn Rep .... Pennsylvania State Reports [*A publication*] (DLA)

Penn Rep .... Penrose and Watts' Pennsylvania Reports [*A publication*] (DLA)

PennsF .... Pennsylvania Folklife [*A publication*]

Penn St ...... Pennsylvania State Reports [*A publication*] (DLA)

PENNSTAC ... Penn State University Automatic Digital Computer

Penn Stat ... Pennsylvania State Reports [*A publication*] (DLA)

Penn State F ... Penn State Farmer [*A publication*]

Penn State Rep ... Pennsylvania State Reports [*A publication*] (DLA)

Penn State Univ Exp Sta Bull ... Pennsylvania State University. Experiment Station. Bulletin [*A publication*]

Penn State Univ Exp Sta Circ ... Pennsylvania State University. Experiment Station. Circular [*A publication*]

Penn St M Q ... Penn State Mining Quarterly [*A publication*]

Penn Stock & F ... Pennsylvania Stockman and Farmer [*A publication*]

Penn St R ... Pennsylvania State Reports [*A publication*] (ILCA)

Penn St Rep ... Pennsylvania State Reports [*A publication*] (DLA)

Penn Super ... Pennsylvania Superior Court Reports [*A publication*] (DLA)

Pennsyl M ... Pennsylvania Magazine of History and Biography [*A publication*]

Pennsylvania Acad Sci Newsletter ... Pennsylvania Academy of Science. Newsletter [*A publication*]

Pennsylvania Acad Sci Proc ... Pennsylvania Academy of Science. Proceedings [*A publication*]

Pennsylvania Bus Survey ... Pennsylvania Business Survey [*A publication*]

Pennsylvania Geol ... Pennsylvania Geology [*A publication*]

Pennsylvania Geol Survey Bull ... Pennsylvania. Geological Survey. Bulletin [*A publication*]

Pennsylvania Geol Survey Inf Circ ... Pennsylvania. Geological Survey. Information Circular [*A publication*]

Pennsylvania Geol Survey Prog Rept ... Pennsylvania. Geological Survey. Progress Report [*A publication*]

PENNTAP ... Pennsylvania Technical Assistance Program [*Pennsylvania State University*] [*University Park, PA*]

Penn Univ Mus Bul ... Pennsylvania University. University Museum. Bulletin [*A publication*]

Penny .... Pennypacker's Pennsylvania Colonial Cases [*A publication*] (DLA)

Penny .... Pennypacker's Unreported Pennsylvania Cases [*A publication*] (DLA)

Penny Col Cas ... Pennypacker's Pennsylvania Colonial Cases [*A publication*] (DLA)

Penny M .... Penny Magazine [*A publication*]

Penny Mech Chem ... Penny Mechanic and the Chemist [*A publication*]

Pennyp .... Pennypacker's Unreported Pennsylvania Cases [*A publication*] (DLA)

Pennyp Col Cas ... Pennypacker's Pennsylvania Colonial Cases [*A publication*] (DLA)

Pennyp (PA) ... Pennypacker's Unreported Pennsylvania Cases [*A publication*] (DLA)

PENOL ...... Penology

Pen P .... Penault's Prerosti de Quebec [*A publication*] (DLA)

Pen Pow ... Penny Power [*A publication*]

PENR .... Pennant Resources Ltd. [*NASDAQ symbol*] (NQ)

PENR .... Penryn [*England*]

PENRAD ... Penetration RADAR

Penr Anal ... Penruddocke's Short Analysis of Criminal Law [*2nd ed.*] [*1842*] [*A publication*] (DLA)

PENRB ...... Professional Engineer [*Washington, DC*] [*A publication*]

Pen Ref ...... Penal Reformer [*1934-39*] [*A publication*] (DLA)

Pen Ref League M Rec ... Penal Reform League Monthly Record [*1909-12*] [*A publication*] (DLA)

Pen Ref League Q Rec ... Penal Reform League Quarterly Record [*1912-20*] [*A publication*] (DLA)

PENREP ... Penetration Report [*National Security Agency*]

Penrose Ann ... Penrose Annual [*A publication*]

Penr & W ... Penrose and Watts' Pennsylvania Reports [*1829-32*] [*A publication*] (DLA)

PENS .... Magic Marker Industries [*NASDAQ symbol*] (NQ)

PENS .... Partido Espanol Nacional Sindicalista [*Political party*] [*Spain*]

PENS .... Polymer Ejection for Noise Suppression

PENSAM .. Penetration Survivability Assessment Model (MCD)

Pensamiento Econ ... Pensamiento Economico [*A publication*]

Pensamiento Polit ... Pensamiento Politico [*A publication*]

PensCr .... Pensamiento Cristiano. Tribuna de Exposicion del Pensamiento Evangelico [*Cordoba, Argentina*] [*A publication*] (BJA)

Pensee Nat ... Pensee Nationale [*A publication*]

Pensez Plast ... Pensez Plastiques [*A publication*]

Pensiero Med ... Pensiero Medico [*A publication*]

Pensiero Polit ... Pensiero Politico [*A publication*]

Pension FA ... Pension Fund Sponsors Ranked by Assets [*A publication*]

Pension Fc ... Pension Facts [*A publication*]

Pension Rep ... Pension Reporter [*Bureau of National Affairs*] [*A publication*] (DLA)

Pensions ..... Pensions and Investments [*Later, Pension & Investment Age*] [*A publication*]

Pensions Investm Age ... Pensions and Investment Age [*A publication*]

Pension Wld ... Pension World [*A publication*]

Pens Plan Guide CCH ... Pension Plan Guide. Commerce Clearing House [*A publication*]

Pens & Profit Sharing (P-H) ... Pension and Profit Sharing (Prentice-Hall, Inc.) [*A publication*] (DLA)

Pens Rep (BNA) ... Pension Reporter (Bureau of National Affairs) [*A publication*] (DLA)

PenST .... Penicillin Skin Test [*Immunology*]

Pen St R ...... Pennsylvania State Reports [*A publication*] (DLA)

PENT .... Penetrate (AABC)

PENT .... Pennsylvania Enterprises, Inc. [*NASDAQ symbol*] (NQ)

PENT........ Pentagon
PENT........ Pentameter
Pent........... Pentateuch (BJA)
PENT........ Pentecost
PENT........ Pentode (AAG)
PENTAC... Penetration for Tactical Aircraft [*Air Force*]
Pentax Photogr ... Pentax Photography [*A publication*]
PENTENG ... Pentagon English [*Pseudotechnical language*]
P Ent S Ont ... Proceedings. Entomological Society of Ontario [*A publication*]
P Ent S Was ... Proceedings. Entomological Society of Washington [*A publication*]
PENVAL... Penetration Evaluation [*Military*] (NVT)
PENVDK... Population and Environment [*A publication*]
PENW .... Penetrating Wound
Pen & W..... Penrose and Watts' Pennsylvania Reports [*1829-32*] [*A publication*] (DLA)
PENW .... PENWEST Ltd. [*Bellevue, WA*] [*NASDAQ symbol*] (NQ)
PENW .... Penwith [*England*]
Pen Wld ..... Pension World [*A publication*]
PENZ........ Penzance [*City in England*] (ROG)
Penz Ped Inst Ucen Zap ... Penzenskii Pedagogiceskii Institut Imeni V. G. Belinskogo. Ucenye Zapiski [*A publication*]
Penz Politehn Inst Ucen Zap Mat Meh ... Penzenskii Politehniceskii Institut. Matematika i Mehanika. Ucenye Zapiski [*A publication*]
Penzuegyi Szemle ... Penzuegyi Szemle [*A publication*]
Penzugyi Szle ... Penzuegyi Szemle [*A publication*]
PEO .... Pankypria Ergatiki Omospondia [*Pancyprian Federation of Labour*] [*The "Old Trade Unions"*] [*Cyprus*]
PEO .... Patrol Emergency Officer [*Nuclear energy*] (NRCH)
PEO .... People
peo.............. Persian, Old [*MARC language code*] [*Library of Congress*] (LCCP)
PEO .... Petroleum & Resources Corp. [*NYSE symbol*] (SPSG)
PEO .... Petrolia Oil & Gas [*Vancouver Stock Exchange symbol*]
PEO .... Philanthropic and Educational Organization [*Facetious translation "Pop Eats Out"*]
PEO .... Planners for Equal Opportunity [*Defunct*] (EA)
PEO .... Plant Engineering Order
PEO .... Plant Equipment Operator [*Nuclear energy*] (NRCH)
PEO .... Poly(ethylene oxide) [*Acronym is trade name owned by Seitetsu Kagaku Co.*]
PEO .... Principal Executive Officer [*Civil Service*] [*British*]
PEO .... Process Engineering Order
PEO .... Product Engineering Office
PEO .... Production Engineering Order
PEO .... Program Evaluation Office [*Army*]
PEO .... Program Executive Office [*or Officer*]
PEO .... Progressive External Ophthalmoplegia
PEO .... Propulsion Engineering Officer (MCD)
PEO .... Prospective Engineer Officer
PEO .... Public Employment Office [*State Employee Security Agency*] (OICC)
PEOC .... Publishing Employees Organizing Committee [*AFL-CIO*]
PEOED...... Proceedings. European Offshore Petroleum Conference and Exhibition [*A publication*]
Peo L Adv .. People's Legal Advisor [*Utica, NY*] [*A publication*] (DLA)
PEOPD7... Perspectives in Ophthalmology [*A publication*]
Peop J .... People's Journal [*A publication*]
People .... People Weekly [*A publication*]
People and Plann ... People and Planning [*A publication*]
Peoples....... Peoples' Reports [*77-97 Georgia*] [*A publication*] (DLA)
People Wkly ... People Weekly [*A publication*]
Peopl Tax..... People and Taxes [*A publication*]
Peoria Med Month ... Peoria Medical Monthly [*A publication*]
PEOS........ Propulsion and Electrical Operating System (IEEE)
PEOUD ..... Petroleum Outlook [*A publication*]
Peo World ... People's World [*A publication*]
PEP.......... All India Reporter, Patiala and East Punjab States Union Series [*A publication*] (ILCA)
PEP........... Charlotte, NC [*Location identifier*] [*FAA*] (FAAL)
PEP........... Packetized Ensemble Protocol [*Data processing*]
PEP........... Paperless Electronic Payment [*Business term*]
PEP........... Paperless Entry Processing User Group [*Defunct*] (CSR)
PEP........... Parenting, Education, and Political Involvement [*Jack and Jill of America*]
PEP........... Parti Evangelique Populaire [*Popular Protestant Party*] [*Switzerland*] [*Political party*] (PPE)
PEP........... Partitioned Emulation Program [*Data processing*] (BUR)
PEP........... Pauli Exclusion Principle [*Physics*]
PEP........... Peak Effective Power
PEP........... Peak Energy Product
PEP........... Peak Envelope Power [*Telecommunications*]
PEP........... Peer Evaluation Program [*College of American Pathologists*]
PEP........... People for Energy Progress (EA)
PEP........... Pepitilla [*Race of maize*]
PEP........... Peppermint (DSUE)
PEP........... PepsiCo Inc. [*NYSE symbol*] (SPSG)
PEP........... Peptide [*Biochemistry*]
PEP........... Performance Effectiveness [*or Evaluation*] Program [*Navy*]
PEP........... Performance Evaluation Procedure [*Joint Commission on Accreditation of Hospitals*] (DHSM)

PEP........... Peripheral Event Processor [*Data processing*]
PEP........... Perkin-Elmer Processor [*Computer*]
PEP........... Personal Employee Profiling [*Information service or system*] (IID)
PEP........... Personal Equity Plan [*Finance*]
PEP........... Personal Exemption Phase-Out [*Income tax*]
PEP........... Personal Exercise Programmer
PEP........... Personality-Profile Exam
PEP........... Personnel Exchange Program [*Military*] (NVT)
PEP........... Pfizer, Inc., Research Center Library, Easton, PA [*Library symbol*] [*Library of Congress*] (LCLS)
PEP........... Phenethyl Propionate [*Insect attractant*] [*Organic chemistry*]
PEP........... Phosphoenolpyruvate [*Biochemistry*]
PEP........... Photoelectric Potential
PEP........... Photoelectrophoresis
PEP........... Photographic Exploitation Products (MCD)
PEP........... Physical Education Program
PEP........... Physiological Evaluation of Primates
PEP........... Pictorial End-Papers [*Publishing*]
PEP........... Pipeline Expanding Polymer
PEP........... Piping Efficiency Program
PEP........... Planar Epitaxial Passivated
PEP........... Planetary Ephemeris Program (IEEE)
PEP........... Planetary Exploration Plan [*NASA*]
PEP........... Plant Equipment Package [*DoD*]
PEP........... Platform Electronic Package
PEP........... Platform Evaluation Program
PEP........... Plessey Electronic Payroll (DEN)
PEP........... Plume Exposure Pathway [*Nuclear emergency planning*]
PEP........... Political and Economic Planning [*A British organization*] [*Later, Policy Studies Institute*]
PEP........... Polyestradiol Phosphate [*Endocrinology*]
PEP........... Polyethylene Powder
PEP........... Polynominal Error Protection (MCD)
PEP........... Porsche Experimental Prototype [*Automotive engineering*]
PEP........... Positive Energy [*Vancouver Stock Exchange symbol*]
PEP........... Positron-Electron Project [*High-energy accelerator*]
PEP........... Positron Electron Proton [*Physics*]
PEP........... Power Evaluation Program
PEP........... Power Extension Package (MCD)
PEP........... Power Extension Plant (MCD)
PEP........... Practical Engineering Paperwork
PEP........... Pratt & Whitney Engine Program [*Aviation*] (NG)
PEP........... Pre-Ejection Period [*Cardiology*]
PEP........... Pre-Employment Program
PEP........... Preamplifier Extension Plug
PEP........... President's Economy Program
PEP........... Preventive Enforcement Patrol [*New York City police*]
PEP........... Primary Education Program [*Child development test*]
PEP........... Primate Equilibrium Platform
PEP........... Princeton Experiment Package [*NASA*]
PeP........... Principal of Pedagogy [*Academic degree*]
PEP........... Printer-Emulation Package [*Software*]
PEP........... Priority Energy Policy [*Environmental Protection Agency*]
PEP........... Processing Enhancing Protein [*Biochemistry*]
PEP........... Procurement Evaluation Panel [*Air Force*] (MCD)
PEP........... Procytox [*Cyclophosphamide*], Epipodophyllotoxin Derivative [*VM-26*], Prednisolone [*Antineoplastic drug regimen*]
PEP........... Producibility Engineering and Planning [*Army*] (AABC)
PEP........... Product Engineering and Production (MCD)
PEP........... Production EAGLE [*Elevation Angle Guidance Landing Equipment*] Package
PEP........... Production Engineering Planning
PEP........... [*The*] Production Engineering and Productivity Exhibition and Conference [*British*] (ITD)
PEP........... Production Equipment Package
PEP........... [*The*] Productivity Effectiveness Program [*Title of a pamphlet by Robert Gedaliah that describes sedentary exercises for desk-bound workers*]
PEP........... Professional Enhancement Project [*American Occupational Therapy Association*]
PEP........... Proficiency Examination Program (MCD)
PEP........... Program Element Plan (AFIT)
PEP........... Program Evaluation Procedure [*Air Force*]
PEP........... Progressive Exercise Program
PEP........... Projects and Exports Policy [*Board of Trade*] [*British*]
PEP........... Promoting Enduring Peace (EA)
PEP........... Promotion Evaluation Pattern
PEP........... Proposal Equipment Packages (MCD)
PEP........... Proposal Evaluation Panel (MCD)
PEP........... Proposal Evaluation Plan [*or Program*] (MCD)
PEP........... Propulsion Evaluation Plan
PEP........... Protection in Evaluation Procedures
PEP........... Proton-Electron-Proton [*Nuclear physics*]
PEP........... Psychoeducational Profile [*Test for autistic children*]
PEP........... Psychoepistemological Profile [*Student personality test*]
PEP........... Pulse Echo Pattern
PEPA........ Peptidase A [*An enzyme*]
PEPA........ Petroleum Electric Power Association [*Later, EUIPA*] (EA)
PEPA........ Protected Environment plus Prophylactic Antibiotics [*Oncology*]

PEPA......... Pulse Echo Pattern Analyzer
PEPAG...... Physical Electronics and Physical Acoustics Group
[*MIT*] (MCD)
Pe de Pal .... Pierre de la Palu [*Deceased, 1342*] [*Authority cited in pre-1607 legal work*] (DSA)
PEPAOP ... (Phenylethyl)phenylacetoxypiperidine [*Organic chemistry*]
PEPAS....... WHO [*World Health Organization*] Western Pacific Regional Centre for the Promotion of Environmental Planning and Applied Studies (EAIO)
PEPC......... Peptidase C [*An enzyme*]
PEPC......... Phosphoenolpyruvate Carboxylase [*An enzyme*]
PEPC......... Polynomial Error Protection Code [*Data processing*]
PEPC......... Potomac Electric Power Company
PEPCK....... Phosphoenolopyruvate Carboxykinase [*An enzyme*]
PEPCO...... Potomac Electric Power Company
PEPD......... Peptidase D [*An enzyme*]
PEPE .... Parallel Element Processing Ensemble [*Burroughs Corp.*] (BUR)
PEPE .... Prolonged Elevated-Pollution Episode [*Environmental Protection Agency*]
PEPG........ Piezoelectric Power Generation
PEPG......... Port Emergency Planning Group [*NATO*] (NATG)
PEPI .... Physical Education Public Information [*Film*]
PEPI .... Piezo Electric Products, Incorporated [*NASDAQ symbol*] (NQ)
PEPI .... Pre-Ejection Period Index [*Cardiology*]
PEPIA .... Physics of the Earth and Planetary Interiors [*A publication*]
Pepinier Hortic Maraichers ... Pepinieristes, Horticulteurs, Maraichers [*France*] [*A publication*]
PEPL .... Peoples Restaurants [*NASDAQ symbol*] (NQ)
PEPL .... Preliminary Engineering Parts List
PEPLAN ... Polaris Executive Plan [*British*]
PEPMC..... Printing Estimators and Production Men's Club [*New York, NY*] (EA)
PEPMIS.... Plant Equipment Packages Management Information System (MCD)
PEPOA...... Philippine Electric Plant Owners Association (DS)
PEPP .... Planetary Entry Parachute Program [*NASA*]
PEPP .... Professional Engineers in Private Practice
PEPPA ...... Preparedness for Emergency Plant Pest Action [*In Animal and Plant Health Inspection Service publication PEPPA Pot*]
Pepperdine LR ... Pepperdine Law Review [*A publication*]
Pepperdine L Rev ... Pepperdine Law Review [*A publication*]
Pepper & L Dig ... Pepper and Lewis' Digest of Laws [*Pennsylvania*] [*A publication*] (DLA)
Pepper & L Dig Laws ... Pepper and Lewis' Digest of Laws [*Pennsylvania*] [*A publication*] (DLA)
Pepp LR ..... Pepperdine Law Review [*A publication*]
PEPR .... Precision Encoding and Pattern Recognition Device [*Data processing*]
PEPS .... National Committee on Public Employee Pension Systems (EA)
PEPS .... Peperomia and Exotic Plant Society (EA)
PEPS .... Peptidase S [*An enzyme*]
PEPS .... Pesticide Enforcement Policy Statement [*Environmental Protection Agency*]
PEPS .... Primary Environmental Prediction System
PEPS .... Production Engineering Productivity System [*Camtek Ltd.*] [*Software package*]
PEPS .... Productivity Environmental Preference Survey [*Test*]
PEPS .... Program Element Plan Supplement
PEPSB....... Perception and Psychophysics [*A publication*]
PEP-SEP ... Peptide Separation [*Biochemistry*]
PEPSI........ Plasma Electron Profiles, Symmetric Integrals (MCD)
PEPSS .... Preschool and Early Primary Skills Survey [*Child development test*]
PEPSS .... Programmable Equipment for Personnel Subsystem Simulation
PEPSU ...... All India Reporter, Patiala and East Punjab States Union [*1950-57*] [*A publication*] (DLA)
PEPSU ...... Patiala and East Punjab States Union
PEPSY....... Precision Earth-Pointing System (MCD)
PEPTDO ... Peptides [*New York*] [*A publication*]
Pept Protein Rev ... Peptide and Protein Reviews [*A publication*]
Pept Res ..... Peptide Research [*A publication*]
PEP/USA ... Parkinson's Educational Program - USA (EA)
PEPUSL.... Pepperdine University School of Law (DLA)
PEpW .... Westinghouse Electric Corp., East Pittsburgh, PA [*Library symbol*] [*Library of Congress*] (LCLS)
PEQ .... Palestine Exploration Quarterly [*A publication*]
PEQ .... Pecos City, TX [*Location identifier*] [*FAA*] (FAAL)
PEQ .... Personal Experience Questionnaire [*Psychology*]
PEQ .... Petroquin Resources Ltd. [*Vancouver Stock Exchange symbol*]
PEQUA ...... Production Equipment Agency [*Army*]
PEQUOD .. Pacific Equatorial Ocean Dynamics
PEr............. Erie Public Library, Erie, PA [*Library symbol*] [*Library of Congress*] (LCLS)
PER........... Par Exchange Rate [*Business term*]
PER........... Parity Error Rate
PER........... Partido Estadista Republicano [*Puerto Rico*] [*Political party*]
PER........... Peak Expiration Rate [*Medicine*]
Pe R........... Pennewill's Delaware Reports [*A publication*] (DLA)

Per con .... Per Contra [*On the Other Side*] [*Latin*]
per .... Perennial [*Botany*]
Per............. Perera's Select Decisions [*Ceylon*] [*A publication*] (DLA)
PER........... Performance Evaluation Report [*DoD*]
PER........... Perhaps (ROG)
Per............. Pericles [*of Plutarch*] [*Classical studies*] (OCD)
Per............. Pericles [*Shakespearean work*]
PER........... Perigee (KSC)
Per............. Periochae [*of Livy*] [*Classical studies*] (OCD)
Per............. Period
PER........... Period [*Record label*]
PER........... Periodical (ROG)
PER........... Permian Airways, Inc. [*Midland, TX*] [*FAA designator*] (FAAC)
PER........... Permission (AABC)
Per............. Perseus [*Constellation*]
PER........... Persia [*Obsolete*]
per .... Persian, Modern [*MARC language code*] [*Library of Congress*] (LCCP)
PER........... Person
PER........... Personnel (KSC)
PER........... Personnel [*A publication*]
Per............. Perspective [*A publication*]
Per............. Perspectives [*A publication*]
PER........... PERT [*Program Evaluation and Review Technique*] Event Report
PER........... Perth [*Australia*] [*Seismograph station code, US Geological Survey*] [*Closed*] (SEIS)
PER........... Perth [*Australia*] [*Airport symbol*] (OAG)
PER........... Peru [*ANSI three-letter standard code*] (CNC)
PER........... Phase Engineering Report
PER........... Physical Examination Rate [*Military*] (AFM)
PER........... Planning, Evaluation, and Reporting [*Education-improvement system*]
PER........... Pominex Ltd. [*Toronto Stock Exchange symbol*]
PER........... Ponca City, OK [*Location identifier*] [*FAA*] (FAAL)
PER........... Pope, Evans & Robbins, Inc. [*AMEX symbol*] (SPSG)
PER........... Port Everglades Railway [*AAR code*]
PER........... Post Engineer Request
PER........... Postelectrophoresis Relaxation
PER........... Preliminary Engineering Report (KSC)
PER........... PressNet Environmental Reports [*Information service or system*] (IID)
PER........... Price Earnings Ratio [*Relation between price of a company's stock and its annual net income*]
PER........... Product Engineering Recommendation [*Automotive engineering*]
PER........... Production Engine Remanufacturers Program [*Automotive engineering*]
PER........... Professional and Executive Recruitment Service [*British*]
PER........... Proficiency Evaluation Review
PER........... Program Event Recording [*Data processing*] (MDG)
PER........... Program Execution Request
PER........... Proposal Evaluation Report (MCD)
PER........... Protein Efficiency Ratio [*Nutrition*]
PER........... Public Employees Roundtable (EA)
PER........... Pyrotechnical Evaluation Range [*Army*] (RDA)
PERA........ Planning and Engineering for Repair and Alteration [*Navy*]
PERA........ Production Engine Remanufacturers Association (EA)
PERA........ Production Engineering Research Association [*Research center*] [*British*] (IRC)
Per AJ........ Performing Arts Journal [*A publication*]
PERAM..... Personnel Action Memorandum [*Military*]
PER AN..... Per Annum [*By the Year*] [*Latin*]
PER ANN ... Per Annum [*By the Year*] [*Latin*]
Per A R ..... Performing Arts Review [*A publication*]
Pe Rave ...... Petrus Ravennas [*Flourished, 1468-1508*] [*Authority cited in pre-1607 legal work*] (DSA)
Per Biol ..... Periodicum Biologorum [*A publication*]
PERC........ Peace on Earth Research Center
PERC........ Perceptronics, Inc. [*NASDAQ symbol*] (NQ)
PERC........ Percolator (DSUE)
PERC........ Percussion (AAG)
PERC........ Pittsburgh Energy Research Center [*Later, PETC*] [*Energy Research and Development Administration*]
PERC........ Political Economy Research Center [*Research center*] (RCD)
PERC........ Processor Emergency Recovery Circuit [*Bell System*]
PERC........ Professional Engineering and Research Consultants
PERC........ Psoriasis Education and Research Centre [*University of Toronto*] [*Canada*] [*Research center*] (RCD)
PERCAM .. Performance and Cost Analysis Model (MCD)
Per Cap ...... Per Capita [*By the Individual*] [*Latin*]
PERCAP..... Persian Gulf Requirements and Capabilities [*Military*]
PERCASREPT ... Personnel Casualty Report [*Military*] (NVT)
PERCENT ... Per Centum [*By the Hundred*] [*Latin*]
Percept Cognit Devel ... Perceptual Cognitive Development [*A publication*]
Percept & Motor Skills ... Perceptual and Motor Skills [*A publication*]
Percept and Mot Sk ... Perceptual and Motor Skills [*A publication*]
Percept Mot Skills ... Perceptual and Motor Skills [*A publication*]
Percept Psychophys ... Perception and Psychophysics [*A publication*]
PERCHLOR ... Perchloride [*Chemistry*] (ROG)

PERCI .... Personnel Contamination Instrumentation
Perc Mot Sk ... Perceptual and Motor Skills [*A publication*]
Perc Notes ... Percussive Notes [*A publication*]
PERCOM ... Peripheral Communications (FAAC)
PERCOM ... Personnel Command [*Army*] (MCD)
PERCOMPASIA ... South East Asian Personal Computer Hardware and
   Software Show (TSPED)
Per Comp T ... Personal Computers Today [*A publication*]
PERCOS ... Performance Coding System
Perc Psych ... Perception and Psychophysics [*A publication*]
Per CS........ Perrault's Conseil Superieur [*Canada*] [*A publication*] (DLA)
PERCUSS & AUSC ... Percussion and Ausculation [*Medicine*] (DHSM)
PERD........ Perdendo [*or Perdendosi*] [*Softer and Slower*] [*Music*]
PERD........ Perdendosi [*Softer and Slower*] [*Music*]
PERD........ Periodic (MSA)
PERD........ Perused (ROG)
PERDA...... Per Diem [*By the Day*] [*Latin*] (NOAA)
Per & Dav .. Perry and Davison's English King's Bench Reports [*1838-41*] [*A
   publication*] (DLA)
PERDDiMS ... Personnel Deployment and Distribution Management System
   [*Military*] (AABC)
PERDEN... Perdendo [*or Perdendosi*] [*Softer and Slower*] [*Music*]
PERDEN... Perdendosi [*Softer and Slower*] [*Music*]
PERDEX ... Permuted Formula Index [*Molecular formula indexing*]
Peredovoi Opyt Stroit Ekspl Shakht ... Peredovoi Opyt v Stroitel'stve i
   Ekspluatatsii Shakht [*A publication*]
Peredovoi Opyt Stroit Eksp Shakht ... Peredovoi Opyt v Stroitel'stve i
   Ekspluatatsii Shakht [*USSR*] [*A publication*]
PEREF...... Personal Effects
PEREF...... Propellant Engine Research Environmental Facility
Pereg.......... Peregrinus Fabius [*Authority cited in pre-1607 legal
   work*] (DSA)
Pererab Gaza Gazov Kondens Nauchno-Tekh Obz ... Pererabotka Gaza i
   Gazovogo Kondensata. Nauchno-Tekhnicheskii Obzor [*A
   publication*]
Pererab Tverd Topl ... Pererabotka Tverdogo Topliva [*USSR*] [*A publication*]
PE Rev .... Physical Education Review [*A publication*]
PERF......... Perfect
PERF......... PerfectData Corp. [*NASDAQ symbol*] (NQ)
PERF......... Perforate (KSC)
PERF......... Perforation (DSUE)
PERF......... Performance (KSC)
PERF......... Police Executive Research Forum (EA)
Perf Art C .. Performing Arts in Canada [*A publication*]
Perf Art J .. Performing Arts Journal [*A publication*]
Perf Art R .. Performing Arts Review [*A publication*]
Perf Arts .... Performing Arts in Canada [*A publication*]
Perf Arts Can ... Performing Arts in Canada [*A publication*]
Perf Arts R ... Performing Arts Review [*A publication*]
PERFCE..... Performance
PERFD..... Performed (ROG)
Perf Eval .... Performance Evaluation [*A publication*]
Perf Eval Rev ... Performance Evaluation Review [*A publication*]
PERFINS .. Perforated Insignia [*Philately*]
PERFM..... Perform (ROG)
Performance Eval ... Performance Evaluation [*A publication*]
Performance Eval Rev ... Performance Evaluation Review [*A publication*]
Performing Arts Rev ... Performing Arts Review [*A publication*]
Perform Instr J ... Performance and Instruction Journal [*A publication*]
Perf Right .. Performing Right [*A publication*]
Perfumer ... Perfumer and Flavorist [*A publication*]
Perfum Essent Oil Rec ... Perfumery and Essential Oil Record [*A publication*]
Perfum Flavorist ... Perfumer and Flavorist [*A publication*]
Perfum Flavour ... Perfumery and Flavouring [*Japan*] [*A publication*]
Perfum J .... Perfumers' Journal [*A publication*]
Perfum Kosmet ... Perfumerie und Kosmetik [*A publication*]
PERFW ..... Perforating Wound
PErG......... Gannon University, Erie, PA [*Library symbol*] [*Library of
   Congress*] (LCLS)
PERG......... Pergola [*Classified advertising*] (ADA)
PERG......... Production Emergency Redistribution Group
PERG......... Production Equipment Redistribution Group [*Army*]
Pergamon Gen Psychol Ser ... Pergamon General Psychology Series [*A
   publication*]
Pergamon Ser Environ Sci ... Pergamon Series on Environmental Science [*A
   publication*]
Pergamon Ser Monogr Lab Tech ... Pergamon Series of Monographs in
   Laboratory Techniques [*A publication*]
Pergamon Texts Inorg Chem ... Pergamon Texts in Inorganic Chemistry [*A
   publication*]
Perg I S Da ... Pergamon International Series on Dance and Related
   Disciplines [*A publication*]
PERGO ..... Project Evaluation and Review with Graphic Output (IEEE)
PERGRA ... Permission Granted [*Military*]
PERH .... Perhaps
PerHi .... Erie County Historical Society, Erie, PA [*Library symbol*]
   [*Library of Congress*] (LCLS)
PERI .... Pacific Energy Resources, Inc. [*NASDAQ symbol*] (NQ)
PERI .... Pea Ridge National Military Park
PERI .... Perigee
PERI .... Perimeter (AABC)

PERI .... Periscope
PERI .... Platemakers Educational and Research Institute [*Later, IAP*]
PERI .... Production Equipment Redistribution Inventory [*Army*]
PERI .... Production Equipment Reserve Inventory [*Navy*] (NG)
PERI .... Protein Engineering Research Institute [*Japanese governmental
   and industrial consortium*]
PERIAP..... Periapical [*Dentistry*]
PERIF....... Peripheral
Pe Rigal...... Petrus Rigaldi [*Flourished, 14th century*] [*Authority cited in
   pre-1607 legal work*] (DSA)
PERIM ...... Perimeter (KSC)
PERIN....... Penalty Enforcement Registration of Infringement Notice
   [*Australia*]
Perinat Med ... Perinatal Medicine [*A publication*]
Perinat Neonat ... Perinatology/Neonatology [*A publication*]
PERINTREP ... Periodic Intelligence Report (NATG)
PERINTREPT ... Periodic Intelligence Report
PERINTSUM ... Periodic Intelligence Summary [*Army*] (AABC)
Period Anim Prod ... Periodical on Animal Production [*A publication*]
Period Biol ... Periodicum Biologorum [*A publication*]
Period Bull Int Sugar Confect Manuf Assoc Int Off Cocoa Choc ... Periodic
   Bulletin. International Sugar Confectionery Manufacturers'
   Association and International Office of Cocoa and
   Chocolate [*A publication*]
Period Mat ... Periodico di Matematiche [*A publication*]
Period Mat 5 ... Periodico di Matematiche. Serie V [*A publication*]
Period Math Hung ... Periodica Mathematica Hungarica [*A publication*]
Period Math Hungar ... Periodica Mathematica Hungarica [*A publication*]
Period Mineral ... Periodico di Mineralogia [*Italy*] [*A publication*]
Periodont Abstr ... Periodontal Abstracts. Journal of the Western Society of
   Periodontology [*A publication*]
Periodont Case Rep ... Periodontal Case Reports [*A publication*]
Period Polytech ... Periodica Polytechnica [*A publication*]
Period Polytech Chem Eng ... Periodica Polytechnica. Chemical Engineering
   [*A publication*]
Period Polytech Civ Eng ... Periodica Polytechnica. Civil Engineering
   [*Hungary*] [*A publication*]
Period Polytech Civ Engng ... Periodica Polytechnica. Civil Engineering [*A
   publication*]
Period Polytech Electr Eng ... Periodica Polytechnica. Electrical Engineering
   [*A publication*]
Period Polytech Eng ... Periodica Polytechnica. Engineering [*A publication*]
Period Polytech Mech Eng ... Periodica Polytechnica. Mechanical Engineering
   [*Hungary*] [*A publication*]
Period Polytech Mech Engng ... Periodica Polytechnica. Mechanical
   Engineering [*A publication*]
Period Polytech Trans Engng ... Periodica Polytechnica. Transportation
   Engineering [*A publication*]
Period Speaking ... Periodically Speaking [*A publication*]
Periopr Nurs Q ... Perioperative Nursing Quarterly [*A publication*]
PERIPH .... Periphery (KSC)
Peripl M Eux ... Periplus Maris Euxini [*of Arrian*] [*Classical studies*] (OCD)
PERIS........ Periscope (KSC)
Periton Dia ... Peritoneal Dialysis Bulletin [*A publication*]
PERJ .... Perjury [*FBI standardized term*]
PERJY...... Perjury (ROG)
PERK........ Payroll Earnings Record Keeping
Perk........... Perkins on Conveyancing [*A publication*] (DLA)
Perk........... Perkins Journal [*A publication*]
Perk........... Perkins on Pleading [*A publication*] (DLA)
Perk........... Perkins' Profitable Book (Conveyancing) [*A
   publication*] (DLA)
PERK........ Perquisite
PERK........ Prospective Evaluation of Radial Keratotomy [*for eye surgery*]
Perkin-Elmer Tech News ... Perkin-Elmer Technical News [*A publication*]
Perkins J.... Perkins School of Theology. Journal [*A publication*]
Perkins Obs Contrib Ser 2 ... Perkins Observatory. Contributions. Series 2 [*A
   publication*]
Per & Kn ... Perry and Knapp's English Election Reports [*1838*] [*A
   publication*] (DLA)
Perk Pr Bk ... Perkins' Profitable Book (Conveyancing) [*A
   publication*] (DLA)
PERL........ Pathologically Eclectic Rubbish Lister
PERL........ Perkin-Elmer Robot Language
PERL........ Perle Systems Ltd. [*Scarborough, ON*] [*NASDAQ
   symbol*] (NQ)
PERL........ Perusal (ROG)
PERL........ Pictorial Engineering and Research Laboratory
PERL........ Prepositioned Equipment Requirements List [*Navy*] (MCD)
PERL........ Public Employee Relations Library [*of International Personnel
   Management Association*]
PERLA ...... Pupils Equal, React to Light and Accommodation [*Medicine*]
PERLS...... Principal Exchange-Rate-Linked Securities [*Investment term*]
PERM....... Permanent
PERM....... Permanent Employee (DSUE)
PERM....... Permeability
PERM....... Permian [*Period, era, or system*] [*Geology*]
PERM....... Permission (MSA)
PERM....... Permutation (DSUE)
PERM....... Program Evaluation for Repetitive Manufacture (IEEE)

PERMACAP ... Personnel Management and Accounting Card Processor [*Military*]
PERMACAPS ... Personnel Management and Accounting Card Processing System (MCD)
PERMAFROST ... Permanent Frost
PerManAb ... Personal Management Abstracts [*A publication*]
PERMAS .. Personnel Management Assistance System [*Military*] (AABC)
PERMB..... Permeability
Permbledhje Stud ... Permbledhje Studimesh [*A publication*]
Permbledhje Stud Inst Kerkimeve Gjeol Miner ... Permbledhje Studimesh. Instituti i Kerkimeve Gjeologijke dhe Minerale [*A publication*]
Permbledhje Stud Inst Stud Kerkimeve Ind Miner ... Permbledhje Studimesh. Instituti i Studimeve dhe Kerkimeve Industirale e Minerale [*A publication*]
PErMC ...... Mercyhurst College, Erie, PA [*Library symbol*] [*Library of Congress*] (LCLS)
PERME..... Propellants, Explosives, and Rocket Motors Establishment [*British*] (RDA)
Perm Found Med Bull ... Permanente Foundation Medical Bulletin [*A publication*]
Perm Gos Ped Inst Ucen Zap ... Permskii Gosudarstvennyi Pedagogiceskii Institut. Ucenye Zapiski [*A publication*]
Perm Gos Univ Ucen Zap ... Permskii Gosudarstvennyi Universitet Imeni A. M. Gor'kogo. Ucenye Zapiski [*A publication*]
PERMIC ... Personnel Management Information Center [*Navy*] (NVT)
PERMINVAR ... Permeability Invariant
PERMIXT ... Permixtus [*Mixed*] [*Pharmacy*] (ROG)
PERMLY .. Permanently
Perm Politehn Inst Sb Naucn Trudov ... Permskii Politehniceskii Institut. Sbornik Naucnyh Trudov [*A publication*]
PERMR..... Permanent Residence
PERMREP ... Permanent Representation to North Atlantic Council [*NATO*] (NATG)
PERMS ..... Process and Effluent Radiological Monitoring System [*Nuclear energy*] (NRCH)
PERMSS... Process and Effluent Radiological Monitoring and Sampling System [*Nuclear energy*] (NRCH)
PERMT ..... Permanent (ROG)
PERMU..... Permanent Magnet Users Association [*Defunct*] (EA)
Perm Way ... Permanent Way [*A publication*]
Pernamb Odont ... Pernambuco Odontologica [*A publication*]
PERNOGRA ... Permission Not Granted [*Military*]
PER OP EMET ... Peracta Operatione Emetici [*When the Operation of the Emetic is Finished*] [*Pharmacy*] (ROG)
Per Or Cas ... Perry's Oriental Cases [*Bombay*] [*A publication*] (DLA)
PEROX...... Peroxide
PERP......... Pan-Ethnic Republican Party of Australia [*Political party*] (ADA)
PERP........ Perpendicular (AAG)
PERP........ Perpetual (ADA)
perp........... Perpetuel [*Irredeemable*] [*Business term*] [*French*]
Per P .... Perrault's Prevoste de Quebec [*A publication*] (DLA)
PERP........ Personnel Processing (MUGU)
Perpet........ Perpetual (DLA)
Per Poly CE ... Periodica Polytechnica. Chemical Engineering [*A publication*]
Per Poly EE ... Periodica Polytechnica. Electrical Engineering [*A publication*]
Per Poly ME ... Periodica Polytechnica. Mechanical Engineering [*A publication*]
Per Pract B ... Personnel Practice Bulletin [*A publication*] (APTA)
PER PROC ... Per Procurationem [*By Proxy, By the Action Of*] [*Legal term*] [*Latin*]
Per Psy....... Personnel Psychology [*A publication*]
PERR........ Premature Engine Removal Rate (AAG)
Perrault....... Perrault's Conseil Superieur [*Canada*] [*A publication*] (DLA)
Perrault...... Perrault's Prevoste de Quebec [*A publication*] (DLA)
Perrault...... Perrault's Quebec Reports [*A publication*] (DLA)
Per Rel St... Perspectives in Religious Studies [*A publication*]
PERRLA ... Pupils Equal, Round, React to Light and Accommodation [*Medicine*]
Perry .... Perry's Oriental Cases [*Bombay*] [*A publication*] (DLA)
Perry .... [*Sir Erskine*] Perry's Reports in Morley's East Indian Digest [*A publication*] (DLA)
Perry & D... Perry and Davison's English King's Bench Reports [*A publication*] (DLA)
Perry & D (Eng) ... Perry and Davison's English King's Bench Reports [*A publication*] (DLA)
Perry Ins .... Perry's English Insolvency Cases [*1831*] [*A publication*] (DLA)
Perry & K... Perry and Knapp's English Election Cases [*A publication*] (DLA)
Perry & Kn ... Perry and Knapp's English Election Cases [*A publication*] (DLA)
Perry OC... Perry's Oriental Cases [*Bombay*] [*A publication*] (DLA)
PERS .... Performance Evaluation Reporting System [*DoD*]
PERS .... Periodical Source Index [*A publication*]
Pers .... Persae [*of Aeschylus*] [*Classical studies*] (OCD)
Pers .... Perseus [*Constellation*]
PERS .... Persia [*Obsolete*]
Pers .... Persius [*34-62AD*] [*Classical studies*] (OCD)
PERS .... Person
PERS .... Personal

PERS .... Personal Diagnostics, Inc. [*NASDAQ symbol*] (NQ)
PERS .... Personal Emergency Response System [*Telecommunications*]
Pers .... Personalist [*A publication*]
Pers .... Personnel [*A publication*]
PERS .... Personnel (AFM)
Pers .... Perspektiv [*A publication*]
PERS .... Preliminary Engineering Reports (MUGU)
PERSACLIT ... Peritus in Sacred Liturgy [*Roman Catholic*]
PERSACS ... Personnel Structure and Accounting System [*Army*]
PERSACS ... Personnel Structure and Composition System [*Military*]
Pers Adm ... Personnel Administration [*A publication*]
Pers Adm ... Personnel Administrator [*A publication*]
Pers Admin ... Personnel Administrator [*A publication*]
Pers Am Hist ... Perspectives in American History [*A publication*]
PERSC....... Public Education Religion Studies Center (EA)
PERSCEN ... Personnel Center
PERSCO ... Personnel Support of Contingency Operations [*Military*]
PersCom .... Personnel Command [*Army*] (INF)
Pers Comput World ... Personal Computer World [*A publication*]
PERSCON ... Personnel Control [*Military*]
PERSD ...... Personnel Department [*Marine Corps*]
PERSDEP ... Personnel Deployment Report [*Military*]
PERSEP..... Pershing Survivability Evaluation Program [*Military*] (MCD)
PERSET..... Personnel Standardization and Evaluation Team [*Military*]
PERSEVCE ... Perseverance (ROG)
PERSEXP ... Personal Expense Money [*Army*]
Pers Finance LQ ... Personal Finance Law Quarterly Report [*A publication*]
Pers Finance LQ Rep ... Personal Finance Law Quarterly Report [*A publication*]
Pers Guid J ... Personnel and Guidance Journal [*A publication*]
Pershad...... Privy Council Judgments [*1829-69*] [*India*] [*A publication*] (DLA)
PERSIL..... Peroxide Silicate [*Detergent and bleach*]
Pers Indiv... Personality and Individual Differences [*A publication*]
Pers Individ Differ ... Personality and Individual Differences [*A publication*]
Pers Inj Ann ... Personal Injury Annual [*A publication*]
Pers Inj Comment'r ... Personal Injury Commentator [*A publication*] (DLA)
Pers Inj Deskbook ... Personal Injury Deskbook [*A publication*]
Pers Inj LJ ... Personal Injury Law Journal [*A publication*] (DLA)
PERSINS .. Personnel Information System [*Army*]
PERSINSCOM ... Personnel Information Systems Command [*Army*] (AABC)
PERSINSD ... Personnel Information Systems Directorate [*Military Personnel Center*] (AABC)
PERSIR .... Personnel Inventory Report [*Army*] (AABC)
Pers J .... Personnel Journal [*A publication*]
Pers Jrl ...... Personnel Journal [*A publication*]
PERSL....... Personal
Pers Man ... Personnel Management [*A publication*]
Pers Manage ... Personnel Management [*A publication*]
Pers Manage Abstr ... Personnel Management Abstracts [*A publication*]
Pers Mgt .... Personnel Management [*A publication*]
PERSNET ... Personnel Network [*Army*]
Pers New Mus ... Perspectives of New Music [*A publication*]
PERSO ...... Personnel Officer [*Air Force*]
PERSOF .... Personnel Officer [*Navy*]
Person .... Personalist [*A publication*]
PERSON... Personnel Simulation On-Line [*Department of State*] [*Computer program*]
Personal & Soc Psychol Bull ... Personality and Social Psychology Bulletin [*A publication*]
Personnel Exec ... Personnel Executive [*A publication*]
Personnel Guidance J ... Personnel and Guidance Journal [*A publication*]
Personnel & Guid J ... Personnel and Guidance Journal [*A publication*]
Personnel J ... Personnel Journal [*A publication*]
Personnel Manag (London) ... Personnel Management (London) [*A publication*]
Personnel Mgmt ... Personnel Management [*A publication*]
Personnel Mgmt P-H ... Personnel Management. Prentice-Hall [*A publication*]
Personnel Mgt Abstracts ... Personnel Management Abstracts [*A publication*]
Personnel Practice B ... Personnel Practice Bulletin [*A publication*]
Personnel Practice Bul ... Personnel Practice Bulletin [*A publication*] (APTA)
Personnel Psych ... Personnel Psychology [*A publication*]
Personnel Psychol ... Personnel Psychology [*A publication*]
Personn Pract Bull ... Personnel Practice Bulletin [*A publication*] (APTA)
Persp......... Perspective [*Record label*]
PERSP....... Perspective (MSA)
Persp......... Perspectives [*A publication*]
PERSPAY ... Personnel and Pay [*Project*] [*Navy*]
Persp Biol .. Perspectives in Biology and Medicine [*A publication*]
Perspec....... Perspective [*A publication*]
Perspec Biol & Med ... Perspectives in Biology and Medicine [*A publication*]
Perspec Ed ... Perspectives on Education [*A publication*]
Perspect Accredit ... Perspectives on Accreditation [*A publication*]
Perspect Am Hist ... Perspectives in American History [*A publication*]
Perspect Biol Med ... Perspectives in Biology and Medicine [*A publication*]
Perspect Biom ... Perspectives in Biometrics [*A publication*]
Perspect Brain Sci ... Perspectives in the Brain Sciences [*A publication*]
Perspect Cardiovasc Res ... Perspectives in Cardiovascular Research [*A publication*]

Perspect Clin Pharmacol ... Perspectives in Clinical Pharmacology [*A publication*]
Perspect Comput ... Perspectives in Computing [*A publication*]
Perspect in Educ ... Perspectives in Education [*A publication*]
Perspect Hum Reprod ... Perspectives in Human Reproduction [*A publication*]
Perspect Ind Psychol ... Perspectives in Industrial Psychology [*A publication*]
Perspect Int ... Perspectives Internationales [*A publication*]
Perspective K ... Perspective (Karachi) [*A publication*]
Perspectives Biol Med ... Perspectives in Biology and Medicine [*A publication*]
Perspectives Civ Rights Q ... Perspectives. The Civil Rights Quarterly [*A publication*]
Perspectives Euro-Afr ... Perspectives Euro-Africaines [*A publication*]
Perspectives Latino-Am ... Perspectives Latino-Americaines [*A publication*]
Perspectives New M ... Perspectives of New Music [*A publication*]
Perspect Med ... Perspectives in Medicine [*A publication*]
Perspect Medicaid Manage ... Perspectives on Medicaid Management [*A publication*]
Perspect Medicaid Medicare Manage ... Perspectives on Medicaid and Medicare Management [*A publication*]
Perspect Nephrol Hypertens ... Perspectives in Nephrology and Hypertension [*A publication*]
Perspect Ophthalmol ... Perspectives in Ophthalmology [*A publication*]
Perspect Pediatr Pathol ... Perspectives in Pediatric Pathology [*A publication*]
Perspect Polon ... Perspectives Polonaises [*A publication*]
Perspect Powder Metall ... Perspectives in Powder Metallurgy [*A publication*]
Perspect Psychiatr ... Perspectives Psychiatriques [*A publication*]
Perspect Psychiatr Care ... Perspectives in Psychiatric Care [*A publication*]
Perspect Vertebr Sci ... Perspectives in Vertebrate Science [*A publication*]
Perspect Virol ... Perspectives in Virology [*A publication*]
Perspekt Phil ... Perspektiven der Philosophie [*A publication*]
Persp N Mus ... Perspectives of New Music [*A publication*]
Persp Pol ... Perspectives Polonaises [*A publication*]
Pers Prac B ... Personnel Practice Bulletin [*A publication*]
Pers Prac Bul ... Personnel Practice Bulletin [*A publication*] (APTA)
Pers Pract Bull ... Personnel Practice Bulletin [*A publication*] (APTA)
PERSPROC ... Personnel Processing [*Army*]
Persp Soc ... Perspectives Socialistes [*A publication*]
Pers Psych ... Personnel Psychology [*A publication*]
Pers Psych C ... Perspectives in Psychiatric Care [*A publication*]
Pers Psychol ... Personnel Psychology [*A publication*]
Persp Teol ... Perspectiva Teologica [*A publication*]
Pers Rep Exec ... Personal Report for the Executive [*A publication*]
PERSSEPCENT ... Personnel Separation Center
PERSSO ... Personnel System Staff Officer
PERSTAT ... Personnel Status Report [*Military*]
PERSTATREP ... Personnel Status Report [*Military*]
PERS & TRACOMD ... Personnel and Training Command
PERSTRAN ... Personal Transportation [*Navy*]
Pers V .... Personalvertretung [*A publication*]
PERT .... Patients Experience of the Relationship with the Therapist Method
PERT .... Performance Evaluation Review Technique
PERT .... Pertain (AABC)
PERT .... Pertussis [*Whooping cough*]
PERT .... Phenol Enhanced Reassociation Technique [*Clinical chemistry*]
PERT .... Program Evaluation Research Task (IEEE)
PERT .... Program Evaluation and Review Technique [*Data processing*] [*Computer performance management*]
PERTCO ... Program Evaluation and Review Technique with Cost
PERTHS ... Perthshire [*County in Scotland*]
Perti .... [*Petrus de*] Bellapertica [*Deceased, 1308*] [*Authority cited in pre-1607 legal work*] (DSA)
Pertica .... [*Petrus de*] Bellapertica [*Deceased, 1308*] [*Authority cited in pre-1607 legal work*] (DSA)
PERTO ..... Pertaining To (NVT)
Per Tr .... Perry on Trusts [*A publication*] (DLA)
PERTRAN ... Perturbation Transport [*NASA*]
PERTSIM ... Program Evaluation and Review Technique Simulation [*Game*]
PERT-TAM ... Program Evaluation and Review Technique Task, Action, and Milestone Items
PERT/TIME ... Program Evaluation and Review Technique/Time Analyzer [*Sperry UNIVAC*]
PERU .... Production Equipment Records Unit (IEEE)
Peru Dir Gen Mineria Bol ... Peru. Ministerio de Fomento y Obras Publicas. Direccion General de Mineria. Boletin [*A publication*]
PERUG ...... Perusing (ROG)
Peru Indig ... Peru Indigena [*A publication*]
Peru Minist Agric Dir Gen Invest Agropecu Bol Tec ... Peru. Ministerio de Agricultura. Direccion General de Investigaciones Agropecuarias. Boletin Tecnico [*A publication*]
Peru Minist Agric Serv Invest Promoc Agrar Bol Tec ... Peru. Ministerio de Agricultura. Servicio de Investigacion y Promocion Agraria. Boletin Tecnico [*A publication*]
PERUSA ... Perspectives - United States of America [*History course*]
Peru Serv Geol Min Bol ... Peru. Servicio de Geologia y Mineria. Boletin [*A publication*]
Peru Serv Geol Min Estud Espec ... Peru. Servicio de Geologia y Mineria. Estudios Especiales [*A publication*]

Peru Serv Geol Min Geodinamica Ing Geol ... Peru. Servicio de Geologia y Mineria. Geodinamica e Ingenieria Geologica [*A publication*]
PERUV ...... Peruvian
PERV .... Pervert [*or Perverted*] [*FBI standardized term*]
PErV .... United States Veterans Administration Hospital, Erie, PA [*Library symbol*] [*Library of Congress*] (LCLS)
PErVM ...... Villa Maria College, Erie, PA [*Library symbol*] [*Library of Congress*] (LCLS)
PERYLENE ... Peri-Dinaphthalene [*A fluorophore*] [*Organic chemistry*]
PES .... IEEE Power Engineering Society (EA)
PES .... Paid Educational Services [*British*]
PES .... Pan European Survey [*A publication*]
PES .... Paraendocrine Syndrome [*Endocrinology*]
PES .... Parent Egg Seed
PES .... Partido Ecuatoriano Socialista [*Ecuadorean Socialist Party*] [*Political party*]
PES .... Parts Engineering Support
PES .... Patent Examining System
PES .... Pecos Resources [*Vancouver Stock Exchange symbol*]
Pes .... Pesahim (BJA)
PES .... Peshawar [*Pakistan*] [*Seismograph station code, US Geological Survey*] [*Closed*] (SEIS)
PES .... Philosophy of Education Society (EA)
PES .... Photoelectric Scanner
PES .... Photoelectron Spectroscopy
PES .... Photojet Edge Sensor
PES .... Physicians Equity Services
PES .... Pictorial Eleven Society [*Formerly, PE*] [*Absorbed by PCS*] (EA)
PES .... Pointing Error Sensor (MCD)
PES .... Polish Economic Survey [*A publication*]
PES .... Polyethersulfone [*Organic chemistry*]
PES .... Polyethylene Sodium Sulfonate [*Anticoagulant*]
PES .... Post-Enumeration Survey [*Bureau of the Census*]
PES .... Postextrasystolic Potentiation [*Cardiology*]
PES .... Potential Energy Source [*Physiology*]
PES .... Potential-Energy Surface [*Chemical kinetics*]
PES .... Poultry and Egg Situation
PES .... Power Engineering Society
PES .... Power Engineering Specification
PES .... Preexcitation Syndrome [*Cardiology*]
Pes .... Pressure, End-Systole [*Cardiology*]
P(ES) .... Probability of Equal Regressive Slopes [*Statistics*]
PES .... Problem-Etiology-Signs [*or Symptoms*] [*Nursing*]
PES .... Production Engineering Service
PES .... Production Engineering Specification (NG)
PES .... Professional Employment Service [*Australia*]
PES .... Professional Examination Service
PES .... Program Element Summary
PES .... Program Emphasis Statement [*US Employment Service*] [*Department of Labor*]
PES .... Program Execution System
PES .... Programmed Electrical Stimulation [*Neurophysiology*]
PES .... Projected Engagement Scheduler [*Military*] (CAAL)
PESA .... Petroleum Electric Supply Association [*Defunct*] (EA)
PESA .... Petroleum Equipment Suppliers Association (EA)
PESA .... Petroleum Exploration Society of Australia
PESA .... Philippine Electrical Suppliers Association (DS)
PESA .... Proton Elastic-Scattering Analysis
PESABC .... Permanent Executive Secretariat of the Andres Bello Convention [*See also SECAB*] (EAIO)
Pe de Sal .... Petrus de Salinis [*Flourished, 13th century*] [*Authority cited in pre-1607 legal work*] (DSA)
Pe de Samp ... Petrus de Sampsone [*Flourished, 1246-58*] [*Authority cited in pre-1607 legal work*] (DSA)
Pesca Mar ... Pesca y Marina [*A publication*]
Pesca Pesqui ... Pesca y Pesquisa [*A publication*]
PESC Rec IEEE Power Electron Spec Conf ... PESC Record. IEEE [*Institute of Electrical and Electronics Engineers*] Power Electronics Specialists Conference [*A publication*]
PESD .... Program Element Summary Data [*DoD*]
PESD .... Program Execution Subdirective (AABC)
PESDC ...... Properties of Electrolyte Solutions Data Center [*National Institute of Standards and Technology*]
PESDS ...... Program Element Summary Data Sheet [*DoD*]
PESGB ...... Petroleum Exploration Society of Great Britain
Pesh .... Peshitta [*Syriac translation of the Bible*] (BJA)
Peshawar ... All India Reporter, Peshawar [*1933-50*] [*A publication*] (DLA)
Peshawar ... Indian Rulings, Peshawar Series [*1933-47*] [*A publication*] (DLA)
Peshawar Univ Dep Geol Geol Bull ... Peshawar. University. Department of Geology. Geological Bulletin [*A publication*]
P & ESI ...... Physical and Engineering Sciences Division [*Army Research Office*]
PESIA .... Postal Employees Salary Increase Act of 1960
PESIC .... Parti du Progres Economique et Social des Independants Congolais Luluabourg [*Party for Economic and Social Progress of the Congolese Independents in Luluabourg*] [*Political party*]
Pesik .... Pesikta de-Rav Kahana (BJA)

Pesikt......... Pesikta de-Rav Kahana (BJA)
PesiktR ...... Pesikta Rabbati (BJA)
PESM .... Photoelectron Spectromicroscope
PeSMoT .... Penn State Microoxidation Test [*Analytical chemistry*]
PESO......... Participation Enriches Science, Music, and Art Organizations
                 [*Orlando, Florida*]
PESO........ Performance Evaluation Support Office
PESO........ Plant Engineering Shop Order (AAG)
PESO........ Product Engineering Services Office [*DoD*]
PESOD...... Proceedings. Electrochemical Society [*A publication*]
PESOS ...... Perkin-Elmer Solvent Optimization System [*Chemistry*]
PESOS ...... Prepare, Explain, Show, Observe, Supervise [*Formula*]
                 [*LIMRA*]
PESPD ...... Periodically Speaking [*A publication*]
Pesqu......... Pesquisas [*A publication*]
Pesqui Agropecuar Brasil Ser Agron ... Pesquisa Agropecuaria Brasileira. Serie
                 Agronomia [*A publication*]
Pesqui Agropecuar Brasil Ser Vet ... Pesquisa Agropecuaria Brasileira. Serie
                 Veterinaria [*A publication*]
Pesqui Agropecu Bras ... Pesquisa Agropecuaria Brasileira [*A publication*]
Pesqui Agropecu Bras Ser Agron ... Pesquisa Agropecuaria Brasileira. Serie
                 Agronomia [*A publication*]
Pesqui Agropecu Bras Ser Vet ... Pesquisa Agropecuaria Brasileira. Serie
                 Veterinaria [*A publication*]
Pesqui Agropecu Bras Ser Zootec ... Pesquisa Agropecuaria Brasileira. Serie
                 Zootecnia [*A publication*]
Pesqui Agropecu Nordeste Recife ... Pesquisas Agropecuarias do Nordeste
                 Recife [*A publication*]
Pesqui Agropecu Pernambucana ... Pesquisa Agropecuaria Pernambucana [*A
                 publication*]
Pesqui Bot (Porto Alegre) ... Pesquisas Botanica (Porto Alegre) [*A publication*]
Pesqui Commun (Porto Alegre) ... Pesquisas Communications (Porto Alegre)
                 [*A publication*]
Pesqui Med ... Pesquisa Medica [*A publication*]
Pesquisa e Planejamento Econ ... Pesquisa e Planejamento Economico [*A
                 publication*]
Pesquisas Antropol ... Pesquisas Antropologia [*A publication*]
Pesqui Secc B Cienc Nat (Porto Alegre) ... Pesquisas. Seccao B. Ciencias
                 Naturais (Porto Alegre) [*A publication*]
Pesqui Zool (Porto Alegre) ... Pesquisas Zoologia (Porto Alegre) [*A
                 publication*]
PesR........... Pesikta Rabbati (BJA)
PESR .... Planning Element System Report (NATG)
PESR .... Precision Echo Sounder Recorder
PESR .... Pseudoequivalent Service Rounds [*Military*] (NVT)
PEsS .... East Stroudsburg State College, East Stroudsburg, PA [*Library
                 symbol*] [*Library of Congress*] (LCLS)
PESS.......... Pessus [*Pessary*] [*Pharmacy*]
PESSO .... Personnel System Staff Officer
PEST .... Parameter Estimation by Sequential Testing [*Computer*]
PEST .... Patterned Elicitation Syntax Test [*Educational test*]
PEST .... Pesticide Evaluation Summary Tabulation
PEST .... Production Evaluation Surveillance Test
PEST .... Reuter Laboratories, Inc. [*Detroit, MI*] [*NASDAQ
                 symbol*] (NQ)
Pest Bioch ... Pesticide Biochemistry and Physiology [*A publication*]
Pest Contr ... Pest Control [*A publication*]
Pest Contro ... Pest Control [*A publication*]
Pest Control Circ ... Pest Control Circular [*A publication*]
PESTD ...... Proceedings. European Society of Toxicology [*A publication*]
PESTDOC ... Pest Control Literature Documentation [*Derwent Publications
                 Ltd.*] [*Bibliographic database*] [*Information service or
                 system*] (IID)
PESTF....... Proton Event Start Forecast [*Solar weather information*]
PESTIC ..... Pesticide
Pestic Abstr ... Pesticides Abstracts and News Summary [*A publication*]
Pestic Abstr News Sum Sect C Herbic ... Pesticides Abstracts and News
                 Summary. Section C. Herbicides [*A publication*]
Pestic Biochem Physiol ... Pesticide Biochemistry and Physiology [*A
                 publication*]
Pestic CIPAC Methods Proc Ser ... Pesticides. CIPAC [*Collaborative
                 International Pesticides Analytical Council*] Methods and
                 Proceedings Series [*A publication*]
Pestic Doc Bull ... Pesticides Documentation Bulletin [*A publication*]
Pesticide A ... Pesticides Annual [*A publication*]
Pestic Monit J ... Pesticides Monitoring Journal [*A publication*]
Pestic Progr ... Pesticide Progress [*A publication*]
Pestic Res Rep Agric Can ... Pesticide Research Report. Agriculture Canada
                 [*A publication*]
Pestic Sci.... Pesticide Science [*A publication*]
Pestic Tech ... Pesticide and Technique [*A publication*]
Pest Toxic Subst Mon Rep ... Pesticides and Toxic Substances Monitoring
                 Report [*A publication*]
Pest Infest Control Lab Rep (Lond) ... Pest Infestation Control. Laboratory
                 Report (London) [*A publication*]
Pest Infest Control (Lond) ... Pest Infestation Control. Laboratory Report
                 (London) [*A publication*]
Pest Infest Res Rep Pest Infest Lab Agric Res Counc ... Pest Infestation
                 Research Report. Pest Infestation Laboratory. Agricultural
                 Research Council [*A publication*]

Pest Leafl Pac For Res Cent ... Pest Leaflet. Pacific Forest Research Centre [*A
                 publication*]
Pest Mon J ... Pesticides Monitoring Journal [*A publication*]
Pest Sci ...... Pesticide Science [*A publication*]
PESY .... People Say. Bimonthly Newsletter [*Canada*] [*A publication*]
PET .... Pacific Enterprises [*NYSE symbol*] (SPSG)
PET .... Panel on Education and Training [*COSATI*]
PET .... Panel on Educational Terminology [*Office of Education*]
PET .... Parent Effectiveness Training [*A course of study*]
PET .... Particle Electrostatic Thruster
PET .... Patterned Epitaxial Technology (IEEE)
PET .... Pelotas [*Brazil*] [*Airport symbol*] (OAG)
PET .... Pentaerythritol [*Organic chemistry*]
PET .... Pentaerythritol Tetranitrate [*Also, PETN*] [*Explosive,
                 vasodilator*]
PET .... Penthouse Entertainment Network [*Cable television system*]
PET .... Performance Efficiency Test [*Employee screening and
                 placement test*]
PET .... Performance Evaluation Team [*Nuclear energy*] (NRCH)
PET .... Performance Evaluation Test
PET .... Periodic Environmental Test
PET .... Periodic Evaluation Test
PET .... Peripheral Equipment Tester [*Data processing*] (BUR)
PET .... Personal Effectiveness Training (MCD)
PET .... Personal Electronic Transactor [*Computer*] [*Commodore
                 Business Machines*]
PET .... Personal Employee Time (DHSM)
PET .... Pet, Inc., Corporate Information Center, St. Louis, MO [*OCLC
                 symbol*] (OCLC)
Pet............. Peter [*New Testament book*]
Pet............. Peters Notes [*A publication*]
Pet............. Peters' Prince Edward Island Reports [*1850-72*] [*Canada*] [*A
                 publication*] (DLA)
Pet............. Peters' United States Circuit Court Reports [*A
                 publication*] (DLA)
Pet............. Peters' United States District Court Reports, Admiralty
                 Decisions [*A publication*] (DLA)
Pet............. Peters' United States Supreme Court Reports [*26-41 United
                 States*] [*A publication*] (DLA)
Pet............. Petihta (BJA)
PET .... Petition
PET .... Petrine [*Of, or relating to, Peter the Apostle or Peter the Great*]
PET .... Petroleum
PET .... Petropavlovsk [*USSR*] [*Seismograph station code, US
                 Geological Survey*] (SEIS)
PET .... Petropavlovsk [*USSR*] [*Geomagnetic observatory code*]
PET .... Petrotech, Inc. [*Toronto Stock Exchange symbol*]
Pet............. Petrus [*Authority cited in pre-1607 legal work*] (DSA)
Pet............. Petrus de Bellapertica [*Deceased, 1308*] [*Authority cited in pre-
                 1607 legal work*] (DSA)
PET .... Phase Elapsed Time (NASA)
PET .... Photoemission Tube
PET .... Phototropic Energy Transfer
PET .... Physical Equipment Table
PET .... Pierre Elliott Trudeau [*Canadian prime minister*] [*Acronymic
                 designation considered derogatory*]
PET .... Point of Equal Time [*Aviation*]
PET .... Polyester
PET .... Poly(ethylene Terephthalate) [*Organic chemistry*]
PET .... Portable Earth Terminal [*NASA*]
PET .... Portable Electronic Telephone
PET .... Position-Event-Time
PET .... Positron-Emission Tomography
PET .... Potential Evapotranspiration
PET .... Pre-Eclamptic Toxemia [*Medicine*]
PET .... Pre-Employment Training (OICC)
PET .... Preliminary Evaluation Team
PET .... Preliminary Examination Team [*NASA*]
PET .... Preprimary Evaluation and Training
PET .... Pressurization Events Trainer
PET .... Probe Ephemeris Tape
PET .... Process Evaluation Tester
PET .... Production Environmental Tests
PET .... Production Evaluation Test
PET .... Program Evaluator and Tester [*Data processing*]
PET .... Property Enterprise Trust [*Investment term*] [*British*] (ECON)
PET .... Prototype Evaluation Test
PET .... Psychiatric Emergency Team
PET .... Pupil Evaluation Team [*Education*]
PETA........ Pentaerythritol Triacrylate [*Organic chemistry*]
PETA........ People for the Ethical Treatment of Animals (EA)
PETA........ Performance Evaluation and Trend Analysis (NASA)
PETA........ Plutonium Equipment Transfer Area [*Nuclear energy*] (NRCH)
PETA........ Portable Electronic Traffic Analyzer [*British*]
Pet Ab .... Petersdorff's Abridgment [*A publication*] (DLA)
Pet Abr ...... Petersdorff's Abridgment [*1660-1823*] [*A publication*] (DLA)
Pet Ad .... Peters' United States District Court Reports, Admiralty
                 Decisions [*A publication*] (DLA)
Pet Ad Dec ... Peters' United States District Court Reports, Admiralty
                 Decisions [*A publication*] (DLA)

Pet Adm ..... Peters' United States District Court Reports, Admiralty Decisions [*A publication*] (DLA)
Pet Adm App ... Peters' United States District Court Reports, Admiralty Decisions (Appendix) [*A publication*] (DLA)
Pet Ad R ..... Peters' United States District Court Reports, Admiralty Decisions [*A publication*] (DLA)
Pet Age ...... Petroleum Age [*A publication*]
Pet de Anch ... Petrus de Ancharano [*Deceased, 1416*] [*Authority cited in pre-1607 legal work*] (DSA)
Pet Aret ...... Petrus Aretinus [*Flourished, 1088-91*] [*Authority cited in pre-1607 legal work*] (DSA)
PETAT ...... Periodic Inspection Turn-Around Time [*Military*] (AFIT)
Pet Bail ...... Petersdorff on Bail [*1824*] [*A publication*] (DLA)
Pet de Bel ... Petrus de Bellapertica [*Deceased, 1308*] [*Authority cited in pre-1607 legal work*] (DSA)
Pet de Bellap ... Petrus de Bellapertica [*Deceased, 1308*] [*Authority cited in pre-1607 legal work*] (DSA)
Pet de Belper ... Petrus de Bellapertica [*Deceased, 1308*] [*Authority cited in pre-1607 legal work*] (DSA)
Pet Br .... Bellewe's Cases Tempore Henry VIII [*Brooke's New Cases*] [*England*] [*A publication*] (DLA)
Pet Br .... Brooke's New Cases (Petit Brooke) [*1515-58*] [*A publication*] (DLA)
PETC .... Pittsburgh Energy Technology Center [*Formerly, PERC*] [*Department of Energy*] [*Pittsburgh, PA*] (GRD)
PETC .... Portable Equipment Test Chamber (MCD)
Pet CC .... Peters' United States Circuit Court Reports [*A publication*] (DLA)
Pet Chem Ind Conf Rec Conf Pap ... Petroleum and Chemical Industry Conference. Record of Conference Papers [*United States*] [*A publication*]
Pet Chem Ind Dev ... Petroleum and Chemical Industry Developments [*India*] [*A publication*]
Pet Chem USSR ... Petroleum Chemistry USSR [*A publication*]
Pet Cir CR ... Peters' Condensed United States Circuit Court Reports [*A publication*] (DLA)
Pet Cond .... Peters' Condensed Reports, United States Supreme Court [*A publication*] (DLA)
Pet Cond Rep ... Peters' Condensed United States Circuit Court Reports [*A publication*] (DLA)
PETD .... Petroleum Development Corp. [*NASDAQ symbol*] (NQ)
Pet Dig ...... Peters' United States Digest [*A publication*] (DLA)
Pet Dig ...... Peticolas' Texas Digest [*A publication*] (DLA)
PETE .... Petersburg National Battlefield
PETE .... Pneumatic End to End
PETE .... Portable Emergency Thermal Environment
PETE .... Product Engineering Tribute to Excellence
PETE .... Proof and Experimental Test Establishment [*Canada*] (MCD)
Pet Econ ..... Petroleum Economist [*A publication*]
Pet Eng ...... Petroleum Engineer [*A publication*]
Pet Eng Int ... Petroleum Engineer International [*A publication*]
Pet Equip ... Petroleum Equipment [*A publication*]
Pet Equip Serv ... Petroleum Equipment and Services [*A publication*]
Peter .... Analysis and Digest of the Decisions of Sir George Jessel, by A. P. Peter [*England*] [*A publication*] (DLA)
Petermanns Geog Mitt ... Petermanns Geographische Mitteilungen [*A publication*]
Petermanns Geogr Mitt ... Petermanns Geographische Mitteilungen [*A publication*]
Petermanns Mitt ... Petermanns. A. Mitteilungen aus J. Perthes Geographischer Anstalt [*A publication*]
Petermanns Mitt Erg ... Petermanns Mitteilungen. Ergaenzungsheft [*Gotha*] [*A publication*]
Peterm Geog ... Petermanns Geographische Mitteilungen [*A publication*]
Peter Phot Mag ... Petersen's Photographic Magazine [*A publication*]
Peters .... Haviland's Prince Edward Island Chancery Reports, by Peters [*1850-72*] [*Canada*] (DLA)
Peters .... Peters' United States Supreme Court Reports [*26-41 United States*] [*A publication*] (DLA)
Peters' Ad .. Peters' United States District Court Reports, Admiralty Decisions [*A publication*] (DLA)
Peters Adm ... Peters' United States District Courts Reports, Admiralty Decisions [*A publication*] (DLA)
Peters' Adm Dec ... Peters' United States District Court Reports, Admiralty Decisions [*A publication*] (DLA)
Peters' Admiralty Dec ... Peters' United States District Court Reports, Admiralty Decisions [*A publication*] (DLA)
Peters' Adm R ... Peters' United States District Court Reports, Admiralty Decisions [*A publication*] (DLA)
Peters Adm Rep ... Peters' United States District Court Reports, Admiralty Decisions [*A publication*] (DLA)
Peters CC ... Peters' United States Circuit Court Reports [*A publication*] (DLA)
Petersd Ab ... Petersdorff's Abridgment [*A publication*] (DLA)
Pet Explor Dev ... Petroleum Exploration and Development [*A publication*]
PETFEM ... Postsecondary Education Task Force on Energy Management [*Canada*]
Pet Gas Process ... Petroleum and Gas Processing [*A publication*]
Pet Gaz ...... Petroleum Gazette [*A publication*] (APTA)
Pet & Gaze ... Petrol si Gaze [*Romania*] [*A publication*]
Pet Gaze Supl ... Petrol si Gaze. Supliment [*Romania*] [*A publication*]

Pet Geogr Mitt ... Petermanns Geographische Mitteilungen [*A publication*]
Pet Geol ...... Petroleum Geology [*A publication*]
Pet Geol Taiwan ... Petroleum Geology of Taiwan [*A publication*]
Petg Pr & Ag ... Petgrave's Principal and Agent [*1857*] [*A publication*] (DLA)
Pet Greg ..... Petrus Gregorius [*Deceased, 1617*] [*Authority cited in pre-1607 legal work*] (DSA)
Peth Dis ..... Petheram's Discovery by Interrogations [*1864*] [*A publication*] (DLA)
Pet Hydrocarbons ... Petroleum and Hydrocarbons [*India*] [*A publication*]
PETI .... Percent of Travel Involved (FAAC)
PETI .... Portable Electronic Typewriter Interface [*Applied Creative Technology, Inc.*]
PETIA .... Particle-Enhanced Turbidometric Immunoassay [*Clinical chemistry*]
Pet Indep .... Petroleum Independent [*A publication*]
Pet Inf .... Petrole Informations [*A publication*]
Pet Int .... Petroleo Internacional [*A publication*]
Pet Interam ... Petroleo Interamericano [*A publication*]
Pet Interamericano ... Petroleo Interamericano [*A publication*]
Pet Int (London) ... Petroleum International (London) [*A publication*]
Petit Br .... Petit Brooke, or Brooke's New Cases, English King's Bench [*1515-58*] [*A publication*] (DLA)
Petit J Brass ... Petit Journal du Brasseur [*A publication*]
PETITN .... Petition
Pet L Nat ... Petersdorff's Law of Nations [*A publication*] (DLA)
Pet Manage ... Petroleum Management [*A publication*]
Pet Mitt .... Petermanns Mitteilungen [*A publication*]
Pet de Mont ... Petrus Piccoli de Monteforte [*Flourished, 14th century*] [*Authority cited in pre-1607 legal work*] (DSA)
Pet M & S .. Petersdorff's Master and Servant [*1876*] [*A publication*] (DLA)
PETN .... Pentaerythritol Tetranitrate [*Also, PET*] [*Explosive, vasodilator*]
PETN .... Petition
Pet News ..... Petroleum News [*Taiwan*] [*A publication*]
Pet Newsl .. Petroleum Newsletter [*A publication*]
PETNR ...... Petitioner
PETOA .... Petrotecnica [*A publication*]
Pet Outlook ... Petroleum Outlook [*A publication*]
PETP .... (Phenylethyl)phenyltetrahydropyridine [*Organic chemistry*]
PETP .... Poly(ethylene Terephthalate) [*Organic chemistry*]
PETP .... Preliminary Engineering Technical Proposal
p et p .... Profits et Pertes [*Profits and Losses*] [*Business term*] [*French*]
Pet Peck Zir ... Petrus Peckius (Ziricaeus) [*Deceased, 1589*] [*Authority cited in pre-1607 legal work*] (DSA)
Pet Petrochem ... Petroleum and Petrochemicals [*Japan*] [*A publication*]
Pet Petrochem Int ... Petroleum and Petrochemical International [*England*] [*A publication*]
Pet Petrochem (Tokyo) ... Petroleum and Petrochemicals (Tokyo) [*Japan*] [*A publication*]
Pet P M ...... Petersen's Photographic Magazine [*A publication*]
Pet Press Serv ... Petroleum Press Service [*England*] [*A publication*]
Pet Press Service ... Petroleum Press Service [*A publication*]
PetPRO ...... Pet Professional Retailers Organization (EA)
Pet Process ... Petroleum Processing [*A publication*]
Pet Process Eng ... Petroleum Process Engineering [*A publication*]
PETQ .... Petro Quest, Inc. [*NASDAQ symbol*] (NQ)
PETR .... Petitioner
PETR .... Petra Resources, Inc. [*NASDAQ symbol*] (NQ)
PETRA .... Positron-Electron Tandem Ring Accelerator [*Nuclear*]
PETRASAFE ... Petroleum Transport Scheme for Assistance in Freight Emergencies [*A publication*] (APTA)
PETRB ...... Petroleum Review [*A publication*]
Petr Bellug ... Petrus Belluga [*Flourished, 1446-68*] [*Authority cited in pre-1607 legal work*] (DSA)
Petr de Benint ... Petrus de Benintendis [*Flourished, 16th century*] [*Authority cited in pre-1607 legal work*] (DSA)
Petr de Bezut ... [*Johannes*] Petrus de Bezutio [*Deceased circa 1582*] [*Authority cited in pre-1607 legal work*] (DSA)
PETRD ...... Petrologie [*A publication*]
Pet Refiner ... Petroleum Refiner [*A publication*]
Pet Refin Petrochem Lit Abstr ... Petroleum Refining and Petrochemicals Literature Abstracts [*A publication*]
PETRES .... Petroleum Reserves [*Navy*]
PETRESO ... Petroleum Reserves Office [*or Officer*]
Pet Rev .... Petrocorp Review [*A publication*]
Pet Rev .... Petroleum Review [*A publication*]
Petr Greg ... Petrus Gregorius [*Deceased, 1617*] [*Authority cited in pre-1607 legal work*] (DSA)
PETRIBURG ... Petriburgensis [*Signature of the Bishops of Peterborough*] [*Latin*] (ROG)
Petr Inde .... Petroleum Independent [*A publication*]
PETRL ...... Petroleum (AABC)
Petr Nuni ... Petrus Nunius de Avendano [*Flourished, 16th century*] [*Authority cited in pre-1607 legal work*] (DSA)
PETRO ...... Petroleum
PETROCH ... Rock Chemical Database [*Ontario Geological Survey*] [*Canada*] [*Information service or system*] (CRD)
Petro/Chem Eng ... Petro/Chem Engineer [*A publication*]
PETRODEG ... Petroleum Degrading [*Agent*]
PETROFERTIL ... PETROBRAS Fertilizantes SA [*State enterprise*] [*Brazil*] (EY)

PETROG... Petrographic
PETROGR ... Petrography
PETROL ... Petroleum
PETROL ... Petrology
Petrol Abstr ... Petroleum Abstracts [*A publication*]
Petrol Eng ... Petroleum Engineer [*A publication*]
Petrol Eng Int ... Petroleum Engineer International [*A publication*]
Petroleo...... Petroleo Internacional [*A publication*]
Petroleos Mexicanos Servicio Inf ... Petroleos Mexicanos Servicio de Informacion [*A publication*]
Petroleum... Petroleum Economist [*A publication*]
Petroleum Gaz ... Petroleum Gazette [*A publication*]   (APTA)
Petrol Gaz ... Petroleum Gazette [*A publication*]   (APTA)
Petrol Geol ... Petroleum Geology [*A publication*]
Petrolieri Int ... Petrolieri International [*A publication*]
Petrol Independ ... Petroleum Independent [*A publication*]
Petrol Inform ... Petrole Informations [*A publication*]
Petrol Int.... Petroleo Internacional [*A publication*]
Petrol News ... Petroleum News [*A publication*]
Petrol Ref... Petroleum Refiner [*A publication*]
Petrol Rev .. Petroleum Review [*A publication*]
Petrol Tech ... Petrole et Techniques [*A publication*]
Petrol Technol ... Petroleum Technology [*A publication*]
Petrol Tecnol ... Petroleo y Tecnologia [*A publication*]
PETROMIN ... General Petroleum & Mineral Organization [*Saudi Arabia state-owned oil company*]
PETROMISA ... PETROBRAS Mineracao Sociedade Anonima [*State enterprise*] [*Brazil*]   (EY)
Petron .... Petronius [*First century AD*] [*Classical studies*]   (OCD)
PETRONET ... Petroleum Network [*Distribution and interdiction model*]   (MCD)
Petron Satyric ... Petronius' [*Titus*] Arbiter, Satyricon, Etc. [*A publication*]   (DLA)
PETROPHIL ... Petroleum Philatelic Society International   (EA)
PETROPOL ... Petropolis [*St. Petersburg*] [*Imprint*] [*Latin*]   (ROG)
Petrozavodsk Gos Univ Ucen Zap ... Petrozavodskii Gosudarstvennyi Universitet. Ucenye Zapiski [*A publication*]
Petr Prog.... Petrole-Progres [*A publication*]
Petr Rave ... Petrus Ravennas [*Flourished, 1468-1508*] [*Authority cited in pre-1607 legal work*]   (DSA)
Petr Sit....... Petroleum Situation [*A publication*]
Petr Techn ... Petroleum Technology [*A publication*]
Petr Times ... Petroleum Times [*A publication*]
Petr Tm R .. Petroleum Times Price Report [*A publication*]
PETS .... Pacific Electronics Trade Show
PETS .... Payload Environmental Transportation System [*NASA*]   (NASA)
PETS .... Peripheral Equipment Test Set
PETS .... POCC [*Payload Operations Control Center*] Experiments Timeline System [*Ground Data Systems Division and Spacelab*] [*NASA*]   (NASA)
PETS .... Polaris Engineering Technical Service [*Missiles*]
PETS .... Positions Equipment Task Summary   (AAG)
PETS .... Prior to Expiration of Term of Service [*Reenlistments*] [*Military*]
PETS .... Programmed Extended Time Sharing [*Data processing*]
Pet de Sam ... Petrus de Sampsone [*Flourished, 1246-58*] [*Authority cited in pre-1607 legal work*]   (DSA)
Pet de Samp ... Petrus de Sampsone [*Flourished, 1246-58*] [*Authority cited in pre-1607 legal work*]   (DSA)
Pet SC........ Peters' United States Supreme Court Reports [*26-41 United States*] [*A publication*]   (DLA)
PETSEC .... Petroleum Section [*Allied Force Headquarters*]
Pet Substitutes ... Petroleum Substitutes [*A publication*]
Pet Suppl ... Supplement to Petersdorff's Abridgment [*A publication*]   (DLA)
PETT .... Pettibone Corp. [*NASDAQ symbol*]   (NQ)
PETT .... Phototropic Energy Transfer Technique
PETT .... Positron Emission Transaxial [*or Transverse*] Tomography [*Roentgenography*]
PETTA ...... Petroleum Times [*A publication*]
Pet Tech..... Petrole et Techniques [*A publication*]
Pet Technol ... Petroleum Technology [*A publication*]
Pet Tech Rev ... Petroleum Technical Review [*A publication*]
Pet Times... Petroleum Times [*A publication*]
Pet Today... Petroleum Today [*A publication*]
Petty SR.... Petty Sessions Review [*A publication*]   (APTA)
PETV......... Planar Epitaxial Tuning Varactor
PETV......... Process Evaluation Test Vehicle
Pet W .... Petroleum Week [*A publication*]
Pet Week.... Petroleum Week [*A publication*]
Pet World... Petroleum World [*London*] [*A publication*]
Pet World (London) ... Petroleum World (London) [*A publication*]
Pet World (Los Angeles) ... Petroleum World (Los Angeles) [*A publication*]
Pet World Oil ... Petroleum World and Oil [*A publication*]
Pet World Oil Age ... Petroleum World and Oil Age [*A publication*]
PETX .... PETX Petroleum [*NASDAQ symbol*]   (NQ)
PEU .... Paneuropa-Union [*Paneuropean Union*]   (EAIO)
PEU .... Paneuropean Union   (EAIO)
PEU .... Port Expander Unit
PEU .... Protected Environment Unit [*Medicine*]

PEUA .... Pelvic Exam under Anesthesia [*Medicine*]
PEUBA...... Publikacije Elektrotehnickog Fakulteta Univerziteta u Beogradu. Serija Matematika i Fizika [*A publication*]
PEUU .... Polyether Polyurethane Urea [*Organic chemistry*]
peV............ Peak Electron Volts
PEV........... Peak Envelope Voltage [*Telecommunications*]   (TEL)
PEV........... Pleasant Valley [*California*] [*Seismograph station code, US Geological Survey*]   (SEIS)
P Evang...... Pentecostal Evangel [*A publication*]
PEVE......... Prensa Venezolana [*Press agency*] [*Venezuela*]
PEVI .... Perry's Victory and International Peace Memorial National Monument
PEVL......... Polyethylene Expanded Video Longitudinal Cable   (MCD)
PEVM....... Personal'naia Elektronnaia Vychislitel'naia Mashina [*Personal Computer*] [*Russian*]
PEVM....... Professional'naia Elektronnaia Vychislitel'naia Mashina [*Professional Computer*] [*Russian*]
PEW .... Passive Electronics Warfare   (NG)
PEW .... Percussion Welding
PEW .... Peshawar [*Pakistan*] [*Airport symbol*]   (OAG)
PEW .... Philosophy East and West [*A publication*]
PE & W ..... Philosophy East and West [*A publication*]
PEW .... Politiek Economisch Weekblad [*A publication*]
PEWO .... Plant Engineering Work Order   (MCD)
PEWR........ Plant Engineering Work Release   (AAG)
PEWS....... Platoon Early Warning System   (RDA)
PEWS....... Plutonium Equipment Warm Shop [*Nuclear energy*]   (NRCH)
PEWV....... Pulmonary Extravascular Water Volume [*Physiology*]
PEX........... People Express [*Newark, NJ*] [*FAA designator*]   (FAAC)
PEX........... Per Example
PEX........... Phenazine Ethosulfate [*Biochemistry*]
PEX........... Pronto Explorations Ltd. [*Vancouver Stock Exchange symbol*]
PEXP .... People Express Airlines, Inc. [*NASDAQ symbol*]   (NQ)
PEXRAD ... Programmed Electronic X-Ray Automatic Diffractometer
PEY........... Pengelly Mines Ltd. [*Vancouver Stock Exchange symbol*]
PEY........... Photoelectric Yield
PEZ........... Pezgold Resource Corp. [*Vancouver Stock Exchange symbol*]
PEZ........... Pleasanton, TX [*FAA*]   (FAAL)
PEZAF ...... Pezamerica Resources Corp. [*NASDAQ symbol*]   (NQ)
PF.............. American First Preparation Fund 2 LP [*AMEX symbol*]   (SPSG)
PF.............. Frankford Public Library, Frankford, PA [*Library symbol*] [*Library of Congress*]   (LCLS)
PF.............. French Polynesia [*ANSI two-letter standard code*]   (CNC)
PF.............. Pacifica Foundation   (EA)
PF.............. Package Freighter [*Shipping*]
PF.............. Paderewski Foundation [*Defunct*]   (EA)
PF.............. Paedagogische Forschungen [*A publication*]
PF.............. Page Footing   (BUR)
PF.............. Page Formatter   (MDG)
PF.............. Paling Fence
PF.............. Panchromatic Film   (ADA)
PF.............. Paper and Foil [*Capacitor*]   (DEN)
pf.............. Paracel Islands [*MARC country of publication code*] [*Library of Congress*]   (LCCP)
PF.............. Parachute Facility   (NASA)
PF.............. Parachute Flare   (NVT)
PF.............. Parafascicular Nucleus [*Neuroanatomy*]
PF.............. Parallel Fiber [*Neuroanatomy*]
PF.............. Parallel Fold
PF.............. Paramount Funding Corp. [*Toronto Stock Exchange symbol*]
PF.............. Parapsychology Foundation   (EA)
PF.............. Partition Factor   (NRCH)
PF.............. Passage Free   (ROG)
PF.............. Path Finder [*British military*]   (DMA)
PF.............. Pathfinder Fund   (EA)
PF.............. Patriotic Front [*Zimbabwe*] [*Political party*]   (PPW)
PF.............. Patrol Vessel, Frigate [*Navy symbol*]
P/F............ Pattern Flight [*Also, P/FLT*]   (MUGU)
PF.............. Payload Forward [*NASA*]   (MCD)
PF.............. Payload Function [*NASA*]   (MCD)
PF.............. Peace and Freedom Party [*Political party*]   (DLA)
PF.............. Peak Flow [*Medicine*]
PF.............. Peak Frequency
PF.............. Peanut Flour
PF.............. Pedal Furrow
PF.............. Pen Friends   (EA)
PF.............. Pennsylvania Folklife [*A publication*]
PF.............. Pensee Francaise [*A publication*]
PF.............. Pension Fund
PF.............. Peregrine Fund   (EA)
PF.............. Perfect
PF.............. Performance Factor
PF.............. Perfusion Fixation [*Histology*]
PF.............. Permanent Fireman
PF.............. Permanent Force [*Canadian Militia before 1940*]
PF.............. Permeability Factor
pf.............. Perofskite [*CIPW classification*] [*Geology*]
PF.............. Personal Fouls [*Basketball*]
PF.............. Personal Security File Number [*British Secret Service*]
PF.............. Personality Factor

P & F	Petroleum and Fuel
Pf	Pfeifferella [*Genus of bacteria*]
PF	Pfennig [*Penny*] [*Monetary unit*] [*German*]
PF	Pfleuger Flug-Betriehs GmbH [*Germany*] [*ICAO designator*] (FAAC)
PF	Phenol-Formaldehyde [*Organic chemistry*]
PF	Philatelic Foundation (EA)
PF	Philosophische Forschungen [*A publication*]
PF	Philosophy Forum [*A publication*]
PF	Photogrammetric Facility [*Army*]
P & F	Photography and Focus [*A publication*]
PF	Physicians Forum (EA)
PF	Pianoforte [*Soft, then Loud*] [*Music*]
pF	Picofarad
P & F	Pike and Fischer's Administrative Law [*A publication*] (DLA)
P & F	Pike and Fischer's Federal Rules Service [*A publication*] (DLA)
P & F	Pike and Fischer's OPA Price Service [*A publication*] (DLA)
PF	Pilgrim Fellowship (EA)
PF	[*The*] Pioneer & Fayette Railroad Co. [*AAR code*]
PF	Piu Forte [*A Little Louder*] [*Music*]
PF	Plain Face [*Construction*]
P & F	Planning and Forecasting (MCD)
PF	Planning Forum (EA)
P & F	Plant and Facilities
PF	Plantar Fasciaitis [*Medicine*]
PF	Plantar Flexion [*Medicine*]
PF	Platelet Factor [*Hematology*]
PF	Plentiful Foods [*A publication*] [*Department of Agriculture*]
PF	Plot Function [*Data processing*]
PF	Pneumatic Float
PF	Poco Forte [*Rather Loud*] [*Music*]
PF	Poe Foundation (EA)
PF	Poesie Francaise [*A publication*]
PF	Point Foundation (EA)
PF	Point of Frog [*Electronics*] (MSA)
PF	Points For [*Football*]
PF	Pole Fittings [*JETDS nomenclature*] [*Military*] (CET)
PF	Police Forces [*British*]
PF	Police Foundation (EA)
PF	POLISARIO [*Frente Popular para la Liberacion de Saguia El Hamra y Rio De Oro*] [*Popular Front for the Liberation of Saguia El Hamra and Rio De Oro*] [*Morocco*] (PD)
PF	Polish Folklore [*A publication*]
PF	Poloidal Field (MCD)
PF	Polyurethane Foam
PF	Pool Frequency [*Pisciculture*]
PF	Poop and Forecastle [*of a ship*] (DS)
PF	Popular Foodservice [*A publication*]
PF	Popular Forces [*ARVN*]
PF	Por Favor [*Please*] [*Portuguese*]
PF	Portal Fibrosis [*Medicine*]
PF	Position Failure
PF	Position Finder [*British military*] (DMA)
P/F	Post Flight (AFIT)
PF	Postage Free (ROG)
PF	Postman's Federation [*A union*] [*British*]
PF	Posture Foundation [*Initialism is used in brand of sneaker shoe, PF Flyers*]
PF	Power Factor [*Radio*]
PF	Power Frame [*Telecommunications*] (TEL)
PF	Powered Flight (NASA)
PF	Prace Filologiczne [*A publication*]
P/F	Practical Factors
PF	Preference
PF	Preferred
PF	Preflight
PF	Pressure Fan (AAG)
PF	Prime Function (NASA)
PF	Prison Fellowship Ministries (EA)
PF	Probability of Failure (NASA)
PF	Procurator Fiscal
PF	Profile (KSC)
PF	Program Function [*Data processing*] (IBMDP)
PF	Programmable Format [*Perforating keyboard*]
PF	Progressive Foundation (EA)
PF	Project Friend (EA)
PF	Projectile Fragment
PF	Proof
PF	Prop Forward
PF	Proposed Finding [*Nuclear energy*] (NRCH)
PF	Protection Factor
PF	Protein-Free
PF	Protoplasmic Fracture [*Freeze etching in microscopy*]
PF	Proximity Fuze [*Bomb, rocket, or shell*]
PF	PsychoHistory Forum (EA)
PF	Psychologische Forschung [*A publication*]
PF	Psynetics Foundation (EA)
P/F	Pteropod/Foramifera [*Ratio in coastal waters*]
PF	Public Finance [*A publication*]
PF	Pulmonary Factor [*Medicine*]
PF	Pulse Frequency
PF	Pulverized Fuel
P F	Pump-Out Facilities [*Nautical charts*]
PF	Punch Off [*Data processing*] (BUR)
PF	Purge Fan [*Nuclear energy*] (NRCH)
PF	Purple Finch [*Ornithology*]
PF	Pygmy Fund (EA)
PFA	Korte Berichten over Buitenlandse Projecten [*A publication*]
PFA	Palmdale Final Assembly [*NASA*] (NASA)
PFA	Panarcadian Federation of America (EA)
PFA	Papermakers Felt Association (EA)
PFA	Para-Fluorophenylalanine [*Biochemistry*]
PFA	Parti de la Federation Africaine [*African Federation Party*] [*Political party*]
PFA	Participating Field Activity [*DoD*]
PFA	Perfluoroalkoxy [*Organic chemistry*]
PFA	Petroflame International [*Vancouver Stock Exchange symbol*]
Pf A	Pfluegers Archiv fuer die Gesamte Physiologie des Menschen und der Tiere [*A publication*]
PFA	Philippine Foundry Association (DS)
PFA	Phosphonoformic Acid [*Antiviral compound*]
PFA	Pianists Foundation of America (EA)
PFA	Pierce Ferry [*Arizona*] [*Seismograph station code, US Geological Survey*] [*Closed*] (SEIS)
PFA	Pierre Fauchard Academy (EA)
PFA	Pioneer Fraternal Association (EA)
PFA	Pitch Follow-Up Amplifier
PFA	Plan for Action (MCD)
PFA	Polish Falcons of America (EA)
PFA	Polyfurfuryl Alcohol [*Organic chemistry*]
PFA	Polyurethane Foam Association (EA)
PFA	Popular Flying Association [*British*]
PFA	Post Flight Analysis
PFA	Prescription Footwear Association (EA)
PFA	Prison Families Anonymous (EA)
PFA	Professional Farmers of America (EA)
PFA	Professional Fraternity Association (EA)
PFA	Program and File Analysis
PFA	Proportional Fluid Amplifier
PFA	Public Finance and Accountancy [*A publication*]
PFA	Pulverized Fuel Ash (IEEE)
PFA	Pure Fluid Amplification
PFAA	Prairie Farm Assistance Act
8PFAB	Eight-Parallel-Form Anxiety Battery [*Psychology*]
PFAC	Panepirotic Federation of America and Canada [*Later, PFACA*] (EA)
PFAC	People for a Change (EA)
PFACA	Panepirotic Federation of America, Canada, and Australia (EA)
P/FACCTL	Pad Facility Controls [*Aerospace*] (AAG)
PFAD	Palm Fatty Acid Distillate [*Organic chemistry*]
PFAE	Perfluoroalkyl Ether [*Organic chemistry*]
Pfaelzer H	Pfaelzer Heimat [*A publication*]
Pfaelz Heimat	Pfaelzer Heimat [*A publication*]
PFAM	Programmed Frequency Amplitude Modulation
PFAP	Poly(fluoroalkoxyphosphazene) [*Organic chemistry*]
PFAR	Popular Front for Armed Resistance [*Pakistan*]
PFAR	Power Fail Automatic Restart [*Data processing*]
PFAR	Preliminary Failure Analysis Report [*NASA*] (KSC)
PFAS	President of the Faculty of Architects and Surveyors [*British*] (DBQ)
PFAT	Preliminary Flight Appraisal Test (MCD)
PFATA	Problemy Fiziki Atmosfery [*A publication*]
PFAW	People for the American Way (EA)
PFAX	Primefax, Inc. [*NASDAQ symbol*] (NQ)
PFB	Partei Freier Buerger [*Free Citizens' Party*] [*Federal Republic of Germany*] [*Political party*] (PPW)
PFB	Passo Fundo [*Brazil*] [*Airport symbol*] (OAG)
PFB	Payload Feedback [*NASA*] (MCD)
PFB	Payload Forward Bus [*NASA*] (MCD)
PFB	Pentafluorobenzyl [*Organic radical*]
PFB	Pentafluorobenzyl Bromide [*Organic chemistry*]
PFB	Photo Flash Battery
PFB	Plasti-Fab Ltd. [*Toronto Stock Exchange symbol*]
PFB	Pneumatic Float Bridge
PFB	Position Feedback (MCD)
PFB	Prefabricated [*Technical drawings*]
PFB	Preformed Beams [*SONAR*]
PFB	Pressure Fed Booster (NASA)
PFB	Pressurized Fluid-Bed [*Chemical engineering*]
PFB	Provisional Frequency Board [*ITU*]
PFB	Pseudofollicutitis Barbae [*Medicine*]
PFBA	Poly(perfluorobutyl Acrylate) [*Organic chemistry*]
PFBC	Pressurized Fluidized-Bed Combustion
PFBFA	Power Farming and Better Farming Digest (Australia) [*A publication*]
PFBHA	Pentafluorobenzylhydroxylamine Hydrochloride [*Analytical biochemistry*]
PFBK	Pioneer Federal Savings Bank [*NASDAQ symbol*] (NQ)
PFBRG	Pneumatic Float Bridge

PFBS......... Ponce Federal Bank FSB [*Ponce, PR*] [*NASDAQ symbol*] (NQ)
PFC........... Pacific City, OR [*Location identifier*] [*FAA*] (FAAL)
PFC........... Parti Feministe du Canada
PFC........... Passed Flying College [*British*]
PFC........... Pathfinder Industries Ltd. [*Formerly, Pathfinder Financial Corporation*] [*Toronto Stock Exchange symbol*]
PFC........... Peak Follower Circuit
PFC........... Peculiar Facility Change (AAG)
PFC........... Pen Fancier's Club (EA)
PFC........... Pennsylvania Public Library Film Center, University Park, PA [*OCLC symbol*] (OCLC)
PFC........... Perfluorocarbon [*Organic chemistry*]
PFC........... Perfluorochemical [*Organic chemistry*]
PFC........... Performance Flight Certification [*NASA*] (NASA)
PFC........... Permanent Families for Children [*Defunct*] (EA)
PFC........... Persistent Fetal Circulation [*Medicine*]
PFC........... Physicians for Choice (EA)
PFC........... Plan Filing Cabinet
PFC........... Plaque-Forming Cell [*Immunochemistry*]
PFC........... Pneumatic Function Controller
PFC........... Police Forces [*British*]
PFC........... Positive Feedback Circuit
PFC........... Postflight Checklist (MCD)
PFC........... Power Factor Corrector (MCD)
PFC........... Prairie Fiction Collection, Alberta Culture [*UTLAS symbol*]
PFC........... Praying for Corporal [*Private First Class desirous of promotion, or female in wartime desirous of a boyfriend*]
PFC........... Preflight Console (MCD)
PFC........... Preliminary Flight Certification [*NASA*]
PFC........... Presley-ites Fan Club (EA)
PFC........... Pressure Function Controller
PFC........... Primary Flight Control
PFC........... Priority Foreign Country [*International trade*] (ECON)
PFC........... Private, First Class [*Army*]
PFC........... Programmed Fuel Computer [*Automotive engineering*]
PFC........... Progressive Fish-Culturist [*A publication*]
PFC........... Pulse-Flow Coulometry
PFC........... Pulsed Flame Combustor
PFCA........ Performance Ford Club of America (EA)
PFCA........ Plastic Food Container Association [*Defunct*]
PFCD........ Primary Flight Control Display
PFCE........ Preface (ROG)
PFCE........ Preference (AAG)
PFCF........ Payload Flight Control Facility [*NASA*] (MCD)
PFCH........ Prefilled Clutch Hydraulic Actuation [*Automotive Products, Inc.*] [*Automotive engineering*]
PFCM........ Pittsburgh Festival of Contemporary Music [*Record label*]
PFCO........ Position Field Classification Officer
PFCO........ Preferred Financial [*NASDAQ symbol*] (NQ)
PFCP........ Perpetual Financial Corporation [*NASDAQ symbol*] (NQ)
PFCS........ Primary Flight Control System [*NASA*] (MCD)
PFCS........ Primary Flow Control System [*Nuclear energy*] (NRCH)
PFCS........ Program and Funds Control System (MCD)
PFCUA...... Progressive Fish-Culturist [*A publication*]
PFD........... Particle [*or Proton*] Flux Density
PFD........... Perfluorodecalin [*Organic chemistry*]
PFD........... Personal, Fatigue, and Delay [*Work measurement factors*]
PFD........... Personal Flotation Device [*Life jacket*]
PFD........... Planning Factors Development (MCD)
PFD........... Position Fixing Device (ADA)
PFD........... Power Flux Density [*Telecommunications*] (TEL)
PFD........... Preferred (AAG)
PFD........... Preferred Income Fund [*NYSE symbol*] (SPSG)
PFD........... Preliminary Functional Description (CINC)
PFD........... Present for Duty
PFD........... Primary Flash Distillate [*Chemical technology*]
PFD........... Primary Flight Display
PFD........... Process Flow Diagram (NRCH)
PFD........... Puffed [*Freight*]
PFD........... Pulse-Frequency Diversity [*Electronics*] (NG)
PFDA........ Perfluorodecanoic Acid [*Organic chemistry*]
PFDA........ Philippine Fisheries Development Authority (DS)
PFDA........ Post Flight Data Analysis
PFDA........ Precision Frequency Distribution Amplifier
PFDA........ Pulse-Frequency Distortion Analyzer
PFDC........ Peoples Federal Savings Bank of DeKalb City [*NASDAQ symbol*] (NQ)
PFDCCA ... Prodemca: Friends of the Democratic Center in the Americas (EA)
PFDF........ Pacific Fisheries Development Foundation (EA)
PFDM........ Preliminary Final Draft Manuscript
PFDR........ Pathfinder [*Aircraft*]
PFDR........ Preferred Risk Life Insurance Co. [*NASDAQ symbol*] (NQ)
PfdrBad...... Pathfinder Badge [*Military decoration*] (AABC)
PFDS........ Pergamon Financial Data Services [*Pergamon Orbit Infoline Ltd.*] [*London, England*] [*Information service or system*] (IID)
PFE........... Pacific Fruit Express Co. [*AAR code*]
PFE........... Paper, Film, and Foil Converter [*A publication*]

PFE........... Partido Feminista de Espana [*Feminist Party of Spain*] [*Political party*] (PPW)
PFE........... Pfizer, Inc. [*NYSE symbol*] (SPSG)
PFE........... Physics of Failure in Electronics [*A publication*] (MCD)
PFE........... Plenum Fill Experiment [*Nuclear energy*] (NRCH)
PFE........... Post Fire Evaluation [*Military*] (CAAL)
PFE........... Post Flight Evaluation
PFE........... Priests for Equality (EA)
PFE........... Pulsed Field Electrophoresis [*Analytical biochemistry*]
PFE........... Purchaser Furnished Equipment (NATG)
PFEC........ Philatelic Friends Exchange Circuit (EA)
PFEFES.... Pacific and Far East Federation of Engineering Societies
PFEL........ Pacific Far East Line
PFEP........ Programmable Front-End Processor [*Data processing*]
PFES........ Pan American Federation of Engineering Societies
PFES........ Proposed Final Environmental Statement [*Department of Energy*]
PFES........ Pure Fluid Encoder System
PFF........... Pathfinder Force [*British RADAR designation which became overall synonym for RADAR*] [*Military*]
PFF........... Permanent Family File [*Navy*] (NG)
PFF........... Planning Factors File (MCD)
PFF........... Police Field Force (CINC)
PFF........... Porcine Follicular Fluid [*Endocrinology*]
PFF........... Primary Focus Feed [*Satellite communications*]
PFF........... Proposed Fabric Flammability Standard [*Consumer Product Safety Commission*]
PFF........... Protein Fat-Free [*Food technology*]
PFF........... Punjab Frontier Force [*British military*] (DMA)
PFFC........ Parallel-Flow Film Cooling
PFFC........ Philadelphia Flyers Fan Club (EA)
PFF Convrt ... Paper, Film, and Foil Converter [*A publication*]
PFF Convt ... Paper, Film, and Foil Converter [*A publication*]
PFF Inc...... Police-FBI Fencing, Incognito [*Phony fencing ring operated by Washington, DC, law enforcement agents during 1976 to identify and arrest area thieves*]
PFFS......... Pacific First Financial Corp. [*Formerly, Pacific First Federal Savings Bank*] [*NASDAQ symbol*] (NQ)
PFFX .... Profiling Fixture
PFG........... Pacific Rim Mining Corp. [*Vancouver Stock Exchange symbol*]
PFG........... Paeoniflorigenone [*Biochemistry*]
PFG........... Pfennig [*Penny*] [*Monetary unit*] [*German*]
PFG........... Piping and Filter Gallery [*Nuclear energy*] (NRCH)
PFG........... Primary Frequency Generator
PFG........... Pulsed Field Gradient [*Electroanalytical chemistry*]
PFG........... Purple Flower Gang (EA)
PFGC........ Parameters from Group Contribution [*Equation of state*]
PFGE........ Pulsed Field Gel Electrophoresis
PFGE........ Pulsed Field Gradient Gel Electrophoresis
PFGGA...... Professional Geographer [*A publication*]
PFGM........ Guided Missile Patrol Escort [*Ship symbol*] (NATG)
PFGX........ Pacific Fruit Growers Express
PFH........... Hudson, NY [*Location identifier*] [*FAA*] (FAAL)
PFH........... Pafco Financial Holdings Ltd. [*Toronto Stock Exchange symbol*]
PfH........... Pfaelzische Heimatblaetter [*A publication*]
PFH........... Pressurized Fluidized-Bed Hydroretorting [*Chemical engineering*]
PFHA .... Paso Fino Horse Association (EA)
PFHEDE... Pfaelzer Heimat [*A publication*]
PFHM....... Protein-Free Hybridoma Medium
PFHS......... Precipitation from Homogeneous Solution [*Catalyst preparation process*]
PFI............ Pacific Forest Industries (EA)
PFI............ People First International (EA)
PFI............ Pet Food Institute (EA)
PFI............ Photo Finishing Institute [*Defunct*] (EA)
PFI............ Physical Fitness Index
PFI............ Picture and Frame Institute [*Defunct*] (EA)
PFI............ Pie Filling Institute [*Defunct*] (EA)
PFI............ Pipe Fabrication Institute (EA)
PFI............ Port Fuel Injector [*Automotive engines*]
PFI............ Position Finding Instrument (DS)
PFI............ Power Failure Indicator [*NASA*] (KSC)
PFI............ Prison Fellowship International (EA)
PFI............ Profile Index. Micromedia Ltd. [*A publication*]
PFIA......... Police and Firemen's Insurance Association (EA)
PFIA......... Prevention of Fraud Investments Act [*British*]
PFIAB....... President's Foreign Intelligence Advisory Board (AFM)
PFIB .... Pentafluoroiodosylbenzene [*Organic chemistry*]
PFIB .... Perfluoroisobutene [*Organic chemistry*]
PFIC......... Passive Foreign Investment Company [*IRS*]
PFIEP....... Perfluorinated Ion-Exchange Polymer [*Organic chemistry*]
PFil.......... Prace Filologiczne [*A publication*]
PFil.......... Przeglad Filozoficzny [*A publication*]
PFIM........ Pure Fluid Impact Modulator
PFIN......... P & F Industries, Inc. [*NASDAQ symbol*] (NQ)
PFI & R.... Part Fill In and Ram [*Construction*]
Pfitzner ...... Hans Pfitzner-Gesellschaft. Mitteilungen [*A publication*]
PFIU......... Plot File Import Utility [*IBM Corp.*]
Pfizer Med Monogr ... Pfizer Medical Monographs [*A publication*]

PFJ .... Patreksfjordur [*Iceland*] [*Airport symbol*] (OAG)
PFJ .... Polar Front Jet Stream (ADA)
PFJR .... Patellofemoral Joint Reaction [*Physiology*]
PFK .... Payload Function Key [*NASA*] (MCD)
PFK .... Perfluorokerosene [*Heat transfer agent*]
PFK .... Phosphofructokinase [*An enzyme*]
PFK .... Programmed Function Keyboard [*Data processing*]
PFL .... Fort Sill, OK [*Location identifier*] [*FAA*] (FAAL)
PFL .... Pacific Cassiar Ltd. [*Toronto Stock Exchange symbol*]
PFL .... Pennsylvania Folklife [*A publication*]
PFL .... People for Life (EA)
PFL .... Pharmacists for Life (EA)
PFL .... Pounds per Lineal Foot [*Technical drawings*]
PFL .... Primary Freon Loop (NASA)
PFL .... Propulsion Field Laboratory
PFL .... Public Facility Loans
PFLA .... Popular Front for the Liberation of Ahvaz [*Iran*]
PFLAB .... Pfluegers Archiv. European Journal of Physiology [*A publication*]
P-FLAG ..... Federation of Parents and Friends of Lesbians and Gays (EA)
Pflanzenschutzber ... Pflanzenschutzberichte [*A publication*]
Pflanzenschutz-Nachr ... Pflanzenschutz-Nachrichten [*A publication*]
Pflanzenschutz-Nachr (Am Ed) ... Pflanzenschutz-Nachrichten (American Edition) [*A publication*]
Pflanzenschutz Nachr Bayer ... Pflanzenschutz-Nachrichten Bayer [*A publication*]
Pflanz-Nach Bayer ... Pflanzenschutz-Nachrichten Bayer [*A publication*]
PflBau PflSchutz PflZucht ... Pflanzenbau, Pflanzenschutz, Pflanzenzucht [*A publication*]
PFLDA ...... Physics of Fluids [*A publication*]
PFLF .... People, Food and Land Foundation (EA)
PFLFT .... Pubblicazioni. Facolta di Lettere e Filosofia. Universita di Torino [*A publication*]
P Flo .... Pandectae Florentinae [*A publication*] (DSA)
PFLO .... Popular Front for the Liberation of Oman [*Political party*] (PD)
PFLOAG ... Popular Front for the Liberation of Oman and the Arabian Gulf [*Political party*] (PD)
PFLOLS .... Portable Fresnel-Lens Optical-Landing System (NG)
P Florent .... Pandectae Florentinae [*A publication*] (DSA)
PFLP .... Popular Front for the Liberation of Palestine [*Political party*] (PD)
PFLP-GC... Popular Front for the Liberation of Palestine - General Command [*Political party*] (PD)
PFLSA .... Physics of Fluids. Supplement [*A publication*]
PFLSH ...... Publications. Faculte des Lettres et Sciences Humaines de Paris [*A publication*]
P/FLT .... Pattern Flight [*Also, P/F*] (MUGU)
PFLTS .... Parquet Floor Layers' Trade Society [*A union*] [*British*]
Pflueg Arch ... Pfluegers Archiv. European Journal of Physiology [*A publication*]
Pfluegers Arch Eur J Physiol ... Pfluegers Archiv. European Journal of Physiology [*A publication*]
Pfluegers Arch Ges Physiol ... Pfluegers Archiv fuer die Gesamte Physiologie [*A publication*]
Pfluegers Archiv Gesamte Physiol Menschen Tiere ... Pfluegers Archiv fuer die Gesamte Physiologie des Menschen und der Tiere [*A publication*]
PFLUS .... Publications. Faculte des Lettres. Universite de Strasbourg [*A publication*]
PFLV .... Pressure Fed Launch Vehicle [*NASA*] (KSC)
PFLY .... Polifly Finance Corp. [*NASDAQ symbol*] (NQ)
PFM .... Little Franciscan Sisters of Mary [*Roman Catholic religious order*]
PFM .... Pacific Minesearch Ltd. [*Vancouver Stock Exchange symbol*]
PFM .... Patriots of Fort McHenry (EA)
PFM .... Physiological Flow Model [*For simulating medical conditions*]
PFM .... Pitch Follow-Up Motor
PFM .... Plan for Maintenance [*Navy*]
PFM .... Planning Factors Management (MCD)
PFM .... Platform (NASA)
PFM .... Political Freedom Movement [*British*]
PFM .... Porcelain Fused to Metal [*Dentistry*]
PFM .... Potato Futures Market [*Finance*]
PFM .... Power Factor Meter
PFM .... Precision Frequency Multivider (KSC)
PFM .... Predictor Frame Memory
PFM .... Pressure Flow Meter
PFM .... Prison Fellowship Ministries (EA)
P & FM ...... Programs and Financial Management [*Navy*]
PFM .... Pulse-Forming Machine
PFM .... Pulse-Frequency Modulation [*RADAR*]
P/FM .... Pylon/Fin Movement
PFM .... University of Pittsburgh, Falk Library - Health Professions, Pittsburgh, PA [*OCLC symbol*] (OCLC)
PFMA .... Pipe Fittings Manufacturers Association [*Later, APFA*] (EA)
PFMA .... Plumbing Fixture Manufacturers Association [*Defunct*] (EA)
PFMC .... Pacific Fishery Management Council (EA)
PFMO .... Planning Factors Management Office
PFMR .... Pasadena Foundation for Medical Research [*California*]
PFMR .... Plug-Flow Membrane Reactor [*Chemical engineering*]

PFMR .... Project Funds Management Record (MCD)
PFN .... Panama City [*Florida*] [*Airport symbol*] (OAG)
PFN .... Pantyffynnon [*British depot code*]
PFN .... Parti des Forces Nouvelles [*New Forces Party*] [*France*] [*Political party*] (PPW)
PFN .... Passamaquoddy Ferry & Navigation Co. [*AAR code*]
PFN .... Permanent File Name
PFN .... Plasma Fibronectin [*Biochemistry*]
PFN .... PMC Corp. [*Toronto Stock Exchange symbol*]
PFN .... Prefinished [*Technical drawings*]
PFN .... Pulse-Forming Network
PFNA .... Pentecostal Fellowship of North America (EA)
PFNC .... Progress Financial Corporation [*Plymouth Meeting, PA*] [*NASDAQ symbol*] (NQ)
PFNS .... Position Fixing Navigation System (AABC)
PFNTU ..... Pathfinder Navigation Training Unit [*Military*]
PFO .... Paphos [*Cyprus*] [*Airport symbol*] (OAG)
PFO .... Partly Filled Out [*Questionnaire*]
PFO .... Patent Foramen Ovale [*Cardiology*]
PFO .... Physical Fitness Officer [*British military*] (DMA)
PFO .... Pitch Follow-Up Operation
PFO .... Pomona Public Library, Pomona, CA [*OCLC symbol*] (OCLC)
PFO .... Postal Finance Officer [*Army*]
PFO .... Procurement Field Office
PFO .... Pyrolysis Fuel Oil [*Petroleum refining*]
PFO .... Spofford, TX [*Location identifier*] [*FAA*] (FAAL)
PFOBA ...... Paso Fino Owners and Breeders Association [*Later, PFHA*] (EA)
PFOD .... Presumed Finding of Death [*DoD*]
PFol .... Ridley Township Public Library, Folsom, PA [*Library symbol*] [*Library of Congress*] (LCLS)
PFouad ...... Les Papyrus Fouad I [*A publication*] (OCD)
PFP .... Partnership for Productivity International (EA)
PFP .... Peace and Freedom Party (EA)
PFP .... Pensions for Professionals, Inc.
PFP .... Pentafluoropropionate [*or Pentafluoropropionyl*] [*Organic chemistry*]
PFP .... Personal Financial Planning (ADA)
PFP .... Pet-Facilitated Psychotherapy [*Psychiatry*]
PFP .... Platelet-Free Plasma [*Hematology*]
PFP .... Pleiades Foundation for Peace [*Later, PFPSE*] (EA)
PFP .... Popular Front Party [*Ghana*] [*Political party*] (PPW)
PFP .... Pore Forming Protein [*Biochemistry*]
PFP .... Post Flight Processor
PFP .... Postage Forward Parcels [*Shipping*]
PFP .... Prime Financial Partnership [*AMEX symbol*] (SPSG)
PFP .... Products for Power [*Automotive components manufacturer*]
PFP .... Program File Processor
PFP .... Program Financial Plan (NASA)
PFP .... Program Forecast Period [*Military*] (AFIT)
PFP .... Programmable Function Panel (NASA)
PFP .... Progressiewe Federale Party [*Progressive Federal Party*] [*South Africa*] [*Political party*] (PPW)
PFP .... Proving for Production (MCD)
PFP .... Publishers for Peace [*An association*]
PFPA .... Pentafluoropropionic Anhydride [*Organic chemistry*]
PFPA .... Pro-Family Press Association (EA)
PFPC .... Passenger Form and Procedures Committee [*IATA*] (DS)
PFPI .... Partnership for Productivity International (EA)
PFPI .... Pentafluoropropionyl Imidazole [*Organic chemistry*]
PFPM .... Production Flight Procedures Manual (MCD)
PFPS .... Potential for Foster Parenthood Scale [*Psychology*]
PFPS .... Progressive French Polishers' Society [*A union*] [*British*]
PFPSE .... Pleiades Foundation for Peace and Space Education (EA)
PFPUT ...... Pension Fund Property Unit Trust [*British*]
PFPXA6 .... Pediatric Continuing Education Courses for the Practitioner [*A publication*]
PFQ .... Preflight Qualification
PFQ .... Public Finance Quarterly [*A publication*]
PFr .... Franklin Public Library, Franklin, PA [*Library symbol*] [*Library of Congress*] (LCLS)
PFR .... Part Failure Rate
PFR .... Peak Flow Rate [*or Reading*] [*Medicine*]
PFR .... Perforator (DEN)
PFR .... Perkins Family Restaurants LP [*NYSE symbol*] (SPSG)
PFR .... Permanent Factory Repairable (MCD)
PFR .... Persistent Fat Retention [*Syndrome*]
PFR .... Personal Financial Record [*Army*] (AABC)
PFR .... Pfarrer [*Pastor*] [*German*] (EY)
PFR .... Photoflash Relay
PFR .... Pike Fry Rhabdovirus
PFR .... Plug-Flow Reactor [*Engineering*]
PFR .... Polarized Frequency Relay
PFR .... Portable Foot Restraint (NASA)
PFR .... Power Fail Recovery System [*Data processing*] (MDG)
PFR .... Power Fail/Restart
PFR .... Power Failure Release
PFR .... Precision Fathometer Recorder [*Raytheon Co.*]
PFR .... Preferred Resources, Inc. [*Vancouver Stock Exchange symbol*]
PFR .... Preflight Review [*NASA*] (KSC)

PFR............ Preheating, Falling-Film, Rising-Film [*Sections of a concentrator*] [*Chemical engineering*]
PFR............ Preliminary Flight Rating [*Air Force*]
PFr............ Presence Francophone [*A publication*]
PFR............ Problem/Failure Report
PFR............ Programmed Film Reader [*System*]
pfr.............. Proofreader [*MARC relator code*] [*Library of Congress*]   (LCCP)
PFR............ Prototype Fast Reactor
PFR............ Pulmonary Blood Flow Redistribution [*Medicine*]
PFR............ Pulse Frequency   (MDG)
PFR............ Punch Feed Read   (CMD)
PFRA........ Percent of Females Reproductively Active [*Ecology*]
PFRA........ Prairie Farm Rehabilitation Administration [*Canada*]
PFRA........ Problem-Focused Research Applications [*of ASRA*] [*National Science Foundation*]
PFRA........ Professional Football Referees Association   (EA)
PFRA........ Professional Football Researchers Association   (EA)
P & F Radio Reg ... Pike and Fischer's Radio Regulation Reporter [*A publication*]
PFRC........ Pacific Forest Research Centre [*Canada*]   (ARC)
PFRD........ Preferred Homecare of America, Inc. [*NASDAQ symbol*]   (NQ)
PFRD........ Preferred Stock [*Investment term*]
PFredY....... Joseph A. Yablonski Memorial Clinic, Fredericktown, PA [*Library symbol*] [*Library of Congress*]   (LCLS)
PFRMG..... Performing   (ROG)
PFRS........ Portable Field Recording System [*NASA*]   (KSC)
PFRT........ Preliminary Flight Rating Test
PFRT........ Preliminary Flight Readiness Test [*NASA*]   (KSC)
PFS........... Parallel Filter System
PFS........... Particles and Fields Subsatellite [*NASA*]
P & FS....... Particles and Fields Subsatellite [*NASA*]   (KSC)
PFS........... Percent Full Scale   (KSC)
PFS........... Peripheral Fixed Shim [*Nuclear energy*]   (NRCH)
PFS........... Personal and Family Survival [*Civil Defense*]
PFS........... Personal Filing System [*Data-base program*] [*Software Publishing Corp.*]
PFS........... Photofragment Spectroscopy
PFS........... Pioneer Financial Services, Inc. [*NYSE symbol*]   (SPSG)
PFS........... Pitch Follow-Up System
PFS........... Pittsburgh, PA [*Location identifier*] [*FAA*]   (FAAL)
PFS........... Plasterers' Friendly Society [*A union*] [*British*]
PFS........... Porous Friction Surface [*Airfield pavement*]
PFS........... Positive Fuel Stop
PFS........... Precision Frequency Source
PFS........... Preflight School [*Military*]
PFS........... Press Fit Socket
PFS........... Primary Flight System   (NASA)
PFS........... Primary Frequency Supply [*Telecommunications*]   (TEL)
PFS........... Programmable Frequency Standard
PFS........... Progress in Filtration and Separation [*Elsevier Book Series*] [*A publication*]
PFS........... Propellant Feed System
PFS........... Propellant Field System
PFS........... Pulmonary Function Score [*Physiology*]
PFS........... Pure Fluid System
PFS........... [*P. F.*] Smith's Pennsylvania State Reports [*51-81 1/2 Pennsylvania*] [*A publication*]   (DLA)
PFSA........ Pour Faire Ses Adieux [*To Say Good-Bye*] [*French*]
PFSB........ Piedmont Federal Corp. [*NASDAQ symbol*]   (NQ)
P Fsch....... Philosophische Forschungen [*A publication*]
PFSCL....... Papers on French Seventeenth Century Literature [*A publication*]
PFSh......... Partia Fashismit e Shqiperise [*Fascist Party of Albania*] [*Political party*]   (PPE)
PFSH........ Porcine Follicle Stimulating Hormone [*Endocrinology*]
PFSL......... Prudential Financial Services Corp. [*NASDAQ symbol*]   (NQ)
P F Smith... [*P. F.*] Smith's Pennsylvania State Reports [*51-81 1/2 Pennsylvania*] [*A publication*]   (DLA)
PFSO........ Postal Finance and Supply Office   (AFM)
PFS/PRS... Patent Family Service/Patent Register Service [*Database*] [*International Patent Documentation Center*] [*Information service or system*]   (CRD)
PFSR........ Program Financial Status Report   (AAG)
PFSS........ Patellofemoral Stress Syndrome [*Medicine*]
PFSV........ Pilot-to-Forecaster Service   (FAAC)
PFT........... Pacific Asia Tech [*Vancouver Stock Exchange symbol*]
PFT........... Page Frame Table   (BUR)
PFT........... Pancreatic Function Test [*Medicine*]
PFT........... Paper, Flat Tape
PFT........... Parafascicular Thalamotomy [*Medicine*]
PFT........... Parallel Fourier Transform   (MCD)
PFT........... Pet-Facilitated Therapy [*Psychiatry*]
PFT........... Phenylalanine mustard [*Melphalan*], Fluorouracil, Tamoxifen [*Antineoplastic drug regimen*]
PFT........... Physical Fitness Test
PFT........... Plastic Fuel Tank
PFT........... Portable Flame Thrower [*Army*]
PFT........... Positive Flight Termination   (MUGU)
PFT........... Preflight Team [*Air Force*]   (AFM)
PFT........... Preflight Tool   (MCD)

PFT........... Professional Football Trainers   (EA)
PFT........... Program Flying Training [*Air Force*]   (AFM)
PFT........... Projective Field Theory
PFT........... Pulmonary Function Test [*Medicine*]
PFT........... Pulse Fourier Transform
PFTA........ Payload Flight Test Article [*NASA*]   (MCD)
PFTB........ Preflight Test Bus   (MCD)
PFTC........ Pestalozzi-Froebel Teachers College [*Illinois*]
PFTE........ Pianoforte [*Soft, then Loud*] [*Music*]
PFTE........ Portable Field Trainer/Evaluator   (MCD)
PFTM....... Preliminary Flight Test Memo
PFTR........ Preliminary Flight Test Report
PFTS........ Permanent Field Training Site
PFTS......... Profit Systems, Inc. [*NASDAQ symbol*]   (NQ)
PFU .... Passive Filtration Unit
PFU .... Plaque-Forming Unit [*Immunochemistry*]
PFU .... Please Follow Up
PFU .... Pock-Forming Unit
PFU .... Preparation for Use
PFU .... Presbyterian Fellowship Union [*Australia*]
PFUA........ Pitch Follow-Up Amplifier
PFUEI....... Prime Focus Universal Extragalactic Instrument [*Astronomy*]
PFUM....... Pitch Follow-Up Motor
PFUO........ Pitch Follow-Up Operation
PFUS........ Pitch Follow-Up System
PFV.......... Pestalozzi-Froebel-Verband [*Pestalozzi-Froebel Association*]
PFV.......... Philippine Forces, Vietnam
PFV.......... Physiological Full Value
PFV.......... Pour Faire Visite [*To Make a Call*] [*French*]
PFVEA ..... Professional Film and Video Equipment Association   (EA)
PFW......... Power, Fulcrum, Weight
PFW......... Progressive Free Wave
PFWA........ Professional Football Writers of America   (EA)
PFwB .... Budd Co., Fort Washington, PA [*Library symbol*] [*Library of Congress*]   (LCLS)
PFWOAD ... Place from Which Ordered to Active Duty [*Military*]
PFwR .... William H. Rorer, Inc., Fort Washington, PA [*Library symbol*] [*Library of Congress*]   (LCLS)
PFX........... Prefix   (ROG)
PFX........... Proflex Ltd. [*Vancouver Stock Exchange symbol*]
PFY........... Prior Fiscal Year   (AFIT)
PFYA........ Predicted First-Year Average [*Law school*]
PFZ........... Polar Front Zone [*Marine science*]   (MSC)
PFZ........... Potassium Hexafluorozirconate [*Inorganic chemistry*]
PF-ZAPU .. Patriotic Front - Zimbabwe African People's Union [*Political party*]   (PD)
PG .... Air Gabon Cargo [*ICAO designator*]   (FAAC)
PG .... Page [*or Pagination*] [*Online database field identifier*]
PG .... Palestine Gazette [*A publication*]
PG .... Papua New Guinea [*ANSI two-letter standard code*]   (CNC)
PG .... Paralysie Generale [*General Paralysis*] [*Medicine*] [*French*]
PG .... Paregoric [*Slang*]
PG .... Parental Guidance Suggested [*Formerly, GP*] [*Some material may not be suitable for preteenagers*] [*Movie rating*]
PG .... Paris Granite
PG .... Paris Group [*See also GP*] [*Saint Cloud, France*]   (EAIO)
PG .... Partial Gum [*Philately*]
PG .... Past Grand [*Freemasonry*]
PG .... Paste Grain [*Bookbinding*]
PG .... Patrol Combatant [*Gunboat*] [*Navy symbol*]
PG .... Patrologia Graeca [*A publication*]
PG .... Patrologiae Cursus. Series Graeca [*A publication*]   (OCD)
PG .... Pay Grade
PG .... Pay Group
PG .... Paying Guest
PG .... PEACE [*Program for Emergency Assistance, Cooperation, and Education*] for Guatemala   (EA)
PG .... Pedal Ganglion
PG .... Pedal Groove
PG .... Pelham Grenville Wodehouse [*British humorist, 1881-1975*]
Pg .... Pentagram [*One million metric tons*]
PG .... Peptidoglycan [*Biochemistry*]
PG .... Permanent Glow [*Telecommunications*]   (TEL)
PG .... Permanent Grade
PG .... Persian Gulf   (MCD)
PG .... Pharmacopoeia Germanica [*German Pharmacopoeia*]
PG .... Phosphatidylglycerol
PG .... Phosphogluconate [*Biochemistry*]
PG .... Phosphogypsum [*Inorganic chemistry*]
PG .... Photogrammetry
PG .... Picogram
PG .... Pine Grosbeak [*Ornithology*]
PG .... Pipers Guild   (EA)
PG .... Placebo Group [*Medicine*]
PG .... Planning Group [*DoD*]
PG .... Planning Guide [*HUD*]
PG .... Plasma Glucose [*Hematology*]
PG .... Plate Glass
PG .... Plate-Glazed [*Paper*]
PG .... Politie-Gids [*A publication*]
PG .... Pollen Grain [*Botany*]

PG .... Polyethylene Glycol [*Organic chemistry*]
PG .... Polygalacturonase [*An enzyme*]
PG .... Polyglycine [*Biochemistry*]
PG .... Pontius Guillelmi [*Authority cited in pre-1607 legal work*]   (DSA)
PG .... Port Group [*Telecommunications*]   (TEL)
PG .... Portugal
PG .... Portuguese [*Language, etc.*]
pg .... Portuguese Guinea [*Guinea-Bissau*] [*MARC country of publication code*] [*Library of Congress*]   (LCCP)
PG .... Position Guide   (MCD)
P/G .... Postagram [*British military*]   (DMA)
PG .... Postgraduate [*Refers to courses or students*] [*Slang*]
PG .... Power Gain
PG .... Power Generation   (MCD)
PG .... Preacher General
PG .... Predicted Grade [*IRS*]
PG .... Pregnanediol Glucuronide [*Endocrinology*]
PG .... Pregnant
PG .... Press Gallery [*US Senate*]
PG .... Pressure Gauge   (KSC)
PG .... Prisonnier de Guerre [*Prisoner of War - POW*] [*French*]
PG .... Pro-German [*Prisoner of war term*] [*World War I*]   (DSUE)
P & G .... Procter & Gamble Co.
PG .... Procter & Gamble Co. [*NYSE symbol*]   (SPSG)
PG .... Procureur Generaal [*Public Attorney*] [*Dutch*]   (ILCA)
PG .... Producers Group   (EA)
PG .... Professional Group   (MCD)
PG .... Program [*Telecommunications*]
PG .... Program Generic [*Data processing*]   (TEL)
PG .... Program Guidance
PG .... Programmer   (AAG)
PG .... Project Group
PG .... Proof Gallon [*Wines and spirits*]
PG .... Propyl Gallate [*Antioxidant*] [*Organic chemistry*]
PG .... Propylene Glycol
PG .... Prostaglandin [*Also, Pg*] [*Biochemistry*]
PG .... Protein Granule
PG .... Proteoglycan [*Biochemistry*]
PG .... Prothoracic Gland [*Insect anatomy*]
PG .... Province Guard [*Cambodia*]   (CINC)
PG .... Proving Ground [*Army*]
PG .... Przeglad Geograficzny [*A publication*]
PG .... Public Gaol [*British*]
PG .... Pulse Gate
PG .... Pulse Generator
PG .... Pure Gum [*of envelopes*]
PG .... Pyoderma Gangrenosum [*Medicine*]
PG .... Pyrolytic Graphite   (MCD)
PG .... Pyrotechnic Gyro   (AAG)
PG-13 .... Parental Guidance Suggested [*Now: Parents Strongly Cautioned. Some material may be inappropriate for children under 13*] [*Movie rating*]
PGA .... Page [*Arizona*] [*Airport symbol*]   (OAG)
PGA .... Paragould [*Arkansas*] [*Seismograph station code, US Geological Survey*]   (SEIS)
P & GA .... Pastoralists' and Graziers' Association of Western Australia
PGA .... Pega Capital Resources Ltd. [*Toronto Stock Exchange symbol*]
PGA .... Pendulous Gyro Accelerometer
PGA .... PGI, Inc. [*AMEX symbol*]   (SPSG)
PGA .... Phosphoglyceric Acid [*Biochemistry*]
PGA .... Pin-Grid-Array [*Motorola, Inc.*]
PGA .... Polyglycolic Acid [*Organic chemistry*]   (RDA)
PGA .... Poly(L-glutamic Acid) [*Organic chemistry*]
PGA .... Power Gain Antenna
PGA .... Power Generating Assembly   (KSC)
PGA .... Pressure Garment Assembly
PGA .... Printing and Graphic Arts [*A publication*]
PGA .... Producers Guild of America   (EA)
PGA .... Professional Golfers' Association of America   (EA)
PGA .... Professional Graphics Adapter [*IBM Corp.*]
PGA .... Professional Group Audio
PGA .... Programmable Gain Amplifier   (MCD)
PGA .... Programmable Gate Array
PGA .... Prostaglandin A [*Biochemistry*]
PGA .... Prostaglandin Analog [*Biochemistry*]
PGA .... Pteroylmonoglutamic Acid [*Folic acid*] [*Also, FA, PteGlu*] [*Biochemistry*]
PGA .... Purchased Gas Adjustment
PGA .... Pyrolysis Gas Analysis
PGA .... Upjohn Co. [*Research code symbol*]
PGAA .... Professional Guides Association of America   (EA)
PGAA .... Prompt Gamma-Ray Activation Analysis
P-GABA .... Phenyl-gamma-aminobutyric Acid [*Tranquilizer*]
PGAC .... Guam/Taguac [*Mariana Islands*] [*ICAO location identifier*]   (ICLI)
PGAC .... Professional Group - Automatic Control
PGAEA ...... Proceedings. Geologists' Association (England) [*A publication*]
PGAH .... Pineapple Growers Association of Hawaii   (EA)
PGAI .... Pension Insurance Group of America, Incorporated [*Valley Forge, PA*] [*NASDAQ symbol*]   (NQ)

PGAM .... Pacific Gamble Robinson Co. [*NASDAQ symbol*]   (NQ)
PGAM .... Phosphoglyceromutase [*An enzyme*]
PGANE ...... Professional Group on Aeronautical and Navigational Electronics
PGA-NOC ... Permanent General Assembly of National Olympic Committees
PGAP .... Professional Group - Antennas and Propagation
PGAPL ...... Preliminary Group Assembly Parts List
PGAR .... Provisional Government of the Algerian Republic
PGase........ Polygalacturonase [*An enzyme*]
PGAZA...... Petrol si Gaze [*A publication*]
Pg B........... Bachelor of Pedagogy
PGB .... Patrol Gunboat [*Navy symbol*]   (NATG)
PGB .... Phoenix Global [*Vancouver Stock Exchange symbol*]
PGB .... Prostaglandin B [*Biochemistry*]
PGB .... Protestant Guild for the Blind   (EA)
PGB .... Pyrographalloy Boron
PGBA........ Piece Goods Buyers Association [*Defunct*]   (EA)
PGBA........ Possum Growers and Breeders Association   (EA)
PGBD .... Pegboard [*Freight*]
PGBM .... Pulse Gate Binary Modulation   (MCD)
PGbSH ..... Seton Hill College, Greensburg, PA [*Library symbol*] [*Library of Congress*]   (LCLS)
PGBTR ...... Professional Group - Broadcast and Television Receivers
PGBTS ...... Professional Group - Broadcast Transmission Systems
PGbU........ University of Pittsburgh at Greensburg, Greensburg, PA [*Library symbol*] [*Library of Congress*]   (LCLS)
PGC .... Geneva College, Beaver Falls, PA [*OCLC symbol*]   (OCLC)
PGC .... Gettysburg College, Gettysburg, PA [*Library symbol*] [*Library of Congress*]   (LCLS)
PGC .... Pacific Geoscience Centre [*Research center*]   (RCD)
PGC .... Pagurian Corp. [*Toronto Stock Exchange symbol*]
PGC .... Past Grand Commander [*Freemasonry*]   (ROG)
PGC .... Pelican Gospel Commentaries [*Harmondsworth*] [*A publication*]
PGC .... Per Gyro Compass [*Navigation*]
PGC .... Persian Gulf Command [*World War II*]
PGC .... Pontine Gaze Center [*Eye anatomy*]
PGC .... Poorly Graphitized Carbon [*Physical chemistry*]
PGC .... Port Group Control [*Telecommunications*]   (TEL)
PGC .... Potassium Gold Cyanide [*Inorganic chemistry*]
PGC .... Potential Gas Committee
PGC .... Primordial Germ Cell
PGC .... Process Gas Chromatography
PGC .... Process Gas Consumers Group   (EA)
PGC .... Professional Graphics Controller [*IBM Corp.*]
PGC .... Program Generation Center [*Military*]   (CAAL)
PGC .... Programmed Gain Control
PGC .... Proving Ground Command [*Air Force*]
PGC .... Pulsed Gas Crymography
PGC .... Pyrolysis Gas Chromatography
PGcC......... Grove City College, Grove City, PA [*Library symbol*] [*Library of Congress*]   (LCLS)
PGCC....... Power Generation Control Complex [*Nuclear energy*]   (NRCH)
PGCE....... Post Graduate Certificate of Education
PGCh .... Past Grand Chaplain [*Freemasonry*]
PGCOA .... Pennsylvania Grade Crude Oil Association   (EA)
PGCP........ Professional Group - Component Parts
PGCRA ..... Professional Golf Club Repairmen's Association   (EA)
PGCS........ Professional Group - Communications Systems
PGCT........ Professional Group - Circuit Theory
PGCU .... International Printing and Graphic Communications Union
PGD .... Pango Gold Mines Ltd. [*Toronto Stock Exchange symbol*]
PGD .... Past Grand Deacon [*Freemasonry*]
PGD .... Personnel and Guidance Journal [*A publication*]
PGD .... Phosphogluconate Dehydrogenase [*Also, PGDH*] [*An enzyme*]
PGD .... Pikwitonei Granulite Domain [*Geology*]
PGD .... Pinion Gear Drive
PGD .... Planar Gas Discharge   (MCD)
PGD .... Prostaglandin D [*Biochemistry*]
PGD .... Pulse Generator Display
PGD .... Punta Gorda [*Florida*] [*Airport symbol*]   (OAG)
PGDB .... Plumbers, Gasfitters, and Drainers' Board [*New South Wales, Australia*]
PGDB .... Propylene Glycol Dibenzoate [*Organic chemistry*]
PGDC .... Provincial Grand Director of Ceremonies [*Freemasonry*]
PGDCS...... Power Generation, Distribution, and Control Subsystem   (MCD)
PGDF........ Pilot Guide Dog Foundation   (EA)
PGDH........ 15-Hydroxyprostaglandin Dehydrogenase [*An enzyme*]
PGDH........ Phosphogluconate Dehydrogenase [*Also, PGD*] [*An enzyme*]
PGDN........ Propylene Glycol Dinitrate [*Organic chemistry*]
PGDS........ Pioneer Ground Data System
PGDS........ Pulse Generator Display System
PG & E....... Pacific Gas and Electric [*Rock music group*]
PG & E....... Pacific Gas & Electric Co.
PGE .... Pacific Great Eastern Railway Co. [*Nicknames: Prince George Eventually, Please Go Easy*] [*Later, British Columbia Railway*] [*AAR code*]
PGE .... Page Petroleum Ltd. [*Toronto Stock Exchange symbol*]   (SPSG)
PGE .... Phenyl Glycidyl Ether [*Organic chemistry*]
PGE .... Platinum Group Element [*Chemistry*]

PGE .... Population Growth Estimation
PGE .... Pore Gradient Electrophoresis
PGE .... Portland General Electric Co., Library, Portland, OR [*OCLC symbol*] (OCLC)
PGE .... Portland Grain Exchange (EA)
PGE .... Precision Gimbal Experiment
PGE .... Prime Group Engineer (AAG)
PGE .... Professional Group - Education
PGE .... Prostaglandin E [*Biochemistry*]
PGE .... Purge (NASA)
PGEC .... Professional Group on Electronic Computers [*IEEE*]
PGED .... Professional Group - Electronic Devices
PGEM .... Professional Group - Engineering Management
PGEN .... Plant Genetics, Inc. [*NASDAQ symbol*] (NQ)
PGEWS ..... Professional Group on Engineering Writing and Speech [*Institute of Radio Engineers; now IEEE*]
PGF .... Pacific Gamefish Foundation (EA)
PGF........... Pengrowth Gas Income Fund Trust Units [*Toronto Stock Exchange symbol*]
PGF........... Perpignan [*France*] [*Airport symbol*] (OAG)
PGF........... Plerocercoid Growth Factor [*Endocrinology*]
PGF........... Portugal Fund [*NYSE symbol*] (SPSG)
PGF........... Presentation Graphic Feature [*Data processing*]
PGF........... Prostaglandin F [*Biochemistry*]
PGFC........ Periodical Guide for Computerists [*Applegate Computer Enterprises*] [*Information service or system*] [*Defunct*] (IID)
PGFS .... Pennsylvania German Folklore Society. Bulletin [*A publication*]
PGFW........ Guam [*Mariana Islands*] [*ICAO location identifier*] (ICLI)
PGG .... Page America Group, Inc. [*AMEX symbol*] (SPSG)
PGG .... Petrogold Financial Corp. [*Vancouver Stock Exchange symbol*]
PGG .... Pneumatic Ground Group
PGG .... Power Generation Group [*Nuclear Regulatory Commission*] (NRCH)
PGG .... Prostaglandin G [*A prostaglandin endoperoxide*] [*Biochemistry*]
PGGJ-A..... Philippine Geographical Journal [*A publication*]
PGGUDU ... Annual Research Reviews. Prostaglandins and the Gut [*A publication*]
PGH.......... Patrol Gunboat (Hydrofoil) [*Navy symbol*]
PGH.......... Pituitary Growth Hormone [*Endocrinology*]
PGH.......... Porcine Growth Hormone [*Biochemistry*]
PGH.......... Port Group Highway [*Telecommunications*] (TEL)
PGH.......... Prostaglandin H [*A prostaglandin endoperoxide*] [*Biochemistry*]
PGHA........ Park Gallatin Hereford Association (EA)
PGHFE...... Professional Group - Human Factors in Electronics
Pgh Leg Journal ... Pittsburgh Legal Journal [*Pennsylvania*] [*A publication*] (DLA)
PGHM....... Payload Ground Handling Mechanism [*NASA*] (MCD)
PGHMPR .. People's Great Hural of the Mongolian People's Republic
PGHS .... Public-General Hospital Section [*American Hospital Association*] (EA)
PGHTA ...... Progress in Hemostasis and Thrombosis [*A publication*]
PGHTS...... Port Group Highway Timeslot [*Telecommunications*] (TEL)
PGI .... Chitato [*Angola*] [*Airport symbol*] [*Obsolete*] (OAG)
PGI .... General Information Programme [*Acronym is based on foreign phrase*] [*UNESCO*]
PGi............ Paragigantocellularis [*Neuroanatomy*]
PGI .... Paris Gestion Informatique [*Paris Informatics Administration*] [*France*] [*Information service or system*] (IID)
PGI .... Peripheral Graphics, Incorporated
PGI .... Phosphoglucoisomerase [*An enzyme*]
PGI .... Ply-Gem Industries, Inc. [*AMEX symbol*] (SPSG)
PGI .... Port Group Interface [*Telecommunications*] (TEL)
PGI .... Professional Group - Instrumentation
PGI .... Project Group, Incorporated [*Advertising agency*] [*Acronym now used as official name of agency*]
PGI .... Prostaglandin I [*Biochemistry*]
PGI .... Provigo, Inc. [*Toronto Stock Exchange symbol*]
PGI .... Pyrotechnics Guild International (EA)
PGIE .... Professional Group - Industrial Electronics
PGiess........ Griechische Papyri im Museum des Oberhessischen Geschichtsvereins zu Giessen [*A publication*] (OCD)
PGIM .... Professional Group on Instrumentation and Measurement [*National Bureau of Standards*]
PGIS .... Project Grant Information System
PGIT........ Professional Group - Information Theory
PGJ........... Personnel and Guidance Journal [*A publication*]
PGJ........... Pipeline Girth Joint
PGJD........ Past Grand Junior Deacon [*Freemasonry*]
PGJN........ Pomegranate Guild of Judaic Needlework (EA)
P & G Jour ... Pipeline and Gas Journal [*A publication*]
P & G Jour BG ... Pipeline and Gas Journal Buyer's Guide Issue Handbook [*A publication*]
PGJW........ Past Grand Junior Warden [*Freemasonry*] (ROG)
PGK .... Pangkalpinang [*Indonesia*] [*Airport symbol*] (OAG)
PGK .... Phosphoglycerate Kinase [*An enzyme*]
PGK .... Preussischer Gesamtkatalog [*A publication*]

PGI............ Glenside Free Library, Glenside, PA [*Library symbol*] [*Library of Congress*] (LCLS)
PGL .... Lutheran Theological Seminary, Gettysburg, PA [*Library symbol*] [*Library of Congress*] (LCLS)
PGL .... Paraglossa of Labium [*Entomology*]
PGL ...... Pascagoula, MS [*Location identifier*] [*FAA*] (FAAL)
PGL ...... Peoples Energy Corp. [*NYSE symbol*] (SPSG)
PGL ...... Persistent Generalized Lymphadenopathy [*Medicine*]
PGL ...... Phosphoglycolipid
PGL ...... Polyglutaraldehyde [*Organic chemistry*]
PGL ...... Portable Gas LASER
PGL ...... Professional Graphics Language [*Software*] [*IBM Corp.*] (BYTE)
PGL ...... Provincial Grand Lodge [*Freemasonry*]
PGL .... Pulsed Gas LASER
PGladM .... Mary J. Drexel Home, Gladwyne, PA [*Library symbol*] [*Library of Congress*] [*Obsolete*] (LCLS)
PGlB .... Beaver College, Glenside, PA [*Library symbol*] [*Library of Congress*] (LCLS)
PGLC........ Pyrolysis Gas Liquid Chromatography
PGL-Hi..... Lutheran Historical Society, Gettysburg, PA [*Library symbol*] [*Library of Congress*] (LCLS)
PGLO .... NV Philips Gloeilampenfabrieken [*NASDAQ symbol*] (NQ)
PGM .... Messiah College Learning Center, Grantham, PA [*OCLC symbol*] (OCLC)
PGM .... Papyri Graecae Magicae [*A publication*] (OCD)
PGM .... Past Grand Master [*Freemasonry*]
PGM .... Patrol Vessel, Motor Gunboat [*Navy symbol*] [*Obsolete*]
PGM .... Perron Gold Mines [*Vancouver Stock Exchange symbol*]
PGM .... Persatuan Geologi Malaysia [*Geological Society of Malaysia*] (EAIO)
PGM .... Petermanns Geographische Mitteilungen [*A publication*]
PGM .... Phosphoglucomutase [*An enzyme*]
PGM .... Planetary Gearhead Motor [*Aerospace*]
PGM .... Platinum Group Metal [*In meteorites*]
PGM .... Port Graham, AK [*Location identifier*] [*FAA*] (FAAL)
PGM .... Postgraduate Medicine [*A publication*]
PGM .... Precision Guided Missile
PGM .... Precision-Guided Munition (MCD)
PGM .... Program
PGM .... Program Guidance Memorandum
PGM .... Program Manager [*A publication*]
PGM .... Putnam Investment Grade Municipal Trust [*NYSE symbol*] (SPSG)
PGMA ...... Poly(glyceryl Methacrylate) [*Organic chemistry*]
PGMA ...... Pulsed Gas Metal Arc (KSC)
PGME ...... Professional Group - Medical Electronics
PGMIL...... Professional Group - Military Electronics (MUGU)
PGMILE ... Professional Group - Military Electronics (AAG)
PGMS........ Professional Grounds Management Society (EA)
PGMSJ ...... Professional Group of Mathematical Symbol Jugglers (MUGU)
PGMT .... Pigment (MSA)
PGMTT..... Professional Group - Microwave Theory and Techniques
PGN......... Paragon Petroleum Ltd. [*Toronto Stock Exchange symbol*]
PGN .... Perigeniculate Nucleus [*Anatomy*]
PGN .... Phi Gamma Nu [*Fraternity*]
PGN .... Pigeon (ADA)
PGN .... Platinum Group Nugget [*In meteorites*]
PGN .... Portland General Corp. [*NYSE symbol*] (SPSG)
PGN .... Proliferative Glomerulonephritis [*Medicine*]
PGNAA ..... Prompt Gamma Neutron Activation Analysis [*Analytical chemistry*]
PGNCS...... Primary Guidance, Navigation, and Control System [*or Subsystem*] [*Apollo*] [*NASA*] (MCD)
PGND........ Propaganda (AABC)
P & G News ... Plants and Gardens News [*A publication*]
PGNGD..... Prace Instytutu Gornictwa Naftowego i Gazownictwa [*A publication*]
PGNMA .... Progress in Nuclear Medicine [*A publication*]
PGNS........ Polar Gas News [*A publication*]
PGNS........ Primary Guidance and Navigation System [*Apollo*] [*NASA*]
PGNS........ Professional Group - Nuclear Science
PGNT .... Sabanettan, Tinian Island [*Mariana Islands*] [*ICAO location identifier*] (ICLI)
PGNW....... Ritidian Point, Guam Island [*Mariana Islands*] [*ICAO location identifier*] (ICLI)
PGO .... Page, OK [*Location identifier*] [*FAA*] (FAAL)
PGO .... Pagecorp, Inc. [*Toronto Stock Exchange symbol*]
PGO .... Past Grand Orient [*Freemasonry*] (ROG)
PGO .... Peroxidase-Glucose Oxidase [*Also, GOD-POD*] [*Enzyme mixture*]
PGO .... Ponto-Geniculate-Occipital [*Electroencephalography*]
PGO .... Positive Grid Oscillator
PGO .... Progressive Grocer [*A publication*]
PGOR .... Payload Ground Operation Requirements [*NASA*] (NASA)
PGORS...... Payload Ground Operation Requirements Study [*NASA*] (MCD)
PGP .... Peace Garden Project [*Later, NPG*] (EA)
PGP .... Phosphoglycolate Phosphatase [*An enzyme*]
PGP .... Pico Glass Pellet
PGP .... Planning Grant Program

PGP .... Precision Gas Products [*Commercial firm*]
PGP .... Prepaid Group Practice [*Insurance*]
PGP .... Programmable Graphics Processor
PGP .... Project on Government Procurement   (EA)
PGP .... Prostaglandin Production
PGP .... Puerta Galera [*Philippines*] [*Seismograph station code, US Geological Survey*]   (SEIS)
PGP .... University of Southern Maine at Portland, Portland, ME [*OCLC symbol*]   (OCLC)
PGPEP ...... Professional Group - Product Engineering and Production
PGPI......... Protein Grain Products International   (EA)
PGPKA...... Problemy Gematologii i Perelivaniya Krovi [*A publication*]
PGPR......... Plant-Growth-Promoting Rhizobacteria
PGPS......... Packaged Gas Pressure System
PGPSDZ ... Pergamon General Psychology Series [*A publication*]
PGPT........ Professional Group - Production Techniques
PGR .... Pakistan Geographical Review [*A publication*]
PGR .... Paragould, AR [*Location identifier*] [*FAA*]   (FAAL)
PGR .... Parental Guidance Recommended [*Movie rating*] [*Australia*]   (ADA)
P Gr........... Patrologia Graeca [*A publication*]
PGR .... Peregrine Petroleum [*Vancouver Stock Exchange symbol*]
PGR .... PGR. Press Gallery Report [*A publication*]   (ADA)
PGR .... [*Spacelab*] Planning and Ground Rule [*NASA*]   (NASA)
PGR .... Plant Growth Regulation [*A publication*]
PGR .... Polymerized Grass Extract [*Immunology*]
PGR .... Precision Graphic Recorder
PgR .... Progesterone Receptor [*Endocrinology*]
PGR .... Progressive Corp. [*NYSE symbol*]   (SPSG)
PGR .... Psychogalvanic Reflex [*or Response*] [*Psychology*]
PGR .... Pyrogallol Red [*Also, PR*] [*An indicator*] [*Chemistry*]
PGRAA ...... Progressive Architecture [*A publication*]
PGraM...... Messiah College, Grantham, PA [*Library symbol*] [*Library of Congress*]   (LCLS)
PGRC........ Plant Gene Resources of Canada [*See also RPC*]
PGRC........ Program Guidance and Review Committee [*Army*]   (AABC)
PGrev........ Greenville Area Public Library, Greenville, PA [*Library symbol*] [*Library of Congress*]   (LCLS)
PGrevT ...... Thiel College, Greenville, PA [*Library symbol*] [*Library of Congress*]   (LCLS)
PGRF........ Pacific Gamefish Research Foundation [*Later, PORF*]   (EA)
PGRF........ Pulse Group Repetition Frequency
PGRFI ...... Professional Group - Radio Frequency Interference
PGRM .... Parti Gerakan Rakyat Malaysia [*People's Action Party of Malaysia*] [*Political party*]   (PPW)
PGRO .... Processors and Growers Research Organisation [*British*]   (IRUK)
PGRO .... Rota/International [*Mariana Islands*] [*ICAO location identifier*]   (ICLI)
PGRQC ..... Professional Group - Reliability and Quality Control
PGRS......... Pergerakan Guerilja Rakyat Sarawak [*Sarawak People's Guerrilla Forces*] [*Malaya*]
PGRSA ...... Plant Growth Regulator Society of America   (EA)
PGRT........ Petroleum Gas and Revenue Tax [*Canada*]
PGRV .... Precision Guided Reentry Vehicle
PGRWG .... Payload Ground Requirements Working Group [*NASA*]   (NASA)
PGS........... Naval Postgraduate School
PGS........... Pagosa Springs [*Colorado*] [*Seismograph station code, US Geological Survey*] [*Closed*]   (SEIS)
PGS........... Papergram System [*Military*]   (CAAL)
PGS........... Parallel Gap Soldering
PGS........... Passive Geodetic Satellite [*NASA*]
PGS........... Passive Gravity Stabilization
PGS........... Peach Springs, AZ [*Location identifier*] [*FAA*]   (FAAL)
PGS........... Pegasus Club [*St. Louis, MO*] [*FAA designator*]   (FAAC)
PGS........... Pennsylvania German Society [*Later, TPGS*]   (EA)
PGS........... Pennsylvania German Society. Proceedings and Addresses [*A publication*]
PGS........... Pikunas Graphoscopic Scale [*Personality development test*] [*Psychology*]
PGS........... Plane Grating Spectrograph
PGS........... Plant Growth Substance
PGS........... Plasma Generator System
PGS........... Polish Genealogical Society   (EA)
PGS........... Polymer Glass Sealant
PGS........... Portable Ground Station
PGS........... Power Generation System [*or Subsystem*]
PGS........... Power Generator Section   (KSC)
PGS........... Precision Gunnery System [*Army training device*]   (INF)
PGS........... Predicted Ground Speed [*Navigation*]
PGS........... President of the Geographical Society [*British*]   (ROG)
PGS........... President of the Geological Society [*British*]
PGS........... Pressure-Gradient Single-Ended [*Microphone*]   (DEN)
PGS........... Pretty Good Stuff [*Liquor*]
PGS........... Professional Guidance Systems, Inc. [*Information service or system*]   (IID)
PGS........... Progenitor Genealogical Society   (EA)
PGS........... Program Generation System [*Data processing*]   (MDG)
PGS........... Propellant Gauging System
PGS........... Prostaglandin Synthase [*An enzyme*]

PGS.......... Provincial Grand Secretary [*Freemasonry*]
PGSB........ Past Grand Sword Bearer [*Freemasonry*]   (ROG)
PGSB........ Provincial Grand Sword-Bearer [*Freemasonry*]
PGSC........ Payload and General Support Computer [*NASA*]
PGSC........ Persian Gulf Service Command
PGSCOL ... Naval Postgraduate School
PGSD........ Past Grand Senior Deacon [*Freemasonry*]
PGSE........ Payload Ground Support Equipment [*NASA*]   (MCD)
PGSE........ Peculiar Ground Support Equipment [*DoD*]
PGSE........ Pulsed Field Gradient Spin-Echo
PGSE........ Pulsed Gradient Spin Echo [*Physics*]
PGSEL ...... Priced Ground Support Equipment List   (AAG)
PGSET ...... Professional Group on Space Electronics and Telemetry   (AAG)
PGSN........ Saipan Island (Obyan)/International [*Mariana Islands*] [*ICAO location identifier*]   (ICLI)
PGSP........ Pennsylvania German Society. Proceedings and Addresses [*A publication*]
PGSR........ Psychogalvanic Skin Resistance [*Otolaryngology*]
PGSTAP.... Pressure, Gas, Start, Turbine, Auxiliary Pump-Drive Assembly [*Pronounced "pigstap"*]
PGSU........ Propellant [*or Propulsion*] Gas Supply Unit
PGSW....... Past Grand Senior Warden [*Freemasonry*]
PGT .... Page Table [*Data processing*]   (IBMDP)
PGT .... Partido Guatemalteco del Trabajo [*Guatemalan Labor Party*] [*Political party*]   (PD)
PGT .... Past Grand Treasurer [*Freemasonry*]
PGT ..... Per Gross Ton [*Shipping*]
PGT .... Photo Glow Tube
PGT .... Pigtail   (MSA)
PGT .... Pollen Grain Trajectory [*Botany*]
PGT .... Potato Extract-Glucose-Thiamine Hydrochloride [*Growth medium*]
PGT .... Power Grid Tube
PGT .... Putnam Intermediate Government Income [*NYSE symbol*]   (SPSG)
PGTAA...... Prager Tieraerztliches Archiv [*A publication*]
PGTO .... Portuguese Government Trade Office   (EA)
PGTS........ Precision Gunnery Training System [*Army*]   (INF)
PGTSND... Puget Sound [*FAA*]   (FAAC)
PGTTT ...... Precision Gear Train Tools and Test
PGTW .... Guam [*Mariana Islands*] [*ICAO location identifier*]   (ICLI)
PGTWA.... Petroleum Geology of Taiwan [*A publication*]
PGU........... Gannon University, Nash Library, Erie, PA [*OCLC symbol*]   (OCLC)
PGU........... Pegasus Gold, Inc. [*AMEX symbol*] [*Toronto Stock Exchange symbol*]
PGU........... Plant Growth Unit [*NASA*]   (MCD)
PGU........... Postgonococcal Urethritis [*Medicine*]
PGU........... Pressure Gas Umbilical   (KSC)
PGU........... Propulsion Gas Umbilical
PGUA .... Andersen Air Force Base, Guam Island [*Mariana Islands*] [*ICAO location identifier*]   (ICLI)
PGUE .... Professional Group - Ultrasonic Engineering
PGUL .... Pegasus Gold, Inc. [*NASDAQ symbol*]   (NQ)
PGUM .... Agana Naval Air Station, Guam Island [*Mariana Islands*] [*ICAO location identifier*]   (ICLI)
PGUT .... Phosphogalactose Uridyltransferase [*An enzyme*] [*Known as Galactose-1-phosphate Uridylyltransferase*]
PGV .... Greenville [*North Carolina*] [*Airport symbol*]   (OAG)
PGV .... Proximal Gastric Vagotomy [*Medicine*]
PGVC........ Professional Group - Vehicular Communications
PGW .... Parallel Gap Welding
PGW .... Past Grand Warden [*Freemasonry*]
PGW .... Pressure Gas Welding
PGW .... Pressurized Stone Groundwood [*Pulp and paper technology*]
PGW .... United Plant Guard Workers of America
PGWG .... Parliamentary Group for World Government
PGWG .... Particles and Gases Working Group [*NASA*]   (NASA)
PGWS .... P. G. Wodehouse Society   (EA)
PGWT .... Peipeinimaru, Tinian Island [*Mariana Islands*] [*ICAO location identifier*]   (ICLI)
PGwvG...... Gwynedd-Mercy College, Gwynedd, PA [*Library symbol*] [*Library of Congress*]   (LCLS)
PGX .... Prostaglandin X [*or Prostacyclin*] [*Biochemistry*]
PGY ...... Global Yield Fund, Inc. [*NYSE symbol*]   (SPSG)
PGY .... Postgraduate Year
PGY ...... San Diego, CA [*Location identifier*] [*FAA*]   (FAAL)
PGZ .... Ponta Grossa [*Brazil*] [*Airport symbol*]   (OAG)
PH.............. Czechoslovakia [*License plate code assigned to foreign diplomats in the US*]
PH.............. Netherlands [*Aircraft nationality and registration mark*]   (FAAC)
Ph............... [*The*] New Testament in Modern English [*1958*] [*J. B. Phillips*] [*A publication*]   (BJA)
PH.............. Paedigogica Historica [*A publication*]
PH.............. Page Heading   (BUR)
PH.............. Pakistan Horizon [*A publication*]
PH.............. Palabra y el Hombre. Revista de la Universidad Veracruzana [*A publication*]
PH.............. Parker-Hannifin Corp. [*NYSE symbol*]   (SPSG)
PH.............. Past History [*Medicine*]

P of H......... Patron of Husbandry
P & H......... Patton, Jr., and Heath's Reports [*Virginia Special Court of Appeals*] [*A publication*]　(DLA)
PH.............. Pearl Harbor, Hawaii
PH.............. Pennsylvania History [*A publication*]
PH.............. Performance History
PH.............. Persistent Hepatitis [*Medicine*]
PH.............. Personal Hygiene　(MCD)
Ph.............. Phallacidin [*Biochemistry*]
PH.............. Phantom Circuit [*Telecommunications*]　(TEL)
Ph.............. Pharmacia AB [*Sweden*] [*Research code symbol*]
Ph.............. Pharmacopoeia
PH.............. Phase　(KSC)
Ph.............. Phenyl [*Organic chemistry*]
PH.............. Phiala [*Bottle*] [*Pharmacy*]
Ph'.............. Philadelphia [*Chromosome*]
Ph.............. Philippians [*New Testament book*]　(BJA)
ph.............. Philippines [*IYRU nationality code*] [*MARC country of publication code*] [*Library of Congress*]　(LCCP)
PH.............. Philippines [*ANSI two-letter standard code*]　(CNC)
Ph.............. Philippus [*Flourished, 13th century*] [*Authority cited in pre-1607 legal work*]　(DSA)
Ph.............. Phillimore's English Ecclesiastical Reports [*A publication*]　(DLA)
Ph.............. Phillips' English Chancery Reports [*1841-49*] [*A publication*]　(DLA)
Ph.............. Phillips' English Election Cases [*1780-81*] [*A publication*]　(DLA)
Ph.............. Philologus. Zeitschrift fuer Klassische Altertum [*A publication*]
Ph.............. Philosophisches Jahrbuch [*A publication*]
Ph.............. Philosophy [*A publication*]
Ph.............. Phoenix [*A publication*]
PH.............. Phone　(MDG)
Ph.............. Phosphate
PH.............. Phot [*Electronics*]　(DEN)
PH.............. Photographer's Mate [*Navy rating*]
PH.............. Photography Program [*Association of Independent Colleges and Schools specialization code*]
Ph.............. Photoreceptor
Ph.............. Photostat　(BJA)
PH.............. Phrase　(ADA)
Ph.............. Physica [*of Aristotle*] [*Classical studies*]　(OCD)
PH.............. Physically Handicapped　(OICC)
Ph.............. Phytane [*Organic chemistry*]
PH.............. Piano Type Hinge
PH.............. Picohenry
P/H............. Pier to House [*Classified advertising*]　(ADA)
Ph.............. Pilot-Helicopter [*Navy*] [*British*]
PH.............. Pilot House
PH.............. Pinch Hitter [*Baseball*]
PH.............. Plane Handler [*Navy*]
PH.............. Plant Height [*Botany*]
PH.............. Polynesian Airlines Ltd. [*ICAO designator*]　(FAAC)
PH.............. Porta Hepatis [*Anatomy*]
PH.............. Porter House [*Initials often used as a pattern on clothing designed by this firm*]
P/H............. Postage and Handling [*Shipping*]
pH.............. Pouvoir Hydrogene [*Hydrogen Power*] [*Negative logarithm of effective H ion concentration*] [*Chemistry*]
PH.............. Powerhouse
PH.............. Practical Homeowner [*A publication*]
PH.............. Practitioner's Handbooks [*A publication*]
PH.............. Precipitation Hardening
P-H............. Prentice-Hall, Inc. [*Publishers*]
PH.............. Presidential Medal of Honour [*Botswana*]
PH.............. Previous History [*Medicine*]
PH.............. Primary Hyperparathyroidism
PH.............. Private Hotel
PH.............. Probability of Hit [*Military*]　(MCD)
PH.............. Project Handclasp　(EA)
PH.............. Prospect Hill [*Vole virus*]
PH.............. Provence Historique [*A publication*]
PH.............. Przeglad Historyczny [*A publication*]
PH.............. Public Health
PH.............. Public House [*A drinking establishment*] [*British*]
PH.............. Purple Heart [*Given to personnel wounded in military service*] [*Military decoration*]
PH1............. Photographer's Mate, First Class [*Navy rating*]
1PH............. Single-Phase
PH2............. Photographer's Mate, Second Class [*Navy rating*]
2PH............. Two-Phase
PH3............. Photographer's Mate, Third Class [*Navy rating*]
3PH............. Three-Phase
PHA............ Chicago, IL [*Location identifier*] [*FAA*]　(FAAL)
PHa............. Hazelton Public Library, Hazelton, PA [*Library symbol*] [*Library of Congress*]　(LCLS)
PHA............ Pachena Industries Ltd. [*Vancouver Stock Exchange symbol*]
PHA............ Palomino Horse Association　(EA)
PHA............ Parts per Hundred of Asphalt [*Chemical technology*]
PHA............ Passive Hemagglutination [*Immunology*]
PHA............ Peripheral Hyperalimentation (Solution) [*Medicine*]

PHA............ Peruvian Heart Association　(EA)
PHA............ Pharmaceutisch Weekblad [*A publication*]
Pha............. Philologica [*A publication*]
PHA............ Philosophia Antiqua [*A publication*]
PHA............ Phytohemagglutinin [*Immunology*]
PHA............ Polyhydroxyalkanoate [*Organic chemistry*]
PHA............ Poly(hydroxystearic Acid) [*Organic chemistry*]
PHA............ Port Heiden [*Alaska*] [*Seismograph station code, US Geological Survey*] [*Closed*]　(SEIS)
PHA............ Poultry Husbandry Adviser [*Ministry of Agriculture, Fisheries, and Food*] [*British*]
PHA............ Preferred Hotels Association [*Also known as Preferred Hotel Worldwide*]　(EA)
PHA............ Prelaunch Hazard Area　(MUGU)
PHA............ Preliminary Hazard Analyses　(NASA)
PHA............ Professional Handlers Association　(EA)
PHA............ Professional Historians Association [*Australia*]
PHA............ Professional Horsemen's Association of America　(EA)
PHA............ Public Health Act　(DAS)
PHA............ Public Housing Administration [*or HHFA; disbanded 1965*]
PHA............ Pulse Height Analysis [*Spectroscopy*]
PHA............ State Library of Pennsylvania, Harrisburg, PA [*OCLC symbol*]　(OCLC)
PHAA......... Airman Apprentice, Photographer's Mate, Striker [*Navy rating*]
PHAA......... Percheron Horse Association of America　(EA)
PHAA......... Photographer's Airman Apprentice [*Navy*]
PHAA......... Positive High-Angle of Attack
PHAA......... Professional Horsemen's Association of America [*Later, PHA*]　(EA)
PHAABO... Purebred Hanoverian Association of American Breeders and Owners　(EA)
PHAB........ Pharmacia AB [*NASDAQ symbol*]　(NQ)
PhAb.......... Photographic Abstracts [*A publication*]
PHAB........ Physically Handicapped and Able Bodied [*Charitable organization*] [*British*]
PHACCK... PHAC. Pathologie Humaine et Animale Comparee [*A publication*]
PHADA..... Public Housing Authorities Directors Association　(EA)
PHAGA..... Philippine Agriculturist [*A publication*]
Phal CC..... Phalen's Criminal Cases [*A publication*]　(DLA)
PHALCM... Phytohemagglutinin Stimulated Leukocyte Conditioned Medium
PHALSE... Phreakers, Hackers, and Laundry Service Employees [*East Coast group of computer trespassers raided by the FBI*]
P-H Am Lab Arb Awards... American Labor Arbitration Awards (Prentice-Hall, Inc.) [*A publication*]　(DLA)
P-H Am Lab Cas... American Labor Cases (Prentice-Hall, Inc.) [*A publication*]　(DLA)
PHAMOS... Premote Hemodynamics and Metabolism in an Orbiting Satellite　(KSC)
PHAN........ Airman, Photographer's Mate, Striker [*Navy rating*]
Phanerogamarum Monogr... Phanerogamarum Monographiae [*A publication*]
PHANT..... Phantom-Glass [*Theater term*]　(DSUE)
PHAOMU... Pianoforte, Harmonium, and American Organ Makers' Union [*British*]
PHAP........ Palmitoyl Hydrolyzed Animal Protein [*Organic chemistry*]
PHAP........ Provincial Health Assistance Program [*Vietnam*]
PHAR........ Pharmacology
PHAR........ PharmaControl Corp. [*NASDAQ symbol*]　(NQ)
PHAR........ Pharmacopoeia　(ROG)
PHAR........ Pharmacy [*or Pharmacist*]　(MSA)
PHarA....... AMP, Inc., Harrisburg, PA [*Library symbol*] [*Library of Congress*]　(LCLS)
PHARA..... Pharmazie [*A publication*]
Phar B....... Pharmaciae Baccalaureus [*Bachelor of Pharmacy*]
PHarC........ Harrisburg Area Community College, Harrisburg, PA [*Library symbol*] [*Library of Congress*]　(LCLS)
PharC........ Pharmaceutical Chemist [*British*]
PHarD....... Dauphin County Library System, Harrisburg, PA [*Library symbol*] [*Library of Congress*]　(LCLS)
Phar D....... Pharmaciae Doctor [*Doctor of Pharmacy*]
PHarH....... Pennsylvania Historical and Museum Commission, Harrisburg, PA [*Library symbol*] [*Library of Congress*]　(LCLS)
PHARM... Pharmaceutical
Phar M....... Pharmaciae Magister [*Master of Pharmacy*]
PHARM... Pharmacist [*or Pharmacy*]
PHARM... Pharmacology
Pharm Abstr... Pharmaceutical Abstracts [*A publication*]
PHARMAC... Pharmacology
Pharmaceutical J... Pharmaceutical Journal and Transactions [*A publication*]
Pharmacochem Libr... Pharmacochemistry Library [*A publication*]
Pharmacog Tit... Pharmacognosy Titles [*A publication*]
PHARMACOL... Pharmacological　(MSA)
Pharmacol... Pharmacology [*A publication*]
Pharmacol Biochem Behav... Pharmacology, Biochemistry, and Behavior [*A publication*]
Pharmacol Clin... Pharmacologia Clinica [*A publication*]
Pharmacolog... Pharmacologist [*A publication*]
Pharmacol Physicians... Pharmacology for Physicians [*A publication*]
Pharmacol R... Pharmacological Research Communications [*A publication*]

Pharmacol Res ... Pharmacological Research [*A publication*]
Pharmacol Res Commun ... Pharmacological Research Communications [*A publication*]
Pharmacol Rev ... Pharmacological Reviews [*A publication*]
Pharmacol Sleep ... Pharmacology of Sleep [*A publication*]
Pharmacol Ther ... Pharmacology and Therapeutics [*A publication*]
Pharmacol Ther (B) ... Pharmacology and Therapeutics. Part B. General and Systematic Pharmacology [*A publication*]
Pharmacol Ther Dent ... Pharmacology and Therapeutics in Dentistry [*A publication*]
Pharmacol Ther Part A Chemother Toxicol Metab Inhibitors ... Pharmacology and Therapeutics. Part A. Chemotherapy, Toxicology, and Metabolic Inhibitors [*A publication*]
Pharmacol Ther Part B Gen Syst Pharmacol ... Pharmacology and Therapeutics. Part B. General and Systematic Pharmacology [*A publication*]
Pharmacol Ther Part C ... Pharmacology and Therapeutics. Part C. Clinical Pharmacology and Therapeutics [*A publication*]
Pharmacol Toxicol (Engl Transl) ... Pharmacology and Toxicology (English Translation of Farmakologiya Toksikologiya) [*Moscow*] [*A publication*]
Pharmacol Toxicol (USSR) ... Pharmacology and Toxicology (USSR) [*A publication*]
Pharm Acta Helv ... Pharmaceutica Acta Helvetiae [*A publication*]
Pharm Act H ... Pharmaceutica Acta Helvetiae [*A publication*]
Pharma Int Engl Ed ... Pharma International (English Edition) [*A publication*]
Pharmakeutickon Delt Epistem Ekodosis ... Pharmakeutikon Deltion. Epistemonike Ekodosis [*A publication*]
Pharmakopsy ... Pharmakopsychiatrie Neuro-Psychopharmakologie [*A publication*]
Pharmakopsychiatr Neuro-Psychopharmakol ... Pharmakopsychiatrie Neuro-Psychopharmakologie [*A publication*]
Pharm Aquitaine ... Pharmacien d'Aquitaine [*A publication*]
Pharm Arch ... Pharmaceutical Archives [*A publication*]
Pharmazie Beih ... Pharmazie. Beihefte [*A publication*]
Pharm Bio B ... Pharmacology, Biochemistry, and Behavior [*A publication*]
Pharm Biol ... Pharmacien Biologiste [*A publication*]
Pharm Bull ... Pharmaceutical Bulletin [*A publication*]
Pharm Bull Nihon Univ ... Pharmaceutical Bulletin. Nihon University [*A publication*]
Pharm Chem J ... Pharmaceutical Chemistry Journal [*A publication*]
Pharm Chem J (Engl Transl Khim Farm Zh) ... Pharmaceutical Chemistry Journal (English Translation of Khimiko-Farmatsevticheskii Zhurnal) [*A publication*]
Pharm Chem J (USSR) ... Pharmaceutical Chemistry Journal (USSR) [*A publication*]
PHARMCL ... Pharmaceutical
Pharm Cosmet ... Pharmaceuticals and Cosmetics [*A publication*]
Pharm Cosmet Rev ... Pharmaceutical and Cosmetics Review [*South Africa*] [*A publication*]
Pharm D .... Doctor of Pharmacy
Pharm Delt Epistem Ekdosis ... Pharmkeutikon Deltion Epistemonike Ekdosis [*A publication*]
Pharm Era ... Pharmaceutical Era [*A publication*]
Pharm Fr ... Pharmacien de France [*A publication*]
Pharm Heute ... Pharmazie Heute [*A publication*]
Pharm Hist ... Pharmacy in History [*A publication*]
Pharm Hosp Fr ... Pharmacie Hospitaliere Francaise [*A publication*]
Pharm Ind ... Pharmazeutische Industrie [*A publication*]
Pharm Ind Yugosl ... Pharmaceutical Industry of Yugoslavia [*A publication*]
Pharm Int... Pharmacy International [*Netherlands*] [*A publication*]
Pharm J ..... Pharmaceutical Journal [*A publication*]
Pharm J NZ ... Pharmaceutical Journal of New Zealand [*A publication*]
Pharm J Pharm ... Pharmaceutical Journal and Pharmacist [*A publication*]
Pharm M ... Master of Pharmacy
Pharm Manage ... Pharmacy Management [*A publication*]
Pharm Manage Comb Am J Pharm ... Pharmacy Management Combined with the American Journal of Pharmacy [*A publication*]
Pharm Manuf Assoc Yearb ... Pharmaceutical Manufacturers Association. Yearbook [*A publication*]
Pharm Med (Hamps) ... Pharmaceutical Medicine (Hampshire) [*A publication*]
Pharm Monatsbl ... Pharmazeutische Monatsblaetter [*A publication*]
Pharm Monatsh ... Pharmazeutische Monatshefte [*A publication*]
Pharm Monogr ... Pharmaceutical Monographs [*A publication*]
Pharm Post ... Pharmazeutische Post [*A publication*]
Pharm Prax ... Pharmazeutische Praxis [*A publication*]
Pharm Presse ... Pharmazeutische Presse [*A publication*]
Pharm Presse Wiss Prakt Hefte ... Pharmazeutische Presse. Wissenschaftlich-Praktische Hefte [*A publication*]
Pharm Prod Pharm ... Pharmacie-Produits Pharmaceutiques [*A publication*]
Pharm Rep (Beijing) ... Pharmacy Reports (Beijing) [*A publication*]
Pharm Res ... Pharmaceutical Research [*A publication*]
Pharm Rev ... Pharmaceutical Review [*A publication*]
Pharm Rev ... Pharmacological Reviews [*A publication*]
Pharm Rundsch ... Pharmazeutische Rundschau [*A publication*]
Pharm Rural ... Pharmacien Rural [*A publication*]
Pharm Soc Jpn J ... Pharmaceutical Society of Japan. Journal [*A publication*]
Pharm Technol ... Pharmaceutical Technology [*A publication*]
Pharm Tijdschr Belg ... Pharmaceutische Tijdschrift voor Belgie [*A publication*]

Pharm Times ... Pharmacy Times [*A publication*]
Pharm Tox ... Pharmacology and Toxicology [*A publication*]
Pharm Unserer Zeit ... Pharmazie in Unserer Zeit [*A publication*]
Pharm Weekbl ... Pharmaceutisch Weekblad [*A publication*]
Pharm Weekbl Ned ... Pharmeceutisch Weekblad voor Nederland [*A publication*]
Pharm Weekbl Sci ... Pharmaceutisch Weekblad. Scientific Edition [*A publication*]
Pharm Zentralhalle ... Pharmazeutische Zentralhalle [*A publication*]
Pharm Zentralhalle Dtl ... Pharmazeutische Zentralhalle fuer Deutschland [*A publication*]
Pharm Zentralhalle Dtschl ... Pharmazeutische Zentralhalle fuer Deutschland [*A publication*]
Pharm Z Russl ... Pharmaceutische Zeitschrift fuer Russland [*A publication*]
Pharm Ztg ... Pharmazeutische Zeitung [*A publication*]
Pharm Ztg (Berl) ... Pharmazeutische Zeitung (Berlin) [*A publication*]
Pharm Ztg Nachr ... Pharmazeutische Zeitung Nachrichten [*A publication*]
Pharm Ztg Ver Apotheker-Ztg ... Pharmazeutische Zeitung. Vereinigt mit Apotheker-Zeitung [*West Germany*] [*A publication*]
Pharos........ Pharos of Alpha Omega Alpha Honor Medical Society [*A publication*]
PHAROS... Phased Array RADAR Operational Simulation [*Army*] (AABC)
PHarP........ Harrisburg Polyclinic Hospital, Harrisburg, PA [*Library symbol*] [*Library of Congress*] (LCLS)
PHAS .... Phaser Systems, Inc. [*NASDAQ symbol*] (NQ)
PHAS .... Pulse Height Analyzer System
PHASR........ Personnel Hazards Associated with Space Radiation [*Satellite*]
PHatfB........ Biblical School of Theology, Hatfield, PA [*Library symbol*] [*Library of Congress*] (LCLS)
PHatU .... Union Library Co., Hatboro, PA [*Library symbol*] [*Library of Congress*] [*Obsolete*] (LCLS)
PHav.......... Haverford Township Free Library, Havertown, PA [*Library symbol*] [*Library of Congress*] (LCLS)
P Hawaii En ... Proceedings. Hawaiian Entomological Society [*A publication*]
Ph B .... Bachelor of Pharmacy
Ph B .... Bachelor of Physical Culture
PHB.......... Para-Hexadecylaminobenzoate [*Clinical chemistry*]
PHB.......... Parliament House Book [*Scotland*] [*A publication*] (DLA)
PHB.......... Parnaiba [*Brazil*] [*Airport symbol*] (OAG)
PhB.......... Philobiblon [*A publication*]
Ph B .... Philosophiae Baccalaureus [*Bachelor of Philosophy*]
PhB.......... Philosophische Bibliothek [*Meiner*] [*A publication*]
PHB.......... Photochemical Hole Burning [*Spectrometry*]
PHB.......... Photographic Bulletin (MCD)
PHB.......... Poly(hydroxybenzoate) [*Organic chemistry*]
PHB.......... Polyhydroxybutyrate [*Organic chemistry*]
PHB.......... Public Health Bibliography
PHB.......... Public Health Service Building
PHBA........ Palomino Horse Breeders of America (EA)
PHBA........ Para-Hydroxybenzoic Acid [*Organic chemistry*]
Ph B in Arch ... Bachelor of Philosophy in Architecture
PHBCD........ Physica B + C [*A publication*]
Ph B in Com ... Bachelor of Philosophy in Commerce
Ph BD .... Doctor of Bible Philosophy
Ph B in Ed ... Bachelor of Philosophy in Education
PHBHA..... Physiology and Behavior [*A publication*]
PHBIA....... Pharmacien Biologiste [*A publication*]
PHBK .... Barking Sands, Kauai Island [*Hawaii*] [*ICAO location identifier*] (ICLI)
PHBK .... People's Heritage Financial Group, Inc. [*NASDAQ symbol*] (NQ)
PHBLA...... Physikalische Blaetter [*A publication*]
PHBOA ..... Physiologia Bohemoslovenica [*Later, Physiologia Bohemoslovaca*] [*A publication*]
PHBRZ...... Phosphor Bronze
PHBV .... Hydroxy Butyric Valeric Acid [*Polymer*]
PHC........... Chief Photographer's Mate [*Navy rating*]
PHC........... Children's Hospital of Pittsburgh, Pittsburgh, PA [*OCLC symbol*] (OCLC)
PHC........... Haverford College, Haverford, PA [*Library symbol*] [*Library of Congress*] (LCLS)
PHC........... Pacific Hurricane Centers [*National Weather Service*]
PHC........... Palmitoyl Homocysteine [*Biochemistry*]
PHC........... Pathonic Network, Inc. [*Toronto Stock Exchange symbol*]
PHC........... Personal Holding Company [*Generic term*]
PHC........... Perturbed-Hardness Chain [*Molecular thermodynamics*]
Ph C........... Pharmaceutical Chemist
Ph C........... Philosopher of Chiropractic
PHC........... Photographic Change (MCD)
PHC........... Population Housing Census (OICC)
PHC........... Port Harcourt [*Nigeria*] [*Airport symbol*] (OAG)
PHC........... Port Hardy [*British Columbia*] [*Seismograph station code, US Geological Survey*] (SEIS)
PHC........... Posthospital Care [*Medicine*]
PHC........... [*A*] Prairie Home Companion [*National Public Radio program*]
PHC........... Pratt Hotel Corp. [*AMEX symbol*] (SPSG)
PHC........... Primary Health Care
PHC........... Primary Health Centre [*British*]
PHC........... Primary Hepatic Carcinoma [*Medicine*]
PHC........... Proliferative Helper Cells [*Immunology*]

Ph¹c.......... Philadelphia Chromosome
PHCA .... Parliament House Construction Authority [*Australia*]
PHCA .... Pig Health Control Association [*British*]
PHCA .... Pleasure Horse Club of America   (EA)
PHCAA ..... Physics in Canada [*A publication*]
PHCAA ..... Public Health Cancer Association of America [*Defunct*]   (EA)
P-H Cas ..... American Federal Tax Reports (Prentice-Hall, Inc.) [*A publication*]   (DLA)
PHCBA ..... Photochemistry and Photobiology [*A publication*]
PHCC .... Punjab High Court Cases [*India*] [*A publication*]   (DLA)
PHCCA ..... Progress in Histochemistry and Cytochemistry [*A publication*]
Ph Ch .... Phillips' English Chancery Reports [*1841-49*] [*A publication*]   (DLA)
PHCI .... Peak Health Care, Incorporated [*NASDAQ symbol*]   (NQ)
PHCIB ...... Plumbing-Heating-Cooling Information Bureau   (EA)
PhCL.......... Pharmacochemistry Library [*Elsevier Book Series*] [*A publication*]
PHCLIS..... Protected Home Circle Life Insurance Society   (EA)
PHCM .... Master Chief Photographer's Mate [*Navy rating*]
P-H Corp ... Corporation [*Prentice-Hall, Inc.*] [*A publication*]   (DLA)
PHCP .... [*International Trade Show for*] Plumbing, Heating, Cooling, and Piping   (ITD)
PHCS........ Pacific Hills Christian School [*Australia*]
PHCS........ Senior Chief Photographer's Mate [*Navy rating*]
PHCSC...... Piers-Harris Children's Self-Concept Scale [*Child development test*] [*Psychology*]
PHCT .... Perturbed Hard Chain Theory [*Equation of state*]
PHCTB...... Photophysiology [*A publication*]
PHCV-SD ... Phase Conversion and Step-Down   (MSA)
PHCYAQ .. Specialist Periodical Reports. Photochemistry [*A publication*]
PHD.......... Dixmont State Hospital, Sewickley, PA [*OCLC symbol*]   (OCLC)
Ph D.......... Doctor of Pharmacy
PH D........ Doctor of Philosophy
PHD.......... Doctor of Public Health [*British*]   (DAS)
PHD.......... Duncan Aviation, Inc. [*Lincoln, NE*] [*FAA designator*]   (FAAC)
PHD.......... New Philadelphia, OH [*Location identifier*] [*FAA*]   (FAAL)
PHD.......... Parallel Head Disk
PhD.......... Perfect Hard Disk [*Century Data Systems*] [*Data processing*]
Phd.......... Phaedo [*of Plato*] [*Classical studies*]   (OCD)
PHD.......... Phase-Shift Driver   (CET)
Ph D .... Philosophiae Doctor [*Doctor of Philosophy*] [*Facetious translation: Piled Higher and Deeper*]
PHD.......... Photoelectron Diffraction [*Spectroscopy*]
PHD.......... Photohydrodynamic [*Astrophysics*]
PHD.......... Pilot's Horizontal Display [*Aviation*]   (CAAL)
PHD.......... Port Huron & Detroit Railroad Co. [*AAR code*]
PH D .... Pre-Pearl Harbor Dad [*A humorous wartime degree*]
PHD.......... Precision High Dose
PHD.......... Pride, Hustle, and Drive
PHD.......... Public Health Department
PHD.......... Public Health Director
PHD.......... Pulse Height Discrimination
PHDDS ..... PSRO [*Professional Standards Review Organization*] Hospital Discharge Data Set
PHDEA ..... Public Housing Drug Elimination Act [*1988*]
PhDEd .... Doctor of Philosophy in Education [*British*]   (ADA)
PHDH .... Dillingham Air Force Base, Oahu Island [*Hawaii*] [*ICAO location identifier*]   (ICLI)
PHDK........ Phi Delta Kappan [*A publication*]
PHDLAQ .. Farmakeftikon Deltion. Edition Scientifique [*A publication*]
PhD(Med) ... Doctor of Philosophy (Medicine)   (ADA)
PhDMH.... Doctor of Philosophy in Mechanics and Hydraulics
PHDr .... Doctor of Philosophy
Phdr .... Phaedrus [*of Plato*] [*Classical studies*]   (OCD)
PHDR........ Preliminary Hardware Design Review
PhD(RCA) ... Doctor of Philosophy (Royal College of Art) [*British*]   (DBQ)
PHDS .... Post-Harvest Documentation Service [*Kansas State University*]   (IID)
PHE .... Aviation POL [*Petroleum, Oil, and Lubrication*] Handling Equipment Programmable   (NATG)
PHE .... Eastern State School and Hospital, Trevose, PA [*OCLC symbol*]   (OCLC)
PHE .... Periodic Health Examination
PHE .... Petroleum Handling Equipment   (MCD)
Phe .... Phenylalanine [*Also, F*] [*An amino acid*]
PHE .... Pheophytin [*Biochemistry*]
Phe .... Phoenix [*Constellation*]
PHE .... Photo Engravers & Electrotypers Ltd. [*Toronto Stock Exchange symbol*]
PHE .... Plate Heat Exchanger [*Chemical engineering*]
PHE .... Port Hedland [*Australia*] [*Airport symbol*]   (OAG)
PHE .... Preflight Heat Exchanger [*NASA*]   (KSC)
PHEA .... Public Health Engineering Abstracts [*A publication*]
Phear Wat ... Phear's Rights of Water [*1859*] [*A publication*]   (DLA)
PHEDA ..... Physics Education [*A publication*]
PHEI .... Penetrator, High-Explosive, Incendiary   (MCD)
PhEJ .... Philippine Economic Journal [*A publication*]
PHEL........ Petroleum Helicopters, Inc. [*NASDAQ symbol*]   (NQ)

P Helm Soc ... Proceedings. Helminthological Society of Washington [*A publication*]
PHeM .... Hershey Medical Center, Hershey, PA [*Library symbol*] [*Library of Congress*]   (LCLS)
PHEMA .... Poly(hydroxyethyl Methacrylate) [*Organic chemistry*]
phen .... o-Phenanthroline [*Organic chemistry*]
PHEN....... Phenolic   (AAG)
Pheney Rep ... Pheney's New Term Reports [*England*] [*A publication*]   (DLA)
PH Eng ...... Public Health Engineer
PHENO...... Phenobarbital [*A drug*]
pheno.......... Phenotype
PHENO...... Precise Hybrid Elements for Nonlinear Operation   (IEEE)
Phen & Ped ... Phenomenology and Pedagogy [*A publication*]
PHEO........ Pheochromocytoma [*Oncology*]
PHERMEX ... Pulsed High-Energy Radiographic Machine Emitting X-Rays
PHESA ..... Proceedings. Hawaiian Entomological Society [*A publication*]
PHESF ..... Private Hospital Employees' Superannuation Fund [*Australia*]
P-H Est Plan ... Estate Planning (Prentice-Hall, Inc.) [*A publication*]
Ph Ev........ Phillips on Evidence [*A publication*]   (DLA)
Ph E W ...... Philosophy East and West [*A publication*]
PHEWA ... Presbyterian Health, Education, and Welfare Association   (EA)
PHF .... Fairview State Hospital, Waymart, PA [*OCLC symbol*]   (OCLC)
PHF .... Newport News [*Virginia*] [*Airport symbol*]   (OAG)
PHF .... Paired Helical Filaments [*Neuroanatomy*] [*Term coined by Dr. Robert Terry to describe the components of neurofibrillary tangles in the brains of Alzheimer's Disease patients*]
PHF .... Patrick Henry Foundation [*Liberty, NY*]   (EA)
PHF .... Peak Hour Factor [*Transportation*]
PHF .... Peanut Hull Flour
PHF .... Pergamon Holding Foundation [*Liechtenstein*]
PHF .... Personal Hygiene Facility [*NASA*]   (NASA)
PHF .... Phoenix House Foundation   (EA)
PHF .... Plug Handling Fixture   (NRCH)
PHF .... Process Holding Fixture   (MCD)
PHF .... Procurement History File [*DoD*]
PHF .... Public Health Foundation [*Information service or system*]   (EISS)
PHF .... USF & G Pacholder Fund, Inc. [*AMEX symbol*]   (CTT)
PHFA .... Potomac Horse Fever Agent
PHFC........ Phoenix Financial Corporation [*Medford, NJ*] [*NASDAQ symbol*]   (NQ)
PHFEA ...... Physica Fennica [*A publication*]
P-H Fed Taxes ... Federal Taxes (Prentice-Hall, Inc.) [*A publication*]   (DLA)
PHFF........ Oahu [*Hawaii*] [*ICAO location identifier*]   (ICLI)
PHFG .... Primary Human Fetal Glial [*Cytology*]
PHFTX...... Prentice-Hall Federal Taxes [*Database*]   (IT)
Ph G .... Graduate in Pharmacy
PHG.......... Phenate-Hexamine Goggle [*British World War I anti-poison-gas helmet*]
PHG.......... Philips NV [*NYSE symbol*]   (SPSG)
PHG.......... Phillipsburg, KS [*Location identifier*] [*FAA*]   (FAAL)
Phg.......... Phytophthora Megasperma Glycinea [*A fungus*]
PHG.......... Prototype Hydrofoil Gunboat
PHG.......... Scranton State General Hospital, Scranton, PA [*OCLC symbol*]   (OCLC)
PHGA .... Pteroylhexaglutamylglutamic [*or Pteroylheptaglutamic*] Acid [*Biochemistry*]
PhGABA ... Phenyl-gamma-aminobutyric Acid [*Tranquilizer*]
Phgly.......... Phenylglycine [*An amino acid*]
Phgn.......... Physiognomonica [*of Aristotle*] [*Classical studies*]   (OCD)
P HGT ...... Package Height [*Freight*]
PHH .... Andrews, SC [*Location identifier*] [*FAA*]   (FAAL)
PHH .... Haverford State Hospital, Haverford, PA [*OCLC symbol*]   (OCLC)
PHH .... PHH Corp. [*NYSE symbol*] [*Toronto Stock Exchange symbol*]   (SPSG)
PHH .... Phillips Head [*Screw*]
PHH .... Puu Huluhulu [*Hawaii*] [*Seismograph station code, US Geological Survey*] [*Closed*]   (SEIS)
PHHA....... Pearl Harbor History Associates   (EA)
PHHC....... Programmable Hand-Held Calculator   (RDA)
PHHI........ Wheeler Air Force Base, Oahu Island [*Hawaii*] [*ICAO location identifier*]   (ICLI)
PHHN .... Hana, Maui Island [*Hawaii*] [*ICAO location identifier*]   (ICLI)
PHHSA ..... Protestant Health and Human Services Assembly   (EA)
PHi............ Historical Society of Pennsylvania, Philadelphia, PA [*Library symbol*] [*Library of Congress*]   (LCLS)
PhI .... International Pharmacopoeia
PHI .... Permanent Health Insurance [*British*]
PHI .... Petroleum Helicopters, Incorporated   (MCD)
PHI .... Philadelphia [*Pennsylvania*] [*Seismograph station code, US Geological Survey*] [*Closed*]   (SEIS)
PHI .... Philippine Long Distance Telephone Co. [*AMEX symbol*]   (SPSG)
Phi............ Philippus [*Flourished, 13th century*] [*Authority cited in pre-1607 legal work*]   (DSA)
Phi.............. Philips [*Holland & International*] [*Record label*]
PHI .... Philipsburg State General Hospital, Philipsburg, PA [*OCLC symbol*] [*Inactive*]   (OCLC)
PHI .... Phillipsite [*A zeolite*]

PHI .... Philosophie Informationsdienst [*Philosophy Information Service*] [*University of Dusseldorf*] [*Information service or system*] (IID)

Phi .... Philosophy [*A publication*]

PHI .... Phosphohexose Isomerase [*An enzyme*]

Phi .... Physeptone [*A narcotic substitute*]

PHI .... Physiological Hyaluronidase Inhibitor [*Biochemistry*]

PHI .... Polarity Health Institute (EA)

PHI .... Position and Homing Indicator

PHI .... Prentice-Hall International [*Publisher*]

PHI .... Programme Hydrologique International [*International Hydrological Program - IHP*] [*UNESCO*] (MSC)

PHI .... Public Health Inspector [*British*]

PHIAL .... Phiala [*Bottle*] [*Pharmacy*]

PHIB .... Amphibious

PHib .... Hibeh Papyri [*A publication*] (OCD)

PHIBB .... Project for Historical Biobibliography [*A publication*]

PHIBCB ... Amphibious Construction Battalion [*Also, ACB*] (NVT)

PHIBCORPAC ... Amphibious Corps, Pacific Fleet [*Marine Corps*]

PHIBCORPS ... Amphibious Corps [*Marine Corps*]

PHIBDET ... Amphibious Detachment

PHIBDETIND ... Amphibious Detachment, India

PHIBEU ... Amphibious Forces, Europe

PHIBEX .... Amphibious Exercise [*NATO*]

PHIBFOR ... Amphibious Forces

PHIBGROUP ... Amphibious Group

PHIBGRU ... Amphibious Group

PHIBLANT ... Amphibious Forces, Atlantic Fleet

PHIBLEX ... Amphibious Landing Exercise [*Navy*] (NVT)

PHIBNAW ... Amphibious Forces, Northwest African Waters

PHIBOPS ... Amphibious Operations [*Navy*] (NVT)

PHIBPAC ... Amphibious Forces, Pacific Fleet

PHIBRAIDEX ... Amphibious Raid Exercise [*Navy*] (NVT)

PHIBRECONEX ... Amphibious Reconnaissance Exercise [*Navy*] (NVT)

PHIBREFTRA ... Amphibious Refresher Training [*Navy*] (CAAL)

PHIBRFT ... Amphibious Refresher Training [*Navy*] (NVT)

PHIBRON ... Amphibious Squadron [*Army*]

PHIBSEU ... Amphibious Forces, Europe

PHIBSFORPAC ... Amphibious Forces, Pacific Fleet

PHIBSKDN ... Amphibious Ship Shakedown Cruise [*Navy*] (NVT)

PHIBSLANT ... Amphibious Forces, Atlantic Fleet

PHIBSPAC ... Amphibious Forces, Pacific Fleet

PHIBSS ..... Amphibious Schoolship [*Navy*] (NVT)

PHIBSTRAPAC ... Training Command Amphibious Forces, US Pacific Fleet

PHIBSUKAY ... Amphibious Bases, United Kingdom

PHIBTF .... Amphibious Task Force [*Navy*] (NVT)

PHIBTRA ... Training Command Amphibious Forces

PHIBTRABASE ... Amphibious Training Base [*Navy*]

PHIBTRAEX ... Amphibious Training Exercise [*Navy*] (NVT)

PHIBTRAINLANT ... Training Command Amphibious Forces, US Atlantic Fleet

PHIBTRAINPAC ... Training Command Amphibious Forces, US Pacific Fleet

PHIBTRALANT ... Training Command Amphibious Forces, US Atlantic Fleet

PHIBTRANS ... Amphibious Transport [*Navy*]

PHIBTRAPAC ... Training Command Amphibious Forces, US Pacific Fleet

PHIBTRBASE ... Amphibious Training Base [*Navy*]

PHIBWARTRACEN ... Amphibious Warfare Training Center [*Navy*]

PHIC .... Pharmaceutical Industries Corporation [*Burma*] (DS)

PHIC .... Poly(hexyl Isocyanate) [*Organic chemistry*]

Phi D .... Doctor of Philanthropy

PHID .... Positive Hostile Identification Device [*Air Force*]

Phi Del Kap ... Phi Delta Kappan [*A publication*]

Phi D K .... Phi Delta Kappan [*A publication*]

PHIGS ...... Programmers Hierarchical Interactive Graphics System [*IBM Corp.*]

PHIK .... Honolulu/Hickam Air Force Base, Oahu Island [*Hawaii*] [*ICAO location identifier*] (ICLI)

Phil .... Orationes Philippicae [*of Cicero*] [*Classical studies*] (OCD)

PHIL .... Philadelphia [*Pennsylvania*]

Phil .... Philadelphia Reports [*A publication*] (DLA)

Phil .... Philemon [*New Testament book*]

Phil .... Philharmonia [*Record label*]

PHIL .... Philharmonic

Phil .... Philippians [*New Testament book*]

Phil .... Philippine Island Reports [*A publication*] (DLA)

PHIL .... Philippines (AFM)

Phil .... Phillimore's English Ecclesiastical Reports [*A publication*] (DLA)

Phil .... Phillips' English Chancery Reports [*1841-49*] [*A publication*] (DLA)

Phil .... Phillips' English Election Cases [*1780-81*] [*A publication*] (DLA)

Phil .... Phillips' Illinois Reports [*152-245 Illinois*] [*A publication*] (DLA)

Phil .... Phillips' North Carolina Law Reports [*A publication*] (DLA)

Phil .... Phillips' Treatise on Insurance [*A publication*] (DLA)

Phil .... Philoctetes [*of Sophocles*] [*Classical studies*] (OCD)

Phil .... Philologus. Zeitschrift fuer Klassische Altertum [*A publication*]

PHIL .... Philology

Phil .... Philopoemen [*of Plutarch*] [*Classical studies*] (OCD)

PHIL .... Philosophy

PHIL .... Programmable Algorithm Machine High-Level Language [*Data processing*]

PHILA ...... Philadelphia [*Pennsylvania*]

Phila .... Philadelphia Reports [*Pennsylvania*] [*A publication*] (DLA)

Phila Bs J .. Philadelphia Business Journal [*A publication*]

Philad .... Philadelphia Reports [*Pennsylvania*] [*A publication*] (DLA)

PHILADA ... Philadelphia (ROG)

Philada R ... Philadelphia Reports [*Pennsylvania*] [*A publication*] (DLA)

Philada Rep ... Philadelphia Reports [*Pennsylvania*] [*A publication*] (DLA)

PHILADEL ... Philadelphia (ROG)

Philadelphia Leg Int ... Philadelphia Legal Intelligencer [*Pennsylvania*] [*A publication*] (DLA)

Philadelphia Med ... Philadelphia Medicine [*A publication*]

Philadelphia Rep ... Philadelphia Reports [*Pennsylvania*] [*A publication*] (DLA)

Phil Ag ...... Philippine Agriculturist [*A publication*]

Phila Geog Soc Bull ... Philadelphia Geographical Society. Bulletin [*A publication*]

Phil Ag R ... Philippine Agricultural Review [*A publication*]

Phila Inqr... Philadelphia Inquirer [*A publication*]

Phila Leg Int ... Philadelphia Legal Intelligencer [*Pennsylvania*] [*A publication*] (DLA)

Phila LJ ..... Philadelphia Law Journal [*A publication*] (DLA)

Phila Med ... Philadelphia Medicine [*A publication*]

Phila Med J ... Philadelphia Medical Journal [*A publication*]

Phila Med Phys J ... Philadelphia Medical and Physical Journal [*A publication*]

Phila Mus Bull ... Philadelphia Museum of Art. Bulletin [*A publication*]

philan .... Philanthropical (BJA)

PHILANTHR ... Philanthropic (ROG)

Philanthrop ... Philanthropist [*A publication*]

Phila Orch ... Philadelphia Orchestra. Program Notes [*A publication*]

Phila (PA) ... Philadelphia Reports [*Pennsylvania*] [*A publication*] (DLA)

Phila Phot ... Philadelphia Photographer [*A publication*]

Phila Reports ... Philadelphia Reports [*Pennsylvania*] [*A publication*] (DLA)

philat........... Philately

Philat Aust ... Philately from Australia [*A publication*] (APTA)

Philat Bul... Philatelic Bulletin [*A publication*] (APTA)

Philately from Aust ... Philately from Australia [*A publication*] (APTA)

Philat Pregl ... Philatelen Pregled [*A publication*]

Phil Books ... Philosophical Books [*A publication*]

Philbro .... Philipp Brothers Ltd. [*Commercial firm*]

Phil Bull....... Philatelic Bulletin [*A publication*] (APTA)

(Phil) Busn ... Business Journal (Philadelphia) [*A publication*]

Phil Bus R ... Philippine Business Review [*A publication*]

Phil C .... Philosophy in Chiropractic

PHILCITE ... Philippine Center for International Trade and Exhibitions (DS)

Phil Civ & Can Law ... Phillimore's Civil and Canon Law [*A publication*] (DLA)

PHILCOM ... Philippine Global Communications, Inc. [*Manila*] [*Telecommunications*] (TSSD)

PHILCON ... Philippine Contingent [*Military*]

Phil Context ... Philosophy in Context [*A publication*]

Phil Cop..... Phillips' Law of Copyright Designs [*A publication*] (DLA)

Phil D........ Philosophiae Doctor [*Doctor of Philosophy*] [*See also Ph D*] [*Latin*]

PHILDANCO ... Philadelphia Dance Company

Phil Dec ..... Philippus Decius [*Deceased circa 1537*] [*Authority cited in pre-1607 legal work*] (DSA)

Phil Dev .... Philippine Development [*A publication*]

Phil Dom..... Phillimore's Law of Domicil [*A publication*] (DLA)

Phil East West ... Philosophy East and West [*A publication*]

Phil Ecc...... Phillimore's Ecclesiastical Judgments [*A publication*] (DLA)

Phil Ecc...... Phillimore's English Ecclesiastical Law [*2 eds.*] [*1873, 1895*] [*A publication*] (DLA)

Phil Ecc...... Phillimore's English Ecclesiastical Reports [*1809-21*] [*A publication*] (DLA)

Phil Ecc Judg ... Phillimore's Ecclesiastical Judgments [*1867-75*] [*A publication*] (DLA)

Phil Ecc Law ... Phillimore's English Ecclesiastical Law [*2 eds.*] [*1873, 1895*] [*A publication*] (DLA)

Phil Ecc R.. Phillimore's English Ecclesiastical Reports [*1809-21*] [*A publication*] (DLA)

Phil Educ Proc ... Proceedings. Far Western Philosophy of Education Society [*A publication*]

Phil El Cas ... Phillips' English Election Cases [*1780-81*] [*A publication*] (DLA)

Philem........ Philemon [*New Testament book*]

Phil Eq....... Phillips' North Carolina Equity Reports [*A publication*] (DLA)

Phil Ev ...... Phillips on Evidence [*A publication*] (DLA)

Phil Ev Cow & H & Edw Notes ... Phillips on Evidence, Notes by Cowen, Hill, and Edwards [*A publication*] (DLA)

PHILEX .... Philadelphia Stock Exchange

Phil Exch ... Philosophic Exchange [*A publication*]

Phil Fam Cas ... Phillips' Famous Cases in Circumstantial Evidence [*A publication*] (DLA)

Phil Forum (Boston) ... Philosophical Forum (Boston) [*A publication*]

Phil Forum (De Kalb) ... Philosophy Forum (De Kalb) [*A publication*]

Phil Geog J ... Philippine Geographical Journal [*A publication*]
Phil Grand ... Phillips' Grandeur of the Law [*A publication*]   (DLA)
Philhar....... Philharmonic [*A publication*]
Phili Fran... Philippus Francus [*Deceased, 1471*] [*Authority cited in pre-1607 legal work*]   (DSA)
Phil ILJ ..... Philippine International Law Journal [*A publication*]   (DLA)
Phil Ind...... Philosopher's Index [*A publication*]
Phil Inq ...... Philosophical Inquiry [*A publication*]
Phil Ins ...... Phillips on Insurance [*A publication*]   (DLA)
Phil Insan .. Phillips on Lunatics [*1858*] [*A publication*]   (DLA)
Phil Int Law ... Phillimore's International Law [*A publication*]   (DLA)
Phil Int LJ ... Philippine International Law Journal [*A publication*]   (DLA)
Phil Int Rom Law ... Phillimore's Introduction to the Roman Law [*A publication*]   (DLA)
Phil Invest ... Philosophical Investigators [*A publication*]
Philip .... Philippines
Philip Abstr ... Philippine Abstracts [*A publication*]
Philip Fran ... Philippus Franchus [*Deceased, 1471*] [*Authority cited in pre-1607 legal work*]   (DSA)
Philipp AEC ... Philippine Atomic Energy Commission. Publications [*A publication*]
Philipp AEC Annu Rep ... Philippine Atomic Energy Commission. Annual Report [*A publication*]
Philipp AEC Rep ... Philippine Atomic Energy Commission. Reports [*A publication*]
Philipp Agric ... Philippine Agriculturist [*A publication*]
Philipp Agric Eng J ... Philippine Agricultural Engineering Journal [*A publication*]
Philipp Agric Rev ... Philippine Agricultural Review [*A publication*]
Philipp At Bull ... Philippine Atomic Bulletin [*A publication*]
Philipp Bur Mines Inf Circ ... Philippines. Bureau of Mines. Information Circular [*A publication*]
Philipp Bur Mines Rep Invest ... Philippines. Bureau of Mines. Report of Investigations [*A publication*]
Philipp Bur Mines Spec Proj Ser Publ ... Philippines. Bureau of Mines. Special Projects Series. Publication [*A publication*]
Philipp Dep Agric Nat Resour Bur Mines Inf Circ ... Philippines. Department of Agriculture and Natural Resources. Bureau of Mines. Information Circular [*A publication*]
Philipp Ent ... Philippine Entomologist [*A publication*]
Philipp Entomol ... Philippine Entomologist [*A publication*]
Philipp For ... Philippine Forests [*A publication*]
Philipp For Prod Res Ind Dev Comm FORPRIDE Dig ... Philippines. Forest Products Research and Industries Development Commission. FORPRIDE Digest [*A publication*]
Philipp Geogr J ... Philippine Geographical Journal [*A publication*]
Philipp Geol ... Philippine Geologist [*A publication*]
Philippine .. Philippine Reports [*A publication*]   (DLA)
Philippine Ag R ... Philippine Agricultural Review [*A publication*]
Philippine Agr ... Philippine Agriculturist [*A publication*]
Philippine Agr Situation ... Philippine Agricultural Situation [*A publication*]
Philippine Co ... Philippine Code [*A publication*]   (DLA)
Philippine Econ J ... Philippine Economic Journal [*A publication*]
Philippine Economy and Ind J ... Philippine Economy and Industrial Journal [*A publication*]
Philippine Farm Gard ... Philippine Farms and Gardens [*A publication*]
Philippine Internat LJ ... Philippine International Law Journal [*Manila, Philippines*] [*A publication*]   (DLA)
Philippine Int'l LJ ... Philippine International Law Journal [*A publication*]   (DLA)
Philippine J Nutr ... Philippine Journal of Nutrition [*A publication*]
Philippine J Plant Ind ... Philippine Journal of Plant Industry [*A publication*]
Philippine J Pub Adm ... Philippine Journal of Public Administration [*A publication*]
Philippine J Pub Admin ... Philippine Journal of Public Administration [*A publication*]
Philippine J Public Admin ... Philippine Journal of Public Administration [*A publication*]
Philippine J Sci ... Philippine Journal of Science [*A publication*]
Philippine LJ ... Philippine Law Journal [*A publication*]   (DLA)
Philippine L Rev ... Philippine Law Review [*A publication*]   (DLA)
Philippine Planning J ... Philippine Planning Journal [*A publication*]
Philippine Rice Corn Progr ... Philippines Rice and Corn Progress [*A publication*]
Philippines Bur Mines Geo-Sci Rep Invest ... Philippines. Bureau of Mines and Geo-Sciences. Report of Investigation [*A publication*]
Philippine Sociol R ... Philippine Sociological Review [*A publication*]
Philippine Stud ... Philippine Studies [*A publication*]
Philipp J Agric ... Philippine Journal of Agriculture [*A publication*]
Philipp J Anim Ind ... Philippine Journal of Animal Industry [*A publication*]
Philipp J Cardiol ... Philippine Journal of Cardiology [*A publication*]
Philipp J Coconut Stud ... Philippine Journal of Coconut Studies [*A publication*]
Philipp J Crop Sci ... Philippine Journal of Crop Science [*A publication*]
Philipp J Food Sci Technol ... Philippine Journal of Food Science and Technology [*A publication*]
Philipp J For ... Philippine Journal of Forestry [*A publication*]
Philipp J Intern Med ... Philippine Journal of Internal Medicine [*A publication*]
Philipp J Nurs ... Philippine Journal of Nursing [*A publication*]
Philipp J Nutr ... Philippine Journal of Nutrition [*A publication*]

Philipp J Ophthal ... Philippine Journal of Ophthalmology [*A publication*]
Philipp J Ophthalmol ... Philippine Journal of Ophthalmology [*A publication*]
Philipp J Pediat ... Philippine Journal of Pediatrics [*A publication*]
Philipp J Pediatr ... Philippine Journal of Pediatrics [*A publication*]
Philipp J Plant Ind ... Philippine Journal of Plant Industry [*A publication*]
Philipp J Pub Admin ... Philippine Journal of Public Administration [*A publication*]
Philipp J Sci ... Philippine Journal of Science [*A publication*]
Philipp J Sci Sect A ... Philippine Journal of Science. Section A. Chemical Sciences [*A publication*]
Philipp J Sci Sect B ... Philippine Journal of Science. Section B. Medical Sciences [*A publication*]
Philipp J Sci Sect C ... Philippine Journal of Science. Section C. Botany [*A publication*]
Philipp J Surg Obstet Gynecol ... Philippine Journal of Surgery, Obstetrics, and Gynecology [*A publication*]
Philipp J Surg Surg Spec ... Philippine Journal of Surgery and Surgical Specialties [*A publication*]
Philipp J Vet Anim Sci ... Philippine Journal of Veterinary and Animal Sciences [*A publication*]
Philipp J Vet Med ... Philippine Journal of Veterinary Medicine [*A publication*]
Philipp Lumberm ... Philippine Lumberman [*A publication*]
Philipp Med Dent J ... Philippine Medical-Dental Journal [*A publication*]
Philipp Med World (1946-1951) ... Philippine Medical World (1946-1951) [*A publication*]
Philipp Med World (1952-1962) ... Philippine Medical World (1952-1962) [*A publication*]
Philipp Min J ... Philippine Mining Journal [*A publication*]
Philipp Nucl J ... Philippines Nuclear Journal [*A publication*]
Philip Popul J ... Philippine Population Journal [*A publication*]
Philipp Phytopathol ... Philippine Phytopathology [*A publication*]
Philipp Popul J ... Philippine Population Journal [*A publication*]
Philipp Q Cult Soc ... Philippine Quarterly of Culture and Society [*A publication*]
Philipp Quart Cult Soc ... Philippine Quarterly of Culture and Society [*A publication*]
Philipp Sci ... Philippine Scientist [*A publication*]
Philipp Sugar Inst Q ... Philippine Sugar Institute. Quarterly [*A publication*]
Philipp Text Inf Dig ... Philippine Textile Information Digest [*A publication*]
Philips....... Philips Music Herald [*A publication*]
PhilipSa....... Philippiana Sacra [*Manila*] [*A publication*]
Philips Ind Eng Bul ... Philips Industrial Engineering Bulletin [*A publication*]   (APTA)
Philips J Res ... Philips Journal of Research [*A publication*]
Philips Res Rep ... Philips Research Reports [*A publication*]
Philips Res Rep Suppl ... Philips Research Reports. Supplements [*A publication*]
Philips Serv Sci Ind ... Philips Serving Science and Industry [*A publication*]
PhilipSt...... Philippine Studies [*Manila*] [*A publication*]
Philips Tech Rev ... Philips Technical Review [*A publication*]
Philips Tech Rundsch ... Philips Technische Rundschau [*A publication*]
Philips Tech Rundschau ... Philips Technische Rundschau [*Netherlands*] [*A publication*]
Philips Tech Tijdschr ... Philips Technisch Tijdschrift [*A publication*]
Philips Telecommun Rev ... Philips Telecommunication Review [*A publication*]
Philips Weld Rep ... Philips Welding Reporter [*A publication*]
Phili S Rev ... Philippine Sociological Review [*A publication*]
Phil J Ag ... Philippine Journal of Agriculture [*A publication*]
Phil Jahr.... Philosophisches Jahrbuch [*A publication*]
Phil J Ling ... Philippine Journal of Linguistics [*A publication*]
Phil J Pub Admin ... Philippine Journal of Public Administration [*A publication*]
Phil Jrl....... Business Journal (Philippines) [*A publication*]
Phil J Sci ... Philippine Journal of Science [*A publication*]
Phil Jud ..... Phillimore's Ecclesiastical Judgments [*1867-75*] [*England*] [*A publication*]   (DLA)
Phil Judg.... Phillimore's Ecclesiastical Judgments [*1867-75*] [*A publication*]   (DLA)
Phill .... Phillips' English Chancery Reports [*1841-49*] [*A publication*]   (DLA)
Phill .... Phillips' English Election Cases [*1780-81*] [*A publication*]   (DLA)
Phill .... Phillips' Illinois Reports [*152-245 Illinois*] [*A publication*]   (DLA)
Phill .... Phillips' North Carolina Equity Reports [*A publication*]   (DLA)
Phill .... Phillips' North Carolina Law Reports [*A publication*]   (DLA)
Phil Lab R ... Philippine Labor Review [*A publication*]
Phil Lab Rel J ... Philippine Labour Relations Journal [*A publication*]   (DLA)
Phil Law..... Phillips' North Carolina Law Reports [*A publication*]   (DLA)
Phill Ch...... Phillips' English Chancery Reports [*1841-49*] [*A publication*]   (DLA)
Phill Ch (Eng) ... Phillips' English Chancery Reports [*1841-49*] [*A publication*]   (DLA)
Phil LD ...... Doctor of Lithuanian Philology
Phill Ecc Judg ... Phillimore's Ecclesiastical Judgments [*1867-75*] [*A publication*]   (DLA)
Phill Ecc R ... Phillimore's English Ecclesiastical Reports [*1809-21*] [*A publication*]   (DLA)

Phill Eq (NC) ... Phillips' North Carolina Equity Reports [*A publication*] (DLA)
Phil Lic ...... Licentiate of Philosophy [*British*]
Phillim .... Phillimore's English Ecclesiastical Reports [*1809-21*] [*A publication*] (DLA)
Phillim Dom ... Phillimore's Law of Domicil [*A publication*] (DLA)
Phillim Eccl ... Phillimore's Ecclesiastical Judgments [*1867-75*] [*A publication*] (DLA)
Phillim Eccl ... Phillimore's English Ecclesiastical Reports [*1809-21*] [*A publication*] (DLA)
Phillim Ecc Law ... Phillimore's English Ecclesiastical Law [*A publication*] (DLA)
Phillim Eccl (Eng) ... [*J.*] Phillimore's English Ecclesiastical Reports [*1809-21*] [*A publication*] (DLA)
Phillim Int Law ... Phillimore's International Law [*A publication*] (DLA)
Phil Ling .... Philosophical Linguistics [*A publication*]
Phill Ins ...... Phillips on Insurance [*A publication*] (DLA)
Phillip J Sci ... Philippine Journal of Science [*A publication*]
Phillips .... Phillips' English Chancery Reports [*1841-49*] [*A publication*] (DLA)
Phillips .... Phillips' English Election Cases [*1780-81*] [*A publication*] (DLA)
Phillips .... Phillips' Illinois Reports [*152-245 Illinois*] [*A publication*] (DLA)
Phillips .... Phillips' North Carolina Equity Reports [*A publication*] (DLA)
Phillips .... Phillips' North Carolina Law Reports [*A publication*] (DLA)
Phillips Dir ... Phillips' Paper Trade Directory of the World [*A publication*]
Phil Lit .... Philosophy and Literature [*A publication*]
Phil LJ .... Philippine Law Journal [*Manila*] [*A publication*] (DLA)
Phill L (NC) ... Phillips' North Carolina Law Reports [*A publication*] (DLA)
Phil Log .... Philosophie et Logique [*A publication*]
Phil L Rev ... Philippine Law Review [*A publication*] (DLA)
Phil Lun ..... Phillips on Lunatics [*1858*] [*A publication*] (DLA)
Philly .... Philadelphia
Phil Mag .... Philosophical Magazine [*A publication*]
Phil Math ... Philosophia Mathematica [*A publication*]
Phil Mech Liens ... Phillips on Mechanics' Liens [*A publication*] (DLA)
philn .... Philanthropy
Phil Natur ... Philosophia Naturalis [*A publication*]
Phil NC ...... Phillips' North Carolina Law Reports [*A publication*] (DLA)
Philo .... Philo Judaeus [*First century AD*] [*Classical studies*] (OCD)
Philol .... Philologus [*A publication*] (OCD)
PHILOL .... Philology
Philologus ZKA ... Philologus. Zeitschrift fuer Klassische Altertum [*A publication*]
Philol Q ...... Philological Quarterly [*A publication*]
Philol Suppl ... Philologus. Supplement [*A publication*] (OCD)
PHILOM .. Philomathes [*Lover of Learning*] (ROG)
PHILOMATH ... Philomathematicus [*Lover of Mathematics*] (ROG)
PHILOS .... Philosophy (EY)
Philos .... Philosophy [*A publication*]
Philos Abhandlungen ... Philosophische Abhandlungen [*A publication*]
Philos Bibliothek ... Philosophische Bibliothek [*Hamburg*] [*A publication*]
Philos Book ... Philosophical Books [*A publication*]
Philos Collect R Soc London ... Philosophical Collections. Royal Society of London [*A publication*]
Philos Curr ... Philosophical Currents [*A publication*]
Philos East & West ... Philosophy East and West [*A publication*]
Philos EW ... Philosophy East and West [*A publication*]
Philos Foru ... Philosophy Forum [*A publication*]
Philos Forum ... Philosophical Forum [*A publication*]
Philos Forum ... Philosophy Forum [*A publication*]
Philos Forum Quart ... Philosophical Forum. A Quarterly [*A publication*]
Philos His .. Philosophy and History [*A publication*]
Philos Hist ... Philosophy and History. German Studies Section I [*A publication*]
PhilosI .... Philosopher's Index [*A publication*]
Philos J .... Philosophical Journal [*A publication*]
Philos Jahr ... Philosophisches Jahrbuch [*A publication*]
Philos Lit ... Philosophy and Literature [*A publication*]
Philos M .... Philosophical Magazine [*A publication*]
Philos Mag ... Philosophical Magazine [*A publication*]
Philos Mag A ... Philosophical Magazine A. Physics of Condensed Matter, Defects, and Mechanical Properties [*A publication*]
Philos Mag B ... Philosophical Magazine B. Physics of Condensed Matter, Electronic, Optical, and Magnetic Properties [*A publication*]
Philos Math ... Philosophia Mathematica [*A publication*]
Philos Med ... Philosophy and Medicine [*A publication*]
Philos Nat ... Philosophia Naturalis [*A publication*]
Philos Natur ... Philosophia Naturalis [*A publication*]
Philosophy of Ed Soc Proc ... Philosophy of Education Society of Great Britain. Proceedings [*A publication*]
Philos Pap ... Philosophical Papers [*A publication*]
Philos Phen ... Philosophy and Phenomenological Research [*A publication*]
Philos Phenomenol Res ... Philosophy and Phenomenological Research [*A publication*]
Philos & Phenom Res ... Philosophy and Phenomenological Research [*A publication*]
Philos Pub ... Philosophy and Public Affairs [*A publication*]
Philos & Pub Affairs ... Philosophy and Public Affairs [*A publication*]

Philos Publ Aff ... Philosophy and Public Affairs [*A publication*]
PhilosQ ...... Philosophical Quarterly [*A publication*]
Philos Quart ... Philosophical Quarterly [*A publication*]
Philos R ..... Philosophical Review [*A publication*]
Philos Rd ... Philosophische Rundschau [*A publication*]
PhilosRdschau ... Philosophische Rundschau [*A publication*]
Philos Rev ... Philosophical Review [*A publication*]
Philos Rhet ... Philosophy and Rhetoric [*A publication*]
Philos Rund ... Philosophische Rundschau [*A publication*]
Philos Sci ... Philosophy of Science [*A publication*]
Philos Soc Sci ... Philosophy of the Social Sciences [*A publication*]
Philos S Sc ... Philosophy of the Social Sciences [*A publication*]
Philos Stud ... Philosophical Studies [*A publication*]
Philos Studies ... Philosophical Studies [*Dordrecht*] [*A publication*]
Philos Stud Ser Philos ... Philosophical Studies Series in Philosophy [*A publication*]
Philo Stds .. Philosophical Studies [*A publication*]
Philos Tod ... Philosophy Today [*A publication*]
Philos Top ... Philosophical Topics [*A publication*]
Philostr .... Philostratus [*Second century AD*] [*Classical studies*] (OCD)
Philos Trans Roy Soc London Ser A ... Philosophical Transactions. Royal Society of London. Series A. Mathematical and Physical Sciences [*A publication*]
Philos Trans R Soc A ... Philosophical Transactions. Royal Society of London. Series A. Mathematical and Physical Sciences [*A publication*]
Philos Trans R Soc Lond A Math Phys Sci ... Philosophical Transactions. Royal Society of London. Series A. Mathematical and Physical Sciences [*A publication*]
Philos Trans R Soc Lond Biol ... Philosophical Transactions. Royal Society of London. Series B. Biological Sciences [*A publication*]
Philos Trans R Soc London ... Philosophical Transactions. Royal Society of London [*A publication*]
Philos Trans R Soc London A ... Philosophical Transactions. Royal Society of London. Series A. Mathematical and Physical Sciences [*A publication*]
Philos Trans R Soc London Ser A ... Philosophical Transactions. Royal Society of London. Series A. Mathematical and Physical Sciences [*A publication*]
Philos Trans R Soc London Ser B ... Philosophical Transactions. Royal Society of London. Series B. Biological Sciences [*A publication*]
Phil (PA) .... Philadelphia Reports [*Pennsylvania*] [*A publication*] (DLA)
Phil Papers ... Philosophical Papers [*A publication*]
Phil Pat ...... Phillips on Patents [*A publication*] (DLA)
Phil Perspekt ... Philosophische Perspektiven [*A publication*]
Phil Phenomenol Res ... Philosophy and Phenomenological Research [*A publication*]
Phil Plan J ... Philippine Planning Journal [*A publication*]
Phil Pln 87 ... Five-Year Philippine Development Plan, 1983-1987 [*A publication*]
Phil Pol Sci J ... Philippine Political Science Journal [*A publication*]
Phil Post .... Philharmonic Post [*A publication*]
Phil Pub Affairs ... Philosophy and Public Affairs [*A publication*]
PHILPUC ... Philippine Presidential Unit Citation Badge [*Military decoration*]
Phil Q .... Philippines Quarterly [*A publication*]
Phil Q .... Philosophical Quarterly [*A publication*]
Phil Q Cult Soc ... Philippine Quarterly of Culture and Society [*A publication*]
Phil Qy ...... Philological Quarterly [*A publication*]
Phil R .... Philadelphia Reports [*Pennsylvania*] [*A publication*] (DLA)
Phil R .... Philosophical Review [*A publication*]
PhilR .... Philosophy and Rhetoric [*A publication*]
Phil R Bus Econ ... Philippine Review of Business and Economics [*A publication*]
Phil Reform ... Philosophia Reformata [*A publication*]
Phil Rep ..... Philadelphia Reports [*Pennsylvania*] [*A publication*] (DLA)
Phil Res Arch ... Philosophy Research Archives [*A publication*]
Phil Res R ... Philips Research Reports [*A publication*]
Phil Rev .... Philosophical Review [*A publication*]
Phil Rev (Taiwan) ... Philosophical Review (Taiwan) [*A publication*]
Phil Rhet .... Philosophy and Rhetoric [*A publication*]
Phil Rom Law ... Phillimore's Private Law among the Romans [*A publication*] (DLA)
Phil Rundsch ... Philosophische Rundschau [*A publication*]
PhilS .... Philosophical Studies [*A publication*]
Phil Sacra .. Philippine Sacra [*A publication*]
Phil Sci ...... Philosophy of Science [*A publication*]
PHILSEAFRON ... Philippine Sea Frontier
Phil Soc ...... Philological Society. Transactions [*A publication*]
Phil Soc Act ... Philosophy and Social Action [*A publication*]
Phil Soc Cr ... Philosophy and Social Criticism [*A publication*]
Phil Soc Crit ... Philosophy and Social Criticism [*A publication*]
Phil Sociol R ... Philippine Sociological Review [*A publication*]
Phil Soc Sci ... Philosophy of the Social Sciences [*A publication*]
Phil Soc Sci Hum R ... Philippine Social Sciences and Humanities Review [*A publication*]
PHILSOM ... Periodical Holdings in the Library of the School of Medicine [*Washington University School of Medicine*] [*Library network*]
Phil St .... Philologische Studien [*A publication*]

Phil St Leg R ... Phillips' Studii Legalis Ratio [*A publication*]　(DLA)
Phil St Tr ... Phillipps' State Trials [*Prior to 1688*] [*A publication*]　(DLA)
Phil Stud .... Philippine Studies [*A publication*]
Phil Stud .... Philosophical Studies [*A publication*]
Phil Stud Educ ... Philosophical Studies in Education [*A publication*]
Phil Stud (Ireland) ... Philosophical Studies (Ireland) [*A publication*]
PHILSUCOM ... Philippines Sugar Commission　(DS)
PhilT ... Philosophy Today [*A publication*]
Phil Techn Rd ... Philips Technische Rundschau [*A publication*]
Phil Techn Rev ... Philips Technical Review [*A publication*]
Phil Tech R ... Philips Technical Review [*A publication*]
Phil Today ... Philosophy Today [*A publication*]
Phil Topics ... Philosophical Topics [*A publication*]
Phil Trans ... Philosophical Transactions [*A publication*]
Phil Trans Royal Soc London Ser A ... Philosophical Transactions. Royal Society of London. Series A. Mathematical and Physical Sciences [*A publication*]
Phil Trans Roy Soc Lond ... Philosophical Transactions. Royal Society of London [*A publication*]
Phil Trans Roy Soc Lond B ... Philosophical Transactions. Royal Society of London. Series B. Biological Sciences [*A publication*]
Phil Trans Roy Soc London Ser A Math Phys Sci ... Philosophical Transactions. Royal Society of London. Series A. Mathematical and Physical Sciences [*A publication*]
Phil Trans R Soc ... Philosophical Transactions. Royal Society of London [*A publication*]
Phil Unters ... Philologische Untersuchungen [*A publication*]　(OCD)
Phil US Pr ... Phillips' United States Practice [*A publication*]　(DLA)
Phil Woch ... Philologische Wochenschrift [*A publication*]
Phil Wochenschr ... Philologische Wochenschrift [*A publication*]　(OCD)
Phil Yb Int'l L ... Philippine Yearbook of International Law [*Manila, Philippines*] [*A publication*]　(DLA)
PHIN .... Position and Homing Inertial Navigator
PHINA ...... Pharmazeutische Industrie [*A publication*]
PHIND ...... Pharmaceutical and Healthcare Industries News Database [*PJB Group Publications Ltd.*] [*Information service or system*]　(IID)
PHIND ...... Pharmacy International [*A publication*]
P-H Ind Rel Lab Arb ... Industrial Relations, American Labor Arbitration (Prentice-Hall, Inc.) [*A publication*]　(DLA)
P-H Ind Rel Union Conts ... Industrial Relations, Union Contracts, and Collective Bargaining (Prentice-Hall, Inc.) [*A publication*]　(DLA)
PHINet ...... Prentice-Hall Information Network [*Prentice-Hall Information Services*] [*Information service or system*]　(IID)
Phip .... Phipson's Digest, Natal Reports [*South Africa*] [*A publication*]　(DLA)
Phip .... Phipson's Reports, Natal Supreme Court [*South Africa*] [*A publication*]　(DLA)
Phip Ev ...... Phipson on Evidence [*12th ed.*] [*1976*] [*A publication*]　(DLA)
Phipson ...... Reports of Cases in the Supreme Court of Natal [*A publication*]　(DLA)
PHIS .... Program Hardware Interface Specification　(CAAL)
PHITAP .... Predesigned [*or Priority*] High-Interest Tactical Air [*Acoustic forecast*] Prediction　(MCD)
PHITAR .... Predesignated High-Interest Tactical Area [*Navy*]　(NVT)
Phi T Roy A ... Philosophical Transactions. Royal Society of London. Series A. Mathematical and Physical Sciences [*A publication*]
Phi T Roy B ... Philosophical Transactions. Royal Society of London. Series B. Biological Sciences [*A publication*]
PHIX .... [*The*] Phoenix Group International, Inc. [*NASDAQ symbol*]　(NQ)
PHJ .... Danville State Hospital, Danville, PA [*OCLC symbol*]　(OCLC)
Ph J .... Philosophical Journal [*A publication*]
Ph J .... Philosophisches Jahrbuch [*A publication*]
Ph J .... Philosophisches Jahrbuch der Goerres-Gesellschaft [*A publication*]
Ph Jb .... Philosophisches Jahrbuch [*A publication*]
Ph Jb .... Philosophisches Jahrbuch der Goerres-Gesellschaft [*A publication*]
PHJC .... Penn Hall Junior College [*Pennsylvania*] [*Closed, 1973*]
PHJC .... Poor Handmaids of Jesus Christ [*Ancilla Domini Sisters*] [*Roman Catholic religious order*]
PHJC .... Port Huron Junior College [*Michigan*]
PHJRD ...... Philips Journal of Research [*A publication*]
PHK .... Pahokee, FL [*Location identifier*] [*FAA*]　(FAAL)
PHK .... Personal Hygiene Kit　(MCD)
PhK .... Phosphorylase Kinase [*An enzyme*]
PHK .... Pootaardappelwereld [*A publication*]
PHK .... Porter [*H. K.*] Co., Inc. [*NYSE symbol*]　(SPSG)
PHK .... Postmortem Human Kidney [*Cells*]
PHKO .... Kona/Ke-Ahole, Hawaii Island [*Hawaii*] [*ICAO location identifier*]　(ICLI)
PHKOA ..... Photographische Korrespondenz (Austria) [*A publication*]
PHKP .... Kaanapali, Maui Island [*Hawaii*] [*ICAO location identifier*]　(ICLI)
PHKU .... Kunia [*Hawaii*] [*ICAO location identifier*]　(ICLI)
PHL .... Allentown State Hospital, Allentown, PA [*OCLC symbol*]　(OCLC)
Ph L .... Licentiate of Pharmacy
Ph L .... Licentiate in Philosophy

PHL .... Periodical Holdings List [*Libraries*]
PHL .... Philadelphia [*Pennsylvania*] [*Airport symbol*]
PHL .... Philippines [*ANSI three-letter standard code*]　(CNC)
PHL .... Philips Industries, Inc. [*NYSE symbol*]　(SPSG)
PHL .... Phillips Michigan City Flying Service [*Michigan City, IN*] [*FAA designator*]　(FAAC)
PHL .... Pressure to Horizontal Locks [*Missiles*]　(AAG)
PHL .... Public Health Law
Ph La .... Philosophischer Literaturanzeiger [*A publication*]
PHLA .... Plasma Postheparin Lipolytic Activity [*Clinical chemistry*]
PHLAG ..... Phillips Petroleum Load and Go [*System*]
Phlb. .... Philebus [*of Plato*] [*Classical studies*]　(OCD)
PHLBA ...... Phlebologie [*A publication*]
Phld. .... Philodemus [*First century BC*] [*Classical studies*]　(OCD)
Phl Freep ... Philadelphia Free Press [*A publication*]
PHLH .... Phillips Head [*Screw*]
PHLI .... Lihue, Kauai Island [*Hawaii*] [*ICAO location identifier*]　(ICLI)
Ph Lit .... Philosophischer Literaturanzeiger [*A publication*]
Phlm. .... Philemon [*New Testament book*]
PHLO .... Phloretin [*Biochemistry*]
PHLODOT ... Phase Lock Doppler Tracking [*System*]　(MUGU)
PHLS .... Public Health Laboratory Service [*British*]
PHLSB ...... Public Health Laboratory Service Board [*British*]
PHLTA ...... Physics Letters [*A publication*]
PHLX .... Philadelphia Stock Exchange
Ph M .... Master in Pharmacy
Ph M .... Master of Philosophy
PHM .... Mayview State Hospital, Bridgeville, PA [*OCLC symbol*]　(OCLC)
PHM .... Patrol Hydrofoil Missile [*Navy symbol*]
PHM .... Patterson-Harker Method [*Physics*]
PHM .... Per Hundred Million　(NASA)
PHM .... Petroleum Helicopters, Inc. [*Lafayette, LA*] [*FAA designator*]　(FAAC)
PHM .... Phantom　(MSA)
PHM .... Pharmacist's Mate [*Navy rating*]
PHM .... Phase Meter
PHM .... Phase Modulation [*Radio data transmission*]　(DEN)
Phm. .... Philemon [*New Testament book*]　(BJA)
PhM .... Philips Minigroove [*Record label*]
PHM .... PHM Corp. [*Formerly, Pulte Home Corp.*] [*NYSE symbol*]　(SPSG)
PHM .... Post-Holiday Movie
PHM .... Posterior Hyaloid Membrane [*Eye anatomy*]
PHM .... Power Hybrid Microcircuit
PHMA ...... Plastic Houseware Manufacturers Association
PHMAA ..... Philosophical Magazine [*A publication*]
Ph Mag ...... Philosophical Magazine [*A publication*]
Phm B .... Bachelor of Pharmacy
PHMB .... Para-Hydroxymercuribenzoate [*Biochemistry*]
PHMBA ..... Physics in Medicine and Biology [*A publication*]
PHMC .... Probe Heater Motor Controller [*NASA*]　(MCD)
PHMDEH ... Pharmaceutical Medicine [*Hampshire*] [*A publication*]
PHMDP ..... Pharmacist's Mate, Dental Prosthetic Technician [*Navy rating*]
Phm G .... Graduate in Pharmacy
PHMGB ...... Pharmacology [*A publication*]
PHMK .... Molokai, Molokai Island [*Hawaii*] [*ICAO location identifier*]　(ICLI)
PHMMA ... Physics of Metals and Metallography [*English Translation*] [*A publication*]
PHMO .... Partially Hydrogenated Menhaden Oil [*Food science*]
PHMODF ... Phanerogamarum Monographiae [*A publication*]
PHMS .... Para-Hydroxymercuriphenylsulfonate [*Organic chemistry*]
PHMS .... Patrol Hydrofoil Missile Ship [*Navy/NATO*]
PHMS .... Polish Historical Military Society　(EA)
PHMT .... PhoneMate, Inc. [*NASDAQ symbol*]　(NQ)
PHMTD ..... Previews of Heat and Mass Transfer [*A publication*]
PHMU .... Waimea-Kohala, Kamuela, Hawaii Island [*Hawaii*] [*ICAO location identifier*]　(ICLI)
PhMV .... Phleum Mottle Virus
PHMWO ... Prospect Hill Millimeter Wave Observatory [*Waltham, MA*] [*Air Force*]
PHN .... Norristown State Hospital, Norristown, PA [*OCLC symbol*]　(OCLC)
PHN .... Phone　(KSC)
PHN .... Port Huron, MI [*Location identifier*] [*FAA*]　(FAAL)
PHN .... Public Health Network [*Information service or system*]　(EISS)
PHN .... Public Health Nurse
PHNA .... Barbers Point Naval Air Station, Oahu Island [*Hawaii*] [*ICAO location identifier*]　(ICLI)
Ph Nat .... Philosophia Naturalis [*A publication*]
PHNC .... Pearl Harbor, Oahu Island [*Hawaii*] [*ICAO location identifier*]　(ICLI)
PHNG .... Kaneohe Bay Marine Corps Air Station, Oahu Island [*Hawaii*] [*ICAO location identifier*]　(ICLI)
PHNL .... Honolulu/International, Oahu Island [*Hawaii*] [*ICAO location identifier*]　(ICLI)
PHNOA .... Physica Norvegica [*A publication*]
PHNTA ..... Phonetica [*A publication*]
PHNX .... Phoenix Medical Technology, Inc. [*Andrews, SC*] [*NASDAQ symbol*]　(NQ)

PHNY .... Lanai City, Lanai Island [*Hawaii*] [*ICAO location identifier*] (ICLI)
PHNY .... Pearl Harbor Navy Yard [*Later, Pearl Harbor Naval Shipyard*]
P-H NYETR ... Prentice-Hall New York Estate Tax Reports [*A publication*] (DLA)
PHO .... Pediatric Hematology-Oncology [*Medical specialty*] (DHSM)
PHO .... Phenolic Heavy Oil
PhO .... Philologia Orientalis [*A publication*]
Pho .... Photographer [*British military*] (DMA)
PHO .... Point Hope [*Alaska*] [*Airport symbol*] (OAG)
PHO .... Polk State School and Hospital, Polk, PA [*OCLC symbol*] (OCLC)
PHO .... Port Health Officer
PHO .... Puu Honuaula [*Hawaii*] [*Seismograph station code, US Geological Survey*] (SEIS)
PHOAC ..... Photographer's Mate, Combat Aircrewman [*Navy rating*] [*Obsolete*]
Phob .... Previous Highroller, on a Budget [*Lifestyle classification*]
PHOBOS .. Photometric Instrument for Biological Optical Sections
PHOC .... Photo Control Corp. [*NASDAQ symbol*] (NQ)
PHOC .... Photocopy (MSA)
PHOD .... Philadelphia Ordnance Depot [*Military*] (AAG)
PHODEC .. Photometric Determination of Equilibrium Constants [*Data processing*]
Phoe .... Phoenix [*Constellation*]
Phoen .... Phoenician (BJA)
Phoen .... Phoenissae [*of Euripides*] [*Classical studies*] (OCD)
PHOENIX ... Plasma Heating Obtained by Energetic Neutral Injection Experiment (IEEE)
Phoenix BJ ... Phoenix Business Journal [*A publication*]
PhoenixC ... Phoenix: The Classical Association of Canada [*A publication*]
Phoenix Ex Or Lux ... Phoenix. Bulletin Uitgegeven door het Vooraziatisch-Egyptisch Genootschap Ex Oriente Lux [*A publication*]
PhoenixK ... Phoenix (Korea) [*A publication*]
Phoenix Q ... Phoenix Quarterly [*A publication*]
Phoe Sh ...... Phoenix Shocker [*A publication*]
PHOFEX ... Photofragment Excitation [*Spectroscopy*]
PHOFL ...... Photoflash (AAG)
PHOG .... Kahului, Maui Island [*Hawaii*] [*ICAO location identifier*] (ICLI)
PHOM .... Photographer's Mate [*Navy rating*] [*Obsolete*]
PHON .... Phoenician
Phon .... Phonetica [*A publication*]
PHON .... Phonetics
PHON .... Phonogram (ROG)
PHON .... Phonograph (AAG)
PHON .... Photon Technology International, Inc. [*NASDAQ symbol*] (NQ)
PHONCON ... Telephone Conversation [*or Conference*]
PHONET .. Phonetics (ROG)
P HONG ..... Ponchong [*Tea trade*] (ROG)
PHONO .... Phonograph (MSA)
PHONOG .. Phonography
PHONOL ... Phonology
PhonPr ...... Phonetica Pragensia [*A publication*]
PHOPD ..... Photobiochemistry and Photobiophysics [*A publication*]
PHOPT ...... Pseudohypoparathyroidism [*Endocrinology*]
Phorm .... Phormio [*of Terence*] [*Classical studies*] (OCD)
PHOS .... Phosphate (KSC)
PHOS .... Phosphorescent (KSC)
PHOS .... Phosphorus [*Chemical symbol is P*]
PHOSCHEM ... Phosphate Chemicals Export Association (EA)
PHOSI .... Preliminary Handbook of Operations and Service Instructions
PHOSIAC ... Photographically Stored Information Analog Comparator
Phospho Potas ... Phosphorus and Potassium [*A publication*]
Phosphore Agric ... Phosphore et Agriculture [*France*] [*A publication*]
Phosphor Sulfur Relat Elem ... Phosphorus and Sulfur and the Related Elements [*A publication*]
Phosphorus ... Phosphorus and Potassium [*A publication*]
Phosphorus Agric ... Phosphorus in Agriculture [*A publication*]
Phot .... Photius [*Ninth century AD*] [*Classical studies*] (OCD)
PHOT .... Photograph
PHOT .... Photographer [*Navy rating*] [*British*]
Phot .... Photon [*A publication*]
PHOT .... Photronics Corp. [*NASDAQ symbol*] (NQ)
PHOTABS ... Photographic Abstracts [*Pergamon*] [*Database*]
Phot Abstr ... Photographic Abstracts [*A publication*]
PHOTAC .. Phototypesetting and Composing [*AT & T*]
Phot Appln Sci ... Photographic Applications in Science, Technology, and Medicine [*A publication*]
Phot Appl Sci Tech Med ... Photographic Applications in Science, Technology, and Medicine [*A publication*]
Phot Arch... Photographisches Archiv [*A publication*]
PHOTEX... [*Day*] Photographic Exercise [*Military*] (NVT)
Phot Industrie ... Photographische Industrie [*A publication*]
PHOTINT ... Photographic Intelligence [*Military*]
Phot J......... Photographic Journal [*A publication*]
Phot J Amer ... Photographic Journal of America [*A publication*]
Phot Ko ...... Photographische Korrespondenz [*A publication*]
Phot Korr ... Photographische Korrespondenz [*A publication*]
PHOTO ..... Photograph (AAG)

Photo .... Photogravure [*Philately*]
Photo Abstr ... Photographic Abstracts [*A publication*]
Photo Art Mon ... Photo Art Monthly [*A publication*]
Photobiochem and Photobiophys ... Photobiochemistry and Photobiophysics [*A publication*]
Photobiochem Photobiophys ... Photobiochemistry and Photobiophysics [*A publication*]
Photobl .... Photoblaetter [*A publication*]
Photo Can .. Photo Canada [*A publication*]
Photo Chem Mach Photo Chem Etching ... Photo Chemical Machining - Photo Chemical Etching [*A publication*]
Photochem P ... Photochemistry and Photobiology [*A publication*]
Photochem Photobiol ... Photochemistry and Photobiology [*A publication*]
Photochem Photobiol Rev ... Photochemical and Photobiological Reviews [*A publication*]
Photo Cine Rev ... Photo-Cine-Review [*A publication*]
Photodermatol ... Photo-Dermatology [*A publication*]
Photoelastic Soil Mech J ... Photoelastic and Soil Mechanics Journal [*A publication*]
Photoelectr Spectrom Group Bull ... Photoelectric Spectrometry Group Bulletin [*A publication*]
Photo Engravers Bull ... Photo-Engravers' Bulletin [*A publication*]
Photo Era Mag ... Photo-Era Magazine [*A publication*]
PHOTOG ... Photographic
Photog Abstr ... Photographic Abstracts [*A publication*]
PHOTOGR ... Photography
Photogr Alle ... Photographie fuer Alle [*A publication*]
Photogram Eng Remote Sensing ... Photogrammetric Engineering and Remote Sensing [*A publication*]
Photogramma ... Photogrammetria [*A publication*]
Photogramm Eng ... Photogrammetric Engineering [*Later, Photogrammetric Engineering and Remote Sensing*] [*A publication*]
Photogramm Eng Remote Sensing ... Photogrammetric Engineering and Remote Sensing [*A publication*]
Photogramm Eng and Remote Sensing ... Photogrammetric Engineering and Remote Sensing [*A publication*]
Photogrammetric Eng ... Photogrammetric Engineering [*Later, Photogrammetric Engineering and Remote Sensing*] [*A publication*]
Photogramm Rec ... Photogrammetric Record [*A publication*]
Photographie Forsch ... Photographie und Forschung [*A publication*]
Photogr Appl Sci Technol Med ... Photographic Applications in Science, Technology, and Medicine [*A publication*]
Photogr Appl Sci Technol and Med ... Photographic Applications in Science, Technology, and Medicine [*A publication*]
Photogr Canadiana ... Photographic Canadiana [*A publication*]
Photogr Chron ... Photographische Chronik [*A publication*]
Photogr Chron Allg Photogr Ztg ... Photographische Chronik und Allgemeine Photographische Zeitung [*A publication*]
Photogr Collector ... Photographic Collector [*A publication*]
Photogr Eng ... Photographic Engineering [*A publication*]
Photogr E R ... Photogrammetric Engineering and Remote Sensing [*A publication*]
Photogr Forsch ... Photographie und Forschung [*A publication*]
Photogr Ind ... Photographische Industrie [*A publication*]
Photogr J ... Photographic Journal [*A publication*]
Photogr J Sect A ... Photographic Journal. Section A. Pictorial and General Photography [*A publication*]
Photogr J Sect B ... Photographic Journal. Section B. Scientific and Technical Photography [*A publication*]
Photogr Korresp ... Photographische Korrespondenz [*A publication*]
Photogr Sci and Eng ... Photographic Science and Engineering [*A publication*]
Photogr Sci Eng ... Photographic Science and Engineering [*A publication*]
Photogr Sci Tech ... Photographic Science and Technique [*A publication*]
Photogr Sensitivity ... Photographic Sensitivity [*A publication*]
Photogr Tech Sci Res ... Photographic Techniques in Scientific Research [*A publication*]
Photogr Welt ... Photographische Welt [*A publication*]
Photogr Wiss ... Photographie und Wissenschaft [*A publication*]
Photo Ind ... Photo-Industrie und -Handel [*A publication*]
Photo Ind ... Photographische Industrie [*A publication*]
Photo Ind ... Wolfman Report on the Photographic Industry in the United States [*A publication*]
Photo Lab Manag ... Photo Lab Management [*A publication*]
PHOTOLITH ... Photolithographic
Photo-M ... Photo-Miniature [*A publication*]
PHOTOM ... Photometry
Photo-Mag ... Photo-Magazin [*A publication*]
Photomethd ... Photomethods [*A publication*]
Photo Methods Ind ... Photo Methods for Industry [*A publication*]
Photo Min ... Photo-Miniature [*A publication*]
Photo Mkt ... Photo Marketing [*A publication*]
Photophysiol Curr Top ... Photophysiology. Current Topics [*A publication*]
Photoplay ... Photoplay, Movies, and Video [*A publication*]
Photo-Rev .. Photo-Revue [*A publication*]
Photo Spec ... Photonics Spectra [*A publication*]
Photosynthe ... Photosynthetica [*A publication*]
Photosynth Res ... Photosynthesis Research [*A publication*]
Photo Tech ... Photo Technique [*A publication*]
PHOTRIPART ... Photo Triangulation Party [*Military*]
PHOTRON ... Photographic Squadron [*Navy*]

Phot Sci En ... Photographic Science and Engineering [*A publication*]
Phot Sci Eng ... Photographic Science and Engineering [*A publication*]
Phot Sci Tech ... Photographic Society of America. Journal. Section B. Photographic Science and Technique [*A publication*]
Phot Tech... Photo Technique [*A publication*]
Phot Tech Wirt ... Photo-Technik und -Wirtschaft [*A publication*]
PHOTUB .. Phototube (KSC)
PHO/TY ... Photo Type [*Deltiology*]
PHP .... Pacific Hawaiian Products Co. [*Later, PHP Co.*]
PHP .... Packing-House Products [*Food industry*]
PHP .... Parents Helping Parents [*An association*]   (EA)
PHP .... Parts, Hybrids, and Packaging   (MCD)
PHP .... Passive Hyperpolarizing Potential [*Neurochemistry*]
PHP .... Payload Handling Panel [*NASA*]   (MCD)
PHP .... Peace, Happiness, Prosperity for All [*A publication*]
PH and P ... Peace, Health, and Prosperity
PHP .... Pennhurst State School and Hospital, Spring City, PA [*OCLC symbol*]   (OCLC)
PHP .... Petroleum Heat & Power Co. [*AMEX symbol*]   (SPSG)
PHP .... Philip, SD [*Location identifier*] [*FAA*]   (FAAL)
PHP .... Phillip Resources, Inc. [*Vancouver Stock Exchange symbol*]
PhP .... Philologica Pragensia [*A publication*]
PhP .... Philologike Protochronia [*A publication*]
PHP .... Philosophia Patrum [*A publication*]   (BJA)
PHP .... Physician's Health Plan
PHP .... Pinane Hydroperoxide [*Organic chemistry*]
PHP .... Planetary Horizon Platform [*Aerospace*]
PHP .... Post-Hostilities Planning Subcommittee of the Chiefs of Staff Committee [*World War II*]
PHP .... Pounds per Horsepower
PHP .... Prentice Hall Press [*Publisher*]
PHP .... Prepaid Health Plan [*Insurance*]
PHP .... Presbyterian Hunger Program   (EA)
PHP .... Propeller Horsepower
PHP .... Pseudohypoparathyroidism [*Endocrinology*]
PHP .... Pump Horsepower
PHPA ...... Pacific Herring Packers Association   (EA)
PHPC ...... Post-Hostilities Planning Committee [*Navy*] [*World War II*]
PHPG ...... Poly(hydroxypropylglutamine) [*Organic chemistry*]
PHPH ...... PHP Healthcare Corp. [*NASDAQ symbol*]   (NQ)
PHPHB ..... P-heptyl-p-hydroxy Benzoate [*A preservative used in the making of American and British beer*]
Ph & Phen R ... Philosophy and Phenomenological Research [*A publication*]
PHPL ...... Parallel Hardware Processing Language [*1977*] [*Data processing*]   (CSR)
PHPLA ...... Physiologia Plantarum [*A publication*]
Ph Prag ...... Philologica Pragensia [*A publication*]
PHPS ...... Post-Hostilities Planning Staff [*World War II*]
PHPT ...... Portable High-Potential Tester
PHPT ...... Primary Hyperparathyroidism
PHPV ...... Persistent Hyperplastic Primary Vitreous [*Ophthalmology*]
PHPXA ...... Pharmazeutische Praxis [*A publication*]
PHQ .... Phenylhydroquinone [*Organic chemistry*]
PhQ .... Philosophical Quarterly [*A publication*]
PHQ .... Postal Headquarters [*British*]
PHR .... Pacific Harbour [*Fiji*] [*Airport symbol*]   (OAG)
PHR .... Pacific Historical Review [*A publication*]
PHR .... Parts per Hundred of Rubber [*Chemical technology*]
PHR .... Payload Hazardous Report   (NASA)
PHR .... Peak Heart Rate [*Cardiology*]
PHR .... Peak Height Ratio
PHR .... Pharmazeutische Industrie [*A publication*]
PHR .... Philippine Historical Review [*A publication*]
PhR .... Philosophical Review [*A publication*]
Ph R .... Philosophische Rundschau [*A publication*]
PHR .... Phorbol [*Organic chemistry*]
PHR .... Photographic Reconnaissance
PHR .... Phrase
Phr .... Phrenomena: an Annual Review [*A publication*]   (APTA)
PHR .... Physical Record [*Data processing*]
PHR .... Physicians for Human Rights   (EA)
PHR .... Pounds per Hour   (AAG)
PHR .... Preheater   (KSC)
PHR .... Process Heat Reactor Program [*Nuclear Regulatory Commission*]
PHR .... Public Health Reports [*A publication*]
PHR .... Pulse-Height Resolution [*By photomultiplier tubes*]
PHR .... Retreat State Hospital, Hunlock Creek, PA [*OCLC symbol*]   (OCLC)
PHRA ...... Poverty and Human Resources Abstracts [*A publication*]
PHRC ...... Palestine Human Rights Campaign   (EA)
Ph Rdschau ... Philosophische Rundschau [*A publication*]
PHRE ...... Public Health Reports [*A publication*]
PHREA ...... Physiological Reviews [*A publication*]
PHREN ..... Phrenology
Ph Rep ...... Philadelphia Reports [*Pennsylvania*] [*A publication*]   (DLA)
Ph Res ...... Philosophy and Phenomenological Research [*A publication*]
Ph Rev ...... Philosophical Phenomenological Review [*A publication*]
PHRF...... Performance Handicap Racing Formula [*Sailing*]
PHRG ...... Parliamentary Human Rights Group   (EAIO)
Ph & Rh ..... Philosophy and Rhetoric [*A publication*]

PHRHD..... Pump, Hydraulic Ram, Hand-Driven   (MSA)
PHRI .... Public Health Research Institute of the City of New York, Inc. [*Research center*]   (RCD)
PHRK ...... Power and Heat Rejection Kit [*NASA*]
PHRM ...... Pharmetics, Inc. [*NASDAQ symbol*]   (NQ)
PHRR ...... Parenchymal Hepatic Resection Rate [*Medicine*]
PHRS...... Paul Harris Stores, Inc. [*NASDAQ symbol*]   (NQ)
PHRS........ Portable Heat Rejection System
Ph Ru .... Philosophische Rundschau [*A publication*]
PHRV ...... Public Health Reviews [*A publication*]
PHRVA .... Physical Review [*A publication*]
PHS .... Packaging, Handling, and Storage   (MCD)
PHS .... Pallottine House of Studies
PHS .... Pathological Human Serum [*Serology*]
PHS .... Payload Handling Station [*NASA*]   (MCD)
PHS .... Peace and Humanity Society [*Australia*]
PHS .... Personal Health Survey [*Psychology*]
PHS .... Personal Hygiene Subsystem [*NASA*]   (KSC)
PhS .... Philologische Studien [*A publication*]
PhS .... Philosophical Studies [*A publication*]
PHS .... Phitsanuloke [*Thailand*] [*Airport symbol*]   (OAG)
PHS .... Photographic Historical Society   (EA)
PHS .... Postal History Society   (EA)
PHS .... Postcard History Society   (EA)
PHS .... Posthypnotic Suggestion [*Psychology*]
PHS .... Prepared Hessian Surfacing [*Air Force*]
PHS .... Presbyterian Historical Society   (EA)
PHS .... Price History System   (MCD)
PHS .... Printing Historical Society [*British*]
PHS .... Probability of Having a Space
PHS .... Progressive Hongkong Society [*Political party*]
PHS .... Public Health Service [*Department of Health and Human Services*]
PHS .... Public Health Service. Publications [*A publication*]
PHS .... Pumped Hydro Storage [*Power source*]
PHS .... Schippersweekblad [*A publication*]
PHS .... Somerset State Hospital, Somerset, PA [*OCLC symbol*]   (OCLC)
PHSA ...... Pearl Harbor Survivors Association   (EA)
PHSA ...... Polyhydroxystearic Acid [*Organic chemistry*]
PHSA ...... Polymerized Human Serum Albumin [*Biochemistry*]
PHS of A... Postal History Society of the Americas   (EA)
PHSBB..... Physics Bulletin [*A publication*]
PHSC........ Pluripotent Hematopoietic Stem Cells [*Cytology*]
PHSC........ Postal History Society of Canada   (EA)
PHSC........ Private Hospital Supplementary Charges   (ADA)
PHSCA .... Philippine Journal of Science [*A publication*]
PHSE........ Phase [*Data processing*]
PHSF........ Bradshaw Field, Hawaii Island [*Hawaii*] [*ICAO location identifier*]   (ICLI)
PHSG........ Postal History Study Group   (EA)
PHSI........ Pearle Health Service [*NASDAQ symbol*]   (NQ)
PHSI........ Plant Health and Seeds Inspectorate [*Ministry of Agriculture, Fisheries, and Food*] [*British*]
PHSIA ...... Physiotherapy [*A publication*]
PHSIG...... Pan Hellenic Society Inventors of Greece in USA   (EA)
PHSNA .... Philosophia Naturalis [*A publication*]
PHSNB.... Physics of Sintering [*A publication*]
PHSNZ........ Postal History Society of New Zealand [*Auckland*]   (EA)
PHSO ...... Partially Hydrogenated Soybean Oil [*Cooking fat*]
PHSO ...... Postal History Society of Ontario [*Later, PHSC*]   (EA)
Ph Soc ...... Philosophy/Social Theory/Sociology [*A publication*]
PHSOC ..... Photographical Historical Society of Canada
Ph Soc Glasgow Pr ... Philosophical Society of Glasgow. Proceedings [*A publication*]
P-H Soc Sec Taxes ... Social Security Taxes (Prentice-Hall, Inc.) [*A publication*]   (DLA)
Ph Soc Wash B ... Philosophical Society of Washington. Bulletin [*A publication*]
PHSP........ Phase-Splitter   (MSA)
PHSP........ Public Health Service Publications
PHSPS ..... Preservation, Handling, Storage, Packaging, and Shipping   (NRCH)
PhSR........ Philippine Sociological Review [*A publication*]
PHSSA ...... Physica Status Solidi [*A publication*]
PHST........ Packaging, Handling, Storage, and Transportation [*Shipping*]
PHS & T .... Packaging, Handling, Storage, and Transportation [*Shipping*]
PhSt .... Philosophical Studies [*A publication*]
PHSTB ..... Physica Scripta [*A publication*]
Ph St Tr ...... Phillipps' State Trials [*A publication*]   (DLA)
PHSWA...... Proceedings. Helminthological Society of Washington [*A publication*]
PHSY........ PacifiCare Health Systems, Inc. [*Cypress, CA*] [*NASDAQ symbol*]   (NQ)
PHSYB..... Photosynthetica [*A publication*]
PHT .... Paris, TN [*Location identifier*] [*FAA*]   (FAAL)
PHT .... Passive Hemagglutination Technique [*Immunology*]
PHT .... Personhistorisk Tidskrift [*A publication*]
PhT .... [*The*] Phoenix and the Turtle [*Shakespearean work*]
pht.............. Photographer [*MARC relator code*] [*Library of Congress*]   (LCCP)

PHT .... Phototube
Pht.............. Phthaloyl [*Also, Phth*] [*Organic chemistry*]
PHT .... Physical Therapy Technician [*Navy*]
PHT .... Pitch, Hit, and Throw [*Youth competition sponsored by professional baseball*]
PHT .... Portal Hypertension [*Medicine*]
PHT .... Preheat
PHT .... Putting Hubby Through [*College "degree" earned by some wives*]
PHT .... Pyridohomotropane [*Organic chemistry*]
PHT .... Torrance State Hospital, Torrance, PA [*OCLC symbol*] (OCLC)
PHTab ...... President's Hundred Tab [*Military decoration*] (AABC)
PHTAT..... Para-Hydroxytriamterene [*Biochemistry*]
PHTATS ... Para-Hydroxytriamterene Sulfate [*Biochemistry*]
P-H Tax ..... Federal Taxes (Prentice-Hall, Inc.) [*A publication*] (DLA)
P-H Tax Ct Mem ... Tax Court Memorandum Decisions (Prentice-Hall, Inc.) [*A publication*] (DLA)
P-H Tax Ct Rep & Mem Dec ... Tax Court Reported and Memorandum Decisions (Prentice-Hall, Inc.) [*A publication*] (DLA)
PHTC .... Pharmatec, Inc. [*NASDAQ symbol*] (NQ)
PHTC .... Pneumatic Hydraulic Test Console (KSC)
PhTD .... Physical Therapy Doctor
PHTEA...... Physics Teacher [*A publication*]
PHTED ...... Physiology Teacher [*A publication*]
PHTF........ Pearl Harbor Training Facility [*Navy*]
Ph TF .... Philologiae Turcicae Fundamenta [*A publication*]
Phth............ Phthaloyl [*Also, Pht*] [*Organic chemistry*]
PHTN........ Photon Sources, Inc. [*NASDAQ symbol*] (NQ)
PHTO........ Hilo/General Lyman Field, Hawaii Island [*Hawaii*] [*ICAO location identifier*] (ICLI)
PHTOA.... Physics Today [*A publication*]
PHTS........ Primary Heat Transport System [*Nuclear energy*] (NRCH)
PHTTA...... Philips Technische Tijdschrift [*A publication*]
PHU.......... Pressure, Hydraulic Unit
PHuJ .... Juniata College, Huntingdon, PA [*Library symbol*] [*Library of Congress*] (LCLS)
PHum......... Przeglad Humanistyczny [*A publication*]
P-H Unrep Tr Cas ... Prentice-Hall Unreported Trust Cases [*A publication*] (DLA)
Phus Plu..... Philippus Puldericus [*Authority cited in pre-1607 legal work*] (DSA)
PHUZA ..... Physik in Unserer Zeit [*A publication*]
PHV.......... Paramount Home Video
PHV.......... Phase Velocity
PHV.......... Pro Haec Vice [*For This Turn*] [*Latin*] (ROG)
PHV.......... Wernersville State Hospital, Wernersville, PA [*OCLC symbol*] (OCLC)
PHVA........ Plasma Homovanillic Acid [*Biochemistry*]
PHVPS...... Primary High-Voltage Power Supply
PHW.......... Pemberton Houston Willoughby Investment Corp. [*Toronto Stock Exchange symbol*] [*Vancouver Stock Exchange symbol*]
PHW.......... Phalaborwa [*South Africa*] [*Airport symbol*] (OAG)
PHW.......... Philatelic Hobbies for the Wounded (EA)
PhW.......... Philologische Wochenschrift [*A publication*]
PHW.......... Warren State Hospital, Warren, PA [*OCLC symbol*] (OCLC)
PHWA....... Professional Hockey Writers' Association (EA)
PHWA....... Protestant Health and Welfare Assembly [*Later, PHHSA*] (EA)
PHWC....... Polish Helsinki Watch Committee [*Address unknown*] (EAIO)
PHWEA .... Pharmaceutisch Weekblad [*A publication*]
PHWFJD.. Partners in Harmony, World Family of John Denver (EA)
PHWR....... Hickam United States Air Force Automatic Weather Switch, Oahu Island [*Hawaii*] [*ICAO location identifier*] (ICLI)
PHWR....... Pressurized Heavy Water Reactor [*Nuclear energy*]
PHX.......... Partial Hepectomy [*Medicine*]
PHX.......... PHL Corp. [*NYSE symbol*] (SPSG)
PHX.......... Phoenix [*Arizona*] [*Airport symbol*] (OAG)
PHX.......... Woodville State Hospital, Carnegie, PA [*OCLC symbol*] (OCLC)
PHXA .... Phoenix American, Inc. [*NASDAQ symbol*] (NQ)
PHXN....... Phoenix Network, Inc. [*NASDAQ symbol*] (NQ)
PHXQA ..... Phoenix Quarterly [*A publication*]
PHY.......... C. Howard Marcy State Hospital, Pittsburgh, PA [*OCLC symbol*] (OCLC)
PHY.......... Norman, OK [*Location identifier*] [*FAA*] (FAAL)
PHY ..... Pharyngitis
Phy............ Phylon [*A publication*]
Phy ..... Physalaemin [*Biochemistry*]
PHY.......... Physical
PHY.......... Physician
PHY.......... Physics
PHY.......... Prospect Street High Income Portfolio, Inc. [*NYSE symbol*] (SPSG)
PHYBA ..... Phyton (Buenos Aires) [*A publication*]
PHYCA ..... Physics [*A publication*]
PHYCOM ... Physicians Communications Service [*Fisher-Stevens, Inc.*] [*Merged into BRS/COLLEAGUE*]
Phyl........... Phylon [*A publication*]
PHYL .... Physiological
PHYLIP .... Phylogeny Inference Package [*Botany*]

PHYMA .... Phytomorphology [*A publication*]
PHYP .... Physicians' Pharmaceutical Services, Inc. [*NASDAQ symbol*] (NQ)
PHYS........ Physical (AFM)
PHYS........ Physician
PHYS........ Physicist (ADA)
PHYS........ Physics (EY)
PHYS........ Physiology
Phys .... Physis [*A publication*]
Phys A .... Physica A. Europhysics Journal [*A publication*]
PHYSA..... Physica (Amsterdam) [*A publication*]
Phys Abstr ... Physics Abstracts [*A publication*]
Phys Acoust ... Physical Acoustics. Principles and Methods [*A publication*]
Phys Act Rep ... Physical Activities Report [*A publication*]
Phys Appl .. Physics and Applications [*A publication*]
Phys Appl .. Physique Appliquee [*A publication*]
Phys Atoms and Molecules ... Physics of Atoms and Molecules [*A publication*]
Phys B........ Physica B. Europhysics Journal. Low Temperature and Solid State Physics [*A publication*]
PHYSBE ... Physiological Simulation Benchmark Experiment
Phys Belustigungen ... Physikalische Belustigungen [*A publication*]
Phys Ber .... Physikalische Berichte [*A publication*]
Phys Bioinorg Chem Ser ... Physical Bioinorganic Chemistry Series [*A publication*]
Phys Bl....... Physikalische Blaetter [*A publication*]
Phys Bohemoslov ... Physiologia Bohemoslovenica [*Later, Physiologia Bohemoslovaca*] [*A publication*]
Phys Briefs ... Physics Briefs [*West Germany*] [*A publication*]
Phys Bull ... Physics Bulletin [*A publication*]
Phys Bull (Peking) ... Physics Bulletin (Peking) [*A publication*]
Phys C........ Physica C. Europhysics Journal. Atomic, Molecular, and Plasma Physics Optics [*A publication*]
Phys Can.... Physics in Canada [*A publication*]
Phys C Glas ... Physics and Chemistry of Glasses [*A publication*]
Phys Chem ... Physical Chemistry [*A publication*]
Phys & Chem ... Physics and Chemistry [*A publication*]
Phys Chem ... Physik und Chemie [*A publication*]
Phys-Chem Biol (Chiba) ... Physico-Chemical Biology (Chiba) [*A publication*]
Phys Chem Centralbl ... Physikalisch-Chemisches Centralblatt [*A publication*]
Phys and Chem Earth ... Physics and Chemistry of the Earth [*A publication*]
Phys Chem Earth ... Physics and Chemistry of the Earth [*A publication*]
Phys Chem Fast React ... Physical Chemistry of Fast Reactions [*A publication*]
Phys Chem Glasses ... Physics and Chemistry of Glasses [*A publication*]
Phys and Chem Glasses ... Physics and Chemistry of Glasses. Section B. Journal. Society of Glass Technology [*A publication*]
Phys Chem Liq ... Physics and Chemistry of Liquids [*A publication*]
Phys and Chem Liq ... Physics and Chemistry of Liquids [*A publication*]
Phys Chem Mater Layered Struct ... Physics and Chemistry of Materials with Layered Structures [*A publication*]
Phys and Chem Miner ... Physics and Chemistry of Minerals [*A publication*]
Phys Chem Miner ... Physics and Chemistry of Minerals [*A publication*]
Phys Chem (NY) ... Physical Chemistry (New York) [*A publication*]
Phys Chem Phys ... Physiological Chemistry and Physics [*A publication*]
Phys Chem Sci Res Rep ... Physical and Chemical Sciences Research Report [*A publication*]
Phys Chem Ser Monogr ... Physical Chemistry. Series of Monographs [*A publication*]
Phys Chem Solids ... Physics and Chemistry of Solids [*A publication*]
Phys Chem Space ... Physics and Chemistry in Space [*A publication*]
Phys Comp ... Physiologia Comparata et Oecologia [*A publication*]
Phys Condens Matter ... Physics of Condensed Matter [*A publication*]
Phys Con Matt ... Physics of Condensed Matter [*A publication*]
Phys D .... Physica D. Nonlinear Phenomena [*A publication*]
Phys Daten ... Physik Daten [*Physics Data*] [*A publication*]
Phys-Diaet Ther ... Physikalisch-Diaetetische Therapie [*West Germany*] [*A publication*]
Phys Didakt ... Physik und Didaktik [*A publication*]
Phys Earth Planetary Interiors ... Physics of the Earth and Planetary Interiors [*A publication*]
Phys Earth and Planet Inter ... Physics of the Earth and Planetary Interiors [*A publication*]
Phys Earth Planet Inter ... Physics of the Earth and Planetary Interiors [*A publication*]
PHYSEC ... Physical Security (MCD)
PHYS ED.. Physical Education
Phys Ed...... Physical Educator [*A publication*]
Phys Ed Bul ... Physical Education Bulletin for Teachers in Secondary Schools [*A publication*] (APTA)
Phys Ed J... Physical Education Journal [*A publication*] (APTA)
Phys Ed News ... Physical Education News [*A publication*]
Phys Educ ... Physical Education [*A publication*]
Phys Educ ... Physical Educator [*A publication*]
Phys Educ Newsl ... Physical Education Newsletter [*A publication*]
Phys Energ Fortis Phys Nucl ... Physica Energiae Fortis et Physica Nuclearis [*People's Republic of China*] [*A publication*]
Phys Energi Fort Phys Nuclear ... Physica Energiae Fortis et Physica Nuclearis [*People's Republic of China*] [*A publication*]
Phys Eng.... Physical Engineer

Phys Environ Rep Dep Archit Sci Syd Univ ... Physical Environment Report. Department of Architectural Science. University of Sydney [*A publication*] (APTA)

Phys E Plan ... Physics of the Earth and Planetary Interiors [*A publication*]

PHYSEXAM ... Physical Examination

Phys Failure Electron ... Physics of Failure in Electronics [*A publication*]

Phys Fenn.. Physica Fennica [*A publication*]

Phys Fit Newsl ... Physical Fitness Newsletter [*A publication*]

Phys Fit Res Dig ... Physical Fitness Research Digest [*A publication*]

Phys Fluids ... Physics of Fluids [*A publication*]

Phys Fluids Suppl ... Physics of Fluids. Supplement [*A publication*]

Phys Grundlagen Med Abh Biophys ... Physikalische Grundlagen der Medizin. Abhandlungen aus der Biophysik [*A publication*]

Physica A... Physica A. Theoretical and Statistical Physics [*A publication*]

Physica B... Physica B. Europhysics Journal. Low Temperature and Solid State Physics [*A publication*]

Physica C... Physica C. Europhysics Journal. Atomic, Molecular, and Plasma Physics Optics [*A publication*]

Physical Educ J ... Physical Education Journal [*A publication*] (APTA)

Physica Status Solidi A ... Physica Status Solidi. Sectio A. Applied Research [*A publication*]

Physica Status Solidi B ... Physica Status Solidi. Sectio B. Basic Research [*A publication*]

Physician Assist ... Physician Assistant [*Later, Physician Assistant/Health Practitioner*] [*A publication*]

Physician Assist Health ... Physician Assistant/Health Practitioner [*A publication*]

Physician Assist Health Pract ... Physician Assistant/Health Practitioner [*A publication*]

Physician Comput Monthly ... Physician Computer Monthly [*A publication*]

Physician Exec ... Physician Executive [*A publication*]

Physicians Manage ... Physicians Management [*A publication*]

Physician Sportsmed ... Physician and Sports Medicine [*A publication*]

Physician and Surg ... Physician and Surgeon [*A publication*]

Physicochem Hydrodyn ... Physicochemical Hydrodynamics [*England*] [*A publication*]

Physics & Chem ... Physics and Chemistry [*A publication*]

Physics Ed ... Physics Education [*A publication*]

Physics Med Biol ... Physics in Medicine and Biology [*A publication*]

Physics Teach ... Physics Teacher [*A publication*]

Physikertag Hauptvortr Jahrestag Verb Dtsch Phys Ges ... Physikertagung. Hauptvortraege der Jahrestagung des Verbandes Deutscher Physikalischer Gesellschaften [*A publication*]

Physikunterr ... Physikunterricht [*A publication*]

PHYSIO.... Physiotherapy [*Medicine*]

PHYSIOG ... Physiognomy [*Slang*] (DSUE)

PHYSIOG ... Physiographic

PHYSIOL ... Physiological (MSA)

PHYSIOL ... Physiology (ROG)

Physiol Abstr ... Physiological Abstracts [*A publication*]

Physiol Behav ... Physiology and Behavior [*A publication*]

Physiol Biochem Cultiv Plants ... Physiology and Biochemistry of Cultivated Plants [*A publication*]

Physiol Biochem Cult Plants (USSR) ... Physiology and Biochemistry of Cultivated Plants (USSR) [*A publication*]

Physiol Bohemoslov ... Physiologia Bohemoslovaca [*A publication*]

Physiol Can ... Physiology Canada [*A publication*]

Physiol Chem Phys ... Physiological Chemistry and Physics [*Later, Physiological Chemistry and Physics and Medical NMR*] [*A publication*]

Physiol Chem Phys Med NMR ... Physiological Chemistry and Physics and Medical NMR [*A publication*]

Physiol Ecol ... Physiology and Ecology [*A publication*]

Physiol Ecol (Jpn) ... Physiology and Ecology (Japan) [*A publication*]

Physiol Ent ... Physiological Entomology [*A publication*]

Physiol Entomol ... Physiological Entomology [*A publication*]

Physiol Menschen ... Physiologie des Menschen [*A publication*]

Physiol Mol Plant Pathol ... Physiological and Molecular Plant Pathology [*A publication*]

Physiologia Comp Oecol ... Physiologia Comparata et Oecologia [*A publication*]

Physiologia Pl ... Physiologia Plantarum [*A publication*]

Physiol Pathophysiol Skin ... Physiology and Pathophysiology of the Skin [*A publication*]

Physiol Pharmacol Physicians ... Physiology and Pharmacology for Physicians [*A publication*]

Physiol Physicians ... Physiology for Physicians [*A publication*]

Physiol Plant ... Physiologia Plantarum [*A publication*]

Physiol Plant Pathol ... Physiological Plant Pathology [*A publication*]

Physiol Plant Suppl ... Physiologia Plantarum. Supplementum [*A publication*]

Physiol Psychol ... Physiological Psychology [*A publication*]

Physiol Rev ... Physiological Reviews [*A publication*]

Physiol Soc Philadelphia Monogr ... Physiological Society of Philadelphia. Monographs [*A publication*]

Physiol Teach ... Physiology Teacher [*A publication*]

Physiol Veg ... Physiologie Vegetale [*A publication*]

Physiol Zool ... Physiological Zoology [*A publication*]

Physiother Can ... Physiotherapy Canada [*A publication*]

Physiother Pract ... Physiotherapy Practice [*A publication*]

Physis Riv Internaz Storia Sci ... Physis. Rivista Internazionale di Storia della Scienza [*A publication*]

Physis Secc A Oceanos Org ... Physis. Seccion A: Oceanos y Sus Organismos [*A publication*]

Physis Secc A Oceanos Sus Org ... Physis. Seccion A: Oceanos y Sus Organismos [*A publication*]

Physis Secc B Aguas Cont Org ... Physis. Seccion B: Aguas Continentales y Sus Organismos [*A publication*]

Physis Secc B Aguas Cont Sus Org ... Physis. Seccion B: Aguas Continentales y Sus Organismos [*A publication*]

Physis Secc C Cont Org Terr ... Physis. Seccion C: Continentes y Organismos Terrestres [*A publication*]

Phys Kondens Mater ... Physik der Kondensierten Materie [*A publication*]

PHYSL...... Physiological (AFM)

Physl Behav ... Physiology and Behavior [*A publication*]

Physl Bohem ... Physiologia Bohemoslovaca [*A publication*]

Physl Chem ... Physiological Chemistry and Physics [*Later, Physiological Chemistry and Physics and Medical NMR*] [*A publication*]

Phys Lett.... Physics Letters [*Netherlands*] [*A publication*]

Phys Lett A ... Physics Letters. Section A [*A publication*]

Phys Lett B ... Physics Letters. Section B [*A publication*]

Phys Lett C ... Physics Letters. Section C [*Netherlands*] [*A publication*]

Phys Letters ... Physics Letters [*A publication*]

Physl Plant ... Physiologia Plantarum [*A publication*]

Physl Pl P .. Physiological Plant Pathology [*A publication*]

Physl Psych ... Physiological Psychology [*A publication*]

Physl Veget ... Physiologie Vegetale [*A publication*]

Physl Zool ... Physiological Zoology [*A publication*]

Phys Med Bi ... Physics in Medicine and Biology [*A publication*]

Phys Med and Biol ... Physics in Medicine and Biology [*A publication*]

Phys Med Biol ... Physics in Medicine and Biology [*A publication*]

Phys Met ... Physics of Metals [*A publication*]

Phys Methods Chem Anal ... Physical Methods in Chemical Analysis [*A publication*]

Phys Methods Macromol Chem ... Physical Methods in Macromolecular Chemistry [*A publication*]

Phys Met Metallogr ... Physics of Metals and Metallography [*A publication*]

Phys Met (USSR) ... Physics of Metals (USSR) [*A publication*]

PHYSN ..... Physician

Phys News ... Physics News Bulletin. Indian Physics Association [*A publication*]

Phys Norv.. Physica Norvegica [*A publication*]

Phys Norveg ... Physica Norvegica [*A publication*]

Phys Occup Ther Geriatr ... Physical and Occupational Therapy in Geriatrics [*A publication*]

Phys Occup Ther Pediatr ... Physical and Occupational Therapy in Pediatrics [*A publication*]

PHYSOG .. Physiognomy [*Slang*] (DSUE)

Phys Pap.... Physics Papers [*A publication*]

Phys Pap Silesian Univ Katowice ... Physics Papers. Silesian University in Katowice [*Poland*] [*A publication*]

Phys Quantum Electron ... Physics of Quantum Electronics [*A publication*]

Phys R........ Physical Review [*A publication*]

Phys Regelm Ber ... Physik in Regelmaessigen Berichten [*A publication*]

Phys Rep.... Physics Reports. Review Section of Physics Letters. Section C [*Netherlands*] [*A publication*]

Phys Rep Kumamoto Univ ... Physics Reports. Kumamoto University [*A publication*]

Phys Rep Phys Lett Sect C ... Physics Reports. Physics Letters. Section C [*A publication*]

Phys Rev .... Physical Review [*A publication*]

Phys Rev .... Physiological Reviews [*A publication*]

Phys Rev A ... Physical Review. Section A. General Physics [*A publication*]

Phys Rev A 3 ... Physical Review. Section A. General Physics. Third Series [*A publication*]

Phys Rev A Gen Phys ... Physical Review. Section A. General Physics [*A publication*]

Phys Rev B 3 ... Physical Review. Section B. Condensed Matter. Third Series [*A publication*]

Phys Rev B Conden Matt ... Physical Review. Section B. Condensed Matter [*A publication*]

Phys Rev B Condens Matter ... Physical Review. Section B. Condensed Matter [*A publication*]

Phys Rev C ... Physical Review. Section C. Nuclear Physics [*A publication*]

Phys Rev C 3 ... Physical Review. Section C. Nuclear Physics. Third Series [*A publication*]

Phys Rev D ... Physical Review. Section D. Particles and Fields [*A publication*]

Phys Rev D 3 ... Physical Review. Section D. Particles and Fields. Third Series [*A publication*]

Phys Rev L ... Physical Review. Letters [*A publication*]

Phys Rev Lett ... Physical Review. Letters [*A publication*]

Phys Rev Sect A ... Physical Review. Section A. General Physics [*A publication*]

Phys Rev Sect B ... Physical Review. Section B. Condensed Matter [*A publication*]

Phys Rev Suppl ... Physical Review. Supplement [*A publication*]

Phys Sci Data ... Physical Sciences Data [*Amsterdam*] [*A publication*]

Phys Scr ... Physica Scripta [*A publication*]

Phys Scripta ... Physica Scripta [*Stockholm*] [*A publication*]

Phys Sintering ... Physics of Sintering [*Yugoslavia*] [*A publication*]

Phys Soc Lond Proc ... Physical Society of London. Proceedings [*A publication*]

Phys Solariterr ... Physica Solariterrestris [*A publication*]
Phys Solid Earth (Engl Ed) ... Physics of the Solid Earth (English Edition) [*A publication*]
Phys Stat Sol A ... Physica Status Solidi. Sectio A. Applied Research [*A publication*]
Phys Stat Sol B ... Physica Status Solidi. Sectio B. Basic Research [*A publication*]
Phys Status Solidi ... Physica Status Solidi [*A publication*]
Phys Status Solidi A ... Physica Status Solidi. Sectio A. Applied Research [*A publication*]
Phys Status Solidi B ... Physica Status Solidi. Sectio B. Basic Research [*A publication*]
Phys St S-A ... Physica Status Solidi. Sectio A. Applied Research [*A publication*]
Phys St S-B .. Physica Status Solidi. Sectio B. Basic Research [*A publication*]
Phys Teach ... Physics Teacher [*A publication*]
Phys Tech Biol Res ... Physical Techniques in Biological Research [*A publication*]
Phys Technol ... Physics in Technology [*A publication*]
PHYSTER ... Physical Therapy (AABC)
Phys Ther .. Physical Therapy [*A publication*]
Phys Therapy ... Physical Therapy [*A publication*]
Phys Therapy Rev ... Physical Therapy Review [*A publication*]
Phys Thin Films ... Physics of Thin Films. Advances in Research and Development [*A publication*]
Phys Today ... Physics Today [*A publication*]
Phys Unserer Zeit ... Physik in Unserer Zeit [*A publication*]
Phys Verh .. Physikalische Verhandlungen [*A publication*]
PHYSY ...... Physiology
Phys Z .... Physikalische Zeitschrift [*East Germany*] [*A publication*]
Phys Zeit .... Physikalische Zeitschrift [*A publication*]
Phys Zool ... Physiological Zoology [*A publication*]
Phys Z Sowjetunion ... Physikalische Zeitschrift der Sowjetunion [*A publication*]
PHYT .... Physio Technology, Inc. [*NASDAQ symbol*] (NQ)
Phyt .... Phytopathology [*A publication*]
PHYTA ..... Phytopathology [*A publication*]
PHYTB ..... Physics in Technology [*A publication*]
Phytiat Phytopharm ... Phytiatrie-Phytopharmacie [*A publication*]
Phytiatr-Phytopharm Rev Fr Med Pharm Veg ... Phytiatrie-Phytopharmacie. Revue Francaise de Medecine et de Pharmacie des Vegetaux [*A publication*]
Phytochem ... Phytochemistry [*Oxford*] [*A publication*]
Phytochem Eff Environ Compd ... Phytochemical Effects of Environmental Compounds [*A publication*]
Phytochemistr (Oxf) ... Phytochemistry (Oxford) [*A publication*]
Phytochem Soc Annu Proc ... Phytochemical Society. Annual Proceedings [*A publication*]
Phytochem Soc Eur Symp Ser ... Phytochemical Society of Europe. Symposia Series [*A publication*]
Phytoma Def Cult ... Phytoma. Defense des Cultures [*France*] [*A publication*]
Phytomorph ... Phytomorphology [*A publication*]
Phytomorphol ... Phytomorphology [*A publication*]
Phyton Ann Rei Bot ... Phyton. Annales Rei Botanicae [*A publication*]
Phyton (Aust) ... Phyton. Annales Rei Botanicae (Austria) [*A publication*]
Phyton Int J Exp Bot ... Phyton. International Journal of Experimental Botany [*A publication*]
Phyton Rev Int Bot Exp ... Phyton. Revista Internacional de Botanica Experimental [*A publication*]
PHYTOPATH ... Phytopathology
Phytopathol ... Phytopathology [*A publication*]
Phytopathol Mediterr ... Phytopathologie Mediterranea [*A publication*]
Phytopathol News ... Phytopathology News [*A publication*]
Phytopathol Z ... Phytopathologische Zeitschrift [*Journal of Phytopathology*] [*A publication*]
Phytopathol ZJ Phytopathol ... Phytopathologische Zeitschrift/Journal of Phytopathology [*A publication*]
Phytopath Z ... Phytopathologische Zeitschrift [*Journal of Phytopathology*] [*A publication*]
Phytoprot ... Phytoprotection [*A publication*]
Phytotronic Newsl ... Phytotronic Newsletter [*A publication*]
PHYVA ..... Physiologie Vegetale [*A publication*]
PHYZA ..... Phytopathologische Zeitschrift [*Journal of Phytopathology*] [*A publication*]
PHZ .... Ashland State General Hospital, Ashland, PA [*OCLC symbol*] (OCLC)
PHZAA ..... Pharmazeutische Zeitung. Vereinigt mit Apotheker-Zeitung [*A publication*]
PHZH .... Honolulu Air Traffic Control Center [*Hawaii*] [*ICAO location identifier*] (ICLI)
PHZIA .... Pharamazeutische Zeitung [*A publication*]
PHZOA ..... Physiological Zoology [*A publication*]
PI .... Package Insert [*Instructional leaflet distributed with certain prescription drugs*] [*Also, PPI*]
PI .... Packaging Institute [*Later, PI/USA*] (EA)
PI .... Paducah & Illinois Railroad [*AAR code*]
PI .... Pagine Istriane [*A publication*]
PI .... Pancreatic Insufficiency [*Gastroenterology*]
Pi .... Pandectae (Pisanae) Florentinae [*A publication*] (DSA)
PI .... Panel Input
PI .... Pansophic Institute (EA)

PI .... Pantera International (EA)
PI .... Paper Insulated
PI .... Paracel Islands [*ANSI two-letter standard code*] (CNC)
PI .... Parallel Input [*Data processing*] (BUR)
PI .... Parental Investment [*Biology*]
PI .... Parity Index [*EEO*]
P & I .... Parole e le Idee [*A publication*]
PI .... Parti Independantiste [*Quebec*]
PI .... Particle Integration (CAAL)
PI .... Partido Independente [*Independent Party*] [*Costa Rica*] [*Political party*]
PI .... Partido Intransigente [*Intransigent Party*] [*Argentina*] [*Political party*] (PD)
P & I .... Passenger and Immigration Lists [*A publication*]
PI .... Patient's Interests [*Medicine*]
PI .... Patrol Inspector [*Immigration and Naturalization Service*]
PI .... Payload Interrogator [*NASA*] (MCD)
PI .... Pen and Ink
PI .... Per Inquiry [*Advertising*]
PI .... Perceptions, Inc. (EA)
PI .... Perceptual Isolation
PI .... Perfect Initials [*Philately*]
PI .... Performance Improvement
PI .... Performance Index
PI .... Performance Indicator (MCD)
P & I .... Performance and Interface [*Specification*] [*NASA*] (NASA)
PI .... Periodic Inspection [*Military*] (AFM)
PI .... Periodicals Institute (EA)
PI .... Peripheral Iridectomy [*Medicine*]
PI .... Perlite Institute (EA)
PI .... Permeability Index [*Clinical chemistry*]
PI .... Personal Identification
PI .... Personal Income
PI .... Personal Injury [*Insurance*]
PI .... Personal Injury Accident [*British police term*]
PI .... Personal Investment [*A publication*] (ADA)
PI .... Personality Inventory [*Psychology*]
PI .... Peru Indigena [*A publication*]
PI .... Petroleum Information Corp. (IID)
PI .... Pharmacopoeia Internationalis [*International Pharmacopoeia*]
PI .... Phenanthroimidazole [*Organic chemistry*]
PI .... Phenyl Isocyanate [*Organic chemistry*]
PI .... Philippine Islands
PI .... Philippines [*Aircraft nationality and registration mark*] (FAAC)
PI .... Philosopher's Index [*A publication*]
Pi. .... Phosphate, Inorganic [*Chemistry*]
PI .... Phosphatidylinositol [*Also, PtdIns*] [*Biochemistry*]
PI .... Photo International (EAIO)
P-I .... Photogrammetric Instrumentation (AAG)
PI .... Photointerpretation [*or Photointerpreter*]
PI .... Photoionization [*Physical chemistry*]
PI .... Physical Inventory (NRCH)
PI .... Physically Impaired
PI .... Piedmont Aviation, Incorporated [*ICAO designator*] (OAG)
PI .... Pig Iron
PI .... Pigeon Trainer [*Navy*]
Pi .... Pillius Medicinensis [*Flourished, 1165-1207*] [*Authority cited in pre-1607 legal work*] (DSA)
PI .... Pilot. Fort Smith and Simpson [*Northwest Territory, Canada*] [*A publication*]
PI .... Pilot International (EA)
PI .... Pilot Item (MCD)
PI .... Pilotless Intercepter [*Air Force*]
PI .... Pink (ROG)
PI .... Pipe [*Freight*]
P & I .... Piping and Instrumentation [*Nuclear energy*] (NRCH)
PI .... Plant Introduction [*Botany*]
PI .... Plaque Index [*Dentistry*]
PI .... Plasma Iron [*Hematology*]
PI .... Plastochron Index [*Botany*]
PI .... Pneumatosis Intestinalis [*Medicine*]
PI .... Point of Impact (AFM)
PI .... Point Initiating
PI .... Point Insulating
PI .... Point of Interception [*Navigation*]
PI .... Point of Intersection
PI .... Poison Ivy [*Campers' slang*]
PI .... Polyimide [*Organic chemistry*]
PI .... Polyisoprene [*Organic chemistry*]
PI .... Polymer International (NS), Inc. [*Toronto Stock Exchange symbol*]
PI .... Pompeiiana, Incorporated (EA)
PI .... Poni Iussit [*Ordered to Be Placed*] [*Latin*]
PI .... Popcorn Institute (EA)
PI .... Population Institute (EA)
PI .... Portfolio Insurance [*Finance*]
PI .... Position Indicator [*Army*]
PI .... Positive Identification Feature
PI .... Positive Interlace [*Television*]
P & I .... Postage and Insurance

PI	Postimpressionist Movement [*Art*]
PI	Postinoculation [*Medicine*]
PI	Postischemic [*Medicine*]
PI	Potash Institute [*Later, PPI*] (EA)
PI	Potomac Institute (EA)
PI	Power Injection
PI	Power Input
PI	Precision Instrument (NVT)
PI	Predicted Impact (MCD)
PI	Pregnancy Induced [*Gynecology*]
PI	Preinduction [*Medicine*]
PI	Preliminary Inspection (MCD)
PI	Preliminary Investigation (NASA)
PI	Preliminary Issue
PI	Preparatory Interval [*Psychometrics*]
PI	Prepositioned Instruction [*DoD*]
PI	Present Illness [*Medicine*]
PI	Pressure Indicator [*Nuclear energy*]
Pi	Pressure of Inspiration [*Medicine*]
PI	Primacord Interstage
PI	Primary Infarction [*Medicine*]
PI	Prime Interest Rate [*Banking*]
P & I	Principal and Interest [*Banking*] (ADA)
PI	Principal Investigator (MCD)
PI	Printer [*Navy*]
PI	Printers' Ink [*A publication*]
PI	Priority Interrupt (IEEE)
PI	Private Institution [*British*]
PI	Private Investigator
PI	Proactive Inhibition [*Psychology*]
PI	Process Instrumentation [*Nuclear energy*] (NRCH)
PI	Processor Interface
PI	Procurement Inspection (MCD)
PI	Procurement Item (NASA)
PI	Product Improvement (MCD)
P/I	Production Illustration (MSA)
PI	Production Interval
PI	Productivity Index (IEEE)
PI	Program Indicator (IEEE)
PI	Program Indicator Code (CMD)
PI	Program Innovations (ADA)
PI	Program Instruction [*Data processing*] (BUR)
PI	Program of Instrumentation (MUGU)
PI	Program Interrupt
PI	Program Introduction
PI	Program Issuances [*Assistance Payments Administration, HEW*]
PI	Programmed Information [*Data processing*]
PI	Programmed Instruction
PI	Programmed Introduction (MCD)
PI	Project Inform (EA)
PI	Project Intrex [*Massachusetts Institute of Technology*] (EA)
PI	Prolactin Inhibitor [*Endocrinology*]
P & I	Properties and Installations
PI	Property Index [*British police term*]
PI	Propidium Iodide [*Fluorescent dye*]
PI	Proportional-Plus Integral [*Digital control*]
PI	Protamine Insulin
Pi	Protease Inhibitor
P & I	Protection and Indemnity [*Insurance*]
PI	Proteinase Inhibitor [*Biochemistry*]
PI	Protocol Internationale
PI	Psychiatric Institute
PI	Psychosynthesis Institute (EA)
PI	Public Information
PI	Publication Instructions
PI	Puebla Institute (EA)
PI	Pulmonary Incompetence [*Medicine*]
PI	Pulmonary Indices [*Medicine*]
PI	Pulmonary Infarction [*Medicine*]
PI	Pulmonary Intervertebral Disc [*Medicine*]
PI	Pulse Induction (ADA)
PI	Purge Isolation [*Nuclear energy*] (NRCH)
PI	Pyritization Index [*Geoscience*]
PI	Trademark for an ophthalmic drug
PI1	Pinedale [*Wyoming*] [*Seismograph station code, US Geological Survey*] [*Closed*] (SEIS)
PI1	State Correctional Institute at Camp Hill, Camp Hill, PA [*OCLC symbol*] (OCLC)
PI2	Pinedale [*Wyoming*] [*Seismograph station code, US Geological Survey*] [*Closed*] (SEIS)
P2I	Planned Product Improvement
PI2	State Correctional Institute at Dallas, Dallas, PA [*OCLC symbol*] (OCLC)
PI3	Pinedale [*Wyoming*] [*Seismograph station code, US Geological Survey*] [*Closed*] (SEIS)
P³I	Preplanned Product Improvement [*DoD*]
PI3	State Correctional Institute at Grateford, Grateford, PA [*OCLC symbol*] (OCLC)
PI4	Pinedale [*Wyoming*] [*Seismograph station code, US Geological Survey*] [*Closed*] (SEIS)

PI4	State Correctional Institute at Huntingdon, Huntingdon, PA [*OCLC symbol*] (OCLC)
PI5	Pinedale [*Wyoming*] [*Seismograph station code, US Geological Survey*] [*Closed*] (SEIS)
PI5	State Correctional Institute at Muncy, Muncy, PA [*OCLC symbol*] (OCLC)
PI6	Pinedale [*Wyoming*] [*Seismograph station code, US Geological Survey*] [*Closed*] (SEIS)
PI6	State Correctional Institute at Pittsburgh, Pittsburgh, PA [*OCLC symbol*] (OCLC)
PI7	Pinedale [*Wyoming*] [*Seismograph station code, US Geological Survey*] [*Closed*] (SEIS)
PI7	State Regional Correctional Facility, Greensburg, PA [*OCLC symbol*] (OCLC)
PIA	Pacific Islands Association (EA)
PIA	Packaged Ice Association (EA)
PIA	Pakistan International Airlines Corp.
PIA	Panel-Information-Air Operation
PIA	Parapsychology Institute of America (EA)
PIA	Particle Impact Analyzer [*Astrophysics*]
PIA	Passive Immunological Agglutination
PIA	Pensions and Investment Age [*A publication*]
PIA	Peoria [*Illinois*] [*Airport symbol*] (OAG)
PIA	Perfumery Importers Association [*Defunct*] (EA)
PIA	Peripheral Interface Adapter [*Data processing*]
PIA	Personnel Inventory Analysis [*Army*]
PIA	Petervin Information Associates [*Also, an information service or system*] (IID)
PIA	Petroleum Incentives Administration [*Canada*]
PIA	Phenylisopropyladenosine [*Biochemistry*]
PIA	Piano [*Softly*] [*Music*]
PIA	Pilots International Association (EA)
PIA	Pitten [*Austria*] [*Seismograph station code, US Geological Survey*] (SEIS)
PIA	Plasma Insulin Activity [*Clinical chemistry*]
PIA	Plastics Institute of America (EA)
PIA	Plug-In Amplifier
PIA	Polycultural Institution of America
PIA	Positive Ion Accelerator
PIA	Positron Intensity Accumulator (MCD)
PIA	Postal Inspectors' Association [*A union*] [*British*]
PIA	Potentiometric Immunoassay [*Clinical chemistry*]
PIA	Preinstallation Acceptance
PIA	Primary Industry Association of Western Australia
PIA	Primary Insurance Account [*Social Security Administration*] (OICC)
PIA	Primary Insurance Amount
PIA	Principal Industry Activity [*IRS*]
PIA	Printing Industries of America (EA)
PIA	Proceedings. Irish Academy [*A publication*]
PIA	Production Inventory Analysis (AAG)
PIA	Professional Insurance Agents [*Alexandria, VA*] (EA)
PIA	Project Impact Analysis (NASA)
PIA	Psychiatric Institute of America [*For-profit network of private psychiatric hospitals*] (EA)
PIA	Public Information Act
PIA	Public Information Adviser [*NATO*] (NATG)
PIA	Pumice Institute of America (EA)
PIA	White Haven Center, White Haven, PA [*OCLC symbol*] (OCLC)
505 PIA	505th Parachute Infantry Association [*Later, 505th Regimental Combat Team Association*] (EA)
PIAA	Pre-Arrangement Interment Association of America [*Later, PAA*] (EA)
PIAAD	Proceedings. Indian Academy of Sciences. Series Chemical Sciences [*A publication*]
PIAC	Permanent International Altaistic Conference (EA)
PIAC	Petroleum Industry Advisory Committee [*British*]
PIAC	Problem Identification and Correction [*DoD*] (AFIT)
PIAC	Public Interest Advocacy Centre [*Australia*]
PIACA	Proceedings. Indiana Academy of Science [*A publication*]
PIACS	Pacific Integrated Automatic Communications Systems [*Military*]
PIACT	Program for the Introduction and Adaptation of Contraceptive Technology (EA)
PIADC	Plum Island Animal Disease Center [*Formerly, PIADL*]
PIADL	Plum Island Animal Disease Laboratory [*of ARS, Department of Agriculture*] [*Later, PIADC*]
Piaget Theor Help Prof	Piagetian Theory and the Helping Professions [*A publication*]
PIAMA	Professional Institute for the American Management Association (OICC)
PIAMD	Proceedings. Indian Academy of Sciences. Series Mathematical Sciences [*A publication*]
PIANC	Permanent International Association of Navigation Congresses [*Brussels, Belgium*] (EAIO)
PIand	Papyri Iandanae [*A publication*] (OCD)
PIAND	Proceedings. Indian Academy of Sciences. Series Animal Sciences [*A publication*]
PIANG	Piangendo [*Plaintive*] [*Music*]
PIANISS	Pianissimo [*Very Softly*] [*Music*]

Piano Q	Piano Quarterly [*A publication*]
Piano Quart	Piano Quarterly [*A publication*]
Piano Tech	Piano Technician [*A publication*]
PIAP	Printing Industries Association of the Philippines (DS)
PIAP	Psychologists Interested in the Advancement of Psychotherapy [*Later, APA*] (EA)
PIAPACS	Psychophysiological Information Acquisition, Processing, and Control System
PIAR	Problem Identification and Analysis Report [*Military*] (CAAL)
PIAR	Project Impact Analysis Report (MCD)
PIARC	Permanent International Association of Road Congresses [*See also AIPCR*] [*Paris, France*] (EAIO)
PIAS	Photographic Inventory and Accountancy System
PIAS	Piaster [*Monetary unit*] [*Spain, Republic of Vietnam, and some Middle Eastern countries*]
PIAS	Precision Intelligence Augmentation System
PIAS	Program Impact Analysis Scenario
PIASA	Polish Institute of Arts and Sciences of America (EA)
P I A Sci A	Proceedings. Indian Academy of Sciences. Section A [*A publication*]
P I A Sci B	Proceedings. Indian Academy of Sciences. Section B [*A publication*]
PIASH	Proceedings. Israel Academy of Sciences and Humanities [*Jerusalem*] [*A publication*]
PIASS	Paris International Aviation and Space Salon (MCD)
PIAT	Peabody Individual Achievement Test [*Education*]
PIAT	Projector Infantry, Antitank [*British shoulder-controlled weapon*]
PIB	George Junior Republic, Grove City, PA [*OCLC symbol*] (OCLC)
PIB	Laurel/Hattiesburg [*Mississippi*] [*Airport symbol*] (OAG)
PIB	Pacific Inland Tariff Bureau, Portland OR [*STAC*]
PIB	Papuan Infantry Battalion
PIB	Parachute Infantry Battalion [*Army*]
PIB	Partial Ileal Bypass [*Medicine*]
PIB	Partido Indio de Bolivia [*Political party*]
PIB	Payload Integration Bay [*NASA*] (KSC)
PIB	Pender Island [*British Columbia*] [*Seismograph station code, US Geological Survey*] (SEIS)
PIB	Periodic Information Briefing (MCD)
PIB	Personal Information Briefing [*of returning POW's*] [*Air Force*]
PIB	Petroleum Information Bureau
PIB	Photo Intelligence Brief (AFM)
PIB	Photo Interpretation Brief (MCD)
PIB	Plug-In Blank
PIB	Polar Ionospheric Beacon
PIB	Polyisobutylene [*Organic chemistry*]
PIB	Polytechnic Institute of Brooklyn [*Later, PINY*] (MCD)
PIB	Preliminary Instruction Book
PIB	Prices and Incomes Board [*British*]
PIB	Processor Interface Buffer [*Telecommunications*] (TEL)
PIB	Product Improvement Bulletin
PIB	Programmable Input Buffer
PIB	Propellant Inspection Building [*NASA*] (KSC)
PIB	Public Information Bulletin [*Australian Taxation Office*] [*A publication*] (APTA)
PIB	Publishers Information Bureau [*New York, NY*] (EA)
PIB	Publishing Information Bulletin [*A publication*]
PIB	Pulse Interference Blanker
PIB	Pyrotechnic Installation Building [*NASA*] (KSC)
PIBA	Primary Industry Bank of Australia Ltd. (ADA)
PIBAC	Permanent International Bureau of Analytical Chemistry of Human and Animal Food
PIBAL	Pilot Balloon Observation
PIBAL	Polytechnic Institute of Brooklyn Aeronautical Laboratory (MCD)
PIBALS	Pilot Balloon Soundings
PIBC	Pacific Inland Bancorp [*Anaheim, CA*] [*NASDAQ symbol*] (NQ)
PIBC	Pacific Institute of Bio-Organic Chemistry
PIBD	Point Initiating, Base Detonating Projectile [*Army*]
PIBL	PEMA Item Baseline List [*Army*]
PIBMM	Permanent International Bureau of Motorcycle Manufacturers
PIBMRI	Polytechnic Institute of Brooklyn, Microwave Research Institute (IEEE)
PIBOL	Pilot Back Up Control
PIBS	Polar Ionospheric Beacon Satellite [*NASA*]
PIBSB	Proceedings. Indian National Science Academy. Part B. Biological Sciences [*A publication*]
PIBTAD	Proceedings. Congress of the International Society of Blood Transfusion [*A publication*]
PIBUC	Pilot Back Up Control
PIC	Calverton, NY [*Location identifier*] [*FAA*] (FAAL)
PIC	Craig House Technoma Workshop, Pittsburgh, PA [*OCLC symbol*] (OCLC)
PIC	Pacific Insurance Conference
PIC	Pacific Intelligence Center (MCD)
PIC	Paired-Ion Chromatography
PIC	Para-iodoclonidine [*Biochemistry*]
PIC	Particle in Cell [*Gas solid*]
PIC	Partners in Change Program [*Department of Labor*]

PIC	Payload Integration Center [*NASA*] (MCD)
PIC	Payload Integration Committee [*NASA*] (NASA)
PIC	Payload Integration Contractor (MCD)
PIC	Peak Identification Computer
PIC	People's Involvement Corporation (EA)
PIC	Peripheral Interface Controller [*Data processing*]
PIC	Pershing Instant Comment [*Donaldson, Lufkin & Jenrette*] [*Database*]
PIC	Personal Identification Code [*Banking*]
PIC	Personality Inventory for Children [*Psychology*]
PIC	Perspectives in Computing [*A publication*]
PIC	Pesticides Information Center [*National Agricultural Library*] [*Terminated, 1969*]
PIC	Petrochemical Industries Corporation [*Burma*] (DS)
PIC	Petrochemical Investing Corporation
PIC	Photographic Industry Council (EA)
PIC	Photographic Interpretation Center (MCD)
PIC	Physical Inorganic Chemistry [*Elsevier Book Series*] [*A publication*]
PIC	Piccadilly Saloon [*London*] (DSUE)
PIC	Piccolo [*Music*] (ROG)
PIC	[*The*] Pickens Railroad Co. [*Later, PICK*] [*AAR code*]
Pic	Picrotoxin [*Biochemistry*]
Pic	Pictor [*Constellation*]
PIC	Picture (AABC)
PIC	Pig Improvement Co. [*British*] (ECON)
PIC	Pilot in Command [*Aviation*] (FAAC)
PIC	Pilot-Integrated Cockpit (AAG)
PIC	Pine Cay [*British West Indies*] [*Airport symbol*] [*Obsolete*] (OAG)
PIC	Planned Insurance Coverage
PIC	Plasma Insulin Concentration [*Clinical chemistry*]
PIC	Plastic Insulated Conductor
PIC	Policy Information Center [*Department of Health and Human Services*] [*Information service or system*] (IID)
PIC	Polyethylene Insulated Conductor [*Telecommunications*]
PIC	Polymer-Impregnated Concrete (KSC)
PIC	Portable Imaging Computer
PIC	Position Independent Code [*Telecommunications*] (TEL)
PIC	Positive Ion Chamber
PIC	Postinflammatory Corticoid [*Medicine*]
PIC	Power Information Center [*Interagency Advanced Power Group*] [*DoD*] [*Washington, DC*]
PIC	Power Integrated Circuit [*Data processing*]
PIC	Preinstallation Calibration (KSC)
PIC	Preinstallation Checkout (NASA)
PIC	Presbyterian Interracial Council (EA)
PIC	Pressure Indicator Controller
PIC	Primate Information Center [*University of Washington*] [*Seattle, WA*]
pic	Prince Edward Island [*Canada*] [*MARC country of publication code*] [*Library of Congress*] (LCCP)
PIC	Printer Interface Cartridge [*Epson America, Inc.*]
PIC	Prior Informed Consent [*For use of pesticides*]
PIC	Priority Interrupt Controller
PIC	Private Industry Council [*Generic term for group that helps provide job training*]
PIC	Procedures for Instrument Calibration
PIC	Process Interface Control
PIC	Processor Input Channel (NVT)
PIC	Procurement Information Center
PIC	Procurement Information for Contracts [*AFSC*]
PIC	Product of Incomplete Combustion
PIC	Product Information Center [*AgriData Resources, Inc.*] [*Information service or system*]
PIC	Professional Instrument Course [*Aeronautics*]
PIC	Professional Interfraternity Conference [*Later, PFA*] (EA)
PIC	Program Identification Code (MUGU)
PIC	Program for Improved Contract Management [*Military*] (AFIT)
PIC	Program Information Center
PIC	Program Initiations and Commitments (AAG)
PIC	Program Instruction, Calibration [*Marine Corps*]
PIC	Program Interrupt Control [*Data processing*]
PIC	Programmable Interrupt Controller [*Data processing*]
PIC	Programmable Interval Clock (NASA)
PIC	Project Information Center
PIC	Promotion Industry Club (EA)
PIC	Pseudo-Isocytidine [*Antineoplastic compound*]
PIC	Public Information Center [*Nuclear energy*] (NRCH)
PIC	Public Information Committee [*of the NATO Military Committee*] (NATG)
PIC	Publishers' Information Card [*Later, IBIS*] [*British*]
PIC	Pulsed Ionization Chamber
PIC	Purpose Identification Code
PIC	Pursuant to Instructions Contained In (MUGU)
PIC	Pyrotechnic Ignition Control (NASA)
PIC	Pyrotechnic Initiator Capacitor (NASA)
PIC	Pyrotechnic Initiator Controller (NASA)
PICA	Palestine Israelite Colonisation Association
PICA	Police Insignia Collector's Association (EA)

PICA	Porch Index of Communicative Ability [*Psychology*]
PICA	Posterior Inferior Cerebellar Artery [*Anatomy*]
PICA	Power Industry Computer Applications (MCD)
PICA	Primary Inventory Control Activity (MCD)
PICA	Printing Industry Computer Associates, Inc.
PICA	Private Investment Company for Asia SA
PICA	Procedures for Inventory Control Afloat [*Navy*]
PICA	Professional Insurance Communicators of America (EA)
PICA	Programming Interpersonal Curricula for Adolescents [*Learning model*] [*Education*]
PICA	Project for Integrated Catalogue Automation [*Royal Netherlands Library*] [*Cataloging cooperative*] (IID)
PICA	Property Services Agency Information on Construction and Architecture [*Property Service Agency Library Service*] [*Great Britain*] [*Information service or system*]
PICA	Public Interest Computer Association (EA)
PICAC	Porch Index of Communicative Ability in Children [*Psychology*]
PICAC	Power Industry Computer Applications Conference (MCD)
PICADAD	Place Identification/Characteristics and Area/Distance and Direction [*Bureau of the Census*]
PICAM	Proceedings. International Congress of Americanists [*A publication*]
PICAO	Provisional International Civil Aviation Organization [*Later, ICAO*]
Picardie Inform	Picardie Information [*A publication*]
PICB	Peabody Institute of the City of Baltimore [*Maryland*]
PICC	Parts for Import Cars Coalition [*Inactive*] (EA)
PICC	Philadelphia International Convention Center [*Pennsylvania*]
PICC	Philippine International Convention Center (DS)
PICC	Piccadilly Cafeterias, Inc. [*NASDAQ symbol*] (NQ)
PICC	Piccolo
PICC	Plastics in Construction Council [*Later, CCS*] (EA)
PICC	Professional Institutions Council for Conservation [*British*]
PICC	Provisional International Computation Center
PICCA	Positive Ion Cluster Composition Analyzer [*Instrumentation*]
PICCED	Pratt Institute Center for Community and Environmental Development [*Research center*] (RCD)
PICCO	Pennsylvania Industrial Chemical Corporation [*Trademark*]
PICDG	Polar Icebreaker Canadian Design Group
PICE	Product Improved Compatibility Electronics (MCD)
PICE	Programmable Integrated Control Equipment
PICED	Proceedings. International Conference on Noise Control Engineering [*A publication*]
PICEE	President's Interagency Committee on Export Expansion [*Absorbed by President's Export Council in 1979*] (EGAO)
PICE/PIA	Printing Industry Credit Exchange/PIA [*of the Printing Industries of America*] (EA)
PICG	Programme International de Correlation Geologique [*International Geological Correlation Programme - IGCP*] (EAIO)
PICGC	Permanent International Committee for Genetic Congresses
PicGPA	Picrylated Guinea Pig Albumin [*Immunochemistry*]
PICI	Polymer International Corporation [*Tampa, FL*] [*NASDAQ symbol*] (NQ)
PICI	Publications. Institut de Civilisation Indienne [*A publication*]
P I Civ E 1	Proceedings. Institution of Civil Engineers. Part 1. Design and Construction [*A publication*]
P I Civ E 2	Proceedings. Institution of Civil Engineers. Part 2. Research and Theory [*A publication*]
PICK	Part Information Correlation Key
PICK	[*The*] Pickens Railroad Co. [*Formerly, PIC*] [*AAR code*]
Pick	Pickering's Massachusetts Supreme Judicial Court Reports [*1822-39*] [*A publication*] (DLA)
PICK	Pickwick [*Refers to an inferior quality cigar*] (DSUE)
Picker Clin Scintil	Picker Clinical Scintillator [*A publication*]
PICKFAIR	[*Mary*] Pickford and [*Douglas*] Fairbanks [*Acronym is name of estate once owned by these early film stars*]
Pickle	Pickle's Reports [*85-108 Tennessee*] [*A publication*] (DLA)
PICKLE	President's Intelligence Checklist [*Daily report prepared by CIA*]
Pickle Pak Sci	Pickle Pak Science [*A publication*]
Pick (Mass)	Pickering's Massachusetts Reports [*18-41 Massachusetts*] [*A publication*] (DLA)
Pick Stat	Pickering's English Statutes [*A publication*] (DLA)
PICKUP	Professional, Industrial and Commercial Updating [*Vocational training*] [*British*]
PICL	Proceedings. International Congress of Linguists [*A publication*]
PICM	Master Chief Precision Instrumentman [*Navy rating*]
PICM	Party of the Independence Congress of Madagascar
PICM	Permanent International Committee of Mothers
PICMME	Provisional Intergovernmental Committee for Movement of Migrants in Europe (NATG)
PICN	Pic 'N' Save Corp. [*NASDAQ symbol*] (NQ)
PIC-NF	Picroindigocarmine-Nuclear Fast Red [*A biological stain*]
PICO	Person in Column One [*1980 census*]
PICO	Physicians Insurance Company of Ohio [*NASDAQ symbol*] (NQ)
PICO	Polar Ice Core Drilling Office [*National Science Foundation*] (MSC)
PICO	Proceedings. International Congress of Orientalists [*A publication*]
PICO	Product Improvement Control Office (AFM)
PICO	Purchasing Internal Change Order (MCD)
PICOE	Programmed Initiations, Commitments, Obligations, and Expenditures [*AFSC*]
PICOMM	Potter Instrument Coordinated Measuring Machine
PICON	Process Intelligent Control [*A data processing system from LISP Machine, Inc.*]
PICORNAVIRUS	Pico Ribonucleic Acid Virus
PICOST	Probability of Incurring Estimated Costs [*Military*] (MCD)
PICP	Proceedings. International Congress of Philosophy [*A publication*]
PICP	Program Interface Control Plan (NASA)
PICPAB	Phenomena Induced by Charged Particle Beams
PICPS	Proceedings. International Congress of Phonetic Sciences [*A publication*]
PICPSA	Permanent International Commission for the Proof of Small-Arms (EAIO)
PICRC	Pesticide and Industrial Chemicals Research Center [*Public Health Service*] (GRD)
PICRS	Program Information Control and Retrieval System (NASA)
PICRS	Program Information Coordination and Review Service [*NASA*] (NASA)
PICS	Finest Hour, Inc. [*NASDAQ symbol*] (NQ)
PICS	Permit Imprint Collectors Society (EA)
PICS	Perpetual Inventory Control System
PICS	Personnel Information Communication [*or Control*] System [*Data processing*]
PICS	Pharmaceutical Information Control System (DIT)
PICS	Photo Index and Cataloging System (NASA)
PICS	Photography in Community Self-Development [*Program of Master Photo Dealers and Finishers Association*]
PICS	Pioneer Image Converter System [*NASA*]
PICS	Plastid Isolation Column System [*Analytical chemistry*]
PICS	Plug-In Inventory Control System [*Bell System*]
PICS	Predefined Input Control Sequence (MCD)
PICS	Procurement Information Control System [*NASA*]
PICS	Production Information and Control System [*IBM Corp.*] [*Software package*]
PICS	Production Inventory Control System
PICS	Productivity Improvement and Control System (BUR)
PICS	Program Information and Control System (MCD)
PICS/DCPR	Plug-In Inventory Control System/Detailed Continuing Property Record [*Telecommunications*] (TEL)
PICT	Perceived Instrumentality of the College Test
Pict	Pictor [*Constellation*]
PICT	Pictorial (ROG)
PICT	Project on the Improvement of College Teaching
Pict Dict Rome	Pictorial Dictionary of Ancient Rome [*A publication*] (OCD)
PICTOMAP	Photographic Image Conversion by Tonal Masking Procedures (MCD)
PictR	Pictorial Review [*A publication*]
PICTUREBALM	[*A*] programming language [*1979*] (CSR)
PICU	Parallel Instruction Control Unit
PICU	Pediatric Intensive Care Unit [*Medicine*]
PICU	Priority Interrupt Control Unit [*Data processing*] (MDG)
PICU	Pulmonary Intensive Care Unit [*Medicine*]
PICUTPC	Permanent and International Committee of Underground Town Planning and Construction
PID	D. T. Watson Home for Crippled Children, Leetsdale, PA [*OCLC symbol*] (OCLC)
PID	Pain Intensity Differences [*Medicine*]
PId	Parole e le Idee [*A publication*]
PID	Partial Initial Decision [*Nuclear energy*] (NRCH)
PID	Partido de Integracion Democrata [*Democratic Integration Party*] [*Argentina*] [*Political party*] (PPW)
PID	Partido Izquierda Democratica [*Democratic Left Party*] [*Political party*] (EAIO)
PID	Passenger Information Display
PID	Patrol Input Device (MCD)
PID	Payload Insertion Device (NASA)
PID	Pelvic Inflammatory Disease [*Medicine*]
PID	Perfect-Gas Isentropic Decompression [*Engineering*]
PID	Phenindione [*or Phenylindandione*] [*Anticoagulant*]
PID	Photointerpretation Department [*Military*]
PID	Photoionization Detector
PID	Photon-Induced Dissociation [*For spectral studies*]
PID	Pictorial Information Digitizer [*Data processing*] (DIT)
PID	Pilot-Induced Deceleration
P & ID	Piping and Instrumentation Diagram [*or Design or Drawing*] [*Calcomp Ltd.*] [*Software package*] [*Nuclear energy*] (NRCH)
PID	Political Intelligence Department [*British*] [*World War II*]
PID	Port Identification [*Telecommunications*] (TEL)
PID	Primary Immunodeficiency Disease [*Medicine*]
PID	Prime Item Development (MCD)
PID	Process Identifier [*Data processing*] (PCM)

P & ID........ Process and Instrumentation Diagram [*Nuclear energy*] (NRCH)
PID .... Procurement Information Digest (AFM)
PID .... Procurement Item/Identification Description [*DoD*]
PID .... Program Information Document [*NASA*] (MCD)
PID .... Program Introduction Document (NASA)
PID .... Project Implementation Directive [*Air Force*]
PID .... Prolapsed Intervertebral Disc [*Medicine*]
PID .... Proportional-Plus Integral-Plus Derivative [*Digital control algorithm*]
PID .... Protruded Intervertebral Disc [*Medicine*]
PID .... Pseudo Interrupt Device
PID .... Public Information Division [*Army*]
PIDA........ Payload Installation and Deployment Aid [*NASA*] (NASA)
PIDA........ Pet Industry Distributors Association (EA)
PIDAS ...... Portable Instantaneous Display and Analysis Spectrometer
PIDC........ Philadelphia Industrial Development Corporation
PIDCOM... Process Instruments Digital Communication System [*Beckman Industries*]
PIDD .... Passive Identification/Detection and Direction (MCD)
PI/DE....... Passive Identification/Direction Finding Equipment (MCD)
PIDE.......... Policia Internacional e de Defesa do Estado [*Police for the Control of Foreigners and Defense of the State*] [*Portugal and Portuguese Africa*]
PI/DE........ Positive Identification and Direction Equipment
PIDEP .... Preinterservice Data Exchange Program
PIDL........ Position Involves Intermittent Duty at Isolated Locations (FAAC)
PIDP......... Pacific Islands Development Program [*East-West Center*] [*Research center*] (RCD)
PIDP......... Pilot Information Display Panel
PIDP......... Programmable Indicator Data Processor [*Military*] (CAAL)
PIDR......... Product Inspection Discrepancy Report (MCD)
PIDRA...... Portable Insulin Dosage-Regulating Apparatus [*Medicine*]
PIDRS ...... Photographic Instrumentation Data Recording System (MCD)
PIDS........ Portable Image Display System (NASA)
PIDS........ Prime Item Development Specification
PIDSA...... Population Information Documentation System for Africa
PIE............ Elwyn Institute, Elwyn, PA [*OCLC symbol*] (OCLC)
PIE............ Pacific Information Exchange [*Information service or system*] (IID)
PIE............ Pacific Islands Ecosystems [*Springfield, VA*] [*Department of the Interior*] [*Information service or system*] [*No longer available online*]
PIE............ Pacing Item Evaluation (MCD)
PIE............ Paedophile Information Exchange [*British*] (ILCA)
PIE............ Pan Island Expressway [*Singapore*] (DS)
PIE............ Parallel Instruction Execution [*Data processing*] (BUR)
PIE............ Parallel Interface Element
PIE............ Patent Information Exploitation [*Canadian Patent Office*]
PIE............ Payload Integration Equipment [*NASA*] (MCD)
PIE............ Payroll Audit, Indexing, and Expiration
PIE............ Photo-Induced Electrochromism
PIE............ Piedmont Aviation, Inc. [*NYSE symbol*] (SPSG)
PIE............ Pietermaritzburg [*South Africa*] [*Seismograph station code, US Geological Survey*] [*Closed*] (SEIS)
PIE............ Pipestone Petroleums, Inc. [*Toronto Stock Exchange symbol*] [*Vancouver Stock Exchange symbol*]
PIE............ Plug-In Electronics
PIE............ Plume Interaction Experiment [*Army*] (RDA)
PIE............ Poly(iminoethylene) [*Organic chemistry*]
PIE............ Portable Information Evaluation
PIE............ Post-Irradiation Examination [*Nuclear energy*] (NRCH)
PIE............ Post-Irradiation Experiment [*Nuclear energy*] (NRCH)
PIE............ Preimplantation Embryo
PIE............ Price in Effect [*Military*]
PIE............ Program for Increased Education [*Military*]
PIE............ Program Interrupt Entry [*Data processing*]
PIE............ Programming and Instrumentation Environment [*Data processing*]
PIE............ Prolog Inference Engine [*Data processing*]
PIE............ Proposal Information Exchange [*Military*]
PIE............ Public Interest Economics Foundation [*Defunct*] (EA)
PIE............ Publications Indexed for Engineering [*A publication*]
PIE............ Pulmonary Infiltration with Eosinophilia [*Medicine*]
PIE............ Pulmonary Interstitial Emphysema [*Medicine*]
PIE............ Pulse Interference Eliminator [*RADAR*]
PIE............ Pulse Interference Emitting (MCD)
PIE............ St. Petersburg [*Florida*] [*Airport symbol*] (OAG)
3PIE......... Three-Pulse Image Photon Echo [*Spectroscopy*]
PIEA........ Pencil Industry Export Association [*Defunct*] (EA)
PIEA........ Petroleum Industry Electrical Association [*Later, ENTELEC*] (EA)
PIEA........ Pre-Arrangement Interment Exchange of America [*Later, PIAA*]
PIE-C........ Public Interest Economics Center (EA)
PIECOST ... Probability of Incurring Estimated Costs [*Military*]
PIECP....... Preliminary Impact Engineering Change Proposal (MCD)
PIED......... Piedmont Mining Co., Inc. [*NASDAQ symbol*] (NQ)
PIEEA ...... Proceedings. Institution of Electrical Engineers [*A publication*]
P IEEE....... Proceedings. Institute of Electrical and Electronics Engineers [*A publication*]

P IEE (Lond) ... Proceedings. Institution of Electrical Engineers (London) [*A publication*]
PIE-F .... Public Interest Economics Foundation [*Defunct*] (EA)
Pieleg Polozna ... Pielegniarka i Polozna [*A publication*]
Pienpuu Toimikun Julk ... Pienpuualan Toimikunnan Julkaisu [*A publication*]
PIEP .... Primary Irritation Evaluation Program
Pierce RR... Pierce on Railroad Law [*A publication*] (DLA)
PIERS........ Port Import/Export Reporting Service [*Journal of Commerce, Inc.*] [*Information service or system*]
PIES .... Packaged Interchangeable Electronic System
PIES .... Penning Ionization Electron Spectroscopy
PIES .... Project Independence Evaluation System [*Energy policy*]
PIESD .... Proceedings. Indian Academy of Sciences. Series Earth and Planetary Sciences [*A publication*]
PIEWD...... Prace Naukowe Instytutu Energoelektryki Politechniki Wroclawskiej [*A publication*]
PIF .... Paris et Ile-De-France. Memoires [*A publication*]
P & IF .... Paris et Ile-De-France. Memoires [*A publication*]
PIF .... Partners in Friendship (EA)
PIF .... Payload Integration Facility [*NASA*] (KSC)
PIF .... Personnel Identification Feature [*Navy*] (NVT)
PIF .... Phase Inversion Formulation [*Chemistry*]
PIF .... Pilot Information File [*Army*]
PIF .... Place in Inactive File [*Army*]
PIF .... Point Initiating Fuze
PIF .... Positive Identification Feature (MCD)
PIF .... Predictive Influence Function [*Statistics*]
PIF .... Preparer Inventory File [*IRS*]
PIF .... Privatization Investment Fund Trust Units [*Toronto Stock Exchange symbol*]
PIF .... Productivity Investment Fund [*Program*] [*Air Force*]
PIF .... Program Information File
PIF .... Prolactin-Release Inhibiting Factor [*Also, PRIH*] [*Endocrinology*]
PIF .... Proliferation Inhibitory Factor [*Immunochemistry*]
PIF .... Provision of Industrial Facilities [*Army*] (AABC)
PIF .... Prudential Intermediate Income [*NYSE symbol*] (SPSG)
PIF .... Pseudo-Identification Feature (MCD)
PIF .... Punjab Irregular Force [*British military*] (DMA)
PIFAO ...... Publications. Institut Francais d'Archeologie Orientale du Caire [*A publication*]
PIFAO BEC ... Publications. Institut Francais d'Archeologie Orientale. Bibliotheque d'Etudes Coptes [*A publication*]
PIFAS....... Publicaciones. Instituto de Filologia. Anejo de Sphinx [*A publication*]
PIFEX....... Programmable Image Feature Extractor [*to provide real-time machine vision for the Martian Rover robot*] [*Jet Propulsion Laboratory*] (BYTE)
PIFF .... Punjab Irregular Frontier Force [*British military*] (DMA)
PIFI .... Piemonte Foods, Inc. [*NASDAQ symbol*] (NQ)
PIFI .... Pressure-Induced Intracranial Focal Ischemia [*Medicine*]
PIFLD .... Problemy Yadernoi Fiziki i Kosmicheskikh Luchei [*A publication*]
PIFMLL.... Proceedings. International Federation for Modern Languages and Literatures [*A publication*]
PIFOV ...... Planet in Field of View [*NASA*]
PIFR .... Peak Inspiratory Flow Rate [*Medicine*]
PIFS.......... Plume-Induced Flow Separation
PIFS.......... Post Infection Fatigue Syndrome [*Medicine*]
PIFS.......... Prime Item Fabrication Specification
PIFT .... Platelet Immunofluorescence Test [*Analytical biochemistry*]
PIFUA ...... Powerplant and Industrial Fuel Use Act of 1978
PIFWD ...... Prace Naukowe Instytutu Fizyki Politechniki Wroclawskiej [*A publication*]
PIG .... Glenn Mills School, Glenn Mills, PA [*OCLC symbol*] (OCLC)
PIG .... Pacific Institute of Geography
PIG .... Passive-Income Generator [*Investment term*]
PIG .... Pendulous Integrating Gyro
PIG .... Phillips Ionization Gauge
PIG .... Phosphatidylinositol Glycan [*Biochemistry*]
PIG .... Photo-Island Grid
Pig............. Pig Iron [*A publication*]
Pig............. Pigott's Common Recoveries [*3 eds.*] [*1739-92*] [*A publication*] (DLA)
PIG .... Pork Industry Gazette [*A publication*]
PIG .... Pride, Integrity, Guts [*Police alternative for the appellation applied to police by radical groups*]
PIG .... Process Ink Gamut [*Printing technology*]
PIG .... Production Image Generator (MCD)
PIG .... Production Installation Group [*Military*] (CAAL)
PIG .... Pulse Inert Gas
PIGA........ Pendulous Integrating Gyro Accelerometer
PIGBA...... Proceedings. Royal Institution of Great Britain [*A publication*]
Pig Judg.... Pigott's Foreign Judgments [*3rd ed.*] [*1908-09*] [*A publication*] (DLA)
PIGLET.... Purchase Information, Gifts, Loans, Exchanges Tracking [*Suggested name for the Library of Congress computer system*]
PIGM .... Pigmentum [*Paint*] [*Pharmacy*]
PIGMA...... Pressurized Inert Gas Metal Arc (KSC)

Pigm Cell ...	Pigment Cell [A publication]
Pigment Resin Tech ...	Pigment and Resin Technology [A publication]
Pigment Resin Technol ...	Pigment and Resin Technology [A publication]
PIGMI.......	Pion Generator for Medical Irradiation [Radiology]
PIGMI.......	Position Indicating General Measuring Instrument
Pig News Inf ...	Pig News and Information [A publication]
Pig & R.......	Pigott and Rodwell's English Registration Appeal Cases [1843-45] [A publication] (DLA)
Pig Rec.......	Pigott's Recoveries [England] [A publication] (DLA)
Pig Rsn Tech ...	Pigment and Resin Technology [A publication]
PIGS.........	Passive Infrared Guidance System [DoD]
PIGS.........	Poles, Italians, Greeks, and Slavs
PIGS.........	Portable Inertial Guidance System
PIGU........	Pendulous Integrating Gyro Unit
PIGWA......	Prace Instytutu Gospodarki Wodnej [A publication]
PIH...........	Permanent Income Hypothesis [Economics]
PIH...........	Phenylisopropylhydrazine [Pharmacology]
PIH...........	Pipeline Induction Heat [Industrial firm] [British]
PIH...........	Pocatello [Idaho] [Airport symbol] (OAG)
PIH...........	Pork Industry Handbook [A publication]
PIH...........	Pregnancy-Induced Hypertension [Gynecology]
PIH...........	Prolactin-Release Inhibiting Hormone [Endocrinology]
PIH...........	Public and Indian Housing [HUD]
PIH...........	St. Gabriel's Hall, Phoenixville, PA [OCLC symbol] (OCLC)
PIHANS...	Publications. Institut Historique et Archeologique Neerlandais de Stamboul [Leiden] [A publication]
PIHCA......	Polyisohexylcyanoacrylate [Antibacterial]
PIHM.......	Polish Institute of Hydrology and Meteorology
PIHUA	Prace Instytutow Hutniczych [A publication]
PII............	Fairbanks, AK [Location identifier] [FAA] (FAAL)
PII............	Pershing II [Army]
PII............	Positive Immittance Inverter (IEEE)
PII............	Primary Irritation Indices [for skin]
PII............	Printing Industry Institute [A graphic arts training school]
PII............	Procurement Instrument Identification (NG)
PII............	Pueblo International, Incorporated [NYSE symbol] (SPSG)
PII............	Sleighton School, Darling, PA [OCLC symbol] (OCLC)
PIIAA	Proceedings. National Institute of Sciences (India). Part A. Physical Sciences [A publication]
PIIC..........	Pergamon International Information Corporation [Information service or system] (IID)
PIIC..........	Pilgrim Intergroup Investment Corporation [NASDAQ symbol] (NQ)
PIICAV......	Convenio IICA-ZN-ROCAP [Instituto Interamericano de Ciencias Agricolas-Zona Norte-Regional Organization for Central America and Panama] Publicacion Miscelanea [A publication]
PIIF	Proteinase Inhibitor Inducing Factor [Biochemistry]
PIIM.........	Planned Interdependency Incentive Method
PIIN..........	Procurement Instruction Identification Number [Army] (AABC)
PIIN..........	Procurement Instrument Identification Number [Military]
PI/INT'L...	Packaging Institute International [Later, IoPP] (EA)
PIJ...........	Pickled-in-Jar [Food technology]
PIJAC.......	Pet Industry Joint Advisory Council (EA)
PIJR	Product Improvement Joint Review [Military]
PIK...........	Glasgow [Scotland] Prestwick Airport [Airport symbol] (OAG)
PIK...........	Payment in Kind
PIK...........	Pic Prospectors [Vancouver Stock Exchange symbol]
PIK...........	Portable Injection Kit
Pike...........	Pike's Reports [1-5 Arkansas] [A publication] (DLA)
Pike & F Adm Law ...	Pike and Fischer's Administrative Law [A publication] (DLA)
Pike & F Fed Rules Service ...	Pike and Fischer's Federal Rules Service [A publication] (DLA)
Pike & Fischer Admin Law ...	Pike and Fischer's Administrative Law [A publication] (DLA)
Pike H of L ...	Pike's History of the House of Lords [A publication] (DLA)
PIKM.......	PIK. Northern Magazine for Children [Northwest Territory, Canada] [A publication]
PIKS	American Sports Advisors, Inc. [NASDAQ symbol] (NQ)
PIL............	Brazos Santiago, TX [Location identifier] [FAA] (FAAL)
PIL............	Pair Inter Langues [Bourg La Reine, France] (EAIO)
PIL............	Papers in Linguistics [A publication]
PIL............	Parti de l'Independance et de la Liberte [Party for Independence and Liberty] [Congo] [Political party]
PIL............	Payment in Lieu
PIL............	Percentage Increase in Loss [Statistics]
PIL............	Petroleum Investors Depositary Receipts Units [NYSE symbol] (SPSG)
PIL...........	Pilar [Argentina] [Geomagnetic observatory code]
PIL...........	Pilar [Cordoba] [Seismograph station code, US Geological Survey] (SEIS)
PIL...........	Pilula [Pill] [Pharmacy]
PIL...........	Pistol Petroleum [Vancouver Stock Exchange symbol]
PIL...........	Pitt Interpretive Language [Data processing] (DIT)
PIL...........	Plastic Impregnated Laminate
PIL...........	Practice Instrument Landing (ADA)
PIL...........	Preferred Item List (RDA)
PIL...........	Processing Information List [Data processing]
PIL...........	Procurement Information Letter (MCD)
PIL............	Publications International Limited
PIL............	Purple Indicating Light (MSA)
PIL............	Purpose in Life [Personality development test] [Psychology]
PILA	Power Industry Laboratory Association (EA)
PILAC.......	Pulsed Ion Linear Accelerator
PILB.........	Passenger and Immigration Lists Bibliography [A publication]
PILC.........	Paper-Insulated, Lead-Covered Cable [Telecommunications]
PILC.........	Pilgrim Holdings Ltd. [Formerly, Pilgrim Coal Corp.] [NASDAQ symbol] (NQ)
PILC.........	Pillared Interlayered Clays [Catalysis technology]
PILC.........	Pregnancy and Infant Loss Center (EA)
PILI.........	Passenger and Immigration Lists Index [A publication]
PILL.........	Newport Dock [British depot code]
PILL.........	Programmed Instruction Language Learning [Data processing]
PILM........	Pillared Interlayered Montmorillonite [Catalysis technology]
PILO........	Public Information Liaison Officer [Military]
PILOA......	Prace Instytutu Lotnictwa [A publication]
PILOT.......	Paton Lyall Tosh [Rock music group]
PILOT	Payment in Lieu of Taxes
PILOT.......	Permutation Indexed Literature of Technology (IEEE)
PILOT.......	Piloted Low-Speed Test [Aerospace]
PILOT.......	Printing Industry Language for Operations of Typesetting
PILP	Parametric Integer Linear Program [Data processing]
PILP	Program of Industry/Laboratory Projects [National Research Council of Canada]
PILP	Pseudoinfinite, Logarithmically Periodic
PILS.........	Pilsener Lager (DSUE)
PILS.........	Precision Instrument Landing System
PILSA.......	Progress in Immunobiological Standardization [A publication]
PIL STA ...	Pilot Station [Nautical charts]
PILTA	Payment in Lieu of Taxes Act
PIm	Immaculata College, Immaculata, PA [Library symbol] [Library of Congress] (LCLS)
PIM	Pacem in Maribus [Secondary name for the International Ocean Institute] (MSC)
PIM	Pacific Islands Monthly [A publication] (APTA)
PIM	Pacific Rim Energy [Vancouver Stock Exchange symbol]
PIM	Parallel Inference Machine [Data processing]
PIM	Partners-in-Mission [Church of England]
PIM	Penalties in Minutes [Hockey]
PIM	Peripheral Interface Module
PIM	Personal Information Manager
Pi M	Pillius Medicinensis [Flourished, 1165-1207] [Authority cited in pre-1607 legal work] (DSA)
PIM	Pine Mountain, GA [Location identifier] [FAA] (FAAL)
PIM	Plan of Intended Movement (MUGU)
PIM	Plated Interconnecting Matrix
PIM	Plug-In Module (MCD)
PIM	Point of Intended Movement [Military]
PIM	Politica Internacional (Madrid) [A publication]
PIM	Polyphase Induction Motor
PIM	Position and Intended Movement [or Maneuver] (NATG)
PIM	Position in Miles (MCD)
PIM	Precision Indicator of the Meridian
PIM	Precision Instrument Mount
PIM	Presa Del Infiernillo [Mexico] [Seismograph station code, US Geological Survey] [Closed] (SEIS)
PIM	Pricing Instructions Memorandum (MCD)
PIM	Processor Interface Module
PIM	Product Information Memoranda
PIM	Program Integration Manual
PIM	Program Interface Module
PIM	Progress in Industrial Microbiology [Elsevier Book Series] [A publication]
PIM	Provincial Institute of Mining
PIM	Pulse Intensity Modulation
PIM	Pulse Interval Modulation
PIM	Putnam Master Intermediate Income Trust [NYSE symbol] (SPSG)
PIM	South Mountain Restoration Center, South Mountain, PA [OCLC symbol] (OCLC)
PiMA	Ateneo de Manila University, Manila, Philippines [Library symbol] [Library of Congress] (LCLS)
PIMA........	Paper Industry Management Association (EA)
PIMA........	Plug-In Module Assembly (MCD)
PIMA........	Polyisocyanurate Insulation Manufacturers Association (EA)
PIMA........	Prime Intermediate Maintenance Activity
PIMA........	Professional Insurance Mass-Marketing Association [Bethesda, MD] (EA)
PIMA Mag ...	PIMA [Paper Industry Management Association] Magazine [United States] [A publication]
PIMA Yrb ...	PIMA [Paper Industry Management Association] Yearbook [A publication]
PIMBel......	Pracy Instytuta Movaznaustva Akademii Nauk Belaruskaj SSR [A publication]
PIMCC	Packards International Motor Car Club (EA)
PIMCO......	Poultry Industry Manufacturers Council [Defunct] (EA)
PIME........	Petrofi Irodalmi Muzeum Evkonyve [A publication]
PIME........	Pontifical Institute for Mission Extension [Roman Catholic men's religious order]
PIMGA......	Production and Inventory Management [A publication]

PIMI.......... Preinactivation Material Inspection [*Military*]   (NVT)
PIMIA....... Potentiometric Ionophore Modulated Immunoassay
            [*Electrochemistry*]
PIMK........ Portable Injection Molding Kit
PIMM....... Pacific International Media Market [*Australia*]
PIMMA...... Professional Insurance Mass-Marketing Association [*Bethesda,
            MD*]   (EA)
PIMNY...... Printing Industries of Metropolitan New York
PIMO .... Presentation of Information for Maintenance and Operation
            [*DoD*]
PIMOS...... Parallel Inference Multiprocessor Operating System [*Data
            processing*]
PIMP........ Peroxisomal Integral Membrane Protein [*Biochemistry*]
PIMP......... Pimperne [*England*]
PIMRA...... Pirmasens Missile Repair Activity [*Federal Republic of
            Germany*] [*Army*]
PIMRA...... Progress in Industrial Microbiology [*A publication*]
PIMS........ Personnel Inventory Management System [*AT & T*]
PIMS........ Photoionization Mass Spectrometry
PIMS........ Profit Impact of Marketing Strategy
PIMS........ Programmable Implantable Medication System
PIMSA...... Prensa Independiente Mexicana Sociedad Anonima [*Press
            agency*] [*Mexico*]
PIMSST .... Pontifical Institute of Mediaeval Studies. Studies and Texts [*A
            publication*]
PIMST ...... Pontifical Institute of Mediaeval Studies. Studies and Texts [*A
            publication*]
PIMTB ...... Proceedings. Annual Technical Meeting. International
            Metallographic Society, Inc. [*A publication*]
Pim Ten ..... Pim on Feudal Tenures [*A publication*]   (DLA)
Pi Mu Epsilon J ... Pi Mu Epsilon Journal [*A publication*]
PIN .... Jasper, TX [*Location identifier*] [*FAA*]   (FAAL)
PIN .... P-Type Intrinsic N-Type [*or Positive-Intrinsic-Negative*]
PIN .... Page and Item Number
PIN .... Parallel Input
PIN .... Patriots Information Network   (EA)
PIN .... Pennsylvania School for the Deaf, Philadelphia, PA [*OCLC
            symbol*]   (OCLC)
PIN .... People in Need [*Food program sponsored by family of
            kidnapped heiress, Patricia Hearst, 1974*]
PIN .... Personal [*or Private*] Identification Number [*Banking*]
PIN .... Personal Information Network [*Indesys, Inc.*]
            [*Telecommunications service*]   (TSSD)
PIN .... Personal Injury Notice   (AAG)
PIN .... Piece Identification Number
PIN .... Pinedale [*Wyoming*] [*Seismograph station code, US Geological
            Survey*] [*Closed*]   (SEIS)
PIN .... Pinion   (MSA)
Pin............. Pinney's Wisconsin Supreme Court Reports [*1839-52*] [*A
            publication*]   (DLA)
PIN .... Plan Identification Number   (AFM)
PIN .... Plant Information Network [*Fish and Wildlife Service*] [*Ceased
            operation*]   (IID)
PIN .... Plastics Industry Notes [*Later, CIN*]
PIN .... Police Information Network [*San Francisco Bay area,
            California*]
PIN .... Policy Review [*A publication*]
PIN .... Position Indicator
PIN .... Positive-Intrinsic-Negative [*or P-Type Intrinsic N-Type*]
PIN .... Preliminary Imagery Nomination File   (MCD)
PIN .... Product Information Network [*McGraw-Hill Information
            Systems Co.*] [*Information service or system*]   (IID)
PIN .... Program Identification Number   (MUGU)
PIN .... Program Integrated Network
PIN .... Property Inheritance Network Computer
PIN .... Proposal Identification Number   (AAG)
PIN .... PSI Resources [*NYSE symbol*]   (SPSG)
PIN .... Public Interest [*A publication*]
PINA .... Parallax in Altitude [*Navigation*]
PINA .... Parenting in a Nuclear Age   (EA)
PINA .... Potash Institute of North America [*Later, PPI*]   (EA)
PINC........ Property Income Certificate [*Investment term*] [*Great Britain*]
PINCCA .... Price Index Numbers for Current Cost Accounting [*Service in
            Information and Analysis*] [*Great Britain*] [*Information
            service or system*]   (IID)
PIND .... Particle Impact Noise Detection
Pind........... Pindar [*518-438BC*] [*Classical studies*]   (OCD)
PINE.......... Passive Infrared Night Equipment   (MCD)
Pineal Res Rev ... Pineal Research Reviews [*A publication*]
Pineapple Q ... Pineapple Quarterly [*A publication*]
PINEDV.... Annual Research Reviews. Pineal [*A publication*]
Pine Inst Am Abstr Chem Sect ... Pine Institute of America. Abstracts.
            Chemical Section [*A publication*]
Pine Inst Am Tech Bull ... Pine Institute of America. Technical Bulletin [*A
            publication*]
Pinell.......... [*Arius*] Pinellus [*Flourished, 1544-59*] [*Authority cited in pre-
            1607 legal work*]   (DSA)
PINES .... Public Information on Nuclear Energy Service [*American
            Nuclear Society*]
PING .... Packet Internet Groper [*Computer program*]   (PCM)

Ping Chat Mortg ... Pingrey's Treatise of Chattel Mortgages [*A
            publication*]   (DLA)
PINGP....... Prairie Island Nuclear Generating Plant   (NRCH)
PINH .... Pyridoxal Isonicotinoylhydrazone [*Biochemistry*]
PINHA3 .... Iraq Natural History Museum. Publication [*A publication*]
PINN .... Pinnacles National Monument
Pinn........... Pinney's Wisconsin Reports [*A publication*]   (DLA)
PINN .... Proposed International Nonproprietary Name [*Drug research*]
Pinney .... Pinney's Wisconsin Reports [*A publication*]   (DLA)
Pinney (sv) ... Pinney's Wisconsin Reports [*A publication*]   (DLA)
PINO .... Positive Input - Negative Output [*Data processing*]
PINS.......... Personnel Information System [*Army*]   (AABC)
PINS.......... Persons in Need of Supervision [*Classification for delinquent
            children*]
PINS......... Point-in-Space   (MCD)
PINS.......... Political Information System [*Databank of political strategist
            Richard Wirthlin*]
PINS.......... Portable Inertial Navigation System
PINS.......... Precise Integrated Navigation System [*Offshore Systems of
            Vancouver*]
PINSAC .... PINS [*Portable Inertial Navigation System*] Alignment Console
PINSTD .... Preinserted
PINT........ Pioneer International Corp. [*NASDAQ symbol*]   (NQ)
PINT........ Purdue Interpretive Programming and Operating
            System   (MCD)
Pint Acabados Ind ... Pinturas y Acabados Industriales [*A publication*]
PINTS .... Ported-Coax Intrusion Sensor [*Military*]   (INF)
PInU .... Indiana University of Pennsylvania, Indiana, PA [*Library
            symbol*] [*Library of Congress*]   (LCLS)
Pin (Wis) .... Pinney's Wisconsin Reports [*A publication*]   (DLA)
Pin Wis R... Pinney's Wisconsin Reports [*A publication*]   (DLA)
PINX........ Pinxit [*He, or She, Painted It*] [*Latin*]
PINXT....... Pinxit [*He, or She, Painted It*] [*Latin*]   (ROG)
PINY........ Polytechnic Institute of New York
PIO .... Palestine Information Office   (EA)
PIO .... Parallel Input/Output
PIO .... Pheniminooxazolidinone [*Pharmacology*]
PIO .... Photo Interpretation Officer [*Air Force*]
PIO .... Pi Omicron National Sorority   (EA)
PIO .... Pielago [*Ship's rigging*]   (ROG)
PIO .... Pilot-Induced Oscillation
PIO .... Pilot Information Office
PIO .... Pinon, NM [*Location identifier*] [*FAA*]   (FAAL)
PIO .... Pioneer Airlines, Inc. [*Denver, CO*] [*FAA designator*]   (FAAC)
PIO .... Pioneer Electronic Corp. [*NYSE symbol*]   (SPSG)
PIO .... Poets International Organisation [*Bangalore, India*]   (EAIO)
PIO .... Position Iterative Operation
PIO .... Precision Interactive Operation [*Data processing*]
PIO .... Private Input/Output [*Telecommunications*]   (TEL)
PIO .... Processor Input-Output [*Data processing*]   (MDG)
PIO .... Programmed Input/Output
PIO .... Provisioned Item Order   (MCD)
PIO .... Public Information Office [*or Officer*]
PIO .... Western Pennsylvania School for the Deaf, Pittsburgh, PA
            [*OCLC symbol*]   (OCLC)
PIOCA...... Progress in Inorganic Chemistry [*A publication*]
PIOCS .... Physical Input-Output Control System [*Data
            processing*]   (BUR)
PIOG .... [*The*] Pioneer Group, Inc. [*NASDAQ symbol*]   (NQ)
PION .... Pioneer   (AABC)
PION .... Pioneer Finance Corp. [*NASDAQ symbol*]   (NQ)
Pioneering Concepts Mod Sci ... Pioneering Concepts in Modern Science [*A
            publication*]
Pioneers' Assoc of SA Pubs ... Pioneers' Association of South Australia.
            Publications [*A publication*]   (APTA)
PIOP......... Pharmacists in Ophthalmic Practice   (EA)
PIOPIC ..... Protection and Indemnity of Oil Pollution Indemnity Clause
            [*Insurance*]   (DS)
PIOS......... Pioneer-Standard Electronics, Inc. [*NASDAQ symbol*]   (NQ)
PIOSA....... Pan-Indian Ocean Science Association   (NOAA)
PIOTA....... Post Irradiation Open Test Assembly [*Nuclear
            energy*]   (NRCH)
PIOTA....... Proximity Instrumented Open Test Assembly [*Nuclear
            energy*]   (NRCH)
PIOU .... Parallel Input-Output Unit [*Data processing*]   (IEEE)
PIP............ Pan-Iranist Party [*Political party*]   (PPW)
PIP............ Para-Isothiocyanatephenethylamine [*Biochemistry*]
PIP............ Partido Independentista Puertorriqueno [*Puerto Rican
            Independence Party*] [*Political party*]   (PPW)
PIP............ Partners in Progress [*Government*] [*Civil rights*]
PIP............ Pasuquin [*Philippines*] [*Seismograph station code, US
            Geological Survey*]   (SEIS)
PIP............ Path Independent Protocol
PIP............ Payload Integration Plan [*NASA*]   (NASA)
PIP............ Payload Interface Plan [*NASA*]   (NASA)
PIP............ Payment in Part [*Business term*]
PIP............ Penny Illustrated Paper [*A publication*]
PIP............ Peripheral Interchange Program [*Data processing*]
PIP............ Peripheral Interface Programmer [*Circuit*] [*Data processing*]
PIP............ Persistent Internal Polarization
PIP............ Personal Identification Project [*Data processing*]

PIP............ Personal Injury Protection [*Insurance*]
PIP............ Personal Innovation Program
PIP............ Personnel Interface Processor   (MCD)
PIP............ Petroleum Incentives Program [*Canada*]
PIP............ Phosphatidylinositol Phosphate [*Biochemistry*]
PIP............ Photo Image Processor   (MCD)
PIP............ Photo Interpretive Program   (BUR)
PIP............ Picture-in-a-Picture [*Multi-Vision Products*] [*Video technology*]
PIP............ Pilot Point [*Alaska*] [*Airport symbol*]   (OAG)
PIP............ Piperacillin [*An antibiotic*]
PIP............ Plant Instrumentation Program
PIP............ Plant-in-Place
PIP............ Policy Improvement Program
PIP............ Policy Integration Program
PIP............ Population Information Program [*Later, CCP*]   (EA)
PIP............ Portable Instrumentation Package [*Military*]   (CAAL)
PIP............ Position Indicating Probe   (IEEE)
PIP............ Postal Instant Press [*AMEX symbol*]   (SPSG)
PIP............ Power Input Panel
PIP............ Prearrival Inspection Procedure
PIP............ Precise Installation Position
PIP............ Predicted Impact Point [*Aerospace*]   (AAG)
PIP............ Predicted Intercept Point
PIP............ Preliminary Information Pamphlet
PIP............ Preparatory Investment Protection [*For the consortia which invested in deep sea mining*]
PIP............ Preparedness and Industrial Planning
PIP............ Pretty Important Person
PIP............ Primary Indicating Position Data Logger   (IEEE)
PIP............ Prior Immobilization and Positioning [*Roentgenology*]
PIP............ Probabilistic Information Processing
PIP............ Problem Identification Program   (MCD)
PIP............ Problem Input Preparation [*Data processing*]   (BUR)
PIP............ Procedural Information Pamphlet
PIP............ Proceedings in Print [*A bibliographic publication*]
PIP............ Product Improvement   (MCD)
PIP............ Product Improvement Plan
PIP............ Product Improvement Program [*Military*]
PIP............ Product Improvement Program [*A publication*]
PIP............ Product Improvement Proposal   (MCD)
PIP............ Product Introductory Presentation
PIP............ Production Implementation Program   (AAG)
PIP............ Production Improvement Program [*Navy*]   (NG)
PIP............ Production Instrumentation Package   (NASA)
PIP............ Productivity Improvement Program [*Department of Labor*]
PIP............ Profile Ignition Pick-Up [*Automotive engineering*]
PIP............ Profit Improvement Program
PIP............ Program Implementation Plan   (MCD)
PIP............ Program Integration Plan
PIP............ Program in Process [*Data processing*]   (BUR)
PIP............ Programmable Integrated Processor   (IEEE)
PIP............ Programmable Interconnect Point [*Data processing*]
PIP............ Programs for the Improvement of Practice [*Washington, DC*] [*Department of Education*]   (GRD)
PIP............ Progressive Inspection Plan [*Navy*]   (NG)
PIP............ Project Implementation Plan
PIP............ Project on Information Processing   (IEEE)
PIP............ Project Initiation Period
PIP............ Projected Impact Point [*Aviation*]
PIP............ Proof in Print
PIP............ Proposal Instruction Package   (MCD)
PIP............ Proprietary Information Protection
PIP............ Prototypic Inlet Piping [*Nuclear energy*]   (NRCH)
PIP............ Prove in Place   (MCD)
PIP............ Proximal Interphalangeal [*Joint*]
PIP............ Psychotic Inpatient Profile [*Psychology*]
PIP............ Public and Institutional Property [*Insurance*]
PIP............ Puerto Rican Independence Party   (PD)
PIP............ Pulse Input Proportional [*Electro-optical system*]
PIP............ Pulse Integrating Pendulum
PIP............ Western Psychiatric Institute and Clinic, University of Pittsburgh, Pittsburgh, PA [*OCLC symbol*]   (OCLC)
PIPA......... Pacific Industrial Property Association   (EA)
PIPA......... Pulse Integrating Pendulum Accelerometer
PIPA......... Pulse Integrating Pendulum Assembly   (NASA)
PIPACE..... Peacetime Intelligence Plan, Allied Central Europe [*NATO*]   (NATG)
Pip & C Mil L ... Pipon and Collier's Military Law [*3rd ed.*] [*1865*] [*A publication*]   (DLA)
PIPE .... IPM, Inc. [*NASDAQ symbol*]   (NQ)
PIPE .... Pipeline. Report of the Northern Pipeline Agency [*A publication*]
PIPE .... Pipestone National Monument
PIPE .... Plumbing Industry Progress and Education Fund
PIPECO .... Photoion-Photoelectron Coincidence [*Spectroscopy*]
Pipeline Contractors Assoc Can ... Pipeline Contractors Association of Canada [*A publication*]
Pipe Line D ... Pipeline Annual Directory and Equipment Guide [*A publication*]
Pipeline Eng ... Pipeline Engineer [*A publication*]

Pipeline Gas J ... Pipeline and Gas Journal [*A publication*]
Pipeline & Gas J ... Pipeline and Gas Journal [*A publication*]
Pipe Line Ind ... Pipe Line Industry [*A publication*]
Pipeline Manage Oper Eng Gas Distrib News ... Pipeline Management, Operations, Engineering, and Gas Distribution News [*A publication*]
Pipeline Underground Util Constr ... Pipeline and Underground Utilities Construction [*A publication*]
Pipeln Ind .. International Pipe Line Industry [*A publication*]
PIPER........ Pulsed Intense Plasma for Exploratory Research
PIPES........ Piperazinediethanesulfonic Acid [*A buffer*]
PIPES........ Program on International Politics, Economics, and Security [*University of Chicago*]
Pipes & Pipelines Int ... Pipes and Pipelines International [*A publication*]
Pipes Pipelines Int ... Pipes and Pipelines International [*A publication*]
PIPICO ..... Panel on International Programs and International Cooperation in Oceans Affairs [*Department of State*]   (NOAA)
PIPIDA ..... Para-Isopropylphenyl(iminodiacetic Acid)
Piping Eng ... Piping Engineering [*A publication*]
Piping Process Mach (Tokyo) ... Piping and Process Machinery (Tokyo) [*A publication*]
PIPJ.......... Proximal Interphalangeal Joint [*Anatomy*]
PIPLC........ Phosphatidylinositol-Specific Phospholipase C [*Biochemistry*]
PIPLD .... Proceedings. Indian Academy of Sciences. Series Plant Sciences [*A publication*]
PIPO.......... Parallel-In Parallel-Out [*Telecommunications*]   (TEL)
PIPO.......... Phase-In, Phase-Out   (MCD)
PIPPAP..... Pile for Producing Power and Plutonium [*Nuclear energy*]   (NRCH)
PIPPS........ Publication Information Processing and Printing System
Pippy.......... Person Inheriting Parents' Property [*Lifestyle classification*] [*British*]
PIPR .... Piper Jaffray, Inc. [*Minneapolis, MN*] [*NASDAQ symbol*]   (NQ)
PIPR .... Plant-in-Place Records
PIPR .... Polytechnic Institute of Puerto Rico
PIPR .... Public Interest Public Relations   (EA)
PIPS........ Paperless Item Processing System [*Banking*]
PIPS........ Pattern Information Processing System
PIPS........ Peabody Intellectual Performance Scale [*Education*]
PIPS........ Postinjection Propulsion Subsystem [*NASA*]
PIPS........ Preschool Interpersonal Problem Solving Test
PIPS........ Professional Institute of the Public Service of Canada [*See also IPFP*]
PIPS.......... Properties of Irregular Parts System   (MCD)
PIPS.......... Science and Technology Policies Information Exchange Programme [*Superseded by SPINES*] [*UNESCO*] [*Information service or system*]   (IID)
PIPSCR ..... Philippine Islands Public Service Commission Reports [*A publication*]   (DLA)
PIPSD........ Preprint. Institut Prikladnoi Matematiki Akademii Nauk SSSR [*A publication*]
PIPUCR .... Philippine Islands Public Utility Commission Reports [*A publication*]   (DLA)
PIPWA ...... Paper Industry and Paper World [*A publication*]
PIPYDX .... Proceedings. International Colloquium on Invertebrate Pathology [*A publication*]
PIQ .... Parallel Instruction Queue
PIQ .... Plant Inspection and Quarantine [*Australia*]
PIQ .... Program Idea Quotient [*Study to determine audience receptivity to new TV program*]
PIQ .... Property in Question
PIQ .... State Regional Correctional Facility at Mercer, Mercer, PA [*OCLC symbol*]   (OCLC)
PIQA .... Proofing, Inspection, and Quality Assurance [*Military*]
PIQSY ...... Probes for the International Quiet Solar Year [*OSS*]
PIQUA ...... Pit and Quarry [*A publication*]
PIR............ Pacific Islands Regiments [*Australia*]
PIR............ Packaging Information Record   (MCD)
PIR............ Parachute Infantry Regiment [*Military*]
PIR............ Paragnostic Information Retrieval [*Parapsychology*]
PIR............ Partido de la Izquierda Revolucionaria [*Party of the Revolutionary Left*] [*Bolivia*] [*Political party*]   (PPW)
PIR............ Past in Review   (EA)
PIR............ Peak Intensity Ratio [*Spectroscopy*]
PiR............ Pecat' i Revoljucija [*A publication*]
PIR............ Pennsylvania Rehabilitation Center, Johnstown, PA [*OCLC symbol*]   (OCLC)
PIR............ Periodic Incremental Release [*Physiology*]
PIR............ Periodic Intelligence Report
PIR............ Periodic Intelligence Review [*Supreme Allied Commander, Atlantic*]   (NATG)
PIR............ Personal Interview Record
PIR............ Personnel Information Roster [*Military*]
PIR............ Pesticide Ingredient Review Program [*Chemical Specialties Manufacturers Association*]
PIR............ Petrolite Irradiation Reactor
PIR............ Philippine Independence Ribbon [*Military decoration*]
PIR............ Phoenix International Raceway
PIR............ Photo Interpretation Report [*Air Force*]   (AFM)
PIR............ Photographic Intelligence Report [*Military*]

PIR............ Pier 1 Imports [*NYSE symbol*] (SPSG)
PIR............ Pierre [*South Dakota*] [*Airport symbol*] (OAG)
PIR............ Pirmasens [*Federal Republic of Germany*] [*Seismograph station code, US Geological Survey*] (SEIS)
PIR............ Plug-In Relay
PIR............ Postinhibitory Rebound [*Physiology*]
PIR............ Precision Instrument Runway [*Aviation*] (FAAC)
PIR............ Precision Instrumentation RADAR
PIR............ Predicted Intercept Range [*Military*] (CAAL)
PIR............ Pressure Ignition Rocket (NATG)
PIR............ Primary Intelligence Requirement [*Military*] (INF)
PIR............ Priority Information Requirement [*Military intelligence*] (INF)
PIR............ Process and Indoctrinate Recruits
PIR............ Procurement Initiation Request (MCD)
PIR............ Product Improvement Review
PIR............ Product Information Release
PIR............ Production Inspection Record
PIR............ Professional Investor Report [*A publication*] (IT)
PIR............ Program Incident Report
PIR............ Project Independence Report
PIR............ Prosopographia Imperii Romani [*A publication*]
PIR............ Protein Identification Resource [*National Biomedical Research Foundation*] [*Georgetown University Medical Center*] [*Information service or system*] (IID)
PIR............ Pure India Rubber [*Cables*]
PIRA.......... Prison Industries Reorganization Administration [*Terminated, 1940*]
PIRA.......... Provisional Irish Republican Army
PIRAD........ Proximity Information, Range, and Disposition
PIRAZ........ Positive Identification RADAR Advisory Zone (NVT)
PIRB.......... Position Indicating Radio Beacon
PIRC.......... Pier 1 Imports, Inc. [*NASDAQ symbol*] (NQ)
PIRC.......... Portable Inflatable Recompression Chamber (MCD)
PIRC.......... Preventive Intervention Research Center for Child Health [*Yeshiva University*] [*Research center*] (RCD)
PIRCS........ Passive Infrared Confirming Sensor (MCD)
PIRD.......... Program Instrumentation Requirements Document [*NASA*]
PIRE.......... Pacific Institute for Research and Evaluation [*Research center*] (RCD)
PIRED........ Power Industry Research [*A publication*]
PI Rep........ Philippine Island Reports [*A publication*] (DLA)
PIREP........ Pilot Report [*Pertaining to meteorological conditions*] [*FAA*]
PIRF.......... Perimeter-Insulated Raised Floor [*Residential construction*]
PIRFC........ Pilot Requests Forecast (FAAC)
PIRG.......... Public Interest Research Group [*Formed by consumer-advocate Ralph Nader*]
PIRI.......... Psychologists Interested in Religious Issues (EA)
PIRID........ Passive Infrared Intrusion Detector (NVT)
PIRINC...... Petroleum Industry Research Foundation (EA)
PIRN.......... Preliminary Interface Revision Notice [*NASA*] (KSC)
PIRO.......... People, Ideas, Resources, Objectives [*Management strategy*] (DHSM)
PIRO.......... Pictured Rocks National Lakeshore [*National Park Service designation*]
PIRP.......... Provisional International Reference Preparation
PIRR.......... Parts Installation and Removal Record [*NASA*] (KSC)
PIRR.......... Problem Investigation and Repair Record [*NASA*] (KSC)
PIRR.......... PWRS [*Prepositioned War Reserve Stock*] Interrogation and Readiness Reporting System [*Navy*]
PIRRB........ Photo Intelligence Requirements Review Board [*Military*]
PIRS.......... Personal Information Retrieval System
PIRS.......... Perspectives in Religious Studies [*A publication*]
PIRS.......... Philosopher's Information Retrieval System [*Bowling Green State University*]
PIRS.......... Pollution Incident Reporting System [*Coast Guard*]
PIRS.......... Poseidon Information Retrieval System [*Missiles*]
PIRS.......... Project Information Retrieval System [*HEW*]
PIRT.......... Precision Infrared Tracking
PIRT.......... Precision Infrared Triangulation
Pis............. In Pisonem [*of Cicero*] [*Classical studies*] (OCD)
PIS............ Parts Identification Service
PIS............ Passenger Information System
PIS............ Passive Infrared System
PIS............ Photographic Interpretation Section
PIS............ Pisa [*Italy*] [*Seismograph station code, US Geological Survey*] [*Closed*] (SEIS)
PIS............ Piscivorous
PIS............ Poitiers [*France*] [*Airport symbol*] (OAG)
PIS............ Position Indicator System
PIS............ Positive Ion Source
PIS............ Postal Inspection Service
PIS............ Preinfarction Syndrome [*Cardiology*]
PIS............ Preinsert Sequencing
PIS............ Pressure-Indicating Switch [*Nuclear energy*] (NRCH)
PIS............ Process Instrument Sheet
PIS............ Process Instrumentation System [*Nuclear energy*] (NRCH)
PIS............ Product Information Specialist
PIS............ Provisional International Standard
PIS............ Pulse Integration System
PIS............ Pulsed Illumination Source
PiS............. Puskin i Ego Sovremenniki [*A publication*]

PIS............ Stevens Trade School, Lancaster, PA [*OCLC symbol*] (OCLC)
PISA.......... Persistent Information Space Architecture [*Data processing*]
PISA.......... Polish Independent Student Association (EA)
PISA.......... Public Interest Satellite Association [*Defunct*] (EA)
PISAA7...... Indian Academy of Sciences. Proceedings. Section A [*A publication*]
PISAB........ Pulse Interference Separation and Blanking [*RADAR*]
PISAD........ Proceedings. International Symposium on Automotive Technology and Automation [*A publication*]
PISBAA..... Indian Academy of Sciences. Proceedings. Section B [*A publication*]
PISC.......... Pacific International Services Corporation [*NASDAQ symbol*] (NQ)
PISC.......... Parris Island, South Carolina [*Marine Corps*]
PISC.......... Petroleum Industry Security Council (EA)
PISC.......... Philippine International Shipping Corp. (DS)
Pisc........... Pisces [*Constellation*]
PISE.......... No Pilot Balloon Observation Due to Unfavorable Sea Conditions [*National Weather Service*] (FAAC)
PISEAJ...... Proceedings. Research Institute of Pomology [*Skierniewice, Poland*]. Series E. Conferences and Symposia [*A publication*]
PISG.......... Pitcairn Islands Study Group (EA)
PISH.......... Program Instrumentation Summary Handbook [*NASA*] (KSC)
Pishch Pererabatyvayushchaya Promst ... Pishchevaya i Pererabatyvayushchaya Promyshlenost' [*A publication*]
Pishch Prom Kaz ... Pishchevaya Promyshlennost Kazakhstana [*A publication*]
Pishch Promst Kaz Mezhved Resp Nauchno Tekh Sb ... Pishchevaya Promyshlennost Kazakhstana Mezhvedomstvennyi Respublikanskii Nauchno Tekhnicheskii Sbornik [*A publication*]
Pishch Prom-St (Kiev 1965) ... Pishchevaya Promyshlennost (Kiev, 1965) [*A publication*]
Pishch Promst (Moscow) ... Pishchevaya Promyshlennost (Moscow) [*A publication*]
Pishch Prom-St' Nauchno-Proizvod Sb ... Pishchevaya Promyshlennost Nauchno-Proizvodstvennyi Sbornik [*A publication*]
Pishch Promst Ser 6 Obz Inf ... Pishchevaya Promyshlennost. Seriya 6. Maslo-Zhirovaya Promyshlennost. Obzornaya Informatsiya [*A publication*]
Pishch Promst Ser 20 Obz Inf ... Pishchevaya Promyshlennost. Seriya 20. Maslo-Zhirovaya Promyshlennost. Obzornaya Informatsiya [*A publication*]
Pishch Promst SSSR ... Pishchevaya Promyshlennost SSSR [*A publication*]
Pis'ma Astron Zh ... Pis'ma v Astronomicheskii Zhurnal [*A publication*]
Pis'ma v Astron Zh ... Pis'ma v Astronomicheskii Zhurnal [*A publication*]
Pis'ma Zh Eksp Teor Fiz ... Pis'ma v Zhurnal Eksperimental'noi i Teoreticheskoi Fiziki [*A publication*]
Pis'ma v Zh Eksp i Teor Fiz ... Pis'ma v Zhurnal Eksperimental'noi i Teoreticheskoi Fiziki [*A publication*]
Pis'ma v Zh Tekh Fiz ... Pis'ma v Zhurnal Tekhnicheskoi Fiziki [*A publication*]
Pis'ma Zh Tekh Fiz ... Pis'ma v Zhurnal Tekhnicheskoi Fiziki [*A publication*]
Pism Pam Vostoka ... Pis'mennye Pamiatniki Vostoka [*A publication*]
PISO.......... Parallel-In Serial-Out [*Telecommunications*] (TEL)
PISO.......... Philippine Investments Systems Organization (DS)
PISP.......... Pipe Springs National Monument
PISSC........ Programme International sur la Securite des Substances Chimiques [*International Programme on Chemical Safety*] (EAIO)
PIST.......... Piston [*Automotive engineering*]
Pist........... Piston's Mauritius Reports [*A publication*] (DLA)
Piston........ Piston's Mauritius Reports [*A publication*] (DLA)
PISW......... Process Interrupt Status Word
PIT............ Pacific Investment Trust [*Finance*] [*British*]
PI/T.......... Parallel Interface/Timer [*Motorola, Inc.*]
PIT............ Part-Time, Intermittent, Temporary [*Nuclear energy*]
PIT............ Parti de l'Independance et du Travail [*Party of Independence and Labor*] [*Senegal*] [*Political party*] (PPW)
PIT............ Performance Improvement Tests
PIT............ Peripheral Input Tape [*Data processing*]
PIT............ Peripheral Interface Tests (MCD)
PIT............ Permanent Income Theory [*Econometrics*]
PIT............ Personal Income Tax
PIT............ Phase Inversion Temperature [*Physical Chemistry*]
PIT............ Photographic Interpretation Technique
PIT............ Picture Identification Test [*Psychology*]
PIT............ Picture Impressions Test [*Psychology*]
PIT............ Pilot Instructor Training [*Aviation*] (FAAC)
PIT............ Pirates Gold Corp. [*Vancouver Stock Exchange symbol*]
PIT............ Pittsburgh [*Pennsylvania*] [*Airport symbol*]
PIT............ Pittsburgh [*Pennsylvania*] [*Seismograph station code, US Geological Survey*] [*Closed*] (SEIS)
PIT............ Plasma Iron Transport [*Hematology*]
PIT............ Polar Ionospheric Trough
PIT............ Polaris Industrial Team [*Missiles*]
PIT............ Pre-Induction Training
PIT............ Preinstallation Test [*NASA*] (KSC)
PIT............ Prevailing-In Torque [*Automotive engineering*]
PIT............ Print Illegal and Trace

PIT............. Processing of Indexing Terms
PIT............. Product Improvement Test
PIT............. Program Instruction Tape [*Data processing*]   (IEEE)
PIT............. Programmable Interval Timer
PIT............. Programmed Instruction Text
PIT............. Projected Inactive Time [*Data processing*]
PIT............. Provincial Institute of Textiles
PIT............. Psychological Insight Test [*Psychometrics*]
PIT............. Public Information Terminal [*Australia*]
PIT............. University of Pittsburgh, Pittsburgh, PA [*OCLC symbol*]   (OCLC)
PITA......... Pacific International Trapshooting Association   (EA)
PITA......... Provincial Institute of Technology and Art
Pitanie Udobr Rast ... Pitanie i Udobrenie Rastenii [*A publication*]
PITB......... Pacific Inland Tariff Bureau
PITB......... PUSH [*People United to Save Humanity*] International Trade Bureau   (EA)
PITBB....... Piano Teachers Journal [*A publication*]
Pitblado Lect ... Isaac Pitblado Lectures on Continuing Legal Education [*A publication*]
Pitblado Lect ... Isaac Pitblado's Lectures on Continuing Legal Education [*A publication*]   (DLA)
PITC......... Phenylisothiocyanate [*Organic chemistry*]
PITC......... Philippine International Trading Corporation   (GEA)
PITC......... Photoinduced Tunnel Current
Pitc............. Pitcairn's Criminal Trials [*1488-1624*] [*Scotland*] [*A publication*]   (DLA)
Pitc Crim Tr ... Pitcairn's Ancient Criminal Trials [*Scotland*] [*A publication*]   (DLA)
Pitch Pine Nat ... Pitch Pine Naturalist [*A publication*]
PITCOM... Parliamentary Information Technology Committee [*Political communications*] [*British*]
Pitc Tr........ Pitcairn's Criminal Trials [*3 Scotland*] [*A publication*]   (DLA)
PITE......... Project on Information Technology and Education   (EA)
PITG......... Payload Integration Task Group [*NASA*]   (NASA)
PITI.......... Principal, Interest, Taxes, Insurance [*Real estate*]
Pitisc Lex ... Pitisci's Lexicon [*A publication*]   (DLA)
PITKA ...... Proceedings. Institut Teknologi Bandung. Supplement [*A publication*]
Pit L .... University of Pittsburgh. Law Review [*A publication*]
Pitm Prin & Sur ... Pitman on Principal and Surety [*A publication*]   (DLA)
PITN......... Polyisothianaphthene [*Organic chemistry*]
Pit & Quar ... Pit and Quarry [*A publication*]
Pit Quarry ... Pit and Quarry [*A publication*]
PITR......... Plasma Iron Transport [*or Turnover*] Rate [*Hematology*]
PITS .... Passive Intercept Tracking System
PITS .... Payload Integration Test Set [*NASA*]   (MCD)
PITS .... Photoinduced Transient Spectroscopy
PITS .... Propulsion Integration Test Stand
Pit Sur........ Pitman on Principal and Surety [*1840*] [*A publication*]   (DLA)
Pitt .... Pittsburgh, PA   (DLA)
PITT .... Polaris Integrated Test Team [*Missiles*]
Pitt Bank.... Pitt's Bankruptcy Acts [*A publication*]   (DLA)
Pitt CC Pr .. Pitt's County Court Practice [*A publication*]   (DLA)
Pitt LJ....... Pittsburgh Legal Journal [*A publication*]   (DLA)
Pitt Rivers Mus Univ Oxford Occas Pap Technol ... Pitt Rivers Museum. University of Oxford. Occasional Papers on Technology [*A publication*]
Pitts............ Pittsburgh, PA   (DLA)
Pitts............ Pittsburgh Reports [*A publication*]   (DLA)
Pittsb.......... Pittsburgh, PA   (DLA)
Pittsb.......... Pittsburgh Reports [*A publication*]   (DLA)
Pittsb Bs T ... Pittsburgh Business Times-Journal [*A publication*]
Pittsbg Bs... Pittsburgh Business Review [*A publication*]
Pittsbg P .... Pittsburgh Press [*A publication*]
Pittsb Leg J ... Pittsburgh Legal Journal [*Pennsylvania*] [*A publication*]   (DLA)
Pittsb Leg J NS ... Pittsburgh Legal Journal, New Series [*Pennsylvania*] [*A publication*]   (DLA)
Pittsb Leg J (OS) ... Pittsburgh Legal Journal, Old Series [*A publication*]   (DLA)
Pittsb Leg J (PA) ... Pittsburgh Legal Journal [*Pennsylvania*] [*A publication*]   (DLA)
Pittsb LJ .... Pittsburgh Legal Journal [*Pennsylvania*] [*A publication*]   (DLA)
Pittsb L Rev ... Pittsburgh Law Review [*A publication*]   (DLA)
Pittsb R (PA) ... Pittsburgh Reporter [*Pennsylvania*] [*A publication*]   (DLA)
Pittsburgh Bus R ... Pittsburgh Business Review [*A publication*]
Pittsburgh Leg J ... Pittsburgh Legal Journal [*Pennsylvania*] [*A publication*]   (DLA)
Pittsburgh Leg Journal ... Pittsburgh Legal Journal [*Pennsylvania*] [*A publication*]   (DLA)
Pittsburgh Sch ... Pittsburgh Schools [*A publication*]
Pittsburgh Univ Bull ... Pittsburgh University. Bulletin [*A publication*]
Pittsburgh Univ Sch Ed J ... Pittsburgh University. School of Education Journal [*A publication*]
Pitts Leg J ... Pittsburgh Legal Journal [*Pennsylvania*] [*A publication*]   (DLA)
Pitts Leg J (NS) ... Pittsburgh Legal Journal, New Series [*Pennsylvania*] [*A publication*]   (DLA)
Pitts Leg Jour ... Pittsburgh Legal Journal [*Pennsylvania*] [*A publication*]   (DLA)

Pitts LJ ..... Pittsburgh Legal Journal [*A publication*]   (DLA)
Pitts LJ (NS) ... Pittsburgh Legal Journal, New Series [*A publication*]   (DLA)
Pitts L Rev ... University of Pittsburgh. Law Review [*A publication*]
Pitts R .... Pittsburgh Reports [*Pennsylvania*] [*A publication*]   (DLA)
Pitts Rep .... Pittsburgh Reports [*A publication*]   (DLA)
Pitts Rep (PA) ... Pittsburgh Reports [*Pennsylvania*] [*A publication*]   (DLA)
Pitt Sym .... Pittsburgh Symphony Orchestra. Program Notes [*A publication*]
Pitture Vern ... Pitture e Vernici [*A publication*]
PITU......... Pipe or Tubing [*Freight*]
PITY-EM .. Principal, Interest, Taxes, Energy, and Maintenance [*Real estate*]
PIU .... East Pennsylvania Psychiatric Institute, Philadelphia, PA [*OCLC symbol*]   (OCLC)
PIU .... Path Information Unit [*Data processing*]
PIU .... Photographic Interpretation Unit [*Marine Corps*]
PIU .... Pilot Information Utilization
PIU .... Piura [*Peru*] [*Airport symbol*]   (OAG)
PIU .... Plug-In Unit
PIU .... Polymerase-Inducing Unit
PIU .... Power Intercept Unit [*Military*]   (CAAL)
PIU .... Power Interface Unit   (MCD)
PIU .... Private Lines Unlimited   (EA)
PIU .... Process Input Unit [*Data processing*]   (BUR)
PIU .... Process Interface Unit
PIU .... Programmer Interface Unit   (MCD)
PIU .... Pyrotechnic Initiator Unit   (MCD)
PiU .... University of the Philippines, Quezon City, Philippines [*Library symbol*] [*Library of Congress*]   (LCLS)
PIUG .... Parti Independantiste de l'Unite Guyanaise [*Pro-Independence Party of Guyanese Unity*] [*Political party*]   (PPW)
PIUMP..... Plug-In Unit Mounting Panel
PIUS.......... Process Inherent Ultimately Safe [*Nuclear reactor*]
PI/USA ..... Packaging Institute, United States of America [*Later, PI/INT'L*]   (EA)
PIUT......... Paiute Oil & Mining [*NASDAQ symbol*]   (NQ)
PIV............ Parainfluenza Virus
PIV............ Peak Inverse Voltage [*RADAR*]
PIV............ Piva [*Solomon Islands*] [*Seismograph station code, US Geological Survey*] [*Closed*]   (SEIS)
PIV............ Pivot [*Automotive engineering*]
PIV............ Planet in View [*NASA*]
PIV............ Plug-In Valve
PIV............ Positive Infinitely Variable
PIV............ Post Indicator Valve
PIV............ Product Inspection Verification
PIV............ Propellant Isolation Valve
PIV............ Scotland School for Veterans' Children, Scotland, PA [*OCLC symbol*]   (OCLC)
PIVADS ... Product Improved Vulcan Air Defense System   (MCD)
PIVD......... Protruded Intervertebral Disc [*Medicine*]
PIVED ...... Plasma-Injection Vacuum Energy Diverter
PIVN........ Public Interest Video Network/New Voices Radio   (EA)
PIVOT...... Planning and Implementing Vocational Readiness in Occupational Therapy
PIVS .... Particle-Induced Visual Sensations
PivS........... Pivnicne Sjajvo [*A publication*]
PIVT......... Production Improvement Verification Test
PIW .... Petroleum Intelligence Weekly [*A publication*]
PIW .... Plastic Insulated Wire
PIW .... Polski Instytut Wydawniczy [*A publication*]
PIW .... Ports and Inland Waterways
PIW .... Program Interrupt Word
PIW .... Woodhaven Center, Philadelphia, PA [*OCLC symbol*]   (OCLC)
PIWC........ Petroleum Industry War Council
PIWCA..... Proceedings. International Waste Conference [*A publication*]
PIWG....... Product Improvement Working Group [*Military*]   (AFIT)
PIWI......... No Pilot Balloon Observation Due to High, or Gusty, Surface Wind [*National Weather Service*]   (FAAC)
PIWSD ..... Proceedings. International Wire and Cable Symposium [*A publication*]
PIWWC..... Planetary Initiative for the World We Choose   (EA)
PIX............ Pico Island [*Azores*] [*Airport symbol*]   (OAG)
PIX............ Picture
PIX............ Picture Rocks, PA [*Location identifier*] [*FAA*]   (FAAL)
PIX............ Pinxit [*He, or She, Painted It*] [*Latin*]   (ROG)
PIX............ Proton-Induced X-Ray Analysis
PIX............ School Pictures, Inc. [*AMEX symbol*]   (SPSG)
PIX............ Youth Development Center, Loysville, Loysville, PA [*OCLC symbol*]   (OCLC)
Pix Aud ...... Pixley on Auditors [*8th ed.*] [*1901*] [*A publication*]   (DLA)
PIXE .... Particle [*or Proton*]-Induced X-Ray Emission
PIXEL........ Picture Element [*Single element of resolution in image processing*]
PIY............ Pembroke Imperial Yeomanry [*British military*]   (DMA)
PIY............ Youth Development Center, New Castle, New Castle, PA [*OCLC symbol*]   (OCLC)
PIZ............ Point Lay [*Alaska*] [*Airport symbol*]   (OAG)
PIZ............ Point Lay, AK [*Location identifier*] [*FAA*]   (FAAL)
PIZ............ Youth Development Center, Waynesburg, Waynesburg, PA [*OCLC symbol*]   (OCLC)

PIZA......... National Pizza Co. [Pittsburg, KS] [NASDAQ symbol]   (NQ)
PIZK........ Pantheon. Internationale Zeitschrift fuer Kunst [A publication]
PIZZ........ Pizzicato [Plucked] [Music]
PJ.............. Bombay High Court Printed Judgments [1869-1900] [India] [A publication]   (DLA)
PJ.............. ICC [Interstate Commerce Commission] Practitioners' Journal [A publication]
PJ.............. Netherlands Antilles [Aircraft nationality and registration mark]   (FAAC)
PJ.............. Pajamas
PJ.............. Palastinajahrbuch. Deutsches Evangelische Institut fuer Altertumswissenschaft des Heiligen Landes zu Jerusalem [Berlin] [A publication]
PJ.............. Panel Jack
PJ.............. Parteijargon [Party Language] [German]
PJ.............. Peregrine Air Services Ltd. [Great Britain] [ICAO designator]   (FAAC)
PJ.............. Peripheral Jet   (AAG)
PJ.............. Personnel Journal [A publication]
PJ.............. Petajoule   (ADA)
PJ.............. Pharmaceutical Journal [A publication]
PJ.............. Philosophisches Jahrbuch [A publication]
PJ.............. Philosophisches Jahrbuch der Goerres-Gesellschaft [A publication]
PJ.............. Picojoule [Logic gate efficiency measure]   (MDG)
PJ.............. Piece Jointe [Enclosure] [French]   (NATG)
PJ.............. Plasma Jet   (AAG)
PJ.............. Plastic Jacket
P & J......... Plaza y Janes [Publisher] [Spain]
PJ.............. Police Justice
PJ.............. Poradnik Jezykowy [A publication]
PJ.............. Possible Jobs [Test] [Psychology]
PJ.............. Presiding Judge
PJ.............. Presiding Probate Judge [British]   (ROG)
PJ.............. Preussische Jahrbuecher [A publication]
PJ.............. Prince of Jerusalem [Freemasonry]
PJ.............. Privacy Journal [A publication]
PJ.............. Probate Judge
PJ.............. Procurement Justification [Navy]
PJ.............. Project Jonah   (EA)
PJ.............. Prudhoe Bay Journal [A publication]
PJ.............. Pulsejet
PJ.............. Purchases Journal [Accounting]
PJ's .... Pajamas [Slang]
PJ's .... Paramedic Jumpers
PJ's .... Physical Jerks [Exercise] [Slang] [British]   (DSUE)
PJA.......... Abington Library Society, Jenkintown, PA [Library symbol] [Library of Congress] [Obsolete]   (LCLS)
PJa .... Papers on Japan [A publication]
PJACA ..... Proceedings. Japan Academy [A publication]
PJAFC...... P. J. Allman Fan Club   (EA)
PJAIA....... Philippine Journal of Animal Industry [A publication]
PJAlG....... Alverthorpe Gallery, Rosenwald Collection, Jenkintown, PA [Library symbol] [Library of Congress]   (LCLS)
P Jap Acad ... Proceedings. Japan Academy [A publication]
PJB .... Pad Journal Bearing
PJB .... Palastinajahrbuch. Deutsches Evangelische Institut fuer Altertumswissenschaft des Heiligen Landes zu Jerusalem [Berlin] [A publication]
PJB .... Premature Junctional Beat [Cardiology]
PJb .... Preussische Jahrbuecher [A publication]
PJBD........ Permanent Joint Board on Defense [US, Canada]
PJBSA...... Pavlovian Journal of Biological Science [A publication]
PJC........... Jean Coutu Group (PJC), Inc. [Toronto Stock Exchange symbol]
PJC........... Paducah Junior College [Kentucky]
PJC........... Paris Junior College [Texas]
PJC........... Pensacola Junior College [Florida]
PJC........... Perkinston Junior College [Mississippi]
PJC........... Post Junior College [Connecticut]
PJC........... Poteau Junior College [Oklahoma]
PJC........... Pratt Junior College [Kansas]
PJC........... University of Pittsburgh, Johnstown, Johnstown, PA [OCLC symbol]   (OCLC)
PJCTL...... Projectile   (MSA)
PJD.......... Pedro Dome [Alaska] [Seismograph station code, US Geological Survey] [Closed]   (SEIS)
PJE.......... Parachute Jumping Exercise
PJE.......... Peabody Journal of Education [A publication]
PJE.......... Project Engineer
PJE.......... Pulse Jet Engine
PJES......... Photojet Edge Sensor
PJez .... Prace Jezykoznawcze Polskiej Akademii Nauk [A publication]
PJF.......... Peripheral Jet (Flat-Bottom)
PJF.......... Pharmaceutical Journal Formulary   (ROG)
PJF.......... Pin Jointed Framework
PJFS........ Philip Jose Farmer Society   (EA)
PJG.......... Panjgur [Pakistan] [Airport symbol]   (OAG)
PJG.......... Potts Junction [Guam] [Seismograph station code, US Geological Survey]   (SEIS)

PJGG........ Philosophisches Jahrbuch der Goerres-Gesellschaft [A publication]
PJGNI .... Persica. Jaarboek van het Genootschap Nederland-Iran [A publication]
PJH .... Piper, Jr., H. E., Philadelphia PA [STAC]
PJHI......... PLRS/JTIDS [Position Location Reporting System/Joint Tactical Information Distribution System] Hybrid Interface
PJHNAW ... Pavlov Journal of Higher Nervous Activity [English translation of Zhurnal Vysshei Nervnoi Deyatelnosti Imeni I. P. Pavlova] [A publication]
PJI .... Parachute Jump Instructor [Military] [British]   (INF)
PJI .... Pattern Jury Instructions [A publication]
PJI .... Personnel Journal Index [Personnel Journal] [Information service or system]   (CRD)
PJI .... Point Judith, RI [Location identifier] [FAA]   (FAAL)
PJILMCC ... Philip C. Jessup International Law Moot Court Competition   (EA)
PJJ............ Provincial Judges Journal [A publication]
PJK........... Prace Jezykoznawcze [A publication]
P Jl........... Pharmaceutical Journal [A publication]   (ROG)
PJL........... Philippine Journal of Linguistics [A publication]
PJLB......... Lower Burma Printed Judgments [A publication]   (DLA)
PJLT......... Philippine Journal of Language Teaching [A publication]
PJM.......... Pennsylvania-Jersey-Maryland [Electric power pool]
PJM.......... Polymer Jell Material
PJM.......... Postjunctional Membrane
PJM.......... Power Jets Memorandum
PJM.......... Project Manager [Military]
PJN........... Fort Lauderdale, FL [Location identifier] [FAA]   (FAAL)
PJN........... Philippine Journal of Nursing [A publication]
PJNEE5 .... Pakistan Journal of Nematology [A publication]
PJNu........ Philippine Journal of Nutrition [A publication]
PJo........... Cambria County Library System, Johnstown, PA [Library symbol] [Library of Congress]   (LCLS)
PJO.......... Pioneer Jupiter Orbit [NASA]
PJON........ Johnston Island/Johnston Atoll [Johnston Island] [ICAO location identifier]   (ICLI)
PJOP........ Preliminary Joint Operation Procedure   (KSC)
PJOPA ...... Pakistan Journal of Psychology [A publication]
PJoU......... University of Pittsburgh at Johnstown, Johnstown, PA [Library symbol] [Library of Congress]   (LCLS)
PJP........... Philippine Journal of Pediatrics [A publication]
PJPA .... Philippine Journal of Public Administration [A publication]
PJPC......... Plug/Jack Patch Cord
PJPI.......... Philippine Journal of Plant Industry [A publication]
PJR........... Peoria, IL [Location identifier] [FAA]   (FAAL)
PJR........... Peterson, J. Robert, New York NY [STAC]
PJR........... Philadelphia Journalism Review [A publication]
PJR........... Port Jersey [AAR code]
PJR........... Power Jets Report
PJRCM ..... Philippine Junior Red Cross Magazine [A publication]
P Jr & H.... Patton, Jr., and Heath's Reports [Virginia Special Court of Appeals] [A publication]   (DLA)
PJS........... Newport News, VA [Location identifier] [FAA]   (FAAL)
PJS........... Peripheral Jet (Skegs)
PJS........... Peutz-Jeghers Syndrome [Oncology]
PJS........... Philippine Journal of Science [A publication]
PJs........... Physical Jerks [Exercise] [Slang] [British]   (DSUE)
PJS........... Piezojunction Sensor
PJS........... Plug and Jack Set
PJS........... Production Job Sheet
PJ Schw E ... Politisches Jahrbuch der Schweizerischen Eidgenoessenschaft [A publication]
PJSRA...... Pakistan Journal of Scientific Research [A publication]
PJSS......... PACAF [Pacific Air Forces] Jungle Survival School   (AFM)
PJSS......... Philippine Journal of Surgical Specialties [A publication]
PJT........... Paroxysmal Junctional Tachycardia [Cardiology]
PJT........... Practical Job Training   (MCD)
PJT........... Pulse Jitter Tester
PJTN........ Projection   (MSA)
PJTP........ Planner Journal. Royal Town Planning Institute [A publication]
PJTR........ Projector   (MSA)
PJU.......... Juniata College, Huntingdon, PA [OCLC symbol]   (OCLC)
PJU.......... Physician's Journal Update [Television program]
P Jur Vj..... Prager Juristische Vierteljahrsschrift [A publication]
PJV.......... Pump Jet Vehicle
PJZSAZ .... Agriculturae Conspectus Scientificus [A publication]
PK .... Indonesia [Aircraft nationality and registration mark]   (FAAC)
pK'........... Negative Log of the Dissociation Constant [Medicine]
PK .... Pack   (AAG)
PK .... Package [Shipping]   (MCD)
pk .... Pakistan [IYRU nationality code] [MARC country of publication code] [Library of Congress]   (LCCP)
PK .... Pakistan [ANSI two-letter standard code]   (CNC)
PK .... Pakistan International Airlines Corp. [ICAO designator]   (FAAC)
PK .... Park [or Parking]
PK .... Peak [Maps and charts]
pK.............. Peak Value [Data processing]
PK .... Peck   (AAG)

P & K......... Perry and Knapp's English Election Cases [*1833*] [*A publication*] (DLA)
PK............. Peter King [*Afro-jazz band*]
PK............. Phileleftheron Komma [*Liberal Party*] [*Greek*] [*Political party*] (PPE)
PK............. Philologike Kypros [*A publication*]
PK............. Pike
PK............. Pink (FAAC)
PK............. Pinkas ha-Kehilot [*Encyclopedia of Jewish Communities*] [*A publication*]
PK............. Plaste und Kautschuk [*A publication*]
PK............. Pole Cat [*Slang*]
PK............. Politicka Knihovna Ceskoslovenske Strany Lidove [*A publication*]
PK............. Position Keeper
PK............. Posta Kutusu [*Postbox*] [*Turkish*] (EY)
PK............. Prausnitz-Kuestner [*Reaction*] [*Immunology*]
PK............. Prawo Kanoniczne [*A publication*]
PK............. Praxis-Kurier [*A publication*]
PK............. Preacher's Kid [*Slang*]
PK............. Pridie Kalendas [*The Day before the Calends*] [*Latin*]
PK............. Principal Keeper [*Slang for a warden*]
PK............. Probability of Kill (MCD)
PK............. Problemy Kibernetiki [*A publication*]
PK............. Prophets and Kings (BJA)
PK............. Protein Kinase [*Also, PKase*] [*An enzyme*]
PK............. Przeglad Klasyczny [*A publication*]
PK............. Przeglad Koscielny [*A publication*]
PK............. Przeglad Kulturalny [*A publication*]
PK............. Psychokinesis
PK............. Pyruvate Kinase [*An enzyme*]
P-K4......... Pawn to King Four [*Standard opening to a game of chess. Pawn is moved to the fourth square in front of the king*]
PKA.......... Napaskiak [*Alaska*] [*Airport symbol*] (OAG)
PKA.......... Napaskiak, AK [*Location identifier*] [*FAA*] (FAAL)
PKA.......... Paul Kagan Associates, Inc. [*Information service or system*] [*Telecommunications*] (IID)
PKA.......... Pi Kappa Alpha [*Fraternity*]
PKA.......... Primary Knock-on-Atom (MCD)
PKA.......... Professional Karate Association (EA)
PKA.......... Protein Kinase A [*An enzyme*]
PkAF......... Pakistani Air Force
PKAFA...... PKA [*Professional Karate Association*] Fighters Association (EA)
PKAS........ Parti Kadazan Asli Sabah [*Political party*] [*Malaysia*] (FEA)
PKase........ Protein Kinase [*Also, PK*] [*An enzyme*]
PKAWA..... Pocket Knife Ancillary Workers' Association [*A union*] [*British*]
PKB.......... Parkersburg [*West Virginia*] [*Airport symbol*] (OAG)
PKB.......... Parkersburg, WV [*Location identifier*] [*FAA*] (FAAL)
PKB.......... Photoelectric Keyboard
PKB.......... Portable Keyboard
PKC.......... Beijing Review [*A publication*]
PKC.......... Cocoa, FL [*Location identifier*] [*FAA*] (FAAL)
PKC.......... Pannill Knitting Company, Inc. [*NYSE symbol*] (SPSG)
PKC.......... Peckham Road [*California*] [*Seismograph station code, US Geological Survey*] (SEIS)
PKC.......... Position Keeping Computer
PKC.......... Protein Kinase C [*An enzyme*]
PKCVA...... Promyshlennost Khimicheskikh Reaktivov i Osobo Chistykh Veshchestv [*A publication*]
PKD.......... Pac Ed Systems Corp. [*Vancouver Stock Exchange symbol*]
PKD.......... Park Rapids, MN [*Location identifier*] [*FAA*] (FAAL)
PKD.......... Parker Drilling Co. [*NYSE symbol*] (SPSG)
PKD.......... Partially Knocked Down [*Consignment*] [*Shipping*] (DS)
PKD.......... Philip K. Dick [*Science fiction writer*]
PKD.......... Pi Kappa Delta [*Society*]
PKD.......... Programmable Keyboard and Display [*Data processing*] (NASA)
PKDOM.... Pack for Domestic Use
PKDR-B.... Pakistan Development Review [*A publication*]
PKDS........ Philip K. Dick Society (EA)
PKE.......... Pacific Kenridge [*Vancouver Stock Exchange symbol*]
PKE.......... Pakistan and Gulf Economist [*A publication*]
PKE.......... Park Electrochemical Corp. [*NYSE symbol*] (SPSG)
PKE.......... Parker, CA [*Location identifier*] [*FAA*] (FAAL)
PKE.......... Parkes [*Australia*] [*Airport symbol*] (OAG)
PKE.......... Public-Key Encryption [*Microcomputer technology*]
PKF.......... Park Falls, WI [*Location identifier*] [*FAA*] (FAAL)
PKF.......... Parkfield Array [*California*] [*Seismograph station code, US Geological Survey*] (SEIS)
PKF.......... Primary Kidney Fold
PKFC........ Princess Kitty Fan Club (EA)
PKG.......... Package [*Shipping*] (AFM)
Pkg............. Packing (DS)
Pkg instr.... Packing Instruction (DS)
PKG.......... Parking (KSC)
PKG.......... Phonocardiogram [*Cardiology*]
PKG.......... Propylaeen Kunstgeschichte [*A publication*]
Pkg Abstr... Packaging Abstracts [*A publication*]
PKGE........ Package

Pkg Eng..... Package Engineering [*A publication*]
Pkg (India) ... Packaging (India) [*A publication*]
P-K GL....... [*A.*] Philippson and [*E.*] Kirsten, Die Griechischen Landschaften [*A publication*] (OCD)
Pkg (London) ... Packaging (London) [*A publication*]
Pkg News... Packaging News [*A publication*]
Pkg Technol ... Packaging Technology and Management [*A publication*]
PKH.......... Park Hill [*California*] [*Seismograph station code, US Geological Survey*] (SEIS)
PKH.......... Publikatieblad van de Europese Gemeenschappen. Handelingen van het Europese Parlement [*A publication*]
PKHO........ Protivo-Khimicheskaia Oborona [*A Chemical Defense*] [*USSR*]
PKHOW.... Pack Howitzer [*Marine Corps*]
PKI........... Parkland Industries Ltd. [*Toronto Stock Exchange symbol*]
PKI........... Partai Katolik Indonesia [*Catholic Party of Indonesia*] [*Political party*]
PKI........... Partai Komunis Indonesia [*Communist Party of Indonesia*] [*Political party*]
PKI........... Partai Kristen Indonesia [*Christian Party of Indonesia*] [*Political party*]
P & KI....... Promisel & Korn, Inc. [*Information service or system*] (IID)
PKI........... Protein Kinase Inhibitor [*Biochemistry*]
PKIKA....... Praxis der Kinderpsychologie und Kinderpsychiatrie [*A publication*]
PKJ........... Pitanja Knjizevnosti a Jezika [*A publication*]
PKK.......... Kurdish Workers' Party [*Turkey*] [*Political party*] (PD)
PKK.......... Pakokku [*Burma*] [*Airport symbol*] (OAG)
PKK.......... Porkkala [*Finland*] [*Seismograph station code, US Geological Survey*] (SEIS)
PKK.......... Protein Kinase K [*An enzyme*]
PkKP........ Pakistan National Scientific and Documentation Center, Karachi, Pakistan [*Library symbol*] [*Library of Congress*] (LCLS)
PKL.......... Parklane Technologies, Inc. [*Vancouver Stock Exchange symbol*]
PKL.......... Pi Kappa Lambda [*Society*]
PKLB........ Pharmakinetics Laboratories, Inc. [*NASDAQ symbol*] (NQ)
PK-LT........ Psychokinesis on Living Targets
PKM.......... Perigee Kick Motor (MCD)
PKMA....... Eniwetok [*Marshall Islands*] [*ICAO location identifier*] (ICLI)
PK-MB....... Psychokinetic Metal-Bending [*Parapsychology*]
PKMJ........ Majuro [*Marshall Islands*] [*ICAO location identifier*] (ICLI)
PKMKA..... Prikladnaya Mekhanika [*A publication*]
PKMKCMD... Perhaps...Kids Meeting Kids Can Make a Difference (EA)
PKMS........ Pertubohan Kebangsaan Melayu Singapura [*Singapore Malays' National Organization*] [*Political party*] (FEA)
PKN.......... Aspen, CO [*Location identifier*] [*FAA*] (FAAL)
PKN.......... Pangkalanbuun [*Indonesia*] [*Airport symbol*] (OAG)
PKN.......... Pauken [*Kettledrums*]
PKN.......... Perkin-Elmer Corp. [*NYSE symbol*] (SPSG)
PKNG HSE ... Packing House [*Freight*]
PKO.......... Parakou [*Benin*] [*Airport symbol*] (OAG)
PKO.......... Parfuemerie und Kosmetik. Internationale Zeitschrift fuer Wissenschaftliche und Technische Grundlagen der Parfuem- und Kosmetika Industrie [*A publication*]
PKO.......... Peace-Keeping Operation (MCD)
PKO.......... Perdant par Knockout [*Losing by a Knockout*] [*French*]
PKOH........ Park-Ohio Industries, Inc. [*NASDAQ symbol*] (NQ)
PKOM....... Publicationen. Kaiserlich Osmanische Museen [*Constantinople*] [*A publication*]
PKOMA..... Physik der Kondensierten Materie [*A publication*]
P Kon Ned A ... Proceedings. Koninklijke Nederlandse Akademie van Wetenschappen. Series A. Mathematical Sciences [*A publication*]
P Kon Ned B ... Proceedings. Koninklijke Nederlandse Akademie van Wetenschappen. Series B. Physical Sciences [*A publication*]
P Kon Ned C ... Proceedings. Koninklijke Nederlandse Akademie van Wetenschappen. Series C. Biological and Medical Sciences [*A publication*]
PKOP........ Piscovee Knigi Obonezskoj Pjatiny [*A publication*]
PKP.......... Palestiner Komunistische Partei [*Palestine Communist Party*] [*Political party*] (BJA)
PKP.......... Partido Komunista ng Pilipinas [*Communist Party of the Philippines*] [*Political party*] (PPW)
PKP.......... Penetrating Keratoplasty [*Ophthalmology*]
PKP.......... Perustuslaillinen Kansanpuolue [*Constitutional People's Party*] [*Finland*] [*Political party*] (PPE)
PKP.......... Polskie Koleje Panstwowe [*Polish State Railways*]
PKP.......... Preknock Pulse
PKP.......... Pukapuka [*French Polynesia*] [*Airport symbol*] (OAG)
PKP.......... Purple-K-Powder
PK/PK........ Peak-to-Peak (MCD)
PKpP......... Pennwalt Corp., King Of Prussia, PA [*Library symbol*] [*Library of Congress*] (LCLS)
PKPS........ [*The*] Poughkeepsie Savings Bank FSB [*Poughkeepsie, NY*] [*NASDAQ symbol*] (NQ)
PKQ.......... Dallas-Fort Worth, TX [*Location identifier*] [*FAA*] (FAAL)
PKR.......... P. K. Le Roux Dam [*South Africa*] [*Seismograph station code, US Geological Survey*] (SEIS)
PKR.......... Picker

PKR	Pokhara [*Nepal*] [*Airport symbol*] (OAG)
PKRDD	Pravitel'stvennaya Komissiya po Raketam Dalnego Deistviya [*State Commission for the Study of the Problems of Long-Range Rockets*] [*USSR*]
PKs...........	Bayard Taylor Memorial Library, Kennett Square, PA [*Library symbol*] [*Library of Congress*] (LCLS)
PKS...........	Packs of Cigarettes Smoked
PKS...........	Phi Kappa Sigma [*Fraternity*]
PKS...........	Publikatieblad van de Europese Gemeenschappen. Serie C. Mededelingen en Bekendmakingen [*A publication*]
PKS...........	Publikatieblad van de Europese Gemeenschappen. Supplement [*A publication*]
PKSCAT....	Parkes Catalogue of Radio Sources [*Australian National Radio Astronomy Observatory*] [*Information service or system*] (IID)
PKSCU	PKS/Communications Uts [*NASDAQ symbol*] (NQ)
PKSEA	Pack for Overseas
PKSh.........	Partia Komuniste e Shqiperise [*Communist Party of Albania*] [*Later, PPSh*] [*Political party*] (PPE)
PKsL.........	Longwood Gardens Library, Kennett Square, PA [*Library symbol*] [*Library of Congress*] (LCLS)
Pks & Rec ..	Parks and Recreation [*A publication*]
PKSS	Probability of Kill Single Shot (MCD)
PKSVAG ...	Pneumokoniosenavorsingseenheid Jaarverslag Pochvoznanie Agrokhimiya i Rastitelna Zashtita [*A publication*]
PKT...........	Packet
PKT...........	Phase Keying Technique
PKT...........	Phi Kappa Tau [*Fraternity*]
PKT...........	Pittsburgh Theological Seminary, Pittsburgh, PA [*OCLC symbol*] (OCLC)
PKT...........	Pocket (MSA)
PKTDA.....	Prace Komisji Technologii Drewna. Poznanskie Towarzystwo Przyjaciol Nauk [*A publication*]
PKU	Pekanbaru [*Indonesia*] [*Airport symbol*] (OAG)
PKU	Phenylketonuria [*Congenital metabolism disorder*] [*Medicine*]
PKU	Pianoforte Keymakers' Union [*British*]
PKU-P	PKU [*Phenylketonuria*] Parents (EA)
PKuS.........	Kutztown State College, Kutztown, PA [*Library symbol*] [*Library of Congress*] (LCLS)
PkV	Peak Kilovolts
PKV	Port Lavaka, TX [*Location identifier*] [*FAA*] (FAAL)
PKVJA	PKV [*Punjabrao Krishi Vidyapeeth*] Research Journal [*A publication*]
PKVL........	Pikeville National Corp. [*NASDAQ symbol*] (NQ)
PKVOA	Produktivnost [*A publication*]
PKV Res J ...	PKV [*Punjabrao Krishi Vidyapeeth*] Research Journal [*A publication*]
PKW	Kenosha, WI [*Location identifier*] [*FAA*] (FAAL)
PKW	Personenkraftwagen [*Automobile*] [*German*]
PKW	Selebi-Phikwe [*Botswana*] [*Airport symbol*] (OAG)
PKWA	Kwajalein [*Marshall Islands*] [*ICAO location identifier*] (ICLI)
PKWAY....	Parkway (MSA)
PKWY.......	Parkway (KSC)
PKWY.......	[*The*] Parkway Co. [*NASDAQ symbol*] (NQ)
PKY	Palangkaraya [*Indonesia*] [*Airport symbol*] (OAG)
PKY	Parkway (MCD)
PKy	Pneumatike Kypros [*A publication*]
PKY	Tri-City Air Taxi [*San Bernardino, CA*] [*FAA designator*] (FAAC)
PKZ...........	Pensacola, FL [*Location identifier*] [*FAA*] (FAAL)
PKZZD......	Problemy Kontrolya i Zashchita Atmosfery ot Zagryazneniya [*A publication*]
PL	Empresade Transporte Aere de Peru [*ICAO designator*] (FAAC)
PL	Front Line [*Revolutionary group*] [*Italy*]
PL	Lancaster County Library, Lancaster, PA [*Library symbol*] [*Library of Congress*] (LCLS)
PL	Packing List
PL	Padlock (AAG)
PL	Pail
PL	Palaeographia Latina [*A publication*]
PL	Palm Leaf [*Reaction*] [*Medicine*]
PL	Pamietnik Literacki [*A publication*]
PL	Pamphlet Laws [*A publication*] (DLA)
PL	Panel Left [*Nuclear energy*] (NRCH)
PL	Paper Life Ltd. [*British*]
PL	Paperleg [*A favored student*] [*Teen slang*]
PL	Papers in Linguistics [*A publication*]
PL	Parish Line R. R. [*AAR code*]
PL	Parti Liberal [*Liberal Party (1974-1979)*] [*Belgium*] [*Political party*] (PPE)
PL	Partial Loss [*Insurance*]
PL	Partido Liberal [*Liberal Party*] [*Honduras*] [*Political party*]
PL	Partido Liberal [*Liberal Party*] [*Portugal*] [*Political party*] (PPE)
PL	Partido Liberal [*Liberal Party*] [*Paraguay*] [*Political party*] (PPW)
PL	Partido Liberal [*Liberal Party*] [*Spain*] [*Political party*] (PPE)
PL	Partido Liberal [*Liberal Party*] [*Panama*] [*Political party*] (PPW)
PL	Partido Libertador [*Brazil*] [*Political party*]
PL	Parting Line [*Castings*] (AAG)
PL	Parts List
PL	Path Loss [*Communications*]
PL	Patrol Land [*Aviation*]
PL	Patrologia Latina [*A publication*]
PL	Patrologiae Cursus. Series Latina [*A publication*] (OCD)
Pl...............	Paul (BJA)
P & L........	Paul and Lisa (EA)
PL	Paulist League (EA)
P de L........	Paulus de Liazaris [*Deceased, 1356*] [*Authority cited in pre-1607 legal work*] (DSA)
PL	Payload [*NASA*] (KSC)
PL	Paymaster-Lieutenant [*Navy*] [*British*]
PL	Peanut Leafspot [*Plant pathology*]
PL	Pectate Lyase [*An enzyme*]
Pl...............	Pelagius [*Deceased, 1232*] [*Authority cited in pre-1607 legal work*] (DSA)
PL	Pelusium Line [*Nile delta*] [*Geology*]
PL	People for Life (EA)
PL	People's Lobby (EA)
PL	Perceived Level [*Noise*]
PL	Perception of Light
P/L............	Personal Lines
PL	Personnel Laboratory [*Air Research and Development Command*] [*Air Force*] (AAG)
PL	Petty Larceny
PL	Phase Line
PL	Philosophical Library [*A publication*]
PL	Philosophischer Literaranzeiger [*A publication*]
P & L........	Philosophy and Literature [*A publication*]
PL	Phospholipid [*Biochemistry*]
PL	Photolocator (MCD)
PL	Photoluminescence
PL	Pilatus Flugzeugwerke AG [*Switzerland*] [*ICAO aircraft manufacturer identifier*] (ICAO)
PL	Pile
PL	Pinelands, Inc. [*NYSE symbol*] (SPSG)
PL	Pipe Lines Act [*Town planning*] [*British*]
PL	Pipeline
PL	Piping Load [*Nuclear energy*] (NRCH)
PL	Pitch Line (MSA)
PL	Place [*Investment term*]
PL	Place
PL	Placebo [*Medicine*]
PL	Placental Lactogen [*Endocrinology*]
Pl...............	Plagioclase [*Lunar geology*]
PL	Plain (MSA)
PL	Plain Language [*As opposed to coded message*] [*Military*]
PL	Plans
Pl...............	Pianta [*A publication*]
PL	Plantagenet [*Genealogy*] (ROG)
pl...............	Plasma
PL	Plastic Laboratory [*Princeton University*] (MCD)
PL	Plastic Limit (IEEE)
PL	Plastic Surgery [*Medicine*]
pl...............	Plastid [*Botany*]
PL	Plate (KSC)
PL	Plateau Length
PL	Platinum [*Chemistry*] (ROG)
Pl...............	Plato [*Fourth century BC*] [*Classical studies*] (OCD)
PL	Platoon (NATG)
PL	Platoon Leader [*Military*] (INF)
PL	Platz [*Square*] [*German*] (EY)
PL	Players League [*Major league in baseball, 1890*]
PL	Pleasure (ROG)
PL	Plimsoll Line [*Shipping*] (DAS)
PL	Ploshchad [*Square*] [*Russian*] (EY)
Pl...............	Plowden's English King's Bench Commentaries [*or Reports*] [*1550-80*] [*A publication*] (DLA)
PL	Plug (AAG)
PL	Plume [*Numismatics*]
PL	Plural
PL	Poet Laureate
PL	Poet Lore [*A publication*]
PL	Poetry London [*A publication*] [*British*]
P & L........	Points and Lines [*Military*] (CAAL)
Pl...............	Poiseuille [*Unit of dynamic viscosity*]
pl...............	Poland [*MARC country of publication code*] [*Library of Congress*] (LCCP)
PL	Poland [*ANSI two-letter standard code*] (CNC)
PL	Polarized Light
PL	Policy Loan
P & L........	Politics and Letters [*A publication*]
PL	Poly-L-lysine [*Also, PLL*] [*Biochemical analysis*]
PL	Poor Law [*A publication*] (DLA)
P of L........	Port of London (ROG)
PL	Portable Low-Power [*Reactor*] (NRCH)
PL	Position Line [*Navigation*]
PL	Position Location [*DoD*]
PL	Post Landing [*NASA*] (KSC)
PL	Post Laundry [*Army*]

P & L	Power and Lighting (MSA)
P & L	Pratt & Lambert, Inc.
PL	Prayers for Life (EA)
PL	Prelaunch (NASA)
PL	Preliminary Leaf [*Bibliography*]
P/L	Presentation Label [*Publishing*]
PL	Presley Labs [*Vancouver Stock Exchange symbol*]
PL	Pressurizer Level (IEEE)
PL	Price Level [*Economics*]
PL	Price List
PL	Princess Louise's Sutherland and Argyll Highlanders [*Military*] [*British*] (ROG)
PL	Private Label [*A publication*]
PL	Private Label [*Business term*]
PL	Private Library [*A publication*]
PL	Private Line
PL	Procedural Language (PCM)
PL	Procedure Library [*Data processing*]
PL	Product Liability [*Insurance*]
PL	Product License
PL	Production Language
PL	Production List (AAG)
P/L	Profit and Loss [*Accounting*]
P & L	Profit and Loss [*Accounting*]
PL	Program Library [*Data processing*]
PL	Program Logic [*Data processing*] (TEL)
PL	Programming Language [*Data processing*]
PL	Programming Languages Series [*Elsevier Book Series*] [*A publication*]
PL	Progressive Labor [*A faction of Students for a Democratic Society*]
PL	Project Leader
PL	Project Lighthawk [*Later, LH*] (EA)
PL	Project Local [*Defunct*] (EA)
PL	Projection Lens [*Microscopy*]
PL	Prolymphocytic Leukemia [*Also, PLL*] [*Oncology*]
PL	Propagation Loss
PL	Propellant Loading [*NASA*] (KSC)
PL	Property Line [*Real estate*] (MSA)
PL	Proportional Limit
P/L	Proprietary Limited (ADA)
PL	Propulsion Laboratory [*Army*] (GRD)
PL	Prospective Loss
PL	Protected Location [*Shipping*] (DS)
PL	Protectively Located [*Plant layout*]
PL	Provisioning List (MCD)
PL	Pseudolumina [*Anatomy*]
PL	Psychological Laboratory (MCD)
PL	Public Law [*An act of Congress*]
PL	Public Liability [*Business term*]
PL	Public Library
PL	Pulpolingual [*Dentistry*]
PL	Pulse Length (NVT)
P/L	Purchased Labor (NASA)
PL	Pyridoxal [*Also, Pxl*] [*Biochemistry*]
P & L	Radio Positioning Land Station [*ITU designation*] (CET)
PL/1	Programming Language, Version One [*Data processing*] (MCD)
PLA	Pakistan Liberation Army (PD)
PLA	Palau [*Palau Islands*] [*Seismograph station code, US Geological Survey*] [*Closed*] (SEIS)
PLA	Palestine Liberation Army
PLA	Parachute Location Aid (MCD)
PLA	Parlamento Latinoamericano [*Latin American Parliament - LAP*] [*Bogota, Colombia*] (EAIO)
PLA	Parlar Resources Ltd. [*Vancouver Stock Exchange symbol*]
PLA	Party of Labor of Albania [*Political party*] (PPW)
PLA	Passengers' Luggage in Advance [*Railway*] (ROG)
PLA	Patriotic Liberation Army [*Burma*] (PD)
PLA	Pedestrian League of America [*Later, APA*] (EA)
PLA	Pedro Leon Abroleda Brigade [*Colombia*] (PD)
Pla	Pelagius [*Deceased, 1232*] [*Authority cited in pre-1607 legal work*] (DSA)
PLA	Pennilane Development [*Vancouver Stock Exchange symbol*]
PLA	People's Liberation Army [*Communist China*]
PLA	People's Liberation Army [*India*] (PD)
PLA	Pet Lovers Association (EA)
PLA	Phase Locked Arrays [*Physics*]
PLA	Philatelic Literature Association [*Later, APRL*] (EA)
PLA	Philosophischer Literaturanzeiger [*A publication*]
PLA	Physiological Learning Aptitude (KSC)
PLA	Pitch Lock Actuator (MCD)
PLA	Place (ADA)
PLA	Placebo [*Medicine*]
Pla	Placentinus [*Deceased, 1192*] [*Authority cited in pre-1607 legal work*] (DSA)
PLA	Placitum [*or Placita*] [*Agreeable, Agreed Upon*] [*Latin*] [*Legal term*] (DLA)
PLA	Plain Language Address [*Telecommunications*] (TEL)
PLA	Plan of Launch Azimuth [*Aerospace*] (AAG)
PLA	Planned Labor Application [*Military*] (AFIT)

PLA	Planned Landing Area [*NASA*]
PLA	Playboy Enterprises, Inc. [*NYSE symbol*] (SPSG)
PLA	Plaza (ADA)
PLA	Poetry League of America (EA)
PLA	Poly-L-arginine [*Biochemistry*]
PLA	Polylactic Acid [*Organic chemistry*] (RDA)
PLA	Polynesian Airways [*Honolulu, HI*] [*FAA designator*] (FAAC)
PLA	Popular Library of Art [*A publication*]
PLA	Port of London Authority [*British*]
PLA	Posterior Left Atrial Wall [*Cardiology*]
PLA	Potential Leaf Area [*Botany*]
PLA	Power Lever Angle
PLA	Practice Landing Approach [*Aviation*]
PLA	Practice Low Approach [*Aviation*] (FAAC)
PLA	Price-Level-Adjusted Accounting (ADA)
PLA	Print Load Analyzer
PLA	Private Libraries Association [*British*]
PLA	Product License Application [*FDA*]
PLA	Professional Legal Assistants (EA)
PLA	Programmable Line Adapter
PLA	Programmable Logic Array [*Data processing*]
PLA	Proton Linear Accelerator
PLA	Psycholinguistic Age [*Education*]
PLA	Psychological Learning Aptitude (MCD)
PLA	Public Library Association (EA)
PLa	Pulpolabial [*Dentistry*]
PLA	Pulpolinguoaxial [*Dentistry*]
PLA	Pulsed LASER Annealing [*Semiconductor technology*]
PLA	Pulverized Limestone Association (EA)
PLA	University of Pittsburgh, Law School, Pittsburgh, PA [*OCLC symbol*] (OCLC)
PLA$_2$	Phospholipase A$_2$ [*An enzyme*]
PLAA	Positive Low Angle of Attack
PLA AEPS	PLA [*Public Library Association*] Alternative Education Programs Section
PLA AFLS	PLA [*Public Library Association*] Armed Forces Library Section
PLAAR	Packaged Liquid Air-Augmented Rocket (MCD)
PLAAS	Plasma Atomic Absorption System [*Spectrometry*]
PLA AV	PLA [*Public Library Association*] Audiovisual
PLAB	Philadelphia Library Association. Bulletin [*A publication*]
PLAB	Philippine Library Association. Bulletin [*A publication*]
PLAB	Photronics, Inc. [*NASDAQ symbol*] (NQ)
PLABED	Plant Breeding [*A publication*]
PLA Bull	PLA [*Pennsylvania Library Association*] Bulletin [*A publication*]
PLAC	Placebo [*Medicine*]
Plac	Placentinus [*Deceased, 1192*] [*Authority cited in pre-1607 legal work*] (DSA)
PLAC	Post-Launch Analysis of Compliance [*NASA*]
Plac Abbrev	Placitorum Abbreviatio [*Latin*] [*A publication*] (DLA)
Plac Angl Nor	Placita Anglo-Normannica Cases [*1065-1195*] [*A publication*] (DLA)
Plac Ang Nor	Bigelow's Placita Anglo-Normanica [*A publication*] (DLA)
PLACE	Position Location and Aircraft Communication Equipment
PLACE	Position Location and Communications Experiment [*NASA*]
PLACE	Positioner Layout and Cell Evaluator [*Robotics*]
PLACE	Post-LANDSAT Advanced Concept Evaluation (MCD)
PLACE	Programa Latinoamericano de Cooperacion Energetica [*Latin American Energy Cooperation Program*] (EAIO)
PLACE	Programming Language for Automatic Checkout Equipment
Placenta Suppl	Placenta. Supplement [*A publication*]
Plac Gen	Placita Generalia [*Latin*] [*A publication*] (DLA)
PLACID	Payload Aboard, Caution in Descent [*NASA*]
PLA CIS	PLA [*Public Library Association*] Community Information Section
PLACO	Planning Committee [*International Organization for Standardization*] (IEEE)
PLAD	Parachute Low-Altitude Delivery [*Air Force*]
PLAD	Plain Language Address Directory
PLAD	Price-Level-Adjusted Deposit
PLADS	Parachute Low-Altitude Delivery System [*Military*]
PLADS	Pulsed LASER Airborne Depth Sounding System [*Naval Oceanographic Office*]
PLAFB	Plattsburgh Air Force Base [*New York*] (AAG)
PLAFSEP	Processing Libraries - Anecdotes, Facetia, Satire, Etc., Periodicals [*A publication*]
Plag	Plagioclase [*Lunar geology*]
PLAGM	Placid, Louisiana Land and Exploration, Amerada Hess, Getty, and Marathon [*Oil-and gas-holding bloc in Alaska*]
PLAI	Preschool Language Assessment Instrument [*Child development test*]
PLAIC	Purdue Laboratory for Applied Industrial Control [*Purdue University*] [*Research center*] (RCD)
PLAID	Programmed Learning Aid
PLAIN	Public Libraries Automated Information Network [*Australia*]
Plain Ra	Plain Rapper [*A publication*]
Plains Anthropol	Plains Anthropologist [*A publication*]
PLAKA	Planovoe Khozyaistvo [*A publication*]
PLAL	Pro-Life Action League (EA)
PLAM	Plastic Laminate [*Technical drawings*]

PLAM........ Practice Limpet Assembly Modular [*Navy*] (CAAL)
PLAM........ Price-Level-Adjusted Mortgage
PLAMED.. Plantas Medicinales [*Ministerio de Sanidad y Consumo*]
　　　　[*Spain*] [*Information service or system*] (CRD)
PLA MLS ... PLA [*Public Library Association*] Metropolitan Libraries
　　　　Section
PLAN .... Parts Logistics Analysis Network
PLAN .... People's Liberation Army of Namibia [*Political party*] (PPW)
PLAN .... Planner Newsletter. NWT [*Northwest Territories, Canada*]
　　　　Land Use Planning Commission [*A publication*]
Plan............ Planning (DLA)
PLAN .... Polska Ludowa Akcja Niepodleglosci [*A publication*]
PLAN .... Positive Locator Aid to Navigation
PLAN .... Problem Language Analyzer [*Data processing*]
PLAN .... Program Language Analyzer [*Data processing*] (IEEE)
PLAN .... Program for Learning in Accordance with Needs [*Westinghouse
　　　　Learning Corp.*]
PLAN .... Programming Language Nineteen-Hundred [*Data processing*]
PLAN .... Protect Life in All Nations (EA)
PLAN .... Public Libraries Automation Network [*California State Library*]
　　　　[*Sacramento, CA*]
PLANA...... Planta [*A publication*]
PLANAT... North Atlantic Treaty Regional Planning Group
Planc.......... Pro Plancio [*of Cicero*] [*Classical studies*] (OCD)
Plan Can ... Plan Canada [*A publication*]
Plan Choz.. Planovoe Chozjajstvo [*A publication*]
PLANCODE ... Planning, Control, and Decision Evaluation System [*IBM
　　　　Corp.*]
Plan & Comp ... Planning and Compensation Reports [*British*] [*A
　　　　publication*] (DLA)
Planeacion Reg ... Planeacion Regional [*A publication*]
Planen Pruef Investieren PPI ... Planen-Pruefen-Investieren. PPI [*West
　　　　Germany*] [*A publication*]
PLANES ... Programmed Language-Based Enquiry System
PLANET ... Planned Logistics Analysis and Evaluation Technique [*Air
　　　　Force*]
PLANET ... Private Local Area Network [*Racal LAN Systems, Inc.*] [*Boca
　　　　Raton, FL*] (TSSD)
Planet Assoc Clean Energy Newsl ... Planetary Association for Clean Energy.
　　　　Newsletter [*Canada*] [*A publication*]
Planet Spac ... Planetary and Space Science [*A publication*]
Planet Space Sci ... Planetary and Space Science [*A publication*]
Planet and Space Sci ... Planetary and Space Science [*A publication*]
PLANEX ... [*The*] Planning Exchange Database [*Pergamon InfoLine*]
　　　　[*Database*] [*Information service or system*] (IID)
PLANEX ... Planning Exercise [*Military*] (NVT)
Pl Ang-Norm ... Placita Anglo-Normannica Cases (Bigelow) [*A
　　　　publication*] (DLA)
Plan Higher Ed ... Planning for Higher Education [*A publication*]
Plan Higher Educ ... Planning for Higher Education [*A publication*]
Plan Hospod ... Planovane Hospodarstvi [*A publication*]
Plan Hoz.... Planovoe Hozjajstvo [*A publication*]
Planif Habitat Inform ... Planification, Habitat, Information [*A publication*]
Plan Inovtn ... Planned Innovation [*A publication*]
PLANIT .... Programming Language for Interaction and Teaching [*1966*]
　　　　[*Data processing*]
Plan Khoz .. Planovoe Khozjaistvo [*A publication*]
PLANN ..... Plant Location Assistance Nationwide Network
Plann Admin ... Planning and Administration [*A publication*]
Plann Build Dev ... Planning and Building Developments [*A publication*]
Planned Innov ... Planned Innovation [*England*] [*A publication*]
PLANNER ... [*A*] programming language (CSR)
PLANNET ... Planning Network
Planning and Adm ... Planning and Administration [*A publication*]
Planning Bul ... Planning Bulletin [*A publication*] (APTA)
Planning Develop Netherl ... Planning and Development in the Netherlands
　　　　[*A publication*]
Planning History Bull ... Planning History Bulletin [*A publication*]
Plann News ... Planning News [*A publication*] (APTA)
Plann Outlook ... Planning Outlook [*A publication*]
Plann Pam Nat Plann Ass ... Planning Pamphlets. National Planning
　　　　Association [*A publication*]
Plann Parenthood Rev ... Planned Parenthood Review [*A publication*]
Plann Transp Abs ... Planning and Transportation Abstracts [*A publication*]
Plan Q........ Planning Quarterly [*A publication*]
Plan Rev..... Planning Review [*A publication*]
PLANS ...... Position Location and Navigation System
PLANS...... Program Logistics and Network Scheduling System (IEEE)
PLANS...... Programming Language for Allocation and Network Scheduling
　　　　[*1975*] [*Data processing*] (CSR)
Planseeberichte ... Planseeberichte fuer Pulvermetallurgie [*A publication*]
Planseeber Pulvermet ... Planseeberichte fuer Pulvermetallurgie [*A
　　　　publication*]
Plant........... De Plantatione [*Philo*] (BJA)
Plant........... Plant Maintenance and Engineering [*A publication*]
PLANT...... Program for Linguistic Analysis of Natural Plants (IEEE)
Planta Med ... Planta Medica [*A publication*]
Plant Bibliogr ... Plant Bibliography [*A publication*]
Plant Biochem J ... Plant Biochemical Journal [*A publication*]
Plant Biol (NY) ... Plant Biology (New York) [*A publication*]
Plant Breed Abstr ... Plant Breeding Abstracts [*A publication*]

Plant Breed Rev ... Plant Breeding Reviews [*A publication*]
Plant Bull Rubber Res Inst Malays ... Planters' Bulletin. Rubber Research
　　　　Institute of Malaysia [*A publication*]
Plant Cell Environ ... Plant Cell and Environment [*A publication*]
Plant Cell Physiol ... Plant and Cell Physiology [*A publication*]
Plant Cell Physiol (Kyoto) ... Plant and Cell Physiology (Kyoto) [*A
　　　　publication*]
Plant Cell Physiol (Tokyo) ... Plant and Cell Physiology (Tokyo) [*A
　　　　publication*]
Plant Cell Rep ... Plant Cell Reports [*A publication*]
Plant Cell Tissue Organ Cult ... Plant Cell Tissue and Organ Culture [*A
　　　　publication*]
Plant Cel P ... Plant and Cell Physiology [*A publication*]
Plant Chron ... Planters' Chronicle [*A publication*]
Plant Cultiv Repub Argent Inst Bot Agric (B Aires) ... Plantas Cultivadas en la
　　　　Republica Argentina. Instituto de Botanica Agricola
　　　　(Buenos Aires) [*A publication*]
Plant Dis.... Plant Disease [*A publication*]
Plant Dis Adv Treatise ... Plant Disease. An Advanced Treatise [*A
　　　　publication*]
Plant Dis Leafl Dept Agr Biol Br (NSW) ... Plant Disease Leaflet. Department
　　　　of Agriculture. Biological Branch (New South Wales) [*A
　　　　publication*]
Plant Dis R ... Plant Disease Reporter [*A publication*]
Plant Dis Rep ... Plant Disease Reporter [*A publication*]
Plant Dis Rep Suppl ... Plant Disease Reporter. Supplement [*A publication*]
Plant Energy Manage ... Plant Energy Management [*A publication*]
Plant Eng... Plant Engineer [*A publication*]
Plant Eng... Plant Engineering [*A publication*]
Plant & Eng Applications ... Plant and Engineering Applications [*A
　　　　publication*] (APTA)
Plant Eng (Lond) ... Plant Engineer (London) [*A publication*]
Plant Engng ... Plant Engineering [*A publication*]
Plant Engng & Maint ... Plant Engineering and Maintenance [*A publication*]
Plant Eng (Tokyo) ... Plant Engineer (Tokyo) [*A publication*]
Planter .... Planter and Sugar Manufacturer [*A publication*]
Planters' Bull ... Planters' Bulletin. Rubber Research Institute of Malaysia [*A
　　　　publication*]
PLANTFACTS ... Steel Plants Information System [*German Iron and Steel
　　　　Engineers Association*] [*Dusseldorf*] [*Information service
　　　　or system*] (IID)
Plant Field Lab Mimeo Rep Fla Univ ... Plantation Field Laboratory Mimeo
　　　　Report. Florida University [*A publication*]
Plant Food Rev ... Plant Food Review [*A publication*]
Plant Foods Hum Nutr ... Plant Foods for Human Nutrition [*A publication*]
Plant Gard ... Plants and Gardens [*A publication*]
Plant Genet Resour Lett ... Plant Genetic Resources Newsletter [*A
　　　　publication*]
Pl Anth....... Plains Anthropologist [*A publication*]
Plant Ind Dig (Manila) ... Plant Industry Digest (Manila) [*A publication*]
Plant Ind Ser Chin-Amer Joint Comm Rural Reconstr ... Plant Industry Series.
　　　　Chinese-American Joint Commission on Rural
　　　　Reconstruction [*A publication*]
Plant Ind Ser J Comm Rural Reconstr China (US Repub China) ... Plant
　　　　Industry Series. Joint Commission on Rural
　　　　Reconstruction in China (United States and Republic of
　　　　China) [*A publication*]
Plant Info Bul ... Plant Information Bulletin [*A publication*]
Plant Maint ... Plant Maintenance [*A publication*]
Plant Maint Import Substitution ... Plant Maintenance and Import
　　　　Substitution [*A publication*]
Plant Manage Eng ... Plant Management and Engineering [*A publication*]
Plant Med J Med Plant Res ... Planta Medica. Journal of Medicinal Plant
　　　　Research [*A publication*]
Plant Med Phytother ... Plantes Medicinales et Phytotherapie [*A publication*]
Plant Mol Biol ... Plant Molecular Biology [*A publication*]
Plant Operations Prog ... Plant/Operations Progress [*A publication*]
Plant Oper Manage ... Plant Operating Management [*A publication*]
Plant Path ... Plant Pathology [*London*] [*A publication*]
Plant Pathol ... Plant Pathology [*A publication*]
Plant Pathol (Lond) ... Plant Pathology (London) [*A publication*]
Plant Physiol ... Plant Physiology [*A publication*]
Plant Physiol (Bethesda) ... Plant Physiology (Bethesda) [*A publication*]
Plant Physiol & Biochem ... Plant Physiology and Biochemistry [*A
　　　　publication*]
Plant Physiol Commun (Shanghai) ... Plant Physiology Communications
　　　　(Shanghai) [*A publication*]
Plant Physiol Suppl ... Plant Physiology. Supplement [*A publication*]
Plant Physl ... Plant Physiology [*A publication*]
Plant & Power Services Eng ... Plant and Power Services Engineer [*A
　　　　publication*]
Plant Propagat ... Plant Propagator [*A publication*]
Plant Prot... Plant Protection [*A publication*]
Plant Prot Bull ... Plant Protection Bulletin [*A publication*]
Plant Prot Bull (Ankara) ... Plant Protection Bulletin (Ankara) [*A publication*]
Plant Prot Bull (New Delhi) ... Plant Protection Bulletin (New Delhi) [*A
　　　　publication*]
Plant Prot Overseas Rev ... Plant Protection Overseas Review [*A publication*]
Plant Prot Q ... Plant Protection Quarterly [*A publication*]
Plant Sci Bull ... Plant Science Bulletin [*A publication*]
Plant Sci L ... Plant Science Letters [*A publication*]

Plant Sci Lett ... Plant Science Letters [*A publication*]
Plant Sci (Lucknow) ... Plant Science (Lucknow, India) [*A publication*]
Plant Sci (Lucknow India) ... Plant Science (Lucknow, India) [*A publication*]
Plant Sci (Shannon) ... Plant Science (Shannon) [*A publication*]
Plant Sci (Sofia) ... Plant Science (Sofia) [*A publication*]
Plants Gard ... Plants and Gardens [*A publication*]
Plant Sugar Manuf ... Planter and Sugar Manufacturer [*A publication*]
Plant Sys E ... Plant Systematics and Evolution [*A publication*]
Plant Syst Evol ... Plant Systematics and Evolution [*A publication*]
Plant Var Seeds ... Plant Varieties and Seeds [*A publication*]
PLANY ...... Protestant Lawyers Association of New York   (EA)
PLAO .... Parts List Assembly Order   (MCD)
PLAP .... Placental Alkaline Phosphatase [*An enzyme*]
PLAP .... Power Lever Angle Position   (MCD)
Pla Par .... Placita Parliamentaria [*Latin*] [*A publication*]   (DLA)
PLapK .... Keystone Junior College, La Plume, PA [*Library symbol*]
     [*Library of Congress*]   (LCLS)
PLA PLSS ... PLA [*Public Library Association*] Public Library Systems
     Section
PLAQ .... PLA [*Private Libraries Association*] Quarterly [*A publication*]
PLARA ...... Plastverarbeiter [*A publication*]
PLARS ...... Position Location and Reporting System [*Military*]   (INF)
PLAS .... Plaster   (AAG)
PLAS .... Private Line Assured Service [*Telecommunications*]   (TEL)
PLAS .... Program Logical Address Space
PLAS .... Programmable Link Adaptation System   (MCD)
PLASCAMS ... Plastics: Computer Aided Materials Selector [*Rapra
     Technology Ltd.*] [*Information service or system*]   (CRD)
Plas Compd ... Plastics Compounding [*A publication*]
Plas Com R ... Plastics Compounding Redbook [*A publication*]
Plas Desgn ... Plastics Design Forum [*A publication*]
Plas Eng ... Plastics Engineering [*A publication*]
Plas Ind ES ... Plastics Industry Europe. Special Report [*A publication*]
Plas Ind Eur ... Plastics Industry Europe [*A publication*]
Plas Ind N ... Plastics Industry News [*A publication*]
PLASMA .. Parents League of American Students of Medicine
     Abroad   (EA)
Plasma Chem ... Plasma Chemistry and Plasma Processing [*A publication*]
Plasma Chem Plasma Process ... Plasma Chemistry and Plasma Processing [*A
     publication*]
Plasma Phys ... Plasma Physics [*A publication*]
Plasma Phys Contr Nucl Fusion Res Conf Proc ... Plasma Physics and
     Controlled Nuclear Fusion Research. Conference
     Proceedings [*A publication*]
Plasma Phys Controlled Fusion ... Plasma Physics and Controlled Fusion [*A
     publication*]
Plasma Phys Index ... Plasma Physics Index [*West Germany*] [*A publication*]
Plas Massy ... Plasticheskie Massy [*A publication*]
PLASMEX ... International Plastics Exhibition   (TSPED)
PLA SMLS ... PLA [*Public Library Association*] Small and Medium-Sized
     Libraries Section
Plas R Surg ... Plastic and Reconstructive Surgery [*A publication*]
Plas Rubbers Text ... Plastics, Rubbers, Textiles [*A publication*]
Plas Rub Int ... Plastics and Rubber International [*A publication*]
Plas Rubr ... Plastics and Rubber Weekly [*A publication*]
PLAST .... Propellant Loading and All Systems Test [*NASA*]   (KSC)
Plast Abstr ... Plastic Abstracts [*A publication*]
Plast Age .... Plastics Age [*A publication*]
Plast Aust .. Plastics in Australia [*A publication*]
Plast Bldg Constr ... Plastics in Building Construction [*A publication*]
Plast Build Constr ... Plastics in Building Construction [*A publication*]
Plast Bull (London) ... Plastics Bulletin (London) [*A publication*]
Plast Busin ... Plastics Business [*A publication*]
Plast Compd ... Plastics Compounding [*A publication*]
Plast Compounding ... Plastics Compounding [*A publication*]
Plast Des Process ... Plastics Design and Processing [*A publication*]
Plast Dig .... Plastics Digest [*A publication*]
PLASTEC ... Plastics Technical Evaluation Center [*Army*] [*Dover, NJ*]
PLASTEC Note ... PLASTEC [*Plastics Technical Evaluation Center*] Note [*A
     publication*]
PLASTEC Rep ... PLASTEC [*Plastics Technical Evaluation Center*] Report
     [*A publication*]
Plaste u Kaut ... Plaste und Kautschuk [*A publication*]
Plaste Kaut ... Plaste und Kautschuk [*A publication*]
Plaste und Kautsch ... Plaste und Kautschuk [*A publication*]
Plast Eng ... Plastics Engineering [*A publication*]
Plast Engng ... Plastics Engineering [*A publication*]
PLASTEUROTEC ... Groupement Europeen des Fabricants de Pieces
     Techniques Plastiques [*European Group of Fabricators of
     Technical Plastics Parts*]   (EAIO)
Plast Flash ... Plastiques Flash [*A publication*]
Plast Hmoty Kauc ... Plasticke Hmoty a Kaucuk [*A publication*]
Plastiche .... Materie Plastiche ed Elastomeri [*A publication*]
Plastic IN ... Plastics Industry News [*A publication*]
Plastico ...... Noticiero del Plastico [*A publication*]
Plastic Prod ... Plastic Products [*A publication*]
Plastics in Aust ... Plastics in Australia [*A publication*]   (APTA)
Plastics Engng ... Plastics Engineering [*A publication*]
Plast Ind .... Plastic Industry [*India*] [*A publication*]
Plast Ind News ... Plastics Industry News [*A publication*]
Plast Ind News (Jap) ... Plastics Industry News (Japan) [*A publication*]

Plast Ind (NY) ... Plastics Industry (New York) [*A publication*]
Plast Ind (Paris) ... Plastiques et Industrie (Paris) [*A publication*]
Plast Inst Trans ... Plastics Institute. Transactions [*A publication*]
Plast Inst Trans J ... Plastics Institute. Transactions and Journal [*A
     publication*]
Plast Inst Trans J Conf Suppl ... Plastics Institute. Transactions and Journal.
     Conference Supplement [*A publication*]
Plast Kauc ... Plasty a Kaucuk [*A publication*]
Plast Massen Wiss Tech ... Plastische Massen in Wissenschaft und Technik
     [*A publication*]
Plast Massy ... Plasticheskie Massy [*A publication*]
Plast Mater (Tokyo) ... Plastics Materials (Tokyo) [*A publication*]
Plast Matr ... Plast. Rivista delle Materie Plastiche [*A publication*]
Plast M & E ... Plastics Machinery and Equipment [*A publication*]
Plast Mod .. Plasticos Modernos [*A publication*]
Plast Mod Elast ... Plastiques Modernes et Elastomeres [*A publication*]
Plast Mod Elastomeres ... Plastiques Modernes et Elastomeres [*A publication*]
Plast Molded Prod ... Plastics and Molded Products [*A publication*]
Plast News ... Plastics News [*A publication*]   (APTA)
Plast News (Aust) ... Plastics News (Australia) [*A publication*]
Plast News Briefs ... Plastics News. Briefs [*A publication*]
Plast Paint Rubber ... Plastics, Paint, and Rubber [*A publication*]
Plast Panorama ... Plast Panorama Scandinavia [*A publication*]
Plast Polym ... Plastics and Polymers [*A publication*]
Plast and Polym ... Plastics and Polymers [*A publication*]
Plast Polym Conf Suppl ... Plastics and Polymers. Conference Supplement [*A
     publication*]
Plast Prod .. Plastic Products [*A publication*]
Plast Prog India ... Plastics Progress in India [*A publication*]
Plast Reconstr Surg ... Plastic and Reconstructive Surgery [*A publication*]
Plast Reconstr Surg Transplant Bull ... Plastic and Reconstructive Surgery
     and the Transplantation Bulletin [*A publication*]
Plast Renf Fibres Verre Text ... Plastiques Renforces Fibres de Verre Textile
     [*A publication*]
Plast Resinas ... Plasticos y Resinas [*Mexico*] [*A publication*]
Plast Resins ... Plastics and Resins [*A publication*]
Plast Retail Packag Bull ... Plastics in Retail Packaging Bulletin [*A
     publication*]
Plast em Rev ... Plasticos em Revista [*A publication*]
Plast Rubber ... Plastics and Rubber [*Later, Plastics and Rubber
     International*] [*A publication*]
Plast and Rubber ... Plastics and Rubber [*Later, Plastics and Rubber
     International*] [*A publication*]
Plast Rubber Int ... Plastics and Rubber International [*A publication*]
Plast and Rubber Int ... Plastics and Rubber International [*A publication*]
Plast Rubber Mater Appl ... Plastics and Rubber. Material and Applications
     [*A publication*]
Plast Rubber News ... Plastics and Rubber News [*South Africa*] [*A
     publication*]
Plast Rubber Proc Appl ... Plastics and Rubber Processing and Applications
     [*A publication*]
Plast Rubber Process ... Plastics and Rubber Processing and Applications [*A
     publication*]
Plast & Rubber Process & Appl ... Plastics and Rubber Processing and
     Applications [*A publication*]
Plast Rubbers Text ... Plastics, Rubbers, Textiles [*A publication*]
Plast Rubber Wkly ... Plastics and Rubber Weekly [*England*] [*A publication*]
Plast Rubb Int ... Plastics and Rubber International [*A publication*]
Plast Rubb News ... Plastics and Rubber News [*South Africa*] [*A publication*]
Plast Rubb Process Appln ... Plastics and Rubber Processing and Applications
     [*A publication*]
Plast Rub Wkly ... Plastics and Rubber Weekly [*A publication*]
Plast (S Afr) ... Plastics (Southern Africa) [*A publication*]
Plast (S Africa) ... Plastics (Southern Africa) [*A publication*]
Plast (Sthn Afr) ... Plastics (Southern Africa) [*A publication*]
Plast Surg Nurs ... Plastic Surgical Nursing [*A publication*]
Plast Tech ... Plastics Technology [*A publication*]
Plast Technol ... Plastics Technology [*A publication*]
Plast Today ... Plastics Today [*A publication*]
Plast Trends ... Plastics Trends [*A publication*]
Plast Univers ... Plasticos Universales [*A publication*]
Plast World ... Plastics World [*A publication*]
PLAT .... Pilot-LOS [*Line of Sight*] Landing Aid Television   (NG)
PLAT .... Plateau [*Board on Geographic Names*]
PLAT .... Platelet [*Hematology*]
PLAT .... Platform   (KSC)
PLAT .... Platinum [*Chemical symbol is Pt*]   (AAG)
PLAT .... Platonic
PLAT .... Platoon
PLAT .... Platt National Park
PLAT .... Present Latitude [*Aviation*]   (FAAC)
PLATA ...... Plating [*A publication*]
Plateau Q Mus North Ariz ... Plateau. Quarterly of the Museum of Northern
     Arizona [*A publication*]
PLATF ...... Platform   (AAG)
Plating & Surface Finish ... Plating and Surface Finishing [*A publication*]
Platinum Met Rev ... Platinum Metals Review [*A publication*]
PLATLDR ... Platoon Leader [*Military*]
PLATN ...... Platinum [*Chemistry*]   (ROG)
PLATO ...... Pennzoil Louisiana and Texas Offshore [*Oil industry group*]
PLATO ...... Platform Observables Subassembly

PLATO...... Pollution Liability Agreement Among Tanker Owners [*Insurance*]   (DS)
PLATO...... Programmed Logic for Automatic Teaching [*or Training*] Operations [*University of Illinois*] [*Programming language*]
Platoon Sch ... Platoon School [*A publication*]
PLATR...... Pawling Lattice Test Rig [*United Nuclear Co.*]
PLatS......... Saint Vincent College, Latrobe, PA [*Library symbol*] [*Library of Congress*]   (LCLS)
Plat Surf Finish ... Plating and Surface Finishing [*A publication*]
Plat and Surf Finish ... Plating and Surface Finishing [*A publication*]
Platt.......... Platt on the Law of Covenants [*1829*] [*A publication*]   (DLA)
Platt........ Platt on Leases [*A publication*]   (DLA)
Platt Cov .... Platt on the Law of Covenants [*A publication*]   (DLA)
Platt Leas... Platt on Leases [*1847*] [*A publication*]   (DLA)
Plaut.......... Plautus [*Third century BC*] [*Classical studies*]   (OCD)
PLAV........ Polish Legion of American Veterans, USA   (EA)
PLAVA...... Polish Legion of American Veterans, USA , Ladies Auxiliary   (EA)
PLAVLA ... Polish Legion of American Veterans, USA, Ladies Auxiliary   (EA)
PLAWA..... Plastics World [*A publication*]
Plaxton....... Plaxton's Canadian Constitutional Decisions [*A publication*]   (DLA)
PLAY........ Players International, Inc. [*NASDAQ symbol*]   (NQ)
PLAY........ [*The*] Playgoer [*A publication*]
Playb.......... Playboy [*A publication*]
Players Mag ... Players Magazine [*A publication*]
Playmate.... Children's Playmate Magazine [*A publication*]
PLAZ........ Plaza Communications [*NASDAQ symbol*]   (NQ)
PLB........... Papyrologica Lugduno-Batava [*A publication*]
PLB........... Payload Bay [*NASA*]   (MCD)
PLB........... Per Pound [*Freight*]
PLB........... Personal Locator Beacon [*Military*]   (AFM)
PLB........... Plattsburgh [*New York*] [*Airport symbol*]   (OAG)
PLB........... Plattsburgh, NY [*Location identifier*] [*FAA*]   (FAAL)
PLB........... Plumbing Mart [*Vancouver Stock Exchange symbol*]
PLB........... Poor Law Board
PLB........... Proctolin-Like Bioactivity [*Neurobiology*]
PLB........... Public Light Bus [*British*]
PLB........... Publisher's Library Binding
PLB........... Pullbutton   (AAG)
PLBD........ Payload Bay Door [*NASA*]   (MCD)
PLBD........ Plugboard   (MSA)
Pl Biochem J ... Plant Biochemical Journal [*A publication*]
PLBK........ Playback   (NASA)
PL-BL........ Plate Block [*Philately*]
PLBLK...... Pillow Block
PLBNDJ.... Faculte des Sciences Agronomiques. Laboratoire de Biochimie de la Nutrition. Publication [*A publication*]
PLBOL...... Position Launch/Bearing Only Launch
PLBPDP.... Contribution on the Paleolimnology of Lake Biwa and the Japanese Pleistocene [*A publication*]
PLBR........ Prototype Large Breeder Reactor [*Also, NCBR*] [*Nuclear energy*]
Pl Breed Abstr ... Plant Breeding Abstracts [*A publication*]
PLBYD...... Plan og Bygg [*A publication*]
PLC........... Pacific Logging Congress   (EA)
PLC........... Palomares Road [*California*] [*Seismograph station code, US Geological Survey*]   (SEIS)
PLC........... Partido Liberal Constitucionalista [*Constitutionalist Liberal Party*] [*Nicaragua*] [*Political party*]   (PPW)
PLC........... Patrice Lumumba Coalition   (EA)
PLC........... Paymaster-Lieutenant-Commander [*Navy*] [*British*]
PLC........... Periventricular Leukomalacia Complex [*Medicine*]
PLC........... Perry-Link Cubmarine [*A submersible vehicle*]
PLC........... Phospholipase C [*An enzyme*]
PLC........... Phospholysine C [*Biochemistry*]
PLC........... Pilot Laboratories Corp. [*Vancouver Stock Exchange symbol*]
PLC........... Placer Development Ltd. [*AMEX symbol*]   (SPSG)
Pl C .... Placita Coronae [*Pleas of the Crown*] [*Latin*] [*Legal term*]   (DLA)
PLC........... Planar Chromatography
PLC........... Platform Control
PLC........... Platoon Leader's Class [*Army*]
PLC........... Pneumatic Lead Cutter
PLC........... Poet Laureatus Caesareus [*Imperial Poet Laureate*] [*Latin*]   (ROG)
PLC........... Point Loma College [*California*]
PLC........... Poor Law Commissioners [*British*]
PLC........... Power Lever Control   (MCD)
PLC........... Power Line Carrier
PLC........... Power Line Communications
PLC........... Predictive Linguistic Constraint
PLC........... Presbyterian Lay Committee   (EA)
PLC........... Primary Leadership Course [*Army*]
PLC........... Primary Location Code [*Data processing*]
PLC........... Prime Level Code
PLC........... Princeton University. Library. Chronicle [*A publication*]
PLC........... Process Liquid Chromatography
PLC........... Production Line Configured [*Military*]   (CAAL)

PLC........... Products List Circular [*Patents*]
PLC........... Program-Length Commercial [*Television*]
PLC........... Program Level Change Tape [*Data processing*]   (IBMDP)
PLC........... Programmable Logic Control [*Data processing*]
PLC........... Programming Language Committee [*CODASYL*]
PLC........... Proinsulin-Like Compound [*Endocrinology*]
PLC........... Pseudophase Liquid Chromatography
PLC........... Public Lands Council   (EA)
PLC........... Public Lighting Commission
PLC........... Public Limited Company [*British*]
PLCA........ Pipe Line Contractors Association   (EA)
PLCAA...... Professional Lawn Care Association of America   (EA)
PLCAI....... Pipe Line Contractors Association, International   (EA)
PLCB........ Pseudoline Control Block [*Data processing*]
PLCC........ Plastic Leadless Chip Carrier [*Computer technology*]   (PCM)
PLCC......... Primary Liver Cell Cancer [*Oncology*]
PLCD........ Product Liability Common Defense [*Later, PLPD*] [*An association*]   (EA)
PLCEA ...... Part-Length Control Element Assembly [*Nuclear energy*]   (NRCH)
PLCEDM .. Part-Length Control Element Drive Mechanism [*Nuclear energy*]   (NRCH)
PLCEDV .. Plant Cell and Environment [*A publication*]
PLCH .... Kiritimati Island [*Christmas Islands*] [*Kiribati*] [*ICAO location identifier*]   (ICLI)
PLCHB...... Physiological Chemistry and Physics [*Later, Physiological Chemistry and Physics and Medical NMR*] [*A publication*]
PLCLAS .... Propagation Loss Classification System [*Navy*]   (NVT)
PLCM........ Propellant Loading Control Monitor [*NASA*]   (KSC)
PLCMC ..... Public Library of Charlotte and Mecklenburg County [*North Carolina*]
PLCM & ND ... Proceedings. Linguistic Circle of Manitoba and North Dakota [*A publication*]
PLCN........ Parts List Change Notice   (MCD)
PLCN-A .... Plan Canada [*A publication*]
PLCNY ..... Publications. Linguistic Circle of New York [*A publication*]
Pl Com .... Plowden's English King's Bench Commentaries [*or Reports*] [*1550-80*] [*England*] [*A publication*]   (DLA)
PL Com...... Poor Law Commissioner [*A publication*]   (DLA)
PLCOP...... Prelaunch Checkout Plan [*NASA*]   (KSC)
PLCPB....... Plant and Cell Physiology [*A publication*]
Pl Cr Con Tr ... Plowden's Criminal Conversation Trials [*A publication*]   (DLA)
PLCS .... Proceedings. London Classical Society [*A publication*]
PLCS .... Propellant Loading Control System [*NASA*]   (AAG)
PLCU .... Propellant Level Control Unit [*NASA*]   (KSC)
PLCWTWU ... Power Loom Carpet Weavers' and Textile Workers' Union [*British*]
PLCY .... Policy   (AFM)
PLD .... All Pakistan Legal Decisions [*A publication*]   (ILCA)
PLD .... Partial Lipodystrophy [*Medicine*]
PLD .... Partido de la Liberacion Dominicana [*Dominican Liberation Party*] [*Dominican Republic*] [*Political party*]   (PPW)
PLd .... Path Loss, Downlink [*Communications*]
PLD .... Payload [*NASA*]
PLD .... Personnel Letdown Device
PLD .... Phase Lock Demodulator
PLD .... Phospholipase D [*An enzyme*]
PLD .... Plaid   (ADA)
PLD .... Plated   (MSA)
PLD .... Played Matches [*Cricket*]   (ROG)
PLD .... Portland, IN [*Location identifier*] [*FAA*]   (FAAL)
PLD .... Posterior Latissimus Dorsi [*Anatomy*]
PLD .... Posterolateral Dendrite [*Neurology*]
PLD .... Potentially Lethal Damage [*Medicine*]
PLD .... Precision LASER Designator   (RDA)
PLD .... Primary Layer Depth [*Military*]   (CAAL)
PLD .... Principle of Limit Design
PLD .... Probable Line of Deployment [*Army*]   (AABC)
PLD ...... Procurement Legal Division [*Later, Office of General Counsel*] [*Navy*]
PLD .... Product Line Development
PLD .... Program Listing Document   (MCD)
PLD .... Programmable Logic Device
PLD .... Protective LASER Devices   (MCD)
PLD .... Public Libraries Division. Reporter [*A publication*]
PLD .... Pulse-Length Discriminator   (IEEE)
PLD .... Pulse Level Detector   (MCD)
PLdaC....... Calvary Baptist School of Theology, Lansdale, PA [*Library symbol*] [*Library of Congress*]   (LCLS)
PLDAL...... Pro-Life Direct Action League   (EA)
PLDC........ Preliminary List of Design Changes
PLDC........ Primary Leadership Development Course [*Army*]   (INF)
PLDC........ Primary Long-Distance Carrier [*Telephone service*]
PLDI......... Payload Data Interleaver [*NASA*]   (MCD)
PLDI......... Plastic Die [*Tool*]   (AAG)
P & L Dig Laws ... Pepper and Lewis' Digest of Laws [*Pennsylvania*] [*A publication*]   (DLA)
PLDK........ Peabody Language Development Kits [*Education*]
PLDM .... Payload Management [*NASA*]   (MCD)

PLDMI...... Precise LASER Distance Measuring Instrument
PLDP......... Parti Liberal Democrate et Pluraliste [*Belgium*] [*Political party*] (PPW)
PLDP......... Public Library Development Plan [*American Library Association, Public Library Association*]
PLD-PACOM ... Petroleum Logistical Data - Pacific Command (CINC)
PLDR........ Potentially Lethal Damage Repair [*Medicine*]
PLDRA...... Plant Disease Reporter [*A publication*]
PLDS........ Payload Support [*NASA*] (MCD)
PLDT........ Philippine Long Distance Telephone Co.
PLDTS ...... Propellant Loading Data Transmission System [*NASA*] (KSC)
PLE........... Encyclopedia of Pennsylvania Law [*A publication*] (DLA)
PLE........... Phased Loading Entry [*Data processing*]
PLE........... Photoluminescence Excitation [*Physics*]
PLE........... [*The*] Pittsburgh & Lake Erie Railroad Co. [*AAR code*]
PLE........... Planned Life Extension [*Pershing*] (MCD)
Ple .... Pleiade [*Record label*] [*France*]
PLE........... Plesetsk [*Satellite launch complex*] [*USSR*]
PLE........... Preliminary Logistics Evaluation
PLE........... Primary Loss Expectancy [*Insurance*]
PLE........... Prudent Limit of Endurance (NVT)
PLE........... Pulse Length Error (MCD)
PLE........... Pulsed LASER Experiment
PLEA........ Pacific Lumber Exporters Association (EA)
PLEA........ Poverty Lawyers for Effective Advocacy
PLEA........ Prototype Language for Economic Analysis [*Data processing*] (IID)
PLEAD...... Place of Last Entered Active Duty [*Military*]
PLEADGS ... Pleadings [*Legal term*] (ROG)
PLEASE.... Parolees, Law-Enforcement Assist Student Education [*Project to reduce drug abuse among junior and senior high school students in California*]
PLeB......... Bucknell University, Lewisburg, PA [*Library symbol*] [*Library of Congress*] (LCLS)
PLEB........ Plebiscitum [*A Decree of the People*] [*Latin*] (DLA)
PLebHi ...... Lebanon County Historical Society, Lebanon, PA [*Library symbol*] [*Library of Congress*] (LCLS)
PLebV....... United States Veterans Administration Hospital, Lebanon, PA [*Library symbol*] [*Library of Congress*] (LCLS)
PLEGA ...... Plant Engineering [*A publication*]
PLEGB ...... Plastics Engineering [*A publication*]
P Leg J .... Pittsburgh Legal Journal [*Pennsylvania*] [*A publication*] (DLA)
P Leg Jour ... Pittsburgh Legal Journal [*Pennsylvania*] [*A publication*] (DLA)
PLEI .... Public Law Education Institute (EA)
PLEN........ Plenipotentiary
PLEN........ Plenum Publishing Corp. [*NASDAQ symbol*] (NQ)
PLEN........ Public Leadership Education Network (EA)
PLENA...... Plant Engineering [*A publication*]
PLENAPS ... Plans for the Employment of Naval and Air Forces of the Associated Powers in the Eastern Theatre in the Event of War with Japan
PLENCH... Pliers and Wrench [*Combination tool*]
PLEND...... Plumbing Engineer [*A publication*]
P & LERR ... [*The*] Pittsburgh & Lake Erie Railroad Co.
PLESA....... Programs for Persons with Limited English-Speaking Ability [*Department of Labor*]
PLEURO... Pleuropneumonia [*Veterinary medicine*] (DSUE)
PLF........... Franklin and Marshall College, Lancaster, PA [*Library symbol*] [*Library of Congress*] (LCLS)
PLF........... Free Library of Philadelphia, Philadelphia, PA [*OCLC symbol*] (OCLC)
PLF........... Pacific Legal Foundation (EA)
PLF........... Page Length Field
PLF........... Palestine Liberation Front [*Political party*] (PD)
PLF........... Parachute Landing Fall [*Military*]
PLF........... Pastel Food [*Vancouver Stock Exchange symbol*]
PLF........... Patient Load Factor (AFM)
PLF........... People's Liberation Forces [*Ethiopia*] [*Political party*]
PLF........... Perilymph Fistula [*Medicine*]
PLF........... Phase Lock Frequency
PLF........... Phone Line Formatter
PLF........... Plaintiff
PLF........... Polar Lipid Fraction [*Biochemistry*]
PLF........... Positive Lock Fastener
PLF........... Power for Level Flight [*Aeronautics*]
PLF........... Private Line Telephone
PLF........... Proposition Letter Formula
PLF........... Public Administration [*A publication*]
PLFA........ Primary Level Field Activity [*Defense Supply Agency*]
PLFA .... Tabueran Island [*Fanning Islands*] [*Kiribati*] [*ICAO location identifier*] (ICLI)
Plf Adv ...... Plaintiff's Advocate [*A publication*]
PLFC .... Pulaski Furniture Corporation [*NASDAQ symbol*] (NQ)
PLFC & A ... Peggy Lee Fan Club and Archives [*Later, OOPLFC & A*] (EA)
PLFE .... Presidential Life Corp. [*NASDAQ symbol*] (NQ)
PLFF......... Plaintiff
PLFS......... Polarforschung [*A publication*]
PLFTR....... Please Furnish Transportation Requests (NOAA)
PLFUR ...... Please Furnish (NOAA)
PLG .... Pakistan Labour Gazette [*A publication*]

PLG .... Piling (MSA)
PLG .... Place Resources Corp. [*Toronto Stock Exchange symbol*]
PLG .... Plane Guard (NVT)
PLG .... Plant Management and Engineering [*A publication*]
PLG .... Pleural Ganglion [*Medicine*]
PLG .... Plug (AAG)
PLG .... Poetae Lyrici Graeci [*A publication*] (OCD)
PLG .... PolyGram NV [*NYSE symbol*] (SPSG)
PLG .... Polygyros [*Greece*] [*Seismograph station code, US Geological Survey*] (SEIS)
PLG .... Poor Law Guardian [*British*]
PLG .... Private-Label and Generic Brands
PLG .... Probleme de Lingvistica Genarala [*A publication*]
PLG .... Progressive Librarians Guild [*American Library Association*]
PLG .... Prolyl(leucyl)glycinamide [*Biochemistry*]
PLG .... Pulsed Light Generator
PLGAA...... Plants and Gardens [*A publication*]
PLGC........ Presbyterians for Lesbian/Gay Concerns (EA)
PLGFA ...... Poligrafiya [*A publication*]
PLGJA ...... Pipeline and Gas Journal [*A publication*]
PLGL........ Plate Glass
PLGM....... NYC Parents of Lesbians and Gay Men (EA)
PLGR........ Plunger (MSA)
PLGS .... Partita Liberale Giovani Somali [*Somali Liberal Youth Party*] [*Political party*]
PLGSS....... Payload Ground Support Systems [*NASA*] (NASA)
PLGT........ Prototype Lunar Geologist Tool
P-LGV ...... Psittacosis-Lymphogranuloma Venereum [*Medicine*]
PLH .... Hamilton Watch Co., Lancaster, PA [*Library symbol*] [*Library of Congress*] [*Obsolete*] (LCLS)
PLH .... Palaemontes-Lightening Hormone
PLH .... Partido Liberal de Honduras [*Liberal Party of Honduras*] [*Political party*] (PPW)
PLH .... Payload Handling [*NASA*] (NASA)
PLH .... Plaser Light [*Vancouver Stock Exchange symbol*]
PLH .... Plymouth [*England*] [*Airport symbol*] (OAG)
PLH .... Punjab Light Horse [*British military*] (DMA)
PLHi .... Lancaster County Historical Society, Lancaster, PA [*Library symbol*] [*Library of Congress*] (LCLS)
PLHID....... Plant Hire [*A publication*]
PLHJA ...... Plumbing and Heating Journal [*A publication*]
PLhS.......... Lock Haven State College, Lock Haven, PA [*Library symbol*] [*Library of Congress*] (LCLS)
PLI............ Leiner [*P.*] Nutritional Products Corp. [*AMEX symbol*] (SPSG)
pli .... Pali [*MARC language code*] [*Library of Congress*] (LCCP)
PLI............ Panarea [*Lipari Islands*] [*Seismograph station code, US Geological Survey*] (SEIS)
PLI............ Partido Liberal Independiente [*Independent Liberal Party*] [*Nicaragua*] [*Political party*] (PPW)
PLI............ Partito Liberale Italiano [*Italian Liberal Party*] [*Political party*] (PPW)
PLI............ Passenger and Immigration Lists Index [*A publication*]
PLI............ Payload Interrogator [*NASA*] (MCD)
PLI............ Phone Line Interface [*IBM Corp.*] (PCM)
PLI............ Pilot Location Indicator
PLI............ PLC Systems [*Vancouver Stock Exchange symbol*]
PLI............ Power Level Indicator
PLI............ Practising Law Institute (EA)
PLI............ Preload Indicating
PLI............ Private Line Interface
PLI............ Proctolin-Like Immunoactivity [*Neurobiology*]
PLI............ Public Lands Institute (EA)
PLI............ Pulsed LASER Interferometry
PLIA .... Pollution Liability Insurance Association [*Downers Grove, IL*] (EA)
PLIANT .... Procedural Language Implementing Analog Techniques [*Data processing*] (IEEE)
PLIB .... Pacific Lumber Inspection Bureau (EA)
PLIB .... Program Library [*Data processing*]
PLIC .... Public Libraries and Information Council [*Proposed*] [*Australia*]
PLIM........ Post Launch Information Message [*NASA*] (KSC)
PLIMC ...... Pipe Line Insurance Managers Conference [*Defunct*] (EA)
PLimT........ Tyler Arboretum, Lima, PA [*Library symbol*] [*Library of Congress*] (LCLS)
PLIN......... Power Line Impedance Network
PLINA....... Pipe Line Industry [*A publication*]
PLing .... Papers in Linguistics [*A publication*]
PLINK .... American People/Link [*American Design and Communication*] [*Information service or system*] (IID)
PLIS......... Preclinical Literature Information System [*Data processing*]
PLISN .... Parts List Item Sequence Number (MCD)
PLISN .... Provisioning List Item Sequence Number (NASA)
PLISP .... [*A*] programming language (CSR)
PLISSIT ... Permission, Limited Information, Specific Suggestions, and Intensive Therapy [*Occupational therapy*]
PLIT .... Petrolite Corp. [*NASDAQ symbol*] (NQ)
PLITTY.... Private Line Teletypewriter Service [*Telecommunications*] (TEL)
PLIW .... Preload Indicating Washer

PLJ .... Pacific Law Journal [*A publication*] (ILCA)
PLJ .... Parliamentary Lobby Journalists [*British*]
PLJ .... Pass Lake Resources Ltd. [*Vancouver Stock Exchange symbol*]
PLJ .... Patna Law Journal [*India*] [*A publication*] (ILCA)
PLJ .... Pennsylvania Law Journal [*A publication*] (DLA)
PLJ .... Philippine Law Journal [*A publication*] (ILCA)
PLJ .... Philippine Library Journal [*A publication*]
PLJ .... Pittsburgh Legal Journal [*Pennsylvania*] [*A publication*] (DLA)
PLJ .... Punjab Law Reporter [*India*] [*A publication*] (DLA)
PLJ .... Pure Lemon Juice
PLJ NS ...... Pittsburgh Legal Journal, New Series [*Pennsylvania*] [*A publication*] (DLA)
PLK .... Branson, MO [*Location identifier*] [*FAA*] (FAAL)
PLK .... Phi Lambda Kappa [*Fraternity*]
PLK .... Plank (AAG)
PLK .... Ploecker-Lee-Kesler [*Equation of state*]
PLK .... Plucky Little King [*Used by Western diplomats in Amman in reference to King Hussein of Jordan*]
PLK .... Poincare-Lighthill-Kuo [*Method*]
PLKAA ..... Plaste und Kautschuk [*A publication*]
PLKR .... Peacoat Locker
PLL .... Pall Corp. [*AMEX symbol*] (SPSG)
PLL .... Pallet [*Building construction*]
PLL .... Papers on Language and Literature [*A publication*]
PLL .... Parts Load List (MCD)
PLL .... Passenger Legal Liability [*Insurance*] (AIA)
PLL .... Peripheral Light Loss
PLL .... Phase-Locked Loop [*NASA*]
Pl L .... Platt on Leases [*1841*] [*A publication*] (DLA)
PLL .... Polo, IL [*Location identifier*] [*FAA*] (FAAL)
PLL .... Poly-L-lysine [*Also, PL*] [*Biochemistry*]
PLL .... Positive Logic Level
PLL .... Prescribed Load List [*Vehicle maintenance operation*] [*Army*]
PLL .... Prolymphocytic Leukemia [*Also, PL*] [*Oncology*]
PLL .... Pseudoalcoholic Liver Lesions [*Medicine*]
PLLAA ...... Royal Society. Proceedings. Series A. Mathematical and Physical Sciences [*A publication*]
P & L Laws ... Private and Local Laws [*A publication*] (DLA)
PLLE .... Prueba de Lectura y Lenguaje Escrito [*Standardized test of reading and writing in Spanish for students in grades 3 through 10*]
PLLL .... Parallel Petroleum Corp. [*NASDAQ symbol*] (NQ)
PLLL .... Posterior Lateral Line Lobe [*Of electric fishes*]
PLLP .... Polish Literature/Litterature Polonaise [*A publication*]
PLLR .... Phase Lock Loop Receiver
PLLRC ..... Public Land Law Review Commission [*Terminated, 1970*]
PLLSA....... Plzensky Lekarsky Sbornik [*A publication*]
PLLT .... Pallet (NATG)
PLLTN ...... Pollution
PLLVM ..... Pennsylvania Farm Museum of Landis Valley, Lancaster, PA [*Library symbol*] [*Library of Congress*] (LCLS)
PLM .... Pacific Law Magazine [*A publication*] (DLA)
PLM .... Packaged Liquid Missile
PLM .... Pakistan Liberation Movement [*Political party*] (PD)
PLM .... Palembang [*Indonesia*] [*Airport symbol*] (OAG)
PLM .... Palomar [*California*] [*Seismograph station code, US Geological Survey*] (SEIS)
PLM .... Papers in Linguistics of Melanesia [*A publication*]
PLM .... Passive Line Monitor [*Datapoint*]
PLM .... Passive Lunar Marker
PLM .... Payload Management [*NASA*] (NASA)
PLM .... Payload Monitoring [*NASA*] (NASA)
PLM .... People's Liberation Movement [*Montserrat*] [*Political party*] (PPW)
PLM .... Percent Labeled Mitosis [*Cytology*]
PLM .... Phleomycin [*Biochemistry*]
PLM .... Plastic Laminating Mold (MCD)
PLM .... PLM International [*AMEX symbol*] (SPSG)
PLM .... Plymouth Financial [*Vancouver Stock Exchange symbol*]
PLM .... Poetae Latini Minores [*A publication*] (OCD)
PLM .... Polarized Light Microscopy
PLM .... Poor Law Magazine [*A publication*] (DLA)
PLM .... Power Line Modulation (AABC)
PLM .... Prelaunch Monitor [*NASA*] (KSC)
PLM .... Preliminary (KSC)
PLM .... Product Line Manager
PLM .... Production Line Maintenance [*Air Force*]
PLM .... Production Line Manufacturing
PL/M .... Programming Language/Microcomputers [*Intel Corp.*] [*1973*] [*Data processing*] (CSR)
PLM .... Programming Logic Manual
PLM .... Pulse-Length Modulation
PLMA .... Private Label Manufacturers Association (EA)
PLMA....... Producers Livestock Marketing Association [*Later, IPLA*] (EA)
PL Mag..... Poor Law Magazine [*1858-1930*] [*Scotland*] [*A publication*] [*A publication*] (DLA)
PLMB....... Plumbing (AAG)
PLMD ...... Payload Mating Dolly
PLME....... Peak Local Mean Error (MCD)
PLMEA ..... Planta Medica [*A publication*]

PLMG....... Publishers' Library Marketing Group (EA)
PLMHi ...... Lancaster Mennonite Conference Historical Society, Lancaster, PA [*Library symbol*] [*Library of Congress*] (LCLS)
PLMN .... Plasmine Corp. [*NASDAQ symbol*] (NQ)
PLMP .... Program Logistic Management Plan (MCD)
PLMPA ..... Permanent Labourers' Mutual Protective Association [*A union*] [*British*]
PLMR....... Paris, Lyons, and Mediterranean Railway (ROG)
PLMR....... Post Launch Memorandum Report
PLMS .... Palms
PLMS .... Plastic Master [*Tool*] (AAG)
PLMS .... Preservation of Library Materials Section [*Resources and Technical Services Division*] [*American Library Association*]
PLMS .... Program Logistics Master Schedule [*NASA*] (NASA)
PLMS .... Public Land Mobile Service Data Base [*Comp Comm, Inc.*] [*Information service or system*] (CRD)
PLMSA ..... Plasticheskie Massy [*A publication*]
PLMX....... PL/M Extended [*Programming language*] (CSR)
PLMX....... PLM Financial Services [*NASDAQ symbol*] (NQ)
PLN .... Flight Plan [*Aviation code*]
PLN .... Partido Liberacion Nacional [*National Liberation Party*] [*Costa Rica*] [*Political party*] (PPW)
PLN .... Partido Liberal Nacionalista [*Nationalist Liberal Party*] [*Nicaragua*]
PLN .... Pellston [*Michigan*] [*Airport symbol*] (OAG)
PLN .... Pellston, MI [*Location identifier*] [*FAA*] (FAAL)
PLN .... Phospholamban [*Biochemistry*]
PLN .... Plain
PLN .... Plan (NASA)
PLN .... Plane (MSA)
PLN .... Planning [*A publication*]
Pln............ Platoon [*British military*] (DMA)
PLN .... Plauen [*German Democratic Republic*] [*Seismograph station code, US Geological Survey*] (SEIS)
PLN .... Popliteal Lymph Node [*Anatomy*]
PLN .... Program Line Number [*DoD*]
PLN .... Program Logic Network (NASA)
PLNAP....... Pro-Life Nonviolent Action Project (EA)
PLNG .... Planning
PLNN .... Planning (MCD)
PLNN-A .... Plan [*A publication*]
PLNO .... Plano Petroleum Corp. [*NASDAQ symbol*] (NQ)
PLNR....... Planar (MSA)
PLNS .... Plains (MCD)
PLNSTD ... Planned Standard Equipment [*Navy*] (AFIT)
PLNSW Staff News ... Public Library of New South Wales. Staff News [*A publication*] (APTA)
PLNT....... Planet (MSA)
PLNTY....... Planetary (MSA)
PLO .... Pacific Launch Operations [*NASA*]
PLO .... Palestine Liberation Organization [*Political party*] (PD)
PLO .... Parliamentary Liaison Officer (ADA)
PLO .... Partial Lunar Orbit [*Planetary science*]
PLO .... Parts List Only (MCD)
PLO .... Passenger Liaison Office [*Military*] (AABC)
PLO .... Payload Officer [*NASA*] (MCD)
PLO .... Pensiero e Linguaggio in Operazioni/Thought and Language in Operations [*A publication*]
PLO .... Pentagon Liaison Office (MCD)
PLO .... Phase-Locked Oscillator
PLO .... Plans Officer
PLO .... Poly-L-ornithine
PLO .... Poor Law Office (ROG)
PLO .... Port Liaison Officer
PLO .... Port Lincoln [*Australia*] [*Airport symbol*] (OAG)
PLO .... Program Line Organization
PLO .... Programmed Local Oscillator
PLO .... Project Line Organization
PLO .... Public Land Order [*Interior*]
PLO .... Pulsed LASER Oscillator
PLO .... Pulsed Locked Oscillator
PLOA .... Proposed Letter of Agreement (MCD)
PLOB....... Patrol Log Observations [*Aviation*] (DSUE)
PLOB....... Place of Birth
PLOCAP ... Post Loss-of-Coolant Accident Protection [*Nuclear energy*] (NRCH)
PLOCSA ... Personnel Liaison Officer, Chief of Staff, Army (AABC)
PLOD .... Periodic List of Data [*Data processing*]
PLOD .... Planetary Orbit Determination (IEEE)
Plodorodie Pochv Karelii Akad Nauk SSSR Karel'sk Filial ... Plodorodie Pochv Karelii. Akademiya Nauk SSSR. Karel'skii Filial [*A publication*]
P Lom......... Petrus Lombardi [*Flourished, 1154-59*] [*Authority cited in pre-1607 legal work*] (DSA)
PLOM .... Prescribed Loan Optimization Model [*Army*] (AABC)
PLOME..... Poor Little Old Me Syndrome [*British*]
P Lond Math ... Proceedings. London Mathematical Society [*A publication*]
PLondon .... Greek Papyri in the British Museum [*A publication*] (OCD)
PLONG ..... Present Longitude [*Aviation*] (FAAC)

PLOO .... Pacific Launch Operations Office [*NASA*]
PLOP........ Planetary Landing Observation Package [*Aerospace*]
PLOP........ Policy Options/Options Politiques [*A publication*]
PLOP........ Pressure Line of Position [*Air Force*]
PLor .... Saint Francis College, Loretto, PA [*Library symbol*] [*Library of Congress*]   (LCLS)
PLOS .... Primary Line of Sight [*Sextants*]
PLOT........ People's Liberation Organization of Tamil Eelam [*Political party*] [*Sri Lanka*]
PLOT........ Plotting
PLOT........ Porous Layer, Open Tubular Column [*Gas chromatography*]
PLOT........ Probability of Launch on Time   (MCD)
Plot........... Vita Plotini [*of Porphyry*] [*Classical studies*]   (OCD)
PLOTE ...... People's Liberation Organization of Tamil Eelam [*Sri Lanka*]
Ploughs ...... Ploughshares [*A publication*]
Plovdiv Univ Naucn Trud ... Plovdivski Universitet. Naucni Trudove [*A publication*]
PLOW .... Petunia Lovers of the World
Plow .... Plowden's English King's Bench Commentaries [*or Reports*] [*A publication*]   (DLA)
Plowd .... Plowden's English King's Bench Commentaries [*or Reports*] [*A publication*]   (DLA)
PLOYREP ... Unit Deployment Report   (CINC)
PLP........... La Palma [*Panama*] [*Airport symbol*]   (OAG)
PLP........... Palo [*Philippines*] [*Seismograph station code, US Geological Survey*]   (SEIS)
PLP........... Palpus [*Arthropod anatomy*]
PLP........... Parliamentary Labour Party [*British*]
PLP........... Parti Liberal Progressiste [*Liberal Progressive Party*] [*Morocco*] [*Political party*]   (PPW)
PLP........... Parti pour la Liberation du Peuple [*People's Liberation Party*] [*Senegal*] [*Political party*]   (PPW)
PLP........... Parti de la Liberte et du Progres [*Party of Liberty and Progress*] [*See also PVV*] [*Belgium*]   (PPE)
PLP........... Partido de los Pobres [*Poor People's Party*] [*Mexico*] [*Political party*]   (PD)
PLP........... Partners for Livable Places   (EA)
PLP........... Parts List Page   (KSC)
PLP........... Pattern Learning Parser
PLP........... People's Liberation Party [*Pakistan*]
PLP........... Periodate Lysine-Paraformaldehyde
PLP........... Personal LASER Printer [*Data processing*]
PLP........... Phillips Petroleum Co. [*Toronto Stock Exchange symbol*]
PLP........... Plains Petroleum Co. [*NYSE symbol*]   (SPSG)
PLP........... Polyoma-Like Particle [*Genetics*]
PLP........... Post Launch Phase
PLP........... Presentation Level Protocol [*AT & T Videotex System*]
PLP........... Principal Locating Point [*Automotive engineering*]
PLP........... Procedural Language Processor
PLP........... Process Layup Procedure
PLP........... Product Liability Prevention [*Conference*]
PLP........... Progressive Labor Party   (EA)
PLP........... Progressive Liberal Party [*Bahamas*] [*Political party*]   (PPW)
PLP........... Proteolipid [*Biochemistry*]
PLP........... Proteolipid Protein [*Biochemistry*]
PLP........... Pyridoxal Phosphate [*Also, PALP*] [*Biochemistry*]
PLPA .... Pageable Link-Pack Area
PLPA .... Palmyra, Palmyra Island [*Line Islands*] [*ICAO location identifier*]   (ICLI)
PLPA .... Permissive Low-Pressure Alarm   (IEEE)
Pl Par........ Placita Parliamentaria [*Latin*] [*A publication*]   (DLA)
Pl Path ...... Plant Pathology [*A publication*]
PLPB .... Petroleum Labor Policy Board [*Abolished, 1936*]
PLPBD ...... Pulpboard
PLPD........ Product Liability Prevention and Defense [*An association*]   (EA)
PL & PD .... Public Liability and Property Damage [*Insurance*]
PLP FOR... Foramen of Labial Palpus [*Arthropod anatomy*]
PLPG .... Publishers' Library Promotion Group [*Later, PLMG*]   (EA)
PLP GRNDG ... Pulp Grinding [*Freight*]
PLPHA...... Plant Physiology [*A publication*]
PLPHB ...... Plasma Physics [*A publication*]
Pl Physics .. Plasma Physics [*A publication*]
Pl Physiol (Lancaster) ... Plant Physiology (Lancaster) [*A publication*]
Pl Physiol (Wash) ... Plant Physiology (Washington) [*A publication*]
PLPLS....... Proceedings. Leeds Philosophical and Literary Society [*A publication*]
PLPLS-LHS ... Proceedings. Leeds Philosophical and Literary Society. Literary and Historical Section [*A publication*]
PLPLS-SS ... Proceedings. Leeds Philosophical and Literary Society. Scientific Section [*A publication*]
PLPP .... Position Location Post Processor   (MCD)
Pl & Pr Cas ... Pleading and Practice Cases [*1837-38*] [*England*] [*A publication*]   (DLA)
Pl Prot (Tokyo) ... Plant Protection (Tokyo) [*A publication*]
PLPS........ Packaged Liquid Propellant System
PLPS........ Propellant Loading and Pressurization System [*NASA*]
PLPSA...... Physiological Psychology [*A publication*]
PLPUA...... Planseeberichte fuer Pulvermetallurgie (Austria) [*A publication*]
PLQ .... Plaque   (MSA)
PLQ .... Tallahassee, FL [*Location identifier*] [*FAA*]   (FAAL)

PLR........... LaRoche College, Pittsburgh, PA [*OCLC symbol*]   (OCLC)
PLR........... Pacific Law Reporter [*A publication*]   (DLA)
PLR........... Pakistan Law Reports [*A publication*]   (DLA)
PLR........... Pakistan Law Review [*A publication*]   (DLA)
PLR........... Palestine Law Reports [*A publication*]
PLR........... Parlake Resources Ltd. [*Toronto Stock Exchange symbol*]
PLR........... Partido Liberal Radical [*Radical Liberal Party*] [*Ecuador*] [*Political party*]   (PPW)
PLR........... Partido Liberal Radical [*Radical Liberal Party*] [*Paraguay*] [*Political party*]   (PPW)
PLR........... Patent Law Review [*A publication*]   (DLA)
PLR........... Patent Log Reading [*Navigation*]
PLR........... Patna Law Reporter [*India*] [*A publication*]   (DLA)
PLR........... Pell City, AL [*Location identifier*] [*FAA*]   (FAAL)
PLR........... Pennsylvania Law Record [*Philadelphia*] [*A publication*]   (DLA)
P-LR .... Pennsylvania Legislative Reference Bureau, Harrisburg, PA [*Library symbol*] [*Library of Congress*]   (LCLS)
PLR........... Periodic Logistical Report
PLR........... Philippine Liberation Ribbon [*Military decoration*]
PLR........... Pillar   (MSA)
PLR........... Plan. Zeitschrift fuer Planen, Bauen, und Umwelt [*A publication*]
PLR........... Planning Review [*A publication*]
PLR........... Pliers   (MSA)
PLR........... Plymouth Rubber Co., Inc. [*AMEX symbol*]   (SPSG)
PLR........... Portable LASER Range-Finder
PL & R .... Postal Laws and Regulations [*Later, Postal Manual*]
PLR........... Power Line Radiation [*Radioscience*]
PLR........... Presentation Loss Rate   (MCD)
PLR........... Pressure Level Recorder
PLR........... Primary Loss Retention [*Insurance*]
PLR........... Private Legislation Reports [*Scotland*] [*A publication*]   (DLA)
PLR........... Program Life Requirement   (NG)
PLR........... Psychological Laboratories [*Harvard University*]   (KSC)
PLR........... Public Law Review [*A publication*]
PLR........... Public Lending Right [*Royalty for books borrowed from public libraries*] [*British*]
PLR........... Puller   (MSA)
PLR........... Pulse Link Relay [*Telecommunications*]   (TEL)
PLR........... Pulse Link Repeater [*Telecommunications*]   (TEL)
PLR........... Punjab Law Reporter [*India*] [*A publication*]   (DLA)
PLR........... University of Pittsburgh. Law Review [*A publication*]
PLRA .... Partido Liberal Radical Autentico [*Authentic Liberal Radical Party*] [*Paraguay*] [*Political party*]   (PD)
PLRACTA ... Position Location, Reporting, and Control of Tactical Aircraft [*Military*]
PLRB .... Property Loss Research Bureau   (EA)
PLRC .... Pulsed LASER Remote Crosswind Sensor   (MCD)
PLRCA ...... Pharmacological Research Communications [*A publication*]
PLRCAE.... Radio Corp. of America, Electron Tube Division, Engineering Section, Lancaster, PA [*Library symbol*] [*Library of Congress*] [*Obsolete*]   (LCLS)
PLRD........ Payload Requirements Document   (NASA)
PLRD........ Pull Rod
PLR Dacca ... Pakistan Law Reports, Dacca Series [*A publication*]   (DLA)
PLRF .... Pediatric Liver Research Foundation [*Inactive*]   (EA)
pLRF.......... Placental Luteinizing Hormone-Releasing Factor [*Endocrinology*]
PLRI .... Posterolateral Rotation Instability [*Sports medicine*]
PLRJ & K.. Punjab Law Reporter, Jammu and Kashmir Section [*India*] [*A publication*]   (DLA)
PLR Kar.... Pakistan Law Reports, Karachi Series [*1947-53*] [*A publication*]   (DLA)
PLR Lah .... Pakistan Law Reports, Lahore Series [*1947-55*] [*A publication*]   (DLA)
PLRPF....... Personnel Loss Rate Planning Factors   (MCD)
PLRS .... Pelorus
PLRS .... Phase Lock Receiving System
PLRS .... Position Location Reporting System [*Military*]
PLRSA ...... Plasticos y Resinas [*A publication*]
Plrs' Bull Rubb Res Inst Malaya ... Planters' Bulletin. Rubber Research Institute of Malaya [*A publication*]
PLRS/TIDS ... Position Location Reporting System/Tactical Information Distribution Systems [*Military*]   (RDA)
PLRSTN.... Pelorus Stand
PLRT........ Polarity   (MSA)
PLRV......... Payload Launch Readiness Verification [*NASA*]   (MCD)
PLRV......... Potato Leafroll Virus
PLRWP ..... Pakistan Law Reports, West Pakistan Series [*A publication*]   (DLA)
PLS........... Palletized Load System [*Army*]   (RDA)
PLS........... Palomar-Leiden Survey
PLS........... Parcels   (MSA)
PLS........... Parsons Language Sample
PLS........... Parti Liberal Suisse [*Liberal Party of Switzerland*] [*Political party*]   (PPE)
PLS........... Partial Least Squares
PLS........... Patrol Locator System [*Army*]
PLS........... Payload Systems [*NASA*]   (MCD)
PLS........... Peerless Tube Co. [*AMEX symbol*]   (SPSG)

PLS .... Peninsula Library System [*Belmont, CA*] [*Library network*]
PLS .... People's Law School　(EA)
PLS .... Peralto Resources Corp. [*Vancouver Stock Exchange symbol*]
PLS .... Periodic Log System
PLS .... Pitch Limit Switch
PLS .... Plaisance [*Mauritius*] [*Geomagnetic observatory code*]
PLS .... Plasma Light Source
PLS .... Plates [*Classical studies*]　(OCD)
PLS .... Please　(AFM)
PLS .... Plugging Switch　(IEEE)
PLS .... Pneumatic Limit Switch
PLS .... Polson, MT [*Location identifier*] [*FAA*]　(FAAL)
PLS .... Polystyrene Latex Sphere
PLS .... Portable Laboratory Salinometer
PLS .... Position Location System [*Army*]
PLS .... Post Landing and Safing [*NASA*]　(NASA)
PLS .... Precautions, Limitations, and Setpoints [*Nuclear energy*]　(NRCH)
PLS .... Preliminary Landing Site　(NASA)
PLS .... Preschool Language Scale [*Child development test*]
PLS .... President of the Linnaean Society [*British*]
PLS .... Primary Landing Site　(MCD)
PLS .... Private Line Service
PLS .... Product Line Simulator
PLS .... Professional Legal Secretary [*Designation awarded by National Association of Legal Secretaries*]
PLS .... Profit-and-Loss-Sharing Account [*Banking*]　(IMH)
PLS .... Programmable Logic Sequencer [*Data processing*]
PLS .... Progressive Learning Systems [*Potomac, MD*]　(TSSD)
PLS .... Propellant Loading Sequencer　(AAG)
PLS .... Propellant Loading System
PLS .... Providenciales [*British West Indies*] [*Airport symbol*]　(OAG)
PLS .... Public Library Service [*Australia*]
PLS .... Pulse　(MSA)
PLS .... Pulsed LASER System
PLS .... Pulsed Light Source
PLS .... Purnell Library Service [*Commercial firm*]
PLSCB ...... Policy Sciences [*A publication*]
PLSCE4 ...... Plant Science [*Shannon*] [*A publication*]
PLSD .... Promotion List Service Date [*Air Force*]
PLSFC .... Part Load Specific Fuel Consumption [*Gas turbine*]
Pls Gds...... Plants and Gardens [*A publication*]
PLSGT .... Platoon Sergeant [*Marine Corps*]
PLSHD ...... Polished [*Freight*]
PLSL.......... Propellants and Life Support Laboratory [*NASA*]　(NASA)
PLSN .... Pulsation　(MSA)
PLSO .... Propellant Life Support and Ordnance [*NASA*]　(KSC)
PLSOA ...... Plant and Soil [*A publication*]
PLSP......... Payload Signal Processor [*NASA*]　(MCD)
PLSP......... Prelaunch Survival Probability　(CINC)
PLSPS .... Performance Levels of a School Program Survey [*Teacher evaluation test*]
PLSR .... Pulsar Oil & Gas [*NASDAQ symbol*]　(NQ)
PLSR .... Pulsator　(MSA)
PLSS .... Portable Life Support System [*or Subsystem*] [*NASA*]
PLSS .... Post-Landing Survival System [*NASA*]
PLSS .... Precision Location Strike System [*Air Force*]
PLSS .... Prelaunch Status Simulator
PLSS .... Primary Life Support System [*or Subsystem*]　(NASA)
PLSSA .... Public Library Systems Section [*Public Library Association*]
PLSSA .... Planetary and Space Science [*A publication*]
PLSSRS ..... Plant and Soil Science Research Station [*Southern Illinois University at Carbondale*] [*Research center*]　(RCD)
PLSSU...... Portable Life Support Stretcher Unit [*Military*]　(CAAL)
PLSTC ...... Plastic　(AAG)
PLSTR ...... Plasterer　(ADA)
PLSV .... Propellant Latching Solenoid Valve
PLT .... Columbus, NE [*Location identifier*] [*FAA*]　(FAAL)
PLT .... Lancaster Theological Seminary of the United Church of Christ, Lancaster, PA [*Library symbol*] [*Library of Congress*]　(LCLS)
PLT .... Lutheran Theological Seminary, Philadelphia, PA [*OCLC symbol*]　(OCLC)
PLT .... Pallet　(AABC)
Plt .... Parliament
PLT .... Partido Liberal Teete [*Teete Liberal Party*] [*Paraguay*] [*Political party*]　(PPW)
PLT .... Patna Law Times [*India*] [*A publication*]　(DLA)
Plt .... Peltier's Orleans Appeals Decisions [*Louisiana*] [*A publication*]　(DLA)
PLT .... Photoluminescent Thermometer
PLT .... Pilot　(AFM)
PLT .... Pilot Knob [*California*] [*Seismograph station code, US Geological Survey*]　(SEIS)
PLT .... Pipeline Time [*Army*]
PLT .... Plaint [*Legal term*]　(ROG)
PLT .... Planar Tube
PLT .... Plant
PLT .... Plate
PLT .... Platelet [*Hematology*]
PLT .... Platoon [*Military*]　(AABC)

PLT .... Port Light
PLT .... Post Loading Test　(NG)
PLT .... Power Line Transient　(IEEE)
PLT .... Primed Lymphocyte Typing [*Hematology*]
PLT .... Princeton Large Torus [*Nuclear reactor*]
PLT .... Private Line Telephone
PLT .... Private Line Teletypewriter
PLT .... Procurement Lead Time [*Army*]
PLT .... Production Lead Time
PLT .... Program Library Tape [*Data processing*]　(IEEE)
PLT .... Programmed Learning Textbook
PLT .... Progress in Low Temperature Physics [*Elsevier Book Series*] [*A publication*]
PLT .... Psittacosis-Lymphogranuloma Venereum Trachoma [*Microbiology*]
PLT .... Pulsed Light Theodolite
PLT .... Punjab Law Times [*India*] [*A publication*]　(DLA)
PLT .... South Carolina Aeronautics Commission [*Columbia, SC*] [*FAA designator*]　(FAAC)
PLTC .... Port Liner Terms Charges [*Shipping*]　(DS)
PLTC .... Propellant Loading Terminal Cabinet　(AAG)
PLTD........ Plated
PLTEA ...... Plastics Technology [*A publication*]
PLTF .... Par Leadership Training Foundation [*Defunct*]　(EA)
PLTF .... Plaintiff [*Legal term*]　(ROG)
PLTF .... Purple Loosestrife Task Force　(EA)
PLTFF .... Plaintiff
PLTFM ...... Platform
PLTG........ Plating
PLT GL ..... Plate Glass [*Freight*]
PLTHS ...... Pilothouse
PLT LT ...... Pilot Light　(MSA)
Plt Off........ Pilot Officer [*British military*]　(DMA)
PLTP .... Phospholipid Transfer Protein [*Biochemistry*]
PLTPA ...... Progress in Low Temperature Physics [*A publication*]
PLTR .... Plan for Long-Range Technical Requirements
PLTR .... Plotter　(MSA)
PLTRY ...... Poultry [*Freight*]
PLTS .... Precision LASER Tracking System　(NASA)
PLTTNG ... Pilot Training [*Air Force*]
PLTTNGSq ... Pilot Training Squadron [*Air Force*]
PLTVA ...... Plastvaerlden [*A publication*]
PLTZ .... Pulitzer Publishing Co. [*St. Louis, MO*] [*NASDAQ symbol*]　(NQ)
PLU .... Partido Liberal Unificado [*Unified Liberal Party*] [*Paraguay*] [*Political party*]　(PPW)
PLu .... Path Loss, Uplink [*Communications*]
PLU .... Phi Lambda Upsilon [*Fraternity*]
PLU U .... Platoon Leaders Unit [*Marine Corps*]
Pl U .... Plowden on Usury [*A publication*]　(DLA)
PLU .... Plural
PLU .... Plutonium [*Chemical symbol is Pu*]　(AAG)
PLU .... Poor Law Union [*British*]
PLU .... Preservation of Location Uncertainty [*Strategy for protecting missiles*] [*Military*]
PLU .... Pressure Lubrication Unit
PLU .... Propellant Loading and Utilization　(AAG)
Plucne Bolesti Tuberk ... Plucne Bolesti i Tuberkuloza [*A publication*]
Plucne Boles Tuberk ... Plucne Bolesti i Tuberkuloza [*A publication*]
PLUCON .. Plutonium Decontamination Emergency Team [*Army*]
PLUDA....... Plutonium-Dokumentation [*A publication*]
PLUG .... ComponentGuard, Inc. [*NASDAQ symbol*]　(NQ)
PLUG .... Propellant Loading and Utilization Group　(AAG)
PLUGE....... Picture Line-Up Generator [*Television*]
PLuL .... Lincoln University, Lincoln University, PA [*Library symbol*] [*Library of Congress*]　(LCLS)
PLUM .... Payload Launch Module
PLUM .... Payload Umbilical Mast　(NASA)
PLUM .... Priority Low-Use Minimal
PLUMB..... Plumbum [*Lead*] [*Pharmacy*]
Plumb Heat J ... Plumbing and Heating Journal [*A publication*]
Plumbing Eng ... Plumbing Engineer [*A publication*]
Plumbing Engr ... Plumbing Engineer [*A publication*]
Plumbing Heat Equip News ... Plumbing and Heating Equipment News [*A publication*]
Plum Contr ... Plumptre on Contracts [*2nd ed.*] [*1897*] [*A publication*]　(DLA)
PLUNA ..... Primeras Lineas Uruguayas de Navegacion Aerea [*Uruguayan National Airlines*]
PLund .... Papyri Lundenses [*A publication*]　(OCD)
PLUP .... Pluperfect [*Grammar*]
PLUPF ...... Pluperfect [*Grammar*]
PLUR........ Jarvis Island [*Line Islands*] [*ICAO location identifier*]　(ICLI)
PLUR........ Photo Lab Usage Reporting　(MCD)
PLUR........ Plural
Plural Soc .. Plural Societies [*The Hague*] [*A publication*]
PLUS .... Parent Loans to Undergraduate Students [*Later, ALAS*] [*Department of Education*]
PLUS .... PERT [*Program Evaluation and Review Technique*] Lifecycle Unified System
PLUS .... Plexus Resources Corp. [*NASDAQ symbol*]　(NQ)
PLUS .... Portable Lightweight Upper Air Sounding System　(MCD)

PLUS......... Potential Long Supply Utilization Screening (NATG)
PLUS......... Precision Loading and Utilization System (AAG)
PLUS......... Prima Leben und Sparen [*Quality Living and Saving*] [*Brand name and discount store chain in West Germany and US*]
PLUS......... Procedures for Long Supply Assets Utilization Screening [*DoD*]
PLUS......... Program Library Update System
PLUS......... Programmed Learning under Supervision
PLUS......... Programming Language for UNIVAC [*Universal Automatic Computer*] Systems [*Data processing*] (CSR)
PLUS......... Project Literacy US [*Joint project of American Broadcasting Company and Public Broadcasting Service*]
Plut............ Plutarch [*First century AD*] [*Classical studies*] (OCD)
Plut............ Plutus [*of Aristophanes*] [*Classical studies*] (OCD)
PLUTA...... Pollution [*A publication*]
PLUTHARCO ... Plutonium, Uranium, Thorium Assembly Reactivity Code
PLUTO..... Pipeline under the Ocean [*British project*] [*World War II*]
PLUTO..... Plutonium [*Loop-Testing*] Reactor [*British*] (DEN)
Plutonium-Dok ... Plutonium-Dokumentation [*West Germany*] [*A publication*]
PLV............ Peak Left Ventricular [*Pressure*] [*Cardiology*]
PLV............ Phu-Lien [*Kien-An*] [*Vietnam*] [*Seismograph station code, US Geological Survey*] (SEIS)
PLV............ Posterior Left Ventricular Wall [*Cardiology*]
PLV............ Postlanding Vent [*or Ventilation*] [*Apollo*] [*NASA*]
PLV............ Power Limiting Valve
PLV............ Production Level Video
PLV............ Sterling Air Service, Inc. [*Sterling, CO*] [*FAA designator*] (FAAC)
PLVC......... Post-Landing Vent Control [*NASA*] (KSC)
PLVDA...... Progress in Liver Diseases [*A publication*]
PLVRZD... Pulverized (MSA)
PLW.......... Palau [*ANSI three-letter standard code*] (CNC)
PLW.......... Palu [*Indonesia*] [*Airport symbol*] (OAG)
PLW.......... Patna Law Weekly [*India*] [*A publication*] (DLA)
PLW.......... Plastic Engine Technology Corp. [*Toronto Stock Exchange symbol*]
PLW.......... Plow (FAAC)
PLW.......... Preload Washer
PLWA........ People Living with AIDS [*Acquired Immune Deficiency Syndrome*] [*Australia*]
PL/WA...... Plain Washer [*Automotive engineering*]
PLX.......... Parallax Developments [*Vancouver Stock Exchange symbol*]
PLX.......... Plains Resources, Inc. [*AMEX symbol*] (SPSG)
PLX.......... Plantronics, Inc. [*NYSE symbol*] (SPSG)
PLX.......... Plexus [*Medicine*]
PLX.......... Position Launch [*Search mode wherein X signifies the launch mode number*] (MCD)
PLX.......... Propellant Loading Exercise (MCD)
PLX.......... Robinson, IL [*Location identifier*] [*FAA*] (FAAL)
PLXS......... Plexus Corp. [*NASDAQ symbol*] (NQ)
PLXX........ Polymerix, Inc. [*NASDAQ symbol*] (NQ)
PLY........... [*The*] Plessey Co. Ltd. [*NYSE symbol*] (SPSG)
Ply............ Plymouth [*Record label*]
PLY........... Plywood
PLY........... Polaris Energy [*Vancouver Stock Exchange symbol*]
PLY........... Prune Extract Lactose Yeast Medium [*Microbiology*]
PLYGA...... Psychologia: An International Journal of Psychology in the Orient [*A publication*]
PLYHD ..... Polyhedron [*A publication*]
PLYINST .. Command Comply Current Instructions
PLYM........ Plymouth [*England*]
PLYMCHAN ... Plymouth Subarea Channel [*NATO*] (NATG)
Plymouth Miner Min Club J ... Plymouth Mineral and Mining Club. Journal [*A publication*]
PLYMP ..... Plympton [*England*]
PLYMT ..... Plymtree [*England*]
Plyn Voda Zdra Tech ... Plyn Voda a Zdravotni Technika [*A publication*]
PLYPASSPORT ... Application for Passport for Self and/or Dependents Accordance BUPERS Manual [*Navy*]
PLYWD..... Plywood (AAG)
Plyw and Plyw Prod ... Plywood and Plywood Products [*A publication*] (APTA)
Plyw Plyw Prod ... Plywood and Plywood Products [*A publication*] (APTA)
PLZ........... Plastics World [*A publication*]
PLZ........... Plaza (MCD)
PLZ........... Please
PLZ........... Polarize (MSA)
PLZ........... Port Elizabeth [*South Africa*] [*Airport symbol*] (OAG)
PLZ........... Programming Languages for the Zilog [*Data processing*] (CSR)
PLZA......... Plaza Commerce Bancorp [*NASDAQ symbol*] (NQ)
Plzen Lek Sb ... Plzensky Lekarsky Sbornik [*A publication*]
Plzen Lek Sb Suppl ... Plzensky Lekarsky Sbornik. Supplementum [*A publication*]
PLZN......... Polarization (MSA)
PLZT......... Pb-based Lanthanum-doped Zirconate Titanates
PM............. Brymon Airways [*British*] [*ICAO designator*] (FAAC)
PM............. [*The*] Chesapeake & Ohio Railway Co. (Pere Marquette District) [*AAR code*]
PM............. Ha-Po'el ha-Mizrahi (BJA)
PM............. International Journal of Psychiatry in Medicine [*A publication*]

P & M .... Law Reports, Probate and Matrimonial Cases [*England*] [*A publication*] (DLA)
PM............. Pacific Mail (ROG)
PM............. Pad Mechanic [*Aerospace*]
PM............. Painting Machine
PM............. Pak [*or Phak*] Mai [*New Party*] [*Political party*]
PM............. Palace of Minos [*A publication*]
PM............. Paleographie Musicale [*A publication*]
PM............. Pamphlet
PM............. Panel Meter (IEEE)
PM............. Paper Maker [*A publication*]
PM............. Paper Money [*A publication*]
PM............. Parachute Mine [*British military*] (DMA)
PM............. Parameter [*Data processing*]
P M .... Paris Match [*A publication*]
PM............. Parlor Maid
PM............. Parole et Mission [*A publication*]
PM............. Particulate Matter
PM............. Partito Monarchico [*Monarchist Party*] [*Italy*] [*Political party*] (PPE)
P/M .... Parts per Million (IEEE)
PM............. Passed Midshipman
PM............. Passed Motion
PM............. Past Master [*Freemasonry*]
PM............. Patriotic Majority [*An association*] (EA)
PM............. Patriotikon Metopon [*Patriotic Front*] [*Greek Cyprus*] [*Political party*] (PPE)
PM............. Patternmaker [*Navy rating*]
PM............. Payload Management [*NASA*] (NASA)
PM............. Payload Midbody [*NASA*] (MCD)
PM............. Paymaster
PM............. Peace Museum (EA)
PM............. Pectoralis Major [*Anatomy*]
PM............. Peculiar Meter
PM............. Penalty Minutes [*Hockey*]
PM............. Pension Mortgage [*British*]
PM............. People Meter [*TV ratings measuring device*] [*Advertising*]
PM............. Per Million
pM............. Per Monat [*Per Month*] [*German*]
PM............. Per Month
PM............. Pere Marquette Railroad
PM............. Perfect Master [*Freemasonry*]
PM............. Performance Monitor [*NASA*] (NASA)
PM............. Periodic Maintenance (AFM)
PM............. Permanent Magnet [*Loudspeaker*]
PM............. Petermanns Geographische Mitteilungen [*A publication*]
PM............. Petit Mal [*Epilepsy*]
PM............. Peuples Mediterraneens [*A publication*]
PM............. Phase Modulation [*Radio data transmission*]
PM............. Phased Maintenance (MCD)
PM............. Philip Morris, Inc.
PM............. Philippine Manager [*A publication*]
PM............. Phorbol Monomyristate [*Organic chemistry*]
PM............. Phosphoramide Mustard [*Antineoplastic drug*]
PM............. Photo Marketing Magazine [*A publication*] (EAAP)
PM............. Photo Master (MCD)
PM............. Photomultiplier
PM............. Phyllosticta maydis [*A toxin-producing fungus*]
PM............. Physical Medicine
P/M .... Physical Medicine [*Medical Officer designation*] [*British*]
PM............. Piae Memoriae [*Of Pious Memory*] [*Latin*]
pm............. Picometer
PM............. Pilot Motor (MSA)
PM............. Pioneer Ministries (EA)
PM............. Pit Membrane [*Paleobotany*]
PM............. Placer Mining Times [*Whitehorse*] [*A publication*]
PM............. Planetary Mission [*NASA*] (NASA)
PM............. Plasma Membrane [*Cytology*]
PM............. Plasmalemma [*Cytology*]
PM............. Plaster Master (MSA)
P/M .... Plastic Mold (MCD)
P/M .... Player/Missile [*Atari computers*]
P or M .... Plus or Minus (MSA)
PM............. Plus Minus [*More or less*]
PM............. PM. Pharmacy Management [*A publication*]
PM............. Polarization Modulation (MCD)
PM............. Police Magistrate
PM............. Police Mutual Assurance Society [*British*]
PM............. Policy Memorandum [*Military*]
PM............. Poliomyelitis [*Medicine*]
PM............. Pollen Mass [*Botany*]
P & M .... Pollock and Maitland's History of English Common Law [*A publication*] (DLA)
PM............. Polymethacrylic [*Organic chemistry*]
PM............. Polymorph [*Hematology*]
PM............. Polymyositis [*Medicine*]
PM............. Pondus Medicinale [*Medicinal Weight*] [*Pharmacy*] (ROG)
PM............. Pontifex Maximus [*Supreme Pontiff*] [*Latin*]
PM............. Poor Metabolism [*Medicine*]
PM............. Pope and Martyr [*Church calendars*]
P & M .... Popular Mechanics [*A publication*]

PM............	Portable Magnetometer [NASA]
PM............	Portable Medium Power Plant [Nuclear energy] (NRCH)
PM............	Post Magazine and Insurance Monitor [A publication]
PM............	Post Meridiem [After Noon] [Latin]
PM............	Post Mortem [After Death] [Latin]
PM............	Postal Manual
PM............	Posterior Mitral Leaflet [Cardiology]
PM............	Postmark [Deltiology]
PM............	Postmaster
PM............	Postmodernist [Architecture]
PM............	Potentiometer (DEN)
PM............	Potting Mold (MCD)
PM............	Pounds per Minute
PM............	Powder Metallurgy
PM............	Power Module (MCD)
PM............	Powlesland & Mason [Railway] [Wales]
PM............	Pratt & Lambert, Inc. [AMEX symbol] (SPSG)
PM............	Pravna Misul [A publication]
PM............	Precious Metal
PM............	Preincubation Mixture
PM............	Premium
PM............	Premolar [Dentistry]
PM............	Preparation Meetings [Quakers]
PM............	Prepared Message
PM............	Presbyterian Men (EA)
PM............	Presentation Manager [Data processing]
PM............	Presidential Memo
PM............	Presse Medicale [A publication]
PM............	Pressure Multiplier [Nuclear energy] (NRCH)
PM............	Presystolic Murmur [Cardiology]
PM............	Preventive Maintenance
PM............	Preventive Material
PM............	Preventive Medicine [Also, PVNTMED] (AFM)
PM............	Priest and Martyr [Church calendars]
PM............	Primary Market [Investment term]
PM............	Primary Munition
PM............	Prime Minister
PM............	Prime Mover (MCD)
PM............	Primitive Methodists (ROG)
PM............	Principal Matron [Navy] [British]
PM............	Principle of Multiplying [New math]
PM............	Prize Money
PM............	Pro Memoria [In Remembrance] [Latin]
PM............	Pro Mense [Per Month] [Latin]
PM............	Pro Mille [Per Thousand] [Latin]
P & M	Probate and Matrimonial [Legal] [British]
PM............	Procedures Manual (IEEE)
PM............	Process Manual
PM............	Process Metallurgy [Elsevier Book Series] [A publication]
P & M	Processes and Materials (NASA)
PM............	Processing Module [Data processing]
PM............	Procurement and Material
PM............	Production Manager
PM............	Production Mode
PM............	Profit Motivated [Housing]
PM............	Program (NG)
PM............	Program Manager (MCD)
PM............	Program Memorandum (MCD)
PM............	Program Milestone [NASA] (NASA)
PM............	Program Monitoring (MUGU)
PM............	Project Magic (EA)
PM............	Project Manager [Military]
Pm............	Promethium [Chemical symbol]
PM............	Propellant Management (KSC)
PM............	Property Management (OICC)
PM............	Propulsion Memorandum
PM............	Propulsion Module [NASA] (KSC)
PM............	Prostatic Massage [Medicine]
PM............	Province du Maine [A publication]
PM............	Provost Marshal [Army]
PM............	Public Management [A publication]
PM............	Publicity Man [Slang]
PM............	Pulmonary Macrophages [Medicine]
PM............	Pulpomesial [Dentistry]
PM............	Pulse Modulation
Pm............	Pumice [Quality of the bottom] [Nautical charts]
PM............	Punjabi Muslim [Pakistan]
PM............	Purchase Memo (MCD)
PM............	Purchase-Money Mortgage [Real estate]
PM............	Purchasing Manager
PM............	Purpose-Made [Construction]
PM............	Push Money [Sales incentive]
P/M...........	Put of More [Stock exchange term]
PM............	Pyridoxamine [Also, Pxm] [Biochemistry]
PM............	St. Pierre and Miquelon [ANSI two-letter standard code] (CNC)
PM............	Sisters of the Presentation of Mary [Roman Catholic religious order]
PM1..........	Patternmaker, First Class [Navy rating]
PM2..........	Patternmaker, Second Class [Navy rating]
PM3..........	Patternmaker, Third Class [Navy rating]

PMA	Allegheny College, Meadville, PA [Library symbol] [Library of Congress] (LCLS)
PMA	Pacific Maritime Association (EA)
PMA	Pan-Macedonian Association (EA)
PMA	Panorama Resources Ltd. [Vancouver Stock Exchange symbol]
PMA	Papillary, Marginal, Attached [With reference to gingivae] [Dentistry]
PMA	Paramethoxyamphetamine
PMA	Parts Manufacturer Approval (MCD)
PMA	Peat Moss Association (EA)
PMA	Pemba Island [Tanzania] [Airport symbol] (OAG)
PMA	Pencil Makers Association (EA)
PMA	Performance Monitor Annunciator [NASA] (MCD)
PMA	Permanent Mailing Address
PMA	Personal Money Allowance
PMA	Personnel Management Abstracts [A publication]
PMA	Personnel Management Advisor (NOAA)
PMA	Personnel Management Assistance
PMA	Petroleum Monitoring Agency [Ministry of Energy, Mines, and Resources] [Canada]
PMA	Pharmaceutical Manufacturers Association (EA)
PMA	Phenylmercuric Acetate [Also, PMAC] [Herbicide and fungicide]
PMA	Philadelphia Musical Academy
PMA	Philippine Mahogany Association [Defunct] (EA)
PMA	Phonograph Manufacturers Association (EA)
PMA	Phorbol Myristate Acetate [Also, PTA, TPA] [Organic chemistry]
PMA	Phosphomolybdic Acid [Organic chemistry]
PMA	Photo Marketing Association International (EA)
PMA	Photonic Multichannel Analyzer
PMA	Physical Memory Address
PMA	Pine Manor College, Chestnut Hill, MA [OCLC symbol] (OCLC)
PMA	Planetary Microbiological Assay [Aerospace]
PMA	Plastic Mock-Up Assembly
PMA	Pole-Mounted Amplifier
PMA	Police Management Association (EA)
PMA	Police Marksman Association (EA)
PMA	Polish Museum of America (EA)
PMA	Poly(methyl Acrylate) [Organic chemistry]
PMA	Polyurethane Manufacturers Association (EA)
PMA	Port Moller [Alaska] [Seismograph station code, US Geological Survey] (SEIS)
PMA	Portable Maintenance Aid [Army] ·
PMA	Positive Mental Attitude
PMA	Power Marketing Administration [Department of Energy]
PMA	Preamplifier Module Assembly
PMA	Precious Metal Adder (Cost) (MCD)
PMA	Precious Metal Anode
PMA	Precision Measurements Association (EA)
PMA	Precision Metalforming Association (EA)
PMA	Premarket Approval Application [Food and Drug Administration]
PMA	Preventive Maintenance Agreement
PMA	Primary Market Area
PMA	Primary Mental Abilities [Test] [Education]
PMA	Priority Memory Access
PMA	Prison Mission Association (EA)
PMA	Probationary Medical Assistant [British military] (DMA)
P M A	Proceedings. Musical Association [A publication]
PMA	Proceedings. Royal Musical Association [A publication]
PMA	Procurement and Management Assistance [Small Business Administration]
PMA	Procurement Methods Analyst (AFM)
PMA	Produce Marketing Association [Newark, DE] (EA)
PMA	Production and Marketing Administration [Department of Agriculture] [Functions dispersed, 1953]
PMA	Professional Managers Association (EA)
PMA	Professional Manufacturers' Agents (EA)
PMA	Professional Mariners Alliance (EA)
PMA	Programa Mundial de Alimentos [World Food Program - WFP] [Italy]
PMA	Progressive Muscular Atrophy [Medicine]
PMA	Project Manager, Air
PMA	Project Manager, Air Systems Command [Navy]
PMA	Project Military Adviser (NATG)
PMA	Property Management Association of America (EA)
PMA	Property Market Analysis [Consulting firm] [British]
PMA	Prorated Mental Age [Psychology]
PMA	Protected Memory Address
PMA	Publications. Mediaeval Academy [A publication]
PMA	Publishers Marketing Association (EA)
PMA	Pulpomesioaxial [Dentistry]
PMA	Pump-Motor Assembly
PMA	Purchase Methods Analyst
PMA	Pyridylmercuric Acetate [Fungicide] [Organic chemistry]
PMA	Pyromellitic Acid [Organic chemistry]
PMAA	Paper Makers Advertising Association (EA)
PMAA	Petroleum Marketers Association of America (EA)

PMAA .... Promotion Marketing Association of America [*New York, NY*] (EA)
PMAA .... Property Management Association of America (EA)
PM-AAH... Project Manager, Advanced Attack Helicopter [*Military*]
PMAC ...... Parallel Memory Address Counter [*Data processing*]
PMAC ...... Phenylmercuric Acetate [*Also, PMA*] [*Herbicide and fungicide*]
PMAC ...... PMA Communications, Inc. [*Boston, MA*] (TSSD)
PMAC ...... Preliminary Maintenance Allocation Chart (MCD)
PMAC ...... Provisional Military Administrative Council [*Ethiopia*] [*Political party*] (PD)
PMAC ...... Purchasing Management Association of Canada
PMACODS ... Project Manager, Army Container Oriented Distribution System (MCD)
PM & ACS ... Procurement Management and Acquisition Control System [*Social Security Administration*]
PMAD ...... Performance Monitor Annunciation Driver [*NASA*] (MCD)
PMAD ...... Personnel Management Authorization Document [*Army*]
PMAD ...... Power Management and Distribution (NASA)
PMadW ..... Westinghouse Electric Corp., Waltz Mill Site Library, Madison, PA [*Library symbol*] [*Library of Congress*] (LCLS)
PMAESA .. Port Management Association of Eastern and Southern Africa (EA)
PMAF....... Polaris Missile Assembly Facility
PMAFS ...... Public Members Association of the Foreign Service (EA)
PMAG ...... Program Manager Assistance Group [*Military*] (MCD)
PMAG ...... Provisional Military Advisory Group
PMAHD3 ... Annual Research Reviews. Peripheral Metabolism and Action of Thyroid Hormones [*A publication*]
PMAI........ Piano Manufacturers Association International (EA)
PMaine ...... Province du Maine [*A publication*]
PMAI News Lett ... PMAI [*Powder Metallurgy Association of India*] News Letter [*A publication*]
P/Maj....... Pipe-Major [*British military*] (DMA)
PMALS .... Prototype Miniature Air-Launched System
PMAMA ... Prikladnaya Matematika i Mekhanika [*A publication*]
PMAN .... Piedmont Management Co., Inc. [*NASDAQ symbol*] (NQ)
PMA News ... PMA [*Pharmaceutical Manufacturers Association*] Newsletter [*A publication*]
PManM ..... Mansfield State College, Mansfield, PA [*Library symbol*] [*Library of Congress*] (LCLS)
PMANY .... Pattern Makers Association of New York (EA)
PMAODO ... Proceedings. American Society of Clinical Oncology. Annual Meeting [*A publication*]
PMAP....... Performance Monitor Annunciation Panel [*NASA*] (MCD)
PMAP....... Photomap
PMAPP ..... Combined International Corp. Conv Pfd [*NASDAQ symbol*] (NQ)
PMAR ...... Page Map Address Register
PMAR ...... Precious Metals Area Representative [*DoD*] (AFIT)
PMAR ...... Preliminary Maintenance Analysis Report [*Aerospace*] (AAG)
PMarhSO ... Sun Oil Co., Marcus Hook, PA [*Library symbol*] [*Library of Congress*] (LCLS)
PMARP..... Peacetime Manpower Allocation Requirements Plan (CINC)
PMAS....... Police Mutual Assurance Society [*British*]
PMAS....... Purdue Master Attitude Scales [*Psychology*]
PMASAL .. Publications. Michigan Academy of Science, Arts, and Letters [*A publication*]
PM-ASE.... Project Manager, Aircraft Survivability Equipment [*Military*]
PM-ASH ... Project Manager, Advanced Scout Helicopter [*Military*]
PMAT....... Page Map Address Table [*NASA*] (NASA)
PMAT....... Primary Mental Abilities Test [*Education*]
PMAT....... Purdue Mechanical Adaptability Test
PMAX ...... Petromax Energy Corp. [*NASDAQ symbol*] (NQ)
PMB .... Pacific Motor Tariff Bureau, Inc., Oakland CA [*STAC*]
PMB .... Paranormal Metal Bending
PMB .... Pembina, ND [*Location identifier*] [*FAA*] (FAAL)
PMB .... Performance Measurement Baseline (MCD)
PMB .... Physical Metallurgy Branch
PMB .... Pilot Make Busy (IEEE)
PMB .... Polish Maritime News [*A publication*]
PMB .... Polychrome Methylene Blue
PMB .... Polymethylbenzene [*Organic chemistry*]
PMB .... Polymorphonuclear Basophilic [*Leucocytes*] [*Hematology*]
PMB .... Postmenopausal Bleeding [*Medicine*]
PMB .... Potato Marketing Board [*British*]
PMB .... Practice Multiple Bomb (MCD)
PMB .... Precision Manned Bomber
PMB .... Print Measurement Bureau [*Founded in 1971*] [*Canada*] [*Also the name of a database*]
PMB .... Program Management Board (AFM)
PMB .... PROM [*Programmable Read-Only Memory*] Memory Board
PMBAA..... Publications. Institut Royal Meteorologique de Belgique. Serie A [*A publication*]
PMBC....... Phuket Marine Biological Center [*Marine science*] (MSC)
PMBIAS.... Percentage Median Bias [*Statistics*]
PMBIDB .. Plant Molecular Biology [*A publication*]
PMBK....... PrimeBank, Federal Savings Bank [*Grand Rapids, MI*] [*NASDAQ symbol*] (NQ)
PMBR....... Practice Multiple Bomb Rack (NG)
PMBRAZ .. Contributions. General Agricultural Research Station [*Bogor*] [*A publication*]

PMBS....... Pelican Man's Bird Sanctuary (EA)
PMBS....... Prime Bancshares, Inc. [*NASDAQ symbol*] (NQ)
PMBU ...... Personal Member of the Baptist Union [*British*]
PMBX....... Private Manual Branch Exchange [*Communications*]
PMC .... Carnegie-Mellon University, Pittsburgh, PA [*OCLC symbol*] (OCLC)
PMC .... Chief Patternmaker [*Navy rating*]
PMC .... Little Missionary Sisters of Charity [*Roman Catholic religious order*]
PMC .... Pacific Marine Center [*National Oceanic and Atmospheric Administration*]
PMC .... Pacific Missile Center [*Marine science*] (MSC)
PMC .... Pan Metal [*formerly, Patton Morgan*] Corporation [*Ammunition manufacturer*]
PMC .... Parents of Murdered Children [*Later, POMC*] (EA)
PMC .... Partially Mission Capable [*Maintenance and supply*] (MCD)
PMC .... Payload Monitoring and Control [*NASA*] (NASA)
PMC .... Penguin Modern Classics [*Book publishing*]
PMC .... Pennsylvania Military College
PMC .... Pentamethyl(hydroxy)chromane [*Organic chemistry*]
PMC .... People's Mandate Committee (EA)
PMC .... Percent Modern Carbon [*In atmosphere*]
PMC .... Peripheral Mononuclear Cell [*Cytology*]
PMC .... Peritoneal Mast Cell
PMC .... Personnel Mobilization Center [*Military*]
PMC .... Phased Maintenance Checklist (MCD)
PMC .... Phenolic Molding Compound
PMC .... Phenylmercuric Chloride [*Antiseptic*]
PMC .... Philatelic Music Circle (EA)
PMC .... Piperidinomethylcyclohexane [*Organic chemistry*]
PM & C..... Plant Monitoring and Control [*IBM Corp.*]
PMC .... Plaster-Molded Cornice [*Construction*]
PMC .... Plutona-Molybdenum CERMET [*Ceramic Metal Element*] (NASA)
PMC .... Pollen Mother Cell [*Botany*]
PMC .... Pollution Engineering [*A publication*]
PMC .... Post Maintenance Check (MCD)
PMC .... Post Manufacturing Checkout (KSC)
PMC .... Posterior Medial Corner of Knee [*Sports medicine*]
PMC .... Powdered Metal Cathode
PMC .... Precision Machining Commercialization (MCD)
PMC .... Predictive Multisensor Correlation
PMC .... Premium Merchandising Club of New York (EA)
PMC .... Premotor Cortex [*Neuroanatomy*]
PMC .... President of the Mess Committee [*Military*] [*British*]
PMC .... Pressurized Membrane Container
PMC .... Prime Mover Control [*Valve*]
PMC .... Princeton Microfilm Corporation
PmC .... Princeton Microfilm Corporation, Princeton, NJ [*Library symbol*] [*Library of Congress*] (LCLS)
PMC .... Private Mailing Card [*Deltiology*]
PMC .... Private Medical Communication
PMC .... Private Meter Check [*Telecommunications*] (TEL)
PMC .... Pro Maria Committee (EA)
PMC .... Pro-Med Capital [*AMEX symbol*] (SPSG)
PMC .... Processed Meats Committee [*Later, DPMC*] (EA)
PMC .... Procurement Committee (MCD)
PMC .... Procurement Management Code [*Military*] (AFIT)
PMC .... Procurement, Marine Corps [*An appropriation*]
PMC .... Procurement Method Coding [*DoD*]
PMC .... Program Management Control
PMC .... Program Management Course [*Army*] (RDA)
PMC .... Program Marginal Checking
PMC .... Programmable Machine Controller (NRCH)
PMC .... Progress in Medicinal Chemistry [*Elsevier Book Series*] [*A publication*]
PMC .... Project Management Course [*Army*]
PMC .... Project Manufacturing Controller (MCD)
PMC .... Propellant Monitor and Control (AFM)
PMC .... Pseudo Machine Code [*Data processing*] (BUR)
PMC .... Pseudomembranous Colitis [*Medicine*]
PMC .... Public Media Center (EA)
PMC .... Puerto Montt [*Chile*] [*Airport symbol*] (OAG)
PMC .... Pumice (MSA)
PMCA ...... Purple Martin Conservation Association (EA)
PM-CAWS ... Project Manager for Cannon Artillery Weapon Systems (RDA)
PMCB....... Partially Mission Capable Both [*Maintenance and supply*] (MCD)
P/MCB ..... Project/Miscellaneous Change Board (MCD)
PMCC....... Peerless Motor Car Club (EA)
PMCC....... Pensky-Martens Closed Cup [*Flash point test*]
PMCC....... Platform Mission Control Center [*NASA*]
PMCC....... Post Mark Collectors Club (EA)
PMCD ...... Post Mortem Core Dump [*Data processing*]
PMCF....... Partial Mission Capability Factor
PMCF....... Post Maintenance Check Flight (MCD)
PMCHi...... Crawford County Historical Society, Meadville, PA [*Library symbol*] [*Library of Congress*] (LCLS)
PM & C-HI ... Plant Monitoring and Control - Host Interface [*IBM Corp.*]
PMCI........ Phosphate Mining Corporation of Christmas Island (EY)

PMC INC .. Precision Management of Concordville, Incorporated [*Media, PA*] (TSSD)
PMck .... Carnegie Free Library of McKeesport, McKeesport, PA [*Library symbol*] [*Library of Congress*] (LCLS)
PMCL .... Periodica de Re Morali Canonica Liturgica [*A publication*]
PMCL .... Posterior Medial Collateral Ligament [*Anatomy*]
PMCL .... Proposed MILSTRIP Change Letters
PMCM ...... Master Chief Patternmaker [*Navy rating*]
PMCM ...... Partially Mission Capable Maintenance [*Maintenance and supply*] (MCD)
PMCM ...... Permanent Mold Casting Mold (MCD)
PMCO .... Pan American Mortgage Corporation [*Miami, FL*] [*NASDAQ symbol*] (NQ)
PMCP .... Photo-Marker Corporation [*NASDAQ symbol*] (NQ)
PMCS .... Partially Mission Capable Supply [*Maintenance and supply*] (MCD)
PMCS .... Phoenix Materials [*NASDAQ symbol*] (NQ)
PMCS .... Preventive Maintenance Checks and Services [*for Army vehicles*] (INF)
PMCS .... Process Monitoring and Control System
PMCS .... Program [*or Project*] Management Control System [*Army*]
PMCS .... Pulse-Modulated Communications System
PMCS .... Senior Chief Patternmaker [*Navy rating*]
PMCT .... PAL [*Permissive Action Link*] Management Control Team [*Army*] (AABC)
PMCU .... Personal Member of the Congregational Union [*British*]
PMCV .... Programmed Multichannel Valve [*Chromatography*]
PMCX .... Polar Molecular Corp. [*NASDAQ symbol*] (NQ)
PMD .... Palmdale, CA [*Location identifier*] [*FAA*] (FAAL)
PMD .... Palmdale/Lancaster [*California*] [*Airport symbol*] (OAG)
PMD .... Palmer Industries Ltd. [*Vancouver Stock Exchange symbol*]
PMD .... Panel-Mounted Display (MCD)
PMD .... Part Manufacturing Design
PMD .... Payload Mating Dolly [*NASA*]
PMD .... Payload Module Decoder [*NASA*]
PMD .... Pharmaco-Medical Documentation, Inc. [*Information service or system*] (IID)
PMD .... Physical Medium Dependent [*Data processing*]
PMD .... Post Mortem Dump [*Data processing*]
PMD .... Preventive Maintenance, Daily (MCD)
PMD .... Preventive Maintenance Division [*Air Force*]
PMD .... Primary Myeloproliferative Disease [*Medicine*]
PMD .... Primary Myocardial Disease [*Medicine*]
PMd .... Private Physician
PMD .... Processing, Marketing, and Distribution
PMD .... Program Management Directive [*Air Force*]
PMD .... Program Management Documentation [*Army*]
PMD .... Program Module Dictionary
PMD .... Program Monitoring and Diagnosis
PMD .... Programmed Multiple Development [*Analytical chemistry*]
PMD .... Progressive Muscular Dystrophy [*Medicine*]
PMD .... Project Manager Development (MCD)
PMD .... Projected Map Display
PMD .... Psychiatric Military Duty
PMDA .... Peace Messenger. Diocese of Athabasca. Peace River [*A publication*]
PMDA .... Photographic Manufacturers and Distributors Association (EA)
PMDA .... Pyromellitic Dianhydride [*Organic chemistry*]
PMDAMT ... Pacific Mobile Depot Activity Maintenance Team (CINC)
PMDC .... Project for Mathematical Development of Children [*National Science Foundation*]
PMDCA ..... Progress in Medicinal Chemistry [*A publication*]
PMDD .... Personnel Management Development Directorate [*Military Personnel Center*] (AABC)
PMDF .... Project Master Data File [*For spacecraft*]
PMDG .... Pentamethylene Diguanidine [*Organic chemistry*]
PMDL .... Palmdale, CA (NASA)
PMDL .... Post M-Day Deployment List [*Military*] (AABC)
PMDL .... Provisional Military Demarcation Line (CINC)
PMDM .... Polyhedra Molecular Demonstration Model
PMDM .... Poly(mellitic Dianhydride Methacrylate) [*Organic chemistry*]
PMDO .... Phased Maintenance During Overhaul
PMDP .... Pavement Marking Demonstration Program [*Federal Highway Administration*]
PMDP .... Project Manager Development Program [*Army*] (RDA)
PMDR .... Parametric Monotone Decreasing Ratio [*Statistics*]
PMDR .... Phosphorescence-Microwave Double Resonance
PMDR .... Provisioning Master Data Record
PMDS .... (Phenylmercury)dodecenyl Succinate [*Antimicrobial agent*]
PMDS .... Pilot Map Display System
PMDS .... Projected Map Display System
PMDS .... Property Management and Disposal Service [*Abolished, 1973*] [*General Services Administration*]
PMDT .... Pentamethyldiethylenetriamine [*Organic chemistry*]
PMDY .... Midway Naval Station [*Henderson Field*], Sand Island [*Midway Islands*] [*ICAO location identifier*] (ICLI)
PME .... Caltech Political Military Exercise [*International relations simulation game*]
PME .... Passive Microelectronic Element
PME .... Peace Movement of Ethiopia (EA)

PME .... Pectin Methylesterase [*Also, PE*] [*An enzyme*]
PME .... Pedal Mode Ergometer
PME .... Performance Management and Evaluation
PME .... Performance Monitoring Equipment (NVT)
PME .... Phosphatidylmonomethylethanolamine [*Biochemistry*]
PME .... Phosphomonoester [*Biochemistry*]
PME .... Phosphorylated Monester [*Organic chemistry*]
PME .... Photomagnetoelectric
PME .... Pinosylvin Methyl Ether [*Organic chemistry*]
PME .... Polymorphonuclear Eosinophile [*Hematology*]
PME .... Prace i Materialy Etnograficzne [*A publication*]
PME .... Precision Measuring Equipment (AFM)
PME .... Primary Mission Equipment
PME .... Prime Ministers of England [*A publication*]
PME .... Process and Manufacturing Engineering (NRCH)
PME .... Processor Memory Enhancement
PME .... Professional Military Education (AFM)
PME .... Professional Military Ethic (MCD)
PME .... Project Manager, Electronics System Command [*Navy*]
PME .... Protective Multiple Earthing [*Electricity*]
PMEA .... Powder Metallurgy Equipment Association (EA)
P/MEA ...... Probationary Marine Engineering Artificer [*British military*] (DMA)
PMEA .... Production and Maintenance Engineering Agent (MCD)
PMEA .... Publishing Manufacturers Executive Association (EA)
PMEAR ..... Preliminary Maintenance Engineering Analysis Requirement (AFM)
PMED .... Pace Medical, Inc. [*NASDAQ symbol*] (NQ)
PMedS ...... Delaware County Institute of Science, Media, PA [*Library symbol*] [*Library of Congress*] (LCLS)
PMEE .... Prime Mission Electronic Equipment [*NASA*] (KSC)
PMEF .... Petroleum Marketing Education Foundation (EA)
PMEL .... Pacific Marine Environmental Laboratory [*National Oceanic and Atmospheric Administration*] [*Seattle, WA*] (GRD)
PMEL .... Precision Measurements Equipment Laboratory [*NASA*]
PMELA ..... Plastiques Modernes et Elastomeres [*A publication*]
PM-ENDOR ... Polarization Modulated Electron Nuclear Double Resonance [*Spectroscopy*]
PMer .... Mercer Free Library, Mercer, PA [*Library symbol*] [*Library of Congress*] (LCLS)
PMES .... Personnel Management Evaluation System [*Department of Labor*]
PMES .... Productivity Measurement and Evaluation System (MCD)
PMES .... Proposed Material Erection Schedule (MCD)
PMEST ..... Personality, Matter, Energy, Space, Time [*Colon classification, S. R. Ranganathan*] [*Library science*]
PMET .... Painter Metal (AAG)
PMEV .... Panel-Mounted Electronic Voltmeter
PMEXPO ... Property Management Exposition [*Bachner Communications*] (TSPED)
PMF .... Paint and Resin News [*A publication*]
PMF .... Pakistan Mazdoor Federation
PMF .... Parts Master File (MCD)
PMF .... Performance Monitor Function [*NASA*] (NASA)
PMF .... Perigee Motor Firing [*Aerospace*] (MCD)
PMF .... Permanent Magnetic Field
PMF .... Permanent Military Force (ADA)
PMF .... Personnel Master File [*Army*] (AABC)
PMF .... Pilot Mortar Fire
PM of F ..... Presidential Medal of Freedom [*Military decoration*] (AABC)
PMF .... Price Master File (MCD)
PMF .... Principle Management Facility (MCD)
PMF .... Pro Media Foundation (EA)
PMF .... Probable Maximum Flood [*Nuclear energy*] (NRCH)
PMF .... Processed Message File (MCD)
PMF .... Professional Medical Film (AABC)
PMF .... Program Management Facility [*NASA*] (MCD)
PMF .... Progressive Massive Fibrosis
PMF .... Proton Motive Force [*Physics*]
PMFA .... Fireman Apprentice, Patternmaker, Striker [*Navy rating*]
PMFAA ..... Pokroky Matematiky, Fyziky, a Astronomie [*A publication*]
PM-FAC ... Prednisone, Methotrexate, Fluorouracil, Adriamycin, Cyclophosphamide [*Antineoplastic drug regimen*]
PMFC .... Pacific Marine Fisheries Commission [*Later, PSMFC*] (EA)
PMFC .... Patsy Montana Fan Club (EA)
PMFG .... Peerless Manufacturing Co. [*NASDAQ symbol*] (NQ)
PM/FL ...... Performance Monitor/Fault Locator [*Military*] (CAAL)
PMFLT ..... Pamphlet (MSA)
PMFN .... Fireman, Patternmaker, Striker [*Navy rating*]
PMFPAC ... Polaris Missile Facility, Pacific Fleet
PMFS .... Pulsed Magnetic Field System
PMFWCMA ... Paper Mill Fourdrinier Wire Cloth Manufacturers Association [*Later, FWC*] (EA)
PMG .... Pall Mall Gazette [*A publication*]
PMG .... Paymaster General [*Navy*]
PMG .... Permanent Magnet Generator
PMG .... Phase Modulation Generator
PMG .... Physiological Measurement Group
PMG .... Phytophthora Megasperma F. Sp. Glycinea [*A fungus*]
PMG .... Pinto Malartic [*Vancouver Stock Exchange symbol*]
PMG .... Polymethylgalacturonase [*An enzyme*]

PMG	Ponta Pora [*Brazil*] [*Airport symbol*] (OAG)
PMG	Port Moresby [*Papua New Guinea*] [*Seismograph station code, US Geological Survey*] (SEIS)
PMG	Port Moresby [*Papua New Guinea*] [*Geomagnetic observatory code*]
PMG	Postmaster General
PMG	Poultry Marketing Guide
PMG	Prediction Marker Generator
PMG	Propodial Mucus Gland [*Zoology*]
PMG	Provisional Military Government [*Ethiopia*]
PMG	Provost Marshal General [*Army*]
P1MG	P1 [*Code*] for Multigroup [*Method*] [*Nuclear energy*] (NRCH)
PMGDINYC ...	Production Men's Guild of the Dress Industry of New York City (EA)
PMGO	Office of the Provost Marshal General [*Army*]
PMGS	Provost Marshal General's School, United States Army
PMGW	Primary Mission Gross Weight
PMH	Past Medical History
PMH	Portsmouth, OH [*Location identifier*] [*FAA*] (FAAL)
PMH	Probable Maximum Hurricane [*Nuclear energy*] (NRCH)
PMH	Production per Man-Hour
PMHB	Pennsylvania Magazine of History and Biography [*A publication*]
PMHBA	Polish Medical Science and History Bulletin [*A publication*]
PMHC	Pyridinylmethylethylene(hydrazinecarbothioamide) [*Organic chemistry*]
P & MHEL ...	Pollock and Maitland's History of English Common Law [*A publication*] (DLA)
PMHL	Preferred Measurement Hardware List [*NASA*] (NASA)
PMH/M	Productive Man-Hours per Month [*Navy*] (NG)
PMHP	Para-Menthane Hydroperoxide [*Organic chemistry*]
PMHS	Polymethylhydrosiloxane [*Organic chemistry*]
PMHS	Proceedings. Massachusetts Historical Society [*A publication*]
PMHSA	Polish Military History Society of America (EA)
PMi	Milton Public Library, Milton, PA [*Library symbol*] [*Library of Congress*] (LCLS)
PMI	Palma [*Mallorca Island*] [*Airport symbol*] (OAG)
PMI	Parmac Mines [*Vancouver Stock Exchange symbol*]
PMI	Past [*or Previous*] Medical Illness
PMI	Patient Medication Instruction
PMI	Pearlitic Malleable Iron (MCD)
PMI	Pennsylvania Muscle Institute [*University of Pennsylvania*] [*Research center*] (RCD)
PMI	Permanent Manufacturing Information (MSA)
PMI	Photo Methods for Industry [*A publication*]
PMI	Photographic Microimage Master [*Reprography*]
PMI	Plant Manager Instruction [*Nuclear energy*] (NRCH)
PMI	Plasma-Materials Interactions (MCD)
PMI	Plumbing Manufacturers Institute (EA)
PMI	Point of Maximal Impulse [*Medicine*]
PMI	Point of Maximum Intensity
PMI	Postmyocardial Infarction [*Syndrome*] [*Medicine*]
PMI	Power Management Inventory [*Test*]
PMI	Preliminary Maintenance Inspection (MCD)
PMI	Premark International, Inc. [*NYSE symbol*] (SPSG)
PMI	Prescriptive Math Inventory
PMI	Present Medical Illness
PMI	Presidential Management Incentives [*Office of Management and Budget*]
PMI	Pressed Metal Institute [*Later, AMSA*]
PMI	Preventive Maintenance Inspection (AFM)
PMI	Preventive Maintenance Instruction (NASA)
PMI	Primary Measurement Instrument
PMI	Principal Maintenance Inspector (NASA)
PMI	Private Mortgage Insurance [*Insurance of mortgages by private insurers*]
PMI	Probe Ministries International (EA)
PMI	Processor Monitoring Instrument [*Data processing*] (ADA)
PMI	Program Management Instruction
PMI	Programmable Machine Interface (MCD)
PMI	Project Management Institute (EA)
PMI	Proposed Military Improvement (CAAL)
PMI	Pseudomatrix Isolation
PMI	Purchased Materials Inspection
PMIA	Parallel Multiplexer Interface Adapter (MCD)
PMIA	Presidential Management Improvement Award
PMIC	Parallel Multiple Incremental Computer
PMIC	Payload Mission Integration Contract (MCD)
PMIC	Periodic Maintenance Information Cards (MCD)
PMIC	Personnel Management Information Center [*Air Force*] (AFM)
PMICA	Proceedings. Institute of Medicine of Chicago [*A publication*]
PMIG	Programmers Minimal Interface to Graphics (MCD)
PMIJ	Pulse-Modulated Infrared Jammer
PMilan	Papiri Milanesi [*A publication*] (OCD)
PMilS	Millersville State College, Millersville, PA [*Library symbol*] [*Library of Congress*] (LCLS)
PM Iowa State Univ Sci Technol Coop Ext Serv ...	PM. Iowa State University of Science and Technology. Cooperative Extension Service [*A publication*]
PMIP	Pan Malayan Islamic Party
PMIP	Postmaintenance Inspection Pilot

PMIR	Program Manager's Integration Review [*NASA*] (NASA)
PMIR	Psi-Mediated Instrumental Response [*Parapsychology*]
PMIRD	Passive Microwave Intercept Receiver Display
PMIS	Passive Microwave Imaging System [*NASA*]
PMIS	Personnel Management Information System
PMIS	Plant Monitoring and Information System [*Nuclear energy*] (NRCH)
PMIS	Precision Mechanisms in Sodium [*Nuclear energy*] (NRCH)
PMIS	Printing Management Information Systems
PMIS	Program Management Information System [*Army*]
PMIS	PSRO [*Professional Standards Review Organization*] Management Information System (DHSM)
PMITS	Post Mobilization Individual Training and Support (MCD)
PMIZ	PM Industries, Inc. [*NASDAQ symbol*] (NQ)
PMJ	Project Management Journal [*A publication*]
PMJ	Pulse-Modulated Jammer
PMK	Panel Marking Kit
PMK	Pitch Mark [*Shipfitting*] (AAG)
PMK	Pointe Molloy [*Kerguelen Islands*] [*Seismograph station code, US Geological Survey*] (SEIS)
PMK	Portable Molding Kit
PMK	Postmark
PMK	Primark Corp. [*NYSE symbol*] (SPSG)
PMK	Primary Monkey Kidney [*Physiology*]
PMKM	Past Master, Knights of Malta [*Freemasonry*] (ROG)
PMKR	Petromark Resources Co. [*Tulsa, OK*] [*NASDAQ symbol*] (NQ)
PMKY	Pittsburgh, McKeesport & Youghiogheny [*AAR code*]
PML	Pakistan Muslim League [*Political party*]
PML	Parts Material List
PML	Pattern Makers' League of North America (EA)
PML	Physical Memory Level
PML	PI Edit's Macro Language [*Iliad Group*] [*Data processing*]
PML	[*The*] Pierpont Morgan Library (BJA)
PML	Plymouth Marine Laboratory [*Natural Environment Research Council*] [*Great Britain*] [*Information service or system*] (IID)
PML	Polymer Microdevice Laboratory [*Case Western Reserve University*] [*Research center*] (RCD)
PML	Polymorphonuclear Leukocyte [*Hematology*]
PML	Port Moller [*Alaska*] [*Airport symbol*] (OAG)
PML	Port Moller, AK [*Location identifier*] [*FAA*] (FAAL)
PML	Posterior Mitral Leaflet [*Cardiology*]
PML	Preliminary Materials List [*NASA*]
PML	Probable Maximum Loss [*Insurance*]
PML	Progressive Multifocal Leukoencephalopathy [*Oncology*]
PML	Promotion Management List [*Pronounced "pemell"*] [*Air Force*]
PML	University of Windsor, Paul Martin Law Library [*UTLAS symbol*]
PMLA	Proceedings of the Modern Language Association [*A publication*]
PMLA	Production Music Libraries Association (EA)
PMLA	Publications. Modern Language Association of America [*Database*] [*A publication*]
PMLAAm ...	Publications. Modern Language Association of America [*A publication*]
PMLC	Pooled Mixed Lymphocyte Culture [*Clinical chemistry*]
PMLC	Programmed Multiline Controller
PMLE	Polymorphous Light Eruption [*Medicine*]
PMLG	Poly(methyl L-Glutamate) [*Organic chemistry*]
PMLM	Photosensitive Membrane Light Modulator
PMLO	Principal Military Landing Offices [*British*]
PMLPC	Permanent Mass Layoffs and Plant Closings Program [*Bureau of Labor Statistics*]
PMLV	Permanent Magnet Latch Valve
PMM	Military Morale Division [*Coast Guard*]
PMM	Pall Mall Magazine [*A publication*]
PMM	Peace Mission Movement (EA)
PMM	Peat Marwick McLintock [*Accounting firm*] [*British*]
PMM	Pedestal-Mounted Manipulator [*Nuclear energy*] (NRCH)
PMM	Penobscot Marine Museum (EA)
PMM	Personnel Management Manual [*A publication*] (ADA)
PMM	Petroleum Marketing Management [*Petroleum Marketers Association of America*] [*A publication*]
PMM	Petroleum Marketing Monthly [*Department of Energy*] [*Information service or system*] (CRD)
PMM	Phytophthora Megasperma F.Sp Medicaginia [*A fungus*]
PMM	Poly(methyl Methacrylate) [*Also, PMMA*] [*Organic chemistry*]
PMM	Pool Maintenance Module [*Telecommunications*] (TEL)
PMM	Portavideo [*Vancouver Stock Exchange symbol*]
PMM	Presa Malpaso [*Mexico*] [*Seismograph station code, US Geological Survey*] (SEIS)
PMM	Procom Emerald [*Vancouver Stock Exchange symbol*]
PMM	Professional Music Men, Inc. (EA)
PMM	Profile Milling Machine
PMM	Programmable Microcomputer Module
PMM	Property Management Manual [*NASA*] (MCD)
PMM	Pullman, MI [*Location identifier*] [*FAA*] (FAAL)
PMM	Pulse Mode Multiplex
PMM	Purchase-Money Mortgage [*Real estate*]

PMM .... Putnam Managed Municipal Income [*NYSE symbol*] (SPSG)
PMMA ...... Pere Marquette Memorial Association (EA)
PMMA ...... Poly Methyl Methacrylate Association [*European Council of Chemical Manufacturers Federations*] [*Brussels, Belgium*] (EAIO)
PMMA ...... Poly(methyl Methacrylate) [*Also, PMM*] [*Organic chemistry*]
PMMA ...... Publications. Metropolitan Museum of Art. Egyptian Expedition [*New York*] [*A publication*]
PMMAP.... Poly(methyl Methacrylate Peroxide) [*Organic chemistry*]
PMMB ...... Parallel Memory-to-Memory Bus
PMMC ...... Permanent Magnetic Movable Coil
PMMEA.... Prensa Medica Mexicana [*A publication*]
PM-MEP.. Project Manager - Mobile Electric Power [*DoD*]
PMMF....... Precious Metals Master File [*DoD*] (AFIT)
PMMF....... Presbyterian Medical Mission Fund [*A publication*]
PMMI ...... Packaging Machinery Manufacturers Institute (EA)
PMMLA.... Papers. Midwest Modern Language Association [*A publication*]
PMMM .... Pall Mall Money Management [*Investment group*] [*British*]
PMMP...... Preventive Maintenance Management Program
PMMR ...... Panel-Mounted Microfilm Reader
PMMR ...... Passive Multichannel Microwave Radiometer [*NASA*]
PMMS ...... Phrenicon Metabolic Monitoring System
PMMS...... Plainsong and Mediaeval Music Society (EA)
PMMS...... Program Master Milestone Schedule (MCD)
PMMU ...... Paged Memory Management Unit [*Computer chip*] (BYTE)
PMN .... Pacific Mountain Network [*Television*]
PMN.......... Pahute Mesa [*Nevada*] [*Seismograph station code, US Geological Survey*] [*Closed*] (SEIS)
PMN .... Panglima Mangku Negara [*Malaysian Honour*]
PMN.......... Permian Resources Ltd. [*Vancouver Stock Exchange symbol*]
PMN .... Phenylmercuric Nitrate [*Antiseptic*]
PMN .... Polymorphonuclear [*Hematology*]
PMN .... Polymorphonuclear Neutrophilic [*Hematology*]
PMN .... Postman (DCTA)
PMN .... Premanufacture Notification [*Environmental Protection Agency*]
PMN .... Premarket Notification [*Requirement for introducing new chemicals into the EEC*]
PMN .... Program Management Network (MCD)
PMN .... Proposed Material Need (MCD)
PMN .... Pullman Co. [*NYSE symbol*] (SPSG)
PMN .... Pumani [*Papua New Guinea*] [*Airport symbol*] (OAG)
PM-NAVCON ... Project Manager, Navigation and Control [*Military*]
PMNL ...... Polymorphonuclear Leukocyte [*Hematology*]
PMNP .... Platform-Mounted Nuclear Plant (NRCH)
PMNR ...... Periadenitis Mucosa Necrotica Recurrens [*Medicine*]
PMN/SFS ... People's Music Network for Songs of Freedom and Struggle (EA)
PM-NUC... Project Manager for Nuclear Munitions [*Army*] (RDA)
PMNV ...... Project Manager, Night Vision (RDA)
PMNWA .. Pressemitteilung Nordrhein-Westfalen [*A publication*]
PMo .... Monessen Public Library, Monessen, PA [*Library symbol*] [*Library of Congress*] (LCLS)
PMO .... Palermo [*Italy*] [*Airport symbol*] (OAG)
PMO .... Palermo Resources, Inc. [*Vancouver Stock Exchange symbol*]
PMO .... Perroni, Martin, O'Reilly [*Commercial firm*]
PMO .... Personnel Management Officer [*Army*] (INF)
PMO .... Perturbation Molecular Orbital [*Theory*]
PMO .... Pianissimo [*Very Softly*] [*Music*] (ROG)
PMO .... Pine Mountain Observatory
PMO .... Polaris Material Office [*Missiles*]
PMO .... Polaris Missile Office
PMO .... Pomariorio [*Tuamotu Archipelago*] [*Seismograph station code, US Geological Survey*] (SEIS)
PMO .... Port Meteorological Office [*National Weather Service*]
PMO .... Postal Money Order [*Military*]
PMO .... Postmenopausal Osteoporosis [*Medicine*]
PMO .... Prime Minister's Office
PMO .... Principal Medical Officer
PMO .... Product Manager's Office (RDA)
PMO .... Product Manufacturing Organization
PMO .... Profit Making Organization
PMO .... Program Management Office [*NASA*] (KSC)
PMO .... Project Management Office [*Army*] (AABC)
PMO .... Property Movement Order
PMO .... Provisional [*Program Management*] Office [*Army*]
PMO .... Provost Marshal's Office
PMO .... Psychiatric Military Officer
PMO .... Public Medical Officer [*Australia*]
PMOA ...... Prospectors and Mine Owners Association (EA)
PMOC ...... Pioneer Mission Operations Center [*NASA*]
PMODA.... Phenyl(mercapto)oxadiazole [*Reagent*]
PMOG....... Plutonium Maintenance and Operating Gallery [*Nuclear energy*] (NRCH)
PMOG....... Proposed Material Ordering Guide (MCD)
PMOGA.... Progress in Medical Genetics [*A publication*]
PMOJ........ Pesticides Monitoring Journal [*A publication*]
PMOLANT ... Polaris Material Office, Atlantic Fleet [*Missiles*]
PMOM...... Performance Management Operations Manual [*NASA*] (NASA)

PMON....... Performance Management Operations Network [*NASA*] (NASA)
PMONDN ... Society of Economic Paleontologists and Mineralogists. Paleontological Monograph [*A publication*]
PMOPAC .. Polaris Material Office, Pacific Fleet [*Missiles*]
PMOS .... Permanent Manned Orbital Station (AAG)
PMOS .... Positive-Channel Metal-Oxide Semiconductor [*Telecommunications*] (TEL)
PMOS .... Primary Military Occupational Specialty [*Army*]
PMOSA.... Perceptual and Motor Skills [*A publication*]
PMOSC.... Primary Military Occupational Specialty Code [*Army*] (AABC)
PMP .... Packed Main Parachute
PMP .... Parallel Microprogrammed Processor [*Data processing*]
PMP .... Parent Mass Peak
PMP .... Parents' Magazine Press
PMP .... Parti du Mouvement Populaire de la Cote Francaise des Somalis [*Popular Movement Party of French Somaliland*] [*Political party*]
PMP .... Partito Monarchico Popolare [*Popular Monarchist Party*] [*Italy*] [*Political party*] (PPE)
PMP .... Parts, Materials, and Packaging (MCD)
PMP .... Parts, Materials, and Processes (MCD)
PMP .... Passive Measurement Program
PMP .... Past Menstrual Period [*Medicine*]
PMP .... Patient Management Problem [*Gerontology*]
PMP .... Performance Management Package [*NASA*] (NASA)
PmP .... Pergamon Press, Inc., Fairview Park, Elmsford, NY [*Library symbol*] [*Library of Congress*] (LCLS)
PMP .... Persistent Mentoposterior [*A fetal position*] [*Obstetrics*]
PMP .... Peter Miller Apparel Group, Inc. [*Toronto Stock Exchange symbol*]
PMP .... Phenyl(methyl)pyrazolone [*An organic pigment*]
PMP .... Pimaga [*Papua New Guinea*] [*Airport symbol*] (OAG)
PMP .... Planned Maintenance Plan (MCD)
PMP .... Poly(metal Phosphinate) [*Organic chemistry*]
PMP .... Poly(methylpentene) [*Organic chemistry*]
PMP .... Pompano Beach, FL [*Location identifier*] [*FAA*] (FAAL)
PMP .... Pompeii [*Italy*] [*Seismograph station code, US Geological Survey*] [*Closed*] (SEIS)
PMP .... Pontifical Mission for Palestine (EA)
PMP .... Position Management Program
PMP .... Powdered Metal Part
PMP .... Power Management Profile [*Test*]
PMP .... Preliminary Mission Profile (MCD)
PMP .... Premodulation Processor
PMP .... Preoperational Maintenance Plan
PMP .... Preoperational Monitoring Program [*Nuclear energy*] (NRCH)
PMP .... Pressure Measurement Package
PMP .... Preventive Maintenance Plan (KSC)
PMP .... Preventive Maintenance Procedure [*Nuclear energy*] (NRCH)
PMP .... Previous Menstrual Period [*Medicine*]
PMP .... Prime Mission Project [*Military*]
PMP .... Prime Motor Inns LP [*NYSE symbol*] (SPSG)
PMP .... Prism-Mirror-Prism [*For electron microscopy*]
PMP .... Probable Maximum Precipitation [*Nuclear energy*] (NRCH)
PMP .... Professor of Moral Philosophy
PMP .... Program Management Plan [*NASA*]
PMP .... Program Monitor Panel
PMP .... Progressive Merger Procedure [*Econometrics*]
PMP .... Project Master Plan [*Army*]
PMP .... Project on Military Procurement [*Later, PGP*] (EA)
PMP .... Protective Mobilization Plan
PMP .... Pulmonary Mean Pressure [*Medicine*]
PMP .... Pulsed Microwave Power
PMP .... Pump (KSC)
PMP .... Pyridoxamine Phosphate [*Biochemistry*]
PMPA........ Permanent Magnet Producers Association [*Later, MMPA*] (EA)
PMPA........ Petroleum Marketing Practices Act
PMPA........ Proximal Main Pulmonary Artery [*Anatomy*]
PMPA........ Publications. Missouri Philological Association [*A publication*]
PMPEA .... Professional Motion Picture Equipment Association [*Later, PFVEA*] (EA)
PMPFR .... Program Manager's Preflight Review [*NASA*] (KSC)
PMPH ...... Pamphlet (DLA)
PMPL........ Preferred Mechanical Parts List [*NASA*] (NASA)
PMPM...... Perpetual Motion Poetry Machine
PMPM...... Phase Margin Performance Measure [*Manual control system*]
PMPM...... Programmable Multiple Position Machine (MCD)
PMPM...... Pulse Mode Performance Model (KSC)
PMPMA.... Plastic and Metal Products Manufacturers Association (EA)
PMPO ...... Postmenopausal Palpable Ovary [*Gynecology*]
PMPP....... Program Management Phase-Out Plan [*Military*] (AFIT)
PMPPEZ... Physiological and Molecular Plant Pathology [*A publication*]
PMPPI ..... Polymethylenepolyphenyl Polyisocyanate [*Organic chemistry*]
PMPQ ...... Professional and Managerial Position Questionnaire [*Test*]
PMQ........ Perito Moreno [*Argentina*] [*Airport symbol*] (OAG)
PMQ........ Permanent Married Quarters [*Canadian Forces*]
PMQ......... Phytylmenaquinone [*Vitamin K*] [*Also, K*] [*Biochemistry*]
PMQ......... Primitive Methodist Quarterly Review [*A publication*] (ROG)
PMR .... Micron Products [*AMEX symbol*] (SPSG)

PMR	Pacific Missile Range [*Later, WTR*]
PMR	Palmer [*Alaska*] [*Seismograph station code, US Geological Survey*] (SEIS)
PMR	Palmerston North [*New Zealand*] [*Airport symbol*] (OAG)
PMR	Parabolic Microwave Reflector
PMR	Partidul Muncitoresc Roman [*Romanian Workers' Party*] [*Political party*]
PMR	Parts Material Requirements File
PMR	Payload Mass Ratio
PMR	Paymaster
PMR	Performance Measurement Report [*NASA*] (NASA)
PMR	Performance Monitoring Receiver
PMR	Perinatal Mortality Rate [*Medicine*]
PMR	Philippine Mining Record [*A publication*]
PM & R	Physical Medicine and Rehabilitation
PMR	Planned Maintenance Requirements
PMR	Polymerization of Monomer Reactants [*Organic chemistry*]
PMR	Polymyalgia Rheumatica [*Medicine*]
PMR	Portable Microfiche Reader [*DASA Corp.*]
PMR	Postmaster (DCTA)
PMR	Potential Military Relevance
PMR	Power Monitor Relay
PMR	Preliminary Materials Review
PMR	Pressure Modulation Radiometer
PMR	Preventive Maintenance and Repair [*Aviation*] (MCD)
PMR	Primary Mission Readiness
PMR	Prime Resources Corp. [*Vancouver Stock Exchange symbol*]
PMR	Priority Monitor Report
PMR	Proceedings. Patristic, Mediaeval, and Renaissance Conference [*A publication*]
PMR	Procurement Management Review [*DoD*]
PMR	Profoundly Mentally Retarded
PMR	Program Management Responsibility (MCD)
PMR	Program Manager's Review [*NASA*] (NASA)
PMR	Programmed Mixture Ratio (KSC)
PMR	Progress in Mutation Research [*Elsevier Book Series*] [*A publication*]
PMR	Project Management Report
PMR	Property Movement Request (MCD)
PMR	Proportionate Mortality Rate [*or Ratio*]
PMR	Proton Magnetic Resonance
PMR	Provisioning Master Record (MCD)
PMR	Pulsational Magnetic Radiation [*Astronomy*]
PMRA	Percent of Males Reproductively Active [*Ecology*]
PMRA	Projected Manpower Requirements Account [*Navy*]
PMRAFNS	Princess Mary's Royal Air Force Nursing Service [*British*]
PMRB	Preliminary Materials Review Board
PMRC	Parents' Music Resource Center (EA)
PMRC	Prepositioned Material Receipt Card [*DoD*]
PMRC	Proctor Maple Research Center [*University of Vermont*] [*Research center*] (RCD)
PMRD	Prepositioned Material Receipt Documents (MCD)
PMRDET	Pacific Missile Range Detachment [*Obsolete*] (MUGU)
PMRF	Pacific Missile Range Facility [*Obsolete*] (MSC)
PMRFAC	Pacific Missile Range Facility [*Obsolete*] (MUGU)
PMRG	Preliminary Materials Review Group [*NASA*] (KSC)
PMRGA	Prace Morski Instytut Rybacki w Gdyni [*A publication*]
PMRI	Posteromedial Rotation Instability [*Sports medicine*]
PMRL	Pulp Manufacturers' Research League
PMRM	Periodic Maintenance Requirements Manual [*Navy*]
PMRMO	Protectable Mobilization Reserve Materiel Objective [*Army*] (AABC)
PMRMR	Protectable Mobilization Reserve Materiel Requirements [*Army*]
PMRN	Parents' Music Resource Network (EA)
PMRO	Popular Magazine Review Online [*EBSCO Subscription Services*] [*Information service or system*]
PMRP	Petroleum Material Requirements Plan (MCD)
PMRP	Precious Metals Recovery Program [*DoD*] (AFIT)
PM-RPV	Project Manager, Remotely Piloted Vehicle [*Military*]
PMRR	Pacific Missile Range Representative [*Obsolete*] (MUGU)
PMRR	Pre-Mate Readiness Review [*NASA*] (KSC)
PMRS	Parachute Medical Rescue Service (EA)
PMRS	Physical Medicine and Rehabilitation Service
PMRS	Progress of Medieval and Renaissance Studies in the United States and Canada [*A publication*]
PMRSG	Pacific Missile Range Study Group [*Obsolete*]
PMRT	Peabody Mathematics Readiness Test [*Educational test*]
PMRT	Program Management Responsibility Transfer (MCD)
PMRT	Progressive Muscle Relaxation Training [*Psychology*]
PMRTD	Program Management Responsibility Transfer Date (AFIT)
PMRTF	Pacific Missile Range Tracking Facility [*Obsolete*] (MUGU)
PMRTP	Program Management Responsibility Transfer Plan (AFIT)
PMRY	Presidio of Monterey [*Military*] (AABC)
PMS	Palmer - Arctic Valley [*Alaska*] [*Seismograph station code, US Geological Survey*] (SEIS)
PMS	Pantone Matching System [*Printing*]
PMS	Paper Manifesting System
PMS	Para-Methylstyrene [*Organic chemistry*]
PMS	Parallel Mass Spectrometer
PMS	Particle Measuring Systems [*Aerosol measurement device*]

PMS	Pedestal-Mounted Stinger [*Army*]
PMS	People's Medical Society (EA)
PMS	People's Message System [*For Apple II computers*] [*Electronic bulletin board*]
PMS	Perceptual and Motor Skills [*A publication*]
PMS	Performance Management System
PMS	Performance Measurement System [*Nuclear Regulatory Commission*] (MCD)
PMS	Performance Monitoring System [*Army*] [*Fort Belvoir, VA*] (NASA)
PMS	Permanent Magnet Speaker
PMS	Personnel Management Series [*Civil Service Commission*]
PMS	Personnel Management System [*Air Force*] (AFM)
PMS	Phenazine Methosulfate [*Biochemistry*]
PMS	Phoenix Missile System
PMS	Phytophthora Megasperma Var. Sojae [*A fungus*]
PMS	Piccola Missione per il Sordomuti [*Little Mission for the Deaf-Mute - LMDM*] [*Rome, Italy*] (EAIO)
PMS	Picturephone Meeting Service [*AT & T*]
PMS	Pitch Microwave System
PMS	Planned Maintenance System [*SNMMS*]
PMS	Planned Missile System
PMS	Plant Monitoring System [*Nuclear energy*] (NRCH)
PMS	Plastic to Metal Seal
PMS	PM Industries, Inc. [*Vancouver Stock Exchange symbol*]
PMS	Polaris Missile System
PMS	Policy Management Systems [*NYSE symbol*] (SPSG)
PMS	Pollution Monitoring Satellite
PMS	Poor Miserable Soul [*Medical slang*]
PMS	Popular Music and Society [*A publication*]
PMS	Portable Monitoring Set (MCD)
PMS	Post-Marketing Surveillance
PMS	Post-Merger Syndrome [*Business term*]
PMS	Post-Mortem Survival [*Parapsychology*]
PMS	Postmeiotic Segregation [*Genetics*]
PMS	Postmenopausal Syndrome [*Medicine*]
PMS	Power Management System
PMS	Prang-Mark Society (EA)
PMS	Pre-Midshipmen School
PMS	Predicted Manning System [*Military*]
PMS	Pregnant Mare's Serum [*Endocrinology*]
PMS	Premature Start [*Yacht racing*] (IYR)
PMS	Premenstrual [*Stress*] Syndrome [*Medicine*]
PMS	President of the Meteorological Society [*British*]
PmS	Preston Microfilming Services Ltd., Toronto, ON, Canada [*Library symbol*] [*Library of Congress*] (LCLS)
PMS	Preventive Maintenance System
PMS	Probability of Mission Success [*Aerospace*] (AAG)
PMS	Probable Maximum Surge [*Nuclear energy*] (NRCH)
PMS	Processors, Memories, and Switches [*Programming language*] (CSR)
PMS	Professor of Military Science
PMS	Program Management Support [*Army*]
PMS	Program Management System [*Data processing*]
PMS	Program Master Schedule (MCD)
PMS	Project Management System [*IBM Corp.*] [*Data processing*]
PMS	Project Manager, Ships
PMS	Proposal Management System
PMS	Public Management Sources [*A publication*]
PMS	Public Message Service [*Western Union Corp.*]
PMSA	Office of the Project Manager Selected Ammunition [*DoD*]
PMSA	PM [*Product Management*] Materiel Systems Assessment (RDA)
PMSA	Posterior Middle Suprasylvian Area [*Anatomy*]
PMSA	Primary Metropolitan Statistical Area [*Census Bureau*]
P/MSA	Project/Major Subcontractor Affected (MCD)
PMSA	Project Manager for Selected Ammunition
PMSA	Project Manager's System Assessment
PMSCD	Proceedings. Microscopical Society of Canada [*A publication*]
PMSD	Parti Mauricien Social-Democrate [*Mauritian Social Democratic Party*] [*Political party*] (PPW)
PMS/DOD	Performance Measurement System/Department of Defense
PMSE	Percentage Mean Squared Error [*Statistics*]
PMSE	Program Management Simulation Exercise [*Aerospace*]
PMSF	Phenylmethylsulfonyl Fluoride [*Analytical chemistry*]
PMSFN	Planetary Manned Space Flight Network [*Aerospace*] (MCD)
PMSG	Peace Movement Study Group [*Colgate University*] (EA)
PMSG	Pregnant Mare's Serum Gonadotrophin [*Endocrinology*]
PMSGT	Paymaster Sergeant [*Marine Corps*]
PMSI	Prime Medical Services, Inc. [*NASDAQ symbol*] (NQ)
PMSN	Permission (FAAC)
PMSO	Project Management Staff Officer [*Military*] (AFIT)
PMSO	Project Management Support Office [*Army*] (RDA)
PMSP	Parallel Modular Signal Processor
PMSP	Photon-Counting Microspectrophotometer
PMSP	Preliminary Maintainability and Spare Parts
PMSPS	Project Management Staffing Practices Study [*Navy*] (NG)
PMSR	Patternmaker, Ship Repair [*Navy rating*]
PMSR	Physical, Mental, Social, Religious [*"Fourfold Life" symbol of American Youth Foundation*]

PMSRC..... Pittsburgh Mining and Safety Research Center [*Bureau of Mines*]
PMSRP..... Physical and Mathematical Sciences Research Paper   (IEEE)
PMSS....... Personnel Mobility Support System [*Military*]
PMSS....... Precision Measuring Subsystem   (KSC)
PMSS....... Progress in Mathematical Social Sciences [*Elsevier Book Series*] [*A publication*]
PMS/SMS ... Planned Maintenance System for Surface Missile Ships
PMST....... Professor of Military Science and Tactics   (MUGU)
PMS & T ... Professor of Military Science and Tactics
PMSTA..... Promyshlennoe Stroitel'stvo [*A publication*]
PMSV....... Pilot-to-Metro Service
PMSX....... Processor Memory Switch Matrix
PMT.......... Medical Photography Technician [*Navy*]
PMT.......... Para-Methoxytoluene [*Organic chemistry*]
PMT.......... Partido Mexicano de los Trabajadores [*Mexican Workers' Party*] [*Political party*]   (PPW)
PMT.......... Payment   (AFM)
PMT.......... Pennsylvania Motor Truck Association, Inc., Harrisburg PA [*STAC*]
PMT.......... Perceptual Maze Test [*Psychology*]
PMT.......... Periodic Maintenance Team
PMT.......... Permanent Magnet Twistor [*Memory*] [*Bell Laboratories*]
PMT.......... Permit   (FAAC)
PMT.......... Personnel Management Team
PMT.......... Phase-Modulated Transmission
PMT.......... Philip Michael Thomas [*Co-star in TV series "Miami Vice"*]
PMT.......... Photomechanical Transfer [*Negative paper*] [*Eastman Kodak*]
PMT.......... Photomultiplier Tube
PMT.......... Pilgrim Airlines [*New London, CT*] [*FAA designator*]   (FAAC)
PMT.......... Pine Mountain [*Oregon*] [*Seismograph station code, US Geological Survey*]   (SEIS)
PMT.......... Planning/Management Team [*NASA*]   (MCD)
PMT.......... PMC Technologies Ltd. [*Vancouver Stock Exchange symbol*]
PMT.......... Polaromicrotribrometry [*Analytical chemistry*]
PMT.......... Portable Magnetic Tape
PMT.......... Potteries Motor Traction Co. [*British*]
PMT.......... Power Microwave Tube
PMT.......... Premenstrual Tension [*Medicine*]
PMT.......... Prepare Master Tape
PMT.......... Preventive Maintenance Time   (MCD)
PMT.......... Production Monitoring Test   (NG)
PMT.......... Products, Marketing, and Technology [*Bank Administration Institute*] [*A publication*]
PMT.......... Program Master Tape
PMT.......... Programmed Math Tutorial [*National Science Foundation*]
PMT.......... Pulse-Modulator Tube
PMT.......... Putnam Master Income Trust [*NYSE symbol*]   (SPSG)
PMTAS..... Pre-Menstrual Tension Advisory Service [*British*]
PMTC....... Pacific Missile Test Center [*Navy*] [*Point Mugu, CA*]
PMTC....... Parametric Technology Corp. [*NASDAQ symbol*]   (NQ)
PMTC....... Pittsburgh Mining Technology Center [*Department of Energy*]   (GRD)
PMTD....... Post Mortem Tape Dump [*Data processing*]
PMTF Zh Prikl Mekh Tekh Fiz ...   PMTF. Zhurnal Prikladnoi Mekhaniki Tekhnickeskio Fiziki [*A publication*]
PMTHP..... Project Mercury Technical History Program [*NASA*]
PMTO....... Project Manager Test Offices [*Military*]
PMTP....... Production Missile Test Program
P/MTR...... Potentiometer [*Automotive engineering*]
PM TRADE ... Office of the Project Manager for Training Devices [*Military*]   (RDA)
PMTS....... Predetermined Motion Time Systems [*Management*]
PMTS....... Premenstrual Tension Syndrome [*Medicine*]
PMTT....... Phase-Modulated Telemetry Transmission
PMU.......... Paimiut, AK [*Location identifier*] [*FAA*]   (FAAL)
PMU.......... Performance Monitor Unit [*Communications*]
PMU.......... Physical Mock-Up
PMU.......... Pierce Mountain [*Vancouver Stock Exchange symbol*]
PMU.......... Plant Makeup [*Nuclear energy*]   (NRCH)
PMU.......... Pontifical Missionary Union [*Later, PMUPR*] [*See also OPM*]   (EA)
PMU.......... Portable Memory Unit [*Data processing*]
PMU.......... Pressure Measuring Unit   (KSC)
PMU.......... Preventive Medicine Unit [*Navy*]   (NVT)
PMU.......... Progress in Medical Ultrasound [*Elsevier Book Series*] [*A publication*]
PMU.......... Pulse Modulation Unit   (NASA)
PMUB....... Presbyterian, Methodist, and United Board [*British military*]   (DMA)
PMUCAH ... Memorias e Noticias Publicacoes. Museu e Laboratorio Mineralogico e Geologico. Universidade de Coimbra e Centro de Estudos Geologicos [*A publication*]
PMUPR..... Pontifical Missionary Union of Priests and Religious   (EA)
PMUS....... Permanently Mounted User Set [*Data processing*]   (ADA)
PMUS....... Polymuse, Inc. [*New York, NY*] [*NASDAQ symbol*]   (NQ)
PM-UTTAS ... Project Manager, Utility Tactical Transport Aircraft System [*Military*]
PMUX....... Programmable Multiplex [*Data processing*]   (TEL)
PMv.......... Monroeville Public Library, Monroeville, PA [*Library symbol*] [*Library of Congress*]   (LCLS)

PMV.......... Panicum Mosaic Virus
PMV.......... Papaya Mosaic Virus
PMV.......... Paramyxovirus
PMV.......... Parcel Mail Vans [*British railroad term*]
PMV.......... Peanut Mottle Virus
PMV.......... Plasma Membrane Vesicle [*Cytology*]
PMV.......... Plate-Motion Vector [*Geology*]
PMV.......... Plattsmouth, NE [*Location identifier*] [*FAA*]   (FAAL)
PMV.......... Politically Motivated Violence   (ADA)
PMV.......... Porlamar [*Venezuela*] [*Airport symbol*]   (OAG)
PMV.......... Prime Mission Vehicle   (MCD)
PMV.......... Pro Mundi Vita [*Brussels, Belgium*]   (EAIO)
PMV.......... Prolapsing Mitral Valve [*Cardiology*]
PMvAC..... Community College of Allegheny County, Boyce Campus, Monroeville, PA [*Library symbol*] [*Library of Congress*]   (LCLS)
PMVI........ Promovision Video Displays Corp. [*Jamaica, NY*] [*NASDAQ symbol*]   (NQ)
PMVIA...... Progress in Medical Virology [*A publication*]
PMvK .... Koppers Co., Inc., Research Department, Monroeville, PA [*Library symbol*] [*Library of Congress*]   (LCLS)
PMVR ...... Prime Mover [*Technical drawings*]
PMvS........ United States Steel Corp., Research Center Library, Monroeville, PA [*Library symbol*] [*Library of Congress*]   (LCLS)
PMW........ Parts Manufacturing Workmanship
PMW........ Pole Mountain [*Wyoming*] [*Seismograph station code, US Geological Survey*] [*Closed*]   (SEIS)
PMW........ Private Microwave [*System*]
PMW........ Progressive Mine Workers of America
PMW........ Project Magic Wand [*Military*]   (MCD)
PMW........ Prompt Mobilization Designation Withdrawn
PMWI........ PACE Membership Warehouse, Incorporated [*Aurora, CO*] [*NASDAQ symbol*]   (NQ)
PMWP...... Probable Maximum Winter Precipitation [*Nuclear energy*]   (NRCH)
PMX .... Packet Multiplexer
PMX .... Palmer, MA [*Location identifier*] [*FAA*]   (FAAL)
PMX .... Pamorex Minerals, Inc. [*Toronto Stock Exchange symbol*]
PMX .... Private Manual Exchange
PMX .... Protected Message Exchange
PMyE .... Evangelical Congregational School of Theology, Myerstown, PA [*Library symbol*] [*Library of Congress*]   (LCLS)
PMYOB .... Please Mind Your Own Business
PMZ .... Plymouth, NC [*Location identifier*] [*FAA*]   (FAAL)
pn---- .... North Pacific [*MARC geographic area code*] [*Library of Congress*]   (LCCP)
PN............. North Pole [*Also, NP*]
PN............. Pacific Communications Net [*Air Force*]
PN............. Pakistan Navy
PN............. Palus Nebularum [*Lunar area*]
PN............. Pan Am Corp. [*Formerly, Pan American Airways, Inc.*] [*See also PA, PAA, PAN-AM*] [*NYSE symbol*]   (SPSG)
pn .... Panama [*MARC country of publication code*] [*Library of Congress*]   (LCCP)
PN............. Papillary or Nodular Hyperplasia [*Medicine*]
PN............. Parenteral Nutrition [*Medicine*]
PN............. Part Number
PN............. Partenavia Construzioni Aeronautiche SpA [*Italy*] [*ICAO aircraft manufacturer identifier*]   (ICAO)
PN............. Parti Nationaliste [*Canada*]
PN............. Partido Nacional [*National Party*] [*Dominican Republic*] [*Political party*]
PN............. Partido Nacional [*Blanco Party*] [*Uruguay*] [*Political party*]   (PPW)
PN............. Partido Nacional [*National Party*] [*Honduras*] [*Political party*]   (PPW)
PN............. Partit Nazzjonalista [*Nationalist Party*] [*Malta*] [*Political party*]   (EAIO)
PN............. Perceived Noise
PN............. Percussion Note [*Physiology*]
PN............. Percussive Notes [*A publication*]
PN............. Performance Number
PN............. Periarteritis [*or Polyarteritis*] Nodosa [*Also, PAN*] [*Medicine*]
PN............. Perigean Range
PN............. Peripheral Nerve [*Anatomy*]
PN............. Peripheral Neuropathy [*Medicine*]
PN............. Personal Names from Cuneiform Inscriptions of the Cassite Period [*A publication*]   (BJA)
PN............. Personnel Navigant
PN............. Personnelman [*Navy rating*]
PN............. Phenolic Nylon
PN............. Philippine Aero Transport, Inc. [*Philippines*] [*ICAO designator*]   (FAAC)
PN............. Philippine Navy   (CINC)
P/N............ Phonogram [*British military*]   (DMA)
pN .... Piconewton [*Unit of force*]
PN............. Piedmont & Northern Railway Co. [*AAR code*]
P/N............ Pin Number   (AAG)
PN............. Pitcairn Islands [*ANSI two-letter standard code*]   (CNC)
PN............. Place-Name

PN.............	Planners Network (EA)
PN.............	Plant Normal [Nuclear energy] (NRCH)
PN.............	Plasticity Number (AAG)
PN.............	Please Note
PN.............	Pneumatic
PN.............	Pneumonia [Medicine]
PN.............	Poe Newsletter [A publication]
PN.............	Poesia Nuova [A publication]
PN.............	Poetry Northwest [A publication]
PN.............	Pontine Nuclei [Neuroanatomy]
PN.............	Portsmouth News [United Kingdom] [A publication]
PN.............	Position Number (ADA)
PN.............	Position Pennant [Navy] [British]
P/N............	Positive/Negative
PN.............	Postal Note (ADA)
PN.............	Postnatal [Medicine]
Pn.............	Poznan [A publication]
PN.............	Practical Nurse
PN.............	Preliminary Notification (NRCH)
PN.............	Press Night
PN.............	Prior Notice Required (FAAC)
PN.............	Pro Nervia [A publication]
PN.............	Processing Negativity [Data processing]
Pn.............	Production [Economics]
PN.............	Production Notice (KSC)
PN.............	Program Notice (KSC)
PN.............	Program Number [Horse racing]
PN.............	Programmable Network
PN.............	Project Note
PN.............	Project Number [Data processing] [Online database field identifier]
PN.............	Promissory Note [Business term]
PN.............	Pronuclei [Embryology]
PN.............	Pseudonoise
PN.............	Pseudorandom Number
PN.............	Psychiatric Nurse
P & N	Psychiatry and Neurology
PN.............	Psychic News [A publication]
PN.............	Psychoneurologist
PN.............	Psychoneurotic [Cases, patients, etc.]
PN.............	Public Network [Telecommunications]
PN.............	Publisher's Name [Online database field identifier]
PN.............	Publishing News [A publication]
PN.............	Pulse Network (KSC)
PN.............	Punch On
PN.............	Putative Neurotransmitter [Biochemistry]
PN.............	Pyridoxine [or Pyridoxol] [Also, Pxn] [Biochemistry]
PN.............	Pyrrolnitrin [Antifungal antibiotic]
PN1...........	Regular Pending Transaction [IRS]
PN1...........	Personnelman, First Class [Navy rating]
PN2...........	Personnelman, Second Class [Navy rating]
PN3...........	Personnelman, Third Class [Navy rating]
PNA..........	Pakistan National Alliance (PD)
PNA..........	Pamplona [Spain] [Airport symbol] (OAG)
PNA..........	Paper Napkin Association
PNA..........	Para-Nitroaniline [Organic chemistry]
PNA..........	Parenting in a Nuclear Age (EA)
PNA..........	Parisiensis Nomina Anatomica [Paris Anatomical Nomenclature] [Medicine]
PNA..........	Partacoona [Australia] [Seismograph station code, US Geological Survey] (SEIS)
PNA..........	Parti Nationale Africain [African National Party] [Chad] [Political party]
PNA..........	Passed, but Not Advanced
PNA..........	Peanut Agglutinin [Immunology]
PNA..........	Pentosenucleic Acid [Biochemistry]
PNA..........	People's News Agency [An association] (EA)
PNA..........	Pinedale, WY [Location identifier] [FAA] (FAAL)
PNA..........	Pioneer Corp. [Formerly, Pioneer Natural Gas Co.] [NYSE symbol] (SPSG)
PNA..........	Polish National Alliance of the United States of North America (EA)
PNA..........	Polish Nobility Association (EA)
PNA..........	Polynuclear Aromatic [Organic chemistry]
PNA..........	Processing Terminal Network Architecture [Data processing] (BUR)
PNA..........	Project Network Analysis
PNAB	Percutaneous Needle Aspiration Biopsy [Medicine]
PNAC	Psychiatric Nurses' Association of Canada
PNAF........	Plan Name and Address File [IRS]
PNAF........	Potential Network Access Facility
PNAF........	Primary Nuclear Airlift Force
PNAH........	Polynuclear Aromatic Hydrocarbon [Environmental chemistry]
PNAP........	Pro-Life Nonviolent Action Project (EA)
PNAS........	Palletized Night Attack System
PNAS........	Proceedings. National Academy of Sciences [A publication]
P NAS (Ind) A ...	Proceedings. National Academy of Sciences (India). Section A. Physical Sciences [A publication]
P NAS (Ind) B ...	Proceedings. National Academy of Sciences (India). Section B. Biological Sciences [A publication]

P NAS (US) ...	Proceedings. National Academy of Sciences (United States of America) [A publication]
PNAvQ	Positive-Negative Ambivalent Quotient [Psychology]
PNazMHi ...	Moravian Historical Society, Nazareth, PA [Library symbol] [Library of Congress] (LCLS)
PNB	North Platte, NE [Location identifier] [FAA] (FAAL)
PNB	Pacific Northwest Ballet
PNB	Particle/Neutral Beam (MCD)
PNB	Partido ng Bayan [Party of the Nation] [Political party] [Philippines]
PNB	Pomio [New Britain] [Seismograph station code, US Geological Survey] [Closed] (SEIS)
PNB	Product National Brut [Gross National Product - GNP] [Romanian]
PNB	Produit National Brut [Gross National Product - GNP] [French]
PNBA	Pennbancorp [NASDAQ symbol] (NQ)
PNBAS	((Para-Nitrophenyl)azo)salicylic Acid [A dye] [Organic chemistry]
PNBC........	Pacific Northwest Bibliographic Center [Library network]
P²NBC²	Physiological and Psychological Effects of NBC [Nuclear, Biological, and Chemical Warfare] and Extended Operations [Army study project] (INF)
PNBF........	Peak Nucleate Boiling Flux
PNBMS	Pacific Northwest Bird and Mammal Society [Later, SNUB] (EA)
PNBS........	Pyridinium(nitro)benzenesulfonate [Organic chemistry]
PNBT........	Para-Nitroblue Tetrazolium
PNBT........	[The] Planters Corp. [NASDAQ symbol] (NQ)
PNC..........	Chief Personnelman [Navy rating]
PNc	New Castle Free Public Library, New Castle, PA [Library symbol] [Library of Congress] (LCLS)
PNC	Northampton County Area Community College, Bethlehem, PA [OCLC symbol] (OCLC)
PNC	Pakistan National Congress [Political party]
PNC	Palestine National Council (PD)
PNC	Parti National Caledonien [Caledonian National Party] [Political party] (PPW)
PNC	Partido Nacional Ceuti [Ceuta National Party] [Political party] (PPW)
PNC	Partidual Nationale Crestine [National Christian Party] [Romania] [Political party] (PPE)
PNC	Passenger Name Check-In (MCD)
PNC..........	Pencrude Resources, Inc. [Vancouver Stock Exchange symbol]
PNC..........	Penicillin
PNC	People's National Congress [Guyana] (PD)
PNC	Personal Names from Cuneiform Inscriptions of Cappadocia [A publication]
PNC	Philatelic-Numismatic Combination [or Commemorative]
PNC	Phosphonitrilic Chloride [Inorganic chemistry]
PNC	Physitest Normalise Canadien [Canadian Standardized Test of Fitness - CSTF]
PNC	Pine Canyon [California] [Seismograph station code, US Geological Survey] (SEIS)
PNC	Plate Number Coil [Philately]
PNC	PNC Financial Corp. [NYSE symbol] (SPSG)
PNC	Police National Computer [British]
PNC	Ponca City [Oklahoma] [Airport symbol] (OAG)
PNC	Ponca City, OK [Location identifier] [FAA] (FAAL)
PNC..........	Postnatal Clinic
PNC..........	Power Reactor and Nuclear Fuel Development Corp. [Japan]
PNC..........	Premature Nodal Contraction [Cardiology]
PNC	Programmed Numerical Control
PNC	Prohibition National Committee (EA)
PNC	Pseudonurse Cells [Cytology]
PNCB........	Para-Nitrochlorobenzene [Organic chemistry]
PNCC	Partial Network Control Center
PNCCA.....	Proceedings. National Cancer Conference [United States] [A publication]
PNCF........	PNC Financial Corp. [NASDAQ symbol] (NQ)
PNCFN......	Permanent Nordic Committee on Food and Nutrition [Copenhagen, Denmark] (EAIO)
PNCH.......	Partido Nacional Conservador de Honduras [National Conservative Party of Honduras] [Political party]
PNCH.......	Pinch or Pound, Inc. [Boca Raton, FL] [NASDAQ symbol] (NQ)
PNCH.......	Proceedings. National Conference on Health Education Goals [A publication]
PNCH.......	Punch
PNCL........	Pinnacle Petroleum, Inc. [NASDAQ symbol] (NQ)
PNCM.......	Master Chief Personnelman [Navy rating]
PNCOC	Primary Noncommissioned Officer Course [Army] (INF)
PNCR	Pancretec, Inc. [NASDAQ symbol] (NQ)
PNCS........	Private Network Communication Systems (MCD)
PNCS........	Senior Chief Personnelman [Navy rating]
PNCTD......	Proceedings. National Conference on Power Transmission [A publication]
PNCU	Police National Computer Unit [British]
PND..........	Paroxysmal Nocturnal Dyspnea [Medicine]
PND..........	Parti des Nationalistes du Dahomey [Dahomean Nationalists Party] [Political party]

PND.......... Partido Nacional Democratico [*National Democratic Party*] [*Dominican Republic*] [*Political party*]
PND.......... Partido Nacional Democratico [*National Democratic Party*] [*Costa Rica*] [*Political party*]   (PPW)
PND.......... Partidul National-Democratic [*National Democratic Party*] [*Romania*] [*Political party*]   (PPE)
PND.......... Passive Navigation Device
PND.......... Pending
PND.......... Postnasal Drip [*Medicine*]
PND........ Premodulation Processor - Near Earth Data   (KSC)
PND.......... Present Next Digit
PND.......... Principal Neutralizing Domain [*Medicine*]
PND.......... Program Network Diagram [*Telecommunications*]   (TEL)
PND.......... Pseudonyms and Nicknames Dictionary [*A publication*]
PND.......... Punta Gorda [*Belize*] [*Airport symbol*]   (OAG)
PNDB........ Pelerinage a Notre Dame de Beauraing [*An association*]   (EAIO)
PNdB........ Perceived Noise Decibels
PNDC........ Parallel Network Digital Computer   (IEEE)
PNDC........ Progressive Neuronal Degeneration of Childhood [*Medicine*]
PNDC........ Provisional National Defence Council [*Ghana*]   (PD)
PNDG........ Pending   (AFM)
PNDI......... Pennsylvania Natural Diversity Inventory [*Bureau of Forestry*] [*Harrisburg*] [*Information service or system*]   (IID)
PNDLR....... Pendular
PNDM....... Project Nondesign Memo
PNDO........ Partial Neglect of Differential Overlap [*Physics*]
PNDT........ Parti Nationale pour la Developpement du Tchad [*National Party for the Development of Chad*]
PNE.......... Pacific National Exhibition Home Show [*Southex Exhibitions*]   (TSPED)
PNE.......... Paine College, Warren A. Candler Library, Augusta, GA [*OCLC symbol*]   (OCLC)
PNE.......... Panhandle Eastern Corp. [*Toronto Stock Exchange symbol*]
PNE.......... Peaceful Nuclear Explosion
PNE.......... Philadelphia [*Pennsylvania*] North Philadelphia [*Airport symbol*]   (OAG)
PNE ..●...... Philadelphia, PA [*Location identifier*] [*FAA*]   (FAAL)
PNE.......... Practical Nurse's Education
PNEC........ Primary Navy Enlisted Classification [*Code*]
PNEC........ Proceedings. National Electronics Conference [*A publication*]
PNECA...... Proceedings. National Electronics Conference [*United States*] [*A publication*]
PNed......... Pharmacopeia Nederlandsche [*Netherlands Pharmacopoeia*]
PNEM-APROME ... Partido Nacionalista Espanol de Melilla - Asociacion pro Melilla [*Political party*] [*Spanish North Africa*]   (MENA)
PNEND..... Progress in Nuclear Energy [*A publication*]
PNERL...... Pacific Northwest Environmental Research Laboratory [*Environmental Protection Agency*]   (MSC)
PNES........ Pines
PNET........ Peaceful Nuclear Explosions Treaty [*Officially, Treaty on Underground Nuclear Explosions for Peaceful Purposes*]
PNET........ Primitive Neuroectodermal Tumor [*Oncology*]
PNET........ ProNet, Inc. [*NASDAQ symbol*]   (NQ)
PNEU....... Parents' National Educational Union [*British*]
PNEU....... Pneumatic   (AAG)
PNEUDZ .. Pneumoftiziologie [*Bucharest*] [*A publication*]
PNEUG..... Pneumatic Pressure Generator   (MCD)
PNEUM .... Pneumatic
Pneum Dig & Druckluft Prax ... Pneumatic Digest and Druckluft Praxis [*A publication*]
PNEUMO ... Pneumothorax [*Medicine*]
Pneumokoniosenavorsingseenheid Jaarversl ... Pneumokoniosenavorsingseenheid Jaarverslag [*A publication*]
Pneumolog Hung ... Pneumologia Hungarica [*Hungary*] [*A publication*]
Pneumol/Pneumol ... Pneumonologie/Pneumonology [*A publication*]
Pneumonol-P ... Pneumonologie/Pneumonology [*A publication*]
Pneumonol Pol ... Pneumonologia Polska [*A publication*]
PNEUROP ... European Committee of Manufacturers of Compressors, Vacuum Pumps, and Pneumatic Tools   (EA)
PNEX .... Phonex, Inc. [*NASDAQ symbol*]   (NQ)
PNF.......... Pacific National Financial Corp. [*Toronto Stock Exchange symbol*] [*Vancouver Stock Exchange symbol*]
PNF.......... Palestine National Front [*Political party*]   (PD)
PNF.......... Palestine National Fund [*Palestine Liberation Organization*]
PNF.......... Partito Nazionale Fascista [*National Fascist Party*] [*Italy*] [*Political party*]   (PPE)
PNF.......... Peierls-Nabarro Force [*Physics*]
PNF.......... Penn Traffic Co. [*AMEX symbol*]   (SPSG)
PNF.......... Phosphonitrilic Fluoroelastomer [*Synthetic rubber*]
PNF.......... Postnuclear Fraction [*Biochemical tissue analysis*]
PNF.......... Prenex Normal Form [*Logic*]
PNF.......... Proprioceptive Neuromuscular Facilitation [*Neurology*]
PNFD .... Present Not for Duty [*Military*]
PNFI......... Petawawa National Forestry Institute [*Canadian Forestry Service*] [*Research center*]   (RCD)
PNFI......... Pinnacle Financial Services, Inc. [*NASDAQ symbol*]   (NQ)
PNG.......... Pacific Northern Gas Ltd. [*Toronto Stock Exchange symbol*] [*Vancouver Stock Exchange symbol*]

PNG.......... Papua New Guinea   (ADA)
PNG.......... Papua New Guinea [*ANSI three-letter standard code*]   (CNC)
PNG.......... Paranagua [*Brazil*] [*Airport symbol*]   (OAG)
PNG.......... Partido Nacional Guevarista [*Ecuador*] [*Political party*]   (PPW)
PNG.......... Penghu [*Hokoto*] [*Republic of China*] [*Seismograph station code, US Geological Survey*]   (SEIS)
PNG.......... Persona Non Grata [*Unacceptable Person*] [*Latin*]
PNG.......... Plant Nitrogen in Grain [*Harvest nitrogen index*]
PNG.......... Professional Numismatists Guild   (EA)
PNG.......... Pseudonoise Generator
PNGCS...... Primary Navigation, Guidance and Control System   (KSC)
PNGFA..... Pacific Northwest Grain and Feed Association   (EA)
PNGL....... Papers in New Guinea Linguistics [*A publication*]
P & NGLR ... Papua and New Guinea Law Reports [*A publication*]   (APTA)
PNGR....... Penguin Group, Inc. [*NASDAQ symbol*]   (NQ)
PNGS........ Primary Navigation System
PNGUA8... Forest Research Institute [*Bogor*]. Communication [*A publication*]
PNH.......... North Hills School District Instructional Materials Center, Pittsburgh, PA [*OCLC symbol*]   (OCLC)
PNH.......... Pan Head [*Design engineering*]
PNH.......... Paroxysmal Nocturnal Hemoglobinuria [*Medicine*]
PNH.......... Parti National d'Haiti [*National Party of Haiti*] [*Political party*]
PNH.......... Partido Nacional Hondureno [*Honduran National Party*] [*Political party*]
PNH.......... Phnom Penh [*Cambodia*] [*Airport symbol*]   (OAG)
PNH.......... Pitcher Mountain [*New Hampshire*] [*Seismograph station code, US Geological Survey*]   (SEIS)
PNH.......... Public Service Co. of New Hampshire [*NYSE symbol*]   (SPSG)
PNHA....... Physicians National Housestaff Association [*Defunct*]
PNHDL..... Panhandle [*FAA*]   (FAAC)
PNHS........ Pacific Northwest Heather Society [*Later, NAHS*]   (EA)
PNHYD.... Perspectives in Nephrology and Hypertension [*A publication*]
PNI .... Part Number Index   (MCD)
PNI .... Partai Nasionalis Indonesia [*Nationalist Party of Indonesia*] [*Political party*]
PNI .... Participate but Do Not Initiate [*Investment term*]
PNI .... Partido Nacional Independiente [*National Independent Party*] [*Costa Rica*] [*Political party*]   (PPW)
PNI .... Pascoe Nally International [*British*]
PNI .... Peer Nomination Inventory [*Psychology*]
PNI .... Pensions and Investment Age [*A publication*]
PNI .... Peripheral Nerve Injury [*Medicine*]
PNI .... Pharmaceutical News Index [*UMI/Data Courier*] [*Information service or system*] [*A publication*]
PNI .... Pinerola [*Italy*] [*Seismograph station code, US Geological Survey*]   (SEIS)
PNI .... Ponape [*Caroline Islands*] [*Airport symbol*]   (OAG)
PNI .... Positive Noninterfering [*Alarm system*]
PNI .... Postnatal Infection [*Medicine*]
PNI .... Principal Neo-Tech, Incorporated [*Toronto Stock Exchange symbol*]
PNI .... Protease Nexin I [*Biochemistry*]
PNI .... Psychoneuroimmunology
PNI .... Publications. Netherlands Institute of Archaeology and Arabic Studies [*Cairo*] [*A publication*]
PNI .... Punjab Native Infantry [*India*]
PNIC........ Pleasure Navigation International Joint Committee [*See also CINP*] [*The Hague, Netherlands*]   (EAIO)
PNID .... Peer Nomination Inventory of Depression [*Child development test*] [*Psychology*]
P-NID....... Precedence Network In-Dialing [*Telecommunications*]   (TEL)
PNII.......... Prentiss Normal and Industrial Institute [*Mississippi*]
PNIIA....... Prace Naukowe Instytutu Inzynierii Ochrony Srodowiska Politechniki Wroclawskiej [*A publication*]
PNIO........ Priority National Intelligence Objectives   (MCD)
PNIP........ Positive-Negative-Intrinsic-Positive [*Electron device*]   (MSA)
PNJ.......... Paterson [*New Jersey*] [*Seismograph station code, US Geological Survey*]   (SEIS)
PNJ.......... Paterson, NJ [*Location identifier*] [*FAA*]   (FAAL)
PNJ.......... Polar Night Jet Stream   (ADA)
PNJHS...... Proceedings. New Jersey Historical Society [*A publication*]
PNK.......... Pink Pages Publication [*Vancouver Stock Exchange symbol*]
PNK.......... Pinkham Creek [*Montana*] [*Seismograph station code, US Geological Survey*] [*Closed*]   (SEIS)
PNK.......... Polynucleotide Kinase [*An enzyme*]
PNK.......... Pontianak [*Indonesia*] [*Airport symbol*]   (OAG)
PNkA........ Aluminum Co. of America, ALCOA Research Laboratories Library, New Kensington, PA [*Library symbol*] [*Library of Congress*]   (LCLS)
pnksh .... Pinkish [*Philately*]
PNL.......... Pacific Northwest Laboratory [*Department of Energy*] [*Richland, WA*]
PNL.......... Pakistan National League [*Political party*]
PNL.......... Panel   (KSC)
PNL.......... Pantelleria [*Italy*] [*Airport symbol*]   (OAG)
PNL.......... Parti National Liberal [*National Liberal Party*] [*Lebanon*] [*Political party*]   (PPW)
PNL.......... Partidul National Liberal [*National Liberal Party*] [*Romania*] [*Political party*]   (PPE)
PNL.......... Passenger Name List [*Travel industry*]

PNL .... Peanut Lectin [*Immunochemistry*]
PNL .... Peninsula [*Alaska*] [*Seismograph station code, US Geological Survey*] (SEIS)
PNL .... Penril Corp. [*AMEX symbol*] (SPSG)
PNL .... Perceived Noise Level
PNL .... Pine Bell Mines [*Vancouver Stock Exchange symbol*]
PNL .... Polytechnic of North London, School of Librarianship, London, England [*OCLC symbol*] (OCLC)
PNL .... Prescribed Nuclear Load [*Military*] (AABC)
PNL .... Przewodnik Naukowy i Literacki [*A publication*]
PNL .... Pulsed Neodymium LASER
PNLA .... Pacific Northwest Library Association
PNLA .... Pacific Northwest Loggers Association (EA)
PNLAADA ... Programme National de Lutte Contre l'Abus de l'Alcohol et des Drogues chez les Autochtones [*Canada*]
PNLA Q..... Pacific Northwest Library Association. Quarterly [*A publication*]
pnlbd .... Panelboard [*National Electrical Code*] (IEEE)
PNLBRG ... Panel Bridge (MUGU)
PNLG .... Phase Nulling LASER Gyroscope
PNLM .... Palestine National Liberation Movement [*Political party*] (BJA)
PNLO .... Principal Naval Liaison Officer [*British*]
PNLT....... Perceived Noise Level, Tone Corrected
PNM.......... Pan-Somali Nationalist Movement [*Political party*]
PNM.......... Partido Nacionalista de Mexicano [*Nationalist Party of Mexico*] [*Political party*]
PNM.......... Partito Nazionale Monarchico [*National Monarchist Party*] [*Italy*] [*Political party*] (PPE)
PNM.......... People's National Movement [*Trinidad and Tobago*] [*Political party*] (PD)
PNM.......... Perinatal Mortality [*Medicine*]
PNM.......... Perspectives of New Music [*A publication*]
Pnm.......... Phantom [*A publication*]
PNM.......... Phenolic Nylon with Microballoon
PNM.......... Price Negotiation Memorandum (MCD)
PNM.......... Public Service Co. of New Mexico [*NYSE symbol*] (SPSG)
PNM.......... Pulse Number Modulation
PNMBA .... Progress in Nucleic Acid Research and Molecular Biology [*A publication*]
PNMC....... Phenyl Methylcarbamate [*Organic chemistry*]
PNMO....... Provided No Military Objection Exists [*Army*]
PNMPA..... Psychiatrie, Neurologie, und Medizinische Psychologie [*A publication*]
PNMRA .... Progress in Nuclear Magnetic Resonance Spectroscopy [*A publication*]
PNMT ...... Phenylethanolamine N-Methyltransferase [*An enzyme*]
PNMUB.... Perspectives of New Music [*A publication*]
PNMUD.... PNM Update [*A publication*]
PNN.......... Penn Engineering & Manufacturing Corp. [*AMEX symbol*] (SPSG)
PNN.......... Pinnacle Mountain [*Alaska*] [*Seismograph station code, US Geological Survey*] (SEIS)
PNN.......... Princeton, ME [*Location identifier*] [*FAA*] (FAAL)
PNNCF..... Pacific Northern Naval Coastal Frontier
PNNT .... Pennant (MSA)
PNo .... Montgomery County-Norristown Public Library, Norristown, PA [*Library symbol*] [*Library of Congress*] (LCLS)
PNO.......... Nashville, TN [*Location identifier*] [*FAA*] (FAAL)
PNO.......... Pancontinental Oil Ltd. [*Toronto Stock Exchange symbol*]
PNO.......... Parti Nationaliste Occitan [*Occitanian Nationalist Party*] [*France*] [*Political party*] (PPE)
PNO.......... Party for National Order [*Political party*] [*Defunct*] [*Turkey*] (MENA)
PNO.......... Pendleton [*Oregon*] [*Seismograph station code, US Geological Survey*] (SEIS)
PNO.......... Piano [*Music*]
PNO.......... Preliminary Notification [*Nuclear energy*] (NRCH)
PNO.......... Premium Notice Ordinary [*Insurance*]
PNO.......... Principal Naval Overseer [*British*]
PNO.......... Principal Nursing Officer
PNOA....... Para-Nitro-ortho-anisidine [*Organic chemistry*]
pnob .... Pencil Note on Back [*Philately*]
PNOC........ Proposed Notice of Change
PNO-CI .... Pair Natural Orbital Configuration Interaction [*Atomic physics*]
PNoH........ Norristown State Hospital, Norristown, PA [*Library symbol*] [*Library of Congress*] (LCLS)
PNohM...... Mary Immaculate Seminary, Northampton, PA [*Library symbol*] [*Library of Congress*] (LCLS)
PNOK....... Primary Next of Kin [*Army*] (AABC)
PNOM....... Procedural Nomenclature (MCD)
PNOPO..... Parliament National Organisations and Public Offices [*British*]
PNortHi..... Historical Society of Montgomery County, Norristown, PA [*Library symbol*] [*Library of Congress*] [*Obsolete*] (LCLS)
PNOT .... Para-Nitro-ortho-toluidine [*Organic chemistry*]
PNotes .... Pynchon Notes [*A publication*]
PNOU-A ... Planning Outlook [*A publication*]
PNP .... Pakistan National Party [*Political party*] (PD)
PNP .... Panache Resources, Inc. [*Vancouver Stock Exchange symbol*]
PNP .... Para-Nitrophenol [*or Nitrophenyl*] [*Organic chemistry*]

PNP .... Parti National Populaire [*National Popular Party*] [*Canada*] [*Political party*] (PPW)
PNP .... Parti National du Progres [*National Progress Party*] [*Congo*] [*Political party*]
PNP .... Partido Nacionalista Popular [*Popular Nationalist Party*] [*Panama*] [*Political party*] (PPW)
PNP .... Partido Nacionalista del Pueblo [*Bolivia*] [*Political party*] (PPW)
PNP .... Partido Nuevo Progresista [*New Progressive Party*] [*Puerto Rico*] [*Political party*] (PPW)
PNP .... Partidul National Poporului [*National People's Party*] [*Romania*] [*Political party*] (PPE)
PNP .... Pay'n Pak Stores, Inc. [*NYSE symbol*] (SPSG)
PNP .... Peake's English Nisi Prius Cases [*1790-1812*] [*A publication*] (DLA)
PNP .... Pediatric Nephrology [*Medical specialty*] (DHSM)
PNP .... Pediatric Nurse Practitioner
PNP .... Penuelas [*Puerto Rico*] [*Seismograph station code, US Geological Survey*] (SEIS)
PNP .... People's National Party [*Ghana*] [*Political party*] (PPW)
PNP .... People's National Party [*Jamaica*] [*Political party*] (PPW)
PNP .... Peripheral Neuropathy [*Medicine*]
PNP .... Popondetta [*Papua New Guinea*] [*Airport symbol*] (OAG)
PNP .... Popular Nationalist Party [*Panama*] [*Political party*] (PD)
PNP .... Positive-Negative-Positive [*Transistor*]
PNP .... Precision Navigation Project
PNP .... Prenegotiation Position (MCD)
PNP .... Progressive National Party [*Turks and Caicos Islands*] [*Political party*] (PPW)
PNP .... Prototype Nuclear Process
PNP .... Psychogenic Nocturnal Polydipsia [*Medicine*]
PNP .... Purine-Nucleoside Phosphorylase [*An enzyme*]
PNP .... Pyridoxine Phosphate [*Biochemistry*]
PNPA .... Para-Nitrophenyl Acetate [*Organic chemistry*]
PNPF....... Piqua Nuclear Power Facility
PNPG .... Para-Nitrophenylglycerine [*Biochemistry*]
PNPH .... Parti National Progressiste d'Haiti [*National Progressive Party of Haiti*] [*Political party*]
PNPL........ Para-Nitrophenyl Laurate [*Organic chemistry*]
PNPN .... Positive-Negative-Positive-Negative [*Transistor*] (MUGU)
PNPP........ Para-Nitrophenyl Phosphate [*Organic chemistry*]
PNPP........ Perry Nuclear Power Plant (NRCH)
PNPR....... Positive-Negative Pressure Respiration
PNPRA..... Progress in Nuclear Energy. Series 3. Process Chemistry [*A publication*]
PNPS....... Palisades Nuclear Power Station (NRCH)
PNPS........ Plant Nitrogen Purge System (IEEE)
PNPSA ..... Progress in Neurology and Psychiatry [*A publication*]
PNPSD..... Prace Naukowe Politechniki Szczecinskiej [*A publication*]
PNQ.......... Pacific Northwest Quarterly [*A publication*]
PNQ.......... Pine Crest Resources [*Vancouver Stock Exchange symbol*]
PNQ.......... Poona [*India*] [*Airport symbol*] (OAG)
PNQ.......... Provincial Newspapers (Queensland) Ltd. [*Australia*]
PNR .... Partido Nacional Republicano [*National Republican Party*] [*Portugal*] [*Political party*] (PPE)
PNR .... Partido Nacional Republicano [*National Republican Party*] [*Paraguay*] [*Political party*]
PNR .... Partido Nacional Revolucionario [*National Revolutionary Party*] [*Venezuela*] [*Political party*]
PNR .... Partido Nacionalista Renovador [*Nationalist Renewal Party*] [*Guatemala*] [*Political party*] (PPW)
PNR .... Partido Nacionalista Revolucionario [*Revolutionary Nationalist Party*] [*Ecuador*] [*Political party*] (PPW)
PNR .... Partij Nationalistische Republiek [*Nationalist Republic Party*] [*Surinam*] [*Political party*] (PPW)
PNR .... Passenger Name Record [*Airlines*]
PNR .... Peninsula Airlines, Inc. [*Port Angeles, WA*] [*FAA designator*] (FAAC)
PNR .... Pennant Resources Ltd. [*Toronto Stock Exchange symbol*]
PNR .... Penrod [*Nevada*] [*Seismograph station code, US Geological Survey*] [*Closed*] (SEIS)
PNR .... Philippine National Railways (DS)
PNR .... Pioneer
PNR .... Pittsburgh Naval Reactors Office [*Energy Research and Development Administration*]
PNR .... PN [*Poetry Nation*] Review [*A publication*]
PNR .... Point of No Return [*Aviation*]
PNR .... Pointe Noire [*Congo*] [*Airport symbol*] (OAG)
PNR .... Popular News and Review [*A publication*]
PNR .... Preliminary Negotiation Reports
PNR .... Primary Navigation Reference (AAG)
PNR .... Prior Notice Required (AFM)
PNR .... Prisoner
PNR .... Proximal Negative Response
PNR .... Pulse Nuclear Radiation (AAG)
PNRBC..... Pacific Northwest River Basin Commission
PNRC .... Pacific Northwest Regional Commission [*Department of Commerce*]
PNRC .... Projet National de Coordination des Ressources dans le Domaine de la Statistiques et de l'Information Judiciaires [*Canada*]

P N Review ... Poetry Nation Review [*A publication*]
PNRG .... PrimeEnergy Corp. [*NASDAQ symbol*] (SPSG)
PNRHSL... Pacific Northwest Regional Health Science Library [*Library network*]
PNRS .... Project Notification and Review System [*Department of Labor*]
PNRSV ...... Prunus Necrotic Ringspot Virus
PNS .... Pansophic Systems, Inc. [*NYSE symbol*] (SPSG)
PNS .... Parasympathetic Nervous System
PNS .... Part Number Specification (MCD)
PNS .... Partial Niche Separation
PNS .... Peculiar and Nonstandard Items (AAG)
PNS .... Penas [*Bolivia*] [*Seismograph station code, US Geological Survey*] (SEIS)
PNS .... Pennington's Stores Ltd. [*Toronto Stock Exchange symbol*]
PNS .... Pensacola [*Florida*] [*Airport symbol*] (OAG)
PNS .... Peripheral Nervous System [*Medicine*]
PNS .... Perkins Nuclear Station (NRCH)
PNS .... Philadelphia & Norfolk Steamship [*AAR code*]
PNS .... Philippines News Service
PNS .... Plate Number Society [*Defunct*] (EA)
PNS .... Portable Navigation System
PNS .... Portsmouth Naval Shipyard [*New Hampshire*]
PNS .... Positive-Negative Selection [*Genetic engineering technique*]
PNS .... Postnuclear Supernatant
PNS .... Prescribed Nuclear Stockage [*Military*] (AABC)
PNS .... Probability of Not Having a Space
PNS .... Professionals for National Security [*Inactive*] (EA)
PNS .... Professor of Naval Science
PNS .... Publishers Newspaper Syndicate
PNSA .... Pacific Northwest Ski Association (EA)
PNSA .... Peanut and Nut Salters Association [*Later, PBNPA*] (EA)
PNSA .... Seaman Apprentice, Personnelman, Striker [*Navy rating*]
PNSC .... Pakistan National Shipping Corp. (DS)
PNSCEI .... National Museum of Natural Sciences [*Ottawa*]. Publications in Natural Sciences [*A publication*]
PNSCP ..... Plan for Navy Satellite Communications Plan
PNSFA ..... Proceedings. National Shellfisheries Association [*United States*] [*A publication*]
PNSI .... Polhemus Navigational Sciences, Incorporated (MCD)
PNSL .... Peninsula Federal Savings & Loan [*NASDAQ symbol*] (NQ)
PNSN .... Seaman, Personnelman, Striker [*Navy rating*]
PNS & T .... Professor of Naval Science and Tactics [*Naval ROTC*]
PNSUS ...... Placename Survey of the US (EA)
PNSY .... Portsmouth Naval Shipyard [*New Hampshire*]
PNt .... Newtown Library Co., Newtown, PA [*Library symbol*] [*Library of Congress*] [*Obsolete*] (LCLS)
PNT .... Paint (MSA)
Pnt .... Panart [*Record label*] [*Cuba, USA*]
PNT .... Pantasote, Inc. [*AMEX symbol*] (SPSG)
PNT .... Para-Nitrotoluene [*Organic chemistry*]
PNT .... Paroxysmal Nodal Tachycardia [*Cardiology*]
PNT .... Patient (AABC)
PNT .... Pentagon
PNT .... Penticton [*British Columbia*] [*Seismograph station code, US Geological Survey*] (SEIS)
PNT .... Petromet Resources Ltd. [*Toronto Stock Exchange symbol*]
PNT .... Point
PNT .... Pontiac, IL [*Location identifier*] [*FAA*] (FAAL)
PNTA .... Pacific Northwest Trade Association
PNTA .... Pentair, Inc. [*NASDAQ symbol*] (NQ)
PNtB .... Bucks County Community College, Newtown, PA [*Library symbol*] [*Library of Congress*] (LCLS)
PNtC .... Council Rock High School, Newtown, PA [*Library symbol*] [*Library of Congress*] (LCLS)
PNTC .... Panatech Research & Development Corporation [*NASDAQ symbol*] (NQ)
PNTC .... Parti National Travailliste Camerounais [*Cameroonese National Workers' Party*]
PNTCENS ... Patient Census Report
PNTD .... Painted
PNTD .... Personnel Neutron Threshold Detector (IEEE)
PN/TDMA ... Pseudo Noise/Time Division Multiple Access (MCD)
PNtE .... Ellis College, Newtown, PA [*Library symbol*] [*Library of Congress*] [*Obsolete*] (LCLS)
PNTEA ...... Progress in Nuclear Energy. Series 4 [*A publication*]
PNTG .... Petromet Resources Ltd. [*NASDAQ symbol*] (NQ)
PNTG .... Printing (ROG)
PNTGN ...... Pentagon (MSA)
PNTK .... Pentech International, Inc. [*NASDAQ symbol*] (NQ)
PNTL .... Phonetel Technologies, Inc. [*NASDAQ symbol*] (NQ)
PNTO .... Portuguese National Tourist Office (EA)
PNTO .... Principal Naval Transport Officer [*British military*] (DMA)
PNTOS ...... Para-Nitrotoluene-ortho-sulfonic Acid [*Organic chemistry*]
PNTR .... Painter (FAAC)
PNTR .... Pinetree Computer Systems, Inc. [*NASDAQ symbol*] (NQ)
PNTR .... Pointer (MCD)
PNts .... Newtown Public Library, Newtown Square, PA [*Library symbol*] [*Library of Congress*] (LCLS)
PNU .... Palestine National Union (BJA)
PNU .... Panguitch [*Utah*] [*Airport symbol*] (OAG)
PNU .... Personennamen der Texte aus Ugarit [*A publication*] (BJA)

PNU .... Platinum Communication System [*Vancouver Stock Exchange symbol*]
PNU .... Pneumatic Scale Corp. [*AMEX symbol*] (SPSG)
PNU .... Protein Nitrogen Units [*Clinical chemistry*]
PNUA .... Partito Nazionale Unito Africa [*National Party of United Africans*] [*Somalia*] [*Political party*]
PNUA .... Polish National Union of America (EA)
PNUD .... Programa de las Naciones Unidas para el Desarrollo [*United Nations Development Program - UNDP*] [*Spanish*] (MSC)
PNUD .... Programme des Nations Unies pour le Developpement [*United Nations Development Program*] [*French*]
PNUE .... Programme des Nations Unies pour l'Environnement [*United Nations Environment Programme - UNEP*] (EAIO)
PNUED ..... Preprint. Akademiya Nauk Ukrainskoi SSR Institut Elektrodinamiki [*A publication*]
PNUMA .... Programa de las Naciones Unidas para el Medio Ambiente [*United Nations Environmental Programme Regional Office for Latin America*] (EAIO)
PNUPA ...... Progress in Nuclear Physics [*A publication*]
PNUS .... Prace Naukowe Uniwersytetu Slaskiego [*A publication*]
PNUT .... Portable Nursing Unit Terminal
PNUT .... Possible Nuclear Underground Test
PNUT .... Specialty Retail Concepts, Inc. [*Winston-Salem, NC*] [*NASDAQ symbol*] (NQ)
P Nutr Soc ... Proceedings. Nutrition Society [*A publication*]
PNUTS ...... Possible Nuclear Test Site [*Pronounced "peanuts"*] [*Air Force intelligence*]
PNV .... National Velasquista Party [*Ecuador*] [*Political party*] (PPW)
PNV .... Parti National Voltaique [*Voltaic National Party*] [*Political party*]
PNV .... Partido Nacional Velasquista [*National Velasquista Party*] [*Ecuador*] [*Political party*] (PPW)
PNV .... Partido Nacionalista Vasco [*Basque Nationalist Party*] [*Spain*] [*Political party*] (PPE)
PNV .... Patino N. V. [*Toronto Stock Exchange symbol*]
PNV .... Perini Investment Properties, Inc. [*AMEX symbol*] (SPSG)
PNVAL ..... Previously Not Available [*Army*] (AABC)
PNVD .... Passive Night Vision Devices [*Army*] (AABC)
PNVS .... Pilot Night Vision System [*Army*] (MCD)
PNVS .... Pilot's Night Vision Sensor
PNVTS ..... Pyrotechnics No-Voltage Test Set
PNW .... Pacific Northwest
PNW .... Pinnacle West Capital Corp. [*NYSE symbol*] (SPSG)
PNW .... [*The*] Prescott & Northwestern Railroad Co. [*AAR code*]
PNWC .... Pacific Northwest Writers' Conference
PNwC .... Westminster College, New Wilmington, PA [*Library symbol*] [*Library of Congress*] (LCLS)
PNWCSC .. Pacific Northwest Canadian Studies Consortium [*University of Oregon*]
PNWL .... Pacific Northwest Laboratory [*AEC*]
PNW Pac Northwest Ext Publ Oreg State Univ Coop Ext Serv ... PNW. Pacific Northwest Extension Publication. Oregon State University. Cooperative Extension Service [*A publication*]
PNWRBC ... Pacific Northwest River Basins Commission [*Water Resources Council*] [*Terminated, 1981*] (NOAA)
PNX .... Imperial Airways, Inc. [*St. Paul, MN*] [*FAA designator*] (FAAC)
PNX .... Pneumothorax [*Medicine*]
PNXT .... Pinxit [*He, or She, Painted It*] [*Latin*]
PNY .... Camp Parks, CA [*Location identifier*] [*FAA*] (FAAL)
PNY .... Piedmont Natural Gas Co., Inc. [*NYSE symbol*] (SPSG)
PNY .... Plattsburgh [*New York*] [*Seismograph station code, US Geological Survey*] (SEIS)
PNY .... Poetry New York [*A publication*]
PNY .... Portuguese Navy
PNYA .... Port of New York Authority [*Later, PANYNJ*]
PNYMD ..... Polytechnic Institute of New York. Department of Mechanical and Aerospace Engineering. Report POLY M/AE [*A publication*]
PNZ .... Pennzoil Co., Exploration Library, Houston, TX [*OCLC symbol*] (OCLC)
PNZ .... Petrolina [*Brazil*] [*Airport symbol*] (OAG)
PO .... Dust Devils [*Aviation code*] (FAAC)
po---- .... Oceanica [*MARC geographic area code*] [*Library of Congress*] (LCCP)
PO .... Officer Personnel Division [*Coast Guard*]
PO .... Oil City Library, Oil City, PA [*Library symbol*] [*Library of Congress*] (LCLS)
PO .... Oscillopolarograph
PO .... Pacific Ocean
P & O .... Paints and Oil
PO .... Palomar Capital [*Vancouver Stock Exchange symbol*]
PO .... Parallel Output [*Data processing*] (BUR)
P:O .... Parent Offspring [*Genetics*]
PO .... Parity Odd
PO .... Parking Orbit [*NASA*]
PO .... Parole Officer
P/O .... Part Of (KSC)
PO .... Passport Office [*Department of State*]
PO .... Patent Office [*Later, PTO*] [*Department of Commerce*]

PO............ Patrologia Orientalis [*A publication*]
P & O .... Peninsular & Oriental Steam Navigation Co. [*Steamship line*]
PO............ Per Os [*By Mouth*] [*Pharmacy*]
PO............ Performance Objectives   (OICC)
P & O .... Performance and Operational [*Test or reports*]
PO............ Period of Onset [*Medicine*]
PO............ Permit Office [*British*]   (ROG)
PO............ Peroxidase [*Also, POD*] [*An enzyme*]
PO............ Personnel Office [*Kennedy Space Center Directorate*]   (NASA)
PO............ Personnel Officer
PO............ Pesticides Office [*Environmental Protection Agency*]
PO............ Petty Officer [*Navy*]
PO............ Philharmonic Orchestra [*Music*]
P/O............ Phone Order [*Medicine*]
PO............ Phymatotrichum omnivorum [*A fungus*]
P & O .... Pickled and Oiled
PO............ Pilot Officer
PO............ Planetary Orbit
PO............ Planning Objectives
P & O .... Planning and Operations
P & O .... Plans and Operations Division [*War Department*] [*World War II*]
PO............ Poco [*Somewhat*] [*Music*]
Po............ Poesie [*A publication*]
PO............ Polarity   (AAG)
PO............ Pole [*Unit of measurement*]
Po............ Polet [*A publication*]
PO............ Police Officer
PO............ Political Officer [*NATO*]   (NATG)
P/O............ Pollen/Ovule Ratio [*Botany*]
Po............ Polonium [*Chemical element*]
PO............ Polskie Zaklady Lotnicze [*Poland*] [*ICAO aircraft manufacturer identifier*]   (ICAO)
PO............ Polyolefin [*Organic chemistry*]
Po............ Polyzoa [*Quality of the bottom*] [*Nautical charts*]
PO............ Poona Orientalist [*A publication*]
PO............ Por Orden [*By Order*] [*Spanish*]
PO............ Port Flag [*Navy*] [*British*]
PO............ Port Officer
P & O .... Portland & Ogdensburgh Railroad
po............ Portugal [*MARC country of publication code*] [*Library of Congress*]   (LCCP)
PO............ Portugal [*NATO*]   (AFM)
Po............ Portuguese [*Language, etc.*]   (DLA)
PO............ Position Offered
P & O .... Positioning and Orientation
Po............ Possible
PO............ Post Flight Inspection [*Air Force*]
PO............ Post Office
PO............ Post Office Department [*Canada*]
PO............ Post Orbit [*NASA*]
PO............ Postal Officer   (DCTA)
PO............ Postal Order
PO............ Postoperative [*Medicine*]
PO............ Postpay Coin Telephone [*Telecommunications*]   (TEL)
PO............ Potential Officer [*British military*]   (DMA)
PO............ Power-Operated
PO............ Power Oscillator [*Electronics*]
PO............ Power Output
PO............ Prairie Overcomer [*A publication*]
PO............ Pre-Authorization Order
PO............ Preoperational   (MCD)
PO............ Preoptic [*Area of the brain*]
PO............ Presbyteri Oratorii [*Oratorians*] [*Roman Catholic religious order*]
PO............ Presbyterorum Ordinis [*Decree on the Ministry and Life of Priests*] [*Vatican II document*]
PO............ Preventive Officer [*British*]   (ROG)
PO............ Previous Orders [*Military*]
PO............ Principal Officer [*Foreign Service*]
PO............ Principal Only Strip [*Mortgage security*]
POAI......... Printout
PO............ Private Office [*Documents issued by the Secretary General, NATO*]   (NATG)
PO............ Privately Owned   (AFM)
PO............ Probation Officer
PO............ Procurement Objective   (NVT)
PO............ Production Offset   (AABC)
PO............ Production Order   (KSC)
PO............ Professor Ordinarius [*Ordinary Professor*] [*Latin*]   (ROG)
PO............ Program Objective
PO............ Program Office [*Air Force*]   (CET)
PO............ Program Originator   (AFM)
PO............ Programmed Oscillator
PO............ Project Office [*or Officer*] [*Military*]
PO............ Project ORBIS   (EA)
PO............ Project Order [*DoD*]
PO............ Project Overcome   (EA)
PO............ Proposals Outstanding
PO............ Proposition One   (EA)
PO............ Propylene Oxide [*Organic chemistry*]

PO............ Protea Lugdiens [*South Africa*] [*ICAO designator*]   (FAAC)
PO............ Province of Ontario [*Canada*]
PO............ Provisioning Order   (AFM)
PO............ Przeglad Orientalistyczny [*A publication*]
PO............ Pseudoadiabatic Operation [*Chemical engineering*]
PO............ Psychological Operation [*Military*]   (CINC)
PO............ Public Offering [*Investment term*]
PO............ Public Office [*British*]   (ROG)
PO............ Public Official
PO............ Pulmonary Valve Opening [*Cardiology*]
PO............ Pulse Output
PO............ Pulsed Carrier without Any Modulation Intended to Carry Information [*IEEE*]
PO............ Punted Over [*Boating*] [*British*]   (ROG)
PO............ Purchase Order
PO............ Purchasing Office [*DoD*]   (AFIT)
PO............ Putout [*Baseball*]
PO............ Radio Positioning Mobile Station [*ITU designation*] [*Telecommunications*]   (CET)
PO1......... Petty Officer, First Class [*Navy*]
PO2......... Petty Officer, Second Class [*Navy*]
PO3......... Petty Officer, Third Class [*Navy*]
PO'd........ Put Out [*i.e., angry*] [*Bowdlerized version*]
PO'ed....... Put Out [*i.e., angry*] [*Bowdlerized version*]
POA........ Pacific Ocean Area [*World War II*]
POA........ Pahoa, HI [*Location identifier*] [*FAA*]   (FAAL)
POA........ Pancreatic Oncofetal Antigen [*Immunochemistry*]
POA........ Panel of Americans [*Defunct*]   (EA)
POA........ Pay-on-Answer [*Telecommunications*] [*British*]
POA........ Peacetime Operating Assets [*DoD*]   (AFIT)
POA........ Petroleum Operating Agreement   (CINC)
POA........ Petty Officer Airman [*British military*]   (DMA)
POA........ Phalangeal Osteoarthritis [*Medicine*]
POA........ Phenoxyacetic Acid [*Organic chemistry*]
POA........ Place of Acceptance [*Business term*]   (DCTA)
POA........ Plan of Action   (NASA)
POA........ Pontifica Opera di Assistenza [*Pontifical Relief Organization*]
POA........ Port of Arrival
POA........ Porto Alegre [*Brazil*] [*Airport symbol*]   (OAG)
POA........ Power of Attorney
POA........ Preoptic Area [*of the brain*]
POA........ Price on Application [*Business term*]   (ADA)
POA........ Primary Optic Afferents
POA........ Primary Optic Atrophy
POA........ Prison Officers' Association [*A union*] [*British*]   (DCTA)
POA........ Privately Owned Aircraft   (FAAC)
POA........ Privately Owned Automobile
POA........ Proof of Accounts
POA........ Provisional Operating Authorization [*for nuclear power plant*]
POA........ Public Order Act
POA........ Purchased on Assembly   (KSC)
POA........ Purgeable Organic Analyzer
POAA...... Planetary Operations Analysis Area [*NASA*]
POAA...... Problems of the Arctic and the Antarctic [*A publication*]
POAA....... Property Owners Association of America [*Defunct*]   (EA)
POAC....... Pony of the Americas Club   (EA)
POAC....... Port and Ocean Engineering Under Arctic Conditions International Committee   (EAIO)
POAC........ Post Office Advisory Committee [*British*]
POA Chronicle ... Professional Officers' Association Chronicle [*A publication*]   (APTA)
POACMN ... Petty Officer Aircrewman [*British military*]   (DMA)
POACS...... Prior Other Active Commissioned Service [*Military*]
POAE .... Port of Aerial Embarkation [*Air Force*]
POAE .... Principal Officer of Aircraft Equipment [*Ministry of Aircraft Production*] [*British*] [*World War II*]
POAES...... Prior Other Active Enlisted Service [*Military*]
POAF........ Petty Officer Air Fitter [*British military*]   (DMA)
POAG........ Petro Oil & Gas, Inc. [*NASDAQ symbol*]   (NQ)
POAG........ Primary Open-Angle Glaucoma [*Ophthalmology*]
POAHEDPEARL ... Pacific Ocean Areas Headquarters Pearl Harbor
POAI .... Properties of America, Inc. [*NASDAQ symbol*]   (NQ)
POALS...... Petty Officers Advanced Leadership School [*Navy*]   (MUGU)
POAM...... Petty Officer Air Mechanician [*Australia*]
POA & M .. Plan of Action and Milestones   (NVT)
POAN...... Procurement of Ordnance and Ammunition - Navy
POAR ...... Problem-Objective-Approach-Response [*System of planning patient care*] [*Medicine*]
POAR ...... Project Order Action Request [*Navy*]   (NG)
poas--- .... American Samoa [*MARC geographic area code*] [*Library of Congress*]   (LCCP)
POAS........ Pankypria Omospondia Anexartiton Syntechnion [*Pancyprian Federation of Independent Trade Unions*] [*Cyprus*]
POAS........ Poems on Affairs of State [*A publication*]
POASP...... Plans and Operations Automated Storage Program [*Military*]
POATSC ... Pacific Overseas Air Technical Service Command
POAU........ Protestants and Other Americans United [*for Separation of Church and State*]
POB........... Fayetteville, NC [*Location identifier*] [*FAA*]   (FAAL)
POB .... Paris Opera Ballet

POB	Parti Ouvrier Belge [*Belgian Workers' Party*] [*Later, Belgian Socialist Party*] [*Political party*] (PPE)
POB	Penicillin, Oil, Beeswax [*Medicine*]
POB	Perfluorooctyl Bromide [*Organic chemistry*]
POB	Persons on Board [*Aviation*]
POB	Phenoxybenzamine [*Later, PBZ*] [*Adrenergic blocking agent*]
POB	Place of Birth
POB	Point of Beginning
POB	Point of Business
POB	Polarboken [*A publication*]
POB	Post Office Box
POB	Postal Bulletin [*A publication*]
POB	Power Outlet Box
POB²	Prepped Out Beyond Belief [*Book title*]
POBAL	Powered Balloon [*System*]
POBATO...	Propellant on Board at Takeoff
POBCOST ...	Probabilistic Budgeting and Forward Costing (MCD)
POBI.........	Polar Biology [*A publication*]
pobp---........	British Solomon Islands [*MARC geographic area code*] [*Library of Congress*] (LCCP)
POBR	Problem-Oriented Basic Research [*National Science Foundation*]
POBS........	Portsmouth Bank Shares, Inc. [*NASDAQ symbol*] (NQ)
POBS........	Proceedings. Oxford Bibliographical Society [*A publication*]
POBUD	Polymer Bulletin [*A publication*]
POBY	Prior Operating Budget Year [*Military*] (AFIT)
POC	Clarion State College, Oil City, PA [*Library symbol*] [*Library of Congress*] (LCLS)
POC	La Pocatiere [*Quebec*] [*Seismograph station code, US Geological Survey*] (SEIS)
POC	La Verne, CA [*Location identifier*] [*FAA*] (FAAL)
POC	Packaged Optimization Control [*Engineering*]
POC	Parallel Optical Computer
POC	Parti d'Opposition Congolais [*Congolese Opposition Party*] [*Political party*]
POC	Particulate Organic Carbon
POC	Particulate Organic Concentration [*Environmental science*]
POC	Payload Operations Center [*NASA*] (NASA)
P & OC.......	Peninsular & Oriental (Steam Navigation) Company Ltd. (ROG)
POC	Personnel Operations Center
POC	Peugeot Owners' Club (EA)
POC	Pick Off, Circuit
POC	Planning Objective Coordinator
POC	Plymouth Owners Club (EA)
POC	Poco Petroleums Ltd. [*Toronto Stock Exchange symbol*]
POC	Pocono Air Lines, Inc. [*East Stroudsburg, PA*] [*FAA designator*] (FAAC)
POC	Poculum [*Cup*] [*Pharmacy*]
POC	Point of Contact (AABC)
POC	Porsche Owners Club (EA)
POC	Port of Call
POc	Porte-Oceane [*Record label*] [*France*]
POC	Post of the Corps
POC	Post Office Corps [*British military*] (DMA)
POC	Post Office Counters Ltd. [*British*]
POCUL	Postoperative Care [*Medicine*]
POC	Postoral Ciliary [*Gland*]
POC	Power Control
POC	Precision Oscillator Crystal
POC	Preliminary Operational Capability [*Military*] (AFIT)
POC	Preservation of Capital [*Investment term*]
POC	Principal Operating Component
POC	Prisoners of Conscience [*File of persons imprisoned for political or religious beliefs kept by Amnesty International*]
POC	Privately Owned Conveyance [*Army*]
PoC	Problems of Communism [*A publication*]
POC	Procarbazine, Oncovin [*Vincristine*], CCNU [*Lomustine*] [*Antineoplastic drug regimen*]
POC	Proceed [*or Proceeding*] on Course [*Aviation*] (FAAC)
POC	Process Operator Console
POC	Proche-Orient Chretien [*A publication*]
POC	Production Operational Capability
POC	Production Order Change (KSC)
POC	Professional Officer Course [*AFROTC*] (AFM)
POC	Programs of Cooperation (MCD)
POC	Proopiocortin [*Biochemistry*]
POC	Purchase Order Closeout (NASA)
POC	Purchase Order Contract
POC	Purgeable Organic Carbon [*Chemistry*]
POCA	Association of Psychiatric Outpatient Centers of America [*Acronym is based on former name, Psychiatric Outpatient Centers of America*] (EA)
POCA	Petty Officer Caterer [*British military*] (DMA)
POCA	Post Office Clerks' Association [*A union*] [*Northern Ireland*]
POCA	Prednisone, Oncovin [*Vincristine*], Cytarabine, Adriamycin [*Antineoplastic drug regimen*]
POCA	Public Offender Counselors Association [*Later, IAAOC*] (EA)
PO Cas.......	Perry's Oriental Cases [*Bombay*] [*A publication*] (DLA)
POCASEA ...	Protection of Children Against Sexual Exploitation Act of 1977
POCB	Philippine Overseas Construction Board (DS)

POCB	Plain Ol' Country Boy
POCC	Payload Operations Control Center [*NASA*] (NASA)
POCC	Procarbazine, Oncovin [*Vincristine*], Cyclophosphamide, CCNU [*Lomustine*] [*Antineoplastic drug regimen*]
POCC	Program Operation Control Center [*Space science*]
Poc Costs ...	Pocock on Costs [*1881*] [*A publication*] (DLA)
POCD	Petty Officer Clearance Diver [*Australia*]
POCE	Proof-of-Concept Experiment [*Solar thermal conversion*]
POCEL	Petty Officer Control Electrician [*British military*] (DMA)
POCH.......	Progressiven Organisationen der Schweiz [*Progressive Organizations of Switzerland*] [*Political party*] (PPE)
P-O Chr	Proche-Orient Chretien [*A publication*]
Poch Urozhai Latv Nauch-Issled Inst Zemled ...	Pochva i Urozhai. Latviiskii Nauchno-Issledovatel'skii Institut Zemledeliya [*A publication*]
Pochv Issled Primen Udobr ...	Pochvennye Issledovaniya i Primenenie Udobrenii [*A publication*]
Pochvoved ..	Pochvovedenie [*A publication*]
Pochvozn Agrokhim ...	Pochvoznanie i Agrokhimiya [*A publication*]
Pochv Usloviya Eff Udobr ...	Pochvennye Usloviya i Effektivnost Udobrenii [*A publication*]
Pochvy Baskh Puti Ratsion Ikh Ispol'z ...	Pochvy Bashkirii i Puti Ratsional'nogo Ikh Ispol'zovaniya [*USSR*] [*A publication*]
Pochvy Yuzhn Urala Povolzhya ...	Pochvy Yuzhnogo Urala i Povolzh'ya [*A publication*]
poci---.........	Caroline Islands [*MARC geographic area code*] [*Library of Congress*] (LCCP)
POCI.........	Pontiac-Oakland Club International (EA)
POCIBO.....	Polar Circling Balloon Observatory
POCIC	POCI, Inc. [*NASDAQ symbol*] (SPSG)
POCIL.......	Pocillum [*Little Cup*] [*Pharmacy*] (ROG)
Pocill........	Pocillum [*Little Cup*] [*Pharmacy*]
POCK	Petty Officer Cook [*British military*] (DMA)
Pocket Pict Guides Clin Med ...	Pocket Picture Guides to Clinical Medicine [*A publication*]
POCL.........	Project Office Change Letter
POCM	Partido Obrero y Campesino de Mexico [*Mexico*] [*Political party*]
POCM	Postal Contracting Manual [*Postal Service*]
POCN	Purchase Order Change Notice
POCO	Physiology of Chimpanzees in Orbit [*NASA*]
Poco..........	Politically Correct
POCO	Power On - Clock On [*Aerospace*]
POCO	Purchase Order Change Order (AAG)
POCO	Purchase Order Closeout (AAG)
POCOA	Post Office Controlling Officers' Association [*A union*] [*British*]
POCOX	Petty Officer Coxswain [*Australia*]
pocp---........	Canton and Enderbury Islands [*MARC geographic area code*] [*Library of Congress*] (LCCP)
POCP........	Program Objectives Change Proposal
POCR	Program Objectives Change Request [*DoD*]
POCS........	Patent Office [*later, PTO*] Classification System
PO & CS	Post Office and Civil Service Committee [*Obsolete*] [*US Senate*]
Po Ct	Police Court (DLA)
POCTA......	Prevention of Cruelty to Animals Society Member (DSUE)
POCUL......	Poculum [*Cup*] [*Pharmacy*] (ROG)
pocw---	Cook Island [*MARC geographic area code*] [*Library of Congress*] (LCCP)
POD..........	Pacific Ocean Division [*Army Corps of Engineers*]
POD..........	Parent Organization Designator (MCD)
POD........	Parents of Diabetics
POD..........	Pay on Delivery [*Shipping*]
POD..........	Payable on Death [*Insurance*]
POD..........	Payload Operations Division [*NASA*] (MCD)
POD..........	Permissible Operating Distance [*Army*] (AFIT)
POD..........	Peroxidase [*Also, PO*] [*An enzyme*]
POD..........	Personal Orientation Dimensions [*Personality development test*] [*Psychology*]
POD..........	Place of Delivery [*Shipping*] (DS)
POD..........	Place of Discharge
POD..........	Plan of the Day
POD..........	Pneumatically Operated Disconnect (KSC)
POD..........	Pocket Oxford Dictionary [*A publication*]
POD..........	Podkamennaya [*USSR*] [*Geomagnetic observatory code*]
POD..........	Podor [*Senegal*] [*Airport symbol*] (OAG)
POD..........	Point-of-Origin Device (IEEE)
POD..........	Polycystic Ovarian Disease [*Medicine*]
POD..........	Port of Debarkation [*Military*]
POD..........	Port of Delivery [*Shipping*]
POD..........	Port of Discharge [*Navy*]
POD..........	Post of Duty
POD..........	Post Office Department [*Later, United States Postal Service*]
POD..........	Post Office Directory
POD..........	Postoperative Day [*Medicine*]
POD..........	Potential Ozone Depleter
POD..........	Precision Orbit Determination (MCD)
POD..........	Preflight Operation Division [*NASA*]
POD..........	Professional and Organizational Development [*In association name Professional and Organizational Development Network in Higher Education*] (EA)

POD........... Program Office Directive
POD........... Program Operation Description
POD........... Programmed Operational Date   (AFIT)
POD........... Proof of Debt [*Business term*]   (DCTA)
POD........... Proof of Delivery [*Shipping*]   (DS)
POD........... Proof of Deposit [*Banking*]
POD........... Proof of Design   (MCD)
POD........... Prosthetics and Orthotics Database [*University of Strathclyde*] [*Glasgow, Scotland*] [*Information service or system*]   (IID)
POD........... Proximity Optical Device   (NASA)
POD........... Pulse Omission Detector   (MCD)
POD........... Purchase Order Deviation   (KSC)
PODA........ Priority-Oriented Demand Assignment
PODAF...... Post Operation Data Analysis Facility
PODAF...... Power Density Exceeding a Specified Level over an Area with an Assigned Frequency Band   (IEEE)
PODAPS... Portable Data Processing System
PODAS...... Portable Data Acquisition System
PODBCA... Post Office Department Board of Contract Appeals   (AFIT)
PODCC...... Plan, Organize, Direct, Coordinate, Control [*Principles of management*]
Pod D........ Doctor of Podiatry
PODE........ Pacific Ocean Division Engineers   (CINC)
PODEX..... [*Night*] Photographic Exercise [*Military*]   (NVT)
PODF........ Post of Duty File
Podgot Koksovanie Uglei ... Podgotovka i Koksovanie Uglei [*A publication*]
Podgot Vosstanov Rud ... Podgotovka i Vosstanovlenie Rud [*A publication*]
PODIM...... Poseidon Design Information Memo [*Missiles*]
P & O Div .. Planning and Operations Division [*Military*]
PODM........ Preliminary Orbit Determination Method [*Computer*] [*NASA*]
PODO........ Profit on Day One [*Classification for new newspaper*]
PODRS...... Patent Office [*later, PTO*] Data Retrieval System [*Department of Commerce*]
PODS........ Parents of Down's Syndrome   (EA)
PODS........ Postoperative Destruct System   (MCD)
PODSC...... Parents of Down's Syndrome Children   (EA)
Podstawowe Probl Wspolczesnej Tech ... Podstawowe Problemy Wspolczesnej Techniki [*A publication*]
Podst Sterow ... Podstawy Sterowania [*A publication*]
PODU........ Praci Odes'koho Derzavnoho Universytetu [*A publication*]
PODUC..... Provided [*Following Named*] Officers Have Not Departed Your Command [*Amend Assignment Instructions as Indicated*] [*Army*]   (AABC)
PODx........ Postoperative Diagnosis [*Medicine*]
PODx........ Preoperative Diagnosis [*Medicine*]
Podzemn Gazif Uglei ... Podzemnaya Gazifikatsiya Uglei [*USSR*] [*A publication*]
Podzemn Gazif Uglei (1934-35) ... Podzemnaya Gazifikatsiya Uglei (1934-35) [*A publication*]
Podzemn Gazif Uglei (1957-59) ... Podzemnaya Gazifikatsiya Uglei (1957-59) [*A publication*]
Podzemn Vody SSSR ... Podzemnye Vody SSSR [*A publication*]
POE........... Fort Polk [*Louisiana*] [*Airport symbol*]   (OAG)
POE........... Fort Polk, LA [*Location identifier*] [*FAA*]   (FAAL)
POE........... Panel on the Environment [*of President's Science Advisory Committee*]
POE........... Payment Option Election   (MCD)
POE........... Peace on Earth [*Australia*] [*Political party*]
POE........... People of the Earth [*Also, RAN*]   (EA)
POE........... Pilot Operational Equipment   (MCD)
POE........... Plank-on-Edge
POE........... Pneumatically Operated Equipment   (AAG)
Poe............ Poetik [*A publication*]
POE........... Point of Entry [*Accounts*]
POE........... Polyoxyethylene [*Organic chemistry*]
POE........... Port of Embarkation [*Shipping*]
POE........... Port of Entry [*Shipping*]
POE........... Post-Operations Evaluation   (MCD)
POE........... Postoperative Endophthalmitis [*Ophthalmology*]
POE........... Predicted Operational Environment [*Military*]   (CAAL)
POE........... Pretesting Orientation Exercises [*US Employment Service*] [*Department of Labor*]
POE........... Primary Organization Element   (NOAA)
POE........... Print Out Effect
POE........... Projected Operational Environment   (NVT)
POE........... Pulsar Energy/Resources [*Vancouver Stock Exchange symbol*]
POE........... Pulse Oriented Electrophoresis [*Analytical biochemistry*]
poea---..... Easter Island [*MARC geographic area code*] [*Library of Congress*]   (LCCP)
POEA....... Poe & Associates, Inc. [*NASDAQ symbol*]   (NQ)
POEA....... Protection of Offshore Energy Assets [*Navy*]   (NVT)
P/OEA3..... Probationary Ordnance Electrical Artificer 3rd Class [*British military*]   (DMA)
POEAS...... Planetary Orbiter Error Analysis Study Program
POE(AW)... Petty Officer Electrician (Air Weapon) [*Australia*]
Poe Chpbk ... Poetry Chapbook [*A publication*]
POED........ Program Organization for Evaluation and Decision
POEER...... Pacific Oceanographic Equipment Evaluation Range   (NOAA)
POEF........ Post Office Engineering Federation [*A union*] [*British*]

POEIT....... Provisional Organization for European Inland Transportation [*World War II*]
POEL(A)... Petty Officer Electrician (Air) [*British military*]   (DMA)
POEL(AW) ... Petty Officer Electrician (Air Weapon) [*British military*]   (DMA)
P O Elect Engrs J ... Post Office Electrical Engineers. Journal [*A publication*]
P O Electr Eng J ... Post Office Electrical Engineers. Journal [*A publication*]
POEM....... Petty Officer Electrical Mechanician [*Australia*]
POEMS..... Polyneuropathy Associated with Organomegaly Endocrine Disorders, Myeloma, and Skin Modifications
POEMS..... Polyoxyethylene Monostearate [*Organic chemistry*]
POENIT.... Poenitentia [*Penance*] [*Latin*]   (ADA)
POEOP..... Polyoxyethyleneoxypropylene [*Organic chemistry*]
Poe Pal....... Poetry Palisade [*A publication*]
Poe Pl........ Poe on Pleading and Practice [*A publication*]   (DLA)
POERD..... Power Engineer [*A publication*]
PoeS......... Poe Studies [*A publication*]
POES......... Polar Orbiting Environmental Satellite
POESID.... Position of Earth Satellite in Digital Display   (MCD)
Poe Stud..... Poe Studies [*A publication*]
Poet......... De Poetis [*of Suetonius*] [*Classical studies*]   (OCD)
POET........ Petty Officer Enroute Training [*Navy*]   (NVT)
Poet......... Poetica [*A publication*]
Poet......... Poetica [*of Aristotle*] [*Classical studies*]   (OCD)
Poet......... Poetry [*A publication*]
POET........ Primed Oscillator Expendable Transponder [*Military*]   (CAAL)
POET........ Psychological Operations Exploitation Team [*Vietnam*]
PoetC........ Poet and Critic [*A publication*]
Poet Crit..... Poet and Critic [*A publication*]
Poetics Tod ... Poetics Today [*A publication*]
Poet L........ Poet Lore [*A publication*]
Poet Mel Gr ... Poetae Melici Graeci [*A publication*]   (OCD)
POETRI .... Programme on Exchange and Transfer of Information on Community Water Supply and Sanitation [*International Reference Center for Community Water Supply and Sanitation*] [*Information service or system*]   (IID)
Poet Rom Vet ... Poetarum Romanorum Veterum Reliquiae [*A publication*]   (OCD)
Poetry Aust ... Poetry Australia [*A publication*]
Poetry Mag ... Poetry Magazine [*A publication*]   (APTA)
Poetry NW ... Poetry Northwest [*A publication*]
Poetry R.... Poetry Review [*London*] [*A publication*]
Poetry Wale ... Poetry Wales [*A publication*]
POETS...... Phooey on Everything, Tomorrow's Saturday [*Bowdlerized version*]
Poets .... Poets in the South [*A publication*]
POETS...... Push Off Early, Tomorrow's Saturday [*Bowdlerized version*]
PoetW .... Poetry Wales [*A publication*]
POEU....... Post Office Engineering Union [*British*]
Poeyana Inst Biol La Habana Ser A ... Poeyana Instituto de Biologia. La Habana. Serie A [*A publication*]
Poeyana Inst Biol La Habana Ser B ... Poeyana Instituto de Biologia. La Habana. Serie B [*A publication*]
Poeyana Inst Zool Acad Cienc Cuba ... Poeyana Instituto de Zoologia. Academia de Ciencias de Cuba [*A publication*]
POF........... American Jurisprudence Proof of Facts [*A publication*]
POF........... Planned Outage Factor [*Electronics*]   (IEEE)
POF........... Point-of-Failure [*Data processing*]   (IBMDP)
POF........... Police Officer, Female
POF........... Poplar Bluff [*Missouri*] [*Airport symbol*]   (OAG)
POF........... Poplar Bluff, MO [*Location identifier*] [*FAA*]   (FAAL)
POF........... Positive Opening Fin   (MCD)
POF........... Postovulatory Follicle [*Endocrinology*]
POF........... Prilozi za Orijentalnu Filologiju [*A publication*]
POF........... Privately Owned Firearm   (MCD)
POF........... Prolific Resources [*Vancouver Stock Exchange symbol*]
POF........... Pyruvate Oxidation Factor [*Biochemistry*]
POFA........ Programmed Operational Functional Appraisal [*Navy*]
POFI........ Pacific Oceanic Fisheries Investigations   (NOAA)
pofj---...... Fiji [*MARC geographic area code*] [*Library of Congress*]   (LCCP)
POFO....... Po Folks, Inc. [*NASDAQ symbol*]   (NQ)
POFOOGUSA ... Protection of Foreign Officials and Official Guests of the United States Act
pofp........... French Polynesia [*MARC geographic area code*] [*Library of Congress*]   (LCCP)
POG.......... Official Gazette. United States Patent Office [*A publication*]
POG.......... Parents of Gays   (EA)
POG.......... Petty Officer's Guide [*A publication*] [*Navy*]
POG.......... Piping Instrumentation and Operating Gallery [*Nuclear energy*]   (NRCH)
Pog............ Pogledi [*A publication*]
POG.......... Port Gentil [*Gabon*] [*Airport symbol*]   (OAG)
POG.......... Position of Germany [*British*] [*World War II*]
POG.......... Post Office Guide [*Book of regulations*] [*British*]
POG.......... Provisional Ordnance Group [*Military*]
POG.......... Tableware International [*A publication*]
POGASIS ... Planetary Observation Geometry and Science Instrument Sequence Program [*Aerospace*]
POGaz....... Post Office Gazette [*British*] [*A publication*]   (DCTA)
POGCA ..... Progress in Organic Coatings [*A publication*]

POGE .... Planning Operational Gaming Experiment [*Game*]
POGE .... Polar Geography and Geology [*A publication*]
pogg--- .... Galapagos Islands [*MARC geographic area code*] [*Library of Congress*] (LCCP)
Poggendorffs Ann ... Poggendorffs Annalen [*A publication*]
pogn--- .... Gilbert and Ellice Islands [*Tuvalu*] [*MARC geographic area code*] [*Library of Congress*] (LCCP)
POGO .... Personal Objectives and Goals (MCD)
Pogo .... Pogonomyrinex Occidentalis [*A genus of ants*]
POGO .... Polar Orbiting Geophysical Observatory [*NASA*]
POGO .... Programmer-Oriented Graphics Operation (IEEE)
POGR .... Poplar Grove National Cemetery
POGS .... National Association of Post Office and General Service Maintenance Employees [*Later, APWU*] [*AFL-CIO*]
POGSI ...... Policy Group on Scientific Information [*Marine science*] (MSC)
POGT .... Power-Operated Gun Turret
pogu--- .... Guam [*MARC geographic area code*] [*Library of Congress*] (LCCP)
POH .... Placed out of Hire
POH .... Planned Outage Hours [*Electronics*] (IEEE)
POH .... Pocahontas, IA [*Location identifier*] [*FAA*] (FAAL)
POH .... Pull-Out Harness
POHC .... Principal Organic Hazardous Constituent [*Environmental chemistry*]
POHI .... Physically or Otherwise Health Impaired
POHM ...... Page-Oriented Holograph Memory [*Data processing*]
POHM ...... Prisoner of His Majesty [*Australia*]
POHMA .... Project for the Oral History of Music in America
POHS .... Presumed Ocular Histoplasmosis Syndrome [*Ophthalmology*]
POHWARO ... Pulsated, Overheated, Water Rocket [*Swiss space rocket*]
POI .... Parking Orbit Injection [*NASA*]
POI .... Parti Oubanguien de l'Independance [*Ubangi Independence Party*] [*Political party*]
POI .... Period of Interest (MCD)
POI .... Personal Orientation Inventory [*Psychology*]
POI .... Personal Outlook Inventory [*Employment test*]
POI .... Plan of Instruction
POI .... Point of Impact
POI .... Point of Interface [*Telecommunications*]
POI .... Poison
POI .... Politique Etrangere [*A publication*]
POI .... Pre-Overhaul Inspection (MCD)
POI .... Pressure-Operated Initiator (MCD)
POI .... Product of Inertia (MCD)
POI .... Program of Instruction
POI .... Public Office of Information (MCD)
POI .... Purchase Order Item (KSC)
POIC .... Petty Officer in Charge [*Navy*] (NVT)
POIC .... Poly(octyl Isocyanate) [*Organic chemistry*]
POIF .... Plan Organization Index File [*IRS*]
Poimennye Pochvy Russ Ravniny ... Poimennye Pochvy Russkoi Ravniny [*A publication*]
POINT ...... Pasadena Online Information Network [*Pasadena Public Library*] (OLDSS)
POINT ...... Pursuing Our Italian Names Together (EA)
POINTER .. Particle Orientation Interferometer [*ASD*]
POINTERM ... Appointment Will Be Regarded as Having Terminated upon This Date
POINTMAIL ... Letter Appointment in Mail
Point Point Commun ... Point-to-Point Communication [*Later, Communication and Broadcasting*] [*A publication*]
Point Point Telecommun ... Point-to-Point Telecommunications [*A publication*]
Points Appui Econ Rhone-Alpes ... Points d'Appui pour l'Economie Rhone-Alpes [*A publication*]
Point Vet .... Point Veterinaire [*A publication*]
POIP .... Potential Offender Identification Program
POIPCD .... Patent Office and Industrial Property and Copyright Department [*British*]
POIQT .... Performance-Oriented Infantry Qualification Test (INF)
POIR .... Project Officers Interim Report [*Air Force*] (MCD)
POIS .... Poisoning [*FBI standardized term*]
POIS .... Procurement Operations Information System (MCD)
POIS .... Prototype On-Line Instrument System [*Data processing*] (NRCH)
POIS .... Purchase Order Information System (MCD)
POISE .... Panel on Inflight Scientific Experiments [*NASA*]
POISE .... Photosynthetic Oxygenation Illuminated by Solar Energy
POISE .... Pointing and Stabilization Platform Element [*Army*] (MCD)
POIT .... Power of Influence Test [*Psychology*]
POJ .... Patent Office Journal [*India*] [*A publication*] (DLA)
POJ .... Selma, AL [*Location identifier*] [*FAA*] (FAAL)
poji--- .... Johnston Atoll [*MARC geographic area code*] [*Library of Congress*] (LCCP)
POK .... Sacramento, CA [*Location identifier*] [*FAA*] (FAAL)
poki--- .... Kermadec Islands [*MARC geographic area code*] [*Library of Congress*] (LCCP)
Pokroky Mat Fyz Astron ... Pokroky Matematiky, Fyziky, a Astronomie [*A publication*]
Pokroky Praskove Metal ... Pokroky Praskove Metalurgie [*A publication*]

Pokroky Praskove Metal VUPM ... Pokroky Praskove Metalurgie VUPM [*Vyzkumny Ustav pro Praskovou Metalurgii*] [*A publication*]
Pokroky Vinohrad Vina- Vysk ... Pokroky vo Vinohradnickom a Vinarskom Vyskume [*A publication*]
Pol .... FS. Political Risk Letter [*A publication*]
POL .... Pacific Ocean Lines (DS)
POL .... Pacific Oceanographic Laboratories [*Later, Pacific Marine Environmental Laboratory*]
POL .... Pair Orthogonalized Lowdin [*Physics*]
POL .... Parents of Large Families
POL .... Paul Otchakovsky-Laurens [*Publishing imprint, named for imprint editor*]
POL .... Pemba [*Mozambique*] [*Airport symbol*] (OAG)
POL .... Petroleum, Oil, and Lubricants [*Military*]
POL .... Physician's Office laboratory
POL .... Pola [*Yugoslavia*] [*Seismograph station code, US Geological Survey*] [*Closed*] (SEIS)
POL .... Polacca [*Ship's rigging*] (ROG)
POL .... Poland [*ANSI three-letter standard code*] (CNC)
POL .... Polar Airways, Inc. [*Anchorage, AK*] [*FAA designator*] (FAAC)
POL .... Polarity [*or Polarize*] (KSC)
POL .... Police
POL .... Policy
POL .... Polish (AAG)
pol .... Polish [*MARC language code*] [*Library of Congress*] (LCCP)
Pol .... Politica [*of Aristotle*] [*Classical studies*] (OCD)
POL .... Political
POL .... Politician
Pol .... Politics [*A publication*]
Pol .... Pollexfen's English King's Bench Reports [*1669-85*] [*A publication*] (DLA)
POL .... Pollution
POL .... Polonium [*Chemical symbol is Po*] (AAG)
Pol .... Polonystyka [*Warsaw*] [*A publication*]
Pol .... [*Epistle of*] Polycarp (BJA)
Pol .... Polydor & Deutsche Grammophon [*Record label*] [*Germany, Europe, etc.*]
POL .... Polymerase [*An enzyme*]
Pol .... Polyphon [*Record label*] [*Denmark, etc.*]
POL .... Port of Loading [*Shipping*]
POL .... Problem-Oriented Language [*Data processing*]
POL .... Procedure-Oriented Language [*Data processing*]
POL .... Process-Oriented Language [*Data processing*] (IEEE)
POL .... Provisional Operating License [*for nuclear power plant*]
POL .... Public Opinion Laboratory [*Northern Illinois University*] [*Research center*] (RCD)
POLA .... Polaris Resources, Inc. [*NASDAQ symbol*] (NQ)
POLA .... Project on Linguistic Analysis
PolAb .... Pollution Abstracts [*A publication*]
Pol Acad Sci Bull Biol ... Polish Academy of Sciences. Bulletin. Biology [*A publication*]
Pol Acad Sci Bull Chem ... Polish Academy of Sciences. Bulletin. Chemistry [*A publication*]
Pol Acad Sci Bull Earth Sci ... Polish Academy of Sciences. Bulletin. Earth Sciences [*A publication*]
Pol Acad Sci Inst Ecol Rep Sci Act ... Polish Academy of Sciences. Institute of Ecology. Report on Scientific Activities [*A publication*]
Pol Acad Sci Inst Fundam Tech Res Nonlinear Vib Probl ... Polish Academy of Sciences. Institute of Fundamental Technical Research. Nonlinear Vibration Problems [*A publication*]
Pol Acad Sci Inst Fundam Tech Res Proc Vib Probl ... Polish Academy of Sciences. Institute of Fundamental Technical Research. Proceedings of Vibration Problems [*A publication*]
Pol Acad Sci Inst Geophys Publ Ser D ... Polish Academy of Sciences. Institute of Geophysics. Publications. Series D. Atmosphere Physics [*A publication*]
Pol Acad Sci Med Sect Ann ... Polish Academy of Sciences. Medical Section. Annals [*A publication*]
Pol Acad Sci Rev ... Polish Academy of Sciences. Review [*A publication*]
POLAD ...... Political Adviser
Pol Affairs ... Political Affairs [*A publication*]
Pol Akad Nauk Inst Geofiz Mater Pr ... Polska Akademia Nauk. Instytut Geofizyki. Materialy i Prace [*A publication*]
Pol Akad Nauk Kom Ceram Pr Ser Ceram ... Polska Akademia Nauk. Komisja Ceramiczna. Prace. Serja Ceramika [*A publication*]
Pol Akad Nauk Kom Krystalogr Biul Inf ... Polska Akademia Nauk. Komisja Krystalografii. Biuletyn Informacyjny [*A publication*]
Pol Akad Nauk Muz Ziemi Pr ... Polska Akademia Nauk. Muzeum Ziemi. Prace [*A publication*]
Pol Akad Nauk Oddzial Krakowie Kom Nauk Geol Pr Geol ... Polska Akademia Nauk. Oddzial w Krakowie. Komisja Nauk Geologicznych. Prace Geologicane [*A publication*]
Pol Akad Nauk Oddzial Krakowie Kom Nauk Mineral Pr Mineral ... Polska Akademia Nauk. Oddzial w Krakowie. Komisja Nauk Mineralogicznych. Prace Mineralogiczne [*A publication*]
Pol Akad Nauk Oddzial Krakowie Nauk Mineral Pr Mineral ... Polska Akademia Nauk. Oddzial w Krakowie. Komisja Nauk Mineralogicznych. Prace Mineralogiczne [*A publication*]

Pol Akad Nauk Oddzial Krakowie Pr Kom Ceram Ceram ... Polska Akademia Nauk. Oddzial w Krakowie. Prace Komisji Ceramicznej. Ceramika [*A publication*]

Pol Akad Nauk Oddzial Krakowie Pr Kom Ceram Ser Ceram ... Polska Akademia Nauk. Oddzial w Krakowie. Prace Komisji Ceramicznej. Serja Ceramika [*A publication*]

Pol Akad Nauk Oddzial Krakowie Pr Kom Metal Odlew Metal ... Polska Akademia Nauk. Oddzial w Krakowie. Prace Komisji Metalurgiczno-Odlewniczej. Metalurgia [*A publication*]

Pol Akad Nauk Oddzial Krakowie Pr Kom Metal-Odlew Metalurg ... Polska Akademia Nauk. Oddzial w Krakowie. Prace Komisji Metalurgiczno-Odlewniczej. Metalurgia [*A publication*]

Pol Akad Nauk Oddzial Krakowie Pr Kom Nauk Tech Ser Ceram ... Polska Akademia Nauk. Oddzial w Krakowie. Prace Komisji Nauk Technicznych. Serja Ceramika [*A publication*]

Pol Akad Nauk Pr Inst Masz Przeplyw ... Polska Akademia Nauk. Prace Instytutu Maszyn Przeplywowych [*A publication*]

Pol Akad Nauk Pr Kom Nauk Tech Metal Fiz Met Stopow ... Polska Akademia Nauk. Prace Komisji Nauk Technicznych Metalurgia Fizyka Metali i Stopow [*A publication*]

Pol Akad Nauk Pr Kom Nauk Tech Ser Ceram ... Polska Akademia Nauk. Prace Komisji Nauk Technicznych. Serja Ceramika [*A publication*]

Pol Akad Nauk Rozpr Wydz Nauk Med ... Polska Akademia Nauk. Rozprawy Wydzialu Nauk Medycznych [*A publication*]

Pol Akad Umiejet Pr Muz Przyr ... Polska Akademia Umiejetnosci. Prace Muzeum Przyrodniczego [*A publication*]

Pol Akad Umiejet Pr Roln Lesne ... Polska Akademia Umiejetnosci. Prace Rolniczo-Lesne [*A publication*]

Polam LJ ... Polamerican Law Journal [*A publication*]   (DLA)

Pol Am Stds ... Polish American Studies [*A publication*]

Poland China ... Poland China World [*A publication*]

Poland Inst Geol Biul ... Poland. Instytut Geologiczny. Biuletyn [*A publication*]

POLANG .. Polarization Angle [*Telecommunications*]

POLAR...... Production Order Location and Reporting [*NASA*]   (NASA)

POLAR...... Projected Operational Logistics Analysis Requirements

Polar Biol... Polar Biology [*A publication*]

Pol Arch Hydrobiol ... Polskie Archiwum Hydrobiologii/Polish Archives of Hydrobiology [*A publication*]

Pol Arch Med Wewn ... Polskie Archiwum Medycyny Wewnetrznej [*A publication*]

Pol Arch Wet ... Polskie Archiwum Weterynaryjne [*A publication*]

Pol Arch Weter ... Polskie Archiwum Weterynaryjne [*A publication*]

POLARIS ... Polar-Motion Analysis by Radio Interferometric Surveying [*Geodetic measuring facilities*]

Polarogr Ber ... Polarographische Berichte [*A publication*]

Polar Rec ... Polar Record [*A publication*]

Polar Res ... Polar Research [*A publication*]

Pol Bildung ... Politische Bildung [*A publication*]

Pol C .... Political Code [*A publication*]   (DLA)

POLCAP ... Petroleum, Oils, and Lubricants Capabilities   (MCD)

POLCOD ... Police Code [*INTERPOL*]

Pol Code..... Political Code [*A publication*]   (DLA)

Pol Communication and Persuasion ... Political Communication and Persuasion [*A publication*]

Pol Cont ..... Pollock on Contracts [*A publication*]   (DLA)

POLDAM ... POL [*Petroleum, Oil, and Lubricants*] Installations Damage Report   (NATG)

Pol Dig Part ... Pollock's Digest of the Laws of Partnership [*A publication*]   (DLA)

Pol Diritto ... Politica del Diritto [*A publication*]

Pol Dokum ... Politische Dokumentation [*A publication*]

POLDPS... Pioneer Off-Line Data-Processing System [*NASA*]

POLE...... Point-of-Last-Environment [*Data processing*]   (IBMDP)

POLEA...... Polski Tygodnik Lekarski [*A publication*]

Pol Ecol Bibliogr ... Polish Ecological Bibliography [*A publication*]

Pol Ecol Stud ... Polish Ecological Studies [*A publication*]

Pol Endocrinol ... Polish Endocrinology [*A publication*]

Pol Endocrinol (Engl Transl Endokrynol Pol) ... Polish Endocrinology (English Translation of Endokrynologia Polska) [*A publication*]

Pol Eng ...... Polish Engineering [*A publication*]

Pol Eng Rev ... Polish Engineering Review [*A publication*]

Pol Etrang ... Politique Etrangere [*Paris*] [*A publication*]

Pol Etrangere ... Politique Etrangere [*A publication*]

POLEX...... Polar Experiment

POLEX...... Political Exercise [*International relations game*]

POLEX-NORTH ... Polar Experiment in the Northern Hemisphere   (MSC)

POLEX-SOUTH ... Polar Experiment in the Southern Hemisphere   (MSC)

POLFA...... Polarforschung [*A publication*]

Pol Fedn Newsl ... Police Federation Newsletter [*A publication*]   (DLA)

POLGEN... Problem-Oriented Language Generator [*Data processing*]   (BUR)

POLI.......... Postal Life [*A publication*]

POLIA........ Polimery [*A publication*]

POLIC....... Petroleum Intersectional Command [*Army*]   (AABC)

Police Fedn Newsl ... Police Federation Newsletter [*A publication*]   (ILCA)

Police J ...... Police Journal [*A publication*]

Police J Ct ... Police Justice's Court [*A publication*]   (ILCA)

Police LQ... Police Law Quarterly [*A publication*]   (ILCA)

Police Mag ... Police Magazine [*A publication*]

Police Mag (Syria) ... Police Magazine (Syria) [*A publication*]

Police Res Bull ... Police Research Bulletin [*A publication*]

Police Rev .... Police Review [*A publication*]

Police Sc Abs ... Police Science Abstracts [*A publication*]

Policlinico Sez Chir ... Policlinico. Sezione Chirurgica [*A publication*]

Policlinico Sez Med ... Policlinico. Sezione Medica [*A publication*]

Policlinico Sez Prat ... Policlinico. Sezione Practica [*A publication*]

Policlin Infant ... Policlinico Infantile [*A publication*]

Policy Anal ... Policy Analysis [*Later, Journal of Policy Analysis and Management*] [*A publication*]

Policy Pol... Policy and Politics [*A publication*]

Policy Polit ... Policy and Politics [*A publication*]

Policy Publ Rev ... Policy Publication Review [*England*] [*A publication*]

Policy R...... Policy Review [*A publication*]

Policy Rev .. Policy Review [*A publication*]

Policy Sci ... Policy Sciences [*A publication*]

Policy Statement R Coll Gen Pract ... Policy Statement. Royal College of General Practitioners [*A publication*]

Policy Stud ... Policy Studies [*A publication*]

Policy Studies J ... Policy Studies Journal [*A publication*]

Policy Studies R ... Policy Studies Review [*A publication*]

Policy Stud J ... Policy Studies Journal [*A publication*]

Policy Stud Rev ... Policy Studies Review [*A publication*]

POLID...... Power Line [*A publication*]

Poligr Proizvod ... Poligraficheskoe Proizvodstvo [*A publication*]

Poligr Promst Obz Inf ... Poligraficheskaya Promyshlennost. Obzornaya Informatsiya [*A publication*]

Polim Mashinostr ... Polimery v Mashinostroenii [*Ukrainian SSR*] [*A publication*]

Polim Mater Ikh Issled ... Polimernye Materialy i Ikh Issledovanie [*A publication*]

Polim Med ... Polimery w Medycynie [*A publication*]

Polim Medziagos Ju Tyrimas ... Polimerines Medziagos ir Ju Tyrimas [*A publication*]

Polim Medziagu Panaudojimas Liaudies Ukyje ... Polimeriniu Medziagu Panaudojimas Liaudies Ukyje [*A publication*]

Polim Sb Tr Nauchnoizsled Inst Kauch Plastmasova Promst ... Polimeri Sbornik ot Trudove na Nauchnoizsledovatelskiya Institut po Kauchukova i Plastmasova Promishlenost [*A publication*]

Polim Sb Tr Nauchnoizsled Inst Prerabotka Plastmasi ... Polimeri Sbornik ot Trudove na Nauchnoizsledovatelskiya Institut po Prerabotkka na Plastmasi [*A publication*]

Polim Tworzwa ... Polimery Tworzywa [*Poland*] [*A publication*]

Polim Tworz Wielk ... Polimery-Tworzywa Wielkoczasteczkowe [*Poland*] [*A publication*]

Polim Tworz Wielkoczast ... Polimery-Tworzywa Wielkoczasteczkowe [*A publication*]

Polim Tworzywa Wielkoczasteczkowe ... Polimery Tworzywa Wielkoczasteczkowe [*A publication*]

Polim Vehomarim Plast ... Polimerim Vehomarim Plastiim [*A publication*]

Pol Inst Geol Bibliogr Geol Pol ... Poland. Instytut Geologiczny. Bibliografia Geologiczna Polski [*A publication*]

Pol Inst Meteorol Gospod Wodnej Pr ... Poland. Instytut Meteorologii i Gospodarki Wodnej. Prace [*A publication*]

Pol Internat ... Politique Internationale [*A publication*]

POLIO...... Poliomyelitis [*Medicine*]

Poliplasti Mater Rinf ... Poliplasti e Materiali Rinforzati [*A publication*]

Poliplasti Plast Rinf ... Poliplasti e Plastici Rinforzati [*A publication*]

Poli Q .... Political Quarterly [*A publication*]

POLIS .... Parliamentary On-Line Information System [*House of Commons Library*] [*Bibliographic database*] [*Information service or system*] [*British*]   (IID)

POLIS .... Petroleum Intersectional Service [*Army*]

POLIS .... Political Institutions Simulation [*Game*]

POLISARIO ... [*Frente*] Popular para la Liberacion de Saguia El Hamra y Rio De Oro [*Popular Front for the Liberation of Saguia El Hamra and Rio De Oro*] [*Morocco*]

Poli Sci...... Political Science [*A publication*]

Poli Sci Q... Political Science Quarterly [*A publication*]

Polish Acad Sci Fluid Flow ... Polish Academy of Sciences. Transactions. Institute of Fluid Flow Machinery [*Warsaw*] [*A publication*]

Polish Acad Sci Inst Philos Sociol Bull Sect Logic ... Polish Academy of Sciences. Institute of Philosophy and Sociology. Bulletin of the Section of Logic [*A publication*]

Polish Am Stud ... Polish American Studies [*A publication*]

Polish F...... Polish Film [*A publication*]

Polish J Chem ... Polish Journal of Chemistry [*A publication*]

Polish J Pharmacol Pharmacy ... Polish Journal of Pharmacology and Pharmacy [*A publication*]

Polish Mus ... Polish Music [*A publication*]

Polish Perspect ... Polish Perspectives [*A publication*]

Polish R ..... Polish Review [*A publication*]

Polish Sociol B ... Polish Sociological Bulletin [*A publication*]

Polish Tech & Econ Abstr ... Polish Technical and Economic Abstracts [*A publication*]

Poli Societ ... Politics and Society [*A publication*]

POLIT .... Political   (EY)

Polit........... Politics [*A publication*]

Polit Aff ..... Political Affairs [*A publication*]
Polit Aujourd ... Politique d'Aujourd'hui [*A publication*]
Polit Belge ... Politique Belge [*A publication*]
POLITBUREAU ... Political Bureau [*of USSR*]
POLITBURO ... Politicheskoe Byuro [*Political Bureau of USSR*]
Polit Dir ..... Politica del Diritto [*A publication*]
Politech Rzeszowska Im Ignacego Lukasiewicza Rozpr ... Politechnika Rzeszowska Imienia Ignacego Lukasiewicza. Rozprawy [*A publication*]
Politech Rzeszowska Zesz Nauk ... Politechnika Rzeszowska. Zeszyty Naukowe [*A publication*]
Politech Warsz Pr Inst Podstaw Konstr Masz ... Politechnika Warszawska. Prace Instytutu Podstaw Konstrukcji Maszyn [*A publication*]
Politech Warsz Pr Nauk Mech ... Politechnika Warszawska. Prace Naukowe. Mechanika [*A publication*]
Polit Eco ..... Review of Radical Political Economics [*A publication*]
Polit Econ .. Politica ed Economia [*A publication*]
Polit ed Econ ... Politica ed Economia [*A publication*]
Polit Ekon ... Politicka Ekonomie [*A publication*]
Polit Etr ..... Politique Etrangere [*A publication*]
Polit Foisk Kozlem ... Politikai Foiskola Kozlemenyei [*A publication*]
Polit Gazdasag Tanulmany ... Politikai Gazdasagtan Tanulmanyok [*A publication*]
Politic St .... Political Studies - London [*A publication*]
Polit Int (Roma) ... Politica Internazionale (Roma) [*A publication*]
Polit Meinung ... Politische Meinung [*A publication*]
Polit Methodol ... Political Methodology [*A publication*]
Polit Perspect ... Politiek Perspectief [*A publication*]
Polit Q .... Political Quarterly [*A publication*]
Polit Quart ... Political Quarterly [*A publication*]
Polit Rdsch ... Politische Rundschau [*A publication*]
Polit Sci ...... Political Science [*A publication*]
Polit Sci Ann ... Political Science Annual [*A publication*]
Polit Scientist ... Political Scientist [*A publication*]
Polit Sci Q ... Political Science Quarterly [*A publication*]
Polit Sci R ... Political Science Review [*A publication*]
Polit Sci R'er ... Political Science Reviewer [*A publication*]
Polit Sci (Wellington) ... Political Science (Wellington) [*A publication*]
Polit and Soc ... Politics and Society [*A publication*]
Polit Soc Econ Rev ... Political, Social, Economic Review [*A publication*]
Polit Spolecz ... Polityka Spoleczna [*A publication*]
Polit Stud ... Politische Studien [*Muenchen*] [*A publication*]
Polit Theor ... Political Theory [*A publication*]
Polit Today ... Politics Today [*A publication*]
Polit Vjschr ... Politische Vierteljahresschrift [*A publication*]
Polit Vjschr Sonderh ... Politische Vierteljahresschrift. Sonderheft [*A publication*]
Polit u Zeitgesch ... Politik und Zeitgeschichte [*A publication*]
Pol J .... Police Journal [*A publication*] (ILCA)
Pol J Anim Sci Technol ... Polish Journal of Animal Science and Technology [*A publication*]
Pol J Chem ... Polish Journal of Chemistry [*A publication*]
Pol J Ecol ... Polish Journal of Ecology [*A publication*]
Poljopriv Pregl ... Poljoprivredni Pregled [*A publication*]
Poljopriv Sumar ... Poljoprivredna i Sumarstvo [*A publication*]
Poljopriv Znan Smotra ... Poljoprivredna Znanstvena Smotra [*A publication*]
Poljopr Sumar ... Poljoprivredna i Sumarstvo [*A publication*]
Poljopr Znan Smotra ... Poljoprivredna Znanstvena Smotra [*A publication*]
Poljopr Znanst Smotra ... Poljoprivredna Znanstvena Smotra [*A publication*]
Pol J Phar ... Polish Journal of Pharmacology and Pharmacy [*A publication*]
Pol J Pharmacol Pharm ... Polish Journal of Pharmacology and Pharmacy [*A publication*]
Pol J Soil Sci ... Polish Journal of Soil Science [*A publication*]
POLK .... Polk Audio, Inc. [*Baltimore, MD*] [*NASDAQ symbol*] (NQ)
POLK of A ... Polka Lovers Klub of America (EA)
Poll .... Pollack's Ohio Unreported Judicial Decisions Prior to 1823 [*A publication*] (ILCA)
POLL .... Pollex [*An Inch*] [*Pharmacy*]
Poll .... Pollexfen's English King's Bench Reports [*1669-85*] [*A publication*] (ILCA)
PolL .... Polonista (Lublin) [*A publication*]
POLL .... Public Opinion Location Library [*The Roper Center for Public Opinion Research*] [*Information service or system*] (CRD)
Poll Abstr ... Pollution Abstracts [*A publication*]
Pollack Mihaly Muesz Foeisk Tud Koezl ... Pollack Mihaly Mueszaki Foeiskola Tudomanyos Koezlemenyei [*A publication*]
Pol Law of Nat ... Polson's Law of Nations [*1848*] [*A publication*] (DLA)
Poll CC Pr ... Pollock's Practice of the County Courts [*A publication*] (ILCA)
Poll Contr Guide ... Pollution Control Guide [*A publication*] (DLA)
POLLD ..... Pollimo [*A publication*]
Pollen Grain US For Serv Southeast Area ... Pollen Grain. United States Forest Service. Southeastern Area [*A publication*]
Pollex .... Pollexfen's English King's Bench Reports [*1669-85*] [*A publication*] (ILCA)
Pollexf .... Pollexfen's English King's Bench Reports [*1669-85*] [*A publication*] (ILCA)
Pollexfen .... Pollexfen's English King's Bench Reports [*1669-85*] [*A publication*] (ILCA)

Pollock & Maitl ... Pollock and Maitland's History of English Common Law [*A publication*] (DLA)
Poll Prod .... Pollock on the Production of Documents [*A publication*] (DLA)
Pol LQ .... Police Law Quarterly [*A publication*] (DLA)
POLLS ...... Parliamentary On-Line Library Study [*Atomic Energy Authority*] [*British*]
POLLUT ... Pollution
Pollut Abstr ... Pollution Abstracts [*A publication*]
Pollut Atmos ... Pollution Atmospherique [*A publication*]
Pollut Control ... Pollution Control [*Japan*] [*A publication*]
Pollut Eng .. Pollution Engineering [*A publication*]
Pollut Eng Technol ... Pollution Engineering and Technology [*A publication*]
Pollution .... Pollution Equipment News [*A publication*]
Pollution Cont Guide (CCH) ... Pollution Control Guide (Commerce Clearing House) [*A publication*] (DLA)
Pollut Monitor ... Pollution Monitor [*A publication*]
Pollut Tech ... Pollution Technology [*A publication*]
POLLY ...... [*A*] programming language [*1973*] (CSR)
Pol Mach Ind ... Polish Machine Industry [*A publication*]
Pol Mach Ind Offers ... Polish Machine Industry Offers [*A publication*]
Pol Med J .. Polish Medical Journal [*A publication*]
Pol Med J (Engl Transl Pol Arch Med Wewn) ... Polish Medical Journal (English Translation of Polskie Archiwum Medycyny Wewnetrznej) [*A publication*]
Pol Med Sci Hist Bull ... Polish Medical Science and History Bulletin [*A publication*]
Pol Meinung ... Politische Meinung [*A publication*]
Pol Methodol ... Political Methodology [*A publication*]
Pol Mil Dig ... Poland's Digest of the Military Laws of the United States [*A publication*] (DLA)
poln--- .... Central and Southern Line Islands [*MARC geographic area code*] [*Library of Congress*] (LCCP)
POLNA ..... Polnohospodarstvo [*A publication*]
Polnohospod ... Polnohospodarstvo [*A publication*]
POLO .... Pacific Command Operations Liaison Office [*Army*] (AABC)
POLO .... Plant and Office Layout (MCD)
POLO .... Polar Orbiting Lunar Observatory [*Satellite*]
POLO .... Polaris Oil & Gas [*NASDAQ symbol*] (NQ)
Pologne Aff Occid ... Pologne et les Affaires Occidentales [*A publication*]
Pologne Contemp ... Pologne Contemporaine [*A publication*]
POLOPS ... Polynomial Operations [*Air Force*]
Pol'ovnicky Zb ... Pol'ovnicky Zbornik [*A publication*]
PolP .... Polish Perspectives [*A publication*]
Pol Part ...... Pollock's Digest of the Laws of Partnership [*A publication*] (DLA)
Pol Perspect ... Polish Perspectives [*A publication*]
Pol Pismo Entomol ... Polskie Pismo Entomologiczne [*A publication*]
Pol Pismo Entomol Ser B Entomol Stosow ... Polskie Pismo Entomologiczne. Seria B. Entomologia Stosowana [*A publication*]
Pol and Polit ... Policy and Politics [*A publication*]
Pol Prod Doc ... Pollock on the Power of Courts to Compel the Production of Documents [*A publication*] (DLA)
Pol Przegl Chir ... Polski Przeglad Chirurgiczny [*A publication*]
Pol Przegl Radiol ... Polski Przeglad Radiologii i Medycyny Nuklearnej [*A publication*]
Pol Przegl Radiol Med Nukl ... Polski Przeglad Radiologii i Medycyny Nuklearnej [*A publication*]
Pol Psych B ... Polish Psychological Bulletin [*A publication*]
Pol Q .... Political Quarterly [*A publication*]
Pol Quar ..... Political Quarterly [*A publication*]
Pol R .... Policy Review [*A publication*]
PolR .... Polish Review [*New York*] [*A publication*]
POLR .... Polymeric Resources Corp. [*NASDAQ symbol*] (NQ)
POLRA ...... Polar Record [*A publication*]
Pol Rev Radiol Nucl Med ... Polish Review of Radiology and Nuclear Medicine [*A publication*]
Pol Sci .... Policy Sciences [*A publication*]
Pol Sci .... Political Science [*A publication*]
Pol Science Q ... Political Science Quarterly [*A publication*]
Pol Sci Q ... Political Science Quarterly [*A publication*]
Pol Sci Quar ... Political Science Quarterly [*A publication*] (ILCA)
Pol Sci R .... Political Science Review [*Jaipur*] [*A publication*]
Polska Akad Nauk Met ... Polska Akademia Nauk. Metalurgia [*A publication*]
Polska Akad Nauk Oddzial Krakowie Pr Kom Nauk Tech Ceram ... Polska Akademia Nauk. Oddzial w Krakowie. Prace Komisji Nauk Technicznych. Serja Ceramika [*A publication*]
Polska Biblio Analit Mech ... Polska Bibliografia Analityczna. Mechanika [*A publication*]
Polska Gaz Lekar ... Polska Gazeta Lekarska [*A publication*]
Polskie Arch Med Wewnetrznej ... Polskie Archiwum Medycyny Wewnetrznej [*A publication*]
Polskie Archwm Wet ... Polskie Archiwum Weterynaryjne [*A publication*]
Polskie Pismo Entomol ... Polskie Pismo Entomologiczne [*A publication*]
Polskie Pismo Entomol Ser B Entomol Stosow ... Polskie Pismo Entomologiczne. Seria B. Entomologia Stosowana [*A publication*]
Polskie Tow Ent Klucze Oznaczania Owadow Pol ... Polskie Towarzystwo Entomologiczne. Klucze do Oznaczania Owadow Polski [*A publication*]

Polski Tygod Lek ... Polski Tygodnik Lekarski [*A publication*]
Pols Nat ..... Polson's Law of Nations [*1848*] [*A publication*] (DLA)
Pol & Soc ... Politics and Society [*A publication*]
Pol Soc .... Politics and Society [*A publication*]
Pol Soc B .... Polish Sociological Bulletin [*A publication*]
Pol Stud ..... Political Studies [*A publication*]
Pol Studien ... Politische Studien [*Muenchen*] [*A publication*]
Pol Studies ... Political Studies [*A publication*]
Pol Stud J .. Policy Studies Journal [*A publication*]
Pol Szt Lud ... Polska Sztuka Ludowa [*A publication*]
Pol Tech Abstr ... Polish Technical Abstracts [*A publication*]
Pol Tech Econ Abstr ... Polish Technical and Economic Abstracts [*A publication*]
Pol Technol News ... Polish Technological News [*A publication*]
Pol Tech Rev ... Polish Technical Review [*A publication*]
Pol Theory ... Political Theory [*A publication*]
POLTHN .. Polyethylene [*Organic chemistry*]
Pol Tijd ...... Polytechnisch Tijdschrift [*A publication*]
POLTL ...... Political (AFM)
Pol Today ... Politics Today [*A publication*]
Pol Tow Entomol Klucze Oznaczania Owadow Pol ... Polskie Towarzystwo Entomologiczne. Klucze do Oznaczania Owadow Polski [*A publication*]
Pol Tow Geol Rocz ... Polskie Towarzystwo Geologiczne. Rocznik [*A publication*]
Pol Trasporti ... Politica dei Trasporti [*A publication*]
Pol Tr Mar ... Poland's Law of Trade Marks [*A publication*] (DLA)
Pol Tyg Lek ... Polski Tygodnik Lekarski [*A publication*]
Pol Tyg Lek Wiad Lek ... Polski Tygodnik Lekarski i Wiadomosci Lekarskie [*A publication*]
Poluch Strukt Svoistv Sorbentov ... Poluchenie, Struktura, i Svoistva Sorbentov [*A publication*]
Poluch Svoistva Tonkikh Plenok ... Poluchenie i Svoistva Tonkikh Plenok [*Ukrainian SSR*] [*A publication*]
Poluprovdn Prib Tekh Elektrosvyazi ... Poluprovodnikovye Pribory v Tekhnike Elektrosvyazi [*A publication*]
Poluprovodn Elektron ... Poluprovodnikovaya Elektronika [*A publication*]
Poluprovodn Ikh Primen Elektrotekh ... Poluprovodniki i Ikh Primenenie v Elektrotekhnike [*A publication*]
Poluprovodn Prib Ikh Primen ... Poluprovodnikovye Pribory i Ikh Primenenie [*A publication*]
Poluprovodn Prib Primen ... Poluprovodnikovye Pribory i Ikh Primenenie [*A publication*]
Poluprovodn Tekh i Mikroelektron ... Poluprovodnikovaya Tekhnika i Mikroelektronika [*A publication*]
Poluprov Prib Ikh Primen Sb Statei ... Poluprovodnikovye Pribory i Ikh Primenenie Sbornik Statei [*USSR*] [*A publication*]
Poluprov Tekh Mikroelektron ... Poluprovodnikovaya Tekhnika i Mikroelektronika [*Ukrainian SSR*] [*A publication*]
POLUT ...... Pollution
Pol Vjschr .. Politische Vierteljahresschrift [*A publication*]
Pol VO .... Polizeiverordnung [*A publication*]
POLWAR ... Political Warfare
POLWARADDIR ... Political Warfare Advisory Directorate
POLX .... Polydex Pharmaceuticals Ltd. [*NASDAQ symbol*] (NQ)
Pol'y .... Policy (DLA)
POLY .... Poly-Tech, Inc. [*NASDAQ symbol*] (NQ)
POLY .... Polyester
POLY .... Polyethylene (DEN)
POLY .... Polygamy [*FBI standardized term*]
POLY .... Polymorphonuclear Leukocyte [*Hematology*]
POLY .... Polytechnic
PolyA .... Polyadenylated
POLY-AE/AM Rep (Polytech Inst NY Dep Aerosp Eng Appl Mech) ... POLY-AE/AM Report (Polytechnic Institute of New York. Department of Aerospace Engineering and Applied Mechanics) [*A publication*]
Polyarn Siyaniya Svechenie Nochnogo Neba ... Polyarnye Siyaniya i Svechenie Nochnogo Neba [*A publication*]
Polyar Siyaniya ... Polyarnye Siyaniya [*USSR*] [*A publication*]
Polyb .... Polybius [*Second century BC*] [*Classical studies*] (OCD)
Pol Yb of Internat L ... Polish Yearbook of International Law [*Warsaw*] [*A publication*] (DLA)
Pol YB Int'l L ... Polish Yearbook of International Law [*Warsaw*] [*A publication*] (DLA)
Polyc .... [*Epistle of*] Polycarp (BJA)
POLYEST ... Polyester
Poly L Rev ... Poly Law Review [*A publication*]
Polym .... Polymusic [*Record label*]
Polym Age ... Polymer Age [*A publication*]
Polym Appl ... Polymer Application [*Japan*] [*A publication*]
POLYMAT ... Polymer Materials [*Deutsches Kunststoff-Institut*] [*Federal Republic of Germany*] [*Information service or system*] (CRD)
Polym Bull ... Polymer Bulletin [*A publication*]
Polym Bull (Berlin) ... Polymer Bulletin (Berlin) [*A publication*]
Polym Commun ... Polymer Communications [*A publication*]
Polym Compos ... Polymer Composites [*A publication*]
Polym Composites ... Polymer Composites [*A publication*]
Polym Degradat Stabil ... Polymer Degradation and Stability [*A publication*]
Polym Engng News ... Polymer Engineering News [*A publication*]

Polym Engng Rev ... Polymer Engineering Reviews [*A publication*]
Polym Engng Sci ... Polymer Engineering and Science [*A publication*]
Polym Eng S ... Polymer Engineering and Science [*A publication*]
Polym Eng and Sci ... Polymer Engineering and Science [*A publication*]
Polym Eng Sci ... Polymer Engineering and Science [*A publication*]
Polymer Engng Science ... Polymer Engineering and Science [*A publication*]
Polymer J ... Polymer Journal [*A publication*]
Polym J ...... Polymer Journal [*A publication*]
Polym J (Jap) ... Polymer Journal (Japan) [*A publication*]
Polym Mech ... Polymer Mechanics [*A publication*]
Polym Monogr ... Polymer Monographs [*A publication*]
Polym News ... Polymer News [*A publication*]
POLYMODE ... Polygon-MODE [*Mid-Ocean Dynamics Experiment*] [*Soviet-US cooperative undersea weather exploration*]
Polym Paint Col J ... Polymers, Paint, and Colour Journal [*A publication*]
Polym Paint Colour J ... Polymers, Paint, and Colour Journal [*A publication*]
Polym Photochem ... Polymer Photochemistry [*A publication*]
Polym-Plast ... Polymer-Plastics Technology and Engineering [*A publication*]
Polym Plast Mater ... Polymers and Plastic Materials [*A publication*]
Polym-Plast Technol Eng ... Polymer-Plastics Technology and Engineering [*A publication*]
Polym Prepr Am Chem Soc Div Polym Chem ... Polymer Preprints. American Chemical Society. Division of Polymer Chemistry [*A publication*]
Polym Preprints ... Polymer Preprints [*A publication*]
Polym Rep ... Polymer Report [*A publication*]
Polym Rev ... Polymer Reviews [*A publication*]
Polym Sci Technol ... Polymer Science and Technology [*American Chemical Society*] [*Information service or system*] [*A publication*]
Polym Sci USSR ... Polymer Science. USSR [*English Translation of Vysokomolekulyarnye Soyedineniya. Series A*] [*A publication*]
Polym Test ... Polymer Testing [*A publication*]
POLYN ..... Polynesia
Polyn Soc J ... Polynesian Society Journal [*A publication*]
POLYOX ... Poly(ethylene Oxide) [*Trademark*]
Polysaccharides Biol Trans Conf ... Polysaccharides in Biology. Transactions of the Conference [*A publication*]
Polysar Prog ... Polysar Progress [*A publication*]
Polyscope Autom und Elektron ... Polyscope. Automatik und Elektronik [*A publication*]
Polyscope Comput und Elektron ... Polyscope. Computer und Elektronik [*A publication*]
Polytech Inst Brooklyn Microwave Res Inst Symp Ser ... Polytechnic Institute of Brooklyn. Microwave Research Institute. Symposia Series [*A publication*]
Polytech Tijdschr Bouwk Wegen- & Waterbouw ... Polytechnisch Tijdschrift Bouwkune Wegen- en Waterbouw [*A publication*]
Polytech Tijdschr Ed A ... Polytechnisch Tijdschrift. Editie A. Werktuigbouwkunde en Elektrotechniek [*A publication*]
Polytech Tijdschr Ed B ... Polytechnisch Tijdschrift. Editie B [*A publication*]
Polytech Tijdschr Elektrotech Elektron ... Polytechnisch Tijdschrift. Elektrotechniek. Elektronica [*A publication*]
Polytech Tijdschr Procestech ... Polytechnisch Tijdschrift. Procestechniek [*A publication*]
Polytech Tijdschr Werktuigbouw ... Polytechnisch Tijdschrift. Werktuigbouw [*A publication*]
Polytech Weekbl ... Polytechnisch Weekblad [*A publication*]
Polytek Revy ... Polyteknisk Revy [*Norway*] [*A publication*]
POLYTRAN ... Polytranslation Analysis and Programming (IEEE)
Polyt Rv ... Polytechnic Review [*A publication*]
POM .... Operation: Peace of Mind [*Later, Runaway Hotline*] [*An association*] (EA)
POM .... Pallet-Only Mode [*NASA*] (NASA)
POM .... Particulate Organic Matter [*Environmental chemistry*]
POM .... Peritronics Med [*Vancouver Stock Exchange symbol*]
POM .... Personnel, Operations, Maintenance (MCD)
POM .... Phenomenon of Man [*Project*] (EA)
POM .... Police Officer, Male
POM .... Polycyclic Organic Matter
POM .... Poly(oxymethylene) [*Organic chemistry*]
POM .... Pomeranian Dog (DSUE)
POM .... Pomona [*California*] [*Seismograph station code, US Geological Survey*] [*Closed*] (SEIS)
POM .... Pomona, CA [*Location identifier*] [*FAA*] (FAAL)
Pom .... Pompon [*Horticulture*]
Pom .... [*Sextus*] Pomponius [*Flourished, 2nd century*] [*Authority cited in pre-1607 legal work*] (DSA)
POM .... Pool Operational Module [*Telecommunications*] (TEL)
POM .... Port Moresby [*Papua New Guinea*] [*Airport symbol*] (OAG)
POM .... Position Modulator (NRCH)
POM .... Potential Officer Material [*British military*] (DMA)
POM .... Potomac Electric Power Co. [*NYSE symbol*] (SPSG)
POM .... Preparation for Overseas Movement [*Military*]
POM .... Prescription Only Medicine [*British*]
POM .... Printer Output Microfilm
POM .... Prior to Overseas Movement [*DoD*]
POM .... Priority of Movements [*Military*] [*British*]
POM .... Program Objectives Memorandum [*Military*]
POM .... Program Operation Mode
POM .... Project Office Memo

POM.......... Project Officers Meeting
POMA .... Petty Officer Medical Assistant [*British military*] (DMA)
POMA .... Petty Officer's Military Academy [*Navy*]
POMAR .... Position Operational, Meteorological Aircraft Report
POMAR .... Preventive Operational Maintenance and Repair
      [*Military*] (NVT)
POMAS..... Procurement Office for Military Automotive Supplies
POMBA .... Parents of Multiple Births Associations of Canada
POM/BES ... Program Objective Memorandum/Budget Estimate
      Submission (MCD)
POMC .... Parents of Murdered Children (EA)
POMC .... Pro-Opiomelanocortin [*Endocrinology*]
Pom Code Rem ... Pomeroy on Code Remedies [*A publication*] (DLA)
Pom Const Law ... Pomeroy's Constitutional Law of the United States [*A
      publication*] (DLA)
Pom Contr ... Pomeroy on Contracts [*A publication*] (DLA)
POMCUS ... Prepositioning of Materiel Configured to Unit Sets
      [*Army*] (AABC)
POMDA .... Postgraduate Medicine [*A publication*]
POMDD.... Poznanskie Roczniki Medyczne [*A publication*]
pome---....... Melanesia [*MARC geographic area code*] [*Library of
      Congress*] (LCCP)
POME .... Principal Ordnance Mechanical Engineer [*British
      military*] (DMA)
POME .... Prisoner of Mother England [*Nineteenth-century convict in
      penal colony of Australia; term is said to have been
      shortened eventually to "pom" or "pommie" as a
      nickname for any Australian. A second theory maintains
      that the nickname is short for "pomegranate," a red fruit,
      and refers to the sunburn that fair-skinned Englishmen
      quickly acquire upon arrival in Australia.*]
POME .... Problems-Objectives-Methods-Evaluation [*Planning method*]
POMEM ... Petty Officer Marine Engineering Mechanic [*British
      military*] (DMA)
Pom Eq Jur ... Pomeroy's Equity Jurisprudence [*A publication*] (DLA)
Pom Eq Juris ... Pomeroy's Equity Jurisprudence [*A publication*] (DLA)
POMERID ... Pomeridianus [*In the Afternoon*] [*Pharmacy*]
Pomeroy..... Pomeroy's Reports [*73-128 California*] [*A publication*] (DLA)
POMF .... Polaris Missile Facility
POMFE4.... Ontario. Ministry of Agriculture and Food. Publication [*A
      publication*]
POMFLANT ... Polaris Missile Facility, Atlantic Fleet
POMFPAC ... Polaris Missile Facility, Pacific Fleet
POMGEN ... Program Objective Memorandum Generator [*Military*]
POMH....... National Association of Post Office Mail Handlers, Watchmen,
      Messengers, and Group Leaders [*Later, NPOMHWMGL*]
POMI .... Preliminary Operating and Maintenance Instructions
      [*Aerospace*] (AAG)
Pomiary Autom Kontrola ... Pomiary Automatyka Kontrola [*A publication*]
POMINS... Portable Mine Neutralization System (MCD)
POMJA..... Polish Medical Journal [*A publication*]
POMM...... Preliminary Operating and Maintenance Manual
      [*Military*] (AABC)
Pomme Terre Fr ... Pomme de Terre Francaise [*A publication*]
Pom Mun Law ... Pomeroy on Municipal Law [*A publication*] (DLA)
POMNDR ... Museo Nacional de Historia Natural. Publicacion Ocasional
      [*Santiago, Chile*] [*A publication*]
POMO....... Partially Occupied Molecular Orbitals [*Physical chemistry*]
POMO....... Personnel Objectives Monitoring Operation
POMO....... Production-Oriented Maintenance Organization (MCD)
POMOL.... POMCUS [*Prepositioning of Materiel Configured to Unit Sets*]
      Objective Levels [*Military*]
POMOL.... Pomology
POMOLA ... Poor Man's Optical Landing System
Pomol Fr .... Pomologie Francaise [*A publication*]
Pomol Fruit Grow Soc Annu Rep ... Pomological and Fruit Growing Society.
      Annual Report [*A publication*]
Pomor Ant ... Pomorania Antiqua [*A publication*]
Pomp.......... Epistula ad Pompeium [*of Dionysius Halicarnassensis*]
      [*Classical studies*] (OCD)
Pomp.......... Pompeius [*of Plutarch*] [*Classical studies*] (OCD)
Pomp.......... [*Sextus*] Pomponius [*Flourished, 2nd century*] [*Authority cited
      in pre-1607 legal work*] (DSA)
POMP .... Pomposo [*Grandly*] [*Music*] (ROG)
POMP .... Prednisone, Oncovin [*Vincristine*], Methotrexate, Purinethol
      [*Mercaptopurine*] [*Antineoplastic drug regimen*]
POMP .... Principal Outer Membrane Protein
POMPA .... Publications. Mississippi Philological Association [*A
      publication*]
Pompebl..... Pompebledon [*A publication*]
POMR .... Problem-Oriented Medical Record
Pom Rem.... Pomeroy on Civil Remedies [*A publication*] (DLA)
Pom Rem & Rem Rights ... Pomeroy on Civil Remedies and Remedial Rights
      [*A publication*] (DLA)
POMR/PST ... Partido Obrero Marxista Revolucionario/Partido Socialista de
      los Trabajadores [*Marxist Revolutionary Workers' Party/
      Socialist Workers' Party*] [*Peru*] [*Political party*] (PPW)
POMS .... Panel on Operational Meteorological Satellites
POMS .... Profile of Mood States [*A questionnaire*]
POMS .... Program Operations Manual System [*Social Security
      Administration*]

POMSA..... Post Office Management Staffs Association [*A union*]
      [*British*] (DCTA)
POMS-BI .. Profile of Mood States-Bipolar Form
POMSEE .. Performance, Operating and Maintenance Standards for
      Electronic Equipment (NG)
POMSIP ... Post Office Management and Service Improvement Program
      [*Obsolete*]
Pom Spec Perf ... Pomeroy on Specific Performance of Contracts [*A
      publication*] (DLA)
POMT .... Planning and Operations Management Team (MCD)
POMV .... National Federation Post Office Motor Vehicle Employees
      [*Later, APWU*] (EA)
POMV .... Privately Owned Motor Vehicle (NATG)
PON.......... Paraoxonase [*An enzyme*]
PON.......... Particulate Organic Nitrogen
PON.......... Ponce [*Puerto Rico*] [*Seismograph station code, US Geological
      Survey*] (SEIS)
PON.......... Ponder Oils Ltd. [*Toronto Stock Exchange symbol*]
Pon .... Ponte [*A publication*]
Pon .... Pontius [*Authority cited in pre-1607 legal work*] (DSA)
PON.......... Pontoon (AAG)
PON.......... Pride of Newark [*Feigenspan beer*]
PON.......... Program Opportunity Notice [*Energy Research and
      Development Administration*]
PON.......... Public Opinion [*A publication*]
PONA .... Paraffins, Olefins, Naphthenes, Aromatics
Pon Ble....... Poncius Blegerii [*Flourished, 14th century*] [*Authority cited in
      pre-1607 legal work*] (DSA)
PONBRG .. Pontoon Bridge (MUGU)
POND....... Parents of Near Drownings [*An association*] (EA)
POND....... Pondere [*By Weight*] [*Latin*]
POND....... Ponderosus [*Heavy*] [*Pharmacy*]
PONE........ Polar News. Japan Polar Research Association [*A publication*]
ponl--- .... New Caledonia [*MARC geographic area code*] [*Library of
      Congress*] (LCCP)
ponn--- .... New Hebrides [*MARC geographic area code*] [*Library of
      Congress*] (LCCP)
pono.......... Peso Neto [*Net Weight*] [*Spanish*]
Po Now...... Poetry Now [*A publication*]
PONS .... Platt's Oilgram News Service
PONS .... Polar Notes [*A publication*]
PONS .... Profile of Nonverbal Sensitivity [*Psychology*]
PONSA ..... Platt's Oilgram News Service [*A publication*]
PONSE...... Personnel of the Naval Shore Establishment [*Report*] (NG)
PONSI...... Program of Noncollegiate Sponsored Instruction (OICC)
Pont............ Epistulae ex Ponto [*of Ovid*] [*Classical studies*] (OCD)
PONT .... Pontiac [*Automotive engineering*]
PONTA ..... Popular New Titles from Abroad [*Book acquisition program for
      libraries*]
Ponte Riv M ... Ponte. Rivista Mensile di Politica e Letteratura [*A
      publication*]
Pontif Acad Sci Acta ... Pontificia Academia Scientiarum. Acta [*A
      publication*]
Pontif Acad Sci Comment ... Pontificia Academia Scientiarum. Commentarii
      [*A publication*]
Pontif Acad Sci Scr Varia ... Pontificia Academia Scientiarum. Scripta Varia
      [*A publication*]
Po Nto .... Peso Neto [*Net Weight*] [*Spanish*]
ponu---........ Nauru [*MARC geographic area code*] [*Library of
      Congress*] (LCCP)
PONUC..... Post Office National Users' Council [*British*]
PONY....... Prostitutes of New York
PONY....... Protect Our Nation's Youth [*Baseball league*] [*Name usually
      written Pony*]
PONY....... Purpose of Neighborhood Youth [*Foundation*]
PONYA ..... Port of New York Authority [*Later, PANYNJ*]
POO.......... Panel on Oceanography
POO.......... Payload Operations Office [*NASA*]
POO.......... Platform of Opportunity Program [*National Oceanic and
      Atmospheric Administration*] (MSC)
POO.......... Pocos De Caldas [*Brazil*] [*Airport symbol*] (OAG)
POO.......... Poona [*India*] [*Seismograph station code, US Geological
      Survey*] (SEIS)
POO.......... Port Operations Officer (DS)
POO.......... Post Office Order
POO.......... Priority Operational Objective [*Military*]
POO.......... Program Operations Officer [*Social Security Administration*]
POOD....... Permanent Officer of the Day [*or Deck*] [*Navy*]
POOD....... Provisioning Order Obligating Document
POOEL...... Petty Officer Ordnance Electrician [*British military*] (DMA)
POOFF...... Preservation of Our Femininity and Finances [*Women's group
      opposing below-the-knee fashions introduced in 1970*]
POOFF...... Professional Oglers of Female Figures [*Men's group opposing
      below-the-knee fashions introduced in 1970*]
POOL .... Poseidon Pools of America, Inc. [*NASDAQ symbol*] (NQ)
Poona Agr Col Mag ... Poona Agricultural College Magazine [*A publication*]
Poona Agric Coll Mag ... Poona Agricultural College Magazine [*A
      publication*]
POOP .... Process Oriented Observation Program [*NORPAX*] (MSC)
POOR........ Prevention of Over-Radiation [*Military*]
Poore Const ... Poore's Federal and State Constitution [*A publication*] (DLA)

Poor L & Local Gov't ... Poor Law and Local Government Magazine [*A publication*] (DLA)
POOS .... Priority Order Output System [*Japan*] (DIT)
POOW....... Petty Officer of the Watch [*Navy*] (NVT)
POP .... Pacific Ocean Perch
POP .... Panoramic Office Planning
POP .... Parallel Output Platform
POP .... Parents of Punkers (EA)
POP .... Paroxypropione [*or Paraoxypropiophenone*] [*Endocrinology*]
POP .... Parti Ouvrier et Paysan du Congo [*Congolese Workers' and Peasants' Party*] [*Political party*] [*Zaire*]
POP .... Parti Ouvrier-Progressiste [*Canada*]
POP .... Particulate Organic Phosphorus
POP .... Partido de Orientacion Popular [*Popular Orientation Party*] [*El Salvador*] [*Political party*] (PPW)
POP .... Pay One Price
POP .... Payload Optimized Program [*NASA*] (KSC)
POP .... Peak Overpressure [*Nuclear energy*] (NRCH)
POP .... Period of Performance (MCD)
POP .... Perpendicular Ocean Platform [*Oceanography*]
POP .... Perpendicular-to-Orbit Plane [*Aerospace*] (KSC)
POP .... Persistent Occipit Posterior [*A fetal position*] [*Obstetrics*]
POP .... Pharmacists in Ophthalmic Practice [*Later, PIOP*] (EA)
POP .... Pipeline Outfit, Petroleum (MCD)
POP .... Plasma Osmotic Pressure [*Medicine*]
POP .... Plaster of Paris
POP .... Point of Purchase [*Advertising*]
PoP .... Political Psychology [*A publication*]
POP .... Pollution and Overpopulation
POP .... Pope & Talbot, Inc. [*NYSE symbol*] (SPSG)
Pop .... Popham's English King's Bench Reports [*1592-1627*] [*A publication*] (DLA)
POP .... Popondetta [*Papua New Guinea*] [*Seismograph station code, US Geological Survey*] [*Closed*] (SEIS)
POP .... Popping [*Mining engineering*]
POP .... Popular
Pop .... Populare [*Record label*] [*Romania*]
POP .... Population (AAG)
Pop .... Population [*A publication*]
POP .... Population Division [*Bureau of the Census*] (OICC)
POP .... Post Office Plan
POP .... Post Office Preferred (DCTA)
POP .... Posterior Odds Processing [*Weather forecasting*] [*National Science Foundation*]
POP .... Postoperative [*Medicine*]
POP .... Power On/Off Protection
POP .... Preburner Oxidizer Pump (MCD)
POP .... Preflight Operations Procedure (MCD)
POP .... Prelaunch Operations Plan [*NASA*] (NASA)
POP .... Premanagement Orientation Program [*LIMRA*]
POP .... Pressurizer Overpressure Protection System [*Nuclear energy*] (IEEE)
POP .... Primary Operation
pop .... Printer of Plates [*MARC relator code*] [*Library of Congress*] (LCCP)
POP .... Printing-Out Paper
POP .... Profit Option Plan [*Retailing*]
POP .... Program Obligation Plan (KSC)
POP .... Program Operating Plan
POP .... Programmed Operators and Primitives [*Data processing*]
POP .... Project Objective Plan (NG)
POP .... Prompt Ordering Plan
POP .... Proof-Of Principle [*Test*]
POP .... Proof of Purchase
POP .... Puerto Plata [*Dominican Republic*] [*Airport symbol*] (OAG)
POP .... Pump Optimizing Program
POPA .... Patent Office Professional Association (EA)
POPA .... Payload Ordnance Processing Area (NASA)
POPA .... Pet Owners' Protective Association
POPA .... Property Owners' Protection Association
POPAE..... Protons on Protons and Electrons [*Physics*]
POPAI...... Point-of-Purchase Advertising Institute [*Fort Lee, NJ*] (EA)
Pop Astron ... Popular Astronomy [*A publication*]
Pop Astronomy ... Popular Astronomy [*A publication*]
Pop B.......... Population Bulletin [*A publication*]
POP & B ... Proposed Operating Program and Budget [*Army*]
Pop Bul ...... Population Bulletin [*A publication*]
Pop Bull Colo State Univ Agr Exp Sta ... Popular Bulletin. Colorado State University. Agricultural Experiment Station [*A publication*]
popc--- .... Pitcairn [*MARC geographic area code*] [*Library of Congress*] (LCCP)
Pop Comput ... Popular Computing [*A publication*]
POP-CON ... Populist Conservative [*Wing of the Republican Party represented by Congressmen Gingrich, Kemp, and Lott*]
POPD .... Power-Operated
POPDA ..... Polish Psychological Bulletin [*A publication*]
POPDA ..... Polyoxypropylenediamine [*Organic chemistry*]
Pop Dev R ... Population and Development Review [*New York*] [*A publication*]

POPE......... Parents for Orthodoxy in Parochial Education [*Group opposing sex education in schools*]
Pope Cust... Pope on Customs and Excise [*11th ed.*] [*1828*] [*A publication*] (DLA)
POP ED.... Popular Edition [*Publishing*]
Pop Educ... Popular Educator [*A publication*]
Pop Electr .. Popular Electronics [*A publication*]
Pope Lun.... Pope on Lunacy [*A publication*] (DLA)
Pop Gard.... Popular Gardening [*A publication*]
Pop Govt.... Popular Government [*A publication*]
POPGUN .. Policy and Procedure Governing the Use of Nicknames [*Army*] (AABC)
Poph.......... Popham's English King's Bench Reports [*1592-1627*] [*A publication*] (DLA)
Poph (2) ..... Cases at the End of Popham's Reports [*A publication*] (DLA)
Popham...... Popham's English King's Bench Reports [*79 English Reprint*] [*1592-1626*] [*A publication*] (DLA)
Poph Insol ... Popham's Insolvency Act of Canada [*A publication*] (DLA)
POPI......... Fast Food Operators, Inc. [*NASDAQ symbol*] (NQ)
PopI .... Population Index [*A publication*]
POPI......... Post Office Position Indicator [*A form of long-range position indicator*] [*British*]
Pop Ind ...... Population Index [*A publication*]
Pop Index ... Population Index [*A publication*]
POPINFORM ... Population Information Network [*UNESCO*]
POPINS .... Population Information System [*UNESCO*]
POPLAB .. International Program of Laboratories for Population Statistics
POPLER ... [*A*] programming language (CSR)
POPLINE ... Population Information On-Line [*Bibliographic database*] (IID)
POPLIT.... Popliteal [*Anatomy*]
Pop Mech... Popular Mechanics Magazine [*A publication*]
Pop Med (Tokyo) ... Popular Medicine (Tokyo) [*A publication*]
POPMIP ... Portable Ocean Platform Motion Instrumentation Package [*Marine science*] (MSC)
Pop Mo L Tr ... Popular Monthly Law Tracts [*1877-78*] [*A publication*] (DLA)
Pop Music S ... Popular Music and Society [*A publication*]
Pop Mus Per Ind ... Popular Music Periodicals Index [*A publication*]
Pop Mus & Soc ... Popular Music and Society [*A publication*]
Popn.......... Population
POPO .... Polar Post. Polar Postal History Society of Great Britain [*A publication*]
POPO .... Poured-On, Passed-Over [*Bowdlerized version*]
POPO .... Push-On, Pull-Off [*Data processing*]
POPOA ..... Phosphorus and Potassium [*A publication*]
POPPD..... Plant/Operations Progress [*A publication*]
Pop Per Ind ... Popular Periodical Index [*A publication*]
Pop Phot .... Popular Photography [*A publication*]
Pop Photog ... Popular Photography [*A publication*]
Pop Plast.... Popular Plastics [*A publication*]
Pop Plast Annu ... Popular Plastics Annual [*A publication*]
POPR........ Pilot Overhaul Provisioning Review
POPR........ Prototype Organic Power Reactor [*Nuclear energy*]
POPS........ Free-Fall Pop-Up Ocean Bottom Seismometer [*Marine science*] (MSC)
POPS........ Pantograph Optical Projection System (IEEE)
POPS........ Parachute Opening Proximity Sensor (MCD)
POPS........ People Opposed to Pornography in Schools [*Group opposing sex education in schools*]
POPS........ Platt's Oilgram Price Service
pops--- .... Polynesia [*MARC geographic area code*] [*Library of Congress*] (LCCP)
POPS........ Preserve Our Presidential Sites (EA)
POPS........ Pressurizer Overpressure Protection System [*Nuclear energy*] (NRCH)
POPS........ Process Operating System [*Toshiba Corp.*] [*Japan*]
POPS........ Procurers of Painted-Label Sodas (EA)
POPS........ Program for Operator Scheduling [*Bell System computer program*]
POPS........ Project Operations [*Navy*] (NVT)
POPS........ Protect Our Pelican Society [*Later, PMBS*] (EA)
POPS........ Pyrotechnic Optical Plume Simulator (MCD)
Pop Sci ...... Popular Science Monthly [*A publication*]
POP SCI MO ... Popular Science Monthly [*A publication*] (ROG)
Pop Sci (Peking) ... Popular Science (Peking) [*A publication*]
Pop Sci R .. Popular Science Review [*A publication*]
POPSE...... Project Office for Physical Security Equipment [*Army*] (RDA)
POPSER.... Polaris Operational Performance Surveillance Engineering Report [*Missiles*]
POPSI .... Precipitation and Off-Path Scattered Interference [*Report*] [*FCC*]
POPSIPT .. Project Operations in Port [*Navy*] (NVT)
Pop Stud ... Population Studies [*London*] [*A publication*]
Pop Stud (Lo) ... Population Studies (London) [*A publication*]
Pop Stud (NY) ... Population Studies (New York) [*A publication*]
POPT......... Petty Officer Physical Trainer [*British military*] (DMA)
POPT......... Pretesting Orientation on the Purpose of Testing [*US Employment Service*] [*Department of Labor*]
Pop Tech Tous ... Popular Technique pour Tous [*A publication*]
POPU .... Push Over Pull Up (NASA)

Popul.......... Population [*A publication*]
Popular Govt ... Popular Government [*A publication*]
Popular M Soc ... Popular Music and Society [*A publication*]
Population Bul ... Population Bulletin [*A publication*]
Population Bul UN ... Population Bulletin. United Nations [*A publication*]
Population R ... Population Review [*A publication*]
Population Research and Policy R ... Population Research and Policy Review [*A publication*]
Popul et Avenir ... Population et Avenir [*A publication*]
Popul Bull .. Population Bulletin [*A publication*]
Popul Bull UN Econ Comm West Asia ... Population Bulletin. United Nations Economic Commission for Western Asia [*A publication*]
Popul B UN Econ Com West Asia ... Population Bulletin. United Nations Economic Commission for Western Asia [*A publication*]
Popul Counc Annu Rep ... Population Council. Annual Report [*A publication*]
Popul Data Inf Serv ... Population Data Information Service [*A publication*]
Popul Dev Rev ... Population and Development Review [*A publication*]
Popul Educ News ... Population Education News [*A publication*]
Popul Environ ... Population and Environment [*A publication*]
Popul et Famille ... Population et Famille [*A publication*]
Popul et Famille/Bevolk en Gezin ... Population et Famille/Bevolking en Gezin [*A publication*]
Popul Forum ... Population Forum [*A publication*]
Popul Geogr ... Population Geography [*A publication*]
Popul Ind ... Population Index [*A publication*]
Popul Newsl ... Population Newsletter [*A publication*]
Popul Policy Compend ... Population Policy Compendium [*A publication*]
Popul Rep A ... Population Reports. Series A. Oral Contraceptives [*A publication*]
Popul Rep B ... Population Reports. Series B. Intrauterine Devices [*A publication*]
Popul Rep C ... Population Reports. Series C. Sterilization. Female [*A publication*]
Popul Rep D ... Population Reports. Series D. Sterilization (Male) [*A publication*]
Popul Rep E ... Population Reports. Series E. Law and Policy [*A publication*]
Popul Rep F ... Population Reports. Series F. Pregnancy Termination [*A publication*]
Popul Rep G ... Population Reports. Series G. Prostaglandins [*A publication*]
Popul Rep H ... Population Reports. Series H. Barrier Methods [*A publication*]
Popul Rep I ... Population Reports. Series I. Periodic Abstinence [*A publication*]
Popul Rep J ... Population Reports. Series J. Family Planning Programs [*A publication*]
Popul Rep K ... Population Reports. Series K. Injectables and Implants [*A publication*]
Popul Rep L ... Population Reports. Series L. Issues in World Health [*A publication*]
Popul Rep M ... Population Reports. Series M. Special Topics [*A publication*]
Popul Rep Spec Top Monogr ... Population Reports. Special Topics. Monographs [*A publication*]
Popul Rev... Population Review [*A publication*]
Popul et Societes ... Population et Societes [*A publication*]
Popul Stud ... Population Studies [*A publication*]
Popul Today ... Population Today [*A publication*]
Populuxe .... Popular Luxury [*Coined by Thomas Hine, design critic for the Philadelphia Inquirer, to describe the period from the mid-1950's to the mid-1960's*]
POPUS...... Post Office Processing Utility Subsystem [*Telecommunications*] (TEL)
POPX......... POP Radio Corp. [*New York, NY*] [*NASDAQ symbol*] (NQ)
POPYA...... Portugaliae Physica [*A publication*]
POQ.......... Production Offset Quantity [*Military*]
POQ.......... Provided Otherwise Qualified [*Military*] (AABC)
POQ.......... Public Opinion Quarterly [*A publication*]
POQ.......... Push Off Quickly [*i.e., Be quick about it*] [*British*]
POR.......... Pacific Ocean Region
POR.......... Pack Report. Fachzeitschrift fuer Verpackungs Marketing und Verpackungs (Technik) [*A publication*]
POR.......... Parking Orbit Rendezvous [*NASA*] (MCD)
POR.......... Partido Obrero Revolucionario [*Revolutionary Workers Party*] [*Argentina*] [*Political party*]
POR.......... Partido Obrero Revolucionario [*Revolutionary Workers Party*] [*Bolivia*] [*Political party*] (PPW)
POR.......... Partido Obrero Revolucionario [*Revolutionary Workers Party*] [*Peru*] [*Political party*]
POR.......... Patent Office Reports [*A publication*] (DLA)
POR.......... Patrol Operations Report
POR.......... Pay on Return [*Business term*]
POR.......... Payable on Receipt [*Business term*]
POR.......... Periodic Operation Report
POR.......... Personnel Occurrence Report [*RAF*] [*British*]
POR.......... Pilot Opinion Rating
POR.......... Plutonium Organic Recycle [*Nuclear energy*] (NRCH)
PoR.......... Poetry Review [*London*] [*A publication*]
POR.......... Pola Resources Ltd. [*Vancouver Stock Exchange symbol*]
POR.......... Pori [*Finland*] [*Airport symbol*] (OAG)
POR.......... Port of Refuge [*Shipping*]
POr.......... Porta Orientale [*A publication*]
POR.......... Portec, Inc. [*NYSE symbol*] (SPSG)

POR.......... Portion
POR.......... Portland [*Maine*] [*Seismograph station code, US Geological Survey*] [*Closed*] (SEIS)
POR.......... Portrait
Por............ Portugale [*A publication*]
POR.......... Portuguese
por............ Portuguese [*MARC language code*] [*Library of Congress*] (LCCP)
POR.......... Position of Responsibility (ADA)
POR.......... Post Office Return
POR.......... Post Office Rifles [*Military*] [*British*] (ROG)
POR.......... Preparation of Overseas Replacement [*Military*] (RDA)
POR.......... Press on Regardless [*Automotive marathon*]
POR.......... Price on Request
POR.......... Problem-Oriented Records [*Medicine*]
POR.......... Problem-Oriented Routine (IEEE)
POR.......... Project Officers Report (MCD)
POR.......... Psychotherapy Outcome Research
POR.......... Purchase Order Request
PORAC...... Peace Officers Research Association of California
PORACC.... Principles of Radiation and Contamination Control [*Nuclear energy*]
PORADD .. Postgraduate Radiology [*A publication*]
Poradnik M ... Poradnik Muzyczny [*A publication*]
PORAM .... Palm Oil Refiners Association of Malaysia (DS)
PORB .... Production Operations Review Board [*NASA*] (NASA)
PORC .... Partido Obrero Revolucionario-Combate [*Revolutionary Struggle Workers' Party*] [*Bolivia*] [*Political party*] (PPW)
PORC .... Plant Operations Review Committee [*Nuclear energy*] (NRCH)
PORC .... Porcelain (AAG)
PORCD ...... Population Reports. Series C [*United States*] [*A publication*]
PORCN ...... Production Order Records Change Notice (KSC)
PORCO ..... Port Control Office
PORD .... Performance and Operations Requirements Document [*NASA*] (NASA)
PORDA .... Personnel Officers of Research and Development Agencies
PORDB .... Ports and Dredging [*A publication*]
PORDIR... Port Director
PORE .... Point Reyes National Seashore [*National Park Service designation*]
PORE .... Polar Record [*A publication*]
POREA...... Post Office Regional Employees' Association [*Defunct*] (EA)
POREEQ.... Polar Research [*A publication*]
POREL(A) ... Petty Officer Radio Electrician (Air) [*British military*] (DMA)
POREP....... Position Report [*Air Force*]
PORES........ Purchase Order Receiving System (MCD)
PORF........ Pacific Ocean Research Foundation (EA)
P de Orfi .... Petrus de Orfila [*Deceased, 1307*] [*Authority cited in pre-1607 legal work*] (DSA)
Porg............ Person of Restricted Growth [*Lifestyle classification*] [*Slang term used to describe a person of limited cultural awareness*]
PORGIE.... Paperback Original [*Award for best original paperback books of the year*]
PORI.......... Polaris Operational Readiness Instrumentation [*Missiles*]
Por Jez...... Poradnik Jezykowy [*A publication*]
PORK .... Sooner State Farms [*NASDAQ symbol*] (NQ)
Pork Ind Gaz ... Pork Industry Gazette [*A publication*]
PORLA...... Practica Oto-Rhino-Laryngologica [*A publication*]
PORM........ Plus or Minus
PORN........ Pornography (DSUE)
PORN........ Protect Our Responsibilities Now [*Book title*]
PORNO..... Pornography (DSUE)
Poroshk Metall ... Poroshkovaya Metallurgiya [*A publication*]
Poroshk Metall (Kiev) ... Poroshkovaya Metallurgiya (Kiev) [*A publication*]
Poroshk Metall (Kuibyshev) ... Poroshkovaya Metallurgiya (Kuibyshev) [*A publication*]
Porosh Met ... Poroshkovaya Metallurgiya [*A publication*]
PORP......... Partial Ossicular Replacement Prosthesis
Porph......... Porphyry [*Third century AD*] [*Classical studies*] (OCD)
PORR .... Preliminary Operations Requirements Review [*NASA*] (NASA)
PORR .... Purchase Order Revision Request
PORS......... Polar Research [*A publication*]
PORS......... Product Output Reporting System
PORS......... Publications in Operations Research Series [*Elsevier Book Series*] [*A publication*]
PORSE...... Post Overhaul Reaction Safeguard Examination [*Navy*] (NVT)
porssi.......... Porssitermi [*Stock Exchange*] [*Finland*]
PORT .... Photo-Optical Recorder Tracker
PORT .... Portable (KSC)
PORT .... Porter (DSUE)
Port .... Porter's Alabama Supreme Court Reports [*1834-39*] [*A publication*] (DLA)
Port .... Porter's Indiana Reports [*3-7 Indiana*] [*A publication*] (DLA)
PORT .... Portland Railroad
PORT .... Portmanteau (DSUE)
PORT .... Portrait
PORT .... Portugal
Port .... Portugale [*A publication*]
PORT .... Prescriptive Objective Reference Testing [*Vocational guidance*]

Port Acta Biol A ... Portugaliae Acta Biologica. A. Morfologia, Fisiologia, Genetica, e Biologia Geral [*A publication*]
Port Acta Biol Ser A ... Portugaliae Acta Biologica. Serie A [*A publication*]
Port Acta Biol Ser B ... Portugaliae Acta Biologica. Serie B [*A publication*]
PORTAL... Process-Oriented Real-Time Algorithmic Language [*1978*] [*Data processing*]   (CSR)
Port (Ala)... Porter's Alabama Reports [*A publication*]   (DLA)
Port Ala R ... Porter's Alabama Reports [*A publication*]   (DLA)
PORTAPAK ... Portable, Self-Contained, Instrument Package
Port Electrochim Acta ... Portugaliae Electrochimica Acta [*A publication*]
Porter........ Porter's Alabama Reports [*A publication*]   (DLA)
Porter........ Porter's Indiana Reports [*3-7 Indiana*] [*A publication*]   (DLA)
Porter (Ala) ... Porter's Alabama Reports [*A publication*]   (DLA)
Porter R ..... Porter's Alabama Reports [*A publication*]   (DLA)
Porter's Ala R ... Porter's Alabama Reports [*A publication*]   (DLA)
Porter's R ... Porter's Alabama Reports [*A publication*]   (DLA)
Porter's Repts ... Porter's Alabama Reports [*A publication*]   (DLA)
Portfo......... Portfolio [*A publication*]
Portfo (Den) ... Portfolio (Dennie's) [*A publication*]
Port Gazette ... Melbourne Harbour Trust Port Gazette [*A publication*]   (APTA)
Portia L J... Portia Law Journal [*A publication*]
Port Ins ...... Porter's Laws of Insurance [*A publication*]   (DLA)
Port Junta Invest Cient Ultramar Estud Ensaios Doc ... Portugal. Junta de Investigacoes Cientificas do Ultramar. Estudos, Ensaios, e Documentos [*A publication*]
Port Lab Nac Eng Civ Mem ... Portugal. Laboratorio Nacional de Engenharia Civil. Memoria [*A publication*]
Portland Cem Ass Advanced Eng Bull ... Portland Cement Association. Advanced Engineering Bulletin [*A publication*]
Portland Cem Ass J PCA Res Develop Lab ... Portland Cement Association. Journal of the PCA Research and Development Laboratories [*A publication*]
Portland Cem Assoc Fellowship Natl Bur Stand Pap ... Portland Cement Association Fellowship at the National Bureau of Standards. Papers [*A publication*]
Portland Cem Assoc Res Dev Lab Dev Dep Bull D ... Portland Cement Association. Research and Development Laboratories. Development Department. Bulletin D [*A publication*]
Portland Soc N H Pr ... Portland Society of Natural History. Proceedings [*A publication*]
Portland UL Rev ... Portland University. Law Review [*A publication*]   (DLA)
Port Melb... Port Of Melbourne [*A publication*]   (APTA)
Port Melbourne Quart ... Port Of Melbourne Quarterly [*A publication*]   (APTA)
Port Melb Q ... Port Of Melbourne Quarterly [*A publication*]   (APTA)
Port Minist Ultramar Junta Invest Ultramar Mem Ser Antropol ... Portugal. Ministerio do Ultramar. Junta de Investigacoes do Ultramar. Memorias. Serie Antropologica e Etnologica [*A publication*]
Port Minist Ultramar Junta Invest Ultramar Mem Ser Botanica ... Portugal. Ministerio do Ultramar. Junta de Investigacoes do Ultramar. Memorias. Serie Botanica [*A publication*]
Port Minist Ultramar Junta Invest Ultramar Mem Ser Geol ... Portugal. Ministerio do Ultramar. Junta de Investigacoes do Ultramar. Memorias. Serie Geologica [*A publication*]
Port Minist Ultramar Mem Junta Invest Ultramar ... Portugal. Ministerio do Ultramar. Memorias da Junta de Investigacoes do Ultramar [*A publication*]
PORTN ..... Portion   (ROG)
Port Of Melbourne Q ... Port Of Melbourne Quarterly [*A publication*]
Port Of Melbourne Quart ... Port Of Melbourne Quarterly [*A publication*]   (APTA)
Port Of Melb Q ... Port Of Melbourne Quarterly [*A publication*]   (APTA)
Port Of Melb Quart ... Port Of Melbourne Quarterly [*A publication*]   (APTA)
Port Of Syd ... Port Of Sydney [*A publication*]   (APTA)
Port Of Sydney J ... Port Of Sydney Journal [*A publication*]   (APTA)
PORTP...... Partido Obrero Revolucionaria Trotskista Posadista [*Bolivia*] [*Political party*]   (PPW)
Port P......... Portuguese Pharmacopoeia [*A publication*]
Port Phillip Gaz ... Port Phillip Gazette [*A publication*]   (APTA)
Port Phy ... Portugaliae Physica [*A publication*]
Port Phys ... Portugaliae Physica [*A publication*]
Port R........ Portland Review [*A publication*]
PORTREP ... Port [*or Anchorage*] Capacity Report [*Navy*]   (NVT)
PORTS .... Portsmouth [*City in England*]
Ports Dredging Oil Rep ... Ports and Dredging and Oil Report [*A publication*]
Port Serv Fom Min Estud Notas Trab ... Portugal. Servico de Fomento Mineiro. Estudos, Notas, e Trabalhos [*A publication*]
Port Serv Geol Mem ... Portugal. Servicos Geologicos. Memoria [*A publication*]
PORTSM .. Portsmouth [*County borough in England*]
Ports NSW Jl ... Ports of New South Wales Journal [*A publication*]
PORTSREP ... Ports Report File   (MCD)
PORTSUM ... Port [*or Anchorage*] Summary Report [*Navy*]   (NVT)
Port Syd ..... Port Of Sydney [*A publication*]   (APTA)
Portug Acta Biol ... Portugaliae Acta Biologica [*A publication*]
Portugal Math ... Portugaliae Mathematica [*A publication*]
Portugal Phys ... Portugaliae Physica [*A publication*]
Port UL Rev ... Portland University. Law Review [*A publication*]   (DLA)
PORV .... Pilot-Operated Relief Valve [*Nuclear energy*]   (NRCH)

PORV .... Power-Operated Relief Valve [*Nuclear energy*]   (NRCH)
PORX .... Porex Technologies Corp. [*NASDAQ symbol*]   (NQ)
POS .... Pacific Ocean Ship   (NASA)
POS .... Pacific Orchid Society of Hawaii   (EA)
POS .... Parent Operating Service   (MCD)
POS .... Patent Office Society   (EA)
POS .... Peacetime Operating Stock [*Military*]   (CINC)
POS .... Period of Service [*Military*]
POS .... Photo Optic System
POS .... Pico Resources [*Vancouver Stock Exchange symbol*]
POS .... Plan of Service   (OICC)
POS .... Plant Operating System [*Nuclear energy*]   (NRCH)
P-O-S .... Point-of-Sale
POS .... Policy Statements [*Australian Broadcasting Tribunal*] [*A publication*]
POS .... Polycystic Ovarian Syndrome [*Also, PCOS*] [*Gynecology*]
POS .... Population Studies [*A publication*]
POS .... Port Of Spain [*Trinidad and Tobago*] [*Airport symbol*]   (OAG)
POS .... Portable Oxygen System   (MCD)
POS .... Position   (KSC)
POS .... Positive   (AFM)
Pos .... Possible
POS .... Post Office Scheme [*Regulations*] [*British*]
POS .... Preferred Overseas Shore Duty
POS .... Pretoria Oriental Series [*A publication*]
POS .... Primary Operating System   (IEEE)
POS .... Primary Oxygen System
POS .... Probability of Survival [*Automotive componant analysis*]
POS .... Problem Oriented System
POS .... Professions and Occupations Sourcebook [*A publication*]
POS .... Program Order Sequence
POS .... Programmable Option Select [*Data processing*]
POS .... Protein, Oil, and Starch [*Pilot manufacturing plant established by the Canadian government*]
POS .... Pskovskij Oblastnoj Slovar's Istoriceskimi Dannymi [*A publication*]
POS .... Pupil Observation Survey [*Education*]
POS .... Purchase Order Supplement
POSA .... Patriotic Order Sons of America   (EA)
POSA .... Payment Outstanding Suspense Accounts   (NATG)
POSA .... Petty Officer Stores Accountant [*British military*]   (DMA)
POSA .... Preliminary Operating Safety Analysis [*Nuclear energy*]   (NRCH)
POSARS ... Plan of Service Automated Reporting System [*Employment and Training Administration*] [*Department of Labor*]
POSB .... Polish Sociological Bulletin [*A publication*]
POSB .... Post Office Savings Bank
posc--- .... Santa Cruz Islands [*MARC geographic area code*] [*Library of Congress*]   (LCCP)
P & OSCC ... Plans and Operations for the Safeguard Communications Command [*Army*]   (RDA)
POSCH ..... Program of Surgical Control of Hyperlipidemia
POSCOR... Position Correct   (CAAL)
POSCORB ... Planning, Organizing, Staffing, Coordinating, Reporting, and Budgeting [*Management*]
POSD .... Personnel on Station Date [*Army*]   (AABC)
POSD .... Program for Optical System Design
POSD .... Project Operation Support Division [*NASA*]
POSDCORB ... Planning, Organizing, Staffing, Directing, Coordinating, Reporting, and Budgeting [*Principles of management*]
POSDSPLT ... Positive Displacement
POSE .... Parents Opposed to Sex Education
POSE .... Photogrammetric Ocean Survey Equipment
POSE .... Power Operational Support Equipment
POSEA ...... Peredovoi Opyt v Stroitel'stve i Ekspluatatsii Shakht [*A publication*]
Posebna Izdan ... Posebna Izdanja [*A publication*]
Posebna Izd Biol Inst N R Srb Beograd ... Posebna Izdanja Bioloski Institut N R Srbije Beograd [*A publication*]
Posebna Izd Geol Glas (Sarajevo) ... Posebna Izdanja Geoloskog Glasnika (Sarajevo) [*A publication*]
Posey......... Posey's Unreported Cases [*Texas*] [*A publication*]   (ILCA)
Posey UC ... Texas Unreported Cases [*A publication*]   (DLA)
Posey Unrep Cas ... Posey's Unreported Cases [*Texas*] [*A publication*]   (DLA)
POSH .... Permuted on Subject Headings [*Indexing technique*]
POSH .... Personal & Organizational Security Handbook [*A publication*]
POSH .... Port Outwardbound, Starboard Homewardbound [*Some claim that this acronym describes the location of shaded cabins on ships carrying British officers to the Far East and back. Many etymologists, however, believe that the origin of the word "posh" is unknown*]
posh............ Samoa Islands [*MARC geographic area code*] [*Library of Congress*]   (LCCP)
POSI .... Positech Corp. [*NASDAQ symbol*]   (NQ)
POSID....... Polyarnye Siyaniya [*A publication*]
POSIP .... Portable Ship's Instrumentation Package
POSIT .... Position   (NVT)
POSIT .... Positive
POSIT .... Positivism   (ROG)
POSITIVE ... Parents of Surrogate-Borne Infants and Toddlers in Verbal Exchange   (EA)

POSITREPS ... Position Reports
POSITRON ... Positive Electron
POSIX .... Portable Operating System Specification [*IEEE*]
POSK .... Polski Osrodek Spoleczno-Kulturalny [*Polish Social and Cultural Association - PSCA*] (EAIO)
POSKP ...... Polski Osrodek Spoleczno-Kulturalny Posk [*Polish Social and Cultural Association - PSCA*] (EAIO)
POsl .... Papyri Osloenses [*A publication*] (OCD)
POSL .... Parti Ouvrier Socialiste Luxembourgeois [*Luxembourg Socialist Workers' Party*] (EAIO)
POSL .... Posi-Seal International [*NASDAQ symbol*] (NQ)
PosLuth ..... Positions Lutheriennes [*Paris*] [*A publication*]
POSM .... National Association of Post Office and General Service Maintenance Employees [*Later, APWU*] [*AFL-CIO*]
POSM ...... Patient-Operated Selector Mechanism [*Pronounced "possum"*]
POSMA ...... Postal Service Manual [*A publication*]
POSN .... Position (AFM)
posn— .... Solomon Islands [*MARC geographic area code*] [*Library of Congress*] (LCCP)
POSNA ..... Pediatric Orthopaedic Society of North America (EA)
POS/NAV ... Position/Navigation [*System*] [*Military*] (INF)
P & OSNCo ... Peninsular & Oriental Steam Navigation Company [*Steamship line*]
POSPB ...... Problemy Osvoeniya Pustyn [*A publication*]
POSR .... Peacetime Operating Stock Requirement [*Military*] (AFIT)
POS R .... Positive Review [*A publication*] (ROG)
POSRIP ..... People Organized to Stop Rape of Imprisoned Persons (EA)
POSS .... Palomar Observatory Sky Survey [*NASA*]
POSS .... Passive Optical Satellite Surveillance [*System*] (NATG)
POSS .... Photo-Optical Surveillance Subsystem
POSS .... Portable Oceanographic Survey System (MCD)
POSS .... Possession [*or Possessive*] (AFM)
POSS .... Possible
POSS .... Possis Corp. [*NASDAQ symbol*] (NQ)
POSS .... Prototype Optical Surveillance System
POSS .... Proximal Over-Shoulder Strap [*Medicine*]
POSSE ...... Parents Opposed to Sex and Sensitivity Education [*An association*]
POSSE ...... Police Operations Systems Support System Elementary
POSSE ...... Progressive Onslaught to Stamp out Stock Errors [*Navy*] (NG)
POSSED ... Possessed (ROG)
Posselt's Text J ... Posselt's Textile Journal [*A publication*]
POSSLQ ... Persons of Opposite Sex Sharing Living Quarters [*Bureau of the Census*]
POSSNC ... Post Office Senior Staff Negotiating Council [*British*]
POSSON... Possession
POSSUB .. Possible Submarine [*Navy*] (NVT)
POSSUM .. Polar Orbiting Satellite System - University of Michigan [*Designed by engineering students*]
Post .... De Posteritate Caini [*of Philo*] (BJA)
POST .... Passive Optical Scan Tracker (MCD)
POST .... Passive Optical Seeker Technique
POST .... Payload Operations Support Team [*NASA*] (MCD)
POST .... Peace Officer Standards and Training
POST .... Peritoneal Ovum Sperm Transfer [*Medicine*]
POST .... Piezoelectric-Oscillator Self-Tuned [*Electric system*]
POST .... Point-of-Sale Terminal [*Business term*]
POST .... Point-of-Sale Transaction
POST .... Polaris Operation Support Task Group [*Missiles*]
POST .... Polymer Science and Technology [*American Chemical Society*] [*Information service or system*] [*A publication*]
POST .... Positive (AAG)
POST .... Postemergence [*Weed control*]
POST .... [*The*] Poster [*A publication*] (ROG)
post .... Posterior
Post .... Post's Reports [*42-64 Missouri*] [*A publication*] (DLA)
Post .... Post's Reports [*23-26 Michigan*] [*A publication*] (DLA)
POST .... Power-On Self Test [*IBM-PC feature*]
POST .... Production-Oriented Scheduling Techniques (MCD)
POST .... Program to Optimize Shuttle [*or Simulated*] Trajectories [*NASA*] (KSC)
POST .... Programmer Operating Standards Technique
POST-A ..... Population Studies [*A publication*]
Postal Bull ... Postal Bulletin. Weekly [*A publication*]
Postal Bull US Postal Serv ... Postal Bulletin. United States Postal Service [*A publication*]
Postal Spvr ... Postal Supervisor [*A publication*]
POST AUR ... Post Aurem [*Behind the Ear*] [*Pharmacy*]
PostB .... Postilla Bohemica [*A publication*]
Post Bioch ... Postepy Biochemii [*A publication*]
POSTD ...... Petty Officer Steward [*British military*] (DMA)
Postdiplom Sem Fiz ... Postdiplomski Seminar iz Fizike [*A publication*]
Postdiplom Sem Mat ... Postdiplomski Seminar iz Matematike [*A publication*]
Post Dir ...... Post's Paper Mill Directory [*A publication*]
POSTE .... Postage (ROG)
POSTEC ... Powder Science and Technology Research Association (EAIO)
Postepy Astron ... Postepy Astronomii [*A publication*]
Postepy Astronaut ... Postepy Astronautyki [*A publication*]
Postepy Biochem ... Postepy Biochemii [*A publication*]
Postepy Biol Komorki ... Postepy Biologii Komorki [*A publication*]

Postepy Cybernet ... Postepy Cybernetyki [*A publication*]
Postepy Fiz ... Postepy Fizyki [*A publication*]
Postepy Fizjol ... Postepy Fizjologii [*A publication*]
Postepy Fiz Med ... Postepy Fizyki Medycznej [*A publication*]
Postepy Ftyz Pneumon ... Postepy Ftyzjatrii i Pneumonologii [*A publication*]
Postepy Hig Med Dosw ... Postepy Higieny i Medycyny Doswiadczalnej [*A publication*]
Postepy Med ... Postepy Medycyny [*A publication*]
Postepy Mikrobiol ... Postepy Mikrobiologii [*A publication*]
Postepy Nauk Roln ... Postepy Nauk Rolniczych [*A publication*]
Postepy Tech Jad ... Postepy Techniki Jadroweki [*A publication*]
Postepy Techn Jadr ... Postepy Techniki Jadrowej [*A publication*]
Postepy Technol Masz Urzadz ... Postepy Technologii Maszyn i Urzadzen [*A publication*]
Postepy Wied Med ... Postepy Wiedzy Medycznej [*A publication*]
Postepy Wiedzy Med ... Postepy Wiedzy Medycznej [*A publication*]
Postepy Wiedzy Roln ... Postepy Wiedzy Rolniczej [*A publication*]
POSTER ... Post Strike Emergency Reporting
Poste's Gai ... Post's Translation of Gaius [*A publication*] (ILCA)
Poste's Gaius Inst ... Post's Translation of Gaius [*A publication*] (DLA)
Poste Telecommun ... Poste e Telecommunicazioni [*A publication*]
POSTFAT ... Postfinal Acceptance Trials [*Navy*] (NVT)
POSTFAX ... Post Office Facsimile [*British*]
Postg Med J ... Postgraduate Medical Journal [*A publication*]
Postgrad Courses Pediatr ... Postgraduate Courses in Pediatrics [*A publication*]
PostgradDipAgr ... Postgraduate Diploma in Agriculture
Postgrad Med ... Postgraduate Medicine [*A publication*]
Postgrad Med J ... Postgraduate Medical Journal [*A publication*]
Postgrad Med J Suppl ... Postgraduate Medical Journal. Supplement [*A publication*]
Postgrad Med Ser ... Postgraduate Medicine Series [*A publication*]
Postgrad MJ ... Postgraduate Medical Journal [*A publication*]
Postgrad Paediatr Ser ... Postgraduate Paediatrics Series [*A publication*]
Postgrad Radiol ... Postgraduate Radiology [*A publication*]
Postgr Med ... Postgraduate Medicine [*A publication*]
POSTH ...... Posthumous
Post Harvest Technol Cassava ... Post Harvest Technology of Cassava [*A publication*]
Post & Ins .. Postage and Insurance (ILCA)
POST-J ..... Polymer Science and Technology - Journals [*A publication*]
Postl Dict ... Postlethwaite's Dictionary of Trade and Commerce [*A publication*] (DLA)
Postmasters Adv ... Postmasters Advocate [*A publication*]
Post-Medieval Arch ... Post-Medieval Archaeology [*A publication*]
Post-Medieval Archaeol ... Post-Medieval Archaeology [*A publication*]
post-obit ..... Post Obitum [*After Death*] [*Latin*]
Post O E E J ... Post Office Electrical Engineers. Journal [*A publication*]
Post Off Electr Eng J ... Post Office Electrical Engineers. Journal [*A publication*]
Post Off (GB) Res Dep Rep ... Post Office (Great Britain). Research Department Report [*A publication*]
Post Office Hist Soc Trans ... Post Office Historical Society. Transactions [*Queensland*] [*A publication*] (APTA)
Post Off Telecommun J ... Post Office Telecommunications Journal [*A publication*]
POSTOP ... Postoperative [*Medicine*]
POST-P ..... Polymer Science and Technology - Patents [*A publication*]
POSTP ...... Posterior Probability [*Computations*]
POSTP ...... Postprocessor [*Data processing*]
POSTPRO ... Postprocessor [*Data processing*]
Post & Reg ... Postage and Registration (DLA)
Post S .... Post Script [*A publication*]
Post Scr ...... Post Script [*A publication*]
POST SING SED LIQ ... Post Singulas Sedes Liquidas [*After Every Loose Stool*] [*Pharmacy*] (ROG)
POSWa ...... Pozprawy Komisji Orientalistycznej Towarzystwa Naukowego Warszawskiego [*A publication*]
POSWG ..... Poseidon Software Working Group [*Missiles*]
POT .... British Telecom Journal [*A publication*]
POT .... Papper och Trae [*A publication*]
POT .... Parallel Output
POT .... Pennsylvania-Ontario Transportation Co. [*AAR code*]
POT .... Piston Operated Transducer
POT .... Pitch-Orthogonal Thrust
POT .... Plain Old Telephone [*Bell System's basic model*]
Po T .... Poetics Today [*A publication*]
POT .... Port Antonio [*Jamaica*] [*Airport symbol*] (OAG)
POT .... Portable Outside Toilet [*A unit of mobility equipment*] [*Military*]
POT .... Post Office Telecommunications [*British*]
POT .... Potable
POT .... Potash Corp. of Saskatchewan [*NYSE symbol*] (SPSG)
POT .... Potassium [*Chemical symbol is K*]
POT .... Potato (ROG)
POT .... Potentate
POT .... Potential (AFM)
POT .... Potentiometer [*or Potentiometric*]
Pot .... Potion
POT .... Potsdam [*German Democratic Republic*] [*Seismograph station code, US Geological Survey*] (SEIS)

POT .... Potsdam [German Democratic Republic] [Later, NGK] [Geomagnetic observatory code]
POT .... Pottle [Unit of measure] (ROG)
POT .... Pottsville Free Public Library, Pottsville, PA [OCLC symbol] (OCLC)
POT .... Potus [A Drink] [Pharmacy]
POT .... Prevailing-Out Torque [Automotive engineering]
POT .... Princess of Tasmania [Ferry between the Mainland Australia and Tasmania] (DSUE)
PotAGT ..... Potential Abnormality of Glucose Tolerance [Medicine]
POTANN.. Potomac Annex [Navy]
Potash 90 ... Potash 1990. Feast or Famine [A publication]
Potash J .... Potash Journal [A publication]
Potash Rev ... Potash Review [A publication]
Potash Trop Agric ... Potash and Tropical Agriculture [A publication]
Potassium Potasio Kalium Symp ... Potassium Potasio Kalium Symposium [A publication]
Potassium Symp ... Potassium. Symposium [A publication]
POTASWG ... Poseidon Test Analysis Software Working Group [Missiles]
Potato Grow ... Potato Grower [A publication]
Potato Handb ... Potato Handbook [A publication]
Potato M .... Potato Magazine [A publication]
Potato Res ... Potato Research [A publication]
Pot Aust ..... Pottery in Australia [A publication] (APTA)
POTC .... PERT [Program Evaluation and Review Technique] Orientation and Training Center
POTCP ...... Partially Oxidized Tetracyanoplatinate Compound [Inorganic, one-dimensional conductor]
POTD .... Player of the Decade [Sports]
Pot Dwar .... Potter's Edition of Dwarris on Statutes [A publication] (DLA)
POTel .... Petty Officer Telegraphist [Australia]
P O Telecommun J ... Post Office Telecommunications Journal [A publication]
Potfuzetek Termeszettud Kozl ... Potfuzetek a Termeszettudomanyi Kozlonyhoz [A publication]
Poth Bail a Rente ... Pothier's Traite du Contrat de Bail a Rente [A publication] (DLA)
Poth Cont... Poultry's Contracts [A publication] (DLA)
Poth Cont de Change ... Pothier's Traite de Change [A publication] (DLA)
Poth Contr Sale ... Pothier's Treatise on the Contract of Sale [A publication] (DLA)
Poth Cont Sale ... Pothier's Treatise on the Contract of Sale [A publication] (DLA)
Pothier Pand ... Pothier's Pandectae Justinianeae, Etc. [A publication] (DLA)
Poth Mar Cont ... Pothier's Treatise on Maritime Contracts [A publication] (DLA)
Poth Ob...... Pothier on the Law of Obligations [A publication] (DLA)
Poth Obl .... Pothier on the Law of Obligations [A publication] (DLA)
Poth Oblig ... Pothier on the Law of Obligations [A publication] (DLA)
Poth Oeuv .. Oeuvres de Pothier [A publication] (DLA)
Poth Pand .. Pothier's Pandects [A publication] (DLA)
Poth Part.... Pothier on Partnership [A publication] (DLA)
Poth Proc Civ ... Pothier. Procedure Civile [A publication] (DLA)
POT & I..... Preoverhaul Tests and Inspections [Navy] (NVT)
POTIB .... Polaris Technical Information Bulletin [Missiles]
potl--- .... Tokelau Islands [MARC geographic area code] [Library of Congress] (LCCP)
Pot LD .... Pott's Law Dictionary [3rd ed.] [1815] [A publication] (DLA)
POTMC..... Protective Outfit Toxicological Microclimate Controlled (RDA)
POTMLD ... Potential Mixed Layer Depth
POTN .... Problems of the North [A publication]
poto--- .... Tonga [MARC geographic area code] [Library of Congress] (LCCP)
POTOMAC ... Patent Office Techniques of Mechanized Access and Classification [Automation project, shut down in 1972]
Potomac Appalachian Trail Club Bull ... Potomac Appalachian Trail Club. Bulletin [A publication]
Potomac L Rev ... Potomac Law Review [A publication]
Potomac R ... Potomac Review [A publication]
Potosi Univ Autonoma Inst Geologia y Metalurgia Fol Tec ... Universidad Autonoma Potosina. Instituto de Geologia y Metalurgia. Folleto Tecnico [A publication]
Potravin Chladici Tech ... Potravinarska a Chladici Technika [A publication]
POTS........ Petty Officer Telegraphist Special (DSUE)
POTS........ Photo-Optical Terrain Simulator (MUGU)
POTS........ Plain Old Telephone Service [Humorous term for Long Lines Department of AT & T] [See also PANS]
POTS........ PORI [Polaris Operational Readiness Instrumentation] Operational Test System [Missiles]
POTS........ Precision Optical Tracking System (KSC)
POTS........ Preoverhaul Tests [Navy] (NVT)
POTS........ Purchase of Telephone Services Contracts
pott--- .... Trust Territory of the Pacific Islands [MARC geographic area code] [Library of Congress] (LCCP)
Pott Corp.... Potter on Corporations [A publication] (DLA)
Pott Dwarris ... Potter's Edition of Dwarris on Statutes [A publication] (DLA)
Potter .... Potter's Reports [4-7 Wyoming] [A publication] (DLA)
Potter Am Mo ... Potter's American Monthly [A publication]
Pottery .... Pottery in Australia [A publication] (APTA)

Pottery Aust ... Pottery in Australia [A publication]
Pottery in Aust ... Pottery in Australia [A publication] (APTA)
Pottery Gaz Glass Trade Rev ... Pottery Gazette and Glass Trade Review [A publication]
Pottery Glass Rec ... Pottery and Glass Record [A publication]
Pottery Glass Trades J ... Pottery and Glass Trades Journal [A publication]
Potts LD..... Potts' Law Dictionary [3rd ed.] [1815] [A publication] (DLA)
POTUS...... President of the United States
Potvrda Valjanosti Broj Inst Meh Poljopr ... Potvrda o Valjanosti Broj-Institut za Mehanizaciju Poljoprivrede [A publication]
POTW .... Potable Water (KSC)
POTWA .... Polimery Tworzywa [A publication]
POU.......... Paramount Resources Ltd. [Toronto Stock Exchange symbol]
POU.......... Placenta, Ovary, Uterus [Medicine]
POU.......... Poughkeepsie [New York] [Airport symbol] (OAG)
POU.......... Poughkeepsie, NY [Location identifier] [FAA] (FAAL)
POU.......... Pouilloux [France] [Seismograph station code, US Geological Survey] (SEIS)
POUCC ..... Post Office Users Coordination Committee [British]
POUDAY.. Poultry Digest [A publication]
POUF .... Projects of Optimum Urgency and Feasibility
Poughkeepsie Soc N Sc Pr ... Poughkeepsie Society of Natural Science. Proceedings [A publication]
POUL .... Poultry
Poult........... Poultry Forum [A publication]
Poult Advis ... Poultry Adviser [A publication]
Poult Bull... Poultry Bulletin [A publication]
Poult Dig... Poultry Digest [A publication]
Poult Egg Situat PES US Dep Agric Econ Res Serv ... Poultry and Egg Situation. PES. United States Department of Agriculture. Economic Research Service [A publication]
Poult Health Symp ... Poultry Health Symposium [A publication]
Poult Ind .... Poultry Industry [A publication]
Poultry Dig ... Poultry Digest [A publication]
Poultry Livestock Comment ... Poultry and Livestock Comment [A publication]
Poultry Process ... Poultry Processing and Marketing [A publication]
Poultry Sci ... Poultry Science [A publication]
Poult Sci... Poultry Science [A publication]
Poult Trib... Poultry Tribune [A publication]
Poult World ... Poultry World [A publication]
POUNC..... Post Office Users' National Council [British] (ILCA)
POUP .... Post Overhaul Upkeep Period
poup---........ United States Miscellaneous Pacific Islands [MARC geographic area code] [Library of Congress] (LCCP)
Pour Sci (Paris) ... Pour la Science (Paris) (Edition Francaise de Scientific American) [A publication]
POUS .... Partido Operario de Unidade Socialista [Workers' Party for Socialist Unity] [Portugal] [Political party] (PPW)
POV .... Peak Operated Valve (MCD)
POV .... Peak Operating Voltage
POV .... Personally Owned Vehicle
POV .... Pinch-Off Voltage
POV .... Pittsburgh & Ohio Valley Railway Co. [AAR code]
POV .... Plane of Vibration
POV .... Pneumatically Operated Valve
POV .... Point of View
POV .... Pressure-Operated Valve (MCD)
POV .... Privately Owned Vehicle (NVT)
POV .... Purchase, Outside Vendors
POV .... Putting-On Voltage [Doppler navigation] (DEN)
Poverkhn Yavleniya Polim ... Poverkhnostnye Yavleniya v Polimerakh [A publication]
Poverkhn Yavleniya Zhidk Zhidk Rastvorakh ... Poverkhnostnye Yavleniya v Zhidkostyakh i Zhidkikh Rastvorakh [A publication]
POVEU ..... Program Operations Vocational Education Unit (OICC)
Pov & Human Resour Abstr ... Poverty and Human Resources Abstracts [A publication]
Pov L Rep .. Poverty Law Reporter [Commerce Clearing House] [A publication] (DLA)
Povolzh Lesotekh Inst Sb Tr ... Povolzhskii Lesotekhnicheskii Institut Sbornik Trudov [A publication]
POVORTAD ... Positive Vorticity Advection [Meteorology] (FAAC)
POVT .... Puerperal Ovarian-Vein Thrombophlebitis [Medicine]
Povysh Plodorodiya Pochv Nechernozemn Polosy ... Povyshenie Plodorodiya Pochv Nechernozemnoi Polosy [A publication]
POW......... Pay Order of Withdrawal
POW......... Paying Their Own Way
POW......... Peoples of the World [A publication]
POW......... Perception of Ward [Scales] [Psychology]
POW......... Petty Officer of the Watch [Navy]
POW......... Powassan Encephalitis [Medicine]
POW......... Power
POW......... Power Corp. of Canada [Toronto Stock Exchange symbol] [Vancouver Stock Exchange symbol]
POW......... Powhatan [Arkansas] [Seismograph station code, US Geological Survey] (SEIS)
POW......... Prince of Wales
POW......... Prisoner of War [Also, PW]
POW......... Progressive Order of the West [Defunct] (EA)
POW......... PSE, Inc. [AMEX symbol] (SPSG)

POWACO ... Portable Water Coolant Circulator
Pow App Proc ... Powell's Law of Appellate Proceedings [*A publication*] (DLA)
PoWBN ..... Biblioteka Narodowa [*National Library*], Warsaw, Poland [*Library symbol*] [*Library of Congress*] (LCLS)
PoWC .... Instytut Informacji Naukowej, Technicznej, i Ekonomicznej, Warsaw, Poland [*Library symbol*] [*Library of Congress*] (LCLS)
Pow Car ..... Powell's Inland Carriers [*2nd ed.*] [*1861*] [*A publication*] (DLA)
Pow Cont .... Powell on Contracts [*A publication*] (DLA)
Pow Conv ... Powell. Conveyancing [*1810*] [*A publication*] (ILCA)
POWD .... Powder [*England*]
POWD .... Powdered
Powder Coat ... Powder Coatings [*A publication*]
Powder Eng ... Powder Engineering [*USSR*] [*A publication*]
Powder Ind Res ... Powder Industry Research [*A publication*]
Powder Met ... Powder Metallurgy [*A publication*]
Powder Metall ... Powder Metallurgy [*A publication*]
Powder Metall Def Technol ... Powder Metallurgy in Defense Technology [*A publication*]
Powder Metall Int ... Powder Metallurgy International [*A publication*]
Powder Technol ... Powder Technology [*A publication*]
Powder Technol (Lausanne) ... Powder Technology (Lausanne) [*A publication*]
Powder Technol (Tokyo) ... Powder Technology (Tokyo) [*A publication*]
Pow Dev ..... Powell's Essay upon the Learning of Devises, Etc. [*A publication*] (DLA)
Powd Metall ... Powder Metallurgy [*A publication*]
POWDR .... Protect Our Wetlands and Duck Resources [*Department of the Interior*] [*Washington, DC*]
Powd Tech ... Powder Technology [*A publication*]
POWER ..... People Organized and Working for Economic Rebirth [*Program for black economic development*] [*Later, Nationway Ventures International Ltd.*]
POWER ..... Professionals Organized for Women's Equal Rights [*Feminist group*]
POWER ..... Programmed Operational Warshot Evaluation and Review
POWER ..... Promote Our Wonderful Energy Resources (EA)
PowerConvers Int ... PowerConversion International [*A publication*]
Power Eng ... Power Engineering [*A publication*]
Power Eng (India) ... Power Engineer (India) [*A publication*]
Power Eng J Acad Sci (USSR) ... Power Engineering Journal. Academy of Sciences [*USSR*] [*A publication*]
Power Eng (NY Eng Transl) ... Power Engineering (New York, English Translation) [*A publication*]
Power Eqp ... Survey of Power Equipment Requirements of the United States Electric Utility Industry [*A publication*]
Power F ...... Power Farming [*A publication*]
Power Farming Aust ... Power Farming in Australia [*A publication*] (APTA)
Power Farming Better Farming Dig Aust NZ ... Power Farming and Better Farming Digest in Australia and New Zealand [*Later, Power Farming*]
Power Farming Mag ... Power Farming Magazine [*A publication*] (APTA)
Power Fuel Bull ... Power and Fuel Bulletin [*A publication*]
Power Gener ... Power Generation [*A publication*]
Power Ind... Power Industry, Including Industrial Power and Industry Power [*A publication*]
Power Ind Res ... Power Industry Research [*England*] [*A publication*]
Power Plant Eng S Afr ... Power and Plant Engineering in South Africa [*A publication*]
Power Plant S Afr ... Power and Plant in Southern Africa [*A publication*]
Power Plant South Afr ... Power and Plant in Southern Africa [*A publication*]
Power Plant Sthn Afr ... Power and Plant in Southern Africa [*A publication*]
Power Pl Eng ... Power Plant Engineering [*A publication*]
Power Reactor Technol ... Power Reactor Technology [*Japan*] [*A publication*]
Power Reactor Technol Reactor Fuel Process ... Power Reactor Technology and Reactor Fuel Processing [*United States*] [*A publication*]
Power Reactor Technol (Tokyo) ... Power Reactor Technology (Tokyo) [*A publication*]
Power React Technol ... Power Reactor Technology [*A publication*]
Powers .... Powers' Reports, New York Surrogate Court [*A publication*] (DLA)
Power Sources Symp Proc ... Power Sources Symposium. Proceedings [*United States*] [*A publication*]
Power's Sur ... Powers' Reports, New York Surrogate Court [*A publication*] (DLA)
Power Trans Des ... Power Transmission Design [*A publication*]
Power Transm Des ... Power Transmission Design [*A publication*]
Power Works Eng ... Power and Works Engineering [*A publication*]
Power & Works Engng ... Power and Works Engineering [*A publication*]
Pow Ev .... Powell on Evidence [*10th ed.*] [*1921*] [*A publication*] (DLA)
powf---........ Wallis and Futuna [*MARC geographic area code*] [*Library of Congress*] (LCCP)
Pow Inl Car ... Powell on the Law of Inland Carriers [*A publication*] (DLA)
powk---....... Wake Island [*MARC geographic area code*] [*Library of Congress*] (LCCP)
POWL .... Powell Industries, Inc. [*NASDAQ symbol*] (NQ)
Powloki Ochr ... Powloki Ochronne [*A publication*]
Pow Mort... Powell on Mortgages [*6th ed.*] [*1826*] [*A publication*] (DLA)

Pow Mortg ... Powell on Mortgages [*A publication*] (DLA)
POWO....... Prince [*or Princess*] of Wales' Own [*Military unit*] [*British*] (DMA)
PoWP......... Biblioteka Glowna Politechniki Warszawsjiej (Warsaw Technical University Central Library), Warsaw, Poland [*Library symbol*] [*Library of Congress*] (LCLS)
POWR .... Environmental Power Corp. [*NASDAQ symbol*] (NQ)
Pow R & D ... Power, Rodwell, and Drew's English Election Cases [*1847-56*] [*A publication*] (DLA)
POWRENAF ... Petty Officer WREN [*Women's Royal Naval Service*] Air Fitter [*British military*] (DMA)
POWRENCINE ... Petty Officer WREN [*Women's Royal Naval Service*] Cinema Operator [*British military*] (DMA)
POWRENCK ... Petty Officer WREN [*Women's Royal Naval Service*] Cook [*British military*] (DMA)
POWRENDHYG ... Petty Officer WREN [*Women's Royal Naval Service*] Dental Hygienist [*British military*] (DMA)
POWRENDSA ... Petty Officer WREN [*Women's Royal Naval Service*] Dental Surgery Assistant [*British military*] (DMA)
POWRENMET ... Petty Officer WREN [*Women's Royal Naval Service*] Meteorological Observer [*British military*] (DMA)
POWRENMT ... Petty Officer WREN [*Women's Royal Naval Service*] Motor Transport Driver [*British military*] (DMA)
POWRENPHOT ... Petty Officer WREN [*Women's Royal Naval Service*] Photographer [*British military*] (DMA)
POWRENQA ... Petty Officer WREN [*Women's Royal Naval Service*] Quarters Assistant [*British military*] (DMA)
POWREN(R) ... Petty Officer WREN [*Women's Royal Naval Service*] (RADAR) [*British military*] (DMA)
POWRENREL ... Petty Officer WREN [*Women's Royal Naval Service*] Radio Electrician [*British military*] (DMA)
POWRENRS(M) ... Petty Officer WREN [*Women's Royal Naval Service*] Radio Supervisor (Morse) [*British military*] (DMA)
POWRENSA ... Petty Officer WREN [*Women's Royal Naval Service*] Stores Accountant [*British military*] (DMA)
POWRENS(C) ... Petty Officer WREN [*Women's Royal Naval Service*] Stores Assistant (Clothes) [*British military*] (DMA)
POWRENS(S) ... Petty Officer WREN [*Women's Royal Naval Service*] Stores Assistant (Stores) [*British military*] (DMA)
POWRENSTD ... Petty Officer WREN [*Women's Royal Naval Service*] Steward [*British military*] (DMA)
POWRENS(V) ... Petty Officer WREN [*Women's Royal Naval Service*] Stores Assistant (Victualling) [*British military*] (DMA)
POWRENTEL ... Petty Officer WREN [*Women's Royal Naval Service*] Telephonist [*British military*] (DMA)
POWRENTSA ... Petty Officer WREN [*Women's Royal Naval Service*] Training Support Assistant [*British military*] (DMA)
POWRENWA ... Petty Officer WREN [*Women's Royal Naval Service*] Weapon Analyst [*British military*] (DMA)
POWRENWTR(G) ... Petty Officer WREN [*Women's Royal Naval Service*] Writer (General) [*British military*] (DMA)
POWRENWTR(P) ... Petty Officer WREN [*Women's Royal Naval Service*] Writer (Pay) [*British military*] (DMA)
POWRENWW ... Petty Officer WREN [*Women's Royal Naval Service*] Welfare Worker [*British military*] (DMA)
POWS....... Project Operating Work Statement [*NASA*] (NASA)
POWS....... Pyrotechnic Outside Warning System (IEEE)
pows--....... Western Samoa [*MARC geographic area code*] [*Library of Congress*] (LCCP)
POW-SIG ... Pagan/Occult/Witchcraft Special Interest Group (EA)
Pow Surr .... Powers' Reports, New York Surrogate Court [*A publication*] (DLA)
POWTECH ... International Powder and Bulk Solids Technology Exhibition and Conference (TSPED)
POWTR..... Petty Officer Writer [*British military*] (DMA)
POWU....... Post Office Work Unit [*Computer performance measure*] [*British Telecom*]
PoWU .... Uniwersytet Warszawski [*University of Warsaw*], Warsaw, Poland [*Library symbol*] [*Library of Congress*] (LCLS)
POWWER ... Power of World Wide Energy Resources [*In organization name "Natural POWWER"*] (EA)
Powys N ..... Powys Newsletter [*A publication*]
Powys Rev ... Powys Review [*A publication*]
POX........... Partial Oxidation [*Organic chemistry*]
POX.......... Point of Exit
P-OX.......... Pressure Oxidation
poxd---........ Mariana Islands [*MARC geographic area code*] [*Library of Congress*] (LCCP)
poxe---........ Marshall Islands [*MARC geographic area code*] [*Library of Congress*] (LCCP)
poxf--- .... Midway Islands [*MARC geographic area code*] [*Library of Congress*] (LCCP)
poxh--- .... Niue [*MARC geographic area code*] [*Library of Congress*] (LCCP)
POxy.......... Oxyrhynchus Papyri [*A publication*]
POY........... Partially Oriented Yarns
POY .... Powell, WY [*Location identifier*] [*FAA*] (FAAL)
POY .... Prairie Oil Royalties Co. Ltd. [*AMEX symbol*] [*Toronto Stock Exchange symbol*] (SPSG)
Poynt M & D ... Poynter on Marriage and Divorce [*2nd ed.*] [*1824*] [*A publication*] (DLA)

POZ .... Poznan [*Poland*] [*Airport symbol*] (OAG)
POZBDM ... Folia Venatoria [*A publication*]
Pozharnaya Okhr ... Pozharnaya Okhrana [*A publication*]
Poznan Rocz Med ... Poznanskie Roczniki Medyczne [*Poland*] [*A publication*]
Poznan Stud ... Poznan Studies [*A publication*]
Poznan Tow Przyj Nauk Pr Kom Biol ... Poznanskie Towarzystwo Przyjaciol
       Nauk. Prace Komisji Biologicznej [*A publication*]
Poznan Tow Przyj Nauk Pr Kom Farm ... Poznanskie Towarzystwo Przyjaciol
       Nauk. Prace Komisji Farmaceutycznej [*A publication*]
Poznan Tow Przyj Nauk Pr Kom Lek ... Poznanskie Towarzystwo Przyjaciol
       Nauk. Prace Komisji Lekarskiej [*A publication*]
Poznan Tow Przyj Nauk Pr Kom Mat Przyr ... Poznanskie Towarzystwo
       Przyjaciol Nauk. Prace Komisji Matematyczno-
       Przyrodniczej [*A publication*]
Poznan Tow Przyj Nauk Pr Kom Mat Przyr Pr Chem ... Poznanskie
       Towarzystwo Przyjaciol Nauk. Prace Komisji
       Matematyczno-Przyrodniczej. Prace Chemiczne [*A
       publication*]
Poznan Tow Przyj Nauk Pr Kom Mat Przyr Ser B ... Poznanskie Towarzystwo
       Przyjaciol Nauk. Prace Komisji Matematyczno-
       Przyrodniczej. Seria B [*A publication*]
Poznan Tow Przyj Nauk Pr Kom Med Dosw ... Poznanskie Towarzystwo
       Przyjaciol Nauk. Prace Komisji Medycyny Doswiadezalnej
       [*A publication*]
Poznan Tow Przyj Nauk Pr Kom Nauk Podstawowych Stosow ... Poznanskie
       Towarzystwo Przyjaciol Nauk. Prace Komisji Nauk
       Podstawowych Stosowanych [*A publication*]
Poznan Tow Przyj Nauk Pr Kom Nauk Roln Kom Nauk Lesn ... Poznanskie
       Towarzystwo Przyjaciol Nauk. Prace Komisji Nauk
       Rolniczych i Komisji Nauk Lesnych [*A publication*]
Poznan Tow Przyj Nauk Wydz Lek Pr Kom Farm ... Poznanskie Towarzystwo
       Przyjaciol Nauk. Wydzial Lekarski. Prace Komisji
       Farmaceutycznej [*A publication*]
Poznan Tow Przyj Nauk Wydz Lek Pr Kom Med Doswi ... Poznanskie
       Towarzystwo Przyjaciol Nauk. Wydzial Lekarski. Prace
       Komisji Medycyny Doswiadczalnej [*Poland*] [*A
       publication*]
Poznan Tow Przyj Nauk Wydz Mat-Przyr Kom Biol Pr ... Poznanskie
       Towarzystwo Przyjaciol Nauk. Wydzial Matematyczno-
       Przyrodniczy. Komisja Biologiczna Prace [*Poland*] [*A
       publication*]
Poznan Tow Przyj Nauk Wydz Mat Przyr Pr Kom Mat Przyr ... Poznanskie
       Towarzystwo Przyjaciol Nauk, Wydzial Matematyczno-
       Przyrodniczy Prace Komisji Matematyczno-Przyrodniczej
       [*A publication*]
Pozn St Teol ... Poznanskie Studie Teologiczne [*A publication*]
PP .... Brazil [*Aircraft nationality and registration mark*] (FAAC)
PP .... Descent through Cloud [*Procedure*] [*Aviation code*] (FAAC)
PP .... Die Palmyrenischen Personennamen [*A publication*]
PP .... Eisai Co. Ltd. [*Japan*] [*Research code symbol*]
PP .... Free Library of Philadelphia, Philadelphia, PA [*Library symbol*]
       [*Library of Congress*] (LCLS)
P & P .... Packing and Preservation
PP .... Page Printer (NVT)
PP .... Pages
PP .... Pages from the Past [*Later, PIR*] [*An association*] (EA)
PP .... Palestine Post [*A publication*]
POZBDM ... Palisades Plant [*Nuclear energy*] (NRCH)
PP .... Palus Putretudinis [*Lunar area*]
P & P .... Pam and Peter Fisher [*Commercial firm*] [*British*]
PP .... Pan Pipes [*A publication*]
PP .... Pancreatic Polypeptide [*Biochemistry*]
PP .... Pandectes Periodiques [*A publication*] (ILCA)
PP .... Panel Point [*Technical drawings*]
PP .... Pangu Pati [*Papua New Guinea*] [*Political party*] (PPW)
PP .... Panstwo i Prawo [*A publication*]
PP .... Papa [*Pope*]
PP .... Paper Profit
P j P .... Paperi ja Puu [*A publication*]
pp .... Papua New Guinea [*MARC country of publication code*]
       [*Library of Congress*] (LCCP)
PP .... Papyrusfunde und Papyrusforschung [*A publication*]
PP .... Paradigm Publishing Ltd. [*British*]
PP .... Parallel Processor
PP .... Parcel Post
PP .... Paris Publications, Inc.
PP .... Parish Priest
PP .... Parliamentary Paper [*A publication*] (APTA)
PP .... Parliamentary Papers [*British*]
PP .... Parola del Passato [*A publication*]
PP .... Part Paid [*Business and trade*]
PP .... Parti du Peuple [*People's Party*] [*Burundi*] [*Political party*]
PP .... Partia Popullore [*Popular Party*] [*Albania*] [*Political
       party*] (PPE)
P/P .... Partial Pay [*Air Force*]
PP .... Partial Pressure
PP .... Partial Program
PP .... Particular [*Named*] Port [*British*] (ROG)
PP .... Partido Panamenista [*Panamanian Party*] [*Political
       party*] (PPW)
PP .... Partido Popular [*Popular Party*] [*Spain*] [*Political party*] (PPE)

PP .... Partido Populista [*Populist Party*] [*Argentina*] [*Political party*]
PP .... Partners in Politics (EA)
PP .... Parts Per
PP .... [*The*] Passionate Pilgrim [*Shakespearean work*]
PP .... Passive Participle
PP .... Past Participle
PP .... Past Patriarch [*Freemasonry*] (ROG)
P & P .... Past and Present [*A publication*]
PP .... Past President
PP .... Pastor Pastorum [*Shepherd of the Shepherds*] [*Latin*] (ROG)
P/P .... Patch Panel (NASA)
PP .... Pater Patriae [*The Father of His Country*] [*Latin*]
PP .... Patres [*Fathers*] [*Latin*]
PP .... Patriarchs and Prophets
PP .... Patriotic Party [*British*]
PP .... Patrol Vessels [*Navy symbol*] (MUGU)
PP .... Pay Period (FAAC)
P and P ...... Payments and Progress Committee [*NATO*] (NATG)
PP .... Peace PAC (EA)
P & P .... Peace and Prosperity Issue [*Politics*]
PP .... Peak-to-Peak
PP .... Peak Pressure
PP .... Peanut Pals (EA)
PP .... Pedal Pulse
PP .... Pellagra Preventive [*Factor*] [*See also PPF*] [*Biochemistry*]
PP .... Pension Plan
PP .... People's Party [*Halkci Partisi*] [*Turkey*] [*Political
       party*] (PPW)
PP .... Pep Pill [*Slang*]
PP .... Per Procurationem [*By Proxy, By the Action Of*] [*Legal term*]
       [*Latin*]
P and P ...... Perception and Psychophysics [*A publication*]
PP .... Periodical Publications [*British Library shelf designation*]
PP .... Peripheral Processor [*Data processing*]
PP .... Periportal [*Anatomy*]
PP .... Periproct [*Invertebrate anatomy*]
PP .... Permanent Party [*Military*]
PP .... Permanent Pasture [*Agriculture*]
PP .... Permanent Press (ADA)
PP .... Permanent Professor
PP .... [*Length between*] Perpendiculars [*Shipbuilding*]
P-P .... Person to Person [*Word processing*]
PP .... Personal Property
PP .... Pet Pride (EA)
PP .... Petroleum Point
PP .... Petrus Piccoli de Monteforte [*Flourished, 14th century*]
       [*Authority cited in pre-1607 legal work*] (DSA)
PP .... Petticoat Peeping [*From one girl to another, in reference to dress
       disarrangement*]
PP .... Peyer's Patch [*Immunology*]
PP .... Philo-Phobe [*Psychological testing*]
PP .... Philologica Pragensia [*A publication*]
PP .... Philosophia Patrum [*A publication*]
PP .... Phoenix Project [*An association*] (EA)
PP .... Phony Peach Bacteria [*Plant pathology*]
PP .... Photosynthetic Panel [*i.e., leaf*] [*Slang*]
PP .... Physical Profile
PP .... Physical Properties
PP .... Phytophthora Parasitica [*A fungus*]
PP .... Pianissimo [*Very Softly*] [*Music*]
PP .... Picked Ports
PP .... Pickpocket
PP .... Picture Peace [*Defunct*] (EA)
P/P .... Pier to Pier (ADA)
PP .... Piers Plowman [*Middle English poem*]
PP .... Piissimus [*Most Holy*] [*Latin*]
PP .... Pilot Parents (EA)
PP .... Pilot Punch
PP .... Pilotless Plane
PP .... Pine Bark Mixed with Peat
PP .... Pinepointer [*A publication*]
PP .... Piping
PP .... Piscataqua Pioneers (EA)
PP .... Piu Piano [*More Softly*] [*Music*]
PP .... PIXEL-Processing [*Data processing*]
PP .... Placental Protein [*Gynecology*]
PP .... Plan Profile
PP .... Plane Parallel
PP .... Plane Polarized [*Telecommunications*] (TEL)
PP .... Planetary Programs [*NASA*]
PP .... Planned Parenthood
PP .... Planning Package [*NASA*] (NASA)
PP .... Planning Purpose
P & P .... Plans and Policies
P & P .... Plans and Programs
PP .... Plant Protection
PP .... Plasma Protein
PP .... Plasmapheresis [*Hematology*]
PP .... Plaster of Paris
P to P .... Plate to Plate (DEN)
PP .... Play or Pay (ROG)

PP .... Please Pay (ROG)
PP .... Pleural Pressure [Medicine]
PP .... Plot Points [Data processing]
PP .... Pluvius Policy [Insurance against rain]
P a P .... Poco a Poco [Little by Little] [Music]
PP .... Poetry Project (EA)
P/P .... Point-to-Point [Air Force]
PP .... Polar Pacific [American air mass]
PP .... Pole Piece (DEN)
PP .... Polizei Pistole [Police Pistol] [Walther Waffenfabrik, German arms manufacturer]
PP .... Polypeptide [Biochemistry]
PP .... Polypropylene [Organic chemistry]
PP .... Polypyrrole [Photovoltaic energy systems]
PP .... Pom-Pom [Gun]
PP .... Pontificum [Of the Popes] [Latin]
PP .... Population (Paris) [A publication]
PP .... Populist Party of America [Political party] (EA)
PP .... Por Poder [Power of Attorney] [Legal term] [Spanish]
pp .... Por Procuracao [By Proxy, By the Action Of] [Legal term] [Portuguese]
pp .... Port Paye [Postage Paid] [French] [Shipping]
PP .... Port Pipe (ADA)
P to P .... Port to Port [Shipping] (DS)
PP .... Porte Pagado [Carriage Paid] [Spanish]
PP .... Posa Piano [Handle with Care] [Italian] [Shipping]
PP .... Position Paper (MCD)
PP .... Post Pagado [Postage Paid] [Spanish] [Shipping]
PP .... Post Partum [After Birth] [Latin] (ADA)
PP .... Post Position [Racing]
P & P .... Postage and Packing [Shipping]
PP .... Postage Paid [Shipping]
PP .... Postavy a Problemy [A publication]
pp .... Posted Price (MENA)
PP .... Posterior Parietal Cortex [Neuroanatomy]
PP .... Posterior Pituitary [Medicine]
pp .... Postpaid
PP .... Postpass
PP .... Postponed
PP .... Postprandial [After Meals] [Pharmacy]
PP .... Pounds Pressure
PP .... Pour Presenter [To Present] [French]
PP .... Power Package
PP .... Power People
PP .... Power Plant
PP .... Power Play [Hockey]
PP .... Power Pole (NASA)
PP .... Power Supplies [JETDS nomenclature] [Military] (CET)
PP .... Prace Polonistyczne [Warsaw] [A publication]
PP .... Praemissis Praemittendis [Omitting Preliminaries] [Latin]
PP .... Praepter Propter [Approximately] [Pharmacy]
PP .... Prasa Polska [A publication]
Pp .... Pratylenchus penetrans [A nematode]
PP .... Prepaid
PP .... Preparative Flag [Navy] [British]
PP .... Preparing, Providing [Pharmacy] (ROG)
PP .... Preposition [Industrial engineering]
PP .... Prepositional Phrase (BYTE)
PP .... Prepregnancy [Medicine]
PP .... Preprinted
PP .... Preprocessor
PP .... Preproduction (KSC)
P/P .... Prescribed Period [Social Security Administration] (OICC)
PP .... Present Participle [Grammar]
PP .... Present Position [Military]
PP .... Press Packed
PP .... Pressure Pattern (MCD)
PP .... Pressure-Proof [Technical drawings]
PP .... Pretty Poor [Slang] [Bowdlerized version]
P & P .... Pride and Prejudice [Novel by Jane Austen]
PP .... Primary Pressure [Nuclear energy] (NRCH)
PP .... Primary Producers (ADA)
PP .... Princess Pat's [Princess Patricia of Connaught's Light Infantry] [Military unit] [Canada]
PP .... Principal
PP .... Principal Point
PP .... Print Positions
PP .... Print-Punch [Data processing] (BUR)
PP .... Printer Page [Data processing]
P/P .... Printer/Plotter (NASA)
PP .... Prior Permission
PP .... Private Jet Services AG [Sweden] [ICAO designator] (ICDA)
PP .... Private Passenger
P/P .... Private Patient [Medicine]
PP .... Private Practice [Chiropody] [British]
PP .... Private Property [Military]
PP .... Privately Printed
PP .... Procurement Plan (MCD)
P & P .... Procurement and Production [Military]
PP .... Producer Price
PP .... Production Processes

P & P .... Production and Procurement [Military]
PP .... Professional Paper
PP .... Professor Publicus [Public Professor] [Latin] (ROG)
PP .... Program Package (MCD)
PP .... Program Paper
PP .... Program Performance (NASA)
PP .... Program Product [Data processing]
PP .... Programming Plan (AFM)
PP .... Progress Payments [Military procurement]
PP .... Project Priesthood (EA)
PP .... Project Proposal (KSC)
PP .... Proletarian Party
PP .... Proodeftiki Parataxis [Progressive Front] [Greek Cyprus] [Political party] (PPE)
PP .... Propeller Pitch
PP .... Proportional Part
PP .... Propulsion Power (KSC)
PP .... Prothrombin-Proconvertin [Hematology]
PP .... Proton-Proton [Nuclear physics]
PP .... Protoporphyria [Medicine]
PP .... Protoporphyrin [Biochemistry]
PP .... Provisional Parish [Church of England in Australia]
PP .... Provisioning Procedures [Corps of Engineers]
PP .... Proximal Phalanx [Anatomy]
PP .... Przeglad Powszechny [A publication]
PP .... Psychic Phenomena
PP .... Psychological Profile
PP .... Psychologists and Psychiatrists [in service] [British]
P/P .... Pterocephaliid-Ptychaspid [Paleogeologic boundary]
PP .... Public Property
PP .... Publie Par [Published By] [French]
P or P .... Publish or Perish [Said of scholars, scientists, etc.]
PP .... Published Price [of a book]
PP .... Pulse Polarography [Analytical chemistry]
PP .... Pulse Pressure [Medicine]
PP .... Pulvis Patrum [The Fathers' Powder (or Jesuits' Powder)] [Pharmacy] (ROG)
PP .... Punctum Proximum [Near Point] [Latin]
PP .... Purchase Power [Commercial firm] (EA)
PP .... Purchase Price
PP .... Purchased Parts
PP .... Push-Pull [Technical drawings]
PP .... Pusher Plane
PP .... Pyrophosphate [Chemistry]
PPA............ Athenaeum of Philadelphia, Philadelphia, PA [Library symbol] [Library of Congress] (LCLS)
PPA............ National Plant Protection Association
PPA............ Paleopathology Association (EA)
PPA............ Palpation, Percussion, and Auscultation [Medicine]
PP & A .... Palpation, Percussion, and Auscultation [Medicine]
PPA............ Pampa, TX [Location identifier] [FAA] (FAAL)
PPA............ Panamerican/Panafrican Association (EA)
PPA............ Paper Pail Association [Defunct] (EA)
PPA............ Paper Plate Association [Later, SSI] (EA)
PPA............ Parcel Post Association [Later, PSA] (EA)
PPA............ Parents for Private Adoption (EA)
PPa............ Parola del Passato [A publication]
PPA............ Partido Patriotico Arubano [Aruban Patriotic Party] [Netherlands Antilles] [Political party] (PPW)
PPA............ Partido Peronista Autentico [Authentic Peronist Party] [Argentina] [Political party] (EY)
PPA............ Pathology Practice Association (EA)
PPA............ Pensioner Party of Australia [Political party] (ADA)
PPA............ Peppa Resources [Vancouver Stock Exchange symbol]
PPA............ Per Power of Attorney [Business term]
PPA............ Perennial Plant Association (EA)
PPA............ Periodical Publishers Association [Later, MCA] (EA)
PPA............ Permian Partnership LP [NYSE symbol] (SPSG)
PPA............ Pesticide Producers Association (EA)
PPA............ Pet Producers of America (EA)
PPA............ Phenylpropanolamine [Organic chemistry]
PPA............ Phenylpropanolamine(hydrochloride) [Also, PPH, PPM] [Decongestant]
PPA............ Phenylpyruvic Acid [Organic chemistry]
PPA............ Phiala Prius Agitata [Having First Shaken the Bottle] [Pharmacy]
PPA............ Philippine Ports Authority (DS)
PPA............ Philippine Posts Authority (DS)
PPA............ Photo Peak Analysis (IEEE)
PPA............ Pictorial Photographers of America (EAIO)
PPA............ Pie De Palo [Argentina] [Seismograph station code, US Geological Survey] (SEIS)
PPA............ Pilots and Passengers Association [Defunct] (EA)
PPA............ Pitch Precession Amplifier
PPA............ Pittsburgh Pneumonia Agent [Microbiology]
PPA............ Plant Patent Act [1930]
PPA............ Plasminogen Proactivator [Hematology]
PPA............ Policyholders Protective Association of America (EA)
PPA............ Polymer Permeation Analyzer
PPA............ Poly(phosphoric Acid) [Inorganic chemistry]
PPA............ Popcorn Processors Association [Later, PI]

PPA........... Popski's Private Army [*Commando force led by Vladimir Peniakoff*] [*World War II*]
PPA........... Postpartum Amenorrhea [*Medicine*]
PPA........... Poultry Publishers Association (EA)
PPA........... Power Plant Automation
PPA........... Powerplant Performance Analysis
PPA........... Preschool Playgrounds Association [*British*]
PPA........... Presidents' Professional Association [*Later, Presidents Association*] (EA)
PPA........... Press and Publications Administration [*China*]
PPA........... Princeton-Pennsylvania Accelerator [*Closed, 1972*] [*AEC*]
PPA........... Principal Port Authority [*British*] (ROG)
PPAW........ Printing Platemakers Association [*Later, GPA*]
PPA........... Priority Problem Areas (MCD)
PPA........... Process Plan Association [*United Kingdom*] (DS)
PPA........... Produce Packaging Association [*Later, PMA*] (EA)
PPA........... Professional Panhellenic Association [*Later, PFA*] (EA)
PP of A...... Professional Photographers of America (EA)
PPA........... Professional Programmers Association (EA)
PPA........... Professional Putters Association (EA)
PPA........... Program Problem Area
PPA........... Progress Presse Agentur GmbH [*Press agency*] [*Federal Republic of Germany*]
PPA........... Progressive Party of America [*Third party in 1948 Presidential race*]
PPA........... Propane-Precipitated Asphalt [*Petroleum technology*]
PPA........... Protestant Press Agency [*British*]
PPA........... Prudent Purchaser Arrangement [*Medical insurance*]
PPA........... Pseudopassive Array
PPA........... Public Personnel Association [*Later, IPMA*] (EA)
PPA........... Publishers' Publicity Association (EA)
PPA........... Pulmonary Artery Pressure [*Cardiology*]
PPA........... Pulse Plasma Accelerator
PPA........... Pulsed Power Amplifier
PPA........... Purple Plum Association [*Defunct*] (EA)
PPAA........ Patres Amplissimi [*Cardinals*] [*Latin*]
PPAA........ Personal Protective Armor Association (EA)
PPAB........ Program and Policy Advisory Board [*UN Food and Agriculture Organization*]
PPABP ...... American Baptist Publication Society, Philadelphia, PA [*Library symbol*] [*Library of Congress*] [*Obsolete*] (LCLS)
PPAC........ Penn-Pacific Corp. [*NASDAQ symbol*] (NQ)
PPAC........ Pesticide Policy Advisory Committee [*Environmental Protection Agency*]
PPAC........ Primary Progress Assessment Chart [*Psychology*]
PPAC........ Private Planning Association of Canada
PPAC........ Product Performance Agreement Center [*Military*]
PPAC........ Progressive Political Action Committee [*Defunct*]
PPACE ...... United States Army, Corps of Engineers, Philadelphia District Library, Custom House, Philadelphia, PA [*Library symbol*] [*Library of Congress*] (LCLS)
PPACHi .... American Catholic Historical Society, Philadelphia, PA [*Library symbol*] [*Library of Congress*] (LCLS)
PPADS ...... Parawing Precision Aerial Delivery System (MCD)
PPAEM ..... Albert Einstein Medical Center, Northern Division, Philadelphia, PA [*Library symbol*] [*Library of Congress*] (LCLS)
PPAFA ...... Pennsylvania Academy of the Fine Arts, Philadelphia, PA [*Library symbol*] [*Library of Congress*] [*Obsolete*] (LCLS)
PPAG........ Personnel Profile - Age by Grade [*Army*]
PPAI.......... Pinpoint Assignment Instructions [*Army*] (INF)
PPAK........ Atwater Kent Museum, Philadelphia, PA [*Library symbol*] [*Library of Congress*] (LCLS)
PPAL........ Principal (ROG)
PPalZ........ New Jersey Zinc Co. [*of Pennsylvania*], Technical Library, Palmerton, PA [*Library symbol*] [*Library of Congress*] (LCLS)
PPAmP ...... American Philosophical Society, Philadelphia, PA [*Library symbol*] [*Library of Congress*] (LCLS)
PPAmS ...... American Sunday School Union, Philadelphia, PA [*Library symbol*] [*Library of Congress*] [*Obsolete*] (LCLS)
PPAmSR ... American Sugar Refining Co., Philadelphia, PA [*Library symbol*] [*Library of Congress*] [*Obsolete*] (LCLS)
PPAmSwM ... American Swedish Historical Foundation, Philadelphia, PA [*Library symbol*] [*Library of Congress*] (LCLS)
PPAN .... Academy of Natural Sciences of Philadelphia, Philadelphia, PA [*Library symbol*] [*Library of Congress*] (LCLS)
PPAp......... Apprentices' Free Library, Philadelphia, PA [*Library symbol*] [*Library of Congress*] [*Obsolete*] (LCLS)
PPAP .... People's Party of Arunachal Pradesh [*India*] [*Political party*] (PPW)
PPAP .... Precedents of Private Acts of Parliament [*A publication*] (DLA)
PPAR........ Paterson Parchment Paper Co. [*Sunnyvale, CA*] [*NASDAQ symbol*] (NQ)
PPAR........ Project Performance Audit Report
PPArmA .... Armstrong Association of Philadelphia, Philadelphia, PA [*Library symbol*] [*Library of Congress*] [*Obsolete*] (LCLS)
PPAS .... Patti Page Appreciation Society (EA)
PPAS .... Portable Public Address System (MCD)

PPAS .... Potassium Picrate Active Substances [*Measure of detergent content of water*]
PPAS .... Probability Proportional to Aggregate Size [*Statistics*]
PPATDQ... Pediatric Pathology [*A publication*]
PPAtR....... Atlantic Refining Co., Philadelphia, PA [*Library symbol*] [*Library of Congress*] (LCLS)
PPATY ...... Preparatory (ROG)
PPAuC....... Automobile Club of Philadelphia, Philadelphia, PA [*Library symbol*] [*Library of Congress*] [*Obsolete*] (LCLS)
PPA Univ KY Coop Ext Serv ... PPA. University of Kentucky. Cooperative Extension Service [*A publication*]
PPAUS ...... Peat Producers Association of the United States (EA)
PPAW ...... Public Policy Affecting Women Task Force (EA)
PP & B ...... Paper, Printing, and Binding [*Publishing*]
PPB........... Parachute Paraglider Building [*NASA*] (KSC)
PPB........... Parts per Billion
PPB........... Petro-Canada Products, Inc. [*Toronto Stock Exchange symbol*] [*Vancouver Stock Exchange symbol*]
PPB........... Philadelphia Bar Association, Philadelphia, PA [*Library symbol*] [*Library of Congress*] (LCLS)
P-P-B .... Planning-Programming-Budgeting [*System*] [*Army*]
PPB........ Political Party Broadcast [*Television*] [*British*]
PPB........... Polybiblion. Partie Litteraire [*A publication*]
PPB........... Poly(para-benzamide) [*Organic chemistry*]
PPB........... Positive Pressure Breathing [*Aerospace*]
PPB........... Power Plant Bulletin (MCD)
PPB........... Precision Pressure Balance
PPB........... Pres Prudente [*Brazil*] [*Airport symbol*] (OAG)
PPB........... Primary Propulsion Branch [*Manned Spacecraft Center*]
PPB........... Private Posting Box
PPB........... Production Parts Breakdown (MCD)
PPB........... Program Performance Baseline (NASA)
PPB........... Program Planning Budget (NOAA)
PPB........... Program-Planning-Budgeting
PPB........... PROM [*Programmable Read-Only Memory*] Programmer Board
PPB........... Provisioning Parts Breakdown
PPB........... Purchasing Power Benefit (ADA)
PPB........... Push-Pull Bearing
PPBB .... Partai Pesaka Bumiputra Bersatu [*United Traditional Bumiputra Party*] [*Malaysia*] [*Political party*] (PPW)
PPBB .... Prime Power Brass Board (MCD)
PPBC .... Pittsburgh Penguins Booster Club (EA)
PPBC .... Plant Pathogenic Bacteria Committee (EA)
PPBC-R ..... Portland Problem Behavior Checklist - Revised [*Educational test*]
P PBD .... Paper or Paperboard [*Freight*]
PPBD........ Port of Palm Beach District [*AAR code*]
PPBERS .... Program Performance and Budget Execution Review System [*Army*]
PPBES...... Planning, Programming, Budgeting, and Execution System [*Army*] (RDA)
PPBES...... Program Planning and Budget Execution System [*Army*]
PPBES...... Program Planning-Budgeting-Evaluation System Project (EA)
PPBESP..... Program Planning-Budgeting-Evaluation System Project (EA)
PPBF .... Pan-American Pharmaceutical and Biochemical Federation
PPBFSPS.. Pen and Pocket Blade Forgers' and Smithers' Protective Society [*A union*] [*British*]
PPBG........ Preliminary Program and Budget Guidance
PPBI .... Balch Institute, Philadelphia, PA [*Library symbol*] [*Library of Congress*] (LCLS)
PPBM....... Pulse Polarization Binary Modulation (MCD)
PPBMIS.... Planning, Programming, and Budgeting Management Information System [*Army*]
PPBR .... Program Plan and Budget Request (OICC)
PPBS .... Planning, Programming, and Budgeting System [*Army*]
PPBS .... Positive Pressure Breathing System [*Aerospace*]
PPBS .... Postprandial Blood Sugar [*Clinical chemistry*]
PPBUA...... Personnel Practice Bulletin [*A publication*]
PPC........... College of Physicians of Philadelphia, Philadelphia, PA [*Library symbol*] [*Library of Congress*] [*OCLC symbol*] (LCLS)
PP-C .... Free Library of Philadelphia, Carson Collection, Philadelphia, PA [*Library symbol*] [*Library of Congress*] (LCLS)
PPC........... Journal of Pension Planning and Compliance [*A publication*]
PPC........... Pan Pacific Centers (EA)
PPC........... Paperboard Packaging Council (EA)
PPC........... Partial Pay Card
PPC........... Partido Popular Cristiano [*Christian Popular Party*] [*Peru*] [*Political party*] (PPW)
PPC........... Parting Post Calls (MCD)
PPC........... Partitu Populare Corsu [*Corsica*] [*Political party*] (PD)
PPC........... Parts Preference Code [*Military*] (AFIT)
PPC........... Patres Conscripti [*Senators*] [*Latin*] (ROG)
PPC........... Patrick Petroleum Company [*NYSE symbol*] (SPSG)
PPC........... Patrol Plane Commander
PPC........... Peak Power Control [*Telecommunications*] (TEL)
PPC........... Per Pupil Cost (AFM)
PPC........... Permission to Photocopy (MCD)
PPC........... Personal Portable Computer
PPC........... Personal Productivity Center
PPC........... Petroleum Planning Committee [*Obsolete*] [*NATO*] (NATG)

PPC............	Phased Provisioning Code (NASA)
PPC............	Philatelic Press Club [*Later, IPPC*]
PPC............	Photographic Processing Cells (AFM)
PpC............	Pick Publishing Corporation, New York, NY [*Library symbol*] [*Library of Congress*] (LCLS)
PP & C	Pickpocket and Confidence [*Police term*]
PPC............	Picture Postcard
PPC............	Pierce's Perpetual Code [*1943*] [*A publication*] (DLA)
PPC............	Pine Pass [*British Columbia*] [*Seismograph station code, US Geological Survey*] [*Closed*] (SEIS)
PPC............	Plain Paper Copier [*Electrophotography*]
PPC............	Plain Plaster Cornice [*Construction*]
PPC............	Plant Pest Control Division [*of ARS, Department of Agriculture*]
PPC............	Platform Position Computer
PPC............	Plug Patch Cord
PPC............	Plutonium Process Cell [*Nuclear energy*] (NRCH)
PPC............	Plutonium Product Cell [*Nuclear energy*] (NRCH)
PPC............	Point of Possible Collision [*Navigation*]
PPC............	Polyphthalate-Polycarbonate
PPC............	Positive Peer Control
PPC............	Posterior Parietal Cortex [*Brain anatomy*]
PPC............	Postpulmonary Complications
PPC............	Potential Points of Collision [*Navigation*]
PPC............	Pour Prendre Conge [*To Take Leave*] [*French*]
PPC............	Power Pack Charger
PPC............	Power Plant Change (NVT)
PPC............	PPC Oil & Gas Corp. [*Toronto Stock Exchange symbol*]
PPC............	Pre-Proposal Conference (MCD)
PPC............	Precision Photomechanical Corporation
PPC............	Preprocessing Center [*NASA*] (NASA)
PPC............	President of the Privy Council [*Canada*]
PPC............	Primary Power Control (MCD)
PPC............	Print Position Counter
PPC............	Priority Placement Certificate [*Military*] (AFM)
PP & C	Production Planning and Control [*Military*] (AABC)
PPC............	Production Planning and Control
PPC............	Professional Personal Computer
PPC............	Program Planning and Control (AAG)
PPC............	Program Planning Coordination Office [*United Nations*]
PPC............	Progressive Patient Care
PPC............	Project Parts Coordinator
PPC............	Project Physics Course [*National Science Foundation*]
PPC............	Project Planning Centre for Developing Countries [*Research center*] [*British*] (IRC)
PP & C	Project Planning and Control (NG)
PPC............	Prospect Creek, AK [*Location identifier*] [*FAA*] (FAAL)
PPC............	Prospective Parliamentary Candidate [*British*]
PPC............	Proximal Palmar Crease [*Anatomy*]
PPC............	Psychorotrophic Plate Count [*Bacteriology*]
PPC............	Publishers Publicity Circle
PPC............	Pulsed Power Circuit (IEEE)
PPCA.........	Plasma [*or Proserum*] Prothrombin Conversion Accelerator [*Factor VII*] [*Also, SPCA*] [*Hematology*]
PPCAA......	Parole and Probation Compact Administrators Association (EA)
PPCAP......	People to People Citizen Ambassador Program (EA)
PPCB........	Page Printer Control Block [*Data processing*]
PPCC.........	Carpenters' Company, Philadelphia, PA [*Library symbol*] [*Library of Congress*] (LCLS)
PPCC.........	Particles per Cubic Centimeter
PPCC.........	Postmolded Plastic Chip Carrier [*Data processing*]
PPCCH......	Chestnut Hill College, Philadelphia, PA [*Library symbol*] [*Library of Congress*] (LCLS)
PPCE........	Portable Pneumatic Checkout Equipment (KSC)
PPCE........	Post-Proline Cleaving Enzyme [*Biochemistry*]
PPCF.........	Plasmin Prothrombin Conversion Factor [*Factor V*] [*Hematology*]
PPCH........	People-to-People Committee for the Handicapped (EA)
PPCH........	Pilot Pouch [*Aviation*] (FAAC)
PPCI.........	Curtis Institute of Music, Philadelphia, PA [*Library symbol*] [*Library of Congress*] (LCLS)
PPCI.........	Pressure Piping Components, Incorporated [*North Hills, NY*] [*NASDAQ symbol*] (NQ)
PPCiC........	Civic Club of Philadelphia, Philadelphia, PA [*Library symbol*] [*Library of Congress*] [*Obsolete*] (LCLS)
PPCIG.......	Personal Property Consignment Instruction Guide (MCD)
PPC Jrl......	Polymers, Paint, and Colour Journal [*A publication*]
PPCLI.......	Princess Patricia of Connaught's Light Infantry [*Military unit*] [*Canada*]
PPCM.......	Philadelphia County Medical Society, Philadelphia, PA [*Library symbol*] [*Library of Congress*] [*Obsolete*] (LCLS)
PPCO.........	Philadelphia College of Osteopathic Medicine, Philadelphia, PA [*Library symbol*] [*Library of Congress*] (LCLS)
PPCoC.......	Community College of Philadelphia, Philadelphia, PA [*Library symbol*] [*Library of Congress*] (LCLS)
PPColP......	Colonial Penn Group, Inc., Marketing Research Library, Philadelphia, PA [*Library symbol*] [*Library of Congress*] (LCLS)
PPComm....	Commercial Museum, Philadelphia, PA [*Library symbol*] [*Library of Congress*] [*Obsolete*] (LCLS)

PPCP.........	Propellant Pneumatic Control Panel (KSC)
PPCPC......	Philadelphia City Planning Commission, Philadelphia, PA [*Library symbol*] [*Library of Congress*] (LCLS)
PPCPSG....	Polish POW Camps Philatelic Study Group (EA)
PPCS........	National Carl Schurz Memorial Foundation, Philadelphia, PA [*Library symbol*] [*Library of Congress*] [*Obsolete*] (LCLS)
PPCS........	Page Printer Control System [*Data processing*]
PPCS........	Person to Person: Collect and Special Instruction [*Telecommunications*] (TEL)
PPCS........	Precision Pointing Control System [*Engineering*]
PPCS........	Production Planning and Control System
PPCS........	Project Planning and Control System [*Social Security Administration*]
PPCuP.......	Curtis Publishing Co., Research Library, Philadelphia, PA [*Library symbol*] [*Library of Congress*] [*Obsolete*] (LCLS)
PPD	Drexel University, Philadelphia, PA [*Library symbol*] [*Library of Congress*] (LCLS)
PPD	Humacao-Palmas [*Puerto Rico*] [*Airport symbol*] (OAG)
PPD	Papered (ROG)
PPD	Parti Populaire Djiboutien [*Djibouti People's Party*] [*Political party*] (PPW)
PPD	Parti Progressiste Dahomeen [*Dahomey Progressive Party*] [*Political party*]
PPD	Partido Popular Democratico [*Popular Democratic Party*] [*Puerto Rico*] [*Political party*] (PPW)
PPD	Parts Provisioning Document
PPD	Party for Peace and Democracy [*South Korea*] [*Political party*]
PPD	Pay Packets Deficiency [*British*]
PPD	Payload Position Data
PPD	Pepsin Pancreatin Digest [*Food protein digestibility assay*]
P & PD......	Percussion and Postural Drainage
PPD	Personnel Planning Data [*Navy*]
PPD	Personnel Priority Designator [*Military*] (AFM)
PPD	Pitch Phase Detector
PPD	Plains Petroleum Co. [*Vancouver Stock Exchange symbol*]
PPD	Point Position Data
PPD	Polish Perspectives [*A publication*]
PPD	Portuguese Popular Democrats
PPD	Postpaid
PPD	Pre-Paid Legal Services, Inc. [*AMEX symbol*] (SPSG)
PPD	Prepaid
PPD	Presidential Protective Division [*US Secret Service*]
PPD	Primary Production Department [*Singapore*] (DS)
PPD	Prime Power Distribution
PPD	Proficiency Pay Designator [*Military*] (AABC)
PPD	Prognostic Prediction Devices
PPD	Program Package Document
PPD	Program Planning Directives [*NASA*] (KSC)
PPD	Program Planning Document (NG)
PPD	Progressive Perceptive Deafness [*Medicine*]
PPD	Project Planning Directive (NG)
PPD	Projectile Pull and Drain [*Machine*] (MCD)
PPD	Propria Pecunia Dedicavit [*With His Own Money He Offered It*] [*Latin*] (ROG)
PPD	Propulsion and Power Division [*Manned Spacecraft Center*] [*NASA*]
PPD	Provisioning Procurement Data
PPD	Pulse-Type Phase Detector
PPD	Purified Protein Derivative [*Tuberculin*]
PPDA.......	Para-Phenylenediamine [*Organic chemistry*]
PPDA.......	Phenyl Phosphorodiamidate [*Fertilizer technology*]
PPDB........	Personnel Planning Data Book [*Navy*]
PPDB........	Point-Positioning Data Base [*Cartography*] (RDA)
PPDC........	Dental Cosmos Library, Philadelphia, PA [*Library symbol*] [*Library of Congress*] [*Obsolete*] (LCLS)
PPDC........	Paraguayan People's Documentation Center [*Mestre, Italy*] (EAIO)
PPDC........	Partido Popular Democratica Cristiana [*Popular Christian Democratic Party*] [*Spain*] [*Political party*] (PPE)
PPDC........	Programming Panels and Decoding Circuits
PPDD	Plan Position Data Display
PPDD	Preliminary Project Design Description (NRCH)
PPDDS.....	Private Practice Dental Delivery System
PPDef-M ...	Defense Personnel Support Center, Directorate of Medical Material Library, Philadelphia, PA [*Library symbol*] [*Library of Congress*] (LCLS)
PPDF........	Poisson Probability Distribution Function [*Mathematics*]
PPDGF	Porcine Platelet-Derived Growth Factor [*Biochemistry*]
PPDIL	Pre-Power-Dependent Insertion Limit [*Nuclear energy*] (NRCH)
PPDio	Diocesan Library, Philadelphia, PA [*Library symbol*] [*Library of Congress*] [*Obsolete*] (LCLS)
PPDM	E. I. Du Pont de Nemours & Co., Marshall Laboratory, Philadelphia, PA [*Library symbol*] [*Library of Congress*] (LCLS)
PPDMG.....	Popular Priced Dress Manufacturers Group [*Later, AMA*] (EA)
PPDO	Personal Paid Days Off
ppdo	Proximo Pasado [*Last Month*] [*Spanish*]
PPDP........	Preliminary Project Development Plan [*NASA*]
PPDP.........	Preprogram Definition Phase

PP-DPH	Free Library of Philadelphia, Library for the Blind and Physically Handicapped, Philadelphia, PA [*Library symbol*] [*Library of Congress*] (LCLS)
PPDR........	Pilot Performance Description Record
PPDR........	Population and Development Review [*A publication*]
PP/DR.......	Preliminary Performance Design Requirements
PPDR........	Production Packing Depth Range (NG)
PPDrop......	Dropsie University, Philadelphia, PA [*Library symbol*] [*Library of Congress*] (LCLS)
PPDS	Physical Property Data Service [*Institution of Chemical Engineers*] [*Databank*] [*Information service or system*] (IID)
PPDS........	Planning Production Data Sheet
PPDS........	Preservation and Packaging Data Sheet [*DoD*]
PPD-S........	Purified Protein Derivative-Standard [*Tuberculin*]
PPDSE	International Plate Printers, Die Stampers, and Engravers' Union of North America
PPDT........	(Phenylpyridyl)diphenyltriazine [*Analytical chemistry*]
PPDT........	Poly(phenyleneterephthalamide) [*Organic chemistry*]
PPE...........	Independent Union of Plant Protection Employees in the Electrical and Machine Industry
PPE...........	Parti Populaire Europeen [*European Peoples' Party - EPP*] (EAIO)
PPE...........	Personal Protective Equipment [*General Motors Corp.*]
PPE...........	Philosophy, Politics, Economics [*Oxford University*]
PPE...........	Pholbe Phillips Editions [*Publisher*] [*British*]
PPE...........	Pipette [*Chemistry*]
PPE...........	Platform Position Equipment
PPE...........	Polyphenylether (IEEE)
PPE...........	Polyphosphate Ether [*Inorganic chemistry*]
PPE...........	Porcine Pancreatic Elastase [*An enzyme*]
PPE...........	Portable Purge Equipment [*NASA*]
PPE...........	Potomac Pacific Engineering, Inc.
PPE...........	Predicted Period-of-Effect [*Meteorology*]
PPE...........	Premodulation Processing Equipment
PPE...........	Preproduction Engineering
PPE...........	Preproduction Evaluation (NG)
PPE...........	Preproenkephalin [*Biochemistry*]
PPE...........	Problem Program Efficiency (IEEE)
PPE...........	Problem Program Evaluator
PPE...........	Program Planning and Evaluation
PPE...........	Prototype Production Evaluation (NG)
PPE...........	Purchasing Power Equivalent
PPE...........	Pyridoxal Phosphate Effect [*Medicine*]
PPEB	Eastern Baptist Theological Seminary, Philadelphia, PA [*Library symbol*] [*Library of Congress*] (LCLS)
PPEB	[*The*] Pottery of Palestine from the Earliest Times to the End of the Early Bronze Age [*A publication*] (BJA)
PPeda........	Problemi della Pedagogia [*A publication*]
PPEF	Public Policy Education Fund (EA)
PPEFH	E. F. Hutton & Co., Philadelphia, PA [*Library symbol*] [*Library of Congress*] [*Obsolete*] (LCLS)
PPEMA	Portable Power Equipment Manufacturers Association (EA)
PPENA	Plant and Power Services Engineer [*A publication*]
PPEng........	Engineers' Club, Philadelphia, PA [*Library symbol*] [*Library of Congress*] [*Obsolete*] (LCLS)
PPEP	Eastern Pennsylvania Psychiatric Institute, Philadelphia, PA [*Library symbol*] [*Library of Congress*] (LCLS)
PPEP	Plasma Physics and Environmental Perturbation (NASA)
P/PEP.......	Progress Performance Evaluation Panel [*Job Corps*]
PPERB	Progress in Pediatric Radiology [*A publication*]
PPES	Physical Performance Evaluation System [*Army*]
PPES	Pilot Performance Evaluation System [*Air Force*]
PPeSchw	Schwenkfelder Historical Library, Pennsburg, PA [*Library symbol*] [*Library of Congress*] (LCLS)
PPESD9	Proceedings. APRES [*American Peanut Research and Education Society*] [*A publication*]
PPET	Pangea Petroleum Co. [*NASDAQ symbol*] (NQ)
PPF...........	Franklin Institute, Philadelphia, PA [*Library symbol*] [*Library of Congress*] [*OCLC symbol*] (LCLS)
PPF...........	Pacific Peace Fund (EA)
PPF...........	Parsons [*Kansas*] [*Airport symbol*] (OAG)
PPF...........	Parsons, KS [*Location identifier*] [*FAA*] (FAAL)
PPF...........	Parti Populaire Francais [*French Popular Party*] [*Political party*] (PPE)
PPF...........	Patriotic People's Front [*Hungary*] [*Political party*]
PPF...........	Payload Processing Facility [*Air Force*] (NASA)
PPF...........	Peacetime Planning Factors
PPF...........	Peak Power Frequency
PPF...........	Pellagra Preventive Factor [*See also PP*] [*Biochemistry*]
PPF...........	People's Police Force (CINC)
PPF...........	Personal Property Floater [*Insurance*]
PPF...........	Phase Pushing Factor
PPF...........	Photophoretic Force [*Pressure exerted by light*]
PPF...........	Plasma Protein Fraction [*Hematology*]
PPF...........	Poetarum Philosophorum Graecorum Fragmenta [*A publication*] (OCD)
PPF...........	Poly(phenolformaldehyde) [*Organic chemistry*]
PPF...........	Porous Polyurethane Foam [*Also, PUF*] [*Plastics technology*]
PPF...........	Presbyterian Peace Fellowship (EA)
PPF...........	Principal Profile Forms [*Soil classification*]

PPF...........	Privatefoeretagarnas Partioganisation i Finland [*Finnish Private Entrepreneurs' Party*] [*Political party*] (PPE)
PPF...........	Production Possibility Frontier [*Economics*]
PPF...........	Provision of Production Facilities [*Military*] (AABC)
PPF...........	United Association of Journeymen and Apprentices of the Plumbing and Pipe Fitting Industry of the United States and Canada
PPFA	Planned Parenthood Federation of America (EA)
PPFA	Plastic Pipe and Fittings Association (EA)
PPFA	Professional Picture Framers Association (EA)
PPFA	United States Army, Frankford Arsenal Library, Philadelphia, PA [*Library symbol*] [*Library of Congress*] (LCLS)
PPFAR	Federal Archives and Records Center, General Services Administration, Philadelphia, PA [*Library symbol*] [*Library of Congress*] (LCLS)
PPFAS......	Past President of the Faculty of Architects and Surveyors [*British*] (DBQ)
PPFC	People's Pearl and Fishery Corporation [*Government corporation*] [*Burma*] (EY)
PPFC	Philadelphia Fellowship Commission, Philadelphia, PA [*Library symbol*] [*Library of Congress*] [*Obsolete*] (LCLS)
PPFC	Priscilla Presley Fan Club (EA)
PPFCDY....	Proceedings. Southern Pasture and Forage Crop Improvement Conference [*A publication*]
PPFD........	Photosynthetically Active Photon Flux Density [*Botany*]
PPFF.........	Poisson Probability Frequency Function [*Mathematics*]
PPF-G.......	Germantown Laboratories, Inc., Philadelphia, PA [*Library symbol*] [*Library of Congress*] (LCLS)
PPFHi.......	Historical Society of Frankford, Philadelphia, PA [*Library symbol*] [*Library of Congress*] [*Obsolete*] (LCLS)
PPFJC	Federation of Jewish Charities, Philadelphia, PA [*Library symbol*] [*Library of Congress*] [*Obsolete*] (LCLS)
PPFML......	Fidelity Mutual Life Insurance Co., Philadelphia, PA [*Library symbol*] [*Library of Congress*] (LCLS)
PPFO........	Paris Procurement Field Office
PPFPR......	F. P. Ristine & Co., Philadelphia, PA [*Library symbol*] [*Library of Congress*] [*Obsolete*] (LCLS)
PPFr..........	Friends' Free Library of Germantown, Philadelphia, PA [*Library symbol*] [*Library of Congress*] (LCLS)
PPFR........	Plutonium Product Filter Room [*Nuclear energy*] (NRCH)
PPFRB......	Federal Reserve Bank of Philadelphia, Philadelphia, PA [*Library symbol*] [*Library of Congress*] (LCLS)
PPFRT......	Prototype Preliminary Flight Rating Test
PPFS........	Pergamon Professional and Financial Services [*Commercial firm*] [*British*]
PPG	German Society of Pennsylvania, Philadelphia, PA [*Library symbol*] [*Library of Congress*] (LCLS)
PPG	Pacific Proving Ground [*AEC*]
PPG	Pago Pago [*Samoa*] [*Airport symbol*] (OAG)
PPG	Pago Pago, AQ [*Location identifier*] [*FAA*] (FAAL)
PPG	PEMA Policy and Guidance [*Military*] (AABC)
PPG	Periodical Press Gallery [*US Senate*]
PPG	Permanent Planning Group [*Military*] [*British*]
PPG	Personnel Processing Group [*Army*]
PPG	Phoenizisch-Punische Grammatik [*A publication*]
PPG	Photoplethysmography [*Medicine*]
PPG	Picopicogram
PPG	Piezoelectric Power Generation
PPG	Pipe Plug
PPG	Planned Procurement Guide
PPG	Planning and Policy Guidance (MCD)
PPG	Planning and Programming Guidance [*Army*] (AABC)
PPG	Plasma Power Generator
PPG	Player Piano Group (EAIO)
PPG	Poly(propylene Glycol) [*Organic chemistry*]
ppg	Pounds per Gallon
PPG	Power-Play Goal [*Hockey*]
PPG	PPG Industries, Inc. [*Formerly, Pittsburgh Plate Glass Co.*] [*NYSE symbol*] (SPSG)
PPG	PPG Industries, Inc., Coatings and Resins Division, Allison Park, PA [*OCLC symbol*] (OCLC)
PPG	Primary Pattern Generator [*Bell Laboratories*]
PPG	Program Planning Guide (OICC)
PPG	Program Policy Guidelines
PPG	Program Pulse Generator (IEEE)
PPG	Propulsion and Power Generation
PPGA........	Personal Producing General Agent [*Insurance*]
PPGA........	Post Pill Galactorrhea-Amenorrhea [*Medicine*]
PPGE........	General Electric Co., Philadelphia, PA [*Library symbol*] [*Library of Congress*] (LCLS)
PPGE-M....	General Electric Co., Missile and Space Vehicle Department, Aerosciences Laboratory, Philadelphia, PA [*Library symbol*] [*Library of Congress*] (LCLS)
PPGen........	Genealogical Society of Pennsylvania, Philadelphia, PA [*Library symbol*] [*Library of Congress*] (LCLS)
PPGenH	Philadelphia General Hospital Laboratories, Philadelphia, PA [*Library symbol*] [*Library of Congress*] [*Obsolete*] (LCLS)
PPGeo.......	Geographical Society of Philadelphia, Philadelphia, PA [*Library symbol*] [*Library of Congress*] [*Obsolete*] (LCLS)
PPGH	Philadelphia General Hospital, Philadelphia, PA [*Library symbol*] [*Library of Congress*] (LCLS)

PPGi .... Girard College, Philadelphia, PA [*Library symbol*] [*Library of Congress*] [*Obsolete*] (LCLS)
PPGJW ..... Past Pro-Grand Junior Warden [*Freemasonry*] (ROG)
PPGM....... Past Provincial Grand Master [*Freemasonry*]
PPGM....... Planning-Programming Guidance Memo [*Navy*]
PPGO .... Past Pro-Grand Organist [*Freemasonry*] (ROG)
PPGO .... Past Pro-Grand Orient [*Freemasonry*] (ROG)
PPGP........ Past Pro-Grand Pursuivant [*Freemasonry*] (ROG)
PPGP........ Prepaid Group Practice [*Insurance*] (DHSM)
PPGraph.... Graphic Sketch Club, Philadelphia, PA [*Library symbol*] [*Library of Congress*] [*Obsolete*] (LCLS)
PPGratz ..... Gratz College, Philadelphia, PA [*Library symbol*] [*Library of Congress*] [*Obsolete*] (LCLS)
PPGRC ..... Public Policy and Government Relations Council
PPGS .... Publications. Pennsylvania German Society [*A publication*]
PPGSB ..... Past Pro-Grand Sword Bearer [*Freemasonry*] (ROG)
PPGSN ..... Past Provincial Grand Senior [*Freemasonry*] (ROG)
PPGSW ..... Past Provincial Grand Senior Warden [*Freemasonry*]
PP Guide.... Prescription Proprietaries Guide [*A publication*] (APTA)
PPGW....... Past Pro-Grand Warden [*Freemasonry*] (ROG)
PPH .... Paid Personal Holiday
PPH .... Pamphlet
PPH .... Parts per Hundred
PPH .... Persistent Pulmonary Hypertension [*Medicine*]
PPH .... Petroleum Pipehead
PPH .... Phenylpropanolamine(hydrochloride) [*Also, PPA, PPM*] [*Decongestant*]
PPH .... Phosphopyruvate Hydratase [*An enzyme*]
PPH .... Postpartum Hemorrhage [*Medicine*]
PPH .... Pounds per Hour (NG)
PPH .... Primary Pulmonary Hypertension [*Medicine*]
PPH .... Prophet Resources Ltd. [*Vancouver Stock Exchange symbol*]
PPH .... Pulses per Hour
PPHa .... Hahnemann Medical College and Hospital, Philadelphia, PA [*Library symbol*] [*Library of Congress*] (LCLS)
PPHA .... Peak Pulse Height Analysis
PPHA .... Private Proprietary Homes for Adults
PPHBA..... Peruvian Paso Half-Blood Association [*Later, PPPBR*] (EA)
PPHBD7..... Plant Physiology and Biochemistry [*A publication*]
PPHFC ...... Holy Family College, Philadelphia, PA [*Library symbol*] [*Library of Congress*] (LCLS)
PPHID...... Plasma Physics Index [*A publication*]
P Ph L .... Papers in Philippine Linguistics [*A publication*] (APTA)
PPHM .... Parts per Hundred Million
P-PH-M..... Pulse Phase Modulation (DEN)
PPHN .... Persistent Pulmonary Hypertension of the Newborn [*Medicine*]
PPHOPT ... Pseudo-Pseudohypoparathyroidism [*Also, PPHP*] [*Endocrinology*]
PPHor........ Pennsylvania Horticultural Society, Philadelphia, PA [*Library symbol*] [*Library of Congress*] (LCLS)
PPHP........ Pseudo-Pseudohypoparathyroidism [*Also, PPHOPT*] [*Endocrinology*]
PPHPB...... Problemy Projektowe Hutnictwa i Przemyslu Maszynowego [*A publication*]
PPHPI....... Henry Phipps Institute, Philadelphia, PA [*Library symbol*] [*Library of Congress*] [*Obsolete*] (LCLS)
PPHR .... Planned Parenthood Review [*A publication*]
PPHRA..... Philosophy and Phenomenological Research [*A publication*]
PPHRD ..... Photochemical and Photobiological Reviews [*A publication*]
PPHRII ..... Parents of Premature and High Risk Infants International (EA)
PPHRNA .. Peruvian Paso Horse Registry of North America (EA)
PPHS......... Partisan Prohibition Historical Society (EA)
PPHSL...... Periodical Publication in Harvard Science Libraries
PPHT........ (Phenylethyl-propylamino)hydroxytetralin [*Biochemistry*]
PPHYA..... Plant Physiology [*English Translation*] [*A publication*]
PPi .... Carnegie Library of Pittsburgh, Pittsburgh, PA [*Library symbol*] [*Library of Congress*] (LCLS)
PPI............ Institute for Psychosomatic and Psychiatric Research and Training [*Research center*] (RCD)
PPI............ Packing, Postage, and Insurance [*Shipping*]
PPI............ Padangpandjang [*Sumatra*] [*Seismograph station code, US Geological Survey*] (SEIS)
PPI............ Pages per Inch [*Publishing*]
PPI............ Pakistan Press International
PPI............ Parallel Peripheral Interface [*Data processing*]
PPI............ Parcel Post, Insured [*Shipping*]
PPI............ Park Practice Index [*A publication*]
PPI............ Particles per Inch
PPI............ Patient Package Insert [*Also, PI*] [*Instructional leaflet distributed with certain prescription drugs*]
PPI............ Pensioners for Peace International (EAIO)
PPI............ Pergamon Press, Incorporated
PPI............ Personality and Personal Illness Questionnaire [*Psychology*]
PPI............ Personnel Planning Information
PPI............ Phoenix Precision Instrument Co.
PPI............ Pickle Packers International (EA)
PPI............ Pico Products, Incorporated [*AMEX symbol*] (SPSG)
PPI............ Pictorial Position Indicator
PPI............ Pilgrim Holdings Ltd. [*Vancouver Stock Exchange symbol*]
PPI............ PIPA [*Pulsed Integrating Pendulous Accelerometer*] Pulse Integrator

PPI............ Piston Position Indicator
PPI............ Plan Position Indicator Mode [*Data processing*] (ADA)
PPI............ Plane Position Indicator [*RADAR*]
PPI............ Planen-Pruefen-Investieren [*A publication*]
PPI............ Plasma Protein Isolate [*Food technology*]
PPI............ Plastics Pipe Institute (EA)
PPI............ Plot Position Indicator
PPI............ Policy Proof of Interest
PPI............ Polyphosphonositides
PPI............ Polyphthalimide [*Organic chemistry*]
PPI............ POM [*Program Objective Memorandum*] Preparation Instructions [*Military*]
PPI............ Popular Periodical Index [*A publication*]
ppi .... Pores per Inch
PPI............ Port Pirie [*Australia*] [*Airport symbol*] (OAG)
PPI............ Postage Paid Impression [*Freight*] (DCTA)
PPI............ Potash and Phosphate Institute (EA)
PPI............ Pounds per Inch [*Lubrication load*]
PPI............ Preceding Preparatory Interval [*Psychometrics*]
PPI............ Preferred Parts Index
PPI............ Preplant Incorporated [*Herbicides*] [*Agriculture*]
PPI............ Prepleading Investigation [*Law*]
PPI............ Present Pain Intensity
PPI............ Present Position Indicator [*Aviation*]
PPI............ Prices Paid Index [*Economics*]
PPI............ Primary Personal Interest [*Personnel study*]
PPI............ Prince Patrick Island [*Canada*]
PPI............ Producer Price Index [*Bureau of Labor Statistics*] [*Information service or system*]
PPI............ Program Position Indicator
PPI............ Programmable Peripheral Interface (MCD)
PPI............ Project Procurement Instructions [*Jet Propulsion Laboratory, NASA*]
PPI............ Property Protection Insurance
PPI............ Public-Private Interface
PPI............ Pulp and Paper International [*A publication*]
PPI............ Pulse Position Indicator (MCD)
PPI............ Pulses per Inch (CMD)
PPI............ Pyrophosphate Index [*Agronomy*]
PPi............ Pyrophosphate, Inorganic [*Chemistry*]
PPi-A .... Carnegie Library of Pittsburgh, Allegheny Regional Branch, Monroeville, PA [*Library symbol*] [*Library of Congress*] (LCLS)
PPIA .... Philippine Poultry Industry Association (DS)
PPIA .... Programme du Pipeline des Iles de l'Arctique [*Canada*]
PPiAC........ Community College of Allegheny County, Pittsburgh, PA [*Library symbol*] [*Library of Congress*] (LCLS)
PPiAL........ Allegheny County Law Library, Pittsburgh, PA [*Library symbol*] [*Library of Congress*] (LCLS)
PPiAM...... Pittsburgh Academy of Medicine, Pittsburgh, PA [*Library symbol*] [*Library of Congress*] (LCLS)
PPIB .... Programmable Protocol Interface Board
PPiC.......... Carnegie-Mellon University, Pittsburgh, PA [*Library symbol*] [*Library of Congress*] (LCLS)
PPIC.......... Pollution Prevention Information Clearinghouse [*Environmental Protection Agency*]
PPiCa........ Carlow College, Pittsburgh, PA [*Library symbol*] [*Library of Congress*] (LCLS)
PPiCa-O .... Carlow College, Our Lady of Mercy Academy, Pittsburgh, PA [*Library symbol*] [*Library of Congress*] (LCLS)
PPiCC .... Chatham College, Pittsburgh, PA [*Library symbol*] [*Library of Congress*] (LCLS)
PPICR .... Institute for Cancer Research, Philadelphia, PA [*Library symbol*] [*Library of Congress*] (LCLS)
PPiD .... Duquesne University, Pittsburgh, PA [*Library symbol*] [*Library of Congress*] (LCLS)
PPID......... Polaris-Poseidon Intelligence Digest (MCD)
PPiD-L...... Duquesne University, School of Law, Pittsburgh, PA [*Library symbol*] [*Library of Congress*] (LCLS)
PPiE......... E. D'Appolonia Consulting Engineers, Pittsburgh, PA [*Library symbol*] [*Library of Congress*] (LCLS)
PPIF .... Photo Processing Interpretation Facility
PPIFC....... Pauline Pinkney International Fan Club (EA)
PPiGulf ...... Gulf Research & Development Co., Pittsburgh, PA [*Library symbol*] [*Library of Congress*] (LCLS)
PPiHB .... Carnegie-Mellon University, Hunt Institute for Botanical Documentation, Pittsburgh, PA [*Library symbol*] [*Library of Congress*] (LCLS)
PPiHi........ Historical Society of Western Pennsylvania, Pittsburgh, PA [*Library symbol*] [*Library of Congress*] (LCLS)
PPiI.......... International Poetry Forum, Pittsburgh, PA [*Library symbol*] [*Library of Congress*] (LCLS)
PPiK......... Ketchum, McLeod & Grove, Inc., Pittsburgh, PA [*Library symbol*] [*Library of Congress*] (LCLS)
PPiL......... LaRoche College, Pittsburgh, PA [*Library symbol*] [*Library of Congress*] (LCLS)
PPIL .... Priced Provisioned Item List (MCD)
PPIL .... Problems in Private International Law [*Elsevier Book Series*] [*A publication*]
PPiM .... Carnegie-Mellon University, Mellon Institute, Pittsburgh, PA [*Library symbol*] [*Library of Congress*] (LCLS)

PPiMS...... Mine Safety Appliances Co., Pittsburgh, PA [*Library symbol*] [*Library of Congress*] (LCLS)
PPIn.......... Independence National Historical Park, Philadelphia, PA [*Library symbol*] [*Library of Congress*] (LCLS)
PPINA...... Insurance Co., of North America, Corporate Archives, Philadelphia, PA [*Library symbol*] [*Library of Congress*] (LCLS)
PPINICI.... Pulsed Positive Ion-Negative Ion Chemical Ionization [*Instrumentation*]
P & P Intnl ... Pulp and Paper International Annual Review [*A publication*]
PPiPP........ Point Park College, Pittsburgh, PA [*Library symbol*] [*Library of Congress*] (LCLS)
PPiPPG ..... PPG Industries, Inc., Glass Research Center, Information Services Library, Pittsburgh, PA [*Library symbol*] [*Library of Congress*] (LCLS)
PPiPT .... Pittsburgh Theological Seminary, Pittsburgh, PA [*Library symbol*] [*Library of Congress*] (LCLS)
PPIR......... Personnel Planning Information Report (MCD)
PPiR.......... Rockwell International Corp., Pittsburgh, PA [*Library symbol*] [*Library of Congress*] (LCLS)
PPIRO...... Planned Position Indicator Readout (NVT)
PPIS.......... Product Profile Information System [*Shell Oil Co.*]
PPIU......... Programmable Peripheral Interface Unit
PPiU .... University of Pittsburgh, Pittsburgh, PA [*Library symbol*] [*Library of Congress*] (LCLS)
PPiU-A ...... University of Pittsburgh, Henry Clay Frick Fine Arts Center, Pittsburgh, PA [*Library symbol*] [*Library of Congress*] (LCLS)
PPiU-BL.... University of Pittsburgh, Blair-Lippincott Library, Eye and Ear Hospital of Pittsburgh, Pittsburgh, PA [*Library symbol*] [*Library of Congress*] (LCLS)
PPiU-H...... University of Pittsburgh, Maurice and Laura Falk Library of the Health Professions, Pittsburgh, PA [*Library symbol*] [*Library of Congress*] (LCLS)
PPiU-L ...... University of Pittsburgh, Law School, Pittsburgh, PA [*Library symbol*] [*Library of Congress*] (LCLS)
PPiU-LS .... University of Pittsburgh, Graduate School of Library and Information Sciences, Pittsburgh, PA [*Library symbol*] [*Library of Congress*] (LCLS)
PPiU-NS ... University of Pittsburgh, Natural Sciences Library, Pittsburgh, PA [*Library symbol*] [*Library of Congress*] (LCLS)
PPiU-PH ... University of Pittsburgh, Graduate School of Public Health, Pittsburgh, PA [*Library symbol*] [*Library of Congress*] (LCLS)
PPiU-PIA .. University of Pittsburgh, Graduate School of Public and International Affairs, Pittsburgh, PA [*Library symbol*] [*Library of Congress*] (LCLS)
PPiUS....... United States Steel Corp., Pittsburgh, PA [*Library symbol*] [*Library of Congress*] (LCLS)
PPiU-SF .... University of Pittsburgh, Stephen Collins Foster Memorial [*Music*] Library, Pittsburgh, PA [*Library symbol*] [*Library of Congress*] (LCLS)
PPiUSM.... United States Department of the Interior, Bureau of Mines, Pittsburgh Research Center, Pittsburgh, PA [*Library symbol*] [*Library of Congress*] (LCLS)
PPiW .... Westinghouse Electric Corp., Research and Development Center, Pittsburgh, PA [*Library symbol*] [*Library of Congress*] (LCLS)
PPiW-N ..... Westinghouse Electric Corp., Nuclear Center Library, Pittsburgh, PA [*Library symbol*] [*Library of Congress*] (LCLS)
PPiWP....... Western Psychiatric Institute and Clinic, University of Pittsburgh, Pittsburgh, PA [*Library symbol*] [*Library of Congress*] (LCLS)
PPJ .... Philippine Planning Journal [*A publication*]
PPJ .... Pressure Plane Joint
PPJ .... Prilozi Proucavanju Jezika [*A publication*]
PPJ .... Pure Pancreatic Juice
PPJ .... Thomas Jefferson University, Philadelphia, PA [*Library symbol*] [*Library of Congress*] (LCLS)
PPJea........ Jeanes Hospital, Philadelphia, PA [*Library symbol*] [*Library of Congress*] [*Obsolete*] (LCLS)
PPJO .... Pli Premier Jour Officiel [*Official First Day Cover - OFDC*] [*Canada Post Corp.*]
P & P Jrl .... Pulp and Paper Journal [*A publication*]
PPJ-S........ Thomas Jefferson University, Scott Memorial Library, Philadelphia, PA [*Library symbol*] [*Library of Congress*] (LCLS)
PPJW .... Past Pro-Junior Warden [*Freemasonry*] (ROG)
PPK.......... Paired Perpendicular Keratotomy [*Procedure to correct astigmatism*]
PPK.......... Paramp Pump Klystron
PPK.......... Parti Progressiste Katangais [*Political party*]
PPK.......... Personal Preference Kit [*Small bag in which astronauts are allowed to take personal mementos*]
PPK.......... Polizei Pistole Kriminal [*Pistol suitable for undercover police or detective use*] [*Walther Waffenfabrik, German arms manufacturer*]
PPK.......... Punt, Pass, and Kick [*Youth competition sponsored by professional football*]
PPKCA ...... Pen and Pocket Knife Cutters' Association [*A union*] [*British*]

PPKCB ...... Prace Komisji Ceramicznej. Polskiej Akademii Nauk. Ceramica [*A publication*]
PPKG......... Power Package (MSA)
PPKGA...... Ponpu Kogaku [*A publication*]
PPL........... Journal of Pension Planning and Compliance [*A publication*]
PPL........... Library Co. of Philadelphia, Philadelphia, PA [*Library symbol*] [*Library of Congress*] (LCLS)
PPL........... Palach Press Ltd. [*London, England*] (EAIO)
PPL........... Palmer Physical Laboratory [*Princeton University*] (MCD)
PPL........... Pembina Resources Limited [*Toronto Stock Exchange symbol*]
PPL........... Penicilloyl Polylysine [*Pharmacology*]
PPL........... Pennsylvania Power & Light Co. [*NYSE symbol*] (SPSG)
PPL........... Per Pupil Limitation (AFM)
PPL........... Peter Peregrinus Limited [*Publisher*]
PPL........... Phenylpropanolamine [*Organic chemistry*]
PPL........... Phonographic Performance Limited [*British*]
PPL........... Physical Properties Laboratory [*Oklahoma State University*] [*Research center*] (RCD)
PPL........... Plan Position Landing (DEN)
PPL........... Planning Parts List
PPL........... Plasma Physics Laboratory [*Also known as PPPL*]
PPL........... Plasma Propulsion Laboratory (MCD)
PPL........... Plus Programming Language [*Data processing*]
PPL........... Plutonium Product Loadout [*Nuclear energy*] (NRCH)
PPL........... Polybiblion. Partie Litteraire [*A publication*]
PPL........... Polymorphic Programming Language [*1971*] [*Data processing*] (CSR)
PPL........... Populated Place [*Board on Geographic Names*]
PPL........... Posterior Pole Plasm [*Insect embryology*]
PPL........... Power Plant Laboratory (MUGU)
PPL........... Prace Polonistyczne (Lodz) [*A publication*]
PPL........... Predictive Period LASER (KSC)
PPL........... Preferential Planning List
PPL........... Preferred Parts List
PPL........... Preliminary Parts List
PPL........... Priced Parts List (NASA)
P/PL .... Primary Payload [*NASA*] (NASA)
PPL........... Princeton Polymer Laboratories
PPL........... Private Pilot's Licence [*British*]
PPL........... Program Production Library [*Data processing*]
PPL........... Project Priority List [*Environmental Protection Agency*]
PPL........... Provisioning Parts List (AAG)
PPL........... Purchased Parts List
PPL........... Pure Prairie League [*Musical group*]
PPL........... Puu Pili [*Hawaii*] [*Seismograph station code, US Geological Survey*] (SEIS)
PpL .... W. & F. Pascoe Proprietory Ltd., Milsons Point, Australia [*Library symbol*] [*Library of Congress*] (LCLS)
PPLA .... Practice Precautionary Landing Approach [*Aviation*]
PPLas .... La Salle College, Philadelphia, PA [*Library symbol*] [*Library of Congress*] (LCLS)
PPlase........ Peptidylprolyl Cis-Trans Isomerase [*An enzyme*]
PPLD........ Pikes Peak Library District [*Internationally recognized computerized library system*]
PPLDF...... Professional Protector and Legal Defense Fund
PPLE .... Partial Preliminary Logistic Evaluation
PPLE .... Participle [*Grammar*]
PPLE .... Principle (ROG)
PPL/H....... Private Pilot's Licence/Helicopters [*British*] (AIA)
PPLI .... Precise Participant Location-Identification [*Navigation*]
PPLI .... Provisioning Parts List Index (MCD)
PPLL........ Military Order of the Loyal Legion of the United States, [*Civil War Library and Museum, Philadelphia, PA* [*Library symbol*] [*Library of Congress*] (LCLS)
PPLN........ Pipeline
PPLO........ Pleuropneumonia-Like Organisms [*Bacteriology*]
PPLP .... Photopolymers Lithograph Plate
P PLPBD... Paper or Pulpboard [*Freight*]
PPLS........ Precision Position Locator System [*Army*]
PPLS........ Preferred Parts List System (MCD)
PPLS........ Propellant and Pressurant Loading System [*NASA*] (KSC)
PPLT .... Lutheran Theological Seminary, Philadelphia, PA [*Library symbol*] [*Library of Congress*] (LCLS)
PPLX .... Section of Populated Place [*Board on Geographic Names*]
PPM .... Aberdeen, MD [*Location identifier*] [*FAA*] (FAAL)
PPM .... Mercantile Library, Philadelphia, PA [*Library symbol*] [*Library of Congress*] [*Obsolete*] (LCLS)
P & PM...... Packing and Packaging Manual (MCD)
PPM .... Pages per Minute [*Printer technology*]
ppm .... Papermaker [*MARC relator code*] [*Library of Congress*] (LCCP)
PPM .... Part Program Manager
PPM .... Parti Pekerja-Pekerja Malaysia [*Workers' Party of Malaysia*] [*Political party*] (PPW)
PPM .... Parti du Peuple Mauritanien [*Mauritania*] [*Political party*]
PPM .... Parti Progressiste Martinquais [*Progressive Party of Martinique*] [*Political party*] (PPW)
PPM .... Particuliere Participatiemaatschappy [*Private Joint Stock Company*] [*Dutch*]
PPM .... Partido del Pueblo Mexicano [*Mexican People's Party*] [*Political party*] (PPW)

PPM .... Parts per Million
PPM .... Parts per Minute   (MCD)
PPM .... Pattani People's Movement [*Political party*] [*Thailand*]
PPM .... Peak Power Meter
PPM .... Peak Program Meter [*Television*]
PPM .... Periodic Permanent Magnet
PPM .... Periodic Pulse Metering [*Telecommunications*]   (TEL)
PPM .... Pershing Project Manager
PPM .... Personnel Priority Model   (MCD)
PPM .... Personnel Program Manager [*Navy*]
PPM .... Phenylpropanolamine(hydrochloride) [*Also, PPA, PPH*] [*Decongestant*]
PPM .... Phosphopentomutase [*An enzyme*]
PPM .... Piecewise Parabolic Method [*Mathematical model of fluid flow*]
PPM .... Pilot Production Model [*Military*]   (CAAL)
PPM .... Pistol Prize Money [*British military*]   (DMA)
PPM .... Planned Preventive Maintenance   (IEEE)
PPM .... Popocatepetl [*Mexico*] [*Seismograph station code, US Geological Survey*]   (SEIS)
PPM .... Position and Pay Management [*Army*]   (AABC)
PPM .... Postage Prepaid in Money
PPM .... Postpass Message
PPM .... Pounds per Minute
PPM .... Prairie Print Makers [*Defunct*]   (EA)
PPM .... Previous Processor Mode
PPM .... Production Planning Memorandum
PPM .... Program, Project Management [*Army*]
PPM .... Project Profile Manual
PPM .... Prudential Portfolio Managers Ltd. [*British*]
PPM .... Public Personnel Management [*A publication*]
PPM .... Pulp and Paper Magazine of Canada [*Later, Pulp and Paper (Canada)*] [*A publication*]
PPM .... Pulse Position Modulation [*Radio data transmission*]
PPM .... Pulses per Minute
PPMA....... Plastic Products Manufacturers Association [*Later, Plastic and Metal Products Manufacturers Association*]   (EA)
PPMA....... Political Products Manufacturers Association   (EA)
PPMA....... Post-Poliomyelitis Muscular Atrophy [*Medicine*]
PPMA....... Precision Potentiometer Manufacturers Association [*Later, Variable Resistive Components Institute*]   (EA)
PPMA....... Pulp and Paper Manufacturers Association [*Later, PPMMA*]   (EA)
PPMC....... People to People Music Committee   (EA)
PPME....... Pacific Plate Motion Experiment   (NASA)
PPMFC ..... Preprints on Precision Measurement and Fundamental Constants [*National Institute of Standards and Technology*]
PPMG....... Professional Publishers Marketing Group   (EA)
PPMI....... Pilot Plant Meat Irradiator
PPMI....... Printed Paper Mat Institute   (EA)
PPMIN..... Pulses per Minute   (MSA)
PPMis........ Misericordia Hospital, Philadelphia, PA [*Library symbol*] [*Library of Congress*] [*Obsolete*]   (LCLS)
PPML....... Preferred Parts and Materials List [*NASA*]
PPMMA.... Problemy Prochnosti v Mashinostroenii [*A publication*]
PPMMA.... Pulp and Paper Machinery Manufacturers Association [*Later, APMA*]   (EA)
PPMMB... Periodica Polytechnica. Mechanical Engineering [*A publication*]
PPMN .... Preliminary Program Management Network [*Military*]
PPMNA..... Polski Przeglad Radiologii i Medycyny Nuklearnej [*A publication*]
PPMO .... Pershing Project Manager's Office   (RDA)
PPMO .... Provisional Program Management Office [*Army*]
PPMoI....... Moore College of Art, Philadelphia, PA [*Library symbol*] [*Library of Congress*]   (LCLS)
PPMR....... Purchased Parts Material Requirements
PPMRC ..... Proceedings. PMR Conference. Annual Publication of the International Patristic, Mediaeval, and Renaissance Conference [*A publication*]
PPMS....... Pitt Press Mathematical Series [*A publication*]
PPMS....... Poly(para-Methylstyrene) [*Organic chemistry*]
PPMS....... Program Performance Measurement Systems   (IEEE)
PPMS....... Purdue Perceptual-Motor Survey [*Kephart Scale*]
PPMV....... Parts per Million by Volume
PPMVA.... Pishchevaya Promyshlennost [*Kiev, 1965*] [*A publication*]
PPN .... Numismatic and Antiquarian Society, Philadelphia, PA [*Library symbol*] [*Library of Congress*] [*Obsolete*]   (LCLS)
PPN .... Papenoo [*Society Islands*] [*Seismograph station code, US Geological Survey*]   (SEIS)
PPN .... Parameterized Post-Newtonian [*Gravity*]
PPN .... Parti Progressiste Nigerien [*Nigerian Progressive Party*] [*Political party*]
PPN .... Partido Progreso Nacional [*National Progress Party*] [*Costa Rica*] [*Political party*]   (PPW)
PPN .... Peak-to-Peak Noise [*Instrumentation*]
PPN .... Peroxypropionyl Nitrate [*Organic chemistry*]
PPN .... Polyphosphonate [*Organic chemistry*]
PPN .... Popayan [*Colombia*] [*Airport symbol*]   (OAG)
PPN .... Portland Public Library, Portland, ME [*OCLC symbol*]   (OCLC)
PPN .... Procurement Program Number [*Military*]

PPN .... Project, Programmer Number
PPN .... Proportion   (ROG)
PPNA .... Peak Phrenic Nerve Activity [*Medicine*]
PP & NA.... Private Plants and Naval Activities
PPNADY.. Pitch Pine Naturalist [*A publication*]
PPNB....... Pre-Pottery Neolithic B Period [*Paleontology*]
PPNC........ Pre-Pottery Neolithic C Phase [*Paleontology*]
PPNCFL.... Proceedings. Pacific Northwest Conference on Foreign Languages [*A publication*]
PPNDG ...... Petition Pending
PPNF......... Price-Pottenger Nutrition Foundation   (EA)
PPNG .... Penicillinase-Producing Neisseria gonorrhoeae
PPNICI.... Pulsed Positive/Negative Ion Chemical Ionization
P/PNL .... Pocket Panel [*Automotive engineering*]
PPNMC..... United States Navy, Naval Regional Medical Center, Philadelphia, PA [*Library symbol*] [*Library of Congress*]   (LCLS)
PPNPD...... Progress in Particle and Nuclear Physics [*A publication*]
PPNSC ...... Preferred Procurement Number Selector Code [*Military*]   (AFIT)
PPNSCA ... Policy Plans and National Security Council Affairs
PPNT....... Proponent
PPNWA..... N. W. Ayer & Son, Philadelphia, PA [*Library symbol*] [*Library of Congress*] [*Obsolete*]   (LCLS)
PPO .... Photographic Program Office [*NASA*]   (KSC)
PPO .... Platelet Peroxidase [*An enzyme*]
PPO .... Pleuropneumonia Organisms [*Bacteriology*]
PPO .... Pollution Prevention Office [*Environmental Protection Agency*]
PPO .... Polyphenol Oxidase [*An enzyme*]
PPO .... Polyphenylene Oxide [*Organic chemistry*]
PPO .... Poly(propylene Oxide) [*Organic chemistry*]
PPO .... Port Postal Office   (AFM)
PPO .... Power Plant Operating
PPO .... Preferred Provider Option [*Insurance*]
PPO .... Preferred-Provider Organization [*Insurance*]
PPO .... Pressed Plutonium Oxide
PPO .... Primary Party Organization [*Politics*]
PPO .... Principal Priority Officer
PPO .... Prior Permission Only   (AFM)
PPO .... Procurement Planning Officer
PPO .... Program Printout   (MCD)
PPO .... Projected Program Objective   (NG)
PPO .... Publications and Printing Office [*Army*]
PPO .... Pure Plutonium Oxide
PPO .... Push-Pull Output   (DEN)
PPO$_2$........ Partial Pressure of Oxygen   (CAAL)
PPOC....... Per Pupil Operating Cost   (ADA)
PPol .... Pensiero Politico [*A publication*]
PPol .... Przeglad Polski [*A publication*]
PPOS......... Saint George United Methodist Church, Philadelphia, PA [*Library symbol*] [*Library of Congress*]   (LCLS)
PPOSN...... Proposition   (ROG)
PPOTA..... Prumysl Potravin [*A publication*]
PPow .... Przeglad Powszechny [*A publication*]
PPOW ..... Psychologists for the Prevention of War [*Australia*]
PPP........... Pacific Peacemaker Project   (EA)
PPP........... Pakistan People's Party [*Political party*]   (PD)
PPP........... Pan Pacific Petroleum [*Vancouver Stock Exchange symbol*]
PPP........... Paper, Printing, Publishing [*Department of Employment*] [*British*]
PPP........... Parallel Pattern Processor
PPP........... Pariser-Parr-Pople [*Physical chemistry*]
PPP........... Partai Persatuan Pembangunan [*United Development Party*] [*Indonesia*] [*Political party*]   (PPW)
PPP........... Partido del Pueblo de Panama [*Panamanian People's Party*] [*Political party*]   (PPW)
PPP........... Peak Pulse Power
PPP........... Pentose-Phosphate Pathway [*Metabolism*]
PPP........... People's Patriotic Party [*Burma*] [*Political party*]   (PD)
PPP........... People's Political Party [*St. Vincent*] [*Political party*]   (PPW)
PPP........... People's Progress Party [*Papua New Guinea*] [*Political party*]   (PPW)
PPP........... People's Progressive Party [*Gambia*] [*Political party*]   (PPW)
PPP........... People's Progressive Party [*Guyana*] [*Political party*]   (PD)
PPP........... People's Progressive Party [*Solomon Islands*] [*Political party*]   (PPW)
PPP........... People's Progressive Party [*Anguilla*] [*Political party*]   (PPW)
PPP........... Permanent Party Personnel   (MCD)
PPP........... Perpex Peristaltic Pump
PPP........... Personal Property Policy [*Insurance*]
PPP........... Personnel Performance Profile
PPP........... Phased Project Planning [*NASA*]   (KSC)
PPP........... Pianississimo [*As Softly As Possible*] [*Music*]
PPP........... Pickford Projective Pictures [*Psychology*]
PPP........... Pipelines, Politics, and People. Capital Communications Ltd. [*A publication*]
PPP........... Plan Position Presentation
PPP........... Planning Purpose Proposal
PPP........... Platelet-Poor Plasma [*Hematology*]
PPP........... Pluripotent Progenitor [*Cytology*]
PPP........... Pogo Producing Co. [*NYSE symbol*]   (SPSG)

PPP........... Polluter Pays Principle
PPP........... Poly(para-phenylene) [*Organic chemistry*]
PPP........... Portable Plotting Package [*Nuclear energy*]   (NRCH)
PPP........... Positive Pressure Paradox
PPP........... Powerful Permutation Procedure [*Meteorology*]
PPP........... Prescriptive Parent Programming [*Education*]
PPP........... Prescriptive Program Plan [*Education*]
PPP........... Pretty Poor Planning
PPP........... Prison Pen Pals   (EA)
PPP........... Private Patients' Plan [*British*]
PPP........... Production Part Pattern   (MCD)
PPP........... Profit and Performance Planning   (DCTA)
PPP........... Progressive People's Party [*Liberia*] [*Political party*]   (PPW)
PPP........... Propria Pecunia Posuit [*Erected at His Own Expense*] [*Latin*]
PPP........... Proserpine [*Australia*] [*Airport symbol*]   (OAG)
PPP........... Province Pacification Plan   (CINC)
PPP........... Provisioning Program Plan   (MCD)
P & PP ...... Pull and Push Plate
PPP........... Pulp and Paper International [*A publication*]
PPP........... Purchasing Power Parity [*Economics*]
PPPA........ Poison Prevention Packaging Act
PPPA........ Professional Pool Players Association   (EA)
PPPA........ Pulp and Paper Prepackaging Association [*Later, SSI*]
PPPBDD ... Iran. Plant Pests and Diseases Research Institute. Department
            of Botany. Publication [*A publication*]
PPPBR...... Peruvian Paso Part-Blood Registry   (EA)
PPPC .... Petroleum Pool Pacific Coast
PPPC .... Pipe Plug Producers Council   (EA)
PPPCA ...... Philadelphia College of Art Library, Philadelphia, PA [*Library
            symbol*] [*Library of Congress*]   (LCLS)
PPPCity..... Philadelphia City Institute Branch Free Library, Philadelphia,
            PA [*Library symbol*] [*Library of Congress*]
            [*Obsolete*]   (LCLS)
PPPCO ...... Pennsylvania College of Optometry, Philadelphia, PA [*Library
            symbol*] [*Library of Congress*]   (LCLS)
PPPCPh.... Philadelphia College of Pharmacy and Science, Philadelphia, PA
            [*Library symbol*] [*Library of Congress*]   (LCLS)
PPPE .... Pennsylvania Economy League, Inc., Eastern Division,
            Philadelphia, PA [*Library symbol*] [*Library of
            Congress*]   (LCLS)
PPPE .... People, Plans, and the Peace. Peace River Planning Commission
            [*A publication*]
PPPEA ...... Pulp, Paper, and Paperboard Export Association of the United
            States   (EA)
PPPEC...... Philadelphia Electric Co., Philadelphia, PA [*Library symbol*]
            [*Library of Congress*]   (LCLS)
PPPEE...... Pulsed Pinch Plasma Electromagnetic Engine   (AAG)
PPPFM...... Free and Accepted Masons of Pennsylvania, Grand Lodge
            Library, Philadelphia, PA [*Library symbol*] [*Library of
            Congress*]   (LCLS)
PPPG .... People's Progressive Party of Guyana [*Political party*]
PPPH........ Pennsylvania Hospital, Philadelphia, PA [*Library symbol*]
            [*Library of Congress*]   (LCLS)
PPPHA...... Philadelphia Housing Association, Philadelphia, PA [*Library
            symbol*] [*Library of Congress*] [*Obsolete*]   (LCLS)
PPPHC...... Philadelphia Tuberculosis and Health Association,
            Philadelphia, PA [*Library symbol*] [*Library of Congress*]
            [*Obsolete*]   (LCLS)
PPPH-I...... Institute of the Pennsylvania Hospital, Philadelphia, PA
            [*Library symbol*] [*Library of Congress*]   (LCLS)
PPPI .... Insurance Society of Philadelphia, Philadelphia, PA [*Library
            symbol*] [*Library of Congress*] [*Obsolete*]   (LCLS)
PPPI .... Personnel Performance Problems Inventory [*Test*]
PPPI .... Plan Positional Plot Indicator
PPPI .... Precision Plan Position Indicator
PPPI .... Private Pay Phones, Inc. [*NASDAQ symbol*]   (NQ)
PPPI .... Projection Plan Position Indicator
PPPI .... Pulp, Paper, and Paperboard Institute USA [*Later, API*]
PPPL .... Philadelphia Board of Public Education, Pedagogical Library,
            Philadelphia, PA [*Library symbol*] [*Library of
            Congress*]   (LCLS)
PPPL .... Princeton Plasma Physics Laboratory [*Also known as PPL -
            Plasma Physics Laboratory*] [*Department of Energy*]
            [*Princeton, NJ*]
PPPL .... Printed Planning Parts List
PPPL .... Program Preferred Parts List
PPPlanP .... Planned Parenthood of Southeast Pennsylvania, Philadelphia,
            PA [*Library symbol*] [*Library of Congress*]   (LCLS)
PPPlay....... Plays and Players Club, Philadelphia, PA [*Library symbol*]
            [*Library of Congress*] [*Obsolete*]   (LCLS)
PPPM....... Philadelphia Museum of Art, Philadelphia, PA [*Library
            symbol*] [*Library of Congress*]   (LCLS)
PPP & M ... Preservation, Packaging, Packing, and Marking
PPPMD..... Pishchevaya Promyshlennost. Seriya 12. Spirtavya i Likero-
            Vodochnaya Promyshlennost [*A publication*]
PPPM-I .... Philadelphia Museum of Art, College of Art, Philadelphia, PA
            [*Library symbol*] [*Library of Congress*] [*Obsolete*]   (LCLS)
PPPP .... Past Performance and Present Posture   (AAG)
PPPP .... People's Peace and Prosperity Party [*Defunct*]   (EA)
PPPP .... Proposed Partial Package Program   (MUGU)
PPPPI....... Photographic Projection Plan Position Indicator   (DEN)

PPPR .... Philadelphia Transportation Co., Philadelphia, PA [*Library
            symbol*] [*Library of Congress*] [*Obsolete*]   (LCLS)
PPPRC ...... Poor Richard Club, Philadelphia, PA [*Library symbol*] [*Library
            of Congress*] [*Obsolete*]   (LCLS)
PPPres....... Presbyterian University of Pennsylvania, Scheie Eye Institute
            Library, Philadelphia, PA [*Library symbol*] [*Library of
            Congress*]   (LCLS)
PPPRF...... Pan Pacific Public Relations Federation [*Thailand*]
PPPRF...... PanPacific Public Relations Federation   (EAIO)
PPPrHi ..... Presbyterian Historical Society, Philadelphia, PA [*Library
            symbol*] [*Library of Congress*]   (LCLS)
PPPrI........ Printing Institute, Philadelphia, PA [*Library symbol*] [*Library
            of Congress*]   (LCLS)
PPProM..... Provident Mutual Life Insurance Co., Philadelphia, PA [*Library
            symbol*] [*Library of Congress*] [*Obsolete*]   (LCLS)
PPPS........ People's Press Printing Society [*British*]
PPPSB....... Philadelphia College of the Bible, Philadelphia, PA [*Library
            symbol*] [*Library of Congress*]   (LCLS)
PPPTe........ Philadelphia College of Textiles and Science, Philadelphia, PA
            [*Library symbol*] [*Library of Congress*]   (LCLS)
PPPYBC.... Physiological Plant Pathology [*A publication*]
PPQ .... Abandoned Police Post [*Board on Geographic Names*]
PPQ .... Parts per Quadrillion
PPQ .... Pittsfield, IL [*Location identifier*] [*FAA*]   (FAAL)
PPQ .... Planning Purpose Quote
PPQ .... Plant Protection and Quarantine Programs [*Department of
            Agriculture*]   (IMH)
PPQ .... Polyphenylquinoxaline [*Resin*]
PPQA....... Pageable Partition Queue Area [*Data processing*]
PPQT........ Preproduction Qualification Test [*Army*]
P & P Qtly ... Pulp and Paper Quarterly Statistics [*A publication*]
PPQUE8.... Plant Protection Quarterly [*A publication*]
PPr............ Paedagogische Provinz [*A publication*]
PPR........... Paid Pensioner Recruiter [*British military*]   (DMA)
PPR........... Palomino Pony Registry
PPR........... Paper
PPR........... Partido Proletariano Revolucionario [*Proletarian
            Revolutionary Party*] [*Portugal*] [*Political party*]   (PPW)
PPR........... Payload Preparation Room [*VAFB*] [*NASA*]   (MCD)
PPR........... Peak Production Rate
PPR........... Periodic Personnel Report
PPR........... Periodicals Publishing Record [*Alberta Public Affairs Bureau*]
            [*Canada*] [*Information service or system*]   (CRD)
PPR........... Permanent Pay Record [*Military*]
PPR........... Peste des Petits Ruminants [*Rinderpest-like disease*]
            [*Veterinary medicine*]   ᛫
PPR........... Philosophy and Phenomenological Research [*A publication*]
PPR........... Photo-Plastic-Recording
PPR........... Photographic Press Review [*A publication*] [*British*]
PPR........... Pilot, Pressure Regulator   (MCD)
P Pr .... Pionerskaja Pravda [*A publication*]
PPR........... Polish People's Republic
PPR........... Politieke Partij Radikalen [*Radical Political Party*]
            [*Netherlands*] [*Political party*]   (PPE)
PPR........... Polska Partia Robotnicza [*Polish Workers' Party*] [*Political
            party*]
PPR........... Portable Propagation Recorder [*Bell System*]
PPR........... Potential Problem Report [*Navy*]   (CAAL)
PPR........... Present Participle [*Grammar*]
PPR........... Price. Procedural Regulation [*United States*] [*A
            publication*]   (DLA)
PPR........... Price's Precipitation Reaction [*Medicine*]
PPR........... Principal Private Residence [*Income tax*] [*British*]
PPR........... Principal Probate Registry   (DLA)
PPR........... Printed Paper Rate [*British*]   (ILCA)
PPR........... Prior Permission Required   (FAAC)
PPR........... Production Parts Release   (KSC)
PPR........... Production Progress Report   (MCD)
PPR........... Program Progress Review
PPR........... Program Proposal Request
PPR........... Project Progress Report   (OICC)
PPR........... Proper [*Heraldry*]
PPR........... Proprietary Procurement Request   (NG)
PPR........... Provisioning Preparedness Review [*Navy*]   (CAAL)
P & PR ...... Psychoanalysis and the Psychoanalytic Review [*A publication*]
PPR........... Public Productivity Review [*A publication*]
PPR........... Purchase Parts Request   (KSC)
PPRA....... Past President of the Royal Academy [*British*]   (EY)
PPRA....... Preliminary Personnel Requirements Analysis [*Navy*]
PPRAA ..... Polski Przeglad Radiologiczny [*A publication*]
PPRBD ..... Paperboard [*Freight*]
PPRC........ Personnel Program Review Committee [*Military*]
PPRC........ Prepositioned Receipt Card   (AABC)
PPRCl........ Rittenhouse Club, Philadelphia, PA [*Library symbol*] [*Library
            of Congress*] [*Obsolete*]   (LCLS)
PPRD....... Pontypool Road [*Welsh depot code*]
PPRDS ...... Products and Process Research and Development
            Support   (DCTA)
PPREC ...... Pulp and Paper Research and Education Center [*Auburn
            University*] [*Research center*]   (RCD)
P Prehist S ... Proceedings. Prehistoric Society [*A publication*]

PPREPT.... Periodic Personnel Report [*Military*] (AABC)
PPRETS.... Reformed Episcopal Seminary, Philadelphia, PA [*Library symbol*] [*Library of Congress*] [*Obsolete*] (LCLS)
PPRF........ Paramedian Pontine Reticular Formation [*Neuroanatomy*]
PPRF........ Pulse Pair Repetition Frequency (MCD)
PPRF........ Rosenbach Foundation, Philadelphia, PA [*Library symbol*] [*Library of Congress*] (LCLS)
PPRFA...... Poliplasti e Plastici Rinforzati [*A publication*]
PPRG........ Precambrian Paleobiology Research Group
PPRGF...... Richard Gimbel Foundation for Literary Research, Philadelphia, PA [*Library symbol*] [*Library of Congress*] [*Obsolete*] (LCLS)
PPRI........ PACOM [*Pacific Command*] Priority Number (CINC)
PPRI........ Poloron Products, Inc. [*NASDAQ symbol*] (NQ)
PPRIBA.... Past President of the Royal Institute of British Architects (EY)
PPRibP...... Phosphoribose Diphosphate [*Biochemistry*]
PPRIC....... Pulp and Paper Research Institute of Canada
PPRL........ Poisonous Plant Research Laboratory [*Agricultural Research Service*] [*Research center*] (RCD)
PPRM........ Population Protection and Resources Management [*Military*] [*British*]
PPRM........ Pure Premium Rating Method [*Insurance*]
PPRN........ Preliminary Publication Revision Notice
PPRN........ Purchased Parts Requirement Notice (KSC)
PPRNCM ... Professional Performance of the Royal Northern College of Music [*British*] (DBQ)
PPRNS...... Pulse-Phased Radio Navigation System
PPRO......... Pattern Processing Technologies, Inc. [*NASDAQ symbol*] (NQ)
PPRO......... Per Procuration [*Business term*]
P Proc Hampshire Field Club ... Papers and Proceedings. Hampshire Field Club and Archaeological Society [*A publication*]
PProv .... Padova e la Sua Provincia [*A publication*]
PPRPA ...... Produits et Problemes Pharmaceutiques [*A publication*]
PPRPF...... Regional Planning Federation, Philadelphia, PA [*Library symbol*] [*Library of Congress*] [*Obsolete*] (LCLS)
PPRRD3.... Peptide and Protein Reviews [*A publication*]
PPRS .... Perceptions of Parental Role Scales
PPRS .... Pharmaceutical Price Regulation Scheme [*British*]
PPRS .... Promotions and Placements Referral System (MCD)
PPrStBrt.... Perspectives in Probability and Statistics: in Honor of M. S. Bartlett [*A publication*]
PPRV .... Peste des Petits Ruminants Virus [*Rinderpest-like disease*] [*Veterinary medicine*]
PPRWP ..... Poor Precordial R-Wave Progression [*Cardiology*]
PPS .... Paco Pharmaceutical Services, Inc. [*NYSE symbol*] (SPSG)
PPS .... Page Printing System [*Honeywell, Inc.*] [*Data processing*]
PPS .... Paper Publications Society [*Amsterdam, Netherlands*] (EA)
PP & S .... Papers on Poetics and Semiotics [*A publication*]
PPS .... Parallel Processing System [*Data processing*] (MDG)
PPS .... Parameter Processing System (CAAL)
PPS .... Parliamentary Private Secretary [*British*]
PPS .... Parti Populaire Senegalais [*Senegalese People's Party*] [*Political party*] (PPW)
PPS .... Parti Populaire Syrien [*Syrian People's Party*] [*Political party*] (BJA)
PPS .... Parti du Progres et du Socialisme [*Party of Progress and Socialism*] [*Morocco*] [*Political party*] (PPW)
PPS .... Parti Progressiste Soudanais [*Sudanese Progressive Party*] [*Political party*]
PPS .... Partia e Punes e Shqiperise [*Party of Labor of Albania - PLA*] [*Political party*] (PPW)
PPS .... Partial Pressure Sensor
PPS .... Partido Popular Salvadoreno [*Salvadoran Popular Party*] [*Political party*] (PPW)
PPS .... Partido Popular Socialista [*Popular Socialist Party*] [*Mexico*] [*Political party*]
PPS .... Partido Popular Socialista [*Popular Socialist Party*] [*Argentina*] [*Political party*] (PPW)
PPS .... Partito Populare Somalo [*Somali People's Party*]
PPS .... Parts Provisioning System (KSC)
PPS .... Patchboard Programming System
PPS .... Payload Power Switch
PPS .... Pension and Profit-Sharing Tax Journal [*A publication*]
PPS .... Peoples Oil Ltd. [*Vancouver Stock Exchange symbol*]
PPS .... Personal Plane Service [*Aircraft restoration firm*] [*British*]
PPS .... Personal Preference Scale [*Psychology*]
PPS .... Personal Printing System [*Data processing*]
PPS .... Personal Protection Squad [*of the London Metropolitan Police*]
PPS .... Personnel/Payroll System
PPS .... Personnel Psychology [*A publication*]
PPS .... Petroleum Press Service
PPS .... Petroleum Production Survey [*Bureau of Mines*]
PPS .... Phantom Phanatics Society (EA)
PPS .... Phosphorous Propellant System (KSC)
PPS .... Photophoretic Spectroscopy
PPS .... Photopolarimeter Spectrometer
PPS .... Photovoltaic Power Supply
PPS .... Piece Part Specification (MCD)
PPS .... Pierpont [*South Carolina*] [*Seismograph station code, US Geological Survey*] (SEIS)

PPS .... Pitt Press Series [*A publication*]
PPS .... Plant Parasitic Systems
PPS .... Plant Protection System [*Nuclear energy*] (NRCH)
PPS .... Plasma Power Supply
PPS .... Plutonium Product Storage [*Nuclear energy*] (NRCH)
PPS .... Pneumatic Power Subsystem (NASA)
PPS .... Policy Processing Sheet [*Insurance*]
PPS .... Polonus Philatelic Society (EA)
PPS .... Polska Partia Socjalistyczna [*Polish Socialist Party*]
PPS .... Poly(para-phenylene Sulfide) [*Organic chemistry*]
PPS .... Post-Polio Sequelae [*Medicine*]
PPS .... Post-Postscriptum [*Further Postscript*] [*Latin*]
PPS .... Post Production Service (AAG)
PPS .... Post Production Support (MCD)
PPS .... Postpartum Sterilization [*Medicine*]
PPS .... Postperfusion Syndrome [*Medicine*]
PPS .... Pounds per Second (AAG)
PPS .... Precise Positioning Service [*Military*]
PPS .... Precision Power Supply
PPS .... Prepositioned Stock (NG)
PPS .... Prescribed Payments System (ADA)
PPS .... Primary Paraffin Sulfonate [*Organic chemistry*]
PPS .... Primary Power Standard
PPS .... Primary Power System [*Nuclear energy*] (NRCH)
PPS .... Primary Pressure Standard
PPS .... Primary Propulsion System [*Spacecraft*]
PPS .... Principal Private Secretary [*British*]
PPS .... Printer/Plotter System (MCD)
PPS .... Prior Preferred Stock
PPS .... Private Practice Section [*American Physical Therapy Association*] (EA)
PPS .... Probability Proportional to Size [*Statistics*]
PPS .... Proceedings. Prehistoric Society [*A publication*]
PPS .... Procurement Planning Schedule [*DoD*]
PPS .... Program Performance Specification (CAAL)
PPS .... Program Planning Summary (OICC)
PPS .... Program Planning System [*DoD*]
PPS .... Program Policy Staff [*UN Food and Agriculture Organization*]
PPS .... Programmable Patch System
PPS .... Programmable Power Supply
PPS .... Programmed Processor System
PPS .... Programming Program Strela [*Data processing*]
PPS .... Progressive Pneumonia of Sheep
PPS .... Project for Public Spaces (EA)
PPS .... Propose (FAAC)
PPS .... Prospective Payment System [*For hospital care*]
PPS .... Provisioning Performance Schedule (AFM)
PPS .... Provisioning Policy Statement (MCD)
PPS .... Prudential Property Services [*Prudential Group*] [*British*]
PPS .... Public and Private [*Nongovernment*] Schools [*Public-performance tariff class*] [*British*]
PPS .... Publications. Philological Society [*A publication*]
PPS .... Puerto Princesa [*Philippines*] [*Airport symbol*] (OAG)
PPS .... Pulses per Second [*Data transmission*]
PPSA .... Pan-Pacific Surgical Association (EA)
PPSA .... Prospect Park Savings & Loan Association [*NASDAQ symbol*] (NQ)
PPSAS...... Program Planning and Status Assessment System [*Nuclear energy*] (NRCH)
PPSB .... Prothrombin, Proconvertin, Stuart Factor, Antihemophilic B Factor [*Blood coagulation factors*] [*Hematology*]
PPSC .... Petroleum Products Supply Corporation [*Burma*] (DS)
PPSC .... Physical Profile Serial Code [*Military*]
PPSC .... Privacy Protection Study Commission [*Government commission*]
PPSCI....... Seamen's Church Institute, Philadelphia, PA [*Library symbol*] [*Library of Congress*] [*Obsolete*] (LCLS)
PPSD .... Polska Partia Socialno-Demokratyczna [*Polish Social-Democrat Party*] [*Political party*]
PPSD .... Proposed
PPSE .... Petroleum Economist [*A publication*]
PPSE .... Purpose
PPSEAWA ... Pan-Pacific and South-East Asia Women's Association [*Tokyo, Japan*] (EAIO)
PPSEAWA-USA ... Pan Pacific and Southeast Asia Women's Association of the USA (EA)
PPSED3 .... Annual Research Reviews. Physiological and Pathological Aspects of Prolactin Secretion [*A publication*]
PPSEE4 .... Postgraduate Paediatrics Series [*A publication*]
PPSEI....... Progres Politique, Social, et Economique de l'Itasy [*Political, Social, and Economic Progress of the Itasy*]
PPSF......... Palestinian Popular Struggle Front [*Political party*] (BJA)
PPS-FR...... Polska Partia Socjalistyczna - Frakcja Rewolucyjna [*Polish Socialist Party - Revolutionary Faction*] [*Political party*] (PPE)
PPSG .... Piston and Pin Standardization Group [*Later, NEPMA*] (EA)
PPSG .... Spring Garden College, Philadelphia, PA [*Library symbol*] [*Library of Congress*] (LCLS)
PPSh......... Partia e Punes e Shqiperise [*Labor Party of Albania*] [*Formerly, PKSh*] [*Political party*] (PPE)
PPSH......... Pseudovaginal Perineoscrotal Hypospadias [*Medicine*]

PPSIA........ "Personal Property Shipping Information" [*Pamphlet*] Is Applicable [*Military*] (AABC)
PPSJ......... Pressure Plane Swivel Joint
PPSJ......... Saint Joseph's College, Philadelphia, PA [*Library symbol*] [*Library of Congress*] (LCLS)
PPSJ-AF ... Saint Joseph's College, Academy of Food Marketing, Philadelphia, PA [*Library symbol*] [*Library of Congress*] (LCLS)
PPSKED.... Provisioning Performance Schedule (MCD)
PPSKF...... SmithKline Corp., Philadelphia, PA [*Library symbol*] [*Library of Congress*] (LCLS)
PPSL......... Program Parts Selection List
PPSL......... Provisioning Parts Selection List (MCD)
PPSMEC... Procurement, Precedence of Supplies, Material and Equipment Committee [*Joint Communications Board*]
PPSN........ Present Position [*Aviation*] (FAAC)
PPSN........ Public Packet Switched Network [*Telecommunications*]
PPSN........ Purchased Part Shortage Notice
PPSO........ Personal Property Shipping Office [*Military*]
PPSOPR.... Sun Oil Co., General Office Library, Philadelphia, PA [*Library symbol*] [*Library of Congress*] [*Obsolete*] (LCLS)
PPSP......... Page Printer Spooling System [*Data processing*]
PPSP......... Ponderosa Pine or Sugar Pine [*Lumber*]
PPSPS ...... Plutonium Product Shipping Preparation Station [*Nuclear energy*] (NRCH)
PPSR .... Periodic Personnel Strength Report [*Army*] (AABC)
PPSS......... Foundation for the President's Private Sector Survey on Cost Control (EA)
PPSSA...... Proceedings. Nuclear Physics and Solid State Physics Symposium [*A publication*]
PPSSCC .... Foundation for the President's Private Sector Survey on Cost Control (EA)
PPStarr...... Starr Center Association, Philadelphia, PA [*Library symbol*] [*Library of Congress*] [*Obsolete*] (LCLS)
PPStCh..... Saint Charles Borromeo Seminary, Philadelphia, PA [*Library symbol*] [*Library of Congress*] (LCLS)
PPSteph..... William B. Stephens Memorial Library, Philadelphia, PA [*Library symbol*] [*Library of Congress*] [*Obsolete*] (LCLS)
PPSV .... Plutonium Product Storage Vault [*Nuclear energy*] (NRCH)
PPS-WRN ... Polska Partia Socjalistyczna - Wolnosc, Rownosc, Niepodleglosc [*Polish Socialist Party - Freedom, Equality, Independence*] [*Political party*] (PPE)
PPSYA ...... Personnel Psychology [*A publication*]
PPT........... Pamatai [*French Polynesia*] [*Geomagnetic observatory code*]
PPT........... Papeete [*Society Islands*] [*Seismograph station code, US Geological Survey*] (SEIS)
PPT........... Papeete [*French Polynesia*] [*Airport symbol*] (OAG)
PPT........... Parti Progressiste Tchadien [*Progressive Party of Chad*] [*Political party*]
PPT........... Partial Prothrombin Time [*Hematology*]
PPT........... Parts per Trillion
p-p-t .... Pay-per-Transaction [*Agreement between video cassette rental stores and owners of film rights*]
PPT........... Pedunculopontine Tegmentum [*Neurology*]
PPT........... Period Pulse Train
PPT........... Periodic Programs Termination [*Data processing*]
PPT........... Peripheral Performance Test (CAAL)
PPT........... Permanent Part-Time (ADA)
PPT........... Pine Point Mines Ltd. [*Toronto Stock Exchange symbol*] [*Vancouver Stock Exchange symbol*]
PPT........... Pitch Precession Torquer
PPT........... Polypurine Tract [*Genetics*]
PPT........... Pooh Property Trust [*A.A. Milne estate*] [*British*]
PPT........... Poppet [*Engineering*]
PPT........... Post Production Test
PPT........... Practical Policy Test [*Psychology*]
PPT........... Praecipitatus [*Precipitated*] [*Pharmacy*]
PPT........... Praeparata [*Prepared*] [*Pharmacy*] (ROG)
PPT........... Precipitate (MSA)
PPT........... Preproduction Test [*Army*]
PPT........... Preprotachykinin [*Biochemistry*]
PPT........... Private Purchasing Tariff [*British*]
PPT........... Process Page Table [*Telecommunications*] (TEL)
PPT........... Product Positioning Time (AFM)
PPT........... Production Prototype
PPT........... Project Planning Technique (MCD)
PPT........... Prompt (ROG)
PPT........... Propyl(thio)uracil [*Biochemistry*]
PPT........... Public and Private Transport
PPT........... Pulse Plasma Thruster
PPT........... Punched Paper Tape [*Data processing*]
PPT........... Putnam Premier Income Trust [*NYSE symbol*] (SPSG)
PPT........... Temple University, Philadelphia, PA [*Library symbol*] [*Library of Congress*] (LCLS)
PPT........... Theosophical Society, Philadelphia, PA [*Library symbol*] [*Library of Congress*] [*Obsolete*] (LCLS)
PPTA J ..... PPTA [*Post-Primary Teachers Association*] Journal [*A publication*]
PPTB .... Pin-Pack Test Board
PPTBA ...... Pattern and Plastic Tool Builders Association (EA)
PPTC......... People-to-People Tennis Committee (EA)

PPTC .... Purchased Part Tab Card
PPTD........ Precipitated
PPT-D....... Temple University, Dental-Pharmacy School, Philadelphia, PA [*Library symbol*] [*Library of Congress*] (LCLS)
PPTEC ...... Polymer-Plastics Technology and Engineering [*A publication*]
PPTF .... Public Policy Task Force [*Defunct*] (EA)
pPTH........ Porcine Parathyroid Hormone [*Endocrinology*]
PPTI .... Passport Travel, Incorporated [*NASDAQ symbol*] (NQ)
PPT-ISA.... Picture Personality Test for Indian South Africans
PPTJ........ Theodore F. Jenkins Memorial Law Library, Philadelphia, PA [*Library symbol*] [*Library of Congress*] (LCLS)
PPTL........ Postpartum Tubal Ligation [*Medicine*]
PPTL........ Pulp and Paper Traffic League [*Defunct*] (EA)
PPT-L....... Temple University, Law School, Philadelphia, PA [*Library symbol*] [*Library of Congress*] (LCLS)
PPT-M...... Temple University, Medical School, Philadelphia, PA [*Library symbol*] [*Library of Congress*] (LCLS)
PPTMR .... Personal Property Traffic Management Regulation
PPTN........ Precipitation
PPTO........ Personal Property Transportation Officer
PPTO......... Principal Professional and Technology Officer [*British*]
PPTR......... Punched Paper Tape Reader [*Data processing*]
PPTri .... Tri-Institutional Library, Philadelphia, PA [*Library symbol*] [*Library of Congress*] (LCLS)
PPTS .... Pianoforte Polishers' Trade Society [*A union*] [*British*]
PPT-T........ Temple University, School of Theology, Philadelphia, PA [*Library symbol*] [*Library of Congress*] (LCLS)
PPTV .... Parts per Trillion by Volume
PPTW .... Permanent Part-Time Work
PPTY .... Property (AFM)
PPU .... Cocoa, FL [*Location identifier*] [*FAA*] (FAAL)
PPU .... Papun [*Burma*] [*Airport symbol*] (OAG)
PPU .... Parti Populaire des Ueles [*Ueles People's Party*] [*Political party*]
PPU .... Payment for Public Use [*Canada*]
PPU .... Peace Pledge Union [*British*]
PPU .... Peninsula Petroleum Corp. [*Vancouver Stock Exchange symbol*]
PPU .... Peoria & Pekin Union Railway Co. [*AAR code*]
PPU .... Peripheral Processing Unit [*Data processing*]
PPU .... Platform Position Unit
PPU .... Preproduction Unit (MCD)
PPU .... Prime Power Unit
PPU .... Professional Psychics United (EA)
PPU .... Promontory Point [*Utah*] [*Seismograph station code, US Geological Survey*] [*Closed*] (SEIS)
PPUAES.... Publications. Princeton University Archaeological Expeditions to Syria in 1904-5 and 1909 [*A publication*]
PPUCA4.... Acta Scientiarum Naturalium. Academiae Scientiarum Bohemoslovacae [*Brno*] [*A publication*]
PPUG .... United Gas Improvement Corp., Philadelphia, PA [*Library symbol*] [*Library of Congress*] [*Obsolete*] (LCLS)
PPULC ...... Union Library Catalogue of Pennsylvania, Philadelphia, PA [*Library symbol*] [*Library of Congress*] (LCLS)
PPUMD3 .. Museum of Paleontology. Papers on Paleontology [*A publication*]
PPUNA ..... United States Naval Aircraft Factory, Philadelphia, PA [*Library symbol*] [*Library of Congress*] [*Obsolete*] (LCLS)
PPUnC...... University Club, Philadelphia, PA [*Library symbol*] [*Library of Congress*] [*Obsolete*] (LCLS)
PPUNH ..... United States Naval Home, Philadelphia, PA [*Library symbol*] [*Library of Congress*] [*Obsolete*] (LCLS)
PPUR-A .... Population Review [*A publication*]
PPUSDA ... United States Department of Agriculture, Agricultural Research Service, Eastern Utilization Research and Development Division, Philadelphia, PA [*Library symbol*] [*Library of Congress*] (LCLS)
PPV........... Pay-per-View [*Pay-television service*]
PPV........... People-Powered Vehicle [*Recreational vehicle powered by pedaling*]
PPV........... Plum Pox Virus [*Plant pathology*]
PPV........... Positive Predictive Value [*Experimentation*]
PPV........... Positive Pressure Ventilation [*Medicine*]
PPV........... Preprogrammed Vehicles (MCD)
P/PV .... Public/Private Ventures [*Philadelphia, PA*] [*Research center*] (RCD)
PPV........... United States Veterans Administration Hospital, Philadelphia, PA [*Library symbol*] [*Library of Congress*] (LCLS)
PPVT........ Peabody Picture Vocabulary Test [*Education*]
PPVT-R..... Peabody Picture Vocabulary Test - Revised [*Education*]
PP-W........ Free Library of Philadelphia, H. Josephine Widener Memorial Branch, Philadelphia, PA [*Library symbol*] [*Library of Congress*] [*Obsolete*] (LCLS)
PPW........... PacifiCorp [*NYSE symbol*] (SPSG)
PPW........... Papa Westray [*Scotland*] [*Airport symbol*] (OAG)
PPW........... Parts per Weight
PPW........... Petitions for Patent Waiver
PPW........... Plane-Polarized Wave
PPW........... Ponderosa Pine Woodwork Association [*Absorbed by NWWDA*] (EA)
PPW........... Potato Processing Waste

PPW........... Prace Polonistyczne (Wroclaw) [*A publication*]
P & PW...... Publicity and Psychological Warfare
PPWA......... Ponderosa Pine Woodwork Association [*Absorbed by NWWDA*]
PPWa......... Wagner Free Institute of Science, Philadelphia, PA [*Library symbol*] [*Library of Congress*] (LCLS)
PPWC........ Pulp, Paper, and Woodworkers of Canada
PPWD........ S. S. White Co., Philadelphia, PA [*Library symbol*] [*Library of Congress*] [*Obsolete*] (LCLS)
PPWe......... Westminster Theological Seminary, Philadelphia, PA [*Library symbol*] [*Library of Congress*] (LCLS)
PPWF........ Pakistan Petroleum Workers' Federation
PPWI......... Wistar Institute of Anatomy and Biology, Philadelphia, PA [*Library symbol*] [*Library of Congress*] (LCLS)
PPWiH...... Wills Eye Hospital, Philadelphia, PA [*Library symbol*] [*Library of Congress*] (LCLS)
PPWM....... Medical College of Pennsylvania, Philadelphia, PA [*Library symbol*] [*Library of Congress*] (LCLS)
PPWMA.... Progress in Powder Metallurgy [*A publication*]
PPWP........ Planned Parenthood - World Population [*Later, PPFA*] (EA)
PPWR........ Prepositioned War Reserves [*Army*]
PPWRS..... Prepositioned War Reserve Stocks [*Army*]
PPX........... Packet Protocol Extension
PPX........... Port Moller, AK [*Location identifier*] [*FAA*] (FAAL)
PPX........... Private Packet Exchange
PPY........... Pages per Year [*Facetious criterion for determining insignificance of Supreme Court Justices*] [*Proposed by University of Chicago professor David P. Currie*]
PPY........... Prophesy Development [*Vancouver Stock Exchange symbol*]
PPYH........ Young Men's and Young Women's Hebrew Association, Philadelphia, PA [*Library symbol*] [*Library of Congress*] [*Obsolete*] (LCLS)
PPYSA...... Plant Physiology. Supplement [*A publication*]
PPYU........ Party of Popular Yemenite Unity [*Political party*] (PD)
PPZ........... Proton Polar Zone
PPZ........... Zoological Society of Philadelphia, PA [*Library symbol*] [*Library of Congress*] [*Obsolete*] (LCLS)
PPZI......... Przeglad Pismiennictwa Zagadnien Informacji [*A publication*]
PQ............. Pack Quickly [*Humorous interpretation for Parti Quebecois*] [*Canada*]
PQ............. Pakistan Quarterly [*A publication*]
PQ............. Panic in Quebec [*Humorous interpretation for Parti Quebecois*] [*Canada*]
PQ............. Parliamentary Question [*British*]
PQ............. Parti Quebecois [*Quebec separatist political party*]
P & Q........ Peace and Quiet
PQ............. Performer Quotient [*TV-performer rating*]
PQ............. Permeability Quotient
PQ............. Personality Quotient [*Psychology*]
PQ............. Philological Quarterly [*A publication*]
PQ............. Philosophical Quarterly [*A publication*]
PQ............. Physically Qualified
PQ............. Piano Quarterly [*A publication*]
PQ............. Planetary Quarantine [*NASA*]
PQ............. Plant Quarantine Division [*of ARS, Department of Agriculture*]
PQ............. Plasma Quad [*Instrumentation*]
PQ............. Plastoquinone [*Biochemistry*]
PQ............. Pollution Quotient
PQ............. Polyquinoxaline [*Organic chemistry*]
P-Q........... Porphyrin-Quinone [*Photochemistry*]
PQ............. PQ Corp. [*Formerly, Philadelphia Quartz Co.*]
PQ............. Premier Quartier [*First Quarter*] [*French*]
PQ............. Premium Quality (MUGU)
PQ............. Preparative Quencher [*Spectroscopy*]
PQ............. Previous Question [*Parliamentary law*]
P and Q...... Prime Quality [*Slang*]
pq............. Pro Querente [*For the Plaintiff*] [*Latin*] [*Legal term*] (DLA)
PQ............. Province Quebec [*Quebec*] [*Canadian province*] [*Postal code*]
PQ............. Psi Quotient [*Parapsychology*]
PQ............. Psychiatric Quarterly [*A publication*]
PQ............. Public Quarters
PQ............. Puerto Rico International Airlines, Inc. [*Prinair*] [*ICAO designator*] (OAG)
PQ............. United States Patent Quarterly [*A publication*] (DLA)
P's & Q's.... Of expression "Mind your P's and Q's." Exact origin unclear, but theories include: admonishment of pub-owners that British drinkers be aware of number of "Pints and Quarts" being marked on their accounts; warning to apprentice typesetters that "p" and "q" fonts be carefully restored to correct case, since each could so easily be mistaken for the other; cautioning of French dancing masters that pupils be aware of position of their "Pieds" [*feet*] and "Queues" [*wigs*] in executing the deep bow of a formal curtsey.
PQA.......... Parts Quality Assurance
PQA.......... Petroleum Quality Assurance
PQA.......... Plant Quality Assurance
PQA.......... Preliminary Quantitative Analysis
PQA.......... Procurement Quality Assurance [*Program*] [*DoD*]
PQA.......... Production Quality Assurance
PQA.......... Project Quality Assurance
PQA.......... Protected Queue Area [*Data processing*] (BUR)

PQAD........ Plant Quality Assurance Director [*Nuclear energy*] (NRCH)
PQAI......... Procurement Quality Assurance Instruction
PQAM....... Project Quality Assurance Manager [*Nuclear energy*] (NRCH)
PQAP........ Planned Quality Assurance Program [*Navy*]
PQAP........ Procurement Quality Assurance Program [*DoD*]
PQB.......... Quebecor, Inc. [*AMEX symbol*] (SPSG)
PQBOAK .. Pesquisas Botanica [*A publication*]
PQC.......... Paul Quinn College [*Texas*]
PQC.......... Paul Quinn College, Waco, TX [*OCLC symbol*] (OCLC)
PQC.......... Precision Quartz Crystal
PQC.......... Production Quality Control
PQCS........ Philippine Quarterly of Culture and Society [*A publication*]
PQCS........ Process Quality Control System
PQCSD6.... Commissione Internazionale per la Protezione delle Acque Italo-Svizzere. Rapporti [*A publication*]
PQD.......... Partido Quisqueyano Democrata [*Quisqueyan Democratic Party*] [*Dominican Republic*] [*Political party*] (PPW)
PQD.......... Percentage Quartile Deviation [*Statistics*]
PQD.......... Predicted Quarterly Demand
PQD.......... Pyroelectric Quad Detector
PQDMB .... Percentage Quartile Deviation Median Bias [*Statistics*]
PQE.......... Parents for Quality Education (EA)
PQE.......... Principal Quality Engineers [*British*] (RDA)
PQE.......... Project Quality Engineering
PQEP........ Product Quality Evaluation Plan [*Military*] (AABC)
PQGS........ Propellant Quantity Gauge [*or Gauging*] System [*Apollo*] [*NASA*]
PQI .... Presque Isle [*Maine*] [*Airport symbol*] (OAG)
PQI .... Presque Isle, ME [*Location identifier*] [*FAA*] (FAAL)
PQI .... Product Quality Improvement [*Program*] [*Chrysler Corp.*]
PQI .... Professional Qualification Index (AFM)
PQI .... Propellant Quantity Indicator (NASA)
PQL .... Prior Quarter Liability [*IRS*]
PQLI .... Physical Quality of Life Index [*Overseas Development Council*]
PQM.......... Pacific Quarterly (Moana): An International Review of Arts and Ideas [*A publication*]
PQM.......... Pilot Qualified in Model (NVT)
PQM.......... Post Quartermaster [*Marine Corps*]
PQM.......... Pulse Quaternary Modulation
PQMC....... Philadelphia Quartermaster Center [*Merged with Defense Clothing and Textile Supply Center*] [*Military*]
PQMD...... Philadelphia Quartermaster Depot [*Military*]
PQMD...... Propellant Quantity Measuring Device
PQMDO.... Proposed Quality Material Development Objective (NATG)
PQMR....... Preliminary Quantitative Material Requirements (MCD)
PQMS....... Process Quality Measurement System [*Chemical process engineering*]
PQN.......... Consolidated Petroquin [*Vancouver Stock Exchange symbol*]
PQN.......... Pahaquarry [*New Jersey*] [*Seismograph station code, US Geological Survey*] (SEIS)
PQN.......... Pipestone, MN [*Location identifier*] [*FAA*] (FAAL)
PQN.......... Principal Quantum Number [*Atomic physics*]
PQO.......... Phoenix, AZ [*Location identifier*] [*FAA*] (FAAL)
PQP .... Planetary Quarantine Plan [*NASA*]
PQP .... Prequalification Prototype (KSC)
PQQ.......... Port Macquarie [*Australia*] [*Airport symbol*] (OAG)
PQQ.......... Pyrroloquinoline Quinone [*Biochemistry*]
PQQPRI .... Provisional Qualitative and Quantitative Personnel Requirements Information [*Army*] (AABC)
PQR.......... Pantan Resources [*Vancouver Stock Exchange symbol*]
PQR.......... Performance Qualification Requirement
PQR.......... Personnel Qualification Roster [*Military*] (AABC)
PQR.......... Peruvian Quarterly Report [*A publication*]
PQR.......... Procedure Qualification Record [*Nuclear energy*] (NRCH)
PQRST...... Personal Questionnaire Rapid Scaling Technique [*Personality development test*] [*Psychology*]
PQRST...... Product-Quality-Routing-Service-Timing [*Industrial engineering*]
PQS.......... Palestine Exploration Fund. Quarterly Statement [*A publication*]
PQS.......... Personnel Qualification Standards [*Military*] (NVT)
PQS........... Pilot Station [*Alaska*] [*Airport symbol*] (OAG)
PQS.......... Production Quotation Support
PQS.......... Progressive Qualification Scheme [*British*]
PQS.......... Promotion Qualification Score [*Military*]
PQSF........ Preparative Quencher Stopped Flow [*Spectroscopy*]
PQT .... Parquet Resources, Inc. [*Toronto Stock Exchange symbol*]
PQT .... Polyquinazolotriazole [*Organic chemistry*]
PQT .... Preliminary Qualification Test (MCD)
PQT .... Production Qualification and Testing
PQT .... Professional Qualification Test [*of the National Security Agency*]
PQT .... Prototype Qualification Testing (RDA)
PQT-C ...... Prototype Qualification Test - Contractor (MCD)
PQT-G ...... Prototype Qualification Test - Government (MCD)
PQT-SE .... Prototype Qualification Test - Service Evaluation (MCD)
P Qu.......... Philippines Quarterly [*A publication*]
PQu........... Salisbury, MD [*Location identifier*] [*FAA*] (FAAL)
PQUE........ Print Queue Processor [*Data processing*]
PQUEA ..... Progress in Quantum Electronics [*A publication*]

PQW	Placita de Quo Warranto, Record Commission [*England*] [*A publication*] (DLA)
PQX	Physically Qualified Except
PQZ	Premium Quality Zinc
PR	Abbott Laboratories [*Research code symbol*]
PR	Aircrew Survival Equipmentman [*Navy rating*]
PR	Pacific Reporter [*A publication*] (DLA)
PR	Painter (ADA)
PR	Pair (KSC)
PR	Pakistan Railways (DCTA)
PR	Panama Red [*Variety of marijuana*]
PR	Panel Receptacle
PR	Pangenesis Related [*Protein chemistry*]
PR	Panthere Rose [*An association*] (EAIO)
PR	Paper Tape Reader
PR	Parachute Rigger [*Navy*] (KSC)
PR	Parallax and Refraction
PR	Parcel Receipt [*Shipping*]
PR	Parents Rights (EA)
PR	Paris Review [*A publication*]
PR	Parish Register
P & R	Parks and Recreation [*A publication*]
PR	Parliamentary Report [*British*]
PR	Parrott Rifle
PR	Parti Republicain [*Republican Party*] [*Martinique*] [*Political party*] (PPW)
PR	Parti Republicain [*Republican Party*] [*France*] [*Political party*] (PPW)
PR	Parti Republicain [*Republican Party*] [*New Caledonia*] [*Political party*] (FEA)
PR	Partial Remission [*Medicine*]
PR	Partial Response [*Oncology*]
PR	Partido Radical [*Radical Party*] [*Chile*] [*Political party*]
PR	Partido Radical [*Radical Party*] [*Spain*] [*Political party*] (PPE)
PR	Partido Reformista [*Reformist Party*] [*Dominican Republic*] [*Political party*] (PPW)
PR	Partido Revolucionario [*Revolutionary Party*] [*Guatemala*] [*Political party*] (PPW)
PR	Partisan Review [*A publication*]
PR	Partito Radicale [*Radical Party*] [*Founded, 1955*] [*Italy*] [*Political party*] (PPE)
PR	Party Raayat [*Leftist organization in Singapore*] (CINC)
PR	Passengers' Risk (ROG)
PR	Past in Review [*Later, PIR*] (EA)
PR	Pastor
PR	Patient Relations [*Medicine*]
PR	Patria Roja [*Red Fatherland*] [*Peru*] (PD)
PR	Patrol Vessel, River Gunboat [*Navy symbol*]
PR	Pattern Recognition (BUR)
PR	Payroll
PR	Peer Review
PR	Peking Review [*A publication*]
P & R	Pelvic and Rectal [*Medicine*]
PR	Peng-Robinson [*Equation of state*]
PR	Penicillium roqueforti [*Toxin*] [*Medicine*]
PR	Pennsylvania Reports (Penrose and Watts) [*A publication*] (DLA)
PR	Penny Resistance (EA)
PR	Per
PR	Per Price [*Business term*]
PR	Per Rectum [*Medicine*]
PR	Percent Recovery [*Plant pathology*]
PR	Percentage Rates
PR	Percentile Rank
PR	Performance Rating (OICC)
PR	Performance Ratio (AAG)
PR	Performance Report (AFM)
PR	Performance Requirement
P & R	Performance and Resources (NASA)
PR	Peripheral Resistance [*Medicine*]
PR	Perirenal [*Nephrology*]
PR	Permanens Rector [*Permanent Rector*]
PR	Permissive Reassignment [*Air Force*] (AFM)
PR	Pershing Rifles [*Honorary military organization*]
PR	Persistency Rater [*LIMRA*]
PR	Personality Record [*Psychological testing*]
PR	Personnel Resources (EA)
PR	Pesikta Rabbati (BJA)
PR	Petroleum Review [*A publication*]
PR	Pharmaceutical Record [*New York*] [*A publication*]
PR	Phenol Red
P & R	Philadelphia & Reading Railway
PR	Philadelphia Reports [*Pennsylvania*] [*A publication*] (DLA)
PR	Philanthropic Roundtable (EA)
PR	Philippine Airlines, Inc. [*PAL*] [*ICAO designator*] (FAAC)
PR	Philippine Island Reports [*A publication*] (DLA)
PR	Philosophical Review [*A publication*]
P & R	Philosophy and Rhetoric [*A publication*]
PR	Phosphate Rock [*Petrology*]
PR	Phosphorylase-Rupturing [*Biochemistry*]
PR	Photographic Reconnaissance [*Military*] (MCD)
PR	Photographic Recorder
PR	Photoreacting [*or Photoreactivation*] [*Biochemistry*]
PR	Photorecorder
PR	Photoresist
P/R	Photosynthesis/Respiration [*Biochemistry*]
PR	Physical Record [*Data processing*]
P & R	Picture and Resume [*Theatre slang*]
P & R	Pigott and Rodwell's Reports in Common Pleas [*1843-45*] [*A publication*] (DLA)
PR	Pilot Rating
PR	Pinch Runner [*Baseball*]
PR	Pineal Recess [*Neuroanatomy*]
PR	Pioneer [*Kumasi*] [*A publication*]
PR	Pipe Rail (AAG)
PR	Pitch Ratio
P/R	Pitch/Roll (MCD)
PR	Pittsburgh Reports [*1853-73*] [*Pennsylvania*] [*A publication*] (DLA)
PR	Pityriasis [*Dermatology*]
PR	Planetary RADAR [*Equipment box*]
PR	Planning Reference
P & R	Planning and Review (MCD)
PR	Plant Recovery [*Nuclear energy*] (NRCH)
PR	Plant Report
PR	Please Return
PR	Plotting and RADAR
PR	Ply Rating [*Tires*] (NATG)
PR	Pneumatic Retinopathy [*Ophthalmology*]
PR	Podravska Revija [*A publication*]
PR	Poetry Review [*A publication*]
PR	Policy Review (MCD)
PR	Polish Register [*Polish ship classification society*] (DS)
PR	Ponceau Red [*Biological stain*]
PR	Poor Rate [*British*] (ROG)
PR	Populus Romanus [*The Roman People*] [*Latin*]
PR	Position Record (NASA)
PR	Position Report [*Air Force*]
P & R	Post and Rail
PR	Post Request
PR	Post-Resuscitation
PR	Postal Regulations (DLA)
PR	Poste Recommandee [*Registered Post*]
PR	Posterior Ridge
PR	Pounder [*Gun*]
PR	Pour Remercier [*To Express Thanks*] [*French*]
PR	Power Range [*Nuclear energy*] (NRCH)
PR	Power Return
Pr	Practice Reports [*Various jurisdictions*] [*A publication*] (DLA)
Pr	Practitioner [*A publication*]
PR	Prairie (MCD)
Pr	Prandtl Number [*IUPAC*]
Pr	Praseodymium [*Chemical element*]
PR	Prayer
PR	Pre-Raphaelite
PR	Preacher
Pr	Preamble (ILCA)
Pr	Precancelled [*Philately*]
PR	Precedence Rating [*Military*] (AFIT)
Pr	Prednisone [*Also, P, PDN, Pred, Pro*] [*Antineoplastic drug*] [*Endocrinology*]
PR	Preferred [*Stock exchange term*] (SPSG)
PR	Prefix [*Indicating a private radiotelegram*] (BUR)
PR	Pregnancy Rate [*Medicine*]
Pr	Preis [*Price*] [*German*]
PR	Preliminary Report
PR	Preliminary Review [*Army*]
PR	Premature Release [*Telecommunications*] (TEL)
PR	Prepare Reply
PR	Preposition
PR	Presbyopia [*Ophthalmology*]
PR	Presbyterian (ROG)
PR	Present
Pr	Presentation [*Gynecology*]
PR	Presidency (ROG)
Pr	Press [*Christchurch, New Zealand*] [*A publication*]
PR	Press Release
PR	Press Releases [*United Kingdom*] [*A publication*]
PR	Pressure
PR	Pressure Ratio
PR	Pressure Recorder (NRCH)
PR	Pressure Regulator (KSC)
Pr	Prevention [*A publication*]
PR	Price [*Online database field identifier*]
PR	Price Communications Corp. [*AMEX symbol*] (SPSG)
PR	Price Received
PR	Price Redetermination [*Economics*]
PR	Price Reduced [*of a book*]
Pr	Price's English Exchequer Reports [*1814-24*] [*A publication*] (DLA)
PR	Priest
PR	Primary (NASA)

PR	Primitive
PR	Prince
PR	Prince Regent (ROG)
PR	Princess Royal's [*Military unit*] [*British*]
Pr	Principal
PR	Principal Register [*Data processing*]
PR	Printed [*or Printer*]
PR	Printing Request (MCD)
PR	Prior
PR	Priority Regulation
PR	Priory
PR	Prism
pr	Prismatic Tank [*Liquid gas carriers*]
Pr	Pristane [*Organic chemistry*]
pr	Private (DLA)
PR	Private Road [*Maps and charts*] [*British*] (ROG)
PR	Prize Ring [*Boxing*]
PR	Pro Rata
PR	Probabilistic Risk Assessment [*Computer-based technique for accident prediction*]
Pr	Probable
PR	Probate Reports [*A publication*] (DLA)
Pr	Probe [*A publication*]
PR	Problem Report (MCD)
Pr	Problemata [*of Aristotle*] [*Classical studies*] (OCD)
Pr	Procarbazine [*Also, P, PC, PCB*] [*Antineoplastic drug*]
PR	Procedural Regulations [*Civil Aeronautics Board*]
PR	Procedures Review [*DoD*]
PR	Proceedings. American Society of University Composers [*A publication*]
PR	Process-Reactive [*Scale*] [*Psychometrics*]
PR	Proctologist
PR	Procurement Regulation [*Military*]
PR	Procurement Request [*or Requisition*]
PR	Producing Region [*Agriculture*]
PR	Production Rate
PR	Production Requirements [*Military*] (AFIT)
P/R	Productivity/Respiration [*Physiology*]
PR	Profile Reliability
P-R	Progesterone Receptor [*Endocrinology*]
P-as-R	Program as Recorded [*Radio*] (DEN)
PR	Program Register [*Data processing*] (BUR)
PR	Program Requirements (KSC)
PR	Progress Report
PR	Progressive Resistance
Pr	Prohemio [*A publication*]
PR	Project Release (EA)
PR	Project Report
PR	Prolactin [*Also, LTH, PRL*] [*Endocrinology*]
PR	Prolonged-Release [*Pharmacy*]
Pr	Prometheus [*A publication*]
PR	Pronominal [*Grammar*] (ROG)
PR	Pronoun
PR	Pronounced
PR	Proper
PR	Proportional Representation [*in legislatures, etc.*]
PR	Proposed Regulation
PR	Proposed Request
PR	Propulsion Range
Pr	Propyl [*Organic chemistry*]
pr	Prose
Pr	Prostor [*Moscow*] [*A publication*]
PR	Protease [*Chemistry*]
PR	Protective Reaction [*Bombing raid*] [*Vietnam*]
PR	Protectorate Regiment [*British military*] (DMA)
PR	Protestant (ADA)
PR	Prototype
PR	Proved
PR	Provencal [*Language, etc.*]
Pr	Proverbs [*Old Testament book*] (BJA)
Pr	Proximal
PR	Pseudorandom
PR	Pseudoresidual
PR	Psychedelic Review [*A publication*]
PR	Psychoanalytic Review [*A publication*]
PR	Psychological Review [*A publication*]
PR	Public Relations
PR	Public Responsibility
PR	Public Roads [*A publication*]
PR	Puerto Rican [*Derogatory term*]
PR	Puerto Rico [*ANSI two-letter standard code*] (CNC)
pr	Puerto Rico [*MARC country of publication code*] [*Library of Congress*] [*IYRU nationality code*] (LCCP)
PR	Puerto Rico [*Postal code*]
PR	Puerto Rico Supreme Court Reports [*A publication*] (DLA)
PR	Pulse Rate
PR	Pulse Ratio (IEEE)
PR	Pulse Regenerator
P & R	Pulse and Respiration [*Medicine*]
PR	Punctum Remotum [*Far Point*] [*Latin*]
PR	Punjab Record [*India*] [*A publication*] (DLA)

PR	Purchase Request
PR	Purple (AAG)
PR	Purplish Red
PR	Pyke's Reports [*Canada*] [*A publication*] (DLA)
pr	Pyrite [*CIPW classification*] [*Geology*]
PR	Pyrogallol Red [*Also, PGR*] [*An indicator*] [*Chemistry*]
PR	Pyrolytic Release
PR+	Reactor Pressure Plus (NRCH)
PR	Reading Public Library, Reading, PA [*Library symbol*] [*Library of Congress*] (LCLS)
PR	River Gunboat [*Navy symbol*]
PR	Upper Canada Practice Reports [*1850-1900*] [*Ontario*] [*A publication*] (DLA)
PR1	Parachute Rigger, First Class [*Navy*]
PR2	Parachute Rigger, Second Class [*Navy*]
PR3	Parachute Rigger, Third Class [*Navy*]
PR's	Partial Responders [*to medication*]
PR's	Planning References (AAG)
PRA	Albright College, Reading, PA [*Library symbol*] [*Library of Congress*] (LCLS)
Pra	Die Praxis des Bundesgerichts [*Basel, Switzerland*] [*A publication*]
PRA	Division of Policy Research and Analysis [*National Science Foundation*]
PRA	Paint Research Association [*British*]
PRA	Parabolic Reflector Antenna
PRA	Parana [*Argentina*] [*Airport symbol*] (OAG)
PRA	Parool (Amsterdam) [*A publication*]
PRA	Parti du Regroupement Africain [*African Regroupment Party*] [*Niger*] [*Political party*] (PD)
PRA	Parti du Regroupement Africain [*African Regroupment Party*] [*Banned, 1974*] [*Upper Volta*] [*Political party*]
PRA	Partido Revolucionario Autentico [*Authentic Revolutionary Party*] [*Bolivia*] [*Political party*] (PPW)
PRA	Pay Readjustment Act [*1942*]
PRA	Pay Record Access
PRA	Paymaster-Rear-Admiral [*Navy*] [*British*]
PRA	Payroll Auditor [*Insurance*]
PRA	Peak Recording Accelerograph [*Accelerometer*] (IEEE)
PRA	Pendulous Reference Axis [*Accelerometer*] (IEEE)
PRA	People's Revolutionary Army [*Grenada*]
PRA	Permanent Restricted Area [*USSR*] (NATG)
PRA	Personnel Research Activity [*Later, NPTRL*] [*Navy*]
PRA	Petrol Retailers' Association [*British*]
PRA	Phosphoribosylamine
PRA	Pilots Rights Association (EA)
PRA	Planetary Radio Astronomy
PRA	Planned Restricted Availability [*Military*] (NVT)
PRA	Plasma Renin Activity [*Hematology*]
PRA	Plutonium Recycle Acid [*Nuclear energy*] (NRCH)
PRA	Policy Research and Analysis
PRA	Popular Rotocraft Association (EA)
PRA	Praha [*Prague*] [*Czechoslovakia*] [*Seismograph station code, US Geological Survey*] (SEIS)
PRA	Prairiefire Rural Action (EA)
pra	Prakrit [*MARC language code*] [*Library of Congress*] (LCCP)
PRA	Precision Axis (KSC)
PRA	Premium Audit
PRA	Prerefund Audit [*IRS*]
PRA	President of the Royal Academy [*British*]
PRA	Primary Reviewing Authority
PrA	Primer Acto [*Madrid*] [*A publication*]
PRA	Print Alphanumerically [*Data processing*] (MDG)
PRA	Probabilistic Risk Assessment [*Computer-based technique for accident prediction*]
PRA	Probation and Rehabilitation of Airmen [*Air Force*] (AFM)
PRA	Production Reader Assembly (KSC)
PRA	Progesterone Receptor Assay [*Clinical chemistry*]
PRA	Program Reader Assembly [*Data processing*]
PRA	Projected Requisition Authority [*Army*] (AABC)
PRA	Proust Research Association (EA)
PRA	Psoriasis Research Association (EA)
PRA	Psychiatric Rehabilitation Association [*British*]
PRA	Psychological Research Associates
PRA	Public Resources Association [*Defunct*] (EA)
PRA	Public Roads Administration
PRA	Puerto Rico Area Office [*AEC*]
PRA	US 1869 Pictorial Research Associates (EA)
PRAA	Airman Apprentice, Parachute Rigger, Striker [*Navy rating*]
PRAB	Prab Robots, Inc. [*NASDAQ symbol*] (NQ)
Pra Bhar	Prabuddha Bharata [*Calcutta*] [*A publication*]
Prac	Practical (DLA)
PRAC	Practice (AABC)
PRAC	Pressure Ratio Acceleration Control [*Gas turbine engine*]
PRAC	Production Research Advisory Committee [*Australia*]
PRAC	Program Resource Advisory Committee [*TRADOC*] (MCD)
PRAC	Public Relations Advisory Committee
PRACA	Practitioner [*A publication*]
PRACA	Problem Reporting and Corrective Action (MCD)
PRACA	Puerto Rican Association for Community Affairs (EA)
Prac Acc.....	Practical Accountant [*A publication*]

Prac Accnt ... Practical Accountant [*A publication*]
Prac Act ..... Practice Act [*A publication*] (DLA)
Prac Anth... Practical Anthropology [*A publication*]
Prac Appr Pat TM and Copyright ... Practical Approach to Patents, Trademarks, and Copyrights [*A publication*]
Pra Cas ...... Prater's Cases on Conflict of Laws [*A publication*] (DLA)
Praca Zabezp Spolecz ... Praca i Zabezpieczenie Spoleczne [*A publication*]
Prace A ...... Prace Archaeologiczne [*A publication*]
Prace Brnenske Zakl Ceskoslov Akad Ved ... Prace Brnenske Zakladny Ceskoslovenske Akademie Ved [*A publication*]
Prace Inst Bad Lesn ... Prace Instytut Badawezy Lesnictwa [*A publication*]
Prace Inst Fiz ... Prace Instytutu Fizyki [*A publication*]
Prace Inst Maszyn Przeplywowych ... Prace Instytutu Maszyn Przeplywowych [*A publication*]
Prace Inst Tech Drewna ... Prace Instytut Technologii Drewna [*A publication*]
Prace Inst Technol Drewna ... Prace Instytut Technologii Drewna [*A publication*]
Prace Mat Lodz ... Prace i Materialy Muzeum Archeologicznego i Etnograficznego w Lodzi [*A publication*]
Prace Nauk Akad Ekon Poznan ... Prace Naukowe Akademii Ekonomicznej w Poznaniu [*A publication*]
Prace Nauk Akad Ekon Wroclaw ... Prace Naukowe Akademii Ekonomicznej we Wroclawiv [*A publication*]
Prace Nauk Inst Cybernet Techn Politech Wroclaw Ser Konfer ... Wroclaw. Politechnika. Instytut Cybernetyki Technicznej. Prace Naukowe. Seria Konferencje [*A publication*]
Prace Nauk Inst Cybernet Techn Politech Wroclaw Ser Monograf ... Wroclaw. Politechnika. Instytut Cybernetyki Technicznej. Prace Naukowe. Seria Monografie [*A publication*]
Prace Nauk Inst Cybernet Techn Wroclaw Ser Stud i Materialy ... Wroclaw. Politechnika. Instytut Cybernetyki Technicznej. Prace Naukowe. Seria Studia i Materialy [*A publication*]
Prace Nauk Inst Mat Politech Wroclaw Ser Konfer ... Wroclaw. Politechnika Wroclawska. Instytutu Matematyki. Prace Naukowe. Seria Konferencje [*A publication*]
Prace Nauk Inst Mat Politech Wroclaw Ser Monograf ... Prace Naukowe Instytutu Matematyki Politechniki Wroclawskiej. Seria Monografie [*A publication*]
Prace Nauk Inst Mat Politech Wroclaw Ser Stud i Materialy ... Politechniki Wroclawskiej. Instytutu Matematyki. Prace Naukowe. Seria Studia i Materialy [*A publication*]
Prace Nauk Inst Mat Politech Wroclaw Ser Stud Materialy ... Politechniki Wroclawskiej. Instytutu Matematyki. Prace Naukowe. Seria Studia i Materialy [*A publication*]
Prace Nauk Inst Ochr Rosl ... Prace Naukowe Instytutu Ochrony Roslin [*A publication*]
Prace Nauk Uniw Slask Katowic ... Prace Naukowe Uniwersytetu Slaskiego w Katowicach [*A publication*]
Prace Stud Vysokej Skoly Doprav Spojov Ziline Ser Mat-Fyz ... Prace a Studie Vysokej Skoly Dopravy a Spojov v Ziline. Seria Matematicko-Fyzikalna [*A publication*]
Prace Stud Vysokej Skoly Doprav Ziline Ser Mat-Fyz ... Prace a Studie Vysokej Skoly Dopravnej v Ziline. Seria Matematicko-Fyzikalna [*A publication*]
Prace Vyzkum Ust Lesn Hosp Mysl ... Prace Vyzkumneho Ustavu Lesneho Hospodarstvi a Myslivosti [*A publication*]
Prace Wroclaw Towarz Nauk Ser A ... Prace Wroclawskiego Towarzystwa Naukowego. Seria A [*A publication*]
Prace Zakr Nauk Roln Lesn (Poznan) ... Prace z Zakresu Nauk Rolniczych i Lesnych (Poznan) [*A publication*]
Prac F......... Practical Farmer [*A publication*]
Prac Forecast ... Practical Forecast for Home Economics [*A publication*]
Prac Home Econ ... Practical Home Economics [*A publication*]
PRACL...... Page-Replacement Algorithm and Control Logic [*Data processing*]
Prac Law.... Practical Lawyer [*A publication*]
Prac Lawyer ... Practical Lawyer [*A publication*]
Prac Lek.... Pracovni Lekarstvi [*A publication*]
PRACSATS ... Practical Satellites
PRACT...... Practical (ROG)
PRACT...... Practitioner
Pract Account ... Practical Accountant [*A publication*]
Pract Adm ... Practising Administrator [*A publication*] (APTA)
Pract Biotechnol ... Practical Biotechnology [*A publication*]
Pract Colloid Chem ... Practical Colloid Chemistry [*A publication*]
Pract Comput ... Practical Computing [*A publication*]
Pract Dig.... Practice Digest [*A publication*]
Pract Electron ... Practical Electronics [*A publication*]
Pract Electronics ... Practical Electronics [*A publication*]
Pract Energy ... Practical Energy [*A publication*]
Pract Eng (Chicago) ... Practical Engineer (Chicago) [*A publication*]
Pract Eng (London) ... Practical Engineering (London) [*A publication*]
Pract Gastroenterol ... Practical Gastroenterology [*A publication*]
Pract House ... Practical Householder [*England*] [*A publication*]
Practical Comput ... Practical Computing [*A publication*]
Practition ... Practitioner [*A publication*]
Pract Law.... Practical Lawyer [*A publication*] (DLA)
Pract M...... Practical Magazine [*A publication*]
Pract Med (Phila) ... Practice of Medicine (Philadelphia) [*A publication*]
Pract Metallogr Spec Issues ... Practical Metallography. Special Issues [*A publication*]

Pract Methods Electron Microsc ... Practical Methods in Electron Microscopy [*A publication*]
Pract Mot... Practical Motorist [*A publication*]
Pract Otol (Kyoto) ... Practica Otologica (Kyoto) [*A publication*]
Pract Otorhinolaryng ... Practica Oto-Rhinolaryngologica [*A publication*]
Pract Oto-Rhino-Laryngol ... Practica Oto-Rhino-Laryngologica [*A publication*]
Pract Pharm (Tokyo) ... Practical Pharmacy (Tokyo) [*A publication*]
Pract Plast ... Practical Plastics [*A publication*]
Pract Plast Aust NZ ... Practical Plastics in Australia and New Zealand [*A publication*]
Pract Power Farming ... Practical Power Farming [*A publication*]
Pract Reg ... Practical Register in the Common Pleas [*England*] [*A publication*] (DLA)
Pract Solar ... Practical Solar [*A publication*]
Pract Spectrosc ... Practical Spectroscopy [*A publication*]
Pract Spectrosc Ser ... Practical Spectroscopy Series [*A publication*]
Pract Surf Technol ... Practical Surface Technology [*Japan*] [*A publication*]
Pract Welder ... Practical Welder [*A publication*] (APTA)
Pract Wireless ... Practical Wireless [*A publication*]
Pract Woodworking ... Practical Woodworking [*England*] [*A publication*]
Prac Wel .... Practical Welder [*A publication*] (APTA)
PRAD .... Pitch Ratio Adjust Device (MCD)
PRADA...... Partido Revolucionario Dominicano Autentico [*Dominican Republic*] [*Political party*]
Pr Adm Dig ... Pritchard's Admiralty Digest [*3rd ed.*] [*1887*] [*A publication*] (DLA)
PRADOR .. PRF [*Pulse Repetition Frequency*] Ranging Doppler RADAR
pr Adr........ Per Adresse [*Care Of*] [*German*]
PRAED...... Practical Energy [*A publication*]
praef.......... Praefatio [*Latin*] (OCD)
PrAeg........ Probleme der Aegyptologie [*Leiden*] [*A publication*]
Praehist Z.. Praehistorische Zeitschrift [*A publication*]
Praem........ De Praemiis et Poenis [*of Philo*] (BJA)
Praep Evang ... Praeparatio Evangelica [*of Eusebius*] [*Classical studies*] (OCD)
Praepo........ Praepositus [*Deceased, 1509*] [*Authority cited in pre-1607 legal work*] (DSA)
Praep Pharmazie ... Praeparative Pharmazie [*A publication*]
PRAF........ Passenger-Reserved Air Freight
PRAG .... Pragma Bio-Tech, Inc. [*Bloomfield, NJ*] [*NASDAQ symbol*] (NQ)
PRAGA...... Probleme Agricole [*Romania*] [*A publication*]
Prager Med Wochenschr ... Prager Medizinische Wochenschrift [*A publication*]
Prag Micro ... Pragmatics Microficke [*A publication*]
PR Agric Exp Stn Bull ... Puerto Rico. Agricultural Experiment Station. Bulletin [*A publication*]
PR Agric Exp Stn Tech Pap ... Puerto Rico. Agricultural Experiment Station. Technical Paper [*A publication*]
Prague Bull Math Linguist ... Prague Bulletin of Mathematical Linguistics [*A publication*]
Prague St ... Studies in English by Members of the English Seminar of the Charles University, Prague [*A publication*]
Prague Stud Math Linguist ... Prague Studies in Mathematical Linguistics [*A publication*]
Pra H & W ... Prater on Husband and Wife [*2nd ed.*] [*1836*] [*A publication*] (DLA)
PRAI......... Phosphoribosyl Anthranilate Isomerase
Prairie Gard ... Prairie Garden [*A publication*]
Prairie Inst Environ Health PIEH ... Prairie Institute of Environmental Health. Report PIEH [*A publication*]
Prairie Nat ... Prairie Naturalist [*A publication*]
Prairie Sch ... Prairie Schooner [*A publication*]
Prairie Schoon ... Prairie Schooner [*A publication*]
Prairie Sch R ... Prairie School Review [*A publication*]
PRAIS .... Passive Ranging Interferometer Sensor
PRAIS .... Pesticide Residue Analysis Information Service [*British*]
PRAJ .... Peace Research Abstracts Journal [*A publication*]
Prakla-Seismo· Rep ... Prakla-Seismos Report [*West Germany*] [*A publication*]
Prakruti Utkal Univ J Sci ... Prakruti Utkal University Journal of Science [*A publication*]
Prakt Akad Athenon ... Praktika tes Akademias Athenon [*A publication*]
Prakt Ak Ath ... Praktika tes Akademias Athenon [*A publication*]
Prakt Anaesth ... Praktische Anaesthesie, Wiederbelebung, und Intensivtherapie [*A publication*]
Prakt Arzt ... Praktische Arzt [*A publication*]
Prakt Bl Pflanzenbau Pflanzenschutz ... Praktische Blaetter fuer Pflanzenbau und Pflanzenschutz [*A publication*]
Prakt Chem ... Praktische Chemie [*A publication*]
Prakt Desinfekt ... Praktische Desinfektor [*A publication*]
Prakt Energiek ... Praktische Energiekunde [*A publication*]
Prakt Hell Hydrobiol Inst ... Praktika. Hellenic Hydrobiological Institute [*A publication*]
Praktika..... Praktika tes en Athenais Arkhaiologikes Hetairias [*A publication*]
Prakt Landtech ... Praktische Landtechnik [*A publication*]
Prakt Lek... Prakticky Lekar [*A publication*]
Prakt Metallogr ... Praktische Metallographie [*A publication*]

Prakt Metallogr Sonderb ... Praktische Metallographie. Sonderbaende [*A publication*]
Prakt Schadlingsbekampf ... Praktische Schadlingsbekampfer [*A publication*]
Prakt Sudebnopsikhiatr Ekspert ... Praktika Sudebnopsikhiatricheskoi Ekspertizy [*A publication*]
Prakt Tier .. Praktische Tieraerzt [*A publication*]
Prakt Tierarzt ... Praktische Tieraerzt [*German Federal Republic*] [*A publication*]
Prakt Tuberk Bl ... Praktische Tuberkulose Blaetter [*A publication*]
Prakt Vet (Moskva) ... Prakticheskaia Veterinariia (Moskva) [*A publication*]
Prakt Wegw Bienenz ... Praktischer Wegweiser fuer Bienenzuechter [*A publication*]
Prakt Yad Fiz ... Praktikum po Yadernoi Fizike [*A publication*]
PRAM .... Parallel Random Access Machine [*Data processing*]
PRAM .... Perambulator [*British*]
PRAM .... Poseidon Random Access Memory [*Missiles*]
PRAM .... Product Reliability and Maintainability
PRAM .... Productivity, Reliability, Availability, and Maintainability Office [*Air Force*]
PRAM .... Program Requirements Analysis Method
PRAM .... Propelled Ascent Mine
PRAMC ..... Pramana [*A publication*]
PRAN .... Airman, Parachute Rigger, Striker [*Navy*]
PRAN .... Proust Research Association. Newsletter [*A publication*]
PRAND ..... Prandium [*Dinner*] [*Pharmacy*]
PRANDM ... Progress in Anesthesiology [*A publication*]
PRANG ..... Puerto Rico Air National Guard
PRAODP ... Agricultural Research Organization. Preliminary Report (Bet-Dagan) [*A publication*]
PRAP .... Patient Resident Assessment Profile [*Geriatrics*]
PRAP .... Provincial/Regional Library Association Presidents [*Canada*]
PRAP .... Provisions of Following Reference Apply [*Army*] (AABC)
PraPol .... Prace Polonistyczne [*Warsaw*] [*A publication*]
PRAR .... Partido Revolucionario Autentico Rios [*Bolivia*] [*Political party*] (PPW)
PRARE ...... Precise Range and Range-Rate Experiment
PRARS ...... Pitch, Roll, Azimuth Reference System (NG)
PRAS .... Pension and Retirement Annuity System
Pra S .... Prairie Schooner [*A publication*]
PRAS .... Prereduced, Anaerobically Sterilized [*Microbiology*]
PRASD ...... Personnel Research Activity, San Diego [*California*] [*Navy*]
PRASD3 .... Alabama. Agricultural Experiment Station. Progress Report Series (Auburn University) [*A publication*]
Prat .... [*Pardulphus*] Pratteius [*Deceased, 1535*] [*Authority cited in pre-1607 legal work*] (DSA)
PRAT .... Predicted Range Against Target [*Military*] (NVT)
PRAT .... Pressure-Retaining Amphipod Trap [*Deep-sea biology*]
PRAT .... Production Reliability Acceptance Test
P RAT AET ... Pro Ratione Aetatis [*According to Age*] [*Pharmacy*] (ROG)
P RAT AETAT ... Pro Rata Aetatis [*According to Age*] [*Pharmacy*]
Pratica Med ... Pratica del Medico [*A publication*]
Prat Ind Mec ... Pratique des Industries Mecanique [*A publication*]
Pratsi Inst Zool Akad Nauk Ukr RSR ... Pratsi Institutu Zoologii Akademiya Nauk Ukrains'koi RSR [*A publication*]
Pratsi Odes Derzh Univ Ser Biol Nauk ... Pratsi Odeskogo Derzhavnogo Universitetu. Seriya Biologichnikh Nauk [*A publication*]
Prat Soudage ... Pratique du Soudage [*A publication*]
Pratt .... Pratt's Contraband-of-War Cases [*A publication*] (DLA)
Pratt .... Pratt's Supplement to Bott's Poor Laws [*1833*] [*A publication*] (DLA)
Pratt BS ..... Pratt's Law of Benefit Building Societies [*A publication*] (DLA)
Pratt Cont .. Pratt's Contraband-of-War Cases [*A publication*] (DLA)
Pratt Cts Req ... Pratt's Statutes Establishing Courts of Request [*A publication*] (DLA)
Pratt Fr Soc ... Pratt on Friendly Societies [*15th ed.*] [*1931*] [*A publication*] (DLA)
Pratt High ... Pratt and Mackenzie on Highways [*21st ed.*] [*1967*] [*A publication*] (DLA)
Pratt PL ..... Pratt's Edition of Bott on the Poor Laws [*A publication*] (DLA)
Pratt Prop T ... Pratt on the Property Tax Act [*A publication*] (DLA)
Pratt Sav B ... Pratt on Savings Banks [*6th ed.*] [*1845*] [*A publication*] (DLA)
Pratt SL ..... Pratt on Sea Lights [*2nd ed.*] [*1858*] [*A publication*] (DLA)
Prat Vet Equine ... Pratique Veterinaire Equine [*A publication*]
PRAUD9 ... Agricultural Research Institute Ukiriguru. Progress Report [*A publication*]
PRAUS ...... Programme de Recherche sur l'Amiante de l'Universite de Sherbrooke [*Asbestos Research Program*] [*University of Sherbrooke*] [*Quebec*] [*Information service or system*] (IID)
PRAVA ...... Pravda [*A publication*]
PRAW .... Personnel Research Activity, Washington, DC [*Obsolete*] [*Navy*]
PRaW .... Wyeth Laboratories, Radnor, PA [*Library symbol*] [*Library of Congress*] (LCLS)
PRAWL ..... Puerto Rican American Women's League
Prax .... Brown's Practice (Praxis) [*or Precedents*] in Chancery [*A publication*] (DLA)
PRAX .... Praxis Pharmaceuticals, Inc. [*Beverly Hills, CA*] [*NASDAQ symbol*] (NQ)
PRAXA ...... Praxis [*A publication*]

Prax Can .... Praxis Almae Curiae Cancellariae (Brown) [*A publication*] (DLA)
Prax Forsch ... Praxis und Forschung [*A publication*]
Praxis .... Praxis des Neusprachlichen Unterrichts [*A publication*]
Praxis Int ... Praxis International [*A publication*]
Praxis Math ... Praxis der Mathematik [*A publication*]
Prax Kinder ... Praxis der Kinderpsychologie und Kinderpsychiatrie [*A publication*]
Prax Kinderpsychol Kinderpsychiatr ... Praxis der Kinderpsychologie und Kinderpsychiatrie [*A publication*]
Prax Klin Pneumol ... Praxis und Klinik der Pneumologie [*A publication*]
Prax Naturw ... Praxis der Naturwissenschaften [*A publication*]
Prax Naturwiss Phy ... Praxis der Naturwissenschaften. Physik [*A publication*]
Prax Naturwiss Phys Unterr Sch ... Praxis der Naturwissenschaften. Physik im Unterricht der Schulen [*A publication*]
Prax Naturwiss Teil 3 ... Praxis der Naturwissenschaften. Teil 3. Chemie [*West Germany*] [*A publication*]
Prax Pneumol ... Praxis der Pneumologie [*A publication*]
Prax Psychother ... Praxis der Psychotherapie [*A publication*]
Prax Psychother Psychosom ... Praxis der Psychotherapie und Psychosomatik [*A publication*]
Prax Schriftenr Phys ... Praxis Schriftenreihe Physik [*A publication*]
Prax Vet ... Praxis Veterinaria [*A publication*]
PRAZ .... Prazosin [*A vasodilator*]
Prazsky Sbor Hist ... Prazsky Sbornik Historicky [*A publication*]
PRB .... Panel Review Board [*NASA*] (KSC)
PRB .... Parabola [*Mathematics*]
PRB .... Parachute Refurbishment Building [*NASA*] (NASA)
PRB .... Paso Robles, CA [*Location identifier*] [*FAA*] (FAAL)
PRB .... Pension Review Board [*Canada*]
PRB .... Personnel Reaction Blank [*Psychology*]
PRB .... Personnel Records Branch [*Army*] (AABC)
PRB .... Personnel Requirements Branch (MUGU)
PRB .... Personnel Research Branch [*Army*] (MCD)
PRB .... Planned Requirements - Bureau Directed
PRB .... Plant Review Board [*Nuclear energy*] (NRCH)
PRB .... Polar Research Board [*National Academy of Sciences*]
PRB .... Population Reference Bureau (EA)
PRB .... Pre-Raphaelite Brotherhood [*A publication*]
PRB .... Procedure Review Board [*Nuclear energy*] (NRCH)
PRB .... Procurement Review Board (MCD)
PRB .... Program Review Board
PRB .... Project Review Board [*NASA*] (NASA)
PRB .... Prosthetics Research Board
PRB .... Public Roads Bureau
PRBA .... Puerto Rican Bar Association (EA)
PRBA(AG) ... Personnel Research Board of the Army, Adjutant General
PrBayA ...... American Junior College of Puerto Rico, Bayamon, PR [*Library symbol*] [*Library of Congress*] (LCLS)
PrBayC ...... Bayamon Central University (Universidad Central de Bayamon), Bayamon, Puerto Rico [*Library symbol*] [*Library of Congress*] (LCLS)
PRBC .... Packed Red Blood Cells [*Medicine*]
PRBC .... Premier Bancorp, Inc. [*NASDAQ symbol*] (NQ)
PRBCA ...... Process Biochemistry [*A publication*]
PRBCB ...... Preparative Biochemistry [*A publication*]
PRBD .... Paraboloid
PRBG .... Puerto Rican Board of Guardians [*Defunct*] (EA)
PRBK .... Provident Bancorp, Inc. [*NASDAQ symbol*] (NQ)
PRBL .... Probable (FAAC)
PRBLC ...... Parabolic
PRBLTY .... Probability (FAAC)
PRBMD ...... Physical Review. Section B. Condensed Matter [*A publication*]
PRBMECAB ... Permanent Regional Bureau of the Middle East Committee for the Affairs of the Blind [*Riyadh, Saudi Arabia*] (EAIO)
PRBNT ...... Prebent
Pr Bot Sadu Kiiv Derzh Univ ... Pratsi Botanichnogo Sadu Kiivs'kii Derzhavnii Universitet [*A publication*]
Pr Brnenske Zakl Cesk Akad Ved ... Prace Brnenske Zakladny Ceskoslovenske Akademie Ved [*A publication*]
PRBS .... Pseudorandom Binary Sequence [*Data processing*]
PRBSG ...... Pseudorandom Binary Sequence Generator [*Data processing*] (NRCH)
PRBT .... Precision Remote Bathythermograph
PRC .... Chief Aircrew Survival Equipmentman [*Formerly, Chief Parachute Rigger*] [*Navy rating*]
PRC .... Park Ridge Center (EA)
PRC .... Part Requirement Card
PRC .... Parti Republicain Caledonien [*Political party*] [*New Caledonia*] (FEA)
PRC .... Partial Response Coding (IEEE)
PRC .... Partido Republicano Calderonista [*Calderonista Republican Party*] [*Costa Rica*] [*Political party*] (PPW)
PRC .... Parts Release Card (KSC)
PRC .... Passaic River Coalition (EA)
PRC .... Passenger Reservation Center [*Army*]
PRC .... Penrose Resources Corp. [*Vancouver Stock Exchange symbol*]
PRC .... Pension Research Council (EA)
PRC .... Pension Rights Center [*Washington, DC*] (EA)
PRC .... People's Redemption Council [*Liberia*] (PD)

PRC............ People's Republic of China [*Mainland China*]
PRC............ People's Republic of the Congo
PRC............ Permanent Regular Commissions [*Army*] [*British*]
PRC............ Personality Research Center [*University of Texas at Austin*] [*Research center*]   (RCD)
PRC............ Personnel Readiness Center [*Air Force*]
PRC............ Personnel Reception Centre [*British military*]   (DMA)
PRC............ Personnel Recovery Center [*Military*]
PRC............ Personnel Reporting Code [*Army*]   (AABC)
PRC............ Phase-Response Curve
PRC............ Philippine Resource Center [*An association*]   (EA)
PRC............ Physical Review Council [*DoD*]
PRC............ Pierce   (MSA)
PRC............ Planned Requirements, Conversion   (NG)
PRC............ Planning Research Corp. [*Telecommunications service*]   (TSSD)
PRC............ Plant Records Center [*of the American Horticultural Society*]   (IID)
PRC............ Plasma Renin Concentration [*Hematology*]
PRC............ Plastic Roller Conveyor
PRC............ Plutonium Rework Cell [*Nuclear energy*]   (NRCH)
PRC............ Point of Reverse Curve   (MSA)
PRC............ Point Reyes [*California*] [*Seismograph station code, US Geological Survey*] [*Closed*]   (SEIS)
PRC............ Policy Review Committee [*Terminated, 1981*] [*National Security Council*]   (EGAO)
PRC............ Polish Resettlement Corps [*British military*]   (DMA)
PRC............ Polymer Research Centre [*Australia*]
PRC............ Population Research Center [*University of Chicago*] [*Research center*]   (RCD)
PRC............ Population Resource Center   (EA)
PRC............ Post Roman Conditam [*After the Founding of Rome*] [*Latin*]
PRC............ Postal Rate Commission [*Federal government*]
PRC............ Poultry Research Centre [*of the Agricultural Research Council*] [*British*]   (ARC)
PRC............ Power Reflection Coefficient [*of RADAR signals*]
PRC............ Prattsburgh Railway Corporation [*AAR code*]
PRC............ Preoral Ciliary [*Gland*]
PRC............ Prescott [*Arizona*] [*Airport symbol*]   (OAG)
PRC............ Prescott, AZ [*Location identifier*] [*FAA*]   (FAAL)
PRC............ Pressure Recorder Controller [*Nuclear energy*]   (NRCH)
PRC............ Pressure Response Cell [*For chemical kinetic studies*]
PRC............ Prevention Research Center [*Pacific Institute for Research and Evaluation*] [*Research center*]   (RCD)
PRC............ Primary Routing Center [*Telecommunications*]   (TEL)
PRC............ Primate Research Center
PRC............ Printer Control
PRC............ Priory Cell
Pr C............ Prize Cases [*A publication*]   (DLA)
PRC............ Problem Resolution Coordinator [*IRS*]
PRC............ Procaterol [*Pharmacology*]
PRC............ Procedure Review Committee   (AAG)
PRC............ Procession Register Clock
PRC............ Proconsul
PRC............ Procurement Request Code [*Military*]   (AFIT)
PRC............ Product Regional Center [*Department of Supply and Service*] [*Canada*]   (IMH)
PRC............ Production Readjustments Committee [*WPB*]
PRC............ Products Research & Chemical Corp. [*NYSE symbol*]   (SPSG)
PRC............ Professional Reference Center [*Los Angeles County Office of Education*] [*Downey, CA*] [*Library network*]
PRC............ Professional Relations Council [*American Chemical Society*]
PRC............ Program Review Committee   (AFM)
PrC............ Proster in Cas [*A publication*]
PRC............ Providence College, Phillips Memorial Library, Providence, RI [*OCLC symbol*]   (OCLC)
PRC............ Pyrotechnic Rocket Container
PRC............ Revolutionary Socialist Party [*Peru*] [*Political party*]   (PD)
Pr Ca......... Great War Prize Cases, by Evans [*England*] [*A publication*]   (DLA)
PRCA........ Palomino Rabbit Co-Breeders Association   (EA)
PRCA........ Parks, Recreation and Cultural Affairs Administration [*New York City*]
PRCA........ People's Republic of China Army   (MCD)
PRCA........ Pitch and Roll Channel Assembly   (MCD)
PRCA........ President of the Royal Canadian Academy
PRCA........ Problem Reporting and Corrective Action   (NASA)
PRCA........ Professional Rodeo Cowboys Association   (EA)
PRCA........ Public Relations Consultants Association   (EAIO)
PRCA........ Puerto Rico Communications Authority
PRCA........ Pure Red Cell Aplasia [*Hematology*]
PrCaC........ Colegio Universitario de Cayey, Cayey, PR [*Library symbol*] [*Library of Congress*]   (LCLS)
PRCAD....... Primary Care [*A publication*]
PRCAFL.... Publications. Research Center in Anthropology, Folklore, and Linguistics [*A publication*]
PRCB........ Program Requirements Change Board [*NASA*]   (NASA)
PRCB........ Program Requirements Control Board [*NASA*]
PRCB........ Program Review Control Board [*NASA*]   (NASA)
PRCBD...... Program Requirements Control Board Directive [*NASA*]   (NASA)

PRCBD...... Program Review Control Board Directive [*NASA*]   (NASA)
PRCC........ Peoria Record Club [*Record label*]
PRCC........ Puerto Rico Cancer Center [*University of Puerto Rico*] [*Research center*]   (RCD)
PRCCh...... Principal Roman Catholic Chaplain [*Navy*] [*British*]
PRCE........ Pierce [*S. S.*] Co., Inc. [*NASDAQ symbol*]   (NQ)
Pr Cent Inst Ochr Pr ... Prace Centralnege Instytutu Ochrony Pracy [*A publication*]
Pr Cesk Vyzk Slevarenskeho ... Prace Ceskoslovenskeho Vyzkumu Slevarenskeho [*A publication*]
PRCESSN ... Processing
PRCF .... Petroleum Resources Communications Foundation [*Canada*]
PRCF .... Plutonium Recycle Critical Facility [*Nuclear energy*]
PR Ch .... Practical Register in Chancery [*England*] [*A publication*]   (DLA)
Pr Ch......... Precedents in Chancery, Edited by Finch [*1689-1722*] [*England*] [*A publication*]   (DLA)
PRCH .... Precharge
PRCH .... Proprietary Chapel [*Church of England*]
Pr Chem..... Prace Chemiczne [*A publication*]
Pr Chem Pr Nauk Uniw Slask Katowic ... Prace Chemiczne. Prace Naukowe Uniwersytetu Slaskiego w Katowicach [*A publication*]
PRCHT...... Parachute   (AFM)
Prcht Bad... Parachutist Badge [*Military decoration*]
Pr CKB ..... Practice Cases, in the King's Bench [*England*] [*A publication*]   (DLA)
PRCLS...... Property Investors of Colorado [*NASDAQ symbol*]   (NQ)
PRCM....... Master Chief Aircrew Survival Equipmentman [*Navy rating*] [*Formerly, Master Chief Parachute Rigger*]
PRCM....... Passive Radiation Countermeasure [*Military*]
PRCM....... Protocom Devices, Inc. [*Bronx, NY*] [*NASDAQ symbol*]   (NQ)
PRCMC..... Percussionist [*A publication*]
PRCMC..... Protective Coatings on Metals [*English Translation*] [*A publication*]
PRCMT..... Procurement   (MSA)
PRCN .... Precision   (MSA)
PR-CNTL ... Product Control Register
PRC & NW ... Pierre, Rapid City & Northwestern Railroad [*Nickname: Plenty Rough Country and No Women*]
PRCO .... Pacific Requisition Control Office [*Navy*]
Pr Co......... Prerogative Court   (DLA)
PRCO .... Pricor, Inc. [*NASDAQ symbol*]   (NQ)
PR Commonw Water Resour Bull ... Puerto Rico Commonwealth. Water Resources Bulletin [*A publication*]
pr compt ..... Pour Compte [*By Cash*] [*Business term*] [*French*]
Pr Cont....... Pratt's Contraband-of-War Cases [*1861*] [*A publication*]   (DLA)
PRCP........ Power Remote Control Panel   (AAG)
PRCP........ Practical Register in the Common Pleas [*A publication*]   (DLA)
PRCP........ President of the Royal College of Physicians [*British*]
PRCP........ President of the Royal College of Preceptors [*British*]   (ROG)
PRCP........ Puerto Rican Communist Party [*Political party*]
PRCPTN ... Precipitin [*Test*] [*Immunology*]
PRCR........ Professional Health Care of America, Inc. [*NASDAQ symbol*]   (NQ)
PRCR........ Protective Cover   (AAG)
PRCS........ Passive and Remote Crosswind Sensor   (MCD)
PRCS........ Personal Radio Communications System [*General Electric Co.*]
PRCS........ Personal Report of Confidence as a Speaker [*Psychology*]
PRCS........ Polish Red Cross Society
PRCS........ President of the Royal College of Surgeons [*British*]
PRCS........ Prevention and Removal of Corrosion and Scale [*Engineering*]
PRCS........ Process   (AFM)
P/RCS .... Propulsion and Reaction Control Subsystem [*NASA*]   (KSC)
PRCS........ Psychological Response Classification System
PRCS........ Purchase Requisition Change Supplement
PRCS........ Senior Chief Aircrew Survival Equipmentman [*Navy rating*] [*Formerly, Senior Chief Parachute Rigger*]
PRCSG...... Processing   (MSA)
PRCST...... Precast   (AAG)
PRCT........ Pool Repair Cycle Time   (MCD)
517 PRCT A ... 517th Parachute Regimental Combat Team Association   (EA)
PRCTN...... Precaution   (FAAC)
PRCU .... Power Regulating and Control Unit   (CET)
PRCUA...... Polish Roman Catholic Union of America   (EA)
PRCY........ ProCyte Corp. [*NASDAQ symbol*]   (NQ)
P and RD ... Decisions of the Department of the Interior, Pension and Retirement Claims [*United States*] [*A publication*]   (DLA)
PRD .... Part Reference Designator
PRD .... Parti Democratique Dahomeen [*Dahomey Democratic Party*] [*Political party*]
PRD .... Parti Radical-Democratique Suisse [*Radical Democratic Party of Switzerland*] [*Political party*]   (PPE)
PRD .... Partial Reaction of Degeneration
PRD .... Partido Reformista Democratico [*Democratic Reformist Party*] [*Spain*] [*Political party*]   (PPW)
PRD .... Partido de Renovacion Democratica [*Democratic Renewal Party*] [*Costa Rica*] [*Political party*]   (PPW)
PRD .... Partido Revolucionario Democratico [*Democratic Revolutionary Party*] [*Panama*] [*Political party*]   (PPW)

PRD .... Partido Revolucionario Dominicano [*Dominican Revolutionary Party*] [*Dominican Republic*] [*Political party*] (PPW)
PRD .... Party of the Democratic Revolution [*Mexico*] [*Political party*]
PRD .... Payroll Deduction
PRD .... Period
PRD .... Periodontics and Restorative Dentistry
PRD .... Personal Radiation Dosimeter (KSC)
PR & D ...... Personal Rest and Delay [*Air Force*] (AFM)
PRD .... Personnel Readiness Date [*Army*] (AABC)
PRD .... Personnel Records Division [*Army*] (AABC)
PRD .... Personnel Requirements Data (AAG)
PRD .... Personnel Research Division [*Navy*] (MCD)
PRD .... Personnel Resources Data
PRD .... Piezoelectric Resonating Device
PRD .... Planned Residential Development
PRD .... Polaroid Corp. [*NYSE symbol*] (SPSG)
PRD .... Political Resource Directory [*A publication*]
PRD .... Polytechnic Research & Development Co. (AAG)
PRD .... Postal Regulating Detachment [*Military*]
PRD .... Postradiation Dysplasia [*Medicine*]
PRD .... Potentially Reportable Deficiency [*Nuclear energy*] (NRCH)
PRD .... Power Range Detector (IEEE)
PRD .... Power Requirement Data
PR & D ...... Power, Rodwell, and Drew's English Election Cases [*1847-56*] [*A publication*] (DLA)
PRD .... Predicted Range of the Day [*Military*] (NVT)
PRD .... Preretro Update Display
PRD .... Princeton Reference Design (MCD)
PRD .... Printer Driver
PRD .... Printer Dump
PRD .... Pro Rate Distribution [*Clause*] [*Insurance*]
PRD .... Process Requirements Drawing (MCD)
PRD .... Procurement Regulation Directive [*NASA*] (NASA)
PRD .... Procurement Requirements Document [*NASA*] (NASA)
PRD .... Production [*A publication*]
PRD .... Production Responsibilities Document (MCD)
PRD .... Productivity Research Division [*Office of Personnel Management*] (GRD)
PRD .... Proficiency Rating Designator [*Military*]
PRD .... Program [*or Project*] Requirement Data [*NASA*] (KSC)
PRD .... Program Requirements Document
PRD .... Projected Rotation Date (NG)
PR & D ...... Public Research and Development
PRD .... Puerto Rico, Decisiones [*A publication*] (DLA)
PRD .... Push Rod [*Mechanical engineering*]
PRDA .... Program Research and Development Announcement [*Energy Research and Development Administration*]
PRDC........ Personnel Research and Development Center [*Office of Personnel Management*] (GRD)
PRDC........ Polar Research and Development Center [*Army*]
PRDDO ..... Partial Retention of Diatomic Differential Overlap [*Physics*]
PRDE......... Preliminary Determination of Epicenters [*A publication*] [*National Oceanic and Atmospheric Administration*]
PRDE......... Pride Petroleum Services, Inc. [*NASDAQ symbol*] (CTT)
PR & D El Cas ... Power, Rodwell, and Drew's English Election Cases [*A publication*] (DLA)
PRDF......... Political Rights Defense Fund (EA)
PRDG .... Princess Royal's Dragoon Guards [*Military unit*] [*British*] (ROG)
PRDIAG.... Primary Diagnosis [*Medicine*]
Pr & Div ..... Law Reports, Probate and Divorce [*England*] [*A publication*] (DLA)
PRDL......... Personnel Research and Development Laboratory [*Navy*] (MCD)
PRDN .... Partido de Reconciliacion Democratica Nacional [*Party of National Democratic Reconciliation*] [*Guatemala*] [*Political party*]
PRDP......... Power Reactor Demonstration Program
PRDR .... Preproduction Reliability Design Review [*Navy*] (CAAL)
PRDR .... Production Request Design Review
PRDV .... Peak Reading Digital Voltmeter
PRDX .... Prediction Program [*NASA*]
Pr Dzialu Zywenia Rosl Nawoz ... Prace Dzialu Zywenia Roslin i Nawozenia [*Poland*] [*A publication*]
PRE........... Bureau for Private Enterprise
PRE........... Federation Europeenne des Fabricants de Produits Refractaires [*Zurich, Switzerland*] (EAIO)
PRE........... Partido Republicano Evolucionista [*Republican Evolutionist Party*] [*Portugal*] [*Political party*] (PPE)
PRE........... Partner-Resisted Exercise [*Army*] (INF)
PRE........... Personal Radio Exchange [*A publication*]
PRE........... Personal Rescue Enclosure (NASA)
PRE........... Petroleum Refining Engineer
PRE........... Photoreactivating
PRE........... Pineridge Capital [*Vancouver Stock Exchange symbol*]
PRE........... Portable RADAR Equipment
PRE........... Precinct
PRE........... Precision Airlines [*North Springfield, VT*] [*FAA designator*] (FAAC)
PRE........... Predecessor (KSC)

PRE........... Prefect
PRE........... Prefix
PRE........... Preliminary
PRE........... Premier Industrial Corp. [*NYSE symbol*] (SPSG)
PRE........... Prepayment Coin Telephone [*Telecommunications*] (TEL)
PRE........... Presbyterian Historical Society, Philadelphia, PA [*OCLC symbol*] (OCLC)
PRE........... President of the Royal Society of Painter-Etchers and Engravers [*British*]
PRE........... Pretoria [*South Africa*] [*Seismograph station code, US Geological Survey*] (SEIS)
PRE........... Pretoria [*South Africa*] (KSC)
PRE........... Processing Refabrication Experiment [*Nuclear energy*] (NRCH)
PRE........... Progesterone [*A hormone*]
PRE........... Progressive Resistive Exercise [*Medicine*]
PRE........... Public Relations Exchange [*Later, PRXI*] (EA)
PRE........... Pulse Radiation Effect
PRE........... Realencyclopaedie fuer Protestantische Theologie und Kirche [*A publication*]
PRE........... Spanish Catalonian Battalion (PD)
PREA........ Pension Real Estate Association (EA)
P/REA .... Probationary Radio Electrical Artificer [*British military*] (DMA)
PREAG...... Photographic Reconnaissance Equipment Advisory Group [*Military*]
PREAMP .. Preamplifier (AAG)
PREAP ...... Prison Research Education Action Project (EA)
PRE-ARM ... People's Rights Enforced Against Riots and Murder [*Vigilante group in New Jersey*]
PREB........ Prebendary
PREB........ Pupil Record of Educational Behavior [*Aptitude test*]
PREBA3 .... Proceedings. Royal Society of Edinburgh. Section B. Biological Sciences [*A publication*]
PREBD...... Population Reports. Series B [*United States*] [*A publication*]
Preb Dig..... Preble. Digest, Patent Cases [*A publication*] (DLA)
Preb Pat Cas ... Preble. Digest, Patent Cases [*A publication*] (DLA)
PREC........ Palestine Research and Educational Center (EA)
PREC........ Precambrian [*Period, era, or system*] [*Geology*]
PREC........ Precedence (AABC)
PREC........ Preceding
PREC........ Precentor (ROG)
PREC........ Precious (ROG)
PREC........ Precision (AABC)
Prec........... Precite [*Supra, Cited Before*] [*French*] (ILCA)
PREC........ Propulsion Research Environmental Chamber
PREC........ Public Revenue Education Council (EA)
PRECA...... Pauly-Wissowas Realencyclopaedie der Classischen Altertumswissenschaft [*A publication*]
Precamb Res ... Precambrian Research [*A publication*]
Precambrian Res ... Precambrian Research [*A publication*]
Precast Concr ... Precast Concrete [*A publication*]
Prec Ch ...... Precedents in Chancery, Edited by Finch [*24 English Reprint*] [*A publication*] (DLA)
Prec in Ch .. Precedents in Chancery, Edited by Finch [*24 English Reprint*] [*1689-1722*] [*A publication*] (DLA)
Prec in Ch (Eng) ... Precedents in Chancery, Edited by Finch [*24 English Reprint*] [*A publication*] (DLA)
PRECD...... Precede (FAAC)
PRECEDE ... Predisposing, Reinforcing, and Enabling Causes in Educational Diagnosis and Evaluation [*Occupational therapy*]
Pre Ch........ Precedents in Chancery, Edited by Finch [*A publication*] (DLA)
Precious Met ... Precious Metals [*A publication*]
PRECIP..... Precipitation
PRECIS ..... Pre-Coordinate Indexing System
PRECIS ..... Preserved Context Index System [*British Library*] [*Information service or system*] [*London, England*]
Precis Eng ... Precision Engineering [*A publication*]
Precis Engng ... Precision Engineering [*A publication*]
Precis Met ... Precision Metal [*A publication*]
Precis Met Molding ... Precision Metal Molding [*A publication*]
PRECO...... Preparatory Commission of the United Nations Organization
PRECOM ... Precommissioning [*Military*]
PRECOM ... Preliminary Communications Search [*Military*] (NVT)
PRECOMDET ... Precommissioning Detail [*Navy*] (NVT)
PRECOMG ... Precommissioning [*Military*] (NVT)
PRECOMM ... Preliminary Communications [*Military*] (NVT)
PRECOMMDET ... Precommissioning Detail [*Navy*]
PRECOMMSCOL ... Precommissioning School [*Navy*]
precomp ..... Precomputed Loan
PRECOMP ... Prediction of Contingency Maintenance and Parts Requirements (MCD)
PRED........ Predicate
PRED........ Predicted
PRED........ Prediction (AFM)
Pred........... Prednisone [*Also, P, PDN, Pr, Pro*] [*Antineoplastic drug*] [*Endocrinology*]
PREDECE ... Predecease (ROG)
Predel no Dopustimye Konts Atmos Zagryaz ... Predel no Dopustimye Kontsentratsii Atmosfernykh Zagryaznenii [*A publication*]

Predi........... Predicasts Special Study [*A publication*]
Predi 161.... Predicasts. Recreational Vehicles Industry Study 161 [*A publication*]
Predi 162.... Predicasts. World Rubber and Tire Markets Industry Study 162 [*A publication*]
Predi 163.... Predicasts. Glass and Advanced Fibers Industry Study 163 [*A publication*]
Predi 165.... Predicasts. Water Treatment Chemicals Industry Study 165 [*A publication*]
Predi 168.... Predicasts. World Housing Industry Study 168 [*A publication*]
PredicadorEv ... El Predicador Evangelico [*Buenos Aires*] [*A publication*]
PREDICT ... Prediction of Radiation Effects by Digital Computer Techniques
Predi P55 ... Predicasts. Industrial Packaging Paper Trends P-55 [*A publication*]
Pr Edw I..... Prince Edward Island   (DLA)
Pr Edw I..... Prince Edward Island Reports [*Canada*] [*A publication*]   (DLA)
Pr Edw Isl.. Prince Edward Island   (DLA)
Pr Edw Isl.. Prince Edward Island Reports [*Canada*] [*A publication*]   (DLA)
PREEB ...... Presence [*A publication*]
PRE-EMPTN ... Pre-Emption   (ROG)
PREF .... Preface
PREF .... Prefecture
PREF .... Preference [*or Preferred*]   (AFM)
PREF .... Preferred   (KSC)
PREF .... Prefix   (AAG)
PREF .... Prefocused
PREF .... Propulsion Research Environmental Facility
PREFAB..... Prefabricated   (KSC)
PREFACE ... Pre-Freshman and Cooperative Education for Minorities in Engineering
PREF-AP... Prefect-Apostolic [*Roman Catholic*]
PREFAT.... Prepare Final Acceptance Trials [*Navy*]   (NVT)
PREFCE.... Preface   (ROG)
PREFLT.... Preflight   (KSC)
PREFLTSCOL ... Preflight School [*Military*]
PREFMD.. Preformed
PREFRAM ... Prepare Fleet Rehabilitation and Modernization Overhaul [*Navy*]   (NVT)
preft............ Prefecture
PREG........ Pregnancy [*or Pregnant*]
PREG........ Pregnenolone [*Endocrinology*]
PREGA...... Promyshlennaya Energetika [*A publication*]
pregang...... Preganglionic [*Anatomy*]
Pregled Naucnoteh Rad Inform Zavod Tehn Drveta ... Pregled Naucnotehnickih Radova i Informacija. Zavod za Tehnologiiu Drveta [*A publication*]
Pregl Probl Ment Retard Osoba ... Pregled Problema Mentalno Retardiranih Osoba [*A publication*]
Preh............ Prehistoire [*A publication*]
Prehist Arieg ... Prehistoire Ariegeoise [*A publication*]
Prehlad Lesnickej Lit ... Prehl'ad Lesnickej. Drevarskej. Celulozovej a Papierenskej Literatury [*A publication*]
Prehl Lesn Mysliv Lit ... Prehled Lesnicke a Myslivecke Literatury [*A publication*]
Prehl Zahr Zemed Lit ... Prehled Zahranicni Zemedelske Literatury [*A publication*]
Prehl Zemed Lit ... Prehled Zemedelske Literatury [*A publication*]
Prehl Zemed Lit Zahr Domaci ... Prehled Zemedelske Literatury Zahranicni i Domaci [*A publication*]
Prehrambeno Tehnol Rev ... Prehrambeno Tehnoloska Revija [*A publication*]
PREINACT ... Prepare Inactivation [*Navy*]   (NVT)
PREINSURV ... Prepare for Board of Inspection and Survey [*Navy*]   (NVT)
Preist Alp... Preistoria Alpina [*Museo Tridentino di Scienze Naturali*] [*A publication*]
PREJ .... Prejudice   (AABC)
PREL........ Pain Relief Level [*Medicine*]
PREL........ Preliminary
PREL........ Preliminary Evaluation [*Orbit identification*]
PREL........ Prelude [*Music*]   (ROG)
PREL........ Priority Reconnaissance Exploitation List   (CINC)
PRELA ...... Prensa Latina, Angencia Informativa Latinoamericana [*Press agency*] [*Cuba*]
PRELA ...... Przeglad Elektroniki [*Poland*] [*A publication*]
PRELIM.... Preliminary   (AFM)
Prelim Rep Dir Gen Mines (Queb) ... Preliminary Report. Direction Generale des Mines (Quebec) [*A publication*]
Prelim Rep Rehovot Nat Univ Inst Agr ... Preliminary Report. Rehovot. National and University Institute of Agriculture [*A publication*]
prelims....... Preliminary Pages [*Frontmatter*] [*Publishing*]
PRELIMY ... Preliminary   (ROG)
PRELOG... People's Revolutionary League of Ghana [*Political party*]   (PPW)
PRELORT ... Precision Long-Range Tracking RADAR
PREM........ Preliminary Reference Earth Model [*Geology*]
PREM........ Premature [*Medicine*]
PREM........ Premier   (ROG)
PREM........ Premier Financial Services, Inc. [*Freeport, IL*] [*NASDAQ symbol*]   (NQ)
PREM........ Premium   (AFM)
PREM........ Probe-Microphone Real Ear Measurement [*Audiology*]

PREMA ..... Pulp Refining Equipment Manufacturers Association   (EA)
PRE-MED ... Previous to Appearance in MEDLINE [*Latham, NY*] [*Bibliographic database*]
PREMEDU ... Preventive Medicine Unit
PREMES.. Premises   (ROG)
Premium/Incentive Bus ... Premium/Incentive Business [*A publication*]
PREMOD ... Premodeling Data Output [*Environmental Protection Agency*]
PREMOD ... Premodulation   (NASA)
PREMODE ... Preliminary Mid-Ocean Dynamics Experiment [*Marine science*]   (MSC)
pre-mRNA ... Precursor-Messenger Ribonucleic Acid
PREMS ..... Premises   (DSUE)
PRENA...... Product Engineering [*New York*] [*A publication*]
Pren Act..... Prentice's Proceedings in an Action [*2nd ed.*] [*1880*] [*A publication*]   (DLA)
prenat......... Prenatal
Prenatal Diagn ... Prenatal Diagnosis [*A publication*]
Prenat Diagn ... Prenatal Diagnosis [*A publication*]
PR Enferm ... Puerto Rico y Su Enferma [*A publication*]
PrEng......... Professional Engineer
Prensa Med Argent ... Prensa Medica Argentina [*A publication*]
Prensa Med Mex ... Prensa Medica Mexicana [*A publication*]
preocc......... Preoccupied [*Biology, taxonomy*]
PREOP....... Preoperative [*Medicine*]
PREOS...... Predicted Range for Electrooptical Systems [*Military*]   (CAAL)
PREOVHL ... Prepare for Shipyard Overhaul [*Navy*]   (NVT)
PREP........ Pacific Range Electromagnetic Platform   (AAG)
PREP........ Parent Readiness Evaluation of Preschoolers [*Child development test*]
PREP........ Peace Research and Education Project
PREP........ Peacetime Requirements and Procedures [*Strategic Air Command*]   (MUGU)
PREP........ Persons Responsive to Educational Problems   (EA)
PREP........ Plan, Rehearse, Edit, and Psych [*Public speaking preparation technique*]
PREP........ Plasma Rotating Electrode Process [*Metallurgy*]
PREP........ Police Recruit Education Program [*Australia*]
PREP........ Population, Resources, and Environment Program [*American Association for the Advancement of Science*]
PREP........ Predischarge Education Program [*DoD*]
PREP........ Preparation [*or Preparatory*]
PREP........ Prepare   (AFM)
PREP........ Preposition
PREP........ Productivity Research and Extension Program [*North Carolina State University*] [*Research center*]   (RCD)
PREP........ Programmed Educational Package
PREP........ Purchasing, Receiving, and Payable System
PREP........ Putting Research into Educational Practice [*Information service of ERIC*]
PREPA ..... Przeglad Epidemiologiczny [*A publication*]
Prepak....... People's Revolutionary Party of Kungleipak [*India*] [*Political party*]   (PD)
PREPARE ... Premarital Personal and Relationship Evaluation
PREPARE ... Project for Retraining of Employable Persons as Relates to EDP
Prep Bioch ... Preparative Biochemistry [*A publication*]
Prep Biochem ... Preparative Biochemistry [*A publication*]
PREPD ...... Prepared
PREPE ...... Prepare   (ROG)
Prep Food D ... Prepared Foods New Food Products Directory [*A publication*]
Prep Foods ... Prepared Foods [*A publication*]
PREPG...... Preparing
Prep Inorg React ... Preparative Inorganic Reactions [*A publication*]
PREPN...... Preparation
Prepo.......... Praepositus [*Deceased, 1509*] [*Authority cited in pre-1607 legal work*]   (DSA)
Prepos........ Praepositus [*Deceased, 1509*] [*Authority cited in pre-1607 legal work*]   (DSA)
PREPOS.... Preposition   (AABC)
PREPOSTOR ... Prepositioned Storage [*Army*]   (AABC)
Prep Prop Solid State Mat ... Preparation and Properties of Solid State Materials [*A publication*]
PREPPSA ... Prepare Postshakedown Availability [*Navy*]   (NVT)
Preppy........ Preparatory School Alumnus [*Lifestyle classification*]
Prepr Am Chem Soc Div Fuel Chem ... Preprints. American Chemical Society. Division of Fuel Chemistry [*A publication*]
Prepr Amer Wood Pres Ass ... Preprint. American Wood Preservers' Association [*A publication*]
Prepr Am Soc Lubr Eng ... Preprints. American Society of Lubrication Engineers [*A publication*]
Prepr Annu Sci Meet Aerosp Med Assoc ... Preprints. Annual Scientific Meeting. Aerospace Medical Association [*A publication*]
Prepr Aust Miner Ind Annu Rev ... Preprints. Australian Mineral Industry. Annual Review [*A publication*]
Prepr Daresbury Lab ... Preprint. Daresbury Laboratory [*A publication*]
Prepr Div Pet Chem Am Chem Soc ... Preprints. American Chemical Society. Division of Petroleum Chemistry [*A publication*]
PREPREG ... Pre-Impregnated Glass Fibers [*Fiberglass production*]
Preprint Inst Eng Aust Conf ... Preprint. Institution of Engineers of Australia. Conference [*A publication*]   (APTA)
PREPRO.... Preprocessor [*Computer*] [*Coast Guard*]
PREPROD ... Preproduction Model [*Military*]   (AFIT)

Prepr Pap Annu Conf Australas Corros Assoc ... Australasian Corrosion Association. Preprinted Papers of the Annual Conference [*A publication*] (APTA)
Prepr Pap Natl Meet Div Environ Chem Am Chem Soc ... Preprints of Papers Presented at National Meeting. Division of Environmental Chemistry. American Chemical Society [*A publication*]
Prepr Pap Natl Meet Div Water Air Waste Chem Am Chem Soc ... Preprints of Papers Presented at National Meeting. Division of Water, Air, and Waste Chemistry. American Chemical Society [*A publication*]
Prepr Pap Oilseed Process Clin ... Preprints of Papers. Oilseed Processing Clinic [*A publication*]
Prepr Sci Program Aerosp Med Assoc ... Preprints. Scientific Program. Aerospace Medical Association [*A publication*]
Prepr Ser.... Preprint Series. University of Oslo. Institute of Mathematics [*A publication*]
Prepr Ser Inst Math Univ Oslo ... Preprint Series. Institute of Mathematics. University of Oslo [*Norway*] [*A publication*]
PREPS....... Predischarge Remedial Education Program [*For servicemen*]
PREPS....... Program of Research and Evaluation in Public Schools [*Mississippi State University*] [*Research center*] (RCD)
PREPSCOL ... Preparatory School
prepub........ Prepublication
PREQUAL ... Prequalified [*NASA*] (KSC)
Prer .... Prerogative Court (DLA)
PRER......... Prevention Resources [*A publication*]
PRERECPAC ... Preplanned Reconnaissance Pacific (CINC)
Prerog Ct.... Prerogative Court, New Jersey (DLA)
PRES .... Precision Resources, Inc. [*Whippany, NJ*] [*NASDAQ symbol*] (NQ)
PRES .... Premises (ROG)
Pres .... Presbyterian [*A publication*]
PRES .... Presbyterian
PRES .... Presence
PRES .... Present (AAG)
PRES .... Preserved
PRE-S........ Preshaving (MSA)
PRES .... President (EY)
PRES .... President of the Royal Entomological Society [*British*]
PRES .... Pressure (FAAC)
PRES .... Preston R. R. [*AAR code*]
PRES .... Presumptive [*Grammar*]
Pres Abs..... Preston's Abstracts of Title [*2nd ed.*] [*1823-24*] [*A publication*] (DLA)
PRESAC.... Photographic Reconnaissance System Analysis by Computer
PresAfr ...... Presence Africaine [*A publication*]
PRESAILEDREP ... Forecast Sailing Report [*Navy*] (NVT)
PRESB....... Presbyterian
PRESB....... Prescribe (AABC)
Presb Q ...... Presbyterian Quarterly Review [*A publication*]
Presb R ...... Presbyterian Review [*A publication*]
Presb & Ref R ... Presbyterian and Reformed Review [*A publication*]
PRESBY.... Presbytery
Presbyt-St. Luke's Hosp Med Bull ... Presbyterian-St. Luke's Hospital. Medical Bulletin [*A publication*]
Presbyt-St. Luke's Hosp Res Rep ... Presbyterian-St. Luke's Hospital. Research Report [*A publication*]
Pres C of E Ch ... Presbyterian Church of England Chaplain [*Navy*] [*British*]
Pre-Sch Years ... Pre-School Years [*A publication*]
Pres Coll Physiol Inst J ... Presidency College. Physiological Institute Journal [*A publication*]
Pres Conv... Preston on Conveyancing [*5th ed.*] [*1819-29*] [*A publication*] (DLA)
PRESCORE ... Program for the Rapid Estimation of Construction Requirements
PRESCR.... Prescription (MSA)
Presence Afr ... Presence Africaine [*A publication*]
PRESERV ... Preservation
Preserv Madeiras ... Preservacao de Madeiras [*A publication*]
Preserv Madeiras Bol Tec ... Preservacao de Madeiras. Boletim Tecnico [*A publication*]
Pres Est...... Preston on Estates [*3rd ed.*] [*1829*] [*A publication*] (DLA)
PRESET.... Preset Spin Echo Technique
Pres Fal...... Falconer's Decisions, Scotch Court of Session [*1744-51*] [*A publication*] (DLA)
Pres Fal...... Gilmour and Falconer's Reports, Scotch Court of Session [*A publication*] (DLA)
Pres Falc.... President Falconer's Scotch Session Cases (Gilmour and Falconer) [*1681-86*] [*A publication*] (DLA)
PRESFR.... Pressure Falling Rapidly [*Meteorology*] (FAAC)
Pres His S ... Presbyterian Historical Society. Journal [*A publication*]
Pres His SJ ... Presbyterian Historical Society. Journal [*A publication*]
PRESIG..... Pressurizing (KSC)
PRESIGN ... Procedure Sign
PRESINSURV ... Inspection and Survey Board [*Navy*]
Pres J......... Presbyterian Journal [*A publication*]
Pres Leg..... Preston on Legacies [*1824*] [*A publication*] (DLA)
Pres Life..... Presbyterian Life [*A publication*] (APTA)
Pres Mem .. Presidential Member [*Australia*]
Pres Mer.... Preston on Merger [*A publication*] (DLA)
PRESNAVWARCOL ... Naval War College

PRESPROC ... Presidential Proclamation
PRESRR.... Pressure Rising Rapidly [*Meteorology*] (FAAC)
PRESS....... Pacific Range Electromagnetic Signature Studies [*or System*] [*Military*] (NG)
PRESS....... Parti Republicain Social du Senegal [*Social Republican Party of Senegal*] [*Political party*]
PRESS....... Prereading Expectancy Screening Scale [*Educational test*]
PRESS...... Pressure (MCD)
PRESS....... Prolog Equation Solving System (BYTE)
PRESS....... Property Record for Equipment Servicing and Sharing (MCD)
PRESSAR ... Presentation Equipment for Slow Scan RADAR
Presse Actual ... Presse Actualite [*A publication*]
Pressedienst Bundesminist Bild Wiss ... Pressedienst. Bundesministerium fuer Bildung und Wissenschaft [*A publication*]
Presse Med ... Presse Medicale [*A publication*]
Presse Med Belge ... Presse Medicale Belge [*A publication*]
Pressemitt Nordrh-Westfalen ... Pressemitteilung Nordrhein-Westfalen [*A publication*]
Presse Therm Clim ... Presse Thermale et Climatique [*A publication*]
Presse-Umsch ... Presse-Umschau [*A publication*]
Pressluft Ind ... Pressluft Industrie [*A publication*]
PRESSO..... Program for Elective Surgical Second Opinion [*Blue Cross/Blue Shield*]
Pres Studies Q ... Presidential Studies Quarterly [*A publication*]
Pres Stud Q ... Presidential Studies Quarterly [*A publication*]
Pressure Eng ... Pressure Engineering [*Japan*] [*A publication*]
PRESSURS ... Pre-Strike Surveillance/Reconnaissance System (MCD)
PREST....... Present (ROG)
PRES'T....... President
PRE-ST ..... Prestart (AAG)
Prest Conv ... Preston on Conveyancing [*A publication*] (DLA)
Prestel D ..... Prestel Directory and Magazine [*A publication*]
Prest Est ..... Preston on Estates [*A publication*] (DLA)
Prestige de la Photogr ... Prestige de la Photographie [*A publication*]
Prest Merg ... Preston on Merger [*A publication*] (DLA)
PRESTMO ... Prestissimo [*Very Fast*] [*Music*] (ROG)
PRESTO .... Personnel Response and Evaluation System for Target Obscuration [*Military*] (RDA)
PRESTO .... Prestissimo [*Very Fast*] [*Music*] (ROG)
PRESTO .... Program for Rapid Earth-to-Space Trajectory Optimization [*NASA*]
PRESTO ... Program Reporting and Evaluation System for Total Operations [*AFSC*]
Prest Shep T ... Sheppard's Touchstone by Preston [*A publication*] (DLA)
PRET........ Preterit [*Past tense*] [*Grammar*] (ROG)
PRET........ Pretoria [*South Africa*] (ROG)
PRETCHREP ... Preliminary Technical Report (MCD)
PRETECHREP ... Preliminary Technical Report [*Army*] (AABC)
PRETOS ... Proofreading Tests of Spelling [*Educational test*]
PRETTYBLUEBATCH ... Philadelphia Regular Exchange Tea Total Young Belles Lettres Universal Experimental Bibliographical Association To Civilize Humanity [*From Edgar Allan Poe essay "How to Write a Blackwood Article"*]
Preuss Jahrb ... Preussische Jahrbuecher [*A publication*]
Preuss Sitzb ... Preussische Akademie der Wissenschaften. Sitzungsbericht [*A publication*]
PREV......... Medical and Psychological Previews [*Database*] [*BRS Information Technologies*] [*Information service or system*] (IID)
P Rev.......... Powys Review [*A publication*]
PREV......... Prevention
PREV......... Previous (AFM)
PREV......... [*The*] Revere Fund, Inc. [*NASDAQ symbol*] (NQ)
PrevAGT ... Previous Abnormality of Glucose Tolerance
Prev Assist Dent ... Prevenzione e Assistenza Dentale [*A publication*]
PREVENT ... Precertification to Verify Necessary Treatment
Prev Fract Conf Aust Fract Group ... Prevention of Fracture. Conference of the Australian Fracture Group [*A publication*] (APTA)
Prev Hum Serv ... Prevention in Human Services [*A publication*]
Previdenza Soc ... Previdenza Sociale [*A publication*]
Previd Soc ... Previdenza Sociale [*A publication*]
Prev L Rep ... Preventive Law Reporter [*A publication*]
PREVLV.... Prevalve
Prev Med ... Preventive Medicine [*A publication*]
PREVMEDU ... Preventive Medicine Unit
Prev Stomatol ... Prevenzione Stomatologica [*A publication*]
PREVT ...... Preventative
Prev Vet M ... Preventive Veterinary Medicine [*A publication*]
Prev Vet Med ... Preventive Veterinary Medicine [*A publication*]
PREW....... Preway, Inc. [*NASDAQ symbol*] (NQ)
PREWI...... Press Wireless [*A radio service for the transmission of news*]
PREXA...... Personal Report for the Executive [*A publication*]
Pr Exch ...... Price's English Exchequer Reports [*1814-24*] [*A publication*] (DLA)
PREXD...... Propellants and Explosives [*A publication*]
PRF............ Palestine Rejection Front (BJA)
PRF............ Parachute Refurbishment Facility [*NASA*] (NASA)
PRF............ Partial Reinforcement [*Training*]
PRF............ Partido Revolucionario Febrerista [*Febrerista Revolutionary Party*] [*Paraguay*] [*Political party*] (PPW)
PRF............ Penetration Room Filtration [*Nuclear energy*] (NRCH)

prf..............	Performer [*MARC relator code*] [*Library of Congress*] (LCCP)
PRF...........	Personality Research Form [*Psychology*]
PRF...........	Personnel Readiness File [*Army*] (AABC)
PRF...........	Petroleum Research Fund
PRF...........	Phenol/Resorcinol/Formaldehyde [*Plastics technology*]
PRF...........	Plastics Recycling Foundation (EA)
PRF...........	Plutonium Reclamation Facility [*Nuclear energy*]
PRF...........	Plymouth Rock Foundation (EA)
PRF...........	Plywood Research Foundation (EA)
PRF...........	Point Response Function [*Of a telescope*]
PRF...........	Pontine Reticular Formation [*Neurophysiology*]
PRF...........	Porpoise Rescue Foundation (EA)
PRF...........	Prefac Enterprises, Inc. [*Toronto Stock Exchange symbol*]
PRF...........	Preformed [*Technical drawings*]
PRF...........	Pride Companies LP [*NYSE symbol*] (SPSG)
PRF...........	Primary Reference Fuel
PRF...........	Pro-Air [*Mountain View, CA*] [*FAA designator*] (FAAC)
PRF...........	Processor Request Flag [*Telecommunications*] (TEL)
PRF...........	Prolactin-Releasing Factor [*Endocrinology*]
PRF...........	Proliferation Regulatory Factor [*Biochemistry*]
PRF...........	Proof (KSC)
PRF...........	Protein Rich Fraction [*Food analysis*]
PRF...........	Psychiatric Research Foundation
PRF...........	Psychical Research Foundation (EA)
PRF...........	Psychosynthesis Research Foundation (EA)
PRF...........	Public Relations Foundation
PRF...........	Public Residential Facility
PRF...........	Publications Reference File [*Government Printing Office*] [*Washington, DC*] [*Database*] (MCD)
PRF...........	Publications Romanes et Francaises [*A publication*]
PRF...........	Puerto Rico Federal Reports [*A publication*] (DLA)
PRF...........	Pulse Rate Frequency (MUGU)
PRF...........	Pulse Recurrence Frequency
PRF...........	Pulse Repetition Frequency [*Data processing*]
PRF...........	Purchase Rate Factor
PRF...........	Purdue Research Foundation [*Purdue University*] [*Research center*] (MCD)
Pr Falc	President Falconer's Scotch Session Cases [*1744-51*] [*A publication*] (DLA)
PRFAW	Personnel Research Field Activity, Washington [*Navy*] (MUGU)
PRFC	Plymouth Rock Fanciers Club (EA)
PRFC	Potomac River Fisheries Commission [*Maryland and Virginia*] (NOAA)
PRFCA	Products Finishing (Cincinnati) [*A publication*]
PRFCN	Purification
PRFCS.......	Prefocus
PRFD........	Pulse Recurrence Frequency Discrimination [*Telecommunications*] (TEL)
PRFE	Polar Reflection Faraday Effect
PR Fed	Puerto Rico Federal Reports [*A publication*] (DLA)
PRFG........	Proofing [*Freight*]
PRFI	Portable Range-Finder/Illuminator
PRFI	Puerto Rican Family Institute (EA)
PRFIA	Phase-Resolved Fluoroimmunoassay
PRFIA	Product Finishing [*London*] [*A publication*]
Pr Fiz Pr Nauk Uniw Slaskiego Katowic ... Prace Fizyczne. Prace Naukowe Uniwersytetu Slaskiego w Katowicach [*Poland*] [*A publication*]	
Pr Fiz Pr Nauk Uniw Slask Katowic ... Prace Fizyczne. Prace Naukowe Uniwersytetu Slaskiego w Katowicach [*A publication*]	
PRFL........	Pressure Fed Liquid (KSC)
PRFM........	Performance (MSA)
PRFM.......	Pseudorandom Frequency Modulated [*Data processing*]
PRFO........	Prairie Forum. Journal. Canadian Plains Research Centre [*A publication*]
PRFR........	Proofer [*Freight*]
PRFRD......	Proofread (MSA)
PRFS........	Phase-Resolved Fluorescence Spectroscopy
PRFT	Partially Relaxed Fourier Transform [*Mathematics*]
PRFT	Press Fit
PRFT	Presser Foot
PRFT	Proffitt's, Inc. [*NASDAQ symbol*] (NQ)
Prft Bldg St ... Profit-Building Strategies [*A publication*]	
PRFU........	Processor Ready for Use [*Telecommunications*] (TEL)
PRG	Gilbert Associates, Inc., Reading, PA [*Library symbol*] [*Library of Congress*] (LCLS)
PRG	Parabolic Radius Gage (MCD)
PRG	Paris, IL [*Location identifier*] [*FAA*] (FAAL)
PRG	Peerless Carpet Corp. [*Toronto Stock Exchange symbol*]
PRG	People's Revolutionary Government [*Grenada*] (PD)
PRG	Perennial Rye Grass [*Immunology*]
PRG	Personnel Requirements Generator
PRG	Perugia [*Italy*] [*Seismograph station code, US Geological Survey*] (SEIS)
PRG	Pick Resources Guide [*ALLM Books*] [*England*] [*Information service or system*] (IID)
PRG	Plastic Radial Grating
PRG	Prague [*Czechoslovakia*] [*Airport symbol*] (OAG)
PRG	Procedure Review Group [*Nuclear energy*] (NRCH)
PRG	Program Regulation Guide
PRG	Program Review Group [*Military*]
PRG	Progresso. Driemaandelijks Tijdschrift van de Nederlands Italiaanse Kamer van Koophandel [*A publication*]
PRG	Provisional Revolutionary Government [*Vietcong*]
PRG	Psychological Readers' Guide [*A publication*]
PRG	Purge (AAG)
PRGC	Past Royal Grand Cross [*Freemasonry*] (ROG)
PRGEA......	Przeglad Geofizyczny [*A publication*]
Pr Geol-Mineral Acta Univ Wratislav ... Prace Geologiczno-Mineralogiczne. Acta Universitatis Wratislaviensis [*A publication*]	
PRG/I	Pick Resources Guide/International [*ALLM Books*] [*Information service or system*] (IID)
PRGLB	Prostaglandins [*A publication*]
Pr Gl Inst Gorn ... Prace Glownego Instytutu Gornictwa [*Poland*] [*A publication*]	
Pr Gl Inst Gorn Komun ... Prace Glownego Instytutu Gornictwa. Komunikat [*A publication*]	
Pr Gl Inst Przem Rolnego Spozyw ... Prace Glownego Instytutu Przemyslu Rolnego i Spozywczego [*A publication*]	
PRGM	Program (AFM)
PRGMG	Programming (MSA)
PRGMR....	Programmer (AFM)
Pr Gory Goretskaga Navuk Tav ... Pratsy Gory Goretskaga Navukov aga Tavarystva [*A publication*]	
PRGR........	ProGroup, Inc. [*NASDAQ symbol*] (NQ)
PRGS........	President of the Royal Geographical Society [*British*]
PRGS........	Prognosis (AABC)
PRGVB.....	Progressive [*A publication*]
PRH...........	Partido Revolucionario Hondureno [*Honduras Revolutionary Party*] [*Political party*] (PPW)
PRH...........	Petrol Railhead
PRH...........	Phrae [*Thailand*] [*Airport symbol*] (OAG)
PrH	Prepositus Hypoglossi [*Neuroanatomy*]
PRH...........	Program Requirements Handbook (MUGU)
PRH...........	Prolactin-Releasing Hormone [*Endocrinology*]
PRHA	President of the Royal Hibernian Academy [*British*]
Pr HC Ch...	Practice of the High Court of Chancery [*A publication*] (DLA)
PR Health Bull ... Puerto Rico Health Bulletin [*A publication*]	
PR Health Sci J ... Puerto Rico Health Sciences Journal [*A publication*]	
PRHi..........	Historical Society of Berks County, Reading, PA [*Library symbol*] [*Library of Congress*] (LCLS)
PrHlit........	Prace Historycznoliterackie [*A publication*]
PRI.............	Farmington, MO [*Location identifier*] [*FAA*] (FAAL)
PRI.............	Pacific Research Institute for Public Policy (EA)
PRI.............	Pain Rating Index
PRI.............	Paint Research Institute (EA)
PRI.............	Paleontological Research Institution (EA)
PRI.............	Partido Revolucionario Institucional [*Party of the Institutionalized Revolution*] [*Mexico*] [*Political party*]
PRI.............	Partito Repubblicano Italiano [*Italian Republican Party*] [*Political party*] (PPW)
PRI.............	Partner Relationship Inventory [*Marital relations test*] [*Psychology*]
PRI.............	Peace Research Institute [*Later, Institute for Policy Studies*] (EA)
PRI.............	Performance Registry International
PRI.............	Personal Reaction Index [*Interpersonal skills and attitudes test*]
PRI.............	Personnel Research, Incorporated [*Information service or system*] (IID)
PRI.............	Petroleum Recovery Institute [*Research center*] (RCD)
PRI.............	Phosphate Rock Institute [*Defunct*] (EA)
PRI.............	Photo RADAR Intelligence
PRI.............	Photographic Reconnaissance and Interpretation (NATG)
PRI.............	Pineapple Research Institute of Hawaii (EA)
PRI.............	Plasticity Retention Index [*Rubber test method*]
PRI.............	Plastics and Rubber Institute [*Formed by a merger of Institution of the Rubber Industry and Plastics Institute*] (EAIO)
PRI.............	Polymer Research Institute [*Polytechnic Institute of New York*] [*Research center*] (RCD)
PRI.............	Polymer Research Institute [*University of Massachusetts*] [*Research center*] (RCD)
PRI.............	Practice Training Index
PRI.............	Praslin Island [*Seychelles Islands*] [*Airport symbol*] (OAG)
PRI.............	Preliminary Rifle Instruction [*Military*]
PRI.............	Prescriptive Reading Inventory
PRI.............	President Regimental Institutes [*British*]
PRI.............	President of the Royal Institute (of Painters in Water Colours) [*British*] (ROG)
PRI.............	President of the Royal Institution (London) (ROG)
PRI.............	Prevention Routiere Internationale [*International Road Safety Organization*] [*Luxembourg*] (EAIO)
Pri	Price's English Exchequer Reports [*1814-24*] [*A publication*] (DLA)
Pri	Price's English Mining Commissioners' Cases [*A publication*] (DLA)
PRI.............	Priest [*California*] [*Seismograph station code, US Geological Survey*] (SEIS)
PRI.............	Primary (KSC)
PRI.............	Primate Research Institute [*New Mexico State University*] [*Hollman, NM*]

PRI............ Prime Computer Inc., Corporation Library, Framingham, MA [*OCLC symbol*]   (OCLC)
PRI............ Princeville Airways, Inc. [*Honolulu, HI*] [*FAA designator*]   (FAAC)
PRI............ Priority   (AFM)
PRI............ Priority Repair Induction [*Code*]
PRI............ Priority Requirement for Information   (AFM)
Pri............. Priroda [*A publication*]
Pri............ Priscianus [*Authority cited in pre-1607 legal work*]   (DSA)
PRI............ Prison
PRI............ Private
PRI............ Prize [*or Prizeman*] [*British*]   (ROG)
PRI............ Processing Research Institute [*Carnegie Mellon University*]
PRI............ Production Records, Incorporated   (EA)
PRI............ Program Revision Intent
PRI............ Promus Companies [*NYSE symbol*]   (SPSG)
PRI............ Proteus Resources, Inc. [*Vancouver Stock Exchange symbol*]
PRI............ Psoriasis Research Institute   (EA)
PRI............ Puerto Rican Independence [*Later, GPRG*] [*An association*]   (EA)
PRI............ Puerto Rico [*ANSI three-letter standard code*]   (CNC)
PRI............ Pulse Rate Increase [*Medicine*]
PRI............ Pulse Rate Indicator
PRI............ Pulse Recurrence [*or Repetition*] Interval   (NATG)
PRI............ Pulse Repetition Internal
PRI............ Pure Research Institute [*Later, BRINC*]   (EA)
PRIA......... Peer Review Improvement Act of 1982
PRIA......... President of the Royal Irish Academy
PRIA......... Priam Corp. [*NASDAQ symbol*]   (NQ)
PRIA......... Proceedings. Royal Irish Academy [*A publication*]
PRIA......... Public Rangelands Improvement Act of 1978
PRIAA....... Proceedings. Royal Irish Academy. Section A. Mathematical and Physical Sciences [*A publication*]
PRIAM...... Precision Range Information Analysis for Missiles   (MCD)
PrIAU-SJ .. Inter-American University of Puerto Rico, San Juan Campus, San Juan, PR [*Library symbol*] [*Library of Congress*]   (LCLS)
PRIB......... Private Brands, Inc. [*NASDAQ symbol*]   (NQ)
PRIBA....... President of the Royal Institute of British Architects
PRIBA....... Proceedings. Royal Irish Academy. Section B. Biological, Geological, and Chemical Science [*A publication*]
PRIBAN.... Proceedings. Royal Irish Academy. Section B. Biological, Geological, and Chemical Science [*A publication*]
Pribliz Metod Resen Differencial Uravnen ... Priblizennye Metody Resenija Differencial nyh Uravnenii [*A publication*]
Prib Metody Anal Izluch ... Pribory i Metody Analiza Izluchenii [*A publication*]
Pribory i Sistemy Avtomat ... Pribory i Sistemy Avtomatiki [*A publication*]
Prib Sist Avtom ... Pribory i Sistemy Avtomatiki [*A publication*]
Prib Sist Upr ... Pribory i Sistemy Upravleniya [*A publication*]
Prib i Sist Upr ... Pribory i Sistemy Upravleniya [*A publication*]
Prib i Tekh Eksp ... Pribory i Tekhnika Eksperimenta [*A publication*]
Prib Tekhn ... Pribory i Tekhnika Eksperimenta [*A publication*]
Prib Ustroistva Sredstv Avtom Telemekh ... Pribory i Ustroistva Sredstv Avtomatiki i Telemekhaniki [*A publication*]
PRIC Dec... Puerto Rico Industrial Commission Decisions [*A publication*]   (DLA)
PRICE ...... Physicians for Research in Cost-Effectiveness   (EA)
Price.......... Price's English Exchequer Reports [*A publication*]   (DLA)
Price.......... Price's English Mining Commissioners' Cases [*A publication*]   (DLA)
PRICE ...... Pricing Review to Intensify Competitive Environment [*Data processing*]
PRICE ...... Programmed Review of Information for Costing and Evaluation   (MCD)
Price Gen Pr ... Price's General Practice [*A publication*]   (DLA)
Price Liens ... Price on Maritime Liens [*1940*] [*A publication*]   (DLA)
Price Min Cas ... Price's Mining Cases [*A publication*]   (DLA)
Price Notes PC ... Price's Notes of Practice Cases in Exchequer [*1830-31*] [*England*] [*A publication*]   (DLA)
Price Notes PP ... Price's Notes of Points of Practice, English Exchequer Cases [*A publication*]   (DLA)
Price PC..... Price's English Practice Cases [*1830-31*] [*A publication*]   (DLA)
Price Pr Cas ... Price's English Practice Cases [*A publication*]   (DLA)
Price R Est ... Price on Acts Relating to Real Estate [*A publication*]   (DLA)
Price & St... Price and Stewart's Trade Mark Cases [*A publication*]   (DLA)
Price Waterhouse R ... Price Waterhouse Review [*A publication*]
Price Waterhouse Rev ... Price Waterhouse Review [*A publication*]
Prickett...... Prickett's Reports [*1 Idaho*] [*A publication*]   (DLA)
PRICOM.... Prison Commission [*British*]
PRID......... Pridie [*The Day Before*] [*Latin*]
PriD .... Princeton Datafilm, Inc., Princeton, NJ [*Library symbol*] [*Library of Congress*]   (LCLS)
Prid & C ... Prideaux and Cole's English Reports [*4 New Sessions Cases*] [*1850-51*] [*A publication*]   (DLA)
Prid Ch W ... Prideaux's Directions to Churchwardens [*10th ed.*] [*1835*] [*A publication*]   (DLA)
Prid & Co ... Prideaux and Cole's English Reports [*4 New Sessions Cases*] [*1850-51*] [*A publication*]   (DLA)
PRIDCO.... Puerto Rico Industrial Development Company

Prid Conv... Prideaux's Forms and Precedents in Conveyancing [*24th ed.*] [*1952*] [*A publication*]   (DLA)
PRIDE....... National Parents' Resource Institute for Drug Education   (EA)
PRIDE....... People for Rehabilitating and Integrating the Disabled through Education [*New York City*]
PRIDE....... Perfection Requires Individual Defect Elimination
PRIDE....... Personal Responsibility in Daily Effort [*Military Airlift Command's acronym for the Zero Defects Program*]
PRIDE....... Preschool and Kindergarten Interest Descriptor [*Educational test*]
PRIDE....... Priority Receiving with Inter-Departmental Efficiency [*Data processing*]
PRIDE....... Production of Reliable Items Demands Excellence [*Navy*]   (NG)
PRIDE....... Productive Rehabilitation Institute of Dallas for Ergonomics [*Research center*]   (RCD)
PRIDE....... Professional Results in Daily Effort [*Strategic Air Command's acronym for the Zero Defects Program*]
PRIDE....... Programmed Reliability in Design Engineering
PRIDE....... Promote Real Independence for the Disabled and Elderly   (EA)
PRIDE....... Prompt Response Insurance Delivery Express
PRIDE....... Protection of Reefs and Islands from Degradation and Exploitation
Pride Inst J Long Term Home Health Care ... Pride Institute. Journal of Long Term Home Health Care [*A publication*]
Prid Judg ... Prideaux's Judgments and Crown Debts [*4th ed.*] [*1854*] [*A publication*]   (DLA)
PRIF .... Prior Year Refund Information File [*IRS*]
PRI-FLY.... Primary Flight Control [*on an aircraft carrier*] [*Navy*]
PRIGA....... Prace Instytutu Geologii [*A publication*]
PRIH .... Prolactin-Release Inhibiting Factor [*Also, PIF*] [*Endocrinology*]
PRIISM..... Pacific Research Institute for Information Systems and Management [*University of Hawaii at Manoa*] [*Research center*]   (RCD)
Prikladnaya Geofiz ... Prikladnaya Geofizika [*A publication*]
Prikl Biokhim Mikrobiol ... Prikladnaya Biokhimiya i Mikrobiologiya [*A publication*]
Prikl Geofiz ... Prikladnaya Geofizika [*A publication*]
Prikl Geom i Inzener Grafika ... Prikladnaja Geometrija i Inzenernaja Grafika [*A publication*]
Prikl Mat ... Prikladnaya Matematika i Mekhanika [*A publication*]
Prikl Mat Mekh ... Prikladnaya Matematika i Mekhanika [*A publication*]
Prikl Mat i Mekh ... Prikladnaya Matematika i Mekhanika [*A publication*]
Prikl Mat i Programmirovanie ... Prikladnaja Matematika i Programmirovanie [*A publication*]
Prikl Meh .. Akademija Nauk Ukrainskoi SSR. Otdelenie Matematiki. Mehaniki i Kibernetiki. Prikladnaja Mehanika [*A publication*]
Prikl Mekh ... Akademiya Nauk Ukrainskoi SSR. Otdelenie Matematiki. Mekhaniki i Kibernetiki. Prikladnaya Mekhanika [*A publication*]
Prikl Mekh ... Prikladnaya Mekhanika [*A publication*]
Prikl Mekh Priborostr ... Prikladnaya Mekhanika v Priborostroenii [*A publication*]
Prikl Problemy Proc i Plast ... Gor'kovskii Gosudarstvennyi Universitet Imeni N. I. Lobacevskogo. Prikladnye Problemy Procnosti i Plasticnosti [*A publication*]
Prikl Yad Fiz ... Prikladnaya Yadernaya Fizika [*A publication*]
Prikl Yad Spektrosk ... Prikladnaya Yadernaya Spektroskopiya [*A publication*]
PrilKJIF .... Prilozi za Knjizevnost, Jezik, Istoriju, i Folklor [*A publication*]
Prilozh Sb Nauchn Rab Med Fak Karlova Univ Gradtse Kralove ... Prilozhenie k Sborniku Nauchnykh Rabot Meditsinskogo Fakul'teta Karlova Universiteta v Gradtse Kralove [*A publication*]
Prilozi........ Prilozi za Knjizevnost, Jezik, Istoriju, i Folklor [*A publication*]
PrilPJ .... Prilozi Proucavanju Jezika [*A publication*]
PRIM......... Plans and Reports Improvement Memorandum [*Military*]   (CAAL)
PRIM......... Plume Radiation Intensity Measurement   (MUGU)
PRIM......... Primages, Inc. [*NASDAQ symbol*]   (NQ)
PRIM......... Primary   (AFM)
PRIM......... Primate
PRIM......... Primitive
PRIM......... Program for Information Managers [*Later, AIM*] [*An association*]
PRIMA...... Pollutant Response in Marine Animals [*Marine science*]   (MSC)
PRIMA...... Public Risk and Insurance Management Association [*Washington, DC*]   (EA)
PRIMAR ... Program to Improve Management of Army Resources   (AABC)
Primary Cardiol ... Primary Cardiology [*A publication*]
Primary Ed ... Primary Education [*A publication*]
Primary Educ ... Primary Education [*A publication*]   (APTA)
Primary J... Primary Journal [*A publication*]   (APTA)
Primary Maths ... Primary Mathematics [*A publication*]
Primary Sci Bull ... Primary Science Bulletin [*A publication*]   (APTA)
PRIMATE ... Personal Retrieval of Information by Microcomputer and Terminal Ensemble
Primate Behav ... Primate Behavior [*A publication*]
Primates Med ... Primates in Medicine [*A publication*]

Primatolog ... Primatologia [*A publication*]
PRIME ...... Planning through Retrieval of Information for Management Extrapolation
PRIME ...... Precision Integrator for Meteorological Echoes   (IEEE)
PRIME ...... Precision Recovery Including Maneuvering Entry [*Air Force*]
PRIME ...... Prescribed Right to Income and Maximum Equity
PRIME ...... Priority Improved Management Effort   (KSC)
PRIME ...... Priority Improvement Effort [*DoD*]
PRIME ...... Priority Management Effort [*Army*]
PRIME ...... Priority Management Evaluation [*Navy*]
PRIME ...... Procarbazine, Ifosfamide, Methotrexate [*Antineoplastic drug regimen*]
PRIME ...... Processing, Research, Inspection, and Marine Extension Program [*National Oceanic and Atmospheric Administration*]   (MSC)
PRIME ...... Profession Related Intern-Mentorship Experience
PRIME ...... Program Independence, Modularity, Economy
PRIME ...... Program Research in Integrated Multiethnic Education [*Defunct*]   (EA)
PRIME ...... Programmed Instruction for Management Education [*American Management Association*]
Prim Ed-Pop Ed ... Primary Education - Popular Educator [*A publication*]
Prim Educ .. Primary Education [*A publication*]
Primenen Mat Ekonom ... Leningradskii Ordena Lenina Gosudarstvennyi Universitet Imeni A. A. Zdanova. Kafedra i Laboratorija Ekonomiko-Matematiceskih Metodov. Primenenie Matematikii v Ekonomike [*A publication*]
Primenen Mat Ekonom ... Primenenie Matematiki v Ekonomike [*A publication*]
Primenen Teor Verojatnost i Mat Statist ... Primenenie Teorii Verojatnostei i Matematiceskoi Statistiki [*A publication*]
PRIMENET ... Prime Network Software Package [*Prime Computer, Inc.*]
Primen Mat Metodov Biol ... Primenenie Matematicheskikh Metodov v Biologii [*A publication*]
Primen Mikroelem Sel-Khoz Akad Nauk UkrSSR ... Primenenie Mikroelementov Sel'skom Khozyaistve Akademiya Nauk Ukrainskoi SSR [*A publication*]
Primen Polim Mater Nar Khoz ... Primenenie Polimernykh Materialov v Narodnom Khozyaistve [*A publication*]
Primen Tsifrovykh Analogovykh Vychisl Mash Yad Fiz Tekh ... Primenenie Tsifrovykh i Analogovykh Vychislitel'nykh Mashin v Yadernoi Fizike i Tekhnike [*A publication*]
Primen Ul'traakust Issled Veshchestva ... Primenenie Ul'traakustiki k Issledovaniyu Veshchestva [*A publication*]
PRIMER ... Patient Record Information for Education Requirements [*Data processing*]
PRIMES .... Productivity Integrated Measurement System [*Army*]
PRIMEX ... Private Message Switching [*Telecommunications*] [*British*]
PRIMIR .... Product Improvement Management Information Report
PRIM LUC ... Prima Luce [*Early in the Morning*] [*Pharmacy*]
PRIM M .... Primo Mane [*Early in the Morning*] [*Pharmacy*]
PRIM METH ... Primitive Methodist [*A publication*]
PRIMO ...... Programmable, Realtime, Incoherent, Matrix, Optical Processor [*Data processing*]
PRIMOS ... Prime Operating System [*Prime Computer, Inc.*]
PRIM & R ... Public Responsibility in Medicine and Research   (EA)
PRIMS ...... Product Requirement Information Management System   (MCD)
PRIMTRA ... Air Primary Training
PRIMUS ... Physician Reservists in Medical Universities and Schools [*Military*]
PRIMUS ... Primary Medical Care for the Uniformed Services [*DoD*]
PRIN .... Partido Revolucionario de la Izquierda Nacionalista [*National Leftist Revolutionary Party*] [*Bolivia*] [*Political party*]   (PPW)
PRIN .... Performance Risk Index Number   (NG)
PRIN .... Powerec International [*NASDAQ symbol*]   (NQ)
PRIN .... Princeton [*New Jersey*] [*Seismograph station code, US Geological Survey*]   (SEIS)
PRIN .... Principal
PRIN .... Principality   (ROG)
PRIN .... Principally   (ROG)
PRIN .... Principia [*Elements*] [*Latin*]   (ROG)
PRIN .... Principle   (ROG)
PRINAIR .. Puerto Rico National Airlines
Princ .... Princeton Review [*A publication*]
PRINC .... Principal
PRINC .... Principle
Princ in Counc ... Principals in Council [*A publication*]
PRINCE .... Parts Reliability Information Center [*NASA*]
PRINCE .... Programmed International Computer Environment [*International relations simulation game*]
PRINCE .... Programmed Reinforced Instruction Necessary to Continuing Education
PRINCE/APIC ... Parts Reliability Information Center/Apollo Parts Information Center [*NASA*]
Prince NML ... Prince's New Mexico Laws [*A publication*]   (DLA)
Prince S B .. Princeton Seminary Bulletin [*A publication*]
Princeton Coll B ... Princeton College. Bulletin [*A publication*]

Princeton Conf Cerebrovasc Dis ... Princeton Conference on Cerebrovascular Diseases [*A publication*]
Princeton Conf Cereb Vasc Dis ... Princeton Conference on Cerebral Vascular Diseases [*Later, Princeton Conference on Cerebrovascular Diseases*] [*A publication*]
Princeton Math Ser ... Princeton Mathematical Series [*A publication*]
Princeton Mus Rec ... Princeton University. Museum of Historic Art. Record [*A publication*]
Princeton Stud Math Econom ... Princeton Studies in Mathematical Economics [*A publication*]
Princeton Univ Lib Chron ... Princeton University. Library. Chronicle [*A publication*]
Princ Food Rice ... Principal Food. Rice [*A publication*]
Principia Cardiol ... Principia Cardiologica [*A publication*]
Pr Incntv .... Premium/Incentive Business [*A publication*]
Princ Pract Pediatr Surg Spec ... Principles and Practice of the Pediatric Surgical Specialities [*A publication*]
PrincSB ...... Princeton Seminary Bulletin [*A publication*]
PrincSemB ... Princeton Seminary Bulletin [*Princeton, NJ*] [*A publication*]
Princ Tech Hum Res Ther ... Principles and Techniques of Human Research and Therapeutics [*A publication*]
Princ Theol R ... Princeton Theological Review [*A publication*]
Princ Univ Bull ... Princeton University. Bulletin [*A publication*]
Princ Viana ... Principe de Viana [*A publication*]
PRIND .... Present Indications Are [*Aviation*]   (FAAC)
PRINDUS ... Prison Industries [*Industries conducted in English prisons*]
PRING .... Partido Revolucionario de Izquierda Nacional Gueiler [*Revolutionary Party of the National Left - Gueiler Wing*] [*Bolivia*] [*Political party*]   (PPW)
PRIN-L ...... Partido Revolucionario de la Izquierda Nacional Laboral [*Political party*]   (PPW)
PRINM ...... Partido Revolucionario de la Izquierda Nacional Moller [*Bolivia*] [*Political party*]   (PPW)
PRINMUS ... Principal Musician [*Marine Corps*]
PRINOBC/NEC ... Primary Navy Officer Billet Classification and Navy Enlisted Classification
Prin PL ...... Eden's Principles of Penal Law [*A publication*]   (DLA)
Prins & Conderlag ... Prins and Conderlag's Reports [*Ceylon*] [*A publication*]   (ILCA)
Pr Inst Badaw Lesn ... Prace Instytutu Badawczego Lesnictwa [*A publication*]
Pr Inst Celul Papier ... Prace Instytutu Celulozowo-Papierniczego [*A publication*]
Pr Inst Cybern PAN ... Prace Instytutu Cybernetyki Stosowanej PAN [*Polska Akademia Nauk*] [*A publication*]
Pr Inst Elektrotech ... Prace Instytutu Elektrotechniki [*A publication*]
Pr Inst Elektrotech (Warsaw) ... Prace Instytutu Elektrotechniki (Warsaw) [*A publication*]
Pr Inst Fiz Politech Warsz ... Prace Instytutu Fizyki Politechnica Warszawska [*A publication*]
Pr Inst Geol Korisnikh Kopalin Akad Nauk Ukr ... Pratsi Institut Geologii Korisnikh Kopalin Akademiya Nauk Ukrains'koi [*A publication*]
Pr Inst Gidrobiol Akad Nauk Ukr RSR ... Pratsi Institutu Gidrobiologii Akademiya Nauk Ukrains'koi RSR [*A publication*]
Pr Inst Gospod Wodnej ... Prace Instytutu Gospodarki Wodnej [*A publication*]
Pr Inst Hutn ... Prace Instytutow Hutniczych [*A publication*]
Pr Inst Inz Chem Politech Warsz ... Prace Instytutu Inzynierii Chemicznej Politechniki Warszawskiej [*A publication*]
Pr Inst Jedwabiu Nat ... Prace Instytutu Jedwabiu Naturalnego [*A publication*]
Pr Inst Lab Badaw Przem Spozyw ... Prace Instytutow i Laboratoriow Badawczych Przemyslu Spozywczego [*A publication*]
Pr Inst Lacznosci ... Prace Instytutu Lacznosci [*A publication*]
Pr Inst Masz Mat ... Prace Instytutu Maszyn Matematycznych [*A publication*]
Pr Inst Masz Przeplyw ... Prace Instytutu Maszyn Przeplywowych [*A publication*]
Pr Inst Masz Przeplyw Pol Akad Nauk ... Prace Instytutu Maszyn Przeplywowych. Polska Akademia Nauk [*Poland*] [*A publication*]
Pr Inst Mech ... Prace Instytutow Mechaniki [*A publication*]
Pr Inst Mech Precyz ... Prace Instytutu Mechaniki Precyzyjnej [*Poland*] [*A publication*]
Pr Inst Met ... Prace Instytutu Metalurgue [*A publication*]
Pr Inst Metal Gliwice (Pol) ... Prace Instytutu Metalurgii. Gliwice (Poland) [*A publication*]
Pr Inst Metal Zelaza ... Prace Instytutu Metalurgii Zelaza [*A publication*]
Pr Inst Meteorol Gospod Wodnej ... Prace Instytutu Meteorologii i Gospodarki Wodnej [*A publication*]
Pr Inst Met Niezelaz ... Prace Instytutu Metali Niezelaznych [*A publication*]
Pr Inst Minist Hutn (Pol) ... Prace Instytutu Ministerstwa Hutnictwa (Poland) [*A publication*]
Pr Inst Naft (Krakow) ... Prace Instytutu Naftowego (Krakow) [*Poland*] [*A publication*]
Pr Inst Obrobki Skrawaniem ... Prace Instytutu Obrobki Skrawaniem [*Poland*] [*A publication*]
Pr Inst Odlew ... Prace Instytutu Odlewnictwa [*A publication*]
Pr Inst Odlew Zesz Spec ... Prace Instytutu Odlewnictwa. Zeszyty Specjalne [*A publication*]

Pr Inst Odlew Zesz Specjalne ... Prace Instytutu Odlewnictwa. Zeszyty Specjalne [*Poland*] [*A publication*]
Pr Inst Przem Cukrow ... Prace Instytutu Przemyslu Cukrowniczego [*A publication*]
Pr Inst Przem Miecz ... Prace Instytutu Przemyslu Mieczarskiego [*A publication*]
Pr Inst Przem Org ... Prace Instytutu Przemyslu Organicznego [*A publication*]
Pr Inst Przem Skorzanego ... Prace Instytutu Przemyslu Skorzanego [*A publication*]
Pr Inst Przem Szkla Ceram ... Prace Instytutu Przemyslu Szkla i Ceramiki [*A publication*]
Pr Inst Przem Wlok Lykowych ... Prace Instytutu Przemyslu Wlokien Lykowych [*A publication*]
Pr Inst Sadow Ser E Mater Zjazdow Konf ... Prace Instytutu Sadownictwa. Seria E. Materialy Zjazdow i Konferencji [*A publication*]
Pr Inst Sadow Skierniew ... Prace Instytutu Sadownictwa w Skierniewicach [*A publication*]
Pr Inst Sadow Skierniewicach ... Prace Instytutu Sadownictwa w Skierniewicach [*A publication*]
Pr Inst Sadow Skierniewicach Ser A Pr Dosw Z Zakresu Sadow ... Prace Instytutu Sadownictwa w Skierniewicach. Seria A. Prace Doswiadczalne Z Zakresu Sadownictwa [*A publication*]
Pr Inst Tech Budow Ser 1 ... Prace Instytutu Techniki Budowlanej. Seria 1. Materialy Budowlane i Ich Zastosowanie [*A publication*]
Pr Inst Tech Budow Ser 2 ... Prace Instytutu Techniki Budowlanej. Seria 2. Konstrukeje Budowlane i Inzynierskie [*A publication*]
Pr Inst Tech Ciepl ... Prace Instytutu Techniki Cieplnej [*Poland*] [*A publication*]
Pr Inst Technol Drewna ... Prace Instytut Technologii Drewna [*A publication*]
Pr Inst Technol Elektron ... Prace Instytutu Technologii Elektronowej [*A publication*]
Pr Inst Tele- & Radiotech ... Prace Instytutu Tele- i Radiotechnicznego [*A publication*]
Pr Inst Wlok ... Prace Instytutu Wlokiennictwa [*A publication*]
Pr Inst Wlok (Lodz) ... Prace Instytutu Wlokiennictwa (Lodz) [*A publication*]
PRINT .... Pre-Edited Interpretive System [*Data processing*]
PRINT .... Public Release of Information and Transcripts [*Student legal action organization*]
Print Art ..... Printing Art [*Massachusetts*] [*A publication*]
Print Art Q ... Printing Art Quarterly [*A publication*]
Print Bookbind Trade Rev ... Printing and Bookbinding Trade Review [*A publication*]
Print Coll Q ... Print Collector's Quarterly [*A publication*]
Print Equip Eng ... Printing Equipment Engineer [*A publication*]
Print Graph Arts ... Printing and Graphic Arts [*A publication*]   (APTA)
Printing .... Printing Impressions [*A publication*]
Printing Abs ... Printing Abstracts [*A publication*]
Printing Abstr ... Printing Abstracts [*A publication*]
Printing Impr ... Printing Impressions [*A publication*]
Printing and Pub ... Printing and Publishing [*A publication*]
Printing Trades J ... Printing Trades Journal [*A publication*]
Print Mag .. Printing Magazine [*A publication*]
Print Mag Natl Lithogr ... Printing Magazine National Lithographer [*A publication*]
Print Manag ... Printing Management [*A publication*]
Print Prod .. Printing Production [*A publication*]
Print & Pub ... Printing and Publishing [*A publication*]
Print R .... Print Review [*A publication*]
Print Rev .... Print Review [*A publication*]
Print Sales ... Printed Salesmanship [*A publication*]
Print Technol ... Printing Technology [*A publication*]
Print Trades J ... Printing Trades Journal [*A publication*]   (APTA)
PRINUL .... Puerto Rico International Undersea Laboratory
PRIO .... International Peace Research Institution, Oslo [*Norway*]
PRIO .... Priority [*Telecommunications*]
PRIOR .... Program for In-Orbital Rendezvous [*Antisatellite system*] [*Air Force*]
PRIP .... Park Restoration and Improvement Program [*National Park Service*]
PRIP .... Parts Reliability Improvement Program
PRIP .... Planned Retirement Income Program [*Institute of Financial Management*]
PRIPACSEVOCAM ... Primary Pacific Secure Voice Communications [*Navy*]   (CAAL)
Pr IPO .... Prace IPO [*Instytutu Przemyslu Organicznego*] [*A publication*]
PRIPP .... Pacific Research Institute for Public Policy   (EA)
PRIRA .... Priroda [*Moscow*] [*A publication*]
P R Ir Ac A ... Proceedings. Royal Irish Academy. Section A. Mathematical, Astronomical, and Physical Science [*A publication*]
P R Ir Ac B ... Proceedings. Royal Irish Academy. Section B. Biological, Geological, and Chemical Science [*A publication*]
P R Ir Ac C ... Proceedings. Royal Irish Academy. Section C. Archaeology, Celtic Studies, History, Linguistics, Literature [*A publication*]
PRIRB .... Priroda (Sofia, Bulgaria) [*A publication*]
Prir Gaz Sib ... Prirodnyi Gaz Sibiri [*A publication*]
Prir-Mat Fak Univ Kiril Metodij (Skopje) God Zb Biol ... Prirodno-Matematicka Fakultet na Univerzitetot Kiril i Metodij (Skopje). Godisen Zbornik. Biologija [*A publication*]

Prir Mat Fak Univ Kiril Metodij (Skopje) God Zb Sek A ... Prirodno-Matematicka Fakultet na Univerzitetot Kiril i Metodij (Skopje). Godisen Zbornik. Sekcja A. Matematika, Fizika, i Hemija [*A publication*]
Prir (Moscow) ... Priroda (Moscow) [*A publication*]
Prirod-Mat Fak Univ Kiril i Metodij (Skopje) Godisen Zb ... Prirodno-Matematicka Fakultet na Univerzitetot Kiril i Metodij (Skopje). Godisen Zbornik [*A publication*]
Prirod-Mat Fak Univ Kiril Metodij (Skopje) Godisen Zb ... Prirodno-Matematicka Fakultet na Univerzitetot Kiril i Metodij (Skopje). Godisen Zbornik [*A publication*]
Prirodonauc Muz Skopje Posebno Izd ... Prirodonaucen Muzej Skopje Posebno Izdanie [*A publication*]
Prirodosl Istraz Acta Biol ... Prirodoslovna Istrazivanja Acta Biologica [*A publication*]
Prirodosl Istraz Acta Geol ... Prirodoslovna Istrazivanja Acta Geologica [*A publication*]
Prirodoved Cas Slezsky ... Prirodovedny Casopis Slezsky [*A publication*]
Prirodoved Pr Ustavu Cesk Akad Ved Brne ... Prirodovedne Prace Ustavu Ceskoslovenske Akademie Ved v Brne [*A publication*]
Prir (Sofia) ... Priroda (Sofia) [*A publication*]
Prir Tr Resur Levoberezhnoi Ukr Ikh Ispolz ... Prirodnye i Trudot ye Resursy Levoberezhnoi Ukrainy i Ikh Ispolzovanie [*A publication*]
Prir Usloviya Zapadn Sib ... Prirodnye Usloviya Zapadnoi Sibiri [*A publication*]
PRIS .... Pacific Range Instrumentation Satellite   (MUGU)
PRIS .... Pest Management Research Information System [*Agriculture Canada*] [*Information service or system*]   (IID)
PRIS .... Physis. Rivista Internazionale di Storia della Scienze [*A publication*]
PRIS .... Prison   (ROG)
PRIS .... Prisoner   (AFM)
PRIS .... Program Resource Information System [*Department of Agriculture*]
PRIS .... Propeller Revolution Indicator System   (MSA)
Prisadki Smaz Maslam ... Prisadki i Smazochnym Maslam [*A publication*]
PRISCO .... Price Stabilization Corporation
PRISD .... Proceedings. Indian Academy of Sciences. Series Engineering Sciences [*A publication*]
PRISE .... Page Reader Input System with Editing   (NVT)
PRISE .... Pennsylvania Resources and Information Center for Special Education [*Montgomery County Intermediate Unit*] [*King of Prussia*] [*Information service or system*]   (IID)
PRISE .... Pennsylvania's Regional Instruction System for Education [*Network of colleges and universities*]
PRISE .... Program for Integrated Shipboard Electronics
PRISIC .... Photographic Reconnaissance Interpretation Section [*Squadron*] Intelligence Center [*JICPOA*]
Pris Jrnl .... Prisoners Journal [*A publication*]
PRISM ...... Parameter Related Internal Standard Method [*Statistical procedure*]
PRISM ...... Pattern Recognition Information Synthesis Modeling [*Market analysis*]
PRISM ...... Personnel Record Information Systems for Management
PRISM ...... Personnel Requirements Information System Methodology   (NVT)
PRISM ...... Power Reactor Inherently Safe Module [*Nuclear energy*]
PRISM ...... Program Reliability Information System for Management [*Polaris*]
PRISM ...... Programmed Integrated System Maintenance   (NG)
PRISM ...... Progressive Refinement of Integrated Supply Management   (AFM)
Prism Int .... Prism International [*A publication*]
PRISNET ... Private Switching Network Service [*Telecommunications*]
Prison L Reptr ... Prison Law Reporter [*A publication*]   (ILCA)
Prison L Rptr ... Prison Law Reporter [*A publication*]   (DLA)
Prison Serv J ... Prison Service Journal [*A publication*]   (DLA)
PrisrAcSci&Hum ... Proceedings. Israel Academy of Sciences and Humanities [*Jerusalem*] [*A publication*]
PRISS .... Plaza Realty Investors SBI [*NASDAQ symbol*]   (NQ)
PRISS .... Post Deployment Software Support Real-Time Interactive Simulation System
PRIST .... Paper Radioimmunosorbent Test [*Analytical biochemistry*]
PRITA ...... Problems of Information Transmission [*A publication*]
Pritch Adm Dig ... Pritchard's Admiralty Digest [*3rd ed.*] [*1887*] [*A publication*]   (DLA)
Pritch M & D ... Pritchard's Divorce and Matrimonial Causes [*3rd ed.*] [*1874*] [*A publication*]   (DLA)
Pritch Quar Sess ... Pritchard's Quarter Sessions [*A publication*]   (DLA)
Pr ITME .... Prace ITME [*Instytut Technologii Materialow Elektronicznych*] [*A publication*]
PRIV .... Private
PRIV .... Privative
PRIV .... Privilege
Privacy Rept ... Privacy Report [*A publication*]
Private Pract ... Private Practice [*A publication*]
PRIVAUTH ... Travel Authorized via Privately-Owned Vehicle with Understanding No Additional Cost to Government Involved
Priv C App ... Privy Council Appeals [*England*] [*A publication*]   (DLA)

Priv CDI .... Indian Privy Council Decisions [*A publication*] (DLA)
Priv Counc App ... Privy Council Appeals [*England*] [*A publication*] (DLA)
Priv Counc Dl ... Privy Council Decisions [*India*] [*A publication*] (DLA)
PRIVE ...... Private (ROG)
Priv Hous Fin ... Private Housing Finance [*A publication*] (DLA)
Priv Lib ...... Private Library [*A publication*]
Priv Libr ..... Private Library [*A publication*]
Priv Lond ... Privilegia Londini [*A publication*] (DLA)
PRIZE .... Program for Research in Information Systems Engineering [*University of Michigan*] [*Research center*] (RCD)
Prize CR ..... Prize Court Reports [*South Africa*] [*A publication*] (DLA)
PRIZM ...... Potential Rating Index by ZIP [*Zone Improvement Plan*] Market [*Advertising*]
PRJ .... American Junior College of Puerto Rico, Bayamon, PR [*OCLC symbol*] (OCLC)
PRJ .... Payroll Journal [*Accounting*]
PRJ .... Port Royal [*Jamaica*] [*Seismograph station code, US Geological Survey*] (SEIS)
PrJ .... Preussische Jahrbuecher [*A publication*]
PRJ .... Public Relations Journal [*A publication*]
PRJC .... Pearl River Junior College [*Poplarville, MS*]
PRJC .... Puerto Rico Junior College
PRJMP ...... Pressure Jump (FAAC)
PR J Public Health Trop Med ... Puerto Rico Journal of Public Health and Tropical Medicine [*A publication*]
PRK .... Democratic People's Republic of Korea [*ANSI three-letter standard code*] (CNC)
PRK .... Paraskevi [*Lesbos*] [*Greece*] [*Seismograph station code, US Geological Survey*] (SEIS)
PRK .... Park
PRK .... Parkside Petroleum, Inc. [*Toronto Stock Exchange symbol*] [*Vancouver Stock Exchange symbol*]
PRK .... People's Republic of Kampuchea [*Formerly, Cambodia*] (PD)
PRK .... Praktijkgids [*A publication*]
PRK .... Pridie Kalendas [*The Day before the Calends*] [*Latin*]
PRK .... Primary Rat Kidney [*Cells*]
PRKG .... Parking
PRKNA ..... Progress in Reaction Kinetics [*A publication*]
Pr Kom Biol (Poznan) ... Prace Komisji Biologicznej (Poznan) [*A publication*]
Pr Kom Biol Poznan Tow Przyj Nauk ... Prace Komisji Biologicznej. Poznanskie Towarzystwo Przyjaciol Nauk [*Poland*] [*A publication*]
Pr Kom Ceram Pol Akad Nauk Ceram ... Prace Komisji Ceramicznej. Polskiej Akademii Nauk. Ceramica [*A publication*]
Pr Kom Krystalogr Pol Akad Nauk Inst Nisk Temp Badan Strukt ... Prace Komitetu Krystalografii. Polska Akademia Nauk. Instytut Niskich Temperatur i Badan Strukturalnych [*A publication*]
Pr Kom Mat-Przyr Poznan Tow Przyj Nauk ... Prace Komisji Matematyczno-Przyrodniczej. Poznanskie Towarzystwo Przyjaciol Nauk [*Poland*] [*A publication*]
Pr Kom Nauk Roln Kom Nauk Lesn Poznan Tow Przyj Nauk ... Prace Komisji Nauk Rolniczych i Komisji Nauk Lesnych. Poznanskiej Towarzystwo Przyjaciol [*A publication*]
Pr Kom Nauk Roln Lesn (Poznan) ... Prace Komisji Nauk Rolniczych i Lesnych. Poznanskie Towarzystwo Przyjaciol Nauk (Poznan) [*A publication*]
Pr Kom Nauk Tech Pol Akad Nauk Ser Ceram ... Prace Komisji Nauk Technicznych. Polska Akademia Nauk. Serja Ceramika [*A publication*]
Pr Kom Technol Drewna Poznan Tow Przyj Nauk ... Prace Komisji Technologii Drewna. Poznanskie Towarzystwo Przyjaciol Nauk [*Poland*] [*A publication*]
PRKPA ...... Probleme der Kosmichen Physik [*A publication*]
PRKRA ...... Parks and Recreation [*A publication*]
PRL .... Pacht, Ross et Al, Los Angeles, CA [*OCLC symbol*] (OCLC)
PRL .... Page Revision Log (NASA)
PRL .... Parallel (MSA)
PRL .... Parti Reformateur Liberal [*Liberal Reform Party*] [*Belgium*] [*Political party*] (PPW)
PRL .... Parti Republicain de la Liberte [*Republican Party for Liberty*] [*France*] [*Political party*] (PPE)
PRL .... Parti Republicain de la Liberte [*Republican Party for Liberty*] [*Upper Volta*] [*Political party*]
PRL .... Partido Radical Liberal [*Radical Liberal Party*] [*Ecuador*] [*Political party*]
PRL .... Parts Requirement List (KSC)
PRL .... Peace Research Laboratory [*Later, LPRL*] [*An association*] (EA)
PRL .... Pesticide Research Laboratory and Graduate Study Center [*Pennsylvania State University*] [*Research center*] (RCD)
PRL .... Petroleum Refining Laboratory [*Pennsylvania State University*] (MCD)
PRL .... Philco Resources [*Vancouver Stock Exchange symbol*]
PRL .... Photoreactivating Light
PRL .... Physiological Research Laboratories [*University of California at San Diego*] [*Research center*]
PRL .... Pioneering Research Laboratory [*Massachusetts*] [*Army*]
PRL .... Planning Requirements List (MCD)
PRL .... Plastics Research Laboratory [*MIT*] (MCD)

PRL .... Political Risk Letter [*Database*] [*Frost & Sullivan, Inc.*] [*Information service or system*] (CRD)
PRL .... Preamble
PRL .... Precision Reduction Laboratory (AFM)
PRL .... Predicted Repair Level (MCD)
PRL .... Pressure Ratio Limiter (MCD)
PRL .... Priority Rate Limiting (MCD)
PRL .... Progressive Republican League
PRL .... Project Research Laboratory
PRL .... Prolactin [*Also, LTH, PR*] [*Endocrinology*]
PRL .... Propulsion Research Laboratory
PRL .... Proton Reference Level [*Chemistry*]
PRL .... Publications Requirements List (NG)
PRLA .... Prairie Religious Library Association
PRLASR .... Population Research Laboratory. University of Alberta. Department of Sociology. Alberta Series Report [*A publication*]
PR Laws Ann ... Laws of Puerto Rico, Annotated [*A publication*] (DLA)
PRLC .... Pittsburgh Regional Library Center [*Chatham College*] [*Pittsburgh, PA*] [*Library network*]
PRLDEF ..... Puerto Rican Legal Defense and Education Fund (EA)
PRLEA ...... Pracovni Lekarstvi [*A publication*]
PRLI .... Purchase Request Line Item [*DoD*]
PRLINK .... Public Relations Society of America Online Information Service (IID)
PrLit .... Prace Literackie [*A publication*]
PRLKA ..... Przeglad Lekarski [*A publication*]
PRLP .... Planetary Rocket Launcher Platform (AAG)
PRLP .... Puerto Rico Legal Project [*of the National Lawyers Guild*] (EA)
PRLS .... Pima Regional Library Service [*Library network*]
PRLS .... Pulsed Ruby LASER System
PRLST ...... Price List
PRLTA ...... Physical Review. Letters [*A publication*]
PRLTRL & M ... Printer, Lithographer, and Multilith Operator [*Navy*]
PRLW .... Parti des Reformes et de la Liberte de Wallonie [*Belgium*] [*Political party*] (PPW)
PRLWCSR ... Population Research Laboratory. University of Alberta. Department of Sociology. Western Canada Series Report [*A publication*]
PRLX .... Parallax (AAG)
PRLX .... Parlex Corp. [*NASDAQ symbol*] (NQ)
PRM .... Panarim Resources, Inc. [*Vancouver Stock Exchange symbol*]
Prm .... Parmenides [*of Plato*] [*Classical studies*] (OCD)
PRM .... Parsons Mountain [*South Carolina*] [*Seismograph station code, US Geological Survey*] (SEIS)
PRM .... Parti de Regroupement Mauritanien [*Mauritanian Regroupment Party*]
PRM .... Partial Response Method
PRM .... Partially Reflecting Mirror
PRM .... Partially Regulated Module
PRM .... Payload Retention Mechanism [*NASA*] (NASA)
PRM .... Personal Radiation Monitor
PRM .... Petition [*or Proposal*] for Rule Making (NRCH)
PRM .... Photoreceptor Membrane [*Of the eye*]
PRM .... Pilots Radio Manual
PRM .... Pit Rib Meristem [*Botany*]
PRM .... Polski Rocznik Muzykologiczny [*A publication*]
PRM .... Posigrade Rocket Motor (NASA)
PRM .... Power Range Monitor (IEEE)
PRM .... PR Magazin. Public Relations und Informationspolitik in Medien und Gesellschaft [*A publication*]
PrM .... Pravna Misul [*A publication*]
PRM .... Preformed Road Markings [*Road markings embedded in the pavement rather than painted on street's surface*]
PRM .... Preliminary Requirements Model [*NASA*]
PRM .... Premium
PRM .... Presbyterian Renewal Ministries (EA)
PRM .... Presidential Review Memorandum [*Jimmy Carter Administration*]
PRM .... Pressure Remanent Magnetization
PRM .... Prime (AAG)
PRM .... Prime Computer, Inc. [*NYSE symbol*] (SPSG)
PRM .... Process Radiation Monitor [*Nuclear energy*] (NRCH)
PRM .... Programmer Reference Manual [*Data processing*]
PRM .... Programming and Resources Management [*NASA*] (MCD)
PRM .... Promote (AABC)
PrM .... Protestantische Monatshefte [*A publication*]
PRM .... Publications Requirements Manager [*DoD*]
PRM .... Pulse Rate Modulation
PRMA ...... Permeator Corp. [*NASDAQ symbol*] (NQ)
PRMA .... Proceedings. Royal Musical Association [*A publication*]
PrMan .... Prayer of Manasses [*Apocrypha*] (BJA)
PR of MAN ... [*The*] Prayer of Manasses, King of Judah [*Apocrypha*]
PRMAR ..... Primary Mission Area [*Military*] (CAAL)
Pr Mater Nauk Inst Matki Dziecka ... Prace i Materialy Naukowe. Instytut Matki i Dziecka [*A publication*]
Pr Mater Pershogo Khark Derzh Med Inst ... Pratsi i Materiali Pershogo Kharkivs'kogo Derzhavnogo Medichnogo Institutu [*A publication*]
Pr Mater Zootech ... Prace i Materialy Zootechniczne [*A publication*]

PRMC....... Periodically Replenished Magma Chambers [*Geology*]
PRMC....... Puerto Rican Migration Consortium   (EA)
PRMCL..... Periodica de Re Morali Canonica Liturgica [*A publication*]
PRMCLS... Papers. Regional Meeting. Chicago Linguistics Society [*A publication*]
PRME........ Prime Capital Corp. [*Rolling Meadows, IL*] [*NASDAQ symbol*]   (NQ)
PRMEA..... Presse Medicale [*A publication*]
Pr Med........ Presse Medicale [*A publication*]
Pr Med Opolskie Tow Przyj Nauk Wyd Nauk Med ... Prace Medyczne. Opolskie Towarzystwo Przyjaciol Nauk. Wydzial 5. Nauk Medycznych [*A publication*]
PRMF........ Petroleum Retail Marketing Franchise Act [*Australia*]
PRMG....... Piston Ring Manufacturers Group [*Later, NEPMA*]   (EA)
Pr Min .... Printed Minutes of Evidence [*A publication*]   (DLA)
Pr Mineral Pol Akad Nauk ... Prace Mineralogiczne Polska Akademia Nauk [*A publication*]
PR/MIPR ... Purchase Request/Military Interdepartmental Purchase Request   (AFIT)
PRMLD..... Premolded [*Technical drawings*]   (MSA)
PRMO....... Primo, Inc. [*Phoenix, AZ*] [*NASDAQ symbol*]   (NQ)
Pr Molodikh Uch Ukr Akad Sil's'kogospod Nauk ... Pratsi Molodikh Uchenikh Ukrains'ka Akademiya Sil's'kogospodars'kikh Nauk [*A publication*]
Pr Moravskoslezske Akad Ved Prir ... Prace Moravskoslezske Akademie Ved Prirodnich [*A publication*]
Pr Morsk Inst Rybackiego Ser A ... Prace Morskiego Instytutu Rybackiego. Seria A. Oceanografia i Biologia Rybacka [*A publication*]
Pr Morsk Inst Rybackiego Ser B ... Prace Morskiego Instytutu Rybackiego. Seria B. Technika Rybacka i Technologia Ryb [*A publication*]
Pr Morsk Inst Rybacki Gdyni ... Prace Morski Instytut Rybacki w Gdyni [*Poland*] [*A publication*]
PRMR....... Primer   (MSA)
PRMSA..... Progress in Materials Science [*A publication*]
PRMSB..... Proceedings. Royal Microscopical Society [*A publication*]
PRMSC..... Proceedings. Annual Reliability and Maintainability Symposium [*A publication*]
PRMSD.... Problemy Mashinostroeniya [*A publication*]
PRMTR.... Parameter   (AAG)
Pr Muz Ziemi ... Prace Muzeum Ziemi [*A publication*]
PRN .... Greenville, AL [*Location identifier*] [*FAA*]   (FAAL)
PRN .... Pahrock Range [*Nevada*] [*Seismograph station code, US Geological Survey*]   (SEIS)
PRN .... Partido Republicano Nacional [*National Republican Party*] [*Costa Rica*] [*Political party*]
PRN .... Partido de la Revolucion Nacional [*Party of the National Revolution*] [*Bolivia*] [*Political party*]   (PPW)
PRN .... Parts Requirement Notice   (KSC)
PRN .... Peace Research Network [*Later, PSA*]   (EA)
PRN .... Physicians Radio Network
PRN .... Playfulness, Revelry, Nonsense [*Quarterly Newsletter of Nurses for Laughter*] [*Title is derived from the pharmaceutical term PRN (Pro Re Nata)*] [*A publication*]
PRN .... PR Newswire [*PR Newswire, Inc.*] [*Information service or system*]   (IID)
PRN .... Pridie Nonas [*The Day before the Nones*] [*Latin*]
PRN .... Print Numerically   (DEN)
PRN .... Printer [*Data processing*]
PRN .... Pristina [*Yugoslavia*] [*Airport symbol*]   (OAG)
PRN .... Pro Re Nata [*Whenever Necessary*] [*Pharmacy*]
PRN .... Procurement Reallocation Notice
PRN .... Program Release Notice [*NASA*]   (NASA)
PRN .... Prominent Resources Corp. [*Vancouver Stock Exchange symbol*]
PRN .... Pronasale [*Anatomy*]
PRN .... Pseudorandom Noise
PRN .... Pseudorandom Number
PRN .... Puerto Rican Cement Co., Inc. [*NYSE symbol*]   (SPSG)
PRN .... Pulse Ranging Navigation
PRN .... Pulse Ranging Network   (KSC)
pRNA........ Ribonucleic Acid, Polysomal [*Biochemistry, genetics*]
Pr Naturwiss Teil 3 ... Praxis der Naturwissenschaften. Teil 3. Chemie [*A publication*]
Pr Nauk Akad Ekon Oskara Langego Wroclaw Chem ... Prace Naukowe Akademii Ekonomicznej Imienia Oskara Langego we Wroclawiu. Chemia [*A publication*]
Pr Nauk Inst Chem Org Fiz Politech Wroclaw ... Prace Naukowe Instytutu Chemii Organicznej i Fizycznej Politechniki Wroclawskiej [*A publication*]
Pr Nauk Inst Chem Org Fiz Politech Wroclaw Ser K ... Prace Naukowe Instytutu Chemii Organicznej i Fizycznej Politechniki Wroclawskiej. Seria. Konferencje [*A publication*]
Pr Nauk Inst Chem Org Fiz Politech Wroclaw Ser Konf ... Prace Naukowe Instytutu Chemii Organicznej i Fizycznej Politechniki Wroclawskiej. Seria Konferencje [*A publication*]
Pr Nauk Inst Chem Org Fiz Politech Wroclaw Ser S ... Prace Naukowe Instytutu Chemii Organicznej i Fizycznej Politechniki Wroclawskiej. Seria Studia i Materialy [*A publication*]

Pr Nauk Inst Chem Technol Nafty Wegla Politech Wroclaw ... Prace Naukowe Instytutu Chemii i Technologii Nafty i Wegla Politechniki Wroclawskiej [*Poland*] [*A publication*]
Pr Nauk Inst Cybern Tech Politech Wroclaw Ser K ... Prace Naukowe Instytutu Cybernetyki Technicznej Politechniki Wroclawskiej. Seria Konferencje [*A publication*]
Pr Nauk Inst Cybern Tech Politech Wroclaw Ser M ... Prace Naukowe Instytutu Cybernetyki Technicznej Politechniki Wroclawskiej. Seria Monografie [*A publication*]
Pr Nauk Inst Cybern Tech Politech Wroclaw Ser S ... Prace Naukowe Instytutu Cybernetyki Technicznej Politechniki Wroclawskiej. Seria Studia i Materialy [*A publication*]
Pr Nauk Inst Fiz Politech Wroclaw ... Prace Naukowe Instytutu Fizyki Politechniki Wroclawskiej [*A publication*]
Pr Nauk Inst Fiz Politech Wroclaw Ser M ... Prace Naukowe Instytutu Fizyki Politechniki Wroclawskiej. Seria Monografie [*A publication*]
Pr Nauk Inst Fiz Politech Wroclaw Ser Monogr ... Prace Naukowe Instytutu Fizyki Politechniki Wroclawskiej. Seria Monografie [*A publication*]
Pr Nauk Inst Fiz Politech Wroclaw Ser S ... Prace Naukowe Instytutu Fizyki Politechniki Wroclawskiej. Seria Studia i Materialy [*A publication*]
Pr Nauk Inst Fiz Tech Politech Wroclaw ... Prace Naukowe Instytutu Fizyki Technicznej Politechniki Wroclawskiej [*A publication*]
Pr Nauk Inst Geotech Politech Wroclaw ... Prace Naukowe Instytutu Geotechniki Politechniki Wroclawskiej [*Poland*] [*A publication*]
Pr Nauk Inst Gorn Politech Wroclaw ... Prace Naukowe Instytutu Gornictwa Politechniki Wroclawskiej [*Poland*] [*A publication*]
Pr Nauk Inst Gorn Wroclaw ... Prace Naukowe Instytutu Gornictwa Politechniki Wroclawskiej [*A publication*]
Pr Nauk Inst Inz Chem Urzadz Ciepl Politech Wroclaw Ser M ... Prace Naukowe Instytutu Inzynierii Chemicznej i Urzadzen Cieplnych Politechniki Wroclawskiej. Seria. Monografie [*A publication*]
Pr Nauk Inst Inz Chem Urzadzen Cieplnych Politech Wroclaw ... Prace Naukowe Instytutu Inzynierii Chemicznej i Urzadzen Cieplnych Politechniki Wroclawskiej [*Poland*] [*A publication*]
Pr Nauk Inst Inz Ladowej Politech Wroclaw ... Prace Naukowe Instytutu Inzynierii Ladowej Politechniki Wroclawskiej [*A publication*]
Pr Nauk Inst Inz Ochr Srodowiska Politech Wroclaw ... Prace Naukowe Instytutu Inzynierii Ochrony Srodowiska Politechniki Wroclawskiej [*Poland*] [*A publication*]
Pr Nauk Inst Inz Ochr Sr Politech Wroclaw ... Prace Naukowe Instytutu Inzynierii Ochrony Srodowiska Politechniki Wroclawskiej [*A publication*]
Pr Nauk Inst Inz Sanit Wodnej Politech Wroclaw ... Prace Naukowe Instytutu Inzynierii Sanitarnej i Wodnej Politechniki Wroclawskiej [*A publication*]
Pr Nauk Inst Materialozn Mech Tech Politech Wroclaw ... Prace Naukowe Instytutu Materialoznawstwa i Technicznej Politechniki Wroclawskiej [*A publication*]
Pr Nauk Inst Materialozn Mech Tech Politech Wroclaw Ser M ... Prace Naukowe Instytutu Materialoznawstwa i Mechaniki Technicznej Politechniki Wroclawskiej. Seria. Monografie [*A publication*]
Pr Nauk Inst Materialozn Mech Tech Politech Wroclaw Ser S ... Prace Naukowe Instytutu Materialoznawstwa i Mechaniki Technicznej Politechniki Wroclawskiej. Seria. Studia i Materialy [*A publication*]
Pr Nauk Inst Mat Politech Wroclaw Ser M ... Prace Naukowe Instytutu Matematyki Politechniki Wroclawskiej. Seria Monografie [*A publication*]
Pr Nauk Inst Mat Politech Wroclaw Ser S ... Prace Naukowe Instytutu Matematyki Politechniki Wroclawskiej. Seria Studia i Materialy [*A publication*]
Pr Nauk Inst Metrol Elektr Politech Wroclaw Ser K ... Prace Naukowe Instytutu Metrologii Elektrycznej Politechniki Wroclawskiej. Seria. Konferencje [*A publication*]
Pr Nauk Inst Metrol Elektr Politech Wroclaw Ser Konf ... Prace Naukowe Instytutu Metrologii Elektrycznej Politechniki Wroclawskiej. Seria Konferencje [*A publication*]
Pr Nauk Inst Metrol Elektr Politech Wroclaw Ser M ... Prace Naukowe Instytutu Metrologii Elektrycznej Politechniki Wroclawskiej. Seria. Monografie [*A publication*]
Pr Nauk Inst Metrol Elektr Politech Wroclaw Ser S ... Prace Naukowe Instytutu Metrologii Elektrycznej Politechniki Wroclawskiej. Seria. Studia i Materialy [*A publication*]
Pr Nauk Inst Ochr Rosl ... Prace Naukowe Instytutu Ochrony Roslin [*A publication*]
Pr Nauk Inst Ochr Rosl (Warsz) ... Prace Naukowe Instytutu Ochrony Roslin (Warszawa) [*A publication*]
Pr Nauk Inst Przem Org (Warsaw) ... Prace Naukowe Instytutu Przemyslu Organicznego (Warsaw) [*A publication*]
Pr Nauk Inst Tech Ciepl Mech Plynow Politech Wroclaw ... Prace Naukowe Instytutu Techniki Cieplnej i Mechaniki Plynow Politechniki Wroclawskiej [*A publication*]

Pr Nauk Inst Tech Ciepl Mech Plynow Politech Wroclaw Ser M ... Prace Naukowe Instytutu Techniki Cieplnej i Mechaniki Plynow Politechniki Wroclawskiej. Seria. Monografie [*A publication*]

Pr Nauk Inst Tech Ciepl Mech Plynow Politech Wroclaw Ser S ... Prace Naukowe Instytutu Techniki Cieplnej i Mechaniki Plynow Politechniki Wroclawskiej. Seria. Studia i Materialy [*A publication*]

Pr Nauk Inst Technol Elektron Politech Wroclaw ... Prace Naukowe Instytutu Technologii Elektronowej Politechniki Wroclawskiej [*A publication*]

Pr Nauk Inst Technol Elektron Politech Wroclaw Ser Monogr ... Prace Naukowe Instytutu Technologii Elektronowej Politechniki Wroclawskiej. Seria Monografie [*A publication*]

Pr Nauk Inst Technol Elektron Politech Wroclaw Ser S ... Prace Naukowe Instytutu Technologii Elektronowej Politechniki Wroclawskiej. Seria. Studia i Materialy [*A publication*]

Pr Nauk Inst Technol Nieorg Nawozow Miner Politech Wroclaw ... Prace Naukowe Instytutu Technologii Nieorganicznej i Nawozow Mineralnych Politechniki Wroclawskiej [*A publication*]

Pr Nauk Inst Technol Org Tworz Sztucz Politech Wroclaw Ser S ... Prace Naukowe Instytutu Technologii Organicznej i Tworzyw Sztucznych Politechniki Wroclawskiej. Seria. Studia i Materialy [*A publication*]

Pr Nauk Inst Technol Org Tworzyw Sztucznych Politech Wroclaw ... Prace Naukowe Instytutu Technologii Organicznej i Tworzyw Sztucznych Politechniki Wroclawskiej [*A publication*]

Pr Nauk Inst Telekomun Akust Politech Wroclaw Ser K ... Prace Naukowe Instytutu Telekomunikacji i Akustyki Politechniki Wroclawskiej. Seria. Konferencje [*A publication*]

Pr Nauk Inst Telekomun Akust Politech Wroclaw Ser M ... Prace Naukowe Instytutu Telekomunikacji i Akustyki Politechniki Wroclawskiej. Seria. Monografie [*A publication*]

Pr Nauk Inst Telekomun Akust Politech Wroclaw Ser S ... Prace Naukowe Instytutu Telekomunikacji i Akustyki Politechniki Wroclawskiej. Seria. Studia i Materialy [*A publication*]

Pr Nauk Inst Ukladow Elektromasz Politech Wroclaw Ser S ... Prace Naukowe Instytutu Ukladow Elektromaszynowych Politechniki Wroclawskiej. Seria. Studia i Materialy [*A publication*]

Pr Nauk Politech Szczecin ... Prace Naukowe Politechniki Szczecinskiej [*Poland*] [*A publication*]

Pr Nauk Politech Warsz Elektron ... Prace Naukowe Politechnika Warszawska Elektronika [*A publication*]

Pr Nauk Politech Wroclaw Ser Konf ... Prace Naukowe Politechniki Wroclawskiej. Seria Konferencje [*A publication*]

Pr Nauk Politech Wroclaw Ser Monogr ... Prace Naukowe Politechniki Wroclawskiej. Seria Monografie [*A publication*]

Pr Nauk Politech Wroclaw Ser Stud Mater ... Prace Naukowe Politechniki Wroclawskiej. Seria Studia i Materialy [*A publication*]

Pr Nauk Politech Wroclaw Ser Wspolpraca ... Prace Naukowe Politechniki Wroclawskiej. Seria Wspolpraca [*A publication*]

Pr Nauk Uniw Slask Katowicach ... Prace Naukowe Uniwersytetu Slaskiego w Katowicach [*A publication*]

Pr Nauk Uniw Slask Katowic Pr Fiz ... Prace Naukowe Uniwersytetu Slaskiego w Katowicach. Prace Fizyczne [*A publication*]

Pr Nauk Wyzsz Szk Ekon Wroclawiu ... Prace Naukowe Wyzszej Szkoly Ekonomicznej we Wroclawiu [*A publication*]

PRNBA...... Proceedings. Research Institute for Nuclear Medicine and Biology [*A publication*]

PRNC .... Potomac River Naval Command [*Washington, DC*]

PRNC .... Puerto Rico Nuclear Center

PRNDL...... Park, Reverse, Neutral, Drive, Low [*Automotive term for automatic gearshift indicator in cars; pronounced "prindle"*]

PRNET...... Packet Radio Network

PRNG .... Purging　(MSA)

PRNHA...... Professional Nursing Home [*A publication*]

PRNJ .... Project North Journal [*A publication*]

PRNN .... Project North Newsletter [*A publication*]

prnnl............ Perennial [*Botany*]

PRNT .... Plaque Reduction Neutralization Test [*Immunochemistry*]

PRNTG...... Printing　(MSA)

PRNTR...... Printer

PRNTV...... Preventive

PRO .... Pacific Research Office　(CINC)

PRO .... Parallel Rod Oscillator

PRO .... Parents Rights Organization　(EA)

PRO .... Particle Reduction Oven

PRO .... Parts Release Order

PRO .... Patients' Rights Organization　(EA)

PRO .... Pay and Records Office [*British military*]　(DMA)

PRO .... Peer Review Organization [*Medicare*]

PRO .... Performing Rights Organization [*Formerly, BMI-Canada Ltd.*] [*Canada*]

PRO .... Perry, IA [*Location identifier*] [*FAA*]　(FAAL)

PRO .... Personnel Relations Officer [*for Shore Stations*] [*Navy*]

PRO .... Pitch Response Operator

PRO .... Planned Requirements, Outfitting [*Navy*]　(NG)

PRO .... Planning Resident Order　(KSC)

PRO .... Plant Representative Officer　(MCD)

PRO .... Population Renewal Office　(EA)

Pro............. Prednisone [*Also, P, PDN, PR, Pred*] [*Antineoplastic drug, Endocrinology*]

PRO .... Principal Public Library [*Library network*]

PRO .... Print Octal　(DEN)

PRO .... Pro Musica [*A publication*]

PRO .... Probate

PRO .... Probation [*or Probationer*]

PRO .... Problem Resolution Office [*IRS*]

PRO .... Procedure　(AABC)

Pro............. Proculus [*Flourished, 1st century*] [*Authority cited in pre-1607 legal work*]　(DSA)

PRO .... Procurement Research Office [*Army*]

PRO .... Production Repair Order

PRO .... Produktnieuws voor Kantoor en Bedrijf. Investeringsinformatie voor Managers [*A publication*]

PRO .... Professional

PRO .... Professional Racing Organization of America [*Later, USCF*]　(EA)

PRO .... Professional Report [*A publication*]

PRO .... Professional Resellers Organization　(EA)

PRO .... Professional Review Organization [*Medicare*]

PRO .... Proficiency

PRO .... Proflavine [*An antiseptic*]

PRO .... Programmable Remote Operation [*Computer Devices, Inc.*]

PRO .... Progressive

Pro............. Proline [*Also, P*] [*An amino acid*]

Pro............. Prolyl [*Biochemistry*]

PRO .... Pronation [*Medicine*]

PRO .... Pronto Explorations Ltd. [*Toronto Stock Exchange symbol*]

PRO .... Propagation [*Military*]

PRO .... Propeller Order

PRO .... Prophylactic　(AABC)

PRO .... Prostitute　(ADA)

Pro............. Protein

PRO .... Protest

Pro............. Prothrombin [*Factor II*] [*Hematology*]

PRO .... Proved

pro .... Provencal [*MARC language code*] [*Library of Congress*]　(LCCP)

Pro............. Proverbs [*Old Testament book*]　(BJA)

PRO .... Province　(ROG)

PRO .... Provost

PRO .... Public Record Office [*British*]

PRO .... Public Relations Office [*or Officer*] [*Usually military*]

PRO .... Puchase Request Order

PROA .... Polymer Research Corp. of America [*NASDAQ symbol*]　(NQ)

PROA .... Puerto Rico Operations Area

Pro Acad Pol Sci (USA) ... Proceedings. Academy of Political Science (USA) [*A publication*]

Pro Am Gas Inst ... Proceedings. American Gas Institute [*A publication*]

ProAOS ..... Proceedings. American Oriental Society [*Baltimore, MD*] [*A publication*]

PROAP...... Principal Regional Office for Asia and the Pacific [*UNESCO*]

Prob............ English Probate and Admiralty Reports for Year Cited [*A publication*]　(DLA)

Prob............ Law Reports, Probate Division [*England*] [*A publication*]　(DLA)

PROB .... Probability　(KSC)

prob............ Probable

PROB .... Probably

Prob............ Probate [*Legal term*]　(DLA)

PROB .... Probation [*FBI standardized term*]

PROB .... Problem

Prob............ Quod Omnis Probus Liber Sit [*of Philo*]　(BJA)

PROB .... Teleprobe Systems, Inc. [*NASDAQ symbol*]　(NQ)

Prob (1891) ... Law Reports, Probate Division [*1891*] [*England*] [*A publication*]　(DLA)

Probab Math Stat ... Probability and Mathematical Statistics [*A publication*]

Probab Math Statist ... Probability and Mathematical Statistics [*A publication*]

Prob Actuels ORL ... Problemes Actuels d'Oto-Rhino-Laryngologie [*A publication*]

Prob & Adm Div ... Probate and Admiralty Division Law Reports [*A publication*]　(DLA)

Prob Agric Ind Mex ... Problemas Agricolas e Industriales de Mexico [*A publication*]

Probat .... Probation [*Legal term*]　(DLA)

Probation & Parole L Rep ... Probation and Parole Law Reports [*A publication*]　(DLA)

Probation & Parole L Summ ... Probation and Parole Law Summaries [*A publication*]　(DLA)

Probat J ..... Probation Journal [*A publication*]　(ILCA)

Prob C .... Probate Code [*A publication*]　(DLA)

Prob Com ... Problems of Communism [*A publication*]

Prob Commun ... Problems of Communism [*A publication*]

PROBCOST ... Probabilistic Budgeting and Forward Costing

Prob Ct Rep ... Probate Court Reporter [*Ohio*] [*A publication*]　(DLA)

PROBDET ... Probability of Detection [*Navy*]　(NVT)

Prob Div..... Probate Division, English Law Reports [*A publication*]　(DLA)

Prob & Div ... Probate and Divorce, English Law Reports [*A publication*] (DLA)
PROBE...... Performance Review of Base Supply Effectiveness [*Air Force*] (AFM)
PROBE...... Program Optimization and Budget Evaluation [*Military*]
PROBE...... Program for Research on Objectives-Based Evaluation [*UCLA*]
Prob Econ ... Problems of Economics [*A publication*]
PROBES ... Processes and Resources of the Bering Sea Shelf [*University of Alaska*]
PROBFOR ... Probability Forecasting [*Computer program*] [*Bell System*]
PROBIT .... Probability Unit [*Statistics*]
Prob J .... Probation Journal [*A publication*] (DLA)
Prob Khig ... Problemi na Khigienata [*A publication*]
Probl Actuels Biochim Appl ... Problemes Actuels de Biochimie Appliquee [*A publication*]
Probl Actuels Endocrinol Nutr ... Problemes Actuels d'Endocrinologie et de Nutrition [*A publication*]
Probl Actuels Ophthal ... Problemes Actuels d'Ophthalmologie [*A publication*]
Probl Actuels Otorhinolaryngol ... Problems Actuels d'Otorhinolaryngologie [*A publication*]
Probl Actuels Paediatr ... Problemes Actuels de Paediatrie [*A publication*]
Probl Actuels Phoniatr Logop ... Problemes Actuels de Phoniatrie et Logopedie [*A publication*]
Probl Actuels Psychotherap ... Problemes Actuels de Psychotherapie [*A publication*]
Probl Afr Centr ... Problemes d'Afrique Centrale [*A publication*]
Probl Agr (Bucharest) ... Probleme Agricole (Bucharest) [*A publication*]
Probl Agric ... Probleme Agricole [*A publication*]
Probl Agrofiz ... Problemy Agrofizyki [*A publication*]
Probl Anal Khim ... Problemy Analiticheskoi Khimii [*A publication*]
Probl Arkt Antarkt ... Problemy Arktiki i Antarktiki [*A publication*]
Probl Arktiki Antarkt ... Problemy Arktiki i Antarktiki [*A publication*]
Probl Arktiki Antarktiki ... Problemy Arktiki i Antarktiki [*USSR*] [*A publication*]
Probl Attuali Sci Cult ... Problemi Attuali di Scienza e di Cultura [*A publication*]
Prob Law.... Probate Lawyer [*A publication*]
Probl Biocybern Biomed Eng ... Problems of Biocybernetics and Biomedical Engineering [*A publication*]
Probl Biol... Problems in Biology [*A publication*]
Probl Biol Krajiny ... Problemy Biologie Krajiny [*A publication*]
Probl Bioniki ... Problemy Bioniki [*A publication*]
Probl Bioniki Resp Mezhved Nauchno-Tekh Sb ... Problemy Bioniki Respublikanskii Mezhvedomstvennyi Nauchno-Tekhnicheskii Sbornik [*A publication*]
Probl Bor'by Protiv Burz Ideol ... Problemy Bor'by Protiv Burzuaznoj Ideologii [*A publication*]
Probl Bot.... Problemy Botaniki [*A publication*]
Probl Commu ... Problems of Communism [*A publication*]
Probl Control Inf Theor ... Problems of Control and Information Theory [*A publication*]
Probl Control and Inf Theory ... Problems of Control and Information Theory [*A publication*]
Probl Control and Inf Theory (Engl Transl Pap Rus) ... Problems of Control and Information Theory (English Translation of the Papers in Russian) [*A publication*]
Probl Cybern ... Problems of Cybernetics [*A publication*]
Probl Cybern (USSR) ... Problems of Cybernetics (USSR) [*A publication*]
Probl Dal'nego Vost ... Problemy Dal'nego Vostok [*A publication*]
Probl Desarr ... Problemas del Desarrollo [*A publication*]
Probl Desert Dev (Engl Transl Probl Osvoeniya Pustyn) ... Problems of Desert Development (English Translation of Problemy Osvoeniya Pustyn) [*A publication*]
Probl Dialektiki ... Problemy Dialektiki [*A publication*]
Probl Drug Depend ... Problems of Drug Dependence [*A publication*]
Probl Ec ..... Problemes Economiques [*A publication*]
Probl Ecol Biocenol ... Problems of Ecology and Biocenology [*A publication*]
Probl Econ ... Problems of Economics [*A publication*]
Probl Econ (Bucharest) ... Probleme Economice (Bucharest) [*A publication*]
Probl Ekol ... Problemy Ekologii [*A publication*]
Probl Ekon Morja ... Problemy Ekonomiki Morja [*A publication*]
Probl Ekon (Warszawa) ... Problemy Ekonomiczne (Warszawa) [*A publication*]
Problemas Bras ... Problemas Brasileiros [*A publication*]
Probleme de Automat ... Probleme de Automatizare [*A publication*]
Probleme Prot Plantelor ... Probleme de Protectia Plantelor [*A publication*]
Problemes Eur ... Problemes de l'Europe [*A publication*]
Problemi Sicurezza Soc ... Problemi della Sicurezza Sociale [*A publication*]
Problemi Tehn Kibernet ... Problemi na Tehniceskata Kibernetika [*Problems of Engineering Cybernetics*] [*A publication*]
Problemi Tekhn Kibernet Robot ... Problemi na Tekhnicheskata Kibernetika i Robotika [*Problems of Engineering Cybernetics and Robotics*] [*A publication*]
Problems Control Inform Theory/Problemy Upravlen Teor Inform ... Problems of Control and Information Theory. Problemy Upravlenija i Teorii Informacii [*Budapest*] [*A publication*]
Problems Econ ... Problems of Economics [*A publication*]
Problems in Geometry ... Problems in Geometry in the Key Word Index [*Moscow*] [*A publication*]

Problems Inform Transmission ... Problems of Information Transmission [*A publication*]
Problemy Jadern Fiz i Kosm Lucei ... Problemy Jadernoi Fiziki i Kosmiceskih Lucei [*A publication*]
Problemy Kibernet ... Problemy Kibernetiki [*A publication*]
Problemy Kosmich Biol Akad Nauk SSSR ... Problemy Kosmicheskoi Biologii Akademiya Nauk SSSR [*A publication*]
Problemy Mat ... Bydgoszcz. Whzsza Szkola Pedagogiczna. Zeszyty Naukowe. Problemy Matematyczne [*A publication*]
Problemy Mat Anal Sloz Sistem ... Problemy Matematiceskogo Analiza Sloznyh Sistem [*A publication*]
Problemy Matematiceskogo Analiza ... Problemy Matematiceskogo Analiza [*Leningrad*] [*A publication*]
Problemy Pered Inf ... Problemy Peredachi Informatsii [*A publication*]
Problemy Slucain Poiska ... Akademija Nauk Latviiskoi SSR. Institut Elektroniki i Vyceslitel'noi Tehniki. Problemy Slucainogo Poiska [*A publication*]
Problemy Teor Gravitacii i Element Castic ... Problemy Teorii Gravitacii i Elementarnyh Castic [*A publication*]
Problemy Yadern Fiz i Kosm Luchei ... Problemy Yadernoi Fiziki i Kosmicheskikh Luchei [*A publication*]
Probl Endokr Gormonot ... Problemy Endokrinologii i Gormonoterapii [*A publication*]
Probl Endokrinol ... Problemy Endokrinologii [*A publication*]
Probl Endokrinol Gormonoter ... Problemy Endokrinologii i Gormonoterapii [*Later, Problemy Endokrinologii*] [*A publication*]
Probl Endokrinol (Mosk) ... Problemy Endokrinologii (Moskva) [*A publication*]
Probl Entrep Agric ... Problemes de l'Enterprise Agricole [*A publication*]
Probl Evol.. Problemy Evolyutsii [*A publication*]
Probl Farine ... Problemes de Farine [*A publication*]
Probl Farm ... Problemy na Farmatsiyata [*A publication*]
Probl Farmakol ... Problemi na Farmakologiyata [*A publication*]
Probl Festkoerperelektron ... Probleme der Festkoerperelektronik [*A publication*]
Probl Filos Nauc Kommunizma ... Problemy Filosofii i Naucnogo Kommunizma [*A publication*]
Probl Fiz Atmos ... Problemy Fiziki Atmosfery [*A publication*]
Probl Fiz Elem Chastits At Yadra ... Problemy Fiziki Elementarnykh Chastits i Atomnogo Yadra [*A publication*]
Probl Fiziol Gipotal ... Problemy Fiziologii Gipotalamusa [*A publication*]
Probl Fiziol Opt ... Problemy Fiziologicheskoj Optiki [*A publication*]
Probl Fiziol Patol Vyssh Nervn Deyat ... Problemy Fiziologii i Patologii Vysshei Nervnoi Deyatel'nosti [*A publication*]
Probl Fiz Khim ... Problemy Fizicheskoi Khimii [*A publication*]
Probl Funkts Morfol ... Problemy Funktsional'noi Morfologii [*A publication*]
Probl Gastroenterol ... Problemy Gastroenterologii [*A publication*]
Probl Gemat ... Problemy Gematologii i Perelivanija Krovi [*A publication*]
Probl Gematol Pereliv Krovi ... Problemy Gematologii i Perelivaniya Krovi [*A publication*]
Probl Geokhim ... Problemy Geokhimii [*A publication*]
Probl Geol Nefti ... Problemy Geologii Nefti [*USSR*] [*A publication*]
Probl Gestione ... Problemi di Gestione [*A publication*]
Probl Gidroenerg Vod Khoz ... Problemy Gidroenergetiki i Vodnogo Khozyaistva [*A publication*]
Probl Glubokikh Mikozov ... Problemy Glubokikh Mikozov [*A publication*]
Probl Gos Prava ... Problemy Gosudarstva i Prava [*A publication*]
Probl Grippa Ostrykh Respir Zabol ... Problemy Grippa i Ostrykh Respiratornykh Zabolevanii [*A publication*]
Probl Hematol Blood Transfus ... Problems of Hematology and Blood Transfusion [*A publication*]
Probl Hematol Blood Transfus (USSR) ... Problems of Hematology and Blood Transfusion (USSR) [*A publication*]
Probl Inf & Doc ... Probleme de Informare si Documentare [*A publication*]
Probl Inf Docum ... Probleme de Informare si Documentare [*A publication*]
Probl Infect Parasit Dis ... Problems of Infectious and Parasitic Diseases [*A publication*]
Probl Influenza Acute Respir Dis ... Problems of Influenza and Acute Respiratory Diseases [*A publication*]
Probl Inf Transm ... Problems of Information Transmission [*A publication*]
Probl Inf Transm (USSR) ... Problems of Information Transmission (USSR) [*A publication*]
Probl Inzh Geol Sev Kavk ... Problemy Inzhenernoi Geologii Severnogo Kavkaza [*A publication*]
Probl Kamen Litya ... Problemy Kamennogo Lit'ya [*A publication*]
Probl Khig ... Problemi na Khigienata [*A publication*]
Probl Kibern ... Problemy Kibernetiki [*A publication*]
Probl Kinet Katal ... Problemy Kinetiki i Kataliza [*A publication*]
Probl Kontrolya Zashch Atmos Zagryaz ... Problemy Kontrolya i Zashchita Atmosfery ot Zagryazneniya [*A publication*]
Probl Kosm Biol ... Problemy Kosmicheskoi Biologii [*A publication*]
Probl Kosm Fiz ... Problemy Kosmicheskoj Fiziki [*A publication*]
Probl Kosm Phys ... Probleme der Kosmichen Physik [*West Germany*] [*A publication*]
Probl Kriolitologii ... Problemy Kriolitologii [*A publication*]
Probl Lek ... Problemy Lekarskie [*A publication*]
Probl Low Temp Phys Thermodyn ... Problems of Low Temperature Physics and Thermodynamics [*A publication*]
Probl Mashinostr ... Problemy Mashinostroeniya [*Ukrainian SSR*] [*A publication*]
Probl Mat Fiz ... Problemy Matematicheskoj Fiziki [*A publication*]

Probl Med Wieku Rozwoj ... Problemy Medycyny Wieku Rozwojowego [*A publication*]
Probl Metalloved Fiz Met ... Problemy Metallovedeniya i Fiziki Metallov [*USSR*] [*A publication*]
Probl Metalloved Term Obrab ... Problemy Metallovedeniya i Termicheskoi Obrabotki [*A publication*]
Probl Metodol Ist-Filos Issled ... Problemy Metodologii Istoriko-Filosofskogo Issledovanija [*A publication*]
Probl Morfopatol ... Probleme de Morfopatologie [*A publication*]
Probl Narodonas Trud Resursov ... Problemy Narodonaselenija i Trudovyh Resursov [*A publication*]
Probl Nauc Kommunizma (Leningrad) ... Problemy Naucnogo Kommunizma (Leningrad) [*A publication*]
Probl Nauc Kommunizma (Moskva) ... Problemy Naucnogo Kommunizma (Moskva) [*A publication*]
Probl Nauc Uprav Soc Processami ... Problemy Naucnogo Upravlenija Social'nymi Processami [*A publication*]
Probl Neftegazonosn Tadzh ... Problemy Neftegazonosnosti Tadzhikistana [*A publication*]
Probl Nefti Gaza Tyumeni ... Problemy Nefti i Gaza Tyumeni [*A publication*]
Probl Neirokhim ... Problemy Neirokhimii [*A publication*]
Probl Neirokhir ... Problemy Neirokhirurgii [*A publication*]
Probl Neirokhir (1955-1963) ... Problemy Neirokhirurgii (1955-1963) [*A publication*]
Probl Neirokhir Resp Mezhved Sb ... Problemy Neirokhirurgii Respublikanskii Mezhvedomstvenhyi Sbornik [*A publication*]
Probl Neirokibern ... Problemy Neirokibernetiki [*A publication*]
Probl Nevrol Psikhiatr Nevrokhir ... Problemi na Nevrologiyata, Psikhiatriyata, i Nevrokhirurgiyata [*A publication*]
Probl Nevrol Resp Mezhved Sb ... Problemy Nevrologii Respublikanskii Mezhvedomstvennyi Sbornik [*A publication*]
Probl North ... Problems of the North [*A publication*]
Probl Obshch Mol Biol ... Problemy Obshchei i Molekulyarnoi Biologii [*A publication*]
Probl Okh Vod ... Problemy Okhrany Vod [*A publication*]
Probl Oncol (Engl Transl Vopr Onkol) ... Problems of Oncology (English Translation of Voprosy Onkologii) [*A publication*]
Probl Onkol (Sofia) ... Problemi na Onkologiyata (Sofia) [*A publication*]
Probl Organ ... Problemy Organizacji [*A publication*]
Probl Ortop Stomatol ... Problemy Ortopedicheskoi Stomatologii [*A publication*]
Probl Osad Geol Dokembr ... Problemy Osadochnoy Geologii Dokembriya [*A publication*]
Probl Osobo Opasnykh Infekts ... Problemy Osobo Opasnykh Infektsii [*A publication*]
Probl Osvoeniya Pustyn ... Problemy Osvoeniya Pustyn [*A publication*]
Probl Osvo Pustyn ... Problemy Osvoeniya Pustyn [*A publication*]
Probl Parazitol ... Problemy Parazitologii [*A publication*]
Probl Patol Comp ... Probleme de Patologie Comparata [*A publication*]
Probl Ped ... Problemi della Pedagogia [*A publication*]
Probl Peredachi Inf ... Problemy Peredachi Informatsii [*A publication*]
Probl Pereda Inf ... Problemy Peredachi Informatsii [*A publication*]
Probl Pnevmol Ftiziatr ... Problemi na Pnevmologiyata i Ftiziatriyata [*A publication*]
Probl Polesya ... Problemy Poles'ya [*A publication*]
Probl Polit Soc ... Problemes Politiques et Sociaux [*A publication*]
Probl Proch Mashinostr ... Problemy Prochnosti v Mashinostroenii [*USSR*] [*A publication*]
Probl Prochn ... Problemy Prochnosti [*A publication*]
Probl Prochn Mashinostr ... Problemy Prochnosti v Mashinostroenii [*A publication*]
Probl Proj .. Problemy Projectowa [*A publication*]
Probl Prot Plant ... Probleme de Protectia Plantelor [*A publication*]
Probl Psychol (Engl Transl Vopr Psikhol) ... Problems of Psychology (English Translation of Voprosy Psikhologii) [*A publication*]
Probl Razrab Polezn Iskop ... Problemy Razrabotki Poleznykh Iskopaemykh [*A publication*]
Probl Rentgenol Radiobiol ... Problemi na Rentgenologiyata i Radiobiologiyata [*A publication*]
Probl Selsk Khoz Priamurya ... Problemy Sel'skogo Khozyaistva Priamur'ya [*A publication*]
Probl Ser .... Problemy Severa [*A publication*]
Probl Sev .... Problemy Severa [*A publication*]
Probl Sicur Soc ... Problemi della Sicurezza Sociale [*A publication*]
Probl Soc Aktivnosti ... Problemy Social'noj Aktivnosti [*A publication*]
Probl Social (Milano) ... Problemi del Socialismo (Milano) [*A publication*]
Probl Soc Prognoz ... Problemy Social'nogo Prognozirovanija [*A publication*]
Probl Soc Zair ... Problemes Sociaux Zairois [*A publication*]
Probl Soc Zairois ... Problemes Sociaux Zairois [*A publication*]
Probl Sov Geol ... Problemy Sovetskoi Geologii [*USSR*] [*A publication*]
Probl Sov Gos Prava ... Problemy Sovetskogo Gosudarstva i Prava [*A publication*]
Probl Sovrem Khim Koord Soedin ... Problemy Sovremennoi Khimii Koordinatsionnykh Soedinenii [*USSR*] [*A publication*]
Probl Sovrem Khim Koord Soedin Leningr Gos Univ ... Problemy Sovremennoj Khimii Koordinatsionnykh Soedinenij Leningradskij Gosudarstvennyj Universitet [*A publication*]
Probl Sovrem Teor Elem Chastits ... Problemy Sovremennmoi Teorii Elementarnykh Chastits [*A publication*]
Probl Stomatol ... Problemi na Stomatologiyata [*A publication*]

Prob LT ...... Probyn on Land Tenure [*4th ed.*] [*1881*] [*A publication*] (DLA)
Probl Tech Med ... Problemy Techniki w Medycynie [*A publication*]
Probl Tekh Elektrodin ... Problemy Tekhnicheskoi Elektrodinamiki [*A publication*]
Probl Tekh Kibern ... Problemy na Tekhnicheskata Kibernetika [*A publication*]
Probl Tekh Kibern na Robotikata ... Problemy na Tekhnicheskata Kibernetika i Robotikata [*A publication*]
Probl Teor Gravitatsii Elem Chastits ... Problemy Teorii Gravitatsii i Elementarnykh Chastits [*USSR*] [*A publication*]
Probl Teploenerg Prikl Teplofiz ... Problemy Teploenergetiki i Prikladnoi Teplofiziki [*USSR*] [*A publication*]
Probl Ter .... Probleme de Terapeutica [*A publication*]
Probl Ter Stomatol ... Problemy Terapeuticheskoi Stomatologii [*A publication*]
Probl Treniya Iznashivaniya ... Problemy Treniya i Iznashivaniya [*A publication*]
Probl Tub ... Problemy Tuberkuleza [*A publication*]
Probl Tuberk ... Problemy Tuberkuleza [*A publication*]
Probl Virol (Engl Transl Vopr Virusol) ... Problems of Virology (English Translation of Voprosy Virusologii) [*A publication*]
Probl Yad Fiz Kosm Luchej ... Problemy Yadernoj Fiziki i Kosmicheskikh Luchej [*A publication*]
Probl Zaraznite Parazit Bolesti ... Problemi na Zaraznite i Parazitnite Bolesti [*A publication*]
Probl Zhivotnovod ... Problemy Zhivotnovodstva [*A publication*]
Probl Zooteh Vet ... Probleme Zootehnice si Veterinare [*A publication*]
Prob & Mat ... Probate and Matrimonial Cases [*A publication*] (DLA)
PROBO ..... Product/Ore/Bulk/Oil Carrier [*Shipping*] (DS)
PROBOUT ... Proceed On or About (MUGU)
Prob Pr Act ... Probate Practice Act [*A publication*] (DLA)
Prob and Prop ... Probate and Property [*A publication*]
Prob R .... Probate Reports [*A publication*] (DLA)
Prob Rep ..... Probate Reports [*A publication*] (DLA)
Prob Rep Ann ... Probate Reports, Annotated [*A publication*] (DLA)
PROBSUB ... Probable Submarine (NVT)
PRO Bull Men ... PROSI [*Public Relations Office of the Sugar Industry*] Bulletin Mensuel [*Port Louis*] [*A publication*]
PROBUS ... Program Budget System [*Military*]
Prob Vostok ... Problemy Vostokovedeniia [*A publication*]
Proby .... Probationary [*British military*] (DMA)
PROC .... Performing Rights Organization of Canada [*See also SDE*]
PROC .... Preliminary Required Operational Capability [*Military*]
PROC .... Pro-Cel International, Inc. [*NASDAQ symbol*] (NQ)
PROC .... Problems of Communism [*A publication*]
PROC .... Procedure (AAG)
PROC .... Proceedings
Proc .... Procellaria [*A publication*]
PROC .... Process (AABC)
PROC .... Procession (ROG)
PROC .... Processor [*or Processing*]
Proc .... Proclamation (DLA)
PROC .... Proctor
PROC .... Procure (AABC)
PROC .... Procurement (MSA)
PROC .... Programming Computer [*Data processing*]
PROC .... Proposed Required Operational Capability [*Military*] (AABC)
P6ROC ...... P6 Rover Owners Club (EAIO)
ProcAAAS ... Proceedings. American Association for the Advancement of Science [*A publication*]
Proc A Biol Colloq ... Proceedings. Annual Biology Colloquium [*A publication*]
Proc 31 A Blueberry Open House ... Proceedings. 31st Annual Blueberry Open House [*A publication*]
Proc Abstr Soc Biol Chem (Bangalore) ... Proceedings and Abstracts. Society of Biological Chemists (Bangalore) [*A publication*]
Proc Acad Man ... Proceedings. Academy of Management [*A publication*]
Proc Acad Nat Sci Phila ... Proceedings. Academy of Natural Sciences of Philadelphia [*A publication*]
Proc Acad Pol Sci ... Proceedings. Academy of Political Science [*A publication*]
Proc Acad Sci Armenian SSR ... Proceedings. Academy of Sciences of the Armenian SSR [*A publication*]
Proc Acad Sci Georgian SSR Biol Ser ... Proceedings. Academy of Sciences. Georgian SSR. Biological Series [*A publication*]
Proc Acad Sci United Prov Agra Oudh India ... Proceedings. Academy of Sciences. United Provinces of Agra and Oudh India [*A publication*]
Proc Acad Sci USSR Geochem Sect ... Proceedings. Academy of Sciences of the USSR. Geochemistry Section [*A publication*]
Proc Acad Sci USSR Sect Agrochem ... Proceedings. Academy of Sciences of the USSR. Section Agrochemistry [*A publication*]
Proc Acad Sci USSR Sect Appl Phys ... Proceedings. Academy of Sciences of the USSR. Section Applied Physics [*A publication*]
Proc A Conv Am Cranberry Growers' Ass ... Proceedings. Annual Convention. American Cranberry Growers' Association [*A publication*]
Proc Afr Cl Ass ... Proceedings. African Classical Associations [*A publication*]
Proc Afr Classical Assoc ... Proceedings. African Classical Association [*A publication*]

Proc Agric Soc (Trinidad Tobago) ... Proceedings. Agricultural Society (Trinidad and Tobago) [*A publication*]
Proc Agron Soc NZ ... Proceedings. Agronomy Society of New Zealand [*A publication*]
Proc Agr Outlook Conf ... Proceedings. Agricultural Outlook Conference [*A publication*]
Proc Agr Pestic Tech Soc ... Proceedings. Agricultural Pesticide Technical Society [*A publication*]
Proc Air Pollut Contr Ass ... Proceedings. Air Pollution Control Association [*A publication*]
Proc Air Pollut Control Assoc ... Proceedings. Air Pollution Control Association [*A publication*]
Proc Alaska Sci Conf ... Proceedings. Alaska Science Conference [*A publication*]
Proc Alberta Sulphur Gas Res Workshop ... Proceedings. Alberta Sulphur Gas Research Workshop [*A publication*]
Proc Alfred Benzon Symp ... Proceedings. Alfred Benzon Symposium [*A publication*]
Proc All Pak Sci Conf ... Proceedings. All Pakistan Science Conference [*A publication*]
Proc Alumni Assoc (Malaya) ... Proceedings. Alumni Association (Malaya) [*A publication*]
Proc Am Acad ... Proceedings. American Academy of Arts and Sciences [*A publication*]
Proc Am Acad Arts Sci ... Proceedings. American Academy of Arts and Sciences [*A publication*]
ProcAmAcAS ... Proceedings. American Academy of Arts and Sciences [*A publication*]
Proc Am Ant Soc ... Proceedings. American Antiquarian Society [*A publication*]
Proc Am Ass Can Res ... Proceedings. American Association for Cancer Research [*A publication*]
Proc Am Assoc Cancer Res ... Proceedings. American Association for Cancer Research [*A publication*]
Proc Am Assoc Cancer Res Am Soc Clin Oncol ... Proceedings. American Association for Cancer Research and American Society of Clinical Oncology [*A publication*]
Proc Am Assoc Cancer Res Annu Meet ... Proceedings. American Association for Cancer Research. Annual Meeting [*A publication*]
Proc Am Assoc Econ Entomol North Cent States Branch ... Proceedings. American Association of Economic Entomologists. North Central States Branch [*A publication*]
Proc Am Assoc State Highw Off ... Proceedings. American Association of State Highway Officials [*A publication*]
Proc Am Chem Soc Symp Anal Calorim ... Proceedings. American Chemical Society Symposium on Analytical Calorimetry [*A publication*]
Proc Am Concr Inst ... Proceedings. American Concrete Institute [*A publication*]
Proc Am Congr Surv Mapp ... Proceedings. American Congress on Surveying and Mapping [*A publication*]
Proc Am Cranberry Grow Assoc ... Proceedings. American Cranberry Growers' Association [*A publication*]
Proc Am Cranberry Growers' Ass ... Proceedings. American Cranberry Growers' Association [*A publication*]
Proc Am Diabetes Assoc ... Proceedings. American Diabetes Association [*A publication*]
Proc Am Doc Inst ... Proceedings. American Documentation Institute [*A publication*]
Proc Am Drug Manuf Assoc Annu Meet ... Proceedings. American Drug Manufacturers Association. Annual Meeting [*A publication*]
Proc A Meet Coun Fertil Applic ... Proceedings. Annual Meeting. Council on Fertilizer Application [*A publication*]
Proc A Meeting Sugar Ind Technicians ... Proceedings. Annual Meeting of Sugar Industry Technicians [*A publication*]
Proc A Meet Pl Physiol Univ MD ... Proceedings. Annual Meeting. American Society of Plant Physiologists at the University of Maryland [*A publication*]
Proc Amer Acad Arts Sci ... Proceedings. American Academy of Arts and Sciences [*A publication*]
Proc Amer Ass State Highw Offic ... Proceedings. American Association of State Highway Officials [*A publication*]
Proc Amer Math Soc ... Proceedings. American Mathematical Society [*A publication*]
Proc Amer Phil Ass ... Proceedings and Addresses. American Philosophical Association [*A publication*]
Proc Amer Philosophical Soc ... Proceedings. American Philosophical Society [*A publication*]
Proc Amer Philos Soc ... Proceedings. American Philosophical Society [*A publication*]
Proc Amer Phil Soc ... Proceedings. American Philosophical Society [*A publication*]
Proc Amer Power Conf ... Proceedings. American Power Conference [*A publication*]
Proc Amer Soc Anim Pro W Sect ... Proceedings. American Society of Animal Production. Western Section [*A publication*]
Proc Amer Soc Anim Sci W Sect ... Proceedings. American Society of Animal Science. Western Section [*A publication*]
Proc Amer Soc Bakery Eng ... Proceedings. American Society of Bakery Engineers [*A publication*]

Proc Amer Soc Brew Chem ... Proceedings. American Society of Brewing Chemists [*A publication*]
Proc Amer Soc Hort Sci ... Proceedings. American Society for Horticultural Science [*A publication*]
Proc Amer Soc of Internat L ... Proceedings. American Society of International Law [*A publication*]   (DLA)
Proc Amer Soc Testing Materials ... Proceedings. American Society for Testing and Materials [*A publication*]
Proc Amer Soc U Composers ... Proceedings. American Society of University Composers [*A publication*]
Proc Amer Wood-Preserv Ass ... Proceedings. American Wood-Preservers' Association [*A publication*]
Proc Am Hortic Congr ... Proceedings. American Horticultural Congress [*A publication*]
Proc Am Inst Electr Eng ... Proceedings. American Institute of Electrical Engineers [*A publication*]
Proc Am Math Soc ... Proceedings. American Mathematical Society [*A publication*]
Proc Am Peanut Res Educ Assoc ... Proceedings. American Peanut Research and Education Association [*A publication*]
Proc Am Pet Inst Div Refining ... Proceedings. American Petroleum Institute. Division of Refining [*A publication*]
Proc Am Pet Inst Refin Dep ... Proceedings. American Petroleum Institute. Refining Department [*A publication*]
Proc Am Pet Inst Sect 1 ... Proceedings. American Petroleum Institute. Section 1 [*A publication*]
Proc Am Pet Inst Sect 2 ... Proceedings. American Petroleum Institute. Section 2. Marketing [*A publication*]
Proc Am Pet Inst Sect 3 ... Proceedings. American Petroleum Institute. Section 3. Refining [*A publication*]
Proc Am Pet Inst Sect 4 ... Proceedings. American Petroleum Institute. Section 4. Production [*A publication*]
Proc Am Pet Inst Sect 5 ... Proceedings. American Petroleum Institute. Section 5. Transportation [*A publication*]
Proc Am Pet Inst Sect 6 ... Proceedings. American Petroleum Institute. Section 6. Interdivisional [*A publication*]
Proc Am Pet Inst Sect 8 ... Proceedings. American Petroleum Institute. Section 8. Science and Technology [*A publication*]
Proc Am Pet Inst Sect 3 Refining ... Proceedings. American Petroleum Institute. Section 3. Refining [*A publication*]
Proc Am Pharm Manuf Assoc Annu Meet ... Proceedings. American Pharmaceutical Manufacturers' Association. Annual Meeting [*A publication*]
Proc Am Pharm Manuf Assoc Midyear East Sect Meet ... Proceedings. American Pharmaceutical Manufacturers' Association. Midyear Eastern Section Meeting [*A publication*]
Proc Am Philos Soc ... Proceedings. American Philosophical Society [*A publication*]
Proc Am Phil Soc ... Proceedings. American Philosophical Society [*A publication*]
Proc Am Phytopathol Soc ... Proceedings. American Phytopathological Society [*A publication*]
Proc Am Power Conf ... Proceedings. American Power Conference [*A publication*]
Proc Am Soc Civ Eng ... Proceedings. American Society of Civil Engineers [*A publication*]
Proc Am Soc Civ Eng Transp Eng J ... Proceedings. American Society of Civil Engineers. Transportation Engineering Journal [*A publication*]
Proc Am Soc Clin Oncol Annu Meet ... Proceedings. American Society of Clinical Oncology. Annual Meeting [*A publication*]
Proc Am Soc Enol ... Proceedings. American Society of Enologists [*A publication*]
Proc Am Soc Hortic Sci ... Proceedings. American Society for Horticultural Science [*A publication*]
Proc Am Soc Hort Sci ... Proceedings. American Society for Horticultural Science [*A publication*]
Proc Am Soc Inf Sci ... Proceedings. American Society for Information Science [*A publication*]
Proc Am Soc Test & Mater ... Proceedings. American Society for Testing and Materials [*A publication*]
Proc Am Vet Med Ass ... Proceedings. American Veterinary Medical Association [*A publication*]
Proc Am Vet Med Assoc ... Proceedings. American Veterinary Medical Association [*A publication*]
Proc Am Water Works Assoc ... Proceedings. American Water Works Association [*A publication*]
Proc Am Wood-Preserv Assoc ... Proceedings. American Wood-Preservers' Association [*A publication*]
Proc Anal Div Chem Soc ... Proceedings. Analytical Division. Chemical Society [*A publication*]
Proc Anim Care Panel ... Proceedings. Animal Care Panel [*A publication*]
Proc Ann Conf High En Nucl Phys ... Proceedings. Annual Conference on High Energy Nuclear Physics [*A publication*]
Proc Ann Conf Rehab Eng ... Proceedings. Annual Conference on Rehabilitation Engineering [*A publication*]
Proc Annu AIChE Southwest Ohio Conf Energy Environ ... Proceedings. Annual AIChE [*American Institute of Chemical Engineers*] Southwestern Ohio Conference on Energy and the Environment [*A publication*]

Proc Annu Allerton Conf Circuit Syst Theory ... Proceedings. Annual Allerton Conference on Circuit and System Theory [*Later, Proceedings. Annual Allerton Conference on Communication, Control, and Computing*] [*A publication*]

Proc Annu Allerton Conf Commun Control Comput ... Proceedings. Annual Allerton Conference on Communication, Control, and Computing [*Formerly, Annual Allerton Conference on Circuit and System Theory*] [*United States*] [*A publication*]

Proc Annu Arkansas Water Works Pollut Control Conf Short Sch ... Proceedings. Annual Arkansas Water Works and Pollution Control Conference and Short School [*A publication*]

Proc Annu Battery Res Dev Conf ... Proceedings. Annual Battery Research and Development Conference [*A publication*]

Proc Annu Biochem Eng Symp ... Proceedings. Annual Biochemical Engineering Symposium [*United States*] [*A publication*]

Proc Annu Biol Colloq (Oreg State Univ) ... Proceedings. Annual Biology Colloquium (Oregon State University) [*A publication*]

Proc Annu Biomed Sci Instrum Symp ... Proceedings. Annual Biomedical Sciences Instrumentation Symposium [*A publication*]

Proc Annu Blueberry Open House ... Proceedings. Annual Blueberry Open House [*A publication*]

Proc Annu Calif Weed Conf ... Proceedings. Annual California Weed Conference [*A publication*]

Proc Annu Cli Spinal Cord Inj Conf ... Proceedings. Annual Clinical Spinal Cord Injury Conference [*A publication*]

Proc Annu Conf Agron Soc NZ ... Proceedings. Annual Conference. Agronomy Society of New Zealand [*A publication*]

Proc Annu Conf Autom Control Pet Chem Ind ... Proceedings. Annual Conference on Automatic Control in the Petroleum and Chemical Industries [*A publication*]

Proc Annu Conf Biol Sonar Diving Mamm ... Proceedings. Annual Conference on Biological Sonar and Diving Mammals [*A publication*]

Proc Annu Conf Biol Sonar Diving Mammals ... Proceedings. Annual Conference on Biological Sonar and Diving Mammals [*A publication*]

Proc Annu Conf Can Nucl Assoc ... Proceedings. Annual Conference. Canadian Nuclear Association [*A publication*]

Proc Annu Conf Energy Convers Storage ... Proceedings. Annual Conference on Energy Conversion and Storage [*A publication*]

Proc Annu Conf Environ Chem Hum Anim Health ... Proceedings. Annual Conference on Environmental Chemicals. Human and Animal Health [*A publication*]

Proc Annu Conf Ind Appl X Ray Anal ... Proceedings. Annual Conference on Industrial Applications of X-Ray Analysis [*A publication*]

Proc Annu Conf Int Symp N Am Lake Manage Soc ... Proceedings. Annual Conference and International Symposium. North American Lake Management Society [*A publication*]

Proc Annu Conf Kidney ... Proceedings. Annual Conference on the Kidney [*A publication*]

Proc Annu Conf Manitoba Agron ... Proceedings. Annual Conference of Manitoba Agronomists [*A publication*]

Proc Annu Conf MD Del Water Sewage Assoc ... Proceedings. Annual Conference. Maryland-Delaware Water and Sewage Association [*A publication*]

Proc Annu Conf Microbeam Anal Soc ... Proceedings. Annual Conference. Microbeam Analysis Society [*A publication*]

Proc Annu Conf Reinf Plast Compos Inst Soc Plast Ind ... Proceedings. Annual Conference. Reinforced Plastics/Composites Institute. Society of the Plastics Industry [*A publication*]

Proc Annu Conf Res Med Educ ... Proceedings. Annual Conference on Research in Medical Education [*A publication*]

Proc Annu Conf Restor Coastal Veg Fla ... Proceedings. Annual Conference on Restoration of Coastal Vegetation in Florida [*A publication*]

Proc Annu Conf Southeast Assoc Fish Wildl Agencies ... Proceedings. Annual Conference. Southeastern Association of Fish and Wildlife Agencies [*A publication*]

Proc Annu Conf Southeast Assoc Game Fish Comm ... Proceedings. Annual Conference. Southeastern Association of Game and Fish Commissioners [*A publication*]

Proc Annu Congr S Afr Sugar Technol Assoc ... Proceedings. Annual Congress. South African Sugar Technologists Association [*A publication*]

Proc Annu Connector Symp ... Proceedings. Annual Connector Symposium [*A publication*]

Proc Annu Conv Assoc Am Pestic Control Off ... Proceedings. Annual Convention Association. American Pesticide Control Officials [*A publication*]

Proc Annu Conv Flavoring Ext Manuf Assoc US ... Proceedings. Annual Convention. Flavoring Extract Manufacturers' Association of the United States [*A publication*]

Proc Annu Conv Gas Process Assoc Meet Pap ... Proceedings. Annual Convention. Gas Processors Association. Meeting Papers [*A publication*]

Proc Annu Conv Gas Process Assoc Tech Pap ... Proceedings. Annual Convention. Gas Processors Association. Technical Papers [*A publication*]

Proc Annu Conv Milk Ind Found ... Proceedings. Annual Convention. Milk Industry Foundation [*A publication*]

Proc Annu Conv Nat Gasoline Assoc Am Tech Pap ... Proceedings. Annual Convention. Natural Gasoline Association of America. Technical Papers [*A publication*]

Proc Annu Conv Nat Gas Process Assoc Tech Pap ... Proceedings. Annual Convention. Natural Gas Processors Association. Technical Papers [*United States*] [*A publication*]

Proc Annu Conv Natur Gas Process Ass Tech Pap ... Proceedings. Annual Convention. Natural Gas Processors Association. Technical Papers [*A publication*]

Proc Annu Conv Oil Technol Assoc ... Proceedings. Annual Convention. Oil Technologists Association [*A publication*]

Proc Annu Conv Philipp Sugar Assoc ... Proceedings. Annual Convention. Philippine Sugar Association [*A publication*]

Proc Annu Conv Sugar Technol Assoc India ... Proceedings. Annual Convention. Sugar Technologists' Association of India [*A publication*]

Proc Annu Conv West Can Water Sewage Conf ... Proceedings. Annual Convention. Western Canada Water and Sewage Conference (1960-1975) [*A publication*]

Proc Annu East Theor Phys Conf ... Proceedings. Annual Eastern Theoretical Physics Conference [*A publication*]

Proc Annu Eng Geol Soils Eng Symp ... Proceedings. Annual Engineering Geology and Soils Engineering Symposium [*A publication*]

Proc Annu Eng Geol Symp ... Proceedings. Annual Engineering Geology Symposium [*A publication*]

Proc Annu Environ Water Resour Eng Conf ... Proceedings. Annual Environmental and Water Resources Engineering Conference [*A publication*]

Proc Annu Fall Meet Calif Nat Gasoline Assoc ... Proceedings. Annual Fall Meeting. California Natural Gasoline Association [*A publication*]

Proc Annu Fall Meet West Gas Process Oil Refin Assoc ... Proceedings. Annual Fall Meeting. Western Gas Processors and Oil Refiners Association [*A publication*]

Proc Annu Fall Meet West Gas Process Oil Refiners Assoc ... Proceedings. Annual Fall Meeting. Western Gas Processors and Oil Refiners Association [*A publication*]

Proc Annu Freq Control Symp ... Proceedings. Annual Frequency Control Symposium [*A publication*]

Proc Annu Hardwood Symp Hardwood Res Counc ... Proceedings. Annual Hardwood Symposium. Hardwood Research Council [*A publication*]

Proc Annu Holm Semin Electr Contacts ... Proceedings. Annual Holm Seminar on Electrical Contacts [*A publication*]

Proc Annu Ind Pollut Conf ... Proceedings. Annual Industrial Pollution Conference [*United States*] [*A publication*]

Proc Annu Instrum Conf ... Proceedings. Annual Instrumentation Conference [*A publication*]

Proc Annu Int Conf Can Nucl Assoc ... Proceedings. Annual International Conference. Canadian Nuclear Association [*A publication*]

Proc Annu Int Conf Fault Tolerant Comput ... Proceedings. Annual International Conference on Fault-Tolerant Computing [*A publication*]

Proc Annu Int Conf High Energy Phys ... Proceedings. Annual International Conference on High Energy Physics [*A publication*]

Proc Annu Int Conf Plasma Chem Technol ... Proceedings. Annual International Conference of Plasma Chemistry and Technology [*A publication*]

Proc Annu Int Game Fish Res Conf ... Proceedings. Annual International Game Fish Research Conference [*A publication*]

Proc Annu Manage Conf Am Dent Assoc ... Proceedings. Annual Management Conference. American Dental Association [*A publication*]

Proc Annu Mar Coat Conf ... Proceedings. Annual Marine Coatings Conference [*A publication*]

Proc Annu Meat Sci Inst ... Proceedings. Annual Meat Science Institute [*A publication*]

Proc Annu Meet Agric Res Inst ... Proceedings. Annual Meeting. Agricultural Research Institute [*A publication*]

Proc Annu Meet Air Pollut Control Assoc ... Proceedings. Annual Meeting. Air Pollution Control Association [*A publication*]

Proc Annu Meet Am Assoc Vet Lab Diagn ... Proceedings. Annual Meeting. American Association of Veterinary Laboratory Diagnosticians [*A publication*]

Proc Annu Meet Amer Soc Hort Sci Caribbean Reg ... Proceedings. Annual Meeting. American Society for Horticultural Science. Caribbean Region [*A publication*]

Proc Annu Meet Am Pet Inst ... Proceedings. Annual Meeting. American Petroleum Institute [*A publication*]

Proc Annu Meet Am Psychopathol Assoc ... Proceedings. Annual Meeting. American Psychopathological Association [*A publication*]

Proc Annu Meet Am Sect Int Sol Energy Soc ... Proceedings. Annual Meeting. American Section. International Solar Energy Society [*A publication*]

Proc Annu Meet Am Soc Anim Sci West Sect ... Proceedings. Annual Meeting. American Society of Animal Science. Western Section [*A publication*]

Proc Annu Meet Am Soc Bak Eng ... Proceedings. Annual Meeting. American Society of Bakery Engineers [*A publication*]

Proc Annu Meet Am Soc Inf Sci ... Proceedings. Annual Meeting. American Society for Information Science [*A publication*]

Proc Annu Meet Am Soybean Assoc ... Proceedings. Annual Meeting. American Soybean Association [*A publication*]

Proc Annu Meet Biochem (Hung) ... Proceedings. Annual Meeting of Biochemistry (Hungary) [*A publication*]

Proc Annu Meet Can Nucl Assoc ... Proceedings. Annual Meeting. Canadian Nuclear Association [*A publication*]

Proc Annu Meet Can Soc Agron ... Proceedings. Annual Meeting. Canadian Society of Agronomy [*A publication*]

Proc Annu Meet Chem Spec Manuf Assoc ... Proceedings. Annual Meeting. Chemical Specialties Manufacturers Association [*A publication*]

Proc Annu Meet Compressed Gas Assoc ... Proceedings. Annual Meeting. Compressed Gas Association [*A publication*]

Proc Annu Meet Conn Pomol Soc ... Proceedings. Annual Meeting. Connecticut Pomological Society [*A publication*]

Proc Annu Meet Electron Microsc Soc Am ... Proceedings. Annual Meeting. Electron Microscopy Society of America [*A publication*]

Proc Annu Meet Fert Ind Round Table ... Proceedings. Annual Meeting. Fertilizer Industry Round Table [*A publication*]

Proc Annu Meet Fla State Hortic Soc ... Proceedings. Annual Meeting. Florida State Horticultural Society [*A publication*]

Proc Annu Meet Hawaii Sugar Plant Assoc ... Proceedings. Annual Meeting. Hawaiian Sugar Planters Association [*A publication*]

Proc Annu Meeting Amer Soc Int Law ... Proceedings. Annual Meeting. American Society of International Law [*A publication*]

Proc Annu Meet Int Magnesium Assoc ... Proceedings. Annual Meeting. International Magnesium Association [*A publication*]

Proc Annu Meet Jpn Endocrinol Soc ... Proceedings. Annual Meeting. Japan Endocrinological Society [*A publication*]

Proc Annu Meet Lightwood Res Conf ... Proceedings. Annual Meeting. Lightwood Research Conference [*A publication*]

Proc Annu Meet Med Sect Am Counc Life Insur ... Proceedings. Annual Meeting. Medical Section. American Council of Life Insurance [*A publication*]

Proc Annu Meet Med Sect Am Life Conv ... Proceedings. Annual Meeting. Medical Section. American Life Convention [*A publication*]

Proc Annu Meet Med Sect Am Life Insur Assoc ... Proceedings. Annual Meeting. Medical Section. American Life Insurance Association [*A publication*]

Proc Annu Meet Met Powder Assoc ... Proceedings. Annual Meeting. Metal Powder Association [*A publication*]

Proc Annu Meet Nat Assoc Corros Eng ... Proceedings. Annual Meeting. National Association of Corrosion Engineers [*A publication*]

Proc Annu Meet Nat Ass Wheat Growers ... Proceedings. Annual Meeting. National Association of Wheat Growers [*A publication*]

Proc Annu Meet Natl Counc Radiat Prot Meas ... Proceedings. Annual Meeting. National Council on Radiation Protection and Measurements [*United States*] [*A publication*]

Proc Annu Meet Natl Jt Comm Fert Appl ... Proceedings. Annual Meeting. National Joint Committee on Fertilizer Application [*A publication*]

Proc Annu Meet Nat Res Counc Agr Res Inst ... Proceedings. Annual Meeting. National Research Council. Agricultural Research Institute [*A publication*]

Proc Annu Meet N Cent Weed Contr Conf ... Proceedings. Annual Meeting. North Central Weed Control Conference [*A publication*]

Proc Annu Meet NJ ... Proceedings. Annual Meeting. New Jersey Mosquito Extermination Association [*A publication*]

Proc Annu Meet Northeast Weed Sci Soc ... Proceedings. Annual Meeting. Northeastern Weed Science Society [*A publication*]

Proc Annu Meet NY State Hort Soc ... Proceedings. Annual Meeting. New York State Horticultural Society [*A publication*]

Proc Annu Meet Pac Coast Fertil Soc ... Proceedings. Annual Meeting. Pacific Coast Fertility Society [*A publication*]

Proc Annu Meet Soc Promot Agric Sci ... Proceedings. Annual Meeting. Society for the Promotion of Agricultural Science [*A publication*]

Proc Annu Meet US Anim Health Assoc ... Proceedings. Annual Meeting. United States Animal Health Association [*A publication*]

Proc Annu Meet Utah Mosq Abatement Assoc ... Proceedings. Annual Meeting. Utah Mosquito Abatement Association [*A publication*]

Proc Annu Meet West Div Am Dairy Sci Assoc ... Proceedings. Annual Meeting. Western Division. American Dairy Science Association [*A publication*]

Proc Annu Meet West Soc Fr Hist ... Proceedings. Annual Meeting. Western Society for French History [*A publication*]

Proc Annu Meet W Farm Econ Ass ... Proceedings. Annual Meeting. Western Farm Economics Association [*A publication*]

Proc Annu Mid-Am Spectrosc Symp ... Proceedings. Annual Mid-America Spectroscopy Symposium [*A publication*]

Proc Annu Midwest Fert Conf ... Proceedings. Annual Midwest Fertilizer Conference [*A publication*]

Proc Annu Nat Dairy Eng Conf ... Proceedings. Annual National Dairy Engineering Conference [*A publication*]

Proc Annu Nat Dairy Food Eng Conf ... Proceedings. Annual National Dairy and Food Engineering Conference [*A publication*]

Proc Annu Northwest Wood Prod Clin ... Proceedings. Annual Northwest Wood Products Clinic [*A publication*]

Proc Annu Power Sources Conf ... Proceedings. Annual Power Sources Conference [*A publication*]

Proc Annu Purdue Air Qual Conf ... Proceedings. Annual Purdue Air Quality Conference [*A publication*]

Proc Annu Recipro Meat Conf Am Meat Sci Assoc ... Proceedings. Annual Reciprocal Meat Conference. American Meat Science Association [*A publication*]

Proc Annu Reliab Maintainability Symp ... Proceedings. Annual Reliability and Maintainability Symposium [*A publication*]

Proc Annu Reliab Maintain Symp ... Proceedings. Annual Reliability and Maintainability Symposium [*A publication*]

Proc Annu Rochester Conf High Energy Nucl Phys ... Proceedings. Annual Rochester Conference on High Energy Nuclear Physics [*A publication*]

Proc Annu Rocky Mount Bioeng Symp ... Proceedings. Annual Rocky Mountain Bioengineering Symposium [*A publication*]

Proc Annu Rocky Mt Bioeng Symp ... Proceedings. Annual Rocky Mountain Bioengineering Symposium [*A publication*]

Proc Annu San Franc Cancer Symp ... Proceedings. Annual San Francisco Cancer Symposium [*A publication*]

Proc Annu Sci Meet Comm Probl Drug Depend US Nat Res Counc ... Proceedings. Annual Scientific Meeting. Committee on Problems of Drug Dependence. United States National Research Council [*A publication*]

Proc Annu Senior Staff Conf USARS ... Proceedings. Annual Senior Staff Conference. United States Agricultural Research Service [*A publication*]

Proc Annu Sess Ceylon Assoc Adv Sci ... Proceedings. Annual Session. Ceylon Association for the Advancement of Science [*A publication*]

Proc Annu Southwest Pet Short Course ... Proceedings. Annual Southwestern Petroleum Short Course [*United States*] [*A publication*]

Proc Annu Symp Eng Geol Soils Eng ... Proceedings. Annual Symposium on Engineering Geology and Soils Engineering [*A publication*]

Proc Annu Symp Eugen Soc ... Proceedings. Annual Symposium of the Eugenics Society [*A publication*]

Proc Annu Symp Freq Control ... Proceedings. Annual Symposium on Frequency Control [*A publication*]

Proc Annu Symp Incremental Motion Control Syst Devices ... Proceedings. Annual Symposium. Incremental Motion Control Systems and Devices [*A publication*]

Proc Annu Tall Timbers Fire Ecol Conf ... Proceedings. Annual Tall Timbers Fire Ecology Conference [*A publication*]

Proc Annu Tech Conf Soc Vac Coaters ... Proceedings. Annual Technical Conference. Society of Vacuum Coaters [*A publication*]

Proc Annu Tech Meet Inst Environ Sci ... Proceedings. Annual Technical Meeting. Institute of Environmental Sciences [*A publication*]

Proc Annu Tech Meet Int Metallogr Soc Inc ... Proceedings. Annual Technical Meeting. International Metallographic Society, Inc. [*A publication*]

Proc Annu Tech Meet Tech Assoc Graphic Arts ... Proceedings. Annual Technical Meeting. Technical Association. Graphic Arts [*A publication*]

Proc Annu Tex Nutr Conf ... Proceedings. Annual Texas Nutrition Conference [*A publication*]

Proc Annu Tung Ind Conv ... Proceedings. Annual Tung Industry Convention [*A publication*]

Proc Annu UMR-MEC Conf Energy ... Proceedings. Annual UMR-MEC [*University of Missouri at Rolla - Missouri Energy Council*] Conference on Energy [*A publication*]

Proc Annu West Tex Oil Lifting Short Course ... Proceedings. Annual West Texas Oil Lifting Short Course [*A publication*]

Proc Annu WWEMA Ind Pollut Conf ... Proceedings. Annual WWEMA [*Water and Wastewater Equipment Manufacturers Association*] Industrial Pollution Conference [*United States*] [*A publication*]

Proc APCA Annu Meet ... Proceedings. APCA [*Air Pollution Control Association*] Annual Meeting [*A publication*]

PRO CAPILL ... Pro Capillis [*For the Hair*] [*Pharmacy*]

Proc APREA ... Proceedings. APREA [*American Peanut Research and Education Association*] [*A publication*]

Proc APRES (Am Peanut Res Educ Soc) ... Proceedings. APRES (American Peanut Research and Education Society) [*A publication*]

Proc Aris Soc ... Proceedings. Aristotelian Society [*A publication*]

Proc Ark Acad Sci ... Proceedings. Arkansas Academy of Science [*A publication*]

Proc Arkansas Acad Sci ... Proceedings. Arkansas Academy of Science [*A publication*]

Proc Arkansas Water Works Pollut Control Conf Short Sch ... Proceedings. Arkansas Water Works and Pollution Control Conference and Short School [*A publication*]

Proc Asian-Pac Congr Cardiol ... Proceedings. Asian-Pacific Congress of Cardiology [*A publication*]

Proc Asiat Soc (Bengal) ... Proceedings. Asiatic Society (Bengal) [*A publication*]

Proc ASIS Annu Meet ... Proceedings. ASIS [*American Society for Information Science*] Annual Meeting [*A publication*]

Proc Ass Asphalt Paving Technol ... Proceedings. Association of Asphalt Paving Technologists [*A publication*]

Proc Ass Econ Biol ... Proceedings. Association of Economic Biologists [*A publication*]
Proc Assoc Asphalt Paving Technol ... Proceedings. Association of Asphalt Paving Technologists [*A publication*]
Proc Assoc Clin Biochem ... Proceedings. Association of Clinical Biochemists [*A publication*]
Proc Assoc Off Seed Anal ... Proceedings. Association of Official Seed Analysts [*A publication*]
Proc Assoc Off Seed Anal (North Am) ... Proceedings. Association of Official Seed Analysts (North America) [*A publication*]
Proc Assoc Plant Prot Kyushu ... Proceedings. Association for Plant Protection of Kyushu [*A publication*]
Proc Assoc South Agric Work ... Proceedings. Association of Southern Agricultural Workers [*A publication*]
Proc Ass Offic Seed Anal ... Proceedings. Association of Official Seed Analysts [*A publication*]
Proc Ass Plant Prot Hokuriku ... Proceedings. Association of Plant Protection of Hokuriku [*A publication*]
Proc Ass Plant Prot Kyushu ... Proceedings. Association for Plant Protection of Kyushu [*A publication*]
Proc Ass Res Nerv Ment Dis ... Proceedings. Association for Research in Nervous and Mental Diseases [*A publication*]
Proc Ass S Agr Workers ... Proceedings. Association of Southern Agricultural Workers [*A publication*]
Proc Ass Sth Agric Wkrs ... Proceedings. Association of Southern Agricultural Workers [*A publication*]
Proc ASTM ... Proceedings. American Society for Testing and Materials [*A publication*]
Proc Astron Soc Aust ... Proceedings. Astronomical Society of Australia [*A publication*]
Proc Astr Soc Aust ... Proceedings. Astronomical Society of Australia [*A publication*]   (APTA)
Proc Aust Ass Clin Biochem ... Proceedings. Australian Association of Clinical Biochemists [*A publication*]   (APTA)
Proc Aust Assoc Neurol ... Proceedings. Australian Association of Neurologists [*A publication*]
Proc Aust Biochem Soc ... Proceedings. Australian Biochemical Society [*A publication*]
Proc Aust Bldg Res Congr ... Australian Building Research Congress. Proceedings [*A publication*]   (APTA)
Proc Aust Build Res Congr ... Australian Building Research Congress. Proceedings [*A publication*]   (APTA)
Proc Aust Ceram Conf ... Australian Ceramic Conference. Proceedings [*A publication*]   (APTA)
Proc Aust Ceramic Conf ... Australian Ceramic Conference. Proceedings [*A publication*]   (APTA)
Proc Aust Clay Miner Conf ... Australian Clay Minerals Conference. Proceedings [*A publication*]   (APTA)
Proc Aust Comput Conf ... Proceedings. Australian Computer Conference [*A publication*]   (APTA)
Proc Aust Conf Nucl Tech Anal ... Australian Conference on Nuclear Techniques of Analysis. Proceedings [*A publication*]   (APTA)
Proc Aust Grasslds Conf ... Proceedings. Australian Grasslands Conference [*A publication*]   (APTA)
Proc Aust Inst Min and Metall ... Australasian Institute of Mining and Metallurgy. Proceedings [*A publication*]   (APTA)
Proc Aust Inst Min Metall ... Proceedings. Australasian Institute of Mining and Metallurgy [*A publication*]
Proc Aust Physiol Pharmacol Soc ... Proceedings. Australian Physiological and Pharmacological Society [*A publication*]
Proc Aust Pulp Pap Ind Tech Assoc ... Proceedings. Australian Pulp and Paper Industry Technical Association [*A publication*]
Proc Australasian Poultry Sci Conv ... Proceedings. Australasian Poultry Science Convention [*A publication*]
Proc Australas Inst Min Eng ... Proceedings. Australasian Institute of Mining Engineers [*A publication*]
Proc Australas Inst Min and Metall ... Australasian Institute of Mining and Metallurgy. Proceedings [*A publication*]   (APTA)
Proc Australas Inst Min Metall ... Proceedings. Australasian Institute of Mining and Metallurgy [*A publication*]
Proc Aust Road Res Bd ... Australian Road Research Board. Proceedings [*A publication*]   (APTA)
Proc Aust Road Research Board ... Australian Road Research Board. Proceedings [*A publication*]   (APTA)
Proc Aust Soc Anim Prod ... Proceedings. Australian Society of Animal Production [*A publication*]
Proc Aust Soc Med Res ... Proceedings. Australian Society for Medical Research [*A publication*]
Proc Aust Soc Sugar Cane Technol ... Proceedings. Australian Society of Sugar Cane Technologists [*A publication*]
Proc Aust Weed Conf ... Proceedings. Australian Weed Conference [*A publication*]
Proc Auto Div Instn Mech Engrs ... Proceedings. Institution of Mechanical Engineers. Auto Division [*A publication*]
Proc Bakish Mater Corp Publ ... Proceedings. Bakish Materials Corporation Publication [*A publication*]
Proc B & B ... Proctor's Bench and Bar of New York [*A publication*]   (DLA)
Proc Beltwide Cotton Prod Res Conf ... Proceedings. Beltwide Cotton Production Research Conferences [*A publication*]

Proc Berkeley Symp Math Stat Probab ... Proceedings. Berkeley Symposium on Mathematical Statistics and Probability [*A publication*]
Proc Bienn Conf Inst Briquet Agglom ... Proceedings. Biennial Conference. Institute for Briquetting and Agglomeration [*A publication*]
Proc Bienn Conf Int Briquet Assoc ... Proceedings. Biennial Conference. International Briqueting Association [*A publication*]
Proc Bienn Gas Dyn Symp ... Proceedings. Biennial Gas Dynamics Symposium [*A publication*]
Proc Bienn Symp Turbul Liq ... Proceedings. Biennial Symposium on Turbulence in Liquids [*A publication*]
Proc Bihar Acad Agric Sci ... Proceedings. Bihar Academy of Agricultural Sciences [*A publication*]
Proc Bihar Acad Agr Sci ... Proceedings. Bihar Academy of Agricultural Sciences [*A publication*]
Proc Biol Soc Wash ... Proceedings. Biological Society of Washington [*A publication*]
Proc Bird Control Semin ... Proceedings. Bird Control Seminar [*A publication*]
Proc Bos Soc ... Proceedings. Bostonian Society [*A publication*]
Proc Bot Soc Br Isles ... Proceedings. Botanical Society of the British Isles [*A publication*]
Proc Br Acad ... Proceedings. British Academy [*A publication*]
Proc Br Acoust Soc ... Proceedings. British Acoustical Society [*A publication*]
Proc Br Assoc Refrig ... Proceedings. British Association for Refrigeration [*A publication*]
Proc Br Ceram Soc ... Proceedings. British Ceramic Society [*A publication*]
Proc Br Crop Prot Conf ... Proceedings. 1980 British Crop Protection Conference. Weeds [*A publication*]
Proc Bristol Nat Soc ... Proceedings. Bristol Naturalists Society [*A publication*]
Proc Brit Ac ... Proceedings. British Academy [*A publication*]
Proc Brit Acad ... Proceedings. British Academy for the Promotion of Historical, Philosophical, and Philological Studies [*A publication*]
Proc Brit Ceram Soc ... Proceedings. British Ceramic Society [*A publication*]
Proc Brit Insectic Fungic Conf ... Proceedings. British Insecticide and Fungicide Conference [*A publication*]
Proc British Asso Ja Stud ... Proceedings. British Association for Japanese Studies [*A publication*]
Proc Brit Weed Contr Conf ... Proceedings. British Weed Control Conference [*A publication*]
Proc Brown Univ Symp Biol Skin ... Proceedings. Brown University Symposium on the Biology of Skin [*A publication*]
Proc Br Paedod Soc ... Proceedings. British Paedodontic Society [*A publication*]
Proc Br Soc Anim Prod ... Proceedings. British Society of Animal Production [*A publication*]
Proc Br Weed Control Conf ... Proceedings. British Weed Control Conference [*A publication*]
Proc Buffalo Milan Symp Mol Pharmacol ... Proceedings. Buffalo-Milan Symposium on Molecular Pharmacology [*A publication*]
Proc Calif Acad Sci ... Proceedings. California Academy of Sciences [*A publication*]
Proc Calif Ann Weed Conf ... Proceedings. California Annual Weed Conference [*A publication*]
Proc Calif Weed Conf ... Proceedings. California Weed Conference [*A publication*]
Proc Calif Zool Club ... Proceedings. California Zoological Club [*A publication*]
Proc Camb Philos Soc ... Proceedings. Cambridge Philosophical Society [*A publication*]
Proc Camb Phil Soc Math Phys Sci ... Proceedings. Cambridge Philosophical Society. Mathematical and Physical Sciences [*A publication*]
Proc Cambridge Antiq Soc ... Proceedings. Cambridge Antiquarian Society [*A publication*]
Proc Cambridge Ant Soc ... Proceedings. Cambridge Antiquarian Society [*A publication*]
Proc Cambridge Philos Soc ... Proceedings. Cambridge Philosophical Society [*A publication*]
Proc Cambridge Phil Soc ... Proceedings. Cambridge Philological Society [*A publication*]
Proc Cambr Phil Soc ... Proceedings. Cambridge Philological Society [*A publication*]
Proc Canad Oto Soc ... Proceedings. Canadian Otolaryngological Society [*A publication*]
Proc Can Cancer Res Conf ... Proceedings. Canadian Cancer Research Conference [*A publication*]
Proc Can Centen Wheat Symp ... Proceedings. Canadian Centennial Wheat Symposium [*A publication*]
Proc Can Fed Biol Soc ... Proceedings. Canadian Federation of Biological Societies [*A publication*]
Proc Can Nat Weed Comm E Sect ... Proceedings. Canadian National Weed Committee. Eastern Section [*A publication*]
Proc Can Nat Weed Comm W Sect ... Proceedings. Canadian National Weed Committee. Western Section [*A publication*]
Proc Can Nucl Assoc Annu Int Conf ... Proceedings. Canadian Nuclear Association Annual International Conference [*A publication*]

Proc Can Phytopathol Soc ... Proceedings. Canadian Phytopathological Society [*A publication*]
Proc Can Rock Mech Symp ... Proceedings. Canadian Rock Mechanics Symposium [*A publication*]
Proc Can Soc Forensic Sci ... Proceedings. Canadian Society of Forensic Science [*A publication*]
Proc Cardiff Med Soc ... Proceedings. Cardiff Medical Society [*A publication*]
Proc Caribb Reg Am Soc Hort Sci ... Proceedings. Caribbean Region. American Society for Horticultural Science [*A publication*]
Proc Cath ... Proceedings. Catholic Theological Society of America [*A publication*]
Proc Cath Phil Ass ... Proceedings. American Catholic Philosophical Association [*A publication*]
Proc Cellul Conf ... Proceedings. Cellulose Conference [*A publication*]
Proc Ch ...... Proceedings in Chancery [*A publication*] (DLA)
Proc Chem Soc ... Proceedings. Chemical Society [*A publication*]
Proc Chem Soc (London) ... Proceedings. Chemical Society (London) [*A publication*]
Proc Chin Physiol Soc Chengtu Branch ... Proceedings. Chinese Physiological Society. Chengtu Branch [*A publication*]
PROCCIR ... Procurement Circular [*Air Force*] (AFIT)
Proc Clin Dial Transplant Forum ... Proceedings. Clinical Dialysis and Transplant Forum [*A publication*]
Proc Coal Mining Inst Amer ... Proceedings. Coal Mining Institute of America [*A publication*]
Proc Coll Med Univ Philipp ... Proceedings. College of Medicine. University of the Philippines [*A publication*]
Proc Coll Nat Sci Sect 4 Biol Sci Seoul Natl Univ ... Proceedings. College of Natural Sciences. Section 4. Biological Sciences. Seoul National University [*A publication*]
Proc Coll Nat Sci Sect 2 Seoul Nat Univ ... Proceedings. College of Natural Sciences. Section 2. Physics, Astronomy. Seoul National University [*A publication*]
Proc Coll Nat Sci Sect 3 Seoul Nat Univ ... Proceedings. College of Natural Sciences. Section 3. Chemistry. Seoul National University [*A publication*]
Proc Coll Nat Sci Sect 4 Seoul Nat Univ ... Proceedings. College of Natural Sciences. Section 4. Life Sciences. Seoul National University [*A publication*]
Proc Coll Nat Sci Sect 5 Seoul Nat Univ ... Proceedings. College of Natural Sciences. Section 5. Geology, Meteorology, and Oceanography. Seoul National University [*A publication*]
Proc Coll Nat Sci (Seoul) ... Proceedings. College of Natural Sciences (Seoul) [*A publication*]
Proc Coll Nat Sci Seoul Natl Univ ... Proceedings. College of Natural Sciences. Seoul National University [*A publication*]
Proc Colloq Int Potash Inst ... Proceedings. Colloquium of the International Potash Institute [*A publication*]
Proc Commonw Min Metall Congr ... Proceedings. Commonwealth Mining and Metallurgical Congress [*A publication*]
Proc Conf Aust Road Res Board ... Proceedings. Conference of the Australian Road Research Board [*A publication*]
Proc Conf Aust Soc Sugar Cane Technol ... Australian Society of Sugar Cane Technologists. Proceedings of the Conference [*A publication*] (APTA)
Proc Conf Eng Med Biol ... Proceedings. Conference of Engineering in Medicine and Biology [*A publication*]
Proc Conf Great Lakes Res ... Proceedings. Conference on Great Lakes Research [*A publication*]
Proc Conf Hot Lab Equip ... Proceedings. Conference on Hot Laboratories and Equipment [*A publication*]
Proc Conf (Int) Solid State Devices ... Proceedings. Conference (International) on Solid State Devices [*A publication*]
Proc Conf Remote Syst Technol ... Proceedings. Conference on Remote Systems Technology [*A publication*]
Proc Conf Silic Ind ... Proceedings. Conference on the Silicate Industry [*A publication*]
Proc Conf Solid State Devices ... Proceedings. Conference on Solid State Devices [*A publication*]
Proc Congenital Anomalies Res Assoc Annu Rep ... Proceedings. Congenital Anomalies. Research Association. Annual Report [*A publication*]
Proc Cong Mediterr Phytopathol Union ... Proceedings. Congress of the Mediterranean Phytopathological Union [*A publication*]
Proc Congr Ann Corp Ingen For (Quebec) ... Proceedings. Congres Annuel. Corporation des Ingenieurs Forestiers (Quebec) [*A publication*]
Proc Congr Eur Soc Haematol ... Proceedings. Congress of the European Society of Haematology [*A publication*]
Proc Congr Fed Int Precontrainte ... Proceedings. Congress of the Federation Internationale de la Precontrainte [*A publication*]
Proc Congr Hung Assoc Microbiol ... Proceedings. Congress of the Hungarian Association of Microbiologists [*A publication*]
Proc Congr Int Assoc Sci Study Ment Defic ... Proceedings. Congress of the International Association for the Scientific Study of Mental Deficiency [*A publication*]
Proc Congr Int Comm Opt ... Proceedings. Congress of the International Commission for Optics [*A publication*]
Proc Congr Int Potash Inst ... Proceedings. Congress of the International Potash Institute [*A publication*]

Proc Congr Int Soc Blood Transf ... Proceedings. Congress of the International Society of Blood Transfusion [*A publication*]
Proc Congr Int Soc Blood Transfus ... Proceedings. Congress of the International Society of Blood Transfusion [*A publication*]
Proc Congr Int Soc Sugar Cane Technol ... Proceedings. Congress of the International Society of Sugar Cane Technologists [*A publication*]
Proc Congr Int Union For Res Organ ... Proceedings. Congress of the International Union of Forest Research Organizations [*A publication*]
Proc Congr Jpn Soc Cancer Ther ... Proceedings. Congress of the Japan Society for Cancer Therapy [*A publication*]
Proc Congr S Afr Genet Soc ... Proceedings. Congress of the South African Genetic Society [*A publication*]
Proc Congr S Afr Sug Technol Ass ... Proceedings. Congress of the South African Sugar Technologists' Association [*A publication*]
Proc Conv Int Assoc Fish Wildl Agencies ... Proceedings. Convention. International Association of Fish and Wildlife Agencies [*A publication*]
Proc Cornell Nutr Conf Feed Mfr ... Proceedings. Cornell Nutrition Conference for Feed Manufacturers [*A publication*]
Proc Cosmic-Ray Res Lab Nagoya Univ ... Proceedings. Cosmic-Ray Research Laboratory. Nagoya University [*A publication*]
Proc Cotteswold Natur Fld Club ... Proceedings. Cotteswold Naturalists' Field Club [*A publication*]
Proc Counc Econ AIME ... Proceedings. Council of Economics. American Institute of Mining, Metallurgical, and Petroleum Engineers [*A publication*]
Proc Coventry Dist Natur Hist Sci Soc ... Proceedings. Coventry District Natural History and Scientific Society [*A publication*]
Proc Crayford Manor House Hist Archaeol Soc ... Proceedings. Crayford Manor House Historical and Archaeological Society [*A publication*]
Proc Crop Sci Chugoku Br Crop Sci Soc ... Proceedings. Crop Science. Chugoku Branch of the Crop Science Society [*A publication*]
Proc Crop Sci Soc Jap ... Proceedings. Crop Science Society of Japan [*A publication*]
Proc Crop Sci Soc Jpn ... Proceedings. Crop Science Society of Japan [*A publication*]
Proc Croydon Nat Hist Sci Soc ... Proceedings. Croydon Natural History Science Society [*A publication*]
ProcCTS .... Proceedings. College Theology Society [*A publication*]
ProcCTSA ... Proceedings. Catholic Theological Society of America [*A publication*]
Proc Cumberland Geol Soc ... Proceedings. Cumberland Geological Society [*A publication*]
PROCD ..... Procedure (AFM)
PROCD ..... Proceed (AFM)
PROCD ..... Processing [*Johannesburg*] [*A publication*]
Proc Dep Hortic Plant Health Massey Univ ... Proceedings. Department of Horticulture and Plant Health. Massey University [*A publication*]
Proc Devon Archaeol Soc ... Proceedings. Devon Archaeological Society [*A publication*]
Proc Devon Arch Soc ... Proceedings. Devon Archaeological Society [*A publication*]
Proc Distill Feed Conf ... Proceedings. Distillers Feed Conference [*A publication*]
Proc Distill Feed Res Counc Conf ... Proceedings. Distillers Feed Research Council Conference [*A publication*]
Proc Divers' Gas Purity Symp ... Proceedings. Divers' Gas Purity Symposium [*A publication*]
Proc Div Refin Am Pet Inst ... Proceedings. Division of Refining. American Petroleum Institute [*A publication*]
Proc Dorset Natur Hist Archaeol Soc ... Proceedings. Dorset Natural History and Archaeological Society [*A publication*]
Proc Dorset Natur Hist Arch Soc ... Proceedings. Dorset Natural History and Archaeological Society [*A publication*]
Proc Dorset Soc ... Dorset Natural History and Archaeological Society. Proceedings [*A publication*]
PROCDRE ... Procedure (ROG)
Proc East Afr Acad ... Proceedings. East African Academy [*A publication*]
Proc Easter Sch Agric Sci Univ Nottingham ... Proceedings. Easter School in Agricultural Science. University of Nottingham [*England*] [*A publication*]
Proc Ecol Soc Aust ... Proceedings. Ecological Society of Australia [*A publication*]
PROCED ... Procedure
Proc Edinburgh Math Soc ... Proceedings. Edinburgh Mathematical Society [*A publication*]
Proc Edinburgh Math Soc 2 ... Proceedings. Edinburgh Mathematical Society. Series 2 [*A publication*]
Proc Edinburgh Math Soc Edinburgh Math Notes ... Proceedings. Edinburgh Mathematical Society. Edinburgh Mathematical Notes [*A publication*]
Proceedings of the IEEE ... Proceedings. Institute of Electrical and Electronics Engineers [*A publication*]
Proceedings NAPEHE ... Proceedings. National Association for Physical Education in Higher Education [*A publication*]

Proceedings NIRSA ... Proceedings. National Intramural Recreational Sports Association [*A publication*]

Proceedngs ... Proceedings. United States Naval Institute [*A publication*]

Proc Egypt Acad Sci ... Proceedings. Egyptian Academy of Sciences [*A publication*]

Proc Eighth Br Weed Control Conf ... Proceedings. Eighth British Weed Control Conference [*A publication*]

Proc Electron Components Conf ... Proceedings. Electronic Components Conference [*A publication*]

Proc Electron Microsc Soc Am ... Proceedings. Electron Microscopy Society of America [*A publication*]

Proc Electron Microsc Soc South Afr ... Proceedings. Electron Microscopy Society of Southern Africa [*A publication*]

Proc Endoc Soc Aust ... Proceedings. Endocrine Society of Australia [*A publication*] (APTA)

Proc Eng Soc Hong Kong ... Proceedings. Engineering Society of Hong Kong [*A publication*]

Proc Eng Soc West PA ... Proceedings. Engineers' Society of Western Pennsylvania [*A publication*]

Proc Entomol Soc Amer N Cent Br ... Proceedings. Entomological Society of America. North Central Branch [*A publication*]

Proc Entomol Soc BC ... Proceedings. Entomological Society of British Columbia [*A publication*]

Proc Entomol Soc Brit Columbia ... Proceedings. Entomological Society of British Columbia [*A publication*]

Proc Entomol Soc Manit ... Proceedings. Entomological Society of Manitoba [*A publication*]

Proc Entomol Soc Manitoba ... Proceedings. Entomological Society of Manitoba [*A publication*]

Proc Entomol Soc Ont ... Proceedings. Entomological Society of Ontario [*A publication*]

Proc Entomol Soc Ontario ... Proceedings. Entomological Society of Ontario [*A publication*]

Proc Entomol Soc Wash ... Proceedings. Entomological Society of Washington [*A publication*]

Proc Entomol Soc Wash DC ... Proceedings. Entomological Society of Washington, DC [*A publication*]

Proc Ent Soc Br Columb ... Proceedings. Entomological Society of British Columbia [*A publication*]

Proc Ent Soc Manitoba ... Proceedings. Entomological Society of Manitoba [*A publication*]

Proc Ent Soc Ont ... Proceedings. Entomological Society of Ontario [*A publication*]

Proc Ent Soc Wash ... Proceedings. Entomological Society of Washington [*A publication*]

Proc Environ Eng Sci Conf ... Proceedings. Environmental Engineering and Science Conference [*A publication*]

Pro CERN Sch Comput ... Proceedings. CERN [*Conseil Europeen pour la Recherche Nucleaire*] School of Computing [*A publication*]

Process Archre ... Process Architecture [*A publication*]

Process Autom ... Process Automation [*A publication*]

Process Bio ... Process Biochemistry [*A publication*]

Process Biochem ... Process Biochemistry [*A publication*]

Process Chem Eng ... Process and Chemical Engineering [*A publication*]

Process Control Autom ... Process Control and Automation [*A publication*]

Process Des Dev ... Process Design and Development [*A publication*]

Process Econ Int ... Process Economics International [*A publication*]

Process Eng ... Process Engineering [*A publication*]

Process Eng Mag ... Process Engineering Magazine [*A publication*]

Process Engng ... Process Engineering [*A publication*]

Process Eng Plant and Control ... Process Engineering. Plant and Control [*A publication*]

Process Engravers Mon ... Process Engravers Monthly [*A publication*]

Process Instrum ... Process Instrumentation [*A publication*]

Process Metall ... Process Metallurgy [*A publication*]

Process Ser Okla State Univ Agr Exp Sta ... Processed Series. Oklahoma State University. Agricultural Experimental Station [*A publication*]

Process St .. Process Studies [*A publication*]

Process Stud ... Process Studies [*A publication*]

Process Technol Int ... Process Technology International [*A publication*]

Proces-Verb Seances Soc Sci Phys Nat Bordeaux ... Proces-Verbaux des Seances. Societe des Sciences Physiques et Naturelles de Bordeaux [*France*] [*A publication*]

Prcc Eur Conf Mixing ... Proceedings. European Conference on Mixing [*A publication*]

Proc Eur Dial Transplant Assoc ... Proceedings. European Dialysis and Transplant Association [*A publication*]

Proc Eur Dial Transplant Assoc Eur Renal Assoc ... Proceedings. European Dialysis and Transplant Association - European Renal Association [*A publication*]

Proc Eur Prosthodontic Assoc ... Proceedings. European Prosthodontic Association [*A publication*]

Proc Eur Soc Toxicol ... Proceedings. European Society of Toxicology [*A publication*]

Proc Fac Agric Kyushu Tokai Univ ... Proceedings. Faculty of Agriculture. Kyushu Tokai University [*A publication*]

Proc Fac Eng Keiogijuku Univ ... Proceedings. Faculty of Engineering. Keiogijuku University [*A publication*]

Proc Fac Eng Tokai Univ ... Proceedings. Faculty of Engineering. Tokai University [*Japan*] [*A publication*]

Proc Fac Sci Tokai Univ ... Proceedings. Faculty of Science. Tokai University [*Japan*] [*A publication*]

Proc Farm Seed Conf ... Proceedings. Farm Seed Conference [*A publication*]

Proc FEBS Meet ... Proceedings. FEBS [*Federation of European Biochemical Societies*] Meeting [*A publication*]

Proc Fertil Soc ... Proceedings. Fertilizer Society [*A publication*]

Proc Finn Dent Soc ... Proceedings. Finnish Dental Society of Washington [*A publication*]

Proc First Livest Ocean Conf ... Proceedings. First Livestock by Ocean Conference [*A publication*]

Proc Fla Acad Sci ... Proceedings. Florida Academy of Sciences [*A publication*]

Proc Fla Anti-Mosq ... Proceedings. Florida Anti-Mosquito Association [*A publication*]

Proc Fla Lychee Grow Ass ... Proceedings. Florida Lychee Growers Association [*A publication*]

Proc Fla State Hortic Soc ... Proceedings. Florida State Horticultural Society [*A publication*]

Proc Fla State Hort Soc ... Proceedings. Florida State Horticultural Society [*A publication*]

Proc Fla St Hort Soc ... Proceedings. Florida State Horticultural Society [*A publication*]

Proc Florida State Hortic Soc ... Florida. State Horticultural Society. Proceedings [*A publication*]

Proc Food ... Processed Prepared Food [*A publication*]

Proc For Microclim Symp Can Dep Fish For ... Proceedings. Forest Microclimate Symposium. Canada Department of Fisheries and Forestry [*A publication*]

Proc For Prod Res Soc ... Proceedings. Forest Products Research Society [*A publication*]

Proc For Symp LA Sch For ... Proceedings. Annual Forestry Symposium. Louisiana State University. School of Forestry and Wildlife Management [*A publication*]

Proc Forum Fundam Surg Probl Clin Congr Am Coll Surg ... Proceedings. Forum on Fundamental Surgical Problems. Clinical Congress of the American College of Surgeons [*A publication*]

Proc Found Orthod Res ... Proceedings. Foundation for Orthodontic Research [*A publication*]

Proc (Fourth) NZ Geogr Conf ... Proceedings. (Fourth) New Zealand Geographical Conference [*A publication*]

Proc FPLC Symp ... Proceedings. FPLC [*Fast Protein, Polypeptide, and Polynucleotide Liquid Chromatography*] Symposium [*A publication*]

Proc FRI Symp For Res Inst NZ For Serv ... Proceedings. FRI Symposium. Forest Research Institute. New Zealand Forest Service [*A publication*]

Proc Front Educ Conf ... Proceedings. Frontiers in Education Conference [*A publication*]

Proc Fujihara Mem Fac Eng Keio Univ ... Proceedings. Fujihara Memorial Faculty of Engineering. Keio University [*A publication*]

Proc Fujihara Mem Fac Eng Keio Univ (Tokyo) ... Proceedings. Fujihara Memorial Faculty of Engineering. Keio University (Tokyo) [*A publication*]

Proc Gas Cond Conf ... Proceedings. Gas Conditioning Conference [*United States*] [*A publication*]

Proc Genet Soc Can ... Proceedings. Genetics Society of Canada [*A publication*]

Proc Gen Meet Soc Ind Microbiol ... Proceedings. General Meeting of the Society for Industrial Microbiology [*A publication*]

Proc Geoinst ... Proceedings. Geoinstitut [*A publication*]

Proc Geol Ass ... Proceedings. Geological Association [*A publication*]

Proc Geol Ass Can ... Proceedings. Geological Association of Canada [*A publication*]

Proc Geol Assoc ... Proceedings. Geologists' Association [*A publication*]

Proc Geol Assoc London ... Proceedings. Geologists Association of London [*A publication*]

Proc Geol Soc China ... Proceedings. Geological Society of China [*Taipei*] [*A publication*]

Proc Geol Soc Lond ... Proceedings. Geological Society of London [*A publication*]

Proc Geol Soc S Afr ... Proceedings. Geological Society of South Africa [*A publication*]

Proc Geophys Soc Tulsa ... Proceedings. Geophysical Society of Tulsa [*A publication*]

Proc Geosci Inf Soc ... Proceedings. Geoscience Information Society [*A publication*]

Proc Ger Soc Neurosurg ... Proceedings. German Society of Neurosurgery [*A publication*]

Proc Ghana Acad Arts Sci ... Proceedings. Ghana Academy of Arts and Sciences [*A publication*]

Proc Grass Breeders Work Plann Conf ... Proceedings. Grass Breeders Work Planning Conference [*A publication*]

Proc Grassl Soc South Afr ... Proceedings. Grassland Society of Southern Africa [*A publication*]

Proc Great Plains Agr Conf ... Proceedings. Great Plains Agriculture Conference [*A publication*]

Proc Gulf Caribb Fish Inst ... Proceedings. Gulf and Caribbean Fisheries Institute [*A publication*]

Proc Hampshire Field Club ... Proceedings. Hampshire Field Club and Archaeological Society [*A publication*]

Proc Hampshire Fld Club Archaeol Soc ... Proceedings. Hampshire Field Club and Archaeological Society [*A publication*]
Proc Hamp Soc ... Proceedings. Hampshire Field Club and Archaeological Society [*A publication*]
Proc Hawaii Acad Sci ... Proceedings. Hawaiian Academy of Science [*A publication*]
Proc Hawaii Entomol Soc ... Proceedings. Hawaiian Entomological Society [*A publication*]
Proc Hawaii Ent Soc ... Proceedings. Hawaiian Entomological Society [*A publication*]
Proc Hawaii Int Conf Syst Sci ... Proceedings. Hawaii International Conference on System Science [*A publication*]
Proc Hawaii Top Conf Part Phys ... Proceedings. Hawaii Topical Conference in Particle Physics [*A publication*]
Proc Health Policy Forum ... Proceedings. Health Policy Forum [*A publication*]
Proc Heat Transfer Fluid Mech Inst ... Proceedings. Heat Transfer and Fluid Mechanics Institute [*A publication*]
Proc Helminthol Soc Wash ... Proceedings. Helminthological Society of Washington [*A publication*]
Proc Helminthol Soc (Wash DC) ... Proceedings. Helminthological Society (Washington, DC) [*A publication*]
Proc Helminth Soc Wash ... Proceedings. Helminthological Society of Washington [*A publication*]
Proc High Lysine Corn Conf ... Proceedings. High Lysine Corn Conference [*A publication*]
Prochn Deform Mater Neravnomernykh Fiz Polyakh ... Prochnost i Deformatsiya Materialov v Neravnomernykh Fizicheskikh Polyakh [*A publication*]
Prochnost Din Aviats Dvigatelei ... Prochnost i Dinamika Aviatsionnykh Dvigatelei [*USSR*] [*A publication*]
Proc Hokkaido Symp Plant Breed Crop Sci Soc ... Proceedings. Hokkaido Symposium of Plant Breeding and Crop Science Society [*A publication*]
Proc Hokuriku Br Crop Sci Soc (Jap) ... Proceedings. Hokuriku Branch of Crop Science Society (Japan) [*A publication*]
Proc Hoshi Coll Pharm ... Proceedings. Hoshi College of Pharmacy [*A publication*]
Proc Huguenot Soc Lond ... Proceedings. Huguenot Society of London [*A publication*]
Proc Hung Annu Meet Biochem ... Proceedings. Hungarian Annual Meeting for Biochemistry [*A publication*]
Proc Hydrol Symp ... Proceedings. Hydrology Symposium [*A publication*]
Proc I Cda ... Process Industries Canada [*A publication*]
Proc ICE .... Proceedings. Institution of Civil Engineers. Parts 1 and 2 [*A publication*]
Proc ICMR Semin ... Proceedings. ICMR [*International Center for Medical Research, Kobe University*] Seminar [*A publication*]
Proc IEE-A ... Institution of Electrical Engineers. Proceedings. A [*A publication*]
Proc IEE-B ... Institution of Electrical Engineers. Proceedings. B [*A publication*]
Proc IEE-C ... Institution of Electrical Engineers. Proceedings. C [*A publication*]
Proc IEE D ... Institution of Electrical Engineers. Proceedings. D [*A publication*]
Proc IEEE ... Proceedings. Institute of Electrical and Electronics Engineers [*A publication*]
Proc IEEE Conf Decis Control ... Proceedings. IEEE Conference on Decision and Control [*A publication*]
Proc IEEE Conf Decis Control Incl Symp Adapt Processes ... Proceedings. IEEE Conference on Decision and Control Including the Symposium on Adaptive Processes [*A publication*]
Proc IEEE Int Symp Circuits Syst ... Proceedings. IEEE International Symposium on Circuits and Systems [*A publication*]
Proc IEE F ... Institution of Electrical Engineers. Proceedings. F [*A publication*]
Proc IEE G ... Institution of Electrical Engineers. Proceedings. G [*A publication*]
Proc IEE H ... Proceedings. Institution of Electrical Engineers. H [*A publication*]
Proc IEE I ... Proceedings. Institution of Electrical Engineers. I [*A publication*]
Proc III Natn Peanut Res Conf ... Proceedings. Third National Peanut Research Conference [*A publication*]
Proc Ill Mining Inst ... Proceedings. Illinois Mining Institute [*A publication*]
Proc Imp Acad Japan ... Proceedings. Imperial Academy of Japan [*A publication*]
Proc Imp Acad (Tokyo) ... Proceedings. Imperial Academy (Tokyo) [*A publication*]
Proc Indiana Acad Sci ... Proceedings. Indiana Academy of Science [*A publication*]
Proc Indian Acad Sci ... Proceedings. Indian Academy of Sciences [*A publication*]
Proc Indian Acad Sci A ... Proceedings. Indian Academy of Sciences. Section A [*A publication*]
Proc Indian Acad Sci Anim Sci ... Proceedings. Indian Academy of Sciences. Animal Sciences [*A publication*]
Proc Indian Acad Sci B ... Proceedings. Indian Academy of Sciences. Section B [*A publication*]

Proc Indian Acad Sci Chem Sci ... Proceedings. Indian Academy of Sciences. Chemical Sciences [*A publication*]
Proc Indian Acad Sci Earth Planetary Sci ... Proceedings. Indian Academy of Sciences. Earth and Planetary Sciences [*A publication*]
Proc Indian Acad Sci Earth Planet Sci ... Proceedings. Indian Academy of Sciences. Earth and Planetary Sciences [*A publication*]
Proc Indian Acad Sci Earth and Planet Sci ... Proceedings. Indian Academy of Sciences. Earth and Planetary Sciences [*A publication*]
Proc Indian Acad Sci Eng Sci ... Proceedings. Indian Academy of Sciences. Engineering Sciences [*A publication*]
Proc Indian Acad Sci Math Sci ... Proceedings. Indian Academy of Sciences. Mathematical Sciences [*A publication*]
Proc Indian Acad Sci Plant Sci ... Proceedings. Indian Academy of Sciences. Plant Sciences [*A publication*]
Proc Indian Acad Sci Sect A ... Proceedings. Indian Academy of Sciences. Section A [*A publication*]
Proc Indian Acad Sci Sect A Chem Sci ... Proceedings. Indian Academy of Sciences. Section A. Chemical Sciences [*A publication*]
Proc Indian Acad Sci Sect A Earth Planetary Sci ... Indian Academy of Sciences. Proceedings. Section A. Earth and Planetary Sciences [*A publication*]
Proc Indian Acad Sci Sect A Math Sci ... Proceedings. Indian Academy of Sciences. Section A. Mathematical Sciences [*A publication*]
Proc Indian Acad Sci Sect B ... Proceedings. Indian Academy of Sciences. Section B [*A publication*]
Proc Indian Acad Sci Sect C ... Proceedings. Indian Academy of Sciences. Section C. Engineering Sciences [*India*] [*A publication*]
Proc Indian Assoc Cultiv Sci ... Proceedings. Indian Association for Cultivation of Sciences [*A publication*]
Proc Indian Natl Sci Acad A ... Proceedings. Indian National Science Academy. Part A. Physical Sciences [*A publication*]
Proc Indian Natl Sci Acad Part A ... Proceedings. Indian National Science Academy. Part A [*A publication*]
Proc Indian Natl Sci Acad Part A Phys Sci ... Proceedings. Indian National Science Academy. Part A. Physical Sciences [*A publication*]
Proc Indian Natl Sci Acad Part B ... Proceedings. Indian National Science Academy. Part B. Biological Sciences [*A publication*]
Proc Indian Natl Sci Acad Part B Biol Sci ... Proceedings. Indian National Science Academy. Part B. Biological Sciences [*A publication*]
Proc Indian Nat Sci Acad Part A ... Proceedings. Indian National Science Academy. Part A. Physical Sciences [*A publication*]
Proc Indian Roads Congr ... Proceedings. Indian Roads Congress [*A publication*]
Proc Indian Sci Congr ... Proceedings. Indian Science Congress [*A publication*]
Proc Ind Waste Conf ... Proceedings. Industrial Waste Conference [*A publication*]
Proc Ind Waste Conf Purdue Univ ... Proceedings. Industrial Waste Conference. Purdue University [*A publication*]
Proc Ind Waste Util Conf ... Proceedings. Industrial Waste Utilization Conference [*A publication*]
Proc Inst Automob Eng (London) ... Proceedings. Institution of Automobile Engineers (London) [*A publication*]
Proc Inst Br Foundrymen ... Proceedings. Institute of British Foundrymen [*A publication*]
Proc Inst Chem (Calcutta) ... Proceedings. Institution of Chemists (Calcutta) [*A publication*]
Proc Inst Civ Eng ... Proceedings. Institution of Civil Engineers [*London*] [*A publication*]
Proc Inst Civ Eng (London) Suppl ... Proceedings. Institution of Civil Engineers (London). Supplement [*A publication*]
Proc Inst Civ Eng Part 1 ... Proceedings. Institution of Civil Engineers. Part 1. Design and Construction [*A publication*]
Proc Inst Civ Eng Part 2 ... Proceedings. Institution of Civil Engineers. Part 2. Research and Theory [*United Kingdom*] [*A publication*]
Proc Inst Criminol Univ Sydney ... University of Sydney. Institute of Criminology. Proceedings [*A publication*]
Proc Inst Elec Eng (London) ... Proceedings. Institution of Electrical Engineers (London) [*A publication*]
Proc Inst Elec Eng Pt B Elec Power Appl ... Proceedings. Institution of Electrical Engineers. Part B. Electric Power Applications [*A publication*]
Proc Inst Elec Eng Pt C Generation Transmission Distribution ... Proceedings. Institution of Electrical Engineers. Part C. Generation-Transmission-Distribution [*A publication*]
Proc Inst Elec Eng Pt E Computers Digital Tech ... Proceedings. Institution of Electrical Engineers. Part E. Computers and Digital Techniques [*A publication*]
Proc Inst Elec Eng Pt F Commun Radar Signal Process ... Proceedings. Institution of Electrical Engineers. Part F. Communications, Radar, and Signal Processing [*A publication*]
Proc Inst Elec Eng Pt G Electron Circuits Syst ... Proceedings. Institution of Electrical Engineers. Part G. Electronics Circuits and Systems [*A publication*]
Proc Inst Elec Eng Pt H Microwaves Opt Antennas ... Proceedings. Institution of Electrical Engineers. Part H. Microwaves, Optics, and Antennas [*A publication*]
Proc Inst Elec Engrs ... Proceedings. Institution of Electrical Engineers [*A publication*]

Proc Inst Elect ... Proceedings. Institution of Electrical Engineers [*A publication*]
Proc Inst Electr Eng ... Proceedings. Institution of Electrical Engineers [*A publication*]
Proc Inst Electr Eng (London) ... Proceedings. Institution of Electrical Engineers (London) [*A publication*]
Proc Inst Electr Eng Part 1 ... Proceedings. Institution of Electrical Engineers. Part 1. General [*A publication*]
Proc Inst Electr Eng Part 2 ... Proceedings. Institution of Electrical Engineers. Part 2. Power Engineering [*A publication*]
Proc Inst Electr Eng Part 3 ... Proceedings. Institution of Electrical Engineers. Part 3. Radio and Communication Engineering [*A publication*]
Proc Inst Electr Eng Part 4 ... Proceedings. Institution of Electrical Engineers. Part 4. Monographs [*A publication*]
Proc Inst Electr Eng Part A ... Proceedings. Institution of Electrical Engineers. Part A. Power Engineering [*A publication*]
Proc Inst Electr Eng Part A Suppl ... Proceedings. Institution of Electrical Engineers. Part A. Supplement [*A publication*]
Proc Inst Electr Eng Part B ... Proceedings. Institution of Electrical Engineers. Part B. Electronic and Communication Engineering Including Radio Engineering [*A publication*]
Proc Inst Electr Eng Part B Suppl ... Proceedings. Institution of Electrical Engineers. Part B. Supplement [*A publication*]
Proc Inst Electr Eng Part C ... Proceedings. Institution of Electrical Engineers. Part C. Monographs [*A publication*]
Proc Inst Environ Sci ... Proceedings. Institute of Environmental Sciences [*A publication*]
Proc Inst Fd Sci Technol ... Proceedings. Institute of Food Science and Technology [*A publication*]
Proc Inst Food Sci Technol UK ... Proceedings. Institute of Food Science and Technology of the United Kingdom [*A publication*]
Proc Institute Med Chicago ... Proceedings. Institute of Medicine of Chicago [*A publication*]
Proc Inst Mech Eng ... Proceedings. Institution of Mechanical Engineers [*A publication*]
Proc Inst Mech Eng (London) ... Proceedings. Institution of Mechanical Engineers (London) [*A publication*]
Proc Inst Mech Eng Part A ... Proceedings. Institution of Mechanical Engineers. Part A. Power and Process Engineering [*A publication*]
Proc Inst Mech Eng Part B ... Proceedings. Institution of Mechanical Engineers. Part B. Management and Engineering Manufacture [*A publication*]
Proc Inst Mech Eng Part C ... Proceedings. Institution of Mechanical Engineers. Part C. Mechanical Engineering Science [*A publication*]
Proc Inst Mech Engrs ... Proceedings. Institution of Mechanical Engineers [*A publication*]
Proc Inst Med Chic ... Proceedings. Institute of Medicine of Chicago [*A publication*]
Proc Inst Med Chicago ... Proceedings. Institute of Medicine of Chicago [*A publication*]
Proc Inst Nat Sci Nihon Univ ... Proceedings. Institute of Natural Sciences. Nihon University [*A publication*]
Proc Instn CE ... Proceedings. Institution of Civil Engineers [*A publication*]
Proc Instn Civ Engrs ... Proceedings. Institution of Civil Engineers [*A publication*]
Proc Instn Civ Engrs 1 2 ... Proceedings. Institution of Civil Engineers. Parts 1 and 2 [*A publication*]
Proc Instn Elect Engrs ... Proceedings. Institution of Electrical Engineers [*A publication*]
Proc Instn Mech Engrs ... Proceedings. Institution of Mechanical Engineers [*A publication*]
Proc Instn Mech Engrs Pt B Mgmt Engng Mf ... Proceedings. Institution of Mechanical Engineers. Part B. Management and Engineering Manufacture [*A publication*]
Proc Instn Mech Engrs Pt C Mech Engng Sci ... Proceedings. Institution of Mechanical Engineers. Part C. Mechanical Engineering Science [*A publication*]
Proc Instn Mech Engrs Pt D Transp Engng ... Proceedings. Institution of Mechanical Engineers. Part D. Transport Engineering [*A publication*]
Proc Instn Radio Electron Engrs Aust ... Proceedings. Institution of Radio and Electronics Engineers of Australia [*A publication*] (APTA)
Proc Instn Radio Engrs Aust ... Proceedings. Institution of Radio Engineers of Australia [*A publication*] (APTA)
Proc Inst Oceanogr Fish Bulg Acad Sci ... Proceedings. Institute of Oceanography and Fisheries. Bulgarian Academy of Sciences [*A publication*]
Proc Inst Pomol (Skierniewice Pol) Ser E Conf Symp ... Proceedings. Research Institute of Pomology (Skierniewice, Poland). Series E. Conferences and Symposia [*A publication*]
Proc Inst Radio Electron Eng Aust ... Proceedings. Institution of Radio and Electronics Engineers of Australia [*A publication*] (APTA)
Proc Inst Railw Signal Eng ... Proceedings. Institution of Railway Signal Engineers [*A publication*]
Proc Inst Refrig ... Proceedings. Institute of Refrigeration [*A publication*]
Proc Inst Rubber Ind ... Proceedings. Institution of the Rubber Industry [*A publication*]

Proc Instrum Soc Am ... Proceedings. Instrument Society of America [*A publication*]
Proc Inst Sewage Purif ... Proceedings. Institute of Sewage Purification [*A publication*]
Proc Inst Statist Math ... Proceedings. Institute of Statistical Mathematics [*A publication*]
Proc Inst Teknol Bandung ... Proceedings. Institut Teknologi Bandung [*Indonesia*] [*A publication*]
Proc Inst Teknol Bandung Suppl ... Proceedings. Institut Teknologi Bandung. Supplement [*Indonesia*] [*A publication*]
Proc Inst Vitreous Enamellers ... Proceedings. Institute of Vitreous Enamellers [*A publication*]
Proc Int Acad Oral Pathol ... Proceedings. International Academy of Oral Pathology [*A publication*]
Proc Int Assoc Milk Dealers ... Proceedings. International Association of Milk Dealers [*A publication*]
Proc Int Assoc Test Mater ... Proceedings. International Association for Testing Materials [*A publication*]
Proc Int Assoc Theor Appl Limnol ... Proceedings. International Association of Theoretical and Applied Limnology [*A publication*]
Proc Int Assoc Vet Food Hyg ... Proceedings. International Association of Veterinary Food Hygienists [*A publication*]
Proc Int Astronaut Congr ... Proceedings. International Astronautical Congress [*A publication*]
Proc Int Barley Genet Symp ... Proceedings. International Barley Genetics Symposium [*A publication*]
Proc Int Bedding Plant Conf ... Proceedings. International Bedding Plant Conference [*A publication*]
Proc Int Bot Congr ... Proceedings. International Botanical Congress [*A publication*]
Proc Int Clean Air Congr ... Proceedings. International Clean Air Congress [*A publication*]
Proc Int Colloq Invertebr Pathol ... Proceedings. International Colloquium on Invertebrate Pathology [*A publication*]
Proc Int Colloq Plant Anal Fert Probl ... Proceedings. International Colloquium on Plant Analysis and Fertilizer Problems [*A publication*]
Proc Int Comm Glass ... Proceedings. International Commission on Glass [*A publication*]
Proc Int Conf Biochem Probl Lipids ... Proceedings. International Conference on Biochemical Problems of Lipids [*A publication*]
Proc Int Conf Cent High Energy Form ... Proceedings. International Conference. Center for High Energy Forming [*A publication*]
Proc Int Conf Cybern Soc ... Proceedings. International Conference on Cybernetics and Society [*A publication*]
Proc Int Conf Fire Saf ... Proceedings. International Conference on Fire Safety [*A publication*]
Proc Int Conf Fluid Sealing ... Proceedings. International Conference on Fluid Sealing [*A publication*]
Proc Int Conf High Energy Phys ... Proceedings. International Conference on High Energy Physics [*A publication*]
Proc Int Conf High Energy Rate Fabr ... Proceedings. International Conference on High Energy Rate Fabrication [*A publication*]
Proc Int Conf Int Assoc Water Pollut Res ... Proceedings. International Conference of the International Association on Water Pollution Research [*A publication*]
Proc Int Conf Lasers ... Proceedings. International Conference on Lasers [*A publication*]
Proc Int Conf New Front Hazard Waste Manage ... Proceedings. International Conference on New Frontiers for Hazardous Waste Management [*A publication*]
Proc Int Conf Noise Control Eng ... Proceedings. International Conference on Noise Control Engineering [*A publication*]
Proc Int Conf Org Coat Sci Technol Technomic Publ ... Proceedings. International Conference in Organic Coatings Science and Technology. Technomic Publication [*A publication*]
Proc Int Conf Peaceful Uses Atomic Energy ... Proceedings. International Conference on the Peaceful Uses of Atomic Energy [*A publication*]
Proc Int Conf Pervaporation Processes Chem Ind ... Proceedings. International Conference on Pervaporation Processes in the Chemical Industry [*A publication*]
Proc Int Conf Plant Growth Regulat ... Proceedings. International Conference on Plant Growth Regulation [*A publication*]
Proc Int Conf Plant Pathog Bact ... Proceedings. International Conference on Plant Pathogenic Bacteria [*A publication*]
Proc Int Conf Sci Aspects Mushroom Grow ... Proceedings. International Conference on Scientific Aspects of Mushroom Growing [*A publication*]
Proc Int Conf Wildl Dis ... Proceedings. International Conference on Wildlife Disease [*A publication*]
Proc Int Cong Phot ... Proceedings. International Congress of Photography [*A publication*]
Proc Int Congr Anim Reprod Artif Insemin ... Proceedings. International Congress on Animal Reproduction and Artificial Insemination [*A publication*]
Proc Int Congr Biochem ... Proceedings. International Congress of Biochemistry [*A publication*]

Proc Int Congr Crop Prot ... Proceedings. International Congress on Crop Protection [*A publication*]

Proc Int Congr Ent ... Proceedings. International Congress of Entomology [*A publication*]

Proc Int Congr Entomol ... Proceedings. International Congress of Entomology [*A publication*]

Proc Int Congr Food Sci Technol ... Proceedings. International Congress of Food Science and Technology [*A publication*]

Proc Int Congr Genet ... Proceedings. International Congress of Genetics [*A publication*]

Proc Int Congr Geront ... Proceedings. International Congress on Gerontology [*A publication*]

Proc Int Congr Gerontol ... Proceedings. International Congress on Gerontology [*A publication*]

Proc Int Congr Hist Sci ... Proceedings. International Congress of the History of Science [*A publication*]

Proc Int Congr Hum Genet ... Proceedings. International Congress of Human Genetics [*A publication*]

Proc Int Congr Ment Retard ... Proceedings. International Congress on Mental Retardation [*A publication*]

Proc Int Congr Microbiol Stand ... Proceedings. International Congress for Microbiological Standardization [*A publication*]

Proc Int Congr Mushroom Sci ... Proceedings. International Congress on Mushroom Science [*A publication*]

Proc Int Congr Nephrol ... Proceedings. International Congress of Nephrology [*A publication*]

Proc Int Congr Nutr (Hamburg) ... Proceedings. International Congress of Nutrition (Hamburg) [*A publication*]

Proc Int Congr Pharmacol ... Proceedings. International Congress on Pharmacology [*A publication*]

Proc Int Congr Photosynth Res ... Proceedings. International Congress on Photosynthesis Research [*A publication*]

Proc Int Congr Primatol ... Proceedings. International Congress of Primatology [*A publication*]

Proc Int Congr Protozool ... Proceedings. International Congress on Protozoology [*A publication*]

Proc Int Congr Psychother ... Proceedings. International Congress of Psychotherapy [*A publication*]

Proc Int Congr Pure Appl Chem ... Proceedings. International Congress of Pure and Applied Chemistry [*A publication*]

Proc Int Congr Radiat Prot ... Proceedings. International Congress of Radiation Protection [*A publication*]

Proc Int Congr Refrig ... Proceedings. International Congress of Refrigeration [*A publication*]

Proc Int Congr Stereol ... Proceedings. International Congress for Stereology [*A publication*]

Proc Int Congr Virol ... Proceedings. International Congress for Virology [*A publication*]

Proc Int Congr Zool ... Proceedings. International Congress of Zoology [*A publication*]

Proc Int Dist Heat Assoc ... Proceedings. International District Heating Association [*A publication*]

Proc Internat School of Phys Enrico Fermi ... Proceedings. International School of Physics "Enrico Fermi" [*A publication*]

Proc Intersoc Energy Conver Eng Conf ... Proceedings. Intersociety Energy Conversion Engineering Conference [*A publication*]

Proc Intersoc Energy Convers Eng Conf ... Proceedings. Intersociety Energy Conversion Engineering Conference [*A publication*]

Proc Interuniv Fac Work Conf ... Proceedings. Interuniversity Faculty Work Conference [*A publication*]

Proc Int Grassland Congr ... Proceedings. International Grassland Congress [*A publication*]

Proc Int Gstaad Symp ... Proceedings. International Gstaad Symposium [*A publication*]

Proc Int Hort Congr ... Proceedings. International Horticultural Congress [*A publication*]

Proc Int Hortic Congr ... Proceedings. International Horticultural Congress [*A publication*]

Proc Int ISA Biomed Sci Instrum Symp ... Proceedings. International ISA [*Instrument Society of America*] Biomedical Sciences Instrumentation Symposium [*A publication*]

Proc Int Meet Biol Stand ... Proceedings. International Meeting of Biological Standardization [*A publication*]

Proc Int Microelectron Symp ... Proceedings. International Microelectronics Symposium [*A publication*]

Proc Int Ornithol Congr ... Proceedings. International Ornithological Congress [*A publication*]

Proc Int Pharmacol Meet ... Proceedings. International Pharmacological Meeting [*A publication*]

Proc Int Pl Propag Soc ... Proceedings. International Plant Propagators' Society [*A publication*]

Proc Int Sch Phys Enrico Fermi ... Proceedings. International School of Physics "Enrico Fermi" [*A publication*]

Proc Int Sci Congr Cultiv Edible Fungi ... Proceedings. International Scientific Congress on the Cultivation of Edible Fungi [*A publication*]

Proc Int Seaweed Symp ... Proceedings. International Seaweed Symposium [*A publication*]

Proc Int Seed Test Ass ... Proceedings. International Seed Testing Association [*A publication*]

Proc Int Seed Test Assoc ... Proceedings. International Seed Testing Association [*A publication*]

Proc Int Shade Tree Conf ... Proceedings. Annual Meetings. International Shade Tree Conference [*A publication*]

Proc Int Soc Citric ... Proceedings. International Society of Citriculture [*A publication*]

Proc Int Soc Soil Sci ... Proceedings. International Society of Soil Science [*A publication*]

Proc Int Soc Sugar Cane Technol ... Proceedings. International Society of Sugar Cane Technologists [*A publication*]

Proc Int Symp Enzyme Chem ... Proceedings. International Symposium on Enzyme Chemistry [*A publication*]

Proc Int Symp Food Irradiation ... Proceedings. International Symposium on Food Irradiation [*A publication*]

Proc Int Symp Fresh Water Sea ... Proceedings. International Symposium on Fresh Water from the Sea [*A publication*]

Proc Int Symp Inst Biomed Res Am Med Assoc Educ Res Found ... Proceedings. International Symposium of the Institute for Biomedical Research. American Medical Association Education and Research Foundation [*A publication*]

Proc Int Symp Med Mycol ... Proceedings. International Symposium on Medical Mycology [*A publication*]

Proc Int Symp Mult Valued Logic ... Proceedings. International Symposium on Multiple-Valued Logic [*A publication*]

Proc Int Symp Poll ... Proceedings. International Symposium on Pollination [*A publication*]

Proc Int Symp Princess Takamatsu Cancer Res Fund ... Proceedings. International Symposium of the Princess Takamatsu Cancer Research Fund [*A publication*]

Proc Int Symp Remote Sens Environ ... Proceedings. International Symposium on Remote Sensing of Environment [*A publication*]

Proc Int Symp Remote Sensing Environ ... Proceedings. International Symposium on Remote Sensing of Environment [*A publication*]

Proc Int Tech Conf APICS ... Proceedings. International Technical Conference. American Production and Inventory Control Society [*A publication*]

Proc Int Union Biol Sci Ser B ... Proceedings. International Union of Biological Sciences. Series B [*A publication*]

Proc Int Union Forest Res Organ ... Proceedings. International Union of Forest Research Organizations [*A publication*]

Proc Int Vet Congr ... Proceedings. International Veterinary Congress [*A publication*]

Proc Int Water Qual Symp ... Proceedings. International Water Quality Symposium [*A publication*]

Proc Int Wheat Genet Symp ... Proceedings. International Wheat Genetics Symposium [*A publication*]

Proc Int Wheat Surplus Util Conf ... Proceedings. International Wheat Surplus Utilization Conference [*A publication*]

Proc Int Wire Cable Symp ... Proceedings. International Wire and Cable Symposium [*A publication*]

Proc Int Workshop Nude Mice ... Proceedings. International Workshop on Nude Mice [*A publication*]

Proc Iowa Acad Sci ... Proceedings. Iowa Academy of Science [*A publication*]

Proc IPI Congr ... Proceedings. IPI [*International Potash Institute*] Congress [*A publication*]

Proc Iraqi Sci Soc ... Proceedings. Iraqi Scientific Societies [*A publication*]

Proc IRE .... Proceedings. IRE [*Institute of Radio Engineers*] [*United States*] [*A publication*]

Proc Irish Ac Section C ... Proceedings. Royal Irish Academy. Section C. Archaeology, Celtic Studies, History, Linguistics, Literature [*A publication*]

Proc ISA .... Proceedings. Instrument Society of America [*A publication*]

Proc Isle Man Natur Hist Antiq Soc ... Proceedings. Isle of Man Natural History and Antiquarian Society [*A publication*]

Proc Isle Wight Natur Hist Archaeol Soc ... Proceedings. Isle of Wight Natural History and Archaeological Society [*A publication*]

Proc Jap Acad ... Proceedings. Japan Academy [*A publication*]

Proc Japan Acad ... Proceedings. Japan Academy [*A publication*]

Proc Japan Acad Ser A Math Sci ... Proceedings. Japan Academy. Series A. Mathematical Sciences [*A publication*]

Proc Japan Acad Ser B Phys Biol Sci ... Proceedings. Japan Academy. Series B. Physical and Biological Sciences [*A publication*]

Proc Jap Soc Civ Eng ... Proceedings. Japan Society of Civil Engineers [*A publication*]

ProcJPES .. Proceedings. Jewish Palestine Exploration Society [*A publication*]

Proc Jpn Acad ... Proceedings. Japan Academy [*A publication*]

Proc Jpn Acad Ser A ... Proceedings. Japan Academy. Series A. Mathematical Sciences [*A publication*]

Proc Jpn Acad Ser B ... Proceedings. Japan Academy. Series B. Physical and Biological Sciences [*A publication*]

Proc Jpn Acad Ser B Phys Biol Sci ... Proceedings. Japan Academy. Series B. Physical and Biological Sciences [*A publication*]

Proc Jpn At Ind Forum Inc ... Proceedings. Japan Atomic Industrial Forum, Incorporated [*A publication*]

Proc Jpn Cem Eng Assoc ... Proceedings. Japan Cement Engineering Association [*A publication*]

Proc Jpn Conf Radioisot ... Proceedings. Japan Conference on Radioisotopes [*A publication*]

Proc Jpn Congr Mater Res ... Proceedings. Japan Congress on Materials Research [*A publication*]

Proc Jpn Congr Test Mater ... Proceedings. Japanese Congress for Testing Materials [*A publication*]

Proc Jpn Pharmacol Soc ... Proceedings. Japanese Pharmacology Society [*A publication*]

Proc Jpn Soc Civ Eng ... Proceedings. Japan Society of Civil Engineers [*A publication*]

Proc Jpn Soc Clin Biochem Metab ... Proceedings. Japan Society of Clinical Biochemistry and Metabolism [*A publication*]

Proc Jpn Soc Med Mass Spectrom ... Proceedings. Japanese Society for Medical Mass Spectrometry [*A publication*]

Proc Jpn Soc Reticuloendothel Syst ... Proceedings. Japan Society of the Reticuloendothelial System [*A publication*]

Proc J US Conf Compos Mater ... Proceedings. Japan-US Conference on Composite Materials [*A publication*]

Proc Kansai Plant Prot Soc ... Proceedings. Kansai Plant Protection Society [*A publication*]

Proc Kanto-Tosan Plant Prot Soc ... Proceedings. Kanto-Tosan Plant Protection Society [*A publication*]

Proc Kimbrough Urol Semin ... Proceedings. Kimbrough Urological Seminar [*A publication*]

Proc Kinki Symp Crop Sci Plant Breed Soc ... Proceedings. Kinki Symposium of Crop Science and Plant Breeding Society [*A publication*]

Proc K Ned Akad Wet ... Proceedings. Koninklijke Nederlandse Akademie van Wetenschappen [*A publication*]

Proc K Ned Akad Wet B ... Proceedings. Koninklijke Nederlandse Akademie van Wetenschappen. Series B. Physical Sciences [*A publication*]

Proc K Ned Akad Wet Ser A ... Proceedings. Koninklijke Nederlandse Akademie van Wetenschappen. Series A. Mathematical Sciences [*A publication*]

Proc K Ned Akad Wet Ser B ... Proceedings. Koninklijke Nederlandse Akademie van Wetenschappen. Series B. Physical Sciences [*A publication*]

Proc K Ned Akad Wet Ser B Palaeontol Geol Phys Chem ... Proceedings. Koninklijke Nederlandse Akademie van Wetenschappen. Series B. Palaeontology, Geology, Physics, and Chemistry [*Later, Proceedings. Koninklijke Nederlandse Akademie van Wetenschappen. Series B. Palaeontology, Geology, Physics, Chemistry, Anthropology*] [*A publication*]

Proc K Ned Akad Wet Ser B Phys Sci ... Proceedings. Koninklijke Nederlandse Akademie van Wetenschappen. Series B. Physical Sciences [*A publication*]

Proc K Ned Akad Wet Ser C ... Proceedings. Koninklijke Nederlandse Akademie van Wetenschappen. Series C. Biological and Medical Sciences [*A publication*]

Proc K Ned Akad Wet Ser C Biol Med Sci ... Proceedings. Koninklijke Nederlandse Akademie van Wetenschappen. Series C. Biological and Medical Sciences [*A publication*]

Proc LA Acad Sci ... Proceedings. Louisiana Academy of Sciences [*A publication*]

Proc LA Ass Agron ... Proceedings. Louisiana Association of Agronomists [*A publication*]

Proc Leatherhead Dist Local Hist Soc ... Proceedings. Leatherhead and District Local History Society [*A publication*]

Proc Lebedev Phys Inst ... Proceedings (Trudy). P. N. Lebedev Physics Institute [*A publication*]

Proc Leeds Phil Lit Soc Sci Sect ... Proceedings. Leeds Philosophical and Literary Society. Scientific Section [*A publication*]

Proc Leeds Philos & Lit Soc ... Proceedings. Leeds Philosophical and Literary Society [*A publication*]

Proc Leeds Philos Lit Soc Lit Hist Sect ... Proceedings. Leeds Philosophical and Literary Society. Literary and Historical Section [*A publication*]

Proc Leeds Philos Lit Soc Sci Sect ... Proceedings. Leeds Philosophical and Literary Society. Scientific Section [*A publication*]

Proc Leucocyte Cult Conf ... Proceedings. Leucocyte Culture Conference [*A publication*]

PROCLIB ... Procedure Library [*Data processing*]

Proc Lincoln Coll Farmers Conf ... Proceedings. Lincoln College. Farmer's Conference [*A publication*]

Proc Linnean Soc NSW ... Proceedings. Linnean Society of New South Wales [*A publication*]

Proc Linn Soc Lond ... Proceedings. Linnean Society of London [*A publication*]

Proc Linn Soc London ... Proceedings. Linnean Society of London [*A publication*]

Proc Linn Soc NSW ... Proceedings. Linnean Society of New South Wales [*A publication*] (APTA)

Proc Linn Soc NY ... Proceedings. Linnean Society of New York [*A publication*]

Proc Liverpool Geol Soc ... Proceedings. Liverpool Geological Society [*A publication*]

Proc London Math Soc ... Proceedings. London Mathematical Society [*A publication*]

Proc London Math Soc 3 ... Proceedings. London Mathematical Society. Third Series [*A publication*]

Proc Lunar Sci Conf ... Proceedings. Lunar Science Conference [*United States*] [*A publication*]

Proc Malacol Soc Lond ... Proceedings. Malacological Society of London [*A publication*]

Proc Mark Milk Conf ... Proceedings. Market Milk Conference [*A publication*]

Proc Mar Safety Council USCG ... Proceedings. Marine Safety Council. United States Coast Guard [*A publication*]

Proc Mass Hist Soc ... Proceedings. Massachusetts Historical Society [*A publication*]

Proc Math Phys Soc (Egypt) ... Proceedings. Mathematical and Physical Society (Egypt) [*A publication*]

Proc Mayo Clin ... Proceedings. Staff Meetings of the Mayo Clinic [*A publication*]

Proc Mayo Clin Staff Meet ... Proceedings. Mayo Clinic Staff Meeting [*A publication*]

Proc MD Del Water Pollut Control Assoc ... Proceedings. Maryland-Delaware Water and Pollution Control Association [*A publication*]

Proc MD Nutr Conf Feed Manuf ... Proceedings. Maryland Nutrition Conference for Feed Manufacturers [*A publication*]

Proc Meat Ind Res Conf ... Proceedings. Meat Industry Research Conference [*A publication*]

Proc Medico-Legal Soc Vict ... Proceedings. Medico-Legal Society of Victoria [*A publication*] (APTA)

Proc Med-Leg Soc Vic ... Medico-Legal Society of Victoria. Proceedings [*A publication*]

Proc Meet Anim Husb Wing Board Agric Anim Husb India ... Proceedings. Meeting of the Animal Husbandry Wing. Board of Agriculture and Animal Husbandry in India [*A publication*]

Proc Meet Jpn Soc Med Mass Spectrom ... Proceedings. Meeting of the Japanese Society for Medical Mass Spectrometry [*A publication*]

Proc Meet West Indies Sugar Technol ... Proceedings. Meeting of West Indies Sugar Technologists [*A publication*]

Proc Microbiol Res Group Hung Acad Sci ... Proceedings. Microbiological Research Group. Hungarian Academy of Science [*A publication*]

Proc Microsc Soc Can ... Proceedings. Microscopical Society of Canada [*A publication*]

Proc Mid-Atl Ind Waste Conf ... Proceedings. Mid-Atlantic Industrial Waste Conference [*United States*] [*A publication*]

Proc Midwest Fert Conf ... Proceedings. Midwestern Fertilizer Conference [*A publication*]

Proc Mid Year Meet Am Pet Inst ... Proceedings. Mid-Year Meeting. American Petroleum Institute [*A publication*]

Proc Mine Med Off Assoc ... Proceedings. Mine Medical Officers Association [*A publication*]

Proc Mine Med Off Assoc SA ... Proceedings. Mine Medical Officers Association of South Africa [*A publication*]

Proc Minn Acad Sci ... Proceedings. Minnesota Academy of Sciences [*A publication*]

Proc Minutes Ann Meet Agric Res Inst ... Proceedings and Minutes. Annual Meeting of the Agricultural Research Institute [*A publication*]

Proc Mont Acad Sci ... Proceedings. Montana Academy of Sciences [*A publication*]

Proc Mont Nutr Conf ... Proceedings. Montana Nutrition Conference [*A publication*]

Proc Montpellier Symp ... Proceedings. Montpellier Symposium [*A publication*]

Proc Mtg Comm For Tree Breeding Can ... Proceedings. Meeting of the Committee on Forest Tree Breeding in Canada [*A publication*]

Proc Mtg Sect Int Union For Res Organ ... Proceedings. Meeting of Section. International Union of Forest Research Organizations [*A publication*]

Proc Nagano Pref Agr Exp Sta ... Proceedings. Nagano Prefectural Agricultural Experiment Station [*A publication*]

Proc NA Sci ... Proceedings. National Academy of Sciences [*A publication*]

Proc NASSH ... Proceedings. North American Society for Sport History [*A publication*]

Proc Nat Acad Sc ... Proceedings. National Academy of Science [*A publication*]

Proc Nat Acad Sci ... Proceedings. National Academy of Sciences [*United States of America*] [*A publication*]

Proc Nat Acad Sci (India) Sect A ... Proceedings. National Academy of Sciences (India). Section A [*A publication*]

Proc Nat Acad Sci (India) Sect B ... Proceedings. National Academy of Sciences (India). Section B. Biological Sciences [*A publication*]

Proc Nat Acad Sci (USA) ... Proceedings. National Academy of Sciences (United States of America) [*A publication*]

Proc Nat Acad Sci (USA) Biol Sci ... Proceedings. National Academy of Sciences (United States of America). Biological Sciences [*A publication*]

Proc Nat Acad Sci (USA) Phys Sci ... Proceedings. National Academy of Sciences (United States of America). Physical Sciences [*A publication*]

Proc Nat Ass Wheat Growers ... Proceedings. National Association of Wheat Growers [*A publication*]

Proc Nat Conf AIAS ... Proceedings. National Conference. Australian Institute of Agricultural Science [*A publication*] (APTA)

Proc Nat Conf Fluid Power Annu Meet ... Proceedings. National Conference on Fluid Power. Annual Meeting [*A publication*]

Proc Nat Electron Conf ... Proceedings. National Electronics Conference [*A publication*]

Proc Nat Food Eng Conf ... Proceedings. National Food Engineering Conference [*A publication*]

Proc Nat Gas Process Assoc Tech Pap ... Proceedings. Natural Gas Processors Association. Technical Papers [*A publication*]

Proc Nat Gas Processors Assoc Annu Conv ... Proceedings. Natural Gas Processors Association. Annual Convention [*A publication*]

Proc Natl Acad Sci ... Proceedings. National Academy of Sciences [*United States of America*] [*A publication*]

Proc Natl Acad Sci (India) ... Proceedings. National Academy of Sciences (India) [*A publication*]

Proc Natl Acad Sci (India) Sect A ... Proceedings. National Academy of Sciences (India). Section A. Physical Sciences [*A publication*]

Proc Natl Acad Sci (India) Sect A Phys Sci ... Proceedings. National Academy of Sciences (India). Section A. Physical Sciences [*A publication*]

Proc Natl Acad Sci (India) Sect B ... Proceedings. National Academy of Sciences (India). Section B. Biological Sciences [*A publication*]

Proc Natl Acad Sci (India) Sect B Biol Sci ... Proceedings. National Academy of Sciences (India). Section B. Biological Sciences [*A publication*]

Proc Natl Acad Sci (USA) ... Proceedings. National Academy of Sciences (United States of America) [*A publication*]

Proc Natl Biomed Sci Instrum Symp ... Proceedings. National Biomedical Sciences Instrumentation Symposium [*A publication*]

Proc Natl Cancer Conf ... Proceedings. National Cancer Conference [*A publication*]

Proc Natl Conf Adm Res ... Proceedings. National Conference on the Administration of Research [*A publication*]

Proc Natl Conf Fluid Power ... Proceedings. National Conference on Fluid Power [*United States*] [*A publication*]

Proc Natl Conf Fluid Power Annu Meet ... Proceedings. National Conference on Fluid Power. Annual Meeting [*A publication*]

Proc Natl Conf Individ Onsite Wastewater Syst ... Proceedings. National Conference for Individual Onsite Wastewater Systems [*A publication*]

Proc Natl Conf Methadone Treat ... Proceedings. National Conference on Methadone Treatment [*A publication*]

Proc Natl Conv Study Inf Doc ... Proceedings. National Convention for the Study of Information and Documentation [*Japan*] [*A publication*]

Proc Natl Counc Radiat Prot Meas ... Proceedings. National Council on Radiation Protection and Measurements [*A publication*]

Proc Natl Counc Sci Dev (Repub China) ... Proceedings. National Council on Science Development (Republic of China) [*A publication*]

Proc Natl Electron Conf ... Proceedings. National Electronics Conference [*A publication*]

Proc Natl Food Eng Conf ... Proceedings. National Food Engineering Conference [*A publication*]

Proc Natl Incinerator Conf ... Proceedings. National Incinerator Conference [*A publication*]

Proc Natl Inst Sci (India) ... Proceedings. National Institute of Sciences (India) [*A publication*]

Proc Natl Inst Sci (India) A ... Proceedings. National Institute of Sciences (India). Part A. Physical Sciences [*A publication*]

Proc Natl Inst Sci (India) Part A ... Proceedings. National Institute of Sciences (India). Part A. Physical Sciences [*A publication*]

Proc Natl Inst Sci (India) Part A Phys Sci ... Proceedings. National Institute of Sciences (India). Part A. Physical Sciences [*A publication*]

Proc Natl Inst Sci (India) Part A Suppl ... Proceedings. National Institute of Sciences (India). Part A. Supplement [*A publication*]

Proc Natl Inst Sci (India) Part B ... Proceedings. National Institute of Sciences (India). Part B. Biological Sciences [*A publication*]

Proc Natl Inst Sci (India) Part B Biol Sci ... Proceedings. National Institute of Sciences (India). Part B. Biological Sciences [*A publication*]

Proc Natl Meet Biophys Biotechnol Finl ... Proceedings. National Meeting on Biophysics and Biotechnology in Finland [*A publication*]

Proc Natl Meet Biophys Med Eng Finl ... Proceedings. National Meeting on Biophysics and Medical Engineering in Finland [*A publication*]

Proc Natl Open Hearth Basic Oxygen Steel Conf ... Proceedings. National Open Hearth and Basic Oxygen Steel Conference [*A publication*]

Proc Natl Sci Counc ... Proceedings. National Science Council [*A publication*]

Proc Natl Sci Counc (Repub China) ... Proceedings. National Science Council (Republic of China) [*A publication*]

Proc Natl Sci Counc (Repub China) Part A Appl Sci ... Proceedings. National Science Council (Republic of China). Part A. Applied Sciences [*A publication*]

Proc Natl Sci Counc (Repub China) Part A Phys Sci Eng ... Proceedings. National Science Council (Republic of China). Part A. Physical Science and Engineering [*A publication*]

Proc Natl Sci Counc (Repub China) Part B Basic Sci ... Proceedings. National Science Council (Republic of China). Part B. Basic Science [*A publication*]

Proc Natl Sci Counc (Repub China) Part B Life Sci ... Proceedings. National Science Council (Republic of China). Part B. Life Sciences[*A publication*]

Proc Natl Shellfish Assoc ... Proceedings. National Shellfisheries Association [*A publication*]

Proc Natl Symp Radioecol ... Proceedings. National Symposium on Radioecology [*A publication*]

Proc Natl Telecommun Conf ... Proceedings. National Telecommunications Conference [*A publication*]

Proc Natn Acad Sci (India) ... Proceedings. National Academy of Sciences (India) [*A publication*]

Proc Natn Acad Sci (USA) ... Proceedings. National Academy of Sciences (United States of America) [*A publication*]

Proc Natn Ent Soc (USA) ... Proceedings. National Entomological Society (United States of America) [*A publication*]

Proc Natn Inst Sci (India) ... Proceedings. National Institute of Sciences (India) [*A publication*]

Proc Nat Silo Ass ... Proceedings. National Silo Association [*A publication*]

Proc Nat Telemetering Conf ... Proceedings. National Telemetering Conference [*A publication*]

Proc Natur Gas Processors Ass ... Proceedings. Natural Gas Processors Association [*A publication*]

Proc N Cent Brch Am Ass Econ Ent ... Proceedings. North Central Branch. American Association of Economic Entomologists [*A publication*]

Proc N Cent Brch Ent Soc Am ... Proceedings. North Central Branch. Entomological Society of America [*A publication*]

Proc ND Acad Sci ... Proceedings. North Dakota Academy of Science [*A publication*]

Proc N Dak Acad Sci ... Proceedings. North Dakota Academy of Science [*A publication*]

Proc Near E S Afr Irrig Pract Semin ... Proceedings. Near East - South Africa Irrigation Practices Seminar [*A publication*]

Proc Nebr Acad Sci ... Proceedings. Nebraska Academy of Sciences [*A publication*]

Proc Nebr Acad Sci Affil Soc ... Proceedings. Nebraska Academy of Sciences and Affiliated Societies [*A publication*]

Proc Ned Akad Wet ... Proceedings. Koninklijke Nederlandse Akademie van Wetenschappen [*A publication*]

Proc N Engl Bioeng Conf ... Proceedings. New England Bioengineering Conference [*A publication*]

Proc N Engl Soils Discuss Grp ... Proceedings. North of England Soils Discussion Group [*A publication*]

Proc News Aust Oil Colour Chem Assoc ... Proceedings and News. Australian Oil and Colour Chemists Association [*A publication*] (APTA)

Proc News Aust Oil Colour Chemists Assoc ... Proceedings and News. Australian Oil and Colour Chemists Association [*A publication*] (APTA)

Proc NH Acad Sci ... Proceedings. New Hampshire Academy of Science [*A publication*]

Proc Ninth Int Grassld Congr ... Proceedings. Ninth International Grassland Congress [*A publication*]

Proc NJ Hist Soc ... Proceedings. New Jersey Historical Society [*A publication*]

Proc NJ Mosq Control Assoc ... Proceedings. New Jersey Mosquito Control Association [*A publication*]

Proc NJ Mosq Control Assoc Suppl ... Proceedings. New Jersey Mosquito Control Association. Supplement [*A publication*]

Proc N Mex W Tex Phil Soc ... Proceedings. New Mexico-West Texas Philosophical Society [*A publication*]

Proc NMFA ... Procedure. National Microfilm Association [*A publication*]

Proc Nord Aroma Symp ... Proceedings. Nordic Aroma Symposium [*A publication*]

Proc North Am Metalwork Res Conf ... Proceedings. North American Metalworking Research Conference [*A publication*]

Proc North Cent Branch Entomol Soc Am ... Proceedings. North Central Branch. Entomological Society of America [*A publication*]

Proc North Cent Weed Control Conf ... Proceedings. North Central Weed Control Conference [*A publication*]

Proc Northeast Weed Contr Conf ... Proceedings. Northeastern Weed Control Conference [*A publication*]

Proc Northeast Weed Control Conf ... Proceedings. Northeastern Weed Control Conference [*A publication*]

Proc Northeast Weed Sci Soc ... Proceedings. Northeastern Weed Science Society [*A publication*]

Proc Northwest Conf Struct Eng ... Proceedings. Northwest Conference of Structural Engineers [*A publication*]

Proc Northwest Wood Prod Clin ... Proceedings. Northwest Wood Products Clinic [*A publication*]

Proc NS Inst Sci ... Proceedings. Nova Scotian Institute of Science [*A publication*]

Proc Ntheast For Tree Impr Conf ... Proceedings. Northeastern Forest Tree Improvement Conference [*A publication*]

Proc Nucl Phys Solid State Phys Symp ... Proceedings. Nuclear Physics and Solid State Physics Symposium [*India*] [*A publication*]

Proc Nurs Theory Conf ... Proceedings. Nursing Theory Conference [*A publication*]

Proc Nutr Soc ... Proceedings. Nutrition Society [*A publication*]
Proc Nutr Soc Aust ... Proceedings. Nutrition Society of Australia [*A publication*]   (APTA)
Proc Nutr Soc Aust Annu Conf ... Proceedings. Nutrition Society of Australia. Annual Conference [*A publication*]
Proc Nutr Soc South Afr ... Proceedings. Nutrition Society of Southern Africa [*A publication*]
Proc NY St Hist Assn ... Proceedings. New York State Historical Association [*A publication*]
Proc NY St Hort Soc ... Proceedings. New York State Horticultural Society [*A publication*]
Proc NZ Ecol Soc ... Proceedings. New Zealand Ecological Society [*A publication*]
Proc NZ Grassl Assoc ... Proceedings. New Zealand Grassland Association [*A publication*]
Proc NZ Grassl Assoc Conf ... Proceedings. New Zealand Grassland Association. Conference [*A publication*]
Proc NZ Grassld Ass ... Proceedings. New Zealand Grassland Association [*A publication*]
Proc NZ Inst Agr Sci ... Proceedings. New Zealand Institute of Agricultural Science [*A publication*]
Proc NZ Soc Anim Proc ... Proceedings. New Zealand Society of Animal Production [*A publication*]
Proc NZ Weed Conf ... Proceedings. New Zealand Weed and Pest Control Conference [*A publication*]
Proc NZ Weed Control Conf ... Proceedings. New Zealand Weed Control Conference [*A publication*]
Proc NZ Weed Pest Contr Conf ... Proceedings. New Zealand Weed and Pest Control Conference [*A publication*]
Proc NZ Weed & Pest Control Conf ... Proceedings. New Zealand Weed and Pest Control Conference [*A publication*]
PROCO ..... Procurement Officer [*Military*]
PROCO ..... Programmed Combustion [*Ford Motor Co.*]
PROCO ..... Projects for Continental Operations [*World War II*]
Proc Ohio State Hortic Soc ... Proceedings. Ohio State Horticultural Society [*A publication*]
Proc Ohio State Hort Soc ... Proceedings. Ohio State Horticultural Society [*A publication*]
Proc Oil Recovery Conf Tex Petrol Res Comm ... Proceedings. Oil Recovery Conference. Texas Petroleum Research Committee [*A publication*]
Proc Okla Acad Sci ... Proceedings. Oklahoma Academy of Science [*A publication*]
PROCOM ... Procedures Committee [*Institute of Electrical and Electronics Engineers*]   (IEEE)
PROCOM ... Procurement Committee
PROCOMEXCHI ... Mexican-Chicano Cooperative Programs on Mexican-US-Chicano Futures   (EA)
PROCOMP ... Process Computer [*Data processing*]
PROCOMP ... Program Compiler [*Data processing*]   (IEEE)
PROCON .. Request Diagnosis, Prognosis, Present Condition, Probable Date and Mode of Disposition of Following Patient Reported in Your Hospital [*Military*]
Proc Ont Ind Waste Conf ... Proceedings. Ontario Industrial Waste Conference [*A publication*]
Procop .... Procopius [*Sixth century AD*] [*Classical studies*]   (OCD)
Proc Oreg Acad Sci ... Proceedings. Oregon Academy of Science [*A publication*]
Proc Oreg Weed Conf ... Proceedings. Oregon Weed Conference [*A publication*]
Proc Organ Inst NSW ... Proceedings. Organ Institute of New South Wales [*A publication*]
Proc Osaka Prefect Inst Public Health Ed Food Sanit ... Proceedings. Osaka Prefecture Institute of Public Health. Edition of Food Sanitation [*A publication*]
Proc Osaka Prefect Inst Public Health Ed Ind Health ... Proceedings. Osaka Prefecture Institute of Public Health. Edition of Industrial Health [*A publication*]
Proc Osaka Prefect Inst Public Health Ed Ment Health ... Proceedings. Osaka Prefecture Institute of Public Health. Edition of Mental Health [*A publication*]
Proc Osaka Prefect Inst Public Health Ed Pharm Aff ... Proceedings. Osaka Prefecture Institute of Public Health. Edition of Pharmaceutical Affairs [*A publication*]
Proc Osaka Prefect Inst Public Health Ed Public Health ... Proceedings. Osaka Prefecture Institute of Public Health. Edition of Public Health [*A publication*]
Proc Osaka Public Health Inst ... Proceedings. Osaka Public Health Institute [*Japan*] [*A publication*]
PROCOTIP ... Promotion Cooperative du Transport Individuel Publique [*Public cars for private use to reduce traffic congestion*] [*Also known as TIP*] [*France*]
Proc PA Acad Sci ... Proceedings. Pennsylvania Academy of Science [*A publication*]
Proc Pac Chem Eng Congr ... Proceedings. Pacific Chemical Engineering Congress [*A publication*]
Proc Pac Coast Gas Ass ... Proceedings. Pacific Coast Gas Association, Inc. [*California*] [*A publication*]
Proc Pac Northwest Fert Conf ... Proceedings. Pacific Northwest Fertilizer Conference [*A publication*]

Proc Pac Northwest Ind Waste Conf ... Proceedings. Pacific Northwest Industrial Waste Conference [*A publication*]
Proc Pac Sci Congr ... Proceedings. Pacific Science Congress [*A publication*]
Proc PA Ger Soc ... Proceedings and Addresses. Pennsylvania-German Society [*A publication*]
Proc Pak Acad Sci ... Proceedings. Pakistan Academy of Sciences [*A publication*]
Proc Pakistan Statist Assoc ... Proceedings. Pakistan Statistical Association [*A publication*]
Proc Pakist Sci Conf ... Proceedings. Pakistan Science Conference [*A publication*]
Proc Pak Sci Conf ... Proceedings. Pakistan Science Conference [*A publication*]
Proc Pap Annu Conf Calif Mosq Control Assoc ... Proceedings and Papers. Annual Conference. California Mosquito Control Association [*A publication*]
Proc Pap Annu Conf Calif Mosq Vector Control Assoc ... Proceedings and Papers. Annual Conference. California Mosquito and Vector Control Association [*A publication*]
Proc Pap Graphic Arts Conf ... Proceedings and Papers. Graphic Arts Conference [*A publication*]
Proc Pap Int Union Conserv Nature Nat Resour ... Proceedings and Papers. International Union for the Conservation of Nature and Natural Resources [*A publication*]
Proc Path Soc Phila ... Proceedings. Pathological Society of Philadelphia [*A publication*]
Proc Paving Conf ... Proceedings. Paving Conference [*A publication*]
Proc Penn Acad Sci ... Proceedings. Pennsylvania Academy of Science [*A publication*]
Proc Peoria Acad Sci ... Proceedings. Peoria Academy of Science [*A publication*]
Proc Pharm Soc Egypt ... Proceedings. Pharmaceutical Society of Egypt [*A publication*]
Proc Phil As ... Proceedings. American Philological Association [*A publication*]
Proc Phil Educ Soc Austl ... Proceedings. Philosophy of Education Society of Australasia [*A publication*]
Proc Phil Educ Soc GB ... Proceedings. Philosophy of Education Society of Great Britain [*A publication*]
Proc Phil Soc ... Proceedings. American Philosophical Society [*A publication*]
Proc Phys Math Soc Jpn ... Proceedings. Physico-Mathematical Society of Japan [*A publication*]
Proc Phys Semin Trondheim ... Proceedings. Physics Seminar in Trondheim [*Norway*] [*A publication*]
Proc Phys Soc ... Proceedings. Physics Society [*A publication*]
Proc Phys Soc Edinb ... Proceedings. Physical Society of Edinburgh [*A publication*]
Proc Phys Soc Jpn ... Proceedings. Physical Society of Japan [*A publication*]
Proc Phys Soc Lond ... Proceedings. Physical Society of London [*A publication*]
Proc Phys Soc London ... Proceedings. Physical Society of London [*A publication*]
Proc Phys Soc London Sect A ... Proceedings. Physical Society of London. Section A [*A publication*]
Proc Phys Soc London Sect B ... Proceedings. Physical Society of London. Section B [*A publication*]
Proc Phytochem Soc ... Proceedings. Phytochemical Society [*A publication*]
Proc Plant Growth Regul Work Group ... Proceedings. Plant Growth Regulator Working Group [*A publication*]
Proc Plant Propagators' Soc ... Proceedings. Plant Propagators' Society [*United States*] [*A publication*]
Proc PN Lebedev Phys Inst ... Proceedings. P. N. Lebedev Physics Institute [*A publication*]
Proc PN Lebedev Phys Inst Acad Sci USSR ... Proceedings. P. N. Lebedev Physics Institute. Academy of Sciences of the USSR [*A publication*]
Proc Porcelain Enamel Inst Tech Forum ... Proceedings. Porcelain Enamel Institute. Technical Forum [*A publication*]
Proc Power Plant Dyn Control Test Symp ... Proceedings. Power Plant Dynamics. Control and Testing Symposium [*A publication*]
Proc Pr .... Proctor's Practice [*A publication*]   (DLA)
Proc Prac ... Proctor's Practice [*A publication*]   (DLA)
Proc Prehist Soc ... Proceedings. Prehistoric Society [*A publication*]
Proc Pr Hist Soc ... Proceedings. Prehistoric Society [*A publication*]
Proc Prod Liability Prev Conf ... Proceedings. Product Liability Prevention Conference [*A publication*]
Proc PS ...... Proceedings. Prehistoric Society [*A publication*]
Proc Public Health Eng Conf ... Proceedings. Public Health Engineering Conference [*Loughborough University of Technology*] [*A publication*]
Proc QD Soc Sug Cane Tech ... Queensland Society of Sugar Cane Technologists. Proceedings [*A publication*]   (APTA)
Proc QD Soc Sug Cane Technol ... Proceedings. Queensland Society of Sugar Cane Technologists [*A publication*]
Proc Queensl Soc Sugar Cane Technol ... Proceedings. Queensland Society of Sugar Cane Technologists [*A publication*]
Proc Queensl Soc Sug Cane Technol ... Queensland Society of Sugar Cane Technologists. Proceedings [*A publication*]   (APTA)
Proc Queens Soc Sugar Cane Technol ... Queensland Society of Sugar Cane Technologists. Proceedings [*A publication*]   (APTA)

Proc Radio Club Am ... Proceedings. Radio Club of America [*A publication*]
Proc Radioisot Soc Philipp ... Proceedings. Radioisotope Society of the Philippines [*A publication*]
Proc R Agric Hort Soc S Aust ... Royal Agricultural and Horticultural Society of South Australia. Proceedings [*A publication*]   (APTA)
Proc Rajasthan Acad Sci ... Proceedings. Rajasthan Academy of Sciences [*A publication*]
Proc R Aust Chem Inst ... Proceedings. Royal Australian Chemical Institute [*A publication*]
Proc R Can Inst ... Proceedings. Royal Canadian Institute [*A publication*]
Proc 3rd Int Conf Peaceful Uses Atom Energy ... Proceedings. Third International Conference on the Peaceful Uses of Atomic Energy [*A publication*]
Proc Refin Dep Am Pet Inst ... Proceedings. Refining Department. American Petroleum Institute [*A publication*]
Proc Reg Conf Int Potash Inst ... Proceedings. Regional Conference. International Potash Institute [*A publication*]
Proc Relay Conf ... Proceedings. Relay Conference [*A publication*]
Proc Reliab Maint Conf ... Proceedings. Reliability and Maintainability Conference [*A publication*]
Proc Remote Syst Technol Div ANS ... Proceedings. Remote Systems Technology Division of the American Nuclear Society [*A publication*]
Proc Rencontre Moriond ... Proceedings. Rencontre de Moriond [*A publication*]
Proc R Entomol Soc Lond Ser A Gen Entomol ... Proceedings. Royal Entomological Society of London. Series A. General Entomology [*A publication*]
Proc R Entomol Soc Lond Ser B Taxon ... Proceedings. Royal Entomological Society of London. Series B. Taxonomy [*A publication*]
Proc R Ent Soc ... Proceedings. Royal Entomological Society [*A publication*]
Proc R Ent Soc Lond A ... Proceedings. Royal Entomological Society of London. A [*A publication*]
Proc Rep Belfast Nat Hist Philos Soc ... Proceedings and Reports. Belfast Natural History and Philosophical Society [*A publication*]
Proc Rep S Seedmen's Ass ... Proceedings and Reports. Southern Seedmen's Association [*A publication*]
Proc Res Conf Res Counc Am Meat Inst Found Univ Chicago ... Proceedings. Research Conference Sponsored by the Research Council of the American Meat Institute Foundation. University of Chicago [*A publication*]
Proc Res Inst Atmos Nagoya Univ ... Proceedings. Research Institute of Atmospherics. Nagoya University [*A publication*]
Proc Res Inst Nucl Med Biol ... Proceedings. Research Institute for Nuclear Medicine and Biology [*A publication*]
Proc Res Inst Nucl Med Biol Hiroshima Univ ... Proceedings. Research Institute for Nuclear Medicine and Biology. Hiroshima University [*Japan*] [*A publication*]
Proc Res Inst Oceanogr Fish (Varna) ... Proceedings. Research Institute of Oceanography and Fisheries (Varna) [*A publication*]
Proc Res Inst Pomol (Skierniewice Pol) Ser E Conf Symp ... Proceedings. Research Institute of Pomology (Skierniewice, Poland). Series E. Conferences and Symposia [*A publication*]
Proc Res Soc Jap Sugar Refin Technol ... Proceedings. Research Society of Japan Sugar Refineries' Technologists [*A publication*]
Proc Res Soc Jpn Sugar Refineries' Technol ... Proceedings. Research Society of Japan Sugar Refineries' Technologists [*A publication*]
Proc R Geogr Soc Australas S Aust Br ... Proceedings. Royal Geographical Society of Australasia. South Australian Branch [*A publication*]   (APTA)
Proc R Geogr Soc Australas South Aust Branch ... Proceedings. Royal Geographical Society of Australasia. South Australian Branch [*A publication*]   (APTA)
Proc R Geog Soc Aust S Aust Br ... Proceedings. Royal Geographical Society of Australasia. South Australian Branch [*A publication*]   (APTA)
Proc R Hortic Soc ... Proceedings. Royal Horticulture Society [*A publication*]
Proc R Inst GB ... Proceedings. Royal Institution of Great Britain [*A publication*]
Proc R Instn Gt Br ... Proceedings. Royal Institution of Great Britain [*A publication*]
Proc Rio Grande Val Hortic Inst ... Proceedings. Rio Grande Valley Horticultural Institute [*A publication*]
Proc R Ir Acad ... Proceedings. Royal Irish Academy [*A publication*]
Proc R Ir Acad A ... Proceedings. Royal Irish Academy. Section A. Mathematical, Astronomical, and Physical Science [*A publication*]
Proc R Ir Acad Sect B ... Proceedings. Royal Irish Academy. Section B. Biological, Geological, and Chemical Science [*A publication*]
Proc R Ir Acad Sect B Biol Geol Chem Sci ... Proceedings. Royal Irish Academy. Section B. Biological, Geological, and Chemical Science [*A publication*]
Proc R Irish Acad Sect A ... Proceedings. Royal Irish Academy. Section A. Mathematical, Astronomical, and Physical Science [*A publication*]
Proc R Irish Acad Sect B ... Proceedings. Royal Irish Academy. Section B. Biological, Geological, and Chemical Science [*A publication*]
Proc R Microsc Soc ... Proceedings. Royal Microscopical Society [*England*] [*A publication*]

Proc RNS ... Proceedings. Royal Numismatic Society [*A publication*]
Proc Robert A Welch Found Conf Chem Res ... Proceedings. Robert A. Welch Foundation. Conferences on Chemical Research [*A publication*]
Proc Rochester Acad Sci ... Proceedings. Rochester Academy of Science [*A publication*]
Proc Rocky Mt Coal Min Inst ... Proceedings. Rocky Mountain Coal Mining Institute [*A publication*]
Proc Royal Aust Chem Inst ... Proceedings. Royal Australian Chemical Institute [*A publication*]   (APTA)
Proc Royal Irish Acad ... Proceedings. Royal Irish Academy [*A publication*]
Proc Royal M Assoc ... Proceedings. Royal Musical Association [*A publication*]
Proc Royal Soc Canad ... Proceedings. Royal Society of Canada [*A publication*]
Proc Royal Soc London Ser A ... Proceedings. Royal Society of London. Series A. Mathematical and Physical Sciences [*A publication*]
Proc Royal Soc London Series A ... Proceedings. Royal Society of London. Series A [*A publication*]
Proc Roy Anthropol Inst ... Proceedings. Royal Anthropological Institute [*A publication*]
Proc Roy Anthropol Inst Gr Brit Ir ... Proceedings. Royal Anthropological Institute of Great Britain and Ireland [*A publication*]
Proc Roy Aust Chem Inst ... Proceedings. Royal Australian Chemical Institute [*A publication*]   (APTA)
Proc Roy Entomol Soc Lond ... Proceedings. Royal Entomological Society of London [*A publication*]
Proc Roy Entomol Soc Lond C ... Proceedings. Royal Entomological Society of London. Series C. Journal of Meetings [*A publication*]
Proc Roy Entomol Soc London Ser A ... Proceedings. Royal Entomological Society of London. Series A [*A publication*]
Proc Roy Geog Soc Austral ... Proceedings. Royal Geographical Society of Australia. South Australian Branch [*A publication*]
Proc Roy Inst ... Proceedings. Royal Institution of Great Britain [*A publication*]
Proc Roy Inst Gr Brit ... Proceedings. Royal Institution of Great Britain [*A publication*]
Proc Roy Ir Acad B C ... Proceedings. Royal Irish Academy. Series B and C [*A publication*]
Proc Roy Irish Acad ... Proceedings. Royal Irish Academy [*A publication*]
Proc Roy Irish Acad Sect A ... Proceedings. Royal Irish Academy. Section A. Mathematical, Astronomical, and Physical Science [*A publication*]
Proc Roy Phys Soc Edinb ... Proceedings. Royal Physical Society of Edinburgh [*A publication*]
Proc Roy Soc ... Proceedings. Royal Society [*A publication*]
Proc Roy Soc B ... Proceedings. Royal Society of London. Series B. Biological Sciences [*A publication*]
Proc Roy Soc Can ... Proceedings. Royal Society of Canada [*A publication*]
Proc Roy Soc Canada ... Proceedings. Royal Society of Canada [*A publication*]
Proc Roy Soc Canada 4 ... Proceedings. Royal Society of Canada. Fourth Series [*A publication*]
Proc Roy Soc Edinb ... Proceedings. Royal Society of Edinburgh [*A publication*]
Proc Roy Soc Edinb B ... Proceedings. Royal Society of Edinburgh. Section B. Biological Sciences [*A publication*]
Proc Roy Soc Edinburgh Sect A ... Proceedings. Royal Society of Edinburgh. Section A. Mathematical and Physical Sciences [*A publication*]
Proc Roy Soc London ... Proceedings. Royal Society of London [*A publication*]
Proc Roy Soc London S B ... Proceedings. Royal Society of London. Series B. Biological Sciences [*A publication*]
Proc Roy Soc London Ser A ... Proceedings. Royal Society of London. Series A. Mathematical and Physical Sciences [*A publication*]
Proc Roy Soc Med ... Proceedings. Royal Society of Medicine [*A publication*]
Proc Roy Soc QD ... Royal Society of Queensland. Proceedings [*A publication*]   (APTA)
Proc Roy Soc Ser A ... Proceedings. Royal Society. Series A [*A publication*]
Proc Roy Soc Vict ... Royal Society of Victoria. Proceedings [*A publication*]   (APTA)
Proc Roy Zool Soc NSW ... Royal Zoological Society of New South Wales. Proceedings [*A publication*]   (APTA)
Proc R Philos Soc Glasgow ... Proceedings. Royal Philosophical Society of Glasgow [*A publication*]
Proc R Physiogr Soc Lund ... Proceedings. Royal Physiograph Society at Lund [*A publication*]
Proc R Phys Soc Edinb ... Proceedings. Royal Physical Society of Edinburgh [*A publication*]
Proc R Soc A ... Proceedings. Royal Society of London. Series A. Mathematical and Physical Sciences [*A publication*]
Proc R Soc B ... Proceedings. Royal Society of London. Series B. Biological Sciences [*A publication*]
Proc R Soc Can ... Proceedings. Royal Society of Canada [*A publication*]
Proc R Soc Edinb Biol ... Proceedings. Royal Society of Edinburgh. Section B. Biology [*A publication*]
Proc R Soc Edinb Nat Environ ... Proceedings. Royal Society of Edinburgh. Section B. Natural Environment [*A publication*]
Proc R Soc Edinb Sect A ... Proceedings. Royal Society of Edinburgh. Section A. Mathematical and Physical Sciences [*Later, Proceedings. Royal Society of Edinburgh. Mathematics*] [*A publication*]

Proc R Soc Edinb Sect A Math Phys Sci ... Proceedings. Royal Society of Edinburgh. Section A. Mathematical and Physical Sciences [*Later, Proceedings. Royal Society of Edinburgh. Mathematics*] [*A publication*]

Proc R Soc Edinb Sect B ... Proceedings. Royal Society of Edinburgh. Section B. Biological Sciences [*A publication*]

Proc R Soc Edinb Sect B Biol ... Proceedings. Royal Society of Edinburgh. Section B. Biology [*A publication*]

Proc R Soc Edinb Sect B Nat Environ ... Proceedings. Royal Society of Edinburgh. Section B. Natural Environment [*A publication*]

Proc R Soc Edinburgh ... Proceedings. Royal Society of Edinburgh [*A publication*]

Proc R Soc Edinburgh B ... Proceedings. Royal Society of Edinburgh. Section B. Biological Sciences [*A publication*]

Proc R Soc Edinburgh Biol Sci ... Proceedings. Royal Society of Edinburgh. Section B. Biological Sciences [*A publication*]

Proc R Soc Edinburgh Sect A ... Proceedings. Royal Society of Edinburgh. Section A. Mathematical and Physical Sciences [*A publication*]

Proc R Soc Lond ... Proceedings. Royal Society of London. Series B. Biological Sciences [*A publication*]

Proc R Soc Lond B Biol Sci ... Proceedings. Royal Society of London. Series B. Biological Sciences [*A publication*]

Proc R Soc Lond Biol ... Proceedings. Royal Society of London. Series B. Biological Sciences [*A publication*]

Proc R Soc London A ... Proceedings. Royal Society of London. Series A. Mathematical and Physical Sciences [*A publication*]

Proc R Soc London Ser A ... Proceedings. Royal Society of London. Series A. Mathematical and Physical Sciences [*A publication*]

Proc R Soc Med ... Proceedings. Royal Society of Medicine [*A publication*]

Proc R Soc Med Suppl ... Proceedings. Royal Society of Medicine. Supplement [*England*] [*A publication*]

Proc R Soc NZ ... Proceedings. Royal Society of New Zealand [*A publication*]

Proc R Soc QD ... Proceedings. Royal Society of Queensland [*A publication*]

Proc R Soc Queensl ... Proceedings. Royal Society of Queensland [*A publication*]

Proc R Soc VIC ... Royal Society of Victoria. Proceedings [*A publication*] (APTA)

Proc R Soc Vict ... Proceedings. Royal Society of Victoria [*A publication*]

Proc R Soc Victoria ... Proceedings. Royal Society of Victoria [*A publication*]

Proc Ruakura Farmers Conf ... Proceedings. Ruakura Farmers' Conference [*A publication*]

Proc Ruakura Farmers Conf Week ... Proceedings. Ruakura Farmers' Conference Week [*A publication*]

Proc Rudolf Virchow Med Soc City NY ... Proceedings. Rudolf Virchow Medical Society in the City of New York [*A publication*]

Proc Rudolph Virchow Med Soc NY ... Proceedings. Rudolph Virchow Medical Society of New York [*A publication*]

Proc R Zool Soc NSW ... Proceedings. Royal Zoological Society of New South Wales [*A publication*]

PROCS ...... Proceedings

Proc S Afr Soc Anim Prod ... Proceedings. South African Society of Animal Production [*A publication*]

Proc S Afr Sugar Technol Assoc Annu Congr ... Proceedings. South African Sugar Technologists Association. Annual Congress [*A publication*]

Proc San Diego Biomed Symp ... Proceedings. San Diego Biomedical Symposium [*A publication*]

Proc SA Scot ... Proceedings. Society of Antiquaries of Scotland [*A publication*]

Proc S Aust Brch R Geogr Soc Australas ... Royal Geographical Society of Australasia. South Australian Branch. Proceedings [*A publication*] (APTA)

Proc SC Hist Assn ... Proceedings. South Carolina Historical Association [*A publication*]

Proc Sci Assoc Nigeria ... Proceedings. Science Association of Nigeria [*A publication*]

Proc Sci Inst Kinki Univ ... Proceedings. Science Institution. Kinki University [*A publication*]

Proc Sci Sect Toilet Goods Assoc ... Proceedings. Scientific Section of the Toilet Goods Association [*A publication*]

Proc Scotts Turfgrass Res Conf ... Proceedings. Scotts Turfgrass Research Conference [*A publication*]

PROCSD ... Processed

Proc SD Acad Sci ... Proceedings. South Dakota Academy of Science [*A publication*]

Proc S Dak Acad Sci ... Proceedings. South Dakota Academy of Science [*A publication*]

Proc Sea Grant Conf ... Proceedings. Sea Grant Conference [*A publication*]

Proc Sec Int Symp Vet Epidemiol Econ ... Proceedings. Second International Symposium on Veterinary Epidemiology and Economics [*A publication*]

Proc Second Malays Soil Conf (Kuala Lumpur) ... Proceedings. Second Malaysian Soil Conference (Kuala Lumpur) [*A publication*]

Proc Sect Sci Is Acad Sci Humanit ... Proceedings. Section of Sciences. Israel Academy of Sciences and Humanities [*A publication*]

Proc Sect Sci K Ned Akad Wet ... Proceedings. Section of Sciences. Koninklijke Nederlandse Akademie van Wetenschappen [*A publication*]

Proc Seed Protein Conf ... Proceedings. Seed Protein Conference [*A publication*]

Proc Semin Biomass Energy City Farm Ind ... Proceedings. Seminar on Biomass Energy for City, Farm, and Industry [*A publication*]

Proc Ser Am Water Resour Assoc ... Proceedings Series. American Water Resources Association [*A publication*]

Proc Serono Clin Colloq Reprod ... Proceedings. Serono Clinical Colloquia on Reproduction [*A publication*]

Proc Serono Symp ... Proceedings. Serono Symposia [*A publication*]

Proc SESA ... Proceedings. Society for Experimental Stress Analysis [*A publication*]

Proc Shikoku Br Crop Sci Soc (Jap) ... Proceedings. Shikoku Branch of Crop Science Society (Japan) [*A publication*]

Proc SID .... Proceedings. SID [*Society for Information Display*] [*A publication*]

Proc Sigatoka Workshop ... Proceedings. Sigatoka Workshop [*A publication*]

Proc Silvic Conf ... Proceedings. Silviculture Conference [*A publication*]

Proc Soc Agric Bacteriol ... Proceedings. Society of Agricultural Bacteriologists [*A publication*]

Proc Soc Am For ... Proceedings. Society of American Foresters [*A publication*]

Proc Soc Anal Chem ... Proceedings. Society for Analytical Chemistry [*A publication*]

Proc Soc Antiq Scot ... Proceedings. Society of Antiquaries of Scotland [*A publication*]

Proc Soc Antiq Scotland ... Proceedings. Society of Antiquaries of Scotland [*A publication*]

Proc Soc Appl Bact ... Proceedings. Society for Applied Bacteriology [*A publication*]

Proc Soc Appl Bacteriol ... Proceedings. Society for Applied Bacteriology [*A publication*]

Proc Soc Biol Chem ... Proceedings. Society of Biological Chemists [*A publication*]

Proc Soc Biol Chem India ... Proceedings. Society of Biological Chemists of India [*A publication*]

Proc Soc Can ... Proceedings. Royal Society of Canada [*A publication*]

Proc Soc Chem Ind (Victoria) ... Proceedings. Society of Chemical Industry (Victoria) [*A publication*]

Proc Soc Exp Biol Med ... Proceedings. Society for Experimental Biology and Medicine [*A publication*]

Proc Soc Exp Biol (NY) ... Proceedings. Society for Experimental Biology and Medicine (New York) [*A publication*]

Proc Soc Exper Biol Med ... Proceedings. Society for Experimental Biology and Medicine [*A publication*]

Proc Soc Exp Stress Anal ... Proceedings. Society for Experimental Stress Analysis [*A publication*]

Proc Soc Exp Stress Analysis ... Proceedings. Society for Experimental Stress Analysis [*A publication*]

Proc Soc Ind Microbiol ... Proceedings. Society for Industrial Microbiology [*A publication*]

Proc Soc Inf Disp ... Proceedings. Society for Information Display [*A publication*]

Proc Soc Lond ... Proceedings. Royal Society of London [*A publication*]

Proc Soc Med ... Proceedings. Royal Society of Medicine [*A publication*]

Proc Soc Photo Opt Instrum Eng ... Proceedings. Society of Photo-Optical Instrumentation Engineers [*A publication*]

Proc Soc Promot Agric Sci ... Proceedings. Society for the Promotion of Agricultural Science [*A publication*]

Proc Soc Protozool ... Proceedings. Society of Protozoologists [*A publication*]

Proc Soc Relay Eng ... Proceedings. Society of Relay Engineers [*A publication*]

Proc Soc Study Fertil ... Proceedings. Society for the Study of Fertility [*A publication*]

Proc Soc Study Ind Med ... Proceedings. Society for the Study of Industrial Medicine [*A publication*]

Proc Soc Vict ... Proceedings. Royal Society of Victoria [*A publication*]

Proc Soc Water Treat Exam ... Proceedings. Society for Water Treatment and Examination [*A publication*]

Proc Soil Crop Sci Soc Fla ... Proceedings. Soil and Crop Science Society of Florida [*A publication*]

Proc Soil Sci Soc Am ... Proceedings. Soil Science Society of America [*A publication*]

Proc Soil Sci Soc Amer ... Proceedings. Soil Science Society of America [*A publication*]

Proc Soil Sci Soc Fla ... Proceedings. Soil Science Society of Florida [*A publication*]

Proc Somerset Arch Natur Hist Soc ... Proceedings. Somerset Archaeology and Natural History Society [*A publication*]

Proc South Afr Electron Microsc Soc Verrigtings ... Proceedings. Southern African Electron Microscopy Society-Verrigtings [*A publication*]

Proc South Conf For Tree Improv ... Proceedings. Southern Conference on Forest Tree Improvement [*A publication*]

Proc Southeast Asian Reg Semin Trop Med Public Health ... Proceedings. Southeast Asian Regional Seminar on Tropical Medicine and Public Health [*A publication*]

Proc Southeastcon Reg 3 (Three) Conf ... Proceedings. Southeastcon Region 3 (Three) Conference [*United States*] [*A publication*]

Proc Southeast Pecan Grow Assoc ... Proceedings. Southeastern Pecan Growers Association [*US*] [*A publication*]

Proc South For Tree Improv Conf ... Proceedings. Southern Forest Tree Improvement Conference [*A publication*]
Proc South Lond Entom and Nat Hist Soc ... Proceedings. South London Entomological and Natural History Society [*A publication*]
Proc South Munic Ind Waste Conf ... Proceedings. Southern Municipal and Industrial Waste Conference [*A publication*]
Proc South Pasture Forage Crop Improv Conf ... Proceedings. Southern Pasture and Forage Crop Improvement Conference [*A publication*]
Proc South Wales Inst Eng ... Proceedings. South Wales Institute of Engineers [*A publication*]
Proc South Water Resour Pollut Control Conf ... Proceedings. Southern Water Resources and Pollution Control Conference [*A publication*]
Proc South Weed Conf ... Proceedings. Southern Weed Conference [*A publication*]
Proc South Weed Sci Soc ... Proceedings. Southern Weed Science Society [*A publication*]
Proc Southwest Agr Trade Farm Policy Conf ... Proceedings. Southwestern Agricultural Trade Farm Policy Conference [*A publication*]
Proc SPE Symp Form Damage Control ... Proceedings. Society of Petroleum Engineers. American Institute of Mining, Metallurgical, and Petroleum Engineers. Symposium on Formation Damage Control [*A publication*]
Proc SPE Symp Improv Oil Recovery ... Proceedings. Society of Petroleum Engineers. American Institute of Mining, Metallurgical, and Petroleum Engineers. Symposium on Improved Oil Recovery [*A publication*]
Proc SPI Annu Struct Foam Conf ... Proceedings. SPI [*Society of the Plastics Industry*] Annual Structural Foam Conference [*A publication*]
Proc SPI Struct Foam Conf ... Proceedings. SPI [*Society of the Plastics Industry*] Structural Foam Conference [*A publication*]
Proc Sprinkler Irrig Assoc Tech Conf ... Proceedings. Sprinkler Irrigation Association. Technical Conference [*A publication*]
Proc SSSA ... Proceedings. Soil Science Society of America [*A publication*]
Proc St .... Process Studies [*A publication*]
Proc Staff Meetings Mayo Clin ... Proceedings. Staff Meetings of the Mayo Clinic [*A publication*]
Proc Staff Meet Mayo Clin ... Proceedings. Staff Meeting. Mayo Clinic [*A publication*]
Proc Staffs Iron Steel Inst ... Proceedings. Staffordshire Iron and Steel Institute [*A publication*]
Proc State Coll Wash Inst Dairy ... Proceedings. State College of Washington. Institute of Dairying [*A publication*]
Proc State Horti Assoc PA ... Proceedings. State Horticultural Association of Pennsylvania [*A publication*]
Proc State Secr Manage Conf Am Dent Assoc ... Proceedings. State Secretaries Management Conference. American Dental Association [*A publication*]
Proc Steel Treat Res Soc ... Proceedings. Steel Treating Research Society [*A publication*]
Proc Steklov Inst Math ... Proceedings. Steklov Institute of Mathematics [*A publication*]
Proc Sth Conf For Tree Impr ... Proceedings. Southern Conference on Forest Tree Improvement [*A publication*]
Proc Sth Weed Control Conf ... Proceedings. Southern Weed Control Conference [*A publication*]
Proc Sth Weed Sci Soc ... Proceedings. Southern Weed Science Society [*A publication*]
Proc Stream Workshop ... Proceedings. Streams Workshop [*A publication*]
Proc Study Fauna Flora USSR Sect Bot ... Proceedings on the Study of the Fauna and Flora of the USSR. Section of Botany [*A publication*]
Proc 1st Vic Weed Conf ... Proceedings. First Victorian Weed Conference [*A publication*] (APTA)
Proc Suff Inst A ... Proceedings. Suffolk Institute of Archaeology [*A publication*]
Proc Suffolk Inst Arch ... Proceedings. Suffolk Institute of Archaeology [*A publication*]
Proc Suffolk Inst Archaeol Hist ... Proceedings. Suffolk Institute of Archaeology and History [*A publication*]
Proc Sugar Beet Res Assoc ... Proceedings. Sugar Beet Research Association [*A publication*]
Proc Sugar Process Res Conf ... Proceedings. Sugar Processing Research Conference [*A publication*]
Proc Summer Comput Simul Conf ... Proceedings. Summer Computer Simulation Conference [*A publication*]
Proc Summer Conf Spectrosc Its Appl ... Proceedings. Summer Conference on Spectroscopy and Its Application [*A publication*]
Proc Summer Inst Part Phys ... Proceedings. Summer Institute on Particle Physics [*A publication*]
Proc S Wales Inst Eng ... Proceedings. South Wales Institute of Engineers [*A publication*]
Proc Symp Appl Math ... Proceedings. Symposia in Applied Mathematics [*A publication*]
Proc Symp Biol Skin ... Proceedings. Symposium on the Biology of Skin [*A publication*]
Proc Symp Chem Data Append R Aust Chem Inst ... Proceedings. Symposium on Chemical Data. Royal Australian Chemical Institute [*A publication*] (APTA)

Proc Symp Chem Physiol Pathol ... Proceedings. Symposium on Chemical Physiology and Pathology [*A publication*]
Proc Symp Effects Ionizing Radiat Seed Signific Crop Impr ... Proceedings. Symposium on the Effects of Ionizing Radiation on Seeds and Their Significance for Crop Improvement [*A publication*]
Proc Symp Eng Probl Fusion Res ... Proceedings. Symposium on Engineering Problems of Fusion Research [*A publication*]
Proc Symp Explos Pyrotech ... Proceedings. Symposium on Explosives and Pyrotechnics [*A publication*]
Proc Symp Fertil Indian Soils ... Proceedings. Symposium on Fertility of Indian Soils [*A publication*]
Proc Symp Isotop Plant Nutr Physiol (Vienna Austria) ... Proceedings. Symposium on Isotopes in Plant Nutrition and Physiology (Vienna, Austria) [*A publication*]
Proc Sympos Appl Math ... Proceedings. Symposia in Applied Mathematics [*A publication*]
Proc Sympos Pure Math ... Proceedings. Symposia in Pure Mathematics [*A publication*]
Proc Symp Particleboard ... Proceedings. Symposium on Particleboard [*A publication*]
Proc Symp Photogr Sensitivity ... Proceedings. Symposium on Photographic Sensitivity [*A publication*]
Proc Symp Rock Mech ... Proceedings. Symposium on Rock Mechanics [*A publication*]
Proc Symp Soc Study Inborn Errors Metab ... Proceedings. Symposium. Society for the Study of Inborn Errors of Metabolism [*A publication*]
Proc Symp Turbul Liq ... Proceedings. Symposium on Turbulence in Liquids [*A publication*]
Proc Symp Use Isotop Weed Res ... Proceedings. Symposium on the Use of Isotopes in Weed Research [*Vienna, Austria*] [*A publication*]
Proc Symp Use Radioisotop Soil Plant Nutr Stud ... Proceedings. Symposium on the Use of Radioisotopes in Soil-Plant Nutrition Studies [*A publication*]
Proc Symp Waste Manage ... Proceedings. Symposium on Waste Management [*A publication*]
Proc Synth Pipeline Gas Symp ... Proceedings. Synthetic Pipeline Gas Symposium [*A publication*]
PROCT ...... Proctology
Proc Tall Timbers Conf Ecol Anim Control Habitat Manage ... Proceedings. Tall Timbers Conference on Ecological Animal Control by Habitat Management [*A publication*]
Proc Tall Timbers Fire Ecol Conf ... Proceedings. Tall Timbers Fire Ecology Conference [*A publication*]
Proc Tech Conf Soc Vac Coaters ... Proceedings. Technical Conference. Society of Vacuum Coaters [*A publication*]
Proc Tech Groups NZ Inst Eng ... Proceedings of Technical Groups. New Zealand Institution of Engineers [*A publication*]
Proc Tech Mtg Int Union Conserv Nature ... Proceedings. Technical Meeting. International Union for Conservation of Nature and Natural Resources [*A publication*]
Proc Tech Program Electro-Opt Laser Conf Exp ... Proceedings. Technical Program. Electro-Optics/Laser Conference and Exposition [*A publication*]
Proc Tech Program Natl Electron Packag Prod Conf ... Proceedings. Technical Program. National Electronic Packaging and Production Conference [*A publication*]
Proc Tech Sess Cane Sugar Refin Res ... Proceedings. Technical Session on Cane Sugar Refining Research [*A publication*]
Proc Tex Conf Comput Syst ... Proceedings. Texas Conference on Computing Systems [*A publication*]
Proc Tex Nutr Conf ... Proceedings. Texas Nutrition Conference [*A publication*]
Proc Tex Water Sewage Works Short Sch ... Proceedings. Texas Water and Sewage Works Short School [*A publication*]
Proc Tex Water Util Short Sch ... Proceedings. Texas Water Utilities Short School [*A publication*]
Proc Therm Power Conf ... Proceedings. Thermal Power Conference [*A publication*]
PROCTO ... Proctoscopy [*Medicine*]
PROCTOR ... Priority Routine Organizer for Computer Transfers and Operations of Registers
PROCTOT ... Priority Routine Organizer for Computer Transfers and Operations and Transfers
Proc Trans Br Entomol Nat Hist Soc ... Proceedings and Transactions. British Entomological and Natural History Society [*A publication*]
Proc Trans Croydon Natur Hist Sci Soc ... Proceedings and Transactions. Croydon Natural History and Scientific Society [*A publication*]
Proc Trans Liverp Biol Soc ... Proceedings and Transactions. Liverpool Biological Society [*A publication*]
Proc and Trans Rhod Sci Assoc ... Proceedings and Transactions. Rhodesia Scientific Association [*A publication*]
Proc Trans Rhod Sci Assoc ... Proceedings and Transactions. Rhodesia Scientific Association [*A publication*]
Proc Trans R Soc Can ... Proceedings and Transactions. Royal Society of Canada [*A publication*]
Proc Tree Wardens Arborists Util Conf ... Proceedings. Tree Wardens, Arborists, and Utilities Conference [*A publication*]

Proc and Tr Liverpool Biol Soc ... Proceedings and Transactions. Liverpool Biological Society [*A publication*]

Proc Tr PN Lebedev Phys Inst ... Proceedings (Trudy). P. N. Lebedev Physics Institute [*A publication*]

Proc (Trudy) P N Lebedev Phys Inst ... Proceedings (Trudy). P. N. Lebedev Physics Institute [*A publication*]

ProCTS...... Proceedings. College Theology Society [*A publication*]

Proc Tub Res Coun ... Proceedings. Tuberculosis Research Council [*A publication*]

Proc Turbomachinery Symp ... Proceedings. Turbomachinery Symposium [*A publication*]

Proc Turfgrass Sprinkler Irrig Conf ... Proceedings. Turfgrass Sprinkler Irrigation Conference [*A publication*]

PROCU ..... Processing Unit

Proc UNESCO Conf Radioisot Sci Res ... Proceedings. UNESCO Conference on Radioisotopes in Scientific Research [*A publication*]

Proc Univ Bristol Spelaeol Soc ... Proceedings. University of Bristol Spelaeological Society [*A publication*]

Proc Univ Durham Phil Soc ... Proceedings. University of Durham. Philosophical Society [*A publication*]

Proc Univ MD Nutr Conf Feed Mfr ... Proceedings. University of Maryland. Nutrition Conference for Feed Manufacturers [*A publication*]

Proc Univ MO Annu Conf Trace Subst Environ Health ... Proceedings. University of Missouri. Annual Conference on Trace Substances in Environmental Health [*A publication*]

Proc Univ Newcastle Upon Tyne Philos Soc ... Proceedings. University of Newcastle-Upon-Tyne Philosophical Society [*A publication*]

Proc Univ Otago Med Sch ... Proceedings. University of Otago Medical School [*A publication*]

Proc USAID Ghana Agr Conf ... Proceedings. USAID [*United States Agency for International Development*]. Ghana Agriculture Conference [*A publication*]

Proc US Natl Mus ... Proceedings. United States National Museum [*A publication*]

Proc US Nat Mus ... Proceedings. United States National Museum [*A publication*]

Proc Ussher Soc ... Proceedings. Ussher Society [*A publication*]

Proc Utah Acad Sci ... Proceedings. Utah Academy of Sciences, Arts, and Letters [*A publication*]

Proc Utah Acad Sci Arts Lett ... Proceedings. Utah Academy of Sciences, Arts, and Letters [*A publication*]

PROCVAL ... Validation Procedures Library [*Social Security Administration*]

Proc Vertebr Pest Conf ... Proceedings. Vertebrate Pest Conference [*A publication*]

Proc Veterans Adm Spinal Cord Inj Conf ... Proceedings. Veterans Administration Spinal Cord Injury Conference [*A publication*]

Proc Vib Probl ... Proceedings of Vibration Problems [*A publication*]

Proc VIC Weeds Conf ... Proceedings. Victorian Weeds Science Society [*A publication*] (APTA)

Proc Virchow-Pirquet Med Soc ... Proceedings. Virchow-Pirquet Medical Society [*A publication*]

Proc Virgil Soc ... Proceedings. Virgil Society [*A publication*]

Proc Vol Bakish Mater Corp Publ ... Proceedings Volume. Bakish Materials Corporation. Publication [*A publication*]

Proc Wash Anim Nutr Conf ... Proceedings. Washington Animal Nutrition Conference [*A publication*]

Proc Wash State Entomol Soc ... Proceedings. Washington State Entomological Society [*A publication*]

Proc Wash State Univ Int Particleboard/Compos Mater Ser ... Proceedings. Washington State University International Particleboard/Composite Materials Series [*A publication*]

Proc Wash State Univ Int Symp Particleboard ... Proceedings. Washington State University International Symposium on Particleboard [*A publication*]

Proc Wash State Univ Symp Particleboard ... Proceedings. Washington State University Symposium on Particleboard [*A publication*]

Proc Wash St Ent Soc ... Proceedings. Washington State Entomological Society [*A publication*]

Proc Wash St Hort Ass ... Proceedings. Washington State Horticultural Association [*A publication*]

Proc Weed Soc NSW ... Proceedings. Weed Society of New South Wales [*A publication*] (APTA)

Proc West Can Weed Control Conf ... Proceedings. Western Canadian Weed Control Conference [*A publication*]

Proc West Chapter Int Shade Tree Conf ... Proceedings. Western Chapter. International Shade Tree Conference [*A publication*]

Proc West Eur Conf Photosyn ... Proceedings. Western Europe Conference on Photosynthesis [*A publication*]

Proc West For Conserv Ass ... Proceedings. Western Forestry Conference. Western Forestry and Conservation Association [*A publication*]

Proc West Found Vertebr Zool ... Proceedings. Western Foundation of Vertebrate Zoology [*A publication*]

Proc West Pharmacol Soc ... Proceedings. Western Pharmacology Society [*A publication*]

Proc West Poult Dis Conf ... Proceedings. Western Poultry Disease Conference [*A publication*]

Proc West Poult Dis Conf Poult Health Symp ... Proceedings. Western Poultry Disease Conference and Poultry Health Symposia [*United States*] [*A publication*]

Proc West Snow Conf ... Proceedings. Western Snow Conference [*A publication*]

Proc West Soc Weed Sci ... Proceedings. Western Society of Weed Science [*A publication*]

Proc West Virginia Acad Sci ... Proceedings. West Virginia Academy of Science [*A publication*]

Proc Wis Hist Soc ... Proceedings. Wisconsin State Historical Society [*A publication*]

Proc Wkly Semin Neurol ... Proceedings. Weekly Seminar in Neurology [*A publication*]

Proc Wld For Congr ... Proceedings. World Forestry Congress [*A publication*]

Proc Wld Orchid Conf ... Proceedings. World Orchid Conference [*A publication*]

Proc Wood Pole Inst Colo State Univ ... Proceedings. Wood Pole Institute. Colorado State University [*A publication*]

Proc World Congr Agr Res ... Proceedings. World Congress of Agricultural Research [*A publication*]

Proc World Congr Fertil Steril ... Proceedings. World Congress on Fertility and Sterility [*A publication*]

Proc World Congr Gastroenterol ... Proceedings. World Congress of Gastroenterology [*A publication*]

Proc World For Congr ... Proceedings. World Forestry Congress [*A publication*]

Proc World Pet Congr ... Proceedings. World Petroleum Congress [*A publication*]

Proc World Poultry Congr ... Proceedings. World Poultry Congress [*A publication*]

Proc W Va Acad Sci ... Proceedings. West Virginia Academy of Science [*A publication*]

Proc Yorks Geol Soc ... Proceedings. Yorkshire Geological Society [*England*] [*A publication*]

Proc Yorkshire Geol Soc ... Proceedings. Yorkshire Geological Society [*A publication*]

Proc Zool Soc ... Proceedings. Zoological Society [*A publication*]

Proc Zool Soc (Calcutta) ... Proceedings. Zoological Society (Calcutta) [*A publication*]

Proc Zool Soc Lond ... Proceedings. Zoological Society of London [*A publication*]

PROD .... Office of Production [*National Security Agency*]

PROD .... Photographic Retrieval from Optical Disk

PROD .... Prisoner Rehabilitation on Discharge [*A publication*] (APTA)

PROD .... Produce

PROD .... Product [*or Production*] (AABC)

PROD .... Professional Drivers Council for Safety and Health

PROD .... Professional Over-the-Road Drivers [*Part of Teamsters Union*]

PRODAC... Programmed Digital Automatic Control [*Data processing*]

Prod Aggregates GB ... Production of Aggregates in Great Britain [*A publication*]

Prod Agric Fr ... Producteur Agricole Francais [*A publication*]

PRODAN .. Propionyl(dimethylamino)naphthalene [*Organic chemistry*]

Prod Anim ... Produzione Animale [*A publication*]

PRODASE ... Protein Database

Prod Aust ... Productivity Australia [*A publication*]

PRODC ...... Production Command [*Army*]

Proden .... Proyecto de Desarrollo Nacional [*Project for National Development*] [*Chile*] (PPW)

Prod Eng ... Product Engineering [*A publication*]

Prod Eng (Cleveland) ... Production Engineering (Cleveland) [*A publication*]

Prod Eng (Lond) ... Production Engineer (London) [*A publication*]

Prod Engng ... Production Engineering [*A publication*]

Prod Engr ... Production Engineer [*London*] [*A publication*]

Pr Odes Gidrometeorol Inst ... Pratsi Odes'kogo Gidrometeorologichnogo Institutu [*A publication*]

Prod Finish ... Product Finishing [*Cincinnati*] [*A publication*]

Prod Finish (Cinci) ... Product Finishing (Cincinnati) [*A publication*]

Prod Finish (Cincinnati) ... Products Finishing (Cincinnati) [*A publication*]

Prod Finish (Lond) ... Product Finishing (London) [*A publication*]

Prod G Am J ... Producers Guild of America. Journal [*A publication*]

Prod Invent Manage ... Production and Inventory Management [*A publication*]

Prod and Inventory Manage ... Production and Inventory Management [*A publication*]

PRODISCO ... Producers Distributing Corporation

Prod Lait Mod ... Production Laitiere Moderne [*A publication*]

Prod Liability Int ... Product Liability International [*A publication*]

Prod Liab Int ... Product Liability International [*A publication*]

Prod Liab Int'l ... Product Liability International [*A publication*] (DLA)

Prod Liab Rep ... Product Liability Reporter [*Commerce Clearing House*] [*A publication*] (DLA)

Prod Liab Rep CCH ... Product Liability Reporter. Commerce Clearing House [*A publication*]

Prod Manage ... Production Management [*A publication*]

Prod Market ... Product Marketing [*A publication*]

Prod Marketing ... Produce Marketing [*A publication*]

Prod Miner Serv Fom Prod Miner Avulso ... Producao Mineral Servico de Fomento da Producao Mineral. Avulso [*A publication*]

Prod Miner Serv Fom Prod Miner Bol ... Producao Mineral Servico de Fomento da Producao Mineral. Boletim [*A publication*]

Prod Mkt ... Product Marketing [*A publication*]
Prod Mktg ... Product Marketing [*A publication*]
Prod Mon... Producers Monthly [*United States*] [*A publication*]
Prodn .... Production
Prodn Engnr ... Production Engineer [*A publication*]
Prodn J ...... Production Journal [*A publication*]
PRODON ... Production
PRO DOS ... Pro Dose [*For a Dose*] [*Pharmacy*]
Prod Pharm ... Produits Pharmaceutiques [*France*] [*A publication*]
Prod Probl Pharm ... Produits et Problemes Pharmaceutiques [*A publication*]
Prod Prod Bull Natl Coal Board Min Dep ... Production and Productivity Bulletin. National Coal Board. Mining Department [*A publication*]
Prod Proj Trends Bldg ... Products, Projects, and Trends in Building [*A publication*] (APTA)
Prod Publ Assoc Off Seed Certifying Agencies ... Production Publication. Association of Official Seed Certifying Agencies [*A publication*]
Prod Publ Int Crop Impr Ass ... Production Publication. International Crop Improvement Association [*A publication*]
PRODR ..... Producer
Prod Res Rep US Dep Agric ... Production Research Report. United States Department of Agriculture [*A publication*]
Prod Res Rep US Dep Agric Sci Educ Adm ... Production Research Report. United States Department of Agriculture. Science and Education Administration [*A publication*]
Prod Rev .... Producers' Review [*A publication*] (APTA)
Prod with Safety ... Production with Safety [*A publication*] (APTA)
Prod Safety & Liab Rep ... Product Safety and Liability Reporter [*A publication*] (DLA)
Prod Safety & Liab Rep BNA ... Product Safety and Liability Reporter. Bureau of National Affairs [*A publication*]
Prod Technol ... Productivity and Technology [*A publication*]
Prod Tech (Osaka) ... Production and Technique (Osaka) [*Japan*] [*A publication*]
Prod Tech (Suita) ... Production and Technique (Suita) [*Japan*] [*A publication*]
Produccion Anim ... Produccion Animal [*A publication*]
Producers R ... Producers' Review [*A publication*] (APTA)
Producers' Rev ... Producers' Review [*A publication*]
Product Eng ... Product Engineering [*A publication*]
Product et Gestion ... Production et Gestion [*A publication*]
Production ... Production Engineering [*A publication*]
PRODUCTN ... Production
Product Res Dev ... Product Research and Development [*A publication*]
Produits Pharm ... Produits et Problemes Pharmaceutiques [*A publication*]
PRODUTAS ... Proceed on Duty Assigned [*Military*]
PRODVAL ... Product Validation (MCD)
Prod Veg Cereale Plante Teh ... Productia Vegetala. Cereale si Plante Tehnice [*A publication*]
Prod Veg Mec Agric ... Productia Vegetala. Mecanizarea Agriculturii [*A publication*]
Prod Yb FAO ... Production Yearbook FAO [*Food and Agriculture Organization*] [*A publication*]
PROE .... Programme Regional Oceanien de l'Environnement [*South Pacific Regional Environmental Programme - SPREP*] (EAIO)
Proefstn Akkerbouw Lelystad Versl Interprov Proeven ... Proefstation voor de Akkerbouw Lelystad. Verslagen van Interprovinciale Proeven [*A publication*]
Proefstn Akkerbouw (Wageningen) Versl Interprov Proeven ... Proefstation voor de Akkerbouw (Wageningen). Verslagen van Interprovinciale Proeven [*A publication*]
Proektn Nauchno-Issled Inst Ural Promstroiniiproekt Tr ... Proektnyi i Nauchno-Issledovatel'skii Institut "Ural'skii Promstroiniiproekt." Trudy [*A publication*]
Pro Engr..... Professional Engineer [*A publication*] (APTA)
Pro Ex .... Protein Exchange [*Dietetics*]
PROEXPA ... Promotora Espanola de Exportadores Alimentarios [*Trade association*] [*Spain*] (EY)
PROEXPO ... Fondo de Promocion de Exportaciones [*Export Promotion Fund*] [*Colombia*]
PROF........ Peace Research Organization Fund
PROF......... Personal Radio Operators Federation [*Inactive*] (EA)
PROF......... Profanity [*FBI standardized term*]
PROF......... Profession [*or Professional*]
PROF......... Professional Investors Insurance Group, Inc. [*NASDAQ symbol*] (NQ)
PROF......... Professional Office System
PROF......... Professor (EY)
Prof .... Profile
PROF......... Pupil Registering and Operational Filing [*Data processing*]
PROFAC... Propulsive Fluid Accumulator
Prof Admin ... Professional Administration [*A publication*]
Prof Admin ... Professional Administrator [*A publication*]
PROFAGTRANS ... Proceed by First Available Government Transportation [*Military*]
Pro Fam Inf ... Pro Familia Informationen [*A publication*]
PROFAT ... Projet des Francophones de l'Atlantique [*Canada*]
Prof Build... Professional Builder [*A publication*]

Prof Build Apartm Bus ... Professional Builder and Apartment Business [*A publication*]
Prof Builder & Apt Bus ... Professional Builder and Apartment Business [*A publication*]
Prof Builder/Apt Bus ... Professional Builder and Apartment Business [*A publication*]
Prof Burd ... Commemoratio Professorum Burdigalensium [*of Ausonius*] [*Classical studies*] (OCD)
Prof Camera ... Professional Camera [*A publication*]
Prof Corp ... Proffatt on Private Corporations in California [*A publication*] (DLA)
Prof Corp Guide (P-H) ... Professional Corporation Guide (Prentice-Hall, Inc.) [*A publication*] (DLA)
PROFCY ... Proficiency
Prof Eng..... Professional Engineer
Prof Eng (Pretoria) ... Professional Engineer (Pretoria) [*A publication*]
Prof Engr ... Professional Engineer [*A publication*]
Prof Eng (Wash DC) ... Professional Engineer (Washington, DC) [*A publication*]
Professional Eng ... Professional Engineer [*A publication*] (APTA)
Profession Med ... Profession Medicale [*A publication*]
Professions et Entr ... Professions et Entreprises [*A publication*]
PROFESSL ... Professional
PROFFIS .. Professional Filler System [*Military*]
Prof Flashes ... Professional Flashes [*A publication*]
Prof Geog... Professional Geographer [*A publication*]
Prof Geogr ... Professional Geographer [*A publication*]
Prof Geologist ... Professional Geologist [*A publication*]
PROFILE ... [*A*] programming language (CSR)
Profile .... Profiles [*A publication*]
PROFILE ... Programmed Functional Indices for Laboratory Evaluation [*RAND Corp.*]
Profile Med Pract ... Profile of Medical Practice [*A publication*]
PROFILES ... Personal Reflection on Family Life and Employment Stressors [*Psychology*]
Profiles Hosp Mark ... Profiles in Hospital Marketing [*A publication*]
Profils Econ Nord-Pas-De-Calais ... Profils de l'Economie Nord-Pas-De-Calais [*A publication*]
Prof Inferm ... Professioni Infermieristiche [*A publication*]
PROFIS..... Programminformationssystem Sozialwissenschaften [*Informationszentrum Sozialwissenschaften*] [*Federal Republic of Germany*] [*Defunct*] [*Information service or system*] (CRD)
PROFIT .... Program for Financed Insurance Techniques
PROFIT .... Programmed Reviewing, Ordering, and Forecasting Inventory Technique
PROFIT .... Propulsion Flight Control Integration Technology (MCD)
Prof Jur...... Proffatt on Trial by Jury [*A publication*] (DLA)
PROFL.... Professional
Prof Med Assist ... Professional Medical Assistant [*A publication*]
Prof Not ..... Proffatt on Notaries [*A publication*] (DLA)
Prof Nurse ... Professional Nurse [*A publication*]
Prof Nurs Home ... Professional Nursing Home [*A publication*]
Prof Nutr... Professional Nutritionist [*A publication*]
Prof Officer ... Professional Officer [*A publication*]
PROFP ...... Proficiency Pay [*Military*]
Prof Pap Deputy Minist Miner Resour (Saudi Arabia) ... Professional Papers. Deputy Ministry for Mineral Resources (Saudi Arabia) [*A publication*]
Prof Pap Geol Surv ... Professional Papers. United States Geological Survey [*A publication*]
Prof Pap Ser Fla Dep Nat Resour Mar Res Lab ... Professional Papers Series. Florida Department of Natural Resources. Marine Research Laboratory [*A publication*]
Prof Pap US Geol Surv ... Professional Papers. United States Geological Survey [*A publication*]
Prof Photogr ... Professional Photographer [*A publication*]
Prof Print... Professional Printer [*A publication*]
Prof Psycho ... Professional Psychology [*A publication*]
Prof Regulation N ... Professional Regulation News [*A publication*]
Prof Rpt ... Professional Report [*A publication*]
PROFS ...... Professional Office System [*IBM Corp.*]
PROFS ...... Program for Regional Observing and Forecasting Services [*Boulder, CO*] [*Department of Commerce*] (GRD)
PROFS ...... Prototype Regional Observation and Forecasting Service [*National Oceanic and Atmospheric Administration*] (GRD)
Prof Saf...... Professional Safety [*A publication*]
Prof Safety .. Professional Safety [*A publication*]
Prof Sanit Manage ... Professional Sanitation Management [*A publication*]
Prof Wills .. Proffatt on Wills [*A publication*] (DLA)
PROG .... Prognosis [*or Prognostication*] (AAG)
PROG .... Program (KSC)
PROG .... Programmer [*or Programming*]
PROG .... Progress (AABC)
Prog.......... Progressive [*A publication*]
Prog Aeronaut Sci ... Progress in Aeronautical Science [*A publication*]
Prog Aerosp Sci ... Progress in Aerospace Sciences [*A publication*]
Prog Agric ... Progresso Agricolo [*A publication*]
Prog Agric Ariz ... Progressive Agriculture in Arizona [*A publication*]
Prog Agric Vitic ... Progres Agricole et Viticole [*France*] [*A publication*]

Prog Agri Fr ... Progres Agricole de France [*A publication*]
Prog Allerg ... Progress in Allergy [*A publication*]
Prog Allergol Jpn ... Progress of Allergology in Japan [*A publication*]
Prog Allergy ... Progress in Allergy [*A publication*]
Prog Anal At Spectrosc ... Progress in Analytical Atomic Spectroscopy [*A publication*]
Prog Anal Chem ... Progress in Analytical Chemistry [*A publication*]
Prog Anat... Progress in Anatomy [*A publication*]
Prog Androl ... Progres en Andrologie [*A publication*]
Prog Anesthesiol ... Progress in Anesthesiology [*A publication*]
Prog Anim Biometeorol ... Progress in Animal Biometeorology [*A publication*]
Prog Appl Mater Res ... Progress in Applied Materials Research [*A publication*]
Prog Appl Microcirc ... Progress in Applied Microcirculation [*A publication*]
Prog Arch... Progressive Architecture [*A publication*]
Prog Archit ... Progressive Architecture [*A publication*]
Prog Astronaut Aeronaut ... Progress in Astronautics and Aeronautics [*A publication*]
Prog Astronaut Rocketry ... Progress in Astronautics and Rocketry [*A publication*]
Prog Astronaut Sci ... Progress in the Astronautical Sciences [*A publication*]
Prog At Med ... Progress in Atomic Medicine [*A publication*]
Prog Batteries Sol Cell ... Progress in Batteries and Solar Cells [*A publication*]
Prog Behav Modif ... Progress in Behavior Modification [*A publication*]
Prog Biochem Biophys ... Progress in Biochemistry and Biophysics [*People's Republic of China*] [*A publication*]
Prog Biochem Pharmacol ... Progress in Biochemical Pharmacology [*A publication*]
Prog Biochim ... Progressi in Biochimica [*A publication*]
Prog Biocybern ... Progress in Biocybernetics [*A publication*]
Prog Biol Sci Relat Dermatol ... Progress in the Biological Sciences in Relation to Dermatology [*A publication*]
Prog Biomass Convers ... Progress in Biomass Conversion [*A publication*]
Prog Biometeorol ... Progress in Biometeorology [*A publication*]
Prog Biometeorol Div A ... Progress in Biometeorology. Division A. Progress in Human Biometeorology [*Netherlands*] [*A publication*]
Prog Biometeorol Div B ... Progress in Biometeorology. Division B. Progress in Animal Biometeorology [*A publication*]
Prog Bioorg Chem ... Progress in Bioorganic Chemistry [*A publication*]
Prog Biophys Biophys Chem ... Progress in Biophysics and Biophysical Chemistry [*A publication*]
Prog Biophys Mol Biol ... Progress in Biophysics and Molecular Biology [*A publication*]
Prog Biophys and Mol Biol ... Progress in Biophysics and Molecular Biology [*A publication*]
PROG BK ... Programmed Book [*Publishing*]
Prog Boron Chem ... Progress in Boron Chemistry [*A publication*]
Prog Bot..... Progress in Botany [*A publication*]
Prog Bot Fortschr Bot ... Progress in Botany-Fortschritt der Botanik [*A publication*]
Prog Brain Res ... Progress in Brain Research [*A publication*]
Prog Build ... Progressive Builder [*A publication*]
Prog Cancer Res Ther ... Progress in Cancer Research and Therapy [*A publication*]
Prog Cardiol ... Progress in Cardiology [*A publication*]
Prog Cardiovasc Dis ... Progress in Cardiovascular Diseases [*A publication*]
Prog Ceram Sci ... Progress in Ceramic Science [*A publication*]
Prog Chem Fats ... Progress in the Chemistry of Fats and Other Lipids [*A publication*]
Prog Chem Fats Other Lipids ... Progress in the Chemistry of Fats and Other Lipids [*A publication*]
Prog Chem Fibrinolysis Thrombolysis ... Progress in Chemical Fibrinolysis and Thrombolysis [*A publication*]
Prog Chem Toxicol ... Progress in Chemical Toxicology [*A publication*]
Prog Clin Biochem Med ... Progress in Clinical Biochemistry and Medicine [*A publication*]
Prog Clin Biol Res ... Progress in Clinical and Biological Research [*A publication*]
Prog Clin Cancer ... Progress in Clinical Cancer [*A publication*]
Prog Clin Immunol ... Progress in Clinical Immunology [*A publication*]
Prog Clin Neurophysiol ... Progress in Clinical Neurophysiology [*A publication*]
Prog Clin Pathol ... Progress in Clinical Pathology [*A publication*]
Prog Clin Pharm ... Progress in Clinical Pharmacy [*A publication*]
Prog Colloid Polym Sci ... Progress in Colloid and Polymer Science [*A publication*]
Prog Coll & Polym Sci ... Progress in Colloid and Polymer Science [*A publication*]
Prog Combus Sci Technol ... Progress in Combustion Science and Technology [*A publication*]
Prog Concept Control ... Progress in Conception Control [*A publication*]
Prog Contracep Delivery Syst ... Progress in Contraceptive Delivery Systems [*A publication*]
Prog Cosmic Ray Phys ... Progress in Cosmic Ray Physics [*A publication*]
Prog Crit Care Med ... Progress in Critical Care Medicine [*A publication*]
Prog Cryog ... Progress in Cryogenics [*A publication*]
Prog Cryst Growth Charact ... Progress in Crystal Growth and Characterization [*A publication*]
Prog Cryst Phys ... Progress in Crystal Physics [*A publication*]
PROGDEV ... Program Device (KSC)
Prog Dielectr ... Progress in Dielectrics [*A publication*]

Prog Drug Metab ... Progress in Drug Metabolism [*A publication*]
Prog Drug Res ... Progress in Drug Research [*A publication*]
Prog Educ .. Progress in Education [*A publication*] (APTA)
Prog Educ .. Progressive Education [*A publication*]
Prog Educ (Poona) ... Progress of Education (Poona) [*India*] [*A publication*]
Prog Elem Part Cosmic Ray Phys ... Progress in Elementary Particle and Cosmic Ray Physics [*A publication*]
Prog Endocr Res Ther ... Progress in Endocrine Research and Therapy [*A publication*]
Prog Energy Combust Sci ... Progress in Energy and Combustion Science [*A publication*]
Prog Explor Tuberc ... Progres de l'Exploration de la Tuberculose [*A publication*]
Prog Exp Pers Res ... Progress in Experimental Personality Research [*A publication*]
Prog Exp Tumor Res ... Progress in Experimental Tumor Research [*A publication*]
Prog Extr Metall ... Progress in Extractive Metallurgy [*A publication*]
Prog Ex Tum ... Progress in Experimental Tumor Research [*A publication*]
Prog F .... Progressive Farmer and Farm Woman [*A publication*]
Prog Farmer West ... Progressive Farmer for the West [*A publication*]
Prog Farming ... Progressive Farming [*A publication*]
Prog Farming/Farmer ... Progressive Farming/Farmer [*A publication*]
Prog Fire Retard Ser ... Progress in Fire Retardancy Series [*A publication*]
Prog Fish-C ... Progressive Fish-Culturist [*A publication*]
Prog Fish-Cult ... Progressive Fish-Culturist [*A publication*]
Prog Food Nutr Sci ... Progress in Food and Nutrition Science [*A publication*]
Prog Fotogr (Barcelona) ... Progresso Fotografico (Barcelona) [*A publication*]
Prog Fotogr (Milan) ... Progresso Fotografico (Milan) [*A publication*]
Prog Gastroenterol ... Progress in Gastroenterology [*A publication*]
Prog Geogr ... Progress in Geography [*A publication*]
Prog Groc... Progressive Grocer [*A publication*]
Prog Grocer ... Progressive Grocer [*A publication*]
Prog Gynecol ... Progress in Gynecology [*A publication*]
Prog Heat Mass Transf ... Progress in Heat and Mass Transfer [*A publication*]
Prog Heat Mass Transfer ... Progress in Heat and Mass Transfer [*A publication*]
Prog Hematol ... Progress in Hematology [*A publication*]
Prog Hemostasis Thromb ... Progress in Hemostasis and Thrombosis [*A publication*]
Prog Hemost Thromb ... Progress in Hemostasis and Thrombosis [*A publication*]
Prog High Polym ... Progress in High Polymers [*A publication*]
Prog High Temp Phys Chem ... Progress in High Temperature Physics and Chemistry [*A publication*]
Prog Histochem Cytochem ... Progress in Histochemistry and Cytochemistry [*A publication*]
Prog Hort... Progressive Horticulture [*India*] [*A publication*]
Prog Hortic ... Progressive Horticulture [*A publication*]
Prog Hum Biometeorol ... Progress in Human Biometeorology [*A publication*]
Prog Hum Nutr ... Progress in Human Nutrition [*A publication*]
Prog Immunobiol Stand ... Progress in Immunobiological Standardization [*A publication*]
Prog Ind Microbiol ... Progress in Industrial Microbiology [*A publication*]
Prog Infrared Spectrosc ... Progress in Infrared Spectroscopy [*A publication*]
Prog Inorg Chem ... Progress in Inorganic Chemistry [*A publication*]
Prog Instr Bul ... Programmed Instruction Bulletin [*A publication*] (APTA)
Prog Instr & Ed Tech ... Programmed Instruction and Educational Technology [*A publication*] (APTA)
Prog Learn ... Programmed Learning and Educational Technology [*A publication*]
Prog Learn Disabil ... Progress in Learning Disabilities [*A publication*]
Prog Leukocyte Biol ... Progress in Leukocyte Biology [*A publication*]
PROGLIB ... Production Program Library [*Social Security Administration*]
Prog Lipid Res ... Progress in Lipid Research [*A publication*]
Prog Liver Dis ... Progress in Liver Diseases [*A publication*]
Prog Low Temp Phys ... Progress in Low Temperature Physics [*A publication*]
PRO GM ... Pro Grand Master [*Freemasonry*]
Prog Mater Sci ... Progress in Materials Science [*A publication*]
Prog Mat Sc ... Progress in Materials Science [*A publication*]
Prog Med ... Progres Medical [*A publication*]
Prog Med Chem ... Progress in Medicinal Chemistry [*A publication*]
Prog Med Ge ... Progress in Medical Genetics [*A publication*]
Prog Med Genet ... Progress in Medical Genetics [*A publication*]
Prog Med (Istanbul) ... Progressus Medicinae (Istanbul) [*A publication*]
Prog Med Parasitol Jpn ... Progress in Medical Parasitology in Japan [*A publication*]
Prog Med Psychosom ... Progres en Medecine Psychosomatique [*A publication*]
Prog Med (Rome) ... Progresso Medico (Rome) [*A publication*]
Prog Med (Tokyo) ... Progress in Medicine (Tokyo) [*A publication*]
Prog Med Vi ... Progress in Medical Virology [*A publication*]
Prog Med Virol ... Progress in Medical Virology [*A publication*]
Prog Met Phys ... Progress in Metal Physics [*A publication*]
PROGMG ... Programming
Prog Mol Subcell Biol ... Progress in Molecular and Subcellular Biology [*A publication*]
Prog Mutat Res ... Progress in Mutation Research [*A publication*]
Prog Neurobiol ... Progress in Neurobiology [*A publication*]
Prog Neurobiol (NY) ... Progress in Neurobiology (New York) [*A publication*]
Prog Neurobiol (Oxf) ... Progress in Neurobiology (Oxford) [*A publication*]

Prog Neurol Psychiatry ... Progress in Neurology and Psychiatry [*A publication*]
Prog Neurol Surg ... Progress in Neurological Surgery [*A publication*]
Prog Neuropathol ... Progress in Neuropathology [*A publication*]
Prog Neuro-Psychopharmacol ... Progress in Neuro-Psychopharmacology [*A publication*]
Prog Neuro-Psychopharmacol & Biol Psychiatry ... Progress in Neuro-Psychopharmacology and Biological Psychiatry [*A publication*]
Prog Neuropsychopharmacol Biol Psychiatry ... Progress in Neuropsychopharmacology and Biological Psychiatry [*A publication*]
PROGNO ... Prognosen-Trends-Entwicklungen [*Forecasts-Trends-Developments*] [*Society for Business Information*] [*Information service or system*] (IID)
Prog Non Destr Test ... Progress in Non-Destructive Testing [*A publication*]
Prog Notes Walter Reed Army Med Cent ... Progress Notes. Walter Reed Army Medical Center [*A publication*]
Prog Nucleic Acid Res ... Progress in Nucleic Acid Research [*A publication*]
Prog Nucleic Acid Res Mol Biol ... Progress in Nucleic Acid Research and Molecular Biology [*A publication*]
Prog Nucl Energy ... Progress in Nuclear Energy [*England*] [*A publication*]
Prog Nucl Energy Anal Chem ... Progress in Nuclear Energy. Analytical Chemistry [*A publication*]
Prog Nucl Energy New Ser ... Progress in Nuclear Energy. New Series [*A publication*]
Prog Nucl Energy Ser 1 ... Progress in Nuclear Energy. Series 1. Physics and Mathematics [*A publication*]
Prog Nucl Energy Ser 2 ... Progress in Nuclear Energy. Series 2. Reactors [*A publication*]
Prog Nucl Energy Ser 3 ... Progress in Nuclear Energy. Series 3. Process Chemistry [*A publication*]
Prog Nucl Energy Ser 4 ... Progress in Nuclear Energy. Series 4. Technology, Engineering, and Safety [*A publication*]
Prog Nucl Energy Ser 5 ... Progress in Nuclear Energy. Series 5. Metallurgy and Fuels [*A publication*]
Prog Nucl Energy Ser 6 ... Progress in Nuclear Energy. Series 6 [*England*] [*A publication*]
Prog Nucl Energy Ser 8 ... Progress in Nuclear Energy. Series 8. The Economics of Nuclear Power Including Administration and Law [*A publication*]
Prog Nucl Energy Ser 9 ... Progress in Nuclear Energy. Series 9 [*England*] [*A publication*]
Prog Nucl Energy Ser 10 ... Progress in Nuclear Energy. Series 10. Law and Administration [*A publication*]
Prog Nucl Energy Ser 11 ... Progress in Nuclear Energy. Series 11. Plasma Physics and Thermonuclear Research [*A publication*]
Prog Nucl Energy Ser 12 ... Progress in Nuclear Energy. Series 12. Health Physics [*A publication*]
Prog Nucl Energy Ser 7 Med Sci ... Progress in Nuclear Energy. Series 7. Medical Sciences [*A publication*]
Prog Nucl Magn Reson Spectrosc ... Progress in Nuclear Magnetic Resonance Spectroscopy [*A publication*]
Prog Nucl Med ... Progress in Nuclear Medicine [*A publication*]
Prog Nucl Phys ... Progress in Nuclear Physics [*A publication*]
Prog Nucl Tech Instrum ... Progress in Nuclear Techniques and Instrumentation [*Netherlands*] [*A publication*]
Prog Nurse ... Progressive Nurse [*A publication*]
Prog Obstet Gynecol ... Progres en Obstetrique et Gynecologie [*A publication*]
Prog Oceanogr ... Progress in Oceanography [*A publication*]
Prog Odontostomatol ... Progres Odonto-Stomatologique [*A publication*]
PROGOFOP ... Program of Operation [*Data processing*]
Prog Ophtalmol ... Progres en Ophtalmologie [*A publication*]
Prog Ophthalmol Otolaryngol ... Progress in Ophthalmology and Otolaryngology [*A publication*]
Prog Opt .... Progress in Optics [*A publication*]
Prog Org Chem ... Progress in Organic Chemistry [*A publication*]
Prog Org Coat ... Progress in Organic Coatings [*A publication*]
Prog Org Coatings ... Progress in Organic Coatings [*A publication*]
Prog Oto-Rhino-Laryngol ... Progres en Oto-Rhino-Laryngologie [*A publication*]
Prog Part Nucl Phys ... Progress in Particle and Nuclear Physics [*England*] [*A publication*]
Prog Pediatr Hematol/Oncol ... Progress in Pediatric Hematology/Oncology [*A publication*]
Prog Pediatr Pueric ... Progresos de Pediatria y Puericultura [*A publication*]
Prog Pediatr Radiol ... Progress in Pediatric Radiology [*Switzerland*] [*A publication*]
Prog Pediatr Surg ... Progress in Pediatric Surgery [*A publication*]
Prog Perfum Cosmet ... Progressive Perfumery and Cosmetics [*A publication*]
Prog Photogr ... Progress in Photography [*A publication*]
Prog Phys .. Progress of Physics [*East Germany*] [*A publication*]
Prog Phys Geogr ... Progress in Physical Geography [*A publication*]
Prog Physiol Psychol ... Progress in Physiological Psychology [*A publication*]
Prog Physiol Sci (Engl Transl Usp Fiziol Nauk) ... Progress in Physiological Sciences (English Translation of Uspekhi Fiziologicheskikh Nauk) [*A publication*]
Prog Physiol Sci (USSR) ... Progress in Physiological Sciences (USSR) [*A publication*]
Prog Phys Org Chem ... Progress in Physical Organic Chemistry [*A publication*]

Prog Phys Ther ... Progress in Physical Therapy [*A publication*]
Prog Phytochem ... Progress in Phytochemistry [*A publication*]
Prog Plann ... Progress in Planning [*A publication*]
Prog Plast .. Progressive Plastics [*A publication*]
Prog Polym Sci ... Progress in Polymer Science [*A publication*]
Prog Powder Metall ... Progress in Powder Metallurgy [*A publication*]
Prog Protozool Proc Int Congr Protozool ... Progress in Protozoology. Proceedings. International Congress on Protozoology [*A publication*]
Prog Psychiatr Drug Treat ... Progress in Psychiatric Drug Treatment [*A publication*]
Prog Psychobiol Physiol Psychol ... Progress in Psychobiology and Physiological Psychology [*A publication*]
Prog Quantum Electron ... Progress in Quantum Electronics [*A publication*]
Prog Radiat Ther ... Progress in Radiation Therapy [*A publication*]
Prog Radiopharmacol ... Progress in Radiopharmacology [*A publication*]
Progr Agr ... Progresso Agricolo [*A publication*]
Progr Agr Ariz ... Progressive Agriculture in Arizona [*A publication*]
Progr Agr Vitic ... Progres Agricole et Viticole [*A publication*]
Progr Allergy ... Progress in Allergy [*A publication*]
Program Abstr Am Soc Parasitol Annu Meet ... Program and Abstracts. American Society of Parasitologists. Annual Meeting [*A publication*]
Program Aid US Dep Agric ... Program Aid. United States Department of Agriculture [*A publication*]
Program Am Dairy Sci Assoc Annu Meet Branch Abstr ... Program. American Dairy Science Association. Annual Meeting and Branch Abstracts [*A publication*]
Program Autom Libr Inf Syst ... Program. Automated Library and Information Systems [*England*] [*A publication*]
Program and Comput Software ... Programming and Computer Software [*A publication*]
Program Learn and Educ Technol ... Programmed Learning and Educational Technology [*A publication*]
Programmed Learning ... Programmed Learning and Educational Technology [*A publication*]
Programming and Comput Software ... Programming and Computer Software [*A publication*]
Programming Lang Ser ... Programming Languages Series [*A publication*]
Programmirovan ... Programmirovanie. Akademija Nauk SSSR [*A publication*]
Program News Comput Libr ... Program. News of Computers in Libraries [*A publication*]
Program Notes Assoc Univ Programs Health Adm ... Program Notes. Association of University Programs in Health Administration [*A publication*]
Program/Proc Natl Horsemen's Semin ... Program/Proceedings. National Horsemen's Seminar [*A publication*]
Progr Bull Alberta Univ Ext Dept ... Progress Bulletin. Alberta University Extension Department [*A publication*]
Progr Card ... Progress in Cardiovascular Diseases [*A publication*]
Progr Cardiovas Dis ... Progress in Cardiovascular Diseases [*A publication*]
Progr Clin Cancer ... Progress in Clinical Cancer [*A publication*]
Progr Contr Eng ... Progress in Control Engineering [*A publication*]
Progr Coop Centroamer Mejor Maiz ... Programa Cooperativo Centroamericano para el Mejoramiento del Maiz [*A publication*]
Prog React Kinet ... Progress in Reaction Kinetics [*A publication*]
Prog Rech Cancer ... Progres dans les Recherches sur le Cancer [*A publication*]
Prog Rech Exp Tumeurs ... Progres de la Recherche Experimentale des Tumeurs [*A publication*]
Prog Rech Pharm ... Progres des Recherches Pharmaceutiques [*A publication*]
Prog Rep Agric Exp Stn Univ Idaho ... Progress Report. Agricultural Experiment Station. University of Idaho [*A publication*]
Prog Rep Ala Agric Exp Stn ... Progress Report. Alabama Agricultural Experiment Station [*A publication*]
Prog Rep Ariz Exp Stn ... Progress Report. Arizona Experiment Station [*A publication*]
Prog Rep Clovers Spec Purpose Legumes Res ... Progress Report. Clovers and Special Legumes Research [*A publication*]
Prog Rep Colo Exp Stn ... Progress Report. Colorado Experiment Station [*A publication*]
Prog Rep Dom Apiarist Canad Dep Agric ... Progress Report. Dominion Apiarist. Canadian Department of Agriculture [*A publication*]
Prog Rep Exp Stn Colorado State Univ ... Colorado State University. Experiment Station. Progress Report [*A publication*]
Prog Rep Exp Stns (Tanzania) ... Progress Reports. Experiment Stations (Tanzania) [*A publication*]
Prog Rep Gen Rev World Coal Ind ... Progress Report. General Review of the World Coal Industry [*A publication*]
Prog Rep KY Agric Exp Stn ... Progress Report. Kentucky Agricultural Experiment Station [*A publication*]
Prog Rep Minist Agric Fish Fd Exp Husb Fms Exp Hort Stns ... Progress Report. Ministry of Agriculture, Fisheries, and Food. Experimental Husbandry Farms and Experimental Horticulture Stations [*A publication*]
Prog Rep NM Bur Mines Miner Resour ... Progress Report. New Mexico Bureau of Mines and Mineral Resources [*A publication*]
Prog Rep Nucl Energy Res Jpn ... Progress Report. Nuclear Energy Research in Japan [*A publication*]

Prog Rep PA Agric Exp Stn ... Progress Report. Pennsylvania Agricultural Experiment Station [*A publication*]
Prog Reprod Biol ... Progress in Reproductive Biology [*A publication*]
Prog Reprod Biol Med ... Progress in Reproductive Biology and Medicine [*A publication*]
Prog Rep Texas Agric Exp Stn ... Progress Report. Texas Agricultural Experiment Station [*A publication*]
Prog Res..... Progress thru Research [*A publication*]
Progres Arch ... Progressive Architecture [*A publication*]
Progres Ed ... Progressive Education [*A publication*]
Prog Res Emphysema Chronic Bronchitis ... Progress in Research in Emphysema and Chronic Bronchitis [*A publication*]
Progres Med (Paris) ... Progres Medical (Paris) [*A publication*]
Progreso Med (Habana) ... Progreso Medico (Habana) [*A publication*]
Prog Respir Res ... Progress in Respiration Research [*A publication*]
Progres Scientif ... Progres Scientifique [*A publication*]
Progressive Archit ... Progressive Architecture [*A publication*]
Progressive Archre ... Progressive Architecture [*A publication*]
Progress in Math ... Progress in Mathematics [*A publication*]
Progres Soc 3e Ser ... Progres Social. Troisieme Serie [*A publication*]
Progresso Fotogr ... Progresso Fotografico [*A publication*]
Progress Organic Coatings ... Progress in Organic Coatings [*A publication*]
Progress in Particle and Nuclear Phys ... Progress in Particle and Nuclear Physics [*A publication*]
Progress in Phys ... Progress in Physics [*A publication*]
Progress Phytochem ... Progress in Phytochemistry [*A publication*]
Progressv ... Progressive [*A publication*]
Progres Techn ... Progres Technique [*A publication*]
Progres Vet ... Progres Veterinaire [*A publication*]
Progr Hemat ... Progress in Hematology [*A publication*]
Progr Hum Geogr ... Progress in Human Geography. International Review of Current Research [*A publication*]
Progr Indust Microbiol ... Progress in Industrial Microbiology [*A publication*]
Progr Learn Educ Technol ... Programmed Learning and Educational Technology [*A publication*]
Progr Mater Sci ... Progress in Materials Science [*A publication*]
Progr Math (Allahabad) ... Progress of Mathematics (Allahabad) [*A publication*]
Progr Med (Paris) ... Progres Medical (Paris) [*A publication*]
Progr Med Virol ... Progress in Medical Virology [*A publication*]
Progr Neurol Psychiat ... Progress in Neurology and Psychiatry [*A publication*]
Progr Nucl Energy Ser 6 ... Progress in Nuclear Energy. Series 6. Biological Sciences [*A publication*]
Progr Nucl Energy Ser 8 Econ ... Progress in Nuclear Energy. Series 8. Economics [*A publication*]
Progr Nucl Energy Ser 10 Law Admin ... Progress in Nuclear Energy. Series 10. Law and Administration [*A publication*]
Progr Nucl Energy Ser 5 Met Fuels ... Progress in Nuclear Energy. Series 5. Metallurgy and Fuels [*A publication*]
Progr Nucl Energy Ser 1 Phys Math ... Progress in Nuclear Energy. Series 1. Physics and Mathematics [*A publication*]
Progr Nucl Energy Ser 11 Plasma Phys Thermonucl Res ... Progress in Nuclear Energy. Series 11. Plasma Physics and Thermonuclear Research [*A publication*]
Progr Nucl Energy Ser 3 Process Chem ... Progress in Nuclear Energy. Series 3. Process Chemistry [*A publication*]
Progr Nucl Energy Ser 2 Reactors ... Progress in Nuclear Energy. Series 2. Reactors [*A publication*]
Progr Nucl Energy Ser 4 Technol Eng ... Progress in Nuclear Energy. Series 4. Technology and Engineering [*A publication*]
Progr Offic Journee Interreg Recolte Mec Mais-Grain ... Programme Officiel. Journee Interregionale de Recolte Mechanique du Mais-Grain [*A publication*]
Progr Particle and Nuclear Phys ... Progress in Particle and Nuclear Physics [*A publication*]
Progr Phys ... Progress in Physics [*A publication*]
Progr Physiol Psych ... Progress in Physiological Psychology [*A publication*]
Progr Phys Sci ... Progress of Physical Sciences [*A publication*]
Progr Plast ... Progressive Plastics [*A publication*]
Progr Polymer Sci ... Progress in Polymer Science [*A publication*]
Progr Powder Met ... Progress in Powder Metallurgy [*A publication*]
Progr Prob Statist ... Progress in Probability and Statistics [*A publication*]
Progr Rep Cereal Breed Lab ... Progress Report. Cereal Breeding Laboratory [*A publication*]
Progr Rep Colo State Univ Agr Exp Sta ... Progress Report. Colorado State University. Agricultural Experiment Station [*A publication*]
Progr Rep Conn Agr Exp Sta ... Progress Report. Connecticut Agricultural Experiment Station [*A publication*]
Progr Rep Idaho Agr Res ... Progress Report. Idaho Agricultural Research [*A publication*]
Progr Rep KY Agr Exp Sta ... Progress Report. Kentucky Agricultural Experiment Station [*A publication*]
Progr Rep PA Agric Exp Sta ... Progress Report. Pennsylvania State University. Agricultural Experiment Station [*A publication*]
Progr Rep PA State Univ Agr Exp Sta ... Progress Report. Pennsylvania State University. Agricultural Experiment Station [*A publication*]

Progr Rep Ser Ala Agr Exp Sta ... Progress Report Series. Alabama Agricultural Experiment Station [*A publication*]
Progr Rep Tex Agr Exp Sta ... Progress Report. Texas Agricultural Experiment Station [*A publication*]
Progr Rep Tohoku Agr Exp Sta ... Progress Report. Tohoku Agricultural Experiment Station [*A publication*]
Progr Rep Univ Nebr Coll Agr Dept Agr Econ ... Progress Report. University of Nebraska. College of Agriculture. Department of Agricultural Economics [*A publication*]
Progr Rev For Prod Lab (Ottawa) ... Program Review. Forest Products Laboratory (Ottawa) [*A publication*]
Progr Rev For Prod Lab (Vancouver) ... Program Review. Forest Products Laboratory (Vancouver) [*British Columbia, Canada*] [*A publication*]
Progr Rubber Technol ... Progress of Rubber Technology [*A publication*]
Progr Sci Comput ... Progress in Scientific Computing [*A publication*]
Progr Soc ... Progres Social [*A publication*]
Progr Stiintei ... Progresele Stiintei [*A publication*]
Progr Surg ... Progress in Surgery [*A publication*]
Progr Ter Clin ... Progresos de Terapeutica Clinica [*A publication*]
Progr Theoret Phys ... Progress of Theoretical Physics [*A publication*]
Progr Theoret Phys Suppl ... Progress of Theoretical Physics. Supplement [*A publication*]
Prog Sci..... Progres Scientifique [*France*] [*A publication*]
Prog Sci Technol Rare Earths ... Progress in the Science and Technology of the Rare Earths [*A publication*]
Prog Semicond ... Progress in Semiconductors [*A publication*]
Prog Sens Physiol ... Progress in Sensory Physiology [*A publication*]
Prog Sep Purif ... Progress in Separation and Purification [*A publication*]
Prog Solid State Chem ... Progress in Solid State Chemistry [*England*] [*A publication*]
Prog Stereochem ... Progress in Stereochemistry [*A publication*]
Prog Surf Membr Sci ... Progress in Surface and Membrane Science [*A publication*]
Prog Surf Sci ... Progress in Surface Science [*A publication*]
Prog Surg... Progress in Surgery [*A publication*]
Prog Tech... Progres Technique [*A publication*]
Prog Technol ... Progress in Technology [*United States*] [*A publication*]
Prog Tekhnol Mashinostr ... Progressivnaya Tekhnologiya Mashinostroeniya [*A publication*]
Prog Ter..... Progresso Terapeutico [*A publication*]
Prog Theor Biol ... Progress in Theoretical Biology [*A publication*]
Prog Theor Org Chem ... Progress in Theoretical Organic Chemistry [*A publication*]
Prog Theor Phys ... Progress of Theoretical Physics [*A publication*]
Prog Theor Phys Suppl ... Progress of Theoretical Physics. Supplement [*A publication*]
Prog Thin-Layer Chromatogr Relat Methods ... Progress in Thin-Layer Chromatography and Related Methods [*A publication*]
Prog Top Cytogenet ... Progress and Topics in Cytogenetics [*A publication*]
Prog T Phys ... Progress of Theoretical Physics [*A publication*]
Prog Underwater Sci ... Progress in Underwater Science [*A publication*]
Prog Vac Microbalance Tech ... Progress in Vacuum Microbalance Techniques [*A publication*]
PROGVAL ... Validation Program Library [*Social Security Administration*]
Progve Agric Ariz ... Progressive Agriculture in Arizona [*A publication*]
Progve Fmg ... Progressive Farming [*A publication*]
Prog Vet ... Progresso Veterinario [*A publication*]
Prog Vet Microbiol Immunol ... Progress in Veterinary Microbiology and Immunology [*A publication*]
Prog Virol Med ... Progres en Virologie Medicale [*A publication*]
Prog Water Technol ... Progress in Water Technology [*A publication*]
PROH........ Prohibit
PROH........ Prohibition [*FBI standardized term*]
PROH........ Promoting Health [*A publication*]
Prohib .... Prohibited
PROI......... President of the Royal Institute of Oil Painters [*British*]
PRO-IF...... Personal Radio Operators International Federation [*Formerly, ARC*] (EA)
PROIMREP ... Proceed Immediately - Report for Purpose Indicated [*Military*]
Pro Indian Soc of Internat L ... Proceedings of the Conference. Indian Society of International Law [*New Delhi, India*] [*A publication*] (DLA)
Proizv Obuc ... Proizvodstvennoe Obucenie [*A publication*]
Proizvod Elektrostali ... Proizvodstvo Elektrostali [*A publication*]
Proizvod Issled Stalei Splavov ... Proizvodstvo i Issledovanie Stalei i Splavov [*A publication*]
Proizvod Koksa ... Proizvodstvo Koksa [*A publication*]
Proizvod Krupnykh Mash ... Proizvodstvo Krupnykh Mashin [*A publication*]
Proizvod Nauchno-Issled Inst Inzh Izyskaniyam Stroit Tr ... Proizvodstvennyi i Nauchno-Issledovatel'skii Institut po Inzhenernym Izyskaniyam v Stroitel'stve Trudy [*A publication*]
Proizvod Smaz Mater ... Proizvodstvo Smazochnykh Materialov [*A publication*]
Proizvod Stochnye Vody ... Proizvodstvennye Stochnye Vody [*A publication*]
Proizvod Svarnykh Besshovnykh Trub ... Proizvodstvo Svarnykh i Besshovnykh Trub [*A publication*]
Proizvod Trub ... Proizvodstvo Trub [*A publication*]
Proizvod Vysokokach Prokata ... Proizvodstvo Vysokokachestvennogo Prokata [*A publication*]

Proizv Shin RTI i ATI ... Proizvodstvo Shin Rezinotekhnicheskikh i Asbestotekhnicheskikh Izdelii [*A publication*]
PROJ......... Project (AFM)
PROJ......... Projectile (AFM)
PROJ......... Projector
Proj Civ Trav Econ ... Projet. Civilisation, Travail, Economie [*France*] [*A publication*]
PROJECT ... Project Engineering Control
Project Hist Biobibliog ... Project for Historical Biobibliography [*A publication*]
Project IUCN/Wld Wildl Fund ... Project. International Union for Conservation of Nature. World Wildlife Fund. Joint Project Operations [*A publication*]
Projektrapp Grafiska Forskningslab ... Projektrapport. Grafiska Forskningslaboratoriet [*A publication*]
PROJENGR ... Project Engineer
PROJID .... Project Identification [*Data processing*]
PROJMGR ... Project Manager [*Military*]
PROJMGRASWS ... Project Manager, Antisubmarine Warfare Systems
PROJMGRFBM ... Project Manager, Fleet Ballistic Missile [*Navy*]
PROJMGRSMS ... Project Manager, Surface Missile Systems [*Navy*]
Proj RADAMBRAS Levantamento Recursos Nat ... Projeto RADAMBRASIL [*Radar da Amazonia, Brasil*]. Levantamento de Recursos Naturais [*A publication*]
Proj Rep Victoria Minist Conserv Environ Stud Program ... Victoria. Ministry for Conservation. Environmental Studies Program. Project Report [*A publication*] (APTA)
PROJTRNS ... Project Transition [*DoD*]
PROL........ Priority Requirement Objective List (AFM)
PROL........ Prologue
PRO L........ Province Laws (DLA)
PROLAMAT ... Programming Languages for Machine Tools [*Conference*]
PROLAN... Processed Language [*Data processing*]
PROLDI.... Annual Research Reviews. Prolactin [*A publication*]
Prolif........ Proliferative [*or Proliferation*]
PROLLAP ... Professional Library Literature Acquisition Program
PRO LOC et TEM ... Pro Loco et Tempore [*For the Place and Time*] [*Latin*] (ROG)
PROLOG .. Program Logistics (NG)
PROLOG .. Programming in Logic [*Programing language*] [*1970*]
Pro LR .... Professional Liability Reporter [*A publication*]
PROLT...... Procurement Lead Time
P Rom .... Papers in Romance [*A publication*]
PROM .... Passive Range of Motion [*Medicine*]
PROM .... Pockels Readout Optical Modulator
PROM .... Premature [*or Prolonged*] Rupture of Membranes [*Gynecology*]
PROM .... Program, Resources, Objectives, Management [*Air Force Systems Command technique*]
PROM .... Programmable Read-Only Memory [*Data processing*]
PROM .... Progressive Range of Motion [*Medicine*]
PROM .... Promenade [*Maps and charts*]
Prom dk ..... Promenade Deck [*of a ship*] (DS)
PROM .... Prominent
Prom .... Promissory [*A publication*] (DLA)
PROM .... Promontory
PROM .... Promote [*or Promotion*] (AFM)
Prom .... Promotion [*A publication*]
PROM .... Promulgate (AABC)
Pro-MACE ... Prednisone, Methotrexate with Leucovorin, Adriamycin, Cyclophosphamide, Epipodophyllin [*Etoposide, VP-16*] [*Antineoplastic drug regimen*]
PROMACE-MOPP ... Procarbazine, Methotrexate, Adriamycin, Cyclophosphamide, Etoposide, Mustargen [*Nitrogen mustard*], Oncovin [*Vincristine*], Procarbazine, Prednisone [*Antineoplastic drug regimen*]
PROMADATA ... Promotions Marketing and Advertising Data [*A publication*]
Prom Aerod ... Promyshlennaya Aerodinamika [*USSR*] [*A publication*]
PROMAG ... Production Management Action Group [*British*]
Pro Managr ... Program Manager [*A publication*]
PROMAP ... Program for the Refinement of the Materiel Acquisition Process [*Army*] (AABC)
Pro Med..... Pro Medico [*A publication*]
Prom Ekon Byull Sov Nar Khoz Ivanov Ekon Adm Raiona ... Promyshlenno-Ekonomicheskii Byulleten Sovet Narodnogo Khozyaistva Ivanovskogo Ekonomicheskogo Administrativnogo Raiona [*A publication*]
Prom Energ ... Promyshlennaya Energetika [*A publication*]
Pro Met....... Pro Metal [*A publication*]
PROMETHEUS ... Program for European Traffic with Highest Efficiency and Unprecedented Safety (ECON)
Prometheus ... Prometheus. Revista Quadrimestrale di Studi Classici [*A publication*]
Promet-Meteorol Fortbild ... Promet-Meteorologische Fortbildung [*West Germany*] [*A publication*]
PROMEX ... Productivity Measurement Experiment [*National Institute of Standards and Technology*]
PROMIM ... Programmable Multiple Ion Monitor
PROMIS ... Problem-Oriented Medical Information System [*Computerized patient-management system*]
PROMIS ... Project-Oriented Management Information System

PROMIS ... Prosecutor's Management Information System [*Law Enforcement Assistance Administration*]
PROML..... Promulgate
PROMO..... Promotion [*Slang*] (DSUE)
Promoclim A Actual Equip Tech ... Promoclim A. Actualites, Equipement, Technique [*France*] [*A publication*]
Promoclim E ... Promoclim E. Etudes Thermiques et Aerauliques [*A publication*]
Promoclim Ind Therm Aerauliques ... Promoclim. Industries Thermiques et Aerauliques [*A publication*]
Prom Org Sint ... Promyslennyj Organiceskij Sintez [*A publication*]
Promot Dent ... Promotion Dentaire [*A publication*]
Promot Health ... Promoting Health [*A publication*]
Promozione Soc ... Promozione Sociale [*A publication*]
PROMPT ... Production, Reviewing, Organizing, and Monitoring of Performance Techniques (BUR)
PROMPT ... Program Monitoring and Planning Techniques (IEEE)
PROMPT ... Program to Record Official Mail Point-to-Point Times [*Postal Service program*]
PROMPT ... Project Management and Production Team Technique [*Data processing*]
PROMPT ... Project Reporting Organization and Management Planning Technique
PROMS..... Procurement Management System (MCD)
PROMS..... Program Monitoring System (MCD)
PROMS..... Programmable Read Only Memory System [*Data processing*]
PROMS..... Projectile Measurement System [*Data processing*] [*Army*]
Prom Sint Kauch ... Promyshlennost Sinteticheskogo Kauchuka [*A publication*]
Promst Arm ... Promyshlennost Armenii [*A publication*]
Prom-St Arm Sov Nar Khoz Arm SSR Tekh-Ekon Byull ... Promyshlennost Armenii Sovet Narodnogo Khozyajstva Armyanskoj SSR Tekhniko-Ekonomicheskij Byulleten [*A publication*]
Promst Beloruss ... Promyshlennost Belorussii [*A publication*]
Prom-St Khim Reaktiv Osobo Chist Veshchestv ... Promyshlennost Khimicheskikh Reaktivov i Osobo Chistykh Veshchestv [*USSR*] [*A publication*]
Promst Khim Reakt Osobo Chist Veshchestv ... Promyshlennost Khimicheskikh Reaktivov i Osobo Chistykh Veshchestv [*A publication*]
Promst Lub Volokon ... Promyshlennost Lubyanykh Volokon [*A publication*]
Prom-St Org Khim ... Promyshlennost Organicheskoi Khimii [*USSR*] [*A publication*]
Prom Stroit ... Promyshlennoe Stroitel'stvo [*A publication*]
Prom Stroit Inzh Sooruzh ... Promyshlennoe Stroitel'stvo i Inzhenernye Sooruzheniya [*A publication*]
Promst Stroit Mater ... Promyshlennost Stroitel'nykh Materialov [*A publication*]
PROMT .... Precision Optimized Measurement Time [*Spectroscopy*]
PROMT .... Predicasts Overviews of Marketing and Technology [*Business database*]
PROMT .... Programmable Miniature Message Terminal (MCD)
Prom Teplotekh ... Promyshlennaya Teplotekhnika [*Ukrainian SSR*] [*A publication*]
Pro Mundi Vita ... Pro Mundi Vita Bulletin [*A publication*]
Pro Mundi Vita Africa Dossier ... Pro Mundi Vita Dossiers. Africa [*A publication*]
Pro Mundi Vita Asia-Australasia Dossier ... Pro Mundi Vita Dossiers. Asia and Australasia [*A publication*]
Pro Mundi Vita Europe N Am Dossier ... Pro Mundi Vita Dossiers. Europe/ North America [*A publication*]
PROMUS ... Provincial-Municipal Simulator [*Computer-based urban management system*]
PROMY .... Promissory (ROG)
Prom Zagryaz Vodoemov ... Promyshlennye Zagryazneniya Vodoemov [*A publication*]
PRON........ Patriotyczny Ruch Odrodzenia Narodowego [*Patriotic Movement for National Rebirth*] [*Poland*] (EY)
PRON....... Procurement Request Order Number [*Army*] (AABC)
PRON....... Pronation
PRON....... Pronominal (ADA)
PRON....... Pronoun
PRON....... Pronounced
PRON....... Pronunciation (ROG)
Pro Nat ...... Pro Natura [*A publication*]
Pro-Nica .... Professionals - Nicaragua (EA)
Pr ONPMP ... Prace ONPMP [*Osrodek Naukowo-Produkcyjny Materialow Polprzewodnikowych*] [*A publication*]
PRONTO .. Program for Numeric Tool Operation [*Data processing*]
PRONTO .. Programmable Network Telecommunications Operating System
prooem .... Prooemium (BJA)
PROOF..... Precision Recording (Optical) of Fingerprints
PROOF..... Projected Return on Open Office Facilities [*Computer program*]
proOLMC ... Pro-Opiolipomelanocortin [*Endocrinology*]
PROP........ Performance Review for Operating Programs (BUR)
PROP........ Pilot Repair Overhaul and Provisioning (MUGU)
PROP........ Planetary Rocket Ocean Platform
PROP........ Prerelease Orientation Program [*Reformatory program*]
PROP........ Preservation of the Rights of Prisoners [*An association*] [*British*]

PROP........ Production Operators Corp. [*NASDAQ symbol*]   (NQ)
PROP........ Profit Rating of Projects
PROP........ Propaganda   (AFM)
Prop .... Propagate [*Botany*]
PROP........ Propellant   (KSC)
PROP........ Propeller
PROP........ Proper
PROP........ Propertius [*Roman poet, c. 29BC*] [*Classical studies*]   (ROG)
PROP........ Property
Prop .... Property [*A publication*]
PROP........ Property Release Option Program [*HUD*]
PROP........ Proportional   (KSC)
PROP........ Proposal   (AAG)
PROP........ Proposed   (AFM)
PROP........ Proposition
PROP........ Proprietor
PROP........ Propulsion   (AAG)
PROP........ Propylthiouracil [*Also, PT, PTU*] [*Thyroid inhibitor*]
PROPA...... Propagation   (FAAC)
PROPAC.... Progressive Political Action Committee [*Defunct*]   (EA)
PROPAC.... Prospective Payment Assessment Commission [*Washington, DC*]   (EGAO)
PROPAKASIA ... International Food Processing and Packaging Technology Exhibition and Conference for South East Asia   (TSPED)
PROPAL ... Proportional
Propane Can ... Propane Canada [*A publication*]
PRO-PAY ... Proficiency Pay [*Military*]
Prop & Comp ... Property and Compensation Reports [*A publication*]   (DLA)
Prop & Comp R ... Property and Compensation Reports [*A publication*]   (DLA)
Propellants Explos ... Propellants and Explosives [*A publication*]
Property Mthly Rev ... Property Monthly Review [*A publication*]
Property Tax J ... Property Tax Journal [*A publication*]
Prop & Ex .. Propellents, Explosives, and Pyrotechnics [*A publication*]
PROPH ..... Prophylactic
PROPHET ... Proactive Rehabilitation of Outside Plant Using Heuristic Expert Techniques [*GTE computer software*]
Proph Sanit Mor ... Prophylaxie Sanitaire et Morale [*A publication*]
PROPIN..... Proprietary Information
PROPL..... Proportional
Prop Law.... Property Lawyer [*1826-30*] [*A publication*]   (DLA)
Prop Law Bull ... Property Law Bulletin [*A publication*]   (DLA)
Prop Law NS ... Property Lawyer, New Series [*England*] [*A publication*]   (DLA)
PROPLING ... Propelling
PROPLOSS ... Propagation Loss   (NVT)
PROPLT ... Propellant   (NASA)
PROPN ..... Proportion   (MSA)
PROPON .. Proportion   (ROG)
Proposte Soc ... Proposte Sociali
PROPR...... Proprietary   (ROG)
PROPR...... Proprietor   (EY)
Propr Agric ... Propriete Agricole [*A publication*]
PROPRE ... Property Press   (DLA)
PROPRSS ... Proprietress   (ROG)
PROPTRY ... Proprietary [*Freight*]
PROPUL... Propulsion
Pro Quer .... Pro Querente [*For the Plaintiff*] [*Latin*]   (ILCA)
PROR .... Predicted Orbit
Pr Or .... Przeglad Orientalistyczny [*A publication*]
PRORA ...... Programs for Research on Romance Authors
PRO RAT AET ... Pro Ratione Aetatis [*According to Age*] [*Pharmacy*]
PrOrChr .... Proche-Orient Chretien [*Jerusalem*] [*A publication*]
PRO RECT ... Pro Recto [*Rectal*] [*Pharmacy*]
PROREP ... Proceed Ship, Command Station Reporting Duty or Purpose Indicated [*Military*]
Pr O S .... Princeton Oriental Series [*A publication*]
PROS........ Professional Reactor Operator Society   (EA)
PROS........ Proscenium [*Theater term*]   (DSUE)
PROS........ Prosecution   (ROG)
PROS........ Prosody
PROS......... [*The*] Prospect Group, Inc. [*New York, NY*] [*NASDAQ symbol*]   (NQ)
Pros........... Prospetti [*A publication*]
PROS........ Prosthetic   (AABC)
PROS........ Prostitute   (DSUE)
PROS........ Prostitutes Rights Organisation for Sexworkers [*Australia*]
PROS........ Prostrate
PROSAM ... Programmed Single-Axis Mount [*Military camera*]
PROSAMO ... Planned Release of Selected and Modified Organisms [*British*]
Pros Atty.... Prosecuting Attorney   (DLA)
PRosC........ Rosemont College, Rosemont, PA [*Library symbol*] [*Library of Congress*]   (LCLS)
PROSE ...... Problem Solution Engineering [*Programming language*] [*Data processing*]   (CSR)
PROSEA ... Plant Resources of South-East Asia [*A publication*]
PROSECON ... Prosecution   (ROG)
PROSI .... Procedure Sign [*Aviation*]   (FAAC)
PROSI .... Public Relations Office of the Sugar Industry
PROSIG .... Procedure Signal [*Navy*]
PROSIGN ... Procedure Sign [*Military*]   (AABC)

PROSIM .... Production System Simulator [*Data processing*]
PROSINE ... Procedure Sign [*Military*]
Pros J Natl Dist Att'y A ... Prosecutor. Journal of the National District Attorneys Association [*A publication*]
ProSoc........ Prometheus Society   (EA)
Pro Soc Water Treat Exam ... Proceedings. Society for Water Treatment and Examination [*A publication*]
Prosop Att ... Prosopographia Attica [*A publication*]   (OCD)
prosp.......... Prospectively   (DLA)
PROSPECT ... Proponent Sponsored Engineer Corps Training [*Army Corps of Engineers*]
Prospect West Aust ... Prospect Western Australia [*A publication*]
Prospettiva ... Prospettiva. Rivista d'Arte Antica e Moderna [*A publication*]
Prospett Merid ... Prospettive Meridionali [*A publication*]
Prosp R ...... Prospective Review [*A publication*]
PROSPRO ... Process Systems Program
Pr Osr Badaw-Rozwoj Elektron Prozniowej ... Prace Osrodka Badawczo-Rozwojowego Elektroniki Prozniowej [*A publication*]
Pr Osr Nauk Prod Mater Polprzewodn ... Prace Osrodek Naukowo-Produkcyjny Materialow Polprzewodnikowych [*A publication*]
Pr Osrodka Badawczo-Rozwojowego Przetwornikow Obrazu ... Prace Osrodka Badawczo-Rozwojowego Przetwornikow Obrazu [*A publication*]
Pr Osrodka Badaw Rozwojowego Elektron Prozniowej ... Prace Osrodka Badawczo-Rozwojowego Elektroniki Prozniowej [*A publication*]
PROST ...... Prostitute [*or Prostitution*] [*FBI standardized term*]
Prostagland ... Prostaglandins [*A publication*]
Prostaglandins Leukotrienes Med ... Prostaglandins, Leukotrienes, and Medicine [*A publication*]
Prostaglandins Med ... Prostaglandins and Medicine [*A publication*]
Prostaglandins Relat Lipids ... Prostaglandins and Related Lipids [*A publication*]
Prostaglandins Ther ... Prostaglandins and Therapeutics [*A publication*]
PROSTH... Prosthesis
Prosthet and Orthotics Int ... Prosthetics and Orthotics International [*A publication*]
Prosthet Orthot Int ... Prosthetics and Orthotics International [*A publication*]
PROSY...... People's Republic of South Yemen   (BJA)
PROT .... Protect [*or Protection*]   (MSA)
PROT .... Protective Life Corp. [*NASDAQ symbol*]   (NQ)
PROT .... Protein
PROT .... Protest   (ROG)
PROT .... Protestant
Prot .... Protestantesimo [*A publication*]
PROT .... Proteus [*Bacterium*]
PROT .... Protinus [*Speedily*] [*Pharmacy*]
Prot .... Protocol   (DLA)
PROT .... Prototype
PROT .... Protractor   (AAG)
PROTA...... Protection Actual [*Probability for avoidance of ship*]
PROTA...... Protoplasma [*Austria*] [*A publication*]
ProTACA... Procurement Technical Assistance Cooperative Agreement Program [*DoD*]
Prot Aer ..... Protection Aerienne [*A publication*]
PROTAP... Professional Opportunities through Academic Partnership [*National War College*]
PROTAP... Protonotary Apostolic [*Roman Catholic*]
Prot Civ Secur Ind ... Protection Civile et Securite Industrielle [*A publication*]
Prot CJ....... Protocol on the Statute of the European Communities Court of Justice [*A publication*]   (DLA)
Prot Coat Met ... Protective Coatings on Metals [*A publication*]
PROTCT... Protective   (AAG)
PROTEC... Protection
Prot Ecol... Protection Ecology [*A publication*]
PROTECT ... Probabilities Recall Optimizing the Employment of Calibration Time   (KSC)
Protein Abnorm ... Protein Abnormalities [*A publication*]
Protein Nucl Acid Enzyme ... Protein Nucleic Acid Enzyme [*A publication*]
Protein Synth ... Protein Synthesis [*A publication*]
Protein Synth Ser Adv ... Protein Syntheses: A Series of Advances [*A publication*]
PRO TEM ... Pro Tempore [*For the Time Being*] [*Latin*]
PRO TEM et LOC ... Pro Tempore et Loco [*For the Time and Place*] [*Latin*]   (ROG)
Prot Epis His M ... Protestant Episcopal Church. Historical Magazine [*A publication*]
Protes Dent ... Protesista Dental [*A publication*]
Protet Stomatol ... Protetyka Stomatologiczna [*A publication*]
PROTEUS ... [*A*] programming language   (CSR)
PROTEUS ... Project to Research Objects Theories, Extraterrrestrials, and Unusual Sightings   (EA)
PROTEUS ... Propulsion Research and Open Water Testing of Experimental Underwater Systems   (MCD)
PROTHROM ... Prothrombin [*Hematology*]
Proth Werkst Kd ... Prothetik und Werkstoffkunde [*A publication*]
Protides Biol Fluids Proc Colloq ... Protides of the Biological Fluids. Proceedings of the Colloquium [*Belgium*] [*A publication*]
Protides Biol Fluids Proc Colloq (Bruges) ... Protides of the Biological Fluids. Proceedings of the Colloquium (Bruges) [*A publication*]

PROTIMEREP ... Proceed in Time Report Not Later Than [*Hour and/or date indicated*] [*Military*]
Prot Met .... Protection of Metals [*A publication*]
Prot Metals ... Protection of Metals [*A publication*]
Prot Met (USSR) ... Protection of Metals (Union of Soviet Socialist Republics) [*A publication*]
PROTN ..... Procedure Turn [*Aviation*] (FAAC)
PROTO ..... Protoporphyrin [*Hematology*]
PROTO ..... Prototype (KSC)
Protok Fischereitech ... Protokolle zur Fischereitechnik [*A publication*]
Protok OS ... Protokoly Obscego Sobranija Akademii Nauk [*A publication*]
Protoplasma Suppl ... Protoplasma Supplementum [*A publication*]
Prot PI .... Protocol on Privileges and Immunities of the European Economic Community [*A publication*] (DLA)
PROTR ...... Protractor (MSA)
Protr .... Protrepticus [*of Clemens Alexandrinus*] [*Classical studies*] (OCD)
Protsessy Khromatogr Kolonkakh ... Protsessy v Khromatograficheskikh Kolonakh [*A publication*]
Prot Vitae ... Protectio Vitae [*A publication*]
Prouchvaniya Mikroelem Mikrotorovete Bulg ... Prouchvaniya vurkhu Mikroelementite i Mikrotorovete v Bulgariya [*A publication*]
Proud Dom Pub ... Proudhon's Domaine Public [*A publication*] (DLA)
Proudf Land Dec ... United States Land Decisions (Proudfit) [*A publication*] (DLA)
PROUS ...... Proceed to a Port in Continental United States [*Military*]
PRO US EXT ... Pro Usu Externo [*For External Use*] [*Pharmacy*]
Prouty .... Prouty's Reports [*61-68 Vermont*] [*A publication*] (DLA)
Prov .... De Providentia [*of Seneca the Younger*] [*Classical studies*] (OCD)
prov .... Provedor [*Purveyor*] [*Portuguese*]
PROV .... Provencal [*Language, etc.*]
PROV .... Provence [*France*] (ROG)
PROV .... Proverb
Prov .... Proverbs [*Old Testament book*]
PROV .... Provide (KSC)
PROV .... Providence Journal-Bulletin [*A publication*]
PROV .... Provident Institute for Savings of Boston [*NASDAQ symbol*] (NQ)
PROV .... Province
Prov .... Provincia [*A publication*]
Prov .... Provincial [*A publication*]
PROV .... Provincial
PROV .... Provinciale [*Provincial*] [*Netherlands*] (EY)
Prov .... Provision [*Commission*] [*German*] [*Business term*]
PROV .... Provision [*or Provisional*] (AFM)
Prov .... Provisional Light [*Navigation signal*]
PROV .... Provost
Prov Buenos Aires Com Invest Cient Inf ... Provincia de Buenos Aires. Comision de Investigaciones Cientificas. Informes [*A publication*]
Prov Buenos Aires Com Invest Cient Mem ... Provincia de Buenos Aires. Comision de Investigaciones Cientificas. Memoria [*A publication*]
Prov Can Stat ... Statutes of the Province of Canada [*A publication*] (DLA)
Prov Cons ... De Provinciis Consularibus [*of Cicero*] [*Classical studies*] (OCD)
PROVCORPV ... Provisional Corps, Vietnam
PROVD ..... Provided
Provebruksmeld Nor Landbruksokonomiske Inst ... Provebruksmelding-Norges Landbruksokonomiske Institutt [*A publication*]
Provence Hist ... Provence Historique [*A publication*]
Provence Univ Ann Geol Mediterr ... Provence Universite. Annales. Geologie Mediterraneenne [*A publication*]
Provence Univ Lab Paleontol Hum Prehist Etud Quat Mem ... Provence Universite. Laboratoire de Paleontologie Humaine et de Prehistoire. Etudes Quaternaires. Memoire [*A publication*]
PROVER ... Procurement for Minimum Total Cost through Value Engineering and Reliability
ProvGM ..... Provincial Grand Master [*Freemasonry*]
PROVGR .... Proving Grounds
Prov Hist .... Provence Historique [*A publication*]
Provid .... De Providentia [*of Philo*] (BJA)
Providence Hosp Detroit Med Bull ... Providence Hospital of Detroit. Medical Bulletin [*A publication*]
Providence Hosp (Southfield Mich) Med Bull ... Providence Hospital (Southfield, Michigan). Medical Bulletin [*A publication*]
Providen JB ... Providence Journal-Bulletin [*A publication*]
Providen SJ ... Providence Sunday Journal [*A publication*]
Providnc J ... Providence Journal [*A publication*]
PROVIMI ... Proteins, Vitamins, and Minerals [*Dutch manufacturing company*]
Provincial Bank Can Econ R ... Provincial Bank of Canada. Economic Review [*A publication*]
Prov Inher & Gift Tax Rep CCH ... Provincial Inheritance and Gift Tax Reporter. Commerce Clearing House [*A publication*]
PROVIS .... Provision
Prov Judges J ... Provincial Judges Journal [*A publication*]
PROVMAAG ... Provisional Military Assistance Advisory Group (CINC)

PROVMAAG-K ... Provisional Military Assistance Advisory Group, Korea (CINC)
PROVMAIN ... Other Provisions Basic Orders Remain in Effect
provns .... Provisions (DLA)
PROVO ..... Proviso [*Contract clause*] (ROG)
PROVO ..... Provocateur (DSUE)
PROVO ..... Provost Marshal [*Australian*] [*World War II*] (DSUE)
PROVONS ... Provisions
provor .... Provisor [*Purveyor*] [*Spanish*]
PROVOST ... Priority Research Objectives for Vietnam Operations Support
Prov St .... Statutes, Laws, of the Province of Massachusetts [*A publication*] (DLA)
PROWDELREP ... Proceed Without Delay Report Duty or Purpose Indicated [*Military*]
PROWLER ... Programmable Robot Observer with Logical Enemy Response [*Developed by Robot Defense Systems of Thornton, CO*]
PROWORD ... Procedure Word
PROX .... Proximity (AABC)
PROX .... Proximo [*In Next Month*] [*Latin*]
PROX ACC ... Proxime Accessit [*Next in Order of Merit*] [*Latin*]
PRO-XAN ... Protein-Xanthophyll [*Alfalfa protein concentrate process*]
PROXI .... Projection by Reflection Optics of Xerographic Images (IEEE)
Proyecto Desarrollo Pesq Publ ... Proyecto de Desarrollo Pesquero. Publicacion [*A publication*]
P Roy Music ... Proceedings. Royal Musical Association [*A publication*]
P Roy S Med ... Proceedings. Royal Society of Medicine [*A publication*]
P Roy Soc A ... Proceedings. Royal Society of London. Series A. Mathematical and Physical Sciences [*A publication*]
P Roy Soc B ... Proceedings. Royal Society of London. Series B. Biological Sciences [*A publication*]
Proz .... Prozent [*or Prozentig*] [*Percent or Percentage*] [*German*]
PRP .... Pamjatniki Russkogo Prava [*A publication*]
PRP .... Panretinal Photocoagulation [*Ophthalmology*]
PRP .... Parent Rule Point (MCD)
PRP .... Parti Republicain du Progres [*Republican Progress Party*] [*Central Africa*] [*Political party*] (PD)
PRP .... Parti de la Revolution Populaire [*People's Revolutionary Party*] [*Zaire*] [*Political party*] (PD)
PRP .... Partido de Representacao Popular [*Brazil*] [*Political party*]
PRP .... Partido Republicano Portugues [*Portuguese Republican Party*] [*Political party*] (PPE)
PRP .... Partido Revolucionario Popular [*Popular Revolutionary Party*] [*Portugal*] [*Political party*] (PPE)
PRP .... Peace Resource Project (EA)
PRP .... Peak Radiated Power (CET)
PRP .... People's Redemption Party [*Nigeria*] [*Political party*] (PPW)
PRP .... People's Revolutionary Party [*Benin*] [*Political party*]
PRP .... People's Revolutionary Party [*North Vietnam*] [*Political party*]
PRP .... Peptide Recognition Protein [*Biochemistry*]
PRP .... Performance, Requirements, Practices [*Military*]
PRP .... Personnel Reliability Program [*Air Force*]
PRP .... Phantom Range Pod (MCD)
PRP .... Phase Review Package (MCD)
PRP .... Pickup-Zone Release Point
PRP .... Platelet-Rich Plasma [*Hematology*]
PRP .... Polyribitol Phosphate [*Organic chemistry*]
PRP .... Position Report Printout
PRP .... Postbuckled Rectangular Plate
PRP .... Potentially Responsible Party [*Environmental Protection Agency*]
PRP .... Power-Deployed Reserve Parachute (MCD)
PRP .... Premature-Removal Period (MCD)
PRP .... Prepare (FAAC)
PRP .... Prerigor Pressurization [*Meat processing*]
PRP .... Pressure Rate Product [*In treadmill test*]
PRP .... Primary Raynaud's Phenomenon [*Medicine*]
PrP .... Prion Protein [*Biochemistry*]
PRP .... Problem Resolution Program [*IRS*]
PRP .... Procurement Requirements Package (MCD)
PRP .... Production Readiness Plan
PRP .... Production Requirements Plan
PRP .... Production Reserve Policy
PRP .... Profit-Related Pay [*Economics*]
PRP .... Program Requirements Package [*Data processing*]
PRP .... Program Review Panel [*Army*] (AABC)
PRP .... Progress in Radiopharmacology [*Elsevier Book Series*] [*A publication*]
PRP .... Progressive Rework Plan
PRP .... Progressive Rubella Panencephalitis [*Medicine*]
PRP .... Proliferative Retinopathy Photocoagulation
PRP .... Proline-Rich Protein [*Biochemistry*]
PRP .... Proper Return Port [*Shipping*]
PRP .... Prospective Reimbursement Plan [*Medicaid*]
PRP .... Protease-Resistant Prion [*Medicine*]
PrP .... Protease-Resistant Protein [*Microbiology*]
PrP .... Protein Phosphatase [*An enzyme*]
PRP .... Pseudorandom Pulse
PRP .... Psychotic Reaction Profile [*Psychology*]
PRP .... Public Relations Personnel [*Navy*]
PRP .... Pulse Recurrence [*or Repetition*] Period (CET)
PRP .... Purchase Request Package [*Shipping*] (MCD)

PRP............ Purple (MSA)
PRP............ Purpose (MSA)
PRP............ Reformed Presbyterian Theological Seminary, Pittsburgh, PA [*OCLC symbol*] (OCLC)
PRPA........ Professional Race Pilots Association [*Later, USARA*] (EA)
PRPB........ Parti de la Revolution Populaire du Benin [*Benin People's Revolutionary Party*] [*Political party*] (PD)
PRPC........ Public Relations Policy Committee [*NATO*] (NATG)
PRPE........ Prairie Pacific Energy Corp. [*NASDAQ symbol*] (NQ)
PRPF........ Planar Radial Peaking Factor [*Network analysis*] (IEEE)
PRPG........ Proportioning
Pr/Ph........ Pristane/Phytane Ratio [*Environmental science*]
PRPHL...... Peripheral
Pr Phys Soc L ... Proceedings. Physical Society of London [*A publication*]
Pr PIT....... Prace PIT [*Przemyslowego Instytutu Telekomunikacji*] [*A publication*]
PRPL........ PACOM [*Pacific Command*] Reconnaissance Priority List (CINC)
PRPL........ People's Democratic Republic of Laos
PRPL........ Procurement Repair Parts List (AAG)
PRPLN...... Propulsion (MSA)
PRPLNT ... Propellant (KSC)
PRPLT...... Propellant (MSA)
PRPNE...... Propane [*Organic chemistry*]
PrPol........ Prace Polonistyczne [*Warsaw*] [*A publication*]
PRPOOS ... Plankton Rate Processes in Oligotrophic Oceans [*Cooperative research project*]
Pr Poznan Tow Przyj Nauk Wydz Nauk Roln Lesn ... Prace-Poznanskie Towarzystwo Przyjaciol Nauk. Wydzial Nauk Rolniczych i Lesnych [*A publication*]
PRPP........ Phosphoribosylpyrophosphate [*Biochemistry*]
PRPP........ Phosphorylribose Pyrophosphate [*Biochemistry*]
PRPP........ Pseudoresidual Plot Program
PRPQ........ Programming Request for Price Quotation [*Data processing*]
Pr PR........ Praeter Propter [*About, Nearly*] [*Latin*] (ROG)
Pr Preh Soc ... Proceedings. Prehistoric Society [*A publication*]
Pr Primer ... Prairie Primer [*A publication*]
Pr Przem Inst Elektron ... Prace Przemyslowego Instytutu Elektroniki [*A publication*]
Pr Przem Inst Elektron (Warsaw) ... Prace Przemyslowego Instytutu Elektroniki (Warsaw) [*A publication*]
Pr Przem Inst Telekomun ... Prace Przemyslowego Instytutu Telekomunikacji [*A publication*]
PRPS .... Pressure Rise per Stage (MCD)
PRPS .... Program Requirement Process Specification [*NASA*] (KSC)
PRPSA...... Petroleum Press Service [*A publication*]
PRPSB...... Progress in Polymer Science [*A publication*]
PRPSD...... Proposed (MSA)
PRPSL....... Proposal (MSA)
PRPT........ Parti Revolutionnaire du Peuple Tunisien [*Revolutionary Party of the Tunisian People*] [*Political party*] (PD)
PRPT........ Prescriptive Reading Performance Test [*Educational test*]
PRPT........ Probe Post [*A publication*]
PRPTA ...... Proceedings. Association of Asphalt Paving Technologists [*A publication*]
PRPUC...... Philippine Republic Presidential Unit Citation [*Military decoration*] (AFM)
PRPUCE ... Philippine Republic Presidential Unit Citation Emblem [*Military decoration*]
PRPYA...... Praxis der Psychotherapie [*A publication*]
PRQ........... Houston, TX [*Location identifier*] [*FAA*] (FAAL)
PRQ........... Problems of Communism [*A publication*]
PRQA........ Passenger Ride Quality Apparatus [*Public transportation*]
PRR .... Parts Replacement Request (KSC)
PRR .... Passenger Reservation Request (NVT)
PRR .... Passive Ranging RADAR
PRR .... Pawling Research Reactor
PRR .... Pennsylvania Railroad Co. [*AAR code*] [*Obsolete*]
PRR .... Performance-Related Remuneration (ADA)
PRR .... Perrine, FL [*Location identifier*] [*FAA*] (FAAL)
PRR .... Perris [*California*] [*Seismograph station code, US Geological Survey*] [*Closed*] (SEIS)
PRR .... Personnel Requirements Report [*Army*]
PRR .... Placement Revision Request
PRR .... Planning Release Record (AAG)
PRR .... Plans and Requirements Review
PRR .... Political Risk Review [*A publication*] (EAAP)
Pr R........... Practice Reports [*Quebec*] [*A publication*] (DLA)
Pr R........... Practice Reports [*Ontario*] [*A publication*] (DLA)
PRR .... Pre-Raphaelite Review [*A publication*]
PRR .... Preliminary Requirements Review [*NASA*] (KSC)
PRR .... Premature Removal Rate
PRR .... Presbyterian and Reformed Renewal Ministries International [*Formerly, PCC*] (EA)
PRR .... Presbyterian and Reformed Review [*A publication*]
PRR .... Pressure Rise Rate [*Nuclear energy*] (NRCH)
PRR .... Prism Resources Ltd. [*Vancouver Stock Exchange symbol*]
PRR .... Producer's Reliability Risk
PRR .... Production Readiness Review
PRR .... Production Research Reports
PR & R....... Professional Rights and Responsibilities

PRR .... Program Requirements Review [*NASA*] (NASA)
PRR .... Program Revision Report (KSC)
PRR .... Proline-Rich Protein [*Biochemistry*]
PRR .... Proton Relaxation Rate
PRR .... Public Relations Review [*A publication*]
PRR .... Publication Revision Request (AAG)
PRR .... Puerto Rico Reactor (NRCH)
PRR .... Puerto Rico Supreme Court Reports [*A publication*] (DLA)
PRR .... Pulse Recurrence [*or Repetition*] Rate (MUGU)
PrRA......... Academia Maria Reina, Rio Piedras, PR [*Library symbol*] [*Library of Congress*] (LCLS)
PRRA........ Puerto Rico Reconstruction Administration [*Terminated, 1955*]
Pr Rady Nauk-Tech Huty Lenina ... Prace Rady Naukowo-Technicznej Huty Imienia Lenina [*A publication*]
PRRB........ Physics Reports. Reprints Book Series [*Elsevier Book Series*] [*A publication*]
PRRB........ Provider Reimbursement Review Board [*Medicare*]
PRRC........ New Mexico Petroleum Recovery Research Center [*New Mexico Institute of Mining and Technology*] [*Research center*] (RCD)
PRRC........ Pitch/Roll Rate Changer Assembly (MCD)
PrRe......... Evangelical Seminary, Rio Piedras, PR [*Library symbol*] [*Library of Congress*] (LCLS)
PRREA ...... Philips Research Reports [*A publication*]
Pr Reg BC ... Practical Register in the Bail Court [*A publication*] (DLA)
Pr Reg Ch .. Practical Register in Chancery [*1 vol.*] [*A publication*] (DLA)
Pr Reg CP .. Practical Register in the Common Pleas [*1705-42*] [*A publication*] (DLA)
Pr Rep .... Practice Reports [*England*] [*A publication*] (DLA)
Pr Rep .... Practice Reports [*Ontario*] [*A publication*] (DLA)
Pr Rep BC ... Lowndes, Maxwell, and Pollock's English Bail Court Practice Reports [*1850-51*] [*A publication*] (DLA)
PRRFC ...... Planar Randomly Reinforced Fiber Composite
PRRI......... Puerto Rico Rum Institute [*Later, PRRPA*]
PRRM....... Presbyterian and Reformed Renewal Ministries International (EA)
PRRM....... Program Review and Resources Management [*NASA*]
PRRM........ Pulse Repetition Rate Modulation [*Data transmission*] [*Data processing*] (TEL)
Pr Roy Soc ... Proceedings. Royal Society [*A publication*]
PRRPA ...... Puerto Rico Rum Producers Association (EA)
PRR & Regs ... Commonwealth of Puerto Rico Rules and Regulations [*A publication*] (DLA)
PRRS .... Positioning Reporting Recording System (RDA)
PRRS .... Problem Reporting and Resolution System [*Military*] (CAAL)
Pr RS Med .. Proceedings. Royal Society of Medicine [*A publication*]
PR-RSV .... Rous Sarcoma Virus, Prague Strain
PRS........... Pacific Railroad Society (EA)
PRS........... Pacific Rocket Society (EA)
PRS........... Padre Resources [*Vancouver Stock Exchange symbol*]
PRS........... Pairs
PRS........... Paraiso [*California*] [*Seismograph station code, US Geological Survey*] (SEIS)
PRS........... Parametric Ruled Surface (MCD)
PRS........... Parasi [*Solomon Islands*] [*Airport symbol*] (OAG)
PRS........... Parliamentary Research Services [*British*]
PRS........... Partei fuer Renten-, Steuer-, und Soziale Gerechtigkeit [*Party for Equitable Pensions, Taxation, and Social Services*] [*Federal Republic of Germany*] [*Political party*] (PPW)
PRS........... Parti de la Revolution Socialiste [*Party of Socialist Revolution*] [*Benin*] [*Political party*]
PRS........... Parti de la Revolution Socialiste [*Party of Socialist Revolution*] [*Senegal*] [*Political party*]
PRS........... Partido de la Revolucion Socialista [*Party of the Socialist Revolution*] [*Cuba*] [*Political party*]
PRS........... Passive RADAR Surveillance [*Military*] (CAAL)
PRS........... Pattern Recognition Society (EA)
PRS........... Pattern Recognition System
PRS........... Payload Retention Subsystem [*NASA*] (NASA)
PRS........... Pennsylvania-Reading Seashore Lines [*Absorbed into Consolidated Rail Corp.*]
PRS........... Perceptual Respresentation System [*Memory*]
PRS........... Performance Rating System (OICC)
PRS........... Performing Right Society [*British*]
PRS........... Personal Recording System
PRS........... Personal Relations Survey [*Managerial skills test*]
PRS........... Personality Rating Scale [*Psychology*]
PRS........... Personnel Readiness System [*Air Force*]
PRS........... Personnel Rescue Service [*NASA*] (NASA)
PRS........... Personnel Rescue System [*NASA*] (MCD)
PRS........... Personnel Research Section [*Army*]
PRS........... Personnel Research Staff [*Department of Agriculture*]
PRS........... Perspectives in Religious Studies [*A publication*]
PRS........... Philatelic Research Society
PRS........... Philosophical Research Society (EA)
PRS........... Photo Resist Spinner
PRS........... Photographic Reconnaissance System
PRS........... Physically Restricted Status [*Military*]
PRS........... Pipe Roll Society (EA)
PRS........... Planar Rider System

PRS........... Planners Referral Service [*Information service or system*]   (EISS)
PRS........... Planning Record Sheet
PRS........... Planning Research & Systems PLC [*British*]
PRS........... Plasma Renin Substrate [*Hematology*]
PRS........... Pneumatic Reading System
PRS........... Pointing Reference System   (KSC)
PRS........... Political Reference Service Group [*Australia*]
PRS........... Population Research Service [*Information service or system*]   (IID)
PRS........... Power Reactant Subsystem [*NASA*]   (NASA)
PRS........... Power Relay Satellite
PrS............ Prairie Schooner [*A publication*]
PRS........... Prayers   (ROG)
PRS........... Precision Ranging System
PRS........... Precision Rotary Stripper
PRS........... President of the Royal Society [*British*]
PRS........... Presidential Airways [*Philadelphia, PA*] [*FAA designator*]   (FAAC)
PRS........... Presidio Oil Co. [*AMEX symbol*]   (SPSG)
PRS........... Presidio, TX [*Location identifier*] [*FAA*]   (FAAL)
PRS........... Press   (MSA)
PRS........... Press Summary [*A publication*]
PRS........... Pressure Reducing Station
PRS........... Pressure Response Spectrum [*Nuclear energy*]   (NRCH)
PRS........... Primary Recovery Ship [*NASA*]
PRS........... Primary Recovery Site [*NASA*]   (KSC)
PRS........... Primary Rescue Site [*NASA*]   (NASA)
PRS........... Procedure Review Section [*Social Security Administration*]
PRS........... Process Radiation Sampler [*Nuclear energy*]   (NRCH)
PRS........... Product Requirement Schedule   (MCD)
PRS........... Production Recording System
PRS........... Production Release System   (MCD)
PRS........... Program Requirements Summary   (MUGU)
PRS........... Property Recovery Section
PRS........... Propodial Sinus [*Zoology*]
PRS........... Prospectors Air [*Vancouver Stock Exchange symbol*]
PRS........... Protestant Reformation Society   (EA)
PRS........... Provide Repair Service [*Navy*]   (NVT)
PRS........... Provisioning Requirements Statement
PRS........... Pseudorandom Sequence
PRS........... Psycholinguistic Rating Scale
PRS........... Public Relations Section [*Library Administration and Management Association*]
PRSA........ Pan-Rhodian Society of America   (EA)
PRSA........ Power Reactant Storage Assembly [*NASA*]   (MCD)
PRSA........ President of the Royal Scottish Academy
PRSA........ Public Relations Society of America   (EA)
PRSA........ Puerto Rico Statehood Commission   (EA)
PrSaC .... Colegio Universitario del Sagrado Corazon [*College of the Sacred Heart*], Santurce, PR [*Library symbol*] [*Library of Congress*]   (LCLS)
Prsb Q....... Presbyterian Quarterly Review [*A publication*]
PRSC........ Plutonium Rework Sample Cell [*Nuclear energy*]   (NRCH)
PRSC........ Puerto Rico Solidarity Committee   (EA)
Pr Schae B ... Praktische Schaedlingsbekaempfer [*Braunschweig*] [*A publication*]
PRSCR ..... Puerto Rico Supreme Court Reports [*A publication*]   (DLA)
PRSD........ Portable Rectilinear Scanning Device
PRSD........ Power Reactant Storage [*or Supply*] and Distribution [*NASA*]   (NASA)
PRSD........ Pressed   (AAG)
PRSDS ...... Power Reactant Storage and Distribution System   (MCD)
PrSE .... El Mundo Publishing Co., San Juan, PR [*Library symbol*] [*Library of Congress*]   (LCLS)
PRSE........ President of the Royal Society of Edinburgh
PRSE........ Proceedings. Royal Society of Edinburgh [*A publication*]
PRSEC...... Payroll Section
P RS Edin A ... Proceedings. Royal Society of Edinburgh. Section A. Mathematical and Physical Sciences [*A publication*]
P RS Edin B ... Proceedings. Royal Society of Edinburgh. Section B. Natural Environment [*A publication*]
PRSG........ Personal Radio Steering Group [*Ann Arbor, MI*] [*Telecommunications service*]   (TSSD)
PRSG........ Pulse-Rebalanced Strapdown Gyro   (MCD)
PRSH........ President of the Royal Society for the Promotion of Health [*British*]
PRSL .... Pennsylvania-Reading Seashore Lines [*Absorbed into Consolidated Rail Corp.*] [*AAR code*]
PRSL .... Progressive Savings & Loan Association [*NASDAQ symbol*]   (NQ)
PRSM .... Proceedings. Royal Society of Medicine [*A publication*]
PRSMA ..... Proceedings. Royal Society of Medicine [*A publication*]
PRSMN..... Pressman   (AABC)
PRSN........ Provisional Relative Sunspot Number [*NASA*]
PRSNG...... Pressing
Prsnrs........ Prisoners [*A publication*]
PRSNT...... Present   (FAAC)
Pr Soc Exp Biol Med ... Proceedings. Society for Experimental Biology and Medicine [*A publication*]
PRSR .... Presser   (MSA)

PRSRV ..... Preservative   (AAG)
PRSRZ ..... Pressurize   (MSA)
PRSS .... Pennsylvania-Reading Seashore Lines [*Absorbed into Consolidated Rail Corp.*]
PRSS .... Problem Report Squawk Sheet [*NASA*]   (NASA)
PRSSA...... Philips Research Reports. Supplements [*A publication*]
PRSSA...... Public Relations Student Society of America   (EA)
PRSSA...... Puerto Rico Mainland US Statehood Students Association   (EA)
PRSSD ..... Pressed
PRST .... Persist   (FAAC)
PRST .... Presstek, Inc. [*NASDAQ symbol*]   (NQ)
PRST .... Probability Reliability Sequential Tests   (MCD)
PRSTA ...... Progress in Stereochemistry [*A publication*]
Pr Stat....... Private Statutes [*Legal term*]   (DLA)
Pr Statneho Geol Ustavu (Bratisl) ... Prace Statneho Geologickeho Ustavu (Bratislava) [*A publication*]
Pr Statneho Geol Ustavu (Bratislava) ... Prace Statneho Geologickeho Ustavu (Bratislava) [*A publication*]
PRSTB....... Progresele Stiintei [*A publication*]
PRSTC...... Prosthetic
Pr Stud Vyzk Ustav Vodohospod ... Prace a Studie. Vyzkumny Ustav Vodohospodarsky [*A publication*]
Pr Stud Zakl Badan Nauk Gorn Okregu Przem Pol Akad Nauk ... Prace i Studia Zakladu Badan Naukowych Gornoslaskiego Okregu Przemyslowego Polskiej Akademii Nauk [*Poland*] [*A publication*]
PRSUA ...... Plastic and Reconstructive Surgery [*A publication*]
PRSUB...... Pribory i Sistemy Upravleniya [*A publication*]
PR Sugar Man ... Puerto Rico Sugar Manual [*A publication*]
PRSVN...... Preservation   (AABC)
PRSW....... President of the Royal Scottish Water Colour Society
PrSW .... World University, San Juan, PR [*Library symbol*] [*Library of Congress*]   (LCLS)
PrSW-I ...... World University, International Institute of the Americas, Barbosa Esq. Guayama, San Juan, PR [*Library symbol*] [*Library of Congress*]   (LCLS)
PRT........... Parr Terminal Railroad [*AAR code*]
PRT........... Part   (AAG)
PRT........... Participating Research Teams [*Department of Energy*]
PRT........... Partido Revolucionario de los Trabajadores [*Workers' Revolutionary Party*] [*Argentina*] [*Political party*]   (PD)
PRT........... Partido Revolucionario de los Trabajadores [*Workers' Revolutionary Party*] [*Peru*] [*Political party*]   (PPW)
PRT........... Partido Revolucionario de los Trabajadores [*Workers' Revolutionary Party*] [*Uruguay*] [*Political party*]   (PD)
PRT........... Pattern Recognition Technique
PRT........... Payroll Tax   (ADA)
PRT........... Periodic Reevaluation Tests
PRT........... Personal Rapid Transit [*Computer-guided transit system*]
PRT........... Personnel Research Test [*Military*]
PRT........... Petroleum Revenue Tax [*British*]
PRT........... Pharmaceutical Research and Testing [*Public Health Service*]   (GRD)
PRT........... Philadelphia Reading Test [*Education*]
PRT........... Phosphoribosyltransferase [*Also, PRTase*] [*An enzyme*]
PRT........... Photoradiation Therapy [*Oncology*]
PRT........... Physical Readiness Training [*Army*]   (INF)
P & RT...... Physical and Recreational Training [*Navy*] [*British*]
PRT........... Pictorial Reasoning Test [*Job screening test*]
PRT........... Platinum Resistance Thermometer
PRT........... Point Retreat, AK [*Location identifier*] [*FAA*]   (FAAL)
PRT........... Port
PRT........... Portable Radiation Thermometer
PRT........... Portable Radio Telephone
PRT........... Portable Remote Terminal
PRT........... Portable Router Template   (MCD)
PRT........... Portugal [*ANSI three-letter standard code*]   (CNC)
PRT........... Power Recovery Turbine
PRT........... Prato [*Italy*] [*Seismograph station code, US Geological Survey*]   (SEIS)
PRT........... Precision Radiation Thermometer
PRT........... Preliminary Reference Trajectory [*NASA*]   (KSC)
PRT........... Pressurized Relief Tank   (NRCH)
PRT........... Printer [*Data processing*]   (MDG)
prt............ Printer [*MARC relator code*] [*Library of Congress*]   (LCCP)
Prt............ Private [*British military*]   (DMA)
PRT........... Problem Resolution Tasking System [*Army*]   (INF)
PRT........... Procurement Review Team
PRT........... Procurement Round Table   (EA)
PRT........... Product Range Testing [*Business term*]
PRT........... Production Reliability Test
PRT........... Production Run Tape
PRT........... Program Reference Table
PRT........... Prompt Relief Trip [*Nuclear energy*]   (NRCH)
Prt............ Protagoras [*of Plato*] [*Classical studies*]   (OCD)
PRT........... Prova di Restituzione Termica [*Italy*] [*Medicine*]
PRT........... Provost
PRT........... Prudential Realty Trust [*NYSE symbol*]   (SPSG)
PRT........... Psychiatric Rehabilitation Team   (EA)
PRT........... Publications Requirements Tables   (AAG)

PRT........... Pulse Recurrence [*or Repetition*] Time (CET)
PRT........... Pulsed RADAR Transmitter
PRTB........ Partido Revolucionario de Trabajadores Bolivianos [*Bolivian Workers' Revolutionary Party*] [*Political party*] (PD)
PRTBR ...... Partido Revolucionario de Bolivia Romero [*Bolivia*] [*Political party*] (PPW)
PRTC........ Partido Revolucionario de los Trabajadores Centroamericanos [*Revolutionary Party of Central American Workers*] [*Guatemala*] [*Political party*] (PPW)
PRTC........ Partido Revolucionario de los Trabajadores Centroamericanos [*Revolutionary Party of Central American Workers*] [*El Salvador*] [*Political party*] (PD)
PRTC......... Pediatric Research and Training Center [*University of Connecticut*] [*Research center*] (RCD)
PRTC........ Ports Canada
PRTC........ Precision Technologies [*NASDAQ symbol*] (NQ)
PRTCD...... Progres Technique [*A publication*]
PRTCD...... Puerto Rico Tax Court Decisions [*A publication*] (DLA)
PRTD........ Portland Traction Co. [*AAR code*]
PRTE......... Profit Technology, Inc. [*New York, NY*] [*NASDAQ symbol*] (NQ)
PRTEA ...... Pribory i Tekhnika Eksperimenta [*A publication*]
PR Tex Agric Exp Stn ... PR. Texas Agricultural Experiment Station [*A publication*]
PRTF......... Pheromone and Receptor Transcription Factor [*Genetics*]
PRTG........ Printing (AFM)
PRTHA ...... Progress in Radiation Therapy [*A publication*]
PrThR........ Princeton Theological Review [*A publication*]
PRTI......... Physical and Recreational Training Instructor [*British military*] (DMA)
PRTK........ Presto-Tek Corp. [*NASDAQ symbol*] (NQ)
PRTKT...... Parts Kit
PRTLS....... Powered Return to Launch Site [*NASA*] (MCD)
PRTLY...... Partially
PRTM........ Printing Response-Time Monitor
PRTN........ Partition
PRTO .... Preservation Research and Testing Office [*Library of Congress*] (EA)
PRTOT...... Prototype Real-Time Optical Tracker [*Data processing*]
PRT Polym Age ... PRT Polymer Age [*A publication*]
PRTR......... Plutonium Recycle Test Reactor [*Nuclear energy*]
PRTR......... Printer
Prt Rep....... Practice Reports [*A publication*] (DLA)
PRTRL...... Printer, Lithographer [*Navy*]
PRTRM..... Printer, Offset Process [*Navy*]
PRTRNS ... Programmable Transformer Converter (MCD)
PRTS......... Personal Rapid Transit System [*Computer-guided transit system*]
PRTS......... Politisch-Religioese Texte aus der Sargonidenzeit [*A publication*]
PRTS......... Pretoria Theological Series [*A publication*] (BJA)
PrtSc......... Print Screen [*Computer keyboard*]
PRTUA...... Problemy Tuberkuleza [*A publication*]
Prtw........... Propeller Twist [*Genetics*]
PRTY........ Priority
PRU .... Packet Radio Unit
PRu .... Paedagogische Rundschau [*A publication*]
PRU .... Peripheral Resistance Unit [*Medicine*]
PRU .... Photographic Reconnaissance Unit [*Aircraft*] [*Marine Corps*]
PRU .... Pneumatic Regulation Unit (AAG)
PRU .... Polarity Reversal Unit [*Electrochemistry*]
Pr U........... Pravda Ukrainy [*A publication*]
PRU .... Primary Replacement Unit
PRU .... Prisoner's Rights Union (EA)
PRU .... Programs Research Unit (KSC)
PRU .... Prome [*Burma*] [*Airport symbol*] (OAG)
PRU .... Provincial Reconnaissance Unit [*Military*]
PRU .... Prudential Property & Casualty Insurance Co., Holmdel, NJ [*OCLC symbol*] (OCLC)
PRU .... Pruhonice [*Czechoslovakia*] [*Seismograph station code, US Geological Survey*] (SEIS)
PrU .... University of Puerto Rico, Rio Piedras, PR [*Library symbol*] [*Library of Congress*] (LCLS)
PRUAA ..... President of the Royal Ulster Academy of Arts
PRUC .... Partido Revolucionario de Union Civico [*Revolutionary Party for Civic Union*] [*Costa Rica*] [*Political party*]
PRUC .... Practice Reports [*1848-1900*] [*Upper Canada*] [*A publication*] (DLA)
PRUD........ Partido Revolucionario de Unificacion Democratica [*Revolutionary Party of Democratic Unification*] [*El Salvador*]
PrU-H........ University of Puerto Rico, Humacao Regional College, Humacao, PR [*Library symbol*] [*Library of Congress*] (LCLS)
PRUL........ Programs Unlimited [*NASDAQ symbol*] (NQ)
PrU-L........ University of Puerto Rico, Law Library, San Juan, PR [*Library symbol*] [*Library of Congress*] (LCLS)
PrU-M....... University of Puerto Rico, School of Medicine, San Juan, PR [*Library symbol*] [*Library of Congress*] (LCLS)

PrU-MA .... University of Puerto Rico, Mayaguez Campus, Mayaguez, Puerto Rico [*Library symbol*] [*Library of Congress*] (LCLS)
Prum Potravin ... Prumysl Potravin [*A publication*]
PrU-MS..... University of Puerto Rico, Department of Marine Sciences, Mayaguez, PR [*Library symbol*] [*Library of Congress*] (LCLS)
PRUND ..... Plastics and Rubber News [*A publication*]
PrU-NS...... University of Puerto Rico, Natural Science Library, Rio Piedras, PR [*Library symbol*] [*Library of Congress*] (LCLS)
PRUS........ Prussia [*Obsolete*]
Prus............ Prussian [*Philately*]
PRUSAF.... Puerto Rico, USA Foundation (EA)
Pr Ustavu Geol Inz ... Prace Ustavu Geologickeho Inzenyrstvu [*A publication*]
Pr Ustavu Naft Vyzk ... Prace Ustavu pro Naftovy Vyzkum [*A publication*]
Pr Ustavu Vyzk Paliv ... Prace Ustavu pro Vyzkum Paliv [*Czechoslovakia*] [*A publication*]
Pr Ustavu Vyzk Vyuziti Paliv ... Prace Ustavu pro Vyzkum a Vyuziti Paliv [*A publication*]
PRV .... Papaya Ringspot Virus
PRV .... Peak Reverse Voltage
PRV .... Pearl River Valley Railroad Co. [*AAR code*]
PRV .... Personnel Review [*A publication*]
PRv .... Philosophical Review [*A publication*]
PRV .... Polycythemia Rubra Vera [*Medicine*]
PRV .... Porvoo [*Finland*] [*Seismograph station code, US Geological Survey*] [*Closed*] (SEIS)
PRV .... Pour Rendre Visite [*To Make a Call*] [*French*]
PRV .... Pressure Reducing [*or Regulation or Relief*] Valve
PRV .... Princess Ventures [*Vancouver Stock Exchange symbol*]
PRV .... Prior Record Variable [*Criminal sentencing*]
PRV .... Propeller Revolution
Prv............. Proverbs [*Old Testament book*]
PRV .... Provisional Reconnaissance Unit
PRV .... Pseudorabies Virus
PRV .... Pseudorelative Velocity
Prv............. Pyruvenol [*Biochemistry*]
PRVD .... Procurement [*or Purchase*] Request for Vendor Data (AAG)
PRVD .... Provide (FAAC)
PRVEP ...... Pattern Reversal Visual Evoked Potential
Pr Vinnits'k Derzh Med Inst ... Pratsi Vinnits'kogo Derzhavnogo Medichnogo Institutu [*A publication*]
PRVNTV.... Preventive
PRVOA ..... Pravda Vostoka [*A publication*]
PRVS .... Penetration Room Ventilation System [*Nuclear energy*] (IEEE)
PRVT........ Product Reliability Validation Test (MCD)
PRVT........ Production Readiness Verification Testing (MCD)
Prvt Label .. Private Label [*A publication*]
PRVW....... Preview (MSA)
PRVYD...... Polyteknisk Revy [*A publication*]
Pr Vyzk Ustavu CS Naft Dolu ... Prace Vyzkumneho Ustavu CS Naftovych Dolu [*A publication*]
Pr Vyzk Ustavu Lesn Hospod Myslivosti (Strnady) ... Prace Vyzkumneho Ustavu Lesneho Hospodarstvi a Myslivosti (Strnady) [*A publication*]
PRW .... Paired Wire [*Telecommunications*] (TEL)
PRW .... Percent Rated Wattage
PRW .... Polymerized Ragweed [*Immunology*]
Pr W.......... Prawda Wostoka [*A publication*]
PRW .... Press Relations Wire [*Commercial firm*] (EA)
PRW .... Promark Software [*Vancouver Stock Exchange symbol*]
PRW .... Prosser [*Washington*] [*Seismograph station code, US Geological Survey*] (SEIS)
PRW .... Purchasing World [*A publication*]
PRW .... World University, San Juan, PR [*OCLC symbol*] (OCLC)
PRWAD .... Professional Rehabilitation Workers with the Adult Deaf [*Later, ADARA*] (EA)
PR Water Resour Bull ... Puerto Rico. Water Resources Bulletin [*A publication*]
PrWCJewSt ... Proceedings. World Congress of Jewish Studies [*Jerusalem*] [*A publication*]
PRWD .... Priority Regular World Day
PRWI......... Prince William Forest Park [*National Park Service designation*]
Pr Winter... Probability Winter School. Proceedings of the Fourth Winter School on Probability [*A publication*]
PRWO .... Puerto Rican Revolutionary Workers Organization
PRWRA ..... Puerto Rican Water Resources Authority
Pr Wroclaw Tow Nauk Ser B ... Prace Wroclawskiego Towarzystwa Naukowego. Seria B [*A publication*]
PRWS........ President of the Royal Society of Painters in Water Colours [*British*]
PRWV........ Peak Reserve Working Voltage
Pr Wydz Nauk Tech Bydgoskie Tow Nauk Ser A ... Prace Wydzialu Nauk Technicznych. Bydgoskie Towarzystwo Naukowe. Seria A. Technologia Chemiczna [*A publication*]
Pr Wydz Nauk Tech Bydgoskie Tow Nauk Ser B ... Prace Wydzialu Nauk Technicznych. Bydogoskie Towarzystwo Naukowe. Seria B [*A publication*]

Pr Wydz Nauk Tech Bydgoskie Tow Nauk Ser C ... Prace Wydzialu Nauk Technicznych. Bydgoskie Towarzystwo Naukowe. Seria C. Elektronika, Elektrotechnika [*A publication*]
PRX .... Par Pharmaceutical, Inc. [*NYSE symbol*]   (SPSG)
PRX .... Paris [*Texas*] [*Airport symbol*]   (OAG)
PRX .... Paris, TX [*Location identifier*] [*FAA*]   (FAAL)
PRX .... Pressure Regulation Exhaust
PRXI .... PRX [*Public Relations Exchange*] International   (EA)
PRXS .... Praxis Biologics, Inc. [*NASDAQ symbol*]   (NQ)
PRY .... Paraguay [*ANSI three-letter standard code*]   (CNC)
PRY .... Parys [*South Africa*] [*Seismograph station code, US Geological Survey*]   (SEIS)
PRY .... Pittway Corp. [*AMEX symbol*]   (SPSG)
P Ryl .... Catalogue of the Greek Papyri in the John Rylands Library at Manchester [*A publication*]   (OCD)
PRZ .... Portales, NM [*Location identifier*] [*FAA*]   (FAAL)
PrZ .... Praehistorische Zeitschrift [*A publication*]
PRZ .... Prism Entertainment Corp. [*AMEX symbol*]   (SPSG)
PRZ .... Przhevalsk [*USSR*] [*Seismograph station code, US Geological Survey*]   (SEIS)
Pr Zakresu Lesn ... Prace z Zakresu Lesnictwa [*Poland*] [*A publication*]
Pr Zakresu Nauk Roln ... Prace z Zakresu Nauk Rolniczych [*A publication*]
Prz Arch ..... Przeglad Archeologiczny [*A publication*]
Przegd St ..... Przeglad Statystyczny [*A publication*]
Przegl A ..... Przeglad Archeologiczny [*A publication*]
Przeglad Bibliot ... Przeglad Biblioteczny [*A publication*]
Przeglad Geog ... Przeglad Geograficzny [*A publication*]
Przeglad Hist ... Przeglad Historyczny [*A publication*]
Przeglad Mech ... Przeglad Mechaniczny [*A publication*]
Przeglad Papier ... Przeglad Papierniczy [*A publication*]
Przeglad Statyst ... Przeglad Statystyczny [*A publication*]
Przeglad Wlok ... Przeglad Wlokienniczy [*A publication*]
Przegl Antrop ... Przeglad Antropologiczny [*A publication*]
Przegl Antropol ... Przeglad Antropologiczny [*A publication*]
Przegl Bibl ... Przeglad Biblioteczny [*A publication*]
Przegl Bibliogr Chem ... Przeglad Bibliograficzny Chemii [*A publication*]
Przegl Budow ... Przeglad Budowlany [*A publication*]
Przegl Dermatol ... Przeglad Dermatologiczny [*A publication*]
Przegl Dermatol Wenerol ... Przeglad Dermatologii i Wenerologii [*A publication*]
Przegl Derm Wener ... Przeglad Dermatologii i Wenerologii [*A publication*]
Przegl Dok Ceram Szlachetnej Szkla ... Przeglad Dokumentacyjny Ceramiki Szlachetnej i Szkla [*A publication*]
Przegl Dok Nafty ... Przeglad Dokumentacyjny Nafty [*A publication*]
Przegl Dokum Chem ... Przeglad Dokumentacyjny Chemii [*A publication*]
Przegl Dosw Roln ... Przeglad Doswiadezalnictwa Rolniczego [*A publication*]
Przegl Elektr ... Przeglad Elektroniki [*A publication*]
Przegl Elektron ... Przeglad Elektroniki [*A publication*]
Przegl Elektrotech ... Przeglad Elektrotechniczny [*A publication*]
Przegl Epidemiol ... Przeglad Epidemiologiczny [*A publication*]
Przegl Geofiz ... Przeglad Geofizyczny [*A publication*]
Przegl Geogr ... Przeglad Geograficzny [*A publication*]
Przegl Geogr Pol Geogr Rev ... Przeglad Geograficzny/Polish Geographical Review [*A publication*]
Przegl Geol ... Przeglad Geologiczny [*A publication*]
Przegl Gorn ... Przeglad Gorniczy [*A publication*]
Przegl Gorn Hutn ... Przeglad Gorniczo Hutniczy [*A publication*]
Przegl Hist ... Przeglad Historyczny [*A publication*]
Przegl Hodowlany ... Przeglad Hodowlany [*A publication*]
Przegl Kom ... Przeglad Komunikacyjny [*A publication*]
Przegl Komunik ... Przeglad Komunikacyjny [*A publication*]
Przegl Lek ... Przeglad Lekarski [*A publication*]
Przegl Mech ... Przeglad Mechaniczny [*A publication*]
Przegl Met Hydrol ... Przeglad Meteorologiczny i Hydrologiczny [*A publication*]
Przegl Morski ... Przeglad Morski [*A publication*]
Przegl Nauk Lit Zootech ... Przeglad Naukowej Literatury Zootechnicznej [*A publication*]
Przegl Nauk Tech Akad Gorn Hutn Krakowie Ser G ... Przeglad Naukowo Techniczny. Akademia Gorniczo Hutnicza w Krakowie. Seria G. Gornictwo [*A publication*]
Przegl Nauk Tech Akad Gorn Hutn Krakowie Ser H ... Przeglad Naukowo Techniczny. Akademia Gorniczo Hutnicza w Krakowie. Seria H. Hutnictwo [*A publication*]
Przegl Odlew ... Przeglad Odlewnictwa [*A publication*]
Przegl Organ ... Przeglad Organizacji [*A publication*]
Przegl Papiern ... Przeglad Papierniczy [*A publication*]
Przegl Przem Olejowego ... Przeglad Przemyslu Olejowego [*A publication*]
Przegl Skorzany ... Przeglad Skorzany [*A publication*]
Przegl Socjol ... Przeglad Socjologiczny [*A publication*]
Przegl Spawalnictwa ... Przeglad Spawalnictwa [*A publication*]
Przegl Stat ... Przeglad Statystyczny [*A publication*]
Przegl Telekomun ... Przeglad Telekomunikacyjny [*A publication*]
Przegl Wlok ... Przeglad Wlokienniczy [*A publication*]
Przegl Wojsk Ladowych ... Przeglad Wojsk Ladowych [*Poland*] [*A publication*]
Przegl Zachod ... Przeglad Zachodni [*A publication*]
Przegl Zboz Mlyn ... Przeglad Zbozowo Mlynarski [*A publication*]
Przegl Zbozowo Mlyn ... Przeglad Zbozowo Mlynarski [*A publication*]
Przegl Zool ... Przeglad Zoologiczny [*A publication*]
Przekazy .... Przekazy/Opinie [*A publication*]

Przem Chem ... Przemysl Chemiczny [*A publication*]
Przem Drzew ... Przemysl Drzewny [*A publication*]
Przem Drzewny ... Przemysl Drzewny [*A publication*]
Przem Ferment ... Przemysl Fermentacyjny [*A publication*]
Przem Ferment Rolny ... Przemysl Fermentacyjny i Rolny [*A publication*]
Przem Naft ... Przemysl Naftowy [*A publication*]
Przem Roln Spozyw ... Przemysl Rolny i Spozywczy [*A publication*]
Przem Spozyw ... Przemysl Spozywczy [*A publication*]
Przem Spozywczy ... Przemysl Spozywczy [*A publication*]
Przem Wlok ... Przemysl Wlokienniczy [*A publication*]
Przemy Chem ... Przemysl Chemiczny [*A publication*]
PRZGA ...... Przeglad Geologiczny [*A publication*]
PrzH .... Przeglad Humanistyczny [*A publication*]
PrzK .... Przeglad Kulturalny [*A publication*]
PrzKl .... Przeglad Klasyczny [*A publication*]
PrzOr .... Przeglad Orientalistyczny [*Cracow/Warsaw*] [*A publication*]
PRZPB .... Przeglad Psychologiczny [*A publication*]
Prz Stat ...... Przeglad Statystyczny [*A publication*]
PrzZ .... Przeglad Zachodni [*A publication*]
PS .... Abbott Laboratories [*Research code symbol*]
PS .... American Political Science Association. Quarterly [*A publication*]
PS .... Chloropicrin [*Poison gas*] [*Army symbol*]
PS .... Pacific Southwest Airlines [*ICAO designator*]   (OAG)
PS .... Pacific Spectator [*A publication*]
PS .... Pacific Star Communication [*Vancouver Stock Exchange symbol*]
P & S .... Packers and Stockyards
PS .... Packet Switching [*Telecommunications*]
PS .... Packing Sheet   (MCD)
PS .... Paddle Steamer   (ADA)
PS .... Paediatric Surgery
PS .... Painting System
PS .... Paleontological Society   (EA)
PS .... Palestinskii Sbornik [*A publication*]
PS .... Palm Society [*Later, IPS*]   (EA)
PS .... Pamietnik Slowianski [*A publication*]
PS .... Pan Salicornia Zone [*Ecology*]
P & S .... Paracentesis and Suction [*Medicine*]
PS .... Parachute Subsystem [*NASA*]   (NASA)
PS .... Paradoxical Sleep
P/S .... Parallel to Serial Converter   (MCD)
PS .... Parents' Section of the Alexander Graham Bell Association for the Deaf   (EA)
PS .... Parents of Suicides   (EA)
PS .... Parity Switch
PS .... Parliamentary Secretary [*British*]
PS .... Parlor Snake [*Slang for "to escort visitors around post"*]
PS .... Parochial School
PS .... Parrot Society   (EA)
ps .... PARSEC [*Parallax Second*] [*See PARSEC*]
PS .... Parti Socialiste [*Socialist Party*] [*Belgium*] [*Political party*]   (PPW)
PS .... Parti Socialiste - Federation de la Reunion [*Reunion Federation of the Socialist Party*] [*Political party*]   (PPW)
PS .... Partially Smutted [*Plant pathology*]
PS .... Partially Synergistic [*Pharmacology*]
PS .... Partido Socialista [*Socialist Party*] [*Chile*] [*Political party*]
PS .... Partido Socialista [*Socialist Party*] [*Uruguay*] [*Political party*]
PS .... Partido Socialista Portuguesa [*Portuguese Socialist Party*] [*Political party*]   (PPE)
PS .... Partido Socialista - Uno [*Socialist Party - One*] [*Also, PS-1*] [*Bolivia*] [*Political party*]   (PPW)
PS .... Partijnaja Shisn [*A publication*]
PS .... Parts Shipper
PS .... Passed School of Instruction [*of Officers*] [*British*]
PS .... Passenger Service
PRZGA ...... Passenger Steamer
PS .... Passing Scuttle
PS .... Pastel Society [*British*]
PS .... Pathologic Stage
PS .... Pathological (Surgical) Staging [*For Hodgkin's Disease*]
PS .... Patient's Serum [*Medicine*]
PS .... Patrol Service [*British military*]   (DMA)
PS .... Patrol Ship   (CINC)
PS .... Patrologia Syriaca   (BJA)
PS .... Patton Society   (EA)
P/S .... Pause/Still [*Video technology*]
PS .... Pavel Stepanek [*Czech ESP performer*]
P & S .... Pay and Supply [*Coast Guard*]
PS .... Payload Shroud   (MCD)
PS .... Payload Specialist [*NASA*]   (MCD)
PS .... Payload Station [*NASA*]   (MCD)
PS .... Payload Support [*NASA*]   (NASA)
PS .... Paymaster Sergeant
PS .... Pedagogical Seminary and Journal of Genetic Psychology [*A publication*]
PS .... Pedal Sinus
PS .... Pellet Size
PS .... Penal Servitude
PS .... Penny Stock [*Investment term*]

PS.............	Pensiero e Scuola [A publication]
PS.............	Peperomia Society [Later, PEPS] (EA)
PS.............	Per Ship
PS.............	Per Speculum [Medicine]
PS.............	Perception Schedule
PS.............	Perceptual Speed (Test) [Psychology]
PS.............	Performance Score
PS.............	Performance Standard
PS.............	Periodic Syndrome [Medicine]
PS.............	Peripheral Shock [Psychology]
P & S.........	Perkins & Squier [Paper manufacturer]
PS.............	Permanent Secretary
PS.............	Permanent Signal [Telecommunications] (TEL)
PS.............	Personal Secretary (DCTA)
PS.............	Personal Skills
PS.............	Personal Survival
PS.............	Personal System [IBM computer introduced in 1987]
PS.............	Personnel Subsystem [Army]
PS.............	Peru Solidarity [An association] (EA)
PS.............	Pet Switchboard (EA)
PS.............	Petty Sessions (DLA)
PS.............	Phase Separation
PS.............	Phase-Shift
PS.............	Phenomenally Speedy Ordinary [Photographic plates] (ROG)
PS.............	Philalethes Society (EA)
PS.............	Philippine Scouts
PS.............	Philippine Studies [A publication]
PS.............	Phillnathean Society (EA)
PS.............	Philolexian Society (EA)
PS.............	Philological Society (EAIO)
PS.............	Philosophical Studies [A publication]
PS.............	Phosphate-Saline [A buffer] [Cell culture]
PS.............	Phosphatidylserine [Biochemistry]
PS.............	Photochemical System
PS.............	Photoemission Scintillation (MCD)
PS.............	Photographic Service
PS.............	Photometer System (KSC)
PS.............	Photosystems
PS.............	Phylaxis Society (EA)
PS.............	Physical Sciences
PS.............	Physical Security
PS.............	Physical Status [Medicine]
PS.............	Picket Ships [Navy]
ps.............	Picosecond
PS.............	Pilgrim Power Station (NRCH)
PS.............	Pilgrim Society (EA)
PS.............	Pine Bark Mixed with Clay Loam Soil
PS.............	Pine Siskin [Ornithology]
PS.............	Pineal Stalk [Neuroanatomy]
PS.............	Pink Sheet [Investment term]
PS.............	Pirandello Society (EA)
PS.............	Pistol Sharpshooter [Army]
P & S.........	[The] Pittsburg & Shawmut Railroad Co.
PS.............	[The] Pittsburg & Shawmut Railroad Co. [AAR code]
PS.............	Pituitary Stalk [Neuroanatomy]
PS.............	Planet Stories [A publication]
PS.............	Planetary Society (EA)
P & S.........	Planking and Strutting [Construction]
PS.............	Planning and Scheduling
PS.............	Planning Study (AAG)
PS.............	Plant Stress [Horticulture]
P & S.........	Plant and Structures [Aviation] (FAAC)
PS.............	Plastic Surgery [Medicine]
PS.............	Platform (Sided) (DCTA)
PS.............	Plea Side (ROG)
PS.............	Pleural Sclerite [Entomology]
PS.............	Plotting System
PS.............	Plus
PS.............	Pneumatic System
PS.............	Poetry Society [British]
P/S.............	Point of Shipment
PS.............	Point of Switch
PS.............	Point of Symmetry
PS.............	Polanyi Society (EA)
PS.............	Polaris Standard [Missiles]
PS.............	Polarity Scale [Psychology]
PS.............	Police Sergeant [Scotland Yard]
PS.............	Policy Statement
PS.............	Polio Society (EA)
PS.............	Political Studies [A publication]
Ps.............	Polyporus sulphureus [A fungus]
PS.............	Polystyrene [Organic chemistry]
PS.............	Polysulfone [Also, PSO] [Organic chemistry]
P/S.............	Polyunsaturated/Saturated [Fatty acid ratio]
PS.............	Pop Shop Magazine [A publication]
PS.............	Popular Science [A publication]
PS.............	Porlock Society (EA)
PS.............	Port Security
P & S.........	Port and Starboard
P/S.............	Port or Starboard
PS.............	Port Store [Telecommunications] (TEL)
PS.............	Port Strobe [Telecommunications] (TEL)
PS.............	Pos-Escrito [Postscript] [Portuguese]
PS.............	Position-Specific Antigen
PS.............	Post Script [A publication]
PS.............	Post Scriptum [Written Afterwards, Postscript] [Latin]
PS.............	Postal Satsang [An association] (EA)
PS.............	Postal Service [US]
PS.............	Poster Society (EA)
PS.............	Potassium Sorbate [Food additive]
PS.............	Potentiometer Synchro
P/S.............	Power Section (NG)
PS.............	Power Source
PS.............	Power-Specific
PS.............	Power Station (MCD)
PS.............	Power Steering [Automobile ads]
PS.............	Power Supply
PS.............	Powys Society (EA)
PS.............	Prairie Schooner [A publication]
PS.............	Prairies Service [Record series prefix] [Canada]
PS.............	Pravoslavnyi Sobesiednik [A publication]
PS.............	Predictive Saccades [Ophthalmology]
PS.............	Preduzece Soko [Yugoslavia] [ICAO aircraft manufacturer identifier] (ICAO)
PS.............	Preferred Stock [Investment term]
PS.............	Prehistoric Society (EA)
PS.............	Preliminary Study
PS.............	Presentation Services [Data processing] (IBMDP)
PS.............	Press Secretary (ILCA)
PS.............	Press to Start (KSC)
PS.............	Pressure [or Propellant] Seal
P-S.............	Pressure-Sensitive
PS.............	Pressure Sensor
PS.............	Pressure Switch
Ps	Pressure, Systolic [Cardiology]
PS.............	Price Spreading [Business term]
PS.............	Primary School (ADA)
PS.............	Prime Select (MCD)
PS.............	Prime Sponsor
PS.............	Principal Sojourner [Freemasonry] (ROG)
PS.............	Principal Subject [In a sonata or rondo] [Music] (ROG)
PS.............	Prior Service [Military]
PS.............	Private Screenings [Cable TV programming service]
PS.............	Private Secretary
PS.............	Private Security Program [Association of Independent Colleges and Schools specialization code]
PS.............	Private Siding [Rail] [Shipping] (DS)
PS.............	Privy Seal [British]
PS.............	Probability of Survival (MCD)
PS.............	Problem Specification
PS.............	Procambial Strand [Botany]
PS.............	Process Solution (MCD)
PS.............	Process Specification
PS.............	Process Studies [A publication]
PS.............	Process Subsystem [Telecommunications] (TEL)
PS.............	Processor Status
PS.............	Procurement Specification (MCD)
PS.............	Product Standards (MCD)
PS.............	Product Support
PS.............	Profit Sharing [Business term]
PS.............	Program Simulation (OICC)
PS.............	Program Specification (MCD)
PS.............	Program Start (KSC)
PS.............	Program Store [Data processing] (IEEE)
PS.............	Program Summary (NG)
PS.............	Programming System
PS.............	Project Slip
PS.............	Project Stock [Military] (AABC)
PS.............	Project Study [British military] (DMA)
PS.............	Proler International Corp. [NYSE symbol] (SPSG)
PS.............	Prolifers for Survival (EA)
PS.............	Prometheus Society (EA)
PS.............	Prompt Side [of a stage] [i.e., the right side] [A stage direction]
PS.............	Proof Shot [Ammunition]
PS.............	Proof Stress
PS.............	Propellant Supply (KSC)
PS.............	Propellant System
PS.............	Prose Studies 1800-1900 [A publication]
PS.............	Prostaglandin Synthetase [An enzyme]
PS.............	Protective Service
PS.............	Protein Synthesis
PS.............	Proto-Semitic (BJA)
PS.............	Proton Synchrotron [Nuclear energy]
PS.............	Protoplasmic Surface [Freeze etching in microscopy]
PS.............	Provost-Sergeant
PS.............	Psalm
Ps	Psalms [Old Testament book]
PS.............	Pseudo [Classical studies] (OCD)
PS.............	Pseudomonas Stutzeri [Bacterium]
PS.............	Psychology Society (EA)
PS.............	Psychometric Society (EA)
PS.............	Psychonomic Society (EA)

PS...............	Psychotic
PS...............	Public Sale
PS...............	Public School
PS...............	Public Services
PS...............	Public Statutes [*Legal term*] (DLA)
PS...............	Public Stenographer
PS...............	Publication Standard
PS...............	Publishing Services [*American Library Association*]
PS...............	Puget Sound [*Also, Puget Sound Naval Shipyard*] [*Washington*]
PS...............	Pull Switch
PS...............	Pulmonary Stenosis [*Medicine*]
PS...............	Pulse Sensor (KSC)
PS...............	Pulse Shaper
PS...............	Pulse Stretcher
PS...............	Pulses per Second [*Data transmission*] (DEN)
PS...............	Pumping Station (NATG)
P & S........	Purchase and Sale [*Business term*]
PS...............	Purdon's Pennsylvania Statutes [*A publication*] (DLA)
PS...............	Purity-Supreme [*Supermarkets*]
PS...............	Pyloric Stenosis [*Medicine*]
ps----	South Pacific [*MARC geographic area code*] [*Library of Congress*] (LCCP)
PS...............	South Pole [*Also, SP*]
PS...............	Static Pressure
PS...............	Swarthmore Public Library, Swarthmore, PA [*Library symbol*] [*Library of Congress*] (LCLS)
PS...............	Transport [*Russian aircraft symbol*]
PS-1	Partido Socialista - Uno [*Socialist Party - One*] [*Also, PS*] [*Bolivia*] [*Political party*] (PD)
PS/2	Personal System/2 [*IBM Corp.*]
PS²	Profound Sensitivity Syndrome [*Psychology*]
PS3............	PROBE [*Program Optimization and Budget Evaluation*] Staff Support System [*Military*]
PS2000.......	Public Service 2000 Program [*Canada*]
PSA............	Pacific Science Association (EA)
PSA............	Pacific Southwest Airlines
P & SA	Packers and Stockyards Administration [*Department of Agriculture*]
PSA............	Papeles de Son Armadans [*A publication*]
PSA............	Parametric Semiconductor Amplifier
PSA............	Parametric Sound Amplifier [*Blaupunkt*]
PSA............	Parcel Shippers Association
PSA............	Parti Socialiste Autonome [*Autonomous Socialist Party*] [*France*] [*Political party*] (PPE)
PSA............	Parti Solidaire Africain [*African Solidarity Party*] [*Congo*] [*Political party*]
PSA............	Particle Size Analyzer
PSA............	Partido Socialista Aponte [*Bolivia*] [*Political party*] (PPW)
PSA............	Partido Socialista Argentino [*Socialist Party of Argentina*] [*Political party*]
PSA............	Partito Socialista Autonomo [*Autonomous Socialist Party*] [*Switzerland*] [*Political party*] (PPW)
PSA............	Past Shakedown Availability [*Military*]
PSA............	Pastel Society of America (EA)
PSA............	Path Selection Algorithm [*Telecommunications*] (TEL)
PSA............	Path of Steepest Ascent [*Statistical design of experiments*]
PSA............	Payload Service Area [*NASA*] (NASA)
PSA............	Payload Support Avionics [*NASA*] (NASA)
PSA............	Peace and Solidarity Alliance (EA)
PSA............	Peace Studies Association (EA)
PSA............	People's Supreme Assembly [*Yemen*] [*Political party*] (PPW)
PSA............	Personal Service Agreements (MCD)
PSA............	Personnel and Service Area [*Nuclear energy*] (NRCH)
PSA............	Petersburg [*Alaska*] [*Seismograph station code, US Geological Survey*] (SEIS)
PSA............	Petites Soeurs de l'Assumption [*Little Sisters of the Assumption - LSA*] [*Paris, France*] (EAIO)
PSA............	Peugeot Societe Anonyme [*France*]
PSA............	Philippine Shipbuilders Association (DS)
PSA............	Philippine Sugar Association [*Later, PSC*] (EA)
PSa............	Philippiniana Sacra [*A publication*]
PSA............	Philosophy of Science Association (EA)
PSA............	Phobia Society of America [*Later, ADAA*] (EA)
PSA............	Photographic Society of America (EA)
PSA............	Phycological Society of America (EA)
PSA............	Pirandello Society of America (EA)
PSA............	Pisa [*Italy*] [*Airport symbol*] (OAG)
PsA	Pisces Austrinus [*Constellation*]
PSA............	Pisces Society of America
PSA............	Play Schools Association (EA)
PSA............	Pleasant Sunday Afternoons
PSA............	Plumeria Society of America (EA)
PSA............	Pneumatic Sensor Assembly
PSA............	Poe Studies Association (EA)
PSA............	Poetry Society of America (EA)
PSA............	Police Science Abstracts [*A publication*]
PSA............	Political Studies Association [*British*]
P Sa............	Polotitscheskoje Samoobrasowanije [*A publication*]
PSA............	Polysilicic Acid [*Organic chemistry*]
PSA............	Port Of Singapore Authority (DS)
PSA............	Port Storage Area [*Telecommunications*] (TEL)

PSA............	Portable Sanitation Association (EA)
PSA............	Portable Sound Analyzer
PSA............	Post Shakedown Availability
PSA............	Post-Sleep Activity
PSA............	Potential Surface Analysis (ADA)
PSA............	Poultry Science Association (EA)
PSA............	Power Servo Amplifier (KSC)
PSA............	Power Servo Assembly (MCD)
PSA............	Power Supply Assembly
PSA............	Power Switching Assembly
PSA............	Pre/Post Sleep Activity (NASA)
PSA............	Prefabricated Surfacing Aluminum
PSA............	Preferred Storage Area (MCD)
PSA............	President of the Society of Antiquaries [*British*]
PSA............	Pressure Sensitive Adhesive [*Trademark*]
PSA............	Pressure Suit Assembly
PSA............	Pressure-Swing Adsorption [*Chemical engineering*]
PSA............	Pressure Switch Assembly (NASA)
PSA............	Presunrise Authority
PSA............	Private Schools Association [*British*]
PSA............	Probabilistic Safety Analysis (NRCH)
PSA............	Procurement Seminar for Auditors [*Army*]
PSA............	Product Safety Association (EA)
PSA............	Product Standards Agency [*Philippines*] (DS)
PSA............	Product Support Administration (MCD)
PSA............	Professional Salespersons of America [*Albuquerque, NM*] (EA)
PSA............	Professional Skills Alliance (EA)
PSA............	Professional Stringers Association (EA)
PSA............	Program Study Authorization (KSC)
PSA............	Prolonged Sleep Apnea
PSA............	Property Services Agency [*Department of the Environment*] [*British*]
PSA............	Prostate-Specific Antigen [*Immunochemistry*]
PSA............	Provisional Site Acceptance (NATG)
PSA............	Provisions Stowage Assembly (NASA)
PSA............	Psalm
Psa	Psalms [*Old Testament book*]
PSA............	Pseudomonic Acid [*Biochemistry*]
PSA............	Psychological Operations Support Activity [*Military*] (MCD)
PSA............	Psychologists for Social Action [*Defunct*] (EA)
PSA............	Psychopharmacology Abstracts [*A publication*]
PSA............	Public Securities Association [*Database producer*] (EA)
PSA............	Public Service Announcement
PSA............	Publication Systems Associates, Inc. [*Information service or system*] (IID)
PSA............	Push Down Stack Automaton [*Data processing*]
PSA............	Storage Properties, Inc. [*AMEX symbol*] (SPSG)
PSAA........	Pacific Special Activities Area [*Military*]
PSAA........	Pakistan Students' Association of America
PSAA........	Polish Singers Alliance of America (EA)
PSAA........	Poststimulatory Auditory Adaptation
PSAB........	Prime Bancorp, Inc. [*NASDAQ symbol*] (CTT)
PSAB........	Production Systems Acceptance Branch [*Social Security Administration*]
PSAC........	Passive Satellite Attitude Control
PSAC........	Pathology Services Advisory Committee [*Australia*]
PSAC........	Personnel Service Company [*Army*] (AABC)
PSAC........	Policy Signing and Accounting Centre [*Insurance firm*] [*British*]
PSAC........	President's Science Advisory Committee [*Terminated, 1973*] [*Executive Office of the President*]
PSAC	Private Security Advisory Council [*Terminated, 1977*] [*Department of Justice*] (EGAO)
PSAC	Product Safety Advisory Council [*Consumer Product Safety Commission*]
PSAC........	Professional Skating Association of Canada
PSAC........	Public Service Alliance of Canada [*Labor union of federal government employees*]
PSAcPh	Prostate-Specific Acid Phosphatase [*An enzyme*]
PSACPOO ...	Presidents Scientific Advisory Committee Panel on Oceanography [*Marine science*] (MSC)
PSAC TD..	Publications. Societe d'Archeologie Copte. Textes et Documents [*A publication*]
PSAD........	Predicted Site Acquisition Data [*NASA*]
PSAD........	Prediction, Simulation, Adaptation, Decision [*Data processing*]
PSAF........	Private Sector Adjustment Factor [*Banking*]
Ps Af	Psychopathologie Africaine [*A publication*]
PSAGN.....	Poststreptococcal Acute Glomerulonephritis [*Medicine*]
PSAI.........	Philippine Shipowners Association, Inc. (DS)
PSAIR	Priority Specific Air Information Request [*Defense Mapping Agency*] (MCD)
PSA Jl.......	Photographic Society of America. Journal [*A publication*]
PSA Journal ...	Photographic Society of America. Journal [*A publication*]
P de Sal	Petrus de Salinis [*Flourished, 13th century*] [*Authority cited in pre-1607 legal work*] (DSA)
PSAL	Programming System Activity Log [*Data processing*]
PSAL	Public Schools Athletic League
PSALI	Permanent Supplementary Artificial Lighting of Interiors (IEEE)
P Salin	Petrus de Salinis [*Flourished, 13th century*] [*Authority cited in pre-1607 legal work*] (DSA)
PSAM........	Partitioned Sequence Access Method

P de Sam .... Petrus de Sampsone [*Flourished, 1246-58*] [*Authority cited in pre-1607 legal work*] (DSA)
PSAM........ Publications. Service des Antiquites du Maroc [*A publication*]
P de Samp ... Petrus de Sampsone [*Flourished, 1246-58*] [*Authority cited in pre-1607 legal work*] (DSA)
PSANDT ... Pay, Subsistence, and Transportation [*Military*]
PSANP ...... Phenol-Soluble Acidic Nuclear Protein[*s*] [*Biochemistry*]
PSAO........ Primary Staff Action Officer [*Military*]
PSAP .... Plane Stress Analysis and Plot [*Data processing*]
PSAP .... Public Safety Answering Point [*Telecommunications*] (TEL)
PSAP .... Pulmonary Surfactant Apoprotein [*Biochemistry*]
PSA/PS ..... Political Studies. Political Studies Association [*United Kingdom*] [*A publication*]
PsaQ .... Psychoanalytic Quarterly [*A publication*]
PSAR........ Platform Shock Attenuation and Realignment System (MCD)
PSAR........ Pneumatic [*or Pressure*] System Automatic Regulator (AAG)
PSAR........ Preliminary Safety Analysis Report
PSAR........ Programmable Synchronous/Asynchronous Receiver (IEEE)
PsaR......... Psychoanalytic Review [*A publication*]
PSarg .... Pre-Sargonic (BJA)
PSAS .... Papers in International Studies. Africa Series. Ohio University [*A publication*]
PSAS .... Prespeech Assessment Scale [*Occupational therapy*]
PSAS .... Proceedings. Society of Antiquaries of Scotland [*A publication*]
PSAS .... Production Systems Acceptance Section [*Social Security Administration*]
PSASS .... Perishable Subsistence Automated Supply System [*DoD*]
PSASV .... Phase-Sensitive Anodic Stripping Voltammetry
PSAT .... Predicted Site Acquisition Table [*NASA*]
PSAT .... Preliminary Scholastic Aptitude Test
PSAT .... Programmable Synchronous/Asynchronous Transmitter (IEEE)
PSAUK ...... Political Studies Association of the United Kingdom
PSAUSA ... Polish Socialist Alliance of the United States of America (EA)
PSAVA ...... Pribory i Sistemy Avtomatiki [*A publication*]
PSAX .... Pacific Southwest Airlines [*Air carrier designation symbol*]
PSB........... Pacific Science Board [*National Academy of Sciences*]
PSb........... Palestinskii Sbornik [*A publication*]
PSB........... Parti Socialiste Belge [*Belgian Socialist Party*]
PSB........... Personeelbeleid [*A publication*]
PSB........... Philatelic Sales Branch [*Later, PSD*] [*US Postal Service*]
PSB........... Philipsburg, PA [*Location identifier*] [*FAA*] (FAAL)
PSB........... Phosphorus-Solubilizing Bacteria [*Microbiology*]
PSB........... Plant Safety Bureau
PSB........... Plant Service Building [*Nuclear energy*] (NRCH)
PSB........... Polski Slownik Biograficzny [*A publication*]
PSB........... Polytechnic of the South Bank [*London, England*]
PSB........... Premium Savings Bond [*British*] (DCTA)
PSB........... Program Specification Block [*IBM Corp.*]
PSB........... Protected Specimen Brush [*Medicine*]
PSB........... Psychiatric BioScience, Inc. [*AMEX symbol*] (SPSG)
PsB........... Psychological Bulletin [*A publication*]
Ps B .... Psychologische Beitraege fuer alle Gebiete der Psychologie [*A publication*]
PSBA .... Power-Specific Biological Activity [*Engine emissions testing*]
PSBA .... Proceedings. Society of Biblical Archaeology [*A publication*]
PSBBF .... Pearl S. Buck Birthplace Foundation (EA)
PSBF......... Pearl S. Buck Foundation (EA)
PSBF......... Pioneer Savings Bank FSB [*NASDAQ symbol*] (NQ)
PSBG........ Pregnancy-Specific beta-Glycoprotein [*Gynecology*]
PSBH......... Pad Safety in Blockhouse
PSBK......... Progressive Bank, Inc. [*Pawling, NY*] [*NASDAQ symbol*] (NQ)
PSBL......... Possible (FAAC)
PSBLS .... Permanent Space Based Logistics System
PSBMA ..... Professional Services Business Management Association [*Later, PSMA*] (EA)
PSBN........ Pioneer Bancorp, Inc. [*Formerly, Pioneer Savings Bank, Inc.*] [*NASDAQ symbol*] (NQ)
PSBNDY ... Sociedade Brasileira de Nematologia. Publicacao [*A publication*]
PSBR .... Pennsylvania State University Breazeale Nuclear Reactor [*Research center*] (RCD)
PSBR .... Public Sector Borrowing Requirement
PSBRA9 .... International Committee for Bird Preservation. Pan American Section. Research Report [*A publication*]
PSBS......... Policy Sciences Book Series [*Elsevier Book Series*] [*A publication*]
PSBT .... Pilot Self-Briefing Terminal (FAAC)
PSBU........ Propeller Shaft Bearing Unit [*Truck engineering*]
PSBU........ Psychopharmacology Bulletin [*A publication*]
PSBUA ..... Psychological Bulletin [*A publication*]
Ps Bull...... Psychological Bulletin [*A publication*]
PSBX .... Peoples Savings Bank FSB [*NASDAQ symbol*] (NQ)
PSC........... Congolese Socialist Party [*Zaire*] [*Political party*] (PD)
PSC........... Isla De Pascua [*Easter Island*] [*Seismograph station code, US Geological Survey*] [*Closed*] (SEIS)
PSC........... Pacific Salmon Commission (EA)
PSC........... Pacific Science Center
PSC........... Pacific Science Council
PSC........... Pacific South Coast Freight Bureau, San Francisco CA [*STAC*]

PSC........... Pacific Studies Center (EA)
PSC........... Palestine Solidarity Committee [*Defunct*] (EA)
PSC........... Palmer Skin Conductance
PSC........... Parallel to Serial Converter
PSC........... Parallel Switch Control (MCD)
PSC........... Parents Sharing Custody (EA)
PSC........... Parti Socialiste Caledonien [*Political party*] [*New Caledonia*] (FEA)
PSC........... Parti Socialiste Camerounais [*Cameroonese Socialist Party*] [*Political party*]
PSC........... Parti Socialiste Centrafricain [*Central African Socialist Party*] [*Political party*] (PD)
PSC........... Partido Social Cristiano [*Social Christian Party*] [*Guatemala*] [*Political party*] (PPW)
PSC........... Partido Social Cristiano [*Social Christian Party*] [*Bolivia*] [*Political party*]
PSC........... Partido Social Cristiano [*Social Christian Party*] [*Ecuador*] [*Political party*] (PPW)
PSC........... Partido Socialcristiano Nicaraguense [*Nicaraguan Social Christian Party*] [*Political party*] (PPW)
PSC........... Partido Socialista de Catalunya [*Catalan Socialist Party*] [*Spain*] [*Political party*] (PPE)
PSC........... Pasco [*Washington*] [*Airport symbol*] (OAG)
PSC........... Pasco, WA [*Location identifier*] [*FAA*] (FAAL)
PSC........... Passed Staff College [*British*]
PSC........... Passenger Services Conference [*IATA*] (DS)
PSC........... Paul Smiths College [*New York*]
PSC........... Peacetime Subcontract
PSC........... Pembroke State College [*North Carolina*]
PSC........... Per Standard Compass [*Navigation*]
PSC........... Percentage of Successful Collisions [*Obstetrics*]
PSC........... Personal Computing [*A publication*]
PSC........... Personal Supercomputer [*Culler Scientific Systems Corp.*]
PSC........... Personnel Service Center [*or Company*] [*Military*] (INF)
PSC........... Personnel Status Change (KSC)
PSC........... Personnel Subsystem Cost
PSC........... Petty Sessional Court [*British*] (ROG)
PSC........... Phase-Sensitive Converter
PSC........... Philadelphia Service Center [*IRS*]
PSC........... Philadelphia Suburban Corporation [*NYSE symbol*] (SPSG)
PSC........... Philander Smith College [*Little Rock, AR*]
PSC........... Philippine Shippers Council (DS)
PSC........... Philippine Sugar Commission (EA)
PSC........... Phonemic Spelling Council (EA)
PSC........... Photography Studies College [*Australia*]
PSC........... Photosensitive Cell (IEEE)
PSC........... Physical Sciences Center
PSC........... Physical Sciences Committee [*Terminated, 1977*] [*NASA*] (EGAO)
PSC........... Physical Security/Pilferage Code (MCD)
Psc............ Pisces [*Constellation*]
PSC........... Pittsburgh Supercomputing Center [*National Science Foundation*] [*Research center*] (RCD)
PSC........... Pittsburgh Superconducting Center [*Pennsylvania*] (GRD)
pSC .... Plasmid Stanley Cohen [*Molecular biology*]
PSC........... Pluripotent Stem Cell [*Cytology*]
PSC........... Plutonium Stripping Concentrate [*Nuclear energy*] (NRCH)
PSC........... Polar Science Center [*University of Washington*] [*Research center*] (RCD)
PSC........... Polar Stratospheric Cloud [*Meteorology*]
PSC........... Polaroid Stereoscopic Chroncyclegraph
PSC........... Population Studies Center [*University of Michigan*] [*Research center*] (RCD)
PSC........... Porcelain on Steel Council [*Defunct*] (EA)
PSC........... Portland Society for Calligraphy (EA)
PSC........... Post-Storage Checkout [*NASA*] (KSC)
PSC........... Postal Service Center (AFM)
PSC........... Posterior Subcapsular Cataracts [*Ophthalmology*]
PSC........... Potentiometer Strip Chart
PSC........... Potomac State College [*of West Virginia University*]
PSC........... Power Supply Calibrator
PSC........... Preparatory Studies Course [*Australia*]
PSC........... Pressure Suit Circuit (KSC)
PSC........... Pressure System Control (AAG)
PSC........... Prestressed Concrete (ADA)
PSC........... Presumptive Hematopoietic Stem Cell
PSC........... Price Signal Code [*Military*] (AABC)
PSC........... Price Stabilization Council [*Philippines*] (DS)
PSC........... Primary Sclerosing Cholangitis [*Medicine*]
PSC........... Principal Subordinate Command (NATG)
PSC........... Private Sector Council (EA)
PS & C ...... Private Siding and Collected One End
PSC........... PROBE [*Program Optimization and Budget Evaluation*] Steering Committee [*Military*]
PSC........... Processing Service Centers [*Social Security Administration*]
PSC........... Processing and Spectral Control
PSC........... Procurement Source Code (AFM)
PSC........... Product Support Confidential (AAG)
PSC........... Professional Services Council [*Washington, DC*] (EA)
PSC........... Program Schedule Chart (NASA)

PSC........... Program Service Center [*Social Security Administration*]　(OICC)
PSC........... Program Standards Checker [*Data processing*]
PSC........... Program Status Chart [*Data processing*]
PSC........... Program Structure Code　(AFM)
PSC........... Programmable Sample Changer [*Spectroscopy*]
PSC........... Project Systems Control　(MCD)
PSC........... Prototype System Characteristics
PSC........... Public Service Careers [*Program*] [*Department of Labor*]
PSC........... Public Service Commission [*Usually, of a specific state*]
PSC........... Public Service Company
PSC........... Pulse Synchronized Contraction [*In the vascular system*] [*Medicine*]
PSC........... Sandoz AG [*Switzerland*] [*Research code symbol*]
PSc........... Scranton Public Library, Scranton, PA [*Library symbol*] [*Library of Congress*]　(LCLS)
PSC........... Swarthmore College, Swarthmore, PA [*Library symbol*] [*Library of Congress*] [*OCLC symbol*]　(LCLS)
PSCA......... Parliamentary Select Committee on Agriculture [*British*]
PscA......... Pisces Austrinus [*Constellation*]
PSCA......... Polish Social and Cultural Association　(EAIO)
PSCA......... Pressure Suit Conditioning Assembly　(MCD)
PSCA......... Profit Sharing Council of America　(EA)
PSCAN...... Purchase Order Scan
PSCB........ Padded Sample Collection Bag [*NASA*]
PSCBG...... Paper Shipping-Containers Buyers Group
PS & CC..... Packaging, Storage, and Containerization Center [*DARCOM*]　(MCD)
PSCC......... Photo Systems Controller Console　(KSC)
PSCC......... Projets de Services Communautaires du Canada
PSCD........ Plutonium Stripping Concentration Distillate [*Nuclear energy*]　(NRCH)
PSCD........ Program for the Study of Crime and Delinquency [*Ohio State University*] [*Research center*]　(RCD)
PSCF........ Personal Security Clearance File
PSCF........ Processor Storage Control Function
PSCFB...... Pacific South Coast Freight Bureau
PSCG........ Power Supply and Control Gear
PSCG........ Power Supply Control Group [*Military*]　(CAAL)
PSCH........ Postoperative Suprachoroidal Hemorrhage [*Medicine*]
P Sch........ Prairie Schooner [*A publication*]
PSC-Hi...... Friends Historical Library of Swarthmore College, Swarthmore, PA [*Library symbol*] [*Library of Congress*]　(LCLS)
PSCHO..... Psychopharmacology [*A publication*]
PSCI......... Plastic Shipping Container Institute　(EA)
PSCIA....... Peuce. Studii si Communicari de Istorie si Arheologie [*A publication*]
PSCJ......... Perseverance Society of Carpenters and Joiners [*A union*] [*British*]
PSCJ......... Progressive Society of Carpenters and Joiners [*A union*] [*British*]
PSCKAR.... Bulletin of National Fisheries. University of Pusan. Natural Sciences [*A publication*]
PSCL........ Papers and Studies in Contrastive Linguistics [*A publication*]
PSCL........ Programmed Sequential Control Language
PSCL........ Propellant Systems Cleaning Laboratory [*NASA*]　(NASA)
PSCL........ Propellants System Components Laboratory [*Kennedy Space Center*] [*NASA*]
PScLL....... Lackawanna Bar Association Law Library, Scranton, PA [*Library symbol*] [*Library of Congress*]　(LCLS)
PScM........ Marywood College, Scranton, PA [*Library symbol*] [*Library of Congress*]　(LCLS)
PSCM....... Process Steering and Control Module [*Telecommunications*]　(TEL)
PSCN........ Partido Socialcristiano Nicaraguense [*Nicaraguan Social Christian Party*] [*Political party*]　(PPW)
PSCN........ Permanent System Control Number　(MCD)
PSCN........ Preliminary Specification Change Notice [*NASA*]　(NASA)
PSCN........ Proposed Specification Change Notice
PSCNET.... Pittsburgh Superconducting Center Network
PSCO........ Pennsylvania State College of Optometry
PSCO........ Personnel Survey Control Officer [*Military*]　(AABC)
PSCOB...... Psychiatric Communications [*A publication*]
P S Conf Co ... Proceedings. Southern Conference on Corrections [*A publication*]
PSCP........ Palestine Symphonic Choir Project　(EA)
PSCP........ Polar Continental Shelf Project [*Canada*]
PSCP........ Public Service Careers Program [*Department of Labor*]
PSC-P....... Swarthmore College Peace Collection, Swarthmore, PA [*Library symbol*] [*Library of Congress*]　(LCLS)
PSCPD...... Philadelphia Signal Corps Procurement District [*Army*]
PSC-PSOE ... Partit dels Socialistes de Catalunya [*Party of Socialists of Catalonia*] [*Political party*]　(PPW)
PSCPT...... Preschool Self-Concept Picture Test [*Psychology*]
PScQ........ Political Science Quarterly [*A publication*]
PSCR........ Permanent Scratch File [*Data processing*]
PSCR........ Photo-Selective Copper Reduction [*For circuit board manufacture*]
PSCR........ Priority System Change Request
PSCR........ Production Schedule Completion Report [*DoD*]
PSCR........ Public Service Commission Reports [*A publication*]　(DLA)

P Scribe...... Portland Scribe [*A publication*]
PSCS......... Pacific Scatter Communications System [*Air Force*]　(CET)
PSCS......... Program Support Control System
PSCU....... Power Supply Control Unit　(CET)
PScU......... University of Scranton, Scranton, PA [*Library symbol*] [*Library of Congress*]　(LCLS)
PSCUS...... Peters' United States Surpeme Court Reports [*26-41 United States*] [*A publication*]　(DLA)
PSCX........ Photographic Sciences Corporation [*NASDAQ symbol*]　(NQ)
PSD......... Destour Socialist Party [*Tunisia*] [*Political party*]　(PD)
PSD......... Doctor of Political Science
Ps D......... Doctor of Psychology
Ps D......... Doctor of Psychology in Metaphysics
PSD......... Doctor of Public Service
PSD......... Packed Switched Data
PSD........... Parti Social-Democrate [*Social Democratic Party*] [*France*] [*Political party*]　(PPW)
PSD........... Parti Social Democrate de Madagascar et des Comores [*Social Democratic Party of Madagascar and Comores*]
PSD......... Particle Size Distribution
PSD......... Partido Social Democrata [*Social Democratic Party*] [*Mexico*] [*Political party*]　(PPW)
PSD......... Partido Social Democrata [*Social Democratic Party*] [*Spain*] [*Political party*]　(PPE)
PSD......... Partido Social Democrata [*Social Democratic Party*] [*Bolivia*] [*Political party*]　(PPW)
PSD......... Partido Social Democratico [*Social Democratic Party*] [*Brazil*]
PSD......... Partido Social Democratico [*Social Democratic Party*] [*El Salvador*]
PSD......... Partido Social Democratico [*Social Democratic Party*] [*Nicaragua*] [*Political party*]　(PPW)
PSD......... Partido Socialista Democratico [*Democratic Socialist Party*] [*Guatemala*] [*Political party*]　(PD)
PSD......... Partido Socialista Democratico [*Democratic Socialist Party*] [*Argentina*] [*Political party*]　(PPW)
PSD......... Passed　(ROG)
PSD......... Passing Scene Display
PSD......... Past Start Date
PSD......... Patient Symptom Diary
PSD......... Permanent Signal Detection [*Telecommunications*]　(TEL)
PSD......... Personal Services Department [*Navy*] [*British*]
PSD......... Personnel Services Division [*Army*]
PSD......... Personnel System [*or Subsystem*] Development　(AAG)
PSD........... Pescadero [*California*] [*Seismograph station code, US Geological Survey*]　(SEIS)
PSD......... Petroleum Safety Data [*American Petroleum Institute*]
PSD......... Petty Session Division [*Legal term*]　(DLA)
PSD......... Phase-Sensitive Demodulator [*or Detector*]
PSD......... Phase Shift Driver
PSD......... Philatelic Sales Division [*Formerly, PSB*] [*US Postal Service*]
PSD......... Photoconductive, Semiconductive Device
PSD......... Photon Stimulated Desorption [*For analysis of surfaces*]
PSD......... Physical Sciences Data [*Elsevier Book Series*] [*A publication*]
PSD......... Pictorialized Scatter Diagram [*Botany*]
PSD......... Pitch Servo Drive
PSD......... Polystyrene, Deuterated [*Organic chemistry*]
PSD......... Post Sending Delay
PSD......... Postsynaptic Density [*Neurophysiology*]
PSD......... Power Spectral [*or Spectrum*] Density
PSD......... Preferred Sea Duty
PSD......... Pressure-Sensitive Devices　(MCD)
PSD........... Prevention of Significant Deterioration [*Environmental Protection Agency*]
PS & D....... Private Siding and Delivered One End
PSD......... Procedural Support Data
PSD........... Processing Status Display [*NASA*]
PSD......... Procurement Surveys Division [*NASA*]　(MCD)
PsD......... Professional Service Dates [*Formerly, ADBD*]
PSD......... Professional Systems Division [*American Institute of Architects Service Corp.*] [*Information service or system*]　(IID)
PSD......... Program Status Documents [*Data processing*]
PSD......... Program Status Doubleword
PSD......... Program Support Document　(MUGU)
PSD......... Programme Support and Development [*British*]
PSD......... Promotion Service Date
PSD......... Propellant Slosh Dynamics
PSD......... Propellant Storage Depot [*NASA*]
PSD......... Proportional Stock Density [*Pisciculture*]
PSD......... Protective Serum Dilution
PSD......... Protective Structures Division [*Office of Civil Defense*]
PSD......... Pseudosingle Domain [*Behavior of grains in rocks*] [*Geophysics*]
PSD......... Puget Sound Power & Light Co. [*NYSE symbol*]　(SPSG)
PSD......... Pulse Shape Discriminator
PSD......... Pure Screw Dislocation
PSDA........ Partial Source Data Automation　(NVT)
PSDA........ Particle Size Distribution Analysis [*Statistics*]
P/SDA....... Power/Signal Distribution Assembly
PSDC........ Pennsylvania State Data Center [*Middletown*] [*Information service or system*]　(IID)

PSDC......... Plant Sciences Data Center [*Formerly, Plant Records Center*] [*American Horticultural Society*] [*Mt. Vernon, VA*]
PSDC......... Power Sprayer and Duster Council   (EA)
PSDC......... Protective Structures Development Center [*Military*]
PSDD........ Preliminary System Design Description [*Nuclear energy*]   (NRCH)
PSDDS..... Pilot [*or Public*] Switched Digital Data Service [*Telecommunications*]   (TEL)
Psdepgr...... Pseudepigrapha   (BJA)
PSDF........ Popular Self-Defense Force [*Local armed units protecting Vietnamese hamlets*]
PSDF........ Propulsion Systems Development Facility   (KSC)
PSDI.......... Partido Social Democratico Independente [*Independent Social Democratic Party*] [*Portugal*] [*Political party*]   (PPE)
PSDI.......... Partito Socialista Democratico Italiano [*Italian Social Democratic Party*]
PSDIAD .... Photostimulated Desorption Ion Angular Distribution [*Surface analysis*]
PSDIS....... Partito Socialista Democratico Indipendente Sammarinese [*Independent Social Democratic Party of San Marino*] [*Political party*]   (PPE)
PSdM........ Mennonite Publishing House, Scottsdale, PA [*Library symbol*] [*Library of Congress*]   (LCLS)
PSDN .... Packet Switched Data Network [*Telecommunications*]
PSDP........ Payload Station Distribution Panel [*NASA*]   (MCD)
PSDP........ Personnel Subsystem Development Plan
PSDP........ Phrase Structure and Dependency Parser   (DIT)
PSDP........ Programmable Signal Data Processor   (MCD)
PSDR........ Planning and Scheduling Document Record [*NASA*]   (NASA)
PSDR........ Public Sector Debt Repayment [*British*]   (ECON)
PSDS........ Packet Switch Data System [*Information retrieval*]   (IID)
PSDS........ Packet Switched Data Service [*Telecommunications*]   (TEL)
PSDS........ Partito Socialista Democratico Sammarinese [*Social Democratic Party of San Marino*] [*Political party*]   (PPE)
PSDS........ Passing Scene Display System
PSDS........ Permanently Separated from Duty Station [*Military*]
PS & DS..... Program Statistics and Data Systems
PSDS........ Public Switched Data Service [*Telecommunications*]
PSDSP...... Pious Society of the Daughters of Saint Paul [*See also FSP*] [*Rome, Italy*]   (EAIO)
PSDT........ President   (ROG)
PSDTC..... Pacific Securities Depository Trust Company
PSDU........ Power Switching Distribution Unit
PSDVB...... Poly(styrene-Divinylbenzene) [*Organic chemistry*]
PSE........... Pacific Stock Exchange   (EA)
PSE........... Packet-Switching Exchange
PSE........... Partido Socialista Ecuatoriano [*Ecuadorean Socialist Party*] [*Political party*]   (PPW)
PSE........... Partido Socialista de Euskadi [*Basque Socialist Party*] [*Spain*] [*Political party*]   (EY)
PSE........... Passive Seismic Experiment [*NASA*]
PSE........... Payload Service Equipment [*NASA*]   (MCD)
PSE........... Payload Support Equipment [*NASA*]   (MCD)
PSE........... Peculiar Support Equipment [*NASA*]   (NASA)
PSE........... Personnel Subsystem Elements [*Army*]   (AABC)
PSE........... Perth Stock Exchange [*Australia*]
PSE........... Phase-Shifter, Electronic
PSE........... Philadelphia Stock Exchange
PS and E .... Photographic Science and Engineering [*A publication*]
PSE........... Physical Security Equipment [*Army*]   (RDA)
PSE........... Phytochemical Society of Europe   (EA)
PSE........... Pitch Steering Error
PS & E .... Plans, Specifications, and Estimates [*Construction*]
PSE........... Pleasant Saturday Evenings
PSE........... Pleasant Sunday Evenings   (ROG)
PSE........... Please   (MDG)
PSE........... Point of Subjective Equality [*Psychology*]
PSE........... Polestar Exploration, Inc. [*Vancouver Stock Exchange symbol*]
PSE........... Ponce [*Puerto Rico*] [*Airport symbol*]   (OAG)
PSE........... Portal Systemic Encephalopathy [*Medicine*]
PSE........... Postshunt Encephalopathy [*Medicine*]
PSE........... Power System Engineering
PSE........... Prague Studies in English [*A publication*]
PSE........... Pressurized Subcritical Experiment [*Nuclear energy*]
PSE........... Prevention of Stripping Equipment   (NATG)
PSE........... Princeton Studies in English [*A publication*]
PSE........... Principal Staff Element [*Defense Supply Agency*]
PSE........... Priority Standardization Effort [*Army*]   (AABC)
PSE........... Probability of Successful Engagement [*Military*]   (CAAL)
PSE........... Process Systems Engineering
PSE........... Producer Subsidy Equivalent [*OECD model for the study of farm-support policies in the EC, Japan, America, Canada, Australia, and New Zealand*]
PSE........... Product Support Engineering   (MCD)
PSE........... Programmed System Evolution   (MCD)
PSE........... Protein Separation Efficiency [*Food technology*]
PSE........... Psychological Stress Evaluator [*Lie detector*]
PSE........... Public Sector [*or Service*] Employment
PSE........... Public Service Electric & Gas Co., Newark, NJ [*OCLC symbol*]   (OCLC)
PSE........... Pulse Sense

3PSE........ Three-Pulse Stimulated Photon Echo [*Spectroscopy*]
PSEA .... Physical Security Equipment Agency [*Army*]
PSEA .... Pleaters, Stitchers, and Embroiderers Association   (EA)
PSEAL...... Papers in South East Asian Linguistics [*A publication*]
PSEB .... Poisoning Surveillance and Epidemiology Branch   (EA)
PSEBA ...... Proceedings. Society for Experimental Biology and Medicine [*A publication*]
PSEBM ..... Proceedings of the Society for Experimental Biology and Medicine [*A publication*]
P/SEC .... Personal Secretary   (DCTA)
PSEC .... Picosecond
PSE & C..... Power Supply Engineering and Construction [*Nuclear energy*]   (NRCH)
PSED .... Preliminary Systems Engineering Design
PSEF........ Pennsylvania Science and Engineering Foundation
PSEF........ Plastic Surgery Educational Foundation   (EA)
PSE & G .... Public Service Electric & Gas Co.
PSEKUT ... Paar Sammukest Eesti Kirjanduse Uurimise Teed [*A publication*]
PSEL .... Publications. Societe Egyptologique a l'Universite d'Etat de Leningrad [*A publication*]
PSelS .... Susquehanna University, Selinsgrove, PA [*Library symbol*] [*Library of Congress*]   (LCLS)
PSEMA ..... Parti Social d'Education des Masses Africaines [*African Party for Social Education of the Masses*] [*Upper Volta*]
PSENA ...... Photographic Science and Engineering [*A publication*]
PSEP .... Passive Seismic Experiments Package [*NASA*]
PSEPB ...... Progress in Separation and Purification [*A publication*]
PSEQ........ Pupil Services Expectation Questionnaire
PS & ER..... Production Support and Equipment Replacement [*Military*]   (AABC)
PSERC...... Public Sector Economics Research Centre [*University of Leicester*] [*British*]   (CB)
PSES........ Pretreatment Standards for Existing Sources [*Environmental Protection Agency*]
Pseud........ Pseudepigrapha   (BJA)
PSEUD...... Pseudonym
Pseudep..... Pseudepigrapha   (BJA)
PSEW .... Project on the Status and Education of Women   (EA)
PSewD ...... Dixmont State Hospital, Sewickley, PA [*Library symbol*] [*Library of Congress*]   (LCLS)
PSF .... Pakistan Science Foundation
PSF .... Panama Sea Frontier
P & SF....... Panhandle & Santa Fe Railway Co.
PSF .... Panhandle & Santa Fe Railway Co. [*AAR code*]
PSF .... Parti Social Francais [*French Social Party*] [*Political party*]   (PPE)
PSF .... Passive Solar Foundation   (EA)
PSF .... Payload Structure Fuel [*Ratio*]
PSF .... Per Square Foot   (ADA)
PSF .... Permanent Signal Finder
PSF .... Philippine Sea Frontier
PSF .... Pittsfield, MA [*Location identifier*] [*FAA*]   (FAAL)
PSF .... Plutonium Stripper Feed [*Nuclear energy*]   (NRCH)
PSF .... Point Spread Function
PSF .... Popular Struggle Front [*Palestine*] [*Political party*]   (PD)
PSF .... Port Stanley [*Falkland Islands*] [*Seismograph station code, US Geological Survey*] [*Closed*]   (SEIS)
PSF .... Pounds per Square Foot
PSF .... Presidio of San Francisco [*Military*]   (AABC)
PSF .... Prime Subframe   (MCD)
PSF .... Probability of Spurious Fire [*Military*]   (CAAL)
PSF .... Processing and Staging Facility [*Solid rocket booster*]   (NASA)
PSF .... Processing and Storage Facility [*NASA*]   (NASA)
PSF .... Program for the Study of the Future   (EA)
PSF .... Progres Social Francais [*French Social Progress*] [*Political party*]   (PPE)
PSF .... Progressive Space Forum   (EA)
PSF .... Provisional Sinn Fein [*Northern Ireland*]
PSF .... Provisional System Feature [*Telecommunications*]   (TEL)
PSF .... Prudential Strategic Income [*NYSE symbol*]   (SPSG)
PSF .... Pseudosarcomatous Fasciitis [*Medicine*]
PSF .... Saint Francis College, Loretto, PA [*OCLC symbol*]   (OCLC)
PSFADF.... Proceedings. Annual Conference. Southeastern Association of Fish and Wildlife Agencies [*A publication*]
PSFAM ..... Parameter Sensitive Frequency Assignment Method   (MCD)
PS/FC........ Power Supply/Fuel Cell   (MCD)
PSFC .... Process Supercritical Fluid Chromatography
PSFC .... Provisional Special Forces Company   (CINC)
PSFC/HIMH ... Pete Shelley Fan Club/Harmony in My Head   (EA)
PSFD .... Public Sector Financial Deficit
PSFL........ Puget Sound Freight Lines [*AAR code*]
PSFM .... Publications. Societe Francaise de Musicologie [*A publication*]
PSFQ........ Pupil Services Fulfillment Questionnaire
PSFS......... Philadelphia Savings Fund Society [*NASDAQ symbol*]   (NQ)
PSG........... Pacific Seabird Group   (EA)
PSG........... Palestine Study Group   (EA)
PSG........... Parachute Study Group   (EA)
PSG........... Parti Socialiste Guyanais [*Guiana Socialist Party*] [*Political party*]   (PPW)
PSG........... Passage   (FAAC)

PSG.......... Passing (FAAC)
PSG.......... Pechiney-Saint-Gobain [*Commercial firm*] [*France*]
PSG.......... Petersburg [*Alaska*] [*Airport symbol*] (OAG)
PSG.......... Petersburg, AK [*Location identifier*] [*FAA*] (FAAL)
PSG.......... Phenol Sector Group [*European Council of Chemical Manufacturers Federations*] [*Brussels, Belgium*] (EAIO)
PSG.......... Phosphate-Saline-Glucose [*A buffer*] [*Cell culture*]
PSG.......... Phosphosilicate Glass (IEEE)
PSG.......... Planning Systems Generator
PSG.......... Platoon Sergeant [*Army*] (AABC)
PSG.......... Post Stall Gyration (MCD)
PSG.......... Power Subsystem Group [*NASA*] (MCD)
PSG.......... Presystolic Gallop [*Cardiology*]
PSG.......... Production System Generator
PSG.......... Professional Specialty Group
PSG.......... Programmable Sound Generator [*Chip*] [*Atari, Inc.*]
PSG.......... Programmable Symbol Generator
PSG.......... PS Group, Inc. [*NYSE symbol*] (SPSG)
PSG.......... Pseudomonas Syringae PV Glycinea [*Plant pathology*]
PSG.......... Psychogalvanometer
PSG.......... Publishing Systems Group [*Later, CPSUG*] (EA)
PSG.......... Pulse Sequence Generation [*Instrumentation*]
PSGA........ Parkinson Support Groups of America (EA)
PSGA........ Pedal Steel Guitar Association (EA)
PSGA........ Professional Skaters Guild of America (EA)
PSGB........ Pharmaceutical Society of Great Britain
PSGD........ Past Senior Grand Deacon [*Freemasonry*]
PSGM........ Past Supreme Grand Master [*Freemasonry*]
PSGN........ Post-Streptococcal Glomerulonephritis [*Medicine*]
PSGR........ Passenger (AFM)
PSGT........ Platoon Sergeant [*Military*]
PSGTCAEI ... Permanent Secretariat of the General Treaty on Central American Economic Integration (EAIO)
PSGW....... Past Senior Grand Warden [*Freemasonry*]
PSH .... Friends Historical Library of Swarthmore College, Swarthmore, PA [*OCLC symbol*] (OCLC)
PSH .... Parshall, ND [*Location identifier*] [*FAA*] (FAAL)
PSH .... Permanent Shift of Hearing
PSH .... Peshawar [*Pakistan*] [*Seismograph station code, US Geological Survey*] (SEIS)
PSH .... Phase Shift (MSA)
PSH .... Polystyrene, Hydrogenous [*Organic chemistry*]
PSH .... Post-Stimulus Histogram [*Psychometrics*]
PSH .... Preselect Heading (NG)
PSH .... Pressure Switch, High [*Nuclear energy*] (NRCH)
PSH .... Program Support Handbook
PSH .... Proximity Sensing Head
PSH .... Public Storage Canadian Properties IIIa Ltd. [*Toronto Stock Exchange symbol*]
PSH .... Publications Statistiques Hongroises [*Hungary*]
PSHADL... Publications. Societe Historique et Archeologique dans le Duche de Limbourg [*A publication*]
PSHAL...... Publications. Societe Historique et Archeologique dans le Duche de Limbourg [*A publication*]
P Shaw ...... Patrick Shaw's Justiciary Cases [*1819-31*] [*Scotland*] [*A publication*] (DLA)
PSHC....... Permanent Secretariat of the Hemispheric Congress (EA)
PSHC....... Public Speaking and Humor Club (EA)
PSHCJ ...... Philanthropic Society of House Carpenters and Joiners [*A union*] [*British*]
PSHD .... Phase-Shift Driver (MSA)
PSHED...... Psychologie Heute [*A publication*]
PSHF........ Polysulfone Hollow Fiber [*Filtration membrane*]
PSHIGDL ... Publications. Section Historique. Institut Grand-Ducal de Luxembourg [*A publication*]
PSHIL ...... Publications. Section Historique. Institut Grand-Ducal de Luxembourg [*A publication*]
PSHL........ Publications. Societe Historique et Archeologique dans le Duche de Limbourg [*A publication*]
PSHP........ Pennsylvania Journal for Health, Physical Education, and Recreation [*A publication*]
PSHPZ...... PSH Master LP I [*NASDAQ symbol*] (SPSG)
PSHR........ Pusher [*Freight*]
PShS.......... Shippensburg State College, Shippensburg, PA [*Library symbol*] [*Library of Congress*] (LCLS)
PSHT........ Powys Self-Help Trust [*British*]
PSI........... Paid Service Indication [*Telecommunications*] (TEL)
PSI........... Paper Stock Institute of America (EA)
PSI........... Parapat [*Sumatra*] [*Seismograph station code, US Geological Survey*] (SEIS)
PSI........... Parapsychological Services Institute (EA)
PSI........... Parenting Stress Index [*Psychology*]
PSI........... Partai Socialis Indonesia [*Socialist Party of Indonesia*]
PSI........... Participation Systems, Incorporated [*Electronics Communications Co.*] [*Winchester, MA*] [*Telecommunications*] (TSSD)
PSI........... Partito Socialista Italiano [*Italian Socialist Party*] [*Political party*] (PPE)
PSI........... Pasni [*Pakistan*] [*Airport symbol*] (OAG)
PSI........... Passive Solar Institute (EA)
P & SI ...... Pay and Supply Instruction [*Coast Guard*]

PSI........... Per Square Inch (ADA)
PSI........... Peripherally Synapsing Interneuron [*Neurology*]
PSI........... Permanent Staff Instructor [*Military*] [*British*]
PSI........... Permuterm Subject Index [*Institute for Scientific Information*] [*A publication*] (IID)
PsI........... Perpetual Storage, Inc., Salt Lake City, UT [*Library symbol*] [*Library of Congress*] (LCLS)
PSI........... Person of Special Importance [*British military*] (DMA)
PSI........... Personal Sequential-Inference Machine [*Data processing*]
PSI........... Personal Service Income
PSI........... Personalized System of Instruction
PSI........... Personnel Security Investigation [*Military*]
PSI........... Personnel Selection Inventory [*Test*]
PSI........... Phenomenological Systems, Incorporated
PSI........... Photo Services Industrial Ltd. [*British*]
PSI........... Photographic Society International (EA)
PSI........... Photometric Sunspot Index
PSI........... Physical, Sensitivity, Intellectual [*Biorhythmics*]
PSI........... Piccole Storie Illustrate [*A publication*]
PSI........... Plan Speed Indicator [*Military*]
PSI........... Planned Start Installation [*Telecommunications*] (TEL)
PSI........... Play Skills Inventory
PSI........... Policy Studies Institute [*Research center*] [*British*] (IRC)
PSI........... Pollutant Standards Index [*Environmental Protection Agency*]
p-Si......... Polycrystalline Silicon [*Photovoltaic energy systems*]
PSI........... Porta Systems Corp. [*AMEX symbol*] (SPSG)
PSI........... Positive Self-Image [*Psychology*]
PSI........... Postpartum Support, International (EA)
PSI........... Pounds per Square Inch
PSI........... Power per Square Inch
PSI........... Power Static Inverter (NASA)
PSI........... Praed Street Irregulars (EA)
PSI........... Pre-Sentence Investigation (OICC)
PSI........... Preprogrammed Self-Instruction [*Data processing*] (IEEE)
PSI........... Present Serviceability Index (IEEE)
PSI........... Preservice Inspection [*Nuclear energy*] (NRCH)
PSI........... Preshipment Inspection [*International trade*]
PSI........... Pressure Sensitive Identification
PSI........... Problem-Solving Information [*Apparatus*]
PSI........... Problem Solving Interpreter [*Computer language*]
PSI........... Process System Index
PSI........... Process Systems, Incorporated
PSI........... Proctorial System of Instruction (IEEE)
PSI........... Product Support Instructions (AAG)
PSI........... Production Stock Item (MCD)
PSI........... Professional Secretaries International [*Kansas City, MO*] (EA)
PSI........... Program Status Information [*Data processing*] (MCD)
PSI........... Program Supply Interest (MCD)
PSI........... Programmed School Input (NVT)
PSI........... Project Starlight International (EA)
PSI........... Protosynthex Index
PSI........... Psychological Screening Inventory [*Personality development test*]
PSI........... Psychosomatic Inventory [*Psychology*]
PSI........... Pubblicazioni. Societa Italiana per la Ricerca dei Papiri Greci e Latini in Egitto [*Florence*] [*A publication*]
PSI........... Public Services International [*See also ISP*] [*Ferney Voltaire, France*] (EAIO)
PSI........... Publications Standing Instruction (AAG)
PSIA........ Paper Stock Institute of America (EA)
PSIA........ Pounds per Square Inch Absolute
PSIA........ President of the Society of Industrial Artists [*British*]
PSIA........ Production System Integration Area
PSIA........ Professional Ski Instructors of America (EA)
PSIA........ Public Security Investigation Agency [*Japan*] (CINC)
PSI Ber .... PSI [*Paul Scherrer Institut*] Bericht [*A publication*]
PSIC .... Passenger Service Improvement Corporation
PSIC .... Passive Solar Industries Council (EA)
PSIC .... Process Signal Interface Controller
PSIC .... Production Scheduling and Inventory Control
PSICD ...... Proceedings. IEEE Computer Society's International Computer Software and Applications Conference [*A publication*]
PSICP....... Program Support Inventory Control Point
PSID .... Partial Seismic Intrusion Device (MCD)
PSID .... Patrol Seismic Intrusion Detector [*DoD*]
PSID .... Pounds per Square Inch Differential (MCD)
PSID .... Preliminary Safety Information Document [*Nuclear energy*] (NRCH)
PS/IDS...... Physical Security/Intrusion Detection System (MCD)
PSIEP....... Project on Scientific Information Exchange in Psychology [*Superseded by Office of Communication*]
PSIFL....... Pan. Studi dell'Istituto di Filologia Latina [*A publication*]
PSIG .... Pounds per Square Inch Gauge
PSIG .... Propulsion Systems Integration Group [*NASA*] (NASA)
PSIL........ Potential Selected Item List (MCD)
PSIL........ Preferred Speech Interference Level
PSI-LOGO ... Listing of Oil and Gas Opportunities [*Online Resource Exchange, Inc.*] [*Database*]
PSIM........ Power System Instrumentation and Measurement (MCD)
PSIM........ Problem-Solving Instructional Material [*National Science Foundation project*]

PSIP.......... Private Sector Initiative Program [*Department of Labor*]
PSIR Bull Monogr ... PSIR [*Pakistan Council of Scientific and Industrial Research*] Bulletin Monograph [*A publication*]
PSIS.......... Pounds per Square Inch Sealed   (NASA)
PSISIG........ Psychic Science International Special Interest Group   (EA)
PSIT........... Property Security Investment Trust [*British*]
PSIUP .... Partito Socialista Italiano di Unita Proletaria [*Italian Socialist Party of Proletarian Unity (1945-1947)*] [*Political party*]   (PPE)
PSIV .... Passive
PSIX .... Peripheral Systems, Incorporated [*Portland, OR*] [*NASDAQ symbol*]   (NQ)
PSJ .... Parallel Swivel Joint
PSJ .... Petites Soeurs de Jesus [*Little Sisters of Jesus - LSJ*] [*Rome, Italy*]   (EAIO)
PSJ .... Philosophical Studies of Japan [*A publication*]
PSJ .... Plane Swivel Joint
PSJ .... Poso [*Indonesia*] [*Airport symbol*]   (OAG)
PSJ .... Pressure Switch Joint
PSJ .... Public Service Job   (OICC)
PSJS.......... Pier and Span Junction Set   (MCD)
PSK........... Dublin, VA [*Location identifier*] [*FAA*]   (FAAL)
PSK........... Phase-Shift Keying [*Data processing*]
PSK........... Power Supply Kit
PSK........... Private Secretary to the King [*British*]
PSK........... Program Selection Key [*Data processing*]   (BUR)
PSK........... Protection Survey Kit
PSK........... Pulse Shift Keying   (CAAL)
PSKAD ..... Promyshlennost Sinteticheskogo Kauchuka [*A publication*]
PSKI .... Pikes Peak Ski Corp. [*NASDAQ symbol*]   (NQ)
PSKJ......... Pitanja Savremenog Knjizevnog Jezika [*A publication*]
PSKM........ Phase-Shift Keying MODEM
Pskov Gos Pedagog Inst Uch Zap ... Pskovskii Gosudarstvennyi Pedagogicheskii Institut. Uchenye Zapiski [*A publication*]
Pskov Ped Inst Fiz-Mat Fak Ucen Zap ... Pskovskii Pedagogiceskii Institut. Fiziko-Matematiceskii Fakul'tet. Ucenye Zapiski [*A publication*]
PSK-PCM ... Phase-Shift Keying - Pulse Code Modulation
PSL........... Palouse Silt Loam [*Agronomy*]
PSL........... Parallel Strand Lumber
PSL........... Paymaster-Sub-Lieutenant [*Navy*] [*British*]
PSL........... Peabody Short Line R. R. [*Army*]
PSL........... Personnel Management [*A publication*]
PSL........... Personnel Skill Levels   (AAG)
PSL........... Petroleum Ether-Soluble Lipid
PSL........... Photographic Science Laboratory [*Navy*]
PSL........... Photostimulated Luminescence [*Physics*]
PSL........... Physical Sciences Laboratory [*University of Wisconsin - Madison, New Mexico State University*] [*Research center*]
PSL........... Physical Sciences Laboratory [*Bethesda, MD*] [*National Institutes of Health*]   (GRD)
PSL........... Pipe Sleeve
PSL........... Pocket Select Language [*Burroughs Corp.*]
PSL........... Polskie Stronnictwo Ludowe [*Polish Peasant Party*] [*Political party*]   (PPE)
PSL........... Polymer Science Library [*Elsevier Book Series*] [*A publication*]
PSL........... Portable Standard List Processing [*Data processing*]
PSL........... Potential Source List   (MCD)
PSL........... Power and Signal List [*Telecommunications*]   (TEL)
PSL........... Power Source Logic
PS & L....... Power Switching and Logic
PSL........... Practical Storage Life
PSL........... Pressure Seal   (NASA)
PSL........... Pressure-Sensitive Label
PSL........... Primary Standards Laboratory
PSL........... Private Sector Liquidity
PSL........... Problem-Solving Language
PSL........... Problem Specification Language
PSL........... Process Simulation Language [*Data processing*]   (TEL)
PSL........... Process Status Longword [*Number*] [*Data processing*]   (BYTE)
PSL........... Program Support Library   (MCD)
PSL........... Project Support Laboratory [*Military*]   (CAAL)
PSL........... Propellant Seal
PSL........... Propulsion Systems Laboratory [*USATACOM*]   (RDA)
PSL........... Public School League [*Sports*]
PSL........... South Hills Library Association, Pittsburgh, PA [*OCLC symbol*]   (OCLC)
PSLA .... Polish Sea League of America   (EA)
PSLA .... Preferred Savings Bank, Inc. [*NASDAQ symbol*]   (NQ)
Psl Admr ... Personnel Administrator [*A publication*]
PSLC .... Pawathy Stare Literatury Ceske [*A publication*]
PSLC .... Post-Schistosomal Liver Cirrhosis [*Medicine*]
PSLC .... Private Security Liaison Council   (EA)
Psl Exec ...... Personnel Executive [*A publication*]
PSLG .... Public Service and Local Government [*A publication*]
Psl & Guid J ... Personnel and Guidance Journal [*A publication*]
PSLI.......... Packet Switch Level Interface
PSLI.......... Partito Socialista dei Lavoratori Italiani [*Socialist Party of Italian Workers*] [*Political party*]   (PPE)
PSLI.......... Penta Systems International, Inc. [*NASDAQ symbol*]   (NQ)
PSLI.......... Physalaemin-Like Immunoreactivity [*Medicine*]

Psl J .... Personnel Journal [*A publication*]
PSL-Lewica ... Polskie Stronnictwo-Lewica [*Polish Peasant Party-Left (1947-1949)*] [*Political party*]
PSL-Lewica ... Polskie Stronnictwo Ludowe-Lewica [*Polish Peasant Party-Left (1913-1920)*] [*Political party*]   (PPE)
PSLLS .... Pulsed Solid-State LASER Light Source
PSL-NW...... Polskie Stronnictwo Ludowe-Nowe Wyzwolenie [*Polish Peasant Party-New Liberation*] [*Political party*]   (PPE)
PSL-Piast .. Polskie Stronnictwo Ludowe-Piast [*Polish Peasant Party-Piast*] [*Political party*]   (PPE)
PSL/PSA... Problem Statement Language/Problem Specification Analyzer [*Data processing*]
Psl Psy .... Personnel Psychology [*A publication*]
Psl R .... Personnel Review [*A publication*]
PSLR .... Product Safety and Liability Reporter [*A publication*]
PSLS.......... Pan Stock Line Station   (MCD)
PSLT .... Picture Story Language Test
PSLT .... Pressurized Sonobuoy Launch Tube [*Navy*]   (CAAL)
PSLV .... Poa Semilatent Virus
PSL-Wyzwolenie ... Polskie Stronnictwo Ludowe-Wyzwolenie [*Polish Peasant Party-Liberation*] [*Political party*]   (PPE)
PSM.......... Mauritian Socialist Party [*Political party*]   (PD)
PSM.......... Pagine di Storia della Medicina [*A publication*]
PSM.......... Parc Saint-Maur [*France*] [*Later, CLF*] [*Geomagnetic observatory code*]
PSM.......... Parcel Sorting Machine [*Freight*]   (DCTA)
PSM.......... Parti Socialiste Monegasque [*Monaco Socialist Party*] [*Political party*]   (PPW)
PSM.......... Passenger Service Manager [*Travel industry*]
PSM.......... Past Savio Movement   (EA)
PSM.......... Peak Selector Memory [*Data processing*]
PSM.......... Pennwalt Corp. [*Formerly, Pennsalt Chemicals Corp.*] [*NYSE symbol*]   (SPSG)
PSM.......... Personal Skills Map [*Career effectiveness test*]
PSM.......... Personnel Subsystem Manager [*Army*]   (AABC)
PS & M ..... Personnel Supervision and Management Division of ASTSECNAV's Office [*Absorbed into SECP, 1944*]
PSM.......... Personnel Systems Management [*Air Force*]   (AFM)
PSM.......... Petroleum Supply Monthly [*Database*] [*Department of Energy*] [*Information service or system*]   (CRD)
PSM.......... Phase-Sensitive Modulator   (MCD)
PSM.......... Phase-Shifter Module
PSM.......... Philippine Studies (Manila) [*A publication*]
PSM.......... Pia Societas Missionum [*Fathers of the Pious Society of Missions, Pallottini*] [*Roman Catholic religious order*]
PSM.......... Pioneer Metals Corp. [*Toronto Stock Exchange symbol*] [*Vancouver Stock Exchange symbol*]
PSM.......... Please See Me
PSM.......... Plymouth State College of the University of New Hampshere, Plymouth, NH [*OCLC symbol*]   (OCLC)
PSM.......... Portsmouth, NH [*Location identifier*] [*FAA*]   (FAAL)
PSM.......... Postal Service Manual [*A publication*]   (AFM)
PSM.......... Postsynaptic Membrane [*Neurology*]
PSM.......... Power Strapping Machine
PSM.......... Power System Module
PSM.......... Presystolic Murmur [*Cardiology*]
PSM.......... Prism   (MSA)
PSM.......... Pro Sanctity Movement   (EA)
P & SM ...... Procurement and Subcontract Management [*NASA*]   (NASA)
PSM.......... Product Support Manual   (AAG)
PSM.......... Program-Sensitive Malfunction
PSM.......... Program Support Management [*NASA*]   (KSC)
PSM.......... Programming Support Monitor [*Texas Instruments, Inc.*]
PSM.......... Propellant Storage Module [*NASA*]
PSM.......... Public School Magazine [*A publication*]
PSM.......... Pyro Substitute Monitor [*NASA*]   (NASA)
PSM.......... Pytannja Slov'jans'koho Movoznavstva [*A publication*]
PSm.......... Thesaurus Syriacus [*R. Paine Smith*] [*A publication*]   (BJA)
PSMA........ Power Saw Manufacturers Association [*Later, CSMA*]   (EA)
PSMA........ President of the Society of Marine Artists [*British*]
PSMA........ Professional Services Management Association [*Alexandria, VA*]   (EA)
PSMA........ Progressive Spinal Muscular Atrophy [*Medicine*]
PSMA........ Pyrotechnic Signal Manufacturers Association   (EA)
PSMD....... Photo Selective Metal Deposition
PSMDC...... Psychological Medicine [*A publication*]
PSMDEQ ... Psychiatric Medicine [*A publication*]
PSME .... Partido Socialista de Melilla [*Political party*] [*See also PSOE*] [*Spanish North Africa*]   (MENA)
PSMEA ...... Psychosomatic Medicine [*A publication*]
PSMF .... Protein Sparing Modified Fast
PSMFC...... Pacific States Marine Fisheries Commission
PSMI .... Phase-Shift Modal Interference
PSMI .... Precise Ship Motion Instrument
PSMIAM .. Pontica. Studii si Materiale de Istorie, Arheologie, si Muzeografie [*Constanta*] [*A publication*]
PSMIT ...... Programming Services for Multimedia Industry Terminals [*IBM Corp.*]
PSML........ Prague Studies in Mathematical Linguistics [*A publication*]
PSML........ Processor System Modeling Language [*1976*] [*Data processing*]   (CSR)

PSMM....... Multimission Patrol Ship [*Symbol*]
PSMMA..... Plastic Soft Materials Manufacturers Association   (EA)
PSMMAF ... Proceedings. Staff Meeting of the Mayo Clinic [*A publication*]
PSMR........ Parts Specification Management for Reliability
PSMR........ Pneumatic [*or Pressure*] System Manifold [*or Manual*]
                Regulator   (AAG)
PSMS .... Permanent Section of Microbiological Standardization   (MCD)
PSMSC...... Psychotherapie und Medizinische Psychologie [*A publication*]
PSMSL...... Permanent Service for Mean Sea Level [*of the Federation of
                Astronomical and Geophysical Data Analysis Services*]
                [*Birkenhead, Merseyside, England*]   (EAIO)
PSMT .... Perishable Sheet Metal Tool   (MCD)
PSMU........ Power Supply and Multiplexer Unit
                [*Telecommunications*]   (TSSD)
PSMUD..... Psychology of Music [*A publication*]
PSN .... Package Sequence Number
PSN .... Packet Switched Network
PSN .... Packet Switching Node
PSN .... Palestine, TX [*Location identifier*] [*FAA*]   (FAAL)
PSN .... Parti de la Solidarite Nationale [*Party of National Solidarity*]
                [*Luxembourg*] [*Political party*]   (PPE)
PSN .... Partial Shipment Number [*DoD*]
PSN .... Partido Socialista Nicaraguense [*Nicaraguan Socialist Party*]
                [*Political party*]   (PPW)
PSN .... Permanent Sort Number [*Data processing*]
PSN .... Position
PSN .... Private Satellite Network, Inc. [*New York, NY*]
                [*Telecommunications*]   (TSSD)
PSN .... Processing Serial Number   (MCD)
PSN .... Program Summary Network   (MCD)
PSN .... Progressive Student Network   (EA)
PSN .... Provisioning Sequence Number   (MCD)
PSN .... Public Switched Network   (BUR)
PSNA........ Phytochemical Society of North America   (EA)
PSNA........ Powys Society of North America   (EA)
PSNB........ Puget Sound Bancorp [*NASDAQ symbol*]   (NQ)
PSNC........ Parti Socialiste de la Nouvelle Caledonie [*Socialist Party of New
                Caledonia*] [*Political party*]   (PPW)
PSNC........ Public Service Company of North Carolina, Inc. [*NASDAQ
                symbol*]   (NQ)
PSNCF ...... Pacific Southern Naval Coastal Frontier
PSNCO...... Personnel Staff Noncommissioned Officer [*Military*]
PSNEB...... Psychiatric Annals [*A publication*]
PSNL........ Personnel   (FAAC)
P & SNP .... Pay and Subsistence of Naval Personnel [*Budget appropriation
                title*]
PSNP........ Pebble Springs Nuclear Plant   (NRCH)
PSNR........ Positioner
PSNR........ Power Signal-to-Noise Ratio
PSNRP ...... Position Report [*Aviation*]   (FAAC)
PSNS .... Physical Science for Nonscience Students
PSNS .... Pretreatment Standards for New Indirect Sources
                [*Environmental Protection Agency*]
PSNS .... Programmable Sampling Network Switch
PSNS........ Puget Sound Naval Shipyard [*Bremerton, WA*]   (MCD)
PSNSR ...... Position Sensor   (MCD)
PSNSY ...... Puget Sound Naval Shipyard [*Bremerton, WA*]
PSNT .... Pismo Swiete Nowego Testamentu [*Posen*] [*A publication*]
PSNT........ Present [*Legal term*]   (ROG)
PSNTA ...... Progres Scientifique [*A publication*]
PSO .... Pad Safety Officer [*Aerospace*]   (MCD)
PSO .... Paint Spray Outfit
PSO .... Pasto [*Colombia*] [*Airport symbol*]   (OAG)
PSO .... Pasto [*Colombia*] [*Seismograph station code, US Geological
                Survey*]   (SEIS)
PSO .... Pauli Spin Operator [*Physics*]
PSO .... Peacetime Stockage Objective [*DoD*]   (AFIT)
PSO .... Penobscot Shoe Co. [*AMEX symbol*]   (SPSG)
PSO .... Personnel Security Officer [*Military*]
PSO .... Personnel Selection Officer [*British military*]   (DMA)
PSO .... Piano-Shaped Object
PSO .... Pilot Systems Operator
PSO .... Planet Sensor Output
PSO .... Polaris Systems Officer [*British military*]   (DMA)
PSO .... Policy Studies Organization   (EA)
PSO .... Political Survey Officers [*Navy*]
PSO .... Polysulfone [*Also, PS*] [*Organic chemistry*]
PSO .... Presidential Security Office [*Republic of Vietnam*]   (CINC)
PSO .... Primary Standardization Office [*Military*]   (AABC)
PSO .... Principal Scientific Officer [*British*]
PSO .... Principal Staff Officer [*British military*]   (DMA)
PSO .... Procurement Services Office
PSO .... Product Support Organization
PSO .... Profco Resources Ltd. [*Vancouver Stock Exchange symbol*]
PSO .... Program Staff Officer
PSO .... Provisions Supply Office [*Military*]
PSO .... Public Safety Officer
PSO .... Public Service Organisation [*Government grant*] [*British*]
PSO .... Publications Supply Officer [*Military*]
PSO .... Publicity Security Officer [*Navy*]
PSOA........ Pro Stock Owners Association   (EA)

PSOB......... Paper Society for the Overseas Blind [*Defunct*]   (EA)
PSoc......... Przeglad Socjologiczny [*A publication*]
P Soc Exp M ... Proceedings. Society for Experimental Biology and Medicine
                [*A publication*]
PSOE......... Partido Socialista Obrero Espanol [*Spanish Socialist Workers'
                Party*] [*See also PSME*] [*Political party*]   (PPE)
PSOLMHT ... Pious Society of Our Lady of the Most Holy Trinity   (EA)
PSom.......... Mary S. Biesecker Public Library, Somerset, PA [*Library
                symbol*] [*Library of Congress*]   (LCLS)
PSomHi ..... Somerset County Historical and Genealogical Society,
                Somerset, PA [*Library symbol*] [*Library of
                Congress*]   (LCLS)
PSON .... Person   (ROG)
PSONAL... Personal   (ROG)
PSOP......... Parti Socialiste des Ouvriers et Paysans [*Socialist Party of
                Workers and Peasants*] [*France*] [*Political party*]
PSOP......... Payload Systems Operating Procedures [*NASA*]   (NASA)
PSOP......... Power System Optimization Program [*Data processing*]
PSOR........ Preliminary System of Requirements
PSP........... Pace-Setting Potential [*Physiology*]
PSp............ Pacific Spectator [*A publication*]
PSP........... Pacifistische Socialistische Partij [*Pacific Socialist Party*]
                [*Political party*] [*Netherlands*]
PSP........... Package Size Proneness [*Marketing*]
PSP .... Packaging Shipping Procedures
PSP........... Packet Switching Processor
PSP........... Pad Safety Plan
PSP........... Palm Springs [*California*] [*Airport symbol*]   (OAG)
PSP .... Palm Springs, CA [*Location identifier*] [*FAA*]   (FAAL)
PSP........... Pancreatic Spasmolytic Peptide [*Biochemistry*]
PSP........... Paralytic Shellfish Poisoning [*Marine biology*]
PSP........... Parathyroid Secretory Protein [*Biochemistry*]
PSP........... Parti Socialiste Polynesien [*Polynesian Socialist Party*]
                [*Political party*]   (PPW)
PSP........... Parti Soudanais Progressiste [*Sudanese Progressive Party*]
                [*Political party*]
PSP .... Partido Social Progresista [*Social Progressive Party*] [*Brazil*]
                [*Political party*]
PSP........... Partido Socialista del Peru [*Socialist Party of Peru*] [*Political
                party*]   (PPW)
PSP........... Partido Socialista Popular [*Popular Socialist Party*] [*Spain*]
                [*Political party*]   (PPE)
PSP........... Partido Socialista Popular [*Popular Socialist Party*] [*Pre-1965*]
                [*Cuba*]   (PPW)
PSP........... Partido Socialista Popular [*Popular Socialist Party*] [*Peru*]
                [*Political party*]   (PPW)
PSP........... Partido Socialista Portuguesa [*Portuguese Socialist Party*]
                [*Political party*]   (PPW)
PSP........... Parts Screening Program
PSP .... Patrol Seaplane
PSP........... Payload Signal Processor [*NASA*]   (NASA)
PSP........... Payload Specialist Panel [*NASA*]   (NASA)
PSP........... Payload Support Plan [*NASA*]   (MCD)
PSP........... Peak Sideband Power   (DEN)
PSP........... Performance Shaping Parameters   (IEEE)
PSP........... Performance Standards Program
PSP........... Personal Success Program
PSP........... Personnel Subsystem Process [*Army*]   (AABC)
PSP........... Pharmacological Sciences Program [*Bethesda, MD*] [*National
                Institute of General Medical Sciences*]   (GRD)
PSP........... Phenolsulfonephthalein [*Chemical indicator*]
PSP........... Pierced Steel Planking [*Military*]
PSP........... Plane Strain Plastometer
PSP........... Planet Scan Platform [*NASA*]   (KSC)
PSP........... Planned Standard Programming [*Data processing*]
PSP........... Plasma Spraying [*Welding*]
PSP........... Plasmon Surface Polariton [*Physics*]
PSP........... Platform Sensor Package
PSP........... Pointed Soft Point [*Ammunition*]
PSP........... Pointed Soft Point Bullet
PSP........... Polyfactorial Study of Personality [*Psychology*]
PSP........... Poly(styrene peroxide) [*Organic chemistry*]
PSP........... Portable Service Processor   (IEEE)
PSP........... Post-Shoring-Polyethylene [*Method of constructing
                underground homes*]
PSP........... Post-Surgical Pain [*Medicine*]
PSP........... Postsynaptic Potential [*Neurophysiology*]
PSP........... Potential for Successful Performance [*Test*]
PSP........... Power System Planning
PSP........... Praja Socialist Party [*India*] [*Political party*]   (PPW)
PSP........... Precision Spot Positioning
PSP........... Predictive Smooth Pursuit [*Ophthalmology*]
PSP........... Presensitized Photoplate
PSP........... Prestart Panel [*Aerospace*]   (AAG)
PSP........... Priced Spare Parts [*Military*]   (AFIT)
PSP........... Primary Sodium Pump [*Nuclear energy*]   (NRCH)
PSP........... Primary Supply Point [*Military*]   (AFM)
PSP........... Primary Support Point [*Military*]   (AFM)
PSP........... Priority Strike Program
PSP........... Product Service Publication [*General Motors Corp.*]
PSP........... Product Support Program   (NG)

PSP............	Program Segment Prefix [*Data processing*]
PSP............	Program Support Plan [*NASA*]
PSP............	Programmable Signal Processor (MCD)
PSP............	Progressive Socialist Party [*Lebanon*] (BJA)
PSP............	Progressive Supranuclear Palsy [*Neurology*]
PSP............	Project Schedule Plan (NASA)
PSP............	Protective Shielding Program
PSP............	Protocol for Specific Purpose
PSP............	Provincia de Sao Pedro [*Brazil*] [*A publication*]
PSP............	Pseudopregnancy [*Gynecology*]
PSP............	Public Storage Canadian Properties [*Limited Partnership Units*] [*Toronto Stock Exchange symbol*]
PSP............	Puerto Rican Socialist Party [*Political party*] (PD)
PSP............	Swarthmore College Peace Collection, Swarthmore, PA [*OCLC symbol*] (OCLC)
PSPA	Pacific Seafood Processors Association (EA)
PSPA	Passive Solar Products Association (EA)
PSPA	Pennview Savings Association [*NASDAQ symbol*] (NQ)
PSPA	Pressure Static Probe Assembly (MCD)
PSPA	Professional School Photographers of America (EA)
PSPAEW...	Psychotherapy Patient [*A publication*]
PSPC	Polystyrene Packaging Council (EA)
PSPC	President's Soviet Protocol Committee [*World War II*]
PSPCD	Proceedings. Annual Southwestern Petroleum Short Course [*A publication*]
PSPCE4.....	Proceedings. Sugar Processing Research Conference [*A publication*]
PSPD	Position-Sensitive Proportional Detector [*For X-ray diffraction*]
PSP & E.....	Product Support Planning and Estimating (AAG)
PSPEN	Primary/Secondary Peace Education Network [*Later, PEN*] (EA)
PSPF.........	Potential Single Point Failures [*NASA*] (KSC)
PSPF.........	Prostacyclin Stimulating Plasma Factor [*Endocrinology*]
PSPFLI......	Pulsed Single Photon Fluorescence Lifetime Instrumentation
PSPGV	Primary Sodium Pump Guard Vesel [*Nuclear energy*] (NRCH)
PSPHA	Psychophysiology [*A publication*]
PSPHDI	Psychopharmacology Series [*A publication*]
PSphR........	Rohm & Haas Co., Research Library Services, Spring House, PA [*Library symbol*] [*Library of Congress*] (LCLS)
PSPI..........	Psychosocial Pain Inventory [*Psychology*]
PSPL.........	Priced Spare Parts List
PSPL.........	Progressive Socialist Party of Lebanon
PSPLR.......	Priced Spare Parts List Revision
PSPM	Procurement Seminar for Project Management [*Army*]
PSPMW	International Brotherhood of Pulp, Sulphite, and Paper Mill Workers [*Later, UPIU*]
PSPOB	Psychiatria Polska [*A publication*]
PSPOS.......	Philological Society. Publications. Occasional Studies [*A publication*]
PSPP.........	Preliminary System Package Plan
PSPP.........	Program System Package Plan
PSPP.........	Proposed System Package Plan [*Military*]
PSPR	Personnel Subsystem Products [*Army*] (AABC)
PSPS.........	Paddle Steamer Preservation Society [*High Wycombe, Buckinghamshire, England*]
PSPS.........	Pesticides Safety Precautions Scheme [*British*]
PSPS.........	Planar Silicon Photoswitch (IEEE)
PSPS.........	Power Steering Pressure Switch [*Automotive engineering*]
PS to PS.....	Private Siding to Private Siding
PSPS.........	Product Support Procurement Summary (MCD)
PSPS.........	Program Support Plan Summary
PSPSB	Psychotherapy and Psychosomatics [*A publication*]
PSPT	Passport (AABC)
PSPT	Planar Silicon Power Transistor
PSQ...........	Personnel Security Questionnaire
PSQ...........	Philologische Studien und Quellen [*A publication*]
PSQ...........	Political Science Quarterly [*A publication*]
PSQA........	Pageable System Queue Area [*Data processing*] (MCD)
PSQAA......	Psychoanalytic Quarterly [*A publication*]
PSQSA	Psychiatric Quarterly. Supplement [*A publication*]
PSQUA......	Psychiatric Quarterly [*A publication*]
PSR...........	Pacific Security Region
PSR...........	Pacific Sociological Review [*A publication*]
PSR...........	Packed Snow on Runway [*Aviation*] (FAAC)
PSR...........	Pad Safety Report [*NASA*]
PSR...........	Page Send-Receive [*Teletypewriter*]
PSR...........	Pain Sensitivity Range [*Biometrics*]
PSR...........	Panoramic Stereo Rectification
PSR...........	Parachute Status Report [*Army*] (AABC)
PSR...........	Partido Socialista Revolucionario [*Revolutionary Socialist Party*] [*Peru*] [*Political party*] (PPW)
PSR...........	Partido Socialista Revolucionario [*Revolutionary Socialist Party*] [*Portugal*] [*Political party*] (PPE)
PSR...........	Partido Socialista Revolucionario [*Revolutionary Socialist Party*] [*Mexico*] [*Political party*] (PPW)
PSR...........	Party Socialiste Revolutionnaire [*Socialist Revolutionary Party*] [*Lebanon*] [*Political party*] (PPW)
psr	Paternal Sex Ratio Gene [*Genetics*]
PSR...........	Paul's Scarlet Rose [*Plant cell line*]
PSR...........	Pennsylvania State Reports [*A publication*] (DLA)

PSR...........	Pennsylvania State University Reactor (NRCH)
PSR...........	Perfectly Stirred Reactor
PSR...........	Performance Summary Report (NG)
PSR...........	Peripheral Shim Rod [*Nuclear energy*] (NRCH)
PSR...........	Personnel Status Report [*Military*]
PSR...........	Pescara [*Italy*] [*Airport symbol*] (OAG)
PSR...........	Petaluma & Santa Rosa Railroad Co. [*AAR code*]
PSR...........	Petrostates Resource Corp. [*Vancouver Stock Exchange symbol*]
PSR...........	Petty Sessions Review [*A publication*] (APTA)
PSR...........	Phase Sequence Relay
PSR...........	Philatelic Societies' Record [*A publication*] [*British*]
PSR...........	Philippine Sociological Review [*A publication*]
PSR...........	Physical Sciences Research Program [*North Carolina State University*] [*Research center*] (RCD)
PSR...........	Physicians for Social Responsibility (EA)
PSR...........	Plow-Steel Rope
PSR...........	Point of Safe Return (MCD)
PSR...........	Policy Status Report [*Insurance*]
PSR...........	Political Science Review [*A publication*]
PSR...........	Political and Social Reform Movement [*British*]
PSR...........	Portable Seismic Recorder
PSR...........	Positive Support Review, Inc. [*Telecommunications service*] (TSSD)
PSR...........	Post-Sinusoidal Resistance
PSR...........	Postal Service Representative [*British*] (DCTA)
PSR...........	Power System Relaying (MCD)
PSR...........	Predicted SONAR Range [*Military*] (NVT)
PSR...........	Price-Sales Ratio [*Economics*]
PSR...........	Primary Surveillance RADAR
PSR...........	Problem Status Report (MCD)
PSR...........	Processor State Register
PSR...........	Procurement Status Report (IEEE)
PSR...........	Program Status Register
PSR...........	Program Status Report [*or Review*]
PSR...........	Program Status Review [*NASA*] (NASA)
PSR...........	Program Study Request (AAG)
PSR...........	Program Summary Record [*Military*] (AFIT)
PSR...........	Program Support Requirements (KSC)
PSR...........	Programming Status Report [*Data processing*]
PSR...........	Programming Support Representative [*IBM Corp.*]
PSR...........	Progress Summary Report
PSR...........	Project Scan Record
PSR...........	Project Summary Report (MCD)
PSR...........	Propeller Shaft Rate [*Navy*] (CAAL)
PSR...........	Proton Storage Ring [*Nuclear physics*]
PSR...........	Prototype Systems Review
PSR...........	Provisioning Support Request [*Military*] (CAAL)
PsR............	Psychoanalytic Review [*A publication*]
PsR............	Psychological Review [*A publication*]
PSR...........	Public Service Co. of Colorado [*NYSE symbol*] (SPSG)
PSR...........	Public Social Responsibility [*Unit of the Anglican Church of Canada General Synod*]
PSR...........	Pulmonary Stretch Receptors [*Medicine*]
PSRA	Professional Soccer Reporter's Association (EA)
PSRAA	Progress in the Science and Technology of the Rare Earths [*A publication*]
PSRAAALAA ...	President's Special Representative and Adviser on African, Asian, and Latin American Affairs [*Department of State*]
PSRC	Plastic Surgery Research Council (EA)
PSRC	Pretrial Services Resource Center (EA)
PSRC	Public Service Research Council (EA)
PSRD........	Personnel Shipment Ready Date [*Army*] (AABC)
PSRD........	Program Support Requirements Document [*NASA*] (KSC)
PSRE	Partido Socialista Revolucionario Ecuatoriano [*Socialist Revolutionary Party of Ecuador*] [*Political party*] (PPW)
PSREA	Psychoanalytic Review [*A publication*]
PSRED	Psychological Research [*A publication*]
PSRF	Product Support Reports and Functions
PSRF	Profit Sharing Research Foundation (EA)
PSRI	Particulate Solid Research Institute
PSRI	Position Subject Return of Incumbent (FAAC)
PSRI	Psycho-Social Rehabilitation International (EAIO)
PSRIA	Papers. Ship Research Institute [*A publication*]
PSRL	Post Strike Reconnaissance List [*Military*] (CINC)
PSRM........	Parti Sosialis Rakyat Malaya [*People's Socialist Party of Malaya*]
PSRM........	Post-Scram Reactivity Monitor [*Nuclear energy*] (NRCH)
PSRM........	Pressurization Systems Regulator Manifold (AAG)
PSRM........	Processor State Register Main [*Data processing*]
PSRMA......	Pacific Southwest Railway Museum Association [*Later, SDRM*] (EA)
PSR-ML/MIR-el Militante ...	Partido Socialista Revolucionario (Marxista-Leninista)/Movimiento de Izquierda Revolucionaria-El Militante [*Revolutionary Socialist Party (Marxist-Leninist)/Militant Movement of the Revolutionary Left*] [*Peru*] [*Political party*] (PPW)
PSRMLS...	Pacific Southwest Regional Medical Library [*Library network*]
PSRMT	Piecewise-Sinusoidal Reaction Matching Technique [*Antenna*] [*Navy*]
PSRO.........	Passenger Standing Route Order [*Army*] (AABC)

PSRO......... Professional Standards Review Organization [*Generic term for groups of physicians who may review the policies and decisions of their colleagues*]
PSRP .... Physical Sciences Research Papers [*Air Force*]   (MCD)
PSRPD ..... Prakla-Seismos Report [*A publication*]
PSRR .... Parachute Supported Radio Relay
PSRR .... Product and Support Requirements Request [*Data processing*]   (IBMDP)
PSRS .... Portable Seismic Recording System
PSRS .... Position Subject to Rotating Shifts   (FAAC)
PSrS.......... Slippery Rock State College, Slippery Rock, PA [*Library symbol*] [*Library of Congress*]   (LCLS)
PSRT .... Passive Satellite Research Terminal
PS-RTP ..... Paper-Substrate Room-Temperature Phosphorescence [*Analytical chemistry*]
PSRU......... Processor State Register Utility [*Data processing*]
PSRVA ...... Psychological Review [*A publication*]
PSRWD.... Policy Studies Review [*A publication*]
PSS .... Hastings, NE [*Location identifier*] [*FAA*]   (FAAL)
PSS .... International Production, Service, and Sales Union
PSS .... Packet Switching Service [*Telecommunications*] [*Information service or system*] [*British*]   (IID)
PSS .... Packet SwitchStream [*British Telecommunications Plc*] [*London*] [*Information service or system*]   (IID)
PSS .... Pad Safety Supervision [*Aerospace*]   (AAG)
PSS .... Palomar Sky Survey [*NASA*]
PSS .... Parti Socialiste Suisse [*Social Democratic Party of Switzerland*] [*Political party*]   (PPE)
PSS .... Parti de Solidarite Senegalaise [*Senegalese Solidarity Party*] [*Political party*]
PSS .... Partially Sighted Society [*British*]
PSS .... Partito Socialista Sammarinese [*Socialist Party of San Marino*] [*Political party*]   (PPE)
PSS .... Partito Socialista Somalo [*Somali Socialist Party*] [*Political party*]
PSS .... Passenger Service Supervisor [*Travel industry*]
PSS .... Passenger Service Systems [*Airlines*]
PSS .... Patent Search System [*Pergamon*] [*Database*] [*Data processing*] [*British*]
PSS .... Pauli Spin Susceptibility [*Physics*]
PSS .... Payload Specialist Station [*NASA*]   (NASA)
PSS .... Payload Support System [*NASA*]   (MCD)
PSS .... Performance Standard Sheet
PSS .... Periscope Simulation System [*Navy*]
PSS .... Personal Signaling System
PSS .... Personnel Subsystem [*Air Force*]   (AFM)
PSS .... Personnel Support System [*Army*]   (AABC)
PSS .... Phase-System Switching [*Physical chemistry*]
PSS .... Physiological Saline Solution [*Physiology*]
PSS .... Planetary Scan System [*or Subsystem*]
PSS .... Planned Systems Schedule   (AAG)
PSS .... Planning Summary Sheets   (AAG)
PSS .... Plant Science Seminar [*Later, ASP*]
PS/S.......... Plumbing Supervisor/Specialist   (AAG)
PSS .... Plunger Snap Switch
PSS .... Pneumatic Supply Subsystem   (AAG)
PSS .... Poly(styrenesulfonate) [*Organic chemistry*]
PSS .... Porcine Stress Syndrome [*Veterinary medicine*]
PSS .... Portable Simulation System   (MCD)
PSS .... Posadas [*Argentina*] [*Airport symbol*]   (OAG)
PSS .... Postal Savings System [*Terminated, 1966*]
PSS .... Postscripts
PSS .... Power Supply Section
PSS .... Power System Synthesizer
PSS .... Precancel Stamp Society   (EA)
PSS .... Presbyteri Sancti Sulpicii [*Sulpicians*] [*Roman Catholic men's religious order*]
P/S/S......... Price/Stern/Sloan Publishers, Inc.
PSS .... Primary Sampling System [*Nuclear energy*]   (NRCH)
PSS .... Princess   (ROG)
PS to S ...... Private Siding to Station
PSS .... Probabilistic Safety Study [*Nuclear energy*]   (NRCH)
PSS .... Process Sampling System [*Nuclear energy*]   (NRCH)
PSS .... Professor of Sacred Scripture
PSS .... Progressive Science Series [*A publication*]
PSS .... Progressive Systemic Sclerosis [*Medicine*]
PSS .... Propellant Supply System [*or Subsystem*]
PSS .... Proprietary Software Systems [*Data processing*]   (IEEE)
PSS .... Propulsion Subsystem Structure
PSS .... Propulsion Support System   (KSC)
PSS .... Protective Security Service
PSS .... Psalms [*Old Testament book*]
PSS .... Pseudo Spread Spectrum   (MCD)
Pss........... Pseudomonas Syringae Syringae [*Plant pathology*]
PSS .... Psychiatric Services Section [*of the American Hospital Association*] [*Later, SCSMHPS*]   (EA)
PSS .... Psychiatric Status Schedules [*Psychology*]
PSS .... Pubblicazioni. Seminario de Semitistica. Istituto Orientale di Napoli [*A publication*]
PSS .... Public Services Satellite

PSS .... Public Storage Canadian Properties II [*Limited Partnership Units*] [*Toronto Stock Exchange symbol*]
PSS .... Push-Button Selection Station
PSSA .... Pitch Starting Synchro Assembly
PSSA .... Professional Ski Shops Association [*Australia*]
PSSA .... Pseudo-Steady-State Approximation [*Chemical engineering*]
PSSA .... Public State Services Association [*Australia*]
PSSAANDPS ... Permanent Secretariat of the South American Agreement on Narcotic Drugs and Psychotropic Substances   (EAIO)
PSSAB......... Physica Status Solidi. Sectio A. Applied Research [*A publication*]
PSSB......... Palm Springs Savings Bank [*Palm Springs, CA*] [*NASDAQ symbol*]   (NQ)
PSSB........ Passing Stopped School Bus [*Traffic offense charge*]
PSSBB....... Public School System Blanket Bond [*Insurance*]
PSSC......... Petroleum Security Subcommittee [*of Foreign Petroleum Supply Committee*] [*Terminated, 1976*]   (EGAO)
PSSC......... Physical Science Study Committee [*National Science Foundation*]
PSSC......... Pious Society of Missionaries of St. Charles [*Later, CS*] [*Roman Catholic men's religious order*]
PSSC......... Public Service Satellite Consortium   (EA)
PSSCC....... Peter Symonds School Cadet Corps [*British military*]   (DMA)
PSSEAS .... Papers in International Studies. Southeast Asia Series. Ohio University [*A publication*]
PSSEP....... Preliminary System Safety Engineering Plan
PSSF........ Petites Soeurs de la Sainte-Famille [*Little Sisters of the Holy Family*] [*Sherbrooke, PQ*]   (EAIO)
PSSFB .... Progress in Surface Science [*A publication*]
PSSG .... Physical Science Study Group
PSSGL....... Penn State Series in German Literature [*A publication*]
PSSHR ..... Philippine Social Sciences and Humanities Review [*A publication*]
PSS-I .... Peace Science Society (International)   (EA)
PSSI.......... Primary Specialty Skill Identifier [*Military*]   (AABC)
PSSIIS....... Partito Socialista: Sezione Italiana del Internazionale Socialista [*Socialist Party: Italian Section of International Socialism*] [*Political party*]   (PPE)
PSS(Int)..... Peace Science Society (International)
PSSK....... Probability of Single Shot Kill [*Of a guided missile*]
PSSM .... Preliminary Science Meeting [*NASA*]
PSSMA ..... Paper Shipping Sack Manufacturers Association   (EA)
PSSMDE... Proceedings. Symposium of the Society for the Study of Inborn Errors of Metabolism [*A publication*]
PSSMLF ... Provincial Society of Spanish and Moroccan Leather Finishers [*A union*] [*British*]
PSSO .... Pass Slip Stitch Over [*Knitting*]
PsSol.......... Psalms of Solomon [*Pseudepigrapha*]   (BJA)
PSSP......... Payload Specialist Station Panel [*NASA*]   (MCD)
PSSP......... Phone Center Staffing and Sizing Program [*Telecommunications*]   (TEL)
PSSP......... Price/Stern/Sloan, Inc. [*Formerly, Price/Stern/Sloan Publishers, Inc.*] [*NASDAQ symbol*]   (NQ)
PSSR .... Parallel-Shaft Speed Reducer
PSSR .... Philippine Social Science Review [*A publication*]
PSSR .... Problem Status and Summary Report [*NASA*]   (KSC)
PSSR .... Provisioning Supply Support Requests [*DoD*]
PSSRA....... Public Service Staff Relations Act [*Canada*]
PSSRB....... Public Service Staff Relations Board [*Canada*]
PSSS .... Philosophic Society for the Study of Sport   (EA)
PSSS .... Proceedings. Shevchenko Scientific Society. Philological Section [*A publication*]
PSSSP .... Proceedings. Shevchenko Scientific Society. Philological Section [*A publication*]
PSST......... Periodic Significant Scheduled Tasks [*NASA*]   (NASA)
PSSTA....... Port Security Station [*Coast Guard*]
PSSTA....... Progress in Solid State Chemistry [*A publication*]
PSSU .... Patch Survey and Switching Unit   (MCD)
PSSUE5... Psychopharmacology. Supplementum [*A publication*]
PSSZAG.... Psychologie. Schweizerische Zeitschrift fuer Psychologie und Ihre Anwendungen [*A publication*]
PST .... Pacific Standard Time
PST .... Pacific Summer Time
PST .... Pair Selected Ternary [*Data processing*]
PST .... Partido Socialista de los Trabajadores [*Socialist Workers' Party*] [*Mexico*] [*Political party*]   (PPW)
PST .... Partido Socialista de los Trabajadores [*Socialist Workers' Party*] [*Colombia*] [*Political party*]   (PPW)
PST .... Pass Time [*Military*]
PST .... Paste
PST .... Pastry   (MSA)
PST .... Pasture Canyon [*Utah*] [*Seismograph station code, US Geological Survey*] [*Closed*]   (SEIS)
PS & T ...... Pay, Subsistence, and Transportation [*Military*]
PSt .... Pennsylvania State University, University Park, PA [*Library symbol*] [*Library of Congress*]   (LCLS)
PST .... Performance Specification Tree
PST .... Periodic Self-Test [*Data processing*]
PST .... Peristimulus Time [*Neurophysiology*]
PST .... Personnel Subsystem Team [*Military*]   (AFIT)
PST .... Peseta [*Monetary unit*] [*Spain and Latin America*]

PST........... Petrie Stores Corp. [*NYSE symbol*] (SPSG)
PST........... Phase Space Theory [*Physical chemistry*]
PST........... Phenol Sulfotransferase [*An enzyme*]
PST........... Philadelphia Suburban Transportation [*AAR code*]
PST........... Philological Society. Transactions [*A publication*]
PST........... Piston Shock Tunnel
PST........... Point of Spiral Tangent (KSC)
PST........... Polaris Star Tracker [*Missiles*]
PST........... Policy Studies Journal. Policy Studies Institute [*London*] [*A publication*]
PST........... Polished Surface Technique (IEEE)
pst .... Pond Sterling [*Pound Sterling*] [*Monetary unit*] [*Netherlands*] (GPO)
PST........... Pontifical Institute of Mediaeval Studies. Studies and Texts [*A publication*]
PST........... Porcine Somatotropin [*Gene-spliced animal hormone*] [*Monsanto Co.*]
PST........... Post-Stimulus Time
PST........... Pressure-Sensitive Tape
PST........... Primary Surge Tank [*Nuclear energy*] (NRCH)
PST........... Prior Service Training [*US Army Reserve*] (INF)
PST........... Priority Selection Table [*Data processing*] (IBMDP)
PST........... Product Support Technician
PST........... Professional, Scientific, and Technical
PST........... Profit Sharing Trustee (DLA)
PST........... Program Synchronization Table (CMD)
PST........... Project ST [*Later, NSTA*] (EA)
PST........... Propeller STOL [*Short Takeoff and Landing*] Transport
PSt........... Prose Studies [*A publication*]
PST........... Shepard's Preparing for Settlement and Trial [*A publication*]
3PST......... Triple-Pole, Single-Throw [*Switch*] (MUGU)
4PST......... Four-Pole, Single-Throw [*Switch*]
PSTA........ Packaging Science and Technology Abstracts [*International Food Information Service*] [*Federal Republic of Germany*] [*Information service or system*]
PSTA........ Partido Socialista Tito Atahuichi [*Bolivia*] [*Political party*] (PPW)
PSt-A .... Pennsylvania State University, Agricultural Library, University Park, PA [*Library symbol*] [*Library of Congress*] (LCLS)
PSta .... Philippine Statistican [*A publication*]
PSTA .... Pre-Sea Trial Audit (MCD)
PSt-All....... Pennsylvania State University, Allentown Campus, Allentown, PA [*Library symbol*] [*Library of Congress*] (LCLS)
PSt-Alt....... Pennsylvania State University, Altoona Campus, Altoona, PA [*Library symbol*] [*Library of Congress*] (LCLS)
PSTAU...... Pastabilities Food Uts [*NASDAQ symbol*] (NQ)
PSt-B .... Pennsylvania State University, Berks Campus, Wyomissing, PA [*Library symbol*] [*Library of Congress*] (LCLS)
PSTB .... Picture Story Test Blank [*Psychology*]
PSTB .... Propulsion System Test Bed [*for ABC helicopters*] (RDA)
PSTB .... Puget Sound Tug & Barge [*AAR code*]
PSt-Be....... Pennsylvania State University, Beaver Campus, Monaca, PA [*Library symbol*] [*Library of Congress*] (LCLS)
PS & TC..... Population Studies and Training Center [*Brown University*] [*Research center*] (RCD)
PSTC .... Pressure Sensitive Tape Council (EA)
PSTC .... Product Support Task Control (AAG)
PSTC .... Public Switched Telephone Circuits [*Telecommunications*] (TEL)
PStcA........ American Philatelic Research Library, State College, PA [*Library symbol*] [*Library of Congress*] (LCLS)
PSt-Ca .... Pennsylvania State University, Capitol Campus, Middletown, PA [*Library symbol*] [*Library of Congress*] (LCLS)
PSTCA ...... Public Services Temporary Clerks' Association [*A union*] [*British*]
PStcH........ HRB-Singer, Inc., Science Park, State College, PA [*Library symbol*] [*Library of Congress*] (LCLS)
PSt-D .... Pennsylvania State University, DuBois Campus, DuBois, PA [*Library symbol*] [*Library of Congress*] (LCLS)
PSTD........ Potato Spindle Tuber Disease
PstdE .... Eastern College, St. Davids, PA [*Library symbol*] [*Library of Congress*] (LCLS)
PSt-De .... Pennsylvania State University, Delaware Campus, Chester, PA [*Library symbol*] [*Library of Congress*] (LCLS)
PSt-E .... Pennsylvania State University, Behrend Campus, Erie, PA [*Library symbol*] [*Library of Congress*] (LCLS)
PSTE .... Personnel Subsystem Test and Evaluation [*Military*]
PST-E........ Priority Selection Table Extension [*Data processing*] (IBMDP)
PSTEP....... Pre-Service Teacher Education Program [*National Science Foundation*]
PSt-F......... Pennsylvania State University, Fayette Campus, Uniontown, PA [*Library symbol*] [*Library of Congress*] (LCLS)
PSTF......... Pioneer Station Training Facility [*NASA*]
PSTF......... Pressure Suppression Test Facility [*Nuclear energy*] (IEEE)
PSTF......... Profit Sharing Trust Fund
PSTF......... Proximity Sensor Test Facility [*Nuclear energy*] (NRCH)
PSTF......... Pump Seal Test Facility [*Nuclear energy*] (NRCH)
PSTGC...... Per Steering Compass [*Navigation*]
PSt-H........ Pennsylvania State University, Hazelton Campus, Hazelton, PA [*Library symbol*] [*Library of Congress*] (LCLS)
PSTH......... Peristimulus Time Histogram

PSTH........ Posthumously
PSTH........ Poststimulus Time Histogram [*Medical statistics*]
PSTI .... Pancreatic Secretory Trypsin Inhibitor [*Biochemistry*]
PSTIAC.... Pavements and Soil Trafficability Information Analysis Center [*Army Corps of Engineers*] (IID)
PSt-KP...... Pennsylvania State University, King of Prussia Graduate Center, King of Prussia, PA [*Library symbol*] [*Library of Congress*] (LCLS)
PSTL .... Pastoral
PSTL .... Pistol (MSA)
PSTL .... Postal (AFM)
PSTM .... Persistent Standoff Target Marker (MCD)
PSTMA .... Paper Stationery and Tablet Manufacturers Association [*Later, PCA*] (EA)
PSt-MA .... Pennsylvania State University, Mont Alto Campus, Mont Alto, PA [*Library symbol*] [*Library of Congress*] (LCLS)
PSt-McK... Pennsylvania State University, McKeesport Campus, McKeesport, PA [*Library symbol*] [*Library of Congress*] (LCLS)
PS & TN .... Pay, Subsistence, and Transportation, Navy
PSTN .... Piston (MSA)
PSTN .... Public Switched Telephone Network
PSt-NK...... Pennsylvania State University, New Kensington Campus, New Kensington, PA [*Library symbol*] [*Library of Congress*] (LCLS)
PSt-O......... Pennsylvania State University, Ogontz Campus, Abington, PA [*Library symbol*] [*Library of Congress*] (LCLS)
PSTO........ Principal Sea Transport Officer
PSTO........ Purdue Student-Teacher Opinionaire [*Test*]
PSTOA...... Psychology Today [*A publication*]
PSt-PiN ..... Pennsylvania State University, School of Nursing, Allegheny General Hospital, Pittsburgh, PA [*Library symbol*] [*Library of Congress*] (LCLS)
PSTR .... Pacesetter Corp. [*NASDAQ symbol*] (NQ)
PSTR .... Penn State TRIGA [*Training Reactor, Isotopes General Atomic*] Reactor
P/STRG..... Power Steering [*Automotive engineering*]
PSTS......... Passive SONAR Tracking System
PSt-S........ Pennsylvania State University, Scranton Campus, Scranton, PA [*Library symbol*] [*Library of Congress*] (LCLS)
PSt-Sk .... Pennsylvania State University, Schuylkill Campus, Schuylkill Haven, PA [*Library symbol*] [*Library of Congress*] (LCLS)
PSt-SV .... Pennsylvania State University, Shenango Valley Campus, Sharon, PA [*Library symbol*] [*Library of Congress*] (LCLS)
PStu .... Philippine Studies [*A publication*]
PSTV .... Potato Spindle Tuber Virus
PSTV .... Private Screening, Inc. [*NASDAQ symbol*] (NQ)
PSt-WB ..... Pennsylvania State University, Wilkes-Barre Campus, Wilkes-Barre, PA [*Library symbol*] [*Library of Congress*] (LCLS)
PSt-WS...... Pennsylvania State University, Worthington Scranton Campus, Dunmore, PA [*Library symbol*] [*Library of Congress*] (LCLS)
PSt-Y .... Pennsylvania State University, York Campus, York, PA [*Library symbol*] [*Library of Congress*] (LCLS)
PSTYY ...... President Steyn Gold Mining ADR [*NASDAQ symbol*] (NQ)
PSTZG ..... Pasteurizing [*Freight*]
PSu........... John R. Kaufman, Jr., [*Sunbury*] Public Library, Sunbury, PA [*Library symbol*] [*Library of Congress*] (LCLS)
PSU........... Package Size Unspecified
PSU........... Packet Switching Unit
PSU........... Parti Socialiste Unifie [*Unified Socialist Party*] [*France*] [*Political party*] (PPW)
PSU........... Partido Socialista Unificado [*Socialist Unification Party*] [*Argentina*] [*Political party*] (PPW)
PSU........... Partido Socialista Uruguayo [*Uruguayan Socialist Party*] [*Political party*] (PD)
PSU........... Partidul Socialist Unitar [*Unitary Socialist Party*] [*Romania*] [*Political party*] (PPE)
PSU........... Partito Socialista Unificato [*Unified Socialist Party*] [*Italy*] [*Political party*] (PPE)
PSU........... Partito Socialista Unitario [*Socialist Unity Party*] [*San Marino*] [*Political party*] (PPW)
PSU........... Partito Socialista Unitario [*Socialist Unity Party*] [*Italy*] [*Political party*] (PPE)
PSU........... Path Setup [*Telecommunications*] (TEL)
PSU........... Pennsylvania State University
PSU........... Pet Services, Unlimited [*Commercial firm*] (EA)
PSU........... Philatelic Sales Unit
PSu........... Photosynthetic Unit
PSU........... Plasma Spray Unit
PSU........... Port Storage Utility [*Telecommunications*] (TEL)
PSU........... Portland State University
PSU........... Power Supply Unit (MSA)
PSU........... Power Switching Unit (MCD)
PSU........... Pressure Status Unit (AAG)
PSU........... Primary Sampling Unit [*Statistics*]
PSU........... Processor Speed Up [*Computer memory core*]
PSU........... Program Storage Unit [*Data processing*] (MDG)
PSU........... Tatoo-a-Pet [*Commercial firm*] (EA)

PSU-ADA ... Pennsylvania State University-Abstracts of Doctoral Dissertations [*A publication*]
PSUB .... Piston-Supported Upper Bearing
PSUC .... Partit Socialista Unificat de Catalunya [*Unified Socialist Party of Catalonia*] [*Spain*] [*Political party*] (PPE)
PSULI .... Partito Socialista Unitario di Lavoratori Italiani [*Unitary Socialist Party of Italian Workers*] [*Political party*] (PPE)
PSUN .... Piper Hydro, Inc. [*NASDAQ symbol*] (NQ)
PSUPB ...... Pribory i Sistemy Upravleniya [*A publication*]
PSuQ .... Philologische Studien und Quellen [*A publication*]
PSUR .... Pennsylvania State University Reactor
PSURA ...... Progress in Surgery [*A publication*]
PSURAO ... Pennsylvania State University Radio Astronomy Observatory
PSurg .... Plastic Surgery [*Medicine*]
PSUSAM .. Philippine Statehood USA Movement [*An association*] (EA)
PSV .... Peanut Stunt Virus
PSV .... Pictorial Study of Values [*Psychology*]
PSV .... Planetary Space Vehicle [*NASA*] (NASA)
PSV .... Portable Sensor Verifier (AAG)
PSV .... Positive Start Voltage
PSV .... Preserve (MSA)
PSV .... Probability State Variable [*Statistics*]
PSV .... Progressieve Surinaamse Volkspartij [*Progressive Suriname People's Party*] [*Political party*] (PPE)
PSV .... Psychological, Social, and Vocational [*Adjustment factors*]
PSV .... Public Service Vehicle
PSV .... Saint Vincent College, Latrobe, PA [*OCLC symbol*] (OCLC)
PSVB .... Penn Savings Bank FSB [*Wyomissing, PA*] [*NASDAQ symbol*] (NQ)
PSvcBad ..... Presidential Service Badge [*Military decoration*] (AABC)
PSVD .... Polystyrene-Divinylbenzene Copolymer [*Organic chemistry*]
PSVM .... Phase-Sensitive Voltmeter
PSVOA ...... Purse Seine Vessel Owners Association (EA)
PSVOMA ... Purse Seine Vessel Owners Marketing Association [*Later, PSVOA*] (EA)
PSVP .... Pilot Secure Voice Project [*NATO Integrated Communications System*] (NATG)
PSVT .... Paroxysmal Supraventricular Tachycardia [*Cardiology*]
PSVT .... Passivate [*Metallurgy*]
PSVTN ...... Preservation (MSA)
PSVTV ...... Preservative (MSA)
PS & W ...... Pacific, Southern & Western Railroad [*Nickname: Play Safe and Walk*]
PSW .... Pacific Southwest Forest and Range Experiment Station [*Berkeley, CA*] [*Department of Agriculture*] (GRD)
PSW .... Pinetree Software Canada Ltd. [*Vancouver Stock Exchange symbol*]
PSW .... Plasma Spray Welder
PSW .... Politically Simulated World [*Computer-assisted political science game*]
PSW .... Potential Switch
PSW .... Potentiometer Slidewire
PSW .... Powerplant Specific Weight
PSW .... Processor Status Word
PSW .... Program Status Word [*Data processing*]
PSW .... Psychiatric Social Worker [*British*]
4PSW .... Four-Pole Switch
PSWA .... Pacific Southwest Airlines [*San Diego, CA*] [*NASDAQ symbol*] (NQ)
PSWA .... Partially Smooth Water Area (DS)
PSWAD ..... Perspective Study of World Agricultural Development [*FAO*] [*United Nations*] (MSC)
PSWB .... Public School Word-Book [*A publication*]
PSWBD ..... Power Switchboard
PSWEA ...... Proceedings. South Wales Institute of Engineers [*A publication*]
PSWG .... Pressure Sine Wave Generator
PSWMOW ... Psychiatric Social Work in Mental Observation Wards [*British*]
PSWO .... Picture and Sound World Organization
PSWO .... Princess of Wales' Own [*Military unit*] [*British*] (ROG)
PSWO .... Product Support Work Order
PSWOPC .. Psychiatric Social Work in Out-Patient Clinics [*British*]
PSWP .... Plant Service Water Pump (IEEE)
PSWR .... Powell Sport Wagon Registry (EA)
PSWR .... Power Standing Wave Ratio
PSWS .... Potable and Sanitary Water System [*Nuclear energy*] (NRCH)
PSwS .... Smith, Kline & French Co. [*Later, SmithKline Corp.*], Swedeland, PA [*Library symbol*] [*Library of Congress*] (LCLS)
PSWT .... Polysonic Wind Tunnel (MCD)
PSWT .... Psychiatric Social Work Training [*British*]
PSWTUF ... Public Service Workers' Trade Union Federation [*Ceylon*]
PSWYA ..... Psychologia Wychowawcza [*A publication*]
PSX .... Pacific Scientific Co. [*NYSE symbol*] (SPSG)
PSX .... Palacios, TX [*Location identifier*] [*FAA*] (FAAL)
PSY .... Persky Air Service [*Valdosta, GA*] [*FAA designator*] (FAAC)
PSY .... Pillsbury Co. [*NYSE symbol*] (SPSG)
PSY .... Port Stanley [*Falkland Islands*] [*Airport symbol*]
PSY .... PSM Technologies, Inc. [*Vancouver Stock Exchange symbol*]
PSY .... Psychiatry
PSY .... Psychological (CINC)

PsyAb .... Psychological Abstracts [*A publication*]
Psy B .... Psychological Bulletin [*A publication*]
PSYBB ..... Psychopharmacology Bulletin [*A publication*]
PSYC .... Psych Systems, Inc. [*NASDAQ symbol*] (NQ)
PSYC .... Psychology
PSYCA ...... Psychiatry [*A publication*]
PSYCD ...... Psychendocrinology [*A publication*]
PSYCH ...... Psychiatrist (DSUE)
PSYCH ...... Psychiatry
PSYCH ...... Psychic (ROG)
PSYCH ...... Psychology (AFM)
Psych Bull ... Psychological Bulletin [*A publication*]
PSYCHEM ... Psychiatric Chemistry
Psychiat ...... Psychiatry [*A publication*]
Psychiat Cl ... Psychiatria Clinica [*A publication*]
Psychiat Digest ... Psychiatry Digest [*A publication*]
Psychiat Fo ... Psychiatric Forum [*A publication*]
Psychiat Me ... Psychiatry in Medicine [*A publication*]
Psychiat Opin ... Psychiatric Opinion [*A publication*]
Psychiat Q ... Psychiatric Quarterly [*A publication*]
Psychiatr Ann ... Psychiatric Annals [*A publication*]
Psychiatr Annals ... Psychiatric Annals [*A publication*]
Psychiatr Clin ... Psychiatria Clinica [*A publication*]
Psychiatr Clin (Basel) ... Psychiatria Clinica (Basel) [*A publication*]
Psychiatr Commun ... Psychiatric Communications [*A publication*]
Psychiatr Dev ... Psychiatric Developments [*A publication*]
Psychiatr Enfant ... Psychiatrie de l'Enfant [*A publication*]
Psychiatr Fenn ... Psychiatria Fennica [*A publication*]
Psychiatr Fenn Monogr ... Psychiatria Fennica. Monografiasarja [*A publication*]
Psychiatr Forum ... Psychiatric Forum [*A publication*]
Psychiatr Hosp ... Psychiatric Hospital [*A publication*]
Psychiatr J Univ Ottawa ... Psychiatric Journal. University of Ottawa [*A publication*]
Psychiatr Med ... Psychiatric Medicine [*A publication*]
Psychiatr Neurol ... Psychiatria et Neurologia [*A publication*]
Psychiatr Neurol Jpn ... Psychiatria et Neurologia Japonica [*A publication*]
Psychiatr Neurol Med Psychol ... Psychiatrie, Neurologie, und Medizinische Psychologie [*A publication*]
Psychiatr Neurol Med Psychol (Leipz) ... Psychiatrie, Neurologie, und Medizinische Psychologie (Leipzig) [*A publication*]
Psychiatr Neurol Neurochir ... Psychiatria, Neurologia, Neurochirurgia [*A publication*]
Psychiatr Neurol Wochenschr ... Psychiatrisch Neurologische Wochenschrift [*A publication*]
Psychiatr News ... Psychiatric News [*A publication*]
Psychiatr Nurs Forum ... Psychiatric Nursing Forum [*A publication*]
Psychiatr Opinion ... Psychiatric Opinion [*A publication*]
Psychiatr Pol ... Psychiatria Polska [*A publication*]
Psychiatr Prax ... Psychiatrische Praxis [*A publication*]
Psychiatr Q ... Psychiatric Quarterly [*A publication*]
Psychiatr Q (NY) ... Psychiatric Quarterly (New York) [*A publication*]
Psychiatr Q Suppl ... Psychiatric Quarterly. Supplement [*A publication*]
Psychiatr Res Rep ... Psychiatric Research Reports [*A publication*]
Psychiatr Res Rep Am Psychiatr Assoc ... Psychiatric Research Reports. American Psychiatric Association [*A publication*]
Psychiatr Soc ... Psychiatrie Sociale [*A publication*]
Psychiatry Dig ... Psychiatry Digest [*A publication*]
Psychiatry Med ... Psychiatry in Medicine [*A publication*]
Psychiatry Res ... Psychiatry Research [*A publication*]
Psychic R ... Psychical Review [*A publication*]
PSYCHL ... Psychological (AFM)
Psych & MLJ ... Psychological and Medico-Legal Journal [*A publication*] (DLA)
Psych of Music ... Psychology of Music [*A publication*]
PSYCHO ... Psychoanalysis (DSUE)
Psychoanal Contemp Sci ... Psychoanalysis and Contemporary Science [*A publication*]
Psychoanal Contemp Thought ... Psychoanalysis and Contemporary Thought [*A publication*]
Psychoanal Q ... Psychoanalytic Quarterly [*A publication*]
Psychoanal R ... Psychoanalytic Review [*A publication*]
Psychoanal Rev ... Psychoanalytic Review [*A publication*]
Psychoanal Stud Child ... Psychoanalytic Study of the Child [*A publication*]
Psychoanal Study Child ... Psychoanalytic Study of the Child [*A publication*]
Psychoanal Study Child Monogr Ser ... Psychoanalytic Study of the Child. Monograph Series [*A publication*]
Psychoan Q ... Psychoanalytic Quarterly [*A publication*]
Psychoan Re ... Psychoanalytic Review [*A publication*]
Psychocultural R ... Psychocultural Review [*A publication*]
Psychohist Rev ... Psychohistory Review [*A publication*]
PSYCHOL ... Psychology
Psychol Absts ... Psychological Abstracts [*A publication*]
Psychol Afr ... Psychologia Africana [*A publication*]
Psychol Africana ... Psychologia Africana [*A publication*]
Psychol Afr Monogr Suppl ... Psychologie Africana. Monograph and Supplement [*A publication*]
Psychol B ... Psychological Bulletin [*A publication*]
Psychol Be ... Psychologische Beitraege [*A publication*]
Psychol Beitr ... Psychologische Beitraege [*A publication*]
Psychol Bel ... Psychologica Belgica [*A publication*]

Psychol Belg ... Psychologica Belgica [*A publication*]
Psychol Bul ... Psychological Bulletin [*A publication*]
Psychol Bull ... Psychological Bulletin [*A publication*]
Psychol Can ... Psychologie Canadienne [*A publication*]
Psychol Clinic ... Psychological Clinic [*A publication*]
Psychol Erz ... Psychologie in Erziehung und Unterricht [*A publication*]
Psychol Forsch ... Psychologische Forschung [*A publication*]
Psychol Fr ... Psychologie Francaise [*A publication*]
Psychol Iss ... Psychological Issues [*A publication*]
Psychol Issues ... Psychological Issues [*A publication*]
Psychol Issues Monogr ... Psychological Issues. Monographs [*A publication*]
Psychol Learn & Motiv ... Psychology of Learning and Motivation [*A publication*]
Psychol Med ... Psychological Medicine [*A publication*]
Psychol Med ... Psychologie Medicale [*A publication*]
Psychol Med Monogr Suppl ... Psychological Medicine. Monograph Supplement [*A publication*]
Psychol Monogr Gen Appl ... Psychological Monographs. General and Applied [*A publication*]
Psychology M ... Psychology of Music [*A publication*]
Psychol Prax ... Psychologische Praxis [*A publication*]
Psychol R ... Psychological Review [*A publication*]
Psychol Rec ... Psychological Record [*A publication*]
Psychol Rep ... Psychological Reports [*A publication*]
Psychol Res ... Psychological Research [*A publication*]
Psychol Rev ... Psychological Review [*A publication*]
Psychol Rundsch ... Psychologische Rundschau [*A publication*]
Psychol Sch ... Psychology in the Schools [*A publication*]
Psychol in the Schs ... Psychology in the Schools [*A publication*]
Psychol Stu ... Psychological Studies [*A publication*]
Psychol Tod ... Psychology Today [*A publication*]
Psychol Today ... Psychology Today [*A publication*]
Psychol Women Q ... Psychology of Women Quarterly [*A publication*]
Psychometri ... Psychometrika [*A publication*]
Psychometrika Monogr Suppl ... Psychometrika. Monograph Supplement [*A publication*]
Psycho Mycol Stud ... Psycho-Mycological Studies [*A publication*]
Psychon Sci ... Psychonomic Science [*A publication*]
Psychon Sci Sect Anim Physiol Psychol ... Psychonomic Science. Section on Animal and Physiological Psychology [*A publication*]
Psychon Sci Sect Hum Exp Psychol ... Psychonomic Science. Section on Human Experimental Psychology [*A publication*]
Psychop Afr ... Psychopathologie Africaine [*A publication*]
Psychopathol Afr ... Psychopathologie Africaine [*A publication*]
Psychopathol Expression Suppl Encephale ... Psychopathologie de l'Expression. Supplement de l'Encephale [*A publication*]
Psychopathol Pict Expression ... Psychopathology and Pictorial Expression [*A publication*]
Psychopharm ... Psychopharmacologia [*A publication*]
Psychopharmacol Abstr ... Psychopharmacology Abstracts [*A publication*]
Psychopharmacol Bull ... Psychopharmacology Bulletin [*A publication*]
Psychopharmacol Commun ... Psychopharmacology Communications [*A publication*]
Psychopharmacology Suppl ... Psychopharmacology. Supplementum [*A publication*]
Psychopharmacol Ser ... Psychopharmacology Series [*A publication*]
Psychopharmacol Serv Cent Bull ... Psychopharmacology Service Center. Bulletin [*A publication*]
Psychopharmacol Suppl ... Psychopharmacology. Supplementum [*A publication*]
Psychopharmacol Suppl Encephale ... Psychopharmacologie. Supplement de l'Encephale [*A publication*]
Psychoph C ... Psychopharmacology Communications [*A publication*]
Psychophysl ... Psychophysiology [*A publication*]
Psychos Med ... Psychosomatic Medicine [*A publication*]
Psychosocial Rehabil J ... Psychosocial Rehabilitation Journal [*A publication*]
Psychosoc Proc Iss Child Ment Health ... Psychosocial Process. Issues in Child Mental Health [*A publication*]
Psychosoc Rehabil J ... Psychosocial Rehabilitation Journal [*A publication*]
Psychosomat ... Psychosomatics [*A publication*]
Psychosom Med ... Psychosomatic Medicine [*A publication*]
Psychother Med Psychol ... Psychotherapie und Medizinische Psychologie [*A publication*]
Psychother Patient ... Psychotherapy Patient [*A publication*]
Psychother Psychosom ... Psychotherapy and Psychosomatics [*A publication*]
Psychother Psychosom Med Psychol ... Psychotherapie, Psychosomatik, Medizinische Psychologie [*A publication*]
Psychother Theory Res Pract ... Psychotherapy: Theory, Research, and Practice [*A publication*]
Psychoth MP ... Psychotherapie und Medizinische Psychologie [*A publication*]
Psychoth Ps ... Psychotherapy and Psychosomatics [*A publication*]
Psychoth/TR ... Psychotherapy: Theory, Research, and Practice [*A publication*]
Psych Prax ... Psychologische Praxis [*A publication*]
Psych Soc ... Psychology and Social Theory [*A publication*]
Psych Stud ... Psychological Studies [*Mysore*] [*A publication*]
Psych Teaching ... Psychology Teaching [*A publication*]
Psych Today ... Psychology Today [*A publication*]
PsycINFO ... Psychological Abstracts Information Services [*American Psychological Association*] (IID)

PSYCTRC ... Psychiatric
PSYCTRY ... Psychiatry
Psycul R ... Psychocultural Review [*A publication*]
PsyD ... Doctor of Psychology
PsyETA ... Psychologists for the Ethical Treatment of Animals (EA)
PSYOP ... Psychological Operation [*Military*]
Psy R ... Proceedings. Society for Psychical Research [*A publication*]
PsyR ... Psychoanalytic Review [*A publication*]
Psy Rund ... Psychologische Rundschau [*A publication*]
PSYS ... Programming and Systems, Inc. [*NASDAQ symbol*] (NQ)
PsyS ... Psychonomic Science [*A publication*]
PSYSA ... Psyche [*A publication*]
PsySR ... Psychologists for Social Responsibility (EA)
P Sy St Carletn ... Proceedings. Symposium on Statistics and Related Topics. Carleton University [*A publication*]
Psy T ... Psychology Today [*A publication*]
PSYU ... Public Sustained Yield Unit [*Forestry*]
PSYWAR ... Psychological Warfare
PSYWPN ... Psychological Weapon [*Military*] (AFM)
PSZ ... Partially-Stabilized Zirconia [*Ceramics*]
PSZ ... Piszkesteto [*Hungary*] [*Seismograph station code, US Geological Survey*] (SEIS)
PSZ ... Pressure Sealing Zipper
PSZ ... Pro Air Services [*Miami, FL*] [*FAA designator*] (FAAC)
PSZ ... Puerto Suarez [*Bolivia*] [*Airport symbol*] (OAG)
PSZBA ... Prace i Studia Zakladu Badan Naukowych Gornoslaskiego Okregu Przemyslowego Polskiej Akademii Nauk [*A publication*]
Pszczelnicze Zesz Nauk ... Pszczelnicze Zeszyty Naukowe [*A publication*]
Pszczel Zesz Nauk ... Pszczelnicze Zeszyty Naukowe [*A publication*]
PSzL ... Polska Sztuka Ludowa [*A publication*]
PSZN ... Pubblicazioni. Stazione Zoologica di Napoli [*A publication*]
PT ... Advanced Planning and Technology Office [*Kennedy Space Center Directorate*] (NASA)
PT ... Brazil [*Aircraft nationality and registration mark*] (FAAC)
PT ... Duffryn Yard [*Welsh depot code*]
PT ... Motor Torpedo Boat [*Navy symbol*] [*Obsolete*]
PT ... Pacific Time
PT ... Pain Threshold
PT ... Pallet Truck (DCTA)
P-T ... Palomero Toluqueno [*Race of maize*]
PT ... Pamietnik Teatralny [*A publication*]
PT ... Paper Tape
PT ... Paper Title [*Business term*]
PT ... Paper Trooper [*One who salvaged paper for war effort*] [*World War II*]
PT ... Para-Terphenyl [*Organic chemistry*]
PT ... Parathyroid [*Medicine*]
PT ... Parcel Ticket [*Freight*]
PT ... Paroxysmal Tachycardia [*Cardiology*]
pt ... Part [*of a deck*] (DS)
PT ... Part [*Online database field identifier*]
PT ... Part Throttle [*Engines*]
P-T ... Part-Time [*Employment*]
PT ... Part Total [*Earnings less than weekly benefit amount*] [*Unemployment insurance*] (OICC)
PT ... Participative Teams (MCD)
PT ... Paschale Tempore [*Easter Time*] [*Latin*]
PT ... Passenger Transport
PT ... Passing Title [*Real estate*]
PT ... Passive Track [*Military*] (CAAL)
PT ... Past Tense
PT ... Pataca [*Monetary unit*] [*Macau*]
PT ... Patellar Tendon [*Anatomy*]
PT ... Patient
PT ... Patrol Torpedo Boat [*Later, PTF*] [*Navy symbol*]
PT ... Pay Tone [*Telecommunications*] (TEL)
PT ... Paying Teller [*Banking*]
PT ... Payment
PT ... Pencil Tube
PT ... Penetrant Test [*Nuclear energy*] (NRCH)
PT ... Penetration Test (NATG)
PT ... Peninsula Terminal Co. [*AAR code*]
PT ... Pennant [*British naval signaling*]
PT ... Pension Trustee (DLA)
PT ... Per Truck
PT ... Perfect Title [*Business term*]
PT ... Performance Test
PT ... Periodic Test [*Nuclear energy*] (NRCH)
P & T ... Permanent and Total [*Disability*] [*Medicine*]
PT ... Persepolis Texts (BJA)
PT ... Perseroan Terbatas [*Limited Company*] [*Indonesian*]
PT ... Persistent Tease [*Slang*] [*Bowdlerized version*]
P/T ... Personal Time [*Employment*]
PT ... Personal Trade [*In some retail establishments, customers are assigned to salesmen in rotation. A customer who is the "PT" or personal client of a salesman is not counted as part of the salesman's share of customers*]
PT ... Personal Transporter
P & T ... Personnel and Training [*Military*] (MUGU)
PT ... Perstetur [*Let It Be Continued*] [*Pharmacy*]

PT	Perturbation Theory [*Physical chemistry*]
PT	Pertussis Toxin [*Pharmacology*]
Pt	Peter [*New Testament book*]
PT	Petrol Tractor [*British*]
PT	Petroleum Times [*A publication*]
PT	Petty Theft
P & T	Pharmacy and Therapeutics
PT	Pheasant Trust (EA)
PT	Phoenix Theatre [*Defunct*] (EA)
PT	Photographic Intelligenceman [*Navy rating*]
PT	Phototherapy [*Medicine*]
PT	Phototoxity [*Medicine*]
PT	Phototransistor (NRCH)
PT	Physical Teardown (MCD)
PT	Physical Therapy [*or Therapist*]
PT	Physical Training [*Military*]
PT	Physiotherapy [*Medicine*]
PT	Piaster [*Monetary unit*] [*Spain, Republic of Vietnam, and some Middle Eastern countries*] (IMH)
PT	Pint
PT	Pipe Tap (MSA)
PT	Pitch Trim (MCD)
PT	Placebo Treated [*Medicine*]
PT	Plain Talk (EA)
PT	Plain Test (MCD)
PT	Planning and Timing [*of Investments*]
PT	Planum Temporale [*Brain anatomy*]
P-T	Plasma Thermocouple Reactor [*Nuclear energy*] (NRCH)
PT	Plastic Tube
PT	Plastics Technology [*A publication*]
Pt	Platinum [*Chemical element*]
PT	Platoon Truck [*British*]
PT	Pleno Titulo [*With Full Title*] [*Latin*]
PT	Plenty Tough [*Slang*]
PT	Plenty Trouble [*Slang*]
PT	Plonia Technica
PT	Plot Titles [*Test*] [*Psychology*]
PT	Plotting Equipment [*JETDS nomenclature*] [*Military*] (CET)
PT	Pneumatic Tube [*Technical drawings*]
PT	Pneumothorax [*Medicine*]
PT	Poetry Treasury [*An association*] [*Inactive*] (EA)
PT	Point
PT	Point [*Maps and charts*]
PT	Point of Tangency
PT	Point of Turn [*Navigation*]
P/T	Pointer/Tracker (MCD)
PT	Polar Times [*A publication*]
PT	Poll-Tax Rolls [*British*]
PT	Pollen Tube [*Botany*]
PT	Polythiophene [*Organic chemistry*]
PT	Pool Temperature [*Nuclear energy*] (NRCH)
PT	Popliteal Tendon [*Anatomy*]
PT	Port
PT	Port Number [*Telecommunications*] (TEL)
PT	Port Talbot Railway [*Wales*]
PT	Portal Tract [*Anatomy*]
PT	Portugal [*ANSI two-letter standard code*] (CNC)
pt	Portuguese Timor [*io (Indonesia) used in records cataloged after January 1978*] [*MARC country of publication code*] [*Library of Congress*] (LCCP)
PT	Positional Tolerancing
PT	Post Town
PT	Postal Telegraph Co. [*Terminated*]
PT	Poste e Telegrafi [*Post and Telegraph Service*] [*Italy*]
PT	Posterior Tibial [*Anatomy*]
P et T	Postes et Telecommunications
P & T	Posts and Timbers [*Technical drawings*]
PT	Potential Transformer
PT	Power Transfer (KSC)
PT	Prachakorn Thai [*Thai Citizens Party*] [*Thailand*] [*Political party*]
PT	Precision Teaching
PT	Preferential Treatment (OICC)
PT	Preoperational Test [*Nuclear energy*] (NRCH)
PT	Press Test [*Psychology*]
P/T	Pressure/Temperature (KSC)
PT	Pressure Test (AAG)
PT	Pressure Time Fuel System [*Cummins Engine Co., Inc.*]
PT	Pressure Transducer (KSC)
PT	Pressure Transmitter (NRCH)
PT	Pressure Tubing
PT	Pretectal [*Neuroanatomy*]
pt	Preterit [*Past tense*] [*Grammar*]
PT	Previous Operating Time (AFIT)
PT	Primal Therapy
PT	Primary Target [*Army*]
PT	Primary Trainer [*Aircraft*]
PT	Print (MSA)
PT	Printed Text
PT	Printer Terminal
PT	Prior Treatment [*Medicine*]
PT	Priority Telegram
PT	Private Terms
PT	Pro Tempore [*For the Time Being*] [*Latin*]
PT	Procedure Turn [*Aviation*] (FAAC)
PT	Processing Tax Division [*United States Internal Revenue Bureau*] (DLA)
PT	Processing Time
PT	Production Techniques (MCD)
PT	Production Test [*Military*]
PT	Productive Time [*Computer order entry*]
P & T	Professional and Technology [*Category*] [*British*]
PT	Proficiency Testing
PT	Profile Template
PT	Profit Taking [*Investment term*]
PT	Program (Exercise) on Treadmill
PT	Programmable Terminal [*Data processing*]
PT	Programmer and Timer
PT	Prohibited Telegrams
PT	Project Tibet (EA)
PT	Project Transition [*DoD*] (OICC)
PT	Project Trust (EAIO)
PT	Prolong Tablets [*Pharmacy*]
PT	Proof Test (AAG)
PT	Propellant Transfer
PT	Propeller Torpedo [*Boat*]
PT	Property Transfer [*Real estate*] (KSC)
PT	Prophet
PT	Propylthiouracil [*Also, PROP, PTU*] [*Thyroid inhibitor*]
PT	Prothrombin Time [*Hematology*]
PT	Provascular Tissue [*Botany*]
PT	Provincetown-Boston Airlines, Inc. and Naples Airlines, Inc. [*ICAO designator*] (FAAC)
PT	Provisioning Team (AAG)
PT	Przeglad Teologiczny [*A publication*]
Pt	Pseudoword Target [*Psychology*]
PT	Psychology Today [*A publication*]
Pt	Pteropods [*Quality of the bottom*] [*Nautical charts*]
PT	PTP Resource Corp. [*Formerly, Petrologic Petroleum Ltd.*] [*Vancouver Stock Exchange symbol*]
PT	Public Trustee
PT	Publication Type [*Online database field identifier*]
P & T	Pugsley and Trueman's New Brunswick Reports [*A publication*] (DLA)
PT	Pull-Through [*Gun cleaning*]
PT	Pulmonary Tuberculosis [*Medicine*]
PT	Pulp Testing [*Dentistry*]
PT	Pulse Timer
PT	Pulse Train
PT	Punched Tape [*Data processing*]
PT	Pupil Teacher
PT	Purchase Tax [*British*]
PT	Pure Telepathy [*Psychical research*]
P & T	Purge-and-Trap [*Technique*] [*Environmental Protection Agency*]
PT	Pyramid Texts (BJA)
PT	Pyramidal Tract [*Anatomy*]
PT	Pytannja Tekstolohiji [*A publication*]
PT	Total Pressure
PT1	Photographic Intelligenceman, First Class [*Navy rating*]
PT2	Photographic Intelligenceman, Second Class [*Navy rating*]
PT3	Photographic Intelligenceman, Third Class [*Navy rating*]
PTA	CareerCom Corp. [*NYSE symbol*] (SPSG)
PTA	Kunststof en Rubber [*A publication*]
PTA	National Postal Transport Association [*Later, APWU*]
PTA	Palatines to America (EA)
PTA	Pantorama Industries, Inc. [*Toronto Stock Exchange symbol*]
PTA	Paper and Twine Association (EA)
PTA	Parallel Tubular Array [*Cytology*]
PTA	Parent-Teacher Association
PTA	Passenger Transport Authorities [*British*]
PTA	People Taking Action
PTA	Percent Time Active (CAAL)
PTA	Percutaneous Transluminal Angioplasty [*Medicine*]
PTA	Periodical Title Abbreviations [*A publication*]
PTA	Personnel and Training Abstracts [*A publication*]
PTA	Peseta [*Monetary unit*] [*Spain and Latin America*]
PTA	Petaluma Aero, Inc. [*Petaluma, CA*] [*FAA designator*] (FAAC)
PTA	Phenyltrimethylammonium [*Also, PTM, PTMA*] [*Organic chemistry*]
PTA	Phorbol Tetradecanoyl Acetate [*Also, PMA, TPA*] [*Organic chemistry*]
PTA	Phosphoryl Triamide [*Organic chemistry*]
PTA	Phosphotransacetylase [*An enzyme*]
PTA	Phosphotungstic Acid [*Inorganic chemistry*]
PTA	Photographers' Telegraph Association
PTA	Phototransistor Amplifier
PTA	Physical Therapy Assistant
PTA	Picatinny Arsenal [*New Jersey*] [*Later, Armament Development Center*] [*Army*]
PTA	Pitch Trim Adjustment
PTA	Pitch Trim Angle

PTA	Planar Turbulence Amplifier (IEEE)
PTA	Plasma Thromboplastin Antecedent [*Factor XI*] [*Hematology*]
PTA	Plasma Transferred Arc [*Metallurgy*]
PTA	Platinized Titanium Anode
PTA	Point of Total Assumption (MCD)
PTA	Port Alsworth [*Alaska*] [*Airport symbol*] (OAG)
PTA	Post-Test Analysis [*NASA*] (NASA)
PTA	Post-Traumatic Amnesia [*Medicine*]
PTA	Potential Toxic Area (NASA)
PTA	Practical Accountant [*A publication*]
PTA	Preferential Trade Agreement
PTA	Preferential Trade Area
PTA	Preferential Trade Arrangements [*ASEAN*] (IMH)
PTA	Premium Transportation Authorization (AAG)
PTA	Prepaid Ticket Advice [*Travel industry*]
PTA	Preparation through Acceptance
PTA	Pressure Transducer Assembly
PTA	Price-Tag Awareness [*See also PTS*]
PTA	Primary Target Area [*Military*]
PTA	Primary Tungsten Association [*London, England*] (EAIO)
PTA	Prior to Admission [*Medicine*]
PTA	Program Time Analyzer
PTA	Programmable Translation Array
PTA	Proposed Technical Approach
PTA	Propulsion Test Article [*NASA*] (NASA)
PTA	Prothrombin Activity [*Hematology*]
PTA	Proton Target Area
PTA	Pulse Torquing Assembly (KSC)
PTA	Punta Arenas [*Chile*] [*Seismograph station code, US Geological Survey*] [*Closed*] (SEIS)
PTA	Purchase Transaction Analysis
PTA	Purified Terephthalic Acid [*Organic chemistry*]
PTAA	Airman Apprentice, Photographic Intelligenceman, Striker [*Navy rating*]
PTA-A	Periodical Title Abbreviations: by Abbreviation [*A publication*]
PTAB	Photographic Technical Advisory Board [*American National Standards Institute*]
PTAC	Penn Treaty American Corp. [*NASDAQ symbol*] (NQ)
PTAC	Plant Transportation Advisory Committee
PTAC	Professional and Technical Advisory Committee [*JCAH*]
PTACV	Prototype Tracked Air-Cushion Vehicle
PTAD	Productivity and Technical Assistance Division [*Mutual Security Agency*] [*Abolished, 1953*]
PT AEQ	Partes Aequales [*Equal Parts*] [*Pharmacy*]
PTAG	Professional Tattoo Artists Guild (EA)
PTAH	Phosphotungstic Acid-Hematoxylin [*A stain*]
PTAIOC ...	Proceedings and Transactions. All-India Oriental Conferences [*A publication*]
PTAL	Para-Tolualdehyde [*Organic chemistry*]
PTA Mag...	PTA [*Parent-Teacher Association*] Magazine [*A publication*]
PTAN	Airman, Photographic Intelligenceman, Striker [*Navy rating*]
PTANYC...	Protestant Teachers Association of New York City (EA)
PTAR	Prime Time Access Rule [*Television*]
PTASB	Photographic Applications in Science, Technology, and Medicine [*A publication*]
PTASE	Phosphatase [*An enzyme*] (DHSM)
PTA-T	Periodical Title Abbreviations: by Title [*A publication*]
PTAVE	Parents and Teachers Against Violence in Education (EA)
PTAWT	Atlantic Wind Test Site, Tignish, Prince Edward Island [*Library symbol*] [*National Library of Canada*] (NLC)
ptB............	Part Bunkers [*Shipping*] (DS)
PTB............	Partido Trabalhista Brasileiro [*Brazilian Labor Party*] [*Political party*] (PPW)
PTB............	Patellar Tendon Bearing [*Medicine*]
PTB............	Payload Timing Buffer [*NASA*] (NASA)
PTB............	Perishables Tariff Bureau, Atlanta GA [*STAC*]
PTB............	Personnel Test Battery
PTB............	Petersburg, VA [*Location identifier*] [*FAA*] (FAAL)
PTB............	Physical Transaction Block
PTB............	Point Barrow [*Alaska*] [*Later, BRW*] [*Geomagnetic observatory code*]
PTB............	Point Barrow [*Alaska*] [*Seismograph station code, US Geological Survey*] [*Closed*] (SEIS)
PTB............	Pounds per Thousand Barrels [*Petroleum technology*]
PTB............	Pressure Test Barrel
PTB............	Prior to Birth [*Medicine*]
PTB............	Process Technical Bulletin (MCD)
PTB............	Program Time Base [*Military*] (AFIT)
PTB............	PT Boats, Inc. (EA)
PTBA.........	Proud to be Australian [*Political party*]
PTBB	Para-tertiary-butylbenzaldehyde [*Organic chemistry*]
PTBBA	Para-tertiary-butylbenzoic Acid [*Organic chemistry*]
PTBC	Pittsburgh Brewing Company [*NASDAQ symbol*] (NQ)
PTBD.........	Percutaneous Transhepatic Biliary Drainage [*Medicine*]
PTBF	Portal Tributary Blood Flow [*Physiology*]
PTBK.........	Partbook [*Music*]
PTBL.........	Portable (AABC)
PTB Mitt ...	PTB [*Physikalisch-Technische Bundesanstalt*] Mitteilungen. Amts- und Mitteilungsblatt der Physikalisch- Technische Bundesanstalt [*Braunschweig-Berlin*] [*A publication*]

PTB Mitt Forsch Pruefen ...	PTB [*Physikalisch-Technische Bundesanstalt*] Mitteilungen. Forschen und Pruefen [*A publication*]
PTBR.........	Processing Tax Board of Review Decisions [*United States Internal Revenue Bureau*] [*A publication*] (DLA)
PTBR.........	Punched Tape Block Reader [*Data processing*]
PtBS..........	Poly(tertiary-butylstyrene) [*Organic chemistry*]
PTBT.........	Para-tertiary-butyltoluene [*Organic chemistry*]
PTC............	Chief Photographic Intelligenceman [*Navy rating*]
PTC............	Motor Boat Subchaser [*Navy symbol*] [*Obsolete*]
PTC............	Pacific Telecommunications Council (EA)
PTC............	Pacific Tuna Conference
PTC............	Packung und Transport in der Chemischen Industrie [*A publication*]
PTC............	PAR Technology Corp. [*NYSE symbol*] (SPSG)
PTC............	Part Through Crack [*Alloy tension*]
PTC............	Parti Travailliste Congolais [*Congolese Labor Party*] [*Political party*]
Ptc............	Participating [*Business term*]
PTC............	Passive Thermal Control
PTC............	Patent, Trademark, and Copyright Institute [*Franklin Pierce College*] (IID)
PTC............	Patrol Vessel, Motor Torpedo Boat, Submarine Chaser [*Navy symbol*]
PTC............	Pentagon Telecommunications Center (MCD)
PTC............	Peoria Terminal Company [*AAR code*]
PTC............	Percutaneous Cholangiography [*Medicine*]
PTC............	Percutaneous Transhepatic Cholangiogram [*Medicine*]
PTC............	Performance Test Chamber (MCD)
PTC............	Performance Test Code
PTC............	Permission to Take Classes [*Education*]
PTC............	Personnel Transfer Capsule [*Undersea technology*]
PTC............	Personnel Transport Carrier
PTC............	Perth Technical College [*Australia*]
PTC............	Phase Transfer Catalysis [*Physical chemistry*]
PTC............	Phenylisothiocyanate [*Organic chemistry*]
PTC............	Phenylthiocarbamide [*or Phenylthiocarbamyl*] [*Organic chemistry*]
PTC............	Photographic Training Centre [*British*] (CB)
PTC............	Photographic Type Composition (ADA)
PTC............	Pipe Tobacco Council (EA)
PTC............	Pipe and Tobacco Council of America [*Defunct*] (EA)
PTC............	Pitch Trim Compensator
PTC............	Pitch Trim Controller (MCD)
PTC............	Plan to Clear [*Aviation*] (FAAC)
PTC............	Plasma Thromboplastin Component [*Factor IX*] [*Also, CF*] [*Hematology*]
PTC............	Plastic Training Cartridge [*Army*] (INF)
PTC............	Pneumatic Temperature Control
PTC............	Pneumatic Test Console
PTC............	Police Training Centre [*British*]
PTC............	Portable Tele-Transaction Computer [*Telxon*]
PTC............	Portable Temperature Control (KSC)
PTC............	Porto Cannone [*Italy*] [*Seismograph station code, US Geological Survey*] (SEIS)
PTC............	Portuguese Trade Commission (EA)
PTC............	Positive Target Control (FAAC)
PTC............	Positive Temperature Coefficient
PTC............	Positive Transmitter Control
PTC............	Post-Tensioned Concrete [*Technical drawings*]
PTC............	Post-Turnover Change [*Nuclear energy*] (NRCH)
PTC............	Postal Telegraph Cable
PTC............	Posterior Trabeculae Carneae [*Heart anatomy*]
PTC............	Posts and Telecommunications Corporation [*Burma*] (DS)
PTC............	Power Testing Code (MCD)
PTC............	Power Transfer Coefficient
PTC............	Power Transmission Council
PTC............	Premium Tax Concession [*Australia*]
PTC............	Preoperative Testing Center
PTC............	Pressure and Temperature Control (KSC)
PTC............	Pressure Transducer Calibrator
PTC............	Primary Technical Course [*Military*]
PTC............	Primary Training Centre [*British military*] (DMA)
PTC............	Princeton Resources Corporation [*Vancouver Stock Exchange symbol*]
PTC............	Programmable Temperature Controls
PTC............	Programmable Test Console
PTC............	Programmed Transmission Control (BUR)
PTC............	Programmer Training Center
PTC............	Promotional Telephone Call [*Marketing*] (OICC)
PTC............	Proof Test Capsule [*NASA*]
PTC............	Propellant Tanking Console (AAG)
PTC............	Propulsion Test Complex (KSC)
PTC............	Prothrombin Complex [*Hematology*]
PTC............	Psychophysical Timing Curve
PTC............	Publishing Technology Corporation [*Information service or system*] (IID)
PTC............	Pulse Time Code
PTCA........	Patience T'ai Chi Association (EA)
PTCA........	Percutaneous Transluminal Coronary Angioplasty [*Medicine*]
PTCA........	Plains Tribal Council of Assam [*India*] [*Political party*] (PPW)
PTCA........	Postal Telegraph Clerks' Association [*A union*] [*British*]

PTCA......... Pressure Technology Corporation of America
PTCA......... Private Truck Council of America (EA)
PTCAA..... Professional Turkey Calling Association of America (EA)
PTCAD..... Provisional Troop Carrier Airborne Division
PTCC........ Pacific Division Transport Control Center
PT/CC....... Problem Tracking and Change Control [Data processing]
PTCCS...... Polaris Target Card Computing System [Missiles]
PtcD.......... Phosphatidylcholine [Biochemistry]
PTCEDJ... Plant Cell Tissue and Organ Culture [A publication]
PTCH........ Pacer Technology [NASDAQ symbol] (NQ)
PTCH .... Patch (FAAC)
PTCI......... Programmable Terminal Communications Interface (MCD)
PTCI......... Pullman Transportation [NASDAQ symbol] (NQ)
PTC J........ Patent, Trademark, and Copyright Journal [A publication]
PTCJB...... Postepy Techniki Jadrowej [A publication]
PTCL........ Peripheral T-Cell Lymphoma [Oncology]
PTCLA...... Presse Thermale et Climatique [A publication]
PTCLD...... Part Called [Stock exchange term] (SPSG)
PTCM....... Master Chief Photographic Intelligenceman [Navy rating]
PTCM....... Pacific Telecom, Inc. [NASDAQ symbol] (NQ)
PTCO .... Petroleum Equipment Tools Company [NASDAQ symbol] (NQ)
Pt Copyright & TM Cas ... Patent, Copyright, and Trade Mark Cases [United States] [A publication] (DLA)
PTCP........ Participate (FAAC)
PTCP........ Positive Turnaround Control Point (MCD)
PTCR........ Pad Terminal Connection Room [NASA]
PTCR........ Payload Terminal Connector Room [NASA] (MCD)
PTCR........ Positive Temperature Coefficient Resistance [Materials science and technology]
PTCRM..... Partial Thermochemical Remanent Magnetization
PTCS .... Passive Thermal Control Section [NASA] (NASA)
PTCS .... Passive Thermal Control System (NASA)
PTCS .... Pax Tibi cum Sanctis [Peace to Thee with the Saints] [Latin]
PTCS .... Planning, Training, and Checkout System [NASA] (MCD)
PTCS .... Pressure Transducer Calibration System
PTCS .... Propellant Tanking Computer System (KSC)
PTCS .... Senior Chief Photographic Intelligenceman [Navy rating]
PTCT......... Protect (MSA)
PTCV........ Pilot-Operated Temperature Control Valve
PTCV........ Plowright Tissue Culture Vaccine [Against rinderpest]
PTD.......... Painted (AAG)
PTD .... Paper Towel Dispenser [Technical drawings]
PTD .... Particle Transfer Device
PTD .... Permanent Total Disability [Medicine]
PTD.......... Phenyltriazolinedione [Organic chemistry]
Ptd........... Phosphatidyl
PTD .... Photodiode Detector [Instrumentation]
PTD .... Photothermal Deflection
PTD .... Physical Teardown (MCD)
PTD .... Pilot to Dispatcher
PTD .... Plant Test Date [Telecommunications] (TEL)
PTD .... Portland [Oregon] [Seismograph station code, US Geological Survey] (SEIS)
PTD .... Posttuning Drift
PTD .... Potsdam, NY [Location identifier] [FAA] (FAAL)
PTD .... Potter Distilleries Ltd. [Toronto Stock Exchange symbol] [Vancouver Stock Exchange symbol]
PTD .... Printed
PTD .... Programmable Threshold Detector (MCD)
PTD .... Programmed Thermal Desorber
PTD .... Provisioning Technical Documentation
PTD .... Provisioning Transcript Documentation (MCD)
PTDA........ Per Task Data Area [Data processing] (BYTE)
PTDA........ Power Transmission Distributors Association (EA)
PTDC........ Pacific Trade and Development Conference [OPTAD] (FEA)
PTDDSS.... Provisioning Technical Documentation Data Selection Sheet [NASA] (NASA)
PTDF........ Pacific Tuna Development Foundation (EA)
PTDF........ Procurement Technical Data File [DoD]
PTDIA....... Professional Truck Driver Institute of America (EA)
PtdIns....... Phosphatidylinositol [Also, PI] [Biochemistry]
P & T Div... Plans and Training Division [Military]
PTDOS...... Processor Technology Disk Operating System
PTDP........ Preliminary Technical Development Plan (AFM)
PTDP........ Proposed Technical Development Plan
PTDQ .... Polymerized Trimethyldihydroquinoline [Organic chemistry]
PtdS.......... Phosphatidylserine [Biochemistry]
PTDS......... Photo Target Detection System
Ptd Salesmanship ... Printed Salesmanship [A publication]
PTDSC ...... Performers and Teachers Diploma, Sydney Conservatorium [Australia]
PTDTL ...... Pumped Tunnel Diode Transistor Logic
PTDU .... Pointing and Tracking Demonstration Unit (MCD)
PTe........... Indian Valley Public Library, Telford, PA [Library symbol] [Library of Congress] (LCLS)
PTE........... International Federation of Professional and Technical Engineers
PTE........... Packet Transport Equipment [Data processing] (PCM)
PTE........... Page Table Entry
PTE........... Parathyroid Extract [Medicine]

PTE........... Partido de Trabajadores Espanoles [Spanish Workers' Party] [Political party] (PPE)
PTE........... Passenger Transport Executive [British]
PTE........... Pectin transeliminase [or Pectate Lyase] [An enzyme]
PTE........... Peculiar Test Equipment
pte........... Perte [Loss] [Bookkeeping] [French]
PTE........... Photographic Tasks and Equipment [NASA]
PT & E ...... Physical Teardown and Evaluation (MCD)
PTE........... Plate (ROG)
PTE........... Port Stephens [Australia] [Airport symbol] (OAG)
PTE........... Portable Test Equipment (AAG)
PTE........... Portage [Alaska] [Seismograph station code, US Geological Survey] (SEIS)
PTE........... Power Transport Equipment
PTE........... Pressure Test Equipment (MCD)
PTE........... Pressure-Tolerant Electronics (IEEE)
PTE........... Pretax Earnings [Employment]
PTE........... Primrose Technology Corp. [Vancouver Stock Exchange symbol]
PTE........... Private [British]
PTE........... Private Trade Entity
PTE........... Problem Trend Evaluation (MCD)
PTE........... Production Test Equipment (MCD)
PT & E .... Progress Tests and Examinations
PTE........... Proxylem Tracheary Element [Botany]
Pte............. Pteroyl [Biochemistry]
PTEAR...... Physical Teardown
PTEAR...... Physical Teardown and Maintenance Allocation Review (MCD)
PTeb.......... Tebtunis Papyri [A publication] (OCD)
PTEC........ Petrotech, Inc. [NASDAQ symbol] (NQ)
PTEC........ Phoenix Technologies Ltd. [NASDAQ symbol] (NQ)
PTEC........ Plastics Technical Evaluation Center [Military]
PTED........ Pulmonary Thromboembolic Disease [Medicine]
PteGlu....... Pteroylmonoglutamic Acid [Folic acid] [Also, FA, PGA] [Biochemistry]
PTEK........ Protectaire Systems Co. [NASDAQ symbol] (NQ)
PTEKAA ... Klucze do Oznaczania Owadow Polski [A publication]
PTEL........ People's Telephone Co., Inc. [NASDAQ symbol] (NQ)
PT & ER .... Physical Teardown and Evaluation Review (MCD)
PTER........ Physical Teardown and Evaluation Review (MCD)
Ptero.......... Pterodactyl [A publication]
PTES .... Productivity Trend Evaluation System (MCD)
PTES .... Purdue Teacher Evaluation Scale
PTETD...... Production Test Engineering Task Description (MCD)
PTETPC.... Party to Expose the Petrov Conspiracy [Australia]
PTETS...... Pioneer Television and Electronic Technicians Society [Defunct] (EA)
PTEV........ Primrose Technology Corp. [Vancouver, BC] [NASDAQ symbol] (NQ)
PText .... Papiere zur Textlinguistik [Papers in Textlinguistics] [A publication]
PTF........... Malololailai [Fiji] [Airport symbol] (OAG)
PTF........... Paralemniscal Tegmental Field [Neuroanatomy]
PTF........... Patch and Test Facility
PTF........... Patrol Torpedo Boat, Fast [Formerly, PT] [Navy symbol]
PTF........... Payload Test Facility [VAFB] [NASA] (MCD)
PTF........... Permit to Fly [Aviation] (AIA)
PTF........... Petersfield Oil & Minerals [Vancouver Stock Exchange symbol]
PTF........... Phase Transfer Function (MCD)
PTF........... Plaintiff [Legal term] (ROG)
PTF........... Plasma Thromboplastin Factor [Factor VIII] [Also, AHF, AHG, TPC] [Hematology]
PTF........... Police Training Foundation
PTF........... Polymer Thick Film
PTF........... Port Task Force
PTF........... Power Test Fail
PTF........... Production Tabulating Form (AAG)
PTF........... Program Temporary Fix [Data processing]
PTF........... Programmable Transversal Filter [SMP]
PTF........... Proof Test Facility [Nuclear energy]
PTF........... Propellant Tank Flow
PTFA........ Preliminary Tool and Facility Analysis (MCD)
PTFC .... Pretty Things Fan Club (EA)
PTFD........ Personnel, Training and Force Development [Army]
PTFDA...... Professional Travel Film Directors Association [Later, Professional Travelogue Sponsors - PTS] (EA)
PTFE........ Polytetrafluoroethylene [Organic chemistry]
PTFHA...... Physician Task Force on Hunger in America (EA)
PTFM........ Platform (AAG)
PTFMA .... Peacetime Force Material Assets [Navy] (AFIT)
PTFMA .... Public Telecommunications Financial Management Association (EA)
PTFMO..... Peacetime Force Materiel Objective [Army]
PTFMPO .. Peacetime Force Materiel Procurement Objective [Army]
PTFMR..... Peacetime Force Materiel Requirements [Army]
PTFMR-A ... Peacetime Force Materiel Requirements - Acquisition [Army] (AABC)
PTFMR-R ... Peacetime Force Materiel Requirements - Retention [Army] (AABC)

PTFP .... Public Telecommunications Facilities Program [*Department of Commerce*]
PTFS......... Pilot-to-Forecaster Service (NOAA)
PTFS......... Publications. Texas Folklore Society [*A publication*]
PTFUR ...... President's Task Force on Urban Renewal (EA)
PTFX .... Plating Fixture (AAG)
PTG .... Parent-Teacher Group
PTG .... Pennington Gap, VA [*Location identifier*] [*FAA*] (FAAL)
PTG .... Piano Technicians Guild (EA)
PTG .... Pietersburg [*South Africa*] [*Airport symbol*] (OAG)
PTG .... Polaris Task Group [*Missiles*]
PTG .... Portage Industries [*AMEX symbol*] (SPSG)
PTG .... Portageville [*Missouri*] [*Seismograph station code, US Geological Survey*] [*Closed*] (SEIS)
PTG .... Portugal, Belgique, Luxembourg. Informations Economiques [*A publication*]
PTG .... Portuguese (ROG)
PTG .... Precise Tone Generator [*Telecommunications*] (TEL)
PTG .... Pressure Test Gauge
PTG .... Pressure Transfer Gauge
PTG .... Printing
PTG .... Professional Technical Group
PTG .... Prothoracic Gland [*Insect anatomy*]
PTG .... Pulse Target Generator
PTGA........ Pteroyltriglutamic Acid [*Pharmacology*]
PTGAP...... Professional Technical Group on Antennas and Propagation [*of the IEEE*]
Ptg Art ..... Printing Art [*A publication*]
PTGBD..... Percutaneous Transhepatic Gallbladder Drainage [*Medicine*]
PTGC........ Programmed Temperature Gas Chromatography
PTGEC ..... Professional Technical Group on Electronic Computers [*Later, IEEE Computer Society*]
PT GEO.... Posted to Geographics
PTGEWS .. Professional Technical Group on Engineering Writing and Speech [*of the IEEE*]
pTGF .... Porcine Transforming Growth Factor
PTGL........ Pyrolysis to Gases and Liquids [*Chemical processing*]
PTGMA.... Photogrammetria [*A publication*]
PTGS .... Paper Trade Golfing Society [*British*]
PTGS .... Portable Telemetry Ground Station
PTGT........ Primary Target [*Military*]
PTH .... Hydrofoil Motor Torpedo Boat [*Ship symbol*] (NATG)
PTH .... Pallet Torque Hook
PTH .... Panther Mines Ltd. [*Vancouver Stock Exchange symbol*]
PTH .... Paper Tape Half-Duplex
PTH .... Parathyroid Hormone [*Endocrinology*]
PTH .... Pathology [*Medical specialty*] (DHSM)
PTH .... Peak Tanning Hours [*Supposedly occurring between 10am and 2pm*] [*See also BROTS, SROTS*]
PTH .... Phenylthiohydantoin [*Organic chemistry*]
PTH .... Plated through Hole
PTH .... Port Heiden [*Alaska*] [*Airport symbol*] (OAG)
PTH .... Port Heiden, AK [*Location identifier*] [*FAA*] (FAAL)
PTH .... Post-Transfusion Hepatitis [*Medicine*]
PTH .... Project Top Hat (EA)
PtHA........ Pinto Horse Association of America (EA)
P Th B....... Bachelor of Practical Theology
PTHEA..... Physical Therapy [*A publication*]
PTHF........ Polytetrahydrofuran [*Organic chemistry*]
PTH-LP..... Parathyroid Hormone-Like Peptide [*Endocrinology*]
PThR .... Princeton Theological Review [*A publication*]
PTHrP....... Parathyroid Hormone-Related Protein [*Biochemistry*]
PTI............ Package Turn In (MCD)
PTI............ Pancreatic Trypsin Inhibitor [*Biochemistry*]
PTI............ Parkes-Tidbinbilla Interferometer [*Astronomy*]
PTI............ Party Identity [*Telecommunications*] (TEL)
PTI............ Pathways to Independence [*An association*] (EA)
PTI............ Penn Telecom, Incorporated [*Gibsonia, PA*] (TSSD)
PTI............ Pennsylvania Transportation Institute [*Pennsylvania State University*] [*Research center*] (RCD)
PTI............ Persistent Tolerant Infection
PTI............ Personnel Tests for Industry
PTI............ Personnel Transaction Identifier [*Air Force*] (AFM)
PTI............ Petroleum Times [*A publication*]
PTI............ Philadelphia Textile Institute
PTI............ Physical-Technical Institute [*USSR*]
PTI............ Physical Training Instructor [*British*]
PTI............ Pictorial Test of Intelligence [*Education*]
PTI............ Pipe Test Insert [*Liquid Metal Engineering Center*] [*Energy Research and Development Administration*] (IEEE)
PTI............ Plugging Temperature Indicator [*Nuclear energy*] (NRCH)
PTI............ Poetry Therapy Institute (EA)
PTI............ Porous Tungsten Ionizer
PTI............ Post-Tensioning Institute (EA)
PTI............ Power Tool Institute (EA)
PTI............ Pre-Trip Inspection [*Shipping*]
PTI............ Precision Technology, Incorporated (AAG)
PTI............ Preliminary Test Information (KSC)
PTI............ [*The*] Press Trust of India
PTI............ Production Training Indicator [*Data processing*]
PTI............ Program Transfer Interface

PTI............ Programmed Test Input (MCD)
PTI............ Promethean Technologies, Inc. [*Vancouver Stock Exchange symbol*]
PTI............ Public Technology, Inc. [*Research center*] (RCD)
PTI............ Publicacoes Tecnicas Internacionais Ltda. [*International Technical Publications Ltd.*] [*Information service or system*] (IID)
PTI............ Puntilla Lake, AK [*Location identifier*] [*FAA*] (FAAL)
PTIA......... Pet Trade and Industry Association (EAIO)
PTIC......... Patent and Trade Mark Institute of Canada
PTIE .... Pet Trade and Industry Exhibition [*British*] (ITD)
PTIL......... Parts Test Information List (KSC)
PTIND....... Paper Technology and Industry [*A publication*]
PTI-ODT... Personnel Tests for Industry - Oral Directions Test
PTIS .... Pacific Triangle Information Services [*Information service or system*] (IID)
PTIS .... Plasma-Therm, Incorporated [*NASDAQ symbol*] (NQ)
PTIS .... Programmed Test Input System (MCD)
PTIS .... Propulsion Test Instrumentation System (KSC)
PTIWU...... Posts and Telegraphs Industrial Workers' Union [*India*]
PTJ .... Part-Time Job
PTJ .... Piano Technician's Journal [*A publication*]
PTJ .... Portland [*Australia*] [*Airport symbol*] (OAG)
PTJ .... Property Tax Journal [*A publication*]
PTJA .... Plan to Join Airways (FAAC)
PTK.......... Polishing Tool Kit
PTK.......... Pontiac, MI [*Location identifier*] [*FAA*] (FAAL)
PTK.......... Potentiometer Tapping Kit
PTK.......... Protein-Tyrosine Kinase [*An enzyme*]
PTKK........ Truk [*Caroline Islands*] [*ICAO location identifier*] (ICLI)
PTL.......... Part Time Legislature
PTL.......... Partial Total Loss [*Insurance*] (DS)
PTL.......... Patrol [*or Patrolman*] (AABC)
PTL.......... Peacetime Losses [*Military*]
PTL.......... Penteli [*Greece*] [*Seismograph station code, US Geological Survey*] (SEIS)
PTL.......... People That Love [*Of television's "PTL Club"*] [*Facetious translations: "Pass the Loot" and "Pay the Lady"*]
PTL.......... Perinatal Telencephalic Leukoencephalopathy [*Medicine*]
PTL.......... Peripheral T-Cell Lymphoma [*Oncology*]
PTL.......... Petroleum Testing Laboratory
PTL.......... Phase Tracking Loop (MCD)
PTL.......... Photographic Technology Laboratory (KSC)
PTL.......... Pintle [*Design engineering*]
PTL.......... Planning Test List
PTL.......... Pocket Testament League (EA)
PTL.......... Praise the Lord [*Of television's "PTL Club"*] [*Facetious translations: "Pass the Loot" and "Pay the Lady"*]
PTL.......... Pressure, Torque, and Load
PTL.......... Pretty Tough Lawyer [*Refers to Melvin Belli, attorney for Tammy and Jim Bakker of the PTL Club*]
PTL.......... Primary Target Line [*Military*]
PTL.......... Process and Test Language
PTL.......... Providence Airline [*Coventry, RI*] [*FAA designator*] (FAAC)
PTL.......... Public Television Library
PTLA .... Praise the Lord Anyway
PTLA .... Publishers' Trade List Annual
PTLC......... Piedmont Triad Library Council [*Library network*]
PT-LD....... Physical Teardown - Logistics Demonstration (MCD)
PTLD......... Post-Transfusion Liver Disease [*Medicine*]
PTLD......... Prescribed Tumor Lethal Dose [*Oncology*]
PTLEF....... Peace through Law Education Fund (EA)
PTLEN...... Petal Length [*Botany*]
PTLF .... Pressure, Temperature, Level, and Flow [*Chemical engineering*]
PTLRS....... Publications and Technical Literature Research Section [*Environmental Protection Agency*] (IID)
PTLV .... Primate T-Lymphotropic Viruses
PTLX......... Patlex Corp. [*NASDAQ symbol*] (NQ)
PTLY......... Partly (FAAC)
PTM .... Palmarito [*Venezuela*] [*Airport symbol*] (OAG)
PTM .... Passenger Traffic Manager
PTM .... Pattern Transformation Memory
PTM .... Petromac Energy, Inc. [*Vancouver Stock Exchange symbol*]
PTM .... Phase Time Modulation
PTM .... Phenyltrimethylammonium [*Also, PTA, PTMA*] [*Organic chemistry*]
PTM .... Physical Teardown and Maintenance (MCD)
PTM .... Pietermaritzburg [*South Africa*] [*Seismograph station code, US Geological Survey*] (SEIS)
PTM .... Pneumatic Telescope Mast
PTM .... Polaris Tactical Missile
PTM .... Portable Traffic Monitor [*Telecommunications*] (TEL)
PTM .... Portland Terminal Co. [*AAR code*]
PTM .... Posttransfusion Mononucleosis [*Medicine*]
PTM .... Practising Manager [*A publication*]
PTM .... Pressure-Transmitting Medium [*Engineering*]
PTM .... Preterm Milk [*Medicine*]
PTM .... Primary Thickening Meristem [*Botany*]
PTM .... Program Timing and Miscellaneous [*Electronics*]
PTM .... Programmable Terminal Multiplexer [*Texas Instruments, Inc.*]
PTM .... Programmable Timer Module

PTM .... Proof Test Model [*NASA*]
PTM .... Pulse Time Modulation [*Radio*]
PTM .... Pulse Time Multiplex
PTM .... Pulse Transmission Mode   (MCD)
PTM .... Southeastern Airways Corp. [*Double Springs, AL*] [*FAA designator*]   (FAAC)
PTMA....... Phenyltrimethylammonium [*Also, PTA, PTM*] [*Organic chemistry*]
PTMA....... Phosphotungstomolybdic Acid [*Inorganic chemistry*]
PTMAS .... Professional, Technical, Managerial, and Administrative Staff
PTMC....... Polaris Tender Management Computer [*Missiles*]
PTMD ...... Propellant Toxicity Monitoring Devices (KSC)
PTMDF ..... Pupils, Tension, Media, Disc, Fundus [*Medicine*]
PT & ME ... Physical Teardown and Maintenance Evaluation [*Army*]
PTMEG..... Polytetramethylene Ether Glycol [*Organic chemistry*]
PTMI........ Precision Target Marketing, Incorporated [*New Hyde Park, NY*] [*NASDAQ symbol*]   (NQ)
PTML........ PNP [*Positive-Negative-Positive*] Transistor Magnetic Logic   (IEEE)
PTMRA..... Platinum Metals Review [*A publication*]
PTMS .... Para-Toluidine-meta-sulfonic Acid [*Also, PTMSA*] [*Organic chemistry*]
PTMS .... Pattern Transformation Memory System
PTMS .... Precision Torque Measuring System   (NASA)
PTMS .... Publication Text Management System   (MCD)
PTMSA ..... Para-Toluidine-meta-sulfonic Acid [*Also, PTMS*] [*Organic chemistry*]
PTMT....... Poly(tetramethylene Terephthalate) [*Organic chemistry*]
PTMTLG .. Pitometer-Log [*Engineering*]
PTMU .... Power and Temperature Monitor Unit   (KSC)
PTMUD ..... Postepy Technologii Maszyn i Urzadzen [*A publication*]
PTMUX..... Pulse Time Multiplex   (MSA)
PTN .... Morgan City/Patterson [*Louisiana*] [*Airport symbol*]   (OAG)
PTN .... Particulate Total Nitrogen [*Analytical chemistry*]
PTN .... Partido Trabalhista Nacional [*National Workers' Party*] [*Brazil*]
PTN .... Partition   (KSC)
PTN .... Patterson, LA [*Location identifier*] [*FAA*]   (FAAL)
PTN .... Phenotemperature Normogram [*Phenology*]
PTN .... Phenytoin [*Anticonvulsant*]
PTN .... Plant Test Number [*Telecommunications*]   (TEL)
PTN .... Pluton Industries Ltd. [*Vancouver Stock Exchange symbol*]
PTN .... Portion   (FAAC)
PTN .... Potsdam [*New York*] [*Seismograph station code, US Geological Survey*]   (SEIS)
PTN .... Procedure Turn [*Aviation*]   (FAAC)
Ptn............ Pterin [*Biochemistry*]
PTNM .... [*The*] Putnam Trust Co. of Greenwich [*NASDAQ symbol*]   (NQ)
PTNMA .... Protection of Metals [*English Translation*] [*A publication*]
PTNR .... Partner   (ROG)
PTNRA8.... Pattern Recognition [*A publication*]
PTNRSHIP ... Partnership   (ROG)
PTNX .... Printronix, Inc. [*NASDAQ symbol*]   (NQ)
PTO .... Pacific Theater of Operations [*World War II*]
PTO .... Packard Truck Organization   (EA)
PTO .... Participating Test Organization [*Air Force*]
PTO .... Partners Oil & Mining [*Vancouver Stock Exchange symbol*]
PTO .... Patent and Trademark Office [*Formerly, PO*] [*Department of Commerce*]
PTO .... Pato Branco [*Brazil*] [*Airport symbol*]   (OAG)
PTO .... People, Topics, Opinions [*A publication*] [*British*]
PTO .... Please Turn Over [*the page*]
PTO .... Port Transportation Officer
PTO .... Porto [*Serro Do Pilar*] [*Portugal*] [*Seismograph station code, US Geological Survey*]   (SEIS)
PTO .... Power Takeoff
PTO .... Power Test Operations   (MCD)
PTO .... Professional and Technology Officer [*British*]
PTO .... Project Type Organization   (AAG)
PTO .... Proof Test Orbiter [*NASA*]
PTO .... Propellant Transfer Operation   (AFM)
PTO .... Protivo-Tankovaia Oborona [*Antitank Defense*] [*USSR*]
PTO .... Public Trustee Office   (DLA)
PTO .... Purdue Teacher Opinionaire [*Test*]
PTO .... Pyridinethiol Oxide [*Pharmacology*]
PTOA .... Projective Tests of Attitudes
PTobA........ United States Army, Tobyhanna Army Depot Library, Tobyhanna, PA [*Library symbol*] [*Library of Congress*]   (LCLS)
PTOC .... Progress in Theoretical Organic Chemistry [*Elsevier Book Series*] [*A publication*]
PToG .... General Telephone & Electronics, GTE Sylvania, Inc., Towanda, PA [*Library symbol*] [*Library of Congress*]   (LCLS)
PTOL........ Peacetime Operating Level   (AFM)
Ptol........... Ptolemaeus Mathematicus [*Second century AD*] [*Classical studies*]   (OCD)
Ptol............ Ptolemaic   (BJA)
PTOP........ Program Test and Operations Plan
PTOS......... Paper Tape Oriented Operating System

PTOS........ Patent and Trademark Office Society   (EA)
PTOS........ Patriot Tactical Operations Simulator [*Army*]
PTOS........ Peacetime Operating Stock [*Military*]
PTOUT .... Printout   (MSA)
PTP........... Paper Tape Perforator [*or Punch*]
PTP........... Parti Togolais du Progres [*Party for Togolese Progress*]
PTP........... Peak-to-Peak [*Nuclear energy*]
PTP........... Pensions for Technical Professionals [*An association*]
PTP........... People to People International   (EA)
PTP........... Percutaneous Transhepatic Selective Portography [*Roentgenography*]
PTP........... Petrologic Petroleum [*Vancouver Stock Exchange symbol*]
PTP........... Phase Transition Phenomena [*Elsevier Book Series*] [*A publication*]
PTP........... Phenyltetrahydropyridine [*Biochemistry*]
PTP........... Platinum Temperature Probe
PTP........... Point Park College, Pittsburgh, PA [*OCLC symbol*] [*Inactive*]   (OCLC)
PTP........... Point-to-Point [*Robotics*] [*Telecommunications*]
PTP........... Pointe-A-Pitre [*Guadeloupe*] [*Airport symbol*]   (OAG)
PTP........... Pollution Transfer Program [*Marine science*]   (MSC)
PTP........... Porous Tungsten Plug
PTP........... Post-Transfusion Purpura [*Medicine*]
PTP........... Posto Telefonico Pubblico [*Public Telephone*] [*Italy*]
PTP........... Posttetanic Potentiation [*Neurophysiology*]
PTP........... Potato Tuber Peroxidase [*An enzyme*]
PTP........... Preferred Target Point   (KSC)
PTP........... Preliminary Task Plan   (MCD)
PTP........... Pretransmission Precautionary Answer to Nature's Call [*Especially before a long program*] [*Television*]
PTP........... Primary Target Point [*NASA*]
PTP........... Production Test Plan   (MCD)
PTP........... Production Test Procedure   (NATG)
PTP........... Professional Tax Planner
PTP........... Program Task Planning   (MCD)
PTP........... Programmable Text Processor [*Programming language*]   (CSR)
PTP........... Programmed Turn Phase
PTP........... Proximity Test Plug [*Nuclear energy*]   (NRCH)
PTP........... Pueblo to People   (EA)
PTPC........ Professional Teaching Practices Commission   (OICC)
PTPD........ Part Paid [*Business term*]
PTP'er........ Prime Time Performer [*In book title, "Vitale: Just Your Average Bald, One-Eyed Basketball Wacko Who Beat the Ziggy and Became a PTP'er"*]
PTPF .... Payee TIN [*Taxpayer Identification Number*] Perfection File [*IRS*]
PTPFA...... Poznanskie Towarzystwo Przyjaciol Nauk. Wydzial Lekarski. Prace Komisji Farmaceutycznej [*A publication*]
Pt Phil Gaz ... Port Phillip Gazette [*A publication*]   (APTA)
PTPI......... Professional and Technical Programs, Incorporated
PTPKA ..... Progress of Theoretical Physics (Kyoto) [*A publication*]
PTPL......... PTP Resource Corp. [*Formerly, Petrologic Petroleum Limited*] [*NASDAQ symbol*]   (NQ)
PTPMA ..... Poznanskie Towarzystwo Przyjaciol Nauk. Wydzial Lekarski. Prace Komisji Medycyny Doswiadczalnej [*A publication*]
PTPN........ Ponape Island [*Caroline Islands*] [*ICAO location identifier*]   (ICLI)
PTPN........ Poznanskie Towarzystwo Przyjaciol Nauk [*A publication*]
PTPRAI..... Poznanskie Towarzystwo Przyjaciol Nauk, Wydzial Matematyczno-Przyrodniczy Prace Komisji Biologicznej [*A publication*]
PT/Procestech ... PT/Procestechniek [*A publication*]
PTPS .... Package Test Power Supply
PTPS .... Propellant Transfer Pressurization System   (KSC)
PTPSC....... People-to-People Sports Committee   (EA)
P-TPT .... Portable Tactual Performance Test [*Child development test*] [*Psychology*]
PTPU........ Program Tape Preparation Unit
PTQ .... Poly(tolyquinoxaline) [*Organic chemistry*]
PTQ .... Pulse-Taking Questionnaire
PTR........... Pacific Test Range   (MUGU)
PTR........... Painter
PTR........... Paper Tape Reader
PTR........... Paper Towel Receptor [*Technical drawings*]
PTR........... Partner
PTR........... Parts Tool Requirements File
PTR........... Patuxent River [*Navy*]   (MCD)
PTR........... Perforated Tape Reader
P/Tr.......... Permian/Triassic [*A geological period boundary*]
PTR........... Personality Tests and Reviews [*A publication*]
PTR........... Peterson [*Alabama*] [*Seismograph station code, US Geological Survey*]   (SEIS)
Ptr .... Petrine [*Of, or relating to, Peter the Apostle or Peter the Great*]   (BJA)
PTR........... Photoelectric Tape Reader
PTR........... Physikalisch-Technische Reichsanstalt
PTR........... Pilot Training Rate [*Navy*]
PTR........... Pleasant Harbor [*Alaska*] [*Airport symbol*]   (OAG)
PTR........... Plug-Type Receptacle
PTR........... Pointer [*Data processing*]
PTR........... Pool Test Reactor [*Nuclear energy*]

PTR............ Pool Training Reactor [*Nuclear energy*]
PTR............ Poor Transmission [*Telecommunications*]   (TEL)
PTR............ Portable Tape Recorder
PTR............ Position Track RADAR
PTR............ Positive Termination Rate [*Job Training and Partnership Act*]   (OICC)
PTR............ Power Transformers   (MCD)
PTR............ Pre-Trial Release   (OICC)
PTR............ Precision Transmitter Receiver
PTR............ Preliminary Technical Report
PTR............ Preliminary Test Report [*NASA*]   (KSC)
PTR............ Pressure Test Record
PTR............ Pressure-Tube Reactor [*Nuclear energy*]
PTR............ Pretransmit Receiving
PTR............ Princeton Theological Review [*A publication*]
PTR............ Printer   (MSA)
P Tr............ Private Trust [*Includes testamentary, investment, life insurance, holding title, etc.*] [*Legal term*]   (DLA)
PTR............ Processor Tape Read
PTR............ Production Test Record
PTR............ Production Test Requirements   (KSC)
PTR............ Professional Tennis Registry, USA   (EA)
PTR............ Proficiency Testing Research   (EA)
PTR............ Program Technical Review   (MCD)
PTR............ Program Trouble Report [*NASA*]   (KSC)
PTR............ Proof Test Reactor [*Nuclear energy*]
PTR............ Property Trust of America SBI [*NYSE symbol*]   (SPSG)
PTR............ Publishing Trade [*A publication*]
PTR............ Punched Tape Reader [*Data processing*]
PTR............ Pupil-Teacher Ratio
PTRA........ Port Terminal Railroad Association
PTRA........ Power Transmission Representatives Association   (EA)
P/TRAC .... Positraction [*Automotive engineering*]
PTrB .... Betz Laboratories, Inc., Trevose, PA [*Library symbol*] [*Library of Congress*]   (LCLS)
PTRC........ Personnel and Training Research Center [*Air Force*]
PTRC......... PTRC. Planning and Transport Research and Computation [*A publication*]
PTRD........ Part Redeemed [*Stock exchange term*]   (SPSG)
PTREA ...... Philips Technical Review [*A publication*]
PTREDQ... Proceedings. Technical Session on Cane Sugar Refining Research [*A publication*]
PTRF .... Peacetime Rate Factor [*Military*]   (AABC)
PTRF .... Peacetime Replacement Factor [*Military*]
PTRI.......... Pharmaceutical and Toxicological Research Institute [*Ohio State University*] [*Research center*]   (RCD)
Ptr Ink....... Printers' Ink [*A publication*]
Ptr Ink Mo ... Printers' Ink Monthly [*A publication*]
PTRJ .... Powered Thermocouple Reference Junction
PTRK........ Preston Corp. [*NASDAQ symbol*]   (NQ)
PTRL........ Petrol Industries, Inc. [*NASDAQ symbol*]   (NQ)
PTRM........ Partial Thermoremanent Magnetization [*Geophysics*]
PTRO .... Koror [*Caroline Islands*] [*ICAO location identifier*]   (ICLI)
PTRO .... Personnel Transaction Register by Originator [*Military*]   (AABC)
PTRO .... Petrominerals Corp. [*NASDAQ symbol*]   (NQ)
PTRO .... Preoverhaul Test Requirement Outline
PTRR .... Port Townsend Railroad, Inc. [*Formerly, PTS*] [*AAR code*]
PTRS .... Philosophical Transactions. Royal Society of London [*A publication*]
PTRSC....... Proceedings and Transactions. Royal Society of Canada [*A publication*]
PT Rulings ... Pay-Roll Tax Rulings [*Australia*] [*A publication*]
PTRY......... Pottery [*Freight*]
PTS............ Pali Text Society   (EA)
PTS............ Paper Tape-to-Magnetic Tape Conversion System   (DIT)
PTS............ Paper Tape Sender
PTS............ Papiertechnische Stiftung [*Database producer*]
PTS............ Para-Toluenesulfonic Acid
PTS............ Parachute Training School [*British military*]   (DMA)
PTS............ Parameter Test Setup
PTS............ Parts
PTS............ Patellar-Tendon Supracondylar [*Anatomy*]
PTS............ Payload Test Set [*NASA*]   (NASA)
PTS............ Payload Transportation System [*NASA*]   (MCD)
PTS............ People's Translation Service   (EA)
PTS............ Permanent Threshold Shift [*Hearing evaluation*]
PTS............ Petro-Sun International, Inc. [*Toronto Stock Exchange symbol*]
PTS............ Photogrammetric Target System [*Air Force*]
PTS............ Photothermal Spectroscopy
PTS........... Pi Tau Sigma [*Society*]
PTS............ Pittsburg, KS [*Location identifier*] [*FAA*]   (FAAL)
PTS............ Player Trade Society [*A union*] [*British*]
PTS............ Pneumatic Test Sequencer   (AFM)
PTS............ Pneumatic Test Set   (KSC)
PTS............ Pod Tail Section
PTS............ Pointing and Tracking Scope
PTS............ Port Townsend Railroad, Inc. [*Later, PTRR*] [*AAR code*]
PTS............ Post-Traumatic Stress [*Medicine*]
PTS............ Power Transfer Switch
PTS............ Power Transient Suppressor   (IEEE)

PTS............ Precision Timing System
PTS............ Predicasts Terminal Systems [*Predicasts, Inc.*] [*Cleveland, OH*] [*Database*]
PTS............ Predicasts Time Series [*Series of databases*] [*Predicasts, Inc.*] [*Cleveland, OH*]
PTS............ Pressurized Thermal Shock [*Nuclear energy*]
PTS............ Price-Tag Shock [*See also PTA*]
PTS............ Prime Time Sunday [*TV program*]
PTS............ Princeton Theological Seminary, Princeton, NJ [*OCLC symbol*]   (OCLC)
PTS............ Private Telecommunications Systems [*Radio-Suisse Ltd.*] [*Switzerland*] [*Telecommunications*]   (TSSD)
PTS............ Proactive TMDE Support   (RDA)
PTS............ Proceed to Select [*Telecommunications*]   (TEL)
PTS............ Proceed to Send [*Telecommunications*]   (TEL)
PTS............ Production Test Specification
PTS............ Professional Travelogue Sponsors   (EA)
PTS............ Program of Technology and Society [*Later, DTS*]   (EA)
PTS............ Program Test System [*Data processing*]   (IEEE)
PTS............ Program Triple Store
PTS............ Programmer Test Station
PTS............ Propellant Transfer System
PTS............ Public Telephone Service [*or System*] [*Telecommunications*]   (TEL)
PTS............ Pure Time Sharing [*Data processing*]   (IEEE)
PTSA .... Kusaie [*Caroline Islands*] [*ICAO location identifier*]   (ICLI)
PTSA .... Para-Toluenesulfonic Acid [*Organic chemistry*]
PTSA .... Parent-Teacher-Student Association [*Nickname: "Pizza"*]
PTSA .... Professional Trucking Services Association   (EA)
PTSC .... Passed Technical Staff College [*Australia*]
PT-S/C ...... Proof Test Spacecraft [*NASA*]
PTSD........ Post-Traumatic Stress Disorder [*Psychiatry*]
PTSE .... Paper Tape Splicing Equipment
pts et pts.... Profits et Pertes [*Profits and Losses*] [*Business term*] [*French*]
PTSI .... PAM Transportation Services, Inc. [*NASDAQ symbol*]   (NQ)
PTSI .... Para-Toluene Sulfonylisocyanate [*Organic chemistry*]
PTSLA....... Plant Science Letters [*A publication*]
PTSO........ Personnel Transaction Summary by Originator [*Military*]   (AABC)
PTSP .... Peacetime Support Period [*DoD*]
PT/SP........ Pressure Tube to Spool Piece [*Nuclear energy*]   (NRCH)
PTS PROMT ... Predicasts Overview of Markets and Technology [*Predicasts, Inc.*] [*Cleveland, OH*] [*Bibliographic database*]
PTSR .... Performance Technical Survey Report
PTSR .... Preliminary Technical Survey Report [*Military*]   (AFIT)
PTSR .... Pressure-Tube Superheat Reactor [*Nuclear energy*]
PTSS .... Photon Target Scoring System   (AAG)
PTSS......... Princeton Time Sharing Services, Inc.
PTSSD5..... US National Park Service. Transactions and Proceedings [*A publication*]
PTST .... Personnel Transaction Summary by Type Transaction [*Military*]   (AABC)
PTST .... Pretransfusion Serologic Testing
PTST .... Prime Time School Television   (EA)
PTT............ Pacific Telephone & Telegraph Co.   (FAAC)
PTT............ Part Task Trainer   (MCD)
PTT............ Partial Thromboplastin Time [*Hematology*]
PTT............ Party Test [*Telecommunications*]   (TEL)
PTT............ Peak Twitch Tension [*Physiology*]
PTT............ Petrotex Resources [*Vancouver Stock Exchange symbol*]
PTT............ Physical Therapist Technician
PTT............ Platform Transmitter Terminal [*Satellite-based tracking system*]
PTT............ Post und Telegraphenverwaltung [*Postal and Telegraph Administration*] [*Austria*] [*Telecommunications*]   (TSSD)
PTT............ Post, Telephon und Telegraphenbetriebe [*Switzerland*] [*Telecommunications*]   (TSSD)
PTT............ Post Ten Tumblers [*Pseudonym used by William Maginn*]
PTT............ Postal, Telegraph, and Telephone Administration   (NATG)
PTT............ Postes, Telegraphes, et Telediffusion [*Post, Telegraph, and Telephone*] [*General Post Office*] [*Facetious translation: Prostitution Telematique et Telephonique*] [*France*]
PTT............ Pratt, KS [*Location identifier*] [*FAA*]   (FAAL)
PTT............ Press to Transmit
PTT............ Private Tombs at Thebes [*Oxford*] [*A publication*]   (BJA)
PTT............ Production Type Test
PTT............ Program Technical Training   (AFM)
PTT............ Program Test Tape [*Data processing*]   (IEEE)
PTT............ Public Telecommunications Trust [*Proposed replacement for Corporation for Public Broadcasting*]
PTT............ Pulmonary Transit Time [*Physiology*]
PTT............ Push to Talk
PTTC......... Pacific Transportation Terminal Command [*Army*]
PTTC......... Paper Tape and Transmission Code
PTTDA...... Petroleum Today [*A publication*]
PTTDAR ... Personnel Training and Training Devices Analysis Report   (MCD)
PTTH .... Prothoracicotropic Hormone
PTTI.......... Postal, Telegraph, and Telephone International [*See also IPTT*] [*Geneva, Switzerland*]   (EAIO)
PTTI.......... Precise Time and Time Interval   (AFM)

PTTI Stud ... PTTI [*Postal, Telegraph, and Telephone International*] Studies [*A publication*]
PTTK .... Kosrae Island [*Caroline Islands*] [*ICAO location identifier*]   (ICLI)
PTTK .... Partial Thromboplastin Time with Kaolin [*Hematology*]
PTTL .... Press-to-Test Light
PTTMC ..... PACOM [*Pacific Command*] Tactical Target Materials Catalog   (CINC)
PTTPD ...... Bandaoti Xuebao [*A publication*]
PTU .... Package Transfer Unit
PTU .... Pallet Transporter Unit [*Military*]   (CAAL)
PTU .... Parallel Transmission Unit   (AAG)
PTU .... Pathology Transcription Unit
PTU .... Phenylthiourea [*Organic chemistry*]
PTU .... Pilot Test Unit [*Air Force*]
PTU .... Planning Tracking Unit   (MCD)
PTU .... Platinum [*Alaska*] [*Airport symbol*]   (OAG)
PTU .... Platinum, AK [*Location identifier*] [*FAA*]   (FAAL)
PTU .... Plumbing Trades Union [*British*]
PTU .... Portable Test Unit
PTU .... Power Transfer Unit
PTU .... Propylthiouracil [*Also, PROP, PT*] [*Thyroid inhibitor*]
PTUC .... Pacific Trade Union Community [*Melbourne, VIC, Australia*]   (EAIO)
Ptuj Zbor .... Ptujski Zbornik [*A publication*]
PTV .... Parachute Test Vehicle
PTV .... Passenger Transfer Vehicle [*Airport transportation*]
PTV .... Passenger Transport Vehicle
PTV .... Pathfinder Test Vehicle [*NASA*]   (MCD)
PTV .... Pay Television
PTV .... Peach Tree Valley [*California*] [*Seismograph station code, US Geological Survey*]   (SEIS)
PTV .... Peak-to-Valley
PTV .... Penetration Test Vehicle [*Aerospace*]
PTV .... Pietas Tutissima Virtus [*Piety Is the Safest Virtue*] [*Latin*] [*Motto of Ernst, Margrave of Brandenburg (1583-1613)*]
PTV .... Pitch Thrust Vector   (KSC)
PTV .... Porous Tungsten Vaporizer
PTV .... Porterville, CA [*Location identifier*] [*FAA*]   (FAAL)
PTV .... Predetermined Time Value   (IEEE)
PTV .... Programmable Temperature Vaporizer
PTV .... Programmed-Temperature Vaporizing [*Analytical chemistry*]
PTV .... Propulsion Technology Validation   (MCD)
PTV .... Propulsion Test Vehicle
PTV .... Prototype Test Vehicle   (MCD)
PTV .... Public Television
PTV .... Punched Tape Verifier [*Data processing*]
PTVA .... Propulsion Test Vehicle Assembly [*NASA*]
PTVC .... Pitch Thrust Vector Control   (KSC)
PTVD .... Portable Toxic Vapor Detector
PTVE .... Propulsion Test Vehicle Engineering [*NASA*]   (MCD)
PTVST .... Port Visit [*Navy*]   (NVT)
PTVV .... Peak-to-Valley Variation   (MCD)
PT & W ...... Physical Training and Welfare [*British military*]   (DMA)
PTW .... Physikalisch-Technische-Werkstatten [*Roentgenology*]
PTW .... Playing to Win   (EA)
PTW .... Point Target Weapon
PTW .... Pottstown, PA [*Location identifier*] [*FAA*]   (FAAL)
PTW .... Pressure-Treated Wood
PTW .... Pressure-Type Window
PTWC .... Pacific Tsunami Warning Center [*National Weather Service*]   (MSC)
PTWC .... Project on Technology, Work, and Character   (EA)
PTWF .... Pakistan Transport Workers' Federation
PTWM ...... Power Transformation Weighting Method [*Mathematics*]
P-TWP ...... Post-Township
PTWT .... Photo-Type Traveling Wave Tube   (NG)
PTX .... Pacific Trans-Ocean Resources Ltd. [*Toronto Stock Exchange symbol*]
PTX .... Palytoxin [*Organic chemistry*]
PTx .... Parathyroidectomy [*Medicine*]
PTX .... Pertussis Toxin [*Pharmacology*]
PTX .... Picrotoxin [*Biochemistry*]
PTX .... Polythiazide [*Organic chemistry*]
PTX .... Pressure-Temperature Composition
PTXB .... Pumiliotoxin B [*Organic chemistry*]
PTY .... Panama City [*Panama*] [*Airport symbol*]   (OAG)
PTY .... Party   (AAG)
PTY .... Proprietary
PTYA .... Yap [*Caroline Islands*] [*ICAO location identifier*]   (ICLI)
PTZ .... Pentylenetetrazole [*CNS stimulant*]
PU .... Pack Unit [*Single title, multiple orders*] [*Publishing*] [*British*]
PU .... Paid Up [*Insurance*]   (EY)
PU .... Parents United   (EA)
PU .... Participating Unit   (NVT)
PU .... Parts Used [*Medicine*]
PU .... Passed Urine [*Medicine*]
PU .... Paste Up   (ADA)
PU .... Peptic Ulcer [*Medicine*]
PU .... Per Urethra [*Medicine*]
PU .... Perbonate Unit [*Analytical biochemistry*]

PU .... Percent Utilization [*Anesthesiology*]
PU .... Peripheral Unit [*Computers*]   (MSA)
PU .... Personnel, Utility [*British military*]   (DMA)
PU .... Peru [*IYRU nationality code*]   (IYR)
PU .... Physical Unit [*Data processing*]   (IBMDP)
PU .... Pick Up [*Business term*]
PU .... Plant Unit
PU .... Players' Union [*Football*] [*British*]
Pu .... Plutonium [*Chemical element*]
PU .... Polyurethane [*Also, PUR*] [*Organic chemistry*]
PU .... Power Equipment [*JETDS nomenclature*] [*Military*]   (CET)
PU .... Power Unit
PU .... Pregnancy Urine [*Medicine*]
PU .... Prilled Urea [*A fertilizer*]
PU .... Primeras Lineas Uruguayas [*ICAO designator*]   (FAAC)
PU .... Princeton University
PU .... Prisoner's Union [*Later, PRU*]   (EA)
PU .... Problemi di Ulisse [*A publication*]
PU .... Processing Unit [*Data processing*]
PU .... Processor Utility [*Telecommunications*]   (TEL)
PU .... Production Unit   (CAAL)
PU .... Propellant Unit   (NASA)
PU .... Propellant Utilization [*Aerospace*]
PU .... Propulsion Unit   (KSC)
PU .... Propyleneurea [*Organic chemistry*]
PU .... Proutist Universal   (EA)
PU .... Publications   (MCD)
PU .... Publisher [*Online database field identifier*]
PU .... Puetzer [*Federal Republic of Germany*] [*ICAO aircraft manufacturer identifier*]   (ICAO)
PU .... Pump Unit   (AAG)
Pu .... Punic   (BJA)
PU .... Purdue University
Pu .... Purine [*Biochemistry*]
PU .... Purple   (ROG)
PU .... University of Pennsylvania, Philadelphia, PA [*Library symbol*] [*Library of Congress*]   (LCLS)
PUA .... Partido de Unificacion Anticomunista [*Anti-Communist Unification Party*] [*Guatemala*] [*Political party*]   (PPW)
PUA .... Plant-Unique Analysis [*Nuclear energy*]   (NRCH)
PUA .... Polish Union of America   (EA)
PUA .... Pride Users' Association [*Defunct*]   (EA)
PUA .... Public Administration [*A publication*]
PU-A .... University of Pennsylvania, Morris Arboretum, Philadelphia, PA [*Library symbol*] [*Library of Congress*]   (LCLS)
PUAA .... Public Utilities Advertising Association [*Later, PUCA*]   (EA)
PUAC .... Propellant Utilization Acoustical Checkout   (AAG)
PU-AC .... University of Pennsylvania, Annenberg School of Communications, Philadelphia, PA [*Library symbol*] [*Library of Congress*]   (LCLS)
PUAD .... Pueblo Army Depot [*Colorado*]   (AABC)
PUADA ..... Pueblo Army Depot Activity   (AABC)
PUAHC ...... Proceedings. Union of American Hebrew Congregations [*A publication*]
PUAR .... Pulse Acquisition RADAR [*Military*]   (MSA)
PUAS .... Postal Union of the Americas and Spain [*See also UPAE*] [*Montevideo, Uruguay*]   (EAIO)
PUASAL ... Proceedings. Utah Academy of Sciences, Arts, and Letters [*A publication*]
PUB .... Pacific University Bulletin [*A publication*]
PUB .... Partido Union Boliviana [*Bolivian Unity Party*] [*Political party*]   (PPW)
PUB .... Phycourobilin [*Biochemistry*]
PUB .... Physical Unit Block [*Data processing*]
PUB .... Puale Bay [*Alaska*] [*Seismograph station code, US Geological Survey*]   (SEIS)
PUB .... Public
PUB .... Public House [*A drinking establishment*] [*British*]
PUB .... Publication   (AFM)
PUB .... Publicity
PUB .... Published   (AABC)
Pub .... Publisher [*A publication*]
PUB .... Publisher
PUB .... Pueblo [*Colorado*] [*Airport symbol*]   (OAG)
PUB .... Pueblo, CO [*Location identifier*] [*FAA*]   (FAAL)
Pub Adm ... Public Administration [*A publication*]
Pub Admin ... Public Administration [*A publication*]   (APTA)
Pub Admin Abstr ... Public Administration Abstracts and Index of Articles [*A publication*]
Pub Admin Survey ... Public Administration Survey [*A publication*]
Pub Adm R ... Public Administration Review [*A publication*]
Pub Adm Rev ... Public Administration Review [*A publication*]
Pub Ad Rev ... Public Administration Review [*A publication*]
Pub Am Stat Assn ... Publications. American Statistical Association [*A publication*]
Pub Archives Can Report ... Public Archives of Canada. Report [*A publication*]
Pub Ast S J ... Publications. Astronomical Society of Japan [*A publication*]
Pub Ast S P ... Publications. Astronomical Society of the Pacific [*A publication*]

Pub Bargaining Cas (CCH) ... Public Bargaining Cases (Commerce Clearing House) [*A publication*] (DLA)
Pubbl (Bergamo) Sta Sper Maiscoltura ... Pubblicazioni (Bergamo) Stazione Sperimentale di Maiscoltura [*A publication*]
Pubbl Centro Sper Agr Forest ENCC ... Pubblicazioni. Centro di Sperimentazione Agricola e Forestale. Ente Nazionale per la Cellulosa e per la Carta [*A publication*]
Pubbl Cent Sper Agric For ... Pubblicazioni. Centro di Sperimentazione Agricola e Forestale [*A publication*]
Pubbl Cent Sper Agric For (Rome) ... Pubblicazioni. Centro di Sperimentazione Agricola e Forestale (Rome) [*A publication*]
Pubbl Cent Stud Citogenet Veg CNR ... Pubblicazioni. Centro di Studio per la Citogenetica Vegetale. Consiglio Nazionale della Ricerche [*A publication*]
Pubbl Chim Biol Med Ist "Carlo Erba" Ric Ter ... Pubblicazioni Chimiche, Biologiche, e Mediche. Istituto "Carlo Erba" per Ricerche Terapeutiche [*A publication*]
Pubbl Ente Naz Cellulosa Carta ... Pubblicazioni. Ente Nazionale per la Cellulosa e per la Carta [*A publication*]
Pubbl Fac Sci Ing Univ Trieste Ser A ... Pubblicazioni. Facolta di Scienze e d'Ingegneria. Universita di Trieste. Serie A [*A publication*]
Pubbl Fac Sci Ing Univ Trieste Ser B ... Pubblicazioni. Facolta di Scienze e d'Ingegneria. Universita di Trieste. Serie B [*A publication*]
Pubbl IAC ... Pubblicazioni. Istituto per le Applicazioni del Calcolo. Consiglio Nazionale delle Ricerche [*A publication*]
Pubbl Ist Chim Agrar Sper Gorizia Nuovi Ann ... Pubblicazioni. Istituto Chimico Agrario Sperimentale di Gorizia. Nuovi Annali [*A publication*]
Pubbl Ist Geol Mineral Univ Ferrara ... Pubblicazioni. Istituto di Geologia e Mineralogia. Universita di Ferrara [*A publication*]
Pubbl Ist Mat Appl Fac Ingegneria Univ Stud Roma ... Pubblicazioni. Istituto di Matematica Applicata. Facolta di Ingegneria. Universita degli Studi di Roma [*A publication*]
Pubbl Ist Sper Selv (Arezzo) ... Pubblicazioni. Istituto Sperimentale per la Selvicoltura (Arezzo, Italy) [*A publication*]
Pubbl Oss Geofis Trieste ... Pubblicazioni. Osservatorio Geofisico di Trieste [*A publication*]
Pubbl Ser III ... Pubblicazione. Serie III [*A publication*]
Pubbl Stn Zool Napoli ... Pubblicazioni. Stazione Zoologica di Napoli [*A publication*]
Pubbl Univ Studi Firenze Fac Sci Mat Fis Nat ... Pubblicazioni. Universita degli Studi di Firenze. Facolta di Scienze Matematiche, Fisiche, e Naturali [*A publication*]
Pubbl Univ Stud Perugia Fac Med Vet ... Pubblicazioni. Universita degli Studi di Perugia. Facolta di Medicina Veterinaria [*A publication*]
PUBC .... Presbyterians United for Biblical Concerns [*Later, PBC*] (EA)
PUBC .... Pubcoa, Inc. [*NASDAQ symbol*] (NQ)
Pubcaster ... Public Broadcaster [*Radio or TV station affiliated with NPR or PBS*]
Pub Circ ..... Publishers' Circular and Booksellers' Record [*A publication*]
Pub Col Soc Mass ... Publications. Colonial Society of Massachusetts [*A publication*]
Pub Cont LJ ... Public Contract Law Journal [*A publication*]
Pub Cont Newsl ... Public Contract Newsletter [*A publication*]
Pub Contract L J ... Public Contract Law Journal [*A publication*]
PUBD .... Published (ROG)
PUB DOC ... Public Documents (ROG)
Pub Dom Ast ... Publications. Dominion Astrophysical Observatory [*A publication*]
Pub Emp .... Public Employee [*A publication*]
Pub Employee Bargaining CCH ... Public Employee Bargaining. Commerce Clearing House [*A publication*]
Pub Employee Bargaining Rep (CCH) ... Public Employee Bargaining Reports (Commerce Clearing House) [*A publication*] (DLA)
Pub Employee Rel Rep ... Public Employee Relations Reports [*A publication*] (DLA)
Pub Ent Advert & Allied Fields LQ ... Publishing, Entertainment, Advertising, and Allied Fields Law Quarterly [*A publication*] (DLA)
Pub Ent Adv LQ ... Publishing, Entertainment, Advertising, and Allied Fields Law Quarterly [*A publication*]
Pub Gen Acts S Austl ... Public General Acts of South Australia [*A publication*] (DLA)
Pub Gen Laws ... Public General Laws [*A publication*] (DLA)
PUB HA .... Public Hall [*Freemasonry*] (ROG)
Pub Health ... United States Public Health Service, Court Decisions [*A publication*] (DLA)
Pub Health Monogr ... Public Health Monographs [*A publication*]
Pub Health Nurs ... Public Health Nursing [*A publication*]
Pub Health Rep ... Public Health Reports [*A publication*]
Pub Health Rept ... Public Health Reports [*A publication*]
Pub Health Rep US Pub Health and Mar Hosp Serv ... Public Health Reports. United States Surgeon-General. Public Health and Marine Hospital Service [*A publication*]
Pub Health Rep US Pub Health Serv ... Public Health Reports. United States Public Health Service [*A publication*]
Pub Health Soc B ... Public Health Society. Bulletin [*Kuala Lumpur*] [*A publication*]
Pub Hist Inst Luxembourg ... Publications. Section Historique. Institut Grand-Ducal de Luxembourg [*A publication*]
PUBINFO ... Office of Public Information [*Formerly, OPR*] [*Navy*]

Pub Interest ... Public Interest [*A publication*]
Pub Intl L ... Public International Law [*A publication*] (DLA)
Pub L .... Public Law [*A publication*]
PUBL .... Publication [*or Published or Publisher*] (EY)
Publ Adm ... Public Administration [*A publication*] (APTA)
Publ Admin ... Public Administration [*A publication*]
Publ Adm R ... Public Administration Review [*A publication*]
Publ Adm Re ... Public Administration Review [*A publication*]
Publ Aff B .. Public Affairs Bulletin [*A publication*]
Publ Agric (Can) ... Publication. Agriculture (Canada) [*A publication*]
Publ Agric Ext Serv N Carol St Univ ... Publication. Agricultural Extension Service. North Carolina State University [*A publication*]
Publ Agric Res Serv US Dep Agric ... Publication. Agricultural Research Service. United States Department of Agriculture [*A publication*]
Publ Alberta Dept Agr ... Publication. Alberta Department of Agriculture [*A publication*]
Publ Allegheny Obs Univ Pittsburgh ... Publications. Allegheny Observatory. University of Pittsburgh [*A publication*]
Publ Amakusa Mar Biol Lab Kyushu Univ ... Publications. Amakusa Marine Biological Laboratory. Kyushu University [*A publication*]
Publ Am Assoc Adv Sci ... Publication. American Association for the Advancement of Science [*A publication*]
Publ Amer Ass Advan Sci ... Publication. American Association for the Advancement of Science [*A publication*]
Publ Amer Univ Beirut Fac Agr Sci ... Publication. American University of Beirut. Faculty of Agricultural Sciences [*A publication*]
Publ Am Inst Biol Sci ... Publication. American Institute of Biological Sciences [*A publication*]
Publ Am Univ Beirut Fac Agric Sci ... Publication. American University of Beirut. Faculty of Agricultural Sciences [*A publication*]
Publ ANARE Data Rep Ser ... Publications. ANARE [*Australian National Antarctic Research Expeditions*] Data Reports Series [*A publication*] (APTA)
Pub Land L Rev ... Public Land Law Review [*A publication*] (DLA)
Pub Land & Res L Dig ... Public Land and Resources Law Digest [*A publication*]
Pub Lands Dec ... Department of the Interior, Decisions Relating to Public Lands [*A publication*] (DLA)
Publ Ass For-Cell ... Publication. Association Foret-Cellulose [*A publication*]
Publ Assoc Etude Paleontol Stratigr Houilleres ... Publication. Association pour l'Etude de la Paleontologie et de la Stratigraphie Houilleres [*A publication*]
Publ Assoc Ing Fac Polytech Mons ... Publications. Association des Ingenieurs. Faculte Polytechnique de Mons [*A publication*]
Publ Astron Soc Jpn ... Publications. Astronomical Society of Japan [*A publication*]
Publ Astron Soc Pac ... Publications. Astronomical Society of the Pacific [*A publication*]
Publ Aust Natl Univ Res Sch Phys Sci Dep Eng Phys ... Australian National University. Research School of Physical Sciences. Department of Engineering Physics. Publication [*A publication*] (APTA)
Publ Avulsa FZB Fund Zoobot Rio Grande Sul ... Publicacao Avulsa FZB. Fundacao Zoobotanica do Rio Grande Do Sul [*A publication*]
Publ Avulsas Cent Pesqui Aggeu Magalhaes (Recife Braz) ... Publicacoes Avulsas. Centro de Pesquisas Aggeu Magalhaes (Recife, Brazil) [*A publication*]
Publ Avulsas Inst Aggeu Magalhaes (Recife Braz) ... Publicacoes Avulsas. Instituto Aggeu Magalhaes (Recife, Brazil) [*A publication*]
Publ Avulsas Mus Nac (Rio De J) ... Publicacoes Avulsas. Museu Nacional (Rio De Janeiro) [*A publication*]
Publ Avuls Rev Bras Malariol ... Publicacoes Avulsas. Revista Brasileira de Malariologia [*A publication*]
Publ BC Minist Agric ... Publications. British Columbia Ministry of Agriculture [*A publication*]
Publ BC Minist Agric Food ... Publications. British Columbia Ministry of Agriculture and Food [*A publication*]
Publ Beaverlodge Res Stn ... Publication. Beaverlodge Research Station [*A publication*]
Publ Biol Dir Gen Invest Cient UANL (Univ Auton Nuevo Leon) ... Publicaciones Biologicas. Direccion General de la Investigacion Cientifica UANL (Universidad Autonoma de Nuevo Leon) [*A publication*]
Publ Biol Univ Navarra Ser Zool ... Publicaciones de Biologia. Universidad de Navarra. Serie Zoologica [*A publication*]
Publ Bot ..... Publications in Botany [*A publication*]
Publ Brit Columbia Dept Agr ... Publication. British Columbia Department of Agriculture [*A publication*]
Publ Bur Etud Geol Minieres Colon (Paris) ... Publications. Bureau d'Etudes Geologiques et Minieres Coloniales (Paris) [*A publication*]
Publ Bur Rech Geol Geophys Minieres (Fr) ... Publications. Bureau de Recherches Geologiques, Geophysiques, et Minieres (France) [*A publication*]
Publ Cairo Univ Herb ... Publications. Cairo University Herbarium [*A publication*]
Publ Calif Dep Agric ... Publication. California Department of Agriculture [*A publication*]
Publ Canada Dep Agric ... Publication. Canada Department of Agriculture [*A publication*]

Publ Canada Dep For ... Publication. Canada Department of Forestry [*A publication*]

Publ Can Dep Agric ... Publication. Canada Department of Agriculture [*A publication*]

Publ Can Dept Agr ... Publication. Canada Department of Agriculture [*A publication*]

Publ Can For Serv ... Publication. Canadian Forestry Service [*A publication*]

Publ Center Medieval Ren Stud UCLA ... Publications. Center for Medieval and Renaissance Studies. UCLA [*University of California at Los Angeles*] [*A publication*]

Publ Cent Estud Entomol Univ Chile ... Publicaciones. Centro de Estudios Entomologicos. Universidad de Chile [*A publication*]

Publ Cent Estud Leprol ... Publicacoes. Centro de Estudos Leprologicos [*A publication*]

Publ Cent Etude Util Sciures de Bois ... Publication. Centre d'Etude pour l'Utilisation des Sciures de Bois [*A publication*]

Publ Cent Natl Exploit Oceans Actes Colloq ... Publications. Centre National pour l'Exploitation des Oceans. Actes de Colloques [*A publication*]

Publ Cent Natl Exploit Oceans Result Campagnes Mer ... Publications. Centre National pour l'Exploitation des Oceans. Resultats des Campagnes a la Mer [*A publication*]

Publ Cent Natl Exploit Oceans Ser Rapp Sci Tech (Fr) ... Publications. Centre National pour l'Exploitation des Oceans. Serie. Rapport Scientifique et Technique (France) [*A publication*]

Publ Cent Natl Geol Houillere ... Publication. Centre National de Geologie Houillere [*A publication*]

Publ Cent Quim Ind (Buenos Aires) ... Publicacion. Centro de Quimicos Industriales (Buenos Aires) [*A publication*]

Publ Cent Rech Zootech Univ Louvain ... Publication. Centre de Recherches Zootechniques. Universite de Louvain [*A publication*]

Publ Centre Recherches Math Pures Ser 3 ... Publications. Centre de Recherches en Mathematiques Pures. Serie 3 [*A publication*]

Publ Centre Rech Math Pures ... Publications. Centre de Recherches en Mathematiques Pures [*A publication*]

Publ Centre Rech Math Pures 1 ... Publications. Centre de Recherches en Mathematiques Pures. Serie 1 [*A publication*]

Publ Centre Rech Math Pures Ser 3 ... Publications. Centre de Recherches en Mathematiques Pures. Serie 3 [*A publication*]

Publ Centre Tech For Trop ... Publication. Centre Technique Forestier Tropical [*A publication*]

Publ Cent Stud Citogenet Veg CNR ... Pubblicazioni. Centro di Studi per la Citogenetica Vegetale. Consiglio Nazionale delle Ricerche [*A publication*]

Publ Cent Tech For Trop (Nogent-Sur-Marne Fr) ... Publication. Centre Technique Forestier Tropical (Nogent-Sur-Marne, France) [*A publication*]

Publ Chile Univ Cent Estud Entomol ... Publicaciones. Chile Universidad. Centro de Estudios Entomologicos [*A publication*]

Publ Choice ... Public Choice [*A publication*]

Publ Cient Univ Austral Chile (Fac Ingen For) ... Publicaciones Cientificas. Universidad Austral de Chile (Facultad de Ingenieria Forestal) [*A publication*]

Publ Clark ... Publications. Clark Library Professorship. University of California at Los Angeles [*A publication*]

Publ Cleans ... Public Cleansing [*A publication*]

Publcoes Avuls Mus Parana ... Publicacoes Avulsas. Museu Paranaense [*A publication*]

Publcoes Cult Co Diam Angola ... Publicacoes Culturais. Companhia de Diamantes de Angola [*A publication*]

Publcoes Dir Ger Servs Flor Aquic ... Publicacoes. Direccao Geral dos Servicos Florestais e Aqueicolas [*A publication*]

Publ Coffee Brew Inst ... Publication. Coffee Brewing Institute [*A publication*]

Publ Com Nac Energ At (Argent) Misc ... Publicaciones. Comision Nacional de Energia Atomica (Argentina). Miscelanea [*A publication*]

Publ Com Nac Energ At (Argent) Ser Fis ... Publicaciones. Comision Nacional de Energia Atomica (Argentina). Serie Fisica [*A publication*]

Publ Com Nac Energ At (Argent) Ser Geol ... Publicaciones. Comision Nacional de Energia Atomica (Argentina). Serie Geologia [*A publication*]

Publ Com Nac Energ At (Argent) Ser Mat ... Publicaciones. Comision Nacional de Energia Atomica (Argentina). Serie Matematica [*A publication*]

Publ Com Nac Energ At (Argent) Ser Quim ... Publicaciones. Comision Nacional de Energia Atomica (Argentina). Serie Quimica [*A publication*]

Publ Cons Recur Nat No Renov (Mex) ... Publicacion. Consejo de Recursos Naturales No Renovables (Mexico) [*A publication*]

Publ Cons Recursos Miner ... Publicacion. Consejo de Recursos Minerales [*A publication*]

Publ Contr LJ ... Public Contract Law Journal [*A publication*]

Publ Coop Ext Serv Miss State Univ ... Publication. Cooperative Extension Service. Mississippi State University [*A publication*]

Publ Coop Ext Serv Wash St Univ ... Publication. Cooperative Extension Service. Washington State University [*A publication*]

Publ Co-Op Ext Univ Calif ... Publication. Cooperative Extension. University of California [*A publication*]

Publ Cult Cia Diamantes Angola ... Publicacoes Culturais. Companhia de Diamantes de Angola [*A publication*]

PUBLD ...... Published (ROG)

Publ Dep Agric (Can) ... Publication. Department of Agriculture (Ottawa, Canada) [*A publication*]

Publ Dep Cristalogr Miner CSIC (Spain) ... Publicaciones. Departamento de Cristalografia y Mineralogia. Consejo Superior de Investigaciones Cientificas (Spain) [*A publication*]

Publ Dep Math Lyon ... Publications. Departement de Mathematiques. Faculte des Sciences de Lyon [*A publication*]

Publ Dept Agr (Can) ... Publications. Department of Agriculture (Canada) [*A publication*]

Publ Dept Agr Conserv (Manitoba) ... Publications. Department of Agriculture and Conservation (Manitoba) [*A publication*]

Publ Dep Zool (Barc) ... Publicaciones. Departamento de Zoologia (Barcelona) [*A publication*]

Publ Dir Gen Geol Minas Repub Ecuador ... Publicacion. Direccion General de Geologia y Minas. Republica del Ecuador [*A publication*]

Publ Dir Gen Invent Nac For (Mex) ... Publicacion. Direccion General del Inventario Nacional Forestal (Coyoacan, Mexico) [*A publication*]

Publ Diverses Mus Natl Hist Nat ... Publications Diverses. Museum National d'Histoire Naturelle [*A publication*]

Publ Dom Astrophys Obs ... Publications. Dominion Astrophysical Observatory [*Victoria, British Columbia*] [*A publication*]

Publ Dom Astrophys Obs (Victoria BC) ... Publications. Dominion Astrophysical Observatory (Victoria, British Columbia) [*A publication*]

Publ Dom Obs (Ottawa) ... Publications. Dominion Observatory (Ottawa) [*A publication*]

Publ Dushanb Inst Epidemiol Gig ... Publikatsiya Dushanbinskogo Instituta Epidemiologii i Gigieny [*A publication*]

Publ Earth Phys Branch (Can) ... Publications. Earth Physics Branch (Canada) [*A publication*]

Publ Earth Phys Branch Dep Energy Mines & Resour ... Publications. Earth Physics Branch. Department of Energy, Mines, and Resources [*A publication*]

Publ Econometriques ... Publications Econometriques [*A publication*]

Publ Elektrote Fak Univ Beogradu Ser Mat Fiz ... Publikacije Elektrotehnickog Fakulteta Univerziteta u Beogradu. Serija Matematika i Fizika [*A publication*]

Publ Elektroteh Fak Ser Elektroenerg ... Publikacije Elektrotehnickog Fakulteta. Serija Elektroenergetika [*A publication*]

Publ Elektroteh Fak Ser Elektron Telekommun Autom ... Publikacije Elektrotehnickog Fakulteta. Serija Elektronika Telekommunikacije. Automatika [*A publication*]

Publ Elektroteh Fak Ser Mat & Fiz ... Publikacije Elektrotehnickog Fakulteta. Serija Matematika i Fizika [*A publication*]

Publ Elektroteh Fak Univ Beogr Ser Mat Fiz ... Publikacije Elektrotehnickog Fakulteta Univerziteta u Beogradu. Serija Matematika i Fizika [*A publication*]

Publ Energ ... Publicacion sobre Energia [*A publication*]

Publ Ent Adv A ... Publishing, Entertainment, Advertising, and Allied Fields Law Quarterly [*A publication*]

Publ E Purdue Univ Coop Ext Serv ... Publication E. Purdue University. Cooperative Extension Service [*A publication*]

Publ Espec Inst Nac Invest Forest (Mex) ... Publicacion Especial. Instituto Nacional de Investigaciones Forestal (Mexico) [*A publication*]

Publ Espec Inst Oceanogr (San Paulo) ... Publicacao Especial. Instituto Oceanografico (San Paulo) [*A publication*]

Publ Espec Serv Nac Trigo Min Agr (Madrid) ... Publicaciones Especiales. Servicio Nacional del Trigo. Ministerio de Agricultura (Madrid) [*A publication*]

Publ Ethnol ... Publications in Ethnology [*A publication*]

Publ Eur Gem ... Publicatieblad van de Europese Gemeenschappen [*A publication*]

Publ Ext Serv Israel Min Agric ... Israel. Ministry of Agriculture. Extension Service Publication [*A publication*]

Pub LF .... Public Law Forum [*A publication*] (DLA)

Publ Fac Agron Univ Teheran ... Publications. Faculte d'Agronomie. Universite de Teheran [*A publication*]

Publ Fac Agr Sci Amer Univ (Beirut) ... Publications. Faculty of Agricultural Sciences. American University (Beirut) [*A publication*]

Publ Fac Cienc Fisicomat Univ Nac La Plata Ser 2 ... Publicaciones. Facultad de Ciencias Fisicomatematicas. Universidad Nacional de La Plata. Serie 2. Revista [*A publication*]

Publ Fac Dr Econ Amiens ... Publications. Faculte de Droit et d'Economie d'Amiens [*A publication*]

Publ Fac Dr Sci Polit Soc Amiens ... Publications. Faculte de Droit et des Sciences Politiques et Sociales d'Amiens [*A publication*]

Publ Fac Sci Univ Clermont Geol Mineral ... Publications. Faculte des Sciences. Universite de Clermont. Geologie et Mineralogie [*A publication*]

Publ FAO/ECE Jt Comm Working Tech ... Publication. FAO [*Food and Agriculture Organization of the United Nations*]/ECE [*Economic Commission for Europe*] Joint Committee on Forest Working Techniques and Training Forest Workers [*A publication*]

Publ Farm (Sao Paulo) ... Publicacoes Farmaceuticas (Sao Paulo) [*A publication*]
Publ Finan ... Public Finance [*A publication*]
Publ Finance ... Public Finance [*A publication*]
Publ Fin Q ... Public Finance Quarterly [*A publication*]
Publ Fond Agathon de Potter ... Publications. Foundation Agathon de Potter [*A publication*]
Publ For Commn NSW ... Publication. Forestry Commission of New South Wales [*A publication*]
Publ Foreign Agric Serv US Dep Agric ... Publication. Foreign Agricultural Service. United States Department of Agriculture [*A publication*]
Publ Forest Res Brch Canada Dep For ... Publication. Forest Research Branch. Canada Department of Forestry [*A publication*]
Publ For Res Inst Finl ... Publications. Forest Research Institute in Finland [*A publication*]
Publ For Serv (Can) ... Publication. Forestry Service. Department of Fisheries and Forestry (Ottawa, Canada) [*A publication*]
Publ Found Sci Res Surinam Neth Antilles ... Publications. Foundation for Scientific Research in Surinam and the Netherlands Antilles [*A publication*]
Publ Geol Dep Ext Serv Univ West Aust ... Publication. Geology Department and the Extension Service. University of Western Australia [*A publication*]
Publ Geol Surv Queensl ... Publication. Geological Survey of Queensland [*A publication*] (APTA)
Publ Great Plains Agric Coun ... Great Plains Agricultural Council. Publication [*A publication*]
Publ Group Adv Psychiatry ... Publication. Groups for the Advancement of Psychiatry [*A publication*]
Publ Group Av Methodes Spectrogr ... Publication. Groupement pour l'Avancement des Methodes Spectrographiques [*A publication*]
Publ Gulf Coast Res Lab Mus ... Publications. Gulf Coast Research Laboratory. Museum [*A publication*]
Publ Haewundae Mar Lab Pusan Fish Coll ... Publications. Haewundae Marine Laboratory. Pusan Fisheries College [*A publication*]
Publ Hannah Inst Hist Med ... Publication. Hannah Institute for the History of Medicine [*A publication*]
Publ Heal... Public Health: The Journal of the Society of Community Medicine [*A publication*]
Publ Heal R ... Public Health Reviews [*A publication*]
Publ Health Lab ... Public Health Laboratory [*A publication*]
Publ Hea Re ... Public Health Reports [*A publication*]
Publ Hlth... Public Health [*A publication*]
Publ Hlth Ne ... Public Health News [*A publication*]
Publ Hlth Rep (Wash) ... Public Health Reports (Washington, DC) [*A publication*]
Publ Hung Min Res Inst ... Publications. Hungarian Mining Research Institute [*A publication*]
Publ Hung Res Inst Mining ... Publications. Hungarian Research Institute for Mining [*A publication*]
Pub Lib ...... Public Libraries [*A publication*]
Pub Lib Op ... Public Library Opinion [*A publication*] (APTA)
Pub Lib Trustee ... Public Library Trustee [*A publication*]
public .... Publicist
Publicaciones Dept Agric Costa Rica ... Publicaciones. Departamento de Agricultura de Costa Rica [*A publication*]
Public Adm ... Public Administration [*A publication*]
Public Adm Bull ... Public Administration Bulletin [*A publication*]
Public Admin ... Public Administration [*A publication*] (APTA)
Public Admin Bull ... Public Administration Bulletin [*A publication*]
Public Admin and Development ... Public Administration and Development [*A publication*]
Public Admin J (Kathmandu) ... Public Administration Journal (Kathmandu) [*A publication*]
Public Admin R ... Public Administration Review [*A publication*]
Public Admin Survey ... Public Administration Survey [*A publication*]
Public Adm R ... Public Administration Review [*A publication*]
Public Adm Rev ... Public Administration Review [*A publication*]
Public Affairs Rept ... Public Affairs Report [*A publication*]
Public Aff Rep ... Public Affairs Report [*A publication*]
Public Anal Assoc J ... Public Analysts Association. Journal [*England*] [*A publication*]
Public Budgeting and Fin ... Public Budgeting and Finance [*A publication*]
Public Fin... Public Finance [*A publication*]
Public Fin Account ... Public Finance and Accountancy [*A publication*]
Public Fin (Berlin) ... Public Finance (Berlin) [*A publication*]
Public Fin Q ... Public Finance Quarterly [*A publication*]
Public Health Eng ... Public Health Engineer [*England*] [*A publication*]
Public Health Eng Abstr ... Public Health Engineering Abstracts [*A publication*]
Public Health Eur ... Public Health in Europe [*A publication*]
Public Health J ... Public Health Journal [*A publication*]
Public Health Lab ... Public Health Laboratory [*United States*] [*A publication*]
Public Health Monogr ... Public Health Monograph [*A publication*]
Public Health Nurs ... Public Health Nursing [*A publication*]
Public Health Pap ... Public Health Papers [*A publication*]
Public Health Rep ... Public Health Reports [*A publication*]

Public Health Rev ... Public Health Reviews [*A publication*]
Public Health Revs ... Public Health Reviews [*A publication*]
Public Hlth Engr ... Public Health Engineer [*A publication*]
Public Land Resour Law Dig ... Public Land and Resources Law Digest [*United States*] [*A publication*]
Public Lib .. Public Libraries [*A publication*]
Public Light ... Public Lighting [*A publication*]
Public Mgt ... Public Management [*A publication*]
Public Opin ... Public Opinion [*A publication*]
Public Opinion Q ... Public Opinion Quarterly [*A publication*]
Public Opin Q ... Public Opinion Quarterly [*A publication*]
Public Pers Manage ... Public Personnel Management [*A publication*]
Public Prod Rev ... Public Productivity Review [*A publication*]
Public Rel... Public Relations Journal [*A publication*]
Public Relations R ... Public Relations Review [*A publication*]
Public Relat J ... Public Relations Journal [*A publication*]
Public Relat Q ... Public Relations Quarterly [*A publication*]
Public Relat Rev ... Public Relations Review [*A publication*]
Public Sect ... Public Sector. New Zealand Institute of Public Administration [*A publication*]
Public Sector Health Care Risk Manage ... Public Sector. Health Care Risk Management [*A publication*]
Public Serv Action ... Public Service Action [*A publication*]
Public TC Review ... Public Telecommunications Review [*A publication*]
Public Util Fortn ... Public Utilities Fortnightly [*A publication*]
Public Welf ... Public Welfare [*A publication*]
Public Works Eng Yearb ... Public Works Engineers' Yearbook [*A publication*]
Public Works Local Gov Eng ... Public Works and Local Government Engineering [*A publication*]
Public Works Rev ... Public Works Review [*Japan*] [*A publication*]
Public Works Roads Transp ... Public Works, Roads, and Transport [*A publication*]
Public Works Ser ... Public Works and Services [*A publication*] (APTA)
Public Work (Syd) ... Public Works and Services (Sydney) [*A publication*] (APTA)
Publ INCAR ... Publicacion INCAR [*Instituto Nacional del Carbon y Sus Derivados "Francisco Pintado Fe"*] [*A publication*]
Publ INED ... Publications INED [*Institut National d'Etudes Demographiques*] [*A publication*]
Publ Inst Antart Argent (B Aires) ... Publicacion. Instituto Antartico Argentino (Buenos Aires) [*A publication*]
Publ Inst Biol Apl (Barc) ... Publicaciones. Instituto de Biologia Aplicada (Barcelona) [*A publication*]
Publ Inst Biol Apl (Barcelona) ... Publicaciones. Instituto de Biologia Aplicada (Barcelona) [*A publication*]
Publ Inst Bot "Dr Goncalo Sampaio" Fac Cienc Univ Porto ... Publicacoes. Instituto de Botanica "Dr. Goncalo Sampaio." Faculdade de Ciencias. Universidade do Porto [*A publication*]
Publ Inst Edafol Hidrol Univ Nac Sur (Bahia Blanca) ... Publicaciones. Instituto de Edafologia e Hidrologia. Universidad Nacional del Sur (Bahia Blanca) [*A publication*]
Publ Inst Fis "Alonso De St Cruz" ... Publicaciones. Instituto de Fisica "Alonso De Santa Cruz" [*A publication*]
Publ Inst Florestal ... Publicacao. Instituto Florestal [*A publication*]
Publ Inst Found Engng Soil Mech Rock Mech Waterways Constr ... Publications. Institute of Foundation Engineering, Soil Mechanics, Rock Mechanics, and Waterways Construction [*A publication*]
Publ Inst Fr Pet Collect Colloq Semin ... Publications. Institut Francais du Petrole. Collection Colloques et Seminaires [*France*] [*A publication*]
Publ Inst Geogr (Bogota) ... Publication. Instituto Geografico Agustin Codazzi (Bogota) [*A publication*]
Publ Inst Geol (Barcelona) ... Publicaciones. Instituto Geologico (Barcelona) [*A publication*]
Publ Inst Geol Topogr ... Publicaciones. Instituto Geologico Topografico [*A publication*]
Publ Inst Geol Univ Chile ... Publicaciones. Instituto de Geologia del Universidade de Chile [*A publication*]
Publ Inst Geophys Pol Acad Sci ... Publication. Institute of Geophysics. Polish Academy of Sciences [*A publication*]
Publ Inst Geophys Pol Acad Sci Ser A ... Publications. Institute of Geophysics. Polish Academy of Sciences. Series A. Physics of the Earth Interior [*A publication*]
Publ Inst Geophys Pol Acad Sci Ser B ... Publications. Institute of Geophysics. Polish Academy of Sciences. Series B. Seismology [*A publication*]
Publ Inst Geophys Pol Acad Sci Ser C ... Publications. Institute of Geophysics. Polish Academy of Sciences. Series C. Earth Magnetism [*A publication*]
Publ Inst Geophys Pol Acad Sci Ser E ... Publications. Institute of Geophysics. Polish Academy of Sciences. Series E. Ionosphere Physics [*A publication*]
Publ Inst Geophys Pol Acad Sci Ser F ... Publications. Institute of Geophysics. Polish Academy of Sciences. Series F. Planetary Geodesy [*A publication*]
Publ Inst Geophys Ser D Pol Acad Sci ... Publications. Institute of Geophysics. Polish Academy of Sciences. Series D. Atmosphere Physics [*A publication*]

Publ Inst Invest Geol Diputacion Barcelona ... Publicaciones. Instituto de Investigaciones Geologicas. Diputacion de Barcelona [*A publication*]

Publ Inst Invest Geol Diputacion Prov Barcelona ... Publicaciones. Instituto de Investigaciones Geologicas. Diputacion Provincial de Barcelona [*A publication*]

Publ Inst Invest Microquim Univ Nac Litoral (Rosario Argent) ... Publicaciones. Instituto de Investigaciones Microquimicas. Universidad Nacional del Litoral (Rosario, Argentina) [*A publication*]

Publ Inst Mar Sci Nat Fish Univ Busan ... Publications. Institute of Marine Sciences. National Fisheries. University of Busan [*A publication*]

Publ Inst Mar Sci Natl Fish Univ Busan ... Publications. Institute of Marine Sciences. National Fisheries University of Busan [*A publication*]

Publ Inst Mar Sci Univ Tex ... Publications. Institute of Marine Science. University of Texas [*A publication*]

Publ Inst Mar Sci Univ Texas ... Publications. Institute of Marine Science. University of Texas [*A publication*]

Publ Inst Math (Belgrade) ... Publications. Institut Mathematique. Nouvelle Serie (Belgrade) [*A publication*]

Publ Inst Math (Belgrad) NS ... Institut Mathematique. Publications. Nouvelle Serie (Belgrade) [*A publication*]

Publ Inst Math Univ Nancago ... Publications. Institut Mathematique. Universite de Nancago [*Paris*] [*A publication*]

Publ Inst Math Univ Strasbourg ... Publications. Institut de Mathematiques. Universite de Strasbourg [*A publication*]

Publ Inst Mex Recursos Nat Renov ... Publicacion. Instituto Mexicano de Recursos Naturales Renovables [*A publication*]

Publ Inst Mineral Paleontol Quat Geol Univ Lund ... Publications. Institutes of Mineralogy, Paleontology, and Quaternary Geology. University of Lund [*A publication*]

Publ Inst Musee Voltaire ... Publications. Institut et Musee Voltaire [*A publication*]

Publ Inst Nac Carbon Sus Deriv "Francisco Pintado Fe" ... Publicacion. Instituto Nacional del Carbon y Sus Derivados "Francisco Pintado Fe" [*A publication*]

Publ Inst Nac Nutr (Argent) Publ Cient ... Publicaciones. Instituto Nacional de la Nutricion (Argentina). Publicaciones Cientificas [*A publication*]

Publ Inst Nat Etude Agron Congo ... Publications. Institut National pour l'Etude Agronomique du Congo [*A publication*]

Publ Inst Nat Etude Agron Congo (INEAC) Serie Scientifique ... Publications. Institut National pour l'Etude Agronomique du Congo (INEAC). Serie Scientifique [*A publication*]

Publ Inst Natl Etude Agron Congo Belge Ser Sci ... Publications. Institut National pour l'Etude Agronomique du Congo Belge. Serie Scientifique [*A publication*]

Publ Inst Natl Etude Agron Congo Ser Sci ... Publications. Institut National pour l'Etude Agronomique du Congo. Serie Scientifique [*A publication*]

Publ Inst Natl Etude Agron Congo Ser Tech ... Publications. Institut National pour l'Etude Agronomique du Congo. Serie Technique [*A publication*]

Publ Inst Opt Madrid ... Publicaciones. Instituto de Optica Daza de Valdes de Madrid [*A publication*]

Publ Inst Pesqui Mar ... Publicacao. Instituto de Pesquisas da Marinha [*A publication*]

Publ Inst Quim Fis Rocasolano ... Publicaciones. Instituto de Quimica Fisica "Rocasolano" [*A publication*]

Publ Inst Rech Sider Ser B ... Publications. Institut de Recherches de la Siderurgie. Serie B [*A publication*]

Publ Inst Rech Siderurg Ser A ... Publications. Institut de Recherches de la Siderurgie [*Saint-Germain-En-Laye*]. Serie A [*A publication*]

Publ Inst R Meteorol Belg A ... Publications. Institut Royal Meteorologique de Belgique. Serie A. Format in-4 [*A publication*]

Publ Inst R Meteorol Belg B ... Publications. Institut Royal Meteorologique de Belgique. Serie B. Format in-8 [*A publication*]

Publ Inst R Meteorol Belg Ser A ... Publications. Institut Royal Meteorologique de Belgique. Serie A. Format in-4 [*A publication*]

Publ Inst R Meteorol Belg Ser B ... Publications. Institut Royal Meteorologique de Belgique. Serie B [*A publication*]

Publ Inst Soil Rock Mech Univ Fridericiana (Karlsruhe) ... Publications. Institute for Soil and Rock Mechanics. University of Fridericiana (Karlsruhe) [*A publication*]

Publ Inst Statist Univ Paris ... Publications. Institut de Statistique. Universite de Paris [*A publication*]

Publ Inst Suflos Agrotec (B Aires) ... Publicacion. Instituto de Suflos y Agrotecnia (Buenos Aires) [*A publication*]

Publ Inst Tecnol Estud Super Monterrey Ser Cienc Biol ... Publicaciones. Instituto Tecnologico y de Estudios Superiores de Monterrey. Serie Ciencias Biologicas [*A publication*]

Publ Inst Zool "Dr Augusto Nobre" Fac Cienc Porto ... Publicacoes. Instituto de Zoologia "Dr. Augusto Nobreda." Faculdade de Ciencias. Universidade do Porto [*A publication*]

Publ Inst Zootec (Rio De J) ... Publicacao. Instituto de Zootecnia (Rio De Janeiro) [*A publication*]

Publ Int ...... Public Interest [*A publication*]

Publ Int Ass Scient Hydrol Symp (Budapest) ... Publication. International Association of Scientific Hydrology. Symposium (Budapest) [*A publication*]

Publ Inter ... Public Interest [*A publication*]

Publ Intern Postgrado ... Publicaciones Internas del Postgrado [*A publication*]

PUBLINX ... Public Links [*Amateur golf*]

Publishers ... Publishers' Weekly [*A publication*]

Publius J F ... Publius. Journal of Federalism [*A publication*]

Publ Junta Nac Prod Pecu Ser A Ser Cient Invest ... Publicacoes. Junta Nacional dos Produtos Pecuarios. Serie A. Serie Cientifica e de Investigacao [*A publication*]

Publ Korean Natl Astron Obs ... Publications. Korean National Astronomical Observatory [*Republic of Korea*] [*A publication*]

Publ L .... Public Law [*A publication*]

Publ Lab Biochim Nutr Univ Cathol Louvain Fac Sci Agron ... Publication. Laboratoire de Biochimie de la Nutrition. Universite Catholique de Louvain. Faculte des Sciences Agronomiques [*A publication*]

Publ Lab Cent Ensayo Mater Constr (Madrid) ... Publication. Laboratorio Central de Ensayo de Materiales de Construccion (Madrid) [*A publication*]

Publ Lab Jefferson Med Coll Hosp ... Publications. Laboratories of the Jefferson Medical College Hospital [*A publication*]

Publ Lab Photoelasticite Ecole Polytech Fed (Zurich) ... Publications. Laboratoire de Photoelasticite. Ecole Polytechnique Federale (Zurich) [*A publication*]

Publ Lab Physiol Chem Univ Amsterdam ... Publications. Laboratory of Physiological Chemistry. University of Amsterdam [*A publication*]

Publ Law (London) ... Public Law (London) [*A publication*]

Publ Ld Capability Surv Trinidad & Tobago ... Publication. Land Capability Survey of Trinidad and Tobago [*A publication*]

Publ Ltg ..... Public Lighting [*A publication*]

Publ Manitoba Beekprs Ass ... Publication. Manitoba Beekeepers' Association [*A publication*]

Publ Mar Biol Stn (Al Ghardaqa) ... Publications. Marine Biological Station (Al Ghardaqa, Red Sea) [*A publication*]

Publ Mar Biol Stn (Ghardaqa Red Sea) ... Publications. Marine Biological Station (Al Ghardaqa, Red Sea) [*A publication*]

Publ Mar Lab Pusan Fish Coll ... Publications. Marine Laboratory. Pusan Fisheries College [*South Korea*] [*A publication*]

Publ Math Debrecen ... Publicationes Mathematicae. Universitatis Debreceniensis [*A publication*]

Publ Math Orsay 80 ... Publications Mathematiques d'Orsay 80 [*A publication*]

Publ Math Orsay 81 ... Publications Mathematiques d'Orsay 81 [*A publication*]

Publ Math Orsay 82 ... Publications Mathematiques d'Orsay 82 [*A publication*]

Publ Math Res Center Univ Wisconsin ... Publications. Mathematics Research Center. University of Wisconsin [*A publication*]

Publ Math Res Cent Univ Wis ... Publication. Mathematics Research Center. University of Wisconsin [*A publication*]

Publ Math Res Inst (Istanbul) ... Publications. Mathematical Research Institute (Istanbul) [*A publication*]

Publ Math Soc Japan ... Publications. Mathematical Society of Japan [*A publication*]

Publ Math Univ Bordeaux ... Publications Mathematiques. Universite de Bordeaux [*A publication*]

Publ Math Univ Paris VII ... Publications Mathematiques. Universite de Paris. VII [*A publication*]

Publ Math Univ Pierre et Marie Curie ... Publications Mathematiques. Universite Pierre et Marie Curie [*A publication*]

Publ Med ... Publicacoes Medicas [*A publication*]

Publ Med Exp Univ Chile ... Publicaciones de Medicina Experimental. Universidad de Chile [*A publication*]

Publ Metaalinst TNO ... Publikatie. Metaalinstituut TNO [*Nederlands Centrale Organisatie voor Toegepast-Natuurwetenschappelijk Onderzoek*] [*A publication*]

Publ Min Agr Ser Premios Nac Invest Agr ... Publicaciones. Ministerio de Agricultura. Serie. Premios Nacionales de Investigacion Agraria [*A publication*]

Publ Minist Agric (Can) ... Publication. Ministry of Agriculture (Canada) [*A publication*]

Publ Misc Agric Univ Chile Fac Agron ... Publicaciones Miscelaneas Agricolas. Universidad de Chile. Facultad de Agronomia [*A publication*]

Publ Misc Estac Exp Agr Tucuman ... Publicaciones Miscelaneas. Estacion Experimental Agricola de Tucuman [*A publication*]

Publ Miss State Univ Agr Ext Serv ... Publication. Mississippi State University. Agricultural Extension Service [*A publication*]

Publ Mod Lang Ass ... Publications. Modern Language Association of America [*A publication*]

Publ Mus Hist Nat "Javier Prado" Ser A Zool ... Publicaciones. Museo de Historia Natural "Javier Prado." Series A. Zoologia [*A publication*]

Publ Mus Hist Nat "Javier Prado" Ser B Bot ... Publicaciones. Museo de Historia Natural "Javier Prado." Series B. Botanica [*A publication*]

Publ Mus Hist Nat Javier Prado Ser C Geol ... Publicaciones. Museo de Historia Natural "Javier Prado." Series C. Geologia [*A publication*]
Publ Mus Lab Mineral Geol Fac Cienc Porto ... Publicacoes. Museu e Laboratorio Mineralogico e Geologico. Faculdade de Ciencias do Porto [*A publication*]
Publ Mus Mich State Univ Biol Ser ... Publications. Museum. Michigan State University. Biological Series [*A publication*]
Publ Nat Acad Sci Nat Res Counc ... Publication. National Academy of Sciences. National Research Council [*A publication*]
Publ Natn Acad Sci Natn Res Coun (Wash) ... Publication. National Academy of Sciences. National Research Council (Washington) [*A publication*]
Publ Natuurhist Genoot Limburg ... Publicaties. Natuurhistorisch Genootschap in Limburg [*A publication*]
Publnes Misc Minist Agric Ganad Repub Argent ... Publicaciones Miscelaneas. Ministerio de Agricultura y Ganaderia. Republica de Argentina [*A publication*]
Publn Inst Nac Tec Agropec (B Aires) ... Publicacion. Instituto Nacional de Tecnologia Agropecuaria (Buenos Aires) [*A publication*]
Publn Inst Suelos Agrotec ... Publicacion. Instituto de Suelos y Agrotecnia [*A publication*]
Publ NMAB Natl Mater Advis Board (US) ... Publication. NMAB. National Materials Advisory Board (US) [*A publication*]
Publ Nor Inst Kosm Fys ... Publikasjoner. Norske Institutt foer Kosmisk Fysikk [*A publication*]
Publ Obs Astr Univ Belgr ... Publications. Observatoire Astronomique. Universite de Belgrade [*A publication*]
Publ Obs Univ Mich ... Publications. Observatory. University of Michigan [*A publication*]
Publ Ocas Mus Cienc Nat (Caracas) Zool ... Publicaciones Ocasionales. Museo de Ciencias Naturales (Caracas). Zoologia [*A publication*]
Publ OECD (Paris) ... Publication. OECD [*Organization for Economic Cooperation and Development*] (Paris) [*A publication*]
Publ Okla State Univ Agr Inform Serv ... Publication. Oklahoma State University. Agricultural Information Service [*A publication*]
Publ Ont Dep Agric ... Publication. Ontario Department of Agriculture and Food [*A publication*]
Publ Opin Q ... Public Opinion Quarterly [*A publication*]
Publ Pacif Nth-West Co-Op Ext Serv ... Publication. Pacific Northwest Cooperative Extension Service [*A publication*]
Publ Palaeontol Inst Univ Upps Spec Vol ... Publications. Palaeontological Institution. University of Uppsala. Special Volume [*A publication*]
Publ Pers M ... Public Personnel Management [*A publication*]
Publ Personnel Manag ... Public Personnel Management [*A publication*]
Publ Phil Soc ... Publications. Philological Society [*A publication*]
Publ Pol ..... Public Policy [*A publication*]
Publ Policy ... Public Policy [*A publication*]
Publ Purdue Univ Sch Civ Eng ... Publication. Purdue University. School of Civil Engineering [*A publication*]
PUBLR ...... Publisher
Publ Ramanujan Inst ... Publications. Ramanujan Institute [*A publication*]
Publ R Coll Physicians Edinburgh ... Publication. Royal College of Physicians of Edinburgh [*A publication*]
Publ Relat Congo Belg Reg Voisines ... Publications Relatives au Congo Belge et aux Regions Voisines [*A publication*]
Publ Rel J .. Public Relations Journal [*A publication*]
Publ Res Inst Math Sci ... Publications. Kyoto University. Research Institute for Mathematical Sciences [*A publication*]
Publ Res Inst Math Sci Ser A ... Publications. Research Institute for Mathematical Sciences. Series A [*Japan*] [*A publication*]
Publ Res Inst Math Sci Ser B ... Publications. Research Institute for Mathematical Sciences. Series B [*Japan*] [*A publication*]
Publ Roads ... Public Roads [*A publication*]
Publ R Obs (Edinburgh) ... Publications. Royal Observatory (Edinburgh) [*A publication*]
Publ Rom Fr ... Publications Romanes et Francaises [*A publication*]
Publ S Afr Inst Med Res ... Publications. South African Institute for Medical Research [*A publication*]
Publs ANARE Data Rep Ser ... Publications. ANARE [*Australian National Antarctic Research Expeditions*] Data Reports Series [*A publication*] (APTA)
Publs ANARE Interim Rep Ser ... Publications. ANARE [*Australian National Antarctic Research Expeditions*] Interim Reports Series [*A publication*] (APTA)
Publs ANARE Sci Rep Ser ... Publications. ANARE [*Australian National Antarctic Research Expeditions*] Scientific Reports Series [*A publication*] (APTA)
Publs Aust Soc Soil Sci ... Publications. Australian Society of Soil Science [*A publication*] (APTA)
Publs Aust Soc Soil Science ... Publications. Australian Society of Soil Science [*A publication*] (APTA)
Publ Scient Univ Alger Ser B ... Publications Scientifiques. Universite d'Alger. Serie B. Sciences Physiques [*A publication*]
Publ Sci For Bois ... Publications Scientifiques Forestieres et du Bois [*A publication*]
Publ Sci Tech Min Air ... Publications Scientifiques et Techniques. Ministere de l'Air [*France*] [*A publication*]

Publ Sci Tech Min Air Bull Serv Tech ... Publications Scientifiques et Techniques. Ministere de l'Air. Bulletins des Services Techniques [*France*] [*A publication*]
Publ Sci Tech Min Air Notes Tech ... Publications Scientifiques et Techniques. Ministere de l'Air [*France*]. Notes Techniques [*A publication*]
Publ Sci Tech Minist Air (Fr) ... Publications Scientifiques et Techniques. Ministere de l'Air (France) [*A publication*]
Publ Sci Tech Minist Air (Fr) Bull Serv Tech ... Publications Scientifiques et Techniques. Ministere de l'Air (France). Bulletin des Services Techniques [*A publication*]
Publs Co-Op Ext Univ Mass Coll Agric ... Publications. Co-Operative Extension Service. University of Massachusetts. College of Agriculture [*A publication*]
Publs Dep Agric (Alberta) ... Publications. Department of Agriculture (Alberta) [*A publication*]
Publs Dep Agric (Can) ... Publications. Department of Agriculture (Canada) [*A publication*]
Publ Sem Geom Univ Neuchatel Ser 2 ... Publications. Seminaire de Geometrie. Universite de Neuchatel. Serie 2 [*A publication*]
Publ Sem Geom Univ Neuchatel Ser 3 ... Publications. Seminaire de Geometrie. Universite de Neuchatel. Serie 3 [*A publication*]
Publ Sem Mat Garcia De Galdeano ... Publicaciones. Seminario Matematico Garcia De Galdeano [*A publication*]
Publ Serv Agric (Mozambique) ... Publicacoes. Servicos de Agricultura. Servicos de Veterinaria (Lourenco Marques, Mozambique) [*A publication*]
Publ Serv Flor Aqueic (Portugal) ... Publicacoes. Direccao Geral dos Servicos Florestais e Aqueicolas (Lisbon, Portugal) [*A publication*]
Publ Serv Geol Alger Bull ... Publications. Service Geologique de l'Algerie. Bulletin [*A publication*]
Publ Serv Geol Luxemb ... Publications. Service Geologique de Luxembourg [*A publication*]
Publ Serv Met Madag ... Publications. Service Meteorologique de Madagascar [*A publication*]
Publ Serv Piscic Ser I-C ... Publicacao. Servico de Piscicultura. Serie I-C [*A publication*]
Publ Serv Plagas For (Madrid) ... Publicacion. Servicio de Plagas Forestales (Madrid) [*A publication*]
Publ Serv Rev ... Public Service Review [*A publication*]
Publ Seto Mar Biol Lab ... Publications. Seto Marine Biological Laboratory [*A publication*]
Publ Seto Mar Biol Lab Spec Publ Ser ... Publications. Seto Marine Biological Laboratory. Special Publication Series [*A publication*]
Publs Geol Surv QD ... Publications. Geological Survey of Queensland [*A publication*] (APTA)
Publs Geol Surv QD Palaeont Pap ... Publications. Geological Survey of Queensland. Palaeontological Papers [*A publication*] (APTA)
PUBLSHG ... Publishing (DCTA)
Publ S Ill Univ Sch Agr ... Publication. Southern Illinois University. School of Agriculture [*A publication*]
Publs Indiana Dep Conserv ... Publications. Indiana Department of Conservation [*A publication*]
Publs Inst Natn Etude Agron Congo Ser Sci ... Publications. Institut National pour l'Etude Agronomique du Congo. Serie Scientifique [*A publication*]
Publs Manitoba Dep Agric ... Publications. Manitoba Department of Agriculture [*A publication*]
Publs Maria Moors Cabot Fdn Bot Res ... Publications. Maria Moors Cabot Foundation for Botanical Research [*A publication*]
Publs Met Dep Melb Univ ... Publications. Meteorology Department. University of Melbourne [*A publication*] (APTA)
Publ Smithson Inst ... Publication. Smithsonian Institution [*A publication*]
Publs Mktg Bd ... Publications. Empire Marketing Board [*A publication*]
Publs Mus Natn Hist Nat ... Publications. Museum National d'Histoire Naturelle [*A publication*]
Publ Soc Geol Nord ... Publication. Societe Geologique du Nord [*A publication*]
Publ Soc Savante Alsace Reg Est ... Publications. Societe Savante d'Alsace et des Regions de l'Est [*A publication*]
Publ Soil Bur (NZ) ... Publication. Soil Bureau. Department of Scientific and Industrial Research (New Zealand) [*A publication*]
Publs Osaka Mus Nat Hist ... Publications. Osaka Museum of Natural History [*A publication*]
Publ SP Am Concr Inst ... Publication SP. American Concrete Institute [*A publication*]
Publs Petrol Search Subsidy Acts ... Publications. Petroleum Search Subsidy Acts. Bureau of Mineral Resources, Geology, and Geophysics [*Australia*] [*A publication*] (APTA)
Publ Sta Fed Essais Agr (Lausanne) ... Publications. Stations Federales d'Essais Agricoles (Lausanne) [*A publication*]
Publ State Inst Agric Chem (Finl) ... Publications. State Institute of Agricultural Chemistry (Finland) [*A publication*]
Publ State Inst Tech Res ... Publications. State Institute for Technical Research [*A publication*]
Publ Stn Fed Essais Agric (Lausanne) ... Publication. Stations Federales d'Essais Agricoles (Lausanne) [*A publication*]
Publ SUG ... Publikace. Statni Ustav Geofysikalni [*A publication*]

Publ Systematics Ass ... Publication. Systematics Association [*A publication*]

Publ Tartu Astrofiz Obs ... Publikatsii Tartuskoi Astrofizicheskoi Observatorii [*Estonian SSR*] [*A publication*]

Publ Tec Estac Exp Agropecuar INTA (Pergamino) ... Publicaciones Tecnicas. Estacion Experimental Agropecuaria. INTA [*Instituto Nacional de Tecnologia Agropecuaria*] (Pergamino) [*A publication*]

Publ Tec Estac Exp Agropecuar Manfredi (Argentina) ... Publicaciones Tecnicas. Estacion Experimental Agropecuaria de Manfredi (Argentina) [*A publication*]

Publ Tech Charbon Fr Inf Tech ... Publications Techniques des Charbonnages de France. Informations Techniques [*A publication*]

Publ Tech Inst Belge Amelior Betterave Tirlemont ... Publications Techniques. Institut Belge pour l'Amelioration de la Betterave Tirlemont [*A publication*]

Publ Technion Israel Inst Technol Agric Eng Fac ... Publication-Technion. Israel Institute of Technology. Agricultural Engineering Faculty [*A publication*]

Publ Tech Pap Proc Annu Meet Sugar Ind Technol Inc ... Publication of Technical Papers and Proceedings. Annual Meeting of Sugar Industry Technologists, Incorporated [*A publication*]

Publ Tech Res Cen Finl Mater Process Technol ... Publication. Technical Research Centre of Finland. Materials and Processing Technology [*A publication*]

Publ Tech Univ Heavy Ind (Miskoic) Ser B Metall ... Publications. Technical University for Heavy Industry (Miskoic). Series B. Metallurgy [*Hungary*] [*A publication*]

Publ Tec Inst Patol Veg (B Aires) ... Publicacion Tecnica. Instituto de Patologia Vegetal (Buenos Aires) [*A publication*]

Publ Tec Patronato Invest Cient Tec "Juan De La Cierva" ... Publicaciones Tecnicas. Patronato de Investigacion Cientifica y Tecnica "Juan De La Cierva" [*A publication*]

Publ Tehn Fak u Sarajevu ... Publikacije Tehnickog Fakulteta u Sarajevu [*A publication*]

Publ Thoresby Soc ... Publications. Thoresby Society [*A publication*]

Publ Trimest Univ Pontif Bolivar ... Publicacion Trimestral. Universidad Pontificia Bolivariana [*A publication*]

Publ UER Math Pures Appl IRMA ... Publications. Unites d'Enseignement et de Recherche de Mathematiques Pures et Appliquees. Institut de Recherche de Mathematiques Avancees [*A publication*]

Publ Univ Auton St Domingo ... Publicaciones. Universidad Autonoma de Santo Domingo [*A publication*]

Publ Univ Calif Agric Ext Serv ... Publication. University of California. Agricultural Extension Service [*A publication*]

Publ Univ Costa Rica Ser Cienc Nat ... Publicaciones. Universidad de Costa Rica. Serie Ciencias Naturales [*A publication*]

Publ Univ Europ ... Publications Universitaires Europeennes [*Frankfurt Am Main*] [*A publication*]

Publ Univ Joensuu Ser B ... Publications. University of Joensuu. Series B [*Finland*] [*A publication*]

Publ Univ Joensuu Ser B-I ... Publications. University of Joensuu. Series B-I [*A publication*]

Publ Univ Joensuu Ser B-II ... Publications. University of Joensuu. Series B-II [*A publication*]

Publ Univ Kuopio Community Health Ser Orig Rep ... Publications. University of Kuopio. Community Health Series. Original Reports [*A publication*]

Publ Univ Laval ... Publications. Universite Laval [*A publication*]

Publ Univ Nac Litoral Inst Fisiogr Geol ... Publicaciones. Universidad Nacional del Litoral. Instituto de Fisiografia y Geologia [*A publication*]

Publ Univ Nac Tucuman Fac Agron Zootec ... Publicacion. Universidad Nacional de Tucuman. Facultad de Agronomia y Zootecnia [*A publication*]

Publ Univ Off Congo Elisabethville ... Publications. Universite Officielle du Congo a Elisabethville [*A publication*]

Publ Univ Off Congo Lubumbashi ... Publications. Universite Officielle du Congo a Lubumbashi [*A publication*]

Publ Univ Pretoria ... Publikasies. Universiteit van Pretoria [*A publication*]

Publ Univ Sevilla Ser Cienc ... Publicaciones. Universidad de Sevilla. Serie Ciencias [*A publication*]

Publ Univ Sevilla Ser Med ... Publicaciones. Universidad de Sevilla. Serie Medicina [*A publication*]

Publ Univ Toronto Dep Civ Eng ... Publication. University of Toronto. Department of Civil Engineering [*A publication*]

Publ Univ Toulouse-Le Mirail Ser A ... Publications. Universite de Toulouse-Le Mirail. Serie A. [*A publication*]

Publ Univ Wis Ext ... Publication. University of Wisconsin Extension [*A publication*]

Publ US Agric Res Serv ... Publication. United States Agricultural Research Service [*A publication*]

Publ US Int Trade Commn ... Publication. United States International Trade Commission [*A publication*]

Publ US Natl Tech Inf Serv ... United States. National Technical Information Service. Publication [*A publication*]

Publ Utah Geol Assoc ... Publication. Utah Geological Association [*A publication*]

Publ Virginia Div Miner Resour ... Publication. Virginia Division of Mineral Resources [*A publication*]

Publ Vulkaninst Immanuel Friedlaender ... Publikationen Herausgegeben von der Stiftung Vulkaninstitut Immanuel Friedlaender [*A publication*]

Publ W ... Publishers' Weekly [*A publication*]

Publ Wagner Free Inst Sci Philadelphia ... Publications. Wagner Free Institute of Science of Philadelphia [*A publication*]

Publ Water Environ Res Inst ... Publications. Water and Environment Research Institute [*A publication*]

Publ Water Res Inst ... Publications. Water Research Institute [*A publication*]

Publ Welfar ... Public Welfare [*A publication*]

Publ Wiss Filmen Sekt Tech Wiss Naturwiss ... Publikationen zu Wissenschaftlichen Filmen. Sektion Technische Wissenschaften. Naturwissenschaften [*A publication*]

Publ W J Barrow Res Lab ... Publication. W. J. Barrow Research Laboratory [*A publication*]

Publ Wkly ... Publishers' Weekly [*A publication*]

Publ Wks ... Public Works [*A publication*] (APTA)

Publ Wks Local Govt Engng ... Public Works and Local Government Engineering [*A publication*] (APTA)

Publ Zoo .... Publications in Zoology [*A publication*]

Pub Manag ... Public Management [*A publication*]

Pub Mgt ..... Public Management [*A publication*]

PUBN .... Publication (MSA)

PUBNET .... American Association of Publishers' electronic ordering system

PUBO .... Pubco Corp. [*NASDAQ symbol*] (NQ)

Pub Opin .... Public Opinion [*A publication*]

Pub Opinion Q ... Public Opinion Quarterly [*A publication*]

Pub Opn Q ... Public Opinion Quarterly [*A publication*]

Pub Op Q ... Public Opinion Quarterly [*A publication*]

Pub Papers ... Public Papers of the President [*A publication*] (DLA)

Pub Pers Mgt ... Public Personnel Management [*A publication*]

Pub Pol .... Public Policy [*A publication*]

Pub Rel ...... Public Relations

Pub Rel Bull ... Public Relations Bulletin [*American Bar Association*] [*A publication*] (DLA)

Pub Rel J ... Public Relations Journal [*A publication*]

Pub Rel Q .. Public Relations Quarterly [*A publication*]

Pub Rel Rv ... Public Relations Review [*A publication*]

Pub Res C .. Public Resources Code [*California*] [*A publication*] (ILCA)

Pub Res No ... Public Resolution Number [*Congress*] (ILCA)

Pub Roads ... Public Roads [*A publication*]

Pub Roch Hist Soc ... Publication Fund Series. Rochester Historical Society [*A publication*]

PUBS .... Percutaneous Umbilical Blood Sampling [*Medicine*]

PUBS .... Pop-Up Bottom Seismograph [*Marine science*] (MSC)

PUBS .... Publication Series

PUBSAT ... Publications Special Assistance Team [*Military*]

Pubs Ceramicas ... Publicaciones Ceramicas [*A publication*]

Pub Sector ... Public Sector [*New Zealand*] [*A publication*]

Pub Ser Comm ... Public Service Commission [*Usually, of a specific state*] (DLA)

Pub Service J Vic ... Public Service Journal of Victoria [*A publication*] (APTA)

Pub Serv Management ... Public Service Management [*A publication*]

Pub Soc Bras Nematol ... Publicacao. Sociedade Brasileira de Nematologia [*A publication*]

Pubs Petrol Search Subsidy Acts ... Publications. Petroleum Search Subsidy Acts. Bureau of Mineral Resources, Geology, and Geophysics [*Australia*] [*A publication*] (APTA)

Pub St .... Public Statutes [*A publication*] (DLA)

Pub U Rep ... Public Utilities Reports [*A publication*] (DLA)

Pub Util ..... Public Utilities Fortnightly [*A publication*]

Pub Util C ... Public Utilities Code [*A publication*] (DLA)

Pub Util Fort ... Public Utilities Fortnightly [*A publication*]

Pub Util Fortnightly ... Public Utilities Fortnightly [*A publication*]

Pub Util L Anthol ... Public Utilities Law Anthology [*A publication*] (DLA)

Pub Util Rep ... Public Utilities Reports [*A publication*] (DLA)

Pub W .... Publishers' Weekly [*A publication*]

Pub Wel ...... Public Welfare [*A publication*]

PU-BZ .... University of Pennsylvania, Biology Library, Philadelphia, PA [*Library symbol*] [*Library of Congress*] (LCLS)

PUC .... Pacific Unicorn [*Vancouver Stock Exchange symbol*]

PUC .... Pacific Union College [*Angwin, CA*]

PUC .... Papers under Consideration

PUC .... Parti de l'Unite Congolaise [*Congolese Unity Party*] [*Political party*]

PUC .... Pediatric Urine Collector [*Medicine*]

PUC .... Permanent Unit Code (NG)

PUC .... Pick-Up Car

PUC .... Planification d'Urgence Canada [*Emergency Planning Canada - EPC*]

PUC .... Player Unit Component (MCD)

PUC .... Pontificia Universidade Catolica [*Rio de Janeiro*]

PUC .... Popular Unity of Chile [*Political party*]

PUC .... Port Utilization Committee

PUC .... Post Urbem Conditam [*After the Building of the City of Rome*] [*Latin*]

PUC .... Presidential Unit Citation [*Military decoration*]

PUC .... Price [*Utah*] [*Airport symbol*] (OAG)

PUC .... Price, UT [*Location identifier*] [*FAA*] (FAAL)

PUC .... Processing Unit Cabinet [*Data processing*]

PUC .... Production Urgency Committee [*WPB*]
PUC .... Program Unit Code [*Military*]   (AFIT)
PUC .... Provided You Concur [*Army*]
PUC .... Pubblicazioni. Universita Cattolica del Sacro Cuore [*A publication*]
PUC .... Public Utilities Commission
PU-C .... University of Pennsylvania, Chemistry Library, Philadelphia, PA [*Library symbol*] [*Library of Congress*]   (LCLS)
PUCA .... Public Utilities Communicators Association [*Later, UCI*] [*New Castle, PA*]   (EA)
PUCalLL ... Publications. University of California. Languages and Literature [*A publication*]
PUCC .... Port Utilities [*AAR code*]
PUCK .... Propellant Utilization Checkout Kit   (KSC)
PUCK .... Pucklechurch [*England*]
PUCM .... Progressive Union of Cabinet Makers [*British*]
PUCODM ... Conseil Scientifique International de Recherches sur les Trypanosomiases et leur Controle [*A publication*]
PUCP/DA ... Debates en Antropologia. Pontificia Universidad Catolica del Peru. Departamento de Ciencias Sociales [*A publication*]
PUCS .... Propellant Utilization Control System   (KSC)
PUCU .... Propellant Utilization Control Unit
PUCVA6 .... Pubblicazioni. Centro di Studi per la Citogenetica Vegetale. Consiglio Nazionale delle Ricerche [*A publication*]
PUD .... Partido Union Democratica [*Political party in Guatemala*]
PUD .... Peptic Ulcer Disease
PU & D ..... Pick Up and Delivery [*Business term*]
PUD .... Pick Up and Delivery [*Business term*]
PUD .... Planned Unit Development [*Housing*]
PUD .... Planned Urban Development
PUD .... Preretro Update Display
PUD .... Prisoner under Detention   (ADA)
PUD .... Public Utility District [*Bonds*]
PUD .... Puerto Deseado [*Argentina*] [*Airport symbol*]   (OAG)
PUD .... Pulmonary Disease [*Medicine*]
PU-D .... University of Pennsylvania, Evans Dental Library, Philadelphia, PA [*Library symbol*] [*Library of Congress*]   (LCLS)
PUDCPAHM ... Poona University and Deccan College Publications in Archaeology and History of Maharashtra [*A publication*]
PUDD .... Programmable Universal Direct Drive
PUDN .... Perpetuation of Unit Documentation Number   (MCD)
PUDOC ..... Centrum voor Landbouwpublikaties en Landbouwdocumentatie [*Center for Agricultural Publishing and Documentation*] [*Ministry of Agriculture and Fisheries*] [*Information service or system*]   (IID)
PUDOC Annu Rep ... PUDOC [*Centre for Agricultural Publishing and Documentation*] Annual Report [*A publication*]
PUDOC (Cent Landbouwpubl Landbouwdoc) Literatuuroverz ... PUDOC (Centrum voor Landbouwpublikaties en Landbouwdocumentatie) Literatuuroverzicht [*A publication*]
PUDT .... Propellant Utilization Data Translator   (AAG)
PUDVM .... Pulsed Ultrasound Doppler Velocity Meter
PUE .... Phosphorus Utilization Efficiency [*Ecology*]
PUE .... Pre-Stock Unit Equipment [*Military*] [*British*]
PUE .... Presidential Unit Emblem [*Military decoration*]   (AABC)
PUE .... Propellant Utilization Exerciser
PUE .... Puebla [*Mexico*] [*Seismograph station code, US Geological Survey*] [*Closed*]   (SEIS)
PUE .... Puerto Obaldia [*Panama*] [*Airport symbol*]   (OAG)
PUE .... Pyrexia of Unknown Etiology [*Medicine*]
PUEE .... Publications. Universite de l'Etat a Elisabethville [*A publication*]
PU-El .... University of Pennsylvania, Moore School of Electrical Engineering, Philadelphia, PA [*Library symbol*] [*Library of Congress*]   (LCLS)
Puer Rico ... Puerto Rico Libre [*A publication*]
Puerto Rico ... Puerto Rico Reports [*A publication*]   (DLA)
Puerto Rico Bus R ... Puerto Rico Business Review [*A publication*]
Puerto Rico Dept Indus Research Bull ... Puerto Rico. Department of Industrial Research. Bulletin [*A publication*]
Puerto Rico F ... Puerto Rico Federal Reports [*A publication*]   (DLA)
Puerto Rico Fed ... Puerto Rico Federal Reports [*A publication*]   (DLA)
Puerto Rico J Publ Hlth ... Puerto Rico Journal of Public Health and Tropical Medicine [*A publication*]
Puerto Rico Rep ... Puerto Rico Supreme Court Reports [*A publication*]   (DLA)
Puerto Rico Univ Agr Expt Sta Tech Paper ... Puerto Rico University. Agricultural Experiment Station. Technical Paper [*A publication*]
Puerto Rico Water Resources Authority Water Resources Bull ... Puerto Rico. Water Resources Authority. Water Resources Bulletin [*A publication*]
PUF .... Partido Union Federal [*Federal Union Party*] [*Argentina*] [*Political party*]
PUF .... Pau [*France*] [*Airport symbol*]   (OAG)
PUF .... People's United Front [*Papua New Guinea*] [*Political party*]   (PPW)
PUF .... People's United Front [*Bangladesh*] [*Political party*]
PUF .... Percent Unaccounted For

PUF .... Pluimveehouderij [*A publication*]
PUF .... Polyurethane Film [*Plastics technology*]
PUF .... Porous Polyurethane Foam [*Also, PPF*] [*Plastics technology*]
PUF .... Presses Universitaires de France [*Publisher*]
PUF .... Prime Underwriting Facility [*Banking*]
PUF .... Public Utilities Fortnightly [*A publication*]
Puf............. Puffendorf's Law of Nature and Nations [*A publication*]   (DLA)
PU-F .... University of Pennsylvania, H. H. Furness Memorial Library, Philadelphia, PA [*Library symbol*] [*Library of Congress*]   (LCLS)
PUFA .... Polyunsaturated Fatty Acid [*Nutrition*]
PU-FA ...... University of Pennsylvania, School of Fine Arts, Philadelphia, PA [*Library symbol*] [*Library of Congress*]   (LCLS)
PUFF .... People United to Fight Frustrations   (EA)
PUFF .... Picofarad   (MDG)
PUFF .... Proposed Uses of Federal Funds [*Health Planning and Resource Development Act of 1974*]
PUFFS ...... Passive Underwater Fire Control Feasibility Study
PUFFS ...... Passive Underwater Fire Control Feasibility System
PUFFT ...... Purdue University Fast FORTRAN [*Formula Translation*] Translator [*Data processing*]
PUFI .... Packed under Federal Inspection
PUFL .... Pump Fed Liquid   (KSC)
PUFO .... Pack Up and Fade Out [*End of military exercise*] [*British*]   (DSUE)
PU Fort ..... Public Utilities Fortnightly [*A publication*]
PUFS .... Programmer's Utility Filing System   (DIT)
PUG .... Partially Underground [*Military*]
PUG .... PASCAL Users' Group   (EA)
PUG .... Penta Users Group   (EA)
PUG .... Port Augusta [*Australia*] [*Airport symbol*]   (OAG)
PUG .... Porzellan und Glas [*A publication*]
PUG .... PRIME Users Group   (EA)
PUG .... Print under Glaze [*Ceramics*]
PUG .... Propellant Utilization and Gauging [*Apollo*] [*NASA*]
PUG .... Przeglad Ustawodawstwa Gospodarczego [*A publication*]
PUG .... Publications. Universite de Grenoble [*A publication*]
PUG .... Pugilist
PUG .... Pugillus [*A Pinch*] [*Pharmacy*]   (ROG)
Pug............. Pugsley's New Brunswick Reports [*14-16 New Brunswick*] [*A publication*]   (DLA)
PUG .... Pulsed Universal Grid
PUG .... Pure Gold Resources, Inc. [*Toronto Stock Exchange symbol*]
Puget Snd ... Puget Sound Business Journal [*A publication*]
Puglia Chir ... Puglia Chirurgica [*A publication*]
PUGS .... Propellant Utilization and Gauging System [*Apollo*] [*NASA*]   (KSC)
Pugs .... Pugsley's New Brunswick Reports [*14-16 New Brunswick*] [*A publication*]   (DLA)
Pugs & Bur ... Pugsley and Burbridge's New Brunswick Reports [*17-20 New Brunswick*] [*A publication*]   (DLA)
Pugs & Burg ... Pugsley and Burbridge's New Brunswick Reports [*17-20 New Brunswick*] [*A publication*]   (DLA)
Pugs & T .... Pugsley and Trueman's New Brunswick Reports [*A publication*]   (DLA)
Pugs & Tru ... Pugsley and Trueman's New Brunswick Reports [*1882-83*] [*A publication*]   (DLA)
PUH.......... Pauahi [*Hawaii*] [*Seismograph station code, US Geological Survey*]   (SEIS)
PUH.......... Pregnancy Urine Hormone [*Endocrinology*]
PUH.......... Purchasing [*A publication*]
PUHCA ..... Public Utility Holding Company Act of 1935
PUHS .... Proceedings. Unitarian Historical Society [*A publication*]
PUI .... Pilot-under-Instruction [*Navy*]
PUI .... Platelet Uptake Index [*Clinical chemistry*]
PUIAA7...... Atas. Instituto de Micologia da Universidade Federal de Pernambuco [*A publication*]
PU-Ind ...... University of Pennsylvania, Industrial Research Department, Philadelphia, PA [*Library symbol*] [*Library of Congress*] [*Obsolete*]   (LCLS)
PUIWP...... People for a United India and World Peace   (EA)
PUJ.......... Punta Cana [*Dominican Republic*] [*Airport symbol*]   (OAG)
PUK .... Parti d'Unite Katangaise [*Katanga Unity Party*] [*Political party*]
PUK .... Patriotic Union of Kurdistan [*Iraq*] [*Political party*]   (PD)
PUK .... Pechiney-Ugine-Kuhlmann [*Commercial firm*] [*France*]
PUK .... Prourokinase [*An enzyme*] [*Thrombolytic*]
PUK .... Pukarua [*French Polynesia*] [*Airport symbol*]   (OAG)
PUKO........ Pan-American Union of Karatedo Organizations   (EA)
PUKOD...... Puresutoresuto Konkurito [*A publication*]
PUKS........ Pivotal Unknowables
PUL .... Percutaneous Ultrasonic Lithotripsy [*Medicine*]
PUL .... Press Union of Liberia
PUL .... Princeton University, Princeton, NJ [*OCLC symbol*] [*Inactive*]   (OCLC)
PUL .... Program Update Library
PUL .... Propellant Utilization and Loading
PUL .... Public Ledger [*A publication*]
PUL .... Publicker Industries, Inc. [*NYSE symbol*]   (SPSG)
PUL .... Pulkovo [*USSR*] [*Seismograph station code, US Geological Survey*]   (SEIS)

PUL .... Pulley (AAG)
PUL .... Pulmonary
PUL .... Pulse Resources [*Vancouver Stock Exchange symbol*]
PU-L .... University of Pennsylvania, Biddle Law Library, Philadelphia, PA [*Library symbol*] [*Library of Congress*] (LCLS)
PULA .... Public Laws
PULC .... Princeton University. Library. Chronicle [*A publication*]
PULL .... Power for Underwater Logistics and Living
PULL .... Pullman-Peabody Co. [*Princeton, NJ*] [*NASDAQ symbol*] (NQ)
Pull Acc ..... Pulling on Mercantile Accounts [*1846*] [*A publication*] (DLA)
Pull Accts ... Pulling's Law of Mercantile Accounts [*A publication*] (DLA)
Pull Att ...... Pulling on Attorneys and Solicitors [*3rd ed.*] [*1862*] [*A publication*] (DLA)
Pull Groupe Etud Rythmes Biol ... Bulletin. Groupe d'Etude des Rythmes Biologiques [*A publication*]
Pull Laws & Cust Lond ... Pulling's Treatise on the Laws, Customs, and Regulations of the City and Port of London [*A publication*] (DLA)
Pull Port of London ... Pulling's Treatise on the Laws, Customs, and Regulations of the City and Port of London [*A publication*] (DLA)
PULM .... Pulmonary
PULO .... Pattani United Liberation Organization [*Thailand*] [*Political party*] (PD)
PULP .... Kingston Systems, Inc. [*NASDAQ symbol*] (NQ)
Pulp & Pa ... Pulp and Paper [*A publication*]
Pulp & Pa Can ... Pulp and Paper Magazine of Canada [*Later, Pulp and Paper (Canada)*] [*A publication*]
Pulp Pap ... Pulp and Paper [*A publication*]
Pulp Pap & Board ... Pulp, Paper, and Board [*A publication*]
Pulp and Pap (Can) ... Pulp and Paper (Canada) [*A publication*]
Pulp Pap (Can) ... Pulp and Paper (Canada) [*A publication*]
Pulp & Pap Eng ... Pulp and Paper Engineering [*A publication*]
Pulp Paper Mag Can ... Pulp and Paper Magazine of Canada [*Later, Pulp and Paper (Canada)*] [*A publication*]
Pulp Paper Manual Can ... Pulp and Paper Manual of Canada [*A publication*]
Pulp Pap Ind ... Pulp and Paper Industry [*A publication*]
Pulp Pap Int ... Pulp and Paper International [*A publication*]
Pulpudeva .. Pulpudeva. Semaines Philippopolitaines de l'Histoire et de la Culture Thrace [*A publication*]
Pulpwood Annu ... Pulpwood Annual [*United States*] [*A publication*]
Pulpwood Prodn ... Pulpwood Production and Sawmill Logging [*A publication*]
PULS .... Poseidon Undersea Launching System (NOAA)
PULS .... Propellant Utilization Loading System (AAG)
PULS .... Pulawski Savings & Loan Association [*South River, NJ*] [*NASDAQ symbol*] (NQ)
PULSAR ... Pulsating Star
PULSAR ... Pulsed Uniform LASER-Stimulated Artificial Radiation [*Proposed acronymic designation for pulsars, in the event they are found to be artificially caused by intelligent life from outer space*]
PULSE ...... Public Urban Locator Service
Pulse .... Pulse. Montana State Nurses Association [*A publication*]
PULSES .... Physical Condition, Upper Extremity Function, Lower Extremity Function, Sensory and Communication Abilities, Excretory Control, Social Support [*A neurological disability profile*]
Pulsifer (ME) ... Pulsifer's Reports [*35-68 Maine*] [*A publication*] (DLA)
PULSTAR ... Pulse Training Assembled Reactor [*Nuclear energy*] (NRCH)
Pult .... Pulton. De Pace Regis [*A publication*] (DLA)
PULV .... Pulverized
PULV .... Pulvis [*Powder*] [*Pharmacy*]
PULV CONSPER ... Pulvis Conspersus [*Dusting Powder*] [*Pharmacy*]
PUM .... Pennsylvania University Museum
PUM .... Pomalaa [*Indonesia*] [*Airport symbol*] (OAG)
PUM .... President of the United Mineworkers
PUM .... Processor Utility Monitor [*Telecommunications*] (TEL)
PUM .... PW. Maandblad voor Personeelswerk en Arbeidsverhoudingen [*A publication*]
PUM .... Pytannja Ukrajins'koho Movoznavstva [*A publication*]
PUMA ...... Powered Ultralight Manufacturers Association (EA)
PUMA ...... Programmable Universal Manipulator for Assembly [*General Motors Corp. assembly robot*]
PUMA ...... Prostitutes' Union of Massachusetts
PU-Math ... University of Pennsylvania, Mathematics-Physics Library, Philadelphia, PA [*Library symbol*] [*Library of Congress*] (LCLS)
PUMCODOXPURSACOMLOPAR ... Pulse-Modulated Coherent Doppler-Effect X-Band Pulse-Repetition Synthetic-Array Pulse Compression Side Lobe Planar Array
PU-Med ..... University of Pennsylvania, Medical School, Philadelphia, PA [*Library symbol*] [*Library of Congress*] (LCLS)
PU-Med-TS ... University of Pennsylvania, Medical School, Hospital Nurses Library, Philadelphia, PA [*Library symbol*] [*Library of Congress*] (LCLS)
PUMF .... Peaceful Uses of Military Forces
PUMGC .... Pious Union of Our Mother of Good Counsel [*See also SMBC*] [*Genazzano, Italy*] (EAIO)

PUMP .... Protesting Unfair Marketing Practices [*Student legal action organization*]
Pump Eng (Tokyo) ... Pump Engineering (Tokyo) [*A publication*]
Pumpen & Verdichter Inf ... Pumpen und Verdichter Information [*A publication*]
Pumps .... Pumps-Pompes-Pumpen [*England*] [*A publication*]
Pumps Their Appl ... Pumps and Their Applications [*England*] [*A publication*]
PUMRL ..... Purdue University. Monographs in Romance Languages [*A publication*]
PUMS .... Permanently Unfit for Military Service [*British*]
PUMST ...... Polish Underground Movement (1939-1945) Study Trust (EA)
PUMTA ...... Trace Substances in Environmental Health [*A publication*]
PU-Mu .... University of Pennsylvania, University Museum, Philadelphia, PA [*Library symbol*] [*Library of Congress*] (LCLS)
PU-Music .. University of Pennsylvania, School of Music, Philadelphia, PA [*Library symbol*] [*Library of Congress*] (LCLS)
Pun .... All India Reporter, Punjab [*A publication*] (DLA)
Pun .... Indian Law Reports, Punjab Series [*A publication*] (DLA)
PUN .... Parti de l'Unite Nationale [*Party of National Unity*] [*Haiti*] [*Political party*] (PPW)
PUN .... Partido Union Nacional [*National Union Party*] [*Costa Rica*] [*Political party*]
PUN .... Plutonyl Nitrate [*Inorganic chemistry*]
PUN .... Precision Underwater Navigation
PUN .... Prepare a New Perforated Tape for Message [*Communications*] (FAAC)
PUN .... Punch
PUN .... Puncheon [*Unit of measurement*]
Pun .... Punica [*of Silius Italicus*] [*Classical studies*] (OCD)
PUN .... Punishment (DSUE)
PUN .... Puno [*Peru*] [*Seismograph station code, US Geological Survey*] (SEIS)
PUN .... Punta [*Flamenco dance term*]
PUNA .... Parti de l'Unite Nationale [*National Unity Party*] [*Congo*]
PUNC .... Practical, Unpretentious, Nomographic Computer
PUNC .... Probable Ultimate Net Cost [*Accounting*]
PUNC .... Program Unit Counter
PUNC .... Punctuation
PUNCT ..... Punctuation (ROG)
PUNGA ..... Parti de l'Unite Nationale Gabonaise [*Party for Gabonese National Unity*] [*Political party*]
Punjab Fruit J ... Punjab Fruit Journal [*A publication*]
Punjab Hortic J ... Punjab Horticultural Journal [*A publication*]
Punjab Med J ... Punjab Medical Journal [*A publication*]
Punjabrao Krishi Vidyapeeth Coll Agric (Nagpur) Mag ... Punjabrao Krishi Vidyapeeth. College of Agriculture (Nagpur). Magazine [*A publication*]
Punjabrao Krishi Vidyapeeth Res J ... Punjabrao Krishi Vidyapeeth. Research Journal [*A publication*]
Punjab Univ J Math (Lahore) ... Punjab University. Journal of Mathematics (Lahore) [*A publication*]
Punj Med J ... Punjab Medical Journal [*A publication*]
Punj Rec ..... Punjab Record [*India*] [*A publication*] (DLA)
PUNS .... Partido de Liberacion Nacional del Sahara [*Western Sahara*] [*Political party*]
PUNS .... Partido de Union Nacional del Sahara [*Western Sahara*] [*Political party*]
PUNS .... Permanently Unfit for Naval Service [*British*]
PUNT .... Partido Unico Nacional de los Trabajadores [*Political party*] [*Equatorial Guinea*]
PUO .... Placed under Observation [*Medicine*]
PUO .... Princeton University Observatory [*New Jersey*]
PUO .... Prudhoe Bay [*Arkansas*] [*Airport symbol*] (OAG)
PUO .... Prudhoe Bay, AK [*Location identifier*] [*FAA*] (FAAL)
Puo .... [*A*] Purine Nucleoside [*Also, R*]
PUO .... Pyrexia [*fever*] of Unknown Origin [*Commonly called Trench Fever*]
P U Otago M ... Proceedings. University of Otago Medical School [*A publication*]
PUP .... Paid-Up Policy [*Insurance*] (DSUE)
PUP .... Partido Union Patriotica [*Patriotic Union Party*] [*Dominican Republic*] [*Political party*] (PPW)
PUP .... Peak Underpressure [*Nuclear energy*] (NRCH)
PUP .... People's United Party [*Belize*] [*Political party*] (PPW)
PUP .... Peripheral Unit Processor [*Data processing*]
PUP .... Pick Up (FAAC)
PUP .... Pious Union of Prayer (EA)
PUP .... Plutonium Utilization Program [*Nuclear Regulatory Commission*] (NRCH)
PUP .... Popular Unity Party [*Bangladesh*] [*Political party*] (PPW)
PUP .... Power Upgrade Program
Pup .... Pre-Urban Professional [*Lifestyle classification*] [*Acronym coined by TeenAge magazine to describe its typical reader*]
PUP .... Progressive Unionist Party [*Northern Ireland*] [*Political party*] (PPW)
PUP .... Public Utilities Panel [*EECE*]
PUP .... Pull Up Point
PUP .... Pupakea [*Hawaii*] [*Seismograph station code, US Geological Survey*] [*Closed*] (SEIS)
PUP .... Pupil (DSUE)

Pup............ Puppis [Constellation]
PUPA......... Polish Union Printers Association [Chicago]
PU-Penn .... University of Pennsylvania, Penniman Library of Education,
　　　　　　Philadelphia, PA [Library symbol] [Library of Congress]
　　　　　　[Obsolete]   (LCLS)
PUPG .... Production Unit Price Goals   (MCD)
PUPID....... Pulp and Paper Industry Division [Instrument Society of
　　　　　　America]
PUPO .... Pull Up Push Over   (NASA)
Pupp........... Puppis [Constellation]
PUPPI .... Pop-Up Pore Pressure Instrument [Oceanography]
Puppie........ Pregnant Urban Professional [Lifestyle classification]
　　　　　　[Terminology used in "The Yuppie Handbook"]
PUPPP ...... Pruritic Urticarial Papules and Plaques of Pregnancy
　　　　　　[Medicine]
PU-PSW.... University of Pennsylvania, Pennsylvania School of Social
　　　　　　Work, Philadelphia, PA [Library symbol] [Library of
　　　　　　Congress]   (LCLS)
PUQ........... Public Relations Quarterly [A publication]
PUQ........... Punta Arenas [Chile] [Airport symbol]   (OAG)
PUR .... Partido de Unificacion Revolucionaria [Party of Revolutionary
　　　　　　Unification] [Guatemala] [Political party]
PUR .... Partido Union Revolucionaria [Cuba]
PUR .... Patch Unit Radio [Bell System]
PUR .... Polyurethane [Also, PU] [Organic chemistry]
PUR .... Program of University Research
PUR .... Program Utility Routines [Data processing]
PUR .... Public Utilities Reports [A publication] [Information service or
　　　　　　system]   (IID)
PUR .... Purari [Papua New Guinea] [Seismograph station code, US
　　　　　　Geological Survey]   (SEIS)
PUR .... Purchase   (AFM)
PUR .... Purchasing [A publication]
PUR .... Purchasing Receipt [Business term]
PUR .... Purdue University Reactor
PUR .... Purdue University Research   (MCD)
PUR .... Purgative [Medicine]   (ROG)
PUR .... Purichlor Technology Ltd. [Vancouver Stock Exchange symbol]
PUR .... Purifier   (AAG)
Pur .... [A] Purine [Biochemistry]
PUR .... Purity [of the Drug] [Pharmacy]   (ROG)
PUR .... Puromycin [Trypanocide] [Antineoplastic drug]
pur............. Purple [Philately]
PUR .... Purpure [Purple] [Heraldry]
PUR .... Purse   (FAAC)
PUR .... Pursuant   (AABC)
PUR .... Pursuit   (AABC)
PURA .... PACOM [Pacific Command] Utilization and Redistribution
　　　　　　Agency
PURA .... Public Utilities Review Act [1934]
PURAC...... Personal Use Radio Advisory Committee [FCC]
　　　　　　[Defunct]   (TSSD)
Pur A Chem ... Pure and Applied Chemistry [A publication]
Pur A Geoph ... Pure and Applied Geophysics [A publication]
PURB........ Purbeck [District in England]
PURBA...... Panjab University. Research Bulletin (Arts) [A publication]
PURC .... Pacific Utilization Research Center [Marine science]   (MSC)
PURC .... Princeton University Research Center [Marine science]   (MSC)
PURC .... Public Utility Research Center [University of Florida]
　　　　　　[Research center]   (RCD)
PURC .... Purchasing
PURCH ..... Purchase
Purch Adm ... Purchasing Administration [A publication]
Purchasing ... Purchasing World [A publication]
PURCHG .. Purchasing   (ROG)
Purch (S Afr) ... Purchasing (South Africa) [A publication]
PUR 3d ...... Public Utilities Reports, Third Series [A publication]   (DLA)
Purd Dig..... Purdon's Digest of Laws [Pennsylvania] [A publication]   (DLA)
Purd Dig Laws ... Purdon's Digest of Laws [Pennsylvania] [A
　　　　　　publication]   (DLA)
Purdue Ag .. Purdue Agriculturist [A publication]
Purdue Air Qual Conf Proc ... Purdue Air Quality Conference. Proceedings [A
　　　　　　publication]
Purdue Univ Agric Exp Stn Res Bull ... Purdue University. Agricultural
　　　　　　Experiment Station. Research Bulletin [A publication]
Purdue Univ Agric Exp Stn Stn Bull ... Purdue University. Agricultural
　　　　　　Experiment Station. Station Bulletin [A publication]
Purdue Univ Dept Agr Ext Mimeo AY ... Purdue University. Department of
　　　　　　Agricultural Extension. Mimeo AY [A publication]
Purdue Univ Eng Bull Eng Ext Ser ... Purdue University. Engineering
　　　　　　Bulletin. Engineering Extension Series [A publication]
Purdue Univ Eng Exp Sta Res Bull ... Purdue University. Engineering
　　　　　　Experiment Station. Research Bulletin [A publication]
Purdue Univ Ext Publ ... Purdue University. Extension Publications [A
　　　　　　publication]
Purdue Univ Sch Aeronaut Astronaut Eng Sci Res Proj ... Purdue University.
　　　　　　School of Aeronautics, Astronautics, and Engineering
　　　　　　Sciences. Research Project [A publication]
Purdue Univ Water Resources Research Center Tech Rept ... Purdue
　　　　　　University. Water Resources Research Center. Technical
　　　　　　Report [A publication]

Purdue Univ Water Resour Res Cent Tech Rep ... Purdue University. Water
　　　　　　Resources Research Center. Technical Report [A
　　　　　　publication]
PURE........ People United for Rural Education   (EA)
PURE........ Present University Research Efforts [Database] [Harperson
　　　　　　Data Services]
Pure Appl Chem ... Pure and Applied Chemistry [A publication]
Pure and Appl Chem ... Pure and Applied Chemistry [A publication]
Pure Appl Cryog ... Pure and Applied Cryogenics [A publication]
Pure and Appl Geophys ... Pure and Applied Geophysics [A publication]
Pure Appl Geophys ... Pure and Applied Geophysics [A publication]
Pure Appl Math ... Pure and Applied Mathematics [A publication]
Pure and Appl Math ... Pure and Applied Mathematics [A publication]
Pure Appl Phys ... Pure and Applied Physics [A publication]
Pure Prod ... Pure Products [A publication]
PUREQ ..... Purchase Requisition   (NOAA)
PUREX...... Plutonium Uranium Extraction [Nuclear energy]
PURGE...... Pearson Universal Random Generator
PURIF ...... Purification
PURM .... Project for Utilization and Redistribution of Materiel [Air
　　　　　　Force]
PURMA .... Purasuchikku Materiaru [A publication]
PUR (NS).. Public Utilities Reports, New Series [A publication]   (DLA)
PURO........ Puroflow, Inc. [NASDAQ symbol]   (NQ)
PURP........ Purpose   (AFM)
Purp .... [Johannes Franciscus] Purpuratus [Flourished, 16th century]
　　　　　　[Authority cited in pre-1607 legal work]   (DSA)
PURP........ Purpure [Purple] [Heraldry]   (ROG)
PURPA...... Public Utilities Regulatory Policy Act [1978]
Purple's St ... Purple's Statutes, Scates' Compilation [A publication]   (DLA)
Purpur....... [Johannes Franciscus] Purpuratus [Flourished, 16th century]
　　　　　　[Authority cited in pre-1607 legal work]   (DSA)
Purpura...... [Johannes Franciscus] Purpuratus [Flourished, 16th century]
　　　　　　[Authority cited in pre-1607 legal work]   (DSA)
PURS......... Partido de la Union Republicana Socialista [Socialist
　　　　　　Republican Union Party] [Bolivia]
PURS........ Program Usage Replenishment System
PURS........ Pursuit
PURSCE ... Pursuance   (ROG)
PURST....... Pursuant
PURT........ Pure Tech International, Inc. [NASDAQ symbol]   (NQ)
PURV .... Powered Underwater Research Vehicle [Navy]
Purv Coll .... Purvis' Collection of the Laws of Virginia [A
　　　　　　publication]   (DLA)
PUS........... Parliamentary Under Secretary [British]
PUS........... Permanent Under Secretary [British]   (RDA)
PUS........... Permanently Unfit for Service [Military]   (ADA)
PUS........... Personnel Utilization Sheet
PUS........... Pharmacopeia of the United States
PUS........... President of the United States
PUS........... Processor Utility Subsystem [Telecommunications]   (TEL)
PUS........... Propellant Utilization System
PUS........... Przeglad Ubezpieczen Spolecznych [A publication]
PUS........... Pusan [South Korea] [Seismograph station code, US Geological
　　　　　　Survey] [Closed]   (SEIS)
PUS........... Pusan [South Korea] [Airport symbol]   (OAG)
pus............. Pushto [MARC language code] [Library of Congress]   (LCCP)
PU-S .... University of Pennsylvania, Edgar Fah Smith Memorial
　　　　　　Library, Philadelphia, PA [Library symbol] [Library of
　　　　　　Congress]   (LCLS)
PUSA........ Perspectives USA [A publication]
PUSAS ..... Proposed United States of America Standard
PUSC........ Pubblicazioni. Universita Cattolica del Sacro Cuore [A
　　　　　　publication]
PU-Sc........ University of Pennsylvania, Towne Scientific School,
　　　　　　Philadelphia, PA [Library symbol] [Library of
　　　　　　Congress]   (LCLS)
PUSE........ Propellant Utilization System Exerciser
PUSEC ...... Polish-US Economic Council   (EA)
PUSH .... People United to Save Humanity [In organization name
　　　　　　"Operation PUSH"]
PUSJD ...... Pious Union of St. Joseph for the Dying   (EA)
PUSJDS.... Pious Union of St. Joseph for Dying Sinners [Later,
　　　　　　PUSJD]   (EA)
PUSMM.... Parti d'Union Socialiste des Musulmans Mauritaniens [Party
　　　　　　for Socialist Unity of Moslems of Mauritania] [Political
　　　　　　party]
PUSO .... Principal Unit Security Officer   (AAG)
PU-SRS ..... University of Pennsylvania, South Asia Regional Studies
　　　　　　Library, Philadelphia, PA [Library symbol] [Library of
　　　　　　Congress]   (LCLS)
PUSS .... Pallet Utility Support Structure [NASA]   (MCD)
PUSS .... Pilots Universal Sighting System
PUT .... Persons Using Television [Television ratings]
PUT .... Program Update Tape
PUT .... Programmable Unijunction Transistor
PUT .... Property Unit Trust [Finance] [British]
PUT .... Punta De Talca [Chile] [Seismograph station code, US
　　　　　　Geological Survey]   (SEIS)
Put............. [Jacobus] Puteus [Deceased, 1453] [Authority cited in pre-1607
　　　　　　legal work]   (DSA)

PUT .... Putnam, CT [*Location identifier*] [*FAA*] (FAAL)
PUT .... Putrescine [*Organic chemistry*]
Puter Ch..... Puterbaugh's Illinois Chancery Pleading [*A publication*] (DLA)
Puter Pl...... Puterbaugh's Illinois Common Law Pleading [*A publication*] (DLA)
Puti Povysh Intensivn Prod Fotosint ... Puti Povysheniya Intensivnosti i Produktivnosti Fotosinteza [*A publication*]
Puti Povysh Intensivn Prod Fotosint Resp Mezhved Sb ... Puti Povysheniya Intensivnosti i Produktivnosti Fotosinteza Respublikanskii Mezhvedomstvennyi Sbornik [*A publication*]
Puti Sint Izyskaniya Protivoopukholevykh Prep ... Puti Sinteza i Izyskaniya Protivoopukholevykh Preparatov [*A publication*]
Putnam...... Putnam's Monthly Magazine [*A publication*]
Putnam...... Putnam's Proceedings before the Justice of the Peace [*A publication*] (DLA)
PUTT........ Portable Underwater Tracking Transducer
PUTT........ Propellant Utilization Time Trace
PUU.......... Piute Reservoir [*Utah*] [*Seismograph station code, US Geological Survey*] (SEIS)
PUU.......... Puerto Asis [*Colombia*] [*Airport symbol*] (OAG)
PU-UH ...... University of Pennsylvania, University Hospital, Philadelphia, PA [*Library symbol*] [*Library of Congress*] (LCLS)
PU-UH-DeS ... University of Pennsylvania, University Hospital, De Schweinitz Collection of Ophthalmology, Philadelphia, PA [*Library symbol*] [*Library of Congress*] (LCLS)
PUUSNA .. Polish Union of the United States of North America (EA)
PUV .... Propellant Utilization Valve [*NASA*] (NASA)
PUV .... Pulaski [*Virginia*] [*Seismograph station code, US Geological Survey*] [*Closed*] (SEIS)
PUV .... Pulp and Paper [*A publication*]
PU-V .... University of Pennsylvania, School of Veterinary Medicine, Philadelphia, PA [*Library symbol*] [*Library of Congress*] (LCLS)
PUVA .... Photochemotherapy with Ultraviolet A [*Oncology*]
PUVA .... Psoralens and Ultraviolet A [*Therapy*] [*Medicine*]
PUVLV..... Propellant Utilization Valve [*NASA*] (AAG)
PuW......... Poesie und Wissenschaft [*A publication*]
PUW........ Pullman [*Washington*] [*Airport symbol*] (OAG)
PUW........ Pullman, WA [*Location identifier*] [*FAA*] (FAAL)
PU-W........ University of Pennsylvania, Wharton School of Finance and Commerce, Philadelphia, PA [*Library symbol*] [*Library of Congress*] (LCLS)
PUWP .... Polish United Workers' Party [*See also PZPR*] [*Political party*] (PD)
PUY .... Pula [*Yugoslavia*] [*Airport symbol*] (OAG)
PUZBAR ... Bulletin. Department of Zoology. University of the Panjab. New Series [*A publication*]
PV .... Eastern Provincial Airways [*Labrador*] [*ICAO designator*] (OAG)
PV .... Pacific Viewpoint [*A publication*]
PV .... Papillomavirus
PV .... Par Value [*Finance*]
PV .... Paravane [*Anti-moored-mine device*] [*Obsolete*]
PV .... Parole Violator
PV .... Paromomycin-Vancomycin [*Blood agar*] [*Microbiology*]
PV .... Path Verification
pv............... Pathovar [*Microbiology*]
PV .... Patrol Vessel
PV .... Paving [*Technical drawings*]
P/V............. Peak-to-Valley
PV .... Pemphigus Vulgaris [*Dermatology*]
PV .... [*The*] People's Voice [*Pre-World War II publication of Adam Clayton Powell, Jr., and Charlie Buchanan*]
PV .... Per Vaginam [*Medicine*]
PV .... Periodieke Verzameling van Administratieve en Rechterlijke Beslissingen Betreffende het Openbaar Bestuur in Nederland [*A publication*]
PV .... Peripheral Vascular [*Medicine*]
PV .... Peripheral Vein [*Anatomy*]
PV .... Peroxide Value [*Food analysis*]
PV .... Petite Vitesse [*Goods train*] [*French*]
PV .... Photographic Vision [*Filter*]
PV .... Photovoltaic
PV .... Physical Vulnerability [*Number*] (NATG)
PV .... Pigment Volume
PV .... Pilot Vessel
PV .... Pioneer Venus [*Spacecraft*]
PV .... Pipe Ventilated
PV .... Plan View (MSA)
PV .... Planetary Vehicle [*NASA*]
PV .... Planuebergang [*Grade Crossing*] [*German military - World War II*]
PV .... Plasma Volume [*Medicine*]
PV .... Plastic Viscosity
PV .... Playback Verifier (MCD)
PV .... Poesia e Verita [*A publication*]
PV .... Pole Vault
PV .... Poliovirus
PV .... Polycythemia Vera [*Also, PCV*] [*Hematology*]
PV .... Polydor/Deutsche-Grammophon Variable Microgroove [*Record label*] [*Germany*]

PV .... Polyoma Virus
PV .... Pore Volume [*Geology*]
PV .... Pornovision [*Television*]
PV .... Portal Vein [*Anatomy*]
PV .... Position Vacant (ADA)
PV .... Position Value
PV .... Positive Volume (IEEE)
PV .... Post Village
PV .... Post-Virgil
PV .... Postvaccination
PV .... Potential Vorticity [*Meteorology*] [*Fluid mechanics*]
PV .... Present Value [*Finance*]
P/V............. Pressure/Vacuum
PV .... Pressure Vessel (MSA)
P-V .... Pressure-Volume
PV .... Pressurization Valve
PV .... Prevailing Visibility
PV .... Prevalve (NASA)
P/V............. Preview
PV .... Priest Vicar
PV .... Primary Valve
PV .... Prime Vertical
PV .... Princess Victoria's Royal Irish Fusiliers [*Military*] [*British*] (ROG)
PV .... Principe de Viana [*A publication*]
PV .... Private Varnish [*Privately owned railroad cars*]
PV .... Problemy Vostokovedenija [*A publication*]
PV .... Production Validation [*Military*] (AABC)
PV .... Professional Virgin (DSUE)
PV .... Professional Volunteer
P/V............. Profit/Volume Ratio
PV .... Project Volunteer (EA)
PV .... Prometheus Vinctus [*of Aeschylus*] [*Classical studies*] (OCD)
PV .... Proteus Vulgaris [*Bacterium*]
PV .... Public Volunteer
PV .... Public Voucher
PV .... Pull and Void (MCD)
PV .... Pulmonary Valvotomy [*Cardiology*]
PV .... Pulmonary Vascularity [*Medicine*]
PV .... Pulmonary Vein [*Medicine*]
PV .... Pulse Voltammetry [*Analytical chemistry*]
P & V......... Pyloroplasty and Vagotomy [*Medicine*]
PV .... Pyrocatechol Violet [*Also, PCV*] [*An indicator*] [*Chemistry*]
Pv.............. Ventral Pressure Neurons [*of a leech*]
PV .... Villanova University, Villanova, PA [*Library symbol*] [*Library of Congress*] (LCLS)
PV1 .... Private E-1 [*Army*]
PV2 .... Private E-2 [*Army*]
PV 4 .... Pickup Trucks, Vans, and Four-Wheel-Drive Vehicles [*Initialism used as title of a publication*]
PVA .... Paralyzed Veterans of America (EA)
PVA .... Personal Values Abstract [*Scale*]
PVA .... Platinova Resources Ltd. [*Toronto Stock Exchange symbol*]
PVA .... Poly(vinyl Alcohol) [*Also, PVAL*] [*Organic chemistry*]
PVA .... Positive Vorticity Advection [*Meteorology*] (FAAC)
PVA .... Preburner Valve Actuator [*NASA*] (NASA)
PVA .... Privacy Act (MCD)
PVA .... Propellant Valve Actuator (MCD)
PVA .... Providencia [*Colombia*] [*Airport symbol*] (OAG)
PVAC....... Peak Volts Alternating Current (KSC)
PVAC....... Poly(vinyl Acetate) [*Organic chemistry*]
PVAC....... Present Value of Annual Charges
PVAE....... Poly(vinyl Acetate) [*Organic chemistry*]
PVAGA..... Pochvoznanie i Agrokhimiya [*A publication*]
PVAHI ...... Augustinian Historical Institute, Villanova University, Villanova, PA [*Library symbol*] [*Library of Congress*] (LCLS)
PVAL....... Poly(vinyl Alcohol) [*Also, PVA*] [*Organic chemistry*]
PVAR....... Percentage Variance [*Statistics*]
PVAS........ Primary Voice Alert System [*NORAD*] (MCD)
PVat II ...... Il Papiro Vaticano Greco II [*A publication*] (OCD)
PVB........... Platinol [*Cisplatin*], Vinblastine, Bleomycin [*Antineoplastic drug regimen*]
PVB........... Platteville, WI [*Location identifier*] [*FAA*] (FAAL)
PVB........... Poly(vinyl Butyral) [*Safety glass laminating material*] [*Organic chemistry*]
PVB........... Portametric Voltmeter Bridge
PVB........... Premature Ventricular Beat [*Cardiology*]
PV-B .... Villanova University, Business and Finance Library, Villanova, PA [*Library symbol*] [*Library of Congress*] (LCLS)
PVBA........ Persoonlijke Vennootschap met Beperkte Aansprakelijkheid [*Limited Company*] [*Netherlands*] (CED)
PVBPA ..... Proceedings of Vibration Problems [*Poland*] [*A publication*]
PVBRDX... Pesquisa Veterinaria Brasileira [*Brazilian Journal of Veterinary Research*] [*A publication*]
PVC .... Pacvest Capital, Inc. [*Toronto Stock Exchange symbol*]
PVC .... Partido de Veteranos Civiles [*Civilian Veterans' Party*] [*Dominican Republic*] [*Political party*] (PPW)
PVC .... Peripheral Vasoconstriction [*Medicine*]
PVC .... Periscope Viewer/Controller (MCD)
PVC .... Permanent Virtual Circuit

PVC	Pigment Volume Concentration
PVC	Point of Vertical Curve
PVC	Points de Vente. Le Magazine des Magasins [*A publication*]
PVC	Poly(vinyl Chloride) [*Organic chemistry*]
PVC	Port Vila [*New Hebrides*] [*Seismograph station code, US Geological Survey*] (SEIS)
PVC	Position and Velocity Computer
PVC	Potential Volume Change
PVC	Premature Ventricular Contraction [*Cardiology*]
PVC	Pressure Vacuum Chamber
PVC	Pressure Volume Compensator (KSC)
pvc	Price Variation Clause (DS)
PVC	Primary Visual Cortex [*Anatomy*]
PVC	Prosthetic Valve (Disk) Closing [*Cardiology*]
PVC	Provincetown [*Massachusetts*] [*Airport symbol*] (OAG)
PVC	Provincetown, MA [*Location identifier*] [*FAA*] (FAAL)
PVC	Pulmonary Venous Congestion [*Medicine*]
PVCBMA	PVC [*Polyvinylchloride*] Belting Manufacturers Association (EA)
PVCC	PVC Container Corp. [*Eatontown, NJ*] [*NASDAQ symbol*] (NQ)
PVCF	Present Value Cash Flow [*Finance*]
PVCI	Peripheral Vision Command Indicator
PVCN	Poly(vinyl Cinnamate) [*Organic chemistry*]
PVCS	Portable Voice Communications System
PVD	Pancreatic Ventral Duct [*Anatomy*]
PVD	Paravisual Director [*British*]
PVD	Peripheral Vascular Disease [*Medicine*]
PVD	Physical Vapor Deposition [*Coating technology*]
PVD	Physical Vulnerability Division [*Air Force*]
PVD	Plan [*or Planned*] View Display [*RADAR*] (AFM)
PVD	Planned Variations Demonstration [*HUD*]
PVD	Portable Vapor Detector
PVD	Posterior Vitreous Detachment [*Ophthalmology*]
PVD	Product Verification Demonstration (MCD)
PVD	Protective Vehicle Division [*US Secret Service*]
PVD	Providence [*Rhode Island*] [*Airport symbol*] (OAG)
PVD	Pulmonary Vascular Disease [*Medicine*]
PV & D	Purge, Vent, and Drain (NASA)
PVD	Purge, Vent, Drain System (MCD)
PvdA	Partij van de Arbeid [*Labor Party*] [*Netherlands*] [*Political party*] (PPE)
PvdA/PTA	Partij van de Arbeid van Belgiee/Parti du Travail de Belgique [*Belgian Labor Party*] [*Political party*] (PPW)
PVDC	Poly(vinylidene Chloride) [*Organic chemistry*]
PVDC	Princeville Corporation [*NASDAQ symbol*] (NQ)
PVDF	Poly(vinylidene Fluoride) [*Organic chemistry*]
PVDL	Precision Variable Delay Line
PVDS	Physical Vulnerability Data Sheets (MCD)
PvdV	Partij van de Vrijheid [*Party of Freedom*] [*Netherlands*] [*Political party*] (PPE)
PVE	Pine Valley Explorers [*Vancouver Stock Exchange symbol*]
PVE	Polyvinyl Ether [*Organic chemistry*]
PVE	Porvenir [*Panama*] [*Airport symbol*] (OAG)
PVE	Prolonged Vacuum Exposure
P & VE	Propulsion and Vehicle Engineering [*A Marshall Space Flight Center laboratory*] (MCD)
PVE	Prosthetic Valve Echogram [*Cardiology*]
PVE	Prosthetic Valve Endocarditis [*Medicine*]
PVE	Provisioning Engineer
PVE	Pulmonary Vascular Effect [*Physiology*]
PVED	Parity Violating Energy Difference [*Physical chemistry*]
PVEPP	Preliminary Value Engineering Program Plan (MCD)
PVF	Peak Visibility Factor
PVF	Peripheral Visual Field [*Optics*]
PVF	Placerville, CA [*Location identifier*] [*FAA*] (FAAL)
PVF	Political Victory Fund [*National Rifle Association*]
PVF	Poly(vinyl Fluoride) [*Organic chemistry*]
PVF	Portal Venous Flow [*Physiology*]
PVF$_2$	Poly(vinylidene Fluoride) [*Organic chemistry*]
PVFD	Pipe Ventilated, Forced Draught
PVfHi	Valley Forge Historical Society, Valley Forge, PA [*Library symbol*] [*Library of Congress*] (LCLS)
PVFHP	Public Voice for Food and Health Policy (EA)
PVfP	Philadelphia Quartz Co., Valley Forge, PA [*Library symbol*] [*Library of Congress*] (LCLS)
PVG	Periventricular Gray [*Neurobiology*]
PVG	Personalvertretungsgesetz [*A publication*]
PVG	Portsmouth, VA [*Location identifier*] [*FAA*] (FAAL)
PVG	Programmable Variations Generator [*Data processing*]
PVG	Project on the Vietnam Generation [*Later, II*] (EA)
PVGC	Pioneer Venus Gas Chromatograph [*NASA*]
PVH	Paraventricular Hypothalmic Nucleus [*Neuroanatomy*]
PVH	Periventricular Hemorrhage [*Medicine*]
PVH	Phillips-Van Heusen Corp. [*NYSE symbol*] (SPSG)
PVH	Pope Valley Holding [*Vancouver Stock Exchange symbol*]
PVH	Porto Velho [*Brazil*] [*Airport symbol*] (OAG)
PVH	Pulmonary Venous Hypertension [*Medicine*]
PVHO	Pressure Vessel for Human Occupancy [*Deep-sea diving*]
PVHS	Photorefractive Volume Holographic Storage
PVI	Pacific Vocational Institute Library [*UTLAS symbol*]

PVI	Peripheral Vascular Insufficiency [*Medicine*]
PVI	Perpendicular Vegetation Index [*Botany*]
PVI	Personal Values Inventory [*Psychology*]
PVI	Picture Vocational Interest Questionnaire for Adults [*Vocational guidance test*]
PVI	Pilot-Vehicle Interface [*Search technology*]
PVI	Point of Vertical Intersection
PVI	Poly(vinyl Isobutyl Ether) [*Organic chemistry*]
PVI	Portal Vein Inflow [*Physiology*]
PVI	Prevulcanization Inhibitor
PVI	Primary Vocational Interest [*Personnel study*]
PVI	Product Verification Inspection [*DoD*]
PVI	Programmable Video Interface
PVID	Pipe Ventilated, Induced Draught
PVIF	Present Value Interest Factor [*Finance*]
PVIFA	Present Value Interest Factor of an Annuity [*Real estate*]
PVIR	Penn Virginia Corp. [*NASDAQ symbol*] (NQ)
P & VIR	Pure and Vulcanized Rubber Insulation
PVIZT	Phenyl(vinyl)imidazolidinethione [*Organic chemistry*]
PvJ	Paleis van Justitie. Nieuwsblad Gewijd aan Binnen- en Buitenlandse Rechtspleging [*A publication*]
PVJ	Pauls Valley, OK [*Location identifier*] [*FAA*] (FAAL)
PVJC	Palo Verde Junior College [*California*]
PVK	Packaged Ventilation Kit [*Civil Defense*]
PVK	Polyvinylcarbazol [*Organic chemistry*] (IEEE)
PVK	Preveza/Lefkas [*Greece*] [*Airport symbol*] (OAG)
P-VL	Panton-Valentine Leukocidin
PVL	Pavlikeny [*Bulgaria*] [*Seismograph station code, US Geological Survey*] (SEIS)
PVL	Periventricular Leukomalacia [*Medicine*]
PVL	Povest' Vremennych Let [*A publication*]
PVL	Pressure to Vertical Locks
PVL	Prevail (FAAC)
PV-L	Villanova University, Law School, Villanova, PA [*Library symbol*] [*Library of Congress*] (LCLS)
PV-2(L)	Poliovirus Type 2, Lansing
PVLT	Prevalent (FAAC)
PVM	Pneumonia Virus of Mice
PVM	Poly(vinyl Methyl Ether) [*Organic chemistry*]
PVM	Posterior Ventral Microtubule [*Anatomy*]
PVM	Potato Virus M [*Plant pathology*]
PVM	Potentiometric Voltmeter
PVM	Pressure Vessel Material
PVM	Progressive Minerals [*Vancouver Stock Exchange symbol*]
PVM	Projection Video Monitor
PVM	Protein, Vitamins, Minerals [*J. B. Williams Co. brand of liquid protein*]
PVM	Proton Vector Magnetometer (NOAA)
PV-1(M)	Poliovirus Type 1, Maloney
PVMA	Pressure Vessel Manufacturers Association (EA)
PVMB	Potential Variation Mixed Basis [*Photovoltaic energy systems*]
PVME	Poly(vinyl Methyl Ether) [*Organic chemistry*]
PVMI	Parish Visitors of Mary Immaculate [*Roman Catholic women's religious order*]
PVMT	Pavement [*Technical drawings*]
PVMTD	Preservation Method
PVN	Paraventricular Nucleus [*Brain anatomy*]
PVN	Peters Valley [*New Jersey*] [*Seismograph station code, US Geological Survey*] [*Closed*] (SEIS)
PVN	Proven Resources Ltd. [*Vancouver Stock Exchange symbol*]
PVNA	Provena Foods, Inc. [*NASDAQ symbol*] (NQ)
PVNGS	Palo Verde Nuclear Generating Station (NRCH)
PVNO	Polyvinylpyridine-N-Oxide [*Organic chemistry*]
PVNPS	Post-Vietnam Psychiatric Syndrome
PVNS	Pigmented Villonodular Synovitis [*Also, PVS*] [*Medicine*]
PVNT	Prevent (AAG)
PVNTMED	Preventive Medicine [*Also, PM*]
PVO	Atlantic City, NJ [*Location identifier*] [*FAA*] (FAAL)
PVO	Phosphorus Vanadium Oxide [*Inorganic chemistry*]
PVO	Pioneer Venus Orbiter [*NASA*]
PVO	Portoviejo [*Ecuador*] [*Airport symbol*] (OAG)
PVO	Principal Veterinary Officer (ROG)
PVO	Private Voluntary Organization
PVO	Prosthetic Valve (Disk) Opening [*Cardiology*]
PVO	Protivo-Voxdushnaia Oborona [*Antiaircraft Defense*] [*USSR*]
PVOD	Peripheral Vascular Occlusive Disease [*Medicine*]
PVOR	Precision VHF Omnirange
PVP	Modern Paint and Coatings [*A publication*]
PV-P	Past Vice-President
PVP	Peripheral Venous Pressure [*Cardiology*]
PVP	Plasma Vaporization Process
PVP	Poly(vinylpyrrolidone) [*Organic chemistry*]
PVP	Portal Venous Pressure [*Physiology*]
PVP	Preferred Vision Provider
PVP	President's Veterans Program [*Employment*]
PVP	Professional Video Productions, Inc. [*Telecommunications service*] (TSSD)
PVP	Pueblo Viejo [*Peru*] [*Seismograph station code, US Geological Survey*] [*Closed*] (SEIS)
PVPA	Plant Variety Protection Act [*1970*]
PVP-I	Poly(vinylpyrrolidone) Iodine Complex

PVPMPC .. Perpetual Vice-President-Member Pickwick Club [*From "The Pickwick Papers" by Charles Dickens*]
PVPO......... Plant Variety Protection Office [*Department of Agriculture*]
P & V Prod ... Paint and Varnish Production [*A publication*]
PVPS......... Plasma Varactor Phase Shifter
PVQ.......... Deadhorse, AK [*Location identifier*] [*FAA*]   (FAAL)
PVQ.......... Personal Value Questionnaire [*Navy*]
PVR .... Palos Verdes [*California*] [*Seismograph station code, US Geological Survey*] [*Closed*]   (SEIS)
PVR .... Peripheral Vascular Resistance [*Cardiology*]
PVR .... Phase Volume Ratio [*Physical chemistry*]
PVR .... Platte Valley Review [*A publication*]
PVR .... Pontefract Volunteer Rifles [*British military*]   (DMA)
PVR .... Postvoiding Residual [*Medicine*]
PVR .... Precision Voltage Reference   (MDG)
PVR .... Premature Voluntary Release [*British military*]   (DMA)
PVR .... Procedure Validation Report   (AAG)
PVR .... Process Variable Record
PVR .... Profit/Volume Ratio
PVR .... Proliferative Vitreoretinopathy [*Ophthalmology*]
PVR .... Puerto Vallarta [*Mexico*] [*Airport symbol*]   (OAG)
PVR .... Pulmonary Vascular Resistance [*Physiology*]
PVR .... Pulse Volume Rate [*Physiology*]
PVR .... Pulse Volume Recording [*Medicine*]
PVRC .... Pressure Vessel Research Committee [*National Institute of Standards and Technology*]
PVRD .... Purge, Vent, Repressurize, and Drain   (NASA)
PVRO .... Plant Variety Rights Office [*Ministry of Agriculture, Fisheries, and Food*] [*British*]
PVS........... [*The*] Pecos Valley Southern Railway Co. [*AAR code*]
PVS........... Performance Verification System
PVS........... Peritoneovenous Shunt [*Medicine*]
PVS........... Persistent Vegetative State [*Medicine*]
PVS........... Personal Videoconferencing Station [*Widcom, Inc.*] [*Los Gatos, CA*] [*Telecommunications service*]   (TSSD)
PVS........... Photovoltaic System
PVS........... Pigmented Villonodular Synovitis [*Also, PVNS*] [*Medicine*]
PVS........... Plant Vent Stack [*Nuclear energy*]   (NRCH)
PVS........... Plexus Visibility Score [*Medicine*]
PVS........... Politische Vierteljahresschrift [*A publication*]
PVS........... Polyvinylsulfonate [*Organic chemistry*]
PVS........... Post-Vietnam Syndrome
PVS........... Postal Vehicle Service
PVS........... Potato Virus S [*Plant pathology*]
PVS........... Present Value Service [*LIMRA*]
PVS........... Pressure Vacuum System
PVS........... Principal Veterinary Surgeon [*British*]
PVS........... Priority Ventures [*Vancouver Stock Exchange symbol*]
PVS........... Private Viewdata System [*Data processing*]
PVS........... Proceedings. Virgil Society [*A publication*]
PVS........... Professional Video Services Corporation [*Telecommunications service*]   (TSSD)
PVS........... Program Validation Services [*Data processing*]
PVS........... Propellant Venting System
PVS........... Pulmonary Valve Stenosis [*Cardiology*]
PVSA .... Parkvale Financial Corp. [*NASDAQ symbol*]   (NQ)
PVSC .... Professional Video Services Corp. [*Telecommunications service*]   (TSSD)
PVSCA ...... Proceedings. Veterans Administration Spinal Cord Injury Conference [*A publication*]
PVSCD5 .... Perspectives in Vertebrate Science [*A publication*]
P-V Seances Com Int Poids Mes ... Proces-Verbaux des Seances. Comite International des Poids et Mesures [*A publication*]
P-V Seances Soc Sci Phys Nat Bord ... Proces-Verbaux des Seances. Societe des Sciences Physiques et Naturelles de Bordeaux [*A publication*]
P-V Seances Soc Sci Phys Nat Bordeaux ... Proces-Verbaux des Seances. Societe des Sciences Physiques et Naturelles de Bordeaux [*A publication*]
PVSG........ Paravertebral Sympathetic Ganglion [*Neuroanatomy*]
PVSG........ Periscope Visual Scene Generation
PV SIg ...... Polyvalent Surface Immunoglobulin [*Immunology*]
P V Soc Linn Bordeaux ... Proces-Verbaux. Societe Linneenne de Bordeaux [*A publication*]
PV/ST....... Premate Verification/System Test [*NASA*]   (KSC)
PVT........... Pacific Vending Technology Ltd. [*Vancouver Stock Exchange symbol*]
PVT........... Page View Terminal [*Typography*] [*Videotex terminal*]
PVT........... Par Voie Telegraphique [*By Telegraph*] [*French*]
PVT........... Paroxysmal Ventricular Tachycardia [*Medicine*]
PVT.......... Performance Verification Test
PV/T......... Photovoltaic/Thermal
PVT........... Physical Vapor Transport [*Materials processing*]
PVT........... Pivot   (MSA)
PVT........... Point of Vertical Tangent
PVT........... Polyvalent Tolerance [*Immunology*]
PVT........... Poly(vinyltoluene) [*Organic chemistry*]
PVT........... Portal Vein Thrombosis [*Physiology*]
PVT........... Position Velocity-Time
PVT........... Precision Verification Team
PVT........... Precision Verification Test   (MCD)

PVT........... Preflight Verification Test   (NASA)
PVT........... Pressure, Volume, Temperature
PVT........... Private [*Military*]   (AFM)
PVT........... Probe Velocity Transducer   (KSC)
PVT........... Product Verification Test   (MCD)
PVT........... Prototype Validation Test   (MCD)
PVT........... Provisioning Technician
PVT........... Pulse Video Thermography [*Nondestructive testing technique*]
PVT........... Pyrotechnic Verification Test [*NASA*]   (NASA)
PVTAP .... Photovoltaic Transient Analysis Computer Program
PVT-C....... Product Verification Test - Contractor   (MCD)
PVT-C....... Production Validation Test - Contractor   (MCD)
PVT-C....... Prototype Validation Test - Contractor   (MCD)
PVTE........ Private
PVT-G .... Production Validation Test - Government
PVT-G .... Prototype Validation Test - Government
PVTI .... Piping and Valve Test Insert [*Nuclear energy*]   (NRCH)
PVTM....... Physical Vulnerability Technical Memorandum   (MCD)
PVTMA..... Preventive Medicine [*A publication*]
PVTOS ..... Physical Vapor Transport of Organic Solutions [*Materials processing*]
PVTR........ Portable Video Tape Recorder
PVU .... Perimeter Ventures Ltd. [*Vancouver Stock Exchange symbol*]
PVU .... PR Revue. Schweizerische Zeitschrift fuer Public Relations [*A publication*]
PVU .... Provo [*Utah*] [*Airport symbol*]   (OAG)
PVU .... Provo, UT [*Location identifier*] [*FAA*]   (FAAL)
PVU .... Villanova University, Villanova, PA [*OCLC symbol*]   (OCLC)
PV Ue........ Pariser Verbandsuebereinkunft zum Schutze des Gewerblichen Eigentums [*A publication*]
PVV .... Fondation Europeenne "Pro Venetia Viva" [*European Foundation "Pro Venetia Viva"*]   (EAIO)
PVV .... Partij voor Vrijheid en Vooruitgang [*Freedom and Progress Party*] [*See also PLP*] [*Belgium*] [*Political party*]   (PPW)
PVV .... Portal Venous Velocity [*Physiology*]
PVV .... Pressure, Vent, and Vacuum
PVW .... Plainview, TX [*Location identifier*] [*FAA*]   (FAAL)
PVW .... Wilson College, Chambersburg, PA [*OCLC symbol*]   (OCLC)
PVWA .... Planned Value of Work Accomplished
PVWS .... Planned Value of Work Scheduled   (MCD)
PVX .... Potato Virus X [*Plant pathology*]
PVY .... Pope Vanoy [*Alaska*] [*Airport symbol*]   (OAG)
PVY .... Potato Virus Y
PVY .... Providence Energy Corp. [*AMEX symbol*]   (SPSG)
PVZ........... Painesville, OH [*Location identifier*] [*FAA*]   (FAAL)
PVZTA ...... Plyn [*A publication*]
PW .... Citizens Library, Washington, PA [*Library symbol*] [*Library of Congress*]   (LCLS)
PW .... Pacific Western Airlines Ltd. [*Canada*] [*ICAO designator*]   (OAG)
PW .... Packed Weight
PW .... Paedagogische Welt [*A publication*]
PW .... Palau [*ANSI two-letter standard code*]   (CNC)
PW .... Paper Wrapper [*ADA*]
PW .... Paraguay Watch   (EA)
PW .... Passing Window   (MSA)
PW .... Password [*Data processing*]
PW .... [*A.*] Pauly, [*G.*] Wissowa, and [*W.*] Kroll, Real-Encyclopaedie der Klassischen Altertumswissenschaft [*A publication*]   (OCD)
PW .... Peere-Williams' English Chancery Reports [*1695-1736*] [*A publication*]   (DLA)
P & W .... Penrose and Watts' Pennsylvania Reports [*1829-32*] [*A publication*]   (DLA)
PW .... Pension World [*A publication*]
PW .... Pension for Wounds [*Navy*] [*British*]   (ROG)
PW .... Per Week
PW .... Pericardium Wall [*Medicine*]
PW .... Petroleum Week [*A publication*]
PW .... Philadelphia & Western Railroad [*AAR code*] [*Terminated*]
PW .... Philologische Wochenschrift [*A publication*]
pW .... Picowatt
PW .... Pilot Wire   (MSA)
PW .... Pine Bark Mixed with Weblite and Peat
PW .... Pittsburgh & West Virginia Railroad [*AMEX symbol*]   (SPSG)
PW .... Pivoted Window   (AAG)
PW .... Plain Washer   (MSA)
PW .... Platoon Weapons [*British military*]   (DMA)
PW .... Poetry Wales [*A publication*]
PW .... Poets and Writers   (EA)
PW .... Ports and Waterways
PW .... Position Wanted [*Employment*]
P & W .... Post and Wire   (ADA)
PW .... Posterior Wall [*Medicine*]
PW .... Postwar
PW .... Poswissel [*Money Order*] [*Afrikaans*]
PW .... Potable Water [*Nuclear energy*]   (NRCH)
PW .... Power
PW .... Power Windows [*Automobile ads*]
P & W .... Pratt & Whitney [*Aircraft*]
PW .... Present Worth [*Economics*]

PW.............	Pressurized Water
PW.............	Prime Western [*Zinc*]
PW.............	Prince of Wales [*Military unit*] [*British*]
PW.............	Printed Wiring (MSA)
PW.............	Prisoner of War [*Also, POW*]
PW.............	Private Wire (NATG)
PW.............	Progesterone Withdrawal [*Endocrinology*]
PW.............	Projected Window (MSA)
PW.............	Projection Welding
PW.............	Protestant World [*A publication*] (APTA)
PW.............	Providence & Worcester Co. [*AAR code*]
PW.............	Psychological Warfare
PW.............	Public Welfare
PW.............	Public Works
PW.............	Publishers' Weekly [*A publication*]
PW.............	Pulpwash [*Byproduct of citrus processing*]
PW.............	Pulse Width [*RADAR*]
PW.............	Purlwise [*Knitting*]
PW.............	Royal Warrant for Pay and Promotion [*British military*] (DMA)
PWA.........	Oklahoma City, OK [*Location identifier*] [*FAA*] (FAAL)
PWA.........	Pacific Western Airlines Ltd. [*Toronto Stock Exchange symbol*] [*Vancouver Stock Exchange symbol*]
PWA.........	Palmer-Houston [*Alaska*] [*Seismograph station code, US Geological Survey*] (SEIS)
PWA.........	Papierwerke Waldhof-Aschaffenburg AG [*Waldhof-Aschaffenburg Paper Works*] [*Business term*] [*Federal Republic of Germany*]
PWA.........	People with AIDS Coalition (EA)
PWA.........	Performance Warehouse Association (EA)
PWA.........	Person with AIDS [*Acquired Immune Deficiency Syndrome*] [*Medicine*]
PWA.........	Pharmaceutical Wholesalers Association [*Later, DWA*]
PWA.........	Please Wait Awhile [*Humorous interpretation for Pacific Western Airlines Corp.*]
PWA.........	Portuguese West Africa [*Angola*]
P & WA.....	Pratt & Whitney Aircraft (KSC)
PWA.........	Pratt & Whitney Aircraft (MCD)
PWA.........	Pray while Aloft [*Humorous interpretation for Pacific Western Airlines Corp.*]
PWA.........	Printed Wire Assembly [*Data processing*]
PWA.........	Private Write Area [*NASA*] (NASA)
PWA.........	Probably Won't Arrive [*Humorous interpretation for Pacific Western Airlines Corp.*]
PWA.........	Product Work Authorization (NASA)
PWA.........	Project Work Authorization
PWA.........	Public Works Administration [*All functions transferred to office of Federal Works Agency, 1943*]
PWA.........	Publishers' Weekly Announcements [*Title changed to Forthcoming Books*] [*A publication*]
PWA.........	PWA Corp. [*Toronto Stock Exchange symbol*] [*Vancouver Stock Exchange symbol*]
PWa.........	Warren Library Association and County Division, Warren, PA [*Library symbol*] [*Library of Congress*] (LCLS)
PWA.........	Waynesburg College, Waynesburg, PA [*OCLC symbol*] (OCLC)
PWAA......	Paint and Wallpaper Association of America [*Later, NDPA*] (EA)
PWAA......	Polish Western Association of America (EA)
PWAA......	Polish Women's Alliance of America (EA)
PWAA......	Professional Women's Appraisal Association (EA)
PWAC......	Periodical Writers Association of Canada
PWAC......	Pratt & Whitney Aircraft (AAG)
PWAC......	Present Worth of Annual Charges [*Pronounced "p-wack"*] [*Bell System*]
PWacD......	David Library of the American Revolution, Washington Crossing, PA [*Library symbol*] [*Library of Congress*] (LCLS)
PWAF.......	Polish Workers' Aid Fund (EA)
PWAFRR ..	Present Worth of All Future Revenue Requirements [*Finance*]
PWAK	Wake Island Air Force Base [*Wake Island*] [*ICAO location identifier*] (ICLI)
PWal........	Helen Kate Furness Free Library, Wallingford, PA [*Library symbol*] [*Library of Congress*] (LCLS)
PWalPH	Pendle Hill Library, Wallingford, PA [*Library symbol*] [*Library of Congress*] (LCLS)
PWA Rep...	PWA. Report fuer Mitarbeiter und Freunde der Papierwerke "Waldhof-Aschaffenburg" [*A publication*]
PWayC	Waynesburg College, Waynesburg, PA [*Library symbol*] [*Library of Congress*] (LCLS)
PWB	Directorate of Post War Building [*British*] (DAS)
PWb..........	Osterhout Free Library, Wilkes-Barre, PA [*Library symbol*] [*Library of Congress*] (LCLS)
PWB	Pacific Western Bancshares [*AMEX symbol*] (SPSG)
PWB	Partial Weight Bearing [*Medicine*]
PWB	Pencil Writing on Back [*Deltiology*]
PWB	Permanent Water Ballast (DS)
PW & B	Philadelphia, Wilmington & Baltimore Railroad
PWB	Pilot Weather Briefing (FAAC)
PWB	Printed Wiring Board
PWB	Psychological Warfare Branch [*Allied Forces*] [*World War II*]
PWB	Pulling Whaleboat
PWBA.......	Pension and Welfare Benefits Administration [*Department of Labor*]
PWBA.......	Plane-Wave Born Approximation
PWBA.......	Printed Wiring Board Assembly (MCD)
PWBA.......	Professional Women Bowlers Association [*Later, LPBT*] (EA)
PWBC.......	Peripheral White Blood Cells [*Medicine*]
PWbH........	Wyoming Historical and Geological Society, Wilkes-Barre, PA [*Library symbol*] [*Library of Congress*] (LCLS)
PWBI........	Posterior Wall of Bronchus Intermedius [*Anatomy*]
PWbK	King's College, Wilkes-Barre, PA [*Library symbol*] [*Library of Congress*] (LCLS)
PWBP........	Pension and Welfare Benefit Programs [*Labor-Management Services Administration*]
PWBS........	Program Work Breakdown Structure (NASA)
PWbW.......	Wilkes College, Wilkes-Barre, PA [*Library symbol*] [*Library of Congress*] (LCLS)
PWC	Chester County District Library Center, Exton, PA [*OCLC symbol*] (OCLC)
PWC	Pacific War Council [*World War II*]
PWC	Peak Work Capacity
PWC	Pentecostal World Conference [*Emmetten, Switzerland*] (EA)
PWC	Personal Watercraft
PWC	Physical Work Capacity
PWC	Physicians Who Care (EA)
PWC	Poland Watch Center (EA)
PWC	Port Workers' Committee [*British*]
PWC	Pratt & Whitney Canada, Inc. [*Montreal, PQ, Canada*] [*FAA designator*] (FAAC)
PWC	Printed Wiring Cards [*Telecommunications*]
PWC	Prisoner of War Cage
PWC	Prisoner of War Camp
PWC	Prisoner of War Command
PWC	Prisoner of War Compound
PWC	Process Water Cooler (MSA)
PWC	Professional Women in Construction (EA)
PWC	Professional Women's Caucus (EA)
PWC	Provincial Warning Center [*NATO*] (NATG)
PWC	Public Works Canada [*See also TPC*]
PWC	Public Works Center [*Navy*]
PWC	Public Works Committee [*Australia*]
PWC	Pulse-Width Coded
PWcC........	Chester County District Library Center, West Chester, PA [*Library symbol*] [*Library of Congress*] (LCLS)
PWCC.......	Political Warfare Coordination Committee [*London*] [*World War II*]
PWCCA.....	Pembroke Welsh Corgi Club of America (EA)
PWCEN.....	Public Works Center [*Navy*]
PWcHi.......	Chester County Historical Society, West Chester, PA [*Library symbol*] [*Library of Congress*] (LCLS)
PW/CI/DET ...	Prisoner of War/Civilian Internees/Detainees (MCD)
PWCJS......	Proceedings. Fifth World Congress of Jewish Studies [*1969*] [*A publication*]
PWCLANT ...	Public Works Center, Atlantic [*Navy*]
PWCMS....	Public Works Center Management System [*Navy*]
PWCOU	Public Workers and Constructional Operatives' Union [*British*]
PWCPAC ..	Public Works Center, Pacific [*Navy*]
PWcS........	West Chester State College, West Chester, PA [*Library symbol*] [*Library of Congress*] (LCLS)
PWD.........	Pan World Ventures, Inc. [*Vancouver Stock Exchange symbol*]
PWD.........	Permanent Wants Directory [*A publication*]
PWD.........	Petroleum Warfare Department [*Ministry of Fuel and Power*] [*British*] [*World War II*]
PWD.........	Plentywood, MT [*Location identifier*] [*FAA*] (FAAL)
PWD.........	Plywood [*Technical drawings*]
PWD.........	Powder (KSC)
PWD.........	Power Distributor (KSC)
PWD.........	Procurement Work Directive [*Army*] (AABC)
PWD.........	Proximity Warning Device (MCD)
PWD.........	Psychological Warfare Division [*SHAEF*] [*World War II*]
PWD.........	Public Works Department [*Navy*]
PWD.........	Pulse-Width Detector [*or Discriminator*] [*RADAR*]
PWDC.......	Philippine War Damage Commission [*Post-World War II*]
PWDCA	Portuguese Water Dog Club of America (EA)
PWDEPT ..	Public Works Department [*Navy*]
PWDG.......	Prince of Wales' Dragoon Guards [*Military*] [*British*] (ROG)
PWDI........	Program with Developing Institutions (EA)
PWDMS....	Public Works Developmental Management System [*Navy*]
PWDP.......	Powder Passing
PWDR	Partial Wave Dispersing Relation
PWDRD ...	Powdered [*Freight*]
PWDS.......	Protected Wireline Distribution System (CET)
PWE	Pauli-Weisskopf Equation [*Physics*]
PWE	Pawnee City, NE [*Location identifier*] [*FAA*] (FAAL)
PWE	Political Warfare Executive [*World War II*]
PWE	Present Worth Expenditures [*Telecommunications*] (TEL)
PWE	Primary Weapons and Equipment
PWE	Prisoner of War Enclosure
PWE	Pulse-Width Encoder
PWEA.......	Printed Wiring and Electronic Assemblies [*NASA*]
PWEDA.....	Public Works and Economic Development Act
PWEDA.....	Public Works and Economic Development Association (EA)

P'well .... Planwell [*A publication*]
PWER......... Power Recovery Systems, Inc. [*Cambridge, MA*] [*NASDAQ symbol*]   (NQ)
PWesAC .... Community College of Allegheny County, South Campus, West Mifflin, PA [*Library symbol*] [*Library of Congress*]   (LCLS)
PWesD....... Dresser Industries, Inc., Harbison-Walker Refractories Co., West Mifflin, PA [*Library symbol*] [*Library of Congress*]   (LCLS)
P West Ph S ... Proceedings. Western Pharmacology Society [*A publication*]
PWF........... Pacific Whale Foundation   (EA)
PWF........... Package Will Follow [*Birthday-card notation*]
PWF........... Pax World Foundation   (EA)
PWF........... Photoelectric Work Function
PWF........... Pop Warner Football   (EA)
PWF........... Power Financial Corp. [*Toronto Stock Exchange symbol*]
PWF........... Present Worth Factor [*Real estate*]
PWF........... Propellant Weight Fraction   (NATG)
PWF........... Pulse Wave Form
PWFG......... Primary Waveform Generator [*Telecommunications*]   (TEL)
PWFN......... Projection Weld Flange Nut
PWFND..... Publikationen zu Wissenschaftlichen Filmen. Sektion Technische Wissenschaften. Naturwissenschaften [*A publication*]
PWFR........ Plantwide Failure Reporting   (MCD)
PWG........... Panzerwagen [*Tank*] [*German military - World War II*]
PWG........... Permanent Working Group   (NATG)
PWG........... Photoelectric Web Guide
PWG........... Plastic Wire Guide
PWG........... Powergem Resources Corp. [*Vancouver Stock Exchange symbol*]
PWH........... Pellet Warhead
PWH........... Poliokeawe [*Pali*] [*Hawaii*] [*Seismograph station code, US Geological Survey*]   (SEIS)
PWH........... Precision Welding-Head
PWH........... Proprietor of Copyright on a Work Made for Hire
PWH........... Prototype Wave Height
PWHA........ Plutonium Waste Handling Area [*Nuclear energy*]   (NRCH)
Pwhe .... Person Who Has Everything [*Lifestyle classification*]
PWhi........... Whitehall Township Public Library, Whitehall, PA [*Library symbol*] [*Library of Congress*]   (LCLS)
PWHQ....... Peace War Headquarters   (NATG)
PWHS .... Public Works Historical Society   (EA)
PWHT .... Post-Weld Heat Treatment [*Nuclear energy*]   (NRCH)
PWI .... Permanent Ware Institute [*Defunct*]   (EA)
PWI .... Permanent Way Institution [*Fleet, Hampshire, England*]   (EAIO)
PWI .... Physiological Workload Index [*Aviation*]
PWI .... Pilot Warning Indicator [*or Instrument*] [*Aviation*]
PWI .... Plasma Wave Instrument [*Physics*]
PWI .... Platoon Weapons Instructor [*British military*]   (DMA)
PWI .... Potable Water Intake
PWI .... Precedence Work Item
PWI .... Prince of Wales' Island   (ROG)
PWI .... Prisoner of War Interrogation
PWI .... Projects with Industry Program [*Department of Education*]
PWI .... Proximity Warning Indicator [*or Instrument*] [*Aviation*]
PWIA........ Personal Watercraft Industry Association   (EA)
PWIB........ Prisoner of War Information Bureau [*Post-World War II*]
PWIF........ Plantation Workers' International Federation [*Later, IFPAAW*]
PWIFC ..... Porter Wagoner International Fan Club   (EA)
PWIN .... Prototype WWMCCS Intercomputer Network   (MCD)
PWJ.......... PaineWebber Group, Inc. [*NYSE symbol*]   (SPSG)
PWJ.......... Pulsating Water-Jet Lavager [*Medicine*]   (RDA)
PWJC .... Paine, Webber, Jackson & Curtis [*Later, Paine Webber, Inc.*]
PWK .... Chicago/Wheeling, IL [*Location identifier*] [*FAA*]   (FAAL)
PWL.......... Piecewise-Linear
PWL.......... Piecework Linear
PWL.......... Port Wells [*Alaska*] [*Seismograph station code, US Geological Survey*]   (SEIS)
PWL.......... Poughkeepsie, NY [*Location identifier*] [*FAA*]   (FAAL)
PWL.......... Power Level
PWL.......... Printed Wiring Laboratory   (MCD)
PWLB....... Public Works Loan Board [*British*]
PWM......... Planar Wing Module   (MCD)
PWM......... Pokeweed Mitogen [*Genetics*]
PWM......... Portable Welding Machine
PWM......... Portland [*Maine*] [*Airport symbol*]   (OAG)
PWM......... Portland, ME [*Location identifier*] [*FAA*]   (FAAL)
PWM......... Printed Wiring Master
PWM......... Pulse-Width Modulation [*Electronic instrumentation*]
PWM......... Pulse-Width Multiplier   (IEEE)
PWMA....... Portable Wear Metal Analyzer [*Air Force*]
PWMD...... Printed Wiring Master Drawing   (NASA)
PWM-FM ... Pulse-Width Modulation - Frequency Modulation [*RADAR*]
PWMIB....... Powder Metallurgy International [*A publication*]
PWmL .... Lycoming College, Williamsport, PA [*Library symbol*] [*Library of Congress*]   (LCLS)
PWML....... Patchy White Matter Lesion [*Medicine*]

PWmP .... James V. Brown Library of Williamsport and Lycoming County, Williamsport, PA [*Library symbol*] [*Library of Congress*]   (LCLS)
P Wms .... Peere-Williams' English Chancery Reports [*1695-1736*] [*A publication*]   (DLA)
PWMS....... Public Works Management System [*Navy*]
PWMSCM ... Pokeweed Mitogen-Stimulated Spleen-Cell-Conditioned Medium [*For growing cells*]
P Wms (Eng) ... Peere-Williams' English Chancery Reports [*1695-1736*] [*A publication*]   (DLA)
PWN.......... Cash America Investments, Inc. [*NYSE symbol*]   (SPSG)
PWN.......... Panstwowe Wydawnictwo Naukowe [*A publication*]
PWN.......... Patna Weekly Notes [*India*] [*A publication*]   (ILCA)
PWN.......... Pinewood Nematode
PWN.......... Polskie Wydawnictwe Naukowe [*A publication*]
PWN.......... Pulsar Wind Nebula [*Astronomy*]
PWN.......... West Plains, MO [*Location identifier*] [*FAA*]   (FAAL)
PW-NWLZOA ... Pioneer Women/Na'amat, the Women's Labor Zionist Organization of America [*Later, MWWV*]   (EA)
PWO.......... Parliamentarians for World Order   (EA)
PWO.......... Prince of Wales' Own [*Military unit*] [*British*]
PWO.......... Principal Welfare Officer [*Navy*] [*British*]
PWO.......... Principle Warfare Officer [*British*]
PWO.......... Production Work Order   (MCD)
PWO.......... Public Works Officer [*Navy*]
PWOC ...... Protestant Women of the Chapel
PWOP ...... Pregnant without Permission [*Military*] [*World War II*]
PWOQD... Psychology of Women Quarterly [*A publication*]
PWOR...... Prince of Wales' Own Royal [*Military unit*] [*British*]
PWP.......... Barrio Florida [*Puerto Rico*] [*Seismograph station code, US Geological Survey*]   (SEIS)
PWP.......... Parents without Partners   (EA)
PWP.......... Past Worthy Patriarch
PWP.......... Peasants' and Workers' Party [*India*] [*Political party*]   (PPW)
PWP.......... Picowatt Power   (CET)
pWp .... Picowatts, Psophometrically Weighted
PWP.......... Planning Work Package   (MCD)
PWP.......... Plasticized White Phosphorus
PWP.......... Polish Workers' Party
PWP.......... Postwar Planning [*World War II*]
PWP.......... Professional Women Photographers   (EA)
PWP.......... Public Watering Place   (ADA)
PWP.......... Pulmonary Wedge Pressure [*Medicine*]
PWP.......... Purchase-with-Purchase [*Sales promotion*]
pW0p .... Picowatts, Psophometrically Weighted at a Point of Zero Reference Level
PWpM .... Merck, Sharp & Dohme [*Later, Merck & Co., Inc.*] Research Laboratories, Library Services, West Point, PA [*Library symbol*] [*Library of Congress*]   (LCLS)
PWPMA.... Politechnika Warszawska, Prace Naukowe. Mechanika [*A publication*]
PWPP........ Professionwide Pension Plan [*American Chemical Society*]
PWPS........ Pure Water Preservation Society [*British*]
PWQ.......... Petersburg, WV [*Location identifier*] [*FAA*]   (FAAL)
PWQ.......... Preferred and Well Qualified [*Candidate designation*]
PWQM ...... Protection Water Quality Management
PWR .... International Power Machines Corp. [*AMEX symbol*]   (SPSG)
PWR .... Pilot Wire Regulator
PWR .... Police War Reserve [*British*]   (DAS)
PWR .... Port Walter, AK [*Location identifier*] [*FAA*]   (FAAL)
PWR .... Power   (KSC)
PWR .... Power Explorations, Inc. [*Toronto Stock Exchange symbol*]
PWR .... Power Wirewound Resistor
PWR .... Pressurized-Water Reactor [*Nuclear energy*]
PWR .... Prevailing Wage Rate [*US Employment Service*] [*Department of Labor*]
PWR .... Prince of Wales' Royal [*Military unit*] [*British*]
PWR .... Program Work Requirement   (MCD)
PWR .... Project Work Review [*Army*]   (AFIT)
PWR .... Public Worship Regulation Act [*1874*] [*British*]   (ROG)
PWR .... Publication Work Request   (MCD)
PWR .... Punjab Weekly Reporter [*India*] [*A publication*]   (ILCA)
PWRC....... Power Conversion [*NASDAQ symbol*]   (NQ)
PWRCB .... President's War Relief Control Board [*World War II*]
PWRE....... Prepositioned War Reserve Equipment [*Army*]
PWREMR ... Prepositioned War Reserve Material Requirements [*Navy*]   (MCD)
PWREMS ... Prepositioned War Reserve Material Stocks [*Navy*]   (MCD)
P W Rev ... Price Waterhouse Review [*A publication*]
Pwr Fmg.... Power Farming [*A publication*]
Pwr Fmg Aust NZ ... Power Farming in Australia and New Zealand and Better Farming Digest [*A publication*]   (APTA)
Pwr Fmg Mag ... Power Farming Magazine [*A publication*]   (APTA)
Pwr Frmg.... Power Farming in Australia and New Zealand [*A publication*]   (APTA)
Pwr Frmg Aust NZ ... Power Farming in Australia and New Zealand [*A publication*]   (APTA)
PWRH....... Powerhouse   (MSA)
PWRIMC.. Prince of Wales Royal Indian Military College [*British military*]   (DMA)
PWRM ...... Prepositioned War Reserve Materiel   (MCD)

PWRMR.... Prepositioned War Reserve Materiel Requirement (NVT)
PWRMRB ... Prepositioned War Reserve Materiel Requirement Balance (AFIT)
PWRMS.... Prepositioned War Reserve Materiel Stock (NVT)
PWRNO.... Power Failure (FAAC)
PWRO...... Pending Work Release Order (MCD)
PWROK .... Power Restored (FAAC)
PWRR....... Prepositioned War Reserve Requirements [Army] (NG)
PWRR....... Providence and Worcester Railroad Co. [NASDAQ symbol] (NQ)
PWRR-MF ... Prepositioned War Reserve Requirements for Medical Facilities [Army] (AABC)
PWRS....... Prepositioned War Reserve Stocks [Army]
PWRS....... Programmable Weapons Release System (IEEE)
PWRS-MF ... Prepositioned War Reserve Stocks for Medical Facilities [Army] (AABC)
Pwr Wks Engng ... Power and Works Engineering [A publication]
PWS.......... Paddle-Wheel Steamer [Shipping] (ROG)
PWS.......... Parallel Working System
PWS.......... Pattern Weavers' Society [A union] [British] (DCTA)
PWS.......... Performance Work Statement [DoD]
PWS.......... Peter Warlock Society (EA)
PWS.......... Petrified Wood Society (EA)
PWS.......... Petroleum and Water Systems [Army] (RDA)
PWS.......... Phoenix Weapons System
PWS.......... Plane-Wave Spectrum
PWS.......... Plasma Wave Source [Physics]
PWS.......... Plasma Wave System [Instrumentation]
PWS.......... Port-Wine Stain
PWS.......... Potable Water System (KSC)
PWS.......... Prader-Willi Syndrome Association (EA)
PWS.......... Predicted Wave Signaling
PWS.......... Preliminary Work Statement (MCD)
PWS.......... Pricing Work Statement (MCD)
PWS.......... Private Wire Service
PWS.......... Private Wire System (AAG)
PWS.......... Program Work Statement (MCD)
PWS.......... Programmer Work Station
PWS.......... Project Work Schedule [Data processing]
PWS.......... Psychological Warfare Service [Allied Forces] [World War II]
PWS.......... Psychological Warfare Society [Birmingham, England] (EA)
PWS.......... Pulau-Weh [Sumatra] [Seismograph station code, US Geological Survey] [Closed] (SEIS)
PWSB....... Peoples Westchester Savings Bank [Hawthorne, NY] [NASDAQ symbol] (NQ)
PWSC....... Post-War Scientific Collaboration [British]
PWSCC ..... Prince William Sound Community College [Alaska]
PWSO....... Pilot Weapons System Officer
PWSP....... Power Spectra, Inc. [NASDAQ symbol] (NQ)
PWsp....... Przeglad Wspotczesny [A publication]
PWSPP...... Payne Whitney Suicide Prevention Program [New York Hospital] (EA)
PWSS....... Port War Signal Station [British military] (DMA)
PWST....... Pacwest Bancorp [NASDAQ symbol] (NQ)
PWST....... Protected Water Storage Tank [Nuclear energy] (NRCH)
PWT .... Bremerton, WA [Location identifier] [FAA] (FAAL)
PWT .... Panstwowe Wydawnictwo Techniczne [A publication]
PWT .... Penn West Petroleum Ltd. [Toronto Stock Exchange symbol]
PWT .... Pennyweight
PWT .... Picture World Test [Psychology]
PWT .... Progressive Wave Tube
PWT .... Propulsion Wind Tunnel Facility [Air Force] [Arnold Air Force Base, TN]
PWTC....... Powertec, Inc. [NASDAQ symbol] (NQ)
PWTC....... Public Works Training Center [Navy]
PWTC....... Public Works Transportation Center (MCD)
PWTCA..... Powder Technology [A publication]
PWTCVA .. Procurement of Weapons and Tracked Combat Vehicles, Army (AABC)
PWTF....... Polish Workers Task Force (EA)
PWTN...... Power Train (AABC)
PWTN-A ... Prace Wroclawskiego Towarzystwa Naukowego. A [A publication]
PWTR...... Pewter (MSA)
PWTR...... Philadelphia War Tax Resistance (EA)
PWTVA..... Procurement of Weapons and Tracked Vehicles, Army (AABC)
PWU........ Political World Union (EA)
PWU........ Postal Workers Union [Australia]
PWV........ Pittsburgh & West Virginia Railroad [AAR code]
P & WV..... Pittsburgh & West Virginia Railroad
PWV .... Precipitable Water Vapor
PWV .... Prince of Wales' Volunteers [Military unit] [British]
PWV .... Pulse Wave Velocity
PWVA ...... Pacific War Veterans of America [Defunct]
PWVS....... Prince of Wales' Volunteer Service [British]
PWW........ Plannar Wing Weapon (MCD)
PWW........ Point Weather Warning
PWW........ Project West Wing (MCD)
PWW........ Washington and Jefferson College, Washington, PA [Library symbol] [Library of Congress] (LCLS)
PWWA...... Provincial Water Works Authority [Thailand] (DS)

PWWC ...... Post War World Council [Defunct] (EA)
PW-WLZOA ... Pioneer Women, the Women's Labor Zionist Organization of America [Later, PW-MWLZOA] (EA)
PWWR ...... Power Wirewound Resistor
PWX .... Permanent Working Staff [NATO] (NATG)
PWX .... Prisoners of War Executive [Branch of SHAEF] [World War II]
PX .... Air Niugini [New Guinea] [ICAO designator] (FAAC)
PX .... Pancreatectomized [Medicine]
PX .... Pedro Ximenez [A blending sherry]
PX .... Peroxidase [Also, PO, POD] [An enzyme]
PX .... Physical Examination
Px............. Plantwax [A fungicide]
PX .... Please Exchange
PX .... Pneumothorax [Medicine]
PX .... Post Exchange [Military]
PX .... Private Exchange
PX .... Production Executive of the War Cabinet [World War II]
PX .... Pyroxene [Also, PYX] [A mineral]
PXA .... Pulsed Xenon Arc
PXD .... Place Index in Decrement
PXD .... Post-Exercise Discussion [NATO] (NATG)
PXD .... Price Ex-Dividend [Stock market]
PXE........... Phenylxylylethane [Organic chemistry]
PXE........... Poly(xylenyl ether) [Organic chemistry]
PXE........... Provinces X Explorations [Vancouver Stock Exchange symbol]
PXE........... Pseudoxanthoma Elasticum [Medicine]
PXF........... Primex Forest Industries Ltd. [Toronto Stock Exchange symbol] [Vancouver Stock Exchange symbol]
PXG .... Phoenix Gold Mines Ltd. [Toronto Stock Exchange symbol]
PXI .... Pax Christi International (EA)
PXI .... Pulsed Xenon Illuminator
PxIMP....... Peroxisomal Integral Membrane Protein [Biochemistry]
PX In.......... Arrival Time [Aviation]
PXL .... Poney Explorations Limited [Vancouver Stock Exchange symbol]
PXL........... Pulsed Xenon LASER
Pxl............ Pyridoxal [Also, PL] [Biochemistry]
PXLS......... Phoenix Laser Systems, Inc. [NASDAQ symbol] (NQ)
PXLS......... Pulsed Xenon Light Source
PXLSS....... Pulsed Xenon Light Source System
PXM .... Projection X-Ray Microscope
Pxm.......... Pyridoxamine [Also, PM] [Biochemistry]
PX Me....... Report My Arrival or Departure [Aviation slang]
PXN .... Panoche, CA [Location identifier] [FAA] (FAAL)
Pxn........... Pyridoxine [Also, PN] [Biochemistry]
PXO .... Porto Santo [Portugal] [Airport symbol] (OAG)
PXO .... Prospective Executive Officer
PX Out....... Takeoff Time [Aviation]
PXPPL....... Pull and Push Plate
PXR .... Paxar Corp. [AMEX symbol] (SPSG)
PXR .... Plus-X-Reversal
PXR .... Praxis Resources Ltd. [Vancouver Stock Exchange symbol]
PXRE......... Phoenix Re Corp. [NASDAQ symbol] (NQ)
PXS .... Plexus Resources Corp. [Toronto Stock Exchange symbol]
PXS .... Pulsed Xenon System
PXSS .... Pulsed Xenon Solar Simulator
PXSTR ...... Phototransistor (IEEE)
PXT........... Patuxent River, MD [Location identifier] [FAA] (FAAL)
PXT........... Pinxit [He, or She, Painted It] [Latin]
PXT........... Praxis Technologies Corp. [Toronto Stock Exchange symbol]
PXU .... Portable X-Ray Unit
PXV .... Evansville, IN [Location identifier] [FAA] (FAAL)
PXV .... Pedro Ximenez Viejo [A blending sherry]
PXXP......... Pacific Express Holding [NASDAQ symbol] (NQ)
PXY .... Milwaukee, WI [Location identifier] [FAA] (FAAL)
Pxy .... Pyridoxyl [Biochemistry]
PY .... Martin Memorial [York City and County] Library, York, PA [Library symbol] [Library of Congress] (LCLS)
PY .... Paraguay [ANSI two-letter standard code] (CNC)
py .... Paraguay [MARC country of publication code] [Library of Congress] [IYRU nationality code] (LCCP)
PY .... Patrol Vessel, Yacht [Navy symbol]
PY .... Pembroke Yeomanry [British military] (DMA)
PY .... Person Years [After radiation exposure]
PY .... Physical Year
P/Y .... Pitch or Yaw
PY .... Polysar Ltd. [Toronto Stock Exchange symbol] [Vancouver Stock Exchange symbol]
PY .... Preferred Health Care [AMEX symbol] (SPSG)
PY .... Prior Year (AABC)
PY .... Professional Year
PY .... Program Year (AFM)
PY .... Project Yedid (EA)
PY .... Proto Yiddish (BJA)
PY .... Publication Year [Online database field identifier]
Py............. Pyridine [Organic chemistry]
Py............. Pyrogen [Medicine]
PY .... Pyrometer (IEEE)
PY .... Pyronin Y [A biological dye]
PY .... Pythium [A fungus]

PY .... Surinaamse Luchtvaart Maatschappij NV [*Surinam*] [*ICAO designator*] (FAAC)
PYA .... Penn Yan, NY [*Location identifier*] [*FAA*] (FAAL)
PYA .... Pioneer Youth of America (EA)
PYA .... Plan, Year, and Age [*Insurance designations*]
PYA .... Psychoanalysis [*Medicine*]
PYA .... Pyatigorsk [*USSR*] [*Seismograph station code, US Geological Survey*] (SEIS)
PYA .... Pyroair Tech [*Vancouver Stock Exchange symbol*]
PYACA...... Psychoanalytic Study of the Child [*A publication*]
PYAFB ..... Psychologia Africana [*A publication*]
PYAIA ...... Postepy Astronomii [*A publication*]
PYarE .... Electric Storage Battery Co., Yardley, PA [*Library symbol*] [*Library of Congress*] (LCLS)
Py B........... Bachelor of Pedagogy
PYB........... Borg-Warner Corp., York Division, York, PA [*Library symbol*] [*Library of Congress*] (LCLS)
PYB........... [*The*] Palestine Year Book [*New York*] [*A publication*] (BJA)
PYB........... Problems of Economics. A Journal of Translations [*A publication*]
PYBT .... [*The*] Prince's Youth Business Trust [*British*]
PYC........... Kuparuk, AK [*Location identifier*] [*FAA*] (FAAL)
PYC........... Pale Yellow Candle [*Baltic coffee-house*] [*London*] (DSUE)
PYC........... Patrol Vessel, Yacht, Coastal [*Navy symbol*] [*Obsolete*]
PYC........... Pay Your Cash [*Australian slang*]
PYC........... Pembroke Yeomanry Cavalry [*British military*] (DMA)
PYC........... Perishability Code [*Military*] (AFIT)
PYC........... Playon Chico [*Panama*] [*Airport symbol*] (OAG)
PYC........... Pope and Young Club (EA)
PYC........... York College of Pennsylvania, York, PA [*Library symbol*] [*Library of Congress*] (LCLS)
PYCG........ Pyrochromatogram [*Analytical chemistry*]
PYCHB...... Psychology [*A publication*]
PYCOA...... Phycologia [*A publication*]
Pyd............ [*A*] Pyrimidine Nucleoside [*Also, Y*]
PYE........... Point Reyes, CA [*Location identifier*] [*FAA*] (FAAL)
PYE........... Progressive Incorporated Equity [*NYSE symbol*] (SPSG)
PYE........... Protect Your Environment [*Groups*]
PYE........... Pryme Energy Resources [*Vancouver Stock Exchange symbol*]
PYF........... French Polynesia [*ANSI three-letter standard code*] (CNC)
PYF........... Pay-Fone Systems, Inc. [*AMEX symbol*] (SPSG)
PYF........... Pyrenees [*France*] [*Seismograph station code, US Geological Survey*] (SEIS)
Py-FD-MS ... Pyrolysis Field Desorption Mass Spectrometry
PYG.......... Peptone-Yeast-Glucose [*Medium*] [*Microbiology*]
PYGC........ Pyrolysis Gas Chromatography
PYGN........ Pyrogen Unit [*Biochemistry*]
PYGS........ Church of Jesus Christ of Latter-Day Saints, Genealogical Society Library, Gettysburg Branch, York, PA [*Library symbol*] [*Library of Congress*] (LCLS)
PYH.......... Puerto Ayacucho [*Venezuela*] [*Airport symbol*] (OAG)
PYH.......... York Hospital, York, PA [*Library symbol*] [*Library of Congress*] (LCLS)
PYHi......... Historical Society of York County, York, PA [*Library symbol*] [*Library of Congress*] (LCLS)
Py-HRMS ... Pyrolysis High-Resolution Mass Spectrometry
PYJ.......... Louisville, KY [*Location identifier*] [*FAA*] (FAAL)
Pyke.......... Pyke's Lower Canada King's Bench Reports [*1809-10*] [*A publication*] (ILCA)
Pyke LC .... Pyke's Lower Canada King's Bench Reports [*1809-10*] [*A publication*] (ILCA)
Pyke's R..... Pyke's Lower Canada King's Bench Reports [*1809-10*] [*A publication*] (ILCA)
PYL........... Perry Island, AK [*Location identifier*] [*FAA*] (FAAL)
PYLR........ Peach Yellow Leaf Roll [*Plant pathology*]
PYM .... Martin Memorial [*York City and County*] Library, York, PA [*OCLC symbol*] (OCLC)
PYM .... Pan-African Youth Movement (EA)
PYM .... Plymouth, MA [*Location identifier*] [*FAA*] (FAAL)
PYM .... Psychosomatic Medicine
PYM .... Putnam High Yield Municipal [*NYSE symbol*] (SPSG)
PYMOA ..... Psychological Monographs. General and Applied [*A publication*]
Py-MS .... Pyrolysis Mass Spectrometry
Pymt.......... Payment
PYN .... Chicago, IL [*Location identifier*] [*FAA*] (FAAL)
PYN .... Poneloya [*Nicaragua*] [*Seismograph station code, US Geological Survey*] (SEIS)
PYNC .... Prior Year Notice [*IRS*]
PYNNA ..... Psychiatria, Neurologia, Neurochirurgia [*A publication*]
PYO .... Pick Your Own [*Fruits and vegetables*] (DSUE)
PYO .... Pyongyang [*Heizo*] [*North Korea*] [*Seismograph station code, US Geological Survey*] [*Closed*] (SEIS)
PYOL........ Pyramid Oil Co. [*NASDAQ symbol*] (NQ)
PYoW .... Westmoreland County Community College, Youngwood, PA [*Library symbol*] [*Library of Congress*] (LCLS)
PYP .... Pyrophosphate [*Scintiscanning*]
PYPH .... Polyphase
PYPYB ..... Psychophysiology (Baltimore) [*A publication*]
P-Y-R .... Pitch-Yaw-Roll (AAG)
PYR .... Player Resources, Inc. [*Vancouver Stock Exchange symbol*]

PYR .... Prior Year Report
PYR .... Prior Year's Return [*IRS*]
Py R .... Pyke's Lower Canada King's Bench Reports [*1809-10*] [*A publication*] (ILCA)
Pyr............ Pyralidae [*Entomology*]
PYR .... Pyramid [*California*] [*Seismograph station code, US Geological Survey*] (SEIS)
PYR .... Pyramid (MSA)
Pyr............ Pyramidal Tract [*Neuroanatomy*]
PYR .... Pyridine [*Organic chemistry*]
Pyr............ [*A*] Pyrimidine [*Biochemistry*]
PYR .... Pyrometer (AAG)
PYR .... Pyruvate [*Biochemistry*]
PYRCA...... Psychological Record [*A publication*]
PYRD .... Pyramid Technology Corp. [*NASDAQ symbol*] (NQ)
PYRETH... Pyrethrum [*Pellitory*] [*Pharmacology*] (ROG)
PYRM... Pyramid Magnetics, Inc. [*Chatsworth, CA*] [*NASDAQ symbol*] (NQ)
PYRMD..... Pyramid [*Freight*]
PYRO........ Pyrogallic Acid (ROG)
PYRO .... Pyrotechnic
PYROM .... Pyrometer [*Engineering*]
PYROTECH ... Pyrotechnical (ROG)
PYROX GN .. Pyroxene Gneisses [*Agronomy*]
PYRR......... Pyrrolidine [*Organic chemistry*]
PYRREC ... Pyrrolidinoethyl Chloride [*Organic chemistry*]
Pyrrh........ Pyrrhus [*of Plutarch*] [*Classical studies*] (OCD)
PYRS......... Pyramids [*Board on Geographic Names*]
PYRTA...... Psychological Reports [*A publication*]
PYS............ Primitive Yolk Sac [*Embryology*]
PYSCB...... Psychology in the Schools [*A publication*]
PYSOA...... Physiologist [*A publication*]
PYSSB...... Psychoanalytic Study of Society [*A publication*]
PYT........... Payment (DCTA)
PYT........... Playitas [*Nicaragua*] [*Seismograph station code, US Geological Survey*] (SEIS)
PYT........... Prentiss, MS [*Location identifier*] [*FAA*] (FAAL)
PYT........... Pretty Young Thing [*In song title from the Michael Jackson album "Thriller"*]
PYT........... Pyng Tech [*Vancouver Stock Exchange symbol*]
PYTCA...... Phytochemistry [*A publication*]
Pyth.......... Pythian [*of Pindar*] [*Classical studies*] (OCD)
Py-TRMS.. Pyrolysis Time-Resolved Mass Spectrometry
PYV .... Payton Ventures [*Vancouver Stock Exchange symbol*]
PyV .... Polyoma Virus
PYV .... Yaviza [*Panama*] [*Airport symbol*] (OAG)
PYX .... Perryton, TX [*Location identifier*] [*FAA*] (FAAL)
PYX .... Pyroxene [*Also, PX*] [*A mineral*]
Pyx........... Pyxis [*Constellation*]
Pyxi.......... Pyxis [*Constellation*]
PZ .... Canal Zone [*ANSI two-letter standard code*] [*Obsolete*] (CNC)
PZ .... Lineas Aereas Paraguayas [*ICAO designator*] (FAAC)
PZ .... Pancreozymin [*Also, CCK*] [*Endocrinology*]
PZ .... Panzerbrechend [*Armor-Piercing*] [*German military - World War II*]
PZ .... Partiinaya Zhizn [*A publication*]
PZ .... Past Z
PZ .... Pastural Zone [*Agriculture*]
PZ .... Paterson Zochonis [*Commercial firm*] [*British*]
PZ .... Penzance [*British depot code*]
PZ .... Peripheral Zone [*Botany*] [*Anatomy*]
PZ .... Phase Zero
Pz .... Phenylazobenzyloxycarbonyl [*Biochemistry*]
PZ .... Phytopathologische Zeitschrift [*Journal of Phytopathology*] [*A publication*]
PZ .... Pick Up Zone [*Shipping*]
PZ .... Pie Zeses [*May You Live Piously*] [*Italian*]
pz............. Pieze [*Unit of pressure*]
PZ .... Poale Zion [*Labor federation*] [*Later, Labor Zionist Alliance*]
PZ .... Poland [*IYRU nationality code*] (IYR)
PZ .... Potez [*Etablissements Henri Potez*] [*France*] [*ICAO aircraft manufacturer identifier*] (ICAO)
PZ .... Praehistorische Zeitschrift [*A publication*]
PZ .... Prazosin [*A vasodilator*]
PZ .... Primary Zone [*Military*]
PZ .... Prisoner of Zion (BJA)
PZ .... Protective Zone
PZ .... Prozone Phenomenon [*Immunology*]
PZ .... Przeglad Zachodni [*A publication*]
PZ .... Psychic Zodiac
PZ .... Pyrazine [*Organic chemistry*]
PZA .... Patrol Zone Area (MCD)
PZA .... Paz De Ariporo [*Colombia*] [*Airport symbol*] (OAG)
PZA .... Piasa Commuter Airlines, Inc. [*St. Louis, MO*] [*FAA designator*] (FAAC)
PZA .... Pizza Inn, Inc. [*AMEX symbol*] (SPSG)
PZA .... Pyrazinamide [*Antibacterial compound*]
PZAA........ Polarized Zeeman Atomic Absorption
PZB........... Pietermaritzburg [*South Africa*] [*Airport symbol*] (OAG)
PZBUA...... Przeglad Budowlany [*Poland*] [*A publication*]

PZC............ Pezamerica Resources Corporation [*Vancouver Stock Exchange symbol*]
PZC............ Point of Zero Charge [*Electrochemistry*]
PZC............ Progressive Zionist Caucus   (EA)
PZCO........ Pickup-Zone Control Officer [*Military*]   (INF)
PZD........... Phase Zero Defense
PZDV........ Panzer-Division [*Armored Division*] [*German military*]
PZE............ Pamietniki Zjazdow Polskiego Zwiazku Entomologicznego [*A publication*]
PZE............ Penzance [*England*] [*Airport symbol*]   (OAG)
PZE............ Piezoelectric
PZELA...... Przeglad Elektrotechniczny [*A publication*]
PZFC......... Pia Zadora Fan Club   (EA)
PZH........... Zhob [*Pakistan*] [*Airport symbol*]   (OAG)
PZI............ Indiana University of Pennsylvania, Indiana, PA [*OCLC symbol*]   (OCLC)
PZI............ Protamine Zinc Insulin
PZKA........ Philologus. Zeitschrift fuer Klassische Altertum [*A publication*]
PZKiOR..... Polish Union of Agricultural Circles and Organizations   (PD)
PZKP........ Philologus. Zeitschrift fuer Klassische Philologie [*A publication*]
PZKPFW... Panzerkampfwagen [*German tank*] [*World War II*]
PZKW....... Panzerkampfwagen [*German tank*] [*World War II*]
PZL............ Pennzoil Co. [*NYSE symbol*] [*Toronto Stock Exchange symbol*]   (SPSG)
PZL............ Progressive Zionist League-Hashomer Hatzair   (EA)
PZLSA...... Prace z Zakresu Lesnictwa [*A publication*]
PZM.......... Pod Znamenem Marksizma [*A publication*]
PZM.......... Pressurized Zone Microphone
PZMEA..... Przeglad Mechaniczny [*A publication*]
PZO........... Peebles, OH [*Location identifier*] [*FAA*]   (FAAL)
PZO........... Podnik Zahranicniho Obchodu [*Foreign Trade Enterprise*] [*Czechoslovakian*]
PZO........... Puerto Ordaz [*Venezuela*] [*Airport symbol*]   (OAG)
PZP........... Phase Zero Program
PZP........... Pregnancy Zone Protein
PZPR........ Polska Zjednoczona Partia Robotnicza [*Polish United Workers' Party - PUWP*] [*Political party*]   (PPW)
PZQ.......... Rogers City, MI [*Location identifier*] [*FAA*]   (FAAL)
PZ(R)........ Penetration Zone (Radius)   (MCD)
PZR........... Pressurizer   (NRCH)
PZS........... President of the Zoological Society [*British*]
PZS........... Przeglad Zagadnien Socjalnych [*A publication*]
PZT........... Lead [*Plumbum*] Zirconate-Titanate [*Piezoelectric transducer*]
PZT........... Photographic Zenith Tube
PZT........... Piezoelectric Translator
PZT........... Piezoelectric Zirconate Titanate
PZT........... Polycrystalline Lead Zirconate Titanate [*Piezoelectricity*]
PZTFD...... Pis'ma v Zhurnal Tekhnicheskoi Fiziki [*A publication*]
PZU.......... Port Sudan [*Sudan*] [*Airport symbol*]   (OAG)
PZV........... New York, NY [*Location identifier*] [*FAA*]   (FAAL)
PZWS....... Panstwowe Zaklady Wydawnictwo Szkolnych [*A publication*]
PZX........... Paragould, AR [*Location identifier*] [*FAA*]   (FAAL)
PZY........... Piestany [*Czechoslovakia*] [*Airport symbol*]   (OAG)
PZZ........... Pizza Patio Ltd. [*Vancouver Stock Exchange symbol*]

Q

Q .... Chicago, Burlington & Quincy Railroad [*Also known as Burlington Route*] [*Slang*]
Q .... Codex Marchalianus   (BJA)
Q .... Coefficient of Association [*Statistics*]
Q .... Coenzyme Q [*Ubiquinone*] [*Also, CoQ, U, UQ*] [*Biochemistry*]
Q .... Combination of Purpose [*JETDS nomenclature*]
Q .... Drone [*Designation for all US military aircraft*]
Q .... Dynamic Pressure [*NASA*]
Q .... Glutamine [*One-letter symbol; see Gln*]
Q .... Heat [*or q*] [*Symbol*] [*IUPAC*]
Q .... Kuwait [*IYRU nationality code*]   (IYR)
Q .... Merit of a Coil or Capacitor [*Electronics*]
q .... Partition Function, Particle [*Symbol*] [*IUPAC*]
Q .... Partition Function, System [*Symbol*] [*IUPAC*]
Q .... Polaris Correction [*Missiles*]
Q .... Promotional Fare [*Also, K, L, V*] [*Airline fare code*]
Q .... Proportion Not in a Specific Class
Q .... Q-Factor   (DEN)
Q .... Qere   (BJA)
Q .... Quadragesms [*Year Books of Edward III*] [*A publication*]   (ILCA)
Q .... Quadrans [*A Farthing*] [*Monetary unit*] [*British*]
Q .... Quadriceps [*Anatomy*]
Q .... Quadrillion BTU's [*Also known as "quads"*]
Q .... Quadrivium [*A publication*]
Q .... Quadruple
Q .... Quadruple Expansion Engine
Q .... Quaere [*Inquire*] [*Latin*]
Q .... Qualifier [*Linguistics*]
Q .... Quality Factor
q .... Quality of Output [*Economics*]
Q .... Quantity
Q .... Quantity of Electricity [*Symbol*] [*IUPAC*]
Q .... Quaque [*Each or Every*] [*Latin*]
Q .... Quark [*Physics*]
Q .... Quart
Q .... Quarter
Q .... Quarter Word Designator [*Data processing*]
Q .... Quarterback [*Football*]
Q .... Quartering [*Military*] [*British*]
Q .... Quarterly
Q .... Quartermaster [*Military*]
Q .... Quarternary [*Geology*]
Q .... Quarters [*Officer's rating*] [*British Royal Navy*]
Q .... Quartile
Q .... Quarto [*Book from 25 to 30 centimeters in height*]
Q .... Quarto Edition [*Shakespearean work*]
Q .... Quartz [*CIPW classification*] [*Geology*]
Q .... Quasi [*Almost, As It Were*] [*Latin*]
Q .... Quebec [*Phonetic alphabet*] [*International*]   (DSUE)
Q .... Queen
Q .... Queen [*Chess*]
Q .... Queen [*Phonetic alphabet*] [*Pre-World War II*] [*World War II*]   (DSUE)
Q .... Queenie [*Phonetic alphabet*] [*Royal Navy*] [*World War I*]   (DSUE)
Q .... Queen's Quarterly [*A publication*]
Q .... Queensland [*Australia*]
Q .... Queensland Fever [*Disease first noted in farmers of Queensland, Australia*]
Q .... Queensway [*Furniture store chain*] [*British*]
Q .... Queer [*Homosexual*] [*Slang*]   (DSUE)
Q .... Quercetin [*Botany*]
Q .... Query
Q .... Query Language [*1975*]   (CSR)
Q .... Question
q .... Questioned [*Soundness of decision or reasoning in cited case questioned*] [*Used in Shepard's Citations*] [*Legal term*]   (DLA)
Q .... Questionnaire
Q .... Quetzal [*Monetary unit*] [*Guatemala*]

Q .... Queue
Q .... Quick
Q .... Quick [*Flashing*] Light [*Navigation signal*]
Q .... Quiescent [*Cytology*]
Q .... Quiescit [*He Rests*] [*Latin*]
Q .... Quiller-Couch [*Sir Arthur, 1863-1944, English man of letters*] [*Letter used as pen name*]
Q .... Quiller Press [*Publisher*] [*British*]
Q .... Quilting
Q .... Quinacrine [*Fluorescent method*] [*Chromosome stain*]
Q .... Quintal [*Unit of weight*]
Q .... Quintar [*Monetary unit*] [*Albania*]
Q .... Quintus [*Fifth*] [*Latin*]
Q .... Quinzaine [*A publication*]
Q .... Quire [*Measure of paper*]
Q .... Quisque [*Each, Every*] [*Pharmacy*]
Q .... Qumran   (BJA)
Q .... Quorum   (DLA)
Q .... Quotient   (ADA)
Q .... Radiant Energy [*Symbol*] [*IUPAC*]
Q .... Receivership [*or Bankruptcy*] [*Designation used with NYSE symbols*]   (SPSG)
Q .... Respiratory Quotient [*Also, RQ*] [*Physiology*]
Q .... San Quentin [*Prison*]
Q .... Semi-Interquartile Range or Quartile Deviation [*Statistics*]
Q .... Sonar [*JETDS nomenclature*]
Q .... Special Purpose [*JETDS nomenclature*]
Q .... Squall [*Meteorology*]   (FAAC)
Q .... Volume Rate [*Heat transmission symbol*]
9Q .... Congo (Leopoldville) [*Aircraft nationality and registration mark*]   (FAAC)
Q (Car)...... Chrysler car made by Maserati
QA.............. Bibliotheque Municipale, Alma, Quebec [*Library symbol*] [*National Library of Canada*]   (NLC)
QA.............. Inter City Airlines [*Great Britain*] [*ICAO designator*]   (FAAC)
QA.............. National Restaurant Association Quality Assurance Study Group   (EA)
QA.............. QANTAS Airways Ltd. [*Australia*]   (DS)
qa.............. Qatar [*MARC country of publication code*] [*Library of Congress*]   (LCCP)
QA.............. Qatar [*ANSI two-letter standard code*] [*IYRU nationality code*]   (CNC)
QA.............. Quadrans [*A Farthing*] [*Monetary unit*] [*British*]   (ROG)
QA.............. Quadripartite Agreement
QA.............. Quality Assurance
QA.............. Quantum Access, Inc. [*Database producer*]   (IID)
QA.............. Quarternary Ammonium [*Chemistry*]
QA.............. Quarters Allowance
QA.............. Quarters Armourer [*British military*]   (DMA)
QA.............. Quarters Assistant [*British military*]   (DMA)
QA.............. Query Analyzer   (IEEE)
QA.............. Query Author [*Proofreader's notation*]
Q & A .... Question and Answer   (MSA)
QA.............. Quick-Acting
QA.............. Quick Assembly [*Furniture*]
QA.............. Quick Asset [*Finance*]
QA.............. Quiescent Aerial [*or Antenna*]
QA.............. Quinic Acid [*Organic chemistry*]
QA.............. Quisqualic Acid [*Biochemistry*]
QAA........... ALCAN International Ltee. [*ALCAN International Ltd.*] Jonquiere, Quebec [*Library symbol*] [*National Library of Canada*]   (NLC)
QAA........... Quality Assurance Assistant [*DoD*]
QAA........... Quality Assurance Audit   (MCD)
QAA........... Queensland Athletic Association [*Australia*]
QAA........... Quinoline Amino Alcohol [*Organic chemistry*]
QAAA........ Queensland Amateur Athletic Association [*Australia*]
QAAS .... Quality Assurance Ammunition Specialist [*or Speciality*]   (MCD)
QAASCAE ... Queensland Association of Academic Staff in Colleges of Advanced Education [*Australia*]

QAB.......... Queen Anne's Bounty
QAB.......... Quick Action Button [*Military*]   (CAAL)
QABA....... Bibliotheque et Audiovisuel, Alma, Quebec [*Library symbol*] [*National Library of Canada*]   (NLC)
Q Abh Mittelrh Kg ... Quellen und Abhandlungen zur Mittelrheinischen Kirchengeschichte [*A publication*]
QAC.......... Quadrant Aimable Charge Warhead   (MCD)
QAC.......... Quadripartite Agreements Committee [*Military*]
QAC.......... Quality Assurance Chart   (MCD)
QAC.......... Quality Assurance Checklist   (NRCH)
QAC.......... Quality Assurance Code
QAC.......... Quality Assurance Criterion [*Nuclear energy*]   (NRCH)
QAC.......... Quarternary Ammonium Compound [*Chemistry*]
QAC.......... Quebec Appeal Cases [*Maritime Law Book Co. Ltd.*] [*Canada*] [*Information service or system*]   (CRD)
QACAD..... Quality Assurance Corrective Action Document   (NASA)
QACC Mot Trader ... QACC [*Queensland Automobile Chamber of Commerce*] Motor Trader [*A publication*]   (APTA)
QACHL..... Centre de Documentation, Centre Hospitalier des Laurentides et Centre d'Accueil et de Readaptation des Hautes-Vallees, L'Annonciation, Quebec [*Library symbol*] [*National Library of Canada*]   (BIB)
Qad .... Qadmoniot [*Jerusalem*]   (BJA)
QAD.......... Quadriceps Active Displacement [*Sports medicine*]
QAD.......... Quality Assurance Data
QAD.......... Quality Assurance Directive
QAD.......... Quality Assurance Directorate [*Materials*] [*British*]
QAD.......... Quick Attach-Detach [*Engine*]
QADC....... Queen's Aide-de-Camp [*Military*] [*British*]
QADK....... Quick Attach-Detach Kit
QADS........ Quality Assurance Data System
QAE.......... Quality Assurance Engineering
QAE.......... Quality Assurance Evaluator [*Military*]
QAE.......... Queen's Awards for Export [*British*]
QAES........ Quality Assurance and Expert Systems [*Data processing*]
QAET........ Quality Assurance Environment Testing [*Military*]   (CAAL)
QAET .... Quality Assurance Evaluation Test   (NG)
QAF.......... Quality Assurance Function
QAFA .... Quality Assurance Field Activity
QAFL....... Queensland Australian Football League
QAFO .... Quality Assurance Field Operations
Q Ag J....... Queensland Agricultural Journal [*A publication*]   (APTA)
QAHD .... Centre de Documentation, Hotel-Dieu d'Arthabaska, Quebec [*Library symbol*] [*National Library of Canada*]   (BIB)
QAHI........ American Healthcare Management, Inc. [*AMEX symbol*]   (SPSG)
QAI.......... Quality Assurance Inspection
QAI.......... Quality Assurance Instruction   (NRCH)
QAIA .... Queen Alia International Airport [*Jordan*]
QAIMNS... Queen Alexandra's Imperial Military Nursing Service [*British*]
QAIMNSR ... Queen Alexandra's Imperial Military Nursing Service Reserve [*British military*]   (DMA)
QAIP .... Quality Assurance Inspection Procedure
QAIRG ...... Quality Assurance Installation Review Group [*Nuclear energy*]   (NRCH)
QA + IS .... Quality Association and Inspection Service [*British*]
QAITAD.... Queensland Aboriginal and Islander Teacher Aide Development [*Australia*]
QAK.......... Quick Attach Kit
QAL.......... Quaderni di Archeologia della Libia [*A publication*]
QAL.......... Quality Assurance Laboratory
QAL.......... Quarterly Acceptance List   (AFIT)
QAL.......... Quarterly Accession List
QAL.......... Quartz Aircraft Lamp
QAL.......... Quebec Airways Limited   (MCD)
QAL.......... Quebec Aviation Ltd. [*Quebec City, PQ, Canada*] [*FAA designator*]   (FAAC)
QALAS...... Qualified Associate of the Land Agents' Society [*British*]
QALC .... College d'Alma, Lac St.-Jean, Quebec [*Library symbol*] [*National Library of Canada*]   (NLC)
QALI .... Quality Assurance Letter of Instructions
QALL........ Quartz Aircraft Landing Lamp
QALTR...... Quality Assurance Laboratory Test Request   (MCD)
QALY's..... Quality Adjusted Life Years
QAM.......... Quadrature Amplitude Modulation
QAM.......... Quality Assurance Manager
QAM.......... Quality Assurance Manual
QAM.......... Quaque Aente Meridiem [*Every Morning*] [*Pharmacy*]
QAM.......... Queued Access Method [*Data processing*]
QAMAA..... Quarterly of Applied Mathematics [*A publication*]
QAMDO..... Quadripartite Agreed Materiel Development Objective [*Military*]
QAMFNS ... Queen Alexandra's Military Family Nursing Service [*British military*]   (DMA)
QAML....... Centre de Documentation, Musee Laurier, Arthabaska, Quebec [*Library symbol*] [*National Library of Canada*]   (NLC)
QAMM...... Quality Assurance Management Meeting [*DoD*]
QAMR...... Quadripartite Agreed Materiel Requirement [*Military*]
QAMR...... Quality Assurance Management Review [*DoD*]
QA Mrh K ... Quellen und Abhandlungen zur Mittelrheinischen Kirchengeschichte [*A publication*]

QAMT...... Queensland Association of Mathematics Teachers [*Australia*]
QAN .... Queensland Air Navigation Co. Ltd. [*Australia*]   (ADA)
QANT........ Quantech Electronics Corp. [*NASDAQ symbol*]   (NQ)
Qantara...... Al-Qantara. Revista de Estudios Arabes [*A publication*]
Qantas........ Quantas Empire Airways [*A publication*]   (APTA)
QANTAS... Queensland & Northern Territory Aerial Service [*Later, QANTAS Airways Ltd.*] [*Australia*]
Qantas E Air ... Qantas Empire Airways [*A publication*]   (APTA)
QAO .... Quality Assurance Office [*Navy*]
QAO .... Quality Assurance Operation
QAO .... Quality Assurance Outline
QAO .... Queen's Awards Office [*British*]
QAOGR...... Queen Alexandra's Own Gurkha Rifles [*British military*]   (DMA)
QAOP........ Quality Assurance Operating Plan
QAP.......... Department of Antiquities in Palestine. Quarterly [*A publication*]
QAP.......... Quadratic Assignment Problem [*Mathematics*]
QAP.......... Qualifications Appraisal Panel   (OICC)
QAP.......... Quality Assurance Plan
QAP.......... Quality Assurance Procedure
QAP.......... Quality Assurance Program [*Nuclear energy*]
QAP.......... Quality Assurance Provision
QAP.......... Quanah, Acme & Pacific Railway Co. [*AAR code*]
QAP.......... Quinine, Atabrine, Plasmoquine [*Treatment for malaria*]
QAPED...... Quadripartite Agreed Plans of Engineering Design [*Military*]
QAPET...... Quadripartite Agreed Plans of Engineering Tests [*Military*]
QAPI .... Quality Assurance Program Index [*Nuclear energy*]   (NRCH)
QAPL........ Queensland Airlines Party Limited
Q Ap Math ... Quarterly of Applied Mathematics [*A publication*]
1QApoc...... [*The*] Genesis Apocryphon from Qumran. Cave One   (BJA)
QAPP........ Quality Assurance Program Plan [*Nuclear energy*]   (NRCH)
Q Appl Math ... Quarterly of Applied Mathematics [*A publication*]
Q App Math ... Quarterly of Applied Mathematics [*A publication*]
QAPST...... Quadripartite Agreed Plans of Service Tests [*Military*]
QAR.......... Quaderni di Archeologia Reggiana [*A publication*]
QAR.......... Quality Assurance Record
QA & R ..... Quality Assurance and Reliability
QAR.......... Quality Assurance Representative
QAR.......... Quality Assurance Requirements   (NRCH)
QAR.......... Quality Assurance Responsible/Witness   (MCD)
QAR.......... Quantitative Autoradiography [*Medicine*]
QAR.......... Quasi-Adiabatic Representation
QAR.......... Questionable Activity Report [*Employment and Training Administration*] [*Department of Labor*]
QAR.......... Quick Access Recording
QARANC.. Queen Alexandra's Royal Army Nursing Corps [*British*]
QARC....... Quality Assurance Record Center   (MCD)
QARC....... Quality Assurance Review Center [*National Cancer Institute*]
QARM....... Bibliotheque Municipale, Arthabaska, Quebec [*Library symbol*] [*National Library of Canada*]   (NLC)
QARNNS.. Queen Alexandra's Royal Navy Nursing Service [*British*]
QARNNSR ... Queen Alexandra's Royal Naval Nursing Service Reserve [*British military*]   (DMA)
QAS.......... Quality Assurance Service [*Medicine*]
QAS.......... Quality Assurance Specialist [*DoD*]
QAS.......... Question-Answering System
QAS.......... Quick Action Shuttle
QASAC...... Quality Assurance Spacecraft Acceptance Center   (MCD)
QASAG ..... Experimental Farm, Agriculture Canada [*Ferme Experimentale, Agriculture Canada*] L'Assomption, Quebec [*Library symbol*] [*National Library of Canada*]   (NLC)
QASAR...... Quality Assurance Systems Analysis Review   (FAAC)
QASAS...... Quality Assurance Specialist, Ammunition Surveillance   (MCD)
QASB........ Bibliotheque Municipale, Asbestos, Quebec [*Library symbol*] [*National Library of Canada*]   (NLC)
QASC .... Quadripartite Armaments Standardization Committee [*Military*]   (AABC)
QASDM..... Quality Assurance, Sample, and Data Management
QASK .... Quadrature Amplitude Shift Keying
QASL........ Quality Assurance Systems List   (IEEE)
QASP........ Quality Assurance Standard Practice   (MCD)
QASPR...... Qualcomm, Inc. Automatic Satellite Position Reporting
Q Assoc Lig Arch Stor Nav ... Quaderni. Associazione Ligure di Archeologia e Storia Navale [*A publication*]
QAST........ Quality Assurance Service [*or Serviceability*] Test [*Nuclear energy*]   (NG)
Qat .... Qatabanian   (BJA)
QAT.......... Qatar [*ANSI three-letter standard code*]   (CNC)
QAT.......... Quaker Oats Co. [*Toronto Stock Exchange symbol*]
QAT.......... Qualification Approval Test   (NATG)
QAT.......... Quality Assurance Team   (MCD)
QATIP...... Quality Assurance Test and Inspection Procedures   (MCD)
QATP........ Quality Assurance Technical Publications   (AAG)
QATT .... Qualification for Acceptance Thermal Testing [*NASA*]   (NASA)
QAU .... Quality Assurance Unit
QAVC........ Quiet Automatic Volume Control
QAVT........ Qualification Acceptance Vibration Test [*NASA*]   (NASA)
QAY.......... Bibliotheque Municipale, Aylmer, Quebec [*Library symbol*] [*National Library of Canada*]   (NLC)

QB............. Bibliotheque Municipale, Brossard, Quebec [*Library symbol*] [*National Library of Canada*] (BIB)
QB............. Qualified Bidder (FAAC)
QB............. Qualified Buyer
QB............. Quarterback [*Football*]
QB............. Quebecair, Inc. [*Airlines*] [*ICAO designator*] (OAG)
QB............. Queen's Bays [*Later, QDG*] [*Military unit*] [*British*]
QB............. Queen's Bench [*Legal*] [*British*]
QB............. Queen's Bench Reports, by Adolphus and Ellis, New Series [*A publication*] (DLA)
QB............. Queen's Bishop [*Chess*]
QB............. Quick Break (MSA)
QB............. Quickbrew [*Brand of tea*] [*British*]
QB............. Quiet Birdmen [*An association*] (EA)
QBA.......... Quality Bakers of America Cooperative (EA)
QBA.......... Quality Brands Associates of America [*Defunct*] (EA)
QBA.......... Quantitative Budget Analysis (MCD)
QBA.......... Quebecair, Inc. [*Airlines*]
QBAC....... Quality Bakers of America Cooperative (EA)
QBAN....... Qui Bixit Annos [*Who Lived ____ Years*] [*Latin*]
Q Bar News ... Queensland Bar News [*A publication*] (APTA)
QBB.......... Queen's Bad Bargain [*Undesirable serviceman*] [*Slang*] [*British*] (DSUE)
QBC.......... Bella Coola [*Canada*] [*Airport symbol*] (OAG)
QBCB .... Quarterly Bulletin of Chinese Bibliography [*A publication*]
QBCCL...... Centre de Documentation, CLSC de l'Aquilon, Baie-Comeau, Quebec [*Library symbol*] [*National Library of Canada*] (BIB)
QBCDP...... Quarterly Bibliography of Computers and Data Processing [*A publication*]
QBCH........ Centre de Documentation, Pavillon St.-Joseph, Centre Hospitalier Regional de Beauceville, Quebec [*Library symbol*] [*National Library of Canada*] (BIB)
QBD.......... Quasi Birth and Death [*Statistics*]
QBD.......... Queen's Bench Division [*Military unit*] [*British*]
QBD.......... Queen's Bench Division, Law Reports [*A publication*]
QBD.......... Queensland Book Depot [*Australia*]
QB Div .... English Law Reports, Queen's Bench Division [*1865-75*] [*A publication*] (DLA)
QBE.......... Beaconsfield Public Library, Quebec [*Library symbol*] [*National Library of Canada*] (NLC)
QBE.......... Query by Example [*Data processing search method*]
QBEAU ..... Bibliotheque Municipale, Beauport, Quebec [*Library symbol*] [*National Library of Canada*] (BIB)
QBEC .... Bibliotheque Municipale, Becancour, Quebec [*Library symbol*] [*National Library of Canada*] (NLC)
QBEHBI.... H. Bergstrom International Ltd., Beaconsfield, Quebec [*Library symbol*] [*National Library of Canada*] (NLC)
QBF .... Query-by-Forms [*Data processing search method*]
QBFJOTF ... [*The*] Quick Brown Fox Jumped over the Fence [*Typing exercise*]
QBFJOTLD ... [*The*] Quick Brown Fox Jumped over the Lazy Dogs [*Typing exercise*]
QBI .... Quite Bloody Impossible [*British slang, applied particularly to flying conditions*]
QBib.......... Quarterly Bibliography of Computers and Data Processing [*A publication*]
QBID .... Queensland Business and Industry Directory [*Australia*] [*A publication*]
QBIO .... Quest Biotechnology, Inc. [*Detroit, MI*] [*NASDAQ symbol*] (NQ)
QBIR .... Quarterly Printing Industry Business Indicator Report [*A publication*] (EAAP)
QBIX .... Qubix Graphic Systems, Inc. [*NASDAQ symbol*] (NQ)
QBJ........... Juniorat des Freres du Sacre-Coeur, Bramptonville, Quebec [*Library symbol*] [*National Library of Canada*] (NLC)
QBKI .... Beker Industries Corp. [*NYSE symbol*] (SPSG)
QBL .... Qualified Bidders List
QBLC........ Queen's Bench Reports, Lower Canada [*A publication*] (DLA)
QBMS .... Mitel Semiconductor, Bromont, Quebec [*Library symbol*] [*National Library of Canada*] (NLC)
QBO........... Bibliotheque Municipale, Boucherville, Quebec [*Library symbol*] [*National Library of Canada*] (NLC)
QBO........... Mail Advertising Service Association International. Quarterly Business Outlook [*A publication*]
QBO........... Quarterly Business Outlook [*A publication*] (EAAP)
QBO........... Quasi-Biennial Oscillation [*Earth science*]
Q-BOP....... Quick Basic Oxygen Process [*Steelmaking*]
QBPL........ Queens Borough Public Library [*New York, NY*]
QBR .... Quebecor, Inc. [*Toronto Stock Exchange symbol*]
QBR .... Queen's Bench Reports [*Legal*] [*British*]
QBR .... Queen's Bench Reports, by Adolphus and Ellis, New Series [*A publication*] (DLA)
QBRA .... ACS Biblio-information, Inc., Brossard, Quebec [*Library symbol*] [*National Library of Canada*] (BIB)
QBRG .... Centre Hospitalier Robert Giffard, Beauport, Quebec [*Library symbol*] [*National Library of Canada*] (NLC)
QBSA........ Centre Hospitalier St.-Augustin, Beauport, Quebec [*Library symbol*] [*National Library of Canada*] (BIB)
QBSM .... Que Besa Sus Manos [*Kissing Your Hands*] [*Spanish*]
QBSP......... Que Besa Sus Pies [*Kissing Your Feet*] [*Spanish*]

QBSPH...... Centre Hospitalier de Charlevoix, Baie St.-Paul, Quebec [*Library symbol*] [*National Library of Canada*] (BIB)
QBU........... Bibliotheque Municipale, Buckingham, Quebec [*Library symbol*] [*National Library of Canada*] (NLC)
QBUC....... Queen's Bench Reports, Upper Canada [*A publication*] (DLA)
Q Building Yrbk ... Queensland Building Yearbook [*A publication*] (APTA)
Q Bull Alp Gdn Soc ... Quarterly Bulletin. Alpine Garden Society [*A publication*]
Q Bull Am Rhodod Soc ... Quarterly Bulletin. American Rhododendron Society [*A publication*]
Q Bull Ass Fd Drug Off (US) ... Quarterly Bulletin. Association of Food and Drug Officials (United States) [*A publication*]
Q Bull Assoc Food Drug Off ... Quarterly Bulletin. Association of Food and Drug Officials [*A publication*]
Q Bull Assoc Food Drug Off US ... Quarterly Bulletin. Association of Food and Drug Officials of the United States [*Later, Quarterly Bulletin. Association of Food and Drug Officials*] [*A publication*]
Q Bull Fac Sci Tehran Univ ... Quarterly Bulletin. Faculty of Science. Tehran University [*A publication*]
Q Bull Fac Sci Univ Tehran ... Quarterly Bulletin. Faculty of Science. University of Tehran [*A publication*]
Q Bull Geo-Heat Util Cent ... Quarterly Bulletin. Geo-Heat Utilization Center [*United States*] [*A publication*]
Q Bull Health Organ League Nations ... Quarterly Bulletin. Health Organisation. League of Nations [*A publication*]
Q Bull IAALD ... Quarterly Bulletin. International Association of Agricultural Librarians and Documentalists [*A publication*]
Q Bull Indiana Univ Med Cent ... Quarterly Bulletin. Indiana University. Medical Center [*A publication*]
Q Bull Int Ass Agric Libr ... Quarterly Bulletin. International Association of Agricultural Librarians and Documentalists [*A publication*]
Q Bull Int Assoc Agric Libr & Doc ... Quarterly Bulletin. International Association of Agricultural Librarians and Documentalists [*A publication*]
Q Bull Mich St Univ Agric Exp Stn ... Quarterly Bulletin. Michigan State University. Agricultural Experiment Station [*A publication*]
Q Bull Natl Res Counc Can Div Mech Eng ... Quarterly Bulletin. National Research Council of Canada. Division of Mechanical Engineering [*A publication*]
Q Bull Natn Counc Women Aust ... National Council of Women of Australia. Quarterly Bulletin [*A publication*]
Q Bull Northwest Univ Med Sch ... Quarterly Bulletin. Northwestern University. Medical School [*A publication*]
Q Bull NWest Univ Med Sch ... Quarterly Bulletin. Northwestern University. Medical School [*A publication*]
Q Bull S Afr Libr ... Quarterly Bulletin. South African Library [*A publication*]
Q Bull S Afr Natl Gall ... Quarterly Bulletin. South African National Gallery [*A publication*]
Q Bull Sea View Hosp ... Quarterly Bulletin. Sea View Hospital [*A publication*]
QC............. Air Zaire SA [*Zaire*] [*ICAO designator*] (ICDA)
QC............. Bibliotheque Municipale, Cowansville, Quebec [*Library symbol*] [*National Library of Canada*] (BIB)
QC............. QC Explorations [*Vancouver Stock Exchange symbol*]
QC............. Quad Center [*Typography*]
QC............. Quaderni della Critica [*A publication*]
QC............. Qualification Course
QC............. Quality Certificate
QC............. Quality Circle [*Labor-management team organized to increase industrial productivity*]
QC............. Quality Control [*or Controller*]
QC............. Quantek Corporation [*Trademark*]
QC............. Quantitative Command
QC............. Quantum Counter
QC............. Quarter of Coverage [*Social Security Administration*] (OICC)
QC............. Quarterly Credit
QC............. Quartz Crystal
QC............. Quasi-Contract [*Business term*]
QC............. Quaternary Carrier [*Biochemistry*]
QC............. Quebec Central Railway Co. [*AAR code*]
QC............. Queen Consort [*British*] (ROG)
QC............. Queen's College [*Oxford and Cambridge Universities*] (ROG)
QC............. Queen's Counsel [*British*]
QC............. Quench Correction
QC............. Quick Cleaning (MSA)
QC............. Quick Connect
QC............. Quick Curl [*Refers to Barbie doll hair*] [*Doll collecting*]
QC............. Quiesce-Completed [*Data processing*] (IBMDP)
QC............. Quiescent Center [*Plant root growth*]
QC............. Quixote Center (EA)
QC............. Societe Air-Zaire [*ICAO designator*] (FAAC)
QCA........... Bibliotheque Municipale, Candiac, Quebec [*Library symbol*] [*National Library of Canada*] (BIB)
QCA........... Quality Control Analysis
QCA........... Quarterly Compilation of Abstracts [*A publication*]
QCA........... Queen Charlotte Airlines Ltd.
QCAG........ Ministere de l'Agriculture, des Pecheries et de l'Alimentation, Chateauguay, Quebec [*Library symbol*] [*National Library of Canada*] (NLC)

QCAI .... Quality Conformance Acceptance Inspection (MCD)
QCAL .... Centre de Documentation, Centre Hospitalier Anna-Laberge, Chateauguay, Quebec [*Library symbol*] [*National Library of Canada*] (BIB)
Q Can Studies ... Quarterly of Canadian Studies [*A publication*]
QCAR .... Queensland Criminal Reports [*A publication*]
Q Case Note ... Queensland Law Reporter Case Note [*A publication*] (APTA)
QCB .... Bibliotheque Municipale, Coaticook, Quebec [*Library symbol*] [*National Library of Canada*] (NLC)
QCB .... Quality Control Board (MCD)
QCB .... Queue Control Block [*Data processing*]
QCBC .... Quick Change Boost Control [*Automotive engineering*]
QCBK .... [*The*] Quincy Co-Operative Bank [*Quincy, MA*] [*NASDAQ symbol*] (NQ)
QCC .... Bibliotheque Gaspesienne, Cap-Chat, Quebec [*Library symbol*] [*National Library of Canada*] (NLC)
QCC .... Quaderni di Cultura Contemporanea [*A publication*]
QCC .... Qualification Correlation Certification
QCC .... Quality Communications Circle (MCD)
QCC .... Quality Control Committee (MCD)
QCC .... Queen Charlotte [*British Columbia*] [*Seismograph station code, US Geological Survey*] (SEIS)
QCC .... Queensland Cricketers' Club [*Australia*]
QCC .... Quenched Carbonaceous Composite [*Plasma technology*]
QCC .... Quick Connect Coupling
QCC .... Quinsigamond Community College [*Worchester, MA*]
QCCA .... Quality Control Council of America (EA)
QCCARS ... Quality Control Collection Analysis and Reporting System
QCCB .... Queen's College Cadet Battalion [*Taunton*] [*British military*] (DMA)
QCCL .... CLSC Albert Samson, Coaticook, Quebec [*Library symbol*] [*National Library of Canada*] (NLC)
QCCRS ...... Conseil Regional de la Sante et des Services Sociaux, Chicoutimi, Quebec [*Library symbol*] [*National Library of Canada*] (NLC)
QCCS .... Cree School Board, Chisasibi, James Bay, Quebec [*Library symbol*] [*National Library of Canada*] (BIB)
QCD .... Quality Control Data
QCD .... Quantum Chromodynamics [*Nuclear physics*]
QCD .... Quick Control Dial [*Photography*]
QCDPA ...... Quality Chekd Dairy Products Association (EA)
QCDR .... Quality Control Deficiency Report (AFM)
QCE .... Quality Control Engineers
QCE .... Quality Control and Evaluation (MCD)
QCEA .... Quaker Council for European Affairs (EA)
Q Census & Statistics Bul ... Australia. Commonwealth Bureau of Census and Statistics. Queensland Office. Bulletin [*A publication*] (APTA)
QCF .... Quality Control [*Tabulating*] Form (AAG)
QCF .... Quarterly Control Contract Factor (MCD)
QCF .... Quartz Crystal Filter
QCF .... Quench Compensation Factor
QCFO .... Quartz Crystal Frequency Oscillator
QCG .... Quartz Creek Gold Mines (BC), Inc. [*Vancouver Stock Exchange symbol*]
QCGAT ..... Quiet, Clean, General Aviation Turbofan [*NASA*]
QCH .... Hopital de Chicoutimi, Inc., Quebec [*Library symbol*] [*National Library of Canada*] (NLC)
QCH .... Quick Connect Handle
QCHJC ...... Health Sciences Information Centre, Jewish Rehabilitation Hospital [*Centre d'Information sur les Sciences de la Sante, Hopital Juif de Readaptation*] Chomedey, Quebec [*Library symbol*] [*National Library of Canada*] (NLC)
QCHM ...... Quaker Chemical Corp. [*NASDAQ symbol*] (NQ)
QCHR .... Quality Control History Record
QCI .... Quality Conformance Inspection (MSA)
QCI .... Quality Control Information (AABC)
QCI .... Quarto Castello [*Italy*] [*Seismograph station code, US Geological Survey*] [*Closed*] (SEIS)
QCI .... Queen's College, Ireland (ROG)
QCI .... Quota Club International [*Later, QI*]
QCI's .... Queen Charlotte Islands
QCIE .... Quality Control Inspection Element (AFIT)
QCIM .... Quarterly Cumulative Index Medicus [*A publication*]
QCIN .... Queensland Curriculum Information Network [*Australia*]
QCIP .... Quality Control Inspection Procedure [*Nuclear energy*] (NRCH)
QCIR .... Queen's University at Kingston Centre for International Relations [*Canada*] [*Research center*] (RCD)
QCJ .... Quality Circles Journal [*A publication*]
QCJJ .... Quaker Committee on Jails and Justice [*Canada*]
QCK .... Quick Connect Kit
Qckslv .... Quicksilver Times [*A publication*]
QCL .... Logilab, Inc., Charlebois, Quebec [*Library symbol*] [*National Library of Canada*] (NLC)
QCL .... Quality Characteristics List (MSA)
QCL .... Quality Checklist
QCL .... Quality Control Level
QCL .... Queensland Conveyancing Library [*A publication*] (APTA)
QCLBS ...... Quarterly Check-List of Biblical Studies [*A publication*]

QCLC .... CLC of America, Inc. [*Formerly, Consolidated Leasing Corporation of America*] [*NYSE symbol*] (SPSG)
QCLE .... Queensland Continuing Legal Education [*Australia*]
QCLLR ..... Queensland Crown Lands Law Reports [*A publication*] (APTA)
QCLPC ..... National Historic Park, Parks Canada [*Parc Historique National, Parcs Canada*] Coteau-du-Lac, Quebec [*Library symbol*] [*National Library of Canada*] (NLC)
QCLRS ...... Quarterly Check-List of Renaissance Studies [*A publication*]
QCM .... Bibliotheque Municipale, Chateauguay, Quebec [*Library symbol*] [*National Library of Canada*] (BIB)
QCM .... Quality Control Manager
QCM .... Quality Control Manual
QCM .... Quality Courts Motels [*Later, QM*]
QCM .... Quantitative Computer Management (IEEE)
QCM .... Quantum Conformal Fluctuation [*Theoretical physics*]
QCM .... Quartz Crystal Microbalance
QCM .... Quartz Crystal Monitor
QCMB ...... Centre de Documentation, Musee Beaulne, Coaticook, Quebec [*Library symbol*] [*National Library of Canada*] (NLC)
QCMM ..... Bibliotheque Municipale, Cap-De-La-Madeleine, Quebec [*Library symbol*] [*National Library of Canada*] (NLC)
QCMPE .... Quantum Chemistry Microcomputer Program Exchange
QCO .... Quality Control Officer (AAG)
QCO .... Quality Control Organization
QCO .... Quantity at Captain's Option [*Shipping*] (DS)
QCO .... Quartz Crystal Oscillator
QCOA .... QCOA: Journal of the Queensland Council on the Ageing [*A publication*] (APTA)
Q Coal Rpt ... Quarterly Coal Report [*A publication*]
Q Colorado Sch Mines ... Quarterly. Colorado School of Mines [*A publication*]
Q Colo Sch Mines ... Quarterly. Colorado School of Mines [*A publication*]
Q Conv R ... Queensland Conveyancing Cases [*Australia*] [*A publication*]
Q Coop ...... Queensland Co-Operator [*A publication*] (APTA)
QCOP .... Quality Control Operating Procedure
Q Countrywoman ... Queensland Countrywoman [*A publication*] (APTA)
QCP .... Quality Check Program [*DoD*]
QCP .... Quality Continuation Plan [*BMW manufacturer's warranty*]
QCP .... Quality Control Procedure
QCP .... Quezon City [*Philippines*] [*Seismograph station code, US Geological Survey*] (SEIS)
QCPCA ..... Queensland Centre for Prevention of Child Abuse [*Australia*]
QCPE .... Quantum Chemistry Program Exchange
QCPI .... Queen's College of Physicians, Ireland (ROG)
QCPMS ..... Quality Control and Performance Monitoring System (MCD)
QCPSA ..... Quaker Center for Prisoner Support Activities (EA)
QCPSK ..... Quaternary Coherent Phase-Shift Keying
QCQ .... Quebec [*Quebec*] [*Seismograph station code, US Geological Survey*] (SEIS)
QCR .... Qualitative Construction Requirement [*Army*]
QCR .... Quality Control/Reliability
QCR .... Quality Control Report
QCR .... Quality Control Reports: the Gold Sheet [*A publication*]
QCR .... Quality Control Representative [*Military*] (AABC)
QCR .... Quality Control Review
QCR .... Quality Control Room
QCR .... Queensland Criminal Reports [*A publication*] (APTA)
QCR .... Quick Change Response [*System*]
QCR .... Quick Connect Relay
QCRCN ..... Campus Notre-Dame-De-Foy, Cap-Rouge, Quebec [*Library symbol*] [*National Library of Canada*] (NLC)
QCRM .... Bibliotheque Municipale, Cap-Rouge, Quebec [*Library symbol*] [*National Library of Canada*] (BIB)
QCRS .... Seminaire St-Augustin, Cap-Rouge, Quebec [*Library symbol*] [*National Library of Canada*] (NLC)
QCS .... Quad-Cities Station [*Nuclear energy*] (NRCH)
QCS .... Quaderni. Centro di Studi sulla Deportazione e l'Internamento [*A publication*]
QCS .... Quality Control Standard (AAG)
QCS .... Quality Control System
QCS .... Quality Cost System
QCS .... Query Control Station (MCD)
QCS .... Service de la Bibliotheque de Ville de Laval, Chomedey, Quebec [*Library symbol*] [*National Library of Canada*] (BIB)
QCSC .... Quadripartite Chemical, Biological, Radiological Standardization Committee [*Military*] (AABC)
QCSEE ...... Quiet, Clean, Short-Haul Experimental Engine [*NASA*]
QCSEL ...... Quality Control Select Vendor (MCD)
QCSH .... Societe Historique du Saguenay, Chicoutimi, Quebec [*Library symbol*] [*National Library of Canada*] (NLC)
QCSM .... Quiescent Command/Service Module (MCD)
QCSMA .... Quarterly. Colorado School of Mines [*A publication*]
QCSS .... Quaderni di Cultura e Storia Sociale [*A publication*]
QCSSP ...... Quality Control Single Source Procurement (MCD)
QCSTL ...... Cote St. Luc Public Library, Quebec [*Library symbol*] [*National Library of Canada*] (NLC)
QCT .... Quantitative Computerized Tomography [*Biomedical engineering*]
QCT .... Quasiclassical Trajectory [*Chemical physics*]
QCT .... Questionable Corrective Task

Q Ct of Cr App ... Queensland Court of Criminal Appeal [*Australia*]
QCTR .... Quality Control Test Report
QCTT .... Quality Control Test Team [*Military*]
QCU .... Quality Courts United [*Later, QM*]　(EA)
QCU .... Quartz Crystal Unit
QCU .... Quick Change Unit　(MCD)
QCU .... Universite du Quebec, Chicoutimi, Quebec [*Library symbol*] [*National Library of Canada*]　(NLC)
QCUG .... Departement de Geographie, Universite du Quebec, Chicoutimi, Quebec [*Library symbol*] [*National Library of Canada*]　(NLC)
QCUGC ..... Cartotheque, Universite du Quebec, Chicoutimi, Quebec [*Library symbol*] [*National Library of Canada*]　(NLC)
Q Cum Index Med ... Quarterly Cumulative Index Medicus [*A publication*]
QCUS .... Quartz Crystal Unit Set
QCVC .... Quick Connect Valve Coupler
QCW .... Quadrant Continuous Wave
QCWA .... Quarter Century Wireless Association　(EA)
QD .... Bibliotheque Municipale, Dorval, Quebec [*Library symbol*] [*National Library of Canada*]　(BIB)
QD .... QData Systems, Inc. [*Vancouver Stock Exchange symbol*]
QD .... Quaderni Dannunziani [*A publication*]
QD .... Quaestiones Disputatae　(BJA)
QD .... Quantity Distance [*Explosives*]
QD .... Quaque Die [*Every Day*] [*Pharmacy*]
QD .... Quarter Distribution [*Parapsychology*]
QD .... Quarterdeck
QD .... Quartile Deviation [*Statistics*]
QD .... Quasi Dicat [*As If One Should Say, or As Though One Should Say*] [*Latin*]
QD .... Quasi Dictum [*As If Said, or As Though It Had Been Said*] [*Latin*]
QD .... Quasi Dixisset [*As If One Had Said*] [*Latin*]
QD .... Quater in Die [*Four Times a Day*] [*Pharmacy*]
QD .... Questioned Document [*Criminology*]
Q & D .... Quick and Dirty [*Data processing*]
QD .... Quick Disconnect
QD .... Quicksilver Data [*Information service or system*]　(IID)
QD .... Transbrasil SA Linhas Aereas [*Brazil*] [*ICAO designator*]　(ICDA)
6QD .... Damascus Document [*or Sefer Berit Damesek*] from Qumran. Cave Six　(BJA)
QDA........... Quantitative Descriptive Analysis
QDA........... Quantity Discount Agreement
QDA........... Quarterly. Department of Antiquities in Palestine [*Jerusalem*] [*A publication*]
Qd Ag J...... Queensland Agricultural Journal [*A publication*]　(APTA)
Qd Agric J ... Queensland Agricultural Journal [*A publication*]　(APTA)
QDAP .... Quarterly. Department of Antiquities in Palestine [*Jerusalem*] [*A publication*]
Qd Bur Invest Tech Bull ... Queensland. Department of Public Lands. Bureau of Investigation. Technical Bulletin [*A publication*]　(APTA)
Qd Bur Sug Exp Stat Tech Commun ... Queensland. Bureau of Sugar Experiment Stations. Technical Communication [*A publication*]　(APTA)
Qd Bur Sug Exp Stn Tech Commun ... Queensland. Bureau of Sugar Experiment Stations. Technical Communication [*A publication*]　(APTA)
QDC........... Quick Dependable Communications
QDC........... Quick Die Change [*Automotive engineering*]
QDC........... Quick Disconnect Cap
QDC........... Quick Disconnect Connector
QDCC .... Quick Disconnect Circular Connector
QDCE .... College Bourgchemin (CEGEP), Drummondville, Quebec [*Library symbol*] [*National Library of Canada*]　(NLC)
QDC & E ... Quartz Devices Conference and Exhibition
Qd Chamber Manufacturers Yb ... Queensland Chamber of Manufacturers. Yearbook [*A publication*]　(APTA)
QDD .... Qualified for Deep Diving Duties [*Navy*] [*British*]
QDD .... Quantized Decision Detection
Qd Dent J .. Queensland Dental Journal [*A publication*]　(APTA)
Qd Dent Mag ... Queensland Dental Magazine [*A publication*]　(APTA)
QDE........... Etablissement Donnacona, Quebec [*Library symbol*] [*National Library of Canada*]　(BIB)
QDE........... Qualified Designated Entities [*Independent counseling groups and churches involved with aiding aliens*] [*Immigration and Naturalization Service term*]
Q Dent Rev ... Quarterly Dental Review [*A publication*]
4QDeut32 .. Manuscript of Deuteronomy 32 from Qumran. Cave 4　(BJA)
QDF .... Quantum Distribution Function
Qd For Dep Adv Leafl ... Queensland. Department of Forestry. Advisory Leaflet [*A publication*]　(APTA)
Qd For Dep Pamph ... Queensland. Department of Forestry. Pamphlet [*A publication*]　(APTA)
Qd Forest Bull ... Queensland Forest Bulletin [*A publication*]　(APTA)
QDG .... Queen's Dragoon Guards [*Formerly, KDG, QB*] [*Military unit*] [*British*]
Qd Geogr J ... Queensland Geographical Journal [*A publication*]　(APTA)
Qd Geol Surv 1:250 000 Geol Ser ... Queensland. Geological Survey. 1:250,000 Geological Series [*A publication*]　(APTA)

Qd Geol Surv Rep ... Queensland. Geological Survey. Report [*A publication*]　(APTA)
Qd Govt Mining J ... Queensland Government Mining Journal [*A publication*]
Qd Govt Min J ... Queensland Government Mining Journal [*A publication*]
Qd Graingrower ... Queensland Graingrower [*A publication*]
QDH .... Quick Disconnect Handle
Qd Heritage ... Queensland Heritage [*A publication*]　(APTA)
QDHSC ..... Hopital Sainte-Croix, Drummondville, Quebec [*Library symbol*] [*National Library of Canada*]　(NLC)
Q Digger .... Queensland Digger [*A publication*]　(APTA)
Qd Ind....... Queensland Industry [*A publication*]
QDISC....... Quick Disconnect
Qd J Agric Anim Sci ... Queensland Journal of Agricultural and Animal Sciences [*A publication*]
Qd J Agric Sci ... Queensland Journal of Agricultural Science [*Later, Queensland Journal of Agricultural and Animal Sciences*] [*A publication*]　(APTA)
QDK.......... Quick Disconnect Kit
Qd L.......... Queensland Lawyer [*Australia*] [*A publication*]
QDL........... Quick Disconnect, Large
Qd Law Soc J ... Queensland Law Society. Journal [*A publication*]
QDLC........ Quadlogic Controls Corp. [*NASDAQ symbol*]
QDM .... Centre d'Information Documentaire Come-Saint-Germain, Drummondville, Quebec [*Library symbol*] [*National Library of Canada*]　(NLC)
QDM .... Magnetic Heading (Zero Wind) [*to steer to reach me*] [*Aviation code*]　(FAAC)
QDM .... Quick Disconnect, Miniature
1QDM .... [*The*] Words of Moses from Qumran. Cave One　(BJA)
QDMBPT ... Quasi-Degenerate Many-Body Perturbation Theory [*Physics*]
QDMC....... Quadratic Matrix Control [*Chemical engineering*] [*Data processing*]
QDN .... Quick Disconnect Nipple
Qd Nat .... Queensland Naturalist [*A publication*]　(APTA)
QDO .... Quadripartite Development Objective [*Military*]　(AABC)
QDO .... Quantitative Design Objective
QDO .... Quick Delivery Order
QDOPH ..... Office des Personnes Handicapees du Quebec, Drummondville, Quebec [*Library symbol*] [*National Library of Canada*]　(NLC)
QDP.......... Quick Disconnect Pivot
Qd Police J ... Queensland Police Journal [*A publication*]
Qd Prod...... Queensland Producer [*A publication*]　(APTA)
QDPSK...... Quaternary Differential Phase-Shift Keying　(TEL)
QDR.......... Dubai Riyal [*Monetary unit*]
QDR.......... Magnetic Bearing [*from me*] [*Aviation code*]　(FAAC)
QDR.......... Qualification Design Review [*NASA*]　(MCD)
QDR.......... Quality Data and Reporting　(MCD)
QDR.......... Quality Deficiency Record [*DoD*]
QDR.......... Quality Deficiency Report [*DoD*]
Qd R.......... Queensland Reports [*A publication*]　(APTA)
QDRI .... Qualitative Development Requirement Information
QDRNT...... Quadrant　(MSA)
QDRT........ Qadrant Corp. [*NASDAQ symbol*]　(NQ)
QDRT........ Quadrant
QDRTR ..... Quadrature
QDRX........ Quadrax Corp. [*NASDAQ symbol*]　(NQ)
QDS.......... Quality Data System　(NASA)
QDS.......... Quarantine Document System [*Information retrieval*] [*NASA*]
QDS.......... Quick Disconnect Series
QDS.......... Quick Disconnect, Small
QDS.......... Quick Disconnect Swivel
Qd Surv...... Queensland Surveyor [*A publication*]　(APTA)
QDT.......... Qualified Domestic Trust
QDT.......... Quintessence of Dental Technology
QDTA....... Quantitative Differential Thermal Analysis
Qd Teach J ... Queensland Teachers' Journal [*A publication*]
QDU .... Dusseldorf-Main RR [*West Germany*] [*Airport symbol*]　(OAG)
Qd Univ Agric Dep Pap ... University of Queensland. Agriculture Department. Papers [*A publication*]　(APTA)
Qd Univ Bot Dep Pap ... University of Queensland. Botany Department. Papers [*A publication*]　(APTA)
Qd Univ Civ Engng Dep Bull ... University of Queensland. Department of Civil Engineering. Bulletin [*A publication*]　(APTA)
Qd Univ Comput Centre Pap ... University of Queensland. Computer Centre. Papers [*A publication*]　(APTA)
Qd Univ Ent Dep Pap ... University of Queensland. Entomology Department. Papers [*A publication*]　(APTA)
Qd Univ Fac Vet Sci Pap ... University of Queensland. Faculty of Veterinary Science. Papers [*A publication*]　(APTA)
Qd Univ Geol Dep Pap ... University of Queensland. Geology Department. Papers [*A publication*]　(APTA)
Qd Univ Pap Zool Dep ... University of Queensland. Zoology Department. Papers [*A publication*]　(APTA)
Qd Univ Zool Dep Pap ... University of Queensland. Zoology Department. Papers [*A publication*]　(APTA)
QDV.......... Quick Disconnect Valve
Qd Vet Proc ... Queensland Veterinary Proceedings [*A publication*]　(APTA)
QDX.......... Quick Decision Exercise [*Training simulation*] [*Army*]

QDXR........ Quadriplexer
QE............. Air Tahiti [*ICAO designator*] (FAAC)
QE............. Bibliotheque Municipale, St.-Eustache, Quebec [*Library symbol*] [*National Library of Canada*] (BIB)
QE............. Journal of Quantum Electronics [*A publication*] (MCD)
QE............. Quadrant Elevation
QE............. Quadruple Expansion (DS)
QE............. Quaestiones et Salutationes in Exodum [*Philo*] (BJA)
QE............. Quality Engineer [*or Engineering*]
QE............. Quality Evaluation (NG)
QE............. Quality Excellence [*Chrysler Corp.*]
QE............. Quantum Electronics [*A publication*]
QE............. Queue Entry
QE............. Quod Est [*Which Is*] [*Latin*]
QE............. Quotation Estimate (MCD)
QE 2.......... Queen Elizabeth 2 [*Luxury liner*]
QEA.......... QANTAS Empire Airways Ltd. [*Later, QANTAS Airways Ltd.*]
QeA........... Questo e Alto [*A publication*]
QEAE........ Quarternary Ethylaminoethyl [*Organic chemistry*]
QEAM........ Quick Erecting Antenna Mast [*Army*] (RDA)
QEAS......... Quantum Electronics and Applications Society (MCD)
QEAV........ Quick Exhaust Air Valve
QEB........... Quality Engineering Bulletin [*NASA*]
QEBG........ Quellen und Eroerterungen zur Bayerischen Geschichte [*A publication*]
QEC........... Quantum Electronics Council
QEC........... Quantum Energy [*Vancouver Stock Exchange symbol*]
QEC........... Queen Elizabeth College [*London, England*]
QEC........... Quick Engine Change
QEC........... Quiesce-at-End-of-Chain [*Data processing*] (IBMDP)
QECA........ Quick Engine Change Assembly (NG)
QECCH..... Compton County Historical and Museum Society [*Societe d'Histoire et du Musee du Comte de Compton*] Eaton Corner, Quebec [*Library symbol*] [*National Library of Canada*] (NLC)
QECK........ Quick Engine Change Kit (NG)
Q Econ Comment ... Quarterly Economic Commentary [*A publication*]
Q Economic Rev of UK ... Quarterly Economic Review of the United Kingdom [*A publication*]
Q Econ R.... Quarterly Economic Review [*Seoul*] [*A publication*]
Q Econ Rev Chile ... Quarterly Economic Review of Chile [*A publication*]
Q Econ Rev Iran ... Quarterly Economic Review of Iran [*A publication*]
Q Econ Rev Oil West Eur ... Quarterly Economic Review. Oil in Western Europe [*A publication*]
QECS......... Quick Engine Change Stand (NG)
QECU........ Quick Engine Change Unit
QED........... Quality Education Data [*Information service or system*] (IID)
QED........... Quantum Electrodynamics [*Theory*]
QED........... Queensland Education Department [*Australia*]
QED........... Quentin E. Deverill [*Protagonist in TV series; initialism also used as title of the series*]
QED........... Quick Erection Dome
QED........... Quick Text Editor
QED........... Quod Erat Demonstrandum [*Which Was the Thing to Be Proved*] [*Latin*]
Q Ed Off Gaz ... Education Office Gazette. Queensland Department of Education [*A publication*] (APTA)
QEDX........ QED Exploration, Inc. [*NASDAQ symbol*] (NQ)
QEEL........ Quality Evaluation and Engineering Laboratory [*Navy*]
QEEL/CO ... Quality Evaluation and Engineering Laboratory, Concord [*California*] [*Navy*]
QEF........... Quod Erat Faciendum [*Which Was to Be Made, or Done*] [*Latin*]
QEH .... Queen Elizabeth Hall [*London, England*]
QEH .... Queen Elizabeth's Hospital School [*England*]
QEI .... Quod Erat Inveniendum [*Which Was to Be Found Out*] [*Latin*]
QEIC......... Quicksilver Enterprises, Inc. [*NASDAQ symbol*] (NQ)
QEKG........ Q-Med, Inc. [*Clark, NJ*] [*NASDAQ symbol*] (NQ)
QEL .... Quality Evaluation Laboratory
QEL .... Queue Element [*Data processing*]
QEL .... Quiet Extended Life
Q Elec Contractor ... Queensland Electrical Contractor [*A publication*] (APTA)
QElecSC .... Quadripartite Electronic Standardization Committee [*Military*] (AABC)
QELS......... Quantitative Evaluation of Library Searching [*Spectra matching technique*]
QELS......... Quasi-Elastic Light Scattering [*Also, QLS, QUELS*] [*Physics*]
QEM.......... Quadrant Electrometer
QEM.......... Qualified Export Manager [*Designation awarded by American Society of International Executives*]
QEM.......... Quality Education for Minorities Project (EA)
QEMM...... Quarterdeck Expanded Memory Manager [*Data processing*]
QEN.......... Quare Executionem Non [*Wherefore Execution Should Not Be Issued*] [*Latin*] [*Legal term*] (DLA)
QEngrSC ... Quadripartite Engineer Standardization Committee [*Military*] (AABC)
QEO.......... Quality Engineering Operations
QEO.......... Queen Elizabeth's Own [*British military*] (DMA)
QEOP........ Quartermaster Emergency Operation Plan [*Army*]
QEP.......... Quality Evaluation Program [*College of American Pathologists*]

QEP .... Quality Examination Program (AFM)
QEPL........ Quality Engineering Planning List (MCD)
QER........... Qualitative Equipment Requirements [*Army*] (AABC)
QER........... Quarterly Economic Review [*A publication*]
QER........... Queen's Edinburgh Rifles [*British military*] (DMA)
QES .... Quadrant Eleventh-Gram Second
QES .... Quaker Esperanto Society (EA)
QESCP ..... Quality Engineering Significant Control Points (MCD)
QEST........ Quality Evaluation System Tests (NG)
QEST........ Query, Update Entry, Search, Time-Sharing System (NVT)
QET .... Quality Expo TIME-International (ITD)
QET .... Quasi-Equilibrium Theory [*Physical chemistry*]
QEV .... Quick Exhaust Valve
QEVY........ Evans Products Co. [*NYSE symbol*] (SPSG)
QEW......... Queen Elizabeth Way [*Canada*]
QEWDA .... Queensland Ethnic Welfare Development Association [*Australia*]
QF .... Qabel Foundation (EA)
QF .... QANTAS Airways Ltd. [*Australia*] [*ICAO designator*] (OAG)
QF .... Qualifying Facility [*Electric power*]
QF .... Quality Factor [*Nuclear energy*]
QF .... Quality Form [*Nuclear energy*] (NRCH)
QF .... Quellen und Forschungen aus Italienischen Archiven und Bibliotheken [*A publication*]
QF .... Quellen und Forschungen zur Sprach- und Kulturgeschichte der Germanischen Voelker [*A publication*]
QF .... Quench Frequency (DEN)
QF .... Queue Full
QF .... Quick-Firing [*Gun*]
QF .... Quick Fix (MCD)
QF .... Quick Freeze
QFA .... Quantitative Fibrinogen Assay [*Clinical chemistry*]
QFAB........ Quellen und Forschungen aus Italienischen Archiven und Bibliotheken [*A publication*]
QFB .... Quiet Fast Boat [*Navy symbol*]
QF-BH....... Quick Fix - Black Hawk
QFC .... Quantitative Flight Characteristics
QFCC........ Quantitative Flight Characteristics Criteria
QFCI......... Quality Food Centers, Inc. [*NASDAQ symbol*] (NQ)
QFCI......... Quartermaster Food and Container Institute for the Armed Forces
QFD .... Quality Function Deployment [*Automotive engineering*]
QFD .... Quantum Flavor Dynamics
QFD .... Quarterly Forecast Demand
QFE .... Atmospheric Pressure at Aerodrome Elevation [*or Runway Threshold*] [*Aviation code*] (FAAC)
QFE .... Columbus [*Georgia*] Fort Benning [*Airport symbol*] (OAG)
QFE .... Query Formulation and Encoding
QFF.......... Atmospheric Pressure Converted to Mean Sea Level Elevation [*Aviation code*] (AIA)
QFF.......... Quadrupole Flip-Flop [*Data processing*]
QFG .... Quaderni di Filologia Germanica. Facolta di Lettere e Filosofia. Universita di Bologna [*A publication*]
QFHS .... Queensland Family History Society [*Australia*]
QFI .... Qualified Flight Instructor
QFI .... Quellen und Forschungen aus Italienischen Archiven und Bibliotheken [*A publication*]
QFIA......... Quantitative Fluorescence Image Analysis [*Medicine*]
QFIAB....... Quellen und Forschungen aus Italienischen Archiven und Bibliotheken [*A publication*]
Q Film Radio TV ... Quarterly of Film, Radio, and Television [*A publication*]
QFINBL.... Queensland. Department of Harbours and Marine. Fisheries Notes [*A publication*]
QFIRC ...... Quick Fix Interference Reduction Capability (AFM)
QFL .... Quasi-Fermi Level
4QFlor....... Florilegium. A Miscellany from Qumran. Cave Four (BJA)
QFLOW .... Quota Flow Control Procedures (FAAC)
QFM .... Quantized Frequency Modulation
QFM .... Quartz-Fayalite-Magnetite [*Geology*]
QFMA .... Queensland Fish Management Authority [*Australia*]
QFMR .... Quantized Frequency Modulation Repeater
QFO.......... Quartz Frequency Oscillator
QFP .... Quartz Fiber Product
QFP .... Quick Fix Program
QFr .... Epistulae ad Quintum Fratrem [*of Cicero*] [*Classical studies*] (OCD)
QFR .... Quarterly Financial Report for Manufacturing, Mining, and Trade Companies [*Information service or system*] [*A publication*]
QFR .... Quarterly Force Revision [*Military*] (NVT)
QFRNAV... Queensland. Department of Forestry. Research Note [*A publication*]
QFRT........ Quarterly of Film, Radio, and Television [*A publication*]
Q Fruit & Veg News ... Queensland Fruit and Vegetable News [*A publication*] (APTA)
QFSK........ Quellen und Forschungen zur Sprach- und Kulturgeschichte der Germanischen Voelker [*A publication*]
QFSM....... Queen's Fire Service Medal for Distinguished Service [*British*]
QFSR........ Quartus Foundation for Spiritual Research (EA)
QFT .... Quantized Field Theory
QFU........... Magnetic Orientation of Runway [*Aviation code*] (FAAC)

Q Fuel Energy Summ ... Quarterly Fuel and Energy Summary [*United States*] [*A publication*]
QG .... Bibliotheque Municipale, Gatineau, Quebec [*Library symbol*] [*National Library of Canada*]   (NLC)
QG .... Quadrature Grid
QG .... Quaestiones et Salutationes in Genesin [*Philo*]   (BJA)
QG .... Qualified in Gunnery [*British military*]   (DMA)
QG .... Quartermaster General [*Military*]
QG .... Quartier General [*Headquarters*] [*French*]
QG .... Seychelles-Kilimanjaro Air Transport Ltd. [*Kenya*] [*ICAO designator*]   (FAAC)
QGAH .... Hotel-Dieu de Gaspe, Quebec [*Library symbol*] [*National Library of Canada*]   (NLC)
QGAP .... Centre de Documentation, Peches Maritimes, Ministere de l'Agriculture, des Pecheries, et de l'Alimentation du Quebec, Gaspe, Quebec [*Library symbol*] [*National Library of Canada*]   (NLC)
QGBF .... Quasi-Grain Boundary Free [*Photovoltaic energy systems*]
QGC .... College de la Gaspesie, Gaspe, Quebec [*Library symbol*] [*National Library of Canada*]   (NLC)
QGCH .... Centre Hospitalier de Gatineau, Quebec [*Library symbol*] [*National Library of Canada*]   (NLC)
QGE .... Queen's Gurkha Engineers [*British military*]   (DMA)
1QGen .... [*The*] Genesis Apocryphon from Qumran. Cave One   (BJA)
Q Geog J .... Queensland Geographical Journal [*A publication*]   (APTA)
Q Geol Notes Geol Surv South Aust ... South Australia. Geological Survey. Quarterly Geological Notes [*A publication*]   (APTA)
QGG .... Queensland Government Gazette [*A publication*]   (APTA)
QGHR .... Quellen zur Geschichte des Humanismus und der Reformation in Facsimile-Ausgaben [*A publication*]
QGI .... Grosse Ile Library, Magdalen Islands, Quebec [*Library symbol*] [*National Library of Canada*]   (NLC)
QGIG .... Queensland Government Industrial Gazette [*A publication*]   (APTA)
QGJD .... Quellen zur Geschichte der Juden in Deutschland [*A publication*]
QGL .... Granby Leader Mail Office, Quebec [*Library symbol*] [*National Library of Canada*]   (NLC)
QGM .... Bibliotheque Municipale, Granby, Quebec [*Library symbol*] [*National Library of Canada*]   (NLC)
QGM .... Queen's Gallantry Medal [*British*]
QGM .... Quellen und Studien zur Geschichte der Mathematik [*A publication*]
QGMath .... Quellen und Studien zur Geschichte der Mathematik [*A publication*]
QGMG .... Musee de la Gaspesie, Gaspe, Quebec [*Library symbol*] [*National Library of Canada*]   (BIB)
QGMJA .... Queensland Government Mining Journal [*A publication*]
QGMM ...... Bibliotheque Municipale, Grand'Mere, Quebec [*Library symbol*] [*National Library of Canada*]   (NLC)
QGNG .... Ecole Secondaire Nicolas-Gatineau, Gatineau, Quebec [*Library symbol*] [*National Library of Canada*]   (BIB)
QGO .... Queen's Gurkha Officer [*Military*] [*British*]
Q Gov Indus Gaz ... Queensland Government Industrial Gazette [*A publication*]   (APTA)
Q Govt Min J ... Queensland Government Mining Journal [*A publication*]   (APTA)
Q Govt PRB News Bul ... Queensland Government. Public Relations Bureau. News Bulletin [*A publication*]   (APTA)
QGP .... Queensland Government Publications [*A publication*]   (APTA)
Q Graingrower ... Queensland Graingrower [*A publication*]   (APTA)
QGS .... Quantity Gauging System   (NASA)
QGSH .... Societe Historique du Comte de Shefford, Granby, Quebec [*Library symbol*] [*National Library of Canada*]   (NLC)
QGV .... Quantized Gate Video [*RADAR*]
QH .... Air Florida, Inc. [*ICAO designator*]   (FAAC)
QH .... Bibliotheque Municipale, Hull, Quebec [*Library symbol*] [*National Library of Canada*]   (NLC)
QH .... Quaker History [*A publication*]
QH .... Quaque Hora [*Every Hour*] [*Pharmacy*]
QH .... Quartz Helix
QH .... Queensland Heritage [*A publication*]   (APTA)
QH .... Quorn Hounds
1QH .... Hodayot. Hymns of Thanksgiving from Qumran. Cave One   (BJA)
Q2H .... Quaque Secunda Hora [*Every Second Hour*] [*Pharmacy*]
Q3H .... Quaque Tertia Hora [*Every Third Hour*] [*Pharmacy*]
Q4H .... Quaque Quartus Hora [*Every Fourth Hour*] [*Pharmacy*]
QHAC .... CEGEP [*College d'Enseignement General et Professionnel*] de Hauterive, Baie Comeau, Quebec [*Library symbol*] [*National Library of Canada*]   (NLC)
QHACR ..... Conseil Regional de la Sante et des Services Sociaux de la Region Cote-Nord, Hauterive, Quebec [*Library symbol*] [*National Library of Canada*]   (NLC)
QHB .... Economics Information Centre, Bell Canada, Hull, Quebec [*Library symbol*] [*National Library of Canada*]   (NLC)
QHB .... Queen's Hard Bargain [*Undesirable serviceman*] [*Slang*] [*British*]   (DSUE)
QHBC .... Bibliotheque Centrale de Pret d'Outaouais, Hull, Quebec [*Library symbol*] [*National Library of Canada*]   (BIB)

QHBEER .. Headquarters Engineering Economics Reference Centre, Bell Canada, Hull, Quebec [*Library symbol*] [*National Library of Canada*]   (NLC)
QHBRM .... Bell Canada Headquarters, Regulatory Matters-Regulatory Information Bank, Hull, Quebec [*Library symbol*] [*National Library of Canada*]   (NLC)
QHC .... CEGEP [*College d'Enseignement General et Professionnel*] de l'Outaouais, Hull, Quebec [*Library symbol*] [*National Library of Canada*]   (NLC)
QHC .... Queen's Honorary Chaplain [*British*]
QHCH ...... Heritage Campus, CEGEP de l'Outaouais, Hull, Quebec [*Library symbol*] [*National Library of Canada*]   (NLC)
QHCL .... Centre de Documentation, CLSC de Hull, Quebec [*Library symbol*] [*National Library of Canada*]   (NLC)
QHCRS ..... Conseil Regional de la Sante et des Services Sociaux de la Region Outaouais-Hull, Hull, Quebec [*Library symbol*] [*National Library of Canada*]   (NLC)
QHDS .... Queen's Honorary Dental Surgeon [*British*]
QHE .... E. B. Eddy Co., Hull, Quebec [*Library symbol*] [*National Library of Canada*]   (NLC)
QHE .... Quantum Hall Effect [*Physics*]
Q Health .... Queensland's Health [*A publication*]   (APTA)
Q Her .... Queensland Heritage [*A publication*]
QHESJ ...... Ecole Secondaire St.-Joseph, Hull, Quebec [*Library symbol*] [*National Library of Canada*]   (BIB)
Q Hist Soc J ... Queensland Historical Society. Journal [*A publication*]
QHM .... Quartz Horizontal Magnetometer   (NOAA)
QHM .... Queen's Harbour Master [*British*]
QHMML .... Micromedia Ltee., Hull, Quebec [*Library symbol*] [*National Library of Canada*]   (BIB)
QHNS .... Queen's Honorary Nursing Sister [*British*]
QHO .... Queen's Hall Orchestra
QHP .... Queen's Honorary Physician [*British*]
QHP .... Quiet Helicopter Program   (RDA)
QHPJ .... Centre Hospitalier Pierre Janet, Hull, Quebec [*Library symbol*] [*National Library of Canada*]   (NLC)
QHQAR .... Centre Regional de l'Outaouais, Archives Nationales du Quebec, Hull, Quebec [*Library symbol*] [*National Library of Canada*]   (BIB)
QHR .... Quality History Record [*Nuclear energy*]   (NRCH)
QHR .... Queensland Historical Review [*A publication*]   (APTA)
QHS .... Qinghaosu [*Antimalarial drug*]
QHS .... Queen's Honorary Surgeon [*British*]
QHSA .... Societe d'Amenagement de l'Outaouais, Hull, Quebec [*Library symbol*] [*National Library of Canada*]   (NLC)
QHSC .... Centre Hospitalier Regional de l'Outaouais, Hull, Quebec [*Library symbol*] [*National Library of Canada*]   (NLC)
QHTA Bull ... QHTA [*Queensland History Teachers Association*] Bulletin [*A publication*]   (APTA)
QHU .... Universite du Quebec, Hull, Quebec [*Library symbol*] [*National Library of Canada*]   (NLC)
QHV .... Quiet Heavy Vehicle [*Automotive engineering*]
QI .... Cimber Air [*Denmark*] [*ICAO designator*]   (FAAC)
QI .... Quaderni Ibero-Americani [*A publication*]
QI .... Quaderni d'Italianistica [*A publication*]
QI .... Qualified Instructor [*British military*]   (DMA)
QI .... Quality Increase   (AABC)
QI .... Quality Index
QI .... Quantity Indicator   (KSC)
QI .... Quarterly Index [*A publication*]
QI .... Quasi-Inertial
QI .... Quota International   (EA)
QIA .... Quaderni Ibero-Americani [*A publication*]
QIA .... Quantitative Infrared Analysis
QIAET .... Quartzsite Integrated Acoustic and Engine Test Site
1QIaIQIsa ... Complete Isaiah Scroll from Qumran. Cave One   (BJA)
QIB .... Queensland Imperial Bushmen [*British military*]   (DMA)
QIB .... Quick Is Beautiful [*NASA project philosophy*]
QIBA .... Quaderni Italiani di Buenos Aires [*A publication*]
QIC .... Quality Information Center
QIC .... Quality Inspection Criteria
QIC .... Quarter Inch Cartridge [*Data processing*]
QIC .... Quarter-Inch Compatibility [*Format*]
QIC .... Quartz Iodine Crystal
QIC .... Queensland Industrial Commission [*Australia*]
QI Ct .... Queensland Industrial Court [*Australia*]
QID .... Quater in Die [*Four Times a Day*] [*Pharmacy*]
QIDN .... Queen's Institute of District Nursing [*British*]
QIE .... Quantitative Immunoelectrophoresis Methods [*Analytical biochemistry*]
QIEA .... Queensland Institute for Educational Administration [*Australia*]
QIE-AF ...... Qualified International Executive - Air Forwarding [*Designation awarded by American Society of International Executives, Inc.*]
QIE-EM .... Qualified International Executive - Export Management [*Designation awarded by American Society of International Executives, Inc.*]
QIE-F .... Qualified International Executive - Forwarding [*Designation awarded by American Society of International Executives, Inc.*]

QIER J ...... QIER [*Queensland Institute for Educational Research*] Journal [*A publication*] (APTA)
QIE-TM .... Qualified International Executive - Traffic Management [*Designation awarded by American Society of International Executives, Inc.*]
QIFL......... Quaderni. Istituto di Filologia Latina. Universita di Padova [*A publication*]
QIFMA...... Archives des Freres Maristes, Iberville, Quebec [*Library symbol*] [*National Library of Canada*] (NLC)
QIG............ Quaderni. Istituto di Glottologia [*Bologna*] [*A publication*]
QIG............ Queensland Industrial Gazette [*A publication*]
QIGB .... Quaderni. Istituto di Glottologia (Bologna) [*A publication*]
QIK .... Quick (MSA)
QIL .... Quad In-Line
QIL .... Quartz Incandescent Lamp
QIL .... Quartz Iodine Lamp
Q Illust ...... Quarterly Illustrator [*A publication*]
QILS......... Quantification of Integrated Logistics Support
QILT......... Pathe Computer Control Systems Corp. [*NASDAQ symbol*] (NQ)
QIMA .... QIMA. Institute of Municipal Administration, Queensland Division [*A publication*] (APTA)
QIMA .... Queensland Institute of Managerial Accountants [*Australia*]
Q Ind......... Queensland Industry [*A publication*] (APTA)
Q Industry ... Queensland Industry [*A publication*] (APTA)
3QInv .... [*The*] Copper Treasure Inventory Scroll from Qumran. Cave Three (BJA)
QIO............ Queue Input/Output
QIP .... PALINET [*Pennsylvania Area Library Network*] Central, Philadelphia, PA [*OCLC symbol*] (OCLC)
QIP .... Quality Improvement Process [*Chrysler Corp.*]
QIP .... Quality Inspection Point (KSC)
QIP .... Quarterly Intercession Paper [*A publication*] (ROG)
QIP .... Quarters Improvement Program (MCD)
QIP .... Quartz Insulation Part
QIP .... Quiescat in Pace [*May He, or She, Rest in Peace*] [*Latin*]
QIP Rep Natl Asphalt Pavement Assoc ... QIP Report. National Asphalt Pavement Association [*A publication*]
QISAM...... Queued Indexed Sequential Access Method [*IBM Corp.*] [*Data processing*]
QIT .... Quality Information and Test [*System*]
QITLJ........ Queensland Institute of Technology. Law Journal [*A publication*]
QJ .... Bibliotheque Municipale, Jonquiere, Quebec [*Library symbol*] [*National Library of Canada*] (BIB)
QJ .... Jordanian World Airways [*ICAO designator*] (FAAC)
QJ .... Quarterly Journal. Library of Congress [*A publication*]
QJ .... Quarterly Journal. University of North Dakota [*A publication*]
QJ .... Quick Junction [*Electronics*]
QJA .... Queensland Justices' Association [*Australia*]
QJAAA...... Queensland Journal of Agricultural and Animal Sciences [*A publication*]
QJ Agric Econ ... Quarterly Journal of Agricultural Economy [*A publication*]
Q Japan Com'l Arb Ass'n ... Quarterly. Japan Commercial Arbitration Association [*A publication*] (DLA)
QJBE......... Quarterly Journal of Business and Economics [*A publication*]
QJC............ College de Joliette, Quebec [*Library symbol*] [*National Library of Canada*] (NLC)
QJCA........ Quarterly Journal of Current Acquisitions [*A publication*]
QJCH .... Centre de Documentation, Departement de Sante Communautaire de Lanaudiere, Joliette, Quebec [*Library symbol*] [*National Library of Canada*] (BIB)
Q J Crude Drug Res ... Quarterly Journal of Crude Drug Research [*A publication*]
QJCSVA.... Archives Provinciales des Clercs de Saint-Viateur, Joliette, Quebec [*Library symbol*] [*National Library of Canada*] (NLC)
QJE........... Quarterly Journal of Economics [*A publication*]
Q J Econ .... Quarterly Journal of Economics [*A publication*]
QJ Eng Geol ... Quarterly Journal of Engineering Geology [*A publication*]
QJEPs .... Quarterly Journal of Experimental Psychology [*A publication*]
Q/JET .... Quadrajet Carburetor [*Automotive engineering*]
QJewR....... Quarterly Jewish Review [*A publication*]
QJewSt ...... Quarterly of Jewish Studies. Jewish Chronicle [*A publication*]
Q J Exp Physiol ... Quarterly Journal of Experimental Physiology and Cognate Medical Sciences [*A publication*]
Q J Exp Physiol Cogn Med Sci ... Quarterly Journal of Experimental Physiology and Cognate Medical Sciences [*A publication*]
Q J Exp Psy ... Quarterly Journal of Experimental Psychology [*A publication*]
Q J Exp Psychol ... Quarterly Journal of Experimental Psychology [*A publication*]
QJ Exp Psychol A Hum Exp Psychol ... Quarterly Journal of Experimental Psychology. A. Human Experimental Psychology [*A publication*]
Q J Exp Psychol B ... Quarterly Journal of Experimental Psychology. B. Comparative and Physiological Psychology [*A publication*]
QJ Exp Psychol B Comp Physiol Psychol ... Quarterly Journal of Experimental Psychology. B. Comparative and Physiological Psychology [*A publication*]
Q J Fla Acad Sci ... Quarterly Journal. Florida Academy of Sciences [*A publication*]

Q J For....... Quarterly Journal of Forestry [*A publication*]
Q J Forestry ... Quarterly Journal of Forestry [*A publication*]
Q J Geol Min Metall Soc (India) ... Quarterly Journal. Geological, Mining, and Metallurgical Society (India) [*A publication*]
Q J Geol Soc Lond ... Quarterly Journal. Geological Society of London [*A publication*]
Q J Geol Soc London ... Quarterly Journal. Geological Society of London [*A publication*]
QJH........... Centre Hospitalier Regional de Lanaudiere, Joliette, Quebec [*Library symbol*] [*National Library of Canada*] (NLC)
Q J Indian Chem Soc ... Quarterly Journal. Indian Chemical Society [*A publication*]
Q J Indian Inst Sci ... Quarterly Journal. Indian Institute of Science [*A publication*]
QJ Int Agric ... Quarterly Journal of International Agriculture [*A publication*]
QJJ .... Seminaire de Joliette, Quebec [*Library symbol*] [*National Library of Canada*] (NLC)
QJL........... Querner, J. L., San Antonio TX [*STAC*]
QJLC .... Quarterly Journal. Library of Congress [*A publication*]
Q J Lib Con ... Quarterly Journal. Library of Congress [*A publication*]
Q J Liverpool Univer Inst Commer Res Trop ... Quarterly Journal. Liverpool University Institute of Commercial Research in the Tropics [*A publication*]
Q Jl Microsc Sci ... Quarterly Journal of Microscopical Science [*A publication*]
Q J Local Self Govt Inst ... Quarterly Journal. Local Self-Government Institute [*Bombay*] [*A publication*]
Q Jl R Met Soc ... Quarterly Journal. Royal Meteorological Society [*A publication*]
Q Jl Rubb Res Inst Ceylon ... Quarterly Journal. Rubber Research Institute of Ceylon [*later, Sri Lanka*] [*A publication*]
QJLSGI.... Quarterly Journal. Local Self-Government Institute [*Bombay*] [*A publication*]
QJLSI........ Quarterly Journal. Local Self-Government Institute [*Bombay*] [*A publication*]
QJMA .... Musee d'Art de Joliette, Quebec [*Library symbol*] [*National Library of Canada*] (NLC)
Q J Math ... Quarterly Journal of Mathematics [*A publication*]
Q J Mech Ap ... Quarterly Journal of Mechanics and Applied Mathematics [*A publication*]
QJ Mech and Appl Math ... Quarterly Journal of Mechanics and Applied Mathematics [*A publication*]
QJ Mech Appl Math ... Quarterly Journal of Mechanics and Applied Mathematics [*A publication*]
Q J Med..... Quarterly Journal of Medicine [*A publication*]
Q J Micro Sc ... Quarterly Journal of Microscopical Science [*A publication*]
Q J Microsc Sci ... Quarterly Journal of Microscopical Science [*A publication*]
QJMP........ Queue Jump Command
QJMS........ Quarterly Journal. Mythic Society [*A publication*]
Q Jnl Speech ... Quarterly Journal of Speech [*A publication*]
QJOC .... College de Jonquiere, Quebec [*Library symbol*] [*National Library of Canada*] (NLC)
Q J Pakistan Lib Assn ... Quarterly Journal. Pakistan Library Association [*Karachi*] [*A publication*]
QJ Pharm Allied Sci ... Quarterly Journal of Pharmacy and Allied Sciences [*A publication*]
Q J Pharm Pharmacol ... Quarterly Journal of Pharmacy and Pharmacology [*A publication*]
QJP (Mag Cas) ... Queensland Justice of the Peace (Magisterial Cases) [*A publication*] (APTA)
QJPR......... Queensland Justice of the Peace. Reports [*A publication*] (APTA)
Q J Pub Speak ... Quarterly Journal of Public Speaking [*A publication*]
QJRAA...... Quarterly Journal. Royal Astronomical Society [*A publication*]
Q J R Astro ... Quarterly Journal. Royal Astronomical Society [*A publication*]
QJR Astron Soc ... Quarterly Journal. Royal Astronomical Society [*A publication*]
QJRMA..... Quarterly Journal. Royal Meteorological Society [*A publication*]
Q J R Meteo ... Quarterly Journal. Royal Meteorological Society [*A publication*]
Q J R Meteorol Soc ... Quarterly Journal. Royal Meteorological Society [*A publication*]
Q J Rubber Res Inst Sri Lanka ... Quarterly Journal. Rubber Research Institute of Sri Lanka [*formerly, Ceylon*] [*A publication*]
QJS........... Quarterly Journal of Speech [*A publication*]
Q J Sc .... Quarterly Journal of Science [*A publication*]
Q J Sc .... Quarterly Journal of Science, Literature, and the Arts [*A publication*]
QJ Sci Lit Arts ... Quarterly Journal of Science, Literature, and the Arts [*A publication*]
QJ Seismol ... Quarterly Journal of Seismology [*A publication*]
QJSp.......... Quarterly Journal of Speech [*A publication*]
QJSPA ...... Quarterly Journal of Speech [*A publication*]
Q J Speech ... Quarterly Journal of Speech [*A publication*]
Q J Stud Al ... Quarterly Journal of Studies on Alcohol [*A publication*]
Q J Stud Alcohol ... Quarterly Journal of Studies on Alcohol [*A publication*]
Q J Stud Alcohol Part A ... Quarterly Journal of Studies on Alcohol. Part A [*A publication*]
QJ Stud Alcohol Suppl ... Quarterly Journal of Studies on Alcohol. Supplement [*A publication*]

QJ Surg Sci ... Quarterly Journal of Surgical Sciences [*A publication*]
Q J Taiwan Mus (Taipei) ... Quarterly Journal. Taiwan Museum (Taipei) [*A publication*]
QJXPA ...... Quarterly Journal of Experimental Psychology [*A publication*]
QK .... Compagnie Aeromaritime [*France*] [*ICAO designator*] (FAAC)
QK .... Kirkland Municipal Library [*Bibliotheque Municipale de Kirkland*] Quebec [*Library symbol*] [*National Library of Canada*] (NLC)
QK .... Queen's Knight [*Chess*]
QK .... Quick (FAAC)
QKB .... Brome County Historical Society, Knowlton, Quebec [*Library symbol*] [*National Library of Canada*] (NLC)
QKBW .... Burroughs Wellcome & Co., Kirkland, Quebec [*Library symbol*] [*National Library of Canada*] (NLC)
QKC .... Aero Taxi Aviation, Inc. [*Lester, PA*] [*FAA designator*] (FAAC)
QKFL .... Quick Flashing Light [*Navigation signal*]
Qk Froz Fd ... Quick Frozen Foods [*A publication*]
QKITA .... Institut de Technologie Agricole, Kamouraska, Quebec [*Library symbol*] [*National Library of Canada*] (NLC)
QKL .... Cologne/Bonn-Main RR [*West Germany*] [*Airport symbol*] (OAG)
QKLN .... Laboratoires Nordic, Inc., Kirkland, Quebec [*Library symbol*] [*National Library of Canada*] (BIB)
QKPC .... Medical Library, Pfizer Canada, Inc., Kirkland, Quebec [*Library symbol*] [*National Library of Canada*] (NLC)
QKT .... Queen's Knight [*Chess*]
QL .... Ethyl 2-(Diisopropylamino)ethylmethylphosphonite [*See EDMP*] [*Army symbol*]
QL .... Lesotho Airways [*ICAO designator*] (FAAC)
QL .... Quad Left [*Typography*]
QL .... Quaderni Linguistici [*A publication*]
QL .... Quality of Living
QL .... Quantum Libet [*As Much as Is Desired*] [*Pharmacy*]
QL .... Quarrel (ROG)
QL .... Quartz-Locked
QL .... Quebec Law [*A publication*] (DLA)
QL .... Queen's Lancers [*Military unit*] [*British*]
QL .... Queensland Lawyer [*A publication*] (APTA)
QL .... Query Language [*Data processing*] (DIT)
QL .... Queue Length [*Telecommunications*] (TEL)
Q/L .... Quick Look (KSC)
QL .... Quintal [*Unit of weight*]
QL .... Quinzaine Litteraire [*A publication*]
QL .... Qumran Literature (BJA)
QLA .... Bibliotheque Municipale, Laval, Quebec [*Library symbol*] [*National Library of Canada*] (NLC)
QLA .... Lasham [*England*] [*Airport symbol*]
QLA/ABO ... Quebec Library Association/Association des Bibliothecaires du Quebec [*Canada*]
QLAB .... Quick Like a Bunny
QLAC .... CEGEP [*College d'Enseignement General et Professionnel*] Montmorency, Laval, Quebec [*Library symbol*] [*National Library of Canada*] (NLC)
QLACS ...... Cite de la Sante de Laval, Quebec [*Library symbol*] [*National Library of Canada*] (NLC)
QLACW .... Canadian Workplace Automation Research Centre [*Centre Canadien de Recherche sur l'Informatisation du Travail*] Laval, Quebec [*Library symbol*] [*National Library of Canada*] (NLC)
QLAG .... Research Station, Agriculture Canada [*Station de Recherches, Agriculture Canada*] Lennoxville, Quebec [*Library symbol*] [*National Library of Canada*] (NLC)
QLAH .... Lennoxville-Ascot Historical Society Museum, Lennoxville, Quebec [*Library symbol*] [*National Library of Canada*] (NLC)
QLAID ...... Ateliers d'Ingenierie Dominion, Lachine, Quebec [*Library symbol*] [*National Library of Canada*] (NLC)
QLAP .... Quick Look Analysis Program
QLAR .... Canadian Arsenals Ltd. [*Arsenaux Canada Ltee.*], Le Gardeur, Quebec [*Library symbol*] [*National Library of Canada*] (BIB)
QLASC ...... College de l'Assomption, Quebec [*Library symbol*] [*National Library of Canada*] (NLC)
QLASGPT ... Federal Training Centre, Penitentiary, Ministry of the Solicitor General [*Centre Federal de Formation, Penitencier, Ministere du Solliciteur General*] Laval, Quebec [*Library symbol*] [*National Library of Canada*] (NLC)
QLAVD ..... Centre de Documentation, Assurance-Vie Desjardins, Levis, Quebec [*Library symbol*] [*National Library of Canada*] (NLC)
Q Law Soc J ... Queensland Law Society. Journal [*A publication*] (APTA)
QLB .... Bishop's University, Lennoxville, Quebec [*Library symbol*] [*National Library of Canada*] (NLC)
QL Beor ..... Beor's Queensland Law Reports [*A publication*] (APTA)
QLBG .... Department of Geography, Bishop's University, Lennoxville, Quebec [*Library symbol*] [*National Library of Canada*] (NLC)
QLC .... College de Levis, Quebec [*Library symbol*] [*National Library of Canada*] (NLC)
QLC .... Quasi-Liquid Crystal [*Organic chemistry*]

QLCCP ...... Service de Documentation et de Reference, Confederation des Caisses Populaires et d'Economie Desjardins du Quebec, Levis, Quebec [*Library symbol*] [*National Library of Canada*] (NLC)
QLCLL .... CEGEP [*College d'Enseignement General et Professionnel*] de Levis-Lauzon, Lauzon, Quebec [*Library symbol*] [*National Library of Canada*] (BIB)
QLCR .... Queensland Land Court Reports [*A publication*] (APTA)
QLCRS .... Conseil Regional de la Sante et des Services Sociaux, Longueuil, Quebec [*Library symbol*] [*National Library of Canada*] (NLC)
QLCS .... Quick Look and Checkout System
QLD .... Queen's Light Dragoons [*British military*] (DMA)
QLD .... Queensland [*Australia*]
QLD .... Quillo Resources, Inc. [*Vancouver Stock Exchange symbol*]
QLDC .... Delmar Chemicals, La Salle, Quebec [*Library symbol*] [*National Library of Canada*] (NLC)
Qlder .... Queenslander [*Australia*]
Qld Geog J ... Queensland Geographical Journal [*A publication*] (APTA)
Qld Govt Indust Gaz ... Queensland Government Industrial Gazette [*A publication*] (APTA)
Qld Health ... Queensland's Health [*A publication*] (APTA)
Qld Heritage ... Queensland Heritage [*A publication*] (APTA)
Qld Ind ...... Queensland Industry [*A publication*]
Qld Law ...... Queensland Lawyer [*A publication*]
Qld Mus Mem ... Queensland Museum. Memoirs [*A publication*] (APTA)
Qld Nat ...... Queensland Naturalist [*A publication*] (APTA)
Qld Nurs ...... Queensland Nurse [*A publication*]
Qld Parl Deb ... Queensland Parliamentary Debates [*A publication*] (APTA)
QLDR .... Quick Look Data Reference (NASA)
QLDS .... Quick Look Data Station [*NASA*] (KSC)
Qld Sci Teach ... Queensland Science Teacher [*A publication*] (APTA)
Qld Teach J ... Queensland Teachers' Journal [*A publication*] (APTA)
Qld Univ Law J ... University of Queensland. Law Journal [*A publication*] (APTA)
QLE .... Bibliotheque Municipale, Levis, Quebec [*Library symbol*] [*National Library of Canada*] (NLC)
QLFCAE ... Fonds de Recherches Forestieres. Universite Laval. Contribution [*A publication*]
QLFCP .... Federation des Caisses Populaires Desjardins, Levis, Quebec [*Library symbol*] [*National Library of Canada*] (NLC)
QLFD .... Qualified (KSC)
QLFECA ... Archives des Freres des Ecoles Chretiennes, Ville de Laval, Quebec [*Library symbol*] [*National Library of Canada*] (NLC)
QLFY .... Qualify (FAAC)
QLG .... Quick-Look Guide
QLHD .... Hotel-Dieu de Levis, Quebec [*Library symbol*] [*National Library of Canada*] (NLC)
QLI .... Quality of Life Index
Q Lib .... Quantum Libet [*As Much as You Please*] [*Pharmacy*]
Q Liberal .... Queensland Liberal [*A publication*] (APTA)
QLing .... Quantitative Linguistics [*A publication*]
Q-Link .... QuantumLink [*Quantum Computer Services, Inc.*] [*Vienna, VA*] [*Information service or system*] (IID)
QLIRS .... Queensland Legal Information Retrieval System [*Australia*]
QLISP .... [*A*] programming language (CSR)
QLit .... Quebec. Litteraire [*A publication*]
QLIT .... Quick Look Intermediate Tape
Q LJ .... Queen's Law Journal [*A publication*]
QLJ .... Queensland Law Journal [*A publication*] (APTA)
QLJ (NC) .. Queensland Law Journal (Notes of Cases) [*A publication*] (APTA)
QLL .... Quaderni di Lingue e Letterature [*A publication*]
QLL .... Quartz Landing Lamp [*Aviation*]
QLM .... Bibliotheque Municipale de Lachine, Quebec [*Library symbol*] [*National Library of Canada*] (NLC)
QLM .... Quasi-Linear Machine
QLNLB ...... Institut Nazareth et Louis-Braille, Longueuil, Quebec [*Library symbol*] [*National Library of Canada*] (NLC)
QLO .... Bibliotheque Municipale, Longueuil, Quebec [*Library symbol*] [*National Library of Canada*] (NLC)
QLOCE ..... College Edouard-Montpetit, Longueuil, Quebec [*Library symbol*] [*National Library of Canada*] (NLC)
QLOCSS ... Centre de Services Sociaux Richelieu, Longueuil, Quebec [*Library symbol*] [*National Library of Canada*] (NLC)
QLOPB ...... Centre de Documentation, Centre Hospitalier Pierre Boucher, Longueuil, Quebec [*Library symbol*] [*National Library of Canada*] (NLC)
QLOU .... Pratt & Whitney Aircraft Ltd., Longueuil, Quebec [*Library symbol*] [*National Library of Canada*] (NLC)
QLP .... Quality Low-Priced [*Art series*]
QLP .... Query Language Processor [*Data processing*]
QLP .... Questions Liturgiques et Paroissiales [*A publication*]
QLP .... Quinoxaline Ladder Polymer [*Organic chemistry*]
QLPED .... Pylon Electronic Development Co. Ltd., Lachine, Quebec [*Library symbol*] [*National Library of Canada*] (NLC)
QLPS .... Petro-Sun International, Inc., Longueuil, Quebec [*Library symbol*] [*National Library of Canada*] (NLC)
QLR .... Quebec Law Reports
QLR .... Queen's Lancashire Regiment [*Military unit*] [*British*]

QLR .... Queensland Law Reporter [*A publication*] (APTA)
QLR .... Queensland Law Reports [*A publication*] (APTA)
QL(R)........ Quick Look (Report)
QLR (Beor) ... Queensland Law Reports (Beor) [*A publication*] (APTA)
QL Rev...... Quarterly Law Review [*A publication*] (DLA)
QLS............ Bibliotheque Municipale, La Salle, Quebec [*Library symbol*] [*National Library of Canada*] (NLC)
QLS............ Quasi-Elastic Light Scattering [*Also, QELS, QUELS*] [*Physics*]
QLS............ Quick Look Station [*NASA*] (MCD)
QLSA......... Queue Line Sharing Adapter [*Data processing*]
QLSAA...... Archives des Soeurs de Sainte-Anne, Lachine, Quebec [*Library symbol*] [*National Library of Canada*] (NLC)
QLSD........ Societe de Developpement International Desjardins, Levis, Quebec [*Library symbol*] [*National Library of Canada*] (BIB)
QLSE........ ESSO Building Products of Canada Ltd., La Salle, Quebec [*Library symbol*] [*National Library of Canada*] (NLC)
QLSHG ..... Bibliotheque Medicale, Hopital General La Salle, Quebec [*Library symbol*] [*National Library of Canada*] (NLC)
QLSJ .... Queensland Law Society. Journal [*A publication*] (APTA)
QLSM........ Quasi-Linear Sequential Machine
QLSO .... L'Octogone, Centre de la Culture, La Salle, Quebec [*Library symbol*] [*National Library of Canada*] (NLC)
QL Soc J .... Queensland Law Society. Journal [*A publication*]
QLSS........ Research Department, J. E. Seagram & Sons Ltd., La Salle, Quebec [*Library symbol*] [*National Library of Canada*] (NLC)
QLT .... Bibliotheque Municipale, La Tuque, Quebec [*Library symbol*] [*National Library of Canada*] (NLC)
QLT .... Quadra Logic Technologies, Inc. [*Vancouver Stock Exchange symbol*] [*Toronto Stock Exchange symbol*]
QLT .... Quantitative Leak Test
QLT .... Quasi-Linear Theory
QLTI.......... Quadra Logic Technologies, Incorporated [*NASDAQ symbol*] (NQ)
QLTV .... LTV Corp. [*Formerly, Ling-Temco-Vought, Inc.*] [*NYSE symbol*] (SPSG)
QLTY........ Quality (AFM)
QLTY........ Quality Mills, Inc. [*NASDAQ symbol*] (NQ)
QLTYCONO ... Quality Control Officer [*Military*]
Qly Land R ... Fitzgibbon's Irish Land Reports [*A publication*] (DLA)
QM .... Air Malawi [*ICAO designator*] (FAAC)
QM .... Bulgaria [*License plate code assigned to foreign diplomats in the US*]
QM .... Quadrature Modulation
QM .... Qualification Motor (MCD)
QM .... Quality Manual [*A publication*] (MCD)
QM .... Quality Memorandum
QM .... Quality of Merit
QM .... Quality Motels (EA)
QM .... Quantitative Methods
QM .... Quantum Mechanics
QM .... Quaque Matin [*Every Morning*] [*Pharmacy*]
QM .... Quarterly Meetings [*Quakers*]
QM .... Quarterly Memorandum
QM .... Quartermaster [*Military*] (AFM)
QM .... Queen Mother [*British*]
QM .... Queen's Messenger [*British*]
QM .... Queensland Museum [*Australia*]
QM .... Query Module (MCD)
QM .... Queue Manager [*Data processing*] (CMD)
QM .... Quinacrine Mustard [*Chromosome stain*]
QM .... Quinonemethide [*Organic chemistry*]
QM .... Qumran Manuscripts (BJA)
QM .... Quo Modo [*In What Manner*] [*Latin*]
1QM .... Milchemet, the War of the Sons of Light and the Sons of Darkness from Qumran. Cave One (BJA)
QM1 .... Quartermaster, First Class [*Navy rating*]
QM2 .... Quartermaster, Second Class [*Navy rating*]
QM3 .... Quartermaster, Third Class [*Navy rating*]
QMA.......... Group Information Centre, Alcan Aluminum Ltd. [*Centre d'Information du Groupe, Alcan Aluminium Ltee*] Montreal, Quebec [*Library symbol*] [*National Library of Canada*] (NLC)
QMA.......... Qualified Military Available
QMA.......... Qualitative Materiel Approach [*Army*] (AABC)
QMA.......... Quartermasters Association [*Later, ALA*]
QMAA....... Archives de la Chancellerie, L'Archeveche de Montreal, Quebec [*Library symbol*] [*National Library of Canada*] (NLC)
QMAA....... Queensland Motel and Accommodation Association [*Australia*]
QMAAC.... Queen Mary's Army Auxiliary Corps [*The WAAC*] [*British*]
QMAB....... Montreal Association for the Blind, Quebec [*Library symbol*] [*National Library of Canada*] (NLC)
QMABB .... TECSULT, Montreal, Quebec [*Library symbol*] [*National Library of Canada*] (NLC)
QMAC....... Macdonald College Library, Ste-Anne-De-Bellevue, Quebec [*Library symbol*] [*National Library of Canada*] (NLC)
QMAC....... Quadripartite Materiel and Agreements Committee [*Military*] (AABC)

QMACL .... Quebec Association for Children with Learning Disabilities [*Association Quebecoise pour les Enfants Souffrant de Troubles d'Apprentissage*] Montreal, Quebec [*Library symbol*] [*National Library of Canada*] (NLC)
QMACM ... Centre des Dossiers et de Documentation, Direction de Montreal, Ministere des Affaires Culturelles du Quebec [*Library symbol*] [*National Library of Canada*] (BIB)
QMACN.... Archives de la Congregation de Notre-Dame, Montreal, Quebec [*Library symbol*] [*National Library of Canada*] (NLC)
QMADMA ... Archives, Diocese of Montreal, Anglican Church of Canada, Quebec [*Library symbol*] [*National Library of Canada*] (NLC)
QMAE....... Aviation Electric Ltd., Montreal, Quebec [*Library symbol*] [*National Library of Canada*] (NLC)
QMAEC .... Atomic Energy of Canada [*L'Energie Atomique du Canada*] Montreal, Quebec [*Library symbol*] [*National Library of Canada*] (NLC)
QMAGB.... Bibliotheque Municipale, Magog, Quebec [*Library symbol*] [*National Library of Canada*] (NLC)
Q(Maint) ... Quartermaster Maintenance [*World War II*]
QMAL....... Air Liquide Canada Ltee., Montreal, Quebec [*Library symbol*] [*National Library of Canada*] (NLC)
QMALL..... Abbott Laboratories Limited, Montreal, Quebec [*Library symbol*] [*National Library of Canada*] (NLC)
QMAM...... Allan Memorial Institute, Montreal, Quebec [*Library symbol*] [*National Library of Canada*] (NLC)
QMAMA... Lavalin Environnement, Montreal, Quebec [*Library symbol*] [*National Library of Canada*] (NLC)
QMAMI.... Minerais LAC Ltee., Malartic, Quebec [*Library symbol*] [*National Library of Canada*] (NLC)
QMAO ...... Qualified for Mobilization Ashore Only [*Navy*]
QMAPO.... Centre de Documentation, APO Quebec, Montreal, Quebec [*Library symbol*] [*National Library of Canada*] (NLC)
QMAPS.... Quebec Aid for the Partially-Sighted [*Aide aux Insuffisants Visuels du Quebec*] Montreal, Quebec [*Library symbol*] [*National Library of Canada*] (NLC)
QMARC.... Archives Provinciales des Capucins, Montreal, Quebec [*Library symbol*] [*National Library of Canada*] (NLC)
QMAS....... Archives du Seminaire de Saint-Sulpice, Montreal, Quebec [*Library symbol*] [*National Library of Canada*] (NLC)
QMASBB ... ASEA [*Allmaenna Svenska Elektriska Aktiebolaget*] Brown Boveri, Inc., Montreal, Quebec [*Library symbol*] [*National Library of Canada*] (BIB)
QMASC.... Bibliotheque Municipale, Mascouche, Quebec [*Library symbol*] [*National Library of Canada*] (BIB)
QMASRC ... Space Research Corp., Mansonville, Quebec [*Library symbol*] [*National Library of Canada*] (NLC)
QMASSAS ... Centre de Documentation, Secteur Affaires Sociales, Association pour la Sante et la Securite du Travail, Montreal, Quebec [*Library symbol*] [*National Library of Canada*] (NLC)
Q Master Plumber ... Queensland Master Plumber [*A publication*] (APTA)
QMATC .... College de Matane, Quebec [*Library symbol*] [*National Library of Canada*] (NLC)
QMAV...... Bibliotheque des Avocats, Barreau de Montreal, Quebec [*Library symbol*] [*National Library of Canada*] (NLC)
QMAX...... Qmax Technology Group, Inc. [*Dayton, OH*] [*NASDAQ symbol*] (NQ)
QMAY...... Ayerst, McKenna & Harrison, Inc. Montreal, Quebec [*Library symbol*] [*National Library of Canada*] (NLC)
QMB.......... Information Resource Centre, Bell Canada [*Centre d'Information Specialisee, Bell Canada*], Montreal, Quebec [*Library symbol*] [*National Library of Canada*] (NLC)
QMB.......... Qualified Mortgage Bond
QMB.......... Queensbury [*England*] [*Seismograph station code, US Geological Survey*] (SEIS)
QMB.......... Quick Make-and-Break [*Contact*] (DEN)
QMBA...... Ecole des Beaux-Arts, Montreal, Quebec [*Library symbol*] [*National Library of Canada*] (NLC)
QMBAE .... Bristol Aero Engines Ltd., Montreal, Quebec [*Library symbol*] [*National Library of Canada*] (NLC)
QMBAN.... Centre de Documentation, Banque Nationale du Canada, Montreal, Quebec [*Library symbol*] [*National Library of Canada*] (NLC)
QMBB ...... College Bois-De-Boulogne, Montreal, Quebec [*Library symbol*] [*National Library of Canada*] (NLC)
QMBBL.... Beauchemin, Beaton, Lapointe, Inc., Montreal, Quebec [*Library symbol*] [*National Library of Canada*] (NLC)
QMBC....... Byers, Casgrain, Montreal, Quebec [*Library symbol*] [*National Library of Canada*] (BIB)
QMBD...... Translation Bureau, Canada Department of the Secretary of State [*Bureau des Traductions, Secretariat d'Etat*] Montreal, Quebec [*Library symbol*] [*National Library of Canada*] (NLC)
QMBE ...... Centre de Documentation, Bureau des Economies d'Energie du Quebec, Montreal, Quebec [*Library symbol*] [*National Library of Canada*] (NLC)
QMBGC.... Bibliotheque d'Ingenierie, BG Checo International Ltee., Montreal, Quebec [*Library symbol*] [*National Library of Canada*] (NLC)

QMBIM .... Bio-Mega, Inc., Montreal, Quebec [*Library symbol*] [*National Library of Canada*]　(NLC)

QMBL .... Law Library, Bell Canada, Montreal, Quebec [*Library symbol*] [*National Library of Canada*]　(NLC)

QMBM ...... Bibliotheque de la Ville de Montreal, Quebec [*Library symbol*] [*National Library of Canada*]　(NLC)

QMBMO... Bank of Montreal [*Banque de Montreal*], Quebec [*Library symbol*] [*National Library of Canada*]　(NLC)

QMBMS ... Management Sciences Library, Bell Canada, Montreal, Quebec [*Library symbol*] [*Obsolete*] [*National Library of Canada*]　(NLC)

QMBN .... Bibliotheque Nationale du Quebec, Montreal, Quebec [*Library symbol*] [*National Library of Canada*]　(NLC)

QMBNR .... Bell Northern Research, Montreal, Quebec [*Library symbol*] [*National Library of Canada*]　(NLC)

QMBP .... Building Products Ltd., Montreal, Quebec [*Library symbol*] [*National Library of Canada*]　(NLC)

QMBR .... Bio-Research Laboratories Ltd., Pointe-Claire, Quebec [*Library symbol*] [*National Library of Canada*]　(NLC)

QMBT .... Montreal Board of Trade [*Chambre de Commerce du District de Montreal*] Quebec [*Library symbol*] [*National Library of Canada*]　(NLC)

QMC......... Chief Quartermaster [*Navy rating*]

QMC......... College de Montreal, Quebec [*Library symbol*] [*National Library of Canada*]　(NLC)

QMC......... James Carson Breckinridge Library, Quantico, VA [*OCLC symbol*]　(OCLC)

QMC......... Quadripartite Materiel Committee [*Military*]

QMC......... Quartermaster Clerk [*Marine Corps*]

QMC......... Quartermaster Corps [*Army*]

QMC......... Queen Mary College [*London*]

QMC......... Quick Modification Concept　(MCD)

QMCA .... Engineering Library, Canadair Ltd., Montreal, Quebec [*Library symbol*] [*National Library of Canada*]　(NLC)

QMCAD.... Centre d'Animation, de Developpement, et de Recherche en Education, Montreal, Quebec [*Library symbol*] [*National Library of Canada*]　(NLC)

QMCADM ... Centre d'Accueil Domremy-Montreal, Ste.-Genevieve, Quebec [*Library symbol*] [*National Library of Canada*]　(NLC)

QMCADQ ... Conservatoire d'Art Dramatique de Montreal, Quebec [*Library symbol*] [*National Library of Canada*]　(NLC)

QMCAE .... CAE Electronics Ltd., Montreal, Quebec [*Library symbol*] [*National Library of Canada*]　(NLC)

QMCAG.... College Andre Grasset, Montreal, Quebec [*Library symbol*] [*National Library of Canada*]　(NLC)

QMCAI ..... Canadian Asbestos Information Centre [*Centre Canadien d'Information sur l'Amiante*] Montreal, Quebec [*Library symbol*] [*National Library of Canada*]　(NLC)

QMCAR .... Carmel de Montreal, Quebec [*Library symbol*] [*National Library of Canada*]　(NLC)

QMCAT .... Commission de la Sante et de la Securite du Travail du Quebec, Montreal [*Library symbol*] [*National Library of Canada*]　(NLC)

QMCAV .... Direction Generale du Cinema et de l'Audio-Visuel, Ministere des Communications du Quebec, Montreal, Quebec [*Library symbol*] [*National Library of Canada*]　(NLC)

QMCB .... Canadian Broadcasting Corp. [*Societe Radio-Canada*] Montreal, Quebec [*Library symbol*] [*National Library of Canada*]　(NLC)

QMCBE .... Engineering Headquarters, Canadian Broadcasting Corp. [*Service de l'Ingenierie, Societe Radio-Canada*] Montreal, Quebec [*Library symbol*] [*National Library of Canada*]　(NLC)

QMCBH.... Catherine Booth Hospital, Montreal, Quebec [*Library symbol*] [*National Library of Canada*]　(NLC)

QMCBM ... Music Library, Canadian Broadcasting Corp. [*Musicotheque et Discotheque, Societe Radio-Canada*], Montreal, Quebec [*Library symbol*] [*National Library of Canada*]　(BIB)

QMCC .... Canada Cement Co., Montreal, Quebec [*Library symbol*] [*National Library of Canada*]　(NLC)

QMCC .... Queensland Multicultural Co-Ordinating Committee [*Australia*]

QMCCA .... Centre Canadien d'Architecture [*Canadian Centre for Architecture*] Montreal, Quebec [*Library symbol*] [*National Library of Canada*]　(NLC)

QMCCL..... Currie, Coopers & Lybrand Ltd., Montreal, Quebec [*Library symbol*] [*National Library of Canada*]　(NLC)

QMCCR .... Canadian Council of Resource Ministers [*Conseil Canadien des Ministres des Ressources*] Montreal, Quebec [*Library symbol*] [*National Library of Canada*]　(NLC)

QMCCS.... Centraide, Montreal, Quebec [*Library symbol*] [*National Library of Canada*]　(NLC)

QMCD....... Centre Documentaire, Centrale des Bibliotheques, Montreal, Quebec [*Library symbol*] [*National Library of Canada*]　(NLC)

QMCDM... College de Maisonneuve, Montreal, Quebec [*Library symbol*] [*National Library of Canada*]　(NLC)

QMCDP .... Caisse de Depot et Placement du Quebec, Montreal, Quebec [*Library symbol*] [*National Library of Canada*]　(NLC)

QMCE .... Celanese Canada Ltd., Montreal, Quebec [*Library symbol*] [*National Library of Canada*]　(NLC)

QMCEA .... Canadian Export Association [*Association Canadienne d'Exportation*] Montreal, Quebec [*Library symbol*] [*National Library of Canada*]　(NLC)

QMCEC .... Catholic School Commission [*Commission des Ecoles Catholiques*] Montreal, Quebec [*Library symbol*] [*National Library of Canada*]　(NLC)

QMCECI... Centre Canadien d'Etudes et de Cooperation Internationale, Montreal, Quebec [*Library symbol*] [*National Library of Canada*]　(NLC)

QMCED .... Centre de Documentation, Ministere du Commerce Exterieur et du Developpement Technologique du Quebec, Montreal, Quebec [*Library symbol*] [*National Library of Canada*]　(BIB)

QMCF .... Merck Frosst Laboratories [*Laboratoires Merck Frosst*] Montreal, Quebec [*Library symbol*] [*National Library of Canada*]　(NLC)

QMCFH .... Centre de Documentation, Charette, Fortier, Hawey, Touche, Ross, Montreal, Quebec [*Library symbol*] [*National Library of Canada*]　(NLC)

QMCGW... Clarkson, Gordon, Woods, Gordon, Montreal, Quebec [*Library symbol*] [*National Library of Canada*]　(NLC)

QMCHC.... Montreal Chest Hospital Centre [*Centre Hospitalier Thoracique de Montreal*] Quebec [*Library symbol*] [*National Library of Canada*]　(NLC)

QMCHF .... Centre de Documentation, Centre Hospitalier Fleury, Montreal, Quebec [*Library symbol*] [*National Library of Canada*]　(NLC)

QMCHL.... Centre Hospitalier de Lachine, Montreal, Quebec [*Library symbol*] [*National Library of Canada*]　(NLC)

QMCICM ... Centre Interculturel Monchanin, Montreal, Quebec [*Library symbol*] [*National Library of Canada*]　(NLC)

QMCIH..... Bibliotheque de Documentation des Archives, Ville de Montreal, Quebec [*Library symbol*] [*National Library of Canada*]　(NLC)

QMCIM .... Canadian Institute of Mining and Metallurgy [*Institut Canadien des Mines et de la Metallurgie*] Montreal, Quebec [*Library symbol*] [*National Library of Canada*]　(NLC)

QMC-IRL ... Queen Mary College Industrial Research Ltd. [*British*]　(IRUK)

QMCJ........ Canadian Jewish Congress [*Congres Juif Canadien*] Montreal, Quebec [*Library symbol*] [*National Library of Canada*]　(NLC)

QMCL .... CanAtom Ltd., Montreal, Quebec [*Library symbol*] [*National Library of Canada*]　(NLC)

QMCLG .... College Lionel Groulx, Ste-Therese, Quebec [*Library symbol*] [*National Library of Canada*]　(NLC)

QMCLK .... Quartermaster Clerk [*Navy rating*]

QMCM...... Canadian Marconi Co., Montreal, Quebec [*Library symbol*] [*National Library of Canada*]　(NLC)

QMCM...... Master Chief Quartermaster [*Navy rating*]

QMCM...... Quartermaster Corporal-Major [*British military*]　(DMA)

QMCN....... Canadian National Railways [*Chemins de fer Nationaux du Canada*] Montreal, Quebec [*Library symbol*] [*National Library of Canada*]　(NLC)

QMCNC.... Chemical Library, Canadian National Railways [*Bibliotheque Chimique, Chemins de fer Nationaux du Canada*] Montreal, Quebec [*Library symbol*] [*Obsolete*] [*National Library of Canada*]　(NLC)

QMCOM... Conservatoire de Musique de Montreal, Quebec [*Library symbol*] [*National Library of Canada*]　(NLC)

QMCP .... Canadian Pacific Ltd. [*Le Canadien Pacifique*] Montreal, Quebec [*Library symbol*] [*National Library of Canada*]　(NLC)

QMCQ....... Cinematheque Quebecoise, Montreal, Quebec [*Library symbol*] [*National Library of Canada*]　(BIB)

QMCR .... Canadian Copper Refiners Ltd., Montreal, Quebec [*Library symbol*] [*National Library of Canada*]　(NLC)

QMCR .... Quartermaster Corps Regulations [*Army*]

QMCRI ..... Centre de Recherche Industrielle du Quebec, Montreal, Quebec [*Library symbol*] [*National Library of Canada*]　(NLC)

QMCRIM ... Centre de Documentation, Centre de Recherche Informatique de Montreal, Quebec [*Library symbol*] [*National Library of Canada*]　(BIB)

QMCRP .... Conference des Recteurs et des Principaux des Universites du Quebec, Montreal, Quebec [*Library symbol*] [*National Library of Canada*]　(NLC)

QMCS .... Christian Science Reading Room, Montreal, Quebec [*Library symbol*] [*National Library of Canada*]　(NLC)

QMCS .... Quality Monitoring Control System [*Military*]　(CAAL)

QMCS .... Senior Chief Quartermaster [*Navy rating*]

QMCSCA ... Archives de la Congregation de Sainte-Croix, Montreal, Quebec [*Library symbol*] [*National Library of Canada*]　(NLC)

QMC & SO ... Quartermaster Cataloging and Standardization Office [*Army*]

QMCSSMM ... CSSMM [*Centre de Services Sociaux du Montreal Metropolitain*], Montreal, Quebec [*Library symbol*] [*National Library of Canada*]　(NLC)

QMCSSS... Service de Reference, Conseil de la Sante et des Services Sociaux de la Region de Montreal Metropolitain, Montreal, Quebec [*Library symbol*] [*National Library of Canada*]　(NLC)

QMCSVA ... Archives des Clercs de Saint-Viateur, Province de Montreal, Outremont, Quebec [*Library symbol*] [*National Library of Canada*]　(NLC)

QMCT .... Commission de Transport de la Communaute Urbaine de Montreal, Quebec [*Library symbol*] [*National Library of Canada*] (NLC)

QMCT .... QMC Technology, Inc. [*NASDAQ symbol*] (NQ)

QMCTC .... Quartermaster Corps Technical Committee [*Army*]

QMCTM ... Canadian Tobacco Manufacturers' Council [*Conseil Canadien des Fabricants des Produits du Tabac*] Montreal, Quebec [*Library symbol*] [*National Library of Canada*] (NLC)

QMCVDDH ... Que Me - Comite Vietnam pour la Defense des Droits de l'Homme [*Que Me - Vietnam Committee on Human Rights*] (EAIO)

QMCVM ... Commission des Valeurs Mobilieres du Quebec, Montreal, Quebec [*Library symbol*] [*National Library of Canada*] (NLC)

QMCW ...... Canada Wire & Cable Co. Ltd., Montreal, Quebec [*Library symbol*] [*National Library of Canada*] (NLC)

QMD .... Institut Genealogique Drouin, Montreal, Quebec [*Library symbol*] [*National Library of Canada*] (NLC)

QMDA....... Daniel Arbour & Associes, Montreal, Quebec [*Library symbol*] [*National Library of Canada*] (NLC)

QMDB....... College Jean-De-Brebeuf, Montreal, Quebec [*Library symbol*] [*National Library of Canada*] (NLC)

QMDC....... Dawson College, Montreal, Quebec [*Library symbol*] [*National Library of Canada*] (NLC)

QMDE....... Dominion Engineering Works Ltd., Montreal, Quebec [*Library symbol*] [*National Library of Canada*] (NLC)

QMDEP .... Quartermaster Depot [*Army*]

QMDH ...... Douglas Hospital Centre [*Centre Hospitalier Douglas*] Montreal, Quebec [*Library symbol*] [*National Library of Canada*] (NLC)

QMDK....... Quick Mechanical Disconnect Kit

QMDL....... Domtar Limited, Montreal, Quebec [*Library symbol*] [*National Library of Canada*] (NLC)

QMDM ..... Montreal Association for the Mentally Retarded [*Association de Montreal pour les Deficients Mentaux*] Quebec [*Library symbol*] [*National Library of Canada*] (NLC)

QMDMR... Groupe DMR, Inc., Montreal, Quebec [*Library symbol*] [*National Library of Canada*] (BIB)

QMDO ...... Qualitative Materiel Development Objective [*Army*]

QMDOM .. Dominion Bridge Co. Ltd., Montreal, Quebec [*Library symbol*] [*National Library of Canada*] (NLC)

QMDPC .... Quartermaster Data Processing Center [*Army*]

QMDT....... Dominion Textile, Montreal, Quebec [*Library symbol*] [*National Library of Canada*] (NLC)

QME......... Quarber Merkur [*A publication*]

QMEA....... Atmospheric Environment Service, Environment Canada [*Service de l'Environnement Atmospherique, Environnement Canada*] Dorval, Quebec [*Library symbol*] [*National Library of Canada*] (NLC)

QMEC....... Monenco Consultants Ltd., Montreal, Quebec [*Library symbol*] [*National Library of Canada*] (NLC)

QMECB .... Centrale des Bibliotheques, Services Documentaires Multimedia, Inc., Montreal, Quebec [*Library symbol*] [*National Library of Canada*] (NLC)

QMECS..... Experts-Conseils Shawinigan, Montreal, Quebec [*Library symbol*] [*National Library of Canada*] (NLC)

QMED....... Quest Medical, Inc. [*NASDAQ symbol*] (NQ)

Q Med Rev ... Quarterly Medical Review [*A publication*]

QMEE .... Environmental Protection Service, Environment Canada [*Service de la Protection de l'Environnement, Environnement Canada*] Montreal, Quebec [*Library symbol*] [*National Library of Canada*] (NLC)

QMEM ...... Bibliotheque Municipale de la Ville de Montreal-Est, Quebec [*Library symbol*] [*National Library of Canada*] (BIB)

QMEN....... Ministere de l'Environnement, Montreal, Quebec [*Library symbol*] [*National Library of Canada*] (NLC)

QMENT .... National Theatre School [*Ecole Nationale de Theatre*] Montreal, Quebec [*Library symbol*] [*National Library of Canada*] (NLC)

QMEP .... Ecole Polytechnique, Montreal, Quebec [*Library symbol*] [*National Library of Canada*] (NLC)

QMEPCC ... Quartermaster Equipment and Parts Commodity Center [*Army*]

QMERS..... E. R. Squibb & Sons Ltd., Montreal, Quebec [*Library symbol*] [*National Library of Canada*] (NLC)

QMES .... Ecole Secondaire Saint-Stanislas, Montreal, Quebec [*Library symbol*] [*National Library of Canada*] (NLC)

QMF......... Fraser-Hickson Institute, Montreal, Quebec [*Library symbol*] [*National Library of Canada*] (NLC)

QMF......... Query Management Facility [*Database*] (BYTE)

QMFA .... Montreal Museum of Fine Arts [*Musee des Beaux-Arts de Montreal*] Quebec [*Library symbol*] [*National Library of Canada*] (NLC)

QMFAC .... Farinon Canada, Dorval, Quebec [*Library symbol*] [*National Library of Canada*] (NLC)

QMFBD .... Federal Business Development Bank [*Banque Federale de Developpement*] Montreal, Quebec [*Library symbol*] [*National Library of Canada*] (NLC)

QMFC .... First Church of Christ, Scientist, Montreal, Quebec [*Library symbol*] [*National Library of Canada*] (NLC)

QMFCIAF ... Quartermaster Food and Container Institute for the Armed Forces

QMFCJ ..... Bibliotheque de Theologie, les Facultes de la Compagnie de Jesus, Montreal, Quebec [*Library symbol*] [*National Library of Canada*] (NLC)

QMFER..... Forest Engineering Research Institute of Canada [*Institut Canadien de Recherches en Genie Forestier*] Pointe-Claire, Quebec [*Library symbol*] [*National Library of Canada*] (NLC)

QMFH....... Frank W. Horner Ltd., Montreal, Quebec [*Library symbol*] [*National Library of Canada*] (NLC)

QMFMO... Federation des Medecins Omnipraticiens du Quebec, Montreal, Quebec [*Library symbol*] [*National Library of Canada*] (NLC)

QMFMS.... Federation des Medecins Specialistes du Quebec, Montreal, Quebec [*Library symbol*] [*National Library of Canada*] (NLC)

QMFR .... Arctic Biological Station, Fisheries and Oceans Canada [*Station Biologique de l'Arctique, Peches et Oceans Canada*] Ste-Anne-De-Bellevue, Quebec [*Library symbol*] [*National Library of Canada*] (NLC)

QMFRA .... Archives des Franciscains, Montreal, Quebec [*Library symbol*] [*National Library of Canada*] (NLC)

QMFRAN ... Studium Franciscain de Theologie, Montreal, Quebec [*Library symbol*] [*National Library of Canada*] (NLC)

QMFSGA ... Archives des Freres de Saint-Gabriel, Montreal, Quebec [*Library symbol*] [*National Library of Canada*] (NLC)

QMG .... QMG Holdings, Inc. [*Toronto Stock Exchange symbol*]

QMG .... Quartermaster General [*Army*]

QMG .... Sir George Williams Campus, Concordia University, Montreal, Quebec [*Library symbol*] [*National Library of Canada*] (NLC)

QMGA...... Montreal Gazette, Quebec [*Library symbol*] [*National Library of Canada*] (NLC)

QMGB...... Grands Ballets Canadiens, Montreal, Quebec [*Library symbol*] [*National Library of Canada*] (NLC)

QMGDH ... Grace Dart Hospital Center, Montreal, Quebec [*Library symbol*] [*National Library of Canada*] (NLC)

QMGF ...... Quartermaster-General to the Forces [*Military*] [*British*]

QMGG...... Department of Geography, Sir George Williams Campus, Concordia University, Montreal, Quebec [*Library symbol*] [*National Library of Canada*] (NLC)

QMGGM... University Map Collection, Department of Geography, Sir George Williams Campus, Concordia University, Montreal, Quebec [*Library symbol*] [*National Library of Canada*] (NLC)

QMGH ...... Montreal General Hospital [*Hopital General de Montreal*] Quebec [*Library symbol*] [*National Library of Canada*] (NLC)

QMGHC ... Community Health Department, Montreal General Hospital [*Departement de Sante Communautaire, Hopital General de Montreal*], Quebec [*Library symbol*] [*National Library of Canada*] (NLC)

QMGHN ... Nurses' Library, Montreal General Hospital [*Bibliotheque des Infirmieres, Hopital General de Montreal*], Quebec [*Library symbol*] [*National Library of Canada*] (NLC)

QMGL...... Genstar Ltd., Montreal, Quebec [*Library symbol*] [*National Library of Canada*] (NLC)

QMGLS..... Library Studies Program, Concordia University, Montreal, Quebec [*Library symbol*] [*National Library of Canada*] (NLC)

QMGM...... Gaz Metropolitain, Montreal, Quebec [*Library symbol*] [*National Library of Canada*] (BIB)

QMGMC... Quartermaster-General of the Marine Corps

QMGO...... Quartermaster-General's Office [*Military*] [*British*] (ROG)

QMGP...... Gerard Parizeau Ltee, Montreal, Quebec [*Library symbol*] [*National Library of Canada*] (NLC)

QMGPA .... Quarry Management and Products [*Later, Quarry Management*] [*A publication*]

QMGS .... Grand Seminaire, Montreal, Quebec [*Library symbol*] [*National Library of Canada*] (NLC)

QMH .... Hydro-Quebec, Montreal, Quebec [*Library symbol*] [*National Library of Canada*] (NLC)

QMH .... Queens Moat Houses [*Hotelier*] [*British*]

QMHC .... Medical Library, Hoechst Canada, Inc., Montreal, Quebec [*Library symbol*] [*National Library of Canada*] (BIB)

QMHCL..... Bibliotheque Medicale, Hopital Charles Lemoyne, Greenfield Park, Quebec [*Library symbol*] [*National Library of Canada*] (NLC)

QMHCLC ... Departement de Sante Communautaire, Hopital Charles Lemoyne, Greenfield Park, Quebec [*Library symbol*] [*National Library of Canada*] (NLC)

QMHD ...... Hotel-Dieu de Montreal, Quebec [*Library symbol*] [*National Library of Canada*] (NLC)

QMHDE..... Centre de Documentation, Direction de l'Environnement, Hydro-Quebec, Montreal, Quebec [*Library symbol*] [*National Library of Canada*] (NLC)

QMHE....... Ecole des Hautes Etudes Commerciales, Montreal, Quebec [*Library symbol*] [*National Library of Canada*] (NLC)

QMHGC ... Centre Hospitalier de Verdun, Quebec [*Library symbol*] [*National Library of Canada*] (NLC)

QMHGF.... Hopital General Fleury, Montreal, Quebec [*Library symbol*] [*National Library of Canada*] (NLC)

QMHI........ Centre de Documentation, Hydro-Quebec International, Montreal, Quebec [*Library symbol*] [*National Library of Canada*] (BIB)

QMHJR..... Centre de Documentation du Personnel, Hopital de Convalescents Julius Richardson [*Staff Library, Julius Richardson Convalescent Hospital, Inc.*], Montreal, Quebec [*Library symbol*] [*National Library of Canada*] (NLC)

QMHJT .... Hopital Jean Talon, Montreal, Quebec [*Library symbol*] [*National Library of Canada*] (NLC)

QMHM ..... Centre Hospitalier Jacques Viger, Montreal, Quebec [*Library symbol*] [*National Library of Canada*] (NLC)

QMHME... Hopital Marie-Enfant, Montreal, Quebec [*Library symbol*] [*National Library of Canada*] (NLC)

QMHMR .. Hopital Maisonneuve-Rosemont, Montreal, Quebec [*Library symbol*] [*National Library of Canada*] (NLC)

QMHND ... Hopital Notre-Dame, Montreal, Quebec [*Library symbol*] [*National Library of Canada*] (NLC)

QMHNDI ... Bibliotheque des Services Infirmiers, Hopital Notre-Dame, Montreal, Quebec [*Library symbol*] [*National Library of Canada*] (NLC)

QMHP....... Qualified Mental Health Professional

QMHRP..... Hopital Riviere-Des-Prairies, Montreal, Quebec [*Library symbol*] [*National Library of Canada*] (NLC)

QMHRT.... Centre de Documentation, Redaction et Terminologie, Hydro-Quebec, Montreal, Quebec [*Library symbol*] [*National Library of Canada*] (BIB)

QMHSC.... Hopital du Sacre-Coeur, Montreal, Quebec [*Library symbol*] [*National Library of Canada*] (NLC)

QMHSCA ... Hopital Santa Cabrini, Montreal, Quebec [*Library symbol*] [*National Library of Canada*] (NLC)

QMHSJ..... Hopital Louis H. LaFonataine, Montreal, Quebec [*Library symbol*] [*National Library of Canada*] (NLC)

QMHSJA ... Hopital Ste-Jeanne-D'Arc, Montreal, Quebec [*Library symbol*] [*National Library of Canada*] (NLC)

QMHSL .... Hopital Saint-Luc, Montreal, Quebec [*Library symbol*] [*National Library of Canada*] (NLC)

QMHSLC ... Departement de Sante Communautaire, Hopital Saint-Luc, Montreal, Quebec [*Library symbol*] [*National Library of Canada*] (NLC)

QMHVG ... Centre de Documentation, Verification Generale, Hydro-Quebec, Montreal, Quebec [*Library symbol*] [*National Library of Canada*] (BIB)

QMI.......... Insurance Institute of the Province of Quebec [*Insitut d'Assurance du Quebec*] Montreal, Quebec [*Library symbol*] [*National Library of Canada*] (NLC)

QMI.......... Qualification Maintainability Inspection

QMIA........ International Air Transport Association [*Association du Transport Aerien International*] Montreal, Quebec [*Library symbol*] [*National Library of Canada*] (NLC)

QMIA........ Quartermaster Intelligence Agency [*Merged with Defense Intelligence Agency*]

QMIAA ..... Institut des Arts Appliques, Montreal, Quebec [*Library symbol*] [*National Library of Canada*] (NLC)

QMIAG .... Institut des Arts Graphiques, Montreal, Quebec [*Library symbol*] [*National Library of Canada*] (NLC)

QMIAP...... Pavillon Albert Prevost, Montreal, Quebec [*Library symbol*] [*National Library of Canada*] (NLC)

QMIC........ International Civil Aviation Organization [*Organisation de l'Aviation Civile Internationale*] Montreal, Quebec [*Library symbol*] [*National Library of Canada*] (NLC)

QMICA ..... Institute of Chartered Accountants of Quebec [*Institut Canadien des Comptables Agrees du Quebec*] Montreal, Quebec [*Library symbol*] [*National Library of Canada*] (NLC)

QMICAV... Institut Culturel Avataq, Montreal, Quebec [*Library symbol*] [*National Library of Canada*] (BIB)

QMICE...... Canadian Institute of Adult Education [*Institut Canadien d'Education des Adultes*] Montreal, Quebec [*Library symbol*] [*National Library of Canada*] (NLC)

QMICM .... Institut de Cardiologie de Montreal, Quebec [*Library symbol*] [*National Library of Canada*] (NLC)

QMIF .... Imasco Foods Ltd., Montreal, Quebec [*Library symbol*] [*National Library of Canada*] (NLC)

QMIFQ ..... Informatech France-Quebec, Montreal, Quebec [*Library symbol*] [*National Library of Canada*] (NLC)

QMIG........ Industrial Grain Products Ltd., Montreal, Quebec [*Library symbol*] [*National Library of Canada*] (NLC)

QMII .... Istituto Italiano di Cultura, Montreal, Quebec [*Library symbol*] [*National Library of Canada*] (NLC)

QMIIS....... Islamic Studies Library, McGill University, Montreal, Quebec [*Library symbol*] [*National Library of Canada*] (NLC)

QMIIST .... International Institute of Stress [*Institut International du Stress*] Montreal, Quebec [*Library symbol*] [*Obsolete*] [*National Library of Canada*] (NLC)

QMIKES ... Quadrupole Mass Analyzed Ion Kinetic Energy Spectroscopy

QMILO ..... International Labour Office [*Bureau International du Travail*] Montreal, Quebec [*Library symbol*] [*National Library of Canada*] (NLC)

QMIM....... Institut Armand-Frappier, Universite du Quebc, Laval, Quebec [*Library symbol*] [*National Library of Canada*] (NLC)

QMIMM ... Ministere des Communautes Culturelles et de l'Immigration, Montreal, Quebec [*Library symbol*] [*National Library of Canada*] (NLC)

QMIMSO ... Quartermaster Industrial Mobilization Services Offices [*Army*]

QMINC..... Institut du Cancer de Montreal, Quebec [*Library symbol*] [*National Library of Canada*] (NLC)

QMINCA .. Institut National Canadien pour les Aveugles, Montreal, Quebec [*Library symbol*] [*National Library of Canada*] (NLC)

QMINP ..... Institut National de Productivite, Montreal, Quebec [*Library symbol*] [*National Library of Canada*] (NLC)

QMIP .... Institute of Parasitoloy, Macdonald College, Ste-Anne-De-Bellevue, Quebec [*Library symbol*] [*National Library of Canada*] (NLC)

QMIPP...... Institut Philippe Pinel de Montreal, Quebec [*Library symbol*] [*National Library of Canada*] (NLC)

QMIRC ..... Institut de Recherches Cliniques, Montreal, Quebec [*Library symbol*] [*National Library of Canada*] (NLC)

QMIRP...... Institute for Research on Public Policy [*Institut de Recherches Politiques*] Montreal, Quebec [*Library symbol*] [*National Library of Canada*] (NLC)

QMIRS...... Informatheque IRSST [*Institut de Recherche en Sante et Securite au Travail*] Montreal, Quebec [*Library symbol*] [*National Library of Canada*] (NLC)

QMIS........ Quality Review Management Information System [*IRS*]

QMISM..... Centre de Documentation, Institut Raymond-Dewar, Montreal, Quebec [*Library symbol*] [*National Library of Canada*] (NLC)

QMIST...... Centre d'Information, IST [*Industriel Services Techniques*], Montreal, Quebec [*Library symbol*] [*National Library of Canada*] (BIB)

QMIT .... Imperial Tobacco Co. of Canada Ltd., Montreal, Quebec [*Library symbol*] [*National Library of Canada*] (NLC)

QMITR...... Research Library, Imperial Tobacco Co. of Canada Ltd., Montreal, Quebec [*Library symbol*] [*National Library of Canada*] (NLC)

QMJ .... Jewish Public Library [*Bibliotheque Juive Publique, Montreal*] Quebec [*Library symbol*] [*National Library of Canada*] (NLC)

QMJB........ Jardin Botanique, Montreal, Quebec [*Library symbol*] [*National Library of Canada*] (NLC)

QMJES ..... Technical Services, Joseph E. Seagram & Sons Ltd., La Salle, Quebec [*Library symbol*] [*National Library of Canada*] (NLC)

QMJG .... Jewish General Hospital, Montreal, Quebec [*Library symbol*] [*National Library of Canada*] (NLC)

QMJGI...... Institute of Community and Family Psychiatry, Jewish General Hospital, Montreal, Quebec [*Library symbol*] [*National Library of Canada*] (NLC)

QMJGL..... Lady Davis Institute for Medical Research, Jewish General Hospital, Montreal, Quebec [*Library symbol*] [*National Library of Canada*] (NLC)

QMJH....... Hopital de Mont-Joli, Inc., Quebec [*Library symbol*] [*National Library of Canada*] (NLC)

QMJHW ... Johnson & Higgins, Willis, Faber Ltd., Montreal, Quebec [*Library symbol*] [*National Library of Canada*] (NLC)

QMJJ .... Johnson & Johnson Ltd., Montreal, Quebec [*Library symbol*] [*National Library of Canada*] (NLC)

QMJL........ John Lovell & Son City Directories Ltd., Montreal, Quebec [*Library symbol*] [*National Library of Canada*] (NLC)

QMJLP...... Laboratoire de Police Scientifique, Montreal, Quebec [*Library symbol*] [*National Library of Canada*] (NLC)

QMJM ...... Canada Department of Justice [*Ministere de la Justice*] Montreal, Quebec [*Library symbol*] [*National Library of Canada*] (NLC)

QMJRH .... James R. Hay & Associates, Pointe Claire, Quebec [*Library symbol*] [*National Library of Canada*] (BIB)

QMJSJ...... Commission des Services Juridiques du Quebec, Montreal, Quebec [*Library symbol*] [*National Library of Canada*] (NLC)

QML......... Loyola Campus, Concordia University, Montreal, Quebec [*Library symbol*] [*National Library of Canada*] (NLC)

QML......... Qayyum Moslem League [*Pakistan*] (PD)

QML......... Qualified Manufacturers List [*DoD*]

QMLA ...... Laboratoires Abbott Ltee, Montreal, Quebec [*Library symbol*] [*National Library of Canada*] (NLC)

QMLAV .... Lavalin, Inc., Montreal, Quebec [*Library symbol*] [*National Library of Canada*] (BIB)

QMLAVE ... Lavalin Environment, Inc., Montreal, Quebec [*Library symbol*] [*National Library of Canada*] (BIB)

QMLBD .... Lafleur, Brown & De Granpre, Montreal, Quebec [*Library symbol*] [*National Library of Canada*] (BIB)

QMLCA .... Lower Canada Arms Collectors Association, Montreal, Quebec [*Library symbol*] [*National Library of Canada*] (NLC)

QMLCC..... Lower Canada College Montreal, Quebec [*Library symbol*] [*National Library of Canada*] (NLC)

QMLCPF .. Bibliotheque de la Faune, Ministere du Loisir, de la Chasse et de la Peche, Montreal, Quebec [*Library symbol*] [*National Library of Canada*] (NLC)

QMLF....... Librairies Flammarion, Montreal, Quebec [*Library symbol*] [*National Library of Canada*] (NLC)

QMLG .... Lakeshore General Hospital [*Hopital General du Lakeshore*] Pointe-Claire, Quebec [*Library symbol*] [*National Library of Canada*] (NLC)

QMLGC .... Community Health Department, Lakeshore General Hospital [*Departement de Sante Communautaire, Hopital General du Lakeshore*], Pointe-Claire, Quebec [*Library symbol*] [*National Library of Canada*] (NLC)

QMLM ...... Bibliotheque Municipale, Mont-Laurier, Quebec [*Library symbol*] [*National Library of Canada*] (BIB)

QMLP .... Centre de Documentation, La Presse Ltee., Montreal, Quebec [*Library symbol*] [*National Library of Canada*] (NLC)

QMLPT ..... Librairie Pointe-Aux-Trembles, Quebec [*Library symbol*] [*National Library of Canada*] (NLC)

QMLQ .... Centre de Documentation, Loto-Quebec, Montreal, Quebec [*Library symbol*] [*National Library of Canada*] (NLC)

QMLR .... Constance-Lethbridge Rehabilitation Centre [*Centre de Readaptation Constance-Lethbridge*] Montreal, Quebec [*Library symbol*] [*National Library of Canada*] (NLC)

QMM .... McLennan Library, McGill University, Montreal, Quebec [*Library symbol*] [*National Library of Canada*] (NLC)

QMMAC ... Musee d'Art Contemporain, Montreal, Quebec [*Library symbol*] [*National Library of Canada*] (NLC)

QMMAQ ... La Magnetotheque, Montreal, Quebec [*Library symbol*] [*National Library of Canada*] (NLC)

QMMAR ... Marianapolis College, Montreal, Quebec [*Library symbol*] [*National Library of Canada*] (NLC)

QMMB ...... Blackader/Lauterman Library of Architecture and Art, McGill University, Montreal, Quebec [*Library symbol*] [*National Library of Canada*] (NLC)

QMMBC ... Molson Breweries of Canada Ltd., Montreal, Quebec [*Library symbol*] [*Obsolete*] [*National Library of Canada*] (NLC)

QMMBG ... Botany-Genetics Library, McGill University, Montreal, Quebec [*Library symbol*] [*National Library of Canada*] (BIB)

QMMBZ ... Blacker-Wood Library of Zoology and Ornithology, McGill University, Montreal, Quebec [*Library symbol*] [*National Library of Canada*] (NLC)

QMMC ...... Miron Co. Ltd., Montreal, Quebec [*Library symbol*] [*National Library of Canada*] (NLC)

QMMCH .. Montreal Children's Hospital, Quebec [*Library symbol*] [*National Library of Canada*] (NLC)

QMMCR ... Musee du Chatau de Ramezay, Montreal, Quebec [*Library symbol*] [*National Library of Canada*] (NLC)

QMMD ..... Religious Studies Library, McGill University, Montreal, Quebec [*Library symbol*] [*National Library of Canada*] (NLC)

QMME ...... Physical Sciences and Engineering Library, McGill University, Montreal, Quebec [*Library symbol*] [*National Library of Canada*] (NLC)

QMMG ...... Map and Air Photo Library, McGill University, Montreal, Quebec [*Library symbol*] [*National Library of Canada*] (NLC)

QMMGS ... Department of Geological Sciences, McGill University, Montreal, Quebec [*Library symbol*] [*National Library of Canada*] (NLC)

QMMH ..... Mental Hygiene Istitute [*Institut de l'Hygiene Mentale*] Montreal, Quebec [*Library symbol*] [*National Library of Canada*] (NLC)

QMMHH ... Maimonides Hospital Geriatric Center [*Centre Hospitalier Geriatrique Maimonides*], Montreal, Quebec [*Library symbol*] [*National Library of Canada*] (NLC)

QMMI .... Atwater Library [*Formerly, Mechanics Institute Library*] Montreal, Quebec [*Library symbol*] [*National Library of Canada*] (NLC)

QMMIQ .... Quebec Regional Office, Employment and Immigration Canada [*Bureau Regional du Quebec, Emploi et Immigration Canada*] Montreal, Quebec [*Library symbol*] [*National Library of Canada*] (NLC)

QMML ...... Law Library, McGill University, Montreal, Quebec [*Library symbol*] [*National Library of Canada*] (NLC)

QMMLS .... Library Science Library, McGill University, Montreal, Quebec [*Library symbol*] [*National Library of Canada*] (NLC)

QMMM ..... Medical Library, McGill University, Montreal, Quebec [*Library symbol*] [*National Library of Canada*] (NLC)

QMMMCM ... McCord Museum, McGill University, Montreal, Quebec [*Library symbol*] [*National Library of Canada*] (NLC)

QMMMDM ... Marvin Duchow Music Library, McGill University, Montreal, Quebec [*Library symbol*] [*National Library of Canada*] (NLC)

QMMMM ... Montreal Military and Maritime Museum, Quebec [*Library symbol*] [*National Library of Canada*] (NLC)

QMMN ..... Nursing/Social Work Library, McGill University, Montreal, Quebec [*Library symbol*] [*National Library of Canada*] (NLC)

QMMO ..... Osler Library, McGill University, Montreal, Quebec [*Library symbol*] [*National Library of Canada*] (NLC)

QMMOC ... Monsanto Canada Ltd., Montreal, Quebec [*Library symbol*] [*National Library of Canada*] (NLC)

QMMOS ... Montreal Star, Quebec [*Library symbol*] [*National Library of Canada*] (NLC)

QMMPB ... MPB Technologies, Dorval, Quebec [*Library symbol*] [*National Library of Canada*] (NLC)

QMMRB ... Department of Rare Books and Special Collections, McGill University, Montreal, Quebec [*Library symbol*] [*National Library of Canada*] (NLC)

QMMRS ... Mendelsohn Rosentzveig Shacter, Montreal, Quebec [*Library symbol*] [*National Library of Canada*] (BIB)

QMMSC ... Howard Ross Library of Management, McGill University, Montreal, Quebec [*Library symbol*] [*National Library of Canada*] (NLC)

QMMSR ... Centre de Documentation, Ministere de la Main-d'Oeuvre et de la Securite du Revenu du Quebec, Montreal, Quebec [*Library symbol*] [*National Library of Canada*] (NLC)

QMN .... Centres Biblio-Culturels de Montreal-Nord, Quebec [*Library symbol*] [*National Library of Canada*] (NLC)

QMNA ...... Canadian Pulp and Paper Asssociation [*Association Canadienne des Producteurs dePates et Papiers*] Montreal, Quebec [*Library symbol*] [*National Library of Canada*] (NLC)

QMNB .... Biotechnology Branch, CISTI [*Canada Institute for Scienctific and Technical Information*] [*Annexe de Biotechnologie, ICIST*], Montreal, Quebec [*Library symbol*] [*National Library of Canada*] (BIB)

QMNDE .... Hopital Notre-Dame-De-L'Esperance-De-St-Laurent, Montreal, Quebec [*Library symbol*] [*National Library of Canada*] (NLC)

QMNE .... Northern Electric Co. Ltd., Montreal, Quebec [*Library symbol*] [*National Library of Canada*] (NLC)

QMNF .... National Film Board, Montreal [*Formerly, Ottawa*] [*Office National du Film, Montreal (Anciennement Ottawa)*] Quebec [*Library symbol*] [*National Library of Canada*] (NLC)

QMNFNI .. National Information/Distribution System, National Film Board [*Systeme d'Information et de Distribution pour les Produits Audio-Visuels Canadiens, Office National du film*] Montreal, Quebec [*Library symbol*] [*National Library of Canada*] (NLC)

QMNHH ... Health Protection Branch, Canada Department of National Health and Welfare [*Direction Generale de la Protection de la Sante, Ministere de la Sante Nationale et du Bien-Etre Social*] Montreal, Quebec [*Library symbol*] [*National Library of Canada*] (NLC)

QMNIH .... Montreal Neurological Institute and Hospital [*Institut et Hopital Neurologiques de Montreal*] Quebec [*Library symbol*] [*National Library of Canada*] (NLC)

QMNOT.... Northern Telecom Canada Ltd., Montreal, Quebec [*Library symbol*] [*National Library of Canada*] (NLC)

QMNR....... Noranda Research Centre, Pointe-Claire, Quebec [*Library symbol*] [*National Library of Canada*] (NLC)

QMNT....... Nesbitt, Thomson & Co. Ltd., Montreal, Quebec [*Library symbol*] [*National Library of Canada*] (NLC)

QMO .... Oratoire Saint-Joseph, Montreal, Quebec [*Library symbol*] [*National Library of Canada*] (NLC)

QMO .... Qualitative Materiel Objective [*Army*] (AABC)

QMO .... Quartz Mountain State Park [*Oklahoma*] [*Seismograph station code, US Geological Survey*] (SEIS)

QMO .... Queen Mary's Own [*British military*] (DMA)

QMOB....... Office de Biologie, Ministere de la Chasse et de la Peche, Montreal, Quebec [*Library symbol*] [*Obsolete*] [*National Library of Canada*] (NLC)

QMobSC ... Quadripartite Mobility Standardization Committee [*Military*] (AABC)

QMOCP .... Canadian Livestock Feed Board [*Office Canadien des Provendes*] Montreal, Quebec [*Library symbol*] [*National Library of Canada*] (NLC)

QMOCQ.... Office de la Construction du Quebec, Montreal, Quebec [*Library symbol*] [*National Library of Canada*] (NLC)

QMOF .... Ogilvie Flour Mills Co. Ltd., Montreal, Quebec [*Library symbol*] [*National Library of Canada*] (NLC)

QMOFJ..... Office Franco-Quebecois pour la Jeunesse, Montreal, Quebec [*Library symbol*] [*National Library of Canada*] (NLC)

QMOI........ Ordre des Infirmieres et Infirmiers du Quebec, Montreal, Quebec [*Library symbol*] [*National Library of Canada*] (NLC)

QMOLF .... Office de la Langue Francaise, Montreal, Quebec [*Library symbol*] [*National Library of Canada*] (NLC)

QMO & O ... Quebec, Montreal, Ottawa & Occidental [*Railway*]

QMOP....... Centre de Documentation, Office de Planification et de Developpement du Quebec, Montreal, Quebec [*Library symbol*] [*National Library of Canada*] (BIB)

QMOR....... Ogilvy, Renaud Law Library, Montreal, Quebec [*Library symbol*] [*National Library of Canada*] (BIB)

QMORC.... Quartermaster Officers' Reserve Corps [*Military*]

Q(Mov) ...... Quartermaster Movements [*World War II*]

QMP .... Qualitative Management Program [*Army*] (INF)

QMP.......... Quarry, Mine, and Pit [*A publication*] (APTA)

QMPA .... Centre de Documentation, Projet Archipel de Montreal, Quebec [*Library symbol*] [*National Library of Canada*] (NLC)

QMPA .... Quartermaster Purchasing Agency [*Army*]

QMPAE .... Paramax Electronics, Montreal, Quebec [*Library symbol*] [*National Library of Canada*] (BIB)

QMPC .... Presbyterian College, Montreal, Quebec [*Library symbol*] [*National Library of Canada*] (NLC)

QMPC .... Quartermaster Petroleum Center [*Army*] (MUGU)
QMPCA .... Agriculture Canada, Montreal, Quebec [*Library symbol*]
  [*National Library of Canada*] (NLC)
QMPCG .... Documentation Centre, George Etienne Cartier House, Parks
  Canada [*Centre de Documentation, Maison George-
  Etienne Cartier, Parcs Canada*], Montreal, Quebec [*Library
  symbol*] [*National Library of Canada*] (NLC)
QMPCUSA ... Quartermaster Petroleum Center, United States Army
QMPE .... Pezaris Electronics Co., Montreal, Quebec [*Library symbol*]
  [*National Library of Canada*] (NLC)
QMPI .... Polish Institute of Arts and Sciences in Canada [*Institut
  Polonais des Arts et des Sciences au Canada*] Montreal,
  Quebec [*Library symbol*] [*National Library of
  Canada*] (NLC)
QMPM ...... Peat, Marwick, Mitchell et Cie., Montreal, Quebec [*Library
  symbol*] [*National Library of Canada*] (NLC)
QMPM ...... Quantitative Methods for Public Management [*Course*]
QMPP .... Pulp and Paper Research Institute of Canada [*Institut Canadien
  de Recherches sur les Pates et Papiers*] Pointe-Claire,
  Quebec [*Library symbol*] [*National Library of
  Canada*] (NLC)
QMPPM ... Montreal Branch, Pulp and Paper Research Institute of Canada
  [*Succursale de Montreal, Centre Canadien de Recherche
  sur les Pates et Papiers*], Quebec [*Library symbol*]
  [*National Library of Canada*] (BIB)
QMPRA .... Archives Providence, Montreal, Quebec [*Library symbol*]
  [*National Library of Canada*] (NLC)
QMPSB..... Protestant School Board of Greater Montreal, Quebec [*Library
  symbol*] [*National Library of Canada*] (NLC)
QMPSR..... P. S. Ross & Partners, Montreal, Quebec (NLC)
QMPTI...... Potton Technical Industries, Mansonville, Quebec [*Library
  symbol*] [*National Library of Canada*] (NLC)
QMPWQ... Quebec Region Library, Public Works Canada [*Bibliotheque de
  la Region du Quebec, Travaux Publics Canada*] Montreal,
  Quebec [*Library symbol*] [*National Library of
  Canada*] (NLC)
QMQ .... Queen Mary Veterans Hospital [*Hopital Reine-Marie (Anciens
  combattants)*] Montreal, Quebec [*Library symbol*]
  [*National Library of Canada*] (NLC)
QMQAR.... Centre Regional de Montreal, Archives Nationales du Quebec,
  Quebec [*Library symbol*] [*National Library of
  Canada*] (NLC)
QMQAR.... Quebec Archives, Montreal, Quebec [*Library symbol*] [*National
  Library of Canada*] (NLC)
QMQB....... Quick-Make, Quick-Break
QMQDP.... Commission des Droits de la Personne du Quebec, Montreal,
  Quebec [*Library symbol*] [*National Library of
  Canada*] (NLC)
QMQE....... Queen Elizabeth Hospital, Montreal, Quebec [*Library symbol*]
  [*National Library of Canada*] (NLC)
QMR......... Qualitative Material Report
QMR......... Qualitative Materiel Requirement [*Army*]
QMR......... Qualitative Military Requirements [*NATO*] (NATG)
QMR......... Quartermaster
QMR......... Queen Mary's Regiment [*British military*] (DMA)
QMR......... Royal Bank of Canada [*Banque Royale du Canada*] Montreal,
  Quebec [*Library symbol*] [*National Library of
  Canada*] (NLC)
QMRA .... Railway Association of Canada, Montreal, Quebec [*Library
  symbol*] [*National Library of Canada*] (NLC)
QMRAD.... Centre de Documentation, Institut de Recherche Appliquee sur
  le Travail, Montreal, Quebec [*Library symbol*] [*National
  Library of Canada*] (NLC)
QMRAQ... Recherches Amerindiennes au Quebec, Montreal, Quebec
  [*Library symbol*] [*National Library of Canada*] (NLC)
QMRC...... Quartermaster Reserve Corps [*Military*]
QMRC....... Royal Canadian Air Force [*Corps d'Aviation Royale du
  Canada*] Montreal, Quebec [*Library symbol*] [*National
  Library of Canada*] (NLC)
QMRCH.... Richmond County Historical Society [*Societe d'Histoire du
  Comte de Richmond*] Melbourne, Quebec (NLC)
QMRCM .. Raymond, Chabot, Martin, Pare, Montreal, Quebec [*Library
  symbol*] [*National Library of Canada*] (NLC)
QMRD....... Reader's Digest of Canada Ltd., Montreal, Quebec [*Library
  symbol*] [*National Library of Canada*] (NLC)
QMRE .... Revenue Canada [*Revenu Canada*] Montreal, Quebec [*Library
  symbol*] [*National Library of Canada*] (NLC)
QMREC .... Quartermaster Research and Engineering Command [*Army*]
QMREFEA ... Quartermaster Research and Engineering Field Evaluation
  Agency [*Merged with Troop Evaluation Test*]
QMREG .... Regie de l'Electricite et du Gaz, Montreal, Quebec [*Library
  symbol*] [*National Library of Canada*] (NLC)
QMREX .... Canada Department of Regional Industrial Expansion
  [*Ministere de l'Expansion Industrielle Regionale*]
  Montreal, Quebec [*Library symbol*] [*National Library of
  Canada*] (NLC)
QMRH ...... Centre de Recherches en Relations Humaines, Montreal,
  Quebec [*Library symbol*] [*National Library of
  Canada*] (NLC)

QMRI .... Rehabilitation Institute of Montreal [*Institut de Rehabilitation
  de Montreal*] Quebec [*Library symbol*] [*National Library
  of Canada*] (NLC)
QMRL ...... Quartermaster Radiation Laboratory [*Army*]
QMRL ...... Regie du Logement, Montreal, Quebec [*Library symbol*]
  [*National Library of Canada*] (NLC)
QMRM...... Reddy Memorial Hospital, Montreal, Quebec [*Library symbol*]
  [*National Library of Canada*] (NLC)
QMROS .... Robinson-Sheppard, Montreal, Quebec [*Library symbol*]
  [*National Library of Canada*] (BIB)
QMRP ...... Qualified Mental Retardation Professional
QMRP ...... Rhone-Poulenc Pharma, Inc., Montreal, Quebec [*Library
  symbol*] [*National Library of Canada*] (NLC)
QMRPA .... Quartermaster Radiation Planning Agency [*Army*]
QMRQ...... Societe de Radio-Television du Quebec, Montreal, Quebec
  [*Library symbol*] [*National Library of Canada*] (NLC)
QMRR ...... Rolls-Royce of Canada Ltd., Montreal, Quebec [*Library
  symbol*] [*National Library of Canada*] (NLC)
QMRRD.... Reginald P. Dawson Library, Town of Mount Royal, Quebec
  [*Library symbol*] [*National Library of Canada*] (NLC)
QMRS ...... Information Centre, Canadian Security Intelligence Service
  [*Centre d'Information, Service Canadien du
  Renseignement de Securite*], Montreal, Quebec [*Library
  symbol*] [*National Library of Canada*] (BIB)
QMRSJA .. Archives des Religieuses Hospitalieres de Saint-Joseph,
  Montreal, Quebec [*Library symbol*] [*National Library of
  Canada*] (NLC)
QMRV ...... Royal Victoria Hospital, Montreal, Quebec [*Library symbol*]
  [*National Library of Canada*] (NLC)
QMRVW ... Women's Pavilion, Royal Victoria Hospital, Montreal, Quebec
  [*Library symbol*] [*National Library of Canada*] (NLC)
QMS .... Quadrupole Mass Spectrometer
QMS .... Quality Management System
QMS .... Quality Micro Systems [*Trademark*]
QMS .... Quality Monitoring System (MCD)
QMS .... Quarterly Journal. Mythic Society [*Bangalore*] [*A publication*]
QMS .... Quartermaster School [*Army*]
QMS .... Quartermaster Sergeant [*Military*]
QMS .... Quartermaster Stores [*Military*]
QMS .... Quicksilver Messenger Service [*Pop music group*]
QMS .... Sun Life of Canada [*Sun Life du Canada*] Montreal, Quebec
  [*Library symbol*] [*National Library of Canada*] (NLC)
QMSA ...... Seaman Apprentice, Quartermaster, Striker [*Navy rating*]
QMSA ...... Service de la Documentation, Ministere de la Sante et des
  Services Sociaux du Quebec, Montreal, Quebec [*Library
  symbol*] [*National Library of Canada*] (NLC)
QMSAC..... Sandoz Canada, Inc., Dorval, Quebec [*Library symbol*]
  [*National Library of Canada*] (NLC)
QMSAP..... Societe des Artistes Professionnels du Quebec, Montreal,
  Quebec [*Library symbol*] [*National Library of
  Canada*] (NLC)
QMSC .... Southern Canada Power Co., Montreal, Quebec [*Library
  symbol*] [*National Library of Canada*] (NLC)
QMSCA..... Statistics Canada [*Statistique Canada*] Montreal, Quebec
  [*Library symbol*] [*National Library of Canada*] (NLC)
QMSCC..... Queen Mary's School Cadet Corps [*British military*] (DMA)
QMSCM ... Canadian Microfilming Co. Ltd. [*Societe Canadienne du
  Microfilm, Inc.*] Montreal, Quebec [*Library symbol*]
  [*National Library of Canada*] (NLC)
QMSD .... Information Resource Centre, Systems Development [*Centre
  d'Information Specialise, Systemes-Applications
  Pratiques*], Montreal, Quebec [*Library symbol*] [*National
  Library of Canada*] (BIB)
QMSDB .... Societe de Developpement de la Baie James, Montreal, Quebec
  [*Library symbol*] [*National Library of Canada*] (NLC)
QMSDI...... Centre de Documentation, SOGIC [*Societe Generale des
  Industries Culturelles du Quebec*], Montreal, Quebec
  [*Library symbol*] [*National Library of Canada*] (BIB)
QMSDL..... Sidbec-Dosco Ltd./Ltee., Montreal, Quebec [*Library symbol*]
  [*National Library of Canada*] (NLC)
QM Segt .... Quartermaster-Sergeant [*British military*] (DMA)
QMSG .... Queue Message [*Data processing*] (PCM)
QMSGA .... Archives Generales des Soeurs Grises, Montreal, Quebec
  [*Library symbol*] [*National Library of Canada*] (NLC)
QMSGE .... Office des Services de Garde a l'Enfance, Montreal, Quebec
  [*Library symbol*] [*National Library of Canada*] (NLC)
QMSGME ... Service General des Moyens d'Enseignement, Ministere de
  l'Education du Quebec, Montreal, Quebec [*Library symbol*]
  [*National Library of Canada*] (NLC)
QMSGT .... Quartermaster Sergeant [*Marine Corps*]
QMSH....... Societe Historique de Montreal, Quebec [*Library symbol*]
  [*National Library of Canada*] (NLC)
QMSHE .... Stadler Hurter, Montreal, Quebec [*Library symbol*] [*National
  Library of Canada*] (NLC)
QMSHQ.... Centre de Documentation, Societe d'Habitation du Quebec,
  Montreal, Quebec [*Library symbol*] [*National Library of
  Canada*] (BIB)
QMSI........ Quality Micro Systems [*NASDAQ symbol*] (NQ)
QMSI........ Quartermaster-Sergeant Instructor [*British military*] (DMA)
QMSI........ Scolasticat de l'Immaculee-Conception, Montreal, Quebec
  [*Library symbol*] [*National Library of Canada*] (NLC)

QMSIL...... Silicart, Inc., Montreal, Quebec [*Library symbol*] [*National Library of Canada*] (NLC)
QMSJ........ St. Joseph's Teachers' College, Montreal, Quebec [*Library symbol*] [*National Library of Canada*] (NLC)
QMSMA ... St. Mary's Hospital, Montreal, Quebec [*Library symbol*] [*National Library of Canada*] (NLC)
QMSN...... Seaman, Quartermaster, Striker [*Navy rating*]
QMSNC .... SNC, Inc., Montreal, Quebec [*Library symbol*] [*National Library of Canada*] (NLC)
QMSO...... Quartermaster Supply Officer [*Army*]
QMSO....... Shell Oil Co. of Canada, Montreal, Quebec [*Library symbol*] [*National Library of Canada*] (NLC)
QMSOB .... Le Groupe SOBECO, Montreal, Quebec [*Library symbol*] [*National Library of Canada*] (NLC)
QMSQC .... Squibb Canada, Inc., Montreal, Quebec [*Library symbol*] [*National Library of Canada*] (NLC)
QMST .... Legal Department, Steinberg, Inc., Montreal, Quebec [*Library symbol*] [*National Library of Canada*] (NLC)
QMSTJ ..... Centre d'Information sur la Sante de l'Enfant, Hopital Sainte-Justine, Montreal, Quebec [*Library symbol*] [*National Library of Canada*] (NLC)
QMSTJS... Departement de Sante Communautaire, Hopital Sainte-Justine, Montreal, Quebec [*Library symbol*] [*National Library of Canada*] (NLC)
QMSU....... Surete du Quebec, Montreal, Quebec [*Library symbol*] [*National Library of Canada*] (NLC)
QMSVM ... Centre de Service Social Ville-Marie [*Ville-Marie Social Service Centre*] Montreal, Quebec [*Library symbol*] [*National Library of Canada*] (NLC)
QMSW...... Quartz Metal Sealed Window
QMSW ...... Sherwin-Williams Co. of Canada Ltd., Montreal, Quebec [*Library symbol*] [*National Library of Canada*] (NLC)
QMSWP.... Shawinigan Engineering Ltd. Co., Montreal, Quebec [*Library symbol*] [*National Library of Canada*] (NLC)
QMT......... Montreal Trust Co., Quebec [*Library symbol*] [*National Library of Canada*] (NLC)
QMTA....... Tomenson Alexander Ltd., Montreal, Quebec [*Library symbol*] [*National Library of Canada*] (NLC)
QMTC....... Air Canada, Montreal, Quebec [*Library symbol*] [*National Library of Canada*] (NLC)
QMTD....... Transportation Development Centre, Transport Canada [*Centre de Developpement des Transports, Transports Canada*] Montreal, Quebec [*Library symbol*] [*National Library of Canada*] (NLC)
QMTGC .... Teleglobe Canada, Montreal, Quebec [*Library symbol*] [*National Library of Canada*] (NLC)
QMTH...... Institut de Tourisme et d'Hotellerie du Quebec, Montreal, Quebec [*Library symbol*] [*National Library of Canada*] (NLC)
QMTMO... Centre de Documentation, Ministere du Travail du Quebec, Montreal, Quebec [*Library symbol*] [*National Library of Canada*] (NLC)
QMTOE.... Quartermaster Table of Organization and Equipment [*Units*] [*Military*]
QMTQ....... Direction des Communications, Tourisme Quebec, Montreal, Quebec [*Library symbol*] [*National Library of Canada*] (BIB)
QMTQM... Trans Quebec & Maritimes, Montreal, Quebec [*Library symbol*] [*National Library of Canada*] (NLC)
QMTR .... Waterways Development, Transport Canada [*Developpement des vois Navigables, Transports Canada*] Montreal, Quebec [*Library symbol*] [*National Library of Canada*] (NLC)
QMTRA .... Centre de Documentation, Ministere des Transports du Quebec, Montreal, Quebec [*Library symbol*] [*National Library of Canada*] (NLC)
QMU .... Universite de Montreal, Quebec [*Library symbol*] [*National Library of Canada*] (NLC)
QMUA...... Service des Archives de l'Universite de Montreal, Quebec [*Library symbol*] [*National Library of Canada*] (NLC)
QMUC...... Union Carbide Canada Ltd., Pointe-Aux-Trembles, Quebec [*Library symbol*] [*National Library of Canada*] (NLC)
QMUDD ... Departement de Demographie, Universite de Montreal, Quebec [*Library symbol*] [*National Library of Canada*] (NLC)
QMUE....... Bibliotheque de l'Institut d'Etudes Medievales, Universite de Montreal, Quebec [*Library symbol*] [*National Library of Canada*] (NLC)
QMUEB.... Ecole de Bibliotheconomie, Universite de Montreal, Quebec [*Library symbol*] [*National Library of Canada*] (NLC)
QMUEC.... L'Ecole de Criminologie, Universite de Montreal, Quebec [*Library symbol*] [*National Library of Canada*] (NLC)
QMUGC.... Cartotheque, Departement de Geographie, Universite de Montreal, Quebec [*Library symbol*] [*National Library of Canada*] (NLC)
QMUGL.... Cartotheque, Institut de Geologie, Universite de Montreal, Quebec [*Library symbol*] [*National Library of Canada*] (NLC)
QMUQ ...... Universite de Quebec, Montreal, Quebec [*Library symbol*] [*National Library of Canada*] (NLC)
QMUQA ... Service des Archives de l'Universite du Quebec a Montreal [*Library symbol*] [*National Library of Canada*] (BIB)

QMUQC.... Cartotheque, Universite du Quebec, Montreal, Quebec [*Library symbol*] [*National Library of Canada*] (NLC)
QMUQEN ... Ecole Nationale d'Administration Publique, Universite du Quebec, Montreal, Quebec [*Library symbol*] [*National Library of Canada*] (NLC)
QMUQET ... Ecole de Technologie Superieure, Universite de Quebec, Montreal, Quebec [*Library symbol*] [*National Library of Canada*] (NLC)
QMUQIC.. Cartotheque, INRS-Urbanisation, Montreal, Quebec [*Library symbol*] [*National Library of Canada*] (NLC)
QMUQIS .. Centre de Documentation, INRS [*Institut National de la Recherche Scientifique*]-Sante, Montreal, Quebec [*Library symbol*] [*National Library of Canada*] (NLC)
QMUQIU ... Centre de Documentation INRS [*Institut National de la Recherche Scientifique*]-Urbanisation, Montreal, Quebec [*Library symbol*] [*National Library of Canada*] (NLC)
QMUQPA ... Pavillon des Arts, Universite du Quebec, Montreal, Quebec [*Library symbol*] [*National Library of Canada*] (NLC)
QMUQS... Bibliotheque des Sciences, Universite du Quebec, Montreal [*Library symbol*] [*National Library of Canada*] (BIB)
QMUQTM ... Tele-Universite, Universite du Quebec, Montreal, Quebec [*Library symbol*] [*National Library of Canada*] (NLC)
Q Museum Memoirs ... Memoirs. Queensland Museum [*A publication*] (APTA)
QMV......... Qualified Majority Voting [*Napoleonic Code*]
QMV.......... RCA Victor Co. Ltd., Montreal, Quebec [*Library symbol*] [*National Library of Canada*] (NLC)
QMVC....... Media Resource Centre, Vanier College, Montreal, Quebec [*Library symbol*] [*National Library of Canada*] (NLC)
QMVR....... Resource Centre, VIA Rail Canada, Inc. [*Centre de Documentation, VIA Rail Canada, Inc.*] Montreal, Quebec [*Library symbol*] [*National Library of Canada*] (NLC)
QMVRM ... Centre de Maintenance, VIA Rail, Montreal, Quebec [*Library symbol*] [*National Library of Canada*] (BIB)
QMW......... Quartz Metal Window
QMW........ Warnock Hersey Co. Ltd., Montreal, Quebec [*Library symbol*] [*National Library of Canada*] (NLC)
QMWM..... William M. Mercer, Montreal, Quebec [*Library symbol*] [*National Library of Canada*] (NLC)
QMY......... Queen Mary's Yeomanry [*British military*] (DMA)
QMY.......... YWCA, Montreal, Quebec [*Library symbol*] [*National Library of Canada*] (NLC)
QMYH ...... YM - YWHA, Montreal, Quebec [*Library symbol*] [*National Library of Canada*] (NLC)
QN .... Kabo Air Travels [*Nigeria*] [*ICAO designator*] (FAAC)
QN .... Quantifier Negation [*Principle of logic*]
QN .... Quantum Number
QN .... Quaque Nocte [*Every Night*] [*Pharmacy*]
QN .... Quarterly Newsletter. American Bar Association [*A publication*] (DLA)
QN .... Quarterly Notes (ILCA)
QN .... Quarternote [*A publication*] (EAAP)
QN .... Queen (ADA)
QN .... Query Normalization
QN .... Question (FAAC)
QN .... Quetzalcoatlus Northropi [*Pterosaur, a model constructed for the Smithsonian Institution and referred to by these initials*]
QN .... Quintuple Screw (DS)
QN .... Quotation [*Investment term*]
QNA .... Qatar News Agency (BJA)
QNA .... Quinuclidinol Atrolactate [*Organic chemistry*]
QNaN .... Quiet Not a Number [*Computer programming*] (BYTE)
QNat .... Quaestiones Naturales [*of Seneca the Younger*] [*Classical studies*] (OCD)
Q Natl Dent Assoc ... Quarterly. National Dental Association [*US*] [*A publication*]
Q Natl Fire Prot Assoc ... Quarterly. National Fire Protection Association [*A publication*]
QNB........... Quinuclidinyl Benzilate [*Also, BZ*] [*Hallucinogen*]
QNC........... New Castle Free Public Library, New Castle, PA [*OCLC symbol*] (OCLC)
QNCCR ..... Quarterly Notes on Christianity and Chinese Religion [*A publication*]
QNCH .... Quenched (MSA)
QNCHRN ... Centre Hospitalier Rouyn-Noranda, Noranda, Quebec [*Library symbol*] [*National Library of Canada*] (NLC)
QNCRS ..... Conseil Regional de la Sante et des Services Sociaux Rouyn-Noranda, Noranda, Quebec [*Library symbol*] [*National Library of Canada*] (NLC)
QND .... Quantum Nondemolition [*Method of measurement*]
QNE........... Height Altimeter Set to 1013.2 Millibars Will Read on Landing [*Aviation code*] (AIA)
Q Newl-Spec Comm Env L ... Quarterly Newsletter. Special Committee on Environmental Law [*A publication*] (DLA)
Q News Bull Geol Soc S Afr ... Quarterly News Bulletin. Geological Society of South Africa [*A publication*]
Q Newsl Rhod Nurses Assoc ... Quarterly Newsletter. Rhodesia Nurses Association [*A publication*]
QNH.......... Altimeter Subscale Setting to Obtain Elevation When on the Ground [*Aviation code*] (FAAC)

QNI............ Queen's Nursing Institute [*British*]
QNICA ...... Soeurs de L'Assomption, Nicolet, Quebec [*Library symbol*] [*National Library of Canada*]   (NLC)
QNICS....... Seminaire de Nicolet, Quebec [*Library symbol*] [*National Library of Canada*]   (NLC)
QNIP .... Institut de Police du Quebec, Nicolet, Quebec [*Library symbol*] [*National Library of Canada*]   (NLC)
QNIS .... Queensland Newspapers Information System [*Australia*]
QNL........... Quarterly News Letter [*Book Club of California*] [*A publication*]
QNM .... Quilter's Newsletter Magazine [*A publication*]
QN MAG... Quilter's Newsletter Magazine [*A publication*]
QNMC....... Quadripartite Nonmateriel Committee [*Military*]   (AABC)
QNO........... Quinidine-N-oxide [*Organic chemistry*]
QNOAG .... Experimental Farm, Agriculture Canada [*Ferme Experimentale, Agriculture Canada*] Normandin, Quebec [*Library symbol*] [*National Library of Canada*]   (NLC)
QNS........... Quantity Not Sufficient [*Pharmacy*]
QNS........... Queensland Numismatic Society [*Australia*]
QNSC .... Qui Nhon Support Command [*Vietnam*]
QNST .... Quick Neurological Screening Test
QNT........... Quantizer   (MDG)
QNT........... Quintet [*Music*]
QNTJB...... Queensland and Northern Territory Judgements Bulletin [*Australia*] [*A publication*]
QNTL........ Quintel Corp. [*Tempe, AZ*] [*NASDAQ symbol*]   (NQ)
QNTM...... Quantum Corp. [*NASDAQ symbol*]   (NQ)
QNTY........ Quantity   (AFM)
QO .... Otrag Range Air Service [*Zaire*] [*ICAO designator*]   (FAAC)
QO .... Quaker Oats [*Trade name*]
QO .... Qualified Optician [*British*]
QO .... Qualified in Ordnance [*Obsolete*] [*Navy*]
QO .... Quartermaster Operation [*Military*]
QO .... Quarters Officer [*British military*]   (DMA)
QO .... Queen's Own [*Military unit*] [*British*]
QO .... Quick Opening [*Nuclear energy*]   (NRCH)
QOBV........ Quick-Opening Blowdown Valve [*Nuclear energy*]   (NRCH)
QOC........... Quality of Conformance
QOC........... Quasi-Optical Circuit
QOCG........ Queen's Own Corps of Guides [*British military*]   (DMA)
QOCH ...... Queen's Own Cameron Highlanders [*Military unit*] [*British*]
QOD .... Quality of Design
QOD .... Quantitative Oceanographic Data
QOD .... Quaque Otra Die [*Every Other Day*] [*Pharmacy*]
QOD .... Quick-Opening Device
QOD & WSY ... Queen's Own Dorset and West Somerset Yeomanry [*British military*]   (DMA)
QODY....... Queen's Own Dorsetshire Yeomanry [*British military*]   (DMA)
QOH.......... Quantity on Hand
QOH.......... Quaque Otra Hora [*Every Other Hour*] [*Pharmacy*]
QOH.......... Queen's Own Hussars [*Military unit*] [*British*]
QOI............ Quality Operating Instruction
Q Oil Stat .. Quarterly Oil Statistics [*France*] [*A publication*]
QOL........... Quality of Life [*Program*] [*Army*]
QOLCPF ... Bibliotheque de la Faune, Ministere du Loisir, de la Chasse, et de la Peche, Orsainville, Quebec [*Library symbol*] [*National Library of Canada*]   (NLC)
QOLUG..... Queensland Online Users' Group [*Australia*]   (ADA)
QOLY .... Queen's Own Lowland Yeomanry [*Military unit*] [*British*]   (DMA)
QOMAC.... Quarter Orbit Magnetic Attitude Control
QOMY....... Queen's Own Mercian Yeomanry [*Military unit*] [*British*]
QON .... Quaque Otra Nocte [*Every Other Night*] [*Pharmacy*]
QON .... Quarter Ocean Net
QONR .... Queen's Own Nigeria Regiment [*British military*]   (DMA)
QOOH....... Queen's Own Oxfordshire Hussars [*British military*]   (DMA)
Q(Ops)....... Quartermaster Operations [*World War II*]
QOR.......... Qualitative Operational Requirement [*Military*]
QOR.......... Quarterly Operating Report
QOR.......... Quebec Official Reports [*A publication*]   (DLA)
QOR.......... Queen's Own Rifles [*Military unit*] [*British*]
QOR.......... Queen's Own Royal [*Military unit*] [*British*]
QORC........ Queen's Own Rifles, Canada [*Military*]   (ROG)
QORGIY ... Queen's Own Royal Glasgow Imperial Yeomanry [*British military*]   (DMA)
QORGS ..... Quasi-Optimal Rendezvous Guidance System
QORGY.... Queen's Own Royal Glasgow Yeomanry [*British military*]   (DMA)
QORR....... Queen's Own Royal Regiment [*British military*]   (DMA)
QORWKR ... Queen's Own Royal West Kent Regiment [*Military unit*] [*British*]
QOS........... Quality of Service [*Telecommunications*]   (TEL)
QOT........... Quasi-Optical Technique
QOT........... Quote   (FAAC)
QOT & E ... Qualification, Operational Test, and Evaluation
QOWH ...... Queen's Own Worcestershire Hussars [*British military*]   (DMA)
QOWVR.... Queen's Own Westminster Volunteer Rifles [*Military*] [*British*]   (ROG)
QOY........... Queen's Own Yeomanry [*British military*]   (DMA)
QP............. Caspair Ltd. [*Kenya*] [*ICAO designator*]   (FAAC)
QP............. Quaderni Portoghesi [*A publication*]

QP............. Quadratic Programming [*Data processing*]   (BUR)
QP............. Quadruple Play   (DEN)
QP............. Qualification Proposal
QP............. Quality People
QP............. Quantum Placet [*As Much as You Please*] [*Pharmacy*]
QP............. Quartered Partition
QP............. Quasi-Peak
QP............. Queen Post
QP............. Queen's Pawn [*Chess*]   (ADA)
QP............. Queen's Pleasure [*British*]
QP............. Query Processing   (MCD)
QP............. Quest for Peace   (EA)
QP............. Quick Processing [*Chemicals*]
QP............. Quoted Price [*Investment term*]
QPA........... Bibliotheque Municipale, Port-Alfred, Quebec [*Library symbol*] [*National Library of Canada*]   (NLC)
QPA........... Quality Product Assurance
QPA........... Quantity per Assembly   (MCD)
QPA........... Queensland Potters Association [*Australia*]
QPAA .... Quality Planning and Administration   (MCD)
QPAG........ Experimental Farm, Agriculture Canada [*Ferme Experimentale, Agriculture Canada*] La Pocatiere, Quebec [*Library symbol*] [*National Library of Canada*]   (NLC)
QPAM .... Quantized Pulsed Amplitude Modulation
QPB........... Quality Paperback Book Club [*Trademark of Book-of-the-Month Club, Inc.*]
QPC........... College de Ste.-Anne, La Pocatiere, Quebec [*Library symbol*] [*National Library of Canada*]   (NLC)
QPC........... Quantity per Equipment/Component
QPC........... Quasi-Propulsive Coefficient   (DS)
QPC........... Quasi-Public Company
QPCAI Report ... Queensland Parliamentary Commissioner for Administration. Investigations Report [*Australia*] [*A publication*]
QPCE........ CEGEP [*College d'Enseignement General et Professionnel*] de La Pocatiere, Quebec [*Library symbol*] [*National Library of Canada*]   (NLC)
QPCM .... Bibliotheque Municipale, Port-Cartier, Quebec [*Library symbol*] [*National Library of Canada*]   (NLC)
QPD........... Bibliotheque Intermunicipale de Pierrefonds et Dollard-Des-Ormeaux, Pierrefonds, Quebec [*Library symbol*] [*National Library of Canada*]   (NLC)
QPD........... Queensland Parliamentary Debates [*A publication*]   (APTA)
QPDM....... Quadpixel Data-Flow Manager [*Data processing*]
QPDOLL... Quarterly Payment Demand on Legal Loan
Q Pediatr Bull ... Quarterly Pediatric Bulletin [*A publication*]
QPEI......... Quantity per End Item   (MCD)
QPES........ Centre de Documentation, Institut de Technologie Agro-Alimentaire de La Pocatiere, Quebec [*Library symbol*] [*National Library of Canada*]   (NLC)
QPET........ Queensland Petroleum Exploration Trust [*Australia*]
QPF .... Quantitative Precipitation Forecast   (NOAA)
QPH.......... Queen's Park Harriers [*British*]   (ROG)
1QpHab ..... Commentary [*or Pesher on Habakkuk*] from Qumran. Cave One   (BJA)
Q Philipp Sugar Inst ... Quarterly. Philippine Sugar Institute [*A publication*]
1QpHos ..... Commentary on Hosea from Qumran. Cave One   (BJA)
1QPhyl....... Phylacteries [*or Tefillin*] from Qumran. Cave One   (BJA)
QPI .... Quadratic Performance Index
QPI .... Quality Productivity Improvement   (MCD)
QPIMC...... Quadratic Programming Internal Model Control [*Chemical engineering*] [*Data processing*]
QPIR......... EBRI [*Employee Benefit Research Institute*] Quarterly Pension Investment Report [*A publication*]
QPIS......... Quality Planning Instruction Sheet   (MCD)
QPIT........ Quantitative Pilocarpine Ionophoresis Test
QPITC....... Queensland Plastics Industry Training Committee [*Australia*]
QPL.......... Qualified Parts List   (AAG)
QPL.......... Qualified Products List [*Military*]
Q PL.......... Quantum Placet [*As Much as You Please*] [*Pharmacy*]
QPLM .... Bibliotheque Municipale, Plessisville, Quebec [*Library symbol*] [*National Library of Canada*]   (NLC)
QPLR........ Queensland Planning Law Reports [*A publication*]   (APTA)
QPL & S ... Qualified Products Lists and Sources
QPLT........ Quiet Propulsion Lift Technology [*NASA*]
QPM......... Quality Practice Manual [*A publication*]
QPM......... Quality Program Manager [*Nuclear energy*]   (NRCH)
QPM......... Quality-Protein Maize
QPM......... Quantized Pulse Modulation
QPM......... Queen's Police Medal [*British*]
QPM......... Queen's [*Victoria*] Prime Ministers [*A publication*]
QPMAA .... Quilted Products Manufacturers Association of Australia
1QpMi .... Pesher [*or Commentary on Micah*] from Qumran. Cave One   (BJA)
1QpNah ..... Pesher [*or Commentary on Nahum*] from Qumran. Cave One   (BJA)
4QpNah ..... Pesher [*or Commentary on Nahum*] from Qumran. Cave Four   (BJA)
Q/PNL....... Quarter Panel [*Automotive engineering*]
QPO........... Quasi-Periodic Oscillation [*Astronomy*]

QPOC........ Pointe-Claire Public Library [*Bibliotheque Publique de Pointe-Claire*] Quebec [*Library symbol*] [*National Library of Canada*] (NLC)
QPOCQ..... Quebec Family History Society, Pointe Claire, Quebec [*Library symbol*] [*National Library of Canada*] (BIB)
Q Police J .. Queensland Police Journal [*A publication*] (APTA)
QPON....... Seven Oaks International, Inc. [*NASDAQ symbol*] (NQ)
Q Population Bul NZ ... Quarterly Population Bulletin (New Zealand) [*A publication*]
Q Poul Bull ... Quarterly Poultry Bulletin [*A publication*]
QPP........... Quality Program Plan (MCD)
QPP........... Quality Program Provision
QPP........... Quantized Pulse Position
QPP........... Quebec Pension Plan [*Canada*]
QPP........... Queensland Parliamentary Papers [*A publication*] (APTA)
QPP........... Queensland People's Party [*Australia*] [*Political party*]
QPP........... Quiescent Push-Pull [*Electronics*] (DEN)
QPPC........ Quarterly Production Progress Conference [*Navy*] (NG)
QPPD .... Queensland Parents of People with a Disability [*Australia*]
QPPL......... Queensland People's Progressive League [*Australia*]
4QpPs37 .... Pesher [*or Commentary on Psalm 37*] from Qumran. Cave Four (BJA)
QPR........... Pittsburgh Regional Library Center - Union List, Pittsburgh, PA [*OCLC symbol*] (OCLC)
QPR........... Qualitative Personnel Requirements [*NASA*] (KSC)
QPR........... Quality Progress [*A publication*]
QPR........... Quality Progress Review (MCD)
QPR........... Quarterly Progress Report
QPR........... Quebec Practice Reports [*A publication*] (DLA)
QPR........... Queensland Practice Reports [*A publication*] (APTA)
1QPrayers ... Liturgical Fragments from Qumran. Cave One (BJA)
QPRD........ Quality Planning Requirements Document [*NASA*] (NASA)
Q Predict.... Quarterly Predictions of National Income and Expenditure [*New Zealand*] [*A publication*]
QPRF........ Quantitative Precipitation Ratio Forecasts [*National Weather Service*]
QPRI......... Qualitative Personnel Requirements Information [*NASA*] (MCD)
QPRI......... Qualitative Personnel Requirements Inventory (MCD)
QPRM .... Bibliotheque Municipale, Princeville, Quebec [*Library symbol*] [*National Library of Canada*] (NLC)
4QPrNab ... [*The*] Prayer of Nabonidus from Qumran. Cave Four (BJA)
QPRS........ Quadrature Partial-Response System [*Telecommunications*] (TEL)
QPRS........ Quarterly Project Reliability Summary [*Navy*] (NG)
QPS........... Quaker Peace and Service [*An association*] (EAIO)
QPS........... Qualified Process Supplies (MCD)
QPS........... Qualified Processing Source
QPS........... Quality Planning Specification [*NASA*] (NASA)
QPS........... Quantitative Physical Science
QPS........... Quantity Planning Specification (NASA)
QPS........... Quiescent Power Supply
QPSC........ Quiescent Power Supply Current
QPSII........ Qualified Possession Source Investment Income [*IRS*]
QPSK........ Quadrature-Phase Shift Key
QPSL........ Qualified Parts and Suppliers List (MCD)
QPT........... Quadrant Power Tilt (IEEE)
QPX........... QPX Minerals, Inc. [*Vancouver Stock Exchange symbol*]
QQ .... Aerovias Quisqueyana [*Airlines*] [*Dominican Republic*] [*ICAO designator*] (OAG)
QQ .... Bibliotheque de Quebec, Quebec [*Library symbol*] [*National Library of Canada*] (NLC)
QQ .... Potential Hijacker [*Airline notation*]
QQ .... Qualitate Qua [*In the Capacity Of*] [*Latin*]
Q-Q .... Quantile-Quantile [*Data processing*]
QQ .... Quaque [*Each or Every*] [*Pharmacy*]
QQ .... Queen's Quarterly [*A publication*]
QQ .... Questionable Questionnaires
QQ .... Questions
Q and Q...... Quill and Quire [*A publication*]
QQ .... Quisque [*Each, Every*] [*Pharmacy*]
QQ .... Quoque [*Also*] [*Pharmacy*]
QQA .... Archives Nationales du Quebec, Quebec [*Library symbol*] [*National Library of Canada*] (NLC)
QQAA....... Archives de l'Archeveche de Quebec, Quebec [*Library symbol*] [*National Library of Canada*] (NLC)
QQAC....... Ministere des Affaires Culturelles du Quebec, Quebec, Quebec [*Library symbol*] [*National Library of Canada*] (NLC)
QQACJ...... Archives de la Compagnie de Jesus, Province du Canada - Francais, Saint-Jerome, Quebec, Quebec [*Library symbol*] [*National Library of Canada*] (NLC)
QQAG........ Centre de Documentation du 200, Ministere de l'Agriculture, des Pecheries, et de l'Alimentation, Quebec, Quebec [*Library symbol*] [*National Library of Canada*] (NLC)
QQAI......... Bibliotheque Administrative, Ministere des Affaires Inter-Gouvernementales du Quebec, Quebec, Quebec [*Library symbol*] [*Obsolete*] [*National Library of Canada*] (NLC)
QQAM....... Centre de Documentation, Ministere des Affaires Municipales du Quebec, Quebec, Quebec [*Library symbol*] [*National Library of Canada*] (NLC)

QQAND .... Archives du Monastere Notre-Dame-Des-Anges, Quebec, Quebec [*Library symbol*] [*National Library of Canada*] (NLC)
QQAPC ..... Cerebral Palsy Association of Quebec, Inc. [*L'Association de Paralysie Cerebrale du Quebec, Inc.*] Quebec, Quebec [*Library symbol*] [*National Library of Canada*] (NLC)
QQAQ .... Bibliotheque des Services Diocesains, Archeveche de Quebec, Quebec [*Library symbol*] [*National Library of Canada*] (BIB)
QQAQS..... Synod Office, Diocese of Quebec, Anglican Church of Canada, Quebec, Quebec [*Library symbol*] [*National Library of Canada*] (NLC)
QQAS........ Archives du Seminaire de Quebec, Quebec, Quebec [*Library symbol*] [*National Library of Canada*] (NLC)
QQASF...... Conseil des Affaires Sociales et de la Famille, Quebec, Quebec [*Library symbol*] [*National Library of Canada*] (NLC)
QQBJNQ .. Bureau de la Baie James et du Nord Quebecois, Ste.-Foy, Quebec [*Library symbol*] [*National Library of Canada*] (NLC)
QQBL........ Bibliotheque des Freres des Ecoles Chretiennes, Quebec [*Library symbol*] [*National Library of Canada*] (NLC)
QQBMC.... Bibliotheque Municipale, Charlesbourg, Quebec [*Library symbol*] [*National Library of Canada*] (BIB)
QQBS .... Bureau de la Statistique du Quebec, Quebec, Quebec [*Library symbol*] [*National Library of Canada*] (NLC)
QQBST...... Centre de Documentation, Ministere de l'Enseignement Superieur et de la Science du Quebec, Ste.-Foy, Quebec [*Library symbol*] [*National Library of Canada*] (NLC)
QQC.......... Defence Research Establishment Valcartier, Canada Department of National Defence [*Centre de Recherches pour la Defense Valcartier, Ministere de la Defense Nationale*] Courcelette, Quebec [*Library symbol*] [*National Library of Canada*] (NLC)
QQC.......... Quantitative Quality Characteristics
QQCAD..... Conservatoire d'Art Dramatique du Quebec, Quebec [*Library symbol*] [*National Library of Canada*] (NLC)
QQCAI ..... Centre de Documentation, Commission d'Acces a l'Information, Quebec, Quebec [*Library symbol*] [*National Library of Canada*] (NLC)
QQCAT..... Commission de la Sante et de la Securite du Travail du Quebec, Quebec, Quebec [*Library symbol*] [*National Library of Canada*] (NLC)
QQCC....... Centre de Documentation, Conseil des Colleges du Quebec, Quebec, Quebec [*Library symbol*] [*National Library of Canada*] (BIB)
QQCDP..... Commission des Droits de la Personne du Quebec, Quebec [*Library symbol*] [*National Library of Canada*] (NLC)
QQCDT..... Centre de Documentation, Commission des Normes du Travail, Quebec [*Library symbol*] [*National Library of Canada*] (NLC)
QQCE........ CEGEP [*College d'Enseignement General et Professionnel*] de Limoilou, Quebec, Quebec [*Library symbol*] [*National Library of Canada*] (NLC)
QQCF .... Centre Francois Charron, Quebec, Quebec [*Library symbol*] [*National Library of Canada*] (BIB)
QQCFP...... Centre de Documentation, Commission de la Fonction Publique du Quebec, Quebec, Quebec [*Library symbol*] [*National Library of Canada*] (BIB)
QQCFX ..... CEGEP [*College d'Enseignement General et Professionnel*] F. X. Garneau, Sillery, Quebec [*Library symbol*] [*National Library of Canada*] (NLC)
QQCGI ...... Centre de Documentation, CGI [*Conseillers en Gestion et Informatique*], Inc., Quebec [*Library symbol*] [*National Library of Canada*] (NLC)
QQCH .... Departement des Archives et Statistiques de la Ville de Quebec, Quebec, Quebec [*Library symbol*] [*National Library of Canada*] (NLC)
QQCHJH ... Centre Hospitalier Jeffery Hale, Quebec, Quebec [*Library symbol*] [*National Library of Canada*] (BIB)
QQCLF...... Conseil de la Langue Francaise, Quebec, Quebec [*Library symbol*] [*National Library of Canada*] (NLC)
QQCM....... College Merici, Quebec, Quebec [*Library symbol*] [*National Library of Canada*] (NLC)
QQCMQ..... Service de la Documentation et de l'Audiovisuel, Conservatoire de Musique de Quebec, Quebec [*Library symbol*] [*National Library of Canada*] (NLC)
QQCOC..... Centre de Documentation - DGTI [*Direction Generale des Technologies de l'Information*], Ministere des Communications du Quebec, Ste.-Foy, Quebec [*Library symbol*] [*National Library of Canada*] (BIB)
QQCOM..... Centre de Documentation, Direction Generale des Medias, Ministere des Communications du Quebec, Quebec [*Library symbol*] [*National Library of Canada*] (BIB)
QQCPQ..... Parks Service, Environment Canada [*Service des Parcs, Environnement Canada*], Quebec [*Library symbol*] [*National Library of Canada*] (BIB)

QQCPS...... Centre de Documentation, Conseil de la Science et de la Technologie du Quebec, Ste.-Foy, Quebec [*Library symbol*] [*National Library of Canada*] (NLC)

QQCR....... Centre Hospitalier Christ-Roi, Quebec, Quebec [*Library symbol*] [*National Library of Canada*] (BIB)

QQCRS..... Conseil Regional de la Sante et des Services Sociaux, Quebec, Quebec [*Library symbol*] [*National Library of Canada*] (NLC)

QQCS .... Service de Documentation et de Bibliotheque, Complexe Scientifique, Ste.-Foy, Quebec [*Library symbol*] [*National Library of Canada*] (NLC)

QQCSF...... Consiel du Statut de la Femme, Quebec, Quebec [*Library symbol*] [*National Library of Canada*] (NLC)

QQCSS..... Centre de Documentation, Centre de Services Sociaux de Quebec, Quebec [*Library symbol*] [*National Library of Canada*] (BIB)

QQCT .... Commission de Toponymie du Quebec, Quebec, Quebec [*Library symbol*] [*National Library of Canada*] (NLC)

QQCU....... Conseil des Universites du Quebec, Ste.-Foy, Quebec [*Library symbol*] [*National Library of Canada*] (NLC)

QQCUQ .... Communaute Urbaine de Quebec [*Library symbol*] [*National Library of Canada*] (BIB)

QQE.......... Wildlife and Inland Waters Library, Environment Canada [*Bibliotheque de la Faune et des Eaux Interieures, Environement Canada*] Ste-Foy, Quebec [*Library symbol*] [*National Library of Canada*] (NLC)

QQED....... Centre de Documentation, Ministere de l'Education du Quebec, Quebec, Quebec [*Library symbol*] [*National Library of Canada*] (BIB)

QQEDOP .. Centre de Documentation, Office des Professions du Quebec, Quebec [*Library symbol*] [*National Library of Canada*] (NLC)

QQEN....... Ministere de l'Environnement, Ste-Foy, Quebec [*Library symbol*] [*National Library of Canada*] (NLC)

QQERE ..... Centre de Documentation-Energie, Ministere de l'Energie et des Ressources du Quebec, Quebec, Quebec [*Library symbol*] [*National Library of Canada*] (NLC)

QQERM .... Centre de Documentation-Mines, Ministere de l'Energie et des Ressources du Quebec, Quebec, Quebec [*Library symbol*] [*National Library of Canada*] (NLC)

QQERT ..... Centre de Documentation-Terres et Forets, Ministere de l'Energie et des Ressources du Quebec, Quebec, Quebec [*Library symbol*] [*National Library of Canada*] (NLC)

QQESE...... Centre de Documentation, Direction Generale de l'Enseignement et de la Recherche Universitaires, Ministere de l'Enseignement Superieur et de la Science du Quebec, Quebec, Quebec [*Library symbol*] [*National Library of Canada*] (BIB)

QQF.......... Bibliotheque Franciscaine, Quebec, Quebec [*Library symbol*] [*National Library of Canada*] (NLC)

QQFPCE ... Direction de la Classification et de l'Evaluation des Emplois, Ministere de la Fonction Publique, Quebec, Quebec [*Library symbol*] [*National Library of Canada*] (NLC)

QQFTI....... Service du Traitement de l'Information, Ministere des Finances, Duberger, Quebec [*Library symbol*] [*National Library of Canada*] (NLC)

QQGR....... Bibliotheque Gabrielle-Roy, Quebec, Quebec [*Library symbol*] [*National Library of Canada*] (BIB)

QQH.......... Quaque Hora [*Every Hour*] [*Pharmacy*]

QQH.......... Quaque Quarta Hora [*Every Fourth Hour*] [*Pharmacy*]

QQHD....... Hotel-Dieu de Quebec, Quebec [*Library symbol*] [*National Library of Canada*] (NLC)

QQHDM ... Musee des Augustines de l'Hotel-Dieu de Quebec, Quebec [*Library symbol*] [*National Library of Canada*] (NLC)

QQHDS..... Hotel-Dieu du Sacre-Coeur, Quebec, Quebec [*Library symbol*] [*National Library of Canada*] (NLC)

QQHEJ ..... Hopital de l'Enfant-Jesus, Quebec, Quebec [*Library symbol*] [*National Library of Canada*] (NLC)

QQHFA..... Hopital St-Francois d'Assise, Quebec, Quebec [*Library symbol*] [*National Library of Canada*] (NLC)

QQ HOR ... Quaque Hora [*Every Hour*] [*Pharmacy*]

QQHSS ..... Hopital du Saint-Sacrement, Quebec, Quebec [*Library symbol*] [*National Library of Canada*] (NLC)

QQHSSC... Centre de Documentation, Departement de Sante Communautaire, Hopital du Saint-Sacrement, Quebec, Quebec [*Library symbol*] [*National Library of Canada*] (BIB)

QQIAS....... Service de la Documentation, Ministere de la Sante et des Services Sociaux du Quebec, Quebec, Quebec [*Library symbol*] [*National Library of Canada*] (NLC)

QQIC......... Ministere de l'Industrie, du Commerce et du Tourisme, Quebec, Quebec [*Library symbol*] [*National Library of Canada*] (NLC)

QQIF......... Inspecteur General des Institutions Financieres, Quebec, Quebec [*Library symbol*] [*National Library of Canada*] (NLC)

QQIN......... Indian and Northern Affairs Canada [*Affaires Indiennes et du Nord Canada*], Quebec [*Library symbol*] [*National Library of Canada*] (BIB)

QQIQRC ... Institut Quebecois de Recherche sur la Culture, Quebec, Quebec [*Library symbol*] [*National Library of Canada*] (NLC)

QQJ .... Ministere de la Justice du Quebec, Ste-Foy, Quebec [*Library symbol*] [*National Library of Canada*] (NLC)

QQL........... Bibliotheque de l'Assemblee Nationale, Quebec, Quebec [*Library symbol*] [*National Library of Canada*] (NLC)

QQLA .... Universite Laval, Quebec, Quebec [*Library symbol*] [*National Library of Canada*] (NLC)

QQLAAA .. Secteur Art et Architecture, Universite Laval, Quebec, Quebec [*Library symbol*] [*National Library of Canada*] (NLC)

QQLAAV .. Ecole des Arts Visuels, Universite Laval, Quebec, Quebec [*Library symbol*] [*National Library of Canada*] (NLC)

QQLACA .. Cartotheque, Universite Laval, Quebec, Quebec [*Library symbol*] [*National Library of Canada*] (NLC)

QQLACH ... Centre Hospitalier de l'Universite Laval, Quebec, Quebec [*Library symbol*] [*National Library of Canada*] (NLC)

QQLACHC ... Centre de Documentation, Departement de Sante Communautaire, Centre Hospitalier, Universite Laval, Quebec [*Library symbol*] [*National Library of Canada*] (NLC)

QQLACHR ... Centre de Recherche, Centre Hospitalier, Universite Laval, Quebec, Quebec [*Library symbol*] [*National Library of Canada*] (BIB)

QQLACHT ... Centre de Toxicologie, Centre Hospitalier, Universite Laval, Quebec, Quebec [*Library symbol*] [*National Library of Canada*] (BIB)

QQLACI.... Centre International de Recherches sur le Bilinguisme, Universite Laval, Quebec, Quebec [*Library symbol*] [*National Library of Canada*] (NLC)

QQLAD..... Faculte de Droit, Universite Laval, Quebec, Quebec [*Library symbol*] [*National Library of Canada*] (NLC)

QQLAG ..... Institut de Geographie, Universite Laval, Quebec, Quebec [*Library symbol*] [*National Library of Canada*] (NLC)

QQLAGM ... Departement de Geologie et de Mineralogie, Universite Laval, Quebec, Quebec [*Library symbol*] [*National Library of Canada*] (NLC)

QQLAI ...... Societa Dante Alighieri, Universite Laval, Quebec, Quebec [*Library symbol*] [*National Library of Canada*] (NLC)

QQLAS...... Bibliotheque Scientifique, Universite Laval, Quebec, Quebec [*Library symbol*] [*National Library of Canada*] (NLC)

QQLCP...... Ministere du Loisir, de la Chasse et de la Peche, Quebec, Quebec [*Library symbol*] [*National Library of Canada*] (NLC)

QQLH........ Literary and Historical Society of Quebec [*Societe Litteraire et Historique de Quebec*] Quebec [*Library symbol*] [*National Library of Canada*] (NLC)

QQLM....... Centre de Documentation, Laurentienne Mutuelle d'Assurance, Quebec, Quebec [*Library symbol*] [*National Library of Canada*] (NLC)

QQMAA.... Archives du Monastere des Augustines, Quebec, Quebec [*Library symbol*] [*National Library of Canada*] (NLC)

QQMAB.... Bibliotheque du Monastere des Augustines, Quebec, Quebec [*Library symbol*] [*National Library of Canada*] (NLC)

QQMAGA ... Archives des Augustines du Monastere de l'Hopital General de Quebec, Quebec [*Library symbol*] [*National Library of Canada*] (NLC)

QQMC...... Forestry Canada [*Forets Canada*], Ste.-Foy, Quebec [*Library symbol*] [*National Library of Canada*] (NLC)

QQMCH ... Bibliotheque Administrative, (Edifice H), Ministere des Communications du Quebec, Quebec [*Library symbol*] [*National Library of Canada*] (NLC)

QQMF....... Laurentian Forestry Centre, Canadian Forestry Service [*Centre de Foresterie des Laurentides, Service Canadien des Forets*] Ste.-Foy, Quebec [*Library symbol*] [*National Library of Canada*] (NLC)

QQMQ ...... Musee du Quebec, Quebec [*Library symbol*] [*National Library of Canada*] (NLC)

QQMR....... Le Mussee du Royal 22e Regiment et la Regie du Royal 22e Regiment, Quebec, Quebec [*Library symbol*] [*National Library of Canada*] (NLC)

QQM & R.. Quantitative, Qualitative, Maintainability, and Reliability

QQMSRD ... Centre de Documentation, Direction Generale des Ressources Informationnelles, Ministere de la Main d'Oeuvre et de la Securite du Revenu du Quebec, Quebec, Quebec [*Library symbol*] [*National Library of Canada*] (NLC)

QQMSRP ... Centre de Documentation, Direction Generale de la Planification, Ministere de la Main-d'Oeuvre et de la Securite du Revenu du Quebec, Quebec [*Library symbol*] [*National Library of Canada*] (BIB)

QQMUC.... Centre de Documentation, Musee de la Civilisation, Quebec [*Library symbol*] [*National Library of Canada*] (BIB)

QQOLF ..... Office de la Langue Francaise, Quebec, Quebec [*Library symbol*] [*National Library of Canada*] (NLC)

QQOPC..... Office de la Protection du Consommateur, Quebec, Quebec [*Library symbol*] [*National Library of Canada*] (NLC)

QQOPD..... Direction de la Documentation, Office des Promotions du Quebec, Quebec, Quebec [*Library symbol*] [*National Library of Canada*] (NLC)

QQP.......... Quick Query Program

QQPCQ ..... Canadian Park Service, Environment Canada [*Service Canadien des Parcs, Environnement Canada*], Quebec, Quebec [*Library symbol*] [*National Library of Canada*] (NLC)

QQPEA ..... Archives des Peres Eudistes, Charlesbourg, Quebec [*Library symbol*] [*National Library of Canada*]   (NLC)
QQPR .... Quantitative and Qualitative Personnel Requirements
QQPRI .... Quantitative and Qualitative Personnel Requirements Information [*Military*]
QQPSM .... Maurice Lamontagne Institute, Fisheries and Oceans Canada [*Institut Maurice Lamontagne, Peches et Oceans Canada*], Mont-Joli, Quebec [*Library symbol*] [*National Library of Canada*]   (NLC)
QQQE .... Centre Quebecois des Sciences de l'Eau, Universite du Quebec, Quebec, Quebec [*Library symbol*] [*National Library of Canada*]   (NLC)
QQR .... Technical Information Centre, Reed Ltd., Quebec, Quebec [*Library symbol*] [*National Library of Canada*]   (NLC)
QQRA .... Roche Associes Ltee., Group-Conseil, Ste.-Foy, Quebec [*Library symbol*] [*National Library of Canada*]   (NLC)
QQRAA ..... Regie de l'Assurance Automobile du Quebec, Sillery, Quebec [*Library symbol*] [*National Library of Canada*]   (NLC)
QQRAMQ ... Regie de l'Assurance-Maladie du Quebec, Sillery, Quebec [*Library symbol*] [*National Library of Canada*]   (NLC)
QQRE .... Ministere du Revenu, Ste.-Foy, Quebec [*Library symbol*] [*National Library of Canada*]   (NLC)
QQRRQ ..... Regie des Rentes du Quebec, Ste.-Foy, Quebec [*Library symbol*] [*National Library of Canada*]   (NLC)
QQRSP ...... Regie des Services Publics, Ste.-Foy, Quebec [*Library symbol*] [*National Library of Canada*]   (NLC)
QQS .... Quality Quest System [*Vancouver Stock Exchange symbol*]
QQS .... Seminaire de Quebec, Quebec [*Library symbol*] [*National Library of Canada*]   (NLC)
QQSAA ..... Centre de Documentation, Secretariat aux Affaires Autochtones, Quebec [*Library symbol*] [*National Library of Canada*]   (BIB)
QQSAJ ...... Secretariat a la Jeunesse, Conseil Executif, Quebec, Quebec [*Library symbol*] [*National Library of Canada*]   (NLC)
QQSC .... Quadripartite Quartermaster Standardization Committee [*Military*]   (AABC)
QQSCA ..... Archives des Soeurs de la Charite de Quebec, Quebec, Quebec [*Library symbol*] [*National Library of Canada*]   (NLC)
QQSCF ...... Centre de Documentation, Secretariat a la Condition Feminine du Quebec, Quebec, Quebec [*Library symbol*] [*National Library of Canada*]   (BIB)
QQSHQ ..... Centre de Documentation, Societe d'Habitation du Quebec, Quebec [*Library symbol*] [*National Library of Canada*]   (BIB)
QQSIP .... Societe Quebecoise d'Initiatives Petrolieres, Ste.-Foy, Quebec [*Library symbol*] [*National Library of Canada*]   (NLC)
QQSP .... Centre de Documentation, Syndicat de Professionnels et de Professionnelles du Gouvernement du Quebec, Quebec [*Library symbol*] [*National Library of Canada*]   (BIB)
QQSS .... Quebec Library, Translation Bureau, Secretary of State Canada [*Bibliotheque de Quebec, Bureau des Traductions, Secretariat d'Etat*], Ste.-Foy, Quebec [*Library symbol*] [*National Library of Canada*]   (NLC)
QQST .... Centre de Documentation, Conseil de la Science et de la Technologie, Quebec [*Library symbol*] [*National Library of Canada*]   (NLC)
QQTCG ..... Canadian Coast Guard [*Garde Cotiere Canadienne*] Quebec, Quebec [*Library symbol*] [*National Library of Canada*]   (NLC)
QQTE .... Tecrad, Inc., Ancienne-Lorette, Quebec [*Library symbol*] [*National Library of Canada*]   (NLC)
QQTO .... Ministere du Tourisme du Quebec, Quebec [*Library symbol*] [*National Library of Canada*]   (NLC)
QQTQ .... Centre de Documentation, Ministere du Travail du Quebec, Quebec [*Library symbol*] [*National Library of Canada*]   (BIB)
QQTR .... Ministere des Transports, Quebec, Quebec [*Library symbol*] [*National Library of Canada*]   (NLC)
QQTRD ..... Centre de Documentation, Ministere des Transports - Rue Dorchester, Quebec [*Library symbol*] [*National Library of Canada*]   (NLC)
QQU .... Couvent des Ursulines, Quebec, Quebec [*Library symbol*] [*National Library of Canada*]   (NLC)
QQUA .... Archives du Monastere des Ursulines de Merici, Quebec, Quebec [*Library symbol*] [*National Library of Canada*]   (NLC)
QQUIE ...... Centre de Documentation, INRS [*Institut National de la Recherche Scientifique*]-Eau, Quebec, Quebec [*Library symbol*] [*National Library of Canada*]   (NLC)
QQUQ .... Universite du Quebec, Quebec, Quebec [*Library symbol*] [*National Library of Canada*]   (NLC)
QQUQEN ... Ecole Nationale d'Administration Publique, Universite du Quebec, Quebec, Quebec [*Library symbol*] [*National Library of Canada*]   (NLC)
QQUQT ..... Tele-Universite, Universite du Quebec, Quebec, Quebec [*Library symbol*] [*National Library of Canada*]   (NLC)
QQV .... Centre de Documentation, le Verificateur General du Quebec, Quebec, Quebec [*Library symbol*] [*National Library of Canada*]   (BIB)
QQ V .... Quae Vide [*Which See*] [*Plural form*] [*Latin*]
QQV .... Quantum Vis [*As Much as You Wish*] [*Pharmacy*]   (ADA)

Q-QY .... Question or Query   (AAG)
QQZ .... Jardin Zoologique de Quebec, Charlesbourg, Quebec [*Library symbol*] [*National Library of Canada*]   (NLC)
QR .... Inter RCA [*Central African Republic*] [*ICAO designator*]   (FAAC)
QR .... Qatar Riyal [*Monetary unit*]   (BJA)
Qr .... Qere   (BJA)
QR .... Quad Right [*Typography*]
QR .... Quadrans [*A Farthing*] [*Monetary unit*] [*British*]   (ROG)
Q & R .... Quality and Reliability
QR .... Quality Review
QR .... Quantitative Restrictions [*International trade*]
QR .... Quantity Requested
QR .... Quantity Required
QR .... Quantum Rectum [*The Quantity Is Correct*] [*Pharmacy*]
QR .... Quantum Resources [*Vancouver Stock Exchange symbol*]
QR .... Quarantine Report [*HEW*]
QR .... Quarter
QR .... Quarterly   (ROG)
QR .... Quarterly Replenishment
QR .... Quarterly Report   (OICC)
QR .... Quarterly Review [*A publication*]
QR .... Quarters Rating [*British military*]   (DMA)
QR .... Quaternary Research [*A publication*]
QR .... Quebec Official Reports [*A publication*]   (DLA)
QR .... Queen's Rangers [*British military*]
QR .... Queen's Regulation [*Military*] [*British*]
QR .... Queen's Rook [*Chess*]   (ADA)
QR .... Queen's Royal [*Military unit*] [*British*]
Q/R .... Query/Response   (MCD)
QR .... Quick Reaction
QR .... Quieting Reflex [*In book title "Q-R: The Quieting Reflex" by Charles F. Stroebel*]
QR .... Quire [*Measure of paper*]
QR .... Quotation Request
QR .... Sources Public Library [*Bibliotheque Municipale des Sources*] Roxboro, Quebec [*Library symbol*] [*National Library of Canada*]   (NLC)
QRA .... Archeveche de Rimouski, Quebec [*Library symbol*] [*National Library of Canada*]   (NLC)
Q & RA ..... Quality and Reliability Assurance
QRA .... Quality and Reliability Assurance   (NG)
QRA .... Quick Reaction Acquisition   (MCD)
QRA .... Quick Reaction Aircraft   (MCD)
QRA .... Quick Reaction Alert [*Military*]   (AFM)
QRA .... Quick Reaction Area   (MCD)
QRA .... Quick Replaceable Assembly
QRAAT ..... Centre de l'Abitibi-Temiscamingue, Archives Nationales du Quebec, Rouyn-Noranda, Quebec [*Library symbol*] [*National Library of Canada*]   (BIB)
QRAC .... Quality and Reliability Assessment Council
QRADA ..... Quaderni di Radiologia [*A publication*]
QR Ag Econ ... Quarterly Review of Agricultural Economics [*A publication*]   (APTA)
Q R Agric Econ ... Quarterly Review of Agricultural Economics [*A publication*]
QRAH .... Robins [*A. H.*] Co., Inc. [*NYSE symbol*]   (SPSG)
QR & AI ..... Queen's Regulations and Admiralty Instructions [*Obsolete*] [*Navy*] [*British*]
QR Air .... Queen's Regulations and Orders for the Royal Canadian Air Force
QRAL .... Quality and Reliability Assurance Laboratory [*NASA*]   (KSC)
QRAN .... Archives Nationales du Quebec, Rimouski, Quebec [*Library symbol*] [*National Library of Canada*]   (BIB)
Q Rass Mus ... Quaderni della Rassegna Musicale [*A publication*]
QR Aust Educ ... Quarterly Review of Australian Education [*A publication*]   (APTA)
QRB .... Quality Review Bulletin [*A publication*]
QRB .... Quarterly Review of Biology [*A publication*]
QRBC .... Bibliotheque Centrale de Pret d'Abitibi-Temiscamingue, Rouyn-Noranda, Quebec [*Library symbol*] [*National Library of Canada*]   (NLC)
QRBIA .... Quarterly Review of Biology [*A publication*]
Q R Biol ..... Quarterly Review of Biology [*A publication*]
Q R Biophys ... Quarterly Review of Biophysics [*A publication*]
QRBM .... Quasi-Random Band Model
QRC .... Quaker Resources Canada Ltd. [*Vancouver Stock Exchange symbol*]
QRC .... Quick Reaction Capability [*Military*]
QRC .... Quick Reaction Change   (MCD)
QRC .... Quick Response Capability [*Military*]
QRCA .... Qualitative Research Consultants Association   (EA)
QRCB .... College Bourget, Rigaud, Quebec [*Library symbol*] [*National Library of Canada*]   (NLC)
QRCC .... Quadripartite Research Coordination Committee [*Military*]   (AABC)
QRCC .... Query Response Communications Console
QRCG .... Quasi-Random Code Generator   (CET)
QRCH .... Centre de Documentation, Centre Hospitalier Regional de Rimouski, Quebec [*Library symbol*] [*National Library of Canada*]   (NLC)

QRCN........ College de l'Abitibi-Temiscamingue, Rouyn, Quebec [*Library symbol*] [*National Library of Canada*] (NLC)
QRCN........ Queen's Regulations and Orders for the Royal Canadian Navy
QRCR........ Quality Reliability Consumption Reports
QRCRS...... Conseil Regional de la Sante et des Services Sociaux, Rimouski, Quebec [*Library symbol*] [*National Library of Canada*] (NLC)
QRD.......... Quick Reaction Development
QRDEA ..... Quartermaster Research and Development Evaluation Agency [*Army*]
QRDS .... Quarterly Review of Drilling Statistics [*American Petroleum Institute*]
QRE .... Bibliotheque Municipale, Repentigny, Quebec [*Library symbol*] [*National Library of Canada*] (NLC)
QRE .... Quarterly Review of Economics and Business [*A publication*]
QRE .... Quick Reaction [*or Response*] Estimate
QREB .... Quarterly Review of Economics and Business [*A publication*]
QREBA ...... Quarterly Review of Economics and Business [*A publication*]
Q R Econ Bu ... Quarterly Review of Economics and Business [*A publication*]
Q R Econ & Bus ... Quarterly Review of Economics and Business [*A publication*]
QRECS...... Centre Regional de Documentation Pedagogique, Commission Scolaire de Le Gardeur, Repentigny, Quebec [*Library symbol*] [*National Library of Canada*] (BIB)
Q Rep Railw Tech Res Inst (Tokyo) ... Quarterly Report. Railway Technical Research Institute (Tokyo) [*A publication*]
Q Rep Univ W Indies Sch Agric ... Quarterly Report. University of the West Indies. School of Agriculture [*A publication*]
QRESA...... Quaternary Research [*New York*] [*A publication*]
Q Rev .... Quarterly Review [*A publication*]
Q Rev Ag Economics ... Quarterly Review of Agricultural Economics [*A publication*] (APTA)
Q Rev Agric Econ ... Quarterly Review of Agricultural Economics [*A publication*] (APTA)
Q Rev Am Electroplat Soc ... Quarterly Review. American Electroplaters' Society [*A publication*]
Q Rev Aust Ed ... Quarterly Review of Australian Education [*A publication*] (APTA)
Q Rev Biol ... Quarterly Review of Biology [*A publication*]
Q Rev Bioph ... Quarterly Reviews of Biophysics [*A publication*]
Q Rev Biophys ... Quarterly Reviews of Biophysics [*A publication*]
Q Rev Chem Soc ... Quarterly Reviews. Chemical Society [*A publication*]
Q Rev Chem Soc (Lond) ... Quarterly Reviews. Chemical Society (London) [*A publication*]
Q Rev DC Nurses Assoc ... Quarterly Review. District of Columbia Nurses Association [*A publication*]
Q Rev Drill Stat US ... Quarterly Review. Drilling Statistics for the United States [*A publication*]
Q Rev Drug Metab Drug Interact ... Quarterly Reviews on Drug Metabolism and Drug Interactions [*A publication*]
Q Rev Econ Bus ... Quarterly Review of Economics and Business [*A publication*]
Q Rev Environ ... Quarterly Review on Environment [*Japan*] [*A publication*]
Q Rev Evan Luth Ch ... Quarterly Review. Evangelical Lutheran Church [*A publication*]
Q Rev Film ... Quarterly Review of Film Studies [*A publication*]
Q Rev F Studies ... Quarterly Review of Film Studies [*A publication*]
Q Rev Harefuah ... Quarterly Review of the Harefuah [*A publication*]
Q Rev Hist S ... Quarterly Review of Historical Studies [*A publication*]
Q Review of F Studies ... Quarterly Review of Film Studies [*A publication*]
Q Rev Juris ... Quarterly Review of Jurisprudence [*1887-88*] [*A publication*] (DLA)
Q Rev Lit.... Quarterly Review of Literature [*A publication*]
Q Rev Med ... Quarterly Review of Medicine [*A publication*]
Q Rev Obstet Gynecol ... Quarterly Review of Obstetrics and Gynecology [*A publication*]
Q Rev Pediatr ... Quarterly Review of Pediatrics [*A publication*]
Q Rev Rural Econ ... Quarterly Review of the Rural Economy [*A publication*]
Q Rev Soil Assoc ... Quarterly Review. The Soil Association [*A publication*]
Q Rev Surg ... Quarterly Review of Surgery [*A publication*]
Q Rev Surg Obstet Gynecol ... Quarterly Review of Surgery. Obstetrics and Gynecology [*A publication*]
Q Rev Surg Surg Spec ... Quarterly Review of Surgery and Surgical Specialities [*A publication*]
Q Rev Urol ... Quarterly Review of Urology [*A publication*]
QRF .... Quadrature Rejection Frequency
QRF .... Quality Review File [*IRS*]
QRF .... Quick Reaction Force [*Military*] (CINC)
Q R Film S ... Quarterly Review of Film Studies [*A publication*]
QRG.......... Quadrupole Residual Gas
QRG.......... Quick Reaction Grooming
QRG.......... Quick Response Graphic
QRGA .... Quadrupole Residual Gas Analyzer
QRGAS ..... Quadrupole Residual Gas Analyzer System
QRGS .... Grand Seminaire de Rimouski, Quebec [*Library symbol*] [*National Library of Canada*] (NLC)
QRH .... Rosemere High School, Quebec [*Library symbol*] [*National Library of Canada*] (BIB)
QRHD .... Bibliotheque Medicale, Hotel-Dieu de Roberval, Quebec [*Library symbol*] [*National Library of Canada*] (NLC)

Q R Higher Ed Among Negroes ... Quarterly Review of Higher Education among Negroes [*A publication*]
QR Higher Ed Negroes ... Quarterly Review of Higher Education among Negroes [*A publication*]
Q R Hist Stud ... Quarterly Review of Historical Studies [*A publication*]
QRI .... Qualitative Requirements Information [*Army*]
QRI .... Quick Reaction Integration (NASA)
QRIA .... Quick Reaction Integration Activity (NASA)
QRIB .... Haskell Free Library, Rock Island, Quebec [*Library symbol*] [*National Library of Canada*] (NLC)
QRIC .... CEGEP [*College d'Enseignement General et Professionnel*] de Rimouski, Quebec [*Library symbol*] [*National Library of Canada*] (NLC)
QRIC .... Quick Reaction Installation Capability (CET)
QRICC...... Quick Reaction Inventory Control Center [*Army*] (MCD)
QRIH........ Queen's Royal Irish Hussars [*Military unit*] [*British*]
QRIM .... Institut Maritime, CEGEP de Rimouski, Quebec [*Library symbol*] [*National Library of Canada*] (NLC)
QR J.......... QR Journal. Indian Association for Quality and Reliability [*A publication*]
QRJOD ..... QR [*Quality and Reliability*] Journal [*A publication*]
QRKB .... Quebec King's Bench Reports [*A publication*] (DLA)
QRKB .... Rapports Judiciaires de Quebec, Cour du Banc du Roi [*Quebec Law Reports, King's Bench*] [*A publication*] (DLA)
QRL .... Bibliotheque Municipale, Riviere-Du-Loup, Quebec [*Library symbol*] [*National Library of Canada*] (BIB)
QRL .... Q-Switch Ruby LASER
QRL .... Quadripartite Research List [*Military*] (AABC)
QRL .... Quarterly Review of Literature [*A publication*]
QRL .... Quaternary Research Laboratory [*University of Michigan*] [*Research center*] (RCD)
QRL .... Quick Reference List
QRL .... Quick Relocate and Link
QRLC .... CEGEP [*College d'Enseignement General et Professionnel*] de Riviere-Du-Loup, Quebec [*Library symbol*] [*National Library of Canada*] (BIB)
QRLH........ Centre de Documentation DSC, Hotel-Dieu de Riviere-Du-Loup, Quebec [*Library symbol*] [*National Library of Canada*] (BIB)
QR of Lit.... Quarterly Review of Literature [*A publication*]
QRLP........ Centre de Recherche, Tourbieres Premier Ltee., Riviere-Du-Loup, Quebec [*Library symbol*] [*National Library of Canada*] (BIB)
QRLY .... Quarterly
QRM.......... Artificial Interference to Transmission or Reception [*Broadcasting*]
QRM.......... Bibliotheque Municipale, Rimouski, Quebec [*Library symbol*] [*National Library of Canada*] (NLC)
QRM.......... Quarterly Review of Marketing [*A publication*]
QRM.......... Quorum Resource Corp. [*Vancouver Stock Exchange symbol*]
QRMC .... Quadrennial Review of Military Compensation [*DoD*]
QRMC .... Quick Response Multicolor Copier (MCD)
QRMF .... Quick Reacting, Mobile Force [*Military*] [*NATO*] (NATG)
QRMP .... Quick-Response Multicolor Printer (RDA)
Qr Mr........ Quartermaster [*British military*] (DMA)
QRN.......... Soeurs de Notre-Dame du Saint-Rosaire, Rimouski, Quebec [*Library symbol*] [*National Library of Canada*] (NLC)
QROA....... Quarter Racing Owners of America (EA)
QR & O (Can) ... Queen's Regulations and Orders for the Canadian Army
QRosc .... Pro Roscio Comoedo [*of Cicero*] [*Classical studies*] (OCD)
QRP .... Query and Reporting Processor
QRP .... Quick Reaction Program [*Army*]
QRPAO ..... Qualified Radium Plaque Adaptometer Operator [*Navy*]
QRPS........ Quick Reaction Procurement System [*Army*] (AABC)
QRQB .... Quebec Queen's Bench Reports [*Canada*] [*A publication*] (DLA)
QRR.......... Quadrature Rejection Ratio
QRR.......... Quadrupole Resonance Response
QRR.......... Qualitative Research Requirement for Nuclear Weapons Effects Information (AABC)
QRR.......... Quality Readiness Review (MCD)
QRR.......... Quarterly Research Review
QRR.......... Queen's Royal Regiment [*Military unit*] [*British*]
QRR.......... Queen's Royal Rifles [*British military*] (DMA)
QRR.......... Quincy Railroad Co. [*AAR code*]
QRRF........ Master Quality Review Report File [*IRS*]
QRRI .... Qualitative Research Requirements Information [*Army*]
QRRK .... Quantum Rice-Ramsperger-Kassel [*Chemical kinetics methodology*]
QRRR........ Distress call for emergency use only by amateur radio stations in an emergency situation
Q R Rural Economy ... Quarterly Review of the Rural Economy [*A publication*]
QRS .... Natural Interference to Transmission or Reception [*Broadcasting*]
QRS .... Qualification Review Sheet (KSC)
QRS .... Qualified Repair Source (AFIT)
QRS .... Quantum Readout System [*Method of measurement*]
QRS .... Quarters
QRS .... Queen's Row Spare
QRS .... Quick Reaction Sortie (NASA)

QRSC........ Quebec Superior Court Reports [*A publication*]   (DLA)
QRSC........ Rapports Judiciaires de Quebec, Cour Superieure [*Quebec Law Reports, Superior Court*] [*A publication*]   (DLA)
QRSL........ Qualified Repair Source List   (AFIT)
QRSL........ Quick Reaction Space Laboratory [*NASA*]   (NASA)
QRT.......... Queue Run-Time [*Data processing*]
QRT.......... Quick Reaction Task   (MCD)
QRT.......... Quick Reaction Team [*Military*]
QRTIA........ Quarterly Report. Railway Technical Research Institute [*A publication*]
QRTLY...... Quarterly   (ROG)
QRTP........ Quick Response Targeting Program [*Lunar*]
QRTZ........ Quartz Engineering & Materials, Inc. [*NASDAQ symbol*]   (NQ)
QRU.......... Queen's Row Unit
QRU.......... Universite du Quebec, Rimouski, Quebec [*Library symbol*] [*National Library of Canada*]   (NLC)
QRUC........ Cartotheque, Universite du Quebec, Rimouski, Quebec [*Library symbol*] [*National Library of Canada*]   (NLC)
QRUQR..... Universite du Quebec en Abitibi-Temiscamingue, Rouyn, Quebec [*Library symbol*] [*National Library of Canada*]   (NLC)
QRUS........ Queen's Row Unit Spare
QRV.......... Qualified Valuer of the Real Estate Institute of New South Wales
QRV.......... Queenstown Rifle Volunteers [*British military*]   (DMA)
QRV.......... Quick Release Valve
QRV.......... Quinn River Valley [*Nevada*] [*Seismograph station code, US Geological Survey*] [*Closed*]   (SEIS)
QRVB........ Queen's Rifle Volunteer Brigade [*British military*]   (DMA)
QRW......... Quail Ridge Winery [*Vancouver Stock Exchange symbol*]
QRXI........ Quarex Industries, Inc. [*NASDAQ symbol*]   (NQ)
QRY......... Quality and Reliability Year
QRY.......... Quarry   (KSC)
QS............. African Safari Airways [*ICAO designator*]   (FAAC)
QS............. Les Quatre Saisons [*Record label*] [*France*]
QS............. Quaderni di Semitistica [*Florence*] [*A publication*]
QS............. Quaderni di Storia [*A publication*]
QS............. Quality Standard
QS............. Quality Stock
QS............. Quantity Share [*Economics*]
QS............. Quantity Surveying
QS............. Quantum Sufficit [*A Sufficient Quantity*] [*Pharmacy*]   (ADA)
QS............. Quarter Section
QS............. Quarter Sessions
QS............. Quartermaster Sergeant [*Military*]
QS............. Queen's Scarf   (ADA)
QS............. Queen's Scholar [*British*]
QS............. Queen's Serjeant [*Military*] [*British*]   (ROG)
Q-S........... Queneau-Schuhmann [*Lead process*]
QS............. Query System [*Data processing*]
QS............. Question Standard   (NATG)
QS............. Queue Select [*Data processing*]
QS............. Quick Service
QS............. Quick Sweep [*Construction*]
QS............. Quiet Sleep [*Physiology*]
QS............. Quota Source   (AABC)
1QS............ Community Rule, Rule of the Congregation [*or Manual of Discipline, Serekh ha-Yahad*] from Qumran. Cave One   (BJA)
1QS........... Divrei Berakhot [*or Blessings*] from Qumran. Cave One   (BJA)
QSA........... Quad Synchronous Adapter [*Perkin-Elmer*]
QSA........... Qualification Site Approval [*NASA*]   (NASA)
QSA........... Qualified in Small Arms [*British military*]   (DMA)
QSA........... Quick Service Assistant   (MCD)
QSABS...... Laboratoire de Sante Publique du Quebec, Ste-Anne-De-Bellevue, Quebec [*Library symbol*] [*National Library of Canada*]   (NLC)
QS AD ...... Quantum Sufficiat Ad [*To a Sufficient Quantity*] [*Pharmacy*]
QSAL........ Quadripartite Standardization Agreements List [*Military*]
QSAM....... Quadrature Sideband Amplitude Modulation
QSAM ...... Queued Sequential Access Method [*IBM Corp.*] [*Data processing*]
(Q)SAR...... Quantitative Structure-Activity Relationship [*Pharmacochemistry*]
QSAR .... Quantitative Structure-Activity Relationships [*A publication*]
QSATS ..... Quiet Short-Haul Air Transportation System
1QSb........ Divrei Berakhot [*or Blessings*] from Qumran. Cave One   (BJA)
QSBR....... Bio-Research Laboratory, Senneville, Quebec [*Library symbol*] [*National Library of Canada*]   (NLC)
QSC......... College de Shawinigan, Quebec [*Library symbol*] [*National Library of Canada*]   (NLC)
QSC .... Quality, Service, Cleanliness [*McDonald's Hamburger stands motto*]
QSC .... Quasi-Sensory Communication [*Parapsychology*]
QSC .... Queen Street Camera, Inc. [*Toronto Stock Exchange symbol*]
QSC .... Questionnaire Service Company [*Information service or system*]   (IID)
QSC .... Quick Set Compound
QSCR........ Queensland. Supreme Court. Reports [*A publication*]

QSCV......... Quality, Service, Cleanliness, and Value [*Formula for successful fast-food restaurants as taught by McDonald's Corp. at its Hamburger University*]
QSD.......... Quality Surveillance Division [*Navy*]
QSDC .... Quantitative Structural Design Criteria [*NASA*]
QSE .... Qualified Scientists and Engineers
QSED .... Research Centre, Domtar Ltd., Senneville, Quebec [*Library symbol*] [*National Library of Canada*]   (NLC)
QSem .... Quaderni di Semantica [*A publication*]
QSEMH .... Missisquoi Historical Society [*Societe d'Histoire de Missisquoi*] Stanbridge-East, Quebec [*Library symbol*] [*National Library of Canada*]   (NLC)
QSF........... Bibliotheque Municipale, Ste.-Foy, Quebec [*Library symbol*] [*National Library of Canada*]   (NLC)
QSF........... Quasi-Static Field
QSF........... Quasi-Stationary Front
QSFAG...... Research Station, Agriculture Canada [*Station de Recherches, Agriculture Canada*] Ste-Foy, Quebec [*Library symbol*] [*National Library of Canada*]   (NLC)
QSFB .... Biorex, Ste.-Foy, Quebec [*Library symbol*] [*National Library of Canada*]   (BIB)
QSFBP ..... Maison Generalice des Soeurs du Bon Pasteur, Ste-Foy, Quebec [*Library symbol*] [*National Library of Canada*]   (NLC)
QSFC........ Centre des Medias, CEGEP [*College d'Enseignement General et Professionnel*] de Ste.-Foy, Quebec [*Library symbol*] [*National Library of Canada*]   (NLC)
QSFC........ College d'Enseignement, Ste.-Foy, Quebec [*Library symbol*] [*National Library of Canada*]   (NLC)
QSFCAE ... Clinique d'Aide a l'Enfance, Ste.-Foy, Quebec [*Library symbol*] [*National Library of Canada*]   (NLC)
QSFCD...... Societe de Cooperation pour le Developpement International, Ste.-Foy, Quebec [*Library symbol*] [*National Library of Canada*]   (BIB)
QSFCM..... College Marguerite d'Youville, Ste.-Foy, Quebec [*Library symbol*] [*National Library of Canada*]   (NLC)
QSFCP ..... Commission de Police du Quebec, Ste.-Foy, Quebec [*Library symbol*] [*National Library of Canada*]   (NLC)
QSFCR ..... Centre de Recherche Industrielle du Quebec, Ste.-Foy, Quebec [*Library symbol*] [*National Library of Canada*]   (NLC)
QSFCRO... Centre de Documentation, Commission Rochon, Ste.-Foy, Quebec [*Library symbol*] [*National Library of Canada*]   (BIB)
QSFCSE.... Centre de Documentation, Conseil Superieur de l'Education du Quebec, Ste.-Foy, Quebec [*Library symbol*] [*National Library of Canada*]   (BIB)
QSFE .... Centre de Documentation, Directeur General des Elections du Quebec, Ste.-Foy, Quebec [*Library symbol*] [*National Library of Canada*]   (BIB)
QSFHL...... Hopital Laval, Ste.-Foy, Quebec [*Library symbol*] [*National Library of Canada*]   (NLC)
QSFIG ...... Centre de Documentation, INRS [*Institut National de la Recherche Scientifique*]-Georessources, Ste.-Foy, Quebec [*Library symbol*] [*National Library of Canada*]   (NLC)
QSFIO....... Institut National d'Optique, Ste.-Foy, Quebec [*Library symbol*] [*National Library of Canada*]   (BIB)
QSFPC ..... Centre de Documentation, Bureau de la Protection Civile du Quebec, Ste.-Foy, Quebec [*Library symbol*] [*National Library of Canada*]   (BIB)
QSFS .... SOQUEM [*Societe Quebecoise d'Exploration Miniere*] Documentation, Ste.-Foy, Quebec [*Library symbol*] [*National Library of Canada*]   (NLC)
QSG .... Quasi-Steady Glide [*NASA*]
QSG .... Quasi-Stellar Galaxy
QSGLL...... Queensland Studies in German Language and Literature [*A publication*]
QSGVT..... Quarter Scale Ground Vibration Test   (MCD)
QSH.......... Stanstead Historial Society, Quebec [*Library symbol*] [*National Library of Canada*]   (NLC)
QSHAG..... Saint-Hyacinthe Food Research Centre, Agriculture Canada [*Centre de Recherches Alimentaires de Saint-Hyacinthe, Agriculture Canada*] Quebec [*Library symbol*] [*National Library of Canada*]   (NLC)
QSHC........ CEGEP [*College d'Enseignement General et Professionnel*] de Shawinigan, Quebec [*Library symbol*] [*National Library of Canada*]   (NLC)
QSHCH...... Centre Hospitalier Regional de La Mauricie, Shawinigan, Quebec [*Library symbol*] [*National Library of Canada*]   (NLC)
QSHCHS .. Departement de Sante Communautaire, Centre Hospitalier Regional de la Mauricie, Shawinigan, Quebec [*Library symbol*] [*National Library of Canada*]   (BIB)
QSHCP...... Hopital Communautaire du Pontiac [*Pontiac Community Hospital*], Shawville, Quebec [*Library symbol*] [*National Library of Canada*]   (NLC)
QSHERAN ... Centre Regional de l'Estrie, Archives Nationales du Quebec, Sherbooke, Quebec [*Library symbol*] [*National Library of Canada*]   (NLC)
QSHERB... Bibliotheque Centrale de Pret de l'Estrie, Sherbrooke, Quebec [*Library symbol*] [*National Library of Canada*]   (BIB)

QSHERC... Bibliotheque des Sciences de la Sante, Universite de Sherbrooke, Quebec [*Library symbol*] [*National Library of Canada*] (NLC)

QSHERCR ... Conseil Regional de la Sante et des Services Sociaux des Cantons de l'Est, Sherbrooke, Quebec [*Library symbol*] [*National Library of Canada*] (NLC)

QSHERD .. Sherbrooke Daily Record, Quebec [*Library symbol*] [*National Library of Canada*] (NLC)

QSHERE... College de Sherbrooke (CEGEP) [*College d'Enseignement General et Professionnel*], Quebec [*Library symbol*] [*National Library of Canada*] (NLC)

QSHERG .. Bibliotheque du Grand Seminaire, Sherbrooke, Quebec [*Library symbol*] [*National Library of Canada*] (NLC)

QSHERH .. Huntingdon Gleaner, Quebec [*Library symbol*] [*National Library of Canada*] (NLC)

QSHERHD ... Centre Hospitalier Hotel-Dieu, Sherbrooke, Quebec [*Library symbol*] [*National Library of Canada*] (NLC)

QSHERM ... Monastere des Peres Redemptoristes, Sherbrooke, Quebec [*Library symbol*] [*Obsolete*] [*National Library of Canada*] (NLC)

QSHERN .. Bibliotheque Municipale, Sherbrooke, Quebec [*Library symbol*] [*National Library of Canada*] (NLC)

QSHERS... Seminaire de Sherbrooke, Quebec [*Library symbol*] [*National Library of Canada*] (NLC)

QSHERSB .. Les Conseillers Samson Belair, Inc., Sherbrooke, Quebec [*Library symbol*] [*National Library of Canada*] (NLC)

QSHERSC ... College du Sacre-Coeur, Sherbrooke, Quebec [*Library symbol*] [*National Library of Canada*] (NLC)

QSHERSF ... Ecole Secondaire St.-Francois, Sherbrooke, Quebec [*Library symbol*] [*National Library of Canada*] (NLC)

QSHERSG ... Societe de Genealogie des Cantons de l'Est, Sherbrooke, Quebec [*Library symbol*] [*National Library of Canada*] (NLC)

QSHERSH ... La Societe d'Histoire des Cantons de l'Est, Sherbrooke, Quebec [*Library symbol*] [*National Library of Canada*] (NLC)

QSHERSV ... Centre Hospitalier St.-Vincent-De-Paul, Sherbrooke, Quebec [*Library symbol*] [*National Library of Canada*] (NLC)

QSHERU .. Bibliotheque Generale, Universite de Sherbrooke, Quebec [*Library symbol*] [*National Library of Canada*] (NLC)

QSHERUA ... Galerie d'Art et Centre Culturel, Universite de Sherbrooke, Quebec [*Library symbol*] [*National Library of Canada*] (NLC)

QSHERUD ... Bibliotheque de Droit, Universite de Sherbrooke, Quebec [*Library symbol*] [*National Library of Canada*] (NLC)

QSHERUG ... Departement de Geographie, Universite de Sherbrooke, Quebec [*Library symbol*] [*National Library of Canada*] (NLC)

QSHERUGC ... Cartotheque, Departement de Geographie, Universite de Sherbrooke, Quebec [*Library symbol*] [*National Library of Canada*] (NLC)

QSHERURA ... Centre de Documentation, Programme de Recherche sur l'Amiante, Universite de Sherbrooke, Quebec [*Library symbol*] [*National Library of Canada*] (NLC)

QSHERUS ... Bibliotheque des Sciences, Universite de Sherbrooke, Quebec [*Library symbol*] [*National Library of Canada*] (NLC)

QSHERY... Centre de Documentation et d'Audio-Visuel, Hopital d'Youville de Sherbrooke, Quebec [*Library symbol*] [*National Library of Canada*] (NLC)

QSHM....... Municipal Library [*Bibliotheque Municipale*] Shawinigan, Quebec [*Library symbol*] [*National Library of Canada*] (NLC)

QSHS .... Seminaire Ste-Marie, Shawinigan, Quebec [*Library symbol*] [*National Library of Canada*] (NLC)

QSI .... Bibliotheque Municipale, Sept-Iles, Quebec [*Library symbol*] [*National Library of Canada*] (NLC)

QSI .... Quality Salary Increase (AFM)

QSI .... Quality Service Indicator

QSI .... Quantum Scalar Irradiance [*Instrumentation*]

QSI .... Quarterly Survey of Intentions [*Became Consumer Buying Expectations Survey*] [*Bureau of the Census*]

QSIA.......... Centre Regional de la Cote-Nord, Archives Nationales du Quebec, Sept-Iles, Quebec [*Library symbol*] [*National Library of Canada*] (BIB)

QSIBCP..... Bibliotheque Centrale de Pret de la Cote-Nord, Sept-Iles, Quebec [*Library symbol*] [*National Library of Canada*] (NLC)

QSIC......... CEGEP [*College d'Enseignement General et Professionnel*] de Sept-Iles, Quebec [*Library symbol*] [*National Library of Canada*] (BIB)

QSIC......... Quality Standard Inspection Criteria

QSIH......... Hopital des Sept-Iles, Quebec [*Library symbol*] [*National Library of Canada*] (NLC)

QSII.......... Quality Systems, Incorporated [*NASDAQ symbol*] (NQ)

QSIIOM.... Mineralogy Laboratory, Iron Ore Co., Sept-Iles, Quebec [*Library symbol*] [*National Library of Canada*] (NLC)

QSILC .... College Jesus-Marie de Sillery, Quebec [*Library symbol*] [*National Library of Canada*] (NLC)

QSJ........... Stanstead Journal, Quebec [*Library symbol*] [*National Library of Canada*] (NLC)

QSJHD...... Hotel-Dieu de Saint-Jerome, Quebec [*Library symbol*] [*National Library of Canada*] (NLC)

QSK........... Quadriphase Shift Keying (MCD)

QSL........... Q-Switch LASER

QSL........... Qualification Status List (KSC)

QSL........... Qualified Source List [*NASA*] (NASA)

QSL........... Quality of School Life Scale [*Educational test*]

QSL........... Quarterly Stock List

QS & L....... Quarters, Subsistence, and Laundry [*Military*]

QSL........... Queue Search Limit [*Data processing*]

QSLCR ...... Campus 1, Champlain Regional College, St.-Lambert, Quebec [*Library symbol*] [*National Library of Canada*] (NLC)

QSLE........ Bibliotheque Municipale, Saint-Leonard, Quebec [*Library symbol*] [*National Library of Canada*] (NLC)

QSM........... Quality Systems Management [*DoD*]

QSM......... Quarter Scale Model (MCD)

QSM......... Quarter Square Multiplier

QSM......... Quasi-Linear Sequential Machine

QSM......... Southmark Corp. [*NYSE symbol*] (SPSG)

QSMC .... Queensland Surveying and Mapping Advisory Council [*Australia*]

QSMVT..... Quarter Scale Model Vibration Testing (NASA)

QSND....... Archer Communications, Inc. [*NASDAQ symbol*] (NQ)

QSNT .... (Quinolinesulfonyl)nitrotriazole [*Organic chemistry*]

QSO........... Bibliotheque Municipale, Sorel, Quebec [*Library symbol*] [*National Library of Canada*] (NLC)

QSO........... Quasi-Biennial Stratospheric Oscillation

QSO........... Quasi-Stellar [*or QUASAR*] Object

QSOCS ... C. Stroemgren, Sorel, Quebec [*Library symbol*] [*National Library of Canada*] (NLC)

QSOCS...... QIT - Fer et Titane, Inc., Sorel, Quebec [*Library symbol*] [*National Library of Canada*] (NLC)

QSOP......... Quadripartite Standing Operating Procedures [*Military*]

QSP........... Quench Spray Pump (IEEE)

QSP........... Quick Search Procedure

QSPS......... Qualification Standards for Postal Field Service

QSR .... Quality Status Review (MCD)

QSR .... Quality Strike Reconnaissance

QSR .... Quality System Review

QSR .... Quarterly Statistical Report (NRCH)

QSR .... Quarterly Status Report

QSR .... Quarterly Summary Report

QSR .... Quasi-Stellar Radio Source

QSR .... Quebec Sturgeon River Mines Ltd. [*Toronto Stock Exchange symbol*]

QSR .... Queensland State Reports [*Australia*] [*A publication*] (DLA)

QSR .... Quick-Start Recording [*Video technology*]

QSR .... Quick Strike Reconnaissance (MCD)

QSR .... Quien Sabe Ranch [*California*] [*Seismograph station code, US Geological Survey*] (SEIS)

QSR .... Quinoline Still Residue [*Coal tar technology*]

QSR .... State Reports (Queensland) [*A publication*] (APTA)

QSRA .... Quiet Short-Haul Research Aircraft [*NASA*]

QSRI......... QSR, Inc. [*NASDAQ symbol*] (NQ)

QSRMC.... Quality Scheme for Ready Mixed Concrete (EAIO)

QSRS........ Quasi-Stellar Radio Source

QSRT........ Quebec Sturgeon River Mines Ltd. [*NASDAQ symbol*] (NQ)

QSS......... Quadratic Score Statistic [*Test*]

QSS......... Quadrupole Screw Ship

QSS......... Quasi-Steady State

QSS......... Quasi-Stellar Source

QSS......... Quench Spray Subsystem (IEEE)

QSS......... Quick Service Supervisor (MCD)

QSS......... Quick Supply Store [*Military*] (AABC)

QSS......... Quill and Scroll Society (EA)

QSS......... Quindar Scanning System (NASA)

QSSA .... Quasi-Stationary State Approximation

QSSP .... Quasi-Solid State Panel

QSSR .... Quarterly Stock Status Report

QSSU........ Queensland State Service Union [*Australia*]

QST .... QSA Tech, Inc. [*Vancouver Stock Exchange symbol*]

QST .... Quarterly Statement [*A publication*]

QST .... Quarterly Statements. Palestine Exploration Fund [*A publication*]

QST .... Queensland Science and Technology Ltd. [*Australia*]

QST .... Questmont Mines [*Vancouver Stock Exchange symbol*]

QSTAG..... Quadripartite Standardization Agreement [*Military*]

QSTAG..... Quality Standardization Agreements (MCD)

QSTAH ..... Ste-Anne's Hospital, Ste-Anne-De-Bellevue, Quebec [*Library symbol*] [*National Library of Canada*] (NLC)

QSTAJ ..... John Abbott College, Ste-Anne-De-Bellevue, Quebec [*Library symbol*] [*National Library of Canada*] (NLC)

QSTAMP.. Quality Stamp

QSTAS ...... Spar Technology Ltd., Ste-Anne-De-Bellevue, Quebec [*Library symbol*] [*National Library of Canada*] (NLC)

QSTB........ Bibliotheque Municipale, Saint-Bruno-De-Montarville, Quebec [*Library symbol*] [*National Library of Canada*] (BIB)

QSTBL ...... Abbaye de Saint-Benoit-Du-Lac, Comte De Brome, Quebec [*Library symbol*] [*National Library of Canada*] (NLC)

QSTC......... Tioxide Canada, Inc., Sorel, Quebec [*Library symbol*] [*National Library of Canada*] (NLC)

QSTFAG ... Centre de Documentation, Ministere de l'Agriculture, des Pecheries, et de l'Alimentation, Ste.-Foy, Quebec [*Library symbol*] [*National Library of Canada*] (NLC)

QSTFCE.... Centre de Documentation, Centrale de l'Enseignement du Quebec, Ste.-Foy, Quebec [*Library symbol*] [*National Library of Canada*] (NLC)

QSTFCR.... Resource Centre, St. Lawrence Campus, Champlain Regional College, Ste.-Foy, Quebec [*Library symbol*] [*National Library of Canada*] (NLC)

QSTFP ...... Protecteur du Citoyen du Quebec, Ste.-Foy [*Library symbol*] [*National Library of Canada*] (BIB)

QSTFR ...... Rexfor, Ste.-Foy, Quebec [*Library symbol*] [*National Library of Canada*] (NLC)

QSTFRA ... Centre de Documentation, Roche Associes Ltee., Ste.-Foy, Quebec [*Library symbol*] [*National Library of Canada*] (NLC)

QSTHHR .. Societe d'Histoire Regionale de St-Hyacinthe, Quebec [*Library symbol*] [*National Library of Canada*] (NLC)

QSTHS...... Seminaire de St-Hyacinthe, Quebec [*Library symbol*] [*National Library of Canada*] (NLC)

QSTHTA... Institut de Technologie Agricole et Alimentaire de St.-Hyacinthe, Quebec [*Library symbol*] [*National Library of Canada*] (NLC)

QSTHUM ... Headquarters Mobile Command, Canada Department of National Defence [*Quartier-General du Commandement de la Defense Nationale*] St-Hubert, Quebec [*Library symbol*] [*National Library of Canada*] (NLC)

QSTHV ..... Faulte de Medecine Veterinaire de l'Universite de Montreal, Saint-Hyacinthe, Quebec [*Library symbol*] [*National Library of Canada*] (NLC)

QSTING.... Quasi-Spectral Time Integration on Nested Grids

QSTJ .... College Militaire Royal de Saint-Jean, Quebec [*Library symbol*] [*National Library of Canada*] (NLC)

QSTJA ...... Bibliotheque Adelard-Berger, St.-Jean-Sur-Richelieu, Quebec [*Library symbol*] [*National Library of Canada*] (BIB)

QSTJAG ... Research Station, Agriculture Canada [*Station de Recherches, Agriculture Canada*] Saint-Jean, Quebec [*Library symbol*] [*National Library of Canada*] (NLC)

QSTJB...... Bibliotheque Municipale, Saint-Jean, Quebec [*Library symbol*] [*National Library of Canada*] (NLC)

QSTJC...... College Saint-Jean-Sur-Richelieu, Saint-Jean, Quebec [*Library symbol*] [*National Library of Canada*] (NLC)

QSTJCF .... Canadian Forces Base St. Jean [*Base des Forces Canadiennes St.-Jean*], Quebec [*Library symbol*] [*National Library of Canada*] (NLC)

QSTJE....... Bibliotheque Municipale, Saint-Jerome, Quebec [*Library symbol*] [*National Library of Canada*] (NLC)

QSTJEC .... CEGEP [*College d'Enseignement General et Professionnel*] de St.-Jerome, Quebec [*Library symbol*] [*National Library of Canada*] (BIB)

QSTJECR ... Conseil Regional de la Sante et des Services Sociaux Laurentides-Lanaudiere, Saint-Jerome, Quebec [*Library symbol*] [*National Library of Canada*] (NLC)

QSTJEJ .... Jesuites/Bibliotheque, Saint-Jerome, Quebec [*Library symbol*] [*National Library of Canada*] (NLC)

QSTJH...... Bibliotheque Medicale, Hopital du Haut-Richelieu, St.-Jean-Sur-Richelieu, Quebec [*Library symbol*] [*National Library of Canada*] (BIB)

QSTJSC .... Centre de Documentation, Departement de Sante Communautaire du Haut-Richelieu, St.-Jean, Quebec [*Library symbol*] [*National Library of Canada*] (NLC)

QSTL........ Bibliotheque Municipale, Saint-Laurent, Quebec [*Library symbol*] [*National Library of Canada*] (NLC)

QSTLD...... Dominion Yarn Co., St. Laurent, Quebec [*Library symbol*] [*National Library of Canada*] (BIB)

QSTNRY... Quasi-Stationary (FAAC)

QSTOL...... Quiet-Short-Takeoff-and-Landing [*Airplane*] [*Japan*]

QSTR........ Bibliotheque Municipale de Saint-Raphael-De-L'Ile-Bizard, Quebec [*Library symbol*] [*National Library of Canada*] (NLC)

QSTTB ...... Engineering Library, Bell Helicopter Textron, Ste. Therese, Quebec [*Library symbol*] [*National Library of Canada*] (NLC)

QSTTH ..... Les Industries Harnois, St-Thomas-De-Joliette, Quebec [*Library symbol*] [*National Library of Canada*] (NLC)

QSTV........ Queensland Satellite Television [*Australia*]

QSTX........ Questronics, Inc. [*NASDAQ symbol*] (NQ)

QS Wkly ... Quantity Surveyor Weekly [*A publication*]

QSY .... Quiet Sun Year

QT............ Aer Turas Teoranta [*Ireland*] [*ICAO designator*] (FAAC)

QT............ Bibliotheque Municipale, Trois-Rivieres, Quebec [*Library symbol*] [*National Library of Canada*] (NLC)

QT............ Qualification Test

QT............ Quantity

QT............ Quarry Tile [*Technical drawings*]

QT............ Quart (AFM)

QT............ Quarters

Qt............. Quartet [*A publication*]

QT............ Quartet [*Music*]

QT............ Quebec-Telephone [*Toronto Stock Exchange symbol*]

QT............ Questioned Trade [*on a stock exchange*]

QT............ Queuing Theory [*Telecommunications*]

QT............ Queuing Time [*Telecommunications*] (TEL)

QT............ Qui Tam [*Who as Well*] [*Latin*] (ILCA)

QT............ Quick Tan [*Trademark of Plough, Inc.*]

QT............ Quick Test

QT............ Quiet [*or sub rosa, as, "On the QT"*]

QT............ Quotation Ticker [*Business term*]

QT............ Quotient

QTA.......... Archives Nationales du Quebec, Trois-Rivieres, Quebec [*Library symbol*] [*National Library of Canada*] (NLC)

QTA.......... Quadrant Transformer Assembly

QTAM....... Quadrature Amplitude Modulation (MCD)

QTAM....... Queued Telecommunications Access Method [*IBM Corp.*] [*Data processing*]

QTAM....... Queued Terminal Access Method [*Data processing*]

QTB.......... Le Boreal Express, Montreal, Quebec [*Library symbol*] [*National Library of Canada*] (NLC)

QTB.......... Quarry-Tile Base [*Technical drawings*]

QTBC .... Bibliotheque Centrale de Pret de la Mauricie, Trois-Rivieres, Quebec [*Library symbol*] [*National Library of Canada*] (NLC)

QTC .... Queensland Treasury Corp. [*Australia*]

QTC .... Quick Transmission Change (MCD)

QTCE .... CEGEP [*College d'Enseignement General et Professionnel*], Trois-Rivieres, Quebec [*Library symbol*] [*National Library of Canada*] (NLC)

QTCHC ..... Centre Hospitalier Cooke, Trois-Rivieres, Quebec [*Library symbol*] [*National Library of Canada*] (NLC)

QTCL........ College Lafleche, Trois-Rivieres, Quebec [*Library symbol*] [*National Library of Canada*] (NLC)

QTCO........ Communication-Quebec, Trois-Rivieres, Quebec [*Library symbol*] [*National Library of Canada*] (NLC)

QTCPB...... Corporation Pierre Boucher, Trois-Rivieres, Quebec [*Library symbol*] [*National Library of Canada*] (NLC)

QTCRD ..... Conseil Regional de Developpement, Trois-Rivieres, Quebec [*Library symbol*] [*National Library of Canada*] (NLC)

QTCRS...... Conseil Regional de la Sante et des Services Sociaux, Trois-Rivieres, Quebec [*Library symbol*] [*National Library of Canada*] (NLC)

QTCSRV ... Commission Scolaire Regionale des Vieilles-Forges, Trois-Rivieres, Quebec [*Library symbol*] [*National Library of Canada*] (NLC)

QTCSS ...... Centre de Services Sociaux, Trois-Rivieres, Quebec [*Library symbol*] [*National Library of Canada*] (NLC)

QTD.......... Quadruple Terminal Digits (AABC)

QTD.......... Quartered

QTD.......... Quasi-Two-Dimensional

QTDG........ Quaker Theological Discussion Group (EA)

QTDM....... Qazaq Tili Tarychi Men Dyalektology Jasinin Moseleleri [*A publication*]

QT DX ...... Quantitas Duplex [*Double Quantity*] [*Pharmacy*]

QTE .... Ecole Normale M. L. Duplessis, Trois-Rivieres, Quebec [*Library symbol*] [*National Library of Canada*] (NLC)

QT & E...... Qualification Test and Evaluation [*Military*]

QTE .... Qualite [*Quality*] [*French*] (ROG)

QTE .... Quote

QTE .... True Bearing [*from me*] [*Aviation code*] (FAAC)

Q Teachers J ... Queensland Teachers' Journal [*A publication*] (APTA)

QTEC .... QuesTech, Inc. [*NASDAQ symbol*] (NQ)

Q-TECH.... Quality-Technology

QTER .... Bibliotheque Municipale, Terrebonne, Quebec [*Library symbol*] [*National Library of Canada*] (NLC)

4QTest ...... [*The*] Testimonia from Qumran. Cave Four (BJA)

QTEV........ Quadruple Turbo-Electric Vessel (DS)

QTF .... Quarry-Tile Floor [*Technical drawings*]

QTH .... Queued Transaction Handling [*Data processing*]

QTHSJ...... Hopital Saint-Joseph, Trois-Rivieres, Quebec [*Library symbol*] [*National Library of Canada*] (NLC)

QTHSM..... Hopital Sainte-Marie, Trois-Rivieres, Quebec [*Library symbol*] [*National Library of Canada*] (NLC)

QTI .... Institut Albert Tessier, Trois-Rivieres, Quebec [*Library symbol*] [*National Library of Canada*] (NLC)

Q Tic Num Ant Clas ... Quaderni Ticinesi. Numismatica e Antichita Classiche [*A publication*]

Q-TIP .... Qualified Terminable Interest Property [*Plan*] [*Tax law*]

QTL .... Quantitative Trait Loci [*Genetics*]

QTL .... Quantum Theory of LASERS

QTL .... Quarterly Title List

QTL .... Quintel Industries Ltd. [*Vancouver Stock Exchange symbol*]

4QTLevi.... Testament of Levi from Qumran. Cave Four (BJA)

Qtly.......... Quarterly

QTM......... Qualification Test Model

QTMC .... College de la Region de l'Amiante (CEGEP), Thetford-Mines, Quebec [*Library symbol*] [*National Library of Canada*] (NLC)

QTMC .... Quantum Diagnostics Ltd. [*Hauppauge, NY*] [*NASDAQ symbol*] (NQ)

QTME .... Ministere de l'Energie et des Ressources du Quebec, Trois-Rivieres, Quebec [*Library symbol*] [*National Library of Canada*] (BIB)

QTMH...... Hopital General de la Regie de l'Amiante, Inc., Thetford Mines, Quebec [*Library symbol*] [*National Library of Canada*] (BIB)

QTNT....... QT & T, Inc. [*Brentwood, NY*] [*NASDAQ symbol*] (NQ)

QTO.......... Qualified Testing Officer [*British military*] (DMA)

QTO.......... Quarto [*Book from 25 to 30 centimeters in height*]

QTOD....... Todd Shipyards Corp. [*NYSE symbol*] (SPSG)

QTOL....... Quiet Takeoff and Landing [*Aviation*]

QTOPDQ.. Centre de Documentation, Office de Planification et de Developpement du Quebec, Trois-Rivieres, Quebec [*Library symbol*] [*National Library of Canada*] (NLC)

QTOW....... Towle Manufacturing Co. [*NYSE symbol*] (SPSG)

QTP .... Qualification Test Plan [*NASA*] (NASA)

QTP .... Qualification Test Procedure

QTP .... Qualification Test Program

QTP .... Quality Test Plan [*Nuclear energy*] (NRCH)

QTP .... Quantum Theory of Paramagnetism

QTP .... Quantum Theory Project [*University of Florida*] [*Research center*] (RCD)

QTPC........ Quadripartite Technical Procedures Committee [*Military*] (AABC)

QTPR........ Quarterly Technical Progress Report

QTR.......... Qualification Test Report

QTR.......... Qualified Tuition Reduction [*IRS*]

QTR.......... Quarry-Tile Roof [*Technical drawings*]

QTR.......... Quarter (AFM)

QTR.......... Quarterly (AFM)

QTR.......... Quarterly Technical Report

QTR.......... Quarterly Technical Review [*Jet Propulsion Laboratory publication*]

QTR.......... Queenstake Resources Ltd. [*Toronto Stock Exchange symbol*]

QTRLY...... Quarterly

QTRRSS.... Centre de Documentation, Regie de la Securite dans les Sports du Quebec, Trois-Rivieres, Quebec [*Library symbol*] [*National Library of Canada*] (NLC)

QTRS........ Quarters

QTS .... Qualification Test Specification

QTS .... Quartz Thermometer Sensor

QTS .... Seminaire de Trois-Rivieres, Quebec [*Library symbol*] [*National Library of Canada*] (NLC)

QTT .... Quartet [*Music*]

QTT .... Trois-Rivieres High School, Quebec [*Library symbol*] [*National Library of Canada*] (NLC)

QTTA .... Quaderni Triestini sul Teatro Antico [*A publication*]

QTTE........ Quartette [*Music*]

QTTF........ Temifibre, Inc., Temiscaming, Quebec [*Library symbol*] [*National Library of Canada*] (NLC)

QTTP........ Q-Tags Test of Personality [*Psychology*]

QTU.......... Qualification Test Unit

QTU.......... Universite du Quebec, Trois-Rivieres, Quebec [*Library symbol*] [*National Library of Canada*] (NLC)

QTUAH..... Archives Historiques, Universite du Quebec, Trois-Rivieres, Quebec [*Library symbol*] [*National Library of Canada*] (NLC)

QTUGC..... Cartotheque, Departement de Geographie, Universite du Quebec, Trois-Rivieres, Quebec [*Library symbol*] [*National Library of Canada*] (NLC)

QTUIH...... Imprimes Historiques, Universite du Quebec, Trois-Rivieres, Quebec [*Library symbol*] [*National Library of Canada*] (NLC)

QTURA ..... Archives des Ursulines, Trois-Rivieres, Quebec [*Library symbol*] [*National Library of Canada*] (NLC)

QTUTH..... Centre de Documentation en Theatre Quebecois, Trois-Rivieres, Quebec [*Library symbol*] [*National Library of Canada*] (NLC)

QTV .... Qualification Test Vehicle

Qty .... Quality (DS)

QTY.......... Quantity (KSC)

QTYDESREQ ... Quantity Desired as Requested [*Military*]

QTZ.......... Quartz (AAG)

QTZ.......... Quartzite [*Lithology*]

QU .... Nicaragua [*License plate code assigned to foreign diplomats in the US*]

QU .... Quaderni dell'Umanesimo [*A publication*]

QU .... Quadrantectomy [*Medicine*]

QU .... Quail Unlimited (EA)

QU .... Quarter (ADA)

QU .... Quartermaster (ROG)

QU .... Quartern (ROG)

QU .... Quasi [*Almost, As It Were*] [*Latin*]

QU .... Quay (ROG)

QU .... Queen

QU .... Queen's University [*Canada*]

QU .... Query

QU .... Question

QU .... Questionnaire

QU .... Quina [*Quinine*] [*Pharmacy*] (ROG)

QU .... Quinto Mining [*Vancouver Stock Exchange symbol*]

QU .... Quotation (ROG)

QU .... Uganda Airlines Corp. [*ICAO designator*] (FAAC)

QUA .... Quabbin [*Massachusetts*] [*Seismograph station code, US Geological Survey*] (SEIS)

QUA .... Quality [*A publication*]

QUA .... Quinterra Resources, Inc. [*Toronto Stock Exchange symbol*] [*Vancouver Stock Exchange symbol*]

QUAC .... Quadriatic Arc Computer

QUAD .... Quadrajet Carburetor [*Automotive engineering*]

QUAD .... Quadrangle (AAG)

QUAD .... Quadrant (KSC)

QUAD .... Quadraphonic

QUAD .... Quadrature (NASA)

QUAD .... Quadrex Corp. [*NASDAQ symbol*] (NQ)

QUAD .... Quadrillion

Quad .... Quadriplegic

Quad .... Quadrivium [*A publication*]

QUAD .... Quadruple

Quad Acta Neurol ... Quaderni di Acta Neurologica [*A publication*]

Quad A Libia ... Quaderni di Archeologia della Libia [*A publication*]

Quad Anat Prat ... Quaderni di Anatomia Pratica [*A publication*]

Quad Azione Soc ... Quaderni di Azione Sociale [*A publication*]

Quad Cat.... Quaderni Catanesi di Studi Classici e Medievali [*A publication*]

Quad Chim CNR (Italy) ... Quaderni di Chimica. Consiglio Nazionale delle Ricerche (Italy) [*A publication*]

Quad Clin Ostet ... Quaderni di Clinica Ostetrica e Ginecologica [*A publication*]

Quad Clin Ostet Ginecol ... Quaderni de Clinica Ostetrica e Ginecologica [*A publication*]

Quad Coagulazione Argomenti Connessi ... Quaderni della Coagulazione e Argomenti Connessi [*A publication*]

Quad Criminol Clin ... Quaderni di Criminologia Clinica [*A publication*]

Quad Econ (Sarda) ... Quaderni dell'Economia (Sarda) [*A publication*]

Quad Emiliani ... Quaderni Emiliani [*A publication*]

Quad Ente Naz Semen Elette ... Quaderno. Ente Nazionale Sementi Elette [*A publication*]

Quaderni della Ra M ... Quaderni della Rassegna Musicale [*A publication*]

Quad Formaz ... Quaderni di Formazione [*A publication*]

Quad Geofis Appl ... Quaderni di Geofisica Applicata [*A publication*]

Quad G Fis ... Quaderni del Giornale di Fisica [*Italy*] [*A publication*]

Quad Ing Chim Ital ... Quaderni dell'Ingegnere Chimico Italiano [*A publication*]

Quad Ist Bot Univ Lab Crittogam (Pavia) ... Quaderni. Istituto Botanico. Universita Laboratorio Crittogamico (Pavia) [*A publication*]

Quad Ist Fil Gr ... Quaderni dell'Istituto di Filologia Greca [*A publication*]

Quad Mathesis Cosenza ... Mathesis di Cosenza. Quaderni [*A publication*]

Quad Merceol Ist Merceol Univ Bari ... Quaderni di Merceologia. Istituto di Merceologia. Universita Bari [*A publication*]

Quad Nutr ... Quaderni della Nutrizione [*A publication*]

Quad Nutr (Bologna) ... Quaderni della Nutrizione (Bologna) [*A publication*]

QUADPAN ... Quadrilateral Element Panel Method [*Aerospace propulsion*]

Quad Pignone ... Quaderni Pignone [*A publication*]

Quadr........ Quadragesms [*Yearbooks of Edward III*] [*A publication*] (DLA)

Quadr........ Quadrant [*A publication*]

QUADR..... Quadruple

QUADRADAR ... Four-Way RADAR Surveillance

Quad Radiol ... Quaderni di Radiologia [*A publication*]

Quadrangle Ser 1:50000 Geol Surv Jap ... Quadrangle Series 1:50,000. Geological Survey of Japan [*A publication*]

Quad Ricerca Sci ... Quaderni de la Ricerca Scientifica [*A publication*]

Quad Ric Progettazione ... Quaderni di Ricerca e Progettazione [*A publication*]

Quad Ric Sci ... Quaderni de la Ricerca Scientifica [*A publication*]

Quadrupl... Quadruplicato [*Four Times as Much*] [*Pharmacy*]

QUADS..... Quality Achievement Data System (NASA)

Quad Sardi Econ ... Quaderni Sardi di Economia [*A publication*]

Quad Sclavo Diagn ... Quaderni Sclavo di Diagnostica Clinica e di Laboratorio [*A publication*]

Quad Sclavo Diagn Clin Lab ... Quaderni Sclavo di Diagnostica Clinica e di Laboratorio [*A publication*]

Quad Ser III ... Quaderni. Serie III [*A publication*]

Quad Sez Perugina Soc Ital Biol Sper ... Quaderni. Sezione Perugina. Societa Italiana di Biologia Sperimentale [*A publication*]

Quad Sociol ... Quaderni di Sociologia [*A publication*]

Quad St Lun ... Quaderni. Centro di Studi Lunesi [*A publication*]

Quad Stor... Quaderni di Storia [*A publication*]

Quad Stor... Quaderni Storici [*A publication*]

Quad Storia Sci Med Univ Studi Ferrara ... Quaderni di Storia della Scienza e della Medicina. Universita degli Studi di Ferrara [*A publication*]

Quad Stor Univ Padova ... Quaderni per la Storia. Universita di Padova [*A publication*]

Quad Tec Sint Spec Org ... Quaderni di Tecniche e Sintesi Speciali Organiche [*A publication*]

Quad Top Ant ... Quaderni. Istituto di Topografia Antica. Universita di Roma [*A publication*]

Quad Urb C ... Quaderni Urbinati di Cultura Classica [*A publication*]

Quad Urbin ... Quaderni Urbinati di Cultura Classica [*A publication*]

Quaest Conv ... Quaestiones Convivales [*of Plutarch*] [*Classical studies*] (OCD)

Quaest Ent ... Quaestiones Entomologicae [*A publication*]

Quaest Entomol ... Quaestiones Entomologicae [*A publication*]
Quaest Geobiol ... Quaestiones Geobiologicae [*A publication*]
Quaest Graec ... Quaestiones Graecae [*of Plutarch*] [*Classical studies*]   (OCD)
Quaest Inf .. Quaestiones Informaticae [*A publication*]
Quaestiones Math ... Quaestiones Mathematicae [*A publication*]
Quaest Plat ... Quaestiones Platonicae [*of Plutarch*] [*Classical studies*]   (OCD)
Quaest Rom ... Quaestiones Romanae [*of Plutarch*] [*Classical studies*]   (OCD)
QuakerH .... Quaker History [*A publication*]
QUAL .... Qualification   (NG)
QUAL .... Qualitative
Qual .... Qualiton &' MHV [*Record label*] [*Hungary*]
QUAL .... Quality   (KSC)
Qual Assur ... Quality Assurance [*A publication*]
Qual Contr Appl Stat ... Quality Control and Applied Statistics [*A publication*]
Qual Eng... Quality Engineer [*A publication*]
Qual Eval ... Quality Evaluation [*A publication*]
Qualitas Pl Pl Fds Human Nutr ... Qualitas Plantarum/Plant Foods for Human Nutrition [*A publication*]
Qualite Rev Prat Controle Ind ... Qualite. Revue Pratique de Controle Industriel [*A publication*]
Quality .... Quality of Sheffield and South Yorkshire [*A publication*]
Quality Prog ... Quality Progress [*A publication*]
QUALN ..... Qualification   (ROG)
Qual Plant ... Qualitas Plantarum/Plant Foods for Human Nutrition [*A publication*]
Qual Plant Mater Veg ... Qualitas Plantarum et Materiae Vegetabiles [*Later, Qualitas Plantarum/Plant Foods for Human Nutrition*] [*A publication*]
Qual Plant Plant Foods Hum Nutr ... Qualitas Plantarum/Plant Foods for Human Nutrition [*A publication*]
Qual Prog... Quality Progress [*A publication*]
Qual Quant ... Quality and Quantity [*A publication*]
Qual Reliab J ... Quality and Reliability Journal [*India*] [*A publication*]
Qual Rev Prat Controle Ind ... Qualite. Revue Pratique de Controle Industriel [*A publication*]
QUALT ..... Queensland University Aphasia and Language Test
QUALTIS ... Quality Technology Information Service [*Atomic Energy Authority*] [*British*]   (IID)
Qual Today ... Quality Today [*A publication*]
Qual Zuverlaessigk ... Qualitaet und Zuverlaessigkeit [*A publication*]
Qual und Zuverlassigkeit ... Qualitaet und Zuverlassigkeit [*A publication*]
QUAM ...... Quadrature Amplitude Modulation   (IEEE)
QUAN ...... Quantity   (KSC)
QUAN ...... Quantronix Corp. [*NASDAQ symbol*]   (NQ)
QUANGO ... Quasi-Autonomous Non-Governmental [*or National Governmental*] Organisation [*British*]
Quan Sociol ... Quantitative Sociology [*A publication*]
QUANT ..... Quantitative [*or Quantity*]
Quant Chem Symp ... Quantum Chemistry Symposia [*A publication*]
Quantitative Appl in the Social Sciences ... Quantitative Applications in the Social Sciences [*A publication*]
Quantitative Meth Unternehmungsplanung ... Quantitative Methoden der Unternehmungsplanung [*A publication*]
Quantity Surv ... Quantity Surveyor [*A publication*]
QUANTRAS ... Question Analysis Transformation and Search [*Data processing*]
QUANT SUFF ... Quantum Sufficiat [*A Sufficient Quantity*] [*Pharmacy*]
Quant Suff ... Quantum Sufficit [*A Sufficient Quantity*] [*Pharmacy*]
Quantum Electron (New York) ... Quantum Electronics (New York) [*A publication*]
QUAOPS .. Quarantine Operations [*Military*]   (NVT)
QUAP .... Quality Assurance Procedures
QUAPP ..... Qu'Appelle [*Canadian river*]   (ROG)
QUAPS ..... Quality Assurance Publications [*Navy*]
QUAR .... Quarantine   (AABC)
QUAR .... Quarter [*Business term*]
QUAR .... Quarterly
Quar .... Quarterly Review [*A publication*]
QUARAM ... Quality and Reliability Management [*DoD*]
Quar Crim Dig ... Quarles' Tennessee Criminal Digest [*A publication*]   (DLA)
Quar Jour Econ ... Quarterly Journal of Economics [*A publication*]
QUARK ..... Quantizer, Analyzer, and Record Keeper [*Telecommunications*]   (TEL)
Quar Law Journal ... Quarterly Law Journal [*Virginia*] [*A publication*]   (DLA)
Quar L Rev ... Quarterly Law Review [*Virginia*] [*A publication*]   (DLA)
QUARLY .. Quarterly   (ROG)
QUARPEL ... Quartermaster Water-Repellent Clothing [*Military*]
Quar R Biol ... Quarterly Review of Biology [*A publication*]
Quar Rev .... Quarterly Review [*A publication*]
Quarries Mines Coal Health Saf .. Quarries and Mines Other than Coal. Health and Safety [*A publication*]
Quarry Manage Prod ... Quarry Management and Products [*Later, Quarry Management*] [*A publication*]
Quarry Mgmt ... Quarry Management [*A publication*]
Quarry Mgmt Products ... Quarry Management and Products [*Later, Quarry Management*] [*A publication*]
Quarry Min News ... Quarry and Mining News [*A publication*]
QUART ..... Quadrantectomy, Axillary Dissection, Radiotherapy [*Oncology*]
QUART ..... Quality Assurance and Reliability Team

QUART ..... Quarterly
QUART ..... Quartetto [*Quartet*] [*Music*]   (ROG)
QUART ..... Quartus [*Fourth*] [*Pharmacy*]
Quart Appl Math ... Quarterly of Applied Mathematics [*A publication*]
Quart Bul Ass Food Drug Offic US ... Quarterly Bulletin. Association of Food and Drug Officials of the United States [*Later, Quarterly Bulletin. Association of Food and Drug Officials*] [*A publication*]
Quart Bull Int Ass Agric Libr Docum ... Quarterly Bulletin. International Association of Agricultural Librarians and Documentalists [*A publication*]
Quart Bull Mich Agric Exp Sta ... Quarterly Bulletin. Michigan State University. Agricultural Experiment Station [*A publication*]
Quart Bull Mich State Univ Agr Exp Sta ... Quarterly Bulletin. Michigan State University. Agricultural Experiment Station [*A publication*]
Quart Bull Northwestern Univ M School ... Quarterly Bulletin. Northwestern University Medical School [*A publication*]
Quart Colo Sch Mines ... Quarterly. Colorado School of Mines [*A publication*]
Quarter Horse Dig ... Quarter Horse Digest [*A publication*]
Quarterly Appl Math ... Quarterly of Applied Mathematics [*A publication*]
Quarterly of F R TV ... Quarterly of Film, Radio, and Television [*A publication*]
Quartermaster Food Container Inst Armed Forces Act Rep ... Quartermaster Food and Container Institute for the Armed Forces. Activities Report [*A publication*]
Quart J Adm ... Quarterly Journal of Administration [*A publication*]
Quart J Agr Econ ... Quarterly Journal of Agricultural Economy [*A publication*]
Quart J Chin For (Taipei) ... Quarterly Journal of Chinese Forestry (Taipei) [*A publication*]
Quart J Crude Drug Res ... Quarterly Journal of Crude Drug Research [*A publication*]
Quart J Econ ... Quarterly Journal of Economics [*A publication*]
Quart J Econom ... Quarterly Journal of Economics [*A publication*]
Quart J Exp Physiol ... Quarterly Journal of Experimental Physiology [*A publication*]
Quart J Exp Psychol ... Quarterly Journal of Experimental Psychology [*A publication*]
Quart J For ... Quarterly Journal of Forestry [*A publication*]
Quart J Indian Inst Sci ... Quarterly Journal. Indian Institute of Science [*A publication*]
Quart J Libr Congress ... Quarterly Journal. Library of Congress [*A publication*]
Quart J Math Oxford Ser 2 ... Quarterly Journal of Mathematics. Oxford. Second Series [*A publication*]
Quart J Mech Appld Math ... Quarterly Journal of Mechanics and Applied Mathematics [*A publication*]
Quart J Mech Appl Math ... Quarterly Journal of Mechanics and Applied Mathematics [*A publication*]
Quart J Med ... Quarterly Journal of Medicine [*A publication*]
Quart J Microsc Sci ... Quarterly Journal of Microscopical Science [*A publication*]
Quart J Micr Sc ... Quarterly Journal of Microscopical Science [*A publication*]
Quart J Roy Meteorol Soc ... Quarterly Journal. Royal Meteorological Society [*A publication*]
Quart J Taiwan Mus ... Quarterly Journal. Taiwan Museum [*A publication*]
Quart J Vet Sc India ... Quarterly Journal of Veterinary Science in India and Army Animal Management [*A publication*]
Quart LJ (VA) ... Quarterly Law Journal [*Virginia*] [*A publication*]   (DLA)
Quart L Rev (VA) ... Quarterly Law Review [*Virginia*] [*A publication*]   (DLA)
QUARTM ... Quartermaster   (ROG)
Quart Nat Dent Ass ... Quarterly. National Dental Association [*A publication*]
Quart Nebr Agr Exp Sta ... Quarterly. Nebraska Agricultural Experiment Station [*A publication*]
Quart Newsl (Dehra Dun) ... Quarterly News Letter. Forest Research Institute and Colleges (Dehra Dun) [*A publication*]
Quart Philippine Sugar Inst ... Quarterly. Philippine Sugar Institute [*A publication*]
Quart R ...... Quarterly Review [*A publication*]
Quart R ...... Quarterly Reviews. Chemical Society [*A publication*]
Quart R Agric ... Quarterly Review of Agricultural Economics [*A publication*]   (APTA)
Quart R Agric Econ ... Quarterly Review of Agricultural Economics [*A publication*]
Quart R Centr Bank Ireland ... Quarterly Review. Central Bank of Ireland [*A publication*]
Quart R Econ Busin ... Quarterly Review of Economics and Business [*A publication*]
Quart Rep Ry Tech Res Inst ... Quarterly Report. Railway Technical Research Institute [*Tokyo*] [*A publication*]
Quart Rev... Quarterly Review [*A publication*]
Quart Rev... Quarterly Reviews. Chemical Society [*A publication*]
Quart Rev Agr Econ ... Quarterly Review of Agricultural Economics [*A publication*]
Quart Rev Agric Econ ... Quarterly Review of Agricultural Economics [*A publication*]   (APTA)
Quart Rev Allergy ... Quarterly Review of Allergy and Applied Immunology [*A publication*]

Quart Rev Biol ... Quarterly Review of Biology [*A publication*]
Quart Rev Chem Soc ... Quarterly Reviews. Chemical Society [*A publication*]
Quart Rev Guernsey Soc ... Quarterly Review. Guernsey Society [*A publication*]
Quart Revs ... Quarterly Reviews. Chemical Society [*A publication*]
Quart Trans Soc Autom Eng ... Quarterly Transactions. Society of Automotive Engineers [*A publication*]
Quart Univ Nebr Coll Agr Home Econ Agr Exp Sta ... Quarterly. University of Nebraska. College of Agriculture and Home Economics. Agricultural Experiment Station [*A publication*]
QUARTZ GR ... Quartzite Granite [*Agronomy*]
QUASAR... Quasi-Stellar Radio Source
QUASAT... Quasar Satellite [*Proposed observatory in space*]
QUASD... Quality Assurance [*A publication*]
QUASER... Quantum Amplification by Stimulated Emission of Radiation
QUASS...... Quassia [*Pharmacology*] (ROG)
QUAT........ Quater [*Four Times*] [*Pharmacy*]
QUAT........ Quaternary [*Period, era, or system*] [*Geology*]
QUAT........ Quaternary Ammonium Compound [*Class of antimicrobial agents*]
QUAT....... Quaternion (NASA)
QUAT........ Quatrefoil [*Numismatics*]
Quaternary Res ... Quaternary Research [*A publication*]
Quatern Res ... Quaternary Research [*A publication*]
QUATIP.... Quality Assurance Test and Inspection Plan [*Military*] (CAAL)
Quat Res (Jap Assoc Quat Res) ... Quaternary Research (Japan Association of Quaternary Research) [*A publication*]
Quat Res (NY) ... Quaternary Research (New York) [*A publication*]
Quat Res (Tokyo) ... Quaternary Research (Tokyo) [*A publication*]
Quat Sci R ... Quaternary Science Reviews [*A publication*]
QUB.......... Queen's University, Belfast [*Ireland*]
QUBMIS... Quantitatively Based Management Information System
Qu Bull...... Quarterly Bulletin [*A publication*]
quc.............. Quebec [*MARC country of publication code*] [*Library of Congress*] (LCCP)
QUCA....... Quality Care, Inc. [*NASDAQ symbol*] (NQ)
QUCC........ Quaderni Urbinati di Cultura Classica [*A publication*]
QUE........... Albuquerque Public Library, Albuquerque, NM [*OCLC symbol*] (OCLC)
QUE........... Quebec [*Canadian province*]
que.............. Quechua [*MARC language code*] [*Library of Congress*] (LCCP)
QUE........... Queenston Gold Mines Ltd. [*Toronto Stock Exchange symbol*]
QUE........... Quetta [*Pakistan*] [*Geomagnetic observatory code*]
QUE........... Quetta [*Pakistan*] [*Seismograph station code, US Geological Survey*] (SEIS)
Quebec Dept Nat Resources Prelim Rept ... Quebec. Department of Natural Resources. Preliminary Report [*A publication*]
Quebec Dept Nat Resources Spec Paper ... Quebec. Department of Natural Resources. Special Paper [*A publication*]
Quebec Dept Trade and Commerce Geog Service Pub ... Quebec. Department of Trade and Commerce. Geographical Service. Publication [*A publication*]
Quebec L (Can) ... Quebec Law Reports [*Canada*] [*A publication*] (DLA)
Quebec Pr (Can) ... Quebec Practice [*Canada*] [*A publication*] (DLA)
Queb KB .... Quebec Official Reports, King's Bench [*Canada*] [*A publication*] (DLA)
Queb Pr...... Quebec Practice Reports [*1897-1943*] [*A publication*] (DLA)
Que BR ...... Quebec Rapports Judiciaires Officiels (Banc de la Reine, Cour Superieure) [*A publication*] (DLA)
Que C A ..... Quebec Official Reports, Court of Appeals [*A publication*]
Que CA ...... Rapports Judiciaires Officiels, Cour d'Appel [*1892-date*] [*Official Law Reports, Court of Appeal*] [*Quebec*] [*A publication*] (DLA)
Que CBR.... Rapports Judiciaires Officiels, Cour du Banc du Roi [*ou de la Reine*] [*Official Law Reports, Court of King's, or Queen's, Bench*] [*Quebec*] [*A publication*] (DLA)
Que Cons Rech Dev For Rapp ... Quebec. Conseil de la Recherche et du Developpement Forestiers. Rapport [*A publication*]
Que Cons Rech Dev For Rapp Annu ... Quebec. Conseil de la Recherche et du Developpement Forestiers. Rapport Annuel [*A publication*]
Que CS....... Rapports Judiciaires Officiels, Cour Superieure [*Official Law Reports, Superior Court*] [*Quebec*] [*A publication*] (DLA)
Que Dep Ind Commer Annu Rep ... Quebec. Department of Industry and Commerce. Annual Report [*A publication*]
Que Dep Lands For Res Serv Res Pap ... Quebec. Department of Lands and Forest Research Service. Research Paper [*A publication*]
Que Dep Natur Resour Geol Rep ... Quebec. Department of Natural Resources. Geological Report [*A publication*]
Que Dep Natur Resour Prelim Rep ... Quebec. Department of Natural Resources. Preliminary Report [*A publication*]
Que Dir Geol Trav Terrain ... Quebec. Direction de la Geologie. Travaux sur le Terrain [*A publication*]
Que Dp Col Mines Br Rp ... Quebec. Department of Colonization, Mines, and Fisheries. Mines Branch. Report on Mining Operations [*A publication*]
Queen Q..... Queen's Quarterly [*A publication*]
Queens .... Queensland [*Australia*]
Queens .... Queensway Studios [*Record label*] [*Great Britain*]
Queens B Bull ... Queens Bar Bulletin [*United States*] [*A publication*] (DLA)

Queens CBA Bull ... Queens County Bar Association. Bulletin [*United States*] [*A publication*] (DLA)
Queens Intra LJ ... Queen's Intramural Law Journal [*1968-70*] [*Canada*] [*A publication*] (DLA)
Queen's Intramural LJ ... Queen's Intramural Law Journal [*A publication*]
Queens JP & Loc Auth Jo ... Queensland Justice of the Peace and Local Authorities' Journal [*A publication*] (DLA)
QUEENSL ... Queensland [*Australia*] (ROG)
Queensl ...... Queensland Reports [*A publication*]
Queensl Acts ... Queensland Public Acts [*A publication*] (DLA)
Queensl Agric J ... Queensland Agricultural Journal [*A publication*]
Queensland Ag J ... Queensland Agricultural Journal [*A publication*]
Queensland Agr J ... Queensland Agricultural Journal [*A publication*]
Queensland Dent Mag ... Queensland Dental Magazine [*A publication*] (APTA)
Queensland Gov Min J ... Queensland Government Mining Journal [*A publication*] (APTA)
Queensland Govt Min Jour ... Queensland Government Mining Journal [*A publication*]
Queensland Hist R ... Queensland Historical Review [*A publication*]
Queensland J Agr Anim Sci ... Queensland Journal of Agricultural and Animal Sciences [*A publication*]
Queensland J Ag Sci ... Queensland Journal of Agricultural Science [*Later, Queensland Journal of Agricultural and Animal Sciences*] [*A publication*] (APTA)
Queensland Land Court Rep ... Queensland Land Court Reports [*A publication*] (APTA)
Queensland L Soc'y J ... Queensland Law Society. Journal [*A publication*]
Queensland Pap in Econ Policy ... Queensland Papers in Economic Policy [*A publication*] (APTA)
Queens Law ... Queensland Lawyer [*Australia*] [*A publication*] (DLA)
Queensl Cr Lands LR ... Queensland Crown Lands Law Reports [*A publication*] (DLA)
Queensl Dent J ... Queensland Dental Journal [*A publication*] (APTA)
Queensl Dep Agric Stock ... Queensland. Department of Agriculture and Stock. Annual Report [*A publication*] (APTA)
Queensl Dep Mines Geol Surv Queensl Publ ... Queensland. Department of Mines. Geological Survey of Queensland. Publication [*A publication*] (APTA)
Queensl Dep Mines Geol Surv Queensl Rep ... Queensland. Department of Mines. Geological Survey of Queensland. Report [*A publication*] (APTA)
Queensl Dep Primary Ind Agric Chem Branch Tech Rep ... Queensland. Department of Primary Industries. Agricultural Chemistry Branch. Technical Report [*A publication*]
Queensl Dep Primary Ind Div Anim Ind Bull ... Queensland. Department of Primary Industries. Division of Animal Industry. Bulletin [*A publication*]
Queensl Dep Primary Ind Div Dairy Bull ... Queensland. Department of Primary Industries. Division of Dairying. Bulletin [*A publication*]
Queensl Dep Primary Ind Div Plant Ind Bull ... Queensland. Department of Primary Industries. Division of Plant Industry. Bulletin [*A publication*]
Queensl Dep Primary Ind Inf Ser ... Queensland. Department of Primary Industries. Information Series [*A publication*]
Queensl Fish Serv Res Bull ... Queensland. Fisheries Service. Research Bulletin [*A publication*]
Queensl Fish Serv Tech Rep ... Queensland. Fisheries Service. Technical Report [*A publication*]
Queensl Geogr J ... Queensland Geographical Journal [*A publication*] (APTA)
Queensl Geol ... Queensland Geology [*A publication*]
Queensl Geol Surv 1:250000 Geol Ser ... Queensland. Geological Survey. 1:250,000 Geological Series [*A publication*] (APTA)
Queensl Geol Surv Publ ... Queensland. Geological Survey. Publication [*A publication*]
Queensl Geol Surv Rep ... Queensland. Geological Survey. Report [*A publication*]
Queensl Gov Min J ... Queensland Government Mining Journal [*A publication*]
Queensl Herit ... Queensland Heritage [*A publication*] (APTA)
Queen's L J ... Queen's Law Journal [*A publication*]
Queens LJ ... Queensland Law Journal and Reports [*A publication*] (APTA)
Queensl J Agric Anim Sci ... Queensland Journal of Agricultural and Animal Sciences [*A publication*]
Queensl J Agric & Anim Sci ... Queensland Journal of Agricultural and Animal Sciences [*A publication*] (APTA)
Queensl J Agric Sci ... Queensland Journal of Agricultural Science [*Later, Queensland Journal of Agricultural and Animal Sciences*] [*A publication*]
Queensl JPR ... Queensland Justice of the Peace. Reports [*A publication*] (DLA)
Queensl JP Rep ... Queensland Justice of the Peace. Reports [*A publication*] (DLA)
Queensl L... Queensland Law [*A publication*] (DLA)
Queensl LJ (Austr) ... Queensland Law Journal (Australia) [*A publication*]
Queensl LJ & R ... Queensland Law Journal and Reports [*A publication*]
Queensl LJ & St R ... Queensland Law Journal and State Reports [*Australia*] [*A publication*] (DLA)

Queensl LR ... Queensland Law Reports [*A publication*]
Queensl LSJ ... Queensland Law Society. Journal [*A publication*] [*A publication*] (DLA)
Queensl L Soc'y J ... Queensland Law Society. Journal [*A publication*]
Queensl Nat ... Queensland Naturalist [*A publication*]
Queensl Nurses J ... Queensland Nurses Journal [*A publication*]
Queensl Pub Acts ... Queensland Public Acts [*A publication*]   (DLA)
Queens LR ... Queensland Law Reports (Beor) [*A publication*]   (APTA)
Queensl R .. Queensland State Reports [*A publication*]   (DLA)
Queensl SC (Austr) ... Queensland. Supreme Court. Reports (Australia) [*A publication*]
Queensl SCR ... Queensland. Supreme Court. Reports [*A publication*]   (DLA)
Queensl S Ct R ... Queensland. Supreme Court. Reports [*A publication*]
Queensl Soc Sugar Cane Technol Proc ... Queensland Society of Sugar Cane Technologists. Proceedings [*A publication*]   (APTA)
Queens L Soc'y J ... Queensland Law Society. Journal [*A publication*]   (DLA)
Queensl Stat ... Queensland Statutes [*Australia*] [*A publication*]   (DLA)
Queensl St (Austr) ... Queensland State Reports [*Australia*] [*A publication*]   (DLA)
Queensl St R ... Queensland State Reports [*Australia*] [*A publication*]   (DLA)
Queensl St Rep ... Queensland State Reports [*Australia*] [*A publication*]   (DLA)
Queensl Univ Dep Civ Eng Bull ... Queensland University. Department of Civil Engineering. Bulletin [*A publication*]
Queensl Univ Dep Geol Pap ... Queensland University. Department of Geology. Papers [*A publication*]
Queensl Vet Proc ... Queensland Veterinary Proceedings (Australian Veterinary Association, Queensland Division) [*A publication*]   (APTA)
Queensl WN (Aus) ... Queensland Law Reporter and Weekly Notes (Australia) [*A publication*]   (DLA)
Queensl WN (Austr) ... Queensland Weekly Notes (Australia) [*A publication*]   (DLA)
Queen's Nurs J ... Queen's Nursing Journal [*A publication*]
Queen's Papers in Pure and Appl Math ... Queen's Papers in Pure and Applied Mathematics [*A publication*]
Queen's Q .. Queen's Quarterly [*A publication*]
Queen's Quart ... Queen's Quarterly [*A publication*]
Queens St R ... Queensland State Reports [*A publication*]   (DLA)
Queens Univ Therm Fluid Sci Group Rep ... Queen's University. Thermal and Fluid Science Group. Report [*A publication*]
Que KB ...... Quebec Official Reports, King's Bench [*A publication*]   (DLA)
Que L .... Quebec Law [*A publication*]   (DLA)
Quellen Stud Philos ... Quellen und Studien zur Philosophie [*A publication*]
Que LR ...... Quebec Law Reports [*Canada*] [*A publication*]   (DLA)
QUELS ...... Quasi-Elastic Light Scattering [*Also, QELS, QLS*] [*Physics*]
Que Minist Agric Pech Aliment Dir Gen Pech Marit Cah Inf ... Quebec. Ministere de l'Agriculture, des Pecheries, et de l'Alimentation. Direction General des Peches Maritimes. Cahier d'Information [*A publication*]
Que Minist Chasse Pech Contrib ... Quebec. Ministere de la Chasse et des Pecheries. Contributions [*A publication*]
Que Minist Energ Ressour Serv Rech For Mem ... Quebec. Ministere de l'Energie et des Ressources. Service de la Recherche Forestiere. Memoire [*A publication*]
Que Minist Energ Ressour Serv Rech Mem ... Quebec. Ministere de l'Energie et des Ressources. Service de la Recherche. Memoire [*A publication*]
Que Minist Ind Commer Dir Rech Cah Inf ... Quebec. Ministere de l'Industrie et du Commerce. Direction de la Recherches Cahiers d'Information [*A publication*]
Que Minist Ind Commer Rapp Pech ... Quebec. Ministere de l'Industrie et du Commerce. Rapport sur les Pecheries [*A publication*]
Que Minist Ind Commer Serv Biol Rapp Annu ... Quebec. Ministere de l'Industrie et du Commerce. Service de Biologie. Rapport Annuel [*A publication*]
Que Minist Richesses Nat Etude Spec ... Quebec. Ministere des Richesses Naturelles. Etude Speciale [*A publication*]
Que Minist Terres For Serv Rech Note ... Quebec. Ministere des Terres et Forets. Service de la Recherche. Note [*A publication*]
Que Pr .... Quebec Practice [*A publication*]   (DLA)
Que PR .... Quebec Practice Reports [*A publication*]   (DLA)
Que Prac .... Quebec Practice Reports [*A publication*]   (DLA)
Que (Prov) Dep Mines Gen Rep Minist Mines ... Quebec (Province). Department of Mines. General Report of the Minister of Mines [*A publication*]
Que (Prov) Minist Richesses Nat Rapp Prelim ... Quebec (Province). Ministere des Richesses Naturelles. Rapport Preliminaire [*A publication*]
Que QB ...... Quebec Official Reports, Queen's Bench [*A publication*]   (DLA)
QUERC ..... Quercus [*Oak*] [*Pharmacology*]   (ROG)
Que Rev Jud ... Quebec Revised Judicial [*A publication*]   (DLA)
Que Rev Regs ... Revised Regulations of Quebec [*A publication*]
Que Rev Stat ... Quebec Revised Statutes [*Canada*] [*A publication*]   (DLA)
Que Rev Stat ... Revised Statutes of Quebec [*A publication*]
Query File Commonw Bur Hortic Plant Crops ... Query File. Commonwealth Bureau of Horticulture and Plantation Crops [*A publication*]
QUES .... Question   (AAG)
QUES .... Question Mark   (AABC)
Que SC .... Quebec Official Reports, Superior Court [*A publication*]   (DLA)

Que Sci .... Quebec Science [*A publication*]
Que Serv Faune Rapp ... Quebec. Service de la Faune. Rapport [*A publication*]
Que Soc Prot Plants Rep ... Quebec Society for the Protection of Plants. Report [*A publication*]
QUEST ...... Qualitative Experimental Stress Tomography
QUEST ...... Quality Electrical Systems Test [*Interpreter*]
QUEST ...... Quality Utilization Effectiveness Statistically Qualified
QUEST ...... Quantitative Environmental Science and Technology [*ULDECO Ltd.*] [*British*]   (IRUK)
QUEST ...... Quantitative Understanding of Explosive Stimulus Transfer
QUEST ...... Quantitative Utility Estimates for Science and Technology [*RAND Corp.*]
QUEST ...... Query Evaluation and Search Technique
QUEST ...... Question
Quest Act Soc ... Questions Actuelles du Socialisme [*A publication*]
Quest Act Socialisme ... Questions Actuelles du Socialisme [*A publication*]
Que Stat ...... Quebec Statutes [*Canada*] [*A publication*]   (DLA)
QUESTER ... Quick and Effective System to Enhance Retrieval [*Data processing*]
Quest For ... Questions of Forestry [*A publication*]
QUESTIIO ... Quaderns d'Estadistica. Sistemes. Informatica i Investigacio Operativa [*A publication*]
QUESTN ... Question
Questn .... Questionnaire   (ADA)
QUESTOL ... Quiet Experimental Short Takeoff and Landing [*Program*] [*NASA*]
Que Super .. Quebec Official Reports, Superior Court [*A publication*]   (DLA)
Que Tax Rep (CCH) ... Quebec Tax Reporter (Commerce Clearing House) [*A publication*]   (DLA)
Quetico-Super Wilderness Res Cent Annu Rep ... Quetico-Superior Wilderness Research Center. Annual Report [*A publication*]
Quetico-Super Wilderness Res Cent Tech Note ... Quetico-Superior Wilderness Research Center. Technical Note [*A publication*]
QUF .... National Bank of Yugoslavia. Quarterly Bulletin [*A publication*]
QU Gazette ... Queensland University. Gazette [*A publication*]   (APTA)
QUH .... Queen's University Highland Battalion [*British military*]   (DMA)
QUI .... Queen's University, Ireland
QUI .... Quincy Railroad Co. [*Later, QRR*] [*AAR code*]
QUI .... Quito [*Ecuador*] [*Seismograph station code, US Geological Survey*] [*Closed*]   (SEIS)
QUI .... Quito, Ecuador, Tracking Station [*NASA*]   (NASA)
QUI .... Thomas Crane Public Library, Quincy, MA [*OCLC symbol*]   (OCLC)
QUIBA ...... Quimica e Industria [*Madrid*] [*A publication*]
QUIC .... Quality Data Information and Control   (NASA)
QUICK ...... Quotation Information Center KK [*Nihon Keizai Shimbun, Inc.*] [*Information service or system*]   (IID)
QUICKTRAN ... Quick FORTRAN [*Programming language*] [*1979*]
QUID .... Quantified Intrapersonal Decision-Making [*In book title*]
QUIES .... Quiescent
QUIJA .... Quintessence International [*A publication*]
QUIK .... Quiksilver, Inc. [*Costa Mesa, CA*] [*NASDAQ symbol*]   (NQ)
QUIL .... Quad in Line [*Electronics*] [*Telecommunications*]   (TEL)
QUILL .... Queen's University Interrogation of Legal Literature [*Queen's University of Belfast*] [*Northern Ireland*] [*Information service or system*]   (IID)
QUILL .... QUILL: Queensland Inter-Library Liaison [*A publication*]   (APTA)
Quill & Q ... Quill and Quire [*A publication*]
Quim Anal ... Quimica Analitica [*A publication*]
Quim Farm ... Quimica y Farmica [*A publication*]
Quim Ind .... Quimica e Industria [*A publication*]
Quim Ind (Barcelona) ... Quimica e Industria (Barcelona) [*A publication*]
Quim Ind (Bogota) ... Quimica e Industria (Bogota) [*A publication*]
Quim Ind (Madrid) ... Quimica e Industria (Madrid) [*A publication*]
Quim Ind (Montevideo) ... Quimica Industrial (Montevideo) [*A publication*]
Quim Ind (Sao Paulo) ... Quimica e Industria (Sao Paulo) [*A publication*]
Quim Nova ... Quimica Nova [*A publication*]
QUIN .... Quina [*Quinine*] [*Pharmacy*]   (ROG)
Quin .... Quincy's Massachusetts Reports [*A publication*]   (DLA)
QUIN .... Quintuple
Quin Bank ... Quin on Banking [*1833*] [*A publication*]   (DLA)
Quinct .... Pro Quinctio [*of Cicero*] [*Classical studies*]   (OCD)
Quincy .... Quincy's Massachusetts Reports [*A publication*]   (DLA)
QUINT ...... Quintetto [*Quintet*] [*Music*]   (ROG)
Quint .... Quintilian [*First century AD*] [*Classical studies*]   (OCD)
QUINT ...... Quintuple
Quintessence Dent Technol ... Quintessence of Dental Technology [*A publication*]
Quintessence Int ... Quintessence International [*A publication*]
Quintessencia Protese Lab ... Quintessencia de Protese de Laboratorio [*A publication*]
Quintessenz J ... Quintessenz Journal [*A publication*]
Quintessenz Zahntech ... Quintessenz der Zahntechnik [*A publication*]
Quinti Quinto ... Year Book 5 Henry V [*England*] [*A publication*]   (DLA)
Quint Smyrn ... Quintus Smyrnaeus [*Classical studies*]   (OCD)
Quinz Lit .... Quinzaine Litteraire [*A publication*]

QUIP .... Quad In-Line Package
QUIP .... Query Interactive Processor (IEEE)
QUIP .... Quipp, Inc. [*NASDAQ symbol*] (NQ)
QUIP .... QUOTA [*Query Online Terminal Assistance*] Input Processor
          [*Data processing*]
QUIV .... Quiver (ROG)
Quix .... Quixote [*A publication*]
QUIX .... Quixote Corp. [*NASDAQ symbol*] (NQ)
Qu Jour Int-Amer Rel ... Quarterly Journal of Inter-American Relations [*A
          publication*] (DLA)
QUK .... Quaker Resources, Inc. [*Vancouver Stock Exchange symbol*]
QUL .... Quillagua [*Chile*] [*Seismograph station code, US Geological
          Survey*] (SEIS)
Qu Lait ...... Quebec Laitier [*A publication*]
QU Law J .. University of Queensland. Law Journal [*A
          publication*] (APTA)
Qu LJ .... Quarterly Law Journal [*A publication*] (DLA)
QULJ .... Queensland University. Law Journal [*A publication*] (APTA)
Qu L Rev .... Quarterly Law Review [*A publication*] (DLA)
QUM .... Queen's University, Medical Library [*UTLAS symbol*]
QUM .... Quillmana [*Peru*] [*Seismograph station code, US Geological
          Survey*] [*Closed*] (SEIS)
QUMDO ... Qualitative Materiel Development Objective [*Army*] (AFIT)
QUME .... Qume Corp. [*NASDAQ symbol*] (NQ)
Qu Minist Ind Commer Serv Rech Cah Inf ... Quebec. Ministere de l'Industrie
          et du Commerce. Service de la Recherche. Cahiers
          d'Information [*A publication*]
Qu Minist Terres For Serv Rech Mem ... Quebec. Ministere des Terres et
          Forets. Service de la Recherche. Memoire [*A publication*]
Qu Minist Terres For Serv Rech Note ... Quebec. Ministere des Terres et
          Forets. Service de la Recherche. Note [*A publication*]
QUMR .... Quality Unsatisfactory Material Report (MCD)
QUMS .... Quasar Microsystems [*NASDAQ symbol*] (NQ)
Q Univ Gaz ... University of Queensland. Gazette [*A publication*] (APTA)
QUNJA ..... Queensland Nurses Journal [*A publication*]
QUNO .... Quaker United Nations Office (EAIO)
QUO .... Quadex Users' Organization (EA)
QUO .... Quote Resources, Inc. [*Vancouver Stock Exchange symbol*]
QUODD ... Quodlibet [*Newsletter of the Southeastern Region*] [*A
          publication*]
Quomodo Adul ... Quomodo Adulescens Poetas Audire Debeat [*of Plutarch*]
          [*Classical studies*] (OCD)
QUON ...... Question (ROG)
Quon Attach ... Quoniam Attachiamenta [*A publication*] (DLA)
QUONBLE ... Questionable (ROG)
QUOR ...... Quorum [*Of Which*] [*Pharmacy*]
QUOT .... Quotation
quot .... Quoted In [*or Quoting*] [*Legal term*] (DLA)
QUOT .... Quotient (MSA)
QUOT .... Quoties [*As Often as Needed*] [*Pharmacy*]
QUOT .... Quotron Systems [*NASDAQ symbol*] (NQ)
QUOTA ..... Query Online Terminal Assistance [*Data processing*]
QUOTID ... Quotidie [*Daily*] [*Pharmacy*]
QUOT OP SIT ... Quoties Opus Sit [*As Often as Necessary*] [*Pharmacy*]
QUP .... Quality Unit Pack
QUP .... Quantity Unit Pack
QUP .... Quonset Point [*Navy*]
Qu (Prov) Dep Mines Gen Rep Minist Mines ... Quebec (Province).
          Department of Mines. General Report. Minister of Mines
          [*A publication*]
Qu (Prov) Dep Mines Prelim Rep ... Quebec (Province). Department of Mines.
          Preliminary Report [*A publication*]
Qu (Prov) Dep Nat Resour Spec Pap ... Quebec (Province). Department of
          Natural Resources. Special Paper [*A publication*]
QUR .... Quinstar Resources [*Vancouver Stock Exchange symbol*]
QURBA ..... Quarterly Reviews of Biophysics [*A publication*]
QUREA ..... Quarterly Reviews. Chemical Society [*A publication*]
QURZ .... Quartz, Inc. [*NASDAQ symbol*] (NQ)
QuSAR ...... Quantitative Structure Activity Relationships [*National
          Institute on Drug Abuse*]
Qu Serv Faune Bull ... Quebec. Service de la Faune. Bulletin [*A publication*]
Qu Serv Faune Rapp ... Quebec. Service de la Faune. Rapport [*A publication*]
QUSZA ..... Quintessenz Journal [*A publication*]
QUT .... Queensland University of Technology [*Australia*]
QUTLJ ...... Queensland University of Technology. Law Journal [*A
          publication*]
QUX .... Quinella Exploration Ltd. [*Vancouver Stock Exchange symbol*]
QUY .... Quest Energy Corp. [*Vancouver Stock Exchange symbol*]
QV .... Bibliotheque Municipale, Victoriaville, Quebec [*Library
          symbol*] [*National Library of Canada*] (NLC)
QV .... Lao Aviation [*Laos*] [*ICAO designator*] (ICDA)
QV .... Quality Verification [*Nuclear energy*] (NRCH)
QV .... Quantum Vis [*or Voleris*] [*As Much as You Wish*] [*Pharmacy*]
QV .... Quatro Ventos [*A publication*]
QV .... Queen Victoria [*British*]
QV .... Qui Vixit [*Who Lived*] [*Latin*]
QV .... Quo Vadis [*A publication*]
QV .... Quod Vide [*or Videte*] [*Which See*] [*Latin*]
Q4V .... Quicker for Victory [*World War II*]
QVAH .... Institut de Recherche d'Hydro-Quebec, Varennes, Quebec
          [*Library symbol*] [*National Library of Canada*] (NLC)

QVAI .... Centre de Documentation, INRS [*Institut National de la
          Recherche Scientifique*]-Energie, Varennes, Quebec
          [*Library symbol*] [*National Library of Canada*] (NLC)
Q Van Weyt ... Q. Van Weytson on Average [*A publication*] (DLA)
QVBFL ...... Bibliotheque Felix-Leclerc, Val-Belair, Quebec [*Library symbol*]
          [*National Library of Canada*] (NLC)
QVC .... College de Victoriaville, Quebec [*Library symbol*] [*National
          Library of Canada*] (NLC)
QVC .... Quality Value Convenience Network, Inc. [*Television*]
QVCEMBO ... Ecole Quebecoise du Meuble et du Bois Ouvre, College de
          Victoriaville, Quebec [*Library symbol*] [*National Library of
          Canada*] (NLC)
QVCN .... QVC Network, Inc. [*West Chester, PA*] [*NASDAQ
          symbol*] (NQ)
QVCSF ...... Queen Victoria's Clergy Sustentation Fund [*British*]
QVE .... Bibliotheque Municipale, Verdun, Quebec [*Library symbol*]
          [*National Library of Canada*] (BIB)
QVEC .... Cultural Centre [*Centre Culturel*] Verdun, Quebec [*Library
          symbol*] [*National Library of Canada*] (NLC)
QVEC .... Qualified Voluntary Employee Contribution
QVFC .... Queensland Volunteer Flying Civilians [*Australia*]
QVGCCQ .. Cree Regional Authority, Grand Council of the Crees (of
          Quebec) [*Administration Regionale Crie, Grand Conseil
          des Cris (du Quebec)*] Val D'Or, Quebec [*Library symbol*]
          [*National Library of Canada*] (NLC)
QVH .... Queen Victoria Hospital [*Australia*]
QVI .... Quality Verification Inspection
Q Vic .... Statutes of Quebec in the Reign of Victoria [*A
          publication*] (DLA)
Q Vit .... Quaderni del Vittoriale [*A publication*]
QVJVVNW ... Quellenverzeichnis der Justizverwaltungsvorschriften des
          Landes Nordrhein-Westfalen [*A publication*]
QVL .... Qualified Vendors List
QVLBI ...... Quasi-Very-Long-Baseline Interferometry
QVO .... Queen Victoria's Own [*British military*] (DMA)
QVP .... Quality Verification Plan
QVPL .... Qualified Verification Procedures List
QVR .... Quality Verification Report
QVR .... Queen Victoria's Rifles [*Military unit*] [*British*]
QVS .... Queen Victoria's School [*British military*] (DMA)
QVSLEA ... Atmospheric Environment Service, Environment Canada
          [*Service de l'Environnement Atmospherique,
          Environnement Canada*] Ville St-Laurent, Quebec
          [*Library symbol*] [*National Library of Canada*] (NLC)
QVT .... Qualified Verification Testing [*NASA*]
QVVT .... Qualified Verification Vibration Testing [*NASA*] (NASA)
QW .... Inter-Island Air Services Ltd. [*Grenada*] [*ICAO
          designator*] (FAAC)
QW .... Poland [*License plate code assigned to foreign diplomats in the
          US*]
QW .... Quantum Well [*Physics*]
QW .... Quarter Wave
Q W .... Quarterly West [*A publication*]
QW .... Waterloo Public Library, Quebec [*Library symbol*] [*National
          Library of Canada*] (NLC)
QWA .... Quarter-Wave Antenna
QWAAA ..... Queensland Women's Amateur Athletic Association [*Australia*]
QWAM ...... Qualified for Warrant Air Mechanic [*British military*] (DMA)
Q WAR ...... Quo Warranto [*Latin*] [*Legal term*] (DLA)
QWASC..... Queensland Women's Amateur Sports Council [*Australia*]
QWASP..... Quebec White Anglo-Saxon Protestant
QWBBA ..... Queensland Women's Basketball Association [*Australia*]
QWBBU .... Queensland Women's Basketball Union [*Australia*]
QWBI .... Quality of Well Being Index
QWBP .... Qualification Standards for Wage Board Positions
QWC......... West Chester State College, West Chester, PA [*OCLC
          symbol*] (OCLC)
QWD .... Quarterly World Day
Q/WDO..... Quarter Window [*Automotive engineering*]
QWE......... Qualified for Warrant Engineer [*British military*] (DMA)
QWERTY ... First six keys in the upper row of letters of a standard
          typewriter's keyboard [*Sometimes used as an informal
          name for a standard keyboard typewriter*]
QWG......... Quadripartite Working Group [*Military*]
QWG/CD .. Quadripartite Working Group on Combat
          Developments (MCD)
QWG/ENG ... Quadripartite Working Group on Engineering (MCD)
QWG/EW ... Quadripartite Working Group on Electronic Warfare (MCD)
QWG/LOG ... Quadripartite Working Group on Logistics [*Military*] (RDA)
QWG/PIQA ... Quadripartite Working Group on Proofing Inspection Quality
          Assurance (MCD)
QWG/STANO ... Quadripartite Working Group on Surveillance and Target
          Acquisition/Night Observation (MCD)
QWHA ...... Queensland Women's Historical Association [*Australia*]
QWIKTRAN ... Quick FORTRAN [*Programming language*] [*1979*] (CSR)
QWL.......... Quality of Work Life [*Anti-recession program of Ford Motor
          Co.*]
QWL.......... Quality of Working Life [*Labour Canada program*]
QWL.......... Quick Weight Loss
QWLD .... Quality of Worklife Database [*Management Directions*]
          [*Information service or system*] (IID)

QWM......... Qualified for Warrant Mechanician [*British military*]   (DMA)
QWMP...... Quadruped Walking Machine Program [*Army*]
QWN .... Weekly Notes. Queensland [*A publication*]   (APTA)
QWP......... Quarter-Wave Plate
QWR......... Que West Resources Ltd. [*Toronto Stock Exchange symbol*]
QWR......... Queen's Westminster Rifles [*British military*]   (DMA)
QWRV .... Queen's Westminster Rifle Volunteers [*British
                  military*]   (DMA)
QWSH....... Congregation Shaar Hashomayim Library-Museum,
                  Westmount, Quebec [*Library symbol*] [*National Library of
                  Canada*]   (NLC)
QWSMM .. Westmount Public Library, Quebec [*Library symbol*] [*National
                  Library of Canada*]   (NLC)
QX.............. Qatar Amiri Flight [*Qatar*] [*ICAO designator*]   (ICDA)
QXE........... Horizon Airlines, Inc. [*Seattle, WA*] [*FAA designator*]   (FAAC)
QY.............. Air Limousin T A [*France*] [*ICAO designator*]   (FAAC)
QY.............. Quantum Yield
QY.............. Quay   (ROG)
QY.............. Query
QY.............. Quota Year [*Pisciculture*]
7QY............ Malawi [*Aircraft nationality and registration mark*]   (FAAC)
QYM.......... SOLINET [*Southeastern Library Network*] Center, Atlanta, GA
                  [*OCLC symbol*]   (OCLC)
QZ.............. Quartz [*Quality of the bottom*] [*Nautical charts*]
QZ.............. Stockholm University Computing Center [*Sweden*]   (TSSD)
QZ.............. Zambia Airways [*ICAO designator*]   (FAAC)
QZM.......... Quartz Mountain Gold Corp. [*Vancouver Stock Exchange
                  symbol*] [*Toronto Stock Exchange symbol*]
QZMG....... Quartz Mountain Gold Corp. [*NASDAQ symbol*]   (NQ)
QZN........... Quan Zhou [*Republic of China*] [*Seismograph station code, US
                  Geological Survey*]   (SEIS)

R

R................ Abstracted Reappraisement Decisions [*A publication*]   (DLA)
R................ Acknowledgment of Receipt [*Message handling*]
　　　　　　　　[*Telecommunications*]
R................ All India Reporter, Rajasthan [*A publication*]   (DLA)
r................ Angular Yaw Velocity   (AAG)
R................ Antenna with Reflector
r----- .... Arctic Ocean and Region [*MARC geographic area code*]
　　　　　　　　[*Library of Congress*]   (LCCP)
R................ Arginine [*One-letter symbol; see Arg*]
R................ Army [*Military aircraft identification prefix*]   (FAAC)
R................ Cilag-Chemie AG [*Switzerland*] [*Research code symbol*]
R................ Denver Laboratories [*Great Britain*] [*Research code symbol*]
R................ Janssen [*Belgium*] [*Research code symbol*]
R................ Kentucky Law Reporter [*A publication*]   (DLA)
R................ Molar Gas Constant [*Symbol*] [*IUPAC*]   (NASA)
R................ Nicolaus Rufulus [*Flourished, 13th century*] [*Authority cited in*
　　　　　　　　pre-1607 legal work]   (DSA)
R................ Product Moment Coefficient of Correlation [*Statistics*]
R................ [*A*] Purine Nucleoside [*One-letter symbol; see Puo*]
R................ R-Register [*Data processing*]
R................ Rabba   (BJA)
R................ Rabbanite   (BJA)
R................ Rabbi
R................ Race
r................ Racemic [*Also, dl, rac*] [*Chemistry*]
R................ RACON [*RADAR Beacon*]
R................ RADAR Contact [*A diagonal line through R indicates RADAR*
　　　　　　　　service terminated; a cross through R indicates RADAR
　　　　　　　　contact lost] [*Aviation*]   (FAAC)
R................ Radfahrabteilung [*Bicycle Battalion*] [*German military - World*
　　　　　　　　War II]
R- .... Radial [*Followed by three digits; for use on instrument*
　　　　　　　　approach charts] [*Aviation*]
R................ Radial   (FAAC)
R................ Radian
R................ Radiancy
R................ Radiation
R................ Radical
R................ Radio
R................ Radio (BBC Monitoring) [*A publication*]
R................ Radiographer [*British military*]   (DMA)
R................ Radiology [*or Radiologist*]   (ADA)
R................ Radiotelegram
R................ Radium [*Chemical symbol is Ra*]   (KSC)
r................ Radius [*Symbol*] [*IUPAC*]
R................ Radius
r................ Radius of Gyration   (AAG)
R................ Rail   (MSA)
R................ Railroad [*or Railway*]
R................ Rain [*Meteorology*]
R dk........... Raised Deck [*of a ship*]   (DS)
R................ Ram
R................ Rand [*Monetary unit*] [*Botswana, Lesotho, South Africa, and*
　　　　　　　　Swaziland]
R................ Random Number
R................ Range
R................ Rank
R................ Rankine [*Temperature scale*]
R................ Raphe Nucleus [*Neuroanatomy*]
R................ Rare [*When applied to species*] [*Biology*]
R................ Rare [*Numismatics*]
R................ Rate
R................ Ratio
R................ Rational Number   (MDG)
R................ Rationing [*British*]
R................ Rawle's Pennsylvania Reports [*1828-35*] [*A*
　　　　　　　　publication]   (DLA)
R................ Rayleigh Wave [*Seismology*]
R................ Raymundus de Pennafort [*Deceased, 1275*] [*Authority cited in*
　　　　　　　　pre-1607 legal work]   (DSA)

R................ Raymundus de Sabanacho [*Authority cited in pre-1607 legal*
　　　　　　　　work]   (DSA)
R................ Rays
R................ Reaction   (AAG)
R................ Read   (AAG)
R................ Readiness Count
r................ Real [*Monetary unit*] [*Spanish*]
R................ Real
R................ Realites [*A publication*]
R................ Ream   (ADA)
R................ Rear
R................ Reasoning Factor [*or Ability*] [*Psychology*]
R................ Reaumur [*Temperature scale*]   (MUGU)
R................ Rebounds [*Basketball, hockey*]
R................ Receipt   (ROG)
R................ Received   (FAAC)
R................ Received Solid [*Amateur radio*]
R................ Receiver
R................ Receptor [*Biochemistry*]
R................ Recessed [*Electrical outlet symbol*]
R................ Recht [*Law*] [*German*]
R................ Rechtsstrijd [*A publication*]
R................ Recipe [*Take*] [*Pharmacy*]
R................ Reciprocating
R................ Recite [*Swell Organ*] [*Music*]
R................ Recluse
R................ Recognition [*Experimentation*]
R................ Reconditioned   (DCTA)
R................ Reconnaissance [*Designation for all US military aircraft*]
R................ Reconstruction Committee [*British*] [*World War II*]
R................ Record
R................ Recreations
R................ Recruit   (ROG)
R................ Rectal [*or Rectum*] [*Medicine*]
r................ Rectangular Tank [*Liquid gas carriers*]
R................ Rectilinear Polarization [*Physics*]   (ECON)
R................ Recto [*Also, RO*]
R................ Rector [*or Rectory*]
(R)............... Rectus [*Clockwise configuration*] [*Biochemistry*] [*See RS*]
R................ Recurrence [*Medicine*]
R................ Red
R................ Redemption Fee [*Finance*]
R................ Redetermination
R................ Redundancy [*Used in correcting manuscripts, etc.*]
R................ Referee [*Football*]
R................ Referred   (OICC)
R................ Refill [*of bract liquid*] [*Botany*]
R................ Reflectance
R................ Reflection [*Angle of*]
R................ Reflector Lamp
R................ Reflexive
R................ Reform [*Judaism*]
R................ Refraction
R................ Refrigerated [*Shipping*]   (DS)
R................ Refrigerated Tank [*Liquid gas carriers*]
R................ Refrigerator
R................ Refuse Disposal [*British Waterways Board sign*]
R................ Refused
R................ Regenerated [*Biology*]
R................ Regiment
R................ Regina [*Queen*] [*Latin*]
R................ Register [*Data processing*]
R................ Registered
R................ Registrar   (ROG)
R................ Regna [*Queen*] [*Latin*]   (DLA)
R................ Regular   (ADA)
R................ Regulating
R................ Reigned
R................ Reiz [*Stimulus*] [*German*] [*Psychology*]
R................ Relation [*Data processing*]
R................ Relative Humidity

R................	Relaxed
R................	Reliability (MCD)
R................	Reluctance
R................	Remote [Telecommunications] (TEL)
R................	Repeal [Legal term] (DLA)
R................	Repetitive [Electronics]
R................	Replaceability (AAG)
R................	Replaced [Dentistry]
R................	Reply (ADA)
R................	Report [Carry Forward] [Bookkeeping] [French]
R................	Reports
R................	[The] Reports, Coke's English King's Bench [A publication] (DLA)
R................	Reprint
R................	Republic
R................	Republican
R................	Republika [Zagreb] [A publication]
R................	Request
R................	Requiescat [He, or She Rests] [Latin]
R................	Rerun [of a television show]
R................	Rescinded [Legal term] (DLA)
R................	Research
R................	Resentment [Psychology]
R................	Reserve
R................	Reset (MDG)
R................	Reside [or Resident]
R................	Resistance [Symbol] [IUPAC]
R................	Resistor
R................	Resolution
R................	Resolved [Legal term] (DLA)
R................	Respectfully [Letter closing]
R................	Respiration
R................	Respond [or Response]
R................	Responder [Strain of mice]
R................	Responsorium [Responsory]
R................	Respublica [Commonwealth] [Latin]
R................	Restricted [Immunology]
R................	Restricted [Military document classification]
R................	Restricted [Persons under eighteen (sixteen in some localities) not admitted unless accompanied by parent or adult guardian] [Movie rating]
R................	Restricted Area [Followed by identification]
R................	Retarder [Slow] [On clock-regulators] [French]
R................	Reticular [Nucleus of thalamus] [Neuroanatomy]
R................	Retired [or Retiree]
R................	Rettie's Scotch Court of Session Reports, Fourth Series [A publication] (DLA)
R................	Returning
R................	Revenue
R................	Reverse
R................	Reverse [Giemsa method] [Chromosome stain]
R................	Revised (MCD)
R................	Revision [Legal term] (DLA)
R................	Revoked [Legal term] (DLA)
R................	Reward
R................	Rex [King] [Latin]
R................	Reynolds Number [Also, Re, RN] [Viscosity]
R................	Rhinitis [Medicine]
R................	Rhizoctonia [A fungus]
R................	Rhode Island State Library, Providence, RI [Library symbol] [Library of Congress] (LCLS)
R................	Rhodesia [Later, Zimbabwe] (ROG)
R$.............	Rhodesian Dollar [Monetary unit]
R................	Rhodium [Chemical element] [Symbol is Rh] (ROG)
R................	Rhodopsin [Visual purple]
R................	Rhythm
R................	Rial [Monetary unit] [Iran, Saudi Arabia, etc.]
r.................	Ribose [One-letter symbol; see Rib]
R................	Ricardus Anglicus [Deceased, 1242] [Authority cited in pre-1607 legal work] (DSA)
R................	Richard (King of England) (DLA)
R................	Richtkreis [Aiming Circle] [Gunnery term] [German military - World War II]
R................	Rickettsia
R................	Riffle
R................	Rifle
R................	Rigger [British military] (DMA)
R................	Right [Direction]
R................	Right [Politics]
R................	Right [side of a stage] [A stage direction]
R................	Right Edge [Skating]
R................	Right-Hand [Music] (DAS)
R................	Riker Laboratories, Inc. [Research code symbol]
R................	Rimus (BJA)
R................	Ring [Technical drawings]
R................	Ring Lead [Telecommunications] (TEL)
R................	Ring Road [Traffic sign] [British]
-R	Rinne's Test Negative [Hearing test]
+R	Rinne's Test Positive [Hearing test]
R................	Rio [River] [Spanish] (ROG)
R................	Rio De Janeiro [A publication]

R................	Rise [Electronics]
R................	Riser [Technical drawings]
R................	Rises
R................	Risk
R................	River [Maps and charts]
R................	Riveted (DS)
R................	Road
R................	Road-Holding [In automobile name Rolls-Royce Bentley Turbo R]
R................	Roan (Leather) [Bookbinding] (ROG)
R................	Robert [Phonetic alphabet] [Royal Navy] [World War I] [Pre-World War II] (DSUE)
R................	Robertus [Authority cited in pre-1607 legal work] (DSA)
R................	Robin Avions [Pierre Robin] [France] [ICAO aircraft manufacturer identifier] (ICAO)
R................	Robotics
R................	Rocket [Missile vehicle type symbol]
R................	Rod [Measurement]
r.................	Roentgen [Also, RU] [Unit measuring X and gamma radiations]
R................	Roger [All right or OK] [Communications slang]
R................	Roger [Phonetic alphabet] [World War II] (DSUE)
R................	Roll
R................	Roller-Skating Rinks [Public-performance tariff class] [British]
R................	Rollout (KSC)
R................	Roman
R................	Roman Catholic School [British]
R................	Romania
R................	Romania [A publication]
R................	Romans [New Testament book] (BJA)
R................	Romeo [Phonetic alphabet] [International] (DSUE)
R................	Rood [Unit of measurement]
R................	Rook [Chess]
R................	Rosary
R................	Roscoe's Cape Of Good Hope [A publication] (DLA)
R................	Rosin [Standard material for soldering]
R................	Rostral [Anatomy]
R................	Rotary Wing [Aircraft designation]
R................	Rothschild & Associes Banque [Bank] [France]
R................	Rotor
R................	Rough [Appearance of bacterial colony]
R................	Rough Sea [Navigation]
R................	Roussel [France] [Research code symbol]
R................	Route
R................	Routine (KSC)
R................	Royal
R................	Royalty Monthly [A publication]
R................	Rubber
R................	Rubidomycin [See also D, Daunorubicin] [Antineoplastic drug]
R................	Ruble [Monetary unit] [USSR]
R................	Rue [Street] [French]
R................	Rule
R................	Ruled [Followed by the dates of a monarch's reign]
r.................	Ruler
R................	Rum (ROG)
R................	Run [Deserted] [Nautical] [British] (ROG)
R................	Run [Distance sailed from noon to noon] [Navy] [British] (ROG)
R................	Runic
R................	Runs [scored] [Baseball or cricket]
R................	Rupee [Monetary unit] [Ceylon, India, and Pakistan]
R................	Rural (MCD)
R................	Rydberg Constant [Spectroscopy] [Symbol] (DEN)
R................	Ryder System, Inc. [NYSE symbol] (SPSG)
R................	Rydge's [A publication] (APTA)
R................	Ryman [Office equipment and furniture store chain] [British]
R................	Ship [Missile launch environment symbol]
R................	Stauffer Chemical Co. [Research code symbol]
R................	Transfer Payments [Economics]
R................	Transport [Naval aircraft designation]
R................	Yaw Control Axis [Symbol]
R2.............	Reporting Responsibility [DoD]
R2.............	Richard II [Shakespearean work]
R3.............	Rearm, Resupply, Refuel [Army]
R³	Relay, Reporter, Responder [Military] (CAAL)
3R.............	Request, Retrieve, and Report [Data processing]
3R.............	Resurfacing, Restoration, and Rehabilitation [Also, RRR] [Later, 4R] [Federal Highway Administration]
3R.............	Rheingold-Rotary-Reciprocating [Motor]
R3.............	Richard III [Shakespearean work]
4R.............	Ceylon [Sri Lanka] [Aircraft nationality and registration mark] (FAAC)
4R.............	Resurfacing, Restoration, Rehabilitation, and Reconstruction [Formerly, 3R, RRR] [Federal Highway Administration]
5R.............	Madagascar [Aircraft nationality and registration mark] (FAAC)
8R.............	Guyana [Aircraft nationality and registration mark] (FAAC)
3R's	Readin', Ritin', and Rithmetic [Also, RRR]
3R's	Recognition, Reassurance, and Relaxation [Military mental health technique] (INF)
3R's	Reduction, Refinement, and Replacement [Animal research]

3R's	Reference and Research Library Resources Systems [*New York State Library*] [*Albany*] [*Information service or system*] (IID)
3R's	Relief, Recovery, Reform [*Elements of the New Deal*]
6R's	Remedial Readin', Remedial Ritin', and Remedial Rithmetic [*Also, RRRRRR*] [*Humorous interpretation of the three R's*]
R (Count)	Readiness Count (MCD)
R (Day)	Redeployment Day [*Military*]
RA	Coast RADAR Station [*Maps and charts*]
RA	High-Powered Radio Range (Adcock)
RA	Rabbinical Assembly (EA)
RA	RADAR Altimeter [*Aviation*] (KSC)
Ra	RADAR Station
RA	Radio Altimeter
RA	Radio Antenna
RA	Radio Authority [*Government regulatory agency*] [*British*]
RA	Radioactive
RA	Radionic Association (EA)
Ra	Radium [*Chemical element*]
RA	Radius of Action (AAG)
Ra	Raduga [*Moscow*] [*A publication*]
RA	Ragweed Antigen [*Immunology*]
RA	Rain [*Meteorology*] (FAAC)
Ra	Rainerius [*Authority cited in pre-1607 legal work*] (DSA)
RA	Rainforest Alliance (EA)
RA	Raise (AAG)
RA	Ramp Actuator
RA	Random Access [*Data processing*] (AAG)
RA	Range [*Aviation*]
RA	Range Area (NASA)
RA	Range Assessor [*British military*] (DMA)
RA	Rape [*Division in the county of Sussex*] [*British*]
RA	Rapid-American Corp.
RA	Rapid Anastigmatic (Lens) [*Photography*] (ROG)
RA	Raritan Arsenal (AAG)
Ra	Rassegna [*A publication*]
Ra	Rastell's Entries [*A publication*] (DSA)
RA	Rate Action (AAG)
RA	Rate of Application
RA	Ratepayers' Association [*British*] (ILCA)
R & A	Rates and Allotments [*Eight-Sheet Outdoor Advertising Association*] [*A publication*]
RA	Rating Appeals [*United Kingdom*] [*A publication*]
RA	Ratio Actuator (MCD)
RA	Ration
RA	Ration Allowance [*British military*] (DMA)
Ra	Rayleigh Number [*IUPAC*]
Ra	Raymundus de Pennafort [*Deceased, 1275*] [*Authority cited in pre-1607 legal work*] (DSA)
RA	Raynaud's Phenomenon [*Medicine*]
RA	Rayon (AAG)
RA	Read Amplifier
RA	Ready-Access [*Telecommunications*] (TEL)
RA	Ready Alert [*Navy*] (NVT)
RA	Rear Admiral [*Also, RADM, RADML*]
RA	Rear Artillery
R/A	Rear Axle [*Automotive engineering*]
RA	Rebuild America (EA)
RA	Receiver Attenuation
RA	Rechtsgeleerde Adviezen [*A publication*]
RA	Recipient Rights Adviser
R/A	Recorded Announcement [*Telecommunications*] (TEL)
RA	Records Administration (MCD)
R	Recreation Aide [*Red Cross*]
RA	Redevelopment Act (OICC)
RA	Redstone Arsenal [*Huntsville, AL*] [*Army*]
RA	Reduced Aperture (MCD)
RA	Reduction of Area
RA	Refer to Accepter [*Banking*]
RA	Refractory Anemia [*Medicine*]
RA	Refugee Agency [*NATO*] (NATG)
RA	Regional Administrator
RA	Regional Associations [*Marine science*] (MSC)
RA	Registration Act
RA	Registration Appeals [*A publication*] (DLA)
RA	Regular Army
RA	Regulation Appeals [*A publication*] (DLA)
RA	Rehabilitation Act (OICC)
RA	Reimbursement Authorization (AFM)
RA	Reims Aviation [*France*] [*ICAO aircraft manufacturer identifier*] (ICAO)
RA	Reinforced Alert (NATG)
RA	Relative Abundance [*Chemistry*]
RA	Relative Activity [*Physiology*]
RA	Relative Address
RA	Release Authorization
RA	Released-Action [*Pharmacy*]
RA	Reliability Analysis (AAG)
RA	Reliability Assessment (KSC)
RA	Reliability Assurance (MCD)

RA	Religious of the Apostolate of the Sacred Heart [*Roman Catholic women's religious order*]
RA	Religious of the Assumption [*Roman Catholic women's religious order*]
RA	Relocation Address
RA	Relocation Assistance [*HUD*]
RA	Remittance Advice (MCD)
RA	Renal Artery [*Anatomy*]
RA	Rental Agreement
RA	Repair Assignment (AAG)
RA	Repeat Action [*Medicine*]
R/A	Repeat Attempt [*Telecommunications*] (TEL)
RA	Repeated Attacks [*Medicine*]
Ra	Repertorio Americano [*A publication*]
RA	Replacement Algorithm
RA	Reporting Activity (MCD)
R & A	Reports and Analysis
RA	Representative Assembly
RA	Republicans Abroad (EA)
RA	Requesting Agency (MUGU)
RA	Research Abstracts [*University Microfilms International*] [*A publication*]
R & A	Research and Analysis
RA	Resident Agent (AFM)
RA	Resident Alien
RA	Resident Assistant [*College housing*]
RA	Resident Auditor
RA	Residual Air
RA	Resistor Assembly
RA	Resource Allocation (MCD)
RA	Respiratory Allergy [*Immunology*]
RA	Respiratory Arrest [*Medicine*]
R-A	Response Errors [*Statistics*]
R & A	Responsibility and Action
RA	Restaurant Associates Industries, Inc. [*AMEX symbol*] (SPSG)
RA	Restricted Account [*Banking*]
RA	Retinal Anlage [*Ophthalmology*]
RA	Retinoic Acid [*Biochemistry*]
RA	Retrograde Amnesia [*Medicine*]
RA	Return Address
RA	Return Air [*Technical drawings*]
R/A	Return to Author [*Bookselling*]
RA	Revenue Act [*1962, 1964, 1971, 1976, 1978*]
RA	Revenue Agent [*IRS*]
RA	Reverendus Admodum [*Very Reverend*] [*Latin*]
R & A	Review and Analysis
R & A	Review and Approval
RA	Reviewing Activity (MCD)
RA	Reviewing Authority
RA	Reviews in Anthropology [*A publication*]
RA	Revue de l'Administration et du Droit Administratif de la Belgique [*A publication*]
RA	Revue Administrative [*A publication*] (ILCA)
RA	Revue Africaine. Bulletin de la Societe Historique Algerienne [*A publication*]
RA	Revue Anglo-Americaine [*A publication*]
RA	Revue Archeologique [*A publication*]
RA	Revue des Arts [*A publication*]
RA	Revue d'Assyriologie [*A publication*]
RA	Rheinisches Archiv [*A publication*]
RA	Rheumatoid Agglutinins [*Clinical chemistry*]
RA	Rheumatoid Arthritis [*Medicine*]
RA	Riders Association [*Commercial firm*] (EA)
RA	Right Aft (MCD)
RA	Right Angle (DEN)
RA	Right Arch [*Freemasonry*]
RA	Right Arm [*Medicine*]
RA	Right Ascension [*Navigation*]
RA	Right Atrium [*Cardiology*]
RA	Right Axilla (KSC)
RA	Ripple Adder
RA	Risk Analysis (MCD)
RA	Robbery Armed
RA	Robustrus Archistriatalis [*Bird brain anatomy*]
RA	Rocket Assist (RDA)
RA	Rokitansky-Aschoff [*Sinus*] [*Gastroenterology*]
RA	Romanistische Arbeitshefte [*A publication*]
RA	Root Apex [*Botany*]
RA	Roquefort Association (EA)
RA	Rosin Acid [*Organic chemistry*]
RA	Rosin Activated [*Standard material for soldering*]
RA	Rotary Assembly
RA	Rotogravure Association
RA	Royal Academician [*or Academy*] [*British*]
RA	Royal Academy of Arts in London [*British*]
R & A	Royal and Ancient Golf Club of St. Andrews [*Recognized as the game's legislative authority in all countries except the US*] [*British*]
RA	Royal Arch [*Freemasonry*]
RA	Royal Armouries [*Tower of London*]
RA	Royal Art

RA .... Royal Artillery [*British*]
RA .... Royal Artist
RA .... Royal Nepal Airlines Corp. [*ICAO designator*]   (FAAC)
RA .... Royal Regiment of Artillery [*Military*] [*British*]
RA .... Rueckwaertiges Armeegebiet [*Rear area of an army*] [*German military*]
R & A .... Rules and Administration Committee [*US Senate*]
RA .... Rules on Appeal [*A publication*]   (DLA)
RA .... Russian Air [*To distinguish call-signs and frequencies*] [*World War II*] [*British*]
RA .... Russian American
RA .... Thermal Resistance of Unit Area [*Heat transmission symbol*]
RAA .... Rabbinical Alliance of America   (EA)
RAA .... Reagan Alumni Association   (EA)
RA(A) .... Rear-Admiral of Aircraft Carriers [*Obsolete*] [*British*]
RAA .... Recueil des Arrets et Avis du Conseil d'Etat [*A publication*]
RAA .... Reeve Aleutian Airways, Inc. [*Air carrier designation symbol*]
RAA .... Regenerative Agriculture Association [*Later, RI*]   (EA)
RAA .... Regional Administrative Assistant   (ADA)
RAA .... Regional Airline Association   (EA)
RAA .... Regional Arts Association [*British*]
RAA .... Reinsurance Association of America [*Washington, DC*]   (EA)
RAA .... Rendiconti. Accademia di Archeologia, Lettere, e Belle Arti [*Napoli*] [*A publication*]
RAA .... Renewal Assistance Administration [*HUD*]
RAA .... Renin-Angiotensin-Aldosterone [*Clinical nephrology*]
RAA .... Research Animal Alliance   (EA)
RAA .... Respiratory Aid Apparatus
RAA .... Revue. Academie Arabe [*A publication*]
RAA .... Revue Anglo-Americaine [*A publication*]
RAA .... Revue de l'Art Ancien et Moderne [*A publication*]
RAA .... Revue des Arts Asiatiques [*A publication*]
RAA .... Revue d'Assyriologie et d'Archeologie Orientale [*A publication*]
RAA .... Right Angle Adapter
RAA .... Right Ascension Angle
RAA .... Right Atrial Appendage [*Medicine*]
RAA .... Rockette Alumnae Association   (EA)
RAA .... Royal Academy of Arts [*British*]   (ROG)
RAA .... Royal Regiment of Australian Artillery   (DMA)
RAA .... Rynes Aviation, Inc. [*Melrose Park, IL*] [*FAA designator*]   (FAAC)
RAAA .... Red Angus Association of America   (EA)
RAAA .... Relocation Assistance Association of America   (EA)
RAAAS ..... Remote Antiarmor Assault System   (MCD)
RAAB .... Remote Amplifier and Adaption Box   (NASA)
RAAB .... Remote Application and Advisory Box   (MCD)
RAABF ..... Royal Artillery Association Benevolent Fund [*British military*]   (DMA)
RAAC .... Rhodesian Air Askari Corps [*British military*]   (DMA)
RAAC .... Rome Allied Area Command [*World War II*]
RAACA ..... Radiochimica Acta [*A publication*]
RAACC ..... Robotics and Automation Applications Consulting Center [*Ford Motor Co.*]
RAACEF ... Rear-Admiral of Aircraft Carriers, Eastern Fleet [*British*]
RAACT ..... Radioactive
RAAD .... Revue. Academie Arabe de Damas [*A publication*]
RAADES ... Relative Antiair Defense Effectiveness Simulation [*Military*]   (CAAL)
RAAEAV ... South Africa. Department of Agriculture. Entomology Memoir [*A publication*]
RAAEC Nletter ... Royal Australian Army. Educational Corps. Newsletter [*A publication*]   (APTA)
RA(A)EF ... Rear-Admiral (Administration) Eastern Fleet [*British*]
RAAF .... Redstone Army Airfield [*Huntsville, AL*]
RAAF .... Royal Australian Air Force
RAAF Reserve ... Royal Australian Air Force Reserve. Magazine [*A publication*]   (APTA)
RAAG .... Regional Aviation Assistance Group [*FAA*]
RAAGA ..... Railway Age [*New York*] [*A publication*]
RAAG Res Notes ... Research Notes and Memoranda of Applied Geometry for Prevenient Natural Philosophy [*Tokyo*] [*A publication*]
RAALC ...... Royal Australian Army Legal Corps
RAAM .... Race Across America [*Annual cycling event*]
RAAM .... Remote Antiarmor Mine   (RDA)
RAAM .... Residual-Area-Analysis Method [*Spectrometry*]
RAAM .... Revue de l'Art Ancien et Moderne [*A publication*]
RAAMC ..... Royal Australian Army Medical Corps
RAAMS ..... Remote Antiarmor Mine System [*Military*]   (AABC)
RAAN .... Rendiconti. Accademia di Archeologia, Lettere, e Belle Arti (Napoli) [*A publication*]
RAAN .... Repair Activity Accounting Number [*Navy*]
RAANES ... Recent Advances in Animal Nutrition [*A publication*]
RAAO .... Revue d'Assyriologie et d'Archeologie Orientale [*A publication*]
RAAP .... Radford Army Ammunition Plant   (AABC)
RAAQ .... Recherches Amerindiennes au Quebec. Bulletin d'Information [*A publication*]
RAAR .... RAM Address Register
RA Art Louvain ... Revue des Archeologues et Historiens d'Art de Louvain [*A publication*]
RAAS .... Royal Amateur Art Society [*British*]
RAAT .... Recombinant Alpha 1-Antitrypsin [*Biochemistry*]

RAAWS..... RADAR Altimeter and Altitude Warning System [*Military*]   (CAAL)
RAB .... Rabaul [*New Britain*] [*Seismograph station code, US Geological Survey*]   (SEIS)
RAB .... Rabaul [*Papua New Guinea*] [*Airport symbol*]   (OAG)
RAB .... Rabbet   (MSA)
RAB .... Rabbinical
RAB .... Rabbit Oil & Gas [*Vancouver Stock Exchange symbol*]
RAB .... Rabelais [*French author, 1494-1553*]   (ROG)
RAB .... Radio Advertising Bureau [*New York, NY*]   (EA)
RAB .... Reactor Auxiliary Building [*Nuclear energy*]   (NRCH)
RAB .... Regional Advisory Board [*American Hospital Association*]
RAB .... Rent Advisory Board [*Cost of Living Council*]
RAB .... Richard Austen Butler [*1902-1982*] [*In book title "RAB: The Life of R. A. Butler"*]
RAB .... Rotating Arm Basin
Raba .... [*Januarius*] Rabaca [*Flourished, 1342-48*] [*Authority cited in pre-1607 legal work*]   (DSA)
RABAC..... Real Americans Buy American Cars [*An association*] [*Defunct*]
RABAL..... Radiosonde Balloon
RABAR..... Radiosonde Balloon Release   (FAAC)
RABAR..... Raytheon Advanced Battery Acquisition RADAR
Rab Azovsko-Chernomorsk Nauchn Rybokhoz Stn ... Raboty Azovsko-Chernomorskoi Nauchnoi Rybokhozyaistvennoi Stantsii [*A publication*]
RABB........ Rabbinical
RABBAR ... Revista. Museo Argentino de Ciencias Naturales Bernardino Rivadavia e Instituto Nacional de Investigacion de las Ciencias Naturales. Ciencias Botanicas [*A publication*]
Rabels Z..... Rabels Zeitschrift fuer Auslaendisches und Internationales Privatrecht [*Tubingen, West Germany*] [*A publication*]   (DLA)
RABET...... RADAR Beacon Transponder
RABFAC.... RADAR Beacon, Forward Air Controller
Rab Fiz Tverd Tela ... Raboty po Fizike Tverdogo Tela [*A publication*]
RABI......... Royal Agricultural Benevolent Institution [*Church of England*]
Rab Issled Inst Meteorol Gidrol Chast 2 ... Raboty i Issledovaniya. Institut Meteorologii i Gidrologii. Chast 2. Gidrologiya [*A publication*]
Rab Khim Rastvorov Kompleksn Soedin ... Raboty po Khimii Rastvorov i Kompleksnykh Soedinenii [*A publication*]
RABM ...... Revista de Archivos, Bibliotecas, y Museos [*A publication*]
RABMA .... Radiobiologia si Biologia Moleculara [*A publication*]
Rab Molodykh Uch Vses Akad Skh Nauk ... Raboty Molodykh Uchenykh Vsesoyuznaya Akademiya Sel'skokhozyaistvennykh Nauk [*A publication*]
Rab Neft..... Rabochii Neftyanik [*A publication*]
RABNVS... Reactor Auxiliary Building Normal Ventilation System [*Nuclear energy*]   (NRCH)
RABOA..... Radiation Botany [*A publication*]
Rabocij Klass Sovrem Mir ... Rabocij Klass i Sovremennyj Mir [*A publication*]
RABol .... Rendiconto. Accademia delle Scienze. Istituto di Bologna [*A publication*]
R Abolit..... Revue Abolitionniste [*A publication*]
RABP........ Renal Artery Bypass [*Medicine*]
Rab Post..... Pro Rabirio Postumo [*of Cicero*] [*Classical studies*]   (OCD)
RABR........ Rainbow Bridge National Monument
RABR........ Right Angle Bulkhead Receptacle
RAbr .... Rivista Abruzzese [*A publication*]
RABS........ Remote Air Battle Station
RABT........ Rabbit Software Corp. [*Malvern, PA*] [*NASDAQ symbol*]   (NQ)
Rab Tyan-Shan Fiz-Geogr Sta ... Raboty Tyan-Shan'skoi Fiziko-Geograficheskoi Stantsii. Akademiya Nauk Kirgizskoi SSR [*A publication*]
Rab Tyan Shan'skoi Fiz Geogr Stn Akad Nauk Kirg SSR ... Raboty Tyan-Shan'skoi Fiziko-Geograficheskoi Stantsii. Akademiya Nauk Kirgizskoi SSR [*A publication*]
RABV .... Reflood Assist Bypass Valve [*Nuclear energy*]   (NRCH)
RABVAL... RADAR Bomb Evaluation   (MCD)
RAC .... IEEE Robotics and Automation Council   (EA)
rac .... Racemic [*Also, dl, r*] [*Chemistry*]
RAC .... Racer Resources Ltd. [*Vancouver Stock Exchange symbol*]
RAC .... Raciborz [*Poland*] [*Seismograph station code, US Geological Survey*]   (SEIS)
RAC .... Racine, WI [*Location identifier*] [*FAA*]   (FAAL)
RAC .... RADAR Address Counter
R & AC..... RADAR and Air Communications
RAC .... RADAR Area Correlator
RAC .... RADAR Azimuth Converter
RAC .... Radio Adaptive Communications
RAC .... Radiological Assessment Coordinator [*Nuclear energy*]   (NRCH)
RAC .... Radiometric Area Correlator   (MCD)
RAC .... RAI Research Corporation [*AMEX symbol*]   (SPSG)
RAC .... Raisin Administrative Committee   (EA)
RAC .... Ram Air Charters Ltd. [*Inuvik, NT, Canada*] [*FAA designator*]   (FAAC)
RAC .... Ram Air Cushion [*Aerospace*]   (AAG)
RAC .... Ramsay's Appeal Cases [*Canada*] [*A publication*]   (DLA)

RAC	Random Access Capability [*Microscopy*]
RAC	Rangefinder with Automatic Compensator [*Firearms*]
RAC	Rapid Action Change [*DoD*]
RAC	Ration Accessory Convenience [*World War II*]
RAC	Rational Activity Coefficient
RAC	Reactor Accident Calculation
RAC	Read Address Counter
RAC	Reallexikon fuer Antike und Christentum [*A publication*] (OCD)
RAC	Rear-Admiral Commanding [*British*]
RAC	Receptor-Affinity Chromatography
RAC	Recessed Annular Connector
RAC	Recombinant DNA Advisory Committee [*National Institutes of Health*]
RAC	Recreation Advisory Council [*Bureau of Outdoor Recreation*]
RAC	Rectified Alternating Current [*Radio*]
RAC	Reflect Array Pulse Compressor (RDA)
RAC	Release and Approval Center (MCD)
RAC	Reliability Action Center [*NASA*] (NASA)
RAC	Reliability Analysis Center [*Griffiss Air Force Base, NY*] [*DoD*] (GRD)
RAC	Reliability Assessment of Components (KSC)
RAC	Renal Arterial Constriction [*Medicine*]
RAC	Repair, Alignment, and Calibration (NVT)
RAC	Reparable Assets Control (AFM)
RAC	Representation des Artistes Canadiens
RAC	Request Altitude Change [*Aviation*] (FAAC)
RAC	Request for Authority to Contract [*Military*]
RAC	Requisition Advice Care [*Military*]
RAC	Research Advisory Committee
RAC	Research Advisory Council
RAC	Research Analysis Corporation [*Nonprofit contract agency*] [*Army*]
RAC	Resource Assessment Commission [*Australia*]
RAC	Retail Advertising Conference (EA)
RAC	Revue de l'Art Chretien [*A publication*]
RAC	Rivista di Archeologia Cristiana [*A publication*]
RAC	Royal Academician (of Canada) (ROG)
RAC	Royal Aero Club [*British*]
RAC	Royal Agricultural College [*British*]
RAC	Royal Air Cambodge [*Cambodian airlines*]
RAC	Royal Arch Chapter [*Freemasonry*]
RACLA	Royal Armoured Corps [*British*]
RAC	Royal Artillery Committee [*British military*] (DMA)
RAC	Royal Automobile Club [*Controlling body of motor racing in Britain*]
RAC	Rubber Allocation Committee
RAC	Rules of the Air and Air Traffic Control [*ICAO Air Navigation Commission*]
Ra Ca	English Railway and Canal Cases [*A publication*] (DLA)
RACA	Recovered Alcoholic Clergy Association (EA)
RACA	Regroupement d'Artistes des Centres Alternatifs [*Association of National Non-Profit Artists' Centres - ANNPAC*] [*Canada*]
RACA	Requiring Activity Contract Administrator [*DoD*]
RACAA	Rural Arts and Crafts Association (EA)
RACAA	Radiocarbon [*A publication*]
R Acad Cienc y Artes Barcelona Mem ...	Real Academia de Ciencias y Artes de Barcelona. Memorias [*A publication*]
R Acad Farm Barcelona Discursos Recepcion ...	Real Academia de Farmacia de Barcelona. Discursos de Recepcion [*A publication*]
R Acad Farm Barcelona Ses Inaug ...	Real Academia de Farmacia de Barcelona. Sesion Inaugural [*A publication*]
RA C Ant Nat ...	Revue Archeologique. Centre Consacree aux Antiquites Nationales [*A publication*]
RACAS	Radiation Automatic Casualty Assessment System [*Military*]
RACathHS ...	Records. American Catholic Historical Society of Philadelphia [*A publication*]
RACC	Radiation and Contamination Control
RACC	Regional Agricultural Credit Corporation
RACC	Remote ARIA [*Apollo Range Instrumentation Aircraft*] Control Center [*NASA*]
RACC	Remotely Activated Command and Control [*Military*] (CAAL)
RACC	Reporting Activity Control Card [*Army*] (AABC)
RACC	Research Aviation Coordinating Committee
R Acc..........	Revue des Accidents du Travail [*A publication*]
RACC	Rituels Accadiens [*A publication*] (BJA)
RACC	Royal Armoured Corps Centre [*British*] (MCD)
RACC	Royal Automobile Club of Canada
RACCA......	Refrigeration and Air Conditioning Contractors Association - National [*Later, National Environmental Systems Contractors Association*] (EA)
Racc Fis-Chim Ital ...	Raccolta Fisico-Chimica Italiana [*A publication*]
R Ac Cienc Habana An ...	Real Academia de Ciencias Medicas, Fisicas, y Naturales de la Habana. Anales [*A publication*]
Raccoglitore Med Forli ...	Raccoglitore Medico Fano Forli [*A publication*]
Raccolta Mem Turin Univ Fac Sci Agr ...	Raccolta di Memorie. Turin. Universita. Facolta di Scienze Agrarie [*A publication*]
Racc Opuscoli Sci Filol ...	Raccolta d'Opuscoli Scientifici e Filologici [*A publication*]
RACD	Royal Army Chaplains' Department [*British*]

RACD	Royal Army Clothing Department [*British*]
RACE	Mid-America Racing Stables, Inc. [*NASDAQ symbol*] (NQ)
Race	Race and Class [*A publication*]
RACE........	Racial Attitudes and Consciousness Exam [*Two-part television program broadcast in 1989*]
RACE........	Radiation Adaptive Compression Equipment
RACE........	Random Access Computer Equipment
RACE........	Random Access Control Equipment (IEEE)
RACE........	Rapid Automatic Checkout Equipment
RACE........	Request Altitude Changes En Route [*Aviation*]
RACE........	Research in Advanced Communications in Europe [*European Commission*]
RACE........	Research on Automatic Computation Electronics
RACE........	Resource Assessment and Conservation Engineering [*Environmental protection*]
RACE........	Restoration of Aircraft to Combat Effectivity [*Army*]
Race Clas ...	Race and Class [*A publication*]
Race Hyg ...	Race Hygiene [*Japan*] [*A publication*]
RACEL......	Record of Access/Eligibility [*DoD*]
RACEP.....	Random Access and Correlation for Extended Performance [*Telecommunications*]
Race Rela L R ...	Race Relations Law Reporter [*A publication*]
Race Rela L Sur ...	Race Relations Law Survey [*A publication*]
Race Rel L Rep ...	Race Relations Law Reporter [*A publication*] (DLA)
RACES	Radio Amateur Civil Emergency Service [*Civil defense*]
RACES	Remote Arming Common Element System
RACF........	Resource Access Control Facility [*IBM Corp.*]
RACF........	Revue Archeologique du Centre de la France [*A publication*]
RACFI	Radio and Communication Facilities Inoperative
RACFOE...	Research Analysis Corporation Field Office, Europe [*Army*] (AABC)
RACG	Radiometric Area Correlation Guidance
RACGP......	Royal Australian College of General Practitioners
RACHA	Rassegna Chimica [*A publication*]
RAChD......	Royal Army Chaplain's Department [*British*]
RACHS......	Records. American Catholic Historical Society of Philadelphia [*A publication*]
RACHSP ...	Records. American Catholic Historical Society of Philadelphia [*A publication*]
RACIC......	Remote Area Conflict Information Center [*Battelle Memorial Institute*]
RACIS	RADAR Computer Interaction Simulator
RACLA	Resource and Action Committee for Latin America [*Australia*]
RACM	Raycomm Transworld Industries, Inc. [*NASDAQ symbol*] (NQ)
RACND3 ...	Annual Research Reviews. Rheumatoid Arthritis and Related Conditions [*A publication*]
RACNE	Regional Advisory Committee on Nuclear Energy
RACNSC...	Religious Activities Committee, National Safety Council (EA)
RACNSW ...	Royal Aero Club of New South Wales [*Australia*]
RACO	RealAmerica Company [*NASDAQ symbol*] (NQ)
RACO	Rear Area Combat Operations (INF)
RACOB(WA) ...	Rear-Admiral Commanding Combined Operational Bases (Western Approaches) [*Great Britain*]
RACOG	Royal Australian College of Obstetricians and Gynaecologists
R A Como...	Rivista Archeologica dell'Antica Provincia e Diocesi di Como [*A publication*]
RACOMS ...	Rapid Combat Mapping Service [*or System*] [*Military*]
RACON.....	RADAR Responder Beacon
Ra (Conspic) ...	RADAR Conspicuous Object
RACOON ...	Radiation Controlled Balloon [*Meteorology*]
RACP	Royal Australasian College of Physicians
RACPAS ...	RADAR Coverage Penetration Analysis
RACR	Resources Allocation Change Request
Rac Rel L Survey ...	Race Relations Law Survey [*A publication*] (DLA)
RACrist......	Rivista di Archeologia Cristiana [*A publication*]
RAC/RJ.....	Religious Action Center of Reform Judaism (EA)
RACS.........	Random Access Communications System
RACS.........	Recruit Allocation Control System [*Navy*] (NVT)
RACS.........	Regenerable Affinity Chromatography Support
RACS........	Remote Access Computing System [*Data processing*]
RACS.........	Remote Automatic Calibration System (NASA)
RACS.........	Remote Automatic Control System (KSC)
RACS.........	Request for Approval of Contractual Support
RACS.........	Rotation Axis Coordinate System (MCD)
RACS.........	Royal Australasian College of Surgeons
RACS.........	Royal Australian Corps of Signals (DMA)
RACSA	Royal Aero Club of South Australia
RACT........	Reasonable Available Control Technology [*Environmental Protection Agency*]
RACT........	Remote Access Computer Technique [*Data processing*] (IEEE)
RACT........	Reverse-Acting
R Action Soc ...	Revue d'Action Sociale [*A publication*]
RACU	Remote Acquisiton and Command Unit [*NASA*] (NASA)
RACUAHC ...	Religious Action Center of the Union of American Hebrew Congregations [*Later, RAC/RJ*] (EA)
Rac Uff.......	Raccolta Ufficiale delle Leggi e dei Decreti della Repubblica Italiana [*A publication*]
RAC(WA) ...	Royal Aero Club (Western Australia)
RACYA......	Reviews in Analytical Chemistry [*A publication*]

RACZA...... Revista. Academia de Ciencias Exactas, Fisico-Quimicas, y Naturales de Zaragoza [*A publication*]
Rad.......... Rad Jugoslavenski Akademija Znanosti i Umjetnosti [*A publication*]
RAD.......... RADAR
RAD.......... RADAR Augmentation Device
RAD.......... Radford Arsenal [*Army*] (AAG)
RAD.......... RADIAC [*Radiation Detection, Indication, and Computation*] Equipment (NATG)
RAD.......... Radial
RAD.......... Radian (MCD)
rad............. Radian [*Symbol*] [*SI unit of plane angle*]
RAD.......... Radiation (KSC)
RAD.......... Radiation Absorbed Dose [*Unit of measurement of radiation energy*]
RAD...... Radiator (AAG)
RADS........ Radical
Rad.......... Radical Teacher [*A publication*]
RAD.......... Radio (AAG)
RAD.......... Radioactivity Detection
RAD.......... Radiogram
Rad.......... Radiola [*Record label*] [*Australia*]
RAD...... Radiology [*or Radiologist*] (ADA)
RADS........ Radium [*Chemical symbol is Ra*]
RAD...... Radius (AAG)
RAD.......... Radix [*Root*] [*Latin*]
RAD.......... Radnorshire [*County in Wales*] (ROG)
RAD.......... Raised Afterdeck [*of a ship*] (DS)
RAD.......... Random Access Data (BUR)
RAD.......... Random Access Device
RAD.......... Random Access Disc (MCD)
RAD.......... Rapid Access Data [*Xerox Corp.*]
RAD.......... Rapid Access Device
RAD.......... Rapid Access Disk
RAD.......... Rapid Access Drive (BUR)
RAD.......... Rapid Automatic Drill
RAD.......... Ratio Adjust Device (MCD)
RAD.......... Ratio Analysis Diagram [*Metallurgy*]
RA(D)........ Rear-Admiral (Destroyers) [*Obsolete*] [*Navy*] [*British*]
RAD.......... Recommendation Approval Document (MCD)
RAD.......... Records Arrival Date [*Bell System*] (TEL)
RAD.......... Recruiting Aids Department [*Navy*]
RAD.......... Reference Attitude Display
RAD.......... Reflex Anal Dilatation [*Medicine*]
RAD.......... Regional Accountable Depot [*Military*]
RAD.......... Regional Administrative Directors
RAD.......... Released from Active Duty [*Navy*]
RAD....... Repair at Depot (MCD)
RAD.......... Reported for Active Duty [*Navy*]
RAD.......... Request for Apollo Documents [*NASA*] (KSC)
RAD.......... Required Availability Date [*Military*]
RAD.......... Requirements Action Directive (AFM)
RAD.......... Research and Advanced Development (MCD)
R & AD ...... Research and Advanced Development
RAD.......... Reservists on Active Duty [*Navy*]
RAD.......... Resource Allocation Display [*Navy*]
RAD.......... Resource Availability Determination (MCD)
RAD.......... Restricted Shipyard Availability Requiring Drydocking [*Navy*] (NVT)
RAD.......... Return to Active Duty [*Military*]
RAD.......... Review and Approval Document (MCD)
RAD.......... Right Anterior Digestive [*Gland*]
RAD.......... Right Axis Deviation [*Medicine*]
RAD.......... Rite Aid Corp. [*NYSE symbol*] (SPSG)
RAD.......... Roentgen Administered Dose
RAD.......... Royal Academy of Dancing [*London, England*] (EAIO)
RAD.......... Royal Academy of Dancing, United States Branch (EA)
RAD.......... Royal Albert Dock [*British*]
RAD.......... Rural Areas Development
RAD.......... Warroad, MN [*Location identifier*] [*FAA*] (FAAL)
RadA.......... Radical Alliance [*British*]
RADA....... Radioactive
RADA........ Random Access Discrete Address [*Army division-level battlefield radio communications system*]
RADA........ Realignment of Airdrop Activities (MCD)
RADA........ Right Acromio-Dorsoanterior [*A fetal position*] [*Obstetrics*]
RADA........ Royal Academy of Dramatic Art [*British*]
RADAC ..... RADAR Analog Digital Data and Control (KSC)
RADAC ..... Rapid Digital Automatic Computing
RADAC ..... Raytheon Automatic Drafting Artwork Compiler
RADACS... Random Access Discrete Address Communications System [*Army*]
RaDaK....... Rabbi David Kimhi [*Biblical scholar, 1160-1235*] (BJA)
RADAL...... Radio Detection and Location
Rad Am...... Radical America [*A publication*]
Rad Amer... Radical America [*A publication*]
RADAN..... RADAR Analysis System (MCD)
RADAN..... RADAR Doppler Automatic Navigator
RADAN..... RADAR Navigation
RADANT .. RADOME [*RADAR Dome*] Antenna (NVT)
Radar .... Radar's Reports [*138-163 Missouri*] [*A publication*] (DLA)

RADAR ..... Radio Association Defending Airwave Rights (EA)
RADAR ..... Radio Detection and Ranging
RADAR ..... Rassemblement des Democrates pour l'Avenir de la Reunion [*Rally of Democrats for the Future of Reunion*] [*Political party*] (PPW)
RADAR ..... Repertoire Analytique d'Articles de Revues de Quebec [*Database*] [*A publication*]
RADAR ..... Reseau d'Approvisionnement et de Debouches d'Affaires [*Business Opportunities Sourcing System - BOSS*] [*Canada*]
RAD-AR.... Risk/Benefit Assessment of Drugs - Analysis and Response [*Post-marketing surveillance*]
RADAR ..... Royal Association for Disability and Rehabilitation [*British*]
RADARC.... Radially Distributed Annular Rocket Chamber
RADAREVALSq ... RADAR Evaluation Squadron [*Air Force*]
RADARSAT ... RADAR Satellite [*Canada*]
RADAS..... Random Access Discrete Address System
RADAT .... RADAR Alignment Designation Accuracy Test (MCD)
RADAT .... RADAR Data Transmission
RADAT .... Radio Direction and Track
RADAT .... Radiosonde Observation Data
RADATA.. RADAR Data Transmission and Assembly (IEEE)
RADATAC ... Radiation Data Acquisition Chart
RADAUS... Radio-Austria AG (TSSD)
RADAY .... Radio Day (CET)
RADB .... Radiometric Age Data Bank [*Geological Survey*] [*Information service or system*] [*Defunct*] (IID)
RADBA ..... Radiobiology [*English Translation*] [*A publication*]
RADBIOL ... Radiobiology
RADBN..... Radio Battalion [*Marine Corps*]
RAD(BPF) ... Rear-Admiral Commanding Destroyers (British Pacific Fleet)
RADC .... RADAR Countermeasures and Deception [*Military*] (MCD)
RADC .... Regiment Air Defense Center (NATG)
RADC .... Rome Air Development Center [*Griffiss Air Force Base, NY*] [*Air Force*]
RADC .... Royal Army Dental Corps [*British*]
RADCAP... Research and Development Contributions to Aviation Progress [*Air Force*]
RADCAS... Radiation Casualty [*Criteria for battlefield targets*] (MCD)
RADCC .... Radiological Control Center [*Army*] (KSC)
RADCC ..... Rear Area Damage Control Center (AABC)
RADC/ETR ... Rome Air Development Center Deputy for Electronic Technology [*ESD*]
RADCHM ... Radiochemistry
Rad Clinica ... Radiologia Clinica [*A publication*]
Rad Clin NA ... Radiologic Clinics of North America [*A publication*]
RADCM... RADAR Countermeasures and Deception [*Military*]
RADCOL... RADC [*Rome Air Development Center*] Automatic Document Classification On-Line [*Air Force*] [*Information service or system*] (IID)
RADCOM ... Radiometric Contrast Matching (MCD)
RADCOM ... Research and Development Command (MCD)
RADCON ... RADAR Control
RADCON ... RADAR Data Converter (AFM)
RADCON ... Radiological Control [*Military*] (AABC)
RADCOT .. Radial Optical Tracking Theodolite (MUGU)
RADDEF... Radiological Defense [*To minimize the effect of nuclear radiation on people and resources*]
Rad Diagn ... Radiologia Diagnostica [*A publication*]
RADDOL.. Raddolcendo [*Gradually Softer*] [*Music*]
RADE .... Research and Development Division [*Obsolete*] [*National Security Agency*]
RADEF...... Radiological Defense [*To minimize the effect of nuclear radiation on people and resources*]
RADEM .... Random Access Delta Modulation
Rad Eng (London) ... Radio Engineering (London) [*A publication*]
RADEP...... RADAR Departure (FAAC)
RADER..... Rassemblement Democratique du Ruanda [*Democratic Rally of Rwanda*]
RADES..... Realistic Air Defense Engagement System [*Army*] (RDA)
RADEX..... RADAR Exercise (NVT)
RADEX..... Radiation Exclusion Plot [*Chart of actual or predicted fallout*]
Radex Rundsch ... Radex Rundschau [*A publication*]
Radex Runsch ... Radex Rundschau [*A publication*]
RADFAC... Radiating Facility
RADFAL... Radiological Prediction Fallout Plot
RADFET... Radiation-Sensing Field Effect Transistor [*Instrumentation*]
RADFO.... Radiological Fallout [*Army*]
Rad Geoinst ... Radovi - Geoinstitut [*A publication*]
RADHAZ.. Radiation Hazards
Rad Hist..... Radical History Review [*A publication*]
Rad Humanist ... Radical Humanist [*A publication*]
RADI .... Rada Electronic Industries Ltd. [*New York, NY*] [*NASDAQ symbol*] (NQ)
RADI .... Radiographic Inspection [*NASA*] (AAG)
Radi........... Radium [*Record label*] [*France*]
RADIA ...... Radiography [*A publication*]
RADIAC.... Radiation Detection, Indication, and Computation [*Radiological measuring instruments*]
RADIAC.... Radioactive Detection and Measurement
RADIAT.... Radiation

Radiata Pine Tech Bull ... Radiata Pine Technical Bulletin (Radiata Pine Association of Australia) [*A publication*]   (APTA)
Radiat Biol ... Radiation Biology [*England*] [*A publication*]
Radiat Bot ... Radiation Botany [*A publication*]
Radiat Data Rep ... Radiation Data and Reports [*A publication*]
Radiat Eff .. Radiation Effects [*A publication*]
Radiat Effects ... Radiation Effects [*A publication*]
Radiat Eff Lett ... Radiation Effects. Letters Section [*A publication*]
Radiat Eff Lett Sect ... Radiation Effects. Letters Section [*A publication*]
Radiat Env ... Radiation and Environmental Biophysics [*A publication*]
Radiat and Environ Biophys ... Radiation and Environmental Biophysics [*A publication*]
Radiat Environ Biophys ... Radiation and Environmental Biophysics [*A publication*]
Radiat Med ... Radiation Medicine [*A publication*]
Radiat Phys and Chem ... Radiation Physics and Chemistry [*A publication*]
Radiat Phys Chem ... Radiation Physics and Chemistry [*A publication*]
Radiat Prot ... Radiation Protection [*Republic of Korea*] [*A publication*]
Radiat Prot Aust ... Radiation Protection in Australia [*A publication*]
Radiat Prot Dosim ... Radiation Protection Dosimetry [*A publication*]
Radiat Prot ICRP Publ ... Radiation Protection. ICRP [*International Commission on Radiological Protection*] Publication [*A publication*]
Radiat Prot (Seoul) ... Radiation Protection (Seoul) [*A publication*]
Radiat Prot (Taiyuan People's Repub China) ... Radiation Protection (Taiyuan, People's Republic of China) [*A publication*]
Radiat Rep ... Radiation Report [*A publication*]
Radiat Res ... Radiation Research [*A publication*]
Radiat Res Polym ... Radiation Research on Polymers [*Japan*] [*A publication*]
Radiat Res Rev ... Radiation Research Reviews [*A publication*]
Radiat Res Suppl ... Radiation Research. Supplement [*A publication*]
Radiats Bezop Zashch AEhS ... Radiatsionnaya Bezopasnost' i Zashchita AEhS. Sbornik Statej [*A publication*]
Radiats Fiz ... Radiatsionnaya Fizika [*A publication*]
Radiats Fiz Akad Nauk Latv SSR Inst Fiz ... Radiatsionnaya Fizika. Akademiya Nauk Latviiskoi SSR. Institut Fiziki [*Latvian SSR*] [*A publication*]
Radiats Fiz Nemet Krist ... Radiatsionnaya Fizika Nemetallicheskikh Kristallov [*A publication*]
Radiats Fiz Tverd Tela Radiats Materialoved ... Radiatsionnaya Fizika Tverdogo Tela i Radiatsionnoe Materialovedenie [*A publication*]
Radiats Gig ... Radiatsionnaya Gigiena [*USSR*] [*A publication*]
Radiat Shielding Inf Cent Rep ... Radiation Shielding Information Center. Report [*A publication*]
Radiats Tekh ... Radiatsionnaya Tekhnika [*A publication*]
Radiaz Alta Energ ... Radiazioni di Alta Energia [*A publication*]
Radiaz Radioisot ... Radiazioni e Radioisotopi [*A publication*]
RADIC....... Radical   (ROG)
RADIC....... Radio Interior Communications
RADIC....... Redifon Analog-Digital Computer [*British*]
RADIC....... Research and Development Information Center   (AFM)
Radical Am ... Radical America [*A publication*]
Radical Commun Med ... Radical Community Medicine [*A publication*]
Radical Ed ... Radical Education [*A publication*]
Radical Ed Dossier ... Radical Education Dossier [*A publication*]
Radical Educ Dossier ... Radical Education Dossier [*A publication*]   (APTA)
Radical His ... Radical History Review [*A publication*]
Radical Scot ... Radical Scotland [*A publication*]
RADIC-LIB ... Radical Liberal
RADIL....... Research Animal Diagnostic and Investigative Laboratory [*University of Missouri-Columbia*] [*Research center*]   (RCD)
Rad Imunol Zavoda (Zagreb) ... Radovi Imunoloskog Zavoda (Zagreb) [*A publication*]
Rad Inst Geol-Rud Istraz Ispit Nukl Drugih Miner Sirovina ... Radovi Instituta za Geolosko-Rudarska Istrazivanja i Ispitivanja Nuklearnih i Drugih Mineralnih Sirovina [*Yugoslavia*] [*A publication*]
Rad Inst Proucavanje Suzbijanje Alkohol Drugih Narkomanija ... Radovi Instituta za Proucavanje i Suzbijanje Alkoholizma i Drugih Narkomanija u Zagrebu [*A publication*]
Rad Inst Prouc Suzbijanje Alkohol Drugih Narkomanija Zagrebu ... Radovi Instituta za Proucavanje i Suzbijanje Alkoholizma i Drugih Narkomanija u Zagrebu [*A publication*]
Rad Inst Sum Istraz ... Radovi Institut za Sumarska Istrazivanja. Sumarskog Fakulteta. Sveucilista u Zagrebu [*A publication*]
RADINT.... RADAR Intelligence
RADIO...... Radiotherapy
Radioact Sea ... Radioactivity in the Sea [*Austria*] [*A publication*]
Radioact Surv Data Jap ... Radioactivity Survey Data in Japan [*A publication*]
Radioact Waste Disposal Res Ser Inst Geol Sci ... Radioactive Waste Disposal. Research Series. Institute of Geological Sciences [*A publication*]
Radioact Waste Manage ... Radioactive Waste Management [*A publication*]
Radioact Waste Manage Nucl Fuel Cycle ... Radioactive Waste Management and the Nuclear Fuel Cycle [*A publication*]
Radioact Waste Manage and Nucl Fuel Cycle ... Radioactive Waste Management and the Nuclear Fuel Cycle [*A publication*]

Radioact Waste Manage (Oak Ridge Tenn) ... Radioactive Waste Management (Oak Ridge, Tennessee) [*A publication*]
Radioact Waste Technol ... Radioactive Waste Technology [*A publication*]
Radioaktiv Zivotn Prostr ... Radioaktivita a Zivotne Prostredie [*A publication*]
Radiobiol.... Radiobiologiya [*A publication*]
RADIOBIOL ... Radiobiology
Radiobiol Biol Mol ... Radiobiologia si Biologia Moleculara [*Romania*] [*A publication*]
Radiobiol Inf Byull ... Radiobiologiya Informatsionnyi Byulleten' [*A publication*]
Radiobiol Lat ... Radiobiologica Latina [*Italy*] [*A publication*]
Radiobiol Radioter Fis Med ... Radiobiologia, Radioterapia, e Fisica Medica [*A publication*]
Radiobiol-Radiother ... Radiobiologia-Radiotherapia [*A publication*]
Radiobiol-Radiother (Berl) ... Radiobiologia-Radiotherapia (Berlin) [*A publication*]
Radiobiol-Radiother (Berlin) ... Radiobiologia-Radiotherapia (Berlin) [*A publication*]
Radioch Act ... Radiochimica Acta [*A publication*]
RADIOCHEM ... Radiochemistry
Radiochem and Radioanal Lett ... Radiochemical and Radioanalytical Letters [*A publication*]
Radiochem Radioanal Lett ... Radiochemical and Radioanalytical Letters [*A publication*]
Radiochim Acta ... Radiochimica Acta [*A publication*]
Radioch Rad ... Radiochemical and Radioanalytical Letters [*A publication*]
Radio Commun ... Radio Communication [*A publication*]
Radioekol Vodn Org ... Radioekologiya Vodnykh Organizmov [*A publication*]
Radio Elec ... Radio-Electronics [*A publication*]
Radio-Electr ... Radio-Electronics [*A publication*]
Radio Electron ... Radio Electronica [*Netherlands*] [*A publication*]
Radio-Electron ... Radio-Electronics [*A publication*]
Radio Electron Commun Syst ... Radio Electronics and Communications Systems [*A publication*]
Radioelectron and Commun Syst ... Radioelectronics and Communication Systems [*A publication*]
Radio & Electron Constructor ... Radio and Electronics Constructor [*A publication*]
Radio Electron Eng ... Radio and Electronic Engineer [*A publication*]
Radio and Electron Eng ... Radio and Electronic Engineer [*A publication*]
Radio Electron Eng (London) ... Radio and Electronic Engineer (London) [*A publication*]
Radio & Electronic Eng ... Radio and Electronic Engineer [*A publication*]
Radio and Electron World ... Radio and Electronics World [*A publication*]
Radio Elec W ... Radio Electrical Weekly [*A publication*]   (APTA)
Radio Elektron ... Radio Elektronica [*A publication*]
Radio Elektroniikkalab Tek Korkeakoulu Kertomus ... Radio- ja Elektroniikkalaboratoriot. Teknillinen Korkeakoulu. Kertomus [*A publication*]
Radio Elektron Schau ... Radio Elektronik Schau [*A publication*]
Radio El En ... Radio and Electronic Engineer [*A publication*]
Radio Eng .. Radio Engineering [*A publication*]
Radio Eng and Electron Phys ... Radio Engineering and Electronic Physics [*A publication*]
Radio Eng Electron Phys ... Radio Engineering and Electronic Physics [*A publication*]
Radio Eng Electron (USSR) ... Radio Engineering and Electronic Physics (USSR) [*A publication*]
Radio Engrg Electron Phys ... Radio Engineering and Electronic Physics [*A publication*]
Radio Eng (USSR) ... Radio Engineering (USSR) [*A publication*]
Radio Fernsehen Elektron ... Radio Fernsehen Elektronik [*A publication*]
Radiogr ...... Radiographer [*A publication*]   (APTA)
Radiogr Today ... Radiography Today [*A publication*]
Radio Hobbies Aust ... Radio and Hobbies Australia [*A publication*]
Radio Ind ... Radio Industria [*A publication*]
Radioind Elettron-Telev ... Radioindustria Elettronica-Televisione [*A publication*]
Radioisot (Praha) ... Radioisotopy (Praha) [*A publication*]
Radioisot (Tokyo) ... Radioisotopes (Tokyo) [*A publication*]
Radiol......... Radiology
Radio Lab Tech Univ Helsinki Intern Rep ... Radio Laboratory. Technical University of Helsinki. Internal Report [*A publication*]
Radiol Austriaca ... Radiologia Austriaca [*A publication*]
Radiol Bras ... Radiologia Brasileira [*A publication*]
Radiol Clin ... Radiologia Clinica [*A publication*]
Radiol Clin (Basel) ... Radiologia Clinica (Basel) [*A publication*]
Radiol Clin Biol ... Radiologia Clinica et Biologica [*A publication*]
Radiol Clin N Am ... Radiologic Clinics of North America [*A publication*]
Radiol Clin North Am ... Radiologic Clinics of North America [*A publication*]
Radiol Clin North America ... Radiologic Clinics of North America [*A publication*]
Radiol Diagn ... Radiologia Diagnostica [*A publication*]
Radiol Diagn (Berlin) ... Radiologia Diagnostica (Berlin) [*A publication*]
Radiol Health Data ... Radiological Health Data [*A publication*]
Radiol Health Data Rep ... Radiological Health Data and Reports [*A publication*]
Radiol Iugosl (Ljubljana) ... Radiologia Iugoslavica (Ljubljana) [*A publication*]
Radiol Kozl ... Radiologiai Kozlemenyek [*A publication*]

Radiol Manage ... Radiology Management [*A publication*]
Radiol Med ... Radiologia Medica [*A publication*]
Radiol Med (Torino) ... Radiologia Medica (Torino) [*A publication*]
Radiological Protect Bull ... Radiological Protection Bulletin [*A publication*]
Radiol Prat ... Radiologia Pratica [*Italy*] [*A publication*]
Radiol Prot Bull ... Radiological Protection Bulletin [*A publication*]
Radiol Rev Miss Val Med J ... Radiological Review and Mississippi Valley Medical Journal [*A publication*]
Radiol Technol ... Radiologic Technology [*A publication*]
Radio Mentor Electron ... Radio Mentor Electronic [*A publication*]
Radio Mntr ... Radio Mentor Electronic [*A publication*]
Radiom Polarogr ... Radiometer Polarographics [*A publication*]
Radio N ...... Radio News [*A publication*]
Radiophysiol Radiother ... Radiophysiologie et Radiotherapie [*A publication*]
Radiophys Quantum Electron ... Radiophysics and Quantum Electronics [*A publication*]
Radiophys & Quantum Electron ... Radiophysics and Quantum Electronics [*A publication*]
Radio Sci .... Radio Science [*A publication*]
Radio Serv Bul ... Radio Service Bulletin [*A publication*]
Radio T ...... Radio Times [*United Kingdom*] [*A publication*]
Radiotehn i Elektron ... Akademija Nauk SSSR. Radiotehnika i Elektronika [*A publication*]
Radiotehn (Kharkov) ... Radiotehnika (Kharkov) [*A publication*]
Radiotek El ... Radiotekhnika i Elektronika [*A publication*]
Radiotekh .. Radiotekhnika [*A publication*]
Radiotekh Elektron ... Radiotekhnika i Elektronika [*A publication*]
Radiotekh i Elektron ... Radiotekhnika i Elektronika [*A publication*]
Radiotekhn ... Khar'kovskii Ordena Trudovogo Krasnogo Znameni Gosudarstvennyi Universitet Imeni A.M. Gor'kogo Radiotekhnika [*A publication*]
Radiotekhn i Elektron ... Radiotekhnika i Elektronika. Akademiya Nauk SSSR [*A publication*]
Radiotekh Proizvod ... Radiotekhnicheskoe Proizvodstvo [*A publication*]
Radio Telev ... Radio Television [*A publication*]
Radio Telev Int Rev ... Radio - Television International Review [*A publication*]
Radio Tel & Hobbies ... Radio, Television, and Hobbies [*A publication*]
Radioter Radiobiol Fis Med ... Radioterapia, Radiobiologia, e Fisica Medica [*A publication*]
Radiother Oncol ... Radiotherapy and Oncology [*A publication*]
Radio-TV-Electron ... Radio-TV-Electronic [*Later, RTE. Radio-TV-Electronic*] [*A publication*]
Radio-TV-Electron Serv ... Radio-TV-Electronic Service [*Later, RTE. Radio-TV-Electronic*] [*Switzerland*] [*A publication*]
Radio TVH ... Radio, Television, and Hobbies [*A publication*] (APTA)
Radio & TV N ... Radio and Television News [*A publication*]
Radio es TV Szle ... Radio es TV Szemle [*A publication*]
RADIQUAD ... Radio Quadrangle [*Military*]
RADIR .... Random Access Document Indexing and Retrieval
RADIST .... RADAR Distance Indicator
RADIT .... Radio Teletype (IEEE)
RADIUS ... Research and Development Institute of the United States [*Research center*] (RCD)
RadJA .... Radovi Jugoslavenske Akademije Znanosti i Umjetnosti [*A publication*]
Rad Jugosl Akad Znan Umjet ... Radovi Jugoslavenske Akademije Znanosti i Umjetnosti [*A publication*]
Rad Jugoslav Akad Znan Umjet ... Radovi Jugoslavenske Akademije Znanosti i Umjetnosti [*A publication*]
Rad Jugoslav Akad Znan Umjet Odjel Prir Nauke ... Radovi Jugoslavenske Akademije Znanosti i Umjetnosti. Odjel za Prirodne Nauke [*A publication*]
RADKA ..... Radiokhimiya [*A publication*]
RADL .... Radial (AAG)
RADL .... Radiological [*or Radiology*] (AAG)
RadL .... Radyans'ske Literaturoznavstvo [*Kiev*] [*A publication*]
RADLA ...... Radiology [*A publication*]
RADLAB ... Radiation Laboratory (AAG)
RADLAC ... Radial Pulse Line Accelerators (MCD)
RADLCEN ... Radiological Center
RADLDEF ... Radiological Defense [*To minimize the effect of nuclear radiation on people and resources*]
RADLDEFLAB ... Radiological Defense Laboratory [*NASA*]
RADLFO ... Radiological Fallout [*Army*] (AABC)
RADLGC ... Radiologic
RADLGCL ... Radiological
RADLGY ... Radiology
RADLMON ... Radiological Monitor [*or Monitoring*] [*Military*]
RADLO ..... Radiological Officer
RADLO ..... Regional Air Defense Liaison Officer (FAAC)
RADLOPS ... Radiological Operations [*Military*] (AABC)
RADLSAFE ... Radiological Safety [*Military*]
RADLSO ... Radiological Survey Officer [*Military*]
RADLSV ... Radiological Survey [*Military*]
RadLV .... Radiation Leukemia Virus
RADLWAR ... Radiological Warfare
RADM .... Rear Admiral [*Also, RA, RADML*] (AAG)
RADM .... Regional Acid Deposition Model [*for acid rain*] [*Environmental Protection Agency*]

R Adm .... Revue de l'Administration et du Droit Administratif de la Belgique [*A publication*]
R Adm .... Revue Administrative [*A publication*]
Rad Med Fak Rijeka ... Radovi Medicinskogo Fakulteta. Rijeka [*A publication*]
Rad Med Fak Zagrebu ... Radovi Medicinskogo Fakulteta u Zagrebu [*A publication*]
R Adm Empresas ... Revista de Administracao de Empresas [*A publication*]
R Admin Empresas ... Revista de Administracao de Empresas [*A publication*]
R Admin (Paris) ... Revue Administrative (Paris) [*A publication*]
R Admin Publica ... Revista de Administracion Publica [*A publication*]
RADMIS ... Research Activities Designators Management Information System
RADML .... Rear Admiral [*Also, RA, RADM*] (FAAC)
R Adm Municip (Rio De Janeiro) ... Revista de Administracao Municipal (Rio De Janeiro) [*A publication*]
RADMON ... Radiological Monitoring (AFM)
R Adm Publ (Madrid) ... Revista de Administracion Publica (Madrid) [*A publication*]
R Adm Publ (Rio De Janeiro) ... Revista de Administracao Publica (Rio De Janeiro) [*A publication*]
RADN .... Radiation (AAG)
RADN .... Radnorshire [*County in Wales*]
RADN .... Radyne Corp. [*NASDAQ symbol*] (NQ)
RADNORS ... Radnorshire [*County in Wales*] (ROG)
RADNOS .. No Radio [*Military*]
RADNOTE ... Radio Note [*Military*]
RADOA ...... Radiobiologiya [*A publication*]
RADOC ..... Regional Air Defense Operations Center (NATG)
RADOC ..... Remote Automatic Detection Contingencies
RADOD ..... Research and Development Objectives Document (MCD)
RADOME ... RADAR Dome [*NASA*]
RADON ... RADAR Beacon
RADON ..... Research and Development Operational Needs (MCD)
RADOP ..... RADAR Doppler [*Missile-tracking system*] (AAG)
RADOP ..... RADAR Operator (CET)
RADOP ..... RADAR/Optical Weapons [*Military*]
RADOPR ..... Radio Operator [*Navy*]
RADOPR ... Radio Operator (AAG)
RADOPWEAP ... RADAR Optical Weapons (IEEE)
RADOSE ... Radiation Dosimeter Satellite [*NASA*]
RADOT ...... Real-Time [*or Recording*] Automatic Digital Optical Tracker
RADP .... Right Acromio-Dorsoposterior [*A fetal position*] [*Obstetrics*]
RADPCO ... Regional ADP [*Automatic Data Processing*] Contact Officer [*Australia*]
Rad Phil ..... Radical Philosophy [*A publication*]
Rad Phil News ... Radical Philosopher's Newsjournal [*A publication*]
RADPLANBD ... Radio Planning Board [*Navy*]
Rad Poljopriv Fak Univ Saraj ... Radovi Poljoprivrednog Fakulteta Univerziteta u Sarajevu [*A publication*]
Rad Poljopriv Fak Univ Sarajevu ... Radovi Poljoprivrednog Fakulteta Univerziteta u Sarajevu [*A publication*]
RADPROPCAST ... Radio Propagation Forecast
RADREF ... RADAR Refraction (MCD)
Rad Reg P & F ... Radio Regulation. Pike and Fischer [*A publication*]
Rad Rel ...... Radical Religion [*A publication*]
RADREL ... Radio Relay [*Military*]
Rad Relig ... Radical Religion [*A publication*]
RADRON ... RADAR Squadron [*Air Force*]
RADS .... RADAR Squadron [*Air Force*]
RAD/S .... Radians per Second
RADS .... Radiation and Dosimetry Services (NRCH)
RADS .... Radiation Systems, Inc. [*NASDAQ symbol*] (NQ)
RADS .... Radius (AAG)
RADS .... Rapid Area Distribution Support [*Air Force*]
RADS .... Raw Data System
RADS .... Ryukyu Air Defense System
RAD/S² ...... Radians per Second Squared
RADSAFE ... Radiological Safety [*Military*]
Rad Sarajevo Univ Poljopr Fak ... Radovi Sarajevo Univerzitet. Poljoprivredni Fakultet [*A publication*]
RADSCAT ... Radiometer/Scatterometer [*Sensor*] [*Meteorology*]
Rad Scien ... Radical Science Journal [*A publication*]
RADSO ..... Radiological Survey Officer (IEEE)
RADSOC ... Request for Authority to Develop a System or Change [*Military*] (AFIT)
RADSTA ... Radio Station
Rad Sumar Fak Inst Sumar Sarajevo ... Radovi Sumarskog Fakulteta i Instituta za Sumarstvo u Sarajevo [*A publication*]
Rad Sum Fak i Inst Sum ... Radovi Sumarski Fakultet i Institut za Sumarstvo [*A publication*]
RadT .... Radiola-Telefunken [*Record label*] [*Australia*]
RADT .... Radtech, Inc. [*Albuquerque, NM*] [*NASDAQ symbol*] (NQ)
Rad Teach ... Radical Teacher [*A publication*]
Rad Ther .... Issues in Radical Therapy [*A publication*]
Rad Thera ... Issues in Radical Therapy [*A publication*]
RADTT .... Radio Teletypewriter (CET)
RADU .... RADAR Analysis and Development Unit [*National Severe Storms Forecast Center*] (NOAA)
RADU .... Ram Air-Driven Unit

RAD-UDRT ... Respect voor Arbeid en Democratie/Union Democratique pour le Respect du Travail [*Respect for Labor and Democracy/Democratic Union for the Respect of Labor*] [*Belgium*] [*Political party*] (PPE)
Rad Voj Muz ... Rad Vojvodanskich Muzeja [*A publication*]
RADVS........ RADAR Altimeter and Doppler Velocity Sensor
RADWA ...... Recreation Association for the Disabled of Western Australia
RADWAR ... Radiological Warfare
RADWASTE ... Radioactive Waste
RADX........ Radionics, Inc. [*NASDAQ symbol*] (NQ)
Rad Zavoda Fiz ... Radovi Zavoda za Fiziku [*A publication*]
RadZSF .... Radovi Zavoda za Slavensku Filologiju [*A publication*]
RAE .... Arar [*Saudi Arabia*] [*Airport symbol*] (OAG)
RA(E)........ Engineer Rear-Admiral [*Navy*] [*British*] (DMA)
RAE .... RADAR Altimeter Equipment
RAE .... Radio Astronomy Explorer [*Satellite*]
RAE .... Radiodifusion Argentina al Exterior [*Broadcasting organization*] [*Argentina*]
RAE .... Range, Azimuth, and Elevation (MCD)
RAE .... Real Academia Espanola. Boletin [*A publication*]
RAE .... Review of Applied Entomology [*Database*] [*Commonwealth Institute of Entomology*] [*Information service or system*] (CRD)
RAE .... Revista Antioquena de Economia [*A publication*]
RAE .... Revista Augustiniana de Espiritualidad [*A publication*]
RAE .... Revue Archeologique de l'Est et du Centre-Est [*A publication*]
RAE........... Revue d'Art et d'Esthetique [*A publication*]
RAE .... Right Arithmetic Element
RAE .... Right Ascension Encoder
RAE .... Right Atrial Enlargement [*Cardiology*]
RAE .... Royal Aircraft Establishment [*British*]
RAE .... Royal Australian Engineers
RAEA .... Regroupement des Auteurs-Editeurs Autonomes [*Canada*]
RAEB........ Refractory Anemia with Excess of Blasts [*Hematology*]
RAEB-T..... Refractory Abemia with Excess of Blasts in Transformation [*Hematology*]
RAEC........ Rabbit Aortic Endothelial Cells
RAEC........ Royal Army Educational Corps [*British*]
RAECO ...... Rare-Earth Cobalt
RAEDOT .. Range, Azimuth, and Elevation Detection of Optical Targets
RAEFB ...... Radiation Effects [*A publication*]
RAELA...... Radiotekhnika i Elektronika [*A publication*]
RAEME...... Royal Australian Electrical and Mechanical Engineers (DMA)
RAEN .... Radio Amateur Emergency Network (IEEE)
Ra Ent........ [*Lord*] Raymond's Entries [*A publication*] (DLA)
RaeRG ...... Reallexikon der Aegyptischen Religionsgeschichte [*Berlin*] [*A publication*] (BJA)
RAES........ Radio Astronomy Experiment Selection Panel
RAES........ Rapid Access with Extensive Search [*Algorithm*]
RAES........ Ratios for Automotive Executives [*Computer software*]
RAES........ Remote Access Editing System [*Data processing*] (IEEE)
RAeS........ Royal Aeronautical Society [*London, England*] (EAIO)
RAET........ Range, Azimuth, Elevation, and Time
RAETDS ... Reciprocating Aircraft Engine Type Designation System
Raevar........ [*Jacobus*] Raevardus [*Deceased, 1568*] [*Authority cited in pre-1607 legal work*] (DSA)
RAF .... Racial Awareness Facilitator [*School*] [*Navy*] (NVT)
Ra F............ Raphael Fulgosius [*Deceased, 1427*] [*Authority cited in pre-1607 legal work*] (DSA)
RAF .... Regular Air Force
RAF .... Requirements Allocation Form
RAF .... Requirements Analysis Form [*NASA*] (NASA)
RAF .... Research Aviation Facility [*National Center for Atmospheric Research*]
RAF .... Reserved Air Freight
RAF .... Resource Allocation Formula
RAf............. Revue Africaine [*A publication*]
RAF .... Reynolds Analogy Factor [*Physics*]
RAF .... Rote Armee Faktion (Baader-Meinhof Group)] [*Terrorist group*] [*Federal Republic of Germany*]
RAF .... Royal Air Force [*British*]
RAF .... Royal Aircraft Factory [*World War I*] [*British*]
RAF .... Sacramento, CA [*Location identifier*] [*FAA*] (FAAL)
RAFA........ Rank Annihilation Factor Analysis [*Data processing*]
RAFA........ Royal Air Forces Association (EAIO)
Ra Fab........ Raymundus Fabri [*Flourished, 14th century*] [*Authority cited in pre-1607 legal work*] (DSA)
Rafair........ Royal Air Force [*Airline call sign*] [*British*]
RAFAR...... Radio Automated Facsimile and Reproduction
RAFAX..... RADAR Facsimile
RAFB........ Randolph Air Force Base [*Texas*]
RAFB......... Rickenbacker Air Force Base [*Formerly, Lockbourne Air Force Base*] [*Ohio*]
RAFB......... Royal Air Force Base [*British*]
RAFBF ..... Royal Air Force Benevolent Fund [*British military*] (DMA)
RAFC........ Richmond Area Film Cooperative [*Library network*]
RAFC........ Royal Air Force Club [*British*]
RAFC........ Royal Air Force College [*British*]
RAFC........ Royal Artillery Flying Club [*British military*] (DMA)
RAFCC...... Royal Air Force Cinema Corporation [*British military*] (DMA)
RAFCC...... Royal Air Force Coastal Command [*British*]

RAFCOR... Rural Adjustment and Finance Corporation of Western Australia
RAFD .... Rome Air Force Depot
RAFES ...... Royal Air Force Educational Service [*British military*] (DMA)
RAFFC ..... Royal Air Force Fighter Command [*British*]
Raff Pens Man ... Raff's Pension Manual [*A publication*] (DLA)
RAFG........ Royal Air Force, Germany [*British military*] (DMA)
RAFI........ Ravenswood Finance Corp. [*NASDAQ symbol*] (NQ)
RAFI .... Rural Advancement Fund International [*Later, RAFI-USA*] (EA)
RAFIA ...... Radiatsionnaya Fizika. Akademiya Nauk Latviiskoi SSR. Institut Fiziki [*A publication*]
RAFL........ Rainfall (FAAC)
RAFME..... Royal Air Force, Middle East [*British military*] (DMA)
RAFMS..... Royal Air Force Medical Service [*British*]
RAFNS...... Royal Air Force Nursing Service [*British military*] (DMA)
RAFO........ Reserve Air Force Officers [*Later, RAFRO*] [*British*]
RAfr.......... Revue Africaine [*A publication*]
RAFR........ Royal Air Force Regiment [*British*]
RAFRC...... Revolutionary Armed Forces of the Republic of Cuba
R African Pol Economy ... Review of African Political Economy [*A publication*]
R Afr Manag ... Revue Africaine de Management [*A publication*]
RAFRO..... Royal Air Force Reserve of Officers [*Formerly, RAFO*] [*British*]
RAFRZ...... Radiosonde Observation - Freezing Levels (FAAC)
RAFS .... R. Austin Freeman Society (EA)
RAFS........ Regional Analysis and Forecast System [*National Meteorological Center*]
RAFS .... Royal Air Force Station [*British*] (MCD)
RAFSAA ... Royal Air Force Small Arms Association [*British military*] (DMA)
RAFSC...... Royal Air Force Staff College [*British*]
RAFSP...... Royal Air Force Service Police [*British military*] (DMA)
RAFSTN.... Royal Air Force Air Station
RAFT........ Racial Awareness Facilitator Training [*Navy program*]
RAFT........ Radially Adjustable Facility Tube (IEEE)
RAFT........ Rear-Admiral Fleet Train [*British Pacific Fleet*]
RAFT........ Recomp Algebraic Formula Translator [*Data processing*]
RAFT........ Regional Accounting and Finance Test [*Military*] (AFM)
RAFT........ Reunion des Amateurs de Fox Terriers [*An association*] (EAIO)
RAFTC...... Royal Air Forces Transport Command [*British*]
Ra Fulgo..... Raphael Fulgosius [*Deceased, 1427*] [*Authority cited in pre-1607 legal work*] (DSA)
RAFVR...... Royal Air Force Volunteer Reserve [*British*]
RAG.......... New South Wales Records Administration Group [*Australia*]
RAG.......... Ragged (FAAC)
Rag............ Ragioniere [*Accountant*] [*Italian*]
Rag............ Ragland's California Superior Court Decisions [*A publication*] (DLA)
RAG.......... Raina un Aspazijas Gadagramata [*A publication*]
RAG.......... Readiness Analysis Group
RAG.......... Recombination-Activating Gene
RAG.......... Regional Advisory Group [*Generic term*] (DHSM)
RAg.......... Related Antigen [*Immunology*]
RAG.......... Religious Arts Guild [*Defunct*] (EA)
RAG.......... Replacement Air Group
RAG.......... Requirements Advisory Group [*Air Force*] (MCD)
RAG.......... Resource Appraisal Group [*US Geological Survey*]
RAG.......... Retail Associates Group, Inc. [*Homesewing industry trade group*]
RAG.......... Returned Ammunition Group (NATG)
RAG.......... Reusable Agena [*NASA*] (NASA)
RAG.......... Ring Airfoil Grenade [*Army*]
RAG.......... River Assault Group [*Military*]
RAG.......... ROM [*Read-Only Memory*] Address Gate [*Data processing*]
RAG.......... Runway Arresting Gear [*Aviation*]
RAG-1........ Rosenberg, Avraham, and Gutnick [*Strain of bacteria named for its researchers: Eugene Rosenberg, Avraham Reisfield, and David Gutnick*]
RAGBRAI ... [*Des Moines*] Register Annual Great Bicycle Race Across Iowa [*Pronounced "ragbray"*]
RAGC........ Rainbows for All God's Children [*Later, RFAGC*] (EA)
RAGC .... Relief General Communications Vessel
RAGC........ Royal Adelaide Golf Club [*Australia*]
RAGC .... Royal and Ancient Golf Club [*Scotland*]
R Ag (Cuba) ... Revista de Agricultura (Cuba) [*A publication*]
R de Ag (Cuba) ... Revista de Agricultura (Cuba) [*A publication*]
RAGE .... Radio Amplification of Gamma Emissions [*Antiguerrilla weapon*]
RAGE .... Read and Get Enjoyment Program [*Australia*]
RAGEA...... Razvedochnaya Geofizika [*A publication*]
RAGEMS ... Radioactive Gaseous Effluent Monitoring System
RAGF........ Remote Air-Ground Facility [*Aviation*]
R Ag France ... Revue des Agriculteurs de France [*A publication*]
Ragg.......... Rheumatoid Agglutinator [*Immunology*]
RagL......... Raguaglio Librario [*A publication*]
RAGN....... Ragen Corp. [*NASDAQ symbol*] (NQ)
RAGOA..... Rivista di Agronomia [*A publication*]

R Agr Econ Mal ... Review of Agricultural Economics of Malaysia [*A publication*]
R Agric .... Revue de l'Agriculture [*A publication*]
R Agric Soc (Cairo) Bull Tech Sect ... Royal Agricultural Society (Cairo). Bulletin. Technical Section [*A publication*]
R Agric Soc Kenya QJ ... Royal Agricultural Society of Kenya. Quarterly Journal [*A publication*]
RAGS .... Coated Sales, Inc. [*Laurence Harbor, NJ*] [*NASDAQ symbol*] (NQ)
Rag Super Ct Dec (Calif) ... Ragland's California Superior Court Decisions [*A publication*] (DLA)
RAH .... Rabbit Anti-Human [*Immunology*]
RAH .... Radiation-Anneal Hardening [*Alloy*]
RAH .... Rafha [*Saudi Arabia*] [*Airport symbol*] (OAG)
RAH .... Receipt, Excess, Adjustment, Due-In History File [*Army*]
RAH .... Receiving Array Hydrophone
RAH .... Recuperation Assistee des Hydrocarbures [*Enhanced Oil Recovery*] [*French*]
RAH .... Regressing Atypical Histiocytosis [*Medicine*]
RAH .... Reviews in American History [*A publication*]
RAH .... Right Atrial Hypertrophy [*Cardiology*]
RAH .... Royal Albert Hall [*London, England*]
Ra de Hacur ... Raoul d'Harcourt [*Deceased, 1307*] [*Authority cited in pre-1607 legal work*] (DSA)
RAHBol ..... Real Academia de la Historia. Boletin [*A publication*]
RAHE .... Review of Allied Health Education [*A publication*]
RAHF .... Research Animal Holding Facility [*NASA*] (NASA)
RaHGBM ... Rabbit Anti-Human Glomerular Basement Membrane [*Immunology*]
RAHO .... Rabbits Against Human Ovary [*Immunology*]
RAHO .... Royal Albert Hall Orchestra
RAHS .... Royal Australian Historical Society. Journal [*A publication*] (APTA)
RAHSJ ...... Royal Australian Historical Society. Journal and Proceedings [*A publication*] (APTA)
RAI .... Praia [*Cape Verde Islands*] [*Airport symbol*] (OAG)
RAI .... RADAR Altimeter Indicator (MCD)
RAI .... Radiation Applications, Incorporated
RAI .... Radioactive Interference [*NASA*]
RAI .... Radioactive Iodine [*Medicine*]
RAI .... Radioactive Isotope [*Roentgenology*]
Rai .... Rainerius [*Authority cited in pre-1607 legal work*] (DSA)
RAI .... Random Access and Inquiry [*Data processing*]
RAI .... Range Azimuth Indicator
RAI .... Raspberry Island [*Alaska*] [*Seismograph station code, US Geological Survey*] (SEIS)
RAI .... Reliability Assurance Instructions (KSC)
RAI .... Rencontre Assyriologique Internationale [*A publication*]
RAI .... Rendiconti. Classe di Scienze Morali e Storiche. Accademia d'Italia [*A publication*]
RAI .... Repair at Intermediate (MCD)
RAI .... Request for Additional Information (NRCH)
RAI .... Roll Attitude Indicator [*NASA*]
RAI .... Royal Albert Institution [*British*] (DAS)
RAI .... Royal Anthropological Institute [*British*]
RAI .... Royal Archaeological Institute [*British*]
RAI .... Royal Artillery Institution [*British military*] (DMA)
RAI .... Runway Alignment Indicator [*Aviation*]
RAI .... Rural America, Incorporated (EA)
RAIA .... Royal Australian Institute of Architects
RAIAA ...... Asociacion de Ingenieros Agronomos. Revista [*A publication*]
RAIAD ...... Reverse Acronyms, Initialisms, and Abbreviations Dictionary [*Formerly, RAID*] [*A publication*]
RAIAM ...... Random Access Indestructive Advanced Memory [*Data processing*] (MSA)
RAIB .... Rendiconti. Accademia delle Scienze. Istituto di Bologna [*A publication*]
RAIC .... Radiological Accident and Incident Control
RAIC .... Red Andina de Informacion Comercial [*Andean Trade Information Network*] (EAIO)
RAIC .... Redstone Arsenal Information Center [*Army*]
RAIC .... Royal Architectural Institute of Canada
RAIC .... Royal Australian Infantry Corps (DMA)
RAICG .... Radiosonde Observation Icing at _____ (FAAC)
RAID .... RADAR Identification and Direction System (NG)
RAID .... Ram Air-Inflated Drogue [*Military*] (CAAL)
RAID .... Recallable Airborne Infrared Display
RAID .... Remote Access Interactive Debugger [*Data processing*] (IEEE)
RAID .... Reverse Acronyms and Initialisms Dictionary [*Later, RAIAD*] [*A publication*]
RAID .... River Assault Interdiction Division [*Navy*] (NVT)
RAIDEX ..... Antisurface Raiders Exercise [*NATO*] (NATG)
RAIDS .... Rapid Acquisition and Identification System
RAIDS .... Rapid Availability of Information and Data for Safety [*NASA*] (KSC)
RAIDS .... Recently Acquired Income Deficiency Syndrome
RAIDS .... Reduced Annual Income Deficiency Syndrome [*British*]
RAIF .... Reseau d'Action et d'Information pour les Femmes [*Canada*]
Raiffeisen-Rundsch ... Raiffeisen-Rundschau [*A publication*]
RAIL .... Railroad Advancement through Information and Law Foundation

RAIL .... Railroad Financial Corp. [*NASDAQ symbol*] (NQ)
RAIL .... Railway (ROG)
RAIL .... Runway Alignment Indicator Light [*or Lighting*] [*Aviation*]
Rail Ca ...... Railway and Canal Cases [*1835-54*] [*A publication*] (DLA)
Rail & Can Cas ... English Railway and Canal Cases [*A publication*] (DLA)
Rail & Can Cas ... Railway and Canal Traffic Cases [*A publication*] (DLA)
Rail Cas ..... Railway Cases [*A publication*] (DLA)
Rail Clerk .. Railway Clerk Interchange [*A publication*]
Rail Eng ..... Railway Engineer [*Later, Railway Engineer International*] [*A publication*]
Rail Eng Int ... Rail Engineering International [*A publication*]
Rail Int ...... Rail International [*A publication*]
Rail M .... Railway Magazine [*A publication*]
Railroad Gaz ... Railroad Gazette [*A publication*]
RAILS .... Remote Area Instrument Landing Sensor [*Army*]
RAILS .... Remote Area Instrument Landing System [*Army*]
RAILS .... Runway Alignment Indicator Light [*or Lighting*] System [*Aviation*] (MCD)
Rail Syst Contr ... Railway Systems Control [*A publication*]
Railw Age .... Railway Age [*A publication*]
Railway & Corp Law J ... Railway and Corporation Law Journal [*A publication*] (DLA)
Railway R ... Railway Review [*A publication*] (APTA)
Railways in Aust ... Railways in Australia [*A publication*] (APTA)
Railways Union Gaz ... Railways Union Gazette [*A publication*] (APTA)
Railway Trans ... Railway Transportation [*A publication*] (APTA)
Railw Cas ... Railway Cases [*A publication*] (DLA)
Railw Dev News ... Railway Development News [*A publication*]
Railw Eng .. Railway Engineer [*Later, Railway Engineer International*] [*A publication*]
Railw Eng Int ... Railway Engineer International [*A publication*]
Railw Eng J ... Railway Engineering Journal [*Incorporated in Railway Engineer International*] [*A publication*]
Railw Eng Maint ... Railway Engineering and Maintenance [*A publication*]
Railw Engr ... Railway Engineer [*Later, Railway Engineer International*] [*A publication*]
Railw Gaz ... Railway Gazette [*Later, Railway Gazette International*] [*England*] [*A publication*]
Railw Gaz Int ... Railway Gazette International [*A publication*]
Railw Locomot Cars ... Railway Locomotives and Cars [*A publication*]
Railw Manage Rev ... Railway Management Review [*A publication*]
Railw Mech Eng ... Railway Mechanical Engineer [*United States*] [*A publication*]
Railw Rev ... Railway Review [*A publication*]
Railw Signal Commun ... Railway Signalling and Communications [*United States*] [*A publication*]
Railw South Afr ... Railways Southern Africa [*A publication*]
Railw Syst Control ... Railway Systems Control [*A publication*]
Railw Track Struct ... Railway Track and Structures [*A publication*]
RAIN .... Relational Algebraic Interpreter
RAIN .... Relief for Africans in Need (EA)
RAIN .... Royal Anthropological Institute News [*Later, Anthropology Today*] [*A publication*]
RAIN .... Royal Anthropological Institute. Newsletter [*A publication*]
RAINB .... Radio Industria [*A publication*]
RAINBO ... Research and Instrumentation for National Bio-Science Operations (MUGU)
RAINPAL ... Recursive Aided Inertial Navigation for Precision Approach and Landing [*NASA*]
RAIP .... Rapport d'Activites. Institut de Phonetique [*A publication*]
RAIP .... Requester's Approval in Principle (NRCH)
RAIPA .... Royal Australian Institute of Public Administration
RAIR .... Random Access Information Retrieval [*Data processing*] (IEEE)
RAIR .... Rapid Advancement in Reading [*Education*]
RAIR .... Recordak Automated Information Retrieval [*System*]
RAIR .... Reflection Absorption Infrared Spectroscopy [*Also, IRAS, IRRAS, RAIRS, RAIS*]
RAIR .... Regent Air Corp. [*NASDAQ symbol*] (NQ)
RAIR .... Remote Access Immediate Response [*Data processing*]
R Aircr Establ List Reports ... Royal Aircraft Establishment. List of Reports [*A publication*]
RAIRO Anal Num ... RAIRO [*Revue Francaise d'Automatique, d'Informatique, et de Recherche Operationnelle*] Analyse Numerique [*A publication*]
RAIRO Anal Numer ... RAIRO [*Revue Francaise d'Automatique, d'Informatique, et de Recherche Operationnelle*] Analyse Numerique [*A publication*]
RAIRO Anal Numer Numer Anal ... RAIRO [*Revue Francaise d'Automatique, d'Informatique, et de Recherche Operationnelle*] Analyse Numerique/Numerical Analysis [*A publication*]
RAIRO Automat ... RAIRO [*Revue Francaise d'Automatique, d'Informatique, et de Recherche Operationnelle*] Automatique [*A publication*]
RAIRO Autom Syst Anal Control ... RAIRO [*Revue Francaise d'Automatique, d'Informatique, et de Recherche Operationnelle*] Automatique/Systems Analysis and Control [*A publication*]

RAIRO Autom/Syst Anal et Control ... RAIRO [*Revue Francaise d'Automatique, d'Informatique, et de Recherche Operationnelle*] Automatique/Systems Analysis and Control [*A publication*]
RAIRO Inf/Comput Sci ... RAIRO [*Revue Francaise d'Automatique, d'Informatique, et de Recherche Operationnelle*] Informatique/Computer Science [*A publication*]
RAIRO Inform ... RAIRO [*Revue Francaise d'Automatique, d'Informatique, et de Recherche Operationnelle*] Informatique [*A publication*]
RAIRO Informat ... RAIRO [*Revue Francaise d'Automatique, d'Informatique, et de Recherche Operationnelle*] Informatique [*A publication*]
RAIRO Informat Theor ... RAIRO [*Revue Francaise d'Automatique, d'Informatique, et de Recherche Operationnelle*] Informatique Theorique [*A publication*]
RAIRO Inform Theor ... RAIRO [*Revue Francaise d'Automatique, d'Informatique, et de Recherche Operationnelle*] Informatique Theorique/Theoretical Informatics [*A publication*]
RAIRO Inf Theor Theor Inf ... RAIRO [*Revue Francaise d'Automatique, d'Informatique, et de Recherche Operationnelle*] Informatique Theorique/Theoretical Informatics [*A publication*]
RAIRO Operations Research ... RAIRO [*Revue Francaise d'Automatique, d'Informatique, et de Recherche Operationnelle*] Recherche Operationnelle/Operations Research [*A publication*]
RAIRO Rech Oper Oper Res ... RAIRO [*Revue Francaise d'Automatique, d'Informatique, et de Recherche Operationnelle*] Recherche Operationnelle/Operations Research [*A publication*]
RAIRS .... Railroad Accident/Incident Reporting System [*Department of Transportation*]
RAIRS .... Reflection Absorption Infrared Spectroscopy [*Also, IRAS, IRRAS, RAIR, RAIS*]
RAIS .... Range Automated Information System (KSC)
RAIS .... Reflection Absorption Infrared Spectroscopy [*Also, IRAS, IRRAS, RAIR, RAIRS*]
RAISA ...... Radioisotopes [*Tokyo*] [*A publication*]
RAISE .... Reliability Accelerated In-Service Echelon (MCD)
RAIST .... Reseau Africain d'Institutions Scientifiques et Technologiques [*African Network of Scientific and Technological Institutions*] (EAIO)
RAIT .... Rendiconti. Reale Accademia d'Italia [*A publication*]
Raith St...... Raithby's English Statutes at Large [*A publication*] (DLA)
Raith St...... Raithby's Study of the Law [*A publication*] (DLA)
RAI-TV...... Radio Audizioni Italiana-Televisione [*Italian Radio Broadcasting and Television Company*]
RAIU .... Radioiodide Uptake [*Endocrinology*]
RAIX......... Rosenbalm Aviation [*Air carrier designation symbol*]
Raj............. All India Reporter, Rajasthan [*A publication*] (DLA)
Raj............. Rajaratam Revised Reports [*Ceylon*] [*A publication*] (DLA)
raj............. Rajasthani [*MARC language code*] [*Library of Congress*] (LCCP)
RAJ.......... Rajkot [*India*] [*Airport symbol*] (OAG)
Ra JAH...... Rackham Journal of the Arts and Humanities [*A publication*]
RAJAM..... RADAR Jamming (FAAC)
Rajasthan... Indian Law Reports, Rajasthan Series [*A publication*] (DLA)
Rajasthan Agric ... Rajasthan Agriculturist [*A publication*]
Rajasthan J Agric Sci ... Rajasthan Journal of Agricultural Sciences [*A publication*]
Rajasthan Med J ... Rajasthan Medical Journal [*A publication*]
Rajasthan Univ Studies Statist ... Rajasthan University. Studies in Statistics. Science Series [*A publication*]
Rajasthan Univ Stud Statist ... Rajasthan University. Studies in Statistics. Science Series [*A publication*]
RAJB .... Recueil Annuel de Jurisprudence Belge [*A publication*]
RAJFC....... Rex Allen, Jr. Fan Club (EA)
RAJPO...... Range Applications Joint Program Office
RAJ Tech Bull ... RAJ [*Rhodesia Agricultural Journal*] Technical Bulletin [*A publication*]
RAK .... Marrakech [*Morocco*] [*Airport symbol*] (OAG)
RAK .... Rakhov [*USSR*] [*Seismograph station code, US Geological Survey*] [*Closed*] (SEIS)
RAK .... Read Access Key
RAK .... Remote Access Key
RaKet........ Rahnema-Ye Ketab [*A publication*]
Raketentech Raumfahrtforsch ... Raketentechnik und Raumfahrtforschung [*A publication*]
RAKO .... Rawson-Koenig, Inc. [*NASDAQ symbol*] (NQ)
Rakstu Krajums Daugavpils Pedagog Inst ... Rakstu Krajums. Daugavpils Pedagogiskais Instituts [*A publication*]
RAKTP...... Royal Arch Knight Templar Priest [*Freemasonry*]
RAL .... Rabalanakaia [*New Britain*] [*Seismograph station code, US Geological Survey*] (SEIS)
RAL .... Radio Astronomy Laboratory [*Research center*] (RCD)
RAL .... Ralston Purina Co. [*NYSE symbol*] (SPSG)
RAL .... Rapid Access Loop
RAL .... Rear-Admiral, Alexandria [*British*]
RAL .... Reenlistment Allowance [*Military*]

RAL .... Register of Additional Locations [*Library of Congress*]
RAL .... Remote Area Landing (NG)
RAL .... Rendiconti. Classe di Scienze Morali e Storiche. Accademia dei Lincei [*A publication*]
RAL .... Reports and Analysis Letter (OICC)
RAL .... Research in African Literatures [*A publication*]
RAL .... Resorcylic Acid Lactone [*Veterinary pharmacology*]
RAL .... Responsibility Assignment List [*NASA*] (NASA)
RAL .... Revista. Academias de Letras [*A publication*]
RAL .... Reynold's Aluminum Co. of Canada Ltd. [*Toronto Stock Exchange symbol*]
RAL .... Riverband Acoustical Laboratory (KSC)
RAL .... Riverside [*California*] [*Airport symbol*] (OAG)
RAL .... Riverside, CA [*Location identifier*] [*FAA*] (FAAL)
RAL .... Robotics & Automation Research Laboratory [*University of Toronto*] [*Research center*] (RCD)
RAL .... Roswell Airlines [*Roswell, NM*] [*FAA designator*] (FAAC)
RAL .... Rubber-Air-Lead [*Tile*]
RAL .... Rutherford and Appleton Laboratory [*Observatory*] [*British*]
RALAB ...... Revue de l'Aluminum et de Ses Applications [*A publication*]
RALAC...... RADAR Altimeter Low-Altitude Control [*Military*] (CAAL)
RALAC...... Repatriation Artificial Limb and Appliance Centre [*Australia*]
RALACS ... RADAR Altimeter Low-Altitude Control System [*Military*] (NG)
RALA-EHF ... Roycrofters-at-Large Association/Elbert Hubbard Foundation (EA)
RAlb.......... Rivista d'Albania [*A publication*]
RALD .... Richmond Area Library Directors [*Library network*]
RALF .... Relocatable Assembly Language Floating Point
RALF........ Repertoire Analytique de Litterature Francaise [*Bordeaux*] [*A publication*]
RALF........ Robotic Assistant Labor Facilitator [*In the movie "Flight of the Navigator" (1986)*]
RALFH...... Random Access Logical File Handler (MCD)
R Algerienne Sciences Juridiques Econs et Pols ... Revue Algerienne des Sciences Juridiques, Economiques, et Politiques [*A publication*]
R Alger Trav ... Revue Algerienne du Travail [*A publication*]
RALI......... Remarried Association of Long Island (EA)
RALI......... Resource and Land Investigation [*Program*] [*Department of the Interior*] (GRD)
R Alicante .. Revista. Instituto de Estudios Alicantinos [*A publication*]
RALinc...... Rendiconti. Classe di Scienze Morali e Storiche. Accademia dei Lincei [*A publication*]
RALincei.... Rendiconti. Classe di Scienze Morali e Storiche. Accademia dei Lincei [*A publication*]
RALL .... Rallentando [*Gradually Slower*] [*Music*]
RALLA ...... Regional Allied Long-Lines Agency [*Formerly, RELLA*] (NATG)
R Allem ...... Revue d'Allemagne [*A publication*]
R Allemagne ... Revue d'Allemagne [*A publication*]
RALLEN ... Rallentando [*Gradually Slower*] [*Music*] (ROG)
RALLO...... Rallentando [*Gradually Slower*] [*Music*] (ROG)
RALPH...... Reduction and Acquisition of Lunar Pulse Heights [*NASA*] (NASA)
RALPH...... Royal Association for the Longevity and Preservation of the Honeymooners (EA)
RALRend... Rendiconti. Classe di Scienze Morali e Storiche. Accademia dei Lincei [*A publication*]
RALS .... Remote Augmented Lift System (MCD)
RALS .... Resources for American Literary Study [*A publication*]
RAls .... Revue d'Alsace [*A publication*]
RALS .... Right Add, Left Subtract [*Army field artillery technique*] (INF)
RALS .... Robotic Ammunition Landing System
RALSA ...... Restraint and Life Support Assembly (MCD)
RAL Scav... Reale Accademia dei Lincei. Atti. Notizie degli Scavi [*A publication*]
RALSH...... Revue Algerienne des Lettres et des Sciences Humaines [*A publication*]
RALT........ RADAR Altimeter [*Aviation*] (NASA)
RALT........ Range Light (AAG)
RALT........ Ranging Airborne LASER Tracker (MCD)
RALT........ Regardless of Altitude [*Aviation*] (FAAC)
RALT........ Routine Admission Laboratory Tests [*Medicine*]
RALU .... Register and Arithmetic/Logic Unit [*Data processing*]
RALU .... Rotary Analog Logic Unit (MCD)
RALV........ Random Access Light Valve
RaLV........ Rasheed (Rat) Leukemia Virus
RALW ...... Radioactive Liquid Waste (IEEE)
Ralw & Corp LJ ... Railway and Corporation Law Journal [*A publication*] (DLA)
RAM.......... Rabbit Alveolar Macrophage [*Clinical chemistry*]
RAM.......... Rabbit Antimouse [*Hematology*]
RAM.......... RADAR-Absorbing Material
RAM.......... Radiation Attenuation Measurement (CET)
RAM.......... Radio-Active Magazine [*A publication*]
RAM.......... Radio Attenuation Measurement [*Spacecraft for testing communications*]
RAM.......... Radioactive Material
RAM.......... Ramada, Inc. [*NYSE symbol*] (SPSG)

RAM......... Raman [*Turkey*] [*Seismograph station code, US Geological Survey*] (SEIS)
Ram........... Ramanathan's Reports [*Ceylon*] [*A publication*] (DLA)
RAM......... Ramcor Resources, Inc. [*Vancouver Stock Exchange symbol*]
RAM......... Ramingining [*Australia*] [*Airport symbol*] (OAG)
Ram........... Ramsey's Quebec Appeal Cases [*A publication*] (DLA)
RAM......... Random Access Measurement [*System*] [*Data processing*]
RAM......... Random Access Memory [*Data processing*]
RAM......... Random Angle Modulation
RAM......... Range-Altitude Monitor
RAM......... Rapid Alternating Movement
RAM......... Rapid Amortization Mortgage
RAM......... Rapid Area Maintenance [*Air Force*]
Ra M......... Rassegna Musicale [*A publication*]
RAM......... Raytheon Airborne Microwave (MCD)
RAM......... Recent Advances in Manufacturing [*Information service or system*] (IID)
RAM......... Recovery Aids Material (MUGU)
RAM......... Red Artillery Model [*Military*]
RAM..... Redeye Air Missile [*System*] (RDA)
RAM......... Reentry Antimissile
RAM......... Reentry Attenuation Measurement [*NASA*]
RAM......... Reform the Armed Forces Movement [*Philippines*]
RAMHR..... Regional Audit Manager
RAM......... Registered Apartment Manager [*Designation awarded by National Association of Home Builders*]
RAM......... Regular Army and Militia [*British*]
RAM......... Releasable Asset Program [*Military*] (AFIT)
RAM......... Reliability Assessment for Management
RAM......... Reliability, Availability, and Maintainability [*Army*]
RAM......... Religions, Ancient and Modern [*A publication*]
RAMIsr..... Remote Access Monitor (MCD)
RAM......... Remote Area Monitoring (KSC)
RAM......... Repeater Amplitude Modulation (MCD)
RAM......... Repeating Antipersonnel Mine
RAM......... Research and Applications Module [*NASA*]
RAM......... Research Aviation Medicine [*Navy program of research into aerospace medical techniques*]
RAM......... Reserve Adjustment Magnitude
RAM......... Resident Access Methods (MCD)
RAM......... Resident Aerospace Medicine [*Physician in specialty training*] [*Military*]
RAM......... Resources Analysis and Management
RAM......... Responsibility Assignment Matrix [*NASA*] (NASA)
RAM......... Restricted Access Memory [*Data processing*] (MCD)
RAM......... Returned Account Mechanical [*Aviation*] (FAAC)
RAM......... Reverse Annuity Mortgage
RAM......... Revolutionary Action Movement
RAM......... Revue de l'Ameublement [*A publication*]
RAM......... Revue d'Ascetique et de Mystique [*A publication*]
RAM......... Right Ascension of the Meridian [*Navigation*]
RAM......... Rock Australia Magazine [*A publication*] (APTA)
RAM......... Rocket and Missile System [*Army*]
RAM......... Rolling Airframe Missile
RAM......... Royal Academy of Music [*British*]
RAM......... Royal Air Maroc [*Morocco*]
RAM......... Royal Arch Mason [*Freemasonry*]
RAM......... Royal Ark Mariners
RAMA...... Railway Automotive Management Association (EA)
RAMA....... Recap and Movement Authorization [*NASA*] (NASA)
RAMA....... Region of Assured Mission Abort [*Military*] (CAAL)
RAMA....... Rome Air Materiel Area [*Deactivated*] [*Air Force*]
RAMAB.... Ready Afloat Marine Amphibious Brigade (CINC)
RAMAC.... Random Access Method of Accounting and Control [*Data processing*]
Ramachandrier A ... Ramachandrier's Cases on Adoption [*1892*] [*India*] [*A publication*] (DLA)
Ramachandrier DG ... Ramachandrier's Cases on Dancing Girls [*1892*] [*India*] [*A publication*] (DLA)
Ramachandrier HML ... Ramachandrier's Cases on Hindu Marriage Law [*1891*] [*India*] [*A publication*] (DLA)
Raman Res Inst Mem ... Raman Research Institute. Memoirs [*A publication*]
RAMARK ... RADAR Marker [*Military*]
Ram Ass..... Ram on Assets, Debts, and Incumbrances [*2nd ed.*] [*1837*] [*A publication*] (DLA)
RAMAZ.... Rabbi Moses Zacuto (BJA)
RAMB....... Random Access Memory Buffer [*Data processing*]
RaM-BaM ... Rabbi Moses ben Maimon [*Maimonides*] [*Jewish philosopher, 1135-1204*]
RAMBAN ... Rabbi Moses ben Nahman [*Spanish Talmudist, 1195-1270*] (BJA)
RAMBO .... Real-Time Acquisitions Management and Bibliographic Order System [*Suggested name for the Library of Congress computer system*]
RAMBO .... Remove Aquino from Malacanang before October [*Operation proposed by rebel military leader "Gringo" Honasan*] [*1987*] [*Philippines*]
RAMBO .... Restore a More Benevolent Order Coalition [*Later, NCAN*] (EA)
RAMC....... Rassegna di Asetica e Mistica S. Caterina da Siena [*A publication*]

RAMC .... Royal Army Medical College [*British*]
RAMC .... Royal Army Medical Corps [*Initialism also facetiously translated during World War I as "Rats after Moldy Cheese," "Rob All My Comrades," or "Run Away, Matron's Coming" British*]
Ram Cas P & E ... Ram's Cases of Pleading and Evidence [*A publication*] (DLA)
RA/MCC... Restricted Area/Military Climb Corridor [*Aviation*] (FAAC)
RAMCT.... Royal Army Medical Corps, Territorials [*British*] (ROG)
RAMD....... Random Access Memory Device [*Data processing*]
RAMD....... Receiving Agency Materiel Division [*Military*]
RAMD....... Reliability, Availability, and Maintainability Demonstration
RAM-D...... Reliability, Availability, Maintainability, and Durability [*Army*] (AABC)
RAMEA.... Radiologia Medica [*A publication*]
RAMEC..... Rapid Action Maintenance Engineering Change [*Navy*] (MCD)
RAMEC..... Rapid Action Minor Engineering Change
RAMED..... Reine und Angewandte Metallkunde in Einzeldarstellungen [*A publication*]
Ram F .... Ram on Facts [*A publication*] (DLA)
RAMFAS .. Reliability Analysis of Microcircuit Failure in Avionic Systems (MCD)
R Am Hist ... Reviews in American History [*A publication*]
RAMHR..... Risk-Adjusted Multiple Hurdle Rates (ADA)
RAMIG ..... Rabbit Antimouse Immunoglobulin G [*Immunology*]
RAMIS...... Rapid Access Management Information System [*Data processing*]
RAMIS...... Rapid Automatic Malfunction Isolation System
RAMIS...... Receiving, Assembly Maintenance, Inspection, Storage [*Military*]
RAMIS..... Repair, Assemble, Maintain, Issue, and Supply (MUGU)
RaMIsr..... Rassegna Mensile di Israel [*Rome*] [*A publication*]
RAMIT..... Rate-Aided Manually Implemented Tracking (NATG)
Ram Leg J ... Ram's Science of Legal Judgment [*2nd ed.*] [*1834*] [*A publication*] (DLA)
Ram Leg Judgm (Towns Ed) ... Ram's Science of Legal Judgment, Notes by Townshend [*A publication*] (DLA)
RAM/LOG ... Reliability, Availability, Maintainability, and Logistics (MCD)
RAMM...... Random Access Memory Module [*Data processing*]
RAMM...... Recording Ammeter (MSA)
RAMMIT ... Reliability, Availability, and Maintenance Management Improvements Technique
RAMMIT ... Reliability and Maintainability Management Improvement Techniques [*Army*]
Ram & Mor ... Ramsey and Morin's Montreal Law Reporter [*A publication*] (DLA)
RAMMS.... Responsive Automated Materiel Management System [*Army*] (AABC)
RAMNAC ... Radio Aids to Marine Navigation Committee [*British*]
RAMOGE ... Regional Pollution Studies in the Ligurian Sea [*Marine science*] (MSC)
RAMONT ... Radiological Monitoring
RAMOS .... Remote Automatic Meteorological Observing Station
RAMP .... RADAR Mapping of Panama
RAMP .... RADAR Modification Program (NG)
RAMP .... Radiation Airborne Measurement Program
RAMP .... Radio Attenuation Measurement Project
Ramp.......... Ramparts Magazine [*A publication*]
RAMP .... Random Access Mechanization of Phosphorus
RAMP .... Rapid Acquisition of Manufactured Parts [*Military*]
RAMP .... Raytheon Airborne Microwave Platform [*Sky station*]
RAMP .... Records and Archives Management Programme [*UNESCO*]
RAMP .... Recovered Allied Military Personnel
RAMP .... Regional Administrative Management Plan [*Department of Labor*]
RAMP .... Reliability and Maintainability Program
RAMP .... Research Association of Minority Professors (EA)
RAMP .... Reserve Associate Manning Program [*Military*]
RAMP .... Review of Army Mobilization Planning (MCD)
R/AMP ...... Rifampin [*Also, RF, RIF, RMP*] [*Bactericide*]
RAMP .... Ring Airfoil Munition Projectile [*Army*]
RAMP .... Rural Abandoned Mine Program [*Department of Agriculture*]
RAMPART ... RADAR Advanced Measurements Program for Analysis of Reentry Techniques [*ARPA - Raytheon*]
RAMPART ... Route to Airlift Mobility through Partnership (MCD)
Ramp Mag ... Ramparts Magazine [*A publication*]
RAMPS..... Rapid Message Preparation System (NATG)
RaMPS..... Rapid Multiple Peptide System [*Biotechnology*]
RAMPS..... Repatriated American Military Personnel [*World War II*]
RAMPS..... Resources Allocation and Multiproject Scheduling
Ram Rep .... Ramanathan's Supreme Court Reports [*Ceylon*] [*A publication*] (ILCA)
RAMS....... RADAR Target Scattering Advanced Measurement System
RAMS....... Random Access Measurement System [*Data processing*]
RAMS....... Random Access Memory Store [*Data processing*] (TEL)
RAMS....... Rascal Avionics Management System (MCD)
RAMS....... Recovery and Modification Services (MCD)
RAMS....... Reduced-Size Antenna Monopulse System
RAMS....... Regional Air Monitoring Station [*or System*] [*Environmental Protection Agency*]

RAMS....... Regulatory Activities Manpower System [*Nuclear energy*]　(NRCH)
RAM-S ...... Reliability, Availability, Maintainability - Supportability　(MCD)
RAMS....... Reliability and Maintainability Studies [*Army*]　(RDA)
RAMS....... Remote Area Mobility Study　(MCD)
RAMS....... Remote Automatic Multipurpose Station
RAMS....... Remotely Accessible Management Systems [*Data processing*]
RAMS....... Repairables Asset Management System [*Military*]　(CAAL)
RAMS....... Requirements Analysis Material Sheet [*or Study*]　(MCD)
RAMS....... Right Ascension Mean Sun [*Navigation*]
RAMS....... Rocket and Missile System [*Army*]
RAMSA..... Radio Aeronautica Mexicana, Sociedad Anonima
Rams App .. Ramsey's Quebec Appeal Cases [*1873-86*] [*A publication*]　(DLA)
Ramsay App Cas ... Ramsay's Appeal Cases [*Canada*] [*A publication*]　(DLA)
Ramsay App Cas (Can) ... Ramsay's Appeal Cases [*Canada*] [*A publication*]　(DLA)
Ram SC...... Ramanathan's Supreme Court Reports [*Ceylon*] [*A publication*]　(DLA)
RAMSES... Reprogrammable Advanced Multimode Shipborne ECM System [*Canadian Navy*]
RAMSEZ .. Records. Australian Museum. Supplement [*A publication*]
RAMSH .... Reliability, Availability, Maintainability, Safety, and Human Factors [*Telecommunications*]　(TEL)
RAMSP..... Revista do Arquivo Municipal (Sao Paulo) [*A publication*]
RAMSS .... Royal Alfred Merchant Seamen's Society [*British*]
RAMT....... Rabbit Antimouse Thymocyte [*Immunology*]
RAMT .... Rudder Angle Master Transmitter
RAMTAC ... Reentry Analysis and Modeling of Target Characteristics
RAMTB..... Revue ATB [*Assistance Technique Belge*] Metallurgie [*Belgium*] [*A publication*]
RAMVAN ... Reconnaissance Aircraft Maintenance Van
Ram W .... Ram on Exposition of Wills of Landed Property [*1827*] [*A publication*]　(DLA)
RAN........... Railway Abidjan-Niger
RAN........... Rainforest Action Network　(EA)
Ran............. Ranae [*Frogs*] [*of Aristophanes*] [*Classical studies*]　(OCD)
RAN........... Rangifer. Nordisk Organ foer Reinforskning [*A publication*]
RAN........... Rangoon [*Burma*] [*Seismograph station code, US Geological Survey*] [*Closed*]　(SEIS)
RAN........... Ranitidine [*An antiulcer drug*]
RAN........... Ransome Air, Inc. [*Philadelphia, PA*] [*FAA designator*]　(FAAC)
RAN........ Read around Number
RAN........... Reconnaissance/Attack Navigator
RAN........... Regional Air Navigation [*ICAO*]
RAN........... Rendiconti. Accademia di Archeologia, Lettere, e Belle Arti (Napoli) [*A publication*]
RAN........... Repair Activity Accounting Number [*Navy*]
RAN........ Reporting Accounting Number　(NG)
RAN........ Request for Authority to Negotiate
RAN........... Requirement Action Number
RAN........... Requisition Account Number
RAN........... Resource-Adjacent Nation [*Ocean fishery management*]
RAN........... Revenue Anticipation Note
RAN........... Royal Australian Navy　(ADA)
RANA........ Rheumatoid Arthritis Nuclear Antigen [*Immunology*]
RANA....... Rhodesia & Nyasaland Airways
RANAM... Recherches Anglaises et Americaines [*A publication*]
RA Narb ... Revue Archeologique de Narbonnaise [*A publication*]
RANAS...... Rear-Admiral, Naval Air Stations [*British military*]　(DMA)
RANBDM ... Institut des Sciences Agronomiques du Burundi [*ISABU*]. Rapport Annuel et Notes Annexes [*A publication*]
RANC........ RADAR Absorption Noise and Clutter　(NASA)
RANCA ..... Retired Army Nurse Corps Association　(EA)
Ranchi Univ J Agric Res ... Ranchi University. Journal of Agricultural Research [*A publication*]
Ranchi Univ Math J ... Ranchi University. Mathematical Journal [*A publication*]
Ranch Mag ... Ranch Magazine [*A publication*]
RANCID.... Real and Not Corrected Input Data [*Data processing*]
RANCOM ... Random Communication Satellite
RAND........ Rand Capital Corp. [*NASDAQ symbol*]　(NQ)
Rand........... Randall's Reports [*62-71 Ohio State*] [*A publication*]　(DLA)
Rand........... Randolph's Reports [*7-11 Louisiana*] [*A publication*]　(DLA)
Rand........... Randolph's Reports [*21-56 Kansas*] [*A publication*]　(DLA)
Rand........... Randolph's Reports [*22-27 Virginia*] [*1821-28*] [*A publication*]　(DLA)
Rand........... Selected Rand Abstracts [*A publication*]
RANDAM ... Random Access Nondestructive Advanced Memory [*Data processing*]
Rand Ann... Randolph Annual [*A publication*]　(DLA)
Rand Com Paper ... Randolph on Commercial Paper [*A publication*]　(DLA)
Rand Corp Pap ... Rand Corporation. Papers [*A publication*]
Rand Corp Rep ... Rand Corporation. Report [*A publication*]
Rand Em Dom ... Randolph on Eminent Domain [*A publication*]　(DLA)
Rand & Fur Poi ... Rand and Furness on Poisons [*A publication*]　(DLA)

R ANDI ..... Revista ANDI [*Asociacion Nacional de Industriales*] [*A publication*]
RANDID ... Rapid Alphanumeric Digital Indicating Device
RANDO..... Radiotherapy Analog Dosimetry
Rand Peak .. Randall's Edition of Peake on Evidence [*A publication*]　(DLA)
Rand Perp .. Randall on Perpetuities [*A publication*]　(DLA)
Rand Revw ... Rand Research Review [*A publication*]
Rane .... Rainerius de Forlivio [*Deceased, 1358*] [*Authority cited in pre-1607 legal work*]　(DSA)
RAN(E)..... Royal Australian Navy (Emergency)
RANEL...... Royal Australian Navy Experimental Laboratory　(MCD)
Raney .... Raney's Reports [*16-20 Florida*] [*A publication*]　(DLA)
RANFR...... Royal Australian Naval Fleet Reserve　(DMA)
RANF Rev ... RANF [*Royal Australian Nursing Federation*] Review [*A publication*]
RANG........ Rangoon [*City in Burma*]　(ROG)
Rang Cr LJ ... Rangoon Criminal Law Journal [*A publication*]　(DLA)
Rang Dec.... Sparks' Rangoon Decisions [*British Burma*] [*A publication*]　(DLA)
Range Improv Notes US For Serv Intermt Reg ... Range Improvement Notes. United States Forest Service. Intermountain Region [*A publication*]
Range Improv Studies Calif Dep Conserv Div For ... Range Improvement Studies. California Department of Conservation. Division of Forestry [*A publication*]
Range Impr Stud Calif Div For ... Range Improvement Studies. California Division of Forestry [*A publication*]
Rang LR..... Rangoon Law Reports [*India*] [*A publication*]　(DLA)
RANK........ [*The*] Rank Organisation PLC [*NASDAQ symbol*]　(NQ)
Rank P ...... Rankin on Patents [*1824*] [*A publication*]　(DLA)
Rank & S Comp L ... Ranking and Spicer's Company Law [*11th ed.*] [*1970*] [*A publication*]　(DLA)
Rank S & P Exec ... Ranking, Spicer, and Pegler on Executorship [*21st ed.*] [*1971*] [*A publication*]　(DLA)
RANL .... Rendiconti. Reale Accademia Nazionale dei Lincei [*A publication*]
RANN....... Research Applied to National Needs [*Formerly, IRRPOS*] [*National Science Foundation*] [*Obsolete*]
RANNS ...... Royal Australian Naval Nursing Service　(DMA)
Rannsoknastofnun Fiskidnadarins Arsskyrs ... Rannsoknastofnun Fiskidnadarins Arsskyrsla [*A publication*]
RANOSP... Radiological North Sea Project [*British*]
rANP .... Rat Atrial Natriuretic Peptide [*Biochemistry*]
RANR(S)... Royal Australian Naval Reserve (Seagoing)
RANS .... Report. Australian Numismatic Society [*A publication*]
RANS .... Revenue Anticipation Notes
RANSA ...... Royal Australian Navy Sailing Association
RANSA ...... Rutas Aereas Nacionales Sociedad Anonima [*Cargo airline*] [*Venezuela*]
RANT .... Reentry Antenna Test
R Anthrop .. Reviews in Anthropology [*A publication*]
R Antropol (Sao Paulo) ... Revista de Antropologia (Sao Paulo) [*A publication*]
RAN(V)R... Royal Australian Naval (Volunteer) Reserve
RANVR(S) ... Royal Australian Naval Volunteer Reserve (Seagoing)
RANXPE... Resident Army Nike-X Project Engineer　(AABC)
RAO........... National Radio Astronomy Observatory, Charlottesville, VA [*OCLC symbol*]　(OCLC)
RAO........... RADAR Operator
RAO........... Radio Astronomy Observatory [*University of Michigan*] [*Research center*]
RAO........... Rado Reef Resources [*Vancouver Stock Exchange symbol*]
RAO........... Raoul [*Raoul Island*] [*Seismograph station code, US Geological Survey*]　(SEIS)
RAO........... Recueil d'Archeologie Orientale [*A publication*]
RAO........... Regimental Amalgamation Officer [*British military*]　(DMA)
RAO........... Regional Accounting Office [*Telecommunications*]　(TEL)
RAO........... Regional Administrative Office
RAO........... Regional Agricultural Officer [*Ministry of Agriculture, Fisheries, and Food*] [*British*]
RAO........... Retired Affairs Officers　(EA)
RAO........... Ribeirao Preto [*Brazil*] [*Airport symbol*]　(OAG)
RAO........... Right Anterior Oblique [*Medicine*]
RAO........... Rudder Angle Order　(MSA)
RAOA .... Railway Accounting Officers Association [*Later, AAR*]
RAOB .... Radiosonde Observation
RAOB .... Royal Antediluvian Order of Buffaloes
RAOC....... Rear Area Operations Center　(MCD)
RAOC....... Regional Air Operations Center　(NATG)
RAOC....... Royal Army Ordnance Corps [*Formerly, AOC*] [*British*]
RAOC(E)... Royal Army Ordnance Corps (Engineering) [*British military*]　(DMA)
Rao DHL ... Rao's Decisions on Hindu Law [*1893*] [*India*] [*A publication*]　(DLA)
RA Oise ..... Revue Archeologique de l'Oise [*A publication*]
RAOMP ...... Report of Accrued Obligations, Military Pay　(AFM)
RAONDT .. Radiotherapy and Oncology [*A publication*]
RAOP .... Regional Air Operations Plan　(NATG)
RAOU Newsl ... RAOU [*Royal Australasian Ornithologists Union*] Newsletter [*A publication*]　(APTA)
RAP .... RADAR Aim Point

RAP .... Radical Alternatives to Prison [*British*]
RAP .... Radio Access Point (MCD)
RAP .... Radio Air Play
RAP .... Radiological Assistance Plan [*AEC*]
RAP .... Random Access Program [*Data processing*]
RAP .... Random Access Projector
RAP .... Rapid (AAG)
RAP .... Rapid City [*South Dakota*] [*Airport symbol*] (OAG)
RAP .... Rapid City, SD [*Location identifier*] [*FAA*] (FAAL)
RAP .... Rapindik [*New Britain*] [*Seismograph station code, US Geological Survey*] [*Closed*] (SEIS)
RAP .... Reactive Atmosphere Process
RAP .... Readiness Action Proposal (MCD)
RAP .... Readiness Assessment Program [*Navy*]
RAP .... Rear Area Protection [*Military*] (AABC)
RAP .... Reduced Acreage Program [*Agriculture*]
RAP .... Redundancy Adjustment of Probability (IEEE)
RAP .... Regimental Aid Post [*British*]
RAP .... Regional Acceleratory Phenomenon [*Physiology*]
RAP .... Reglement d'Administration Publique [*Administrative Regulation*] [*French*] (ILCA)
RAP .... Regression Analysis Program [*Military*]
RAP .... Regression-Associated Protein [*Biochemistry*]
RAP .... Regulatory Accounting Practices [*or Principles*] [*Business term*]
RAP .... Regulatory Analysis Program [*Federal government*]
RAP .... Relational Associative Processor (IEEE)
RAP .... Relationship Anecdotes Paradigm Method [*Psychology*]
RAP .... Relative Accident Probability
RAP .... Releasable Assets Program
RAP .... Reliability Assessment Prediction
RAP .... Reliability Assessment Program
RAP .... Reliable Acoustic Path
RAP .... Remedial Action Program [*or Projects*] (MCD)
RAP .... Remote Access Point [*Telecommunications*]
RAP .... Renal Artery Pressure [*Medicine*]
RAP .... Rental Assistance Payment Program [*HUD*]
RAP .... Requirements Analysis Package [*Data processing*]
RAP .... Resident Assembler Program
RAP .... Resident Assessment Protocol [*Occupational therapy*]
RAP .... Resident Associate Program [*Smithsonian Institution*]
RAP .... Residual Analysis Program [*Space Flight Operations Facility, NASA*]
RAP .... Resource Allocation Processor (CMD)
RAP .... Response Analysis Program [*Data processing*] (IBMDP)
RAP .... Results Analysis Plan (MCD)
RAP .... Review and Analysis Process
RAP .... Revised Accounting Procedures
RAP .... Revolutionary Action Power [*A publication*] (APTA)
RAP .... Revue de l'Action Populaire [*Later, Projet*] [*A publication*]
RAp .... Revue Apologetique [*A publication*]
RAP .... Revue d'Archeologie Polonaise [*A publication*]
RAP .... Revue de l'Assistance Publique et de la Prevoyance Sociale [*A publication*]
RAP .... Rhodesian Action Party
RAP .... Right Angle Plug
RAP .... Right Atrial Pressure [*Cardiology*]
RAP .... Ring-Around Programming (CAAL)
RAP .... Rocket-Assisted Projectile (RDA)
RAP .... "Round Up" Administration Planning Staff [*for the invasion of France*] [*World War II*]
RAP .... Rubidium Acid Phthalate [*Organic chemistry*]
RAP .... Rules for Admission to Practice [*A publication*] (DLA)
RA-P .... Rumex Acetosa Polysaccharide [*Antineoplastic drug*]
RAP .... Rupees, Annas, Pies [*Monetary units*] [*India*]
RAP .... Smithsonian Resident Associate Program (EA)
RAPAC .... Research Applications Policy Advisory Committee [*National Science Foundation*] (EGAO)
RAPAD...... Research Association for Petroleum Alternative Development
Rapalje & L ... Rapalje and Lawrence's Law Dictionary [*A publication*] (DLA)
Rapal & L... Rapalje and Lawrence's American and English Cases [*A publication*] (DLA)
RAPBPPI.. Research Association for the Paper and Board, Printing, and Packaging Industries [*United Kingdom*] [*Research center*] (IRC)
Rap Bur Nutr Anim Elev ... Rapport. Bureau de la Nutrition Animale et de l'Elevage [*A publication*]
RAPC......... Radio Administration Plenipotentiary Conference
RAPC......... Right Angle Pressure Cartridge
RAPC......... Royal Army Pay Corps [*Formerly, APC*] [*British*]
RAPCAP ... RADAR Picket Combat Air Patrol (NVT)
RAPCC...... RADAR Approach Control Center (MCD)
RAPCO...... Regional Air Priorities Control Office [*Army*] (AABC)
RAPCOE... Random Access Programming and Checkout Equipment
RAPCON .. RADAR Approach Control [*Air Force*]
Rap Contempt ... Rapalje on Contempt [*A publication*] (DLA)
RAPD......... Relatively Afferent Pupillary Defect [*Ophthalmology*]
RAPD .... Response Amplitude Probability Data
RAPE......... RADAR Arithmetic Processing Element [*Navy*]
RAPEC...... Rocket-Assisted Personnel Ejection Catapult

RAPECA ... Rassemblement du Peuple Camerounais [*Camerounese People's Rally*]
RAP-EX..... Rear Area Protection Operations Extended (MCD)
Rap Fed Ref Dig ... Rapalje's Federal Reference Digest [*A publication*] (DLA)
Raph........... Raphael Fulgosius [*Deceased, 1427*] [*Authority cited in pre-1607 legal work*] (DSA)
RAPH .... Recherches d'Archeologie, de Philologie,et d'Histoire [*Cairo*] [*A publication*]
Raph Cum ... Raphael Cumanus [*Deceased, 1427*] [*Authority cited in pre-1607 legal work*] (DSA)
RAPIC .... Remedial Action Program Information Center [*Department of Energy*] [*Also, an information service or system*] (IID)
RAPID...... Random Access Personnel Information Dissemination
RAPID...... Reactor and Plant Integrated Dynamics [*Data processing*] (KSC)
RAPID...... Reader-to-Advertiser Phone Inquiry Delivery System [*Chilton Corp.*]
RAPID...... Real-Time Acquisition and Processing of Inflight Data
RAPID...... Relative Address Programming Implementation Device [*Data processing*]
RAPID...... Reliability Assessment Program with In-Plant Data
RAPID...... Remote Access Planning for Institutional Development [*Data processing*]
RAPID...... Remote Access Procedure for Interactive Design [*General Motors Corp.*]
RAPID...... Research in Automatic Photocomposition and Information Dissemination
RAPID...... Retrieval through Automated Publication and Information Digest [*Data processing*] (DIT)
RAPID...... Retrieval and Processing Information for Display
RAPID...... Retrorocket-Assisted Parachute in Flight Delivery
RAPID...... Rocketdyne Automatic Processing of Integrated Data [*Data processing*]
RAPID...... Ryan Automatic Plot Indicator Device
RAPIDS .... Random Access Personnel Information Dissemination System [*Army*] (AABC)
RAPIDS .... Rapid Automated Problem Identification System [*DoD*]
RAPIDS .... Real-Time Automated Personnel Identification System [*DoD*]
RAPIER .... Rapid Emergency Reconstitution Team [*Military*]
Rap Inst Fiz Tech Jad AGH ... Raport. Instytut Fizyki i Techniki Jadrowej AGH [*Akademia Gorniczo-Hutnicza*] [*A publication*]
Rap Inst Nat Etude Agron Congo (INEAC) ... Rapport. Institut National pour l'Etude Agronomique du Congo (INEAC)
Rap Inst Tech Jad AGH ... Raport. Instytut Techniki Jadrowej AGH [*Akademia Gorniczo-Hutnicza*] [*A publication*]
Rap Jud QBR ... Rapports Judiciaires de Quebec, Cour du Banc de la Reine [*Quebec Law Reports, Queen's Bench*] [*A publication*] (DLA)
Rap Jud QCS ... Rapports Judiciaires de Quebec. Cour Superieure [*Quebec Law Reports, Superior Court*] [*A publication*] (DLA)
Rap Jud Quebec CS (Can) ... Rapports Judiciaires de Quebec [*Quebec Law Reports*] [*Canada*] [*A publication*] (DLA)
Rap Jud Quebec KB (Can) ... Rapports Judiciaires de Quebec [*Quebec Law Reports*] [*Canada*] [*A publication*] (DLA)
Rap Jud Quebec QB (Can) ... Rapports Judiciaires de Quebec [*Quebec Law Reports*] [*Canada*] [*A publication*] (DLA)
Rap & L...... Rapalje and Lawrence's American and English Cases [*A publication*] (DLA)
Rap Lar...... Rapalje on Larceny [*A publication*] (DLA)
Rap & Law ... Rapalje and Lawrence's American and English Cases [*A publication*] (DLA)
Rap & L Law Dict ... Rapalje and Lawrence's Law Dictionary [*A publication*] (DLA)
RAPLOC... Rapid Passive Localization (MCD)
RAPLOC-LSI ... Rapid Passive Localization - Low-Ship Impact [*Navy*] (CAAL)
RAPLOC-WAA ... Rapid Passive Localization - Wide Aperture Array [*Military*] (CAAL)
RAPM .... Reliability Assessment Prediction Model
RAPM .... Risk-Adjusted Profitability Measure [*Banking*] (ECON)
Rap NY Dig ... Rapalje's New York Digest [*A publication*] (DLA)
RAPO .... Rabbit Antibodies to Pig Ovary [*Immunology*]
RAPO .... Resident Apollo Project Office [*NASA*] (KSC)
Rapp........... Rapport [*A publication*]
RAPP......... Reconciliation and Purification Program [*Air Force*]
RAPP......... Registered Air Parcel Post
RAPP's ...... Radiologists, Anesthesiologists, Pathologists, and Physiatrists
Rapp Act Bur Voltaique Geol Mines ... Rapport. Activite du Bureau Voltaique de le Geologie et des Mines [*A publication*]
Rapp Act Serv Geol (Madagascar) ... Rapport d'Activite. Service Geologique (Madagascar) [*A publication*]
Rapp Act Serv Geol (Malagasy) ... Rapport d'Activite. Service Geologique (Malagasy) [*A publication*]
Rapp Act Stn Amelior Plant Maraicheres ... Rapport d'Activite. Station d'Amelioration des Plants Maraicheres [*A publication*]
Rapp Anal Phys Chim Eau Rhin ... Rapport sur les Analyses Physico-Chimiques de l'Eau du Rhin [*A publication*]
Rapp Annu AFOCEL (Assoc For Cellul) ... Rapport Annuel. AFOCEL (Association Foret-Cellulose) [*A publication*]

Rapp Annu Fed Chambres Synd Miner Met Non Ferreux ... Rapport Annuel. Federation des Chambres Syndicales des Minerais et des Metaux Non Ferreux [*A publication*]

Rapp Annu Serv Geol (Malagasy) ... Rapport Annuel. Service Geologique (Malagasy) [*A publication*]

Rapp Assoc Int Chim Cerealiere ... Rapports. Association Internationale de Chimie Cerealiere [*A publication*]

Rapp BIPM ... Rapport. BIPM [*Bureau International des Poids et Mesures*] [*A publication*]

Rapp Bount ... Rapp on the Bounty Laws [*A publication*] (DLA)

Rapp Comm Int Mer Mediter ... Rapport. Commission Internationale pour la Mer Mediterranee [*France*] [*A publication*]

Rapp Commissar Energie Atom ... Rapport. Commissariat a l'Energie Atomique [*France*] [*A publication*]

Rapp Cons Exp Rech Agron Insp Gen Agric (Algeria) ... Rapport. Conseil de l'Experimentation et des Recherches Agronomiques. Inspection Generale de l'Agriculture (Algeria) [*A publication*]

Rapp Final Conf Tech OCEAC ... Rapport Final. Conference Technique. OCEAC [*Organisation de Coordination pour la Lutte Contre les Endemies en Afrique Centrale*] [*A publication*]

Rapp Fonct Tech Inst Pasteur Dakar ... Rapport sur le Fonctionnement Technique. Institut Pasteur de Dakar [*A publication*]

Rapp Geol Minist Energie Ressour (Quebec) ... Rapport Geologique. Ministere de l'Energie et des Ressources (Quebec) [*A publication*]

Rapp Gronl Geol Unders ... Rapport. Gronlands Geologiske Undersogelse [*A publication*]

RAPPI ... Random Access Plan-Position Indicator [*Air Force*]

Rapp Inst Bodemvruchtbaar ... Rapport. Instituut voor Bodemvruchtbaarheid [*A publication*]

Rapp Instn Virkeslara Skogshogsk ... Rapporter. Institutionen for Virkeslara. Skogshogskolan [*A publication*]

Rapp Inter Etude Lab J Dedek Raffinerie Tirlemontoise ... Rapport Interieur d'une Etude Effectuee au Laboratoire J. Dedek Raffinerie Tirlemontoise [*A publication*]

Rapp ISTISAN ... Rapporti ISTISAN [*Istituto Superiore di Sanita*] [*A publication*]

Rapp Korrosionsinst ... Rapport. Korrosionsinstitutet [*A publication*]

Rapp Lab Prod For Est (Can) ... Rapport. Laboratoire des Produits Forestiers de l'Est (Canada) [*A publication*]

Rapp Off Int Epizoot ... Rapport. Office International des Epizooties [*A publication*]

Rapport Conjonct ... Rapport de Conjoncture [*A publication*]

Rapp Prelim Minist Richesses Nat (Que) ... Rapport Preliminaire. Ministere des Richesses Naturelles (Quebec) [*A publication*]

Rapp Proefstn Groenteteelt Vollegrond Ned ... Rapport. Proefstation voor de Groenteteelt in de Vollegrond in Nederland [*A publication*]

Rapp P-V Reun Cons Int Explor Mer ... Rapports et Proces-Verbaux des Reunions. Conseil International pour l'Exploration de la Mer [*A publication*]

Rapp Rech Lab Cent Ponts Chaussees ... Rapport de Recherche. Laboratoire Central des Ponts et Chaussees [*A publication*]

Rapp Sci Tech CNEXO (Fr) ... Rapports Scientifiques et Techniques. CNEXO [*Centre National pour l'Exploitation des Oceans*] (France) [*A publication*]

Rapp Stat Can Hydrogr Sci Oceaniques ... Rapport Statistique Canadien sur l'Hydrographie et les Sciences Oceaniques [*A publication*]

Rapp Sven Livsmedel-Sinstitutet ... Rapport. Svenska Livsmedelsinstitutet [*A publication*]

Rapp Uppsats Avd Skogsekol Skogshogsk ... Rapporter och Uppsatser. Avdelningen foer Skogsekologi. Skogshogskolan [*A publication*]

Rapp Uppsats Instn Skoglig Mat Statist Skogshogsk ... Rapporter och Uppsatser. Institutionen foer Skoglig Matematisk Statistik. Skogshogskolan [*A publication*]

Rapp Uppsats Instn Skogsforyngr Skogshogsk ... Rapporter och Uppsatser. Institutionen foer Skogsforyngring. Skogshogskolan [*A publication*]

Rapp Uppsats Instn Skogsgenet Skogshogsk ... Rapporter och Uppsatser. Institutionen foer Skogsgenetik. Skogshogskolan [*A publication*]

Rapp Uppsats Instn Skogsprod Skogshogsk ... Rapporter och Uppsatser. Institutionen foer Skogsproduktion. Skogshogskolan [*A publication*]

Rapp Uppsats Instn Skogstax Skogshogsk ... Rapporter och Uppsatser. Institutionen foer Skogstaxering. Skogshogskolan [*A publication*]

Rapp Uppsats Instn Skogstek Skogshogsk ... Rapporter och Uppsatser. Institutionen foer Skogsteknik. Skogshogskolan [*A publication*]

RAPR ... RADAR Processor (CET)

RAPR ... Right Angle Panel Receptacle

RAPRA ... RAPRA Technology [*Formerly, Rubber and Plastics Research Association*] (EA)

RAPRA Abst ... RAPRA [*Rubber and Plastics Research Association*] Abstract [*A publication*]

RAPRA Members J ... RAPRA [*Rubber and Plastics Research Association*] Members Journal [*England*] [*A publication*]

RAPRB ... Radioprotection [*A publication*]

RAPRENOx ... Rapid Reduction of Nitrogen Oxides [*Automotive engineering*]

RAPS ... RADAR-Absorbing Primary Structure (MCD)

RAPS ... RADAR Prediction System (MCD)

RAPS ... RADAR Proficiency Simulator

RAPS ... Radioactive Argon Processing System (NRCH)

RAPS ... Regional Air Pollution Study [*Environmental Protection Agency*]

RAPS ... Regulated Air Pressure System (MCD)

RAPS ... Regulatory Affairs Professionals Society (EA)

RAPS ... Reliable Acoustic Path SONAR (MCD)

RAPS ... Retired Army Personnel System

RAPS ... Retiree Annuitant Pay System

RAPS ... Retrieval Analysis and Presentation System [*Data processing*]

RAPS ... Risk Appraisal of Programs System

RAPS ... Role Activity Performance Scale [*Mental health*]

RAPSAG ... Rapid Sealift Acquisition Group [*Navy*]

RAPSG ... Rapsgate [*England*]

RAPSI ... Remote Area Power Supply Investigation Branch [*Australia*]

RAPT ... Reusable Aerospace Passenger Transport (MCD)

RAPTAP ... Random Access Parallel Tape

RAP-TAP ... Releasable Assets Program - Transferable Assets Program [*Navy*] (NG)

RAPTN ... RAPRA Trade Names [*RAPRA Technology Ltd.*] [*Information service or system*] (IID)

Raptor Res ... Raptor Research [*A publication*]

RAPTUS ... Rapid Thorium-Uranium System [*Nuclear energy*]

RAPUD ... Revenue Analysis from Parametric Usage Descriptions [*Telecommunications*] (TEL)

RAPWI ... Organization for the Recovery of Allied Prisoners of War and Internees [*Initially in Headquarters of Allied Land Forces, Southeast Asia*] [*World War II*]

Rap Wit ... Rapalje's Treatise on Witnesses [*A publication*] (DLA)

RAQ ... Raha [*Indonesia*] [*Airport symbol*] (OAG)

RAQ ... Regional Air Quality

RAQ ... Reglements sur l'Assurance de la Qualite [*Quality Assurance Regulation*] [*French*]

RAQ ... Wirtschaft und Produktivitaet [*A publication*]

RAR ... RADAR Augmentation Reliability (MCD)

RAR ... Radio Acoustic Ranging

RAR ... Random Age Replacement

RAR ... Rapid Access Recording (IEEE)

Rar ... Rare Records [*Record label*]

RAR ... Rarotonga [*Cook Islands*] [*Airport symbol*] (OAG)

RAR ... Rarotonga [*Cook Islands*] [*Seismograph station code, US Geological Survey*] (SEIS)

RAR ... Read around Ratio

RAR ... Real Aperture RADAR

RAR ... Reallexikon der Aegyptischen Religionsgeschichte [*Berlin*] [*A publication*] (BJA)

RAR ... Reasonable Assumed [*or Assured*] Resources [*Minerals*]

RAR ... Record and Report

RAR ... Redevelopment Area Resident

RAR ... Reduced Aspect Ratio

RAR ... Regular Army Reserve

RAR ... Relative Accumulation Rate [*Ecology*]

RAR ... Reliability Action Report [*or Request*]

RAR ... Remote Arm Reset (MCD)

RAR ... Remove Audible Ring

RAR ... Renaissance and Reformation [*A publication*]

RAR ... Repair as Required (AAG)

RAR ... Report Authorization Record [*or Request*] (AAG)

RAR ... Request RADAR Blip Identification Message [*Communications*] (FAAC)

RAR ... Reserve Asset Ratio [*Banking*] (ADA)

RAR ... Resource Allocation Recommendations [*Military*]

RAR ... Restricted Articles Regulation (DS)

RAR ... Retinoic Acid Receptor [*Biochemistry*]

RAR ... Return Address Register

RAR ... Revenue Agent's Report [*IRS*]

RAR ... Revise as Required (MCD)

R Ar ... Revue Archeologique [*A publication*]

R-Ar ... Rhode Island State Archives, Providence, RI [*Library symbol*] [*Library of Congress*] (LCLS)

RAR ... Rhodesian African Rifles [*Military unit*]

RAR ... ROM [*Read-Only Memory*] Address Register

RAR ... Royal Army Reserve [*British*]

RAR ... Royal Australian Regiment

RAR ... Rural Area Redevelopment

RARAD ... RADAR Advisory (FAAC)

R Ar Av C Et ... Recueil des Arrets et Avis du Conseil d'Etat [*A publication*]

RARB ... Raritan Bancorp, Inc. [*NASDAQ symbol*] (NQ)

R Arb ... Recht der Arbeit [*Right to Work*] [*German*] (DLA)

RARC ... Revoked Appointment and Returned to Civilian Status [*Navy*]

R Arch Bibl Mus ... Revista de Archivos, Bibliotecas, y Museos [*A publication*]

RArchCr ... Rivista di Archeologia Cristiana [*Rome*] [*A publication*]

R Archeol ... Revue Archeologique [*A publication*]

R Archeom ... Revue d'Archeometrie [*A publication*]

R Arch Hist Art Louvain ... Revue des Archeologues et Historiens d'Art de Louvain [*A publication*]

RARDE...... Royal Armament Research and Development Establishment [*British*]
RARDEN .. Royal Armament Research and Development Establishment, Enfield [*British military*]　(DMA)
RARE........ Ram Air Rocket Engine
RARE........ Rare Animal Relief Effort
RARE......... Rare Antigen/Antibody Resource Exchange Program [*American Association of Blood Banks*]
RARE........ Rehabilitation of Addicts by Relatives and Employers
RARE........ Reinforcement and Resupply of Europe　(MCD)
RARE........ Retinoic Acid Responsive Element [*Biochemistry*]
RARE........ Roadless Area Resource Evaluation
RARE........ Ronne Antarctic Research Expedition [*1947-48*]
RAREA...... Radiation Research [*A publication*]
Ra Ref....... RADAR Reflector
RAREF...... Radiation and Repair Engineering Facility [*Nuclear energy*]　(NRCH)
Rarefied Gas Dyn Proc Int Symp ... Rarefied Gas Dynamics. Proceedings of the International Symposium [*A publication*]
RAREP...... RADAR Report [*FAA*]
RARF........ RADOME [*RADAR Dome*], Antenna, and Radio Frequency [*Array*] [*Electronics*]
RARG .... Regulatory Analysis Review Group [*Comprising several federal agencies*]
RARI......... Reporting and Routing Instructions [*Navy*]
RARMB..... Razrabotka Rudnykh Mestorozhdenii [*A publication*]
RARNEB.... Recent Achievements in Restorative Neurology [*A publication*]
RARO........ Regular Army Reserve of Officers [*British*]
RAROC ..... Risk-Adjusted Return on Capital [*Economics*]
RAR OCC ... Raro Occurrit [*Rarely Occurs*] [*Latin*]　(ROG)
RARP......... Radio Affiliate Replacement Plan [*Canadian Broadcasting Corporation*]
RARPC...... Roczniki Akademii Rolniczej w Poznaniu [*A publication*]
RArq......... Revista de Arqueologia [*A publication*]
RArqueol.... Revista de Arqueologia [*A publication*]
RARR .... Reinstallation and Removal Record　(KSC)
RARS........ Refractory Anemia with Ringed Sideroblasts [*Hematology*]
RARSA..... Radiation Research. Supplement [*A publication*]
RArt .... Revue de l'Art [*A publication*]
RArt .... Royal Artillery [*British*]
RArte .... Rivista d'Arte [*A publication*]
R Arts........ Revue des Arts [*A publication*]
R des Arts .. Revue des Arts [*A publication*]
RARU .... Rackham Arthritis Research Unit [*University of Michigan*] [*Research center*]　(RCD)
RARU .... Radio Range Station Reported Unreliable [*Message abbreviation*]
RAS........... Rabbonim Aid Society
RAS........... RADAR-Absorbing Structures
RAS........... RADAR Advisory Service
RAS........... RADAR Assembly Spares　(NG)
RAS........... RADAR Augmentation System　(MCD)
RAS........... Radio Science [*A publication*]
RAS........... RADOME [*RADAR Dome*] Antenna Structure
RAS........... Radula Sinus
RAS........... Rasht [*Iran*] [*Airport symbol*]　(OAG)
RAS........... Rassegna. Archivi di Stato [*A publication*]
RAS........... Rassegna della Letteratura Italiana [*A publication*]
RAS........... Reaction Augmentation System
RAS........... Reactor Alarm System　(IEEE)
RAS........... Reactor Analysis and Safety [*Nuclear energy*]　(NRCH)
RAS........... Readers Advisory Service [*A publication*]
RAS........... Rear Area Security [*Army*]　(AABC)
RAS........... Recirculation Actuation Signal [*Nuclear energy*]　(NRCH)
RAS........... Record Assigned System　(MCD)
RAS........... Records and Analysis Subsystem　(TEL)
RASL......... Recruiting Analysis Service [*LIMRA*]
RAS........... Rectified Air Speed [*Navigation*]
RAS........... Recurrent Aphthous Stomatitis [*Medicine*]
RAS........... Reflector Antenna System
RAS........... Refractory Anemia with Ringed Sideroblasts [*Hematology*]
RAS........... Regional Automated Systems
RAS........... Relay Antenna Subsystem [*NASA*]
RAS........... Reliability, Availability, and Serviceability [*IBM Corp. slogan*]　(MCD)
RAS........... Remote Acquisition Station [*Nuclear energy*]　(NRCH)
RAS........... Remote Active Spectrometer
RAS........... Remote Area Support　(MCD)
RAS........... Remote Arm Set　(MCD)
RAS........... Renin-Angiotensin System [*Endocrinology*]
RAS........... Replenishment at Sea [*Navy*]
RAS........... Report Audit Summary　(AAG)
RAS........... Reproduction Assembly Sheet　(MCD)
RAS........... Requirements Allocation Sheet
RAS........... Requirements Analysis Sheet [*NASA*]　(KSC)
RAS........... Requirements Audit System
RAS........... Reticular Activating System [*Diffuse network of neurons in the brain*]
RAS........... Revue Archeologique Syrienne [*A publication*]
RAS........... Rheumatoid Arthritis Serum [*Factor*] [*Medicine*]
RAS........... River Assault Squadron [*Navy*]　(NVT)

RAS........... Riverside Air Service [*Riverside, CA*] [*FAA designator*]　(FAAC)
RAS........... Rockhampton Aerial Services [*Australia*]
RAS........... Route Accounting Subsystem [*Telecommunications*]　(TEL)
RAS........... Row-Address Strobe　(IEEE)
RAS........... Royal Accounting System [*United States Geological Survey*]
RAS........... Royal Aeronautical Society [*British*]
RAS........... Royal African Society　(EAIO)
RAS........... Royal Agricultural Society [*British*]　(DAS)
RAS........... Royal Asiatic Society [*British*]
RAS........... Royal Astronomical Society [*British*]
RAS........... Royal International Agricultural Show [*British*]　(ITD)
RAS........... Rural Adjustment Scheme [*Australia*]
RASA........ Railway and Airline Supervisors Association [*AFL-CIO*]
RASA........ Rassegna Abruzzese di Storia ed Arte [*A publication*]
RASA........ Realignment of Supply Activities　(MCD)
RASA........ Redstone Arsenal Support Activity　(MCD)
RASA........ Regional Aeronautical Support Activity　(AFIT)
RASC........ Rear Area Security Controller [*Military*]
RASC........ Religious Altered State of Consciousness [*Psychology*]
RASC........ Rome Air Service Command [*Air Force*]
RASC........ Royal Agricultural Society of the Commonwealth　(EAIO)
RASC........ Royal Army Service Corps [*Formerly, ASC; later, RCT*] [*British*]
RASC........ Royal Astronomical Society of Canada
RASCA ..... Radio Science [*A publication*]
RASCAL ... Random Access Secure Communications Antijam Link
RASCAL ... Royal Aircraft Establishment Sequence Calculator [*British*]　(DEN)
RASCAP ... Replenishment at Sea Corrective Action Program　(MCD)
RASCC ...... Rear Area Security Control Center [*Military*]
RASC/DC ... Rear Area Security and Area Damage Control [*Military*]
R Ascetique & Mystique ... Revue d'Ascetique et de Mystique [*A publication*]
Raschet Konstr Issled Oborud Proizvod Istochnikov Toka ... Raschet. Konstruirovanie i Issledovanie Oborudovaniya Proizvodstva Istochnikov Toka [*A publication*]
Raschet Konstr Neftezavod Oborud ... Raschet i Konstruirovanie Neftezavodskogo Oborudovaniya [*A publication*]
Raschet Konstr Neftezvod Oborudovaniya ... Raschet i Konstruirovanie Neftezavodskogo Oborudovaniya [*A publication*]
Raschety Prochn ... Raschety na Prochnost [*A publication*]
RASCORE ... RADAR Scorer　(MCD)
RASC/RCT ... Royal Army Service Corps/Royal Corps of Transport [*British*]
RASD......... Reference and Adult Services Division [*American Library Association*]　(EA)
RASD BRASS ... RASD [*Reference and Adult Services Division*] Business Reference Services Section
RASD CODES ... RASD [*Reference and Adult Services Division*] Collection Development and Evaluation Section
RASD HS ... RASD [*Reference and Adult Services Division*] History Section
RASD MARS ... RASD [*Reference and Adult Services Division*] Machine-Assisted Reference Section
RASE........ Rapid Automatic Sweep Equipment [*Air Force*]
RASE........ Royal Agricultural Society of England
RASER...... Radio Amplification by Stimulated Emission of Radiation
RASER...... Random-to-Serial Converter
RASER...... Range and Sensitivity Extending Resonator [*Electronics*]
RasF.......... Rassegna di Filosofia [*A publication*]
RASGN...... Reassignment
RASH......... Rain Showers [*Meteorology*]
RASHA...... RAS. Rohr-Armatur-Sanitaer-Heizung [*A publication*]
RaSHI....... Rabbi Solomon Bar Isaac　(BJA)
RasI.......... Rassegna Italiana [*A publication*]
RASIB .... Rendiconto. Accademia delle Scienze. Istituto di Bologna [*A publication*]
RASIDS..... Range Safety Impact Display System
RASL......... Royal Apex Silver, Inc. [*NASDAQ symbol*]　(NQ)
RASM....... Remote Analog Submultiplexer　(MCD)
RASMA..... Revue Agricole et Sucriere de l'Ile Maurice [*A publication*]
rASMC ..... Rat Aortic Smooth Muscle Cells
RAsMyst ... Revue d'Ascetique et de Mystique [*Paris*] [*A publication*]
RASN .... Rain and Snow [*Sleet*] [*Meteorology*]
RASO .... Radiological Affairs Support Office [*Obsolete*] [*Navy*]
RASO .... Rear Airfield Supply Organization [*Military*]
RASO .... Regional Aviation Supply Officer [*Navy*]　(AFIT)
RASONDE ... Radiosonde Observation
RASP........ Receiver Active Signal Processor [*Military*]　(CAAL)
RASP........ Refined Aeronautical Support Program　(NG)
RASP........ Reliability and Aging Surveillance Program [*Air Force*]
RASP........ Remote Access Switching and Patching
RASP......... Retrieval and Sort Processor [*Data processing*]
RASPE ...... Resident Army SENSCOM [*Sentinel Systems Command*] Project Engineer　(AABC)
RASPO...... Resident Apollo Spacecraft Program Office [*NASA*]　(KSC)
RASR......... Regular Army Special Reserve　(ADA)
RASS .... RADAR Acoustic Sounding System [*National Oceanic and Atmospheric Administration*]
RASS .... RADAR Attitude Sensing System　(MCD)
RASS .... Radio Acoustic Sounding System
RASS .... Rapid Area Supply Support [*Military*]　(AFM)
RAss........... Revue d'Assyriologie et d'Archeologie Orientale [*A publication*]

RASS .... Rock Analysis Storage System [*United States Geological Survey*] [*Information service or system*] (IID)
RASS .... Ruggedized Airborne Seeker Simulator (MCD)
Rass Agr Ital ... Rassegna dell'Agricoltura Italiana [*A publication*]
RASSAN... RADAR Sea State Analyzer [*Marine science*] (MSC)
Rass Arch Chir ... Rassegna ed Archivio di Chirurgia [*A publication*]
Rass Chim ... Rassegna Chimica [*A publication*]
Rass Clin Sci ... Rassegna Clinico-Scientifica [*A publication*]
Rass Clin Sci Ist Biochim Ital ... Rassegna Clinico-Scientifica. Istituto Biochimico Italiano [*A publication*]
Rass Clin Ter Sci Affini ... Rassegna di Clinica Terapia e Scienze Affini [*A publication*]
RassCult .... Rassegna di Cultura [*A publication*]
Rass Dermatol Sifilogr ... Rassegna di Dermatologia e di Sifilografia [*A publication*]
Rass Ec ...... Rassegna Economica [*A publication*]
Rass Econ .. Rassegna Economica [*A publication*]
Rass Econ Afr Ital ... Rassegna Economica dell'Africa Italiana [*A publication*]
Rass Econ Cam Commer Ind Agr Alessandria ... Rassegna Economica. Camera di Commercio, Industria, e Agricoltura di Alessandria [*A publication*]
Rass Econ Colon ... Rassegna Economica delle Colonie [*A publication*]
Rass Econ (Napoli) ... Rassegna Economica (Napoli) [*A publication*]
Rassegna Ital Sociol ... Rassegna Italiana di Sociologia [*A publication*]
Rassegna M Curci ... Rassegna Musicale Curci [*A publication*]
RassFilos ... Rassegna di Filosofia [*A publication*]
Rass Fisiopat Clin Ter ... Rassegna di Fisiopatologia Clinica e Terapeutica [*A publication*]
Rass Fisiopatol Clin Ter ... Rassegna di Fisiopatologia Clinica e Terapeutica [*A publication*]
Rass Giuliana Med ... Rassegna Giuliana di Medicina [*A publication*]
Rass Giur Sard ... Rassegna Giuridica Sarda [*A publication*]
RASSH ...... Radiosondes Shipped From (NOAA)
Rass IGI ..... Rassegna Indo-Greco-Italica [*A publication*]
Rass Int Clin ... Rassegna Internazionale di Clinica e Terapia [*A publication*]
Rass Int Clin Ter ... Rassegna Internazionale di Clinica e Terapia [*A publication*]
Rass Int Stomatol Prat ... Rassegna Internazionale di Stomatologia Pratica [*A publication*]
Rass d'It ..... Rassegna d'Italia [*A publication*]
Rass Ital Chir Med ... Rassegna Italiana di Chirurgia e Medicina [*A publication*]
Rass Ital Gastro-Enterol ... Rassegna Italiana di Gastro-Enterologia [*A publication*]
Rass Ital Gastro-Enterol Suppl ... Rassegna Italiana di Gastro-Enterologia. Supplemento [*A publication*]
Rass Ital Ottalmol ... Rassegna Italiana d'Ottalmologia [*A publication*]
Rass Ital Soc ... Rassegna Italiana di Sociologia [*A publication*]
Rass Ital Sociol ... Rassegna Italiana di Sociologia [*A publication*]
Rass del Lav ... Rassegna del Lavoro [*A publication*]
Rass Lav Pubbl ... Rassegna dei Lavori Pubblici [*A publication*]
Rass Let It ... Rassegna della Letteratura Italiana [*A publication*]
Rass Med... Rassegna Medica [*A publication*]
Rass Med Appl Lav Ind ... Rassegna di Medicina Applicata al Lavoro Industriale [*A publication*]
Rass Med Convivium Sanit ... Rassegna Medica - Convivium Sanitatis [*A publication*]
Rass Med Cult ... Rassegna Medica e Culturale [*A publication*]
Rass Med Ind ... Rassegna di Medicina Industriale [*A publication*]
Rass Med Ind Ig Lav ... Rassegna di Medicina Industriale e di Igiene del Lavoro [*A publication*]
Rass Med Sarda ... Rassegna Medica Sarda [*A publication*]
Rass Med Sarda Suppl ... Rassegna Medica Sarda. Supplemento [*A publication*]
Rass Med Sper ... Rassegna di Medicina Sperimentale [*A publication*]
Rass Med Sper Suppl ... Rassegna di Medicina Sperimentale. Supplemento [*A publication*]
Rass Mens Clin Patol Ter Vita Prof Med Condotto Med Prat ... Rassegna Mensile di Clinica, di Patologia, di Terapia, e di Vita Professionale del Medico Condotto e del Medico Pratico [*A publication*]
Rass Mens Israel ... Rassegna Mensile di Israel [*A publication*]
Rass Min Metall Chim ... Rassegna Mineraria, Metallurgia, e Chimica [*A publication*]
Rass Min Metall Ital ... Rassegna Mineraria e Metallurgica Italiana [*A publication*]
Rass Mus... Rassegna Musicale [*A publication*]
Rass Mus Curci ... Rassegna Musicale Curci [*A publication*]
Rass Neurol Veg ... Rassegna di Neurologia Vegetativa [*A publication*]
Rass Neuropsich ... Rassegna di Neuropsichiatria e Scienze Affini [*A publication*]
Rass Neuropsichiatr Sci Affini ... Rassegna di Neuropsichiatria e Scienze Affini [*A publication*]
R Assoc Canad Educ Langue Franc ... Revue. Association Canadienne d'Education de Langue Francaise [*A publication*]
Rass Odontotec ... Rassegna Odontotecnica [*A publication*]
Rass Patol Appar Respir ... Rassegna di Patologia dell'Apparato Respiratorio [*A publication*]
Rass Propr Ind Lett Art ... Rassegna della Proprieta Industriale, Letteraria, e Artistica [*A publication*]

Rass Psicol Gen Clin ... Rassegna di Psicologia Generale e Clinica [*A publication*]
Rass Pubbl ... Rassegna di Diritto Pubblico [*A publication*]
RASSR ...... Reliable Advanced Solid-State RADAR
R Ass Resp ... Revue Generale des Assurances et des Responsabilites [*A publication*]
Rass Serv Soc ... Rassegna di Servizio Sociale [*A publication*]
Rass Sind Quad ... Rassegna Sindacale. Quaderni [*A publication*]
Rass Statis Lav ... Rassegna di Statistiche del Lavoro [*A publication*]
Rass Stor R ... Rassegna Storica del Risorgimento [*A publication*]
Rass Studi Psichiatr ... Rassegna di Studi Psichiatrici [*A publication*]
RAS-STADES ... Records Association System - Standard Data Elements System (MCD)
Rass Ter Patol Clin ... Rassegna di Terapia e Patologia Clinica [*A publication*]
Rass Trimest Odontoiatr ... Rassegna Trimestrale di Odontoiatria [*A publication*]
Rass Urol Nefrol ... Rassegna di Urologia e Nefrologia [*A publication*]
RASSW ..... Radical Alliance of Social Service Workers (EA)
RAssyr .... Revue d'Assyriologie [*A publication*]
R Assyr ...... Revue d'Assyriologie et d'Archeologie Orientale [*A publication*]
RAST .... Radioallergosorbent Test [*Immunochemistry*]
Rast .... Rastell's Entries and Statutes [*England*] [*A publication*] (DLA)
RAST .... Recovery, Assist, Secure, and Traverse System [*Navy*]
RAST .... Reliability and System Test
RASTA ..... Radiant Augmented Special Test Apparatus (MCD)
RASTA ...... Radio Station [*Coast Guard*]
Rast Abr..... Rastell's Abridgment of the Statutes [*A publication*] (DLA)
RASTAC ... Random Access Storage and Control [*Data processing*]
RASTAD ... Random Access Storage and Display [*Data processing*]
RASTAS.... Radiating Site Target Acquisition System (MCD)
Rasteniev'd Nauki ... Rasteniev'dni Nauki [*A publication*]
Rastenievud Nauk ... Rastenievudni Nauki [*A publication*]
Rastenievud Nauki ... Rastenievudni Nauki [*A publication*]
Rast Ent ..... Rastell's Entries and Statutes [*A publication*] (DLA)
RaStEt .... Rassegna di Studi Etiopici [*Rome*] [*A publication*]
RASTI .... Rapid Speech Transition Index [*Acoustics*]
RASTIC..... Rail, Automatic Straightening, Intrinsically Controlled [*Railroad maintenance device*] [*British*]
Rastit Belki ... Rastitel'nye Belki [*A publication*]
Rastit Krainego Sev Ee Osvoenie ... Rastitel'nost Krainego Severa i Ee Osvoenie [*A publication*]
Rastit Krainego Sev SSSR Ee Osvoenie ... Rastitel'nost Krainego Severa SSSR i Ee Osvoenie [*A publication*]
Rastit Latv SSR ... Rastitel'nost Latviiskoi SSR [*A publication*]
Rastit Resur ... Rastitel'nye Resursy [*A publication*]
Rastit Zasht ... Rastitelna Zashtita [*Plant Protection*] [*A publication*]
Rastit Zasht Plant Prot ... Rastitelna Zashtita/Plant Protection [*A publication*]
Rast Nauki ... Rastenievudni Nauki [*A publication*]
RASTR ...... Recorded Acoustic Signal Target Repeater
Rast Resursy ... Rastitel'nye Resursy [*A publication*]
R Astron Soc Can Pr ... Royal Astronomical Society of Canada. Selected Papers and Proceedings [*A publication*]
Rast Zashch ... Rastitelna Zashchita [*A publication*]
RASU .... Rangoon Arts and Science University [*Later, Rangoon University*] [*Burma*] (DS)
RaSV......... Rasheed (Rat) Sarcoma Virus
RASV .... Reusable Aerodynamic Space Vehicle
RASyr .... Revue Archeologique Syrienne [*A publication*]
RAT .... Radiological Assessment Team [*Nuclear energy*] (NRCH)
RAT .... Ram Air Temperature
RAT .... Ram Air Turbine (MCD)
RAT .... Ranges, Ammunition, and Targets (MCD)
RAT .... Rat Island [*Alaska*] [*Seismograph station code, US Geological Survey*] [*Closed*] (SEIS)
RAT .... Rat Resources [*Vancouver Stock Exchange symbol*]
RAT .... Rated
RAT .... Rating (AABC)
RAT .... Ratio (AAG)
RAT .... Rations [*Military*] (AABC)
RAT .... Raynaud's Association Trust (EA)
RAT .... Regular Associated Troupers (EA)
RAT .... Reliability Assurance Test
RAT .... Remote Area Terminal
RAT .... Remote Associates Test [*Psychology*]
RAT .... Repeat Action Tablet [*Pharmacology*]
R & AT...... Research and Advanced Technology
RAT .... Reseau des Amis de la Terre [*Network of Friends of the Earth*] [*France*] [*Political party*] (PPE)
RAT .... Reserve Auxiliary Transformer (IEEE)
RAT .... Resistance Armee Tunisienne [*Tunisian Armed Resistance*] (PD)
RAT .... Restricted Articles Tariff
RAT .... Revue. Academie Internationale du Tourisme [*A publication*]
RAT .... Revue des Accidents du Travail et de Droit Industriel et Social [*A publication*]
RAT .... Right Anterior Thigh [*Anatomy*]
RAT .... Rocket-Assisted Torpedo [*Antisubmarine warfare*]
RAT .... Rotational Autonomic Tester
RATA .... Rankine Cycle Air Turboaccelerator
RA/TA....... Restricted Availability/Technical Availability (NVT)

RATAC...... RADAR Analog Target Acquisition Computer
RATAC...... Raytheon Acoustic Telemetry and Control
RATAC...... Remote Airborne Television Display of Ground RADAR
                Coverage via TACAN (CET)
RATAN ..... RADAR and Television Aid to Navigation
RATAV...... RADAR Terrain Avoidance
RATBP...... Revised Appendix to Be Published (MCD)
RATC........ Rate-Aided Tracking Computer
RATC........ Rhodesian Air Training Centre [*British military*] (DMA)
RATCC..... RADAR Air Traffic Control Center [*Later, RATCF*] [*Navy*]
RATCC..... Regional Air Traffic Control Center (NATG)
RATCF...... RADAR Air Traffic Control Facility [*Formerly, RATCC*]
                [*Navy*] (FAAC)
RATCON .. RADAR Terminal Control
RATD........ RADAR Automatic Target Detection [*Military*] (CAAL)
RATE........ Rate Analysis and Transportation Evaluation [*Student legal
                action organization*]
RATE........ Record and Tape Exchange (EA)
RATE........ Remote Automatic Telemetry Equipment
RATE........ Retention and Transfer Enhancement [*Military*]
RATEA..... Radiotekhnika [*Moscow*] [*A publication*]
RATEL...... Radiotelephone
RATEL...... Raytheon Automatic Test Equipment Language [*Data
                processing*] (CSR)
RATELO... Radiotelephone Operator (AABC)
RATER...... Response Analysis Tester [*NASA*]
RATES ...... Rapid Access Tariff Expediting Service [*Journal of Commerce,
                Inc.*] [*Database*]
RATEX...... Rational Expectations [*Economics*]
RATF........ Radio Aids Training Flight [*British military*] (DMA)
RATFOR... Rational FORTRAN [*Data processing*]
RA-TFR.... RADAR Altimeter - Terrain Following RADAR (MCD)
RATG........ Rabbit Antithymocyte Globulin [*Immunochemistry*]
RATG........ Radiotelegram [*or Radiotelegraph*]
RATG........ Rhodesian Air Training Group [*British military*] (DMA)
RATHQ..... Rath Packing [*NASDAQ symbol*] (NQ)
RATIB...... Radiologic Technology [*A publication*]
RATIG...... Robert A. Taft Institute of Government [*Later, TTI*] (EA)
RATIO...... Radio Telescope in Orbit (IEEE)
Rationalisierung ... Monatsschrift des Rationalisierungs [*A publication*]
Ration Drug Ther ... Rational Drug Therapy [*A publication*]
RATN........ Ratners Group PLC [*NASDAQ symbol*] (NQ)
Rat News Lett ... Rat News Letter [*A publication*]
RATO........ Rocket-Assisted Takeoff [*Aerospace*]
RATOG.... Rocket-Assisted Takeoff Gear [*Aviation*] (IEEE)
RATP......... Regie Autonome des Transports Parisiens [*Paris Transport
                Authority*]
RATR........ Reliability Abstracts and Technical Reviews [*NASA*]
RATS........ RADAR Acquisition and Tracking System (MCD)
RATS........ RADAR Altimeter Target Simulator (MCD)
RATS........ Ram Air Turbine System
RATS........ Rapid Area Transportation Support [*Air Force*] (MCD)
RATS........ Rate and Track Subsystem
RATS........ Reconnaissance and Tactical Security [*Teams*] [*Military*]
RATS........ Reform of the Australian Taxation System [*1985*] [*A
                publication*]
RATS........ Remote Alarm Transmission System
RATS........ Remote Area Tactical [*Location and Landing*] System
RATS........ Remote Area Television Service [*Australia*] (ADA)
RATS........ Remote Area Terminal System
RATS........ Resolver Alignment Test Set
RATS........ Restricted Articles Terminal System [*IATA*] (DS)
RATSC...... Rome Air Technical Service Command [*Air Force*]
RATSCAT .. RADAR Target Scatter [*RADAR program*]
RATSEC.... Robert A. Taft Sanitary Engineering Center (AABC)
Rat Sel Cas ... Rattigan's Select Hindu Law Cases [*A publication*] (DLA)
RATT........ Radio Airborne Teletype (MCD)
RATT........ Radioteletype
RATTC...... Radio and Teletype Control Center
Rattigan ..... Rattigan's Select Hindu Law Cases [*India*] [*A
                publication*] (DLA)
Ratt LC ...... Rattigan's Leading Cases on Hindu Law [*A publication*] (DLA)
Rat Unrep Cr ... Ratanlal's Unreported Criminal Cases [*India*] [*A
                publication*] (DLA)
RATV........ Remote Access Television Service [*Australia*]
RATWUS ... Research and Technology Work Unit Summary
RAU.......... Radion Access Unit [*Army*]
RAU.......... Railway African Union
RAU.......... Recurrent Aphthous Ulceration [*Medicine*]
RAU.......... Regional Acquisition Unit [*NASA*] (NASA)
RAU.......... Remote Acquisition Unit [*NASA*] (NASA)
RAU.......... River Assault Unit [*Navy*]
Rauch Pnt .. Rauch Guide to the United States Paint Industry Data [*A
                publication*]
RAug.......... Revue Augustinienne [*A publication*]
RAUIC....... Repair Activity Unit Identification Code (MCD)
RAUIS .... Remote Acquisition Unit Interconnecting Station
                [*NASA*] (NASA)
RAUK........ Rear-Admiral of the United Kingdom [*Navy*] [*British*] (ROG)
Raumforsch u-Ordnung ... Raumforschung und Raumordnung [*A
                publication*]

Raumforsch und Raumordnung ... Raumforschung und Raumordnung [*A
                publication*]
R Aust Chem Inst ... Royal Australian Chemical Institute [*A publication*]
R Aust Chem Inst J Proc ... Royal Australian Chemical Institute. Journal and
                Proceedings [*A publication*] (APTA)
R Aust Chem Inst J Proc Suppl ... Royal Australian Chemical Institute.
                Journal and Proceedings. Supplement [*A
                publication*] (APTA)
R Aust Chem Inst Proc ... Royal Australian Chemical Institute. Proceedings
                [*A publication*]
R Aust Plan Inst J ... Royal Australian Planning Institute. Journal [*A
                publication*]
R Aust Plann Inst J ... RAPIJ: Royal Australian Planning Institute. Journal [*A
                publication*] (APTA)
RAUT .... Republic Automotive Parts, Inc. [*NASDAQ symbol*] (NQ)
RAut & L.... Revue des Auteurs et des Livres [*A publication*]
RAUU........ [*The*] Renabie Gold Trust [*NASDAQ symbol*] (NQ)
RAuv.......... Revue d'Auvergne [*A publication*]
R Aux AF.... Royal Auxiliary Air Force [*Formerly, AAF*] [*British*]
RAV .... Cravo Norte [*Colombia*] [*Airport symbol*] (OAG)
RAV .... Ramm Venture [*Vancouver Stock Exchange symbol*]
RAV .... Random Access Viewer
RAV .... Raven Industries, Inc. [*AMEX symbol*] (SPSG)
RAV .... Ravensburg [*Federal Republic of Germany*] [*Seismograph
                station code, US Geological Survey*] (SEIS)
RAV .... Ravine, PA [*Location identifier*] [*FAA*] (FAAL)
RAV .... Reduced Availability (MCD)
RAV .... Remotely Augmented Vehicle [*Aircraft*]
RAV .... Restricted Availability (NG)
RAVC........ Royal Army Veterinary Corps [*Formerly, AVC*] [*British*]
RAVE .... RADAR Acquisition Visual-Tracking Equipment
RAVE .... Random Access Video Editing [*Computerized film editing*]
RAVE .... Random Access Viewing Equipment
RAVE .... Readjustment Assistance Act 74 for Vietnam Era
                Veterans (OICC)
RAVE .... Research Aircraft for the Visual Environment [*Helicopters*]
                [*Army*]
RAVEC..... RADAR Vector
RAVEN .... Ranging and Velocity Navigation
Ravena .... [*Petrus*] Ravennas [*Flourished, 1468-1508*] [*Authority cited in
                pre-1607 legal work*] (DSA)
RAVES ...... Rapid Aerospace Vehicle Evaluation System [*Grumman Corp.*]
RAVIR...... RADAR Video Recorder (NVT)
RAVPRO... Resource Allocation and Validation Program
RAVU....... Radiosonde Analysis and Verification Unit
RAW.......... Airway Resistance [*Medicine*]
RAW.......... Arawa [*Papua New Guinea*] [*Airport symbol*] (OAG)
RAW.......... Raad van Advies voor het Wetenschapsbeleid. Informatiebank.
                Tweekbericht [*A publication*]
RAW.......... Rapid American Withdrawal [*Antiwar march sponsored by
                Vietnam Veterans Against the War*] (EA)
Raw .... Rawle's Pennsylvania Reports [*5 vols.*] [*A publication*] (DLA)
RAW........ Read Alter Wire
RAW........ Read after Write
RAW........ Ready and Waiting [*or Willing*] [*Slang*]
RAW........ Reconnaissance Attack Wing [*Navy*] (NVT)
RAW.......... Record of the Arab World [*Beirut*] [*A publication*]
RAW.......... Redmond, OR [*Location identifier*] [*FAA*] (FAAL)
RAW.......... Reliability Assurance Warranty (MCD)
RAW.......... Rent-a-Wreck Industries Corp. [*Vancouver Stock Exchange
                symbol*]
RAW.......... Return America to Work [*Also translated as "Reaganomics
                Ain't Working"*] [*UAW bumper sticker slogan*]
RAW.......... Rifleman's Assault Weapon (MCD)
RAW.......... Right Attack Wing [*Women's lacrosse position*]
RAW.......... Rural American Women (EA)
RAWA ...... Rail-Water [*Shipping*]
RAWA .... Renaissance Artists and Writers Association (EA)
RAWA .... Rent-a-Wreck of America, Inc. [*Los Angeles, CA*] [*NASDAQ
                symbol*] (NQ)
RAWARA ... Rail-Water-Rail [*Shipping*]
RAWARC ... RADAR and Warning Coordination [*Teletypewriter circuit*]
RAWB .... Railroad and Airline Wage Board [*Terminated, 1953*]
RAWC .... Republic American Corporation [*Encino, CA*] [*NASDAQ
                symbol*] (NQ)
Raw Const ... Rawle on the Constitution of the United States [*A
                publication*] (DLA)
Raw Cov ..... Rawle on Covenants for Title [*A publication*] (DLA)
RAWEB...... Refractory Anemia without Excess of Blasts [*Hematology*]
Raw Eq..... Rawle's Equity in Pennsylvania [*A publication*] (DLA)
RAWIE...... Radio Weather Intercept Element
RAWIN...... RADAR Wind [*Upper air observation*]
RAWIND .. RADAR Wind [*Upper air observation*]
RAWINDS ... RADAR Wind Sounding [*Upper air observation*] (MSA)
RAWINS... RADAR Winds [*Upper air observation*]
RAWINSONDE ... RADAR Wind Sounding and Radiosonde [*Upper air
                observation*]
RAWIT...... RNA [*Ribonucleic Acid*] Amplification with In/Vitro
                Translation [*Genetics*]
Rawle .... Rawle's Pennsylvania Supreme Court Reports [*1828-35*] [*A
                publication*] (DLA)

Rawle Const US ... Rawle on the Constitution of the United States [*A publication*]   (DLA)
Rawle Cov .. Rawle on Covenants for Title [*A publication*]   (DLA)
Rawle Pen & W ... Rawle, Penrose, and Watts' Pennsylvania Reports [*1828-40*] [*A publication*]   (DLA)
Rawl Mun Corp ... Rawlinson's Municipal Corporations [*10th ed.*] [*1910*] [*A publication*]   (DLA)
Raw Mater ... Raw Material [*A publication*]
Raw Materials Survey Res Rept ... Raw Materials Survey. Resource Report [*A publication*]
Raw Mater Rep ... Raw Materials Report [*Sweden*] [*A publication*]
RAWO .... Reliability Assurance Work Order   (MCD)
RAWP ...... Resource Allocation Working Party [*British*]
RAWS .... RADAR Altimeter Warning Set   (MCD)
RAWS .... RADAR Automatic Weather System
RAWS .... Remote Area Weather Station   (MCD)
RAWS .... Remote Automatic Weather Station
RAWS .... Role Adaptable Weapons System [*Military*]
RAWTS ..... RNA [*Ribonucleic Acid*] Amplification with Transcript Sequencing [*Genetics*]
RAWX ...... Returned Account Weather [*Aviation*]   (FAAC)
RAX .... Remote Access [*Data processing*] [*Telecommunications*]
RAX .... Rio Alto Exploration Ltd. [*Toronto Stock Exchange symbol*]
RAX .... Rosenbalm Aviation, Inc. [*Ypsilanti, MI*] [*FAA designator*]   (FAAC)
RAX .... Rural Automatic Exchange   (DEN)
RAXR .... Rax Restaurants, Inc. [*NASDAQ symbol*]   (NQ)
RAXRA ..... Radex Rundschau (Austria) [*A publication*]
Ray .... Raymundus de Pennafort [*Deceased, 1275*] [*Authority cited in pre-1607 legal work*]   (DSA)
Ray .... Raynerius de Forlivio [*Deceased, 1358*] [*Authority cited in pre-1607 legal work*]   (DSA)
RAY .... Rayrock Yellowknife Resources, Inc. [*Toronto Stock Exchange symbol*]
RAY .... Raytech Corp. [*NYSE symbol*]   (SPSG)
RAY .... Rothesay [*Scotland*] [*Airport symbol*]   (OAG)
RAY .... Royale Airlines, Inc. [*Shreveport, LA*] [*FAA designator*]   (FAAC)
Ray B Ex .... Raymond's Bill of Exceptions [*A publication*]   (DLA)
RAYCI ...... Raytheon Controlled Inventory [*Data processing*]
RAY-COM ... Raytheon Communications Equipment [*Citizens band radio*]
RAYDAC ... Raytheon Digital Automatic Computer   (MUGU)
Rayden ...... Rayden on Divorce [*A publication*]   (DLA)
RAYDIST ... Ray-Path Distance   (MUGU)
Ray de For ... Raynerius de Forlivio [*Deceased, 1358*] [*Authority cited in pre-1607 legal work*]   (DSA)
Ray Ins .... Ray's Medical Jurisprudence of Insanity [*A publication*]   (DLA)
RAYM .... [*The*] Raymond Corp. [*NASDAQ symbol*]   (NQ)
Raym .... [*Sir Thomas*] Raymond's King's Bench Reports [*83 English Reprint*] [*1660-84*] [*A publication*]   (DLA)
Raym B Ex ... Raymond's Bill of Exceptions [*A publication*]   (DLA)
Raym Ch Dig ... Raymond's Digested Chancery Cases [*A publication*]   (DLA)
Ray Med Jur ... Ray's Medical Jurisprudence of Insanity [*A publication*]   (DLA)
Ray Men Path ... Ray's Mental Pathology [*A publication*]   (DLA)
Raym Ent .... [*Lord*] Raymond's Entries [*A publication*]   (DLA)
Raym Ld .... Lord Raymond's English King's Bench Reports [*3 vols.*] [*A publication*]   (DLA)
Raymond .... Raymond's Reports [*81-89 Iowa*] [*A publication*]   (DLA)
Raymond W Brink Selected Math Papers ... Raymond W. Brink Selected Mathematical Papers [*A publication*]
Raym Sir T ... [*Sir Thomas*] Raymond's English King's Bench Reports [*A publication*]   (DLA)
Raym T ...... [*Sir Thomas*] Raymond's English King's Bench Reports [*A publication*]   (DLA)
Rayn .... Rayner's English Tithe Cases [*3 vols.*] [*A publication*]   (DLA)
Rayn Ti Cas ... Rayner's English Tithe Cases [*1575-1782*] [*A publication*]   (DLA)
RAYOF ...... Raymac Oil Corp. [*NASDAQ symbol*]   (NQ)
Rayon .... Rayon and Synthetic Textiles [*A publication*]
Rayon J .... Rayon Journal [*A publication*]
Rayon J Cellul Fibers ... Rayon Journal and Cellulose Fibers [*A publication*]
Rayon Melliand Text Mon ... Rayon and Melliand Textile Monthly [*A publication*]
Rayonne Fibres Synth ... Rayonne et Fibres Synthetiques [*A publication*]
Rayonnem Ionis ... Rayonnements Ionisants [*A publication*]
Rayonnem Ionis Tech Mes Prot ... Rayonnements Ionisants. Techniques de Mesures et de Protection [*A publication*]
Rayon Rayon J ... Rayon and the Rayon Journal [*A publication*]
Rayon Rec ... Rayon Record [*A publication*]
Rayon Rev ... Rayon Revue [*A publication*]
Rayon Synth Text ... Rayon and Synthetic Textiles [*A publication*]
Rayon Synth Yarn J ... Rayon and Synthetic Yarn Journal [*A publication*]
Rayon Text Mon ... Rayon Textile Monthly [*A publication*]
Ray de Saba ... Raymundus de Sabanacho [*Authority cited in pre-1607 legal work*]   (DSA)
Ray Sir T .... [*Sir Thomas*] Raymond's English King's Bench Reports [*83 English Reprint*] [*1660-84*] [*A publication*]   (DLA)
RAYSISTOR ... Raytheon Resistor [*Electro-optical control device*]
RAYSPAN ... Raytheon Spectrum Analyzer
RAY-TEL .. Raytheon Telephone [*Citizens band radio*]

Ray Ti Cas ... Rayner's English Tithe Cases [*1575-1782*] [*A publication*]   (DLA)
RAZ .... Rolled Alloyed Zinc
RAZEL ...... Range, Azimuth, and Elevation
RazFe .... Razon y Fe [*Madrid*] [*A publication*]
Raziskave Stud Kmetijski Inst Slov ... Raziskave in Studije-Kmetijski Institut Slovenije [*A publication*]
RAZON ..... Range and Azimuth Only
RAZPE ...... Resident ARGMA [*Army Rocket and Guided Missile Agency*] Zeus Project Engineer   (AAG)
Razpr Slov Akad Znan Umet IV ... Razprave. Slovenska Akademija Znanosti in Umetnosti. IV [*A publication*]
Razpr Slov Akad Znan Umet Razred Mat Fiz Teh Vede Ser A ... Razprave. Slovenska Akademija Znanosti in Umetnosti. Razred za Matematicne, Fizikalne, in Tehnicne Vede. Serija A. Matematicni, Fizikalni, in Kemicne Vede [*A publication*]
Razrab Ehkspl Gazov Gazokondens Mestorozhd ... Razrabotka i Ehksplutatsiya Gazovykh i Gazokondensatnykh Mestorozhdenij [*A publication*]
Razrab Mestorozhd Polezn Iskop (Kiev) ... Razrabotka Mestorozhdenii Poleznykh Iskopaemykh (Kiev) [*A publication*]
Razrab Mestorozhd Polezn Iskop (Tiflis) ... Razrabotka Mestorozhdenii Poleznykh Iskopaemykh (Tiflis) [*A publication*]
Razrab Neft Gazov Mestorozhd ... Razrabotka Neftyanykh i Gazovykh Mestorozhdenii [*A publication*]
Razrab Rudn Mestorozhd ... Razrabotka Rudnykh Mestorozhdenii [*Ukrainian SSR*] [*A publication*]
Razred Mat Fiz Teh Vede Dela ... Razred za Matematicne, Fizikalne in Tehnicne Vede Dela [*Ljubliana*]
RAZS .... Rolled Alloyed Zinc Sheet
Raz SAZU ... Razprave Razreda za Filoloske in Literarne vede Slovenske Akademije Znanoste in Umetnosti [*A publication*]
Razved Geofiz ... Razvedochnaya Geofizika [*A publication*]
Razved Geofiz (Leningrad) ... Razvedochnaya Geofizika (Leningrad) [*A publication*]
Razved Nedr ... Razvedka Nedr [*USSR*] [*A publication*]
Razved Okhr Nedr ... Razvedka i Okhrana Nedr [*A publication*]
Razved i Okhr Nedr ... Razvedka i Okhrana Nedr [*A publication*]
Razved Promysl Geofiz ... Razvedochnaya i Promyslovaya Geofizika [*A publication*]
Razved Razrab Neft Gazov Mestorozhd ... Razvedka i Razrabotka Neftyanykh i Gazovykh Mestorozhdenii [*A publication*]
R/B .... ASE [*National Institute for Automotive Service Excellence*] Test Registration Booklet [*A publication*]   (EAAP)
RB .... Botswana [*IYRU nationality code*]   (IYR)
RB .... RADAR Beacon
R/B .... Radio Beacon
RB .... Radio Bearing   (DEN)
RB .... Radio Brenner [*Radio network*] [*Federal Republic of Germany*]
RB .... Rate Beacon   (AAG)
RB .... Rated Boost
RB .... Ration Book
RB .... Reactor Building [*Nuclear energy*]   (NRCH)
RB .... Read Back [*Communications*]   (FAAC)
RB .... Read Backward
RB .... Read Buffer
RB .... Reading & Bates Corp. [*NYSE symbol*]   (SPSG)
RB .... Recherches Bibliques [*A publication*]
RB .... Rechtsgeleerd Bijblad [*A publication*]
RB .... Reconnaissance Bomber
RB .... Recovery Beacon
R & B .... Red and Blue   (KSC)
RB .... Red Book [*Full name is "Drug Topics Red Book," a pharmacist's guide*] [*A publication*]
RB .... Red Brigades [*Revolutionary group*] [*Italy*]
RB .... Redeemable Bond [*Investment term*]
RB .... Reentry Body
RB .... Regular Budget [*United Nations*]
RB .... Relative Bearing [*Navigation*]
RB .... Relay Block   (MSA)
RB .... Religious Broadcasting [*A publication*]
R & B .... Remington and Ballinger's Code [*1910*] [*A publication*]   (DLA)
RB .... Renaut's Bodies [*Neurology*]
RB .... Renegotiation Board [*Terminated, 1979*] [*Federal government*]
RB .... Renegotiation Bulletins [*A publication*]   (DLA)
RB .... Repeated Back [*Communications*]   (FAAC)
RB .... Report Bibliography
RB .... Request Block
RB .... Rescue Boat   (FAAC)
RB .... Research Bulletin
RB .... Reserve Bank   (ADA)
RB .... Resistance Brazing
RB .... Restiform Body [*Neuroanatomy*]
RB .... Restricted Bulletin
RB .... Retail Business [*A publication*]
Rb. .... Retinoblastoma [*Oncology*]
RB .... Retractable Boom
RB .... Retraining Benefits [*Employment*]   (OICC)
RB .... Return to Bias
RB .... Revenue Bond [*Investment term*]
RB .... Reverse Blocked

RB	Revision Block (MSA)
RB	Revista Bibliotecilor [*Bucharest*] [*A publication*]
RB	Revue de la Banque [*A publication*]
R du B	Revue du Barreau [*A publication*]
RB	Revue Benedictine [*A publication*]
RB	Revue Biblique [*A publication*]
RB	Revue Bossuet [*A publication*]
R & B	Rhythm and Blues [*Music*]
RB	Rich Bitch [*Slang*]
RB	Rifle Brigade
RB	Right Border [*Genetics*]
RB	Right Buttock [*Anatomy*]
RB	Right Fullback [*Soccer*]
RB	Rigid Boat
RB	Rigid Body
Rb	Risicobank [*A publication*]
RB	Ritzaus Bureau [*Press agency*] [*Denmark*]
RB	Rivista Biblica [*Rome*] [*A publication*]
RB	Road Bend
RBT	Roast Beef [*Restaurant slang*]
Rb	Rock Bass [*Ichthyology*]
RB	Rocket Branch (AAG)
RB	Rohon-Beard (Cells) [*Neurology*]
RB	Rollback [*Telecommunications*] (TEL)
RB	Rollback Disability Claims [*Social Security Administration*] (OICC)
RB	Roller Bearing
RB	Roman-British
R & B	Room and Board
RB	Rose Bengal [*A dye*]
RB	Round Bobbin [*A publication*] (EAAP)
RB	Royal Burgh
RB	Rubber Band (ADA)
RB	Rubber Base [*Technical drawings*]
RB	Rubber Bearing (DS)
Rb	Rubidium [*Chemical element*]
RB	Run Back [*Typography*]
RB	Running Back [*Football*]
RB	Rural Bank (ADA)
RB	Russell Bodies [*Medicine*]
RB	Russet-Burbank Potato
RB	Syrian Arab Airlines [*Syrian Arab Republic*] [*ICAO designator*] (FAAC)
RBa	Barrington Public Library, Barrington, RI [*Library symbol*] [*Library of Congress*] (LCLS)
RBA	Rabat [*Morocco*] [*Seismograph station code, US Geological Survey*] (SEIS)
RBA	Rabat [*Morocco*] [*Airport symbol*] (OAG)
RBA	RADAR Beacon Antenna
RBA	Radial Blanket Assembly [*Nuclear energy*] (NRCH)
RBA	Radio Beacon Array
RBA	Radiobinding Assay [*Analytical chemistry*]
RBA	Raisin Bargaining Association (EA)
RBA	Ranger Battalions Association (EA)
RBA	Recovery Beacon Antenna [*NASA*] (KSC)
RBA	Reentry Body Assembly
RBA	Rehoboth Baster Association [*Namibia*] (PPW)
RBA	Relative Binding Affinity [*Chemistry*]
RBA	Relative Byte Address [*Data processing*] (MCD)
RBA	Religious Booksellers Association (EA)
RBA	Rescue Breathing Apparatus
RBA	Reserve Bank Bulletin [*Database*] [*Australia*]
RBA	Retail Bakers of America (EA)
RBA	Retail, Book, Stationery, and Allied Trades Employees' Association [*A union*] [*British*]
RBA	Revista de Bellas Artes [*A publication*]
RBA	Revue Belge d'Archeologie et d'Histoire de l'Art [*A publication*]
RBA	Roadside Business Association (EA)
RBA	Rotary Beam Antenna
RBA	Rotor Blade Antenna
RBA	Royal Brunei Airlines (DS)
RBA	Royal Society of British Architects
RBA	Royal Society of British Artists
RBAA	Religious Booksellers Association of Australia
RBAA	Revue Belge d'Art et d'Archeologie [*A publication*]
RBAADT...	Ain Shams University. Faculty of Agriculture. Research Bulletin [*A publication*]
RBAAP......	Riverbank Army Ammunition Plant (AABC)
RBaB........	Barrington College, Barrington, RI [*Library symbol*] [*Library of Congress*] (LCLS)
RBAB........	Revue des Bibliotheques et des Archives de la Belgique [*A publication*]
RBACB.....	Revista Brasileira de Analises Clinicas [*A publication*]
RBAF........	Royal Belgian Air Force
RBAHA.....	Revue Belge d'Archeologie et d'Histoire de l'Art [*A publication*]
RBAL........	Reprocessing Building Analytical Laboratory [*Nuclear energy*] (NRCH)
RBAM	Revista. Biblioteca, Archivo, y Museo del Ayuntamiento de Madrid [*A publication*]
RBAMM ...	Revista. Biblioteca, Archivo, y Museo del Ayuntamiento de Madrid [*A publication*]

RBAN........	Rainier Bancorporation [*NASDAQ symbol*] (NQ)
R Bancaria ...	Revista Bancaria [*A publication*]
R Bancaria Bras ...	Revista Bancaria Brasileira [*A publication*]
R Banco Republ ...	Revista. Banco de la Republica [*A publication*]
RBAP........	Repetitive Bursts of Action Potential [*Electrophysiology*]
RBAPA.....	Revue du Bois et de Ses Applications [*A publication*]
RBArch.....	Revue Belge d'Archeologie et d'Histoire de l'Art [*A publication*]
RBArg.......	Revista Biblica con Seccion Liturgica [*Buenos Aires*] [*A publication*]
RBAUSC ...	Romanian Baptist Association of United States and Canada [*Inactive*] (EA)
RBA WWII ...	Ranger Battalions Association World War II (EA)
RBB	Reference Books Bulletin [*A publication*]
RBB	Revue Bibliographique Belge [*A publication*]
RBBB........	Right Bundle-Branch Block [*Cardiology*]
RBBRD......	Revista de Biblioteconomia de Brasilia [*A publication*]
RBBS	Remote Bulletin Board System [*For IBM computers*] [*Telecommunications*]
RBBSB	Right Bundle-Branch System Block [*Cardiology*]
RBBT........	Rebabbit
RBC	Radio Beam Communications
RBC	Radio Bureau of Canada
RBC	Rail-Borne Crane [*British*]
RBC	Reactive Bias Circuit (MCD)
RBC	Real Estate Brokerage Council (EA)
RBC	Red Badge of Courage (EA)
RBC	Red Blood Cell [*or Corpuscle*] [*Medicine*]
RBC	Red Blood Count [*Medicine*]
RBC	Redundant Battery Charger (KSC)
RBC	Regal-Beloit Corporation [*AMEX symbol*] (SPSG)
RBC	Regional Blood Center [*Red Cross*]
RBC	Regulations of British Columbia [*Attorney General's Ministry*] [*No longer available online*] [*Information service or system*] (CRD)
RBC	Remote Balance Control
RBC	Retortable Barrier Container [*For food*]
RBC	Return Beam Camera
RBC	Revista Bimestre Cubana [*A publication*]
RBC	Rhodesia Broadcasting Corporation
RBC	Rio Blanco [*Colorado*] [*Seismograph station code, US Geological Survey*] [*Closed*] (SEIS)
RBC	Roller Bearing Corporation (MCD)
RBC	Ropec Industries, Inc. [*Vancouver Stock Exchange symbol*]
RBC	Rotating Beam Ceilometer [*Aviation*]
RBC	Rotating Biological Contractors [*Processing equipment*]
RBC	Royal Bank of Canada [*UTLAS symbol*]
RBC	Royal British Colonial Society of Artists
RBCA........	Rhodes Bantam Class Association (EA)
RBCalb.....	Revista Biblica. Villa Calbada [*Argentina*] [*A publication*]
R du B Can ...	Revue. Barreau Canadien [*A publication*] (DLA)
RBCC........	Reentry Body Coordination Committee
RBCCW.....	Reactor Building Closed Cooling Water [*Nuclear energy*] (NRCH)
RBCM	Red Blood Cell Mass [*in circulation*]
RBCM	Reference Book of Corporate Managements [*Dun's Marketing Services*] [*Information service or system*] (CRD)
RBCN........	Rubicon Corp. [*Richardson, TX*] [*NASDAQ symbol*] (NQ)
RBCNO.....	Rotating Beam Ceilometer Inoperative [*Aviation*] (FAAC)
RBCO	Ryan, Beck & Company, Inc. [*West Orange, NJ*] [*NASDAQ symbol*] (NQ)
RBCPDG...	Canadian Forestry Service. Pacific Forest Research Centre. Report BC-X [*A publication*]
RBCR........	Reprocessing Building Control Room [*Nuclear energy*] (NRCH)
RBCS........	Radio Beam Communications Set
RBCS........	Reactor Building Cooling System [*Nuclear energy*] (NRCH)
RBCU	Reactor Building Cooling Unit [*Nuclear energy*] (NRCH)
RBCV........	Red Blood Cell Volume [*Hematology*]
RBCWS	Reactor Building Cooling Water System (IEEE)
RBD	Dallas, TX [*Location identifier*] [*FAA*] (FAAL)
RBD	Recurrent Brief Depression [*Psychology*] (ECON)
RBD	Refined, Bleached, and Deodorized [*Vegetable oil technology*]
RBD	Reliable Block Diagram (MCD)
RBD	REM [*Rapid Eye Movement*] Behavior Disorder [*Medicine*]
RBD	Reserve Bank of India. Bulletin [*A publication*]
RBD	Revista Bibliografica y Documental [*Madrid*] [*A publication*]
RBD	Rice Blast Disease [*Fungal disease of crop plants*]
RBD	Right Border of Dullness [*Cardiology*]
RBD	Rubbermaid, Inc. [*NYSE symbol*] (SPSG)
RBDE	RADAR Bright Display Equipment [*FAA*]
RBdeF.......	Revista Brasileira de Filosofia [*A publication*]
RBDI........	Revue Belge de Droit International [*A publication*]
RBDNRQ ..	Received but Did Not Return Questionnaire (AABC)
RBDP........	Rocket Booster Development Program [*Aerospace*] (AAG)
RBDS........	RADAR Bomb Directing Systems
RBE	Bassett, NE [*Location identifier*] [*FAA*] (FAAL)
RBE	Radiation Biological Equivalent
RBE	Red Ball Express [*Military*]
RBE	Relative Biological Effectiveness [*or Efficiency*] [*of stated types of radiation*]
RBE	Remote Batch Entry (CMD)

RBE .... Renabie Mines (1981) Ltd. [*Toronto Stock Exchange symbol*]
RBE .... Replacement Battery Equipment
RBE .... Review of Business and Economic Research [*A publication*]
RBEB........ Ribbon Bridge Erection Boat   (MCD)
RBEC........ Roller Bearing Engineers Committee   (EA)
RBEDT....... Reactor Building Equipment Drain Tank [*Nuclear energy*]   (NRCH)
R Belge Archeol ... Revue Belge d'Archeologie et d'Histoire de l'Art [*A publication*]
R Belge Dr Int ... Revue Belge de Droit International [*A publication*]
R Belge Droit Internat ... Revue Belge de Droit International [*A publication*]
R Belge Mus ... Revue Belge de Musicologie [*A publication*]
R Belge Musicol ... Belgisch Tijdschrift voor Muziek-Wetenschap/Revue Belge de Musicologie [*A publication*]
R Belge Philol & Hist ... Revue Belge de Philologie et d'Histoire [*A publication*]
R Belge Securite Soc ... Revue Belge de Securite Sociale [*A publication*]
R Belge Secur Soc ... Revue Belge de Securite Sociale [*A publication*]
RBelPhH ... Revue Belge de Philogogie et d'Histoire [*A publication*]
RBen .... Revue Benedictine [*A publication*]
RB/ER .... Reduced Blast/Enhanced Radiation
RBER......... Review of Business and Economic Research [*A publication*]
RBESI....... Reactor Building Exhaust System Isolation [*Nuclear energy*]   (NRCH)
RBF........... Radial Basis Function [*Mathematics*]
RBF........... Red Lake Buffalo Resources Ltd. [*Toronto Stock Exchange symbol*]
RBF........... Regional Blood Flow [*Physiology*]
RBF........... Remote Batch Facility
RBF........... Renal Blood Flow [*Medicine*]
RBF........... Retarded Bomb Fuze
RBF........... Revista Brasileira de Filosofia [*A publication*]
RBF........... Revista Brasileira de Folclore [*A publication*]
RBF........... Roberson, Fred, Louisville KY [*STAC*]
RBFC........ Razzy Bailey Fan Club   (EA)
RBFC........ Retract Before Firing Contractor   (NG)
RBFI......... Revista Brasileira de Filologia [*A publication*]
RBFI......... Richard Barrie Fragrances, Inc. [*NASDAQ symbol*]   (NQ)
RBFilol...... Revista Brasileira de Filologia [*A publication*]
RBFPP...... Rocket Booster Fuel Pod Pickup   (MUGU)
RBFSA ...... Revista Brasileira de Fisica [*A publication*]
RBFT........ Romanian Bank of Foreign Trade   (IMH)
RBG .... British Guiana Reports of Opinions [*A publication*]   (DLA)
RBG .... Ransburg Corp. [*AMEX symbol*]   (SPSG)
RBG .... Right Buccal Ganglion [*Dentistry*]
RBG .... Roseburg, OR [*Location identifier*] [*FAA*]   (FAAL)
RBGCA...... Revista Brasileira de Geociencias [*A publication*]
RBGd........ Rocznik Biblioteki Gdanskiej Pan [*A publication*]
RBGED3.... Brazilian Journal of Genetics [*A publication*]
RBGS........ Radio Beacon Guidance System   (AAG)
RBH .... Regimental Beachhead [*Army*]
RBH .... Royal Bucks Hussars [*British military*]   (DMA)
RBH .... Rutherford Birchard Hayes [*US president, 1822-1893*]
RBHA .... Rotor Blade Homing Antenna
RBHB .... Red and Black Horizontal Bands [*Navigation markers*]
RBHC .... Regional Bell Holding Co.   (BYTE)
RBHGPV... Rheinische Beitraege und Hilfsbuecher zur Germanischen Philologie und Volkskunde [*A publication*]
RBHPC...... Rutherford B. Hayes Presidential Center   (EA)
RBHPF...... Reactor Building Hydrogen Purge Fan   (IEEE)
RBHS........ Reactor Building Heating System [*Nuclear energy*]   (NRCH)
RBI........... Rabi [*Fiji*] [*Airport symbol*]   (OAG)
RBI........... RADAR Blip Identification Message
RBI........... Radio Berlin International
RBI........... Railway Benevolent Institution [*British*]
RBI........... Range Bearing Indicator   (MCD)
RBI........... RB Industries, Inc. [*NYSE symbol*]   (SPSG)
RBI........... Recherches Bibliques [*A publication*]
RBI........... Reply by Indorsement
RBi........... Revue Biblique [*A publication*]
RBI........... Revue Biblique Internationale [*A publication*]
RBI........... Ripple-Blanking Input   (IEEE)
RBI........... Rivista Biblica Italiana [*Rome*] [*A publication*]
RBI........... Root Beer Institute [*Defunct*]
RBI........... Runs Batted In [*Baseball*]
RBIB........ Reserve Bank of India. Bulletin [*Bombay*] [*A publication*]
RBib........ Revue Biblique [*A publication*]
RBibIT....... Rivista Biblica Italiana [*Rome*] [*A publication*]
RBibl....... Revue des Bibliotheques [*A publication*]
R Bibl .... Revue Biblique [*A publication*]
R Bible .... Revue Biblique [*A publication*]
R Biblio Brasilia ... Revista de Biblioteconomia de Brasilia [*A publication*]
R Bibl Nac (Cuba) ... Revista. Biblioteca Nacional de Cuba [*A publication*]
RBiCalz...... Revista Biblica. Rafael Calzada [*Argentina*] [*A publication*]   (BJA)
RBIF .... Red Basic Intelligence File   (MCD)
RBilt......... Rivista Biblica Italiana [*Rome*] [*A publication*]
RBILA .... Rivista di Biologia [*A publication*]
RBIMBZ ... Bio-Mathematics [*A publication*]

R Bimestr Inform Banque Maroc Com Ext ... Revue Bimestrielle d'Informations. Banque Marocaine du Commerce Exterieur [*A publication*]
RBJ............ Rebun [*Japan*] [*Airport symbol*] [*Obsolete*]   (OAG)
RBJ............ Tucson, AZ [*Location identifier*] [*FAA*]   (FAAL)
RBK .... RBK NT Corp. [*Toronto Stock Exchange symbol*]
RBK .... Reebok International Ltd. [*NYSE symbol*]   (SPSG)
RBK .... Right Bank
RBK & C...... Royal Borough of Kensington and Chelsea [*England*]
RBKr......... Rocznik Biblioteki Pan w Krakowie [*A publication*]
R Bk Rel...... Review of Books and Religion [*A publication*]
RBL........... Radiation Biology Laboratory [*Smithsonian Institution*]
RBL........... Range and Bearing Launch [*Navy*]   (CAAL)
RBL........... Rat Basophilic Leukemia [*Cell line*]
RBL........... Rebroadcast Link [*Aerial*]
RBL........... Red Bluff, CA [*Location identifier*] [*FAA*]   (FAAL)
RBL........... Reid's Base Line [*Neuroanatomy*]
RBL........... Resource Based Learning   (ADA)
RBL........... Revista Brasileira de Linguistica [*A publication*]
RBL........... Revue Bleue [*A publication*]
RBL........... Rifled Breech-Loading [*Gun*]
RBL........... Right Buttock Line   (MCD)
RBL........... Rio Blanco Resources Limited [*Vancouver Stock Exchange symbol*]
RBL........... Royal British Legion [*British military*]   (DMA)
RBL........... Rubblestone [*Technical drawings*]
RBL........... Ruble [*Monetary unit*] [*USSR*]
RBL........... Ruch Biblijny i Liturgiczny   (BJA)
R Black Pol Econ ... Review of Black Political Economy [*A publication*]
R Black Pol Economy ... Review of Black Political Economy [*A publication*]
RBLC......... Renaissance Business and Law Center, Inc. [*Detroit, MI*]   (TSSD)
RBLI......... Rassegna Bibliografica della Letteratura Italiana [*A publication*]
RBLL......... Revista Brasileira de Lingua e Literatura [*A publication*]
RBLR......... Red-Banded Leaf Roller [*Entomology*]
RBLS......... River Bend Library System [*Library network*]
RBM .... Range Betting Method
RBM .... Real-Time Batch Monitor [*Xerox Corp.*]
RBM .... Regional Bone Mass
R-B-M...... Reinforced Brick Masonry
RBM .... Remote Batch Module
RBM .... Resistance to Bending Moment [*Automotive engineering*]
RBM .... Retractor Bulb Motoneuron [*Neurology*]
RBM .... Revue Belge de Musicologie [*A publication*]
RBM .... Rod-Block Monitor [*Nuclear energy*]   (NRCH)
RBMA .... Radiologists Business Managers Association   (EA)
RBME........ Richard [*Cragun*], Birgit [*Keil*], Marcia [*Haydee*], Egon [*Madsen*] [*In ballet title, "Initials RBME." Refers to the four starring dancers.*]
RBMECAB ... Regional Bureau of the Middle East Committee for the Affairs of the Blind [*An association*]   (EAIO)
RBML........ Rare Books and Manuscripts Librarianship [*A publication*]
RBML........ Repertorium fuer Biblische und Morgenlaendische Litteratur [*Leipzig*] [*A publication*]
RBMR .... Rotating Bubble Membrane Radiator [*Battelle Pacific Northwest Laboratories*]
RBMR .... Royal Brunei Malay Regiment   (DS)
RBM Rev Eur Biotechnol Med ... RBM. Revue Europeenne de Biotechnologie Medicale [*A publication*]
RBMS........ Rare Books and Manuscripts Section [*Association of College and Research Libraries*]
RBMT........ Retrospective Bibliographies on Magnetic Tape   (NASA)
RBMU .... Regions Beyond Missionary Union [*Later, Regions Beyond Missionary Union International*]   (EA)
RBMUDD ... Research Bulletin. Marathwada Agricultural University [*A publication*]
RBMus ...... Revue Belge de Musicologie [*A publication*]
RBN .... Brown University, Providence, RI [*OCLC symbol*]   (OCLC)
RBN .... PTS [*Predicasts*] Regional Business News [*Cleveland, OH*] [*Database*] [*Information service or system*]   (IID)
RBN .... Radiobeacon [*Maps and charts*]
RBN .... Random Block Number [*Data processing*]
R B v N...... Rechtskundig Blad voor het Notaris-Ambt [*A publication*]
R Bn .... Red Beacon [*Nautical charts*]
RBN .... Retrobulbar Neuritis [*Medicine*]
RBN .... Revista de Bibliografia Nacional [*Madrid*] [*A publication*]
RBN .... Revue Belge de Numismatique [*A publication*]
RBN .... Ribbon   (MSA)
RBN .... Rybnik [*Poland*] [*Seismograph station code, US Geological Survey*]   (SEIS)
RBNC .... Republic Bancorp, Inc. [*NASDAQ symbol*]   (NQ)
RBNC .... Revista. Biblioteca Nacional de Cuba [*A publication*]
RBNH........ Revista. Biblioteca Nacional de Cuba [*A publication*]
RBNH........ Rockingham Bancorp [*NASDAQ symbol*]   (NQ)
RBNK .... Regent Bancshares Corp. [*NASDAQ symbol*]   (NQ)
RBNS........ Revue Belge de Numismatique et de Sigillographie [*A publication*]
R B Num .... Revue Belge de Numismatique et de Sigillographie [*A publication*]
RBO .... Relationship by Objective [*Management technique*]
RBO .... Ripple-Blanking Output   (IEEE)

RBO............ Russian Brotherhood Organization of the United States of America
RBOA........ Richardson Boat Owners Association (EA)
RBOBDY... Bardsey Observatory Report [*A publication*]
RBOC........ Rapid Bloom Offboard Chaff [*Navy ship system*]
RBOC........ Regional Bell Operating Company
RBOF........ Receiving Basin for Off-Site Fuel [*Nuclear energy*]
RBOK........ Rinderpest Bovine Old Kabete [*A virus*]
R Bolsa Comer Rosario ... Revista. Bolsa de Comercio de Rosario [*A publication*]
RBOT .... Robotics Information [*EIC/Intelligence, Inc.*] [*Information service or system*] (IID)
R Bot Garden Edinb Notes ... Royal Botanical Garden of Edinburgh. Notes [*A publication*]
R Bot Gard (Kew) Notes Jodrell Lab ... Royal Botanic Gardens (Kew). Notes from the Jodrell Laboratory [*A publication*]
RBOUSA... Russian Brotherhood Organization of the USA (EA)
RBP............ Raba Raba [*Papua New Guinea*] [*Airport symbol*] (OAG)
RBP............ Ratio Balance Panel
RBP............ Ration Breakdown Point [*Military*] (AABC)
RBP............ Reactor Building Protection [*Nuclear energy*] (NRCH)
RBP............ Registered Business Programmer [*Offered earlier by Data Processing Management Association, now discontinued*] (IEEE)
RBP............ Retinol-Binding Protein [*Biochemistry*]
RBP............ Retractable Bow Propeller
RBP............ Return Battery Pack (KSC)
RBP............ Riboflavin-Binding Protein [*Biochemistry*]
RBP............ Ribose Binding Protein [*Biochemistry*]
RBP............ Rocket Branch Panel (AAG)
RBP............ RUBISCO [*Ribulosebisphosphate Carboxylase/Oxygenase*] Binding Protein [*Biochemistry*]
RBPA....... Royal Bank of Pennsylvania [*NASDAQ symbol*] (NQ)
RBPC........ Revised Behavior Problem Checklist [*Test*]
RBPCA ...... Rare Breeds Poultry Club of America (EA)
RBPCase.... Ribulosebisphosphate Carboxylase [*Also, RUBISCO*] [*An enzyme*]
RBPD........ Religious Book Publishing Division [*of Association of American Publishers*] [*Superseded by RPG*]
RBPh .... Revue Belge de Philologie et d'Histoire [*A publication*]
RBPhil .... Revue Belge de Philologie et d'Histoire [*A publication*]
RBPMA..... Revue Belge de Pathologie et de Medecine Experimentale [*A publication*]
RBPP .... Rotor Burst Protection Program [*NASA*]
RBQ .... Revue de la Banque [*Bruxelles*] [*A publication*]
RBQ .... Rurrenabaque [*Bolivia*] [*Airport symbol*] (OAG)
RBQSA ...... Revista Brasileira de Quimica (Sao Paulo) [*A publication*]
RBques....... Revue des Bibliotheques [*A publication*]
RBR .... RADAR Boresight Range (KSC)
RBR .... Rambler Exploration [*Vancouver Stock Exchange symbol*]
RBR .... Refracted Bottom-Reflected Ray
RBR .... Renegotiation Board Regulation [*or Ruling*]
RBr............. Revista Brasiliense [*A publication*]
RBR .... Ricerche Bibliche e Religiose [*A publication*]
RBR .... Rio Branco [*Brazil*] [*Airport symbol*] (OAG)
RBr............. Rogers Free Library, Bristol, RI [*Library symbol*] [*Library of Congress*] (LCLS)
RBR .... Rotor Blade RADAR
RBR .... Rubber
rbr .... Rubricator [*MARC relator code*] [*Library of Congress*] (LCCP)
R Bras Ec ... Revista Brasileira de Economia [*A publication*]
R Bras Econ ... Revista Brasileira de Economia [*A publication*]
R Bras Estatistica ... Revista Brasileira de Estatistica [*A publication*]
R Bras Estud Pol ... Revista Brasileira de Estudos Politicos [*A publication*]
R Brasil Econ ... Revista Brasileira de Economia [*A publication*]
R Brasil Estatist ... Revista Brasileira de Estatistica [*A publication*]
R Brasil Estud Polit ... Revista Brasileira de Estudos Politicos [*A publication*]
R Brasil Geogr ... Revista Brasileira de Geografia [*A publication*]
R Brasil Polit Int ... Revista Brasileira de Politica Internacional [*A publication*]
R Bras Mercado Capitais ... Revista Brasileira de Mercado de Capitais [*A publication*]
R Bras Pol Internac ... Revista Brasileira de Politica Internacional [*A publication*]
RBRC......... RB Robot Corporation [*NASDAQ symbol*] (NQ)
RBrHi......... Bristol Historical and Preservation Society, Bristol, RI [*Library symbol*] [*Library of Congress*] (LCLS)
RBRI......... Reference Book Review Index [*A publication*]
RBRIZED ... Rubberized
RBRJ .... Revista Brasileira (Rio De Janeiro) [*A publication*]
RBRLA ...... Revue Bryologique et Lichenologique [*A publication*]
RBRRS ...... Rhythm and Blues Rock and Roll Society [*Later, RBRRSI*] (EA)
RBRRSI.... Rhythm and Blues Rock and Roll Society, Inc. (EA)
RBrRW ...... Roger Williams College, Bristol, RI [*Library symbol*] [*Library of Congress*] (LCLS)
RBRV........ Resource-Based Relative Value [*Health insurance*]
RBRVS ...... Resource-Based Relative Value Scale [*Medicare*]
R Bryol & Lichenol ... Revue Bryologique et Lichenologique [*A publication*]
RBS............ RADAR Beacon Sequencer
RBS............ RADAR Beacon System

RBS............ RADAR Beam Sharpening
RBS............ RADAR Bomb Scoring
RBS............ RADAR Bombardment System (NATG)
RBS............ RADAR Bombsight
RBS............ Random Barrage System [*Military*]
RBS............ Rare Books Section [*Association of College and Research Libraries*]
RBS............ Reactor Building Spray [*Nuclear energy*] (NRCH)
RBS............ Recoverable Booster System
RBS............ Reformer's Book Shelf [*A publication*]
RBS............ Regional Briefing Station
RBS............ Regulae Benedicti Studia [*A publication*]
RBS............ Remote Batch System
RBS............ Remote Battle System
RBS............ Research for Better Schools, Inc. [*Department of Education*] [*Philadelphia, PA*]
RBS............ River Bend Station [*Nuclear energy*] (NRCH)
RBS............ Roberts, IL [*Location identifier*] [*FAA*] (FAAL)
RBS............ Royal Society of British Sculptors
RBS............ Rutherford Backscattering Spectroscopy
RBSA......... [*Member of the*] Royal Birmingham Society of Artists [*British*]
RBSC .... RADAR Bomb Scoring Central (NG)
RBSc .... Royal Society of British Sculptors
RBSCD ...... Rare Book and Special Collections Division [*Library of Congress*]
RBSE .... RADAR Beam Sharpening Element
RBSEBR.... Radiologia [*Madrid*] [*A publication*]
rBSF........... Recombinant B-Cell Stimulatory Factor [*Biochemistry*]
RBSF .... Retail Branch Stores Forum (EA)
RBSL .... Regensburger Beitrage zur Deutschen Sprach- und Literaturwissenschaft [*A publication*]
RBSN........ Reaction Bonded Silicon Nitride [*Materials science and technology*]
RBSN........ Robeson Industries Corp. [*NASDAQ symbol*] (NQ)
RBSR........ Reprocessing Building (Cable) Spreading Room [*Nuclear energy*] (NRCH)
RBSRA ...... Red Berkshire Swine Record Association (EA)
RBSS .... Recoverable Booster Support System
RBSS .... Revue Belge de Securite Sociale [*A publication*]
RBST .... Rare Breeds Survival Trust [*British*]
RBST .... Remedial and Basic Skills Training (OICC)
RBSTARO ... Revue Belge de Statistique, d'Informatique, et de Recherche Operationnelle [*A publication*]
R & B Supp ... Remington and Ballinger's Code, Supplement [*1913*] [*A publication*] (DLA)
R v B S V .... Raad van Beroep. Sociale Verzekering [*A publication*]
RBT .... Rabbet [*Technical drawings*]
RBT .... Radial Beam Tube [*Electronics*]
RBT .... Rainbow Trout
RBT .... Random Breath Testing (ADA)
RBT .... Rational Behavior Therapy
RBT .... Rebate [*Technical drawings*]
RBT .... Rebuilt (DS)
RBT .... Remote Batch Terminal
RBT .... Resistance Bulb Thermometer
RBT .... Reviews in Biochemical Toxicology [*Elsevier Book Series*] [*A publication*]
RBT .... Ribbon Bridge Transporter (MCD)
RBT .... Ringback Tone [*Telecommunications*] (TEL)
RBT .... Rough Blanking Template (MCD)
RBT .... Rubber Tile [*Technical drawings*]
RBT .... Rutland Biotech Ltd. [*Vancouver Stock Exchange symbol*]
RBTA........ Road Builders Training Association (EA)
RBTE .... Replacement Battery Terminal Equipment
RBTL .... RADAR Beacon Tracking Level [*FAA*]
RBTNA....... Revista Brasileira de Tecnologia [*A publication*]
RBTS .... Rider Block Tagline System [*Military*] (CAAL)
RBTWT.... Radial Beam Traveling Wave Tube [*Electronics*]
RBU .... Buro und EDV. Zeitschrift fuer Buroorganisation und Datentechnik [*A publication*]
RBU .... Red Butte Canyon [*Utah*] [*Seismograph station code, US Geological Survey*] (SEIS)
Rbu............. Ribulose [*Biochemistry*]
RB Ue .... Revidierte Berner Uebereinkunft [*A publication*]
RBUPC...... Research in British Universities, Polytechnics, and Colleges [*Formerly, SRBUC*] [*British Library*]
R Bus & Econ Res ... Review of Business and Economic Research [*A publication*]
R Bus and Econ Research ... Review of Business and Economic Research [*A publication*]
R Bus St John's Univ ... Review of Business. St. John's University [*A publication*]
RBV .... Reactor Building Vent (IEEE)
RBV .... Relative Biological Value [*Food science*]
RBV .... Return Beam Vidicon [*Satellite camera*]
RBV .... Robbinsville, NJ [*Location identifier*] [*FAA*] (FAAL)
RBVC........ Return Beam Vidicon Camera
RBVI......... Reactor Building Ventilation Isolation [*Nuclear energy*] (NRCH)
RBVPRM .. Reactor Building Vent Process Radiation Monitor [*Nuclear energy*] (NRCH)

RBW .... RB & W Corp. [*Formerly, Russell, Burdsaw & Ward Corp.*] [*AMEX symbol*] (SPSG)
RBW .... Walterboro, SC [*Location identifier*] [*FAA*] (FAAL)
RBWCD9 .. Washington State University. Agricultural Research Center. Research Bulletin [*A publication*]
RBX .... Manteo, NC [*Location identifier*] [*FAA*] (FAAL)
Rby .... Ribitol [*or Ribityl*] [*Biochemistry*]
RBY .... Rotterdam Europoort Delta [*A publication*]
RBY .... Royal Bucks Yeomanry [*British military*] (DMA)
RBY .... Ruby [*Alaska*] [*Airport symbol*] (OAG)
RBY .... Ruby Resources Ltd. [*Vancouver Stock Exchange symbol*]
RBYC .... Royal Berkshire Yeomanry Cavalry [*British*] (ROG)
RBYOA ..... Rinsho Byori [*A publication*]
RBZ .... Rabat Zaers [*Morocco*] [*Seismograph station code, US Geological Survey*] (SEIS)
RBZ .... Rotterdam [*A publication*]
RBZ .... Rubidazone [*An antibiotic*]
RC .... Circular Radio Beacon
RC .... Congregation de Notre Dame de la Retraite au Cenacle [*Congregation of Our Lady of the Retreat in the Cenacle*] (EAIO)
RC .... Congregation of Our Lady of the Retreat in the Cenacle [*Roman Catholic women's religious order*] [*Italy*]
RC .... Cuba [*IYRU nationality code*] (IYR)
RC .... [*The*] Item Requested Has Been Rescinded. All Stock Has Been Destroyed. Copies Are Not Available [*Advice of supply action code*] [*Army*]
RC .... La Revue du Caire [*Cairo*] [*A publication*]
RC .... Missouri Revised Statutes [*1855*] [*A publication*] (DLA)
RC .... Nicholl, Hare, and Carrow's Railway Cases [*1835-55*] [*A publication*] (DLA)
RC .... Nondirectional Radio Beacon [*ITU designation*] (CET)
RC .... RADAR Computer (MCD)
RC .... RADAR Control (DEN)
RC .... Radio Car [*British*]
RC .... Radio Code Aptitude Area [*Military*]
R/C ...... Radio Command [*or Control*] (KSC)
RC .... Radio Compass
R/C ...... Radio Control [*British military*] (DMA)
RC .... Radix Complement [*Mathematics*]
R & C .... Rail and Canal
RC .... Railway Cases [*A publication*] (DLA)
RC .... Rainbow Coalition [*Named for the 1984 political campaign of Rev. Jesse Jackson*] [*Later, NRCI*] (EA)
RC .... Rainform Compressed (MCD)
R/C ...... Range Clearance [*NASA*] (KSC)
RC .... Range Command [*NASA*] (NASA)
RC .... Range Contractor [*NASA*] (KSC)
RC .... Range Control [*NASA*] (KSC)
RC .... Range Correction
RC .... Rapid Change (MCD)
RC .... Rapid Curing [*Asphalt grade*]
RC .... Rassemblement Congolais [*Congolese Rally*] [*Buakvu*]
RC .... Rate Center [*Telecommunications*] (TEL)
RC .... Rate of Change
R/C ...... Rate of Climb [*Aviation*]
RC .... Rate Command
R/C ...... Ratio Command (MCD)
RC .... Ray Control
RC .... Rayon and Cotton [*Freight*]
RC .... Reaction Center
RC .... Reaction Control
RC .... Reactor Cavity [*Nuclear energy*] (NRCH)
RC .... Reactor Compartment (MSA)
RC .... Reactor Coolant [*Nuclear energy*] (NRCH)
RC .... Read and Compute
RC .... Reader Code
RC .... Ready Calendar
RC .... Real Circuit
RC .... Rear Commodore [*Navy*] (NVT)
RC .... Rear Connection (MSA)
RC .... Rearwin Club (EA)
R & C .... Reasonable and Customary [*Refers to medical charges*] [*Insurance*]
RC .... Receipt
RC .... Receiver Card
RC .... Reception Center [*Army*]
RC .... Receptor-Chemoeffector [*Biochemistry*]
RC .... Recirculating Cooler
RC .... Recirculatory Air (AAG)
RC .... Reconnaissance Car [*British*]
R/C ...... Reconsign
RC .... Reconstruction Committee [*British*] [*World War II*]
RC .... Record Change [*or Changer*] (AAG)
RC .... Record Commissioners [*British*] (DLA)
RC .... Record Count [*Data processing*]
RC .... Recording Completing [*Trunk*] [*Telecommunications*] (TEL)
RC .... Recording Controller [*Nuclear energy*] (NRCH)
RC .... Records Check (AFM)
R & C .... Records and Control
R/C ...... Recovered

RC .... Recovery Controller [*NASA*] (MCD)
R/C ...... Recredited
RC .... Recruiting Center
RC .... Recurring Cost (NASA)
RC .... Red Cell [*or Corpuscle*] [*Hematology*]
RC .... Red China
RC .... Red Cross
RC .... Reduced Capability (MCD)
RC .... Reduced Cuing
RC .... Reels [*JETDS nomenclature*] [*Military*] (CET)
RC .... Reference Cavity
RC .... Reference Clock [*Telecommunications*] (TEL)
RC .... Referred Care [*Medicine*]
RC .... Reformed Church
RC .... Refrigerated Centrifuge
RC .... Regiment of Cavalry [*British military*] (DMA)
RC .... Regional Center
RC .... Regional Commandant [*Air Force*] [*British*]
RC .... Regional Commissioner [*Social Security Administration*]
RC .... Regional Council
RC .... Register of Copyrights [*US*]
RC .... Registered Check
RC .... Registered Criminologist
RC .... Registration Cases [*A publication*] (DLA)
RC .... Regulatory-Catalytic Unit [*Physiology*]
RC .... Regulatory Council [*FAA*] (MCD)
RC .... Rehabilitation Center
RC .... Rehabilitation Counselor
RC .... Reinforced Concrete [*Technical drawings*]
RC .... Rekishi Chiri [*A publication*]
RC .... Relative [*Force*] Cost (MCD)
RC .... Relative Covariance [*Statistics*]
RC .... Relay Computer (BUR)
RC .... Release Card
RC .... Release Clause [*Real estate*]
RC .... Relief Claim
R & C .... Religion y Cultura [*A publication*]
R & C .... Religioni e Civitia [*A publication*]
RC .... Remington's Code [*A publication*] (DLA)
RC .... Remote Computer
RC .... Remote Concentrator
RC .... Remote Control
RC .... Rent Charge
RC .... Reopened Claim [*Unemployment insurance*] (OICC)
RC .... Reorder Cycle
RC .... Repair Costs [*Technical drawings*]
RC .... Replacement Cost [*Insurance*]
RC .... Reply Coupon [*Advertising*]
RC .... Report of Contact [*Social Security Administration*] (OICC)
RC .... Republic Airlines, Inc. [*ICAO designator*] (FAAC)
R/C ...... Request for Checkage [*Navy*]
RC .... Requirements Contract
RC .... Rescriptum [*Counterpart*] [*Latin*]
RC .... Research Center (IEEE)
RC .... Research-Cottrell, Inc. [*NYSE symbol*] (SPSG)
RC .... Reserve Components [*Military*]
RC .... Reserve Corps
RC .... Reserve Currency
RC .... Resin Coated (MCD)
RC .... Resistance-Capacitance
RC .... Resistance Coupled
R-C .... Resistor-Capacitor
RC .... Resolver Control
RC .... Resource Capital International Ltd. [*Toronto Stock Exchange symbol*]
RC .... Resources Council (EA)
RC .... Respiration Ceased [*Medicine*]
RC .... Respiratory Care [*Medicine*]
RC .... Respiratory Care [*A publication*]
RC .... Respiratory Center [*Medicine*]
RC .... Responsibility Center [*Air Force*] (AFM)
RC .... Rest Camp
R & C .... Rest and Convalescence (ADA)
RC .... Rest Cure
RC .... Restrictive Cardiomyopathy [*Cardiology*]
RC .... Retail Consortium [*British*]
RC .... Retention Catheter [*Medicine*]
r/c .... Return Cargo [*Shipping*] (DS)
RC .... Revenue Canada
RC .... Revenue Cutter [*Coast Guard*]
RC .... Reverse Course [*Aviation*]
RC .... Reverse Current
RC .... Reversing Gear Clutch (DS)
RC .... Review of the Churches [*A publication*]
R & C .... Review and Comment [*Aerospace*]
RC .... Review Cycle [*Military*] (AFIT)
RC .... Revised Code
RC .... Revista Contemporanea [*A publication*]
RC .... Revista Cubana [*A publication*]
RC .... Revue Celtique [*A publication*]
RC .... Revue Charlemagne [*A publication*]

RC .... Revue Critique [*A publication*]
RC .... Revue Critique de Legislation et de Jurisprudence de Canada [*A publication*]　(DLA)
RC .... Rib Cage [*Anatomy*]
RC .... Ribbon-Frame Camera　(MUGU)
RC .... Richard of Cashel [*Pseudonym used by Richard Laurence*]
RC .... Rider Club [*Commercial firm*]　(EA)
RC .... Right Center [*Position in soccer, hockey*]
RC .... Right Center [*A stage direction*]
RC .... Right Chest [*Medicine*]
RC .... Ring Counter
RC .... Risk Capital [*Finance*]
RC .... Rivista delle Colonie [*A publication*]
RC .... Road Reconnaissance　(FAAC)
RC .... Robert & Carriere [*France*] [*Research code symbol*]
RC .... Roll Channel
RC .... Roller Coating
RC .... Rolls Court [*Legal*] [*British*]
RC .... Roman Catholic
RC .... Root Canal [*Dentistry*]
rc .... Root Cast [*Archaeology*]
RC .... Rosin Core [*Foundry technology*]
RC .... Rosslyn Connecting Railroad Co. [*AAR code*]
RC .... Rotary Combustion [*Automobile*]
RC .... Rotation Control　(NASA)
RC .... Rough Cast　(ADA)
RC .... Rough Cutting [*Construction*]
R/C .... Round Corners [*Bookselling*]
RC .... Rounding Control [*Computer programming*]　(BYTE)
R/C .... Routing and Clipping　(MCD)
RC .... Royal Commission [*British*]
RC .... Royal Crest [*British*]
RC .... Royal Crown [*Soft drink brand*]
R/C .... Rubber-Capped
RC .... Rudder Club　(EA)
RC .... Rules Committee [*House of Representatives*]　(OICC)
RC .... Ruling Cases [*A publication*]　(DLA)
RC .... Ruperto-Carola [*A publication*]
RC .... Rural Coalition　(EA)
RC .... Rural Construction
RC .... Rushlight Club　(EA)
R & C .... Russell and Chesley's Nova Scotia Equity Reports [*A publication*]　(DLA)
R & C .... Russell and Chesley's Nova Scotia Reports [*A publication*]　(DLA)
RCA .... Alimentation Moderne. Revue de la Conserve [*A publication*]
RCA .... Rabbinical Council of America　(EA)
RCA .... RADAR Controlled Approach　(NVT)
RCA .... Radiative-Convective-Atmospheric [*Meteorology*]
RCA .... Radio Club of America　(EA)
RCA .... Radio Collectors of America　(EA)
RCA .... Radio Corp. of America　(NASA)
RCA .... Radiological Control Area　(MCD)
RCA .... Rapid City, SD [*Location identifier*] [*FAA*]　(FAAL)
RCA .... Rate Change Authorization　(NVT)
RCA .... Ration Cash Allowance [*British military*]　(DMA)
RCA .... Reach Cruising Altitude [*Aviation*]　(FAAC)
RCA .... Reaction Control Assembly
RCA .... Red Cell Aggregate [*or Aggregation*] [*Hematology*]
RCA .... Red Cross Act
RCA .... Reformed Church in America　(ROG)
RCA .... Remote Control Amplifier　(MCD)
RCA .... Renault Club of America　(EA)
RCA .... REO [*Rawson E. Olds*] Club of America　(EA)
RCA .... Replacement Cost Accounting　(ADA)
RCA .... Republican Communications Association　(EA)
RCA .... Request for Corrective Action　(AAG)
RCA .... Resident Care Aide
RCA .... Residential Care Alternatives
RCA .... Residential Care Association [*British*]
RCA .... Review and Concurrence Authority
RCA .... Revista Colombiana de Antropologia [*A publication*]
RCA .... Ricinus communis Agglutinin [*Immunology*]
RCA .... Right Coronary Artery [*Anatomy*]
RCA .... Riot Control Agent　(NVT)
RCA .... Rocket Cruising Association　(EA)
RCA .... Rodeo Cowboys Association [*Later, PRCA*]　(EA)
RCA .... Root Canal Anterior [*Dentistry*]
RCA .... Root Cause Analysis　(MCD)
RCA .... Royal Cambrian Academy [*British*]
RCA .... Royal Cambrian Academy of Art [*British*]
RCA .... Royal Canadian Academy
RCA .... Royal Canadian Academy of Arts
RCA .... Royal Canadian Army　(MCD)
RCA .... Royal Canadian Artillery
RCA .... Royal College of Art [*British*]
RCA .... Rozpravy Ceskoslovenske Akademie Ved [*A publication*]
RCA .... Soil and Water Resources Conservation Act [*1977*]
R-19/CA ... Rhodes 19 Class Association　(EA)
RCAA .... Rocket City Astronomical Association [*Later, VBAS*]　(EA)
RCAB......... Review and Concurrence Advisory Board

RCAC .... Radio Corporation of America Communications　(MCD)
RCAC .... Remote Computer Access Communications Service
RCAC .... Reserve Component Assistance Coordinator　(MCD)
RCAC .... Royal Canadian Armoured Corps
Rc Accad Lincei Cl di Sci Mor Stor Fil ... Rendiconti. Accademia Nazionale dei Lincei. Classe di Scienze Morali. Storiche e Filologiche [*A publication*]
RCACS ...... USREDCOM [*United States Readiness Command*] Command and Control System　(AABC)
RCADI....... Recueil des Cours. Academie de Droit International de La Haye [*A publication*]
RCADV ..... Reverse Course and Advise [*Aviation*]　(FAAC)
RCAE......... Royal Correspondence of the Assyrian Empire [*A publication*]　(BJA)
RCAEB...... RCA [*Radio Corporation of America*] Engineer [*A publication*]
RCA Eng.... RCA [*Radio Corporation of America*] Engineer [*A publication*]
RCAF........ Rail Cost Adjustment Factor [*Interstate Commerce Commission*]
RCAF........ Royal Canadian Air Force
RCAFA...... Revista Cafetalera [*Spain*] [*A publication*]
RCAFA...... Royal Canadian Air Force Association
RCAF(WD) ... Royal Canadian Air Force, Women's Division
RCAG .... Remote Center Air/Ground Facility [*NASA*]
RCAG .... Remote-Controlled Air-Ground Communication Site　(MCD)
RCAG .... Replacement Carrier Air Group [*Military*]　(AFIT)
RCAI........ Railroadiana Collectors Association Incorporated　(EA)
RCAJ .... Royal Central Asian Society. Journal [*A publication*]
R/CAL...... Resistance Calibration　(MCD)
RCal .... Revista Calasancia [*A publication*]
RCAls .... Revue Catholique d'Alsace [*A publication*]
RCALT ..... Reach Cruising Altitude [*Aviation*]　(FAAC)
RCam .... Revista Camoniana [*Sao Paulo*] [*A publication*]
RCamA ..... [*Member of the*] Royal Cambrian Academy [*Formerly, RCA*] [*British*]
RCAMC.... Royal Canadian Army Medical Corps
RCAN........ Recorded Announcement [*Telecommunications*]　(TEL)
RCan .... Revue Canonique [*A publication*]
R Canad-Amer Et Slaves ... Revue Canadienne-Americaine d'Etudes Slaves [*A publication*]
R Canad Biol ... Revue Canadienne de Biologie [*A publication*]
R Canad Et Afr ... Revue Canadienne des Etudes Africaines [*A publication*]
R Canad Geogr ... Revue Canadienne de Geographie [*A publication*]
R & Can Cas ... Railway and Canal Cases [*England*] [*A publication*]　(DLA)
R Can Dent Corps Q ... Royal Canadian Dental Corps. Quarterly [*A publication*]
R Can Etud Nationalisme ... Revue Canadienne des Etudes sur le Nationalisme [*A publication*]
R Can Sciences Info ... Revue Canadienne des Sciences de l'Information [*A publication*]
R & Can Tr ... Railway and Canal Traffic Cases [*England*] [*A publication*]　(DLA)
R & Can Tr Cas ... Railway and Canal Traffic Cases [*England*] [*A publication*]　(DLA)
RCAP........ Rural Community Assistance Program　(EA)
RCAPA...... Revista de Ciencia Aplicada [*A publication*]
RCAPC...... Royal Canadian Army Pay Corps
RCAPDD... Revista de Ciencias Agrarias [*A publication*]
RCAPDR... Revolutionary Council of the Algerian People's Democratic Republic
RCAPS ...... Roosevelt Center for American Policy Studies　(EA)
RCA R....... RCA [*Radio Corporation of America*] Review [*A publication*]
RCAR .... Religious Coalition for Abortion Rights　(EA)
RCARC...... RCA [*Radio Corporation of America*] Review [*A publication*]
RCA Rev .... RCA [*Radio Corporation of America*] Review [*A publication*]
RCAS........ Requirements for Close Air Support [*Army*]　(MCD)
RCAS........ Research Center for Advanced Study [*University of Texas at Arlington*] [*Research center*]　(RCD)
RCAS........ Reserve Component Automation System [*DoD*]
RCAS........ Royal Central Asian Society [*British*]
RCASC...... Royal Canadian Army Service Corps
RCAT........ Radio Code Aptitude Test
RCAT........ Radio-Controlled Aerial Target [*Military*]
RCAT........ Remote-Controlled Aerial Target　(NATG)
RCat.......... Revista de Catalunya [*A publication*]
RCAT........ Ridgetown College of Agricultural Technology [*Canada*]　(ARC)
RCA Tech Not ... RCA [*Radio Corporation of America*] Technical Notes [*A publication*]
RCA Tech Notes ... RCA [*Radio Corporation of America*] Technical Notes [*A publication*]
Rc Atti Accad Naz Lincei ... Rendiconti e Atti. Accademia Nazionale dei Lincei [*A publication*]
RCAV .... Rozpravy Ceskoslovenske Akademie Ved [*A publication*]
RCAVA...... Rozpravy Ceskoslovenske Akademie Ved. Rada Matematickych a Prirodnich Ved [*A publication*]
RCAY .... Gangshan [*China*] [*ICAO location identifier*]　(ICLI)
RCB .... Radiation Control Board　(AAG)
RCB .... Randomized Complete Block [*Statistical design*]
RCB .... Reactor Containment Building [*Nuclear energy*]　(NRCH)
RCB .... Ready Crew Building　(NATG)
RCB .... Reflection Coefficient Bridge
RCB .... Region Control Block [*Data processing*]　(BUR)

RCB .... Regular Commissions Board [*British military*] (DMA)
RCB .... Regulations of the Civil Aeronautics Board
RCB .... Releases Control Branch [*Edison, NJ*] [*Environmental Protection Agency*] (GRD)
RCB .... Remote Circuit Breaker (MCD)
RCB .... Remote Control Bandwidth
RCB .... Representative Church Body [*Ireland*] [*Church of England*]
RCB .... Requirements Control Board (MCD)
RCB .... Resource Control Block [*Data processing*] (IBMDP)
RCB .... Revista de Cultura Biblica [*Rio De Janeiro/Sao Paulo, Brazil*] [*A publication*]
RCB .... Revista de Cultura Brasilena [*A publication*]
RCB .... Richards Bay [*South Africa*] [*Airport symbol*] (OAG)
RCB .... Right Cornerback [*Football*]
RCB .... Root Canal Bicuspid [*Dentistry*]
RCB .... Rubber Control Board
RCBA........ Ratio Changers and Boosters Assembly (MCD)
RCBA........ Relative Basal Area of Conifer Species [*Ecology*]
RCBA........ Royal Crown Bottlers Association (EA)
RCBBDA... Revue de Cytologie et de Biologie Vegetales - La Botaniste [*A publication*]
RCBC........ Red Cross Blood Center
rCBF .... Regional Cerebral Blood Flow [*Medicine*]
RCBHT ..... Reactor Coolant Bleed Holdup Tank [*Nuclear energy*] (NRCH)
RCBI .... Brown [*Robert C.*] & Co., Incorporated [*NASDAQ symbol*] (NQ)
RCBIA ...... Revue Canadienne de Biologie [*A publication*]
RCBOA ..... Radiologia Clinica et Biologica [*A publication*]
RCBPEJ ... Reviews in Clinical and Basic Pharmacology [*A publication*]
RCBR........ Rotating Catalytic Basket Reactor [*Chemical engineering*]
RCBS........ Jinmen [*China*] [*ICAO location identifier*] (ICLI)
RCBT .... Reactor Coolant Bleed Tank [*Nuclear energy*] (NRCH)
RCBW .... Radiological-Chemical-Biological Warfare
RCC .... Belleville, IL [*Location identifier*] [*FAA*] (FAAL)
RCC .... International Society of Reply Coupon Collectors (EA)
RCC .... Rachel Carson Council (EA)
RCC .... Rack Clearance Center [*Association of American Publishers*]
RCC .... RADAR Control Clouds
RCC .... RADAR Control Computer (MCD)
RCC .... RADAR Control Console [*Military*] (CAAL)
RCC .... Radio Common Carrier
RCC .... Radio Common Channels
RCC .... Radio Communications Center
RCC .... Radiochemical Centre [*United Kingdom*] (NRCH)
RCC .... Radiological Control Center [*Army*]
RCC .... Rag Chewers' Club [*Amateur radio*]
R & CC ...... Railway and Canal Cases [*1835-54*] [*A publication*] (DLA)
RCC .... Range Commanders Council [*White Sands Missile Range*] (KSC)
RCC .... Range Communications Component (MCD)
RCC .... Range Control Center [*NASA*]
RCC .... Rape Crisis Center (EA)
RCC .... Ratio of Charges to Costs
RCC .... RCA Corporation Communications
RCC .... Re Capital Corporation [*AMEX symbol*] (SPSG)
RCC .... Reaction Control Center (KSC)
RCC .... Reactor Closed Cooling [*Nuclear energy*] (NRCH)
RCC .... Read Channel Continue
RCC .... Reader Common Contact
RCC .... Real-Time Computer Complex
RCC .... Recco Corp. [*Vancouver Stock Exchange symbol*]
RCC .... Receptor-Chemoeffector Complex [*Biochemistry*]
RCC .... Record Collectors' Club (EA)
R & CC ...... Recorder and Communications Control (NASA)
RCC .... Recovery Control Center
RCC .... Red Carpet Clubs [*United Airlines' club for frequent flyers*] (EA)
RCC .... Red Cross of Constantine (EA)
RCC .... Reduced Crude Conversion [*Petroleum refining*]
RCC .... Regional Control Center [*North American Air Defense*] (FAAC)
RCC .... Regional Coordination Committee [*Department of Health and Human Services*]
RCC .... Reinforced Carbon-Carbon (MCD)
RCC .... Relative Casein Content [*Food analysis*]
RCC .... Remote Center Compliance [*Data processing*]
RCC .... Remote Communications Central
RCC .... Remote Communications Complex
RCC .... Remote Communications Concentrator
RCC .... Remote Communications Console
RCC .... Remote Computer Center (MCD)
RCC .... Renal Cell Carcinoma [*Medicine*]
RCC .... Representative Church Council [*Episcopalian*]
RCC .... Rescue Control Center
RCC .... Rescue Coordination Center [*Coast Guard*]
RCC .... Rescue Crew Commander (AFM)
RCC .... Research Computing Center [*University of New Hampshire*] [*Research center*] (RCD)
RCC .... Reset Control Circuit
RCC .... Resistor Color Code (DEN)
RCC .... Resource Category Code [*Military*] (CAAL)

RCC .... Resource Control Center [*Military*] (AFIT)
RCC .... Resources for Community Change [*Defunct*] (EA)
RCC .... Reusable Carbon-Carbon (MCD)
RCC .... Revolutionary Command Council [*Iraq*] (PD)
RCC .... Revue des Cours et Conferences [*A publication*]
RCC .... Rio Carpintero [*Cuba*] [*Seismograph station code, US Geological Survey*] (SEIS)
R & CC...... Riot and Civil Commotion
RCC .... Riverside City College [*California*]
RCC .... Robotic Command Center [*Army*]
RCC .... Rochester Community College, Rochester, MN [*OCLC symbol*] (OCLC)
RCC .... Rockefeller Center Cable
RCC .... Rod Cluster Control [*Nuclear energy*] (NRCH)
RCC .... Roller-Compacted Concrete
RCC .... Roman Catholic Church
RCC .... Roman Catholic Church Curate (ROG)
RCC .... Rough Combustion Cutoff [*NASA*]
RCC .... Rubber Covered Cable (MSA)
RCC .... Rural Construction Cadre [*Military*]
RCC .... Russian Corps Combatants (EA)
R & C Ca .... Railway and Canal Cases [*England*] [*A publication*] (DLA)
RCCA .... Record Carrier Competition Act [*1981*]
RCCA .... Rickenbacker Car Club of America (EA)
RCCA .... Rod Cluster Control Assembly [*Nuclear energy*] (NRCH)
RCCA .... Rogers Cablesystems of America, Inc. [*NASDAQ symbol*] (NQ)
RCCA .... Rough Combustion Cutoff Assembly [*NASA*] (KSC)
RCCA .... Route Capacity Control Airline (DS)
R & C Cas .. Railway and Canal Cases [*England*] [*A publication*] (DLA)
RCCB........ Remote Control Circuit Breaker (NASA)
RCCC....... Range Communications Control Center [*Military*] (MCD)
RCCC....... Regional Communications Control Center [*FAA*] (FAAC)
RCCC....... Regular Common Carrier Conference (EA)
RCCC....... Reserve Component Career Counselor [*Military*] (AABC)
RCCC....... Reserve Component Coordination Council (MCD)
RC/CC...... Responsibility Center/Cost Center [*Military*] (AFIT)
RCCC....... Return Critical Control Circuit
RCCC....... Royal Caledonia Curling Club
RCCC....... Royal Commission on Corporate Concentration [*Canada*]
RCCC....... Royal Curling Club of Canada
RCCE....... Regional Congress of Construction Employers (EA)
RC-CE...... Revenue Canada, Customs and Excise
RCCE....... Rotating Cylinder-Collector Electrode [*Electrochemistry*]
RCCES ...... Research Centre for Canadian Ethnic Studies [*University of Calgary*] [*Research center*] (RCD)
RCCF....... Reserve Components Contingency Force [*Military*]
RCCFB ..... Revista CENIC [*Centro Nacional de Investigaciones Cientificas*]. Ciencias Fisicas [*Cuba*] [*A publication*]
RCCh .... Roman Catholic Chaplain [*Navy*] [*British*]
RCCH .... Roman Catholic Church
RCCL........ Royal Caribbean Cruise Line
RCCLS ..... Resource Center for Consumers of Legal Services [*Later, NRCCLS*] (EA)
RCCM .... Research Council for Complementary Medicine [*British*] (IRUK)
RCCM .... Rivista di Cultura Classica e Medioevale [*A publication*]
RCCMA...... Rivista Critica di Clinica Medica [*A publication*]
RCCMEF .. Revista Costarricense de Ciencias Medicas [*A publication*]
RCC/MG... Range Commanders Council Meteorological Group [*White Sands Missile Range*]
RCCO .... RADAR Control Console Operator [*Military*] (CAAL)
RCCOW .... Return Channel Control Orderwire [*Military*] (CAAL)
RCCP........ Recorder and Communications Control Panel (NASA)
RCCP........ Reinforced Concrete Culvert Pipe [*Technical drawings*]
RCCPLD ... Resistance-Capacitance Coupled
RC & CR .... Revenue, Civil, and Criminal Reporter [*Calcutta*] [*A publication*] (DLA)
RCCRA...... Rough Combustion Cutoff Replaceable Assembly [*NASA*] (KSC)
RCCS........ Rate Command Control System (AAG)
RCCS........ Reactor Cavity Cooling System [*Nuclear energy*]
RCCS........ Revista Catolica de las Cuestiones Sociales [*A publication*]
RCC & S .... Riots, Civil Commotions, and Strikes [*Insurance*]
RCCS........ Royal Canadian Corps of Signals
RCCUS...... Republican Citizens Committee of the United States (EA)
RCD.......... RADAR Cloud Detection Report [*Meteorology*] (FAAC)
RCD.......... Rapid City [*South Dakota*] [*Seismograph station code, US Geological Survey*] (SEIS)
RCD.......... Rassemblement Constitutionnel Democratique [*Tunisia*] [*Political party*] (ECON)
RCD.......... Received
RCD.......... Receiver-Carrier Detector
RCD.......... Reconnaissance Cockpit Display
RCD.......... Record
RCD.......... Redox Chemiluminescence Detector [*Instrumentation*] [*Sievers*]
RCD.......... Reduced Crude Desulfurization [*Petroleum refining*]
RCD.......... Regent's Canal Dock [*British*]
RCD.......... Reinforcement Control Depot [*Air Force*]
RCD.......... Relative Cardiac Dullness [*Medicine*]

RCD........... Research Centers Directory [*A publication*]
RC & D ...... Resource Conservation and Development [*Department of Agriculture*]
RCD........... Retrofit Configuration Drawing (MCD)
RCD........... Reverse Circulation Drilling [*Mining technology*]
RCD........... Reverse Current Device [*Electronics*] (MSA)
RCD........... Rock Coring Device
RCD........... Rocket Cushioning Device (NG)
RCD........... Route Control Digit [*Telecommunications*] (TEL)
RCD........... Royal Canadian Dragoons [*Military*]
RCD........... Rural Civil Defense
RCD........... Sisters of Our Lady of Christian Doctrine [*Roman Catholic religious order*]
RCDA .... Religion in Communist Dominated Areas [*A publication*]
RCDA .... Research Career Development Awards [*Department of Health and Human Services*]
RCDC .... Pingdong (South) [*China*] [*ICAO location identifier*] (ICLI)
RCDC .... RADAR Course-Directing Central [*Military*]
RCDC .... RADAR Course-Directing Control (MUGU)
RCDC .... Radiation Chemistry Data Center [*Notre Dame, IN*] [*Department of Commerce*]
RCDC .... Ross Cosmetics Distribution Centers, Inc. [*NASDAQ symbol*] (NQ)
RCDC .... Royal Canadian Dental Corps
RCDCB..... Regional Civil Defense Coordination Boards [*DoD*] (AABC)
RCDD........ Registered Communications Distribution Designer [*Designation awarded by Building Industry Consulting Service International*] (TSSD)
RCDEP...... Rural Civil Defense Education Program
RCDG........ Recording (MSA)
RCDHS ..... Rehabilitation and Chronic Disease Hospital Section [*American Hospital Association*] (EA)
RCDI .... Longtan [*China*] [*ICAO location identifier*] (ICLI)
RCDIP....... Revue Critique de Droit International Prive [*A publication*]
RCDIW...... Royal Commission on the Distribution of Income and Wealth [*British*]
RCDMB .... Regional Civil and Defense Mobilization Boards
RCDMS..... Reliability Central Data Management System [*Air Force*] (DIT)
RCDNA ..... RADAR Cloud Detection Report Not Available [*Meteorology*] (FAAC)
RCDNE ..... RADAR Cloud Detection Report No Echoes Observed [*Meteorology*] (FAAC)
RCDNO..... RADAR Cloud Detector Inoperative Due to Breakdown Until [*Followed by time*] [*Meteorology*] (FAAC)
RCDOM.... RADAR Cloud Detector Inoperative Due to Maintenance Until [*Followed by time*] [*Meteorology*] (FAAC)
RCDP........ Record Parallel (MCD)
RCDR .... Recorder (KSC)
RCDS......... Records
RCDS......... Royal College of Defence Studies [*British*]
RCDS......... Rural Community Development Service [*Abolished, 1970*] [*Department of Agriculture*]
RCDT .... Reactor Coolant Drain Tank [*Nuclear energy*] (NRCH)
RCE .... Radio Communications Equipment
RCE .... Railway Construction Engineer [*British military*] (DMA)
RCE .... Rapid Changing Environment (AAG)
RCE .... Rapid Circuit Etch
RC de l'E... Rapports de la Cour de l'Echiquier [*Exchequer Court Reports*] [*Canada*] [*A publication*] (DLA)
RCE .... Reaction Control Engine
RCE .... Reactor Compatibility Experiment [*Nuclear energy*] (NRCH)
rce............. Recording Engineer [*MARC relator code*] [*Library of Congress*] (LCCP)
RCE .... Reece Corp. [*NYSE symbol*] (SPSG)
RCE .... Reentry Control Electronics
RCE .... Reliability Control Engineering (AAG)
RCE .... Religious of Christian Education [*Roman Catholic women's religious order*]
RCE .... Remote Control Equipment (DIT)
RCE .... Repertoire Canadien sur l'Education [*See also CEI*] [*A publication*]
RCE .... Reviews in Cancer Epidemiology [*Elsevier Book Series*] [*A publication*]
RCE .... Revue Catholique des Eglises [*A publication*]
RCE .... Rice University, Fondren Library, Houston, TX [*OCLC symbol*] (OCLC)
RCE .... Roche Harbor [*Washington*] [*Airport symbol*] (OAG)
RCE .... Ross Consumer Electronics [*British*]
RCE .... Royal Canadian Engineers
RCE .... Union Restaurants Collectifs Europeens [*European Catering Association*] (EAIO)
RCEA....... Recreational Coach and Equipment Association [*Later, MHI*]
RCEA....... Research Council Employees' Association [*Canada*]
RCEAC...... Regional Civil Emergency Advisory Committee [*Formerly, JRCC*] [*Civil defense*]
RCEE........ Revista. Centro de Estudios Extemoenos [*A publication*]
RCEEA...... Radio Communications and Electronic Engineers Association
RCEH .... Revista Canadiense de Estudios Hispanicos [*A publication*]
RCEI......... Range Communications Electronics Instructions [*NASA*] (KSC)

RCEI......... Revista Canaria de Estudios Ingleses [*A publication*]
RCel.......... Revue Celtique [*A publication*]
RCEME..... Royal Canadian Electrical and Mechanical Engineers
RCENDR... Revista Colombiana de Entomologia [*A publication*]
R Centroam Econ ... Revista Centroamericana de Economia [*A publication*]
RCEP........ Royal Commission on Environmental Pollution [*British*]
RCEP........ Rural Concentrated Employment Program [*Department of Labor*]
RCERA...... Religious Committee for the ERA [*Equal Rights Amendment*] (EA)
RCERB..... Ricerche di Termotecnica [*A publication*]
RCERIP.... Reserve Component Equipment Readiness Improvement Program [*Military*] (AABC)
RCEUSA ... Romanian Catholic Exarchy in the United States of America (EA)
RCEVH ..... Research Centre for the Education of the Visually Handicapped [*University of Birmingham*] [*British*] (CB)
RCF.......... Radcliffe Resources Ltd. [*Vancouver Stock Exchange symbol*]
RCF.......... Radiocommunication Failure Message [*Aviation*]
RCF.......... Ratio Correction Factor
RCF.......... Reader's Comment Form (IBMDP)
RCF.......... Recall Finder
RCF.......... Regenerated Cellulose Film [*Organic chemistry*]
RCF.......... Relative Centrifugal Force
RCF.......... Relative Cumulative Frequency
RCF.......... Remain on Company Frequency [*Aviation*] (FAAC)
RCF.......... Remote Call Forwarding [*Bell System*]
RCF.......... Repair Cost Factor [*Navy*]
RCF.......... Repair Cycle Float [*Military*] (AABC)
RCF.......... Retail Computer Facilities
RCF.......... Review of Contemporary Fiction [*A publication*]
RCF.......... Revista Colombiana de Folclor [*A publication*]
RCF.......... Revue du Clerge Francais [*A publication*]
RCF.......... River Conservation Fund [*Later, ARCC*] (EA)
RCF.......... Rosicrucian Fellowship (EA)
RCF.......... Rotating Cylinder Flap
RCF.......... Royal Carmarthen Fusiliers [*British military*] (DMA)
RCFA........ Religious Communities for the Arts (EA)
RCFA........ Royal Canadian Field Artillery [*Military*]
RCFC........ Ray Coble Fan Club [*Defunct*] (EA)
RCFC........ Reactor Containment Fan Cooler [*Nuclear energy*] (NRCH)
RCFC........ Ron Craddock Fan Club (EA)
RCFC........ Rosanne Cash Fan Club (EA)
RCFC........ Roy Clark Fan Club (EA)
RCFC........ Roy Clayborne Fan Club (EA)
RCFC(U).. Reactor Core Fan Cooling (Unit) (IEEE)
RCFF .... Repair Cycle Float Factor (MCD)
RCFN........ Taidong/Fengnian [*China*] [*ICAO location identifier*] (ICLI)
RCFNA...... Revista. Real Academia de Ciencias Exactas, Fisicas, y Naturales de Madrid [*A publication*]
RCFP .... Reporters Committee for Freedom of the Press (EA)
RCFR........ Red Cross Field Representative
RCFR........ Royal Canadian Fleet Reserve
RCFS .... Jiadong [*China*] [*ICAO location identifier*] (ICLI)
RCFT .... Randomized Controlled Field Trial [*Statistics*]
RCFU........ Rotary Carton Feed Unit
RCFZ........ Fengshan [*China*] [*ICAO location identifier*] (ICLI)
RCG .... Radiation Concentration Guide [*Formerly, MPC*]
RCG .... Radio Command Guidance (AAG)
RCG .... Radioactivity Concentration Guide (KSC)
rCG .... Rat Chorionic Gonadotropin
RCG .... Reaction Cured Glass [*Ceramic technology*]
RCG .... Receiving (AAG)
RCG .... Recommended Concentration Guide [*Nuclear energy*] (NRCH)
RCG .... Restricted Categorical Grammar
RCG .... Resurgens Communications Group [*AMEX symbol*] (SPSG)
RCG .... Retail Credit Group [*British*]
RCG .... Reverberation Control of Gain
RCG .... Revue du Chant Gregorien [*A publication*]
RCG .... Right Cerebral Ganglion [*Anatomy*]
RCGA .... Royal Canadian Garrison Artillery [*Military*]
RCGD........ Research Center for Group Dynamics [*University of Michigan*] [*Research center*] (RCD)
RCGI......... Ludao [*China*] [*ICAO location identifier*] (ICLI)
RCGJA...... Royal College of General Practitioners. Journal [*A publication*]
RCGM....... Reactor Cover Gas Monitor [*Nuclear energy*] (NRCH)
RCGM....... Taoyuan [*China*] [*ICAO location identifier*] (ICLI)
RCGP........ Royal College of General Practitioners [*British*]
rCGRP....... Rat Calcitonin Gene-Related Peptide [*Biochemistry*]
RCGS........ RADAR Correlation Guidance Study
RCH .... Reach (FAAC)
RCh........... Revue Charlemagne [*A publication*]
RCH........... Rich Resources Ltd. [*Vancouver Stock Exchange symbol*]
RCH........... Riohacha [*Colombia*] [*Airport symbol*] (OAG)
RCH........... Rotary Clothes Hoist (ADA)
RCH........... Rural Cooperative Housing
RCHA....... Rachel Carson Homestead Association (EA)
RCHA....... Royal Canadian Horse Artillery
R Ch Com Franc Canada ... Revue. Chambre de Commerce Francaise au Canada [*A publication*]

R Ch Comm Marseille ... Revue. Chambre de Commerce de Marseille [*A publication*]
RCHCS ...... Regenerable Carbon Dioxide and Humidity Control System (NASA)
RCHE .... Recherche [*A publication*]
RCHF .... Richfood Holdings, Inc. [*NASDAQ symbol*] (NQ)
RCHG .... Reduced Charge (AAG)
RCHG .... Revista Chilena de Historia y Geografia [*A publication*]
RCHI .... Rauch Industries, Inc. [*NASDAQ symbol*] (NQ)
R Chil Hist Geogr ... Revista Chilena de Historia y Geografia [*A publication*]
R Ch J .... Rencontre. Chretiens et Juifs [*A publication*]
RChL .... Revista Chilena de Literatura [*A publication*]
RCHL .... Revue Critique d'Histoire et de Litterature [*A publication*]
RCHM .... Royal Commission on Historical Monuments [*British*]
RChr .... Revue Chretienne [*A publication*]
RCHRA .... Regional Council on Human Rights in Asia (EAIO)
RCHRA ..... Revue de Chimie. Academie de la Republique Populaire Roumaine [*A publication*]
RchScR ...... Recherches de Science Religieuse [*A publication*]
RCHT .... Ratchet [*Design engineering*]
RCH/TCH ... Receive Channel/Transmit Channel [*Telecommunications*] (MCD)
RCI .... RADAR Coverage Indication [*or Indicator*]
RCI .... Radio Canada International
RCI .... Radio Communications Instruction (MUGU)
RCI .... Range Communications Instructions [*NASA*] (KSC)
RCI .... Read Channel Initialize
RCI .... Recommended Course Indicator
RCI .... Regesta Chartarum Italiae [*A publication*]
RCI .... Reggio Calabria [*Italy*] [*Seismograph station code, US Geological Survey*] (SEIS)
RCI .... Reichhold Chemicals, Incorporated [*NYSE symbol*] (SPSG)
RCI .... Religious of Christian Instruction [*Roman Catholic religious order*]
RCI .... Remote Control Indicator (CAAL)
RCI .... Remote Control Interface
RCI .... Request for Contract Investigation (MCD)
RCI .... Resident Cost Inspector
RCI .... Resort Condominiums International (EA)
RCI .... Respiratory Control Index [*Biochemistry*]
RCI .... Retail Confectioners International (EA)
RCI .... Revista delle Colonie Italiane [*A publication*]
RCI .... Rivista del Clero Italiano [*A publication*]
RCI .... Rochester Commercial and Industrial [*Database*]
RCI .... Rogers Communications, Inc. [*Toronto Stock Exchange symbol*] [*Vancouver Stock Exchange symbol*]
RCI .... Roof Consultants Institute (EA)
RCI .... Routing Control Indicator [*Telecommunications*] (TEL)
RCI .... Royal Colonial Institute [*British*]
RCIA .... Retail Clerks International Association [*Later, UFCWIU*] (EA)
RCIA .... Retail Credit Institute of America [*Later, NFCC*]
RCIA .... Rite for Christian Initiation of Adults [*Australia*]
RCIBDB .... Revista de Ciencias Biologicas [*Belem*] [*A publication*]
RCIC .... Reactor Core Isolation Cooling [*Nuclear energy*] (NRCH)
RCIC .... Red Cross International Committee
RCIC .... Regional Coastal Information Center [*National Marine Advisory Service*] (MSC)
RCIC .... Reserve Component Issues Conference [*Military*] (MCD)
RCIC .... Royal Canadian Infantry Corps
RCICDE .... International Whaling Commission. Report of the Commission [*A publication*]
RCICS .... Reactor Core Isolation Cooling System [*Nuclear energy*] (NRCH)
RCID .... Recruiter Code Identification [*Army*] (AABC)
RCID .... Revue Catholique des Institutions et de Droit [*A publication*]
RCIE .... Regional Council for International Education [*University of Pittsburgh*]
R Cienc Ec ... Revista de Ciencias Economicas [*A publication*]
R Ciencia Pol ... Revista de Ciencia Politica [*A publication*]
R Ciencias Econs ... Revista de Ciencias Economicas [*A publication*]
R Ciencias Juridicas ... Revista de Ciencias Juridicas [*A publication*]
R Ciencias Socs (Costa Rica) ... Revista de Ciencias Sociales (Costa Rica) [*A publication*]
R Ciencias Socs (Puerto Rico) ... Revista de Ciencias Sociales (Puerto Rico) [*A publication*]
R Cienc Polit ... Revista de Ciencia Politica [*A publication*]
R Cienc Soc (Ceara) ... Revista de Ciencias Sociales (Ceara) [*A publication*]
R Cienc Soc (Puerto Rico) ... Revista de Ciencias Sociales (Puerto Rico) [*A publication*]
RCIFDN .... Revista de Ciencias Farmaceuticas [*A publication*]
RCIL .... Reliability Critical Item List (AAG)
R Cin .... Revue du Cinema [*A publication*]
R Cin .... Revue du Cinema/Image et Son [*A publication*]
RCINA .... Revista Chilena de Ingenieria [*A publication*]
R Cinematografo ... Rivista del Cinematografo [*A publication*]
RCIPDJ ..... Revista Cubana de Investigaciones Pesqueras [*A publication*]
RCIRR .... Reserve Components, Individual Ready Reserve [*Military*]
RCIS .... Research Conference on Instrumentation Science
Rc Ist Lomb Sci Lett ... Rendiconti. Istituto Lombardo di Scienze e Lettere [*A publication*]
Rc Ist Sup Sanita ... Rendiconti. Istituto Superiore di Sanita [*A publication*]

RCIU .... Remote Computer Interface Unit
RCivB .... Revista Civilizacao Brasileira [*Rio De Janeiro*] [*A publication*]
RCIVS .... Regional Conference on International Voluntary Service [*Commercial firm*] (EAIO)
RCJ .... RCJ Resources Ltd. [*Vancouver Stock Exchange symbol*]
RCJ .... Reaction Control Jet
RCJ .... Reinforced Composite Joint
RCJ .... Reports of Certain Judgments of the Supreme Court, Vice-Admiralty Court, and Full Court of Appeal, Lagos [*1884-92*] [*Nigeria*] [*A publication*] (DLA)
RC(J) .... Rettie, Crawford, and Melville's Session Cases, Fourth Series [*1873-98*] [*Scotland*] [*A publication*] (DLA)
RCJ .... Revue Critique de Jurisprudence Belge [*A publication*]
RCJ .... Royal Courts of Justice [*British*]
RCJS .... Revista de Ciencias Juridicas y Sociales [*A publication*]
RCK .... Radio Check [*Aviation*] (FAAC)
RCK .... Ramp Check [*Aviation*] (FAAC)
RCK .... Rockdale, TX [*Location identifier*] [*FAA*] (FAAL)
RCKH .... Gaoxiong [*China*] [*ICAO location identifier*] (ICLI)
RCKT .... Rocket (FAAC)
RCKU .... Jiayi [*China*] [*ICAO location identifier*] (ICLI)
RCKW .... Hengchun [*China*] [*ICAO location identifier*] (ICLI)
RCKY .... Rockies [*FAA*] (FAAC)
RCKY .... Rocky Mountain Exploration [*NASDAQ symbol*] (NQ)
RCL .... Radial Collateral Ligament [*Anatomy*]
RCL .... Radiation Counter Laboratories, Inc.
RCL & .... Radio Command Linkage (AAG)
RC & L .... Rail, Canal, and Lake [*Transportation*]
RCL .... Ramp Craft Logistic [*Navy*] [*British*]
RCL .... Ramped Cargo Lighter
RCL .... Ramsey County Public Library, St. Paul, MN [*OCLC symbol*] (OCLC)
RCL .... Rationalist Concept of Logic
RCL .... Reactor Coolant Loop [*Nuclear energy*] (NRCH)
RCL .... Reading-Canada-Lecture [*A publication*]
RCL .... Recall (MSA)
RCL .... Recleared [*Aviation*] (FAAC)
RCL .... Recoil (MSA)
RCL .... Redcliff [*Vanuatu*] [*Airport symbol*] (OAG)
RCL .... Regional Container Line (DS)
RCL .... Reichhold Ltd. [*Toronto Stock Exchange symbol*]
RCL .... Reliability Component List (MCD)
RCL .... Reliability Control Level (KSC)
RCL .... Remote Control Location
RCL .... Research Computation Laboratory [*University of Houston*] [*Research center*] (RCD)
RCL .... Reserved Commodity List [*World War II*]
RCL .... Review of Contemporary Law [*A publication*]
RCl .... Rivista Clasica [*A publication*]
RCL .... Royal Canadian Legion
RCL .... Royal Caribbean Line (DS)
RCL .... Rubber Continuous Liner (DS)
RCL .... Ruby Crystal LASER
RCL .... Ruling Case Law
RCL .... Runway Centerline [*Aviation*]
RCLA .... Regis College Lay Apostolate (EA)
RCLAD ...... Ricerca in Clinica e in Laboratorio [*A publication*]
RCLADN .... Investigacion en la Clinica y en el Laboratorio [*A publication*]
RCLB .... Revolutionary Communist League of Britain [*Political party*] (PPW)
RCLC .... Reactor Coolant Leakage Calculation (IEEE)
RCLC .... Reactor Coolant Letdown Cooler [*Nuclear energy*] (NRCH)
RCLC .... Republican Congressional Leadership Council (EA)
RCLC .... Xiao Liu Qiu [*China*] [*ICAO location identifier*] (ICLI)
RCLD .... Reclined (MSA)
RClFr .... Revue du Clerge Francais [*A publication*]
RCLG .... Recoilless Gun (AABC)
RCLG .... Taizhong [*China*] [*ICAO location identifier*] (ICLI)
RCLGGL ... Royal Commission on Local Government in Greater London [*British*]
RCLI .... Rassegna Critica della Letteratura Italiana [*A publication*]
RCLJ .... Revue Critique de Legislation et de Jurisprudence [*A publication*] (DLA)
RCLL .... Revista de Critica Literaria Latinoamericana [*A publication*]
RCLM .... Reclaim (AABC)
RCLM .... Runway Centerline Marking [*Aviation*]
RCLMG ...... Reclaiming
RCLO .... Reports Control Liaison Officer [*Army*] (AABC)
RCLR .... Radio Communications Link Repeater (FAAC)
RCLR .... Recoilless Rifle (AABC)
RCLS .... Lishan [*China*] [*ICAO location identifier*] (ICLI)
RCLS .... Ramapo Catskill Library System [*Library network*]
RCLS .... Recoilless
RCLS .... Runway Centerline Lights System [*Aviation*] (FAAC)
RCLT .... Radio Communications Link Terminal (FAAC)
RCLU .... Jilong [*China*] [*ICAO location identifier*] (ICLI)
RCLWUNE ... Regional Commission on Land and Water Use in the Near East (EA)
RCLY .... Lanyu [*China*] [*ICAO location identifier*] (ICLI)
RCM .... ARCO Chemical Co. [*NYSE symbol*] (SPSG)

RCM .... Aviation Radio and RADAR Countermeasures Technician [*Navy*]
RCM .... La Republique des Citoyens du Monde [*Commonwealth of World Citizens*]
RCM .... RADAR [*or Radio*] Countermeasures [*Military*] (AAG)
RCM .... Radial Compression Model [*Chromatography*]
RCM .... Radiative-Convective Model [*Meteorology*]
RCM .... Radio-Controlled Mine [*Military*]
RCM .... Radio Counter-Measures [*British military*] (DMA)
RCM .... Radiocontrast Media [*Clinical chemistry*]
RCM .... Random Coefficient Model [*Mathematics*]
RCM .... Random Coincidence Monitor [*Beckman Instruments, Inc.*] [*Instrumentation*]
RCM .... Range Change Method [*Aircraft*]
RCM .... Rassemblement Chretien de Madagascar [*Christian Rally of Madagascar*]
RCM .... Reactor Materials [*A publication*]
RCM .... Receipt of Classified Material (AAG)
RCM .... Recent Crustal Movements [*Geology*] (NOAA)
RCM .... Red Cell Mass [*Hematology*]
RCM .... Reduced Casualties and Mishaps
RCM .... Refurbished Command Module [*NASA*] (KSC)
RCM .... Regimental Corporal-Major [*British*]
RCM .... Regimental Court-Martial
RCM .... Reinforced Clostridial Medium [*Microbiology*]
RCM .... Reliability-Centered Maintenance [*DoD*]
RCM .... Reliability Corporate Memory (IEEE)
RCM .... Religious Conceptionist Missionaries [*Roman Catholic women's religious order*]
RCM .... Repair Cycle Monitor
RCM .... Replacement Culture Medium [*Microbiology*]
RCM .... Revised Code of Montana [*A publication*]
RCM .... Rhode Island College, Providence, RI [*OCLC symbol*] (OCLC)
RCM .... Richmond [*Australia*] [*Airport symbol*] (OAG)
RCM .... Right Costal Margin [*Medicine*]
RCM .... Root Canal Molar [*Dentistry*]
RCM .... Rosmac Resources Ltd. [*Vancouver Stock Exchange symbol*]
RCM .... Rotor Current Meter
RCM .... Rous Conditioned Medium
RCM .... Royal Canadian Mint
RCM .... Royal College of Midwives [*British*]
RCM .... Royal College of Music [*British*]
RCM .... Royal College of Music. Magazine [*A publication*]
RCM .... Royal Conservatory of Music [*Leipzig*]
RCMA .... Radio Communications Monitoring Association (EA)
RCMA .... Railroad Construction and Maintenance Association [*Later, NRC/MAI*] (EA)
RCMA .... Religious Conference Management Association (EA)
RCMA .... Reservist Clothing Maintenance Allowance [*Military*]
RCMA .... Roof Coatings Manufacturers Association (EA)
RCMAC... Raw Cotton Marketing Advisory Committee [*Australia*]
RCMASA.. Russian Consolidated Mutual Aid Society of America (EA)
RCMAT..... Radio-Controlled Miniature Aerial Target [*Military*] (MCD)
RCMD....... Recommend (FAAC)
RCMD .... Rice Council for Market Development (EA)
RCM and E ... Radio Control Models and Electronics [*A publication*]
RCMF........ Royal Commonwealth Military Forces (ADA)
RCMI........ Research Centers in Minority Institutions Program [*Bethesda, MD*] [*National Institutes of Health*] (GRD)
RCMIS ..... Reserve Components Management Information System [*Army*]
RCMJ........ Donggang [*China*] [*ICAO location identifier*] (ICLI)
RCMLAO ... Revista. Facultad de Ciencias Medicas. Universidad Nacional del Litoral Rosario [*A publication*]
RCMLDR ... Australia. Commonwealth Scientific and Industrial Research Organisation. Marine Laboratories. Report [*A publication*]
RCMM ...... Registered Competitive Market Maker [*Stock exchange term*] (SPSG)
RCMP........ RCMP [*Royal Canadian Mounted Police*] Quarterly [*A publication*]
RCMP........ Royal Canadian Mounted Police [*Formerly, RNWMP*]
RCMPQ .... Royal Canadian Mounted Police Quarterly [*A publication*]
RCMPRS .. Recompression
RCMQ....... Qingquangang [*China*] [*ICAO location identifier*] (ICLI)
rCMR .... Regional Cerebral Metabolic Rate [*Brain research*]
RCMS........ Ilan [*China*] [*ICAO location identifier*] (ICLI)
RCMS........ Reliability Centered Maintenance Strategy (MCD)
RCMT .... RCM Technologies, Inc. [*NASDAQ symbol*] (NQ)
RCMTA..... Ricerche di Matematica [*A publication*]
RCMUH.... Ruperto-Carola. Mitteilungen der Vereinigung der Freunde der Studentenschaft der Universitaet Heidelberg [*A publication*]
RCN .... Energiespectrum [*A publication*]
RCN .... Receipt of Change Notice
RCN .... Reconnaissance
RCN .... Record Control Number [*Military*] (AFM)
RCN .... Record Number [*Online database field identifier*]
RCN .... Recovery Communications Network
RCN .... Recreation (MSA)
RCN .... Report Change Notice (MCD)
RCN .... Report Control Number (MCD)
RCN .... Requirements Change Notice [*NASA*] (NASA)

RCN .... Resource Center for Nonviolence (EA)
RCN .... Rimacan Resources Ltd. [*Vancouver Stock Exchange symbol*]
RCN .... Royal Canadian Navy [*Obsolete*]
RCN .... Royal College of Nursing [*British*]
RCNAA ..... Radiologic Clinics of North America [*A publication*]
RCNAS...... Royal Canadian Naval Air Station
RCN Bull .. RCN [*Reactor Centrum Nederland*] Bulletin [*A publication*]
RCNC .... Royal Canadian Naval College [*1943-1948*]
RCNC .... Royal Corps of Naval Constructors [*British*]
RCNCOES ... Reserve Components Noncommissioned Officer Education System [*Army*]
RCNDT ..... Recondition
RCNLR..... Reconnaissance Long Range [*Army*]
RCN Meded ... Reactor Centrum Nederland. Mededeling [*A publication*]
RCNMR .... Royal Canadian Navy. Monthly Review [*A publication*]
RCNN....... Tainan [*China*] [*ICAO location identifier*] (ICLI)
RCNO........ Dongshi [*China*] [*ICAO location identifier*] (ICLI)
RCNR .... Royal Canadian Naval Reserve
RCN Rep.... Reactor Centrum Nederland. Report [*A publication*]
R & C N Sc ... Russell and Chesley's Nova Scotia Reports [*A publication*] (DLA)
RCNSS ..... Reserve Component National Security Seminar (MCD)
RCNTR..... Ring Counter (MSA)
RCNV .... Resource Center for Nonviolence (EA)
RCNVR .... Royal Canadian Naval Volunteer Reserve [*1923-1945*]
RCO.......... RADAR Control Officer
RCO.......... Radio Control Operator
RCO.......... Range Control Office [*or Officer*] [*NASA*] (KSC)
RCO.......... Range Cutoff (MCD)
RCO.......... Reactor Core (IEEE)
RCO.......... Receiver Cuts Out [*Telecommunications*] (TEL)
RCO.......... Reclamation Control Officer [*Military*] (AFIT)
RCO.......... Regional Catering Officer [*British*] (DCTA)
RCO.......... Remote Communication Outlet [*ATCS*]
RCO.......... Remote Control Office
RCO.......... Remote Control Oscillator
RCO.......... Rendezvous Compatible Orbit [*Aerospace*]
RCO.......... Reports Control Officer [*Army*] (AABC)
RCO.......... Representative Calculating Operation
RCO.......... Research Contracting Officer
RCO.......... Resistance-Controlled Oscillator
RCo.......... Ristocetin Cofactor
RCO.......... Rococco Resources Ltd. [*Vancouver Stock Exchange symbol*]
RCO.......... Royal College of Organists [*British*]
RCOA .... Radio Club of America
RCOA .... Record Club of America [*Defunct*]
RCOA .... Retailing Corp. of America [*NASDAQ symbol*] (NQ)
RCOBA ..... Revista Chilena de Obstetricia y Ginecologia [*A publication*]
RCOC .... Regional Communications Operations Center [*Military*] (MCD)
RC/OC ...... Reverse Current/Overcurrent (KSC)
RCOC .... Royal Canadian Ordnance Corps
RCOCB..... Research Communications in Chemical Pathology and Pharmacology [*A publication*]
RCOG....... Royal College of Obstetricians and Gynaecologists [*British*]
RCOGB .... Revista Cubana de Obstetricia y Ginecologia [*A publication*]
RCol.......... Rassegna di Coltura [*A publication*]
R Collect Loc ... Revue des Collectivites Locales [*A publication*]
R Coll For Dep Refor Res Notes ... Royal College of Forestry. Department of Reforestation. Research Notes [*A publication*]
R Coll Sci Technol (Glasg) Res Rep ... Royal College of Science and Technology (Glasgow). Research Report [*A publication*]
RColt.......... Rassegna di Coltura [*A publication*]
R Com .... Revue Communale de Belgique [*A publication*]
RCOMD6 ... Recent Advances in Community Medicine [*A publication*]
R Comitato G Italia B ... Reale Comitato Geologico d'Italia. Bolletino [*A publication*]
R Commer ... Revue Commerce [*A publication*]
RCON....... Reconfiguration (FAAC)
RCOND.... Resources and Conservation [*A publication*]
RCong .... Revue Congolaise [*A publication*]
R Cong ...... Revue Juridique du Congo Belge [*A publication*]
R/CONT .... Remote Control [*Automotive engineering*]
RCONT ..... Rod Control
R Contemp Sociol ... Review of Contemporary Sociology [*A publication*]
R Coop Int ... Revue de la Cooperation Internationale [*A publication*]
R Coree ...... Revue de Coree [*A publication*]
RCOSDO .. Revista de Chirurgie, Oncologie, ORL, Radiologie, Oftalmologie, Stomatologie. Seria Stomatologie [*A publication*]
RCOT .... Recoton Corp. [*NASDAQ symbol*] (NQ)
RCOT .... Rolling Contour Optimization Theory [*Bridgestone Corp.*]
RCP.......... RADAR Control Panel (MCD)
RCP.......... RADAR Conversion Program
RCP.......... Radiation Constraints Panel [*NASA*] (MCD)
RCP.......... Radiative-Convective-Photochemical [*Meteorology*]
RCP.......... Radical Caucus in Psychiatry (EA)
RCP.......... Radiological Control Program [*Nuclear energy*] (NRCH)
RCP.......... Rapid City Public Library, Rapid City, SD [*OCLC symbol*] (OCLC)
RCP.......... Reactor Characterization Program [*Nuclear energy*] (NRCH)

RCP........... Reactor Coolant Pump [*Nuclear energy*] (NRCH)
RCP........... Receive Clock Pulse
rcp............ Recipient [*MARC relator code*] [*Library of Congress*] (LCCP)
RCP........... Recognition and Control Processor [*Data processing*] (IBMDP)
RCP........... Reconciling Congregation Program (EA)
RCP........... Recording Control Panel
RCP........... Recovery Command Post
RCP........... Recrea Plus [*A publication*]
RCP........... Recruiting Command Post
RCP........... Rectangular Coordinate Plotter
RCP........... Reflector-cum-Periscope [*British military*] (DMA)
RCP........... Regimental Command Post
RCP........... Regional Conservation Program
RCP........... Register Clock Pulse
RCP........... Registry of Comparative Pathology (EA)
RCP........... Reinforced Concrete Pavement
RCP........... Reinforced Concrete Pipe [*Technical drawings*]
RCP........... Relative Competitive Preference [*Marketing*]
RCP........... Reliability Critical Problem (AAG)
RCP........... Remote Control Panel
RCP........... Request for Contractual Procurement
RCP........... Requirements Change Proposal
RCP........... Restartable Cryogenic Propellant
RCP........... Restoration Control Point [*Telecommunications*] (TEL)
RCP........... Returns Compliance Program [*Internal Revenue Service*]
RCP........... Revolutionary Communist Party of India [*Political party*] (PPW)
RCP........... Riboflavin Carrier Protein [*Immunology*]
RCP........... Right Circular Polarization
RCP........... Rockefeller Center Properties, Inc. [*NYSE symbol*] (SPSG)
RCP........... Roman Catholic Priest (ROG)
RCP........... Romanian Communist Party [*Political party*]
RCP........... Rotation Combat Personnel
RCP........... Royal College of Pathologists [*British*]
RCP........... Royal College of Physicians of London [*British*]
RCP........... Royal College of Preceptors [*British*] (ROG)
RCP........... Royal Commission on the Press [*British*]
RCPA........ Reserve Components Program of the Army (AABC)
RCPA........ Rural Cooperative Power Association
RCPAC...... Reserve Components Personnel and Administration Center [*Army*] (AABC)
RCPath..... Royal College of Pathologists [*British*]
RCPB........ Reactor Coolant Pressure Boundary [*Nuclear energy*] (NRCH)
RCP(B)..... Romanian Communist Party (Bolshevik) [*Political party*]
RCP(b)....... Russian Communist Party (Bolsheviks) [*Political party*]
RCPBO...... Research Communications in Psychology, Psychiatry, and Behavior [*A publication*]
RCPC........ Regional Check Processing Centers
RCPC........ Royal Canadian Postal Corps [*Formerly, CPC*]
RCPD........ Reserve Components Personnel Directorate [*Office of Personnel Operations*] [*Army*]
RCPE........ Radiological Control Practices Evaluation (MCD)
RCPE........ Royal College of Physicians, Edinburgh
RCPEA...... Revista Chilena de Pediatria [*A publication*]
RCPEd....... Royal College of Physicians, Edinburgh
RCPGlas.... Royal College of Physicians and Surgeons of Glasgow
RCPI.......... Revolutionary Communist Party of India [*Political party*] (PPW)
RCPI.......... Royal College of Physicians, Ireland
RCPJA ...... Royal College of Physicians of London. Journal [*A publication*]
RCPL........ Right Circularly Polarized Light
RCPL........ Royal College of Physicians, London (ROG)
RCPO .... Regional Contract Property Officer
RCPO .... Xinzhu [*China*] [*ICAO location identifier*] (ICLI)
RCPP........ Reinforced Concrete Pressure Pipe
RCPRA...... Record of Chemical Progress [*A publication*]
RCPS........ Royal College of Physicians and Surgeons of Glasgow
RCPS........ Royal College of Physicians and Surgeons (of United States of America) (EA)
RCPS(C).... Royal College of Physicians and Surgeons of Canada
RCPS(Glasg) ... Royal College of Physicians and Surgeons of Glasgow (DBQ)
RCPT........ Receipt (AFM)
RCPT........ Receptacle (MSA)
RCPT........ Reception (AABC)
RCPTN...... Reception (MSA)
RCPV........ Riot Control Patrol Vehicle
RCQ.......... Reconquista [*Argentina*] [*Airport symbol*] (OAG)
RCQ.......... Rich Capital Corp. [*Vancouver Stock Exchange symbol*]
RCQC .... Magong [*China*] [*ICAO location identifier*] (ICLI)
RCQFAQ... Revista Colombiana de Ciencias Quimico-Farmaceuticas [*A publication*]
RCQS........ Taidong/Zhihang [*China*] [*ICAO location identifier*] (ICLI)
RCQUD..... Revista de Ciencias Quimicas [*A publication*]
RCR.......... Rabbinical Council Record [*New York*] [*A publication*]
RCR .... RADAR Control Room
RCR .... Ramsbottom Carbon Residue [*Analysis of petroleum products*]
RCR .... Rated Capacity Report [*Army*]
RCR .... Reactor Control Room
RCR .... Reader Control Relay
RCR .... Reciprocating Cryogenic Refrigerator
RCR .... Regenerative Cyclic Reactor [*Chemical engineering*]

RCR .... Relative Consumption Rate [*Entomology*]
RCR .... Required Carrier Return Character [*Data processing*]
RCR .... Respiratory Control Ratio [*Medicine*]
RCR .... Restitution of Conjugal Rights [*Legal*] [*British*] (ROG)
RCR .... Retrofit Configuration Record [*NASA*] (NASA)
RC-R .... Revista Chicano-Riquena [*A publication*]
RCr .... Revue Critique [*A publication*]
RCr............ Revue Critique d'Histoire et de Litterature [*A publication*]
RCR .... Rochester, IN [*Location identifier*] [*FAA*] (FAAL)
RCR .... Room Cavity Ratio [*Lighting*]
RCR .... Royal Canadian Regiment [*Military*]
RCR .... Royal Canadian Rifles [*Military unit*]
RCR .... Royal College of Radiologists [*British*]
RCR .... Runway Condition Reading [*or Report*] [*Aviation*] (FAAC)
RCRA .... Refrigeration Compressor Rebuilders Association (EA)
RCRA .... Resort and Commercial Recreation Association (EA)
RCRA .... Resource Conservation and Recovery Act [*Pronounced "rickra"*] [*1976*]
RCRA .... Rural Cooperative and Recovery Act (OICC)
RCRA .... Zouying [*China*] [*ICAO location identifier*] (ICLI)
RCRADJ ... Revista Cubana de Reproduccion Animal [*A publication*]
R-CRAS.... Rogers Criminal Responsibility Assessment Scales [*Personality development test*] [*Psychology*]
RCRBSJ .... Research Council on Riveted and Bolted Structural Joints [*Later, RCSC*] (EA)
RCRC........ Rabbinic Center for Research and Counseling (EA)
RCRC........ Reinforced Concrete Research Council (EA)
RCRC........ Revoked Commission, Returned to Civilian Status [*Navy*]
RCRD........ Record (AFM)
RCRF........ Rei Cretariae Romanae Fautores (EAIO)
RCRF........ Rei Cretariae Romanae Fautorum Acta [*A publication*]
RCRHRCS ... Research Center for Religion and Human Rights in Closed Societies (EA)
RCrit .... Ragioni Critiche. Rivista di Studi Linguistici e Letterari [*A publication*]
R Crit Dr Int Prive ... Revue Critique de Droit International Prive [*A publication*]
R Crit Jpd B ... Revue Critique de Jurisprudence Belge [*A publication*]
RCRL......... Reliability Critical Ranking List (AAG)
R1 Cro........ Croke's English King's Bench Reports Tempore Elizabeth [*1582-1603*] [*A publication*] (DLA)
R2 Cro........ Croke's English King's Bench Reports Tempore James [*Jacobus*] I [*A publication*] (DLA)
R3 Cro........ Croke's English King's Bench Reports Tempore Charles I [*1625-41*] [*A publication*] (DLA)
RCRP........ Regional Centers for Radiological Physics [*National Cancer Institute*]
RCRR........ Roster Chaplain - Ready Reserve [*Army*]
RCRS........ Regenerative Carbon-Dioxide Removal System (MCD)
RCRS........ Remote Commercial Radio Services [*Australia*]
RCRS........ Remote Control Radio Service [*Australia*]
RcRt .... Romantic Reassessment [*A publication*]
RCRUA ..... Revista. Consejo de Rectores. Universidades Chilenas [*A publication*]
RCRVA...... Russian Chemical Reviews [*English Translation*] [*A publication*]
RCS........... Conditionnement Embouteillage. Revue Mensuelle de l'Embouteillage et des Industries du Conditionnement, Traitement, Distribution, Transport [*A publication*]
RCS........... Rabbit Aorta Contracting Substance [TA_2 - *see TA, Thromboxane*] [*Biochemistry*]
RCS........... RADAR Calibration Sphere
RCr........... RADAR Collimator System
RCS........... RADAR Control Ship
RCS........... RADAR Cross Section
RCS........... Radio Command System
RCS........... Radio Communications Set
RCS........... Radio Communications System [*Military*] (CAAL)
RCS........... Radio Control System
R & CS ...... Radiological and Chemical Support [*Nuclear energy*] (NRCH)
RCS........... Range Control Station [*or System*] [*Army*]
RCS........... Rapports de la Cour Supreme du Canada [*Database*] [*Federal Department of Justice*] [*Information service or system*] (CRD)
RCS........... Rate Command System (AAG)
RCS........... Reaction Control System [*or Subsystem*] [*Steering system in spacecraft*] [*NASA*]
RCS........... Reactive Current Sensing (MCD)
RCS........... Reactor Coolant System [*Nuclear energy*] (NRCH)
RCS........... Rearward Communications System (MDG)
RCS........... Reentry Control System [*Aerospace*] (AFM)
RCS........... Refurbishment Cost Study (KSC)
RCS........... Regional Control Station [*Military*] (MCD)
RCS........... Reliability Control Specification
RCS........... Reliable Corrective Action Summary (AAG)
RCS........... Reloadable Control Storage [*Data processing*]
RCS........... Remington's Compiled Statutes [*1922*] [*A publication*] (DLA)
RCS........... Remote Computing Service
RCS........... Remote Control Set
RC(S)........ Remote Control (System) (DEN)
RCS........... Reports Control Symbol [*Military*]

RCS............ Representative Conflict Situations [*Army*]
RCS............ Request for Consultation Service (MCD)
RCS............ Requirement Clearance Symbol [*Military*] (AFM)
RCS............ Requirements Control Symbol [*Military*] (MCD)
RCS............ Residential Conservation Service [*Offered by major electric and gas utilities*]
RCS............ Reticulum Cell Sarcoma [*Medicine*]
RCS............ Retrofit Configuration System (MCD)
RCS............ Revenue Cutter Service [*Coast Guard*]
RCS............ Revue Catholique Sociale et Juridique [*A publication*]
RCS............ Rich Coast Sulphur Ltd. [*Vancouver Stock Exchange symbol*]
RCS............ Ride-Control Segment [*or System*] [*Aviation*]
RCS............ Rizzoli Corriere della Sera [*Publisher*]
RCS............ Royal Choral Society
RCS............ Royal College of Science [*British*]
RCS............ Royal College of Surgeons [*British*]
RCS............ Royal Commonwealth Society [*British*]
RCS............ Royal Corps of Signals [*British*]
RCSADO... Research Communications in Substances of Abuse [*A publication*]
RCSAV...... Rozpravy Ceskoslovenske Akademie Ved [*A publication*]
RCSB......... [*The*] Rochester Community Savings Bank [*Rochester, NY*] [*NASDAQ symbol*] (NQ)
RCSBP....... Reserve Components Survivor Benefits Plan [*Military*]
RCSC........ Huwei [*China*] [*ICAO location identifier*] (ICLI)
RCSC........ Radio Component Standardization Committee [*British*]
RCSC........ Reaction Control System [*or Subsystem*] Controller [*Apollo*] [*NASA*] (NASA)
RCSC........ Research Council on Structural Connections (EA)
RCSC........ Royal Canadian Sea Cadets
RCSCC....... Royal Canadian Sea Cadets Corps
RCSCSPL ... Russian, Croatian and Serbian, Czech and Slovak, Polish Literature [*A publication*]
RCSDE...... Reactor Coolant System Dose Equivalent (IEEE)
RCSDP...... League of Red Cross Societies Development Program
RCSE......... Remote Control and Status Equipment (MCD)
RCSE......... Royal College of Surgeons, Edinburgh
R2CSE...... Relaxed Two-Color Stimulated Echo [*Spectroscopy*]
RCSEd....... Royal College of Surgeons, Edinburgh
RCSEng..... Royal College of Surgeons, England
RCSF .... Rivista Critica di Storia della Filosofia [*A publication*]
RCSH .... Revue Congolaise des Sciences Humaines [*A publication*]
RCSHSB ... Red Cedar Shingle and Handsplit Shake Bureau [*Later, CSSB*] (EA)
RCSI......... Receipt for [*or of*] Classified Security Information (AAG)
RCSI......... Rede CONSISDATA de Servicos Integrados [*CONSISDATA Integrated Services Network*] [*Consultoria, Sistemas, e Processamento de Dados Ltda.*] [*Brazil*] [*Information service or system*] (CRD)
RCSI......... Royal College of Surgeons, Ireland
RCSIS....... Radio/Cable Switching Integration System (MCD)
RCSL........ Rich Coast Sulphur Limited [*NASDAQ symbol*] (NQ)
RCSM....... Ri Yue Tan [*China*] [*ICAO location identifier*] (ICLI)
RCSMC..... Recent Advances in Studies on Cardiac Structure and Metabolism [*A publication*]
RCSO........ Research Contract Support Office
RCSQ........ Pingdong (North) [*China*] [*ICAO location identifier*] (ICLI)
RCSS .... Radial Compression Separation System [*Chromatography*]
RCSS .... Random Communication Satellite System
RCSS .... Reduced Chi-Square Statistic
RCSS .... Taibei/Songshan [*China*] [*ICAO location identifier*] (ICLI)
RCSSA...... Regional Centre for Seismology for South America (EAIO)
RCS Supp .. Remington's Compiled Statutes, Supplement [*A publication*] (DLA)
RCSU........ Repair Cycle Support Unit
RCSX........ North American Car Corp. [*AAR code*]
RCT .... RADAR Control Trailer [*Military*] (AABC)
RCT .... Radiation/Chemical Technician (IEEE)
RCT .... Radiobeacon Calibration Transmitter
RCT .... Randomized Clinical Trial [*Medicine*]
RCT .... Randomized Control Trial [*Statistics*]
RCT .... Real Estate Investment Trust, California [*NYSE symbol*] (SPSG)
RCT .... Receipts [*Stock exchange term*] (SPSG)
RCT .... Received Copy of Temporary Pay Record
RCT .... Recruit
RCT .... Reed City, MI [*Location identifier*] [*FAA*] (FAAL)
RCT .... Regimental Combat Team
RCT .... Region Control Task [*Data processing*] (BUR)
RCT .... Registered Care Technician [*Proposed by American Medical Association to alleviate nursing shortage*]
RCT .... Regular Care Technologist
RCT .... Rehabilitation and Research Center for Torture Victims (EAIO)
RCT .... Remote Control [*Systems*] (MCD)
RCT .... Remote Control Terminal (MCD)
RCT .... Repair Cycle Time (MCD)
RCT .... Repeat Cycle Timer
RCT .... Resolver Control Transformer
RCT .... Resource Consulting Teacher
RCT .... Response Coordination Team [*Nuclear energy*] (NRCH)

RCT .... Retention Control Training [*Medicine*]
RC-T......... Revenue Canada, Taxation
RCT .... Reversible Counter
RCT .... Revista Catalana de Teologia [*A publication*]
RCT .... Rework/Completion Tag [*Nuclear energy*] (NRCH)
RCT .... Ridgecrest Resources [*Vancouver Stock Exchange symbol*]
RCT .... Roll Call Training
RCT .... Root Canal Therapy [*Dentistry*]
RCT .... Rorschach Content Test [*Psychology*]
RCT .... Royal Clinical Teacher [*British*]
RCT .... Royal Corps of Transport [*Army*] [*British*]
RCT .... Royal Cosmic Theology [*British*]
RCTA........ Resource Centre Teachers Association [*Australia*]
RCTB........ Reserve Components Troop Basis [*Army*] (AABC)
RCTC........ Regeneratively-Cooled Thrust Chamber
RCTC........ Reserve Components Training Center [*Military*]
RCTC........ Union of Rail Canada Traffic Controllers [*See also CCFC*]
RCTCA...... Recherche Technique [*A publication*]
RCTDPOVALCAN ... Request Concurrent Travel of Dependents by Privately Owned Vehicle [*ALCAN Highway or Via Route Required*] [*Army*] (AABC)
RCTEA...... Rubber Chemistry and Technology [*A publication*]
RCTG .... Recruiting (AABC)
RCTL........ Resistance-Coupled Transistor Logic
RCTL........ Resistor-Capacitor Transistor Logic
RCTM .... Regional Center for Tropical Meteorology [*National Hurricane Center*]
RCTN .... Reaction (MSA)
RCTP........ Reserve Components Troop Program [*Army*]
RCTP........ Taibei City/Taibei International Airport [*China*] [*ICAO location identifier*] (ICLI)
RCTPA...... Russian Castings Production [*English Translation*] [*A publication*]
RCTPS....... Revue Canadienne de Theorie Politique et Sociale [*A publication*]
RCTRANSMOD ... Reserve Components Transition to Modernization
R & C Tr Cas ... Railway and Canal Traffic Cases (Neville) [*England*] [*A publication*] (DLA)
RCTS .... Railway Correspondence and Travel Society [*British*]
RCTS .... Reactor Coolant Treatment System [*Nuclear energy*] (NRCH)
R (Ct of Sess) ... Rettie, Crawford, and Melville's Session Cases, Fourth Series [*1873-98*] [*Scotland*] [*A publication*] (DLA)
RCTSR ...... Radio Code Test, Speed of Response [*Military*]
RCTV........ RCA Cable and Rockefeller Center Cable Pay-TV Program Service
RCTV........ Remote Controlled Target Vehicle [*Military*] (INF)
RCU .... RADAR Calibration Unit
RCU .... RADAR Control Unit [*Military*] (CAAL)
RCU .... Rate Construction Unit [*Hypothetical basic currency unit*] (DCTA)
RCU .... Reference Control Unit (MCD)
RCU .... Relay Control Unit (AAG)
RCU .... Remote Control Unit
RCU .... Requisition Control Unit
RCU .... Research into Chronic Unemployment [*British*]
RCU .... Research Coordinating Unit [*Oklaholma State Department of Vocational and Technical Education*] [*Stillwater, OK*]
R/CU .... Research and Curriculum Unit [*Mississippi State University*] [*Research center*] (RCD)
RCU .... Reserve Component Unit [*Army*] (AABC)
RCU .... Respiratory Care Unit [*Medicine*]
RCU .... Revolution Control Unit [*Automotive engineering*]
RCU .... Rio Cuarto [*Argentina*] [*Airport symbol*] (OAG)
RCU .... Rocket Countermeasure Unit
RCUA........ Remote Checkout Umbilical Array
RCuBib ...... Revista de Cultura Biblica [*Rio De Janeiro/Sao Paulo, Brazil*] [*A publication*]
RCUEP...... Research Center for Urban and Environmental Planning [*Princeton University*]
RCUK .... Bakuai [*China*] [*ICAO location identifier*] (ICLI)
RCUL .... Reference Control Unit Launch (MCD)
R Cul Cl Medioev ... Rivista di Cultura Classica e Medioevale [*A publication*]
RCUR .... Recurrent (MSA)
R Current Activities Tech Ed ... Review of Current Activities in Technical Education [*A publication*] (APTA)
RCuTeol..... Revista de Cultura Teologica [*Sao Paulo, Brazil*] [*A publication*]
RCV .... RADAR Control Van (NATG)
RCV .... Radiation Control Valve [*Nuclear energy*] (NRCH)
RCV .... Reaction-Control Valve
RCV .... Receive (AFM)
RCV .... Receiver
RCV .... Receiver/Exciter Subsystem [*Deep Space Instrumentation Facility, NASA*]
RCV .... Recreatievoorzieningen. Maandblad voor Recreatie, Milieu, en Landschap [*A publication*]
RCV .... Red Cell Volume [*Hematology*]
RCV .... Relative Conductor Volume
RCV .... Remote-Controlled Vehicle (MCD)
RCV .... Replacement Cost Valuation [*Insurance*]
RCV .... Restartable Cryogenic Vehicle

RCV	Reversed Circular Vection [*Optics*]
RCV	Revised Claim Valuation [*Insurance*]
RCV	Rich Cut Virginia [*Tobacco*] (ROG)
RCV	Riot Control Vehicle
RCV	Robotic Combat Vehicle [*Army*]
RCV	Routine Coefficient of Variation [*Statistics*]
RCVD	Received (MSA)
RCVG	Receiving (MSA)
RCVG	Replacement Carrier Fighter Group [*V is Navy code for Fighter*]
RCVMV.....	Red Clover Vein Mosaic Virus
RCVR........	Receiver (AAG)
RCVRB......	Royal Military College of Canada. Civil Engineering Research Report [*A publication*]
RCVS........	Rassegna di Cultura e Vita Scolastica [*A publication*]
RCVS........	Remote Control Video Switch (MCD)
RCVS........	Royal College of Veterinary Surgeons [*British*]
RCVSG......	Readiness Antisubmarine Warfare Carrier Air Wing [*Navy*] (NVT)
RCVTA......	Rozpravy Ceskoslovenske Akademie Ved. Rada Technickych Ved [*A publication*]
RCVTB......	Recherches Veterinaires [*A publication*]
RCVV	Rear Compressor Variable Vane
RCVW	Readiness Attack Carrier Air Wing [*Navy*] (NVT)
RCVY	Recovery (MSA)
RCW	Raw Cooling Water [*Nuclear energy*] (NRCH)
RCW	Reactor Cooling Water [*Nuclear energy*] (NRCH)
RCW	Record Control Word [*Data processing*]
RCW	Reformed Church Women [*An association*] (EA)
RCW	Register Containing Word
RCW	Research Center on Women (EA)
RCW	Resident Careworker
RCW	Return Control Word
RCWA	Revised Code of Washington Annotated [*A publication*] (DLA)
RCWI........	Right Ventricular Cardiac Work Index [*Cardiology*]
RCWK.......	Xinshe [*China*] [*ICAO location identifier*] (ICLI)
RCWP.......	Rural Clean Water Program [*Department of Agriculture*]
RCWS.......	Remote Control Water Sampler
RCWS.......	Russian Children's Welfare Society - Outside of Russia (EA)
RCX	Ladysmith, WI [*Location identifier*] [*FAA*] (FAAL)
RCXY........	Guiren [*China*] [*ICAO location identifier*] (ICLI)
RCY	Recovery (NASA)
RCY	Red Cross and Red Crescent Youth [*Geneva, Switzerland*]
RCY	Remaining Cycles (MCD)
RCY	Rotating Coil Yoke
RCY	Royal Crystal [*Vancouver Stock Exchange symbol*]
RCYRA......	Rooster Class Yacht Racing Association (EA)
RCYU	Hualian [*China*] [*ICAO location identifier*] (ICLI)
RCZ	Radiation Control Zone
RCZ	Rear Combat Zone (NATG)
RCZ	Rockingham, NC [*Location identifier*] [*FAA*] (FAAL)
RD.............	Airlift International, Inc. [*ICAO designator*]
Rd..............	Albert Rolland [*France*] [*Research code symbol*]
RD.............	Boots Pure Drug Co. [*Great Britain*] [*Research code symbol*]
RD.............	Directional Radio Beacon [*ITU designation*] (CET)
RD.............	Distribution Is Restricted to Government Agencies Only [*Advice of supply action code*] [*Army*]
RD.............	Indian Revenue Decisions [*A publication*] (DLA)
rd..............	Rad [*Non-SI unit; preferred unit is Gy, Gray*]
RD.............	RADAR (DEN)
RD.............	RADAR Data
RD.............	RADAR Display
RD.............	RADARman [*Also, RDM*] [*Navy rating*]
RD.............	Radiation Detection
Rd..............	Radiolaria [*Quality of the bottom*] [*Nautical charts*]
RD.............	Radiological Defense [*To minimize the effect of nuclear radiation on people and resources*]
Rd..............	Rainbow Darter [*Ichthyology*]
RD.............	Random Drift
RD.............	Random Driver [*Nuclear energy*] (NRCH)
RD.............	Range Development (MUGU)
R/D............	Rate of Descent [*Aviation*] (MCD)
RD.............	Raynaud's Disease [*Medicine*]
RD.............	Reaction of Degeneration [*Physiology*]
RD.............	Read (AAG)
RD.............	Read Data
R & D	Read and Destroy
RD.............	Read Direct
RD.............	Reader's Digest [*A publication*]
RD.............	Readiness Data
RD.............	Readiness Date
RD.............	Reappraisement Decisions [*A publication*] (DLA)
RD.............	Rear Door
RD.............	Receipt Day (NRCH)
RD.............	Received Data (IEEE)
RD.............	Recemment Degorgee [*Recently Disgorged*] [*Refers to aging of wine*] [*French*]
RD.............	Recognition Differential
RD.............	Record Description [*Data processing*]
RD.............	Recorders-Reproducers [*JETDS nomenclature*] [*Military*] (CET)

RD.............	Recording Demand (DEN)
RD.............	Red
RD.............	Red Pennant [*Navy*] [*British*]
RD.............	Refer to Drawer [*Banking*]
RD.............	Reference Designator (NASA)
RD.............	Reference Document
RD.............	Reference Drawing (NATG)
RD.............	Regio Decreto [*Royal Decree*] [*Latin*] (DLA)
RD.............	Regional Director
RD.............	Register Drive (MSA)
RD.............	Registered (ROG)
RD.............	Registered Dietitian
RD.............	Reinforcement Designee [*Air Force*] (AFM)
RD.............	Relative Density
RD.............	Relaxation Delay
RD.............	Relay Drawer
RD.............	Relay Driver
RD.............	Remove Directory [*Data processing*]
RD.............	Renaissance Drama [*A publication*]
RD.............	Renal Disease [*Medicine*]
RD.............	Rendered (ROG)
RD.............	Replacement Detachment [*Army*]
RD.............	Replenishable Demand
RD.............	Reply Delay (MUGU)
R of D........	Reporter of Debate [*US Senate*]
RD.............	Required Date
R & D	Requirements and Distribution (AFM)
RD.............	Requirements Document [*NASA*] (KSC)
R & D	Research and Demonstration [*Labor training*]
R & D	Research and Development
RD.............	Research and Development
RD.............	Reserve Decoration [*Navy*] [*British*]
RD.............	Resource Development
RD.............	Respiratory Disease
RD.............	Restricted Data [*Security classification*]
RD.............	Retention and Disposal
RD.............	Retinal Detachment [*Ophthalmology*]
RD.............	Revision Directive [*Drawings*]
RD.............	Revista de Dialectologia y Tradiciones Populares [*A publication*]
RD.............	Revolutionary Development [*South Vietnam*]
R du D........	Revue du Droit [*A publication*] (DLA)
R de D	Revue de Droit. Universite de Sherbrooke [*A publication*]
RD.............	Revue Historique de Droit Francais et Etranger [*A publication*]
RD.............	Reye's Disease [*Medicine*]
RD.............	Right Defense
RD.............	Right Deltoid [*Medicine*]
RD.............	Right Door [*Theater*]
RD.............	Rights in Data (OICC)
RD.............	Ringdown [*Telecommunications*] (TEL)
RD.............	Rive Droite [*Right Bank*] [*French*]
RD.............	Rivista Dalmatica [*A publication*]
RD.............	Rix-Dollar
RD.............	Road [*Maps and charts*] (AAG)
RD.............	Rod
RD.............	Romanovsky Dye [*Biological stain*]
RD.............	Rood [*Unit of measurement*]
RD.............	Roof Drain (AAG)
RD.............	Root Diameter (MSA)
R/D............	Rotary to Digital (MCD)
RD.............	Rotodrome
RD.............	Round (AAG)
RD.............	Royal Dragoons [*British*]
RD.............	Royal Dutch Petroleum Co. [*NYSE symbol*] (SPSG)
RD.............	Royal Naval Reserve Decoration [*British*]
RD.............	Ruling Date [*IRS*]
RD.............	Run Down [*Typography*]
RD.............	Running Days
RD.............	Rupture Disk (KSC)
RD.............	Rural Deacon [*or Deaconry*] [*Church of England*]
RD.............	Rural Dean [*Church of England*]
RD.............	Rural Delivery
RD.............	Rural Development
RD.............	Rural District
rd..............	Rutherford [*Unit of strength of a radioactive source*]
RD1............	RADARman, First Class [*Navy rating*]
RD2............	RADARman, Second Class [*Navy rating*]
RD3............	RADARman, Third Class [*Navy rating*]
RDA...........	Racial Discrimination Act [*Australia*]
RDA...........	Radioactive Dentin Abrasion [*Dentistry*]
RDA...........	Railway Development Association [*British*]
RDA...........	Ranging Demodulator Assembly [*Deep Space Instrumentation Facility, NASA*]
RDA...........	Rassemblement Democratique Africain [*Niger*] [*Political party*] (PD)
RDA...........	Rassemblement Democratique Africain [*Ivory Coast*] [*Political party*] (PPW)
RDA...........	Read Data Available
RDA...........	Readers Digest Association [*Commercial firm*] (EA)
RDA...........	Reader's Digest Association Class A [*NYSE symbol*] (SPSG)
RDA...........	Real-Time Debugging Aid

RDA.......... Recirculation Duct Assembly
RDA.......... Recommended Daily Allowance [*Dietary*]
RDA.......... Recommended Duty Assignment　(AFM)
RDA.......... Regional Dance America　(EA)
RDA.......... Regional Dance Association
RDA.......... Regional Data Associates [*Information service or system*]　(IID)
RDA.......... Regional Dental Activity　(AABC)
RDA.......... Register Display Assembly
RDA.......... Reliability Design Analysis　(MCD)
RDA.......... Remote Data Access　(NASA)
RDA.......... Request for Deviation Approval　(MCD)
RDA.......... Research and Development Abstracts [*A publication*]
RD & A ..... Research, Development, and Acquisition [*DoD*]
RD & A ..... Research, Development, and Acquisition [*A publication*]
RDA.......... Research and Development, Army
R & DA ...... Research and Development Associates for Military Food and Packaging Systems　(EA)
RDA.......... Resent, Demand, Appreciate [*In Sidney Simon, Leland Howe, and Howard Kirschenbaum's book "Values Clarification"*]
RDA.......... Resident Data Area　(NASA)
RDA.......... Reverse Diels-Alder [*Organic chemistry*]
RDA.......... Riding for the Disabled Association　(EAIO)
RDA.......... Right Dorso Anterior [*Medicine*]　(ROG)
Rd A .... Rivista di Archeologia [*A publication*]
RDA.......... Rod Drop Accident　(IEEE)
RDA.......... Rome Daily American [*An English-language newspaper in Italy*] [*A publication*]
RDA.......... Royal Danish Army　(NATG)
RDA.......... Royal Defence Academy [*British*]
RDA.......... Rules for the Discipline of Attorneys [*A publication*]　(DLA)
RDA.......... Rural Development Abstracts [*Database*] [*Commonwealth Bureau of Agricultural Economics*] [*Information service or system*]　(CRD)
RDA.......... Rural Development Academy [*Bogra, Bangladesh*]　(ECON)
RDA.......... Rural Development Act [*1972*]　(OICC)
RDA.......... Rural Doctors' Association [*Australia*]
RDAC........ Report. Department of Antiquities of Cyprus [*A publication*]
RDAC........ Research and Development Acquisition Committee [*Military*]
RDAF .... Revue de Droit Administratif et de Droit Fiscal [*Lausanne, Switzerland*] [*A publication*]　(DLA)
RDAF .... Royal Danish Air Force
RDAFCI .... Research and Development Associates, Food and Container Institute　(EA)
RDAISA .... Research, Development, and Acquisition Information Systems Agency [*Army*]　(AABC)
RDAL .... Representation Dependent Accessing Language
RDAQ....... Riding for Disabled Association of Queensland [*Australia*]
RDAR .... Reliability Design Analysis Report　(AAG)
RDARA ..... Regional and Domestic Air Route Area
RDAS........ Reflectivity Data Acquisition System
RDAT .... RADAR Data　(FAAC)
RDAT .... Registered Designs Appeal Tribunal　(DLA)
RDAT .... Remote Data Acquisition Terminal　(NRCH)
RDAT .... Research and Development Acceptance Test
RDAT .... Research, Development, and Test
RDAT .... Rotary Digital Audio Tape
RDAU .... Remote Data Acquisition Unit
RDAVS..... Recovered Doppler Airborne Vector Scorer
RDB .... RADAR Decoy Balloon [*Air Force*]
RDB .... Ramped Dump Barge
RDB .... Rapidly Deployable Barge [*Military*]　(MCD)
RDB .... Rare Disease Database [*National Organization for Rare Disorders*] [*Information service or system*]　(IID)
RDB .... Relational Database
RDB .... Research and Development Board [*Abolished, 1953, functions transferred to Department of Defense*]
RDB .... Resistance Decade Box
RDB .... Revue du Bois et de Ses Applications [*A publication*]
RDB .... Round Die Bushing
RDB .... Royal Danish Ballet
RDB .... Rural Development Board [*British*]
RDBA .... Roll Drive and Brake Assembly
RDBel .... Revue de Droit Belge [*A publication*]
RDBGA .... Radiobiologia-Radioterapia [*A publication*]
RDBL........ Readable
RDBMD .... Review on the Deformation Behavior of Materials [*A publication*]
RDBMS..... Relational Database Management System [*Data processing*]　(BYTE)
Rdbr Kraftanl ... Rundbrief Kraftanlagen [*A publication*]
RDC.......... Chief RADARman [*Navy rating*]
RDC.......... RADAR Data Converter　(MCD)
RDC.......... RADAR Design Corporation
RDC.......... RADAR Display Console
RDC.......... Radiac [*Nucleonics*]
RDC.......... Radiation Density Constant
RDC.......... Radioactivity Decay Constant
RDC.......... Rail Diesel Car
RDC.......... Rapaport Diamond Corporation [*Information service or system*]　(IID)

RDC.......... Rapid Development Capability [*Military*]　(NG)
RDC.......... Rassemblement Democratique Caledonien [*Caledonian Democratic Rally*] [*Political party*]　(PPW)
RDC.......... Rassemblement Democratique Centrafricain [*Political party*] [*Central African Republic*]
RDC.......... Rate Damping Control
RDC.......... Read Data Check　(CMD)
RDC.......... Real Decisions Corporation [*Information service or system*]　(IID)
RDC .... Reduce　(MSA)
RDC.......... Reference Designator Code　(NASA)
RDC.......... Reflex Digital Control
RDC.......... Refugee Documentation Centre [*Information service or system*]　(IID)
RDC.......... Regional Data Center [*Marine science*]　(MSC)
RDC.......... Regional Dissemination Center [*NASA*]
RDC.......... Regional Distribution Center [*TRW Automotive Aftermarket Group*]
RDC.......... Reliability Data Center　(KSC)
RDC.......... Remote Data Collection　(MCD)
RDC.......... Remote Data Concentrator
RDC.......... Remote Detonation Capability
RDC.......... Reply Delay Compensation　(MUGU)
RDC.......... Request for Document Change　(NASA)
RDC.......... Research and Development Command [*Military*]
RDC.......... Research Diagnostic Criteria [*Medicine, psychiatry*]
RdC .... Resto del Carlino [*A publication*]
RDC.......... Revolutionary Development Cadre [*South Vietnam*]
RDC.......... Revue de Droit Canonique [*A publication*]
RDC.......... Revue de Droit Compare. Association Quebecoise pour l'Etude Comparative du Droit [*A publication*]
RDC.......... Rochester Diocesan Chronicle [*A publication*]
RDC.......... Rotary Dispersion Colorimeter
RDC.......... Rotating Diffusion Cell [*Chemistry*]
RDC.......... Rotating Disk Contractor [*Chemical engineering*]
RDC.......... Rowan Companies, Inc. [*NYSE symbol*]　(SPSG)
RDC.......... Royal Defence Corps [*British*]
RDC.......... Rubber Development Corporation [*Expired, 1947*]
RDC.......... Running-Down Clause [*Business term*]
RDC.......... Rural Development and Conservation [*Department of Agriculture*]
RDC.......... Rural District Council [*British*]
RDC.......... Sisters of Divine Compassion [*Roman Catholic religious order*]
R2DC3 .... Rapid Reaction, Deployable Command, Control, and Communications
RDCA .... Rural District Councils Association [*British*]
RDCC .... Regional Distributors and Carriers Conference　(EA)
RD-CCSA ... Reciprocal Derivative Constant-Current Stripping Analysis [*Analytical electrochemistry*]
RDCEHCY ... Research and Demonstration Center for the Education of Handicapped Children and Youth　(EA)
RDCEO ..... Rural District Council Executive Officer [*British*]
RDCF........ Restricted Data Cover Folder　(AAG)
RDCHE.... Rene Dubos Center for Human Environments　(EA)
RDCM...... Master Chief RADARman [*Navy rating*]
RDCM...... Reduced Delta Code Modulation [*Digital memory*]
RDCN....... Reduction　(MSA)
RDCO....... Reliability Data Control Office　(AAG)
R & D Con Mn ... Research and Development Contracts Monthly [*A publication*]
RDCP....... Remote Display Control Panel　(MCD)
RDCR .... Reducer　(MSA)
RDCS........ Reconfiguration Data Collection System [*or Subsystem*]　(MCD)
RDCS........ Senior Chief RADARman [*Navy rating*]
RDCTD8 ... Australia. Commonwealth Scientific and Industrial Research Organisation. Division of Chemical Technology. Research Review [*A publication*]
R & DCTE ... Research and Development Center for Teacher Education [*Department of Education*]　(GRD)
RDCU .... Receipt Delivery Control Unit [*Social Security Administration*]
RDD.......... Random Digit Dialing [*Telecommunications*]
RDD.......... Rapid Demolition Device
RDD.......... Rassemblement Democratique Dahomeen [*Dahomean Democratic Rally*]
RDD.......... Reactor Development Division [*of AEC*]
RDD.......... Redding [*California*] [*Airport symbol*]　(OAG)
RDD.......... Reference Design Document　(KSC)
RDD.......... Required Delivery Date　(AABC)
RDD.......... Requirements Definition Document [*NASA*]　(NASA)
RDD.......... Requisition Due Date　(TEL)
RD & D ..... Research, Development, and Demonstration
RDD.......... Research and Development Directorate [*Army*]
RDD.......... Return Due Date [*IRS*]
RDD.......... Routine Dynamic Display　(MCD)
RDDA....... Recommended Daily Dietary Allowance
RDDCS..... Range Drone Data Control System [*Military*]　(CAAL)
RDD & E.... Research, Development, Diffusion [*or Dissemination*], and Evaluation
RDDM....... Reactor Deck Development Mock-Up [*Nuclear energy*]　(NRCH)

RdDM....... Revue des Deux Mondes [*A publication*]
RDDMI..... Radio Digital Distance Magnetic Indicator (MCD)
RDDP .... RNA [*Ribonucleic Acid*]-Directed DNA [*Deoxyribonucleic Acid*] Polymerase [*Formerly, RIDP*] [*An enzyme*]
RDDR .... Rod Drive
RDDS .... RADAR Data Distribution Switchboard [*Military*] (CAAL)
RDDS .... Retail Dental Delivery System [*Dentistry*]
RdDxM...... Revue des Deux Mondes [*A publication*]
RDE .... RADAR Display Equipment
RDE .... Radial Defect Examination (IEEE)
RDE .... Receptor-Destroying Enzyme [*A neuraminidase*] [*Immunochemistry*]
RDE .... Recommended Distribution of Effort [*Civil defense*]
RDE .... Reliability Data Extractor (MCD)
RD & E...... Research, Development, and Engineering
RDE .... Research and Development Establishment [*British*]
RDE .... Research Development Exchange (OICC)
RdE .... Revista de las Espanas [*A publication*]
Rd'E .... Revue d'Egyptologie [*Cairo*] [*A publication*]
RDE .... Revue d'Esthetique [*A publication*]
RdE .... Rivista di Estetica [*A publication*]
RDE .... Rotating Disc Electrode
RDE & A.... Research, Development, Engineering, and Acquisition (RDA)
RDEB .... Recessive Dystrophic Epidermolysis Bullosa [*Also, EBDR*] [*Dermatology*]
RDEEA...... Radio and Electronic Engineer [*A publication*]
RdeIE........ Revista de Ideas Esteticas [*A publication*]
RdeInd ...... Revista de las Indias [*A publication*]
R & DELSEC ... Research and Development Electronic Security [*Military*] (AABC)
RDEP........ Recruit Depot [*Navy*]
R Der Cienc Polit ... Revista de Derecho y Ciencias Politicas. Universidad de San Marcos [*A publication*]
R Der (Concepcion) ... Revista de Derecho (Concepcion) [*A publication*]
R Derechos Humanos ... Revista de Derechos Humanos [*A publication*]
R Der Int Cienc Diplom ... Revista de Derecho Internacional y Ciencias Diplomaticas [*A publication*]
RD & ES .... Requirements Determination and Exercise System [*Military*] (MCD)
RdEt.......... Revista de Etnografia [*A publication*]
R Deux Mondes ... Revue des Deux Mondes [*A publication*]
R Developpement Internat ... Revue du Developpement International [*A publication*]
RDF .... RADAR Direction Finder [*or Finding*] (CET)
RDF .... Radial Distribution Function [*X-ray diffraction*]
RDF .... Radio Direction Finder [*or Finding*] (AABC)
RDF .... Rapid Deployment Force [*Military*]
RDF .... Record Definition Field [*Data processing*] (BUR)
RDF .... Redford Resources, Inc. [*Vancouver Stock Exchange symbol*]
RDF .... Reflection Direction Finding
RDF .... Refuse-Derived Fuel
RDF .... Repeater Distribution Frame (NATG)
RDF .... Research, Development, and Facilities (NOAA)
RDF .... Reserve Defense Fleet [*Navy*]
RDF .... Resource Data File (MCD)
RDF .... Revue de France [*A publication*]
RdF .... Rivista di Filosofia [*A publication*]
RDF .... Robotech Defense Force (EA)
RDF .... Roger Wyburn-Mason and Jack M. Blount Foundation for the Eradication of Rheumatoid Disease (EA)
RDF .... Royal Dublin Fusiliers [*British*]
RDF-A .... Rapid Deployment Force - Army
RDFDF...... Redford Resources, Inc. [*NASDAQ symbol*] (NQ)
RDFI........ Receiving Depository Financial Institution
RDFL........ Reflection Direction Finding, Low Angle (MCD)
RDF/LT.... Rapid Deployment Force/Light Tank [*Military*] (MCD)
RDFQ .... Recueil de Droit Fiscal Quebecois [*A publication*] (DLA)
RDFSTA.... Radio Direction Finder Station
RDFU .... Research and Development Field Unit [*Military*]
RDFU-V .... Research and Development Field Unit - Vietnam [*Military*] (MCD)
RDG.......... Reading [*British depot code*]
RDG.......... Reading [*Pennsylvania*] [*Airport symbol*] (OAG)
RDG.......... Reading
RDG.......... Reference Drawing Group [*NATO*] (NATG)
RDG.......... Regional Development Grant [*British*] (DCTA)
RDG.......... Registrar Data Group [*Information service or system*] (IID)
RDG.......... Relative Disturbance Gain [*Control engineering*]
RDG.......... Research Discussion Group (EA)
RDG.......... Resolver Differential Generator
RDG.......... Resource Development Group Ltd. [*British*]
RDG.......... Ridge (MSA)
RDG.......... Right Digestive Gland
RDG.......... Rounding
RDG.......... Rover P4 Drivers Guild [*An association*] (EAIO)
RDGC....... Reading Company [*NASDAQ symbol*] (NQ)
RDGE .... Resorcinol Diglycidyl Ether [*Organic chemistry*]
RDGF .... Retina-Derived Growth Factor [*Biochemistry*]
RDGNA..... Radiologia Diagnostica [*A publication*]
RDGRA ..... Radiographer [*A publication*]
RDGTA ..... Rational Drug Therapy [*A publication*]

RDH .... Radioactive Drain Header [*Nuclear energy*] (NRCH)
RDH .... Rapid Displacement Heating [*Pulp and paper technology*]
RDH .... Red Hill Marketing Group Ltd. [*Vancouver Stock Exchange symbol*]
RDH .... Registered Dental Hygienist
RDH .... Resource Dispersion Hypothesis [*Animal ecology*]
RdH .... Revista de Historia [*A publication*]
RDH .... Round Head
RDH .... Royal Deccan Horse [*British military*] (DMA)
RDHER ..... Revolutionary Development Hamlet Evaluation Report [*South Vietnam*]
RDI .... Radio Doppler Inertial
RDI .... Rassemblement Democratique pour l'Independance [*Quebec*]
RDI .... Reference Daily Intake [*FDA*]
RDI .... Reference Designation Index (MCD)
RDI .... Rejection and Disposition Item
RDI .... Released Data Index
RDI .... Relief and Development Institute [*Formerly, International Disaster Institute*] (EA)
RDI .... Remote Data Input
RDI .... Research and Development Institute, Inc. [*Montana State University*] [*Research center*] (RCD)
RDI .... Research and Development of Instrumentation [*Program*] [*Army*]
RDI .... Riley's Datashare International Ltd. [*Toronto Stock Exchange symbol*]
RDI .... Route Digit Indicator [*Telecommunications*] (TEL)
RDI .... Royal Designer for Industry [*British*]
RDI .... Rupture Delivery Interval [*Obstetrics*]
RDIA .... Regional Development Incentives Act
R Dialect & Tradic Popul ... Revista de Dialectologia y Tradiciones Populares [*A publication*]
RDI et Comp ... Revue de Droit International et de Droit Compare [*A publication*]
RdiE.......... Rivista di Estetica [*A publication*]
RdiF .... Rivista di Filosofia [*A publication*]
RDIGA ...... Reader's Digest [*A publication*]
RDIn.......... Rivista di Diritto Internazionale [*A publication*]
RDInt......... Revue de Droit International et de Legislation Comparee [*A publication*]
RDIntel...... Revue de Droit Intellectuel [*A publication*]
RDIPP .... Rivista di Diritto Internazionale Privato e Processuale [*A publication*] (DLA)
R Dir Adm ... Revista de Direito Administrativo [*A publication*]
RDIS.......... Radiation Disposal Systems, Inc. [*Charlotte, NC*] [*NASDAQ symbol*] (NQ)
RDIS.......... Replenishment Demand Inventory System
RDIS.......... Research and Development Information System [*Later, EPD/RDIS*] [*Electric Power Research Institute*] [*Information service or system*] (IID)
RDISSS ..... Royal Dockyard Iron and Steel Shipbuilders' Society [*A union*] [*British*]
RDIU .... Remote Device Interface Unit
R 1 DIY...... Royal 1st Devon Imperial Yeomanry [*British military*] (DMA)
RDJ........... Readjustment
RDJ........... Rio De Janeiro [*Brazil*] [*Seismograph station code, US Geological Survey*] (SEIS)
RDJ........... Rio De Janeiro [*Brazil*] [*Later, VSS*] [*Geomagnetic observatory code*]
RdJB.......... Recht der Jugend und des Bildungswesens [*Neuwied, West Germany*] [*A publication*] (DLA)
RDJC......... Revue de Doctrine et de Jurisprudence Coloniales et Financieres [*A publication*]
RDJCT ...... Register, Department of Justice and the Courts of the United States [*A publication*]
RDJTF....... Rapid Deployment Joint Task Force [*Military*] (RDA)
RDK.......... Red Oak, IA [*Location identifier*] [*FAA*] (FAAL)
RDK.......... Research and Development Kit
RDK.......... Ruddick Corp. [*AMEX symbol*] (SPSG)
RDKN........ Redken Laboratories, Inc. [*NASDAQ symbol*] (NQ)
RDL.......... Radial (MSA)
RDL.......... Radioactive Decay Law
RDL........... Radiological Defense Laboratory [*NASA*] (KSC)
RDL........... Rail Dynamics Laboratory
RDL........... Random Dynamic Load
RDL........... [*The*] Reactor Development Laboratory [*UKAEA*] [*British*]
RDL........... Reallexikon der Deutschen Literaturgeschichte [*A publication*]
RDL........... Rear Defence Locality [*British military*] (DMA)
RDL........... Reciprocal Detection Latency
RDL........... Recurring Document Listing (MCD)
RDL .... Redlaw Industries, Inc. [*AMEX symbol*] [*Toronto Stock Exchange symbol*] (SPSG)
RDL........... Regional Development Laboratory [*Philadelphia, PA*]
RDL........... Remote Display Link
RDL........... Replaceable Display Light
RDL........... Resistor Diode Logic
RdL .... Revista de Letras [*A publication*]
RdL .... Revista do Livro [*A publication*]
RDL .... Rim of Dorsal Lip
RDL........... Rocket Development Laboratory [*Air Force*]
RdLet .... Revista de Letras. Serie Literatura [*A publication*]

RDLGB...... Radiologe [*A publication*]
RDLGE...... Reunion Democratica para la Liberacion de Guinea Ecuatorial [*Democratic Movement for the Liberation of Equatorial Guinea*] [*Political party*] (PD)
RDLI......... Royal Durban Light Infantry [*British military*] (DMA)
RDLN .... Retrodorsolateral Nucleus [*Neuroanatomy*]
RDLP........ Research and Development Limited Partnership [*Tax-shelter investment*]
RDLX .... Airlift International, Inc. [*Air carrier designation symbol*]
RdM.......... Die Religionen der Menschheit [*A publication*] (BJA)
RDM.......... Nouvelle Revue des Deux Mondes [*A publication*]
RDM.......... RADARman [*Also, RD*]
RDM.......... Radial Distribution Method
RDM........ Real-Time Data Manager (MCD)
RDM........ Recording Demand Meter
RDM........ Redmond [*Oregon*] [*Airport symbol*] (OAG)
RDM........ Relay Driver Module
RDM........ Remote Data Management
RDM........ Remote Digital Multiplexer (MCD)
RDM........ Retail and Distribution Management [*A publication*]
RDM........ Revue des Deux Mondes [*A publication*]
RdM.......... Revue de la Mediterranee [*A publication*]
RdM.......... Revue de Musicologie [*Paris*] [*A publication*]
RDMAA .... R and D [*Research and Development*] Management [*A publication*]
R and D Manage ... R and D [*Research and Development*] Management [*A publication*]
R & D Mangt ... R and D [*Research and Development*] Management [*A publication*]
RDMC .... Research and Development Management Course [*Army*]
R de D McGill ... Revue de Droit de McGill [*A publication*] (DLA)
RDME .... Range and Distance Measuring Equipment
RDMF .... Rapidly Deployable Medical Facilities
RDMGA .... Railway Dock and Marine Grades Association [*A union*] [*British*]
RDMI .... Roof Drainage Manufacturers Institute [*Defunct*] (EA)
RDMin....... Revue de Droit Minier [*A publication*]
RDMOA.... Repatriation Department Medical Officers' Award [*Australia*]
RDMS ...... Range Data Measurement Subsystem (MCD)
RDMS ...... Registered Diagnostic Medical Sonologist
RDMS ...... Retail Development Management Services [*British*]
RDMS ...... Retrospective Data Management System
RDMTR ..... Radiometer (NASA)
RDMU....... Range-Drift Measuring Unit
RDN.......... Real de Minas Mine [*Vancouver Stock Exchange symbol*]
RDN.......... Rejection Disposition Notice
RDN.......... Revue du Nord [*A publication*]
RDN.......... Royal Danish Navy (NATG)
RDN.......... Rural Deanery [*Church of England*]
rDNA .... Deoxyribonucleic Acid, Recombinant [*Biochemistry, genetics*]
rDNA .... Deoxyribonucleic Acid, Ribosomal [*Biochemistry, genetics*]
RDNamur .. Revue Diocesaine de Namur [*A publication*]
R & DNET ... Research and Development Network [*Formerly, ARPANET*]
RDNG........ Reading (MSA)
RDNGB.... Ryukyu Daigaku Nogakubu Gakujutsu Hokoku [*A publication*]
RDNP .... Rassemblement Democratique Nationaliste et Progressiste [*Progressive Nationalist and Democratic Assembly*] [*Haiti*] (PD)
RDNS .... Readiness (MSA)
RDO.......... Radio (AABC)
RDO........... Radio Readout
RDO........... Radiological Defense Officer [*Civil defense*]
RDO........... Range Development Officer (MUGU)
RDO........... Rechnungswesen, Datentechnik, Organisation [*A publication*]
RDO........... Reconnaissance Duty Officer
RDO........... Redistribution Order [*Military*] (AFM)
RDO........... Regional Disbursing Office
RDO........... Research and Development Objectives [*Military*] (AFM)
RDO........... Research, Development, and Operation [*Military appropriation*]
R & DO ...... Research and Development Operations [*Marshall Space Flight Center*] [*NASA*] (NASA)
RDO........... River District Office [*National Weather Service*]
RDO........... Rodeo Resources Ltd. [*Vancouver Stock Exchange symbol*]
RDO........... Rostered Day Off [*Australia*]
RDO........... Runway Duty Officer [*Aviation*] (MCD)
RDOC........ Reference Designation Overflow Code (NASA)
RDOM....... Restructured Division Operations Manual (MCD)
R Dom Cult ... Revista Dominicana di Cultura [*A publication*]
RDON .... Radon Testing Corporation of America, Inc. [*NASDAQ symbol*] (NQ)
RDON .... Road Octane Number [*Fuel technology*]
RDOS .... Real-Time Disk-Operating System [*Data processing*]
RDOUT..... Readout
RDP .... RADAR Data Processing
RDP .... RADAR Digital Probe
RDP .... Radiation Degradation Product
RDP .... Range Data Processor (MCD)
RDP .... Range Deflection Protractor [*Weaponry*] (INF)
RDP .... Ration Distributing Point [*Military*]

RDP .... Reactor Development Program [*Nuclear Regulatory Commission*] (NRCH)
RDP .... Receiver and Data Processor (MCD)
RDP .... Rectifying-Demodulating Phonopneumograph [*Medicine*]
RDP .... Remote Data Processor
RDP .... Requirements Data Plan (NASA)
RDP .... Requirements Development Plan [*NASA*] (NASA)
RDP .... Research Data Publication [*Center*]
RDP .... Research and Development Plan
RD & P....... Research, Development, and Production [*NATO*] (NATG)
RDP .... Reunification Democracy Party [*Political party*] [*Republic of Korea*]
RDP .... Revolutionary Development Program [*South Vietnam*]
RDP .... Revue de Droit Penal et de Criminologie [*A publication*]
RdP .... Revue de Paris [*A publication*]
RDP .... Ribulosediphosphate [*Also, RuBP*] [*Biochemistry*]
RDP .... Right Dorso Posterior [*Medicine*] (ROG)
RDP .... Rocca Di Papa [*Italy*] [*Seismograph station code, US Geological Survey*] (SEIS)
RdPac....... Revista del Pacifico [*A publication*]
RDPB........ RADAR Data Plotting Board
RDPB........ Research and Development Planning and Budgeting (AFIT)
RDPC........ RADAR Data Processing Center [*Military*]
RDPE........ RADAR Data Processing Equipment (AABC)
RDPJ........ Rail Discharge Point Jet (NATG)
RDPM .... Rail Discharge Point Mogas (NATG)
RDPM .... Revised Draft Presidential Memorandum
RDPM .... Rotary Drive Piston Motor
R & DPP .... Research and Development Program Planning [*Database*] [*DTIC*]
RDPR .... Refer to Drawer Please Represent [*Business term*] (DCTA)
RDPS .... RADAR Data Processing System
RDPS......... Remote Docking Procedures Simulator (MCD)
RDPS......... Research and Development Planning Summary
RdQ........... Reading Quotient
RDR .... Grand Forks, ND [*Location identifier*] [*FAA*] (FAAL)
RDR .... RADAR (AAG)
RDR .... Raider
RDR .... Rapid Canadian Resource Corp. [*Vancouver Stock Exchange symbol*]
RDR .... Raw Data Recorder (NASA)
RDR .... Reader (MSA)
R/DR .... Rear Door [*Automotive engineering*]
RDR .... Receive Data Register [*Data processing*] (MDG)
RDR .... Rejection Disposition Report [*NASA*] (KSC)
RDR .... Relative Digestion Rate [*Nutrition*]
RDR .... Reliability Design Review
RDR .... Reliability Diagnostic Report (AAG)
RDR .... Remote Digital Readout
RDR .... Research and Development Report
RDR .... Research Division Report
RDR .... Ribonucleoside Diphosphate Reductase [*An enzyme*]
RDR .... Risk Data Report [*Insurance*]
RDR .... Rudder (NASA)
RDR .... Ryukoku Daigaku Ronshu [*A publication*]
RDRBCN.. RADAR Beacon (KSC)
RDRC .... Road Design and Road Costs [*British*]
R Dr Cont ... Revue de Droit Contemporain [*A publication*]
RDRD .... Remote Digital Readout
R/D Res/Develop ... R/D. Research/Development [*A publication*]
R Dr Fam ... Revue de Droit Familial [*A publication*]
R Dr Homme ... Revue des Droits de l'Homme [*A publication*]
RDRIA....... Radiazioni e Radioisotopi [*A publication*]
RDRINT.... RADAR Intermittent (IEEE)
R Dr Int Dr Comp ... Revue de Droit International et de Droit Compare [*A publication*]
R Dr Int Sci Dipl ... Revue de Droit International de Sciences Diplomatiques et Politiques [*A publication*]
RDRKB...... Ritsumeikan Daigaku Rikogaku Kenkyusho Kiyo [*A publication*]
R Droit Can ... Revue de Droit Canonique [*A publication*]
R Droit Int Sci Dipl Pol ... Revue de Droit International de Sciences Diplomatiques et Politiques [*A publication*]
R Droit Public ... Revue du Droit Public et de la Science Politique en France et a l'Etranger [*A publication*]
R Droits Homme ... Revue des Droits de l'Homme [*A publication*]
R Droit Soc ... Revue de Droit Social [*A publication*]
R Dr Pen Crim ... Revue de Droit Penal et de Criminologie [*A publication*]
R Dr Publ Sci Polit ... Revue du Droit Public et de la Science Politique en France et a l'Etranger [*A publication*]
R Dr Rur .... Revue de Droit Rural [*A publication*]
RDRSMTR ... RADAR Transmitter (AAG)
R Dr Soc .... Revue de Droit Social [*A publication*]
RDRV .... Rhesus Diploid-Cell-Strain Rabies Vaccine
RDR XMTR ... RADAR Transmitter
RDS .... RADAR Distribution Switchboard
RDS .... RADAUS [*Radio-Austria AG*] Data-Service [*Telecommunications*] (TSSD)
RDS .... Radio Digital System [*Telecommunications*] (TEL)
RDS .... Radius (FAAC)
RDS .... Random Dot Stereogram

RDS .... Range Destruct System
RDS .... Rate of Dispersal Success [*Ecology*]
RDS .... Raytheon Data Systems Co.
RDS .... Read Strobe
RDS .... Records Data Services [*Australia*]
RDS .... Reeds [*Music*]
RDS .... Relative Detector Sensitivity [*Robotics technology*]
RDS .... Rendezvous Docking Simulator [*Aerospace*]
RDS .... Reperimento Documentazione Siderurgica [*Iron and Steel Documentation Service*] [*Information service or system*] (IID)
RDS .... Request for Data Services
RDS .... Required Number of Days of Stock
RDS .... Requisition Distribution System
RDS .... Research Defence Society [*British*]
RDS .... Research and Development Service [*Army-Ordnance*]
RDS .... Research, Development, and Standardization [*Groups*] [*Army*] (RDA)
RD & S ..... Research, Development, and Studies [*Marine Corps*]
RDS .... Research and Development Survey
RDS .... Research Documentation Section [*Public Health Service*] [*Information service or system*] (IID)
RDS .... Research Documents Search [*Information service or system*] (EISS)
RDS .... Resistive Divider Standard
RDS .... Resource Development Services (EA)
RDS .... Respiratory Distress Syndrome [*Formerly, HMD*] [*Medicine*]
RdS .... Responsabilita del Sapere [*A publication*]
RDS .... Retail Distribution Station [*Military*] (AFM)
RDS .... Revolutionary Development Support [*South Vietnam*]
RDS .... Revolving Discussion Sequence
RdS .... Revue de Synthese [*A publication*]
RDS .... Rhode Island Department of State Library Services, Providence, RI [*OCLC symbol*] (OCLC)
RDS .... Richard D. Siegrest [*Alaska*] [*Seismograph station code, US Geological Survey*] (SEIS)
RDS .... Robotic Deriveter System
RDS .... Rocketdyne Digital Simulator [*NASA*] (NASA)
RDS .... Rokeach Dogmatism Scale
RDS .... Rounds [*of ammunition*] [*Military*]
RDS .... Royal Drawing Society [*British*]
RDS .... Royal Dublin Society
RDS .... Rural Development Service [*Department of Agriculture*]
RDS .... Russkaja Demokraticeskaja Satira XVII Veka [*A publication*]
RDSA........ Seaman Apprentice, RADARman Striker [*Navy rating*]
RD/SB ...... Rudder Speed Brake [*Aviation*] (MCD)
RDSD .... Reliability Design Support Document [*Nuclear energy*] (NRCH)
RDSD .... Revolutionary Development Support Division [*South Vietnam*]
RDSG .... Roczniki Dziejow Spoleczno-Gospodarczych [*A publication*]
RDSM .... Remote Digital Submultiplexer (KSC)
RDSM .... Research Development Safety Management [*Air Force*]
RDS/M...... Rounds per Minute [*Military*]
RDSN .... RADARman, Seaman [*Navy rating*]
RDSN .... Seaman, RADARman, Striker [*Navy rating*]
RdSO .... Rivista degli Studi Orientali [*A publication*]
RDSP .... Revolutionary Development Support Plan [*or Program*] [*South Vietnam*]
Rds Rd Constn ... Roads and Road Construction [*A publication*]
RDSS......... Radio Determination Satellite Service [*Geostar Corp.*]
RDSS .... Rapid Deployable Surveillance Systems [*Military*] (NVT)
RD Sup ...... Revenue Decisions, Supplement [*India*] [*A publication*] (DLA)
RDT .... Radio Digital Terminal [*Bell System*]
RDT .... Rapid Decompression Test
RDT .... Reactor Development and Technology [*Nuclear energy*] (MCD)
RDT .... Reactor Drain Tank [*Nuclear energy*] (NRCH)
RDT .... Recreatie-Documentatie. Literatuuroverzicht Inzake Dagrecreatie, Verblijfsrecreatie, en Toerisme [*A publication*]
RDT .... Redoubt [*Alaska*] [*Seismograph station code, US Geological Survey*] (SEIS)
RDT .... Regular Dialysis Treatment [*Medicine*]
RDT .... Reliability Demonstration Test
RDT .... Reliability Design Test
RDT .... Reliability Development Testing (CAAL)
RDT .... Remote Data Transmitter
RDT .... Renal Dialysis Treatment [*Nephrology*]
RDT .... Repertory Dance Theatre [*Salt Lake City, UT*]
RD & T...... Research, Development, and Testing
RDT .... Reserve Duty Training [*Military*]
RDT .... Resource Definition Table [*Data processing*] (IBMDP)
RDT .... Retinal Damage Threshold [*Ophthalmology*]
RdT .... Revista de Teatro [*A publication*]
RDT .... Revue de Droit du Travail [*A publication*] (DLA)
RDT .... Richard-Toll [*Senegal*] [*Airport symbol*] (OAG)
RDT .... Rotational Direction Transmission
RDT & E.... Research, Development, Test, and Evaluation [*DoD*]
RDTE .... Research, Development, Test, and Evaluation [*DoD*]
RDTEA...... Research, Development, Test, and Evaluation, Army

RDT & EN ... Research, Development, Test, and Evaluation, Navy
RDTF........ Revolutionary Development Task Force [*South Vietnam*]
RDTL........ Resistor Diode Transistor Logic (IEEE)
RDTLC...... Rotating Disc Thin-Layer Chromatography
RDTM .... Rated Distribution and Training Management
RDTournai ... Revue Diocesaine de Tournai [*A publication*]
RDTP........ Revista de Dialectologia y Tradiciones Populares [*A publication*]
RDTR .... Radiator (MSA)
RDTR .... Research Division Technical Report
RDTSR ...... Rapid Data Transmission System for Requisitioning [*Navy*]
RDU.......... RADAR Display Unit
RDU.......... Raleigh/Durham [*North Carolina*] [*Airport symbol*]
RDU.......... Receipt and Despatch Unit [*Aircraft*]
RDU.......... Remote Display Unit [*American Solenoid Co.*] [*Somerset, NJ*]
RDU.......... Rideau Resources Corp. [*Vancouver Stock Exchange symbol*]
R Dublin Soc J Sc Pr ... Royal Dublin Society. Journal. Scientific Proceedings [*A publication*]
R Dublin Soc Rep ... Royal Dublin Society. Report [*A publication*]
RDUC........ Receiver Data from Unit Control (MCD)
R D U S...... Revue de Droit. Universite de Sherbrooke [*A publication*]
RDV.......... Rechentechnik-Datenverarbeitung [*A publication*]
RDV.......... Recoverable Drop Vehicle (MCD)
RDV.......... Red Devil [*Alaska*] [*Airport symbol*] (OAG)
RDVA........ Radva Corp. [*Radford, VA*] [*NASDAQ symbol*] (NQ)
RDVT........ Reliability Design Verification Test
RDVU........ Rendezvous (AABC)
RDW.......... Red Cell Size Distribution Width [*Hematology*]
RDW.......... Redwood Resources, Inc. [*Vancouver Stock Exchange symbol*]
RDW.......... Response Data Word (MCD)
RDW.......... Return Data Word (MCD)
RDW.......... Right Defense Wing [*Women's lacrosse position*]
RDWA........ Returned Development Workers Association (EAIO)
RDWCA .... Royal Dockyard Wood Caulkers' Association [*A union*] [*British*]
RDWI........ Roadway Motor Plazas, Incorporated [*Rochester, NY*] [*NASDAQ symbol*] (NQ)
RDWND.... RADAR Dome Wind [*Meteorology*] (FAAC)
RDWS .... Radiological Defense Warning System
RDWW...... United Slate Tile and Composition Roofers, Damp and Waterproof Workers Association [*Later, UURWAW*]
RDX.......... Cocoa, FL [*Location identifier*] [*FAA*] (FAAL)
RDX.......... Research Department Explosive [*Cyclonite*]
RDY.......... Aspen, CO [*Location identifier*] [*FAA*] (FAAL)
RDY.......... Ready (AAG)
RDY.......... Roadway
RDY.......... Royal Devon Yeomanry [*British military*] (DMA)
RDY.......... Royal Dockyard [*British*]
RDYA........ Royal Devon Yeomanry Artillery [*British military*] (DMA)
RDyTP...... Revista de Dialectologia y Tradiciones Populares [*A publication*]
RDZ.......... Ringier Dokumentationszentrum [*Ringier Documentation Center*] [*Switzerland*] [*Information service or system*] (IID)
RDZ.......... Rodez [*France*] [*Airport symbol*] (OAG)
Re .... Earth or Geocentric Radius (AAG)
RE .... Fellow of the Royal Society of Painter-Etchers and Engravers [*British*]
RE .... Nordeste Linhas Aereas Regionais SA [*Brazil*] [*ICAO designator*] (FAAC)
Re .... Ohio Decisions Reprint [*A publication*] (DLA)
RE .... Radiated Emission (IEEE)
RE .... Radiation Effects (AAG)
RE .... Radiation Equipment (NRCH)
RE .... Radio-Eireann [*Eire*] [*Record label*]
RE .... Radio Electrician
RE .... Radio Exposure (AAG)
RE .... Radium Emanation
RE .... Railway Executive [*British*]
Re .... Rainerius [*Authority cited in pre-1607 legal work*] (DSA)
RE .... Rainform Expanded (MCD)
RE .... Rare Earth
RE .... Rate Effect (IEEE)
R of E .... Rate of Exchange
RE .... Rate of Exchange
RE .... Rational Expectations [*Economics*] (ECON)
RE .... Rattus Exulans [*The Polynesian rat*]
RE .... Reactive Evaporation [*Coating technology*]
RE .... Reading-Ease [*Score*] [*Advertising*]
Re .... Real [*Mathematics*]
RE .... Real-Encyclopaedie der Klassischen Altertumswissenschaft [*A publication*]
RE .... Real Estate
RE .... Real Estate Program [*Association of Independent Colleges and Schools specialization code*]
RE .... Real Number (DEN)
Re .... Realidad [*A publication*]
RE .... Receiver/Exciter
RE .... Recent [*Used to qualify weather phenomena*]
RE .... Reconnaissance Experimental [*British military*] (DMA)
RE .... Rectal Examination [*Medicine*]

RE .... Red Edges
RE .... Redman Industries, Inc. [*NYSE symbol*]   (SPSG)
RE .... Reel   (MSA)
R/E .... Reentry [*Aerospace*]   (KSC)
RE .... Reference [*Online database field identifier*]
RE .... Reference Equivalent [*Telecommunications*]   (TEL)
RE .... Reflux
Re .... Reforme [*A publication*]
RE .... Reformed Episcopal [*Church*]
RE .... Refrigeration Effect
RE .... Regarding
RE .... Regional Enteritis [*Medicine*]
RE .... Rehearsal Engineer   (MCD)
RE .... Reinforced [*Technical drawings*]
Re .... Reinsurance [*A publication*]
RE .... Relative Effectiveness [*or Efficiency*]   (MCD)
RE .... Relay Assemblies [*JETDS nomenclature*] [*Military*]   (CET)
RE .... Release
RE .... Religious Education [*A publication*]
RE .... Religious Education [*Secondary school course*] [*British*]
RE .... Religious of the Eucharist [*Roman Catholic women's religious order*]
RE .... Renewal Registration [*US Copyright Office class*]
RE .... Renovacion Espanola [*Spanish Renovation*]   (PPE)
RE .... Repair Equipment for F-15 and Subsequent Programs [*Military*]   (MCD)
RE .... Repayable to Either
RE .... Repetitive Extrasystole [*Cardiology*]
Re .... Republic [*Quezon City*] [*A publication*]
RE .... Republication [*NASA*]
RE .... Request for Estimate
RE .... Research and Engineering
R & E .... Research and Engineering
RE .... Research and Experiments Department [*Ministry of Home Security*] [*British*] [*World War II*]
RE .... Reset   (MDG)
RE .... Resolution Enhancement [*Computer graphics*]
Re .... Response [*A publication*]
RE .... Responsible Engineer   (NASA)
RE .... Rest [*or Resting*] Energy [*Medicine*]
RE .... Restriction Endonuclease [*An enzyme*]
RE .... Reticuloendothelial [*or Reticuloendothelium*] [*Medicine*]
RE .... Retinal Equivalent [*For Vitamin A*]
RE .... Retinyl Ester [*Organic chemistry*]
re .... Reunion [*MARC country of publication code*] [*Library of Congress*]   (LCCP)
RE .... Reunion [*ANSI two-letter standard code*]   (CNC)
RE .... Reversal of Prior Entry [*Banking*]
RE .... Review of Ethnology [*A publication*]
RE .... Review and Expositor [*A publication*]
RE .... Revised Edition [*Publishing*]
RE .... Revista Eclesiastica [*A publication*]
RE .... Revue d'Egyptologie [*A publication*]
RE .... Revue Egyptologique [*A publication*]
RE .... Revue d'Esthetique [*A publication*]
Re .... Reynolds Number [*Also, R, RN*] [*Viscosity*] [*IUPAC*]
Re .... Rhenium [*Chemical element*]
RE .... Rifle Expert
RE .... Right Eminent [*Freemasonry*]
RE .... Right End
RE .... Right Excellent
RE .... Right Eye
RE .... Risk Evaluation [*Insurance*]
RE .... Risk Exercise
RE .... Riviera Explorations Ltd. [*Vancouver Stock Exchange symbol*]
RE .... Rotary Engine [*Automotive engineering*]
RE .... Royal Engineers [*Military*] [*British*]
RE .... Royal Exchange [*British*]
RE .... Royal Society of Painter-Etchers and Engravers [*British*]
RE .... Rupee [*Monetary unit*] [*Ceylon, India, and Pakistan*]
RE .... Rural Electrification
R2E .... Realisations et Etudes Electronique [*Computer manufacturer*] [*France*]
REA .... RADAR Echoing Area
REA .... Radiation Emergency Area
REA .... Radiative Energy Attenuation [*Analytical chemistry*]
REA .... Radio Electrical Artificer [*British military*]   (DMA)
REA .... Radioenzymatic Assay [*Analytical biochemistry*]
REA .... Railroad Evangelistic Association   (EA)
REA .... Railway Express Agency [*Later, REA Express*] [*Defunct*]
REA .... Range Error Average   (MUGU)
REA .... Rare-Earth Alloy
REA .... Rauchgasentschwefelungs-Anlage [*Flue Gas Desulfurization Unit*] [*German*]
R & EA ...... Readiness and Emergency Action [*Red Cross Disaster Services*]
REA .... Realcap Holdings Ltd. [*Toronto Stock Exchange symbol*]
REA .... Reao [*French Polynesia*] [*Airport symbol*]   (OAG)
REA .... Recycle Acid [*Nuclear energy*]   (NRCH)
REA .... Reentry Angle
REA .... Religious Education Association   (EA)
REA .... Renaissance Educational Associates   (EA)

REA .... Renal Anastomosis [*Medicine*]
REA .... Request for Engineering Authorization
REA .... Request for Equitable Adjustment [*Navy*]
REA .... Research and Education Association
REA .... Research Engineering Authorization   (AAG)
REA .... Reserve Enlisted Association   (EA)
REA .... Responsible Engineering Activity
REA .... Revue de l'Egypte Ancienne [*Paris*] [*A publication*]
REA .... Revue des Etudes Anciennes [*A publication*]
REA .... Revue des Etudes Armeniennes [*A publication*]
REA .... Revue des Etudes Augustiniennes [*A publication*]
REA .... Rice Export Association
REA .... Ridihalgh, Eggers & Associates, Columbus, OH [*OCLC symbol*]   (OCLC)
REA .... Rocket Engine Assembly
REA .... Rubber Export Association [*Defunct*]   (EA)
REA .... Rural Education Association [*Later, NREA*]   (EA)
REA .... Rural Electrification Administration [*Department of Agriculture*]
REA et A.... Rite Ecossais Ancien et Accepte [*Ancient and Accepted Scottish Rite*] [*French*] [*Freemasonry*]
REA Bull ... REA [*Rural Electrification Administration*] Bulletin [*A publication*]
REA Bull ... Rural Electrification Administration. Bulletin [*A publication*]   (DLA)
REAC........ Reaction   (AAG)
REAC........ Reactive
REAC........ Reactor   (AAG)
REAC........ Real Estate Aviation Chapter   (EA)
REAC........ Reeves Electronic Analog Computer
REAC........ Regional Educational Advisory Council [*British*]
REACCS .... Reaction Access System [*Computer program*]
REACDU .. Recalled to Active Duty
REACH ..... Reassurance to Each [*To help families of the mentally ill*]
REACH ..... Research, Education, and Assistance for Canadians with Herpes
REACH ..... Responsible Educated Adolescents Can Help   (EA)
REACH ..... Rural Employment Action and Counseling Help [*Project*]
REACK ..... Receipt Acknowledged
REACQ ..... Reacquire
REACT ...... RADAR Electrooptical Area Correlation Tracker [*Military*]   (CAAL)
REACT ...... Radio Emergency Associated Citizens Teams [*Acronym alone is now used as official association name*]   (EA)
RE ACT ..... Reconnaissance/Reaction   (MCD)
REACT ...... Register Enforced Automated Control Technique [*Cash register-computing system*]
REACT ...... Reliability Evaluation and Control Technique
REACT ...... Rese Engineering Automatic Core Tester
REACT ...... Resource Allocation and Control Technique [*Management*]
React Cent Ned Rep ... Reactor Centrum Nederland. Report [*A publication*]
React Fuel Process ... Reactor Fuel Processing [*A publication*]
React Fuel-Process Technol ... Reactor and Fuel-Processing Technology [*A publication*]
React Intermed ... Reactive Intermediates [*A publication*]
React Kin C ... Reaction Kinetics and Catalysis Letters [*A publication*]
React Kinet ... Reaction Kinetics [*Later, Gas Kinetics and Energy Transfer*] [*A publication*]
React Kinet Catal Lett ... Reaction Kinetics and Catalysis Letters [*A publication*]
Reactor Fuel Process ... Reactor Fuel Processing [*A publication*]
Reactor Mater ... Reactor Materials [*A publication*]
React Polym ... Reactive Polymers [*The Netherlands*] [*A publication*]
React Res Soc News ... Reaction Research Society. News [*A publication*]
React Res Soc Rep ... Reaction Research Society. Report [*A publication*]
REAC/TS ... Radiation Emergency Assistance Center/Training Site [*Department of Energy*]
REACTS.... Reader Action Service [*ZIP code computer*]
REACTS.... Regional Educators Annual Chemistry Teaching Symposium
React Struct Concepts Org Chem ... Reactivity and Structure Concepts in Organic Chemistry [*A publication*]
React Technol ... Reactor Technology [*A publication*]
REACTVT ... Reactivate
READ .... American Learning Corp. [*Chicago, IL*] [*NASDAQ symbol*]   (NQ)
READ .... RADAR Echo Augmentation Device
READ .... Readability Ease Assessment Device   (MCD)
READ .... Reading [*County borough in England*]
READ .... Reading Efficiency and Delinquency [*Program*]
READ .... Real-Time Electronic Access and Display [*System*] [*Data processing*]
READ .... Remedial Education for Adults
READ .... Remote Electronic Alphanumeric Display [*Data processing*]   (IEEE)
READ .... Research and Economic Analysis Division [*Office of Transportation*]   (GRD)
READ .... Reserve on Extended Active Duty [*Military*]
Read Dec.... Read's Declarations and Pleadings [*A publication*]   (DLA)
Read Dig .... Reader's Digest [*A publication*]
Read Digest ... Reader's Digest [*A publication*]
Read Educ ... Reading Education [*A publication*]   (APTA)
Reader........ Reader Magazine [*A publication*]

Readers D .. Reader's Digest [*A publication*] (APTA)
Reader's Dig ... Reader's Digest [*A publication*]
Readex .... Readex Microprint Corp., New York, NY [*Library symbol*] [*Library of Congress*] (LCLS)
Read Glass Hist ... Readings in Glass History [*A publication*]
READI .... Rocket Engine Analyzer and Decision Instrumentation
READIMP ... Readiness Improvement (MCD)
Read Improv ... Reading Improvement [*A publication*]
Reading Educ ... Reading Education [*A publication*]
Reading Univ Geol Rep ... Reading University. Geological Reports [*A publication*]
READJ ...... Readjusted
READJP ...... Readjustment Pay [*Military*]
READL ...... Railway Employers' Association Defence League [*British*]
Read Man .. Reading Manitoba [*A publication*]
Read PL ..... Read's Declarations and Pleadings [*A publication*] (DLA)
Read Psychol ... Reading Psychology [*A publication*]
READR ...... Remain in Effect after Discharge and Reenlistment [*Refers to orders*] [*Army*]
Read Res Q ... Reading Research Quarterly [*A publication*]
READS ...... Reader Enrollment and Delivery System [*Library of Congress*] [*Washington, DC*] [*Information service or system*] (IID)
READS ...... Reentry Air Data System (ADA)
READS ...... Reno Air Defense Sector [*ADC*]
Read Teach ... Reading Teacher [*A publication*]
Read Time ... Reading Time [*A publication*] (APTA)
Read Today Int ... Reading Today International [*A publication*]
READU ...... Ready Duty (NVT)
READU ..... Ready Unit (NVT)
Read World ... Reading World [*A publication*]
READYREP ... Ready-to-Sail Report [*Navy*] (NVT)
REAF .... Resources Exchange Association Foundation [*Also known as REA Foundation*] (EA)
REAF .... Revised Engineer Active Force (MCD)
R E Ag .... Revue des Etudes Augustiniennes [*A publication*]
REAIU ...... Revue des Ecoles de l'Alliance Israelite Universelle [*A publication*]
Reakt Bull ... Reaktor Bulletin [*A publication*]
Reaktortag (Fachvortr) ... Reaktortagung (Fachvortraege) [*West Germany*] [*A publication*]
Reakt Osobo Chist Veshchestva ... Reaktivy i Osobo Chistye Veshchestva [*A publication*]
Reakts Metody Issled Org Soedin ... Reaktsii i Metody Issledovaniya Organicheskikh Soedinenii [*USSR*] [*A publication*]
Reakts Sposobn Koord Soedin ... Reaktsionnaya Sposobnost' Koordinatsionnykh Soedinenii [*A publication*]
Reakts Sposobn Mekh Reakts Org Soedin ... Reaktsionnaya Sposobnost' i Mekhanizmy Reaktsii Organicheskikh Soedinenii [*A publication*]
Reakts Sposobn Org Soedin ... Reaktsionnaya Sposobnost' Organicheskikh Soedinenij [*A publication*]
Reakts Sposobnost' Org Soedin Tartu Gos Univ ... Reaktsionnaya Sposobnost' Organicheskikh Soedinenij. Tartuskij Gosudarstvennyj Universitet [*A publication*]
ReAL .... Re Artes Liberales [*A publication*]
REAL .... Re: Arts and Letters [*A publication*]
R/EAL .... Reading/Everyday Activities in Life [*Educational test*]
REAL .... Reliability, Inc. [*NASDAQ symbol*] (NQ)
REAL .... Research-Extension Analytical Laboratory [*Ohio State University*] [*Research center*] (RCD)
REAL .... Routine Economic Air Lift [*Army*]
Real Anal Exchange ... Real Analysis Exchange [*A publication*]
REALB ...... REAL. The Yearbook of Research in English and American Literature [*A publication*]
REALCOM ... Real-Time Communications [*RCA*]
Real Econ ... Realta Economica [*A publication*]
Real-Encycl Ges Heilk ... Real-Encyclopaedie der Gesammten Heilkunde Medicinisch-Chirurgisches Handwoerterbuch fuer Praktische Aerzte [*A publication*]
Real Estate Appraiser & Anal ... Real Estate Appraiser and Analyst [*A publication*]
Real Estate J ... Real Estate Journal [*A publication*] (APTA)
Real Estate L J ... Real Estate Law Journal [*A publication*]
Real Estate R ... Real Estate Review [*A publication*]
Real Estate Rev ... Real Estate Review [*A publication*]
Real Estate & Stock J ... Real Estate and Stock Journal [*A publication*] (APTA)
Real Est L .. Real Estate Law Journal [*A publication*]
Real Est LJ ... Real Estate Law Journal [*A publication*]
Real Est L Rep ... Real Estate Law Report [*A publication*] (DLA)
Real Est Re ... Real Estate Review [*A publication*]
Real Est Rec ... Real Estate Record [*New York*] [*A publication*] (DLA)
Real Est Rev ... Real Estate Review [*A publication*]
REAL FAMMIS ... Real-Time Finance and Manpower Management Information System [*Marine Corps*] (MCD)
Realidad Econ ... Realidad Economica [*A publication*]
Real Ist Veneto Mem ... Reale Istituto Veneto di Scienze, Lettere, ed Arti. Memorie [*A publication*]
REALIZN ... Realization (ROG)
Reallexikon ... Reallexikon der Aegyptischen Religionsgeschichte [*A publication*]

Real M .... Realta del Mezzogiorno. Mensile di Politica, Economia, Cultura [*A publication*]
RealN .... Realta Nuova [*A publication*]
Real Pr Cas ... Real Property Cases [*England*] [*A publication*] (DLA)
Real Prop Acts ... Real Property Actions and Proceedings [*A publication*] (DLA)
Real Prop Cas ... Real Property Cases [*1843-47*] [*A publication*] (DLA)
Real Prop P ... Real Property, Probate, and Trust Journal [*A publication*]
Real Prop Probate & Trust J ... Real Property, Probate, and Trust Journal [*A publication*]
Real Prop Prob and Tr J ... Real Property, Probate, and Trust Journal [*A publication*]
Real Prop Prob & Trust J ... Real Property, Probate, and Trust Journal [*A publication*] (DLA)
Real Prop Rep ... Real Property Reports [*A publication*]
Realta Econ ... Realta Economica [*A publication*]
Realta Mezzogiorno ... Realta del Mezzogiorno [*A publication*]
Real Wr ...... Realist Writer [*A publication*] (APTA)
REAM .... Rapid Excavation and Mining [*Project*] [*Bureau of Mines*]
REAMS ...... Resources Evaluation and Management System [*Army*]
REAN .... Royal East African Navy [*British military*] (DMA)
REAnc .... Revue des Etudes Anciennes [*A publication*]
Reanim Med Urgence ... Reanimation et Medecine d'Urgence [*A publication*]
Reanim Organes Artif ... Reanimation et Organes Artificiels [*A publication*]
REAP .... Read, Encode, Annotate, Ponder [*Reading improvement method*]
REAP .... Remote Entry Acquisition Package
REAP .... Reutilization Expedite Assets Program [*DoD*]
REAP .... Rural Environmental Assistance Program [*Department of Agriculture*]
Reap Dec .... United States Customs Court Reports, Reappraisement Decision [*A publication*] (DLA)
REAPOR ... Real Estate Accounts Payable and Operating Reports
Reapp Dec ... United States Customs Court Reports, Reappraisement Decision [*A publication*] (DLA)
REAPS ...... Rotary Engine Antipollution System
REAPT ...... Reappoint (AFM)
REAR .... Reliability Engineering Analysis Report (IEEE)
REARA .... Recherche Aerospatiale [*A publication*]
REARM .... Renovation of Armament Manufacturing Program [*Army*] (MCD)
REArm ...... Revue des Etudes Armeniennes [*A publication*]
REARM ...... Underway Rearming [*Navy*] (NVT)
REArmen ... Revue des Etudes Armeniennes [*A publication*]
REArmNS ... Revue des Etudes Armeniennes. Nouvelle Serie [*A publication*]
REART .... Restricted Articles [*IATA*] (DS)
REA (Rural Electr Adm) Bull (US) ... REA (Rural Electrification Administration) Bulletin (United States) [*A publication*]
REAS .... Real Estate Appraisal School [*Federal Home Loan Bank Board*]
REAS .... Reasonable (ROG)
REAS .... Register of Environment Assessments and Statements (MCD)
REAS .... Resources, Entities Accounting Subsystem (MCD)
REASM ...... Reassemble (AAG)
REASN ...... Reason (ROG)
REASSCE ... Reassurance (ROG)
REASSEM ... Reassemble (MSA)
REASSN ... Reassign (ROG)
REASSND ... Reassigned (ROG)
REASST .... Reassignment (ROG)
REASSY .... Reassembly (MSA)
REASTAN ... Renton Electrical Analog for Solution of Thermal Analogous Networks
REAT .... Radiological Emergency Assistance Team [*AEC*]
REAT .... Realty Industries [*NASDAQ symbol*] (NQ)
REAug .... Revue des Etudes Augustiniennes [*A publication*]
REAUM .... Reaumur (ROG)
REB .... R. E. Blake [*Record label*]
REB .... RADAR Evaluation Branch [*ADC*]
REB .... Real Estate Business [*Realtors National Marketing Institute*] [*A publication*]
REB .... Reba Resources Ltd. [*Vancouver Stock Exchange symbol*]
REB .... Rebecca/Eureka [*Navigation*] (AIA)
REB .... Rebel
REB .... Rebounds [*Basketball, hockey*]
Reb .... [*Petrus*] Rebuffus [*Deceased, 1557*] [*Authority cited in pre-1607 legal work*] (DSA)
REB .... Rebuilt
REB .... Reentry Body
REB .... Regional Education Board of the Christian Brothers (EA)
REB .... Relativistic Electron Beam (MCD)
REB .... Research Earth Borer
REB .... Resultaten van de Conjunctuurenquete bij het Bedrijfsleven in de Gemeenschap [*A publication*]
REB .... Review of Regional Economics and Business [*A publication*]
ReB .... Revista Biblica [*A publication*]
REB .... Revista Eclesiastica Brasiliera [*A publication*]
ReB .... Revue Biblique [*A publication*]
REB .... Revue des Etudes Byzantines [*A publication*]
REB .... Revue Internationale des Etudes Balkaniques [*A publication*]
REB .... Rocket Engine Band
REB .... Rod End Bearing [*Army helicopter*]

REB .... Roentgen-Equivalent-Biological [*Irradiation unit*]
REBA........ Relativistic Electron Beam Accelerator
REBAR...... Reinforcing Bar (AAG)
REBAT...... Restricted Bandwidth Techniques (NG)
REBC........ Real Estate Brokerage Council (EA)
R-EBD-HS ... Recessive Epidermolysis Bullosa Dystrophia-Hallopeaun
       Siemens [*Dermatology*]
REBE........ Recovery Beacon Evaluation
REBECCA ... RADAR Responder Beacon [*System*] (MUGU)
REBIA .... Regional Educational Building Institute for Africa
REBK......... Repertoire des Banques de Donnees en Conversationnel
       [*Association Nationale de la Recherche Technique*]
       [*Information service or system*]
REBras ...... Revista Eclesiastica Brasileira [*A publication*]
REBS .... Royal Engineers Balloon School [*British military*] (DMA)
REBUD ..... Rehabilitation Budgeting Program
       [*Telecommunications*] (TEL)
REBUD ..... Renewable Energy Bulletin [*A publication*]
Rebuf.......... [*Petrus*] Rebuffus [*Deceased, 1557*] [*Authority cited in pre-1607
       legal work*] (DSA)
Rebuff .... [*Petrus*] Rebuffus [*Deceased, 1557*] [*Authority cited in pre-1607
       legal work*] (DSA)
REBUS...... Reseau des Bibliotheques Utilisant SIBIL [*Library Network of
       SIBIL Users*] [*University of Lausanne*] [*Switzerland*]
       [*Information service or system*] (IID)
REBUS...... Routine for Executing Biological Unit Simulations [*Computer
       program*]
REByz........ Revue des Etudes Byzantines [*A publication*]
REC .... Clarion State College, Clarion, PA [*OCLC symbol*] (OCLC)
REC .... Radiant Energy Conversion
REC .... Radio Electronic Combat [*Communications*]
REC .... Railway Executive Committee [*British*]
REC .... Rain Erosion Coating
REC .... Real Estate Council
REC .... Receipt
REC .... Received (DS)
REC .... Receiver (AAG)
REC .... Recens [*Fresh*] [*Pharmacy*]
REC .... Recent (ROG)
REC .... Reception
REC .... Recess (MSA)
REC .... Recherches sur l'Origine de l'Ecriture Cuneiforme [*A
       publication*] (BJA)
REC .... Recife [*Brazil*] [*Airport symbol*] (OAG)
REC .... Recipe
REC .... Recognition Equipment, Inc. [*NYSE symbol*] (SPSG)
REC .... Recommendation (AFM)
REC .... Record (AAG)
Rec .... Recordati [*Italy*] [*Research code symbol*]
REC .... Recorder
REC .... Recover [*or Recovery*]
REC .... Recreation
REC .... Recreational and Educational Computing [*A publication*]
REC .... Recreo [*Guatemala*] [*Seismograph station code, US Geological
       Survey*] (SEIS)
Rec .... Recruiter [*British military*] (DMA)
RECUT...... Rectifier (IEEE)
Rec .... Recueil (BJA)
Rec .... Recurrence [*A publication*]
REC .... Recurring (MCD)
REC .... Regional Evaluation Center (NVT)
REC .... Regroupement des Etudiants Camerounais [*Regrouping of
       Cameroonese Students*]
REC .... Rehabilitation Engineering Center for the Hearing Impaired
       [*Gallaudet College*] [*Research center*] (RCD)
REC .... Rehabilitation Engineering Centers [*Department of Health and
       Human Services*]
REC .... REM [*Roentgen-Equivalent-Man*] Equivalent Chemical
       [*Irradiation unit*]
REC .... Request for Engineering Change (MCD)
REC .... Reserve Equalization Committee [*Military*]
REC .... Residual Evaluation Center (MCD)
REC .... Retail Control [*A publication*]
REC .... Revista de Estudios Clasicos [*A publication*]
REC .... Revloc, PA [*Location identifier*] [*FAA*] (FAAL)
REC .... Ripling Electrochemical
REC .... Rudge Enthusiasts Club (EA)
RECA........ Residual Capabilities Assessment (MCD)
RECA........ Revenue and Expenditure Control Act of 1968
Rec Agric Res (Belfast) ... Record of Agricultural Research (Belfast) [*A
       publication*]
Rec Agric Res Minist Agric (Nth Ire) ... Record of Agricultural Research.
       Ministry of Agriculture (Northern Ireland) [*A publication*]
Rec Agr Res (N Ireland) ... Record of Agricultural Research (Northern
       Ireland) [*A publication*]
Rec Ak Inst Mus ... Records. Auckland Institute and Museum [*New Zealand*]
       [*A publication*]
RECALC ... Recalculated
Rec Am Cath Hist Soc ... Records. American Catholic Historical Society of
       Philadelphia [*A publication*]

Rec Annu Conv Br Wood Preserv Assoc ... Record of the Annual Convention.
       British Wood Preserving Association [*A publication*]
RECAP...... Real Estate Cost Analysis Program
RECAP...... Recapitulation (AABC)
RECAP...... Reliability Engineering and Corrective Action Program
RECAP...... Reliability Evaluation Continuous Analysis Program
RECAP...... Research and Education Center for Architectural Preservation
       [*University of Florida*] [*Research center*] (RCD)
RECAP...... Resource and Capabilities Model (KSC)
RECAP...... Review and Command Assessment of Project [*Military*]
RECAPS.... Regionalized Civilian Automated Pay System [*Air Force*]
Rec Asilomar Conf Circuits Syst Comput ... Record. Asilomar Conference on
       Circuits, Systems, and Computers [*A publication*]
Rec Ass'n Bar City of NY ... Record. Association of the Bar of the City of New
       York [*A publication*]
RECAT...... Ad Hoc Committee on the Cumulative Regulatory Effects on
       the Cost of Automotive Transportation [*Terminated,
       1972*] (EGAO)
RECAU ..... Receipt Acknowledged and Understood
Rec Auckland Inst ... Records. Auckland Institute and Museum [*A
       publication*]
Rec Auckl Inst Mus ... Records. Auckland Institute and Museum [*A
       publication*]
RecAug....... Recherches Augustiniennes [*A publication*]
Rec Aust Acad Sci ... Records. Australian Academy of Science [*A publication*]
Rec Aust Mus ... Records. Australian Museum [*A publication*]
Rec Aust Museum ... Records. Australian Museum [*A publication*] (APTA)
Rec Aust Mus Suppl ... Records. Australian Museum. Supplement [*A
       publication*]
RECBKS.... Receiving Barracks
Rec Bot Surv India ... Records. Botanical Survey of India [*A publication*]
Rec Buckinghamshire ... Records of Buckinghamshire [*A publication*]
RECC........ Rhine Evacuation and Control Command [*NATO*] (NATG)
Rec Canterbury Mus ... Records. Canterbury Museum [*Christchurch, New
       Zealand*] [*A publication*]
RECCB ...... Regional Education Committee of the Christian Brothers [*Later,
       REB*] (EA)
RECCE....... Reconnaissance (CINC)
Rec CEDH ... Recueil des Decisions de la Commission Europeenne de Droits
       de l'Homme [*A publication*]
RECCEXREP ... Reconnaisance Exploitation Report (MCD)
Rec Changer ... Record Changer [*A publication*]
Rec Chem Prog ... Record of Chemical Progress [*A publication*]
RECCO...... Reconnaissance (NVT)
Rec Coll...... Record Collector [*A publication*]
REC COM ... Record Commissioner [*British*] (DLA)
Rec Conv Brit Wood Pres Ass ... Record of the Annual Convention. British
       Wood Preserving Association [*A publication*]
RECD .... Received (AAG)
Rec Dec ...... Vaux's Recorder's Decisions [*1841-45*] [*Philadelphia, PA*] [*A
       publication*] (DLA)
Rec Dom Mus (Wellington) ... Records. Dominion Museum (Wellington, New
       Zealand) [*A publication*]
Recd Res Fac Agr Univ Tokyo ... Records of Researches. Faculty of
       Agriculture. University of Tokyo [*A publication*]
RECDUINS ... Received for Duty under Instruction
RECDUT... Received for Duty
RECE........ Cuban Representation of Exiles [*Also known as Representacion
       Cubana del Exilio*] (EA)
RECE........ Relativistic Electron Coil Experiment (MCD)
Rec Electr Commun Eng Conversat Tohoku Univ ... Record of Electrical and
       Communication Engineering Conversation. Tohoku
       University [*Japan*] [*A publication*]
Rec Eng N ... Recovery Engineering News [*A publication*]
RECENT... Recentis [*Fresh*] [*Pharmacy*] (ROG)
Recent Achiev Restorative Neurol ... Recent Achievements in Restorative
       Neurology [*A publication*]
Recent Adv Aerosp Med ... Recent Advances in Aerospace Medicine [*A
       publication*]
Recent Advanc Bot ... Recent Advances in Botany [*A publication*]
Recent Advanc Invert Physiol ... Recent Advances in Invertebrate Physiology
       [*A publication*]
Recent Adv Anim Nutr ... Recent Advances in Animal Nutrition [*A
       publication*]
Recent Adv Biol Psychiatry ... Recent Advances in Biological Psychiatry [*A
       publication*]
Recent Adv Clin Nucl Med ... Recent Advances in Clinical Nuclear Medicine
       [*A publication*]
Recent Adv Clin Pathol ... Recent Advances in Clinical Pathology [*A
       publication*]
Recent Adv Community Med ... Recent Advances in Community Medicine [*A
       publication*]
Recent Adv Endocrinol Metab ... Recent Advances in Endocrinology and
       Metabolism [*A publication*]
Recent Adv Eng Sci ... Recent Advances in Engineering Science [*A
       publication*]
Recent Adv Food Sci ... Recent Advances in Food Science [*A publication*]
Recent Adv Gastroenterol ... Recent Advances in Gastroenterology [*A
       publication*]
Recent Adv Gut Horm Res ... Recent Advances in Gut Hormone Research [*A
       publication*]

Recent Adv Phytochem ... Recent Advances in Phytochemistry [*A publication*]
Recent Adv Renal Dis ... Recent Advances in Renal Disease [*A publication*]
Recent Adv RES Res ... Recent Advances in RES [*Reticuloendothelial System*] Research [*A publication*]
Recent Adv Stud Card Struct Metab ... Recent Advances in Studies on Cardiac Structure and Metabolism [*A publication*]
Recent Dev Alcohol ... Recent Developments in Alcoholism [*A publication*]
Recent Dev Chem Nat Carbon Compd ... Recent Developments in the Chemistry of Natural Carbon Compounds [*A publication*]
Recent Dev Neurobiol Hung ... Recent Developments of Neurobiology in Hungary [*A publication*]
Recenti Prog Med ... Recenti Progressi in Medicina [*A publication*]
Recent Lit Hazard Environ Ind ... Recent Literature on Hazardous Environments in Industry [*A publication*]
Recent Med ... Recentia Medica [*A publication*]
Recent Prog Horm Res ... Recent Progress in Hormone Research [*A publication*]
Recent Prog Med (Roma) ... Recenti Progressi in Medicina (Roma) [*A publication*]
Recent Prog Microbiol ... Recent Progress in Microbiology [*A publication*]
Recent Prog Nat Sci Jap ... Recent Progress of Natural Sciences in Japan [*A publication*]
Recent Prog Psychiatry ... Recent Progress in Psychiatry [*A publication*]
Recent Progr Hormone Res ... Recent Progress in Hormone Research [*A publication*]
Recent Progr Natur Sci Japan ... Recent Progress of Natural Sciences in Japan [*A publication*]
Recent Prog Surf Sci ... Recent Progress in Surface Science [*A publication*]
Recent Publ Gov Probl ... Recent Publications on Governmental Problems [*United States*] [*A publication*]
Recent Pubns Governmental Problems ... Recent Publications on Governmental Problems [*A publication*]
Recent Results Cancer Res ... Recent Results in Cancer Research [*A publication*]
RECEP ...... Reception (ADA)
Recept Biochem Methodol ... Receptor Biochemistry and Methodology [*A publication*]
Recept Ligands Intercell Commun ... Receptors and Ligands in Intercellular Communication [*A publication*]
RECERT ... Recertification (NASA)
RECETED ... Receipted (ROG)
RECFD ...... Revista Cubana de Fisica [*A publication*]
RECFM ...... Record Format [*Data processing*]
RECG .... Radioelectrocardiograph
RECG .... Reciting
RECGA ...... Research and Engineering Council of the Graphic Arts Industry
RECGAI .... Research and Engineering Council of the Graphic Arts Industry (EA)
Rec Gen Enr et Not ... Recueil General de l'Enregistrement et du Notariat [*A publication*]
Rec Geol Surv Br Guiana ... Records. Geological Survey of British Guiana [*A publication*]
Rec Geol Surv Dep North Rhod ... Records. Geological Survey Department. Northern Rhodesia [*A publication*]
Rec Geol Surv Guyana ... Records. Geological Survey of Guyana [*A publication*]
Rec Geol Surv India ... Records. Geological Survey of India [*A publication*]
Rec Geol Surv Malawi ... Records. Geological Survey of Malawi [*A publication*]
Rec Geol Surv New South Wales ... Records. Geological Survey of New South Wales [*A publication*]
Rec Geol Surv Niger ... Records. Geological Survey of Nigeria [*A publication*]
Rec Geol Surv NSW ... Records. Geological Survey of New South Wales [*A publication*]
Rec Geol Surv Pak ... Records. Geological Survey of Pakistan [*A publication*]
Rec Geol Surv Tanganyika ... Records. Geological Survey of Tanganyika [*A publication*]
Rec Geol Surv Tasm ... Tasmania. Geological Survey. Record [*A publication*] (APTA)
Rec Geol Surv (Zambia) ... Records. Geological Survey (Zambia) [*A publication*]
RECGP ...... Recovery Group [*Air Force*]
Rech .... Recherche [*A publication*]
RecH .... Recusant History [*A publication*]
RECH .... Reformed Episcopal Church
RechA .... Recherches Augustiniennes [*A publication*]
Rech A Crac ... Recherches Archeologiques. Institut d'Archeologie. Universite de Cracovie [*A publication*]
Rech Aeronaut ... Recherche Aeronautique [*A publication*]
Rech Aerosp ... Recherche Aerospatiale [*A publication*]
Rech Aerospat ... Recherche Aerospatiale [*A publication*]
Rech Aerospat English ... La Recherche Aerospatiale. English Edition [*A publication*]
Rech Agron ... Recherches Agronomiques [*A publication*]
Rech Agron (Quebec) ... Recherches Agronomiques (Quebec) [*A publication*]
Rech Amerind ... Recherches Amerindiennes [*A publication*]
RECHAR ... Recombiner Charcoal Adsorber [*Nuclear energy*] (NRCH)
RechBib ..... Recherches Bibliques. Journees du Colloque Biblique de Louvain [*A publication*]

RechBibl .... Recherches Bibliques. Journees du Colloque Biblique de Louvain [*A publication*]
Rech Chir Eur ... Recherches Chirurgicales Europeennes [*A publication*]
Rech Clin Lab ... Recherche dans la Clinique et le Laboratoire [*A publication*]
Rech Econ Louvain ... Recherches Economiques de Louvain [*A publication*]
Rechentech Datenverarb ... Rechentechnik-Datenverarbeitung [*A publication*]
Recherche Aerospat ... La Recherche Aerospatiale [*A publication*]
Recherches ... Recherches sur la Musique Francaise Classique [*A publication*]
Recherche Soc (Paris) ... Recherche Sociale (Paris) [*A publication*]
Recher Sc Rel ... Recherches de Science Religieuse [*A publication*]
RECHG ...... Recharge (NASA)
Rech Geol Afr ... Recherches Geologiques en Afrique [*A publication*]
Rech Graphique ... Recherche Graphique [*A publication*]
Rech Graphique Commun ... Recherche Graphique. Communications [*A publication*]
Rech Hydrobiol Cont ... Recherches d'Hydrobiologie Continentale [*A publication*]
Rech Int ..... Recherches Internationales a la Lumiere du Marxism [*A publication*]
Rech Invent ... Recherches et Inventions [*A publication*]
Rechn Transp ... Rechnoi Transport [*A publication*]
Rech Prod Foret ... Recherches sur les Produits de la Foret [*A publication*]
RECHRG .. Recharger
Rech Sci Rel ... Recherches de Science Religieuse [*A publication*]
Rech Sci Relig ... Recherches de Science Religieuse [*A publication*]
RechScR ...... Recherches de Science Religieuse [*A publication*]
Rech Soc Anonyme Etabl Roure Bertrand Fils Justin Dupont ... Recherches. Societe Anonyme des Etablissments Roure Bertrand Fils et Justin Dupont [*A publication*]
Rech Sociogr ... Recherches Sociographiques [*A publication*]
Rech Sociographiques ... Recherches Sociographiques [*A publication*]
Rech Sociol ... Recherches Sociologiques [*A publication*]
Rech Soc (Paris) ... Recherche Sociale (Paris) [*A publication*]
Rech Spat ... Recherche Spatiale [*A publication*]
Rech Spatiale ... Recherche Spatiale [*A publication*]
RechSR ...... Recherches de Science Religieuse [*A publication*]
Rech Tech .. Recherche Technique [*A publication*]
Recht Elektrizitaetswirtsch ... Recht der Elektrizitaetswirtschaft [*West Germany*] [*A publication*]
RechTh ...... Recherches de Theologie Ancienne et Medievale [*A publication*]
Recht Landwirtsch ... Recht der Landwirtschaft [*A publication*]
Recht u Polit ... Recht und Politik. Vierteljahreshefte fuer Rechts- und Verwaltungspolitik [*Berlin, West Germany*] [*A publication*] (DLA)
Rechtsk T Belg ... Rechtskundig Tijdschrift voor Belgie [*A publication*]
Recht Steuern Gas-Wasserfach ... Recht und Steuern im Gas- und Wasserfach [*West Germany*] [*A publication*]
Rechtstheor ... Rechtstheorie. Zeitschrift fuer Logik, Methodenlehre, Kybernetik, und Soziologie des Rechts [*Berlin, West Germany*] [*A publication*] (DLA)
Rec Hung Agric Exp Stn A ... Records. Hungarian Agricultural Experiment Stations. A. Plant Production [*A publication*]
Rec Hung Agric Exp Stn C ... Records. Hungarian Agricultural Experiment Stations. C. Horticulture [*A publication*]
Rec Huntingdonshire ... Records of Huntingdonshire [*A publication*]
Rech Vet ..... Recherches Veterinaires [*A publication*]
Rech Vet (Paris) ... Recherches Veterinaires (Paris) [*A publication*]
RECIFS ..... Recherches et Etudes Comparatistes Ibero-Francaises de la Sorbonne Nouvelle [*A publication*]
Rec Indian Mus ... Records. Indian Museum [*A publication*]
Rec Indian Mus (Calcutta) ... Records. Indian Museum (Calcutta) [*A publication*]
Rec Intersoc Energy Convers Eng Conf ... Records. Intersociety Energy Conversion Engineering Conference [*A publication*]
RECIP .... Recipient
RECIP .... Reciprocate (AAG)
RECIPE ..... Recomp Computer Interpretive Program Expediter [*Data processing*]
RECIR .... Recirculating [*Automotive engineering*]
RECIRC .... Recirculate (AAG)
RECIT .... Recitation
RECIT .... Recitative [*Music*]
Rec Jur T A Ni ... Recueil de Jurisprudence des Tribunaux de l'Arrondissement de Nivelles [*A publication*]
REC L .... Recent Law (DLA)
RECL .... Recital (ROG)
RECL .... Reclamation
RECL .... Reclose
Rec L .... Recovering Literature [*A publication*]
REcL .... Revue Ecclesiastique de Liege [*A publication*]
Reclam Era ... Reclamation Era [*A publication*]
Reclam Rev ... Reclamation Review [*A publication*]
Reclam Reveg Res ... Reclamation and Revegetation Research [*A publication*]
Rec Laws .... Recent Laws in Canada [*A publication*] (DLA)
Recl Med Vet ... Recueil de Medecine Veterinaire [*A publication*]
Recl Med Vet Ec Alfort ... Recueil de Medecine Veterinaire. Ecole d'Alfort [*A publication*]
Recl Trav Bot Neerl ... Recueil des Travaux Botaniques Neerlandais [*A publication*]

Recl Trav Chim Pays Bas ... Recueil des Travaux Chimiques des Pays-Bas [*A publication*]
Recl Trav Chim Pays-Bas Belg ... Recueil des Travaux Chimiques des Pays-Bas et de la Belgique [*A publication*]
Recl Trav Inst Biol (Beogr) ... Recueil des Travaux. Institut Biologique (Beograd) [*A publication*]
Recl Trav Inst Ecol Biogeogr Acad Serbe Sci ... Recueil des Travaux. Institut d'Ecologie et de Biogeographie. Academie Serbe des Sciences [*A publication*]
Recl Trav Inst Rech Struct Matiere (Belgrade) ... Recueil de Travaux. Institut de Recherches sur la Structure de la Matiere (Belgrade) [*A publication*]
Recl Trav Stn Mar Endoume Fac Sci Mars ... Recueil des Travaux. Station Marine d'Endoume. Faculte des Sciences de Marseille [*A publication*]
Recl Trav Stn Mar Endoume Marseille Fasc Hors Ser Suppl ... Recueil des Travaux. Station Marine d'Endoume-Marseille. Fascicule Hors Serie. Supplement [*A publication*]
Recl Trav Stn Mar Endoume-Mars Fasc Hors Ser Suppl ... Recueil des Travaux. Station Marine d'Endoume-Marseille. Fascicule Hors Serie. Supplement [*A publication*]
RECM .... Recommend (KSC)
Rec Malar Surv India ... Records of the Malaria Survey of India [*A publication*]
REC MAN ... Recreation Management Exhibition [*British*] (ITD)
RECMD .... Recommend (AAG)
Recmd .... Recommissioned (DS)
RECMECH ... Recoil Mechanism (AAG)
Rec Med Vet ... Recueil de Medecine Veterinaire [*A publication*]
Rec Med Vet Ecole Alfort ... Recueil de Medecine Veterinaire. Ecole d'Alfort [*A publication*]
Rec Med Vet Exot ... Recueil de Medecine Veterinaire Exotique [*A publication*]
Rec Mem Med Mil ... Recueil des Memoires de Medecine, de Chirurgie, et de Pharmacie Militaires [*A publication*]
Rec Mem et Obs Hyg et Med Vet Mil ... Recueil des Memoires et Observations sur l'Hygiene et la Medecine Veterinaires Militaires [*A publication*]
RECMF ..... Radio and Electronic Component Manufacturers' Federation
RECMN .... Recommendation
RECMPT .. Recomputation
RECN .... Reconnaissance
RECNCLN ... Reconciliation (AABC)
RECNO ..... This Office Has No Record Of [*Army*] (AABC)
RECNUM ... Record Number [*Online database field identifier*]
RECO .... Remote Command and Control (MCD)
Rec Obs Med Hop Mil ... Recueil des Observations de Medecine des Hopitaux Militaires [*A publication*]
Rec Obs Scripps Inst Oceanogr ... Records of Observations. Scripps Institution of Oceanography [*A publication*]
Rec Oceanogr Works Jpn ... Records of Oceanographic Works in Japan [*A publication*]
Rec Oceanogr Works Jpn Sp Number ... Records of Oceanographic Works in Japan. Special Number [*A publication*]
RECODEX ... Report Collection Index [*Studsvik Energiteknik AB*] [*Database*] [*Nykoping, Sweden*]
RECOG ..... Recognition [*or Recognize*] (AAG)
RECOGE... Recognisance (ROG)
RECOGN .. Recognizance
RECOGS... Recognisances (ROG)
RECOL...... Retrieval Command Language [*Computer search language*]
Recomb DNA Tech Bull ... Recombinant DNA Technical Bulletin [*A publication*]
Recomb DNA Tech Bull Suppl ... Recombinant DNA Technical Bulletin. Supplement [*A publication*]
RECOMMTRANSO ... Upon Receipt of These Orders Communicate with Transportation Officer for Priority Designator via Government Air If Available to _____
RECOMP ... Recommended Completion
RECOMP ... Recomplement
RECOMP ... Redstone Computer
RECOMP ... Repairs Completed [*Military*] (NVT)
RECOMP ... Retrieval and Composition (DIT)
RECON ..... Readiness Condition [*Military*]
RECON ..... Reconciliation
RECON ..... Reconnaissance (NATG)
RECON ..... Reference Conversation (FAAC)
RECON ..... Reliability and Configuration Accountability System
RECON ..... Remote Console [*NASA computer*]
RECON ..... Remote Control (KSC)
RECON ..... Resources Conservation (MCD)
RECON ..... Retrospective Conversion of Bibliographic Records [*Library of Congress*]
R Econ Agr ... Rivista di Economia Agraria [*A publication*]
R Econ Banque Nat Paris ... Revue Economique. Banque Nationale de Paris [*A publication*]
RECONCE ... Reconveyance (ROG)
R Econ Centre-Est ... Revue de l'Economie du Centre-Est [*A publication*]
Reconciliation Quart ... Reconciliation Quarterly [*A publication*]
RECONCO ... Reconnaissance Company [*Military*]

R Econ Conditions Italy ... Review of the Economic Conditions in Italy [*A publication*]
R Econ Condit Italy ... Review of the Economic Conditions in Italy [*A publication*]
R Econ (Cordoba) ... Revista de Economia (Cordoba) [*A publication*]
RECOND .. Recondition (AABC)
RECONDO ... Reconnaissance Commando Doughboy [*Military*] (AABC)
R Econ Dr Immob ... Revue d'Economie et de Droit Immobilier [*A publication*]
R Econ Estadist ... Revista de Economia y Estadistica [*A publication*]
R Econ y Estadistica ... Revista de Economia y Estadistica [*A publication*]
RECONEX ... Raid/Reconnaissance Exercise [*Military*] (NVT)
RECONFIG ... Reconfiguration (NASA)
R Econ et Fin ... Revue Economique et Financiere Ivoirienne [*A publication*]
R Econ Fr... Revue Economique Francaise [*A publication*]
R Econ Franc ... Revue Economique Francaise [*A publication*]
R Econ Franc-Comtoise ... Revue de l'Economie Franc-Comtoise [*A publication*]
R Econ Franco-Suisse ... Revue Economique Franco-Suisse [*A publication*]
R Econ Fr-Suisse ... Revue Economique Franco-Suisse [*A publication*]
R Econ Gestion ... Revue d'Economie et de Gestion [*A publication*]
R Econ Latinoam ... Revista de Economia Latinoamericana [*A publication*]
R Econ Latinoamer ... Revista de Economia Latinoamericana [*A publication*]
R Econ Merid ... Revue de l'Economie Meridionale [*A publication*]
RECONN .. Reconnaissance (AAG)
R Econ Nordeste ... Revista Economica do Nordeste [*A publication*]
R Econ (Paris) ... Revue Economique (Paris) [*A publication*]
R Econ e Pol Ind ... Rivista di Economia e Politica Industriale [*A publication*]
R Econ Polit (Madrid) ... Revista de Economia Politica (Madrid) [*A publication*]
R Econ Polit (Paris) ... Revue d'Economie Politique (Paris) [*A publication*]
R Econ Pol (Madrid) ... Revista de Economia Politica (Madrid) [*A publication*]
R Econ Pol (Paris) ... Revue d'Economie Politique (Paris) [*A publication*]
R Econ Pol (Sao Paulo) ... Revista de Economia Politica (Sao Paulo) [*A publication*]
R Econ S .... Royal Economic Society [*British*]
R Econ et Soc ... Revue Economique et Sociale [*A publication*]
R Econ Soc ... Revue Economique et Sociale [*A publication*]
Recons Surg ... Reconstruction Surgery and Traumatology [*A publication*]
RECONST ... Reconstruct (AABC)
R Econ Stat ... Review of Economics and Statistics [*A publication*]
R Econ Statist ... Review of Economics and Statistics [*A publication*]
R Econ Statistics ... Review of Economics and Statistics [*A publication*]
Reconstr Surg Traumatol ... Reconstruction Surgery and Traumatology [*A publication*]
R Econ Stud ... Review of Economic Studies [*A publication*]
R Econ Sud-Ouest ... Revue Economique du Sud-Ouest [*A publication*]
Recontr Surg Traumatol ... Reconstruction Surgery and Traumatology [*A publication*]
RECONVCE ... Reconveyance (ROG)
Record .... Record. Association of the Bar of the City of New York [*A publication*]
Record Broward County Med Assoc ... Record. Broward County Medical Association [*Florida*] [*A publication*]
Recorder Columbia Med Soc ... Recorder. Columbia Medical Society of Richland County [*South Carolina*] [*A publication*]
Recorder M Magazine ... Recorder and Music Magazine [*A publication*]
Recorder and Mus ... Recorder and Music [*A publication*]
Recorder & Mus Mag ... Recorder and Music Magazine [*A publication*]
Record of NYCBA ... Record. Association of the Bar of the City of New York [*A publication*]
Records Buck ... Records of Buckinghamshire [*A publication*]
Records Queen Museum ... Records. Queen Victoria Museum [*A publication*] (APTA)
Records SA Museum ... Records. South Australian Museum [*A publication*] (APTA)
RECorses... Revue des Etudes Corses [*A publication*]
RECOV ..... Recovery (KSC)
RECOVER ... Remote Continual Verification [*Telephonic monitoring system*]
RECOVER ... Remote Control Verification [*Nuclear safeguards*]
Recovery Eng News ... Recovery Engineering News [*A publication*]
RECOVY... Recovery
RECP........ International College of Real Estate Consulting Professionals [*Minneapolis, MN*] (EA)
RECP........ Real Estate Consulting Professional [*Designation awarded by International College of Real Estate Consulting Professionals*]
RECP........ Receptacle
RECP........ Receptech Corp. [*NASDAQ symbol*] (NQ)
RECP........ Reciprocal (AAG)
RECP........ Release Engineering Change Proposal (MCD)
RECP........ Request for Engineering Change Proposal [*NASA*]
RECP........ Rural Environmental Conservation Program
RecPap....... Recherches de Papyrologie [*A publication*]
Rec Papua New Guinea Mus ... Records. Papua New Guinea Museum [*A publication*]
Rec Past ..... Records of the Past [*A publication*]
RecPh......... Recherches Philosophiques [*A publication*]

RecPhL...... Recherches de Philologie et de Linguistique [*Louvain*] [*A publication*]
RECPOM ... Resource Constrained Procurement Objectives for Munitions Model [*Army*]
RECPT ...... Receipt
RECPT ...... Receptacle (AAG)
RECPT ...... Reception (AAG)
Rec Queen Vic Mus ... Records. Queen Victoria Museum [*A publication*] (APTA)
Rec Queen Vict Mus ... Records. Queen Victoria Museum [*A publication*] (APTA)
Rec Queen Victoria Mus ... Records. Queen Victoria Museum [*A publication*]
Rec Queen Victoria Mus Launceston ... Records. Queen Victoria Museum of Launceston [*A publication*]
Rec Q Vict Mus ... Records. Queen Victoria Museum [*A publication*] (APTA)
RECR......... Receiver
RECR......... Reclamation Review [*A publication*]
Rec R......... Record Review [*A publication*]
RECR......... Recreation (AABC)
RECRAS ... Retrieval System for Current Research in Agricultural Sciences [*Japan*]
RECRC...... Recirculate (NASA)
RECRE...... Recreation
Rec Res ...... Record Research [*A publication*]
Rec Res Fac Agric Univ Tokyo ... Records of Researches. Faculty of Agriculture. University of Tokyo [*A publication*]
RECRN...... Recreation
Recr Sci...... Recreative Science [*A publication*]
RECRT ...... Recruit (AFM)
RECRYST ... Recrystallized
RECS......... Radiological Emergency Communications System [*Nuclear energy*] (NRCH)
RECS......... Reconstitutable Emergency Communications System
RecS........... Recorded Sound [*A publication*]
RECS......... Representative Shuttle Environmental Control System [*NASA*] (MCD)
RECSAM .. Southeast Asian Regional Center for Education in Science and Mathematics [*Malaysia*]
RECSAT.... Reconnaissance Satellite (NVT)
Rec S Aust Mus ... Records. South Australian Museum [*A publication*] (APTA)
Rec S Aust Mus (Adelaide) ... Records. South Australian Museum (Adelaide) [*A publication*]
Rec Sci Rel ... Recherches de Science Religieuse [*A publication*]
Rec Scott Church Hist Soc ... Records. Scottish Church History Society [*A publication*]
RECSG...... Renewable Energy Congressional Staff Group (EA)
RECSHIP ... Receiving Ship
Rec Sound .. Recorded Sound [*A publication*]
Rec South Aust Mus ... Records. South Australian Museum [*A publication*] (APTA)
Rec South Aust Mus (Adelaide) ... Records. South Australian Museum (Adelaide) [*A publication*]
RECSQUAD ... Reconnaissance Squadron [*Military*]
RecSR .... Recherches de Science Religieuse [*A publication*]
RECSTA..... Receiving Station [*Military*]
RECSYS.... Recreation Systems Analysis [*Data processing*]
RECT......... Receipt
RECT......... Rectangle (AAG)
RECT........ Rectificatus [*Rectified*] [*Pharmacy*]
RECT........ Rectify (AAG)
RECT........ Rectisel Corp. [*NASDAQ symbol*] (NQ)
RECT........ Rector
RECT........ Rectus [*Muscle*] [*Anatomy*]
RECTAD... Received for Temporary Additional Duty
RECTADINS ... Received for Temporary Additional Duty under Instruction
RECTAS.... Regional Centre for Training in Aerial Surveys (EAIO)
RECTD...... Received for Temporary Duty
RECTD...... Recited (ROG)
RECTEMDUINS ... Received for Temporary Duty under Instruction
RECTENNA ... Rectifying Antenna [*Microwave power transmission*]
RECTG...... Reciting (ROG)
RecTh......... Recherches de Theologie Ancienne et Medievale [*A publication*]
RECTIFON ... Rectification (ROG)
RECTIL..... Rectilineal [*Geometry*] (ROG)
RECTON... Reduction (ROG)
RECTR...... Recommend Transfer Of (NOAA)
RECTR...... Rectifier
RECTR...... Restoration and Eighteenth Century Theatre Research [*A publication*]
Rec Trav..... Recueil des Travaux Relatifs a la Philologie et a l'Archeologie Egyptiennes et Assyriennes [*A publication*]
Rec Trav Bot Neerl ... Recueil des Travaux Botaniques Neerlandais [*Netherlands*] [*A publication*]
Rec Trav Chim ... Recueil des Travaux Chimiques des Pays-Bas [*A publication*]
Rec Trav Chim Pays-Bas ... Recueil des Travaux Chimiques des Pays-Bas [*A publication*]
Rec Trav Inst Nat Hyg ... Recueil des Travaux. Institut National d'Hygiene [*A publication*]

Rec Trav Lab Physiol Veg Fac Sci Bordeaux ... Recueil des Travaux. Laboratoire de Physiologie Vegetale. Faculte des Sciences de Bordeaux [*A publication*]
Rec Trav Sci Med ... Recueil de Travaux de Sciences Medicales au Congo Belge [*A publication*]
Rec Tr Chim ... Recueil des Travaux Chimiques des Pays-Bas [*A publication*]
RECTREAT ... Received for Treatment
Recu de l'Acad de Legis ... Recueil. Academie de Legislation [*Toulouse, France*] [*A publication*] (DLA)
Recu des Cours ... Recueil des Cours. Academie de Droit International [*Collected Courses of the Hague Academy of International Law*] [*Leiden, Netherlands*] [*A publication*] (DLA)
Recueil .... Recueil des Cours. Academie de Droit International [*A publication*]
Recu de Jurispr du Droit Admin ... Recueil de Jurisprudence du Droit Administratif et du Conseil d'Etat [*Brussels, Belgium*] [*A publication*] (DLA)
RECUR...... Recurrence [*or Recurrent*] [*Medicine*]
Recur Hidraul ... Recursos Hidraulicos [*A publication*]
Recursos Hidraul ... Recursos Hidraulicos [*Mexico*] [*A publication*]
Recursos Min ... Recursos Minerales [*A publication*]
Rec US Dep State ... Record. United States Department of State [*A publication*]
Recu de la Soc Internat de Droit Penal Mil ... Recueil. Societe Internationale de Droit Penal Militaire et de Droit de la Guerre [*Strasbourg, France*] [*A publication*] (DLA)
RECV......... Receive (NASA)
RECVD...... Received
RECVG...... Receiving
RECVR...... Receiver (NASA)
Rec West Aust Mus Suppl ... Records. Western Australian Museum. Supplement [*A publication*]
RECY........ Recovery (AAG)
RECYA...... Revue Roumaine d'Embryologie et de Cytologie. Serie d'Embryologie [*A publication*]
Recycling Waste Disposal ... Recycling and Waste Disposal [*A publication*]
Recycl Weltkongr Konf Niederschr ... Recycling Weltkongress. Konferenz-Niederschriften [*A publication*]
Recycl World Congr Congr Proc ... Recycling World Congress. Congress Proceedings [*A publication*]
Rec Zool Surv India ... Records. Zoological Survey of India [*A publication*]
Rec Zool Surv Pak ... Records. Zoological Survey of Pakistan [*A publication*]
RED .... A'Beckett's Reserved Judgements [*New South Wales*] [*A publication*] (APTA)
RED .... New South Wales Reserved Equity Decisions [*A publication*] (DLA)
RED .... R and D (Research and Development) Management [*A publication*]
RED .... Radiation Experience Data [*Food and Drug Administration*] [*Database*]
RED .... Radical Education Dossier [*A publication*] (ADA)
RED .... Radio Equipment Department [*British military*] (DMA)
RED .... Railroad Employees' Department [*of AFL-CIO*]
RED .... Range Error Detector
RED .... Rapid Excess Disposal [*Military*] (AABC)
RED .... Rare-Earth Device
RED .... Red Lion Inns LP [*AMEX symbol*] (SPSG)
RED .... Red Lodge, MT [*Location identifier*] [*FAA*] (FAAL)
RED .... Redeemed
Red .... Redfield's New York Surrogate Reports [*A publication*] (DLA)
Red .... Redington's Reports [*31-35 Maine*] [*A publication*] (DLA)
RED .... Redoubt Volcano [*Alaska*] [*Seismograph station code, US Geological Survey*] (SEIS)
RED .... Reduce [*or Reduction*] (AAG)
RED .... Redundant (KSC)
Red .... Redwar's Comments on Ordinances of the Gold Coast Colony [*1889-1909*] [*Ghana*] [*A publication*] (DLA)
RED .... Reflection Electron Diffraction [*For surface structure analysis*]
RED .... Registered Expected Death
R Ed .... Religious Education [*A publication*]
RED .... Repairable Equipment Depot [*British military*] (DMA)
RE & D..... Research, Engineering, and Development
RED .... Restructured Expanded Data (MCD)
RED .... Resume Entry Device
RED .... Review, Evaluation, Disposition Board (AAG)
RED .... Ritchie's Equity Decisions (Russell) [*Canada*] [*A publication*] (DLA)
REDA .... Rural Educational and Development Association [*Canada*]
REDAC...... Real-Time Data Acquisition
Red Am R Cas ... Redfield's American Railway Cases [*A publication*] (DLA)
Red Am RR Cas ... Redfield's Leading American Railway Cases [*A publication*] (DLA)
REDAP...... Reentrant Data Processing
REDAS...... Reduced to Apprentice Seaman [*Navy*]
REDB .... Redbourne [*England*]
REDBA...... Redbook [*A publication*]
Red Bail ...... Redfield on Carriers and Bailments [*A publication*] (DLA)
Red & Big Cas B & N ... Redfield and Bigelow's Leading Cases on Bills and Notes [*A publication*] (DLA)
REDBR...... Redbridge [*England*]

REDC .... Regional Economic Development Center [*Memphis State University*] [*Research center*]　(RCD)
REDC .... Revista Espanola de Derecho Canonico [*A publication*]
REDCAP ... Real-Time Electromagnetic Digitally Controlled Analyser and Processor
REDCAPE ... Readiness Capability [*Military*]
Red Car ..... Redfield on Carriers and Bailments [*A publication*]　(DLA)
Red Cas RR ... Redfield's Leading American Railway Cases [*A publication*]　(DLA)
Red Cas Wills ... Redfield's Leading Cases on Wills [*A publication*]　(DLA)
REDCAT ... Racial and Ethnic Category [*Army*]　(INF)
REDCAT ... Readiness Category [*Military*]
REDCN ..... Reducing　(ROG)
REDCOM ... Readiness Command [*Army*]
REDCON .. Readiness Condition [*Military*]
Red Cross M ... Red Cross Magazine [*A publication*]
REDD .... Reduced　(ROG)
REDEA ...... Research/Development [*A publication*]
Redem .... Redemption　(DLA)
RE Der Can ... Revista Espanola de Derecho Canonico [*A publication*]
Redes Pl ..... Redesdale's Treatise upon Equity Pleading [*A publication*]　(DLA)
Redf .... Redfield's New York Surrogate Reports [*A publication*]　(DLA)
Redf Am Railw Cas ... Redfield's American Railway Cases [*A publication*]　(DLA)
Redf & B .... Redfield and Bigelow's Leading Cases [*England*] [*A publication*]　(DLA)
Redf Carr ... Redfield on Carriers and Bailments [*A publication*]　(DLA)
Redf (NY) .. Redfield's New York Surrogate Reports [*A publication*]　(DLA)
Redf Railways ... Redfield on Railways [*A publication*]　(DLA)
Redf R Cas ... Redfield's Railway Cases [*England*] [*A publication*]　(DLA)
Redf Sur (NY) ... Redfield's New York Surrogate Court Reports [*A publication*]　(DLA)
Redf Surr ... Redfield's New York Surrogate Reports [*A publication*]　(DLA)
Redf Surr (NY) ... Redfield's New York Surrogate Court Reports [*5 vols.*] [*A publication*]　(DLA)
Redf Wills ... Redfield's Leading Cases on Wills [*A publication*]　(DLA)
RED HORSE ... Rapid Engineer Development, Heavy Operational Repair Squadron, Engineering [*Air Force*]　(AFM)
REDI .... ReadiCare, Inc. [*NASDAQ symbol*]　(NQ)
REDI .... Real Estate Data, Incorporated [*Information service or system*]　(IID)
REDI .... Remote Electronic Delivery of Information [*Library science*]
REDI .... Revue Egyptienne de Droit International [*A publication*]
Redia G Zool ... Redia Giornale di Zoologia [*A publication*]
REDICORT ... Readiness Improvement through Correspondence Training　(MCD)
REDIG IN PULV ... Redigatur In Pulverent [*Let It Be Reduced to Powder*] [*Pharmacy*]　(ROG)
Redington... Redington's Reports [*31-35 Maine*] [*A publication*]　(DLA)
Red Int L..... Reddie's Inquiries in International Law [*2nd ed.*] [*1851*] [*A publication*]　(DLA)
REDIS .... Reference Dispatch　(NOAA)
REDISC ..... Rediscount [*Banking*]
REDIST ..... Redistilled
REDISTR ... Redistribution　(AFM)
Redk Elem ... Redkie Elementy [*A publication*]
Redk Met ... Redkie Metally [*A publication*]
REDL .... Redlane [*England*]
REDLOG .. Logistic Readiness Report [*Navy*]　(CINC)
Redman ...... Redman on Landlord and Tenant [*A publication*]　(DLA)
Redm Arb... Redman on Arbitration [*A publication*]　(DLA)
Red Mar Com ... Reddie's Law of Maritime Commerce [*1841*] [*A publication*]　(DLA)
Red Mar Int L ... Reddie's Researches in Maritime International Law [*1844-45*] [*A publication*]　(DLA)
Red Menac ... Red Menace [*A publication*]
REDN .... Reduction
REDNON ... Operational Readiness Report (Nonatomic)　(CINC)
REDNT ...... Redundant　(AAG)
REDO .... RADAR Engineering Design Objectives　(NG)
REDO .... Red Documental [*Ministerio de Educacion Publica*] [*Chile*] [*Information service or system*]　(CRD)
Redog ForsknStift Skogsarb ... Redogorelse. Forskningsstiftelsen Skogsarbeten [*A publication*]
REDOPS ..... Ready for Operations [*Reporting system*] [*DoD*]
REDOX ..... Reduction and Oxidation
REDP......... Redondo Peak [*New Mexico*] [*Seismograph station code, US Geological Survey*]　(SEIS)
Red Pop...... Post Reditum ad Populum [*of Cicero*] [*Classical studies*]　(OCD)
Red Pr .... Redfield's New York Practice Reports [*A publication*]　(DLA)
RED in PULV ... Redactus in Pulverem [*Reduce to a Powder*] [*Pharmacy*]
REDR......... Redruth [*England*]
REDREP .... Redeployment Report [*Military*]
R Ed Res .... Review of Educational Research [*A publication*]
Red RL....... Reddie's Roman Law [*A publication*]
Red RR........ Redfield on the Law of Railroads [*A publication*]　(DLA)
Red RR Cas ... Redfield's Leading American Railway Cases [*A publication*]　(DLA)
REDS......... Royal Engineers Diving School [*British military*]　(DMA)

Red Sc L..... Reddie's Science of Law [*2nd ed.*] [*A publication*]　(DLA)
Red Sen..... Post Reditum in Senatu [*of Cicero*] [*Classical studies*]　(OCD)
REDSG...... Redesignate　(AFM)
redsh .... Reddish [*Philately*]
REDSO...... Regional Economic Development Services Office [*USAID*]
REDSOD.... Repetitive Explosive Device for Soil Displacement
REDSO/ESA ... Regional Economic Development Services Office for East and Southern Africa
RED-T....... Remote Electric Drive Turret
REDTOP.... Reactor Design from Thermal-Hydraulic Operating Parameters [*NASA*]
REDTRAIN ... Readiness Training　(MCD)
REDUC ..... Reduction　(KSC)
R Educ .... Review of Education [*A publication*]
REDUCE... Reduction of Electrical Demand Using Computer Equipment [*Energy management system designed by John Helwig of Jance Associates, Inc.*]
R Educ (Madrid) ... Revista de Educacion (Madrid) [*A publication*]
R Educ Res ... Review of Educational Research [*A publication*]
REDUN...... Redundancy　(NASA)
REDUPL... Reduplication
REDV .... Resource Development. Incorporating Northern Development and Oceanic Industries [*A publication*]
REDW ...... Redwood National Park
Redwar....... Redwar's Comments on Ordinances of the Gold Coast Colony [*1889-1909*] [*Ghana*] [*A publication*]　(DLA)
Red Wills ... Redfield on the Law of Wills [*A publication*]　(DLA)
REDWN ... Redrawn
REDX .... Red Eagle Resources Corp. [*NASDAQ symbol*]　(NQ)
REDY .... Recirculating Dialyzate [*Artificial kidney dialysis system*]
REDYP...... Reentry Dynamics Program
REE .... Lubbock, TX [*Location identifier*] [*FAA*]　(FAAL)
REE .... Rapid Extinction Effect [*Electrophysiology*]
REE .... Rare-Earth Element [*Chemistry*]
REE .... Rational Expectations Equilibrium [*Economics*]
REE .... Red Earth Energy Ltd. [*Vancouver Stock Exchange symbol*]
REE .... [*Department of*] Regional Economic Expansion [*Canada*]
REE .... Resources and Energy [*A publication*]
REE .... Respiratory Energy Expenditure [*Physiology*]
REE .... Resting Energy Expenditure
REE .... Revista de Estudios Extremenos [*A publication*]
REEA........ Real Estate Educators Association [*Chicago, IL*]　(EA)
REEC........ Radical Environmental Education Collective [*Australia*]
REEC........ Regional Export Expansion Council [*Department of Commerce*]
REECO...... Reynolds Electrical & Engineering Company
Reed .... Reed on Bills of Sale [*A publication*]　(DLA)
REED .... Reeds Jewelers, Inc. [*Wilmington, NC*] [*NASDAQ symbol*]　(NQ)
REED .... Resources on Educational Equity for the Disabled
Reed Am LS ... Reed's American Law Studies [*A publication*]　(DLA)
Reed BS .... Reed on Bills of Sale [*A publication*]　(DLA)
Reed Car .... Reed on Railways as Carriers [*A publication*]　(DLA)
Reed Fraud ... Reed's Leading Cases on Statute of Frauds [*A publication*]　(DLA)
REEDN ..... Records of Early English Drama. Newsletter [*A publication*]
Reed PA Black ... Reed's Pennsylvania Blackstone [*A publication*]　(DLA)
Reed Pr Sug ... Reed's Practical Suggestions for the Management of Lawsuits [*A publication*]　(DLA)
Reed's Mar Equip News Mar Dig ... Reed's Marine and Equipment News and Marine Digest [*A publication*]
Reeduc Orthophon ... Reeducation Orthophonique [*A publication*]
REEFER.... Refrigerator, Refrigerated, or Cold Storage [*Airplane, railway car, truck*]
REEG........ Radioelectroencephalograph
REEI......... Russian and East European Institute [*Indiana University*] [*Research center*]　(RCD)
REEL........ Recessive-Expressive Emergent Language Scores [*For the hearing-impaired*]
REELB ...... Revista Electricidade [*A publication*]
REEM....... Reserves Embarked [*Navy*]　(NVT)
REEN .... Regional Energy Education Network [*National Science Teachers Association*]
REENA...... Refrigerating Engineering [*A publication*]
REENL...... Reenlist [*Military*]　(AFM)
REENLA ... Reenlistment Allowance [*Military*]
REENLB ... Reenlistment Bonus [*Military*]
REEP........ Range Estimating and Evaluation Procedure [*Data processing*]
REEP .... Regression Estimation of Event Probabilities　(IEEE)
REEP .... Revista. Escuela de Estudios Penitenciarios [*A publication*]
REES .... Center for Russian and East European Studies [*University of Pittsburgh*] [*Research center*]　(RCD)
REES .... Reactive Electronic Equipment Simulator　(RDA)
REES .... Russian and East European Studies Area Program [*University of Pittsburgh*] [*Research center*]　(RCD)
Rees' Cyclopaedia ... [*Abraham*] Rees' English Cyclopaedia [*A publication*]　(DLA)
Reese.......... Reporter of Vols. 5 and 11, Heiskell's Tennessee Reports [*A publication*]　(DLA)

REETA ...... Rural Extension, Education and Training Abstracts [*Database*] [*Commonwealth Bureau of Agricultural Economics*] [*Information service or system*]　(CRD)

REETS ...... Radiological Effluent and Environmental Technical Specifications [*Nuclear Regulatory Commission*]　(NRCH)

Reeve Des .. Reeve on Descents [*A publication*]　(DLA)

Reeve Dom Rel ... Reeve on Domestic Relations [*A publication*]　(DLA)

Reeve Eng L ... Reeve's History of the English Law [*A publication*]　(DLA)

Reeve Eng Law ... Reeve's History of the English Law [*A publication*]　(DLA)

Reeve Hist Eng Law ... Reeve's History of the English Law [*A publication*]　(DLA)

Reeve Sh .... Reeve on the Law of Shipping [*A publication*]　(DLA)

Reeves HEL ... Reeve's History of the English Law [*A publication*]　(DLA)

Reeves Hist Eng Law ... Reeve's History of the English Law [*A publication*]　(DLA)

Reeves J ..... Reeves Journal [*A publication*]

REF .... Range Error Function [*Aerospace*]　(AAG)

REF .... Rat Embryo Fibroblast [*Cells*]

REF .... Refectory　(DSUE)

REF .... Refer　(EY)

REF .... Referee

REF .... Reference [*Online database field identifier*]　(NATG)

REF .... Referendum

REF .... Refinery [*or Refining*]

REF .... Reflection Resources [*Vancouver Stock Exchange symbol*]

REF .... Reflector

Ref .... Reformatio [*A publication*]

REF .... Reformation

REF .... Reformed

REF .... Refresher　(AABC)

REF .... Refrigerant [*Cooling*] [*Medicine*] [*British*]　(ROG)

REF .... Refund [*or Refunding*]

REF .... Refurbishment　(NASA)

REF .... Refused　(ADA)

REF .... Release of Excess Funds

REF .... Renal Erythropoietic Factor [*Medicine*]

REF .... Revista de Etnografie si Folclor [*A publication*]

REF .... Unclear Pronoun Reference [*Used in correcting manuscripts, etc.*]

REFA .... Real Estate Fund of America

REFAA4 .... Research and Farming [*North Carolina Agricultural Research Service*] [*A publication*]

REFA Nachr ... REFA [*Reichsausschuss fuer Arbeitsstudien*] Nachrichten [*A publication*]

Ref Aust ..... Reference Australia [*A publication*]

REFC .... REFAC Technology Development Corp. [*NASDAQ symbol*]　(NQ)

REFC .... Reference　(ROG)

REFC .... Reflections of Elvis Fan Club　(EA)

REFC .... Richard Eden Fan Club　(EA)

REFCD ...... Research and Education Foundation for Chest Disease　(EA)

Ref Chem Ind ... Referate aus dem Gebiet der Chemischen Industrie [*A publication*]

Ref Ch R .... Reformed Church Review [*A publication*]

REFCO ...... Resolution Funding Corporation [*Established by the Financial Institutions Reform, Recovery, and Enforcement Act of 1989*]

RefCorp ...... Resolution Funding Corporation [*Established by the Financial Institutions Reform, Recovery, and Enforcement Act of 1989*]

REFD .... Referred

REFD .... Refined

REFD .... Refund　(AFM)

REFD CON ... Reinforced Concrete [*Freight*]

Ref Dec ..... Referee's Decision [*Legal term*]　(DLA)

REF/DES .. Reference Designator Number　(MCD)

REFD MTL ... Reinforced Metal [*Freight*]

Ref Dokl Nauchno-Issled Rab Aspir Ukr Skh Akad ... Referaty Dokladov o Nauchno-Issledovatel'skoi Rabote Aspirantov. Ukrainskaya Sel'skokhozyaistvennaya Akademiya [*A publication*]

Ref Dok Mosk Skh Akad ... Referaty Dokladov Moskovskaya Sel'skokhozyaistvennaya Akademiya Imeni K. A. Timiryazeva [*A publication*]

Ref Dopov Nauk Dosl Rob Aspir Ukr Akad Sil's'kogospod Nauk ... Referati Dopovidei pro Naukovo-Doslidnu Robotu Aspirantiv. Ukrains'ka Akademiya Sil's'kogospodars'kikh Nauk [*A publication*]

REFD PLYWD ... Reinforced Plywood [*Freight*]

REFEC ...... Refectory　(DSUE)

RefEgyhaz ... Reformatus Egyhaz [*Budapest*] [*A publication*]

Referatebl zur Raumentwicklung ... Referateblatt zur Raumentwicklung [*A publication*]

Referatebl zur Raumordnung ... Referateblatt zur Raumordnung [*A publication*]

Referat Z.... Referativnyi Zhurnal [*A publication*]

Referat Zh Biol ... Referativnyi Zhurnal. Biologiya [*A publication*]

Referat Zh Fotokinotekh ... Referat Zhurnal Fotokinotekhnika [*A publication*]

Referat Zh Zhivot Vet ... Referativnyi Zhurnal. Zhivotnovodstvo i Veterinariya [*A publication*]

REFG .... Refrigerating [*or Refrigeration*]

Ref Girl ...... Refractory Girl [*A publication*]

REFGR ...... Refrigerator

Refin Eng ... Refining Engineer [*A publication*]

Refiner Nat Gasoline Manuf ... Refiner and Natural Gasoline Manufacturer [*A publication*]

Ref J .... National Association of Referees in Bankruptcy. Journal [*A publication*]

Ref J .... Reformed Journal [*A publication*]

REFL .... Reference Librarian [*A publication*]

REFL .... Reference Line　(AAG)

REFL .... Reflectance [*or Reflector*]　(AAG)

REFL .... Reflex

REFL .... Reflexive

REFLD ...... Reflected

REFLES ...... Reference Librarian Enhancement System [*University of California*] [*Online microcomputer system*]

Reflets Econ Franc-Comtoise ... Reflets de l'Economie Franc-Comtoise [*A publication*]

Reflets et Perspectives ... Reflets et Perspectives de la Vie Economique [*A publication*]

Reflets Perspect Vie Econ ... Reflets et Perspectives de la Vie Economique [*A publication*]

REFLEX.... Reserve Flexibility [*Military*]　(MCD)

Ref Libr...... Reference Librarian [*A publication*]

Ref Lit Music ... Reformed Liturgy and Music [*A publication*]

Refl Persp Vie Ec ... Reflets et Perspectives de la Vie Economique [*A publication*]

REFM........ Revista de Estudios Franceses (Madrid) [*A publication*]

Ref Mag ..... Referee Magazine [*A publication*]

REFMCHY ... Refrigerating Machinery

Ref Med ..... Reforma Medica [*A publication*]

REFMS ..... Recreation and Education for Multiple Sclerosis

REFMT .... Reinforcement

REFNA ...... REFA [*Reichsausschuss fuer Arbeitsstudien*] Nachrichten [*A publication*]

REFNO ..... Reference Number　(CINC)

Ref NRE ..... Refused, Not Reversible Error [*Legal term*]　(DLA)

REFONE ..... Reference Our Telephone Conversation　(FAAC)

REFORGER ... Return of Forces to Germany [*Military*]

REFORM ... Reference Form　(FAAC)

REFORM ... Reformatory　(ROG)

REFORMA ... National Association to Promote Library Services to the Spanish-Speaking

Refor Mon ... Reforestation Monthly [*A publication*]

REFP .... Reference Papers [*Army*]　(AABC)

Ref Pres W ... Reformed and Presbyterian World [*A publication*]

Ref Q.......... Reformed Quarterly Review [*A publication*]

Ref R .... Reformed Review [*A publication*]

REFR........ Refractory　(AAG)

REFR........ Refrigerate　(KSC)

REFR........ Research Frontiers, Inc. [*NASDAQ symbol*]　(NQ)

RE Fr .... Revue d'Histoire de l'Eglise de France [*A publication*]

REFRA ...... Refractories [*English Translation*] [*A publication*]

REFRACDUTRA ... Release from Active Duty for Training [*Army*]　(AABC)

Refract Inst Tech Bull ... Refractories Institute. Technical Bulletin [*A publication*]

Refract J .... Refractories Journal [*A publication*]

Refract Mater ... Refractory Materials [*A publication*]

Refractor J ... Refractories Journal [*A publication*]

REFRAD .... Release from Active Duty [*Army*]

REFRADT ... Release from Active Duty for Training [*Army*]　(AABC)

REFRANACDUTRA ... Release from Annual Active Duty for Training [*Army*]　(AABC)

REFRAT ... Release from Annual Training [*Army*]　(AABC)

REFRD..... Refrigerated　(AAG)

Refr G .... Refractory Girl [*A publication*]

REFRG ...... Refrigerate　(AAG)

REFRIG .... Refrigerated Service [*Shipping*] [*British*]

Refrig .... Refrigeration [*A publication*]

REFRIG .... Refrigerator

Refrig A ...... Refrigeration Annual [*A publication*]　(APTA)

Refrig Air... Refrigeration and Air Conditioning [*A publication*]

Refrig Air Cond & Heat ... Refrigeration Journal, Incorporating Air Conditioning and Heating [*A publication*]　(APTA)

Refrig Air Condit ... Refrigeration and Air Conditioning [*A publication*]

Refrig Air Condit Heat Recovery ... Refrigeration, Air Conditioning, and Heat Recovery [*A publication*]

Refrig Ann ... Refrigeration Annual [*A publication*]　(APTA)

Refrig Annual ... Refrigeration Annual [*A publication*]　(APTA)

Refrig Cold Stor ... Refrigeration, Cold Storage, and Air-Conditioning [*A publication*]　(APTA)

Refrig Cold Storage Air Cond ... Refrigeration, Cold Storage, and Air-Conditioning [*A publication*]　(APTA)

Refrig Eng ... Refrigerating Engineering [*A publication*]

Refrigeration J ... Refrigeration Journal [*A publication*]　(APTA)

Refrig J ...... Refrigeration Journal [*A publication*]

REFRIGN ... Refrigeration

Refrig Sci Technol ... Refrigeration Science and Technology [*A publication*]

Refrig W .... Refrigerating World [*A publication*]

Ref Sc Lit Fire ... References to Scientific Literature on Fire [*A publication*]

Ref Serv R ... Reference Services Review [*A publication*]
Ref Serv Rev ... Reference Services Review [*A publication*]
Ref Shelf .... Reference Shelf [*A publication*]
REFSMMAT ... Reference Stable Member Matrix (KSC)
REFSRV .... [*The*] Reference Service [*Mead Data Central, Inc.*] [*Information service or system*] (IID)
REFT .... Release for Experimental Flight Test (NG)
REFTEL .... Reference Telegram (NATG)
Ref Theol R ... Reformed Theological Review [*A publication*]
Ref Th R .... Reformed Theological Review [*A publication*]
REFTO ...... Reference Travel Order (NOAA)
RefTR .... Reformed Theological Review [*Australia*] [*A publication*]
REFTRA ..... Refresher Training (NVT)
REFTS ...... Resonant Frequency Tracking System
REFUL ...... Refueling
REFURB ..... Refurbished
REFURDIS ... Reference Your Dispatch
REFURLTR ... Reference Your Letter
Refu Vet ..... Refuah Veterinarith [*A publication*]
Ref W .... Reformed World [*A publication*]
RefWID ...... Refugee Women in Development (EA)
Ref WM ..... Refused, Want of Merit [*Legal term*] (DLA)
REFY .... Refinery
Ref Z .... Referativnyi Zhurnal [*A publication*]
Ref Zh .... Referativnyi Zhurnal [*A publication*]
Ref Zh Astron ... Referativnyi Zhurnal. Astronomiya [*A publication*]
Ref Zh Astron Geod ... Referativnyi Zhurnal. Astronomiya. Geodeziya [*A publication*]
Ref Zh Biol ... Referativnyi Zhurnal. Biologiya [*A publication*]
Ref Zh Biol Khim ... Referativnyi Zhurnal. Biologicheskaya Khimiya [*A publication*]
Ref Zh Faramakol Khimioter Sredstva Toksikol ... Referativnyi Zhurnal. Farmakologiya. Khimioterapeuticheskie Sredstva. Toksikologiya [*A publication*]
Ref Zh Fiz ... Referativnyi Zhurnal. Fizika [*A publication*]
Ref Zh Fiz-Khim Biol Biotekhnol ... Referativnyi Zhurnal. Fiziko-Khimicheskaya Biologiya i Biotekhnologiya [*A publication*]
Ref Zh Fotokinotekh ... Referativnyi Zhurnal. Fotokinotekhnika [*A publication*]
Ref Zh Geod ... Referativnyi Zhurnal. Geodeziya [*A publication*]
Ref Zh Geod Aerosemka ... Referativnyi Zhurnal. Geodeziya i Aeros'emka [*A publication*]
Ref Zh Geof ... Referativnyi Zhurnal. Geofizika [*A publication*]
Ref Zh Geol ... Referativnyi Zhurnal. Geologiya [*A publication*]
Ref Zh Inf .. Referativnyi Zhurnal. Informatika [*A publication*]
Ref Zh Khim ... Referativnyi Zhurnal. Khimiya [*A publication*]
Ref Zh Khim Biol Khim ... Referativnyi Zhurnal. Khimiya. Biologicheskaya Khimiya [*A publication*]
Ref Zh Korroz ... Referativnyi Zhurnal. Korroziya [*A publication*]
Ref Zh Legk Promst ... Referativnyi Zhurnal. Legkaya Promyshlennost [*A publication*]
Ref Zh Mekh ... Referativnyi Zhurnal. Mekhanika [*A publication*]
Ref Zh Metall ... Referativnyi Zhurnal. Metallurgiya [*USSR*] [*A publication*]
Ref Zh Metrol Izmer Tekh ... Referativnyi Zhurnal. Metrologiya i Izmeritel'naya Tekhnika [*A publication*]
Ref Zh Nasosostr Kompressorostr Kholod Mashinostr ... Referativnyi Zhurnal. Nasosostroenie i Kompressorostroenie. Kholodil'noe Mashinostroenie [*A publication*]
Ref Zh Obshch Vop Patol Onkol ... Referativnyi Zhurnal. Obshchie Voprosy Patologii. Onkologiya [*A publication*]
Ref Zh Okhr Prir Vosproizvod Prir Resur ... Referativnyi Zhurnal. Okhrana Prirody i Vosproizvodstvo Prirodnykh Resursov [*USSR*] [*A publication*]
Ref Zh Pochvoved Agrokhim ... Referativnyi Zhurnal. Pochvovedenie i Agrokhimiya [*A publication*]
Ref Zh Radiats Biol ... Referativnyi Zhurnal. Radiatsionnaya Biologiya [*USSR*] [*A publication*]
Ref Zh Rastenievod ... Referativnyi Zhurnal. Rastenievodstvo [*A publication*]
Ref Zh Teploenerg ... Referativnyi Zhurnal. Teploenergetika [*A publication*]
Ref Zh Yad Reakt ... Referativnyi Zhurnal. Yadernye Reaktory [*A publication*]
Ref Zh Zhivotnovod Vet ... Referativnyi Zhurnal. Zhivotnovodstvo i Veterinariya [*A publication*]
RefZtg .... Reform Zeitung [*Berlin*] [*A publication*]
REG .... Aircraft Nationality and Registration Marks
Reg .... Daily Register [*New York City*] [*A publication*] (DLA)
REG .... Radiation Exposure Guide
REG .... Radioencephalogram
REG .... Random Event Generator [*Psychology*]
REG .... Range Extender with Gain [*Bell System*]
REG .... Reeves Entertainment Group [*Television*]
Reg .... Regal, Branch of EMI [*Record label*] [*Spain*]
REG .... Regarding
REG .... Regency Resources [*Vancouver Stock Exchange symbol*]
REG .... Regent
REG .... Reggio Calabria [*Italy*] [*Airport symbol*] (OAG)
REG .... Regiment
REG .... Regina [*Queen*] [*Latin*]
REG .... Region (AAG)
REG .... Regional Science and Urban Economics [*A publication*]

REG .... Regis College, Weston, MA [*OCLC symbol*] (OCLC)
REG .... Register (AAG)
REG .... Registered [*Stock exchange term*] (SPSG)
REG .... Registrar (ROG)
Reg .... Registration Cases [*A publication*] (DLA)
Reg .... Registrum Omnium Brevium [*Register of Writs*] [*Latin*] [*A publication*] (DSA)
REG .... Registry
REG .... Regular (AAG)
REG .... Regulate (AAG)
REG .... Regulating [*Duties*] [*Navy*] [*British*]
REG .... Regulation
REG .... Regulator (DEN)
REG .... Repair-Evacuator Group [*USSR*]
REg .... Revue Egyptologique [*A publication*]
REG .... Revue des Etudes Grecques [*A publication*]
REG .... Rheoencephalography [*Medicine*]
REG .... Rock Eagle [*Georgia*] [*Seismograph station code, US Geological Survey*] (SEIS)
REgA .... Revue de l'Egypte Ancienne [*A publication*]
REGAF ..... Regular Air Force
REGAL ...... Range and Elevation Guidance for Approach and Landing [*Aviation*] (FAAC)
REGAL ...... Remotely Guided Autonomous Lightweight Torpedo (MCD)
Reg Anaesth ... Regional Anaesthesia [*A publication*]
Regan Rep Nurs Law ... Regan Report on Nursing Law [*A publication*]
Reg App ...... Registration Appeals [*England*] [*A publication*] (DLA)
Reg Arch ..... Registered Architect
REGARD .... Ruby, Emerald, Garnet, Amethyst, Ruby, Diamond [*Jewelry*]
REGB .... Regional Bancorp, Inc. [*NASDAQ symbol*] (NQ)
Reg Bl .... Regierungsblatt [*Government Gazette*] [*A publication*] (ILCA)
Reg Brev ..... Registrum Omnium Brevium [*Register of Writs*] [*Latin*] [*A publication*] (DLA)
REGC .... Right Eminent Grand Commander [*Freemasonry*]
REG/CAN ... Registry Number/Chemical Abstracts Number [*American Chemical Society information file*]
Reg Cas ...... Registration Cases [*England*] [*A publication*] (DLA)
Reg Cat Earthquakes ... Regional Catalogue of Earthquakes [*A publication*]
Reg Conf Ser Appl Math ... Regional Conference Series in Applied Mathematics [*A publication*]
REGD .... Registered (EY)
Reg Deb ..... Gales and Seaton's Register of Debates in Congress [*1824-37*] [*A publication*] (DLA)
Reg Deb (Gales) ... Register of Debates in Congress (Gales) [*1789-91*] [*A publication*] (DLA)
Reg Deb (G & S) ... Gales and Seaton's Register of Debates in Congress [*1824-37*] [*A publication*] (DLA)
Reg Dev ...... Regional Development News [*New Zealand*] [*A publication*]
Reg Dolg ..... Regeszeti Dolgozatok az Eoetvoes Lorand Tudomanyegyetem Regeszeti Lutezeteboel [*A publication*]
R Eg Dr Int ... Revue Egyptienne de Droit International [*A publication*]
Regelungstech ... Regelungstechnik [*A publication*]
Regelungstech Prax ... Regelungstechnische Praxis [*A publication*]
Regelungstech Prax und Prozess-Rechentech ... Regelungstechnische Praxis und Prozess-Rechentechnik [*A publication*]
Regelungstech Prax Prozess-Rechentech ... Regelungstechnische Praxis und Prozess-Rechentechnik [*A publication*]
Regelungstech Prozess-Datenverarb ... Regelungstechnik und Prozess-Datenverarbeitung [*A publication*]
Regelungstech und Prozess-Datenverarb ... Regelungstechnik und Prozess-Datenverarbeitung [*A publication*]
Regelungstech Prozess-Datenverarbeitung ... Regelungstechnik und Prozess-Datenverarbeitung [*A publication*]
Regelungstech RT ... Regelungstechnik. RT [*West Germany*] [*A publication*]
REGEM ..... Release of Genetically Engineered Microorganisms [*A conference*]
REGEN ..... Regeneration (AAG)
Regensb Univ-Ztg ... Regensburger Universitaets-Zeitung [*A publication*]
Regensburger Math Schriften ... Regensburger Mathematische Schriften [*A publication*]
Reger .... Mitteilungen. Max Reger Institut [*Bonn*] [*A publication*]
Reg Erzb Koeln ... Regesten der Erzbischoefe von Koeln im Mittelalter [*A publication*]
Reg Fuez .... Regeszeti Fuezetek [*A publication*]
Reg Gen ...... Regulae Generales [*A publication*] (DLA)
Reg Genet Mineral ... Regional'naya i Geneticheskaya Mineralogiya [*A publication*]
Reg Geol Ser NC Div Resour Plann Eval Miner Resour Sect ... Regional Geology Series. North Carolina Division of Resource Planning and Evaluation. Mineral Resources Section [*A publication*]
Reg Geol Ser NC Miner Resour Sect ... Regional Geology Series. North Carolina Mineral Resources Section [*A publication*]
REGI .... [*The*] Regina Co., Inc. [*Rahway, NJ*] [*NASDAQ symbol*] (NQ)
Regia Soc Sci Upsal Nova Acta ... Regia Societas Scientiarum Upsaliensis. Nova Acta [*A publication*]
Regia Stn Chim Agrar Sper Roma Pubbl ... Regia Stazione Chimico-Agraria Sperimentale di Roma. Pubblicazione [*A publication*]
Regia Stn Sper Seta Boll Uffic (Italy) ... Regia Stazione Sperimentale per la Seta. Bollettino Ufficiale (Italy) [*A publication*]
REGIM ...... Regimental (ROG)

REGING.... Registering (ROG)
Regional Development J ... Regional Development Journal [*A publication*] (APTA)
Regional Rail Reorg Ct ... Special Court Regional Railroad Reorganization Act [*A publication*] (DLA)
Regional Science and Urban Econ ... Regional Science and Urban Economics [*A publication*]
Regional Stud ... Regional Studies [*Oxford*] [*A publication*]
Region Develop J ... Regional Development Journal [*A publication*] (APTA)
Region Urb Econ ... Regional and Urban Economics Operational Methods [*A publication*]
REGIS .... Regency Investors [*NASDAQ symbol*] (NQ)
REGIS .... Register (AABC)
REGIS .... Relational General Information System
Register of Kentucky Hist Soc ... Register. Kentucky Historical Society [*A publication*]
Regist KY Hist Soc ... Register. Kentucky Historical Society [*A publication*]
Reg Jb Aerztl Fortbild ... Regensburger Jahrbuch fuer Aerztliche Fortbildung [*A publication*]
Reg J Energy Heat Mass Transfer ... Regional Journal of Energy, Heat, and Mass Transfer [*India*] [*A publication*]
Reg J Social Issues ... Regional Journal of Social Issues [*A publication*]
REGL........ Regimental
Regl .... Reglement [*Administrative Ordinance or Rule of Procedure*] [*French*] (ILCA)
Reg Lib...... Register Book [*A publication*] (DLA)
Reg Lib...... Registrar's Book, Chancery [*A publication*] (DLA)
REGLN..... Regulation (AAG)
REGLON .. Regulation (ROG)
REGLOS ... Reserve and Guard Logistic Operations-Streamline [*Army*] (AABC)
Reg Maj ..... Books of Regiam Majestatem [*Scotland*] [*A publication*] (DLA)
REGN....... Registry Number
REG-NEG ... Regulatory Negotiation
Regnum Veg ... Regnum Vegetabile [*A publication*]
REGO .... Registration [*Of a motor vehicle*] [*Australia*] (DSUE)
Reg Om Brev ... Registrum Omnium Brevium [*Register of Writs*] [*Latin*] [*A publication*] (DLA)
Reg Orig..... Registrum Originale [*Latin*] [*A publication*] (DLA)
Reg Plac..... Regula Placitandi [*A publication*] (DLA)
REGPOWREN ... Regulating Petty Officer WREN [*Women's Royal Naval Service*] [*British military*] (DMA)
RegProf...... Regius Professor [*The King's Professor*] [*British*]
REGR .... Register (ROG)
REGR .... Registrar
REGR .... Regulator (AAG)
REGR .... Resources Group Review. Suncor, Inc. [*A publication*]
REGr........ Revue des Etudes Grecques [*A publication*]
Reg Rep New Hebrides Geol Surv ... Regional Report. New Hebrides Geological Survey [*A publication*]
REGS........ Regulations
REGS-A..... Regional Studies [*A publication*]
Reg Soc Sci Upsal Nova Acta ... Regia Societas Scientiarum Upsaliensis. Nova Acta [*A publication*]
REGSTD ... Registered
REGSTR ... Registrar
REGSTRTN ... Registration
Reg Stud..... Regional Studies [*A publication*]
Reg Stud Assoc Newsl ... Regional Studies Association. Newsletter [*A publication*]
REGT........ Regent
REGT........ Regiment (AABC)
REGT........ Regulator
Reg Tech Meet Am Iron Steel Inst ... Regional Technical Meetings. American Iron and Steel Institute [*A publication*]
REGTL...... Regimental
REGUL...... Regular (ROG)
REGULAT ... Regulation
Regulatory Action Net ... Regulatory Action Network [*A publication*]
Regul Bull KY Agr Exp Sta ... Regulatory Bulletin. Kentucky Agricultural Experiment Station [*A publication*]
Regul Bull Univ KY Coll Agric Agric Exp Stn ... Regulatory Bulletin. University of Kentucky. College of Agriculture. Agricultural Experiment Station [*A publication*]
Regul y Mando Autom ... Regulacion y Mando Automatico [*A publication*]
Regul Pept ... Regulatory Peptides [*A publication*]
Regul Pept Suppl ... Regulatory Peptides. Supplement [*A publication*]
Regul Toxicol Pharmacol ... Regulatory Toxicology and Pharmacology [*A publication*]
Regul Tox P ... Regulatory Toxicology and Pharmacology [*A publication*]
Reg Umb.... Regio Umbilici [*Region of the Umbilicus*] [*Pharmacy*]
Reg Urban Econ ... Regional and Urban Economics [*Netherlands*] [*A publication*]
Reg Urb Econ ... Regional Science and Urban Economics [*A publication*]
Reg Veg...... Regnum Vegetabile [*A publication*]
Reg Writ ..... Register of Writs [*A publication*] (DLA)
REGY .... Registry (ROG)
R Egypt ...... Revue d'Egyptologie [*A publication*]
R Egypt Dr Int ... Revue Egyptienne de Droit International [*A publication*]
REH........... Random Evolutionary Hits

REH.......... Rational Expectations Hypothesis [*Economics*]
REH.......... Rehoboth Beach, DE [*Location identifier*] [*FAA*] (FAAL)
REH.......... Revista de Estudios Hispanicos [*A publication*]
REH.......... Revue des Etudes Historiques [*A publication*]
REH.......... Revue des Etudes Hongroises [*A publication*]
REHAB .... Rehabilitate [*or Rehabilitation*] (AFM)
Rehab........ Rehabilitation [*A publication*]
Rehab Aust ... Rehabilitation in Australia [*A publication*]
Rehab Couns ... Rehabilitation Counseling Bulletin [*A publication*]
REHABIL ... Rehabilitation
Rehabil Aust ... Rehabilitation in Australia [*A publication*] (APTA)
Rehabil Lit ... Rehabilitation Literature [*A publication*]
Rehabil Nurs ... Rehabilitation Nursing [*A publication*]
Rehabil Psychol ... Rehabilitation Psychology [*A publication*]
Rehabil Rec ... Rehabilitation Record [*A publication*]
Rehabil SA ... Rehabilitation in South Africa [*A publication*]
Rehabil S Afr ... Rehabilitation in South Africa [*A publication*]
Rehabil Suppl (Bratisl) ... Rehabilitacia Supplementum (Bratislava) [*A publication*]
REHABIT ... Reitan Evaluation of Hemispheric Abilities and Brain Improvement Training [*Neuropsychology test*]
Rehab Lit ... Rehabilitation Literature [*A publication*]
Reh Allowed ... Rehearing Allowed [*Used in Shepard's Citations*] [*Legal term*] (DLA)
REHC........ Random Evolutionary Hits per Codon
Reh Den ..... Rehearing Denied [*Used in Shepard's Citations*] [*Legal term*] (DLA)
Reh Dis ...... Rehearing Dismissed [*Used in Shepard's Citations*] [*Legal term*] (DLA)
Reh'g.......... Rehearing [*Legal term*] (DLA)
REHID .... Recursos Hidraulicos [*A publication*]
REHIS....... Royal Environmental Health Institute of Scotland [*British*]
Re Hist De ... Revue d'Histoire de la Deuxieme Guerre Mondiale [*A publication*]
REHNRAP ... Recreational, Entertainment, and Health Naturally Radioactive Products (NRCH)
REHom...... Revue des Etudes Homeriques [*A publication*]
REH-PR .... Revista de Estudios Hispanicos (Rio Piedras, Puerto Rico) [*A publication*]
REHT .... Reheat (KSC)
REHVA ..... Representatives of European Heating and Ventilating Associations
REI............ Range from Entry Interface (NASA)
REI............ Rat der Europaeischen Industrieverbaende [*Council of European Industrial Federations*]
REI............ Real Estate Issues [*American Society of Real Estate Counselors*] [*A publication*]
REI............ Recycling [*Den Haag*] [*A publication*]
REI............ Reidovoe [*USSR*] [*Seismograph station code, US Geological Survey*] (SEIS)
REI............ Religion and Ethics Institute (EA)
REI............ Renewable Energy Index [*Energy Information Service*] [*Information service or system*] [*Australia*] (ADA)
REI............ Request for Engineering Information (NG)
REI............ Request for Engineering Investigation [*Nuclear energy*] (NRCH)
REI............ Research-Engineering Interaction (IEEE)
REI............ Reusable External Insulation [*of space shuttle*] [*NASA*]
REI............ Revue Economique Internationale [*A publication*]
REI............ Revue des Etudes Indo-Europeennes [*A publication*]
REI............ Revue des Etudes Islamiques [*A publication*]
REI............ Revue des Etudes Italiennes [*A publication*]
REI............ Runway-End Identification [*Aviation*] (NASA)
REI............ Rural Economics Institute (OICC)
REIC........ Radiation Effects Information Center [*Defunct*] [*Battelle Memorial Institute*]
REIC........ Renewable Energy Info Center (EA)
REIC........ Research Industries Corporation [*NASDAQ symbol*] (NQ)
Reichhold-Albert-Nachr ... Reichhold-Albert-Nachrichten [*A publication*]
Reichsber Phys ... Reichsberichte fuer Physik [*A publication*]
Reichstoff Ind Kosmet ... Reichstoff Industrie und Kosmetik [*A publication*]
REIC (Radiat Eff Inf Cent) Rep ... REIC (Radiation Effects Information Center) Report [*A publication*]
Rei Cret Rom Faut Acta ... Rei Cretariae Romanae Fautorum Acta [*A publication*]
REID.......... Reid-Provident Laboratories [*NASDAQ symbol*] (NQ)
Reid PL Dig ... Reid's Digest of Scotch Poor Law Cases [*A publication*] (DLA)
REIE......... Revue des Etudes Indo-Europeennes [*A publication*]
Reihe Informat ... Reihe Informatik [*A publication*]
REIL.......... Real Estate Investing Letter [*Harcourt Brace Jovanovich, Inc.*] [*No longer available online*] [*Information service or system*] (CRD)
REIL.......... Runway-End Identification Lights [*Aviation*]
Reilly.......... Reilly's English Arbitration Cases [*A publication*] (DLA)
Reilly EA ... Reilly's European Arbitration. Lord Westbury's Decisions [*A publication*] (DLA)
REIM........ Reimburse (AABC)
REIMB..... Reimburse (MSA)
REIMD.... Revista da Imagem [*A publication*]
REIN .... Raymond Engineering [*NASDAQ symbol*] (NQ)

REIN .... Real Estate Information Network [*Database*]
REIN .... Reinforce
Rein .... Reinstated [*Regulation or order reinstated*] [*Used in Shepard's Citations*] [*Legal term*] (DLA)
Reine Angew Metallkd Einzeldarst ... Reine und Angewandte Metallkunde in Einzeldarstellungen [*A publication*]
REINET .... Real Estate Information Network [*National Association of Realtors*] [*Information service or system*] (IID)
REINF ...... Refund Information File [*IRS*]
REINF ...... Reinforce (AAG)
REINFD ... Reinforced (AAG)
REINFG ... Reinforcing (AAG)
REINFM ... Reinforcement (AAG)
Rein Foie Mal Nutr ... Rein et Foie. Maladies de la Nutrition [*France*] [*A publication*]
Reinf Plast ... Reinforced Plastics [*A publication*]
Reinf Plast (London) ... Reinforced Plastics (London) [*A publication*]
REINIT ..... Reinitialize (MCD)
REINS ...... RADAR-Equipped Inertial Navigation System
REINS ...... Requirements Electronic Input System [*NASA*] (KSC)
REINSR .... Reinsurance
REINV ...... Reference Invoice (FAAC)
REIPS .... Real Estate Investment Properties [*NASDAQ symbol*] (NQ)
REIS .... Readiness Information System [*Army*]
REIS .... Reconstitutable and Enduring Intelligence System
REIS .... Regional Economic Information System [*Department of Commerce*] [*Information service or system*] (IID)
REIS .... Regional Energy Information System [*Minnesota State Department of Energy and Economic Development*] [*St. Paul*] [*Information service or system*] (IID)
REIS .... Research and Engineering Information Services [*Exxon Research & Engineering Co.*] (IID)
REIS .... Reseau Europeen Integre d'Image et de Services [*European Integrated Network of Image and Services*] (EAIO)
REIsl .... Revue des Etudes Islamiques [*A publication*]
Reiss-Davis Clin Bull ... Reiss-Davis Clinic. Bulletin [*A publication*]
REIT .... Real Estate Investment Trust [*Generic term*]
REIT .... REIT of California [*Los Angeles, CA*] [*NASDAQ symbol*] (NQ)
REIT .... Reiteration [*Printing*] (ROG)
REIV .... Real Estate Institute of Victoria [*Australia*]
REIV .... Rocket Engine Injector Valve
REJ .... Redig, SD [*Location identifier*] [*FAA*] (FAAL)
REJ .... Reject (MSA)
REJ .... Religious Education Journal of Australia [*A publication*] (APTA)
REJ .... Revue des Etudes Juives [*A publication*]
Re de J ...... Revue de Jurisprudence [*Montreal*] [*A publication*] (DLA)
REJASE .... Reusing Junk as Something Else [*Conversion of junk into reusable items*]
REJIS .... Regional Justice Information Service [*St. Louis, MO*]
REJN .... Rejoin (AABC)
REJOD ..... Reeves Journal [*A publication*]
REJU .... Reject Unit [*IRS*]
REJuiv ...... Revue des Etudes Juives [*A publication*]
REJuivHJud ... Revue des Etudes Juives et Historia Judaica [*Paris*] [*A publication*]
REK .... Reykjavik [*Iceland*] [*Airport symbol*] (OAG)
REKY .... Royal East Kent Yeomanry [*Military unit*] [*British*]
REL .... Radiation Evaluation Loop [*Nuclear energy*] (NRCH)
REL .... Radio Electrician [*Navy*] [*British*]
REL .... Radio Engineering Laboratories
REL .... Rapidly Extensible Language System [*Data processing*] (CSR)
REL .... Rare-Earth LASER
REL .... Rassemblement Europeen de la Liberte [*European Liberty Rally*] [*France*] [*Political party*] (PPE)
REL .... Rate of Energy Loss
REL .... Reactor Equipment Limited [*Nuclear energy*] (NRCH)
REL .... Real Estate Law Journal [*A publication*]
REL .... Regional Education Laboratory
REL .... Related
REL .... Relations
REL .... Relative
REL .... Relativity
Rel .... Relatore [*Reporter*] [*Italian*] (ILCA)
REL .... Relay (AAG)
REL .... Release (AAG)
REL .... Reliability
REL .... Reliance Group Holdings, Inc. [*Formerly, Leasco Corp.*] [*NYSE symbol*] (SPSG)
REL .... Relic
REL .... Relie [*Bound*] [*Publishing*] [*French*]
REL .... Relief (AAG)
Rel .... Religion [*A publication*]
REL .... Religion
REL .... Reliquary and Illustrated Archaeologist [*A publication*] (ROG)
REL .... Reliquiae [*Remains*] [*Latin*]
Rel .... Reliquiae [*of Suetonius*] [*Classical studies*] (OCD)
REL .... Relizane [*Algeria*] [*Seismograph station code, US Geological Survey*] [*Closed*] (SEIS)
REL .... Relocatable [*Data processing*]

REL .... Reluctance (DEN)
REL .... Rescue Equipment Locker (AAG)
REL .... Restricted Energy Loss
REL .... Review of English Literature [*A publication*]
REL .... Revue Ecclesiastique de Liege [*A publication*]
REL .... Revue des Etudes Latines [*A publication*]
Re de L .... Revue de Jurisprudence et Legislation [*Montreal*] [*A publication*] (DLA)
REL .... Trelew [*Argentina*] [*Airport symbol*] (OAG)
RELA .... Real Estate Leaders of America [*Montgomery, AL*] (EA)
RELAA ...... Recht der Landwirtschaft [*A publication*]
RelAb .... Religious and Theological Abstracts [*A publication*]
Relac Int ..... Relaciones Internacionales [*A publication*]
RELACS .... RADAR Emission Location Attack Control System
Relais .... Relais Statistiques de l'Economie Picarde [*A publication*]
Relais Econ Picarde ... Relais Statistiques de l'Economie Picarde [*A publication*]
RELAT ...... Related
RELat .... Revue des Etudes Latines [*A publication*]
Relat Annu Inst Geol Publ Hung ... Relationes Annuae. Instituti Geologici Publicii Hungarici [*A publication*]
Relata Tech Chim Biol Appl ... Relata Technica di Chimica e Biologia Applicata [*A publication*]
Relat Cient Esc Super Agric Luiz Queiroz Dep Inst Genet ... Relatorio Cientifico. Escola Superior de Agricultura Luiz de Queiroz. Departamento e Instituto de Genetica [*A publication*]
Relat DNOCS ... Relatoria. DNOCS [*Departamento Nacional de Obras Contra as Secas*] [*A publication*]
Relat Ind .... Relations Industrielles [*A publication*]
Relat Industr ... Relations Industrielles [*A publication*]
Relat Int ...... Relations Internationales [*A publication*]
Relat Int (Geneve) ... Relations Internationales (Geneve) [*A publication*]
Relations Inds (Quebec) ... Relations Industrielles (Quebec) [*A publication*]
RELATN ... Relation (ROG)
Relay Eng ... Relay Engineer [*A publication*]
Relaz Attiv Stn Sper Pratic Lodi ... Relazione sull'Attivita della Stazione Sperimentale di Praticoltura di Lodi [*A publication*]
Relaz Clin Sci ... Relazione Clinico Scientifiche [*A publication*]
Relazione Comm Dirett Ist Zootec Laziale (Roma) ... Relazione. Commissione Direttiva. Istituto Zootecnico Laziale (Roma) [*A publication*]
Relaz Soc ... Relazioni Sociali [*A publication*]
RelB .... Religion och Bibel [*Uppsala*] [*A publication*]
RelBib .... Religion och Bibel [*Uppsala*] [*A publication*]
RELBL ...... Reliability
RELBY ...... When Relieved By [*Army*]
RELC .... Regional Language Centre [*SEAMEO*] [*Research center*] [*Singapore*] (IRC)
RELC .... RELC [*Regional English Language Centre*] Journal [*Singapore*] [*A publication*]
RELC .... Reliability Committee [*NASA*]
Rel Cab ...... Religious Cabinet [*A publication*]
Rel Comm Lands ... Religion in Communist Lands [*A publication*]
RELCT .... Relocate (FAAC)
RELCTD ... Relocated
RELCV .... Regional Educational Laboratory for the Carolinas and Virginia
RELD .... Rare-Earth LASER Device
RELDET ... When Relieved Detached [*Duty Indicated*]
RELDIRDET ... When Relieved and When Directed Detached [*Duty Indicated*]
RELE .... Radio Electrician
RELE .... Release (ROG)
Rel Ed .... Religious Education [*A publication*]
RELET .... Reference Letter (FAAC)
Relevance Logic Newslett ... Relevance Logic Newsletter [*A publication*]
Relev Log News ... Relevance Logic Newsletter [*A publication*]
Rel d Griech ... Die Religion der Griechen [*A publication*] (OCD)
RELHA ...... Revista Espanola de Literatura, Historia, y Arte [*A publication*]
RELI .... Religion Index [*American Theological Library Association*] [*Information service or system*]
RELIA .... Rehabilitation Literature [*A publication*]
Reliab Eng ... Reliability Engineering [*A publication*]
Reliability Eng ... Reliability Engineering [*A publication*]
Reliable P J ... Reliable Poultry Journal [*A publication*]
RELiege ...... Revue Ecclesiastique de Liege [*Belgium*] [*A publication*]
RELIG .... Religion [*or Religious*]
Relig Ed ..... Religious Education [*A publication*]
Relig Educ ... Religious Education [*A publication*]
Relig Hum ... Religious Humanism [*A publication*]
Relig in Life ... Religion in Life [*A publication*]
Relig Soc .... Religion and Society [*A publication*]
Relig Sthn Afr ... Religion in Southern Africa [*A publication*]
Relig Stud .. Religious Studies [*A publication*]
Relig T J ..... Religion Teacher's Journal [*A publication*]
Rel Ind .... Relations Industrielles [*A publication*]
Rel Ind One ... Religion Index One [*A publication*]
RELing ...... Revista Espanola de Linguistica [*A publication*]
RELIQ .... Reliquiae [*Remains*] [*Latin*]
RELIQ .... Reliquum [*The Remainder*] [*Pharmacy*]
RELL .... Reinforced Education Learning Laboratory (EA)
RELL .... Richardson Electronics Limited [*NASDAQ symbol*] (NQ)

RELLA ...... Regional European Long-Lines Agency [*Later, RALLA*] (NATG)
Rel Life ...... Religion in Life [*A publication*]
RELMA..... Robert E. Lee Memorial Association (EA)
RELMAT.. Relative Matrix (MCD)
RELO .... Revue. Organisation Internationale pour l'Etude des Langues Anciennes par Ordinateur [*A publication*]
RELOC...... Relocate (AAG)
RELP .... Real Estate Limited Partnership
RELPAS.... Restricted Express Lists/Physiological Activity Section [*National Science Foundation*]
RelPerI..... Religious Periodicals Index [*A publication*]
Rel & Pub Order ... Religion and the Public Order [*A publication*] (DLA)
RELQ........ Release-Quiesce [*Data processing*]
REL-R....... Reliability Report (AAG)
RELR........ Revised and Expurgated Law Reports [*India*] [*A publication*] (DLA)
RELS .... Real Estate Listing Service [*Database*] [*MDR Telecom*] [*Information service or system*] (CRD)
RELS .... Redeye Launch Simulator (MCD)
RELS .... Relations
RelS .... Religious Studies [*A publication*]
RELSA .... Radio Elektronik Schau [*A publication*]
Rel So Africa ... Religion in Southern Africa [*A publication*]
Rel Soc ...... Religion and Society [*A publication*]
Rel St .... Religious Studies [*A publication*]
Rel St R ..... Religious Studies Review [*A publication*]
Rel St Rev .. Religious Studies Review [*A publication*]
Rel Stud .... Religious Studies [*London*] [*A publication*]
RELT........ Reltron Corp. [*NASDAQ symbol*] (NQ)
RelTAbstr ... Religious and Theological Abstracts [*Myerstown, PA*] [*A publication*]
RELTD...... Related
Rel & Theol Abstr ... Religious and Theological Abstracts [*A publication*]
Rel Trad..... Religious Traditions [*A publication*]
RELV .... Revue de l'Enseignement des Langues Vivantes [*A publication*]
RELX........ Realex Corp. [*NASDAQ symbol*] (NQ)
RELY........ Ingres Corp. [*NASDAQ symbol*] (NQ)
REM .... C & M Aviation, Inc. [*Inyokern, CA*] [*FAA designator*] (FAAC)
REM .... Radio Electrical Mechanic [*British military*] (DMA)
REM .... Radioactivity Environmental Monitoring [*Information service or system*] (EISS)
REM .... Random Entry Memory (ADA)
REM .... Range Evaluation Missile
REM .... Rapid Eye Movement
REM .... Rare Earth Metal [*Inorganic chemistry*]
REM .... Raster Elektron Mikroskopie [*Scanning Electron Microscopy*] [*German*]
REM .... Raumbildentfernungsmesser [*Stereoscopic range-finder*] [*German military - World War II*]
REM .... Reaction Engine Module [*NASA*] (KSC)
REM .... Recognition Memory [*Semionics Associates*] [*Data processing*]
REM .... Recovery Exercise Module (MCD)
REM .... Reentry Module
REM .... Reflection Electron Microscopy
REM .... Registered Equipment Management [*Air Force*] (AFM)
REM .... Release-Engage [*or Engagement*] Mechanism (NASA)
REM .... Release Engine Mechanism (NASA)
REM .... Release Engine Module (MCD)
REM .... Release Escape Mechanism (MCD)
REM .... Reliability Engineering Model (KSC)
REM .... Remainder (MSA)
REM .... Remark
Rem .... Remigius [*Flourished, 841-908*] [*Authority cited in pre-1607 legal work*] (DSA)
Rem........... Remington [*Record label*] [*USA, Europe, etc.*]
Rem........... Remise [*Remittance*] [*Business term*] [*French*]
REM .... Remit (AABC)
Rem........... Remittance (DLA)
REM .... Remote [*Alaska*] [*Seismograph station code, US Geological Survey*] (SEIS)
REM .... Remote Event Module [*Data processing*]
REM .... Remove [*or Removal*] (AAG)
REM .... Repertoire d'Epigraphie Meroitique [*A publication*]
REM .... Research Management [*A publication*]
REM .... Reserves Embarked [*Navy*] (NVT)
REM .... Revue Ecclesiastique de Metz [*A publication*]
Re M .... Revue Musicale [*A publication*]
REM .... Rocket Engine Module (MCD)
REM .... Roentgen-Equivalent-Mammal [*Irradiation unit*]
REM .... Roentgen-Equivalent-Man [*Later, Sv*] [*Irradiation unit*]
REMA .... Refrigeration Equipment Manufacturers Association [*Later, ARI*] (MCD)
REMAB..... Radiation Equivalent Manikin Absorption
REMAB..... Remote Marshalling Base (MCD)
Rem Actual ... Remedes-Actualites [*A publication*]
REMAD .... Remote Magnetic Anomaly Detection
Rem Am ..... Remedia Amoris [*of Ovid*] [*Classical studies*] (OCD)
REMAP..... Record Extraction, Manipulation, and Print

REMARC ... Retrospective Machine Readable Catalog [*Carrollton Press, Inc.*] [*Arlington, VA*] [*Bibliographic database*] [*Online version of the US Library of Congress Shelflist*]
Remarques Afr ... Remarques Africaines [*A publication*]
REMAS.... Radiation Effects Machine Analysis System (AAG)
REMAT..... Research Centre for Management of New Technology [*Wilfrid Laurier University*] [*Canada*] [*Research center*] (RCD)
REMBASS ... Remotely Monitored Battlefield Area Sensor System (MCD)
REMBJTR .. Reimbursement in Accordance with Joint Travel Regulations
Rembt........ Remboursement [*Reimbursement*] [*Business term*] [*French*]
REMC .... Radio and Electronics Measurements Committee [*London, England*] (DEN)
REMC .... Resin-Encapsulated Mica Capacitor
REMC .... Revista de Estudios Musicales. Departamento de Musicologia. Universidad Nacional de Cuyo [*A publication*]
REMCA..... Reliability, Maintainability, Cost Analysis (MCD)
REMCAL... Radiation Equivalent Manikin Calibration
REMCE..... Remittance (ROG)
REMCO .... Committee on Reference Materials [*ISO*] (DS)
REMCO .... Rear Echelon Maintenance Combined Operation [*Military*]
Rem Corps Ames ... Remedes des Corps et des Ames [*A publication*]
Rem Cr Tr .. Remarkable Criminal Trials [*A publication*] (DLA)
REMD....... Rapid Eye Movement Deprivation
Rem'd........ Remanded [*Legal term*] (DLA)
REME....... Royal Electrical and Mechanical Engineers [*Acronym is also humorously interpreted as "Rarely Electrically or Mechanically Efficient"*] [*Military*] [*British*]
REMED ..... Remedium [*Remedy*] [*Pharmacy*] (ROG)
Remedial Ed ... Remedial Education [*A publication*]
Remedial Educ ... Remedial Education [*A publication*]
Rem Educ... Remedial Education [*A publication*]
REMES ..... Reference Message (FAAC)
REMG .... Radioelectromyograph
Rem'g........ Remanding [*Legal term*] (DLA)
REMI .... Reliability Engineering and Management Institute (EA)
REMI .... Remington Diversified Industries Corp. [*NASDAQ symbol*] (NQ)
REMIC...... Real Estate Mortgage Investment Conduit [*Federal National Mortgage Association*]
REMIDS ... Remote Minefield Identification and Deployment [*or Display*] System (MCD)
Remigi........ Remigius de Gonni [*Deceased, 1554*] [*Authority cited in pre-1607 legal work*] (DSA)
REMILOC ... Required Inservice Manyears in Lieu of Controls [*Military*]
REMIS ...... Real Estate Management Information System (BUR)
REMIT..... Remittance (DSUE)
REMIT..... Research Effort Management Information Tabulation
Remitt .... Remittance (DLA)
REML....... Radiation Effects Mobile Laboratory
REML....... Removal (ROG)
REML....... Restricted Maximum Likelihood [*Statistics*]
REM-M..... Rapid Eye Movement-Movement Period
Remma...... Reese, "Musik in the Middle Ages" [*A publication*]
REMMPS ... Reserve Manpower Management and Pay System [*Marine Corps*]
REMN .... Radio Electrical Mechanician [*British military*] (DMA)
REMN .... Remain (ROG)
REMOA .... Revista. Escola de Minas [*Brazil*] [*A publication*]
REMOBE ... Readiness for Mobilization Evaluation (MCD)
REMOS..... Real-Time Event Monitor [*Data processing*] (IEEE)
Remote Sens Earth Resour Environ ... Remote Sensing of Earth Resources and Environment [*A publication*]
Remote Sens Environ ... Remote Sensing of Environment [*A publication*]
Remote Sensing Earth Resour ... Remote Sensing of Earth Resources [*A publication*]
Remote Sensing Environ ... Remote Sensing of Environment [*A publication*]
REMP........ Radiological Environmental Monitoring Program [*Nuclear energy*] (NRCH)
REMP........ Research, Engineering, Mathematics, and Physics Division [*Obsolete*] [*National Security Agency*]
REMP........ Research and Evaluation Methods Program [*University of Massachusetts*] [*Research center*] (RCD)
REMP........ Research Group for European Migration Problems
REMPAC .. Reflectivity Measurements Pacific
REMPI...... Resonance Enhanced Multiple Photon Ionisation [*Physics*]
REMPI...... Resonant Enhanced Multiphoton Ionization [*Spectroscopy*]
REM-Q..... Rapid Eye Movement - Quiescent Period
REMR .... Remainder
REMR .... Remington Rand Corp. [*NASDAQ symbol*] (NQ)
Rem R .... Remington Review [*A publication*]
REMR .... Repair, Evaluation, Maintenance, Rehabilitation
REM-RAND ... Remington Rand Corp. [*Later, a division of Sperry-Rand*]
REMRO .... Remote RADAR Operator (MCD)
REMS........ Rapid Eye Movement State
REMS........ Reentry Measurement System
REMS........ Registered Equipment Management System [*Air Force*]
ReMS........ Renaissance and Modern Studies [*A publication*]
REMSA..... Railway Engineering Maintenance Suppliers Association (EA)
REMSTA .. Remote Electronic Microfilm Storage Transmission and Retrieval
REMT........ Radiological Emergency Medical Team [*Military*] (AABC)

REMT........ Relief Electronic Maintenance Technician
REMT........ Remote
REMTDS.. Rocket Engine and Motor Type Designation System
Rem Tr....... Cummins and Dunphy's Remarkable Trials [*A publication*] (DLA)
Rem Tr No Ch ... Benson's Remarkable Trials and Notorious Characters [*A publication*] (DLA)
REMUDY ... Records. Western Australian Museum [*A publication*]
Remy.......... Remy's Reports [*145-162 Indiana*] [*15-33 Indiana Appellate*] [*A publication*] (DLA)
REN .... Real Estate Newsletter [*A publication*]
REN .... Religion and Ethics Network (EA)
REN .... Remote Enable (IEEE)
Ren .... Renaissance [*Record label*]
REN .... Renaissance
Ren .... Renaissance [*A publication*]
REN .... Rename File [*Data processing*]
Ren .... Renascence [*A publication*]
REN .... Rencon Mining Co. [*Vancouver Stock Exchange symbol*]
REN .... Renewable
REN .... Renewal
REN .... Renin [*An enzyme*]
Ren .... Renner's Gold Coast Colony Reports [*A publication*] (DLA)
REN .... Reno [*Nevada*] [*Seismograph station code, US Geological Survey*] [*Closed*] (SEIS)
REN .... Revue des Etudes Napoleoniennes [*A publication*]
REN .... Ringer Equivalence Number [*Telephones*]
REN .... Rollins Environmental Services, Inc. [*NYSE symbol*] (SPSG)
REN .... Rural Equipment News [*A publication*] (APTA)
Rena .... Renascence [*A publication*]
Renais News ... Renaissance News [*A publication*]
Renaissance Q ... Renaissance Quarterly [*A publication*]
Renaiss Dr ... Renaissance Drama [*A publication*]
Renaiss Q... Renaissance Quarterly [*A publication*]
Renaiss Ref ... Renaissance and Reformation [*A publication*]
Renal Physiol ... Renal Physiology [*A publication*]
Renal Physiol Biochem ... Renal Physiology and Biochemistry [*A publication*]
RENAMO ... Resistencia Nacional Mocambicana [*Mozambique*]
RENAT...... Revolutsiya, Nauka, Trud [*Revolution, Science, Labor*] [*Given name popular in Russia after the Bolshevik Revolution*]
Ren B .... Renaissance Bulletin [*A publication*]
RenBib........ Rencontres Biblique [*A publication*]
RencAssyrInt ... Recontre Assyriologique Internationale. Compte Rendu [*A publication*]
RENCB........ Revue d'Electroencephalographie et de Neurophysiologie Clinique [*A publication*]
Rencontre Biol ... Rencontre Biologique [*A publication*]
RenD.......... Renaissance Drama [*A publication*]
REND........ Rendered (ADA)
Rend.......... Rendezvous [*A publication*]
Rend.......... Rendiconti [*Bologna*] [*A publication*]
Rend Accad Naz 40 (Quaranta) ... Rendiconti. Accademia Nazionale dei 40 (Quaranta) [*A publication*]
Rend Accad Naz XL ... Rendiconti. Accademia Nazionale dei XL [*A publication*]
Rend Accad Naz XL 4 ... Accademia Nazionale dei XL. Rendiconti. Serie 4 [*A publication*]
Rend Accad Naz XL 5 ... Accademia Nazionale dei XL. Rendiconti. Serie 5 [*A publication*]
Rend Accad Sci Fis Mat (Napoli) ... Rendiconto. Accademia delle Scienze Fisiche e Matematiche (Napoli) [*A publication*]
Rend Accad Sci Fis Mat Napoli 4 ... Societa Nazionale di Scienze, Lettere, ed Arti in Napoli. Rendiconto dell'Accademia delle Scienze Fisiche e Matematiche. Serie 4 [*A publication*]
Rend Acc It ... Atti. Reale Accademia d'Italia. Rendiconti. Classe di Scienze Morali [*A publication*]
Rend Acc (Napoli) ... Rendiconti. Accademia di Archeologia, Lettere, e Belle Arti (Napoli) [*A publication*]
Rend Atti Accad Sci Med Chir ... Rendiconti e Atti. Accademia di Scienze Mediche e Chirurgiche [*A publication*]
Rend Bologna ... Atti. Accademia delle Scienze. Istituto di Bologna. Rendiconti [*A publication*]
Rend Circ Mat Palermo ... Rendiconti. Circolo Matematico di Palermo [*A publication*]
Rend Circ Mat Palermo 2 ... Rendiconti. Circolo Matematico di Palermo. Serie II [*A publication*]
RENDD..... Rendered (ROG)
Rend Gastro ... Rendiconti di Gastro-Enterologia [*A publication*]
Rendic Accad Sc Fis e Mat (Napoli) ... Rendiconto. Accademia delle Scienze Fisiche e Matematiche (Napoli) [*A publication*]
Rendic R Accad Sc Ist Bologna ... Rendiconto. Reale Accademia delle Scienze. Istituto di Bologna [*A publication*]
Rend Istit Mat Univ Trieste ... Rendiconti. Istituto di Matematica. Universita di Trieste [*A publication*]
Rend Ist Lomb ... Rendiconti. Istituto Lombardo. Accademia di Scienze e Lettere [*A publication*]
Rend Ist Lomb Accad Sci Lett A ... Rendiconti. Istituto Lombardo. Accademia di Scienze e Lettere. Sezione A. Scienze Matematiche, Fisiche, e Geologiche [*Italy*] [*A publication*]

Rend Ist Lomb Accad Sci Lett A Sci Mat Fis Chim Geol ... Rendiconti. Istituto Lombardo. Accademia di Scienze e Lettere. Sezione A. Scienze Matematiche, Fisiche, Chimiche, e Geologiche [*A publication*]
Rend Ist Lomb Accad Sci Lett B ... Rendiconti. Istituto Lombardo. Accademia di Scienze e Lettere. Sezione B. Scienze Biologiche e Mediche [*Italy*] [*A publication*]
Rend Ist Lomb Accad Sci Lett Parte Gen Atti Uffic ... Rendiconti. Istituto Lombardo. Accademia di Scienze e Lettere. Parte Generale e Atti Ufficiali [*A publication*]
Rend Ist Lomb Sci Lett A ... Rendiconti. Istituto Lombardo di Scienze e Lettere. Sezione A. Scienze Matematiche, Fisiche, Chimiche, e Geologiche [*A publication*]
Rend Ist Lomb Sci Lett A Sci Mat Fis Chim Geol ... Rendiconti. Istituto Lombardo di Scienze e Lettere. Sezione A. Scienze Matematiche, Fisiche, Chimiche, e Geologiche [*A publication*]
Rend Ist Lomb Sci Lett Parte Gen Atti Uffic ... Rendiconti. Istituto Lombardo. Accademia di Scienze e Lettere. Parte Generale e Atti Ufficiali [*A publication*]
Rend Ist Mat Univ Trieste ... Rendiconti. Istituto di Matematica. Universita di Trieste [*A publication*]
Rend Ist Sanita Pubblica ... Rendiconti. Istituto di Sanita Pubblica [*A publication*]
Rend Ist Sci Univ Camerino ... Rendiconti. Istituti Scientifici. Universita di Camerino [*A publication*]
Rend Ist Super Sanita ... Rendiconti. Istituto Superiore di Sanita [*A publication*]
Rend Linc... Rendiconti. Reale Accademia dei Lincei [*A publication*]
Rend Mat... Rendiconti di Matematica [*A publication*]
Rend Mat 6 ... Rendiconti di Matematica. Serie VI [*A publication*]
Rend Mat 7 ... Rendiconti di Matematica. Serie VII [*A publication*]
Rend (Nap) ... Rendiconti. Reale Accademia di Archeologia, Lettere, ed Arti (Naples) [*A publication*]
RENDOCK ... Rendezvous and Docking [*Aerospace*] (MCD)
Rend Pont .. Rendiconti. Pontificia Accademia Romana di Archeologia [*A publication*]
Rend Pont Acc ... Rendiconti. Pontificia Accademia Romana di Archeologia [*A publication*]
Rend R Ist Lomb Sci Lett ... Rendiconti. Reale Istituto Lombardo di Scienze e Lettere [*A publication*]
Rend Riun Annu Assoc Elettrotec Ital ... Rendiconti. Riunione Annuale. Associazione Elettrotecnica Italiana [*Italy*] [*A publication*]
Rend Riunione Assoc Elettrotec Ital ... Rendiconti. Riunione Annuale. Associazione Elettrotecnica Italiana [*A publication*]
Rend Rom Gastroenterol ... Rendiconti Romani di Gastroenterologia [*Italy*] [*A publication*]
Rend Sc Int Fis Enrico Fermi ... Rendiconti. Scuola Internazionale di Fisica "Enrico Fermi" [*A publication*]
Rend Sc Int Fis Fermi ... Rendiconti. Scuola Internazionale di Fisica "Enrico Fermi" [*A publication*]
Rend Scu Int Fis Enrico Fermi ... Rendiconti. Scuola Internazionale di Fisica "Enrico Fermi" [*Italy*] [*A publication*]
Rend Sem Fac Sci Univ Cagliari ... Rendiconti. Seminario della Facolta di Scienze. Universita di Cagliari [*A publication*]
Rend Semin Fac Sci Univ Cagliari ... Rendiconti. Seminario della Facolta di Scienze. Universita di Cagliari [*A publication*]
Rend Semin Mat Fis Milano ... Rendiconti. Seminario Matematico e Fisico di Milano [*A publication*]
Rend Sem Mat Brescia ... Rendiconti. Seminario Matematico di Brescia [*A publication*]
Rend Sem Mat Fis Milano ... Rendiconti. Seminario Matematico e Fisico di Milano [*A publication*]
Rend Sem Mat Univ Padova ... Rendiconti. Seminario Matematico. Universita di Padova [*A publication*]
Rend Sem Mat Univ Politec Torino ... Rendiconti. Seminario Matematico gia Conferenze di Fisica e di Matematica. Universita e Politecnico di Torino [*A publication*]
Rend Sem Mat Univ e Politec Torino ... Rendiconti. Seminario Matematico. Universita e Politecnico di Torino [*A publication*]
Rend Soc Chim Ital ... Rendiconti. Societa Chimica Italiana [*A publication*]
Rend Soc Ital Mineral Petrol ... Rendiconti. Societa Italiana di Mineralogia e Petrologia [*A publication*]
Rend Soc Ital Sci Accad XL ... Rendiconti. Societa Italiana delle Scienze detta Accademia dei XL [*A publication*]
Rend Soc Mineral Ital ... Rendiconti. Societa Mineralogica Italiana [*A publication*]
RENDZ ..... Rendezvous (KSC)
RenE .... Reinare en Espana [*A publication*]
RENE .... Rocket Engine/Nozzle Ejector
RENEA...... Revue Neurologique [*A publication*]
RENEC...... Regroupement National des Etudiants Camerounais [*National Regrouping of Cameroonese Students*]
R Energie ... Revue de l'Energie [*A publication*]
Renew........ Renewal [*A publication*]
Renew Energy Bull ... Renewable Energy Bulletin [*England*] [*A publication*]
REnf.......... Revue Mensuelle de l'Oeuvre Nationale de l'Enfance [*A publication*]
RENFE...... Red Nacional de los Ferrocariles Espanoles [*Spanish National Railways*] (EY)
Ren Funct... Renal Function [*A publication*]

R ENG .... Royal Engineers [*Military*] [*British*]   (ROG)
R Eng J ...... Royal Engineers Journal [*A publication*]
R Engl Lit .. Review of English Literature [*A publication*]
R Engl Stud ... Review of English Studies [*A publication*]
REngS .... Review of English Studies [*A publication*]
R Eng Stud ... Review of English Studies [*A publication*]
R Eng Stud ns ... Review of English Studies. New Series [*A publication*]
RENH .... Revue des Etudes Neo-Helleniques [*A publication*]
RENID3 .... Annual Research Reviews. Renin [*A publication*]
RENJA .... Russian Engineering Journal [*A publication*]
RENL .... REN Corp - USA [*Formerly, Renal System, Inc.*] [*NASDAQ symbol*]   (NQ)
RENLO ..... Revue. Ecole Nationale des Langues Orientales [*A publication*]
Ren M .... Renaissance Monographs [*A publication*]
RENM .... Request for Next Message
Ren Mod St ... Renaissance and Modern Studies [*A publication*]
Ren Mod Stud ... Renaissance and Modern Studies [*A publication*]
RENMR .... Reconnaissance Medium Range [*Army*]
Ren MS ...... Renaissance and Modern Studies [*A publication*]
RenN .... Renaissance News [*A publication*]
Renn .... Renner's Reports, Notes of Cases, Gold Coast Colony and Colony of Nigeria [*1861-1914*] [*A publication*]   (DLA)
Ren News ... Renaissance News [*A publication*]
RENO .... Research on Norway [*A publication*]
RENOT ..... Regional Notice [*FAA*]
RENOVAND ... Renovandus [*To Be Renewed*] [*Pharmacy*]   (ROG)
RenP .... Renaissance Papers [*A publication*]
RENPA ...... Radio Engineering and Electronic Physics [*English Translation*] [*A publication*]
RENPE ...... Rare and Endangered Native Plant Exchange   (EA)
RenQ .... Renaissance Quarterly [*A publication*]
Ren & R ..... Renaissance and Reformation [*A publication*]
RENRA ..... Rentgenologiya i Radiologiya [*A publication*]
RENRAD .. Rendezvous RADAR [*NASA*]   (NASA)
Ren & Ref ... Renaissance and Reformation [*A publication*]
RENS .... Radiation Effects on Network Systems
RENS .... Reconnaissance, Electronic Warfare, and Naval Intelligence System
REN SEM ... Renovetur Semel [*Renew Once*] [*Pharmacy*]
RENSONIP ... Reconnaissance Electronic Warfare, Special Operations, and Naval Intelligence Processing   (MCD)
Rensselaer Polytech Inst Eng Sci Ser ... Rensselaer Polytechnic Institute. Engineering and Science Series [*A publication*]
R Ens Sup .. Revue de l'Enseignement Superieur [*A publication*]
RENT .... Reentry Nose Tip [*Air Force*]
RENT .... Rentrak Corp. [*NASDAQ symbol*]   (NQ)
Rental .... Rental Product News [*A publication*]
Rent Equip ... Rental Equipment Register [*A publication*]
Rentgenogr Miner Syr'ya ... Rentgenografiya Mineral'nogo Syr'ya [*A publication*]
Rentgenol Radiol ... Rentgenologiya i Radiologiya [*A publication*]
R Entomol Soc London Symp ... Royal Entomological Society of London. Symposia [*A publication*]
RENU .... Reconstruction Education for National Understanding [*An association*]   (EA)
RENUNCN ... Renunciation   (ROG)
RENV .... Renovate   (AABC)
RENX .... Renaissance GRX, Inc. [*NASDAQ symbol*]   (NQ)
REO .... Ransom Eli Olds [*Acronym used as name of automobile manufactured by Ransom E. Olds Co.*]
REO .... Rare-Earth Oxide
REO .... Rea Gold Corp. [*Toronto Stock Exchange symbol*] [*Vancouver Stock Exchange symbol*]
REO .... Real Estate Owned [*Banking*]
REO .... Receptive-Expressive Observation [*Sensorimotor skills test*]
REO .... Regenerated Electrical Output
REO .... Regional Executive Officer [*British*]
REO .... Reinforcements   (DSUE)
REO .... Responsible Engineering Office [*Military*]   (AFIT)
REO .... Rio Airways [*Killeen, TX*] [*FAA designator*]   (FAAC)
REO .... Rome, OR [*Location identifier*] [*FAA*]   (FAAL)
Reo .... Te Reo. Linguistic Society of New Zealand [*A publication*]
REOC .... Report When Established on Course [*Aviation*]   (FAAC)
REOC .... Royal Enfield Owners Club   (EA)
REOG .... Rea Gold Corp. [*Vancouver, BC*] [*NASDAQ symbol*]   (NQ)
REON .... Rocket Engine Operations - Nuclear   (IEEE)
REOP .... Reopening [*Investment term*]
REOPT ...... Reorder Point [*Army*]
REORG ..... Reorganize   (EY)
REOS .... Racal Electronic Optical System [*Software package*] [*Racal Imaging Systems*]
REOS .... Rare-Earth Oxysulfide
REOS .... Reflective Electron Optical System
REOT .... Right-End-of-Tape
REOU .... Radio and Electronic Officers' Union [*British*]   (DCTA)
Rep .... Coke's English King's Bench Reports [*1572-1616*] [*A publication*]
Rep .... De Republica [*of Cicero*] [*Classical studies*]   (OCD)
REP .... Die Republikaner [*Republican Party*] [*Federal Republic of Germany*] [*Political party*]   (PPW)

Rep .... Knapp's Privy Council Reports [*England*] [*A publication*]   (DLA)
REP .... RADAR Effects Processor   (MCD)
REP .... RADAR Evaluation Pod [*Spacecraft*]
REP .... Radical Education Project [*Students for a Democratic Society*]
REP .... Radiological Emergency Plan [*Nuclear energy*]   (NRCH)
REP .... Railway Equipment and Publication Company, The, New York NY [*STAC*]
REP .... Range Error Probable [*Military*]
REP .... Range Estimation Program   (MCD)
REP .... Rapid Electrophoresis
REP .... Reaction Energy Profile
REP .... Recovery and Evacuation Program [*Marine Corps*]
REP .... Reentrant Processor [*Telecommunications*]
REP .... Reentry Physics Program
REP .... Regional Employment Premium [*British*]
REP .... Regional Environmental Plan [*Australia*]
REP .... Relativistic Electron Precipitation [*Meteorology*]
REP .... Rendezvous Evaluation Pad [*NASA*]   (KSC)
REP .... Repair   (AAG)
REP .... Repeal   (ROG)
REP .... Repeat   (AAG)
Rep .... Repertoire   (DLA)
REP .... Repertory   (ADA)
REP .... Repertory Theater   (DSUE)
REP .... Repetatur [*Let It Be Repeated*] [*Pharmacy*]
REP .... Repetition   (DSUE)
REP .... Replace   (NVT)
REP .... Replication [*Telecommunications*]   (TEL)
REP .... Report   (AAG)
REP .... Reporter
REP .... Reporting Point [*Aviation*]
REP .... Representative   (AAG)
Rep .... Representing   (DLA)
REP .... Reprimand   (DSUE)
Rep .... Reprint   (DLA)
REP .... Reproductive Endocrinology Program [*University of Michigan*] [*Research center*]   (RCD)
REP .... Repsol SA ADS [*NYSE symbol*]   (SPSG)
REP .... Republic   (EY)
REP .... Republican
Rep .... Republika [*Zagreb*] [*A publication*]
REP .... Repulsion
REP .... Reputation   (DSUE)
REP .... Request for Proposal   (MUGU)
REP .... Research and Economic Programs [*Department of the Treasury*]   (GRD)
REP .... Research Expenditure Proposal
REP .... Research Project   (FAAC)
REP .... Reserve Enlisted Program [*Military*]
REP .... Resonance Escape Probability [*Nuclear energy*]   (NRCH)
REP .... Retrograde Pyelogram [*Medicine*]
REP .... Revista de Estudios Politicos [*A publication*]
REP .... Revue d'Economie Politique [*A publication*]
REP .... Richardson Emergency Psychodiagnostic Summary [*Psychology*]
REP .... Rocket Engine Processor
REP .... Roentgen-Equivalent-Physical [*Irradiation unit*]
REP .... Unnecessary Repetition [*Used in correcting manuscripts, etc.*]
Rep .... Wallace's "The Reporters" [*A publication*]   (DLA)
REP 63 .... Reserve Enlistment Program 1963   (MCD)
Rep AAS (Austral) ... Report. Meeting. Association for the Advancement of Science (Australia) [*A publication*]
Rep Acad Sci Ukr SSR ... Reports. Academy of Sciences of the Ukrainian SSR [*A publication*]
Rep Acad Sci Ukr SSR (Engl Transl Dopov Akad Nauk Ukr RSR) ... Reports. Academy of Sciences. Ukrainian SSR (English Translation of Dopovidi Akademii Nauk Ukrains'koi RSR) [*A publication*]
Rep Acc Natl Coal Board ... Report and Accounts. National Coal Board [*United Kingdom*] [*A publication*]
Rep Activ Dan Atom Energy Commn ... Report. Activities of the Danish Atomic Energy Commission [*A publication*]
Rep Aeromed Lab ... Reports. Aeromedical Laboratory [*A publication*]
Rep Aeronaut Res Inst ... Report. Aeronautical Research Institute [*A publication*]
Rep Aeronaut Res Inst Univ Tokyo ... Report. Aeronautical Research Institute. University of Tokyo [*A publication*]
Rep AFL Univ Cincinnati Dep Aerosp Eng ... Report AFL. University of Cincinnati. Department of Aerospace Engineering [*A publication*]
Rep Agric Coll Swed Ser A ... Reports. Agricultural College of Sweden. Series A [*A publication*]
Rep Agric Hort Res Stn Univ Bristol ... Report. Agricultural and Horticultural Research Station. University of Bristol [*A publication*]
Rep Agric Res Coun Radiobiol Lab ... Report. Agricultural Research Council. Radiobiological Laboratory [*A publication*]
Rep Agron Branch Dep Agric South Aust ... Report. Agronomy Branch. Department of Agriculture and Fisheries. South Australia [*A publication*]   (APTA)

Rep Aichi Inst Public Health ... Report. Aichi Institute of Public Health [*Japan*] [*A publication*]
REPAIRS .. Readiness Evaluation Program for Avionics Intermediate Repair Simulation (MCD)
Rep Akita Prefect Inst Public Health ... Report. Akita Prefecture. Institute of Public Health [*Japan*] [*A publication*]
Rep Alfalfa Improv Conf ... Report. Alfalfa Improvement Conference [*A publication*]
REPAML .. Reply by Airmail (FAAC)
Rep Am Mus Nat Hist ... Report. American Museum of Natural History [*A publication*]
Rep Am Univ Field Staff ... Reports. American Universities Field Staff [*A publication*]
Rep Anal Chem Unit Inst Geol Sci ... Report. Analytical Chemistry Unit. Institute of Geological Sciences [*A publication*]
Rep Anim Breed Res Organ ... Report. Animal Breeding Research Organisation [*A publication*]
Rep Anim Hlth Serv G Br ... Report on Animal Health Services in Great Britain [*A publication*]
Rep Anim Res Div (NZ) ... Report. Animal Research Division. Department of Agriculture (New Zealand) [*A publication*]
Rep Annu Conf Hawaii Sugar Technol ... Reports. Annual Conference. Hawaiian Sugar Technologists [*A publication*]
Rep Annu Conf Ontario Dept Agr Ext Br ... Report. Annual Conference. Ontario Department of Agriculture. Extension Branch [*A publication*]
Rep Annu Date Grow Inst ... Report. Annual Date Growers Institute [*A publication*]
Rep Annu Gen Meet Scott Soc Res Plant Breed ... Report. Annual General Meeting. Scottish Society for Research in Plant Breeding [*A publication*]
Rep Appl Geophys Unit Inst Geol Sci ... Report. Applied Geophysics Unit. Institute of Geological Sciences [*A publication*]
Rep Archit Sci Unit Univ Queensl ... Report. Architectural Science Unit. University of Queensland [*A publication*] (APTA)
Rep Ariz Agr Exp Sta ... Report. Arizona Agricultural Experiment Station [*A publication*]
Rep Ariz Agric Exp Stn ... Report. Arizona Agricultural Experiment Station [*A publication*]
Rep Ark Agric Exp Stn ... Report. Arkansas Agricultural Experiment Station [*A publication*]
Rep Army Res Test Lab ... Report. Army Research and Testing Laboratory [*South Korea*] [*A publication*]
REPAS ...... Research, Evaluation, and Planning Assistance Staff [*AID*]
Rep Ass Occup Ther ... Report. Association of Occupational Therapists [*A publication*]
Rep Assoc Hawaii Sugar Technol ... Reports. Association of Hawaiian Sugar Technologists [*A publication*]
Rep Ass Y .. Clayton's English Reports, York Assizes [*A publication*] (DLA)
REPAT ...... Repatriate (AABC)
Rep Aust Acad Sci ... Reports. Australian Academy of Science [*A publication*]
Rep Aust At Energy Comm ... Report. Australian Atomic Energy Commission [*A publication*] (APTA)
Rep Aust CSIRO Div Text Ind ... Australia. Commonwealth Scientific and Industrial Research Organisation. Division of Textile Industry. Report [*A publication*] (APTA)
Rep Aust Def Stand Lab ... Report. Australia Defence Standards Laboratories [*A publication*]
REPB .... Republic (MSA)
REPB .... Republic Resources Corp. [*NASDAQ symbol*] (NQ)
Rep Basic Sci Chungnam Nat Univ ... Reports of Basic Sciences. Chungnam National University [*A publication*]
Rep BC-X Can For Serv Pac For Res Cent ... Report BC-X. Canadian Forestry Service. Pacific Forest Research Centre [*A publication*]
Rep Bd Health Calif ... Reports. State Board of Health of California [*A publication*]
Rep Bd Health Ohio ... Reports. State Board of Health of Ohio [*A publication*]
Rep Bibl Phil ... Repertoire Bibliographique de la Philosophie [*A publication*]
RepBibPhil ... Repertoire Bibliographique de la Philosophie [*A publication*]
Rep Biochem Res Found Franklin Inst ... Reports. Biochemical Research Foundation. Franklin Institute [*A publication*]
Rep Biomed ... Repertoire Biomed [*A publication*]
Rep BISRA ... Report. BISRA [*British Iron and Steel Research Association*] [*A publication*]
Rep Bot Inst Univ Aarhus ... Reports. Botanical Institute. University of Aarhus [*A publication*]
Rep Bot Surv Ind ... Report. Botanical Survey of India [*A publication*]
Rep Bot Surv India ... Report. Botanical Survey of India [*A publication*]
Rep Br Beekprs Ass ... Report. British Beekeepers Association [*A publication*]
Rep Brit Ass Adv Sc ... Report. British Association for the Advancement of Science [*A publication*]
Rep Brit Assoc Adv Sci ... Report. British Association for the Advancement of Science [*A publication*]
Rep Brit Canc Camp ... Report. British Empire Cancer Campaign [*A publication*]
Rep Brit El All Ind Res Ass ... Report. British Electrical and Allied Industries Research Association [*A publication*]
Rep Brit Mus Natur Hist ... Report. British Museum. Natural History [*A publication*]
Rep Br Palaeobot & Palynol ... Report on British Palaeobotany and Palynology [*A publication*]

Rep Bull Agr Exp Sta S Manchuria Ry Co ... Research Bulletin. Agricultural Experiment Station. South Manchuria Railway Company [*A publication*]
Rep Bur Miner Resour Geol Geophys ... Report. [*Australia*] Bureau of Mineral Resources. Geology and Geophysics [*A publication*] (APTA)
Rep Bur Miner Resour Geol Geophys (Aust) ... Report. Bureau of Mineral Resources, Geology, and Geophysics (Australia) [*A publication*]
Rep Bur Mines Miner Resour Geol Geophys Microform ... Report. Bureau of Mines and Mineral Resources. Geology and Geophysics Microform [*A publication*]
Rep BWRA ... Report BWRA [*British Welding Research Association*] [*A publication*]
REPC .... Regional Economic Planning Council [*British*]
REPC .... Representation Commissioner [*Canada*]
REPC .... Research and Educational Planning Center [*University of Nevada - Reno*] [*Research center*] (RCD)
REPC .... Research and Engineering Policy Council [*DoD*]
Rep in CA .. Court of Appeal Reports [*New Zealand*] [*A publication*] (DLA)
Rep in C of A ... Reports in Courts of Appeal [*New Zealand*] [*A publication*] (DLA)
Rep Cacao Res Reg Cent Br Caribb ... Report on Cacao Research. Regional Research Centre of the British Caribbean [*A publication*]
Rep in Can ... Reports in Chancery [*21 English Reprint*] [*A publication*] (DLA)
Rep Cant Agric Coll ... Report. Canterbury Agricultural College [*A publication*]
Rep Cas Eq ... Gilbert's English Chancery Reports [*1705-27*] [*A publication*] (DLA)
Rep Cas Inc Tax ... Reports of Cases Relating to Income Tax [*1875*] [*A publication*] (DLA)
Rep Cas Madr ... Reports of Cases, Diwani Adalat, Madras [*A publication*] (DLA)
Rep Cas Pr ... Cooke's Practice Cases [*1706-47*] [*England*] [*A publication*] (DLA)
Rep Cast Res Lab ... Report. Castings Research Laboratory [*A publication*]
Rep Cast Res Lab Waseda Univ ... Report. Castings Research Laboratory. Waseda University [*A publication*]
REPCAT ... Report Corrective Action Taken [*Military*]
Rep Cent Res Inst Electr Power Ind Agric Lab ... Report. Central Research Institute. Electric Power Industry Agricultural Laboratory [*A publication*]
Rep Cent Res Inst Electr Power Ind Tech Lab ... Report. Central Research Institute. Electric Power Industry Technical Laboratory [*A publication*]
Rep Cent Res Lab Nippon Suisan Co ... Reports. Central Research Laboratory. Nippon Suisan Company [*A publication*]
Rep CE Technion-Isr Inst Technol Dep Chem Eng ... Report CE. Technion-Israel Institute of Technology. Department of Chemical Engineering [*A publication*]
Rep in Ch ... Reports in Chancery [*21 English Reprint*] [*A publication*] (DLA)
Rep Ch .... Reports in Chancery [*1615-1710*] [*England*] [*A publication*] (DLA)
Rep in Cha ... Bittleston's Chamber Cases [*1883-84*] [*A publication*] (DLA)
Rep Chem Branch Mines Dep (West Aust) ... Report. Chemical Branch. Mines Department (Western Australia) [*A publication*]
Rep Chem Lab Am Med Assoc ... Reports. Chemical Laboratory. American Medical Association [*A publication*]
Rep Chem Lab (West Aust) ... Report. Chemical Laboratory (Western Australia) [*A publication*]
Rep in Ch (Eng) ... Reports in Chancery [*21 English Reprint*] [*A publication*] (DLA)
Rep Chiba Inst Technol ... Report. Chiba Institute of Technology [*A publication*]
Rep Chiba Inst Technol Sci Ser ... Report. Chiba Institute of Technology. Scientific Series [*A publication*]
Rep Chief US Forest Serv ... Report of the Chief. United States Forest Service [*A publication*]
Rep Ch Pr .. Reports on Chancery Practice [*England*] [*A publication*] (DLA)
Rep Class Research ... Reporting Classroom Research [*A publication*]
Rep Com Cas ... Commercial Cases, Small Cause Court [*1851-60*] [*Bengal, India*] [*A publication*] (DLA)
Rep Com Cas ... Report of Commercial Cases [*1895-1941*] [*A publication*] (DLA)
REPCOMDESPAC ... Representative of Commander Destroyers, Pacific Fleet
Rep Comm Accredit Rehabil Facil ... Report. Commission on Accreditation of Rehabilitation Facilities [*A publication*]
Rep Commonw Conf Plant Pathol ... Report. Commonwealth Conference on Plant Pathology [*A publication*]
Rep Commonwealth Entomol Conf ... Report. Commonwealth Entomological Conference [*A publication*]
Rep Commonwealth Mycol Conf ... Report. Commonwealth Mycological Conference [*A publication*]
Rep Commonw Mycol Conf ... Report. Commonwealth Mycological Conference [*A publication*]
Rep Comput Centre Univ Tokyo ... Report. Computer Centre. University of Tokyo [*A publication*]

Rep Conf Role Wheat World Food Supply ... Report. Conference on the Role of Wheat in the World's Food Supply [*A publication*]

Rep Congr Eur Ass Res Plant Breed ... Report. Congress of the European Association for Research on Plant Breeding [*A publication*]

Rep Congr Eur Orthod Soc ... Report. Congress. European Orthodontic Society [*A publication*]

Rep Const Ct ... South Carolina Constitutional Court Reports [*A publication*] (DLA)

Rep Constr Eng Res Inst Found (Kobe) ... Reports. Construction Engineering Research Institute Foundation (Kobe) [*Japan*] [*A publication*]

Rep Coop Res Chugoku Reg ... Report of the Cooperative Research in Chugoku Region [*A publication*]

Rep Cr L Com ... Reports of Criminal Law Commissioners [*England*] [*A publication*] (DLA)

Rep Crop Res Lesotho ... Report on Crop Research in Lesotho [*A publication*]

Rep CSIRO Div Fish Oceanogr ... Australia. Commonwealth Scientific and Industrial Research Organisation. Division of Fisheries and Oceanography. Report [*A publication*] (APTA)

Rep CSIRO Div Text Ind Aust ... Australia. Commonwealth Scientific and Industrial Research Organisation. Division of Textile Industry. Report [*A publication*] (APTA)

Rep CSIRO Sol Energy Stud ... Report. Commonwealth Scientific and Industrial Research Organisation. Solar Energy Studies [*A publication*] (APTA)

REPCY ...... Repair Cycle

Rep Def Stand Lab Aust ... Australia. Defence Standards Laboratories. Report [*A publication*] (APTA)

Rep Deir-Alla Res Sta ... Report. Deir-Alla Research Station [*Jordan*] [*A publication*]

Rep Del Nurses Assoc ... Reporter. Delaware Nurses Association [*A publication*]

Rep Dep Agric Econ Univ Nebr Agric Exp Stn ... Report. Department of Agricultural Economics. University of Nebraska. Agricultural Experiment Station [*A publication*]

Rep Dep Agric NSW ... Report. Department of Agriculture of New South Wales [*A publication*]

Rep Dep Fish Fauna West Aust ... Report. Department of Fisheries and Fauna. Western Australia [*A publication*] (APTA)

Rep Dep Fish Wildl West Aust ... Report. Department of Fisheries and Wildlife. Western Australia [*A publication*] (APTA)

Rep Dep Mines Energy Gov Newfoundland Labrador ... Report. Department of Mines and Energy. Government of Newfoundland and Labrador [*A publication*]

Rep Dep Nucl Tech Univ Oulu (Finl) ... Reports. Department of Nuclear Technics. University of Oulu (Finland) [*A publication*]

Rep Dep Phys Univ Oulu ... Report. Department of Physics. University of Oulu [*A publication*]

Rep Dept Agric (Brit East Africa) ... Report. Department of Agriculture (British East Africa) [*A publication*]

Rep Dept Antiquities Cyprus ... Report. Department of Antiquities of Cyprus [*A publication*]

Rep Director Vet Serv Dept Agric (Union South Africa) ... Report. Director of Veterinary Services and Animal Industry. Department of Agriculture (Union of South Africa) [*A publication*]

Rep Dir Gov Chem Lab (West Aust) ... Report. Director of Government Chemical Laboratories (Western Australia) [*A publication*]

Rep Dir Mines (Tasmania) ... Report. Director of Mines (Tasmania) [*A publication*]

Rep Dir Vet Serv Anim Ind (Onderstepoort) ... Report. Director of Veterinary Services and Animal Industry (Onderstepoort) [*A publication*]

Rep Div Bldg Res CSIRO ... Report. Division of Building Research. Commonwealth Scientific and Industrial Research Organisation [*A publication*] (APTA)

Rep Div Build Res CSIRO ... Report. Division of Building Research. Commonwealth Scientific and Industrial Research Organisation [*A publication*] (APTA)

Rep Div Chem Eng CSIRO ... Report. Division of Chemical Engineering. Commonwealth Scientific and Industrial Research Organisation [*A publication*] (APTA)

Rep Div Chem Engng CSIRO ... Report. Division of Chemical Engineering. Commonwealth Scientific and Industrial Research Organisation [*A publication*] (APTA)

Rep Div Fish Oceanogr CSIRO ... Report. Division of Fisheries and Oceanography. Commonwealth Scientific and Industrial Research Organisation [*A publication*] (APTA)

Rep Div Hort Res CSIRO ... Report. Division of Horticultural Research. Commonwealth Scientific and Industrial Research Organisation [*A publication*] (APTA)

Rep Div Mech Engng CSIRO ... Report. Division of Mechanical Engineering. Commonwealth Scientific and Industrial Research Organisation [*A publication*] (APTA)

Rep Div Miner CSIRO ... Report. Division of Mineralogy. Commonwealth Scientific and Industrial Research Organisation [*A publication*] (APTA)

Rep Div Text Ind CSIRO ... Report. Division of Textile Industry. Commonwealth Scientific and Industrial Research Organisation [*A publication*] (APTA)

REPDN ..... Reproduction (AFM)

REPDU ...... Report for Duty [*Military*]

REPEA ...... Research and Engineers Professional Employees Association

Rep Earth Sci Coll Gen Educ Kyushu Univ ... Reports on Earth Science. College of General Education. Kyushu University [*A publication*]

Rep Earth Sci Dep Gen Educ Kyushu Univ ... Reports on Earth Science. Department of General Education. Kyushu University [*A publication*]

Rep East For Prod Lab (Can) ... Report. Eastern Forest Products Laboratory (Canada) [*A publication*]

Rep ED Eng Sect CSIRO ... Report ED. Engineering Section. Commonwealth Scientific and Industrial Research Organisation [*A publication*] (APTA)

Rep Eg Expl Soc ... Report for the Year. Egypt Exploration Society [*A publication*]

Rep E Malling Res Stn ... Annual Report. East Malling Research Station [*A publication*]

Rep Eng Inst Fac Eng Tokyo Univ ... Report. Engineering Institute. Faculty of Engineering. Tokyo University [*Japan*] [*A publication*]

Rep Eng Res Lab Obayashi-Gumi Ltd ... Report. Engineering Research Laboratory. Obayashi-Gumi Limited [*Japan*] [*A publication*]

Rep Ent Soc Ont ... Report. Entomological Society of Ontario [*A publication*]

Rep Environ Sci Inst Hyogo Prefect ... Report. Environmental Science Institute of Hyogo Prefecture [*A publication*]

Rep Environ Sci Mie Univ ... Report of Environmental Science. Mie University [*A publication*]

Rep Environ Sci Res Cent Shiga Prefect ... Report. Environmental Science Research Center of Shiga Prefecture [*A publication*]

Rep Environ Sci Technol Lab Nippon Bunri Univ ... Reports. Environmental Science and Technology Laboratory. Nippon Bunri University [*A publication*]

Rep Eq .... Gilbert's Reports in Equity [*England*] [*A publication*] (DLA)

Reperes-Econ Languedoc-Roussillon ... Reperes-Economie du Languedoc-Roussillon [*A publication*]

REPERF .... Reperforator [*Telecommunications*] (TEL)

REPERMSG ... Report in Person or by Message to Command or Person Indicated

Repertoire Anal Litt Francaise ... Repertoire Analytique de Litterature Francaise [*Bordeaux*] [*A publication*]

Repertorium der Phot ... Repertorium der Photographie [*A publication*]

Repert Pharm ... Repertoire de Pharmacie [*A publication*]

Repert Plant Succulentarum ... Repertorium Plantarum Succulentarum [*A publication*]

REPET ...... Repetatur [*Let It Be Repeated*] [*Pharmacy*]

Rep Europe ... Report from Europe [*A publication*]

Rep Evol Comm Roy Soc Lond ... Report to the Evolution Committee. Royal Society of London [*A publication*]

Rep Exp Res Stn (Cheshunt) ... Report. Experimental and Research Station. Nursery and Market Garden Industries Development Society, Ltd. (Cheshunt) [*A publication*]

Rep F .... Repertoire Fiscal [*A publication*]

Rep Fac Agr Shizuoka Univ ... Reports. Faculty of Agriculture. Shizuoka University [*A publication*]

Rep Fac Eng Nagasaki Univ ... Reports. Faculty of Engineering. Nagasaki University [*A publication*]

Rep Fac Engrg Kanagawa Univ ... Kanagawa University. Faculty of Engineering. Reports [*A publication*]

Rep Fac Engrg Oita Univ ... Oita University. Faculty of Engineering. Reports [*A publication*]

Rep Fac Eng Shizuoka Univ ... Reports. Faculty of Engineering. Shizuoka University [*A publication*]

Rep Fac Eng Yamanashi Univ ... Reports. Faculty of Engineering. Yamanashi University [*A publication*]

Rep Fac Fish Prefect Univ Mie ... Report. Faculty of Fisheries. Prefectural University of Mie [*A publication*]

Rep Fac Sci Engrg Saga Univ Math ... Reports. Faculty of Science and Engineering. Saga University. Mathematics [*A publication*]

Rep Fac Sci Kagoshima Univ ... Reports. Faculty of Science. Kagoshima University [*A publication*]

Rep Fac Sci Kagoshima Univ (Earth Sci Biol) ... Reports. Faculty of Science. Kagoshima University. Earth Sciences and Biology [*A publication*]

Rep Fac Sci Shizuoka Univ ... Reports. Faculty of Science. Shizuoka University [*A publication*]

Rep Fac Sci Technol Meijyo Univ ... Reports. Faculty of Science and Technology. Meijyo University [*A publication*]

Rep Fac Tech Kanagawa Univ ... Kanagawa University. Faculty of Technology. Reports [*A publication*]

Rep Fam L ... Reports of Family Law [*A publication*]

Rep FAO/IAEA Tech Meet (Brunswick-Volkenrode) ... Report. FAO [*Food and Agriculture Organization of the United Nations*]/IAEA [*International Atomic Energy Agency*] Technical Meeting (Brunswick-Volkenrode) [*A publication*]

Rep Fd Res Inst (Tokyo) ... Report. Food Research Institute (Tokyo) [*A publication*]

Rep Fed Railroad Adm ... Report. Federal Railroad Administration [*United States*] [*A publication*]

Rep Ferment Ind ... Report on the Fermentation Industries [*A publication*]

Rep Ferment Res Inst ... Report. Fermentation Research Institute [*A publication*]

Rep Ferment Res Inst (Chiba) ... Report. Fermentation Research Institute (Chiba) [*A publication*]

Rep Ferment Res Inst (Yatabe) ... Report. Fermentation Research Institute (Yatabe) [*A publication*]

Rep Field Act Miner Resour Div (Manitoba) ... Report of Field Activities. Mineral Resources Division (Manitoba) [*A publication*]

Rep Fire Res Inst Jpn ... Report. Fire Research Institute of Japan [*A publication*]

Rep Fish Board Swed Inst Mar Res ... Report. Fishery Board of Sweden. Institute of Marine Research [*A publication*]

Rep Fish Res Lab Kyushu Univ ... Report. Fishery Research Laboratory. Kyushu University [*A publication*]

Rep Fla Agric Exp Stn ... Report. Florida Agricultural Experiment Station [*A publication*]

Rep Food Ind Exp Stn Hiroshima Prefect ... Report. Food Industrial Experiment Station. Hiroshima Prefecture [*A publication*]

Rep Food Res Inst (Tokyo) ... Report. Food Research Institute (Tokyo) [*A publication*]

Rep Forest Dep (Tanganyika) ... Report. Forest Department (Tanganyika Territory) [*A publication*]

Rep Forest Exp Stn Hokkaido ... Annual Report. Hokkaido Branch. Government Forest Experiment Station [*A publication*]

Rep For Game Manage Res Inst ... Reports. Forestry and Game Management Research Institute [*A publication*]

REPFORMAINT ... Representative of Maintenance Force

Rep For Prod Res Inst (Hokkaido) ... Report. Hokkaido Forest Products Research Institute (Asahikawa, Hokkaido) [*A publication*]

Rep For Res ... Report on Forest Research [*A publication*]

Rep For Resour Reconn Surv Malaya ... Report. Forest Resources Reconnaissance Survey of Malaya [*A publication*]

Rep Forsknstift Skogsarb ... Report. Redogorelse. Forskningsstiftelsen Skogsarbeten [*A publication*]

Rep FPM-X For Pest Manage Inst ... Report FPM-X. Forest Pest Management Institute [*A publication*]

Rep Freedom Hunger Campaign ... Report. Freedom from Hunger Campaign. FAO [*Food and Agriculture Organization of the United Nations*] [*A publication*]

Rep Fukushima Prefect Public Health Inst ... Report. Fukushima Prefectural Public Health Institute [*Japan*] [*A publication*]

Rep Fys Lab I Tek Hoejsk (Lyngby) ... Report. Fysisk Laboratorium I. Danmarks Tekniske Hoejskole (Lyngby) [*A publication*]

REPGA ...... Reprographics [*A publication*]

Rep GA For Res Coun ... Report. Georgia Forest Research Council [*A publication*]

Rep Gen Fish Counc Mediterr ... Report. General Fisheries Council for the Mediterranean [*A publication*]

Rep Geol Min Explor ... Report of Geological and Mineral Exploration [*South Korea*] [*A publication*]

Rep Geol Surv Dep (Guyana) ... Report. Geological Survey Department (Guyana) [*A publication*]

Rep Geol Surv Dep (Zambia) ... Report. Geological Survey Department (Zambia) [*A publication*]

Rep Geol Surv Hokkaido ... Report. Geological Survey of Hokkaido [*Japan*] [*A publication*]

Rep Geol Surv Jpn ... Report. Geological Survey of Japan [*A publication*]

Rep Geol Surv Kenya ... Report. Geological Survey of Kenya [*A publication*]

Rep Geol Surv Malays ... Report. Geological Survey of Malaysia [*A publication*]

Rep Geol Surv Mines Dep (Uganda) ... Report. Geological Survey and Mines Department (Uganda) [*A publication*]

Rep Geol Surv NSW ... Report. Geological Survey of New South Wales [*A publication*]   (APTA)

Rep Geol Surv Qd ... Report. Geological Survey of Queensland [*A publication*]   (APTA)

Rep Geol Surv Queensl ... Report. Geological Survey of Queensland [*A publication*]   (APTA)

Rep Geol Surv Tasm ... Report. Geological Survey of Tasmania [*A publication*]   (APTA)

Rep Geol Surv Uganda ... Report. Geological Survey of Uganda [*A publication*]

Rep Geol Surv Vic ... Report. Geological Survey of Victoria [*A publication*]   (APTA)

Rep Geol Surv Vict ... Report. Geological Survey of Victoria [*A publication*]   (APTA)

Rep Geol Surv West Aust ... Western Australia. Geological Survey. Report [*A publication*]   (APTA)

Rep Geol Surv Zambia ... Report. Geological Survey of Zambia [*A publication*]

Rep Geophys Geochem Explor Geol Surv Korea ... Report of Geophysical and Geochemical Exploration. Geological Survey of Korea [*A publication*]

Rep Geophys Res Stn Kyoto Univ ... Reports. Geophysical Research Station. Kyoto University [*A publication*]

Rep Geosci Miner Resour ... Report on Geoscience and Mineral Resources [*Republic of Korea*] [*A publication*]

Rep Ghana Geol Surv ... Report. Ghana Geological Survey [*A publication*]

Rep Glasshouse Crops Res Inst ... Report. Glasshouse Crops Research Institute [*A publication*]

Rep Gov Chem Ind Res Inst (Tokyo) ... Reports. Government Chemical Industrial Research Institute (Tokyo) [*A publication*]

Rep Gov Chem Lab (West Aust) ... Report. Government Chemical Laboratories (Western Australia) [*A publication*]

Rep Gov For Exp Stn ... Report. Government Forest Experiment Station [*A publication*]

Rep Gov Ind Res Inst (Kyushu) ... Reports. Government Industrial Research Institute (Kyushu) [*Japan*] [*A publication*]

Rep Gov Ind Res Inst (Nagoya) ... Reports. Government Industrial Research Institute (Nagoya) [*A publication*]

Rep Gov Ind Res Inst (Osaka) ... Reports. Government Industrial Research Institute (Osaka) [*A publication*]

Rep Gov Ind Res Inst (Shikoku) ... Reports. Government Industrial Research Institute (Shikoku) [*A publication*]

Rep Gov Ind Res Inst (Tohoku) ... Reports. Government Industrial Research Institute (Tohoku) [*A publication*]

Rep Gov Mineral Anal Chem (West Aust) ... Report. Government Mineralogist, Analyst, and Chemist (Western Australia) [*A publication*]

Rep Govt Inst Vet Research (Fusan Chosen) ... Report. Government Institute for Veterinary Research (Fusan, Chosen) [*A publication*]

Rep Govt Mech Lab (Tokyo) ... Report. Government Mechanical Laboratory (Tokyo) [*A publication*]

Rep Gr Brit Agr Res Counc ... Report. Great Britain Agricultural Research Council [*A publication*]

Rep Gr Brit Colon Pestic Res Unit CPRU/Porton ... Report. Great Britain Colonial Pesticides Research Unit. CPRU/Porton [*A publication*]

Rep Group Adv Psychiatry ... Report. Group for the Advancement of Psychiatry [*A publication*]

Rep Gt Brit Trop Pestic Res Unit TPRU/Porton ... Report. Great Britain Tropical Pesticides Research Unit. TPRU/Porton [*A publication*]

REPH .... Republic Health Corp. [*NASDAQ symbol*]   (NQ)

REPh .... Revue de l'Enseignement Philosophique [*A publication*]

Rep Hawaii Att'y Gen ... Hawaii Attorney General Report [*A publication*]   (DLA)

Rep Health Soc Subj (Lond) ... Reports. Health and Social Subjects (London) [*A publication*]

Rep Himeji Inst Technol ... Reports. Himeji Institute of Technology [*A publication*]

REPHO ..... Reference Telephone Conversation   (NOAA)

Rep Hokkaido For Prod Res Inst ... Report. Hokkaido Forest Products Research Institute [*Japan*] [*A publication*]

Rep Hokkaido Inst Public Health ... Report. Hokkaido Institute of Public Health [*A publication*]

Rep Hokkaido Nat Agr Exp Sta ... Report. Hokkaido National Agricultural Experiment Station [*A publication*]

Rep Hokkaido Natn Agric Exp Stn ... Report. Hokkaido National Agricultural Experiment Station [*A publication*]

Rep Hokkaido Pref Agr Exp Sta ... Report. Hokkaido Prefectural Agricultural Experiment Station [*A publication*]

Rep Hokkaido Prefect Agric Exp Stn ... Report. Hokkaido Prefectural Agricultural Experiment Stations [*A publication*]

Rep Horace Lamb Inst Oceanogr ... Report. Horace Lamb Institute of Oceanography [*A publication*]   (APTA)

Rep Hort Exp Sta (Ontario) ... Report. Horticultural Experiment Station (Ontario) [*A publication*]

Rep Hort Exp Stn Prod Lab (Vineland) ... Report. Horticultural Experiment Station and Products Laboratory (Vineland Station) [*Ontario*] [*A publication*]

Rep H Phipps Inst Tuberc ... Report. Henry Phipps Institute for the Study, Treatment, and Prevention of Tuberculosis [*A publication*]

Rep Hung Acad Sci Cent Res Inst Phys ... Report. Hungarian Academy of Sciences. Central Research Institute for Physics. Koezponti Fizikai Kutato Intezet [*A publication*]

Rep Hybrid Corn Ind Res Conf ... Report. Hybrid Corn Industry. Research Conference [*A publication*]

Rep Hyogo Prefect For Exp Stn ... Report. Hyogo Prefectural Forest Experiment Station [*A publication*]

Rep IA St Apiar ... Report of Iowa State Apiarist [*A publication*]

Rep ICJ ...... International Court of Justice. Reports of Judgements, Advisory Opinions, and Orders [*A publication*]

REPIDISCA ... Pan American Information & Documentation Network on Sanitary Engineering & Environmental Sciences [*Pan American Health Organization*] [*Information service or system*]   (IID)

REpigr .... Revue Epigraphique [*A publication*]

Rep Ill Beekeep Ass ... Report. Illinois Beekeeping Association [*A publication*]

Rep Imp Coun Agric Res ... Report. Imperial Council of Agricultural Research [*A publication*]

Rep Imp Mycol Conf ... Report. Imperial Mycological Conference [*A publication*]

REPIN .... Reply If Negative [*Military*]

Rep Ind Coun Agric Res ... Report. Indian Council of Agricultural Research [*A publication*]

Rep Ind Educ Res Cent Chungnam Natl Univ ... Report. Industrial Education Research Center. Chungnam National University [*Republic of Korea*] [*A publication*]

Rep Ind Hlth Res Bo ... Report. Industrial Health Research Board [*A publication*]

Rep India Min Rur Dev ... Report. India Ministry of Rural Development [*A publication*]

Rep Ind Res Inst Hyogo Prefect ... Reports. Industrial Research Institute. Hyogo Prefecture [*A publication*]

Rep Ind Res Inst Ishikawa ... Report. Industrial Research Institute of Ishikawa [*A publication*]

Rep Ind Res Inst Osaka Prefect ... Reports. Industrial Research Institute. Osaka Prefecture [*Japan*] [*A publication*]

Rep Inf Cent Jt Inst Lab Astrophys ... Report. Information Center. Joint Institute for Laboratory Astrophysics [*A publication*]

Rep Inst Agric Res Tohoku Univ ... Reports. Institute for Agricultural Research. Tohoku University [*A publication*]

Rep Inst Agr Res (Korea) ... Report. Institute of Agricultural Research (Korea) [*A publication*]

Rep Inst Appl Microbiol Univ Tokyo ... Reports. Institute of Applied Microbiology. University of Tokyo [*A publication*]

Rep Inst Bas Med Sci ... Report. Institute of Basic Medical Sciences [*A publication*]

Rep Inst Chem Res Kyoto Univ ... Reports. Institute for Chemical Research. Kyoto University [*A publication*]

Rep Inst Clin Res Exp Med ... Report. Institute of Clinical Research and Experimental Medicine. Middlesex Hospital Medical School [*A publication*]

Rep Inst Fish Biol Minist Econ Aff Natl Taiwan Univ ... Report. Institute of Fishery Biology. Ministry of Economic Affairs. National Taiwan University [*A publication*]

Rep Inst Freshwater Res (Drottningholm) ... Report. Institute of Freshwater Research (Drottningholm) [*A publication*]

Rep Inst Geol Sci ... Report. Institute of Geological Sciences [*A publication*]

Rep Inst Geol Sci (UK) ... Report. Institute of Geological Sciences (United Kingdom) [*A publication*]

Rep Inst High Speed Mech Tohoku Univ ... Reports. Institute of High Speed Mechanics. Tohoku University [*A publication*]

Rep Inst Ind Sci Univ Tokyo ... Report. Institute of Industrial Science. University of Tokyo [*A publication*]

Rep Inst Ld Wat Mgmt Res ... Report. Institute for Land and Water Management Research [*A publication*]

Rep Inst Mar Res Fish Board Swed ... Report. Institute of Marine Research. Fishery Board of Sweden [*A publication*]

Rep Inst Med Vet Sci (SA) ... Report. Institute of Medical and Veterinary Science (South Australia) [*A publication*]

Rep Inst Min Res Univ Rhod ... Report. Institute of Mining Research. University of Rhodesia [*A publication*]

Rep Inst Min Res Univ Zimbabwe ... Report. Institute of Mining Research. University of Zimbabwe [*A publication*]

Rep Inst Phys Chem Res ... Reports. Institute of Physical and Chemical Research [*A publication*]

Rep Inst Sci Labour (Tokyo) ... Reports. Institute for Science of Labour (Tokyo) [*A publication*]

Rep Inst Sci Technol ... Report. Institute of Science and Technology [*Republic of Korea*] [*A publication*]

Rep Inst Sci Technol Sung Kyun Kwan Univ ... Report. Institute of Science and Technology. Sung Kyun Kwan University [*A publication*]

Rep Inst Soc Med ... Report. Institute of Social Medicine [*A publication*]

Rep Inst Syst Des Optim Kans State Univ ... Report. Institute for Systems Design and Optimization. Kansas State University [*A publication*]

Rep Int Assoc Cereal Chem ... Reports. International Association of Cereal Chemistry [*A publication*]

Rep Int Counc Scient Un ... Report. International Council of Scientific Unions [*A publication*]

Rep Int Pac Halibut Comm ... Report. International Pacific Halibut Commission [*A publication*]

Rep Int Whaling Comm ... Report. International Whaling Commission [*A publication*]

Rep Int Whaling Comm Spec Issue ... Report. International Whaling Commission. Special Issue [*A publication*]

Rep Invest Aust Gov Anal Lab ... Australian Government Analytical Laboratories. Report of Investigations [*A publication*] (APTA)

Rep Invest Bur Econ Geol (Texas) ... Report of Investigations. Bureau of Economic Geology (Texas) [*A publication*]

Rep Invest Bur Mines Philipp ... Report of Investigations. Bureau of Mines of the Philippines [*A publication*]

Rep Invest Delaware Geol Surv ... Report of Investigations. Delaware Geological Survey [*A publication*]

Rep Invest Div Miner Resour (VA) ... Report of Investigations. Division of Mineral Resources (Virginia) [*A publication*]

Rep Invest Fla Bur Geol ... Report of Investigations. Florida Bureau of Geology [*A publication*]

Rep Invest Geol Surv Finl ... Report of Investigation. Geological Survey of Finland [*A publication*]

Rep Invest Geol Surv MO ... Report of Investigations. Geological Survey of Missouri [*A publication*]

Rep Invest Geol Surv S Aust ... Report of Investigations. Geological Survey of South Australia [*A publication*]

Rep Invest Geol Surv South Aust ... Report of Investigations. Geological Survey of South Australia [*A publication*] (APTA)

Rep Invest Geol Surv Wyoming ... Report of Investigations. Geological Survey of Wyoming [*A publication*]

Rep Invest Gov Chem Labs West Aust ... Report of Investigations. Government Chemical Laboratories. Western Australia [*A publication*] (APTA)

Rep Invest Ill State Geol Surv ... Report of Investigations. Illinois State Geological Survey [*A publication*]

Rep Invest Minnesota Geol Surv ... Report of Investigations. Minnesota Geological Survey [*A publication*]

Rep Invest ND Geol Surv ... Report of Investigations. North Dakota Geological Survey [*A publication*]

Rep Invest US Bur Mines ... Report of Investigations. United States Bureau of Mines [*A publication*]

Rep Invest WA Govt Chem Labs ... Report of Investigations. Government Chemical Laboratories. Western Australia [*A publication*] (APTA)

Rep Ionos Res Jpn ... Report of Ionosphere Research in Japan [*Later, Report of Ionosphere and Space Research in Japan*] [*A publication*]

Rep Ionos & Space Res Jap ... Report of Ionosphere and Space Research in Japan [*A publication*]

Rep Ionos and Space Res Jpn ... Report of Ionosphere and Space Research in Japan [*A publication*]

Rep Ion Spa ... Report of Ionosphere and Space Research in Japan [*A publication*]

Rep Iowa St Hort Soc ... Report. Iowa State Horticultural Society [*A publication*]

REPISIC ... Report Immediate Superior in Command [*Navy*]

Rep Jur ...... Repertorium Juridicum [*Latin*] [*A publication*] (DLA)

Rep de Jur Com ... Repertoire de Jurisprudence Commerciale [*Paris*] [*A publication*] (DLA)

Rep Kansas Agric Exper Station ... Report. Kansas Agricultural Experiment Station [*A publication*]

Rep Kans State Board Agr ... Report. Kansas State Board of Agriculture [*A publication*]

Rep Kevo Subarct Res Stn ... Reports. Kevo Subarctic Research Station [*A publication*]

Rep Kihara Inst Biol Res ... Reports. Kihara Institute for Biological Research [*Japan*] [*A publication*]

Rep Kunst W ... Repertorium fuer Kunstwissenschaft [*A publication*]

Rep KY Agric Exp Stat ... Report. Kentucky Agricultural Experiment Station. University of Kentucky [*A publication*]

Rep Kyushu Br Crop Sci Soc Jap ... Report. Kyushu Branch. Crop Science Society of Japan [*A publication*]

Rep Kyushu Univ For ... Reports. Kyushu University Forests [*A publication*]

REPL .... Replace (AAG)

repl .... Replacement (DLA)

REPLAB .... Responsive Environment Programmed Laboratory (IEEE)

Rep Lab Soils Fert Fac Agric Okayama Univ ... Reports. Laboratory of Soils and Fertilizers. Faculty of Agriculture. Okayama University [*A publication*]

Rep Lawrence Livermore Lab ... Report. Lawrence Livermore Laboratory. University of California [*Livermore*] [*A publication*]

Rep Lib Arts Sci Fac Shizuoka Univ ... Report. Liberal Arts and Science Faculty. Shizuoka University [*A publication*]

Rep Lib Arts Sci Fac Shizuoka Univ Nat Sci ... Reports. Liberal Arts and Science Faculty. Shizuoka University. Natural Science [*A publication*]

Rep Liberal Arts Sci Fac Shizuoka Univ Nat Sci ... Reports. Liberal Arts and Science Faculty. Shizuoka University. Natural Science [*Japan*] [*A publication*]

Rep Liv Med Inst ... Report. Liverpool Medical Institution [*A publication*]

REPLN ...... Replenish (AABC)

Rep Local Govt Bd (London) ... Reports. Local Government Board (London) [*A publication*]

Rep Long Ashton Res Stn ... Report. Long Ashton Research Station. University of Bristol [*A publication*]

REPLTR .... Report by Letter (NVT)

REPM .... Rare Earth Permanent Magnet

REPM .... Repairman (NATG)

REPM .... Representatives of Electronic Products Manufacturers [*Later, ERA*]

Rep Malta ... Report on the Working of the Museum Department for the Year. Malta Department of Information [*A publication*]

Rep Mar Pollut Lab ... Report. Marine Pollution Laboratory [*A publication*]

Rep Mass Att'y Gen ... Report of the Attorney General of the State of Massachusetts [*A publication*] (DLA)

Rep Mater Res Lab Aust ... Australia. Materials Research Laboratories. Report [*A publication*] (APTA)

Rep Mathematical Phys ... Reports on Mathematical Physics [*A publication*]

Rep Math Log ... Reports on Mathematical Logic [*A publication*]

Rep Math Logic ... Reports on Mathematical Logic [*Warsaw/Krakow*] [*A publication*]

Rep Math Phys ... Reports on Mathematical Physics [*A publication*]

Rep Maurit Sug Ind Res Inst ... Report. Mauritius Sugar Industry Research Institute [*A publication*]

Rep MC ..... Reports of Municipal Corporations [*A publication*] (DLA)

REPMC ..... Representative to the Military Committee [*NATO*]

Rep MD Agr Soc ... Report. Maryland Agricultural Society [*A publication*]

Rep MD Beekprs Ass ... Report. Maryland Beekeepers' Association [*A publication*]

Rep Mech Developm Comm For Comm (Lond) ... Report. Mechanical Development Committee. Forestry Commission (London) [*A publication*]
Rep Med and Health Dept (Mauritius) ... Report. Medical and Health Department (Mauritius) [*A publication*]
Rep Med and Health Work Sudan ... Report on Medical and Health Work in the Sudan [*A publication*]
Rep Med Res Probl Jpn Anti-Tuberc Assoc ... Reports on Medical Research Problems of the Japan Anti-Tuberculosis Association [*A publication*]
Rep Meet Aust NZ Assoc Adv Sci ... Report. Meeting. Australian and New Zealand Association for the Advancement of Science [*A publication*]
Rep Melb Metrop Board Works ... Report. Melbourne and Metropolitan Board of Works [*A publication*] (APTA)
REPMES... Reply by Message (FAAC)
Rep Mich Dept Conserv Game Div ... Report. Michigan Department of Conservation. Game Division [*A publication*]
Rep Miner Bur (S Afr) ... Report. Minerals Bureau. Department of Mines (South Africa) [*A publication*]
Rep Miner Dev Div (Newfoundland) ... Report. Mineral Development Division. Department of Mines (Newfoundland) [*A publication*]
Rep Miner Res Lab CSIRO ... Report. Division of Mineralogy. Minerals Research Laboratory. Commonwealth Scientific and Industrial Research Organisation [*A publication*] (APTA)
REPMIS.... Reserve Personnel Management Information System [*Military*]
Rep Miss Agr Exp Sta ... Report. Mississippi Agricultural Experiment Station [*A publication*]
REPML..... Reply by Mail (FAAC)
Rep MRL NC State Univ Miner Res Lab ... Report MRL. North Carolina State University. Minerals Research Laboratory [*A publication*]
Rep Nat Inst Nutr ... Report. National Institute of Nutrition [*A publication*]
Rep Natl Food Res Inst ... Report. National Food Research Institute [*A publication*]
Rep Natl Food Res Inst (Tokyo) ... Report. National Food Research Institute (Tokyo) [*A publication*]
Rep Natl Ind Res Inst (Korea) ... Report. National Industrial Research Institute (Korea) [*A publication*]
Rep Natl Ind Stand Res Inst (Korea) ... Report. National Industrial Standards Research Institute (Korea) [*A publication*]
Rep Natl Inst Health (Repub Korea) ... Report. National Institute of Health (Republic of Korea) [*A publication*]
Rep Natl Inst Metall ... Report. National Institute for Metallurgy [*A publication*]
Rep Natl Mus Victoria ... Reports. National Museum of Victoria [*A publication*]
Rep Natl Radiol Prot Board ... Report. National Radiological Protection Board [*A publication*]
Rep Natl Res Inst Met ... Report. National Research Institute for Metals [*Tokyo*] [*A publication*]
Rep Natl Res Inst Police Sci (Jpn) Res Forensic Sci ... Reports. National Research Institute of Police Science (Japan). Research on Forensic Science [*A publication*]
Rep Natl Res Inst Pollut Resour (Kawaguchi Jpn) ... Report. National Research Institute for Pollution and Resources (Kawaguchi, Japan) [*A publication*]
Rep Natl Res Lab Metrol ... Report. National Research Laboratory of Metrology [*A publication*]
Rep Natl Water Resour Counc Repub Philipp ... Report. National Water Resources Council. Republic of the Philippines [*A publication*]
Rep Natn Fd Res Inst (Jap) ... Report. National Food Research Institute (Japan) [*A publication*]
Rep Natn Inst Genet (Misima) ... Report. National Institute of Genetics (Misima) [*A publication*]
Rep Natn Inst Metall (S Afr) ... Report. National Institute of Metallurgy (South Africa) [*A publication*]
Rep Nat Res Inst Police Sci ... Reports. National Research Institute of Police Science [*A publication*]
Rep NC Att'y Gen ... North Carolina Attorney General Reports [*A publication*] (DLA)
Rep Neb Att'y Gen ... Report of the Attorney General of the State of Nebraska [*A publication*] (DLA)
Rep N Engl Assoc Chem Teach ... Report. New England Association of Chemistry Teachers [*A publication*]
Rep Nevada Bur Mines Geol ... Report. Nevada Bureau of Mines and Geology [*A publication*]
Rep New Hebrides Geol Surv ... Report. New Hebrides Geological Survey [*A publication*]
Rep NIM ... Report NIM [*National Institute of Metallurgy, South Africa*] [*A publication*]
Rep NJ St Agric Exp Stat ... Report. New Jersey State Agricultural Experiment Station [*A publication*]
Rep Northeast Corn Impr Conf ... Report. Northeastern Corn Improvement Conference [*A publication*]
Rep Norw Fish Mar Invest Rep Technol Res ... Reports on Norwegian Fishery and Marine Investigation. Reports on Technological Research [*A publication*]

Rep Norw For Res Inst ... Reports. Norwegian Forest Research Institute [*A publication*]
Rep de Not ... Repertoire de Notariae [*Paris*] [*A publication*] (DLA)
Rep Nottingham Univ Sch Agr ... Report. Nottingham University. School of Agriculture [*A publication*]
Rep Nova Scotia Dep Mines Energy ... Report. Nova Scotia Department of Mines and Energy [*A publication*]
Rep NRL Prog ... Report of NRL [*Naval Research Laboratory*] Progress [*A publication*]
Rep NY State Vet Coll Cornell Univ ... Report. New York State Veterinary College at Cornell University [*A publication*]
Rep NZ Geol Surv ... Report. New Zealand Geological Survey [*A publication*]
Rep NZ Sci Cong ... Report. New Zealand Science Congress [*A publication*]
REPO .... Reporting Officer [*Navy*]
REPO .... Repossess
REPO .... Repurchase Agreement [*Also, RP*] [*Investment term*]
Rep Ohara Inst Agr Biol ... Report. Ohara Institute of Agricultural Biology [*A publication*]
Rep Ohara Inst Agric Biol ... Report. Ohara Institute of Agricultural Biology [*A publication*]
Rep Ontario Geol Surv ... Report. Ontario Geological Survey [*A publication*]
Rep Ont Dep Agric ... Report. Ontario Department of Agriculture [*A publication*]
Rep Ont Dep Mines ... Reports. Ontario Department of Mines [*A publication*]
Rep Ont Vet Coll ... Report. Ontario Veterinary College [*A publication*]
REP-OP..... Repetitive Operation [*Data processing*] (MDG)
Rep & Ops Atty Gen Ind ... Indiana Attorney General Reports [*A publication*] (DLA)
Rep Ore For Res Lab ... Report. Oregon State University. Forest Research Laboratory [*A publication*]
Rep Oreg Agric Exp Stat ... Report. Oregon Agricultural Experiment Station [*A publication*]
Rep Oreg Wheat Comm ... Report. Oregon Wheat Commission [*A publication*]
Reporter Aust Inst of Crim Qrtly ... Reporter. Australian Institute of Criminology. Quarterly [*A publication*] (APTA)
Reportr D... Reporter Dispatch [*A publication*]
Reports....... Coke's English King's Bench Reports [*1572-1616*] [*A publication*] (DLA)
Reports Inst High Speed Mech Tohoku Univ ... Reports. Institute of High Speed Mechanics. Tohoku University [*A publication*]
Reports Res Inst Appl Mech Kyushu Univ ... Reports. Research Institute for Applied Mechanics. Kyushu University [*A publication*]
Rep Osaka Prefect Ind Res Inst ... Reports. Osaka Prefectural Industrial Research Institute [*Japan*] [*A publication*]
Repos Trab LNIV Port Lab Nac Inves Vet ... Repositorio de Trabalhos do LNIV-Portugal. Laboratorio Nacional de Investigacao Veterinaria [*A publication*]
Rep Overseas Div Inst Geol Sci ... Report. Overseas Division. Institute of Geological Sciences [*A publication*]
REPPAC.... Repetitively Pulsed Plasma Accelerator
Rep Pap Northamptonshire Antiq Soc ... Reports and Papers. Northamptonshire Antiquarian Society [*A publication*]
Rep Pat Cas ... Reports of Patent, Design, and Trade Mark Cases [*England*] [*A publication*] (DLA)
Rep Pat Des & Tr Cas ... Reports of Patent, Design, and Trade Mark Cases [*A publication*] (DLA)
Rep Phil ..... Reports on Philosophy [*A publication*]
Rep Plann Conf Strategy Virus Manage Potato II ... Report. Planning Conference on the Strategy for Virus Management in Potatoes. II [*A publication*]
Rep Popul-Fam Plann ... Reports on Population-Family Planning [*A publication*]
Rep Prat ..... Repertoire Pratique du Droit Belge [*A publication*]
Rep Prefect Ind Res Inst (Shizuoka) ... Reports. Prefectural Industrial Research Institute (Shizuoka) [*Japan*] [*A publication*]
Rep Proc Br Soc Anim Prod ... Report of Proceedings. British Society of Animal Production [*A publication*]
Rep Proc Int Assoc Ice Cream Manuf ... Report of Proceedings. International Association of Ice Cream Manufacturers [*A publication*]
Rep Prog Phys ... Reports on Progress in Physics [*A publication*]
Rep Prog Polym Phys (Jpn) ... Reports on Progress in Polymer Physics (Japan) [*A publication*]
Rep Progr Appl Chem ... Reports on the Progress of Applied Chemistry [*A publication*]
Rep Progr Chem ... Report on the Progress of Chemistry [*A publication*]
Rep Progr Kans Agr Exp Sta ... Report of Progress. Kansas Agricultural Experiment Station [*A publication*]
Rep Progr Kansas Agric Exp Stn ... Report of Progress. Kansas Agricultural Experiment Station [*A publication*]
Rep Progr Phys ... Reports on Progress in Physics [*A publication*]
Rep Proj LA Agr Exp Sta Dept Agron ... Report of Projects. Louisiana Agricultural Experiment Station. Department of Agronomy [*A publication*]
Rep Pr Ph .. Reports on Progress in Physics [*A publication*]
Rep Pr Phys ... Reports on Progress in Physics [*A publication*]
Rep Publ Hlth Comm Ind ... Report. Public Health Commissioner, India [*A publication*]
Rep Public Health Med Subj (Lond) ... Reports on Public Health and Medical Subjects (London) [*A publication*]

Rep QA ...... Reports Tempore Queen Anne [*11 Modern*] [*A publication*] (DLA)
Rep Quebec Soc Prot Plant ... Report. Quebec Society for the Protection of Plants [*A publication*]
REPR .... Real Estate Planning Report [*Military*] (AABC)
REPR .... Repair (ROG)
REPR .... Reports on Polar Research. Berichte zur Polarforschung [*A publication*]
REPR .... Representative
REPR .... Repressurization (MCD)
REPR .... Reprinted
REPR .... Repro Med Systems, Inc. [*NASDAQ symbol*] (NQ)
Repr Acts W Austl ... Reprinted Acts of Western Australia [*A publication*] (DLA)
Rep Rain Making Jpn ... Report of Rain-Making in Japan [*A publication*]
Repr BRA .. Reprint. Bee Research Association [*A publication*]
Repr Bull Bk R ... Reprint Bulletin. Book Reviews [*A publication*]
Rep Rd Res Lab Minist Transp ... Report. Road Research Laboratory. Ministry of Transport [*A publication*]
Rep React Cent (Ned) ... Report. Reactor Centrum (Nederlandse) [*A publication*]
Rep Reelfoot Lake Biol Stn Tenn Acad Sci ... Report. Reelfoot Lake Biological Station. Tennessee Academy of Science [*A publication*]
Rep Reg Res Cent ICTA (Trinidad) ... Report. Regional Research Centre of the British Caribbean. Imperial College of Tropical Agriculture (Trinidad) [*A publication*]
Rep Res Cent Assoc Am Railroads ... Report. Research Center. Association of American Railroads [*A publication*]
Rep Res Dept Kyushu Electr Power Co Inc ... Report. Research Department. Kyushu Electric Power Company, Incorporated [*Japan*] [*A publication*]
Rep Res Grantees Minist Educ (Jpn) ... Reports on Researches by Grantees. Ministry of Education (Japan) [*A publication*]
Rep Res Inst Appl Mech ... Reports. Research Institute for Applied Mechanics [*A publication*]
Rep Res Inst Appl Mech Kyushu Univ ... Reports. Research Institute for Applied Mechanics. Kyushu University [*A publication*]
Rep Res Inst Brew ... Report. Research Institute of Brewing [*A publication*]
Rep Res Inst Electr Commun Tohoku Univ ... Reports. Research Institute of Electrical Communication. Tohoku University [*A publication*]
Rep Res Inst Ind Saf ... Reports. Research Institute of Industrial Safety [*Japan*] [*A publication*]
Rep Res Inst Ind Sci Kyushu Univ ... Reports. Research Institute of Industrial Science. Kyushu University [*A publication*]
Rep Res Inst Nat Sci ... Report. Research Institute of Natural Sciences [*Republic of Korea*] [*A publication*]
Rep Res Inst Nat Sci Chungnam Natl Univ ... Reports. Research Institute of Natural Sciences. Chungnam National University [*A publication*]
Rep Res Inst Sci Ind Kyushu Univ ... Reports. Research Institute of Science and Industry. Kyushu University [*Japan*] [*A publication*]
Rep Res Inst Sci Technol Nihon Univ ... Report. Research Institute of Science and Technology. Nihon University [*A publication*]
Rep Res Inst Strength and Fract Mater ... Reports. Research Institute for Strength and Fracture of Materials [*A publication*]
Rep Res Inst Strength Fract Mater Tohoku Univ ... Reports. Research Institute for Strength and Fracture of Materials. Tohoku University [*A publication*]
Rep Res Inst Strength Fracture Mater Tohoku Univ (Sendai) ... Reports. Research Institute for Strength and Fracture of Materials. Tohoku University (Sendai) [*Japan*] [*A publication*]
Rep Res Inst Underground Resour Min Coll Akita Univ ... Report. Research Institute of Underground Resources. Mining College. Akita University [*Japan*] [*A publication*]
Rep Res Lab Asahi Glass Co Ltd ... Report. Research Laboratory. Asahi Glass Company Limited [*A publication*]
Rep Res Lab Eng Mater Tokyo Inst Technol ... Report. Research Laboratory of Engineering Materials. Tokyo Institute of Technology [*A publication*]
Rep Res Lab Kirin Brew Co ... Report. Research Laboratories of Kirin Brewery Company [*A publication*]
Rep Res Lab Kirin Brewery Co Ltd ... Report. Research Laboratories of Kirin Brewery Company Limited [*Japan*] [*A publication*]
Rep Res Lab Shimizu Constr Co Ltd ... Reports. Research Laboratory of Shimizu Construction Company Limited [*Japan*] [*A publication*]
Rep Res Lab Snow Brand Milk Prod Co ... Reports. Research Laboratory. Snow Brand Milk Products Company [*A publication*]
Rep Res Lab Surf Sci Okayama Univ ... Reports. Research Laboratory for Surface Science. Okayama University [*A publication*]
Rep Res Lab Tohoku Electr Power Co Ltd ... Report. Research Laboratory. Tohoku Electric Power Company Limited [*Japan*] [*A publication*]
Rep Res Nippon Inst Technol ... Report of Researches. Nippon Institute of Technology [*A publication*]
Rep Resour Res Inst (Kawaguchi) ... Report. Resource Research Institute (Kawaguchi) [*Japan*] [*A publication*]
Rep Res Progr Ill Agr Exp Sta ... Report. Research Progress at the Illinois Agricultural Experiment Station [*A publication*]

Rep Res Proj Dis Ornam Pl ... Report. Research Project for Diseases of Ornamental Plants (Victorian Plant Research Institute) [*A publication*] (APTA)
Rep Res Worcester Found Exp Biol ... Report of Research. Worcester Foundation for Experimental Biology [*A publication*]
Repr For Prod (Aust) ... Reprint. Division of Forest Products (Melbourne, Australia) [*A publication*]
Rep Rheum Dis ... Reports on Rheumatic Diseases [*A publication*]
Rep Rheum Dis Ser 2 Pract Probl ... Reports on Rheumatic Diseases. Series 2. Practical Problems [*A publication*]
Rep Rheum Dis Ser 2 Top Rev ... Reports on Rheumatic Diseases. Series 2. Topical Reviews [*A publication*]
Reprint .... English Reports, Full Reprint [*A publication*] (DLA)
Reprint Bull Bk R ... Reprint Bulletin. Book Reviews [*A publication*]
Repr NZ For Serv ... Reprint. New Zealand Forest Service [*A publication*]
REPRO ...... Reproduce (KSC)
REPROC ... Reprocess (MCD)
Reprocess Newsl ... Reprocessing Newsletter [*A publication*]
Rep Rock Found ... Report. Rockefeller Foundation [*A publication*]
REPROD ... Receiver Protective Device (DEN)
REPROD ... Reproduction
Reprod Fertil Dev ... Reproduction, Fertility, and Development [*A publication*]
Reprodn Paper News Bull ... Reproduction Paper News. Bulletin [*A publication*]
Reprodn Rev ... Reproductions Review and Methods [*A publication*]
Reprod Nutr Dev ... Reproduction, Nutrition, Developpement [*A publication*]
Reprod Rev ... Reproductions Review [*A publication*]
Reproduccio ... Reproduccion [*A publication*]
Reproduction Eng ... Reproduction Engineering [*A publication*]
Reprographics Q ... Reprographics Quarterly [*A publication*]
Reprography Newsl ... Reprography Newsletter [*A publication*]
Reprogr Q .. Reprographics Quarterly [*A publication*]
REPROM ... Reprogrammable Programmable Read-Only Memory [*Data processing*] (TEL)
REPRON ... Representation (ROG)
Rep Ross Conf Pediatr Res ... Report. Ross Conference on Pediatric Research [*A publication*]
Rep Rothamsted Exp Sta ... Report. Rothamsted Experimental Station [*A publication*]
Rep Rothamsted Exp Stn ... Report. Rothamsted Experimental Station [*A publication*]
REPROTOX ... Reproductive Toxicology Center [*Database*] [*Washington, DC*]
Rep Rowett Inst ... Report. Rowett Institute [*A publication*]
Repr Res SP ... Representative Research in Social Psychology [*A publication*]
Rep RRL GB Dep Sci Ind Res Road Res Lab ... Report RRL. Great Britain Department of Scientific and Industrial Research. Road Research Laboratory [*A publication*]
Repr Stat NZ ... Reprint of the Statutes of New Zealand [*A publication*] (DLA)
REPS .... Regional Economic Projections Series [*NPA Data Services, Inc.*] [*Information service or system*] (CRD)
REPS .... Regional Emissions Projection System [*Environmental Protection Agency*]
REPS .... Repetitive Electromagnetic Pulse Simulator [*Army*] (RDA)
REPS .... Representative
REPS .... Royal Engineers Postal Section [*British military*] (DMA)
REPSA ...... Revista de Psicoanalisis [*A publication*]
Rep Sado Mar Biol Stn Niigata Univ ... Report. Sado Marine Biological Station. Niigata University [*A publication*]
Rep S Afr Ass Adv Sci ... Report. South African Association for the Advancement of Science [*A publication*]
Rep S Afr Assoc Adv Sci ... Report. South African Association for the Advancement of Science [*A publication*]
Rep S Afr Inst Med Res ... Report. South African Institute for Medical Research [*A publication*]
Rep Saskatchewan Energy Mines ... Report. Saskatchewan Energy and Mines [*A publication*]
Rep Sask Dep Miner Resour ... Report. Saskatchewan Department of Mineral Resources [*A publication*]
Rep Sch Agric Univ Nottingham ... Report. School of Agriculture. University of Nottingham [*A publication*]
Rep Sci Ind Forum ... Report. Science and Industry Forum. Australian Academy of Science [*A publication*] (APTA)
Rep Sci Indust Forum ... Report. Science and Industry Forum. Australian Academy of Science [*A publication*] (APTA)
Rep Sci Indust Forum Aust Acad Sci ... Report. Science and Industry Forum. Australian Academy of Science [*A publication*] (APTA)
Rep Sci Living ... Reports of the Science of Living [*A publication*]
Rep Sci Res Inst ... Reports. Scientific Research Institute [*A publication*]
Rep Scott Beekprs Ass ... Report. Scottish Beekeepers Association [*A publication*]
Rep Sea Fish Inst Ser B (Gdynia Pol) ... Reports. Sea Fisheries Institute. Series B. Fishing Technique and Fishery Technology (Gdynia, Poland) [*A publication*]
Rep Sel Cas Ch ... [*William*] Kelynge's English Chancery Reports [*A publication*] (DLA)
Rep of Sel Cas in Ch ... [*William*] Kelynge's Select Cases in Chancery [*A publication*] (DLA)

Rep Ser Ark Agr Exp Sta ... Report Series. Arkansas Agricultural Experiment Station [*A publication*]

Rep Ser Ark Agric Exp Stn ... Report Series. Arkansas Agricultural Experiment Station [*A publication*]

Rep Ser Geol Surv Irel ... Report Series. Geological Survey of Ireland [*A publication*]

Rep Ser Phys Univ Helsinki ... Report Series in Physics. University of Helsinki [*A publication*]

REPSHIPS ... Reports of Shipments [*Military*]

Rep Shizuoka Prefect Ind Res Inst ... Reports. Shizuoka Prefectural Industrial Research Institute [*A publication*]

Rep Silk Sci Res Inst ... Reports. Silk Science Research Institute [*Japan*] [*A publication*]

Rep SIPRE ... Report SIPRE [*Snow, Ice, and Permafrost Research Establishment*] [*A publication*]

Rep (Sixth) Conf Int Ass Quatern Res ... Report. Sixth Conference. International Association on Quaternary Research [*A publication*]

Rep Smithson Instn ... Report. Smithsonian Institution [*A publication*]

REPSNO ... Report through Senior Naval Officer

Rep Soc Lib St ... Society of Libyan Studies. Annual Report [*A publication*]

Rep Soc Naut Res ... Report. Society for Nautical Research [*A publication*]

Rep Soc Res City Futu ... Report of the Social Research on the City of Futu [*A publication*]

Rep Sol Energy Stud CSIRO ... Report. Solar Energy Studies. Commonwealth Scientific and Industrial Research Organisation [*A publication*] (APTA)

Rep South Conf Geront ... Report. Southern Conference on Gerontology [*A publication*]

Rep South Corn Impr Conf ... Report. Southern Corn Improvement Conference [*A publication*]

Rep Stanford Univ John A Blume Earthquake Eng Cent ... Report. Stanford University. John A. Blume Earthquake Engineering Center [*A publication*]

Rep Stat Appl Res UJSE ... Reports of Statistical Application Research. Union of Japanese Scientists and Engineers [*A publication*]

Rep Stat Appl Res Union Jpn Sci Eng ... Reports of Statistical Application Research. Union of Japanese Scientists and Engineers [*A publication*]

Rep State Bd Health Iowa ... Report. State Board of Health of Iowa [*A publication*]

Rep State Biol Surv Kans ... Reports. State Biological Survey of Kansas [*A publication*]

Rep State Energy Comm WA ... Report. State Energy Commission of Western Australia [*A publication*] (APTA)

Rep Statist Appl Res Un Japan Sci Engrs ... Reports of Statistical Application Research. Union of Japanese Scientists and Engineers [*A publication*]

Rep Steno Mem Hosp Nord Insulinlab ... Reports. Steno Memorial Hospital and the Nordisk Insulinlaboratorium [*A publication*]

Rep Stud Tokyo Coll Domest Sci ... Reports of Studies. Tokyo College of Domestic Science [*A publication*]

Rep Stud Upland Farming Kawatabi Farm Tohoku Univ ... Report of the Studies on Upland Farming in Kawatabi Farm. Tohoku University [*A publication*]

Rep Sugar Exp Sta (Taiwan) ... Report. Sugar Experimental Station (Taiwan) [*A publication*]

Rep Suginami Ward Inst Public Health Res ... Report. Suginami Ward Institute of Public Health Research [*A publication*]

Rep Surg-Gen US Army ... Report. Surgeon-General. United States Army [*A publication*]

Rep Surg Gen US Navy ... Report. Surgeon General. United States Navy [*A publication*]

Rep Surv Thirty-Two NSW River Valleys ... Report. Survey of Thirty-Two New South Wales River Valleys [*A publication*] (APTA)

Rep Swed Deep Sea Exped 1947-1948 ... Reports. Swedish Deep-Sea Expedition, 1947-1948 [*A publication*]

Rep Swed Univ Agric Sci Dep Agric Eng ... Report. Swedish University of Agricultural Sciences. Department of Agricultural Engineering [*A publication*]

Rep Swed Univ Agric Sci Dep Farm Build ... Report. Swedish University of Agricultural Sciences. Department of Farm Buildings [*A publication*]

Rep Swed Univ Agric Sci Dep For Prod ... Report. Swedish University of Agricultural Sciences. Department of Forest Products [*A publication*]

Rep Swed Weed Conf ... Reports. Swedish Weed Conference [*A publication*]

REPT ... Receipt

REPT ... Repeat (ADA)

REPT ... Repetatur [*Let It Be Repeated*] [*Pharmacy*]

REPT ... Report

REPT ... Represent (ROG)

rept ... Reprint (BJA)

Rep Taiwan Sugar Exp Stn ... Report. Taiwan Sugar Experiment Station [*A publication*]

Rep Taiwan Sugar Res Inst ... Report. Taiwan Sugar Research Institute [*A publication*]

Rep Tech Coll Hosei Univ (Tokyo) ... Report. Technical College. Hosei University (Tokyo) [*A publication*]

Rep Technol Iwate Univ ... Report on Technology. Iwate University [*Japan*] [*A publication*]

Rep Technol Res Norw Fish Ind ... Reports on Technological Research Concerning Norwegian Fish Industry [*A publication*]

Rep Tech Res Inst Taisei Corp ... Reports. Technical Research Institute. Taisei Corporation [*A publication*]

Rep Teleph Eng ... Reports on Telephone Engineering [*A publication*]

Rep Tenn Agric Exp Stat ... Report. Tennessee Agricultural Experiment Station [*A publication*]

Rep Tex Agric Exp Stn ... Report. Texas Agricultural Experiment Station [*A publication*]

Rep Tex Water Dev Board ... Report. Texas Water Development Board [*A publication*]

Rep T F ... Reports, Court of Chancery Tempore Finch [*1673-81*] [*A publication*] (DLA)

Rep T Finch ... Reports, Court of Chancery Tempore Finch [*1673-81*] [*A publication*] (DLA)

Rep T Finch (Eng) ... Reports, Court of Chancery Tempore Finch [*1673-81*] [*England*] [*A publication*] (DLA)

Rep T Hard ... Lee's English King's Bench Reports Tempore Hardwicke [*1733-38*] [*A publication*] (DLA)

Rep T Hardw ... Lee's English King's Bench Reports Tempore Hardwicke [*1733-38*] [*A publication*] (DLA)

Rep T Holt ... Reports Tempore Holt, English Cases of Settlement [*A publication*] (DLA)

REPTO ... Rear Engine Power-Take-Off [*Automotive engineering*]

Rep T O Br ... Carter's English Common Pleas Reports Tempore Orlando Bridgman [*A publication*] (DLA)

Rep Tob Res Inst (Taiwan) ... Annual Report. Tobacco Research Institute (Taiwan) [*A publication*]

Rep Tob Res Inst Taiwan Tob Wine Monop Bur ... Report. Tobacco Research Institute. Taiwan Tobacco and Wine Monopoly Bureau [*A publication*]

REPTOF ... Reporting Officer (NATG)

Rep Tohoku Br Crop Sci Soc Jap ... Report. Tohoku Branch. Crop Science Society of Japan [*A publication*]

Rep Tokai Br Crop Sci Soc Jap ... Report. Tokai Branch. Crop Science Society of Japan [*A publication*]

Rep Tokushima Agr Exp Sta ... Report. Tokushima Agricultural Experiment Station [*A publication*]

Rep Tokyo Industr Res Inst ... Report. Tokyo Industrial Research Institute [*A publication*]

Rep Tokyo Metrop Ind Res Inst ... Reports. Tokyo Metropolitan Industrial Research Institute [*A publication*]

Rep Tokyo Metrop Ind Tech Inst ... Report. Tokyo Metropolitan Industrial Technic Institute [*A publication*]

Rep Tokyo Univ Fish ... Report. Tokyo University. Fisheries [*A publication*]

Rep Tottori Mycol Inst ... Reports. Tottori Mycological Institute [*A publication*]

Rept Progr Appl ... Reports on the Progress of Applied Chemistry [*A publication*]

Rept Progr Phys ... Reports on Progress in Physics [*A publication*]

Rept Progr Polymer Phys (Japan) ... Reports on Progress in Polymer Physics (Japan) [*A publication*]

Rep T QA ... Reports Tempore Queen Anne [*11 Modern*] [*A publication*] (DLA)

Reptr ... [*The*] Reporter [*Boston, Los Angeles, New York, Washington*] [*A publication*] (DLA)

Rep Train Inst Eng Teach Kyoto Univ ... Report. Training Institute for Engineering Teachers. Kyoto University [*Japan*] [*A publication*]

REPTRANS ... Report for Transportation

Rep Trans (Devonshire) ... Report and Transactions (Devonshire) [*A publication*]

Rep Trans Devonshire Ass ... Reports and Transactions. Devonshire Association for the Advancement of Science, Literature, and Art [*A publication*]

Rep Transp Tech Res Inst (Tokyo) ... Report. Transportation Technical Research Institute (Tokyo) [*A publication*]

Rep Trans Soc Guernesiaise ... Report and Transactions. Societe Guernesiaise [*A publication*]

Rept Res ... Reporting Research [*Queensland, Department of Education, Research Branch*] [*A publication*]

Rept Statist Appl Res ... Report on Statistical Applications Research [*A publication*]

Rep T Talb ... Reports Tempore Talbot, English Chancery [*A publication*] (DLA)

Rept T Finch ... Cases Tempore Finch, English Chancery [*1673-81*] [*23 English Reprint*] [*A publication*] (DLA)

Rept T Holt ... Cases Tempore Holt, English King's Bench [*A publication*] (DLA)

Rep T Wood ... Manitoba Reports Tempore Wood [*Canada*] [*A publication*] (DLA)

REPTWX ... Reply by TWX [*Teletypewriter communications*] (FAAC)

REPUB ... Republican

Repubb Ital Minist Agri For Collana Verde ... Repubblica Italiana Ministero dell'Agricoltura e delle Foreste Collana Verde [*A publication*]

Repub Malagasy Ann Geol Madagascar ... Republique Malagasy. Annales Geologiques de Madagascar [*A publication*]

Repub Malgache Doc Bur Geol ... Republique Malgache. Documentation du Bureau Geologique [*A publication*]

Repub Malgache Rapp Annu Serv Geol ... Republique Malgache. Rapport Annuel du Service Geologique [*A publication*]
Repub Philipp Dep Agric Nat Resour Bur Mines Inf Circ ... Republic of the Philippines. Department of Agriculture and Natural Resources. Bureau of Mines. Information Circular [*A publication*]
Repub Rwandaise Bull Serv Geol ... Republique Rwandaise. Bulletin du Service Geologique [*A publication*]
Repub S Afr Dep Agric Tech Serv Entomol Mem ... Republic of South Africa. Department of Agricultural Technical Services. Entomology Memoirs [*A publication*]
Repub S Afr Dep Agric Tech Serv Sci Bull ... Republic of South Africa. Department of Agricultural Technical Services. Science Bulletin [*A publication*]
Repub S Afr Dep Agric Tech Serv Tech Commun ... Republic of South Africa. Department of Agricultural Technical Services. Technical Communication [*A publication*]
Repub S Afr Geol Opname Bull ... Republiek van Suid-Afrika. Geologiese Opname. Bulletin [*A publication*]
Repub S Afr Geol Opname Handb ... Republiek van Suid-Afrika. Geologiese Opname. Handboek [*A publication*]
Repub S Afr Geol Surv Mem ... Republic of South Africa. Geological Survey. Memoir [*A publication*]
Repub Venezuela Bol Acad Cienc Fis Mat Natur ... Republica de Venezuela. Boletin. Academia de Ciencias Fisicas, Matematicas, y Naturales [*A publication*]
Repub Venezuela Bol Acad Ci Fis Mat Natur ... Republica de Venezuela. Boletin. Academia de Ciencias Fisicas, Matematicas, y Naturales [*A publication*]
REPUD...... Repudiate
Rep Univ Alaska Inst Mar Sci ... Report. University of Alaska. Institute of Marine Science [*A publication*]
Rep Univ Calif Berkeley Sanit Eng Res Lab ... Report. University of California, Berkeley. Sanitary Engineering Research Laboratory [*A publication*]
Rep Univ Calif Davis Calif Water Resour Cent ... Report. University of California, Davis. California Water Resources Center [*A publication*]
Rep Univ Electro-Comm ... Reports. University of Electro-Communications [*A publication*]
Rep Univ Electro-Commun ... Reports. University of Electro-Communications [*A publication*]
Rep USA Mar Biol Inst Kochi Univ ... Reports. USA Marine Biological Institute. Kochi University [*A publication*]
Rep USA Mar Biol Stn ... Reports. USA Marine Biological Station [*A publication*]
Rep US Dep Agric For Serv North Reg State Priv For ... Report. United States Department of Agriculture Forest Service. Northern Region. State and Private Forestry [*A publication*]
REPVE...... Representative (ROG)
Rep VT Wood Prod Conf ... Report. Vermont Wood Products Conference [*A publication*]
Rep Waite Agric Res Inst ... Report. Waite Agricultural Research Institute [*A publication*]
Rep Water Res Found Aust ... Report. Water Research Foundation of Australia [*A publication*] (APTA)
Rep Water Res Found Aust Ltd ... Report. Water Research Foundation of Australia Limited [*A publication*] (APTA)
Rep Water Res Lab NSW Univ ... Report. Water Research Laboratory. University of New South Wales [*A publication*] (APTA)
Rep Water Resour Res Inst Univ NC ... Report. Water Resources Research Institute. University of North Carolina [*A publication*]
Rep Water Resour Surv ... Report. Water Resources Survey. Tasmania [*A publication*] (APTA)
Rep Wat Res Fdn ... Report. Water Research Foundation of Australia [*A publication*] (APTA)
Rep Wat Res Fdn Aust ... Report. Water Research Foundation of Australia [*A publication*] (APTA)
Rep Wat Res Lab NSW Univ ... Report. Water Research Laboratory. University of New South Wales [*A publication*] (APTA)
Rep Wellcome Research Lab ... Report. Wellcome Research Laboratories [*A publication*]
Rep Wellcome Trop Research Lab ... Report. Wellcome Tropical Research Laboratories [*A publication*]
Rep Welsh Pl Breed Stn ... Report. Welsh Plant Breeding Station [*A publication*]
Rep Welsh Soils Discuss Grp ... Report. Welsh Soils Discussion Group [*A publication*]
Rep Wheat Qual Conf ... Report. Wheat Quality Conference [*A publication*]
Rep World Aff ... Report on World Affairs [*A publication*]
Rep World Congr Agr Res ... Report. World Congress on Agricultural Research [*A publication*]
Rep World Fertil Surv ... Reports on the World Fertility Survey [*A publication*]
Rep W Scot Agr Coll Econ Dept ... Report. West of Scotland Agricultural College. Economics Department [*A publication*]
Rep Wye Agric Coll ... Report. Wye Agricultural College [*A publication*]
Rep Wye Coll Dep Hop Res ... Report. Wye College. Department of Hop Research [*A publication*]
REPYB ...... Research Policy [*Netherlands*] [*A publication*]

Rep Yeungnam Univ Inst Ind Technol ... Report. Yeungnam University. Institute of Industrial Technology [*A publication*]
Rep Yeungnam Univ Inst Nat Prod ... Report. Yeungnam University. Institute of Natural Products [*A publication*]
Rep York Ass ... Clayton's English Reports, York Assizes [*A publication*] (DLA)
Rep Yr Dublin Univ Coll Agr Dept ... Report of the Year. Dublin University College. Agricultural Department [*A publication*]
REQ.......... Request (AAG)
REQ.......... Require (AAG)
REQ.......... Requisition
REQAFA... Request Advise as to Further Action [*Army*] (AABC)
REQANS... Request Answer By [*Date*] [*Military*]
REQAURQN ... Request Authority to Requisition [*Army*] (AFIT)
REQCAPS ... Requirements and Capabilities Automated Planning System (MCD)
REQD........ Required (AAG)
REQDI ...... Request Disposition Instructions [*Army*] (AABC)
REQFOLINFO ... Request Following Information Be Forwarded This Office [*Army*] (AABC)
REQIBO... Request Item Be Placed on Back Order [*Army*]
REQID ...... Request If Desired (FAAC)
REQINT.... Request Interim Reply By [*Date*] [*Military*] (AABC)
REQMAD ... Request Mailing Address (FAAC)
REQMNT ... Requirement (NVT)
REQMT ... Requirement
REQN....... Requisition (AAG)
REQNOM ... Request Nomination
REQPER... Request Permission [*Navy*] (NVT)
REQRCM ... Request Recommendation (FAAC)
REQRE...... Require (ROG)
REQREC... Request Recommendation (NVT)
REQS....... Requires
REQSI ...... Request Shipping Instructions [*Military*]
REQSSD ... Request Supply Status and Expected Delivery Date [*Army*] (AABC)
REQSTD... Requested (FAAC)
REQSUPSTAFOL ... Request Supply Status of Following [*Army*] (AABC)
REQT .... Request (ROG)
REQT .... Requirement (AAG)
REQTAT... [*It Is*] Requested That [*Military*] (AABC)
REQTRAC ... Request Tracer Be Initiated [*Military*]
REQUAL... Requalify
REQUCHRD ... Request Unit of Issue Be Changed to Read [*Army*] (AABC)
REQUEL... Revue d'Entomologie du Quebec [*A publication*]
REQUONS ... Requisitions
REQVER... Requirements Verification (IEEE)
RER .... RADAR Effects Reactor
RER .... Radiation Effects Reactor [*Nuclear energy*]
RER .... Railway Equipment Register
RER .... Real Estate Review [*A publication*]
RER .... Receiver/Exciter Ranging [*NASA*]
ReR .... Remington Rand Corp., Blue Bell, PA [*Library symbol*] [*Library of Congress*] (LCLS)
RER .... Representatives for Experiment Review [*Nuclear energy*] (NRCH)
RER .... Rerun (AAG)
RER .... Reseau Express Regional [*Paris subway*]
RER .... Residual Error Rate
RER .... Resource Evaluation Report (MCD)
RER .... Respiratory Exchange Rate
RER .... Retlaw Resources, Inc. [*Vancouver Stock Exchange symbol*]
RER .... Reusable-Expendable-Reusable
RER .... Review of Educational Research [*A publication*]
RER .... Revue des Etudes Rabelaisiennes [*A publication*]
RER .... Revue des Etudes Roumaines [*A publication*]
RER .... Rough [*Surfaced*] Endoplasmic Reticulum [*Cytology*]
RER .... Rubberized Equipment Repair
RERA........ Reclamation Era [*A publication*]
RERA........ RERA: Official Monthly Journal. Radio and Electrical Retailers' Association of New South Wales [*A publication*] (APTA)
RERAA...... Reclamation Era [*A publication*]
RERAD...... Reference Radio
RERAD...... Reradiation
RERC......... Radiological Emergency Response Coordination [*Nuclear energy*] (NRCH)
RERC......... Rare Earth Research Conference (EA)
RERC......... Real Estate Research Corporation
RER & D.... Rehabilitative Engineering Research and Development Service [*Veterans Administration*] (GRD)
REREPS.... Repair and Rehabilitation of Paved Surfaces (MCD)
REREQ...... Reference Requisition (NOAA)
REREX...... Remote Readout Experiment
RERF........ Radiation Effects Research Foundation [*Formerly, ABCC*]
RERI......... Radiation Effect Research Institute
RERIC....... Regional Energy Resources Information Center [*Asian Institute of Technology*] [*Great Britain*] [*Information service or system*] (IID)
RERIF .... Rainier Energy Resources [*NASDAQ symbol*] (NQ)
RERL......... Residual Equivalent Return Loss

Rer Nat Scr Graec Min ... Rerum Naturalium Scriptores Graeci Minores [*A publication*] (OCD)
RERO .... Radiological Emergency Response Operation [*Nuclear energy*] (NRCH)
RERo .... Revue des Etudes Roumaines [*A publication*]
RERO .... Royal Engineers Reserve of Officers [*British*]
RERP .... Radiological Emergency Response Planning (NRCH)
RERTD ...... Regelungstechnik. RT [*A publication*]
RERTR ...... Reduced Enrichment in Research and Test Reactions [*Department of Energy*]
RERTR ...... Research Enrichment in Research and Test Reactors Program [*Department of Energy*]
RES .... Eastman School of Music, Rochester, NY [*OCLC symbol*] (OCLC)
RES .... Hawaiian Air Tour Service [*Honolulu, HI*] [*FAA designator*] (FAAC)
RES .... Office of Nuclear Regulatory Research [*Nuclear Regulatory Commission*]
RES .... Office of Research [*Washington, DC*] [*Bureau of Intelligence and Research*] [*Department of State*] (GRD)
RES .... On Reserved List [*Army*] [*British*] (ROG)
RES .... RADAR Environment Simulation (NATG)
RES .... RADAR Evaluation Squadron [*Military*]
RES .... Radiation Exposure State (NATG)
RES .... Radio-Echo Sounding [*Geophysics*]
RES .... Recent Economic Developments [*Jerusalem*] [*A publication*]
RES .... Record Element Specification [*Data processing*]
RES .... Record Evaluation System
RES .... Reentry System (ADA)
RES .... Rehabilitation Evolution System [*Medicine*]
ReS .... Reinare en Espana [*A publication*]
RES .... Relief Electronics Specialist
ReS .... Religion et Societes [*A publication*]
RES .... Remote Entry Services (MCD)
RES .... Renaissance Energy Ltd. [*Toronto Stock Exchange symbol*]
RES .... Repertoire d'Epigraphie Semitique [*Paris*] [*A publication*]
RES .... Reprint Expediting Service
RES .... Research (AAG)
Res .... Researcher [*Samar*] [*A publication*]
RES .... Reserve (EY)
RES .... Reservoir (AAG)
RES .... Reset
RES .... Residence
RES .... Resident
RES .... Residual (KSC)
RES .... Residue
RES .... Resigned
RES .... Resilient [*Technical drawings*]
RES .... Resistance [*or Resistor*] (AAG)
RES .... Resistencia [*Argentina*] [*Airport symbol*] (OAG)
RES .... Resistor
Res .... Resolu [*Resolved, Decided*] [*French*] (ILCA)
RES .... Resolute [*Northwest Territories*] [*Seismograph station code, US Geological Survey*] (SEIS)
RES .... Resolute Bay [*Northwest Territories*] [*Geomagnetic observatory code*]
RES .... Resolution
Res .... Resolved [*Legal term*] (DLA)
RES .... Resonator [*Automotive engineering*]
RESo .... Resources
RES .... Restaurant (DSUE)
RES .... Restore
Res .... Resurrection (BJA)
RES .... Reticuloendothelial Society (EA)
RES .... Reticuloendothelial System [*Medicine*]
RES .... Review of Economics and Statistics [*A publication*]
RES .... Review of English Studies [*A publication*]
RES .... Revue de l'Enseignement Superieur [*A publication*]
RES .... Revue des Etudes Semitiques [*A publication*]
RES .... Revue des Etudes Slaves [*A publication*]
RES .... Romance of Empire Series [*A publication*]
RES .... Royal Economic Society [*British*]
RES .... Royal Empire Society [*British*]
RES .... Royal Entomological Society [*British*]
RES .... RPC Energy Services, Inc. [*NYSE symbol*] (SPSG)
ResA .... R & E Research Associates, Palo Alto, CA [*Library symbol*] [*Library of Congress*] (LCLS)
RESA .... Regional Education Service Agency
RESA .... Ring-Infected Erythrocyte Surface Antigen [*Immunochemistry*]
RESA .... Scientific Research Society of America (EA)
Res/Accel ... Research/Accelerators [*A publication*]
Res Act Fac Sci Engrg Tokyo Denki Univ ... Research Activities. Faculty of Science and Engineering of Tokyo Denki University [*A publication*]
Res Act For Comm (Victoria Aust) ... Research Activity. Forests Commission (Victoria, Australia) [*A publication*]
RESAD ...... Revista Saude [*A publication*]
Res Adv Alcohol Drug Probl ... Research Advances in Alcohol and Drug Problems [*A publication*]
RESAF ...... Reserve of the Air Force
Res African Lit ... Research in African Literatures [*A publication*]

Res Afric Lit ... Research in African Literatures [*A publication*]
Res Afr Lit ... Research in African Literatures [*A publication*]
Res Aging ... Research on Aging [*A publication*]
RESALIFT ... Reserve Airlift (NVT)
Res Annu Nihon Nosan Kogyo ... Research Annual. Nihon Nosan Kogyo [*A publication*]
Res Appl Ind ... Research Applied in Industry [*A publication*]
Res Appl Natl Needs Rep NSF/RA (US) ... Research Applied to National Needs. Report. NSF/RA [*National Science Foundation/ Research Applied*] (United States) [*A publication*]
Res Appl Technol Symp Mined-Land Reclam Pap ... Research and Applied Technology Symposium on Mined-Land Reclamation. Papers [*A publication*]
RESAR ...... Reference Safety Analysis Report [*Nuclear energy*] (NRCH)
Res Assoc Br Paint Colour Varn Manuf Bull ... Research Association of British Paint, Colour, and Varnish Manufacturers. Bulletin [*A publication*]
Res Bib ...... Research Service Bibliographies [*A publication*] (APTA)
Res Bk .... Reserve Bank Bulletin [*New Zealand*] [*A publication*]
Res Bk NZ ... Reserve Bank of New Zealand. Bulletin [*A publication*]
Res Brch Rep Can Dep Agric ... Research Branch Report. Canada Department of Agriculture [*A publication*]
Res Briefs ... Research Briefs [*A publication*]
Res Briefs Sch For Resour PA St Univ ... Research Briefs. School of Forest Resources. Pennsylvania State University [*A publication*]
Res Bull Agr Home Econ Exp Sta Iowa State Coll ... Research Bulletin. Agricultural and Home Economics Experiment Station. Iowa State College [*A publication*]
Res Bull Agric Exp Stn Univ Idaho ... Research Bulletin. Agricultural Experiment Station. University of Idaho [*A publication*]
Res Bull Agric Exp Stn Univ Nebr ... Research Bulletin. Agricultural Experiment Station. University of Nebraska [*A publication*]
Res Bull Agric Exp Stn Univ Wis ... Research Bulletin. Agricultural Experiment Station. College of Agriculture. University of Wisconsin [*A publication*]
Res Bull Aichi-Ken Agric Res Cent Ser B Hortic ... Research Bulletin. Aichi-Ken Agricultural Research Center. Series B. Horticulture [*Japan*] [*A publication*]
Res Bull Birla Archaeol Cult Res Inst ... Research Bulletin. Birla Archaeological and Cultural Research Institute [*A publication*]
Res Bull CIMMYT ... Research Bulletin. Centro Internacional de Mejoramiento de Maiz y Trigo [*A publication*]
Res Bull Coll Exp For Hokkaido Univ ... Research Bulletins. College Experiment Forests. Hokkaido University [*A publication*]
Res Bull Coll Expt Forest Hokkaido Univ ... Research Bulletins. College Experiment Forests. Hokkaido University [*A publication*]
Res Bull Coll Gen Educ Nagoya Univ Nat Sci Psychol ... Research Bulletin. College of General Education. Nagoya University. Natural Sciences and Psychology [*A publication*]
Res Bull East Panjab Univ ... Research Bulletin. East Panjab University [*A publication*]
Res Bull Electr Power Dev Co Ltd ... Research Bulletin. Electric Power Development Company Limited [*Japan*] [*A publication*]
Res Bull Exp For Hokkaido Univ ... Research Bulletin. College Experiment Forests. Hokkaido University [*A publication*]
Res Bull Fac Agr Gifu Univ ... Research Bulletin. Faculty of Agriculture. Gifu University [*A publication*]
Res Bull Fac Agric Ain Shams Univ ... Research Bulletin. Faculty of Agriculture. Ain Shams University [*A publication*]
Res Bull Fac Agric Gifu-Ken Prefect Univ ... Research Bulletin. Faculty of Agriculture. Gifu-Ken Prefectural University [*A publication*]
Res Bull Fac Agric Gifu Univ ... Research Bulletin. Faculty of Agriculture. Gifu University [*A publication*]
Res Bull Fac Ed Oita Univ ... Research Bulletin. Faculty of Education. Oita University [*A publication*]
Res Bull Fac Educ Oita Univ Nat Sci ... Research Bulletin. Faculty of Education. Oita University. Natural Science [*A publication*]
Res Bull Fac Lib Arts Oita Univ ... Research Bulletin. Faculty of Liberal Arts. Oita University [*A publication*]
Res Bull For Res Lab Oreg State Univ ... Research Bulletin. Forest Research Laboratory. Oregon State University [*A publication*]
Res Bull Gifu Imp Coll Agr ... Research Bulletin. Gifu Imperial College of Agriculture [*A publication*]
Res Bull Hiroshima Inst Technol ... Research Bulletin. Hiroshima Institute of Technology [*A publication*]
Res Bull Hokkaido Nat Agr Exp Sta ... Research Bulletin. Hokkaido National Agricultural Experiment Station [*A publication*]
Res Bull Hokkaido Natl Agric Exp Stn ... Research Bulletin. Hokkaido National Agricultural Experiment Station [*A publication*]
Res Bull Hokkaido Natn Agric Exp Stn ... Research Bulletin. Hokkaido National Agricultural Experiment Station [*A publication*]
Res Bull Iida Women's Jr Coll ... Research Bulletin. Iida Women's Junior College [*A publication*]
Res Bull Indiana Agr Exp Sta ... Research Bulletin. Indiana Agricultural Experiment Station [*A publication*]

Res Bull Int Cent Impr Maize Wheat ... Research Bulletin. International Center for the Improvement of Maize and Wheat [*A publication*]

Res Bull Iowa Agric Exp Stn ... Research Bulletin. Iowa Agricultural Experiment Station [*A publication*]

Res Bull Iowa Agric Home Econ Exp Stn ... Research Bulletin. Iowa Agricultural and Home Economics Experiment Station [*A publication*]

Res Bull Iowa St Univ Agric Home Econ Exp Stn ... Research Bulletin. Iowa State University Agricultural and Home Economics Experiment Station [*A publication*]

Res Bull Kangweon Natl Univ ... Research Bulletin. Kangweon National University [*Republic of Korea*] [*A publication*]

Res Bull Marathwada Agric Univ ... Research Bulletin. Marathwada Agricultural University [*A publication*]

Res Bull Mass Agric Exp Stn ... Research Bulletin. Massachusetts Agricultural Experiment Station [*A publication*]

Res Bull Meguro Parasitol Mus ... Research Bulletin. Meguro Parasitological Museum [*A publication*]

Res Bull Meisei Univ ... Research Bulletin. Meisei University [*A publication*]

Res Bull Meisei Univ Phys Sci Eng ... Research Bulletin. Meisei University. Physical Sciences and Engineering [*A publication*]

Res Bull Missouri Agric Exp Stn ... Research Bulletin. Missouri Agricultural Experiment Station [*A publication*]

Res Bull MO Agric Exp Sta ... Research Bulletin. Missouri Agricultural Experiment Station [*A publication*]

Res Bull Nat Hist Parks Site Branch ... Research Bulletin. National Historic Parks and Site Branch [*A publication*]

Res Bull Neb Agric Exp Stn ... Research Bulletin. Nebraska Agricultural Experiment Station [*A publication*]

Res Bull Obihiro Univ Ser I ... Research Bulletin. Obihiro University. Series I [*A publication*]

Res Bull Obihiro Zootech Univ ... Research Bulletin. Obihiro Zootechnical University. Series I [*A publication*]

Res Bull Obihiro Zootech Univ Ser I ... Research Bulletin. Obihiro Zootechnical University. Series I [*A publication*]

Res Bull Ohio Agric Res Dev Center ... Research Bulletin. Ohio Agricultural Research and Development Center [*A publication*]

Res Bull Ohio Agric Res Developm Cent ... Research Bulletin. Ohio Agricultural Research and Development Center [*A publication*]

Res Bull Ore For Res Lab ... Research Bulletin. Oregon State University. Forest Research Laboratory [*A publication*]

Res Bull Panjab Univ ... Research Bulletin. Panjab University [*A publication*]

Res Bull Panjab Univ NS ... Research Bulletin. Panjab University. New Series [*A publication*]

Res Bull Panjab Univ Sci ... Research Bulletin. Panjab University. Science [*A publication*]

Res Bull PCSIR Lab ... Research Bulletin. PCSIR [*Pakistan Council of Scientific and Industrial Research*] Laboratories [*A publication*]

Res Bull Plant Prot Serv (Jap) ... Research Bulletin. Plant Protection Service (Japan) [*A publication*]

Res Bull Plant Prot Serv (Jpn) ... Research Bulletin. Plant Protection Service (Japan) [*A publication*]

Res Bull Printing Bur (Tokyo) ... Research Bulletin. Printing Bureau. Ministry of Finance (Tokyo) [*A publication*]

Res Bull Purdue Univ Agr Exp Sta ... Research Bulletin. Purdue University. Agricultural Experiment Station [*A publication*]

Res Bull Reg Eng Coll (Warangal) ... Research Bulletin. Regional Engineering College (Warangal) [*A publication*]

Res Bull Saitama Agr Exp Sta ... Research Bulletin. Saitama Agricultural Experiment Station [*A publication*]

Res Bull Univ Calcutta ... Research Bulletin. University of Calcutta [*A publication*]

Res Bull Univ Farm Hokkaido Univ ... Research Bulletin. University Farm. Hokkaido University [*A publication*]

Res Bull Univ GA Exp Stn ... Research Bulletin. University of Georgia. Experiment Stations [*A publication*]

Res Bull Univ MO Coll Agr Exp Sta ... Research Bulletin. University of Missouri. College of Agriculture. Experiment Station [*A publication*]

Res Bull Univ Nebr Coll Agr Home Econ Agr Exp Sta ... Research Bulletin. University of Nebraska. College of Agriculture and Home Economics. Agricultural Experiment Station [*A publication*]

Res Bull West Scotl Agric Coll ... Research Bulletin. West of Scotland Agricultural College [*A publication*]

Res Bull Wis Agr Exp Sta ... Research Bulletin. Wisconsin Agricultural Experiment Station [*A publication*]

Res Bull W Scotl Coll Agric ... Research Bulletin. West of Scotland College of Agriculture [*A publication*]

RESC .... Regional Educational Service Center

RESC .... Rescind   (AAG)

RESC .... Rescue   (AFM)

RESC .... Resource

RESC .... Roanoke Electric Steel Corporation [*NASDAQ symbol*]   (NQ)

RESCAN ... Reflecting Satellite Communication Antenna

RESCAP .... Rescue Combat Air Patrol [*Army*]

Res Cas ...... Reserved Cases [*Ireland*] [*A publication*]   (DLA)

Res Circ Ohio Agric Exp Stn ... Research Circular. Ohio Agricultural Experiment Station [*A publication*]

Res Circ Ohio Agr Res Develop Cent ... Research Circular. Ohio Agricultural Research and Development Center [*A publication*]

Res Clin Lab ... Research in Clinic and Laboratory [*A publication*]

Res Clin Stud Headache ... Research and Clinical Studies in Headache [*A publication*]

Res Comm C P ... Research Communications in Chemical Pathology and Pharmacology [*A publication*]

Res Commun Chem Pathol Pharmacol ... Research Communications in Chemical Pathology and Pharmacology [*A publication*]

Res Commun Inst Ferment (Osaka) ... Research Communications. Institute for Fermentation (Osaka) [*A publication*]

Res Commun Psychol Psychiatry Behav ... Research Communications in Psychology, Psychiatry, and Behavior [*A publication*]

Res Communs Chem Path Pharmac ... Research Communications in Chemical Pathology and Pharmacology [*A publication*]

Res Commun Subst Abuse ... Research Communications in Substances of Abuse [*A publication*]

Res Constructs Peaceful Uses Nucl Energy ... Research Constructs on Peaceful Uses of Nuclear Energy [*Japan*] [*A publication*]

Res Corresp ... Research Correspondence [*A publication*]

Res Counc Alberta Bull ... Research Council of Alberta. Bulletin [*A publication*]

Res Counc Alberta (Can) Inform Ser ... Research Council of Alberta (Canada). Information Series [*A publication*]

Res Counc Alberta Econ Geol Rep ... Research Council of Alberta. Economic Geology Report [*A publication*]

Res Counc Alberta Geol Div Bull ... Research Council of Alberta. Geological Division. Bulletin [*A publication*]

Res Counc Alberta Geol Div Mem ... Research Council of Alberta. Geological Division. Memoir [*A publication*]

Res Counc Alberta Mimeogr Circ ... Research Council of Alberta. Mimeographed Circular [*A publication*]

Res Counc Alberta Rep ... Research Council of Alberta. Report [*A publication*]

Res Counc Isr Annu Rep ... Research Council of Israel. Annual Report [*A publication*]

RESCRU ... Reserve Cruise [*Navy*]   (NVT)

RESCU ...... Radio Emergency Search Communications Unit

RESCU ...... Rocket-Ejection Seat Catapult Upward [*Aviation*]

RESCUE ... Recovery Employing Storage Chute Used in Emergencies [*Inflatable aircraft wing*]

RESCUE ... Referring Emergency Service for Consumers' Ultimate Enjoyment [*Service plan of Recreational Vehicle Dealers of America*]   (EA)

RESCUE ... Remote Emergency Salvage and Clean Up Equipment

Rescue Archaeol Hampshire ... Rescue Archaeology in Hampshire [*A publication*]

R Escuela Def Nac ... Revista. Escuela de Defensa Nacional [*A publication*]

RESD .... Reentry Environmental Systems Division [*General Electric Co.*]   (MCD)

RESD .... Resigned

RESD .... Resolved   (ROG)

RESDAT ... Restricted Data [*Atomic Energy Act of 1954*]

Res Dep Rep Post Off Res Cent (UK) ... Research Department Report. Post Office Research Centre (United Kingdom) [*A publication*]

Res Des ...... Research and Design [*A publication*]

Res Dev ...... Research/Development [*A publication*]

Res & Dev .. Research and Development [*A publication*]

Res Dev Bull Portland Cem Assoc ... Research and Development Bulletin. Portland Cement Association [*A publication*]

Res/Develop ... Research/Development [*A publication*]

Res Developm Pap For Comm (Lond) ... Research and Development Paper. Forestry Commission (London) [*A publication*]

Res Dev Lab Portland Cem Assoc Res Dep Bull ... Research and Development Laboratories. Portland Cement Association. Research Department Bulletin [*A publication*]

Res Disclosure ... Research Disclosure [*A publication*]

RESDIST .. Reserve District

RESE .... Reseaux [*A publication*]

Research Bul ... Liberal Party of Australia. New South Wales Division. Research Bulletin [*A publication*]   (APTA)

Research Council Alberta Bull ... Research Council of Alberta. Bulletin [*A publication*]

Research Council Alberta Rept ... Research Council of Alberta. Report [*A publication*]

Research in Ed ... Research in Education [*A publication*]

Researches Popul Ecol Kyoto Univ ... Researches on Population Ecology. Kyoto University [*A publication*]

Research F ... Research Film [*A publication*]

Research L & Econ ... Research in Law and Economics [*A publication*]   (DLA)

Research Mgt ... Research Management [*A publication*]

RESEB ...... Resources in Education [*A publication*]

Res Econ Hist ... Research in Economic History [*A publication*]

Res Educ .... Research in Education [*England*] [*A publication*]

ResEduc .... Resources in Education [*A publication*]

RESEE ...... Revue des Etudes Sud-Est Europeennes [*A publication*]

Res Electrotech Lab ... Researches. Electrotechnical Laboratory [*Japan*] [*A publication*]

Res Electrotech Lab (Tokyo) ... Researches. Electrotechnical Laboratory (Tokyo) [*A publication*]

RESem....... Revue des Etudes Semitiques [*A publication*]

Res Eng...... Research Engineer [*A publication*]

Res Eng Jeonbug Natl Univ ... Research of Engineering. Jeonbug National University [*Republic of Korea*] [*A publication*]

Res Eng Res Inst Ind Technol Jeonbug Natl Univ ... Research of Engineering. Research Institute of Industrial Technology. Jeonbug National University [*Republic of Korea*] [*A publication*]

Res Environ Disruption Interdiscip Coop ... Research on Environmental Disruption toward Interdisciplinary Cooperation [*Japan*] [*A publication*]

RESEP....... Reentry System Environmental Protection

Res & Eq J ... Reserved and Equity Judgements [*New South Wales*] [*A publication*] (APTA)

Res & Eq Jud ... Reserved and Equity Judgements [*New South Wales*] [*A publication*]

Res & Eq Judg ... A'Beckett's Reserved Judgements [*New South Wales*] [*A publication*]

Res & Eq Judgm ... Reserved and Equity Judgements [*New South Wales*] [*A publication*]

RESER ...... Reentry Systems Evaluation RADAR [*Aerospace*]

reserva...... Reservation

Reserv Cas ... Reserved Cases [*1860-64*] [*A publication*] (DLA)

Reserve Bank Australia Statis Bul ... Reserve Bank of Australia. Statistical Bulletin [*A publication*]

Reserve Bank India B ... Reserve Bank of India. Bulletin [*A publication*]

Reserve Bank NZ Bul ... Reserve Bank of New Zealand. Bulletin [*A publication*]

RESERVON ... Reservation (ROG)

Res Esst Oils Aust Flora ... Researches on Essential Oils of the Australian Flora [*A publication*]

Res Establ Risoe Rep Risoe-M (Den) ... Research Establishment Risoe. Report. Risoe-M (Denmark) [*A publication*]

Res Establ Risoe Risoe Rep (Den) ... Research Establishment Risoe. Risoe Report (Denmark) [*A publication*]

RESET ...... Regression Specification Error Test [*Statistics*]

Res Exp Econ ... Research in Experimental Economics [*A publication*]

Res Exp Med ... Research in Experimental Medicine [*A publication*]

Res Exp Med (Berlin) ... Research in Experimental Medicine (Berlin) [*A publication*]

Res Exp Rec Minist Agric (Nth Ire) ... Research and Experimental Record. Ministry of Agriculture (Northern Ireland) [*A publication*]

RESF .... Research and Engineering Support Facility (MCD)

Res & Farm ... Research and Farming [*North Carolina Agricultural Experiment Station*] [*A publication*]

Res Farmers ... Research for Farmers [*A publication*]

Res Farming ... Research and Farming [*North Carolina Agricultural Experiment Station*] [*A publication*]

Res Farming (NC Agric Exp Stn) ... Research and Farming (North Carolina Agricultural Experiment Station) [*A publication*]

Res Farming NC Agric Res Serv ... Research and Farming. North Carolina Agricultural Research Service [*A publication*]

RESFDJ .... Rivista Europea per le Scienze Mediche e Farmacologiche [*A publication*]

Res Film..... Research Film [*A publication*]

Res Fish Annu Rep Coll Fish Univ Wash ... Research in Fisheries. Annual Report. College of Fisheries. University of Washington [*A publication*]

Res Fish Annu Rep Sch Fish Univ Wash ... Research in Fisheries. Annual Report. School of Fisheries. University of Washington [*A publication*]

Res Fish (Seattle) ... Research in Fisheries (Seattle) [*A publication*]

RESFLD..... Residual Field (AAG)

RESFLY .... Respectfully (ROG)

RESFOR .... AUTODIN CRT for Secure Reserve Force (MCD)

Res Futures ... Research Futures [*A publication*]

RESFV....... Renaissance Editions. San Fernando Valley State College [*A publication*]

RESG......... Research Engineering Standing Group [*DoD*]

Res Gamma Eta Gamma ... Rescript of Gamma Eta Gamma [*A publication*] (DLA)

RESGD...... Resigned

RESGND... Resigned

RESHAPE ... Resource Self-Help/Affordability Planning Effort [*Program*] [*Federal government*] (RDA)

Res Health Econ ... Research in Health Economics [*A publication*]

Res High Educ Abstr ... Research into Higher Education. Abstracts [*A publication*]

Res Higher Educ ... Research in Higher Education [*A publication*]

RESHUS... Reseau Documentaire en Sciences Humaines de la Sante [*Network for Documentation in the Human Sciences of Health*] [*Institut de l'Information Scientifique et Technique*] [*Information service or system*] (IID)

RES I .... Research EMP [*Electromagnetic Pulse*] Simulator I [*Air Force*]

RESIC .... Redstone Scientific Information Center [*Army*]

RES/IC...... Reserve - In Commission [*Vessel status*]

resid .... Residency

RESID .... Residual (AAG)

Resid Group Care & Treat ... Residential Group Care and Treatment [*A publication*]

Resid Staff Physician ... Resident and Staff Physician [*A publication*]

Residue Rev ... Residue Reviews [*A publication*]

RESIG .... Resignation (AFM)

RESIL........ Resilient

Res Immunochem Immunobiol ... Research in Immunochemistry and Immunobiology [*A publication*]

Res Immunol ... Research in Immunology [*A publication*]

RESIN .... Resina [*Resin*] [*Pharmacy*] (ROG)

Res Ind....... Research and Industry [*A publication*]

Res Indicat Petrol ... Resumos Indicativos do Petroleo [*A publication*]

Res Ind (New Delhi) ... Research and Industry (New Delhi) [*A publication*]

Res Indus ... Research and Industry [*A publication*]

Resin Rev ... Resin Review [*A publication*]

Res Inst Appl Mech Kyushu Univ Report ... Research Institute for Applied Mechanics. Kyushu University. Reports [*A publication*]

Res Inst Fund Information Sci Res Rep ... Research Institute of Fundamental Information Science. Research Report [*A publication*]

Res Inst Fund Inform Sci Res Rep ... Kyushu University. Research Institute of Fundamental Information Science. Research Report [*A publication*]

Res Inst Nedri As (Hveragerdi Icel) Rep ... Research Institute Nedri As (Hveragerdi, Iceland). Report [*A publication*]

Res Int........ Residential Interiors [*A publication*]

Res Intell News ... Research and Intelligence News [*A publication*]

Res & Invt .. Research and Invention [*A publication*]

Res Ipsa ..... Res Ipsa Loquitur [*The Thing Speaks for Itself*] [*Latin*] (DLA)

RES/IS........ Reserve - In Service [*Vessel status*]

RESIS........ Resistance

RESIST ..... Replace Essential Supplies in Sufficient Time [*Navy*] (NVT)

RESIST ..... Resistant

RESIST ..... Reusable Surface Insulation Stresses [*NASA computer program*]

Resistencia (Ser Econ e Gestao) ... Resistencia (Serie de Economia e Gestao) [*A publication*]

RESJA....... RES. Journal of the Reticuloendothelial Society [*A publication*]

Res J Dir Higher Educ (Indones) ... Research Journal. Directorate of Higher Education (Indonesia) [*A publication*]

Res J Fac Sci Kashmir Univ ... Research Journal. Faculty of Science. Kashmir University [*A publication*]

Res J Kanpur Agr Coll ... Research Journal. Kanpur Agricultural College [*A publication*]

Res J Mahatma Phule Agric Univ ... Research Journal. Mahatma Phule Agricultural University [*A publication*]

Res J Philo Soc Sci ... Research Journal of Philosophy and Social Sciences [*Meerut Cantt, India*] [*A publication*]

Res J Phys Educ ... Research Journal of Physical Education [*A publication*]

RES J Reticuloendothel Soc ... RES. Journal of the Reticuloendothelial Society [*A publication*]

Res Jud ...... Res Judicatae [*A publication*] (APTA)

Res Judic ... Res Judicatae [*A publication*] (DLA)

Res J Univ Wyo Agric Exp Stn ... Research Journal. University of Wyoming. Agricultural Experiment Station [*A publication*]

RESL .... Radiological and Environmental Sciences Laboratory [*Nuclear energy*] (NRCH)

RESL .... Revue des Etudes Slaves [*A publication*]

RESLAB.... Research Laboratory

Res Lab Commun Sci Univ Electro-Commun Annu Rep ... Research Laboratory of Communication Science. University of Electro-Communications. Annual Report [*A publication*]

Res Lab Precis Mach Electron ... Research Laboratory Precision Machinery and Electronics [*A publication*]

Res Lab Rec ... Research Laboratory Record [*A publication*]

RESlaves ... Revue des Etudes Slaves [*A publication*]

Res L Deviance and Soc Control ... Research in Law, Deviance, and Social Control [*A publication*]

Res Leafl For Res Inst NZ For Serv ... Research Leaflet. Forest Research Institute. New Zealand Forest Service [*A publication*]

Res Leafl Sav For Res Sta ... Research Leaflet. Savanna Forestry Research Station [*A publication*]

Res L & Econ ... Research in Law and Economics [*A publication*]

Res Libnship ... Research in Librarianship [*A publication*]

Res Librarianship ... Research in Librarianship [*A publication*]

Res Life Sci ... Research in Life Sciences [*A publication*]

Res Life Sci Maine Life Sci Agric Exp Stn ... Research in the Life Sciences. Maine Life Sciences and Agriculture Experiment Station [*A publication*]

Res Lit........ Respublica Literaria [*A publication*]

Res L and Soc ... Research in Law and Sociology [*A publication*]

RESLV ...... Resolve (KSC)

RESM........ Restaurant Management Services, Inc. [*Macon, GA*] [*NASDAQ symbol*] (NQ)

RESMA..... Railway Electric Supply Manufacturers Association [*Later, RSA*]

RESMA..... Research Management [*A publication*]

Res Manag ... Research Management [*A publication*]

Res Management ... Research Management [*A publication*]

Res McGill ... Research McGill [*A publication*]

Res Mech... Res Mechanica [*A publication*]

Res Mech Lett ... Res Mechanica Letters [*A publication*]

Res Memo Int Inst Appl Syst Anal ... Research Memorandum. International Institute for Applied Systems Analysis [*A publication*]

Res Meth Neurochem ... Research Methods in Neurochemistry [*A publication*]
Res Methods Neurochem ... Research Methods in Neurochemistry [*A publication*]
Res Mgt ..... Research Management [*A publication*]
Res Microbiol ... Research in Microbiology [*A publication*]
Res Mol Biol ... Research in Molecular Biology [*A publication*]
Res Monogr Cell Tissue Physiol ... Research Monographs in Cell and Tissue Physiology [*A publication*]
Res Monogr Immunol ... Research Monographs in Immunology [*A publication*]
Res Monogr Ser Natl Inst Drug Abuse (US) ... Research Monograph Series. National Institute on Drug Abuse (United States) [*A publication*]
RESN......... Resonant
RESNA...... RESNA [*Rehabilitation Engineering Society of North America*]: Association for the Advancement of Rehabilitation Technology [*Association retains acronym from former name*]   (EA)
Res Natl Mus (Bloemfontein) ... Researches. National Museum (Bloemfontein) [*A publication*]
RESND...... Resources and Energy [*A publication*]
Res News Off Res Adm Univ Mich (Ann Arbor) ... Research News. Office of Research Administration. University of Michigan (Ann Arbor) [*A publication*]
Res Norw Agric ... Research in Norwegian Agriculture [*A publication*]
Res Note BC For Serv ... Research Notes. British Columbia Forest Service [*A publication*]
Res Note Bur For (Philippines) ... Research Note. Bureau of Forestry (Philippines) [*A publication*]
Res Note Colo Coll For Nat Resour ... Research Note. Colorado State University. College of Forestry and Natural Resources [*A publication*]
Res Note Div For Res (Zambia) ... Research Note. Division of Forest Research (Zambia) [*A publication*]
Res Note Fac For Univ BC ... Research Note. Faculty of Forestry. University of British Columbia [*A publication*]
Res Note For Comm NSW ... Research Note. Forestry Commission of New South Wales [*A publication*]
Res Note For Mgmt Res Ore For Res Lab ... Research Note. Forest Management Research. Oregon State University. Forest Research Laboratory [*A publication*]
Res Note FPL For Prod Lab ... Research Note FPL. Forest Products Laboratory [*United States*] [*A publication*]
Res Note N Cent Forest Exp Stn US Dep Agric ... Research Note. North Central Forest Experiment Station. US Department of Agriculture [*A publication*]
Res Note Oreg State Univ Sch For For Res Lab ... Research Notes. Oregon State University. School of Forestry. Forest Research Laboratory [*A publication*]
Res Note Pacif SW For Exp Stn ... Research Note. Pacific Southwest Forest and Range Experiment Station. US Department of Agriculture [*A publication*]
Res Note Prov BC Minist For ... Research Note. Province of British Columbia. Ministry of Forests [*A publication*]
Res Note Qd For Serv ... Research Notes. Queensland Forest Service [*A publication*]
Res Note Res Prod Counc (NB) ... Research Note. Research and Productivity Council (New Brunswick) [*A publication*]
Res Notes in Math ... Research Notes in Mathematics [*A publication*]
Res Notes Memoranda Appl Geom Post-RAAG ... Research Notes and Memoranda of Applied Geometry in Post-RAAG [*Research Association of Applied Geometry*] [*A publication*]
Res Notes NSW For Comm ... New South Wales. Forestry Commission. Research Notes [*A publication*]   (APTA)
Res Notes Qd Dep For ... Research Notes. Queensland Department of Forestry [*A publication*]   (APTA)
Res Note Tex For Serv ... Research Note. Texas Forest Service [*A publication*]
Res Note UBC For Club ... Research Notes. University of British Columbia. Forest Club [*A publication*]
Res Note Univ Tex Austin Bur Econ Geol ... Research Note. University of Texas at Austin. Bureau of Economic Geology [*A publication*]
Res Not Ford For Cent ... Research Note. Ford Forestry Center [*A publication*]
RESNS ...... Review of English Studies. New Series [*A publication*]
Res Nurs Health ... Research in Nursing and Health [*A publication*]
Res Nurs Hlth ... Research in Nursing and Health [*A publication*]
RESO......... Resoluta [*Music*]   (ROG)
RESO......... Resources Bulletin. Man and Resources Conference Program [*A publication*]
RESOC...... Research Sonobuoy Configuration   (NG)
RES/OC...... Reserve - Out of Commission [*Vessel status*]
Resoconti Assoc Min Sarda ... Resoconti. Associazione Mineraria Sarda [*A publication*]
RESOJET ... Resonant Pulse Jet
RESOLN... Resolution   (MSA)

RESORS ... Remote Sensing On-Line Retrieval System [*Canada Centre for Remote Sensing*] [*Department of Energy, Mines, and Resources*] [*Database*] [*Information service or system*]   (IID)
RES/OS..... Reserve - Out of Service [*Vessel status*]
Resour Am L ... Resources for American Literary Study [*A publication*]
Resour Biomed Res Educ ... Resources for Biomedical Research and Education [*A publication*]
Resour Biosphere (USSR) ... Resources of the Biosphere (USSR) [*A publication*]
Resour Book Publ ... Resources for Book Publishers [*United States*] [*A publication*]
Resources Conserv ... Resources and Conservation [*Netherlands*] [*A publication*]
Resources Pol ... Resources Policy [*A publication*]
Resour Conserv ... Resources and Conservation [*A publication*]
Resour Conserv Recycl ... Resources, Conservation, and Recycling [*A publication*]
Resour and Energy ... Resources and Energy [*A publication*]
Resour Energy ... Resources and Energy [*Netherlands*] [*A publication*]
Resour Ind ... Resources Industry [*A publication*]
Resour Manage Optim ... Resource Management and Optimization [*United States*] [*A publication*]
Resour Manage and Optimiz ... Resource Management and Optimization [*A publication*]
Resour Manage Optimization ... Resource Management and Optimization [*A publication*]
Resour Policy ... Resources Policy [*A publication*]
Resour Recovery Conserv ... Resource Recovery and Conservation [*Netherlands*] [*A publication*]
Resour Recovery Energy Rev ... Resource Recovery and Energy Review [*A publication*]
Resour Rep Coop Ext Univ Wis ... Resource Report. Cooperative Extension. University of Wisconsin [*A publication*]
Resour Sharing and Libr Networks ... Resource Sharing and Library Networks [*A publication*]
Res Outlook ... Research Outlook [*A publication*]
Resp .... De Respiratione [*of Aristotle*] [*Classical studies*]   (OCD)
RESP .... Registered Education Savings Plan [*Canada*]
RESP .... Regulated Electrical Supply Package
ResP.......... Research and Progress [*A publication*]
ResP.......... Research Publications, Inc., New Haven, CT [*Library symbol*] [*Library of Congress*]   (LCLS)
RESP .... Respectively
RESP .... Respiration   (KSC)
RESP .... Respirator
RESP .... Respironics, Inc. [*NASDAQ symbol*]   (NQ)
RESP .... Respondent
RESP .... Response   (AAG)
RESP .... Responsible   (AFM)
Resp .... Republica [*of Plato*] [*Classical studies*]   (OCD)
RESPA ...... Real Estate Settlement Procedures Act of 1974
Res Pam (Div For Res Zambia) ... Research Pamphlet (Division of Forest Research, Zambia) [*A publication*]
Res Pam For Res Inst (Kepong) ... Research Pamphlet. Forest Research Institute (Kepong) [*A publication*]
Res Pamphl For Res Inst (Malaya) ... Research Pamphlet. Forest Research Institute (Malaya) [*A publication*]
Res Pap Dep For (Qd) ... Research Paper. Department of Forestry (Queensland) [*A publication*]   (APTA)
Res Pap Dep For (Queensl) ... Research Paper. Department of Forestry (Queensland) [*A publication*]   (APTA)
Res Paper Horace Lamb Centre Oceanogr Res ... Research Paper. Horace Lamb Centre for Oceanographical Research. Flinders University [*South Australia*] [*A publication*]   (APTA)
Res Pap Fac For Univ BC ... Research Paper. Faculty of Forestry. University of British Columbia [*A publication*]
Res Pap For Dep (West Aust) ... Research Paper. Forests Department (Western Australia) [*A publication*]   (APTA)
Res Pap Forests Dep (West Aust) ... Research Paper. Forests Department (Western Australia) [*A publication*]   (APTA)
Res Pap (Forest Ser) Fed Dep Forest Res (Niger) ... Research Paper (Forest Series). Federal Department of Forest Research (Nigeria) [*A publication*]
Res Pap GA For Res Coun ... Research Paper. Georgia Forest Research Council [*A publication*]
Res Pap Geogr Univ Newcastle ... Research Papers in Geography. University of Newcastle [*A publication*]   (APTA)
Res Pap Horace Lamb Centre Oceanogrl Res ... Research Paper. Horace Lamb Centre for Oceanographical Research. Flinders University [*South Australia*] [*A publication*]   (APTA)
Res Pap Ore For Res Lab ... Research Paper. Oregon State University. Forest Research Laboratory [*A publication*]
Res Pap Phys Educ ... Research Papers in Physical Education [*A publication*]
Res Pap PNW (Pac Northwest For Range Exp Stn) ... Research Paper PNW (Pacific Northwest Forest and Range Experiment Station) [*A publication*]
Res Pap Sav For Res Sta ... Research Paper. Savanna Forestry Research Station [*A publication*]
Res Pap Sch For Resour PA St Univ ... Research Paper. School of Forest Resources. Pennsylvania State University [*A publication*]

Res Pap Ser Int Rice Res Inst ... Research Paper Series. International Rice Research Institute [*A publication*]
Res Pap US Forest Serv Lake St Forest Exp Stn ... Research Paper. United States Forest Service. Lake States Forest Experiment Station [*A publication*]
Res Pap (West Aust) For Dep ... Research Paper (Western Australia). Forests Department [*A publication*]
Resp C .... Respiratory Care [*A publication*]
Resp Care ... Respiratory Care [*A publication*]
RESPD ...... Revue d'Epidemiologie et de Sante Publique [*A publication*]
R Esp Der Int ... Revista Espanola de Derecho Internacional [*A publication*]
Res Phenomenol ... Research in Phenomenology [*A publication*]
REspir .... Revista de Espiritualidad [*A publication*]
Respiration Suppl ... Respiration. Supplement [*Switzerland*] [*A publication*]
Respir Care ... Respiratory Care [*A publication*]
Respir Circ ... Respiration and Circulation [*A publication*]
Respir Med ... Respiratory Medicine [*A publication*]
Respir Physiol ... Respiration Physiology [*A publication*]
Respir Technol ... Respiratory Technology [*A publication*]
Respir Ther ... Respiratory Therapy [*A publication*]
REspL .... Revista Espanola de Linguistica [*A publication*]
RESPLY .... Respectively
Resp Merid ... Responsa Meridiana [*South Africa*] [*A publication*]   (DLA)
RESPO ...... Responsible Property Officer [*Army*]   (AABC)
Res Pol ...... Research Policy [*A publication*]
RESPOND ... Respondere [*To Answer*] [*Pharmacy*]   (ROG)
RESPONSA ... Retrieval of Special Portions from Nuclear Science Abstracts   (DIT)
R Esp Opinion Publica ... Revista Espanola de la Opinion Publica [*A publication*]
R Esp Opin Publ ... Revista Espanola de la Opinion Publica [*A publication*]
Res Popul Ecol ... Researches on Population Ecology [*A publication*]
Res Popul Ecol (Kyoto) ... Researches on Population Ecology (Kyoto) [*A publication*]
Resp Physl ... Respiration Physiology [*A publication*]
Res Pract Forensic Med ... Research and Practice in Forensic Medicine [*A publication*]
Res Preview ... Research Previews [*A publication*]
Res Prog Lithogr Tech Found ... Research Progress. Lithographic Technical Foundation [*A publication*]
Res Prog Org-Biol Med Chem ... Research Progress in Organic-Biological and Medicinal Chemistry [*A publication*]
Res Prog Rep Purdue Univ Agric Exp Stn ... Research Progress Report. Purdue University. Agricultural Experiment Station [*Indiana*] [*A publication*]
Res Prog Rep Tokai-Kinki Natn Agric Exp Stn ... Research Progress Report. Tokai-Kinki National Agricultural Experiment Station [*A publication*]
Res Prog Rep UK At Energy Res Establ Health Phys Med Div ... Research Progress Report. United Kingdom Atomic Energy Research Establishment. Health Physics and Medical Division [*A publication*]
Res Progr Rep Indiana Agr Exp Sta ... Research Progress Report. Indiana Agricultural Experiment Station [*A publication*]
Res Progr Rep Purdue Agric Exp Sta ... Research Progress Report. Purdue University. Agricultural Experiment Station [*Indiana*] [*A publication*]
Res Progr Rep Purdue Univ Agr Exp Sta ... Research Progress Report. Purdue University. Agricultural Experiment Station [*Indiana*] [*A publication*]
Res Progr Rep Tokai-Kinki Nat Agr Exp Sta ... Research Progress Report. Tokai-Kinki National Agricultural Experiment Station [*A publication*]
Res Progr Rep West Weed Control Conf ... Research Progress Report. Western Weed Control Conference [*A publication*]
Res Proj Ser Victoria Dep Agric ... Victoria. Department of Agriculture. Research Project Series [*A publication*]   (APTA)
Res Prostaglandins ... Research in Prostaglandins [*A publication*]
RESPT .... Respondent
REspT .... Revista Espanola de Teologia [*Madrid*] [*A publication*]
Respta .... Respuesta [*Answer*] [*Spanish*]
Resp Technol ... Respiratory Technology [*A publication*]
Resp Ther .. Respiratory Therapy [*A publication*]
Res Pub ...... Res Publica [*A publication*]   (ILCA)
Res Publ ..... Res Publica [*A publication*]
Res Publ Assoc Res Nerv Ment Dis ... Research Publications Association for Research in Nervous and Mental Disease [*A publication*]
Res Publ Gen Mot Corp Res Lab ... Research Publication. General Motors Corporation. Research Laboratories [*A publication*]
Res Publ Kan Agric Exp Stn ... Research Publication. Kansas Agricultural Experiment Station [*A publication*]
RESPY ...... Respectfully   (ROG)
Res Q .... Research Quarterly [*A publication*]
Res Q (AAHPER) ... Research Quarterly. American Association for Health, Physical Education, and Recreation [*A publication*]
Res Q Am Alliance Health Phys Educ Recreat ... Research Quarterly. American Alliance for Health, Physical Education, and Recreation [*A publication*]
Res Q Am Assoc Health Phys Educ Recreat ... Research Quarterly. American Association for Health, Physical Education, and Recreation [*A publication*]

Res Q Am Assoc Health Phys Educ Recreation ... Research Quarterly. American Association for Health, Physical Education, and Recreation [*A publication*]
Res Q Exercise Sport ... Research Quarterly for Exercise and Sport [*A publication*]
Res Q Exerc Sport ... Research Quarterly for Exercise and Sport [*A publication*]
Res Q Ont Hydro ... Research Quarterly. Ontario Hydro [*A publication*]
Res Quart ... Research Quarterly [*A publication*]
ReSR .... Recherches de Science Religieuse [*A publication*]
RESR .... Research, Inc. [*NASDAQ symbol*]   (NQ)
Res R .... Research in Review [*A publication*]
RESR .... Resources   (AABC)
RESRC .... Resources
Resrce Recv ... Resource Recovery Update [*A publication*]
Res Rec Malawi For Res Inst ... Research Record. Malawi Forest Research Institute [*A publication*]
Res Relat Child ... Research Relating to Children [*A publication*]
RESREP .... Resident Representative   (MUGU)
Res Rep Agric Exp Stn Mich St Univ ... Research Report. Agricultural Experiment Station. Michigan State University [*A publication*]
Res Rep Agric Exp Stn Univ Wisc ... Research Report. Agricultural Experiment Station. University of Wisconsin [*A publication*]
Res Rep Agric Exp Stn Utah St Univ ... Research Report. Agricultural Experiment Station. Utah State University [*A publication*]
Res Rep Anan Tech College ... Research Reports. Anan Technical College [*A publication*]
Res Rep Autom Control Lab Fac Eng Nagoya Univ ... Research Reports. Automatic Control Laboratory. Faculty of Engineering. Nagoya University [*A publication*]
Res Rep Biotech Fac Univ Edvard Kardelj (Ljublj) Vet Issue ... Research Reports. Biotechnical Faculty. University of Edvard Kardelj (Ljubljana). Veterinary Issue [*A publication*]
Res Rep Biotech Fac Univ Ljublj Agric Issue ... Research Reports. Biotechnical Faculty. University of Ljubljana. Agricultural Issue [*A publication*]
Res Rep Can Dept Agr Nat Weed Comm West Sect ... Research Report. Canada Department of Agriculture. National Weed Committee. Western Section [*A publication*]
Res Rep Cent Highw Res Univ Tex Austin ... Research Report. Center for Highway Research. University of Texas at Austin [*A publication*]
Res Rep Coll Agric Korea Univ ... Research Reports. College of Agriculture. Korea University [*A publication*]
Res Rep Coll Agric Univ Wis ... Research Report. Experiment Station. College of Agriculture. University of Wisconsin [*A publication*]
Res Rep Coll Agric Vet Med Nihon Univ ... Research Reports. College of Agriculture and Veterinary Medicine. Nihon University [*Japan*] [*A publication*]
Res Rep Coll Eng Busan Natl Univ ... Research Report. College of Engineering. Busan National University [*A publication*]
Res Rep DAE LA St Univ Agric Exp Stn ... Research Report. Department of Agricultural Economics and Agri-Business. Louisiana State University and Agricultural Experiment Station [*A publication*]
Res Rep Dep Crop Sci NC State Univ ... Research Report. Department of Crop Science. North Carolina State University. Agricultural Experiment Station [*A publication*]
Res Rep Dep Electl Engng Melb Univ ... Research Report. Department of Electrical Engineering. University of Melbourne [*A publication*]   (APTA)
Res Rep Dep Electr Eng Melb Univ ... Research Report. Department of Electrical Engineering. University of Melbourne [*A publication*]   (APTA)
Res Rep Div Appl Org Chem CSIRO ... Research Report. Division of Applied Organic Chemistry. Commonwealth Scientific and Industrial Research Organisation [*A publication*]   (APTA)
Res Rep East Sect Nat Weed Comm Can ... Research Report. Eastern Section. National Weed Committee of Canada [*A publication*]
Res Rep Electron Gen Res Inst ... Research Report. Electronics General Research Institute [*Japan*] [*A publication*]
Res Rep Fac Biotech Univ Ljublj Vet Issue ... Research Reports. Faculty of Biotechnics. University of Ljubljana. Veterinary Issue [*A publication*]
Res Rep Fac Eng Kagoshima Univ ... Research Reports. Faculty of Engineering. Kagoshima University [*Japan*] [*A publication*]
Res Rep Fac Eng Meiji Univ ... Research Reports. Faculty of Engineering. Meiji University [*A publication*]
Res Rep Fac Eng Nagoya Univ ... Research Reports. Faculty of Engineering. Nagoya University [*A publication*]
Res Rep Fac Eng Niigata Univ ... Research Report. Faculty of Engineering. Niigata University [*A publication*]
Res Rep Fac Engrg Tokyo Denki Univ ... Research Reports. Faculty of Engineering. Tokyo Denki University [*A publication*]
Res Rep Fac Eng Tokyo Denki Univ ... Research Reports. Faculty of Engineering. Tokyo Denki University [*A publication*]
Res Rep Fac Eng Toyo Univ ... Research Reports. Faculty of Engineering. Toyo University [*A publication*]

Res Rep Fac Sci and Technol Meijyo Univ ... Research Reports. Faculty of Science and Technology. Meijyo University [*A publication*]

Res Rep Fac Text Seric Shinshu Univ ... Research Reports. Faculty of Textiles and Sericulture. Shinshu University [*A publication*]

Res Rep Fish Comm Oreg ... Research Reports. Fish Commission of Oregon [*A publication*]

Res Rep Fish Wildl Serv (US) ... Research Report. Fish and Wildlife Service (United States) [*A publication*]

Res Rep Fla Agric Exp Stn ... Research Report. Florida Agricultural Experiment Station [*A publication*]

Res Rep Fla Sch For ... Research Report. University of Florida. School of Forestry [*A publication*]

Res Rep Flinders Inst Atmos Mar Sci ... Research Report. Flinders Institute of Atmospheric and Marine Sciences. Flinders University [*A publication*]   (APTA)

Res Rep For Prod Util Lab Miss St Univ ... Research Report. Forest Products Utilization Laboratory. Mississippi State University [*A publication*]

Res Rep For Res Inst ... Research Reports. Forest Research Institute [*A publication*]

Res Rep Fukui Tech Coll Nat Sci Eng ... Research Reports. Fukui Technical College. Natural Science and Engineering [*Japan*] [*A publication*]

Res Rep Fukuoka Agr Exp Sta ... Research Report. Fukuoka Agricultural Experiment Station [*A publication*]

Res Rep Fukuoka Agric Exp Stn ... Research Report. Fukuoka Agricultural Experiment Station [*A publication*]

Res Rep GA Agr Exp Sta ... Research Report. Georgia Agricultural Experiment Station [*A publication*]

Res Rep Hanyang Res Inst Ind Sci ... Research Reports. Hanyang Research Institute of Industrial Sciences [*A publication*]

Res Rep Hawaii Agric Exp Stn ... Research Report. Hawaii Agricultural Experiment Station [*A publication*]

Res Rep Helsinki Univ Technol Lab Phys ... Research Report. Helsinki University of Technology. Laboratory of Physics [*A publication*]

Res Rep Hokkaido Natl Agric Exp Stn ... Research Report. Hokkaido National Agricultural Experiment Station [*A publication*]

Res Rep Hunter Valley Res Fdn ... Research Report. Hunter Valley Research Foundation [*A publication*]   (APTA)

Res Rep Hunter Valley Res Found ... Research Report. Hunter Valley Research Foundation [*A publication*]   (APTA)

Res Rep Inst For Genet ... Research Report. Institute of Forest Genetics [*A publication*]

Res Rep Inst For Genet (Korea) ... Research Report. Institute of Forest Genetics (Suwon, Korea) [*A publication*]

Res Rep Inst For Genet (Suwon) Imop Sihomjang ... Research Report. Institute of Forest Genetics (Suwon). Imop Sihomjang [*A publication*]

Res Rep Inst Industr Res (Nigeria) ... Research Report. Federal Institute of Industrial Research (Lagos, Nigeria) [*A publication*]

Res Rep Inst Inform Sci Tech Tokyo Denki Univ ... Tokyo Denki University. Institute of Information Science and Technology. Research Reports [*A publication*]

Res Rep Inst Inf Sci and Technol Tokyo Denki Univ ... Research Reports. Institute of Information Science and Technology. Tokyo Denki University [*A publication*]

Res Rep Inst Plasma Phys Nagoya Univ ... Research Report. Institute of Plasma Physics. Nagoya University [*A publication*]

Res Rep Int Food Policy Res Inst ... Research Report. International Food Policy Research Institute [*A publication*]

Res Rep Kasetsart Univ ... Research Reports. Kasetsart University [*A publication*]

Res Rep Kitakyushu Tech Coll ... Research Report. Kitakyushu Technical College [*A publication*]

Res Rep Kochi Univ Agric Sci ... Research Reports. Kochi University. Agricultural Science [*A publication*]

Res Rep Kogakuin Univ ... Research Reports. Kogakuin University [*Japan*] [*A publication*]

Res Rep Korea Min Agr Forest Office Rural Develop ... Research Reports. Republic of Korea Ministry of Agriculture and Forestry. Office of Rural Development [*A publication*]

Res Rep Kurume Tech Coll ... Research Reports. Kurume Technical College [*A publication*]

Res Rep Kushiro Tech College ... Research Reports. Kushiro Technical College [*A publication*]

Res Rep Lab Nucl Sci Tohoku Univ ... Research Report. Laboratory of Nuclear Science. Tohoku University [*A publication*]

Res Rep Lab Nucl Sci Tohoku Univ Suppl ... Research Report. Laboratory of Nuclear Science. Tohoku University. Supplement [*Japan*] [*A publication*]

Res Rep MAFES ... Research Report. MAFES [*Mississippi Agricultural and Forestry Experiment Station*] [*A publication*]

Res Rep Maizuru Tech Coll ... Research Reports. Maizuru Technical College [*A publication*]

Res Rep Mich State Univ Agric Exp Stn ... Research Report. Michigan State University. Agricultural Experiment Station [*A publication*]

Res Rep Miss Agric For Exp Stn ... Research Report. Mississippi Agricultural and Forestry Experiment Station [*A publication*]

Res Rep Miyagi Tech College ... Research Reports. Miyagi Technical College [*A publication*]

Res Rep Miyakonojo Tech Coll ... Research Report. Miyakonojo Technical College [*A publication*]

Res Rep Mont Agric Exp Stn ... Research Report. Montana Agricultural Experiment Station [*A publication*]

Res Rep Nagano Tech Coll ... Research Report. Nagano Technical College [*Japan*] [*A publication*]

Res Rep Nagaoka Tech Coll ... Research Reports. Nagaoka Technical College [*A publication*]

Res Rep Nagoya Ind Sci Res Inst ... Research Reports. Nagoya Industrial Science Research Institute [*Japan*] [*A publication*]

Res Rep Nara Tech Coll ... Research Reports. Nara Technical College [*Japan*] [*A publication*]

Res Rep Natl Geogr Soc ... Research Reports. National Geographic Society [*A publication*]

Res Rep Natl Inst Nutr ... Research Report. National Institute of Nutrition [*Japan*] [*A publication*]

Res Rep Nat Sci Council Math Res Center ... Research Reports. National Science Council. Mathematics Research Center [*A publication*]

Res Rep NC Agr Exp Sta Dept Crop Sci ... Research Report. North Carolina Agricultural Experiment Station. Department of Crop Science [*A publication*]

Res Rep NC Agr Exp Sta Dept Field Crops ... Research Report. North Carolina Agricultural Experiment Station. Department of Field Crops [*A publication*]

Res Rep N Cent Weed Contr Conf ... Research Report. North Central Weed Control Conference [*A publication*]

Res Rep N Dak Agr Exp Sta ... Research Report. North Dakota Agricultural Experiment Station [*A publication*]

Res Rep New Mex Agr Exp Stn ... Research Report. New Mexico Agricultural Experiment Station [*A publication*]

Res Rep NH Agric Exp Stn ... Research Report. New Hampshire Agricultural Experiment Station [*A publication*]

Res Rep N Mex Agr Exp Sta ... Research Report. New Mexico Agricultural Experiment Station [*A publication*]

Res Rep Norfolk Agr Exp Sta ... Research Report. Norfolk Agricultural Experiment Station [*A publication*]

Res Rep North Cent Weed Control Conf ... Research Report. North Central Weed Control Conference [*A publication*]

Res Rep Nth Cent Weed Control Conf ... Research Report. North Central Weed Control Conference [*A publication*]

Res Rep Numazu Tech Coll ... Research Reports. Numazu Technical College [*A publication*]

Res Rep Office Rur Dev Minist Agric For (Korea) ... Research Reports. Office of Rural Development. Ministry of Agriculture and Forestry (Suwon, South Korea) [*A publication*]

Res Rep Off Rural Dev Agric Eng Farm Manage & Seric (Suweon) ... Research Reports. Office of Rural Development. Agricultural Engineering, Farm Management, and Sericulture (Suweon) [*A publication*]

Res Rep Off Rural Dev Crop (Suwon) ... Research Reports. Office of Rural Development. Crop (Suwon, South Korea) [*A publication*]

Res Rep Off Rural Dev Hortic Agric Eng (Korea Repub) ... Research Reports. Office of Rural Development. Horticulture and Agricultural Engineering (Korea Republic) [*A publication*]

Res Rep Off Rural Dev Hortic (Suwon) ... Research Reports. Office of Rural Development. Horticulture (Suwon, South Korea) [*A publication*]

Res Rep Off Rural Dev Livest (Korea Republic) ... Research Reports. Office of Rural Development. Livestock (Korea Republic) [*A publication*]

Res Rep Off Rural Dev Livest Seric (Suwon) ... Research Reports. Office of Rural Development. Livestock, Sericulture (Suwon, South Korea) [*A publication*]

Res Rep Off Rural Dev Livest (Suwon) ... Research Reports. Office of Rural Development. Livestock (Suwon, South Korea) [*A publication*]

Res Rep Off Rural Dev Livest & Vet (Suweon) ... Research Reports. Office of Rural Development. Livestock and Veterinary (Suweon) [*A publication*]

Res Rep Off Rural Dev Plant Environ (Suwon) ... Research Reports. Office of Rural Development. Plant Environment (Suwon, South Korea) [*A publication*]

Res Rep Off Rural Dev Seric-Vet (Suwon) ... Research Reports. Office of Rural Development. Sericulture-Veterinary (Suwon, South Korea) [*A publication*]

Res Rep Off Rural Dev (Suwon) ... Research Reports. Office of Rural Development (Suwon, South Korea) [*A publication*]

Res Rep Off Rural Dev (Suwon) Livestock ... Research Reports. Office of Rural Development (Suwon, South Korea). Livestock [*A publication*]

Res Rep Off Rural Dev Vet Seric (Korea Republic) ... Research Reports. Office of Rural Development. Veterinary and Sericulture (Korea Republic) [*A publication*]

Res Rep Off Rural Dev Vet (Suwon) ... Research Reports. Office of Rural Development. Veterinary (Suwon, South Korea) [*A publication*]

Res Rep Oklahoma Agric Exp St ... Oklahoma. Agricultural Experiment Station. Research Report [*A publication*]

Res Rep Ore St Univ Forest Res Lab ... Research Report. Oregon State University. Forest Research Laboratory [*A publication*]
Res Reports Fac Engng Meiji Univ ... Research Reports. Faculty of Engineering. Meiji University [*A publication*]
Res Rep Oyama Natl Coll Technol ... Research Reports. Oyama National College of Technology [*A publication*]
Res Rep Oyama Tech Coll ... Research Reports. Oyama Technical College [*A publication*]
Res Rep P Agric Exp Stn Okla State Univ ... Research Report P. Agricultural Experiment Station. Oklahoma State University [*A publication*]
Res Rep Res Inst Ind Saf ... Research Report. Research Institute of Industrial Safety [*A publication*]
Res Reprod ... Research in Reproduction [*A publication*]
Res Rep Rural Dev Adm (Suweon) ... Research Reports. Rural Development Administration (Suweon) [*A publication*]
Res Rep Sasebo Tech Coll ... Research Reports. Sasebo Technical College [*A publication*]
Res Rep Sch Civ Engng Syd Univ ... Research Report. School of Civil Engineering. University of Sydney [*A publication*]　(APTA)
Res Rep Shibaura Inst Technol ... Research Reports. Shibaura Institute of Technology [*Japan*] [*A publication*]
Res Rep Taiwan Sugar Exp Stn ... Research Report. Taiwan Sugar Experiment Station [*A publication*]
Res Rep Timber Dev Assoc (London) ... Research Report. Timber Development Association (London) [*A publication*]
Res Rep Timb Res Developm Ass ... Research Report. Timber Research and Development Association [*A publication*]
Res Rep Tokyo Denki Univ ... Research Reports. Tokyo Denki University [*A publication*]
Res Rep Tokyo Electr Eng Coll ... Research Reports. Tokyo Electrical Engineering College [*A publication*]
Res Rep Tokyo Electr Engrg College ... Research Reports. Tokyo Electrical Engineering College [*A publication*]
Res Rep Tokyo Electrical Engrg College ... Research Reports. Tokyo Electrical Engineering College [*A publication*]
Res Rep Tokyo Natl Tech Coll ... Research Reports. Tokyo National Technical College [*A publication*]
Res Rep Univ Arkansas Eng Exp Stn ... Research Report. University of Arkansas. Engineering Experiment Station [*A publication*]
Res Rep Univ Fla Sch For Resour Conserv ... Research Report. University of Florida. School of Forest Resources and Conservation [*A publication*]
Res Rep Univ GA Coll Agric Exp Stn ... Research Report. University of Georgia. College of Agriculture. Experiment Stations [*A publication*]
Res Rep Univ Tex Austin Cent Highw Res ... Research Report. University of Texas at Austin. Center for Highway Research [*A publication*]
Res Rep US Army Eng Waterw Exp Stn ... Research Report. US Army Engineers. Waterways Experiment Station [*A publication*]
Res Rep US Army Mater Command Cold Reg Res Engng Lab ... Research Report. United States Army Material Command. Cold Regions Research and Engineering Laboratory [*A publication*]
Res Rep US Bur Sport Fish Wildl ... Research Report. United States Bureau of Sport Fisheries and Wildlife [*A publication*]
Res Rep US Fish Wildl Serv ... Research Report. United States Fish and Wildlife Service [*A publication*]
Res Rep VA Agr Exp Sta ... Research Report. Virginia Agricultural Experiment Station [*A publication*]
Res Rep Vet Issue ... Research Reports. Veterinary Issue [*A publication*]
Res Rep West Sect Nat Weed Comm Can ... Research Report. Western Section. National Weed Committee of Canada [*A publication*]
Res Rep Winnipeg Manitoba Res Sta ... Research Report. Winnipeg, Manitoba Research Station [*A publication*]
Res Rep Wis Agr Exp Sta ... Research Report. Wisconsin Agricultural Experiment Station [*A publication*]
Res Results Dig ... Research Results Digest [*A publication*]
ResRev ... Research Review [*A publication*]
Res Rev Bur Hort Plantat Crops ... Research Review. Commonwealth Bureau of Horticulture and Plantation Crops [*A publication*]
Res Rev Can Res Stn (Agassiz BC) ... Research Review. Canada Research Station. (Agassiz, British Columbia) [*A publication*]
Res Rev Chung-Buk Natl Univ ... Research Review. Chung-Buk National University [*A publication*]
Res Rev CSIRO Div Chem Technol ... Australia. Commonwealth Scientific and Industrial Research Organisation. Division of Chemical Technology. Research Review [*A publication*]　(APTA)
Res Rev Div Chem Technol CSIRO ... Research Review. Division of Chemical Technology. Commonwealth Scientific and Industrial Research Organisation [*A publication*]
Res Rev Florida State Univ Bull ... Research in Review. Florida State University. Bulletin [*A publication*]
Res Rev Kyungpook Univ ... Research Review. Kyungpook University [*A publication*]
Res Rev (Off Aerosp Res) ... Research Review (Office of Aerospace Research) [*A publication*]
RESRT ...... Resort

RESRT ...... Restart [*Data processing*]
RESS ...... RADAR Echo Simulation Study [*or Subsystem*]
Res Ser Appl Geogr New Engl Univ ... Research Series in Applied Geography. University of New England [*A publication*]　(APTA)
Res Ser Fowlers Gap Arid Zone Res Stn ... Research Series. Fowlers Gap Arid Zone Research Station. University of New England [*A publication*]　(APTA)
Res Ser ICAR ... Research Series ICAR. Indian Council of Agricultural Research [*A publication*]
RESSI .... Real Estate Securities and Syndication Institute　(EA)
Res Stat Note ... Research and Statistics Note. Social Security Administration. Office of Research and Statistics [*A publication*]
Res Stat Note Health Care Financ Adm Off Policy Plann Res ... Research and Statistics Note. Health Care Financing Administration. Office of Policy, Planning, and Research [*A publication*]
Res Steroids ... Research on Steroids [*A publication*]
Res Stud ..... Research Studies [*A publication*]
Res Stud Udaipur Univ Coll Agr ... Research Studies. Udaipur University. College of Agriculture [*A publication*]
Res Stud Wash State Univ ... Research Studies. Washington State University [*Pullman*] [*A publication*]
Res Sum Ohio Agr Res Develop Cent ... Research Summary. Ohio Agricultural Research and Development Center [*A publication*]
REST .... RADAR Electronic Scan Technique
REST .... Rain Erosion Seed Test
REST .... Range Endurance Speed and Time [*Computer*]
REST .... Reentry Environment and Systems Technology
REST .... Reentry System Test Program
REST .... Reporting System for Training [*Navy*]　(NG)
REST .... Residence in Science and Technology
REST .... Restaurant　(ROG)
REST .... Restored
REST .... Restrict　(AAG)
REST .... Restricted Environmental Stimulation Technique
REST .... Retail Employees Superannuation Trust [*Australia*]
RESt .... Review of English Studies [*A publication*]
R Est .... Revue de l'Est [*A publication*]
RESTA ...... Reconnaissance, Surveillance, and Target Acquisition [*Military*]　(AABC)
RESTA ...... Revue de Stomatologie [*Later, Revue de Stomatologie et de Chirurgie Maxillo-Faciale*] [*A publication*]
RESTAS .... Reception Station System [*Army*]
RESTAT .... Reserve Components Status Reporting [*Army*]　(AABC)
RESTAT .... Review of Economics and Statistics [*A publication*]
Restau Bus ... Restaurant Business [*A publication*]
Restau & Inst ... Restaurants and Institutions [*A publication*]
Restaur Bus ... Restaurant Business and Economic Research [*A publication*]
Restaurnt B ... Restaurant Business [*A publication*]
RESTD ...... Real Estate Today [*A publication*]
RESTD ...... Restricted [*Security classification*] [*Military*]
Res Teach Engl ... Research in the Teaching of English [*A publication*]
Res Tech Instrum ... Research Techniques and Instrumentation [*A publication*]
R Esthet ..... Revue d'Esthetique [*A publication*]
R d'Esthetique ... Revue d'Esthetique [*A publication*]
Rest Inst ..... Restaurants and Institutions [*A publication*]
R Est LJ .... Real Estate Law Journal [*A publication*]
RESTO ...... Restaurant
Res Today .. Research Today [*A publication*]
Res Topics Physiol ... Research Topics in Physiology [*A publication*]
Restoration Q ... Restoration Quarterly [*A publication*]
Restorative Dent ... Restorative Dentistry [*A publication*]
Restor Eigh ... Restoration and Eighteenth Century Theatre Research [*A publication*]
RESTR ...... Restorer
RESTR ...... Restrict　(AABC)
RESTRACEN ... Reserve Training Center
RESTRAFAC ... Reserve Training Facility
Res Trends ... Research Trends [*A publication*]
Restric Prac ... Reports of Restrictive Practices Cases [*A publication*]　(DLA)
Restr Mgt ... Restaurant Management [*A publication*]
Restrnt H ... Restaurant Hospitality [*A publication*]
RESTS ...... Restoration Survey
R E Stud ..... Review of Economic Studies [*A publication*]
R Estud Agro-Soc ... Revista de Estudios Agro-Sociales [*A publication*]
R Estud Penitenciarios ... Revista de Estudios Penitenciarios [*A publication*]
R Estud Pol ... Revista de Estudios Politicos [*A publication*]
R Estud Sindic ... Revista de Estudios Sindicales [*A publication*]
R Estud Soc ... Revista de Estudios Sociales [*A publication*]
R Estud Vida Loc ... Revista de Estudios de la Vida Local [*A publication*]
R Estud Vida Local ... Revista de Estudios de la Vida Local [*A publication*]
RESUB ...... Resources [*A publication*]
RESUB ...... Resublimed
RESUDU ... Records. Western Australian Museum. Supplement [*A publication*]
Resultate Math ... Resultate der Mathematik [*A publication*]
Resultats ..... Resultats Statistiques du Poitou-Charentes [*A publication*]
Result Exped Cient Buque Oceanogr "Cornide de Saavedra" ... Resultados Expediciones Cientificas del Buque Oceanografico "Cornide de Saavedra" [*A publication*]

Results Norw Sci Exped Tristan Da Cunha 1937-1938 ... Results of the Norwegian Scientific Expedition to Tristan Da Cunha 1937-1938 [*A publication*]
Results Probl Cell Differ ... Results and Problems in Cell Differentiation [*A publication*]
Results Res Annu Rep Univ KY Agr Exp Sta ... Results of Research. Annual Report. University of Kentucky. Agricultural Experiment Station [*A publication*]
Resumenes Invest INP-CIP ... Resumenes de Investigacion. INP-CIP [*Instituto Nacional de la Pesca-Centro de Investigaciones Pesqueras*] [*A publication*]
RESUP ...... Resupply   (AABC)
Resur Biosfery ... Resursy Biosfery [*A publication*]
RESURR ... Resurrection
RESUS ..... Resuscitation
RESV .... Reserve Fleet [*Navy*]
RESVD ...... Reserved
Res Vet Sci ... Research in Veterinary Science [*United Kingdom*] [*A publication*]
Res Virol .... Research in Virology [*A publication*]
Res Vol Surrey Archaeol Soc ... Research Volumes. Surrey Archaeological Society [*A publication*]
RESVON ... Reservation   (ROG)
RESVR ...... Reservoir   (AAG)
Res Wks Georgian Beekeep Res Stn (Tbilisi) ... Research Works. Georgian Beekeeping Research Station (Tbilisi) [*A publication*]
Res Works Grad Sch Dong A Univ ... Research Works of the Graduate School. Dong-A University [*A publication*]
RESY .... Residuary   (ROG)
RET .... Rad-Equivalent Therapy [*Radiology*]
RET .... RADAR Equipment Trailer   (MCD)
R-ET .... Rational-Emotive Psychotherapy [*Also known as R-EP, RT*]
RET .... Readiness Enhancement Technology [*Military*]
RET .... Reiteration [*Printers' term*]   (DSUE)
RET .... Reitman's (Canada) Ltd. [*Toronto Stock Exchange symbol*]
RET .... Relay Extractor Tool
RET .... Reliability Evaluation Test
RET .... Repetitive Extrasystole Threshold [*Cardiology*]
RE & T ...... Research Engineering and Test [*NASA*]
RET .... Resonance Energy Transfer [*Physical chemistry*]
RET .... Retain   (AAG)
RET .... Retard   (AAG)
Ret............ Reticulum [*Constellation*]
RET .... Retired   (AFM)
RET .... Retired after Finishing [*Yacht racing*]   (IYR)
RET .... Retract
RET .... Return [*or Returnable*]   (AAG)
RET .... Revista Espanola de Teologia [*Madrid*] [*A publication*]
RET .... Right Esotropia [*Ophthalmology*]
RET .... Ring Emitter Transistor
RET .... Rost [*Norway*] [*Airport symbol*]   (OAG)
RET .... Roster of Employees Transferred [*Army*]
RETA .... Refrigerating Engineers and Technicians Association   (EA)
RETA .... Retrieval of Enriched Textual Abstracts [*Information retrieval program*]
RETAC ..... Regional Educational Television Advisory Council
RETACT ... Real-Time Advanced Core and Thermohydraulic
RETAI .... Real Estate Trainers Association, International   (EA)
Retail Dist Mgmt ... Retail and Distribution Management [*A publication*]
Retailer of Q ... Retailer of Queensland [*A publication*]   (APTA)
Retail Packag ... Retail Packaging [*A publication*]
Retail Pkg .. Retail Packaging [*A publication*]
RETAIN .... Remote Technical Assistance and Information Network [*Data processing*]
R Et Arm .... Revue des Etudes Armeniennes [*A publication*]
RETAT ...... [*It Is*] Requested That   (NVT)
RET BREV ... Retorna Brevium [*The Return of Writs*] [*Latin*] [*Legal term*]   (DLA)
RETC .... Railroad Equipment Trust Certificate
RETC .... Rat Embryo Tissue Culture
RETC .... Regional Emergency Transportation Center [*Military*]
RETCO ...... Regional Emergency Transportation Coordinator [*Military*]
R Et Comp Est-Ouest ... Revue d'Etudes Comparatives Est-Ouest [*A publication*]
R Et Coop ... Revue des Etudes Cooperatives [*A publication*]
RETD .... Recueil d'Etudes Theologiques et Dogmatiques [*A publication*]
RETD .... Red Especial de Transmision de Datos [*Spanish telephone co.*]   (TEL)
RETD .... Retained
RETD .... Retired   (EY)
RETD .... Returned
RETEN ..... Retention [*Insurance*]   (MCD)
RETF .... Retired Document File [*IRS*]
RETG .... Retaining
R Ethnol ..... Review of Ethnology [*A publication*]
RETI .... Communaute de Travail des Regions Europeennes de Tradition Industrielle [*Association of Traditional Industrial Regions of Europe*] [*Lille, France*]   (EAIO)
Reti............ Reticulum [*Constellation*]
RETIC .... Reticulocyte [*Hematology*]
RETIMP ... Raleigh-Edwards Tensile Impact Machine Pendulum

Retina Found Inst Biol Med Sci Monogr Conf ... Retina Foundation. Institute of Biological and Medical Sciences. Monographs and Conferences [*A publication*]
RETIREX ... Retirement Exhibition [*British*]   (ITD)
RETL .... Retail
RETL .... Rocket Engine Test Laboratory [*Air Force*]
Ret Liv .... Retirement Living [*A publication*]
RETMA ..... Radio-Electronics-Television Manufacturers Association [*Later, Electronic Industries Association*]
RETMOB ... Requirements for Total Mobilization Study
RETN .... Return   (ROG)
RETNA ...... Reactor Technology [*A publication*]
Ret News .... Retail News [*A publication*]
RETNG ..... Retraining
RETNN ..... Retention [*Insurance*]
R Etnografie Folclor ... Revista de Etnografie si Folclor [*A publication*]
RETNR ...... Retainer   (ADA)
RETO .... Review of Education and Training for Officers [*Military*]   (RDA)
RETORC ... Research Torpedo Configuration   (NG)
RETP .... Reliability Evaluation Test Procedure
RETP .... Reserve Entry Training Plan [*Canada*]
RETP .... Retape
RETR .... Retainer   (ROG)
RETR .... Retention Register [*Data processing*]
RETR .... Retraced
RETR .... Retract   (AAG)
RETR .... Retrieve   (KSC)
RETRA ...... Radio, Electrical, and Television Retailers' Association [*British*]
Retract .... Retractationes [*of Augustine*] [*Classical studies*]   (OCD)
RETRAN ... Refined Trajectory Analysis
RETRANS ... [*For*] Return Transportation [*To*]
RETRD ...... Retarded
RETREAD ... Retiree Training for Extended Active Duty [*Military*]   (MCD)
RETREP ..... Regional Emergency Transportation Representative
RETRF ...... Rural Electrification and Telephone Revolving Fund [*Department of Agriculture*]
RETRO ...... Regional Environmental Training and Research Organization [*Retraining program for unemployed space-industry workers*]
RETRO ...... Retro-Rocket   (AAG)
RETRO ...... Retroactive   (AAG)
RETRO ...... Retrofire   (KSC)
RETRO ...... Retrofire Officer
RETRO ...... Retrofit
RETRO ...... Retrograde
RETROG ... Retrogressive
Retros .... Retrospective Review [*A publication*]
Retrosp .... Retrospectively   (DLA)
RETRV ...... Retrieve   (MCD)
RETS .... Radiological Environmental Technical Specifications [*Nuclear energy*]   (NRCH)
RETS .... Reconfigurable Electrical Test Stand   (NASA)
RETS .... Remoted Targets System   (MCD)
RETS .... Renaissance English Text Society   (EA)
RETSCP .... Rocket Engine Thermal Strains with Cyclic Plasticity [*Propellant*]
RETSIE ...... Renewable Energy Technologies Symposium and International Exposition [*Renewable Energy Institute*]   (TSPED)
RETSPL .... Reference Equivalent Threshold Sound Pain [*or Pressure*] Level
R Et Sud-Est Europ ... Revue des Etudes Sud-Est Europeennes [*A publication*]
RETT .... Relatively Easy to Test [*Audiology*]
Rett .... Rettie's Scotch Court of Session Cases, Fourth Series [*A publication*]   (DLA)
Rettie .... Rettie's Scotch Court of Session Cases, Fourth Series [*A publication*]   (DLA)
RETUA ...... Revue de Tuberculose [*A publication*]
R Etud Byzantines ... Revue des Etudes Byzantines [*A publication*]
R Etud Coops ... Revue des Etudes Cooperatives [*A publication*]
R Etud Grecques ... Revue des Etudes Grecques [*A publication*]
R Etud Islamiques ... Revue des Etudes Islamiques [*A publication*]
R Etud Juives ... Revue des Etudes Juives [*A publication*]
RETULSIGN ... Retain on Board until Ultimate Assignment Received
RETVE5 .... Revue d'Ecologie; la Terre et la Vie [*A publication*]
RETXEB ... Reviews in Environmental Toxicology [*A publication*]
REU .... AREUEA [*American Real Estate and Urban Economics Association*] Journal [*A publication*]
REU .... Rectifier Enclosure Unit [*Power supply*] [*Telecommunications*]   (TEL)
REU .... Reunion [*ANSI three-letter standard code*]   (CNC)
REU .... Reunion Island [*Reunion Island*] [*Seismograph station code, US Geological Survey*]   (SEIS)
REU .... Reus [*Spain*] [*Airport symbol*]   (OAG)
REUMA ...... Reumatismo [*A publication*]
Reun Annu Sci Terre (Programme Resumes) ... Reunion Annuelle des Sciences de la Terre (Programme et Resumes) [*A publication*]
Reun A Soc Bras Genet ... Reuniao Anual. Sociedade Brasileira de Genetica [*A publication*]
Reunion Latinoam Prod Anim ... Reunion Latinoamericana de Produccion Animal [*A publication*]

Reun Latinoamer Fitotec Actas ... Reunion Latinoamericana de Fitotecnia. Actas [*A publication*]
REUR .... Reference Your
REURAD .. Reference Your Radio
REURD ..... Reuse/Recycle [*A publication*]
R Europ Sci Soc ... Revue Europeenne des Sciences Sociales. Cahiers Vilfredo Pareto [*A publication*]
REURTWX ... Reference Your TWX [*Teletypewriter communications*] (AAG)
REUSE ...... Revitalize Effective Utilization of Supply Excess [*Navy*] (NG)
REUT .... Reuter, Inc. [*NASDAQ symbol*] (NQ)
Rev .... Cour de Revision [*Monaco*] (DLA)
REV .... Ratio of Earth-to-Vehicle Radii
REV .... Reentry Vehicle [*Aerospace*]
REV .... Regulator of Virion-Protein Expression [*Genetics*]
REV .... Reticuloendotheliosis Virus
Rev .... Revelation [*New Testament book*]
REV .... Revelstoke Companies Ltd. [*Toronto Stock Exchange symbol*]
REV .... Reventador [*Race of maize*]
REV .... Revenue
REV .... Reverend (EY)
REV .... Reverse (AAG)
REV .... Review (AFM)
Rev .... Review [*A publication*]
REV .... Revise [*or Revision*] (AAG)
REV .... Revlon Group, Inc. [*NYSE symbol*] (SPSG)
REV .... Revocable [*Business term*]
REV .... Revolution (AAG)
REV .... Rotor Entry Vehicle [*Aerospace*]
REVA .... Recommended Vehicle Adjustment [*Military*] (AABC)
Rev A .... Revue A [*Revue Trimestrielle d'Automatique*] [*Belgium*] [*A publication*]
RevA .... Revue d'Allemagne [*A publication*]
REVAB ...... Relief Valve Augmented Bypass [*Nuclear energy*] (NRCH)
Rev ABIA/SAPRO ... Revista. ABIA/SAPRO [*Associacao Brasileira das Industrias da Alimentacao/Setor de Alimentos Calorico-Proteicos*] [*A publication*]
RevAC .... Revue de l'Art Chretien [*A publication*]
Rev Acad Cienc Exactas Fis-Nat Zaragoza ... Revista. Academia de Ciencias Exactas, Fisico-Quimicas, y Naturales de Zaragoza [*A publication*]
Rev Acad Cienc (Zaragoza) ... Revista. Academia de Ciencias (Zaragoza) [*A publication*]
Rev Acad Cienc Zaragoza 2 ... Revista. Academia de Ciencias Exactas, Fisico-Quimicas, y Naturales de Zaragoza. Serie 2 [*A publication*]
Rev Acad Ci Zaragoza ... Revista. Academia de Ciencias Exactas, Fisico-Quimicas, y Naturales de Zaragoza [*A publication*]
Rev Acad Colomb Cienc Exactas Fis Nat ... Revista. Academia Colombiana de Ciencias Exactas Fisicas y Naturales [*A publication*]
Rev Acoust ... Revue d'Acoustique [*A publication*]
Rev d'Acoustique ... Revue d'Acoustique [*A publication*]
Rev Act Metallges ... Review of Activities. Metallgesellschaft [*A publication*]
Rev Act Metallges AG ... Review of Activities. Metallgesellschaft AG [*A publication*]
Rev de l'Adm ... Revue de l'Administration et du Droit Administratif de la Belgique [*A publication*]
Rev Adm Nac Agua (Argent) ... Revista. Administracion Nacional del Agua (Argentina) [*A publication*]
Rev Aeronaut ... Revista de Aeronautica [*A publication*]
Rev Agr ...... Revue de l'Agriculture [*A publication*]
Rev Agr France ... Revue Agricole de France [*A publication*]
Rev Agri ..... Revista de Agricultura [*Brazil*] [*A publication*]
Rev Agric (Bogota) ... Revista Agricola (Bogota) [*A publication*]
Rev Agric (Bruss) ... Revue de l'Agriculture (Brussels) [*A publication*]
Rev Agric Econ Hokkaido Univ ... Review of Agricultural Economics. Hokkaido University [*A publication*]
Rev Agric Fr ... Revue des Agriculteurs de France [*A publication*]
Rev Agric Ile Maurice ... Revue Agricole de l'Ile Maurice [*A publication*]
Rev Agricola (Chicago) ... Revista Agricola (Chicago) [*A publication*]
Rev Agric (Piracicaba) ... Revista de Agricultura (Piracicaba) [*A publication*]
Rev Agric (Piracicaba) (S Paulo) ... Revista de Agricultura (Piracicaba) (Estado de Sao Paulo) [*A publication*]
Rev Agric (PR) ... Revista de Agricultura (Puerto Rico) [*A publication*]
Rev Agric (Recife) ... Revista de Agricultura (Recife) [*A publication*]
Rev Agric Sucr Ile Maurice ... Revue Agricole et Sucriere de l'Ile Maurice [*A publication*]
Rev Agricultura ... Revista de Agricultura [*A publication*]
Rev Agr (Mocambique) ... Revista Agricola (Mocambique) [*A publication*]
Rev Agron .. Revista Agronomica [*A publication*]
Rev Agron (Lisb) ... Revista Agronomica (Lisbon) [*A publication*]
Rev Agron Noroeste Argent ... Revista Agronomica del Noroeste Argentino [*A publication*]
Rev Agroquim Tecnol Aliment ... Revista de Agroquimica y Tecnologia de Alimentos [*A publication*]
Rev Agr (Piracicaba) ... Revista de Agricultura (Piracicaba) [*A publication*]
Rev Alcool ... Revue de l'Alcoolisme [*A publication*]
Rev Algol ... Revue Algologique [*A publication*]
Rev Allergy ... Review of Allergy and Applied Immunology [*A publication*]
Rev Alteneo Paraguayo ... Revista del Alteneo Paraguayo [*A publication*]
Rev Alum ... Revue de l'Aluminum [*A publication*]

Rev Alum Ses Appl ... Revue de l'Aluminum et de Ses Applications [*France*] [*A publication*]
Rev Amersham Corp ... Review. Amersham Corporation [*A publication*]
Rev Am Hist ... Reviews in American History [*A publication*]
Rev AMRIGS ... Revista. AMRIGS [*Associacao Medica do Rio Grande Do Sul*] [*A publication*]
Rev Anal Chem ... Reviews in Analytical Chemistry [*A publication*]
Rev Anal Chem Euroanal ... Reviews on Analytical Chemistry. Euroanalysis [*A publication*]
Rev Anal Numer Teoria Aproximatiei ... Revista de Analiza Numerica si Teoria Aproximatiei [*A publication*]
Rev Anal Numer Theor Approx ... Revue d'Analyse Numerique et de la Theorie de l'Approximation [*A publication*]
Rev Anal Numer Theorie Approximation ... Revue d'Analyse Numerique et de la Theorie de l'Approximation [*A publication*]
Rev Anat Morphol Exp ... Revues d'Anatomie et de Morphologie Experimentale [*A publication*]
Rev Ang-Am ... Revue Anglo-Americaine [*A publication*]
Rev Annu Chimiother Physiatr Cancer ... Revue Annuelle de Chimiotherapie et de Physiatrie du Cancer [*A publication*]
Rev Annu Chimiother Prophyl Cancer ... Revue Annuelle de Chimiotherapie et de Prophylaxie du Cancer [*A publication*]
Rev Annu Physiatr Prophyl Cancer ... Revue Annuelle de Physiatrie et de Prophylaxie du Cancer [*A publication*]
Rev Annu Soc Odontostomatol Nordest ... Revue Annuelle. Societe Odonto-Stomatologique du Nord-Est [*A publication*]
Rev Anthropol (Paris) ... Revue Anthropologique (Paris) [*A publication*]
Rev Antropol (Sao Paulo) ... Revista de Antropologia (Sao Paulo) [*A publication*]
Rev Appl Elect ... Revue des Applications de l'Electricite [*A publication*]
Rev Appl Ent ... Review of Applied Entomology [*A publication*]
Rev Appl Mycol ... Review of Applied Mycology [*A publication*]
Rev Aquat Sci ... Reviews in Aquatic Sciences [*A publication*]
REVAR ...... Authorized Revisit Above-Mentioned Places and Vary Itinerary as Necessary
Rev Arch .... Revue Archeologique [*A publication*]
Rev Arch Bibl Mus ... Revista de Archivos, Bibliotecas, y Museos [*A publication*]
Rev Arch ECE ... Revue Archeologique de l'Est et du Centre-Est [*A publication*]
Rev Archeol ... Revue Archeologique [*A publication*]
Rev Archit Sci Unit Univ Queensl ... Review. Architectural Science Unit. University of Queensland [*A publication*] (APTA)
Rev Arch Narbonn ... Revue Archeologique de Narbonnaise [*A publication*]
Revard .... [*Jacobus*] Raevardus [*Deceased, 1568*] [*Authority cited in pre-1607 legal work*] (DSA)
Rev Argent Agron ... Revista Argentina de Agronomia [*A publication*]
Rev Argent Alerg ... Revista Argentina de Alergia [*A publication*]
Rev Argent Angiol ... Revista Argentina de Angiologia [*A publication*]
Rev Argent Cancerol ... Revista Argentina de Cancerologia [*A publication*]
Rev Argent Cardiol ... Revista Argentina de Cardiologia [*A publication*]
Rev Argent Cir ... Revista Argentina de Cirugia [*A publication*]
Rev Argent Endocrinol Metab ... Revista Argentina de Endocrinologia y Metabolismo [*A publication*]
Rev Argent Implantol Estomatol ... Revista Argentina de Implantologia Estomatologica [*A publication*]
Rev Argent Microbiol ... Revista Argentina de Microbiologia [*A publication*]
Rev Argent Neurol ... Revista Argentina de Neurologia, Psiquiatria, y Medicina Legal [*A publication*]
Rev Argent Neurol Psiquiat y Med Leg ... Revista Argentina de Neurologia, Psiquiatria, y Medicina Legal [*A publication*]
Rev Argent Pueric Neonatol ... Revista Argentina de Puericultura y Neonatologia [*A publication*]
Rev Argent Radiol ... Revista Argentina de Radiologia [*A publication*]
Rev Argent Reumatol ... Revista Argentina de Reumatologia [*A publication*]
Rev Argent Tuberc Enferm Pulm ... Revista Argentina de Tuberculosis y Enfermedades Pulmonares [*A publication*]
Rev Argent Tuberc Enferm Pulm Salud Publica ... Revista Argentina de Tuberculosis, Enfermedades, Pulmonares, y Salud Publica [*A publication*]
Rev Argent Urol Nefrol ... Revista Argentina de Urologia y Nefrologia [*A publication*]
Rev Arhiv ... Revista Arhivelor [*A publication*]
Rev Art .... Revue de l'Art [*A publication*]
Rev Art Anc ... Revue de l'Art Ancien et Moderne [*A publication*]
Rev Asoc Argent Criad Cerdos ... Revista. Asociacion Argentina Criadores de Cerdos [*A publication*]
Rev Asoc Argent Dietol ... Revista. Asociacion Argentina de Dietologia [*A publication*]
Rev Asoc Argent Microbiol ... Revista. Asociacion Argentina de Microbiologia [*A publication*]
Rev Asoc Bioquim Argent ... Revista. Asociacion Bioquimica Argentina [*A publication*]
Rev Asoc Cienc Nat Litoral ... Revista. Asociacion de Ciencias Naturales del Litoral [*A publication*]
Rev Asoc Geol Argent ... Revista. Asociacion Geologica Argentina [*A publication*]
Rev Asoc Med Argent ... Revista. Asociacion Medica Argentina [*A publication*]
Rev Asoc Med Mex ... Revista. Asociacion Medica Mexicana [*A publication*]

Rev Asoc Odontol Argent ... Revista. Asociacion Odontologica Argentina [*A publication*]
Rev Asoc Odontol Costa Rica ... Revista. Asociacion Odontologica de Costa Rica [*A publication*]
Rev Asoc Prof Hosp Nac Odontol ... Revista. Asociacion de Profesionales. Hospital Nacional de Odontologia [*A publication*]
Rev Asoc Rural Urug ... Revista. Asociacion Rural del Uruguay [*A publication*]
Rev Asoc Rural Uruguay ... Revista. Asociacion Rural del Uruguay [*A publication*]
Rev Assoc Fr Tech Pet ... Revue. Association Francaise des Techniciens du Petrole [*A publication*]
Rev Assoc Med Bras ... Revista. Associacao Medica Brasileira [*A publication*]
Rev Assoc Med Minas Gerais ... Revista. Associacao Medica de Minas Gerais [*A publication*]
Rev Assoc Med Rio Grande Do Sul ... Revista. Associacao Medica do Rio Grande Do Sul [*A publication*]
Rev Assoc Paul Cir Dent ... Revista. Associacao Paulista de Cirurgioes Dentistas [*A publication*]
Rev Ass Resp ... Revue des Assurances et des Responsabilites [*A publication*]
Rev Assyriol ... Revue d'Assyriologie et d'Archeologie Orientale [*A publication*]
Rev Astron ... Revista Astronomica [*A publication*]
Rev Asturiana Cien Med ... Revista Asturiana de Ciencias Medicas [*A publication*]
Rev Ateneo Catedra Tec Oper Dent ... Revista. Ateneo de la Catedra de Tecnica de Operatoria Dental [*A publication*]
Rev Atheroscler ... Revue de l'Atherosclerose [*France*] [*A publication*]
Rev Atheroscler Arteriopathies Peripheriques ... Revue de l'Atherosclerose et des Arteriopathies Peripheriques [*A publication*]
Rev At Ind ... Review of Atomic Industries [*Japan*] [*A publication*]
Rev AUPELF ... Revue de l'AUPELF. Association des Universites Partiellement ou Entierement de Langue Francaise [*A publication*]
Rev Autom ... Revista de Automatica [*A publication*]
Rev Auvergne ... Revue d'Auvergne [*A publication*]
RevB.......... Revista (Barcelona) [*A publication*]
Rev du B..... Revue. Barreau de la Province de Quebec [*A publication*]
RevBAM.... Revista. Biblioteca, Archivo, y Museo del Ayuntamiento de Madrid [*A publication*]
Rev Bank London South Am ... Review. Bank of London and South America [*A publication*]
Rev Bank NSW ... Review. Bank of New South Wales [*A publication*]
Rev Banque ... Revue de la Banque [*A publication*]
Rev Bar ...... Revue du Barreau [*A publication*]
Rev Barreau Que ... Revue. Barreau de Quebec [*A publication*]
Rev Belge ... Revue Belge de Philologie et d'Histoire [*A publication*]
Rev Belge du C ... Revue Belge du Cinema [*A publication*]
Rev Belge Dr Int'l ... Revue Belge de Droit International [*A publication*]
Rev Belge de Droit Internat ... Revue Belge de Droit International [*A publication*]
Rev Belge Hist Mil ... Revue Belge d'Histoire Militaire [*A publication*]
Rev Belge Hist Milit ... Revue Belge d'Histoire Militaire [*A publication*]
Rev Belge Homoeopath ... Revue Belge d'Homoeopathie [*A publication*]
Rev Belge Matieres Plast ... Revue Belge des Matieres Plastiques [*A publication*]
Rev Belge Med Dent ... Revue Belge de Medecine Dentaire [*A publication*]
Rev Belge Pathol Med Exp ... Revue Belge de Pathologie et de Medecine Experimentale [*A publication*]
Rev Belge Phil Hist ... Revue Belge de Philologie et d'Histoire [*A publication*]
Rev Belge Philol Hist ... Revue Belge de Philologie et d'Histoire [*A publication*]
Rev Belge Stat Inf et Rech Oper ... Revue Belge de Statistique, d'Informatique, et de Recherche Operationnelle
Rev Belge Transp ... Revue Belge des Transports [*Belgium*] [*A publication*]
Rev Belg Pathol Med Exp ... Revue Belge de Pathologie et de Medecine Experimentale [*A publication*]
Rev Bel Ph ... Revue Belge de Philologie et d'Histoire [*A publication*]
Rev Bened.. Revue Benedictine [*A publication*]
Rev Bib....... Revista Bibliotecilor [*Bucharest*] [*A publication*]
Rev Bibl ..... Revue Biblique [*A publication*]
Rev Biochem Toxicol ... Reviews in Biochemical Toxicology [*A publication*]
Rev Biol Acad Rep Pop Roumaine ... Revue de Biologie. Academie de la Republique Populaire Roumaine [*A publication*]
Rev Biol (Buchar) ... Revue de Biologie (Bucharest) [*A publication*]
Rev Biol For Limnol ... Revista de Biologia Forestal y Limnologia [*A publication*]
Rev Biol (Lisb) ... Revista de Biologia (Lisbon) [*A publication*]
Rev Biol Mar ... Revista de Biologia Marina [*A publication*]
Rev Biol Med Nucl ... Revista de Biologia y Medicina Nuclear [*A publication*]
Rev Biol Oral ... Revista de Biologia Oral [*A publication*]
Rev Biol Res Aging ... Review of Biological Research in Aging [*A publication*]
Rev Biol Trop ... Revista de Biologia Tropical [*A publication*]
Rev Biol Urug ... Revista de Biologia del Uruguay [*A publication*]
Rev Bio-Math ... Revue de Bio-Mathematique [*A publication*]
Rev Bl Pol.. Review of Black Political Economy [*A publication*]
RevBN .... Revista de Bibliografia Nacional [*Madrid*] [*A publication*]
Rev Bois Appl ... Revue du Bois et de Ses Applications [*A publication*]
Rev Bolsa Cereal ... Revista. Bolsa de Cereales [*A publication*]
Rev Bolsa Comer Rosario ... Revista. Bolsa de Comercio de Rosario [*A publication*]

Rev Bot Appl Agric Trop ... Revue de Botanique Appliquee et d'Agriculture Tropicale [*A publication*]
Rev Bot Appl Agr Trop ... Revue de Botanique Appliquee et d'Agriculture Tropicale [*A publication*]
Rev Bra Ec ... Revista Brasileira de Economia [*A publication*]
Rev Bras Anal Clin ... Revista Brasileira de Analises Clinicas [*A publication*]
Rev Bras Anestesiol ... Revista Brasileira de Anestesiologia [*A publication*]
Rev Bras Armazenamento ... Revista Brasileira de Armazenamento [*A publication*]
Rev Bras Biol ... Revista Brasileira de Biologia [*A publication*]
Rev Bras Cancerol ... Revista Brasileira de Cancerologia [*A publication*]
Rev Bras Cardiovasc ... Revista Brasileira Cardiovascular [*A publication*]
Rev Bras Cienc Solo ... Revista Brasileira de Ciencia do Solo [*A publication*]
Rev Bras Cir ... Revista Brasileira de Cirurgia [*A publication*]
Rev Bras Cirurg ... Revista Brasileira de Cirurgia [*A publication*]
Rev Bras Clin Ter ... Revista Brasileira de Clinica e Terapeutica [*A publication*]
Rev Bras Defic Ment ... Revista Brasileira de Deficiencia Mental [*A publication*]
Rev Bras Enferm ... Revista Brasileira de Enfermagem [*A publication*]
Rev Bras Eng Quim ... Revista Brasileira de Engenharia Quimica [*A publication*]
Rev Bras Ent ... Revista Brasileira de Entomologia [*A publication*]
Rev Bras Entomol ... Revista Brasileira de Entomologia [*A publication*]
Rev Bras Fis ... Revista Brasileira de Fisica [*A publication*]
Rev Bras Gastroenterol ... Revista Brasileira de Gastroenterologia [*A publication*]
Rev Bras Genet ... Revista Brasileira de Genetica [*A publication*]
Rev Bras Geocienc ... Revista Brasileira de Geociencias [*A publication*]
Rev Bras Geogr ... Revista Brasileira de Geografia [*A publication*]
Rev Brasil Geogr ... Revista Brasileira de Geografia [*A publication*]
Rev Brasil Quim ... Revista Brasileira de Quimica [*A publication*]
Rev Bras Leprol ... Revista Brasileira de Leprologia [*A publication*]
Rev Bras Malariol Doencas Trop ... Revista Brasileira de Malariologia e Doencas Tropicais [*A publication*]
Rev Bras Malariol Doencas Trop Publ Avulsas ... Revista Brasileira de Malariologia e Doencas Tropicais. Publicacoes Avulsas [*A publication*]
Rev Bras Med ... Revista Brasileira de Medicina [*A publication*]
Rev Bras Odont ... Revista Brasileira de Odontologia [*A publication*]
Rev Bras Odontol ... Revista Brasileira de Odontologia [*A publication*]
Rev Bras Oftalmol ... Revista Brasileira de Oftalmologia [*A publication*]
Rev Bras Patol Clin ... Revista Brasileira de Patologia Clinica [*A publication*]
Rev Bras Pesqui Med Biol ... Revista Brasileira de Pesquisas Medicas e Biologicas [*A publication*]
Rev Bras Psiquiatr ... Revista Brasileira de Psiquiatria [*A publication*]
Rev Bras Quim (Sao Paulo) ... Revista Brasileira de Quimica (Sao Paulo) [*A publication*]
Rev Bras Reprod Anim ... Revista Brasileira de Reproducao Animal [*A publication*]
Rev Bras Tecnol ... Revista Brasileira de Tecnologia [*A publication*]
Rev Bras Tuberc Doencas Torac ... Revista Brasileira de Tuberculose e Doencas Toracicas [*A publication*]
Rev Bras Zool ... Revista Brasileira de Zoologia [*A publication*]
Rev Bryol Lichenol ... Revue Bryologique et Lichenologique [*A publication*]
Rev Bulg Geol Soc ... Review. Bulgarian Geological Society [*A publication*]
Rev Bus Econ Res ... Review of Business and Economic Research [*A publication*]
RevC.......... Revista Camoniana [*Sao Paulo*] [*A publication*]
Rev C Abo PR ... Revista. Colegio de Abogados de Puerto Rico [*A publication*]
Rev C Abo PR ... Revista de Derecho. Colegio de Abogados de Puerto Rico [*A publication*] (DLA)
Rev Cafetalera (Guatem) ... Revista Cafetalera (Guatemala) [*A publication*]
Rev Cafetera Colomb ... Revista Cafetera de Colombia [*A publication*]
Rev Can...... Revue Canadienne [*Quebec*] [*A publication*] (DLA)
Rev Canadienne Geographie ... Revue Canadienne de Geographie [*A publication*]
Rev Can Bio ... Revue Canadienne de Biologie [*A publication*]
Rev Can Biochim Biol Cell ... Revue Canadienne de Biochimie et Biologie Cellulaire [*A publication*]
Rev Can Biol ... Revue Canadienne de Biologie [*A publication*]
Rev Can Biol Exp ... Revue Canadienne de Biologie Experimentale [*A publication*]
Rev Can D Fam ... Revue Canadienne de Droit Familial [*A publication*] (DLA)
Rev Can Dr Com ... Revue Canadienne de Droit Communautaire [*A publication*] (DLA)
Rev Can Econ Publique Coop Can J Public Coop Econ ... Revue Canadienne d'Economie Publique et Cooperative. Canadian Journal of Public and Cooperative Economy [*A publication*]
Rev Can Gen Electr ... Revue Canadienne de Genie Electrique [*Canada*] [*A publication*]
Rev Can Med Comp ... Revue Canadienne de Medecine Comparee [*A publication*]
Rev Can Psychol ... Revue Canadienne de Psychologie [*A publication*]
Rev Can Sante Publique ... Revue Canadienne de Sante Publique [*A publication*]
Rev Can Sci Comportement ... Revue Canadienne des Sciences du Comportement [*A publication*]
Rev Can Sci Sol ... Revue Canadienne de la Science du Sol [*A publication*]

Rev Cas ...... Revenue Cases [*A publication*] (DLA)
Rev Cas (Ind) ... Revised Cases [*India*] [*A publication*] (DLA)
Rev Catarinense Odontol ... Revista Catarinense de Odontologie [*A publication*]
Rev d Caucho ... Revista del Caucho [*A publication*]
Rev C & C Rep ... Revenue, Civil, and Criminal Reporter [*Calcutta*] [*A publication*] (DLA)
Rev CENIC Cienc Biol ... Revista CENIC [*Centro Nacional de Investigaciones Científicas*]. Ciencias Biologicas [*A publication*]
Rev CENIC Cienc Fis ... Revista CENIC [*Centro Nacional de Investigaciones Científicas*]. Ciencias Fisicas [*Cuba*] [*A publication*]
Rev Cent Cienc Biomed Univ Fed Santa Maria ... Revista. Centro de Ciencias Biomedicas. Universidade Federal de Santa Maria [*A publication*]
Rev Cent Cienc Rurais ... Revista. Centro de Ciencias Rurais [*A publication*]
Rev Cent Ed ... Revista. Centro de Estudios Educativos [*A publication*]
Rev Cent Estud Cabo Verde Ser Cienc Biol ... Revista. Centro de Estudos de Cabo Verde. Serie de Ciencias Biologicas [*A publication*]
Rev Cent Nac Patol Anim ... Revista. Centro Nacional de Patologia Animal [*A publication*]
Rev Centr Estud Med Vet ... Revista. Centro de Estudiantes de Medicina Veterinaria [*A publication*]
Rev Centroam Nutr Cienc Aliment ... Revista Centroamericana de Nutricion y Ciencias de Alimentos [*A publication*]
Rev Centro Estud Agronom y Vet Univ Buenos Aires ... Revista. Centro de Estudiantes de Agronomia y Veterinaria. Universidad de Buenos Aires [*A publication*]
Rev Ceres ... Revista Ceres [*A publication*]
Rev CETHEDEC ... Revue. Centre d'Etudes Theoriques de la Detection et des Communications [*A publication*]
Rev CETHEDEC Cahier ... Revue. Centre d'Etudes Theoriques de la Detection et des Communications. Cahier [*Paris*] [*A publication*]
Rev C Genie Civil Constr ... Revue C. Genie Civil. Construction [*A publication*]
Rev Chapingo ... Revista Chapingo [*A publication*]
Rev Chil Anest ... Revista Chilena de Anestesia [*A publication*]
Rev Chilena Ing ... Revista Chilena de Ingenieria [*A publication*]
Rev Chil Entomol ... Revista Chilena de Entomologia [*A publication*]
Rev Chil Hist Nat ... Revista Chilena de Historia Natural [*A publication*]
Rev Chil Obstet Ginecol ... Revista Chilena de Obstetricia y Ginecologia [*A publication*]
Rev Chil Ortop Traum ... Revista Chilena de Ortopedia y Traumatologia [*A publication*]
Rev Chil Pediatr ... Revista Chilena de Pediatria [*A publication*]
Rev Chim ... Revista de Chimie [*A publication*]
Rev Chim Acad Repub Pop Roum ... Revue de Chimie. Academie de la Republique Populaire Roumaine [*Romania*] [*A publication*]
Rev Chim (Bucharest) ... Revista de Chimie (Bucharest) [*A publication*]
Rev Chim Mi ... Revue de Chimie Minerale [*A publication*]
Rev Chim Miner ... Revue de Chimie Minerale [*France*] [*A publication*]
Rev Chir ..... Revista de Chirurgie. Stomatologie [*A publication*]
Rev Chir Oncol Radiol ORL Oftalmol Stomatol ... Revista de Chirurgie, Oncologie, Radiologie, ORL, Oftalmologie, Stomatologie [*A publication*]
Rev Chir Oncol Radiol ORL Oftalmol Stomatol Ser Chir ... Revista de Chirurgie, Oncologie, Radiologie, ORL, Oftalmologie, Stomatologie. Seria Chirurgie [*A publication*]
Rev Chir Oncol Radiol ORL Oftalmol Stomatol Ser Radiol ... Revista de Chirurgie, Oncologie, Radiologie, ORL, Oftalmologie, Stomatologie. Seria Radiologie [*A publication*]
Rev Chir Or ... Revue de Chirurgie Orthopedique et Reparatrice de l'Appareil Moteur [*A publication*]
Rev Chir Orthop ... Revue de Chirurgie Orthopedique et Reparatrice de l'Appareil Moteur [*A publication*]
Rev Cie Gen Electr ... Review of Compagnie Generale d'Electricite [*France*] [*A publication*]
Rev Cienc ... Revista de Ciencias [*Lima*] [*A publication*]
Rev Cienc Agrar ... Revista de Ciencias Agrarias [*A publication*]
Rev Cienc Agron ... Revista de Ciencias Agronomicas [*A publication*]
Rev Cienc Agron Ser A ... Revista de Ciencias Agronomicas. Serie A [*A publication*]
Rev Cienc Agron Ser B ... Revista de Ciencias Agronomicas. Serie B [*A publication*]
Rev Cienc Apl ... Revista de Ciencia Aplicada [*A publication*]
Rev Cienc Apl (Madrid) ... Revista de Ciencias Aplicadas (Madrid) [*A publication*]
Rev Cienc Biol ... Revista de Ciencias Biologicas [*A publication*]
Rev Cienc Biol (Belem) ... Revista de Ciencias Biologicas (Belem) [*A publication*]
Rev Cienc Biol (Havana) ... Revista de Ciencias Biologicas (Havana) [*A publication*]
Rev Cienc Biol Ser A (Lourenco Marques) ... Revista de Ciencias Biologicas. Serie A (Lourenco Marques) [*A publication*]
Rev Cienc Biol Ser B (Lourenco Marques) ... Revista de Ciencias Biologicas. Serie B (Lourenco Marques) [*A publication*]
Rev Cienc Mat Univ Lourenco Marques ... Revista de Ciencias Matematicas. Universidade de Lourenco Marques [*A publication*]
Rev Cienc Med (Lourenco Marques) ... Revista de Ciencias Medicas. Serie A (Lourenco Marques) [*A publication*]

Rev Cienc Med Ser A (Lourenco Marques) ... Revista de Ciencias Medicas. Serie A (Lourenco Marques) [*A publication*]
Rev Cienc Med Ser B (Lourenco Marques) ... Revista de Ciencias Medicas. Serie B (Lourenco Marques) [*A publication*]
Rev Cienc Psicol Neurol (Lima) ... Revista de Ciencias Psicologicas y Neurologicas (Lima) [*A publication*]
Rev Cienc Quim ... Revista de Ciencias Quimicas [*A publication*]
Rev Cienc Univ Nac Mayor San Marcos ... Revista de Ciencias. Universidad Nacional Mayor de San Marcos [*A publication*]
Rev Cienc Vet ... Revista de Ciencias Veterinarias [*A publication*]
Rev Cien Econ ... Revista de Ciencias Economicas [*A publication*]
Rev Cient CASL ... Revista Cientifica. CASL [*Centro Academico Sarmento Leite*] [*A publication*]
Rev Cient Invest Mus Hist Nat San Rafael (Mendoza) ... Revista Cientifica de Investigaciones del Museo de Historia Natural de San Rafael (Mendoza) [*A publication*]
Rev Cien Vet ... Revista de Ciencias Veterinarias [*A publication*]
Rev Ci (Lima) ... Revista de Ciencias (Lima) [*A publication*]
Rev Ci Mat Univ Lourenco Marques ... Revista de Ciencias Matematicas. Universidade de Lourenco Marques [*A publication*]
Rev Ci Mat Univ Lourenco Marques Ser A ... Revista de Ciencias Matematicas. Universidade de Lourenco Marques. Serie A [*A publication*]
Rev Cinema ... Revue du Cinema/Image et Son. Ecran [*A publication*]
Rev Cir .... Revista de Cirugia [*A publication*]
Rev Circ Argent Odontol ... Revista. Circulo Argentino de Odontologia [*A publication*]
Rev Circ Eng Mil ... Revista. Circulo de Engenharia Militar [*Brazil*] [*A publication*]
Rev Circ Odontol Cordoba ... Revista del Circulo Odontologico de Cordoba [*A publication*]
Rev Circ Odontol Sur ... Revista. Circulo Odontologico del Sur [*A publication*]
Rev Cir (Mex) ... Revista de Cirugia (Mexico) [*A publication*]
Rev Cir Urug ... Revista de Cirugia del Uruguay [*A publication*]
Rev Civ Code ... Revised Civil Code [*A publication*] (DLA)
Rev Civ St .. Revised Civil Statutes [*A publication*] (DLA)
Rev Clin Basic Pharm ... Reviews in Clinical and Basic Pharmacology [*A publication*]
Rev Clin Basic Pharmacol ... Reviews in Clinical and Basic Pharmacology [*A publication*]
Rev Clin Esp ... Revista Clinica Espanola [*Spain*] [*A publication*]
Rev Clin Esp Eur Med ... Revista Clinica Espanola. Europa Medica [*A publication*]
Rev Clin Inst Matern (Lisb) ... Revista Clinica. Instituto Maternal (Lisbon) [*A publication*]
Rev Clin Med ... Revista de Clinica Medica [*A publication*]
Rev Clin Sao Paulo ... Revista Clinica de Sao Paulo [*A publication*]
Rev Coat Corros ... Reviews on Coatings and Corrosion [*A publication*]
Rev Code Civ Proc ... Revised Code of Civil Procedure [*A publication*] (DLA)
Rev Code Cr Proc ... Revised Code of Criminal Procedure [*A publication*] (DLA)
Rev Col Med Guatem ... Revista. Colegio Medico de Guatemala [*A publication*]
Rev Col Nac Enferm ... Revista. Colegio Nacional de Enfermeras [*A publication*]
Rev Colomb Cienc Quimico-Farm ... Revista Colombiana de Ciencias Quimico-Farmaceuticas [*A publication*]
Rev Colomb Fis ... Revista Colombiana de Fisica [*A publication*]
Rev Colombiana Mat ... Revista Colombiana de Matematicas [*A publication*]
Rev Colomb Obstet Ginecol ... Revista Colombiana de Obstetricia y Ginecologia [*A publication*]
Rev Colomb Pediatr Pueric ... Revista Colombiana de Pediatria y Puericultura [*A publication*]
Rev Col Quim Ing Quim Costa Rica ... Revista. Colegio de Quimicos e Ingenieros Quimicos de Costa Rica [*A publication*]
REVCOM ... Revolutionary Committee [*People's Republic of China*]
Rev Comm ... Revue Communale [*A publication*]
Rev Commer ... Revue Commerce [*A publication*]
REVCON .. Review Conference
Rev Confed Med Panam ... Revista. Confederacion Medica Panamericana [*A publication*]
Rev Conserve ... Revue de la Conserve [*France*] [*A publication*]
Rev Conserve Aliment Mod ... Revue de la Conserve. Alimentation Moderne [*A publication*]
Rev Conserve Fr Outre-Mer ... Revue de la Conserve de France et d'Outre-Mer [*A publication*]
Rev Conserve Fr Union Fr ... Revue de la Conserve de France et de l'Union Francaise [*A publication*]
Rev Consor Cent Agr Manabi ... Revista. Consorcio de Centros Agricolas de Manabi [*A publication*]
Rev Cons Rectores Univ Chilenas ... Revista. Consejo de Rectores. Universidades Chilenas [*A publication*]
Rev Contemp L ... Review of Contemporary Law [*A publication*] (DLA)
Rev Cont L ... Review of Contemporary Law [*A publication*]
Rev Coroz ... Revista de Coroziune [*Romania*] [*A publication*]
Rev Corps Sante Armees ... Revue des Corps de Sante des Armees [*A publication*]
Rev Corros Prot Mater ... Revista de Corrosao e Proteccao de Materiais [*A publication*]
Rev Cr Code ... Revised Criminal Code [*A publication*] (DLA)

Rev CREA (Asoc Argent Consorcios Reg Exp Agric) ... Revista. CREA (Asociacion Argentina de Consorcios Regionales de Experimentacion Agricola) [*A publication*]
Rev Crestera Anim ... Revista de Crestera Animalelor [*A publication*]
Rev Criad ... Revista dos Criadores [*A publication*]
Rev Criadores ... Revista dos Criadores [*A publication*]
Rev Crit ...... Revue Critique de Legislation et de Jurisprudence de Canada [*A publication*] (DLA)
Rev Crit de Droit Internat Prive ... Revue Critique de Droit International Prive [*A publication*]
Rev Crit de Jurispr Belge ... Revue Critique de Jurisprudence Belge [*A publication*]
Rev Crit L .. Revista de Critica Literaria Latinoamericana [*A publication*]
Rev Crit de Leg ... Revue Critique de Legislation [*Paris*] [*A publication*] (DLA)
Rev Crit de Legis et Jur ... Revue Critique de Legislation et de Jurisprudence [*Montreal*] [*A publication*] (DLA)
Rev C Tijdschr Civ Tech Genie Civ ... Revue C. Tijdschrift Civiele Techniek. Genie Civil [*A publication*]
Rev Cubana Cardiol ... Revista Cubana de Cardiologia [*A publication*]
Rev Cubana Cienc Agric ... Revista Cubana de Ciencia Agricola [*A publication*]
Rev Cubana Cienc Vet ... Revista Cubana de Ciencias Veterinarias [*A publication*]
Rev Cubana Cir ... Revista Cubana de Cirugia [*A publication*]
Rev Cubana de Derecho ... Revista Cubana de Derecho [*Havana, Cuba*] [*A publication*] (DLA)
Rev Cubana Enferm ... Revista Cubana de Enfermeria [*A publication*]
Rev Cubana Estomatol ... Revista Cubana de Estomatologia [*A publication*]
Rev Cubana Fis ... Revista Cubana de Fisica [*A publication*]
Rev Cubana Hig Epidemiol ... Revista Cubana de Higiene y Epidemiologia [*A publication*]
Rev Cubana Invest Biomed ... Revista Cubana de Investigaciones Biomedicas [*A publication*]
Rev Cubana Lab Clin ... Revista Cubana de Laboratorio Clinico [*A publication*]
Rev Cubana Med ... Revista Cubana de Medicina [*A publication*]
Rev Cubana Med Trop ... Revista Cubana de Medicina Tropical [*A publication*]
Rev Cubana Oftal ... Revista Cubana de Oftalmologia [*A publication*]
Rev Cubana Pediatr ... Revista Cubana de Pediatria [*A publication*]
Rev Cubana Reprod Anim ... Revista Cubana de Reproduccion Animal [*A publication*]
Rev Cub Cienc Vet ... Revista Cubana de Ciencias Veterinarias [*A publication*]
REVCUR ... Reverse Current (AAG)
Rev Current Activities Tech Ed ... Review of Current Activities in Technical Education [*A publication*] (APTA)
Rev Cytol Biol Veg ... Revue de Cytologie et de Biologie Vegetales [*France*] [*A publication*]
Rev Cytol Biol Veg Bot ... Revue de Cytologie et de Biologie Vegetales -La Botaniste [*A publication*]
Rev Czech Med ... Review of Czechoslovak Medicine [*A publication*]
REVD .... Reverend (ROG)
Rev'd .... Reversed [*Legal term*] (DLA)
Rev Data Sci Resour ... Reviews of Data on Science Resources [*United States*] [*A publication*]
Rev Data Sci Resour Natl Sci Found ... Reviews of Data on Science Resources. National Sciences Foundation [*A publication*]
Rev Def Natl ... Revue de Defense Nationale [*France*] [*A publication*]
Rev Deform Behav Mater ... Reviews on the Deformation Behavior of Materials [*A publication*]
Rev Dent Liban ... Revue Dentaire Libanaise [*A publication*]
Rev Dent (San Salv) ... Revista Dental (San Salvador) [*A publication*]
Rev Dent (St Domingo) ... Revista Dental (Santo Domingo) [*A publication*]
Rev de Derecho y Cienc Polit ... Revista de Derecho y Ciencias Politicas. Organo de la Facultad de Derecho. Universidad Nacional Mayor de San Marcos [*A publication*]
Rev de Derecho Esp y Amer ... Revista de Derecho Espanol y Americano [*Madrid, Spain*] [*A publication*] (DLA)
Rev de Derecho Internac y Cienc Diplom ... Revista de Derecho Internacional y Ciencias Diplomaticas [*A publication*]
Rev de Derecho Jurispr y Admin ... La Revista de Derecho, Jurisprudencia, y Administracion [*A publication*] (DLA)
Rev de Derecho Jurispr y Cienc Soc ... Revista de Derecho, Jurisprudencia, y Ciencias Sociales y Gaceta de los Tribunales [*A publication*] (DLA)
Rev de Derecho Publ ... Revista de Derecho Publico. Universidad de Chile. Escuela de Derecho [*A publication*]
Rev Deux Mondes ... Revue des Deux Mondes [*A publication*]
REV DEV .. Revolutionary Development [*South Vietnam*]
Rev Diagn Biol ... Revista de Diagnostico Biologico [*A publication*]
Rev de Direito Adm (Coimbra) ... Revista de Direito Administrativo (Coimbra) [*A publication*]
Rev de Direito Adm (Rio De Janeiro) ... Revista de Direito Administrativo (Rio De Janeiro) [*A publication*]
Rev Dir Gen Geol Minas (Ecuador) ... Revista. Direccion General de Geologia y Minas (Ecuador) [*A publication*]
Rev Doc ...... Revue de la Documentation [*A publication*]
Rev D P ...... Revista de Derecho Puertorriqueno [*A publication*]
Rev DPR .... Revista de Derecho Puertorriqueno [*A publication*]

Rev du Dr ... Revue du Droit [*Quebec*] [*A publication*] (DLA)
Rev Dr Contemp ... Revue de Droit Contemporain ou des Juristes Democrates [*A publication*]
Rev Dr Intern et Dr Comp ... Revue de Droit International et de Droit Compare [*A publication*]
Rev de Dr Int'l de Sci Dip et Pol ... Revue de Droit International de Sciences Diplomatiques et Politiques [*A publication*]
Rev de Droit ... Revue de Droit. Universite de Sherbrooke [*A publication*]
Rev de Droit Canonique ... Revue de Droit Canonique [*A publication*]
Rev de Droit Compare ... Revue de Droit International et de Droit Compare [*A publication*]
Rev de Droit Contemp ... Revue de Droit Contemporain [*Brussels, Belgium*] [*A publication*] (DLA)
Rev de Droit Hong ... Revue de Droit Hongrois [*A publication*] (DLA)
Rev de Droit Internat et de Droit Compare ... Revue de Droit International et de Droit Compare [*A publication*]
Rev de Droit Internat de Sci Diplom ... Revue de Droit International de Sciences Diplomatiques et Politiques [*A publication*]
Rev Droit Int'l Moyen-Orient ... Revue de Droit International pour le Moyen-Orient [*A publication*] (DLA)
Rev de Droit Penal et de Criminologie ... Revue de Droit Penal et de Criminologie [*A publication*]
Rev de Droit Penal Mil et de Droit de la Guerre ... Revue de Droit Penal Militaire et de Droit de la Guerre [*A publication*] (DLA)
Rev Droit Penal Militaire et Dr de la Guerre ... Revue de Droit Penal Militaire et de Droit de la Guerre [*A publication*] (DLA)
Rev Droit Public Sci Polit ... Revue du Droit Public et de la Science Politique en France et a l'Etranger [*A publication*]
Rev du Droit Publ et de la Sci Polit en France ... Revue du Droit Public et de la Science Politique en France et a l'Etranger [*A publication*]
Rev des Droits de l'Homme ... Revue des Droits de l'Homme. Droit International et Droit Compare [*A publication*]
Rev de Droit Unif ... Revue de Droit Uniforme [*A publication*] (DLA)
Rev de Droit Uniforme ... Revue de Droit Uniforme [*A publication*] (DLA)
Rev Droit U Sher ... Revue de Droit. Universite de Sherbrooke [*A publication*]
Rev Dr Soc ... Revue de Droit Social [*A publication*]
Rev Drug Metabol Drug Interact ... Reviews on Drug Metabolism and Drug Interactions [*A publication*]
Rev D US ... Revue de Droit. Universite de Sherbrooke [*A publication*] (DLA)
Rev E .... Revue E. Electricite, Electrotechnique Generale, Courants Forts, et Applications [*Belgium*] [*A publication*]
Rev East Med Sci ... Review of Eastern Medical Sciences [*A publication*]
Rev Eccl ..... Revue d'Histoire Ecclesiastique [*A publication*]
Rev Ecol Biol Sol ... Revue d'Ecologie et de Biologie du Sol [*A publication*]
Rev Ecol BS ... Revue d'Ecologie et de Biologie du Sol [*A publication*]
Rev Ecol Terre Vie ... Revue d'Ecologie; la Terre et la Vie [*A publication*]
Rev Econ .... Revue Economique [*A publication*]
Rev Econ Co ... Review of the Economic Conditions in Italy [*A publication*]
Rev Econom Statist ... Review of Economics and Statistics [*A publication*]
Rev Econom Stud ... Review of Economic Studies [*A publication*]
Rev Economy Emplyment ... Review of the Economy and Employment [*A publication*]
Rev Econ Polit ... Revue d'Economie Politique [*A publication*]
Rev Econ S ... Review of Economic Studies [*A publication*]
Rev Econ Soc ... Revue Economique et Sociale [*A publication*]
Rev Econ St ... Review of Economics and Statistics [*A publication*]
Rev Econ Stat ... Review of Economic Statistics [*A publication*]
Rev Econ Stat ... Review of Economics and Statistics [*A publication*]
Rev Econ Stud ... Review of Economic Studies [*A publication*]
Rev Ecuat Entomol Parasitol ... Revista Ecuatoriana de Entomologia y Parasitologia [*A publication*]
Rev Ecuat Ent Parasit ... Revista Ecuatoriana de Entomologia y Parasitologia [*A publication*]
Rev Ecuat Hig Med ... Revista Ecuatoriana de Higiene y Medicina Tropical [*A publication*]
Rev Ecuat Hig Med Trop ... Revista Ecuatoriana de Higiene y Medicina Tropical [*A publication*]
Rev Ecuat Med Cienc Biol ... Revista Ecuatoriana de Medicina y Ciencias Biologicas [*A publication*]
Rev Ecuat Pediatr ... Revista Ecuatoriana de Pediatria [*A publication*]
Rev Ed .... Revista de Educacion [*A publication*]
Rev Educational Res ... Review of Educational Research [*A publication*]
Rev Educ Re ... Review of Educational Research [*A publication*]
Rev Educ Res ... Review of Educational Research [*A publication*]
Rev E Elec Electrotech Gen ... Revue E. Electricite, Electrotechnique Generale, Courants Forts, et Applications [*A publication*]
Rev Eg .... Revue d'Egyptologie [*A publication*]
Rev Egypt ... Revue d'Egyptologie [*A publication*]
Rev Egypt de Droit Internat ... Revue Egyptienne de Droit International [*A publication*]
Rev Egyptol ... Revue Egyptologique [*A publication*]
REVEL ...... Reverberation Elimination
Rev El Comm ... Review. Electrical Communication Laboratory [*Tokyo*] [*A publication*]
Rev Elec Commun Lab (Tokyo) ... Review. Electrical Communication Laboratory (Tokyo) [*A publication*]
Rev Electr .. Revista Electricidade [*Portugal*] [*A publication*]
Rev Electr Commun Lab ... Review. Electrical Communication Laboratory [*A publication*]

Rev Electr Commun Lab (Tokyo) ... Review. Electrical Communication Laboratory (Tokyo) [*A publication*]
Rev Electr & Mec ... Revue d'Electricite et de Mecanique [*A publication*]
Rev Electr Mecan ... Revue d'Electricite et de Mecanique [*France*] [*A publication*]
Rev Electroencephalogr Neurophysiol Clin ... Revue d'Electroencephalographie et de Neurophysiologie Clinique [*A publication*]
Rev Electrotec ... Revista Electrotecnica [*A publication*]
Rev Electrotec (Buenos Aires) ... Revista Electrotecnica (Buenos Aires) [*A publication*]
Rev Electrotech Energ Acad Repub Pop Roum ... Revue Electrotechnique et Energetique. Academie de la Republique Populaire Roumaine [*Romania*] [*A publication*]
Rev Elevage ... Revue de l'Elevage. Betail et Basse Cour [*A publication*]
Rev Elev Med Vet Pays Trop ... Revue d'Elevage et de Medecine Veterinaire des Pays Tropicaux [*A publication*]
Rev El Mecan ... Revue d'Electricite et de Mecanique [*A publication*]
Rev Empresas Publicas Medellin ... Revista Empresas Publicas de Medellin [*Columbia*] [*A publication*]
Rev Energ .. Revue de l'Energie [*A publication*]
Rev Energie ... Revue de l'Energie [*A publication*]
Rev Energ Primaire ... Revue de l'Energie Primaire [*Belgium*] [*A publication*]
Rev Enferm (Lisboa) ... Revista de Enfermagem (Lisboa) [*A publication*]
Rev Enferm Nov Dimens ... Revista Enfermagem em Novas Dimensoes [*A publication*]
Rev Eng Geol ... Reviews in Engineering Geology [*United States*] [*A publication*]
Rev Engl St ... Review of English Studies [*A publication*]
Rev Engl Stu ... Review of English Studies [*A publication*]
Rev Engl Stud ... Review of English Studies [*A publication*]
Rev Enr ...... Revue de l'Enregistrement et des Douanes [*A publication*]
Rev Ens Phil ... Revue de l'Enseignement Philosophique [*A publication*]
Rev Ens Sup ... Revue de l'Enseignement Superieur [*A publication*]
Rev Entomol Mocambique ... Revista de Entomologia de Mocambique [*A publication*]
Rev Entomol Mocambique Supl ... Revista de Entomologia de Mocambique. Suplemento [*A publication*]
Rev Entomol (Rio De J) ... Revista de Entomologia (Rio De Janeiro) [*A publication*]
Rev Environ Health ... Reviews on Environmental Health [*A publication*]
Rev Environ Toxicol ... Reviews in Environmental Toxicology [*A publication*]
Rev Ep .... Revue Epigraphique [*A publication*]
Rev Epidem ... Revue d'Epidemiologie, Medecine Sociale, et Sante Publique [*Later, Revue d'Epidemiologie et de Sante Publique*] [*A publication*]
Rev Epidemiol Med Soc Sante Publique ... Revue d'Epidemiologie, Medecine Sociale, et Sante Publique [*Later, Revue d'Epidemiologie et de Sante Publique*] [*A publication*]
Rev Epidemiol Sante Publique ... Revue d'Epidemiologie et de Sante Publique [*A publication*]
RevEpigr .... Revue Epigraphique [*A publication*]
RevER .... Revue des Etudes Roumaines [*A publication*]
REVERB ... Reverberator [*Automotive engineering*]
REVERSY ... Reversionary (ROG)
Rev Esc Agron Vet Univ Rio Grande Do Sul (Porto Alegre) ... Revista. Escola de Agronomia e Veterinaria da Universidade do Rio Grande Do Sul (Porto Alegre) [*A publication*]
Rev Esc Enferm USP ... Revista. Escola de Enfermagem. Universidade de Sao Paulo [*A publication*]
Rev Esc Minas ... Revista. Escola de Minas [*A publication*]
Rev Esc Odontol Tucuman ... Revista. Escuela de Odontologia. Universidad Nacional de Tucuman. Facultad de Medicina [*A publication*]
Rev Esp Anest ... Revista Espanola de Anestesiologia [*A publication*]
Rev Esp Anestesiol ... Revista Espanola de Anestesiologia [*A publication*]
Rev Esp Anestesiol Reanim ... Revista Espanola de Anestesiologia y Reanimacion [*A publication*]
Rev Espan Fisiol ... Revista Espanola de Fisiologia [*A publication*]
Rev Espanola Micropaleontologia ... Revista Espanola de Micropaleontologia [*A publication*]
Rev Esp Antropol Amer ... Revista Espanola de Antropologia Americana [*A publication*]
Rev Esp Cardiol ... Revista Espanola de Cardiologia [*A publication*]
Rev Esp Der Can ... Revista Espanola de Derecho Canonico [*A publication*]
Rev Esp de Derecho Canonico ... Revista Espanola de Derecho Canonico [*A publication*]
Rev Esp de Derecho Internac ... Revista Espanola de Derecho Internacional [*A publication*]
Rev Esp de Derecho Mil ... Revista Espanola de Derecho Militar [*A publication*]
Rev Esp Doc Cient ... Revista Espanola de Documentacion Cientifica [*A publication*]
Rev Espec... Revista de Especialidades [*A publication*]
Rev Esp Electron ... Revista Espanola de Electronica [*A publication*]
Rev Esp Enferm Apar Dig ... Revista Espanola de las Enfermedades del Aparato Digestivo [*A publication*]
Rev Esp Enferm Apar Dig Nutr ... Revista Espanola de las Enfermedades del Aparato Digestivo y de la Nutricion [*A publication*]
Rev Esp Estomatol ... Revista Espanola de Estomatologia [*A publication*]
Rev Esp Fis ... Revista Espanola de Fisiologia [*A publication*]

Rev Esp Fisiol ... Revista Espanola de Fisiologia [*A publication*]
Rev Esp Lech ... Revista Espanola do Lecheria [*A publication*]
Rev Esp Med Cirug Guerra ... Revista Espanola de Medicina y Cirugia de Guerra [*A publication*]
Rev Esp Micropaleontol ... Revista Espanola de Micropaleontologia [*A publication*]
Rev Esp Obstet Ginecol ... Revista Espanola de Obstetricia y Ginecologia [*A publication*]
Rev Esp Obstet Ginecol Supl ... Revista Espanola de Obstetricia y Ginecologia. Suplemento [*A publication*]
Rev Esp Oncol ... Revista Espanola de Oncologia [*A publication*]
Rev Esp Oto Neu Oft ... Revista Espanola de Oto-Neuro-Oftalmologia y Neurocirugia [*A publication*]
Rev Esp Oto-Neuro-Oftalmol Neurocir ... Revista Espanola de Oto-Neuro-Oftalmologia y Neurocirugia [*A publication*]
Rev Esp Pediatr ... Revista Espanola de Pediatria [*A publication*]
Rev Esp Reum Enferm Osteoartic ... Revista Espanola de Reumatismo y Enfermedades Osteoarticulares [*A publication*]
Rev Esp Tuberc ... Revista Espanola de Tuberculosis [*A publication*]
Rev Est...... Revue de l'Est [*A publication*]
Rev Esth...... Revue d'Esthetique [*A publication*]
Rev Est His ... Revista de Estudios Hispanicos [*A publication*]
Rev Estud Extremenos ... Revista de Estudios Extremenos [*A publication*]
Rev Estud Gerais Univ Mocambique Ser 3 Cienc Med ... Revista de Estudos Gerais Universitarios de Mocambique. Serie 3. Ciencias Medicas [*A publication*]
Rev Et Anc ... Revue des Etudes Anciennes [*A publication*]   (OCD)
Rev Et Armen ... Revue des Etudes Armeniennes [*A publication*]
Rev Et Grec ... Revue des Etudes Grecques [*A publication*]   (OCD)
Rev Et Lat ... Revue des Etudes Latines [*A publication*]   (OCD)
Rev Et SE Eur ... Revue des Etudes Sud-Est Europeennes [*A publication*]
Rev Etud Augustin ... Revue des Etudes Augustiniennes [*A publication*]
Rev Etud Byz ... Revue des Etudes Byzantines [*A publication*]
Rev Etud Comp Est Ouest ... Revue d'Etudes Comparatives Est-Ouest [*A publication*]
Rev Etud Grec ... Revue des Etudes Grecques [*A publication*]
Rev Etud It ... Revue des Etudes Italiennes [*A publication*]
Rev Etud Juives ... Revue des Etudes Juives et Historia Judaica [*A publication*]
Rev Etud Sud Est Eur ... Revue des Etudes Sud-Est Europeennes [*A publication*]
Rev Eur Endocrinol ... Revue Europeenne d'Endocrinologie [*A publication*]
Rev Eur Etud Clin Biol ... Revue Europeenne d'Etudes Cliniques et Biologiques [*France*] [*A publication*]
Rev Europ Papiers Cartons Complexes ... Revue Europeenne des Papiers Cartons-Complexes [*A publication*]
Rev Eur Pomme Terre ... Revue Europeenne de la Pomme de Terre [*A publication*]
Rev Eur Sci Med Pharmacol ... Revue Europeenne pour les Sciences Medicales et Pharmacologiques [*A publication*]
Rev Exist Psychol Psychiat ... Review of Existential Psychology and Psychiatry [*A publication*]
Rev Exist Psych Psychiat ... Review of Existential Psychology and Psychiatry [*A publication*]
RevExp ...... Review and Expositor [*A publication*]
Rev Exp Agrar ... Revista de Extension Agraria [*A publication*]
Rev and Expositor ... Review and Expositor [*A publication*]
Rev F.......... Revue Fiscale [*A publication*]
Rev Fac Agrar Minist Educ Univ Nac Cuyo (Mendoza) ... Revista. Facultad de Ciencias Agrarias. Ministerio de Educacion. Universidad Nacional de Cuyo (Mendoza) [*Argentina*] [*A publication*]
Rev Fac Agron Alcance (Maracay) ... Revista. Facultad de Agronomia Alcance (Maracay) [*A publication*]
Rev Fac Agron (Maracay) ... Revista. Facultad de Agronomia (Maracay) [*A publication*]
Rev Fac Agron Univ Cent Venezuela ... Revista. Facultad de Agronomia. Universidad Central de Venezuela [*A publication*]
Rev Fac Agron Univ Fed Rio Grande Sul ... Revista. Faculdade de Agronomia. Universidade Federal do Rio Grande Do Sul [*A publication*]
Rev Fac Agron Univ Nac La Plata ... Revista. Facultad de Agronomia. Universidad Nacional de La Plata [*A publication*]
Rev Fac Agron Univ Repub (Montevideo) ... Revista. Facultad de Agronomia. Universidad de la Republica (Montevideo) [*A publication*]
Rev Fac Agron Vet (Buenos Aires) ... Revista. Facultad de Agronomia y Veterinaria (Buenos Aires) [*A publication*]
Rev Fac Agron Vet Univ B Aires ... Revista. Facultad de Agronomia y Veterinaria. Universidad de Buenos Aires [*A publication*]
Rev Fac Agron Vet Univ Rio Grande Do Sul ... Revista. Faculdade de Agronomia e Veterinaria. Universidade do Rio Grande Do Sul [*A publication*]
Rev Fac Agron Vet Univ Rio Grande Sul ... Revista. Faculdade de Agronomia e Veterinaria. Universidade do Rio Grande Do Sul [*A publication*]
Rev Fac Agron (Zulia Venez) Univ ... Revista. Facultad de Agronomia (Zulia, Venezuela). Universidad [*A publication*]
Rev Fac Cienc Agrar Minist Educ Univ Nac Cuyo (Mendoza) ... Revista. Facultad de Ciencias Agrarias. Ministerio de Educacion. Universidad Nacional de Cuyo (Mendoza) [*A publication*]
Rev Fac Cienc Agrar Univ Nac Cuyo ... Revista. Facultad de Ciencias Agrarias. Universidad Nacional de Cuyo [*A publication*]

Rev Fac Cienc Agr Univ Nac Cuyo ... Revista. Facultad de Ciencias Agrarias. Universidad Nacional de Cuyo [*A publication*]

Rev Fac Cienc 2a Ser A Cienc Mat ... Revista. Faculdade de Ciencias. Universidade de Lisboa. 2a Serie A. Ciencias Matematicas [*Portugal*] [*A publication*]

Rev Fac Cienc Med Buenos Aires ... Revista. Facultad de Ciencias Medicas de Buenos Aires [*A publication*]

Rev Fac Cienc Med Cordoba ... Revista. Facultad de Ciencias Medicas de Cordoba [*A publication*]

Rev Fac Cienc Med Univ Catol Parana ... Revista. Faculdade de Ciencias Medicas. Universidade Catolica do Parana [*A publication*]

Rev Fac Cienc Med Univ Cent Ecuador ... Revista. Facultad de Ciencias Medicas. Universidad Central del Ecuador [*A publication*]

Rev Fac Cienc Med Univ Nac Cordoba ... Revista. Facultad de Ciencias Medicas. Universidad Nacional de Cordoba [*A publication*]

Rev Fac Cienc Med Univ Nac Litoral Rosario ... Revista. Facultad de Ciencias Medicas. Universidad Nacional del Litoral Rosario [*A publication*]

Rev Fac Cienc Med Univ Nac Rosario ... Revista. Facultad de Ciencias Medicas. Universidad Nacional de Rosario [*A publication*]

Rev Fac Cienc Nat Salta Univ Nac Tucuman ... Revista. Facultad de Ciencias Naturales de Salta. Universidad Nacional de Tucuman [*A publication*]

Rev Fac Cienc Quim Univ Nac La Plata ... Revista. Facultad de Ciencias Quimicas. Universidad Nacional de La Plata [*A publication*]

Rev Fac Cienc Univ Coimbra ... Revista. Faculdade de Ciencias. Universidade de Coimbra [*A publication*]

Rev Fac Cienc Univ Lisboa B ... Revista. Faculdade de Ciencias. Universidade de Lisboa. Serie B. Ciencias Fisico-Quimicas [*A publication*]

Rev Fac Cienc Univ Lisboa Ser B ... Revista. Faculdade de Ciencias. Universidade de Lisboa. Serie B. Ciencias Fisico-Quimicas [*A publication*]

Rev Fac Cienc Univ Lisboa Ser C ... Revista. Faculdade de Ciencias. Universidade de Lisboa. Serie C. Ciencias Naturais [*A publication*]

Rev Fac Cienc Univ Lisb Ser C Cienc Nat ... Revista. Faculdade de Ciencias. Universidade de Lisboa. Serie C. Ciencias Naturais [*A publication*]

Rev Fac Cienc Univ Oviedo ... Revista. Facultad de Ciencias. Universidad de Oviedo [*A publication*]

Rev Fac Cienc Vet La Plata ... Revista. Facultad de Ciencias Veterinarias de La Plata [*A publication*]

Rev de la Fac de Derecho (Caraboba) ... Revista. Facultad de Derecho. Universidad de Caraboba [*Valencia, Venezuela*] [*A publication*] (DLA)

Rev de la Fac de Derecho (Caracas) ... Revista. Facultad de Derecho. Universidad Catolica Andres Bello (Caracas) [*A publication*] (DLA)

Rev de la Fac de Derecho y Cienc Soc ... Revista. Facultad de Derecho y Ciencias Sociales [*Montevideo, Uruguay*] [*A publication*] (DLA)

Rev de la Fac de Derecho de Mex ... Revista. Facultad de Derecho de Mexico [*A publication*]

Rev da Fac de Direito (Lisbon) ... Revista. Faculdade de Direito. Universidade de Lisboa (Lisbon) [*A publication*] (DLA)

Rev de Fac de Direito (Sao Paulo) ... Revista. Faculdade de Direito. Universidade de Sao Paulo [*Sao Paulo, Brazil*] [*A publication*] (DLA)

Rev Fac Eng Univ Porto ... Revista. Faculdade de Engenharia. Universidade do Porto [*A publication*]

Rev Fac Farm Bioquim Univ Cent Ecuador ... Revista. Facultad de Farmacia y Bioquimica. Universidad Central del Ecuador [*A publication*]

Rev Fac Farm Bioquim Univ Fed St Maria ... Revista. Faculdade de Farmacia e Bioquimica. Universidade Federal de Santa Maria [*A publication*]

Rev Fac Farm Bioquim Univ Nac Mayor San Marcos ... Revista. Facultad de Farmacia y Bioquimica. Universidad Nacional Mayor de San Marcos [*A publication*]

Rev Fac Farm Bioquim Univ Nac Mayor San Marcos (Lima) ... Revista. Facultad de Farmacia y Bioquimica. Universidad Nacional Mayor de San Marcos (Lima) [*A publication*]

Rev Fac Farm Bioquim Univ Sao Paulo ... Revista. Faculdade de Farmacia e Bioquimica. Universidade de Sao Paulo [*A publication*]

Rev Fac Farm Odontol Araraquara ... Revista. Faculdade de Farmacia e Odontologia de Araraquara [*A publication*]

Rev Fac Farm Odontol Ribeirao Preto ... Revista. Facultade de Farmacia e Odontologia de Ribeirao Preto [*A publication*]

Rev Fac Farm Univ Cent Venez ... Revista. Facultad de Farmacia. Universidad Central de Venezuela [*A publication*]

Rev Fac Ing Quim Univ Nac Litoral ... Revista. Facultad de Ingenieria Quimica. Universidad Nacional del Litoral [*Argentina*] [*A publication*]

Rev Fac Med (Maracaibo) ... Revista. Facultad de Medicina (Maracaibo) [*A publication*]

Rev Fac Med (Mex) ... Revista. Facultad de Medicina (Mexico) [*A publication*]

Rev Fac Med (Tucuman) ... Revista. Facultad de Medicina (Tucuman) [*A publication*]

Rev Fac Med Univ Fed Ceara ... Revista. Faculdade de Medicina. Universidade Federal do Ceara [*A publication*]

Rev Fac Med Univ Fed Santa Maria ... Revista. Faculdade de Medicina. Universidade Federal de Santa Maria [*A publication*]

Rev Fac Med Univ Nac Colomb (Bogota) ... Revista. Facultad de Medicina. Universidad Nacional de Colombia (Bogota) [*A publication*]

Rev Fac Med Vet Univ Nac Mayor San Marcos ... Revista. Facultad de Medicina Veterinaria. Universidad Nacional Mayor de San Marcos [*A publication*]

Rev Fac Med Vet Univ Sao Paulo ... Revista. Faculdade de Medicina Veterinaria. Universidade de Sao Paulo [*A publication*]

Rev Fac Med Vet Zootec (Bogota) ... Revista. Facultad de Medicina, Veterinaria, y Zootecnia (Bogota) [*A publication*]

Rev Fac Med Vet Zootec Univ San Carlos ... Revista. Facultad de Medicina, Veterinaria, y Zootecnia. Universidad de San Carlos [*A publication*]

Rev Fac Med Vet Zootec Univ Sao Paulo ... Revista. Faculdade de Medicina Veterinaria e Zootecnia. Universidade de Sao Paulo [*A publication*]

Rev Fac Med Vet Zoot Univ Nac Colomb ... Revista. Facultad de Medicina, Veterinaria, y Zootecnia. Universidad Nacional de Colombia [*A publication*]

Rev Fac Nac Agron (Medellin) ... Revista. Facultad Nacional de Agronomia (Medellin) [*A publication*]

Rev Fac Nac Agron Univ Antioquia ... Revista. Facultad Nacional de Agronomia. Universidad de Antioquia [*A publication*]

Rev Fac Nac Agron Univ Nac (Colombia) ... Revista. Facultad Nacional de Agronomia. Universidad Nacional (Colombia) [*A publication*]

Rev Fac Odontol Aracatuba ... Revista. Faculdade de Odontologia de Aracatuba [*A publication*]

Rev Fac Odontol (P Alegre) ... Revista. Faculdade de Odontologia (Porto Alegre) [*A publication*]

Rev Fac Odontol Pernambuco ... Revista. Faculdade de Odontologia de Pernambuco [*A publication*]

Rev Fac Odontol Port Alegre ... Revista. Faculdade de Odontologia de Port Alegre [*A publication*]

Rev Fac Odontol Sao Jose Dos Campos ... Revista. Faculdade de Odontologia de Sao Jose Dos Campos [*A publication*]

Rev Fac Odontol Sao Paulo ... Revista. Faculdade de Odontologia. Universidade de Sao Paulo [*A publication*]

Rev Fac Odontol Tucuman ... Revista. Facultad de Odontologia. Universidad Nacional de Tucuman [*A publication*]

Rev Fac Odontol Univ Fed Bahia ... Revista. Faculdade de Odontologia. Universidade Federal da Bahia [*A publication*]

Rev Fac Odontol Univ Nac Colomb ... Revista. Facultade de Odontologia. Universidad Nacional de Colombia [*A publication*]

Rev Fac Odontol Univ Sao Paulo ... Revista. Faculdade de Odontologia. Universidade de Sao Paulo [*A publication*]

Rev Fac Quim Farm Univ Cent Ecuador ... Revista. Facultad de Quimica y Farmacia. Universidad Central del Ecuador [*A publication*]

Rev Fac Quim Ind Agric Univ Nac Litoral ... Revista. Facultad de Quimica Industrial y Agricola. Universidad Nacional del Litoral [*A publication*]

Rev Fac Quim Univ Nac Mayor San Marcos ... Revista. Facultad de Quimica. Universidad Nacional Mayor de San Marcos [*A publication*]

Rev Fac Sci Univ Istanbul C ... Revue. Faculte des Sciences. Universite d'Istanbul. Serie C [*A publication*]

Rev Fac Sci Univ Istanbul Ser B Sci Nat ... Revue. Faculte des Sciences. Universite d'Istanbul. Serie B. Sciences Naturelles [*A publication*]

Rev Fac Sci Univ Istanbul Ser C ... Review. Faculty of Science. University of Istanbul. Series C [*Istanbul Universitesi fen Fakultesi Mecmuasi. Serie C*] [*A publication*]

Rev Faill..... Revue des Faillites, Concordats, et Liquidations [*A publication*]

Rev Farm Bahia ... Revista Farmaceutica da Bahia [*A publication*]

Rev Farm (B Aires) ... Revista Farmaceutica (Buenos Aires) [*A publication*]

Rev Farm Bioquim ... Revista de Farmacia e Bioquimica [*A publication*]

Rev Farm Bioquim Amazonia ... Revista de Farmacia e Bioquimica da Amazonia [*A publication*]

Rev Farm Bioquim Univ Sao Paulo ... Revista de Farmacia e Bioquimica. Universidade de Sao Paulo [*A publication*]

Rev Farm (Bucharest) ... Revista Farmaciei (Bucharest) [*A publication*]

Rev Farm Cuba ... Revista Farmaceutica de Cuba [*A publication*]

Rev Farm Odontol ... Revista de Farmacia e Odontologia [*A publication*]

Rev Farm Peru ... Revista Farmaceutica Peruana [*A publication*]

Rev Farm Quim ... Revista de Farmacia y Quimica [*A publication*]

Rev F de C ... Revue des Fonds de Commerce [*A publication*]

Rev Fed Am Health Syst ... Review. Federation of American Health Systems [*A publication*]

Rev Fed Am Hosp ... Review. Federation of American Hospitals [*A publication*]

Rev Fed Doct Cienc Filos Let (Havana) ... Revista. Federacion de Doctors en Ciencias en Filosofia y Letras (Havana) [*A publication*]

Rev Fed Fr Soc Sci Nat ... Revue. Federation Francaise des Societes de Sciences Naturelles [*A publication*]

Rev Fed Odontol Colomb ... Revista. Federacion Odontologica Colombiana [*A publication*]
Rev Ferment Ind Aliment ... Revue des Fermentations et des Industries Alimentaires [*A publication*]
Rev F Gy Ob ... Revue Francaise de Gynecologie et d'Obstetrique [*A publication*]
Rev Filip Med Farm ... Revista Filipina de Medicina y Farmacia [*A publication*]
Rev Filol Istr Cl ... Revista di Filologia e di Isturzione Classica [*A publication*]
Rev Filosof (Argentina) ... Revista de Filosofia (Argentina) [*A publication*]
Rev Filosof Costa Rica ... Revista de Filosofia. Universidad de Costa Rica [*A publication*]
Rev Filosof (Mexico) ... Revista de Filosofia (Mexico) [*A publication*]
Rev Filosof (Spain) ... Revista de Filosofia (Spain) [*A publication*]
Rev Filoz .... Revista de Filozofie [*A publication*]
Rev Fis .... Revista de Fisica [*A publication*]
Rev Fis Quim Eng ... Revista de Fisica, Quimica, e Engenharia [*A publication*]
Rev Fis Quim Eng Ser A ... Revista de Fisica, Quimica, e Engenharia. Serie A [*A publication*]
Rev FITCE ... Revue FITCE [*Federation des Ingenieurs des Telecommunications de la Communaute Europeenne*] [*A publication*]
Rev Fiz Chim Ser A ... Revista de Fizica si Chimie. Seria A [*A publication*]
Rev Fiz Chim Ser B ... Revista de Fizica si Chimie. Seria B [*A publication*]
Rev Fiziol Norm Patol ... Revista de Fiziologie Normala si Patologica [*A publication*]
Rev Flora Med ... Revista da Flora Medicinai [*A publication*]
Rev Foie ..... Revue du Foie [*A publication*]
Rev Fonderie Mod ... Revue de Fonderie Moderne [*A publication*]
Rev Food Sci Technol (Mysore) ... Reviews in Food Sciences and Technology (Mysore) [*A publication*]
Rev Food Technol (Mysore) ... Reviews in Food Technology (Mysore) [*A publication*]
Rev Forest Venezolana ... Revista Forestal Venezolana [*A publication*]
Rev For Franc ... Revue Forestiere Francaise [*A publication*]
Rev For Fr (Nancy) ... Revue Forestiere Francaise (Nancy) [*A publication*]
Rev For Peru ... Revista Forestal del Peru [*A publication*]
Rev Fort Argent ... Revista Forestal Argentina [*A publication*]
Rev For Venez ... Revista Forestal Venezolana [*A publication*]
Rev Fr Alle ... Revue Francaise d'Allergologie [*Later, Revue Francaise d'Allergologie et d'Immunologie Clinique*] [*A publication*]
Rev Fr Allerg ... Revue Francaise d'Allergie [*A publication*]
Rev Fr Allergol ... Revue Francaise d'Allergologie [*Later, Revue Francaise d'Allergologie et d'Immunologie Clinique*] [*A publication*]
Rev Fr Allergol Immunol Clin ... Revue Francaise d'Allergologie et d'Immunologie Clinique [*A publication*]
Rev Franc Agr ... Revue Francais de l'Agriculture [*A publication*]
Rev Francaise Automat Inform Rech Oper Ser Bleue ... Revue Francaise d'Automatique, d'Informatique, et de Recherche Operationnelle. Serie Bleue [*A publication*]
Rev Francaise Automat Inform Rech Oper Ser Jaune ... Revue Francaise d'Automatique, d'Informatique, et de Recherche Operationnelle. Serie Jaune [*A publication*]
Rev Francaise Automat Inform Rech Oper Ser Rouge Anal Numer ... Revue Francaise d'Automatic, d'Informatique, et de Recherche Operationnelle. Serie Rouge. Analyse Numerique [*A publication*]
Rev Francaise Automat Inform Rech Oper Ser Verte ... Revue Francaise d'Automatique, d'Informatique, et de Recherche Operationnelle. Serie Verte [*A publication*]
Rev Franc de Droit Aer ... Revue Francaise de Droit Aerien [*A publication*]
Rev Franc Phot ... Revue Francaise de Photographie [*A publication*]
Rev Fr Astronaut ... Revue Francaise d'Astronautique [*France*] [*A publication*]
Rev Fr Aut Inf Rech Oper Anal Num ... Revue Francaise d'Automatic, d'Informatique, et de Recherche Operationnelle. Serie Analyse Numerique [*A publication*]
Rev Fr Autom Inf Rech Oper ... Revue Francaise d'Automatique, d'Informatique, et de Recherche Operationnelle [*A publication*]
Rev Fr de C ... Revue Francaise de Communication [*A publication*]
Rev Fr Corps Gras ... Revue Francaise des Corps Gras [*A publication*]
Rev Fr Dommage Corpor ... Revue Francaise du Dommage Corporel [*A publication*]
Rev Fr Electr ... Revue Francaise de l'Electricite [*A publication*]
Rev Fr Endocrinol ... Revue Francaise d'Endocrinologie [*A publication*]
Rev Fr Endocrinol Clin Nutr Metab ... Revue Francaise d'Endocrinologie Clinique, Nutrition, et Metabolisme [*A publication*]
Rev Fr Energ ... Revue Francaise de l'Energie [*A publication*]
Rev Fr Entomol ... Revue Francaise d'Entomologie [*A publication*]
Rev Fr Etud Clin Biol ... Revue Francaise d'Etudes Cliniques et Biologiques [*A publication*]
Rev Fr Geotech ... Revue Francaise de Geotechnique [*A publication*]
Rev Fr Gerontol ... Revue Francaise de Gerontologie [*A publication*]
Rev Fr Gynecol Obstet ... Revue Francaise de Gynecologie et d'Obstetrique [*A publication*]
Rev Fr Hist ... Revue Francaise d'Histoire d'Outre-Mer [*A publication*]
Rev Fr Hist Outre Mer ... Revue Francaise d'Histoire d'Outre Mer [*A publication*]
Rev Fr Inf and Rech Oper ... Revue Francaise d'Informatique et de Recherche Operationnelle [*A publication*]

Rev Frio ..... Revista del Frio [*A publication*]
Rev Fr Mal Respir ... Revue Francaise des Maladies Respiratoires [*A publication*]
Rev Fr Mec ... Revue Francaise de Mecanique [*A publication*]
Rev Fr Mkt ... Revue Francaise du Marketing [*A publication*]
Rev Fr Odonto Stomatol (Paris) ... Revue Francaise d'Odonto-Stomatologie (Paris) [*A publication*]
Rev Fr Pediatr ... Revue Francaise de Pediatrie [*A publication*]
Rev Fr Photogr Cinematogr ... Revue Francaise de Photographie et de Cinematographie [*A publication*]
Rev Fr Psychanal ... Revue Francaise de Psychanalyse [*A publication*]
Rev Fr Sci Polit ... Revue Francaise de Science Politique [*A publication*]
Rev Fr Sc P ... Revue Francaise de Science Politique [*A publication*]
Rev Fr Soc ... Revue Francaise de Sociologie [*A publication*]
Rev Fr Tel .. Revue Francaise des Telecommunications [*A publication*]
Rev Fr Trait Inf ... Revue Francaise de Traitement de l'Information [*A publication*]
Rev Fr Tran ... Revue Francaise de Transfusion [*Later, Revue Francaise de Transfusion et Immuno-Hematologie*] [*A publication*]
Rev Fr Transfus ... Revue Francaise de Transfusion [*Later, Revue Francaise de Transfusion et Immuno-Hematologie*] [*A publication*]
Rev Fr Transfus Immuno-Hematol ... Revue Francaise de Transfusion et Immuno-Hematologie [*A publication*]
Rev Fuerzas Armadas Venez ... Revista de las Fuerzas Armadas de Venezuela [*A publication*]
Rev Fund Serv Saude Publica (Braz) ... Revista. Fundacao Servicos de Saude Publica (Brazil) [*A publication*]
Rev Fund SESP ... Revista. Fundacao Servicos de Saude Publica [*Brazil*] [*A publication*]
Rev Fund SESP (Braz) ... Revista. Fundacao Servicos de Saude Publica (Brazil) [*A publication*]
rev'g .... Reversing [*Legal term*] (DLA)
Rev Gastroenterol ... Review of Gastroenterology [*A publication*]
Rev Gastroenterol Mex ... Revista de Gastroenterologia de Mexico [*A publication*]
Rev Gaucha Odontol ... Revista Gaucha de Odontologia [*A publication*]
Rev Gemmol AFG ... Revue de Gemmologie. Association Francaise de Gemmologie [*A publication*]
Rev Gen ...... Revue Generale de Droit [*A publication*] (DLA)
Rev Gen Agron ... Revue Generale Agronomique [*A publication*]
Rev Gen Ass Terr ... Revue Generale des Assurances Terrestres [*A publication*]
Rev Gen Assur Terr ... Revue Generale des Assurances Terrestres [*A publication*]
Rev Gen Bot ... Revue Generale de Botanique [*A publication*]
Rev Gen Caoutch ... Revue Generale du Caoutchouc [*A publication*]
Rev Gen Caoutch Plast ... Revue Generale des Caoutchoucs et Plastiques [*A publication*]
Rev Gen Caoutch Plast Ed Plast ... Revue Generale des Caoutchoucs et Plastiques. Edition Plastiques [*A publication*]
Rev Gen Chem Fer ... Revue Generale des Chemins de Fer [*A publication*]
Rev Gen Chemins de Fer ... Revue Generale des Chemins de Fer [*A publication*]
Rev Gen Chemins Fer ... Revue Generale des Chemins de Fer [*A publication*]
Rev Gen Chim Pure Appl ... Revue Generale de Chimie Pure et Appliquee [*A publication*]
Rev Gen Clin et Therap ... Revue Generale de Clinique et de Therapeutique [*A publication*]
Rev Gen Colloides ... Revue Generale des Colloides [*A publication*]
Rev Gen D ... Revue Generale de Droit [*A publication*] (DLA)
Rev Gen de Droit ... Revue Generale de Droit [*A publication*]
Rev Gen Droit ... Revue Generale de Droit [*A publication*]
Rev Gen Elec ... Revue Generale de l'Electricite [*A publication*]
Rev Gen Electr ... Revue Generale de l'Electricite [*A publication*]
Rev Generale de Droit ... Revue Generale de Droit [*A publication*]
Rev Geneve ... Revue de Geneve [*A publication*]
Rev Gen Froid ... Revue Generale du Froid [*A publication*]
Rev Gen Gaz ... Revue Generale du Gaz [*A publication*]
Rev Gen Ind Text ... Revue Generale de l'Industrie Textile [*A publication*]
Rev Gen Lait ... Revue Generale de Lait [*A publication*]
Rev Gen de Legis y Jurispr ... Revista General de Legislacion y Jurisprudencia [*Madrid, Spain*] [*A publication*] (DLA)
Rev Gen Mar ... Revista General de Marina [*A publication*]
Rev Gen Matieres Color Blanchiment Teint Impress Apprets ... Revue Generale des Matieres Colorantes du Blanchiment de la Teinture de l'Impression et des Apprets [*A publication*]
Rev Gen Matieres Plast ... Revue Generale des Matieres Plastiques [*A publication*]
Rev Gen Mec ... Revue Generale de Mecanique [*A publication*]
Rev Gen Mec Electr ... Revue Generale de Mecanique. Electricite [*A publication*]
Rev Gen Med Vet (Toulouse) ... Revue Generale de Medecine Veterinaire (Toulouse) [*A publication*]
Rev Gen Nucl ... Revue Generale Nucleaire [*A publication*]
Rev Gen Reg ... Revised General Regulation, General Accounting Office [*United States*] [*A publication*] (DLA)
Rev Gen Sci Appl ... Revue Generale des Sciences Appliquees [*A publication*]
Rev Gen Sci Pures Appl ... Revue Generale des Sciences Pures et Appliquees [*A publication*]

Rev Gen Sci Pures Appl Bull Assoc Fr Av Sci ... Revue Generale des Sciences Pures et Appliquees et Bulletin de l'Association Francaise pour l'Avancement des Sciences [*A publication*]

Rev Gen Sci Pures Appl Bull Soc Philomath ... Revue Generale des Sciences Pures et Appliquees et Bulletin de la Societe Philomathique [*A publication*]

Rev Gen Sc Pures et Appliq ... Revue Generale des Sciences Pures et Appliquees [*A publication*]

Rev Gen Tech ... Revue Generale des Techniques [*France*] [*A publication*]

Rev Gen Therm ... Revue Generale de Thermique [*A publication*]

Rev Geofis ... Revista de Geofisica [*A publication*]

Rev Geog.... Revista Geografica [*A publication*]

Rev Geog Ph ... Revue de Geographie Physique et de Geologie Dynamique [*A publication*]

Rev Geogr Alpine ... Revue de Geographie Alpine [*A publication*]

Rev Geographie Alpine ... Revue de Geographie Alpine [*A publication*]

Rev Geographie Montreal ... Revue de Geographie de Montreal [*A publication*]

Rev Geogr Maroc ... Revue de Geographie du Maroc [*A publication*]

Rev Geogr Phys Geol Dyn ... Revue de Geographie Physique et de Geologie Dynamique [*A publication*]

Rev Geogr Pyrenees Sud-Ouest ... Revue Geographique des Pyrenees et du Sud-Ouest [*A publication*]

Rev Geol Chile ... Revista Geologica de Chile [*A publication*]

Rev Geol Dyn Geogr Phys ... Revue de Geologie Dynamique et de Geographie Physique [*A publication*]

Rev Geol Minas Ecuador Dir Gen Geol Minas ... Revista de Geologia y Minas. Ecuador. Direccion General de Geologia y Minas [*A publication*]

Rev Geologia ... Revista de Geologia [*A publication*]

Rev Geomorphol Dyn ... Revue de Geomorphologie Dynamique [*A publication*]

Rev Geophys ... Reviews of Geophysics [*Later, Reviews of Geophysics and Space Physics*] [*A publication*]

Rev Geophys ... Reviews of Geophysics and Space Physics [*A publication*]

Rev Geophysics ... Reviews of Geophysics [*Later, Reviews of Geophysics and Space Physics*] [*A publication*]

Rev Geophys Space Phys ... Reviews of Geophysics and Space Physics [*A publication*]

Rev Geophys and Space Phys ... Reviews of Geophysics and Space Physics [*A publication*]

Rev Geriatr ... Revue de Geriatrie [*A publication*]

Rev Germ .. ... Revue Germanique [*A publication*]

Rev Gerontol Expression Fr ... Revue de Gerontologie d'Expression Francaise [*A publication*]

Rev Ghana L ... Review of Ghana Law [*A publication*]   (DLA)

Rev of Ghana L ... Review of Ghana Law [*A publication*]

Rev Ginecol Obstet ... Revista de Ginecologia e d'Obstetricia [*A publication*]

Rev Goiana Med ... Revista Goiana de Medicina [*A publication*]

Rev Gospod Agr Stat (Bucharest) ... Revista Gospodariilor Agricole de Stat (Bucharest) [*A publication*]

Rev G Therm ... Revue Generale de Thermique [*A publication*]

Rev Guatem Estomatol ... Revista Guatemalteca de Estomatologia [*A publication*]

Rev Guimaraes ... Revista de Guimaraes [*A publication*]

Rev Gynae et Chir Abd ... Revue de Gynaecologie et de Chirurgie Abdominale [*A publication*]

Rev Gynecol Obstet ... Revista de Gynecologia e d'Obstetricia [*A publication*]

RevH.......... Revista de Historia [*Lisbon*] [*A publication*]

REVHA ..... Reviews on Environmental Health [*A publication*]

Rev Haute Auvergne ... Revue de la Haute Auvergne. Societe des Sciences et Arts [*A publication*]

Rev Hautes Temp Refract ... Revue des Hautes Temperatures et des Refractaires [*A publication*]

Rev Hebd Laryngol Otol Rhinol ... Revue Hebdomadaire de Laryngologie, d'Otologie, et de Rhinologie [*A publication*]

Rev HE Fr ... Revue d'Histoire de l'Eglise de France [*A publication*]

Rev Hell Dr Int ... Revue Hellenique de Droit International [*A publication*]

Rev Hellen de Droit Internat ... Revue Hellenique de Droit International [*A publication*]

Rev Hellenique de Dr Int'l ... Revue Hellenique de Droit International [*A publication*]

Rev Hemat ... Revue d'Hematologie [*A publication*]

Rev Hematol ... Revue d'Hematologie [*A publication*]

Rev HF Electron Telecommun ... Revue HF, Electronique, Telecommunications [*A publication*]

Rev High-Temp Mater ... Reviews on High-Temperature Materials [*A publication*]

Rev Hig Med Esc ... Revista de Higiene y Medicina Escolares [*A publication*]

Rev Hig y San Pecuarias ... Revista de Higiene y Sanidad Pecuarias [*A publication*]

Rev Hig y San Vet (Madrid) ... Revista de Higiene y Sanidad Veterinaria (Madrid) [*A publication*]

Rev His A F ... Revue d'Histoire de l'Amerique Francaise [*A publication*]

Rev Hispan ... Revista Hispanica Moderna [*A publication*]

RevHist...... Revista de Historia [*Sao Paulo*] [*A publication*]

Rev Hist ... Revue Historique [*A publication*]

Rev Hist Am ... Revista de Historia de America [*A publication*]

Rev Hist Am ... Revue d'Histoire de l'Amerique Francaise [*A publication*]

Rev Hist Am Fr ... Revue d'Histoire de l'Amerique Francaise [*A publication*]

Rev Hist Armees ... Revue Historique des Armees [*A publication*]

Rev Hist Bordeaux Dep Gironde ... Revue Historique de Bordeaux et du Departement de la Gironde [*A publication*]

Rev Hist Canaria ... Revista de Historia Canaria [*A publication*]

Rev Hist Di ... Revue d'Histoire Diplomatique [*A publication*]

Rev Hist Dipl ... Revue d'Histoire Diplomatique [*A publication*]

Rev Hist Doctr Econ ... Revue d'Histoire des Doctrines Economiques [*A publication*]

Rev Hist Dr Fr et Etrang ... Revue d'Histoire du Droit Francais et Etranger [*A publication*]

Rev Hist Droit ... Revue d'Histoire du Droit [*A publication*]

Rev Hist Eccl ... Revue d'Histoire Ecclesiastique [*A publication*]

Rev Hist Econ Soc ... Revue d'Histoire Economique et Sociale [*A publication*]

Rev Hist L ... Revue d'Histoire Litteraire de la France [*A publication*]

Rev Hist M ... Revue d'Histoire Moderne et Contemporaine [*A publication*]

Rev Hist Maghrebine ... Revue d'Histoire Maghrebine [*A publication*]

Rev Hist Med Hebr ... Revue d'Histoire de la Medecine Hebraique [*A publication*]

Rev Hist Mil ... Revista de Historia Militar [*A publication*]

Rev Hist Mod ... Revue d'Histoire Moderne [*A publication*]

Rev Hist Mod Cont ... Revue d'Histoire Moderne et Contemporaine [*A publication*]

Rev Hist Mod Contemp ... Revue d'Histoire Moderne et Contemporaine [*A publication*]

Rev Hist Nat Appliq ... Revue d'Histoire Naturelle Appliquee [*A publication*]

Rev Histoire Sci Appl ... Revue d'Histoire des Sciences et de Leurs Applications [*A publication*]

Rev Hist Ph ... Revue d'Histoire et de Philosophie Religieuses [*A publication*]

Rev Hist Pharm ... Revue d'Histoire de la Pharmacie [*A publication*]

Rev Hist R ... Revue de l'Histoire des Religions [*A publication*]

Rev Hist Rel ... Revue de l'Histoire des Religions [*A publication*]   (OCD)

Rev Hist Relig ... Revue de l'Histoire des Religions [*A publication*]

Rev Hist Sci ... Revue d'Histoire des Sciences [*A publication*]

Rev Hist Sci Applic ... Revue d'Histoire des Sciences et de Leurs Applications [*A publication*]

Rev Hist Sci Leurs Appl ... Revue d'Histoire des Sciences et de Leurs Applications [*A publication*]

Rev Hist Textes ... Revue d'Histoire des Textes [*A publication*]

Rev Hist Th ... Revue d'Histoire du Theatre [*A publication*]

RevHL ... Revista de Historia. La Laguna de Tenerife [*A publication*]

RevHL .... Revista de Historia (Lisbon) [*A publication*]

Rev Hong Mines Metall Mines ... Revue Hongroise de Mines et Metallurgie. Mines [*A publication*]

Rev Hort .... Revue Horticole [*A publication*]

Rev Hortic ... Revue Horticole [*A publication*]

Rev Hortic (Paris) ... Revue Horticole (Paris) [*A publication*]

Rev Hortic Suisse ... Revue Horticole Suisse [*A publication*]

Rev Hortic Vitic ... Revista de Horticultura si Viticultura [*A publication*]

Rev Hort Viticult ... Revista de Horticultura si Viticultura [*Romania*] [*A publication*]

Rev Hosp Clin Fac Med Univ Sao Paulo ... Revista. Hospital das Clinicas. Faculdade de Medicina. Universidade de Sao Paulo [*A publication*]

Rev Hosp Clin Fac Med Univ Sao Paulo Supl ... Revista. Hospital das Clinicas. Faculdade de Medicina. Universidade de Sao Paulo. Suplemento [*A publication*]

Rev Hosp Clin Sao Paulo ... Revista. Hospital das Clinicas. Faculdade de Medicina. Universidade de Sao Paulo [*A publication*]

Rev Hosp Nino (Lima) ... Revista. Hospital del Nino (Lima) [*A publication*]

Rev Hosp Ninos (B Aires) ... Revista. Hospital de Ninos (Buenos Aires) [*A publication*]

Rev Hosp Psiquiatr Habana ... Revista. Hospital Psiquiatrico de la Habana [*A publication*]

Rev Hosp San Juan De Dios (Bogota) ... Revista. Hospital de San Juan de Dios (Bogota) [*A publication*]

Rev Hosp S Juan ... Revista. Hospital de San Juan de Dios [*Bogota*] [*A publication*]

RevHS........ Revista de Historia (Sao Paulo) [*A publication*]

Rev H Text ... Revue d'Histoire des Textes [*A publication*]

Rev Huis .... Revue des Huissiers [*A publication*]

Rev Hyg ..... Revue d'Hygiene [*A publication*]

Rev Hyg Med Infant Ann Polyclin H de Rothschild ... Revue d'Hygiene et de Medecine Infantiles et Annales de la Polyclinique H. de Rothschild [*A publication*]

Rev Hyg et Med Prevent ... Revue d'Hygiene et de Medecine Preventive [*A publication*]

Rev Hyg Med Sc Univ ... Revue d'Hygiene et Medecine Scolaire et Universitaire [*A publication*]

Rev Hyg Med Soc ... Revue d'Hygiene et de Medecine Sociale [*A publication*]

Rev Hyg Prof ... Revue de l'Hygiene Professionnelle [*A publication*]

Rev Hyg Trav ... Revue d'Hygiene du Travail [*A publication*]

Rev/I.......... Revista/Review Interamericana [*A publication*]

RevIb.......... Revista Iberoamericana [*A publication*]

Rev Iber Endocr ... Revista Iberica de Endocrinologia [*A publication*]

Rev Iber Endocrinol ... Revista Iberica de Endocrinologia [*A publication*]

Rev Iber Micol ... Revista Iberica de Micologia [*A publication*]

Rev Iberoam ... Revista Iberoamericana [*A publication*]

Rev Iberoam Educ Quim ... Revista Iberoamericana de Educacion Quimica [*A publication*]

Rev Iberoam Segur Soc ... Revista Iberoamericana de Seguridad Social [*A publication*]

Rev Iber Parasitol ... Revista Iberica de Parasitologia [*A publication*]

Rev IBYS ... Revista. IBYS [*Instituto de Biologia y Sueroterapia*] [*A publication*]

Rev ICIDCA ... Revista. ICIDCA [*Instituto Cubano de Investigaciones de los Derivados de la Cana de Azucar*] [*A publication*]

Rev IDIEM ... Revista. IDIEM [*Instituto de Investigaciones de Engoyes de Materiales*] [*A publication*]

RevIE .... Revista de Ideas Esteticas [*A publication*]

REVIEW ... Recording and Video Playback of Electronic Warfare Information

Review .... Weekly Review [*A publication*]

Review Inst Nucl Power Oper ... Review. Institute of Nuclear Power Operations [*A publication*]

Rev I F Pet ... Revue. Institut Francais du Petrole [*A publication*]

Rev Ig .... Revista. Igiena, Bacteriologie, Virusologie, Parazitologie, Epidemiologie, Pneumoftiziologie [*A publication*]

Rev Ig Bacteriol Virusol Parazitol Epidemiol Pneumoftiziol ... Revista. Igiena, Bacteriologie, Virusologie, Parazitologie, Epidemiologie, Pneumoftiziologie [*A publication*]

Rev Ig Soc .. Revista de Igiena Sociala [*A publication*]

RevIMA ..... Review of Indonesian and Malayan Affairs [*A publication*]

Rev Imagem ... Revista da Imagem [*A publication*]

Rev IMESC (Inst Med Soc Criminol Sao Paulo) ... Revista. IMESC (Instituto de Medicina Social e de Criminologia de Sao Paulo) [*A publication*]

Rev Immunoassay Technol ... Reviews on Immunoassay Technology [*A publication*]

Rev Immunol ... Revue d'Immunologie [*A publication*]

Rev Immunol Ther Antimicrob ... Revue d'Immunologie et de Therapie Antimicrobienne [*A publication*]

Rev Ind .... Revue Industrielle [*A publication*]

Rev Ind Agr ... Revista de Industria Agricola [*A publication*]

Rev Ind Agric (Tucuman) ... Revista Industrial y Agricola (Tucuman) [*A publication*]

Rev Ind Aliment Prod Anim ... Revista Industriei Alimentare. Produse Animale [*A publication*]

Rev Ind Aliment Prod Veg ... Revista Industriei Alimentare. Produse Vegetale [*A publication*]

Rev Ind Anim ... Revista de Industria Animal [*A publication*]

Rev Ind Chim ... Revue Hebdomadaire des Industries Chimiques [*A publication*]

Rev Ind Elec ... Revue Hebdomadaire de l'Industrie Electrique et Electronique [*A publication*]

Rev Ind Fabril ... Revista Industrial y Fabril [*France*] [*A publication*]

Rev Indias ... Revista de las Indias [*A publication*]

Rev Ind Miner ... Revue de l'Industrie Minerale [*A publication*]

Rev Ind Miner Mines ... Revue de l'Industrie Minerale. Mines [*A publication*]

Rev Indon & Malayan Affairs ... Review of Indonesian and Malayan Affairs [*A publication*]   (APTA)

Rev Ind S Paulo ... Revista Industrial de Sao Paulo [*A publication*]

Rev Industr Agric (Tucuman) ... Revista Industrial y Agricola (Tucuman) [*A publication*]

Rev Inf & Autom ... Revista de Informatica y Automatica [*A publication*]

Rev Infect Dis ... Review of Infectious Diseases [*A publication*]

Rev Infirm ... Revue de l'Infirmiere [*A publication*]

Rev Infirm Infirm Aux Que ... Revue des Infirmieres et Infirmiers Auxiliaires du Quebec [*A publication*]

Rev Inf Med ... Revue d'Informatique Medicale [*A publication*]

Rev Ing .... Revue des Ingenieurs des Ecoles Nationales Superieures des Mines [*A publication*]

Rev Ing (Buenos Aires) ... Revista de Ingenieria (Buenos Aires) [*A publication*]

Rev Ing Ind ... Revista de Ingenieria Industrial [*A publication*]

Rev Ing (Montevideo) ... Revista de Ingenieria (Montevideo) [*A publication*]

Rev Ing (Montreal) ... Revue de l'Ingenierie (Montreal) [*A publication*]

Rev Ing Quim ... Revista de Ingenieria Quimica [*A publication*]

Rev Ingr ..... Universidad Catolica Argentina. Facultad de Ciencias Fisicomatematicas e Ingenieria. Revista da Ingenieria [*A publication*]

Rev In Haut ... Revue Internationale des Hautes Temperatures et des Refractaires [*A publication*]

Rev Inst Adolfo Lutz ... Revista. Instituto Adolfo Lutz [*A publication*]

Rev Inst Agr Catalan San Isidro ... Revista. Instituto Agricola Catalan de San Isidro [*A publication*]

Rev Inst Antibiot (Recife) ... Revista. Instituto de Antibioticos. Universidade Federal de Pernambuco (Recife) [*A publication*]

Rev Inst Antibiot Univ Fed Pernambuco ... Revista. Instituto de Antibioticos. Universidade Federal de Pernambuco [*A publication*]

Rev Inst Antibiot Univ Recife ... Revista. Instituto de Antibioticos. Universidade do Recife [*A publication*]

Rev Inst Antropol Univ Cordoba ... Revista. Instituto de Antropologia. Universidad Nacional de Cordoba [*A publication*]

Rev Inst Bacteriol Dep Nac Hig (Argent) ... Revista. Instituto Bacteriologico. Departamento Nacional de Higiene (Argentina) [*A publication*]

Rev Inst Bacteriol Malbran ... Revista. Instituto Bacteriologico Malbran [*A publication*]

Rev Inst Colomb Agropecu ... Revista. Instituto Colombiano Agropecuario [*A publication*]

Rev del Inst de Derecho Comparado ... Revista. Instituto de Derecho Comparado [*Barcelona, Spain*] [*A publication*]   (DLA)

Rev Inst Franc Petrol ... Revue. Institut Francais du Petrole [*A publication*]

Rev Inst Fr Pet ... Revue. Institut Francais du Petrole [*A publication*]

Rev Inst Fr Pet ... Revue. Institut Francais du Petrole et Annales des Combustibles Liquides [*Later, Revue. Institut Francais du Petrole*] [*A publication*]

Rev Inst Fr Pet Ann Combust Liq ... Revue. Institut Francais du Petrole et Annales des Combustibles Liquides [*Later, Revue. Institut Francais du Petrole*] [*A publication*]

Rev Inst Geogr Geol (Sao Paulo) ... Revista. Instituto Geografico e Geologico (Sao Paulo) [*A publication*]

Rev Inst Geol Min Univ Nac Tucuman ... Revista. Instituto de Geologia y Mineria. Universidad Nacional de Tucuman [*A publication*]

Rev Inst Geol Univ Nac Auton Mex ... Revista. Instituto de Geologia. Universidad Nacional Autonoma de Mexico [*A publication*]

Rev Inst Hist Geogr Bras ... Revista. Instituto Historico e Geografico Brasileiro [*A publication*]

Rev Inst Hyg Mines ... Revue. Institut d'Hygiene des Mines [*A publication*]

Rev Inst Hyg Mines (Hasselt) ... Revue. Institut d'Hygiene des Mines (Hasselt) [*A publication*]

Rev Inst Invest Tecnol (Bogota) ... Revista. Instituto de Investigaciones Tecnologicas (Bogota) [*A publication*]

Rev Inst Malbran ... Revista. Instituto Malbran [*A publication*]

Rev Inst Med Leg Estado Guanabara ... Revista. Instituto Medico-Legal do Estado da Guanabara [*A publication*]

Rev Inst Med Trop Sao Paulo ... Revista. Instituto de Medicina Tropical de Sao Paulo [*A publication*]

Rev Inst Mex Pet ... Revista. Instituto Mexicano del Petroleo [*A publication*]

Rev Inst Mex Petrol ... Revista. Instituto Mexicano del Petroleo [*A publication*]

Rev Inst Munic Bot (B Aires) ... Revista. Instituto Municipal de Botanica (Buenos Aires) [*A publication*]

Rev Inst Nac Geol Min (Argent) ... Revista. Instituto Nacional de Geologia y Mineria (Argentina) [*A publication*]

Rev Inst Nac Hig ... Revista. Instituto Nacional de Higiene [*A publication*]

Rev Inst Nacl Cancerol (Mex) ... Revista. Instituto Nacional de Cancerologia (Mexico) [*A publication*]

Rev Inst Nac Med Leg Colombia ... Revista. Instituto Nacional de Medicina Legal de Colombia [*A publication*]

Rev Inst Napoleon ... Revue. Institut Napoleon [*A publication*]

Rev Inst Pasteur Lyon ... Revue. Institut Pasteur de Lyon [*A publication*]

Rev Inst Salubr Enferm Trop ... Revista. Instituto de Salubridad y Enfermedades Tropicales [*A publication*]

Rev Inst Sociol ... Revue. Institut de Sociologie [*A publication*]

Rev Int Bois ... Revue Internationale du Bois [*A publication*]

Rev Int Bois Matieres Premieres Prod Ind Origine Veg ... Revue Internationale du Bois et des Matieres Premieres et Produits Industriels d'Origine Vegetale [*A publication*]

Rev Int Bot Appl Agric Trop ... Revue Internationale de Botanique Appliquee et d'Agriculture Tropicale [*A publication*]

Rev Int Brass Malt ... Revue Internationale de Brasserie et de Malterie [*A publication*]

Rev Int Choc ... Revue Internationale de la Chocolaterie [*A publication*]

Rev Int Crim ... Revue Internationale du Criminalistique [*A publication*]

Rev Int Criminol Police Tech ... Revue Internationale de Criminologie et de Police Technique [*A publication*]

Rev Int Doc ... Revue Internationale de la Documentation [*A publication*]

Rev Interamer Cienc Soc ... Revista Interamericana de Ciencias Sociales [*A publication*]

Rev Interam Radiol ... Revista Interamericana de Radiologia [*A publication*]

Rev Inter B ... Revista Interamericana de Bibliografia [*Inter-American Review of Bibliography*] [*A publication*]

Rev Internac y Diplom ... Revista Internacional y Diplomatica. Publicacion Mensual [*Mexico*] [*A publication*]   (DLA)

Rev Internat de Droit Compare ... Revue Internationale de Droit Compare. Continuation du Bulletin de la Societe de Legislation Comparee [*A publication*]

Rev Internat de Droit Penal ... Revue Internationale de Droit Penal. Bulletin de l'Association Internationale de Droit Penal [*A publication*]

Rev Internat Franc du Droit des Gens ... Revue Internationale Francaise du Droit des Gens [*A publication*]   (DLA)

Rev Internat Philos ... Revue Internationale de Philosophie [*A publication*]

Rev Intern Crim et Pol Tech ... Revue Internationale de Criminologie et de Police Technique [*A publication*]

Rev Intern Dr Ant ... Revue Internationale des Droits de l'Antiquite [*A publication*]

Rev Intern Dr Comp ... Revue Internationale de Droit Compare [*A publication*]

Rev Intern Sc Adm ... Revue Internationale des Sciences Administratives [*A publication*]

Rev Int Falsif ... Revue Internationale des Falsifications [*A publication*]

Rev Int Falsif Anal Matieres Aliment ... Revue Internationale des Falsifications et d'Analyse des Matieres Alimentaires [*A publication*]

Rev Int Hautes Temp Refract ... Revue Internationale des Hautes Temperatures et des Refractaires [*A publication*]

Rev Int Hautes Temp et Refract ... Revue Internationale des Hautes Temperatures et des Refractaires [*A publication*]

Rev Int Heliotech ... Revue Internationale d'Heliotechnique [*France*] [*A publication*]

Rev Int Hepatol ... Revue Internationale d'Hepatologie [*A publication*]

Rev Int Hist Banque ... Revue Internationale d'Histoire de la Banque [*A publication*]

Rev Int Ind Agric ... Revue Internationale des Industries Agricoles [*A publication*]

Rev Int Ind Min Metall Electrotherm Electrochim ... Revue Internationale des Industries Minieres, Metallurgiques, Electrothermiques, et Electrochimiques [*A publication*]

Rev Int'l Comm Jur ... Review. International Commission of Jurists [*A publication*]   (DLA)

Rev Int'l Comm Jurists ... Review. International Commission of Jurists [*A publication*]

Rev Int'l Dr Auteur ... Revue Internationale du Droit d'Auteur [*A publication*]   (DLA)

Rev Int'l Droit Comp ... Revue Internationale de Droit Compare [*A publication*]   (DLA)

Rev Int'l des Droits de l'Antiquite ... Revue Internationale des Droits de l'Antiquite [*A publication*]   (DLA)

Rev Int'l Dr Penal ... Revue Internationale de Droit Penal [*A publication*]   (DLA)

Rev Int Mus ... Revue Internationale de Musique [*A publication*]

Rev Int Oceanogr Med ... Revue Internationale d'Oceanographie Medicale [*A publication*]

Rev Int Pediatr ... Revue Internationale de Pediatrie [*A publication*]

Rev Int Ph ... Revue Internationale de Philosophie [*A publication*]

Rev Int Pharm ... Revue Internationale de Pharmacie [*A publication*]

Rev Int Phil ... Revue Internationale de Philosophie [*A publication*]

Rev Int Philos ... Revue Internationale de Philosophie [*A publication*]

Rev Int Prod Colon Mater Colon ... Revue Internationale des Produits Coloniaux et du Materiel Colonial [*A publication*]

Rev Int Prod Trop Mater Trop ... Revue Internationale des Produits Tropicaux et du Materiel Tropical [*A publication*]

Rev Int Psy ... Revue Internationale de Psychologie Appliquee [*A publication*]

Rev Int Renseign Agric ... Revue Internationale de Renseignements Agricoles [*A publication*]

Rev Int Sc... Revista Internazionale di Scienze Economiche e Commerciali [*A publication*]

Rev Int Serv Sante Armees Terre Mer Air ... Revue Internationale des Services de Sante des Armees de Terre, de Mer, et de l'Air [*A publication*]

Rev Int Soja ... Revue Internationale du Soja [*A publication*]

Rev Int Tab ... Revue Internationale des Tabacs [*A publication*]

Rev Int Trach ... Revue Internationale du Trachome [*A publication*]

Rev Int Trach Pathol Oculaire Trop Subtrop Sante Publique ... Revue Internationale du Trachome et de Pathologie Oculaire Tropicale et Subtropicale et de Sante Publique [*A publication*]

Rev Int Trach Pathol Ocul Trop Subtrop ... Revue Internationale du Trachome et de Pathologie Oculaire Tropicale et Subtropicale [*A publication*]

Rev Int Trach Pathol Ocul Trop Subtrop Sante Publique ... Revue Internationale de Trachome et de Pathologie Oculaire Tropicale et Subtropicale et de Sante Publique [*A publication*]

Rev Inv Cli ... Revista de Investigacion Clinica [*A publication*]

Rev Invest .. Revista de Investigacion [*A publication*]

Rev Invest Agr ... Revista de Investigaciones Agricolas [*A publication*]

Rev Invest Agric ... Revista de Investigaciones Agricolas [*A publication*]

Rev Invest Agropec Ser ... Revista de Investigaciones Agropecuarias. Serie [*A publication*]

Rev Invest Agropecuar Ser 2 ... Revista de Investigaciones Agropecuarias. Serie 2. Biologia y Produccion Vegetal [*A publication*]

Rev Invest Agropecuar Ser 5 ... Revista de Investigaciones Agropecuarias. Serie 5. Patologia Vegetal [*A publication*]

Rev Invest Agropecu Ser 1 ... Revista de Investigaciones Agropecuarias. Serie 1. Biologia y Produccion Animal [*A publication*]

Rev Invest Agropecu Ser 3 ... Revista de Investigaciones Agropecuarias. Serie 3. Clima y Suelo [*A publication*]

Rev Invest Agropecu Ser 4 ... Revista de Investigaciones Agropecuarias. Serie 4. Patologia Animal [*A publication*]

Rev Invest Agropecu Ser 6 ... Revista de Investigaciones Agropecuarias. Serie 6. Economia y Administracion Rural [*A publication*]

Rev Invest Agropecu Ser 1 Biol Prod Anim ... Revista de Investigaciones Agropecuarias. Serie 1. Biologia y Produccion Animal [*A publication*]

Rev Invest Agropecu Ser 2 Biol Prod Veg ... Revista de Investigaciones Agropecuarias. Serie 2. Biologia y Produccion Vegetal [*A publication*]

Rev Invest Agropecu Ser 3 Clima Suelo ... Revista de Investigaciones Agropecuarias. Serie 3. Clima y Suelo [*A publication*]

Rev Invest Agropecu Ser 4 Patol Anim ... Revista de Investigaciones Agropecuarias. Serie 4. Patologia Animal [*A publication*]

Rev Invest Agropecu Ser 5 Patol Veg ... Revista de Investigaciones Agropecuarias. Serie 5. Patologia Vegetal [*A publication*]

Rev Invest Clin ... Revista de Investigacion Clinica [*A publication*]

Rev Invest For ... Revista de Investigaciones Forestales [*A publication*]

Rev Invest Ganad ... Revista de Investigaciones Ganaderas [*A publication*]

Rev Invest Inst Nac Pesca ... Revista de Investigaciones. Instituto Nacional de la Pesca [*A publication*]

Rev Invest Mar ... Revista de Investigaciones Marinas [*A publication*]

Rev Invest Salud Publica ... Revista de Investigacion en Salud Publica [*A publication*]

Rev Invest Univ Guadalajara (Mex) ... Revista de Investigacion. Universidad de Guadalajara (Mexico) [*A publication*]

Rev Ion....... Revista Ion [*A publication*]

Rev I Psych ... Revue Internationale de Psychologie Appliquee [*A publication*]

Rev IRE ..... Revue. IRE [*Institut National des Radioelements*] [*A publication*]

Revised Rep ... Revised Reports [*England*] [*A publication*]   (DLA)

Rev I Soc.... Revue. Institut de Sociologie [*A publication*]

Revista CF ... Revista Colombiana de Folclor [*A publication*]

Rev Ivoirienne de Droit ... Revue Ivoirienne de Droit [*A publication*]   (DLA)

Rev Jeumont-Schneider ... Revue Jeumont-Schneider [*A publication*]

Rev JFF ..... Revue Juridique, Fiscale, et Financiere [*A publication*]

Rev J Phil Soc Sci ... Review Journal of Philosophy and Social Science [*A publication*]

Rev J & PJ ... Revenue, Judicial, and Police Journal [*Bengal*] [*A publication*]   (DLA)

Rev Jud & Police J ... Revenue, Judicial, and Police Journal [*A publication*]   (DLA)

Rev Jur....... Revista Juridica [*A publication*]

Rev de Jur ... Revue de Jurisprudence [*Quebec*] [*A publication*]   (DLA)

Rev Jur d'Alsace et de Lorraine ... Revue Juridique d'Alsace et de Lorraine [*A publication*]   (DLA)

Rev Jur de Buenos Aires ... Revista Juridica de Buenos Aires [*A publication*]   (DLA)

Rev Jur du Congo ... Revue Juridique du Congo [*A publication*]   (DLA)

Rev Jur del Peru ... Revista Juridica del Peru [*A publication*]

Rev Jur Themis ... Revue Juridique Themis [*A publication*]

Rev Jur U Inter PR ... Revista Juridica. Universidad Interamericana de Puerto Rico [*A publication*]

Rev Jur de la Univ de Puerto Rico ... Revista Juridica. Universidad de Puerto Rico [*A publication*]

Rev Jur UPR ... Revista Juridica. Universidad de Puerto Rico [*A publication*]

Rev Kobe Univ Merc Mar Part 2 ... Review. Kobe University of Mercantile Marine. Part 2 [*Japan*] [*A publication*]

Rev Kobe Univ Merc Mar Part 2 Marit Stud Sci Eng ... Review. Kobe University of Mercantile Marine. Part 2. Maritime Studies, and Science and Engineering [*A publication*]

Rev Kuba Med Trop Parasitol ... Revista Kuba de Medicina Tropical y Parasitologia [*A publication*]

RevL.......... Revista de Letras [*A publication*]

RevLA........ Revista de Letras (Assis) [*A publication*]

Rev Lang R ... Revue des Langues Romanes [*A publication*]

Rev Lang V ... Revue des Langues Vivantes/Tijdschrift voor Levende Talen [*A publication*]

Rev Lang Viv ... Revue des Langues Vivantes [*A publication*]

Rev Laryngol Otol Rhinol ... Revue de Laryngologie, Otologie, Rhinologie [*A publication*]

Rev Laryngol Otol Rhinol (Bord) ... Revue de Laryngologie, Otologie, Rhinologie (Bordeaux) [*A publication*]

Rev Laryngol Otol Rhino Suppl ... Revue de Laryngologie, Otologie, Rhinologie. Supplement [*France*] [*A publication*]

Rev Laser Eng ... Review of Laser Engineering [*Japan*] [*A publication*]

Rev Latam Microbiol ... Revista Latinoamericana de Microbiologia [*A publication*]

Rev Latam P ... Revista Latinoamericana de Psicologia [*A publication*]

Rev Latam Patol ... Revista Latinoamericana de Patologia [*A publication*]

Rev Lat Am Psiquiat ... Revista Latinoamericana de Psiquiatria [*A publication*]

Rev Latin de Filosof ... Revista Latinoamericana de Filosofia [*A publication*]

Rev Latinoam Anat Patol ... Revista Latinoamericana de Anatomia Patologica [*A publication*]

Rev Latinoam Cienc Agric ... Revista Latinoamericana de Ciencias Agricolas [*A publication*]

Rev Latinoam Cir Plast ... Revista Latinoamericana de Cirurgia Plastica [*A publication*]

Rev Latinoam Ing Quim Quim Apl ... Revista Latinoamericana de Ingenieria Quimica y Quimica Aplicada [*A publication*]

Rev Latinoam Microbiol ... Revista Latinoamericana de Microbiologia [*A publication*]

Rev Latinoam Microbiol Parasitol ... Revista Latinoamericana de Microbiologia y Parasitologia [*Later, Revista Latinoamericana de Microbiologia*] [*A publication*]

Rev Latinoam Microbiol Supl ... Revista Latinoamericana de Microbiologia. Suplemento [*A publication*]

Rev Latinoam Patol ... Revista Latinoamericana de Patologia [*A publication*]

Rev Latinoam Psicol ... Revista Latinoamericana de Psicologia [*A publication*]

Rev Latinoam Quim ... Revista Latinoamericana de Quimica [*A publication*]

Rev Latinoam Sider ... Revista Latinoamericana de Siderurgia [*A publication*]

Rev Leg ...... Revue Legale [*Canada*] [*A publication*]   (DLA)

Rev de Leg ... Revue de Legislation et de Jurisprudence [*Montreal*] [*A publication*]   (DLA)

Rev Leg ...... Revue de Legislation et de Jurisprudence [*Quebec*] [*A publication*]   (DLA)

Rev Legale ... Revue Legale [*A publication*]   (DLA)

Rev de Legis ... Revue de Legislation [*Canada*] [*A publication*]   (DLA)

Rev Leg NS ... Revue Legale. New Series [*Canada*] [*A publication*]   (DLA)

Rev Leg (OS) ... Revue Legale (Old Series) [*A publication*]   (DLA)

Rev Leprol Dermatol Sifilogr ... Revista de Leprologia, Dermatologia, y Sifilografia [*A publication*]
Rev Leprol Sao Paulo ... Revista de Leprologia de Sao Paulo [*A publication*]
Rev Lettr Mod ... Revue des Lettres Modernes [*A publication*]
Rev Liberale ... Revue Liberale [*A publication*]
Rev Ling Rom ... Revue de Linguistique Romane [*A publication*]
Rev Lit ...... Revista de Literatura [*A publication*]
Rev Lit ...... Revue de Litterature Comparee [*A publication*]
Rev de Lit Comp ... Revue de Litterature Comparee [*A publication*]
Rev Lit Comp ... Revue de Litterature Comparee [*A publication*]
Rev Litigation ... Review of Litigation [*A publication*]
Rev Litt Comp ... Revue de Litterature Comparee [*A publication*]
Rev Livro.... Revista do Livro [*A publication*]
RevLR .... Revista do Livro (Rio) [*A publication*]
Rev L & Soc ... Review of Law and Social Change [*A publication*]   (DLA)
Rev Lyon Med ... Revue Lyonnaise de Medecine [*A publication*]
RevM .... Revista (Madrid) [*A publication*]
Rev M .... Revue M [*Belgium*] [*A publication*]
Rev M .... Revue de la Mecanique [*A publication*]
Rev Macromol Chem ... Reviews in Macromolecular Chemistry [*A publication*]
Rev Madeira (Sao Paulo) ... Revista da Madeira (Sao Paulo) [*A publication*]
Rev Maigret ... Revue Henri Maigret [*A publication*]
Rev Mal Respir ... Revue des Maladies Respiratoires [*A publication*]
Rev du Marche Commun ... Revue du Marche Commun [*A publication*]
Rev Marit... Revue Maritime [*A publication*]
Rev Market & Ag Econ ... Review of Marketing and Agricultural Economics [*A publication*]   (APTA)
Rev Market Agric Econ ... Review of Marketing and Agricultural Economics [*A publication*]   (APTA)
Rev Market Agric Econ (Sydney) ... Review of Marketing and Agricultural Economics (Sydney) [*A publication*]   (APTA)
Rev Marketing Agr Econ ... Review of Marketing and Agricultural Economics [*A publication*]
Rev Marq Parfum Savonn ... Revue des Marques de la Parfumerie et de la Savonnerie [*A publication*]
Rev Marques Parfums Fr ... Revue des Marques des Parfums de France [*A publication*]
Rev Mater Constr Trav Publics ... Revue des Materiaux de Construction et de Travaux Publics [*A publication*]
Rev Mater Constr Trav Publics Ed B ... Revue des Materiaux de Construction et de Travaux Publics. Edition B. Brique, Tuile, Ceramique [*A publication*]
Rev Mat Hisp-Amer ... Revista Matematica Hispano-Americana [*A publication*]
Rev Mat Hisp-Amer 4 ... Revista Matematica Hispano-Americana. Serie 4 [*A publication*]
Rev Math Phys ... Revue de Mathematiques et de Physique [*A publication*]
Rev Math Pures Appl ... Revue de Mathematiques Pures et Appliquees [*A publication*]
Rev MBLE ... Revue MBLE [*Manufacture Belge de Lampes et de Materiel*] [*Belgium*] [*A publication*]
Rev Mecan ... Revue de la Mecanique [*A publication*]
Rev Mec Appl ... Revue de Mecanique Appliquee [*A publication*]
Rev Mec Tijdsch ... Revue Mecanique Tijdschrift [*Belgium*] [*A publication*]
Rev Med..... Revista Medica [*A publication*]
Rev Med..... Revista Medicala [*A publication*]
Rev Med..... Revista de Medicina [*A publication*]
Rev Med Accidents Mal Prof ... Revue de Medecine des Accidents et des Maladies Professionnelles [*A publication*]
Rev Med Accid Mal Prof ... Revue de Medecine des Accidents et des Maladies Professionnelles [*A publication*]
Rev Med Aero ... Revista Medica da Aeronautica [*A publication*]
Rev Med Aeronaut ... Revista Medica da Aeronautica [*A publication*]
Rev Med Aeronaut (Paris) ... Revue de Medecine Aeronautique (Paris) [*Later, Medecine Aeronautique et Spatial - Medecine Subaquatique et Hyperbare*] [*A publication*]
Rev Med Aeronaut Spat ... Revue de Medecine Aeronautique et Spatiale [*Later, Medecine Aeronautique et Spatial - Medecine Subaquatique et Hyperbare*] [*A publication*]
Rev Med Aeronaut Spat Med Subaquat Hyperbare ... Revue de Medecine Aeronautique et Spatiale - Medecine Subaquatique et Hyperbare [*A publication*]
Rev Med Aliment ... Revista de Medicina y Alimentacion [*A publication*]
Rev Med Angola ... Revista Medica de Angola [*A publication*]
Rev Med ATM ... Revista de Medicina. ATM [*Associacao da Turma Medica*] [*A publication*]
Rev Med Bahia ... Revista Medica de Bahia [*A publication*]
Rev Med Bogota ... Revista Medica de Bogota [*A publication*]
Rev Med Bras ... Revista Medica Brasileira [*A publication*]
Rev Med Brux ... Revue Medicale de Bruxelles [*A publication*]
Rev Med Bruxelles ... Revue Medicale de Bruxelles [*A publication*]
Rev Med Brux Nouv Ser ... Revue Medicale de Bruxelles. Nouvelle Serie [*A publication*]
Rev Med Chi ... Revista Medica de Chile [*A publication*]
Rev Med Chil ... Revista Medica de Chile [*A publication*]
Rev Med Chile ... Revista Medica de Chile [*A publication*]
Rev Med Chir ... Revista Medico-Chirurgicala [*A publication*]
Rev Med Chir ... Revue Medico-Chirurgicale [*A publication*]
Rev Med-Chir (Iasi) ... Revue Medico-Chirurgicale (Iasi) [*A publication*]

Rev Med-Chir Mal Foie ... Revue Medico-Chirurgicale des Maladies du Foie [*A publication*]
Rev Med-Chir Mal Foie Rate Pancreas ... Revue Medico-Chirurgicale des Maladies du Foie, de la Rate, et du Pancreas [*France*] [*A publication*]
Rev Med-Chir Soc Med Nat din Iasi ... Revista Medico-Chirurgicala. Societatii de Medici si Naturalisti din Iasi [*A publication*]
Rev Med-Chir Soc Med Nat Iasi ... Revista Medico-Chirurgicala. Societatii de Medici si Naturalisti din Iasi [*A publication*]
Rev Med Cienc Afines ... Revista de Medicina y Ciencias Afines [*A publication*]
Rev Med Cir Habana ... Revista de Medicina y Cirugia de La Habana [*A publication*]
Rev Med Cir Sao Paulo ... Revista de Medicina e Cirurgia de Sao Paulo [*A publication*]
Rev Med y Cirug (Caracas) ... Revista de Medicina y Cirugia (Caracas) [*A publication*]
Rev Med y Cirug Habana ... Revista de Medicina y Cirugia de La Habana [*A publication*]
Rev Med Cirurg Brasil ... Revista Medico-Cirurgica do Brasil [*A publication*]
Rev Med Cordoba ... Revista Medica de Cordoba [*A publication*]
Rev Med Costa Rica ... Revista Medica de Costa Rica [*A publication*]
Rev Med Cubana ... Revista Medica Cubana [*A publication*]
Rev Med Dijon ... Revue Medicale de Dijon [*A publication*]
Rev Med Est ... Revue Medicale de l'Est [*A publication*]
Rev Med Estado Guanabara ... Revista Medica do Estado da Guanabara [*A publication*]
Rev Med Estado Rio De J ... Revista Medica do Estado do Rio De Janeiro [*A publication*]
Rev Med Estud Gen Navarro ... Revista de Medicina del Estudio General de Navarro [*A publication*]
Rev Med Exp ... Revista de Medicina Experimental [*A publication*]
Rev Med Exp (Lima) ... Revista de Medicina Experimental (Lima) [*A publication*]
Rev Med Fr ... Revue Medicale Francaise [*A publication*]
Rev Med Galicia ... Revista Medica de Galicia [*A publication*]
Rev Med (Hanoi) ... Revue Medicale (Hanoi) [*A publication*]
Rev Med Hondur ... Revista Medica Hondurena [*A publication*]
Rev Med Hosp Cent Empl (Lima) ... Revista Medica. Hospital Central del Empleado (Lima) [*A publication*]
Rev Med Hosp Colon ... Revista Medica. Hospital Colonia [*A publication*]
Rev Med Hosp Colon (Mex) ... Revista Medica. Hospital Colonia (Mexico) [*A publication*]
Rev Med Hosp Ernesto Dornelles ... Revista de Medicina. Hospital Ernesto Dornelles [*A publication*]
Rev Med Hosp Esp ... Revista Medica. Hospital Espanol [*A publication*]
Rev Med Hosp Gen (Mex) ... Revista Medica. Hospital General (Mexico) [*A publication*]
Rev Med Hosp Gen (Mexico City) ... Revista Medica. Hospital General (Mexico City) [*A publication*]
Rev Med Hosp Obrero ... Revista Medica. Hospital Obrero [*A publication*]
Rev Med Hosp Servidores Estado ... Revista Medica. Hospital dos Servidores do Estado [*A publication*]
Rev Med HSE ... Revista Medica. Hospital dos Servidores do Estado [*A publication*]
Rev Med Inst Mex Seguro Soc ... Revista Medica. Instituto Mexicano del Seguro Social [*A publication*]
Rev Med Inst Previdencia Serv Estado Minas Gerais ... Revista Medica. Instituto de Previdencia dos Servidores do Estado de Minas Gerais [*A publication*]
Rev Med Inst Previdencia Servidores Estado Minas Gerais ... Revista Medica. Instituto de Previdencia dos Servidores do Estado de Minas Gerais [*A publication*]
Rev Med Interna Med Interna ... Revista de Medicina Interna, Neurologie, Psihiatrie, Neurochirurgie, Dermato-Venerologie. Seria Medicina Interna [*A publication*]
Rev Med Interna Neurol Psihiatr ... Revista de Medicina Interna, Neurologie, Psihiatrie, Neurochirurgie, Dermato-Venerologie. Neurologie, Psihiatrie, Neurochirurgie [*A publication*]
Rev Med Interna Neurol Psihiatr Neurochir Dermato ... Revista de Medicina-Interna, Neurologie, Psihiatrie, Neurochirurgie, Dermato-Venerologie. Seria Medicina Interna [*A publication*]
Rev Med Interna Neurol Psihiatr Neurochir Dermato-Venerol ... Revista de Medicina Interna, Neurologie, Psihiatrie, Neurochirurgie, Dermato-Venerologie [*A publication*]
Rev Med Interne ... Revue de Medecine Interne [*A publication*]
Rev Mediterr Sci Med ... Revue Mediterraneenne des Sciences Medicales [*A publication*]
Rev Med Juiz de Fora ... Revista Medica de Juiz de Fora [*A publication*]
Rev Med Leg Colomb ... Revista de Medicina Legal de Colombia [*A publication*]
Rev Med Liege ... Revue Medicale de Liege [*A publication*]
Rev Med Liege Suppl ... Revue Medicale de Liege. Supplement [*A publication*]
Rev Med Limoges ... Revue de Medecine de Limoges [*A publication*]
Rev Med Louvain ... Revue Medicale de Louvain [*A publication*]
Rev Med Mil ... Revista de Medicina Militar [*A publication*]
Rev Med Min ... Revue Medicale Miniere [*A publication*]
Rev Med Miniere ... Revue Medicale Miniere [*A publication*]
Rev Med Moyen-Orient ... Revue Medicale du Moyen-Orient [*A publication*]
Rev Med Nancy ... Revue Medicale de Nancy [*A publication*]

Rev Med Nav ... Revue de Medecine Navale (Metropole et Outre-Mer) [*A publication*]
Rev Med Normandes ... Revues Medicales Normandes [*A publication*]
Rev Med Panama ... Revista Medica de Panama [*A publication*]
Rev Med Parag ... Revista Medica del Paraguay [*A publication*]
Rev Med (Paris) ... Revue de Medecine (Paris) [*A publication*]
Rev Med Pharmacol ... Review of Medical Pharmacology [*A publication*]
Rev Med Prev ... Revue de Medecine Preventive [*A publication*]
Rev Med Psychosomat Psychol Med ... Revue de Medecine Psychosomatique et de Psychologie Medicale [*France*] [*A publication*]
Rev Med-Quir (Buenos Aires) ... Revista Medico-Quirurgica (Buenos Aires) [*A publication*]
Rev Med Quir Patol Femenina ... Revista Medico-Quirurgica de Patologia Femenina [*A publication*]
Rev Med Quir Teguelgalpa ... Revista Medico-Quirurgica Teguelgalpa [*A publication*]
Rev Med Rio Grande Do Sul ... Revista de Medicina do Rio Grande Do Sul [*A publication*]
Rev Med Rosario ... Revista Medica del Rosario [*A publication*]
Rev Med d Rosario ... Revista Medica del Rosario [*A publication*]
Rev de Med (Rosario) ... Revista de Medicina (Rosario) [*A publication*]
Rev Med (Sao Paulo) ... Revista de Medicina (Sao Paulo) [*A publication*]
Rev Med Sevilla ... Revista Medica de Sevilla [*A publication*]
Rev Med de S Paulo ... Revista Medica de Sao Paulo [*A publication*]
Rev de Med (S Paulo) ... Revista de Medicina (Sao Paulo) [*A publication*]
Rev Med Suisse Romande ... Revue Medicale de la Suisse Romande [*A publication*]
Rev Med (Tirgu-Mures) ... Revista Medicala (Tirgu-Mures) [*Romania*] [*A publication*]
Rev Med Toulouse ... Revue de Medecine de Toulouse [*A publication*]
Rev Med Toulouse Suppl ... Revue de Medecine de Toulouse. Supplement [*A publication*]
Rev Med Tours ... Revue de Medecine de Tours [*A publication*]
Rev Med Trav ... Revue de Medecine du Travail [*France*] [*A publication*]
Rev Med Trop ... Revista de Medicina Tropical [*A publication*]
Rev Med Univ Fed Ceara ... Revista de Medicina. Universidade Federal do Ceara [*A publication*]
Rev Med Univ Montr ... Revue Medicale. Universite de Montreal [*A publication*]
Rev Med Univ Navarra ... Revista de Medicina. Universidad de Navarra [*A publication*]
Rev Med Uruguay ... Revista Medica del Uruguay [*A publication*]
Rev Med (Valparaiso) ... Revista de Medicina (Valparaiso) [*A publication*]
Rev Med Veracruz ... Revista Medica Veracruzana [*A publication*]
Rev Med Vet ... Revista de Medicina Veterinaria [*A publication*]
Rev Med Vet ... Revue de Medecine Veterinaire [*A publication*]
Rev Med Vet (B Aires) ... Revista de Medicina Veterinaria (Buenos Aires) [*A publication*]
Rev Med Vet (Bogota) ... Revista de Medicina Veterinaria (Bogota) [*A publication*]
Rev Med Vet Escuela Montevideo ... Revista de Medicina Veterinaria. Escuela de Montevideo [*A publication*]
Rev Med Vet (Montev) ... Revista de Medicina Veterinaria (Montevideo) [*A publication*]
Rev Med Vet Mycol ... Review of Medical and Veterinary Mycology [*A publication*]
Rev Med Vet Parasit ... Revista de Medicina Veterinaria y Parasitologia [*A publication*]
Rev Med Vet Parasitol (Maracay) ... Revista de Medicina Veterinaria y Parasitologia (Maracay) [*A publication*]
Rev Med Vet (Santiago) ... Revista de Medicina Veterinaria (Santiago) [*A publication*]
Rev Med Vet (Sao Paulo) ... Revista de Medicina Veterinaria (Sao Paulo) [*A publication*]
Rev Med Vet (Toulouse) ... Revue de Medecine Veterinaire (Toulouse) [*A publication*]
Rev Med Yucatan ... Revista Medica de Yucatan [*A publication*]
Rev Mens Asoc Rural Urug ... Revista Mensual. Asociacion Rural del Uruguay [*A publication*]
Rev Mens Blanchissage Blanchiment Apprets ... Revue Mensuelle de Blanchissage, du Blanchiment, et des Apprets [*A publication*]
Rev Mens Mal Enf ... Revue Mensuelle des Maladies de l'Enfance [*A publication*]
Rev Mens Med Cirug ... Revista Mensual de Medicina e Cirugia [*A publication*]
Rev Mens Pediat ... Revue Mensuelle de Pediatrie [*A publication*]
Rev Mens Sui Odont ... Revue Mensuelle Suisse d'Odontologie [*A publication*]
Rev Mens Suisse Odonto-Stomatol ... Revue Mensuelle Suisse d'Odonto-Stomatologie [*A publication*]
Rev Metal .. Revista de Metalurgia [*A publication*]
Rev Metall ... Revue de Metallurgie [*Paris*] [*A publication*]
Rev Metall Cah Inf Tech ... Revue de Metallurgie. Cahiers d'Informations Techniques [*A publication*]
Rev Metall (Paris) ... Revue de Metallurgie (Paris) [*A publication*]
Rev Metall (Paris) Part 1 ... Revue de Metallurgie (Paris) Part 1. Memoires [*A publication*]
Rev Metall (Paris) Part 2 ... Revue de Metallurgie (Paris) Part 2. Extraits [*A publication*]
Rev Metal (Madrid) ... Revista de Metalurgia (Madrid) [*A publication*]

Rev Metaph ... Review of Metaphysics [*A publication*]
Rev Metaph Mor ... Revue de Metaphysique et de Morale [*A publication*]
Rev Metaph Morale ... Revue de Metaphysique et de Morale [*A publication*]
Rev Metaphy ... Review of Metaphysics [*A publication*]
Rev Metaphys Morale ... Revue de Metaphysique et de Morale [*A publication*]
Rev Meteorol ... Revista Meteorologica [*A publication*]
Rev Met Lit ... Review of Metal Literature [*A publication*]
Rev Met (Madrid) ... Revista de Metalurgia (Madrid) [*A publication*]
Rev Met Mor ... Revue de Metaphysique et de Morale [*A publication*]
Rev Met (Paris) ... Revue de Metallurgie (Paris) [*A publication*]
Rev Metrol Prat Leg ... Revue de Metrologie Pratique et Legale [*A publication*]
Rev Met Technol ... Review of Metals Technology [*A publication*]
RevMex ..... Revolutionary Mexican Historical Society (EA)
Rev Mex Anestesiol ... Revista Mexicana de Anestesiologia [*A publication*]
Rev Mex Astron Astrof ... Revista Mexicana de Astronomia y Astrofisica [*A publication*]
Rev Mex Astron y Astrofis ... Revista Mexicana de Astronomia y Astrofisica [*A publication*]
Rev Mex Astron Astrofis ... Revista Mexicana de Astronomia y Astrofisica [*A publication*]
Rev Mex Cienc Med Biol ... Revista Mexicana de Ciencias Medicas y Biologicas [*A publication*]
Rev Mex Cir Ginecol Cancer ... Revista Mexicana de Cirugia, Ginecologia, y Cancer [*A publication*]
Rev Mex Cirug Ginec Canc ... Revista Mexicana de Cirugia, Ginecologia, y Cancer [*A publication*]
Rev Mex Constr ... Revista Mexicana de la Construccion [*A publication*]
Rev Mex Electr ... Revista Mexicana de Electricidad [*A publication*]
Rev Mex Fis ... Revista Mexicana de Fisica [*A publication*]
Rev Mex Fis Supl Ensenanza ... Revista Mexicana de Fisica. Suplemento de Ensenanza [*A publication*]
Rev Mex Fis Supl Fis Apl ... Revista Mexicana de Fisica. Suplemento de Fisica Aplicada [*A publication*]
Rev Mex Fis Supl Reactor ... Revista Mexicana de Fisica. Suplemento del Reactor [*A publication*]
Rev Mexicana Astronom Astrofis ... Revista Mexicana de Astronomia y Astrofisica [*A publication*]
Rev Mexicana Fis ... Revista Mexicana de Fisica [*A publication*]
Rev Mex Lab Clin ... Revista Mexicana de Laboratorio Clinico [*A publication*]
Rev Mex Pediatr ... Revista Mexicana de Pediatria [*A publication*]
Rev Mex Psiquiat Neurol Med Leg ... Revista Mexicana de Psiquiatria, Neurologia, y Medicina Legal [*A publication*]
Rev Mex Radiol ... Revista Mexicana de Radiologia [*A publication*]
Rev Mex Soc ... Revista Mexicana de Sociologia [*A publication*]
Rev Mex Sociol ... Revista Mexicana de Sociologia [*A publication*]
Rev Mex Tuberc Apar Respir ... Revista Mexicana de Tuberculosis y Aparto Respiratorio [*A publication*]
Rev Mex Tuber Enferm Apar Respir ... Revista Mexicana de Tuberculosis y Enfermedades del Aparato Respiratorio [*A publication*]
Rev Mex Urol ... Revista Mexicana de Urologia [*A publication*]
Rev Micr El ... Revista de Microscopia Electronica [*A publication*]
Rev Microbiol ... Revista de Microbiologia [*A publication*]
Rev Microbiol Appl Agric Hyg Ind ... Revue de Microbiologie Appliquee a l'Agriculture, a l'Hygiene, a l'Industrie [*A publication*]
Rev Micropal ... Revue de Micropaleontologie [*A publication*]
Rev Micropaleontol ... Revue de Micropaleontologie [*A publication*]
Rev Mil ... Revista Militar [*A publication*]
Rev Mil Med Vet ... Revista Militar de Medicina Veterinaria [*A publication*]
Rev Mil Remonta Vet ... Revista Militar de Remonta e Veterinaria [*A publication*]
Rev Mil Vet ... Revista Militar de Veterinaria [*A publication*]
Rev Mil Vet (Rio De Janeiro) ... Revista Militar de Veterinaria (Rio De Janeiro) [*A publication*]
Rev Min ..... Revista Mineria [*A publication*]
REV/MIN ... Revolutions per Minute [*e.g., in reference to phonograph records*]
Rev Minas ... Revista de Minas [*A publication*]
Rev Minas Hidrocarburos ... Revista de Minas e Hidrocarburos [*A publication*]
Rev Minelor ... Revista Minelor [*A publication*]
Rev Minelor (Bucharest) ... Revista Minelor (Bucharest) [*A publication*]
Rev Min Eng ... Revista Mineira de Engenharia [*A publication*]
Rev Minera Geol Mineral ... Revista Minera, Geologia, y Mineralogia [*A publication*]
Rev Mineral ... Reviews in Mineralogy [*A publication*]
Rev Minera y Petrolera ... Revista Minera y Petrolera [*A publication*]
Rev Min Geol Mineral ... Revista Minera, Geologia, y Mineralogia [*A publication*]
Rev Mktg Agric Econ (Sydney) ... Review of Marketing and Agricultural Economics (Sydney) [*A publication*]
Rev M Mec ... Revue M - Mecanique [*A publication*]
Rev Modern Phys ... Reviews of Modern Physics [*A publication*]
Rev Mod Phys ... Reviews of Modern Physics [*A publication*]
Rev Morpho-Phys Hum ... Revue de Morpho-Physiologie Humaine [*A publication*]
Rev Moyen A ... Revue du Moyen-Age Latin [*A publication*]
Rev du Moyen-Age Latin ... Revue du Moyen-Age Latin [*A publication*]
Rev M Phys ... Reviews of Modern Physics [*A publication*]

Revm Resp Mezhved Sb ... Revmatizm Republikanskii Mezhvedomstvennyi Sbornik [*A publication*]
Rev Munic Eng ... Revista Municipal de Engenharia [*A publication*]
Rev Mus..... Revue Musicale [*A publication*]
Rev Mus Chilena ... Revista Musical Chilena [*A publication*]
Rev Mus Hist Nat Mendoza ... Revista. Museo de Historia Natural de Mendoza [*A publication*]
Rev Music ... Revue de Musicologie [*A publication*]
Rev Musical ... Revue Musicale [*A publication*]
Rev Music Chilena ... Revista Musical Chilena [*A publication*]
Rev Mus La Plata ... Revista. Museo de La Plata [*A publication*]
Rev Mus La Plata Secc Antropol ... Revista. Museo de La Plata. Seccion Antropologia [*A publication*]
Rev Mus La Plata Secc Bot ... Revista. Museo de La Plata. Seccion Botanica [*A publication*]
Rev Mus La Plata Secc Geol ... Revista. Museo de La Plata. Seccion Geologia [*A publication*]
Rev Mus La Plata Secc Paleontol ... Revista. Museo de La Plata. Seccion Paleontologia [*A publication*]
Rev Mus La Plata Secc Zool ... Revista. Museo de La Plata. Seccion Zoologia [*A publication*]
Rev Muz..... Revista Muzeelor [*A publication*]
Rev Muz M Mon ... Revista Muzeelor si Monumentelor. Seria Monumente Istorice si Arta [*A publication*]
Rev Muz M Muz ... Revista Muzeelor si Monumentelor. Seria Muzee [*A publication*]
Rev Muz Monum Muz ... Revista Muzeelor si Monumentelor. Seria Muzee [*A publication*]
Rev Mycol ... Revue de Mycologie [*A publication*]
Rev Mycol (Paris) ... Revue de Mycologie (Paris) [*A publication*]
Rev Mycol (Paris) Suppl Colon ... Revue de Mycologie. Supplement Colonial (Paris) [*A publication*]
REVN .... Reversion (ROG)
RevN .... Revue Nouvelle [*Paris*] [*A publication*]
Rev Nac Agr ... Revista Nacional de Agricultura [*A publication*]
Rev Nac Agric (Bogota) ... Revista Nacional de Agricultura (Bogota) [*A publication*]
Rev Nac Hosp ... Revista Nacional de Hospitales [*A publication*]
Rev Nat ...... Revue Nationale [*A publication*]
Rev Nat Lit ... Review of National Literatures [*A publication*]
Rev Nat Res Counc Can ... Review. National Research Council of Canada [*A publication*]
Rev Neurol ... Revue Neurologique [*A publication*]
Rev Neurol B Aires ... Revista Neurologica de Buenos Aires [*A publication*]
Rev Neurol Buenos Aires ... Revista Neurologica de Buenos Aires [*A publication*]
Rev Neurol Clin (Madrid) ... Revista de Neurologia Clinica (Madrid) [*A publication*]
Rev Neurol (Paris) ... Revue Neurologique (Paris) [*A publication*]
Rev Neurops ... Revue de Neuropsychiatrie Infantile et d'Hygiene Mentale de l'Enfance [*A publication*]
Rev Neuro-Psiquiatr ... Revista de Neuro-Psiquiatria [*A publication*]
Rev Neuropsychiatr Infant ... Revue de Neuropsychiatrie Infantile et d'Hygiene Mentale de l'Enfance [*A publication*]
Rev Neuropsychiatr Infant Hyg Ment Enfance ... Revue de Neuropsychiatrie Infantile et d'Hygiene Mentale de l'Enfance [*A publication*]
Rev Neurosci ... Reviews of Neuroscience [*A publication*]
Rev Nickel ... Revue du Nickel [*A publication*]
Rev Nord.... Revue du Nord [*A publication*]
Rev Nordestina Biol ... Revista Nordestina de Biologia [*A publication*]
Rev Not ...... Revue du Notariat [*A publication*]
Rev du Not ... Revue du Notariat [*A publication*]
Rev Notariat ... Revue du Notariat [*A publication*]
Rev du Notariat ... Revue du Notariat [*A publication*]
Rev Nouv.... Revue Nouvelle [*Belgium*] [*A publication*]
REVNRY... Revolutionary
RevNum..... Revue Numismatique [*A publication*]
Rev Num Arg ... Revista Numismatica Argentina [*A publication*]
Rev Nutr Anim ... Revista de Nutricion Animal [*A publication*]
REVO .... Revoke (AABC)
REVO .... Revolution (DSUE)
Rev Oak Ridge Natl Lab (US) ... Review. Oak Ridge National Laboratory (United States) [*A publication*]
Rev Obras Pub ... Revista de Obras Publicas [*A publication*]
Rev Obras Publicas ... Revista de Obras Publicas [*A publication*]
Rev Obras Sanit Nac (Argent) ... Revista de Obras Sanitarias de la Nacion (Argentina) [*A publication*]
Rev Obras Sanit Nac (B Aires) ... Revista de Obras Sanitarias de la Nacion (Buenos Aires) [*A publication*]
Rev Obstet Ginecol Venez ... Revista de Obstetricia y Ginecologia de Venezuela [*A publication*]
Rev Oc........ Revista de Occidente [*A publication*]
Rev Occidente ... Revista de Occidente [*A publication*]
Rev O Chr ... Revue de l'Orient Chretien [*A publication*]
REVOCN .. Revocation (ROG)
REVOCON ... Remote Volume Control
REVOCON ... Revocation
Rev Ocrotirea Mediului Inconjurator Nat Terr Nat ... Revista Ocrotirea Mediului Inconjurator Natura. Terra Natura [*A publication*]
Rev Odontoestomatol ... Revista Odonto-Estomatologica [*A publication*]

Rev Odontoimplantol ... Revue Odonto-Implantologique [*A publication*]
Rev Odontol Circ Odontol Parag ... Revista Odontologica. Circulo de Odontologos del Paraguay [*A publication*]
Rev Odontol (Cordoba) ... Revista Odontologica (Cordoba) [*A publication*]
Rev Odontol Costa Rica ... Revista Odontologica de Costa Rica [*A publication*]
Rev Odontol Ecuat ... Revista Odontologica Ecuatoriana [*A publication*]
Rev Odontol Parana ... Revista Odontologica do Parana [*A publication*]
Rev Odontol PR ... Revista Odontologica de Puerto Rico [*A publication*]
Rev Odontol St Catarina ... Revista de Odontologia. Universidade Federal de Santa Catarina [*A publication*]
Rev Odonto Stomatol ... Revue d'Odonto-Stomatologie [*A publication*]
Rev Odonto-Stomatol (Bord) ... Revue d'Odonto-Stomatologie (Bordeaux) [*A publication*]
Rev Odonto-Stomatol Midi Fr ... Revue d'Odonto-Stomatologie du Midi de la France [*A publication*]
Rev Odontostomatol Nordest ... Revue Odonto-Stomatologique du Nord-Est [*A publication*]
Rev Odonto-Stomatol (Paris) ... Revue d'Odonto-Stomatologie (Paris) [*A publication*]
Rev Of Fed Med Ecuador ... Revista Oficial. Federacion Medica del Ecuador [*A publication*]
Rev Oka..... Revue d'Oka [*A publication*]
Revol Wld .. Revolutionary World [*A publication*]
Revol World ... Revolutionary World [*A publication*]
REVON..... Reversion
REVOP..... Random Evolutionary Operation
Rev Opt...... Revue d'Optique Theorique et Instrumentale [*A publication*]
Rev d'Optique ... Revue d'Optique [*A publication*]
Rev Opt Theor Instrum ... Revue d'Optique Theorique et Instrumentale [*France*] [*A publication*]
Rev Ord...... Revised Ordinances [*A publication*] (DLA)
Rev Ord NWT ... Revised Ordinances, Northwest Territories [*1888*] [*Canada*] [*A publication*] (DLA)
Rev Orl....... Revista de Otorrinolaringologia [*A publication*]
Rev Orthop Dento-Faciale ... Revue d'Orthopedie Dento-Faciale [*A publication*]
Rev Ortop Traumatol Latinoam ... Revista de Ortopedia y Traumatologia Latinoamericana [*A publication*]
Rev Oto-Neuro-Oftalmol Cir Neurol Sud-Am ... Revista de Oto-Neuro-Oftalmologica y de Cirugia Neurologica Sud-Americana [*A publication*]
Rev Oto-Neuro-Ophtalmol ... Revue d'Oto-Neuro-Ophtalmologie [*A publication*]
Rev Oto-Neuro-Ophtalmol (Paris) ... Revue d'Oto-Neuro-Ophtalmologie (Paris) [*A publication*]
Rev Otorrinolaringol ... Revista de Otorrinolaringologia [*A publication*]
Rev Padurilor ... Revista Padurilor [*A publication*]
Rev Padurilor Ind Lemnului Celul Hirtie Ind Lemnului ... Revista Padurilor-Industria Lemnului. Celuloza si Hirtie. Industria Lemnului [*A publication*]
Rev Padurilor Ind Lemnului Celul Hirtie Silvic Exploatarea ... Revista Padurilor-Industria Lemnului. Celuloza si Hirtie. Silvicultura si Exploatarea Padurilor [*A publication*]
Rev Padurilor-Ind Lemnului Ser Ind Lemnului ... Revista Padurilor-Industria Lemnului. Seria Industria Lemnului [*Hungary*] [*A publication*]
Rev Padurilor-Ind Lemnului Ser Silvic Exploatarea Padurilor ... Revista Padurilor-Industria Lemnului. Seria Silvicultura si Exploatarea Padurilor [*A publication*]
Rev Padurilor Ind Lemnului Ser Silvic Exploat Padurilor ... Revista Padurilor-Industria Lemnului. Seria Silvicultura si Exploatarea Padurilor [*A publication*]
Rev Palaeobot Palynol ... Review of Palaeobotany and Palynology [*A publication*]
Rev Palaeobot Palynology ... Review of Palaeobotany and Palynology [*A publication*]
Rev Palae P ... Review of Palaeobotany and Palynology [*A publication*]
Rev Palais Decouv ... Revue du Palais de la Decouverte [*France*] [*A publication*]
Rev Palud Med Trop ... Revue du Paludisme et de Medecine Tropicale [*A publication*]
Rev Path Comp ... Revue de Pathologie Comparee [*A publication*]
Rev Path Gen Physiol Clin ... Revue de Pathologie Generale et de Physiologie Clinique [*A publication*]
Rev Pathol Comp ... Revue de Pathologie Comparee [*A publication*]
Rev Pathol Comp Hyg Gen ... Revue de Pathologie Comparee et Hygiene Generale [*A publication*]
Rev Pathol Comp Med Exp ... Revue de Pathologie Comparee et de Medecine Experimentale [*France*] [*A publication*]
Rev Pathol Gen Comp ... Revue de Pathologie Generale et Comparee [*A publication*]
Rev Pathol Gen Physiol Clin ... Revue de Pathologie Generale et de Physiologie Clinique [*A publication*]
Rev Pathol Veg Entomol Agr France ... Revue de Pathologie Vegetale et d'Entomologie Agricole de France [*A publication*]
Rev Pathol Veg Entomol Agric Fr ... Revue de Pathologie Vegetale et d'Entomologie Agricole de France [*A publication*]
Rev Path Veg et Entom Agric ... Revue de Pathologie Vegetale et d'Entomologie Agricole [*A publication*]

Rev Patronato Biol Anim ... Revista del Patronato de Biologia Animal [*A publication*]
Rev Pau Bearn ... Revue de Pau et du Bearn [*A publication*]
Rev Paul Endodontia ... Revista Paulista de Endodontia [*A publication*]
Rev Paul Med ... Revista Paulista de Medicina [*A publication*]
Rev Paul Tisiol Torax ... Revista Paulista de Tisiologia e do Torax [*A publication*]
Rev Pedag .. Revista de Pedagogia [*A publication*]
Rev Pediatr ... Revue de Pediatrie [*A publication*]
Rev Pediatr Obstet Ginecol ... Revista de Pediatrie, Obstetrica, si Ginecologie [*A publication*]
Rev Pediatr Obstet Ginecol Pediatr ... Revista de Pediatrie, Obstetrica, si Ginecologie. Pediatria [*A publication*]
Rev Pediatr Obstet Ginecol Ser Obstet Ginecol ... Revista de Pediatrie, Obstetrica, si Ginecologie. Seria Obstetrica si Ginecologie [*A publication*]
Rev Pediatr Obstet Ginecol Ser Pediatr ... Revista de Pediatrie, Obstetrica, si Ginecologie. Seria Pediatria [*A publication*]
Rev Pen Code ... Revised Penal Code [*A publication*]   (DLA)
Rev Per Ent Agric ... Revista Peruana de Entomologia Agricola [*A publication*]
Rev Perinat Med ... Reviews in Perinatal Medicine [*A publication*]
Rev Pernambucana Odontol ... Revista Pernambucana de Odontologia [*A publication*]
Rev Per Tuberc ... Revista Peruana de Tuberculosis y Enfermedades Respiratorias [*A publication*]
Rev Peru Entomol ... Revista Peruana de Entomologia [*A publication*]
Rev Peru Entomol Agr ... Revista Peruana de Entomologia Agricola [*A publication*]
Rev Peru Entomol Agric ... Revista Peruana de Entomologia Agricola [*A publication*]
Rev Peru Salud Publica ... Revista Peruana de Salud Publica [*A publication*]
Rev Peru Tuberc Enferm Respir ... Revista Peruana de Tuberculosis y Enfermedades Respiratorias [*A publication*]
Rev Petrolifere ... Revue Petrolifere [*A publication*]
Rev Petrol Technol ... Review of Petroleum Technology [*A publication*]
Rev Pet Technol (London) ... Reviews of Petroleum Technology (London) [*A publication*]
RevPF .... Revista Portuguesa de Filosofia [*A publication*]
Rev Pharm ... Revue Pharmaceutique [*A publication*]
Rev Pharmacol Ter Exp ... Revue de Pharmacologie et de Therapeutique Experimentale [*A publication*]
Rev Pharm Liban ... Revue Pharmaceutique Libanaise [*A publication*]
Rev Ph Ch J ... Review of Physical Chemistry of Japan [*A publication*]
Rev Phil ..... Revue de Philologie, de Litterature, et d'Histoire Anciennes [*A publication*]
Rev Phil Fr ... Revue Philosophique de la France et de l'Etranger [*A publication*]
Rev Phil Louvain ... Revue Philosophique de Louvain [*A publication*]
Rev Philol .. Revue de Philologie, de Litterature, et d'Histoire Anciennes [*A publication*]
Rev Philos ... Revue Philosophique de Louvain [*A publication*]
Rev Philos Fr Etrang ... Revue Philosophique de la France et de l'Etranger [*A publication*]
Rev Philos Louv ... Revue Philosophique de Louvain [*A publication*]
Rev Phonet Appl ... Revue de Phonetique Appliquee [*A publication*]
Rev Phys .... Revue de Physique [*A publication*]
Rev Phys Acad Repub Pop Roum ... Revue de Physique. Academie de la Republique Populaire Roumaine [*Romania*] [*A publication*]
Rev Phys Ap ... Revue de Physique Appliquee [*A publication*]
Rev Phys Appl ... Revue de Physique Appliquee [*A publication*]
Rev Phys Appl (Suppl J Phys) ... Revue de Physique Appliquee (Supplement to Journal de Physique) [*A publication*]
Rev Phys B ... Reviews of Physiology, Biochemistry, and Pharmacology [*A publication*]
Rev Phys Chem Jpn ... Review of Physical Chemistry of Japan [*A publication*]
Rev Physiol Biochem Exp Pharmacol ... Reviews of Physiology, Biochemistry, and Experimental Pharmacology [*A publication*]
Rev Physiol Biochem Pharmacol ... Reviews of Physiology, Biochemistry, and Pharmacology [*A publication*]
Rev Physiother Chir Rad ... Revue de Physiotherapie Chirurgicale et de Radiologie [*A publication*]
Rev Phys Technol ... Review of Physics in Technology [*United Kingdom*] [*A publication*]
Rev Phytother ... Revue de Phytotherapie [*A publication*]
Rev Planeacion Desarrollo ... Revista de Planeacion y Desarrollo [*A publication*]
Rev Plant Path ... Review of Plant Pathology [*A publication*]
Rev Plant Pathol ... Review of Plant Pathology [*A publication*]
Rev Plant Prot Res ... Review of Plant Protection Research [*A publication*]
Rev Plasma Phys ... Reviews of Plasma Physics [*A publication*]
Rev Plast (Madrid) ... Revista de Plasticos (Madrid) [*A publication*]
Rev Plast Mod ... Revista de Plasticos Modernos [*A publication*]
Rev Pneumol Clin ... Revue de Pneumologie Clinique [*A publication*]
Rev Pol .... Review of Politics [*A publication*]
Rev Pol .... Revista de Estudios Politicos [*A publication*]
Rev Pol Acad Sci ... Review. Polish Academy of Sciences [*A publication*]
Rev Polarogr ... Review of Polarography [*A publication*]
Rev Polarogr (Jpn) ... Review of Polarography (Japan) [*A publication*]
Rev Pol Code ... Revised Political Code [*A publication*]   (DLA)

Rev Policlin (Caracas) ... Revista de la Policlinica (Caracas) [*A publication*]
Rev of Polish Law and Econ ... Review of Polish Law and Economics [*Warsaw, Poland*] [*A publication*]   (DLA)
Rev Polit .... Review of Politics [*A publication*]
Rev Politec ... Revista Politecnica [*A publication*]
Rev Pol L ... Review of Polish Law [*A publication*]   (DLA)
Rev Polym Technol ... Reviews in Polymer Technology [*A publication*]
Rev Polytech ... Revue Polytechnique [*Switzerland*] [*A publication*]
Rev Po Quim ... Revista Portuguesa de Quimica [*A publication*]
Rev Port Bioquim Apl ... Revista Portuguesa de Bioquimica Aplicada [*A publication*]
Rev Port Cienc Vet ... Revista Portuguesa de Ciencias Veterinarias [*A publication*]
Rev Port Estomat ... Revista Portuguesa de Estomatologia e Cirurgia Maxilofacial [*A publication*]
Rev Port Estomatol Cir Maxilofac ... Revista Portuguesa de Estomatologia e Cirurgia Maxilofacial [*A publication*]
Rev Port Farm ... Revista Portuguesa de Farmacia [*A publication*]
Rev Port Filosof ... Revista Portuguesa de Filosofia [*A publication*]
Rev Port Med ... Revista Portuguesa de Medicina [*A publication*]
Rev Port Med Milit ... Revista Portuguesa de Medicina Militar [*A publication*]
Rev Port Obstet ... Revista Portuguesa de Obstetricia, Ginecologia, e Cirurgia [*A publication*]
Rev Port Pediatr ... Revista Portuguesa de Pediatria [*A publication*]
Rev Port Quim ... Revista Portuguesa de Quimica [*A publication*]
Rev Port Quim (Lisbon) ... Revista Portuguesa de Quimica (Lisbon) [*A publication*]
Rev Port Zool Biol Geral ... Revista Portuguesa de Zoologia e Biologia Geral [*A publication*]
Rev Powder Metall Phys Ceram ... Reviews on Powder Metallurgy and Physical Ceramics [*A publication*]
Rev PR .... Revista de Derecho Puertorriqueno [*A publication*]
Rev Prat ..... Revue du Praticien [*A publication*]
Rev Prat Biol Appl Clin Ther ... Revue Pratique de Biologie Appliquee a la Clinique et a la Therapeutique [*A publication*]
Rev Prat Connaiss Med ... Revue Pratique des Connaissances Medicales [*A publication*]
Rev Prat Controle Ind ... Revue Pratique du Controle Industriel [*France*] [*A publication*]
Rev Prat Dr Soc ... Revue Pratique de Droit Social [*A publication*]
Rev Prat Froid ... Revue Pratique du Froid [*Later, Journal RPF*] [*A publication*]
Rev Prat Froid Cond Air ... Revue Pratique du Froid et du Conditionnement de l'Air [*Later, Journal RPF*] [*A publication*]
Rev Prat Mal Pays Chands ... Revue Pratique des Maladies des Pays Chands [*A publication*]
Rev Prat Quest Com et Econom ... Revue Pratique des Questions Commerciales et Economiques [*A publication*]
Rev Presse Econ Min ... Revue de Presse d'Economie Miniere [*A publication*]
REV PROC ... Revenue Procedure [*Internal Revenue Service*]
Rev Prod Chim ... Revue des Produits Chimiques [*A publication*]
Rev Prod Chim Actual Sci Reunis ... Revue des Produits Chimiques et l'Actualite Scientifique Reunis [*A publication*]
Rev Prog Color Relat Top ... Review of Progress in Coloration and Related Topics [*A publication*]
Rev Prot ..... Revue de la Protection [*France*] [*A publication*]
Rev Prum Obchodu ... Revue Prumyslu a Obchodu [*Czechoslovakia*] [*A publication*]
Rev Psicol .. Revista de Psicologia [*A publication*]
Rev Psicol Gen Apl ... Revista de Psicologia General y Aplicada [*A publication*]
Rev Psihol ... Revista de Psihologie [*A publication*]
Rev Psiquiat Psicol Med ... Revista de Psiquiatria y Psicologia Medica de Europeo y America Latina [*A publication*]
Rev Psiquiatr ... Revista de Psiquiatria [*A publication*]
Rev Psiquiatr Peru ... Revista Psiquiatrica Peruana [*A publication*]
Rev Psy App ... Revue de Psychologie Appliquee [*A publication*]
Rev Psych Appl ... Revue de Psychologie Appliquee [*A publication*]
Rev Pub Dat ... Review of Public Data Use [*A publication*]
Rev Pub Data Use ... Review of Public Data Use [*A publication*]
Rev Pure Appl Chem ... Reviews of Pure and Applied Chemistry [*A publication*]
Rev Pure Appl Pharmacol Sci ... Reviews in Pure and Applied Pharmacological Sciences [*A publication*]
Rev Questions Sci ... Revue des Questions Scientifiques [*A publication*]
Rev Quest Sci ... Revue des Questions Scientifiques [*A publication*]
Rev Quim ... Revista Quimica [*A publication*]
Rev Quim Farm (Rio De Janeiro) ... Revista de Quimica e Farmacia (Rio De Janeiro) [*A publication*]
Rev Quim Farm (Santiago) ... Revista Quimico-Farmaceutica (Santiago) [*A publication*]
Rev Quim Farm (Tegucigalpa) ... Revista de Quimica y Farmacia (Tegucigalpa) [*A publication*]
Rev Quim Ind (Buenos Aires) ... Revista de Quimica Industrial (Buenos Aires) [*A publication*]
Rev Quim Ind (Rio De Janeiro) ... Revista de Quimica Industrial (Rio De Janeiro) [*A publication*]
Rev Quim Ing Quim ... Revista de Quimica e Ingenieria Quimica [*A publication*]
Rev Quim Pura Apl ... Revista de Quimica Pura e Aplicada [*A publication*]

Rev Quim Text ... Revista de Quimica Textil [*A publication*]
RevQum ..... Revue de Qumran [*A publication*]
REVR........ Receiver (AAG)
REVR........ Reversioner (ROG)
REVR........ Reviewer (AFM)
Rev R......... Revised Reports [*1759-1866*] [*England*] [*A publication*] (DLA)
RevR .... Revue Romane [*A publication*]
Rev R Acad Cienc Exactas Fis Nat Madr ... Revista. Real Academia de Ciencias Exactas, Fisicas, y Naturales de Madrid [*A publication*]
Rev R Acad Farm Barcelona ... Revista. Real Academia de Farmacia de Barcelona [*A publication*]
Rev Radic Polit Econ ... Review of Radical Political Economics [*A publication*]
Rev Radiochem Cent (Amersham Eng) ... Review. Radiochemical Centre (Amersham, England) [*A publication*]
Rev Radio Res Lab ... Review. Radio Research Laboratories [*A publication*]
Rev React Species Chem React ... Reviews on Reactive Species in Chemical Reactions [*A publication*]
Rev Real Acad Cienc Exact Fis Natur Madrid ... Real Academia de Ciencias Exactas, Fisicas, y Naturales de Madrid. Revista [*A publication*]
Rev Real Acad Ci Exact Fis Natur Madrid ... Revista. Real Academia de Ciencias Exactas, Fisicas, y Naturales de Madrid [*A publication*]
Rev Reh ...... Reversed [*or Reversing*] on Rehearing [*Used in Shepard's Citations*] [*Legal term*] (DLA)
Rev Relig.... Review for Religious [*A publication*]
Rev Rel Res ... Review of Religious Research [*A publication*]
Rev Rep ...... Revised Reports [*England*] [*A publication*] (DLA)
Rev Rep Inf Cent Pol AEC ... Review Report Information Center. Polish Atomic Energy Commission [*A publication*]
Rev Rev (A) ... Review of Reviews. Australian Edition [*A publication*]
Rev Revs Australas Ed ... Review of Reviews. Australasian Edition [*A publication*] (APTA)
Rev Rhum .. Revue du Rhumatisme et des Maladies Osteo-Articulaires [*A publication*]
Rev Rhum Mal Osteo-Artic ... Revue du Rhumatisme et des Maladies Osteo-Articulaires [*A publication*]
Rev River Plate ... Review of the River Plate [*A publication*]
Rev Ro Bioc ... Revue Roumaine de Biochimie [*A publication*]
Rev "Roche" Farm ... Revista "Roche" de Farmacia [*A publication*]
Rev Ro Chim ... Revue Roumaine de Chimie [*A publication*]
Rev Roman ... Revue Romane [*A publication*]
Rev Romande Agric Vitic Arboric ... Revue Romande d'Agriculture, de Viticulture, et d'Arboriculture [*A publication*]
Rev Romande Agr Viticult Arboricult ... Revue Romande d'Agriculture, de Viticulture, et d'Arboriculture [*A publication*]
Rev Ro Phys ... Revue Roumaine de Physique [*A publication*]
Rev Roumaine Linguist ... Revue Roumaine de Linguistique [*A publication*]
Rev Roumaine Math Pures Appl ... Revue Roumaine de Mathematiques Pures et Appliquees [*A publication*]
Rev Roumaine Phys ... Revue Roumaine de Physique [*A publication*]
Rev Roumaine Sci Soc ... Revue Roumaine des Sciences Sociales. Serie de Sciences Juridiques [*A publication*]
Rev Roumaine Sci Tech Ser Electrotech Energet ... Revue Roumaine des Sciences Techniques. Serie Electrotechnique et Energetique [*A publication*]
Rev Roumaine Sci Tech Ser Mec Appl ... Revue Roumaine des Sciences Techniques. Serie de Mecanique Appliquee [*A publication*]
Rev Roum Biochim ... Revue Roumaine de Biochimie [*A publication*]
Rev Roum Biol ... Revue Roumaine de Biologie [*A publication*]
Rev Roum Biol Ser Biol Anim ... Revue Roumaine de Biologie. Serie de Biologie Animale [*A publication*]
Rev Roum Biol Ser Biol Veg ... Revue Roumaine de Biologie. Serie Biologie Vegetale [*Romania*] [*A publication*]
Rev Roum Biol Ser Bot ... Revue Roumaine de Biologie. Serie Botanique [*A publication*]
Rev Roum Biol Ser Zool ... Revue Roumaine de Biologie. Serie Zoologie [*A publication*]
Rev Roum Chim ... Revue Roumaine de Chimie [*A publication*]
Rev Roum Embryol ... Revue Roumaine d'Embryologie [*A publication*]
Rev Roum Embryol Cytol Ser Embryol ... Revue Roumaine d'Embryologie et de Cytologie. Serie d'Embryologie [*A publication*]
Rev Roum Endocrinol ... Revue Roumaine d'Endocrinologie [*A publication*]
Rev Roum Geol Geophys Geogr Ser Geogr ... Revue Roumaine de Geologie, Geophysique, et Geographie. Serie de Geographie [*A publication*]
Rev Roum Geol Geophys Geogr Ser Geol ... Revue Roumaine de Geologie, Geophysique, et Geographie. Serie de Geologie [*A publication*]
Rev Roum Geol Geophys Geogr Ser Geophys ... Revue Roumaine de Geologie, Geophysique, et Geographie. Serie de Geophysique [*A publication*]
Rev Roum H ... Revue Roumaine d'Histoire [*A publication*]
Rev Roum Hist ... Revue Roumaine d'Histoire [*A publication*]
Rev Roum Inframicrobiol ... Revue Roumaine d'Inframicrobiologie [*A publication*]
Rev Roum Math Pures Appl ... Revue Roumaine de Mathematiques Pures et Appliquees [*A publication*]
Rev Roum Med ... Revue Roumaine de Medecine [*A publication*]

Rev Roum Med Endocrinol ... Revue Roumaine de Medecine. Endocrinologie [*A publication*]
Rev Roum Med Interne ... Revue Roumaine de Medecine Interne [*Later, Revue Roumaine de Medecine. Medecine Interne*] [*A publication*]
Rev Roum Med Med Interne ... Revue Roumaine de Medecine. Medecine Interne [*A publication*]
Rev Roum Med Neurol Psychiatr ... Revue Roumaine de Medecine. Neurologie et Psychiatrie [*A publication*]
Rev Roum Med Virol ... Revue Roumaine de Medecine. Virologie [*A publication*]
Rev Roum Metall ... Revue Roumaine de Metallurgie [*A publication*]
Rev Roum Morphol Embryol ... Revue Roumaine de Morphologie et d'Embryologie [*A publication*]
Rev Roum Morphol Embryol Physiol Morphol Embryol ... Revue Roumaine de Morphologie, d'Embryologie, et de Physiologie. Serie Morphologie et Embryologie [*A publication*]
Rev Roum Morphol Embryol Physiol Physiol ... Revue Roumaine de Morphologie, d'Embryologie, et de Physiologie. Serie Physiologie [*A publication*]
Rev Roum Morphol Physiol ... Revue Roumaine de Morphologie et du Physiologie [*A publication*]
Rev Roum Neurol ... Revue Roumaine de Neurologie [*Later, Revue Roumaine de Medecine. Serie Neurologie et Psychiatrie*] [*A publication*]
Rev Roum Neurol Psychiatr ... Revue Roumaine de Neurologie et de Psychiatrie [*Later, Revue Roumaine de Medecine. Serie Neurologie et Psychiatrie*] [*A publication*]
Rev Roum Phys ... Revue Roumaine de Physique [*A publication*]
Rev Roum Physiol ... Revue Roumaine de Physiologie [*Later, Revue Roumaine de Morphologie, d'Embryologie, et de Physiologie*] [*A publication*]
Rev Roum Sci Soc Philos Logique ... Revue Roumaine des Sciences Sociales. Serie de Philosophie et de Logique [*A publication*]
Rev Roum Sci Tech Mec Appl ... Revue Roumaine des Sciences Techniques. Serie de Mecanique Appliquee [*Romania*] [*A publication*]
Rev Roum Sci Tech Ser Electrotech Energ ... Revue Roumaine des Sciences Techniques. Serie Electrotechnique et Energetique [*A publication*]
Rev Roum Sci Tech Ser Mec Appl ... Revue Roumaine des Sciences Techniques. Serie de Mecanique Appliquee [*A publication*]
Rev Roum Sci Tech Ser Met ... Revue Roumaine des Sciences Techniques. Serie de Metallurgie [*A publication*]
Rev Roum Virol ... Revue Roumaine de Virologie [*A publication*]
REV RUL.. Revenue Ruling [*Internal Revenue Service*]
REVS........ Reconnaissance Electro-Optical Viewing System
REVS........ Requirements Engineering and Validation System
REVS........ Rotor Entry Vehicle System [*Aerospace*]
Rev Salud Anim ... Revista de Salud Animal [*A publication*]
Rev Sanid Aeronaut ... Revista de Sanidad de Aeronautica [*A publication*]
Rev Sanid Fuerzas Policiales ... Revista de la Sanidad de las Fuerzas Policiales [*A publication*]
Rev Sanid Hig Publica ... Revista de Sanidad e Higiene Publica [*A publication*]
Rev Sanid Hig Publica (Madr) ... Revista de Sanidad e Higiene Publica (Madrid) [*A publication*]
Rev Sanid Mil (Argent) ... Revista de la Sanidad Militar (Argentina) [*A publication*]
Rev Sanid Polic ... Revista de la Sanidad de Policia [*A publication*]
Rev Sanit Mil ... Revista Sanitara Militara [*A publication*]
Rev San Mil (Buenos Aires) ... Revista de la Sanidad Militar (Buenos Aires) [*A publication*]
Rev Sao Paulo Braz Univ Fac Med Vet Zootec ... Revista. Sao Paulo Universidade. Faculdade de Medicina Veterinaria e Zootecnia [*A publication*]
Rev Saude .. Revista Saude [*A publication*]
Rev Saude Publica ... Revista de Saude Publica [*A publication*]
Rev Sc Crim ... Revue de Science Criminelle et de Droit Penal Compare [*A publication*]
Rev Sci .... Revue Scientifique [*A publication*]
Rev Sci Bourbonnais Cent Fr ... Revue Scientifique du Bourbonnais et du Centre de la France [*A publication*]
Rev de Sci Criminelle et de Droit Penal Compare ... Revue de Science Criminelle et de Droit Penal Compare [*Paris, France*] [*A publication*] (DLA)
Rev Sci Ed ... Revue des Sciences de l'Education [*A publication*]
Rev Scient (Paris) ... Revue Scientifique (Paris) [*A publication*]
Rev Sci Hum ... Revue des Sciences Humaines [*A publication*]
Rev Sci Ins ... Review of Scientific Instruments [*A publication*]
Rev Sci Instr ... Review of Scientific Instruments [*A publication*]
Rev Sci Instrum ... Review of Scientific Instruments [*A publication*]
Rev Sci Med ... Revue des Sciences Medicales [*A publication*]
Rev Sci Nat Auvergne ... Revue des Sciences Naturelles d'Auvergne [*A publication*]
Rev Sci Natur Auvergne ... Revue des Sciences Naturelles d'Auvergne [*A publication*]
Rev Sci Ph ... Revue des Sciences Philosophiques et Theologiques [*A publication*]
Rev Sci Phil Theol ... Revue des Sciences Philosophiques et Theologiques [*A publication*]
Rev Sci Rel ... Revue des Sciences Religieuses [*A publication*]

Rev Sc Leg Fin ... Revue de Science et de Legislation Financiere [*A publication*]
RevScPhTh ... Revue des Sciences Philosophiques et Theologiques [*A publication*]
RevScR ...... Regue des Sciences Religieuses [*Strasbourg/Paris*] [*A publication*]
RevScRel .... Revue des Sciences Religieuses [*Strasbourg/Paris*] [*A publication*]
Rev Sec Reg ... Review of Securities Regulation [*A publication*]
Rev Sec Soc ... Revue Belge de Securite Sociale [*A publication*]
Rev Sel Code Leg ... Review of Selected Code Legislation [*A publication*]   (DLA)
Rev Ser IAEA ... Review Series. International Atomic Energy Agency [*A publication*]
Rev Serv Espec Saude Publica ... Revista. Servicio Especial de Saude Publica [*A publication*]
Rev Serv Nac Min Geol (Argent) ... Revista. Servicio Nacional Minero Geologico (Argentina) [*A publication*]
Rev Serv Nac Salud ... Revista. Servicio Nacional de Salud [*A publication*]
Rev SESDA ... Revue du SESDA [*Secretariat de Sante Dentaire de l'Afrique*] [*A publication*]
Rev SESP .. Revista. Servicio Especial de Saude Publica [*A publication*]
Revs Geophys Space Phys ... Reviews of Geophysics and Space Physics [*A publication*]
Rev Shorthorn ... Revista Shorthorn [*A publication*]
Rev Sifilogr Leprol Dermatol ... Revista de Sifilografia, Leprologia, y Dermatologia [*A publication*]
Rev Silicon Germanium Tin Lead Compd ... Reviews on Silicon, Germanium, Tin, and Lead Compounds [*A publication*]
Rev Sind Estad ... Revista Sindical de Estadistica [*A publication*]
Rev SNCASO ... Revue SNCASO [*Societe Nationale de Constructions Aeronautiques du Sud-Ouest*] [*A publication*]
Rev Soc ...... Revue Pratique des Societes Civiles et Commerciales [*A publication*]
Rev Soc ...... Revue des Societes [*A publication*]
Rev Soc Argent Biol ... Revista. Sociedad Argentina de Biologia [*A publication*]
Rev Soc Argent Neurol y Psiquiat ... Revista. Sociedad Argentina de Neurologia y Psiquiatria [*A publication*]
Rev Soc Biom Hum ... Revue. Societe de Biometre Humaine [*A publication*]
Rev Soc Boliv Hist Nat ... Revista. Sociedad Boliviana de Historia Natural [*A publication*]
Rev Soc Bras Agron ... Revista. Sociedade Brasileira de Agronomia [*A publication*]
Rev Soc Bras Med Trop ... Revista. Sociedade Brasileira de Medicina Tropical [*A publication*]
Rev Soc Bras Quim ... Revista. Sociedade Brasileira de Quimica [*A publication*]
Rev Soc Bras Zootec ... Revista. Sociedade Brasileira de Zootecnia [*A publication*]
Rev Soc Cient Parag ... Revista. Sociedad Cientifica del Paraguay [*A publication*]
Rev Soc Colomb Endocrinol ... Revista. Sociedad Colombiana de Endocrinologia [*A publication*]
Rev Soc Cubana Bot ... Revista. Sociedad Cubana de Botanica [*A publication*]
Rev Soc Cubana Ing ... Revista. Sociedad Cubana de Ingenieros [*A publication*]
Rev Soc Cub Hist Med ... Revista. Sociedad Cubana de la Historia de Medicina [*A publication*]
Rev Soc Ec ... Review of Social Economy [*A publication*]
Rev Soc Econ ... Review of Social Economy [*A publication*]
Rev Soc Entomol Argent ... Revista. Sociedad Entomologica Argentina [*A publication*]
Rev Soc Geol Argent ... Revista. Sociedad Geologica Argentina [*A publication*]
Rev Soc Hist Theatre ... Revue. Societe d'Histoire du Theatre [*A publication*]
Rev Soc L ... Review of Socialist Law [*A publication*]
Rev Soc Lun Int ... Revista. Sociedad Lunar Internacional [*A publication*]
Rev Soc Malacol Carlos Torre ... Revista. Sociedad Malacologica Carlos de la Torre [*A publication*]
Rev Soc Med Argent ... Revista. Sociedad Medica Argentina [*A publication*]
Rev Soc Med Cir Sao Jose Rio Preto ... Revista. Sociedade de Medicina e Cirurgia de Sao Jose Do Rio Preto [*A publication*]
Rev Soc Med Int ... Revista. Sociedad de Medicina Interna [*A publication*]
Rev Soc Med Vet (Buenos Aires) ... Revista. Sociedad de Medicina Veterinaria (Buenos Aires) [*A publication*]
Rev Soc Med Vet Chile ... Revista. Sociedad de Medicina Veterinaria de Chile [*A publication*]
Rev Soc Mex Hig ... Revista. Sociedad Mexicana de Higiene [*A publication*]
Rev Soc Mex Hist Nat ... Revista. Sociedad Mexicana de Historia Natural [*A publication*]
Rev Soc Mex Hist Natur ... Revista. Sociedad Mexicana de Historia Natural [*A publication*]
Rev Soc Mex Lepid AC ... Revista. Sociedad Mexicana de Lepidopterologia. AC [*A publication*]
Rev Soc Mex Lepidopterol AC ... Revista. Sociedad Mexicana de Lepidopterologia. AC [*A publication*]
Rev Soc Obstet Ginec ... Revista. Sociedad de Obstetricia y Ginecologia de Buenos Aires [*A publication*]
Rev Soc Pediat ... Revista. Sociedad de Pediatria [*A publication*]

Rev Soc Pediatr Litoral ... Revista. Sociedad de Pediatria del Litoral [*A publication*]
Rev Soc Peru Endocrinol ... Revista. Sociedad Peruana de Endocrinologia [*A publication*]
Rev Soc Quim Mex ... Revista. Sociedad Quimica de Mexico [*A publication*]
Rev Soc R Belge Ing Ind ... Revue. Societe Royale Belge des Ingenieurs et des Industriels [*A publication*]
Rev Soc Rural Rosario ... Revista. Sociedad Rural de Rosario [*A publication*]
Rev Soc Savantes Haute Normandie ... Revue des Societes Savantes de Haute-Normandie [*A publication*]
Rev Soc Sci Hyg Aliment Aliment Ration Homme ... Revue. Societe Scientifique d'Hygiene Alimentaire et de l'Alimentation Rationnelle de l'Homme [*A publication*]
Rev Soc Venez Cardiol ... Revista. Sociedad Venezolana de Cardiologia [*A publication*]
Rev Soc Venez Hist Med ... Revista. Sociedad Venezolana de Historia de la Medicina [*A publication*]
Rev Soc Venez Quim ... Revista. Sociedad Venezolana de Quimica [*A publication*]
Rev Soldadura ... Revista de Soldadura [*A publication*]
Rev Solid State Sci ... Reviews of Solid State Science [*A publication*]
Rev Soudre Lastijdschrift ... Revue de la Soudure/Lastijdschrift [*A publication*]
Rev Soudure ... Revue de la Soudure/Lastijdschrift [*Brussels*] [*A publication*]
Rev Soudure Autogene ... Revue de la Soudure Autogene [*A publication*]
Rev Soudure/Lastijdschrift ... Revue de la Soudure/Lastijdschrift [*A publication*]
Rev Sov Med ... Review of Soviet Medicine [*A publication*]
Rev Sov Med Sci ... Review of Soviet Medical Sciences [*A publication*]
Rev Sport Leisure ... Review of Sport and Leisure [*A publication*]
RevSR .... Revue des Sciences Religieuses [*Strasbourg/Paris*] [*A publication*]
Rev St .... Revised Statutes [*A publication*]   (DLA)
Rev Stat .... Revised Statutes [*Various jurisdictions*] [*A publication*]   (DLA)
Rev Stat Ap ... Revue de Statistique Appliquee [*A publication*]
Rev Statist Appl ... Revue de Statistique Appliquee [*A publication*]
Rev Stiint "V Adamachi" ... Revista Stiintifica "V. Adamachi" [*A publication*]
Rev Stomat ... Revue de Stomatologie [*Later, Revue de Stomatologie et de Chirurgie Maxillo-Faciale*] [*A publication*]
Rev Stomatol ... Revue de Stomatologie [*Later, Revue de Stomatologie et de Chirurgie Maxillo-Faciale*] [*A publication*]
Rev Stomatol Chir Maxillo-Fac ... Revue de Stomatologie et de Chirurgie Maxillo-Faciale [*A publication*]
Rev Stomato-Odontol Nord Fr ... Revue Stomato-Odontologique du Nord de la France [*A publication*]
Rev Sudam Bot ... Revista Sudamericana de Botanica [*A publication*]
Rev Sud-Am Cien Med ... Revista Sud-Americana de Ciencias Medicas [*A publication*]
Rev Sud-Am Endocrin ... Revista Sud-Americana de Endocrinologia [*A publication*]
Rev Sud-Am Endocrinol Immunol Quimioter ... Revista Sud-Americana de Endocrinologia, Immunologia, y Quimioterapia [*A publication*]
Rev Sudam Morfol ... Revista Sudamericana de Morfologia [*A publication*]
Rev Suisse Agric ... Revue Suisse d'Agriculture [*A publication*]
Rev Suisse Dr Int'l Concurrence ... Revue Suisse du Droit International de la Concurrence [*Swiss Review of International Antitrust Law*] [*A publication*]   (DLA)
Rev Suisse Gynecol Obstet ... Revue Suisse de Gynecologie et d'Obstetrique [*A publication*]
Rev Suisse Gynecol Obstet Suppl ... Revue Suisse de Gynecologie et d'Obstetrique. Supplementum [*A publication*]
Rev Suisse Hydrol ... Revue Suisse d'Hydrologie [*A publication*]
Rev Suisse Med Sport ... Revue Suisse de Medecine des Sports [*A publication*]
Rev Suisse Med Sports ... Revue Suisse de Medecine des Sports [*A publication*]
Rev Suisse Pathol Gen Bact ... Revue Suisse de Pathologie Generale et de Bacteriologie [*A publication*]
Rev Suisse Psychol Pure Appl ... Revue Suisse de Psychologie Pure et Appliquee [*A publication*]
Rev Suisse Tuberc Pneum ... Revue Suisse de la Tuberculose et de Pneumonologie [*A publication*]
Rev Suisse Vitic Arboric ... Revue Suisse de Viticulture et Arboriculture [*A publication*]
Rev Suisse Vitic Arboric Hortic ... Revue Suisse de Viticulture et Arboriculture. Horticulture [*A publication*]
Rev Suisse Zool ... Revue Suisse de Zoologie [*A publication*]
Rev Surg ... Review of Surgery [*A publication*]
Rev Sw Dig ... Revision of Swift's Digest of Connecticut Laws [*A publication*]   (DLA)
Rev Syniatrica ... Revista Syniatrica [*A publication*]
Revta Agric (Habana) ... Revista de Agricultura (Habana) [*A publication*]
Revta Agric (Piracicaba) ... Revista de Agricultura (Piracicaba) [*A publication*]
Revta Agron NE Argent ... Revista Agronomica del Noroeste Argentino [*A publication*]
Revta Biol .. Revista de Biologia [*A publication*]
Revta Biol Trop ... Revista de Biologia Tropical [*A publication*]
Revta Bras Biol ... Revista Brasileira de Biologia [*A publication*]
Revta Bras Ent ... Revista Brasileira de Entomologia [*A publication*]

Revta Bras Pesquisas Med Biol ... Revista Brasileira de Pesquisas Medicas e Biologicas [*A publication*]
Revta Chil Ent ... Revista Chilena de Entomologia [*A publication*]
Revta Ent (Rio De J) ... Revista de Entomologia (Rio De Janeiro) [*A publication*]
Revta Esp Fisiol ... Revista Espanola de Fisiologia [*A publication*]
Revta Fac Agron Univ Cent Venez ... Revista. Facultad de Agronomia. Universidad Central de Venezuela [*A publication*]
Revta Fac Agron Univ Nac La Plata ... Revista. Facultad de Agronomia y Veterinaria. Universidad Nacional de La Plata [*A publication*]
Revta Fac Agron Univ Repub (Urug) ... Revista. Facultad de Agronomia. Universidad de la Republica (Uruguay) [*A publication*]
Revta Fac Agron Vet Univ B Aires ... Revista. Facultad de Agronomia y Veterinaria. Universidad de Buenos Aires [*A publication*]
Revta Fac Cienc Agrar Univ Nac Cuyo ... Revista. Facultad de Ciencias Agrarias. Universidad Nacional de Cuyo [*A publication*]
Revta Fac Farm Bioquim S Paulo ... Revista. Faculdade de Farmacia e Bioquimica. Universidade de Sao Paulo [*A publication*]
Revta Floresta ... Revista Floresta [*A publication*]
Revta Hort Vitic ... Revista de Horticultura si Viticultura [*A publication*]
Revta Ind Agric (Tucuman) ... Revista Industrial y Agricola (Tucuman) [*A publication*]
Revta Interam Psicologia ... Revista Interamericana de Psicologia [*A publication*]
Revta Invest Agropec (B Aires) ... Revista de Investigaciones Agropecuarias (Buenos Aires) [*A publication*]
Revta Med Vet Parasit (Caracas) ... Revista de Medicina Veterinaria y Parasitologia (Caracas) [*A publication*]
Revta Mus Argent Cienc Nat Bernardina Rivadavia Zool ... Revista. Museo Argentino de Ciencias Naturales Bernardino Rivadavia. Zoologia [*A publication*]
Revta Padur ... Revista Padurilor [*A publication*]
Revta Peru Ent Agric ... Revista Peruana de Entomologia Agricola [*A publication*]
Revta Psicol Norm Patol ... Revista de Psicologia Normal e Patologica [*A publication*]
RevTar .... Revenue Tariff [*Australia*] [*Political party*]   (ADA)
Revta Stiint Vet ... Revista Stiintelor Veterinare [*A publication*]
Revta Univ Auton G R Moreno ... Revista. Universidad Autonoma Gabriel Rene Moreno [*A publication*]
Revta Univ Univ Catol Chile ... Revista Universitaria. Universidad Catolica de Chile [*A publication*]
Rev Tax Indiv ... Review of Taxation of Individuals [*A publication*]
Rev Tax'n Indiv ... Review of Taxation of Individuals [*A publication*]   (DLA)
Rev & TC ... Revenue and Taxation Code [*A publication*]   (DLA)
Rev Tec ...... Revista Tecnica [*A publication*]
Rev Tec Col Ing Agron Mex ... Revista Tecnica. Colegio de Ingenieros Agronomos de Mexico [*A publication*]
Rev Tech Batim Constr Ind ... Revue Technique du Batiment et des Constructions Industrielles [*France*] [*A publication*]
Rev Tech Ind Aliment ... Revue Technique de l'Industrie Alimentaire [*A publication*]
Rev Tech Ind Cuir ... Revue Technique des Industries du Cuir [*A publication*]
Rev Tech Luxemb ... Revue Technique Luxembourgeoise [*A publication*]
Rev Techn Ind Cuir ... Revue Technique des Industries du Cuir [*A publication*]
Rev Tech Thomson CSF ... Revue Technique Thomson - CSF [*A publication*]
Rev Tec Inst Nac Electron ... Revista Tecnica. Instituto Nacional de Electronica [*A publication*]
Rev Tec INTEVEP ... Revista Tecnica INTEVEP [*Instituto de Tecnologia Venezolana del Petroleo*] [*A publication*]
Rev Tecn Fac Ingr Univ Zulia ... Revista Tecnica. Facultad de Ingenieria. Universidad del Zulia [*A publication*]
Rev Tecnol Med ... Revista de Tecnologia Medica [*A publication*]
Rev Tec Sulzer ... Revista Tecnica Sulzer [*Switzerland*] [*A publication*]
Rev Tec Text Vestido ... Revista Tecnica Textil-Vestido [*A publication*]
Rev Tec Yacimientos Pet Fiscales Boliv ... Revista Tecnica. Yacimientos Petroliferos Fiscales Bolivianos [*A publication*]
Rev Tec Zulia Univ ... Revista Tecnica. Zulia University [*A publication*]
Rev Teilhard de Chardin ... Revue Teilhard de Chardin [*A publication*]
Rev Telecom ... Revista de Telecomunicacion [*A publication*]
Rev Telecommun ... Revue des Telecommunications [*France*] [*A publication*]
Rev Telecomun (Madrid) ... Revista de Telecomunicacion (Madrid) [*A publication*]
Rev Telegr Electron ... Revista Telegrafica Electronica [*A publication*]
Rev Text (Ghent) ... Revue Textilis (Ghent) [*A publication*]
Rev Textile Progr ... Review of Textile Progress [*A publication*]
Rev Text (Paris) ... Revue Textile (Paris) [*A publication*]
Rev Text Progr ... Review of Textile Progress [*A publication*]
Rev Text Tiba ... Revue Textile Tiba [*A publication*]
Rev Theobroma ... Revista Theobroma [*A publication*]
Rev Theol Phil ... Revue de Theologie et de Philosophie [*A publication*]
Rev Theol Philos ... Revue de Theologie et de Philosophie [*A publication*]
Rev Ther .... Revue Therapeutique [*A publication*]
Rev Therap ... Revue Therapeutique [*A publication*]
Rev Therap Bibliogr Med ... Revue Therapeutique et Bibliographie Medicale [*A publication*]
Rev Therap Med-Chir ... Revue de Therapeutique Medico-Chirurgicale [*A publication*]
Rev Thomiste ... Revue Thomiste [*A publication*]

Rev Tisiol Neumonol ... Revista de Tisiologia y Neumonologia [*A publication*]
Rev Trab .... Revista de Trabajo [*A publication*]
Rev Trach .. Revue du Trachome [*A publication*]
Rev Transp Telecomun ... Revista Transporturilor si Telecomunicatiilor [*Romania*] [*A publication*]
Rev Trav ..... Revue du Travail [*A publication*]
Rev Trav ..... Revue du Travail et du Bien-Etre Social [*A publication*]
Rev Trav Inst Peches Marit ... Revue des Travaux. Institut des Peches Maritimes [*A publication*]
Rev Trav Inst Sci Tech Peches Marit ... Revue des Travaux. Institut Scientifique et Technique des Peches Maritimes [*A publication*]
Rev Tr Dr Civ ... Revue Trimestrielle de Droit Civil [*A publication*]
Rev Trimest Can ... Revue Trimestrielle Canadienne [*A publication*]
Rev Trimestr de Droit Eur ... Revue Trimestrielle de Droit Europeen [*A publication*]
Rev Trimestrielle Canadienne ... Revue Trimestrielle Canadienne [*A publication*]
Rev Trimestr de Jurispr ... Revista Trimestral de Jurisprudencia [*Rio De Janeiro, Brazil*] [*A publication*]   (DLA)
Rev Troup Colon ... Revue des Troupes Coloniales [*A publication*]
Rev Tuberc ... Revue de Tuberculose [*A publication*]
Rev Tuberc Pneumol ... Revue de Tuberculose et de Pneumologie [*Later, Revue Francaise des Maladies Respiratoires*] [*A publication*]
Rev Tunisienne de Droit ... Revue Tunisienne de Droit [*Tunis, Tunisia*] [*A publication*]   (DLA)
Rev Tunis Sci Soc ... Revue Tunisienne de Sciences Sociales [*A publication*]
Rev Turq Hyg Biol Exp ... Revue Turque d'Hygiene et de Biologie Experimentale [*A publication*]
Rev Turque Hyg Biol Exp ... Revue Turque d'Hygiene et de Biologie Experimentale [*A publication*]
Rev Tussock Grassl Mt Lands Inst ... Review. Tussock Grasslands and Mountain Lands Institute [*A publication*]
Rev UDEM ... Revista. Universidad de Medellin [*A publication*]
Revue Agric (Brux) ... Revue de l'Agriculture (Bruxelles) [*A publication*]
Revue Agric Nouv Caled ... Revue Agricole de la Nouvelle-Caledonie et Dependances [*A publication*]
Revue Can Biol ... Revue Canadienne de Biologie [*A publication*]
Revue Comp Anim ... Revue du Comportement Animal [*A publication*]
Revue Ferment Ind Aliment ... Revue des Fermentations et des Industries Alimentaires [*A publication*]
Revue For Fr ... Revue Forestiere Francaise [*A publication*]
Revue Fr Allergol ... Revue Francaise d'Allergologie [*Later, Revue Francaise d'Allergologie et d'Immunologie Clinique*] [*A publication*]
Revue Fr Allergol Immunol Clin ... Revue Francaise d'Allergologie et d'Immunologie Clinique [*A publication*]
Revue Fr Apic ... Revue Francaise d'Apiculture [*A publication*]
Revue Fr Geront ... Revue Francaise de Gerontologie [*A publication*]
Revue Gen Bot ... Revue Generale de Botanique [*A publication*]
Revue Gen Gaz ... Revue Generale du Gaz [*Belgium*] [*A publication*]
Revue Geogr Phys Geol Dyn ... Revue de Geographie Physique et de Geologie Dynamique [*A publication*]
Revue Geol Dyn Geogr Phys ... Revue de Geologie Dynamique et de Geographie Physique [*France*] [*A publication*]
Revue Int Apic ... Revue Internationale d'Apiculture [*A publication*]
Revue Lux .. Revue Trimestrielle d'Etudes Linguistiques, Folkloriques, et Toponymiques (Luxembourg) [*A publication*]
Revue Med Liege ... Revue Medicale de Liege [*A publication*]
Revue Med Vet ... Revue Medicale et Veterinaire [*A publication*]
Revue Oka ... Revue d'Oka. Agronomie. Medicine. Veterinaire [*A publication*]
Revue Path Comp ... Revue de Pathologie Comparee [*A publication*]
Revue Path Comp Hyg Gen ... Revue de Pathologie Comparee et Hygiene Generale [*A publication*]
Revue Path Gen Physiol Clin ... Revue de Pathologie Generale et de Physiologie Clinique [*A publication*]
Revue Path Veg Ent Agric Fr ... Revue de Pathologie Vegetale et d'Entomologie Agricole de France [*A publication*]
Revue Quest Scient ... Revue des Questions Scientifiques [*A publication*]
Revue Romande Agric Vitic Arboric ... Revue Romande d'Agriculture, de Viticulture, et d'Arboriculture [*A publication*]
Revue Roum Biochim ... Revue Roumaine de Biochimie [*A publication*]
Revue Roum Biol Ser Bot ... Revue Roumaine de Biologie. Serie Botanique [*A publication*]
Revue Suisse Zool ... Revue Suisse de Zoologie [*A publication*]
Revue Zool Afr ... Revue de Zoologie Africaine [*A publication*]
Revue Zool Agric Appl ... Revue de Zoologie Agricole et Appliquee [*A publication*]
Revue Zool Bot Afr ... Revue de Zoologie et de Botanique Africaines [*A publication*]
Rev Un B .... Revue. Universite de Bruxelles [*A publication*]
Rev Uni ...... Revue Universitaire [*A publication*]
Rev Uniao Pharm (Sao Paulo) ... Revista Uniao Pharmaceutica (Sao Paulo) [*A publication*]
Rev Union Mat Argent ... Revista. Union Matematica Argentina [*A publication*]
Rev Union Mat Argent Asoc Fis Argent ... Revista. Union Matematica Argentina y Asociacion Fisica Argentina [*A publication*]
Rev Univ Al I Cuza Inst Politeh Iasi ... Revista Universitati "Al. I. Cuza" si a Institutului Politehnic din Iasi [*A publication*]

Rev Univ Brux ...   Revue. Universite de Bruxelles [*A publication*]
Rev Univ Burundi ...   Revue. Universite du Burundi [*A publication*]
Rev Univ Cauca ...   Revista. Universidad del Cauca [*A publication*]
Rev Univ C I Parhon Politeh Bucuresti Ser Stiint Nat ...   Revista Universitatii "C. I. Parhon" si a Politehnicii Bucuresti. Seria Stiintelor Naturii [*A publication*]
Rev Univers Mines Metall Mec ...   Revue Universelle des Mines, de la Metallurgie, de la Mecanique, des Travaux Publics, des Sciences, et des Arts Appliques a l'Industrie [*A publication*]
Rev Univ Fed Para Ser II ...   Revista. Universidade Federal do Para. Serie II [*A publication*]
Rev Univ Ind Santander ...   Revista. Universidad Industrial de Santander [*A publication*]
Rev Univ Ind Santander Invest ...   Revista. Universidad Industrial de Santander. Investigaciones [*A publication*]
Rev Univ Ind Santander Tecnolo ...   Revista. Universidad Industrial de Santander. Tecnologia [*A publication*]
Rev Univ Los Andes (Bogota) ...   Revista. Universidad de Los Andes (Bogota) [*A publication*]
Rev Univ Madrid ...   Revista. Universidad de Madrid [*Spain*] [*A publication*]
Rev Univ Nac Cordoba ...   Revista. Universidad Nacional de Cordoba [*A publication*]
Rev Univ Nac Tucuman Ser A ...   Revista. Universidad Nacional de Tucuman. Serie A. Matematica y Fisica Teorica [*Argentina*] [*A publication*]
Rev Univ Natl Zaire Campus Lubumbashi Ser B ...   Revue. Universite Nationale du Zaire. Campus de Lubumbashi. Serie B. Sciences [*A publication*]
Rev Univ Norte (Chile) ...   Revista. Universidad del Norte (Chile) [*A publication*]
Rev Univ Ottawa ...   Revue. Universite d'Ottawa [*A publication*]
Rev Univ Univ Nac Cuzco ...   Revista Universitaria. Universidad Nacional del Cuzco [*A publication*]
Rev Univ Zulia ...   Revista. Universidad del Zulia [*A publication*]
Rev Univ Zulia (Maracaibo) ...   Revista. Universidad del Zulia (Maracaibo) [*A publication*]
Rev Un Mat Argentina ...   Revista. Union Matematica Argentina [*A publication*]
Rev Urol (Caracas) ...   Revista de Urologia (Caracas) [*A publication*]
Rev Usem ...   Revista Usem [*A publication*]
Rev Venez Cir ...   Revista Venezolana de Cirugia [*A publication*]
Rev Venez Sanid Asist Soc ...   Revista Venezolana de Sanidad y Asistencia Social [*A publication*]
Rev Venez Urol ...   Revista Venezolana de Urologia [*A publication*]
Rev Ven Filosof ...   Revista Venezolana de Filosofia [*A publication*]
Rev Ver Soie ...   Revue du Ver a Soie [*A publication*]
Rev Vervietoise Hist Nat ...   Revue Vervietoise d'Histoire Naturelle [*A publication*]
Rev Vet Can ...   Revue Veterinaire Canadienne [*A publication*]
Rev Vet Milit ...   Revista de Veterinaria Militar [*A publication*]
Rev Vet Venez ...   Revista Veterinaria Venezolana [*A publication*]
Rev Vet Zootec (Manizales) ...   Revista de Veterinaria y Zootecnia (Manizales) [*A publication*]
Rev Viernes Med ...   Revista del Viernes Medico [*A publication*]
Rev Vitic ....   Revue de Viticulture [*A publication*]
Rev Vivarais ...   Revue du Vivarais [*A publication*]
Rev V Tr .....   Revue des Ventes et Transports [*A publication*]
REVW ....   Review   (NVT)
Rev Warren Spring Lab (UK) ...   Review. Warren Spring Laboratory (United Kingdom) [*A publication*]
Rev World ...   Revolutionary World [*A publication*]
Rev X ....   Revue X [*Belgium*] [*A publication*]
REVY ....   Reversionary   (ROG)
Rev Zair Sci Nucl ...   Revue Zairoise des Sciences Nucleaires [*Zaire*] [*A publication*]
Rev Zoo Agr ...   Revue de Zoologie Agricole et de Pathologie Vegetale [*A publication*]
Rev Zooiatr ...   Revista Zooiatria [*A publication*]
Rev Zool Afr ...   Revue de Zoologie Africaine [*A publication*]
Rev Zool Agric Appl ...   Revue de Zoologie Agricole et Appliquee [*A publication*]
Rev Zool Agric Pathol Veg ...   Revue de Zoologie Agricole et de Pathologie Vegetale [*A publication*]
Rev Zool Bot Afr ...   Revue de Zoologie et de Botanique Africaines [*A publication*]
Rev Zootec (B Aires) ...   Revista Zootecnica (Buenos Aires) [*A publication*]
Rev Zooteh Med Vet ...   Revista de Zootehnie si Medicina Veterinara [*A publication*]
REW ....   Recycle Water [*Nuclear energy*]   (NRCH)
REW ....   Redwood Valley, CA [*Location identifier*] [*FAA*]   (FAAL)
REW ....   Reward   (AFM)
REW ....   Rewind   (MDG)
REW ....   Russisch-Etymologisches Woerterbuch [*A publication*]
REWDAC ...   Retrieval by Title Words, Descriptors, and Classification   (DIT)
REWK ....   Rework   (MSA)
REWRC .....   Report When Established Well to Right of Course [*Aviation*]   (FAAC)
REWS ....   Radio Electronic Warfare Service   (MCD)
REWSON ...   Reconnaissance, Electronic Warfare, Special Operations, and Naval Intelligence Processing Systems

REX ....   Ram Air Freight, Inc. [*Hillsborough, NC*] [*FAA designator*]   (FAAC)
REX ....   Rapid Text Search [*Data processing*]   (IT)
REX ....   Rare-Earth Exchanged [*Faujasite, a zeolite*]
REX ....   Reactor Experimental [*USSR*]   (DEN)
REX ....   Real-Time Executive Routine [*Data processing*]
REX ....   Rechtswissenschaftliche Experten und Gutachter [*NOMOS Datapool*] [*Database*]
REX ....   Reduced Exoatmospheric Cross Section
REX ....   Reentry Experiment
REX ....   Reflector Erosion Experiment [*NASA*]
REX ....   Regression Expert [*Data processing*]
REX ....   Requisition Exception Code [*Air Force*]   (AFIT)
R EX ....   Review and Expositor [*A publication*]
REX ....   Rex Silver Mines [*Vancouver Stock Exchange symbol*]
REX ....   Rexburg [*Idaho*] [*Seismograph station code, US Geological Survey*]   (SEIS)
REX ....   Rexnord [*NYSE symbol*]   (SPSG)
REX ....   Reynosa [*Mexico*] [*Airport symbol*]   (OAG)
REX ....   Robot Excavation [*Carnegie-Mellon Robotics Institute*]
REX ....   Run Executive [*Data processing*]
REXC ....   Reserve Exploration Company [*NASDAQ symbol*]   (NQ)
REXI ....   Resource Exploration, Incorporated [*NASDAQ symbol*]   (NQ)
R Exist Psych Psych ...   Review of Existential Psychology and Psychiatry [*A publication*]
REXL ....   Rexhall Industries, Inc. [*NASDAQ symbol*]   (NQ)
REXMIT ...   Retransmitted   (AABC)
REXN ....   Rexon, Inc. [*NASDAQ symbol*]   (NQ)
Rexroth Inf ...   Rexroth Informationen [*A publication*]
REXS ....   Radio Exploration Satellite [*Japan*]
REXW ....   Rexworks, Inc. [*NASDAQ symbol*]   (NQ)
REY ....   Reentry
REY ....   Reyes [*Bolivia*] [*Airport symbol*]   (OAG)
REY ....   Reykjavik [*Iceland*] [*Seismograph station code, US Geological Survey*]   (SEIS)
REY ....   Reynolds & Reynolds Co. [*NYSE symbol*]   (SPSG)
REY ....   Rush Ventures, Inc. [*Vancouver Stock Exchange symbol*]
Reyn ....   Reynolds, Reports [*40-42 Mississippi*] [*A publication*]   (DLA)
REYN ....   [*The*] Reynolds and Reynolds Co. [*NASDAQ symbol*]   (NQ)
Reyn L Ins ...   Reynold's Life Insurance [*A publication*]   (DLA)
Reynolds ....   Reynolds, Reports [*40-42 Mississippi*] [*A publication*]   (DLA)
Reynolds' Land Laws ...   Reynolds' Spanish and Mexican Land Laws [*A publication*]   (DLA)
Reyon Synth Zellwolle ...   Reyon, Synthetica, Zellwolle [*A publication*]
Reyon Zellwolle Andere Chem Fasern ...   Reyon, Zellwolle, und Andere Chemie Fasern [*A publication*]
Reyrolle Parsons Rev ...   Reyrolle Parsons Review [*A publication*]
REZ ....   Mary Esther, FL [*Location identifier*] [*FAA*]   (FAAL)
Rezanie Instrum ...   Rezanie i Instrument [*A publication*]
Re Zh Khim Neftepererab Polim Mashinostr ...   Referativnyi Zhurnal. Khimicheskoe. Neftepererabatyuayushchee i Polimerjnoe Mashinostroenie [*A publication*]
Rezul't Issled Mezhdunar Geofiz Proektam ...   Rezul'taty Issledovanyi po Mezhdunarodny Geofizicheskim Proektam [*USSR*] [*A publication*]
RF ....   Fournier [*France*] [*ICAO aircraft manufacturer identifier*]   (ICAO)
RF ....   Franc [*Monetary unit*] [*Rwanda*]
RF ....   Radial Fibers [*Ear anatomy*]
RF ....   Radial Flow   (AAG)
RF ....   Radical Force   (EA)
RF ....   Radio Facility
RF ....   Radio Frequency [*Transmission*]
RF ....   Rainfed [*Agriculture*]
RF ....   Rainform   (MCD)
RF ....   Raised Face   (MSA)
RF ....   Range-Finder [*Gunnery*]
R & F ....   Rank and File
RF ....   Rapeseed Flour [*Food technology*]
RF ....   Rapid-Fire
RF ....   Rapports des Fouilles [*A publication*]
RF ....   Rating Factor   (IEEE)
RF ....   Razon y Fe [*A publication*]
RF ....   Read Forward
RF ....   Reason Foundation   (EA)
RF ....   Reception Fair [*Radio logs*]
RF ....   Receptive Field [*of visual cortex*]
RF ....   Reconnaissance Fighter   (MUGU)
RF ....   Reconnaissance Force
RF ....   Recovery Forces
RF ....   Recovery Forecast
RF ....   Recruitment for the Armed Forces [*British*]
RF ....   Red Fumes   (NATG)
RF ....   Reducing Flame
RF ....   Reef
RF ....   Reference [*Online database field identifier*]
RF ....   Reflight
RF ....   Refunding
RF ....   Regional Forces [*ARVN*]
RF ....   Register File
RF ....   Register Finder

RF .... Relative Flow [Rate]
Rf .... Relative to the Solvent Front [Paper chromatography] [Analytical chemistry]
RF .... Release Factor   (NRCH)
RF .... Releasing Factor [Also, RH] [Endocrinology]
RF .... Reliability Factor
RF .... Renal Failure [Medicine]
RF .... Rent Free
RF .... Replacement Factor [Military]
RF .... Replicative Factor [or Form] [Genetics]
RF .... Reply Finding [Nuclear energy]   (NRCH)
RF .... Reporting File
RF .... Representative Fraction
RF .... Republique Francaise [French Republic]
RF .... Republique Francaise [A publication]
RF .... Reserve Flight [British military]   (DMA)
RF .... Reserve Force
RF .... Resistance Factor
RF .... Respectable Frere [Worshipful Brother] [French] [Freemasonry]   (ROG)
RF .... Response Factor
RF .... Retardation Factor
RF .... Retention File [IRS]
RF .... Reticular Formation [Sleep]
RF .... Retroperitoneal Fibromatosis [Oncology]
RF .... Reverse Free
RF .... Revista de Filologie [A publication]
RF .... Revista Forense [Brazil] [A publication]
RF .... Revolving Fund [Finance]
RF .... Revue Fiscale [A publication]
RF .... Revue de France [A publication]
RF .... Rex Francorum [King of the Franks] [Latin]
RF .... RFG Reiseflug und Industrieflug GmbH [West Germany] [ICAO designator]   (FAAC)
RF .... Rheumatic Fever [Medicine]
RF1 .... Rheumatoid Factor [Also known as IgM] [Immunology]
RF .... Rhinal Fissure [Anatomy]
RF .... Rhodesian Front [Later, Republican Front]
RF .... Riboflavin [Biochemistry]
RF .... Richmond Fellowship   (EAIO)
RF .... Rifampin [Also, R/AMP, RIF, RMP] [Bactericide]
RF .... Riffle Frequency
RF .... Rigging Fixtures   (MCD)
RF .... Right Field [or Fielder] [Baseball]
RF .... Right Foot
RF .... Right Forward [Football]
RF .... Right Front
RF .... Right Fullback [Soccer]
RF .... Rinforzando [With Special Emphasis] [Music]
RF .... Ring Frame
RF .... Ripple Factor
rf............. Rise of Floor   (DS)
RF .... Rivista di Filologia e di Istruzione Classica [A publication]
RF .... Rivista di Filosofia [A publication]
RF .... Rockefeller Foundation
RF .... Rodeo Foundation   (EA)
RF .... Roll Film [Photography]
RF .... Romanische Forschungen [A publication]
RF .... Rosicrucian Fellowship   (EA)
RF .... Rosicrucian Fraternity   (EA)
RF .... Rough Finish
RF .... Royal Fusiliers [Military unit] [British]
RF .... Royal Windsor Foresters [British military]   (DMA)
RF .... Ruch Filozoficzny [A publication]
RF .... Running Forward
Rf .... Rutherfordium [Proposed name for chemical element 104] [See also Ku]
RF .... Sisters of St. Philip Neri Missionary Teachers [Roman Catholic religious order]
RF1 .... Federal Reserve Bank of Boston, Boston, MA [OCLC symbol]   (OCLC)
RFA .... RADAR Filter Assembly
RFA .... Radiation Field Analyzer
RFA .... Radio Frequency Allocation   (MCD)
RFA .... Radio Frequency Amplifier
RFA .... Radio Frequency Attenuator   (MCD)
RFA .... Radio Frequency Authorizations [Air Force]
RFA .... Raleigh Flying Service, Inc. [Morrisville, NC] [FAA designator]   (FAAC)
RFA .... Rapid Flow Analysis
RFA .... Recommendation for Acceptance   (AAG)
RFA .... Recurrent Fault Analysis [Telecommunications]   (TEL)
RFA .... Registered Fitness Appraiser [Canadian Association of Sports Sciences]
RFA .... Regulatory Flexibility Act
RFA .... Relieved from Assigned [Military]
RFA .... Remote File Access
RFA .... Renewable Fuels Association   (EA)
RFA .... Request for Action   (KSC)
RFA .... Request for Alteration   (AAG)

RFA .... Request for Analysis
RFA .... Request for Application
RFA .... Request Further Airways [Aviation]   (FAAC)
RFA .... Request for Grant Applications
RFA .... Reserve Forces Act
RFA .... Restrictive Fire Area [Military]   (AABC)
RFA .... Revue de l'Energie [Paris] [A publication]
RFA .... Revue de la Franco-Ancienne [A publication]
RFA .... Right Femoral Artery [Anatomy]
RFA .... Right Frontoanterior [A fetal position] [Obstetrics]
RFA .... Rimfire Adapter   (MCD)
RFA .... Risley Family Association   (EA)
RFA .... Roll Follow-Up Amplifier
RFA .... Royal Field Artillery [Military] [British]
RFA .... Royal Fleet Auxiliary [British]
RFA .... Rural Forestry Assistance [Program] [Forest Service]
RFAA .... Relieved from Attached and Assigned [Army]
RFAAD...... Revue Francaise d'Automatique, d'Informatique, et de Recherche Operationnelle. Serie Automatique [A publication]
RFAC........ Royal Fine Art Commission [British]
RFACA...... Revista. Facultad de Ciencias Agrarias. Universidad Nacional de Cuyo [A publication]
R Fac Cienc Ec Com ... Revista. Facultad de Ciencias Economicas y Comerciales [A publication]
R Fac Der (Caracas) ... Revista. Facultad de Derecho (Caracas) [A publication]
R Fac Der Mexico ... Revista. Facultad de Derecho de Mexico [A publication]
RFAD .... Released from Active Duty Not Result of Demobilization [Navy]
RFAD .... Request for Accelerated Delivery   (MCD)
RFAED...... Readiness Forecast Authorization Equipment Data [Air Force]   (AFM)
RFAF........ Request for Additional Fire   (MCD)
RF/AFG .... Radio Frequency/Acoustic Firing Group [Military]   (CAAL)
RFAGB...... Riforma Agraria [A publication]
RFAGC...... Rainbows for All God's Children   (EA)
RFALA ...... Revue Francaise d'Allergie [A publication]
RFALROU ... Request Follow-Up Action on Listed Requisitions Indicated Still Outstanding in Unit [Army]   (AABC)
RFAND ..... Revue Francaise d'Automatique, d'Informatique, et de Recherche Operationnelle. Serie Analyse Numerique [A publication]
RFAO .... Rocky Flats Area Office [Energy Research and Development Administration]
RFAPA ...... Revista. Facultad de Agronomia. Universidad Nacional de La Plata [A publication]
RFAS........ Radio Frequency Attitude Sensor
RFASIX..... Reserve Forces Act of 1955, Six Months Trainee
RFASS....... Rapid Fire Artillery Support System   (MCD)
RFAT........ Relieved from Attached [Army]   (AABC)
RFATE...... Radio Frequency Automatic Test Equipment   (MCD)
RFATHREE ... Reserve Forces Act of 1955, Three Months Trainee
RFB........... Air-Cushion Vehicle built by Rhein Flugzeugbau [Federal Republic of Germany] [Usually used in combination with numerals]
RFB........... Rabobank [A publication]
RFB........... Ready for Baseline   (NASA)
RFB........... Reason for Backlog [Telecommunications]   (TEL)
RFB........... Recording for the Blind   (EA)
RFB........... Recording for the Blind, Bethesda, MD [OCLC symbol]   (OCLC)
RFB........... Reliability Functional Block
RFB........... Request for Bid   (AFM)
RFB........... Retained Foreign Body [Medicine]
RFB........... Right Fullback [Soccer]
RFBA........ Reserve Forces Benefit Association [Later, REA]   (EA)
RFBABQ ... Anais. Reuniao de Fitossanitarisatas do Brasil [A publication]
RFBC........ River Forest Bancorp [NASDAQ symbol]   (NQ)
RFBI........ Regional Federal Bancorp, Inc. [NASDAQ symbol]   (NQ)
RFBK........ RS Financial Corp. [Formerly, Raleigh Federal Savings Bank] [NASDAQ symbol]   (NQ)
RFBUB...... Revista de Farmacia e Bioquimica. Universidade de Sao Paulo (Brazil) [A publication]
RFC........... Radio Facility Charts   (MCD)
RFC........... Radio Frequency Chart   (AAG)
RFC........... Radio Frequency Choke   (AAG)
RFC........... Radio Frequency Communications
RFC........... Radio Frequency Compatibility
RFC........... Radio Frequency Crystal
RFC........... Railroad Freight Classification
RFC........... Ranger Fan Club   (EA)
RFC........... Rare Fruit Council [Later, RFCI]   (EA)
RFC........... Ravan Fan Club   (EA)
RFC........... Reason for Change   (MCD)
RFC........... Recirculation Flow Control [Nuclear energy]   (NRCH)
RFC........... Reconstruction Finance Corporation [Abolished, 1957]
RFC........... Regenerative Fuel Cell
RFC........... Relative Force Capability   (NATG)
RFC........... Religious Formation Conference   (EA)
RFC........... Remote Food Carriers [Army]   (INF)

RFC............ Request for Change (KSC)
RFC............ Request for Confirmation (MCD)
RFC............ Required Functional Capability [*Navy*]
RFC............ Research Facilities Center [*National Oceanic and Atmospheric Administration*] (GRD)
RFC............ Residual Functional Capacity [*Social Security Administration*] (OICC)
RFC............ Residuum Fluid Cracking [*Petroleum refining*]
RFC............ Resolution Funding Corp. [*Established by the Financial Institutions Reform, Recovery, and Enforcement Act of 1989*]
RFC............ Resources for Communication [*Information service or system*] (IID)
RFC............ Retirement-for-Cause [*Program*] [*Air Force*]
RFC............ Revista de Folklore (Colombia) [*A publication*]
RFC............ RFC Resource Finance Corp. [*Toronto Stock Exchange symbol*]
RFC............ RFC Resources Corp. [*Vancouver Stock Exchange symbol*]
RFC............ River Forecast Center [*National Weather Service*] (NOAA)
RFC............ Rivista di Filologia Classica [*A publication*]
RFC............ Rivista di Filologia e di Istruzione Classica [*A publication*]
RFC............ Rosette-Forming Cell [*Immunochemistry*]
RFC............ Royal Flying Corps [*Later, RAF*] [*British*]
RFC............ Rugby Football Club
RFC............ Rural Finance Corp. [*Australia*]
RFCA........ Racing Fans Club of America (EA)
RFCA........ Reconstruction Finance Corporation Act [*Obsolete*]
RFCA........ Retail Floor Coverings Association of New South Wales [*Australia*]
RFCC........ Revista de Folklore. Organo de la Comision Nacional de Folklore (Colombia) [*A publication*]
RFCEA...... Revival Fires (Christian Evangelizers Association) (EA)
RF (Cern).. Revista de Filologie (Cernauti) [*A publication*]
RFCFDE.... Revista. Faculdade de Ciencias Farmaceuticas [*Araraquara*] [*A publication*]
RFCG........ Radio Frequency Command Generator (MCD)
RFCI......... Rare Fruit Council International (EA)
RFCI......... Resilient Floor Covering Institute (EA)
RFCM....... Radio Frequency Control Monitor [*Formerly, RFU*] (MCD)
RFCMC..... Reconstruction Finance Corporation Mortgage Company
RFCO........ Radio Frequency Checkout (AAG)
RFCO........ Revue des Facultes Catholiques de l'Ouest [*A publication*]
RFCP........ Radio Frequency Compatibility Program
RFCP........ Request for Computer Program (NASA)
RFCP........ Requests for Contractual Procurement (MUGU)
RFCR........ Refacer
RFCS........ Radio Frequency Carrier Shift (NVT)
RFCS........ Recirculation Flow Control System [*Nuclear energy*] (NRCH)
RFCS......... Regenerative Fuel Cell Subsystem
RFCSEUSG ... Retirement Federation of Civil Service Employees of the United States Government [*Defunct*] (EA)
RFCT........ Report of Federal Cash Transactions (OICC)
RFCTA...... Rassegna di Fisiopatologia Clinica e Terapeutica [*A publication*]
RFCVET.... Revista. Facultad de Ciencias Veterinarias [*A publication*]
RFD .... Radiation Flux Density
RFD .... Radio Frequency Demodulator
RFD .... Raised Face Diameter (MSA)
RFD .... Raised Foredeck [*of a ship*] (DS)
RFD .... Reactor Flight Demonstration
RFD .... Ready for Data (IEEE)
RFD .... Ready for Delivery (MUGU)
RFD .... Ready for Duty
RFD .... Reentry Flight Demonstration
RfD .... Reference Dose [*Environmental science*]
RFD .... Refurbish for Delivery (MCD)
RFD .... Released for Delivery (NG)
RFD .... Reporting for Duty [*Air Force*]
RFD .... Request for Delivery
RFD .... Request for Deviation
RFD .... Request for Parts Disposition (MCD)
RFD .... Requirements Formulation Document [*NASA*] (NASA)
RFD .... Reserve Forces Decoration [*Australia*] (ADA)
RFD .... Reserve Forces Duty [*Military*] (MCD)
RFD .... Residual Flux Density
RFD .... Reverse-Flow Diverter [*Engineering*]
RFD .... Rockford [*Illinois*] [*Airport symbol*] (OAG)
RFD .... Rockford Minerals, Inc. [*Toronto Stock Exchange symbol*]
RFD .... Rural Free Delivery [*of mail*]
RFDA .... Request for Deviation Approval
RFDL........ Radio Frequency Data Link (MCD)
RFDS........ Royal Flying Doctor Service [*Australia*]
RFDT........ Reliability Failure Diagnostic Team (AAG)
RFDU .... Reconfiguration and Fault Detection Unit
RFE........... Radio Free Europe [*A publication*]
RFE........... Radio Free Europe
R Fe........... Razon y Fe [*A publication*]
RFE........... Request for Effectivity (MCD)
RFE........... Request for Estimate (KSC)
RFE........... Request for Expenditure
RFE........... Revista de Filologia Espanola [*A publication*]
RFE........... Rotating Field Electrophoresis [*Analytical biochemistry*]

RFE........... Rutherfordton, NC [*Location identifier*] [*FAA*] (FAAL)
RFEA........ Radio Frequency Equipment Analyzer
RFEA........ Regular Forces Employment Association [*British military*] (DMA)
RFEA........ Revue Francaise d'Etudes Americaines [*A publication*]
RFECA...... Revue Francaise d'Etudes Cliniques et Biologiques [*A publication*]
RFED........ Research Facilities and Equipment Division [*NASA*] (MCD)
RFED........ Roosevelt Financial Group, Inc. [*NASDAQ symbol*] (NQ)
RFEHB..... Retired Federal Employees Health Benefits Program (MCD)
RFEI........ Request for Engineering Information (KSC)
RFELB...... Radio Fernsehen Elektronik [*A publication*]
RF/EMI.... Radio Frequency and Electromagnetic-Interference [*Telecommunications*]
RFEN........ Reef Energy Corp. [*NASDAQ symbol*] (NQ)
RFERB ..... Radio Free Europe. Research Bulletin [*A publication*]
RFE/RL.... Radio Free Europe/Radio Liberty (EA)
RFF........... Radio Frequency Filter
RFF........... Radio Frequency Finder (NVT)
RFF........... Radio Frequency Fuze
RFF........... Random Force Field
RFF........... Ready for Ferry [*Navy*] (NVT)
RFF........... Recirculative Fluid Flow
RFF........... REFF, Inc. [*Toronto Stock Exchange symbol*]
RFF........... Refuge from Flood (ADA)
RFF........... Relative Failure Frequency
RFF........... Remote Fiber Fluorometer [*Instrumentation*]
RFF........... Request for Form
RFF........... Research Flight Facility [*Air Force*]
RFF........... Resources for the Future
RFF........... Rift-Fracture-Fracture [*Geology*]
RFF........... Royal Filling Factory [*British military*] (DMA)
RFFC........ Randy Floyd Fan Club (EA)
RFFD........ Radio Frequency Fault Detection
RFFH........ Revista. Facultad de Filosofia y Humanidades [*A publication*]
RFFID4 .... Canadian Forestry Service. Forest Pest Management Institute. Information Report. FPM-X [*A publication*]
RFFLUP.... Revista. Faculdade de Filosofia e Letras. Universidade do Parana [*A publication*]
RFFO........ Request for Factory Order (MCD)
RFFSA...... Rede Ferroviaria Federal Sociedade Anonima [*Federal Railway Corporation*] [*Brazil*] (EY)
RFG .... RADAR Field Gradient (IEEE)
RFG .... Radio Frequency Generator
RFG .... Rapid-Fire Gun
RFG .... Rate and Free Gyro
RFG .... Receive Format Generator
RFG .... Referendum First Group [*Australia*]
RFG .... Refugio, TX [*Location identifier*] [*FAA*] (FAAL)
RFG .... Refunding [*Business term*]
RFG .... Reise und Industrieflug [*Airline*] [*Federal Republic of Germany*]
RFG .... Report Format Generator
RFG .... Rhodesian Financial Gazette [*A publication*]
RFG .... Rifle Fine Grain [*British military*] (DMA)
RFG .... Roofing (AAG)
RFG .... Royscot Finance Group [*Royal Bank of Scotland*]
RFGN........ Refrigeration [*Charges*]
RFGND ..... RoeFo. Fortschritte auf dem Gebiete der Roentgenstrahlen und der Nuklearmedizin [*A publication*]
RFGT........ Refrigerant (MSA)
RFH......... Radio Frequency Heating
RFH .... Raised Face Height (MSA)
RFH .... Reichsfinanzhof [*Reich Finance Court*] [*German*] (ILCA)
RFH .... Revista de Filologia Hispanica [*A publication*]
RFH .... Roof Hatch [*Technical drawings*]
RFH .... Royal Festival Hall [*London*]
RFH .... Royal Free Hospital (ROG)
RFHC........ Revista. Facultad de Humanidades y Ciencias [*A publication*]
RFHCO .... Rocket Fuel Handler Clothing Outfit [*Protective suit*]
RFHI .... Real Fire Heating International Exhibition [*Great Britain*] (ITD)
RFHL........ Revue Francaise d'Histoire du Livre [*A publication*]
RFHOM.... Revue Francaise d'Histoire d'Outre-Mer [*A publication*]
RFHSP...... Revista de Filologia e Historia (Sao Paulo) [*A publication*]
RFHT .... Radio Frequency Horn Technique
RFI........... RADAR Frequency Interferometer (MCD)
RFI........... Radio Frequency Indicator
RFI........... Radio Frequency Interchange (MDG)
RFI........... Radio Frequency Interference
RFI........... Rajneesh Foundation International (EA)
RFI........... Ready for Installation (MCD)
RFI........... Ready for Issue [*Military*]
RFI........... Regionalism and the Female Imagination [*A publication*]
RFI........... Relative Fluorescent Intensity [*Analytical chemistry*]
RFI........... Release for Issue (MCD)
RFI........... Remote Facility Inquiry [*NASA*] (KSC)
RFI........... Remote File Inquiry [*NASA*] (NASA)
RFI........... Request for Information
RFI........... Request for Investigation
RFI........... Request for Issue

RFI............ Requested for Information
RFI............ Retail Floorcovering Institute [*Later, AFA*] (EA)
RFi............ Revista de Filosofia [*A publication*]
RFI............ Revue Juridique, Fiscale, et Financiere [*A publication*]
RFIAAQ.... Revue des Fermentations et des Industries Alimentaires [*A publication*]
RFIC......... Rivista di Filologia e di Istruzione Classica [*A publication*]
RFID......... Radio Frequency Identification
RFIF......... Refund Information File [*IRS*]
R Fil......... Revista de Filosofia [*A publication*]
RFil.......... Russkaja Filologija [*A publication*]
RF Illus...... RF [*Rockefeller Foundation*] Illustrated [*A publication*]
R Filol Esp ... Revista de Filologia Espanola [*A publication*]
RFilos....... Rivista di Filosofia [*A publication*]
R Filoz....... Revista de Filozofie [*A publication*]
RFIM........ Radio Frequency Interference Meter
RFIN......... Rock Finance Corp. [*NASDAQ symbol*] (NQ)
R Fins Publicas ... Revista de Financas Publicas [*A publication*]
RFIOA....... Revue Francaise d'Informatique et de Recherche Operationnelle [*A publication*]
RFIP......... Radio Frequency Impedance Probe
RF/IR....... RADAR Frequency/Infrared Frequency (IEEE)
RFISA....... Revista de Fisica [*A publication*]
RFIT........ Radio Frequency Interference Tests (KSC)
RFIT......... THE Fitness Centers, Inc. [*Coral Springs, FL*] [*NASDAQ symbol*] (NQ)
RFJ.......... Radio Free Jazz [*A publication*]
RFJ.......... Radio Frequency Joint
RFJI......... Research Foundation for Jewish Immigration (EA)
RFK......... Anguilla, MS [*Location identifier*] [*FAA*] (FAAL)
RFK......... Radio Free Kabul [*London, England*] (EAIO)
RFK......... Reflets et Perspectives de la Vie Economique [*A publication*]
RFK......... Robert Francis Kennedy [*American politician, 1925-68*]
RFKM....... Robert F. Kennedy Memorial (EA)
RFKUL...... Roczniki Filozoficzne. Towarzystwo Naukowe Katolickiego Uniwersytetu Lubelskiego [*A publication*]
RFL.......... Radio Frequency Laboratories
RFL.......... Radio Frequency Lens
RFL.......... Radio-Frequency LINAC (SDI)
RFL.......... Reduced Focal Length
RFL.......... Reflect (NASA)
RFL.......... Reflector [*or Reflected*]
RFL.......... Refuel (AAG)
RFL.......... Reports of Family Law [*A publication*]
RFL.......... Requested Flight Level
RFL.......... Reset Flux Level
RFL.......... Resorcinol-Formaldehyde-Latex
RFL.......... Restrictive Fire Line [*Military*] (AABC)
RFL.......... Revista. Faculdade de Letras. Universidade de Lisboa [*A publication*]
RFL.......... Rough Field Landing
RFLD........ Radio Frequency Leakage Detector
RFL 2d...... Reports of Family Law. Second Series [*A publication*]
RFLHGA... Revue. Faculte de Langues, d'Histoire, et de Geographie. Universite d'Ankara [*A publication*]
RFLL........ Revista. Faculdade de Letras. Universidade de Lisboa [*A publication*]
RFLMN..... Rifleman (AABC)
RFLP........ Restriction Fragment Length Polymorphism [*Genetics*]
R/FLR....... Rear Floor [*Automotive engineering*]
RFLUL...... Revista. Faculdade de Letras. Universidade de Lisboa [*A publication*]
RFLX........ Reflex (MSA)
RFM .... Radio Frequency Management (NOAA)
RFM .... Radio Frequency Monitoring [*Military*] (CAAL)
RFM .... Reactive Factor Meter
RFM .... Red Fox Minerals [*Vancouver Stock Exchange symbol*]
RFM .... Refueling Mission [*Air Force*]
RFM .... Reserve Force Medal [*Military decoration*] [*Australia*]
RFM .... Reserve Forces Modernization (MCD)
RFM .... Revista de Filosofia (Madrid) [*A publication*]
RFM .... Revue Francaise du Marketing [*A publication*]
RFM .... Roll Follow-Up Motor
RFM .... Roll Forming Machine
RFM .... Runway Friction Measurement [*Aviation*]
RFM .... Rural Financial Market
RFMA........ Reliability Figure of Merit Analysis
RFMC....... Regional Fishery Management Council [*National Oceanic and Atmospheric Administration*] (MSC)
RFMNB.... Rein et Foie. Maladies de la Nutrition [*A publication*]
RFMO ...... Radio Frequency Management Office (MCD)
RFM Rev Fr Mec ... RFM. Revue Francaise de Mecanique [*A publication*]
RFMS........ Remote File Management System
RFMT........ Runway Friction Measurement Test [*Aviation*]
RFN .... Radio Frequency Noise
RFN .... Raufarhofn [*Iceland*] [*Airport symbol*] (OAG)
RFN .... Registered Reserve Nurse
RFN .... Remote Filter Niche [*Nuclear energy*] (NRCH)
RFN .... Rifleman
RFN .... Rivista di Filosofia Neo-Scolastica [*A publication*]
RFNA .... Red Fuming Nitric Acid

RFNCC...... Regional Nuclear Fuel Cycle Centers
RFND .... Refined (MSA)
RFNG .... Roofing
RFNM .... Ready for Next Message
RFNS........ Rivista di Filosofia Neo-Scolastica [*A publication*]
RFO .... Radio Frequency Oscillator
RFO .... Ready for Occupancy (MCD)
RFO .... Reason for Outage (FAAC)
RFO .... Regional Field Officer [*Civil Defense*]
RFO .... Request for Factory Order (MCD)
RFO .... Request for Orders [*Military*]
RFO .... Retrofire Officer [*NASA*] (KSC)
RFO .... Roll Follow-Up Operation
RFOFD6.... Revista. Faculdade de Odontologia de Araraquara [*A publication*]
RFOFM..... Records for Our Fighting Men [*Collected phonograph records during World War II*]
RFolc........ Revista de Folclor [*A publication*]
R Fomento Soc ... Revista de Fomento Social [*A publication*]
R Fom Soc ... Revista de Fomento Social [*A publication*]
RF & OOA ... Railway Fuel and Operating Officers Association [*Later, IAROO*] (EA)
RFOP........ Regional Financial Operating Plan
RFORE9.... Rivista di Frutticoltura e di Ortofloricoltura [*A publication*]
R For Franc ... Revue Forestiere Francaise [*A publication*]
R Format Perm ... Revue de la Formation Permanente [*A publication*]
RForsch ..... Romanische Forschungen [*A publication*]
RFOSA....... Revue Francaise d'Odonto-Stomatologie [*A publication*]
RFP.......... Radio Finger Printing [*Identification of wireless radio operators by individual keying characteristics*]
RFP.......... Radio Free People [*An association*] [*Defunct*]
RFP.......... Radio Frequency Plasma
RFP.......... Radio Frequency Pulse (MCD)
RFP.......... Raiatea [*French Polynesia*] [*Airport symbol*] (OAG)
RFP.......... Reactor Feed Pump [*Nuclear energy*] (NRCH)
RFP.......... Registered Financial Planner [*Designation awarded by International Association of Registered Financial Planners*]
RFP.......... Relative Frass Production [*Ecology*]
RFP.......... Remaining Force Potential (MCD)
RFP.......... Reproductive Freedom Project [*ACLU*] [*Attempts to enforce the Supreme Court decisions guaranteeing a woman's right to choose abortion*] (EA)
RFP.......... Republicans for Progress [*Defunct*]
RFP.......... Request for Price Quotation
RFP.......... Request for Programming [*Data processing*]
RFP.......... Request for Proposal
RFP.......... Request for Purchase
RFP.......... Requirements and Formulation Phase (MCD)
RFP.......... Requirements for Production [*Army*] (RDA)
RFP.......... Requisition for Procurement [*DoD*]
RFP.......... Retired on Full Pay [*Military*] [*British*]
RFP.......... Reversed Field Pinch [*Plasma physics*] (NRCH)
RFP.......... Reviews for Physicians [*Elsevier Book Series*] [*A publication*]
RFP.......... Revista de Filologia Portuguesa [*A publication*]
RFP.......... Richmond, Fredericksburg & Potomac Railroad Co. [*AAR code*]
RFP.......... Right Frontoposterior [*A fetal position*] [*Obstetrics*]
RFPA........ Request for Part Approval (MCD)
RFPA........ Request for Proposal Authorization [*NASA*] (NASA)
RFPA........ Right to Financial Privacy Act
RFPB........ Reserve Forces Policy Board [*DoD*]
RFPC........ Reserve Flag Officer Policy Council [*Navy*]
RFPC......... RF & P Corporation [*NASDAQ symbol*] (NQ)
RF/PF....... Regional Forces - Popular Forces [*Republic of Vietnam*] [*Army*] (AABC)
RFPI .... Registered Financial Planners Institute (EA)
RFPP .... Radio Frequency Propagation Program (NG)
RFPR .... Radiant Flash Pyrolysis Reactor [*Chemical engineering*]
RFPRA ...... Reactor Fuel Processing [*A publication*]
RFPRS....... Retail Food Price-Reporting System
RFPS .... Royal Faculty of Physicians and Surgeons of Glasgow
RFPT .... Reactor Feed Pump Turbine [*Nuclear energy*] (NRCH)
RFQ .... Radio-Frequency Quadrupole [*Accelerator for subatomic physics study*]
RFQ .... Request for Qualifications (OICC)
RFQ .... Request for Quotation
RFR.......... Radial Flow Reactor [*Chemical engineering*]
RFR.......... Radio Frequency Receiver
RFR.......... Radio Frequency Relay
RFR.......... Redfern Resources [*Vancouver Stock Exchange symbol*]
RFR.......... Reject Failure Rate
RFR.......... Required Freight Rate (DS)
RFr.......... Revolution Francaise [*A publication*]
RFr.......... Revue Francaise [*A publication*]
RFR.......... Rio Frio [*Costa Rica*] [*Airport symbol*] (OAG)
RFR.......... Royal Fleet Reserve [*British*]
R Fr Affaires Socs ... Revue Francaise des Affaires Sociales [*A publication*]
R Franc Aff Soc ... Revue Francaise des Affaires Sociales [*A publication*]
R Francaise Hist Livre ... Revue Francaise d'Histoire du Livre [*A publication*]

R Francaise Hist Outre-Mer ... Revue Francaise d'Histoire d'Outre-Mer [*A publication*]
R Francaise Sci Pol ... Revue Francaise de Science Politique [*A publication*]
R Francaise Sociol ... Revue Francaise de Sociologie [*A publication*]
R Franc Comptab ... Revue Francaise de Comptabilite [*A publication*]
R Franc Dr Aer ... Revue Francaise de Droit Aerien [*A publication*]
R Franc En ... Revue Francaise de l'Energie [*A publication*]
R Franc Et Amer ... Revue Francaise d'Etudes Americaines [*A publication*]
R Franc Et Polit Afr ... Revue Francaise d'Etudes Politiques Africaines [*A publication*]
R Franc Et Polit Medit ... Revue Francaise d'Etudes Politiques Mediterraneennes [*A publication*]
R Franc Gestion ... Revue Francaise de Gestion [*A publication*]
R Franc Hist O Mer ... Revue Francaise d'Histoire d'Outre-Mer [*A publication*]
R Franc Hist Outre-Mer ... Revue Francaise d'Histoire d'Outre-Mer [*A publication*]
R Franc Mkting ... Revue Francaise du Marketing [*A publication*]
R Franc Pedag ... Revue Francaise de Pedagogie [*A publication*]
R Franc Psych ... Revue Francaise de Psychoanalyse [*A publication*]
R Franc Sci Polit ... Revue Francaise de Science Politique [*A publication*]
R Franc Soc ... Revue Francaise de Sociologie [*A publication*]
R Franc Sociol ... Revue Francaise de Sociologie [*A publication*]
RFRC .... Refractory   (MSA)
R Fr Energ ... Revue Francaise de l'Energie [*A publication*]
R Fr Etud Pol Afr ... Revue Francaise d'Etudes Politiques Africaines [*A publication*]
R Fr Etud Pol Mediterraneennes ... Revue Francaise d'Etudes Politiques Mediterraneennes [*A publication*]
RFRG .... Revista de Filologie Romanica si Germanica [*Bucarest*] [*A publication*]
R Fr Gestion ... Revue Francaise de Gestion [*A publication*]
RFrign .... Rassegna Frignanese [*A publication*]
RFRJ .... Radio Frequency Rotary Joint
R Fr Marketing ... Revue Francaise du Marketing [*A publication*]
RFRO .... Raumforschung und Raumordnung [*A publication*]
RFRR-A ..... Raumforschung und Raumordnung [*A publication*]
R Fr Science Pol ... Revue Francaise de Science Politique [*A publication*]
RFRSH ...... Refresh [*Computer graphics*]
R Fr Sociol ... Revue Francaise de Sociologie [*A publication*]
RFS .... R. F. Scientific, Inc. [*Telecommunications service*]   (TSSD)
RFS .... Radio Frequency Seal
RFS .... Radio-Frequency Shift   (IEEE)
RFS .... Radio Frequency Subsystem [*NASA*]
RFS .... Random Filing System
RFS .... Range Frequency Synthesizer
RFS .... Ready for Sea [*Navy*]
RFS .... Ready for Service
RFS .... Reduced Friction Strut [*Suspension system*] [*Automotive engineering*]
RFS .... Refuse   (FAAC)
RFS .... Regardless of Feature Size [*Manufacturing term*]
RFS .... Regional Field Specialist [*Civil Defense*]
RFS .... Regional Frequency Supplies [*Telecommunications*]   (TEL)
RFS .... Registry of Friendly Societies [*British*]   (ILCA)
RFS .... Relapse-Free Survival [*Oncology*]
RFS .... Religion and Family Life Section   (EA)
RFS .... Remote File Service [*or System*] [*Data processing*]   (PCM)
RFS .... Remote File Sharing [*Data processing*]
RFS .... Renal Function Studies [*Medicine*]
RFS .... Render, Float, and Set [*Construction*]
RFS .... Request for Services [*Social Security Administration*]
RFS .... Request for Shipment   (MCD)
RFS .... Resources Forecasting System
RFS .... Response Feedback System [*NASA*]
RFS .... Revue Francaise de Sociologie [*A publication*]
RFS .... Roll Follow-Up System
RFS .... Rossendorfer Forschungs-Reaktor [*Rossendorf Research Reactor*] [*German*]
RFS .... Rotational Flight Simulator [*Air Force*]
RFS .... Rover Flight Safety
RFS .... Royal Forestry Society of England [*British*]
RFSB .... Regional Forward Scatter Branch [*Supreme Allied Commander, Europe*]   (NATG)
RFSB .... Reisterstown Federal Savings Bank [*NASDAQ symbol*]   (NQ)
RFSE .... Radio Frequency Shielded Enclosure
RFS/ECM ... Radio Frequency Surveillance/Electronic Countermeasures   (MCD)
RFSEDN ... French Journal of Water Science [*A publication*]
RFSH .... Refresh [*Computer graphics*]
RFSHA ...... Reports. Liberal Arts and Science Faculty. Shizuoka University. Natural Science [*A publication*]
RFS/ISE .... Ready for Sea/Individual Ship Exercise   (MCD)
RFSO-A ..... Revue Francaise de Sociologie [*A publication*]
RFSP .... Radioactive Fallout Study Program [*Canada*]
RFSP .... Revue Francaise de Science Politique [*A publication*]
RFSP .... Rigid Frame Selection Program
RFSS .... Radio Frequency Simulation System   (MCD)
RFSS .... Radio Frequency Surveillance Subsystem
RFSS .... Reichsfuehrerschutzstaffel   (BJA)
RFST .... Research Foundation for the Study of Terrorism [*British*]

RFSTF ...... Radio Frequency Systems Test Facility   (KSC)
RFSU .... Rugby Football Schools Union [*British*]
RFT .... Rapid Fermentation Technique
RFT .... Ready for Training [*Military*]
RFT .... Ready for Typesetter [*Publishing*]
RFT .... Real Fourier Transform
RFT .... Reflectance, Fluorescence, Transmittance [*Densitometer*] [*Instrumentation*]
RFT .... Refresher Training [*Navy*]   (NVT)
RFT .... Regge Field Theory [*Particle Physics*]
RFT .... Regional Film Theatre [*British*]
RFT .... Reinforcement
RFT .... Request for Tender   (ADA)
RFT .... Revisable Form Text [*Data processing*]   (PCM)
RFT .... Revue Francaise de Transfusion [*A publication*]
RFT .... Right Frontotransverse [*A fetal position*] [*Obstetrics*]
RFT .... Rotary Feed-Through
RFTC .... Radio Frequency Test Console
RFTD .... Radial Flow Torr Deposition System   (IEEE)
RFTDS ...... RADAR Frequency Target Discrimination System   (MCD)
RFTF .... Radio Frequency Test Facility [*Oak Ridge National Laboratory*]
RF-TK .... Radio Frequency Tracking [*Military*]   (MCD)
RFTL .... Radio Frequency Transmission Line
RFTN .... Reflectone, Inc. [*NASDAQ symbol*]   (NQ)
RFTO .... Ready for Takeoff [*Aviation*]
RFTOI .... Request for Test or Inspection   (MCD)
RFTP .... Request for Technical Proposal
RFTRA ..... Revue Francaise de Traitement de l'Information [*A publication*]
RFTS .... Radio Frequency Test Set   (AABC)
RFTW .... Ready for the World [*Rhythm and Blues recording group*]
RFTY .... Reformatory   (AABC)
RFU .... Radio Frequency Unit [*Later, RFCM*]   (MCD)
RFU .... Ready-for-Use   (NG)
RFU .... Reliability Field Unit
RFU .... Remote Firing Unit   (MCD)
RFU .... Returns File Unit [*IRS*]
RFU .... Rugby Football Union [*British*]
RFUA .... Roll Follow-Up Amplifier
RFUM .... Roll Follow-Up Motor
RFUO .... Roll Follow-Up Operation
RFUS .... Reversible Follow-Up System
RFUS .... Roll Follow-Up System
RFUSA4 ... Clinical Gynecology and Obstetrics [*Tokyo*] [*A publication*]
RFV .... RADAR Film Viewer
RFV .... Ragado Fino Virus
RFV .... Regressing Friend Virus
RFV .... Resonant Frequency Vibration
RFVC .... Reason for Visit Classification [*Medicine*]   (DHSM)
R-FVII .... Reading Free Vocational Interest Inventory [*Vocational guidance test*]
RFVM .... Radio Frequency Voltmeter
RFW .... Radio Free Women   (EA)
RFW .... Radio Frequency Wave
RFW .... Rapid Filling Wave [*Cardiology*]
RFW .... Reactor Feedwater [*Nuclear energy*]   (NRCH)
RFW .... Refrigerated Fresh Water Medium [*Microbiology*]
RFW .... Request for Waiver   (MCD)
RFW .... Reserve Feed Water [*Technical drawings*]
RFW .... Reversible Full Wave
RFWAC .... Reversible Full-Wave Alternating Current
RFWAR .... Requirements for Work and Resources   (MUGU)
RFWDC .... Reversible Full-Wave Direct Current
RFWF .... Radio Frequency Wave Form
RFX .... East Hartford, CT [*Location identifier*] [*FAA*]   (FAAL)
RFX .... Reversed Field Experiment [*Nuclear energy*]   (NRCH)
RFZ .... Restrictive Fire Zone [*Military*]
RFZ .... Rinforzando [*With Special Emphasis*] [*Music*]
RG .... Radial Glial Guide [*Neurology*]
R/G .... Radiation Guidance   (MUGU)
RG .... Radio Direction Finding Station [*ITU designation*]   (CET)
RG .... Radio Frequency Cables; Bulk [*JETDS nomenclature*] [*Military*]   (CET)
RG .... Radio Guidance   (AAG)
RG .... Radiogram   (DEN)
R-G .... Radiologist-General
RG .... Range   (AAG)
RG .... Ranging Gun [*British military*]   (DMA)
RG .... Rate Grown
RG .... Rate Gyroscope   (KSC)
RG .... Readers' Guide to Periodical Literature [*A publication*]
RG .... Readiness Group [*Military*]   (AABC)
RG .... Reagent Grade
RG .... Real Gas
R/G .... Rear Gunner [*British military*]   (DMA)
RG .... Rebuilding Grade [*Automotive engineering*] [*Polymer Steel Corp.*]
RG .... Reception Good [*Radio logs*]
RG .... Recherches Germaniques [*A publication*]
RG .... Rechtsgeschichte [*German*]   (ILCA)

RG............. Rectangular Guide (DEN)
R/G........... Red and Gold (Edges) [*Bookbinding*] (ROG)
RG............. Red-Green
RG............. Reduction Gear [*or Gearbox*] (NG)
RG............. Register (CET)
RG............. Regula Generalis [*General Rule or Order of Court*] [*Latin*] [*A publication*] (DLA)
RG............. Regulated Gallery [*Nuclear energy*] (NRCH)
RG............. Regulatory Guide [*Nuclear energy*] (NRCH)
RG............. Regummed [*Philately*]
RG............. Reichsgericht [*Reich Supreme Court*] [*German*] (ILCA)
RG............. Release Guard [*Telecommunications*] (TEL)
RG............. Remak's Ganglion [*Neurology*]
RG............. Remedial Gymnast [*British*]
RG............. Renabie Gold Trust [*Formerly, Barrick-Cullation Gold Trust*] [*Toronto Stock Exchange symbol*]
RG............. Report Generator (CMD)
RG............. Report Guide
RG............. Reserve Grade [*Military*]
RG............. Reset Gate
RG............. Resettlement Grants [*British*] [*World War II*]
RG............. Resolving Gel [*Biochemistry*]
RG............. Reticulated Grating (AAG)
RGA........... Reverse Gate
RG............. Revista de Guimaraes [*A publication*]
RG............. Revolutionary Government [*Vietnam*]
RG............. Revue Generale [*A publication*]
RG............. Revue Germanique [*A publication*]
RG............. Right Gluteus [*Anatomy*]
RG............. Right Guard [*Football*]
RG............. Right Gun
RG............. Ringing Generator [*Telecommunications*] (TEL)
R-G............ [*Alain*] Robbe-Grillet [*French author and film director*]
RG............. Robert Graham [*Designer's mark on US 1984 $1 Olympic commemorative coin*]
RG............. Rogers Group (EA)
RG............. Rogue's Gallery (EA)
RG............. Rolled Gold
RG............. Romana Gens [*A publication*]
RG............. Rueckgang [*Return*] [*Music*]
R & G........ Russell and Geldert's Nova Scotia Reports [*A publication*] (DLA)
RG............. VEB Fahlberg-List [*East Germany*] [*Research code symbol*]
RG............. Viacao Aerea Rio-Grandense [*VARIG*] [*Brazil*] [*ICAO designator*] (FAAC)
RGA........... Rate Gyro Assembly
RGA........... Regal Petroleum Ltd. [*Vancouver Stock Exchange symbol*]
RGA........... Relative Gain Array [*Control engineering*]
RGA........... Republican Governors Association (EA)
RGA........... Residual Gas Analyzer
RGA........... Ring Guild of America [*Defunct*] (EA)
RGA........... Rio Grande [*Argentina*] [*Airport symbol*] (OAG)
RGA........... Royal Garrison Artillery [*British*]
RGA........... Royal Guernsey Artillery [*British military*] (DMA)
RGA........... Rubber Growers' Association [*Later, TGA*] (EAIO)
RGAA....... Radiochemical Gamma Activation Analysis
R Gabonaise Etud Pols Econs et Juridiques ... Revue Gabonaise d'Etudes Politiques. Economiques et Juridiques [*A publication*]
R Gad........ Raina Gadagramata [*A publication*]
RGAL....... Rate Gyro Assembly - Left Solid Rocket Booster (MCD)
RGand....... Romanica Gandensia [*A publication*]
RGAO....... Rate Gyro Assembly - Orbiter (MCD)
RGAP....... Rate Gyro Accelerometer Package (MCD)
RGAR....... Rate Gyro Assembly - Right Solid Rocket Booster (MCD)
RGAR....... Revue Generale des Assurances et des Responsabilites [*A publication*]
RGAS........ Rocky Mountain Natural Gas Co. [*NASDAQ symbol*] (NQ)
RGB.......... Barry [*R. G.*] Corp. [*AMEX symbol*] (SPSG)
RGB.......... Red Green Blue [*Video monitor*]
RGB.......... Refractory Grade Bauxite [*Geology*]
RGB.......... Revue Generale Belge [*A publication*]
RGB.......... River Gunboat
RGBI......... Red Green Blue Intensity [*Video monitor*]
RGC.......... Radio-Gas Chromatography
RGC.......... Rangely [*Colorado*] [*Seismograph station code, US Geological Survey*] (SEIS)
RGC.......... Reconstructed Gas Chromatogram
RGC.......... Reigate Resources (Canada) Ltd. [*Toronto Stock Exchange symbol*]
RGC.......... Repair Group Category [*Military*] (AFIT)
RGC.......... Repository for Germinal Choice [*A sperm bank*]
RGC.......... Republic Gypsum Company [*NYSE symbol*] (SPSG)
RGC.......... Retinal Ganglion Cell [*Neurochemistry*]
RGC.......... Rio Grande College [*Ohio*]
RGC.......... Rio Grande College, Rio Grande, OH [*OCLC symbol*] (OCLC)
RGC.......... Royal Greenwich Conservatory [*British*]
RGC.......... Rural Governments Coalition [*Defunct*] (EA)
RGCR .... Renner's Gold Coast Colony Reports [*1868-1914*] [*Ghana*] [*A publication*] (DLA)
RGCT .... Residential Group Care and Treatment [*A publication*]

RGCY .... RELM Communications, Inc. [*Formerly, Regency Electronics, Inc.*] [*NASDAQ symbol*] (NQ)
RGD.......... Ragged (FAAC)
RGD.......... Rarefied Gas Dynamics
RGD.......... Regis Development Corp. [*Vancouver Stock Exchange symbol*]
RGD.......... Regular Geophysical Day
RGD.......... Revue Generale de Droit [*A publication*]
RGD.......... Revue de Geomorphologie Dynamique [*A publication*]
RGD.......... Rigid (MSA)
RGda......... Radio Grenada
RGDIP...... Revue Generale de Droit International Public [*A publication*]
RGDPD ..... Revue de Geologie Dynamique et de Geographie Physique [*A publication*]
RGDT........ Reliability Growth/Development Test
RGE .... Porgera [*Papua New Guinea*] [*Airport symbol*] (OAG)
RGE .... Range [*Maps and charts*] (MDG)
RGE .... Rat der Gemeinden Europas [*Council of European Municipalities*]
RGE .... Red under Gold Edges [*Books*]
RGE .... Reduced Gravity Environment
RGE .... Regroupement des Guineens a l'Exterieur [*Rally of Guineans Abroad*] (PD)
RGE .... Rotating Gel Electrophoresis
RGEFA ...... Revue Generale du Froid [*A publication*]
RGEN........ Repligen Corp. [*Cambridge, MA*] [*NASDAQ symbol*] (NQ)
R Gen .... Revue Generale [*A publication*]
R Gen .... Revue Generale de Droit [*A publication*]
R Gen Air Espace ... Revue Generale de l'Air et de l'Espace [*A publication*]
R Gen Assur Terr ... Revue Generale des Assurances Terrestres [*A publication*]
RGenBelge ... Revue General Belge [*A publication*] (BJA)
R Gen Chem de Fer ... Revue Generale des Chemins de Fer [*A publication*]
R Gen Dr Int Publ ... Revue Generale de Droit International Public [*A publication*]
R Gen Sci ... Revue Generale des Sciences Pures et Appliquees [*A publication*]
R Gen Sci Pures et Ap ... Revue Generale des Sciences Pures et Appliquees [*A publication*]
R Geog .... Revista Geografica [*A publication*]
R de Geog de Mtl ... Revue de Geographie de Montreal [*A publication*]
R Geogr Alpine ... Revue de Geographie Alpine [*A publication*]
R Geogr Est ... Revue Geographique de l'Est [*A publication*]
RGeogrH ... Revue de Geographie Humaine et d'Ethnologie [*A publication*]
R Geogr Lyon ... Revue de Geographie de Lyon [*A publication*]
R Geogr Maroc ... Revue de Geographie du Maroc [*A publication*]
R Geogr Pyrenees ... Revue Geographique des Pyrenees et du Sud-Ouest [*A publication*]
R Geogr (Rio De Janeiro) ... Revista Geografica (Rio De Janeiro) [*A publication*]
R Geog Soc Pr ... Royal Geographical Society. Proceedings [*A publication*]
RGEPS ..... Rucker-Gable Educational Programming Scale [*Psychology*]
RGEQ........ Regency Equities Corp. [*NASDAQ symbol*] (NQ)
RGer......... Recherches Germaniques [*A publication*]
RGF .... Range Gated Filter
RGF .... Rarefied Gas Field [*or Flow*]
RGF .... Roemisch-Germanische Forschungen [*A publication*]
RGF .... Royal Gun Factory [*British military*] (DMA)
RGFC........ Ray Griff Fan Club (EA)
RGFC........ Remote Gas Filter Correlation (KSC)
RGFC........ Robin George Fan Club (EA)
RGFil........ Romano-Germanskaja Filologija [*A publication*]
RGFRD4.... Ghana. Fishery Research Unit. Information Report [*A publication*]
RGG.......... Religion in Geschichte und Gegenwart [*A publication*]
RGG.......... Rotating Gravity Gradiometer
RGG.......... Royal Grenadier Guards [*British*]
RGH .... Rare Gas Halogen [*Inorganic chemistry*]
RGH .... Rat Growth Hormone [*Endocrinology*]
RGH .... Rough (AAG)
R Ghana Law ... Review of Ghana Law [*A publication*]
RGHE....... Revue de Geographie Humaine et d'Ethnologie [*A publication*]
RGHSDH ... Annual Research Reviews. Regulation of Growth Hormone Secretion [*A publication*]
RGI .... Rangiroa [*French Polynesia*] [*Airport symbol*] (OAG)
RGI .... Rivista Geografica Italiana [*A publication*]
RGI .... Royal Glasgow Institute of Fine Arts [*Scotland*]
RGICC....... Region Internal Computer Code [*Data processing*]
RGIFA ...... Royal Glasgow Institute of Fine Arts [*Scotland*]
RGIRAG.... Rivista Generale Italiana di Chirurgia [*A publication*]
RGIS........ Regis Corp. [*NASDAQ symbol*] (NQ)
RGIT........ Representative for German Industry and Trade [*An association*] (EA)
RGIT........ Robert Gordon Institute of Technology [*Scotland*]
RGJ.......... Richmond, VA [*Location identifier*] [*FAA*] (FAAL)
RGJ.......... Royal Green Jackets [*Military unit*] [*British*]
RGJLond ... Royal Green Jackets, London [*Military unit*] [*British*]
RGJTAVR ... Royal Green Jackets Territorial and Army Volunteer Reserve [*Military unit*] [*British*]
RGK.......... Red Wing, MN [*Location identifier*] [*FAA*] (FAAL)
RGK.......... Reserv Glavnogo Komandovaniia [*Reserve of the High Command*] [*USSR*]

RGKAI....... Roemisch-Germanische Kommission des Archaeologischen
            Instituts [*A publication*]
RGKNA ..... Rikagaku Kenkyusho Kenkyu Nempo [*A publication*]
RGL .... Rate Gyroscope Limit
RGL .... Reading Grade Level
RGL .... Regal International, Inc. [*NYSE symbol*] (SPSG)
RGL .... Regional Resources Ltd. [*Toronto Stock Exchange symbol*]
            [*Vancouver Stock Exchange symbol*]
RGL .... Regulate (MSA)
RGL .... Reihe Germanistische Linguistik [*A publication*]
RGL .... Report Generator Language [*Data processing*] (IEEE)
RGL .... Resources Policy [*A publication*]
RGL .... Review of Ghana Law [*A publication*]
RGL .... Revue de Geographie de Lyon [*A publication*]
RGL .... Rio Gallegos [*Argentina*] [*Airport symbol*] (OAG)
RGL .... Wrangell, AK [*Location identifier*] [*FAA*] (FAAL)
RGLD .... Royal Gold, Inc. [*NASDAQ symbol*] (NQ)
RGLR....... Regular (MSA)
RGLT....... Regulating (MSA)
RGLTD..... Regulated (MSA)
RGLTR..... Regulator (MSA)
RGM........ Radiogas Monitor [*Nuclear energy*] (NRCH)
RGM........ Recorder Group Monitor
RGM........ Redundant Gyro Monitor (NASA)
RGM........ Reliability Growth Management (MCD)
RGM........ Remote Geophysical Monitor (MCD)
RGM........ Reversible Gelatin Matrix
RGM........ Rounds per Gun per Minute
RGM........ Royex Gold Mining Corp. [*Toronto Stock Exchange symbol*]
            [*Vancouver Stock Exchange symbol*]
RGMI .... Regulations Governing the Meat Inspection [*of the USDA*]
RGMNA .... Chijil Kwangmul Chosa Yongu Pokoso [*A publication*]
RGMS .... Reversible Gelatin Matrix System
RGN.......... Rangoon [*Burma*] [*Airport symbol*] (OAG)
RGN.......... Region (AFM)
RGN.......... Registered General Nurse
RGN.......... Riggins Resources [*Vancouver Stock Exchange symbol*]
RGNEB ..... Review of Compagnie Generale d'Electricite [*A publication*]
RGNG....... Rigging (MSA)
RGNL .... Regional
R & G N Sc ... Russell and Geldert's Nova Scotia Reports [*A
            publication*] (DLA)
RGNUD..... Revue Generale Nucleaire [*A publication*]
RGO.......... Akron, OH [*Location identifier*] [*FAA*] (FAAL)
RGO.......... Ranger Oil Ltd. [*NYSE symbol*] [*Toronto Stock Exchange
            symbol*] (SPSG)
RGO.......... Regulation [*A publication*]
RGo.......... Romanica Gothoburgensia [*A publication*]
RGO.......... Royal Greenwich Observatory [*British*]
RGP .... Rate Gyro Package
RGP .... Regina Public Library [*UTLAS symbol*]
RGP .... Remote Graphics Processor
RGP .... Retired Greyhounds as Pets (EA)
RGP .... Rhodesian Government Party
RGP .... Rigid Gas Permeable [*Contact lens*]
RGP .... Rijks Geschiedkundige Publicaties [*A publication*]
RGP .... Rolled Gold Plate [*Metallurgy*]
RGPF .... Royal Gunpowder Factory [*British*]
RGPGD ..... Revue de Geographie Physique et de Geologie Dynamique [*A
            publication*]
RG PH ...... Registered Pharmacist
RGPO .... Range Gate Pull Off (NVT)
RGPS........ Razor Grinders' Protection Society [*A union*] [*British*]
RGR .... Oklahoma City, OK [*Location identifier*] [*FAA*] (FAAL)
RGR .... Range Gated Receiver
RGR .... Ranger
RGR .... Rare-Gas Recovery [*Nuclear energy*] (NRCH)
RGr .... Rassegna Gregoriana [*A publication*]
RGR .... Rassemblement des Gauches Republicaines [*Assembly of the
            Republican Left*] [*France*] [*Political party*]
RGR .... Receipt of Goods Received
RGR .... Regionair, Inc. [*Canada*] [*FAA designator*] (FAAC)
RGR .... Regulus Resources, Inc. [*Vancouver Stock Exchange symbol*]
RGR .... Relative Growth Rate [*Entomology*]
RGR .... Revista Germanistilor Romani [*A publication*]
RGr .... Revue Gregorienne [*A publication*]
RGR .... Royal Garrison Regiment [*Military*] [*British*] (ROG)
RGR .... Royal Gurkha Regiment [*British military*] (DMA)
RGR .... Sturm Ruger & Co. [*NYSE symbol*] (SPSG)
RGRCD ..... Geothermal Resources Council. Special Report [*A publication*]
R Greenwich Obs Bull ... Royal Greenwich Observatory. Bulletins [*A
            publication*]
R Gregor .... Revue Gregorienne [*A publication*]
RGRMA .... Rate Gyro Redundancy Management Algorithm (NASA)
RgrT.......... Ranger Tab [*Military decoration*]
RGS .... RADAR Ground Stabilization
RGS .... Radio Guidance System
RGS .... Rate Gyro System
RGS .... Remote Ground Switching
RGS .... Rene Guyon Society (EA)
RGS .... Restructured General Support [*Military*]

RGS .... River Gauging Station
RGS .... Rochester Gas & Electric Corp. [*NYSE symbol*] (SPSG)
RGS .... Rocket Guidance System (KSC)
RGS .... Royal Geographical Society [*British*]
RGS .... Royal Gold Enterprises, Inc. [*Toronto Stock Exchange symbol*]
RGS .... Ruffed Grouse Society (EA)
RGS .... Sisters of Our Lady of Charity of the Good Shepherd [*Roman
            Catholic religious order*]
RGSAT...... Radio Guidance Surveillance and Automatic Tracking (AAG)
RGS Austsia SA Br Proc ... Royal Geographical Society of Australasia. South
            Australian Branch. Proceedings [*A publication*] (APTA)
RGSC........ Ramp Generator and Signal Converter (IEEE)
RGSDLR .. Rigsdaler [*Numismatics*]
RGSIA ...... Records. Geological Survey of India [*A publication*]
R G Soc Cornwall Tr ... Royal Geological Society of Cornwall. Transactions [*A
            publication*]
R G Soc Ireland J ... Royal Geological Society of Ireland. Journal [*A
            publication*]
RGSU .... Restructured General Support Unit (MCD)
RGSWA..... Records. Geological Survey of New South Wales [*A
            publication*]
Rgt............ Regent [*Record label*]
RGT .... Regent College Library [*UTLAS symbol*]
RGT .... Regiment
RGT .... Rengat [*Indonesia*] [*Airport symbol*] (OAG)
RGT .... Resonant Gate Transistor [*Data processing*]
RGT .... Reverse Garbage Truck (ADA)
RGT .... Rigging Template (MCD)
RGT .... Right
RGTHA ..... Revue Generale de Thermique [*A publication*]
RGTP........ Reseau Gouvernemental de Transmission par Paquets
            [*Government Packet Network - GPN*] [*Canada*]
RGTP........ Rough Template (AAG)
RGTR .... Register
RGU.......... Rate Gyroscope Unit
R Guardia Fin ... Rivista della Guardia di Finanza [*A publication*]
RGuim....... Revista de Guimaraes [*A publication*]
R Guimar .. Revista de Guimaraes [*A publication*]
RGUMD... Argument [*A publication*]
RGV .... Relative Gas Vacuolation [*In algae*]
RGV .... Rio Grande Ventures Ltd. [*Vancouver Stock Exchange symbol*]
R-GVB ...... Resonating-Generalized Valence Bond [*Physical chemistry*]
RGVV .... Religionsgeschichtliche Versuche und Vorarbeiten [*A
            publication*]
RGW .... Ramp Gross Weight [*Aviation*]
RGW .... Reagent Grade Water
RGWS ...... RADAR Guided Weapon System (MCD)
RGY .... Regency Airlines [*Chicago, IL*] [*FAA designator*] (FAAC)
RGZ .... Recommended Ground Zero [*Military*] (AABC)
RGZM ...... Roemisch-Germanische Zentralmuseum (Mainz) [*A
            publication*]
RGZTA...... Railway Gazette [*Later, Railway Gazette International*] [*A
            publication*]
RH .... 1st Nottinghamshire (Robin Hood) Rifle Volunteer Corps
            [*British military*] (DMA)
RH .... Air Rhodesia [*ICAO designator*] (FAAC)
RH .... Air Zimbabwe [*Zimbabwe*] [*ICAO designator*] (ICDA)
RH .... Rabbinic Hebrew (BJA)
RH .... Radiant Heat
RH .... Radiation Homing (AAG)
RH .... Radiological Health (KSC)
r/h .... RADs [*Radiation Absorbed Doses*] per Hour (DEN)
RH .... Railhead [*British military*] (DMA)
RH .... Rankine-Hugoniot [*Physics*]
RH .... Reactive Hyperemia [*Medicine*]
RH .... Receive Hub [*Telegraph*] [*Telecommunications*] (TEL)
RH .... Red Herring [*Investment term*]
RH .... Regional Headquarters (NOAA)
RH .... Relative Humidity
RH .... Releasing Hormone [*Also, RF*] [*Endocrinology*]
RH .... Religious Humanism [*A publication*]
RH .... Remotely Handled
r/h .... REMs [*Roentgen Equivalents, Man*] per Hour (DEN)
RH .... Report Heading (BUR)
RH .... Request-Response Header [*Data processing*] (BUR)
RH .... Requesta Regni Hierosolymitani [*A publication*] (BJA)
RH .... Research Highlights [*A publication*] (DIT)
RH .... Residential Hotels [*Public-performance tariff class*] [*British*]
RH .... Restaurant Hospitality [*A publication*]
RH .... Revisionist History [*Taby, Sweden*] (EAIO)
R/H .... Revolutions per Hour (DEN)
RH .... Revue Hebdomadaire [*A publication*]
RH .... Revue Hispanique [*A publication*]
RH .... Revue Historique [*A publication*]
RH .... Rheostat (IEEE)
Rh.............. Rhesus [*Blood factor*]
Rh.............. Rhetorica [*of Aristotle*] [*Classical studies*] (OCD)
Rh.............. Rheumatism [*Medicine*]
RH .... Rhinitis [*Medicine*]
RH .... Rhinoceros (ROG)

rh .... Rhodesia [*Southern Rhodesia*] [*MARC country of publication code*] [*Library of Congress*]   (LCCP)
Rh .... Rhodium [*Chemical element*]
Rh .... Rhodopsin [*Visual Purple*]
RH .... Right Halfback [*Soccer*]
RH .... Right Hand
RH .... Right Hyperphoria [*Medicine*]
RH .... Road Haulage
RH .... Rochester History [*A publication*]
RH .... Rockwell Hardness
RH .... Roczniki Humanistyczne [*A publication*]
r/h .... Roentgens per Hour   (DEN)
RH .... Roger Houghton Ltd. [*Publisher*] [*British*]
RH .... Rosh Hashanah [*New Year*]   (BJA)
RH .... Rotuli Hundredorum [*Latin*] [*A publication*]   (DLA)
RH .... Round Head
RH .... Round House [*Maps and charts*]
RH .... Royal Highlanders [*Military unit*] [*British*]
RH .... Royal Highness
RH .... Royal Hospital [*London*]
RH .... Royal Hospital [*Chelsea*] [*British military*]   (DMA)
RH .... Royal Hussars [*Military unit*] [*British*]
RH .... Rueckwaertiges Heeresgebiet [*Rear area of a group of armies*] [*German military*]
RH .... Runaway Hotline   (EA)
RH .... Ryan's Hope [*Television program*]
RH .... Southern Rhodesia [*ANSI two-letter standard code*] [*Obsolete*]   (CNC)
RHA .... Ranching Heritage Association   (EA)
RHA .... Records Holding Area [*Military*]
RHA .... Regional Health Authority [*British*]
RHA .... Reichold [*Alabama*] [*Seismograph station code, US Geological Survey*]   (SEIS)
RHA .... Reindeer Herders Association   (EA)
RHA .... Religious Heritage of America   (EA)
RHA .... Renewal and Housing Assistance Report [*HUD*]
RHA .... Respiratory Health Association   (EA)
RHA .... Revista de Historia de America [*A publication*]
RHA .... Revue Hittite et Asiatique [*A publication*]
RHA .... Reykholar [*Iceland*] [*Airport symbol*] [*Obsolete*]   (OAG)
RHA .... Road Haulage Association [*British*]
RHA .... Rohm & Haas Co., Spring House, PA [*OCLC symbol*]   (OCLC)
RHA .... Rolled Homogeneous Armor [*Weaponry*]   (INF)
RHA .... Roman High Avoidance [*Behavior trait*]
RHA .... Rose Hybridizers Association   (EA)
RHA .... Royal Hawaiian Air Service [*Honolulu, HI*] [*FAA designator*]   (FAAC)
RHA .... Royal Hellenic Army   (NATG)
RHA .... Royal Hibernian Academy
RHA .... Royal Horse Artillery [*British*]
RHA .... Rural Housing Alliance [*Later, RAI*]   (EA)
RHAB .... Random House AudioBooks [*Publisher*]
RHAB .... Rehab Hospital Services [*NASDAQ symbol*]   (NQ)
R Hacienda ... Revista de Hacienda [*A publication*]
RHAF .... Revue d'Histoire de l'Amerique Francaise [*A publication*]
RHAF .... Royal Hellenic Air Force
Rh Al .... Rhetorica ad Alexandrum [*of Aristotle*] [*Classical studies*]   (OCD)
RHAM .... Rhammus [*Pharmacology*]   (ROG)
R Hanazono Coll ... Review of Hanazono College [*A publication*]
RHASS ..... Royal Highland and Agricultural Society of Scotland [*British*]
RHA(T) ..... Regional Health Authority (Teaching) [*British*]
RHAV ...... Rat Hepatoma-Associated Virus
RHAW ...... RADAR Homing and Warning   (MCD)
RHAWR .... RADAR Homing and Warning Receiver   (MCD)
RHAWS ..... RADAR Homing and Warning System
RHB .... RADAR Homing Bomb [*Air Force*]
RHB .... Regional Hospital Boards [*British*]
RhB .... Rheinische Blaetter [*A publication*]
RHB .... Rheinische Heimatblaetter [*A publication*]
RHB .... Right Halfback [*Soccer*]
RHB .... Round Hole Broach
RHBA .... Racking Horse Breeders Association of America   (EA)
R & H Bank ... Roche and Hazlitt's Bankruptcy Practice [*2nd ed.*] [*1873*] [*A publication*]   (DLA)
RHBNA ..... Rehabilitation [*A publication*]
RHC .... Reactive Hydrocarbon [*Environmental science*]
RHC .... Reactor Head Cooling [*Nuclear energy*]   (NRCH)
RHC .... Regional Holding Co.
RHC .... Resetting Half-Cycle
RHC .... Resin Hemoperfusion Column
RHC .... Respirations Have Ceased [*Medicine*]
RHC .... Revue d'Histoire Comparee [*A publication*]
RHC .... Right-Hand Circular [*NASA*]   (KSC)
RHC .... Right-Hand Console
RHC .... Right Hypochondrium [*Medicine*]
RHC .... Riverside Methodist Hospital Library, Columbus, OH [*OCLC symbol*]   (OCLC)
RHC .... Road Haulage Cases [*1950-55*] [*England*] [*A publication*]   (DLA)
RHC .... Rosary Hill College [*New York*]

RHC .... Rotational Hand Controller [*NASA*]
RHC .... Royal Highlanders of Canada [*Military unit*] [*World War I*]
RHC .... Rubber Hydrocarbon
Rh CA .... Rhodesian Court of Appeal Law Reports [*1939-46*] [*A publication*]   (DLA)
RHCA .... Roller Hockey Coaches Association   (EA)
RHCC .... Reproductive Health Care Center
RHCC .... Rocking Horse Child Care Centers of America, Inc. [*NASDAQ symbol*]   (NQ)
RHCC/PP ... Reproductive Health Care Center/Planned Parenthood
RHCF .... Residential Health Care Facility [*Medicine*]   (DHSM)
RHCFA ..... Revista. Hospital das Clinicas. Faculdade de Medicina. Universidade de Sao Paulo [*A publication*]
RHCI .... Radiant Heating and Cooling Institute
RHCI .... Ramsay Health Care, Inc. [*NASDAQ symbol*]   (NQ)
RHCM ...... Relative Humidity Control/Monitor   (NASA)
RHCM ...... Revue d'Histoire et de Civilisation du Maghreb [*A publication*]
RHComp .... Revue d'Histoire Comparee [*A publication*]
RHCP .... Right-Hand Circularly Polarized [*LASER waves*]
RHCS .... Rocznik Historii Czasopismiennictwa Polskiego [*A publication*]
RHCSA ..... Regional Hospitals Consultants' and Specialists' Association
RHD .... Archangelos [*Greece*] [*Seismograph station code, US Geological Survey*]   (SEIS)
RHD .... Radiological Health Data
RHD .... Railhead
RHD .... Random House Dictionary [*A publication*]
RHD .... Regional Health Director [*HEW*]
RHD .... Relative Hepatic Dullness [*Medicine*]
RHD .... Renal Hypertensive Disease [*Medicine*]
RHD .... Required Hangar Depth   (MCD)
RHD .... Return Head
RHD .... Revue d'Histoire Diplomatique [*A publication*]
RHD .... Revue d'Histoire du Droit [*A publication*]
RHD .... Revue Historique de Droit Francais et Etranger [*A publication*]
RHD .... Rheumatic Heart Disease [*Medicine*]
RHD .... Rhodes, Inc. [*NYSE symbol*]   (SPSG)
RHD .... Right Hand Drive [*Automotive engineering*]
RHD .... Rural Housing Disaster
RHDEL-II ... [*The*] Random House Dictionary of the English Language: Second Edition - Unabridged [*A publication*]
RHDFE ..... Revue Historique de Droit Francais et Etranger [*A publication*]
RHDGM.... Revue d'Histoire de la Deuxieme Guerre Mondiale [*A publication*]
R & H Dig ... Robinson and Harrison's Digest [*Ontario*] [*A publication*]   (DLA)
RHD-II ...... [*The*] Random House Dictionary of the English Language: Second Edition - Unabridged [*A publication*]
RHDip .... Revue d'Histoire Diplomatique [*A publication*]
RHD & R ... Radiological Health Data and Reports [*A publication*]
RHDRA .... Radiological Health Data and Reports [*A publication*]
RHE .... Radiation Hazard Effects   (KSC)
RHE .... Random House Encyclopedia [*A publication*]
RHE .... Record Handling Electronics
RHE .... Reims [*France*] [*Airport symbol*]   (OAG)
RHE .... Reliability Human Engineering   (AAG)
RHE .... Remote Hellfire Electronics [*Army*]
RHE .... Reversible Hydrogen Electrode
RHE .... Revue d'Histoire Ecclesiastique [*A publication*]
RHEA .... Reentry Heating Energies Analyzer [*Air Force*]
RHEA .... Research into Higher Education. Abstracts [*A publication*]
RHEAA ..... Rheologica Acta [*A publication*]
RHeb .... Revue Hebdomadaire [*A publication*]
RHEB .... Right-Hand Equipment Bay [*Apollo*] [*NASA*]
RHEED ..... Reflected High-Energy Electron Diffraction [*Spectroscopy*]
RHEF .... Revue d'Histoire de l'Eglise de France [*A publication*]
Rhein Bienenztg ... Rheinische Bienenzeitung [*A publication*]
Rheinisches Mus Philol ... Rheinisches Museum fuer Philologie [*A publication*]
Rheinisch-Westfael Akad Wiss Nat- Ing- Wirtschaftswiss Vort ... Rheinisch-Westfaelische Akademie der Wissenschaften Natur-, Ingenieur-, und Wirtschaftswissenschaften. Vortraege [*A publication*]
Rheinisch Westfael Z Volkskd ... Rheinisch-Westfaelische Zeitschrift fuer Volkskunde [*A publication*]
Rhein Mus (Bonn) ... Rheinische Landesmuseum (Bonn) [*A publication*]
Rheinstahl Tech ... Rheinstahl Technik [*A publication*]
Rhein Vb .... Rheinische Vierteljahresblaetter [*A publication*]
Rhein Viert Jbl ... Rheinische Vierteljahrsblaetter [*A publication*]
Rhein-Westfael Akad Wiss Vortr N ... Rheinisch-Westfaelische Akademie der Wissenschaften Natur-, Ingenieur-, und Wirtschaftswissenschaften. Vortraege [*A publication*]
RHel .... Romanica Helvetica [*A publication*]
RHEL .... Rutherford High Energy Laboratory   (MCD)
R Hell Dr Int ... Revue Hellenique de Droit International [*A publication*]
RHEM .... Rheometrics, Inc. [*Piscataway, NJ*] [*NASDAQ symbol*]   (NQ)
RHEO .... Rheostat   (AAG)
Rheol Abstr ... Rheology Abstracts [*A publication*]
Rheol Act ... Rheologica Acta [*A publication*]
Rheol Acta ... Rheologica Acta [*A publication*]
Rheol Bull ... Rheology Bulletin [*A publication*]
Rheol Leafl ... Rheology Leaflet [*A publication*]

Rheol Mem ... Rheological Memoirs [*A publication*]
Rheol Texture Food Qual ... Rheology and Texture in Food Quality [*A publication*]
RHES .... Revue d'Histoire Economique et Sociale [*A publication*]
Rhes .... Rhesus [*of Euripides*] [*Classical studies*]   (OCD)
Rhet .... Ars Rhetorica [*of Dionysius Halicarnassensis*] [*Classical studies*]   (OCD)
Rhet .... De Rhetoribus [*of Suetonius*] [*Classical studies*]   (OCD)
Rhet .... Rhetores Graeci [*A publication*]   (OCD)
RHET .... Rhetoric
Rhet Her .... Rhetorica ad Herennium [*First century BC*] [*Classical studies*]   (OCD)
Rhet Lat Min ... Rhetores Latini Minores [*A publication*]   (OCD)
RHEUM .... Rheumatism [*Medicine*]
Rheumatol Balneo Allergol ... Rheumatologia, Balneologia, Allergologia [*A publication*]
Rheumatol Int ... Rheumatology International [*A publication*]
Rheumatol Phys Med ... Rheumatology and Physical Medicine [*A publication*]
Rheumatol Rehabil ... Rheumatology and Rehabilitation [*A publication*]
Rheum Intl ... Rheumatology International [*A publication*]
RHF .... Rarefied Hypersonic Flow
RHF .... Remembrance of the Holocaust Foundation   (EA)
RHF .... Restricted Hartree-Fock [*Quantum mechanics*]
RHF .... Retired History File [*Army*]
RHF .... Revue d'Histoire Franciscaine [*A publication*]
RHF .... Right Heart Failure [*Medicine*]
RHF .... Roller Hockey Federation   (EA)
RHF .... Royal Highland Fusiliers [*Military unit*] [*British*]
RHFC .... Richard Hatch Fan Club   (EA)
RHFC .... Robyn Hitchcock Fan Club   (EA)
RHFEB ..... Right-Hand Forward Equipment Bay [*NASA*]   (KSC)
RHFF .... Richard Hatch Fan Fellowship   (EAIO)
RHFS .... Receiving Hospital Field Station
RHFS .... Round Hill Field Station [*MIT*]   (MCD)
RHG .... Royal Horse Guards [*British*]
RHG-CSF ... Recombinant Human Granulocyte, Colony Stimulating Factor [*Hematology*]
RHG1D ..... Royal Horse Guards and 1st Dragoons [*British military*]   (DMA)
RHGH .... Recombinant Human Growth Hormone [*Biochemistry*]
rhGRF .... Rat Hypothalamus Growth Hormone-Releasing Factor [*Endocrinology*]
RHGSA ..... Russian Historical and Genealogical Society in America [*Later, RNAA*]   (EA)
RHH .... Right-Hand Head
RHH .... Robertson-Ceco Corp. [*NYSE symbol*]   (SPSG)
RHI .... Halmi [*Robert*], Incorporated [*AMEX symbol*]   (SPSG)
RHI .... RADAR Height Indicator   (CET)
RHI .... Range-Height Indicator [*RADAR*]
RHI .... Relative Humidity Indicator   (AAG)
RHI .... Responsible Hospitality Institute   (EA)
RHi .... Revue Hispanique [*A publication*]
RHI .... Rhinelander [*Wisconsin*] [*Airport symbol*]   (OAG)
RHI .... Rhinology [*Medicine*]   (DHSM)
RHI .... Rhode Island
RHI .... Rhode Island Historical Society Library, Providence, RI [*OCLC symbol*]   (OCLC)
RHi .... Rhode Island Historical Society, Providence, RI [*Library symbol*] [*Library of Congress*]   (LCLS)
Rh I .... Rhode Island Reports [*A publication*]   (DLA)
Rh I .... Rhode Island Supreme Court Reports [*A publication*]   (DLA)
RHI .... Rigid-Hull Inflatable [*US Coast Guard vessel*]
RHI .... Robert Half International, Inc. [*NYSE symbol*]   (SPSG)
RHIA .... Radiation-Hardened Interfacing Amplifier
RHIB .... Rain and Hail Insurance Bureau [*Defunct*]   (EA)
RHIC .... Relativistic Heavy Ion Collider [*Nuclear physics*]
RHIDEC .... [*The*] Restaurant/Hotel International Design Exposition   (ITD)
RHIFC .... Ray Heatherton Irish Friends Club   (EA)
RHIG .... RH [*or Rhesus*] Immune Globulin [*Immunology*]
RHiM .... Revista Hispanica Moderna [*A publication*]
RHIMO ..... Agency for Navigation on the Rhine and the Moselle   (NATG)
Rhin .... Rhinology [*Medicine*]
RHINO ...... Range-Height Indicator Not Operating [*Aviation*]   (FAAC)
Rhino .... Really Here in Name Only [*Education*] [*British*]
RHINO ...... Rhinoceros   (DSUE)
RHINOL .... Rhinology [*Medicine*]
RHIO .... Rank Has Its Obligations [*Military slang*]
RHIP .... Radiation Health Information Project   (EA)
RHIP .... Rank Has Its Privileges [*Military slang*]
RHIR .... Rank Has Its Responsibilities [*Military slang*]
RHis .... Revue Historique [*A publication*]
RHi-Sh ...... Rhode Island Historical Society, George L. Shepley Collection, Providence, RI [*Library symbol*] [*Library of Congress*]   (LCLS)
RHisp .... Revue Hispanique [*A publication*]
R Hispan Mod ... Revista Hispanica Moderna [*A publication*]
R Hist .... Revista de Historia [*A publication*]
R d'Hist ...... Revue d'Histoire de l'Amerique Francaise [*A publication*]
R Hist .... Revue Historique [*A publication*]
RHist .... Roczniki Historyczne [*A publication*]

R Hist Am ... Revista de Historia de America [*A publication*]
R Hist Ard ... Revue Historique Ardennaise [*A publication*]
R Hist Bul ... Revue Historique. Bulletins Critiques [*A publication*]
R Hist Deuxieme Geurre Mondiale ... Revue d'Histoire de la Deuxieme Guerre Mondiale [*A publication*]
R Hist Diplom ... Revue d'Histoire Diplomatique [*A publication*]
R Hist Droit ... Revue Historique de Droit Francais et Etranger [*A publication*]
R Hist Eccl ... Revue d'Histoire Ecclesiastique [*A publication*]
R Hist Fascisme ... Revue d'Histoire du Fascisme [*A publication*]
R Hist Litt France ... Revue d'Histoire Litteraire de la France [*A publication*]
RHistM ..... Roemische Historische Mitteilungen [*A publication*]
R Hist Mem ... Revue Historique. Memoires et Etudes [*A publication*]
R Hist Mod & Contemp ... Revue d'Histoire Moderne et Contemporaine [*A publication*]
RHistorique ... Revue Historique [*Paris*] [*A publication*]
R Hist & Philos Rel ... Revue d'Histoire et de Philosophie Religieuses [*A publication*]
R Hist Ph Rel ... Revue d'Histoire et de Philosophie Religieuses [*A publication*]
R Hist Rel .. Revue de l'Histoire des Religions [*A publication*]
RHistS ...... Royal Historical Society [*British*]
R Hist Sci & Ap ... Revue d'Histoire des Sciences et de Leurs Applications [*A publication*]
R Hist Spiritualite ... Revue d'Histoire de la Spiritualite [*A publication*]
RhITC .... Rhodamine Isothiocyanate [*Biochemistry*]
RHittAs ..... Revue Hittite et Asianique [*Paris*] [*A publication*]   (BJA)
RHJ .... Rubber Hose Jacket   (MSA)
RhJbV .... Rheinisches Jahrbuch fuer Volkskunde [*A publication*]
RHJE .... Revue de l'Histoire Juive en Egypte [*A publication*]
RHK .... Radio Hong Kong
RHK .... Reefing Hook
RHKUL ..... Roczniki Humanistyczne. Towarzystwo Naukowe Katolickiego Uniwersytetu Lubelskiego [*A publication*]
RHL .... Radiological Health Laboratory
RHL .... Rat Hepatic Lectin [*Biochemistry*]
RHL .... Residual Hazards List [*NASA*]   (NASA)
RHL .... Rettie's Scotch Court of Session Cases, Fourth Series [*House of Lords' Part*] [*A publication*]   (DLA)
RHL .... Reverse Half-Line [*Feed*]
RHL .... Revista de Historia. La Laguna de Tenerife [*A publication*]
RHL .... Revue d'Histoire Litteraire de la France [*A publication*]
RHL .... Richland Mine, Inc. [*Vancouver Stock Exchange symbol*]
RHL .... Right Hepatic Lobe [*Anatomy*]
RHLB .... Revue d'Histoire Litteraire (Bucharest) [*A publication*]
RHLE .... Revista Critica de Historia y Literatura Espanolas [*A publication*]
RHLF .... Revue d'Histoire Litteraire de la France [*A publication*]
RHLG .... Radiometric Homing Level Gauge
RHLI .... Royal Hamilton Light Infantry [*British military*]   (DMA)
Rh LJ .... Rhodesian Law Journal [*A publication*]   (DLA)
RHLK .... Reihe Hanser Literatur-Kommentare [*A publication*]
RHLP .... Revista de Historia Literaria de Portugal [*A publication*]
RHLR .... Revue d'Histoire et de Litterature Religieuse [*A publication*]
RHM .... Ranks Hovis McDougall [*Commercial firm*] [*British*]   (ECON)
RHM .... Refractory Heavy Minerals [*In sands used for glass making*]
RHM .... Renewal and Housing Management [*HUD*]
RHM .... Revista Hispanica Moderna [*A publication*]
RHM .... Revue d'Histoire Moderne [*A publication*]
RHM .... Rhabdomyosarcoma [*Also, RMS*] [*Oncology*]
RhM .... Rheinische Merkur [*A publication*]
RhM .... Rheinisches Museum fuer Philologie [*A publication*]
RHM .... Rio Hardy [*Mexico*] [*Seismograph station code, US Geological Survey*]   (SEIS)
RHM .... Roemische-Historische Mitteilungen [*A publication*]
RHM .... Roentgen per Hour at One Meter
RHMC ...... Revue d'Histoire Moderne et Contemporaine [*A publication*]
RHMH ...... Revue d'Histoire de la Medicine Hebraique [*Paris*] [*A publication*]
RHMis .... Revue d'Histoire des Missions [*A publication*]
RhMP .... Rheinisches Museum fuer Philologie [*A publication*]
Rh M Ph ... Rheinisches Museum fuer Philologie [*A publication*]
RHMS .... Royal Hibernian Military School [*Dublin*]
RHMSA .... Revue d'Hygiene et de Medecine Sociale [*A publication*]
RHMTA ..... Rhumatologie [*Paris*] [*A publication*]
Rh Mus ..... Rheinisches Museum fuer Philologie [*A publication*]   (OCD)
RHN .... Royal Hellenic Navy [*Obsolete*]   (NATG)
RHNB .... RHNB Corp. [*Rock Hill, SC*] [*NASDAQ symbol*]   (NQ)
RHNL .... Reindeer Herders Newsletter. Institute of Arctic Biology. University of Alaska [*A publication*]
RHO .... Railhead Officer [*Military*] [*Obsolete*]
RHO .... Rhodes [*Greece*] [*Seismograph station code, US Geological Survey*] [*Closed*]   (SEIS)
RHO .... Rhodes Island [*Greece*] [*Airport symbol*]   (OAG)
RHO .... Rhodesia [*Later, Zimbabwe*]
RHO .... Rhombic [*Antenna*]
RHO .... Southern Rhodesia [*ANSI three-letter standard code*] [*Obsolete*]   (CNC)
RHOB .... Rayburn House Office Building [*Washington, DC*]   (DLA)
Rhod .... Rhodesia
RHOD .... Rhodium [*Chemistry*]

RHODA .... Rhodora [*A publication*]
Rhod Agric J ... Rhodesia Agricultural Journal [*A publication*]
Rhod Agric J Tech Handb ... Rhodesia Agricultural Journal. Technical Handbook [*A publication*]
Rhod Beekeeping ... Rhodesian Beekeeping [*A publication*]
Rhod Bee News ... Rhodesian Bee News [*A publication*]
Rhod Bull For Res ... Rhodesia. Bulletin of Forestry Research [*A publication*]
Rhod Chibero Coll Agric Annu Rep ... Rhodesia. Chibero College of Agriculture. Annual Report [*A publication*]
Rhod Cotton Res Inst Annu Rep ... Rhodesia Cotton Research Institute. Annual Report [*A publication*]
Rhod Div Livest Pastures Annu Rep ... Rhodesia. Division of Livestock and Pastures. Annual Report [*A publication*]
Rhode Isl Agric ... Rhode Island Agriculture [*A publication*]
Rhode Island Med J ... Rhode Island Medical Journal [*A publication*]
Rhode Island Rep ... Rhode Island Reports [*A publication*] (DLA)
Rhod Eng ... Rhodesian Engineer [*A publication*]
Rhodesia Ag J ... Rhodesia Agricultural Journal [*A publication*]
Rhodesia Agric J ... Rhodesia Agricultural Journal [*A publication*]
Rhodesia Agr J ... Rhodesia Agricultural Journal [*A publication*]
Rhodesian J Agr Res ... Rhodesian Journal of Agricultural Research [*A publication*]
Rhodesian J Econ ... Rhodesian Journal of Economics [*A publication*]
Rhodesian LJ ... Rhodesian Law Journal [*A publication*] (DLA)
Rhodesian Min Jour ... Rhodesian Mining Journal [*A publication*]
Rhodesian Tob J ... Rhodesian Tobacco Journal [*A publication*]
Rhodesia Zambia Malawi J Agr Res ... Rhodesia, Zambia, and Malawi Journal of Agricultural Research [*A publication*]
Rhod Esigodini Agric Inst Annu Rep ... Rhodesia. Esigodini Agricultural Institute. Annual Report [*A publication*]
Rhodes Univ Dep Ichthyol Ichthyol Bull ... Rhodes University. Department of Ichthyology. Ichthyological Bulletin [*A publication*]
Rhodes Univ Dep Ichthyol Occas Pap ... Rhodes University. Department of Ichthyology. Occasional Paper [*A publication*]
Rhodes Univ J L B Smith Inst Ichthyol Spec Publ ... Rhodes University. J. L. B. Smith Institute of Ichthyology. Special Publication [*A publication*]
Rhod Fmr ... Rhodesian Farmer [*A publication*]
Rhod Geol Surv Bull ... Rhodesia. Geological Survey. Bulletin [*A publication*]
Rhod Geol Surv Miner Resour Ser ... Rhodesia. Geological Survey. Mineral Resources Series [*A publication*]
Rhod Geol Surv Short Rep ... Rhodesia. Geological Survey. Short Report [*A publication*]
Rhod Grassl Res Stn Annu Rep ... Rhodesia Grasslands Research Station. Annual Report [*A publication*]
Rhod Hist .. Rhodesian History [*A publication*]
Rhod J Agric Res ... Rhodesia Journal of Agricultural Research [*A publication*]
Rhod Jl Agric Res ... Rhodesian Journal of Agricultural Research [*A publication*]
Rhod Librn ... Rhodesian Librarian [*A publication*]
Rhod Lowveld Res Stn Annu Rep ... Rhodesia. Lowveld Research Station. Annual Report [*A publication*]
Rhod Minist Agric Dep Res Spec Serv Seed Serv Annu Rep ... Rhodesia. Ministry of Agriculture. Department of Research and Specialist Services. Seed Services. Annual Report [*A publication*]
Rhod Minist Agric Gatooma Res Stn Annu Rep ... Rhodesia. Ministry of Agriculture. Gatooma Research Station. Annual Report [*A publication*]
Rhod Minist Agric Grassl Res Stn Annu Rep ... Rhodesia. Ministry of Agriculture. Grasslands Research Station. Annual Report [*A publication*]
Rhod Nurse ... Rhodesian Nurse [*A publication*]
Rhod Prehist ... Rhodesian Prehistory [*A publication*]
Rhod Salisbury Res Stn Annu Rep ... Rhodesia. Salisbury Research Station. Annual Report [*A publication*]
Rhod Sci News ... Rhodesia Science News [*A publication*]
Rhod Tob ... Rhodesian Tobacco [*A publication*]
Rhod Zambia Malawi J Agric Res ... Rhodesia, Zambia, and Malawi Journal of Agricultural Research [*A publication*]
RHOGI...... RADAR Homing Guidance Investigation (MCD)
RHOJ .... RADAR Home on Jam
Rho L .... Rhodian Law [*A publication*] (DLA)
RHOMB.... Rhomboid [*Mathematics*]
RHOSA ...... Rinsho Hoshasen [*A publication*]
RHOSP ...... Registered Home Ownership Savings Plan
R Hospital France ... Revue Hospitaliere de France [*A publication*]
RHP .... Radiant Heat Pump
RHP .... Rated Horsepower
RHP .... Reduced Hard Pressure (MSA)
RHP .... Resource Holding Potential
RHP .... Resource Holding Power [*Fighting ability - animal defense*]
RHP .... Revue d'Histoire de la Philosophie et d'Histoire Generale de la Civilisation [*A publication*]
RHP .... Right Hand Panel (MCD)
RHP .... Right-Handed Pitcher [*Baseball*]
RHP .... Rural Health Program [*Military*] (CINC)
RHPA .... Reverse Hemolytic Plaque Assay [*Clinical chemistry*]
RHPC .... Rapid-Hardening Portland Cement
rhPF........... Recombinant Human Platelet Factor [*Biochemistry*]

RHPH .... Revue d'Histoire de la Philosophie et d'Histoire Generale de la Civilisation [*A publication*]
RHPhC ...... Revue d'Histoire de la Philosophie et d'Histoire Generale de la Civilisation [*A publication*]
RHPhR ...... Revue d'Histoire et de Philosophie Religieuses [*A publication*]
RHPhRel ... Revue d'Histoire et de Philosophie Religieuses [*A publication*]
RH PL .... Rhodium Plate (MSA)
RHPLC ...... Radio-High-Performance Liquid Chromatography
RHPR .... Revue d'Histoire et de Philosophie Religieuses [*A publication*]
RHPS .... Radiation-Hardened Power Supply
RHQ .... Regimental Headquarters
RHR.......... Receiver Holding Register
RHR.......... Reheater (AAG)
RHR.......... Rejectable Hazard Rate (IEEE)
RHR.......... Residual Heat Removal [*Nuclear energy*] (NRCH)
RHR.......... Resting Heart Rate [*Cardiology*]
RHR.......... Revue de l'Histoire des Religions [*A publication*]
r/hr.......... Roentgens per Hour (AABC)
RHR.......... Rohr Industries, Inc. [*NYSE symbol*] (SPSG)
RHR.......... Roughness Height Rating (MSA)
RHR.......... Royal Highland Regiment [*Military unit*] [*British*]
RHRCA ..... Rehabilitation Record [*A publication*]
RHRP .... Residual Heat Removal Pump [*Nuclear energy*] (NRCH)
RHRS .... Residual Heat Removal System [*Nuclear energy*] (NRCH)
RHRSW .... Residual Heat Removal Service Water [*Nuclear energy*] (NRCH)
RHS .... Rectangular Hollow Section [*Metal industry*]
RHS .... Retirement History Survey
RHS .... Revue d'Histoire des Sciences et de Leurs Applications [*A publication*]
RHS .... Revue d'Histoire de la Spiritualite [*A publication*]
RHS .... Right-Hand Side
RHS .... Rocketdyne Hybrid Simulator [*NASA*] (NASA)
RHS .... Rodeo Historical Society (EA)
RHS .... Rolled Hollow Section
RHS .... Rough Hard Sphere [*Model of liquids*]
RHS .... Royal Historical Society [*British*]
RHS .... Royal Historical Society. Transactions [*A publication*]
RHS .... Royal Horticultural Society [*British*] (ARC)
RHS .... Royal Humane Society [*British*]
RHSA .... Revue d'Histoire des Sciences et de Leurs Applications [*A publication*]
RHSC .... Richmond Hill School Company [*British military*] (DMA)
RHSC .... Right-Hand-Side by Centroid
RHSC .... Right-Hand Side Console [*NASA*] (KSC)
RHSCH ..... Rhodes Scholar
RHSE .... Revue Historique du Sud-Est Europeen [*A publication*]
RHSEE ...... Revue Historique du Sud-Est Europeen [*A publication*]
RhSh .... Rosh Hashanah [*New Year*] (BJA)
RHSI........... Rubber Heel and Sole Institute [*Defunct*] (EA)
RHSJ .... Religious Hospitallers of St. Joseph [*Roman Catholic women's religious order*]
RhSNA ...... National Archives of Rhodesia, Salisbury, Rhodesia [*Library symbol*] [*Library of Congress*] (LCLS)
RHSQ .... Royal Historical Society of Queensland. Journal [*A publication*] (APTA)
RHSQJ ...... Royal Historical Society of Queensland. Journal [*A publication*] (ADA)
RHSTr .... Royal Historical Society. Transactions [*A publication*]
RHT.......... Radiant Heat Temperature (NASA)
RHT.......... Revue d'Histoire des Textes [*A publication*]
RHT.......... Revue d'Histoire du Theatre [*A publication*]
RHT.......... Reynolds Hydrodynamic Theory [*Physics*]
RHT.......... Richton International Corp. [*AMEX symbol*] (SPSG)
RHT.......... Right Hypertropia [*Ophthalmology*]
RHTe .... Revue d'Histoire des Textes [*A publication*]
RHTKA ..... Rheinstahl Technik [*A publication*]
RHTM........ Regional Highway Traffic Model [*Database*] [*Obsolete*]
RHTMA ..... Reviews on High-Temperature Materials [*A publication*]
RHTPS ...... Razor Hafters' Trade Protection Society [*A union*] [*British*]
RHTRB ..... Revue des Hautes Temperatures et des Refractaires [*A publication*]
RHTS .... Reactor Heat Transport System (NRCH)
RHU .... Radioisotope Heater Unit (NASA)
RHU .... Registered Health Underwriter [*NAHU*]
RHU .... Residuum Hydrocracking Unit [*Petroleum refining*]
RHU .... Rheumatology [*Medical specialty*] (DHSM)
RHUEA ..... Rheumatism [*England*] [*A publication*]
rHuEPO .... Recombinant Human Erythropoietin [*Biochemistry*]
RHUL .... Revista de Historia. Universidad de La Laguna [*A publication*]
RHUL .... Roczniki Humanistyczne Uniwersytetu Lubelskiego [*A publication*]
RHUMA ..... Rhumatologie [*A publication*]
RHV .... Registered Health Visitor [*British*]
RHV .... Remnant Hepatic Volume [*Hematology*]
RHV .... Revue Historique Vaudoise [*A publication*]
RhV .... Rheinische Vierteljahresblaetter [*A publication*]
RhV .... Rheinische Vorzeit in Wort und Bild [*A publication*]
RHV .... RHYS Industries Ltd. [*Vancouver Stock Exchange symbol*]
RHV .... Road Haulage Vehicle (DCTA)
RHV .... San Jose, CA [*Location identifier*] [*FAA*] (FAAL)

RhVJ.........	Rheinische Vierteljahresblaetter [*A publication*]
RHW.........	Required Hangar Width (MCD)
RHW.........	Reversible Half-Wave
RHW.........	Right Half Word
RHW.........	Router Header Word (NASA)
RHWAC....	Reversible Half-Wave Alternating Current
RHWACDC ...	Reversible Half-Wave Alternating Current - Direct Current
RHWB.......	[*The*] Reverend Henry Ward Beecher [*American clergyman, 1813-1887*]
RHWDC....	Reversible Half-Wave Direct Current
RHWR.......	RADAR Homing and Warning Receiver (MCD)
RHX.........	Atlanta, GA [*Location identifier*] [*FAA*] (FAAL)
RHX.........	Regenerative Heat Exchanger [*Nuclear energy*] (NRCH)
RHY.........	Rhyolite Resources [*Vancouver Stock Exchange symbol*]
RHYTHM ...	Remember How You Treat Hazardous Materials [*E. I. Du Pont De Nemours & Co. program*]
Rhythm	Rhythmica [*of Aristoxenus*] [*Classical studies*] (OCD)
Rhythmes Monde ...	Rhythmes du Monde [*A publication*]
RI	Indonesia [*IYRU nationality code*] (IYR)
RI	Member of the Royal Institute of Painters in Water Colours [*British*]
RI	RADAR Input
RI	Radiation Indicator [*Nuclear energy*] (NRCH)
RI	Radiation Intensity (AABC)
R & I..........	Radical and Intense [*Extremely great*] [*Slang*]
RI	Radicalist International (EA)
RI	Radio Inertial (MCD)
RI	Radio Influence
RI	Radio Inspector
RI	Radio Interference (MCD)
RI	Radioisotope
RI	Radix Institute (EA)
RI	Rampart Institute (EA)
RI	Random Interlace [*Television*]
RI	Range Instrumentation (MCD)
RI	Ranger Instructor [*Army*] (INF)
RI	Rassegna Italiana [*A publication*]
R/I...........	Rate of Interest [*Economics*]
RI	REACT International (EA)
RI	Reactor Island [*Nuclear energy*] (NRCH)
RI	Read-In (DEN)
RI	Readers International [*Subscription book club*] [*British*]
RI	Reallocation Inventory (AFIT)
R & I..........	Receiving and Inspection (KSC)
RI	Receiving Inspection (AAG)
RI	Recipe Index [*A publication*]
RI	Recombinant Inbred [*Genetics*]
RI	Recovery, Incorporated
RI	Recruit Induction [*Military*]
RI	Recruit Instruction [*Navy*]
RI	Redheads International (EA)
RI	Reflective Insulation [*Technical drawings*]
RIAA	Refractive Index
RI	Refugees International (EA)
RI	Regimental Institute [*British military*] (DMA)
R et I	Regina et Imperatrix [*Queen and Empress*] [*Latin*]
RI	Regina Imperatrix [*Queen Empress*] [*Latin*]
RI	Regional Ileitis [*Medicine*]
RI	Registro Italiano [*Italian ship classification society*] (DS)
RI	Rehabilitation International (EA)
RI	Reimplantation [*Dentistry*]
RI	Reinsurance (ADA)
RI	Reissue [*of a book or periodical*] [*Publishing*]
RI	Relative Intensity
RI	Relaxation Instruction [*Psychology*]
RI	Reliability Index
RI	Religion Indexes [*A publication*]
RI	Religious Instruction (ADA)
RI	Remission Induction [*Oncology*]
R & I..........	Removal and Installation (NRCH)
RI	Repeat Indication [*Telecommunications*] (TEL)
RI	Replaceable Item
RI	Report of Investigation
RI	Repulsion Induction [*Motor*]
RI	Request for Information (MCD)
RI	Require Identification
RI	Rescue, Incorporated (EA)
RI	Research Institute [*Fort Belvoir, VA*] [*United States Army Engineer Topographic Laboratories*] (GRD)
RI	Resistance Index
RI	Resistance Inductance (IEEE)
RI	Resistance International (EA)
RI	Resolve, Incorporated
RI	Resonance Integral [*Nuclear energy*] (NRCH)
RI	Respiratory Illness [*Medicine*]
R & I..........	Restaurants and Institutions [*A publication*]
RI	Retention Index
RI	Retirement Income
RI	Retreats International (EA)
RI	Retroactive Inhibition [*Psychology*]
RI	Reunite, Incorporated (EA)
RI	Reverberation Index
RI	Revista Iberoamericana [*A publication*]
RI	Revista de las Indias [*A publication*]
R et I	Rex et Imperator [*King and Emperor*] [*Latin*]
RI	RHEMA [*Restoring Hope through Educational and Medical Aid*] International (EA)
RI	Rhode Island [*Postal code*]
RI	Rhode Island Music Educators Review [*A publication*]
RI	Rhode Island Supreme Court Reports [*A publication*] (ILCA)
RI	Ribosomal [*Protein*] [*Cytology*]
Ri..............	Ricardus Anglicus [*Deceased, 1242*] [*Authority cited in pre-1607 legal work*] (DSA)
RI	Rice Institute Pamphlet [*A publication*]
Ri..............	Richardson Number [*Physics*]
RI	Rigorous Imprisonment [*British military*] (DMA)
RI	Ring Index [*of chemical compounds*] [*A publication*]
RI	Rio-Sul, Servicos Aereos Regionais SA [*Brazil*] [*ICAO designator*] (ICDA)
RI	Risorgimento Italiano [*A publication*]
RI	Rivista Israelitica [*A publication*]
RI	Rivista d'Italia [*A publication*]
RI	Rock Island Lines [*Railroad*]
RI	Rockwell International Corp. (MCD)
RI	Rodale Intstitute (EA)
RI	Rolf Institute (EA)
RI	Rotary International (EA)
RI	Routing Identifier [*or Indicator*] (AFM)
RI	Royal Institution [*British*]
RI	Royal Irish [*Military unit*] [*British*]
RI	Rubber Insulation [*Technical drawings*]
RI	Rulers of India [*A publication*]
RI	Rutherford Institute (EA)
RIA	Radioimmunoassay [*Clinical chemistry*]
RIA	Rain in Area (ADA)
RIA	Reactivity Initiated Accident [*Nuclear energy*] (NRCH)
RIA	Registered Industrial and Cost Accountant
RIA	Registered Investment Adviser [*Securities*]
RIA	Regulatory Impact Analysis [*or Assessment*]
RIA	Religious Instruction Association [*Later, PERSC*]
RIA	Remote Intelligence Acquisition
RIA	Removable Instrument Assembly [*Nuclear energy*] (NRCH)
RIA	Research Institute of America [*New York, NY*] [*Information service or system*] (IID)
RIA	Revista Iberoamericana [*A publication*]
RIA	Rich International Airways, Inc. [*Miami, FL*] [*FAA designator*] (FAAC)
RIA	Rivista. Istituto Nazionale d'Archeologia e Storia dell'Arte [*A publication*]
RIA	Robotic Industries Association (EA)
RIA	Rock Island Arsenal [*Illinois*] [*Army*]
RIA	Royal Irish Academy
RIA	Santa Maria [*Brazil*] [*Airport symbol*] (OAG)
RIAA	Recording Industry Association of America (EA)
RIAB..........	Revista Interamericana de Bibliografia [*A publication*]
RIAC..........	Regional Industry Advisory Committee [*Civil Defense*]
RIAC..........	Royal Irish Automobile Club (EAIO)
RIACS	Research Institute for Advanced Computer Science [*University Space Research Association*] [*Research center*] (RCD)
RIAD	Rencontres Internationales des Assureurs Defense [*Genoa, Italy*] (EA)
RIA-DA	Radioimmunoassay Double Antibody [*Test*] [*Clinical chemistry*]
RIADAG....	Radovi Instituta za Proucavanje i Suzbijanje Alkoholizma i Drugih Narkomanija u Zagrebu [*A publication*]
RIAEC.......	Rhode Island Atomic Energy Commission
RIAES	Rhode Island Agricultural Experiment Station [*University of Rhode Island*] [*Research center*] (RCD)
RIAF..........	Royal Indian Air Force
RIAF..........	Royal Iraqi Air Force
RI Ag.........	Rhode Island Agriculture [*A publication*]
RI Ag Exp ...	Rhode Island. Agricultural Experiment Station. Publications [*A publication*]
RI Agr	Rhode Island Agriculture. Rhode Island Agricultural Experiment Station [*A publication*]
RI Agric	Rhode Island Agriculture [*A publication*]
RI Agric Exp Stn Bull ...	Rhode Island. Agricultural Experiment Station. Bulletin [*A publication*]
RI Agric Exp Stn Res Q Rev ...	Rhode Island. Agricultural Experiment Station. Research Quarterly Review [*A publication*]
RIAI..........	Royal Institute of the Architects of Ireland
RIAIAD.....	Reverse International Acronyms, Initialisms, and Abbreviations Dictionary [*A publication*]
RIAL..........	Religion in American Life (EA)
RIAL..........	Revised Individual Allowance List [*Navy*] (NVT)
RIALF	Flair Resources Ltd. [*NASDAQ symbol*] (NQ)
RIAM	Royal Irish Academy of Music
RIAND........	Risk Analysis [*A publication*]
RIAR........	Requirements Inventory Analysis Report (AFM)
RIA-R	Rock Island Arsenal General Thomas J. Rodman Laboratory [*Army*]

RIA Rev Econ Tech Ind Aliment Eur ... RIA. Revue Economique et Technique de l'Industrie Alimentaire Europeenne [*A publication*]
RIAS .... Research Initiation and Support [*National Science Foundation program*]
RIAS .... Research Institute for Advanced Studies [*Martin Marietta Corp.*]
RIAS .... Royal Incorporation of Architects in Scotland
RIAS .... Rundfunk im Amerikanischen Sektor Berlins [*Radio in American Sector*] [*Federal Republic of Germany*]
RIASB ...... Richerche Astronomiche [*A publication*]
RIASC ...... Royal Indian Army Service Corps [*British*]
RIA Tax ..... Research Institute of America Tax Coordinator [*A publication*]   (DLA)
RIAX .... Rich International Airways, Inc. [*Air carrier designation symbol*]
RIB .... Racing Information Bureau [*British*]   (CB)
RIB .... Railway Information Bureau
RIB .... Recoverable Item Breakdown
RIB .... Recyclable, Incineratable, Biodegradable [*Food packaging*]
RIB .... Review of International Affairs. Politics, Economics, Law, Science, Culture [*A publication*]
RIB .... Review of International Broadcasting [*A publication*]
RIB .... Revista Iberoamericana de Bibliografia [*A publication*]
RIB .... Revista Interamericana de Bibliografia. Organization of American States [*A publication*]
RIB .... Revue de l'Instruction Publique en Belgique [*A publication*]
RIB .... Ribbed   (AAG)
RIB .... Riberalta [*Bolivia*] [*Airport symbol*]   (OAG)
Rib .... Ribose [*Also, r*] [*A sugar*]
RIB .... Right Inboard   (MCD)
RIB .... Right Intermediate Bronchus [*Anatomy*]
Ri B .... Rivista Biblica [*A publication*]
RIB .... [*The*] Roman Inscriptions of Britain [*A publication*]   (OCD)
RIB .... Rural Industries Bureau
RIBA .... Recombinant Immunobioassay
RIBA .... Royal Institute of British Architects   (IID)
RIBA J ...... Royal Institute of British Architects. Journal [*A publication*]
RI Bd RC ... Rhode Island Board of Railroad Commission Reports [*A publication*]   (DLA)
R Iber .... Rassegna Iberistica [*A publication*]
R Iberoamer Segur Soc ... Revista Iberoamericana de Seguridad Social [*A publication*]
R Iberoam Seguridad Soc ... Revista Iberoamericana de Seguridad Social [*A publication*]
RIBI .... Ribi Immunochem Research, Inc. [*NASDAQ symbol*]   (NQ)
RIBIB .... Revista Interamericana de Bibliotecologia [*A publication*]
RIBJ .... Rhode Island Bar Journal [*A publication*]
RIBJD .... RIBA [*Royal Institute of British Architects*] Journal [*A publication*]
RIBLIM..... Reduction in Benefit Limitation
RIBS .... Restructured Infantry Battalion System   (AABC)
RIBS .... Royal Institute of British Sculptors
RIBSS .... Research Institute for the Behavioral and Social Sciences [*Army*]
RI Bur Industrial Statistics An Rp Nat Res S B ... Rhode Island Bureau of Industrial Statistics. Annual Report. Natural Resources Survey. Bulletin [*A publication*]
RIC .... RADAR Indicating Console [*FAA*]
RIC .... RADAR Input Control
RIC .... RADAR Intercept Calculator
RIC .... RADAR Intercept Control
RIC .... Radio Industry Council [*British*]
RIC .... Radioimmunoconjugate
RIC .... Rafter Input Converter
RIC .... Rainforest Information Centre [*Lismore, NSW, Australia*]   (EAIO)
RIC .... Range Instrumentation Conference   (MUGU)
RIC .... Range Instrumentation Coordination   (KSC)
RIC .... Raptor Information Center   (EA)
RIC .... Rare-Earth Information Center   (EA)
RIC .... Read-In Counter
RIC .... Reconstituted Ion Current [*Chromatography*]
RIC .... Reconstructed Ion Chromatogram
RIC .... Record Identification Code [*Navy*]
RIC .... Recruiter Identification Code [*Military*]
RIC .... Regolamento Internazionale Carrozze [*International Carriage and Van Union*]
RIC .... Remote Information Center
RIC .... Remote Interactive Communications [*Xerox Corp.*]
RIC .... Repair Induction Code [*Module Maintenance Facility*]
RIC .... Repairable Identification Code
RIC .... Repairable Item Code
RIC .... Repertoire Bibliographique des Institutions Chretiennes [*Bibliographical Repertory of Christian Institutions*] [*Centre de Recherche et de Documentation des Institutions Chretiennes*] [*France*] [*Information service or system*]   (CRD)
RIC .... Replaceable Item Code
RIC .... Request for Instrumentation Clarification [*NASA*]   (KSC)
RIC .... Resident Inspector-in-Charge

RIC .... Resistance, Inductance, and Capacitance   (NASA)
RIC .... Resource Identification Code [*Navy*]
RIC .... Resource Information Center System [*Search system*]
RIC .... Retirement Income Credit
RIC .... Review of International Cooperation [*A publication*]
RIC .... Revue de Droit Intellectuel "l'Ingenieur Conseil" [*A publication*]
Ric .... Ricardus Malumbra [*Deceased, 1334*] [*Authority cited in pre-1607 legal work*]   (DSA)
Ric .... Richard (King of England)   (DLA)
RIC .... Richmond [*Florida*] [*Seismograph station code, US Geological Survey*] [*Closed*]   (SEIS)
RIC .... Richmond [*Virginia*] [*Airport symbol*]
RIC .... Ricks College, David O. McKay Learning Resources Center, Rexburg, ID [*OCLC symbol*]   (OCLC)
RIC .... Road Information Center [*Arab Contractors Co.*]   (IID)
RIC .... Rockwell International Corporation   (NASA)
RIC .... Rodeo Information Commission   (EA)
RIC .... Roman Imperial Coinage [*A publication*]   (OCD)
RIC .... Routing Identification Code   (NATG)
RIC .... Royal Institute of Chemistry [*Later, RSC*] [*British*]
RIC .... Royal Irish Constabulary
RIC .... Rural Information Center [*Department of Agriculture*] [*Information service or system*]   (IID)
RICA .... Railway Industry Clearance Association   (EA)
RICA .... Research Institute for Consumer Affairs [*British*]
RICAL ...... Research Information Center and Library [*Foster Wheeler Corp.*] [*Information service or system*]   (IID)
Ricar .... Ricardus [*Authority cited in pre-1607 legal work*]   (DSA)
RICASIP ... Research Information Center and Advisory Service on Information Processing [*National Bureau of Standards - National Science Foundation*]
Ric Autom .. Ricerche di Automatica [*A publication*]
RicBibRel... Ricerche Bibliche e Religiose [*Milan*] [*A publication*]
Ric Biol Selvaggina ... Ricerche di Biologia della Selvaggina [*A publication*]
RICC .... Regional Interagency Coordinating Committee [*Department of Labor*]
RICC .... Remote Intercomputer Communications Interface   (MCD)
RICC .... Reportable Item Control Code [*Army*]   (AABC)
Ric Clin Lab ... Ricerca in Clinica e in Laboratorio [*A publication*]
Ric Demos ... Ricerche Demoscopiche [*A publication*]
Ric Doc Tess ... Ricerca e Documentazione Tessile [*A publication*]
RICE .... American Rice, Inc. [*NASDAQ symbol*]   (NQ)
RICE .... Recreational Industries Council on Exporting   (EA)
RICE .... Regional Information and Communications Exchange [*Rice University Library*] [*Houston, TX*]
RICE .... Relative Index of Combat Effectiveness [*Military*] [*British*]
RICE .... Research and Information Centre on Eritrea   (EA)
RICE .... Resources in Computer Education [*Northwest Regional Educational Laboratory Microcomputer Software and Information for Teachers*] [*Information service or system*] [*No longer available online*]
RICE .... Rest, Ice, Compression, Elevation [*Medicine*]
Rice .... Rice's South Carolina Law Reports [*1838-39*] [*A publication*]   (DLA)
RICE .... Right to a Comprehensive Education   (EAIO)
Ric Ch .... Rice's South Carolina Equity Reports [*A publication*]   (DLA)
Ric Econ ..... Ricerche Economiche [*A publication*]
Rice Dig ..... Rice's Digest of Patent Office Decisions [*A publication*]   (DLA)
Rice Eq .... Rice's South Carolina Equity Reports [*1838-39*] [*A publication*]   (DLA)
Rice Ev .... Rice's Law of Evidence [*A publication*]   (DLA)
Rice Inst P ... Rice Institute Pamphlet [*A publication*]
Rice Inst Pam ... Rice Institute Pamphlet [*A publication*]
Rice J .... Rice Journal [*A publication*]
Rice L (SC) ... Rice's South Carolina Law Reports [*A publication*]   (DLA)
Ricerca Scient ... Ricerca Scientifica [*A publication*]
Ricerca Scient Rc ... Ricerca Scientifica. Rendiconti [*A publication*]
Ricerche Automat ... Ricerche di Automatica [*A publication*]
Ricerche Mat ... Ricerche di Matematica [*A publication*]
Rice's Code ... Rice's Code of Practice [*Colorado*] [*A publication*]   (DLA)
Rice Univ Aero-Astronaut Rep ... Rice University. Aero-Astronautic Report [*A publication*]
Rice Univ Stud ... Rice University. Studies [*A publication*]
Rice Univ Studies ... Rice University. Studies [*A publication*]
RiceUS .... Rice University. Studies [*A publication*]
RicF .... Ricerche Filosofiche [*A publication*]
RICH .... Radiation-Induced Color Halo [*Physics*]
Rich .... Richard (King of England)   (DLA)
Rich .... Richardson's Reports [*2-5 New Hampshire*] [*A publication*]   (DLA)
Rich .... [*J. S. G.*] Richardson's South Carolina Law Reports [*A publication*]   (DLA)
RICH .... Richmond Hill Savings Bank [*Floral Park, NY*] [*NASDAQ symbol*]   (NQ)
RICH .... Richmond National Battlefield Park
Richardson Law Practice ... Richardson's Establishing a Law Practice [*A publication*]   (DLA)
Richardson's S Ca Rep ... [*J. S. G.*] Richardson's South Carolina Law Reports [*A publication*]   (DLA)

Rich Cas..... [*J. S. G.*] Richardson's South Carolina Cases [*1831-32*] [*A publication*] (DLA)
Rich Cas (SC) ... [*J. S. G.*] Richardson's South Carolina Equity Cases [*A publication*] (DLA)
Rich Ch...... [*J. S. G.*] Richardson's South Carolina Equity Reports [*A publication*] (DLA)
Rich Ch Pr ... Richardson's Chancery Practice [*1838*] [*A publication*] (DLA)
Rich CP...... Richardson's Practice Common Pleas [*England*] [*A publication*] (DLA)
Rich Ct Cl.. Richardson's Court of Claims Reports [*A publication*] (DLA)
RICHD...... Reviews in Inorganic Chemistry [*A publication*]
Richd E Repts ... [*J. S. G.*] Richardson's South Carolina Equity Reports [*A publication*] (DLA)
Rich Dict.... Richardson's New Dictionary of the English Language [*A publication*] (DLA)
Rich'd Law R ... [*J. S. G.*] Richardson's South Carolina Law Reports [*A publication*] (DLA)
RICHEL.... Richmond - Cape Henry Environmental Laboratory [*NASA/ USGS*]
Rich Eq ...... [*J. S. G.*] Richardson's South Carolina Equity Reports [*1844-46, 1850-68*] [*A publication*] (DLA)
Rich Eq Cas ... [*J. S. G.*] Richardson's South Carolina Equity Reports [*A publication*] (DLA)
Rich Eq Ch ... [*J. S. G.*] Richardson's South Carolina Equity Reports [*A publication*] (DLA)
Rich & H.... Richardson and Hook's Street Railway Decisions [*A publication*] (DLA)
Rich Land A ... Richey's Irish Land Act [*A publication*] (DLA)
Rich Law (SC) ... [*J. S. G.*] Richardson's South Carolina Law Reports [*A publication*] (DLA)
Rich L (SC) ... [*J. S. G.*] Richardson's South Carolina Law Reports [*A publication*] (DLA)
Richmd T-D ... Richmond Times-Dispatch [*A publication*]
Richmond Cty Hist ... Richmond County History [*A publication*]
Rich NH..... Richardson's Reports [*3-5 New Hampshire*] [*A publication*] (DLA)
Rich NS ..... [*J. S. G.*] Richardson's South Carolina Reports, New Series [*A publication*] (DLA)
Rich PRCP ... Richardson's Practical Register of English Common Pleas [*A publication*] (DLA)
Rich Pr KB ... Richardson's Attorney's Practice in the Court of King's Bench [*8th ed.*] [*1792*] [*A publication*] (DLA)
Rich Pr Reg ... Richardson's Practical Register of English Common Pleas [*A publication*] (DLA)
Rich & S..... Richardson and Sayles' Select Cases of Procedure without Writ [*Selden Society Publication 60*] [*A publication*] (DLA)
Rich & W ... Richardson and Woodbury's Reports [*2 New Hampshire*] [*A publication*] (DLA)
Rich Wills ... Richardson's Law of Testaments and Last Wills [*A publication*] (DLA)
RICJA .... Rice Journal [*A publication*]
Rick Eng St ... Rickard's English Statutes [*A publication*] (DLA)
Rickia Arq Bot Estado Sao Paulo Ser Criptogam ... Rickia. Arquivos de Botanica do Estado de Sao Paulo. Serie Criptogamica [*A publication*]
Rickia Arq Bot Estado Sao Paulo Ser Criptogam Supl ... Rickia. Arquivos de Botanica do Estado de Sao Paulo. Serie Criptogamica [*A publication*]
Rickia Supl ... Rickia. Suplemento [*A publication*]
Rick & M ... Rickards and Michael's English Locus Standi Reports [*A publication*] (DLA)
Rickmansworth Hist ... Rickmansworth Historian [*A publication*]
Rick & S..... Rickards and Saunders' English Locus Standi Reports [*A publication*] (DLA)
RicLing ...... Ricerche Linguistiche [*A publication*]
RICM........ Registre International des Citoyens du Monde [*International Registry of World Citizens*]
RicM......... Ricerche Musicali [*A publication*]
RICM........ Right Intercostal Margin [*Medicine*]
Ric Mat...... Ricerche di Matematica [*A publication*]
RICMO .... RADAR Input Countermeasures Officer [*Air Force*]
Ric Morfol ... Ricerche di Morfologia [*A publication*]
RICMT..... RADAR Input Countermeasures Technician [*Air Force*]
RICO .... Racketeer-Influenced and Corrupt Organizations [*Nickname of a 1970 law used by federal prosecutors to indict organized crime leaders*]
RICOA ...... Rivista dei Combustibili [*A publication*]
RI Comp of Rules of St Agencies ... Rhode Island Compilation of Rules of State Agencies [*A publication*] (DLA)
RI Const..... Rhode Island Constitution [*A publication*] (DLA)
RICP......... Revista. Instituto de Cultura Puertorriquena [*A publication*]
RicR .... Ricerche Religiose [*A publication*]
RicRel........ Ricerche Religiose [*A publication*]
RICRS .... Rockford Institute Center on Religion and Society (EA)
Ric Ruf....... Ricardus Rufulus [*Authority cited in pre-1607 legal work*] (DSA)
RICS......... Range Instrumentation Control System
RICS......... Remote Image Confirming Sensor
RICS......... Reports Index Control (MCD)
RICS......... Respiratory Intensive Care System [*Medicine*]

Ric & S....... Rickards and Saunders' English Locus Standi Reports [*1890-94*] [*A publication*] (DLA)
RICS.......... Royal Institution of Chartered Surveyors [*British*]
RICS Abs Rev ... RICS [*Royal Institution of Chartered Surveyors*] Abstracts and Review [*A publication*]
Ric Sci........ Ricerca Scientifica [*A publication*]
Ric Sci Parte 1 ... Ricerca Scientifica. Parte 1. Rivista [*A publication*]
Ric Sci Parte 2 Sez A ... Ricerca Scientifica. Parte 2. Rendiconti. Sezione A. Biologica [*A publication*]
Ric Sci Parte 2 Sez B ... Ricerca Scientifica. Parte 2. Rendiconti. Sezione B. Biologica [*A publication*]
Ric Sci Prog Tec ... Ricerca Scientifica ed il Progresso Tecnico [*A publication*]
Ric Sci Quad ... Ricerca Scientifica. Quaderni [*A publication*]
Ric Sci Rend Sez B ... Ricerca Scientifica. Serie Seconda. Parte II. Rendiconti. Sezione B. Biologica [*A publication*]
Ric Sci Ricostr ... Ricerca Scientifica e Ricostruzione [*A publication*]
Ric Sci Suppl ... Ricerca Scientifica. Supplemento [*A publication*]
RicSL......... Ricerche Slavistiche [*A publication*]
Ric Spettrosc ... Ricerche Spettroscopiche [*A publication*]
Ric Spettros Lab Astrofis Specola ... Ricerche Spettroscopiche. Laboratorio Astrofisico della Specola Vaticana [*A publication*]
RicSRel...... Ricerche di Storia Religiosa [*A publication*]
Ric St (Brindisi) ... Ricerche e Studi. Museo Provinciale Francesco Ribezzo (Brindisi) [*A publication*]
RicStRel..... Ricerche di Storia Religiosa [*Rome*] [*A publication*]
Ric Studi Med Sper ... Ricerche e Studi di Medicina Sperimentale [*A publication*]
Ric Termotecnica ... Ricerche di Termotecnica [*Italy*] [*A publication*]
RI Ct Rec ... Rhode Island Court Records [*A publication*] (DLA)
RICU .... Respiratory Intensive Care Unit [*Medicine*]
Ric Zool Appl Caccia ... Ricerche di Zoologia Applicata alla Caccia [*A publication*]
Ric Zool Appl Caccia Suppl ... Ricerche di Zoologia Applicata alla Caccia. Supplemento [*A publication*]
RID .... RADAR Input Drum
RID .... Radial Immunodiffusion [*Analytical biochemistry*]
RID .... Radio Intelligence Division [*of the Federal Communications Commission*]
RID .... Radioisotope Detection
RID .... Range Instruments Development (MCD)
RID .... Real-Fluid Isentropic Decompression [*Engineering*]
RID .... Record Identity [*Military*] (AFIT)
RID .... Records Issue Date [*Bell System*] (TEL)
RID .... Reduced Ignition Relay (MCD)
RID .... Refractive Index Detector [*Instrumentation*]
RID .... Regimented Inmate Discipline [*Mississippi State Penitentiary*]
RID .... Registry of Interpreters for the Deaf (EA)
RID .... Reglement International Concernant le Transport des Marchandises Dangereuses [*International Regulation Governing the Carriage of Dangerous Goods*]
RID .... Released to Inactive Duty
RID .... Reliability Index Determination (MCD)
RID .... Remove Intoxicated Drivers [*An association*]
RID .... Research Institutes and Divisions [*of National Institutes of Health*]
RID .... Reset Inhibit Drive
RID .... Reset Inhibit Drum
RID .... Retrofit Installation Data (MCD)
RID .... Reversible Intravas Device
RID .... Review Item Discrepancy (MCD)
RID .... Review Item Disposition [*NASA*] (NASA)
RID .... Richmond, IN [*Location identifier*] [*FAA*] (FAAL)
RID .... Rider College Library, Lawrenceville, NJ [*OCLC symbol*] (OCLC)
Rid............ Ridotto [*A publication*]
RID .... Rivista Italiana di Dialettologia [*A publication*]
RID .... Rivista Italiana del Drama [*A publication*]
RID .... Royal Irish Dragoons [*British military*] (DMA)
RID .... Royal Irrigation Department [*Thailand*] (DS)
RIDA .... Reverse Isotope Dilution Assay [*Chemical analysis*]
RIDA .... Revue Internationale des Droits de l'Antiquite [*A publication*]
RIDAC...... Range Interference Detecting and Control
RIDAURA ... Remission Inducing Drug, Au [*Chemical symbol for gold*], Rheumatoid Arthritis [*Gold-based drug manufactured by SmithKline Beckman Corp.*]
RIDC .... Revue Internationale de Droit Compare [*A publication*]
RIDC .... Ryerson International Development Centre [*Ryerson Polytechnical Institute*] [*Canada*] [*Research center*] (RCD)
RIDD .... Rivista Italiana di Drammaturgia. Trimestrale dell'Istituto del Dramma Italiano [*A publication*]
Riddle's Lex ... Riddle's Lexicon [*A publication*] (DLA)
RIDDOR ... Reporting of Injuries, Diseases, and Dangerous Occurrences Regulations [*British*]
RIDE......... People Ridesharing Systems, Inc. [*Newark, NJ*] [*NASDAQ symbol*] (NQ)
RIDE......... Research Institute for Diagnostic Engineering
RI Dec........ Rhode Island Decisions [*A publication*] (DLA)
RI Dent J ... Rhode Island Dental Journal [*A publication*]
RIdeP......... Revue Internationale de Philosophie [*A publication*]
RIDEQ ...... Revista Iberoamericana de Educacion Quimica [*A publication*]

RIDES .... Rockford Infant Developmental Scales [*Child development test*]
RI Dev Counc Geol Bull ... Rhode Island Development Council. Geological Bulletin [*A publication*]
RI Devel Council Geol Bull Sci Contr ... Rhode Island Development Council. Geological Bulletin. Scientific Contribution [*A publication*]
RIDEX .... Ridexchange (EA)
RIDF .... Random Input Describing Function [*Data processing*]
Ridg .... Ridgeway's Reports Tempore Hardwicke, Chancery and English King's Bench [*A publication*] (DLA)
RIDG .... Royal Inniskilling Dragoon Guards [*Military unit*] [*British*]
RIDG .... Royal Irish Dragoon Guards [*British military*] (DMA)
Ridg Ap ...... Ridgeway's Irish Appeal (or Parliamentary) Cases [*A publication*] (DLA)
Ridg App .... Ridgeway's Irish Appeal (or Parliamentary) Cases [*A publication*] (DLA)
Ridg Cas..... Ridgeway's Reports Tempore Hardwicke, Chancery and English King's Bench [*A publication*] (DLA)
RIDGE .... Ridge Interdisciplinary Global Experiments [*NOAA, NSF, ONR, and USGS*]
Ridgew .... Ridgeway's Reports Tempore Hardwicke, Chancery and English King's Bench [*A publication*] (DLA)
Ridgew Ir PC ... Ridgeway's Irish Parliamentary Reports [*1784-96*] [*A publication*] (DLA)
Ridgew L & S (Ir) ... Ridgeway, Lapp, and Schoales' Irish Term Reports [*A publication*] (DLA)
Ridgew L & S (Ire) ... Ridgeway, Lapp, and Schoales' Irish Term Reports [*A publication*] (ILCA)
Ridgew T Hardw ... Ridgeway's Reports Tempore Hardwicke, Chancery [*27 English Reprint*] [*1744-46*] [*A publication*] (DLA)
Ridgew T Hardw (Eng) ... Ridgeway Tempore Hardwicke [*27 English Reprint*] [*A publication*] (DLA)
Ridg & Hard ... Ridgeway's Reports Tempore Hardwicke, Chancery and English King's Bench [*A publication*] (DLA)
Ridg L & S ... Ridgeway, Lapp, and Schoales' Irish Term Reports [*A publication*] (DLA)
Ridg Parl Rep ... Ridgeway's Irish Parliamentary Reports [*1784-96*] [*A publication*] (DLA)
Ridg PC...... Ridgeway's Irish Appeal (or Parliamentary) Cases [*A publication*] (DLA)
Ridg Pr Rep ... Ridgeway's Irish Appeal (or Parliamentary) Cases [*A publication*] (DLA)
Ridg Rep .... Ridgeway's Reports of State Trials in Ireland [*A publication*] (DLA)
Ridg St Tr .. Ridgeway's (Individual) Reports of State Trials in Ireland [*A publication*] (DLA)
Ridg Temp H ... Ridgeway's Reports Tempore Hardwicke, Chancery [*27 English Reprint*] [*1744-46*] [*A publication*] (DLA)
Ridg T H .... Ridgeway's Reports Tempore Hardwicke, Chancery [*27 English Reprint*] [*1744-46*] [*A publication*] (DLA)
Ridg T Hard ... Ridgeway's Reports Tempore Hardwicke, Chancery and English King's Bench [*27 English Reprint*] [*A publication*] (DLA)
Ridg T Hardw ... Ridgeway's Reports Tempore Hardwicke, Chancery and English King's Bench [*27 English Reprint*] [*A publication*] (DLA)
Ridgw Ir PC ... Ridgeway's Irish Parliamentary Cases [*A publication*] (DLA)
RIDI.......... Receiving Inspection Detail Instruction [*NASA*] (NASA)
RIDIC....... Radiopharmaceutical Internal Dose Information Center [*Oak Ridge, TN*] [*Department of Energy*] (GRD)
RIDIT .... Relative to an Identified Distribution Transformation [*Pharmacology*]
RIDL......... Radiation Instrument Development Laboratory
RIDL......... Ridge Instrument Development Laboratory [*Navy*]
Ridley Civil & Ecc Law ... Ridley's Civil and Ecclesiastical Law [*A publication*] (DLA)
RIDP......... RADAR-IFF Data Processor (MCD)
RIDP......... RNA [*Ribonucleic Acid*]-Instructed DNA [*Deoxyribonucleic Acid*] Polymerase [*Later, RDDP*] [*An enzyme*]
RIDPE3 ..... Bulletin of Fisheries Research and Development [*A publication*]
RIDS......... Radio Information Distribution System (MCD)
RIDS......... Range Information Display System (MCD)
RIDS......... Receiving Inspection Data Status [*Report*] [*Nuclear energy*] (NRCH)
RIDS......... Regional Operations Control Centre Information Display System [*NORAD*]
RIDS......... Regulatory Information Distribution System [*Nuclear energy*] (NRCH)
Rid Sup Proc ... Riddle's Supplementary Proceedings [*New York*] [*A publication*] (DLA)
RIE........... RADAR Intercept Event
RIE........... Range of Incentive Effectiveness
RIE........... Reactive Ion Etching [*Semiconductor technology*]
RIE........... Recognised Investment Exchange [*British*]
RIE........... Research in Education [*Monthly publication of ERIC*]
RIE........... Resources in Education [*Formerly, Research in Education*] [*National Institute of Education*] [*Database*]
RIE........... Retirement Income Endowment [*Insurance*]
RIE........... Revista de Ideas Esteticas [*A publication*]
RIE........... Revue Internationale de l'Enseignement [*A publication*]

RIE........... Rice Lake [*Wisconsin*] [*Airport symbol*] (OAG)
RIE........... Riedel Environmental Technologies, Inc. [*AMEX symbol*] (SPSG)
RIE........... Right Inboard Elevon [*Aviation*] (MCD)
RIE........... Royal Institute of Engineers [*British*]
RIEAA .... Rivista di Economia Agraria [*A publication*]
RIEB......... Revista. Instituto de Estudos Brasileiros [*A publication*]
RIEC......... Royal Indian Engineering College [*British*]
Riech Aromen Kosmet ... Riechstoffe, Aromen, Kosmetica [*A publication*]
Riechst Aromen ... Riechstoffe und Aromen [*A publication*]
Riechst Aromen Koerperpflegem ... Riechstoffe, Aromen, Koerperpflegemittel [*Later, Riechstoffe, Aromen, Kosmetica*] [*A publication*]
Ried .... Riedell's Reports [*68, 69 New Hampshire*] [*A publication*] (DLA)
RIEDA....... Reseau d'Innovations Educatives pour le Developpement en Afrique [*Network of Educational Innovation for Development in Africa*] (EAIO)
RIEDAC.... Research in International Economics of Disarmament and Arms Control [*A program of Columbia University School of International Affairs*]
RIEEC .... Research Institute for the Education of Exceptional Children [*A publication*]
RIEF......... Recycling Isoelectric Focusing [*Preparative electrophoresis*]
RIEI......... Roofing Industry Educational Institute (EA)
RIEM........ Research Institute for Environmental Medicine [*Army*] (MCD)
RIEMA...... Rapports et Proces-Verbaux des Reunions. Conseil International pour l'Exploration de la Mer [*A publication*]
RIES......... Research Institute for Engineering Sciences [*Wayne State University*] [*Research center*] (RCD)
RIES .... Resonance Ionization Emission Spectroscopy
RIETCOM ... Regional Interagency Emergency Transportation Committee
RIETDJ..... Institut d'Elevage et de Medecine Veterinaire des Pays Tropicaux. Rapport d'Activite [*A publication*]
RIEtnN ...... Revista. Instituto Etnologico Nacional [*A publication*]
RIEV.......... Revista Internacional de Estudios Vascos [*A publication*]
RIF........... Radio-Influence Field (IEEE)
RIF........... Radio Interference Filter
RIF........... Rate Input Form (NVT)
RIF........... Readiness Index Factor
RIF........... Reading Is Fundamental (EA)
RIF........... Real Estate Securities Income Fund, Inc. [*AMEX symbol*] (CTT)
RIF........... Reduced Injury Factor Baseball
RIF........... Reduction in Force [*Military*]
RIF........... Refund Information File [*IRS*]
RIF........... Relative Importance Factor (NASA)
RIF........... Release-Inhibiting Factor [*Endocrinology*]
RIF........... Reliability Improvement Factor
RIF........... Reportable Item File [*Military*] (AFIT)
RIF........... Resistance Inducing Factor (ADA)
RIF........... Richfield [*Utah*] [*Airport symbol*] (OAG)
RIF........... Richfield, UT [*Location identifier*] [*FAA*] (FAAL)
RIF........... Rifampin [*Also, R/AMP, RF, RMP*] [*Bactericide*]
RIF........... Rifle
RIF........... Right Iliac Fossa [*Medicine*]
RIF........... Rodeo Information Foundation [*Later, Rodeo News Bureau*]
RIF........... Royal Inniskilling Fusiliers [*Military unit*] [*British*]
RIF........... Royal Irish Fusiliers [*Military unit*] [*British*]
RIFAA ...... Revista Industrial y Fabril [*A publication*]
RIFBAZ.... Ching Chi Pu Kuo Li Taiwan Ta Hsueh Ho Pan Yu Yeh Sheng Wu Shih Yen So Yen Chiu Pao Kao [*A publication*]
RIFC......... Radio In-Flight Correction
RIFC......... Radioactive Illuminated Fire Control (MCD)
RIFC......... Rat Intrinsic Factor Concentrate
RIFD......... Rivista Internazionale di Filosofia del Diritto [*A publication*]
RIFFED..... Forced Out by a Reduction in Force
RIFI......... Radio Interference Field Intensity [*Meter*] (NG)
RIFI......... Radio-Interference-Free Instrument
RIFIM....... Radio Interference Field Intensity Meter
RIFL......... Random Item File Locater
RIFM........ Research Institute for Fragrance Materials (EA)
RIFMA...... Roentgen-Isotope-Fluorescent Method of Analysis
RIFN......... Recombinant Interferon [*Biochemistry*]
Riforma Agrar ... Riforma Agraria [*Italy*] [*A publication*]
Riforma Med ... Riforma Medica [*A publication*]
RIFPA .... Revue. Institut Francais du Petrole et Annales des Combustibles Liquides [*Later, Revue. Institut Francais du Petrole*] [*A publication*]
RIFRAF..... Institute of Freshwater Research (Drottningholm). Report [*A publication*]
RIFS .... Radioisotope Field Support
RI/FS........ Remedial Investigation and Feasibility Study [*Environmental Protection Agency*]
RIFT .... Reactor-in-Flight Test [*NASA*]
RIFT/S ...... Reactor-in-Flight Test/System [*NASA*] (AAG)
RIG .... Bouwadviseur Opinievormend Beroepstijdschrift voor Adviseurs [*A publication*]
RIG .... Rabies Immune Globulin [*Immunology*]
RIG .... Radio Inertial Guidance (AAG)
RIG .... Radio Interference Guard
RIG .... Rate Integrating Gyro

RIG .... Reference Interest Group [*Australia*]
RIG .... Ridgeling [*Horse racing*]
RIG .... Rigging (ROG)
RIG .... Rio Grande [*Brazil*] [*Airport symbol*] (OAG)
RIG .... Roll-Imitation Gold
RIGAA....... Rinsho Ganka [*A publication*]
Rigasche Ind Ztg ... Rigasche Industrie Zeitung [*A publication*]
Rigas Med Inst Zinat Rakstu Krajums ... Rigas Medicinas Instituta
         Zinatnisko Rakstu Krajums [*A publication*]
Rigas Politeh Inst Zinat Raksti ... Rigas Politehniskais Instituts. Zinatniskie
         Raksti [*A publication*]
RIGB.......... Royal Institution of Great Britain
RI Gen Laws ... General Laws of Rhode Island [*A publication*] (DLA)
RIGFET..... Resistive Insulated-Gate Field Effect Transistor
Rigg............ Select Pleas, Starrs, and Other Records from the Rolls of the
         Exchequer of the Jews, Edited by J. M. Riggs [*Selden
         Society Publications, Vol. 15*] [*A publication*] (DLA)
RIGGS....... Ross Ice Shelf Geophysical and Glaciological Survey [*Ross Ice
         Shelf Project*]
RIGHTS.... Reforming Institutions to Guarantee Humane Treatment
         Standards [*Student legal action organization*]
RIGI.......... Receiving Inspection General Instruction [*NASA*] (NASA)
RIGI.......... Rivista Indo-Greco-Italico [*A publication*]
RiGI .... Romanskoe i Germanskoe Iazykoznanie [*Minsk*] [*A
         publication*]
RIGIB .... Radovi Instituta za Geolosko-Rudarska Istrazivanja i
         Ispitivanja Nuklearnih i Drugih Mineralnih Sirovina [*A
         publication*]
RIGPA .... Rezul'taty Issledovanyi po Mezhdunarodny Geofizicheskim
         Proektam [*A publication*]
RI Grad Sch Oceanogr Occas Publ ... Rhode Island Graduate School of
         Oceanography. Occasional Publication [*A publication*]
RIGS.......... Radio Inertial Guidance System
RIGS.......... Resonant Infrasonic Gauging System
RIGS.......... Riggs National Corp. [*NASDAQ symbol*] (NQ)
RIGS.......... Runway Identifiers with Glide Slope [*Aviation*]
RIH........... Rhode Island History [*A publication*]
RIH........... Rhode Island Hospital, Providence, RI [*OCLC
         symbol*] (OCLC)
RIH........... Right Inguinal Hernia [*Medicine*]
RIHAA ...... Rivers and Harbors [*A publication*]
Rihaknonjip Res Inst Appl Sci Kon-Kuk Univ ... Rihaknonjip. Research
         Institute of Applied Science. Kon-Kuk University
         [*Republic Of Korea*] [*A publication*]
RIHANS.... River and Harbor Aid to Navigation System [*Coast Guard*]
RIHED ...... Regional Institute of Higher Education and Development
RIHGSP .... Revista. Instituto Historico e Geografico de Sao Paulo [*A
         publication*]
RI His S..... Rhode Island Historical Society. Collections [*A publication*]
RI Hist....... Rhode Island History [*A publication*]
RI Hist Soc Coll ... Rhode Island Historical Society. Collections [*A
         publication*]
RiHM .... Riemann, "Handbuch der Musikgeschichte" [*A publication*]
RIHPC....... Revue Internationale d'Histoire Politique et Constitutionnelle
         [*A publication*]
RIHS.......... Royal International Horse Show [*British*]
RIHT .... RIHT Financial Corp. [*NASDAQ symbol*] (NQ)
RIHTA ...... Revue Internationale des Hautes Temperatures et des
         Refractaires [*A publication*]
RIHYA ...... Rinsho Hinyokika [*A publication*]
RII............. RADAR Intelligence Information
RII............. Receiving Inspection Instruction [*Nuclear energy*] (NRCH)
RII............. Resort Income Investors, Inc. [*AMEX symbol*] (CTT)
RII............. Rivista Inguana et Intemelia [*A publication*]
RIIA.......... Royal Institute of International Affairs [*British*]
RIIA/IA..... International Affairs. Royal Institute of International Affairs [*A
         publication*]
RIIA/WT... World Today. Royal Institute of International Affairs [*A
         publication*]
RIIC........... Research Institute on International Change [*Columbia
         University*]
RIIES........ Research Institute on Immigration and Ethnic Studies
         [*Smithsonian Institution*]
RIIGA....... Rivista Italiana d'Igiene [*A publication*]
RIISA .... Report. Institute of Industrial Science. University of Tokyo [*A
         publication*]
RIISE......... Research Institute for Information Science and Engineering,
         Inc. [*Information service or system*] (IID)
Riista-Kalataloudes Tutkimuslaitos Kalantutkimusosasto Tied ... Riista- ja
         Kalataloudes Tutkimuslaitos Kalantutkimusosasto
         Tiedonantoja [*A publication*]
Riistatiet Julkaisuja ... Riistatieteellisia Julkaisuja [*A publication*]
RIJ .... Right Internal Jugular [*Vein*] [*Anatomy*]
RIJ .... Rioja [*Peru*] [*Airport symbol*] (OAG)
RIJ .... Romano Internacionalno Jekhethanibe [*International Romani
         Union*] (EA)
RIJAZ .... Radovi Instituta Jugoslavenske Akademije Znanosti i
         Umjetnosti u Zadru [*A publication*]
RIJAZUZ ... Radovi Instituta Jugoslavenske Akademije Znanosti i
         Umjetnosti u Zadru [*A publication*]
RIJC .... Rhode Island Junior College [*Later, CCRI*]

RI Jew Hist Note ... Rhode Island Jewish Historical Notes [*A publication*]
RI Jewish Historical Notes ... Rhode Island Jewish Historical Notes [*A
         publication*]
RIJHN....... Rhode Island Jewish Historical Notes [*A publication*]
Rijks Geol Dienst Meded Nieuwe Ser (Neth) ... Rijks Geologische Dienst.
         Mededelingen. Nieuwe Serie (Netherlands) [*A publication*]
Rijksuniv Utrecht Jaarversl Wet Deel ... Rijksuniversiteit Utrecht. Jaarverslag
         Wetenschappelijk Deel [*A publication*]
Rijkswaterstaat Commun ... Rijkswaterstaat Communications [*A publication*]
Rijksw Commun ... Rijkswaterstaat Communications [*A publication*]
RIJU .... Riistatieteellisia Julkaisuja. Finnish Game Research [*A
         publication*]
RIK .... Replacement in Kind (NG)
RIKAA...... Rinsho Kagaku [*A publication*]
RIKEB ...... Rinsho Ketsueki [*A publication*]
RIKES ...... Raman-Induced Kerr Effect Scattering [*Spectroscopy*]
RIL............ Radio Influence Level
RIL............ Radio Interference Level
RIL............ Radiology and Imaging Letter [*A publication*]
RIL............ Recombinant Interleukin [*Immunotherapy*]
RIL............ Recoverable Item List
RIL............ Red Indicator Light
RIL............ Reduction in Leadtime (MCD)
RIL............ Reliability Intensity Level (CAAL)
RIL............ Religion in Life [*A publication*]
RIL............ Rendiconti. Istituto Lombardo di Scienze e Lettere [*A
         publication*]
RIL............ Repairable Item List (CAAL)
RIL............ Rifle, CO [*Location identifier*] [*FAA*] (FAAL)
Ril .... Riley's South Carolina Chancery Reports [*1836-37*] [*A
         publication*] (DLA)
Ril .... Riley's South Carolina Equity Reports [*A publication*] (DLA)
RIL............ University of Rhode Island, Graduate Library School,
         Kingston, RI [*OCLC symbol*] (OCLC)
RILA .... Rassegna Italiana di Linguistica Applicata [*A publication*]
RILA .... Repertoire International de la Litterature de l'Art [*International
         Repertory of the Literature of Art*] [*Information service or
         system*] [*A publication*]
RILAMAC ... Research in Laboratory Animal Medicine and Care
RILD........ Rivista Italiana di Letteratura Dialettale [*A publication*]
RILEM ...... Reunion Internationale des Laboratoires d'Essais et de
         Recherches sur les Materiaux et les Constructions
         [*International Union of Testing and Research Laboratories
         for Materials and Structures*] (EAIO)
Riley.......... Riley's Reports [*37-42 West Virginia*] [*A publication*] (DLA)
Riley.......... Riley's South Carolina Chancery Reports [*A
         publication*] (DLA)
Riley.......... Riley's South Carolina Law Reports [*A publication*] (DLA)
Riley Ch .... Riley's South Carolina Equity Reports [*A publication*] (DLA)
Riley Eq ..... Riley's South Carolina Equity Reports [*A publication*] (DLA)
Riley Eq (SC) ... Riley's South Carolina Equity Reports [*A
         publication*] (DLA)
Riley L (SC) ... Riley's South Carolina Law Reports [*A publication*] (DLA)
RILFC....... Rhode Island Library Film Cooperative [*Library network*]
Ril Harp..... Riley's Edition of Harper's South Carolina Reports [*A
         publication*] (DLA)
RILKO...... Research into Lost Knowledge Organisation Trust (EAIO)
RILM........ RILM [*Repertoire International de la Litterature Musicale*]
         Abstracts of Music Literature [*City University of New
         York*] [*Database*] [*A publication*]
RiLM .... Rivista di Letteratura Moderne [*A publication*]
RILOB .... Recherches Publiees sous la Direction de l'Institut de Lettres
         Orientales de Beyrouth [*A publication*]
RILOP .... Reclamation in Lieu of Procurement [*Navy*] (NG)
RILS .... Ranging Interaction Logic System
RILS .... Rapid Integrated Logistic Support System [*Military*] (AABC)
RILSA .... Resident Integrated Logistics Support Activity
         [*Military*] (AFIT)
RILSD .... Resident Integrated Logistics Support Detachment
         [*Military*] (MCD)
RILSL........ Rendiconti. Istituto Lombardo. Classe di Lettere, Scienze
         Morali, e Storiche [*A publication*]
RILST....... Remote Integrated Logistics Support Team [*Military*] (MCD)
RILT......... Rabbit Ileal Loop Test [*for enterotoxins*]
RILWAS.... Regionalized Integrated Lake-Watershed Acidification Study
         [*Adirondack mountains*]
RIM .... RADAR Input Mapper
RIM .... RADAR Input Monitor (CET)
RIM .... RADAR Intelligence Map
RIM .... Radial Inlet Manifold
RIM .... Radiant Intensity Measurements (MUGU)
RIM .... Radioisotope Medicine
RIM .... Radioisotope Method [*Analytical chemistry*]
RIM .... Railroad Interdiction Mine [*DoD*]
RIM .... Rate Improvement Mortgage [*Banking*]
RIM .... Reaction Injection Molding [*Plastics technology*]
RIM .... Read-In Mode
RIM .... Read Interrupt Mask [*Data processing*]
RIM .... Readiness Indicator Model (MCD)
RIM .... Receipt, Inspection, and Maintenance [*Military*]
RIM .... Receiver Intermodulation [*Telecommunications*] (TEL)

RIM .... Recreation Information Management System [*Department of Agriculture*] [*Washington, DC*] [*Information service or system*] (IID)
RIM .... Regulation Interpretation Memorandum [*Environmental Protection Agency*]
RIM .... Relational Information Management [*Acronym is title of a book by Wayne Erickson*] (PCM)
RIM .... Relative Intensity Measures [*of nursing care*]
RIM .... Research in Marketing [*A publication*]
RIM .... Resident Industrial Manager
RIM .... Resource Interface Module [*Datapoint*]
RIM .... Rim [*Hawaii*] [*Seismograph station code, US Geological Survey*] (SEIS)
Rim.......... Rimesse [*Remittance*] [*Business term*] [*German*]
RIM .... Rimrock Airlines, Inc. [*Spokane, WA*] [*FAA designator*] (FAAC)
RIM .... Rivista Italiana di Musicologia [*A publication*]
RIM .... Rockridge Mining [*Vancouver Stock Exchange symbol*]
RIM .... Rotors in Motion [*Aviation*] (AIA)
RIM .... Royal Indian Marine
RIM .... RSU [*Remote Subscriber Unit*] Interface Module [*Telecommunications*]
RIM .... Rubber Insulation Material
RIMAD ..... Refractive Index Matched Anomalous Diffraction [*Light measurement*]
RIMAS...... Russian Independent Mutual Aid Society (EA)
RiMB........ Riemann, "Musikgeschichte in Beispielen" [*A publication*]
RIMB........ Roche Institute of Molecular Biology
Rimba Indones ... Rimba Indonesia [*A publication*]
RIMC........ Reparable Item Movement Control [*Military*] (AFIT)
RIMC........ Reportable Items of Major Combinations [*Army*] (AABC)
RIMCS...... Reparable Item Movement Control System [*Military*] (AFIT)
RIMD........ Resources and Institutional Management Division [*NASA*]
RIME........ Radio Inertial Missile Equipment
RIME........ Radio Inertial Monitoring Equipment (KSC)
RIME........ Research Institute for Management Executives [*Washington, DC*]
RI Med J.... Rhode Island Medical Journal [*A publication*]
RIMF........ Reportable Item Master File [*Military*] (AFIT)
RIMI .... Research Improvement in Minority Institutions [*Program*] [*National Science Foundation*]
Rimini Stor Art Cult ... Rimini Storia Arte e Cultura [*A publication*]
RIMJA ...... Rhode Island Medical Journal [*A publication*]
RiML .... Riemann, "Musik Lexikon" [*A publication*]
RIMLF ...... Rostral Interstitial Nucleus of Medial Longitudinal Fasciculus [*Neuroanatomy*]
RIMM .... Report on Improved Manpower Management
RIMMS.... RVNAF [*Republic of Vietnam Air Force*] Improvement and Modernization Management System
RIMOB ..... Reserve Indication of Mobilization [*Army*] (AABC)
RIMP........ Minimum Range to Avoid Plumb Impingement (MCD)
RIMP........ Remote Input Message Processor
RIMP........ Risk Management Program (MCD)
RIMPA ..... Rivista degli Infortuni e delle Malattie Professionali [*A publication*]
RIMPAC ... Rim of the Pacific [*Naval exercise; name refers to the four participating countries: Australia, Canada, New Zealand, and the United States*]
RIMPTF.... Recording Industries Music Performance Trust Funds [*Later, MPTF*] (EA)
RIMR .... Rockefeller Institute for Medical Research
RIMS........ RADAR In-Flight Monitoring System
RIMS........ Radiant Intensity Measuring System
RIMS........ Radio Interference Measuring System
RIMS........ Record Information Movement Study (KSC)
RIMS........ Remote Information Management System
RIMS........ Replacement Inertial Measurement System
RIMS........ Requirements Inventory Management System (MCD)
RIMS........ Resonance Ionization Mass Spectrometry
RIMS........ Retarding Ion Mass Spectrometer [*Instrumentation*]
RIMS........ Risk and Insurance Management Society [*Database producer*] (EA)
RIMSE ...... Relative Integrated Mean Square Error [*Statistics*]
RIMSTOP ... Retail Inventory Management/Stockage Policy [*DoD*]
RIMTech ... Research Institute for the Management of Technology [*Southern California Technology Executives Network*] [*Research center*] (RCD)
RIN .... Radio Inertial (MSA)
RIN .... Rassemblement pour l'Independance Nationale [*Quebec separatist party, 1960-1968*] [*Canada*]
RIN .... Rat Insulinoma [*A cell line*]
RIN .... Record Identification Number
RIN .... Redpath Industries Ltd. [*Toronto Stock Exchange symbol*]
RIN .... Reference Indication Number
RIN .... Regular Inertial Navigator (MCD)
RIN .... Regulatory Identifier Number [*Environmental Protection Agency*]
RIN .... Report Identification Number [*Military*] (AABC)
RIn .... Revista de las Indias [*A publication*]
RIN .... Revue Internationale du Notariat [*A publication*]
Rin.......... Rinascimento [*A publication*]

Rin.......... Rinascita [*A publication*]
Rin.......... Riner's Reports [*2 Wyoming*] [*A publication*] (DLA)
RIN .... Ringi Cove [*Solomon Islands*] [*Airport symbol*] (OAG)
RIN .... Rivista Italiana di Numismatica e Scienze Affini [*A publication*]
RIN .... Rotor Impulsive Noise [*Helicopters*]
RIN .... Royal Indian Navy
RIN .... Royal Institute of Navigation (DS)
RIN .... Springfield, MO [*Location identifier*] [*FAA*] (FAAL)
RINA .... Resident Inspector of Naval Aircraft
RINA .... Royal Institution of Naval Architects [*British*]
RINAB...... Research Institute Nedri As (Hveragerdi, Iceland). Bulletin [*A publication*]
RINAL...... RADAR Inertial Altimeter
RINASA .... Rivista. Istituto Nazionale d'Archeologia e Storia dell'Arte [*A publication*]
Rinascenza Med ... Rinascenza Medica [*A publication*]
R Income Wealth ... Review of Income and Wealth [*A publication*]
RIND .... Reversible Ischemic Neurological Deficit [*or Disability*] [*Medicine*]
R Ind .... Revista de las Indias [*A publication*]
RINDA ...... Revue Industrielle [*A publication*]
Rindertuberk Brucell ... Rindertuberkulose und Brucellose [*A publication*]
R Indias...... Revista de las Indias [*A publication*]
RIndM....... Revista de las Indias (Madrid) [*A publication*]
R Indo Mal Aff ... Review of Indonesian and Malayan Affairs [*Australia*] [*A publication*]
R Indones Malay Aff ... Review of Indonesian and Malayan Affairs [*A publication*]
R Indones Malayan Aff ... Review of Indonesian and Malayan Affairs [*A publication*] (APTA)
RINEEK .... Rivista Italiana di Nutrizione Parenterale ed Enterale [*A publication*]
Riner .... Riner's Reports [*2 Wyoming*] [*A publication*] (DLA)
RINF........ Rinforzando [*With Special Emphasis*] [*Music*]
R Info Legis ... Revista de Informacao Legislativa [*A publication*]
RINFZ....... Rinforzando [*With Special Emphasis*] [*Music*]
RING .... Ringer
Ring Bank ... Ringwood's Principles of Bankruptcy [*18th ed.*] [*1947*] [*A publication*] (DLA)
RINGDOC ... Pharmaceutical Literature Documentation [*Derwent Publications Ltd.*] [*Great Britain*] [*Information service or system*] (IID)
Ringing Migr ... Ringing and Migration [*A publication*]
R Ing Intem ... Rivista Ingauna e Intemelia [*A publication*]
Ring Int Ornithol Bull ... Ring. International Ornithological Bulletin [*A publication*]
RINM .... Resident Inspector of Naval Material
RINN........ Recommended International Nonproprietary Name [*Drug research*]
RINPA...... Rivista di Istochimica Normale e Patologica [*A publication*]
RINR .... Royal Indian Naval Reserve [*British military*] (DMA)
RINRBM... Berichte aus der Forschungsstelle Nedri As Hveragerdi Island [*A publication*]
RINS........ Rand Information Systems, Inc. [*NASDAQ symbol*] (NQ)
RINS........ Research Institute for the Natural Sciences
RINS........ Resident Inspector
Rin S .... Rinascenza Salentina [*A publication*]
RINS........ Rotorace Inertial Navigation System (MCD)
RINSE ...... Records Information Service [*Australia*]
RINSMAT ... Resident Inspector of Naval Material (MUGU)
RINSORD ... Resident Naval Inspector of Ordnance
RINSPOW ... Resident Naval Inspector of Powder
R Ins (Solv) ... Revue. Institut de Sociologie (Solvay) [*A publication*]
R Inst Antropol Cordoba ... Revista. Instituto de Antropologia. Universidad de Cordoba [*A publication*]
R Inst Chem Lect Monogr Rep ... Royal Institute of Chemistry. Lectures, Monographs, and Reports [*A publication*]
R Inst Chem Lect Ser ... Royal Institute of Chemistry. Lecture Series [*A publication*]
R Inst Cienc Soc ... Revista. Instituto de Ciencias Sociales [*A publication*]
R Instit Europ ... Revista de Instituciones Europeas [*A publication*]
R Inst Nav Archit (London) Suppl Pap ... Royal Institution of Naval Architects (London). Supplementary Papers [*A publication*]
R Inst Nav Archit Q Trans ... Royal Institution of Naval Architects [*London*]. Quarterly Transactions [*A publication*]
R Inst Nav Archit Suppl Pap ... Royal Institution of Naval Architects [*London*]. Supplementary Papers [*A publication*]
R Inst Pr .... Royal Institution of Great Britain. Proceedings [*A publication*]
R Inst Public Health Hyg J ... Royal Institute of Public Health and Hygiene. Journal [*A publication*]
R Inst Sociol ... Revue. Institut de Sociologie [*A publication*]
RINSUL.... Rubber Insulation
RINT .... RADAR Intermittent (MSA)
RINT .... Radiation Intelligence
RINT .... Revista. Instituto Nacional de la Tradicion [*A publication*]
R Int Commiss Jurists ... Review. International Commission of Jurists [*A publication*]
R Int Coop ... Review of International Cooperation [*A publication*]
R Int Croix Rouge ... Revue Internationale de la Croix Rouge [*A publication*]

R Int Cr Rouge ... Revue Internationale de la Croix Rouge [*A publication*]
R Int Dr Comp ... Revue Internationale de Droit Compare [*A publication*]
R Int Droits Ant ... Revue Internationale des Droits de l'Antiquite [*A publication*]
R Int Dr Penal ... Revue Internationale de Droit Penal [*A publication*]
RINTDU ... Reactive Intermediates [*A publication*]
R Integr ...... Revista de la Integracion [*A publication*]
R Integracion ... Revista de la Integracion [*A publication*]
R Integracion y Desarrollo Centroam ... Revista de la Integracion y el Desarrollo de Centroamerica [*A publication*]
R Interam Bibl ... Revista Interamericana de Bibliografia [*A publication*]
R Interam Bibliog ... Revista Interamericana de Bibliografia [*A publication*]
R Interam Cienc Soc ... Revista Interamericana de Ciencias Sociales [*A publication*]
R Interam Sociol ... Revista Interamericana de Sociologia [*A publication*]
R Internac Sociol ... Revista Internacional de Sociologia [*A publication*]
R Internat Affairs ... Review of International Affairs [*A publication*]
R Internat Hist Banque ... Revue Internationale d'Histoire de la Banque [*A publication*]
R Internat Rech Urbaine et Reg ... Revue Internationale de Recherche Urbaine et Regionale [*A publication*]
R Internaz Econ Trasporti ... Revista Internazionale del Trasporti [*A publication*]
R Internaz Scienze Econ e Commer ... Rivista Internazionale di Scienze Economiche e Commerciali [*A publication*]
R Internaz Scienze Soc ... Rivista Internazionale di Scienze Sociali [*A publication*]
R Int'l Arb Awards ... United Nations Reports of International Arbitral Awards [*A publication*]   (DLA)
RIntMS ...... Rivista Internazionale di Musica Sacra [*A publication*]
R Int Pol Crim ... Revue Internationale de Police Criminelle [*A publication*]
R Int Sci Adm ... Revue Internationale des Sciences Administratives [*A publication*]
R Int Sci Soc ... Revue Internationale des Sciences Sociales [*A publication*]
R Int Secur Soc ... Revue Internationale de la Securite Sociale [*A publication*]
R Int Sociol ... Revue Internationale de Sociologie [*International Review of Sociology*] [*Rome*] [*A publication*]
R Int Sociol (Madrid) ... Revista Internacional de Sociologia (Madrid) [*A publication*]
R Int Stat ... Revue Internationale de Statistique [*A publication*]
R Int Trav .. Revue Internationale du Travail [*A publication*]
RINUA ...... Rivista di Ingegneria Nucleare [*A publication*]
RINV .... Reliable Investors Corp. [*NASDAQ symbol*]   (NQ)
RINVR .... Royal Indian Naval Volunteer Reserve [*British military*]   (DMA)
RIO .... RADAR-Intercept Operator
RIO .... Ramus Infraorbitalis [*Anatomy*]
RIO .... Registry of Italian Oddities   (EA)
RIO .... Relocatable Input/Output
RIO .... Remain Intact Organization   (EA)
RIO .... Reporting In and Out [*Military*]
RIO .... Research Industry Office   (MCD)
RIO .... Reshaping the International Order [*Title of Club of Rome report*]
RIO .... Resident Inspector Office [*Coast Guard*]
RIO .... Resident Inspector of Ordnance   (AAG)
RIO .... Retail Issue Outlets   (NG)
RIO .... Revue Internationale d'Onomastique [*A publication*]
RIO .... Ride-It-Out
RIO .... Rio De Janeiro [*Brazil*] [*Airport symbol*]   (OAG)
RIO .... Rio Grant [*Caja Del Rio*] [*New Mexico*] [*Seismograph station code, US Geological Survey*] [*Closed*]   (SEIS)
RIO .... Rio Sierra Silver [*Vancouver Stock Exchange symbol*]
RIO .... Royal International Optical Corp. [*NYSE symbol*]   (SPSG)
RIO .... Royal Italian Opera
RIO .... Russkoe Istoriceskoe Obscestvo [*A publication*]
Rio De Janeiro Univ Federal Inst Geociencias Bol Geologia ... Universidade Federal do Rio De Janeiro. Instituto de Geociencias. Boletim Geologia [*A publication*]
RIOE .... Research in Ocean Engineering. University Sources and Resources [*A publication*]
RIOGD ...... Rio Grande [*FAA*]   (FAAC)
Rio Grande Do Sul Inst Geocien Mapa Geol ... Universidade Federal do Rio Grande Do Sul. Instituto de Geociencias. Mapa Geologico da Folha de Morretes [*A publication*]
Rio Grande Do Sul Inst Pesqui Zootec Bol Tec ... Rio Grande Do Sul. Instituto de Pesquisas Zootecnicas. Boletim Tecnico [*A publication*]
RIOMETER ... Relative Ionospheric Opacity Meter
RIOno .... Revue Internationale d'Onomastique [*A publication*]
RIOPR .... Rhode Island Open Pool Reactor
RIO-RIT-RIM ... Religion Index Database - Religion Index One; Religion Index Two; Research in Ministry [*American Theological Library Association*] [*Information service or system*]   (CRD)
RIOS .... Joint Working Group on River Inputs to Ocean Systems [*Marine science*]   (MSC)
RIOS .... ROM [*Read-Only Memory*] BIOS [*Pronounced "rye-ose"*] [*Data processing*]
RIOS .... Rotating Image Optical Scanner
RIOT .... RAM Input/Output Timer

RIOT .... Real-Time Input-Output Transducer [*or Translator*] [*Data processing*]
RIOT .... Remote Input/Output Terminal [*Data processing*]
RIOT .... Resolution of Initial Operational Techniques
RIOT .... Retrieval of Information by On-Line Terminal [*Atomic Energy Authority*] [*Data processing*] [*British*]
RIOTE2 ..... Rivista Italiana di Ortopedia e Traumatologia [*Italian Review of Orthopaedics and Traumatology*] [*A publication*]
RIOV .... Rio Verde Energy Corp. [*NASDAQ symbol*]   (NQ)
RIP .... RADAR Identification Point   (AFM)
RIP .... RADAR Improvement Plan   (NATG)
RIP .... RADAR Improvement Program
RIP .... Radioimmunoprecipitation [*Clinical chemistry*]
RIP .... Radioisotopic Pathology [*Medical specialty*]   (DHSM)
RIP .... Radiological Information Plot   (NATG)
RIP .... Random Input Sampling [*Data processing*]
RIP .... Rapid Installation Plan
RIP .... Raster Image Processor [*Printer technology*]
RIP .... Rate-Invariant Path [*Economic theory*]
RIP .... Rays Initiating from a Point   (MCD)
RIP .... Reactive Ion Plating [*Coating technology*]
RIP .... Reactor Instrument Penetration Valve   (IEEE)
RIP .... Readiness Improvement Program [*Military*]   (CAAL)
RIP .... Rearrangement Induced Premeiotically [*Genetics*]
RIP .... Receiving Inspection Plan [*Nuclear energy*]   (NRCH)
RIP .... Recoverable Item Program [*Marine Corps*]
RIP .... Reduction Implementation Panel [*DoD*]
RIP .... Register Indicator Panel
RIP .... Register of Intelligence Publications   (MCD)
RIP .... Reliability Improvement Program
RIP .... Remain in Place   (MCD)
RIP .... Remote Indicator Panel   (CAAL)
RIP .... Renin Inhibitory Peptide [*Biochemistry*]
RIP .... Repeat-Induced Point Mutation [*Genetic engineering technique*]
RIP .... Report on Individual Personnel   (MCD)
RIP .... Requiescat [*or Requiescant*] in Pace [*May He (She, or They) Rest in Peace*] [*Latin*]   (GPO)
RIP .... Research in Parapsychology [*A publication*]
RIP .... Research in Progress   (MCD)
RIP .... Respiratory Inversion Point [*Physiology*]
RIP .... Retired in Place [*Telecommunications*]   (TEL)
RIP .... Retirement Improvement Program [*Air Force*]   (AFM)
RIP .... Retirement Income Plan [*Insurance*]   (MCD)
RIP .... Revue Internationale de Philosophie [*A publication*]
RIP .... Ribosome Inactivating [*or Inhibiting*] Protein [*Biochemistry*]
RIP .... Rice Institute Pamphlet [*A publication*]
Rip .... [*Johannes Franciscus de*] Ripa [*Deceased, 1534*] [*Authority cited in pre-1607 legal work*]   (DSA)
RIP .... Ripieno [*Additional*] [*Music*]
RIP .... Ripple Resources Ltd. [*Vancouver Stock Exchange symbol*]
RIP .... Routing Information Process [*Telecommunications*]   (TEL)
RIP .... Rural Industrialization Program [*Department of Agriculture*]
RIPA .... Radioimmunoprecipitation Assay [*Clinical chemistry*]
RIPA .... Royal Institute of Public Administration [*British*]
RIPB .... Revue de l'Instruction Publique en Belgique [*A publication*]
RIPC .... Rassegna Italiana di Politica e di Cultura [*A publication*]
RIPC .... Regroupement des Independants et Paysans Camerounais [*Regrouping of Independents and Farmers of the Cameroons*]
RIPD .... RLG [*Research Libraries Group, Inc.*] Research-in-Progress Database [*Information service or system*]   (CRD)
RIPE .... Range Instrumentation Performance Evaluation   (MUGU)
RIPEH ...... Review of Iranian Political Economy and History [*A publication*]
RIPFCOMTF ... Rapid Item Processor to Facilitate Complex Operations on Magnetic Tape Files [*Data processing*]
RIPh .... Revue Internationale de Philosophie [*A publication*]
RIPH & H ... Royal Institute of Public Health and Hygiene [*British*]
RIPIA .... Revue Internationale de la Propriete Industrielle et Litteraire [*A publication*]
RIPILS ...... Recently Immigrated Professional Irish Legals [*Lifestyle classification*]
RIPIS .... Rhode Island Pupil Identification Scale [*Psychology*]
RIPL .... Representation-Independent Programming Language
RIPMA ...... Revue des Travaux. Institut des Peches Maritimes [*A publication*]
RIPOAM ... Rivista Italiana delle Essenze dei Profumi e delle Piante Officinali Aromi Saponi Cosmetici Aerosol [*A publication*]
RIPOM ...... Report [*command indicated*] If Present, Otherwise by Message [*Navy*]
RI Port Indus Devel Comm Geol Bull Sci Contr ... Rhode Island. Port and Industrial Development Commission. Geological Bulletin. Scientific Contribution [*A publication*]
RIPOSTE ... Restitution Incentive Program Operationalized as a Strategy Toward an Effective Learning Environment [*HEW*]
RIPP .... RADAR Intelligence Photo Product
RIPP .... Regulatory Information on Pesticide Products [*Database*]   (IT)
RIPPLE ..... Radioactive Isotope-Powered Pulse Light Equipment   (IEEE)
RIPPLE ..... Radioisotope-Powered Prolonged Life Equipment   (IEEE)
RIPPLE ...... Ripplesmere [*England*]

RIPR .... Recommended Immediate Procurement Records (MCD)
RIPS .... RADAR Impact Prediction System (CET)
RIPS .... Radio-Isotope Power Supply [*or System*] [*Nuclear energy*] (NG)
RIPS .... Range Instrumentation Planning Study [*AFSC*]
RIPS .... Remote Image Processing System
RIPSD3 ..... Annual Report. Institute of Physics. Academia Sinica [*A publication*]
RI Pub Laws ... Public Laws of Rhode Island [*A publication*] (DLA)
RIPV .... Reactor Isolation Pressure Valve (IEEE)
RIPWC ...... Royal Institute of Painters in Water-Colours [*British*]
RIPY .... Ripley Co., Inc. [*NASDAQ symbol*] (NQ)
RIQAP .... Reduced Inspection Quality Assurance Program
RIQS .... Remote Information Query System [*Information retrieval service*] [*Data processing*]
RIR .... RADAR Interface Recorder (MCD)
RIR .... Range Illumination RADAR
RIR .... Receiving Inspection Report
RIR .... Redgrave Information Resources Corp. [*Publisher*]
RiR .... Redgrave Information Resources Corp., Westport, CT [*Library symbol*] [*Library of Congress*] (LCLS)
RIR .... Reduction in Requirement [*Air Force*] (AFM)
RIR .... Regimental Inquiry Regulations [*British military*] (DMA)
RIR .... Rehabilitation Information Round Table (EA)
RIR .... Reliability Investigation Requests (KSC)
RIR .... Reportable Item Report [*NASA*] (NASA)
RIR .... Revista Istorica Romana [*A publication*]
RIR .... Rhode Island Red [*Poultry*]
RIR .... Riverside/Rubidoux, CA [*Location identifier*] [*FAA*] (FAAL)
RIR .... ROM [*Read-Only Memory*] Instruction Register
RIR .... Royal Irish Rifles [*British military*] (DMA)
RIRAA .... Russian Immigrants' Representative Association In America
RIRAB ...... Rivista di Radiologia [*A publication*]
R Ir Acad Proc Sect B ... Royal Irish Academy. Proceedings. Section B [*A publication*]
R Iranienne Relations Internat ... Revue Iranienne des Relations Internationales [*A publication*]
R Iran Relat Int ... Revue Iranienne des Relations Internationales [*A publication*]
RIRB .... Railway Insurance Rating Bureau [*Defunct*] (EA)
RIRCA ...... Rhode Island Red Club of America (EA)
RIRED .... Revue. IRE [*Institut National des Radioelements*] [*Belgium*] [*A publication*]
RI Rep .... Rhode Island Reports [*A publication*] (DLA)
RI Resour ... Rhode Island Resources [*A publication*]
RIrF .... Royal Irish Fusiliers [*Military unit*] [*British*] (DMA)
RIRF .... Rural Industry Research Funds [*Australia*]
RIRIG .... Reduced-Excitation Inertial Reference Integrating Gyro
R Irish Ac Pr ... Royal Irish Academy. Proceedings [*A publication*]
RIRJ .... Research Institute of Religious Jewry (EA)
RIRMS ...... Remote Information Retrieval and Management System [*Data processing*] (BUR)
RIRO .... Roll-In/Roll-Out [*Storage allocation*] [*Data processing*]
RIRS .... Reliability Information Retrieval System (MCD)
RIRT .... Rehabilitation Information Round Table (EA)
RIRT .... Rhodium-Iron Resistance Thermometer
RIRTI .... Recording Infrared Tracking Instrument
RIS .... Kansas City, MO [*Location identifier*] [*FAA*] (FAAL)
RIS .... RADIAC [*Radiation Detection, Indication, and Computation*] Instrument System
RIS .... Radio Interference Service [*Department of Trade*] [*British*]
RIS .... Radiology Information System [*Data processing*]
RIS .... Ramjet Inlet System
RIS .... Range Information System [*For aircraft*] (MCD)
RIS .... Range Instrumentation Ship
RIS .... Range Instrumentation Station
RIS .... Rassegna Italiana di Sociologia [*A publication*]
RIS .... Reblooming Iris Society (EA)
RIS .... Receiving Inspection Segment
RIS .... RECON Information System (MCD)
RIS .... Record Input Subroutine
RIS .... Recorded Information Service [*Telecommunications*] (TEL)
RIS .... Redwood Inspection Service (EA)
RIS .... Regulatory Information Service [*Congressional Information Service, Inc.*] [*Information service or system*] [*Defunct*]
RIS .... Reliability Information System
RIS .... Remote Information System
RIS .... Reports Identification Symbol
RIS .... Research Information Service [*John Crerar Library*] [*Information service or system*] (IID)
RIS .... Research Information Services [*Georgia Institute of Technology*] [*Atlanta*] [*Information service or system*] (IID)
RIS .... Research Information System [*Rehabilitation Services Administration*] (IID)
RIS .... Resonance Ionization Spectroscopy
RIS .... Retail Information System
RIS .... Retarded Infants Services [*Later, CFS*] (EA)
RIS .... Retransmission Identity Signal [*Telecommunications*] (TEL)
RIS .... Revista Internacional de Sociologia [*A publication*]
RIS .... Revolution Indicating System (MSA)

RIS .... Revue. Institut de Sociologie [*A publication*]
RIS .... Revue Internationale du Socialisme [*A publication*]
RIS .... Rise Resources, Inc. [*Vancouver Stock Exchange symbol*]
RIS .... Rishiri [*Japan*] [*Airport symbol*] [*Obsolete*] (OAG)
Ris .... Risorgimento [*A publication*]
RIS .... Rivista Italiana di Sociologia [*A publication*]
RIS .... Rotatable Initial Susceptibility
RIS .... Rotating Image Scanner
RIS .... Routine Interest Shipping (MCD)
RIS .... Russian Intelligence Service
RISA .... Radioimmunosorbent Assay [*Clinical chemistry*]
RISA .... Radioiodinated Serum Albumin [*Medicine*]
RISA .... Railway and Industrial Spring Association [*Later, RISRI*]
RISA .... Romani Imperii Semper Auctor [*Continual Increaser of the Roman Empire*] [*Latin*]
RISAA .... Rivista Italiana della Saldatura [*A publication*]
RIS-ALEX ... Research Information Services - Alexander Library
RISB .... Rotter Incomplete Sentences Blank [*Psychology*]
RISC .... Reduced Instruction Set Computer
RISC .... Refractive Index Sounding Central
RISC .... Remote Information Systems Center
RISC .... Research Institute of Scripps Clinic [*Research center*] (RCD)
RISCA .... Rockwell International Science Center
RISCA .... Ricerca Scientifica [*A publication*]
RI Sch Des Bul ... Rhode Island School of Design. Bulletin [*A publication*]
RISD .... Requisition and Invoice Shipping Document
RISD .... Rhode Island School of Design
RISE .... Catch a Rising Star, Inc. [*NASDAQ symbol*] (NQ)
RISE .... National Institute for Resources in Science and Engineering (EA)
RISE .... Radiation-Induced Surface Effect
RISE .... RAM [*Reliability, Availability, and Maintainability*] Improvement of Selected Equipment [*Military*] (MCD)
RISE .... Readiness Improvement Status Evaluation (MCD)
RISE .... Readiness Improvement Summary Evaluation (MCD)
RISE .... Reform of Intermediate and Secondary Education (OICC)
RISE .... Register for International Service in Education [*Institute of International Education*] (IID)
RISE .... Reliability Improvement Selected Equipment (AABC)
RISE .... Research and Information Services for Education [*Montgomery County Intermediate Unit*] [*King of Prussia, PA*]
RISE .... Research Institute for Studies in Education [*Iowa State University*] [*Research center*] (RCD)
RISE .... Research in Science Education [*National Science Foundation*] (GRD)
RISE .... Research in Supersonic Environment
RISE .... Reusable Inflatable Salvage Equipment
RISE .... Rivista Internazionale di Scienze Economiche e Commerciali [*A publication*]
RISE .... Rulings Information System, Excise [*Revenue Canada - Customs and Excise*] [*Information service or system*] (CRD)
RISEAP ..... Regional Islamic Da'Wah Council of Southeast Asia and the Pacific (EAIO)
RISEB8 ...... Clinical Orthopaedic Surgery [*A publication*]
RISG .... Rivista Italiana di Scienze Giuridiche [*A publication*]
RISHB .... Rinsho Shinkeigaku [*A publication*]
RISHBH .... Clinical Neurology [*Tokyo*] [*A publication*]
RISHE .... Research Institute for Supersensic Healing Energies
RISI .... Review. International Statistical Institute [*A publication*]
RISID .... Revista Padurilor-Industria Lemnului. Seria Industria Lemnului [*A publication*]
Rising Up ... Rising Up Angry [*A publication*]
RISK .... George Risk Industries, Inc. [*NASDAQ symbol*] (NQ)
RISK .... Rock Is Stoning Kids [*Defunct*] (EA)
RISKAC ... Risk Acceptance (NASA)
Risk Anal ... Risk Analysis [*A publication*]
Risk Bk Ser ... Risk. Book Series [*A publication*]
Risk Manage ... Risk Management [*A publication*]
Risk Mgmt ... Risk Management [*A publication*]
Risk Mgt .... Risk Management [*A publication*]
RISL .... Residual Item Selection List
RiSL .... Rossija i Slavjanstvo [*A publication*]
RISM .... Reference Interaction Site Model [*Chemical physics*]
RISM .... Repertoire International des Sources Musicales [*A publication*]
RISM .... Research Institute for the Study of Man [*Army*] (MCD)
RI/SME ..... Robotics International of SME [*Society of Manufacturing Engineers*] (EA)
RISO .... Range Instrumentation Systems Office [*White Sands Missile Range*]
RISO .... Revista Internacional de Sociologia [*A publication*]
RISoc .... Revue. Institut de Sociologie [*Solvay*] [*A publication*]
Risoe Inf .... Risoe Information [*Denmark*] [*A publication*]
Risoe Natl Lab Rep Risoe-M (Den) ... Risoe National Laboratory. Report Risoe-M (Denmark) [*A publication*]
Risoe Rep (Den) Res Establ Risoe ... Risoe Report. (Denmark) Research Establishment Risoe [*A publication*]
RISOL .... Risoluto [*Resolutely*] [*Music*] (ROG)
RISOP .... Red Integrated Strategic Offensive Plan [*Army*] (AABC)
Riso Rep ..... Risoe Report [*A publication*]
Risorgiment ... Risorgimento [*A publication*]

RISP .... Robotics and Intelligent Systems Program [*Oak Ridge National Laboratory*]
RISP .... Ross Ice Shelf Project [*International cooperative research project*]
RISPT .... Ross Ice Shelf Project. Technical Reports [*A publication*]
RISR .... Rassegna d'Informazioni. Istituto di Studi Romani [*A publication*]
RI-SR .... Removal Item - Ship's Record (MCD)
RiSR .... Ricerche di Storia Religiosa [*A publication*]
RISRA .... Report of Ionosphere and Space Research in Japan [*A publication*]
RISRI .... Railway and Industrial Spring Research Institute [*Defunct*] (EA)
RISS .... Range Instrumentation and Support Systems
RISS .... Refractive Index Sounding System
RISS .... Regional Information Sharing System [*Department of Justice*]
RISS .... Revue Internationale des Sciences Sociales [*A publication*]
RISS .... Rivista Internazionale di Scienze Sociali e Discipline Ausiliari [*A publication*]
RISS .... Rockwell International Suspension Systems Co.
RISSB .... Research Institute on the Sino-Soviet Bloc (EA)
RIST .... RADAR Installed System Tester (KSC)
RIST .... Radioimmunosorbent Technique [*or Test*] [*Clinical chemistry*]
RIST .... Radioisotopic Sand Tracer [*Marine science*] (MSC)
RISTA .... Rivista Italiana di Stomatologia [*A publication*]
R Istituto Veneto Memorie ... Reale Istituto Veneto di Scienze, Lettere, ed Arti. Memorie [*A publication*]
R Ist Lomb ... Rendiconti. Istituto Lombardo di Scienze e Lettere [*A publication*]
Ri St V .... Richtlinien fuer das Strafverfahren [*A publication*]
RISULB ..... Revue. Institut de Sociologie. Universite Libre de Bruxelles [*A publication*]
RISVD .... Risvegliato [*Reanimated*] [*Music*] (ROG)
RISW .... Registered Industrial Social Worker [*Designation awarded by the American Association of Industrial Social Workers*]
RISW .... Royal Institution of South Wales [*British*]
RISWR ...... Regional Institute of Social Welfare Research (EA)
RIT .... RADAR Inputs Test
RIT .... Radio Information Test
RIT .... Radio Network for Inter-American Telecommunications
RIT .... Railway Inclusive Tour (DCTA)
RIT .... Rate of Information Throughput [*Data processing*] (BUR)
R & IT .... Rating and Income Tax Reports [*England*] [*A publication*] (DLA)
RIT .... Readiness Initiative Team [*Military*]
RIT .... Receiver Incremental Tuning
RIT .... Reclamation Insurance Type [*Military*] (AFIT)
RIT .... Refining in Transit
RIT .... Relative Ignition Temperature
RIT .... Request for Interface Tool [*NASA*] (NASA)
RIT .... Retrieval Injury Threshold
RIT .... Revue Internationale du Travail [*A publication*]
RIT .... Rio Tigre [*Panama*] [*Airport symbol*] (OAG)
RIT .... Ritardando [*Gradually Slower*] [*Music*]
RIT .... Ritenuto [*Immediately Slower*] [*Music*]
rit .... Ritual (BJA)
RIT .... Rivista Italiana del Teatro [*A publication*]
RIT .... Rochester Institute of Technology [*New York*]
RIT .... Rochester Institute of Technology Library [*UTLAS symbol*]
RIT .... Rocket Interferometer Tracking
RIT .... Rotary Indexing Table
RIT .... Rothschild Investment Trust
RITA .... Rand Intelligent Terminal Agent
RITA .... Recoverable Interplanetary Transport Approach
RITA .... Refundable Income Tax Account
RITA .... Reseau Integre de Transmission Automatique [*French*]
RITA .... Reservation, Information, Tourist Accommodation [*Computerized system for booking hotel rooms*] [*British*]
RITA .... Resist Inside the Army [*Peace-movement slang*]
RITA .... Reusable Interplanetary Transport Approach Vehicle
RITA .... Rivera and Tamayo Fault Exploration [*Marine science*] (MSC)
RITA .... Romance Is Treasured Always [*Annual award bestowed by Romance Writers of America. Acronym selected to honor cofounder, Rita Clay Estrada*]
RITA .... Rural Industrial Technical Assistance [*Latin American building program*]
RITAA .... Revue d'Immunologie et de Therapie Antimicrobienne [*A publication*]
RITAC .... Retail Industry Trade Action Coalition [*Washington, DC*] (EA)
RitAcc .... Rituels Accadiens [*A publication*] (BJA)
RITAD .... Radiation-Induced Thermally Activated Depolarization [*Radiation dosimetry technique*]
R Ital Diritto Lav ... Rivista Italiana di Diritto del Lavoro [*A publication*]
R Ital Econ Demografia e Statis ... Rivista Italiana di Economia. Demografia e Statistica [*A publication*]
R Italiana Musicol ... Rivista Italiana di Musicologia [*A publication*]
R Ital Mus ... Nuova Rivista Musicale Italiana [*A publication*]
R Ital Mus ... Rivista Italiana di Musicologia [*A publication*]
RITAR .... Ritardando [*Gradually Slower*] [*Music*]
RITARD .... Ritardando [*Gradually Slower*] [*Music*]

RITARO.... Ritardando [*Gradually Slower*] [*Music*] (ROG)
RITB .... Road Transport Industry Training Board [*British*]
RITC .... Rhodamine Isothiocyanate [*Biochemistry*]
Ritch.......... Ritchie's Cases Decided by Francis Bacon [*1617-21*] [*A publication*] (DLA)
Ritch.......... Ritchie's Equity Reports [*1872-82*] [*Nova Scotia*] [*A publication*] (DLA)
Ritch Eq Dec ... Ritchie's Equity Decisions [*Nova Scotia*] [*A publication*] (DLA)
Ritch Eq Rep ... Ritchie's Equity Reports [*Nova Scotia*] [*A publication*] (DLA)
Ritchie....... Ritchie's Equity [*Canada*] [*A publication*] (DLA)
RITE.......... Rapid Information Technique for Evaluation
RITE.......... Rapidata Interactive Text Editor (IEEE)
RITE.......... Rent Rite Reservation Network, Inc. [*NASDAQ symbol*] (NQ)
RITEA ...... Rock Island Railroad Transportation and Employee Assistance Act [*1980*]
RITEN....... Ritenuto [*Immediately Slower*] [*Music*]
RITENA .... Reunion Internacional de Tecnicos de la Nutricion Animal [*International Meeting of Animal Nutrition Experts*] (EAIO)
RITENO.... Ritenuto [*Immediately Slower*] [*Music*] (ROG)
RiTh.......... Revue Internationale de Theologie [*A publication*]
RITI .... Resident Inspection Test Instruction
RITL.......... Revista de Istorie si Theori Literara [*A publication*]
RITLS........ Rhode Island Test of Language Structure
RITMB....... Rayonnements Ionisants [*A publication*]
RITOP....... Red Integrated Tactical Operational Plan (CINC)
RITQ .... Revised Infant Temperament Questionnaire
RITR.......... Rework Inspection Team Report
RITREAD ... Rapid Iterative Reanalysis for Automated Design [*Computer program*]
RITS .... Radiatively Important Trace Substances
RITS .... Rapid Information Transmission System
RITS .... Reconnaissance Intelligence Technical Squadron
Rits Cts Leet ... Ritson's Jurisdiction of Courts-Leet [*A publication*] (DLA)
Rits Int .... Ritso's Introduction to the Science [*A publication*] (DLA)
RITSL........ Reconfigured Integrated Two-Stage Liquefaction [*Chemical engineering*]
RITSq .... Reconnaissance Intelligence Technical Squadron [*Air Force*]
RITU .... Research Institute of Temple University (KSC)
RITZ.......... Ritzy's [*G.*], Inc. [*NASDAQ symbol*] (NQ)
RIU .... Andalusia, AL [*Location identifier*] [*FAA*] (FAAL)
RIU .... RADAR Interface Unit [*Military*] (CAAL)
RIU .... Radioactive Iodine Uptake [*Medicine*]
RIU .... Railroad Insurance Underwriters [*Later, RTI*] (EA)
RIU .... Refractive Index Unit
RIU .... Remote Interface Unit [*NASA*] (NASA)
riu.............. Rhode Island [*MARC country of publication code*] [*Library of Congress*] (LCCP)
RIU .... University of Rhode Island, Kingston, RI [*OCLC symbol*] (OCLC)
Riun Annu Assoc Elettrot Elettron Ital Rend ... Riunione Annuale della Associazione Elettrotecnica ed Elettronica Italiana. Rendiconti [*A publication*]
RI Univ Agric Exp Stn Bull ... Rhode Island University. Agricultural Experiment Station. Bulletin [*A publication*]
RI Univ Div Eng Res Dev Eng Repr ... Rhode Island University. Division of Engineering. Research and Development Engineering Reprint [*A publication*]
RI Univ Div Eng Res Dev Leafl ... Rhode Island University. Division of Engineering. Research and Development Leaflet [*A publication*]
RI Univ Eng Exp Stn Bull ... Rhode Island University. Engineering Experiment Station. Bulletin [*A publication*]
RI Univ Eng Exp Stn Eng Repr ... Rhode Island University. Engineering Experiment Station. Engineering Reprint [*A publication*]
RI Univ Mar Tech Rep ... Rhode Island University. Marine Technical Report [*A publication*]
RIUPDJ .... US National Institute on Drug Abuse. Research Issues [*A publication*]
RIUSA .... Rehabilitation International USA
RIV .... Radio Influence Voltage
RIV .... Ramus Interventricularis [*First-order branch of coronary artery*] [*Medicine*]
RIV .... Recirculation Isolation Valve (NASA)
RIV .... Regolamento Internazionale Veicoli [*Italian generic term meaning "International Regulation of Vehicles"*] [*Initialism also refers to International Wagon Union*]
RIV .... River
RIV .... Riverbend International [*AMEX symbol*] (SPSG)
RIV .... Riverside, CA [*Location identifier*] [*FAA*] (FAAL)
RIV .... Riverview [*Australia*] [*Seismograph station code, US Geological Survey*] (SEIS)
RIV .... Rivet (AAG)
Riv............. Riviera [*Record label*] [*France*]
Riv............. Rivista [*Review*] [*Italian*] (BJA)
Riv A .... Rivista d'Arte [*A publication*]
Riv AC .... Rivista di Archeologia Cristiana [*A publication*]
Riv Aeronaut ... Rivista Aeronautica [*A publication*]

Riv Aeronaut-Astronaut-Missil ... Rivista Aeronautica-Astronautica-Missilistica [*Italy*] [*A publication*]
Riv Aeronaut Astronaut Missil Suppl Tec ... Rivista Aeronautica-Astronautica-Missilistica. Supplemento Tecnico [*A publication*]
Riv Agric.... Rivista di Agricoltura [*A publication*]
Riv Agric Subtrop Trop ... Rivista di Agricoltura Subtropicale e Tropicale [*A publication*]
Riv Agron ... Rivista di Agronomia [*A publication*]
Riv Agr Subtrop Trop ... Rivista di Agricoltura Subtropicale e Tropicale [*A publication*]
Riv d'Alb.... Rivista d'Albania [*A publication*]
Riv Anat Patol Oncol ... Rivista di Anatomia Patologica e di Oncologia [*A publication*]
Riv Ann Reg ... Rivington's Annual Register [*A publication*]　(DLA)
Riv Antrop ... Rivista di Antropologia [*A publication*]
Riv Antropol ... Rivista di Antropologia [*A publication*]
Riv Arch Crist ... Rivista di Archeologia Cristiana [*A publication*]
Riv d Arch Crist ... Rivista di Archeologia Cristiana [*A publication*]　(OCD)
Riv Arte...... Rivista d'Arte [*A publication*]
Riv B .... Rivista Biblica [*A publication*]
RivB .... Rivista Bibliografica [*A publication*]
RivBA .... Rivista delle Biblioteche e degli Archivi [*A publication*]
RIVBEA .... [*Sam*] Rivers and Bea [*Rivers*] [*As in Rivbea Festival, jazz event named for saxophonist Sam Rivers and his wife, Bea*]
RivBibl....... Rivista Biblica [*A publication*]
Riv Bibl ...... Rivista delle Biblioteche e degli Archivi [*A publication*]
Riv Biol ...... Rivista di Biologia [*A publication*]
Riv Biol Colon ... Rivista di Biologia Coloniale [*A publication*]
Riv Biol Norm Patol ... Rivista di Biologia Normale e Patologica [*A publication*]
Riv Biol (Perugia) ... Rivista di Biologia (Perugia) [*A publication*]
Riv Chim Sci Ind ... Rivista di Chimica Scientifica e Industriale [*A publication*]
Riv Chir (Como) ... Rivista di Chirurgia (Como) [*A publication*]
Riv Chir Med ... Rivista di Chirurgia e Medicina [*A publication*]
Riv Chir Pediat ... Rivista di Chirurgia Pediatrica [*A publication*]
Riv Civ ...... Rivista di Diritto Civile [*A publication*]
Riv Clin Bologna ... Rivista Clinica di Bologna [*A publication*]
Riv Clin Med ... Rivista di Clinica Medica [*A publication*]
Riv Clin Pediat ... Rivista di Clinica Pediatrica [*A publication*]
Riv Clin Pediatr ... Rivista di Clinica Pediatrica [*A publication*]
Riv Clin Tossicol ... Rivista di Clinica Tossicologia [*A publication*]
Riv Clin Univ Napoli ... Rivista Clinica. Universita di Napoli [*A publication*]
Riv Colore Verniciatura Ind ... Rivista del Colore-Verniciatura Industriale [*A publication*]
Riv Combust ... Rivista dei Combustibili [*A publication*]
Riv Comm .. Rivista del Diritto Commerciale e del Diritto Generale delle Obbligazioni [*A publication*]
Riv Coniglicolt ... Rivista di Coniglicoltura [*A publication*]
Riv Crit Clin Med ... Rivista Critica di Clinica Medica [*A publication*]
Riv Crit St ... Rivista Critica di Storia della Filosofia [*A publication*]
Riv Crit Stor Filos ... Rivista Critica di Storia della Filosofia [*A publication*]
Riv Cult Class Med ... Rivista di Cultura Classica e Medioevale [*A publication*]
Riv Cult Mar ... Rivista di Cultura Marinara [*A publication*]
RivDal........ Rivista Dalmatica [*A publication*]
Riv Dif Soc ... Rivista di Difesa Sociale [*A publication*]
Riv Dir Agr ... Rivista di Diritto Agrario [*A publication*]
Riv Dir Civ ... Rivista di Diritto Civile [*A publication*]
Riv Dir Comm ... Rivista del Diritto Commerciale e del Diritto Generale delle Obbligazioni [*A publication*]
Riv Dir Europ ... Rivista di Diritto Europeo [*A publication*]
Riv Dir Finanz ... Rivista di Diritto Finanziaro e Scienza delle Finanze [*A publication*]
Riv Dir Ind ... Rivista di Diritto Industriale [*A publication*]
Riv Dir Int ... Rivista di Diritto Internazionale [*A publication*]
Riv Dir Int e Comp del Lavoro ... Rivista di Diritto Internazionale e Comparato del Lavoro [*Bologna, Italy*] [*A publication*]　(DLA)
Riv Dir Int'le ... Rivista di Diritto Internazionale [*A publication*]
Riv Dir Int'le Priv & Proc ... Rivista di Diritto Internazionale Privato e Processuale [*Padova, Italy*] [*A publication*]　(DLA)
Riv di Diritto Internaz ... Rivista di Diritto Internazionale [*A publication*]
Riv di Diritto Internaz e Comparato del Lavoro ... Rivista di Diritto Internazionale e Comparato del Lavoro [*Padua, Italy*] [*A publication*]　(DLA)
Riv Dir Proc Civ ... Rivista di Diritto e Procedura Civile [*A publication*]
Riv Dir Sport ... Rivista di Diritto Sportivo [*A publication*]
RIVDIV..... River Assault Division [*Military*]
RIVE.......... Resources in Vocational Education [*Database*] [*National Center for Research in Vocational Education*] [*Information service or system*]　(CRD)
RIVE.......... Riverside Properties [*NASDAQ symbol*]　(NQ)
Riv Ecol...... Rivista di Ecologia [*A publication*]
Riv Econ Agr ... Rivista di Economia Agraria [*A publication*]
Riv Emoter Immunoematol ... Rivista di Emoterapia ed Immunoematologia [*A publication*]
River Plat... Review of the River Plate [*A publication*]
Riv Et .... Rivista di Etnografia [*A publication*]

Riv Etnogr ... Rivista di Etnografia [*A publication*]
Riv Eur Sci Med Farmacol ... Rivista Europea per le Scienze Mediche e Farmacologiche [*A publication*]
Riv Farmacol Ter ... Rivista di Farmacologia e Terapia [*A publication*]
RivFC........ Rivista di Filologia e di Istruzione Classica [*A publication*]
Riv Fil .... Rivista di Filologia e di Istruzione Classica [*A publication*]
Riv Fil .... Rivista di Filosofia [*A publication*]
Riv Fil Class ... Rivista di Filologia e di Istruzione Classica [*A publication*]
Riv Filol Istruz Classica ... Rivista di Filologia e di Istruzione Classica [*A publication*]
Riv Filos..... Rivista di Filosofia [*A publication*]
Riv Filos Neo Scolast ... Rivista di Filosofia Neo-Scolastica [*A publication*]
Riv Filosof ... Rivista di Filosofia [*A publication*]
Riv Filosof Neo-Scolas ... Rivista di Filosofia Neo-Scolastica [*A publication*]
Riv Fin Loc ... Rivista della Finanza Locale [*A publication*]
Riv Fis Mat Sci Nat ... Rivista di Fisica, Matematica, e Scienze Naturali [*A publication*]
Riv Fitosanit ... Rivista Fitosanitaria [*A publication*]
RIVFLOT ... River Flotilla [*Military*]
RIVFLOTONE ... River Flotilla One [*Military*]
Riv Fotogr Ital ... Rivista Fotografica Italiana [*A publication*]
Riv Freddo ... Rivista del Freddo [*A publication*]
Riv Frutti ... Rivista di Frutticoltura [*A publication*]
Riv Fruttic ... Rivista di Frutticoltura [*A publication*]
Riv Gastro Enterol ... Rivista di Gastro-Enterologia [*A publication*]
Riv Gen Ital Chir ... Rivista Generale Italiana di Chirurgia [*A publication*]
Riv Geofis Appl ... Rivista di Geofisica Applicata [*A publication*]
Riv Geogr Ital ... Rivista Geografica Italiana [*A publication*]
Riv Geront Geriat ... Rivista di Gerontologia e Geriatria [*A publication*]
Riv Gerontol Geriatr ... Rivista di Gerontologia e Geriatria [*A publication*]
Riv Guard Fin ... Rivista della Guardia di Finanza [*A publication*]
Riv Idrobiol ... Rivista di Idrobiologia [*A publication*]
Riviera Sci ... Riviera Scientifique [*A publication*]
RivIGI........ Rivista Indo-Greco-Italico di Filologia, Lingua, Antichita [*A publication*]
Riv Ig e San Pubb ... Rivista d'Igiene e Sanita Pubblica [*A publication*]
Riv Ind .... Rivista di Diritto Industriale [*A publication*]
Riv Inf........ Rivista di Informatica [*A publication*]
Riv Inf........ Rivista dell'Informazione [*A publication*]
Riv Infort Mal Prof ... Rivista degli Infortuni e delle Malattie Professionali [*A publication*]
Riv Ing .... Rivista di Ingegneria [*A publication*]
Riv Ing Int ... Rivista Inguana et Intemelia [*A publication*]
Riv Ing Nucl ... Rivista di Ingegneria Nucleare [*A publication*]
Riv Int .... Rivista di Diritto Internazionale [*A publication*]
Riv Int Agric ... Rivista Internazionale di Agricoltura [*A publication*]
Riv Int Ec ... Rivista Internazionale di Scienze Economiche e Commerciali [*A publication*]
Riv Internaz di Filos del Diritto ... Rivista Internazionale di Filosofia del Diritto [*A publication*]
Riv Intern Sci Ec Comm ... Rivista Internazionale di Scienze Economiche e Commerciali [*A publication*]
Riv Intern Sci Soc ... Rivista Internazionale di Scienze Sociali [*A publication*]
Riv Int Filosof Diritto ... Rivista Internazionale di Filosofia del Diritto [*A publication*]
Riv Int Filos Polit Soc Dir Comp ... Rivista Internazionale di Filosofia Politica e Sociale e di Diritto Comparato [*A publication*]
Riv Int Sci Econ Com ... Rivista Internazionale di Scienze Economiche e Commerciali [*A publication*]
Riv Int Sci Soc ... Rivista Internazionale di Scienze Sociali [*A publication*]
Riv Ist Arch ... Rivista. Reale Istituto d'Archeologia e Storia dell'Arte [*A publication*]
Riv Istochim Norm Patol ... Rivista di Istochimica Normale e Patologica [*A publication*]
Riv Ist Sieroter Ital ... Rivista. Istituto Sieroterapico Italiano [*A publication*]
Riv Ist Vaccinogeno Consorzi Prov Antituberc ... Rivista. Istituto Vaccinogeno e Consorzi Provinciali Antitubercolari [*A publication*]
Riv Ital Amm Ec ... Rivista Italiana di Amministrazione dell'Economia e Sociologia Industriale [*A publication*]
Riv Ital Dir Proc Pen ... Rivista Italiana di Diritto e Procedura Penale [*A publication*]
Riv Ital Dir Soc ... Rivista Italiana di Diritto Sociale [*A publication*]
Riv Ital Essenze ... Rivista Italiana delle Essenze [*A publication*]
Riv Ital Essenze Profumi ... Rivista Italiana delle Essenze e Profumi [*A publication*]
Riv Ital Essenze Profumi Piante Off ... Rivista Italiana delle Essenze dei Profumi e delle Piante Officinali [*A publication*]
Riv Ital Essenze Profumi Piante Off Aromi Saponi Cosmet ... Rivista Italiana delle Essenze dei Profumi e delle Piante Officinali Aromi Saponi Cosmetici [*A publication*]
Riv Ital Essenze Profumi Piante Offic Aromi Saponi Cosmet ... Rivista Italiana delle Essenze dei Profumi e delle Piante Officinali Aromi Saponi Cosmetici [*A publication*]
Riv Ital Essenze Profumi Piante Offic Olii Veg Saponi ... Rivista Italiana delle Essenze dei Profumi e delle Piante Officinali Olii Vegetali Saponi [*A publication*]
Riv Ital Ge ... Rivista Italiana di Geofisica e Scienze Affini [*A publication*]
Riv Ital Geofis ... Rivista Italiana di Geofisica [*Italy*] [*A publication*]
Riv Ital Geotec ... Rivista Italiana di Geotecnica [*A publication*]
Riv Ital Ginecol ... Rivista Italiana di Ginecologia [*A publication*]

Riv Italiana Paleontologia e Stratigrafia ... Rivista Italiana di Paleontologia e Stratigrafia [*A publication*]
Riv Ital Ig... Rivista Italiana d'Igiene [*A publication*]
Riv Ital Metano ... Rivista Italiana de Metano [*A publication*]
Riv Ital Num ... Rivista Italiana di Numismatica e Scienze Affini [*A publication*]
Riv Ital Nutr Parenter Enterale ... Rivista Italiana di Nutrizione Parenterale ed Enterale [*A publication*]
Riv Ital Ornitol ... Rivista Italiana di Ornitologia [*A publication*]
Riv Ital Ortop Traumatol ... Rivista Italiana di Ortopedia e Traumatologia [*A publication*]
Riv Ital Paleontol Stratigr ... Rivista Italiana di Paleontologia e Stratigrafia [*A publication*]
Riv Ital Radiol Clin ... Rivista Italiana di Radiologia Clinica [*A publication*]
Riv Ital Saldatura ... Rivista Italiana della Saldatura [*A publication*]
Riv Ital per le Sc Giur ... Rivista Italiana per le Scienze Giuridiche [*A publication*] (OCD)
Riv Ital Sci Giur ... Rivista Italiana per le Scienze Giuridiche [*A publication*]
Riv Ital Sci Polit ... Rivista Italiana di Scienza Politica [*A publication*]
Riv Ital Sostanze Grasse ... Rivista Italiana delle Sostanze Grasse [*A publication*]
Riv Ital Sost Grasse ... Rivista Italiana delle Sostanze Grasse [*A publication*]
Riv Ital Stomatol ... Rivista Italiana di Stomatologia [*A publication*]
Riv Ital Trac Patol Ocul Virale Esotica ... Rivista Italiana del Tracoma e di Patologia Oculare, Virale, ed Esotica [*A publication*]
Riv It Num ... Rivista Italiana di Numismatica e Scienze Affini [*A publication*]
RIVL......... Regesten van de Aanwinsten van het Institut voor Vergelijkend Literatuuronderzoek aan de Rijksuniversiteit te Utrecht [*A publication*]
RIVL.......... Rival Manufacturing [*NASDAQ symbol*] (NQ)
RivL .... Rivista Letteraria. Licei Classico, Scientifico, Artistico, e Istituto Magistrale [*A publication*]
Riv Let Mod ... Rivista di Letteratura Moderne e Comparate [*A publication*]
Riv Lett Class ... Rivista di Letteratura Classiche [*A publication*]
Riv Lett Mod ... Rivista di Letteratura Moderne [*A publication*]
Riv Lig ...... Rivista di Studi Liguri [*A publication*]
Riv Liturg... Rivista Liturgica [*A publication*]
Riv Malariol ... Rivista Malariologia [*A publication*]
Riv Maritt ... Rivista Marittima [*A publication*]
Riv Mat Sci Econom Social ... Rivista di Matematica per le Scienze Economiche e Sociali [*A publication*]
Riv Mat Univ Parma ... Rivista di Matematica. Universita di Parma [*A publication*]
Riv Mat Univ Parma 4 ... Rivista di Matematica. Universita di Parma. Serie 4 [*A publication*]
Riv Mecc.... Rivista di Meccanica [*A publication*]
Riv Med Aer ... Rivista di Medicina Aeronautica e Spaziale [*A publication*]
Riv Med Aeronaut ... Rivista di Medicina Aeronautica e Spaziale [*A publication*]
Riv Med Aeronaut Spaz ... Rivista di Medicina Aeronautica e Spaziale [*A publication*]
Riv Med Vet Zootec ... Rivista di Medicina Veterinaria e Zootecnica [*A publication*]
Riv Mens Svizz Odontol Stomatol ... Rivista Mensile Svizzera di Odontologia e Stomatologia [*A publication*]
Riv Meteo A ... Rivista di Meteorologia Aeronautica [*A publication*]
Riv Meteorol Aeronaut ... Rivista di Meteorologia Aeronautica [*A publication*]
Riv Mineral Cristallogr Ital ... Rivista di Mineralogia e Cristallografia Italiana [*A publication*]
Riv Mineraria Sicil ... Rivista Mineraria Siciliana [*Italy*] [*A publication*]
Riv Min Sicil ... Rivista Mineraria Siciliana [*A publication*]
Riv Mus Italiana ... Rivista Musicale Italiana [*A publication*]
Riv Neurobiol ... Rivista di Neurobiologia [*A publication*]
Riv Neurol ... Rivista di Neurologia [*A publication*]
Riv Neuropsichiatr Sci Affini ... Rivista di Neuropsichiatria e Scienze Affini [*A publication*]
Riv Nuovo Cim ... Rivista del Nuovo Cimento [*A publication*]
Riv Nuovo Cimento ... Rivista del Nuovo Cimento [*A publication*]
Riv Nuovo Cimento 2 ... Rivista del Nuovo Cimento. Serie 2 [*A publication*]
Riv Nuovo Cimento 3 ... Rivista del Nuovo Cimento. Serie 3 [*A publication*]
Riv Nuovo Cimento Ser 1 ... Rivista del Nuovo Cimento. Serie 1 [*A publication*]
Riv Nuovo Cimento Soc Ital Fis ... Rivista del Nuovo Cimento. Societa Italiana di Fisica [*Italy*] [*A publication*]
Riv Odontostomatol Implantoprotesi ... Rivista de Odontostomatologia e Implantoprotesi [*A publication*]
Rivoluzione Ind ... Rivoluzione Industriale [*Italy*] [*A publication*]
Riv Ortoflorofruttic Ital ... Rivista della Ortoflorofrutticoltura Italiana [*A publication*]
Riv Osp Roma ... Rivista Ospedaliera Roma [*A publication*]
Riv Ostet Ginecol (Flor) ... Rivista di Ostetricia e Ginecologia (Florence) [*A publication*]
Riv Ostet Ginecol Prat ... Rivista di Ostetricia e Ginecologia Pratica [*A publication*]
Riv Ostet Ginecol Prat Med Perinat ... Rivista di Ostetricia e Ginecologia Pratica e di Medicina Perinatale [*A publication*]
Riv Oto-Neuro-Oftalmol ... Rivista Oto-Neuro-Oftalmologica [*A publication*]
Riv Oto-Neuro-Oftalmol Radio-Neuro-Chir ... Rivista Oto-Neuro-Oftalmologica e Radio-Neuro-Chirurgica [*A publication*]

Riv Parassit ... Rivista di Parassitologia [*A publication*]
Riv Parassitol ... Rivista di Parassitologia [*A publication*]
Riv Patol Appar Respir ... Rivista Patologia dell'Apparato Respiratorio [*A publication*]
Riv Patol Clin ... Rivista di Patologia e Clinica [*A publication*]
Riv Patol Clin Sper ... Rivista di Patologia Clinica e Sperimentale [*A publication*]
Riv Patol Clin Tuberc ... Rivista di Patologia e Clinica della Tubercolosi [*A publication*]
Riv Patol Clin Tuberc Pneumol ... Rivista di Patologia e Clinica della Tubercolosi e di Pneumologia [*A publication*]
Riv Patol Nerv Ment ... Rivista di Patologia Nervosa e Mentale [*A publication*]
Riv Patol Sper ... Rivista di Patologia Sperimentale [*A publication*]
Riv Patol Veg ... Rivista di Patologia Vegetale [*A publication*]
RivPed........ Rivista Pedagogica [*A publication*]
Riv Pediatr Sicil ... Rivista Pediatricia Siciliana [*A publication*]
Riv Per Lav Accad Sc Lett ed Arti Padova ... Rivista Periodica del Lavori. Accademia di Scienze, Lettere, ed Arti di Padova [*A publication*]
Riv Polit Agr ... Rivista di Politica Agraria [*A publication*]
Riv Polit Econ ... Rivista di Politica Economica [*A publication*]
RivR .... Rivista delle Religioni [*A publication*]
Riv Radiol .. Rivista di Radiologia [*A publication*]
Riv Rosmin Filos Cult ... Rivista Rosminiana di Filosofia e di Cultura [*A publication*]
Riv Sci Tecnol Alimenti Nutr Um ... Rivista di Scienza e Tecnologia degli Alimenti e di Nutrizione Umana [*A publication*]
Riv Sci Tecnol Aliment Nutr Umana ... Rivista di Scienza e Tecnologia degli Alimenti e di Nutrizione Umana [*A publication*]
Riv Sc Pr ... Rivista di Scienze Preistoriche [*A publication*]
Riv Sicil Tuberc Mal Respir ... Rivista Siciliana della Tubercolosi e delle Malattie Respiratorie [*A publication*]
Riv Sociol ... Rivista di Sociologia [*A publication*]
Riv Sper Freniatr Med Leg Alienazioni Ment ... Rivista Sperimentale di Freniatria e Medicina Legale delle Alienazioni Mentali [*A publication*]
Riv St Lig... Rivista di Studi Liguri [*A publication*]
Riv Stor...... Rivista Storica Italiana [*A publication*]
Riv St Or... Rivista degli Studi Orientali [*A publication*]
Riv Stor Chiesa Ital ... Rivista di Storia della Chiesa in Italia [*A publication*]
Riv Stor It .. Rivista Storica Italiana [*A publication*]
Riv Stor Ital ... Rivista Storica Italiana [*A publication*]
Riv Stor Med ... Rivista di Storia della Medicina [*A publication*]
Riv Stud Croci ... Rivista di Studi Crociani [*A publication*]
Riv Studi Cl ... Rivista di Studi Classici [*A publication*]
Riv Studi Polit Int ... Rivista di Studi Politici Internazionali [*A publication*]
RivStudOr ... Rivista degli Studi Orientali [*A publication*]
Riv Stud Orient ... Rivista degli Studi Orientali [*A publication*]
Riv Suinicolt ... Rivista di Suinicoltura [*A publication*]
Riv Svizz Apic ... Rivista Svizzera di Apicoltura [*A publication*]
Riv Svizz Med Sport ... Rivista Svizzera di Medicina dello Sport [*A publication*]
RIVT......... RECO International [*AMEX symbol*] (SPSG)
RIVT......... Rivulet (ADA)
Riv Tec Elettr ... Rivista Tecnica d'Elettricita [*A publication*]
Riv Tec Ferrovie Ital ... Rivista Tecnica delle Ferrovie Italiane [*A publication*]
Riv Tess ...... Rivista Tessile [*A publication*]
Riv Tossicol Sper Clin ... Rivista di Tossicologia Sperimentale e Clinica [*A publication*]
Riv Trim Dir Pubbl ... Rivista Trimestrale di Diritto Pubblico [*A publication*]
Riv Trimest di Diritto Pubbl ... Rivista Trimestrale di Diritto Pubblico [*A publication*]
Riv Tuberc Mal Appar Respir ... Rivista della Tubercolosi e delle Malattie dell'Apparato Respiratorio [*A publication*]
Riv Tuberc Mal App Resp ... Rivista della Tubercolosi e delle Malattie dell'Apparato Respiratorio [*A publication*]
Riv Veneta Sc Med ... Rivista Veneta di Scienze Mediche [*A publication*]
Riv Vet....... Rivista di Veterinaria [*A publication*]
Riv Vitic Enol ... Rivista di Viticoltura e di Enologia [*A publication*]
Riv World .. River World [*A publication*]
Riv Zootec ... Rivista di Zootecnia e Veterinaria [*A publication*]
Riv Zootec Vet ... Rivista di Zootecnia e Veterinaria [*A publication*]
RIW .... Recht der Internationalen Wirtschaft [*German*] [*A publication*] (DLA)
RIW .... Reliability Improvement Warranty [*Navy*]
RIW .... Repaired in Works [*British military*] (DMA)
RIW .... Review of Income and Wealth [*A publication*]
RIW .... Riverton [*Wyoming*] [*Airport symbol*] (OAG)
RI Water Res Coordinating Board Geol Bull Hydrol Bull ... Rhode Island. Water Resources Coordinating Board. Geological Bulletin. Hydrologic Bulletin [*A publication*]
RI Water Resour Cent Annu Rep ... Rhode Island. Water Resources Center. Annual Report [*A publication*]
RI Water Resour Coord Board Geol Bull ... Rhode Island. Water Resources Coordinating Board. Geological Bulletin [*A publication*]
RIWC........ Royal Institute of Painters in Water-Colours [*British*] (ROG)
Riwt........... Rich International White Trash [*Lifestyle classification*]
RIX .... Riga [*USSR*] [*Airport symbol*] (OAG)
RIX .... University of Rhode Island, Extension Division Library, Providence, RI [*OCLC symbol*] (OCLC)

RIXT.........	Remote Information Exchange Terminal (MCD)
RIY	Renaissance of Italian Youth (EA)
RIZ............	Radio Industry Zagreb [*Yugoslavia*]
RIZ............	Rio Alzucar [*Panama*] [*Airport symbol*] (OAG)
Rizh Med Inst Sb Nauchn Rab ... Rizhskii Meditsinskii Institut. Sbornik Nauchnykh Rabot [*A publication*]
Riz Rizi ...... Riz et Riziculture [*A publication*]
Riz Rizicult Cult Vivr Trop ... Riz et Riziculture et Cultures Vivrieres Tropicales [*A publication*]
Rizsk Inst Inz Grazdan Aviacii ... Rizskii Institut Inzenerov Grazdanskoi Aviacii Imeni Leninskogo Komsomola [*A publication*]
RJ..............	A'Beckett's Reserved Judgements [*Port Phillip*] [*A publication*] (ILCA)
R(J)...........	Justiciary Cases [*Scotland*] [*A publication*] (DLA)
RJ..............	La Reveil Juif. Sfax [*A publication*] (BJA)
RJ..............	New South Wales, Port Phillip District Judgments [*Australia*] [*A publication*] (DLA)
R & J	Rabkin and Johnson's Federal, Income, Gift, and Estate Taxation [*A publication*] (DLA)
RJ..............	RADAR/Jimsphere
R & J	Rafique and Jackson's Privy Council Decisions [*India*] [*A publication*] (DLA)
RJ..............	Ramjet
RJ..............	Reform Judaism (BJA)
RJ..............	Reformed Journal [*A publication*]
RJ..............	Reject
RJ..............	Revista Javeriana [*A publication*]
RJ..............	Revue Judiciaire, by Bruzard [*1843-44*] [*Mauritius*] [*A publication*]
R de J	Revue de Jurisprudence [*Quebec*] [*A publication*] (DLA)
RJ..............	Revue de Jurisprudence [*A publication*] (DLA)
RJ..............	[*The*] River Jordan [*A publication*] (BJA)
RJ..............	Road Junction [*Maps and charts*]
RJ..............	Romanistisches Jahrbuch [*A publication*]
R & J	Romeo and Juliet [*Shakespearean work*]
RJ..............	Rotary Joint
RJ..............	Royal Jordanian Airlines Co. [*Arab Air Cargo*] [*Jordan*] [*ICAO designator*] (FAAC)
RJ..............	Rusky Jazyk [*A publication*]
RJ11..........	Standard modular telephone jack for a single line instrument (TSSD)
RJ 500.......	Rolls-Japan 500 [*Type of Rolls-Royce engine*]
RJA............	Ramjet Addition (AAG)
RJA............	Reform Jewish Appeal (EA)
RJA............	Retail Jewelers of America [*Later, JA*] (EA)
RJA............	Rotary Joint Assembly
RJA............	Royal Jersey Artillery [*Military unit*] [*British*]
RJA............	Russko-Jewrejsky Archiw [*A publication*] (BJA)
RJAA.........	Tokyo/New Tokyo International [*Japan*] [*ICAO location identifier*] (ICLI)
RJAC.........	Revue Juridique de l'Afrique Centrale [*A publication*]
RJAF.........	Matsumoto [*Japan*] [*ICAO location identifier*] (ICLI)
RJAF.........	Royal Jordanian Air Force
RJAH........	Hyakuri [*Japan*] [*ICAO location identifier*] (ICLI)
RJAI.........	Ichigaya [*Japan*] [*ICAO location identifier*] (ICLI)
RJAK........	Kasumigaura [*Japan*] [*ICAO location identifier*] (ICLI)
RJAM........	Minamitorishima [*Japan*] [*ICAO location identifier*] (ICLI)
RJAO........	Chichijima [*Japan*] [*ICAO location identifier*] (ICLI)
RJaS.........	Russkij Jazyk v Skole [*A publication*]
RJAT.........	Takigahara [*Japan*] [*ICAO location identifier*] (ICLI)
RJav..........	Revista Javeriana [*A publication*]
RJAW........	Iwo Jima [*Japan*] [*ICAO location identifier*] (ICLI)
RJaz..........	Rusky Jazyk [*A publication*]
Rjazansk Gos Ped Inst Ucen Zap ... Rjazanskii Gosudarstvennyi Pedagogiceskii Institut. Ucenye Zapiski [*A publication*]
RJB...........	Rajbiraj [*Nepal*] [*Airport symbol*] [*Obsolete*] (OAG)
RJB...........	Relay Junction Box (KSC)
RJb............	Romanistisches Jahrbuch [*A publication*]
RJB...........	Ruby Jewel Bearing
RJBD.........	Nanki-Shirahama [*Japan*] [*ICAO location identifier*] (ICLI)
RJBE.........	Relative Jostle Biological Effectiveness
RJC...........	Ranger Junior College [*Texas*]
RJC...........	Reaction Jet Control [*NASA*] (NASA)
RJC...........	Revue Juridique du Congo [*A publication*]
RJC...........	Robinson Jeffers Committee (EA)
RJC...........	Rochester Junior College [*Minnesota*] [*Later, Rochester Community College*]
RJCA.........	Asahikawa [*Japan*] [*ICAO location identifier*] (ICLI)
RJCB.........	Obihiro [*Japan*] [*ICAO location identifier*] (ICLI)
RJCB.........	Revue Juridique du Congo Belge [*A publication*]
RJCC.........	Sapporo/Chitose [*Japan*] [*ICAO location identifier*] (ICLI)
RJCG.........	Sapporo [*Japan*] [*ICAO location identifier*] (ICLI)
RJCH........	Hakodate [*Japan*] [*ICAO location identifier*] (ICLI)
RJCK........	Kushiro [*Japan*] [*ICAO location identifier*] (ICLI)
RJCM........	New Memanbetsu [*Japan*] [*ICAO location identifier*] (ICLI)
RJCN........	Nakashibetsu [*Japan*] [*ICAO location identifier*] (ICLI)
RJCO.........	Sapporo/Okadama [*Japan*] [*ICAO location identifier*] (ICLI)
RJCR.........	Rebun [*Japan*] [*ICAO location identifier*] (ICLI)
RJCS.........	Kushiro/Kenebetsu [*Japan*] [*ICAO location identifier*] (ICLI)
RJCT.........	Tokachi [*Japan*] [*ICAO location identifier*] (ICLI)
RJCW........	Wakkanai [*Japan*] [*ICAO location identifier*] (ICLI)
RJCY.........	Muroran/Yakumo [*Japan*] [*ICAO location identifier*] (ICLI)
RJD...........	Reaction Jet Device [*NASA*] (NASA)
RJD...........	Reaction Jet Driver [*NASA*] (NASA)
RJDA.........	Rassemblement des Jeunesses Democratiques Africaines [*Rally of African Democratic Youth*]
RJDA.........	Reaction Jet Driver - Aft [*NASA*] (NASA)
RJDB.........	Iki [*Japan*] [*ICAO location identifier*] (ICLI)
RJDC.........	Yamaguchi-Ube, Honshu Island [*Japan*] [*ICAO location identifier*] (ICLI)
RJDF.........	Reaction Jet Driver - Forward [*NASA*] (NASA)
RJDG.........	Fukuoka [*Japan*] [*ICAO location identifier*] (ICLI)
R & J Dig...	Robinson and Joseph's Digest [*Ontario*] [*A publication*] (DLA)
RJDK.........	Kamigoto [*Japan*] [*ICAO location identifier*] (ICLI)
RJDM........	Metabaru [*Japan*] [*ICAO location identifier*] (ICLI)
RJDO.........	Ojika [*Japan*] [*ICAO location identifier*] (ICLI)
RJDT.........	Tsushima [*Japan*] [*ICAO location identifier*] (ICLI)
RJE...........	Ramjet Engine
RJE...........	Rayleigh-Jeans Equation [*Physics*]
RJE...........	Remote Job Entry [*Data processing*]
RJEB.........	Monbetsu [*Japan*] [*ICAO location identifier*] (ICLI)
RJEC.........	Asahikawa [*Japan*] [*ICAO location identifier*] (ICLI)
RJ/EC........	Reaction Jet/Engine Control [*NASA*] (NASA)
RJEO.........	Okushiri [*Japan*] [*ICAO location identifier*] (ICLI)
RJER.........	Rishiri Island [*Japan*] [*ICAO location identifier*] (ICLI)
RJETS.......	Remote Job Entry Terminal System [*Data processing*] (MCD)
RJF...........	Les Rejaudoux [*France*] [*Seismograph station code, US Geological Survey*] (SEIS)
RJF...........	Raymond James Financial, Inc. [*NYSE symbol*] (SPSG)
RJFA.........	Ashiya [*Japan*] [*ICAO location identifier*] (ICLI)
RJFA.........	Roumanian Jewish Federation of America (EA)
RJFB.........	Gannosu/Brady [*Japan*] [*ICAO location identifier*] (ICLI)
RJFC.........	Yakushima [*Japan*] [*ICAO location identifier*] (ICLI)
RJFE.........	Fukue [*Japan*] [*ICAO location identifier*] (ICLI)
RJFF.........	Fukuoka [*Japan*] [*ICAO location identifier*] (ICLI)
RJFG.........	Tanegashima [*Japan*] [*ICAO location identifier*] (ICLI)
RJFK.........	Kagoshima [*Japan*] [*ICAO location identifier*] (ICLI)
RJFM........	Miyazaki [*Japan*] [*ICAO location identifier*] (ICLI)
RJFN........	Nyutabaru [*Japan*] [*ICAO location identifier*] (ICLI)
RJFN........	RJ Financial Corp. [*NASDAQ symbol*] (NQ)
RJFO.........	Oita [*Japan*] [*ICAO location identifier*] (ICLI)
RJFR.........	Kitakyushu [*Japan*] [*ICAO location identifier*] (ICLI)
RJFT.........	Kumamoto [*Japan*] [*ICAO location identifier*] (ICLI)
RJFU.........	Nagasaki [*Japan*] [*ICAO location identifier*] (ICLI)
RJFY.........	Kanoya [*Japan*] [*ICAO location identifier*] (ICLI)
RJFZ.........	Tsuiki [*Japan*] [*ICAO location identifier*] (ICLI)
RJICA	Russian Journal of Inorganic Chemistry [*English Translation*] [*A publication*]
RJIS..........	Regional Justice Information System
RJK...........	Rijeka [*Yugoslavia*] [*Airport symbol*] (OAG)
RJKA.........	Amami [*Japan*] [*ICAO location identifier*] (ICLI)
RJKB.........	Okierabu [*Japan*] [*ICAO location identifier*] (ICLI)
RJKI.........	Kikai/Kikaigashima Island [*Japan*] [*ICAO location identifier*] (ICLI)
RJKN........	Tokunoshima Island [*Japan*] [*ICAO location identifier*] (ICLI)
RJL...........	Revue Juive de la Lorraine [*A publication*]
RJLI.........	Royal Jersey Light Infantry [*Military unit*] [*British*]
RJM..........	Reed, John M., San Antonio TX [*STAC*]
RJM..........	Religious of Jesus-Mary [*Roman Catholic women's religious order*]
RJM..........	Royal Jersey Militia [*Military unit*] [*British*]
RJM..........	Warner Robins, GA [*Location identifier*] [*FAA*] (FAAL)
RJMBA	Roczniki Akademii Medycznej Imienia Juliana Marchlewskiego w Bialymstoku [*A publication*]
RJN..........	Robinson Jeffers Newsletter [*A publication*]
RJNF........	Fukui [*Japan*] [*ICAO location identifier*] (ICLI)
RJNG........	Gifu [*Japan*] [*ICAO location identifier*] (ICLI)
RJNH........	Hamamatsu [*Japan*] [*ICAO location identifier*] (ICLI)
RJNK........	Kanazawa/Komatsu [*Japan*] [*ICAO location identifier*] (ICLI)
RJNN........	Nagoya [*Japan*] [*ICAO location identifier*] (ICLI)
RJNO........	Oki [*Japan*] [*ICAO location identifier*] (ICLI)
RJNT........	Toyama [*Japan*] [*ICAO location identifier*] (ICLI)
RJNY........	Yaizu/Shizuhama [*Japan*] [*ICAO location identifier*] (ICLI)
RJO..........	Rapports Judiciaires Officiels de Quebec [*Quebec Official Law Reports*] [*A publication*] (ILCA)
RJO	Remote Job Output [*Data processing*]
RJO	Revolutionary Justice Organization [*Lebanese terrorist group*]
RJOA........	Hiroshima [*Japan*] [*ICAO location identifier*] (ICLI)
RJOB........	Okayama [*Japan*] [*ICAO location identifier*] (ICLI)
RJOC........	Izumo [*Japan*] [*ICAO location identifier*] (ICLI)
RJOD........	Reaction Jet OMS [*Orbital Maneuvering Subsystem*] Driver [*NASA*] (NASA)
RJOE........	Akeno [*Japan*] [*ICAO location identifier*] (ICLI)
RJOF........	Hofu [*Japan*] [*ICAO location identifier*] (ICLI)
RJOH........	Miho [*Japan*] [*ICAO location identifier*] (ICLI)
RJOI.........	Iwakuni [*Japan*] [*ICAO location identifier*] (ICLI)
RJOK........	Kochi [*Japan*] [*ICAO location identifier*] (ICLI)
RJOM........	Matsuyama [*Japan*] [*ICAO location identifier*] (ICLI)
RJOO	Osaka/International [*Japan*] [*ICAO location identifier*] (ICLI)
RJOP........	Komatsujima [*Japan*] [*ICAO location identifier*] (ICLI)

RJOQ (BR) ... Rapports Judiciaires Officiels de Quebec, Cour du Banc du Roi [*Quebec Official Law Reports, King's Bench*] [*A publication*]   (ILCA)
RJOQ (CS) ... Rapports Judiciaires Officiels de Quebec, Cour Superieure [*Quebec Official Law Reports, Superior Court*] [*A publication*]   (ILCA)
RJOR........ Tottori [*Japan*] [*ICAO location identifier*]   (ICLI)
RJOS........ Tokushima [*Japan*] [*ICAO location identifier*]   (ICLI)
RJOT........ Takamatsu [*Japan*] [*ICAO location identifier*]   (ICLI)
RJOY........ Osaka/Yao [*Japan*] [*ICAO location identifier*]   (ICLI)
RJOZ........ Ozuki [*Japan*] [*ICAO location identifier*]   (ICLI)
RJP............ Reaction Jet Pipe
RJP............ Realistic Job Preview
RJP............ Remote Job Processing [*Data processing*]
RJP............ RJP Electronics [*Vancouver Stock Exchange symbol*]
RJP............ Rocket Jet Plume
RJPCA...... Russian Journal of Physical Chemistry [*English Translation*] [*A publication*]
RJPIC....... Revue Juridique et Politique. Independance et Cooperation [*A publication*]
RJ & PJ ..... Revenue, Judicial, and Police Journal [*Calcutta*] [*A publication*]   (DLA)
RJQ .... Rapports Judiciaires [*Quebec Law Reports*] [*A publication*]   (DLA)
RJQ BR ..... Rapports Judiciaires de Quebec, Cour du Banc du Roi [*Quebec Law Reports, King's Bench*] [*A publication*]   (DLA)
RJQ CS...... Rapports Judiciaires de Quebec, Cour Superieure [*Quebec Law Reports, Superior Court*] [*A publication*]   (DLA)
RJR............ Mathieu's Quebec Revised Reports [*A publication*]   (DLA)
RJR............ R. J. Reynolds Tobacco Co.
RJR............ RJR Nabisco, Inc. [*NYSE symbol*]   (SPSG)
RJR............ Rotary Joint Reed
RJR............ Russkij Jazyk za Rubezom [*A publication*]
RJRA......... Rotary Joint Reed Assembly
RJRB......... Revue Juridique du Rwanda et du Burundi [*A publication*]
RJRQ......... Mathieu's Quebec Revised Reports [*A publication*]   (DLA)
RJS............ Reaction Jet System   (KSC)
RJS............ Remote Job System [*Data processing*]   (MCD)
RJS............ Richard Jeffries Society   (EAIO)
RJS............ Roberta Jo Society   (EA)
RJS............ Russkij Jazyk v Skole [*A publication*]
RJS............ Ruth Jackson Society   (EA)
RJSA......... Aomori [*Japan*] [*ICAO location identifier*]   (ICLI)
RJSC......... Yamagata [*Japan*] [*ICAO location identifier*]   (ICLI)
RJSCA....... Revue Jeumont-Schneider [*A publication*]
RJSD......... Sado [*Japan*] [*ICAO location identifier*]   (ICLI)
RJSFC....... R. J. Sutton Fan Club   (EA)
RJSH........ Hachinohe [*Japan*] [*ICAO location identifier*]   (ICLI)
RJSHDQ... Jugoslovanski Simpozij za Hmeljarstvo Referati [*A publication*]
RJSI.......... Hanamaki [*Japan*] [*ICAO location identifier*]   (ICLI)
RJSK......... Akita [*Japan*] [*ICAO location identifier*]   (ICLI)
RJSM .... Misawa [*Japan*] [*ICAO location identifier*]   (ICLI)
RJSN......... Niigata [*Japan*] [*ICAO location identifier*]   (ICLI)
RJSO......... Ominato [*Japan*] [*ICAO location identifier*]   (ICLI)
RJSS......... Sendai [*Japan*] [*ICAO location identifier*]   (ICLI)
RJST......... Matsushima [*Japan*] [*ICAO location identifier*]   (ICLI)
RJSU......... Kasuminome [*Japan*] [*ICAO location identifier*]   (ICLI)
RJT............ Rassemblement des Jeunes Togolais [*Togolese Youth Rally*]
RJT............ Reference Jet Transport
RJT............ Rejection Message [*Communications*]   (FAAC)
RJT............ Revue Juridique Themis [*A publication*]
RJT............ Royal Jubilee Trust [*Provides financial aid to start new businesses*] [*British*]
RJTA......... Atsugi [*Japan*] [*ICAO location identifier*]   (ICLI)
RJTC......... Tachikawa [*Japan*] [*ICAO location identifier*]   (ICLI)
RJTD......... Tokyo [*Japan*] [*ICAO location identifier*]   (ICLI)
RJTE......... Tateyama [*Japan*] [*ICAO location identifier*]   (ICLI)
RJTF......... Chofu [*Japan*] [*ICAO location identifier*]   (ICLI)
RJTG......... Tokyo [*Japan*] [*ICAO location identifier*]   (ICLI)
RJTH......... Hachijojima [*Japan*] [*ICAO location identifier*]   (ICLI)
RJTI.......... Tokyo [*Japan*] [*ICAO location identifier*]   (ICLI)
RJTJ.......... Iruma [*Japan*] [*ICAO location identifier*]   (ICLI)
RJTK......... Kisarazu [*Japan*] [*ICAO location identifier*]   (ICLI)
RJTL......... Shimofusa [*Japan*] [*ICAO location identifier*]   (ICLI)
RJTO......... Oshima [*Japan*] [*ICAO location identifier*]   (ICLI)
RJTQ......... Miyakejima [*Japan*] [*ICAO location identifier*]   (ICLI)
RJTR......... Zama/Rankin [*Japan*] [*ICAO location identifier*]   (ICLI)
RJTT......... Tokyo/International [*Japan*] [*ICAO location identifier*]   (ICLI)
RJTU......... Utsunomiya [*Japan*] [*ICAO location identifier*]   (ICLI)
RJTV......... Ramjet Test Vehicle
RJTW........ Zama [*Japan*] [*ICAO location identifier*]   (ICLI)
RJTY......... Yokota [*Japan*] [*ICAO location identifier*]   (ICLI)
RJTZ......... Fuchu [*Japan*] [*ICAO location identifier*]   (ICLI)
R Jur......... Revue Juridique [*A publication*]
R de Jur...... Revue de Jurisprudence [*Quebec*] [*A publication*]   (DLA)
R Juridique ... Revue Juridique [*A publication*]
R Juridique et Econ Sud-Ouest Ser Econ ... Revue Juridique et Economique du Sud-Ouest. Serie Economique [*A publication*]
R Juridique et Pol ... Revue Juridique et Politique [*A publication*]
R Jur Polit ... Revue Juridique et Politique. Independance et Cooperation [*A publication*]

RJV............ Rheinisches Jahrbuch fuer Volkskunde [*A publication*]
RK.............. Air Afrique [*Ivory Coast*] [*ICAO designator*]   (ICDA)
RK.............. Ark Restaurants Corp. [*AMEX symbol*]   (SPSG)
RK.............. Rabbit Kidney
RK.............. Rack
RK.............. Radial Keratotomy [*Ophthalmology*]
RK.............. Rassemblement Katangais [*Katanga Rally*]
RK.............. Rat Kidney
RK.............. Realkatalog der Aegyptologie [*A publication*]   (BJA)
R-K............ Redlich-Kwong [*Physics*]
R/K............ Rekening-Koerant [*Current Account*] [*Business term*] [*Afrikaans*]
RK.............. Republic of Korea [*IYRU nationality code*]   (IYR)
RK.............. Rhodopsin Kinase [*An enzyme*]
RK.............. Right Kidney
RK.............. Right to Know   (EA)
RK.............. Rock [*Maps and charts*]   (MCD)
RK.............. Royal Knight [*British*]
RK.............. Rubbing Keel [*of a ship*]   (DS)
RK.............. Run of Kiln
RK.............. Societe Air Afrique [*Cameroon*] [*ICAO designator*]   (FAAC)
RKA.......... Rockdale, NY [*Location identifier*] [*FAA*]   (FAAL)
RKAF........ Royal Khmer Air Force [*Cambodia*]   (CINC)
RKANA...... Rost Kristallov [*A publication*]
RKB.......... Red Kidney Bean
RKCC........ Right to Know Committee of Correspondence [*Defunct*]   (EA)
RKCLA...... Reaction Kinetics and Catalysis Letters [*A publication*]
RKCSN...... Rospravy Kralovske Ceske Spolecnosti Nauk [*A publication*]
RKD.......... Rockland [*Maine*] [*Airport symbol*]   (OAG)
RKE.......... Roskilde [*Denmark*] [*Airport symbol*]   (OAG)
RKFC........ Ray Kirkland Fan Club   (EA)
RKFJ......... Rad Kongresa Folklorista Jugoslavije [*A publication*]
RKG.......... Radiocardiogram
RKG.......... Rockingham R. R. [*AAR code*]
RKG.......... Royal Khmer Government [*Cambodia*]
RKH.......... Rock Hill [*South Carolina*] [*Airport symbol*]   (OAG)
RKH.......... Rockingham Resources, Inc. [*Vancouver Stock Exchange symbol*]
RKHLit...... Rocznik Komisji Historycznoliterackiej Pan [*A publication*]
RKHS........ Register. Kentucky Historical Society [*A publication*]
RK II......... Runge-Kutta Second Order [*Mathematics*]
RKJ........... Ramsey, Kenneth J., Pittsburgh PA [*STAC*]
RKJ........... Rozprawy Komisji Jezykowej Lodzkiego Towarzystwa Naukowego [*A publication*]
RKJJ......... Kwangju [*Republic of Korea*] [*ICAO location identifier*]   (ICLI)
RKJK......... Kunsan [*Republic of Korea*] [*ICAO location identifier*]   (ICLI)
RKJL......... Rozprawy Komisji Jezykowej Lodzkiego Towarzystwa Naukowego [*A publication*]
RKJM........ Mokpo [*Republic of Korea*] [*ICAO location identifier*]   (ICLI)
RKJO......... Hongjungri [*Republic of Korea*] [*ICAO location identifier*]   (ICLI)
RKJU........ Jhunju [*Republic of Korea*] [*ICAO location identifier*]   (ICLI)
RKJW........ Rozprawy Komisji Jezykowej Wroclawskiego Towarzystwa Naukowego [*A publication*]
RKJY .... Yeosu [*Republic of Korea*] [*ICAO location identifier*]   (ICLI)
RKKA........ Raboche-Krest'ianskaia Krasnaia Armiia [*Workers' and Peasants' Red Army*] [*Redesignated Soviety Army*] [*USSR*]
RKKHA ..... Rikagaku Kenkyusho Hokoku [*A publication*]
RKL........... Right Knee Left [*Guitar playing*]
RKL........... Ruskin Developments Ltd. [*Vancouver Stock Exchange symbol*]
RKLM ...... Ruskin Developments Ltd. [*NASDAQ symbol*]   (NQ)
RKM.......... Risk Management [*A publication*]
RKM.......... Runge-Kutta Method [*Mathematics*]
RKN.......... Root Knot Nematode [*Plant pathology*]
RKN.......... Runge-Kutta-Nystroem [*Formula*] [*Mathematics*]
RKNC........ Chunchon [*Republic of Korea*] [*ICAO location identifier*]   (ICLI)
RKND........ Sokcho [*Republic of Korea*] [*ICAO location identifier*]   (ICLI)
RKNFSYS ... Rock Information System [*National Science Foundation*] [*Carnegie Institution*] [*Databank*]   (IID)
RKNH........ Heongsung [*Republic of Korea*] [*ICAO location identifier*]   (ICLI)
RKNI......... Injae [*Republic of Korea*] [*ICAO location identifier*]   (ICLI)
RKNK........ Kwandaeri [*Republic of Korea*] [*ICAO location identifier*]   (ICLI)
RKNKA ..... Rakuno Kagaku No Kenkyu [*A publication*]
RKNN........ Kangnung [*Republic of Korea*] [*ICAO location identifier*]   (ICLI)
RKNW........ Wonju [*Republic of Korea*] [*ICAO location identifier*]   (ICLI)
RKNY........ Yangku [*Republic of Korea*] [*ICAO location identifier*]   (ICLI)
RKO.......... Radio-Keith-Orpheum [*Motion picture production and exhibition firm, also active in broadcasting*]
RKO.......... Range Keeper Operator [*Navy*]
RKP........... Rockport, TX [*Location identifier*] [*FAA*]   (FAAL)
RKP........... Routledge & Kegan Paul [*British publisher*]
RKPC......... Cheju/International [*Republic of Korea*] [*ICAO location identifier*]   (ICLI)
RKPD .... Chedong [*Republic of Korea*] [*ICAO location identifier*]   (ICLI)

RKPE.........	Chinhae [*Republic of Korea*] [*ICAO location identifier*] (ICLI)
RKPK........	Kimhae/International [*Republic of Korea*] [*ICAO location identifier*] (ICLI)
RKPM	Cheju/Mosulpo [*Republic of Korea*] [*ICAO location identifier*] (ICLI)
RKPN	Rooms Katholieke Partij Nederland [*Roman Catholic Party of the Netherlands*] [*Political party*] (PPE)
RKPP........	Busan [*Republic of Korea*] [*ICAO location identifier*] (ICLI)
RKPS........	Sachon [*Republic of Korea*] [*ICAO location identifier*] (ICLI)
RKPU........	Ulsan [*Republic of Korea*] [*ICAO location identifier*] (ICLI)
RKR	Poteau, OK [*Location identifier*] [*FAA*] (FAAL)
RKr	Rakstu Krajums [*A publication*]
RKR	Rocker (AAG)
RKR	Rockspan Resources [*Vancouver Stock Exchange symbol*]
RKRA	Rocker Arm [*Mechanical engineering*]
RKS...........	Reko [*Solomon Islands*] [*Seismograph station code, US Geological Survey*] (SEIS)
RKS...........	Rock Springs [*Wyoming*] [*Airport symbol*] (OAG)
RKS...........	Rocket Stories [*A publication*]
RKSA........	Ascom City [*Republic of Korea*] [*ICAO location identifier*] (ICLI)
RKSB........	Uijeongbu [*Republic of Korea*] [*ICAO location identifier*] (ICLI)
RKSC........	Cheongokri [*Republic of Korea*] [*ICAO location identifier*] (ICLI)
RKSD........	Kanamni [*Republic of Korea*] [*ICAO location identifier*] (ICLI)
RKSE........	Paekryoungdo Beach [*Republic of Korea*] [*ICAO location identifier*] (ICLI)
RKSF	Republic of Korea Air Force Headquarters [*Republic of Korea*] [*ICAO location identifier*] (ICLI)
RKSG........	Pyongtaek [*Republic of Korea*] [*ICAO location identifier*] (ICLI)
RKSH	Kwanak [*Republic of Korea*] [*ICAO location identifier*] (ICLI)
RKSI	Chajangni [*Republic of Korea*] [*ICAO location identifier*] (ICLI)
RKSK........	Susaek [*Republic of Korea*] [*ICAO location identifier*] (ICLI)
RKSL........	Seoul City [*Republic of Korea*] [*ICAO location identifier*] (ICLI)
RKSM........	Seoul East [*Sinchonri*] [*Republic of Korea*] [*ICAO location identifier*] (ICLI)
RKSO	Osan [*Republic of Korea*] [*ICAO location identifier*] (ICLI)
RKSP........	Paekryoungdo Site [*Republic of Korea*] [*ICAO location identifier*] (ICLI)
RKSP........	Rooms Katholieke Staatspartij [*Roman Catholic State Party*] [*Netherlands*] [*Political party*] (PPE)
RKSR........	Yeongdongri [*Republic of Korea*] [*ICAO location identifier*] (ICLI)
RKSS	Seoul/Kimpo International [*Republic of Korea*] [*ICAO location identifier*] (ICLI)
RKST........	Tongoucheon [*Republic of Korea*] [*ICAO location identifier*] (ICLI)
RKSU........	Yeoju [*Republic of Korea*] [*ICAO location identifier*] (ICLI)
RKSW........	Suwon [*Republic of Korea*] [*ICAO location identifier*] (ICLI)
RKSX........	Song San-Ri [*Republic of Korea*] [*ICAO location identifier*] (ICLI)
RKSY........	Seoul/Yungsan [*Republic of Korea*] [*ICAO location identifier*] (ICLI)
RKT	Ras Al Khaymah [*United Arab Emirates*] [*Airport symbol*] (OAG)
RKT	Rikitea [*Tuamotu Archipelago*] [*Seismograph station code, US Geological Survey*] (SEIS)
RKT	Rocket (AAG)
RKTA	Andong [*Republic of Korea*] [*ICAO location identifier*] (ICLI)
RKTC........	Chungju [*Republic of Korea*] [*ICAO location identifier*] (ICLI)
RKTD........	Taejon [*Republic of Korea*] [*ICAO location identifier*] (ICLI)
RKTEA......	Rakennustekniikka [*A publication*]
RKTH	Pohang [*Republic of Korea*] [*ICAO location identifier*] (ICLI)
RKTJ	Kyungju [*Republic of Korea*] [*ICAO location identifier*] (ICLI)
RKTM.......	Seosan [*Republic of Korea*] [*ICAO location identifier*] (ICLI)
RKTN	Taegu [*Republic of Korea*] [*ICAO location identifier*] (ICLI)
RKTO	Nonsan [*Republic of Korea*] [*ICAO location identifier*] (ICLI)
RKTR.......	Rocketeer
RKTS	Sangju [*Republic of Korea*] [*ICAO location identifier*] (ICLI)
Rk Ts B......	Rechtskundig Tijdschrift voor Belgie [*A publication*]
RKTSTA ...	Rocket Station
RKTT	Taegu [*Republic of Korea*] [*ICAO location identifier*] (ICLI)
RKTY.......	Yechon [*Republic of Korea*] [*ICAO location identifier*] (ICLI)
RKU..........	Yule Island [*Papua New Guinea*] [*Airport symbol*] (OAG)
RKV	Rabbit Kidney Vacuolating Virus
RKV	Rose Knot Victor [*Gemini tracking ship*]
RKVA	Reactive Kilovolt-Ampere
RKVAM	Recording Kilovolt-Ampere Meter (MSA)
RKVP........	Rooms Katholieke Volkspartij [*Roman Catholic People's Party*] [*Netherlands*] [*Political party*] (PPE)
RKW	Repertorium fuer Kunstwissenschaft [*A publication*]
RKW	Rockwood, TN [*Location identifier*] [*FAA*] (FAAL)
RKWD.......	Rockwood Holding Co. [*NASDAQ symbol*] (NQ)
Rk Wkbl	Rechtskundig Weekblad [*A publication*]
RKX..........	Maxton, NC [*Location identifier*] [*FAA*] (FAAL)
RKY	Rockaway Corp. [*NYSE symbol*] (SPSG)

Rky.............	Rocky [*Quality of the bottom*] [*Nautical charts*]
RKY	Roentgen Kymography
RKY	Rokeby [*Australia*] [*Airport symbol*] [*Obsolete*] (OAG)
RKZ	Reformierte Kirchenzeitung [*A publication*]
R & L........	Bureau for Reference and Loan Services [*Library network*]
RL	LAR [*Liniile Aeriene Romane*] [*ICAO designator*] (FAAC)
RL	Master Cross-Reference List
RL	Radiation Laboratory
RL	Radio Liberty [*A publication*]
RL	Radio Liberty [*Board for International Broadcasting*]
RL	Radiolocation
RL	Radioluminescent
RL	Radionavigation land station using two separate loop antennas, and a single transmitter, and operating at a power of 150 watts or more [*ITU designation*] (CET)
RL	Rahmana Litslan (BJA)
RL	Rail (AAG)
R & L........	Rail and Lake
RL	Ralph Lauren [*Fashion designer, 1939-*]
RL	Raman LASER
RL	Random Lengths [*Lumber*]
RL	Random Logic
R/L............	Rate/Limited (MCD)
RL	Rated Load
RL	Reactor Licensing [*Nuclear energy*] (NRCH)
RL	Reader's Library [*A publication*]
RL	Reading List
RL	Receive Leg [*Telecommunications*] (TEL)
RL	Receptor-Ligand Complex
R d L	Recht der Landwirtschaft [*A publication*]
RL	Record Length
R/L............	Redline (KSC)
RL	Reduced [*or Reduction*] Level
RL	Reel
RL	Reeling Machines [*JETDS nomenclature*] [*Military*] (CET)
RL	Reference Library
RL	Reference List
RL	Reflection Loss [*Telecommunications*] (TEL)
RL	Reiz-Limen [*Stimulus threshold*] [*Psychology*]
RL	Relativen Luftfeuchtigkeit [*Relative Humidity*] [*German*]
RL	Relay Logic
RL	Release Load
RL	Religion in Life [*A publication*]
R and L	Religion and Literature [*A publication*]
R/L............	Remote/Local (NASA)
RL	Report Immediately upon Leaving [*Aviation*] (FAAC)
RL	Research Laboratory
RL	Reserve List (ADA)
RL	Residential Lease [*Real estate*] (ADA)
RL	Resistor Logic (IEEE)
RL	Respectable Loge [*Worshipful Lodge*] [*French*] [*Freemasonry*] (ROG)
RL	Restaurant Liquor [*License*]
RL	Restricted Line Officer
RL	Retarded Learner [*Education*]
RL	Reticular Lamina [*Ear anatomy*]
RL	Retired List
RL	Retirement Loss
R/L............	Return Link (MCD)
RL	Return Loss
RL	Revised Laws [*A publication*] (DLA)
RL	Revista de Letras [*A publication*]
RL	Revista de Literatura [*A publication*]
RL	Revista Lusitana [*A publication*]
RL	Revue Legale [*Canada*] [*A publication*] (DLA)
R de L.........	Revue de Legislation et de Jurisprudence [*Canada*] [*A publication*] (DLA)
RL	Revue de Lille [*A publication*]
RL	Rhumb Line
RL	Rial [*Monetary unit*] [*Iran, Saudi Arabia, etc.*]
RL	Ricerche Linguistiche [*A publication*]
RL	Richland Operations Office [*Energy Research and Development Administration*]
RL	Richtlinien [*Instructions, Directions*] [*German*] (ILCA)
R/L............	Right and Left
RL	Right to Left
RL	Right Leg
RL	Right Line
RL	Right Lower [*Medicine*]
RL	Right Lung
RL	Ring Level (BUR)
RL	Ringer Lactated [*Medicine*]
RL	Rive'on Le-Khalkalah [*Tel Aviv*] (BJA)
RL	River Lines, Inc. [*AAR code*]
RL	Rivista Letteraria [*A publication*]
RL	Road Locomotive [*British*]
RL	Rocket Launcher
RL	Roll
RL	Roll Lift [*NASA*] (KSC)
RL	Rolland, Inc. [*Toronto Stock Exchange symbol*]
RL	Roman Law (DLA)

RL	Roof Leader (MSA)
RL	Round Lot [*Unit of trading*]
RL	Royal (ROG)
RL	Royal Lancers [*British military*] (DMA)
RL	Royal Licence [*British*]
RL	Ruch Literacki [*Krakow*] [*A publication*]
RL	Run Length [*Data processing*]
RL	Russian Literature [*A publication*]
RLA	Aeronautical Marker Beacon [*ITU designation*] (CET)
RLA	Reallexikon der Assyriologie [*Berlin*] [*A publication*] (BJA)
RLA	Receptive Language Age [*of the hearing-impaired*]
RLA	Redevelopment Land Agency [*Washington, DC*]
RLA	Regional Land Agent [*Ministry of Agriculture, Fisheries, and Food*] [*British*]
RLA	Relay (FAAC)
RLA	Religious Leaders of America [*A publication*]
RLA	Remote Line Adapter
RLA	Remote Loop Adapter [*Telecommunications*]
RLA	Repair Level Analysis [*Military*] (AFIT)
RLA	Repair Line Agreement (NASA)
RLA	Research Laboratory for Archeology [*British*]
RLA	Responsible Local Agencies (OICC)
RLA	Restricted Landing Area [*Aviation*]
RLA	Revista de Letras. Faculdade de Filosofia, Ciencias, e Letras (Assis) [*A publication*]
RLA	Revista Liturgica Argentina [*A publication*]
RLA	Roll Lock Actuator (MCD)
RLA	Royal Lao Army [*Laos*]
RLA	Rui Lopes Associates, Inc. [*Sunnyvale, CA*] [*Telecommunications*] (TSSD)
RLA	Rural Land Alliance (EA)
RLAB........	Royce Laboratories, Inc. [*Miami, FL*] [*NASDAQ symbol*] (NQ)
RLAC........	Reallexikon fuer Antike und Christentum [*A publication*]
RLAC........	Recycling Legislation Action Coalition (EA)
RLADD......	RADAR Low-Angle Drogue Delivery (AFM)
RLAF........	Royal Laotian Air Force
R Lang Rom ...	Revue des Langues Romanes [*A publication*]
RLANO	Relay Equipment Out of Operation [*Aviation*] (FAAC)
RLAOK	Relay Equipment Resumed Operation [*Aviation*] (FAAC)
RLAQA	Revista Latinoamericana de Quimica [*A publication*]
RLaR........	Revue des Langues Romanes [*A publication*]
RLAS........	Rocket Lunar Attitude System
RLAss........	Reallexikon der Assyriologie [*Berlin*] [*A publication*] (BJA)
R Latinoamer Psicol ...	Revista Latinoamericana de Psicologia [*A publication*]
R Latinoamer Sociol ...	Revista Latinoamericana de Sociologia [*A publication*]
R Latinoam Estud Urbano Reg ...	Revista Latinoamericana de Estudios Urbano Regionales [*A publication*]
RLaV........	Revue des Langues Vivantes [*A publication*]
RLB...........	RACON Station [*ITU designation*] (CET)
RLB...........	Reliability [*or Reliable*] (AAG)
RLB...........	United States Railroad Labor Board Decisions [*A publication*] (DLA)
RLBCD......	Right Lower Border of Cardiac Dullness [*Cardiology*]
RLB Dec ...	Railroad Labor Board Decisions [*A publication*] (DLA)
RLBG........	Relative Bearing [*Navigation*] (FAAC)
RLBL........	Regional Laser and Biotechnology Laboratories [*University of Pennsylvania*] [*Research center*] (RCD)
RLBM........	Rearward Launched Ballistic Missile
RLC...........	Radio Launch Control System (IEEE)
RLC...........	Radio Liberty Committee [*Later, RFE/RL*] (EA)
RLC...........	Rassegna Italiana di Lingue e Letterature Classiche [*A publication*]
RLC...........	Receive Logic Chassis
RLC...........	Refund Litigation Coordinator [*IRS*]
RLC...........	Regulatory Light Chain [*Physiology*]
RLC...........	Remote Line Concentrator
RLC...........	Remote Load Controller [*NASA*] (MCD)
RLC...........	Report Landing Completed [*Aviation*] (FAAC)
RLC...........	Residual Lung Capacity [*Medicine*]
RLC...........	Resistance Inductance Capacitance (MSA)
RLC...........	Revue de Litterature Comparee [*A publication*]
RLC...........	Ribosome-Lamella Complex [*Physiology*]
RLC...........	Right Line Contactor (MCD)
RLC...........	Robinson Little & Company Ltd. [*Toronto Stock Exchange symbol*]
RLC...........	Rollins Truck Leasing [*NYSE symbol*] (SPSG)
RLC...........	ROM [*Read-Only Memory*] Location Counter
RLC...........	Rotating Litter Chair [*NASA*] (KSC)
RLC...........	Run Length Coding
RLCA........	National Rural Letter Carriers' Association
RLCA........	Reaction-Limited Cluster Aggregation
RLCA........	Religion and Labor Council of America [*Defunct*] (EA)
RLCAA......	Railway Locomotives and Cars [*A publication*]
RLCAD......	Revista Latinoamericana de Ciencias Agricolas [*A publication*]
RLCD........	Relocated
RLCM........	Rat Lung-Conditioned Medium [*Culture media*]
RLCP........	Redfern Legal Centre Publishing Ltd. [*Australia*]
RLCR........	Railcar (MSA)
RLCS.........	Radio Launch Control System

RLCU	Reference Link Control Unit [*Telecommunications*] (TEL)
RLD	RADAR Laydown Delivery (AFM)
RLD	Related Living Donor [*Medicine*]
RLD	Relocation Dictionary
RLD	Relocation List Directory
RLD	Repetitive LASER Desorption
RLD	Retail Liquor Dealer
RLD	Richland [*Washington*] [*Airport symbol*] [*Obsolete*] (OAG)
RLD	Rolled (AAG)
RLD	Run Length Discriminator (MCD)
RLD	Ruptured Lumbar Disc [*Medicine*]
RLDS.........	Reorganized Church of Jesus Christ of Latter-Day Saints
RLE...........	Raleigh Energy [*Vancouver Stock Exchange symbol*]
RLE...........	Relative Luminous Efficiency (NATG)
RLE...........	Request Loading Entry [*Data processing*]
RLE...........	Research Laboratory of Electronics [*MIT*] [*Research center*]
RLE...........	Resorts Leisure Exchange [*Commercial firm*] [*British*]
RLE...........	Right Lower Extremity [*Medicine*]
RLE...........	Run-Length Encoding [*Data processing*]
RLEA........	Railway Labor Executives' Association (EA)
RLeIt........	Rassegna della Letteratura Italiana [*A publication*]
RLEO	Request Liaison Engineering Order [*NASA*] (NASA)
R Let	Revista de Letras [*A publication*]
RLETFL......	Report Leaving Each Thousand-Foot Level [*Aviation*] (FAAC)
R Lett Mod ...	Revue des Lettres Modernes [*A publication*]
RLEW........	Research Library for Edward Woodward (EA)
RLF...........	Relief (AAG)
RLF...........	Religion and Labor Foundation
RLF...........	Religious Liberty Foundation (EA)
RLF...........	Remote Lift Fan [*Aviation*]
RLF...........	Retrograde Lipid Flow [*Hypothesis for biological cell movement*]
RLF...........	Retrolental Fibroplasia [*Eye disease in premature babies*]
RLF...........	Rhizoctonia-Like Fungus
RLF...........	Right Lateral Femoral [*Site of injection*] [*Medicine*]
RLF...........	Royal Laotian Forces
RLF...........	Royal Literary Fund [*British*]
RLFC........	Rebel Lee Fan Club (EA)
RLFE........	Revista. Laboratorio de Fonetica Experimental [*A publication*]
RLG...........	Glidepath [*Slope*] Station [*ITU designation*] (CET)
RLG...........	Kremmling, CO [*Location identifier*] [*FAA*] (FAAL)
RLG...........	Railing (AAG)
RLG...........	Regimental Landing Group
RLG...........	Regional Liaison Group (CINC)
RLG...........	Release Guard [*Telecommunications*] (TEL)
RLG...........	Relief Landing Ground [*British military*] (DMA)
RLG...........	Research Libraries Group [*An association*] [*Also, an information service or system*] (EA)
RLG...........	Rifle Large Grain [*British military*] (DMA)
RLG...........	Ring LASER Gyro [*Navy*]
RLG...........	Royal Laotian Government
RLG...........	Royal Lepage Ltd. [*Toronto Stock Exchange symbol*] [*Vancouver Stock Exchange symbol*]
RLGD	Realigned
RLGM	Remote Look Group Multiplexer (MCD)
RLGM-CD ...	Remote Look Group Multiplexer Cable Drive (MCD)
R & LH	Right and Left Hands [*Work-factor system*]
RLH	Run Like Hell [*Slang*]
RLHAS.....	Revue de Litterature, Histoire, Arts, et Sciences [*A publication*]
RLHIT.......	Royal Life High Income Trust [*British*]
RLHS........	Railway and Locomotive Historical Society (EA)
RLHTE......	Research Laboratory of Heat Transfer in Electronics [*MIT*] (MCD)
RLI.............	Anniston, AL [*Location identifier*] [*FAA*] (FAAL)
RLI.............	Radiation Level Indicator
RLI.............	Rand Light Infantry [*British military*] (DMA)
RLI.............	Rassegna della Letteratura Italiana [*A publication*]
RLI.............	Realtors Land Institute (EA)
RLI.............	Retirement Life Item
RLI.............	Revista de las Indias [*A publication*]
RLi.............	Revue de Linguistique [*A publication*]
RLI.............	Rhodesian Light Infantry [*Military unit*]
RLI.............	Right/Left Indicator (NVT)
RLI.............	RLI Corp. [*NYSE symbol*] (SPSG)
RLI.............	Rostral Length Index
RLIB.........	Relocatable Library [*Data processing*]
RLIBD6	Swedish University of Agricultural Sciences. Department of Farm Buildings. Report [*A publication*]
RLIC..........	Revue des Lois, Decrets, Traites de Commerce. Institut International du Commerce [*A publication*]
RLIEVDP ...	Request Line Items Be Expedited for Vehicles [*or Equipment*] Deadlined for Parts [*Army*] (AABC)
RLIF..........	[*The*] Reliable Life Insurance Co. [*NASDAQ symbol*] (NQ)
RLIN.........	Research Libraries Information Network [*Pronounced "arlen"*] [*Formerly, BALLOTS*] [*Research Libraries Group, Inc.*] [*Stanford, CA*] [*Library network*] [*Information service or system*]
RLing	Revue de Linguistique [*A publication*]
RLing	Ricerche Linguistiche [*A publication*]
RLing	Russian Linguistics [*A publication*]
RLir...........	Realismo Lirico [*A publication*]

RLiR .... Revue de Linguistique Romane [*A publication*]
RLit .... Revista de Literatura [*A publication*]
RLit .... Russkaja Literatura [*A publication*]
RLitC .... Readings in Literary Criticism [*A publication*]
RLITDQ .... Swedish University of Agricultural Sciences. Department of
 Agricultural Engineering. Report [*A publication*]
R Litt Comp ... Revue de Litterature Comparee [*A publication*]
RLIV .... Retirement Living Tax-Exempt Mortgage Fund LP [*NASDAQ
 symbol*] (NQ)
RLiv .... Rivista di Livorno [*A publication*]
R de L et de J ... Revue de Legislation et de Jurisprudence [*A
 publication*] (DLA)
RLJ .... Rhodes-Livingstone Journal [*A publication*]
RLJ .... Rhodesian Law Journal [*A publication*] (DLA)
RLJ .... Russian Language Journal [*A publication*]
RLKBAD ... Report. Research Laboratories of Kirin Brewery Company
 Limited [*A publication*]
RLL .... Localizer Station [*ITU designation*] (CET)
RLL .... Religion in Literature and Life [*A publication*]
RLL .... Relocating Linking Loader
RLL .... Representation-Language Language [*Data processing*]
RLL .... Reviews in Leukemia and Lymphoma [*Elsevier Book Series*] [*A
 publication*]
RLL .... Right Lower Limb [*Medicine*]
RLL .... Right Lower Lobe [*Lungs*]
RLL .... Rim of Lateral Lip
RLL .... Rocket Launcher Locator
RLL .... Rolla, ND [*Location identifier*] [*FAA*] (FAAL)
RLL .... Run-Length-Limited [*Data processing*]
RLLB .... Right Long Leg Brace [*Medicine*]
RLLB .... Right Lower Leg Brace [*Medicine*]
RLLD .... Registered Laundry and Linen Director [*Designation awarded
 by National Association of Institutional Linen
 Management*]
RLLO .... Revue de Langue et Litterature d'Oc [*A publication*]
RLLP .... Revue de Langue et Litterature Provencales [*A publication*]
RLLProv ... Revue de Langue et Litterature Provencales [*A publication*]
RLLR .... Revue de Louisiane/Louisiana Review [*A publication*]
RLLSC .... Right to Life League of Southern California (EA)
R & LL & T ... Redman and Lyon on Landlord and Tenant [*8th ed.*] [*1924*] [*A
 publication*] (DLA)
RLLY .... Rally's, Inc. [*NASDAQ symbol*] (NQ)
RLM .... Marine Radio Beacon Station [*ITU designation*] (CET)
RLM .... Rearward Launched Missile
RLM .... Regional Library of Medicine [*Pan American Health
 Organization*]
RLM .... Reichsleftfahrt Ministerium [*German Air Ministry*] [*World
 War II*]
RLM .... Remote Line Module [*Telecommunications*]
RLM .... Return to Land and Management [*Agriculture*]
RLM .... Revista di Letterature Moderne e Comparate [*A publication*]
RLM .... Revue des Langues Modernes [*A publication*]
RLM .... Revue des Lettres Modernes [*A publication*]
RLM .... Reynolds Metals Co. [*NYSE symbol*] (SPSG)
RLM .... Rivista di Letteratura Moderne e Comparate [*A publication*]
RLM .... Roy-L Merchant Group, Inc. [*Toronto Stock Exchange symbol*]
RLM .... Royal American Airways [*Tucson, AZ*] [*FAA
 designator*] (FAAC)
RLM .... Royal Lancashire Militia [*British military*] (DMA)
RLM .... Royal London Militia
RLMA .... Roll Label Manufacturers Association (EA)
RLMBA ..... Rendiconti. Istituto Lombardo. Accademia di Scienze e Lettere.
 Sezione B. Scienze Biologiche e Mediche [*A publication*]
RLMC .... Rivista di Letteratura Moderne e Comparate [*A publication*]
RLMF .... Revue du Louvre et des Musees de France [*A publication*]
RLMM ...... Research Laboratory for Mechanics of Materials (MCD)
RLMod ...... Revue des Lettres Modernes [*A publication*]
RLMPA ..... Revista Latinoamericana de Microbiologia y Parasitologia
 [*Later, Revista Latinoamericana de Microbiologia*] [*A
 publication*]
RLMPB ..... Proceedings. Reliability and Maintainability Conference [*A
 publication*]
RLMS .... RADAR Land Mass Simulation
RLMS .... Reproduction of Library Materials Section [*Resources and
 Technical Services Division of ALA*]
RLN .... LORAN Station [*ITU designation*] (CET)
RLND .... Regional Lymph Node Dissection [*Medicine*]
RLNS .... Revue Legale. New Series [*Canada*] [*A publication*] (DLA)
RLO .... Omnidirectional Range Station [*ITU designation*] (CET)
RLO .... RADAR Lock-On
RLO .... Regional Liaison Office [*Military*] (AFM)
R & LO ..... Reliability and Launch Operations (MCD)
RLO .... Repairs Liaison Officer [*Landing craft and barges*] [*Navy*]
R/LO .... Response/Lockout (MCD)
RLO .... Returned Letter Office
RLO .... Richland Operations Office [*Energy Research and Development
 Administration*]
RLO .... Rose Lookout Tower [*Oklahoma*] [*Seismograph station code,
 US Geological Survey*] (SEIS)
RLOCK...... Record Lock
RLOE .... Roemische Limes in Oesterreich [*A publication*]

RLOP........ Reactor Licensing Operating Procedure [*Nuclear
 energy*] (NRCH)
RLORA ..... Revue de Laryngologie, Otologie, Rhinologie [*A publication*]
RLOS........ Retention Level of Supply [*Navy*] (NG)
RLOS........ Revue Legale (Old Series) [*Canada*] [*A publication*] (DLA)
RLOSA ...... Revue de Laryngologie, Otologie, Rhinologie. Supplement [*A
 publication*]
R Louvre .... Revue du Louvre et des Musees de France [*A publication*]
R du Louvre ... Revue du Louvre et des Musees de France [*A publication*]
RLP........... Rail Loading Point (NATG)
RLP........... Remote Line Printer (MCD)
RLP........... Ribosome-Like Particle [*Cytology*]
RLP........... Roads and Landscape Planning [*British*]
RLP........... Rosella Plains [*Australia*] [*Airport symbol*] [*Obsolete*] (OAG)
RLP........... Rotatable Log Periodic Antenna (MCD)
RLP........... Rotating Linear Polarization
RLP........... Ruby LASER Pulse
RLPA .... Retail Loss Prevention Association [*New York, NY*] (EA)
RLPA .... Rotating Log Periodic Antenna
RLPH .... Reflected Light Photohead
RLPL .... Railway Labor's Political League
RLPNLP.... Retired League Postmasters of the National League of
 Postmasters (EA)
RLQ .... Right Lower Quadrant [*of abdomen*] [*Medicine*]
RLQB........ Revue Legale Reports, Queen's Bench [*Canada*] [*A
 publication*] (DLA)
RLR .... Radio Range Station [*ITU designation*] (CET)
RLR .... Radioactive Lighting Rod [*Nuclear energy*] (NRCH)
RL & R...... Rail, Lake, and Rail
RLR .... Record Length Register
RLR .... Retired Lives Reserve [*Insurance*]
RLR .... Revue des Langues Romanes [*A publication*]
R d LR....... Revue des Langues Romanes [*A publication*]
RLR .... Revue de Linguistique Romane [*A publication*]
RLR .... Right Larval Retractor
RLR .... Right Lateral Rectus [*Eye anatomy*]
RLR .... Right Lateral Rotation [*Medicine*]
RLR .... Riverina Library Review [*A publication*]
RLR .... Roller (MSA)
RLR .... Rutgers Law Review [*A publication*]
RLRB .... Radio Liberty Research Bulletin [*A publication*]
RLRF .... RLR Financial Services, Inc. [*Lauderhill, FL*] [*NASDAQ
 symbol*] (NQ)
RLRIU .... Radio Logic Routing Interface Unit (MCD)
RLS........... Person who stammers, unable to enunciate the letters R, L, and
 S
RLS........... RADAR Line of Sight
RLS........... Radius of Landing Site [*NASA*] (KSC)
RLS........... Raman LASER Source
RLS........... Ranfurly Library Service [*An association*] (EAIO)
RLS........... Recursive Least Squares [*Mathematics*]
RLS........... Regional Language Studies [*Newfoundland*] [*A publication*]
RLS........... Regional Library Service [*Australia*]
RLS........... Release (FAAC)
RLS........... Remote Line Switch [*Telecommunications*] (TEL)
RLS........... Research in the Life Sciences Committee [*National Academy of
 Sciences*]
RLS........... Reservoir Level Sensor (MCD)
RLS........... Resonance Light Scattering [*Physics*]
RLS........... Restricted Least Squares [*Statistics*]
RL & S ...... Ridgeway, Lapp, and Schoales' Irish King's Bench Reports
 [*1793-95*] [*A publication*] (DLA)
RLS........... Rim Latch Set
RLS........... Ringer's Lactate Solution [*Physiology*]
RLS........... Riolos of Patras [*Greece*] [*Seismograph station code, US
 Geological Survey*] (SEIS)
RLS........... Robert Louis Stevenson [*Nineteenth-century Scottish author*]
RLS........... Rocket Launching System
RLS........... Roll Limit Switch
RLS........... Rotary Limit Switch
RLS........... Ruby LASER System
RLS........... Rustenburg Layered Suite [*or Sequence*] [*Bushveld Complex,
 South Africa*] [*Geology*]
RLS........... Surveillance RADAR Station [*ITU designation*] (CET)
RLS........... Westerly, RI [*Location identifier*] [*FAA*] (FAAL)
RLSA .... Republican Law Students Association of New York (EA)
RLSA NY .. Republican Law Students Association of New York (EA)
RLSC .... Revue Legale Reports, Supreme Court [*Canada*] [*A
 publication*] (DLA)
RLSCA ...... Research in Life Sciences [*A publication*]
RLSD........ Received Line Signal Detector
RLSD........ Research and Laboratory Services Division [*Health and Safety
 Executive*] [*British*] (IRUK)
RLSE .... Release (MSA)
RLSP .... Ruby LASER Single Pulse
RLSS .... Regenerative Life Support System [*NASA*] (NASA)
RLSS .... Royal Life Saving Society [*Studley, Warwickshire,
 England*] (EAIO)
R L St........ Rackham Literary Studies [*A publication*]
RLST........ Realist, Inc. [*NASDAQ symbol*] (NQ)
RLST .... Release Timer [*Telecommunications*] (TEL)

RLSTA ...... Regelungstechnik [*A publication*]
RLSTN ...... Relay Station (FAAC)
RLSWA ..... Royal Life Saving Society of Western Australia
RLT .... Arlit [*Niger*] [*Airport symbol*] (OAG)
RLT .... Regimental Landing Team [*Military*]
RLT .... Relating To (AABC)
RLT .... Reliability Life Test
RLT .... Reorder Lead Time [*Navy*] (NG)
RLT .... Repair Lead Time
RLT .... Return Line Tether [*NASA*] (MCD)
RLT .... Right Lateral Thigh [*Medicine*]
RLT .... Ring LASER Technique
RLT .... Rolling Liquid Transporter [*Army*]
RLT .... Russian Literature Triquarterly [*A publication*]
RLTA .... Reenlistment Leave Travel Allowance [*Military*]
RLTA .... Rhodesian Lawn Tennis Association
RLTK .... Rhumb Line Track (FAAC)
RLTM .... Research Laboratories Technical Memorandum
RLTN .... Relation (MSA)
RLTO .... Regional Lime Technical Officer [*Ministry of Agriculture, Fisheries, and Food*] [*British*]
RLTS .... Radio Linked Telemetry System
RLTV .... Relative (AFM)
RLU .... RADAR Logic Unit (MCD)
RLu .... Rassegna Lucchese [*A publication*]
RLU .... Relative Light Units [*Analysis of light intensity*]
RLU .... Remote Line Unit [*Telecommunications*]
RLU .... Waterville, ME [*Location identifier*] [*FAA*] (FAAL)
RLub .... Rocznik Lubelski [*A publication*]
RLuc .... Rassegna Lucchese [*A publication*]
RLux .... Revue Trimestrielle d'Etudes Linguistiques, Folkloriques, et Toponymiques (Luxembourg) [*A publication*]
RLV .... Rauscher [*Murine*] Leukemia Virus
RLV .... Reallexikon der Vorgeschichte [*Berlin*] [*A publication*] (BJA)
RLV .... Relieve (AFM)
RLV .... Reusable Launch Vehicle [*Aerospace*]
RLV .... Revue des Langues Vivantes [*A publication*]
RLV .... Roving Lunar Vehicle (AAG)
RLVD .... Relieved
RLVDT ...... Rotary Linear Variable Differential Transformer
RLVS .... Recoverable Launch Vehicle Structure (KSC)
RLW .... Rajasthan Law Weekly [*India*] [*A publication*] (DLA)
RLW .... Real West Airlines [*Fargo, ND*] [*FAA designator*] (FAAC)
RL & W ...... Roberts, Leaming, and Wallis' County Court Reports [*1849-51*] [*A publication*] (DLA)
RLWL .... Reactor Low-Water Level (IEEE)
RLWY .... Railway (AAG)
RLXN .... Relaxation (MSA)
RLY .... Railway
Rly .... Railway [*A publication*]
RLY .... Relay (AAG)
RLY .... Worland, WY [*Location identifier*] [*FAA*] (FAAL)
Rly Engng .. Railway Engineering Journal [*Incorporated in Railway Engineer International*] [*A publication*]
Rly Gaz ...... Railway Gazette [*Later, Railway Gazette International*] [*A publication*]
Rly Mag ..... Railway Magazine [*A publication*]
R Lz .... Radjans'ke Literaturoznavstvo. Naukovo-Teoretycnyj Zurnal [*A publication*]
RM .... Journal of Recreational Mathematics [*A publication*]
RM .... Lab. Roland-Marie [*France*] [*Research code symbol*]
R & M .... Law Reporter, Montreal [*Canada*] [*A publication*] (DLA)
RM .... Maritime Radionavigation Mobile Station [*ITU designation*] (CET)
RM .... McAlpine Aviation [*Great Britain*] [*ICAO designator*] (FAAC)
RM .... Mitteilungen des Deutschen Archaeologischen Instituts. Roemische Abteilung [*A publication*]
RM .... Office of Resource Management [*Nuclear energy*] (NRCH)
RM .... RADAR Mapper
RM .... RADAR Missile (MUGU)
RM .... Radiation Measurement
R/M .... Radiation/Meteoroid [*NASA satellite*]
RM .... Radiation Monitor (NRCH)
RM .... Radical Mastectomy [*Medicine*]
RM .... Radio Marti [*Cuba*]
RM .... Radio Material Officer (MCD)
RM .... Radio Monitor
RM .... Radioman [*Navy rating*]
RM .... Range Marks
RM .... Range of Movement [*Medicine*]
RM .... Rassegna Monetaria [*A publication*]
RM .... Rassegna Musicale [*A publication*]
RM .... Raw Material
RM .... Reaction Mass
RM .... Reactor Manufacturer [*Nuclear energy*] (NRCH)
R/M .... Read/Mostly [*Data processing*] (TEL)
RM .... Readiness Manager [*DARCOM*] [*Army*]
RM .... Readout Matrix
RM .... Ready Money (ROG)
RM .... Ream
RM .... Reasoning Module [*Data processing*]

RM .... Receiver, Mobile
RM .... Receiving Memo
RM .... Rechtsgeleerd Magazijn [*A publication*]
RM .... Record Mark (BUR)
RM .... Record Mirror [*A publication*]
RM .... Red Marrow [*Hematology*]
R & M .... Redistribution and Marketing (AFM)
RM .... Redundancy Management (MCD)
RM .... Reference Material
RM .... Reference Memory [*Psychology*]
RM .... Reference Method
RM .... Reference Mission [*NASA*] (NASA)
RM .... Refresh Memory (MCD)
R & M .... Refurbishment and Modification
RM .... Regeneration Medium [*Biology*]
RM .... Regional Manager
RM .... Regional Meetings [*Quakers*]
RM .... Register Memory
RM .... Registered Midwife [*British*] (DBQ)
RM .... Reichsmark [*Later, DM*] [*Monetary unit*] [*German*]
RM .... Relais Musique [*Phonorecord series*] [*Canada*]
RM .... Relative Mobility [*of ions*] [*Chemistry*]
R & M .... Release and Material (MCD)
R & M .... Reliability and Maintainability [*Navy*]
RLu .... Religionen der Menschheit [*A publication*]
RM .... Remedial Maintenance (AFM)
Rm .... Remission [*Medicine*]
RM .... Remote Manipulator [*NASA*] (NASA)
RM .... Remote Manual (NRCH)
RM .... Remote Multiplexer [*Data processing*] (CAAL)
RM .... Rendezvous Maneuver (MCD)
RM .... Repair Manual
RM .... Repetition Maximum [*Medicine*]
RM .... Replaceable Module
R & M .... Reports and Memorandum (MCD)
RM .... Rescue Module [*NASA*] (NASA)
RM .... Research Materials [*National Institute of Standards and Technology*]
RM .... Research Memorandum
RM .... Resident Magistrate
RM .... Resident Minister [*Church of England in Australia*]
RM .... Residential Member [*Designation awarded by American Institute of Real Estate Appraisers of the National Association of Realtors*]
RM .... Resource Manager
RM .... Respiratory Movement
RM .... Response Memoranda [*Jimmy Carter administration*]
RM .... Retail Manager
RM .... Retrospective Method [*Insurance*]
RM .... Return Material [*Navy*] (NG)
RM .... Review of Metaphysics [*A publication*]
R/M .... Revolutions per Minute
RM .... Revue de la Mediterranee [*A publication*]
RM .... Revue de Metaphysique et de Morale [*A publication*]
RM .... Revue Mondiale [*A publication*]
RM .... Revue Musicale [*A publication*]
RM .... Rheinisches Museum fuer Philologie [*A publication*]
RM .... Rhesus Monkey
RM .... Richmark Resources Ltd. [*Vancouver Stock Exchange symbol*]
RM .... Riding Master [*British*]
RM .... Right Mid
RM .... Ring Micrometer
RM .... Risk Management [*A publication*]
RM .... Rocket Management (MCD)
RM .... Rocky Mountains
RM .... Rollback Module [*Telecommunications*] (TEL)
RM .... Roman Martyrology
rm .... Romania [*MARC country of publication code*] [*Library of Congress*] (LCCP)
RM .... Romans [*New Testament book*]
RM .... Room (AAG)
RM .... Roumania [*IYRU nationality code*] (IYR)
RM .... Routine Maintenance (AAG)
RM .... Routing Manager
RM .... Rowley Mile [*Horseracing*] [*British*]
RM .... Rowohlts Monographien [*A publication*]
RM .... Royal Mail [*British*]
RM .... Royal Marines [*British*]
RM .... Royal Mint [*British*] (DAS)
RM .... Rubber Mold (MCD)
RM .... Rule Making [*Nuclear energy*] (NRCH)
RM .... Ruptured Membrane [*Medicine*]
RM .... Rural Municipality (DLA)
R & M .... Russell and Mylne's English Chancery Reports [*A publication*] (DLA)
RM .... Russian Military [*World War II*]
RM .... Russkaja Mysl' [*A publication*]
R & M .... Ryan and Moody's English Nisi Prius Reports [*A publication*] (DLA)
RM .... RYMAC Mortgage Investment Corp. [*AMEX symbol*] (CTT)
RM1 .... Radioman, First Class [*Navy rating*]

RM2.......... Radioman, Second Class [*Navy rating*]
R & M/2... RON [*Research Octane Number*] and MON [*Motor Octane Number*] Averaged [*Antiknock index*] [*Fuel technology*]
RM3.......... Radioman, Third Class [*Navy rating*]
RM³ .... Remote Multimedia Mode [*Army*]
RMA........ Racquetball Manufacturers Association (EA)
RMA........ Radio-Labeled Monoclonal Antigloblin [*Clinical chemistry*]
RMA........ Radio Manufacturers Association [*Later, Electronic Industries Association*]
RMA........ Radiometric Microbiological Assay
RMA........ Random Multiple Access
RMA........ Reactive Modulation Amplifier
RMA........ Rear Maintenance Area [*Military*] [*British*]
RMA........ Receiver Measurement Adapter (MCD)
RMA........ Reclaim Managers Association [*Defunct*] (EA)
RMA........ Regional Manpower Administration
RMA........ Registered Medical Assistants [*Later, ARMA*] (EA)
RMA........ Reliability, Maintainability, and Availability [*Standards*]
RMA........ Reliability and Maintenance Analysis (CAAL)
RMA........ Remote Manipulator Arm [*NASA*] (MCD)
RMA........ Research and Marketing Act [*1946*]
RMA........ Reserve Military Aviator
RMA........ Retail Merchants' Association of Canada
RMA........ Rhythmic Motor Activity [*Physiology*]
RMA........ Rice Millers' Association (EA)
RMA........ Right Mentoanterior [*A fetal position*] [*Obstetrics*]
RMA........ Robert Morris Associates [*National Association of Bank Loan and Credit Officers*] [*Philadelphia, PA*] (EA)
RMA........ Rockefeller Mountains [*Antarctica*] [*Seismograph station code, US Geological Survey*] [*Closed*] (SEIS)
RMA........ Rocky Mountain Airways [*Denver, CO*] [*FAA designator*] (FAAC)
RMA........ Rocky Mountain Arsenal [*Army*] (AABC)
RMA........ Rodeo Media Association (EA)
RMA........ Roma [*Australia*] [*Airport symbol*] (OAG)
RMA........ Rosin Mildly Activated [*Standard material for soldering*]
RMA........ Royal Mail Aircraft [*Australia*]
RMA........ Royal Malta Artillery [*Military unit*] [*British*]
RMA........ Royal Marine Academy [*British*]
RMA........ Royal Marine Artillery [*Obsolete*] [*British*]
RMA........ Royal Marines Association [*British military*] (DMA)
RMA........ Royal Military Academy [*For cadets of Royal Engineers and Royal Artillery; frequently referred to as Woolwich*] [*British*]
RMA........ Royal Military Asylum [*British*]
RMA........ Royal Musical Association [*British*]
RMA........ Royal Musical Association. Proceedings [*A publication*]
RMA........ Rubber Manufacturers Association (EA)
RMAAD.... Revista Mexicana de Astronomia y Astrofisica [*A publication*]
RMAAS..... Reactivity Monitoring and Alarm System [*Nuclear energy*] (NRCH)
RMab........ Revue Mabillon [*A publication*]
RMAB ...... Royal Marines Auxiliary Brigade [*British military*] (DMA)
RMAC ...... Remote Master Aircraft (MCD)
RMACHA ... Rocky Mountain Automated Clearing House Association
R-MAD..... Reactor Maintenance, Assembly, and Disassembly
RMAF....... Royal Moroccan Air Force
RMAFA..... Revista. Union Matematica Argentina y Asociacion Fisica Argentina [*A publication*]
RMAL ...... Revised Master Allowance List [*Military*] (AFIT)
RMAL ...... Revue du Moyen-Age Latin [*Strasbourg*] [*A publication*]
RMALAN ... Royal Malaysian Navy
RMA Proc ... Royal Musical Association. Proceedings [*A publication*]
RMARC .... Royal Musical Association. Research Chronicle [*A publication*]
R Marche Commun ... Revue du Marche Commun [*A publication*]
RMARDL ... Revista Medico-Quirurgica. Asociacion Medica del Hospital Rivadavia [*A publication*]
RMA Res Chron ... RMA [*Royal Musical Association*] Research Chronicle [*A publication*]
RMA Research ... Royal Musical Association. Research Chronicle [*A publication*]
RMA Research Chron ... RMA [*Royal Musical Association*] Research Chronicle [*A publication*]
R Mark Agric Econ ... Review of the Marketing and Agricultural Economy [*A publication*]
R Marketing & Ag Econ ... Review of Marketing and Agricultural Economics [*A publication*] (APTA)
R Marketing and Agric Econ ... Review of Marketing and Agricultural Economics [*A publication*]
RMA Rubber ... RMA [*Rubber Manufacturers Association*] Industry Rubber Report [*A publication*]
RMAS........ Royal Military Academy Sandhurst [*British*]
R MAST ... Radio Mast
RMAT ...... Royal Marine Advisory Team [*British military*] (DMA)
RMA Tire .. RMA [*Rubber Manufacturers Association*] Tire and Innertube Statistical Report [*A publication*]
RMATS-1 ... Remote Maintenance, Administration, and Traffic System-1 [*Telecommunications*] (TEL)
RMAX .... Range, Maximum

RMAZDB ... Revista. Museo Argentino de Ciencias Naturales Bernardino Rivadavia e Instituto Nacional de Investigacion de las Ciencias Naturales. Zoologia [*A publication*]
RMB .... Radio Marker Beacon
RMB .... Radio Marketing Bureau [*British*] (CB)
RMB .... Rambler Oil Co. [*Toronto Stock Exchange symbol*]
RMB .... Rand Merchant Bank [*South Africa*]
RMB .... Raw Materials Board [*of the Reconstruction Finance Corp.*]
RMB .... Renminbi [*Monetary unit*] [*China*]
RMB .... Roadside Mailbox (ADA)
RMB .... Rocky Mountain Motor Tariff Bureau, Inc., Denver CO [*STAC*]
RMB .... Rombauer [*Missouri*] [*Seismograph station code, US Geological Survey*] (SEIS)
RMB .... Royal Marine Bands [*British military*] (DMA)
RMB .... Royal Marines Badge [*British*]
RMBC .... Regional Marine Biological Centre [*UNESCO*] (MSC)
RMBC .... Rocky Mountain Beverage Co. [*NASDAQ symbol*] (NQ)
RMBF....... Required Myocardial Blood Flow [*Cardiology*]
RMBI........ Canadian Risk Management and Business Insurance [*A publication*]
RM Bl .... Reichministerialblatt [*A publication*]
R-MBP-A .. Rat-Mannose-Binding Protein A
R-MBP-C .. Rat-Mannose-Binding Protein C
RMBPD.... Royal Marine Boom Patrol Detachment [*World War II*]
RMBRDQ ... Revue Medicale de Bruxelles. Nouvelle Serie [*A publication*]
RMC .... American Restaurant Partnership [*AMEX symbol*] (SPSG)
RMC .... Captain of Royal Marines [*Military*] [*British*]
RMC .... [*Robert M.*] Charlton's Georgia Reports [*1811-37*] [*A publication*] (DLA)
RMC .... Chief Radioman [*Navy rating*]
RMC .... Radiation Management Corporation (NRCH)
RMC .... Radiation Material Corporation
RMC .... Randolph-Macon College [*Virginia*]
RMC .... Rat Mast Cell
RMC .... Raytheon Manufacturing Company (MCD)
RM & C ..... Reactor Monitoring and Control [*Nuclear energy*] (NRCH)
RMC .... Ready Mixed Cement [*Commercial firm*] [*British*]
RMC .... Ready Mixed Concrete (ADA)
RMC .... Recursive Monte Carlo Method
RMC .... Reduced Material Condition (NVT)
RMC .... Redundancy Management Control (MCD)
RMC........ Regional Media Center
RMC .... Regular Military Compensation (AABC)
RMC .... Regulated Motor Carriers
RMC .... Relative-Motion Control [*Microcopy*]
RMC .... Remote Manual Control (NRCH)
RMC .... Remote Multiplexer Combiner (MCD)
RMC .... Rendezvous Mercury Capsule [*NASA*] (AAG)
RMC .... Repair Manufacturer Codes
RMC .... Representative in Medical Council [*Royal College of Physicians*] [*British*] (ROG)
RMC .... Republican Mainstream Committee (EA)
RMC .... Resident Management Corporation [*Public housing*]
RMC .... Residential Manpower Center [*Job Corps*]
RMC .... Resource Management Consultants [*Salem, NH*] [*Telecommunications*] (TSSD)
RMC .... Resource Materials Centre [*Australia*]
RMC .... Return to Military Control (AABC)
RMC .... Revista Musical Chilena [*A publication*]
RMC .... Revolutionary Military Council [*Grenada*]
RMC .... Revue du Marche Commun [*Review of the Common Market*] [*French*]
RMC .... Revue des Materiaux de Construction et de Travaux Publics [*A publication*]
RMC .... Revue Musicale [*A publication*]
RMC .... Rocket Motor Case
RMC .... Rocky Mountain College [*Billings, MT*]
RMC .... Rod Memory Computer [*NCR Corp.*]
RMC .... Rosemont College, Rosemont, PA [*OCLC symbol*] (OCLC)
RMC .... Rotary Mirror Camera
RMC .... Rotating Modulation Collimator
RMC .... Royal Marine Commandos [*British*]
RMC .... Royal Military College [*For army cadets; often referred to as Sandhurst*] [*British*]
RMC .... Rural Manpower Center [*Michigan State University*]
RMCA ...... Right Middle Cerebral Artery [*Anatomy*]
RMCAT..... Ralph Mayer Center for Artists' Techniques [*University of Delaware*] [*Newark*] [*Information service or system*] (IID)
RMCB ...... Registered Mail Central Bureau [*Later, RMIA*] (EA)
RMCB ...... Reserve Mobile Construction Battalion
RMCB ...... Royal Marine Commando Brigade [*British*]
RMCC ...... RADAR Monitor and Control Console [*Military*] (CAAL)
RMCC ...... Royal Military College of Canada [*British military*] (DMA)
RMCC .... Ryan and Moody's English Crown Cases [*A publication*] (DLA)
R & MCC... Ryan and Moody's English Crown Cases Reserved [*A publication*] (DLA)
RMCCR..... Ryan and Moody's English Crown Cases [*A publication*] (DLA)

RMCCSC .. Raw Materials Committee of the Commonwealth Supply Council [*British*] [*World War II*]
RMCDC .... Rocky Mountain Child Development Center [*University of Colorado*] [*Research center*]　(RCD)
RM-CEAAL ... Red de Mujeres del Consejo de Educacion de Adultos de Americana Latina [*Women's Network of the Council for Adult Education in Latin America - WN-CAELA*] [*Quito, Ecuador*]　(EAIO)
RMCF....... Rocky Mountain Chocolate Factory, Inc. [*Durango, CO*] [*NASDAQ symbol*]　(NQ)
R & McG.... Income Tax Decisions of Australasia (Ratcliffe and McGrath) [*A publication*]　(APTA)
R & McG Ct of Rev ... Court of Review Decisions (Ratcliffe and McGrath) [*A publication*]
R M Ch ...... [*Robert M.*] Charlton's Georgia Reports [*1811-37*] [*A publication*]　(DLA)
R M Ch ...... Revista Musical Chilena [*A publication*]
R M Charlt (GA) ... [*Robert M.*] Charlton's Georgia Reports [*1811-37*] [*A publication*]　(DLA)
RM Chilena ... Revista Musical Chilena [*A publication*]
RMCI........ Right Management Consultants, Incorporated [*Philadelphia, PA*] [*NASDAQ symbol*]　(NQ)
RMCL....... Recommended Maximum Contaminant Level [*Environmental Protection Agency*]
RMCLB.... Revue Medico-Chirurgicale [*A publication*]
RMCM ...... Master Chief Radioman [*Navy rating*]
RMCM ...... Reduced Material Condition Maintenance　(MCD)
RMCM ...... Return Material Credit Memo
RMCM ...... Royal Manchester College of Music [*British*]
RMCMI..... Rocky Mountain Coal Mining Institute　(EA)
RMCO....... Raymond Manufacturing Company
RMCOEH ... Rocky Mountain Center for Occupational and Environmental Health [*University of Utah*] [*Research center*]　(RCD)
RMCP....... Rat Mast Cell Protease [*An enzyme*]
RMcraftN... Registered Mothercraft Nurse [*Australia*]
RMCS....... Range Monitoring and Control Subsystem　(MCD)
RMCS....... Reactor Manual Control System [*Nuclear energy*]　(NRCH)
RMCS....... Remote Monitoring and Control System [*Telecommunications*]
RMCS....... Royal Medical and Chirurgical Society [*British*]　(ROG)
RMCS....... Royal Military College of Science [*British*]
RMCS....... Senior Chief Radioman [*Navy rating*]
RMCSF ..... Recombinant Macrophage Colony-Stimulating Factor [*Biochemistry*]
RMCT .... Research Monographs in Cell and Tissue Physiology [*Elsevier Book Series*] [*A publication*]
RMCUSA ... Riley Motor Club USA　(EA)
RMD.......... Raw Materials Department [*Ministry of Supply*] [*British*]
RMD.......... Ready Money Down [*Immediate payment*]
RMD.......... Repair and Modification Directive　(AAG)
RMD.......... Resident Medical Doctor [*Australia*]
RMD.......... Retromanubrial Dullness [*Medicine*]
RMD.......... Rhine-Main-Danube Navigation System　(DS)
RMDA....... Request for Manufacturing Development Authorization　(AAG)
RMDAB ..... Revue de Medecine Aeronautique [*A publication*]
RMDI........ Radio Magnetic Deviation Indicator　(AAG)
RM Dig...... Rapalje and Mack's Digest of Railway Law [*A publication*]　(DLA)
RMDIR ..... Remove Directory [*Data processing*]
RMDMDL ... Revista Medica de Mocambique [*A publication*]
RMDP....... Rural Manpower Development Program
Rmdr......... Remainder　(DLA)
RMDSA...... Rivista di Medicina Aeronautica e Spaziale [*A publication*]
RME .... Radiation Monitoring Equipment
RME .... Railway Age [*A publication*]
RME .... Raw Materials　(MCD)
RME .... Receptor Mediated Endocytosis [*Biochemistry*]
RME .... Relay Mirror Experiment
RME .... Request Monitor Entry [*Data processing*]
RME .... Resident Maintenance Engineer　(NATG)
RME .... Rocket Mission Evaluator　(MCD)
RME .... Rocky Mountain Energy [*Vancouver Stock Exchange symbol*]
RME .... Rome, NY [*Location identifier*] [*FAA*]　(FAAL)
RME .... Royal Marine Engineers [*British*]
RMEA .... Revista Mexicana de Estudios Antropologicos y Historicos [*A publication*]
RMEC .... Refractory Metals Electrofinishing Corporation
RMED .... R-Med International, Inc. [*NASDAQ symbol*]　(NQ)
RMED .... Recruit, Retrain, Reemploy Medics [*Program*]
RMed........ Revue de la Mediterranee [*A publication*]
RMED .... Rocky Mountain Medical Corp. [*Greenwood Village, CO*] [*NASDAQ symbol*]　(NQ)
R Mediterr ... Revue de la Mediterranee [*A publication*]
RMedSoc... Royal Medical Society, Edinburgh
RMEF....... Rocky Mountain Elk Foundation　(EA)
RMEIDE... Revista de Medicina Interna, Neurologie, Psihiatrie, Neurochirurgie, Dermato-Venerologie. Seria Neurologia, Psihiatrie, Neurochirurgie [*A publication*]
RMEL........ Rocky Mountain Educational Laboratory [*Closed*]
RMELB ..... Radio Mentor Electronic [*A publication*]
R Melb Hosp Q ... Royal Melbourne Hospital. Quarterly [*A publication*]

R Melbourne Hosp Clin Rep ... Royal Melbourne Hospital. Clinical Reports [*A publication*]
RMEMAN ... Revue Medicale Miniere [*A publication*]
RMEMD ... Revue Roumaine de Morphologie, d'Embryologie, et de Physiologie. Serie Morphologie et Embryologie [*A publication*]
RMEPD..... Revue Roumaine de Morphologie, d'Embryologie, et de Physiologie. Serie Physiologie [*A publication*]
RMEPDZ ... Romanian Journal of Morphology, Embryology, and Physiology [*A publication*]
RMER .... Resource Management Expense Reporting System　(MCD)
RMERA..... Rumanian Medical Review [*A publication*]
R Mercados ... Revista dos Mercados [*A publication*]
R Metaph Mor ... Revue de Metaphysique et de Morale [*A publication*]
R Metaphys ... Review of Metaphysics [*A publication*]
R Met S...... Royal Meteorological Society [*British*]
R Mex Agr ... Revista del Mexico Agrario [*A publication*]
R Mex Ciencias Pols y Socs ... Revista Mexicana de Ciencias Politicas y Sociales [*A publication*]
R Mexic Sociol ... Revista Mexicana de Sociologia [*A publication*]
R Mexic Trab ... Revista Mexicana del Trabajo [*A publication*]
RMF .... RAC Income Fund [*NYSE symbol*]　(SPSG)
RMF .... Raw Materials Finance Department [*Ministry of Supply*] [*British*]
RMF .... RCS [*Reaction Control System*] Module Forward [*NASA*]　(NASA)
RMF .... Reactivity Measurement Facility [*Nuclear energy*]
RMF .... Reamfixture　(MCD)
RMF .... Reflectivity Measuring Facility
RMF .... Research Management. The International Journal of Research Management [*A publication*]
RMF .... Residual Master File [*Data processing*]
RMF .... Resource Measurement Facility [*Data processing*]
RMF .... Reymann Memorial Farms [*West Virginia University*] [*Research center*]　(RCD)
RMF .... Royal Munster Fusiliers [*Military unit*] [*British*]
RMFA....... Royal Malta Fencible Artillery [*British military*]　(DMA)
RMFC....... Rachel Minke Fan Club　(EA)
R M F C ... Recherches sur la Musique Francaise Classique [*A publication*]
RMFC....... Ronnie McDowell Fan Club　(EA)
RMFC....... Ronnie Milsap Fan Club　(EA)
RMFEB..... Revista Mexicana de Fisica. Suplemento de Ensenanza [*A publication*]
RMFFA ..... Raumfahrtforschung [*A publication*]
RMFIEK ... Revista Mexicana de Fitopatologia [*A publication*]
RMFMA..... Rock Mechanics [*A publication*]
RMFSA ..... Revista Mexicana de Fisica. Suplemento del Reactor [*A publication*]
RMFVR..... Royal Marine Forces Volunteer Reserve [*Obsolete*] [*British*]
RMFZA..... Radovi Medicinskogo Fakulteta u Zagrebu [*A publication*]
RMG .... RADAR Mapper Gapfiller
RMG.......... RAL Marketing Group, Inc. [*Vancouver Stock Exchange symbol*]
RMG.......... Ranging Machine Gun [*British military*]　(DMA)
RMG.......... Recommended for Medal and Gratuity [*British*]
RMG.......... Relative-Motion Gauge
RMG.......... Right Main Gear　(MCD)
RMG.......... Rome [*Georgia*] [*Airport symbol*] [*Obsolete*]　(OAG)
RMG.......... Rome [*Georgia*] [*Seismograph station code, US Geological Survey*]　(SEIS)
RMG.......... Ronald Martin Groome [*Commercial firm*] [*British*]
RMG.......... Royal Marine Gunner [*British*]
RMG.......... Russkaya Muzikal'naya Gazeta [*A publication*]
RMGCA .... Rocky Mountain Association of Geologists. Field Conference [*A publication*]
RMGF ...... RADAR Mapper, Gap Filler　(MSA)
RMGO...... Regional Military Government Officer [*World War II*]
RMGQA ... Records Management Quarterly [*A publication*]
RMH .... Rabbit-Mouse Hybridomas [*Immunochemistry*]
RMH .... Refrigerator Mechanical Household　(MSA)
RMH .... Reserve Bank of Malawi. Financial and Economic Review [*A publication*]
RMH .... Riemann's Metrical Hypothesis [*Mathematics*]
RMHA....... Rocky Mountain Horse Association　(EA)
RMHCSDI ... Robert Maynard Hutchins Center for the Study of Democratic Institutions
RMHDDHG ... Regiere Mich Herr durch Deinen Heiligen Geist [*Rule Me, Lord, Through Thy Holy Spirit*] [*German*] [*Motto of Ann, Margravine of Brandenburg (1575-1612)*]
RMHI....... Religious and Mental Health Inventory
RMHPB .... Reports on Mathematical Physics [*A publication*]
RMI .... Merrell-National Laboratories [*Research code symbol*]
RMI .... Rack Manufacturers Institute　(EA)
RMI .... Radio Magnetic Indicator
RMI .... Radiological Monitoring for Instructors [*Civil Defense*]
RMI .... Rassegna Mensile di Israel [*A publication*]
RMI .... Reich Ministry of Interior
RMI .... Release of Material for Issue
RMI .... Reliability Maturity Index [*Polaris*]
RMI .... Reliability Monitoring Index

RMI .... Religious of Mary Immaculate [*Roman Catholic women's religious order*]
RMI .... Remote Magnetic Indication
RMI .... Renewable Materials Institute [*College of Environmental Science and Forestry at Syracuse*] [*Research center*] (RCD)
RMI .... Repair and Maintenance Instruction [*Military*]
RMI .... Republic of the Marshall Islands
RMI .... Research Monographs in Immunology [*Elsevier Book Series*] [*A publication*]
RMI .... Residential Mortgage Investments, Inc. [*AMEX symbol*] (SPSG)
RMI .... Richardson-Merrell, Incorporated [*Later, Richardson-Vicks, Inc.*]
RMI .... Rivista Mensile di Israel [*A publication*]
RMI .... Rivista Musicale Italiana [*A publication*]
RMI .... Rocket Motor Igniter
RMI .... Roll Manufacturers Institute (EA)
RMI .... Route Monitoring Information [*Telecommunications*] (TEL)
RMI .... Rural Ministry Institute (EA)
RMIA .... Rattan Manufacturers and Importers Association
RMIA .... Registered Mail Insurance Association (EA)
RMIC .... Research Materials Information Center [*ORNL*]
RMICBM ... Road Mobile Intercontinental Ballistic Missile
RMIDDJ ... Revista de Medicina Interna, Neurologie, Psihiatrie, Neurochirurgie, Dermato-Venerologie. Seria Dermato-Venerologia [*A publication*]
RMIFC ...... Reba McEntire International Fan Club (EA)
RMII .... Reference Method Item Identification [*DoD*]
RMIIA .... Rassegna di Medicina Industriale e di Igiene del Lavoro [*A publication*]
RMIIDY .... Revista de Medicina Interna, Neurologie, Psihiatrie, Neurochirurgie, Dermato-Venerologie. Seria Medicina Interna [*A publication*]
R Mil Coll Can Civ Eng Res Rep ... Royal Military College of Canada. Civil Engineering Research Report [*A publication*]
RMIMDC ... Research Monographs in Immunology [*Elsevier Book Series*] [*A publication*]
R/MIN ...... Revolutions per Minute
RMIND ..... Reviews in Mineralogy [*A publication*]
RMIP .... Reentry Measurements Instrumentation Package
RMIs .... Rassegna Mensile di Israel [*A publication*]
RMIS .... Readiness Management Information System [*Military*] (AABC)
RMIS .... Resource Management Information System [*Environmental Protection Agency*]
RMIT .... Remittance Technologies Corp. [*NASDAQ symbol*] (NQ)
RMIT .... Rolland Maintenance Institutional Trainer [*Army*]
RMJ .... Ramjet (MSA)
RMJ .... Rumoi [*Japan*] [*Seismograph station code, US Geological Survey*] (SEIS)
RMJM .... Recluse Missionaries of Jesus and Mary [*Roman Catholic women's religious order*]
RMJMA .... Rocky Mountain Journal of Mathematics [*A publication*]
RMJSA ..... Roczniki Akademii Medycznej Imienia Juliana Marchlewskiego w Bialymstoku. Suplement [*A publication*]
RMK .... Remark (AFM)
RMK .... Renmark [*Australia*] [*Airport symbol*] (OAG)
RMK .... Retrofit Modification Kit
RMK .... Rhesus Monkey Kidney [*Medicine*]
RMK .... Robert-Mark [*AMEX symbol*] (SPSG)
RMK .... Roxmark Mines Ltd. [*Toronto Stock Exchange symbol*]
R Mkting Agric Econ ... Review of Marketing and Agricultural Economics [*A publication*]
RMKUA .... Report. Research Institute for Applied Mechanics (Kyushu University) [*A publication*]
RML .... Lieutenant, Royal Marines [*Navy*] [*British*] (ROG)
RML .... RADAR Mapper, Long Range
RML .... RADAR Microwave Link (IEEE)
RML .... Range Measurements Laboratory [*Air Force*]
RML .... Refresher Maintenance Lab
RML .... Regional Medical Library
RML .... Relational Machine Language
RML .... Remote Maintenance Line [*Bell Laboratories*]
RML .... Remote Measurements Laboratory
RML .... Rescue Motor Launch [*Air/sea rescue*] [*Navy*]
RML .... Restricted Maximum Likelihood [*Statistics*]
RML .... Review of Metal Literature [*American Society for Metals*] [*A publication*]
RML .... Revista Mexicana de Literatura [*A publication*]
R MI .... Revue de Musicologie [*A publication*]
RML .... Rifled Muzzle-Loading [*Gun*]
RML .... Right Mediolateral [*Episiotomy*] [*Obstetrics*]
RML .... Right Mentolateral [*Episiotomy*] [*Obstetrics*]
RML .... Right Middle Lobe [*Lungs*]
RML .... Rock Mechanics Laboratory [*Pennsylvania State University*] [*Research center*] (RCD)
RML .... Rocky Mountain Laboratories [*National Institutes of Health*]
RML .... Rotating Mirror LASER
RML .... Russell Corp. [*NYSE symbol*] (SPSG)
RMLA .... Rocky Mountain Lama Association (EA)

RMLC .... Royal Marine Labour Corps [*British military*] (DMA)
RMLI .... Royal Marine Light Infantry [*Obsolete*] [*British*]
RML IV ..... Mid-Atlantic Regional Medical Library Program [*Library network*]
RMLMA ... Revue MBLE [*Manufacture Belge de Lampes et de Materiel*] [*A publication*]
RMLMDR ... Revue de Medecine du Limousin [*A publication*]
RMLO .... Reports Management Liaison Officer [*Defense Supply Agency*]
RMLP .... Regional Medical Library Program [*Department of Health and Human Services*]
RMLR .... RADAR Mapper, Long Range (MSA)
RMLR .... RADAR Microwave Link Repeater (FAAC)
RMLR .... Rocky Mountain Law Review [*Later, University of Colorado. Law Review*] [*A publication*]
RMLT .... RADAR Microwave Link Terminal (FAAC)
RMM .... RADAR Map Matching
RMM .... Rapid Micromedia Method [*Analytical biochemistry*]
RMM .... Read-Mostly Memory [*Data processing*]
RMM .... Read-Mostly Mode [*Data processing*]
RMM .... Remote Maintenance Monitor [*Data processing*] (MCD)
RMM .... Revue de Metaphysique et de Morale [*A publication*]
RMM .... Revue du Monde Musulman [*A publication*]
RMM .... Rifle Marksman
RMM .... Ripple Mark Meter
RMM .... Rosedale Mennonite Missions (EA)
RMMC ...... Regiment Materiel Management Center [*Military*] (AABC)
RMMC ...... Rocky Mountain Mapping Center [*Colorado*]
RMMDBO ... Royal Marine Mobile Defended Base Organisation [*British military*] (DMA)
RMMEA ... Rolling Mill Machinery and Equipment Association [*Defunct*] (EA)
RMMFA .... Revue Medico-Chirurgicale des Maladies du Foie, de la Rate, et du Pancreas [*A publication*]
RMMI .... Rocky Mountain Minerals, Incorporated [*NASDAQ symbol*] (NQ)
RMMID ... Revue Roumaine de Medecine. Medecine Interne [*A publication*]
RMMJA .... Rocky Mountain Medical Journal [*A publication*]
RMMLF .... Rocky Mountain Mineral Law Foundation (EA)
RMMLR ... Rocky Mountain Mineral Law Review [*A publication*] (DLA)
RMMND... Rocky Mountain Mineral Law Newsletter [*A publication*]
RMMP ...... Riceland Mosquito Management Plan [*Department of Agriculture*]
RM/MS & C ... Redundancy Management/Moding, Sequencing, and Control (MCD)
RMMTB .... Rocky Mountain Motor Tariff Bureau, Inc.
RMMU ...... Removable Media Memory Units
RMN .... Registered Mental Nurse
RMN .... Remain (FAAC)
RMN .... Reserve Material [*Account*] Navy
RMN .... Richard Milhous Nixon [*US president, 1913-*]
RMN .... Roman Corp. Ltd. [*Toronto Stock Exchange symbol*]
RMNac ..... Revista. Museo Nacional [*A publication*]
R & MNP ... Ryan and Moody's English Nisi Prius Reports [*A publication*] (DLA)
RMNS .... Royal Malayan Navy Ship [*British military*] (DMA)
RMNUBP ... Research Methods in Neurochemistry [*A publication*]
RMNZA ... Rudy i Metale Niezelazne [*A publication*]
RMO......... RADAR Master Oscillator
RMO......... RADAR Material Office [*Navy*] (MCD)
RMO......... Radio Material Office [*or Officer*] [*Navy*] (IEEE)
RMO......... Records Management Office [*or Officer*] [*Military*] (AFM)
RMO......... Recruitment and Manning Organization [*WSA*]
RMO......... Refined Menhaden Oil [*Food science*]
RMO......... Regimental Medical Officer (NATG)
RMO......... Regimental Munitions Officer [*Army*]
RMO......... Regional Management Officer [*Social Security Administration*]
RMO......... Regional Medical Officer [*British*]
RMO......... Reports Management Officer [*DoD*]
RMO......... Resident Medical Officer [*British*]
RMO......... Resources Management Office [*NASA*] (KSC)
RMO......... Rochester-Mercier [*New York*] [*Seismograph station code, US Geological Survey*] [*Closed*] (SEIS)
RMO......... Rocket Management Office [*Army*] (RDA)
RMO......... Royal Marine Office [*British*]
RM Obs ..... Royal Marine Observer [*British military*] (DMA)
RMOC .... Reaction Mechanisms in Organic Chemistry [*Elsevier Book Series*] [*A publication*]
RMOC .... Recommended Maintenance Operation Chart [*Army*] (AABC)
RMod .... Revue Moderne [*A publication*]
RMOKHS ... Religious and Military Order of Knights of the Holy Sepulchre (EA)
RMON .... Resident Monitor
R MON RE(M) ... Royal Monmouthshire Royal Engineers (Militia) [*British military*] (DMA)
R Montceau ... Revue Periodique de "La Physiophile." Societe d'Etudes des Sciences Naturelles et Historiques de Montceau-Les-Mines [*A publication*]
RMOS .... Refractory Metal-Oxide Semiconductor (IEEE)
RMP .... International Migration [*A publication*]
RMP .... Radio Motor Patrol [*New York police cars*]

RMP .... Rainform Message Processing   (MCD)
RMP .... Raman Microprobe [*Spectrometer*]
RMP .... Rampart [*Alaska*] [*Airport symbol*]   (OAG)
RMP .... Rampart Resources Ltd. [*Vancouver Stock Exchange symbol*]
RMP .... Range Maintenance Plan   (MCD)
RMP .... Reduction of the Membrane Potential
RMP .... Reentry Measurement Program [*Military*]
RMP .... Refiner Mechanical Pulp [*Papermaking*]
RMP .... Regional Medical Program
RMP .... Registered Medical Practitioner [*British*]   (ROG)
RMP .... Reprogrammable Microprocessor
RMP .... Research Management Plan
RMP .... Research and Microfilm Publications
RMP .... Resting Membrane Potential [*Neuroelectrochemistry*]
RMP .... Rheinisches Museum fuer Philologie [*A publication*]
RMP .... Rifampin [*Also, R/AMP, RF, RIF*] [*Bactericide*]
RMP .... Right Mentoposterior [*A fetal position*] [*Obstetrics*]
RMP .... RMP: Rural Marketing and Policy [*A publication*]
RMP .... Rocket Motor Plume
RMP .... Rocket Motor Propellant   (MUGU)
RMP .... Rome [*Monte Porzio Catone*] [*Italy*] [*Seismograph station code, US Geological Survey*]   (SEIS)
RMP .... Round Maximum Pressure   (NATG)
RMP .... Royal Marine Police [*British military*]   (DMA)
RMP .... Royal Military Police [*British*]
RMPA ...... Rocky Mountain Psychological Association   (MCD)
RMPA ...... Royal Medico-Psychological Association [*British*]
RMPaul ..... Revista. Museu Paulista [*A publication*]
RMPE........ Root Mean Percentage Error [*Statistics*]
RMPF........ Rocky Mountain Poison Foundation
RMPI........ Remote Memory Port Interface
RMPIA ...... Razrabotka Mestorozhdenii Poleznykh Iskopaemykh [*A publication*]
RMPM ...... Rich Man, Poor Man [*Book title*]
RMPM ...... Royal Mail Parcels Marketing [*British Post Office*]
RMPO .... Ramapo Financial Corp. [*NASDAQ symbol*]   (NQ)
RM & PP ... Raw Material and Purchase Parts   (MCD)
RMPP........ Risk Management and the Prevention Plan [*Hazardous materials*]
RMPPA ..... Revue de Medecine Psychosomatique et de Psychologie Medicale [*A publication*]
RMPR........ Rassemblement Mahorais pour la Republique [*Mayotte Rally for the Republic*] [*Political party*]   (PPW)
RMPR........ Rated Mobilization and Professional Resource   (MUGU)
RMPR........ Revised Maximum Price Regulation [*World War II*]
RMPS........ Regional Medical Programs Service [*Health Services and Mental Health Administration, HEW*]
RMPTC..... Royal Military Police Training Centre [*British*]
RMQ......... Records Management Quarterly [*A publication*]
RMQM...... Quarter-Master, Royal Marines [*Navy*] [*British*]   (ROG)
RMR .... Malraux Society   (EAIO)
RMR .... RAC Mortgage Investment [*NYSE symbol*]   (SPSG)
RMR .... Rapid Memory Reload   (MCD)
RMR .... Reamer [*Design engineering*]
RMR .... Reference Mixture Radio   (KSC)
RMR .... Reflector Moderated Reactor   (AAG)
RMR .... Regional Maintenance Representative [*Military*]
RMR .... Remote Map Reader
RMR .... Reserve Minority Report [*Army*]
RMR .... Resource Management Review [*Military*]
RMR .... Resting Metabolic Rate [*Physiology*]
RMR .... Right Medial Rectus [*Eye anatomy*]
RMR .... Rocky Mountain Law Review [*Later, University of Colorado. Law Review*] [*A publication*]
RMR .... Rocky Mountain Review [*A publication*]
RMR .... Rocky Mountain Review of Language and Literature [*A publication*]
RMR .... Rotation Magnitude Ratio
RMR .... Rotational Magnetic-Dipole Radiation [*Astronomy*]
RMR .... Royal Malayan Regiment [*British military*]   (DMA)
RMR .... Royal Marines Reserve [*British*]
RMR .... Royal Montreal Regiment [*Military unit*]
RMRA ...... Royal Marines Rifle Association [*British military*]   (DMA)
RMREEY .. Revue des Maladies Respiratoires [*A publication*]
RMRHB .... Rheumatology and Rehabilitation [*A publication*]
RMRM ...... Radioactive Materials Reference Manual   (NRCH)
RMRMA ... Revue M - Mecanique [*Belgium*] [*A publication*]
RMRO ...... Royal Marine Routine Orders [*British military*]   (DMA)
RMROCK ... Rocket Motors Records Office Center [*Navy*]
RMRS........ Remote Meter Resetting System [*Postage meter*]
RMRS........ Repeatable Maintenance and Recall System   (NASA)
RMS .... RADAR Maintenance Spares   (NG)
RMS .... RADAR Mapping Set [*or System*]
RMS .... Radian Means per Second   (NASA)
RMS .... Radiation and Meteoroid Satellite [*NASA*]
RMS .... Radio Marker Station
RMS .... Radiological Monitoring System
RMS .... Radiology Management System
RMS .... Radiometric Sextant Subsystem
RMS .... Rail Mail Steamer
RMS .... Railway Mail Service

RMS .... Random Mass Storage [*Data processing*]
RMS .... Random Motion Simulator [*NASA*]   (NASA)
RMS .... Range Measuring System [*Air Force*]
RMS .... Range Modification System
RMS .... Rapid Multistream
RMS .... Rathkamp Matchcover Society   (EA)
RMS .... Reactor Monitor System   (IEEE)
RMS .... Reconnaissance Management System
RMS .... Record Management System
RMS .... Recovery Management Support [*Data processing*]
RMS .... Recruiting Main Station [*Military*]
RMS .... Redundancy Management System [*NASA*]   (MCD)
RMS .... Reentry Measurement System
RMS .... Regulatory Manpower System [*Nuclear energy*]   (NRCH)
RMS .... Regulatory Monitoring System   (NRCH)
RMS .... Rehabilitation Medicine Service [*Veterans Administration*]
RMS .... Reliability and Maintainability Simulator
RMS .... Remote Maintenance System
RMS .... Remote Manipulator Subsystem [*NASA*]   (NASA)
RMS .... Remote Manual Switch [*Nuclear energy*]   (NRCH)
RMS .... Remote Master Station   (MCD)
RMS .... Remote Missile Select
RMS .... Renaissance and Modern Studies [*A publication*]
RMS .... Reports Management System [*Office of Management and Budget*] [*Database*]
RMS .... Resources Management System [*Army*]
RMS .... Respiratory Muscle Strength [*Physiology*]
RMS .... Retromotor Simulator
RMS .... Revised Magnetic Standard
RMS .... Revista Mexicana de Sociologia [*A publication*]
RMS .... Rhabdomyosarcoma [*Also, RHM*] [*Oncology*]
RMS .... Rheometrics Mechanical Spectrometer
RMS .... RMS International [*AMEX symbol*]   (SPSG)
RMS .... Rocket Management System   (MCD)
RMS .... Roll Microwave Sensor
RMS .... Romanian Missionary Society   (EA)
RMS .... Root Mean Square [*Physics, statistics*]
RMS .... Royal Mail Service [*British*]
RMS .... Royal Mail Steamship [*British*]
RMS .... Royal Marine Signaller [*British military*]   (DMA)
RMS .... Royal Meteorological Society [*British*]
RMS .... Royal Microscopical Society [*British*]
RMS .... Royal Museum of Scotland
RMS .... Royal Society of Miniature Painters, Sculptors, and Gravers [*British*]
RMS .... Rural Manpower Services   (OICC)
RMSA....... Rural Music Schools Association [*British*]
RMSA....... Seaman Apprentice, Radioman, Striker [*Navy rating*]
RMSCA...... Rivista Mineraria Siciliana [*A publication*]
RMSchMus ... Royal Marines School of Music [*British*]
RMSD ...... Root Mean Square Deviation [*Statistics*]
RMSD .... Royal Mail Special Delivery [*British Post Office facility*]   (DCTA)
RMSDS ..... Reserve Merchant Ship Defense System [*Navy*]   (MCD)
RMSE........ Relative Mean Square Error [*Statistics*]
RMSE........ Root Mean Square Error
RMSF .... Rocky Mountain Spotted Fever
RMSFA ..... Revista Mexicana de Fisica. Suplemento de Fisica Aplicada [*A publication*]
RMSG .... Resource Management Study Group [*Military*]
RMSI .... Royal Marine Signalling Instructor [*British military*]   (DMA)
RMSM ...... Royal Military School of Music [*British*]
RMSN .... Seaman, Radioman, Striker [*Navy rating*]
RMSP....... Refractory Metal Sheet Program [*Navy*]   (NG)
RMSP........ Resource and Mission Sponsor Plan [*Navy*]
RMSP........ Royal Mail Steam Packet Co.
RMSRA ..... Revue Medicale de la Suisse Romande [*A publication*]
RMSS........ Range Meteorological Sounding System   (MCD)
RMSS........ Religious Mercedarians of the Blessed Sacrament [*Roman Catholic women's religious order*]
RMSSJ ..... Rocky Mountain Social Science Journal [*A publication*]
RMSt........ Reading Medieval Studies [*A publication*]
RMSU .... Remote Monitoring Sensor Unit   (MCD)
RM Suisse ... Schweizerische Musikzeitung/Revue Musicale Suisse [*A publication*]
RM Suisse Romande ... Revue Musicale de Suisse Romande [*A publication*]
RMSVP ..... Remote Manipulation Subsystem Verification Plan [*NASA*]   (MCD)
RMT .... Radiometric Moon Tracer
RMT .... Rapid Mass Transfer [*Physics*]
RMT .... Rapidly Moving Telescope [*Astronomy*]
RMT .... Rectangular Midwater Trawl   (ADA)
RMT .... Registered Massage Therapist
RMT .... Registered Music Teacher
RMT .... Registered Music Therapist
RMT .... Registry of Medical Technologists
RMT .... Remote [*Telecommunications*]   (MSA)
RMT .... Research Methods and Techniques
RMT .... Reserve Mechanical Transport [*British military*]   (DMA)
RMT .... Resource Management Team   (MCD)
RMT .... Rework Monitoring Test

RMT .... Right Mentotransverse [*A fetal position*] [*Obstetrics*]
RMTAA .... Rivista di Meteorologia Aeronautica [*A publication*]
RMTB....... Reconfiguration Maximum Theoretical Bandwidth
RMTC ...... RADAR Maintenance and Test Control   (MCD)
RMTC ...... Regional Medical Training Center
RMTC .... Rider Motorcycle Touring Club [*Commercial firm*] [*Later, RC*]   (EA)
RMTC ...... Royal Melbourne Technical College [*Australia*]
RMTE....... Remote   (AAG)
RMTF....... Ready Missile Test Facility [*Military*]   (CAAL)
RM Th ...... Rechtsgeleerd Magazijn Themis [*A publication*]
RMTH....... Regular Member of the Third House [*Pseudonym used by Dr. Francis Bacon*]
RMTH....... River Mouth [*Board on Geographic Names*]
RMTK ...... Ramtek Corp. [*NASDAQ symbol*]   (NQ)
RMTO ...... Regional Motor Transport Officer [*British*]   (DCTA)
RMTOB3 .. Revue Medicale de Tours [*A publication*]
RMTR .... Redesigned Missile Tracking RADAR [*Army*]   (AABC)
RMTRD .... Revue de Medicine du Travail [*A publication*]
RMTS....... Research Member of the Technical Staff
RMTSA ..... Revista. Instituto de Medicina Tropical de Sao Paulo [*A publication*]
RMTSDH ... Texas. Agricultural Experiment Station. Research Monograph [*A publication*]
RMU......... Radio Maintenance Unit   (DEN)
RMU......... Rainbow Monument [*Utah*] [*Seismograph station code, US Geological Survey*]   (SEIS)
RMU......... Reference Measuring Unit   (MCD)
RMU......... Remote Maneuvering Unit [*NASA*]
RMU......... Remote Multiplexer Unit [*Data processing*]   (KSC)
RMu......... Revue Musicale [*A publication*]
R de MU ... Revue de Musicologie [*Paris*] [*A publication*]
RMUC....... Reference Measuring Unit Computer
RMUC....... Rocky Mount Undergarment Company, Inc. [*Rocky Mount, NC*] [*NASDAQ symbol*]   (NQ)
R-MuLV ... Rauscher Murine Leukemia Virus
RMUNA.... Revista de Medicina. Universidad de Navarra [*A publication*]
R Mus....... Revue Musicale [*A publication*]
R de Mus... Revue de Musicologie [*A publication*]
R Mus Art Archeol ... Revue. Musee d'Art et d'Archeologie [*A publication*]
R Mus Chile ... Revista Musical Chilena [*A publication*]
R Musicol ... Revue de Musicologie [*A publication*]
R Mus Ital ... Nuova Rivista Musicale Italiana. Trimestrale di Cultura e Informazione Musicale [*A publication*]
R Mus Ital ... Rivista Musicale Italiana [*A publication*]
R Mus La Plata Antropol ... Revista. Museo de La Plata. Seccion Antropologia [*A publication*]
R Mus Nac ... Revista. Museo Nacional [*A publication*]
R Mus de Suisse Romande ... Revue Musicale de Suisse Romande [*A publication*]
RMV .... Reentry Measurement Vehicle [*Military*]
RMV .... Remotely Manned Vehicle
RMV .... Remove   (AAG)
RMV .... Respiratory Minute Volume [*Physiology*]
RMVBL..... Removable   (AAG)
RMVD...... Removed   (AAG)
RMVG...... Removing   (AAG)
RMVL ...... Removal   (AAG)
RMVM ...... Review of Medical and Veterinary Mycology [*Database*] [*Commonwealth Mycological Institute*] [*Information service or system*]   (CRD)
RMVT ...... Repetitive Monomorphic Ventricular Tachycardia [*Cardiology*]
RMW......... Rattlesnake Mountain [*Washington*] [*Seismograph station code, US Geological Survey*]   (SEIS)
RMW......... Reactor Makeup Water [*Nuclear energy*]   (NRCH)
R/M/W..... Read/Modify/Write
RMWAA ... Roadmasters and Maintenance of Way Association of America   (EA)
RMWC..... Randolph-Macon Woman's College [*Virginia*]
RMWO..... Warrant Officer, Royal Marines [*Navy*] [*British*]   (ROG)
RMWR..... Religious, Morale, Welfare, and Recreation [*Military*]   (AFM)
RMWS..... Reactor Makeup Water Storage [*Nuclear energy*]   (NRCH)
RMWT..... Reactor Makeup Water Tank [*Nuclear energy*]   (NRCH)
RMX......... Resource Management Executive   (MCD)
R & My ..... Russell and Mylne's English Chancery Reports [*A publication*]   (DLA)
RMZBA..... Rudarsko-Metalurski Zbornik [*A publication*]
RN.............. Compagnia d'Exploitation de Lignes Aeriennes Interieures - Royal Air Inter [*Morocco*] [*ICAO designator*]   (FAAC)
RN.............. Neptune Radii [*Astronomy*]
RN.............. Newport Public Library, Newport, RI [*Library symbol*] [*Library of Congress*]   (LCLS)
RN.............. Rada Narodowa [*A publication*]
RN.............. Radio Navigation
RN.............. Radionuclide [*Radiology*]
Rn.............. Radon [*Chemical element*]
RN.............. Random Number   (IEEE)
RN.............. Rassemblement National [*Canada*] [*Political party*]   (PPW)
RN.............. Rattus Norvegicus [*The Norway or brown rat*]
RN.............. Real Name [*British Library indexing for pseudonymous author*]
RN.............. Realta Nuova [*A publication*]

RN.............. Reception Nil [*Radio logs*]
RN.............. Reception Node
RN.............. Record Number [*Online database field identifier*]
RN.............. Red Nucleus [*Brain anatomy*]
RN.............. Reference Noise [*Telecommunications*]
RN.............. Reference Number
RN.............. Registered Nurse
RN.............. Registered Nurse [*A publication*]
RN.............. Registry Number
RN.............. Rejection Notice   (AAG)
RN.............. Release Note [*Shipping*]   (DS)
RN.............. Removable Needle [*Medicine*]
RN.............. Renaissance News [*A publication*]
RN.............. Renastera Noastra [*Rumania*] [*A publication*]   (BJA)
Rn.............. Renumbered [*Existing article renumbered*] [*Used in Shepard's Citations*] [*Legal term*]   (DLA)
RN.............. Research Note
RN.............. Revision Notice   (KSC)
RN.............. Revue du Nord [*A publication*]
R du N........ Revue du Notariat [*A publication*]
RN.............. Revue Nouvelle [*A publication*]
RN.............. Revue Numismatique [*A publication*]
RN.............. Reynolds Number [*Also, R, Re*] [*Viscosity*]
R & N .... Rhodesia and Nyasaland Law Reports [*1956*] [*A publication*]   (DLA)
RN.............. Richard Nixon [*In book title "RN - The Memoirs of Richard Nixon"*]
RN.............. River Name   (BJA)
RN.............. Roan (Leather) [*Bookbinding*]   (ROG)
RN.............. Root Tip Necrosis [*Plant pathology*]
RN.............. Rough Notes [*A publication*]
RN.............. Royal Name   (BJA)
RN.............. Royal Navy [*British*]
RN.............. Rubber Non-Continuous Liner   (DS)
RN.............. Ruin   (ROG)
RN.............. Ruritan National   (EA)
RNA.......... Radio Naval Association [*British*]
RNA.......... Radio Navigational Aids   (NATG)
RNA.......... Rassemblement National Arabe [*Arab National Rally*] [*Tunisia*]   (PD)
RNA.......... Rations Not Available [*Military*]   (AABC)
RNA.......... Recurring Nuisances Act [*British*]
RNA.......... Regina Resources [*Vancouver Stock Exchange symbol*]
RNA.......... Registered Nurse Anesthetist
RNA.......... Registered Nursing Assistant
RNA.......... Religion Newswriters Association   (EA)
RNA.......... Republic of New Africa   (EA)
RNA.......... Research Natural Area [*National Science Foundation*]
RNA.......... Ribonucleic Acid [*Biochemistry, genetics*]
RNA.......... Robbery Not Armed
RNA.......... Romantic Novelists' Association [*British*]
RNA.......... Rotatable Nozzle Assembly
RNA.......... Rough, Noncapsulated, Avirulent [*With reference to bacteria*]
RNA.......... Royal Naval Association [*British military*]   (DMA)
RNA.......... Royal Neighbors of America   (EA)
RNA.......... Royal Netherlands Army   (NATG)
RNA.......... Royal Norwegian Army   (MCD)
RNAA....... Radiochemical Neutron Activation Analysis
RNAA....... Radiometric Neutron Activation Analysis
R/NAA ..... Rocketdyne - North American Aviation [*Later, Rockwell International Corp.*]   (AAG)
RNAA....... Russian Nobility Association in America   (EA)
RNAAC.... Reference Number Action Activity Code   (MCD)
RNAAF.... Royal Norwegian Army and Air Force
RNABC News ... RNABC (Registered Nurses Association of British Columbia) News [*A publication*]
RNAC....... Remote Network Access Controller
RNAC....... Royal Nepal Airlines Corporation
RNAC....... Royal Newcastle Aero Club [*Australia*]
RNAD....... Royal Naval Armament Depot [*British*]
RNAEC .... Rhodesia and Nyasaland Army Educational Corps [*British military*]   (DMA)
RNAF .... Royal Naval Air Force [*British*]
RNAF .... Royal Netherlands Air Force
RNAF .... Royal Norwegian Air Force
RNAH....... Royal Naval Auxiliary Hospital [*British military*]   (DMA)
RNAL .... Radionuclear Applications Laboratory [*Pennsylvania State University*] [*Research center*]   (RCD)
RNAM....... Regional Network for Agricultural Machinery [*Pasay City, Metro Manila, Philippines*]   (EAIO)
RNAMY .... Royal Naval Aircraft Maintenance Yard [*British*]
RNAO News ... RNAO (Registered Nurses Association of Ontario) News [*A publication*]
RNap......... Revue Napoleonienne [*A publication*]
RNAP .... Ribonucleic Acid Polymerase [*An enzyme*]
RNar......... Ragioni Narrative [*A publication*]
RNAS .... Royal Naval Air Service [*Precursor of Fleet Air Arm*] [*British*] [*Initialism also facetiously translated during World War I as "Really Not a Sailor"*]
RNAS .... Royal Naval Air Station [*British

RNASBR...	Royal Naval Auxiliary Sick Berth Reserve [*British military*] (DMA)
RNase.......	Ribonuclease [*An enzyme*]
RNaseP.....	Ribonuclease-P [*An enzyme*]
RNasin......	Ribonuclease Inhibitor [*Biochemistry*]
R Nat........	Revue Nationale [*A publication*]
RNATE.....	Royal Naval Air Training Establishment [*British*]
RNAV.......	Area Navigation
R-NAV......	Random Navigation
RNAV.......	Royal Naval Artillery Volunteers [*British*]
R Navig Fluv Europ ...	Revue de la Navigation Fluviale Europeenne [*A publication*]
RNAW.......	Royal Naval Aircraft Workshop [*British*]
RNAY.......	Royal Naval Aircraft Yard [*British*]
RNaz..........	Rassegna Nazionale [*A publication*]
RNB........	Millville, NJ [*Location identifier*] [*FAA*] (FAAL)
RNB...........	Received, Not Billed (AFM)
RNB...........	Renegotiation Board [*Terminated, 1979*] [*Federal government*]
RNB...........	Republic New York Corp. [*NYSE symbol*] (SPSG)
RNB...........	Resonant Nuclear Battery
RNB...........	Ronneby [*Sweden*] [*Airport symbol*] (OAG)
RNB...........	Royal Naval Barracks [*British*]
RNBC.......	Royal Naval Beach Commando [*British*]
RNBD.......	Royal North British Dragoons [*British military*] (DMA)
RNBF.......	Royal North British Fusiliers [*British military*] (DMA)
RNBLA.....	Rivista di Neurobiologia [*A publication*]
RNBM......	Radio Noise Burst Monitor (MCD)
RNBM......	Royal Navy Ballistic Missile [*British*]
RNBO......	Rainbow Technologies, Inc. [*NASDAQ symbol*] (NQ)
RNBT........	Royal Naval Benevolent Trust [*British*]
RNBWS.....	Royal Naval Bird Watching Society [*British*]
RNC...........	Little Raleigh [*North Carolina*] [*Seismograph station code, US Geological Survey*] (SEIS)
RNC...........	McMinnville, TN [*Location identifier*] [*FAA*] (FAAL)
RNC...........	Radio Noncontingent
RNC...........	Rainbow Network Communications [*Floral Park, NY*] [*Telecommunications*] (TSSD)
RNC........	Republican National Committee (EA)
RNC........	Request Next Character
RNC...........	Revista Nacional de Cultura [*A publication*]
RNC...........	Romanian National Council (EA)
RNC...........	Royal Naval College [*For future officers; often spoken of as Dartmouth*] [*British*]
RNC...........	Rumanian National Committee [*Later, Romanian National Tourist Office*] (EA)
RNCA.......	Rhodesia and Nyasaland Court of Appeal Law Reports [*A publication*] (DLA)
RNCC.......	Reference Number Category Code (MCD)
RNCC.......	Royal Naval College of Canada [*1911-1922*]
RNCF........	Read Natural Childbirth Foundation (EA)
RNCH.......	Ranch (MCD)
RNCM......	Royal Northern College of Music [*British*]
RNColl......	Royal Naval College, Greenwich [*British*]
RN & CR...	Ryde, Newport & Cowes Railway [*British*]
RNCSIR ...	Royal Norwegian Council for Scientific and Industrial Research (EAIO)
RNCT........	Reports of the Working Committees. Northeast Conference on the Teaching of Foreign Languages [*A publication*]
RNCV.......	Royal Navy Coast Volunteers [*British military*] (DMA)
RNCVR	Royal Naval Canadian Volunteer Reserve [*World War I*]
RND...........	Radical Neck Dissection [*Medicine*]
RND...........	Random
RND...........	Rassemblement National Democratique [*National Democratic Rally*] [*Senegal*] [*Political party*] (PPW)
RND...........	Real-Fluid Nonisentropic Decompression [*Engineering*]
RND...........	Rocznik Naukowo-Dydaktyczny [*A publication*]
RND..........	Round
RND...........	Royal Naval Division [*British*]
RND...........	San Antonio, TX [*Location identifier*] [*FAA*] (FAAL)
RNDH.......	Royal North Devon Hussars [*British military*] (DMA)
RNDM......	Random (MSA)
RNDM......	Random Access, Inc. [*NASDAQ symbol*] (NQ)
RNDPD	Roundup [*United States*] [*A publication*]
RNDr........	Doctor of Natural Sciences
RNDZ.......	Rendezvous (KSC)
RNE...........	Aspen, CO [*Location identifier*] [*FAA*] (FAAL)
RNE...........	Register of the National Estate [*Australia*]
RNE...........	Roanne [*France*] [*Airport symbol*] (OAG)
RNEC.......	Royal Naval Engineering College [*British*]
RNEColl....	Royal Naval Engineering College [*British*]
RNEE.......	Royal Navy Equipment Exhibition [*British*]
RNEIAF ...	Royal Netherlands East Indies Air Force
RNEIN	Royal Netherlands East Indies Navy
RNEMDX ...	Revue de Nematologie [*A publication*]
RNeosc.....	Revue Neo-Scolastique de Philosophie [*A publication*]
RNERL......	Radiochemistry and Nuclear Engineering Research Laboratory [*National Environmental Research Center*]
RNES........	Royal Naval Engineering Service [*British*]
RNETA.....	Royal Naval Endurance Triathlon Association [*British*]
RNEW.......	Religious Network for Equality for Women (EA)
RNF	Radial Nerve Factor [*of sea urchin*]
RNF	Radio Noise Figure (CET)
RNF	Receiver Noise Figure
RNF	Refracted Near Field [*Optics*]
RNF	Royal Naval Fund [*British*] (DAS)
RNF	Royal Northumberland Fusiliers [*Military unit*] [*British*]
RNFC........	Reference Number Format Code (MCD)
RNFC........	Royal Naval Film Corporation [*British military*] (DMA)
RNFL........	Rainfall (FAAC)
RNFP........	RADAR Not Functioning Properly [*Military*] (AFIT)
RNG...........	Army National Guard (FAAC)
RNG...........	Radio Range
RNG...........	Random Number Generator [*Parapsychology*]
RNG...........	Range [*or Ranging*] (AAG)
RNG...........	Ranging Noise Generator
RNG...........	Reference Noise Generator
RNG...........	Regulations under the Natural Gas Act
RNG...........	Running
RNGG.......	Ringing (MSA)
RNGHQ	Royal Navy General Headquarters [*British*]
RNGLND..	Rangeland
RNGM......	Royal North Gloucestershire Militia [*British military*] (DMA)
RNGMA....	Refiner and Natural Gasoline Manufacturer [*A publication*]
RNGT.......	Renegotiate
RNGYA	Rhinology [*A publication*]
RNH	New Richmond, WI [*Location identifier*] [*FAA*] (FAAL)
RNH	Royal Naval Hospital [*British*]
RNH	Royal Newcastle Hospital [*Australia*]
RNHA	Republican National Hispanic Assembly of the United States (EA)
RNHi	Newport Historical Society, Newport, RI [*Library symbol*] [*Library of Congress*] (LCLS)
RN-HSG...	Radionuclide Hysterosalpingogram [*Medicine*]
RNI	Kansas City, MO [*Location identifier*] [*FAA*] (FAAL)
RNI	Research Notes (Ibadan) [*A publication*]
RNI	Research Policy. A Journal Devoted to Research Policy, Research Management, and Planning [*A publication*]
RNI	Resident Navy Inspector
RNIB	Royal National Institute for the Blind [*British*]
RNIC	Robinson Nugent, Incorporated [*NASDAQ symbol*] (NQ)
RN ID	RN Idaho [*A publication*]
RNID	Royal National Institute for the Deaf [*British*]
RNIE	Royal Netherlands Institute of Engineers
RNIM	Rotors Not in Motion [*Aviation*] (AIA)
RNIO	Resident Naval Inspector of Ordnance
RNIR	Reduction to Next Inferior Rank
RNIT	Radio Noise Interference Test
RNJ	Ramapo College of New Jersey, Mahwah, NJ [*OCLC symbol*] (OCLC)
RNJ	Rektorskommitten for de Nordiska Journalist Hogskolorna [*Committee for Nordic Universities of Journalism - CNUJ*] (EAIO)
RNJ	Yoron-Jima [*Japan*] [*Airport symbol*] (OAG)
RNk	North Kingstown Free Library, North Kingstown, RI [*Library symbol*] [*Library of Congress*] (LCLS)
RNKID	Rikuyo Nainen Kikan [*A publication*]
RNL	Rainelle, WV [*Location identifier*] [*FAA*] (FAAL)
RNL	Renewal (MSA)
RNL	Rennell Island [*Solomon Islands*] [*Airport symbol*] (OAG)
RNL	Retail Newsletter [*A publication*]
RNL	Review of National Literatures [*A publication*]
RNLAF......	Royal Netherlands Air Force
RNLBI	Royal National Life-Boat Institution [*British*]
RNLC	Rosary Novena for Life Committee (EA)
RNLI.........	Royal National Life-Boat Institution [*British*]
RNLJ	Rhodesia and Nyasaland Law Journal [*A publication*] (DLA)
RNLO	Royal Naval Liaison Officer [*British*]
R & NLR....	Rhodesia and Nyasaland Law Reports [*1956-64*] [*A publication*] (DLA)
RNLT........	Running Light
RNM..........	Radio-Navigation Mobile
RNM..........	Radionuclide Migration
RNM..........	Rassemblement National Malgache [*National Malagasy Rally*]
RNM..........	Resistencia Nacional Mocambicana [*Mozambican National Resistance*] (PD)
RNM..........	Revista Nacional (Montevideo) [*A publication*]
RNM..........	University of Rochester, Miner Medical Library, Rochester, NY [*OCLC symbol*] (OCLC)
RN Mag.....	RN Magazine [*A publication*]
RNMBR	Royal Naval Motor Boat Reserve [*British military*] (DMA)
RNMC	Royal Netherlands Marine Corps (CINC)
RNMCC	Reference Number Mandatory Category Code [*DoD*]
RNMD......	Registered Nurse for Mental Defectives
RNMDSF ...	Royal National Mission to Deep Sea Fishermen [*British*]
RNMH	Registered Nurse for the Mentally Handicapped [*British*] (DBQ)
RNMI	Realtors National Marketing Institute [*Chicago, IL*] (EA)
RNMS	Registered Nurse for the Mentally Subnormal [*British*]
RNMS	Royal Naval Minewatching Service [*British military*] (DMA)
RNMTA	Rendiconti di Matematica [*A publication*]
RNMVDW ..	Reports. National Museum of Victoria [*A publication*]

RNN........... Naval War College, Newport, RI [*Library symbol*] [*Library of Congress*] (LCLS)
RNN........... Ronne [*Denmark*] [*Airport symbol*] (OAG)
RNN........... Royal Netherlands Navy
RNN........... Royal Norwegian Navy
RNNAS .... Royal Netherlands Naval Air Service
RNNU .... United States Navy, Naval Underwater Systems Center, Technical Library, Newport, RI [*Library symbol*] [*Library of Congress*] (LCLS)
RN and O... Raleigh News and Observer [*A publication*]
RNO .... Regional Nuclear Option (MCD)
RNO .... Regional Nursing Officer [*British*]
RNO .... Reno [*Nevada*] [*Airport symbol*] (OAG)
RNO .... Resident Naval Officer [*Followed by place name*] (NATG)
RNO .... Rhino Resources [*Vancouver Stock Exchange symbol*]
RNO .... Riddare of Nordstjerne [*Knight of the Order of the Polar Star*] [*Norway*] (DAS)
RNO .... Roan Selection Trust Ltd. [*Formerly, RHO; later, RST*] [*NYSE symbol*] (SPSG)
RNO .... Rough Notes [*A publication*]
RNOA .... Royal Norwegian Army (NATG)
RNOAF ..... Royal Norwegian Air Force (AFM)
RNOBDG ... Revista Nordestina de Biologia [*A publication*]
RNOC........ Royal Naval Officers Club [*Defunct*] (EA)
RNODC..... Responsible National Oceanographic Data Center [*Marine science*] (MSC)
RNON .... Royal Norwegian Navy (NATG)
RNORA ..... Royal Norwegian Army (NATG)
R Nord .... Revue du Nord [*A publication*]
RNORN.... Royal Norwegian Navy (NATG)
R du Not..... Revue du Notariat [*A publication*]
RNOUD ... Revue Nouvelle [*A publication*]
R Nouv .... Revue Nouvelle [*A publication*]
RNP .... Radio Navigation Point [*Military*] (MCD)
RNP .... Rassemblement National Populaire [*National People's Rally*] [*France*]
RNP .... Remote Network Processor
RNP .... Revue Neo-Scolastique de Philosophie [*A publication*]
RNP .... Ribonucleoprotein [*Biochemistry*]
RNP .... RNA [*Ribonucleic Acid*] Nuclear Protein
RNP .... Rongelap [*Marshall Islands*] [*Airport symbol*] (OAG)
RNP .... Roscoe's Nisi Prius Evidence [*20th ed.*] [*1934*] [*A publication*] (DLA)
RNP .... Royal Naval Personnel Research Committee [*British*]
RNPA .... Regional Nuclear Power Authority
RNPC .... Regional Nuclear Power Company
RNPC .... Required Navigation Performance Capability
RNPL........ Royal Naval Physiological Laboratory [*Later, AMTE (PL)*] [*British*]
RNPR .... Relative Net Protein Ratio [*Nutrition*]
RNPRC..... Royal Naval Personnel Research Committee [*British*] (MCD)
RNPS........ Royal Naval Patrol Service [*Obsolete*] [*British*]
RNPS........ Royal Navy Polaris School [*British*]
RNQ.......... Waycross, GA [*Location identifier*] [*FAA*] (FAAL)
RNR.......... Rate Not Reported (DS)
RNR.......... Receive Not Ready [*Data processing*] (IEEE)
RNR.......... Redwood Library and Athenaeum, Newport, RI [*Library symbol*] [*Library of Congress*] (LCLS)
RNR.......... Registru Naval Roman (DS)
RNR.......... Renewal Not Required (AIA)
RNR.......... Resonant Nuclear Reaction [*Physics*]
RNR.......... Robinson River [*Papua New Guinea*] [*Airport symbol*] (OAG)
RNR.......... Royal Naval Reserve [*British*]
RNR.......... Runner (MSA)
RNRA .... Royal Naval Rifle Association [*British military*] (DMA)
RNRB .... Relative Navigational Reference Beacon [*Military*] (CAAL)
RNRC .... Riverside National Bank [*NASDAQ symbol*] (NQ)
RNRE .... Refused, Not Reversible Error [*Legal term*] (ILCA)
RNRF .... Renewable Natural Resources Foundation (EA)
RNRLA...... Report of Naval Research Laboratory Progress [*United States*] [*A publication*]
RNR(T)..... Royal Naval Reserve (Trawlers) [*British military*] (DMA)
RNRVAK .. Feddes Repertorium. Specierum Novarum Regni Vegetabilis [*A publication*]
RNS .... RADAR Netting Station [*Military*] (AABC)
RNS .... Ransom Resources Ltd. [*Vancouver Stock Exchange symbol*]
RNS .... Religious News Service (EA)
RNS .... Rennes [*France*] [*Airport symbol*] (OAG)
RNS .... Reusable Nuclear Shuttle [*NASA*]
RNS .... Reusable Nuclear Stage [*Aerospace*]
RNS .... Revue Neo-Scolastique de Philosophie [*A publication*]
RNS .... Ribonuclease S [*An enzyme*]
RNS .... Romani Naval School [*British*]
RNS .... Royal Numismatic Society [*British*]
RNS .... Russian Numismatic Society (EA)
RNSA .... Royal Naval Sailing Association [*British*]
RNSC........ Reference Number Status Code (MCD)
RNSC........ Rocket/Nimbus Sounder Comparison [*NASA*]
RNSC........ Royal Naval Staff College [*British*]
RNSD .... Royal Naval Stores Depot [*British*]
RNSH........ Royal National Scottish Hospital

RNSJA ...... Rinsho Seijinbyo [*A publication*]
RNS of M .. Royal Naval School of Music [*British military*] (DMA)
RNSP........ Revue Neo-Scolastique de Philosophie [*A publication*]
RNSP........ Round-Nose Soft-Point Bullet
RNSQ .... Royal Naval Sick Quarters [*British*]
RNSR........ Royal Naval Special Reserve [*British military*] (DMA)
RNSR........ Royal Nova Scotia Regiment [*Military unit*]
RNSS........ Royal Naval Scientific Service [*British*] (DEN)
RNSS........ Royal Norwegian Society of Sciences
RNSTS ...... Royal Naval Supply and Transport Service [*British*]
RNSYS ...... Royal Nova Scotia Yacht Squadron
RNT .... Regensburger Neues Testament [*A publication*] (BJA)
RNT .... Registered Nurse Tutor [*British*]
RNT .... Renton, WA [*Location identifier*] [*FAA*] (FAAL)
RNTE .... Royal Naval Training Establishment [*British military*] (DMA)
RNTL .... Rockwood National Corp. [*NASDAQ symbol*] (NQ)
rNTP .... Ribonucleoside Triphosphate [*Biochemistry*]
RNTU........ Royal Naval Training Unit [*British military*] (DMA)
RNTWPA ... Radio-Newsreel-Television Working Press Association (EA)
RNU.......... RADAR Netting Unit [*Military*] (AABC)
RNU.......... Ranau [*Malaysia*] [*Airport symbol*] (OAG)
RNUCA ..... Rivista del Nuovo Cimento. Societa Italiana di Fisica [*A publication*]
RNum........ Rassegna Numismatica [*A publication*]
RNum........ Revue Numismatique [*A publication*]
RNV.......... Cleveland, MS [*Location identifier*] [*FAA*] (FAAL)
RNV.......... Radio Noise Voltage
RNV.......... Radionuclide Ventriculography [*Medicine*]
RNV.......... Random Noise Voltmeter
RNV.......... Relative Nutritive Value [*Nutrition*]
RNV.......... Replacement Naval Vessels
RNV.......... Resistive Null Voltage
RNV.......... Reusable Nuclear Vehicle [*Aerospace*] (KSC)
RNV.......... Royal Naval Volunteer (Reserve) [*British*] (ROG)
RNVC........ Reference Number Variation Code (MCD)
RN(V)R..... Royal Naval (Volunteer) Reserve [*Obsolete*] [*World War II*] [*British*]
RNVR(A)... Royal Naval Volunteer Reserve (Air) [*British military*] (DMA)
RNVSDY... Kongelige Norske Videnskabers Selskab. Museet. Botanisk Avdeling Rapport [*A publication*]
RNVSR...... Royal Naval Volunteer Supplementary Reserve [*Obsolete*] [*World War II*] [*British*]
RNV(W)R ... Royal Naval Volunteer (Wireless) Reserve [*British military*] (DMA)
RNWAR .... Royal Naval Wireless Auxiliary Reserve [*British military*] (DMA)
RNWBL.... Renewable (MSA)
RNWMP ... Royal North West Mounted Police [*Later, RCMP*] [*Canada*]
RNWSD .... Research News [*A publication*]
RNWY....... Runway (AABC)
RNX.......... Renox Creek Resources [*Vancouver Stock Exchange symbol*]
RNX.......... Rex-Noreco, Inc. [*AMEX symbol*] (SPSG)
RNXS........ Royal Naval Auxiliary Service [*British*]
RNY.......... Rainier Energy Resources [*Vancouver Stock Exchange symbol*]
RNY.......... Runway Lights [*Aviation*] (AIA)
RNZ.......... Radio New Zealand
RNZ.......... Reserve Bank of New Zealand. Bulletin [*A publication*]
RNZ.......... Rhein-Neckar-Zeitung [*A publication*]
RNZ.......... Royal New Zealand
RNZA .... Royal Regiment of New Zealand Artillery (DMA)
RNZAC...... Royal New Zealand Armoured Corps (DMA)
RNZAEC... Royal New Zealand Army Educational Corps (DMA)
RNZAF...... Royal New Zealand Air Force
RNZAMC ... Royal New Zealand Army Medical Corps (DMA)
RNZAOC .. Royal New Zealand Army Ordnance Corps (DMA)
RNZASC... Royal New Zealand Army Service Corps (DMA)
RNZChD ... Royal New Zealand Chaplains Department (DMA)
RNZCS...... Royal New Zealand Corps of Signals (DMA)
RNZDC ..... Royal New Zealand Dental Corps (DMA)
RNZE .... Royal New Zealand Engineers
RNZEME ... Corps of Royal New Zealand Electrical and Mechanical Engineers (DMA)
RNZIR....... Royal New Zealand Infantry Regiment (DMA)
RNZN....... Royal New Zealand Navy
RNZNC ..... Royal New Zealand Nursing Corps (DMA)
RNZN(V)R ... Royal New Zealand Naval (Volunteer) Reserve
RNZOD8... Polish Journal of Animal Science and Technology [*A publication*]
RNZPC...... Royal New Zealand Pay Corps (DMA)
Ro............. Hoffmann-La Roche, Inc. [*Switzerland, USA*] [*Research code symbol*]
RO............ Observer (Radio) [*British military*] (DMA)
RO............ Omani Rial [*Monetary unit*] (IMH)
RO............ RADAR Observer
RO............ RADAR Operator
RO............ Radiation Office [*Environmental Protection Agency*]
RO............ Radio Officer [*Australia*]
RO............ Radio Operator
RO............ Radio Orchestra
RO............ Radionavigation Mobile Station [*ITU designation*] (CET)
RO............ Radioopaque

R & O.........	Rail and Ocean
RO..............	Railway Office [*British*] (ROG)
RO..............	Range Only (CAAL)
RO..............	Range Operation (AAG)
RO..............	Rank Organisation PLC [*Toronto Stock Exchange symbol*]
RO..............	Reactor Operator [*Nuclear energy*] (NRCH)
RO..............	Read Only [*Data processing*] (IBMDP)
RO..............	Readout (KSC)
RO..............	Reality Orientation
RO..............	Receive Only
RO..............	Receiving Office [*or Officer*]
RO..............	Receiving Order [*Business term*] (DCTA)
RO..............	Reconnaissance Officer
RO..............	Recorders [*JETDS nomenclature*] [*Military*] (CET)
RO..............	Records Office [*or Officer*] [*Air Force*] (AFM)
RO..............	Recovery Operations [*NASA*]
RO..............	Recruiting Officer [*Military*]
RO..............	Recto [*Also, R*]
RO..............	Recueil Officiel des Lois et Ordonnances de la Confederation Suisse [*A publication*]
RO..............	Reddish Orange
RO..............	Regimental Orders [*Army*]
RO..............	Regional Office [*or Officer*]
RO..............	Register Output
R/O...........	Regular Order
RO..............	Regulated Output (FAAC)
RO..............	Relieving Officer (ROG)
RO..............	Relocatable Output [*Data processing*]
RO..............	Rent Officer [*British*] (ILCA)
RO..............	Repair Order
R/O...........	Repair and Overhaul (MCD)
RO..............	Reportable Occurrence [*Nuclear energy*] (NRCH)
RO..............	Reporting Officer [*Army*] (AABC)
RO..............	Requirements Objective
R & O.........	Requirements and Objectives
RO..............	Requisitioning Objective [*Military*] (AABC)
R/O...........	Requisitions/Objectives (CINC)
RO..............	Research Objective (MCD)
RO..............	Research Officer [*British*]
R of O........	Reserve of Officers [*British*]
RO..............	Reserve of Officers [*British*]
RO..............	Reserve Order
RO..............	Responding Officer [*Police term*]
RO..............	Restriction Orifice [*Nuclear energy*] (NRCH)
RO..............	Retired Officer [*Military*] [*British*]
RO..............	Retrofit Order [*Navy*] (NG)
RO..............	Returning Officer (ROG)
RO..............	Revenue Officer [*IRS*]
RO..............	Reverse-Osmosis [*Physical chemistry*]
RO..............	Revista de Occidente [*A publication*]
RO..............	Revue Orientale [*A publication*]
RO..............	Rework Order (MCD)
Ro..............	Rhodium [*Correct symbol is Rh*] [*Chemical element*]
RO..............	Right Outboard (MCD)
RO..............	Rimoil Corp. [*Toronto Stock Exchange symbol*]
RO..............	Roan [*Thoroughbred racing*]
RO..............	Rock [*Federal Republic of Germany*] [*ICAO aircraft manufacturer identifier*] (ICAO)
RO..............	Rocznik Orientalistyczny [*A publication*]
Ro..............	Rodoicus [*Authority cited in pre-1607 legal work*] (DSA)
RO..............	Roemisches Oesterreich. Jahresschrift der Oesterreichischen Gesellschaft fuer Archaeologie [*A publication*]
Ro..............	Roffredus Beneventanus [*Flourished, 1215-43*] [*Authority cited in pre-1607 legal work*] (DSA)
Ro..............	Rolandus Bandinelli [*Deceased, 1181*] [*Authority cited in pre-1607 legal work*] (DSA)
RO..............	Roll
Ro..............	Rolle's Abridgment [*A publication*] (DLA)
R/O...........	Rollout (MCD)
R & O.........	Roma e l'Oriente [*A publication*]
Ro..............	Romania [*A publication*]
RO..............	Romania [*ANSI two-letter standard code*] (CNC)
RO..............	Romanian Air Transport [*ICAO designator*] (FAAC)
RO..............	Rood [*Unit of measurement*]
RO..............	Room Only
RO..............	Roper Organization (EA)
RO..............	Rose (ROG)
RO..............	Rough
RO..............	Rough Opening [*Technical drawings*]
RO..............	Route Order [*Military*]
RO..............	Routine Order
RO..............	Routing Office [*or Officer*] [*Navy*]
RO..............	Rowed Over [*Rowing*] [*British*] (ROG)
RO..............	Royal Observatory [*British*]
RO..............	Royal Octavo
RO..............	Royal Ordnance Factory [*British*]
R/O...........	Rule Out [*Medicine*]
R-O...........	Run-On [*Used in correcting manuscripts, etc.*]
RO..............	Runoff Election
RO..............	Runout (MSA)
RO..............	Runover [*Publishing*]

RO..............	Russian Obuckhoff Rifle
ROA...........	Altimeter Station [*ITU designation*] (CET)
ROA...........	Radiation Oncology Administrators [*Later, SROA*] (EA)
ROA...........	Radio Operator's Aptitude Test [*Military*]
ROA...........	Radius of Action (CAAL)
ROA...........	Raman Optical Activity [*Spectrometry*]
ROA...........	RAS. Rohr-Armatur-Sanitaer-Heizung Informationsblatt fuer den Fachhandel und das Sanitaerfach und Heizungsfach [*A publication*]
ROA...........	Reference Optical Alignment
ROA...........	Rehabilitation of Offenders Act [*1974*] [*British*] (DCTA)
ROA...........	Reinsurance Offices Association [*British*] (AIA)
ROA...........	Report on the ORT Activities [*Paris/Geneva*] [*A publication*]
ROA...........	Reserve Officers Association of the United States (EA)
ROA...........	Return on Assets [*Finance*]
ROA...........	Right Occipitoanterior [*A fetal position*] [*Obstetrics*]
ROA...........	Roanoke [*Virginia*] [*Airport symbol*]
ROA...........	Robert Owen Association (EA)
roa	Romance [*MARC language code*] [*Library of Congress*] (LCCP)
ROA...........	Rules of the Air (AFM)
ROA...........	Russian Orchestra of the Americas
Ro Abr.......	Rolle's Abridgment [*A publication*] (ILCA)
ROAC.......	Railways of Australia Committee
ROAD.......	Inroads [*Database*] [*Australia*]
ROAD.......	Reorganization Objectives, Army Division [*Military*]
ROAD.......	Retires on Active Duty [*Military*] (MCD)
ROAD.......	Roadway Services, Inc. [*NASDAQ symbol*] (NQ)
Road Abstr ...	Road Abstracts [*A publication*]
Road A R....	Road Apple Review [*A publication*]
Road Maps ...	Economic Road Maps [*A publication*]
Road Note Road Res Lab (UK) ...	Road Note. Road Research Laboratory (United Kingdom) [*A publication*]
Road Res Bull ...	Road Research Bulletin [*A publication*]
Road Res Lab (UK) RRL Rep ...	Road Research Laboratory (United Kingdom). RRL Report [*A publication*]
Road Res Monogr ...	Road Research Monographs [*A publication*]
Road Res Notes ...	Road Research Notes [*A publication*]
Road Res Pap ...	Road Research Papers [*A publication*]
Road Res Techn Pap ...	Road Research Technical Papers [*A publication*]
ROADS	Real-Time Optical Alignment and Diagnostic System [*Module*]
ROADS	Roadway Analysis and Design System [*Data processing*]
Road Saf	Road Safety [*A publication*] (APTA)
Roads & Bridges ...	Roads and Bridges [*A publication*]
Roads & Constr ...	Roads and Construction [*A publication*]
Roads & Eng Constr ...	Roads and Engineering Construction [*A publication*]
Roads Road Constr ...	Roads and Road Construction [*A publication*]
Roads St.....	Roads and Streets [*A publication*]
Road Transp Aust ...	Road Transporter of Australia [*A publication*] (APTA)
Road Transp of Aust ...	Road Transporter of Australia [*A publication*] (APTA)
ROAH	Naha [*Ryukyu Islands*] [*ICAO location identifier*] (ICLI)
ROAM......	RAN Energy, Inc. [*NASDAQ symbol*] (NQ)
ROAM......	Return on Assets Managed [*Finance*]
ROAMA....	Rome Air Materiel Area [*Deactivated*] [*Air Force*]
ROANA....	Rover Owners' Association of North America [*Defunct*] (EA)
ROAP	Rubidazone [*Zorubicin*], Oncovin [*Vincristine*], ara-C [*Cytarabine*], Prednisone [*Antineoplastic drug regimen*]
ROAR.......	Radio Operated Auto Racing
ROAR.......	Regional Organization for Airways Restudy
ROAR.......	Restore Our Alienated Rights [*Boston antibusing group*]
ROAR.......	Return of Army Repairables (AABC)
ROAR.......	Royal Optimizing Assembly Routing [*Royal McBee Corp.*] [*Data processing*]
ROAR.......	Run for Aquino and Resignation [*Event organized by Philippine joggers to protest the assassination of Benigno Aquino*]
ROARE	Reduction of Attitudes and Repressed Emotions [*Treatment given to sex offenders*] [*Psychology*]
ROARS.....	Rutgers Online Automated Retrieval Service [*Rutgers University*] (OLDSS)
ROAT	Radio Operator's Aptitude Test [*Military*]
ROB...........	Monrovia [*Liberia*] Roberts International Airport [*Airport symbol*] (OAG)
ROB...........	RADAR Order of Battle
ROB...........	RADAR Out of Battle (CET)
ROB...........	Recovery Operations Branch [*NASA*] (KSC)
ROB...........	Regional Office Building
ROB...........	Relieve of Booty [*Crime term*]
RoB	Religion och Bibel [*A publication*]
ROB...........	Remaining on Board
ROB...........	Report on Board [*Navy*]
ROB...........	Report on Business (IT)
ROB...........	Reserve on Board
ROB...........	Reserveoffizier-Bewerber [*Reserve officer applicant*] [*German military - World War II*]
ROB...........	Review of Business [*A publication*]
ROB...........	Right of Baseline (MCD)
ROB...........	Right Outboard (MCD)
ROB...........	Rijksdienst voor het Oudheidkundig Bodemonderzoek [*A publication*]

Rob............ Robards' Reports [12, 13 Missouri] [A publication] (DLA)
Rob............ Robards' Texas Conscript Cases [A publication] (DLA)
ROB.......... Robert Morris College, Coraopolis, PA [OCLC symbol] (OCLC)
ROB.......... Roberts Airways [Dallas, TX] [FAA designator] (FAAC)
Rob............ Roberts' Reports [29-31 Louisiana Annual] [A publication] (DLA)
ROB.......... Robertsfield [Liberia] [Airport symbol]
Rob............ Robertson's English Ecclesiastical Reports [A publication] (DLA)
Rob............ Robertson's Reports [24-30 New York Superior Court] [1863-68] [A publication] (DLA)
Rob............ Robertson's Reports [1 Hawaii] [A publication] (DLA)
Rob............ Robertson's Scotch Appeal Cases [1707-27] [A publication] (DLA)
ROB.......... Robin International, Inc. [Toronto Stock Exchange symbol]
Rob............ Robinson's English Admiralty Reports [1799-1809, 1838-1852] [A publication] (DLA)
Rob............ Robinson's English Ecclesiastical Reports [1844-53] [A publication] (DLA)
Rob............ Robinson's Louisiana Reports [1-4 Louisiana Annual] [1841-46] [A publication] (DLA)
Rob............ Robinson's Reports [1-8 Ontario] [A publication] (DLA)
Rob............ Robinson's Reports [2-9, 17-23 Colorado Appeals] [A publication] (DLA)
Rob............ Robinson's Reports [1 Nevada] [A publication] (DLA)
Rob............ Robinson's Reports [40, 41 Virginia] [A publication] (DLA)
Rob............ Robinson's Reports [38 California] [A publication] (DLA)
Rob............ Robinson's Scotch Appeal Cases [1840-41] [A publication] (DLA)
Rob............ Robinson's Upper Canada Reports [A publication] (DLA)
ROB.......... Roborough [England]
ROB.......... Robotic Operating Buddy [Nintendo video game system accessory]
ROB.......... Robotics Age [A publication]
ROB.......... Roburent [Italy] [Seismograph station code, US Geological Survey] (SEIS)
ROB.......... Roburent [Italy] [Geomagnetic observatory code]
ROB.......... Round of Beam (DS)
ROB.......... Waco, TX [Location identifier] [FAA] (FAAL)
RoBA........ Academia R.S. Romania [Academy of Romania], Bucharest, Romania [Library symbol] [Library of Congress] (LCLS)
Rob A........ [C.] Robinson's Admiralty Reports [1799-1809] [A publication] (DLA)
Rob Adm.... [C.] Robinson's Admiralty Reports [England] [A publication] (DLA)
Rob Adm.... [W.] Robinson's English Admiralty Reports [A publication] (DLA)
Rob Adm & Pr ... Roberts on Admiralty and Prize [A publication] (DLA)
ROBAMP ... Rotational Base for Aviation Maintenance Personnel
Rob App..... Robinson's Scotch Appeal Cases [1840-41] [A publication] (DLA)
Robards...... Robards' Reports [12, 13 Missouri] [A publication] (DLA)
Robards...... Robards' Texas Conscript Cases [1862-65] [A publication] (DLA)
Robards & Jackson ... Robards and Jackson's Reports [26-27 Texas] [A publication] (DLA)
ROBAT ..... Robotic Obstacle-Breaching Assault Tank
Robb.......... Robbins' New Jersey Equity Reports [67-70 New Jersey] [A publication] (DLA)
Robb.......... Robb's United States Patent Cases [A publication] (DLA)
Rob Bank ... Robertson's Handbook of Bankers' Law [A publication] (DLA)
Rob Bank ... Robson on Law and Practice in Bankruptcy [7th ed.] [1894] [A publication] (DLA)
RoBBC...... Biblioteca Centrala de Stat a R.S. Romania [Central State Library of Romania], Bucharest, Romania [Library symbol] [Library of Congress] (LCLS)
Robb (NJ).. Robbins' New Jersey Equity Reports [A publication] (DLA)
Robb Pat Cas ... Robb's United States Patent Cases [A publication] (DLA)
ROBC........ Robec, Inc. [NASDAQ symbol] (NQ)
Rob Cal..... Robinson's Reports [38 California] [A publication] (DLA)
Rob Car V .. Robertson's History of the Reign of the Emperor Charles V [A publication] (DLA)
Rob Cas...... Robinson's Scotch Appeal Cases [1840-41] [A publication] (DLA)
Rob Chr...... Robinson's Reports [2-9, 17-23 Colorado Appeals] [A publication] (DLA)
ROBCO..... Readiness Objective Code [Military] (AABC)
ROBCO..... Requirement Objective Code
Rob Colo .... Robinson's Reports [2-9, 17-23 Colorado Appeals] [A publication] (ILCA)
Rob Cons Cas (Tex) ... Robards' Texas Conscript Cases [A publication] (DLA)
Rob Consc Cas ... Robards' Texas Conscript Cases [A publication] (DLA)
ROBD........ Robot Defense Systems [NASDAQ symbol] (NQ)
Rob Dig...... Robert's Digest [Lower Canada] [A publication] (DLA)
Rob Dig...... Robert's Digest of Vermont Reports [A publication] (DLA)
Rob E......... Robertson's English Ecclesiastical Reports [2 vols.] [1844-53] [A publication] (DLA)
Rob Ecc...... Robertson's English Ecclesiastical Reports [2 vols.] [A publication] (DLA)

Rob Eccl..... Robertson's English Ecclesiastical Reports [2 vols.] [1844-53] [A publication] (DLA)
ROBECO .. Rotterdamsch Beleggingsconsortium, NV [Business term]
Rob El Law ... Robinson's Elementary Law [A publication] (DLA)
Rob Ent...... Robinson's Book of Entries [A publication] (DLA)
ROBEPS ... RADAR Operating below Prescribed Standards (FAAC)
Rob Eq....... Roberts' Principles of Equity [A publication] (DLA)
Rober.......... Robertus [Authority cited in pre-1607 legal work] (DSA)
Rober Maran ... Robertus Maranta [Flourished, 16th century] [Authority cited in pre-1607 legal work] (DSA)
Robert........ Robertson's Scotch Appeal Cases [1707-27] [A publication] (DLA)
Robert App ... Robertson's Scotch House of Lords Appeals [A publication] (DLA)
Robert App Cas ... Robertson's Scotch House of Lords Appeals [A publication] (DLA)
Robert A Taft Sanit Eng Cent Tech Rep ... Robert A. Taft Sanitary Engineering Center. Technical Report [A publication]
Robert A Taft Water Res Cent Rep ... Robert A. Taft Water Research Center. Report [A publication]
Robert A Welch Found Res Bull ... Robert A. Welch Foundation. Research Bulletin [A publication]
Robert Morris Associates Bull ... Robert Morris Associates. Bulletin [A publication]
Roberts....... Roberts' Reports [29-31 Louisiana Annual] [A publication] (DLA)
Roberts Emp Liab ... Roberts on Federal Liabilities of Carriers [A publication] (DLA)
Robertson... Robertson's English Ecclesiastical Reports [A publication] (DLA)
Robertson... Robertson's Reports [New York Marine Court] [A publication] (DLA)
Robertson... Robertson's Reports [1 Hawaii] [A publication] (DLA)
Robertson... Robertson's Reports [24-30 New York Superior Court] [A publication] (DLA)
Robertson... Robertson's Scotch Appeal Cases [1707-27] [A publication] (DLA)
Robertson's Rep ... Robertson's Reports [24-30 New York Superior Court] [A publication] (DLA)
Rob Forms ... Robinson's Virginia Forms [A publication] (DLA)
Rob Fr........ Roberts on Frauds [1805] [A publication] (DLA)
Rob Fr Conv ... Roberts on Fraudulent Conveyances [A publication] (DLA)
Rob Gav..... Robinson's Common Law of Kent, or Custom on Gavelkind [5th ed.] [1897] [A publication] (DLA)
Rob Hawaii ... Robinson's Reports [1 Hawaii] [A publication] (DLA)
ROBIN...... Remote On-Line Business Information Network [Data processing] (IEEE)
ROBIN...... Rocket Balloon Instrument [Air Force]
Robin App ... Robinson's Scotch House of Lords Appeals [A publication] (DLA)
ROBINS.... Roberts Information Services, Inc. [Information service or system] (IID)
Robin Sc App ... Robinson's Scotch Appeal Cases [1840-41] [A publication] (DLA)
Robinson.... [W.] Robinson's English Admiralty Reports [A publication] (DLA)
Robinson.... Robinson's English Ecclesiastical Reports [1844-53] [A publication] (DLA)
Robinson.... Robinson's Louisiana Reports [1-12 Louisiana] [A publication] (DLA)
Robinson.... Robinson's Ontario Reports [A publication] (DLA)
Robinson.... Robinson's Reports [1 Nevada] [A publication] (DLA)
Robinson.... Robinson's Reports [38 California] [A publication] (DLA)
Robinson.... Robinson's Reports [17-23 Colorado] [A publication] (DLA)
Robinson.... Robinson's Reports [40-41 Virginia] [A publication] (DLA)
Robinson.... Robinson's Scotch House of Lords Appeals [A publication] (DLA)
Robinson.... [J. L.] Robinson's Upper Canada Reports [A publication] (DLA)
Robinson Sc App Cas ... Robinson's Scotch Appeal Cases [1840-41] [A publication] (DLA)
Rob & J...... Robards and Jackson's Reports [26, 27 Texas] [A publication] (DLA)
Rob Jun...... William Robinson's English Admiralty Reports [1838-52] [A publication] (DLA)
Rob Jus...... Robinson's Justice of the Peace [1836] [A publication] (DLA)
Rob LA....... Robinson's Louisiana Reports [1-4 Louisiana Annual] [1841-46] [A publication] (DLA)
Rob (LA Ann) ... Robinson's Louisiana Reports [1-4 Louisiana Annual] [A publication] (DLA)
Rob Leg...... Robertson's Legitimation by Subsequent Marriage [1829] [A publication] (DLA)
Rob Louis... Robinson's Louisiana Reports [1-12 Louisiana] [A publication] (DLA)
Rob L & W ... Roberts, Leaming, and Wallis' County Court Reports [1849-51] [A publication] (DLA)
Rob Mar (NY) ... Robertson and Jacob's New York Marine Court Reports [A publication] (DLA)
Rob MO..... Robards' Reports [12, 13 Missouri] [A publication] (DLA)
ROBN........ Robbins & Myers, Inc. [NASDAQ symbol] (NQ)
Rob Nev..... Robinson's Reports [1 Nevada] [A publication] (DLA)

Rob (NY).... Robertson's Reports [*24-30 New York Superior Court*] [*A publication*] (DLA)
ROBO....... Robotool Ltd. [*NASDAQ symbol*] (NQ)
ROBO....... Rocket Orbital Bomber
ROBOMB ... Robot Bomb [*Air Force*]
Rob Ont .... Robinson's Reports [*1-8 Ontario*] [*A publication*] (DLA)
Robot Age .. Robotics Age [*A publication*]
Robot Eng .. Robotics Engineering [*A publication*]
Robotics T ... Robotics Today [*A publication*]
Robotron Tech Commun ... Robotron Technical Communications [*A publication*]
Robot Wld ... Robotics World [*A publication*]
Rob Pat ...... Robinson on Patents [*A publication*] (DLA)
Rob Per Suc ... Robertson's Law of Personal Succession [*1836*] [*A publication*] (DLA)
Rob Pr .... Robinson's Practice [*A publication*] (DLA)
Rob Prior ... Robertson's Law of Priority of Incumbrances [*A publication*] (DLA)
R Obs Ann ... Royal Observatory. Annals [*A publication*]
Robs Bank ... Robson on Law and Practice in Bankruptcy [*7th ed.*] [*1894*] [*A publication*] (DLA)
Robs Bankr ... Robertson's Handbook of Bankers' Law [*A publication*] (DLA)
R Obs Bull ... Royal Observatory. Bulletins [*A publication*]
Rob Sc App ... Robinson's Scotch Appeal Cases [*A publication*] (DLA)
Rob SI .... Robertson's Sandwich Island Reports [*1 Hawaii*] [*A publication*] (DLA)
Robson .... Robson on Law and Practice in Bankruptcy [*7 eds.*] [*1870-94*] [*A publication*] (DLA)
Rob Sr Ct ... Robertson's New York Superior Court Reports [*24-30*] [*A publication*] (DLA)
Rob Succ .... Roberts on the Law of Personal Succession [*A publication*] (DLA)
Rob Super Ct ... Robertson's Reports [*24-30 New York Superior Court*] [*A publication*] (DLA)
Robt Eccl.... Robertson's English Ecclesiastical Reports [*163 English Reprint*] [*1844-53*] [*A publication*] (DLA)
Robt Eccl (Eng) ... Robertson's English Ecclesiastical Reports [*163 English Reprint*] [*A publication*] (DLA)
Robt (NY) .. Robertson's Reports [*24-30 New York Superior Court*] [*A publication*] (DLA)
Robt Sc App Cas ... Robertson's Scotch Appeal Cases [*A publication*] (DLA)
Rob UC .... Robinson's Upper Canada Reports [*A publication*] (DLA)
ROBV .... Robotic Vision Systems, Inc. [*NASDAQ symbol*] (NQ)
Rob VA ...... Robinson's Reports [*40, 41 Virginia*] [*A publication*] (DLA)
Rob W .... Roberts. Wills and Codicils [*1826*] [*A publication*] (ILCA)
Rob Wm Adm ... [*William*] Robinson's English Admiralty Reports [*3 vols.*] [*1838-50*] [*A publication*] (DLA)
Roc .... New Hampshire Reports [*A publication*] (DLA)
ROC.......... Railton Owners Club (EA)
ROC.......... Range Operations Center [*Western Test Range*] (MCD)
ROC.......... Range Operations Conference [*NASA*] (KSC)
ROC.......... Rapid Omnidirectional Compaction [*Materials technology*] [*Dow Chemical Co.*]
ROC.......... Rate of Climb [*Aviation*]
ROC.......... Rate of Convergence (IEEE)
R/OC .... Receive-Only Center (FAAC)
ROC.......... Receiver [*or Relative*] Operating Characteristics [*Signal detection*] [*Graph for assessing diagnostic tests*]
ROC.......... Recommended Operating Condition [*Data processing*]
ROC.......... Reconnaissance and Operations Center (NATG)
ROC.......... Reconnaissance Optique de Caracteres [*Optical Character Recognition*] [*French*]
ROC.......... Record of Comments (NASA)
ROC.......... Redeem Our Country (EA)
ROC.......... Reduce Operating Costs [*Air Force project*]
ROC.......... Reduced Operational Capability Program [*Navy*] (NVT)
ROC.......... Region One Cooperative Library Service Unit [*Library network*]
ROC.......... Regional Operating Center [*NATO Integrated Communications System*] (NATG)
ROC.......... Regroupement des Officiers Communistes [*Burkina Faso*] [*Political party*] (EY)
ROC.......... Relative Operating Characteristics (MCD)
ROC.......... Reliability Operating Characteristic
ROC.......... Remote Operator's Console
ROC.......... Republic of China (CINC)
ROC.......... Republican Organizing Committee [*Political organization in opposition to the NPL of North Dakota*]
ROC.......... Request of Change (NASA)
ROC.......... Required Operational Capability [*Military*] (RDA)
ROC.......... Reserve Officer Candidate
RO in C ... Resident Officer-in-Charge [*Navy*]
ROC.......... Return on Capital [*Finance*]
ROC.......... Reusable Orbital Carrier [*Aerospace*] (MCD)
ROC.......... Revue de l'Orient Chretien [*A publication*]
ROC.......... ROC Taiwan Fund SBI [*NYSE symbol*] (SPSG)
ROC.......... Rochester [*New York*] [*Airport symbol*] (OAG)
ROC.......... Rochester-Odenbach [*New York*] [*Seismograph station code, US Geological Survey*] (SEIS)

ROC.......... Rochester Public Library, Rochester, MN [*OCLC symbol*] (OCLC)
Roc .... Rochus Curtius [*Flourished, 1470-1515*] [*Authority cited in pre-1607 legal work*] (DSA)
Roc .... Rococo Records [*Record label*] [*Canada, USA*]
ROC.......... Rotatable Optical Cube
ROC.......... Rothmans Inc. [*Formerly, Rothmans of Pall Mall Canada*] [*Toronto Stock Exchange symbol*] [*Vancouver Stock Exchange symbol*]
ROC.......... Royal Observer Corps [*British civilian aircraft observers*] [*World War II*]
ROC.......... Royal Ordnance Corps [*British*]
ROCAF...... Republic of China Air Force (CINC)
Rocaf .... [*Bernardus de*] Rocafixa [*Flourished, 14th century*] [*Authority cited in pre-1607 legal work*] (DSA)
ROCALDIS ... Routine Calls May Be Dispensed With
ROCAP...... Regional Office [*or Officer*] for Central American Programs [*Department of State*]
ROCAPPI ... Research on Computer Applications for the Printing and Publishing Industries
Rocas Miner ... Rocas y Minerales [*A publication*]
ROCAT ..... Rocket Catapult
ROCC .... Range Operations Conference Circuit (MUGU)
ROCC .... Range Operations Control Center (MCD)
ROCC .... Receptor-Operated Calcium Channel [*Physiology*]
ROCC .... Regional Oil Combating Center [*United Nations Environment Programme*] (MSC)
ROCC .... Regional Operations Control Center [*AT & T*]
Rocc............ Roccus. De Navibus et Naulo [*Maritime law*] [*A publication*] (DLA)
ROCC .... Russell's Owl Collectors Club (EA)
Rocc De Nav et Nau ... Roccus. De Navibus et Naulo [*Maritime law*] [*A publication*] (DLA)
R Occid Musul Mediterr ... Revue de l'Occident Musulman et de la Mediterranee [*A publication*]
Roccus Ins ... Roccus on Insurance [*A publication*] (DLA)
ROCE .... Return on Capital Employed [*Accounting term*]
ROCF .... [*The*] Rockies Fund, Inc. [*NASDAQ symbol*] (NQ)
ROCH........ Rochester [*Municipal borough in England*] (ROG)
Roch .... Rochus Curtius [*Flourished, 1470-1515*] [*Authority cited in pre-1607 legal work*] (DSA)
ROCH........ Ruch Oporu Chlopskiego [*Movement of Peasant Resistance*] [*Poland*] [*Political party*] (PPE)
ROCHA..... Roczniki Chemii [*A publication*]
Roch Curt... Rochus Curtius [*Flourished, 1470-1515*] [*Authority cited in pre-1607 legal work*] (DSA)
Roche D & K ... Roche, Dillon, and Kehoe's Irish Land Reports [*1881-82*] [*A publication*] (DLA)
Roche & H Bank ... Roche and Hazlitt's Bankruptcy Practice [*2nd ed.*] [*1873*] [*A publication*] (DLA)
Roche Image Med Res ... Roche Image of Medicine and Research [*A publication*]
Roche Med Image Comment ... Roche Medical Image and Commentary [*A publication*]
Rochester Acad Sci Proc ... Rochester Academy of Science. Proceedings [*A publication*]
Rochester Conf Data Acquis Processing Biol Med Proc ... Rochester Conference on Data Acquisition and Processing in Biology and Medicine. Proceedings [*A publication*]
Rochester Hist ... Rochester History [*A publication*]
Rochester Hist Soc Publ Fund Ser ... Rochester Historical Society. Publication Fund Series [*A publication*]
Rochester Univ Lib Bul ... University of Rochester. Library Bulletin [*A publication*]
Roch Patr ... Rochester Patriot [*A publication*]
Roch Phil ... Rochester Philharmonic Orchestra. Program Notes [*A publication*]
ROCI .... Rahim Organizational Conflict Inventories [*Interpersonal skills and attitudes test*]
ROCI .... Rauschenberg Overseas Cultural Interchange [*Retrospective exhibit of artist Robert Rauschenberg's work*]
ROCI .... Rickman Owners Club International (EA)
ROCIA ..... Rozhledy v Chirurgii [*A publication*]
ROCID ...... Reorganization of Combat Infantry Division [*Army*] (AABC)
Roc Ins ...... Roccus on Insurance [*A publication*] (DLA)
Rock .... New Hampshire Reports [*A publication*] (DLA)
ROCK .... Rocket (MCD)
ROCK .... Rockor, Inc. [*NASDAQ symbol*] (NQ)
Rock .... Smith's New Hampshire Reports [*A publication*] (DLA)
ROCKET... Rand's Omnibus Calculator of the Kinetics of Earth Trajectories
Rocket News Lett ... Rocket News Letter [*A publication*]
Rocket Propul Technol ... Rocket Propulsion Technology [*A publication*]
ROCKEX... Rocket Exercise [*Military*] (NVT)
ROCKF...... Rockford [*England*]
Rockingham ... Smith's New Hampshire Reports [*A publication*] (DLA)
Rock Magn Paleogeophys ... Rock Magnetism and Paleogeophysics [*A publication*]
Rock Mech ... Rock Mechanics [*A publication*]
Rock Mech Felsmech Mec Roches ... Rock Mechanics/Felsmechanik/ Mecanique des Roches [*A publication*]
Rock Min ... Rockwell on Mines [*A publication*] (DLA)

ROCKOON ... Rocket Balloon [*Navy*]
Rock Prod .. Rock Products [*A publication*]
Rocks Miner ... Rocks and Minerals [*A publication*]
Rock Sp Law ... Rockwell's Spanish and Mexican Law Relating to Mines [*A publication*] (DLA)
ROCKSTORE ... Rock Storage [*Storage in excavated rock caverns*]
Rocky Mountain J Math ... Rocky Mountain Journal of Mathematics [*A publication*]
Rocky Mountain MJ ... Rocky Mountain Medical Journal [*A publication*]
Rocky Mount Med J ... Rocky Mountain Medical Journal [*A publication*]
Rocky Mt Assoc Geol ... Rocky Mountain Association of Geologists [*A publication*]
Rocky Mt B ... Rocky Mountain Business Journal [*A publication*]
Rocky Mt Bioeng Symp Proc ... Rocky Mountain Bioengineering Symposium. Proceedings [*A publication*]
Rocky Mt J Math ... Rocky Mountain Journal of Mathematics [*A publication*]
Rocky Mt L Rev ... Rocky Mountain Law Review [*Later, University of Colorado. Law Review*] [*A publication*]
Rocky Mt Med J ... Rocky Mountain Medical Journal [*A publication*]
Rocky Mt Miner Law Inst Annu Inst Proc ... Rocky Mountain Mineral Law Institute. Annual Institute. Proceedings [*A publication*]
Rocky Mt Miner L Rev ... Rocky Mountain Mineral Law Review [*A publication*] (DLA)
Rocky Mt Min L Inst ... Rocky Mountain Mineral Law Institute. Proceedings [*A publication*]
Rocky Mt Min L Inst Proc ... Rocky Mountain Mineral Law Institute. Proceedings [*A publication*]
Rocky Mtn L Rev ... Rocky Mountain Law Review [*Later, University of Colorado. Law Review*] [*A publication*]
Rocky Mtn Med J ... Rocky Mountain Medical Journal [*A publication*]
Rocky Mtn Oil Reporter ... Rocky Mountain Oil Reporter [*A publication*]
Rocky Mtn Soc Sci J ... Rocky Mountain Social Science Journal [*A publication*]
Rocky Mt R ... Rocky Mountain Review of Language and Literature [*A publication*]
Rocky Mt So ... Rocky Mountain Social Science Journal [*A publication*]
Rocky Mt Soc Sci J ... Rocky Mountain Social Science Journal [*A publication*]
Rocky Mt Spectrosc Conf Program Abstr ... Rocky Mountain Spectroscopy Conference. Program and Abstracts [*A publication*]
ROCL .... Rockwell Drilling Co. [*NASDAQ symbol*] (NQ)
Rocla Pipes Ltd Tech J ... Rocla Pipes Limited. Technical Journal [*A publication*] (APTA)
ROCMAGV ... Republic of China, Military Assistance Group, Vietnam
ROCMAS ... Russian Orthodox Catholic Mutual Aid Society of USA (EA)
ROCMC .... Republic of China Marine Corps (CINC)
ROCMM .... Regional Office of Civilian Manpower Management
ROCN .... Republic of China Navy (CINC)
ROCN .... Retraining Objective Control Number [*Air Force*] (AFM)
RocO .... Rocznik Orientalistyczny [*Warszawa*] [*A publication*]
ROCOA ..... Renault Owners Club of America (EA)
ROCOB ..... Rocketsonde Observation (NOAA)
ROCOMP ... Radio or Computer Operated Mobile Platform [*Army*]
ROCP .... RADAR Out of Commission for Parts [*ADC*]
ROCP .... Regional Occupation Center Program (OICC)
ROCPEX .... Republic of China Philatelic Exhibition
ROCR .... Recovery Operations Control Room [*NASA*] (KSC)
ROCR .... Remote Optical Character Recognition [*Data processing*]
Roc T Kan .. Roczniki Teologiczno-Kanoniczne [*A publication*]
ROCU .... Remote Operational Control Unit [*Military*] (CAAL)
ROCWMAS ... Russian Orthodox Catholic Women's Mutual Aid Society (EA)
Rocz Akad Med Bialymstoku ... Roczniki Akademii Medycznej Imienia Juliana Marchlewskiego w Bialymstoku [*A publication*]
Rocz Akad Med Bialymstoku Supl ... Roczniki Akademii Medycznej Imienia Juliana Marchlewskiego w Bialymstoku. Suplement [*A publication*]
Rocz Akad Med Juliana Marchlewskiego Bialymstoku ... Roczniki Akademii Medycznej Imienia Juliana Marchlewskiego w Bialymstoku [*A publication*]
Rocz Akad Med Juliana Marchlewskiego Bialymstoku Supl ... Roczniki Akademii Medycznej Imienia Juliana Marchlewskiego w Bialymstoku. Suplement [*A publication*]
Rocz Akad Roln Poznaniu ... Roczniki Akademii Rolniczej w Poznaniu [*Poland*] [*A publication*]
Rocz Akad Roln Poznaniu Pr Habilitacyjne ... Roczniki Akademii Rolniczej w Poznaniu. Prace Habilitacyjne [*A publication*]
Rocz Bial .... Rocznik Bialostocki [*A publication*]
Rocz Bialostocki ... Rocznik Bialostocki [*A publication*]
Rocz Chem ... Roczniki Chemii [*A publication*]
Rocz Glebozn ... Roczniki Gleboznawcze [*A publication*]
RoczH .... Roczniki Humanistyczne Katolickiego Uniwersytetu [*A publication*]
Rocz Hist ... Roczniki Historyczne [*A publication*]
Rocz Inst Przem Mlecz ... Roczniki Instytutu Przemyslu Mleczarskiego [*Poland*] [*A publication*]
Rocz Jeleniogorski ... Rocznik Jeleniogorski [*A publication*]
Rocz Krakowski ... Rocznik Krakowski [*A publication*]
Rocz Muz Etnogr ... Rocznik Muzeum Etnograficznego w Krakowie [*A publication*]

Rocz Muz Narod Warszawie ... Rocznik Muzeum Narodowego w Warszawie [*A publication*]
Rocz Muz Swiet ... Rocznik Muzeum Swietokrzyskiego [*A publication*]
Rocz Muz Toruniu ... Rocznik Muzeum w Toruniu [*A publication*]
Rocz Muz Warsz ... Rocznik Muzeum Narodowego w Warszawie [*A publication*]
Roczn Akad Roln Poznan ... Roczniki Akademii Rolniczej w Poznaniu [*A publication*]
Rocz Nauk Roln ... Roczniki Nauk Rolniczych [*A publication*]
Rocz Nauk Roln Les ... Roczniki Nauk Rolniczych i Lesnych [*A publication*]
Rocz Nauk Roln Lesn ... Roczniki Nauk Rolniczych i Lesnych [*A publication*]
Rocz Nauk Roln Ser A ... Roczniki Nauk Rolniczych. Seria A [*A publication*]
Rocz Nauk Roln Ser A Prod Rosl ... Roczniki Nauk Rolniczych. Seria A. Produkcja Roslinna [*A publication*]
Rocz Nauk Roln Ser B ... Roczniki Nauk Rolniczych. Seria B. Zootechniczna [*A publication*]
Rocz Nauk Roln Ser B Zootech ... Roczniki Nauk Rolniczych. Seria B. Zootechniczna [*A publication*]
Rocz Nauk Roln Ser C Mech Roln ... Roczniki Nauk Rolniczych. Seria C. Mechanizacja Rolnictwa [*A publication*]
Rocz Nauk Roln Ser C Tech Roln ... Roczniki Nauk Rolniczych. Seria C. Technika Rolnicza [*Continues Seria C. Mechznizacja Rolnictwa*] [*A publication*]
Rocz Nauk Roln Ser D ... Roczniki Nauk Rolniczych. Seria D. Monografie [*A publication*]
Rocz Nauk Roln Ser D Monogr ... Roczniki Nauk Rolniczych. Seria D. Monografie [*A publication*]
Rocz Nauk Roln Ser E 1953-60 ... Roczniki Nauk Rolniczych. Seria E. Weterynarii 1953-60 [*A publication*]
Rocz Nauk Roln Ser E Ochr Rosl ... Roczniki Nauk Rolniczych. Seria E. Ochrona Roslin [*A publication*]
Rocz Nauk Roln Ser F ... Roczniki Nauk Rolniczych. Seria F. Melioracji i Vzytkow Zielonych [*A publication*]
Rocz Nauk Roln Ser F Melio Vzytkow Zielonych ... Roczniki Nauk Rolniczych. Seria F. Melioracji i Vzytkow Zielonych [*A publication*]
Rocz Nauk Roln Ser H Rybactwo ... Roczniki Nauk Rolniczych. Seria H. Rybactwo [*A publication*]
Rocz Nauk Zootech ... Roczniki Naukowe Zootechniki [*A publication*]
Rocz Nauk Zootech Monogr Rozpr ... Roczniki Naukowe Zootechniki. Monografie i Rozprawy [*A publication*]
Rocz Nauk Zootech Pol J Anim Sci Technol ... Rocznik Naukowe Zootechniki. Polish Journal of Animal Science and Technology [*A publication*]
Roczn Bibl ... Roczniki Biblioteczne [*A publication*]
Roczn Bibliot Narodowe ... Rocznik Bibliotek Narodowe [*A publication*]
Roczn Chem ... Roczniki Chemii [*A publication*]
Roczn Dendrol Polsk Tow Bot ... Rocznik Sekcji Dendrologicznej Polskiego Towarzystwa Botanicznego [*A publication*]
Roczniki Glebozn ... Roczniki Gleboznawcze [*A publication*]
Roczn Inst Handlu Wewn ... Roczniki Instytutu Handlu Wewnetrznego [*A publication*]
Roczn Nauk Roln A ... Roczniki Nauk Rolniczych. A. Produkcja Roslinna [*A publication*]
Roczn Panst Zakl Hig ... Roczniki Panstwowego Zakladu Higieny [*A publication*]
Roczn T Ch AT ... Rocznik Teologiczne Chrzescijanskiej Akademii Teologicznej [*A publication*]
Roczn Uniw Marie Curie Lubl ... Roczniki Uniwersytetu Marie Curie-Sklodowskiej w Lublinie [*A publication*]
Roczn Wyz Szk Roln Poznan ... Rocznik Wyzszej Szkoly Rolniczej Poznaniu [*A publication*]
RoczOr .... Rocznik Orientalistyczny [*Warsaw*] [*A publication*]
Rocz Panstw Zakl Hig ... Roczniki Panstwowego Zakladu Higieny [*A publication*]
Rocz Panst Zakl Hig (Warszawa) ... Roczniki Panstwowego Zakladu Higieny (Warszawa) [*A publication*]
Rocz Pol Tow Geol ... Rocznik Polskiego Towarzystwa Geologicznego [*A publication*]
Rocz Pomor Akad Med ... Rocznik Pomorska Akademia Medyczna Imienia Generala Karola Swierczewskiego w Szczecinie [*A publication*]
Rocz Pomor Akad Med Im Gen Karola Swierczewskiego Szczecin ... Rocznik Pomorska Akademia Medyczna Imienia Generala Karola Swierczewskiego w Szczecinie [*A publication*]
Rocz Pomor Akad Med Szczecinie ... Rocznik Pomorskiej Akademii Medycznej Imienia Generala Karola Swierczewskiego w Szczecinie [*Poland*] [*A publication*]
Rocz Pomor Akad Med Szczecinie Supl ... Roczniki Pomorskiej Akademii Medycznej w Szczecinie. Suplement [*A publication*]
Rocz Sekc Dendrol Pol Tow Bot ... Rocznik Sekcji Dendrologicznej Polskiego Towarzystwa Botanicznego [*A publication*]
RoczSl .... Rocznik Slawistyczny [*A publication*]
Rocz Stat Pow Zot ... Rocznik Statystyczny Powiatu Zotow [*A publication*]
Rocz Technol Chem Zywn ... Roczniki Technologii Chemii Zywnosci [*A publication*]
Rocz Uniw Marij Curi-Sklodowskiej Dzial AA ... Roczniki Uniwersytetu Marij Curie-Sklodowskiej. Dzial AA. Fizyka i Chemia [*A publication*]
Rocz Wojsk Inst Hig Epidemiol ... Rocznik Wojskowego Instytutu Higieny i Epidemiologii [*Poland*] [*A publication*]

Rocz Wyzs Szkoly Roln Poznaniu ... Roczniki Wyzszej Szkoly Rolniczej w Poznaniu [*A publication*]
Rocz Wyzsz Roln Poznaniu ... Roczniki Wyzszej Szkoly Rolniczej w Poznaniu [*A publication*]
Rocz Wyzsz Szk Roln Poznaniu Pr Habilitacyjne ... Roczniki Wyzszej Szkoly Rolniczej w Poznaniu. Prace Habilitacyjne [*A publication*]
ROD........... Railway Operating Department [*British military*] (DMA)
ROD........... Range of the Day [*Military*] (CAAL)
ROD........... Range Operations Directorate [*White Sands Missile Range*]
ROD........... Rate of Descent (KSC)
ROD........... Record of Decision [*Environmental Protection Agency*]
ROD........... Record of Discussion (MCD)
ROD........... Recorder on Demand
ROD........... Release Order Directive [*Later, ERO*] (NRCH)
ROD........... Remote Operated Door (MCD)
ROD........... Repair and Overhaul Directive (AAG)
ROD........... Report of Discrepancies
ROD........... Required on Dock (KSC)
ROD........... Required Operational Date
ROD........... Reverse-Osmosis Desalination
R-O-D........ Rise-Off-Disconnect (AAG)
ROD........... Roddy Resources, Inc. [*Toronto Stock Exchange symbol*]
Rod............. Rodericus Suarez [*Flourished, 15th century*] [*Authority cited in pre-1607 legal work*] (DSA)
ROD........... Rosewood, OH [*Location identifier*] [*FAA*] (FAAL)
ROD........... Route Opening Detachment (MCD)
RODA....... Regardless of Destination Airport (FAAC)
RODA....... Sisters Oblates to Divine Love [*Roman Catholic religious order*]
RODAC..... Reorganization Objectives, Army Division, Army and Corps [*Military*] (AABC)
RODATA .. Registered Organization Data Bank
RODC....... Regional Oceanographic Data Center [*Marine science*] (MSC)
RODC........ Registered Organization Development Consultant [*Designation awarded by Organization Development Institute*]
RODE........ Iejima United States Air Force Base [*Ryukyu Islands*] [*ICAO location identifier*] (ICLI)
Rod and Gun and Canad Silver Fox News ... Rod and Gun and Canadian Silver Fox News [*A publication*]
RO-DI........ Reverse Osmosis - Deionization System [*Water purification*]
RODIAC ... Rotary Dual Input for Analog Computation
R-O Dis...... Reality-Oriented Discussion
RODM....... Rodime PLC [*NASDAQ symbol*] (NQ)
Rodm.......... Rodman's Reports [*78-82 Kentucky*] [*A publication*] (DLA)
Rodman...... Rodman's Reports [*78-82 Kentucky*] [*A publication*] (DLA)
RODN .... Kadena Air Base [*Ryukyu Islands*] [*ICAO location identifier*] (ICLI)
RODO .... Range Operations Duty Officer (MUGU)
Rodo........... Rodoicus [*Authority cited in pre-1607 legal work*] (DSA)
Rodo Kenky Kenky ... Rodoeisei Kenkyujo Kenkyuhokoku [*A publication*]
Rodopskii Zbor ... Rodopskii Zbornik [*A publication*]
RODS .... American Steel & Wire Corp. [*NASDAQ symbol*] (CTT)
RODS .... Real-Time Operations, Dispatching, and Scheduling [*System*] [*TRW, Inc.*]
RODSB...... Revue d'Odonto-Stomatologie [*A publication*]
ROE........... Birmingham, AL [*Location identifier*] [*FAA*] (FAAL)
ROE........... Rate of Exchange [*Finance*]
ROE........... Reflector Orbital Equipment
ROE........... Return on Equity [*Finance*]
ROE........... Review of Economics and Statistics [*A publication*]
ROE........... Roemisches Oesterreich [*A publication*]
ROE........... Roster of Exception [*Military*] (AABC)
ROE........... Round Off Error
ROE........... Royal Observatory, Edinburgh [*Scotland*]
ROE........... Rules of Engagement [*Military*] (AABC)
ROED....... Ridgeway Exco, Inc. [*NASDAQ symbol*] (NQ)
RoeFo Fortschr Geb Roentgenstr Nuklearmed ... RoeFo. Fortschritte auf dem Gebiete der Roentgenstrahlen und der Nuklearmedizin [*West Germany*] [*A publication*]
Roelk Man ... Roelker's Manual for Notaries and Bankers [*A publication*] (DLA)
Roemische Quartalschrift ... Roemische Quartalschrift fuer Christliche Altertumskunde und fuer Kirchengeschichte [*A publication*]
Roem Jahr Kunstges ... Roemisches Jahrbuch fuer Kunstgeschichte [*A publication*]
Roem Mitt ... Mitteilungen. Deutsches Archaeologische Institut. Abteilung Rome [*A publication*]
Roem Oe .... Roemisches Oesterreich. Jahresschrift der Oesterreichischen Gesellschaft fuer Archaeologie [*A publication*]
Roem Q ...... Roemische Quartalschrift fuer Christliche Altertumskunde und fuer Kirchengeschichte [*A publication*]
Roem Qu .... Roemische Quartalschrift fuer Christliche Altertumskunde und fuer Kirchengeschichte [*A publication*]
ROEND..... Roentgenstrahlen [*A publication*]
Roent.......... Roentgenology [*Radiology*]
Roentgen Ber ... Roentgen Berichte [*A publication*]
Roentgen-Bl ... Roentgen-Blaetter [*A publication*]
Roentgen Laboratoriumsprax ... Roentgen Laboratoriumspraxis [*A publication*]
Roentgenprax ... Roentgenpraxis [*A publication*]

Roentgen Technol ... Roentgen Technology. Official Journal of the Indian Association of Radiological Technologists [*A publication*]
Roent M ..... Master of Roentgenology
Roe Q .... Roemische Quartalschrift fuer Christliche Altertumskunde und fuer Kirchengeschichte [*A publication*]
Roe US Com ... Roe's Manual for United States Commissioners [*A publication*] (DLA)
ROF .... Rate of Fire [*In rounds per minute*] [*Military*]
ROF .... Reformed Ogboni Fraternity [*Nigeria*]
ROF .... Remote Operator Facility [*Honeywell, Inc.*]
ROF .... Reporting Organizational File [*Military*] (AFM)
Rof............. Roffredus Beneventanus [*Flourished, 1215-43*] [*Authority cited in pre-1607 legal work*] (DSA)
ROF .... Romanische Forschungen [*A publication*]
ROF .... Royal Oak Foundation (EA)
ROF .... Royal Ordnance Factory [*British*] (NATG)
Rof Bn .... Roffredus Beneventanus [*Flourished, 1215-43*] [*Authority cited in pre-1607 legal work*] (DSA)
ROFF........ Retail Office Furniture Forum (EA)
ROFF........ Roffler Industries [*NASDAQ symbol*] (NQ)
Roffe Be ..... Roffredus Beneventanus [*Flourished, 1215-43*] [*Authority cited in pre-1607 legal work*] (DSA)
ROFFEN ... Roffensis [*Signature of Bishop of Rochester*] [*Latin*] (ROG)
ROFL........ Russian Orthodox Fraternity Lubov (EA)
ROFOR ..... Route Forecast [*Aviation*] (FAAC)
ROFR .... Repair of Repairables (MCD)
ROFT........ RADAR Off Target
ROFT........ Rapid Optics Fabrication Technology (MCD)
RofThPh .... Review of Theology and Philosophy [*A publication*]
ROG........... Reactive Organic Gas [*Environmental chemistry*]
ROG........... Receipt of Goods
ROG........... Residency Operations Group
R-O-G........ Rise-Off-Ground [*Model airplane*] (AAG)
ROG........... Rodale's Organic Gardening [*A publication*]
Rog............. Rogerius Beneventanus [*Flourished, 12th century*] [*Authority cited in pre-1607 legal work*] (DSA)
ROG........... Rogers, AR [*Location identifier*] [*FAA*] (FAAL)
ROG........... Rogers Corp. [*AMEX symbol*] (SPSG)
ROG........... Roggianite [*A zeolite*]
ROG........... Rothchild Gold [*Vancouver Stock Exchange symbol*]
RO1(G)...... Radio Operator (General) 1st Class [*British military*] (DMA)
RO2(G)...... Radio Operator (General) 2nd Class [*British military*] (DMA)
ROGAR ..... Review of Guard and Reserve Task Force (MCD)
Rog CHR ... Rogers' City Hall Recorder [*1816-22*] [*New York*] [*A publication*] (DLA)
Rog Ecc L ... Rogers' Ecclesiastical Law [*5th ed.*] [*1857*] [*A publication*] (DLA)
Rog Ecc Law ... Rogers' Ecclesiastical Law [*A publication*] (DLA)
Rog Elec..... Rogers on Elections and Registration [*A publication*] (DLA)
Rogers .... Rogers on Elections [*A publication*] (DLA)
Rogers .... Rogers' Reports [*47-51 Louisiana Annual*] [*A publication*] (DLA)
Rog Hov ..... Roger De Hoveden's Chronica [*A publication*] (DLA)
ROGI .... Roberts Oil & Gas, Incorporated [*NASDAQ symbol*] (NQ)
Rog Jud Acts ... Rogers on the Judicature Acts [*A publication*] (DLA)
ROGLA ..... Roczniki Gleboznawcze [*A publication*]
Rog Min ..... Rogers on Mines and Minerals [*A publication*] (DLA)
Rog Min ..... Rogers. Mines, Minerals, and Quarries [*A publication*] (ILCA)
ROGNA ..... Rivista di Ostetricia e Ginecologia [*A publication*]
ROGOPAG ... Rossellini, Jr.; Godard, Pasolini, Gregoretti [*Title of episodic motion picture formed from surnames of its directors*]
Rog Rec...... Rogers' New City Hall Recorder [*A publication*] (DLA)
Rog Trav .... Rogers' Wrongs and Rights of a Traveller [*A publication*] (DLA)
R-O-H........ Receiver Off the Hook
ROH .... Regular Overhaul [*Navy*] (NG)
ROH .... Returned on Hire
roh.............. Rhaeto-Romance [*MARC language code*] [*Library of Congress*] (LCCP)
ROH .... Robinhood [*Australia*] [*Airport symbol*] [*Obsolete*] (OAG)
ROH .... Rohm & Haas Co. [*NYSE symbol*] (SPSG)
ROH .... Rohtak [*India*] [*Seismograph station code, US Geological Survey*] [*Closed*] (SEIS)
RoH........... Roumeliotiko Hemerologio [*A publication*]
ROH .... Royal Opera House [*Covent Garden, London*]
Rohm Haas Rep ... Rohm and Haas Reporter [*A publication*]
Rohm & Haas Reptr ... Rohm and Haas Reporter [*A publication*]
ROHRA..... Rohre, Rohrleitungsbau, Rohrleitungstransport [*A publication*]
Rohre Rohrleitungsbau Rohrleitungstransp ... Rohre, Rohrleitungsbau, Rohrleitungstransport [*West Germany*] [*A publication*]
Rohst Landerber ... Rohstoffwirtschaftliche Landerberichte [*A publication*]
RoHum ...... Roczniki Humanistyczne [*A publication*]
ROI .... Member of the Royal Institute of Oil Painters [*British*]
ROI .... Radio, Optical, Inertial
ROI .... Range Operations Instruction [*NASA*] (KSC)
ROI .... Reactive Oxygen Intermediate [*Biochemistry*]
ROI .... Region of Interest [*Nuclear energy*] (NRCH)
ROI .... Reliability Organization Instruction (AAG)
ROI........... Religious Observance Index (BJA)
ROI .... Remnant of Israel (EA)
ROI .... Rendezvous Orbit Insertion [*Aerospace*]

ROI............ Report of Investigation [*Military*]   (AFM)
ROI............ Resource Objectives, Incorporated [*Ridgewood, NJ*]   (TSSD)
ROI............ Return on Investment [*Finance*]
ROI............ River Oaks Industries, Inc. [*NYSE symbol*]   (SPSG)
ROI............ Rotating Optical Interferometer
ROI............ Royal Institute of Oil Painters [*British*]
ROIC......... Resident Officer-in-Charge [*Military*]
ROICC....... Resident Officer-in-Charge of Construction [*Military*]
ROID......... Report of Item Discrepancy [*Army*]   (AABC)
ROIG......... Ishigaki Jima [*Ryukyu Islands*] [*ICAO location identifier*]   (ICLI)
ROIL......... Reserve Industries Corp. [*NASDAQ symbol*]   (NQ)
ROINST..... Range Operations Instruction [*NASA*]   (MUGU)
ROIP......... Remaining Oil in Place [*Petroleum industry*]
ROIS......... Radio Operational Intercom System   (KSC)
ROITL....... Reports of Interest to Lawyers [*Merton Allen Associates*] [*Information service or system*]   (CRD)
ROJ.......... Range of Jamming
ROJ.......... Romanistisches Jahrbuch [*A publication*]
ROJ.......... Royal Order of Jagie Ilo [*Later, SHOSJ*]   (EA)
ROK.......... Republic of Korea
ROK.......... Rockhampton [*Australia*] [*Airport symbol*]   (OAG)
ROK.......... Rockwell International Corp. [*NYSE symbol*] [*Toronto Stock Exchange symbol*]   (SPSG)
ROKA....... Republic of Korea Army   (AABC)
ROKAA..... Rodo Kagaku [*A publication*]
ROKAF..... Republic of Korea Air Force
ROKAP..... Republic of Korea Civic Action Program   (CINC)
ROKDTF... Republic of Korea Division Task Force
ROKF....... Republic of Korea Forces
ROKFV..... Republic of Korea Forces in Vietnam   (CINC)
ROKG....... Republic of Korea Government   (CINC)
ROKG....... Rocking
ROKIT...... Republic of Korea Indigenous Tank Program   (MCD)
ROKJ....... Kume Jima [*Ryukyu Islands*] [*ICAO location identifier*]   (ICLI)
ROKMC.... Republic of Korea Marine Corps   (CINC)
ROKN....... Republic of Korea Navy   (CINC)
ROKOA5... Folia Entomologica Hungarica [*A publication*]
ROKPTN... Rockhampton   (ROG)
ROKPUC... Republic of Korea Presidential Unit Citation Badge [*Military decoration*]
ROKPUCE ... Republic of Korea Presidential Unit Citation [*Military decoration*]
ROKUSCFC ... Republic of Korea and US Combined Forces Command   (MCD)
ROKW....... Yomitan [*Ryukyu Islands*] [*ICAO location identifier*]   (ICLI)
ROL.......... RADAR Observer License
ROL.......... Record of Oral Language   (ADA)
ROL.......... Reduction-Option Loan [*Banking*]
ROL.......... Remote Operating Location   (MCD)
ROL.......... Reordering Level
ROL.......... Revue de l'Orient Latin [*A publication*]
ROL.......... Right Occipitolateral [*Obstetrics*]
ROL.......... Rolla [*Missouri*] [*Seismograph station code, US Geological Survey*]   (SEIS)
Rol........... Rolle's Abridgment [*A publication*]   (DLA)
Rol........... Rolle's English King's Bench Reports [*2 vols.*] [*A publication*]   (DLA)
ROL.......... Rollins, Inc. [*NYSE symbol*]   (SPSG)
ROL.......... Rotate Left [*Data processing*]
ROL.......... Royal Oak Resources Ltd. [*Toronto Stock Exchange symbol*]
ROL.......... Royal Overseas League   (EAIO)
Rol Ab...... Rolle's Abridgment [*A publication*]   (DLA)
ROLAC...... Regional Organization of Liaison for Allocation of Circuit   (NATG)
ROLAC...... Registry of Life Assurance Commission [*British*]
ROLAC...... UNEP [*United Nations Environment Programme*] Regional Office for Latin America and the Caribbean   (EAIO)
ROLADES ... Roland Air Defense System   (MCD)
ROLE .... Receive Only Link Eleven [*Naval datalink system*] [*British*]
ROLET...... Reference Our Letter   (NOAA)
ROLF........ Remotely Operated Longwall Face   (IEEE)
ROLF........ Rolfite Co. [*NASDAQ symbol*]   (NQ)
RoLit........ Romania Literara [*A publication*]
Roll.......... Rolle's Abridgment [*A publication*]   (DLA)
Roll.......... Rolle's English King's Bench Reports [*2 vols.*] [*A publication*]   (DLA)
Roll Abr..... Rolle's Abridgment [*A publication*]   (DLA)
Rolle......... Rolle's Abridgment [*A publication*]   (DLA)
Rolle......... Rolle's English King's Bench Reports [*2 vols.*] [*1614-25*] [*A publication*]   (DLA)
Rolle Abr.... Rolle's Abridgment of the Common Law [*A publication*]   (DLA)
Rolle R ...... Rolle's English King's Bench Reports [*2 vols.*] [*1614-25*] [*A publication*]   (DLA)
Roll Rep..... Rolle's English King's Bench Reports [*2 vols.*] [*1614-25*] [*A publication*]   (DLA)
Rolls Ct Rep ... Rolls' Court Reports [*A publication*]   (DLA)
Roll Stone .. Rolling Stone [*A publication*]
Ro/Lo....... Roll-On, Roll-Off/Lift-On, Lift-Off [*Shipping*]   (DS)

ROLR .... Receiving Objective Loudness Rating [*Telephones*]   (IEEE)
ROLS........ Recoverable Orbital Launch System
ROLSIM ... Roland Simulation   (MCD)
ROM....... Priest, CA [*Location identifier*] [*FAA*]   (FAAL)
ROM....... Range of Motion [*or Movement*]
ROM....... Read-Only Memory [*Computer memory*] [*Data processing*]
ROM....... Read-Only Men [*On Board car window sign's version of the computer term, Read-Only Memory*]
ROM....... Readout Memory   (IEEE)
ROM....... Return on Market Value [*Finance*]
ROM....... Rio Algom Ltd. [*AMEX symbol*] [*Toronto Stock Exchange symbol*]   (SPSG)
Rom......... Roemisch [*Roman*] [*German*]   (OCD)
Rom......... [*Ludovicus Pontanus de*] Roma [*Deceased, 1439*] [*Authority cited in pre-1607 legal work*]   (DSA)
ROM....... Roman [*Type*] [*Publishing*]
ROM....... Romance
ROM....... Romania [*ANSI three-letter standard code*]   (CNC)
Rom......... Romania [*A publication*]
Rom......... Romans [*New Testament book*]
rom......... Romany [*MARC language code*] [*Library of Congress*]   (LCCP)
Rom......... Romany Records [*Record label*]
ROM....... Romberg [*Medicine*]
ROM....... Rome [*Italy*] [*Seismograph station code, US Geological Survey*] [*Closed*]   (SEIS)
ROM......... Rome [*Italy*] [*Airport symbol*]   (OAG)
Rom......... Romeo and Juliet [*Shakespearean work*]
Rom......... Romilly's Notes of English Chancery Cases [*1767-87*] [*A publication*]   (DLA)
Rom......... Romulus [*of Plutarch*] [*Classical studies*]   (OCD)
ROM....... Rough Order of Magnitude [*Army*]   (AABC)
ROM....... Royal Ontario Museum [*Toronto, ON*] [*Research center*]
ROM....... Run of Mine
ROM......... Rupture of Membranes [*Medicine*]
ROMA..... Return on Managed Assets [*Business term*]
ROMAA ... Rom-Amer Pharmaceuticals [*NASDAQ symbol*]   (NQ)
ROMAC ... Range Operations Monitor Analysis Center   (MCD)
ROMAC ... Range Operations Monitoring and Control
ROMAC ... Robotic Muscle Activator
ROMACC ... Range Operational Monitoring and Control Center
ROMAD.... Radio Operator/Maintenance Driver
Rom Adelsparteien ... Roemische Adelsparteien und Adelsfamilien [*A publication*]   (OCD)
Roma Econ ... Roma Economica [*A publication*]
Romagna Med ... Romagna Medica [*A publication*]
Romance Philol ... Romance Philology [*A publication*]
Roman Forsc ... Romanische Forschungen [*A publication*]
Roman Forsch ... Romanische Forschungen [*A publication*]
Romanian F ... Romanian Film [*A publication*]
Romanian R ... Romanian Review [*A publication*]
Romania P ... Romania during the 1981-1985 Development Plan [*A publication*]
Roman Note ... Romance Notes [*A publication*]
Romanobarbar ... Romanobarbarica. Contributi allo Studio dei Rapporti Culturali tra il Mondo Latino e Mondo Barbarico [*A publication*]
Roman Phil ... Romance Philology [*A publication*]
Roman Philol ... Romance Philology [*A publication*]
Roman R .... Romanic Review [*A publication*]
Roman Rev ... Romanic Review [*A publication*]
ROMANS ... Range-Only Multiple Aircraft Navigation System [*Air Force*]
ROMANS ... Remote Manipulation Systems [*NASA*]
Roman Z Lit ... Romanistische Zeitschrift fuer Literaturgeschichte [*Cahiers d'Histoire des Litteratures Romanes*] [*A publication*]
RO(M)B .... Reduction of (Military) Budgets
ROMBI ..... Results of Marine Biological Investigations [*Marine science*]   (MSC)
ROMBUS ... Reusable Orbital Module Booster and Utility Shuttle [*Aerospace*]
Rom Cas..... Romilly's Notes of English Chancery Cases [*1767-87*] [*A publication*]   (DLA)
Rom Com Geol Dari Seama Sedin ... Romania Comitetul de Stat al Geologiei. Institutul Geologic. Dari de Seama ale Sedintelor [*A publication*]
Rom Con .... Romana Contact. Organe Trimestriel de la Societe d'Archeologie [*A publication*]
Rom Cr Law ... Romilly's Observations on the Criminal Law [*3rd ed.*] [*1813*] [*A publication*]   (DLA)
ROMD....... Minami Daito Jima [*Ryukyu Islands*] [*ICAO location identifier*]   (ICLI)
ROMD....... Remote Operations and Maintenance Demonstration [*Nuclear energy*]
ROME .... Resource Organizations and Meetings for Educators [*National Center for Research in Vocational Education*] [*Information service or system*] [*Defunct*]   (CRD)
ROMEMO ... Reference Our Memorandum   (FAAC)
ROMES...... Reference Our Message   (FAAC)
RomF .... Romanische Forschungen [*A publication*]
Rom Fgn Tr ... Romanian Foreign Trade [*A publication*]
Rom Forsch ... Roemische Forschungen [*A publication*]   (OCD)
Rom G .... Romanica Gandensia [*A publication*]

Rom Gesch ... Grundriss der Romischen Geschichte [*A publication*]   (OCD)
Rom Gesch ... Romische Geschichte bis zum Beginn der Punischen Kriege [*A publication*]   (OCD)
ROMI .... Rule Out Myocardial Infarction [*Medicine*]
Romilly NC (Eng) ... Romilly's Notes of English Chancery Cases [*A publication*]   (DLA)
Rom Inst Geol Dari Seama Sedin ... Romania Institutul Geologic. Dari de Seama ale Sedintelor [*A publication*]
Rom Inst Geol Mem ... Romania Institutul Geologic. Memorii [*A publication*]
Rom Inst Geol Stud Teh Econ Ser B ... Romania Institutul Geologic. Studii Tehnice si Economice. Seria B. Prepararea Minereurilor [*A publication*]
Rom Inst Geol Stud Teh Econ Ser D ... Romania Institutul Geologic. Studii Tehnice si Economice. Seria D. Prospectiuni Geofizice [*A publication*]
Rom Inst Geol Stud Teh Econ Ser E ... Romania Institutul Geologic. Studii Tehnice si Economice. Seria E [*A publication*]
Rom Inst Geol Stud Teh Econ Ser I ... Romania Comitetul de Stat al Geologiei. Institutul Geologic. Studii Tehnice si Economice. Seria I. Mineralogie-Petrografie [*A publication*]
Rom Inst Meteorol Hidrol Stud Hidrogeol ... Romania Institutul de Meteorologie si Hidrologie. Studii de Hidrogeologie [*A publication*]
RomJ .... Romanistisches Jahrbuch [*A publication*]
Rom J Chem ... Romanian Journal of Chemistry [*A publication*]
Rom J Med Endocrinol ... Romanian Journal of Medicine. Endocrinology [*A publication*]
Rom J Med Intern Med ... Romanian Journal of Medicine. Internal Medicine [*A publication*]
Rom J Med Neurol Psychiatry ... Romanian Journal of Medicine. Neurology and Psychiatry [*A publication*]
Rom J Med Virol ... Romanian Journal of Medicine. Virology [*A publication*]
Rom J Morphol Embryol Physiol Physiol ... Romanian Journal of Morphology, Embryology, and Physiology. Physiology [*A publication*]
Rom Law .... Mackeldey's Handbook of the Roman Law [*A publication*]   (DLA)
RomLit .... Romania Literara [*Bucharest*] [*A publication*]
ROMM ..... Read-Only Memory Module [*Data processing*]
ROMM ...... Revue de l'Occident Musulman et de la Mediterranee [*A publication*]
Rom Med Rev ... Romanian Medical Review [*A publication*]
RomN .... Romance Notes [*A publication*]
ROMO ..... Rocky Mountain National Park
ROMON ... Receiving-Only Monitor
ROMOSS ... Revised Officer Military Occupational Speciality System   (MCD)
ROMOTAR ... Range-Only Measurement of Trajectory and Recording
ROMP ...... Recovery of Male Potency   (EA)
ROMP ...... Report of Obligation Military Pay   (AFM)
ROMP ...... Review of Management Practices [*or Processes*]
ROMP ...... Ring Opening Metathesis Polymerization [*Organic chemistry*]
RomPh ...... Romance Philology [*A publication*]
Rom Pol ... Roman Politics 220-150BC [*A publication*]   (OCD)
ROMPS ..... Regional Office Monthly Personnel Status [*Department of Labor*]
RomR .... Romanic Review [*A publication*]
Rom Rev .... [*The*] Roman Revolution [*1939*] [*A publication*]   (OCD)
Rom Rule Asia Min ... Roman Rule in Asia Minor [*A publication*]   (OCD)
ROMS .... Remote Ocean Surface Measuring System [*Navy*]   (CAAL)
RomSl .... Romanoslavica [*A publication*]
Rom Staatsr ... Roemisches Staatsrecht [*A publication*]   (OCD)
Rom Strafr ... Roemisches Strafrecht [*A publication*]   (OCD)
Rom Stud ... Roemische Studien [*A publication*]   (OCD)
Rom Today ... Romania Today [*A publication*]
ROMW ..... Recreation Opportunities for Migrant Women [*Australia*]
ROMY ...... Miyako [*Ryukyu Islands*] [*ICAO location identifier*]   (ICLI)
RON .... Receiving Only   (FAAC)
RON .... Remaining [*or Rest*] Overnight [*Aviation*]
RON .... Remote [*Alaska*] [*Seismograph station code, US Geological Survey*] [*Closed*]   (SEIS)
RON .... Research-Octane-Number [*Fuel technology*]
RON .... Rest Overnight [*or Rest-of-Night*] [*Pronounced "ron"*] [*Chance for a candidate to catch some sleep during a traveling political campaign*]
RoN .... Romance Notes [*A publication*]
RON .... Rondon [*Colombia*] [*Airport symbol*] [*Obsolete*]   (OAG)
RON .... Squadron   (MUGU)
RONA .... Naha United States Naval Base [*Ryukyu Islands*] [*ICAO location identifier*]   (ICLI)
RONA .... Return on Net Assets
RONAG ..... Reserve Officers Naval Architecture Group
RONB .... Research-Octane-Number-Barrels [*Fuel technology*]
RONC .... Ronson Corporation [*Somerset, NJ*] [*NASDAQ symbol*]   (NQ)
Ronchegall ... [*Johannes*] Ronchegallus [*Flourished, 1559-80*] [*Authority cited in pre-1607 legal work*]   (DSA)
RONCO ...... Rock-Oldies-News-Commercials Operation [*Formula radio*]
RONCOM ... Ronald Como, Inc. [*Perry Como's production firm; Ronald is his son*]
RONEO ..... Rotary and Neostyle [*Duplicating machine*] [*Acronym is trademark*]

RONLY ..... Receiver Only [*Radio*]
RONOA ..... Revue d'Oto-Neuro-Ophtalmologie [*A publication*]
RONS .... Reserve Officers of the Naval Service [*Later, ROA*]
R Ont Mus J ... Royal Ontario Museum. Journal [*A publication*]
R Ont Mus Life Sci Contrib ... Royal Ontario Museum. Life Sciences. Contributions [*A publication*]
R Ont Mus Life Sci Misc Publ ... Royal Ontario Museum. Life Sciences. Miscellaneous Publications [*A publication*]
R Ont Mus Life Sci Occas Pap ... Royal Ontario Museum. Life Sciences. Occasional Paper [*A publication*]
R Ont Mus Zool Paleontol Contrib ... Royal Ontario Museum of Zoology and Paleontology. Contributions [*A publication*]
RONWT .... Revised Ordinances, Northwest Territories [*Canada*] [*A publication*]   (DLA)
ROO .... Radio Optical Observatory
ROO .... Railhead Ordnance Officer
ROO .... Range Operations Officer
ROO .... Reserve of Officers [*British*]
ROO .... Resident Obstetric Officer [*British*]
ROO .... Richland Operations Office [*Energy Research and Development Administration*]
ROO .... Rondonopolis [*Brazil*] [*Airport symbol*]   (OAG)
ROOPH ..... Readily Operative Overhead Protection by Hippos [*Facetious proposal for protection against nuclear attack*]
ROORD3 ... Radiologia [*Bucharest*] [*A publication*]
Roorkee Univ Res J ... Roorkee University. Research Journal [*A publication*]
ROOS .... Roosevelt National Investment Co. [*NASDAQ symbol*]   (NQ)
ROOSCH .. Royal Order of Sputnik Chasers
Roosevelt Wild Life Bull ... Roosevelt Wild Life Bulletin [*A publication*]
ROOST ..... Reusable One-Stage Orbital Space Truck [*Aerospace*]
ROOT .... Mr. Rooter Corp. [*Oklahoma City, OK*] [*NASDAQ symbol*]   (NQ)
ROOT .... Relaxation Oscillator Optically Tuned
Root .... Root's Connecticut Reports [*1774-89*] [*A publication*]   (DLA)
Root .... Root's Connecticut Supreme Court Reports [*1789-98*] [*A publication*]   (DLA)
Root Bt Laws ... Root's Digest of Law and Practice in Bankruptcy [*1818*] [*A publication*]   (DLA)
Root R .... Root's Connecticut Reports [*A publication*]   (DLA)
Roots .... Root's Connecticut Reports [*A publication*]   (DLA)
Root's Rep ... Root's Connecticut Reports [*A publication*]   (DLA)
ROP .... Raster Operation
ROP .... Rate of Pay [*British military*]   (DMA)
ROP .... Rate of Penetration [*Drilling technology*]
ROP .... Receive-Only Printer [*Data processing*]
ROP .... Receiving Operations Package [*DoD*]
ROP. .... Record of Performance
ROP .... Record of Production
ROP .... Record of Purchase   (NRCH)
ROP .... Refined Oil Products
ROP .... Regional Operating Plan [*Department of Labor*]
ROP .... Registered Options Principal
ROP .... Reorder Point [*Navy*]   (NG)
ROP .... Reorder Price
ROP .... Repeat Offenders Project
ROP .... Republic of Panama
ROP .... Republic of the Philippines   (CINC)
ROP .... Retinopathy of Prematurity [*Medicine*]
ROP .... Right Occipitoposterior [*A fetal position*] [*Obstetrics*]
ROP .... Right Outside Position [*Dancing*]
ROP .... Rites of Passage
ROP .... Robson Petroleum Ltd. [*Toronto Stock Exchange symbol*]
ROP .... Roll-Over Protection Equipment   (MCD)
ROP .... Romance Philology [*A publication*]
ROP .... Roper Corp. [*NYSE symbol*]   (SPSG)
Rop .... Roper on Legacies [*4 eds.*] [*1799-1847*] [*A publication*]   (DLA)
ROP .... Rota [*Mariana Islands*] [*Airport symbol*]   (OAG)
ROP .... Royal Order of Piast   (EA)
ROP .... Run of Paper [*Business term*]
ROP .... Run of Press [*i.e., on an unspecified page or plate in web press set-up*] [*Printing*]
ROP₃ .... Revision of Procurement Policy and Procedures
ROPA .... Reserve Officer Personnel Act of 1954
ROPAR .... Regional Operators Program for Aircraft Reliability
ROPB .... Reserve Officers Promotion Board [*Air Force*]
ROPE .... Remotely Operated Platform Electronic [*Submarine technology*]
ROPE .... Reunion of Professional Entertainers   (EA)
ROPER ..... Regional Operators Program for Engine Reliability
ROPES ...... Remote Online Print Executive System
ROPEVAL ... Readiness/Operational Evaluation   (NVT)
ROPEVAL ... Rim of the Pacific Evaluation   (MCD)
ROPF .... Research into One-Parent Families [*British*]
ROPHO ..... Reference Our Telephone Call   (NOAA)
Rop Husb & Wife ... Roper's Law of Property between Husband and Wife [*A publication*]   (DLA)
Rop H & W ... Roper's Law of Property between Husband and Wife [*2nd ed.*] [*1826*] [*A publication*]   (DLA)
ROPIS .... Response of Plants to Interacting Stress Program [*Electric Power Research Institute*]
ROPK .... Ropak Corp. [*NASDAQ symbol*]   (NQ)

Rop Leg ...... Roper on Legacies [*A publication*] (DLA)
ROPM .... Revue. Ordre de Premontre et de Ses Missions [*A publication*]
ROPMA .... Reserve Officers Personnel Management Act [*Proposed*]
ROPME ..... Regional Organization for the Protection of the Marine
     Environment [*Safat, Kuwait*] (EAIO)
ROPP .... Receive-Only Page Printer
ROPP .... Review of Plant Pathology [*Database*] [*Commonwealth
     Mycological Institute*] [*Information service or
     system*] (CRD)
Rop Prop .... Roper's Law of Property between Husband and Wife [*2nd ed.*]
     [*1826*] [*A publication*] (DLA)
ROPRA ..... Reserve Officer Performance Recording Activity
ROPRA ..... Rock Products [*A publication*]
Rop Rev ..... Roper on Revocation of Wills [*A publication*] (DLA)
ROPS .... Range Operation Performance Summary
ROPS .... Roll Over Protection System [*for tractors*]
ROPS .... Roll Over Protective Structures [*NASA*] (KSC)
ROPT .... Remaining Number of Operations
ROPT .... Robson Petroleum Ltd. [*NASDAQ symbol*] (NQ)
ROPU .... RADAR Overheat Protection Unit (MCD)
ROPXA .... Roentgenpraxis [*A publication*]
ROQ .... Houghton Lake, MI [*Location identifier*] [*FAA*] (FAAL)
ROQ .... Reordering Quality
ROR .... Koror [*Palau Islands*] [*Airport symbol*] (OAG)
ROR .... Range-Only RADAR [*Military*] (AABC)
ROR .... Rate of Read
ROR .... Rate of Return (MCD)
ROR .... Released on Own Recognizance [*Law*]
ROR .... Repair, Overhaul, Restoration (MCD)
ROR .... Repair of Repairables (MCD)
ROR .... Residual Oil Remover [*Lens cleaner*] [*V-Vax Products*]
ROR .... Return of Repairables
RoR .... Review of Religion [*A publication*]
ROR .... Right of Rescission [*Business term*]
ROR .... Rochester Minerals [*Vancouver Stock Exchange symbol*]
ROR .... Rocket on Rotor
ROR .... Rockton & Rion Railway [*AAR code*]
RoR .... Romanian Review [*A publication*]
ROR .... Romanic Review [*A publication*]
ROR .... Rorschach [*Test*]
ROR .... Rotate Right [*Data processing*]
RORA .... Aguni [*Ryukyu Islands*] [*ICAO location identifier*] (ICLI)
RORA .... Reliable Operate RADAR Altimeter
RORA .... Reserve Officer Recording Activity
RORC .... Royal Ocean Racing Club [*British*]
RORCE ..... Rate of Return on Capital Employed (DS)
RORD .... Research Opportunities in Renaissance Drama [*A publication*]
RORD .... Return on Receipt of Document [*Business term*]
RORE .... Iejima [*Ryukyu Islands*] [*ICAO location identifier*] (ICLI)
ROREF ..... Rosmac Resources Ltd. [*NASDAQ symbol*] (NQ)
Ro Rep .... Robards' Texas Conscript Cases [*1862-65*] [*A
     publication*] (DLA)
Ro Rep ...... Rolle's English King's Bench Reports [*A publication*] (DLA)
ROREQ ..... Reference Our Requisition (NOAA)
Rorer Jud Sales ... Rorer on Void Judicial Sales [*A publication*] (DLA)
Rorer RR .... Rorer on Railways [*A publication*] (DLA)
RORET ..... Authorized Rotational Retention [*Navy*]
RORG .... Naha [*Ryukyu Islands*] [*ICAO location identifier*] (ICLI)
RORH .... Hateruma [*Ryukyu Islands*] [*ICAO location identifier*] (ICLI)
RO/RI .... Redistribution Out/Redistribution In (CINC)
Ror Int St L ... Rorer on Inter-State Law [*A publication*] (DLA)
RORIS ...... Remote Operated Radiographic Inspection System
Ror Jud Sal ... Rorer on Void Judicial Sales [*A publication*] (DLA)
RORK .... Kitadaito [*Ryukyu Islands*] [*ICAO location identifier*] (ICLI)
RO/RO .... Roll-On/Roll-Off [*Shipping*] (AFM)
RO-RO .... Rolls Royce [*Automobile*] [*Slang*] (DSUE)
RORQN ..... Reference Our Requisition (FAAC)
RORS .... Realignment of Resources and Services (MCD)
RORS .... Shimojishima [*Ryukyu Islands*] [*ICAO location
     identifier*] (ICLI)
RORSAT ... RADAR Ocean Reconnaissance Satellite (MCD)
RORT .... Report on Reimbursable Transactions [*DoD*]
RORT .... Tarama [*Ryukyu Islands*] [*ICAO location identifier*] (ICLI)
RORU .... Rest of Route Unchanged (FAAC)
RORY .... Yoron [*Ryukyu Islands*] [*ICAO location identifier*] (ICLI)
ROS .... RADAR Order Switch
ROS .... Range Operation Station
ROS .... Range Operations Supervisor (MUGU)
ROS .... Range of Spares (MCD)
ROS .... Rat Osteosarcoma [*Cell line*]
ROS .... Rate of Speed (MCD)
ROS .... Reactive Oxygen Species
ROS .... Read-Only Storage [*Data processing*]
ROS .... Reduced Operational Status [*Military*]
ROS .... Reed Organ Society (EA)
ROS .... Regulated Oxygen Supply (MCD)
ROS .... Regulated Oxygen System (NASA)
ROS .... Remote Optical Sight [*Military*] (CAAL)
ROS .... Remote Optical System
ROS .... Removable Overhead Structure (MCD)
ROS .... Report Originator System [*Military*] (CAAL)

ROS .... Representative Observation Site [*Weather observing facility*]
     [*Air Force*]
ROS .... Requisition on Stores [*Nuclear energy*] (NRCH)
ROS .... Resident Operating System
ROS .... Restored Oil Shales
ROS .... Return from Overseas [*Military*]
ROS .... Return on Sales
ROS .... Review of Systems [*Medicine*]
ROS .... Robotics Operating System
ROS .... Rod Outer Segments [*of the retina*]
ROS .... Rosa [*Rose*] [*Pharmacology*] (ROG)
ROS .... Rosario [*Argentina*] [*Airport symbol*] (OAG)
ROS .... Rosary
ROS .... Rose Resources Corp. [*Vancouver Stock Exchange symbol*]
ROS .... Roseneath [*New Zealand*] [*Seismograph station code, US
     Geological Survey*] [*Closed*] (SEIS)
ROS .... Ross Aviation, Inc. [*Tulsa, OK*] [*FAA designator*] (FAAC)
ROS .... Roswell Public Library, Roswell, NM [*OCLC symbol*] (OCLC)
ROS .... Rotary on Stamps Fellowship (EA)
ROS .... Rotating Optical Scanner
ROS .... Royal Order of Scotland (EA)
ROS .... Run of Schedule [*Commercial announcement to be broadcast
     throughout the program schedule*] [*Advertising*]
ROS .... Rush Order Service
ROSA .... Record One Stop Association [*Defunct*] (EA)
ROSA .... Recording Optical Spectrum Analyzer (MCD)
ROSA .... Report of Supply Activity (MCD)
ROSAR ...... Read-Only Storage Address Register
ROSAT ...... RADAR Ocean Surveillance Satellite (NVT)
ROSAT ..... Roentgen Satellite [*Space research*]
ROSC .... Reserve Officers Sanitary Corps
ROSC .... Restoration of Spontaneous Circulation
ROSC .... Review of Scottish Culture [*A publication*]
ROSC .... Road Operators Safety Council [*British*]
Rosc .... Roscoe's Reports of the Supreme Court [*1861-78*] [*South
     Africa*] [*A publication*] (DLA)
ROSC .... Roscommon [*County in Ireland*] (ROG)
Rosc Act ..... Roscoe on Actions [*1825*] [*A publication*] (DLA)
Rosc Adm ..... Roscoe's Admiralty Jurisdiction and Practice [*A
     publication*] (DLA)
Rosc Am ..... Pro Sexto Roscio Amerino [*of Cicero*] [*Classical
     studies*] (OCD)
Rosc Bdg Cas ... Roscoe's Digest of Building Cases [*4th ed.*] [*1900*] [*A
     publication*] (DLA)
Rosc Bills ... Roscoe's Bills of Exchange [*2nd ed.*] [*1843*] [*A
     publication*] (DLA)
Rosc Civ Pr ... Roscoe's Outlines of Civil Procedure [*2nd ed.*] [*1880*] [*A
     publication*] (DLA)
Rosc Cr ...... Roscoe's Law of Evidence in Criminal Cases [*16 eds.*] [*1835-
     1952*] [*A publication*] (DLA)
Rosc Crim Ev ... Roscoe's Law of Evidence in Criminal Cases [*16 eds.*] [*1835-
     1952*] [*A publication*] (DLA)
Rosc Ev ...... Roscoe's Nisi Prius Evidence [*20th ed.*] [*1934*] [*A
     publication*] (DLA)
Rosc Jur ..... Roscoe's Jurist [*England*] [*A publication*] (DLA)
Rosc Light ... Roscoe's Law of Light [*4th ed.*] [*1904*] [*A publication*] (DLA)
Rosc NP ..... Roscoe's Law of Evidence at Nisi Prius [*20 eds.*] [*1827-1934*] [*A
     publication*] (DLA)
ROSCOE ... RADAR and Optical Systems Code
Roscoe .... Roscoe's Reports of the Supreme Court of Cape Of Good Hope
     [*South Africa*] [*A publication*] (DLA)
Roscoe Bldg Cas ... Roscoe's Digest of Building Cases [*England*] [*A
     publication*] (DLA)
Roscoe Cr Ev ... Roscoe's Law of Evidence in Criminal Cases [*16 eds.*] [*1835-
     1952*] [*A publication*] (DLA)
Roscoe's BC ... Roscoe's Digest of Building Cases [*England*] [*A
     publication*] (DLA)
ROSCOM ... Roscommon [*County in Ireland*]
ROSCOP ... Report of Observations/Samples Collected by Oceanographic
     Programs [*Intergovernmental Oceanographic
     Commission*] (MSC)
Rosc PC ..... Roscoe's English Prize Cases [*1745-1859*] [*A
     publication*] (DLA)
Rosc Pl .... Roscoe's Pleading [*1845*] [*A publication*] (DLA)
ROSDR ..... Read-Only Storage Data Register
ROSE .... Reconstruction by Optimized Series Expansion [*Of large
     molecules*]
ROSE .... Remote Optical Sensing of Emissions [*Instrumentation*]
ROSE .... Remotely Operated Special Equipment [*Nuclear energy*]
ROSE .... Residuum Oil Supercritical Extraction [*Petroleum refining*]
ROSE .... Retrieval by Online Search [*Data processing*]
ROSE .... Rising Observational Sounding Equipment
ROSE .... Rivera Ocean Seismic Experiment
Rose .... Rose's English Bankruptcy Reports [*A publication*] (DLA)
Rose Annu R Natl Rose Soc ... Rose Annual. Royal National Rose Society [*A
     publication*]
Rose Bankr ... Rose's English Bankruptcy Reports [*1810-16*] [*A
     publication*] (DLA)
Rose Bankr (Eng) ... Rose's English Bankruptcy Reports [*A
     publication*] (DLA)
Rose BC ..... Rose's English Bankruptcy Reports [*A publication*] (DLA)

Rose Dig..... Rose's Digest of Arkansas Reports [*A publication*] (DLA)
Rosenberger ... Street Railway Law [*United States*] [*A publication*] (DLA)
Rosenberger Pock LJ ... Rosenberger's Pocket Law Journal [*A publication*] (DLA)
Rose Notes ... Rose's Notes on United States Reports [*A publication*] (DLA)
Rose RA ..... Roscoe on Real Actions [*A publication*] (DLA)
Rose St D ... Roscoe on Stamp Duties [*A publication*] (DLA)
ROSET...... Register of Solicitors Employing Trainees (ILCA)
Rose WC..... Rose. Will Case [*New York*] [*A publication*] (DLA)
ROSIE....... Reconnaissance by Orbiting Ship-Identification Equipment
ROSIE....... Rooters Organized to Stimulate Interest and Enthusiasm
[*Women baseball fans, Cincinnati*]
ROSIE....... Rule Oriented System for Implementing Expertise (MCD)
Roskills Lett China ... Roskill's Letter from China [*A publication*]
RoSlaw....... Rocznik Slawistyczny [*A publication*]
ROSMAR ... Rosmarinus [*Rosemary*] [*Pharmacology*] (ROG)
ROSO........ Relay-Operated Sampling Oscilloscope
RoSPA .... Royal Society for the Prevention of Accidents [*British*]
ROSS......... Ross Exploration, Inc. [*Ridgefield Park, NJ*] [*NASDAQ symbol*] (NQ)
Ross Conf Med Res Rep ... Ross Conference on Medical Research. Report [*A publication*]
Ross Cont... Ross on Contracts [*A publication*] (DLA)
Ross Conv .. Ross' Lectures on Conveyancing, Etc. [*Sc.*] [*A publication*] (DLA)
Ross LC ..... Ross's Leading Cases on Commercial Law [*England*] [*A publication*] (DLA)
Ross LC ..... Ross's Leading Cases in the Law of Scotland (Land Rights) [*1638-1840*] [*A publication*] (DLA)
Ross Ldg Cas ... Ross's Leading Cases on Commercial Law [*A publication*] (DLA)
Ross Ldg Cas ... Ross's Leading Cases in the Law of Scotland (Land Rights) [*A publication*] (DLA)
Ross Lead Cas ... Ross' Leading Cases [*England*] [*A publication*] (DLA)
Ross Lead Cas ... Ross's Leading Cases in the Law of Scotland (Land Rights) [*1638-1840*] [*A publication*] (DLA)
Ross V & P ... Ross on Vendors and Purchasers [*2nd ed.*] [*1826*] [*A publication*] (DLA)
ROST......... Regional Office of Science and Technology [*UNESCO*] (MSC)
ROST......... Ross Stores, Inc. [*Newark, CA*] [*NASDAQ symbol*] (NQ)
ROSTA...... Roads and Streets [*A publication*]
ROSTA Bull ... ROSTA [*Victoria. Road Safety and Traffic Authority*] Bulletin [*A publication*] (APTA)
ROSTAS ... Regional Office of Science and Technology for the Arab States [*UNESCO*] (IRC)
Rost Krist... Rost Kristallov [*A publication*]
Rostl Vyroba ... Rostlinna Vyroba [*A publication*]
Rostl Vyroba Cesk Akad Zemed Ustav Vedeckotech Inf Zemed ... Rostlinna Vyroba-Ceskoslovenska Akademie Zemedelska. Ustav Vedeckotechnickych Informaci pro Zemedelstvi [*A publication*]
Rostocker Phys Manuskr ... Rostocker Physikalische Manuskripte [*A publication*]
Rostock Math Kolloq ... Rostocker Mathematisches Kolloquium [*A publication*]
Rostov Gidrometeorol Obs Sb Rab ... Rostovskaya Gidrometeorologicheskaya Observatoriya. Sbornik Rabot [*A publication*]
Rostov-Na Donu Gos Ped Inst Fiz Mat Fak Ucen Zap ... Rostovskii-Na-Donu Gosudarstvennyi Pedagogiceskii Institut. Fiziko-Matematiceskii Fakultet Ucenye Zapiski [*A publication*]
Rostov-Na-Donu Gos Univ Ucen Zap ... Rostovskii-Na-Donu Gosudarstvennyi Universitet. Ucenyi Zapiski [*A publication*]
ROSTSCA ... Regional Office of Science and Technology for South and Central Asia [*UNESCO*] (IRC)
ROSTSEA ... Regional Office of Science and Technology for Southeast Asia [*UNESCO*] (IRC)
Rost Ustoich Rast ... Rost i Ustoichivost Rastenii [*A publication*]
Rost Ustoich Rast Respub Mezhved Sb ... Rost i Ustoichivost Rastenii Respublikanskii Mezhvedomstvennyi Sbornik [*A publication*]
ROSX .... Ross Industries, Inc. [*Midland, VA*] [*NASDAQ symbol*] (NQ)
ROT.......... RADAR on Target
ROT.......... Range on Target
ROT.......... Rate of Turn
ROT.......... Rechtsinformation. Berichte und Dokumente zum Auslaendischen Wirtschafts- und Steuerrecht [*A publication*]
ROT.......... Red Oak Tannins [*in leaves*]
ROT.......... Reference Our Telex (DS)
ROT.......... Remaining Operating Time (NASA)
ROT.......... Remedial Occupation Therapy
ROT.......... Reserve Oil Tank (MSA)
ROT.......... Reusable Orbital Transport [*Aerospace*]
ROT.......... Right Occipitotransverse [*A fetal position*] [*Obstetrics*]
ROT.......... Right Outer Thigh [*Injection site*]
ROT.......... Rotary (AAG)
ROT.......... Rotate (AAG)
ROT.......... Rotating Light [*Navigation signal*]
ROT.......... Rotor (ADA)

ROT.......... Rotorua [*New Zealand*] [*Seismograph station code, US Geological Survey*] [*Closed*] (SEIS)
ROT.......... Rotorua [*New Zealand*] [*Airport symbol*] (OAG)
ROT.......... Rule of Thumb
ROTA .... Rats of Tobruk Association [*Australia*]
ROTAA ...... Road Tar [*A publication*]
ROTAB ...... Rotable Table
ROT ABCCC ... Rotational Airborne Command and Control Center (CINC)
ROTAC ...... Rotary Oscillating Torque Actuators
ROTAD ...... Round Table [*A publication*]
Rotation Method Crystallogr ... Rotation Method in Crystallography [*A publication*]
Rotavapor .. Rotary Evaporator
ROT AWS ... Rotational Air Weather Squadron (CINC)
ROT BS ..... Rotational Bomb Squadron (CINC)
ROTC .... Reserve Officers' Training Corps [*Separate units for Army, Navy, Air Force*]
ROTC .... RoTech Medical Corp. [*Orlando, FL*] [*NASDAQ symbol*] (NQ)
ROTCC..... Receiver-Off-Hook Tone Connecting Circuit
Rot Chart ... Rotulus Chartarum [*Charter Roll*] [*Latin*] [*A publication*] (DLA)
Rot Claus ... Rotuli Clause [*Close Roll*] [*Latin*] [*A publication*] (DLA)
ROTCM ..... Reserve Officers' Training Corps Manual (AABC)
ROTCR...... Reserve Officers' Training Corps Region (AABC)
Rot Cur Reg ... Rotuli Curiae Regis [*1194-99*] [*Latin*] [*A publication*] (DLA)
ROTE .... Range Optical Tracking Equipment (AAG)
ROTE .... Role of Occupational Therapy with the Elderly [*Project*]
ROTE AREFS ... Rotating Air Refueling Squadron (CINC)
ROTEL...... Reference Our Telegram (FAAC)
ROTEL...... Rolling Hotel [*European bus-tour system*]
ROTEL...... Rotational Telemetry
Rotenburg Schr ... Rotenburger Schriften [*A publication*]
ROTERO .. Roterodamum [*Rotterdam*] (ROG)
ROTF......... Russian Orthodox Theological Fund (EA)
ROT FIS..... Rotating Fighter Interceptor Squadron (CINC)
ROT FIS DET ... Rotating Fighter Interceptor Squadron Detachment (CINC)
Rot Flor...... Rotae Florentine [*Reports of the Supreme Court of Florence*] [*Latin*] [*A publication*] (DLA)
ROTG......... Rotating (FAAC)
ROTH........ Read-Only Tape Handler
Rothamsted Exp Stn Rep ... Rothamsted Experimental Station. Report [*A publication*]
Rothamsted Exp Stn Rep Part 1 ... Rothamsted Experimental Station. Report. Part 1 [*A publication*]
Rothamsted Exp Stn Rep Part 2 ... Rothamsted Experimental Station. Report. Part 2 [*A publication*]
Rothmill Q ... Rothmill Quarterly [*A publication*]
ROTHR..... Relocatable Over-the-Horizon RADAR
ROTI .... Range Optical Tracking Instrument
ROTI .... Recording Optical Tracking Instrument [*Missiles*]
ROTI .... Reinforced Oxide Throat Insert
RoTKan ..... Roczniki Teologiczno-Kanoniczne [*Lubin*] [*A publication*]
ROTL .... Remote Office Test Line [*Bell Laboratories*]
ROTLT/BCN ... Rotating Light or Beacon
ROTM....... Futema [*Ryukyu Islands*] [*ICAO location identifier*] (ICLI)
ROTN........ Rotation (FAAC)
ROTO........ Roto-Rooter, Inc. [*Cincinnati, OH*] [*NASDAQ symbol*] (NQ)
ROTOB ..... Romania Today [*A publication*]
ROTOMT ... Rotometer
ROTOR...... Rotorcraft Helicopter [*Pilot rating*] (AIA)
Rotor & W .... Rotor and Wing International [*A publication*]
ROTP......... Regular Officer Training Plan [*Canada*]
Rot Parl...... Rotulae Parliamentariae [*Latin*] [*A publication*] (DLA)
Rot Pat....... Rotuli Patenes [*Latin*] [*A publication*] (DLA)
Rot Plac..... Rotuli Placitorum [*Latin*] [*A publication*] (DLA)
ROTR .... Receive-Only Typing Reperforator
ROTR .... Rotator [*Electromagnetics*]
ROT RCS .. Rotational RADAR Calibration Squadron (CINC)
ROTR-S/P ... Receive-Only Typing Reperforator - Series to Parallel
ROTS........ RADAR Observer Testing System
ROTS........ Range on Target Signal
ROTS........ Remote Operator Task Station [*Air Force*]
ROTS........ Rotary Out Trunk Switch [*Telecommunications*] (TEL)
ROTSAL ... Rotate and Scale [*Data processing*]
ROTT .... Rate of Turntable
ROTT .... Reorder Tone Trunks [*Telecommunications*] (TEL)
ROT TAS .. Rotational Tactical Assault Squadron (CINC)
ROT TBS .. Rotational Tactical Bomber Squadron (CINC)
ROT TCS .. Rotational Troop Carrier Squadron (CINC)
ROTTER... Rotterdam (ROG)
ROT TX..... Rotating Transformer
Rotuli Curiae Reg ... Rotuli Curiae Regis [*1194-99*] [*Latin*] [*A publication*] (DLA)
ROTV .... Reusable Orbital Transport Vehicle [*Aerospace*]
ROTWX .... Reference Our TWX [*Teletypewriter communications*] (FAAC)
ROU.......... Radio Officers Union [*British*]
ROU.......... Rougiers [*France*] [*Seismograph station code, US Geological Survey*] [*Closed*] (SEIS)

ROU.......... Rouyn Ressources Minieres, Inc. [*Toronto Stock Exchange symbol*]
ROU.......... Russe [*Bulgaria*] [*Airport symbol*] (OAG)
ROUHA .... Ropa a Uhlie [*A publication*]
ROUL....... Rouletted (ROG)
Roum P ...... Roumanian Pharmacopoeia [*A publication*]
Round Dom ... Round's Law of Domicil [*1861*] [*A publication*] (DLA)
Round L & A ... Round's Right of Light and Air [*1868*] [*A publication*] (DLA)
Round Lien ... Round's Law of Lien [*1863*] [*A publication*] (DLA)
Round Tab ... Round Table [*A publication*]
ROUS....... [*The*] Rouse Co. [*NASDAQ symbol*] (NQ)
Rouse Conv ... Rouse's Practical Conveyancer [*3rd ed.*] [*1867*] [*A publication*] (DLA)
Rouse Cop ... Rouse's Copyhold Enfranchisement Manual [*3rd ed.*] [*1866*] [*A publication*] (DLA)
Rouse Pr Mort ... Rouse's Precedents and Conveyances of Mortgaged Property [*A publication*] (DLA)
R-OUT....... Rollout (NASA)
ROUT....... Routine (AABC)
Roux Archiv EntwMech Organ ... Roux Archiv fuer Entwicklungsmechanik der Organismen [*A publication*]
Roux's Arch Dev Biol ... Roux's Archives of Developmental Biology [*A publication*]
ROV.......... Refined Oil of Vitriol
ROV.......... Remote Operated Valve (KSC)
ROV.......... Remote Optical Viewing
ROV.......... Remotely Operated Vehicle [*Underwater robot*]
ROV.......... Repairs to Other Vessels
ROV.......... Report Over (FAAC)
ROV.......... Report of Visit [*LIMRA*]
ROV.......... Restricted Overhaul (MCD)
ROV.......... Risk, Originality, and Virtuousity [*Scoring considerations in gymnastics competition*]
ROV.......... Rostov [*USSR*] [*Airport symbol*] (OAG)
ROVA....... Returned Overseas Volunteers of Australia
ROVAC ..... Rotary Vane Air Cycle (MCD)
ROVD........ Relay-Operated Voltage Divider
Rov Koezlem ... Rovartani Koezlemenyek [*A publication*]
ROVNITE ... Remaining Overnight
ROVS .... Remote Optical Viewing System
ROVYA ..... Rostlinna Vyroba [*A publication*]
ROW.......... Randstrom Manufacturing Corp. [*Vancouver Stock Exchange symbol*]
ROW.......... Relocate Out of Washington [*Navy*] (NG)
ROW.......... Requisition on Warehouse [*Nuclear energy*] (NRCH)
ROW.......... Rest of World [*Newly industrialized countries of Asia*]
ROW.......... Right of Way
ROW.......... Risk of War
ROW.......... Roll Welding
ROW.......... Romanian Engineering [*A publication*]
ROW.......... Roswell [*New Mexico*] [*Airport symbol*] (OAG)
ROW.......... Rowe Furniture Corp. [*AMEX symbol*] (SPSG)
ROW.......... Rowesville [*South Carolina*] [*Seismograph station code, US Geological Survey*] (SEIS)
RO1(W) ..... Radio Operator (Warfare) 1st Class [*British military*] (DMA)
RO2(W) ..... Radio Operator (Warfare) 2nd Class [*British military*] (DMA)
ROWB....... Rowberrow [*England*]
Rowe.......... Rowe's Interesting Cases [*England and Ireland*] [*1798-1823*] [*A publication*] (DLA)
Rowe........... Rowe's Interesting Parliamentary and Military Cases [*A publication*] (DLA)
Rowell .... Rowell's Reports [*45-52 Vermont*] [*A publication*] (DLA)
Rowell El Cas ... Rowell's Contested Election Cases [*A publication*] (DLA)
Row Eng Const ... Rowland's Manual of the English Constitution [*1859*] [*A publication*] (DLA)
Rowe Rep ... Rowe's Irish Reports [*A publication*] (DLA)
Rowe Sci Jur ... Rowe's Scintilla Juris [*A publication*] (DLA)
Rowett Res Inst Annu Rep Stud Anim Nutr Allied Sci ... Rowett Research Institute. Annual Report. Studies in Animal Nutrition and Allied Sciences [*A publication*]
ROW/FEPA ... Riders of the Wind, the Field Events Player's Association (EA)
ROWJ .... Records of Oceanographic Works in Japan [*A publication*]
ROWJA..... Records of Oceanographic Works in Japan [*A publication*]
ROWPE..... Reverse Osmosis Water Purification Equipment (MCD)
ROW & PF ... Rake Out, Wedge, and Point Flashings [*Construction*]
ROWPS..... Reverse Osmosis Water Purification System (MCD)
ROWPU .... Reverse Osmosis Water Purification Unit [*Army*] (RDA)
ROWPVT ... Receptive One-Word Picture Vocabulary Test [*Educational test*]
ROWS .... RADAR Ocean Wave Spectrometer
ROX.......... Roseau, MN [*Location identifier*] [*FAA*] (FAAL)
ROX.......... Roxburgh [*New Zealand*] [*Seismograph station code, US Geological Survey*] (SEIS)
ROXB .... Roxburghe [*Style of bookbinding*] (ROG)
ROXB .... Roxburghshire [*County in Scotland*]
ROXL .... Rotate through X Left [*Data processing*]
ROXR .... Rotate through X Right [*Data processing*]
ROY.......... Moultonboro, NH [*Location identifier*] [*FAA*] (FAAL)
ROY.......... Rio Mayo [*Argentina*] [*Airport symbol*] (OAG)
ROY.......... Royal

Roy............ Royale & Allegro-Royale [*Record label*]
Roy Aeronaut Soc J ... Royal Aeronautical Society. Journal [*A publication*]
Royal.......... [*The*] Royal Magazine [*A publication*]
Royal Agric Soc England J ... Journal. Royal Agricultural Society of England [*A publication*]
Royal Astron Soc Canada Jour ... Royal Astronomical Society of Canada. Journal [*A publication*]
Royal Astron Soc Geophys Jour ... Royal Astronomical Society. Geophysical Journal [*A publication*]
Royal Astron Soc Monthly Notices Geophys Supp ... Royal Astronomical Society. Monthly Notices. Geophysical Supplements [*A publication*]
Royal Astron Soc Quart Jour ... Royal Astronomical Society. Quarterly Journal [*A publication*]
Royal Aust Army Ed Corps News ... Royal Australian Army. Educational Corps. Newsletter [*A publication*] (APTA)
Royal Aust Chem Inst J & Proc ... Royal Australian Chemical Institute. Journal and Proceedings [*A publication*] (APTA)
Royal Aust Chem Inst Proc ... Royal Australian Chemical Institute. Proceedings [*A publication*] (APTA)
Royal Aust Hist Soc J ... Royal Australian Historical Society. Journal and Proceedings [*A publication*] (APTA)
Royal Aust Hist Soc J & Proc ... Royal Australian Historical Society. Journal and Proceedings [*A publication*] (APTA)
Royal Aust Hist Soc J Proc ... Royal Australian Historical Society. Journal and Proceedings [*A publication*]
Royal Australian Planning Inst Jnl ... Royal Australian Planning Institute. Journal [*A publication*]
Royalauto... Royalauto [*Royal Automobile Club of Victoria*] Journal [*A publication*] (APTA)
Royal Bank Can Mo Letter ... Royal Bank of Canada. Monthly Letter [*A publication*]
Royal Empire Soc News ... Royal Empire Society. News [*A publication*] (APTA)
Royal Geog Soc Asia SA Branch Proc ... Royal Geographical Society of Australasia. South Australian Branch. Proceedings [*A publication*] (APTA)
Royal Hist Soc Q Hist Misc ... Royal Historical Society of Queensland. Historical Miscellanea [*A publication*] (APTA)
Royal Hist Soc QJ ... Royal Historical Society of Queensland. Journal [*A publication*] (APTA)
Royal Hist Soc Trans ... Royal Historical Society. Transactions [*A publication*]
Royal Hort Soc J ... Royal Horticultural Society. Journal [*A publication*]
Royal Inst of British Archts Trans ... Royal Institute of British Architects. Transactions [*A publication*]
Royal Microscopical Soc Proc ... Royal Microscopical Society. Proceedings [*A publication*]
Royal Ontario Mus Div Zoology and Palaeontology Contr ... Royal Ontario Museum. Division of Zoology and Palaeontology. Contributions [*A publication*]
Royal Perth Hospital J ... Royal Perth Hospital. Journal [*A publication*] (APTA)
Royal Prince Alfred Hospital J ... Royal Prince Alfred Hospital. Journal [*A publication*] (APTA)
Royal Soc Arts Jnl ... Royal Society of Arts. Journal [*A publication*]
Royal Soc Canada Proc ... Royal Society of Canada. Proceedings [*A publication*]
Royal Soc of Health Jnl ... Royal Society of Health. Journal [*A publication*]
Royal Soc Hlth J ... Royal Society of Health. Journal [*A publication*]
Royal Soc NSW J & Proc ... Royal Society of New South Wales. Journal and Proceedings [*A publication*] (APTA)
Royal Soc Q Proc ... Royal Society of Queensland. Proceedings [*A publication*] (APTA)
Royal Soc SA Trans ... Royal Society of South Australia. Transactions [*A publication*] (APTA)
Royal Soc Tasmania Papers and Proc ... Royal Society of Tasmania. Papers and Proceedings [*A publication*]
Royal Soc Tas Papers & Proc ... Royal Society of Tasmania. Papers and Proceedings [*A publication*] (APTA)
Royal Soc Vic Proc ... Royal Society of Victoria. Proceedings [*A publication*]
Royal Soc Victoria Proc ... Royal Society of Victoria. Proceedings [*A publication*]
Royal Statis Soc J Ser A Gen ... Journal. Royal Statistical Society. Series A. General [*A publication*]
Royalton R ... Royalton Review [*A publication*]
Royal Zoological Soc NSW Proc ... Royal Zoological Society of New South Wales. Proceedings [*A publication*] (APTA)
Roy Arch Inst Can J ... Royal Architectural Institute of Canada. Journal [*A publication*]
Roy Astron Soc Mem ... Royal Astronomical Society. Memoirs [*A publication*]
Roy Aust Hist J ... Royal Australian Historical Society. Journal [*A publication*]
Roy Aust Hist Soc J Proc ... Royal Australian Historical Society. Journal and Proceedings [*A publication*] (APTA)
Roy Can Inst Trans ... Royal Canadian Institute. Transactions [*A publication*]
RoyCom ..... Royal Commission [*Australia*]
Roy Dig ...... Royall's Digest Virginia Reports [*A publication*] (DLA)
Roy Eng J .. Royal Engineers Journal [*A publication*]

ROYG........ Royal Business Group, Inc. [*NASDAQ symbol*] (NQ)
ROYGBIV ... Red, Orange, Yellow, Green, Blue, Indigo, Violet [*Primary Colors*] [*Mnemonic aid*]
Roy His S... Royal Historical Society. Transactions [*A publication*]
Roy Hist Soc Qld Hist Misc ... Royal Historical Society of Queensland. Historical Miscellanea [*A publication*] (APTA)
Roy Hist Soc Qld J ... Royal Historical Society of Queensland. Journal [*A publication*] (APTA)
Roy Hist Soc Trans ... Royal Historical Society. Transactions [*A publication*]
Roy Hist Soc Vic News ... Royal Historical Society of Victoria. Newsletter [*A publication*] (APTA)
Roy Hort Soc J ... Royal Horticultural Society. Journal [*A publication*]
Roy Inst Brit Arch J ... Royal Institute of British Architects. Journal [*A publication*]
Roy Inst Nav Architects Quart Trans ... Royal Institution of Naval Architects [*London*]. Quarterly Transactions [*A publication*]
Roy Inst Ph ... Royal Institute of Philosophy. Lectures [*A publication*]
ROYL .... Royalpar Industries, Inc. [*NASDAQ symbol*] (NQ)
Royle Stock Sh ... Royle on the Law of Stock Shares, Etc. [*A publication*] (DLA)
Roy Meteorol Soc Q J ... Royal Meteorological Society. Quarterly Journal [*A publication*]
Roy Microscop Soc Proc ... Royal Microscopical Society. Proceedings [*A publication*]
Roy Micros Soc J ... Royal Microscopical Society. Journal [*A publication*]
ROYN........ Yonagunijima [*Ryukyu Islands*] [*ICAO location identifier*] (ICLI)
Roy Soc Arts J ... Royal Society of Arts. Journal [*A publication*]
Roy Soc Can ... Royal Society of Canada. Proceedings and Transactions [*A publication*]
Roy Soc of Canada Trans ... Royal Society of Canada. Proceedings and Transactions [*A publication*]
Roy Soc Edinb Trans ... Royal Society of Edinburgh. Transactions [*A publication*]
Roy Soc of Edinburgh Trans ... Royal Society of Edinburgh. Transactions [*A publication*]
Roy Soc Hea ... Royal Society of Health. Journal [*A publication*]
Roy Soc of London Philos Trans ... Royal Society of London. Philosophical Transactions [*A publication*]
Roy Soc Lond Philos Trans ... Royal Society of London. Philosophical Transactions [*A publication*]
Roy Soc of New South Wales Jour and Proc ... Royal Society of New South Wales. Journal and Proceedings [*A publication*]
Roy Soc NSW J ... Royal Society of New South Wales. Journal [*A publication*] (APTA)
Roy Soc NSW J & Proc ... Royal Society of New South Wales. Journal and Proceedings [*A publication*]
Roy Soc NZ J ... Royal Society of New Zealand. Journal [*A publication*]
Roy Soc NZ Proc ... Royal Society of New Zealand. Proceedings [*A publication*]
Roy Soc NZ Trans ... Royal Society of New Zealand. Transactions [*A publication*]
Roy Soc NZ Trans Bot ... Royal Society of New Zealand. Transactions. Botany [*A publication*]
Roy Soc NZ Trans Earth Sci ... Royal Society of New Zealand. Transactions. Earth Sciences [*A publication*]
Roy Soc NZ Trans Gen ... Royal Society of New Zealand. Transactions. General [*A publication*]
Roy Soc NZ Trans Geol ... Royal Society of New Zealand. Transactions. Geology [*A publication*]
Roy Soc NZ Trans Zool ... Royal Society of New Zealand. Transactions. Zoology [*A publication*]
Roy Soc Proc ... Proceedings. Royal Society [*A publication*]
Roy Soc Qld Proc ... Royal Society of Queensland. Proceedings [*A publication*] (APTA)
Roy Soc SA Trans ... Royal Society of South Australia. Transactions [*A publication*] (APTA)
Roy Soc Tas Papers ... Royal Society of Tasmania. Papers and Proceedings [*A publication*] (APTA)
Roy Soc Vic Proc ... Royal Society of Victoria. Proceedings [*A publication*] (APTA)
Roy Soc WA J ... Royal Society of Western Australia. Journal [*A publication*] (APTA)
Roy Stat Soc J ... Royal Statistical Society. Journal [*A publication*]
Roy Telev Soc J ... Royal Television Society. Journal [*A publication*]
Roy Town Plan Inst ... Royal Town Planning Institute. Journal [*A publication*]
Roy West Aust Hist Soc J Proc ... Royal Western Australian Historical Society. Journal and Proceedings [*A publication*] (APTA)
Roy Zool Soc NSW Proc ... Royal Zoological Society of New South Wales. Proceedings [*A publication*] (APTA)
Roz Cesk Akad ... Rozpravy Ceskoslovenske Akademie Ved [*A publication*]
Rozhl Chir ... Rozhledy v Chirurgii [*A publication*]
Rozhl Tuberk Nemocech Plicn ... Rozhledy v Tuberkulose a v Nemocech Plicnich [*A publication*]
Roz Narod Tech Muz Praze ... Rozpravy Narodniho Technickeho Muzea v Praze [*A publication*]
Rozpr Akad Roln Szczecinie ... Rozprawy. Akademia Rolnicza w Szczecinie [*A publication*]
Rozpravy CSAV ... Rozpravy Ceskoslovenske Akademie Ved [*A publication*]

Rozprawy Elektrotech ... Rozprawy Elektrotechniczne. Polska Akademia Nauk. Instytut Technologii Elektronowej. [*A publication*]
Rozprawy Politech Poznan ... Rozprawy. Politechnika Poznanska [*A publication*]
Rozpr Cesk Akad Rada Tech Ved ... Rozpravy Ceskoslovenske Akademie Ved. Rada Technickych Ved [*Czechoslovakia*] [*A publication*]
Rozpr Cesk Akad Ved Rada Mat Prir Ved ... Rozpravy Ceskoslovenske Akademie Ved. Rada Matematickych a Prirodnich Ved [*A publication*]
Rozpr Cesk Akad Ved Rada Tech Ved ... Rozpravy Ceskoslovenske Akademie Ved. Rada Technickych Ved [*A publication*]
Rozpr Elektrotech ... Rozprawy Elektrotechniczne [*A publication*]
Rozpr Hydrotech ... Rozprawy Hydrotechniczne [*A publication*]
Rozpr Inz ... Rozprawy Inzynierskie [*A publication*]
Rozpr Politech Poznan ... Rozprawy. Politechnika Poznanska [*A publication*]
Rozpr Politech Rzeszowska Im Ignacego Lukasiewicza ... Rozprawy. Politechnika Rzeszowska Imienia Ignacego Lukasiewicza [*A publication*]
Rozpr Ustred Ustavu Geol ... Rozpravy Ustredniho Ustavu Geologickeho [*A publication*]
Rozpr Wydz 3 Nauk Mat Przyr Gdansk Tow Nauk ... Rozprawy Wydzialu 3. Nauk Matematyczno-Przyrodniczych. Gdanskie Towarzystwo Naukowe [*A publication*]
Rozpr Wydz Nauk Med Pol Akad Nauk ... Rozprawy Wydzialu Nauk Medycznych Polska Akademia Nauk [*A publication*]
RP .... Bristol-Myers Co. [*Research code symbol*]
RP .... Problems of Reconstruction [*British*] [*World War II*]
RP .... Providence Public Library, Providence, RI [*Library symbol*] [*Library of Congress*] (LCLS)
RP .... RADAR Plot (DEN)
RP .... Radial Artery Pressure [*Medicine*]
RP .... Radial Pulse [*Medicine*]
RP .... Radiation Pressure
RP .... Radiation Protection
RP .... Radio Phone (DS)
R-P .... Radiologist-Pediatric
RP .... Raid Plotter
RP .... Rally Point [*Air Force*]
RP .... Ranchers for Peace (EA)
RP .... Raphe Pallidus [*Anatomy*]
RP .... Rate Package (AAG)
RP .... Rated Pressure (NATG)
RP .... Raynaud's Phenomenon [*Medicine*]
RP .... Re-Geniusing Project (EA)
RP .... Reactor Pressure [*Nuclear energy*] (NRCH)
RP .... Reactor Project [*Nuclear energy*] (NRCH)
RP .... Reader Printer
RP .... Reader Punch
RP .... Readiness Potential
RP .... Real Part [*of complex number*] (DEN)
RP .... Real Property
RP .... Rear Projection [*Television*]
RP .... Receipt Pass (AAG)
RP .... Receive Processor
RP .... Received Pronunciation [*of the English language*]
RP .... Reception Poor [*Radio logs*]
RP .... Receptor Potential
RP .... Recette Principale [*Principal Returns*] [*French*]
RP .... Recommended Practice
RP .... Recorder Point (MCD)
RP .... Records of the Past [*A publication*] (BJA)
RP .... Recovery Phase (IEEE)
R & P......... Recruitment and Placement (MCD)
RP .... Red Phosphorus [*Military*] (RDA)
RP .... Reddish Purple
RP .... Reference Paper
RP .... Reference Pattern (NATG)
RP .... Reference Point
RP .... Reference Publication (MCD)
RP .... Reference Pulse
RP .... Refilling Point
RP .... Reformed Presbyterian
RP .... Refractory Period [*Medicine*]
RP .... Regeneration Project [*Later, CR*] (EA)
RP .... Regimental Paymaster [*British military*] (DMA)
RP .... Regimental Police [*British*]
RP .... Registered Plumbers [*British*]
RP .... Regius Professor [*The King's Professor*] [*British*]
RP .... Regulatory Peptides [*A publication*]
RP .... Reinforced Plastic [*Packaging*]
RP .... Relative Pressure (KSC)
RP .... Relay Panel
RP .... Release Point [*Ground traffic*] [*Military*]
RP .... Relief Pitcher [*Baseball*]
RP .... Remote Pickup
RP .... Remote Printer (BUR)
RP .... Renaissance Papers [*A publication*]
RP .... Rent Regulation (Office of Price Stabilization) [*Economic Stabilization Agency*] [*A publication*] (DLA)
RP .... Reorder Point [*Army*]

RP	Repair Period (NASA)
RP	Repeater
RP	Repetitively Pulsed (MCD)
RP	Replaceable Pad (MCD)
RP	Replacement Pilot [*Navy*]
RP	Replenishment Park [*British*]
RP	Reply Paid
RP	Report Immediately upon Passing [*Fix altitude*] [*Aviation*] (FAAC)
RP	Reporting Post [*RADAR*]
RP	Reprint
RP	Reproducers [*JETDS nomenclature*] [*Military*] (CET)
RP	Republic of Panama
RP	Republic of the Philippines
RP	Republican Party [*Iraq*] [*Political party*] (BJA)
RP	Republikeinse Party van Suidwesafrika [*Republican Party of South West Africa*] [*Namibia*] [*Political party*] (PPW)
RP	Repurchase Agreement [*Also, REPO*] [*Investment term*]
RP	Res Publica [*A publication*]
RP	Research Paper
RP	Research Publications
RP	Reserve Personnel [*Air Force*] (AFM)
R & P	Reserve and Process (NASA)
RP	Reserve Purchase
RP	Resist Pressure [*Industrial engineering*]
RP	Resistance Plate (AAG)
RP	Resolving Power [*of a lens*]
RP	Resource Processor [*Telecommunications*] (TSSD)
RP	Respiratory Rate:Pulse Rate [*Index*] [*Medicine*]
RP	Resting Pulse [*Physiology*]
RP	Restoration Priority (CET)
RP	Restriction of Privileges [*British military*] (DMA)
RP	Resupply Provisions [*NASA*] (KSC)
RP	Retained Personnel [*Military*]
RP	Retinitis Pigmentosa [*Eye disease*] [*Ophthalmology*]
RP	Retinyl Palmitate [*Organic chemistry*]
RP	Retrograde Pyelography [*Medicine*]
RP	Retroperitoneal [*Medicine*]
R/P	Return to Port [*for Orders*] (DS)
RP	Return of Post
RP	Return Premium
RP	Revealed Preference Analysis [*Economics*]
RP	Reverend Pere [*Reverend Father*] [*French*]
RP	Reverendus Pater [*Reverend Father*] [*Latin*]
R-P	Reversed Phase [*Chromatography*]
RP	Revertive Pulsing
RP	Review of Politics [*A publication*]
RP	Revision Proposal (NG)
RP	Revista de Portugal [*A publication*]
Rp	Revoked or Rescinded in Part [*Existing regulation or order abrogated in part*] [*Used in Shepard's Citations*] [*Legal term*] (DLA)
RP	Revue de Paris [*A publication*]
R d P	Revue de Philologie, de Litterature, et d'Histoire Anciennes [*A publication*]
RP	Revue de Philologie, de Litterature, et d'Histoire Anciennes [*A publication*]
RP	Revue Philosophique [*A publication*]
RP	Revue de Phonetique [*Paris*] [*A publication*]
R/P	Reward/Penalty
RP	Rhone-Poulenc [*France*] [*Research code symbol*]
RP	Right Traffic Pattern [*Aviation*] (FAAC)
R/P	Rise/Passive (MCD)
RP	Ristocetin-Polymyxin [*Antibacterial mixture*]
RP	Rocket Projectile
RP	Rocket Propellant
RP	Rockland and Pollin [*Scale*] [*Psychology*]
RP	Rodent Potency Dose
RP	Roll Pad (MCD)
RP	Rollback Process [*Telecommunications*] (TEL)
RP	Romance Philology [*A publication*]
RP	Ron Pair
RP	Room and Pillar [*Coal mining*]
RP	Root Primordia [*Botany*]
RP	Rotatable Pool Quantity
RP	Rotuli Parliamentorum [*1278-1533*] [*Latin*] [*A publication*] (DLA)
RP	Round Punch
RP	Route Package (CINC)
RP	Royal Panopticon (ROG)
RP	Royal Provincials [*British military*] (DMA)
RP	[*Member of*] Royal Society of Portrait Painters [*British*]
RP	Rules of Procedure
R & P	Rules and Procedures (MSA)
RP	Rupiah [*Monetary unit*] [*Indonesia*]
RP	Russow Aviation GmbH & Co. Luftfahrtunternehmen, Frankfurt [*West Germany*] [*ICAO designator*] (FAAC)
RP	Rust Preventive
RP	Specia [*France*] [*Research code symbol*]
R2P2	Rapid Retargeting and Precision Pointing [*Strategic Defense Initiative*]

RPA	British Plastics and Rubber [*A publication*]
RPA	Executive Air Travel [*Denver, CO*] [*FAA designator*] (FAAC)
RPA	Providence Athenaeum, Providence, RI [*Library symbol*] [*Library of Congress*] (LCLS)
RPA	RADAR Performance Analyzer
RPA	Radium Plaque Adaptometer [*Navy*]
RPA	Random Phase Approximation
RPA	Rationalist Press Association [*London, England*] (EAIO)
RPA	Real Property Administrator [*Designation awarded by Building Owners and Managers Institute*]
RPA	Record and Playback Assembly (MCD)
RPA	Record of Procurement Action (MCD)
RPA	Redundancy Payments Act [*1965*] [*British*] (DCTA)
RPA	Reentrant Process Allocator [*Telecommunications*] (TEL)
RPA	Regional Plan Association (EA)
RPA	Regional Ports Authority [*British*]
RPA	Registered Public Accountant
RPA	Relative Peak Area [*Medicine*]
RPA	Renal Physicians Association (EA)
RPA	Renewal Projects Administration [*HUD*]
RPA	Replacement Price Accounting (ADA)
RPA	Republican Party of Australia [*Political party*]
RPA	Request Present Altitude [*Aviation*] (FAAC)
RPA	Request for Procurement Action [*Authorization*] [*NASA*] (NASA)
RPA	Reserve Personnel Appropriation
RPA	Reserve Personnel, Army
RPA	Resident Programmer Analyst [*Data processing*]
RPA	Resource Planning Associates, Cambridge, MA [*OCLC symbol*] (OCLC)
RPA	Response Profile Analysis [*National Demographics & Lifestyles, Inc.*]
RPA	Resultant Physiological Acceleration
RPA	Retarding Potential Analyzer [*NASA*]
RPA	Retinoylphorbolacetate [*Biochemistry*]
RPA	Retired Philosphers Association (EA)
RPA	Retired Police Association [*Australia*]
RPa	Revue de Paris [*A publication*]
RPA	Revue de Phonetique Appliquee [*Paris*] [*A publication*]
RPA	Revue Pratique d'Apologetique [*A publication*]
RPA	Right Pulmonary Artery [*Medicine*]
RPA	Rolpa [*Nepal*] [*Airport symbol*] (OAG)
RPA	Royal Pakistan Artillery [*British military*] (DMA)
RPA	RPA [*Royal Prince Alfred Hospital*] Magazine [*A publication*] (APTA)
RPA	Rubber Peptizing Agent
RPA	Rural Preservation Association [*British*]
RPA	Rust Prevention Association [*Later, Crop Quality Council*]
RPAA	Rendiconti. Pontificia Accademia di Archeologia [*A publication*]
RPAA	Rotating Phase Array Antenna
RPAB	Brown University, Annmary Brown Memorial Library, Providence, RI [*Library symbol*] [*Library of Congress*] (LCLS)
RPAC	Research Policy Advisory Committee [*Department of Agriculture*] [*South Australia*]
R Pac	Revue du Pacifique. Etudes de Litterature Francaise [*A publication*]
RPACA	Reports on the Progress of Applied Chemistry [*A publication*]
RPACDV	Australia. Commonwealth Scientific and Industrial Research Organisation. Division of Applied Organic Chemistry. Research Report [*A publication*]
RPAE	Retarding Potential Analyzer Experiment [*NASA*]
RPAG	Retired Professionals Action Group [*Later, Gray Panthers*]
RPAH	Royal Prince Alfred Hospital [*Australia*]
RPAL	Royal Palm Savings Bank [*NASDAQ symbol*] (NQ)
R Palaeobot & Palynol	Review of Palaeobotany and Palynology [*A publication*]
RPall	Revue Palladienne [*A publication*]
RPAM	American Mathematical Society, Providence, RI [*Library symbol*] [*Library of Congress*] (LCLS)
RPAM	Regional Public Affairs Manager [*Nuclear energy*] (NRCH)
RPAM	Research in Public Administration and Management [*British*]
RPAO	Radium Plaque Adaptometer Operator [*Navy*]
RPAODS	Remotely Piloted Aerial Observation Detection System (MCD)
RPAP	Repap Enterprises Corp., Inc. [*NASDAQ symbol*] (NQ)
RPAPC	Religious Press Associations Postal Coalition (EA)
RPAPL	Real Property Actions and Proceedings Law [*New York, NY*] [*A publication*]
RPAR	Rebuttable Presumption Against Regulation [*of pesticides*] [*Environmental Protection Agency*]
R Paraguaya Sociol	Revista Paraguaya de Sociologia [*A publication*]
R de Paris	Revue de Paris [*A publication*]
RPAS	Audubon Society of Rhode Island, Providence, RI [*Library symbol*] [*Library of Congress*] (LCLS)
RPAS	Reactor Protection Actuating Signal [*Nuclear energy*] (NRCH)
RPAS	Review. Polish Academy of Sciences [*A publication*]
RPASC	Royal Pakistan Army Service Corps [*British military*] (DMA)
RPASDB	Reviews in Pure and Applied Pharmacological Sciences [*A publication*]

RPASMC .. Rubber and Plastic Adhesive and Sealant Manufacturers Council [*Later, Adhesive and Sealant Council*]   (EA)
R Pat Cas ... Reports of Patent, Design, and Trade Mark Cases [*A publication*]   (DLA)
RP-ATLF... Roscoe Pound - American Trial Lawyers Foundation   (EA)
RPaw.......... Pawtucket Public Library, Pawtucket, RI [*Library symbol*] [*Library of Congress*]   (LCLS)
RPAYC...... Royal Prince Alfred Yacht Club [*Australia*]
R Pays Est ... Revue des Pays de l'Est [*A publication*]
RPB............ Belleville, KS [*Location identifier*] [*FAA*]   (FAAL)
RPB............ Brown University, Providence, RI [*Library symbol*] [*Library of Congress*]   (LCLS)
RPB............ RADAR Plotting Board
RPB............ Recognised Professional Body [*Marketing of Investments Board Organising Committee, London Stock Exchange*] [*Finance*]
RPB............ Regional Preparedness Board [*Military*]   (AABC)
RPB............ Research to Prevent Blindness   (EA)
RPB............ Resources Protection Board
RPB............ River Purification Board [*British*]   (DCTA)
RPB............ Royal Palm Beach Colony Ltd. [*AMEX symbol*]   (SPSG)
RPB............ Royal Protection Branch [*of the London Metropolitan Police*]
Rp B Bk R ... Reprint Bulletin. Book Reviews [*A publication*]
RPBG......... Revised Program and Budget Guidance [*Military*]
RPBH .... Butler Health Center, Providence, RI [*Library symbol*] [*Library of Congress*]   (LCLS)
RPB-JH..... Brown University, John Hay Library of Rare Books annd Special Collections, Providence, RI [*Library symbol*] [*Library of Congress*]   (LCLS)
RPB-S........ Brown University, Sciences Library, Providence, RI [*Library symbol*] [*Library of Congress*]   (LCLS)
RPBS .... Repatriation Pharmaceutical Benefits Scheme [*Australia*]
RPBSC....... Rules Peculiar to the Business of the Supreme Court [*A publication*]   (DLA)
RPC............ Baltimore Regional Planning Commission [*Library network*]
RPC............ RADAR Planning Chart
RPC............ RADAR Processing Center
RPC............ Radiological Physics Center [*National Cancer Institute*]
RPC............ Rapeseed Protein Concentrate [*Food technology*]
RPC............ Real Property Cases [*1843-48*] [*England*] [*A publication*]   (DLA)
RPC............ Real Property Commissioner's Report [*1832*] [*England*] [*A publication*]   (DLA)
RPC............ Records Processing Center [*Veterans Administration*]
RPC............ Recruiting Publicity Center [*Military*]
RPC............ Reefed Parachute Canopy
RPC............ Refugee Processing Center   (MCD)
RPC............ Regional Personnel Center
RPC............ Regional Planning Commission
RPC............ Regional Preparedness Committee [*Civil Defense*]
RPC............ Registered Protective Circuit
RPC............ Registered Publication Clerk [*or Custodian*] [*Navy*]
RPC............ Reliability Policy Committee   (AAG)
RPC............ Remote Position Control
RPC............ Remote Power Controller
RPC............ Remote Procedure Call [*Data processing*]
RPC............ Remote Process Cell [*Nuclear energy*]   (NRCH)
RPC............ Remotely Piloted Craft [*Navy*]
RPC............ Remount Purchasing Commission [*British military*]   (DMA)
RPC............ Remuneration Planning Corporation [*Australia*]
RPC............ Renopericardial Canal [*Medicine*]
RPC............ Repair Parts Catalog
RPC............ Repair Parts Cost   (MCD)
RPC............ Repairable Provisioning Center
RPC............ Reparable Processing Center   (AFM)
RPC............ Reply Postcard
RPC............ Report to Commander [*Military*]
RPC............ Reported Post Coastal   (NATG)
RPC............ Reports of English Patent Cases [*A publication*]   (DLA)
RPC............ Reports of Patent Cases [*Legal*] [*British*]
RPC............ Reports of Patent, Design, and Trade Mark Cases [*A publication*]   (DLA)
RPC............ Republican Policy Committee
RPC............ Request the Pleasure of Your Company [*On invitations*]   (DSUE)
RPC............ Requisition Processing Cycle   (MCD)
RPC............ Research Planning Conference [*LIMRA*]
RPC............ Resource Policy Center [*Dartmouth College*] [*Research center*]   (RCD)
RPC............ Ressources Phytogenetiques du Canada [*Plant Gene Resources of Canada - PGRC*]
RPC............ Restrictive Practices Court [*Legal*] [*British*]
RPC............ Restructured Pork Chop [*Food industry*]
RPC............ Reticularis Pontis Caudalis [*Brain anatomy*]
RPC............ Revenue Properties Ltd. [*AMEX symbol*] [*Toronto Stock Exchange symbol*]   (SPSG)
RPC............ Reverse-Phase Chromatography
RPC............ Reverse-Phase Column
RPC............ River Patrol Craft [*Military*]   (CINC)
RPC............ Romanian Philatelic Club   (EA)
RPC............ Row Parity Check   (IEEE)

RPC............ Royal Parks Constabulary [*British*]
RPC............ Royal Pioneer Corps [*British*]
RPC............ Rules of Practice in Patent Cases [*A publication*]
RPC............ Rural Political Cadre [*Vietnam*]
RPC............ Russian People's Center   (EA)
RPCA...... Remotely Programmable Conference Arranger [*Telecommunications*]   (TSSD)
RPCA...... Reverse Passive Anaphylaxis [*Immunology*]
RPCAS ...... Requisition Priority Code Analysis System [*Army*]
RPCC......... Reactor Physics Constants Center [*Argonne National Laboratory*]
RPCC......... Remote Process Crane Cave [*Nuclear energy*]   (NRCH)
RPCCA ...... Red Poll Cattle Club of America [*Later, ARPA*]   (EA)
RPCF......... Reiter Protein Complement Fixation [*Obsolete test for syphilis*]
RPCH .... Reformed Presbyterian Church
RPCH .... Rospatch Corp. [*NASDAQ symbol*]   (NQ)
RPCI......... Regroupement des Partis de la Cote-D'Ivoire [*Regroupment of the Parties of the Ivory Coast*]
RP/CI .... Reinforced Plastics/Composites Institute [*Later, SPICI*]   (EA)
RPCK........ Renopericardial Canal, Kidney [*Medicine*]
RP/CL........ Reporting Post, Coastal Low [*RADAR*]
RPCM........ Rassemblement Populaire Caledonien et Metropolitain [*Caledonian and Metropolitan Popular Rally*] [*Political party*]   (PPW)
RP/CM...... Reporting Post, Coastal Medium [*RADAR*]
RPCO .... Reclamation Program Control Officer [*Military*]   (AFIT)
RPCO .... Repco, Inc. [*NASDAQ symbol*]   (NQ)
RPCP .... Radioisotope-Powered Cardiac Pacemaker   (MCD)
RPCP .... Renopericardial Canal, Pericardium [*Medicine*]
RPCR .... Rassemblement pour la Caledonie dans la Republique [*Popular Caledonian Rally for the Republic*] [*Political party*]   (PPW)
RPCRAAIO ... Receive and Process Complaints and Requests for Assistance, Advice, or Information Only [*Army*]   (AABC)
RPC Rep .... Real Property Commissioner's Report [*1832*] [*England*] [*A publication*]   (DLA)
RPCRS ...... Reactor Protection Control Rod System   (IEEE)
RPCS .... Reactor Plant Control System [*Nuclear energy*]   (NRCH)
RPCSB....... Rivista di Patologia Clinica e Sperimentale [*A publication*]
RPCV........ Returned Peace Corps Volunteer
RPCVCCA ... Returned Peace Corps Volunteers Committee on Central America   (EA)
RPD .... RADAR Planning Device
RPD .... RADAR Prediction Device
RPD .... Radiation Protection Dosimetry [*A publication*]
RPD .... Radioisotope Power Device
RPD .... Rapid   (AAG)
RPD .... Reactive Plasma Deposition
RPD .... Reactor Plant Designer [*Nuclear energy*]   (NRCH)
RPD .... Reflex Plasma Discharge
RPD .... Regius Professor of Divinity   (ROG)
RPD .... Relative Power Density
RPD .... Renewal Parts Data   (MSA)
RPD .... Repadre Resources Ltd. [*Vancouver Stock Exchange symbol*]
RPD .... Repatriation Pension Decisions [*Australia*] [*A publication*]
RPD .... Rerum Politicarum Doctor [*Doctor of Political Science*]
RPD .... Reserves Available to Support Private, Noninterbank Deposits [*Federal Reserve System*]
RPD .... Resistance Pressure Detector
RPD .... Respiratory Protective Device [*Medicine*]
RPD .... Retarding Potential Difference   (IEEE)
RPD .... Retired Pay Defense   (NVT)
RPD .... Review of Public Data Use [*A publication*]
RPD .... Rhode Island School of Design, Providence, RI [*Library symbol*] [*Library of Congress*]   (LCLS)
RPD .... Rocket Propulsion Department [*Royal Aircraft Establishment*] [*British*]
RPDB........ Repertoire Pratique de Droit Belge [*A publication*]   (ILCA)
RPDC......... Revue Pratique de Droit Commercial, Financier, et Fiscal [*A publication*]
RPDED...... Revue du Palais de la Deouverte [*A publication*]
RPDES ...... Research Program Development and Evaluation Staff [*Department of Agriculture*]
RPDF........ Radiation Protection Design Features   (NRCH)
RPDH........ Reserve Shutdown Planned Derated Hours [*Electronics*]   (IEEE)
RPDL........ Radioisotope Process Development Laboratory [*ORNL*]
RPDL........ Rensselaer Polytechnic Institute Plasma Dynamics Laboratory [*Research center*]   (RCD)
RPDL........ Repair Parts Decision List [*Military*]   (CAAL)
RPDMRC ... Reference or Partial Description Method Reason Code   (MCD)
RPDO........ Repair Parts Directive Order
RPDQDK .. Queensland. Department of Forestry. Research Paper [*A publication*]
RPDR .... Reproducer   (MSA)
RPDR .... Rotating Packed Disk Reactor [*Chemical engineering*]
RPDS........ Rapids   (MCD)
RPDS........ Retired Personnel Data System [*Air Force*]
RPDt......... Registered Professional Dietitian
RPD & TM ... Reports of Patent, Design, and Trade Mark Cases [*United Kingdom*] [*A publication*]

RPDTMC ... Reports of Patent, Design, and Trade Mark Cases [*Australia*] [*A publication*]
RPD & TM Cas ... Reports of Patent Design and Trade Mark Cases [*United Kingdom*] [*A publication*] (DLA)
RPDWR..... Revised Primary Drinking Water Regulations
RPE............ Elmwood Public Library, Providence, RI [*Library symbol*] [*Library of Congress*] (LCLS)
RPE............ Radial Probable Error (IEEE)
RPE............ Range Planning Estimate (MUGU)
RPE............ Range Probable Error [*Formerly, Range Error Probable*] [*Air Force*] (NATG)
RPE............ Rating of Perceived Exertion
RPE............ Reformed Protestant Episcopal
RPE............ Registered Professional Engineer (IEEE)
RPE............ Related Payroll Expense
RPE............ Relative Price Effect
RPE............ Reliability Project Engineer (NASA)
RPE............ Remote Peripheral Equipment (IEEE)
RPE............ Repair Parts Estimate (MCD)
RPE............ Report of Patients Evacuated [*Aeromedical evacuation*]
RPE............ Required Page-End Character [*Data processing*]
RPE............ Resource Planning and Evaluation [*Nuclear energy*] (NRCH)
RPE............ Retinal Pigment Epithelium
RPE.... Revue d'Etudes Comparatives Est-Ouest [*A publication*]
RPE............ Rocket Propulsion Establishment [*British*] (KSC)
RPE............ Ron Pair Enterprises [*Division of Wilson, Inc.*]
RPE............ Rotating Platinum Electrode [*Electrochemistry*]
RPE............ Royal Pakistan Engineers [*British military*] (DMA)
RPEA......... Regional Planning and Evaluation Agency [*California State Board of Education*]
RPed .... Revue Pedagogique [*A publication*]
RPEng........ Providence Engineering Society, Providence, RI [*Library symbol*] [*Library of Congress*] (LCLS)
RPEP......... Register of Planned Emergency Procedures [*Military*]
R Pernambucana Desenvolvimento ... Revista Pernambucana de Desenvolvimento [*A publication*]
R Peruana Derecho Internac ... Revista Peruana de Derecho Internacional [*A publication*]
RPET......... Royal Dutch Petroleum Co. [*NASDAQ symbol*] (NQ)
RPEV......... Roadway Powered Electric Vehicle
RPEYC ...... Royal Prince Edward Yacht Club [*Australia*]
RPF............ Radio Position Finding [*A term for RADAR before early 1942*]
RPF............ Radio Proximity Fuze
RPF............ Radiometer Performance Factor
RPF............ Rassemblement du Peuple Francais [*Rally of the French People*]
RPF............ Real Property Facilities [*Army*] (AABC)
RPF............ Reduced Physical Fidelity (MCD)
RPF............ Reference Point Foundation (EA)
RPF............ Reformatorische Politieke Federatie [*Reformist Political Federation*] [*Netherlands*] [*Political party*] (PPE)
RPF............ Region Peaking Factor [*Nuclear energy*] (NRCH)
RPF............ Registered Professional Forester
RPF............ Relaxed Pelvic Floor [*Medicine*]
RPF............ Remote Processing Facility (MCD)
RPF.... Renal Plasma Flow [*Medicine*]
RPF............ Repair Parts Facility (MCD)
rpf............. Reperforated [*Philately*]
RPF............ Revista Portuguesa de Filologia [*A publication*]
RPF............ Revue de la Pensee Francaise [*A publication*]
RPF............ Right Panel Front [*Nuclear energy*] (NRCH)
RPF............ Rotable Pool Factor (MCD)
RPF............ Royal Pacific Sea Farms Ltd. [*Toronto Stock Exchange symbol*] [*Vancouver Stock Exchange symbol*]
RPFADG ... Forests Department of Western Australia. Research Paper [*A publication*]
RPFC......... Ray Price Fan Club (EA)
RPFC......... Recurrent Peak Forward Current
RPFCA ...... Revue Pratique du Froid et du Conditionnement de l'Air [*Later, Journal RPF*] [*A publication*]
RPFE......... Revue Philosophique de la France et de l'Etranger [*A publication*]
RPFFB....... RP [*Retinitis Pigmentosa*] Foundation Fighting Blindness (EA)
RPFilos ...... Revista Portuguesa de Filosofia [*A publication*]
RPFL......... Revue de Philologie Francaise et de Litterature [*A publication*]
RPFOD...... Reported for Duty (FAAC)
RPFUB...... Radovi Poljoprivrednog Fakulteta Univerziteta u Sarajevu [*A publication*]
RPFWDE .. US Fish and Wildlife Service. Resource Publication [*A publication*]
RPG .... Radiation Protection Guide [*AEC*]
RPG .... Radioisotopic Power Generator [*Navy*]
RPG .... Rampage Resources Ltd. [*Vancouver Stock Exchange symbol*]
RPG .... Rebounds per Game [*Basketball, hockey*]
RPG .... Reflection Phase Grating [*Acoustics*]
RPG .... Refugee Policy Group (EA)
RPG .... Regional Planning Group (NATG)
RPG .... Religion Publishing Group (EA)
RPG .... Report Processor Generator (MCD)
RPG .... Report Program Generator [*Programming language*] [*1962*]

RPG .... Research Planning Guide (MCD)
RPG .... Retrograde Pyelogram [*Medicine*]
RPG .... Right Pedal Ganglion
RPG .... Rocket-Propelled Grenade
RPG .... Role-Playing Game [*Video game*]
RPG .... Rotary Pulse Generator
RPG .... Rounds per Gun
RPGN .... Rapidly Progressive Glomerular Nephritis [*Medicine*]
RPGPA...... Recent Publications on Governmental Problems [*A publication*]
RPGPM..... Rounds per Gun per Minute
RPH......... Radio for the Print Handicapped [*Australia*]
RPH......... Raypath Resources Ltd. [*Vancouver Stock Exchange symbol*]
RPH......... Registered Pharmacist
RPH......... Remember Pearl Harbor [*Group*] [*World War II*]
RPH......... Remotely Piloted Helicopter
RP/H......... Repairs, Heavy
RPH......... Revista Portuguesa de Historia [*A publication*]
RPH......... Revolutions per Hour (MCD)
RPh .... Revue de Philologie [*A publication*]
RPh .... Revue de Philologie, de Litterature, et d'Histoire Anciennes [*A publication*]
RPh .... Revue de Philosophie [*A publication*]
RPH........... Rhode Island Hospital, Peters House Medical Library, Providence, RI [*Library symbol*] [*Library of Congress*] (LCLS)
RPH .... Rideout Pyrohydrolysis
RPh........... Romance Philology [*A publication*]
RPHA .... Reverse Passive Hemagglutination [*Clinical chemistry*]
R Ph F E .... Revue Philosophique de la France et de l'Etranger [*A publication*]
RPhil......... Revue de Philosophie [*A publication*]
R Phil Louvain ... Revue Philosophique de Louvain [*A publication*]
R Philos ..... Revue Philosophique [*A publication*]
RPHJ......... Royal Perth Hospital. Journal [*A publication*] (ADA)
RPhL......... Revue Philosophique de Louvain [*A publication*]
RphLH....... Revue de Philologie, de Litterature, et d'Histoire Anciennes [*A publication*]
RP-HPLC ... Reversed-Phase High-Performance Liquid Chromatography
RPHRA ...... Recent Progress in Hormone Research [*A publication*]
RPHST...... Research Participation for High School Teachers [*National Science Foundation*]
R Phys Soc Edinb Pr ... Royal Physical Society of Edinburgh. Proceedings [*A publication*]
RPI............ RADAR Precipitation Integrator [*National Weather Service*]
RPI............ Railway Progress Institute (EA)
RPI............ Rapeseed Protein Isolate [*Food technology*]
RPI............ Rassemblement Populaire pour l'Independance [*People's Rally for Independence*] [*Djibouti*] [*Political party*] (PPW)
RPI............ Rated Position Identifier (AFM)
RPI............ Read, Punch, and Interpret
RPI............ Real Property Inventory [*Military*]
RPI............ Registro de la Propiedad Industrial [*Spanish Patent Office*] [*Information service or system*] (IID)
RPI............ Relative Position Indication (NRCH)
RPI............ Relay Position Indicator
RPI............ Remarried Parents, Incorporated (EA)
RPI............ Rensselaer Polytechnic Institute [*Troy, NY*] (MCD)
RPI............ Republican Party of India [*Political party*] (PPW)
RPI............ Research Price Index
RPI............ Resource Policy Institute (EA)
RPI............ Responsive Production Inventory
RPI............ Retail Prices Index [*British*]
RPI............ Reticulocyte Production Index [*Hematology*]
RPI............ Richmond Professional Institute [*Virginia*]
RPI............ Rimpac Industries [*Vancouver Stock Exchange symbol*]
RPI............ Rod Position Indicator [*Nuclear energy*] (NRCH)
RPI............ Roll Position Indicator (MCD)
RPI............ Rose Polytechnic Institute [*Indiana*]
RPI............ Royal Polytechnic Institute (ROG)
R & PI .... Rubber and Plastics Industry (MCD)
RPIA......... Rocket Propellant Information Agency (MCD)
RPIA......... Roll Position Indicator Assembly
RPIAC....... Retail Prices Index Advisory Committee [*Department of Employment*] [*British*]
RPIC......... Reagan Political Items Collectors (EA)
RPIC......... Republic Pictures Corp. [*Los Angeles, CA*] [*NASDAQ symbol*] (NQ)
RPIC......... Rock Properties Information Center [*Purdue University*] [*National Science Foundation*] (IID)
RPIE......... Real Property Installed Equipment [*Air Force*] (MCD)
RPIE......... Replacement of Photography Imagery Equipment (RDA)
RPIF......... Real Property Industrial Fund
RPIFC....... Robert Plant International Fan Club (EA)
RPIFC....... Ronnie Prophet International Fan Club (EA)
RPIO......... Registered Publication Issuing Office [*Military*]
RPIS......... Rod Position Indication System [*Nuclear energy*] (NRCH)
RPIS......... Rod Position Information System [*Nuclear energy*] (NRCH)
RPJ........... Revue de la Pensee Juive [*A publication*]
RPJ .... [*The*] Rise of Provincial Jewry [*A publication*] (BJA)
RPJ .... Rotary Pressure Joint

RPJCB....... John Carter Brown Library, Providence, RI [*Library symbol*] [*Library of Congress*]   (LCLS)
RPK .... Revenue Passenger Kilometer   (AIA)
RPK .... Ribophosphate Pyrophosphokinase [*An enzyme*]
RPK .... Roosevelt [*Washington*] [*Seismograph station code, US Geological Survey*]   (SEIS)
RPL............ RADAR Processing Language [*Data processing*]   (IEEE)
RPL............ Radiation Physics Laboratory [*National Institute of Standards and Technology*]   (MCD)
RPL............ Radio-Photo Luminescent [*Dosimetry*]
RPL............ Ram Petroleums Ltd. [*Toronto Stock Exchange symbol*]
RPL............ Ramped Powered Lighter [*British military*]   (DMA)
RPL............ Ramseur Pilot Light Teaching System
RPL............ Rapid Pole Line [*A type of pole line construction*]
RPL............ Rated Power Level   (NASA)
RPL............ Reactor Primary Loop
RPL............ Reading Public Library, Reading, PA [*OCLC symbol*]   (OCLC)
RPL............ Receive Replenishment From [*Navy*]   (NVT)
RPL............ Recommended Provisioning List
RPL............ Remote Program Load
RPL............ Renewal Parts Leaflet   (MSA)
RPL............ Repair Parts List [*Army*]   (AABC)
RP/L.......... Repairs, Light
RPL............ Repetitive Flight Plan [*Aviation*]   (FAAC)
RPL............ Replenish   (NVT)
RPL............ Request Parameter List [*Data processing*]   (BUR)
RPL............ Requested Privilege Level [*Data processing*]
RPL............ Resident Pulmonary Lymphocyte [*Immunology*]
RPL............ Review of the River Plate [*A publication*]
RPL............ Revue Philosophique de Louvain [*A publication*]
RPL............ Rhode Island State Law Library, Providence, RI [*Library symbol*] [*Library of Congress*]   (LCLS)
RPL............ Richmond Public Library [*UTLAS symbol*]
RPL............ Ripe Pulp Liquid [*A banana substrate*]
RPL............ Ripple
RPL............ Robot Programming Language [*Data processing*]
RPL............ Rocket Propulsion Laboratory [*Air Force*]
RPL............ Running Program Language [*Data processing*]
RPLAA ...... Reinforced Plastics [*A publication*]
R Plan Desarr (Bogota) ... Revista de Planeacion y Desarrollo (Bogota) [*A publication*]
R Planeacion y Desarrollo ... Revista de Planeacion y Desarrollo [*A publication*]
R Plastiq .... Revue Generale des Caoutchoucs et Plastiques [*A publication*]
RPLC......... Replace   (FAAC)
RPLC......... Reversed-Phase Liquid Chromatography
RPLHA...... Revue de Philologie, de Litterature, et d'Histoire Anciennes. Troisieme Serie [*A publication*]
RPLHD ..... Revista Padurilor-Industria Lemnului. Celuloza si Hirtie. Seria Celuloza si Hirtie [*A publication*]
RPLit .... Res Publica Litterarum [*A publication*]
RPLLD ...... Revista Padurilor-Industria Lemnului. Celuloza si Hirtie. Seria Industria Lemnului [*A publication*]
RPLN......... Retroperitoneal Lymph Nodes [*Medicine*]
RPLNG...... Replenishing
RPLO......... Regal Petroleum Limited [*NASDAQ symbol*]   (NQ)
RPLPA ...... Reviews of Plasma Physics [*English Translation*] [*A publication*]
RPLR......... Repeller   (MSA)
RPLS .... Radionuclide Perfusion Lung Scan
RPLS .... Reactor Protection Logic System   (IEEE)
RPLSN ...... Repulsion   (MSA)
RPLT......... Repellent   (MSA)
RPLV......... Reentry Payload Launch Vehicle
RPM .... RADAR Performance Monitor
RPM .... Radiation Polarization Measurement
RPM .... Radio Programas de Mexico [*Radio network*]
RPM .... Rate per Minute
RPM .... Read Program Memory [*Data processing*]   (MDG)
RPM .... Real Property Management
RPM .... Reclamation Program Manager [*Military*]   (AFIT)
RPM .... Registered Publications Manual [*Navy*]
RPM .... Registered Publications Memorandum
RPM .... Registrants Processing Manual [*Selective Service System*]
RPM .... Regulated Power Module
RPM .... Relaxation Potential Model [*Physics*]
RPM .... Reliability Performance Measure [*QCR*]
RPM .... Reliability Planning and Management   (MCD)
RPM .... Remote Performance Monitoring   (CET)
RPM .... Remote Program Management
RPM .... Remotely Piloted Munitions [*Army*]
RPM .... Resale Price Maintenance
R & PM..... Research and Program Management [*NASA*]
RPM .... Research and Program Management [*NASA*]
R & PM..... Resources and Program Management [*NASA*]
RPM .... Response-per-Thousand [*Marketing*]
RPM .... Resupply Provisions Module [*NASA*]   (KSC)
RPM .... Retail Price Maintenance   (DCTA)
RPM .... Returns Program Manager [*IRS*]
RPM .... Revenue per Mile
RPM .... Revenue Passenger Mile

RPM .... Revolutions per Minute [*e.g., in reference to phonograph records*]
RPM .... Rhode Island Medical Society, Providence, RI [*Library symbol*] [*Library of Congress*]   (LCLS)
RPM .... Rifle Prize Money [*British military*]   (DMA)
RPM .... Rocket-Propelled Mines   (NATG)
RPM .... Roll Position Mechanism   (MCD)
RPM .... Rotations per Minute
RPM .... Rounds per Minute [*Military*]   (INF)
RPM .... Royalty Payment Mechanism
RPMa .... Masonic Temple Library, Providence, RI [*Library symbol*] [*Library of Congress*]   (LCLS)
RPMA .... Real Property Maintenance Activities [*or Administration*] [*Army*]   (AABC)
RPMB....... Cubi Naval Air Station, Bataan [*Philippines*] [*ICAO location identifier*]   (ICLI)
RPMC....... Cebu/Lahug, Cebu [*Philippines*] [*ICAO location identifier*]   (ICLI)
RPMC....... Remote Performance Monitoring and Control
RPMC....... Reserve Personnel, Marine Corps   (MCD)
RPMD .... Resources Planning and Mobilization Division [*of OEP*]
RPMDA ..... Recenti Progressi in Medicina [*A publication*]
RPMDDQ ... Malaysia. Ministry of Agriculture and Rural Development. Risalah Penerangan [*A publication*]
RPMF........ Reserve Personnel Master File [*Military*]
RPMI........ Radiant Power Measuring Instrument [*Geophysics*]
RPMI........ Revolutions-per-Minute Indicator
RPMI........ Roswell Park Memorial Institute [*State University of New York at Buffalo*] [*Research center*]   (RCD)
RPMIO...... Registered Publication Mobile Issuing Office [*Military*]
RPMK .... Clark Air Base, Pampanga [*Philippines*] [*ICAO location identifier*]   (ICLI)
RPMKA..... Rocznik Pomorskiej Akademii Medycznej Imienia Generala Karola Swierczewskiego w Szczecinie [*A publication*]
RPMKAA ... Annales Academiae Medicae Stetinensis [*A publication*]
RPML........ Laoag/International, Ilocos Norte [*Philippines*] [*ICAO location identifier*]   (ICLI)
RPMM ...... Manila/International [*Philippines*] [*ICAO location identifier*]   (ICLI)
RPMN .... Repairman   (AABC)
RPMO .... Radio Projects Management Office
RPMOR .... Rounds per Mortar
RPMORPM ... Rounds per Mortar per Minute
RPMP........ Legazpi, Albay [*Philippines*] [*ICAO location identifier*]   (ICLI)
RPMP........ Register of Plan Mobilization Producers
RPMR....... Romblon, Tablas Island [*Philippines*] [*ICAO location identifier*]   (ICLI)
RPMS .... Real Property Management System   (MCD)
RPM/S ...... Revolutions per Minute/Second   (DEN)
RPMS .... Royal Postgraduate Medical School [*British*]
RPMS .... Sangley Point Naval Station, Cavite [*Philippines*] [*ICAO location identifier*]   (ICLI)
RPMSBZ... Rocznik Pomorska Akademia Medyczna Imienia Generala Karola Swierczewskiego w Szczecinie. Suplement [*A publication*]
RPMT....... Lapu-Lapu/Mactan International [*Philippines*] [*ICAO location identifier*]   (ICLI)
RPMZ........ Zamboanga/International [*Philippines*] [*ICAO location identifier*]   (ICLI)
RPN .... Registered Professional Nurse
RPN .... Reserve Personnel, Navy [*An appropriation*]
RPN .... Reverse Polish Notation [*Arithmetic evaluation*] [*Data processing*]   (IEEE)
RPN .... Revue Pratique du Notariat [*A publication*]
RPN .... Rosh-Pina [*Israel*] [*Airport symbol*]   (OAG)
RPN .... Royal Pakistan Navy [*British military*]   (DMA)
RPNB .... Revue Pratique du Notariat Belge [*A publication*]
RPND .... Reprinting, No Date [*Publishing*]
R & P News ... Rubber and Plastics News [*A publication*]
R & P News 2 ... Rubber and Plastics News. 2 [*A publication*]
RPNSM..... Replenishment
RPNVR...... Royal Pakistan Naval Volunteer Reserve [*British military*]   (DMA)
RPO .... Radiation Protection Officer [*NASA*]   (NASA)
RPO .... Radiophare Omnidirectionnel [*Omnidirectional Radio Beacon*]   (NATG)
RPO .... Railway Post Office
RPO .... Range Planning Office   (MUGU)
RPO .... Readiness Project Officer
RPO .... Regional Personnel Officer [*Social Security Administration*]
RPO .... Regional Pests Officer [*Ministry of Agriculture, Fisheries, and Food*] [*British*]
RPO .... Regional Program [*or Project*] Officer   (OICC)
RPO .... Regional Purchasing Office [*Defense Supply Agency*]
RPO .... Regular Production Option [*Automotive engineering*]
RPO .... Regulating Petty Officer [*British*]
RPO .... Rejection Purchase Order   (MCD)
RPO .... Repair Parts Order [*Navy*]
RPO .... Replacement Purchase Order
RPO .... Responsible Property Officer [*Military*]   (AFIT)
RPO .... Retired Pay Operations [*Army*]

RPO .... Revolution per Orbit
RPO .... Rotor Power Output
RPO .... Royal Philharmonic Orchestra [*British*]
RPOA .... Recognized Private Operating Agencies   (NATG)
RPOC .... Remote Payload Operations Center [*NASA*]   (MCD)
RPOC .... Report Proceeding on Course [*Aviation*]   (FAAC)
RPOC .... Residual Particulate Organic Carbon [*Environmental science*]
RPOCN ..... Request for Purchase Order Change Notice   (AAG)
R Pol .... Review of Politics [*A publication*]
R Pol Agr ... Rivista di Politica Agraria [*A publication*]
R Pol Econ Terza Ser ...   Revista di Politica Economica. Terza Serie [*A publication*]
R Pol Internac ...   Revista de Politica Internacional [*A publication*]
R Polit .... Review of Politics [*A publication*]
R Politics.... Review of Politics [*A publication*]
R Polit Int .. Revue de Politique Internationale [*A publication*]
R Polit Int (Madrid) ...   Revista de Politica Internacional (Madrid) [*A publication*]
R Polit et Litt ...   Revue Politique et Litteraire [*A publication*]
R Polit Parl ...   Revue Politique et Parlementaire [*A publication*]
R Polit Soc ...   Revista de Politica Social [*A publication*]
R Pol et Litt ...   Revue Politique et Litteraire [*A publication*]
R Pol et Parlementaire ...   Revue Politique et Parlementaire [*A publication*]
R Pol Soc.... Revista de Politica Social [*A publication*]
RPOP......... Rover Preflight Operations Procedures [*NASA*]   (KSC)
RPorP .... Portsmouth Priory, Portsmouth, RI [*Library symbol*] [*Library of Congress*]   (LCLS)
R Porto....... Revista. Faculdade de Letras. Serie de Historia. Universidade do Porto [*A publication*]
RPOW .... RPM, Inc. [*NASDAQ symbol*]   (NQ)
RPP........... RADAR Power Programmer
RPP........... Radiation Protection Plan [*Nuclear energy*]   (NRCH)
RPP........... Radiochemical Processing Plant [*Oak Ridge National Laboratory*]
RPP........... Rassemblement Populaire pour le Progres [*Popular Rally for Progress*] [*Djibouti*] [*Political party*]   (PPW)
RPP........... Rate Pressure Product [*Cardiology*]
RPP........... Real Property Practice [*A publication*]
RPP........... Real Property, Probate, and Trust Journal [*A publication*]
RPP........... Rechargeable Power Pack
RPP........... Recovered Polypropylene [*Organic chemistry*]
R & PP ...... Recreation and Public Purposes Act
RPP........... Reductive Pentose Phosphate [*Photosynthesis cycle*]
RPP........... Regional Priority Program [*Army*]   (AABC)
RPP........... Regional Promotion Plan [*FAA*]   (FAAC)
RPP........... Registered Postal Packet
RPP........... Reinforced Pyrolytic Plastic   (NASA)
RPP........... Reliability Program Plan   (MCD)
RPP........... Removable Patch Panel
RPP........... Rendezvous Point Position [*Aerospace*]
RPP........... Repair Parts Provisioning
RPP........... Repap Enterprises Corp., Inc. [*Toronto Stock Exchange symbol*] [*Vancouver Stock Exchange symbol*]
RPP........... Reply Paid Postcard
RPP........... Republican People's Party [*Cumhuriyet Halk Partisi - CHP*] [*Turkey*] [*Political party*]   (PPW)
RPP........... Request Present Position [*Aviation*]   (FAAC)
RPP........... Requisition Processing Point [*Military*]
RPP........... Retrograde Processing Point   (MCD)
RPP........... Retropubic Prostatectomy [*Medicine*]
RPP........... Reverse Pulse Polarography [*Analytical chemistry*]
RPP........... Review of Public Personnel Administration [*A publication*]
RPP........... Revue des Pays de l'Est [*A publication*]
RPP........... Revue Politique et Parlementaire [*A publication*]
RPP........... Rivers Pollution Prevention   (ROG)
RPP........... Roll-Pitch Pickoff
RP and P.... Romanticism Past and Present [*A publication*]
RPP........... Rules of Practices and Procedure
RPP........... Rural Practice Project [*An association*] [*Defunct*]   (EA)
RPPA........ Republican Postwar Policy Association [*Encouraged Republican Party to drop its isolationist viewpoint and take a stand for an American share in international collaboration after the war*] [*World War II*]
RPPA........ Revue Politique et Parlementaire [*A publication*]
RPPC......... Providence College, Providence, RI [*Library symbol*] [*Library of Congress*]   (LCLS)
RPPE........ Research, Program, Planning, and Evaluation
RPPHA...... Reports on Progress in Physics [*A publication*]
RPPI......... Remote Plan Position Indicator   (MCD)
RPPI......... Repeater Plan Position Indicator   (NVT)
RPPI......... Role Perception Picture Inventory
RPPJA....... Reports on Progress in Polymer Physics (Japan) [*A publication*]
RPPL........ Repair Parts Price List
RPPL........ Repair Parts Provisioning List
RPPM........ Park Museum Reference Library, Providence, RI [*Library symbol*] [*Library of Congress*]   (LCLS)
RPPMP ..... Repair Parts Program Management Plans
RPPO........ Regional Printing Procurement Office [*Army*]
RPPP........ Repair Parts Program Plan [*Army*]
RPPP .... Rules of Pleading, Practice, and Procedure [*A publication*]   (DLA)

RPPR........ Rooney, Pace Group, Inc. [*NASDAQ symbol*]   (NQ)
RPPS .... Robotnicza Partia Polskich Socjalistow [*Workers Party of Polish Socialists*] [*Political party*]   (PPE)
RPPS-Lewica ...   Robotnicza Partia Polskich Socjalistow - Lewica [*Workers Party of Polish Socialists - Left*] [*Political party*]   (PPE)
RPPTF....... Rotatable Porous-Prism Test Fixture
RPQ .... Rapports de Pratique de Quebec [*Quebec Practice Reports*] [*Canada*] [*A publication*]   (DLA)
RPQ .... Request for Price Quotation
RPQ .... Rutter Parent Questionnaire
RPQEA...... Radiophysics and Quantum Electronics [*English Translation*] [*A publication*]
RPR .... Federation Guadeloupeenne du Rassemblement pour la Republique [*Guadeloupe Federation of the Rally for the Republic*] [*Political party*]   (PPW)
RPR .... Radio Physics Research
RPR .... Railway Pioneer Regiment [*British military*]   (DMA)
RPR .... Raipur [*India*] [*Airport symbol*]   (OAG)
RPR .... Rapid Plasma Reagin [*Card test for venereal disease*]
RPR .... Rapid Power Reduction   (IEEE)
RPR .... Rassemblement pour la Republique [*Rally for the Republic*] [*Martinique*] [*Political party*]   (PPW)
RPR .... Rassemblement pour la Republique [*Rally for the Republic*] [*Wallis and Futuna Islands*] [*Political party*]   (PD)
RPR .... Rassemblement pour la Republique [*Rally for the Republic*] [*Reunion*] [*Political party*]   (PPW)
RPR .... Rassemblement pour la Republique [*Rally for the Republic*] [*France*] [*Political party*]   (ECON)
RPR .... Rassemblement pour la Republique [*Rally for the Republic*] [*French Polynesia*] [*Political party*]   (PPW)
RPR .... Rassemblement pour la Republique [*Rally for the Republic*] [*French Guiana*] [*Political party*]   (PPW)
RPR .... Read Printer
RPR .... Real Property Reports [*A publication*]
RPR .... Rear Projection Readout
RPR .... Rectangular Parallelepiped Resonant Method [*Crystal elasticity*]
RPR .... Red Blood Cell Precursor Production Rate [*Hematology*]
RPR .... Rent Procedural Regulation (Office of Rent Stabilization) [*Economic Stabilization Agency*] [*A publication*]   (DLA)
RPR .... Repair   (MSA)
RPR .... Repair Parts Requisition
RPR .... Research Project Report [*A publication*]   (EAAP)
RPR .... Rhone-Poulenc Rorer [*NYSE symbol*]   (SPSG)
RPR .... Rockport Resources Ltd. [*Vancouver Stock Exchange symbol*]
RPR .... Roger Williams College, Providence Campus, Providence, RI [*Library symbol*] [*Library of Congress*]   (LCLS)
RPR .... Roll-Pitch Resolver
RPRA........ Railroad Public Relations Association   (EA)
R Prac Patent Cases ...   Rules of Practice in Patent Cases [*A publication*]   (DLA)
RPrag........ Romanistica Pragensia [*A publication*]
RPrat......... Revue Pratique d'Apologetique [*A publication*]
R Prat Dr Soc ...   Revue Pratique de Droit Social [*A publication*]
R Pratique Questions Commer et Econs ...   Revue Pratique des Questions Commerciales et Economiques [*A publication*]
RPRC......... Regional Primate Research Centers
RPRC......... Religious Public Relations Council   (EA)
RPRC......... Retired and Pioneer Rural Carriers of United States   (EA)
RPRC......... Rhode Island College, Providence, RI [*Library symbol*] [*Library of Congress*]   (LCLS)
RPR-CT..... Rapid Plasma Reagin Card Test [*Clinical chemistry*]
RPRD........ Research Policy and Review Division [*of OEP*]
RPRFA ...... Revue Pratique du Froid [*Later, Journal RPF*] [*A publication*]
rPRL.......... Rat Prolactin [*Biochemistry*]
RPRL......... Regional Parasite Research Laboratory [*US Department of Agriculture*] [*Research center*]   (RCD)
RPRL......... Regional Poultry Research Laboratory [*East Lansing, MI*] [*Department of Agriculture*]   (GRD)
RPRMN..... Repairman
RPRO .... ReproTech, Inc. [*Sweetwater, TN*] [*NASDAQ symbol*]   (NQ)
RPRODG .. Annual Research Reviews. Renal Prostaglandins [*A publication*]
RPROP...... Receiving Proficiency Pay [*Military*]
R Prop Prob and Tr J ...   Real Property, Probate, and Trust Journal [*A publication*]
RPRRA...... Revue de Physique. Academie de la Republique Populaire Roumaine [*A publication*]
RPRRB ..... Real Property Resource Review Board   (AFM)
RPRS .... Random-Pulse RADAR System   (AAG)
RPRS .... Roll-Pitch Resolver System
RPRT........ Report   (AFM)
RPRV........ Remotely Piloted Research Vehicle [*NASA*]
RPRWP..... Reactor Plant River Water Pump   (IEEE)
RPS........... Racial Preservation Society [*British*]
RPS........... RADAR Position Symbol   (FAAC)
RPS........... Radical Philosophy Society [*British*]
RPS........... Radio Program Standard [*Australia*]
RPS........... Radiological Protection Service   (DEN)
RPS........... Range Pad Service
RPS........... Range Positioning System

RPS............	Rapid Patent Service [*Research Publications, Inc.*] [*Information service or system*] (IID)
RPS............	Rapid Photo Screening
RPS............	Rare Poultry Society [*British*]
RPS............	Reactor Protection System [*Nuclear energy*] (NRCH)
RPS............	Real-Time Programming System [*Data processing*] (IEEE)
RPS............	Record and Playback Subsystem (NASA)
RPS............	Records per Sector [*Data processing*]
RPS............	Registered Publications System
RPS............	Regulated Power Supply
RPS............	Regulatory Performance Summary [*Report*] [*Nuclear energy*] (NRCH)
RPS............	Reinforced Porcelain System [*Dentistry*]
RPS............	Relative Performance Score [*Telecommunications*] (TEL)
RPS............	Relay Power Supply (MCD)
RPS............	Remittance Processing Systems [*IRS*]
RPS............	Remote Printing System
RPS............	Remote Processing Service (BUR)
RPS............	Renal Pressor Substance [*Medicine*]
RPS............	Requirements Planning System [*Data processing*]
RPS............	Response-Produced Stimulation
RPS............	Retired Persons Services (EA)
RPS............	Return Pressure Sensing (MCD)
RPS............	Revolutions per Second (AFM)
rps.............	Rhodopseudomonas Virides [*A bacterium*]
RPS............	Right Pedal Sinus
RPS............	Rigid Proctosigmoidoscopy [*Proctoscopy*]
RPS............	Ripe Pulp Solid [*A banana substrate*]
RPS............	Rochester Public Schools, Library Processing Center, Rochester, MN [*OCLC symbol*] (OCLC)
RPS............	Role Performance Scale [*Occupational therapy*]
RPS............	Rotary Precision Switch
RPS............	Rotating Passing Scuttle
RPS............	Rotational Position Sensing [*Data processing*]
RPS............	Royal Philharmonic Society (EAIO)
RPS............	Royal Photographic Society of Great Britain (DEN)
RPS............	RPS Realty Trust [*NYSE symbol*] (SPSG)
RPS............	Rutile-Paper-Slurry [*Grade of titanium dioxide*]
RPSA........	Resources Pension Shares 1 [*New York, NY*] [*NASDAQ symbol*] (NQ)
RPSA........	Rudder Pedal Sensor Assembly (MCD)
RPSB........	Resources Pension Shares 2 [*NASDAQ symbol*] (NQ)
RPSC........	Resources Pension Shares 3 [*New York, NY*] [*NASDAQ symbol*] (NQ)
RPSC........	Royal Philatelic Society of Canada
RPSCTDY ...	Return to Proper Station Upon Completion of Temporary Duty [*Military*]
RPS-DL.....	Registered Publications Section - District Library [*Navy*]
R & P SEC ...	Radio and Panel Section [*Navy*]
RPSGB	Royal Pharmaceutical Society of Great Britain (EAIO)
RPSGB	Royal Photographic Society of Great Britain (EAIO)
RP (Ships) ...	Registered Ships' Plumbers [*British*]
RPSI	Roche Psychiatric Service Institute
R Psicol Gen Apl ...	Revista de Psicologia General y Aplicada [*A publication*]
RPSIO	Registered Publications Subissuing Office [*Military*] (NVT)
RPSL	Repair Parts Selective List
RPSL	Rhode Island Department of State Library Services, Providence, RI [*Library symbol*] [*Library of Congress*] (LCLS)
RPSM.......	Registered Publication Shipment Memorandum
RPSM.......	Resources Planning and Scheduling Method
RPSMG....	Reactor Protective System Motor Generator (IEEE)
RPSML	Repair Parts Support Material List
RPSoc	Revue Pratique des Societes Civiles et Commerciales [*A publication*]
RPSP	RADAR Programmable Signal Processor
RPsP	Revue de Psychologie des Peuples [*A publication*]
RPS-PL.....	Registered Publications Section - Personnel Library [*Navy*]
RPSS	Ryukyu Philatelic Specialist Society (EA)
RPS Subj Cat ...	Royal Photographic Society of Great Britain. Library Catalogue. Part 2. Subject Catalogue [*A publication*]
RPST	Reaction Products Separator Tank [*Nuclear energy*] (NRCH)
RPST	Recombinant Porcine Somatotropin
RPSTA	Rivista di Parassitologia [*A publication*]
RPSTL......	Repair Parts and Special Tools List [*Army*] (AABC)
RPSY	Rapitech Systems, Inc. [*Suffern, NY*] [*NASDAQ symbol*] (NQ)
R Psych	Reading Psychology [*A publication*]
RPT............	Congregation Sons of Israel and David, Temple Beth-El, Providence, RI [*Library symbol*] [*Library of Congress*] (LCLS)
RPT............	Raluana Point [*New Britain*] [*Seismograph station code, US Geological Survey*] (SEIS)
RPT............	Rapid Pull Through [*Gastroenterology*]
RPT............	Rassemblement du Peuple Togolais [*Rally of the Togolese People*] [*Political party*] (PPW)
RPT............	Reactor for Physical and Technical Investigations [*USSR*] [*Nuclear energy*] (DEN)
RPT............	Recirculation Pump Trip [*Nuclear energy*] (NRCH)
RPT............	Reference Point Tracking
RPT............	Registered Physical Therapist
RPT............	Regular Public Transport (ADA)
RPT............	Relative Prime Transform
RPT............	Repair Parts Transporter (MCD)
RPT............	Repeat (AAG)
RPT............	Reply Paid Telegram
RPT............	Report
RPT............	Reprint
RPT............	Request Programs Termination [*Data processing*]
RPT............	Resident Provisioning Team [*NASA*]
R & PT	Rifle and Pistol Team [*Navy*]
RPT............	Rocket-Powered Target
RPT............	Rocket Propulsion Technician [*Air Force*]
RPT............	Rotary Power Transformer
RPT............	Rudder Pedal Transducer (NASA)
RPTA........	Rudder Pedal Transducer Assembly (NASA)
RPTC........	Repeating Coil (MSA)
RPTD........	Repeated
RPTD........	Reported
RPTD........	Ruptured
RPTEA	Reviews of Petroleum Technology [*A publication*]
RPTF........	Republican Presidential Task Force (EA)
RPTF........	Rotatable Porro-Mirror Test Fixture
RPTGA......	Rocznik Polskiego Towarzystwa Geologicznego [*A publication*]
RPTL........	Real Property Tax Law [*New York, NY*] [*A publication*]
RPTLC......	Reverse Phase Thin-Layer Chromatography
RPTN........	Repetition (AAG)
RPTOW....	Rocznik Polskiego Towarzystwa [*A publication*]
RPTR........	Repeater (MSA)
RPU	RADAR Prediction Uncertainty
RPU	Radio Phone Unit [*Navy*]
RPU	Radio Propagation Unit [*Army*] (MCD)
RPU	Railway Patrolmen's International Union [*Later, BRAC*] (EA)
RPu	Rassegna Pugliese [*A publication*]
RPU	Receiver Processor Unit [*Electronics*]
RPU	Rectifier Power Unit
RPU	Regional Planning Unit (OICC)
RPU	Regional Processing Unit
RPU	Registered Publication Unit
RPU	Remote Pickup Unit
RPU	Remote Processing Unit (KSC)
RPU	Retention Pending Use [*Air Force*]
RPU	Rhone-Poulenc (Unit) [*NYSE symbol*] (SPSG)
RPUA	Aparri, Cagayan [*Philippines*] [*ICAO location identifier*] (ICLI)
RPUB........	Baguio, Benguet [*Philippines*] [*ICAO location identifier*] (ICLI)
R Public Data Use ...	Review of Public Data Use [*A publication*]
RPUC	Cabanatuan, Nueva Ecija [*Philippines*] [*ICAO location identifier*] (ICLI)
RPUC	Reprint under Consideration [*Publishing*]
RPUD	Daet, Camarines Norte [*Philippines*] [*ICAO location identifier*] (ICLI)
RPUE........	Lucena, Quezon [*Philippines*] [*ICAO location identifier*] (ICLI)
RPUF........	Floridablanca Air Base, Pampanga [*Philippines*] [*ICAO location identifier*] (ICLI)
RPUG	Lingayen, Pangasinan [*Philippines*] [*ICAO location identifier*] (ICLI)
RPUH	San Jose, Occidental Mindoro [*Philippines*] [*ICAO location identifier*] (ICLI)
RPUI..........	Iba, Zambales [*Philippines*] [*ICAO location identifier*] (ICLI)
RPUJ	Castillejos, Zambales [*Philippines*] [*ICAO location identifier*] (ICLI)
RPUK	Calapan, Oriental Mindoro [*Philippines*] [*ICAO location identifier*] (ICLI)
RPUL.........	Lipa/Fernando Air Base, Batangas [*Philippines*] [*ICAO location identifier*] (ICLI)
RPUM	Mamburao, Occidental Mindoro [*Philippines*] [*ICAO location identifier*] (ICLI)
RPUN	Naga, Camarines Sur [*Philippines*] [*ICAO location identifier*] (ICLI)
RPUO	Basco, Batanes Island [*Philippines*] [*ICAO location identifier*] (ICLI)
RPUP........	Jose Panganiban/PIM, Camarines Norte [*Philippines*] [*ICAO location identifier*] (ICLI)
RPUQ	Vigan, Ilocos Sur [*Philippines*] [*ICAO location identifier*] (ICLI)
RPUR	Baler, Aurora Sub-Province [*Philippines*] [*ICAO location identifier*] (ICLI)
RPUS.........	San Fernando, La Union [*Philippines*] [*ICAO location identifier*] (ICLI)
RPUSSR....	Research Program of the USSR. New York Series [*A publication*]
RPUT.........	Tuguegarao, Cagayan [*Philippines*] [*ICAO location identifier*] (ICLI)
RPUU	Bulan, Sorsogon [*Philippines*] [*ICAO location identifier*] (ICLI)
RPUV	Virac, Catanduanes [*Philippines*] [*ICAO location identifier*] (ICLI)
RPUW	Marinduque/Gasan, Marinduque [*Philippines*] [*ICAO location identifier*] (ICLI)

RPUX .... Plaridel, Bulacan [*Philippines*] [*ICAO location identifier*] (ICLI)
RPUY .... Cauayan, Isabela [*Philippines*] [*ICAO location identifier*] (ICLI)
RPUZ .... Bagabag, Neuva Viscaya [*Philippines*] [*ICAO location identifier*] (ICLI)
RPV .... Reactor Pressure Vessel [*Nuclear energy*] (NRCH)
RPV .... Real Program Value (CAAL)
RPV .... Recorder Processor Viewer
RPV .... Reduced Product Verification [*DoD*]
RPV .... Remote Positioning Valve
RPV .... Remotely Piloted Vehicle [*Aircraft*]
RPV .... Residual Pressure Valve [*Automotive engineering*]
RPV .... Rhopalosiphum padi Virus
RPV .... Right Pulmonary Vein [*Medicine*]
RPV .... Rinderpest Virus
RPV .... United States Veterans Administration Hospital, Davis Park, Providence, RI [*Library symbol*] [*Library of Congress*] (LCLS)
RPVA .... Tacloban/Daniel Z. Romualdez, Leyte [*Philippines*] [*ICAO location identifier*] (ICLI)
RPVB .... Bacolod, Negros Occidental [*Philippines*] [*ICAO location identifier*] (ICLI)
RPVC .... Calbayog, Western Samar [*Philippines*] [*ICAO location identifier*] (ICLI)
RPVD .... Dumaguete/Sibulan Negros Oriental [*Philippines*] [*ICAO location identifier*] (ICLI)
RPVE .... Caticlan, Aklan [*Philippines*] [*ICAO location identifier*] (ICLI)
RPVF .... Catarman, Northern Samar [*Philippines*] [*ICAO location identifier*] (ICLI)
RPVG .... Guiuan, Eastern Samar [*Philippines*] [*ICAO location identifier*] (ICLI)
RPVH .... Hilongos, Leyte Del Norte [*Philippines*] [*ICAO location identifier*] (ICLI)
RPVI .... Iloilo, Iloilo [*Philippines*] [*ICAO location identifier*] (ICLI)
RPVI-AIAF ... Remotely Piloted Vehicle Investigation - Adjustment of Indirect Artillery Fire
RPVI-ES.... Remotely Piloted Vehicle Investigation - Emerging Sensors (MCD)
RPVIO....... Registered Publication Van Issuing Office [*Military*] (NVT)
RPVK....... Kalibo, Aklan [*Philippines*] [*ICAO location identifier*] (ICLI)
RPVL........ Roxas/Del Pilar, Palawan [*Philippines*] [*ICAO location identifier*] (ICLI)
RPVM .... Masbate [*Philippines*] [*ICAO location identifier*] (ICLI)
RPVN .... Medellin, Cebu [*Philippines*] [*ICAO location identifier*] (ICLI)
RPVNTV... Rust Preventative
RPVO .... Ormoc, Leyte [*Philippines*] [*ICAO location identifier*] (ICLI)
RPVP........ Puerto Princesa, Palawan [*Philippines*] [*ICAO location identifier*] (ICLI)
RPVR........ Roxas, Capiz [*Philippines*] [*ICAO location identifier*] (ICLI)
RPVS .... San Jose De Buenavista/Antique [*Philippines*] [*ICAO location identifier*] (ICLI)
RPVT........ Relative Position Velocity Technique
RPVT........ Tagbilaran, Bohol [*Philippines*] [*ICAO location identifier*] (ICLI)
RPVX........ Remote-Piloted Vehicle Experiment
RPW .... Rawle, Penrose, and Watts' Pennsylvania Reports [*1828-40*] [*A publication*] (DLA)
RP & W...... Rawle, Penrose, and Watts' Pennsylvania Reports [*1828-40*] [*A publication*] (DLA)
RPW .... Resistance Projection Welding [*Manufacturing term*]
RPWA .... Surallah/Allah Valley, Cotabato (South) [*Philippines*] [*ICAO location identifier*] (ICLI)
RPWB........ Buayan/General Santos, Cotabato (South) [*Philippines*] [*ICAO location identifier*] (ICLI)
RPWC........ Cotabato, North Cotabato [*Philippines*] [*ICAO location identifier*] (ICLI)
RPWD .... Davao/Francisco Bangoy International [*Philippines*] [*ICAO location identifier*] (ICLI)
RPWDA ..... Retail Paint and Wallpaper Distributors of America [*Later, NDPA*]
RPWE........ Butuan, Agusan [*Philippines*] [*ICAO location identifier*] (ICLI)
RPWG .... Dipolog, Zamboanga Del Norte [*Philippines*] [*ICAO location identifier*] (ICLI)
RPWI........ Ozamis, Misamis Oriental [*Philippines*] [*ICAO location identifier*] (ICLI)
RPWJ .... Jolo, Sulu [*Philippines*] [*ICAO location identifier*] (ICLI)
RPWK........ Tacurong/Kenram, Cotabato [*Philippines*] [*ICAO location identifier*] (ICLI)
RPWL........ Cagayan De Oro, Misamis Oriental [*Philippines*] [*ICAO location identifier*] (ICLI)
RPWM ...... Malabang, Lanao Del Sur [*Philippines*] [*ICAO location identifier*] (ICLI)
RPWN ...... Bongao/Sanga-Sanga, Sulu [*Philippines*] [*ICAO location identifier*] (ICLI)
RPWP........ Pagadian, Zamboanga Del Sur [*Philippines*] [*ICAO location identifier*] (ICLI)
RPWS........ Surigao, Surigao Del Norte [*Philippines*] [*ICAO location identifier*] (ICLI)

RPWT........ Del Monte, Bukidnon [*Philippines*] [*ICAO location identifier*] (ICLI)
RPWV........ Buenavista, Agusan [*Philippines*] [*ICAO location identifier*] (ICLI)
RPWW ...... Tandag, Surigao Del Sur [*Philippines*] [*ICAO location identifier*] (ICLI)
RPWX........ Iligan, Lanao Del Norte [*Philippines*] [*ICAO location identifier*] (ICLI)
RPWY........ Malaybalay, Bukidon [*Philippines*] [*ICAO location identifier*] (ICLI)
RPWZ........ Bislig, Surigao Del Sur [*Philippines*] [*ICAO location identifier*] (ICLI)
RPX .... Roundup, MT [*Location identifier*] [*FAA*] (FAAL)
RPXC........ Tarlac (Crow Valley) [*Philippines*] [*ICAO location identifier*] (ICLI)
RPXG........ Lubang, Occidental Mindoro [*Philippines*] [*ICAO location identifier*] (ICLI)
RPXI .... Itbayat, Batanes [*Philippines*] [*ICAO location identifier*] (ICLI)
RPXJ .... Jomalig, Quezon [*Philippines*] [*ICAO location identifier*] (ICLI)
RPXM........ Fort Magsaysay, Nueva Ecija [*Philippines*] [*ICAO location identifier*] (ICLI)
RPXP........ Poro Point, La Union [*Philippines*] [*ICAO location identifier*] (ICLI)
RPXR........ Corregidor, Cavite [*Philippines*] [*ICAO location identifier*] (ICLI)
RPXT........ Alabat, Quezon [*Philippines*] [*ICAO location identifier*] (ICLI)
RPXU .... Sorsogon, Sorsogon [*Philippines*] [*ICAO location identifier*] (ICLI)
RPY .... Blythe, CA [*Location identifier*] [*FAA*] (FAAL)
RPY .... Roll, Pitch, and Yaw
RPZ........... Rada Pomocy Zydom [*A publication*]
RPZDA ..... Regelungstechnik und Prozess-Datenverarbeitung [*A publication*]
RPZHA ..... Roczniki Panstwowego Zakladu Higieny [*A publication*]
RQ............. Arab Wing Nigeria Ltd. [*Nigeria*] [*ICAO designator*] (FAAC)
RQ............. RASD Quarterly [*American Library Association*] [*A publication*]
RQ............. Recovery Quotient
RQ............. Reference Quarterly [*A publication*]
RQ............. Renaissance Quarterly [*A publication*]
RQ............. Reportable Quantity [*Hazardous substance emergency response*]
RQ............. Request (FAAC)
R/Q........... Request for Quotation (AAG)
R/Q........... Resolver/Quantizer (IEEE)
RQ............. Respiratory Quotient [*Also, Q*] [*Physiology*]
RQ............. Restoration Quarterly [*A publication*]
RQ............. Revue des Questions Historiques [*A publication*]
RQ............. Revue de Qumran [*A publication*]
RQ............. Riverside Quarterly [*A publication*]
RQ............. Roemische Quartalschrift fuer Christliche Altertumskunde und fuer Kirchengeschichte [*A publication*]
RQ............. RQ. Reference Quarterly [*American Library Association. Reference Services Division*] [*A publication*]
RQA........... Recursive Queue Analyzer (IEEE)
R & QA ..... Reliability and Quality Assurance
RQA........... Roemische Quartalschrift fuer Christliche Altertumskunde und fuer Kirchengeschichte [*A publication*]
RQAC .... Royal Queensland Aero Club [*Australia*]
RQAHA.... Research Quarterly. American Association for Health, Physical Education, and Recreation [*A publication*]
RQAK........ Roemische Quartalschrift fuer Christliche Altertumskunde und fuer Kirchengeschichte [*A publication*]
RQAO........ Reliability and Quality Assurance Office [*NASA*]
RQAS .... Royal Queensland Art Society [*Australia*]
RQC........... RADAR Quality Control
RQC........... Reliability and Quality Control (MCD)
RQCAK .... Roemische Quartalschrift fuer Christliche Altertumskunde und fuer Kirchengeschichte [*A publication*]
RQCAKG .. Roemische Quartalschrift fuer Christliche Altertumskunde und fuer Kirchengeschichte [*A publication*]
R Q Ch A K ... Roemische Quartalschrift fuer Christliche Altertumskunde und fuer Kirchengeschichte [*A publication*]
RQCL .... Request Clearance [*Aviation*] (FAAC)
RQD.......... Raised Quarter Deck [*of a ship*] (DS)
RQD.......... Rock Quality Designation [*Nuclear energy*] (NRCH)
RQDCZ ..... Request Clearance to Depart Control Zone [*Aviation*] (FAAC)
RQDP........ Request, Quandary and Deferment Plan
RQECZ ..... Request Clearance to Enter Control Zone [*Aviation*] (FAAC)
RQH .... Revue des Questions Historiques [*A publication*]
RQHist ...... Revue des Questions Historiques [*A publication*]
RQIAC....... Requires Immediate Action (NOAA)
RQIRA....... Revista de Quimica Industrial (Rio De Janeiro) [*A publication*]
RQK........... Roemische Quartalschrift fuer Kirchengeschichte [*A publication*]
RQL........... Reference Quality Level (IEEE)
RQL........... Rejectable Quality Level
RQMC....... Regimental Quartermaster-Corporal [*British*]

RQMD.......	Richmond Quartermaster Depot [*Virginia*] [*Merged with Defense General Supply Center*]
RQMS	Regimental Quartermaster-Sergeant [*British*]
RQMT.......	Requirement (AFM)
RQN..........	Radial Quantum Number
RQN..........	Requisition (AFM)
RQO..........	River Quality Objective [*British*] (DCTA)
RQP	Request Permission (FAAC)
RQP	Resistor Qualification Program
RQPAA	Revista de Investigaciones Agropecuarias. Serie 4. Patologia Animal [*A publication*]
RQQPRI....	Recommended Qualitative and Quantitative Personnel Requirements Information [*Military*] (MCD)
RQR..........	Require (AAG)
RQRD.......	Required
RQRP	Request Reply (FAAC)
RQS	Rate Quoting System
RQS	Ready Qualified for Standby [*Military*]
RQS	Request Supplementary Flight Plan Message [*Aviation code*]
RQS	Revue des Questions Scientifiques [*A publication*]
RQS	River Quality Standard [*British*] (DCTA)
RQS	Roemische Quartalschrift fuer Christliche Altertumskunde und fuer Kirchengeschichte [*A publication*]
RQT	Reenlistment Qualification Test [*Military*] (MCD)
RQT	Reliability Qualification Test (CAAL)
RQT	Resistor Qualification Test
RQTAO	Request Time and Altitude Over [*Aviation*] (FAAC)
RQTO.......	Request Travel Order (NOAA)
RQTP	Resistor Qualification Test Program
R/QTR......	Rear Quarter [*Automotive engineering*]
RQTS........	Requirements (KSC)
RQTV	Requirements Volatility
RQu	Revue de Qumran [*A publication*]
R QUM.....	Revue de Qumran [*A publication*]
RQUS	Remote Query Update System [*Data processing*]
RQY..........	Elkins, WV [*Location identifier*] [*FAA*] (FAAL)
RQY..........	Relative Quantum Yield
RQZ..........	Huntsville, AL [*Location identifier*] [*FAA*] (FAAL)
RR..............	Naval Research Reviews [*A publication*]
RR..............	Pike and Fischer's Radio Regulations [*A publication*] (DLA)
RR..............	RADAR Range Station (FAAC)
RR..............	Radiation Reaction [*Cells*] [*Medicine*]
RR..............	Radiation Response
RR..............	Radiation Retinopathy [*Ophthalmology*]
R/R............	Radio and RADAR
RR..............	Radio Range
RR..............	Radio Recognition
RR..............	Radio Regulations
RR..............	Radio Relay (CINC)
RR..............	Radio Research
RR..............	Radioreceptor [*Assay method*] [*Clinical chemistry*]
RR..............	RAF-1 Group [*Air Transport*] [*Great Britain*] [*ICAO designator*] (FAAC)
RR..............	Railroad
RR..............	Rand Rifles [*British military*] (DMA)
RR..............	Range Rate (NASA)
RR..............	Rapid Rectilinear
RR..............	Rarely Reversed [*Decisions in law*]
RR..............	Rarissime [*Very Rare*]
RR..............	Raritan River Rail Road Co. [*AAR code*]
RR..............	Rate Ratio
RR..............	Rate Rebate [*British*]
R & R	Rate and Rhythm [*of pulse*]
RR..............	Rattus Rattus [*The ship or black rat*]
RR..............	Readiness Region [*Military*]
RR..............	Readiness Review (KSC)
RR..............	Readout and Relay
RR..............	Ready Reference
RR..............	Rear (AABC)
RR..............	Receive Ready [*Data processing*] (IEEE)
RR..............	Receiver Room [*Navy*] (CAAL)
RR..............	Receiving Report (AAG)
RR..............	Recipient Rights
RR..............	Recoilless Rifle
RR..............	Recommended for Re-Engagement [*British*]
RR..............	Record Rarities [*Record label*]
RR..............	Record Research [*A publication*]
R/R............	Record/Retirement
R/R............	Record/Retransmit (IEEE)
RR..............	Record Review [*A publication*]
RR..............	Records and Recording [*A publication*]
R & R	Records and Reports
RR..............	Recovery Reliability (MCD)
RR..............	Recovery Room
RR..............	Recruit Roll [*Navy*]
RR..............	Recurrence Rate
RR..............	Rediscount Rate
RR..............	Redstone Resources, Inc. [*Toronto Stock Exchange symbol*]
RRu...........	Redundancy Reduction (AAG)
RR..............	Reentry Range
RR..............	Reference Register [*Data processing*]
RR..............	Reflectors [*JETDS nomenclature*] [*Military*] (CET)
RR..............	Reformed Review [*A publication*]
R & R	Refueling and Rearming [*Air Force*]
RR..............	Regional Railroad
RR..............	Register to Register (MCD)
RR..............	Registered Representative [*Wall Street stock salesman*]
R & R	Regurgitate and Reingest [*Animal behavior*]
RR..............	Rehabilitation Record
R & R	Reinstatement and Replacement (ADA)
RR..............	Relative Rank
RR..............	Relative Response
RR..............	Relative Risk [*Medicine*]
RR..............	Relay Rack [*Telecommunications*] (TEL)
RR..............	Relief Radii (MSA)
RR..............	Religious Roundtable (EA)
RR..............	Removal-Replacement
R & R	Remove and Replace (KSC)
RR..............	Rendezvous RADAR [*NASA*]
R & R	Rendezvous and Recovery (NASA)
RR..............	Renegotiation Regulations
RR..............	Rent Regulation (Office of Rent Stabilization) [*Economic Stabilization Agency*] [*A publication*] (DLA)
R/R............	Repair/Rebuild (MCD)
R/R............	Repair or Replacement
R & R	Repair and Return
RR..............	Repeatedly Reactive
RR..............	Repetition Rate
RR..............	Report Immediately upon Reaching [*Aviation*] (FAAC)
R & R	Reporting and Requisitioning [*Air Force*]
RR..............	Required Reserves
RR..............	Requirements Review [*NASA*] (NASA)
RR..............	Reroute [*Telecommunications*] (TEL)
RR..............	Research Report
R & R	Research and Reporting Committee [*Interstate Conference of Employment Security Agencies*] (OICC)
RR..............	Reservatis Reservandis [*With All Reserve*] [*Latin*]
RR..............	Reserve Regiment [*British military*] (DMA)
RR..............	Resonance Raman
RR..............	Resource Report
RR..............	Respiratory Rate [*Medicine*]
RR..............	Responsible Receiver
R & R	Rest and Recreation
R & R	Rest and Recuperation [*Military*]
R & R	Rest and Rehabilitation [*Marine Corps*]
RR..............	Retired Reserve [*Military*]
RR..............	Retro-Rocket [*Army*] (AABC)
RR..............	Return Rate (IEEE)
RR..............	Return Register
RR..............	Revenue Release [*A publication*] (DLA)
RR..............	Reverse Recovery [*Electronics*]
RR..............	Reverse Reduction (DS)
RR..............	Review of Religion [*A publication*]
RR..............	Review for Religious [*A publication*]
RR..............	Review of Reviews [*London*] [*A publication*]
RR..............	Revised Reports [*Legal*] [*British*]
RR..............	Revision Record (MSA)
RR..............	Rhodesia Regiment [*British military*] (DMA)
RR..............	Rhymney Railway [*Wales*]
RR..............	Ricerche Religiose [*A publication*]
R & R	Rich & Rare Canadian Whisky [*Gooderham's*]
RR..............	Ridge Regression [*Statistics*]
RR..............	Rifle Range
RR..............	Right Rear
RR..............	Right Reverend [*Of an abbot, bishop, or monsignor*]
RR..............	Rights Reserved
RR..............	Rigid-Rotor [*Calculations*]
RR..............	Risk Ratio
R & R	Rock and Roll [*Music*]
R & R	Rock and Rye
RR..............	Rodman & Renshaw Capital Group [*NYSE symbol*] (SPSG)
RR..............	Roemische Religions-Geschichte [*A publication*] (OCD)
RR..............	Roll Radius (MCD)
RR..............	Roll Roofing (AAG)
RR..............	Rolls-Royce [*Automobile*]
RR..............	Romanic Review [*A publication*]
RR..............	Ronald Reagan [*US president, 1911-*]
RR..............	Root Rot [*Plant pathology*]
RR..............	Rough Riders [*The City of London Yeomanry*] [*Military unit*] [*British*]
RR..............	Round Robin (IEEE)
RR..............	Routine Relay (KSC)
R & R	Routing and Record Sheet [*Air Force*]
RR..............	Rumanian Register of Shipping (DS)
RR..............	Running Reverse
RR..............	Rural Resident (OICC)
RR..............	Rural Route
RR..............	Rush Release
R & R	Russell and Ryan's English Crown Cases [*A publication*] (DLA)
RR..............	Very Rare [*Numismatics*]
R of R's	Review of Reviews [*A publication*]

RRA .... Dallas-Fort Worth, TX [*Location identifier*] [*FAA*]   (FAAL)
RRA .... Race Relations Act [*1976*] [*British*]   (DCTA)
RRA .... Radiation Research Associates, Inc.   (NRCH)
RRA .... Radio Relay Aircraft   (CET)
RRA .... Radioreceptor Assay [*Clinical chemistry*]
RRA .... RAM [*Reliability, Availability, and Maintainablity*] Rationale Annex [*Army*]
RRA .... Ranger Regimental Association   (EA)
RRA .... Record Retention Agreement [*IRS*]
RRA .... Redmond, R. A., Los Angeles CA [*STAC*]
RRA .... Registered Record Administrator [*American Medical Record Association*] [*Medicine*]
RRA .... Religious Research Association   (EA)
RRA .... Remote Record Address
RRA .... Reserve Recognition Accounting [*Securities and Exchange Commission*]
RRA .... Resident Research Associate
R & RA ...... Retraining and Reemployment Administration [*Terminated, 1947*]
RRA .... Review of Reviews [*United States*] [*A publication*]
RRA .... Rubber Reclaimers Association [*Later, NARI*]   (EA)
RRA .... Rubber Recyclers Association   (EA)
RRAC .... Race Relations Advisory Committee [*Trades Union Congress*] [*British*]   (DCTA)
RRAC .... Reactor Review and Audit Committee [*Oak Ridge National Laboratory*]
RRAC .... Regional Resources Advisory Committee [*Army*]   (AABC)
RR et AC.... Rosea Rubeae et Aureae Crucis [*The Order of the Rose of Ruby and the Cross of Gold*]
RRACD ..... Ciencia e Cultura (Sao Paulo). Suplemento [*A publication*]
RRAD .... Red River Army Depot [*Texas*]   (AABC)
RRAD .... Roll Ratio Adjust Device   (MCD)
R Radical Pol Econ ... Review of Radical Political Economics [*A publication*]
R Radic Polit Econ ... Review of Radical Political Economics [*A publication*]
R Rad Pol Econ ... Review of Radical Political Economics [*A publication*]
RRAEA...... Rendiconti. Riunione Annuale. Associazione Elettrotecnica Italiana [*A publication*]
RRAF........ Ready Reserve of the Armed Forces
RRAF........ Royal Rhodesian Air Force
RRALA...... Radiochemical and Radioanalytical Letters [*A publication*]
RRAP........ Residential Rehabilitation Assistance Program [*Canada*]
RRAR .... ROM Return Address Register
RRB .... R. R. Bowker Co. [*Publisher*]
RRB .... RAAF [*Royal Australian Air Force*] Radio Butterworth
RRB .... RADAR Reflective Balloon
RRB .... Radio Research Board   (DEN)
RRB .... Railroad Retirement Board
RRB .... Regular Reenlistment Bonus [*Military*]
RRB .... Rubber Reserve Board [*of the Reconstruction Finance Corp.*]
RRBBA...... Revue Roumaine de Biologie. Serie Botanique [*A publication*]
RRBC........ Rat Red Blood Cell
RRBFC ...... Red River Boys Fan Club [*Inactive*]   (EA)
RRBLB ...... United States Railroad Retirement Board. Law Bulletin [*A publication*]   (DLA)
RRBN .... Round Robin   (FAAC)
RRBODI.... Brazilian Journal of Botany [*A publication*]
RRB Q Rev ... RRB [*Railroad Retirement Board*] Quarterly Review [*A publication*]
RRB (Railroad Retirement Bd) Q R ... RRB (Railroad Retirement Board) Quarterly Review [*A publication*]
RRBVD...... Revue Roumaine de Biologie. Serie Biologie Vegetale [*A publication*]
RRBZA ..... Revue Roumaine de Biologie. Serie Zoologie [*A publication*]
RRC .... RADAR Return Code
RRC .... Radiation Recorder Controller   (NRCH)
RRC .... Radiation Resistance Cable
RRC .... Radio Receptor Company
RRC .... Radio Relay Center   (NATG)
RRC .... Radio Research Company
RRC .... Railroad Record Club [*Commercial firm*]   (EA)
RRC .... Rainy River Community College, International Falls, MN [*OCLC symbol*]   (OCLC)
RRC .... Ravenroc Resources Ltd. [*Vancouver Stock Exchange symbol*]
RRC .... Reactor Recirculation Cooling [*Nuclear energy*]   (NRCH)
R & RC....... Reactors and Reactor Control   (MCD)
RRC .... Receiving Report Change   (AAG)
RRC .... Reconstructionist Rabbinical College [*Pennsylvania*]
RR & C........ Records, Reports, and Control   (AFM)
RRC .... Recreation Resources Center [*University of Wisconsin*] [*Research center*]   (RCD)
RRC .... Recruit Reception Center
RRC .... Red River Community College [*UTLAS symbol*]
RRC .... Reentry Rate Command [*NASA*]
RRC .... Refractories Research Center [*Ohio State University*] [*Research center*]   (RCD)
RRC .... Refugee Resource Center [*Defunct*]   (EA)
RRC .... Regional Resource Center
RRC .... Regional Review Consultants [*American Occupational Therapy Association*]
RRC .... Regular Route Carrier
R/RC.......... Removal/Recertification

RRC .... Report Review Committee [*National Academy of Sciences*]
RRC .... Reports of Rating Cases [*Legal*] [*British*]
RRC .... Requirements Review Committee [*Navy*]
RRC .... Research Registration Centre [*Australia*]
RRC .... Research Resources Center [*University of Illinois at Chicago*] [*Research center*]   (RCD)
RRC .... Residency Review Committee [*Medicine*]
RRC .... Resuscitation Research Center [*University of Pittsburgh*] [*Research center*]   (RCD)
RRC .... Retrograde River Crossing   (MCD)
RRC .... Retrovirus Research Center [*Veterans Administration Medical Center*] [*Baltimore, MD*]
RRC .... Rheology Research Center [*University of Wisconsin - Madison*] [*Research center*]   (RCD)
RRC .... Rigid Raiding Craft [*British military*]   (DMA)
RRC .... Road Runners Club of America
RRC .... Rocket Research Corporation   (MCD)
RRC .... Rodale Research Center [*Horticulture*]
RRC .... Roll Ratio Controller   (MCD)
RRC .... Rollin' Rock Club   (EA)
RRC .... Roof Research Center [*Oak Ridge, TN*] [*Oak Ridge National Laboratory*] [*Department of Energy*]   (GRD)
RRC .... Routine Respiratory Care [*Medicine*]
RRC .... Royal Red Cross [*British*]
RRC .... Rubber Reserve Committee [*Navy*]
RRC .... Rubber Reserve Company [*Dissolved, 1935, functions transferred to Reconstruction Finance Corporation*]
RRC .... Rural Referral Center [*Health care*]
RRC .... Russell Research Center [*Department of Agriculture*]
RRC .... Russian Research Center [*Harvard University*] [*Research center*]   (RCD)
RRC .... Ryde's Rating Cases [*A publication*]   (DLA)
RRCA .... Rhinelander Rabbit Club of America   (EA)
RRCA .... Road Runners Club of America   (EA)
RR & Can Cas ... Railway and Canal Cases [*England*] [*A publication*]   (DLA)
RRCC........ Reduced Rate Contribution Clause [*Insurance*]
R & RCC .... Russell and Ryan's English Crown Cases Reserved [*A publication*]   (DLA)
RRCCC...... Regional Recreation and Conservation Consultative Committee [*Thames Water Authority*] [*British*]
RRCEF ...... Redwood Records Cultural and Educational Fund   (EA)
RRCEM..... Residency Review Committee for Emergency Medicine   (EA)
RRCGDX... Australia. Commonwealth Scientific and Industrial Research Organisation. Division of Animal Genetics. Research Report [*A publication*]
RRCHA ..... Revue Roumaine de Chimie [*A publication*]
RRCM .... Roberts Radio Current Meter   (NOAA)
RRCN .... Receiving Report Change Notice   (AAG)
RR & Cn Cas ... Railway and Canal Cases [*1835-54*] [*A publication*]   (DLA)
RRCO .... Radio Research Coordination Officer [*Air Force*]
RRCO .... Royal Resources Corporation [*NASDAQ symbol*]   (NQ)
RRCOD ..... Resource Recovery and Conservation [*A publication*]
RRCOTAAOSOCOTWAOS ... Rollin' Rock Club of Texas and Any Other State or Country of the World and Outer Space
RRCRB...... Recent Results in Cancer Research [*A publication*]
RR Cr R ..... Revised Reports, Criminal Rulings [*1862-75*] [*India*] [*A publication*]   (DLA)
RRCS .... Railroad Communication System
RRCS .... Reentry RADAR Cross Section
RRCS......... Revenue Receipts Control Sheets [*IRS*]
RRCU .... Remote Range Control Unit   (MCD)
RRCUS...... Rhodesian Ridgeback Club of the US   (EA)
RRCVR...... Remote Receiver   (FAAC)
RRD .... Reactor Radiation Division [*National Institute of Standards and Technology*]
RRD .... Reactor Research and Development
RRD .... Receive, Record, Display
RRD .... Reliability Requirements Directive
RR & D .... Reparations, Removal, and Demolition [*Section*] [*Industry Branch, US Military Government, Germany*]
RRD .... Replacement Regulating Detachment [*Army*]
RRD .... Requisition Received Date [*Bell System*]   (TEL)
RRD .... Resonant Reed Decoder
RRD .... Retendering Receipt Day   (NRCH)
RRD .... Roosevelt Roads [*Puerto Rico*] [*Seismograph station code, US Geological Survey*]   (SEIS)
RRD .... Route/Route Destination [*Telecommunications*]   (TEL)
RRDA .... Rendezvous Retrieval, Docking, and Assembly [*of space vehicle or orbital station*] [*NASA*]   (AAG)
RRDA .... Repetitive Report Distribution Audit   (AAG)
RRDB .... Research Results Data Base [*Department of Agriculture*] [*Information service or system*]   (IID)
RRDE .... Radio Research and Development Establishment   (MCD)
RRDE .... Rotating Ring Disk Electrode
RRDECA.... Roy Rogers - Dale Evans Collectors Association   (EA)
RRDFCS.... Redundant Reconfigurable Digital Flight Control System   (MCD)
RRDO........ Register of Rivers Discharging into the Oceans [*United Nations Environment Programme*]   (MSC)
RRDR .... Raw RADAR Data Recorder
RRDS......... Regents Renaissance Drama Series [*A publication*]

RRDS......... Relative Record Data Set
RRDU........ Recreation Research Demonstration Unit   (RDA)
RRE .... Marree [*Australia*] [*Airport symbol*] [*Obsolete*]   (OAG)
RRE .... RADAR Research Establishment [*British*]
R & RE...... Radiation and Repair Engineering [*Nuclear energy*]   (NRCH)
RRE .... Railroad Enthusiasts   (EA)
RRE .... Range Rate Error
RRE .... Ras Responsive Element [*Genetics*]
RRE .... Receive Reference Equivalent [*Telecommunications*]   (TEL)
RRE .... Reg Resources Corp. [*Vancouver Stock Exchange symbol*]
RRE .... Review of Regional Economics and Business [*A publication*]
RRE .... Rolls-Royce Enthusiasts   (EA)
RR & E...... Round, Regular, and Equal [*With reference to pupils of eyes*]
RRE .... Royal RADAR Establishment [*British*] [*Research center*]
RREA........ Rendezvous RADAR Electronics Assembly [*NASA*]   (MCD)
RREAS..... Race Relations Employment Advisory Service [*British*]
RREC........ Reading Research and Education Center [*Champaign, IL*]
                [*Department of Education*]   (GRD)
RREC........ Rehabilitation Record
RREC........ Rice Research and Extension Center [*University of Arkansas*]
                [*Research center*]   (RCD)
R Regional Econ and Bus ... Review of Regional Economics and Business [*A
                publication*]
RRel .... Review of Religion [*A publication*]
R Rel .... Review for Religious [*A publication*]
R of Religion ... Review of Religion [*A publication*]
R Relig Res ... Review of Religious Research [*A publication*]
R Rel Res ... Review of Religious Research [*A publication*]
RRENA ..... Revue Roumaine d'Endocrinologie [*A publication*]
RR/EO....... Race Relations/Equal Opportunity [*Military*]   (AABC)
RRep .... Records Repository [*Air Force*]   (AFM)
RRERD....... Resource Recovery and Energy Review [*A publication*]
RRESA ...... Rastitel'nye Resursy [*A publication*]
R Rest DS .. Regents Restoration Drama Series [*A publication*]
RRET........ Rainier Realty Investors [*Seattle, WA*] [*NASDAQ
                symbol*]   (NQ)
RRETA...... Reports. Research Institute of Electrical Communication.
                Tohoku University [*A publication*]
RREU .... Rendezvous RADAR Electronics Unit [*NASA*]   (MCD)
RRev .... Records Review [*Air Force*]   (AFM)
RRev .... Rijecka Revija [*A publication*]
RREVA ...... Residue Reviews [*A publication*]
RRF............ Racing Research Fund [*Defunct*]   (EA)
RRF............ Ragged Red Fibers [*Muscle pathology*]
RRF............ Rapid Reaction Forces [*Army*]   (AABC)
RRF............ Raptor Research Foundation   (EA)
RRF............ Reading Reform Foundation   (EA)
RRF............ Ready Reserve Fleet
RRF............ Ready Reserve Force [*Military*]
RRF............ Realty Refund Trust SBI [*NYSE symbol*]   (SPSG)
RRF............ Reconnaissance Reporting Facility
RRF............ Red Resistance Front [*Netherlands*]
RRF............ Reed Reactor Facility [*Reed College*] [*Research center*]   (RCD)
RRF............ Rehabilitation Research Foundation   (EA)
RRF............ Resonant Reed Filter
RRF............ Revised Recommended Findings
RRF............ Rift-Rift-Fracture [*Geology*]
RRF............ Riot Relief Fund   (EA)
RRF............ Royal Regiment of Fusiliers [*Military unit*] [*British*]
RRFC........ Rivista Rosminiana di Filosofia e di Cultura [*A publication*]
RRFC........ Robert Redford Fan Club   (EA)
RRFC........ Robin Right Fan Club   (EA)
RRFIA ...... Radiobiologia, Radioterapia, e Fisica Medica [*A publication*]
RRFO .... Rhine River Field Organization [*Post-World War II*]
RRFS .... Range Rate Frequency Synthesizer
RRG .... Point Mugu, CA [*Location identifier*] [*FAA*]   (FAAL)
RRG .... RADAR Range Gate
RRG .... Requirements Review Group [*Air Staff*] [*Air Force*]   (MCD)
RRG .... Research Review Group   (NRCH)
RRG .... Resource Request Generator
RRG .... Rodrigues Island [*Mauritius*] [*Airport symbol*]   (OAG)
RRG .... Roll Reference Gyro   (AAG)
RRGA .... Revue Roumaine de Geologie, Geophysique, et Geographie.
                Serie de Geographie [*Rumania*] [*A publication*]
RRGAB...... Rendiconti Romani di Gastroenterologia [*A publication*]
RRH........... Rural Rental Housing [*Loans*] [*Farmers Home Administration*]
RRHDAC.. Reports on Rheumatic Diseases [*A publication*]
RRHFF...... Rock and Roll Hall of Fame Foundation   (EA)
RRHPF...... Ronald Reagan Home Preservation Foundation   (EA)
RRI .... Barora [*Solomon Islands*] [*Airport symbol*]   (OAG)
RRI .... Radio Republik Indonesia [*Radio network*]
RRI .... Range Rate Indicator
RRI .... Refugee Relief International   (EA)
RRI .... Reimbursement Refund Indicator [*Military*]   (AFIT)
RRI .... Rendezvous RADAR Indicator [*NASA*]   (NASA)
RRI .... Reroute Inhibit [*Telecommunications*]   (TEL)
RRI .... Resident Reactor Inspector [*Nuclear energy*]   (NRCH)
RRI .... Revised Ring Index [*A publication*]
RRI .... Revista/Review Interamericana [*A publication*]
RRI .... Riverside Research Institute   (MCD)
RRI .... Rocket Research Institute

RRI .... Romex Resources, Incorporated [*Vancouver Stock Exchange
                symbol*]
RRIC......... Race Relations Information Center [*Defunct*]
RRIC......... RADAR Repeater Indicator Console
RRIC (Rubber Res Inst Ceylon) Bull ... RRIC (Rubber Research Institute of
                Ceylon) Bulletin [*A publication*]
RRIF......... Registered Retirement Investment Fund [*Canada*]
RRIHS....... Regional Research Institute for Human Services [*Portland State
                University*] [*Research center*]
RRIL.......... Rendiconti. Reale Istituto Lombardo di Scienze e Lettere
                [*Milan*] [*A publication*]
RR-IM .... Office of Research and Reports, Intelligence Memoranda [*CIA*]
RRIM .... Reinforced Reaction Injection Molding [*Plastics technology*]
RRIM .... Rubber Research Institute of Malaysia   (DS)
RRIMA...... Revue Roumaine d'Inframicrobiologie [*A publication*]
RRIN .... Readiness Risk Index Number   (NG)
RRIP .... Rural Research in Progress [*CSIRO*] [*Australia*] [*Information
                service or system*]
RRIPM...... Rapid Response Interference Prediction Model   (MCD)
RRIS .... Radiological Release Information System   (MCD)
RRIS .... Railroad Research Information Service [*National Academy of
                Sciences*] [*Information service or system*]
RRIS .... Remote RADAR Integration Station [*Military*]
RRISL Bull ... RRISL [*Rubber Research Institute of Sri Lanka*] Bulletin [*A
                publication*]
RRI Sri Lanka Bull ... RRISL (Rubber Research Institute of Sri Lanka)
                Bulletin [*A publication*]
RRI & StL ... Rockford, Rock Island & St. Louis Railroad
RRITA .... Report. Research Institute of Science and Technology. Nihon
                University [*A publication*]
R River Plate ... Review of the River Plate [*A publication*]
RRJaNS .... Rodnoj i Russkij Jazyki v Nacional'noj Skole [*A publication*]
RRK .... Redaurum Red Lake Mines Ltd. [*Toronto Stock Exchange
                symbol*]
RRK .... Retaining Ring Kit
RRKM .... Rice, Ramsperger, Kassel, Marcus [*Developers of a theorem in
                chemical kinetics, designated by the initial letters of their
                last names*]
RRL .... Merrill, WI [*Location identifier*] [*FAA*]   (FAAL)
RRL .... Rabbit Reticulocyte Lysate [*Biochemistry*]
RRL .... Radio Relay Link   (NATG)
RRL .... Radio Research Laboratory
RRL .... Ralston Purina Co., Corporate Library, St. Louis, MO [*OCLC
                symbol*]   (OCLC)
RRL .... Ranchmen's Resources Ltd. [*Toronto Stock Exchange symbol*]
RRL .... Rayleigh Radiation Law [*Physics*]
RRL .... Regimental Reserve Line
RRL .... Registered Record Librarian [*Medicine*]
RRL .... Reserve Retired List [*Military*]
RRL .... Revue Roumaine de Linguistique [*A publication*]
RRL .... Road Research Laboratory [*British*]
RRL .... Rocket Research Laboratories   (KSC)
RRL .... Ruby Rod LASER
RRL .... Rudder Reference Line [*NASA*]   (NASA)
RRL .... Runway Remaining Lights [*Aviation*]
RRLC........ Radiation-Resistant Linear Circuit
RRLC........ Redwood Region Logging Conference   (EA)
RRLC........ Rochester Regional Library Council [*Information service or
                system*]   (IID)
RRLR........ Road Race Lincoln Register   (EA)
RRLTD...... Report. Research Laboratory of Engineering Materials. Tokyo
                Institute of Technology [*A publication*]
RRM .... Rate of Return Method [*Insurance*]
RRM .... Rayleigh-Ritz Method [*Physics*]
RRM .... Red Resource Monitoring   (MCD)
RRM .... Reliant Resources Ltd. [*Vancouver Stock Exchange symbol*]
RRM .... Renegotiated-Rate Mortgage
RRM .... Reports, Reviews, Meetings
RRM .... Runaway Rotating Machine
RRMC........ Royal Roads Military College [*Royal Roads, BC*]
RRMF........ RADAR Reflectivity Measuring Facility
RRMG .... Reactor Recirculation Motor Generator   (IEEE)
RRMIA...... Revue Roumaine de Medecine Interne [*Later, Revue Roumaine
                de Medecine. Medecine Interne*] [*A publication*]
RRMN....... Railroadmen's Federal Savings & Loan Association [*NASDAQ
                symbol*]   (NQ)
RRMPB...... Revue Roumaine de Mathematiques Pures et Appliquees [*A
                publication*]
RRMRP.... Ready Reserve Mobilization Reinforcement Pool [*Army*]
RRMRS.... Ready Reserve Mobilization Reinforcement System [*Army*]
RRMTA..... Reactor Materials [*A publication*]
RRN .... Rapid Reinforcement of NATO   (MCD)
RRN .... Relative Record Number [*Data processing*]
RRN .... Running Research News [*A publication*]
RRN .... Serra Norte [*Brazil*] [*Airport symbol*]   (OAG)
rRNA .... Ribonucleic Acid, Ribosomal [*Biochemistry, genetics*]
RRNC........ Ranger Rick's Nature Club   (EA)
RRNGA ..... Razvedka i Razrabotka Neftyanykh i Gazovykh
                Mestorozhdenii [*A publication*]
RRNN........ Reproductive Rights National Network   (EA)
RRNS......... Redundant Residue Number System   (IEEE)

RRNS......... Related Returns Notification System [*IRS*]
RRNUA..... Revue Roumaine de Neurologie [*Later, Revue Roumaine de Medecine. Serie Neurologie et Psychiatrie*] [*A publication*]
RRO.......... Recipient Rights Officer
RRO.......... Regimental Reserve Officer   (ADA)
RRO.......... Renegotiation Regional Office
RRO.......... Responsible Reporting Office [*Telecommunications*]   (TEL)
RRO.......... Richport Resources Ltd. [*Vancouver Stock Exchange symbol*]
RRo.......... Rivista Rosminiana [*A publication*]
RROA........ Railroadians of America   (EA)
RROC....... Rolls-Royce Owners' Club   (EA)
RROO....... Richport Resources Ltd. [*Vancouver, BC*] [*NASDAQ symbol*]   (NQ)
RROS .... Resistive Read-Only Storage
R & ROTC ... Reserve and Reserve Officers' Training Corps [*Army*]
RROU........ Remote Readout Unit
R Roumaine ... Revue Roumaine d'Histoire de l'Art [*A publication*]
R Roumaine Hist ... Revue Roumaine d'Histoire [*A publication*]
R Roumaine Hist Art ... Revue Roumaine d'Histoire de l'Art [*A publication*]
R Roumaine Sciences Socs Ser Sciences Econs ... Revue Roumaine des Sciences Sociales. Serie de Sciences Economiques [*A publication*]
R Roumaine Sciences Socs Ser Sciences Juridiques ... Revue Roumaine des Sciences Sociales. Serie de Sciences Juridiques [*A publication*]
R Roum Et Int ... Revue Roumaine d'Etudes Internationales [*A publication*]
R Roum Hist ... Revue Roumaine d'Histoire [*A publication*]
R Roum Sci Soc ... Revue Roumaine des Sciences Sociales [*A publication*]
R Roum Sci Soc Ser Philos Logique ... Revue Roumaine des Sciences Sociales. Serie de Philosophie et de Logique [*A publication*]
R Roum Sci Soc Ser Sci Econ ... Revue Roumaine des Sciences Sociales. Serie de Sciences Economiques [*A publication*]
R Roum Sci Soc Ser Sci Jur ... Revue Roumaine des Sciences Sociales. Serie de Sciences Juridiques [*A publication*]
R Roum Sci Soc Ser Sociol ... Revue Roumaine des Sciences Sociales. Serie de Sociologie [*A publication*]
RRP .... Radio Relay Pod
RRP .... Range Ring Profile   (MCD)
RRP .... Reactor Refueling Plug   (NRCH)
RRP .... Ready Replacement Pilot
RRP .... Recommended Retail Price
RRP .... Recoverable Repair Parts
RRP .... Regional Project Research Program   (EA)
RRP .... Regular Retail Price
RRP .... Relative Refractory Period [*Medicine*]
RRP .... Relay Rack Panel
RRP .... Religious Requirements and Practices [*A publication*]
RRP .... Republican Reliance Party [*Cumhuriyetci Guven Partisi - CGP*] [*Turkey*] [*Political party*]   (PPW)
RRP .... Reverse Repurchase Agreement [*Investment term*]
RRP .... Reviews of Research and Practice. Institute for Research into Mental and Multiple Handicap [*Elsevier Book Series*] [*A publication*]
RRP .... Rock Hill, SC [*Location identifier*] [*FAA*]   (FAAL)
RRP .... Roosevelt Roads [*Puerto Rico*] [*Seismograph station code, US Geological Survey*] [*Closed*]   (SEIS)
RRP .... Rotterdam-Rhine Pipeline [*Oil*]
RRP .... Rough River Petroleum Corp. [*Vancouver Stock Exchange symbol*]
RRP .... Rudder Reference Plane [*NASA*]   (NASA)
RRP .... Runway Reference Point [*Aviation*]   (FAAC)
RRPA........ Relativistic Random-Phase Approximation [*Electrodynamics*]
RRPA........ Ruhr Regional Planning Authority [*Post-World War II*]
RRPB........ Retraining and Reemployment Policy Board
RRPC........ Reserve Reinforcement Processing Center [*Army*]   (AABC)
RRPD .... Runway Reference Point Downwind [*Aviation*]   (FAAC)
RRPE........ Union for Radical Review of Radical Political Economics [*A publication*]   (EAAP)
RRPHA ..... Revue Roumaine de Physiologie [*A publication*]
RRPI........ Relative Rod Position Indication [*Nuclear energy*]   (NRCH)
RRPI........ Rotary Relative Position Indicator [*Nuclear energy*]   (NRCH)
RRPL........ Recommend Repair Parts List
RRPP........ Reverends Peres [*Reverend Fathers*] [*French*]
RRPQA...... Revue Roumaine de Physique [*A publication*]
RRPRD...... RTP. Regelungstechnische Praxis [*A publication*]
RRPS .... Ready Reinforcement Personnel Section [*Air Force*]   (AFM)
RRPS .... Ronald Reagan Philatelic Society   (EA)
RRPSDW .. Reading Psychology [*A publication*]
RRPU .... Runway Reference Point Upwind [*Aviation*]   (FAAC)
RRQ.......... Rock Rapids, IA [*Location identifier*] [*FAA*]   (FAAL)
RRQ.......... Romanic Review Quarterly [*A publication*]
RRR .... Exceedingly Rare [*Numismatics*]
RRR .... RADAR Radiation Receiver
RRR .... Railroad Reports [*United States*] [*A publication*]   (DLA)
RRR .... Raleigh Research Reactor
RRR .... RAM [*Reliability, Availability, and Maintainability*] Rationale Report [*Army*]
RRR .... Range and Range Rate
RRR .... Range Rover Register [*An association*]   (EAIO)
RRR .... Rapid Runway Repair
RRR .... Reader Railroad [*AAR code*]

RRR .... Readin', Ritin', and Rithmetic [*Also, 3R's*]
RRR .... Records, Racing, and Rallying [*Sporting aviation*]
RRR .... Red Red Rose   (EA)
RRR .... Reduced Residual Radiation
RRR .... Relief, Recovery, Reform [*Elements of the New Deal*]
RRR .... Required Rate of Return [*Finance*]
RRR .... Residential Resources Mortgage Investment [*AMEX symbol*]   (SPSG)
RRR .... Residual Resistance Ratio [*Metal purity*]
RRR .... Resistor-Reactor Rectifier
RRR .... Resource Requirements Request [*Military*]   (MCD)
RRR .... Resurfacing, Restoration, and Rehabilitation [*US Federal Highway Administration*]
RRR .... Review of Religious Research [*A publication*]
RRR .... Rework Removal Rate
RRR .... Riverton Resources Corp. [*Vancouver Stock Exchange symbol*]
RRR .... Royal Rhodesia Regiment [*British military*]   (DMA)
RRR .... Rum, Romanism, and Rebellion [*Phrase coined during the Presidential campaign of 1884 to describe the Democratic party*]
RRR .... University of Rochester, Rochester, NY [*OCLC symbol*]   (OCLC)
RRRC........ Regulatory Requirements Review Committee [*Nuclear energy*]   (NRCH)
RRRC........ TRI-R Systems Corporation [*NASDAQ symbol*]   (NQ)
RRRE....... RADAR Range-Rate Error
RRREA...... Radiation Research Reviews [*A publication*]
RRRED...... Reclamation and Revegetation Research [*A publication*]
RR Rep...... Railroad Reports [*A publication*]   (DLA)
RRRLC...... Rochester Regional Research Library Council [*Rochester, NY*] [*Library network*]
RRRPD...... Reseau de Radio Rurale des Pays en Developpement [*Developing Countries Farm Radio Network*]   (EAIO)
RRRR....... Railroad Revitalization and Regulatory Reform Act [*1976*]
RRRRR..... Receipt [*British naval signaling*]
RRRRRR... Remedial Readin', Remedial Ritin', and Remedial Rithmetic [*Also, 6R's*] [*Humorous interpretation of the three R's*]
RRRS........ Route Relief Requirements System [*Telecommunications*]   (TEL)
RRRV........ Rate of Rise of Restriking Voltage   (IEEE)
RRS........... Dothan, AL [*Location identifier*] [*FAA*]   (FAAL)
RRS........... RADAR Ranging System
RRS........... Radiation Research Society   (EA)
RRS........... Radio Receiver Set
RRS........... Radio Recording Spectrophotometer
RRS........... Radio Relay Station
RRS........... Radio Relay System
RRS........... Radio Remote Set   (CAAL)
RRS........... Radio Research Station [*British*]
RRS........... Range Rate Search   (MCD)
RRS........... Reaction Research Society   (EA)
RRS........... Reactor Recirculating System   (NRCH)
RRS........... Reactor Refueling System   (NRCH)
RRS........... Reactor Regulating System   (NRCH)
RRS........... Readiness Reportable Status   (NVT)
RRS........... Ready Reportable Status   (MCD)
RRS........... Reconnaissance Reporting System
RRS........... Red River Settlement [*Canada*]
RRS........... Reed Relay Scanner
RRS........... Relay Radio Subsystem [*NASA*]
RRS........... Remaining Radiation Service   (NATG)
RRS........... Remington's Revised Statutes [*A publication*]   (DLA)
RRS........... Rendezvous RADAR System [*NASA*]   (MCD)
RRS........... Required Response Spectrum   (IEEE)
RRS........... Research Referral Service [*International Federation for Documentation*] [*Information service or system*]   (IID)
RRS........... Resin Regeneration Subsystem [*Nuclear energy*]   (NRCH)
RRS........... Resonance Raman Scattering [*Spectroscopy*]
RRS........... Resonance Raman Spectroscopy
RRS........... Resources and Referral Services   (OICC)
RRS........... Restraint Release System   (KSC)
RRS........... Retired Reserve Section
RRS........... Retransmission Request Signal [*Telecommunications*]   (TEL)
RRS........... Retrograde Rocket System
RRS........... Revised Statutes of Nebraska, Reissue
RRS........... River and Rainfall Station [*National Weather Service*]   (NOAA)
RRS........... Roll Rate Sensor
RRS........... Roo Rat Society   (EA)
RRS........... Roros [*Norway*] [*Airport symbol*]   (OAG)
RRS........... Royal Research Ship [*British*]
RRS........... Rural Reconstruction Scheme [*Australia*]
RRSCS...... Rate Stabilization and Control System   (MCD)
RRSM....... Rough Riding Sergeant-Major [*British military*]   (DMA)
RRSP........ Registered Retirement Savings Plan [*Canada*]
RRSSM...... Rough Riding Staff Sergeant-Major [*British military*]   (DMA)
RRSTRAF ... Ready Reserve Strategic Army Forces
RRSV........ Red Ringspot Virus [*of blueberry*]
RRT .... Railroad Retirement Tax [*IRS*]
RRT .... Railroad Transport   (NATG)
RRT .... Randomized Response Technique [*Statistics*]
RRT .... Ready Round Transporter   (NATG)

RRT .... Reentry Reference Time [*NASA*]
RRT .... Registered Recreation Therapist
RRT .... Registered Respiratory Therapist
RRT .... Relative Retention Time
RRT .... Rendezvous RADAR Transducer [*NASA*]   (NASA)
RR/T......... Rendezvous RADAR/Transponder [*NASA*]   (KSC)
RRT .... Repatriation Review Tribunal [*Australia*]
RRT .... Request for Review of Tooling
RRT .... Requirements Review Team
RRT .... Resource Recycling Technology [*AMEX symbol*]   (SPSG)
RRT .... Ring-Ring Trip [*Telecommunications*]   (TEL)
RRT .... Robert Mines Ltd. [*Vancouver Stock Exchange symbol*]
RRTA......... Railroad Retirement Tax [*IRS*]
RRTCD..... Tokyo Denki Daigaku Kenkyu Hokoku [*A publication*]
RRTD .... Rural Rehabilitation Technologies Database [*University of North Dakota*] [*Information service or system*]   (IID)
RRTE........ Reroute   (FAAC)
RRTIS ...... Renewable Resources Technical Information System [*Forest Service*]
RRTS........ Radiometer Recording Titration System [*Experimentation*]
RRTS........ Range-Rate Tracking System
RRU.......... Cedar Rapids, IA [*Location identifier*] [*FAA*]   (FAAL)
RRU.......... Radio Research Unit [*Army*]   (AABC)
RRU.......... Radiobiological Research Unit   (IEEE)
RRU.......... Remington-Rand UNIVAC
RRU.......... Remote Readout Unit
RRU.......... Remote Request Unit   (CAAL)
RRU.......... Resource Recycling Unit
RRU.......... Retro-Rocket UNIVAC   (MUGU)
R RUL....... Renegotiation Rulings   (DLA)
RRUSEO... University of Miami. Rosenstiel School of Marine and Atmospheric Science. Research Review [*A publication*]
RRV .... Denver, CO [*Location identifier*] [*FAA*]   (FAAL)
RRV .... Rotor Reentry Vehicle
RRVRA..... Revue Roumaine de Virologie [*A publication*]
RRVSGA ... Red River Valley Sugarbeet Growers Association   (EA)
RRV & W... Red River Valley & Western Railroad [*North Dakota*]
RRW .... Jacksonville, FL [*Location identifier*] [*FAA*]   (FAAL)
RRW .... Radiation-Resistant Wire
RRW .... Royal Regiment of Wales [*Military unit*] [*British*]
RRWBDG ... Report of Research. Worcester Foundation for Experimental Biology [*A publication*]
RRWL....... Renaissance and Renascences in Western Literature [*A publication*]
RRWU ...... Rhodesia Railway Workers' Union
RRX .... Railroad Crossing [*Telecommunications*]   (TEL)
RRX .... Ronrico Explorations Ltd. [*Vancouver Stock Exchange symbol*]
R & Ry CC ... Russell and Ryan's English Crown Cases [*A publication*]   (DLA)
RS .... Aerotransportes [*Argentina*] [*ICAO designator*]   (FAAC)
RS .... IEEE Reliability Society   (EA)
RS .... Rabbinic Supervisor   (BJA)
RS .... Rabbinical School   (BJA)
RS .... Rabbinical Seminary   (BJA)
R & S......... Raben & Sjogren [*Publisher*] [*Sweden*]
RS .... Raccolta Sistematica del Diritto Federale [*Switzerland*] [*A publication*]
RS .... Rachmaninoff Society [*Record label*]
RS .... RADAR Scanner
RS .... RADAR Scattering
RS .... RADAR Selector   (MCD)
RS .... RADAR Set
RS .... RADAR Simulator   (CET)
RS .... RADAR Start   (CET)
RS .... Radiated Susceptibility   (IEEE)
RS .... Radiation Sensitive [*Physiology*]
RS .... Radiation Source   (NRCH)
RS .... Radio Duties - Special
RS .... Radio Simulator
RS .... Radio Station [*Maps and charts*]
RS .... Radio Supervisor [*British*]
RS .... Radio Switchboard   (CAAL)
RS .... Radius of Safety   (MCD)
RS .... Radular Sac
RS .... Ragtime Society   (EA)
RS .... Railway Station   (ROG)
RS .... Rain and Snow [*Sleet*] [*Meteorology*]
RS .... Raman Scattering [*Spectroscopy*]
RS .... Raman Spectroscopy
RS .... Random Saccades [*Ophthalmology*]
RS .... Random Splice [*Telecommunications*]   (TEL)
R & S......... Range and Safety   (AAG)
RS .... Range Safety [*NASA*]   (KSC)
RS .... Range Selector
R/S............. Range Surveillance
RS .... Rapid Setting [*Asphalt grade*]
RS .... Ras Shamra   (BJA)
RS .... Raster Suppression [*of color images*]
RS .... Rating Sheet [*Psychometrics*]
RS .... Rauwolfia Serpentina [*A plant, the root extract of which is used medicinally*]

RS .... Raw Stock
RS .... RAWINSONDE [*Radiosonde and RADAR Wind Sounding*] [*Upper air observation*]   (NASA)
RS .... Ray Society   (EA)
RS .... Reactor Safeguards   (NRCH)
RS .... Reader Stop [*Data processing*]   (BUR)
RS .... Reading of Standard
RS .... Ready Service   (AAG)
RS .... Real Storage
RS .... Realites Secretes [*A publication*]
RS .... Rearranging Sequence [*Genetics*]
RS .... Rebuild Standard [*Marine Corps*]
RS .... Receiver Station
RS .... Receiving Ship [*or Station*]
RS .... Reception Station
RS .... Recipient's Serum [*In blood matching*]
RS .... Reciprocating Steam   (MCD)
RS .... Reclaimed Wheat Grass/Shrub Cover [*Agriculture*]
RS .... Recognition Structure [*Immunochemistry*]
RS .... Recommended Standard [*Telecommunications*]   (TEL)
RS .... Reconfiguration System   (MCD)
RS .... Reconnaissance Satellite
RS .... Reconnaissance Squadron [*Military*]
RS .... Reconnaissance-Strike [*Military*]
RS .... Reconnaissance Strip [*Military*]   (AFM)
R & S......... Reconnaissance and Surveillance   (MCD)
RS .... Reconstitution Site   (NVT)
RS .... Record Separator [*Control character*] [*Data processing*]
RS .... Recording Secretary
RS .... Recreation Supervisor [*Red Cross*]
RS .... Recruiting Service
RS .... Recruiting Station
RS .... Recruitment Surveys [*Army*] [*British*]
RS .... Rectal Sinus
RS .... Rectal Suppository [*Medicine*]
RS .... Rectified Spirits   (ROG)
RS .... Rectus-Sinister [*Nomenclature system*] [*Biochemistry*]
RS .... Recueil Systematique du Droit Federal [*Switzerland*] [*A publication*]
RS .... Redeemable Stock
RS .... Reduced Strength   (MCD)
RS .... Reducing Sugar
RS .... Redundancy Status [*NASA*]   (MCD)
RS .... Redundant Set [*NASA*]   (MCD)
RS .... Reel Sequence [*Data processing*]
R & S......... Reenlistment and Separation [*Military*]   (AFM)
R & S......... Reentry System   (AFM)
RS .... Reference Serum [*Clinical chemistry*]
RS .... Reference Standard
RS .... Reformed Spelling
RS .... Refrigeration System   (MCD)
RS .... Refurbishment Spare   (NASA)
RS .... Regional Authorities (Scotland)
RS .... Register Select
RS .... Register of Shipping of the USSR [*Ship classification society*]   (DS)
RS .... Register and Storage   (MCD)
RS .... Registered Sanitarian
RS .... Regular Savings
RS .... Regular Station [*Military*]
RS .... Regularly Scheduled [*Red Cross Volunteer*]
RS .... Regulating Station [*Military*]
RS .... Regulation Station [*Air Force*]
RS .... Reinforcing Stimulus
RS .... Reiter's Syndrome [*Medicine*]
R/S............. Rejection Slip   (ADA)
RS .... Relative Sweetness
R/S............. Relay Set [*Telecommunications*]   (TEL)
RS .... Reliability Summary   (KSC)
RS .... Religious Studies [*A publication*]
RS .... Religious Studies [*Secondary school course*] [*British*]
RS .... Relocation Site   (NVT)
RS .... Reminder Shock
R/S............. Remote Site [*NASA*]   (KSC)
RS .... Remote Station
RS .... Remotely Settable Fuze   (MCD)
RS .... Renal Specialist [*Medicine*]
RS .... Renin Substrate [*Biochemistry*]
R & S......... Renovation and Storage [*Military*]   (AFIT)
RS .... Rephael Society   (EA)
RS .... Report of Survey [*Military*]
R & S......... Reports and Statistics Branch [*US Military Government, Germany*]
RS .... Reprint of the Statutes of New Zealand [*A publication*]
RS .... Reproductive Success [*Genetics*]
RS .... Republicains Sociaux [*Social Republicans*] [*France*] [*Political party*]   (PPE)
RS .... Request to Send
RS .... Request for Services [*Social Security Administration*]
RS .... Request for Support   (MCD)
RS .... Research Scientist   (ADA)

R & S......... Research and Statistics   (IEEE)
RS .... Research on Steroids [*Elsevier Book Series*] [*A publication*]
RS .... Research Studies [*Pullman*] [*A publication*]
R & S......... Research and Study
RS .... Research Summary
RS .... Research Systems   (MCD)
RS .... Reserve Section [*Military*]
RS .... Reset
RS .... Reset-Set [*Data processing*]
RS .... Reset Steering
RS .... Resident School   (MUGU)
RS .... Resistance Soldering
RS .... Resistant Sporangia [*Botany*]
RS .... Resources Section [*Resources and Technical Services Division*] [*American Library Association*]
RS .... Respiratory Syncytial [*Virus*]
RS .... Respiratory System [*Medicine*]
RS .... Response-Stimulus
RS .... Responsus [*To Answer*] [*Latin*]
RS .... Resume Sheet
RS .... Retail Shops and Stores [*Public-performance tariff class*] [*British*]
RS .... Return to Saturation
RS .... Revenue Sharing
RS .... Reverberation Strength
RS .... Reversal Shift [*Psychometrics*]
RS .... Review of Symptoms [*Medicine*]
RS .... Revised Statutes
R/S............. Revolutions per Second
RS .... Revue Suisse [*A publication*]
RS .... Revue de Synthese [*A publication*]
RS .... Reye's Syndrome [*Medicine*]
RS .... Rheinflugzeugbau [*Federal Republic of Germany*] [*ICAO aircraft manufacturer identifier*]   (ICAO)
R de S........ Ricardus Petronius de Senis [*Deceased, 1314*] [*Authority cited in pre-1607 legal work*]   (DSA)
RS .... Ricerche Slavistiche [*A publication*]
RS .... Right Sacrum [*Medicine*]   (KSC)
RS .... Right Safety [*Sports*]
RS .... Right Side
RS .... Ringer's Solution [*Physiology*]
RS .... Ripon Society   (EA)
R/S............. Road Service
RS .... Road Space [*Military*]
RS .... [*The*] Roberval & Saguenay Railway Co. [*AAR code*]
RS .... Rochelle Salt [*Potassium Sodium Tartrate*] [*Organic chemistry*]
RS .... Rocket System   (MCD)
RS .... Rocznik Slawistyczny [*A publication*]
RS .... Roll Stabilization
RS .... Roller Shutter
RS .... Rolling Stone [*A publication*]
RS .... Rolls Series [*A publication*]   (DLA)
RS .... Romanische Studien [*A publication*]
R San I ...... Romanische Studien [*A publication*]
RS .... Root Stock [*Botany*]
RS .... Route Selector
RS .... Route Switching [*Telecommunications*]   (TEL)
RS .... Routing Slip [*Military*]
RS .... Royal Scots [*Military unit*]
RS .... Royal Society [*British*]
RS .... Rubble Stone   (AAG)
RS .... Rudder Station   (MCD)
RS .... Rural Sociology [*A publication*]
Rs .... Sri Lanka Rupee [*Monetary unit*]   (IMH)
RS .... Syntex Laboratories, Inc. [*Research code symbol*]
RSA............ American Railway and Airline Supervisors Association   (EA)
RSA............ Rabbit Serum Albumin [*Immunology*]
RSA............ Rack Service Association   (EA)
RSA............ RADAR Service Area
RSA............ RADAR Signature Analysis [*Air Force*]
RSA............ Railway Supply Association   (EA)
RSA............ Range Safety Approval   (MUGU)
RSA............ Rat Serum Albumin [*Immunology*]
RSA............ Rate Subsystem Analyst   (MUGU)
RSA............ Rational Self-Analysis [*Psychology*]   (DHSM)
RSA............ Redstone Arsenal [*Huntsville, AL*] [*Army*]
RSA............ Reference Satellite A   (NASA)
RSA............ Regional Science Association   (EA)
RSA............ Regional Studies Association [*London, England*]   (EAIO)
RSA............ Regular Spiking Activity [*Electrophysiology*]
RSA............ Rehabilitation Services Administration [*Office of Special Education and Rehabilitive Services, Department of Education*]
RSA............ Relative Specific Activity
RSA............ Relative Standard Accuracy [*Testing methodology*]
RSA............ Remote Station Alarm
RSA............ Remote Storage Activities
RSA............ Renaissance Society of America   (EA)
RSA............ Renal Society for Australasia
RSA............ Rental Service Association   (EA)
RSA............ Repair Sevice Attendant [*Telecommunications*]   (TEL)
RSA............ Report from South Africa [*A publication*]

RSA............ Republic of South Africa
RSA............ Requirements Statement Analyzer
RSA............ Research Security Administrators
RSA............ Research Society on Alcoholism   (EA)
RSA............ Resource Sharing Alliance [*Library consortium*]   (IT)
RSA............ Respiratory Sinus Arrhythmia [*Medicine*]
RSA............ Retire to Staging Area [*Military*]
RSA............ Retirement Savings Account [*Australia*]
RSA............ Returned Services Association [*Australia*]
RSA............ Revised Statutes of Alberta [*Canada*] [*A publication*]   (DLA)
RSA............ Revised Statutes Annotated [*A publication*]   (DLA)
RSA............ Revue Internationale des Sciences Administratives [*A publication*]
RSA............ Rheometrics Sound Analyzer
RSA............ Rhetoric Society of America   (EA)
RSA............ Rhythmic Slow Activity [*Electroencephalography*]
RSA............ Ridden Standardbred Association   (EA)
RSA............ Right Sacroanterior [*A fetal position*] [*Obstetrics*]
RSA............ Rivest-Shamir-Adelman [*Cryptography*]
RSA............ Rivista di Storia Antica [*A publication*]
RSA............ Rotary Servo Actuator
RSA............ Royal Scottish Academician
RSA............ [*The*] Royal Scottish Academy
RSA............ Royal Society of Antiquaries
RSA............ Royal Society of the Arts [*London, England*]
RSA............ Rubber Shippers Association [*Defunct*]
RSA............ Rural Sanitary Authority [*British*]
RSA............ Santa Rosa [*Argentina*] [*Airport symbol*]   (OAG)
RSAA......... Revue Suisse d'Art et d'Archeologie [*A publication*]
RSAA......... Romanian Studies Association of America   (EA)
RSAAF ...... Royal South African Air Force
RSABA....... Revista. Sociedad Argentina de Biologia [*A publication*]
RSABA....... Royal South Australia Bowling Association
RSAC......... RADAR Significance Analysis Code
RSAC......... Radiological Safety Analysis Computer   (MCD)
RSAC......... Recueil des Notices et Memoires. Societe Archeologique de Constantine [*A publication*]
RSAC......... Region, State, Area, County [*Code*] [*DoD*]
RSAC......... Remote Slave Aircraft   (MCD)
RSAF .... Royal Saudi Air Force
RSAF .... Royal Small Arms Factory [*British*]
RSAF .... Royal Swedish Air Force
RSAG........ Reserve Storage Activity, Germersheim, West Germany [*Military*]
RSAI .... Royal Society of Antiquaries of Ireland
RSAI .... Rutgers Social Attribute Inventory [*Psychology*]
R Saintonge ... Revue de la Saintonge et de l'Aunis [*A publication*]
RSAK........ Reserve Storage Activity, Kaiserslautern, West Germany [*Military*]
RSAL......... Reserve Storage Activity, Luxembourg [*Military*]
RSALT ...... Running, Signal, and Anchor Lights
RSAMC.... Royal Society of Arts, Manufacturing and Commerce [*London*]
R San I ...... Royal Sanitary Institute [*Later, RSH*] [*British*]
R Sanit Inst J ... Royal Sanitary Institute. Journal [*A publication*]
RSAP........ Regional Science Association. Papers and Proceedings [*A publication*]
RSAP........ Revolutionaire Socialistische Arbeiders Partij [*Revolutionary Socialist Workers' Party*] [*Netherlands*] [*Political party*]   (PPE)
RSARR...... Republic of South Africa Research Reactor
RSAS......... Revenue Sharing Advisory Service   (EA)
RSAS......... Royal Sanitary Association of Scotland
RSASA ...... Royal Society of Arts of South Australia
RSAT........ Recueil. Societe de Prehistoire et d'Archeologie de Tebessa [*A publication*]
RSav......... Revue de Savoie [*A publication*]
RSB........... Range Safety Beacon [*NASA*]   (AAG)
RSB........... Ravensbos [*Netherlands*] [*Seismograph station code, US Geological Survey*]   (SEIS)
RSB........... Reactor Service Building   (NRCH)
RSB........... Reconnaissance Strike Bomber
RSB........... Reduced-Size Blueprint   (NG)
RSB........... Reference Standards Book [*Military*]
RSB........... Regimental Stretcher-Bearer
RSB........... Regional Shipping Boards [*NATO*]   (NATG)
RSB........... Repair Service Bureau [*Telecommunications*]   (TEL)
RSB........... Retail Sales Battery [*Employment test*]
RSB........... Reticulocyte Standard Buffer
RSB........... Revista. Sociedad Bolivariana [*A publication*]
RSB........... Rhondda & Swansea Bay Railway [*Wales*]
RSB........... Right Sternal Border [*Medicine*]
RSB........... Rivista Storica Benedettina [*A publication*]
RSB........... Rochester Subway Co. [*AAR code*]
RSB........... Roller Skating Business Magazine [*A publication*]   (EAAP)
RSB........... Roseberth [*Australia*] [*Airport symbol*] [*Obsolete*]   (OAG)
RSB........... Royal Swedish Ballet
RSB........... Rudder Speed Brake   (MCD)
RSBA........ Rail Steel Bar Association [*Later, SMA*]   (EA)
RSBC........ Revised Statutes of British Columbia [*A publication*]   (ILCA)
RSB(E)....... Regional Shipping Board (East) [*NATO*]

RSBEI....... Registered Student of the Institution of Body Engineers [*British*] (DBQ)
R Sb Ekonom Promysl D ... Referativnyi Sbornik. Ekonomika Promyslennosti. D. Primenenie Matematiceskih Metodov v Ekonomiceskih Issledovanijah i Planirovanii [*A publication*]
RSBKDD... Reports. State Biological Survey of Kansas [*A publication*]
RSBN........ Rivista di Studi Bizantini e Neoellenici [*A publication*]
RSBO........ Refined Soybean Oil
RSBRC...... Reference and Subscription Books Review Committee [*American Library Association*]
RSBS .... RADAR Safety Beacon System (MCD)
RSBTA3 .... Rio Grande Do Sul. Departamento Producao Animal. Divisao de Zootecnia. Servico de Experimentacao Zootecnia. Boletim Tecnico [*A publication*]
RSB(W) ..... Regional Shipping Board (West) [*NATO*]
RSC........... RADAR Scan Converter [*Military*] (CAAL)
RSC........... RADAR Sea Clutter
RSC........... RADAR Set Control
RSC........... RADAR System Console [*Military*] (CAAL)
RSC........... RADAR System Controller [*Military*] (CAAL)
RSC........... Radiation Shielding Computer Codes [*Database*] [*Oak Ridge National Laboratory*] [*Department of Energy*] [*Information service or system*] (CRD)
RSC........... Railway Systems Control [*A publication*]
RSC........... Range Safety Command [*or Control*] [*NASA*]
RSC........... Rat Skin Collagen
RSC........... Rational Self-Counseling [*Psychology*] (DHSM)
RSC........... Reactor Safety Commission [*Federal Republic of Germany*]
RSC........... Reactor Safety Coordinator [*Nuclear energy*] (NRCH)
RSC........... Reactor Steam Cycle
RSC........... Reader Service Card
RSC........... Record Status Code [*Military*] (AABC)
RSC........... Referee Stops Contest [*Amateur boxing*]
RSC........... Regional Service Center [*Military*] (CINC)
RSC........... Regular, Slotted, Corrugated [*Container*]
RSC........... Reinforcement Support Category [*DoD*]
RSC........... Relative System Capability
RSC........... Religious Sisters of Charity [*Roman Catholic religious order*]
RSC........... Remote Sensing Center [*Texas A & M University*] [*Research center*] (RCD)
RSC........... Remote Store Controller
RSC........... Replacement and School Command [*Military*]
R & SC....... Replacement and School Command [*Military*]
RSC........... Rescue Subcenter [*Aviation*] (FAAC)
RSC........... Reserve Service Control [*Navy*]
RSC........... Residential Sales Council (EA)
RSC........... Residential Support Center (OICC)
RSC........... Resort Air Service, Inc. [*Southern Pines, NC*] [*FAA designator*] (FAAC)
RSC........... Restart Capability (AAG)
RSC........... Reversible Sickled Cell [*Hematology*]
RSC........... Revised Statutes of Canada [*Canada Department of Justice*] [*Information service or system*] (CRD)
RSC........... Riga [*USSR*] Skulte Airport [*Airport symbol*] [*Obsolete*] (OAG)
RSC........... Right-Sided Colon Cancer [*Medicine*]
RSC........... Right Stage Center [*A stage direction*]
RSC........... Rivista di Studi Classici [*A publication*]
RSC........... Rivista di Studi Crociani [*A publication*]
RSC........... Road Safety Committee [*British police*]
RSC........... Royal Shakespeare Company [*British*]
RSC........ Royal Society of Canada
RSC........... Royal Society of Chemistry [*Formed by a merger of Chemical Society and Royal Institute of Chemistry*] (EAIO)
RSC........... Rules of the Supreme Court [*A publication*] (DLA)
RSC........... Runway Surface Condition [*Aviation*] (MCD)
RSC........... Rural Service Center [*Agency for International Development*]
RSC........ Russell Sage College [*New York*]
RSC........... Saint Charles Borromeo Seminary, Overbrook, PA [*OCLC symbol*] (OCLC)
RSCA........ Religious Speech Communication Association (EA)
RScA......... Right Scapulo-Anterior [*A fetal position*] [*Obstetrics*]
RSCAA...... Radio Shack Computer Alumni Association (EA)
RSCAAL ... Remote Sensing Chemical Agent Alarm [*Army*] (INF)
RSCC........ Remote-Site Command Computer [*NASA*]
RSCC........ Remote-Site Computer Complex [*NASA*]
RSCC........ Republican Senatorial Campaign Committee
RSCCDS.... Reactivity and Structure Concepts in Organic Chemistry [*A publication*]
RSCD........ Report Series Codes Dictionary [*A publication*]
RSCD........ Request to Start Contract Definition
RSCDSA ... Religion and Socialism Commission of the Democratic Socialists of America (EA)
R Sc Eco..... Revue des Sciences Economiques [*A publication*]
RSCG........ Radio Set Control Group
RSCH .... Range Scheduling (MUGU)
RSCH .... Ready Spares Chassis
RSCH .... Research (AFM)
RSCH .... Rowley-Scher Reprographics, Inc. [*Beltsville, MD*] [*NASDAQ symbol*] (NQ)

RSCHM .... Royal School of Church Music [*British*]
R Sch Mines J ... Royal School of Mines. Journal [*England*] [*A publication*]
R Sci.......... Revue Scientifique [*A publication*]
RSCI .... Rivista di Storia della Chiesa in Italia [*A publication*]
RSCIE .... Remote Station Communication Interface Equipment
R Science Fin ... Revue de Science Financiere [*A publication*]
R Sciences Econs ... Revue des Sciences Economiques [*A publication*]
R Sci Financ ... Revue de Science Financiere [*A publication*]
R Sci Hum ... Revue des Sciences Humaines [*A publication*]
R Sci Instr ... Review of Scientific Instruments [*A publication*]
R Sci Philos & Theol ... Revue des Sciences Philosophiques et Theologiques [*A publication*]
R Sci Ph Th ... Revue des Sciences Philosophiques et Theologiques [*A publication*]
R Sci Pol .... Revue des Sciences Politiques [*A publication*]
R Sci Rel .... Revue des Sciences Religieuses [*A publication*]
R Sci Soc France Est ... Revue des Sciences Sociales de la France de l'Est [*A publication*]
RSCJ .... Society of the Sacred Heart [*Roman Catholic women's religious order*]
RSCL......... Radioactive Sodium Chemistry Loop
RSCL......... Rivista di Studi Classici [*A publication*]
RSCM........ Royal School of Church Music [*British*]
RSCN........ Registered Sick Children's Nurse [*British*]
RSCO........ Rules of the Supreme Court, Order [*Number*] (ILCA)
R Scolaire... Revue Scolaire [*A publication*]
RSCom...... Revue Belge des Sciences Commerciales [*A publication*]
RS Comp.... Statutes of Connecticut, Compilation of 1854 [*A publication*] (DLA)
R Scott Mus Inf Ser Geol ... Royal Scottish Museum. Information Series. Geology [*A publication*]
RScP.......... Right Scapuloposterior [*A fetal position*] [*Obstetrics*]
RScPhilT ... Revue des Sciences Philosophiques et Theologiques [*Paris*] [*A publication*]
RscPhTh.... Revue des Sciences Philosophiques et Theologiques [*Paris*] [*A publication*]
RSCQAX... Riviera Scientifique [*A publication*]
RSCR........ Range Safety Command Receiver [*NASA*] (KSC)
RSCR........ Reserve Special Commendation Ribbon
RScR......... Revue des Sciences Religieuses [*A publication*]
RScRel....... Revue des Sciences Religieuses [*A publication*]
RSCS .... Range Safety Command System [*NASA*] (AAG)
RSCS .... Rate Stabilization and Control System
RSCS .... Remote Spooling Communications Subsystem [*IBM Corp.*] [*Data processing*] (IBMDP)
RSCS .... Rod Sequence Control System [*Nuclear energy*] (NRCH)
RSCSA ...... Railway Signal and Communications Suppliers Association [*Later, RSS*] (EA)
RSCST...... Rivista Storico-Critica delle Scienze Teologiche [*A publication*]
RSCT........ Rohde Sentence Completions Test [*Psychology*]
RSCT........ Royal Society of Canada. Transactions [*A publication*]
RSCU........ Rescue (FAAC)
RSCW....... Research Reactor, State College of Washington (NRCH)
RSD .... Radiance Spectral Distribution
RSD .... Raised (MSA)
RSD .... Raised Shelter Deck (DS)
RSD .... Rassemblement des Socialistes et des Democrates [*Rally of Socialists and Democrats*] [*Reunion*] [*Political party*] (PPW)
RSD .... Ratoon Stunting Disease [*of sugarcane*]
RS & D ...... Receipt, Storage, and Delivery [*Business term*]
RSD .... Reentry Systems Department
RSD .... Reference Services Division [*of ALA*] [*Later, RASD*] (EA)
RSD .... Reflex Sympathetic Dystrophy [*Medicine*]
RSD .... Refueling Shutdown (IEEE)
RSD .... Relative Standard Deviation [*Statistics*]
RSD .... Relative Stock Density [*Pisciculture*]
RSD .... Requirements and Specifications Document [*NASA*] (NASA)
RSD .... Research Services Department [*United Way of Greater Indianapolis*] [*Indiana*] [*Information service or system*] (IID)
RSD .... Research Services Directory [*A publication*]
RSD .... Resigned
RSD .... Responsible System Designer (NRCH)
RSD .... Roadside Delivery (ADA)
RSD .... Rock Sound [*Bahamas*] [*Airport symbol*] (OAG)
RSD .... Rolling Steel Door [*Technical drawings*]
RSD .... Rosehaugh Stanhope Developments [*Commercial firm*] [*British*]
RSD .... Royal Society, Dublin
RSDA........ Reflex Sympathetic Dystrophy Association (EA)
RSDB........ SCB [*Statistika Centralbyran*] Regional Statistical Data Base [*Sweden*] [*Information service or system*] (CRD)
RSDC........ Radiation Subprogramme Data Center [*Marine science*] (MSC)
RSDG .... Raster Scan Display Generator (MCD)
RSDG .... Royal Scots Dragoon Guards [*British military*] (DMA)
RSDI.......... Rivista di Storia del Diritto Italiano [*A publication*]
RSDL........ Resdel Industries [*NASDAQ symbol*] (NQ)
RSDLP...... Russian Social-Democratic Labor Party [*Political party*]
RSDLP(B) ... Russian Social-Democratic Labor Party (Bolsheviks) [*Political party*]

RSDNT...... Resident
RSDP........ Remote Shutdown Panel (IEEE)
RSDP........ Remote-Site Data Processor [NASA]
RSDr......... Doctor of Social Sciences
RSDRP...... Rossiiskaia Sotsial-Demokraticheskaia Rabochaya Partiia [Russian Social Democratic Workers' Party] [Political party] (PPE)
RSDS........ RADAR Systems Design Section
RSDS........ Range Safety Destruct System
RSDT........ Regulations of Office of the Secretary, Department of Transportation
RSDT........ Remote Station Data Terminal
RSDU ...... RADAR Storm Detection Unit
RSDW ...... Ross Sea Deep Water [Marine science] (MSC)
RSDWP..... Russian Social-Democratic Workers Party
RSE.......... RADAR Search Equipment
RSE.......... Raid Size Estimate
RSE.......... Rassegna di Studi Etiopici [A publication]
RSE.......... Receiving Site Equipment [NASA]
RSE.......... Reference Standards Equipment [Deep Space Instrumentation Facility, NASA]
rse........... Remise [Remittance] [Business term] [French]
RSE.......... Renewable Sources of Energy [A publication]
RSE.......... Request Select Entry [Data processing]
RSE.......... Resistance Soldering Equipment
RSE.......... Resource Engineering, Inc. [AMEX symbol] (SPSG)
RSE.......... Review of Social Economy [A publication]
RSE.......... Revue des Sciences Ecclesiastiques [A publication]
RSE.......... Revue. Societe d'Etudes et d'Expansion [A publication]
RSE.......... Rivista di Storia Economica [A publication]
RSE.......... Royal Society of Edinburgh
RSE.......... Rutgers Studies in English [A publication]
RSE.......... Sydney-Rose Bay [Australia] [Airport symbol] (OAG)
RSEA........ Reference Sensing Element Amplifier
RSEA........ Revue de Sud-Est Asiatique [A publication]
R Se As Stud ... Review of Southeast Asian Studies [Singapore] [A publication]
RSEC........ Regional Science Experience Center
RSEC........ Regional Solar Energy Center
RSEC........ Representative Shuttle Environmental Control [System] [NASA]
RSEc......... Revue des Sciences Economiques [A publication]
RSECS...... Representative Shuttle Environmental Control System [NASA] (MCD)
RSED........ Refund Statute Expiration Date [IRS]
RSEEA ..... Remote Sensing of Environment [A publication]
R Seneg Dr ... Revue Senegalaise de Droit [A publication]
RSEP........ Restraint System Evaluation Program [Department of Transportation]
RSEP........ [H. B.] Robinson Steam Electric Plant (NRCH)
RSER........ Remote Sensing of Earth Resources
RSER........ Rotary Stylus Electronics Recorder
R Servizio Soc ... Rivista di Servizio Sociale [A publication]
RSES .... Refrigeration Service Engineers Society (EA)
RSES .... Rosenberg Self-Esteem Scale
RSEt .... Rassegna di Studi Etiopici [A publication]
RSEU........ Remote Scanner-Encoder Unit [Bell Laboratories]
RSEW........ Resistance Seam Welding
RSEW-HF ... Resistance Seam Welding - High Frequency
RSEW-I..... Resistance Seam Welding - Induction
RSF.......... Radial Structure Function [of solid catalysts]
RSF.......... Rassegna di Scienze Filosofiche [A publication]
RSF.......... Rassegna di Studi Francesi [A publication]
RSF.......... Receiving-Safing Facility [NASA] (MCD)
RSF.......... Reciprocal Cross Sterile Females [Genetics]
RSF.......... Refurbish and Subassemblies Facilities [NASA] (NASA)
RSF.......... Reject Suspense File [Army]
RSF.......... Relative Sensitivity Factor [Analytical chemistry]
RSF.......... Relative Substitution Frequency [of amino acids in proteins]
RSF.......... Remote Support Facility
RSF.......... Research Systems Facility
RSF.......... Residual Support Force [After main force redeployment] [Military]
RSF.......... Retail Stores Forum (EA)
RSF.......... Rhododendron Species Foundation (EA)
RSF.......... Risk Studies Foundation (EA)
RSF.......... Rivista di Storia della Filosofia [A publication]
RSF.......... Roll Sheet Feeder
RSF.......... Rough Sunk Face [Construction]
RSF.......... Royal Scots Fusiliers [Military unit]
RSF.......... Russian Student Fund [Defunct] (EA)
RSFA........ Roller Skating Foundation of America (EA)
RSFC........ Republic Savings Financial Corp. [NASDAQ symbol] (NQ)
RSFC........ Ricky Skaggs International Fan Club (EA)
RSFC........ Rolling Stones Fan Club (EA)
RSFC........ Ronnie Smith Fan Club (EA)
RSFFA...... Rendiconti. Scuola Internazionale di Fisica "Enrico Fermi" [A publication]
RSFMA ..... Rivista Sperimentale di Freniatria e Medicina Legale delle Alienazioni Mentali [A publication]

RSFPA....... Revista de la Sanidad de las Fuerzas Policiales del Peru [A publication]
RSFPP....... Retired Servicemen's Family Protection Plan [Military]
RSFR .... Rivista di Studi Filosofici e Religiosi [A publication]
RSFSA....... Rendiconti. Seminario della Facolta di Scienze. Universita di Cagliari [A publication]
RSFSR...... Republique Socialiste Federative Sovietique de Russie
RSFSR...... Russian Soviet Federated Socialist Republic
RSG .... Rabbi Saadia Gaon [Jewish scholar, 882-942] (BJA)
RSG .... RADAR Set Group [HAWK missile] (MCD)
RSG .... RADAR Signal Generator (MCD)
RSG .... RADAR Systems Group [of General Motors Corp.]
RSG .... Rate Signal Generator (AAG)
RSG .... Rate Support Grant [British]
RSG .... Rate Switching Gyro (MCD)
RSG .... Reassign (AABC)
RSG .... Receiving Stolen Goods
RSG .... Reenlistment Steering Group [Military] (MCD)
RSG .... Reference Signal Generator
RSG .... Regional Seat of Government
RSG .... Relay Switch Group
RSG .... Research Study Group (NATG)
RSG .... Resident Study Group [Army] (MCD)
RSG .... Resource Service Group Ltd. [Toronto Stock Exchange symbol]
RSG .... Rising (FAAC)
RSG .... Rocksprings, TX [Location identifier] [FAA] (FAAL)
RSG .... Royal Scots Greys [Military unit]
RSGB........ Radio Society of Great Britain [Potters Bar, Hertfordshire, England] (EAIO)
RSGI......... Riverside Group, Incorporated [Jacksonville, FL] [NASDAQ symbol] (NQ)
RSGMT..... Reassignment
RSGN .... Reassign
RSGPB ...... Rinsan Shikenjo Geppo [A publication]
RSGS .... Ranges and Space Ground Support (AAG)
RSGS .... Royal Scottish Geographical Society
RSH .... RADAR Status History
RSH .... Resin Sluice Header (NRCH)
RSh .... Revista Shell [A publication]
RSH .... Revue des Sciences Humaines [A publication]
RSH .... Revue de Synthese Historique [A publication]
RSH .... Ring Systems Handbook [American Chemical Society] [A publication]
RSH .... Royal Society of Health [Formerly, R San I] [British]
RSH .... Russian Mission [Alaska] [Airport symbol] (OAG)
RSHA .... Reichssicherheitshauptampt [Central Security Office of the Reich] [NAZI Germany]
RSHC........ Research in the Sociology of Health Care [A publication]
RSHEA...... Royal Society of Health. Journal [A publication]
RSHF........ Room Sensible Heat Factor
RSHG .... Revue. Societe Haitienne d'Histoire, de Geographie, et de Geologie [A publication]
RSHKA6 ... Bulletin. Forestry and Forest Products Research Institute [A publication]
RSHM ...... Religious of the Sacred Heart of Mary [Roman Catholic women's religious order]
RSHNDI ... Annual Report. Hokkaido Branch. Forestry and Forest Products Research Institute [A publication]
RSHS........ Railroad Station Historical Society (EA)
RSHum...... Revue des Sciences Humaines [A publication]
RSHX .... Recirculation Spray Heat Exchanger [Nuclear energy] (NRCH)
RSI........... Air Sunshine, Inc. [Ft. Lauderdale, FL] [FAA designator] (FAAC)
RSI........... East-West Resource Systems Institute [Research center] (RCD)
rsi .... Race Specific Incompatibility
RSI........... RADAR Scope Interpretation (AAG)
RSI........... Radiation Shielding Information Data Base [Oak Ridge National Laboratory] [Department of Energy] [Information service or system] (CRD)
RSI........... Rationalization, Standardization, and Integration [or Interoperability] [Program] [Army] (INF)
RSI........... Reactor Siting Index (NRCH)
RSI........... Realty South Investors, Inc. [AMEX symbol] (SPSG)
RSI........... Receipt, Storage, and Issue [Army] (AABC)
R(SI)......... Reconstruction, Social Insurance [British] [World War II]
RSI........... Record Status Indicator [Military] (AABC)
RSI........... Reflected Signal Indication [Air Force]
RSI........... Regional Safety Inspector [Ministry of Agriculture, Fisheries, and Food] [British]
RSI........... Register Sender Inward [Telecommunications] (TEL)
RSI........... Religious Science International (EA)
RSI........... Remote Sensing Institute [South Dakota State University] [Research center] (RCD)
RSI........... Repetitive Strain Injury (PCM)
RSI........... Replacement Stream Input [Military]
RSI........... Repressor-Sensitizer Index [Psychology]
RSI........... Repubblica Sociale Italiana [Italian Socialist Republic] [Founded by Mussolini] [1943-1945]
RSI........... Research Studies Institute
RSI........... Reusable Surface Insulation [NASA]
RSI........... Rio Sidra [Panama] [Airport symbol] (OAG)

RSI............. Rivista Storica Italiana [*A publication*]
RSI............. Roll Stability Indicator [*NASA*] (KSC)
RSI............. Roofing/Siding/Insulation [*A publication*]
RSI............. Rotary Shaft Indicator
RSI............. Royal Sanitary Institute (ROG)
RSI............. Royal Signals Institution [*British*] (DEN)
RS & I .... Rules, Standards, and Instructions
RSIC......... Radiation Shielding Information Center [*Department of Energy*] [*Oak Ridge, TN*]
RSIC......... Redstone Scientific Information Center [*Army*]
RSIC......... Responding Superior in Command (MCD)
RSIC......... RSI [*Resource Services, Inc.*] Corporation [*NASDAQ symbol*] (NQ)
RSID......... Resource Identification Table [*Data processing*]
RSIDA...... Research and Industry [*A publication*]
R SIGS..... Royal Corps of Signals [*British*] (DMA)
RSIH........ RSI Holdings, Inc. [*NASDAQ symbol*] (NQ)
RSIHM...... Reparation Society of the Immaculate Heart of Mary (EA)
RSIJA....... Journal. Royal College of Surgeons in Ireland [*A publication*]
RSIM........ RADAR Simulator (MSA)
RSIM........ Retrospective Single Ion Monitoring [*Analytical chemistry*]
R Sind Estadist ... Revista Sindical de Estadistica [*A publication*]
R Sindical Estadistica ... Revista Sindical de Estadistica [*A publication*]
RSIPR........ Reactor System with Interstage Product Removal [*Chemical engineering*]
RSIR......... International Statistical Institute. Review [*A publication*]
RSIS .... Radical Science Information Service [*News service attempting to interrelate radical politics and scientific issues*]
RSIS .... Reed Stenhouse Investment Services [*British*]
RSIS .... Rotorcraft Systems Integration Simulator [*Joint Army-NASA program*] (RDA)
RSITA .... Reglement du Service International des Telecommunications de l'Aeronautique
RSITD .... Revue Francaise d'Automatique, d'Informatique, et de Recherche Operationnelle. Serie Informatique Theorique [*A publication*]
R/SITU ..... Respiratory/Surgical Intensive Therapy Unit [*of a hospital*]
RSIUFL..... Release Suspension for Issue and Use of Following Lots [*Military*]
RSIVP....... Rapid Sequence Intravenous Pyelogram [*Medicine*]
RSJ .... Rolled-Steel Joist
RSJ .... Rolling-Stock Jigsaws [*British*]
RSKERL.... Robert S. Kerr Environmental Research Laboratory [*Ada, OK*] [*Environmental Protection Agency*] (GRD)
RSKU........ Reza Shah Kibur University [*Iran*]
RS KY Agric Exp Stn ... RS. Kentucky Agricultural Experiment Station [*A publication*]
RSL........... Radio Standards Laboratory [*National Institute of Standards and Technology*]
RS or L....... Rated Same or Lower
RSL........... Reading on Statute Law [*A publication*] (DLA)
RSL........... Received Signal Level [*Telecommunications*] (TEL)
RSL........... Reconnaissance and Security Line
RSL........... Red Suspender League (EA)
RSL........... Reference Standards Laboratory [*Deep Space Instrumentation Facility, NASA*]
RSL........... Relative Sea Level
RSL........... Remote Sensing Laboratory [*University of Kansas, University of Minnesota*] [*Research center*] (MCD)
RSL........... Remote Sprint Launching [*Military*]
RSL........... Requirements Statement Language
RSL........... Research Services Limited [*Database producer*] [*Wembley, Middlesex, England*]
RSL........... Resource Support List [*NASA*] (MCD)
RSL........... Returned Servicemen's League [*British military*] (DMA)
RSL........... Revolutionary Socialist League (EA)
RSl........... Revue des Etudes Slaves [*A publication*]
RSL........... Ricerche Slavistiche [*A publication*]
RSL........... Ripe Skin Liquid [*A banana substrate*]
RSL........... Rivista di Sintesi Litteraria [*A publication*]
RSL........... Rivista di Studi Liguri [*A publication*]
RSL........... Road Service Licence [*British*] (DCTA)
RSl........... Rocznik Slawistyczny [*A publication*]
RSL........... Roselend [*France*] [*Seismograph station code, US Geological Survey*] (SEIS)
RSL........... Royal Society of Literature [*British*]
RSL........... Royal Society, London [*British*]
RSL........... RSI Retail Solutions, Inc. [*Vancouver Stock Exchange symbol*]
RSL........... Rumsford Sandy Loam [*Type of soil*]
RSL........... Russell, KS [*Location identifier*] [*FAA*] (FAAL)
RSLA........ Range Safety Launch Approval (AFM)
RSLA........ Republic Capital Group, Inc. [*NASDAQ symbol*] (NQ)
RSlav........ Ricerche Slavistiche [*A publication*]
RSlav........ Romanoslavica [*A publication*]
RSLB .... Right Short Leg Brace [*Medicine*]
RSLF .... Revue de Science et de Legislation Financiere [*A publication*]
RSlI........... Radovi Slavenskog Instituta [*A publication*]
RSLig........ Rivista di Studi Liguri [*A publication*]
RSLit .... Riverside Studies in Literature [*A publication*]
RSLMDZ .. Swedish University of Agricultural Sciences. Department of Microbiology. Report [*A publication*]

RSLR .... Rivista di Storia e Letteratura Religiosa [*A publication*]
RSLS .... Receiver Side Lobe Suppression (MCD)
RSLTDM .. Swedish University of Agricultural Sciences. Department of Horticultural Science. Report [*A publication*]
RSLTS........ Results
RSIU........ Rocenka Slovanskeho Ustavu v Praze [*A publication*]
RSLV......... Resolve (NASA)
RSLVDS...... Swedish University of Agricultural Sciences. Department of Plant Husbandry. Report [*A publication*]
RSLVR .... Resolver (MSA)
RSM .... Radiation Signature Measurement
RSM .... Radiation Survey Meter [*NASA*]
RSM .... Radio Squadron Mobile (MUGU)
RSM .... Rapeseed Meal
RSM .... Rapidly Solidified Materials
RSM .... Real Storage Management [*Data processing*] (IBMDP)
RSM .... Reconnaissance Strategic Missile
RSM .... Reed Switching Matrix
RSM .... Regimental Sergeant Major [*Army*]
RSM .... Response Surface Methodology
RSM .... Resume (NASA)
RSM .... Revised Statutes of Manitoba [*Canada*] [*A publication*] (DLA)
RSM .... Rivet Setting Machine
RSM .... Rivista Storico-Critica delle Scienze Mediche e Naturali [*A publication*]
RSM .... Robert Strange McNamara [*US Secretary of Defense, 1961-68*]
RS & M ...... Royal Sappers and Miners [*British military*] (DMA)
RSM .... Royal School of Mines [*British*]
RSM .... Royal School of Musketry [*Hythe*] [*Military*] [*British*] (ROG)
RSM .... Royal Society of Medicine [*British*]
RSM .... Royal Society of Musicians of Great Britain
RSM .... Royal Surrey Militia [*British military*] (DMA)
RSM .... Sisters of Mercy [*Roman Catholic religious order*]
RSMA........ Radiological Systems Microfilm Associates (EA)
RSMA........ Railway Supply Manufacturers Association (EA)
RSMA........ Railway Systems and Management Association (EA)
RSMA........ Royal Society of Marine Artists [*Formerly, SMA*] [*British*]
RSMAS .... Rosenstiel School of Marine and Atmospheric Science [*University of Miami*] [*Research center*] (RCD)
RSmB......... Bryant College, Smithfield, RI [*Library symbol*] [*Library of Congress*] (LCLS)
RS & MD ... Riots, Strikes, and Malicious Damage [*Insurance*] (ADA)
RSME .... Royal School of Military Engineering [*British military*] (DMA)
RSMF .... Royal Society of Medicine Foundation (EA)
RSMFA ..... Rendiconti. Seminario Matematico e Fisico di Milano [*A publication*]
RSMG .... Rotorcraft Simulator Motion Generator [*Army*] (RDA)
RSMGB..... Royal Society of Musicians of Great Britain (EAIO)
RSMJA ..... Royal School of Mines. Journal [*A publication*]
RSMLC ..... Red de Salud de las Mujeres Latinoamericanas y del Caribe [*Latin American and Caribbean Women's Health Network*] (EAIO)
RSMM ...... Redundant System Monitor Model [*NASA*] (MCD)
Rs Mod Physics ... Reviews of Modern Physics [*A publication*]
RSMR........ Raw Stock Material Requirements
RSMR........ Rayleigh Scattering of Moessbauer Resonance [*Physics*]
RSMS .... Radio Spectrum Measurement System [*National Telecommunications and Information Administration*]
RSMT........ Ras Shamra Mythological Texts (BJA)
RSMT........ Red Sea Mission Team (EA)
RSMT........ Reliability Safety Margin Test
RSN .... Radiation Surveillance Network [*Public Health Service*]
RSN .... Radio Supernovae [*Astrophysics*]
RSN .... Rassemblement pour le Salut National [*Rally for National Salvation*] [*Senegal*] (PD)
RSN .... Ready, Soon, Now (Approach) [*Marketing*]
RSN .... Reason (AFM)
RSN .... Reference Sequence Number [*Online bibliographies*]
RSN .... Reject Sequence Number [*Data processing*]
RSN .... Report Serial Number [*Army*]
RSN .... Research Surveillance Network
RSN .... Resonate (KSC)
RSN .... Revised Statutes of Newfoundland [*Canada*] [*A publication*] (DLA)
RSN .... Revue Suisse de Numismatique [*A publication*]
RSN .... Royal School of Needlework [*British*]
RSN .... Ruston, LA [*Location identifier*] [*FAA*] (FAAL)
RSNA .... Radiological Society of North America (EA)
RSNA .... Royal Society of Northern Antiquaries (ROG)
RSNB .... Revised Statutes of New Brunswick [*Canada*] [*A publication*] (DLA)
RSNC........ Royal Society for Nature Conservation (EAIO)
RSNF........ Royal Saudi Arabian Navy Forces (MCD)
RSNGS ...... Rancho Seco Nuclear Generating Station (NRCH)
RSNO........ Referral Service Network Office
RSNP........ Registered Student Nurse Program [*Military*] (AABC)
RSNS........ Revised Statutes of Nova Scotia [*Canada*] [*A publication*] (DLA)
RSNT........ Revised Single Negotiating Text [*UN Law of the Sea Conference*]
RSO .... Radiation Safety Officer [*Nuclear energy*] (NRCH)

RSO .... Radio Symphony Orchestra
RSO .... Radiological Safety Office [*or Officer*] (NASA)
RSO .... Radiosonde Observation (MUGU)
RSO .... Railway Sorting Office
RSO .... Railway Suboffice
RSO .... Ramus Supraorbitalis [*Anatomy*]
RSO .... Range Safety Officer [*Military*]
RSO .... Range Support Operation
RSO .... Reactor Standards Office [*Oak Ridge National Laboratory*]
RSO .... Reactor System Outline [*Nuclear energy*] (NRCH)
RSO .... Reconnaissance and Survey Officer [*Military*] (AABC)
RSO .... Reconnaissance System Officer (MCD)
RSO .... Regimental Supply Officer [*Army*]
RSO .... Regional Safety Officer [*British*] (DCTA)
RSO .... Regional Security Officer [*Foreign Service*]
RSO .... Register Sender Outward [*Telecommunications*] (TEL)
RSO .... Research Ship of Opportunity
RSO .... Resident Surgical Officer [*British*]
RSO .... Resonans [*A publication*]
RSO .... Revenue Sharing Office [*Treasury*] (OICC)
RSO .... Revised Statutes of Ontario [*Canada*] [*A publication*] (DLA)
RSO .... Revolutionaere Sozialisten (Oesterreichs) [*Revolutionary Socialists (Austria)*] [*Political party*] (PPE)
RSO .... Right Salpingo-Oophorectomy [*Medicine*]
RSO .... Rivista degli Studi Orientali [*A publication*]
RSO .... Runway Supervisory Officer [*Aviation*] (MCD)
RSO .... Rural Suboffice [*British*]
RSOB........ Russell Senate Office Building [*Also, OSOB*] [*Washington, DC*] (DLA)
RSOC........ Remote Sensing Oceanography [*Navy*]
RSoc........ Revue Socialiste [*A publication*]
R Soc........ Revue des Societes [*A publication*]
R Soc Can .. Royal Society of Canada. Transactions [*A publication*]
R Soc Can Proc ... Royal Society of Canada. Proceedings [*A publication*]
R Soc Can Proc Trans ... Royal Society of Canada. Proceedings and Transactions [*A publication*]
R Soc Chem Spec Publ ... Royal Society of Chemistry. Special Publication [*A publication*]
R Soc Econ ... Review of Social Economy [*A publication*]
R Soc Edinb Proc Sect B ... Royal Society of Edinburgh. Proceedings. Section B. Biology [*A publication*]
R Soc Esp Fis Quim Reun Bienal ... Real Sociedad Espanola de Fisica y Quimica. Reunion Bienal [*A publication*]
R Soc Et Expans ... Revue. Societe d'Etudes et d'Expansion [*A publication*]
R Soc Health J ... Royal Society of Health. Journal [*A publication*]
R Social Economy ... Review of Social Economy [*A publication*]
R Sociol........ Revija za Sociologiju [*A publication*]
R Soc London Proc ... Royal Society of London. Proceedings [*A publication*]
R Soc Lond Philos Trans ... Royal Society of London. Philosophical Transactions [*A publication*]
R Soc Lond Philos Trans Ser A ... Royal Society of London. Philosophical Transactions. Series A [*A publication*]
R Soc Lond Philos Trans Ser B ... Royal Society of London. Philosophical Transactions. Series B [*A publication*]
R Soc Lond Proc Ser B ... Royal Society of London. Proceedings. Series B. Biological Sciences [*A publication*]
R Soc NZ Bull ... Royal Society of New Zealand. Bulletin [*A publication*]
R Soc NZ J ... Royal Society of New Zealand. Journal [*A publication*]
R Soc Queensl Proc ... Royal Society of Queensland. Proceedings [*A publication*]
R Soc S Afr Trans ... Royal Society of South Africa. Transactions [*A publication*]
R Soc S Aust Trans ... Royal Society of South Australia. Transactions [*A publication*]
R Soc Tasmania Pap Proc ... Royal Society of Tasmania. Papers and Proceedings [*A publication*]
R Soc Theory ... Review of Social Theory [*A publication*]
R Soc Victoria Proc ... Royal Society of Victoria. Proceedings [*A publication*]
R Soc West Aust J ... Royal Society of Western Australia. Journal [*A publication*]
RSOG........ Reserve Special Operations Group [*Army*]
RSOHJ...... Royal Society of Health. Journal [*A publication*]
RSOLB...... Research Outlook [*A publication*]
RSONA ..... Revue Stomato-Odontologique du Nord de la France [*A publication*]
RSOP........ Range Safety Operational Plan (MUGU)
RSOP........ Readiness Standing Operating Procedures [*Military*] (INF)
RSOP........ Reconnaissance, Selection, and Occupation of Position [*Military*]
RSOPN...... Resumed Operation (FAAC)
RSOR........ Range Safety Operations Requirement
RSov.......... Rassegna Sovietica [*A publication*]
RSP .... RADAR Signal Processor
RSP .... Radii of Standard Parallels
RSP .... Radio Switch Panel
RSP .... Random Smooth Pursuit [*Ophthalmology*]
RSP .... Range Solar Panel
RSP .... Range Sorting Program
RSP .... Range Support Plan (MUGU)
RSP........... Rapid Site Preparation
RSP........... Rapid Solidification Process (MCD)

RSP........... Rate Sensing Package (AAG)
RSP........... Reactive Soil Pool [*Agriculture*]
RSP........... Reactivity Surveillance Procedures [*Nuclear energy*] (NRCH)
RSP........... Reader/Sorter Processor
RSP........... Real-Time Signal Processor (MCD)
RSP........... Receiving Stolen Property
RSP........... Reconnaissance and Security Positions [*Military*]
RSP........... Record Select Program [*Data processing*]
RSP........... Recoverable Sparoair Probe (MUGU)
RSP........... Reinforced Structural Plastic
RSP........... Remote Sensor Platoon
RSP........... Remote Shutdown Panel [*Nuclear energy*] (NRCH)
RSP........... Render Safe Procedure [*Military*]
RSP........... Rendezvous Station Panel [*NASA*] (MCD)
RSP........... Replenishment Spare Part
RSP........... Replication Synchronization Process [*Telecommunications*] (TEL)
RSP........... Required Space Character [*Data processing*]
RSP........... Reserve Stock Point
RSP........... Respirable Suspended Particulates
RSP........... Responder Beacon
RSP........... Restoration Priority [*Telecommunications*] (TEL)
RSP........... Retail Stockage Policy
RSP........... Revolutionaire Socialistische Partij [*Revolutionary Socialist Party*] [*Netherlands*] [*Political party*] (PPE)
RSP........... Revolutionary Socialist Party [*India*] [*Political party*] (PPW)
RSP........... Revue des Sciences Politiques [*A publication*]
RSP........... Right Sacroposterior [*A fetal position*] [*Obstetrics*]
RSP........... Rivista di Studi Pompeiani [*A publication*]
RSP........... Robotic Sample Processor [*Automation*]
RSP........... Rocky Slope Pipeline
RSP........... Roll Stabilization Platform
RSP........... Roscoe, Snyder & Pacific Railway Co. [*AAR code*]
RSP........... Rotating Shield Plug [*Nuclear energy*] (NRCH)
RSP........... Rotation in a Selected Plane
RSP........... Rural Satellite Program [*US Agency for International Development*] [*Washington, DC*] [*Telecommunications*] (TSSD)
RSPA .... Railway Systems and Procedures Association [*Later, RSMA*]
RSPA .... Research and Special Programs Administration [*Department of Transportation*] [*Washington, DC*] (GRD)
RSPA .... Royal Society for the Prevention of Accidents [*British*]
RSPB .... Retail Stockage Policy, Bulk Supplies (MCD)
RSPB .... Royal Society for the Protection of Birds [*British*]
RSPCA ...... Royal Society for the Prevention of Cruelty to Animals [*British*]
RSPD........ Rapid Solidification Plasma Deposition [*Metallurgy*]
RSPD........ Research and Special Project Division [*Bureau of National Affairs*] [*Information service or system*] (IID)
RSPD........ Respond (MSA)
RSPE .... RADAR Signalling Processing Equipment
RSPE .... Retail Stockage Policy, Evaluation (MCD)
RSPEI........ Revised Statutes of Prince Edward Island [*Canada*]
RSPh.......... Revue des Sciences Philosophiques et Theologiques [*A publication*]
RSPhTh..... Revue des Sciences Philosophiques et Theologiques [*A publication*]
RSPI .... Residential Space Planners International (EA)
RSPK......... Recurrent Spontaneous Psychokinesis [*Poltergeist*] [*Parapsychology*]
RSPL .... RADAR Significant Power Line
RSPL .... Recommended Spare Parts List [*NASA*]
RS/PM .... Rapid Solidification/Powder Metallurgy
RSPMB ..... Research in the Psychology of Music [*A publication*]
RSPMP .... Ready Store Positive Maintenance Program (MCD)
RSPO......... Rail Services Planning Office [*Interstate Commerce Commission*]
RSPO......... Railway Station Police Officer [*British*]
RSPP .... Radio Simulation Patch Panel (CET)
RSPP .... Royal Society of Portrait Painters [*British*]
Rspr .... Rechtspraak [*Case Law, Judicial Decisions*] [*Netherlands*] (ILCA)
Rspr .... Rechtsprechung [*Court Practice*] [*German*] (ILCA)
Rspr Arb .... Rechtsprechung in Arbeitssachen [*Labor Court Reports*] [*German*] (ILCA)
RSPRT ...... Robust Sequential Probability Ratio Test [*Navy*]
RSPS .... Range Solar Panel Substrate
RSPS .... Response (MSA)
RSPT .... Rayleigh-Schrodinger Perturbation Theory [*Physical chemistry*]
RSPT .... Real Storage Page Table [*Data processing*] (BUR)
RSPT .... Revue des Sciences Philosophiques et Theologiques [*A publication*]
RSPTA ...... Recherche Spatiale [*A publication*]
RSPTR ...... Respirator (MSA)
RSPUB9 .... Journal of Public Health [*A publication*]
RSPV .... Respective (AABC)
RSPWC ..... Royal Society of Painters in Water-Colours [*British*]
RSQ .... Rescue (AAG)
RSQ .... Revised Statutes of Quebec [*Canada*] [*A publication*] (DLA)
RSQ .... Rhetoric Society. Quarterly [*A publication*]
RSQBT ..... Rescue Boat
RSQC........ Reliability, Safety, and Quality Control

RSR............ Congregation of Our Lady of the Holy Rosary [*Roman Catholic women's religious order*]
RSR............ En Route Surveillance RADAR
RSR............ Radiological Safety Review [*Nuclear energy*]   (NRCH)
RSR............ Raiding Support Regiment [*British Royal Marines*] [*World War II*]
RSR............ Range Safety Report [*NASA*]   (AAG)
RSR............ Rapid Solidification Rate   (IEEE)
RSR............ Rassegna Storica del Risorgimento [*A publication*]
RSR............ Reactor Safety Research [*Nuclear energy*]
RSR............ Ready Service Ring   (NG)
RSR............ Recherches de Science Religieuse [*A publication*]
RSR............ Red Sulfhydryl Reagent
RSR............ Reference Services Review [*A publication*]
RSR............ Refracted Surface-Reflected Ray
RSR............ Regular Sinus Rhythm [*Physiology*]
RSR............ Republica Socialista Romania [*Socialist Republic of Romania*]   (EY)
RSR............ Request for Scientific Research   (AAG)
RSR............ Required Supply Rate [*Military*]   (AABC)
RSR............ Research Study Requests
RSR............ Residue Solvent Refining [*Lummus Crest, Inc. process*]
RSR............ Resorufin [*Organic chemistry*]
RSR............ Resources Status Report
RSR............ Revised Supplementary Regulation
RSR............ Revue des Sciences Religieuses. Universite de Strasbourg [*A publication*]
RSR............ Riser Foods, Inc. [*AMEX symbol*]   (SPSG)
RSR............ Rivista di Studi Religiosi [*A publication*]
RSR............ Rocket Scoring Reliability   (MCD)
RSR............ Rocket Stabilized Rod
RSR............ Rod Select Relay   (IEEE)
RSR............ Rotary Seal Ring
RSR............ Route Surveillance RADAR
RSR............ Rover Sports Register [*An association*]   (EAIO)
RSR............ Royal Sussex Regiment [*Military unit*] [*British*]
RSR............ Worcester, MA [*Location identifier*] [*FAA*]   (FAAL)
RSRA......... Rotor Systems Research Aircraft [*Army/NASA*]
RSRC......... RSR Corporation [*NASDAQ symbol*]   (NQ)
RSRE......... Royal Signals and RADAR Establishment [*Computer chip designer*] [*England*]
RSRel........ Revue des Sciences Religieuses. Universite de Strasbourg [*A publication*]
RSRF .... Riser Foods, Inc. [*NASDAQ symbol*]   (NQ)
RSRis........ Rassegna Storica del Risorgimento [*A publication*]
RSRM........ Raiding Squadron Royal Marines [*British military*]   (DMA)
RSRM........ Reduced Smoke Rocket Motor   (MCD)
RSROA...... Roller Skating Rink Operators Association   (EA)
RSROD ..... Revue Francaise d'Automatique, d'Informatique, et de Recherche Operationnelle. Serie Recherche Operationnelle [*A publication*]
RSRP......... Remote Sensing Research Program [*University of California*]
RSRP......... Rossica Society of Russian Philately   (EA)
RSRPB ...... Research and the Retarded [*A publication*]
RSRS......... Radio and Space Research Station [*Later, Appleton Laboratory*] [*British*]   (MCD)
RSRS......... Range Safety Receiving Station
RSRS......... Reser's Fine Foods, Inc. [*NASDAQ symbol*]   (NQ)
Rsrt .... Resort
RSRUS ...... Revue des Sciences Religieuses. Universite de Strasbourg [*A publication*]
RSRV......... Rotor Systems Research Vehicle
RSRW........ Remote Short Range Wind Sensor   (MCD)
RSS............ RADAR Seeker Simulator [*Military*]   (CAAL)
RSS............ RADAR Sensing System [*Military*]   (CAAL)
RSS............ RADAR Signal Simulator
RSS............ Radiated Simulation System   (MCD)
RSS............ Radio Security Service [*British*]
RSS............ Radio Subsystem
RS(S) .... Radio Supervisor (Special) [*British military*]   (DMA)
RSS............ Railway Systems Suppliers   (EA)
RSS............ Range Safety Switch [*NASA*]   (MCD)
RSS............ Range Safety System [*NASA*]
RSS............ Range Slaving System
RSS............ Rapid Scanning of Spectra [*Instrumentation*]
RSST.......... Rashtriya Swayamsevak Sangh [*National Union of Selfless Servers*] [*Militant Hindu organization*] [*India*]
RSS............ Rassegna Storica Salernitana [*A publication*]
RSS............ Reactant Service System
RSS............ Reactants Supply System [*NASA*]   (KSC)
RSS............ Reactor Safety Study [*Nuclear energy*]
RSS............ Reactor Shutdown System [*Nuclear energy*]   (NRCH)
RSS............ Ready Service Spares
RSS............ Real-Time Switching System
RS & S .... Receiving, Shipping, and Storage   (NASA)
RSS............ Recombination Signal Sequence [*Immunology*]
RSS............ Reed Stenhouse Companies Ltd. [*Toronto Stock Exchange symbol*]
RSS............ Reference Sound Source
RSS............ Refrigeration System [*or Subsystem*] [*Skylab*] [*NASA*]
RSS............ Refrigeration System Shield   (MCD)

RSS............ Regiae Societatis Sodalis [*Fellow of the Royal Society*]
RSS............ Registered Shoeing Smith [*Blacksmith*] [*Scotland*]
RSS............ Rehabilitation Service Series
RSS............ Rehabilitation Support Schedule   (AFM)
RSS............ Relative System Sensitivity
RSS............ Relaxed Static Stability [*Aviation*]
RSS............ Remote Safing Switch
RSS............ Remote Sensing Society [*Nottingham, England*]   (EAIO)
RSS............ Remote Shutdown System   (IEEE)
RSS............ Remote Slave Station   (MCD)
RSS............ Remote Switching System [*Telecommunications*]
RSS............ Repeat Squawk Sheet   (MCD)
RSS............ Requirements Status System [*NASA*]
RSS............ Residual Sum of Squares [*Statistics*]
RSS............ Resource Survey Satellite
RSS............ Restricted Stepsize [*Statistics*]
RSS............ Retention Spermatemia Syndrome [*Medicine*]
RSS............ Retentive Substrate Shield [*i.e., saucer*] [*Slang*]
RSS............ Revised Statutes of Saskatchewan [*Canada*] [*A publication*]   (DLA)
RSS............ Revue de Securite Sociale [*A publication*]
RSS............ Revue du Seizieme Siecle [*A publication*]
RSS............ Reye's Syndrome Society [*Later, NRSF*]   (EA)
RSS............ Rib Structure Station [*NASA*]   (MCD)
RSS............ Ribbed Smoke Sheet [*Natural rubber*]
RSS............ Ride Smoothing System [*Aviation*]
RSS............ Rifle Sharpshooter
RSS............ Rigid Space Structure
RSS............ Ripe Skin Solid [*A banana substrate*]
RSS............ Rivista di Scienze Storiche [*A publication*]
RSS............ Rockdale, Sandow & Southern Railroad Co. [*AAR code*]
RSS............ Roger Sessions Society   (EA)
RSS............ Roland International Corp. Sound Space [*Electronic music*]
RSS............ Romance of Science Series [*A publication*]
RSS............ Rome and the Study of Scripture [*A publication*]   (BJA)
RSS............ Root-Sum-Square
RSS............ Roseires [*Sudan*] [*Airport symbol*]   (OAG)
RSS............ Rotary Shaft Seal
RSS............ Rotary Stepping Switch
RSS............ Rotary Symbol Switch   (MCD)
RSS............ Rotating Service Structure [*Kennedy Space Center*]   (MCD)
RSS............ Routing and Switching System
RSS............ Rural Sociological Society   (EA)
RSSAA ..... Revue Internationale des Services de Sante des Armees de Terre, de Mer, et de l'Air [*A publication*]
RSSAILA .. Returned Sailors', Soldiers', Airmen's Imperial League of Australia [*British military*]   (DMA)
RSSal........ Rassegna Storica Salernitana [*A publication*]
RSSC .... Remote-Site Simulator Console [*NASA*]
RSSCW ..... Research Studies. State College of Washington [*Pullman*] [*A publication*]
RSSE .... Russian Spring-Summer Encephalitis [*Medicine*]
RSSEL....... Recommended Special Support Equipment List
RSSF.......... Retrievable Surface Storage Facility [*Nuclear energy*]
RSSF.......... Roller Speed Skating Federation   (EA)
RSSI .... Railway Systems Suppliers   (EA)
RSSJ.......... Researches in the Social Sciences on Japan. East Asian Institute. Columbia University [*A publication*]
RSSJA .... Journal. Royal Statistical Society. Series C. Applied Statistics [*A publication*]
RSSK .... Rigid Seat Survival Kit   (NG)
RSSLI....... Radovi Staroslavenskog Instituta [*A publication*]
RSSMAP... Reactor Safety Study Methodology Application Program [*Nuclear energy*]   (NRCH)
RSSME3 ... Swedish University of Agricultural Sciences. Reports in Forest Ecology and Forest Soils [*A publication*]
RSSMN..... Rivista di Storia delle Scienze Mediche e Naturali [*A publication*]
RSSN........ Research Space Surveillance Network
RSSND..... Roessing [*A publication*]
RSSP .... Range Single Shot Probability [*Military*]
RSSPCC.... Royal Scottish Society for Prevention of Cruelty to Children
RSSPL....... Recommended Spares and Spare Parts List
RSSPO ..... Resident Space Shuttle Project Office [*NASA*]   (NASA)
R & S SQ ... Repair and Salvage Squadron [*Military*]
RSSRT....... Russell Sage Social Relations Test [*Psychology*]
RSSS.......... Rashtriya Swayamseyak Sangh [*National Union of Selfless Servers*] [*Militant Hindu organization*] [*India*]   (PD)
RSSS.......... Reusable Space Shuttle System [*Aerospace*]   (KSC)
RSST.......... Reserve Station Service Transformer [*Nuclear energy*]   (NRCH)
RSSU........ Remote-Site Simulation Unit [*Navy*]   (NVT)
RS Supp..... Supplement to the Revised Statutes [*A publication*]   (DLA)
RSSW .... Ross Sea Shelf Water [*Ross Ice Shelf Project*]
RSSZ .... Rung Sat Special Zone [*Vietnam*]
RST............ RADAR Start   (MSA)
RST............ RADAR Systems Technician   (MCD)
RST............ Radiometric Sun Tracer
RST............ Range Search and Track   (MCD)
RST............ Rapid Solidification Technology [*Metallurgy*]
RST............ Read Symbol Table
RST............ Readability, Strength, Tone

RST........... Recessed Selectromatic Terminal   (NASA)
RST........... Recognition Suppression Technique
RST........... Recovery Sequence Tester
RST........... Reentry System Technology [Aerospace]
RST........... Reflector Support Truss
RST........... Register and Self-Test
RST........... Reinforcing Steel [Technical drawings]
RST........... Religious of St. Andrew [Roman Catholic religious order]
RST........... Remote Station [Data processing]
RST........... Requirements for Scheduled Test   (MUGU)
RSt............ Research Studies [A publication]
RST........... Research Study Team
RST........... Reset [Telecommunications]   (TEL)
RST........... Reset-Set Trigger
RST........... Resin Skived Tape
RST........... Resistance   (AABC)
RST........... Resort Airlines [Baltimore, MD] [FAA designator]   (FAAC)
RST........... Rest
RST........... Restore   (MSA)
RST........... Rework/Scrap Tag   (MCD)
RST........... Right Sacrotransverse [A fetal position] [Obstetrics]
RST........... Rivista Storica Ticinese [A publication]
RST........... Rivista di Studi Teatrali [A publication]
RST........... Rochester [Minnesota] [Airport symbol]   (OAG)
RST........... Rolling Stock   (CINC)
RST........... Rough Saw Template   (MCD)
RST........... Routine Sequence Table
RST........... Royal Scot Resources [Vancouver Stock Exchange symbol]
RST........... Royal Society of Teachers [British]
R Sta .... Radio Telegraph Station
RSTA........ Reconnaissance, Surveillance, and Target Acquisition Center [Army] [Fort Monmouth, NJ]   (MCD)
RStA .... Rivista di Storia Antica [A publication]
RSTAA ..... Reconnaissance, Surveillance, and Target Acquisition Aircraft   (MCD)
RSTA & E ... Reconnaissance, Surveillance, Target Acquisition, and Engagement   (MCD)
R Statis Quebec ... Revue Statistique du Quebec [A publication]
R Statist (Bucuresti) ... Revista de Statistica (Bucuresti) [A publication]
R St Biz Neoell ... Rivista di Studi Bizantini e Neoellenici [A publication]
RSTC........ RADAR Ship Target Classification [Military]   (CAAL)
RSTC........ Recreational Scuba Training Council   (EA)
RSTC........ Remote-Site Telemetry Computer [NASA]
RStCr........ Rivista Storico-Critica delle Scienze Teologiche [A publication]
RSTD........ Restricted
R St Fen ..... Rivista di Studi Fenici [A publication]
RSTG........ Roasting   (MSA)
RSTK........ Relay Servicing Tool Kit
RSTL......... Red Status Timeline
RSTL......... Relaxed Skin Tension Line [Dermatology]
R St Lig ..... Rivista di Studi Liguri [A publication]
R St March ... Rivista di Studi Marchigiani [A publication]
RSTMH .... Royal Society of Tropical Medicine and Hygiene [London, England]   (EAIO)
RSTN........ Radio Solar Telescope Network   (MCD)
RSTN........ Regional Seismic Test Network [Nuclear explosion detection]
RSTN........ Resource Technology [A publication]
R St O .... Rivista degli Studi Orientali [A publication]
RSTO........ Rose's Stores, Inc. [NASDAQ symbol]   (NQ)
R/STOL .... Reduced/Short Takeoff and Landing [Aircraft]
R Stor Ant ... Rivista Storica dell'Antichita [A publication]
R Storia Contemporanea ... Rivista di Storia Contemporanea [A publication]
RStorLettRel ... Rivista di Storia e Letteratura Religiosa [Florence] [A publication]   (BJA)
RSTP .... Real-Time Statistical and Terminal Profile [IRS]
RSTP .... Remote-Site Telemetry Processor [NASA]   (KSC)
RSTPF...... Rustproof   (MSA)
R St Pomp ... Rivista di Studi Pompeiani [A publication]
RSTR........ Resistor
RSTR........ Restrict   (MSA)
RSTRD..... Restricted
RSTRT ..... Restart   (NASA)
RSTS .... Resource-Sharing Time-Sharing System
RSTS .... Retirement Systems Testing Section [Social Security Administration]
RSTS .... Sunresorts Ltd. NV [New York, NY] [NASDAQ symbol]   (NQ)
R Stuart Pap ... Royal Stuart Papers [A publication]
RSTUD...... Rivista di Scienza e Tecnologia degli Alimenti e di Nutrizione Umana [A publication]
R Stud .... Romanische Studien [A publication]
R Studi Eur ... Rivista di Studi Europei [A publication]
R Stud Liguri ... Rivista di Studi Liguri [A publication]
R Stud Or... Rivista degli Studi Orientali [Rome] [A publication]
R St Wi ...... Recht, Staat, Wirtschaft [A publication]
RSTY .... Rusty Pelican Restaurants, Inc. [NASDAQ symbol]   (NQ)
RSU .... Rating Scale Unit [Acoustics]
RSU .... Recorder Switch Unit
RSU .... Regional Science and Urban Economics [Netherlands] [A publication]
RSU .... Register Storage Unit
RSU .... Relay Storage Unit

RSU .... Remote Service Unit   (NASA)
RSU .... Remote Subscriber Unit [Telecommunications]
RSU .... Remote Switching Unit [Telecommunications]
RSU .... Repair and Salvage Unit [British military]   (DMA)
RSU .... Rescue Support Umbilical   (MCD)
RSU .... Rocenka Slovanskeho Ustavu [A publication]
RSU .... Runway Supervisory Unit [Aviation]   (FAAC)
RSUED..... Regional Science and Urban Economics [A publication]
R Suisse Zool ... Revue Suisse de Zoologie [A publication]
RSUNAC... Rassegna di Urologia e Nefrologia [A publication]
RSUSEV.... Arkansas. Agricultural Experiment Station. Research Series [A publication]
RSUTA...... Reconstruction Surgery and Traumatology [A publication]
RSV......... Armored Reconnaissance Scout Vehicle [Army]   (RDA)
RSV......... Diesel Run Control Solenoid Valve   (IEEE)
RSV......... Random Sine Vibration
RSV......... Rat Sarcoma Virus
RSV......... Rat Seminal Vesicle
RSV......... Recently Separated Veteran
RSV......... Reconnaissance Scout Vehicle   (MCD)
RSV......... Red Lake & Sun Valley [Vancouver Stock Exchange symbol]
RSV......... Remove Shutoff Valve   (KSC)
RSV......... Research Safety Vehicle [Department of Transportation]
RSV......... Reserve   (MSA)
RSV......... Reservoir [Board on Geographic Names]
RSV......... Respiratory Syncytial Virus
RSV......... Revised Standard Version [of the Bible, 1952]
RSV......... Revista Signos de Valparaiso [A publication]
RSV......... Right Subclavian Vein [Anatomy]
RSV......... Robinson, IL [Location identifier] [FAA]   (FAAL)
RSV......... Rous Sarcoma Virus [Same as ASV]
RSVA....... Randolph-Sheppard Vendors of America   (EA)
RSV-Br ..... Rous Sarcoma Virus, Bryan [Strain]
RSVC....... Resident Supervisor Call   (BUR)
RSVE....... Reconstituted Sendai Virus Envelope [Immunology]
RSVN....... Reservation   (FAAC)
RSVP........ Radiation Spectral Visual Photometer
RSVP........ Rapid Sampling Vertical Profiler [Oceanography]
RSVP........ Rapid Serial Visual Presentation [Data processing]
RSVP........ Remote System Verification Program
RSVP........ Repondez, s'il Vous Plait [The Favor of an Answer Is Requested] [French]
RSVP........ Research Selected Vote Profile [Election poll]
RSVP........ Research Society for Victorian Periodicals   (EA)
RSVP........ Response Segmentation and Validation Program [Donnelley Marketing Information Services] [Information service or system]   (IID)
RSVP........ Restartable Solid Variable Pulse [Motor]   (MCD)
RSVP........ Retired Senior Volunteer Program   (EA)
RSVP........ Ride Shared Vehicle Paratransit [Transportation system]
RSVPI....... Retired Senior Volunteer Program International   (EA)
RSVR....... Reservoir   (AAG)
RSVR....... Resolver   (AAG)
RSVR....... Roma. Rivista di Studi e di Vita Romana [A publication]
RSV(RV) .. Revised Standard Version of the Bible [A publication]   (BJA)
RSV-SR ..... Rous Sarcoma Virus, Schmidt-Ruppin [Strain]
RSVT....... Stetson Reading-Spelling Vocabulary Test [Educational test]
RSVTN..... Reservation
RSW .... Fort Myers [Florida] [Airport symbol]   (OAG)
RSW .... Fort Myers, FL [Location identifier] [FAA]   (FAAL)
RS(W)....... Radio Supervisor (Warfare) [British military]   (DMA)
RSW .... Rattlesnake Hills [Washington] [Seismograph station code, US Geological Survey]   (SEIS)
RSW .... Raw Service Water [Nuclear energy]   (NRCH)
RSW .... Refrigerated Seawater
RSW .... Repeating Slide Wire
RSW .... Resistance Spot Welding
RSW .... Retarded Surface Wave
RSW .... Royal Scottish Society of Painters in Water Colours
RSWB....... Raumordnung, Stadtebau, Wohnungswesen, Bauwesen [Fraunhofer Society] [Federal Republic of Germany]   (IID)
RSWC....... Right Side Up with Care
RSWC....... Royal Society of Painters in Water-Colours [British]   (ROG)
RSWD....... Regiment South Western District [British military]   (DMA)
RSWPS..... Repetitive Square Wave Potential Signal [Electrochemistry]
RSWS....... Royal Scottish Water-Colour Society   (ROG)
RSWSU ..... Research Studies. Washington State University [Pullman] [A publication]
RSWW....... Ross Sea Winter Water [Marine science]   (MSC)
RSY......... Lumberton, NC [Location identifier] [FAA]   (FAAL)
RSY......... Rigelyn Security [Vancouver Stock Exchange symbol]
RSYCA..... Railway Systems Control [A publication]
RSYCS..... Rosy Cross [Freemasonry]
RSYN....... Reactor Synthesis
RSyn .... Revue de Synthese [A publication]
R Synd Suisse ... Revue Syndicale Suisse [A publication]
RSYS........ Responsible System   (NASA)
RSYS........ Restaurant Systems, Inc. [NASDAQ symbol]   (NQ)
RSZ.......... Phoenix, AZ [Location identifier] [FAA]   (FAAL)
RSZOA...... Revue Suisse de Zoologie [A publication]

RT	Air Tungaru (Gilbert Islands) [*United Kingdom*] [*ICAO designator*] (ICDA)
RT	Electric Current Relay
RT	Rachidian Tooth
RT	RADAR Transparency (MCD)
R/T	RADAR Trigger (CET)
RT	Radiation Therapy [*Medicine*]
RT	Radio Technician
RT	Radio Telegraphy (ADA)
RT	Radio Telephone (MSA)
RT	Radio/Television Repair Program [*Association of Independent Colleges and Schools specialization code*]
RT	Radio Times [*A publication*]
RT	Radio Tracking (KSC)
RT	Radio Transmitter
RT	Radiographic Test [*Nuclear energy*] (NRCH)
RT	Radiologic Technologist
RT	Radiotelegraphy
RT	Radiotelephone
R/T	Radiotelephony
RT	Radular Teeth
RT	Rail Tractor [*British*]
RT	Rail Transport
RT	Raintight (MSA)
RT	Randomized Trial [*Statistics*]
RT	Range-to-Target (NASA)
RT	Range Timing (AAG)
RT	Range Tracking
RT	Ranger Tab [*Military decoration*]
RT	Rangetaker [*British military*] (DMA)
RT	Rangoon Institute of Technology [*Burma*] (DS)
RT	Rate (AAG)
RT	Rate Transmitter
RT	Rated Time (IEEE)
RT	Ratio Transformer [*Unit*]
RT	Rational Therapy [*Short form for rational-emotive therapy*]
RT	Reaction Time
RT	Reactor Trip [*Nuclear energy*] (NRCH)
RT	Read Tape [*Data processing*]
RT	Reading Teacher [*A publication*]
RT	Reading Test
RT	Readout Technique
RT	Real Time [*Computer*] [*Data processing*]
RT	Receive-Transmit [*Radio*]
RT	Received Text (ROG)
R/T	Receiver/Transmitter [*Radio*] (KSC)
RT	Receiving Tube
RT	Recherches Theatrales [*A publication*]
R & T	Recherches et Travaux [*A publication*]
RT	Record Transfer
R/T	Record of Trial [*Army*] (AABC)
RT	Recovery Time [*Military*] (AFIT)
RT	Recreational Therapist [*or Therapy*]
RT	Recueil des Travaux Relatifs a la Philologie et a l'Archeologie Egyptiennes et Assyriennes [*A publication*]
RT	Recueillis Temporaires [*Temporarily Taken In*] [*Of unadoptable children*] [*French*]
RT	Red Tetrazolium [*Also, TPTZ, TTC*] [*Chemical indicator*]
RT	Reduced Tillage System [*Agriculture*]
RT	Reduction Tables
RT	Reference Trajectory [*NASA*] (KSC)
RT	Refrigerated Trap [*Biotechnology*]
Rt	Regelungstechnik [*A publication*]
RT	Regional Treasurer [*British*]
RT	Register Ton
RT	Register Traffic [*Telecommunications*] (TEL)
RT	Register Transfer [*Data processing*]
R/T	Register Translator [*Telecommunications*] (TEL)
RT	Registered Technician [*American Registry of X-ray Technicians*]
RT	Regression Testing [*Data processing*] (IEEE)
RT	Rehabilitation Therapist [*or Therapy*]
RT	Rejection Tag (AAG)
RT	Related Term [*Indexing*]
RT	Relaxation Time
RT	Relaxation Training [*Psychology*]
RT	Relay Tester
RT	Relay Transmitter
RT	Release Transmittal (MCD)
RT	Released Time
RT	Religious Theatre [*A publication*]
RT	Remote Terminal [*Data processing*]
RT	Renal Transplant [*Nephrology*]
R/T	Reperforator/Transmitter [*Teletypewriter*] [*Data processing*]
R & T	Research and Technology
RT	Research and Technology
RT	Reserve Training
RT	Reset Trigger
RT	Residence Time [*Chemistry*]
R-T	Resistance Test (NASA)
RT	Resistor Tolerance
RT	Resistor Transistor
RT	Resorts International, Inc. [*AMEX symbol*] (SPSG)
RT	Respiratory Therapy [*Medicine*]
RT	Response Time [*Data processing*]
RT	Resting Tension [*Biology*]
RT	Resuscitation Team
RT	Resuscitation Therapy
RT	Retention Time [*Data processing*]
RT	Retraining (OICC)
RT	Retro Table [*NASA*]
RT	Retroviral Transcript [*Genetics*]
RT	Return Ticket
RT	Reverse Transcriptase [*An enzyme*]
RT	Revista dos Tribunais [*Brazil*] [*A publication*]
RT	Revolving Radio Beacon [*ITU designation*] (CET)
RT	Revue Theatrale [*A publication*]
RT	Revue Thomiste [*Brussels*] [*A publication*]
RT	Revue Tunisienne [*A publication*]
R/T	Rho/Theta
RT	Rigging Tool (MCD)
RT	Right (EY)
RT	Right Tackle [*Football*]
RT	Right Time of Departure/Arrival (DS)
RT	Right Turn after Takeoff [*Aviation*] (FAAC)
RT	Ring Trip [*Telecommunications*] (TEL)
RT	Ringing Tone [*Telecommunications*] (TEL)
RT	RISC [*Reduced-Instruction Set Computer*] Technology [*IBM Corp.*]
RT	Rise Time (DEN)
RT	[*The*] River Terminal Railway Co. [*AAR code*]
R & T	Road and Track [*A publication*]
RT	Road Traffic
RT	Road Transport (NATG)
RT	Road Truck [*Shipping*] (DCTA)
RT	Rocket Target
RT	Romain de Tirtoff [*Also known as ERTE*] [*Couturier*]
RT	Room Temperature
RT	Root [*Mathematics*] (ROG)
RT	Rotation Discrete Rate
rt	Rotten [*Quality of the bottom*] [*Nautical charts*]
RT	Rough Terrain [*Military*] (AABC)
RT	Rough Times [*Formerly, Radical Therapist*] [*A publication*]
R & T	Rough and Tumble Engineers' Historical Association (EA)
RT	Round Table [*Australia*] [*A publication*]
RT	Round Trip
RT	Route (AABC)
RT	Route Treatment [*Telecommunications*] (TEL)
RT	Router Template
RT	Royalty Trust
RT	Rufous-Sided Towhee [*Ornithology*]
RT	Running Title
RT	Runnymead Trust [*An association*] (EAIO)
RT	Runup and Taxi [*Air Force*]
R & T	Rush & Tomkins [*Commercial firm*] [*British*]
RT	Ruth [*Old Testament book*]
RT	Rye Terms
Rt	Tetrachoric Correlation [*Psychology*]
RT	Total Reserves
RT	Transportes Aereos de Timor [*Portugal*] [*ICAO designator*] [*Obsolete*] (FAAC)
rT₃	Reverse Triiodothyronine [*Endocrinology*]
RTA	RADAR Terrain Analysis
RTA	Radically Tapered Antenna
RTA	Radix Teachers Association (EA)
RTA	Rail Travel Authorization [*Military*]
RTA	Railway Tie Association (EA)
RTA	Rattler Resources [*Vancouver Stock Exchange symbol*]
RTA	Reactivity Test Assembly [*Nuclear energy*]
RTA	Ready-to-Assemble
RTA	Real-Time Accumulator
RTA	Real-Time Analyzer [*Electronics*]
RTA	Reciprocal Trade Agreement
RTA	Refrigeration Trade Association of America
RTA	Reliability Test Assembly
RTA	Reliable Test Analyzer [*Data processing*]
RTA	Religious and Theological Abstracts [*A publication*]
RTA	Remote Test Access [*Telecommunications*] (TEL)
RTA	Remote Trunk Arrangement [*Telecommunications*] (TEL)
RTA	Renal Tubule Acidosis [*Medicine*]
RTA	Request for Technical Action (MCD)
RTA	Returned to Australia
RTA	Riberalta [*Bolivia*] [*Seismograph station code, US Geological Survey*] [*Closed*] (SEIS)
RTA	Rise-Time Analyzer
RTA	Road Traffic Accident [*British*]
RTA	Road Traffic Act [*1962*] [*British*] [*A publication*] (DLA)
RTA	Road Trains of Australia
RTA	Roads and Traffic Authority [*New South Wales, Australia*]
RTA	Rotor Test Apparatus (MCD)
RTA	Rotuma [*Fiji*] [*Airport symbol*] (OAG)
RTA	Royal Thai Army

RTA .... Rubber Trade Association of New York   (EA)
RTAC........ Real-Time Adaptive Control
RTAC........ Regional Technical Aid Center [*Agency for International Development*]
RTAC........ Research and Technology Advisory Council [*Terminated, 1977*] [*NASA*]   (EGAO)
RTAC........ Roads and Transportation Association of Canada [*Ottawa, ON*] [*Formerly, Canadian Good Roads Association*] [*Research center*]
RTACF ..... Real-Time Auxiliary Computing Facility [*Apollo*] [*NASA*]
RTACS ..... Real-Time Adaptive Control System [*Military*]   (CAAL)
RTAD .... Router Adapter
RTAF .... Report to Armed Forces
RTAF .... Royal Thai Air Force
RTAFB ...... Royal Thai Air Force Base   (CINC)
RTAFCONV ... Royal Thai Air Force Contingent, Vietnam
RTAG .... Range Technical Advisory Group
RTAM .... Recherches de Theologie Ancienne et Medievale [*A publication*]
RTAM .... Remote Telecommunications Access Method [*Data processing*]
RTAM .... Remote Terminal Access Method [*Data processing*]   (BUR)
RTAM .... Resident Terminal Access Method [*Data processing*]
RTANG ..... Right Angle
RTAPS ...... Real-Time Terminal Application Program System [*Data processing*]
RTARF ..... Royal Thai Armed Forces   (CINC)
RTARP...... Royal Thai Army Rebuild Plant   (MCD)
RTASM..... Revue des Travaux. Academie des Sciences Morales et Politiques [*A publication*]
RTATD8.... Annual Report. Tokyo University of Agriculture and Technology [*A publication*]
RTAV .... Retail Traders Association of Victoria [*Australia*]
R Taxation Individuals ... Review of Taxation of Individuals [*A publication*]
RTB .... Radial Time Base
RTB .... Radio Television Brunei
RTB .... Radiodiffusion-Television Belge [*Belgian Radio Broadcasting and Television System*]
RTB .... Read Tape Binary [*Data processing*]   (IEEE)
RTB .... Reason to Believe   (ECON)
RTB .... Rechtskundig Tijdschrift voor Belgie [*A publication*]
RTB .... Resistance Temperature Bulb [*NASA*]
RTB .... Resolver Tracking Bridge
RTB .... Response/Throughput Bias [*Data processing*]   (BUR)
RTB .... Return to Base [*Military*]
RTB .... Roatan [*Honduras*] [*Airport symbol*]   (OAG)
RTB .... Rocket Test Base
RTB .... Rural Telephone Bank [*Department of Agriculture*]
RTBA......... Rate to Be Agreed [*Business term*]   (DCTA)
RTBCA...... Revue Technique du Batiment et des Constructions Industrielles [*A publication*]
RTBISC..... Radiodiffusion-Television Belge - Institut des Services Comuns [*Belgian Radio Broadcasting and Television - Common Services Institute*]
RTBM........ Real-Time BIT [*Binary Digit*] Mapping
RTBM........ Recoverable Test Bed Missile
RTBNA...... Recueil des Travaux Botaniques Neerlandais [*A publication*]
RTBT .... Resonant Tunneling Bipolar Transistor [*Electronics*]
RTC .... RADAR Tracking Center [*or Control*]
RTC .... Radio Tecnica Colombiana
RTC .... Radio Transmission Control   (NATG)
RTC .... Radio Tuned Circuit   (DEN)
RTC .... Radiodiffusion-Television Congolaise [*Congolese Radio and Television*]
RTC .... Rails-to-Trails Conservancy   (EA)
RTC .... Range Telemetry Central [*Aerospace*]
RTC .... Ratchet   (AAG)
RTC .... Reader Tape Contact
RTC .... Real-Time Captioning [*for the deaf*]
RTC .... Real-Time Clock [*Data processing*]   (MCD)
RTC .... Real-Time Command [*Data processing*]
RTC .... Real-Time Computer
RTC .... Real-Time Conference [*GEnie*] [*Telecommunications*]
RTC .... Real-Time Control [*Data processing*]   (MCD)
RTC .... Real-Time Counter [*Data processing*]
RTC .... Reconstruction of Town and Country [*British*] [*World War II*]
RTC .... Recruit Training Center
RTC .... Recueil Tablettes Chaldeennes [*A publication*]
RTC .... Reference Test Chart
RTC .... Regional Term Contract
RTC .... Regional Transport Commissioner
RTC .... Rehabilitation Research and Training Centers [*Department of Health and Human Services*]
RTC .... Relative Time Clock [*Data processing*]   (MDG)
RTC .... Remote Terminal Controller
RTC .... Removable Top Closure [*Nuclear energy*]   (NRCH)
RTC .... Replacement Training Center [*Military*]
RTC .... Reproductive Toxicology Center [*Database*]   (EISS)
RTC .... Required Technical Characteristic [*Military*]   (CAAL)
RTC .... Requirements Type Contract [*Military*]   (AABC)
RTC .... Reserve Training Corps
RTC .... Residential Training College [*for disabled people*] [*British*]

RTC .... Resolution Trust Corporation [*Federal government instrumentality, established in 1989*]
RTC .... Resort Timesharing Council   (EA)
RTC .... Responsible Training Center [*Air Training Command*]   (MCD)
RTC .... Return to Clinic [*Nursing*]
RTC .... Return to Control
RTC .... Reverse Transfer Capacitance
RTC .... Revue Trimestrielle Canadienne [*A publication*]
RTC .... Ridiculous Theatrical Company
RTC .... Rochester Telephone Corporation [*NYSE symbol*]   (SPSG)
RTC .... Rocket Technique Committee
RTC .... Room Temperature Cure   (NASA)
RTC .... Royal Tank Corps [*Military unit*] [*British*]
RTC-30 ...... Rehabilitation Research and Training Center in Blindness and Low Vision [*Mississippi State University*] [*Research center*]   (RCD)
RTCA........ Race Track Chaplaincy of America   (EA)
RTCA........ Radio Technical Commission for Aeronautics   (EA)
RTCA........ Radio-Television Correspondents Association   (EA)
RTCA........ Real-Time Casualty Assessment   (MCD)
RTCA........ Ribofuranosyltriazolecarboxamide [*Ribavirin*] [*Antiviral compound*]
RTCANI.... Rav Tov Committee to Aid New Immigrants [*Later, RTIJRO*]   (EA)
RTCB........ ROTI [*Recording Optical Tracking Instrument*] Tracker - Cocoa Beach [*NASA*]   (KSC)
RTCB........ Run to Cladding Breach [*Nuclear energy*]   (NRCH)
RTCC........ Radiant Technology Corporation [*NASDAQ symbol*]   (NQ)
RTCC........ Real-Time Command Controller [*Data processing*]   (NASA)
RTCC........ Real-Time Computer Center [*NASA*]   (NASA)
RTCC........ Real-Time Computer Command [*NASA*]   (NASA)
RTCC........ Real-Time Computer Complex [*NASA*]
RTCDS ..... Real-Time Cinetheodolite Data System
RtCE .... Right to a Comprehensive Education [*British*]
RTCE......... Rotation/Translation Control Electronics   (NASA)
RTCF .... Real-Time Combined File [*IRS*]
RTCF .... Real-Time Computer Facility
RTCH .... Radiation Technology, Inc. [*NASDAQ symbol*]   (NQ)
RTCH .... Rough Terrain Container Handler   (MCD)
RTCIL .... Research and Training Center on Independent Living   (EA)
RTCL......... Reticle [*Optics*]
RTCM .... Radio Technical Commission for Maritime Services   (TSSD)
RTC Met Cl J ... RTC [*Royal Technical College*] Metallurgical Club. Journal [*A publication*]
RTCO .... Record Time Compliance Order
RTCOD ..... [*The*] Research and Technology Coordinating Document [*Army*]   (RDA)
RTCP......... Radio Transmission Control Panel   (NATG)
RTCP......... Real-Time Communications Processor   (NASA)
RTCP......... Resident Training and Counseling Programs   (OICC)
RTCPA ...... Recueil des Travaux Chimiques des Pays-Bas [*A publication*]
RTCS .... Real-Time Calling Standards [*Chromatography*]
RTCS .... Real-Time Communication System
RTCS .... Real-Time Computer System
RTCTO..... Record Time Compliance Technical Order   (AAG)
RTCU .... Real-Time Control Unit
RTCU .... Router Cutter [*Tool*]   (AAG)
RTD .... Delayed [*Indicates delayed meteorological message*]   (FAAC)
RTD .... Radiodiffusion-Television de Djibouti
RTD .... Range Time Decoder
RTD .... Rate Damping   (NASA)
RTD .... Rate Dumping   (MCD)
RTD .... Read Tape Decimal
RTD .... Real-Time Decoder
RTD .... Real Time Developments [*Commercial firm*] [*British*]
RTD .... Real-Time Display
RTD .... Reliability Technical Directive   (AAG)
RTD .... Remote Temperature Detector
RTD .... Replacement Task Distribution
RTD .... Replacement Training Detachment   (MCD)
RTD .... Research and Technology Division [*Air Force*]
RTD .... Research Thrust Division [*Washington, DC*] [*DoD*]   (GRD)
RTD .... Residence Time Distribution [*Chemical engineering*]
RTD .... Resistance Temperature Detector [*Nuclear energy*]
RTD .... Resistance Temperature Device [*Nuclear energy*]   (NRCH)
RTD .... Retard   (MSA)
RTD .... Retired
RTD .... Return to Duty [*Military*]
RTD .... Returned [*Medicine*]   (DHSM)
RTD .... Road Traffic Division [*British police*]
RTD .... Routine Test Dilution [*Analysis*]
RTDA .... Radio and Television Dealers' Association
RTDA .... Retail Tobacco Dealers of America   (EA)
RTDA .... Returned Absentees
RTDAP...... RADAR Target Data Analog Processor   (MCD)
RTDB .... Research Training and Development Branch [*Bethesda, MD*] [*National Heart, Lung, and Blood Institute*]   (GRD)
RTDC .... Real-Time Data Channel   (IEEE)
RTDC .... Retardation Coil   (MSA)
RTDC .... Rocket-Thrown Depth Charge   (NG)
RTDD .... Real-Time Data Distribution

RTDD .... Remote Timing and Data Distribution
RTDDC ..... Real-Time Digital Data Correction   (MUGU)
RTDE .... Range Time Data Editor [*NASA*]   (KSC)
RTDE .... Revue Trimestrielle de Droit Europeen [*A publication*]
RTDF .... Real-Time Data File   (NOAA)
RTDG .... Radio and Television Directors Guild [*Later, DGA*]
RTDHS ...... Real-Time Data Handling System
RTDP .... RADAR Target Data Processor   (MCD)
RTDR .... Reliability Test Data Report
RTDS .... Real-Time Data System
RTDT .... Real-Time Data Translator
RTDVA ..... Rechentechnik-Datenverarbeitung [*A publication*]
RTE .... Radio Telefis Eireann [*Radio and television network*] [*Ireland*]
RTE .... Radio Trans-Europe
RTE .... Radio Trunk Extension   (NATG)
RTE .... RADOME [*RADAR Dome*] Test Equipment
RTE .... Railway Transport Establishment [*British military*]   (DMA)
RTE .... Ready to Eat [*Cereals*]
RTE .... Real-Time Executive [*Data processing*]
RTE .... Receiver Test Equipment
RTE .... Recovery Techniques Evaluation [*NASA*]   (KSC)
RTE .... Regenerative Turboprop Engines
RTE .... Reliability Test Evaluation   (AAG)
RTE .... Remote Terminal Emulator [*For teleprocessing validation*]
RTE .... Request to Expedite
RTE .... Research Training and Evaluation   (OICC)
RTE .... Resident Training Equipment   (MCD)
RTE .... Residual Total Elongation [*Nuclear energy*]   (NRCH)
RTE .... Responsible Test Engineer [*NASA*]   (NASA)
RTE .... Return to Earth [*NASA*]
RTE .... Return from Exception [*Data processing*]
RTE .... Route   (AFM)
RTE .... Royal Trust Energy Income Fund Trust Units [*Toronto Stock Exchange symbol*]
RTE .... RTE Corp. [*NYSE symbol*]   (SPSG)
RTE .... RTE. Radio-TV-Electronics [*A publication*]
RTE-B........ Real-Time Basic [*Data processing*]   (MDG)
RTEC......... Restec Systems, Inc. [*NASDAQ symbol*]   (NQ)
RTECS ...... Registry of Toxic Effects of Chemical Substances [*Department of Health and Human Services*] [*Information service or system*] [*A publication*]
RTED .... Return-to-Earth Digital [*NASA*]
RTEEA ...... Revue Roumaine des Sciences Techniques. Serie Electrotechnique et Energetique [*A publication*]
RTEG......... River Transport Escort Group   (CINC)
RTEID....... Revista Tecnica INTEVEP [*Instituto de Tecnologia Venezolana del Petroleo*] [*A publication*]
RTEK......... Rise Technology, Inc. [*NASDAQ symbol*]   (NQ)
RTel .... Radio Telemetry
RTEL......... Radio Telephony   (MSA)
R Telev Soc J ... Royal Television Society. Journal [*A publication*]
RTEM........ RADAR Tracking Error Measurement
RTEMB5.... Revista Espanola de Micropaleontologia [*A publication*]
RT & EPS ... Rapid Transit and Electrical Power Systems
RTES .... Radio and Television Executives' Society [*Later, IRTS*]
RTES .... Real-Time Engine Simulation   (MCD)
RTES .... Real-Time Executive System [*SEMIS*]
RTESB ...... Radio-TV-Electronic Service [*Later, RTE. Radio-TV-Electronic*] [*A publication*]
RTF........... Radio Transmission Facility
RTF........... Radiodiffusion-Television Francaise [*French Radio Broadcasting and Television System*]
RTF........... Radiotelephone
RTF........... Razor Trade Federation [*A union*] [*British*]
RTF........... Ready to Fire   (MCD)
RTF........... Real-Time FORTRAN [*Data processing*]
RTF........... Reconnaissance Task Force   (AFM)
RTF........... Reliability Task Force   (MCD)
RTF........... Religious Task Force   (EA)
RTF........... Reports Tempore Finch, English Chancery [*A publication*]   (DLA)
RTF........... Resistance Task Force   (EA)
RTF........... Resistance Transfer Factor [*of microorganisms to drugs*]
RTF........... Respiratory Tract Fluid [*Medicine*]
RTF........... Revue Theologique Francaise [*A publication*]
RTF........... Rich Text Format [*Data processing*]   (BYTE)
RTF........... Rocket Test Facility
RTF........... Room Temperature Fluorescence [*Physics*]
RTF........... Rotational Test Facility [*NASA*]
RTF........... Rubber-Tile Floor [*Technical drawings*]
RTFC......... Randy Travis Fan Club   (EA)
RTFC......... Retired Teamsters Fellowship Club   (EA)
RTFCA....... Religious Task Force on Central America   (EA)
RTFES....... Religious Task Force on El Salvador   (EA)
RTFFRJ .... Research Task Force for the Future of Reform Judaism   (EA)
RTFL......... Rough Terrain Fork Lift
RTFL......... Rough Terrain Front Loader   (MCD)
RTFLT....... Rough Terrain Forklift Truck   (MCD)
RTFM........ Router Form
RTFMS....... Radio Transmission Frequency Measuring System
RTFR......... Reliability Trouble and Failure Report

RTFR.......... Revista de Jurisprudencia do Tribunal Federal de Recursos [*Brazil*] [*A publication*]
RTFS......... Razor Trade Forgers' Society [*A union*] [*British*]
RTFT........ Rough Terrain Forklift Truck
RTFV........ RADAR Target Folder Viewer
RTG .... Racal Telecom PLC [*NYSE symbol*]   (CTT)
RTG .... Radioactive Thermoelectric Generator [*Nuclear energy*]   (NRCH)
RTG .... Radiodiffusion-Television Gabonaise [*Gabonese radio and television network*]
RTG .... Radiodiffusion-Television Guineenne [*Guinean radio and television network*]
RTG .... Radioisotope Thermoelectric Generator
RTG .... Radiotelegraph
RTG .... Range to Go
RTG .... Range to Ground   (MCD)
RTG .... Rare Tube Gas
RTG .... Rating   (MUGU)
RTG .... Reglement Telegraphique [*Telegraph Regulations*] [*French*]
RTG .... Requirements Tape Generator [*NASA*]
RTG .... Reusable Training Grenade
RTG .... Routing
RTG .... Royal Thai Government
RTG .... Ruteng [*Indonesia*] [*Airport symbol*]   (OAG)
RTGB........ Reactor Turbine Generator Board [*Nuclear energy*]   (NRCH)
RTGD .... Real-Time Graphic Display
RTGD .... Room Temperature Gamma Detector
RTGF .... Rat Transforming Growth Factor [*Biochemistry*]
RTGp .... Reconnaissance Technical Group [*Air Force*]   (AFM)
RTGp .... Reconnaissance Training Group [*Air Force*]   (AFM)
RTGp .... Retraining Group [*Air Force*]   (AFM)
RTGU .... Router Guide
RTGV .... Real-Time Generation of Video
RTH.......... Houston Oil Royalty Trust UBI [*NYSE symbol*]   (SPSG)
RTH.......... New York, NY [*Location identifier*] [*FAA*]   (FAAL)
RTh.......... Radio-Telephone (High Frequency) [*Telecommunications*]   (DS)
RTH.......... Regional Telecommunications Hub [*Telecommunications*]   (TEL)
RTH.......... Relay Transformer Header
RTH.......... Reports of Cases Concerning Settlements Tempore Holt [*England*] [*A publication*]   (DLA)
RTH.......... Reports Tempore Hardwicke [*England*] [*A publication*]   (DLA)
RTH.......... Retail Business. A Monthly Journal Concerned with Consumer Goods Markets, Marketing and Management, and Distribution in the United Kingdom [*A publication*]
RTh.......... Revue de Theologie et de Philosophie [*A publication*]
RTh.......... Revue Thomiste [*A publication*]
RTH.......... Ridgeway's Reports Tempore Hardwicke, Chancery and English King's Bench [*A publication*]   (DLA)
RThAbstr.. Religious and Theological Abstracts [*A publication*]
RThAM ..... Recherches de Theologie Ancienne et Medievale [*A publication*]
R T Hardw ... Reports Tempore Hardwicke, English King's Bench [*A publication*]   (DLA)
RTHC .... Rotation Translation Hand Controller   (NASA)
R Theol Louvain ... Revue Theologique de Louvain [*A publication*]
RTHK .... Radio Television Hong Kong
RThL .... Revue Theologique de Louvain [*A publication*]
R T Holt..... Reports Tempore Holt, English King's Bench [*A publication*]   (DLA)
RThom ...... Revue Thomiste [*A publication*]
RtHon .... Right Honourable   (EY)
RThPh .... Revue de Theologie et de Philosophie [*A publication*]
RThQr .... Revue de Theologie et des Questions Religieuses [*A publication*]   (BJA)
R Th R .... Reformed Theological Review [*A publication*]
RTHS .... Real-Time Hybrid System   (NASA)
RTI........... RADAR Target Identification
RTI........... Radiation Transfer Index
RTI........... Radiodiffusion-Television Ivoirienne [*Ivory Coast Radio and Television*]
RTI........... Railroad Transportation Insurers [*Defunct*]   (EA)
RTI........... Referred-to-Input
RTI........... Related Technical Instruction [*Bureau of Apprenticeship and Training*] [*Department of Labor*]
RTI........... Renault Truck Industries [*British subsidiary of Renault Vehicules Industriels*]
RTI........... Request for Technical Information [*Military*]
RTI........... Research Triangle Institutes [*Duke University, University of North Carolina at Chapel Hill, and North Carolina State University at Raleigh*] [*Research center*]
RTI........... Resilient Tile Institute [*Later, RFCI*]   (EA)
RTI........... Respiratory Tract Infection [*Medicine*]
RTI........... Review of Taxation of Individuals [*A publication*]
RTI........... Right Turn, International   (EA)
RTI........... Rise-Time Indicator
RTI........... RMI Titanium [*NYSE symbol*]   (SPSG)
RTI........... Role Taking Inventory
RTI........... Room, Tax, and Incidentals
RTI........... Root Tolerance Index [*Botany*]

RTI............ Roti [*Indonesia*] [*Airport symbol*]   (OAG)
RTI............ Round Table International   (EA)
RTIA.......... RTIA. Revue Technique de l'Industrie Alimentaire [*A publication*]
RTIC......... Rotor Temperature Indicator and Control [*Instrumentation*]
RTICBT..... Communication. Department of Agricultural Research. Royal Tropical Institute [*Amsterdam*] [*A publication*]
R Tiers-Monde ... Revue Tiers-Monde [*A publication*]
RTIF......... Real-Time Interface [*Data processing*]   (NASA)
RTII.......... RTI, Inc. [*NASDAQ symbol*]   (NQ)
RTIJRO .... Rav Tov International Jewish Rescue Organization   (EA)
RTIO .... Real-Time Input/Output Interface Subsystem [*Space Flight Operations Facility, NASA*]
RTIO .... Remote Terminal Input/Output
RTI/OC ..... Real-Time Input/Output Controller [*Data processing*]   (IEEE)
RTIP......... RADAR Target Identification Point   (AFM)
RTIP......... Real-Time Interactive Processor   (MCD)
RTIP......... Remote Terminal Interactive Processor   (MCD)
RTIP......... Remote Terminal Interface Package
RTIR......... Reliability and Trend Indicator Reports   (AAG)
RTIRS ...... Real-Time Information Retrieval System
RTIS .... Rockwell Technical Information System [*Rockwell International Corp.*] [*Information service or system*]   (IID)
RTITB .... Road Transport Industry Training Board [*British*]   (DCTA)
RTK .... Range Tracker   (KSC)
RTK .... Receptor Tyrosine Kinase [*Biochemistry*]
RTK .... Record Test Kit
RTK .... Response Technologies [*AMEX symbol*]   (SPSG)
RTK .... Right to Know [*Laws*]
RTK .... Roanoke Rapids, NC [*Location identifier*] [*FAA*]   (FAAL)
RTK .... Roczniki Teologiczno-Kanoniczne [*A publication*]
RTKHA ...... Radiotekhnika (Kharkov) [*A publication*]
RTKKUL... Roczniki Teologiczno-Kanoniczne. Katolickiego Uniwersytetu Lubelskiego [*A publication*]
RTKL......... Roczniki Teologiczno-Kanoniczne. Katolickiego Uniwersytetu Lubelskiego [*A publication*]
RTL........... RADAR Threshold Lobe Limit   (CET)
RTL........... Radial Transmission Line
RTL........... Radio Television Luxembourgeoise [*Radio Television Luxembourg*] [*French*]
RTL........... Radioisotope Transport Loop [*Nuclear energy*]   (NRCH)
RTL........... Radiomaritime Telex Letter
RTL........... Real-Time Language [*Data processing*]   (IEEE)
RTL........... Refrigerated Transmission Line
RTL........... Regeneration Thermoluminescence
RTL........... Regimental Training Line [*Army*]
RTL........... Register Transfer Language [*Data processing*]   (CSR)
RTL........... Register Transfer Level
RTL........... Register-Transistor Logic [*Data processing*]
RTL........... Reinforced Tile Lintel [*Technical drawings*]
RTL........... Relative Transcription Level [*Genetics*]
RTL........... Research and Technology Laboratories [*Army*]   (RDA)
RTL........... Resin-Treated Liner
RTL........... Resistor-Transistor Logic [*Data processing*]   (BUR)
RTL........... Resource Tie Line [*An association*]
RTL........... Run-Time Library [*Interdata*]
Rt Law Rep ... Rent Law Reports [*India*] [*A publication*]   (DLA)
RTLF........ Association of Railway Trainmen and Locomotive Firemen
RTLG........ Radio Telegraph   (MSA)
RTLO .... Regional Training Liaison Officer [*Ministry of Agriculture, Fisheries, and Food*] [*British*]
RTLP......... Reference Transmission Level Point [*Telecommunications*]
RTLS .... Return to Launch Site [*NASA*]
RTLT......... Round-Trip Light Time
RTLXA ..... Revue Technique Luxembourgeoise [*A publication*]
RTM .... RADAR Target Materiel   (AFM)
RTM .... Radiation Test Model
RTm .... Radio-Telephone (Medium Frequency) [*Telecommunications*]   (DS)
RTM .... Radio Television Malaysia
RTM .... Radio-Television Malgache [*Malagasy Radio and Television*]
RTM .... Radio-Television Marocaine [*Moroccan Radio and Television*]
RTM .... [*The*] Railway Transfer Co. of the City of Minneapolis [*AAR code*]
RTM .... Rapid Tuning Magnetron
RTM .... Real-Time Metric
RTM .... Real-Time Monitor [*Systems Engineering Labs*]
RTM .... Receiver-Transmitter-Modulator
RTM .... Reconnaissance Tactical Missile
RTM .... Recording Tachometer   (IEEE)
RTM .... Recovery Termination Management [*Data processing*]
RTM .... Register Transfer Module [*Data processing*]   (MDG)
RTM .... Registered Trademark   (DEN)
RTM .... Regulatory Technical Memorandum [*Nuclear energy*]   (NRCH)
RTM .... Representative Town Meeting
RTM .... Requirements Traceability Matrix
RTM .... Research Technical Memorandum
RTM .... Resin Transfer Molding [*Plastics technology*]
RTM .... Response Time Module
RTM .... Revenue Ton-Miles

RTM .... Rivista di Teologia Morale [*A publication*]
RTM .... Rotterdam [*Netherlands*] [*Airport symbol*]   (OAG)
RTM .... Royal Trust Co. Mortgage Corp. [*Toronto Stock Exchange symbol*]
RTM .... Running Time Meter   (AAG)
RTMA .... Radio and Television Manufacturers Association
RTMAA ..... Revue Roumaine des Sciences Techniques. Serie de Mecanique Appliquee [*A publication*]
RTMAGV ... Royal Thai Military Assistance Group, Vietnam
RTMC .... Royal Thai Marine Corps   (CINC)
RTMD .... Real-Time Multiplexer Display
RTMOS..... Real-Time Multiprogramming Operating System [*Data processing*]   (IEEE)
RTMP....... Routing Maintenance Protocol   (BYTE)
RTMS....... RADAR Target Measuring System   (MCD)
RTMS....... Real-Time Memory System
RTMS....... Real-Time Multiprogramming System
RTMS....... Rocket Thrust Measuring System
RTMSW.... Real-Time DSN [*Deep Space Network*] Monitor Software Assembly [*NASA*]
RTMTA..... Revue Roumaine des Sciences Techniques. Serie de Metallurgie [*A publication*]
RTMTR..... Remote Transmitter   (FAAC)
RTN .... North Country Library System, Watertown, NY [*OCLC symbol*]   (OCLC)
RTN .... Radial, Tangential, Normal
RTN .... Radio Telescope Network
RTN .... Raton, NM [*Location identifier*] [*FAA*]   (FAAL)
RTN .... Raytheon Co. [*NYSE symbol*]   (SPSG)
RTN .... Recursive Transition Network [*Language analysis*]   (BYTE)
RTN .... Registered Trade Name
RTN .... Relative Threat Number [*Military*]   (CAAL)
RTN .... Remote Terminal Network
RTN .... Remote Tracking Network
RTN .... Renal Tubule Necrosis [*Medicine*]
RTN .... Report Test Number [*NASA*]
RTN .... Resistor Terminating Network
RTN .... Retain   (KSC)
RTN .... Return   (AAG)
RTN .... Return to Neuter
RTN .... Rota [*Nicaragua*] [*Seismograph station code, US Geological Survey*]   (SEIS)
RTN .... Routine
RTN .... Royal Thai Navy   (CINC)
RTN .... RTN: Radio Television News [*A publication*]   (APTA)
RTNA .... Regional Television News Australia
RTNC .... Radio-Television Nationale Congolaise
RTND .... Retained   (FAAC)
RTND .... Returned
RTNDA ..... Radio-Television News Directors Association   (EA)
RTNE .... Routine   (FAAC)
RTNEE...... Returnee [*Military*]
RTNF........ Recombinant Tumor Necrosis Factor [*Biochemistry*]
RTNG .... Retaining   (MSA)
RTNLB...... Rationalisierung [*Munich*] [*A publication*]
RTNOBE... Round Table of National Organizations for Better Education   (EA)
RTNP .... Red Tag News Publications [*Later, RTNPA*]   (EA)
RTNPA...... Red Tag News Publications Association   (EA)
RTNR .... Retainer   (MSA)
RTNR .... Ringtone No Reply [*Telecommunications*]   (TEL)
RTNS....... Rotating Target Neutron Source [*Nuclear physics*]
RTNT .... Roczniki Towarzystwa Naukowego w Toruniu [*A publication*]
RTO .... Radiotelephone Operator
RTO .... Rail Transportation Officer [*Military*]
RTO .... Railway Traffic Officer [*Military*]
RTO .... Range Training Officer   (MCD)
RTO .... Reactor Trip Override [*Nuclear energy*]   (NRCH)
RTO .... Real-Time Operation
rto.............. Recto   (BJA)
RTO .... Referred-to-Output
RTO .... Regional Team of Officers [*British*]
RTO .... Regional Telecommunications Office [*DoD*]
RTO .... Regional Training Officer   (OICC)
RTO .... Rejected Takeoff [*Aviation*]   (MCD)
RTO .... Reliability Test Outline   (AAG)
RTO .... Report Time Over [*Aviation*]   (FAAC)
RTO .... Request to Off-Load [*Shipping*]   (DS)
RTO .... Responsible Test Organization [*NASA*]   (MCD)
RTO .... Revue de Tourisme [*Berne*] [*A publication*]
RTO .... Road Traffic Officer [*British police*]
RTODA ..... Rassegna Trimestrale di Odontoiatria [*A publication*]
RTOG .... Radiation Therapy Oncology Group   (EA)
RTOK .... Retest OK   (MCD)
RTOL .... Reduced Takeoff and Landing [*Aviation*]
RTOL .... Rotary Takeoff and Landing [*Aviation*]   (AIA)
RTOP .... Research and Technology Objectives and Plans [*NASA*]   (NASA)
RTOP .... Research and Technology Operating [*or Operations*] Plan [*NASA*]

RTOPS......	Research and Technology Objectives and Plans Summary [*NASA*] [*Information service or system*] (CRD)
RTOR..........	Right Turn on Red [*i.e., on red traffic signal*]
RTor..........	Rocznik Torunski [*A publication*]
RTOS.........	Real-Time Operating System [*Control Data Corp.*]
RTOSA......	Revue de Medecine de Toulouse. Supplement [*A publication*]
RTOT	Range Track on Target [*Air Force*]
R Tourisme ...	Revue de Tourisme [*A publication*]
RTOW	Regulated [*or Restricted*] Takeoff Weight (MCD)
RTP..........	Radio Televisao Portuguesa [*Portuguese Radio-Television System*]
RTP..........	Reactor Thermal Power (IEEE)
RTP..........	Real-Time Peripheral (IEEE)
RTP..........	Real-Time Position (AAG)
RTP..........	Real-Time Profiler [*Instrumentation*]
RTP..........	Recruitment and Training Program
RTP..........	Reebok Tennis Professional [*Shoes*]
RTP..........	Reference Telephonic Power (DEN)
RTP..........	Reich & Tang LP [*NYSE symbol*] (SPSG)
RTP..........	Reinforced Theatre Plan [*Military*] [*British*]
RTP..........	Reinforced Thermoplastics
RTP..........	Relative Threat Priority [*Military*] (CAAL)
RTP..........	Reliability Test Plan (MCD)
RTP..........	Remote Transfer Point
RTP..........	Republican Turkish Party [*Cyprus*]
RTP..........	Request to Purchase
RTP..........	Request for Technical Proposal [*Military*]
RTP..........	Requirement and Test Procedures
RTP..........	Research Triangle Park [*North Carolina*]
RTP..........	Resistor Test Program
RTP..........	Resource Teaching Program (OICC)
RTP..........	Reverse Tie Point (KSC)
RTP..........	Revue de Theologie et de Philosophie [*A publication*]
RTP..........	Room-Temperature Phosphorimetry [*Spectrometry*]
RTP..........	Rotex Turret Punch
RTP..........	Rutland Plains [*Australia*] [*Airport symbol*] [*Obsolete*] (OAG)
RTPA..........	Rail Travel Promotion Agency [*Defunct*] (EA)
RTPC.........	Restrictive Trade Practices Commission
RT-PCR....	Reverse Transcription-Polymerase Chain Reaction
RTPh........	Revue de Theologie et de Philosophie [*A publication*]
RTPH.......	Round Trips per Hour (MSA)
RTPhil.......	Revue de Theologie et de Philosophie [*A publication*]
RTPI........	Royal Town Planning Institute [*British*]
RTPI J........	Royal Town Planning Institute. Journal [*A publication*]
RTPL........	Real-Time Procedural Language [*Data processing*] (MDG)
RTPLRS....	Real-Time Position Location Reporting System (MCD)
RTPM.......	Real-Time Program Management
RTPM.......	Revista de Tradiciones Populares (Madrid) [*A publication*]
RTPR........	Reference Theta Pinch Reactor
RTQ..........	Real-Time Quotes [*Information retrieval*]
RTQ..........	Rutter Teacher Questionnaire
RTQA.......	Reports Tempore Queen Anne [*11 Modern*] [*England*] [*A publication*] (DLA)
RTQC.......	Real-Time Quality Control
RTR..........	Le Regiment de Trois-Rivieres [*British military*] (DMA)
R TR..........	Radio Tower
RTR	Reading Test and Reviews [*A publication*]
RTR	Real-Time Readout
RTR	Recovery Temperature Ratio
RTR	Recreational Therapist Registered
RTR	Red Blood Cell Turnover Rate [*Hematology*]
RTR	Reformed Theological Review [*A publication*]
RTR	Reliability Test Requirements (AAG)
RTR	Remote Transmitter
RTR	Repeater Test Rack (DEN)
RTR	Resonance Test Reactor
RTR	Response Time Reporting
RTR	Restoration and Eighteenth Century Theatre Research [*A publication*]
RTR	Return and Restore Status Register [*Data processing*]
RTR	Returning to Ramp [*Aviation*] (FAAC)
RTR	Ribbon-to-Ribbon Regrowth [*Of silicon for photovoltaic cells*]
RTr...........	Rivista della Tripolitania [*A publication*]
RTR	Road Traffic Reports [*A publication*] (DLA)
RTR	Rotor (MSA)
RTR	Royal Tank Regiment [*Military unit*] [*British*]
Rtr.............	Ruth Rabbah (BJA)
RTR	Ryder Truck Rental
RTRA........	Road Traffic Regulation Act [*Town planning*] [*British*]
R Trab (Madrid) ...	Revista de Trabajo (Madrid) [*A publication*]
R Trav........	Revue du Travail [*A publication*]
R Trav Acad Sci Mor Polit ...	Revue des Travaux. Academie des Sciences Morales et Politiques [*A publication*]
R Trav (Bruxelles) ...	Revue du Travail (Bruxelles) [*A publication*]
RTRC.........	Radio and Television Research Council (EA)
RTRC.........	Radiotelemetry and Remote Control (MCD)
RTRC.........	Regional Technical Report Centers [*Department of Commerce*]
RTRCDS ...	Real-Time Reconnaissance Cockpit Display System [*or Subsystem*]
RTRD	Retard (FAAC)
RT Regelungstech ...	RT. Regelungstechnik [*West Germany*] [*A publication*]

R Tres	Revue du Tresor [*A publication*]
R Tresor	Revue du Tresor [*A publication*]
RTREV......	Right Reverend [*Of an abbot, bishop, or monsignor*]
R Trim Dr Com ...	Revue Trimestrielle de Droit Commercial [*A publication*]
R Trim Dr Europ ...	Revue Trimestrielle de Droit Europeen [*A publication*]
R Trim Droit Eur ...	Revue Trimestrielle de Droit Europeen [*A publication*]
R Trim Dr Sanit Soc ...	Revue Trimestrielle de Droit Sanitaire et Social [*A publication*]
RTRN	Return (FAAC)
RTRO	Real-Time Readout
RTRPAEA ...	Recueil des Travaux Relatifs a la Philologie et a l'Archeologie Egyptiennes et Assyriennes [*Paris*] [*A publication*]
RTRPhAEA ...	Recueil des Travaux Relatifs a la Philologie et a l'Archeologie Egyptiennes et Assyriennes [*Paris*] [*A publication*]
RTRS	Real-Time Rescheduling Subsystem
RTRS	Reuters Holdings PLC [*New York, NY*] [*NASDAQ symbol*] (NQ)
RTRSW	Rotary Switch (MSA)
RTRV.........	Retrieve (MSA)
RT RV........	Right Reverend [*Of an abbot, bishop, or monsignor*]
RTRY........	Rotary
RTS..........	RADAR Target Simulator
RTS..........	RADAR Test Set
RTS..........	RADAR Test Station (MCD)
RTS..........	RADAR Test System
RTS..........	RADAR Tracking Station [*Military*]
RTS..........	RADAR Tracking System
RTS..........	Radial Tuned Suspension (ADA)
RTS..........	Radio-Television Scolaire [*French*]
RTS..........	Radio Television Seychelles
RTS..........	Radio-Television Singapore
RTS..........	Radio Wire Broadcasting Network
RTS..........	Radiodiffusion-Television du Senegal [*Radio and television network*] [*Senegal*]
RTS..........	Radiotelemetry Subsystem
RTS..........	Radioteletypewriter Set
RTS..........	Rail Transfer System (KSC)
RTS..........	Range Time Signal
RTS..........	Range Timing System
RTS..........	Rapid Transit System (DCTA)
RTS..........	Rapid Transmission and Storage [*Goldmark Corp.*] [*TV system*]
RTS..........	Ratio Test Set
RTS..........	Reactive Terminal Service [*International Telephone & Telegraph computer*]
RTS..........	Reactor Trip System [*Nuclear energy*] (NRCH)
RTS..........	Readiness Training Squadron [*Military*] (NVT)
RTS..........	Real-Time Simulation
RTS..........	Real-Time Subroutines
RTS..........	Real-Time Supply [*NASA*] (MCD)
RTS..........	Real-Time System
RTS..........	Reconnaissance Technical Squadron [*Air Force*] (CINC)
RTS..........	Recorded Time Signal
RT/S..........	Refrigeration Technician/Specialist (AAG)
RTS..........	Refueling Water Transfer and Storage [*Nuclear energy*] (NRCH)
RTres	Regional Technical Support [*Military*]
RTS..........	Relay Telemetry Subsystem [*NASA*]
RTS..........	Relay Test System
RTS..........	Religious Tract Society [*British*]
RTS..........	Remember That Song (EA)
RTS..........	Remote Targeting System
RTS..........	Remote Terminal Supervisor (CMD)
RTS..........	Remote Test System [*Bell System*]
RTS..........	Remote Tracking Site [*Military*]
RTS..........	Remote Tracking Station [*NASA*]
RTS..........	Repaired This Station (AFM)
RTS..........	Reparatur-Technische Station [*Repair and Technical Station*] [*German*]
RTS..........	Request to Send
RTS..........	Research and Technical Services [*Military*]
RTS..........	Research Test Site (AAG)
RTS..........	Resolute Resources [*Vancouver Stock Exchange symbol*]
RTS..........	Resolve through Sharing (EA)
RTS..........	Return to Search
RTS..........	Return to Sender
RTS..........	Return to Service [*Aviation*]
RTS..........	Return to Stores
RTS..........	Return from Subroutine [*Data processing*]
RTS..........	Return to Supplier (MCD)
RTS..........	Rights [*Stock market term*]
RTS..........	River Thames Society [*British*]
RTS..........	Rosner Television Systems, Inc. [*New York, NY*] [*Telecommunications*] (TSSD)
RTS..........	Rotary Thumbwheel Switch
RTS..........	Rottnest Island [*Australia*] [*Airport symbol*] (OAG)
RTS..........	Royal Television Society [*British*]
RTS..........	Royal Toxophilite Society [*British*]
RTS..........	Russ Togs, Inc. [*NYSE symbol*] (SPSG)
RTSA........	RADAR Target Signature Analysis
RTSA........	Radio Tracking System Analyst (MUGU)

RTSC .... Recommended Test Sequence Chart (MCD)
RTSC .... Replacement and Training School Command [*Military*]
RTSD .... Resources and Technical Services Division [*American Library Association*] [*Later, ALCTS*] (EA)
RTSD .... Royal Thai Survey Department (CINC)
RTSD CCS ... RTSD [*Resources and Technical Services Division*] Cataloging and Classification Section
RTSD LRTS ... RTSD [*Resources and Technical Services Division*] Library Resources and Technical Services [*A publication*]
RTSD PLMS ... RTSD [*Resources and Technical Services Division*] Preservation of Library Materials Section
RTSD RLMS ... RTSD [*Resources and Technical Services Division*] Reproduction of Library Materials Section
RTSD RS... RTSD [*Resources and Technical Services Division*] Resources Section
RTSDS ...... Real-Time Scheduling Display System
RTSD SS ... RTSD [*Resources and Technical Services Division*] Serials Section
RTSF .... Real-Time Simulation Facility [*NASA*] (MCD)
RTSFR .... Rivista Trimestrale di Studi Filosofici e Religiosi [*A publication*]
RTSM .... Return to Stock Memo
RTSP .... Real-Time Signal Processor (NVT)
RTSq .... Reconnaissance Technical Squadron [*Air Force*] (AFM)
RTSS .... Real-Time Scientific System
RTSS .... Returning to School Syndrome
RTSS .... Revue Tunisienne de Sciences Sociales [*A publication*]
RTST .... Radio Technician Selection Test [*Military*]
RTSTA ...... Railway Track and Structures [*A publication*]
RTSZA ...... Revista Tecnica Sulzer [*A publication*]
RTT .... Radet for Teknisk Terminologi [*Norwegian Council for Technical Terminology*] [*Oslo*] [*Information service or system*] (IID)
RTT .... Radiation Therapy Technician
RTT .... Radiation Tracking Transducer
RTT .... Radio Television Tunisien [*Tunisian Radio and Television*]
RTT .... Radiotelemetric Theodolite
RTT .... Radioteletypewriter
RTT .... Rate of Turntable
RTT .... Receiver Threshold Test (CET)
RTT .... Rectangular Tongue Terminal
RTT .... Regie des Telegraphes et des Telephones [*Belgium*] [*Telecommunications service*] (TSSD)
RTT .... Remote Tuning Technique
RTT .... Requirements Traceability Tool [*Data processing*]
RTT .... Research in Text Theory/Untersuchungen zur Text-Theorie [*A publication*]
RTT .... Resonant Tunneling Transistor [*Electronics*]
RTT .... Return Trip Time
RTT .... Ring Tongue Terminal
RTT .... Rocket-Thrown Torpedo
RTT .... Role-Taking Task
RTTA .... Range Tower Transfer Assembly (KSC)
RTTA .... Ranging Tone Transfer Assembly
RTTAA ...... Railway Telegraph and Telephone Appliance Association
RTTC .... Road Time Trials Council [*Bicycle racing competition*] [*British*]
RTTCB ...... Revue Technique Thomson - CSF [*A publication*]
RTTD .... Real-Time Telemetry Data (MCD)
RTTDS ...... Real-Time Telemetry Data System
RTTL .... Rattail [*Metallurgy*]
RTTL .... Running Telltale Light (MSA)
RTTLA ...... Revista Transporturilor si Telecomunicatiilor [*A publication*]
RTTOS ...... Real-Time Tactical Operating System (MCD)
RTTP .... Router Template (AAG)
RTTS .... RADAR Telephone Transmission System
RTTS .... Reaction Torque Temperature Sensitivity
RTTS .... Real-Time Telemetry System
RTTV .... Real-Time Television
RTTV .... Research Target and Test Vehicle
RTTY .... Radioteletypewriter
RTU .... RADAR Timing Unit
RTU .... Railroad Telegraphers Union
RTU .... Range Transfer Unit (MCD)
RTU .... Ready to Use
RTU .... Receiver/Transmitter Unit
RTU .... Recovery Task Unit
RTU .... Reinforcement Training Unit [*Army*] (AABC)
RTU .... Remote Terminal Unit
RTU .... Replacement Training Unit [*Military*]
RTU .... Reserve Training Unit (MCD)
RTU .... Response Test Unit
RTU .... Return to Unit [*Military*] [*British*]
RTU .... Right to Use [*Telecommunications*] (TEL)
RT₃U .... Resin T₃ Uptake [*Endocrinology*]
RT₄U .... Resin T₄ Uptake [*Endocrinology*]
RTUA .... Recognition Technologies Users Association (EA)
RTUM .... Revolutionary Trade Union Movement [*Czechoslovakia*]
R Tunisienne Sciences Socs ... Revue Tunisienne de Sciences Sociales [*A publication*]
R Tunis Sci Soc ... Revue Tunisienne de Sciences Sociales [*A publication*]

RTv .... Radio-Telephone (Very-High Frequency) [*Telecommunications*] (DS)
RTV .... Radiodiffusion-Television (Upper Volta) [*Radio and television network*]
RTV .... Real-Time Video
RTV .... Recovery Test Vehicle
RTV .... Reentry Test Vehicle [*Air Force*]
RTV .... Research Test Vehicle
RTV .... Retrieve Resources Ltd. [*Vancouver Stock Exchange symbol*]
RTV .... Returned to Vendor (AAG)
RTV .... Rhodesian Television
RTV .... Rice Tungro Virus
RTV .... Rocket Test Vehicle (MCD)
RTV .... Room Temperature Vulcanizing (MCD)
RTV .... Rough-Terrain Vehicle
RTVD .... Radiotelevision Dominicana [*Dominican Radio and Television*] [*Dominican Republic*]
RTVE .... Radiotelevision Espanola [*Spanish*]
RTVP .... Real-Time Video Processing
RTVS .... Radio/Television Services [*Washington State University*] [*Pullman*] [*Telecommunications service*] (TSSD)
RTVS .... Real Time Velocimeter System [*Army*] (RDA)
RTVS .... Relay Test and Verification System (MCD)
RTW .... Manitoba Reports Tempore Wood [*Canada*] [*A publication*] (DLA)
RTW .... Railway Tank Wagon [*British military*] (DMA)
RTW .... Ready-to-Wear [*Clothing*]
RTW .... Right to Work
RTW .... Right Worshipful
RTW .... Round the World
RTWB .... Richardson's Theological Word Book [*A publication*] (BJA)
RTWO .... R-2000 Corp. [*Neptune, NJ*] [*NASDAQ symbol*] (NQ)
RTWS .... Raw Type Write Submodule
R & T WUIS ... Research and Technology Work Unit Information System [*Database*] [*Defense Technical Information Center*] (CRD)
RTWUS ...... Research and Technology Work Unit Summary
RTX .... Rapid Transit Experimental [*Gas-turbine bus*]
RTX .... Real-Time Executive
RTX .... Report Time Crossing [*Aviation*] (FAAC)
RTX .... Revenue Canada Taxation Library [*UTLAS symbol*]
RTY .... Merty [*Australia*] [*Airport symbol*] [*Obsolete*] (OAG)
RTY .... Muscatine, IA [*Location identifier*] [*FAA*] (FAAL)
RTYC .... Royal Thames Yachting Club [*British*]
RTZ .... Radio Tanzania Zanzibar
RTZ .... Return-to-Zero [*Recording scheme*]
RTZ .... Rio Tinto Zinc Corp. [*Uranium mining company*] [*British, Namibian*]
RTZ .... Ritz Resources Ltd. [*Vancouver Stock Exchange symbol*]
RTZ .... RTZ Corp. [*NYSE symbol*] (SPSG)
RU .... Are You? [*Communication*]
RU .... Compagnie de Transports Aeriens [*Switzerland*] [*ICAO designator*] (FAAC)
Ru .... Gosudarstvennaia Biblioteka SSR Imeni V. I. Lenina [*Lenin State Library of the USSR*], Moscow, Soviet Union [*Library symbol*] [*Library of Congress*] (LCLS)
RU .... RADAR Unit (MCD)
RU .... Railway Underwriter
RU .... Rain Umbrella [*An association*] (EA)
RU .... Range Unit
RU .... Range User
RU .... Rat Unit
RU .... Reading of Unknown
RU .... Ready Use [*British*]
RU .... Refrigeration Unit (KSC)
RU .... Regular Unleaded [*Shell Oil Co.*]
RU .... Reinforcement Unit [*British military*] (DMA)
RU .... Relative Unit [*Typography*]
RU .... Release Unit [*Army*] (AABC)
RU .... Remote Unit (NASA)
RU .... Renaissance Universal (EA)
R & U .... Repairs and Upkeep [*Military*]
R & U .... Repairs and Utilities [*Military*]
RU .... Repeat Unit [*Genetics*]
RU .... Replaceable Unit
RU .... Reproducing Unit
RU .... Request/Response Unit [*Data processing*]
RU .... Reserve Unit [*Equal to one US dollar*] [*International finance*] [*USSR*]
RU .... Resin Uptake [*Endocrinology*]
RU .... Respiratory Unit [*Medicine*]
RU .... Retransmission Unit [*RADA*] [*Army*] (RDA)
RU .... Revista Universitaria. Universidad Catolica de Chile [*A publication*]
RU .... Right Upper [*Medicine*]
RU .... Roentgen Unit [*Also, r*] [*Measuring X and gamma radiations*]
RU .... Roussel [*France*] [*Research code symbol*]
Ru .... Rufinus [*Flourished, 1150-86*] [*Authority cited in pre-1607 legal work*] (DSA)
RU .... Rugby Union [*Controlling body of British rugby football*]
Ru .... Ruins

RU.............. Runic [*Language, etc.*] (ROG)
Ru.............. Rural
Ru.............. Ruth [*Old Testament book*]
Ru.............. Ruthenium [*Chemical element*]
ru.............. Rutile [*CIPW classification*] [*Geology*]
RU.............. Unborrowed Reserves
RU.............. University of Rhode Island, Kingston, RI [*Library symbol*]
               [*Library of Congress*] (LCLS)
RU.............. Ursuline Nuns of the Congregation of Tildonk, Belgium
               [*Roman Catholic religious order*]
RU.............. Zeitschrift fuer die Praxise des Religionsunterrichts [*A
               publication*]
RU-486 ...... Roussel Uclaf "Once-a-Month" Pill [*Contraceptive*]
RUA........... Arua [*Uganda*] [*Airport symbol*] (OAG)
RUA........... Retailer's Uniform Agency
RUA........... Right Upper Arm [*Medicine*]
RUA........... Royal Ulster Academy of Painting, Sculpture, and Architecture
               [*Ireland*]
RUAC....... Remote User Access System [*Telecommunications*]
RUAGA ..... Rubber Age [*A publication*]
Ruakura Farm Conf Proc ... Ruakura Farmers' Conference. Proceedings [*New
               Zealand*] [*A publication*]
Ruakura Farmers Conf Proc ... Ruakura Farmers' Conference. Proceedings [*A
               publication*]
RUAT....... Report upon Arrival Threat [*Army*] (AABC)
RUB.......... Revue. Universite de Bruxelles [*A publication*]
RUB.......... Rich Urban Biker [*Lifestyle classification*]
RUB........ Rubber (AAG)
RUB.......... Rubefacient [*Producing Heat and Redness of the Skin*]
               [*Medicine*] (ROG)
RUB.......... Ruber [*Red*] [*Pharmacy*]
RUB.......... Ruble [*Monetary unit*] [*USSR*]
RUB.......... Rubric (DLA)
RUB.......... Ruby Mountain Mines [*Vancouver Stock Exchange symbol*]
RuB.......... Russkoe Bogatstvo [*A publication*]
RUBA........ Revista. Universidad de Buenos Aires [*A publication*]
RUBAC ..... Relative Universal Business Automation Code
Rubb Board Bull ... Rubber Board. Bulletin [*India*] [*A publication*]
Rubb Chem ... Rubber Chemistry and Technology [*A publication*]
Rubb Dev ... Rubber Developments [*A publication*]
Rubber Age Synth ... Rubber Age and Synthetics [*A publication*]
Rubber Bul ... Rubber Statistical Bulletin [*A publication*]
Rubber Chem & Tech ... Rubber Chemistry and Technology [*A publication*]
Rubber Chem Technol ... Rubber Chemistry and Technology [*A publication*]
Rubber Dev ... Rubber Developments [*A publication*]
Rubber Devs ... Rubber Developments [*A publication*]
Rubber Devts ... Rubber Developments [*A publication*]
Rubber Ind ... Rubber Industry [*A publication*]
Rubber Ind (London) ... Rubber Industry (London) [*A publication*]
Rubber J .... Rubber Journal [*A publication*]
Rubber J Int Plast ... Rubber Journal and International Plastics [*A
               publication*]
Rubber Plast Age ... Rubber and Plastics Age [*A publication*]
Rubber Plast Wkly ... Rubber and Plastics Weekly [*A publication*]
Rubber Res Inst Ceylon Advis Circ ... Rubber Research Institute of Ceylon.
               Advisory Circular [*A publication*]
Rubber Res Inst Ceylon Annu Rep ... Rubber Research Institute of Ceylon.
               Annual Report [*A publication*]
Rubber Res Inst Ceylon Annu Rev ... Rubber Research Institute of Ceylon.
               Annual Review [*A publication*]
Rubber Res Inst Ceylon Bull ... Rubber Research Institute of Ceylon. Bulletin
               [*A publication*]
Rubber Res Inst Ceylon Q Circ ... Rubber Research Institute of Ceylon.
               Quarterly Circular [*A publication*]
Rubber Res Inst Ceylon Q J ... Rubber Research Institute of Ceylon. Quarterly
               Journal [*A publication*]
Rubber Res Inst Malaya Annu Rep ... Rubber Research Institute of Malaya.
               Annual Report [*A publication*]
Rubber Res Inst Malaya Plant Bull ... Rubber Research Institute of Malaya.
               Planters' Bulletin [*A publication*]
Rubber Res Inst Malaya Plant Man ... Rubber Research Institute of Malaya.
               Planting Manual [*A publication*]
Rubber Res Inst Malaya Q J ... Rubber Research Institute of Malaya.
               Quarterly Journal [*A publication*]
Rubber Res Inst Malaya Rep ... Rubber Research Institute of Malaya. Report
               [*A publication*]
Rubber Res Inst Malays Annu Rep ... Rubber Research Institute of Malaysia.
               Annual Report [*A publication*]
Rubber Res Inst Malays Plant Bull ... Rubber Research Institute of Malaysia.
               Planters' Bulletin [*A publication*]
Rubber Res Inst (Sri Lanka) Advis Circ ... Rubber Research Institute (Sri
               Lanka). Advisory Circular [*A publication*]
Rubber Res Inst (Sri Lanka) Annu Rev ... Rubber Research Institute (Sri
               Lanka). Annual Review [*A publication*]
Rubber Res Inst (Sri Lanka) Q J ... Rubber Research Institute (Sri Lanka).
               Quarterly Journal [*A publication*]
Rubber Wld ... Rubber World [*A publication*]
Rubb (India) ... Rubber (India) [*A publication*]
Rubb J........ Rubber Journal and International Plastics [*A publication*]
Rubb News ... Rubber News [*A publication*]
Rubb Plast Age ... Rubber and Plastics Age [*A publication*]

Rubb Plast Fire Flamm Bull ... Rubber and Plastics Fire and Flammability
               Bulletin [*A publication*]
Rubb Plast News ... Rubber and Plastics News [*A publication*]
Rubb Plast News 2 ... Rubber and Plastics News. 2 [*A publication*]
Rubb Statist Bull ... Rubber Statistical Bulletin [*A publication*]
Rubb Trends ... Rubber Trends [*A publication*]
Rubb World ... Rubber World [*A publication*]
Rub Conv ... Rubinstein on Conveyancing [*5th ed.*] [*1884*] [*A
               publication*] (DLA)
RUBD....... Rubberized (AAG)
RuBeMiA .. Akademiia Nauk Belorusskaia SSR, Fundamemtalnaia
               Biblioteka Imeni Ia. Kolasa [*Academy of Sciences of the
               Belorussian SSR, J. Kolasa Fundamental Library*], Minsk,
               Belorussian SSR, Soviet Union [*Library symbol*] [*Library
               of Congress*] (LCLS)
Rubey Vol .. Rubey Volume [*A publication*]
RuBi.......... Ruch Biblijny i Liturgiczny [*Cracow*] [*A publication*]
RUBIDIC .. Rubidazone [*Zorubicin*]/DIC [*Dacarbazine*] [*Antineoplastic
               drug regimen*]
RUBISCO ... Ribulosebisphosphate Carboxylase/Oxygenase [*An enzyme*]
RUBN........ Russian, Ukrainian, and Belorussian Newspapers [*A
               bibliographic publication*]
RuBP.......... Ribulosebisphosphate [*Also, RDP*] [*Biochemistry*]
RuBPCase ... Ribulosebisphosphate Carboxylase [*An enzyme*]
RuBPC/O .. Ribulosebisphosphate Carboxylase/Oxygenase [*Also,
               RUBISCO*] [*An enzyme*]
RUBR .... Rubber Research Elastomerics, Inc. [*NASDAQ symbol*] (NQ)
RU Brux ... Revue. Universite de Bruxelles [*A publication*]
RUBruxelles ... Revue. Universite de Bruxelles [*Brussels*] [*A publication*]
RUBSG...... Recovery Unit and Base Support Group [*Air Force*]
RUBSH ..... Rubbish
RUBSSO ... Rossendale Union of Boot, Shoe, and Slipper Operatives
               [*British*] (DCTA)
Rub Trends ... Rubber Trends [*A publication*]
RUBWA .... Rubber World [*A publication*]
RUC.......... Reporting Unit Code [*Data processing*]
RUC.......... Revista. Universidad de Cordoba [*A publication*]
RUC.......... Riverine Utility Craft [*Vehicle for transporting through shallow
               water and snow*] [*Navy symbol*]
RUC.......... Royal Ulster Constabulary [*British*]
RuC.......... Ruperto-Carola [*A publication*]
RUCA .... Russell Cave National Monument
RUCAG ..... Residential Utility Consumer Action Group
RuchBL..... Ruch Biblijny i Liturgiczny [*Cracow*] [*A publication*]
Ruch L........ Ruch Literacki [*A publication*]
RuchM .... Ruch Muzyczny [*A publication*]
Ruch Muz .. Ruch Muzyczny [*A publication*]
Ruch Prawn Ekon Socjol ... Ruch Prawniczy Ekonomiczny i Socjologiczny [*A
               publication*]
Rucker....... Rucker's Reports [*43-46 West Virginia*] [*A publication*] (DLA)
RUCP........ Revista. Universidad Catolica del Peru [*A publication*]
RUCS........ Racial Unconscious [*Psychiatry*]
RUCS......... Remote or Underserved Communities Scheme [*Australia*]
RUD.......... Rudder (AAG)
RUDAEE... Report of Unsatisfactory or Defective Airborne Electronic
               Equipment [*Navy*]
RUDAOE.. Report of Unsatisfactory or Defective Aviation Ordnance
               Equipment [*Navy*]
Rud Glas .... Rudarski Glasnik [*A publication*]
RUDH .... Reserve Shutdown Unplanned Derated Hours
               [*Electronics*] (IEEE)
RUDI .... Regional Urban Defense Intercept
RUDI .... Report of Unsatisfactory or Defective Instrumentation [*Navy*]
RUDIM ..... Rudimentary (ROG)
RUDIS....... Reference Your Dispatch (NOAA)
RUDM....... Report of Unsatisfactory or Defective Material [*Aircraft*]
               [*Navy*]
Rud-Metal Zb ... Rudarsko-Metalurski Zbornik [*A publication*]
Rud-Met Zb ... Rudarsko-Metalurski Zbornik [*A publication*]
RUDMIN .. Report of Unsatisfactory or Defective Mine [*Navy*] (NG)
RUDMINDE ... Report of Unsatisfactory or Defective Mine, Depth Charge,
               or Associated Equipment [*Navy*] (NG)
Rudodobiv Metal ... Rudodobiv i Metalurgiya [*A publication*]
Rudodobiv Metal (Sofia) ... Rudodobiv i Metalurgiya (Sofia) [*Bulgaria*] [*A
               publication*]
Rudodob Metal ... Rudodobiv i Metalurgiya [*Bulgaria*] [*A publication*]
Rudolstaedter Heimath ... Rudolstaedter Heimathefte Beitraege zur
               Heimatkunde des Kreises Rudolstaedt [*A publication*]
Rudoobraz Procesi Miner Nakhodisha ... Rudoobrazuvatelni Procesi i
               Mineralni Nakhodisha [*Sofia*] [*A publication*]
RUDTORPE ... Report of Unsatisfactory or Defective Torpedo Equipment
               [*Navy*] (NG)
RUDVA ..... Rubber Developments [*A publication*]
RUDY....... Rudy's Restaurant Group, Inc. [*NASDAQ symbol*] (NQ)
Rudy Met Niezelaz ... Rudy i Metale Niezelazne [*A publication*]
RUE .... Right Upper Entrance [*A stage direction*]
RUE .... Right Upper Extremity [*Medicine*]
RUE .... Russellville, AR [*Location identifier*] [*FAA*] (FAAL)
Ruegg Emp L ... Ruegg on Employer's Liability [*9th ed.*] [*1922*] [*A
               publication*] (DLA)

RUER .... SSRC [*Social Science Research Council*] Research Unit on Ethnic Relations [*Research center*] [*British*]   (IRC)
RUF .... Minocqua-Woodruff, WI [*Location identifier*] [*FAA*]   (FAAL)
RUF .... Radiation Usage Factor   (MCD)
RUF .... Resource Utilization Factor
RUF .... Revolving Underwriting Facility [*Finance*]
RUF .... Rigid Urethane Foam
RUF .... Rough   (FAAC)
Ruf .... Rufinus [*Flourished, 1150-86*] [*Authority cited in pre-1607 legal work*]   (DSA)
RUFAS ...... Remote Underwater Fisheries Assessment System [*National Oceanic and Atmospheric Administration*]
RUFC .... Rugby Union Football Club [*British*]   (DAS)
RUFE .... Zeitschrift fuer Rundfunk und Fernsehen [*Journal for Radio and Television*] [*NOMOS Datapool*] [*Information service or system*]
Ruff ..˙........ Ruffhead's Edition of the Statutes, by Serjeant Runnington [*1235-1785*] [*A publication*]   (DLA)
Ruff .... Ruffin and Hawks' Reports [*8 North Carolina*] [*A publication*]   (DLA)
Ruff .... Statutes at Large, Ruffhead's Edition [*England*] [*A publication*]   (DLA)
Ruff & H .... Ruffin and Hawks' Reports [*8 North Carolina*] [*A publication*]   (DLA)
Ruffh St ...... Ruffhead's English Statutes [*A publication*]   (DLA)
Ruff St .... Ruffhead's English Statutes [*A publication*]   (DLA)
RUFORM ... Reference Your Form   (FAAC)
RUFP .... Regulations under the Federal Power Act
RUG .... Coronet Carpets, Inc. [*Toronto Stock Exchange symbol*]
RUG .... Recomp Users Group [*Data processing*]
RUG .... Regional User Group [*Data processing*]
RUG .... Resource Utilization Group (DHSM)
RUG .... Retrograde Ureterogram [*Medicine*]
RUG .... ROSCOE User Group [*Princeton, NJ*]   (CSR)
RUG .... Rugby, ND [*Location identifier*] [*FAA*]   (FAAL)
RUG .... Rutgers-[*The*] State University, Graduate School of Library and Information Science, New Brunswick, NJ [*OCLC symbol*]   (OCLC)
RUGED ..... Rural Georgia [*A publication*]
RUGLA ..... Rudarski Glasnik [*A publication*]
RUH .... Range Users Handbook
RUH .... Riyadh [*Saudi Arabia*] [*Airport symbol*]   (OAG)
RUHP .... Rescue Unit Home Port [*Navy*]   (NVT)
RUI .... Research in Undergraduate Institutions [*A National Science Foundation program*]
RUI .... Royal University of Ireland
RUI .... Ruidoso [*New Mexico*] [*Airport symbol*]   (OAG)
RUI .... Ruidoso, NM [*Location identifier*] [*FAA*]   (FAAL)
RUIMB...... Ruimtevaart [*A publication*]
RUIN........ Regional and Urban Information Network [*Washington, DC*]
Ruin........... [*Carolus*] Ruinus [*Deceased, 1530*] [*Authority cited in pre-1607 legal work*]   (DSA)
RUISA ...... Revista. Universidad Industrial de Santander [*A publication*]
RuJ........... Rusky Jazyk [*A publication*]
RUKBA ..... Royal United Kingdom Benevolent Institution
RuKiFrA .... Akademiia Nauk Kirgizskoi SSR, Tsentralnaia Nauchaia Biblioteka [*Academy of Sciences of the Kirghiz SSR, Central Scientific Library*], Frunze, Kirghiz SSR, Soviet Union [*Library symbol*] [*Library of Congress*]   (LCLS)
RuL .... Gosudarstvennaia Publichnaia Biblioteka Imeni Saltykova-Shchedrina [*State Saltikov-Shchedrin Public Library*], Leningrad, Soviet Union [*Library symbol*] [*Library of Congress*]   (LCLS)
RUL .... Representative of the Senate of the University of London   (ROG)
RUL .... Revue. Universite Laval [*Quebec*] [*A publication*]
RUL .... Revue. Universite de Lyon [*A publication*]
RUL .... Right Upper Eyelid [*Medicine*]
RUL .... Right Upper Limb [*Medicine*]
RUL .... Right Upper Lobe [*of lung*] [*Medicine*]
RUL .... Rikkyo University Library [*UTLAS symbol*]
RUL .... Rule Resources Limited [*Vancouver Stock Exchange symbol*]
RUL .... Ruled
RuLA .... Akademiia Nauk SSSR [*Academy of Sciences of the USSR*], Leningrad, Soviet Union [*Library symbol*] [*Library of Congress*]   (LCLS)
Rul Cas ...... Campbell's Ruling Cases [*England*] [*A publication*]   (DLA)
RULE........ Restructuring the Undergraduate Learning Environment [*National Science Foundation*]
RULE........ Rule Industries, Inc. [*NASDAQ symbol*]   (NQ)
Rules Sup Ct ... Rules of the Supreme Court [*A publication*]   (DLA)
RULET...... Reference Your Letter   (NOAA)
RULet .... Revista Universitaria de Letras [*A publication*]
RuLit .... Ruch Literacki [*Krakow*] [*A publication*]
RULP .... Revista. Universidad de La Plata [*A publication*]
Ru L T .... Russian Literature Triquarterly [*A publication*]
RuLU-N.... Leningradskii Universitet, Nauchnaia Biblioteka Imeni Gor'kogo [*Leningrad State University, Gor'kii Scientific Library*], Leningrad, Soviet Union [*Library symbol*] [*Library of Congress*]   (LCLS)
RUM.......... Railwaymen's Union of Malaya

RUM.......... Remote Underwater Manipulator [*Oceanography*]
RUM.......... Remote Unit Monitor   (MCD)
RUM.......... Resource Unit Management
RUM.......... Resource Utilization Monitor
RUM.......... Revista. Universidad de Madrid [*A publication*]
rum............ Romanian [*MARC language code*] [*Library of Congress*]   (LCCP)
RUM.......... Rotary Ultrasonic Machining [*Manufacturing term*]
RUM.......... Rumangabo [*Zaire*] [*Seismograph station code, US Geological Survey*]   (SEIS)
RUM......... Rumania
RUM.......... Rumjartar [*Nepal*] [*Airport symbol*] [*Obsolete*]   (OAG)
RUM.......... San Marcos, TX [*Location identifier*] [*FAA*]   (FAAL)
RUMC........ Ruby Mining Co. [*NASDAQ symbol*]   (NQ)
RUMEA .... Rudodobiv i Metalurgiya [*A publication*]
RUMEM ... Reference Your Memorandum   (NOAA)
RUMEMO ... Reference Your Memorandum   (FAAC)
RUMES ..... Reference Your Message   (FAAC)
RuMG........ Gosudarstvennaia Publichnaia Nauchno-Tekhnicheskaia Biblioteka SSSR [*State Public Scientific and Technical Library*], Moscow, Soviet Union [*Library symbol*] [*Library of Congress*]   (LCLS)
RUMG....... Revista. Universidade de Minas Gerais [*A publication*]
RuMHi ...... State Public Historical Library, Moscow, Soviet Union [*Library symbol*] [*Library of Congress*]   (LCLS)
RUMIA ..... Rundfunktechnische Mitteilungen [*A publication*]
RuMIN ...... Institut Nauchnoi Informatsii po Obshchestvennym Naukam, Akademiia Nauk SSSR [*Institute of Scientific Information on Social Sciences, Academy of Sciences of the USSR*], Moscow, Soviet Union [*Library symbol*] [*Library of Congress*]   (LCLS)
RUMIN ..... Ruminant
RuMLit...... Vsesoiuznaia Gosudarstvennaia Biblioteka Inostrannoi Literatury [*All-Union State Library of Foreign Literature*], Moscow, Soviet Union [*Library symbol*] [*Library of Congress*]   (LCLS)
RUMMA ... Russian Metallurgy [*English Translation*] [*A publication*]
Rum Med Rev ... Rumanian Medical Review [*A publication*]
RUMOD.... Regional Underground Monolith Disposal [*Hazardous wastes*]
RuMoKisA ... Akademiia Nauk Moldavskoi SSR, Tsentralnaia Nauchnaia Biblioteka [*Academy of Sciences of the Moldavian SSR, Central Scientific Library*], Kishivev, Moldavian SSR, Soviet Union [*Library symbol*] [*Library of Congress*]   (LCLS)
RUMP .... Radio-Controlled Ultraviolet Measurement Program   (MUGU)
RUMR....... Routine Unsatisfactory Material Report   (MCD)
RUMRA .... Revue Universelle des Mines, de la Metallurgie, de la Mecanique, des Travaux Publics, des Sciences, et des Arts Appliques a l'Industrie [*A publication*]
RUM Rev Univers Mines ... RUM. Revue Universelle des Mines, de la Metallurgie, de la Mechanique, des Travaux Publics, des Sciences [*A publication*]
Rum Sci Abstr ... Rumanian Scientific Abstracts [*A publication*]
RUMUDA ... Reports. USA Marine Biological Institute. Kochi University [*A publication*]
RUN.......... Reduction Unlimited
RUN.......... Reunion Island [*Airport symbol*]   (OAG)
RUN.......... Rewind and Unload
RUN.......... Rockmaster Resources [*Vancouver Stock Exchange symbol*]
run............ Rundi [*MARC language code*] [*Library of Congress*]   (LCCP)
RUN.......... Runstream [*Data processing*]
RUN.......... Ruthven [*California*] [*Seismograph station code, US Geological Survey*]   (SEIS)
RUNAA ..... Revista. Universidad Nacional de Tucuman. Serie A. Matematica y Fisica Teorica [*A publication*]
RUnBrux .... Revue. Universite de Bruxelles [*A publication*]
RUNC........ Revista. Universidad Nacional de Cordoba [*A publication*]
RUNCIBLE ... Revised Unified New Compiler with Its Basic Language Extended [*Data processing*]
Rundfunk & F ... Rundfunk und Fernsehen [*A publication*]
Rundfunktech Mitt ... Rundfunktechnische Mitteilungen [*A publication*]
RUNDH .... Reserve Shutdown Unit Derated Hours [*Electronics*]   (IEEE)
RUNEL ...... Runway-End Lighting [*Aviation*]
RUNID...... Run Identification [*Data processing*]
R Union Ind ... Revista de la Union Industrial [*A publication*]
RUniv......... Revue Universelle [*A publication*]
R Univ .... Revue Universitaire [*A publication*]
R Univ Bruxelles ... Revue. Universite de Bruxelles [*A publication*]
R de l'Univ Laval ... Revue. Universite Laval [*A publication*]
R de l'Univ d'Ott ... Revue. Universite d'Ottawa [*A publication*]
R Univ Ottawa ... Revue. Universite d'Ottawa [*A publication*]
R de l'Univ de Sherbrooke ... Revue. Universite de Sherbrooke [*A publication*]
RUnLav ..... Revue. Universite Laval [*A publication*]
Runn.......... Runnell's Reports [*38-56 Iowa*] [*A publication*]   (DLA)
Runn.......... Statutes at Large, Runnington's Edition [*England*] [*A publication*]   (DLA)
Runn Eject ... Runnington on Ejectment [*2nd ed.*] [*1820*] [*A publication*]   (DLA)
Runnell....... Runnell's Reports [*38-56 Iowa*] [*A publication*]   (DLA)
Runn Stat ... Runnington on Statutes [*A publication*]   (DLA)

Runn Times ... Running Times [*A publication*]
Runn World ... Runner's World [*A publication*]
RUnOtt...... Revue. Universite d'Ottawa [*A publication*]
RUNT....... Russian Underground Nuclear Test (MCD)
RUO.......... Revista. Universidad de Oviedo [*A publication*]
RUO.......... Revue. Universite d'Ottawa [*A publication*]
RUO.......... Right Ureteral Orifice [*Medicine*]
RUOQ .... Right Upper Outer Quadrant [*Site of injection*] [*Medicine*]
RUOt .... Revue. Universite d'Ottawa [*A publication*]
RU Ottawa ... Revue. Universite d'Ottawa [*A publication*]
RUP .... Raza Unida Party (EA)
RUP .... Rupertsland Resources Co. Ltd. [*Toronto Stock Exchange symbol*]
RUPAA ..... Rubber and Plastics Age [*A publication*]
Rupert J ..... Rupert Journal [*A publication*]
Rupert Newsl ... Rupert Newsletter [*A publication*]
RUPHO....... Reference Your Telephone Call (NOAA)
RUPPERT ... Reserve Unit Personnel Performance Report
Ruppie........ Republican Urban Professional [*Lifestyle classification*]
RUPT........ Interrupt (NASA)
RUPT........ Rupture (NASA)
RUQ.......... Rifle Unqualified [*Military*]
RUQ.......... Right Upper Quadrant [*of abdomen*] [*Medicine*]
RUQ.......... Salisbury, NC [*Location identifier*] [*FAA*] (FAAL)
RUR.......... Resin Uptake Ratio [*Endocrinology*]
RUR.......... Rossum's Universal Robots [*Acronym is title of play by Karel Capek*]
RUR.......... Royal Ulster Rifles [*Military unit*] [*British*]
RUR.......... Rurutu Island [*French Polynesia*] [*Airport symbol*] (OAG)
rur .... Russian SFSR [*MARC country of publication code*] [*Library of Congress*] (LCCP)
RUR.......... Russkaja Rech' [*A publication*]
Rur Advis Leafl Edinb Sch Agric ... Rural Advisory Leaflet. Edinburgh School of Agriculture [*A publication*]
Rur Afr....... Rural Africana [*A publication*]
Rural Am ... Rural America [*A publication*]
Rural Develop ... Rural Development [*A publication*]
Rural Dev Res Educ ... Rural Development. Research and Education [*A publication*]
Rural Dev Res Rep US Dep Agric Econ Stat Coop Serv ... Rural Development Research Report. United States Department of Agriculture. Economics, Statistics, and Cooperatives Service [*A publication*]
Rural Elec N ... Rural Electrification News [*A publication*]
Rural GA ... Rural Georgia [*United States*] [*A publication*]
Rural Life Res ... Rural Life Research [*A publication*]
Rural Newsl ... Rural Newsletter. Central Coast Agricultural Research and Extension Committee [*A publication*] (APTA)
Rural N Y... Rural New Yorker [*A publication*]
Rural Res ... Rural Research. Commonwealth Scientific and Industrial Research Organisation [*A publication*] (APTA)
Rural Res CSIRO ... Rural Research. Commonwealth Scientific and Industrial Research Organisation [*A publication*]
Rural Socio ... Rural Sociology [*A publication*]
Rural Sociol ... Rural Sociology [*A publication*]
RURAX ..... Rural Automatic Exchange [*Telecommunications*] (TEL)
RURCA ..... Rural Research [*A publication*]
RUREQ ...... Reference Your Requisition (NOAA)
Rur Ind....... Rural India [*A publication*]
RURLAM ... Replacement Unit Repair Level Analysis Model
Rur Newsl.. Rural Newsletter [*A publication*] (APTA)
RURP .... Realised Ultimate Reality Piton [*Mountain climbing*]
RURPOP... Rural Population File (MCD)
RURQN..... Reference Your Requisition (FAAC)
Rur Res....... Rural Research [*A publication*] (APTA)
Rur Res CSIRO ... Rural Research. Commonwealth Scientific and Industrial Research Organisation [*A publication*] (APTA)
Rur Res CSIRO (Aust) ... Rural Research. Commonwealth Scientific and Industrial Research Organisation (Australia) [*A publication*]
Rur Sociol .. Rural Sociology [*A publication*]
RURTI....... Recurrent Upper Respiratory Tract Infection [*Medicine*] (ADA)
R Uruguaya Ciencias Socs ... Revista Uruguaya de Ciencias Sociales [*A publication*]
RUS .... Marau [*Solomon Islands*] [*Airport symbol*] (OAG)
RUS .... Rapid City, SD [*Location identifier*] [*FAA*] (FAAL)
RUS .... Rice University. Studies [*A publication*]
RUS .... Rural Uplook Service [*Ithaca, NY*]
RUS .... Russ Berrie & Co. [*NYSE symbol*] (SPSG)
Rus .... Russell's Election Cases [*1874*] [*Nova Scotia*] [*A publication*] (DLA)
Rus .... Russell's English Chancery Reports [*A publication*] (DLA)
RUS .... Russia
rus .... Russian [*MARC language code*] [*Library of Congress*] (LCCP)
RUS .... Rust College, Holly Springs, MS [*OCLC symbol*] (OCLC)
RUSC....... Rusco Industries, Inc. [*NASDAQ symbol*] (NQ)
RUSCA ...... Rural Sociology [*A publication*]
Rus & C Eq Cas ... Russell and Chesley's Nova Scotia Equity Cases [*A publication*] (DLA)
RUSDIC.... Russian Dictionary [*A publication*]

RUSE........ Rutgers University. Studies in English [*A publication*]
RUSEC...... Romanian-US Economic Council (EA)
Rus EC....... Russell's Contested Election Cases [*Massachusetts*] [*A publication*] (DLA)
Rus EC....... Russell's Irish Election Reports [*A publication*] (DLA)
RUSEF ...... Rational Use of the Sea Floor Program [*National Oceanic and Atmospheric Administration*] (MSC)
Rus Elec Rep ... Russell's Election Cases [*1874*] [*Nova Scotia*] [*A publication*] (DLA)
RUSEng..... Rajasthan University. Studies in English [*A publication*]
Rus Eq Rep ... Russell's Nova Scotia Equity Decisions [*A publication*] (DLA)
Rus ER....... Russell's Election Cases [*1874*] [*Nova Scotia*] [*A publication*] (DLA)
RusF.......... Russkij Fol'klor [*A publication*]
RUSH .... Remote User Shared Hardware [*Data processing*]
Rush-Presbyt-St Luke's Med Bull ... Rush-Presbyterian-St. Luke's Medical Center. Bulletin [*A publication*]
Rush-Presbyt-St Luke's Med Cent Res Rep ... Rush-Presbyterian-St. Luke's Medical Center. Research Report [*A publication*]
Rushw .... Rushworth's Historical Collections [*A publication*] (DLA)
RUSI......... Journal. Royal United Services Institute for Defence Studies [*A publication*]
RUSI......... Royal United Services Institute for Defence Studies [*British*]
Rusk N ...... Ruskin Newsletter [*A publication*]
RusL .... Russkaja Literatura [*A publication*]
Rus Ling.... Russian Linguistics [*A publication*]
Rus LT ...... Russian Literature Triquarterly [*A publication*]
RUSM .... Royal United Service Museum [*British military*] (DMA)
RUSNO .... Resident United States Naval Officer
Rus P......... Russian Pharmacopoeia [*A publication*]
RusR .... Russian Review [*A publication*]
RusR .... Russkaja Rech' [*A publication*]
Rus Re .... Russkaja Rech' [*A publication*]
RUSS........ Remote User Service Station (MCD)
Russ .... Russell's Contested Election Cases [*Massachusetts*] [*A publication*] (DLA)
Russ .... Russell's Election Cases [*1874*] [*Nova Scotia*] [*A publication*] (DLA)
Russ .... Russell's English Chancery Reports [*A publication*] (DLA)
RUSS........ Russet
RUSS........ Russia
Russ Arb .... Russell on Arbitrators [*A publication*] (DLA)
Russ & C .... Russell and Chesley's Nova Scotia Reports [*10-12 Nova Scotia Reports*] [*1875-79*] [*A publication*] (DLA)
Russ Cast Prod ... Russian Castings Production [*A publication*]
Russ & C Eq Cas ... Russell and Chesley's Nova Scotia Equity Cases [*A publication*] (DLA)
Russ Ch...... Russell's English Chancery Reports [*A publication*] (DLA)
Russ Chem Pharm J ... Russian Chemico-Pharmaceutical Journal [*A publication*]
Russ Chem Rev ... Russian Chemical Reviews [*A publication*]
Russ & Ches ... Russell and Chesley's Nova Scotia Reports [*A publication*] (DLA)
Russ & Ches Eq ... Russell and Chesley's Nova Scotia Equity Reports [*A publication*] (DLA)
Russ Con El (Mass) ... Russell's Contested Election Cases [*Massachusetts*] [*A publication*] (DLA)
Russ Cr ...... Russell on Crimes and Misdemeanors [*A publication*] (DLA)
Russ Crim .. Russell on Crime [*12th ed.*] [*1964*] [*A publication*] (DLA)
Russ Crimes ... Russell on Crimes and Misdemeanors [*A publication*] (DLA)
Russ El Cas ... Russell's Election Cases [*1874*] [*Nova Scotia*] [*A publication*] (DLA)
Russ Elect Cas ... Russell's Contested Election Cases [*Massachusetts*] [*A publication*] (DLA)
Russ Elect Cas ... Russell's Election Cases [*Nova Scotia*] [*A publication*] (DLA)
Russell .... Russell's Nova Scotia Equity Decisions [*A publication*] (DLA)
Russell-Cotes Mus Bul ... Russell-Cotes Art Gallery and Museum. Bulletin [*A publication*]
Russell NS ... Russell's Nova Scotia Equity Decisions [*A publication*] (DLA)
Russ Eng J ... Russian Engineering Journal [*A publication*]
Russ En J... Russian Engineering Journal [*A publication*]
Russ & Eq .. Russell and Chesley's Nova Scotia Equity Reports [*A publication*] (DLA)
Russ Eq...... Russell's Nova Scotia Equity Cases [*A publication*] (DLA)
Russ Eq Cas ... Russell's Nova Scotia Equity Cases [*A publication*] (DLA)
Russ Eq Rep ... Russell's Nova Scotia Equity Decisions [*A publication*] (DLA)
Russ Fact ... Russell on Factors and Brokers [*A publication*] (DLA)
Russ & G.... Russell and Geldert's Nova Scotia Reports [*13-27 Nova Scotia Reports*] [*1879-95*] [*Canada*] [*A publication*] (DLA)
Russ & Geld ... Russell and Geldert's Nova Scotia Reports [*A publication*] (DLA)
Russ Hist ... Russian History [*A publication*]
Russian J Physical Chem ... Russian Journal of Physical Chemistry [*A publication*]
Russian Math Surveys ... Russian Mathematical Surveys [*A publication*]
Russian R... Russian Review [*A publication*]
Russian Rev ... Russian Review [*A publication*]
Russ & Jap PC ... Russian and Japanese Prize Cases [*London*] [*A publication*] (DLA)

Russ J Inorg Chem ... Russian Journal of Inorganic Chemistry [*A publication*]
Russ J Phys Chem ... Russian Journal of Physical Chemistry [*A publication*]
Russkaia L ... Russkaia Literatura [*A publication*]
Russk Arkh Protist ... Russkii Arkhiv Protistologii [*A publication*]
Russk Med ... Russkaia Meditsina [*A publication*]
Russ-K Min Ges St Petersburg Verh ... Russisch-Kaiserliche Mineralogische Gesellschaft zu St. Petersburg. Verhandlungen [*A publication*]
Russk Vestnik Dermat ... Russkii Vestnik Dermatologii [*A publication*]
Russk Zhurnal Trop Med ... Russkii Zhurnal Tropicheskoi Meditsiny [*A publication*]
Russk Zool Zhurnal ... Russkii Zoologicheskii Zhurnal [*A publication*]
Russ Lit...... Russkaja Literatura [*A publication*]
Russ Lit Tr ... Russian Literature Triquarterly [*A publication*]
Russ & M ... Russell and Mylne's English Chancery Reports [*1829-33*] [*A publication*] (DLA)
Russ Math Surv ... Russian Mathematical Surveys [*A publication*]
Russ Merc Ag ... Russell on Mercantile Agency [*A publication*] (DLA)
Russ Met.... Russian Metallurgy [*A publication*]
Russ Metall ... Russian Metallurgy [*A publication*]
Russ & My ... Russell and Mylne's English Chancery Reports [*1829-33*] [*A publication*] (DLA)
Russ N Sc... Russell's Nova Scotia Equity Cases [*A publication*] (DLA)
Russ Pharmacol Toxicol ... Russian Pharmacology and Toxicology [*A publication*]
Russ & R .... Russell and Ryan's English Crown Cases Reserved [*1799-1823*] [*A publication*] (DLA)
Russ R........ Russian Review [*A publication*]
Russ & RCC ... Russell and Ryan's English Crown Cases Reserved [*168 English Reprint*] [*1799-1823*] [*A publication*] (DLA)
Russ & RCC (Eng) ... Russell and Ryan's English Crown Cases Reserved [*1799-1823*] [*A publication*] (DLA)
Russ & R Cr Cas ... Russell and Ryan's English Crown Cases Reserved [*A publication*] (DLA)
Russ Rev .... Russian Review [*A publication*]
Russ Rev Biol ... Russian Review of Biology [*A publication*]
Russ & Ry .. Russell and Ryan's English Crown Cases Reserved [*A publication*] (DLA)
Russ T Eld ... Russell's English Chancery Reports Tempore Elden [*A publication*] (DLA)
RUSSWO ... Revised Uniform Summary of Surveyed Weather Observations (MCD)
Rust............ De Re Rustica [*of Varro*] [*Classical studies*] (OCD)
RUSTA...... Rustica [*A publication*]
RUSTIC .... Regional and Urban Studies Information Center [*Department of Energy*] (IID)
RUT .... Remote User Terminal [*Data processing*] (CAAL)
RUT .... Resource Utilization Time (NASA)
RUT .... Room Usage Time
RUT .... Rooms Using Television [*Television ratings*]
RUT .... Rubber Trends [*A publication*]
RUT .... Ruta [*Rue*] [*Pharmacy*] (ROG)
RUT .... Ruth [*Nevada*] [*Seismograph station code, US Geological Survey*] [*Closed*] (SEIS)
RUT .... Rutland [*Vermont*] [*Airport symbol*] (OAG)
RUT .... Rutland Railway Corp. [*AAR code*] [*Terminated*]
RUT .... Standard Regional Route Transmitting Frequencies [*Communications*] (FAAC)
Rut-Cam LJ ... Rutgers-Camden Law Journal [*A publication*]
RUTD....... Rutlandshire [*County in England*] (ROG)
RUTEL...... Reference Your Telegram (FAAC)
Rutg Cas .... Rutger-Waddington Case [*1784*] [*New York City*] [*A publication*] (DLA)
Rutgers Camden L J ... Rutgers-Camden Law Journal [*A publication*]
Rutgers Comput and Technol Law J ... Rutgers Computer and Technology Law Journal [*A publication*]
Rutgers J Comp & L ... Rutgers Journal of Computers and the Law [*A publication*]
Rutgers J Computers & Law ... Rutgers Journal of Computers and the Law [*A publication*]
Rutgers J Computer Tech and L ... Rutgers Journal of Computers, Technology, and the Law [*A publication*]
Rutgers J Comput & Law ... Rutgers Journal of Computers and the Law [*A publication*]
Rutgers J Comput Technol and Law ... Rutgers Journal of Computers, Technology, and the Law [*A publication*]
Rutgers Jrnl ... Rutgers Computer and Technology Law Journal [*A publication*]
Rutgers LJ ... Rutgers Law Journal [*A publication*]
Rutgers L Rev ... Rutgers Law Review [*A publication*]
Rutgers State Univ Coll Eng Eng Res Bull ... Rutgers State University. College of Engineering. Engineering Research Bulletin [*A publication*]
Rutgers UL Rev ... Rutgers University. Law Review [*A publication*] (DLA)
Rutgers Univ Bur Biol Res Serol Mus Bull ... Rutgers University. Bureau of Biological Research. Serological Museum. Bulletin [*A publication*]
Rutgers Univ Bur Eng Res Eng Res Publ ... Rutgers University. Bureau of Engineering Research. Engineering Research Publication [*A publication*]

Rutgers Univ Bur Miner Res Bull ... Rutgers University. Bureau of Mineral Research. Bulletin [*A publication*]
Rutgers Univ Coll Eng Eng Res Bull ... Rutgers University. College of Engineering. Engineering Research Bulletin [*A publication*]
Rutg L Rev ... Rutgers Law Review [*A publication*]
Rutherford Lab Rep ... Rutherford Laboratory. Report [*A publication*]
Ruth Inst.... Rutherford's Institutes of Natural Law [*A publication*] (DLA)
RuthR........ Ruth Rabbah (BJA)
Rut J Comp L ... Rutgers Journal of Computers, Technology, and the Law [*A publication*]
RUTLDS ... Rutlandshire [*County in England*]
Rut LJ .... Rutgers Law Journal [*A publication*]
Rut LR ...... Rutgers Law Review [*A publication*]
RUTOP ..... Rutowski Optimization [*Computer program*]
RuTuAsA... Akademiia Nauk Turkmenskoi SSR, Tsentralnaia Nauchnaia Biblioteka [*Academy of Sciences of Turkmen SSR, Central Scientific Library*], Ashkhabad, Turkmen, SSR, Soviet Union [*Library symbol*] [*Library of Congress*] (LCLS)
RUTWX .... Reference Your TWX [*Teletypewriter Communications*] (FAAC)
RUU.......... Rijksuniversiteit Utrecht [*Netherlands*]
RuUk .... Gosudartsvennaia Publichnaia Biblioteka Ukrainskoi SSR [*State Public Library of the Ukrainian SSR*], Kiev, Soviet Union [*Library symbol*] [*Library of Congress*] (LCLS)
RUUR........ Regrade Unclassified Upon Receipt [*Air Force*]
RUV.......... Bellefontaine, OH [*Location identifier*] [*FAA*] (FAAL)
RUV .... Rauvai [*Tuamotu Archipelago*] [*Seismograph station code, US Geological Survey*] (SEIS)
RUWS .... Remote Unmanned Work System [*Navy*]
RUX.......... Baltimore, MD [*Location identifier*] [*FAA*] (FAAL)
RUY.......... Revista. Universidad de Yucatan [*A publication*]
RV .... Israel Aircraft Industries Ltd. [*ICAO aircraft manufacturer identifier*] (ICAO)
RV .... Rabies Virus
RV .... Radikale Venstre [*Radical Liberals*] [*Denmark*] [*Political party*] (PPE)
RV .... Radio Vehicle (DEN)
RV .... Rahway Valley R. R. [*AAR code*]
RV .... Random Variable [*Statistics*]
R/V .... Range to Velocity [*Ratio of the RADAR platform*]
RV .... Rassegna Volterrana [*A publication*]
RV .... Rateable Value [*Property value*] [*British*]
RV .... Rated Voltage
RV .... Raven [*A publication*]
RV .... Reaction Voltage
RV .... Reactor Vessel [*Nuclear energy*]
RV .... Reading and Vocabulary Test [*Also, R VT*] [*Military*]
RV .... Realizable Value (ADA)
R/V ...... Rear View (AAG)
RV .... Rear View [*Technical drawings*]
RV .... Recirculation Valve (MCD)
RV .... Recovery Vehicle [*NASA*] (NASA)
RV .... Recovery Vessel [*NASA*] (NASA)
RV .... Recreational Vehicle
RV .... Recycling Valve
RV .... Reentry Vehicle [*Aerospace*]
RV .... Reeve Aleutian Airways, Inc. [*ICAO designator*] (OAG)
RV .... Reeves MacDonald Mines [*Vancouver Stock Exchange symbol*]
RV .... Reference Voltage
RV .... Refugee Voices, a Ministry with Uprooted Peoples (EA)
RV .... Reinforcement Value [*Psychology*]
RV .... Release Valve [*Nuclear energy*] (NRCH)
RV .... Released Value [*Freight*]
RV .... Relief Valve
RV .... Remaining Velocity [*Ballistics*]
RV .... Renal Vessel [*Medicine*]
RV .... Rendezvous
RV .... Rendezvous Vehicle [*NASA*] (KSC)
RV .... Rescue Vessel
RV .... Research Vehicle
RV .... Research Vessel
RV .... Residual Variance
RV .... Residual Volume [*Physiology*]
RV .... Retrieval Vessel (NASA)
RV .... Retroversion
RV .... Retrovirus
Rv .... Revelation [*New Testament book*]
RV .... Reverberation Time
Rv .... Revised [*Regulation or order revised*] [*Used in Shepard's Citations*] [*Legal term*] (DLA)
RV .... Revised Version [*of the Bible, 1881*]
RV .... Rheinische Vierteljahresblaetter [*A publication*]
RV .... Rifle Volunteers
RV .... Right Ventricle [*of heart*] [*Cardiology*]
RV .... Rod Valgallianse [*Red Electoral Alliance*] [*Norway*] (PPE)
RV .... Roving Vehicle [*NASA*]
RV .... Rubella Virus
RV .... Runway Visibility [*Aviation*] (AFM)
RV .... RV: Recreational Vehicles [*A publication*] (APTA)
RVA .... Farafangana [*Madagascar*] [*Airport symbol*] (OAG)
RVA .... Raven Air [*Anchorage, AK*] [*FAA designator*] (FAAC)

RVA .... Reactive Volt-Ampere Meter
RVA .... Recorded Voice Announcement
    [*Telecommunications*] (IBMDP)
RVA .... Regular Veterans Association of the United States (EA)
RVA .... Relative Virtual Address
RVA .... Relative Volt-Ampere
RVA .... Reliability Variation Analysis
RVA .... Remote Voltage Adjustment
RVA .... Rib-Vertebra Angle [*Anatomy*]
RVA .... Right Ventricular Assistance [*Cardiology*]
RVA .... Right Visual Acuity [*Medicine*]
RVA .... Roberts Wesleyan College, K. B. Keating Library, Rochester,
    NY [*OCLC symbol*] (OCLC)
RVAAP...... Ravenna Army Ammunition Plant (AABC)
RVAC .... Royal Victorian Aero Club [*Australia*]
RVACS...... Reactor Vessel Auxiliary Cooling System
RVAD .... Rib-Vertebra Angle Difference [*Anatomy*]
RVAEA...... Rivista Aeronautica [*A publication*]
RVAH........ Reconnaissance Attack Squadron [*Navy*] (NVT)
RVAHA..... Revue d'Acoustique [*A publication*]
RVAHJ...... Royal Victorian Association of Honorary Justices [*Australia*]
RVANCS... Remote View Airborne Night Classification System
RVARM .... Recording Varmeter (MSA)
RVAS........ Records. Victorian Archaeological Survey [*A
    publication*] (APTA)
RVASA...... Revue de l'Atherosclerose [*A publication*]
RVAT .... Retinal Visual Acuity Tester [*Ophthalmology*]
RVAV .... Regulating Valve Actuating Valve (KSC)
RVAW .... Readiness Patrol Squadron [*Navy*] (NVT)
RVB .... RADAR Video Buffer
RVB .... Rear Vacuum Break [*Automotive engineering*]
RVB .... Resonating Valence Bond [*Physical chemistry*]
RVB .... Rheinische Vierteljahresblaetter [*A publication*]
RVB .... Rochester Gas & Electric Corp., TIC Library, Rochester, NY
    [*OCLC symbol*] (OCLC)
RVB .... Royal Veteran Battalion [*British military*] (DMA)
RVBR........ Riveting Bar [*Tool*] (AAG)
RV Bsns ..... Recreational Vehicle Business [*A publication*]
RVBTA...... Revue Belge des Transports [*A publication*]
RVC .... RADAR Video Controller [*Military*] (CAAL)
RVC .... Ramakrishna - Vivekananda Center (EA)
RVC .... Random Vibration Control
RVC .... Relative Velocity Computer
RVC .... Remote-Voice Control
RVC .... Reticulated Vitreous Carbon
RVC .... Review of Economic Studies [*Edinburgh*] [*A publication*]
RVC .... Rifle Volunteer Corps [*Military unit*] [*British*]
RVC .... RNA [*Ribonucleic Acid*] Virus Capsid
RVC .... Rochester General Hospital Library, Rochester, NY [*OCLC
    symbol*] (OCLC)
RVC .... Rotary Voice Coil [*Computer technology*]
RVC .... Royal Veterinary College [*British*]
RVC .... Royal Victorian Chain
RVCC........ Reeves Communication Corporation [*NASDAQ
    symbol*] (NQ)
RVCCB...... Reviews on Coatings and Corrosion [*A publication*]
RVCDA ..... Recreational Vehicle Club Directors of America (EA)
RVCF........ Remote Vehicle Checkout Facility [*NASA*] (NASA)
RVCI......... Royal Veterinary College of Ireland
RVCM .... Recent Vertical Crustal Movement [*Geology*]
RVCM .... Republic of Vietnam Campaign Medal [*Military
    decoration*] (AFM)
RVCZA...... Revista de Coroziune [*A publication*]
RVD .... Dutchess County Mental Health Center, Poughkeepsie, NY
    [*OCLC symbol*] [*Inactive*] (OCLC)
RVD .... RADAR Video Digitizer
RVD .... Relative Vertebral Density
RVD .... Remote Virtual Disk [*Data processing*]
RVD .... Residual Vapor Detector (NATG)
RVD .... Right Ventricular Dimension [*Cardiology*]
RVD .... Right Ventricular Dysfunction [*Medicine*]
RVD .... Royal Victoria Dock [*British*] (ROG)
RVDA........ Recreation Vehicle Dealers Association of North America (EA)
RV Dealer.. Recreational Vehicle Dealer [*A publication*]
RVDP .... RADAR Video Data Processor
RVDP .... Relief Valve Discharge Piping [*Nuclear energy*] (NRCH)
RVDSB...... Revue Medicale de Liege. Supplement (Belgium) [*A
    publication*]
RVDT .... Rotary Variable Differential Transducer [*or Transformer*]
RVE .... RADAR Video Extractor
RVE .... Representative Volume Element
RVE .... Right Ventricular Enlargement [*Cardiology*]
RVE .... Rochester Institute of Technology, Wallace Memorial Library,
    Rochester, NY [*OCLC symbol*] (OCLC)
RVE .... Royce Ventures Ltd. [*Vancouver Stock Exchange symbol*]
RVE .... Saravena [*Colombia*] [*Airport symbol*] (OAG)
RVEAAG... Escuela Nacional de Agricultura [*Chapingo*]. Revista [*A
    publication*]
RVED-CMP ... Right Ventricular End-Diastolic Compliance [*Cardiology*]
RVEDP...... Right Ventricular End-Diastolic Pressure [*Cardiology*]
RVEDPI .... Right Ventricular End-Diastolic Pressure Index [*Cardiology*]

RVEDV...... Right Ventricle End-Diastolic Volume [*Cardiology*]
RVEE........ Holiday RV Superstores, Inc. [*NASDAQ symbol*] (NQ)
RVELA...... Revista Electrotecnica [*A publication*]
RVENA ..... Rivista di Viticoltura e di Enologia [*A publication*]
R Venez Folk ... Revista Venezolana de Folklore [*A publication*]
R Venezolana Estud Municipales ... Revista Venezolana de Estudios
    Municipales [*A publication*]
R Venezolana Folklore ... Revista Venezolana de Folklore [*A publication*]
R Venezolana Sanidad y Asistencia Soc ... Revista Venezolana de Sanidad y
    Asistencia Social [*A publication*]
RVER........ Regional Veterans Employment Representative [*Department of
    Labor*]
RVESV ..... Right Ventricular End-Systolic Volume [*Cardiology*]
RVETA5.... Refuah Veterinarith [*A publication*]
R Vet Agric Univ Steril Res Inst Annu Rep ... Royal Veterinary and
    Agricultural University. Sterility Research Institute.
    Annual Report [*A publication*]
RvEx .... Review and Expositor [*A publication*]
RVF........... Rate Variance Formula [*Air Force*]
RVF........... Revista Valenciana de Filologia [*A publication*]
RVF........... Revista Venezolana de Folklore [*A publication*]
RVF........... Rift Valley Fever
RVF........... Right Visual Field [*Psychometrics*]
RVF........... Rochester Psychiatric Center Library, Rochester, NY [*OCLC
    symbol*] (OCLC)
RVFN .... Report of Visit of Foreign Nationals (AAG)
RVFO .... Revista Venezolana de Folklore [*A publication*]
RVFV .... Rift Valley Fever Virus [*Medicine*]
RVFX........ Rivet Fixture (AAG)
RVG .... Chicago, IL [*Location identifier*] [*FAA*] (FAAL)
RVG .... Reference-Voltage Generator
RVG .... Right Ventral Gluteal [*Injection site*]
RVG .... Right Visceral Ganglion [*Medicine*]
RVG .... Rotating Vertical Gradiometer
RVG .... Rumrill-Hoyt Corp., Library, Rochester, NY [*OCLC
    symbol*] (OCLC)
RVGA-A .... Revue de Geographie Alpine [*France*] [*A publication*]
RV/GC....... Reentry Vehicle and Ground Control [*NASA*] (KSC)
Rv Gen Sciences ... Revue Generale des Sciences Pures et Appliquees [*A
    publication*]
RVGG .... Rotating Vertical Gravity Gradiometer
RVGPA...... Reviews of Geophysics [*Later, Reviews of Geophysics and
    Space Physics*] [*A publication*]
RVH.......... Renovascular Hypertension [*Medicine*]
RVH.......... Reserve Veterinary Hospital [*British military*] (DMA)
RVH.......... Right Ventricular Hypertrophy [*Cardiology*]
RVH.......... St. Bernard's Seminary and College Library, Rochester, NY
    [*OCLC symbol*] (OCLC)
RVI .... Recorded Video Imaging (MCD)
RVI .... Recreational Vehicle Institute
RVI .... Renault Vehicules Industriels
RVI .... Reverse Interrupt Character [*Keyboard*]
RVI .... Saint Mary's Hospital, Medical Library, Rochester, NY [*OCLC
    symbol*] (OCLC)
RVIA........ Recreation Vehicle Industry Association (EA)
RVIAJ .... Royal Victorian Institute of Architects. Journal [*A publication*]
RVIMI....... Rubella Virus-Induced Mitotic Inhibitor
RVIS .... Reactor and Vessel Instrumentation System [*Nuclear
    energy*] (NRCH)
RVJ........... Reidsville, GA [*Location identifier*] [*FAA*] (FAAL)
RVJ........... Sear-Brown Associates Information Center Library, Rochester,
    NY [*OCLC symbol*] (OCLC)
RVJS......... Reentry Vehicle Jamming Simulator [*Army*]
RVK .... Sybron Corp., Medical Products Division Library, Rochester,
    NY [*OCLC symbol*] (OCLC)
RVL .... Reedsville, PA [*Location identifier*] [*FAA*] (FAAL)
RVL .... Revere Resources [*Vancouver Stock Exchange symbol*]
RVL .... Revue Economique et Sociale (Lausanne) [*A publication*]
RVL .... Rolling Vertical Landing (MCD)
RVL .... Royal Viking Line [*Kloster Cruises of Norway*]
RVL .... Sybron Corp., Pfaudler Division Technical Library, Henrietta,
    NY [*OCLC symbol*] (OCLC)
RVLA........ Roanoke Valley Library Association [*Library network*]
RVLG .... Revolving
RVLG .... Right Ventrolateral Gluteal [*Site of injection*] [*Medicine*]
RVLI......... Raksti. Latvijas PSR Zinatnu Akademija. Valodas und
    Literaturas Instituta [*A publication*]
RVLIS....... Reactor Vessel Water Level Indication System (IEEE)
RVLR........ Revolver [*Military*] (AABC)
RVLV........ Revolve (MSA)
RVM .... Reactive Voltmeter
RVM .... Reentry Vehicle Module [*NASA*] (KSC)
RVM .... Repertoire de Vedettes-Matiere [*Laval Subject Authority
    Records*] [*UTLAS symbol*]
RVM .... Residual Volatile Matter [*Chemistry*]
RVm.......... Revised Version [*of the Bible*], Margin
RVM .... Rio Vista Mine [*California*] [*Seismograph station code, US
    Geological Survey*] (SEIS)
RVM .... Sybron Corp., Taylor Division Research Library, Rochester,
    NY [*OCLC symbol*] (OCLC)
RVMCA .... Rivista di Meccanica [*A publication*]

RVN.......... Republic of Vietnam
RVN.......... Requirements Verification Network [*NASA*]　(NASA)
RVN.......... Retrolabyrinthine Vestibular Neurectomy [*Medicine*]
RVN.......... Rogersville, TN [*Location identifier*] [*FAA*]　(FAAL)
RVN.......... Rovaniemi [*Finland*] [*Airport symbol*]　(OAG)
RVN.......... Women's Career Center Library, Rochester, NY [*OCLC symbol*]　(OCLC)
RVNAF..... Republic of Vietnam Air Force　(AFM)
RVNAF..... Republic of Vietnam Armed Forces
RVNAFHMFC ... Republic of Vietnam Armed Forces Honor Medal, First Class [*Military decoration*]　(AABC)
RVNAFHMSC ... Republic of Vietnam Armed Forces Honor Medal, Second Class [*Military decoration*]
RVNCAMFC ... Republic of Vietnam Civil Actions Medal, First Class [*Military decoration*]　(AABC)
RVNCAMSC ... Republic of Vietnam Civil Actions Medal, Second Class [*Military decoration*]　(AABC)
RVNCM .... Republic of Vietnam Campaign Medal [*Military decoration*]　(AABC)
RVNF .... Republic of Vietnam Forces
RVNGCUCW/P ... Republic of Vietnam Gallantry Cross Unit Citation with Palm [*Military decoration*]　(AABC)
RVNMC .... Republic of Vietnam Marine Corps　(CINC)
RVNN........ Republic of Vietnam Navy　(CINC)
RVO.......... Aquinas Institute Library, Rochester, NY [*OCLC symbol*]　(OCLC)
RVO.......... Lubbock, TX [*Location identifier*] [*FAA*]　(FAAL)
RVO.......... Regional Veterinary Officer [*British*]
RVO.......... Relaxed Vaginal Outlet [*Medicine*]
RVO.......... Royal Victorian Order
RVO.......... Runway Visibility Observer [*Aviation*]　(FAAC)
RVOMA .... Revue Internationale d'Oceanographie Medicale [*A publication*]
RVOOA..... Rivista Oto-Neuro-Oftalmologica [*A publication*]
RVOT .... Right Ventricular Outflow Tract [*Cardiology*]
RVP .... Avon Junior/Senior High School Library, Avon, NY [*OCLC symbol*]　(OCLC)
RVP .... RADAR Video Processor [*Military*]　(CAAL)
RVP .... Raster-to-Vector Processor [*Computer graphics technology*]
RVP .... RCA Video Productions
RVP .... Reid Vapor Pressure
RVP .... Reutilization Value Percentage [*DoD*]
RVP .... Rotary Vacuum Pump
RVPA........ Rivet Pattern　(AAG)
RVPMB..... Review of Psychology of Music [*A publication*]
RVPTB ...... Revue Polytechnique [*A publication*]
RVQ.......... Benjamin Franklin High School Library, Rochester, NY [*OCLC symbol*]　(OCLC)
RVR .... Bishop Kearney High School Library, Rochester, NY [*OCLC symbol*]　(OCLC)
RVR .... Cruise America [*AMEX symbol*]　(SPSG)
RVR .... RADAR Video Recorder
R & VR...... Rating and Valuation Reporter [*A publication*]
RVR .... Renal Vascular Resistance [*Medicine*]
RVR .... Reverse Velocity Rotor
RVR .... Rim Vent Release [*Safety device for aerosol containers*]
RVR .... River　(FAAC)
RVR .... Riverside [*California*] [*Seismograph station code, US Geological Survey*]　(SEIS)
RVR .... Runway Visual Range [*Aviation*]
RVRA .... Recreation Vehicle Rental Association　(EA)
RV/RA....... Renal Vein/Renal Activity [*Ratio*] [*Medicine*]
RVRA .... Runway Visual Range Average [*Aviation*]　(FAAC)
RVRANO .. Runway Visual Range Average Not Available [*Aviation*]　(FAAC)
RVRC........ Renal Vein Renin Concentration [*Medicine*]
RVRM ...... Runway Visual Range Midpoint [*Aviation*]
RVRNO..... Runway Visual Range Not Available [*Aviation*]　(FAAC)
RVRR .... Runway Visual Range Rollout [*Aviation*]　(FAAC)
RVRRNO .. Runway Visual Range Rollout Not Available [*Aviation*]　(FAAC)
RVRT........ Runway Visual Range Touchdown [*Aviation*]　(FAAC)
RVRTNO .. Runway Visual Range Touchdown Not Available [*Aviation*]　(FAAC)
RVRU .... RADAR Video Recorder Unit
RVS........... Brighton High School Library, Rochester, NY [*OCLC symbol*]　(OCLC)
RVS........... Radius Vector Subroutine
RVS........... Reentry Vehicle Separation [*Aerospace*]　(MUGU)
RVS........... Reentry Vehicle Simulator [*Aerospace*]　(AAG)
RVS........... Relative Value Scale [*or Schedule or Study*] [*Medicine*]
RVS........... Remote Viewing System
RVS........... Requirements Validation Study　(MCD)
RVS........... Research Vessel Service [*British*]　(IRUK)
RVS........... Reverse　(MSA)
RVS........... Revise　(FAAC)
RVS........... Riverside Mountains [*California*] [*Seismograph station code, US Geological Survey*]　(SEIS)
RVS........... Rocketborne Vacuum System
RVS........... Tulsa, OK [*Location identifier*] [*FAA*]　(FAAL)
RVSBL ...... Reversible　(MSA)

Rv Scient.... Revue Scientifique [*A publication*]
RVSE......... Reverse　(AABC)
RVSFC ...... Ricky and Vince Smith Fan Club　(EA)
RVSMB ..... Revista Sanitara Militara [*A publication*]
RVSS .... Reactor Vessel Support System　(IEEE)
RVSSC....... Reverse Self Check　(AAG)
RVST .... Russel Viper Serum Time [*Clinical chemistry*]
RVSVP ...... Repondez Vite, S'il Vous Plait [*Please Reply at Once*] [*French*]
RVSW....... Right Ventricular Stroke Work [*Cardiology*]
RVSWI ...... Right Ventricular Stroke Work Index [*Cardiology*]
RVSZ .... Riveting Squeezer [*Tool*]　(AAG)
RVT .... Brockport High School Library, Brockport, NY [*OCLC symbol*]　(OCLC)
RVT .... Reading and Vocabulary Test [*Also, RV*] [*Military*]
RVT .... Reliability Verification Tests
RVT .... Renal Vein Thrombosis [*Medicine*]
RVT .... Resource Vector Table [*Data processing*]　(IBMDP)
RVT .... Rivet　(MSA)
RVT .... Royce Value Trust, Inc. [*NYSE symbol*]　(SPSG)
RVTC........ Rochester Volunteer Training Corps [*British military*]　(DMA)
RVTD .... Riveted　(MSA)
RVTK........ Revotek, Inc. [*NASDAQ symbol*]　(NQ)
RVTO .... Reentry Vehicle Test and Observables [*Air Force*]
RVTOL...... Rolling Vertical Takeoff and Landing [*Aviation*]　(MCD)
Rv Trim Can ... Revue Trimestrielle Canadienne [*A publication*]
RVTSA ...... Research in Veterinary Science [*A publication*]
RVU .... Caledonia-Mumford Junior/Senior High School Library, Caledonia, NY [*OCLC symbol*]　(OCLC)
RVU .... Relative Value Unit
RVU .... Relief Valve Unit
RVU .... Revue Economique [*Paris*] [*A publication*]
RVUHA..... Revue HF, Electronique, Telecommunications [*Brussels*] [*A publication*]
RVUXA ..... Revue X [*Belgium*] [*A publication*]
RVV .... Cardinal Mooney High School Library, Rochester, NY [*OCLC symbol*]　(OCLC)
RVV .... Regional Vascular Volume [*Hematology*]
RVV .... Religionsgeschichtliche Versuche und Vorarbeiten [*A publication*]
RVV .... Romanistische Versuche und Vorarbeiten [*A publication*]
RVV .... Runway Visibility Values [*Aviation*]
RVVNO..... Runway Visibility Not Available [*Aviation*]　(FAAC)
RVW .... Charles H. Roth High School Library, Henrietta, NY [*OCLC symbol*]　(OCLC)
RVW .... Ralph Vaughan Williams [*British composer, 1872-1958*]
RVW .... Right Ventricular Weight [*Cardiology*]
RVX .... Charlotte Junior/Senior High School Library, Rochester, NY [*OCLC symbol*]　(OCLC)
RVX .... Reentry Vehicle, Experimental [*Aerospace*]
RVY .... Churchville-Chili Senior High School Library, Rochester, NY [*OCLC symbol*]　(OCLC)
RVY .... Clarksville Flying Service, Inc. [*Clarksville, AR*] [*FAA designator*]　(FAAC)
RVY .... Rivera [*Uruguay*] [*Airport symbol*]　(OAG)
RVZ .... Dansville Senior High School Library, Dansville, NY [*OCLC symbol*]　(OCLC)
RW............ Hughes Air Corp. [*ICAO designator*]　(ICDA)
RW............ R. Warren [*Pseudonym used by Charles Ashton*]
RW............ Race Weight [*of a horse*]
RW............ Radiation Weapon　(AAG)
RW............ Radical Women　(EA)
RW............ Radiological Warfare
RW............ Radiological Warhead
RW............ Radiological Weapons
RW............ Ragweed [*Immunology*]
RW............ Rail and Water [*Shipping*]
R & W .... Rail and Water [*Shipping*]
RW............ Railway
RW............ Rain Showers [*Meteorology*]　(FAAC)
RW............ Ramo Wooldridge [*Later, TRW, Inc.*]
R/W .... Ramo-Wooldridge-Thompson Corp. [*Later, TRW, Inc.*]　(AAG)
RW............ Random Walk
RW............ Random Widths [*Lumber*]
RW............ Raw Water [*Nuclear energy*]
RW............ RAWINSONDE [*Radiosonde and RADAR Wind Sounding*] [*Upper air observation*]
R-W.......... Read-Write [*Data processing*]　(MSA)
RW............ Real Wages [*Economics*]
R d W .... Rechtsarchiv der Wirtschaft [*A publication*]
RW............ Rechtswissenschaft [*Jurisprudence*] [*German*]　(ILCA)
RW............ Reclaimed Wheat Grass Cover [*Agriculture*]
R(W) .... Reconstruction, Workmen's Compensation [*British*] [*World War II*]
RW............ Recreation and Welfare [*Navy*]
RW............ Recruiting Warrant
RW............ Red-Bellied Woodpecker [*Ornithology*]
RW............ Reduced Weight [*DCTA*]
RW............ Reel and Wheel [*Freight*]
RW............ Reformed World [*A publication*]
RW............ Region Wide [*Forestry*]

RW............	Regions of the World [*A publication*]
RW............	Relative Worth (MCD)
R/W..........	Report Writer [*Data processing*]
RW............	Republic Airlines West, Inc. [*ICAO designator*] (FAAC)
RW............	Resistance Welding (IEEE)
RW............	Response Word (NASA)
RW............	Restaurant Wine [*License*]
R/W..........	Returned to Work
RW............	Reverse Wound (MCD)
RW............	Review
RW............	Rewind
RW............	Richardsons Westgarth [*Commercial firm*] [*British*]
RW............	Rideal-Walter Coefficient [*Pharmacy*]
RW............	Right of Way
R of W........	Right of Way
RW............	Right Wing
RW............	Right Worshipful
RW............	Right Worthy
RW............	River Water [*Nuclear energy*] (NRCH)
RW............	Riveted and Welded [*Shipping*] (DS)
RW............	Rotary Wing [*Aircraft designation*]
RW............	Rough Weather [*A publication*]
R & W........	Routing and Work [*Military*]
RW............	Rowa-Wagner KG [*Germany*] [*Research code symbol*]
RW............	Royal Warrant [*British*] (ADA)
RW............	Royal Warwickshire Regiment [*Military unit*] [*British*]
RW............	Runner's World [*A publication*]
RW............	Runway [*Aviation*]
rw	Rwanda [*MARC country of publication code*] [*Library of Congress*] (LCCP)
RW............	Rwanda [*ANSI two-letter standard code*] (CNC)
RWA..........	E. J. Wilson High School Library, Spencerport, NY [*OCLC symbol*] (OCLC)
RWa...........	George Hail Free Library, Warren, RI [*Library symbol*] [*Library of Congress*] (LCLS)
RWA..........	RADWASTE [*Radioactive Waste*] Area [*Nuclear energy*] (NRCH)
RWA..........	Railway Wheel Association [*Defunct*] (EA)
RWA..........	Raoul Wallenberg Association [*See also RWF*] (EA)
RWA..........	Reaction Wheel Assembly (MCD)
RWA..........	Rectangular Wave-Guide Assembly
RWA..........	Regional Water Authority [*British*]
RWA..........	Rippled Wall Amplifier
RWA..........	Romance Writers of America (EA)
RWA..........	Rotary Wing Aircraft
RWA..........	Royal West of England Academy
RWA..........	Rwanda [*ANSI three-letter standard code*] (CNC)
RWAFF......	Royal West African Frontier Force [*Military unit*] [*British*]
RWAG.......	Rural Women's Access Grants [*Australia*]
RWAGE ...	Ragweed Antigen E [*Immunology*]
RWAH.......	Rotor Wing Agricultural Hours [*Aviation*] (AIA)
RWAHSJ ..	Royal Western Australian Historical Society. Journal [*A publication*] (ADA)
RWAMD...	Radioactive Waste Management [*A publication*]
RWar	Warwick Public Library, Warwick, RI [*Library symbol*] [*Library of Congress*] (LCLS)
RWARF.....	Royal Warwickshire Fusiliers [*British military*] (DMA)
RWarR.......	Rhode Island Junior College, Knight Campus, Warwick, RI [*Library symbol*] [*Library of Congress*] (LCLS)
R War R.....	Royal Warwickshire Regiment [*Military unit*] [*British*] (DMA)
RWAVA	Rheinisch-Westfaelische Akademie der Wissenschaften Natur-, Ingenieur-, und Wirtschaftswissenschaften. Vortraege [*A publication*]
RWAW......	United Union of Roofers, Waterproofers, and Allied Workers
RWB..........	Rear Wheel Brake
RWB..........	Rod Withdrawal Block [*Nuclear energy*] (NRCH)
RWB..........	Roger Williams College, Bristol, RI [*OCLC symbol*] (OCLC)
RWB..........	Royal Winnipeg Ballet
RWBH.......	Records Will Be Handcarried [*Army*] (AABC)
RWBN.......	Red and White Beacon [*Nautical charts*]
RWC..........	East Junior/Senior High School Library, Rochester, NY [*OCLC symbol*] (OCLC)
RWC..........	Radioactive Waste Campaign (EA)
RWC..........	Rainwater Conductor (AAG)
RWC..........	Raw Water Cooling
RWC..........	Reactor Water Cleanup [*Nuclear energy*] (NRCH)
RWC..........	Read, Write, and Compute
RWC..........	Read-Write-Continue [*Data processing*]
RWC..........	Relative Water Content
RWC..........	Remote Workcenter
RWC..........	Residential Wood Combustion
RWC..........	Roberts Wesleyan College [*Rochester, NY*]
RWC..........	Rural Water Commission [*Australia*]
RWCH.......	Republican Women of Capitol Hill (EA)
RWCNEC ...	Reports of the Working Committees. Northeast Conference [*A publication*]
RWCS........	Reactor Water Cleanup System [*Nuclear energy*] (NRCH)
RWCS........	Red Wing Collectors Society (EA)
RWCS........	Report Writer Control System [*COBOL*] [*Data processing*]
RWCU	Reactor Water Cleanup [*Nuclear energy*] (NRCH)
RWCUS.....	Raoul Wallenberg Committee of the United States (EA)

RWD..........	Eastridge High School Library, Rochester, NY [*OCLC symbol*] (OCLC)
RWD..........	Rear Wheel Drive
RWD..........	Regular Way Delivery
RWD..........	Regular World Day
RWD..........	Rewind
RWD..........	Right Wing Down [*Aviation*]
RWDCA	Red and White Dairy Cattle Association (EA)
RWDGM...	Right Worshipful Deputy Grand Master [*Freemasonry*]
R/WDO	Rear Window [*Automotive engineering*]
RWDS	RADWASTE [*Radioactive Waste*] Disposal System [*Nuclear energy*] (NRCH)
RWDSU	Retail, Wholesale, and Department Store Union (EA)
RWE	Edison Technical and Occupational Educational Center Library, Rochester, NY [*OCLC symbol*] (OCLC)
RWE	Radio Warfare Establishment [*British military*] (DMA)
RWE	Ralph Waldo Emerson [*Initials used as pseudonym*]
RWE	Review of World Economics [*A publication*]
RWE	REWE Echo. Fachzeitschrift fuer Modernen Handel [*A publication*]
RWE	Rheinisch-Westfaelisches Electrizitaetswerk AG [*Rheine-Westphalian Electricity Co.*] [*Germany*]
RWe	Westerly Public Library, Westerly, RI [*Library symbol*] [*Library of Congress*] (LCLS)
RWEA	Royal West of England Academy
RWED	Read/Write Extend Delete
R Week	Rechtskundig Weekblad [*A publication*]
RWEL........	Rockwell Oil Co. [*NASDAQ symbol*] (NQ)
RWEMA ..	Ralph Waldo Emerson Memorial Association (EA)
RWES.......	Ralph Waldo Emerson Society (EA)
RWES.......	Resources West, Inc. [*NASDAQ symbol*] (NQ)
RWF	Fairport High School Library, Fairport, NY [*OCLC symbol*] (OCLC)
RWF	Raoul Wallenberg Foreningen [*Raoul Wallenberg Association - RWA*] (EAIO)
RWF	Redwood Falls, MN [*Location identifier*] [*FAA*] (FAAL)
RWF	Roundtable for Women in Foodservice [*Later, RWFBH*] (EA)
RWF	Roush, W. F., Miami FL [*STAC*]
RWF	Royal Welch [*or Welsh*] Fusiliers [*Military unit*] [*British*]
RWF	Rozprawy Wydzialu Filologicznego Polskiej Akademyi Umiejetnosci [*A publication*]
RwF............	Rwandan Franc [*Monetary unit*] (IMH)
RWFBH	Roundtable for Women Food-Beverage-Hospitality (EA)
RWFC.......	Randy Wade Fan Club (EA)
RWFC.......	Red Wings For'Em Club (EA)
RWFSDH ...	Reports on the World Fertility Survey [*A publication*]
RWG	Bakersfield Aviation Services [*Bakersfield, CA*] [*FAA designator*] (FAAC)
RWG.........	Gates-Chili Senior High School Library, Rochester, NY [*OCLC symbol*] (OCLC)
RWG.........	Radio Writers' Guild [*Later, WGA*]
RWG.........	Redwing Resources, Inc. [*Vancouver Stock Exchange symbol*]
RWG.........	Reliability Working Group (AAG)
RWG.........	Rigid Waveguide
RWG.........	Roebling Wire Gauge
RWGM......	Right Worshipful Grand Master [*Freemasonry*]
RWGR......	Right Worthy Grand Representative [*Freemasonry*]
RWGS.......	Right Worthy Grand Secretary [*Freemasonry*] (ADA)
RWGT	Right Worthy Grand Templar [*Freemasonry*]
RWGT	Right Worthy Grand Treasurer [*Freemasonry*]
RWGW......	Right Worthy Grand Warden [*Freemasonry*]
RWGW......	Right Worthy Grand Worshipful [*Freemasonry*] (ROG)
RWH.........	Geneseo Junior/Senior High School Library, Geneseo, NY [*OCLC symbol*] (OCLC)
RWH.........	RADAR Warning and Homing
RWH.........	Rainwater Head
RWH.........	Rotor Wing Hours [*Aviation*] (AIA)
RWHD.......	Rawhide (MSA)
RWI	Greece-Arcadia Junior/Senior High School Library, Rochester, NY [*OCLC symbol*] (OCLC)
RWI	RADAR Warning Installation (NATG)
RWI	Radio Wire Integration [*Military*]
RWI	Read-Write-Initialize [*Data processing*]
RWI	Regular World Interval
RWI	Remote Weight Indicator
RWI	Rocky Mount [*North Carolina*] [*Airport symbol*] (OAG)
RWIB........	Rioja Wine Information Bureau (EA)
RWIY.......	Royal Wiltshire Imperial Yeomanry [*British military*] (DMA)
RWJ..........	Greece-Athena Junior/Senior High School Library, Rochester, NY [*OCLC symbol*] (OCLC)
RWJ..........	Robert Wood Johnson Medical School [*New Jersey*]
RWJGW....	Right Worthy Junior Grand Warden [*Freemasonry*]
RWK	Greece-Olympia High School Library, Rochester, NY [*OCLC symbol*] (OCLC)
RWK	Queen's Own Royal West Kent Regiment [*Military unit*] [*British*]
RWK	Remaining Work
RWK	Renwick Explorations Ltd. [*Vancouver Stock Exchange symbol*]
RWK	Rework (AAG)

RWkEPA... United States Environmental Protection Agency, National Marine Water Quality Laboratory, West Kingston, RI [*Library symbol*] [*Library of Congress*] (LCLS)
RWL .... H. W. Schroeder Junior/Senior High School Library, Webster, NY [*OCLC symbol*] (OCLC)
RWL .... Rawlins, WY [*Location identifier*] [*FAA*] (FAAL)
RWL .... Relative Water Level
RWL .... Revolutionary Workers League [*Canada*]
RWLB....... Richwell Resources Ltd. [*Vancouver Stock Exchange symbol*]
RWLB....... Regional War Labor Board
RWLR....... Relative Water-Level Recorder
RWM......... Hilton High School Library, Hilton, NY [*OCLC symbol*] (OCLC)
RWM......... Radioactive Waste Management
RWM........ Read-Write Memory [*Data processing*] (MCD)
RWM........ Rectangular Wave Modulation (IEEE)
RWM........ Resistance Welding Machine
RWM........ Right Worshipful Master [*Freemasonry*] (ROG)
RWM........ Rod Worth Minimizer [*Nuclear energy*] (NRCH)
RWM......... Roll Wrapping Machine
RWMA....... Resistance Welder Manufacturers Association (EA)
RWMEB... Railway Mechanical Engineer [*A publication*]
RWN......... Holly Junior/Senior High School Library, Holly, NY [*OCLC symbol*] (OCLC)
RWN......... Rawdon Resources Ltd. [*Vancouver Stock Exchange symbol*]
RWN......... Winamac, IN [*Location identifier*] [*FAA*] (FAAL)
RWNBH... Records Will Not Be Handcarried [*Army*] (AABC)
RWND...... Rewind (MSA)
RWNF....... Ryan White National Fund (EA)
RWO......... Honeoye Falls-Lima Senior High School Library, Honeoye Falls, NY [*OCLC symbol*] (OCLC)
RWO......... Kodiak, AK [*Location identifier*] [*FAA*] (FAAL)
RWO......... Reconnaissance Watch Officer (MCD)
RWO......... Regional Works Officer [*British*]
RWO......... Reimbursable Work Order [*Navy*] (NG)
RWO......... Riddare af Wasa Order [*Knight of the Order of Vasa*] [*Sweden*]
RWO......... Routine Work Order (KSC)
RWoH....... Harris Institute, Woonsocket, RI [*Library symbol*] [*Library of Congress*] (LCLS)
RWoU....... Union Saint-Jean-Baptiste d'Amerique, Woonsocket, RI [*Library symbol*] [*Library of Congress*] (LCLS)
RWP .... James Madison High School Library, Rochester, NY [*OCLC symbol*] (OCLC)
RWP .... Radiation Work Permit [*Nuclear energy*] (NRCH)
RWP .... Radio Wave Propagation
RWP .... Radio Working Party
RWP .... RADWASTE [*Radioactive Waste*] Work Permit [*Nuclear energy*] (NRCH)
RWP .... Rainwater Pipe [*Construction*]
RWP .... Rawalpindi/Islamabad [*Pakistan*] [*Airport symbol*] [*Obsolete*] (OAG)
RWP .... Reactor Work Permit (IEEE)
RWP .... Reformacja w Polsce [*A publication*]
RWP .... Regiment Western Province [*British military*] (DMA)
RWP .... Rifle and Weapons Platoon [*Army*] [*Obsolete*] (AABC)
RWP .... Romanian Workers' Party
RWPC....... RADWASTE [*Radioactive Waste*] Process Cell [*Nuclear energy*] (NRCH)
RWPG ...... Real World Problem Generation
RWPH....... River Water Pumphouse [*Nuclear energy*] (NRCH)
RWPI........ Ridgewood Properties, Incorporated [*Atlanta, GA*] [*NASDAQ symbol*] (NQ)
RWQ......... James Monroe High School Library, Rochester, NY [*OCLC symbol*] (OCLC)
RWR .... James Sperry High School Library, Henrietta, NY [*OCLC symbol*] (OCLC)
RWR .... RADAR Warning Receiver (MCD)
RWR .... Radioactive Waste Reduction [*Nuclear energy*] (NRCH)
R-W-R ...... Rail-Water-Rail [*Shipping*]
RWR .... Read/Write Register
RWR .... Relative Weight Response
RWR .... Reward Resources Ltd. [*Vancouver Stock Exchange symbol*]
RWR .... Romance Writers Report [*A publication*] (EAAP)
RWR .... Ronald Wilson Reagan [*US president, 1911-*]
RWRC .... Remain Well to Right of Course [*Aviation*] (FAAC)
RWRSq... Rescue and Weather Reconnaissance Squadron [*Air Force*]
RWS .... Camp Springs, MD [*Location identifier*] [*FAA*] (FAAL)
RWS .... John Marshall High School Library, Rochester, NY [*OCLC symbol*] (OCLC)
RWS .... RADAR Warning System (MCD)
RWS .... Radioactive Waste System [*Nuclear energy*] (NRCH)
RWS .... Range While Search
RWS .... Reaction Wheel Scanner
RWS .... Reaction Wheel Systems (AAG)
RWS .... Regional Warning System
RWS .... Regional Weather Service (NOAA)
RWS .... Release with Service (OICC)
RWS .... Religionswissenschaftliche Studien [*A publication*]
RWS .... Royal Society of Painters in Water-Colours [*British*]
RWS .... Royal West Surrey [*Regiment*] [*Military unit*] [*British*]
RWS .... Royal West Sussex [*Regiment*] [*Military unit*] [*British*]

RWSF .... RADWASTE [*Radioactive Waste*] Solidification Facility [*Nuclear energy*] (NRCH)
RWSF .... Revolutionary War Studies Forum (EA)
RWSF .... Roosevelt Warm Springs Foundation (EA)
RWSGW.... Right Worshipful Senior Grand Warden [*Freemasonry*]
RWSS .... RADWASTE [*Radioactive Waste*] Sample Station [*Nuclear energy*] (NRCH)
RWSS .... River Water Supply System (IEEE)
RWST .... Refueling Water Storage Tank [*Nuclear energy*] (NRCH)
RWT .... Kendall High School Library, Kendall, NY [*OCLC symbol*] (OCLC)
RWT .... RADAR Warning Trainer (MCD)
RWT .... Read-Write Tape [*Data processing*]
RWT .... Refueling Water Tank [*Nuclear energy*] (NRCH)
RWTA ...... River Water Treatment Area [*Nuclear energy*] (NRCH)
RWTH...... Rotary Wing Turbine Hours [*Aviation*] (AIA)
RWTI........ RW Technology, Inc. [*NASDAQ symbol*] (NQ)
RWTS .... Regenerant Waste Treatment Subsystem [*Nuclear energy*] (NRCH)
RWU......... Keshequa Junior/Senior High School Library, Nunda, NY [*OCLC symbol*] (OCLC)
RWU......... Rural Workers Union [*Australia*]
RWV......... L. C. Obourn High School Library, East Rochester, NY [*OCLC symbol*] (OCLC)
RWV......... Radioactive Waste Vent [*Nuclear energy*] (NRCH)
RWV......... Read-Write-Verify [*Data processing*]
RWV......... Rubbery Wood Virus
RWV......... Rustad/Wickhem/Video, Inc. [*Madison, WI*] (TSSD)
RWVD....... Real World Visual Display
RWVR ...... Real World Vehicular Rate
RWW......... Lester B. Forman Central Library, Fairport, NY [*OCLC symbol*] (OCLC)
RWX .... Letchworth Junior/Senior High School Library, Gainesville, NY [*OCLC symbol*] (OCLC)
RWY .... Livonia High School Library, Livonia, NY [*OCLC symbol*] (OCLC)
RWY .... Railway
RWY .... Royal Wiltshire Yeomanry [*Military unit*] [*British*]
RWY .... Runway (AAG)
Rwy Age ... Railway Age [*A publication*]
RWZ......... McQuaid Jesuit High School Library, Rochester, NY [*OCLC symbol*] (OCLC)
RX .... Comite International de la Croix-Rouge [*International Committee of the Red Cross*] [*ICAO designator*] (FAAC)
RX .... Excess Reserves
RX .... Rank Xerox
RX .... Receiver [*or Reception*] [*Radio*] (NATG)
Rx............. Recipe [*Used as a symbol for medical prescriptions*]
RX .... Reconnaissance-Experimental Aircraft
RX .... Register and Indexed Storage (MCD)
RX .... Remote Exchange [*Telecommunications*] (TEL)
RX .... Report Crossing [*Aviation*] (FAAC)
RX .... Resolver-Transmitter
RX .... Rix-Dollar [*British*] (ROG)
RX .... Rupees [*Monetary unit*] [*Ceylon, India, and Pakistan*] (ROG)
RX .... Rush [*on teletype messages*]
RXA .... Mount Morris Junior/Senior High School Library, Mount Morris, NY [*OCLC symbol*] (OCLC)
RXA .... Roxana Resources Ltd. [*Vancouver Stock Exchange symbol*]
RXB .... Nazareth Academy Library, Rochester, NY [*OCLC symbol*] (OCLC)
RXC .... Our Lady of Mercy High School Library, Rochester, NY [*OCLC symbol*] (OCLC)
RXCH .... Rexco Industries, Inc. [*NASDAQ symbol*] (NQ)
RXD .... Penfield High School Library, Penfield, NY [*OCLC symbol*] (OCLC)
RXE .... Perry Junior/Senior High School Library, Perry, NY [*OCLC symbol*] (OCLC)
RXF .... Pittsford-Medon High School Library, Pittsford, NY [*OCLC symbol*] (OCLC)
RXF.......... Rexford [*Montana*] [*Seismograph station code, US Geological Survey*] (SEIS)
RXG .... Pittsford-Sutherland High School Library, Pittsford, NY [*OCLC symbol*] (OCLC)
RXH.......... R. L. Thomas High School Library, Webster, NY [*OCLC symbol*] (OCLC)
RXH.......... Rexham Corp. [*NYSE symbol*] (SPSG)
RXI .... Rexplore Resources International Ltd. [*Vancouver Stock Exchange symbol*]
RXI .... St. Agnes High School Library, Rochester, NY [*OCLC symbol*] (OCLC)
RXJ........... Thomas Jefferson Junior/Senior High School Library, Rochester, NY [*OCLC symbol*] (OCLC)
RXK .... Newark, OH [*Location identifier*] [*FAA*] (FAAL)
RXK .... Warsaw High School Library, Warsaw, NY [*OCLC symbol*] (OCLC)
RXL .... Rank Xerox Limited [*Xerox subsidiary*]
RXL .... Wayland Senior High School Library, Wayland, NY [*OCLC symbol*] (OCLC)
RXLI......... Recessive X-Linked Ichthyosis [*Medicine*]
RXM.......... Rexford Minerals Ltd. [*Vancouver Stock Exchange symbol*]

RXM .... West Irondequoit High School Library, Rochester, NY [*OCLC symbol*] (OCLC)
RXN .... Islip, NY [*Location identifier*] [*FAA*] (FAAL)
RXN .... Rexene Corp. [*NYSE symbol*] (SPSG)
RXN .... Wheatland-Chili Junior/Senior High School Library, Scottsville, NY [*OCLC symbol*] (OCLC)
RXO .... York High School Library, Retsof, NY [*OCLC symbol*] (OCLC)
RXP .... American Baptist Historical Society Library, Rochester, NY [*OCLC symbol*] (OCLC)
RXP .... Radix Point
RXQ .... Lincoln First Bank of Rochester Library Service, Rochester, NY [*OCLC symbol*] (OCLC)
RXQ .... Washington, DC [*Location identifier*] [*FAA*] (FAAL)
RXR .... Rainex Industries [*Formerly, Rainex Resources Ltd.*] [*Vancouver Stock Exchange symbol*]
RXS .... RADAR Cross Section
RXS .... Roxas City [*Philippines*] [*Airport symbol*] (OAG)
RXSC .... Rexcom Systems Corporation [*Houston, TX*] [*NASDAQ symbol*] (NQ)
RXT .... Right Exotropia [*Ophthalmology*]
RxTV .... Prescription Television
R du XVIe S ... Revue du Seizieme Siecle [*A publication*]
RXW .... Roxwell Gold Mines [*Vancouver Stock Exchange symbol*]
RXW .... Watersmeet, MI [*Location identifier*] [*FAA*] (FAAL)
RXX .... Reako Exploration [*Vancouver Stock Exchange symbol*]
RXY .... Roxy Petroleum Ltd. [*Toronto Stock Exchange symbol*]
RXZ .... Chicago, IL [*Location identifier*] [*FAA*] (FAAL)
RY .... Railway (AFIT)
RY .... Redcoat Air Cargo Ltd. [*United Kingdom*] [*ICAO designator*] (ICDA)
RY .... Relative Yield [*Agriculture*]
RY .... Relay (DEN)
RY .... Riley Aeronautics Corp. [*ICAO aircraft manufacturer identifier*] (ICAO)
RY .... Roll Yoke
RY .... Rotterdam Airlines [*Netherlands*] [*ICAO designator*] (FAAC)
RY .... Royal (ROG)
RY .... Royal Bank of Canada [*Toronto Stock Exchange symbol*] [*Vancouver Stock Exchange symbol*]
RY .... Royal Yeomanry [*Military unit*] [*British*]
RY .... Runway (FAAC)
ry .... Rydberg [*Unit of energy*] [*Atomic physics*] [*Symbol*]
ry .... Ryukyu Islands, Southern [*ja (Japan)* used in records cataloged after January 1978] [*MARC country of publication code*] [*Library of Congress*] (LCCP)
RYA .... Railroad Yardmasters of America (EA)
RYA .... Royal Yachting Association [*British*]
RYa .... Russkii Yazyk v Shkole [*Moscow*] [*A publication*]
Ry Age .... Railway Age [*A publication*]
RYAL .... Royale Airlines, Inc. [*NASDAQ symbol*] (NQ)
RYALM ...... Relay Alarm (AAG)
RYAN .... Ryan's Family Steak Houses, Inc. [*NASDAQ symbol*] (NQ)
Ryan Advis Health Serv Gov Boards ... Ryan Advisory for Health Services Governing Boards [*A publication*]
Ryan & M .. Ryan and Moody's English Nisi Prius Reports [*171 English Reprint*] [*A publication*] (DLA)
Ryan & M (Eng) ... Ryan and Moody's English Nisi Prius Reports [*171 English Reprint*] [*A publication*] (DLA)
RYB .... Raymond, MS [*Location identifier*] [*FAA*] (FAAL)
RYB .... Rybachye [*USSR*] [*Seismograph station code, US Geological Survey*] (SEIS)
RYBF .... Royal Business Group, Inc. [*NASDAQ symbol*] (NQ)
Ryb Khoz ... Rybnoe Khozyaistvo [*A publication*]
Rybn Khoz ... Rybnoe Khozyaistvo [*A publication*]
Rybn Khoz (Kiev) ... Rybnoe Khozyaistvo (Kiev) [*A publication*]
Rybn Khoz Resp Mezhved Temat Nauchn Sb ... Rybnoe Khozyaistvo Respublikanskii Mezhvedomstvennyi Tematicheskii Nauchnyi Sbornik [*A publication*]
Rybn Prom-St Dal'n Vost ... Rybnaya Promyshlennost' Dal'nego Vostoka [*A publication*]
Rybokhoz Issled Basseine Balt Morya ... Rybokhozyaistvennye Issledovaniya v Basseine Baltiiskogo Morya [*A publication*]
RYC .... Raychem Corp. [*NYSE symbol*] (SPSG)
RYC .... Raymac Oil Corporation [*Vancouver Stock Exchange symbol*]
RyC .... Religion y Cultura [*A publication*]
RYC .... Royal Yacht Club [*Australia*]
RYC .... Rural Youth Corps [*Defunct*] (EA)
Ry & Can.... Reports of Railway and Canal Traffic Cases [*1855-1950*] [*A publication*]
Ry & Can Cas ... Railway and Canal Cases [*England*] [*A publication*] (DLA)
Ry & Can Traf Ca ... Railway and Canal Traffic Cases [*A publication*] (DLA)
Ry & Can Traf Cas ... Reports of Railway and Canal Traffic Cases [*1855-1950*] [*A publication*] (ILCA)
Ry & Can Traffic Cas ... Railway and Canal Traffic Cases [*England*] [*A publication*] (DLA)
Ry & Can Tr Cas ... Reports of Railway and Canal Traffic Cases [*1855-1950*] [*A publication*] (DLA)
Ry Cas........ Reports of English Railway Cases [*A publication*] (DLA)
Ry Cas........ Reports of Railway and Canal Traffic Cases [*1855-1950*] [*A publication*]

Ry & C Cas (Eng) ... Railway and Canal Cases [*England*] [*A publication*] (DLA)
RYCO .... Rynco Scientific Corp. [*NASDAQ symbol*] (NQ)
Ry & Corp Law J ... Railway and Corporation Law Journal [*A publication*] (DLA)
Ry Corp Law Jour ... Railway and Corporation Law Journal [*A publication*] (DLA)
Ry & Corp Law Jour ... Railway and Corporation Law Journal [*A publication*] (DLA)
Ry & C Traffic Cas (Eng) ... Railway and Canal Traffic Cases [*England*] [*A publication*] (DLA)
RYD .... Real Year Dollars (NASA)
Ryde .... Ryde's Rating Appeals [*1871-1904*] [*A publication*] (DLA)
Ryde & K.... Ryde and Konstam's Reports of Rating Appeals [*1894-1904*] [*A publication*] (DLA)
Ryde & K Rat App ... Ryde and Konstam's Reports of Rating Appeals [*1894-1904*] [*A publication*] (DLA)
Ryde Rat App ... Ryde's Rating Appeals [*1871-1904*] [*A publication*] (DLA)
Rydge's ...... Rydge's Business Journal [*A publication*] (APTA)
Rydge's Constr Civ Eng & Min Rev ... Rydge's Construction, Civil Engineering, and Mining Review [*A publication*] (APTA)
Rydges Mgmt Serv ... Rydge's Management Service [*A publication*]
RYDMAR ... Reaction-Yield-Detected Magnetic Resonance [*Also, RYDMR*] [*Spectroscopy*]
RYDMR ... Reaction-Yield-Detected Magnetic Resonance [*Also, RYDMAR*] [*Spectroscopy*]
RYE .... Retirement Year Ending [*Army*] (AABC)
RYE .... Royalon Petroleum [*Vancouver Stock Exchange symbol*]
RYEJA ...... Royal Engineers Journal [*A publication*]
RyF .... Razon y Fe [*A publication*]
Ry F........... Rymer's Foedera [*20 vols.*] [*1704-35*] [*A publication*] (DLA)
RyFab .... Razon y Fabula [*A publication*]
RYFL .... Family Steak Houses of Florida, Inc. [*Neptune Beach, FL*] [*NASDAQ symbol*] (NQ)
Ry Gaz Int ... Railway Gazette International [*A publication*]
RYHY .... Ryerson & Haynes, Inc. [*Jackson, MI*] [*NASDAQ symbol*] (NQ)
RYK .... Relay Creek Resources Ltd. [*Vancouver Stock Exchange symbol*]
RYK .... Romulus, NY [*Location identifier*] [*FAA*] (FAAL)
RYK .... Rykoff-Sexton, Inc. [*NYSE symbol*] (SPSG)
RYKA .... Ryka, Inc. [*NASDAQ symbol*] (NQ)
RYKHA ..... Rybnoe Khozyaistvo [*A publication*]
RYKOD ..... Ryutai Kogaku [*A publication*]
ryl............. Royal [*Philately*]
RYL .... Royal Trustco Limited [*Toronto Stock Exchange symbol*] [*Vancouver Stock Exchange symbol*]
RYL .... Ryland Group, Inc. [*NYSE symbol*] (SPSG)
Ry Loco & Cars ... Railway Locomotives and Cars [*A publication*]
Ryl Plac Parl ... Ryley's Placita Parliamentaria [*1290-1307*] [*England*] [*A publication*] (DLA)
RYM........ Reference Your Message [*Military*] (AABC)
RYM .... Revolutionary Youth Movement [*Factions of Students for a Democratic Society. See RYM-I and RYM-II*]
Ry & M ...... Ryan and Moody's English Nisi Prius Reports [*A publication*] (DLA)
Ry MCC..... Ryan and Moody's English Crown Cases [*A publication*] (DLA)
Ry & MCC ... Ryan and Moody's English Crown Cases Reserved [*A publication*] (DLA)
Ry Mech & Elec Eng ... Railway Mechanical and Electrical Engineer [*A publication*]
Ry Mech Eng ... Railway Mechanical Engineer [*A publication*]
Ry Med Jur ... Ryan's Medical Jurisprudence [*A publication*] (DLA)
Rym F .... Rymer's Foedera [*20 vols.*] [*1704-35*] [*A publication*] (DLA)
RYM-I .... Revolutionary Youth Movement I [*Also known as "Weatherman"*] [*A faction of Students for a Democratic Society*]
RYM-II...... Revolutionary Youth Movement II [*A faction of Students for a Democratic Society*]
Ry & MNP ... Ryan and Moody's English Nisi Prius Reports [*A publication*] (DLA)
Ry Mo .... Rythmes du Monde [*A publication*]
Ry & Moo .. Ryan and Moody [*1823-26*] [*A publication*] (DLA)
RYN.......... Rayon
RYN.......... Ryan Aviation Corp. [*Wichita, KS*] [*FAA designator*] (FAAC)
RYN.......... Ryan Homes, Inc. [*NYSE symbol*] (SPSG)
RYN.......... Tucson, AZ [*Location identifier*] [*FAA*] (FAAL)
RYNA .... Railroad Yardmasters of North America [*Absorbed by RYA*] (EA)
RYNM....... Arlington Realty Investors [*Formerly, Ryan Marketing Investors*] [*NASDAQ symbol*] (NQ)
RYO .... Rio Turbio [*Argentina*] [*Airport symbol*] (OAG)
Ryojun Coll Eng Publ ... Ryojun College of Engineering. Publications [*A publication*]
RYP .... Cumberland, MD [*Location identifier*] [*FAA*] (FAAL)
R-Y-P....... Roll, Yaw, Pitch (MCD)
RYPAAO... Annals. Royal College of Physicians and Surgeons of Canada [*A publication*]
RYPFA ...... Revista YPF [*Yacimientos Petroliferos Fiscales*] (Argentina) [*A publication*]

RYQ.......... Royalstar Resources [*Vancouver Stock Exchange symbol*]
RYR .... Radyr Junction [*Cardiff*] [*Welsh depot code*]
Ry R .... Railway Review [*A publication*]
RYR .... Royal Yeomanry Regiment [*British military*]   (DMA)
RYR .... Rymer Foods, Inc. [*NYSE symbol*]   (SPSG)
RYRKF ..... Rayrock Resources [*NASDAQ symbol*]   (NQ)
RYRQD ..... Reply Requested   (NOAA)
RYS........ Railway Stations [*Public-performance tariff class*] [*British*]
RYS........... Royal Yacht Squadron [*British*]
RYS.......... Ryan Resources Ltd. [*Vancouver Stock Exchange symbol*]
RYT .... Ray-Net Communications Systems, Inc. [*Vancouver Stock Exchange symbol*]
RYT .... Relative Yield Total [*Agriculture*]
Ryt............ Rytmi [*Record label*] [*Finland*]
RYTC........ Raytech Corp. [*NASDAQ symbol*]   (NQ)
Ry Track Struct ... Railway Track and Structures [*A publication*]
RYU.......... Rosanky, TX [*Location identifier*] [*FAA*]   (FAAL)
RYU .... Ryukoku University [*UTLAS symbol*]
RYUSA...... Ryusan To Kogyo [*A publication*]
RYV .... Watertown, WI [*Location identifier*] [*FAA*]   (FAAL)
RYY .... Marietta, GA [*Location identifier*] [*FAA*]   (FAAL)
RZ.............. Air Anjou Transports [*France*] [*ICAO designator*]   (FAAC)
RZ.............. Rada Zydowska [*A publication*]
RZ.............. Radostna Zeme [*A publication*]
RZ.............. Radovi (Filozofski Fakultet-Zadar) [*A publication*]
R & Z .... Range and Zero [*NASA*]   (KSC)
RZ.............. Reaction Zone
RZ.............. Reconnaissance Zone
RZ.............. Recovery Zone   (MCD)
RZ.............. Referativnyi Zhurnal. Informatika [*A publication*]
RZ.............. Regal-Zonophone [*Record label*] [*Great Britain*]
RZ.............. Regiment de Zouaves
RZ.............. Resistance Zone
RZ.............. Return-to-Zero Recording [*Data processing*]
Rz.............. Retzius [*Neuron*]
RZ.............. Revista Zurita Saragosse [*A publication*]
RZ.............. Revolutionary Cells [*Revolutionary group*] [*West Germany*]
Rz.............. Rhizome [*Botany*]
RZ.............. Rueckenfallschirm mit Zwangsausloesung [*Static-line, backpack parachute*] [*German military - World War II*]
RZA .... Religious Zionists of America   (EA)
RZA .... Santa Cruz [*Argentina*] [*Airport symbol*]   (OAG)
R Z Avtomat Telemeh i Vycisl Tehn ... Referativnyi Zhurnal. Avtomatika. Telemehanika i Vycislitelnaja Tehnika [*A publication*]
RZBLA ...... Referativnyi Zhurnal. Biologiya [*A publication*]
RZC .... Fayetteville, AR [*Location identifier*] [*FAA*]   (FAAL)
RZE .... Chemiefasern/Textil-Industrie. Zeitschrift fuer die Gesamte Textil Industrie [*A publication*]
RZE .... Rzeszow [*Poland*] [*Airport symbol*]   (OAG)
RZETA...... Rozprawy Elektrotechniczne [*A publication*]
RZF............ Riemann Zeta Function [*Mathematics*]
R Z Fiz...... Referativnyi Zhurnal. Fizika [*A publication*]
RZFZA ...... Referativnyi Zhurnal. Fizika [*A publication*]
RZh Avtomat Telemekh i Vychisl Tekhn ... Akademiya Nauk SSSR. Institut Nauchnoi Informatsii. Referativnyi Zhurnal. Avtomatika. Telemekhanika i Vychislitel'naya Tekhnika [*A publication*]
RZh Mat.... Akademiya Nauk SSSR. Institut Nauchnoi Informatsii. Referativnyi Zhurnal. Matematika [*A publication*]
RZh Tekhn Kibernet ... Akademiya Nauk SSSR. Institut Nauchnoi i Tekhnicheskoi Informatsii. Referativnyi Zhurnal. Tekhnicheskaya Kibernetika [*A publication*]
RZINA....... Rozprawy Inzynierskie [*A publication*]
RZInformat ... Referativnyi Zhurnal. Informatika [*A publication*]
RZKibernet ... Referativnyi Zhurnal. Kibernetika [*A publication*]
RZL............ Rensselaer, IN [*Location identifier*] [*FAA*]   (FAAL)
RZL............ Return-to-Zero Level
RZM .... Return-to-Zero Mark
RZMA .... Rolled Zinc Manufacturers Association [*Defunct*]   (EA)
RZMat....... Referativnyi Zhurnal. Matematika [*A publication*]
RZMeh..... Referativnyi Zhurnal. Mehanika [*A publication*]
RZMTA..... Referativnyi Zhurnal. Metallurgiya [*A publication*]
RZMVA .... Revista de Zootechnic si Medicina Veterinara [*A publication*]
RZNDA..... Razvedka Nedr [*A publication*]
RZ(NP)...... Nonpolarized Return-to-Zero Recording [*Data processing*]   (IBMDP)
RZO.......... Demopolis, AL [*Location identifier*] [*FAA*]   (FAAL)
RZONA..... Razvedka i Okhrana Nedr [*A publication*]
RZOOA.... Rivista di Zootecnia [*A publication*]
RZ(P)........ Polarized Return-to-Zero Recording [*Data processing*]   (IBMDP)
RZP........... Provincetown, MA [*Location identifier*] [*FAA*]   (FAAL)
RZS........... Rolled Zinc Sheet
RZS........... Royal Zoological Society [*British*]
RZSF........ Radovi Zavoda za Slavensku Filologiju [*A publication*]
RZSND...... Revue Zairoise des Sciences Nucleaires [*A publication*]
RZSS .... Royal Zoological Society of Scotland   (EAIO)
RZT........... Chillicothe, OH [*Location identifier*] [*FAA*]   (FAAL)
RzW .... Rechtsprechung zum Wiedergutmachungsrecht [*Reports on Restitution Law*] [*1949/50-*] [*A publication*]   (ILCA)
RZZ .... Roanoke Rapids, NC [*Location identifier*] [*FAA*]   (FAAL)

S

S	Aerospatiale [*Societe Nationale Industrielle Aerospatiale*] (Sud Aviation) [*France*] [*ICAO aircraft manufacturer identifier*] (ICAO)
S	Antisubmarine [*Designation for all US military aircraft*]
S	Apparent Power [*Symbol*] (DEN)
S	Boltzmann Constant [*Statistical mechanics*]
S	Codex Sinaiticus (BJA)
S	Detecting [*JETDS nomenclature*]
S	Entropy [*Symbol*] [*IUPAC*]
S	Esses [*Phonetic alphabet*] [*Pre-World War II*] (DSUE)
S	Expenditure Saved [*Economics*]
S	Fun Fairs [*Public-performance tariff class*] [*British*]
S	Isis-Chemie KG [*Germany*] [*Research code symbol*]
S	Magnetic Solar Daily Variation
S	New York Supplement [*A publication*] (DLA)
s	Path, Length of Arc [*Symbol*] [*IUPAC*]
(S)	Paymaster [*Navy*] [*British*]
S	Permissible Working Stress
S	Pitman-Moore Co. [*Research code symbol*]
S	Pounds per Square Inch (AAG)
S	Poynting Vector [*Symbol*] [*Electromagnetism*] (DEN)
S	Range Bearing [*JETDS nomenclature*]
S	Reluctance [*Symbol*] (DEN)
s/	Sa [*Their, Your*] [*French*]
S	Sabbath
S	Sabin [*Unit of acoustic measurement*] (DEN)
S	Sable [*Heraldry*]
S	Sacral
S	Sacred
S	Sacrifice [*Baseball*]
S	Sacrum
S	Saduccus [*Flourished, 13th century*] [*Authority cited in pre-1607 legal work*] (DSA)
S	Saeculum
(S)	Safe [*Task classification*] [*NASA*] (NASA)
S	Safety [*Football*]
S	Sailing Ship
S	Saint
s	Saldo [*Balance*] [*Afrikaans*]
S	[*Bartholomaeus de*] Saliceto [*Deceased, 1411*] [*Authority cited in pre-1607 legal work*] (DSA)
S	Saline
S	Salvageable (AAG)
S	Same Case [*Same case as case cited*] [*Used in Shepard's Citations*] [*Legal term*] (DLA)
S	Sample
S	Samuel [*Old Testament book*] (BJA)
S	San Francisco [*California*] [*Mint mark, when appearing on US coins*]
S	Sand [*Quality of the bottom*] [*Nautical charts*]
S	Sandra [*Genotype of Phlox paniculata*]
S	Sapwood [*Forestry*]
S	Satang [*Monetary unit in Thailand*]
S	Saturday
S	Saturn
S	Savanna Zone Soil [*Agriculture*]
S	Savings [*Economics*]
S	Saxon
S	Scalar [*Mathematics*] (ROG)
S	Scanning
S	Scarce [*Numismatics*]
S	Scattering Coefficient [*Photometry*]
S	Schedule
S	Schilling [*Monetary unit*] [*Austria*]
S	[*Wolfgang*] Schmieder [*When used in identifying J. S. Bach's compositions, refers to cataloging of his works by musicologist Schmieder*]
S	School
S	Scilicet [*Namely*] [*Latin*] (DLA)
S	Scot
S	Scouting [*Naval aircraft designation*]
S	Scribe
S	Scuttle
S	Scythian [*Geology*]
S	Sea (ADA)
S	Sea-Air Temperature Difference Correction
S	Seaman [*Navy*]
S	Seaplane [*Navy*]
S	Search
S	Searle's Cape Of Good Hope Reports [*South Africa*] [*A publication*] (DLA)
S	Searle's Cases in the Supreme Court [*1850-67*] [*South Africa*] [*A publication*] (DLA)
S	Sears, Roebuck & Co. [*NYSE symbol*] (SPSG)
S	Seasonal [*Business term*] (OICC)
S	Second [*or Secondary*]
s	Second [*Symbol*] [*SI unit of time*]
s	Secondary [*Preferred form is sec*] [*Chemistry*]
S	Secondary Modern School [*British*]
S	Secondary [*or Shake*] Wave [*Earthquakes*]
S	Secret [*Security classification*]
S	Secretary
S	Secretin [*Endocrinology*]
S	Secretory Substance [*Botany*]
S	Section
S	Sedentary [*Biology*]
S	Seder of Triennial Cycle (BJA)
s	Sedimentation Coefficient [*Physical chemistry*]
S	See
S	Seelenlaenge [*Barrel length*] [*German military - World War II*]
S	Seguente [*And Following*] [*Italian*] (ILCA)
S	Sehen [*See*] [*German*]
S	Seite [*Page*] [*German*]
S	Self-Pollinated [*Botany*]
S	Selvi [*Italy*] [*Research code symbol*]
S	Semi
S	Semi-Registered Tank [*Liquid gas carriers*]
S	Semiannually
S	Semis [*One-Half*] [*Pharmacy*]
S	Sen [*Monetary unit in Japan*]
S	Senate
S	Senate Bill [*with number*] (GPO)
S	Senor [*Mister*] [*Spanish*]
S	Sensation [*Psychology*]
S	Sensitivity (DEN)
S	Sent [*Communications*] (FAAC)
S	Sentence [*Linguistics*]
S	Senza [*Without*] [*Music*]
S	Separation
S	September
S	September [*A publication*]
S	Sepulchrum [*Sepulchre*] [*Latin*]
S	Sepultus [*Buried*] [*Latin*]
S	Serial
S	Series
S	Serine [*One-letter symbol; see Ser*]
S	Sermon
S	Serum
S	Service [*Military document classification*] (INF)
S	Servicing
S	Servier [*France*] [*Research code symbol*]
s/	Ses [*Their, Your*] [*French*]
S	Sesquiplane [*Navy*]
S	Set
S	Set Meals [*School meals*] [*British*]
S	Seven (ROG)
S	Seventy (ROG)
S	Severity
S	Sewage Disposal [*British Waterways Board sign*]
S	Sezatoarea. Revista de Folklor [*A publication*]
S	Shaft Horsepower
S	Shaft Main Engine

S .... Shape Descriptor [*S-curve, for example. The shape resembles the letter for which it is named*]
S .... Shape Factor of a Structure [*Heat transmission symbol*]
S .... Shares [*Following a figure, indicates number of 100-share lots in a transaction; e.g., 4s indicates 400 shares*] [*NYSE symbol*] (SPSG)
S .... Sharp
S .... Shaw, Dunlop, and Bell's Scotch Court of Session Reports, First Series [*A publication*] (DLA)
S .... Shaw's Scotch Appeal Cases, House of Lords [*A publication*] (DLA)
S .... Shaw's Scotch Court of Session Cases [*A publication*] (DLA)
S .... Shear [*Type of seismic wave*]
S .... Sheep (ROG)
S .... Sheet [*Genetics*]
S .... Shell
S .... Shelter [*Bureau of the Census*]
S .... Sheltered [*Takeoff area for seaplanes*] [*For chart use only*]
S .... Shelters [*JETDS nomenclature*] [*Military*] (CET)
S .... Shilling [*Monetary unit in Britain*] [*Obsolete*]
S .... Ship
S .... Shire (ADA)
S .... Short Circuit
S .... Shrub [*Botany*]
S .... Shunt Ahead [*Railroad signal arm*] [*British*]
S .... Sick
S .... Side
S .... Sidrah (BJA)
S .... Siecle [*Century*] [*French*]
S .... Siemens [*Symbol*] [*SI unit of electric conductance*]
S .... Sierra [*Phonetic alphabet*] [*International*] (DSUE)
S .... Sigma Mines (Quebec) Ltd. [*Toronto Stock Exchange symbol*]
S .... Sign [*or Signed*]
S .... Signa [*Write*] [*Pharmacy*]
S .... Signal [*Telecommunications*] (TEL)
S .... Signal Strength [*Broadcasting*]
S .... Signaller [*British military*] (DMA)
S .... Signature
/S/ .... Signed [*Before signature on typed copy of a document, original of which was signed*]
S .... Signetur [*Let It Be Entitled*] [*Pharmacy*] (ROG)
S .... Signor [*Mister*] [*Italian*]
S .... Silent [*Dance terminology*]
S .... Silicate
S .... Silk (AAG)
S .... Silver
S .... Silversmith
S .... Simes [*Italy*] [*Research code symbol*]
S .... Similarity Index
S .... Simon de Bisignano [*Flourished, 1174-79*] [*Authority cited in pre-1607 legal work*] (DSA)
S .... Simon de Paris [*Deceased, 1273*] [*Authority cited in pre-1607 legal work*] (DSA)
S .... Simplex
S .... Simultaneous Transmission of Range Signals and Voice
S .... Sine [*Without*] [*Latin*]
S .... Single
S .... Single [*One way fare*] [*British*]
S .... Single Silk [*Wire insulation*]
S .... Singular
(S) .... Sinister [*Counterclockwise configuration*] [*Biochemistry*]
S .... Sinister [*Left*] [*Latin*]
S .... Sinistra [*Left Hand*] [*Music*]
S .... Sink
S .... Sire
S .... Sister
S .... Site [*Archaeology*]
S .... Situs [*Placed*] [*Latin*]
S .... Sixteenmo [*Book from 15 to 17-1/2 centimeters in height*]
S .... Sixth Word Designator [*Data processing*]
s .... Sjieling [*Shilling*] [*Monetary unit*] [*Afrikaans*]
S .... Skid (AAG)
S .... Slate (KSC)
S .... Slave [*LORAN stations*]
S .... Slavia [*A publication*]
S .... Sleeping [*Medicine*]
S .... Slewed [*Antenna*]
S .... Slip
S .... Slipped Up [*Horse racing*]
S .... Slope [*Technical drawings*]
S .... Slow
S .... Slow Muscle [*Skeletal muscle pharmacology*]
S .... Small [*Size designation for clothing, etc.*]
S .... Smooth [*Appearance of bacterial colony*]
S .... Smooth Sea [*Navigation*]
S .... Sniper [*British military*] (DMA)
S .... Snow [*Meteorology*]
S .... Socialist
S .... Society
S .... Socius [*or Sodalis*] [*Fellow*]
S .... Soft

S .... Software [*Data processing*]
S .... Soiled [*Deltiology*]
S .... Sol [*Monetary unit in Peru*]
S .... Solar (ADA)
S .... Solco Basel AG [*Switzerland*] [*Research code symbol*]
S .... Soldering
S .... Solicitor's Opinion [*A publication*] (DLA)
S .... Solid
(s) .... Solid [*Chemistry*]
S .... Solidus [*Shilling*] [*Latin*]
S .... Solitary [*Biology*]
S .... Solo [*Music*]
S .... Solubility
S .... Somaliland Scouts [*Military unit*] [*British*]
S .... Son
s/ .... Son [*Their, Your*] [*French*]
S .... SONAR [*Sonic Azimuth and Ranging*] [*British military*] (DMA)
S .... Song (ROG)
S .... Soprano
S .... Sou [*Monetary unit in France*]
S .... Sough (AAG)
S .... Sound [*Audiology*]
S .... Sound Tape [*Films, television, etc.*]
S .... Source
S .... South [*or Southern*]
s----- .... South America [*MARC geographic area code*] [*Library of Congress*] (LCCP)
S .... Southern Reporter [*A publication*] (DLA)
S .... Spacer
S .... Spade (ADA)
S .... Spar [*Buoy*]
S .... Spares
S .... Spatial Ability [*Psychology*]
S .... Speak
S .... Special
s .... Special Abilities of an Individual [*Symbol*] [*Psychology*]
S .... Special Air Mission [*Military aircraft identification prefix*] (FAAC)
S .... Special Types [*JETDS nomenclature*]
S .... Specialist [*Ecology*]
S .... Species
S .... Specific Factor
S .... Specific Surface
S .... Specification
S .... Spectator [*A publication*]
S .... Speculum [*A publication*]
S .... Speech
S .... Speed
S .... Sphere [*or Spherical*]
s .... Spin Quantum Number [*Atomic physics*] (DEN)
S .... Spinster
S .... Split [*In stock listings of newspapers*]
S .... Spoilers in Nozzle
S .... Sponsored
S .... Spontaneous
S .... Spool
S .... Sport [*In automobile model name "Honda Civic S"*]
S .... Spring-Burned [*Ecology*]
S .... Spurs [*Horse racing*]
S .... Squadron
S .... Staatsblad van het Koninkrijk der Nederlanden [*A publication*]
S .... Stack
S .... Stackable Container (DCTA)
S .... Staff [*License plate code assigned to foreign diplomats in the US*]
S .... Staff
S .... Stand
S .... Standard
s .... Standard Deviation [*Also, SD*] [*Statistics*]
S .... Star (NASA)
S .... Starboard
S .... Start (KSC)
s .... Stat [*Unit of radioactive disintegration rate*]
S .... State [*Telecommunications*]
S .... Static
S .... Station
S .... Statue (ADA)
S .... Status Required [*Civil Service*]
S .... Statute
S .... Steamer
S .... Steamship (DS)
S .... Steel
S .... Stem
S .... Stephanus Provincialis [*Flourished, 1290-97*] [*Authority cited in pre-1607 legal work*] (DSA)
S .... Stere [*Metric measure of volume*]
S .... Stereo Broadcast [*British*]
S .... Stimulus
S .... Stock
S .... Stockbroker

S	Stolen Base [*Baseball*]
S	Stopping Power
S	Storage
S	Stores [*British military*] (DMA)
S	Straight
S	Straight-In [*Aviation*] (FAAC)
s	Strange [*Quark*] [*Atomic physics*]
S	Stratum (BJA)
S	Stratus [*Meteorology*]
S	Street [*Bureau of the Census*]
S	Strength (DS)
S	Streptomycin [*An antibiotic*]
S	Streptozocin [*Antineoplastic drug*]
S	Stroke of Piston in Inches [*Railroad term*]
S	Studio [*A publication*]
S	Stung [*by bees*] [*Medicine*]
s/	Su [*Your*] [*Spanish*]
S	Subcompact [*Car size*]
S	Subito [*Immediately; Suddenly*] [*Music*]
S	Subject [*Psychology*]
S	Subject [*of a proposition in logic*]
S	Subluxation [*Chiropractic*]
S	Submarine
s	Submerged Pump [*Liquid gas carriers*]
S	Substantive
S	Substrate, Free [*Enzyme kinetics*]
S	Subtitled
S	Succeeded
S	Successor
S	Sucre [*Monetary unit*] [*Ecuador*]
S	Sud [*South*] [*French*] (ROG)
S	Sugar [*Phonetic alphabet*] [*Royal Navy*] [*World War I*] [*Pre-World War II*] [*World War II*] (DSUE)
S	Suit
S	Suitability (CAAL)
S	Sulfamethoxazole [*Also, SMX, SMZ*] [*Antibacterial compound*]
S	Sulfate
S	Sulfur [*Chemical element*]
S	Sumendus [*To Be Taken*] [*Pharmacy*]
S	Summary
S	Summer [*Vessel load line mark*]
S	Summit Books [*Publisher's imprint*]
S	Sun
S	Sunday
S	Sunny [*Meteorology*] (ADA)
S	Super
S	Superb
S	Superficial
S	Superior
S	Supernatant [*Protein*] [*Cytology*]
S	Superseded [*New regulation or order substituted for an existing one*] [*Used in Shepard's Citations*] [*Legal term*] (DLA)
S	Supply [*Department aboard a carrier*] [*Navy*]
S	Supply [*Economics*]
S	Supreme Court Reporter [*A publication*] (DLA)
S	Sur [*On*] [*French*]
S	Surface Area
S	Surfaced
S	Surgeon [*Navy*] [*British*] (ROG)
S	Surgery [*Medical Officer designation*] [*British*]
S	Surplus
S	Surrogate
S	Survey
S	Survival
S	Susceptible
S	Suus [*His*] [*Latin*]
S	Svedberg Unit [*Physical chemistry*]
S	Sweden [*IYRU nationality code*]
S	Switch
S	Switchboard [*Telecommunications*] (TEL)
s	Symmetrical [*Also, sym*] [*Chemistry*]
s	Symmetry Number [*Symbol*] [*IUPAC*]
S	Symposium [*A publication*]
S	Synchronized Sleep
S	Synchronous
S	Synoptic [*Meteorology*]
S	Synthesis [*Phase in mitosis*] [*Cytology*]
S	System
s	Thio [*or Mercapto*] [*As substituent on nucleoside*] [*Biochemistry*]
S	Thiouridine [*One-letter symbol; see Srd*]
S	Water Surface Craft [*JETDS nomenclature*]
S	Wyeth Laboratories [*Research code symbol*]
S-1	Personnel Section [*in Army brigades or smaller units, and in Marine Corps units smaller than a brigade; also, the officer in charge of this section. Also refers to adjutant - 1st staff section, brigades, and lower units*]
S-2	Intelligence Section [*in Army brigades or smaller units, and in Marine Corps units smaller than a brigade; also, the officer in charge of this section*]

2-S	Selective Service Class [*for Registrant Deferred Because of Activity in Study*]
S-3	Operations and Training Section [*in Army brigades or smaller units, and in Marine Corps units smaller than a brigade; also, the officer in charge of this section*]
S3	Signal Selection Switchboard (CAAL)
3S	Simplification, Standardization, Specialization [*Economics*]
S3	Simulation in the Service of Society
S³	Small Scientific Satellite [*NASA*]
3S	Standard Supply System [*Army*] (RDA)
S3	Synergistic Strike System
S3	Systems and Software Simulator
S-4	Logistics Section [*in Army brigades or smaller units, and in Marine Corps units smaller than a brigade; also, the officer in charge of this section*]
4S	Society for Social Studies of Science (EA)
S4	Stanford School Scheduling System
S4	Supply Officer [*Army*]
S5	Civil Affairs Officer [*Army*] (AABC)
S7	Seller's Delivery in Seven Days [*Stock exchange term*]
S/40	Sex Over Forty [*A publication*]
4S's	Sex, Silk, Swords, and Swash [*Elements of historical romances*]
4S's	Stealth Aircraft, Sea-Launched Cruise Missiles, SDI [*Strategic Defense Initiative*]-Like Devices, Space Systems [*High-tech weaponry*]
4S's	Sun, Sand, Sea, Sex [*Used in advertising by travel agencies*]
S (Day)	Day on which deployment to war stations of submarines is ordered [*NATO exercises*] (NATG)
S (Test)	Suitability Test [*Military*] (CAAL)
SA	Air-Cushion Vehicle built by Societe National Industrielle Aerospatiale [*France*] [*Usually used in combination with numerals*]
sa----	Amazon River and Basin [*MARC geographic area code*] [*Library of Congress*] (LCCP)
S & A	Bureau of Supplies and Accounts [*Later, NSUPSC*] [*Navy*]
SA	Le Syllabaire Accadien [*A publication*] (BJA)
SA	Missionary Sisters of Our Lady of Africa [*White Sisters*] [*Roman Catholic religious order*]
SA	Sable [*Heraldry*]
S/A	Safe Arm
S & A	Safe-and-Arm (KSC)
S/A	Safe Arrival
SA	Safety Analysis [*Nuclear energy*] (NRCH)
S & A	Safety and Arming Device
SA	Safety Assessment
SA	Safing Area [*NASA*] (NASA)
SA	Sail Area
SA	Salicylic Acid [*Organic chemistry*]
SA	Salt Acid
SA	Salt Added
SA	Salvation Army (EA)
Sa	Samarium [*Obsolete form; see Sm*] [*Chemical element*]
SA	Sample Array
SA	Sample Assembly (MCD)
Sa	Samtiden [*A publication*]
SA	Sandstorm
Sa	Sanguinarine [*Biochemistry*]
SA	Sanitary Authority [*British*] (ROG)
SA	Sarcastics Anonymous (EA)
SA	Sarcoma [*Medicine*]
SA	Saturday
SA	Saturn Apollo [*NASA*] (KSC)
SA	Saudi Arabia [*ANSI two-letter standard code*] (CNC)
SA	Saunders Aircraft Corp. Ltd. [*Canada*] [*ICAO aircraft manufacturer identifier*] (ICAO)
S & A	Saunders and Austin's Locus Standi Reports [*1895-1904*] [*A publication*] (DLA)
SA	Sausage Aerial [*Radio*]
SA	Savannah & Atlanta Railway Co. [*AAR code*]
SA	Savings Account
SA	Sawmakers' Association [*A union*] [*British*]
SA	Scaling Amplifier
SA	Scenic America (EA)
S/A	Scheduled/Actual (NASA)
SA	Schizophrenics Anonymous (EA)
S of A	School of Artillery [*British military*] (DMA)
SA	Science Abstracts [*A publication*]
SA	Science Advisors [*Army*] (RDA)
S & A	Science and Application (NASA)
SA	Scientific American [*A publication*]
SA	Scientific Assistant [*Ministry of Agriculture, Fisheries, and Food*] [*British*]
SA	Scleroderma Association (EA)
SA	Scoliosis Association (EA)
SA	Scout Association (EAIO)
SA	Seaman Apprentice [*Navy rating*]
SA	Second Attack [*Men's lacrosse position*]
SA	Secretary of the Army
SA	Secundum Artem [*According to the Art*] [*Latin*]
SA	Security Alarm Technician Program [*Association of Independent Colleges and Schools specialization code*]

SA	Security Assistance (MCD)
SA	See Also [*Indexing code*]
SA	Seiners Association [*Later, PSVOA*]
SA	Select Address
SA	Selected Ammunition (RDA)
SA	Selective Availability
SA	Self-Administered [*Drugs*]
SA	Semen Analysis
SA	Semiannual
SA	Semiautomatic
SA	Senior Advisor [*Military*]
SA	Sense Amplifier
SA	Sensitized Activated
SA	Separat-Abdruck (BJA)
SA	Separated Atom [*Atomic physics*]
SA	Sequential Automated
SA	Serendipity Association (EA)
SA	Serra
SA	Serum Albumin [*Serology*]
SA	Servant Allowance [*British military*] (DMA)
S/A	Service Action (AAG)
SA	Service Adviser [*or Attache*] [*British*]
SA	Service Air [*Nuclear energy*] (NRCH)
S/A	Service Application [*Military*] (AFIT)
SA	Service Arm (KSC)
SA	Service Assistant [*Telecommunications*] (TEL)
SA	Serviced Apartment
SA	Servo Amplifier
SA	Seventh Avenue [*New York City*]
SA	Sex Appeal [*Slang*]
SA	Sexaholics Anonymous (EA)
SA	Sexual Abuse
SA	Shaft Angle [*Technical drawings*]
SA	Shell Analysis
SA	Shift Advance Driver
SA	Ship Abstracts [*Helsinki University of Technology*] [*Bibliographic database*]
SA	Ship to Aircraft (DEN)
S/A	Ship Alteration (MCD)
S/A	Shipped Assembled
SA	Shipping Authority
SA	Shock Attenuation (AAG)
SA	Shop Accessory [*Drawing*] (NG)
SA	Shops Act [*1950*] [*British*] (ILCA)
SA	Shortening Allowance [*Carpentry*]
SA	Sicanna Industries Ltd. [*Vancouver Stock Exchange symbol*]
S & A	Sickness and Accident [*Insurance*]
SA	Sideroblastic Anemia [*Hematology*]
SA	Siegfried AG [*Switzerland*] [*Research code symbol*]
SA	Sierra
SA	Signal Analyzer
SA	Signal Attenuation (AAG)
SA	Signature Analysis
SA	Simple Alert (NATG)
sa	Sin Ano [*Without Year*] [*Publishing*] [*Spanish*]
SA	Sine Anno [*Without Date of Publication*] [*Latin*]
SA	Single Access (MCD)
SA	Single Action [*Firearm*]
SA	Single Armor [*Telecommunications*] (TEL)
SA	Sinoatrial [*Medicine*]
SA	Sinoauricular [*Medicine*]
SA	Sinus Aestuum [*Bay of Billows*] [*Lunar area*]
SA	Sister of Arts
SA	Site Activation [*NASA*] (MCD)
SA	Situation Audit (MCD)
SA	Slow-Acting [*Pharmacy*]
SA	Slugging Average [*Baseball*]
SA	Small Arms [*All firearms other than cannon*]
SA	Smithsonian Associates [*Later, Smithsonian Resident Associate Program*]
SA	Snap Action
SA	Sociedad Anonima [*Stock company*] [*Spanish*]
S/A	Societa Anonima [*Stock company*] [*Italian*]
SA	Societas Adunationis [*Franciscan Friars or Sisters of the Atonement*] [*Roman Catholic religious order*]
SA	Societe Anonyme [*Stock company*] [*French*]
SA	Society of Actuaries
SA	Society of Alexandria [*Defunct*] (EA)
SA	Society of Antiquaries [*British*]
SA	Society of Archivists [*British*]
SA	Society of Arts [*British*]
SA	Sociological Abstracts [*Sociological Abstracts, Inc.*] [*Information service or system*] [*A publication*]
SA	Sociological Analysis [*A publication*]
SA	Software Applications
SA	Soil Association [*Bristol, England*] (EAIO)
SA	Solar Array (KSC)
SA	Sols Africains [*A publication*]
SA	Soluble in Alkaline Solution
SA	Son Altesse [*His or Her Highness*] [*French*]
SA	Sonderabdruck (BJA)
SA	Soprano, Alto
SA	Source Address
sa	South Africa [*MARC country of publication code*] [*Library of Congress*] (LCCP)
SA	South Africa [*IYRU nationality code*]
SA	South African Airways [*ICAO designator*]
SA	South African Law Reports [*A publication*]
SA	South America
SA	South Arabian (BJA)
SA	South Atlantic
SA	South Australia (ADA)
SA	South Australiana [*A publication*] (APTA)
SA	Southbank Aviation [*Australia*]
SA	Southern Association [*Baseball league*]
SA	Sovietskaia Archeologiia [*A publication*]
SA	Space Aeronautics [*A publication*]
S/A	Space Available (ADA)
SA	Spacecraft Adapter [*NASA*]
SA	Speaker Amplifier
SA	Special Access
SA	Special Action [*Military*] (AFM)
S/A	Special Activities [*Air Force*]
SA	Special Agent (AFM)
SA	Special Application [*Lift truck*]
SA	Special Area [*RADAR*]
SA	Special Artificer [*Navy*]
SA	Special Assignment [*Navy*]
SA	Specialty Advertising Business [*A publication*] (EAAP)
SA	Specific Activity
SA	Specific Antigen [*Immunology*]
SA	Spectrograph Assembly (KSC)
SA	Spectrum Analysis
SA	Speech Activities [*A publication*]
SA	Sperm Aster [*Cytology*]
SA	Speronara [*Ship's rigging*] (ROG)
SA	Spin Axis (AAG)
SA	Splice Acceptor [*Genetics*]
SA	Splitting Amplifier (AFM)
SA	Sponsored [*or Sponsoring*] Agency (MCD)
SA	Sports Ambassadors (EA)
SA	Spouse's Allowance [*Canada*]
SA	Springfield Armory [*Army*]
SA	Stage II Apparel [*AMEX symbol*] (SPSG)
SA	Standard Accuracy [*Analytical chemistry*]
SA	Standard Addition
SA	Standard Agena [*NASA*] (KSC)
SA	Staphylococcus Aureus [*Microbiology*]
sA	Statampere [*Also, statA*] [*Unit of electric current*]
SA	State Agency [*Formerly, the Disability Determination Services*] [*Social Security Administration*] (OICC)
S/A	State Agent [*Insurance*]
SA	State's Attorney
SA	Station Address [*Data processing*] (BUR)
SA	Statocyst Anlage
S/A	Status and Alert (AAG)
SA	Statutes of Alberta [*Canada*] [*Information service or system*] (IID)
SA	Stokes-Adams [*Syndrome*] [*Medicine*]
SA	Stone Arch [*Bridges*]
SA	Storage Allocator [*Telecommunications*] (TEL)
S/A	Storage Area (KSC)
SA	Store Address
SA	Store Automation
SA	Stores Accountant [*British military*] (DMA)
SA	Stores Assistant [*British military*] (DMA)
S on A	Stratford-On-Avon, England
SA	Stress Anneal (KSC)
SA	Stretch-Activated Ion Channel
SA	Structured Analysis [*Programming language*] [*1977*] (CSR)
SA	Students for America (EA)
SA	Studi Americani [*Roma*] [*A publication*]
SA	Studies in Astronautics [*Elsevier Book Series*] [*A publication*]
SA	Sturmabteilung [*German*] [*Political party*] (PPE)
SA	Styrene-Acrylonitrile [*Also, SAN*] [*Organic chemistry*]
SA	Sub Anno [*Under the Year*] [*Latin*]
SA	Subaccount (NASA)
SA	Subarachnoid [*Medicine*]
SA	Subassembly
SA	Subcontract Agreement (MCD)
SA	Subject to Approval
SA	Subsequent Access (BYTE)
SA	Subsistence Allowance
SA	Substitution Authorization (AAG)
SA	Successive Approximation (IEEE)
S/A	Such As
S & A	Sugar and Acetone [*Medicine*]
SA	Sugar Association
SA	Sulfonamide
SA	Summing Amplifier
SA	Supervisory Authority

SA .... Superwomen Anonymous [*Later, Overachievers Anonymous*] (EA)
SA .... Supplemental Agreement   (NG)
S & A .... Supplies and Accounts
SA .... Supply Accountant [*Navy*] [*British*]
SA .... Supply Activity
SA .... Support Activity   (MCD)
SA .... Support Agency [*NASA*]   (KSC)
SA .... Support Area [*NASA*]   (MCD)
SA .... Supporting Arms [*Navy*] [*A publication*]
SA .... Surface/Air   (NATG)
SA .... Surface Area
SA .... Surgeon's Assistant [*Medicine*]
SA .... Surgical Anastomosis [*Medicine*]
S & A .... Surveillance and Accountability   (NRCH)
SA .... Surveillance Approach   (FAAC)
S/A .... Survivorship Agreement [*Legal term*]   (DLA)
SA .... Sustained Action [*Pharmacy*]
SA .... Sweep, Acoustic [*British military*]   (DMA)
SA .... Sweet Adelines   (EA)
SA .... Swing Arm   (KSC)
SA .... Switching Devices [*JETDS nomenclature*] [*Military*]   (CET)
SA .... Symbolae Arctoae [*A publication*]
SA/AC .... Symbolic Assembler   (IEEE)
SA .... Sympathetic Activity [*Physiology*]
SA .... Synchro Amplifier
SA .... System Administrator [*Data processing*]
SA .... System Assessment
SA .... Systemic Antibiotic [*Medicine*]
SA .... Systems Address
SA .... Systems Analysis
SA .... Systems Analyst
SA .... VEB Farbenfabrik Wolfen [*East Germany*] [*Research code symbol*]
SAA .... S-Band Acquisition Antenna [*Deep Space Instrumentation Facility, NASA*]
SAA .... Saatchi & Saatchi Co. PLC [*NYSE symbol*]   (SPSG)
SAA .... Safety Assurance Analysis   (NASA)
SAA .... Sakai [*Japan*] [*Seismograph station code, US Geological Survey*] [*Closed*]   (SEIS)
SAA .... Santiago Capital [*Vancouver Stock Exchange symbol*]
SAA .... Saratoga, WY [*Location identifier*] [*FAA*]   (FAAL)
SAA .... Satellite Attitude Acquisition
SAA .... Saturn Apollo Applications [*NASA*]   (KSC)
SAA .... Schweizer Anglistische Arbeiten [*A publication*]
SA-A .... Scientific Adviser - Army [*Australia*]
SAA .... Senior Army Advisor
SAA .... Serum Amyloid A [*Clinical chemistry*]
SAA .... Service Action Analysis   (AAG)
SAA .... Servo-Actuated Assembly
SAA .... Severe Aplastic Anemia [*Hematology*]
SAA .... Sex Addicts Anonymous   (EA)
SAA .... Sexual Abuse Anonymous   (EA)
SAA .... Shakespeare Association of America   (EA)
SAA .... Shelter Advertising Association [*Minneapolis, MN*]   (EA)
SAA .... Signal Appliance Association [*Later, RSS*]
SAA .... Simulated Accelerometer Assembly
SAA .... Single Article Announcement [*American Chemical Society publication*]
SAA .... Slot Array Antenna
SAA .... Small Arms Ammunition
SAA .... Social Administration Association [*British*]
SAA .... Society for Academic Achievement   (EA)
SAA .... Society for American Archaeology   (EA)
SAA .... Society of American Archivists   (EA)
SAA .... Society of Animal Artists   (EA)
SAA .... Society of Archer-Antiquaries   (EA)
SAA .... Society of Architectural Administrators   (EA)
SAA .... Society for Asian Art   (EA)
SAA .... Society of Automotive Analysts   (EA)
SAA .... Some American Artists [*An association*]   (EA)
SAA .... South African Airways
SAA .... South African Alliance   (PPW)
SAA .... South Atlantic Anomaly [*NASA*]   (KSC)
SAA .... South Australian Artillery [*British military*]   (DMA)
SAA .... Southern Africa Association   (EAIO)
SAA .... Southern Ash Association [*Defunct*]   (EA)
SAA .... Special Arbitrage Account
SAA .... Special Assignment Airlift [*Air Force*]   (AFM)
SAA .... Specialty Advertising Association [*Later, SAAI*]
SAA .... Speech Association of America [*Later, SCA*]   (EA)
SAA .... Sri Aurobindo Association   (EA)
SAA .... Staff Administrative Assistant [*Army*]   (AABC)
SAA .... Standards Association of Australia
SAA .... State Approving Agency [*Bureau of Apprenticeship and Training*] [*Department of Labor*]
SAA .... Static Allegation Analyzer [*Data processing*]
SAA .... Step Adjustable Antenna
SAA .... Stepfamily Association of America   (EA)
SAA .... Summary Activity Account [*Army*]   (AABC)
SAA .... Sunflower Association of America [*Later, NSA*]   (EA)

SAA .... Sunglass Association of America   (EA)
SAA .... Supima Association of America   (EA)
SAA .... Surety Association of America [*Iselin, NJ*]   (EA)
SAA .... Surface Active Agents   (ADA)
SAA .... Survival Air-to-Air   (MCD)
SAA .... Suzuki Association of the Americas   (EA)
SAA .... Syrian Arab Airlines
SAA .... System Application Architecture [*IBM Corp.*]
SAAA .... San Antonio De Areco [*Argentina*] [*ICAO location identifier*]   (ICLI)
SAAA........ Scottish Amateur Athletic Association
SAA/AA ... American Antiquity. Society for American Archaeology [*A publication*]
SAAARNG ... Senior Army Advisor, Army National Guard   (AABC)
SAAB........ Saudi Arabian Agricultural Bank
SAAB........ South African Archaeological Bulletin [*A publication*]
SAAB........ Svenska Aeroplan Aktiebolaget [*Swedish automobile manufacturer; acronym used as name of its cars*]
SAABA...... South Australian Amateur Basketball Association
SAABL ..... South Australian Amateur Basketball League
SAAC........ Concordia/Commodoro Pierrest Egui [*Argentina*] [*ICAO location identifier*]   (ICLI)
SAAC........ Schedule Allocation and Control   (NASA)
SA/AC .... Scientific Adviser to the Army Council [*World War II*]
SAAC........ Security Assistance Accounting Center [*Military*]   (AFIT)
SAAC........ Seismic Array Analysis Center [*IBM Corp.*]
SAAC........ Shelby American Automobile Club   (EA)
SAAC........ Simulator for Air-to-Air Combat [*Air Force*]
SAAC........ Society for the Advancement of Ambulatory Care   (EA)
SAAC........ South American Athletic Confederation   (EAIO)
SAAC........ Space Applications Advisory Committee
SAAC........ Special Assistant for Arms Control [*Military*]
SAACI ...... Salesmen's Association of the American Chemical Industry [*Later, SACI*]   (EA)
SAACONS ... Standard Army Automated Contracting System   (RDA)
SAACT ..... Surveillance and Accountability Control Team   (MCD)
SAAD .... Sacramento Army Depot [*California*]   (AABC)
SAAD .... San Antonio Air Depot [*Air Force*]
SAAD .... Small Arms Ammunition Depot
SAAD .... Societe des Amis d'Alexandre Dumas   (EA)
SAAD .... Society for the Advancement of Anaesthesia in Dentistry   (EAIO)
SAAD .... Sperry Air Arm Division
SAAD Dig ... SAAD [*Society for the Advancement of Anaesthesia in Dentistry*] Digest [*A publication*]
SA Advertiser (Newspr) ... South Australian Advertiser Reports (Newspaper) [*A publication*]   (APTA)
SAAEB ...... South African Atomic Energy Board
SAAELC.... South Australian Agricultural Equipment Liaison Committee
SAAF........ Saudi Arabian Air Force
SAAF........ Sherman Army Airfield [*Fort Leavenworth, KS*]
SAAF........ Sino-American Amity Fund   (EA)
SAAF........ Small Arms Alignment Fixture [*Weaponry*]   (INF)
SAAF....... South African Air Force
SAAFA...... Astrometriya i Astrofizika [*A publication*]
SAAFL ...... South Australian Amateur Football League
SAAG .... Gualeguaychu [*Argentina*] [*ICAO location identifier*]   (ICLI)
SAAG .... Science and Applications Advocacy Group
SAA/HO ... Human Organization. Society for Applied Anthropology [*A publication*]
SAAHS...... Stability Augmentation Attitude Hold System [*Aviation*]
SAAI....... Punta Indio [*Argentina*] [*ICAO location identifier*]   (ICLI)
SAAI.......... Specialty Advertising Association International [*Irving, TX*]   (EA)
SAAJ .... Junin [*Argentina*] [*ICAO location identifier*]   (ICLI)
SAAJA ...... Soviet Astronomy [*English Translation*] [*A publication*]
SAAL........ Single Address Assembly Machine Language [*Data processing*]   (MCD)
SAAL........ Single-Axis Acoustic Levitator
Saalb Jb..... Saalburg-Jahrbuch. Bericht des Saalburg-Museums [*A publication*]
SA-ALC..... San Antonio Air Logistics Center [*Formerly, SAAMA*] [*Air Force*]   (NASA)
SAALCK ... State Assisted Academic Library Council of Kentucky [*Library network*]
SAAM .... Mazaruca [*Argentina*] [*ICAO location identifier*]   (ICLI)
SAAM .... Simulation Analysis and Modeling
SAAM .... Small-Animal Anesthesia Machine [*Instrumentation*]
SAAM .... Special Air Force Airlift Mission   (NASA)
SAAM .... Special Assignment Air Mission [*Navy*]   (NVT)
SAAM .... Special Assignment Airlift Movement [*Army*]   (AABC)
SAAMA..... San Antonio Air Materiel Area [*Later, SA-ALC*] [*Air Force*]
SAAMI...... Sporting Arms and Ammunition Manufacturers Institute   (EA)
SAAMS ..... Special Airlift Assignment Missions [*Military*]
SAAMS ..... Special Application Alarm Monitoring System
SAAN .... Pergamino [*Argentina*] [*ICAO location identifier*]   (ICLI)
SAAN .... South African Associated Newspapers
SAANAn .. Societe Archeologique de l'Arrondissement de Nivelles. Annales [*A publication*]
SAAO .... South African Astronomical Observatory

SAAP......... Parana/Gral Urquiza [*Argentina*] [*ICAO location identifier*] (ICLI)
SAAP........ Saranton Army Ammunition Plant (AABC)
SAAP........ Saturn Apollo Applications Program [*NASA*]
SAAP........ Society for the Advancement of American Philosophy (EA)
SAAP........ South Atlantic Anomaly Probe [*NASA-CNAE*]
SAAP........ Supported Accommodation Assistance Program [*Australia*]
SAAPCC ... South African Administrative Pay and Clerical Corps [*British military*] (DMA)
SAA/R....... Relaciones. Sociedad Argentina de Antropologia [*A publication*]
SAAR........ Rosario [*Argentina*] [*ICAO location identifier*] (ICLI)
SAAR........ Saw Arbor [*Tool*]
SAARC.... South Asian Association for Regional Cooperation
SA Arch J .. SA [*South African*] Archives Journal [*A publication*]
SAARF ...... Special Allied Airborne Reconnaissance Force [*Teams parachuted into POW areas to take supplies to prisoners or to help them get out*] [*World War II*]
SAAS........ School of Applied Aerospace Sciences [*Air Force*]
SAAS........ Science Achievement Awards for Students
SAAS........ Shuttle Aerosurface Actuator Simulator [*NASA*] (MCD)
SAAS........ Society for the Advancement of Agricultural Studies [*British*]
SAAS........ Society of African and Afro-American Students
SAAS........ Something about the Author Autobiography Series [*A publication*]
SAAS........ Southern Association of Agricultural Scientists (EA)
SAAS........ Standard Army Ammunition System (AABC)
SAAS Bull Biochem Biotechnol ... SAAS [*Southern Association of Agricultural Scientists*] Bulletin. Biochemistry and Biotechnology [*A publication*]
SAASC ...... San Antonio Air Service Command [*Air Force*]
SAAST ...... Self-Administered Alcoholism Screening Test
SAASW ..... Sub-Antarctic Surface Water [*Marine science*] (MSC)
SAAT........ Satellite Attitude Acquisition Technique
SAAT........ Systems Analyst Aptitude Test
SAATAS.... South Australia & Territory Air Services (FAAC)
Saatgut-Wirt ... Saatgut-Wirtschaft [*A publication*]
Saatgut-Wirtsch ... Saatgut-Wirtschaft [*A publication*]
SAATMS .. Satellite-Based Advanced Air Traffic Management System [*Department of Transportation*]
SAATSC.... San Antonio Air Technical Service Command [*Air Force*]
SAAU .... Selfreliance Association of American Ukrainians (EA)
SAAU .... Swiss Association of Autonomous Unions
SAAU .... Villaguay [*Argentina*] [*ICAO location identifier*] (ICLI)
SAAUSAR ... Senior Army Advisor, United States Army Reserve (AABC)
SAAV......... Santa Fe/Sauce Viejo [*Argentina*] [*ICAO location identifier*] (ICLI)
SAAVS ...... Submarine Acceleration and Velocity System
SAAWA..... Schweizer Archiv fuer Angewandte Wissenschaft und Technik [*A publication*]
SAAWC..... Sector Antiair Warfare Coordinator [*Center*] (NVT)
SAAX......... Saturn Airways, Inc. [*Air carrier designation symbol*]
SAB........... Saba [*Netherlands Antilles*] [*Airport symbol*] (OAG)
SAB........... Sabbath
SAB........... Sabhawala [*India*] [*Geomagnetic observatory code*]
SAB........... Sabine Corp. [*NYSE symbol*] (SPSG)
Sab .... Sabinus [*Flourished, 5th or 6th century*] [*Authority cited in pre-1607 legal work*] (DSA)
SAB........... Sabotage [*FBI standardized term*]
SAB........... Sabouraud Dextrose Agar [*Microbiology*]
SAB........... Same as Above
SAB........... Same as Basic (KSC)
SAB........... Satellite Assembly Building (MCD)
SAB........... School of American Ballet [*New York*]
SAB........... Science Advisory Board [*Environmental Protection Agency*]
SAB........... Scientific Advisory Board [*Air Force*]
SAB........... Sealed Argon Bubbling [*Steelmaking*]
SAB........... Shakespeare Association. Bulletin [*A publication*]
SAB........ Shuttle Avionics Breadboard [*NASA*] (NASA)
SAB........... Signal Aviation Branch
SAB........... Silk Association of Great Britain (EAIO)
SAARB........ Site Activation Board [*NASA*] (KSC)
SAB........... Sitzungsberichte. Deutsche (Preussische) Akademie der Wissenschaften zu Berlin. Philosophisch-Historische Klasse [*Berlin*] [*A publication*]
SAB........... Snap Action Bimetal [*Automotive engineering*]
SAB........... Societe Anonyme Belge d'Exploitation de la Navigation Aerienne [*Sabena Belgian World Airlines*]
SAB........... Society of American Bacteriologists [*Later, ASM*]
SAB........... Society for Applied Bacteriology (EA)
SAB........... Solar Array Batteries
SAB........... Solid Assembly Building
SAB........... Soprano, Alto, Bass
SAB........... South Atlantic Bulletin [*A publication*]
SAB........... Space Applications Board [*National Academy of Engineering*]
SAB........... Spacecraft Assembly Building [*NASA*] (MCD)
SAB........... Special Assessment Bond
SAB........... Stack Access Block
SAB........... Statistics and Analysis Branch [*Public Health Service*] [*Information service or system*] (IID)
SAB........... Storage and Assembly Building [*NASA*] (NASA)

SAB........... Structural Adhesive Bond
SAB........... Subject as Above [*Military*] (AABC)
SAB........... Support Activities Building [*National Security Agency*]
SAB........... Supporting Assistance Bureau [*Agency for International Development*]
SAB........... System Advisory Board
SABA........ Buenos Aires [*Argentina*] [*ICAO location identifier*] (ICLI)
SABA........ Serbian-American Bar Association (EA)
SABA........ Small, Able Battlefield Aircraft [*Military*] [*British*]
SABA........ Small Agile Battlefield Aircraft [*British Aerospace PLC*]
SABA........ Societe Archeologique de Bruxelles. Annales [*A publication*]
SABA........ Society for the Advancement of Behavior Analysis (EA)
SABA........ South African Black Alliance [*Political party*] (PPW)
SABA........ Swimmer's Air Breathing Apparatus [*Deep-sea diving*]
Sabah For Rec ... Sabah Forest Record [*A publication*]
Sabah Soc J ... Sabah Society. Journal [*A publication*]
SA Bank Officials J ... South Australian Bank Officials' Journal [*A publication*] (APTA)
SABAR...... Satellites, Balloons, and Rockets [*Air Force program*]
SABC......... Buenos Aires (Edificio Condor) [*Argentina*] [*ICAO location identifier*] (ICLI)
SABC......... South African Broadcasting Corporation
Sabchota Med ... Sabchota Meditsina [*A publication*]
SABCO....... Society for the Area of Biological and Chemical Overlap
SABE....... Buenos Aires/Aeroparque, Jorge Newbery [*Argentina*] [*ICAO location identifier*] (ICLI)
SABE......... Society for Automation in Business Education [*Later, SDE*] (EA)
SABENA ... Societe Anonyme Belge d'Exploitation de la Navigation Aerienne [*Belgian World Airlines*] [*Facetious translation: Such a Bad Experience, Never Again*]
SABER ...... SECNAV [*Secretary of the Navy*] Advisory Board on Educational Requirements (NG)
SABET ...... SECNAV [*Secretary of the Navy*] Advisory Board on Education and Training [*Pensacola, FL*] (EGAO)
SABEW ..... Society of American Business Editors and Writers [*Columbia, MO*] (EA)
SABH .... Simultaneous Automatic Broadcast Homer (FAAC)
SABHI....... Sabouraud Dextrose Agar and Brain-Heart Infusion [*Microbiology*]
SaBi .... La Sacra Bibbia [*Turin*] [*A publication*] (BJA)
SABIC .... Saudi Basic Industries Corporation
SABIR .... Semiautomatic Bibliographic Information Retrieval
SABIRS..... Semiautomatic Bibliographic Information Retrieval System (DIT)
SABLE ...... Semiautomatic BOMARC Local Environment (MCD)
SABM....... Buenos Aires (Servicio Meteorologico Nacional) [*Argentina*] [*ICAO location identifier*] (ICLI)
SABM....... Set Asynchronous Balanced Mode
SA/BM ...... Systems Analysis and Battle Management [*Military*] (RDA)
SABMAR.. Service-Craft and Boats Machine Accounting Report [*Navy*] (NG)
SABMIS... Seaborne [*or Ship-Launched*] Antiballistic Missile Intercept System [*Navy*]
SABNWTR ... Science Advisory Board of the Northwest Territories. Report [*Canada*] [*A publication*]
SABNWTRP ... Science Advisory Board of the Northwest Territories. Research Paper [*Canada*] [*A publication*]
SABNWTWP ... Science Advisory Board of the Northwest Territories. Working Paper [*A publication*]
SABO .... Sense Amplifier Blocking Oscillator
SABOA...... Sabouraudia [*A publication*]
SABOD ...... Same as Basic Operations Directive (KSC)
SABOJ ...... South Australian Bank Officials' Journal [*A publication*] (APTA)
SABOR..... Same as Basic Or (MUGU)
SABP .... Skeletal Axis of Basal Piece
SABP .... Spontaneous Acute Bacterial Peritonitis [*Medicine*]
SABR........ Society for American Baseball Research (EA)
SABR........ Symbolic Assembler for Binary Relocatable Programs
Sabrao Newslett ... Sabrao Newsletter [*A publication*]
SABRB ...... Siemens-Albis Berichte [*A publication*]
SABRE ...... SAGE [*Semiautomatic Ground Environment*] Battery Routing Equipment
SABRE ...... Sales and Business Reservations Done Electronically
SABRE ...... Secure Airborne RADAR Equipment
SABRE ...... Self-Aligning Boost and Reentry [*Air Force*]
SABRE ...... Semiautomated Business Research Environment [*Computerized reservation network*] [*American Airlines*]
SABRE ...... Store Access Bus Recording Equipment [*Telecommunications*] (TEL)
SABRE ...... Sweden and Britain RADAR Auroral Experiment [*Ionospheric physics*]
SABRE ...... System for Autonomous Bodies Reporting and Evaluation [*Joint project of the Government of Bangladesh and United Nations Department of Technical Co-operation for Development*] [*Information service or system*]
SABRF ...... Skeletal Axis of Branchial Filament
SABRI .... Serikat Buruh Rokok Indonesia [*Cigarette Workers' Union of Indonesia*]

SABS	Congregation of the Sisters of the Adoration of the Blessed Sacrament [*Kerala, India*] (EAIO)
S/ABS	Shock Absorber [*Automotive engineering*]
SABS	South African Bureau of Standards [*National standards organization*]
SABS	Stabilizing Automatic Bomb Sight
SABS Bull ...	SABS [*South African Bureau of Standards*] Bulletin [*A publication*]
SABU	Self-Adjusting Ball-Up [*A state of confusion which may, or may not, clear up of itself*] [*Military slang*]
SABW	Society of American Business Writers [*Later, SABEW*]
Sac	De Sacrificiis Abelis et Caini [*Philo*] (BJA)
SAC	Saccharin [*Sweetening agent*]
SAC	Sacramento, CA [*Location identifier*] [*FAA*] (FAAL)
SAC	Sacrifice [*Baseball*]
Sac	Sacris Erudiri. Jaarboek voor Godsdienstwetenschappen [*A publication*]
SAC	Sacristan
SAC	Safety Advisory Committee (MCD)
SAC	Sahali Resources, Inc. [*Vancouver Stock Exchange symbol*]
SAC	Saint Ambrose College [*Davenport, IA*]
SAC	Saint Anselm's College [*Manchester, NH*]
SAC	Saint Anselm's College, Manchester, NH [*OCLC symbol*] (OCLC)
SAC	Saint Augustine's College [*Raleigh, NC*]
SAC	Salute America Committee (EA)
SAC	San Andreas Lake [*California*] [*Seismograph station code, US Geological Survey*] (SEIS)
SAC	San Antonio College [*Texas*]
SAC	Santa Ana College [*California*]
SAC	Scene-of-Action Commander [*Navy*] (NVT)
SAC	School of Army Co-Operation [*Air Force*] [*British*]
SAC	Scientific Advisory Committee [*Presidential*] [*Terminated*]
SAC	Scientific Advisory Council [*Ministry of Supply*] [*British*] [*World War II*]
SAC	Scottish Arts Council (EAIO)
SAC	Secondary Accountability Center (AAG)
SAC	Secondary Address Code
SAC	Sectional Aeronautical Chart (NOAA)
SAC	Security Access Control [*Data processing*]
SAC	Self-Adjusting Clutch
SAC	Semiautomatic Coding
SAC	Semiautomatic Controller (CAAL)
SAC	Senate Appropriations Committee (NVT)
SAC	Senior Aircraftman [*British military*] (DMA)
SAC	Service Application Code [*Navy*]
SAC	Serving Area Concept [*Bell System*]
SAC	Servo Adapter Coupler
SAC	Shipbuilding Advisory Council [*British*]
SAC	Ships Air Coordinator (MCD)
SAC	Side-Arm Controller [*Aviation*]
SAC	Signature Authorization Card [*or Chart*] (AAG)
SAC	Single Acting Cylinder
SAC	Single Address Code (AAG)
SAC	Sisters of the Holy Guardian Angels [*Roman Catholic religious order*]
SAC	Soaring Association of Canada
SAC	Social and Athletic Club
SAC	Sociedad Anglo-Chilena [*Anglo-Chilean Society*] (EAIO)
SAC	Societe Africaine de Culture [*Society of African Culture*]
SAC	Society for American Cuisine [*Later, SCA*] (EA)
SAC	Society for Analytical Chemistry [*British*]
SAC	Society for Analytical Cytology (EA)
SAC	Society of the Catholic Apostolate [*Pallottines*] [*Roman Catholic men's religious order*]
SAC	South-African Constabulary [*Military*] [*British*] [*Defunct*] (ROG)
SAC	South Atlantic Coast
SAC	South Carolina Electric & Gas Co. [*NYSE symbol*] (SPSG)
SAC	Southern Africa Committee (EA)
SAC	Southwest Athletic Conference (EA)
SAC	Special Agent in Charge [*FBI*]
SAC	Special Area Code [*Bell System*]
SAC	Specific Acoustic Capacitance
SAC	Spectrum Analyzer Component (MCD)
SAC	Spiritual Advisory Council (EA)
SAC	Sport for All Clearing House (EAIO)
SAC	Sprayed Acoustical Ceiling [*Technical drawings*]
S/AC	Stabilization/Attitude Control [*NASA*] (NASA)
SAC	Standard Agena Clamshell [*NASA*] (KSC)
SAC	Standard Aircraft Characteristics
SAC	Standing Armaments Committee [*NATO*] (NATG)
SAC	Staphylococcus Aureus Cervan [*Microbiology*]
SAC	Starting Air Compressor (CAAL)
SAC	State Advisory Committee [*Department of Education*]
SAC	State Apprenticeship Council [*Bureau of Apprenticeship and Training*] [*Department of Labor*]
SAC	Statistical Advisory Committee [*UN Food and Agriculture Organization*]
SAC	Statistical Analysis Center (OICC)
SAC	Storage Access Channel (CMD)
SAC	Storage Access Control [*Data processing*]
SAC	Store and Clear
SAC	Store and Clear Accumulator [*Data processing*]
SAC	Strategic Air Command [*Air Force*]
SAC	Strategic Alert Cadre (NVT)
SAC	Structural Adjustment Committee [*Commonwealth Cabinet*] [*Australia*]
SAC	Studies in the Age of Chaucer [*A publication*]
SAC	Studies in Ancient Civilization [*Elsevier Book Series*] [*A publication*]
SAC	Subarea Advisory Council [*Generic term*] (DHSM)
SAC	Submitting Activity Code
SAC	Sudanese African Congress [*Political party*] (MENA)
SAC	Sugar Association of the Caribbean [*Port Of Spain, Trinidad*] (EAIO)
SAC	Sulfuric Acid Concentrate (MCD)
SAC	Sunbeam Alpine Club (EA)
SAC	Suore Missionarie dell'Apostolato Cattolico [*Missionary Sisters of the Catholic Apostolate*] [*Rome, Italy*] (EAIO)
SAC	Supplemental Air Carrier (MCD)
SAC	Supply Administration Center [*DoD*] (MCD)
SAC	Supply Availability Card (MCD)
SAC	Support Action Center [*NASA*] (MCD)
SAC	Supporting Arms Coordinator [*Air Force*] (NVT)
SAC	Supreme Allied Command [*or Commander*] [*Headquarters in London*] [*World War II*]
SAC	Surveyors Appointments Consultancy [*Royal Institute of Chartered Surveyors*] [*British*]
SAC	Sussex Archaeological Collections [*A publication*]
SAC	Sustained Abdominal Compression [*Gastroenterology*]
SAC	Sveriges Arbetares Centralorganisation [*Central Organization of Swedish Workers*]
SAC	Sydney Airport Centre [*Australia*]
SAC	Synchro Azimuth Converter
SAC	System Automation Corporation [*Information service or system*] (IID)
SAC	Systems Acquisition Career
SAC	Systems Auditability and Control [*Data processing*]
SACA	Cordoba/Area de Material [*Argentina*] [*ICAO location identifier*] (ICLI)
SACA	Service Action Change Analysis (AAG)
SACA	Special Assistant for Consumer Affairs [*White House*] [*Obsolete*]
SACA	Steam Automobile Club of America (EA)
SACA	Studebaker Automobile Club of America (EA)
SACA	Student Action Corps for Animals (EA)
SACA	Study Advisory Committee on Aeronautics [*National Academy of Engineering*]
SACA	Subversive Activities Control Act of 1950
SACACCS ...	Strategic Air Command Automated Command Control System (AFM)
SACAM	Ship Acquisition Contract Administration Manual (MCD)
SACAY	SECNAV [*Secretary of the Navy*] Advisory Commission on Youth (NG)
SACB	Subversive Activities Control Board [*Later, Federal Internal Security Board*]
SACBC	Southern African Catholic Bishops' Conference (EAIO)
SACBC-JPC ...	Southern African Catholic Bishops' Conference - Justice and Peace Commission (EAIO)
SACBS	South Australian Cell Biology Society
SACC	La Cumbre [*Argentina*] [*ICAO location identifier*] (ICLI)
S/ACC	Scientific/Academic Computing Center [*State University of New York Health Science Center at Brooklyn*] [*Research center*] (RCD)
SACC	Slovak-American Cultural Center (EA)
SACC	Society for Anthropology in Community Colleges (EA)
SACC	State Auditors Coordinating Committee (EA)
SACC	Supplemental Air Carrier Conference [*Defunct*] (EA)
SACC	Supporting Arms Coordination Center [*Air Force*]
SACCD	Saccharum [*A publication*]
SACCEI	Strategic Air Command Communications-Electronics Instruction
SACCH	Saccharatae [*Sugar-Coated*] [*Pharmacy*]
SACCHS ...	Scottish Advisory Committee on Computers in the Health Service
SACCOM ...	Strategic Air Command Communications (MCD)
SACCOMNET ...	Strategic Air Command Communications Network
SACCON...	Strategic Air Command Command Control Network
SACCP	Strategic Air Command Command Post
SACCS	Strategic Air Command Communications [*or Control*] System [*Military*]
SACD	Coronel Olmedo [*Argentina*] [*ICAO location identifier*] (ICLI)
Sac D	Sacra Doctrina. Quaderni Periodici di Teologia e di Filosofia [*A publication*]
SACD	Societe des Auteurs et Compositeurs Dramatiques [*Society of Dramatic Authors and Composers*] [*Paris, France*] (EAIO)
SACD	Society of Americans of Colonial Descent (EA)
SACD	South African Container Depot (DS)
SACDA	Surplus Agricultural Commodities Disposal Act of 1982
SACDEF....	Strategic Avionics Crewstation Design Evaluation Facility

SACDIN.... Strategic Air Command Digital Information Network (MCD)
SACDM.... Study and Action Course in District Management [*LIMRA*]
SACDNU .. Sudan African Closed Districts National Union
SAC(DP) ... Scientific Advisory Committee, Defence Services Panel [*British*] [*World War II*]
SACDRS .. Standard Air Carrier Delay Reporting System
SACE......... Cordoba [*Argentina*] [*ICAO location identifier*] (ICLI)
SacE........... Sacris Erudiri. Jaarboek voor Godsdienstwetenschappen [*A publication*]
SACE......... Semiautomatic Checkout Equipment [*DoD*]
SACE......... Serum Angiotensin Converting Enzyme [*Activity*] [*Serology*]
SACE......... Sezione Special per l'Assicurazione del Credito all'Exportazione [*Export credit agency*] [*Italian*]
SACE......... Shore-Based Acceptance Checkout Equipment
SACE......... Social and Cultural Education [*Northern Territory, Australia*]
SACE......... South Australian College of English
SACEA ...... Sino-American Cultural and Economic Association
SACED...... South African Journal of Continuing Medical Education [*A publication*]
SACEM..... Society for the Advancement of Continuing Education for Ministry (EA)
SA Census & Statistics Bul ... Australia. Commonwealth Bureau of Census and Statistics. South Australian Office. Bulletin [*A publication*] (APTA)
SA Cereb Palsy J ... SA [*South African*] Cerebral Palsy Journal [*A publication*]
SACEUR ... Supreme Allied Commander, Europe [*NATO*]
SACEUREP ... Supreme Allied Commander, Europe Representative [*NATO*] (NATG)
SACF......... Cordoba [*Argentina*] [*ICAO location identifier*] (ICLI)
SACFI....... Scholars and Citizens for Freedom of Information (EA)
SACG........ Cordoba [*Argentina*] [*ICAO location identifier*] (ICLI)
SACH........ Solid Ankle Cushion Heel [*Foot prosthesis*]
SACh .... Studies in Analytical Chemistry [*Elsevier Book Series*] [*A publication*]
SACHC...... Soviet-American Committee on Health Cooperation
SACHQ ..... Strategic Air Command Headquarters (AAG)
Sachs Akad d Wiss Philol-Hist Kl Ber u d Verhandl ... Saechsische Akademie der Wissenschaften. Philologisch-Historische Klasse. Berichte ueber die Verhandlungen [*A publication*]
Sachse NM ... Sachse's Minutes, Norwich Mayoralty Court [*A publication*] (DLA)
SACI......... Pilar [*Argentina*] [*ICAO location identifier*] (ICLI)
SACI......... Sales Association of the Chemical Industry (EA)
SACI......... Secondary Address Code Indicator
SACI......... South Atlantic Cooperative Investigations [*Military*]
SACL........ Laguna Larga [*Argentina*] [*ICAO location identifier*] (ICLI)
SACL........ South African Confederation of Labour
SACL........ Space and Component Log
SACL........ Standards and Calibration Laboratory (KSC)
SACLA ...... Srpski Arhiv za Celokupno Lekarstvo [*A publication*]
SACLAMP ... Strategic Air Command Low-Altitude Missile Program [*Air Force*]
SACLANT ... Supreme Allied Commander, Atlantic [*NATO*]
SACLANTCEN ... Supreme Allied Commander, Atlantic, Antisubmarine Warfare Research Center [*NATO*] (AABC)
SACLANTREPEUR ... Supreme Allied Commander, Atlantic, Representative in Europe [*NATO*] (AABC)
SACLAU ... SACLANT [*Supreme Allied Commander, Atlantic*] Authentification System [*NATO*] (NATG)
SACLEX.... SACLANT [*Supreme Allied Commander, Atlantic*] Standing Exercise Orders [*NATO*] (NATG)
Sac Lit D.... Doctor of Sacred Literature
SACLO...... Strategic Air Command Liaison Officer
SACLOS.... Semiautomatic Command to Line of Sight [*Military*]
Sac M........ Sacred Music [*A publication*]
SACM........ School of Acquisition Management [*Army*]
SACM........ Simulated Aerial Combat Maneuver
SACM........ Statistical Adiabatic Channel Model [*Physical chemistry*]
SACM........ Villa Gral, Mitre [*Argentina*] [*ICAO location identifier*] (ICLI)
SACMA..... Suppliers of Advanced Composite Materials Association [*Arlington, VA*] (EA)
SACMAP .. Selective Automatic Computational Matching and Positioning (MCD)
SACMAPS ... Selective Automatic Computational Matching and Positioning System
SACMDR ... Site Activation Commander [*Army*] (AABC)
SACMED ... Supreme Allied Commander, Mediterranean [*World War II*]
SAC/MEP ... Strategic Air Command/Minuteman Education Program (AFM)
SACMP..... South African Corps of Military Police [*British military*] (DMA)
SACMPC .. Systems Acquisition Career Management Personnel Center [*DoD*]
SACN .... Ascochinga [*Argentina*] [*ICAO location identifier*] (ICLI)
SACNA...... South Africa Club of North America [*Defunct*] (EA)
SACNAS.... Society for Advancement of Chicanos and Native Americans in Science (EA)
SACNET ... Secure Automatic Communications Network
SACO .... Cordoba [*Argentina*] [*ICAO location identifier*] (ICLI)
SACO .... Select Address and Contract Operate

SACO .... Service Administratif Canadien Outre-Mer [*Canadian Executive Service Overseas - CESO*]
SACO .... Sino American Cooperative Organization (EA)
SACO .... Supporting Administrative Contracting Officer (AFIT)
SACO .... Sveriges Akademikers Centralorganisation [*Swedish Confederation of Professional Associations*]
SACOA ...... Southern Appalachian Coal Operators Association (EA)
SAC-OA .... Strategic Air Command Office of Operations Analysis
SACOD ..... South African Congress of Democrats
SACOM .... SECNAV [*Secretary of the Navy*] Advisory Commission on Manpower (NG)
SACOM .... Southern Area Command [*Military*] (AABC)
SACON ..... Shock-Absorbing Concretes (RDA)
SACON ..... Shock Attenuating Cellular Concrete [*Army*]
SACON ..... Structural Analysis Consultant (MCD)
SACOPD.. Smoking-Attributable Chronic Obstructive Pulmonary Disease
SACOPS.... Strategic Air Command Operational Planning System (MCD)
SACP........ Chepes [*Argentina*] [*ICAO location identifier*] (ICLI)
SACP........ Society for Asian and Comparative Philosophy (EA)
SACP........ South African Communist Party
SACP........ Strategic Air Command Project Office (AAG)
SACPAN .. Stemming and Closure Panel [*Terminated, 1975*] [*DoD*] (EGAO)
SACPB ...... South African Chemical Processing [*A publication*]
SACPG...... Senior Arms Control Planning Group [*Pronounced "sack pig"*] [*DoD*]
SACPO...... Saigon Area Civilian Personnel Office [*Vietnam*]
SACPO...... South African Colored People's Organization
SACPPL.... Standing Advisory Committee on Private Pilot Licensing [*British*] (AIA)
SACQ .... Monte Quemado [*Argentina*] [*ICAO location identifier*] (ICLI)
SACR........ Sacrament (ROG)
SACR........ Sacred (ROG)
SACR........ Sacrifice (ROG)
SACR........ Sacrist
SACR........ Strategic Air Command Regulations (AAG)
SACRA ...... Student Alliance for Christian Renewal in America
Sacramnt B ... Sacramento Bee [*A publication*]
Sacred Mus ... Sacred Music [*A publication*]
SACROC... Scurry Area Canyon Reef Operators Committee
SACS .... Satellite Attitude-Control Simulator [*NASA*]
SACS .... Selective High-Frequency Antenna Coupler System [*Military*] (CAAL)
SACS .... Sensor Accuracy Check Site (MCD)
SACS .... Services After-Care Scheme [*British*]
SACS .... Ship Alteration Completion System
SACS .... Shipyard Accuracy Checksite (MCD)
SACS .... Sino-American Cultural Society (EA)
SACS .... Software Avionics Command Support (NASA)
SACS .... Solar Altitude Control System
SACS .... SONAR Accuracy Check Site (NVT)
SACS .... Southern Association of Colleges and Schools (EA)
SACS .... Structure and Composition System [*Military*] (AABC)
SACS .... Synchronous Altitude Communications Satellite
SACS .... Systems Software Avionics Command Support (MCD)
SACS .... Villa De Soto [*Argentina*] [*ICAO location identifier*] (ICLI)
SACSA ...... Special Assistant for Counterinsurgency and Special Activities [*Military*] (AFM)
SACSA ...... Standing Advisory Committee for Scientific Advice [*Oslo Commission*] (DCTA)
SACSEA .... Supreme Allied Command [*or Commander*], Southeast Asia
SACSIR .... South African Council for Scientific and Industrial Research
SACSOS.... South Australian Coloured Sheep Owners Society
SAC/SSW ... Special Assistant to the Chief of Staff for Special Warfare [*Army*]
SACT......... Gobernador Gordillo [*Argentina*] [*ICAO location identifier*] (ICLI)
SACT........ Sinoatrial Conduction Time [*Cardiology*]
SACTO....... Sacramento Test Operations (MCD)
SACTTYNET ... Strategic Air Command Teletype Network
SACTU...... South African Congress of Trade Unions
SACTW...... South African Council of Transport Workers
SACU .... Cordoba [*Argentina*] [*ICAO location identifier*] (ICLI)
SACU .... Society for Anglo-Chinese Understanding [*London, England*] (EAIO)
SACU .... South African Customs Union
SACUS...... Southern Association on Children under Six (EA)
SACV........ Villa Maria Del Rio Seco [*Argentina*] [*ICAO location identifier*] (ICLI)
SACVAR ... Ship Alteration Cost Variance Account Report
SACW....... Senior Aircraftwoman [*British military*] (DMA)
SACW....... South Australian Creative Workshops
SAD .... Saddle (AAG)
SAD .... Saddleback Community College District, Mission Viejo Campus, Mission Viejo, CA [*OCLC symbol*] (OCLC)
Sad .... Sadler's Pennsylvania Cases [*A publication*] (DLA)
SAD .... Safety Analysis [*or Assurance*] Diagram [*Nuclear energy*] (NRCH)
SAD .... Safety, Arming, and Destruct (MCD)
SAD .... Safety and Arming Device [*Military*] (AABC)
SAD .... Safford, AZ [*Location identifier*] [*FAA*] (FAAL)

sad	Sandawe [*MARC language code*] [*Library of Congress*] (LCCP)
S & AD	Science and Applications Directorate [*NASA*]
SAD	Search and Destroy (MCD)
SAD	Seasonal Affective Disorder [*Type of depression caused by long nights, short days*]
SAD	Selected Area [*Electron*] Diffraction [*Also, SAED*] [*Analysis of solids*]
SAD	Semiconductor Anticoincidence Detector
SAD	Sentence Appraiser and Diagrammer
SAD	Service Action Drawing (AAG)
SAD	Ship Acoustics Department [*David W. Taylor Naval Ship Research and Development Center*]
SAD	Shuttle Authorized Document [*NASA*] (NASA)
SAD	Silverado Mines Ltd. [*Vancouver Stock Exchange symbol*]
SAD	Simple, Average, or Difficult (AAG)
SAD	Single Administrative Document [*European trade contract*] [*1986*] (DCTA)
SAD	Sinoaortic Deafferentation [*Medicine*]
SAD	Sinoaortic Denervation [*Physiology*]
SAD	Situation Attention Display
S-A-D	Sleep Disturbance with Anxiety and Depression [*Combat behavior disorder*] [*Military*] (INF)
SAD	Social Avoidance Distress [*Scale*]
SAD	Society of the Ark and the Dove (EA)
SAD	South American Datum
SAD	South Atlantic Division [*Army Corps of Engineers*]
SAD	Soviet Air Defense
SAD	Soviet Air Demonstration
SAD	Space Antennae Diversity [*Telecommunications*] (TEL)
SAD	Spacecraft Attitude Display (MCD)
SAD	Special Artificer, Special Synthetic Training Devices [*Navy*]
SAD	Station Address Directory [*Army*]
SAD	Store Address Director
SAD	Submarine Anomaly Detection [*Navy*] (NVT)
SAD	Sugar, Acetone, Diacetic Acid [*Test*] [*Medicine*]
SAD	Supervisory Aptitude Development [*In George Lee Walker novel "The Chronicles of Doodah"*]
SAD	Support Air Direction [*Navy*]
SAD	Surface Area Decay [*Plant pathology*]
SAD	Survival Assistance Director [*Federal disaster planning*]
SAD	Sympathetic Aerial Detonation [*Air Force*]
SAD	System Allocation Document [*NASA*] (NASA)
SAD	System Analysis Drawing
SAD	Systems Analysis Document (MCD)
SADA	Seismic Array Data Analyzer (IEEE)
SADA	Southern Appalachian Dulcimer Association (EA)
SADAP	Simplified Automatic Data Plotter
SADAP	State Alcoholism and Drug Abuse Profile [*Public Health Service*] [*Information service or system*] (IID)
SADAR	Satellite Data Reduction [*Processor system*]
SADARM	Selected Armor Defeating Artillery Munition
SADARM	Sense [*or Search*] and Destroy Armor Munition
SAD Beng	Select Cases, Sadr Diwani [*Bengal*] [*A publication*] (DLA)
SAD Bom	Sadr Diwani Adalat Reports [*Bombay, India*] [*A publication*] (DLA)
SADBU	Small and Disadvantaged Business Utilization [*Department of Commerce*]
SADC	Sector Aid Defense Commander (NATG)
SADC	Sequential Analog-Digital Computer (DIT)
SADC	Sneak Attack Defense Coordinator [*Military*] (CAAL)
SADCA	South African Defence Campaign of Australia
SADCC	South African Development Coordination Conference
SADD	Buenos Aires/Don Torcuato [*Argentina*] [*ICAO location identifier*] (ICLI)
SADD	Semiautomatic Detection Device
SADD	Students Against Driving Drunk (EA)
SaDDC	Durban City Council, Durban, South Africa [*Library symbol*] [*Library of Congress*] (LCLS)
SADE	Specialized Armoured Development Establishment [*British military*] (DMA)
SADE	Superheat Advanced Demonstration Experiment [*Nuclear energy*]
SADE	Symbolic Application Debugging Environment
SADEC	Spin Axis Declination [*Aerospace*] (MCD)
SADELCA	Sociedad Aerea del Caqueta [*Airline*] [*Colombia*]
SA Dep Agric Tech Bull	South Australia. Department of Agriculture. Technical Bulletin [*A publication*] (APTA)
SADEYA	Sociedad Astronomica de Espana y America [*Hispano-American Astronomical Society*] (EAIO)
SADF	San Fernando [*Argentina*] [*ICAO location identifier*] (ICLI)
SADF	South African Defence Forces
SADG	Monte Grande [*Argentina*] [*ICAO location identifier*] (ICLI)
SADH	Succinic Acid - Dimethylhydrazide [*Plant growth retardant*]
SADI	Secretarial Automated Data Index
SADIC	Solid-State Analog-to-Digital Computer
SADID4	Annual Research Reviews. Sphingolipidoses and Allied Disorders [*A publication*]
SADIE	Scanning Analog-to-Digital Input Equipment [*National Institute of Standards and Technology*]
SADIE	Secure Automatic Data Information Exchange [*System*]

SADIE	Semiautomatic Decentralized Intercept Environment [*Air Force*]
SADIE	Sterling and Decimal Invoicing Electronically (IEEE)
SADIS	Shipboard Automated Decoy Integration System [*Navy*]
Sadivn Resp Mizhvid Nauk-Temat Zb	Sadivnytstvo Respublikanskyi Mizhvidomchyi Naukovo-Tematychnyi Zbirnik [*A publication*]
SADJ	Jose C. Paz/Dr. Mariano More [*Argentina*] [*ICAO location identifier*] (ICLI)
SADL	La Plata [*Argentina*] [*ICAO location identifier*] (ICLI)
SADL	Sadlier [*William H.*], Inc. [*NASDAQ symbol*] (NQ)
SADL	Ships Authorized Data List
SADL	Spares Application Data List
SADL	Special Automated Distribution List (AFIT)
SADL	Sterilization Assembly Development Laboratory [*NASA*]
SADL	Synchronous Automatic Dial Language
Sadler	Sadler's Pennsylvania Cases [*A publication*] (DLA)
Sadler (PA)	Sadler's Pennsylvania Cases [*A publication*] (DLA)
SADM	Moron [*Argentina*] [*ICAO location identifier*] (ICLI)
SADM	Secretary of the Army Decision Memorandum [*Army*] (RDA)
SADM	Solar Array Drive Motor
SADM	Special Atomic Demolition Munitions [*Military*] (AABC)
SADM	System Acquisition Decision Memorandum (MCD)
SADMG	Special Artificer, Special Devices, Machine Gun Trainer [*Navy*]
SADNWF	Sadr Diwani Adalat Cases, Northwest Frontier [*Pakistan*] [*A publication*] (DLA)
SaDo	Sacra Doctrina [*A publication*]
SADOAJ	Sadovodstvo [*Moscow*] [*A publication*]
Sado Mar Biol Stn Niigata Univ Spec Publ	Sado Marine Biological Station. Niigata University. Special Publication [*A publication*]
Sadovod	Sadovodstvo [*A publication*]
Sadovod Vinograd Vinodel Mold	Sadovodstvo Vinogradarstvo i Vinodelia Moldavii [*A publication*]
SADP	El Palomar [*Argentina*] [*ICAO location identifier*] (ICLI)
SADP	Scales of Attitudes toward Disabled Persons [*Occupational therapy*]
SADP	Scandinavian Association of Directory Publishers (EAIO)
SADP	Selected Area Electron Diffraction Pattern [*Analysis of solids*]
SADP	Small Area Direct Path [*Military*] (CAAL)
SADP	Structured Analysis, Design, and Programming [*Data processing*]
SADP	Synthetic Array Data Processor
SADP	System Architecture Design Package
Sad PA Cas	Sadler's Pennsylvania Cases [*1885-88*] [*A publication*] (DLA)
Sad PA Cs	Sadler's Pennsylvania Cases [*1885-88*] [*A publication*] (DLA)
SADPO	Systems Analysis and Data Processing Office
SADQ	Quilmes [*Argentina*] [*ICAO location identifier*] (ICLI)
SADQ	Severity of Alcohol Dependence Questionnaire
SADR	Merlo [*Argentina*] [*ICAO location identifier*] (ICLI)
SADR	Saharan Arab Democratic Republic [*Morocco*] (PD)
SADR	Secure Acoustic Data Relay (NVT)
SADR	Severity Adjusted Death Rate [*Medicine*] (DHSM)
SADR	Six Hundred Megacycle Air Defense RADAR
SADRAM	Seek and Destroy RADAR-Assisted Mission (MCD)
SADRI	Social and Demographic Research Institute [*University of Massachusetts*] [*Research center*] (RCD)
SADRT	Secure Acoustic Data Relay Terminal (MCD)
SADS	San Justo/Aeroclub Argentino [*Argentina*] [*ICAO location identifier*] (ICLI)
SADS	Schedule for Affective Disorders and Schizophrenia [*Psychological interview*]
SADS	Semiautomatic Defense System (NG)
SADS	Semiconductor Anticoincidence Detection System
SADS	Senate Appropriations Defense Subcommittee
SADS	Simulated Air Defense System [*RADAR*]
SADS	Single Application Data Sheet
SADS	Social Avoidance and Distress Scale [*Psychology*]
SADS	Solar Array Drive System
SADS	Submarine Active Detection System
SADS	Swiss Air Defense System
SADS	System Architecture Development Study [*NATO Integrated Communications System*] (NATG)
SADSAC	Sampled Data Simulator and Computer
SADSAC	Seiler ALGOL Digitally Simulated Analog Computer
SADSAC	Small Acoustic Device Simulating Aircraft Carrier (NVT)
SADSACT	Self-Assigned Descriptors from Self and Cited Titles [*Automatic indexing*]
SADSC	San Antonio Data Services Center [*Military*]
SADS-C	Schedule for Affective Disorders and Schizophrenia - Change Version [*Personality development test*] [*Psychology*]
SADS-L	Schedule for Affective Disorders and Schizophrenia - Lifetime Version [*Personality development test*] [*Psychology*]
SADT	Self-Accelerating Decomposition Temperature
SADT	Special Active Duty for Training [*Military*] (AABC)
SADT	Structured Analysis and Design Technique [*Programming language*] [*1978*]
SADT	Surface Alloy Diffused-Base Transistor
SADTC	SHAPE [*Supreme Headquarters Allied Powers Europe*] Air Defense Technology Center [*Later, STC*] [*NATO*] (MCD)
Sadtler Commer Spectra	Sadtler Commercial Spectra [*United States*] [*A publication*]

SADU .... Sea Search Attack Development Unit
SADV .... Semiannual Density Variation [*Geophysics*]
SADZ......... Matanza/Aeroclub Universita Rio [*Argentina*] [*ICAO location identifier*] (ICLI)
SAE........... Ogallala, NE [*Location identifier*] [*FAA*] (FAAL)
SAE........... Sable Resources Ltd. [*Vancouver Stock Exchange symbol*]
SaE........... Sanguinarine Extract [*Biochemistry*]
SAE........... School of Audio Engineering [*Australia*]
SAE........... Self-Addressed Envelope
SAE........... Semi-Actuator Ejector (MCD)
SAE........... Senior Assistant Editor [*Publishing*]
SAE........... Service Acquisition Executive [*DoD*]
SAE........... Shaft Angle Encoder (KSC)
SAE........... Simple Arithmetic Expression
SAE........... Site Acceptance Evaluation [*Army*] (AABC)
SAE........... Society for the Advancement of Education (EA)
SAE........... Society for the Anthropology of Europe (EA)
SAE........... Society of Automotive Engineers [*Acronym is now organization's official name*] (EA)
SAE........... Son Altesse Electorale [*His Highness the Elector*] [*French*] (ROG)
SAE........... Soviet Antarctic Expedition
SAE........... Specialized Armoured Establishment [*British military*] (DMA)
SAE........... Spiral Aftereffect [*Aerospace*]
SAE........... Stamped Addressed Envelope
SAE........... Standard Average European
SAE........... Steering Angle Error
SAE........... Stop at Expiration [*Magazine subscriptions*]
SAE........... Student Action for Education [*Defunct*] (EA)
SAE........... Subcortical Arteriosclerotic Encephalopathy [*Medicine*]
SAEWS........ Supersonic Aircraft Engine
SAEA........ Southwest Atomic Energy Associates
SAE Australas ... SAE [*Society of Automotive Engineers*] Australasia [*A publication*]
SAEB........ Self-Adjusting Electric Brake
SAEB........ Special Army Evaluation Board (AABC)
SAEBA...... Soviet Antarctic Expedition. Information Bulletin [*English Translation*] [*A publication*]
SAEC........ Saeculum [*Age, Century, Generation, Lifetime*] [*Latin*] (ROG)
SAEC........ South African Exchange Control (IMH)
SAEC........ South American Explorers Club (EA)
SAEC........ South Australian Energy Council
SAEC........ Southern Agricultural Energy Center
SAEC........ State Administration of Exchange Control [*People's Republic of China*]
SAEC........ Sumitomo Atomic Energy Commission [*Japan*]
Saechs Heimatbl ... Saechsische Heimatblaetter [*A publication*]
SAECS...... Southern African Europe Container Service (DS)
Saeculum.... Saeculum. Jahrbuch fuer Universalgeschichte [*A publication*]
SAED........ Selected Area Electron Diffraction [*Also, SAD*] [*Surface analysis*]
SAED........ Societe des Amis d'Eugene Delacroix (EAIO)
SAED........ South Australia Education Department
SA Ed........ South Australian Education [*A publication*] (APTA)
SAED........ Systems Analysis and Engineering Development [*Naval Air Development Center*] (MCD)
SAEDA...... Subversion and Espionage Directed Against US Army and Deliberate Security Violations (AABC)
SAEDE...... Sensory Aids Evaluation and Development Center [*MIT*]
SAEDFR ... Scholars Against the Escalating Danger of the Far Right (EA)
SA Ed Gaz ... Education Gazette. South Australia Department of Education [*A publication*] (APTA)
SAED Info ... SAED [*Societe Africaine d'Etudes et de Developpement*] Information [*A publication*]
SAEF........ Ezeiza [*Argentina*] [*ICAO location identifier*] (ICLI)
SAEF .... SEAQ Automated Execution Facility [*Software package*]
SAEF .... Small-Order Automatic Execution Facility [*London Stock Exchange*] [*British*]
SAEF .... Spacecraft Assembly and Encapsulation Facility [*NASA*] (NASA)
SAEF .... State Administrative Expense Funds
SAEH .... Society for Automation in English and the Humanities [*Later, SDE*]
SAE Handb ... SAE [*Society of Automotive Engineers*] Handbook [*A publication*]
SAEI........ Sumitomo Atomic Energy Industries Ltd. [*Japan*]
SAE J........ SAE [*Society of Automotive Engineers*] Journal [*A publication*]
SAEJA...... SAE [*Society of Automotive Engineers*] Journal [*A publication*]
SAE J Automot Eng ... SAE [*Society of Automotive Engineers*] Journal of Automotive Engineering [*A publication*]
SAE Journ ... SAE [*Society of Automotive Engineers*] Journal [*A publication*]
SAE Meet Pap ... Society of Automotive Engineers. Meeting. Papers [*A publication*]
SAEMR..... Small Arms Expert Marksmanship Ribbon [*Military decoration*] (AFM)
SAEND...... Save Energy [*A publication*]
Saenger Musikanten Z ... Saenger- und Musikantenzeitung [*A publication*]
SAEP........ South African Education Program [*New York, NY*]
SAE Prepr ... SAE [*Society of Automotive Engineers*] Preprints [*A publication*]
SAE Proc ... Society of Automotive Engineers. Proceedings [*A publication*]

SAE Prog Technol ... SAE [*Society of Automotive Engineers*] Progress in Technology [*United States*] [*A publication*]
SAE Q Trans ... SAE [*Society of Automotive Engineers*] Quarterly Transactions [*A publication*]
SAE Quart Trans ... SAE [*Society of Automotive Engineers*] Quarterly Transactions [*A publication*]
SAERB ...... South African Electrical Review [*A publication*]
SAES .... Scanning Auger Electron Spectroscopy
SAES .... Special Assistant for Environmental Services [*Military*]
SAES .... Stand-Alone Engine Simulator (NASA)
SAES .... State Agricultural Experiment Station
SAESA ...... SAE [*Society of Automotive Engineers*] Special Publications [*A publication*]
SAE (Soc Automot Eng) Tech Pap ... SAE (Society of Automotive Engineers) Technical Papers [*A publication*]
SAE Spec Publ ... SAE [*Society of Automotive Engineers*] Special Publications [*A publication*]
SAETA ...... SA Ecuatoriana de Transportes Aereos [*Airline*] [*Ecuador*]
SAETB ...... SAE [*Society of Automotive Engineers*] Technical Progress Series [*A publication*]
SAE Tech Lit Abstr ... SAE [*Society of Automotive Engineers*] Technical Literature Abstracts [*A publication*]
SAE Tech Prog Ser ... SAE [*Society of Automotive Engineers*] Technical Progress Series [*A publication*]
SAETO ...... Sociedad Aereo del Tolina [*Colombia*]
SAE Trans ... SAE [*Society of Automotive Engineers*] Transactions [*A publication*]
Saeugetierkd Mitt ... Saeugetierkundliche Mitteilungen [*A publication*]
SAEV .... Ezeiza [*Argentina*] [*ICAO location identifier*] (ICLI)
SAEW........ Ship's Advanced Electronic Warfare (MCD)
SAEWS ...... Ship's Advanced Electronic Warfare System (NVT)
SAEZ........ Buenos Aires [*Argentina*]/Ezeiza [*Argentina*] [*ICAO location identifier*] (ICLI)
SAF........... SAF [*Society of American Florists*]- The Center for Commercial Floriculture (EA)
SAF........... Safed [*Israel*] [*Seismograph station code, US Geological Survey*] [*Closed*] (SEIS)
SAF........... Safety (KSC)
SAF........... Sample Air Filter
SAF........... San Andreas Fault
SAF........... Santa Fe [*New Mexico*] [*Airport symbol*] (OAG)
SAF........... Scandinavian American Fraternity (EA)
SAF........... School of Aerial Fighting [*British military*] (DMA)
SAF........... Scrapie-Associated Fibrils [*Neuroanatomy*]
SAF........... Scudder New Asia Fund [*NYSE symbol*] (SPSG)
SAF........... Second Amendment Foundation (EA)
SAF........... Secretary of the Air Force
SAF........... Secure Automated Fabrication [*Line*] [*Nuclear energy*]
SAF........... Segment Address Field
SAF........... Self-Articulating Femoral [*Medicine*]
SAF........... Shielding Analysis Form [*Civil Defense*]
SAF........... Single Action [*Maintenance*] Form (NVT)
SAF........... Small Arms Factory [*Australia*]
SAF........... Society of American Florists (EA)
SAF........... Society of American Foresters (EA)
SAF........... Source Acquisitions File (MCD)
SAF........... South Africa (EY)
SAF........... South Africa Foundation (EA)
SA & F .... Southern Airlines and Freighters [*Australia*]
SAF........... Southern Attack Force [*Navy*]
SAF........... Spacecraft Assembly Facility [*NASA*]
SAF........... Spanish Air Force
SAF........... Special Action Force [*Military*]
SAF........... Specification Approval Form (MCD)
SAF........... Spin Armed Fuze
SAF........... Star Alliance Foundation (EA)
SAF........... Stem Cell Activating Factor [*Biochemistry*]
SAF........... Sterilization Assembly Facility
SAF........... Strategic Air Force
SAF........... Structural Adjustment Facility [*Finance*]
SAF........... Students Against Fires [*International student engineering project for 1972-73 sponsored by Student Competitions on Relevant Engineering - SCORE*]
SAF........... Studies in American Fiction [*A publication*]
SAF........... Subject Authority File, Washington, DC [*UTLAS symbol*]
SAF........... Subject to the Availability of Funds (MCD)
SAF........... Super Abrasion Furnace [*Carbon black manufacture*]
SAF........... Support Action Form (MCD)
SAF........... Suppressor Activating Factor [*Immunology*]
SAF........... Svenska Arbetsgivareforeningen [*An employers' confederation*] [*Sweden*]
SAF........... Swedish Air Force
SAF........... Switchable Acoustic Filter
SAF........... Symmetry-Adapted Function
SAF........... Symposium on Applications of Ferroelectrics [*IEEE*]
SAF........... Syrian Air Force (BJA)
SAFA .... School Assistance in Federally Affected Areas
SAFA .... Service d'Aide aux Forces Alliees [*World War II*]
SAFA........ Society of Air Force Anesthesiologists [*Later, DMEF*] (EA)
SAFA .... Society for Automation in the Fine Arts [*Later, SDE*]
SAFA .... Solar Array Failure Analysis

SAFA .... Soluble Antigen Fluorescent-Antibody [*Immunology*]
SAFAA ...... Secretary of the Air Force, Administrative Assistant
SAFAD ...... Small Arms for Air Defense (MCD)
Saf Air Ammonia Plants ... Safety in Air and Ammonia Plants [*A publication*]
SAF/AL ..... Assistant Secretary of the Air Force (Research, Development, and Logistics)
SAFARI.... Semiautomatic Failure Anticipation Recording Instrumentation
SAFARI.... South African Fundamental Atomic Reactor Installation
SAFARI.... Spiro Agnew Fans and Rooters, Incorporated
SAFB .... Scott Air Force Base [*Illinois*]
SAFB .... Shaw Air Force Base [*South Carolina*]
SAFB .... Sheppard Air Force Base [*Texas*] (AAG)
SAFC........ SAFECO Corp. [*NASDAQ symbol*] (NQ)
SAFCA ...... Safeguard Communications Agency [*Army*]
SAFCB...... Secretary of the Air Force Correction Board
SAFCMD . Safeguard Command [*Army*] (AABC)
SAFCO ...... Standing Advisory Committee on Fisheries of the Caribbean Organization
SAFCOM .. Safeguard System Command [*Obsolete*] [*Army*]
SAFCPM... Safeguard Communications Program Manager [*Army*] (AABC)
SAFCPMO ... Safeguard Communications Program Management Office [*Army*] (AABC)
SAFCTF .... Safeguard Central Training Facility [*Army*] (AABC)
SAFD......... Plastics (Southern Africa) [*A publication*]
SAFD .... Society of American Fight Directors (EA)
Saf Dig .... Safety Digest [*Japan*] [*A publication*]
SAFDL ...... Specified Acceptable Fuel Design Limit [*Nuclear energy*] (NRCH)
SAFE .... Safe Access to Files of Estate [*Howrex Corp.*] [*Information service or system*] (IID)
SAFE .... Safeguards Analysis for Effluents
SAFE .... Safeguards Automated Facility Evaluation [*Nuclear energy*] (NRCH)
SAFE .... Safety and Functional Evaluation [*Occupational therapy*]
SAFE .... San Andreas Fault Experiment
SAFE .... Santa Fe [*Argentina*] [*ICAO location identifier*] (ICLI)
SAFE .... Satellite Alert Force Employment
SAFE .... Save Animals from Extinction [*An association*] [*Later, WPTI*]
SAFE .... Security American Finance Enterprises, Inc. [*NASDAQ symbol*] (NQ)
SAFE .... Security, Aptitude, Fitness Evaluation [*Test*]
S/AFE........ Seismic/Acoustic Feature Extraction (MCD)
SAFE .... Selected Areas for Evasion [*Military*] (MCD)
SAFE .... Self-Acceptance, Faulty Information, Effectiveness Counselling or Training [*Sex therapy*]
SAFE .... Sequential Analysis for Force Development (MCD)
SAFE .... Settlement and Accelerated Funds Exchange [*Chicago, IL*]
SAFE .... Shelter Available for Emergency
SAFE .... Simulation-Aided Fault Evaluation (MCD)
SAFE .... Society to Advance Foreclosure Education (EA)
SAFE .... Society for the Advancement of Fission Energy (EA)
SAFE .... Society for the Application of Free Energy (EA)
SAFE .... Society of Associated Financial Executives
SAFE .... Software Abstracts for Engineers [*CITIS Ltd.*] [*Ireland*] [*Information service or system*] (CRD)
SAFE .... Solvent Abuse Foundation for Education (EA)
SAFE .... South America and Far East
SAFE .... Spectronix Automatic Fire Extinguishing [*System*] [*For armored vehicles*]
SAFE .... Stationary Attachment and Flexible Endoskeleton
SAFE .... Stock Assessment and Fishery Investigations [*National Marine Fisheries Service*] (NOAA)
SAFE .... Store and Forward Element [*Telecommunications*] (TEL)
SAFE .... Straits Air Freight Express [*Australia*]
SAFE .... Strategy and Force Evaluation (MCD)
SAFE .... Students Against Famine Everywhere (EA)
SAFE .... Suntanning Association for Education (EA)
SAFE .... Support for the Analysts' File Environment (MCD)
SAFE .... Survival [*formerly, Space*] and Flight Equipment Association [*Later, SAFE Association*]
SAFE .... System, Area, Function, Equipment
SAFEA ...... Safety [*A publication*]
SAFEA ...... Survival and Flight Equipment Association [*Later, SAFE Association*] (EA)
Safe Manag ... Safety Management [*A publication*]
SAFER ...... Sequential Action Flow Routine [*Military*] [*British*]
SAFER ...... Special Aviation Fire and Explosion Reduction (EGAO)
SAFER ...... Systematic Aid to Flow on Existing Roads [*Traffic-control system*]
SAFE TRIP ... Students Against Faulty Tires Ripping in Pieces [*Student legal action organization*]
SAFETY.... Safety Always Follows Everything You Do [*Sign*]
Safety Ed ... Safety Education [*A publication*]
Safety Educ ... Safety Education [*A publication*]
Safety Eng ... Safety Engineering [*A publication*]
Safety Maint ... Safety Maintenance [*A publication*]
Safety Maint & Prod ... Safety Maintenance and Production [*A publication*]
Safety Surv ... Safety Surveyor [*A publication*]
SAFF .... Safing, Arming, Fusing, and Firing [*Military*] (MCD)
SAFF .... Store and Forward Facsimile
SAFFA....... SpA Fabbriche Fiammiferi ed Affini-Saffa [*Italian*]

SAFFE....... Society of Americans for Firearms Elimination (EA)
SAFFI........ Special Assembly for Fast Installations [*Telecommunications*] (TEL)
SAFFM ..... Secretary of the Air Force, Financial Management
SAFFUC... Sudan African Freedom Fighters' Union of Conservatives
SAFFWALD ... Saffron Walden [*Municipal borough in England*]
SAFGC ...... Secretary of the Air Force General Counsel
Saf Health Welfare ... Safety, Health, and Welfare [*A publication*]
Saf Hlth Bull ... Safety and Health Bulletin [*A publication*]
Saf Hyg (Osaka) ... Safety and Hygiene (Osaka) [*Japan*] [*A publication*]
SAFI .... Semiautomatic Flight Inspection [*FAA*]
SAFI .... Senior Air Force Instructor
SAFI .... Sholem Aleichem Folk Institute (EA)
SAFIE........ Secretary of the Air Force, Special Assistant for Installations
SAFIL........ Secretary of the Air Force (Installations and Logistics)
SAFIM ...... Separated Associated Fluid Interaction Model [*Chemical engineering*]
SAFIMDA ... School Aid to Federally Impacted and Major Disaster Areas (OICC)
SAFIN ...... Secretary of the Air Force, Special Assistant for Intelligence
SAFIRE ..... Systems Analysis for Integrated Relief Variation [*Engineering*]
SAFIS........ Secretary of the Air Force, Office of Information Services
SAFISC ..... South Australian Film Industry Standing Committee
SAFISY ..... Space Agency Forum on International Space Year
SAFITP ..... Safeguard Integrated Training Plan [*Army*] (AABC)
SAFJB .... South African Forestry Journal [*A publication*]
S Af J Econ ... South African Journal of Economics [*Suid-Afrikaanse Tydskrif vir Ekonomie*] [*A publication*]
SAFLL....... Secretary of the Air Force, Office of Legislative Liaison
SAFLOG ... Safeguard Logistics Command [*Army*] (AABC)
SAFM........ Sanderson Farms, Inc. [*NASDAQ symbol*] (NQ)
Saf Manage ... Safety Management [*A publication*]
SAFMem ... Societe Nationale des Antiquaires de France. Memoires [*A publication*]
Saf Mines... Safety in Mines [*A publication*]
SAFMP ..... Assistant Secretary of the Air Force (Manpower and Personnel)
SAFMR ..... Secretary of the Air Force, Manpower and Reserve Affairs
SAFMSC... Safeguard Materiel Support Command [*Army*] (AABC)
Saf News Bull ... Safety News Bulletin [*A publication*] (APTA)
Saf Newsl... Safety Newsletter [*A publication*]
SAFNGS ... Small Arms Flash, Noise Gunfire Simulator [*Army*]
SAFO........ Secretary of the Air Force Order (AFM)
SAFO........ Senior Acting Field Officer [*Military*] [*British*] (ROG)
SAFO........ Senior Air Force Officer [*Present*] (AFM)
SAFOAT ... South African Avifauna Series. Percy Fitzpatrick Institute of African Ornithology. University of Cape Town [*A publication*]
SAFOC...... Semiautomatic Flight Operations Center
SAFOC...... Syndicat Autonome des Fonctionnaires d'Oubangi-Chari [*Autonomous Union of the Workers of Ubangi-Shari*]
SAFOH ..... Society of American Florists and Ornamental Horticulturists [*Later, SAF*]
SAFOI .... Secretary of the Air Force, Office of Information
SAFP .... Society of Air Force Physicians (EA)
SAFPACC ... Safeguard Public Affairs Coordinating Committee [*Army*] (AABC)
SAFPC...... Secretary of the Air Force Personnel Council
SAFPD ...... Safety Practitioner [*A publication*]
SAFPLAN ... Submarine Area Frequency Plan [*Navy*]
SAFPO ...... Safeguard Project Office (MCD)
Saf Pract ... Safety Practitioner [*A publication*]
SAFR........ Senior Air Force Representative (AFM)
SAFR .... Social Assessment of Fisheries Resources
SAFR .... Sodium Advanced Fast Reactor
SAFR .... Source Application of Funds Report (MCD)
S Afr.......... South Africa
SAFR .... Supplementary Application Forms Required [*Civil Service*]
S Afr Annu Insur Rev ... South African Annual Insurance Review [*A publication*]
S Afr AR .... Annual Economic Report. South African Reserve Bank [*A publication*]
S Afr Archaeol Bull ... South African Archaeological Bulletin [*A publication*]
S Afr Archaeol Soc Goodwin Ser ... South African Archaeological Society. Goodwin Series [*A publication*]
S Afr Archit J ... South African Architectural Journal [*A publication*]
S Afr Archit Rec ... South African Architectural Record [*A publication*]
S Afr Arch Ophthalmol ... South African Archives of Ophthalmology [*A publication*]
S-Afr Argief Oftalmol ... Suid-Afrikaanse Argief vir Oftalmologie [*A publication*]
SAFRAS.... Self-Adaptive Flexible Format Retrieval and Storage System [*Data processing*] (IID)
S Afr Assoc Adv Sci Spec Publ ... South African Association for the Advancement of Science. Special Publication [*A publication*]
S Afr Assoc Mar Biol Res Bull ... South African Association for Marine Biological Research. Bulletin [*A publication*]
S Afr Bank ... South African Reserve Bank. Quarterly Bulletin [*A publication*]
S Afr Bankers J ... South African Bankers' Journal [*Cape Town, South Africa*] [*A publication*] (DLA)
S Afr Bee J ... South African Bee Journal [*A publication*]

S-Afr Bosbou Tydskr ... Suid-Afrikaanse Bosbou Tydskrif [*A publication*]

S Afr Build ... South African Builder [*A publication*]

S Afr Bur Stand Bull ... South African Bureau of Standards. Bulletin [*A publication*]

S Afr Cancer Bull ... South African Cancer Bulletin [*A publication*]

S Afr (Cape Good Hope) Dep Nat Conserv Rep ... South Africa (Cape Of Good Hope) Department of Nature. Conservation Report [*A publication*]

S Afr Chart Account ... South African Chartered Accountant [*A publication*]

S Afr Chem Process ... South African Chemical Processing [*A publication*]

S Afr Constr World ... South African Construction World [*A publication*]

S Afr Corros J ... South African Corrosion Journal [*A publication*]

S Afr Counc Sci Ind Res Nat Bldg Res Inst Bull ... South Africa. Council for Scientific and Industrial Research. National Building Research Institute. Bulletin [*A publication*]

S Afr CSIR Air Pollut Group Annu Rep ... South Africa CSIR [*Council for Scientific and Industrial Research*] Air Pollution Group. Annual Report [*A publication*]

S Afr CSIR Air Pollut Res Group Annu Rep ... South Africa CSIR [*Council for Scientific and Industrial Research*] Air Pollution Research Group. Annual Report [*A publication*]

S Afr CSIR Air Pollut Res Group Rep APRG ... South African Council for Scientific and Industrial Research. Air Pollution Research Group. Report APRG [*A publication*]

S Afr CSIR Annu Rep ... South Africa CSIR [*Council for Scientific and Industrial Research*] Annual Report [*A publication*]

S Afr CSIR Res Rep ... South Africa CSIR [*Council for Scientific and Industrial Research*] Research Report [*A publication*]

S Afr CSIR Spec Rep ... South Africa CSIR [*Council for Scientific and Industrial Research*] Special Report [*A publication*]

SAFRD ...... Assistant Secretary of the Air Force (Research and Development)

SAFRD ...... South African Food Review [*A publication*]

S Afr Dent J ... South African Dental Journal [*A publication*]

S Afr Dep Agric Entomol Mem ... South Africa. Department of Agriculture. Entomology Memoir [*A publication*]

S Afr Dep Agric Fish Entomol Mem ... South Africa. Department of Agriculture and Fisheries. Entomology Memoir [*A publication*]

S Afr Dep Agric Fish Tech Commun ... South Africa. Department of Agriculture and Fisheries. Technical Communication [*A publication*]

S Afr Dep Agric Tech Serv Bot Surv Mem ... South Africa. Department of Agricultural Technical Services. Botanical Survey Memoir [*A publication*]

S Afr Dep Agric Tech Serv Bull ... South Africa. Department of Agricultural Technical Services. Bulletin [*A publication*]

S Afr Dep Agric Tech Serv Entomol Mem ... South Africa. Department of Agricultural Technical Services. Entomology Memoirs [*A publication*]

S Afr Dep Agric Tech Serv Sci Bull ... South Africa. Department of Agricultural Technical Services. Scientific Bulletin [*A publication*]

S Afr Dep Agric Tech Serv Tech Commun ... South Africa. Department of Agricultural Technical Services. Technical Communication [*A publication*]

S Afr Dep Agric Water Supply Entomol Mem ... South Africa. Department of Agriculture and Water Supply. Entomology Memoir [*A publication*]

S Afr Dep Agric Water Supply Tech Commun ... South Africa. Department of Agriculture and Water Supply. Technical Communication [*A publication*]

S-Afr Dep Bosbou Jaarversl ... Suid-Afrika. Departement van Bosbou Jaarverslag [*A publication*]

S Afr Dep For Annu Rep ... South Africa. Department of Forestry. Annual Report [*A publication*]

S Afr Dep For Bull ... South Africa. Department of Forestry. Bulletin [*A publication*]

S-Afr Dep Landbou-Teg Dienste Teg Meded ... Suid-Afrika. Departement van Landbou-Tegniese Dienste Tegniese Mededeling [*A publication*]

S Afr Dep Landbou Visserye Teg Meded ... Suid-Afrika. Departement van Landbou Visserye Tegniese Mededeling [*A publication*]

S Afr Dep Landbou Viss Teg Meded ... Suid-Afrika. Departement van Landbou en Visserye. Tegniese Mededeling [*A publication*]

S Afr Dep Mines Quart Inform Circ Miner ... South Africa. Department of Mines. Quarterly Information Circular. Minerals [*A publication*]

S Afr Div Sea Fish Annu Rep ... South Africa. Division of Sea Fisheries. Annual Report [*A publication*]

S Afr Div Sea Fish Fish Bull ... South Africa. Division of Sea Fisheries. Fisheries Bulletin [*A publication*]

S Afr Div Sea Fish Invest Rep ... South Africa. Division of Sea Fisheries. Investigational Report [*A publication*]

S Afr Electr Rev ... South African Electrical Review [*A publication*]

S Afr Eng Electr Rev ... South African Engineer and Electrical Review [*A publication*]

S Afr Food Rev ... South African Food Review [*A publication*]

S Afr For J ... South African Forestry Journal [*A publication*]

S Afr Friesland J ... South African Friesland Journal [*A publication*]

S Afr Geogr ... South African Geographer [*A publication*]

S Afr Geogr J ... South African Geographical Journal [*A publication*]

S Afr Geol Surv Bibliogr Subj Index S Afr Geol ... South Africa. Geological Survey. Bibliography and Subject Index of South African Geology [*A publication*]

S Afr Geol Surv Bull ... South Africa. Department of Mines. Geological Survey. Bulletin [*A publication*]

S Afr Geol Surv Mem ... South Africa. Department of Mines. Geological Survey. Memoir [*A publication*]

S Afr Geol Surv Seismol Ser ... South Africa. Geological Survey. Seismologic Series [*A publication*]

S Afr Geol Surv South-West Afr Ser ... South Africa. Geological Survey. South-West Africa Series [*A publication*]

S Afr Hist J ... South African Historical Journal [*A publication*]

S African J Commun Disorders ... South African Journal of Communication Disorders [*A publication*]

S African J Psychol ... South African Journal of Psychology [*A publication*]

S African Lib ... South African Libraries [*A publication*]

S African Lib Q Bull ... South African Library Quarterly Bulletin [*A publication*]

S Afr Ind Chem ... South African Industrial Chemist [*A publication*]

S Afr Inst Mech Eng J ... South African Institution of Mechanical Engineers. Journal [*A publication*]

S Afr Inst Med Res Annu Rep ... South African Institute for Medical Research. Annual Report [*A publication*]

S Afr Inst Min Metall J ... South African Institute of Mining and Metallurgy. Journal [*A publication*]

S Afr Insur Mag ... South African Insurance Magazine [*A publication*]

S Afr Int ..... South Africa International [*A publication*]

S Afr J Agric Ext ... South African Journal of Agricultural Extension [*A publication*]

S Afr J Agric Sci ... South African Journal of Agricultural Science [*A publication*]

S Afr J Agr Sci ... South African Journal of Agricultural Science [*A publication*]

S Afr J Anim Sci ... South African Journal of Animal Science [*A publication*]

S Afr J Antarct Res ... South African Journal of Antarctic Research [*A publication*]

S Afr J Antarct Res Suppl ... South African Journal of Antarctic Research. Supplement [*A publication*]

S Afr J Bot ... South African Journal of Botany [*A publication*]

S Afr J Bus Manage ... South African Journal of Business Management [*A publication*]

S Afr J Chem ... South African Journal of Chemistry [*A publication*]

S Afr J Chem/S Afr Tydskr Chem ... South African Journal of Chemistry/ Suid-Afrikaanse Tydskrif vir Chemie [*A publication*]

S Afr J Clin Sci ... South African Journal of Clinical Science [*A publication*]

S Afr J Comm Disorders ... South African Journal of Communication Disorders [*A publication*]

S Afr J Commun Disord ... South African Journal of Communication Disorders [*A publication*]

S Afr J Contin Med Educ ... South African Journal of Continuing Medical Education [*A publication*]

S Afr J Crim L ... South African Journal of Criminal Law and Criminology [*A publication*]

S Afr J Crim Law Criminol ... South African Journal of Criminal Law and Criminology [*A publication*]

S Afr J Dairy Technol ... South African Journal of Dairy Technology [*A publication*]

S Afr J Ec .. South African Journal of Economics [*Suid-Afrikaanse Tydskrif vir Ekonomie*] [*A publication*]

S Afr J Econ ... South African Journal of Economics [*Suid-Afrikaanse Tydskrif vir Ekonomie*] [*A publication*]

S Afr J Educ ... South African Journal of Education [*A publication*]

S Afr J Enol Vitic ... South African Journal for Enology and Viticulture [*A publication*]

S Afr Jersey ... South African Jersey [*A publication*]

S Afr J Ethnol ... South African Journal of Ethnology [*A publication*]

S Afr J Hosp Med ... South African Journal of Hospital Medicine [*A publication*]

S Afr J Ind ... South African Journal of Industries [*A publication*]

S Afr J Lab Clin Med ... South African Journal of Laboratory and Clinical Medicine [*A publication*]

S Afr J Labour Relat ... South African Journal of Labour Relations [*A publication*]

S Afr J Libr Inf Sci ... South African Journal for Librarianship and Information Science [*A publication*]

S Afr J Mar Sci ... South African Journal of Marine Science [*A publication*]

S Afr J Med Lab Technol ... South African Journal of Medical Laboratory Technology [*A publication*]

S Afr J Med Sci ... South African Journal of Medical Sciences [*A publication*]

S Afr J Musicology ... South African Journal of Musicology [*A publication*]

S Afr J Music Therap ... South African Journal of Music Therapy [*A publication*]

S Afr J Nutr ... South African Journal of Nutrition [*A publication*]

S Afr J Nutr/S Afr Tydskr Voeding ... South African Journal of Nutrition/ Suid-Afrikaanse Tydskrif vir Voeding [*A publication*]

S Afr J Obstet Gynaecol ... South African Journal of Obstetrics and Gynaecology [*A publication*]

S Afr J Occup Ther ... South African Journal of Occupational Therapy [*A publication*]

S Afr J Philos ... South African Journal of Philosophy [*A publication*]

S Afr J Photogramm Remote Sensing Cartogr ... South African Journal of Photogrammetry. Remote Sensing and Cartography [*A publication*]
S Afr J Phys ... South African Journal of Physics [*A publication*]
S Afr J Physiother ... South African Journal of Physiotherapy [*A publication*]
S Afr J Plant Soil ... South African Journal of Plant and Soil [*A publication*]
S Afr J Psychol ... South African Journal of Psychology [*A publication*]
S Afr J Radiol ... South African Journal of Radiology [*A publication*]
S Afr J Sci ... South African Journal of Science [*A publication*]
S Afr J Surg ... South African Journal of Surgery [*A publication*]
S Afr J Surg/S Afr Tydskr Chir ... South African Journal of Surgery/Suid-Afrikaanse Tydskr vir Chirurgie [*A publication*]
S Afr J Wildl Res ... South African Journal of Wildlife Research [*A publication*]
S Afr J Wild Res ... South African Journal of Wildlife Research [*A publication*]
S Afr J Zool ... South African Journal of Zoology [*A publication*]
S Afr Kankerbull ... Suid-Afrikaanse Kankerbulletin [*A publication*]
SAfrL .... Studies in African Literature [*A publication*]
S Afr Labour Bull ... South African Labour Bulletin [*A publication*]
S Afr Lapid Mag ... South African Lapidary Magazine [*A publication*]
S Afr Law J ... South African Law Journal [*A publication*]
S Afr Libr... South African Libraries [*A publication*]
S Afr LJ ..... South African Law Journal [*A publication*]
S Afr LR ... South African Law Reports [*A publication*]
S Afr LR App ... South African Law Reports, Appellate [*A publication*] (DLA)
S Afr L Rev ... South African Law Review [*A publication*] (DLA)
S Afr LT..... South African Law Times [*A publication*] (DLA)
S Afr Mach Tool Rev ... South African Machine Tool Review [*A publication*]
S Afr Mater Handl News ... South African Materials Handling News [*A publication*]
S Afr Mech Eng ... South African Mechanical Engineer [*A publication*]
S Afr Mech Engr ... South African Mechanical Engineer [*A publication*]
S Afr Med Equip News ... South African Medical Equipment News [*A publication*]
S Afr Med J ... South African Medical Journal [*A publication*]
S Afr Med Tim ... South African Medical Times [*A publication*]
S-Afr Med Tydskr ... Suid-Afrikaanse Mediese Tydskrif [*A publication*]
S Afr Min Eng J ... South African Mining and Engineering Journal [*A publication*]
S Afr Min J ... South African Mining Journal [*A publication*]
S Afr Min Rev ... South African Mining Review [*A publication*]
S Afr Min World ... South African Mining World [*A publication*]
S Afr Music Teach ... South African Music Teacher [*A publication*]
S Afr Mus Rep ... South African Museum Report [*A publication*]
S Afr Numis J ... South African Numismatic Journal [*A publication*]
S Afr Nurs J ... South African Nursing Journal [*A publication*]
S AFS ... South African Optometrist [*A publication*]
S Afr Outl .. South African Outlook [*A publication*]
S Afr Outlook ... South African Outlook [*A publication*]
S Afr Panorama ... South African Panorama [*A publication*]
S Afr Pat Trade Marks Off Pat J Incl Trade Marks Des ... South Africa. Patent and Trade Marks Office. Patent Journal, Including Trade Marks and Designs [*A publication*]
S Afr Pharm J ... South African Pharmaceutical Journal [*A publication*]
S Afr Pneumoconiosis Rev ... South African Pneumoconiosis Review [*A publication*]
S Afr Poult Bull ... South African Poultry Bulletin [*A publication*]
S Afr Pract ... South African Practitioner [*A publication*]
SAFRR ...... Secretary of the Air Force, Requirements Review
S Afr Radiogr ... South African Radiographer [*A publication*]
S Afr Railw ... South African Railways [*A publication*]
S Afr Rep Secr Water Affairs ... South Africa. Report of the Secretary for Water Affairs [*A publication*]
S Afr Sci..... South African Science [*A publication*]
S Afr Sea Fish Branch Invest Rep ... South Africa. Sea Fisheries Branch. Investigational Report [*A publication*]
S Afr Sea Fish Inst Invest Rep ... South Africa. Sea Fisheries Institute. Investigational Report [*A publication*]
S Afr Sea Fish Res Inst Invest Rep ... South Africa. Sea Fisheries Research Institute. Investigational Report [*A publication*]
S Afr Shipp News Fish Ind Rev ... South African Shipping News and Fishing Industry Review [*A publication*]
S-Afr Spoorwee ... Suid-Afrikaanse Spoorwee [*South Africa*] [*A publication*]
S Afr Stat... South African Statistical Journal [*A publication*]
S Afr Stat J ... South African Statistical Journal [*A publication*]
S Afr Sugar Assoc Exp Stn Annu Rep ... South African Sugar Association Experiment Station. Annual Report [*A publication*]
S Afr Sugar Assoc Exp Stn Bull ... South African Sugar Association Experiment Station. Bulletin [*A publication*]
S Afr Sugar J ... South African Sugar Journal [*A publication*]
S Afr Sug J ... South African Sugar Journal [*A publication*]
S Afr Surv J ... South African Survey Journal [*A publication*]
S Afr Tax ... South African Tax Cases [*A publication*] (DLA)
S Afr Tax Cas ... South African Tax Cases [*A publication*] (DLA)
S Afr Text.. South African Textiles [*A publication*]
S Afr Transp ... South African Transport [*A publication*]
S Afr Treas ... South African Treasurer [*A publication*]
S Afr Tunnel ... South African Tunnelling [*A publication*]
S Afr Tunnelling ... South African Tunnelling [*A publication*]

S-Afr Tydsk Natuurwet Tegnol ... Suid-Afrikaanse Tydskrif vir Natuurwetenskap en Tegnologie [*A publication*]
S-Afr Tydskr Antarkt Navors ... Suid-Afrikaanse Tydskrif vir Antarktiese Navorsing [*A publication*]
S Afr Tydskr Chem ... Suid-Afrikaanse Tydskrif vir Chemie [*A publication*]
S-Afr Tydskr Chir ... Suid-Afrikaanse Tydskrif vir Chirurgie [*A publication*]
S Afr Tydskr Dierkd ... Suid-Afrikaanse Tydskrif vir Dierkunde [*A publication*]
S-Afr Tydskr Geneeskd ... Suid-Afrikaanse Tydskrif vir Geneeskunde [*A publication*]
S-Afr Tydskr Lab Kliniekwerk ... Suid-Afrikaanse Tydskrif vir Laboratorium en Kliniekwerk [*A publication*]
S-Afr Tydskr Landbouwet ... Suid-Afrikaanse Tydskrif vir Landbouwetenskap [*A publication*]
S Afr Tydskr Med Lab Tegnol ... Suid-Afrikaanse Tydskrif vir Mediese Laboratorium-Tegnologie [*A publication*]
S-Afr Tydskr Natuurwet Tegnol ... Suid-Afrikaanse Tydskrif vir Natuurwetenskap en Tegnologie [*A publication*]
S-Afr Tydskr Obstet Ginekol ... Suid-Afrikaanse Tydskrif vir Obstetrie en Ginekologie [*A publication*]
S Afr Tydskr Plant Grond ... Suid-Afrikaanse Tydskrif vir Plant en Grond [*A publication*]
S-Afr Tydskr Radiol ... Suid-Afrikaanse Tydskrif vir Radiologie [*A publication*]
S Afr Tydskr Seewetenskap ... Suid-Afrikaanse Tydskrif vir Seewetenskap [*A publication*]
S-Afr Tydskr Suiweltegnol ... Suid-Afrikaanse Tydskrif vir Suiweltegnologie [*A publication*]
S-Afr Tydskr Veekd ... Suid-Afrikaanse Tydskrif vir Veekunde [*A publication*]
S-Afr Tydskr Voeding ... Suid-Afrikaanse Tydskrif vir Voeding [*A publication*]
S-Afr Tydskr Wet ... Suid-Afrikaanse Tydskrif vir Wetenskap [*A publication*]
S Afr Tydskr Wysbegeerte ... Suid-Afrikaanse Tydskrif vir Wysbegeerte [*A publication*]
S-Afr Wet Nywerheid-Navorsingsraad Navorsingsversl ... Suid-Afrikaanse Wetenskaplike en Nywerheidnavorskingsraad. Navorsingsverslag [*A publication*]
S-Afr Wet Nywerheid-Navorsingsraad Spes Versl ... Suid-Afrikaanse Wetenskaplike en Nywerheidnavorskingsraad. Spesiale Verslag [*A publication*]
S Afr Wool Text Res Inst Annu Rep ... South African Wool Textile Research Institute. Annual Report [*A publication*]
S Afr Wool Text Res Inst Tech Rep ... South African Wool Textile Research Institute. Technical Report [*A publication*]
S Afr Yearb Int Law ... South African Yearbook of International Law [*A publication*]
S Afr YIL... South African Yearbook of International Law [*A publication*]
SAFS ... Secondary Air Force Specialty
Saf Sci Abstr ... Safety Science Abstracts Journal [*A publication*]
SAFSCOM ... Safeguard System Command [*Obsolete*] [*Army*] (AABC)
SAFSEA .... Safeguard System Evaluation Agency [*Army*] (AABC)
Saf Ser IAEA ... Safety Series. IAEA [*International Atomic Energy Agency*] [*A publication*]
SAFSIM .... Safeguard System Simulation [*Missile system evaluation*] [*Army*] (RDA)
SAFSL....... Secretary of the Air Force Space Liaison (MCD)
SAFSM..... Safeguard System Manager [*Army*]
SAFSO ...... Safeguard System Office [*Army*] (AABC)
SAFSP...... Secretary of the Air Force, Special Projects
SAFSR...... Society for the Advancement of Food Service Research (EA)
Saf Surv ..... Safety Surveyor [*United Kingdom*] [*A publication*]
SAFT........ Safety
SAFT........ Society for the Advancement of the Field Theory (EA)
SAFTAC.... Semiautomatic Facility for Terminal Area Control
SAFTCP.... Safeguard Tactical Communications Plan [*Army*] (AABC)
SAFTCS.... Safeguard Tactical Communications System [*Army*] (AABC)
SAFTO...... South African Foreign Trade Organisation
SAFTRANS ... Safeguard Transportation System [*Army*] (AABC)
SAFTU ...... South African Federation of Trade Unions
Safugetierkd Mitt ... Safugetierkundliche Mitteilungen [*A publication*]
SAFUS ...... Under Secretary of the Air Force
SAFWA ..... Southeastern Association of Fish and Wildlife Agencies (EA)
SAFX........ Saw Fixture [*Tool*] (AAG)
s-ag---........ Argentina [*MARC geographic area code*] [*Library of Congress*] (LCCP)
SAG .... Saga [*Japan*] [*Seismograph station code, US Geological Survey*] (SEIS)
SAG .... Sage Energy Co. [*AMEX symbol*] (SPSG)
Sag .... Saggiatore [*A publication*]
SAG .... Sagwon, AK [*Location identifier*] [*FAA*] (FAAL)
SAG .... Saint Anthony's Guild
SAG .... St. Apollonia Guild (EA)
SAG .... Salicyl Acyl Glucuronide [*Organic chemistry*]
sag............ Sango [*MARC language code*] [*Library of Congress*] (LCCP)
SAG .... Screen Actors Guild (EA)
SAG .... Secretaria de Agricultura y Ganaderia [*Mexico*]
SAG .... Seismic Air Gun
SAG .... Semiautogenous Grinding System [*Ore-crushing process*]
SAG .... Service Advisory Group (NATG)
SAG .... Signal Actuated Gate

SAG .... Significant Air Gap
SAG .... Society of Arthritic Gardeners
SAg .... Soluble Antigen [*Immunochemistry*]
SAG .... Sowjetische Aktiengesellschaften [*Soviet Corporations*]
        [*German Democratic Republic*]
SAG .... Standard Address Generator (IEEE)
SAG .... Statistical Advisory Group [*Cultural Advisory Council*]
        [*Australia*]
SAG .... Strategic Communications Ltd. [*Vancouver Stock Exchange
        symbol*]
SAG .... Study Advisory Group [*Army*]
SAG .... Stuttgarter Arbeiten zur Germanistik [*A publication*]
SAG .... Submarine Analysis Group [*Navy*] (CAAL)
S/Ag .... Supervised Agency (DLA)
SAG .... Surface Action Group [*Military*] (NVT)
SAG .... Surface Attack Group [*Navy*] (CAAL)
SAG .... Systems Analysis Group
SAGA .... Saint-Gaudens National Historic Site
SAGA .... Sand and Gravel Association of Great Britain
SAGA .... Short-Arc Geodetic Adjustment [*Geophysics*]
SAGA .... Smocking Arts Guild of America (EA)
SAGA .... Society of American Graphic Artists (EA)
SAGA .... Software AG Systems, Inc. [*NASDAQ symbol*] (NQ)
SAGA .... Stage and Arena Guild of America
SAGA .... Students Against Greiner's Attacks [*Australia*]
SAGA .... Studies, Analysis, and Gaming Agency [*Military*]
SAGA .... System for Automatic Generation and Analysis
Saga-Book ... Saga-Book. Viking Society for Northern Research [*A
        publication*]
SAGA Bull ... SAGA [*Sand and Gravel Association Ltd.*] Bulletin [*A
        publication*]
Saga S .... Saga och Sed [*A publication*]
SAGB .... Sage Broadcasting Corp. [*NASDAQ symbol*] (NQ)
SAGB .... Schizophrenia Association of Great Britain
SAGB .... Senior Advisory Group on Biotechnology [*British*]
SAGB .... Spiritualist Association of Great Britain
SAGE .... Sage Drilling Co., Inc. [*NASDAQ symbol*] (NQ)
SAGE .... Scientific Advisory Group on Effects [*DoD*] [*Washington,
        DC*] (EGAO)
SAGE .... Semiautomatic Ground Environment [*Military*]
SAGE .... Senior Action in a Gay Environment (EA)
SAGE .... Skylab Advisory Group for Experiments [*NASA*]
SAGE .... Society for the Advancement of the George Economy
        [*Defunct*] (EA)
SAGE .... Society for the Advancement of Good English (EA)
SAGE .... Solar-Assisted Gas Energy [*Water heating*] [*NASA*]
SAGE .... South African General Electric Co.
SAGE .... Soviet-American Gallium Experiment [*Particle physics*]
SAGE .... Special Assistant for Growing Enterprises [*Division of National
        American Wholesale Grocer's Association*]
SAGE .... Sterilization Aerospace Ground Equipment (KSC)
SAGE .... Strategic Analysis Guidance and Estimate (MCD)
SAGE .... Stratospheric Aerosol Gas Experiment
Sage Annu R Communic Res ... Sage Annual Reviews of Communication
        Research [*A publication*]
Sage Elect Stud Yb ... Sage Electoral Studies Yearbook [*A publication*]
Sage Int Yb For Pol Stud ... Sage International Yearbook of Foreign Policy
        Studies [*A publication*]
Sage/JIAS ... Journal of Inter-American Studies and World Affairs. Sage
        Publication for the Center for Advanced International
        Studies. University of Miami [*A publication*]
SAGEM ..... Societe d'Applications Generals d'Electricite et de Mecanique
        [*France*]
SA Geol Atlas Ser ... South Australia. Geological Survey. Atlas Series [*A
        publication*] (APTA)
SA Geol Surv Bull ... South Australia. Geological Survey. Bulletin [*A
        publication*] (APTA)
SA Geol Surv Geol Atlas 1 Mile Ser ... South Australia. Geological Survey.
        Geological Atlas. 1 Mile Series [*A publication*] (APTA)
SA Geol Surv Rep Invest ... South Australia. Geological Survey. Report of
        Investigations [*A publication*] (APTA)
Sage Pap CP ... Sage Professional Papers in Comparative Politics [*A
        publication*]
Sage Pub Admin Abstr ... Sage Public Administration Abstracts [*A
        publication*]
SAGES ...... Society American Gastrointestinal Endoscopic Surgeons (EA)
Sage Urban Abs ... Sage Urban Abstracts [*A publication*]
Sage Urb Stud Abstr ... Sage Urban Studies Abstracts [*A publication*]
Sage Yb Polit Publ Pol ... Sage Yearbooks in Politics and Public Policy [*A
        publication*]
Sage Yb Women's Pol ... Sage Yearbook in Women's Policy Studies [*A
        publication*]
SAGFC ...... Southeastern Association of Game and Fish Commissioners
        [*Later, SAFWA*] (EA)
SAGGBS ... Salvation Army Guides and Guards, Brownies, and
        Sunbeams (EAIO)
SAGGE ...... Synchronous Altitude Gravity Gradient Experiment
Sagg Fen .... Saggi Fenici [*A publication*]
Saggi .... Saggi e Ricerche di Letteratura Francese [*A publication*]
SAGI .... South-African Garrisons Institutes [*Military*] [*British*] (ROG)
SAGI .... Specialty Advertising Guild International [*Later, SAA*] (EA)

SAGJ .... South African Geographical Journal [*A publication*]
SAGLBQ ... Acta Geographica Lodziensia [*A publication*]
SAGM .... Separate Absorption, Grading, and Multiplication Layers
        [*Semiconductor technology*]
SAGMI ...... Surface Attack Guided Missile (MCD)
SAGMN .... Sudhoffs Archiv fuer Geschichte der Medizin und der
        Naturwissenschaften [*A publication*]
SAGMOS ... Self-Aligning Gate Metal Oxide Semiconductor (IEEE)
SAGN .... Sagkeeng News [*Fort Alexander, MB*] [*A publication*]
SA-GOR .... Security Assistance - General Operational Requirement
        [*Military*] (AFIT)
SAGP .... Society for Ancient Greek Philosophy (EA)
SAGP .... Streptococcal Acidic Glycoprotein [*Antineoplastic drug*]
SAGS .... Scandinavian-American Genealogical Society (EA)
SAGS .... Semiactive Gravity-Gradient System [*NASA*]
SAGSET .... Society for Academic Gaming and Simulation in Education and
        Training
SAGT .... Scottish Association of Geography Teachers [*British*]
SAGTA ..... School and Group Travel Association (EAIO)
SAGU .... Saguaro National Monument
Sague Med ... Saguenay Medical [*A publication*]
SAGW .... Surface-to-Air Guided Weapon [*British*]
SAH .... S-Adenosylhomocysteine [*Biochemistry*]
SaH .... Saat auf Hoffnung (BJA)
SAH .... Sachem Exploration [*Vancouver Stock Exchange symbol*]
Sah .... Sahara
SAH .... Sahara Casino Partnership [*NYSE symbol*] (SPSG)
SAH .... Sanaa [*Yemen Arab Republic*] [*Airport symbol*] (OAG)
SaH .... Sandoz Pharmaceuticals [*Research code symbol*]
SAH .... School of Applied Health [*University of Texas*]
SAH .... Security Archives Holdings [*Data storage company*] [*British*]
SAH .... Semiactive Homer [*Missiles*]
SAH .... Sitzungsberichte. Heidelberg Akademie der Wissenschaften.
        Philosophisch-Historische Klasse [*A publication*]
SAH .... Society of Aeronautical Historians [*See also LHV*]
        [*Defunct*] (EAIO)
SAH .... Society of American Historians (EA)
SAH .... Society of Architectural Historians (EA)
SAH .... Society of Automotive Historians (EA)
SAH .... Standard Allowed Hours
SAH .... Stratford-On-Avon Herald [*A publication*]
SAH .... Subarachnoid Hemorrhage [*Medicine*]
SAH .... Supreme Allied Headquarters [*World War II*]
SAH .... Svenska Akademiens Handlingar [*A publication*]
SAHA .... Society of American Historical Artists (EA)
SAHA .... South Australia Hockey Association
SAHARA... Synthetic Aperture High Altitude RADAR (AAG)
SAHC .... Chosmadal [*Argentina*] [*ICAO location identifier*] (ICLI)
SAHC .... S-Adenosylhomocysteine [*Biochemistry*]
SAHC .... Self-Aligning Hydraulic Cylinder
Sah de Dem ... Sahara de Demain [*A publication*]
SAHEA ..... Sanitaer- und Heizungstechnik [*A publication*]
SAHF .... Semiautomatic Height Finder
SAHG .... Die Sumerischen und Akkadischen Hymnen und Gebete
        [*Zurich/Stuttgart*] [*A publication*]
SAH(GB)... Society of Architectural Historians (of Great Britain)
SAHH........ Society for Austrian and Habsburg History (EA)
SAHI .... Sagamore Hill National Historic Site
SAHJ .... Society of Automotive Historians. Journal [*A publication*]
SAHL .... Salvation Army Home League [*See also LF*] (EAIO)
SAHLBull ... Societe d'Art et d'Histoire du le Diocese de Liege. Bulletin [*A
        publication*]
SaHMI ...... Sachs, "History of Musical Instruments" [*A publication*]
SAHOA ..... Saiko To Hoan [*A publication*]
SA Homes & Gardens ... South Australian Homes and Gardens [*A
        publication*] (APTA)
SAHPS ..... Solar Energy Assisted Heat Pump System
SAHR .... Fuerte Gral Roca [*Argentina*] [*ICAO location identifier*] (ICLI)
SAHS........ Swedish-American Historical Society (EA)
SAHS........ Swiss-American Historical Society (EA)
SAHS........ Swiss American Historical Society. Newsletter [*A publication*]
SAHSA...... Servicio Aereo de Honduras Sociedad Anonima
SAHYB..... Simulation of Analog and Hybrid Computers
SAI .... Allstar Inns LP [*AMEX symbol*] (SPSG)
SAI .... Saigo [*Japan*] [*Seismograph station code, US Geological
        Survey*] (SEIS)
SAI .... Schizophrenics Anonymous International [*Later, Canadian
        Schizophrenia Foundation*] (EA)
SAI .... Science Applications, Incorporated (NRCH)
SAI .... Science Associates/International [*Publisher*] (EA)
SAI .... Scientific Aid to Indochina [*Task force established 1973 by
        Scientists' Institute for Public Information*]
SAI .... Scientific Associates, Incorporated (AAG)
SAI .... Scottish Agricultural Industries [*Commercial firm*]
SAI .... Scriptwriters' Association International [*Defunct*] (EA)
SAI .... Self-Actualization Inventory [*Test*]
SAI .... Self-Analysis Inventory [*Psychology*]
SAI .... Seltene Assyrische Ideogramme [*A publication*]
SAI .... Senior Advocates International [*Defunct*] (EA)
SAI .... Senior Army Instructor
SAI .... Shoplifters Anonymous International (EA)

SAI............	Sigma Alpha Iota [*International professional music fraternity for women*] (EA)
SAI............	Social Adequacy Index
SAI............	Societa Anonima Italiana [*Stock company*] [*Italian*]
SAI............	Society of American Inventors (EA)
SAI............	Software Access International, Inc. [*Information service or system*] (IID)
SAI............	Sold as Is [*Philately*]
SAI............	Son Altesse Imperiale [*His or Her Imperial Highness*] [*French*]
sai............	South American Indian [*MARC language code*] [*Library of Congress*] (LCCP)
SAI............	Southern Alberta Institute of Technology [*UTLAS symbol*]
SAI............	Special Accident Insurance (MCD)
SAI............	Specific Acoustic Impedance
SAI............	Spherical Attitude Indicator (MCD)
SAI............	Standby Airspeed [*or Attitude*] Indicator (MCD)
SAI............	State Agency Issuance [*Employment and Training Administration*] (OICC)
SAI............	Statistical Abstracts of Israel [*A publication*]
SAI............	Steering Axis Inclination [*Automotive engineering*]
SAI............	Stern Activities Index [*Psychology*]
SAI............	Subarchitectural Interface
SAI............	Suburban Action Institute [*Later, MAI*] (EA)
SAI............	Sudden Auroral Intensity
SAI............	Sugar Association, Incorporated (EA)
SAI............	Sun Air International [*Ft. Lauderdale, FL*] [*FAA designator*] (FAAC)
SAI............	Surveillance Aided Intercept (NVT)
SAI............	System Analysis Indicator (MCD)
SAIA..........	Survival of American Indians Association (EA)
SAIAS	Ship Aircraft Inertial Alignment System (NG)
SAIB	Safe Area Intelligence Brief (MCD)
SAIB	Societe Arabe Internationale de Banque [*Bank*] [*Egyptian*]
SAIB	Sucrose Acetate Isobutyrate [*Organic chemistry*]
Saibanshu ..	Saiko Saibansho Saibanshu [*A publication*]
SAIBB	Soil Association. Information Bulletin and Advisory Service [*A publication*]
SAIC..........	School of the Art Institute of Chicago
SAIC........	Science Applications International Corp.
SAIC........	Small Arms Interpost Competition [*Military*]
SAIC........	South African Indian Congress (PD)
SAIC........	South Australian Industrial Commission
SAIC........	Special Agent in Charge [*Department of the Treasury*]
SAIC..........	State Administration for Industry and Commerce [*People's Republic of China*] (IMH)
SAIPL	Switch Action Interrupt Count
SAICAR	Succinoaminoimidazolecarboxamide Ribonucleotide [*Biochemistry*]
SAICDB	Israel. Institute of Field and Garden Crops. Scientific Activities [*A publication*]
SAICETT ..	South African Institute of Civil Engineering Technicians and Technologists (EAIO)
SAICt........	South Australian Industrial Court
SAID..........	Safe Area Intelligence Description (MCD)
SAID..........	Safety Analysis Input Data [*Nuclear energy*] (NRCH)
SAID..........	Semiautomatic Integrated Documentation
SAID..........	Specific Adaptation to Improved Demands [*Sports medicine*]
SAID..........	Speech Auto-Instructional Device
SAID..........	Supplementary Aviation Information Display
SAIDET	Single-Axis Inertial Drift Erection Test
Said Med J ...	Said Medical Journal [*A publication*]
SAIDS	Simian Acquired Immunodeficiency Syndrome [*Animal pathology*]
SAIDS	Space Analyst Intervention Display System (MCD)
SAIE	Source and Application Inspection Equipment
SAIE	Special Acceptance Inspection Equipment
SAIEDH....	Israel. Institute of Agricultural Engineering. Scientific Activities [*A publication*]
SAIF	Savings Association Insurance Fund [*Functions transferred from FSLIC, 1989*] [*Pronounced "safe"*]
SAIF	Standard Avionics Integrated Fuzing [*Air Force*]
SAIFER.....	Safe Arm Initiation from Electromagnetic Radiation
SAIG..........	SAI Group, Inc. [*NASDAQ symbol*] (NQ)
SAIG..........	South Australian Industrial Gazette [*A publication*] (APTA)
SAIGA.......	Saishin Igaku [*A publication*]
SAIGB.......	Sangyo Igaku [*A publication*]
SAIHDO ...	Israel. Institute of Horticulture. Scientific Activities [*A publication*]
SAII	Sage Analytics International, Incorporated [*Provo, UT*] [*NASDAQ symbol*] (NQ)
SAIIC	South and Central American Indian Information Center (EA)
SA III VC ..	3rd Sussex Artillery Volunteer Corps [*British military*] (DMA)
SAIL..........	Sea-Air Interaction Laboratory [*Oceanography*]
SAIL..........	Ship's Armament Inventory List [*Navy*]
SAIL..........	Shuttle Avionics Integration Laboratory [*NASA*]
SAIL..........	Simple Analytical Interactive Language [*Data processing*]
SAIL..........	Stanford Artificial Intelligence Laboratory [*Stanford University*]
SAIL..........	Survey of Australian Interlibrary Lending
SAILA	Sail Assist International Liaison Associates (EA)
SAILA	Sault Area International Library Association [*Library network*]
SAILEDREP ...	Sailing Report [*Navy*] (NVT)
SAILER.....	Staffing of African Institutions for Legal Education and Research [*An association*] [*Later, International Legal Center*]
SAILORD ...	Sailing Order [*Navy*] (NVT)
SAILREP ..	Sailing Report [*Navy*]
SAILS.......	Seagoing Assembly-Integration-Launch System
SAILS.......	Simplified Aircraft Instrument Landing System
SAILS.......	Standard Army Intermediate Level Supply System [*or Subsystem*]
SAIM........	Scottish Amicable Investment Managers [*Finance*]
SAIM........	South America Indian Mission [*Later, SAM*] (EA)
SAIM........	Systems Analysis and Integration Model (MCD)
SAIMR......	South African Institute for Medical Research
SAIMS	Selected Acquisitions, Information, and Management System
SAIMS	Supersonic Airborne Infrared Measurement System (MCD)
SAIN........	Society for Advancement in Nursing (EA)
SAIN..........	Systems Associates, Incorporated [*NASDAQ symbol*] (NQ)
Sainan-G-D ...	Sainan-Gakuin-Daigaku (BJA)
Sains Malays ...	Sains Malaysiana [*Malaysia*] [*A publication*]
SA Inst J	South Australian Institutes. Journal [*A publication*] (APTA)
Saint........	Saint's Digest of Registration Cases [*England*] [*A publication*] (DLA)
SAINT	Salzburg Assembly: Impact of the New Technology
SAINT	Satellite Array for International and National Telecommunications (MCD)
SAINT	Satellite Inspection Technique (MCD)
SAINT	Satellite Inspector and Satellite Interceptor [*Air Force spacecraft program*]
SAINT	Satellite Interceptor (KSC)
SAINT	Strategic Artificially Intelligent Nuclear Transport [*Robot series designation in 1986 movie "Short Circuit"*]
SAINT	Symbolic Automatic Integrator
SAINT	Systems Analysis of an Integrated Network of Tasks [*Air Force*]
Saint Lawrence Univ Geol Inf and Referral Service Bull ...	Saint Lawrence University. Geological Information and Referral Service. Bulletin [*A publication*]
Saint Louis Univ LJ ...	St. Louis University. Law Journal [*A publication*]
SAINTS......	Single Attack Integrated System
SAIORG....	Supreme Assembly, International Order of Rainbow for Girls [*Freemasonry*] (EA)
SAIP	Ship Acquisition and Improvement Panel [*Navy*] (CAAL)
SAIP	Societe d'Applications Industrielle de la Physique
SAIP	Spares Acquisition Integrated with Production
SAIPL	Submarine Antenna Improvement Program [*Military*]
SAIPL	Spares Acquisition Incorporated with Production List (MCD)
SAIPMS ...	Science Applications Incorporated Plan Monitoring System
SAIR.........	Saugus Ironworks National Historic Site
SAIR.........	Semiannual Inventory Report [*Military*] (AFM)
SAIR.........	South Australian Industrial Reports [*A publication*] (APTA)
Sairaanh Vuosik ...	Sairaanhoidon Vuosikirja [*A publication*]
SAIRR	South African Institute of Racial Relations
SAIS	School of Advanced International Studies
SAIS	Societa Agricola Italo-Somala [*Italo-Somali Agricultural Society*]
SAIS	Society for American Indian Studies (EA)
SAIS	Southwestern American Indian Society [*Later, SAISR*] (EA)
SAISA	South Atlantic Intercollegiate Sailing Association
SAISAC.....	Ship's Aircraft Inertial System Alignment Console
SAISB.......	South African Individual Scale for the Blind [*Intelligence test*]
SAISDP.....	Israel. Institute of Animal Science. Scientific Activities [*A publication*]
SAISR........	Society for American Indian Studies and Research [*Formerly, SAIS*] (EA)
SAIS Rev ...	SAIS [*School of Advanced International Studies*] Review [*A publication*]
SAIT	Southern Alberta Institute of Technology [*Calgary, AB*]
SAIT News ...	SAIT [*South Australian Institute of Teachers*] Newsletter [*A publication*] (APTA)
Sait Not......	Saitabi. Noticiario de Historia, Arte, y Arqueologia de Levante [*A publication*]
Saito Ho-On Kai Mus Nat Hist Res Bull ...	Saito Ho-On Kai Museum of Natural History. Research Bulletin [*A publication*]
Saito Ho-On Kai Mus Res Bull ...	Saito Ho-On Kai Museum Research Bulletin [*A publication*]
SAITR	Special Artificer, Instruments, Typewriter, and Office Equipment Repairman [*Navy*]
SAIW.........	Sun Artificial Intelligence Workstation
SAIWR.......	Special Artificer, Instruments, Watch Repairman [*Navy*]
SAJ............	Golden Eagle Aviation [*Bedford, MA*] [*FAA designator*] (FAAC)
SA/J	Journal. Societe des Americanistes [*A publication*]
SAJ............	St. Joseph Light & Power Co. [*NYSE symbol*] (SPSG)
SAJ............	Saints Alive in Jesus (EA)
SAJ............	Salon Resources Corp. [*Vancouver Stock Exchange symbol*]
SAJ............	Society for the Advancement of Judaism (EA)
SAJ............	South African Journal of Economics [*Suid-Afrikaanse Tydskrif vir Ekonomie*] [*A publication*]
SAJA	Special Approaches to Juvenile Assistance [*Defunct*] (EA)
SAJAA	South African Journal of African Affairs [*A publication*]
SAJAC.......	South African Journal of Animal Science [*A publication*]

SAJAR ...... South African Journal of Antarctic Research [*A publication*]
SAJBDD ... Suid-Afrikaanse Tydskrif vir Plantkunde [*A publication*]
SAJCD ..... South African Journal of Chemistry [*A publication*]
SAJE .... South African Journal of Economics [*Suid-Afrikaanse Tydskrif vir Ekonomie*] [*A publication*]
SA J Educ Res ... South Australian Journal of Education Research [*A publication*] (APTA)
SAJER....... South Australian Journal of Education Research [*A publication*] (APTA)
SAJH........ San Juan Island National Historic Park
SAJI.......... Saw Jig [*Tool*]
SAJIB....... Societe d'Animation du Jardin et de l'Institut Botaniques [*Canada*]
SAJL........ Studies in American Jewish Literature [*A publication*]
SAJMA ..... South African Journal of Medical Sciences [*A publication*]
SAJPA...... South African Journal of Physiotherapy [*A publication*]
SAJPEM... Suid-Afrikaanse Tydskrif vir Wysbegeerte [*A publication*]
SAJRA...... South African Journal of Radiology [*A publication*]
SAJ Res Sport Phys Educ Recreat ... SA [*South African*] Journal for Research in Sport. Physical Education and Recreation [*A publication*]
SAJS......... School for Advanced Jewish Studies (BJA)
SAJS......... South African Journal of Science [*A publication*]
SAJSA ...... South African Journal of Science [*A publication*]
SAJSB ...... South African Journal of Surgery [*A publication*]
SAJSEV .... Suid-Afrikaanse Tydskrif vir Plant en Grond [*A publication*]
SAJTA...... South African Journal of Medical Laboratory Technology [*A publication*]
SAJZD ...... South African Journal of Zoology [*A publication*]
SAK .... Die Sumerischen und Akkadischen Koeningsinschriften [*A publication*] (BJA)
SAK .... Kalispell, MT [*Location identifier*] [*FAA*] (FAAL)
SAK .... Sakata [*Japan*] [*Seismograph station code, US Geological Survey*] (SEIS)
SAK .... Saudarkrokur [*Iceland*] [*Airport symbol*] (OAG)
SAK .... Stall Lake Mines [*Vancouver Stock Exchange symbol*]
SAK .... Stop Acknowledge (CMD)
SAK .... Sveriges Arbetarepartiet Kommunisterna [*Swedish Workers' Communist Party*] [*Political party*] (PPW)
SAK .... University of Saskatchewan Libraries [*UTLAS symbol*]
SAKAD...... Sangyo To Kankyo [*A publication*]
SAKB........ Suider Afrikaanse Katolieke Biskopsraad [*Southern African Catholic Bishops' Conference - SACBC*] (EAIO)
Sakharth SSR Mecn Akad Gamothvl Centr Srom ... Sakharthvelos SSR Mecnierebatha Akademia Gamothvlithi Centris Sromebi [*A publication*]
Sakharth SSR Mecn Akad Marthw Sistem Inst Srom ... Sakharthvelos SSR Mecnierebatha Akademia Marthwis Sistemebis Instituti Sromebi [*A publication*]
Sakharth SSR Mecn Akad Math Inst Srom ... Sakharthvelos SSR Mecnierebatha Akademia A. Razmadzis Sahelobis Thbilsis Mathematikis Institutis Sromebi [*A publication*]
Sakharth SSR Mecn Akad Moambe ... Sakharthvelos SSR Mecnierebatha Akademia Moambe [*A publication*]
SAKHB...... Sangyo Anzen Kenkyusho Hokoku [*A publication*]
Sakh Prom ... Sakharnaya Promyshlennost [*A publication*]
Sakh Promst ... Sakharnaya Promyshlennost [*A publication*]
Sakh Svekla ... Sakharnaya Svekla [*A publication*]
SAKI......... Solatron Automatic Keyboard Instructor
SAKOD ..... Sangyo Kogai [*A publication*]
SAKSO...... Collective name of Soren Frandsen, Asbjorn Jensen, Kurt Frederiksen, Soren Lundh, and Ole Rud Nielsen when writing in collaboration
Sakura X-Ray Photogr Rev ... Sakura X-Ray Photographic Review [*Japan*] [*A publication*]
SAL........... Anderson County Library, Anderson, SC [*OCLC symbol*] (OCLC)
SAL........... Saharan Air Layer [*Meteorology*]
SAL........... Salary (ADA)
SAL........... Sales and Marketing Management [*A publication*]
Sal .... Salesianum [*A publication*]
Sal .... [*Bartholomaeus de*] Saliceto [*Deceased, 1411*] [*Authority cited in pre-1607 legal work*] (DSA)
sal.............. Salicylate [*Medicine*]
SAL........... Saline
Sal .... Salinger's Reports [*88-117 Iowa*] [*A publication*] (DLA)
SAL........... Salinometer (KSC)
sal.............. Salishan [*MARC language code*] [*Library of Congress*] (LCCP)
SAL........... Salivation [*Treatment for syphilis*] [*Slang*] [*British*] (DSUE)
sal.............. Salmon [*Philately*]
Sal .... Salmonella [*Bacteriology*]
SAL........... Salo [*Italy*] [*Seismograph station code, US Geological Survey*] (SEIS)
SAL........... Saluting (MSA)
SAL........... Salvation Army Shelter (DSUE)
SAL........... Salvex Resources Ltd. [*Vancouver Stock Exchange symbol*]
SAL........... San Salvador [*El Salvador*] [*Airport symbol*] (OAG)
SAL........... Sandhills Agriculture Laboratory [*University of Nebraska - Lincoln*] [*Research center*] (RCD)
SAL........... Saperstein & Associates Limited [*Vancouver, BC*] [*Telecommunications*] (TSSD)

SAL........... School of Australian Linguistics [*Darwin Community College*] [*Australia*]
SAL........... Scientific Airlock (MCD)
SAL........... Seaboard Air Line R. R. [*Later, SCL*] [*AAR code*]
SAL........... Secundum Artis Leges [*According to the Rules of the Art*] [*Latin*] (ADA)
SAL........... Selected Altitude Layer [*Decoder*]
SAL........... Semiactive LASER [*Military*] (CAAL)
SAL........... Sensorineural Acuity Level [*Medicine*]
SAL........... Service Action Log (AAG)
SAL........... Ship Authorized Leave (NG)
SAL........... Shipboard Allowance List (MSA)
SAL........... Short Approach Light [*Aviation*]
SAL........... Shuttle Avionics Laboratory [*NASA*] (NASA)
SAL........... Solar Age. A Magazine of the Sun [*A publication*]
SAL........... Solar Arc Lamp
SAL........... Solar Array Leaf
SAL........... Sons of the American Legion (EA)
SAL........... South Atlantic League [*Nickname: Sally*] [*Baseball*]
SAL........... Southern Airlines [*Australia*]
SAL........... Southwestern American Literature [*A publication*]
SAL........... Space Astronomy Laboratory [*University of Florida*] [*Research center*] (RCD)
SAL........... Special Ammunition Load [*Army*] (AABC)
SAL........... Standard Acceptance Limits
SAL........... Station Allowance Unit (NATG)
SAL........... Strategic Arms Limitation
SAL........... Structural Adjustment Loan [*World Bank*]
SAL........... Structured Assembly Language
SAL........... Studies in African Linguistics [*A publication*]
SAL........... Subject Authority List [*NASA*]
SAL........... Submarine Alerting and Loading System
SAL........... Suid-Afrikaanse Lugmag [*South African Air Force*] [*See also SALM, SAAF*]
SAL........... Supersonic Aerophysics Laboratory (MCD)
SAL........... Surface Mail Air Lifted (ADA)
SAL........... Symbolic Assembly Language [*Data processing*] (DIT)
SAL........... System Access Layer [*Data processing*]
SAL........... Systems Assembly Language [*Data processing*] (IEEE)
SALA .... Sammenslutningen af Landbrugets Arbejdsgiverforeninger [*Agricultural Employers' Federation*] [*Denmark*] (EY)
SALA .... Scientific Assistant Land Agent [*Ministry of Agriculture, Fisheries, and Food*] [*British*]
SALA .... Servicios Aeronauticos Latina America
SALA .... Solar Arc Lamp Assembly
SALA .... Southwest Alliance for Latin America (EA)
SALALM .. Seminar on the Acquisition of Latin American Library Materials (EA)
SA Law Reports CP ... South African Law Reports, Cape Provincial Division [*1910-46*] [*A publication*] (DLA)
SA Law Reports CPD ... South African Law Reports, Cape Provincial Division [*1910-46*] [*A publication*] (DLA)
SA Law Reports NPD ... South African Law Reports, Natal Province Division [*1910-46*] [*A publication*] (DLA)
SA Law Reports SWA ... Reports of the High Court of South-West Africa [*A publication*] (DLA)
SA Law Soc Bull ... South Australian Law Society. Bulletin [*A publication*] (APTA)
SALB .... Studia Albanica [*A publication*]
SALC .... Sacramento Air Logistics Center (NASA)
SALC .... SAL Cable Communications [*NASDAQ symbol*] (NQ)
SALC .... Special Associated Logistics Course (MCD)
Sal Comp Cr ... Salaman's Liquidation and Composition with Creditors [*2nd ed.*] [*1882*] [*A publication*] (DLA)
SALCR ...... South Australian Licensing Court. Reports [*A publication*] (APTA)
SALCV ...... Solanum Apical Leaf-Curling Virus
Saldat Auto ... Saldatura Autogena [*A publication*]
SALDV ...... Salvage Dive [*Military*] (MUGU)
SALE .... Safeguards Analytical Laboratory Evaluation [*Nuclear energy*]
SALE .... Silicon Avalanche Light Emitter
SALE .... Simple Algebraic Language for Engineers [*Data processing*]
SALE .... Special Ammunition Logistical Element
SALEA ...... Sanshi Kenkyu [*A publication*]
SALES ...... Ship Aircraft Locating Equipment
Sales Mgt... Sales Management [*Later, Sales and Marketing Management*] [*A publication*]
Sales & Mkt Mgt ... Sales and Marketing Management [*A publication*]
Sales TC .... Sales Tax Cases [*A publication*] (APTA)
SALF .... Society of American Legion Founders (EA)
SALF .... Somali Abo Liberation Front [*Ethiopia*] (PD)
SALF .... Sudan African Liberation Front
SALG .... South American Liaison Group (CINC)
SALGEP.... Scottish Association of Local Government to Educational Psychologists [*British*]
SAL-GP..... Semiactive LASER-Guided Projectile (MCD)
SALH .... South Alberta Light Horse (DMA)
Sali .... [*Bartholomaeus de*] Saliceto [*Deceased, 1411*] [*Authority cited in pre-1607 legal work*] (DSA)
SALI .... Selected Abstracts: Library, Information [*Australia*] [*A publication*]

SALI .... Suburban Airlines, Incorporated [*NASDAQ symbol*]   (NQ)
SALI .... Surface Analysis by LASER Ionization
SALIA7 ..... Ernaehrungswissenschaft [*A publication*]
Salic .... [*Bartholomaeus de*] Saliceto [*Deceased, 1411*] [*Authority cited in pre-1607 legal work*]   (DSA)
SALIC .... Salicional [*Music*]
Salice.......... [*Bartholomaeus de*] Saliceto [*Deceased, 1411*] [*Authority cited in pre-1607 legal work*]   (DSA)
SALINET ... Satellite Library Information Network
SALIS .... Salisbury [*England*]
SALIS........ Substance Abuse Librarians and Information Specialists   (EA)
Salisbury Med Bull ... Salisbury Medical Bulletin [*A publication*]
Salisbury Rev ... Salisbury Review [*A publication*]
SALit .... Studies in American Literature [*Chu Shikoku*] [*A publication*]
SA L J .... South African Law Journal [*A publication*]
Salk .... Salkeld's English King's Bench Reports [*91 English Reprint*] [*A publication*]   (DLA)
Salk (Eng) ... Salkeld's English King's Bench Reports [*91 English Reprint*] [*A publication*]   (DLA)
SALL .... Sallust [*Roman historian, 86-34BC*] [*Classical studies*]   (ROG)
SALL .... Shore Activity Load List
SALLB....... South Australian Law Librarians Bulletin [*A publication*]
SALLIE MAE ... Student Loan Marketing Association [*See also SLMA*]
Salm .... Salmagundi [*A publication*]
Salm .... Salmanassar   (BJA)
Salm .... Salmanticensis [*A publication*]
SALM....... Salvation Army League of Mercy [*London, England*]   (EAIO)
SALM....... Single Anchor Leg Mooring [*Oil platform*]
SALM....... Society of Air Line Meteorologists
Salm Abr.... Salmon's Abridgment of State Trials [*A publication*]   (DLA)
Salmant...... Salmanticensis [*Salmanca, Spain*] [*A publication*]   (BJA)
Salmon Trou Mag ... Salmon and Trout Magazine [*A publication*]
Salmon Trout Mag ... Salmon and Trout Magazine [*A publication*]
Salm St R... Salmon's Edition of the State Trials [*A publication*]   (DLA)
SALN......... Sahlen & Associates, Inc. [*Deerfield Beach, FL*] [*NASDAQ symbol*]   (NQ)
SALO......... State Aviation Liaison Official   (NOAA)
SALO......... Stop Authorization and Lift Order   (AAG)
SALOP ...... Shrewsbury [*British depot code*]
SALOP ...... Shropshire [*County in England*]
SALORS ... Structural Analysis of Layered Orthotropic Ring-Stiffened Shells [*Computer program*] [*NASA*]
SALP .... Sodium Aluminum Phosphate [*Inorganic chemistry*]
SALP .... South African Labour Party
SALP .... Systematic Assessment of Licensee Performance [*Nuclear energy*]   (NRCH)
Sal Publ ..... Salud Publica [*A publication*]
SALR .... Saturation Adiabatic Lapse Rate [*Meteorology*]   (ADA)
SALR .... South African Law Reports [*A publication*]
SALR .... South Australian Law Reports [*A publication*]   (APTA)
SALR .... Synthetic Aperture LASER RADAR
SALRA ...... Schweizer Aluminium Rundschau [*A publication*]
SALRCP.... South African Law Reports, Cape Provincial Division [*1910-46*] [*A publication*]   (DLA)
SAL Reports OPD ... South African Law Reports, Orange Free State Provincial Division [*1910-46*] [*A publication*]   (DLA)
SALR SWA ... South African Law Reports, South West African Reports [*A publication*]   (DLA)
SALS .... Short Approach Light System [*Aviation*]
SALS .... Small-Angle Light Scattering
SALS .... Solid-State Acoustoelectric Light Scanner
SALS .... Southern Adirondack Library System [*Library network*]
SALS .... Southern African Literature Society   (EAIO)
SALS .... Standard Army Logistics System
SALSF....... Short Approach Light System with Sequenced Flashers [*Aviation*]
SALS-K ..... Single Ammunition Logistics System - Korea   (MCD)
SALSSAH ... Serials in Australian Libraries: Social Sciences and Humanities [*A publication*]   (APTA)
SALSSAH/NRT ... Serials in Australian Libraries: Social Sciences and Humanities/Newly Reported Titles [*A publication*]   (APTA)
SALSU ...... Singapore Admiralty Local Staff Union
SaLSUA .... Sierra Leone Students Union of the Americas   (EA)
Salt............. De Saltatione [*of Lucian*] [*Classical studies*]   (OCD)
SALT .... Saltash [*England*]
SALT .... Salvation and Laughter Together   (EA)
SALT .... Self-Contained All-Weather Landing and Taxiing   (MCD)
SALT .... Serum Alanine Aminotransferase [*An enzyme*]
SALT .... Sisters All Learning Together [*Feminist group*]
SALT .... Skin-Associated Lymphoid Tissue [*Dermatology*]
SALT .... Society of American Law Teachers   (EA)
SALT .... Society for Applied Learning Technology   (EA)
SALT .... South African Law Times [*A publication*]   (DLA)
SALT .... South Australian Library Technicians [*Committee*]
SALT .... State Agency Libraries of Texas [*Library network*]
SALT .... Subscribers' Apparatus Line Tester [*Telecommunications*]   (TEL)
SALT .... Symbolic Algebraic Language Translator [*Data processing*]
SALTA ...... South Australian Lawn Tennis Association
Salt C R...... New Salt Creek Reader [*A publication*]

SALTE ...... Semiautomatic Line Test Equipment   (NG)
SalTerz ...... Sal Terrae. Revista Hispanoamericana de Cultura Ecclesiastica [*Santander, Spain*] [*A publication*]   (BJA)
SALTHQ... Strike Command Alternate Headquarters [*Military*]   (AABC)
SALTI........ Summary Accounting for Low-Dollar Turnover Items [*Army*]
Salt Lake Min Rev ... Salt Lake Mining Review [*A publication*]
Salt Lake M Rv ... Salt Lake Mining Review [*A publication*]
Salt Lk Tr .. Salt Lake City Tribune [*A publication*]
SALT-P ...... Slosson Articulation, Language Test with Phonology [*Child development test*]
Salt Res Ind ... Salt Research and Industry [*A publication*]
Salt Res Ind J ... Salt Research and Industry Journal [*A publication*]
SALTS........ Systems Alterations Status
Salud Ocup ... Salud Ocupacional [*A publication*]
Salud Publica Mex ... Salud Publica de Mexico [*A publication*]
SALUT....... Sea, Air, Land, and Underwater Targets [*Navy*]
SALUTE ... Size, Activity, Location, Unit, Time, Equipment   (MCD)
Salute Italia Med ... Salute Italia Medica [*A publication*]
SALV .... Duty Salvage Ship [*Navy*]   (NVT)
SALV .... Salvador [*Brazil*]   (ROG)
SALV .... Salvage [*Military*]   (AFM)
Salvav........ Salvavidas [*A publication*]
Salv Div Bad ... Salvage Diver Badge [*Military decoration*]
SALVDV ... Salvage Dives [*Army*]
SALVEX ... Salvage Exercise   (MCD)
SALVOPS ... Salvage Operations [*Navy*]   (NVT)
SALVTNG ... Salvage Training [*Navy*]   (NVT)
SALWIS.... Shipboard Air-Launched Weapons Installation System   (NG)
SALX .... Shamrock Airlines [*Air carrier designation symbol*]
SALY .... Salary   (ROG)
Salzburger Beitr Paracelsusforsch ... Salzburger Beitraege zur Paracelsusforschung [*A publication*]
Salzburger Jrbh Phil ... Salzburger Jahrbuch fuer Philosophie [*A publication*]
Salzburg Haus Nat Ber Abt B Geol-Mineral Samml ... Salzburg Haus der Natur. Berichte. Abteilung B. Geologisch-Mineralogische Sammlungen [*A publication*]
Salz St Ang ... Salzburger Studien zur Anglistik und Amerikanistik [*A publication*]
SAM .... S-Adenosylmethionine [*Also, AdoMet, SAMe*] [*Biochemistry*]
SAM .... Safety Activation Monitor   (IEEE)
SAM .... Salamo [*Papua New Guinea*] [*Airport symbol*]   (OAG)
SAM .... Salicylamide [*Analgesic compound*]
SAM .... SAM [*Society for Advancement of Management*] Advanced Management Journal [*A publication*]
Sam .... Samaria   (BJA)
Sam .... Samaritan   (BJA)
sam .... Samaritan Aramaic [*MARC language code*] [*Library of Congress*]   (LCCP)
SAM .... Samarkand [*USSR*] [*Seismograph station code, US Geological Survey*]   (SEIS)
Sam .... Samisdat [*A publication*]
Sam .... Sammlung [*A publication*]
SAM .... Sample and Analysis Management System [*Data processing*]
SAM .... Sampling and Analytical Method
Sam .... Samson   (BJA)
SAM .... Samson Energy Co. LP [*AMEX symbol*]   (SPSG)
SAM .... Samsville, IL [*Location identifier*] [*FAA*]   (FAAL)
Sam .... Samuel [*Old Testament book*]
SAM .... Scanning Acoustic Microscope
SAM .... Scanning Auger Microscopy
SAM .... School of Aerospace Medicine [*Formerly, School of Aviation Medicine*]
SAM .... School in Agency Management [*LIMRA*]
SAM .... School Apperception Method [*Psychology*]
SAM .... School of Assets Management [*Army*] [*Later, School of Materiel Readiness*]
SAM .... School Attitude Measure [*Test*] [*Canadian Comprehensive Assessment Program*]
S Am .... Scientific American [*A publication*]
SAM .... Screen Activated Machine [*Parimutuel wagering*]
SAM .... Script Applier Mechanism [*Programming language*] [*1975*]   (CSR)
SAM .... Sea Air Mariner
SAM .... Selective Automatic Monitoring
SAM .... Self-Assembled Monolayer [*Physical chemistry*]
SAM .... Self-Propelled Anthropomorphic Manipulator [*Moon machine*]
SAM .... Semantic Analyzing Machine
SAM .... Semiautomatic Mathematics   (IEEE)
SAM .... Semiautomatic Mounter [*3M Co.*]
SAM .... Send-a-Message   (MCD)
SAM .... Sensing with Active Microwave
SAM .... Sequential Access Memory [*Data processing*]   (IEEE)
SAM .... Sequential Access Method [*IBM Corp.*] [*Data processing*]
SAM .... Serial Access Memory [*Data processing*]
SAM .... Service Aggregated Module
SAM .... Service Attitude Measurement [*Bell System*]
Sam .... Serving Advertising in the Midwest [*Later, Adweek*] [*A publication*]
SAM .... Sex Arousal Mechanism [*Medicine*]
SAM .... Shared Appreciation Mortgage [*Banking*]
SAM .... Shuttle Attachment Manipulator [*NASA*]

SAM .... Signal Analyzing Monitor   (KSC)
SAM .... Signal [*System*] for Assessment and Modification [*of behavior*] [*Patented*]
SAM .... Simple Architecture Microprocessor
SAM .... Simulated Assignment Model
SAM .... Simulation of Analog Methods [*Data processing*]
SAM .... Single Application Method [*College admissions*]
SAM .... Sinusoidal Amplitude Modulation [*Physics*]
SAM .... Sitzungsberichte. Bayerische Akademie der Wissenschaften [*Munich*] [*A publication*]
SAM .... Sociedad Aeronautica de Medellin Consolidada [*Colombia*]
SAM .... Societe des Americanistes
SAM .... Society for Adolescent Medicine   (EA)
SAM .... Society for Advancement of Management [*Cincinnati, OH*]   (EA)
SAM .... Society of American Magicians   (EA)
SAM .... Society of Americanists [*Paris, France*]   (EA)
SAM .... Society of Antique Modelers   (EA)
SAM .... Society for Asian Music   (EA)
SAM .... Soldier, Sailor, Airman, Marine [*A publication*]
SAM .... Sort and Merge
SAM .... Sound Absorption Material [*Aviation*]
SAM .... Sourcebook in Applied Mathematics [*National Science Foundation project*]
SAM .... South America Mission   (EA)
SAM .... South American   (AIA)
SAM .... Southern Appalachian Migrant [*Cincinnati slang*]
SAM .... Space Available Mail [*Military*]   (AABC)
SAM .... Special Advisory Message
SAM .... Special Air Mission [*Aircraft*] [*Military*]
SAM .... Spills, Accidents, and Mixtures [*of Exxon Corp.'s "Stop SAM" safety program*]
SAM .... Spinal Analysis Machine
SAM .... Squarewave Amplitude Modulation
SAM .... Stabilized Assay Meter   (NRCH)
SAM .... Stage Assembly and Maintenance [*Building*]
SAM .... Standard Addition Method [*Mathematics*]
SAM .... Standard Assembly Module [*Eastman Kodak Co.*]
SAM .... Stimuli and Measurements   (KSC)
SAM .... Strachey and McIlroy [*in SAM/76, a programming language named after its authors and developed in 1976*]   (CSR)
SAM .... Stratospheric Aerosol Measurement [*or Monitor*] [*Meteorology*]
SAM .... Strela Antiaircraft Missiles
SAM .... Stroboscopic Analyzing Monitor [*Instrumentation*]
SAMCU ..... Structural Acoustic Monitor
SAM .... Structural Assembly Model [*NASA*]
SAM .... Student Achievement Monitoring [*Vocational guidance*]
SAM .... Studies in Applied Mechanics [*Elsevier Book Series*] [*A publication*]
SAM .... Study of American Markets [*US News and World Report*]
SAM .... Subject Activity Monitor [*Device used in biological research*]
SAM .... Subsequent Address Message [*Telecommunications*]   (TEL)
SAM .... Substitute Alloy Material [*Nuclear energy*]
SAM .... Substrate Adhesion Molecule [*Cytology*]
SAM .... Substrate-Attached Material [*Cytology*]
SAM .... Subsynoptic Advection Model
SAM .... Subtraction, Addition, Multiplication
SAM .... Sulfur-Asphalt Module [*Road-paving technology*]
SAM .... Surface-Active Material
SAM .... Surface-to-Air Missile
SAM .... Symbolic and Algebraic Manipulation   (IEEE)
SAM .... Synchronous Amplitude Modulation
SAM .... System Accuracy Model
SAM .... System Activity Monitor [*Data processing*]
SAM .... System for Automatic Message Switching [*Telecommunications*]   (TSSD)
SAM .... Systems Adapter Module
SAM .... Systems Analysis Module   (IEEE)
SAM .... Systolic Anterior Motion [*Cardiology*]
SAMA .... Gral Alvear [*Argentina*] [*ICAO location identifier*]   (ICLI)
SAMA .... Sacramento Air Materiel Area
SAMA .... Salem Maritime National Historic Site
SAMA .... Saudi Arabian Monetary Agency [*Riyadh*]
SAMA .... Scientific Apparatus Makers Association [*Later, SAMAGA*]   (EA)
SAMA .... Serum Agar Measuring Aid
SAMA .... Site Approval and Market Analysis [*FHA*]
SAMA .... South Australian Mining Association
SAMA .... Specialty Automotive Manufacturers Association [*Newport Beach, CA*]   (EA)
SAMA .... Student American Medical Association [*Later, AMSA*]   (EA)
SAMA .... Survey of Adults and Markets of Affluence [*Monroe Mendelsohn Research, Inc.*] [*Information service or system*]   (CRD)
SAMAA..... Special Assistant for Military Assistance Affairs [*Army*]   (AABC)
SAMAC..... Scientific and Management Advisory Committee [*Terminated, 1973*] [*Army Computer Systems Command*]
SAMAC..... Swedish American Museum Association of Chicago   (EA)

SAM Advanced Mgt J ... SAM [*Society for Advancement of Management*] Advanced Management Journal [*A publication*]
SAM Adv Man ... SAM [*Society for Advancement of Management*] Advanced Management Journal [*A publication*]
SAMAE..... Southern Air Materiel Area, Europe
SAMAGA ... SAMA [*Scientific Apparatus Makers Association*] Group of Associations   (EA)
SAMANTHA ... System for the Automated Management of Text from a Hierarchical Arrangement
SAMAP..... Southern Air Materiel Area, Pacific [*Army*]   (AFIT)
SAMAR..... Ship Activation, Maintenance, and Repair
SAMAR..... Surface-to-Air Missile Availability Report   (NG)
Samaru Agric Newsl ... Samaru Agricultural Newsletter [*A publication*]
Samaru Agr Newslett ... Samaru Agricultural Newsletter [*A publication*]
Samaru Inst Agric Res Soil Surv Bull ... Samaru Institute for Agricultural Research. Soil Survey Bulletin [*A publication*]
Samaru Misc Pap ... Samaru Miscellaneous Paper [*A publication*]
Samaru Res Bull ... Samaru Research Bulletin [*A publication*]
SAMAS..... Security Assistance Manpower Accounting System   (MCD)
SA Mast Build ... South Australian Master Builder [*A publication*]
SAM-B..... School of Aviation [*later, Aerospace*] Medicine - Brooks
SAMB....... Secondary Aircraft Maintenance Base
SAMBA..... Saudi American Bank
SAMBA..... Special Agents Mutual Benefit Association [*FBI standardized term*]
SAMBA..... Systems Approach to Managing BUSHIPS [*Bureau of Ships; later, NESC or ESC*] Acquisition [*Navy*]   (MCD)
Sambalpur Univ J Sci Technol ... Sambalpur University. Journal of Science and Technology [*A publication*]
SAMBHist ... Societe des Antiquaires de la Morinie. Bulletin Historique [*A publication*]
Sam BN...... Samuel Butler Newsletter [*A publication*]
SAMBO..... Strategic Antimissile Barrage Objects
SAMBUD ... System for Automation of Materiel Plan for Army Materiel/ Budget   (AABC)
SAMC....... Cristo Redentor [*Argentina*] [*ICAO location identifier*]   (ICLI)
SAMC....... Solar Age Industries, Inc. [*Albuquerque, NM*] [*NASDAQ symbol*]   (NQ)
SAMC....... South African Medical Corps
SAMC....... Southern Africa Media Center   (EA)
SamChron ... Samaritan Chronology   (BJA)
SAMCO .... Sales Associates Management Corporation [*Palm Springs, CA*]   (EA)
SAMCOS .. Senior Army Materiel Command Orientation Seminar
SAMCTT .. School of Aerospace Medicine Color Threshold Test
SAMCU..... Special Airborne Medical Care Unit   (MCD)
SAMD ...... Surface-to-Air Missile Development
SAM-DC..... S-Adenosylmethionine Decarboxylase [*An enzyme*]
SAME....... Mendoza/El Plumerillo [*Argentina*] [*ICAO location identifier*]   (ICLI)
SAMe....... S-Adenosylmethionine [*Also, AdoMet, SAM*] [*Biochemistry*]
SAME....... [*The*] S & M Co. [*NASDAQ symbol*]   (NQ)
SAME....... Sensory-Afferent/Motor-Efferent [*Neurology*]
SAME....... Society of American Military Engineers   (EA)
SAME....... South Australian Matriculation Examination
SAME....... Students Against Misleading Enterprises [*Student legal action organization*]
SAMEA..... South African Mechanical Engineer [*A publication*]
SAMEB..... SA [*South African*] Mining and Engineering Journal [*A publication*]
SAMED..... South African Medical Literature [*South African Research Council*] [*Information service or system*]   (CRD)
Same Day Surg ... Same-Day Surgery [*A publication*]
SA Methodist ... South Australian Methodist [*A publication*]   (APTA)
SAMEX..... Shuttle Active-Microwave Experiments   (MCD)
SAMEX..... Surface-to-Air Missile Exercise   (NVT)
SAMF....... Mendoza [*Argentina*] [*ICAO location identifier*]   (ICLI)
SAMF....... Salvation Army Medical Fellowship   (EAIO)
SAMF....... Seaborne Army Maintenance Facilities
SAMF....... Ship's Air Maintenance Facility [*Navy*]   (NVT)
SAmF....... Studies in American Fiction [*A publication*]
SAMF....... Switchable Acoustic Matched Filter
SAMFU..... Self-Adjusting Military Foul-Up [*Slang*]
SA & MGS ... Small Arms and Machine Gun School [*British military*]   (DMA)
SAMH....... Scottish Association for Mental Health [*British*]
SAmH....... Studies in American Humor [*A publication*]
SAMH....... Valle Hermoso [*Argentina*] [*ICAO location identifier*]   (ICLI)
SAMHSJ .. South Australian Methodist Historical Society. Journal [*A publication*]   (ADA)
SAMI......... Sales and Marketing Information Ltd. [*Database producer*]   (IID)
SAMI......... San Martin [*Argentina*] [*ICAO location identifier*]   (ICLI)
SAMI......... Selling Areas-Marketing, Incorporated [*New York, NY*] [*Originator and database*] [*Information service or system*]   (IID)
SAMI......... Sequential Assessment of Mathematics Inventory
SAMI......... Single Action Maintenance Instruction   (NG)
SAMI......... Socially Acceptable Monitoring Instruments [*Medicine*]
SAMI......... Systems Acquisition Management Inspection
SAMI......... United Satellite/America, Inc. [*NASDAQ symbol*]   (NQ)

SAMICS.... Solar Array Manufacturing Industry Costing Standards
SAMICS.... Systems Applications of Millimeter Wave Contact Seeker (MCD)
SAMID...... Ship Antimissile Integrated Defense [*Program*] [*Navy*]
SAMID...... Surface-to-Air Missile Intercept Development
SAMIDF ... Systematic and Applied Microbiology [*A publication*]
SA Min Eng J ... SA [*South African*] Mining and Engineering Journal [*A publication*]
SAMIP ...... Surface-to-Air Missile Improvement Program (MCD)
SAMIS ...... Security Assistance Management Information System (MCD)
SAMIS ...... Ship Alteration Management Information System [*Navy*] [*Discontinued*]
SAMIS ...... Solar Array Manufacturing Industry Simulation
SAMIS ...... Standard Army Management Information System (MCD)
SAMIS ...... Structural Analysis and Matrix Inversion System [*Nuclear energy*] (NRCH)
SAMJ .... Jachal [*Argentina*] [*ICAO location identifier*] (ICLI)
SAMJ .... Sami Medica. Journal. Sami Medical Association [*A publication*]
SAMJA ..... South African Medical Journal [*A publication*]
SAML........ Nationella Samlingspartiet [*National Coalition Party*] [*Finland*] [*Political party*] (PPE)
Saml.......... Samlaren [*A publication*]
SAML........ Sinus Histiocytes with Massive Lymphadenopathy [*Clinical chemistry*]
SAML........ Standard Army Management Language (AABC)
SAML........ Studies in American Literature [*The Hague*] [*A publication*]
SAMLA ..... Southern Atlantic Modern Language Association
SAMM ...... Malargue [*Argentina*] [*ICAO location identifier*] (ICLI)
SAMM ...... Standard Automated Material Management System [*DoD*]
SAMMA ... Stores Account Material Management Afloat (NG)
Sammel Bl Ingolstadt ... Sammelblatt der Historischen Verein Ingolstadt [*A publication*]
SAMMI..... Signature Analysis Methods for Mission Identification
SAMMIE .. Scheduling Analysis Model for Mission Integrated Experiments [*NASA*] (KSC)
Samml Geol Fuehrer ... Sammlung Geologischer Fuehrer [*A publication*]
Samml Goeschen ... Sammlung Goeschen [*A publication*]
Sammlung Wichmann NF ... Sammlung Wichmann. Neue Folge [*A publication*]
Samml Vergiftungsfaellen ... Sammlung von Vergiftungsfaellen [*A publication*]
Samml Zwangl Abh Geb Psychiatr Neurol ... Sammlung Zwangloser Abhandlungen aus dem Gebiete der Psychiatrie und Neurologie [*A publication*]
SAMMS.... Ship Alteration Material Management System
SAMMS.... Standard Automated Materiel Management System [*DoD*]
SAMNAM ... Samradet for Nordisk Amatormusik [*Arhus, Denmark*] (EAIO)
SAMO .... Simulated Ab Initio Molecular Orbitals [*Atomic physics*]
SAMOA ... Systematic Approach to Multidimensional Occupational Analysis (MCD)
Samoan Pac LJ ... Samoan Pacific Law Journal [*A publication*]
Samoan PLJ ... Samoan Pacific Law Journal [*A publication*] (DLA)
SAMOD ... Secretary of the Army's Mobility, Opportunity, and Development Program (MCD)
Samoletostr Tekh Vozdushn Flota ... Samoletostroenie i Tekhnika Vozdushnogo Flota [*A publication*]
SAMOS..... Satellite-Missile Observation Satellite [*or System*]
SAMOS..... Silicon and Aluminum Metal-Oxide Semiconductor (ADA)
SA Motor... South Australian Motor [*A publication*] (APTA)
SAMP....... La Paz [*Argentina*] [*ICAO location identifier*] (ICLI)
SAMP........ Sample (AAG)
SAMP........ Shuttle Automated Mass Properties [*NASA*] (MCD)
SAMP........ Stuntmen's Association of Motion Pictures (EA)
SAMP........ Stuntwomen's Association of Motion Pictures (EA)
SAMPAC .. Society of Advertising Musicians, Producers, Arrangers, and Composers
SAMPAM ... System for Automation of Materiel Plans for Army Material (MCD)
SAMPAP .. Security Assistance Master Planning and Phasing
SAMPD..... Science Analysis and Mission Planning Directorate [*NASA*]
SAMPE..... Society for the Advancement of Material and Process Engineering (EA)
SAMPE J .. SAMPE [*Society for the Advancement of Material and Process Engineering*] Journal [*A publication*]
SAMPE Q ... SAMPE [*Society for the Advancement of Material and Process Engineering*] Quarterly [*A publication*]
SAMPE Qtly ... SAMPE [*Society for the Advancement of Material and Process Engineering*] Quarterly [*A publication*]
SAMPF ..... Sampford [*England*]
SAMPLE... Single Assignment Mathematical Programming Language [*1971*] [*Data processing*] (CSR)
SAMPSP... Security Assistance Master Planning and Phasing (MCD)
SAMQ .... Mendoza Aeroparque [*Argentina*] [*ICAO location identifier*] (ICLI)
SAMQA .... SAMPE [*Society for the Advancement of Material and Process Engineering*] Quarterly [*A publication*]
SAMR........ San Rafael [*Argentina*] [*ICAO location identifier*] (ICLI)
SAM & R... Ship Activation, Maintenance, and Repair
SAMR........ Special Assistant for Material Readiness [*Army*]

SAMRA ..... Sino-American Medical Rehabilitation Association
SAMRAF .. South African Military Refugee Aid Fund (EA)
SAMRD..... South African Machine Tool Review [*A publication*]
SAMREF... South Australian Mines Reference [*Database*]
SAMRT..... Shared Aperture Medium-Range Tracker (MCD)
SAMS........ Sample Method Survey [*for family housing requirements*] [*Military*] (AABC)
SAMS........ Sampling Analog Memory System
SAMS........ San Carlos [*Argentina*] [*ICAO location identifier*] (ICLI)
SAMS........ Sandia Air Force Material Study (MCD)
SAMS........ Satellite Automatic Monitoring System [*Programming language*]
SAMS........ Ship's Alteration Management System [*Navy*]
SAMS........ Shore Activity Management Support [*Navy*] (NVT)
SAMS........ Shuttle Attachment Manipulator System [*NASA*]
SAMS........ Society for Advanced Medical Systems [*Later, AMIA*]
SAMS........ Standard Army Maintenance System (AABC)
SAMS........ Stratospheric and Mesospheric Sounder
SAMS........ Study Attitudes and Methods Survey [*Study skills test*]
SAMSA ..... Standard Army Management System - Supply Support Arrangement
SAM-SAC ... Specialized Aircraft Maintenance - Strategic Air Command (AAG)
SAM/SAR ... South America/South Atlantic Region [*DoD*]
SAMSARS ... Satellite-Based Maritime Search and Rescue System [*Telecommunications*] (TEL)
SAM/SAT ... South America/South Atlantic Region [*Aviation*]
SAMSAT .. Surface-to-Air Missile Servicing, Assembly, and Test
SAMSEM ... Ship Antimissile System Engagement Model [*Navy*] (CAAL)
SAMSI ...... Spacecraft Array for Michelson Spectral Inferometry
SAMSIM ... Surface-to-Air Missile Simulation Model (MCD)
SAMSO..... Space and Missile Systems Office [*Air Force*]
SAMSO..... Space and Missile Systems Organization [*Merger of Ballistic Systems Division and Space Systems Division*] [*Air Force*]
SAMSO..... Systems Analysis of Manned Space Operations (MCD)
SAMSOM ... Support Availability Multisystem Operational Model
SAMSON ... Strategic Automatic Message-Switching Operational Network [*Canada*] (MCD)
SAMSON ... System Analysis of Manned Space Operations (MCD)
SAMSOR.. Space and Missile Systems Organization Regulation [*Later, SDR*] [*Air Force*] (NASA)
SAMSOT .. SAMID [*Ship Antimissile Integrated Defense*] System Operational Test [*Navy*] (NVT)
SAMSq...... Special Air Mission Squadron [*Vietnam Air Force*] (AFM)
SAMS-USA ... South American Missionary Society of the Episcopal Church (EA)
SAMT........ Simulated Aircraft Maintenance Trainer (MCD)
SAMT........ State-of-the-Art Medium Terminal
SAMTA..... South Australian Music Teachers Association
SAMTEC ... Space and Missile Test Center [*Air Force*]
SAMTECM ... Space and Missile Test Center Manual [*Air Force*] (MCD)
SAMTO..... Space and Missile Test Organization [*Air Force*] [*Vandenberg Air Force Base, CA*]
SAMU .... Uspallata [*Argentina*] [*ICAO location identifier*] (ICLI)
SA Museum Rec ... South Australian Museum. Records [*A publication*] (APTA)
SA Mus Tcr ... South Africa Music Teacher [*A publication*]
SAMV........ Mendoza [*Argentina*] [*ICAO location identifier*] (ICLI)
Samv .... Samvirke [*A publication*]
SAN .... Gato, CA [*Location identifier*] [*FAA*] (FAAL)
SAN .... San Carlos Milling Co., Inc. [*AMEX symbol*] (SPSG)
SAN .... San Diego [*California*] [*Airport symbol*] (OAG)
SAN .... San Francisco Helicopter Airlines [*Air carrier designation symbol*]
SAN .... San Francisco Operations Office [*Energy Research and Development Administration*]
SAN .... SAN: Journal of the Society for Ancient Numismatics [*A publication*]
SAN .... Sanatorium
SAN .... Sandersville Railroad Co. [*AAR code*]
SAN .... Sandwich (MSA)
San .... Sanford's Reports [*59 Alabama*] [*A publication*] (DLA)
SAN .... Sanitary (AAG)
san............. Sanskrit [*MARC language code*] [*Library of Congress*] (LCCP)
SAN .... Santiago [*Chile*] [*Seismograph station code, US Geological Survey*] (SEIS)
SAN .... School of Air Navigation [*British*]
SAN .... Servicios Aereos Nacionales [*Airline*] [*Ecuador*]
SAN .... Severe Acoustic Noise
SAN .... Ship Account Number [*Navy*]
SAN .... Shipping Accumulation Numbers (AAG)
SAN .... Sinoatrial Node [*Medicine*]
SAN .... Society for Ancient Numismatics (EA)
SAN .... South Australian Navy
SAN .... Space Age News (AAG)
SAN .... Srpska Akademija Nauka i Umetnosti [*Belgrade, Yugoslavia*]
SAN .... Standard Address Number [*Publishing*]
SAN .... Styrene-Acrylonitrile [*Also, SA*] [*Organic chemistry*]
SAN .... Subsidiary Account Number
SAN .... System Advisory Notice
SANA .... Scientists Against Nuclear Arms [*Australia*]

SANA .... Slavic American National Association (EA)
SANA .... Societa Anonima Navigazione Aerea [*Italy*]
SANA .... Soycrafters Association of North America (EA)
SANA .... Soyfoods Association of North America (EA)
SANA .... Specialty Advertising National Association [*Later, SAA*] (EA)
SANA .... State, Army, Navy, Air (AABC)
SANA .... Syrian Arab News Agency
SANAA ..... Servicio Autonomo Nacional de Acueductos y Alcantarillados [*Honduras*]
SANACC... State-Army-Navy-Air Force Coordinating Committee [*Terminated, 1949*] (EGAO)
SANAE...... South African National Antarctic Expedition
SANAFREQ ... Safety/NATOPS Frequency (MCD)
SANAn ...... Societe Archeologique de Namur. Annales [*A publication*]
San Anto E ... San Antonio Executive [*A publication*]
SANAT...... Sanatorium
SA Nat .... South Australian Naturalist [*A publication*] (APTA)
SA Naturalist ... South Australian Naturalist [*A publication*] (APTA)
SANB........ South African National Bibliography
SANBAR... Sanders Barotropic
SANBB...... Sankhya. Series B. Indian Journal of Statistics [*A publication*]
Sanb & B Ann St ... Sanborn and Berryman's Annotated Statutes [*Wisconsin*] [*A publication*] (DLA)
San Bernardino County Med Soc Bull ... San Bernardino County Medical Society. Bulletin [*California*] [*A publication*]
SANC .... Catamarca [*Argentina*] [*ICAO location identifier*] (ICLI)
SANC .... Sanctuary [*Naval cadet's hiding place for smoking*] [*Slang*] [*British*] (DSUE)
SANC .... Slovak-American National Council (EA)
SANCAD... Scottish Association for National Certificates and Diplomas
SANCAR... South African National Council for Antarctic Research (NOAA)
San Ch .... Sandford's New York Chancery Reports [*A publication*] (DLA)
SANCIP .... SACLANT [*Supreme Allied Commander, Atlantic*] Approved NATO Common Infrastructure Program (NATG)
San D .... Doctor of Sanitation
SAND........ Sampling Aerospace Nuclear Debris
SAND........ Sandata, Inc. [*NASDAQ symbol*] (NQ)
Sand .... Sandford's New York Superior Court Reports [*3-7 New York*] [*A publication*] (DLA)
SAND........ Site Activation Need Date [*NASA*] (NASA)
SAND........ Sorting and Assembly of New Data
SANDA ..... Supplies and Accounts
SANDAC... Sandia Airborne Computer
Sandal........ Sandalion. Quaderni di Cultura Classica, Cristiana, e Medievale [*A publication*]
Sandars Just Inst ... Sandars' Edition of Justinian's Institutes [*A publication*] (DLA)
SANDASO ... Bureau of Supplies and Accounts Shipment Order [*Obsolete*] [*Navy*]
Sand Ch ..... Sandford's New York Chancery Reports [*A publication*] (DLA)
Sand Ch R ... Sandford's New York Chancery Reports [*A publication*] (DLA)
Sand Chy ... Sandford's New York Chancery Reports [*A publication*] (DLA)
Sand Dune Res ... Sand Dune Research [*A publication*]
Sand Essays ... Sanders' Essays on Uses and Trusts [*5th ed.*] [*1844*] [*A publication*] (DLA)
Sandf.......... Sandford's New York Superior Court Reports [*3-7 New York*] [*A publication*] (DLA)
Sandf Ch .... Sandford's New York Chancery Reports [*A publication*] (DLA)
Sandf Ch (NY) ... Sandford's New York Superior Court Reports [*3-7 New York*] [*A publication*] (DLA)
Sandf Ch Rep ... Sandford's New York Chancery Reports [*A publication*] (DLA)
Sandf (NY) ... Sandford's New York Superior Court Reports [*3-7 New York*] [*A publication*] (ILCA)
Sandf (NY) R ... Sandford's New York Superior Court Reports [*A publication*] (DLA)
Sandford .... Sandford's New York Superior Court Reports [*A publication*] (DLA)
Sandford's SCR ... Sandford's New York Superior Court Reports [*A publication*] (DLA)
Sandford's Sup Ct R ... Sandford's New York Superior Court Reports [*A publication*] (DLA)
Sandf R ...... Sandford's New York Superior Court Reports [*A publication*] (DLA)
Sandf SC.... Sandford's New York Superior Court Reports [*A publication*] (DLA)
Sandf SCR ... Sandford's New York Superior Court Reports [*A publication*] (DLA)
Sandf Suc ... Sandford's Heritable Succession in Scotland [*A publication*] (DLA)
Sandf Sup CR ... Sandford's New York Superior Court Reports [*A publication*] (DLA)
Sandf Sup Ct ... Sandford's New York Superior Court Reports [*A publication*] (DLA)
Sandf Superior Court R ... Sandford's New York Superior Court Reports [*A publication*] (DLA)
Sand & H Dig ... Sandels and Hill's Digest of Statutes [*Arkansas*] [*A publication*] (DLA)
Sandia SN ... Sandia Science News [*A publication*]
San Diego B ... San Diego Business Journal [*A publication*]

San Diego L Rev ... San Diego Law Review [*A publication*]
San Diego Soc Nat Hist Mem ... San Diego Society of Natural History. Memoirs [*A publication*]
San Diego Soc Nat History Occasional Paper Trans ... San Diego Society of Natural History. Occasional Papers. Transactions [*A publication*]
San Diego Soc Nat History Trans ... San Diego Society of Natural History. Transactions [*A publication*]
San Diego Soc N H Tr ... San Diego Society of Natural History. Transactions [*A publication*]
San Diego U ... San Diego Union [*A publication*]
Sand Inst Just Introd ... Sandars' Edition of Justinian's Institutes [*A publication*]
Sand I Rep ... Sandwich Islands Reports [*Hawaii*] [*A publication*] (DLA)
Sand Isls .... Sandwich Islands
San DLR.... San Diego Law Review [*A publication*]
Sandl St Pap ... Sandler's State Papers [*A publication*] (DLA)
SANDOCC ... San Diego Oceanic Coordinating Committee
Sandoz Bull ... Sandoz Bulletin [*A publication*]
Sand R .... Sandford's New York Superior Court Reports [*A publication*] (DLA)
SANDRA... Structure and Reference Analyzer [*IBM Corp.*] [*Chemistry*]
SANDS...... Structural Analysis Numerical Design System
Sand SC ..... Sandford's New York Superior Court Reports [*A publication*] (DLA)
Sands Ch.... Sandford's New York Chancery Reports [*A publication*] (DLA)
Sand SCR .. Sandford's New York Superior Court Reports [*A publication*] (DLA)
Sandst .... Sandstone [*Lithology*]
Sand Sup Ct Rep ... Sandford's New York Superior Court Reports [*A publication*] (DLA)
Sand Supr Ct R ... Sandford's New York Superior Court Reports [*A publication*] (DLA)
Sand Uses and Trusts ... Sanders' Essays on Uses and Trusts [*A publication*] (DLA)
SANE......... National Committee for a Sane Nuclear Policy [*"SANE" alone now used as organization name*] (EA)
San E.......... Sanitary Engineer [*Academic degree*]
SANE........ Santiago Del Estero [*Argentina*] [*ICAO location identifier*] (ICLI)
SANE........ Schizophrenia: a National Emergency [*An association*] [*British*]
SANE........ Severe Acoustic Noise Environment
SANE........ Standard Apple Numerics Environment [*Software*] [*Apple Computers, Inc.*]
SANE........ Students Aware of the Natural Environment [*Australia*]
SANET...... Supplement to Ancient Near Eastern Texts [*A publication*]
SANF......... Salvation Army Nurses' Fellowship (EAIO)
SanF......... San Francisco Magazine [*A publication*]
SANF........ Sanford Corp. [*Bellwood, IL*] [*NASDAQ symbol*] (NQ)
SANF........ Sanford Recreation Area
Sanf.......... Sanford's Reports [*59 Alabama*] [*A publication*] (DLA)
SANF........ South African Naval Forces
San Fernando Val Dent Soc Bull ... San Fernando Valley Dental Society. Bulletin [*US*] [*A publication*]
San Fern Val LR ... San Fernando Valley Law Review [*A publication*]
San Fern VL Rev ... San Fernando Valley Law Review [*A publication*]
San FLJ ..... San Francisco Law Journal [*A publication*] (DLA)
Sanf (NY)... Sandford's New York Superior Court Reports [*3-7 New York*] [*A publication*] (DLA)
Sanford's Ch R ... Sandford's New York Chancery Reports [*A publication*] (DLA)
San Fran B ... San Francisco Business Journal [*A publication*]
San Francisco Bus ... San Francisco Business [*A publication*]
San Francisco Med ... San Francisco Medicine [*A publication*]
San Francisco Micro Soc Tr ... San Francisco Microscopical Society. Transactions [*A publication*]
San Fran Cro ... San Francisco Chronicle [*A publication*]
San Fran Law Bull ... San Francisco Law Bulletin [*A publication*] (DLA)
San Fran LB ... San Francisco Law Bulletin [*A publication*] (ILCA)
San Fran LJ ... San Francisco Law Journal [*A publication*] (DLA)
San Fran Opera ... San Francisco Opera Magazine [*A publication*]
San Fr LB .. San Francisco Law Bulletin [*A publication*] (DLA)
San Fr LJ... San Francisco Law Journal [*A publication*] (DLA)
Sang .... Sangre [*A publication*]
SANG .... Saudi Arabian National Guard (RDA)
SANG .... Standardized Aeronautical Navigation/Guidance [*Program*] [*Air Force*]
San Gabriel Val Dent Soc Bull ... San Gabriel Valley Dental Society. Bulletin [*A publication*]
SANGB...... Selfridge Army/Air National Guard Base (MCD)
SANGFPT ... Spherical Angles from Points (MCD)
Sang Natak ... Sangeet Natak [*New Delhi*] [*A publication*]
SANGruz... Soobscenija Akademiji Nauk Gruzinskoj SSR [*A publication*]
SANH........ Rio Hondo/Las Termas [*Argentina*] [*ICAO location identifier*] (ICLI)
Sanh .... Sanhedrin (BJA)
Sanh .... Sanherib (BJA)
SANH....... Somerset Archaeology and Natural History [*A publication*]
SANI......... Tinogasta [*Argentina*] [*ICAO location identifier*] (ICLI)
Sanid Aeronaut ... Sanidad Aeronautica [*A publication*]
Sanid Benef Munic ... Sanidad y Beneficiencia Municipal [*A publication*]

SANINSP ... Sanitation Inspector [*Military*]   (AABC)
Sanit........... Sanitarium
Sanit........... Sanitary
Sanitary & Heat Eng ... Sanitary and Heating Engineering [*A publication*]
Sanit Eng Pap Colo State Univ ... Sanitary Engineering Papers. Colorado State
    University [*A publication*]
Sanit Heiz Tech ... Sanitaer- und Heizungstechnik [*A publication*]
Sanit Heizungstech (Duesseldorf) ... Sanitaer- und Heizungstechnik
    (Duesseldorf) [*A publication*]
Sanit Heizungstechnik ... Sanitaer- und Heizungstechnik [*West Germany*] [*A
    publication*]
Sanit Nytt .. Sanitets Nytt Utgitt av Forsvarets Sanitet [*A publication*]
Sanit Okh Vodoemov Zagryaz Prom Stochnymi Vodami ... Sanitarnaya
    Okhrana Vodoemov ot Zagryazneniya Promyshlennymi
    Stochnymi Vodami [*A publication*]
Sanit Tekh ... Sanitarnaya Tekhnika [*A publication*]
SANJA ...... South African Nursing Journal [*A publication*]
San Jose Bus ... San Jose Business Journal [*A publication*]
San Jose M ... San Jose Mercury News [*A publication*]
San Jose Stud ... San Jose Studies [*A publication*]
San Just ..... Sandars' Edition of Justinian's Institutes [*A
    publication*]   (DLA)
SANKA...... Sans Caffeine [*Acronym used as brand name*]
Sankhya A ... Sankhya. Series A. Indian Journal of Statistics [*A publication*]
Sankhya B ... Sankhya. Series B. Indian Journal of Statistics [*A publication*]
Sankhya C ... Sankhya. Series C. Indian Journal of Statistics [*A publication*]
Sankhya Indian J Stat Ser B ... Sankhya. Series B. Indian Journal of Statistics
    [*A publication*]
Sankhya Ser A ... Sankhya. Series A. Indian Journal of Statistics [*A
    publication*]
Sankhya Ser B ... Sankhya. Series B. Indian Journal of Statistics [*A
    publication*]
SANL........ La Rioja/Cap. V. Almandos Almonacid [*Argentina*] [*ICAO
    location identifier*]   (ICLI)
SANLF ...... Saudi Arabian National Liberation Front [*Political
    party*]   (BJA)
SANM .... Synthetic Algal Nutrient Medium
SAN MIG ... San Miguel Beer   (DSUE)
SANNA ..... Schweizer Archiv fuer Neurologie, Neurochirurgie, und
    Psychiatrie [*A publication*]
SANNAW ... Archives Suisses de Neurologie, Neurochirurgie, et de
    Psychiatrie/Archivio Svizzero di Neurologia,
    Neurochirurgia, e Psichiatria [*A publication*]
SANO .... Chilecito [*Argentina*] [*ICAO location identifier*]   (ICLI)
SANOVA .. Simultaneous Analysis of Variance
SANP........ Secondary Auxiliary Nuclear Power
SANR .... Subject to Approval No Risk
SANROC... South African Non-Racial Olympic Committee   (EAIO)
SANS......... Schedule for the Assessment of Negative Symptoms
    [*Psychometrics*]
SANS........ Simplified Account - Numbering System
SANS......... Small-Angle Neutron Scattering
SANS......... South African Naval Service
SANS......... Students Against Nuclear Suicide   (EA)
SAns......... Studia Anselmiana [*A publication*]
SANS........ Swimmer and Navigation System [*Navy*]   (CAAL)
SANSAN... San Francisco, San Diego [*Proposed name for possible "super-
    city" formed by growth and mergers of other cities*]
SANSC ...... Sanscrit
SANSK ..... Sanskrit [*Language, etc.*]
SANSS ...... Structure and Nomenclature Search System [*Formerly, SSS*]
    [*Chemical Information Systems, Inc.*] [*Information service
    or system*]
SANT......... Santa Monica Bank [*NASDAQ symbol*]   (NQ)
SANT......... Studien zum Alten und Neuen Testament [*A publication*]
S Ant .... Suomen Antropologi/Antropologi i Finland [*A publication*]
SANT......... Tucuman/Teniente Benjamim Matienzo [*Argentina*] [*ICAO
    location identifier*]   (ICLI)
SANTA...... Souvenir and Novelty Trade Association   (EA)
Santa Barbara Mus Nat History Dept Geology Bull ... Santa Barbara Museum
    of Natural History. Department of Geology. Bulletin [*A
    publication*]
Santa Barbara Soc N H B ... Santa Barbara Society of Natural History.
    Bulletin [*A publication*]
Santa Clara L ... Santa Clara Lawyer [*A publication*]
Santa Clara Law ... Santa Clara Lawyer [*A publication*]
Santa Clara LR ... Santa Clara Law Review [*A publication*]   (ILCA)
Santa Clara L Rev ... Santa Clara Law Review [*A publication*]
Sant Cl LR ... Santa Clara Law Review [*A publication*]
Sante........... Sante Mentale au Canada [*A publication*]
Sante Publique (Bucur) ... Sante Publique. Revue Internationale (Bucuresti) [*A
    publication*]
Santerna De Ass ... Santerna. De Asse Curationibus et Sponsionibus
    Mercatorum [*A publication*]   (DLA)
Sante Secur Soc ... Sante Securite Sociale [*A publication*]
Santo Domingo Univ Anales Pub ... Santo Domingo Universidad. Anales.
    Publicaciones [*A publication*]
Santo Tomas J Med ... Santo Tomas Journal of Medicine [*A publication*]
SANU .... San Juan [*Argentina*] [*ICAO location identifier*]   (ICLI)
SANU .... Sudan African National Union [*Political party*]
SANUM .... South Africa National Union for Mineworkers

SA Nurs J .. South African Nursing Journal [*A publication*]
SANW .... Ceres [*Argentina*] [*ICAO location identifier*]   (ICLI)
SANWFZ .. South Asia Nuclear Weapons-Free Zone
SANY .... Sanyo Electric Co. Ltd. [*NASDAQ symbol*]   (NQ)
Sanyal .... Sanyal's Criminal Cases between Natives and Europeans [*1796-
    1895*] [*India*] [*A publication*]   (DLA)
SANYD ..... Sanitets Nytt [*A publication*]
SAO .... Saharan Air Outbreak [*Meteorology*]
SAO .... San Andreas Geological Observatory [*California*] [*Seismograph
    station code, US Geological Survey*]   (SEIS)
SAO .... Sandia Area Office [*Energy Research and Development
    Administration*]
SAO .... Sao Paulo [*Brazil*] [*Airport symbol*]   (OAG)
SAO .... Scottish Association of Opticians   (DAS)
SAO .... Secret Army Organization [*English initialism for OAS, terrorist
    group in Algeria and metropolitan France*]
SAO .... Secretin-Stimulated Acid Output [*Clinical chemistry*]
SAO .... Select Address and Operate
SAO .... Selected Attack Option   (MCD)
SAO .... Senior Administrative Officer [*British military*]   (DMA)
SAO .... Single Airlift Organization   (CINC)
SAO .... Single Attack Option
SAO .... Smithsonian Astrophysical Observatory [*Cambridge, MA*]
SAO .... Smithsonian Institution. Astrophysical Observatory [*A
    publication*]
SAO .... Social Actions Office [*or Officer*] [*Air Force*]   (AFM)
SAO .... Sonobuoy Acoustic Operator [*Navy*]   (CAAL)
SAO .... Special Access Only   (MCD)
SAO .... Special Action Office [*Phased out, 1975*] [*Department of
    Justice*]
SAO .... Special Activities Office [*Air Force*]   (AFM)
SAO .... Special Air Operations
SAO .... Special Artificer, Optical [*Navy*]
SAO .... Special Astrophysics Observatory
SAO .... Splanchnic Artery Occlusion [*Medicine*]
SAO .... Squadron Accountant Officer [*Navy*] [*British*]
SAO .... Staff Administrative Office [*Military*]
SAO .... Studia et Acta Orientalia [*A publication*]
SAO .... Subsidiary/Affiliate Order   (MCD)
SAO .... Support Air Observation [*Navy*]
SAO .... Survey of Agency Opinion [*LIMRA*]
SAO .... Survival Assistance Officer [*Army*]   (AABC)
SAO .... Systems Acquisition Officer [*Military*]   (AFIT)
SAO .... Systems Analysis Office
SAOAAW ... Sbornik Nauchnykh Rabot Arkhangel'skogo Otdeleniya
    Vsesoyuznogo Nauchnogo Obshchestva Anatomov,
    Gistologov, i Embriologov [*A publication*]
SAOABX... Archivos. Sociedad Americana de Oftalmologia y Optometria
    [*A publication*]
SAOAS..... Secretary of the Army, Office of the Assistant Secretary
SAOAS..... Staff Association of the Organization of American States   (EA)
SAOB .... Svenska Akademiens Ordbok [*A publication*]
SAOC .... Rio Cuarto/Area de Material [*Argentina*] [*ICAO location
    identifier*]   (ICLI)
SAOC .... Scottish Association of Operative Coachmakers [*A union*]
SAOC .... Space and Astronautics Orientation Course   (NG)
SAOC .... Studies in Ancient Oriental Civilization. The Oriental Institute
    of the University of Chicago [*A publication*]
SAOCS..... Submarine Air Optical Communications System   (MCD)
SAOD .... Villa Dolores [*Argentina*] [*ICAO location identifier*]   (ICLI)
SAODAP... Special Action Office for Drug Abuse Prevention [*Terminated,
    1975*] [*FDA*]
SAOE .... Embalse Rio Tercero [*Argentina*] [*ICAO location
    identifier*]   (ICLI)
SAOL........ Laboulaye [*Argentina*] [*ICAO location identifier*]   (ICLI)
SAOM .... Marcos Juarez [*Argentina*] [*ICAO location identifier*]   (ICLI)
SAO/MEX ... Special Action Office for Mexico [*Drug Enforcement
    Administration*]
Sao Paulo Brazil Inst Pesqui Tecnol Bol ... Sao Paulo, Brazil. Instituto de
    Pesquisas Tecnologicas. Boletin [*A publication*]
Sao Paulo Inst Agron (Campinas) Bol ... Sao Paulo. Instituto Agronomico
    (Campinas). Boletin [*A publication*]
Sao Paulo Inst Agron (Campinas) Bol Tec ... Sao Paulo. Instituto Agronomico
    (Campinas). Boletim Tecnico [*A publication*]
Sao Paulo Inst Agron (Campinas) Circ ... Sao Paulo. Instituto Agronomico
    (Campinas). Circular [*A publication*]
Sao Paulo Inst Geogr Geol Bol ... Sao Paulo. Instituto Geografico e Geologico.
    Boletim [*A publication*]
Sao Paulo Inst Geogr Geol Relat ... Sao Paulo. Instituto Geografico e
    Geologico. Relatorio [*A publication*]
Sao Paulo Univ Inst Geocienc Bol ... Sao Paulo. Universidade. Instituto de
    Geociencias. Boletim [*A publication*]
Sao Paulo Univ Inst Geogr Geogr Planejamento ... Sao Paulo. Universidade.
    Instituto de Geografia. Geografia e Planejamento [*A
    publication*]
Sao Paulo Univ Inst Geogr Geomorfol ... Sao Paulo. Universidade. Instituto de
    Geografia. Geomorfologia [*A publication*]
Sao Paulo Univ Inst Geogr Ser Teses Monogr ... Sao Paulo. Universidade.
    Instituto de Geografia. Serie Teses e Monografias [*A
    publication*]
SAOR .... Villa Reynolds [*Argentina*] [*ICAO location identifier*]   (ICLI)

SA Ornithol ... South Australian Ornithologist [*A publication*] (APTA)
SA Ornithologist ... South Australian Ornithologist [*A publication*] (APTA)
SAOS .... Select Address [*and Provide*] Output Signal
SAOT .... Semiactive on Target
SAOTA ..... Shrimp Association of the Americas (EA)
SAOU .... San Luis [*Argentina*] [*ICAO location identifier*] (ICLI)
SAP .... ASAP Air, Inc. [*Fort Worth, TX*] [*FAA designator*] (FAAC)
SAP .... San Antonio Public Library, San Antonio, TX [*OCLC symbol*] (OCLC)
SAP .... San Pedro Sula [*Honduras*] [*Airport symbol*] (OAG)
SAP .... Sapporo [*Japan*] [*Seismograph station code, US Geological Survey*] (SEIS)
SAP .... Scientific Advisory Panel [*Arlington, VA*] [*Environmental Protection Agency*] (EGAO)
SAP .... Scorched Aluminum Powder
SAP .... Scouting and Amphibian Plane [*Coast Guard*]
SAP .... Scruple Apothecaries
SAP .... Seaborne Aircraft Platform (ADA)
SAP .... Second Audio Program
SAP .... Security Assistance Program (MCD)
SAP .... Semi-Armor-Piercing [*Projectile*] [*Nickname: Sex-Appeal Pete*] [*Military*]
SAP .... Seminal Acid Phosphatase [*An enzyme*]
SAP .... Separate Audio Program [*Television broadcasting*]
SAP .... Serum Alkaline Phosphatase [*Clinical chemistry*]
SAP .... Serum Amyloid P [*Clinical chemistry*]
SAP .... Service Access Point
SAP .... Share Assembly Program [*Data processing*]
SAP .... Ship Acquisition Plan [*Navy*]
SAP .... Shipboard Acoustic Processor [*Navy*] (CAAL)
SAP .... Shipboard Antenna Pedestal
SAP .... Simple Assembly Plan
SAP .... Single-Axis Platform
SAP .... Sintered Aluminum Powder
SAP .... Skeletal Axis of Pinnule
SAP .... Social Action Party [*Thailand*] [*Political party*] (FEA)
SAP .... Socialistische Arbeidspartij [*Socialist Workers' Party*] [*Netherlands*] [*Political party*] (PPW)
SAP .... Society for Adolescent Psychiatry (EA)
SAP .... Society for American Philosophy [*Defunct*] (EA)
SAP .... Sodium Acid Pyrophosphate [*Also, SAPP*] [*Leavening agent, meat additive*]
SAP .... Soon as Possible
SAP .... South African Party [*Political party*] (PPW)
SAP .... South African Police Force
SAP .... Soysal Adelet Partisi [*Social Justice Party*] [*Turkish Cyprus*] [*Political party*] (PPE)
SAP .... Special and Administrative Provisions [*of the Tariff Act of 1930*]
SAP .... Sphingolipid Activator Protein [*Biochemistry*]
SAP .... Spot Authorization Plan [*WPB*] [*Obsolete*]
SAP .... Spy Against Pollution [*An association*]
SAP .... Squadron Aid Post (ADA)
SAP .... Staphylococcus aureus Protease [*An enzyme*]
SAP .... State Association President [*American Occupational Therapy Association*]
SAP .... Steroidogenesis Activator Polypeptide
SAP .... Strain Arrestor Plate [*NASA*] (NASA)
SAP .... Strategic Advantages Profile
SAP .... Strong Anthropic Principle [*Term coined by authors John Barrow and Frank Tipler in their book, "The Anthropic Cosmological Principle"*]
SAP .... Structural Analysis Program (MCD)
SAP .... Student Aid Project
SAP .... Studia Anglica Posnaniensia [*A publication*]
SAP .... Subassembly Precision (MCD)
SAP .... Subject Access Project
SAP .... Sumerian Animal Proverbs (BJA)
SAP .... Supervisory Airplane Pilot
SAP .... Surface Aligned Photochemistry [*Physics*]
SAP .... Sveriges Socialdemokratiska Arbetareparti [*Swedish Social Democratic Labor Party*] [*Political party*] (PPW)
SAP .... Symbolic Address Program
SAP .... Symbolic Assembly Program [*Data processing*]
SAP .... System Alignment Procedure (NATG)
SAP .... Systemic Arterial Pressure [*Medicine*]
SAP .... Systems Assurance Program [*IBM Corp.*]
SAPA .... Sciences - A Process Approach [*National Science Foundation*]
SapA .... Societa in Accomandita per Azioni [*Limited Partnership with Shares*] [*Italian*] (IMH)
SAPA .... South African Press Association
SAPAA3 .... Escuela Nacional de Agricultura [*Chapingo*]. Serie de Apuntes [*A publication*]
SAPAI .... Salesmen's Association of Paper and Allied Industries (EA)
SA Parl Deb ... South Australia. Parliamentary Debates [*A publication*] (APTA)
SA Parl Parl Deb ... South Australia. Parliament. Parliamentary Debates [*A publication*] (APTA)
SAPAT ...... South African Picture Analysis Test [*Psychology*]
SAPC .... Shipowners Association of the Pacific Coast [*Defunct*] (EA)
SAPC .... Small Arms Post Competition

SAPC .... Substance Abuse Problem Checklist
SAPC .... Supported Aqueous-Phase Catalysis [*Chemistry*]
SAPC .... Suspended Acoustical-Plaster Ceiling [*Technical drawings*]
SAPCHE ... Semiautomatic Program Checkout Equipment (AAG)
SAPCO ..... Security Assistance Policy Coordinating Office [*Military*]
SAPCO ..... Single-Asset Property Company [*British*]
SAPD .... South Australia. Parliamentary Debates [*A publication*]
SAPDF ..... Social Activist Professors Defense Foundation (EA)
SAPDO ..... Special Accounts Property Disposal Officer [*Military*]
SAPE .... Society for Automation in Professional Education [*Later, SDE*]
SAPE .... Solenoid Array Pattern Evaluator
SAPEA ..... Sapere [*A publication*]
SAPEC ..... Savings Associations Political Education Committee
SAPED ..... Salt 'n' Pepper [*A publication*]
SAPENF .... Societe Americaine pour l'Etude de la Numismatique Francaise (EA)
SAPF .... Suider-Afrika Padfederasie [*Southern Africa Road Federation - SARF*] [*Johannesburg, South Africa*] (EAIO)
SAPFU ...... Surpassing All Previous Foul Ups [*Military slang*] [*Bowdlerized version*]
saph .... Sapphire [*Philately*]
SAPhA ...... Student American Pharmaceutical Association [*Later, APhA-ASP*] (EA)
SAPHD .... South African Journal of Physics [*A publication*]
SAPHE ...... Semi-Armor-Piercing High Explosive [*Projectile*] (MCD)
SAPHYDATA ... Panel on the Acquisition, Transmission, and Processing of Hydrological Data [*Marine science*] (MSC)
SAPI .... Sales Association of the Paper Industry [*New York, NY*] (EA)
SAPI .... Semi-Armor-Piercing Incendiary [*Projectile*] (NATG)
SAPIENS .. Spreading Activation Processor for Information Encoded in Network Structure [*Department of Education*]
SAPIR ...... System of Automatic Processing and Indexing of Reports
SAPIS .... State Alcoholism Profile Information System [*Public Health Service*] (IID)
SAPL .... Seacoast Anti-Pollution League (EA)
SAPL .... Service Action Parts List (AAG)
SAPL .... Society for Animal Protective Legislation (EA)
SAPM .... Spartan-Approved Parts List [*Missiles*] (MCD)
SAPM .... Scottish Association of Plane Makers [*A union*]
SAPNA ..... South African Panorama [*A publication*]
SAPNA ..... Succinyl-Alanyl-para-Nitroanilide [*Biochemistry*]
SaPNFB .... National Film Board, Pretoria, South Africa [*Library symbol*] [*Library of Congress*] (LCLS)
SAPO .... Sarawak People's Organization [*Malaysia*] [*Political party*] (PPW)
SAPO .... Silicoaluminophosphate [*Inorganic chemistry*]
SAPO .... Special Aircraft Project Office (AAG)
SAPO .... Subarea Petroleum Office [*Military*]
SAPOA ..... Savremena Poljoprivreda [*A publication*]
SAPOAB .. Contemporary Agriculture [*A publication*]
SAPON ..... Saponaria [*Soapwort*] [*Pharmacology*] (ROG)
SAPON ..... Saponification [*Analytical chemistry*]
SAPOV ..... Subarea Petroleum Office, Vietnam [*Military*]
SAPP .... Security, Accuracy, Propriety, and Policy
S App .... Shaw's Scotch Appeal Cases, House of Lords [*1821-24*] [*A publication*] (DLA)
SAPP .... Skeletal Axis of Palp
SAPP .... Sodium Acid Pyrophosphate [*Also, SAP*] [*Leavening agent, meat additive*]
SAPP .... Soul Assurance Prayer Plan (EA)
SAPP .... Special Airfield Pavement Program (NATG)
SAPPHIRE ... Synthetic Aperture Precision Processor High Reliability (MCD)
SAPPMA .. San Antonio Procurement and Production Materiel Area [*Air Force*]
Sapporo Med J ... Sapporo Medical Journal [*A publication*]
SAPR .... Semiannual Progress Report
SAPR .... South Australian Planning Reports [*A publication*] (APTA)
SAPR .... Summary Area Problem Report (AAG)
SAPRA ..... Sakharnaya Promyshlennost [*A publication*]
SAPRC ..... Security Assistance Program Review Commission
SAPS .... Scandinavian Association of Paediatric Surgeons (EAIO)
SAPS .... Scandinavian Association of Plastic Surgeons [*See also NPF*] (EAIO)
SAPS .... Selected Alternate Processing Separation (MCD)
SAPS .... Servico de Alimentacao da Providencia Social [*Brazil*]
SAPS .... Shippingport Atomic Power Station (NRCH)
SAPS .... Signal Algorithmic Processing System [*Navy*]
SAPS .... Small Area Plotting Sheet
SaPS .... South African Council for Scientific and Industrial Research, Pretoria, South Africa [*Library symbol*] [*Library of Congress*] (LCLS)
SAPS .... Surety Agents Promotional Society [*Defunct*] (EA)
SaPSL .... State Library, Pretoria, South Africa [*Library symbol*] [*Library of Congress*] (LCLS)
SAPST .... Special Assistant to the President for Science and Technology
SAPT .... South Africa/Department of Posts and Telecommunications (TSSD)
SAPT .... Symmetry-Adapted Perturbation Theory [*Physical chemistry*]
SAPTA ...... SAE [*Society of Automotive Engineers*] Progress in Technology [*A publication*]

SA Pub Serv R ... South Australian Public Service Review [*A publication*] (APTA)
SAPUC ...... Sintered Aluminum Powder-Clad Uranium Carbide
SAPW .... United Stone and Allied Products Workers of America [*Later, USWA*]
SAQ .... Pittsburgh, PA [*Location identifier*] [*FAA*] (FAAL)
SAQ .... San Andros [*Bahamas*] [*Airport symbol*] (OAG)
SAQ .... Short Arc Quads [*Medicine*]
SAQ .... South Atlantic Quarterly [*A publication*]
SAQ .... Springbank Aviation Ltd. [*Canada*] [*FAA designator*] (FAAC)
SAQC .... Statistical Analysis and Quality Control
SAQS .... Single Agency Qualification Standards [*Aviation*] (FAAC)
SAQT .... Sociedad Panamericana de Quimioterapia de la Tuberculosis [*Pan American Society for Chemotherapy of Tuberculosis - PASCT*] (EA)
SAR .... National Society, Sons of the American Revolution (EA)
SAR .... Safety Analysis Report [*Nuclear energy*]
SAR .... Safety Assessment Report (MCD)
SAR .... Sales Authorization Request
SAR .... Sample Acceptance Rate [*Statistics*]
SAR .... Santa Anita Realty Enterprises, Inc. [*NYSE symbol*] (SPSG)
SAR .... Santa Rosa Junior College, Santa Rosa, CA [*OCLC symbol*] (OCLC)
SAR .... Sarajevo [*Yugoslavia*] [*Seismograph station code, US Geological Survey*] (SEIS)
SAR .... Sarcoidosis [*Medicine*]
Sar .... Sarcosine [*Biochemistry*]
Sar .... Sarcosyl [*Biochemistry*]
SAR .... Sardinia [*Italy*] (ROG)
Sar .... Sarswati's Privy Council Judgments [*India*] [*A publication*] (DLA)
SAR .... Saudi Arabian Riyal [*Monetary unit*] (DS)
SAR .... Schedule Allocation Requirements (AAG)
SAR .... Schedule and Request (MCD)
SAR .... School of American Research [*Research center*] (RCD)
SAR .... Sea-Air Rescue
SAR .... Search and Release (AAG)
SAR .... Search and Rescue Program [*Coast Guard*]
SAR .... Segment Address Register [*Telecommunications*]
SAR .... Selected Acquisition Report [*Military*]
SAR .... Semiactive RADAR (MCD)
SAR .... Semiannual Report
SAR .... Semiautomatic Rifle [*Army*]
SAR .... Senior Army Representative
SAR .... Service Analysis Report [*Telecommunications*] (TEL)
SAR .... Service Analysis Request [*Telecommunications*] (TEL)
SAR .... Service Aptitude Rating [*Military*] (NVT)
SAR .... Service Assigned Requests (MCD)
SAR .... Sexual Attitude Reassessment [*Medicine*]
SAR .... Siemens Agronaut Reactor [*Germany*]
SAR .... Significant Action Report [*Military*] (MCD)
SAR .... Silver Acorn Developments [*Vancouver Stock Exchange symbol*]
SAR .... Simulated Acid Rain
SAR .... Single-Axis Reference
SAR .... Single-BIT [*Binary Digit*] Alternation Recording
SAR .... Site Acceptance Review [*Military*]
SAR .... Society for Animal Rights [*Later, ISAR*] (EA)
SAR .... Society of Authors' Representatives (EA)
SAR .... Sodium-Adsorption-Ratio
SAR .... Software Acceptance Review
SAR .... Son Altesse Royale [*His or Her Royal Highness*] [*French*]
SAR .... SONAR Acoustique Remorque [*Acoustic imaging system*] [*French*]
SAR .... Sons of the American Revolution
SAR .... Source Address Register [*Telecommunications*]
SAR .... South African Railways
SAR .... South African Republic
SAR .... South African Republic High Court Reports [*A publication*] (DLA)
SAR .... South Asian Review [*A publication*]
SAR .... South Australian Government Railways
SAR .... South Australian Industrial Reports [*A publication*] (APTA)
SAR .... South Australian Reports [*A publication*] (DLA)
SAR .... Spacecraft Acceptance Review (MCD)
SAR .... Sparta, IL [*Location identifier*] [*FAA*] (FAAL)
SAR .... Special Access Required
SAR .... Special Aeronautical Requirement [*Navy*] (NG)
SAR .... Specific Absorption Rate
SAR .... Specific Acoustic Resistance
SAR .... Specific Activity Report
SAR .... Specifically Authorized Representative [*Air Force*]
SAR .... Specification Approval Record (MCD)
SAR .... Stable Auroral Red [*Arc*] [*Geophysics*]
SAR .... Standardized Admissions Ratios [*Hospital activity analysis*]
SAR .... Standing Authority Release [*For perishables*] [*Business term*]
SAR .... Start Action Request [*Environmental Protection Agency*]
SAR .... Starting Air Receiver (AAG)
SAR .... Stock Appreciation Relief [*British*]
SAR .... Stock Appreciation Rights [*Method of compensation for top executives*]

SAR .... Storage Address Register [*Telecommunications*]
SAR .... Street Address Record [*Telecommunications*] (TEL)
SAR .... Structure Activity Relationship
SAR .... Student Aid Report [*Department of Education*]
SAR .... Studies in the American Renaissance [*A publication*]
SAR .... Study and Review [*Reports*] (RDA)
SAR .... Subauroral Red [*Arc*] [*Geophysics*]
SAR .... Submarine Advanced Reactor
SAR .... Subsequent Application Review
SAR .... Substitution Approval Request (MCD)
SAR .... Successive Accelerated Replacement
SAR .... Successive Approximation Register [*Data processing*]
SAR .... Sulfuric Acid Regenerator (MCD)
SAR .... Sum of Absolute Residuals [*Mathematics*]
SAR .... Summary Analysis Report (NASA)
SAR .... Super-Abrasion-Resistant [*LUCITE glazing material*]
SAR .... Support Air Request [*Net*] [*Navy communications*]
SAR .... Symbol Acquisition Routine
SAR .... Synthetic Aperture RADAR
SAR .... Syrian Arab Republic
SAR .... System Analysis Report
SAR .... System Array RADAR (KSC)
SAR .... System Availability Report
SAR .... Systemic Arterial Resistance [*Medicine*]
SAR .... Systemic Availability Ratio [*Physiology*]
SAR .... Systems Assessment Review [*NASA*] (KSC)
SARA .... Saralasin [*Antihypertensive*]
SARA .... Saratoga Mines, Inc. [*NASDAQ symbol*] (NQ)
SARA .... Saratoga National Historical Park
SARA .... Saratoga Trunk (DSUE)
SARA .... Satellite Angular Radiometer (NOAA)
SARA .... Saturates, Aromatics, Resins, and Asphaltenes [*Crude oil analysis*]
SARA .... Search and Rescue Aid
SARA .... Sequential Automatic Recorder and Annunciator
SARA .... Sexual Assault Research Association (EA)
SARA .... Society of American Registered Architects (EA)
SARA .... Still Another Response Averager
SARA .... Superfund Amendment and Reauthorization Act [*1986*]
SARA .... System for Anesthetic and Respiratory Analysis
SARA .... Systems Analysis and Resource Accounting [*Data processing system*]
Sarabhai M Chem Tech News Serv ... Sarabhai M. Chemicals. Technical News Service [*A publication*]
SARAC ...... Steerable Array for RADAR and Communications (CET)
SARAD ...... South African Rates and Data [*A publication*] (IMH)
SARAH ..... Search and Range Homing
SARAH ..... Search and Rescue Aid to Homing [*Australia*]
SARAH ..... Search and Rescue and Homing
SARAH ..... Semiactive RADAR Alternate Head
SARAH ..... Semiautomatic Range Azimuth and Height [*Subsystem*]
SA Railways ... South Australian Railways Institute. Magazine [*A publication*] (APTA)
SA Railways Institute Mag ... South Australian Railways Institute. Magazine [*A publication*] (APTA)
SARARC ... Subauroral Red Arc [*Geophysics*]
Sarat Ch Sent ... Saratoga Chancery Sentinel [*1841-47*] [*New York*] [*A publication*] (DLA)
Saratov Gos-Ped Inst Ucen Zap ... Saratovskii Gosudarstvennyi-Pedagogiceskii Institut. Ucenye Zapiski [*A publication*]
SARAW ..... Sarawak [*Malaysia*] (ROG)
SarawakMJ ... Sarawak Museum. Journal [*A publication*]
Sarawak Mus J ... Sarawak Museum. Journal [*A publication*]
Sarawak Res Branch Dep Agric Annu Rep ... Sarawak. Research Branch. Department of Agriculture. Annual Report [*A publication*]
SARB .... State Air Resources Board
Sarbah .... Sarbah's Fanti Law Reports [*Gold Coast*] [*A publication*] (DLA)
Sarbah FC ... Sarbah's Fanti Customary Laws [*Ghana*] [*A publication*] (DLA)
SARBE ...... Search and Rescue-Beacon Equipment (MCD)
SARBICA ... Southeast Asian Regional Branch of the International Council on Archives (EAIO)
SARC .... Corrientes [*Argentina*] [*ICAO location identifier*] (ICLI)
SARC .... Sarcasm (DSUE)
SARC .... Search and Rescue Center (CINC)
SARC .... Secure Airborne RADAR Control
SARC .... System Acquisition Review Council [*Army*]
SARC .... Systems Analysis and Research Corporation
SARCALM ... Synthetic Array RADAR Command Air-Launched Missile
SARCAP ... Search and Rescue - Civil Air Patrol (MCD)
SARCAR ... Smithsonian Archaeometric Research Collection and Records [*Facility*]
SARCC ...... Search and Rescue Coordination Center [*Air Force*]
SARCCUS ... South African Regional Committee for Conservation and Utilization of Soil
SARCEN ... Search and Rescue Central [*Navy*]
Sar Ch Sen ... Saratoga Chancery Sentinel [*New York*] [*A publication*] (DLA)
SARCOM ... Search and Rescue Communicator [*Navy*]
SARCUP ... Search and Rescue Capability Upgrade Project [*Canadian Navy*]

SARD........ Resistencia (Ciudad) [*Argentina*] [*ICAO location identifier*] (ICLI)
SARD........ Sardinia
SARD........ Simulated Aircraft RADAR Data
SARD........ Solar Array Release and Deployment (MCD)
SARD........ Special Airlift Requirement Directive [*Air Force*] (AFM)
SARD........ Special Airlift Requirement Document [*Army*]
SARD........ Statistical Analysis and Reports Division [*Washington, DC*] [*Administrative Office of the US Courts*] (GRD)
SARD........ Support and Range Development (MUGU)
SARD........ Synchronized Accumulating Radioisotope Detection
SARDA...... Society for Aid and Rehabilitation of Drug Addicts [*Hong Kong*]
SARDA...... State and Regional Defense Airlift Plan [*FAA, Civil Defense*]
SARDC...... Small Arms Research and Development Center [*Army*]
SARDEC ... Societe des Auteurs, Recherchistes, Documentalistes, et Compositeurs [*Canada*]
Sardegna Econ ... Sardegna Economica [*A publication*]
SARDET ... Search and Rescue Detachment [*Navy*] (NG)
SARDIP .... Stricken Aircraft Reclamation and Disposal Program [*Navy*] (NG)
SARDPO... San Antonio Research and Development Procurement Office [*Air Force*]
SARDS..... Special Air Route Designators (CINC)
SARDX...... Sardonyx [*Gemstone*] (ROG)
SARE........ Resistencia [*Argentina*] [*ICAO location identifier*] (ICLI)
SARE........ Safety Review [*A publication*]
SARE........ Southeast Asian Review of English [*A publication*]
SARE-A..... Saturday Review [*A publication*]
SAREA...... Sinus Area of Leaf [*Botany*]
SARED...... Supporting Applied Research and Exploratory Development [*National Weather Service*]
SAREF ...... Safety Research Experiment Facility [*Nuclear energy*]
SA Regr ..... South Australian Register [*A publication*] (APTA)
SA Regr (Newspr) ... South Australian Register Reports (Newspaper) [*A publication*] (APTA)
SAREP ...... Speech and Reading Enrichment Program
SA Res Service Bibliog ... South Australia. Public Library. Research Service. Bibliographies [*A publication*] (APTA)
SARev .... South Asian Review [*A publication*]
SARev .... South Atlantic Review [*A publication*]
SAREX ..... Search and Rescue Exercise (MCD)
SARF........ Formosa [*Argentina*] [*ICAO location identifier*] (ICLI)
SARF........ Semiautomated Reconstruction Facility [*Military*] (CAAL)
SARF........ Southeast Asia Rescue Foundation (EA)
SARF........ Southern Africa Road Federation [*See also SAPF*] [*Johannesburg, South Africa*] (EAIO)
Sar FCL ..... Sarbah's Fanti Customary Laws [*Ghana*] [*A publication*] (DLA)
Sar FLR ..... Sarbah's Fanti Law Cases [*1845-1903*] [*Ghana*] [*A publication*] (DLA)
Sar FNC..... Sarbah's Fanti National Constitution [*Ghana*] [*A publication*] (DLA)
SARFS...... Subordinate Army Field Services
Sarg............ Sargonic (BJA)
SARG........ Synthetic Aperture RADAR Guidance (MCD)
Sar Gaz ...... Sarawak Gazette [*Kuching*] [*A publication*]
Sarget........ Sargetia. Acta Musei Devensis [*A publication*]
Sargetia Ser Sci Nat ... Sargetia [*Acta Devensis*]. Series Scientia Naturae [*A publication*]
SARGUN .. Synthetic Aperture RADAR Gun [*NASA*]
SARI......... Iguazu/Cataratas Del Iguazu [*Argentina*] [*ICAO location identifier*] (ICLI)
SARI......... Share-a-Ride International (EA)
SARI......... Standby Altitude Reference Indicator (MCD)
SARIE....... Semiautomatic RADAR Identification Equipment (MCD)
SARIHHWP ... Serendipity Association for Research and Implementation of Holistic Health and World Peace (EA)
SARIPADI ... Serikat Pamong Desa Indonesia [*Village Officials' Union of Indonesia*]
SARIS........ Synthetic Aperture RADAR Interpretation System [*NASA*] (MCD)
SARISA..... Surface Analysis by Resonance Ionization of Sputtered Atoms
SARK........ Saville Advanced Remote Keying (MCD)
SARL........ Paso De Los Libres [*Argentina*] [*ICAO location identifier*] (ICLI)
SARL........ Societa a Responsabilita Limitata [*Limited Liability Company*] [*Italian*]
SARL........ Societe a Responsabilite Limitee [*Private Limited Company*] [*French*]
SARL........ South Australia Rugby League
SARL........ Subtropical Agricultural Research Laboratory [*Weslaco, TX*] [*Department of Agriculture*] (GRD)
SARLA...... South African Rock Lobster Association [*Defunct*]
SARLANT ... Search and Rescue, Atlantic [*Coast Guard*]
SARM........ Monte Caseros [*Argentina*] [*ICAO location identifier*] (ICLI)
SARM........ Set Asynchronous Response Mode
SARM........ Standard Antiradiation Missile (MCD)
SARM........ System Acquisition Review Memorandum [*Army*]
SARMIT ... Sport and Recreation Association of RMIT [*Royal Melbourne Institute of Technology*] Union

Sar Mus J .. Sarawak Museum. Journal [*Kuching*] [*A publication*]
SARNI....... Serikat Nelajan Indonesia [*Sailors' Union of Indonesia*]
SARO .... Ituzaingo [*Argentina*] [*ICAO location identifier*] (ICLI)
SAROAD... Storage and Retrieval of Aerometric Data [*Database*] [*Sigma Data Services Corp.*] [*Information service or system*] (CRD)
Sarot Otd Gos Nauchno-Issled Inst Ozern Rechn Rybn Khoz Tr ... Sarotovskoe Otdelenie Gosudarstvennogo Nauchno-Issledovatel'skogo Instituta Ozernogo i Rechnogo Rybnogo Khozyaistva. Trudy [*A publication*]
SARP........ Posadas [*Argentina*] [*ICAO location identifier*] (ICLI)
SARP........ Safety Analysis Report for Packaging [*NASA*] (NASA)
SARP........ Schedule, Analysis, and Review Procedure [*NASA*] (KSC)
SARP........ Schedule and Resources Procedure [*NASA*] (KSC)
SARP........ Scheduling and Reporting [*or Review*] Procedure [*NASA*] (KSC)
SARP........ Severe Accident Research Plan [*Nuclear energy*] (NRCH)
SARP........ Ship Alteration and Repair Package [*Navy*] (CAAL)
SARP........ Shuttle Astronaut Recruitment Program [*NASA*] (MCD)
SARP........ Signal Automatic RADAR Processing
SARP........ Small Autonomous Research Package
SARP........ Space Allocation Requirement Procedures (MCD)
SARP........ Space Allocation and Reservation Program (MCD)
SARP........ Standards and Recommended Practices
SARP........ Storage and Retrieval Processor (MCD)
SARPA...... South Australian Revolver and Pistol Association
SARPF...... Strategic Air Relocatable Photographic Facility (CINC)
SARPMA .. San Antonio Real Property Maintenance Agency [*Military*]
SARPS...... Standards and Recommended Practices [*International Civil Aviation Organization*]
SARR........ Resistencia [*Argentina*] [*ICAO location identifier*] (ICLI)
SARRA...... Short-Arc Reduction of RADAR Altimetry
SARRC...... South Australian Road Runners Association
SARRP ...... Severe Accident Risk Reduction Program [*Nuclear energy*] (NRCH)
SARS........ Presidencia R. Saenz Pena [*Argentina*] [*ICAO location identifier*] (ICLI)
SaRS......... Safety and Reliability Society [*British*]
SARS........ Secretary of the Army Research and Study [*Fellowship*]
SARS........ Semiautomated Reconstruction System [*Military*] (CAAL)
SARS........ Sensor Analog Relay System
SARS........ Ship Attitude Record System
SARS........ Simulated Airborne RADAR System (MCD)
SARS........ Single Allocation and Reservation Study (MCD)
SARS........ Single-Axis Reference System
SARS........ Solar Array Reorientation System
SARS........ Spares Accounting Replenishment System [*NASA*] (KSC)
SARS........ Stellar Attitude Reference Study
SARS........ Synthetic Array RADAR System
SARSA...... Social Affairs Recreation and Sports Association
SARSAT... Search and Rescue Satellite [*Navy*]
SARSAT.... Search and Rescue Satellite-Aided Tracking [*NASA*]
SARSEX.... Synthetic Aperture RADAR Signature Experiment [*Oceanography*]
SARSIM... Search and Rescue Simulation [*Coast Guard*]
SARSS...... Search and Rescue Satellite System [*Navy*] (MCD)
SARSS...... Standard Army Retail Supply System
SART........ St. Alban's Repertory Theater [*Washington, DC*]
SART........ Seattle Army Terminal
SART........ Society for Assisted Reproductive Technology (EA)
SART........ Special Army Review Team (MCD)
SART........ Standard Acid Reflux Test [*Clinical chemistry*]
SART........ Stimuli Analog Refresh Table [*NASA*] (MCD)
SARTACK ... Search AntiRADAR Tactical Aircraft, K-Band
SARTEL... Search and Rescue, Telephone [*Coast Guard*]
SARTITC... South Australian Road Transport Industry Training Committee
SARTOC... Southern Africa Regional Tourism Council (EAIO)
SARTS...... Satisfaction of Army Requirements through Space (MCD)
SARTS...... Small Arms Readiness Training Section [*National Guard*]
SARTS...... Small Arms Remote Target System (MCD)
SARTS...... Switched Access Remote Test System [*Bell System*]
SARU .... Resistencia [*Argentina*] [*ICAO location identifier*] (ICLI)
SARU .... System Analysis Research Unit
SARUM ... Bishop of Salisbury [*British*]
SARUS ..... Search and Rescue Using Satellites [*Air Force*]
SARV........ Satellite Aeromedical Research Vehicle
SAS........... Lithuanian Catholic Students' Association "Ateitis" (EA)
SAS........... St. Andrew Goldfields Ltd. [*Toronto Stock Exchange symbol*]
SAS........... St. Andrew Society [*Edinburgh, Scotland*] (EAIO)
SAS........... Salicylazosulfapyridine [*Antibacterial*]
SAS........... Salton City, CA [*Location identifier*] [*FAA*] (FAAL)
SAS........... Sample Array System (KSC)
SAS........... Sand-Asphalt-Sulfur [*Road paving material*]
SAS........... Saskatoon [*Saskatchewan*] [*Seismograph station code, US Geological Survey*] [*Closed*] (SEIS)
SAS........... Satellite Attack Sensor
SAS........... Scandinavian Airlines System [*Sweden*]
SAS........... Schiapparelli [*Italy*] [*Research code symbol*]
SAS........... SEAL [*Subsea Equipment Associates Limited*] Atmospheric System
SAS........... Sealed Authentication System [*Military*]

SAS	Secondary Alarm Station [*Nuclear energy*] (NRCH)
SAS	Sections Administratives Specialisees [*French Army*]
SAS	Security Agency Study [*Nuclear energy*] (NRCH)
SAS	Segment Arrival Storage Area (KSC)
SAS	Self-Adaptive System
SAS	Sensor and Source
SAS	Service Activity System
SAS	Service Air System (NRCH)
SASA	Sex Attitudes Survey [*Psychology*]
SAS	Shakespearean Authorship Society [*Later, SAT*] (EA)
SAS	Sherwood Anderson Society (EA)
SAS	Ship Alteration Suite [*Navy*] (CAAL)
SASCOM	Side-Angle-Side (Rule) [*Geometry*]
SAS	Signal Airways Service
SAS	Signal Analysis System
SAS	Silicon Avalanche Suppressor [*Telecommunications*]
SASDT	Single Angle Scattering
SAS	Single Anomalous Scattering [*Crystallography*]
SAS	Single Audio System (CAAL)
SAS	Sklar Aphasia Scale [*Psychology*]
SAS	Sleep Apnea Syndrome [*Medicine*]
SaS	Slovo a Slovesnost [*A publication*]
SAS	Small Applications Satellite (KSC)
SAS	Small Arms School [*British military*] (DMA)
SAS	Small Astronomy Satellite
SAS	Small-Probe Atmospheric Structure [*NASA*]
SAS	Snake Approach Scale [*Psychology*]
SAS	Snap Action Switch
SAS	Societatis Antiquariorum Socius [*Fellow of the Society of Antiquaries*] [*British*]
SAS	Society of American Silversmiths (EA)
SAS	Society for Applied Sociology (EA)
SAS	Society for Applied Spectroscopy (EA)
SAS	Society for Armenian Studies (EA)
SAS	Society of Australasian Specialists [*Later, SASO*]
SAS	Sodium Alkane Sulfonate [*Detergent intermediate*]
SAS	Sodium Aluminum Sulfate [*Organic chemistry*]
SAS	Solar Array Structure
SAS	Solar Array System (MCD)
SAS	Solar Aspect Sensor
SAS	Solomons Ano Sagufenua [*Political party*] [*Solomon Islands*] (FEA)
SAS	Son Altesse Serenissime [*His or Her Serene Highness*] [*French*]
SAS	Sound Amplification System
SAS	South American Series [*A publication*]
SASK	Southern Anthropological Society
SAS	Southern Appalachian Studies [*Defunct*] (EA)
SAS	Soviet Academy of Sciences
SAS	Space Activity Suit
SAS	Space Adaptation Syndrome [*NASA*]
SAS	Spacecraft Antenna System
SAS	Special Access Space (CAAL)
SAS	Special Air Service [*British commando unit*]
SAS	Special Ammunition Section [*Picatinny Arsenal*] [*Army*]
SAS	Special Ammunition Site [*Army*]
SAS	Special Ammunition Stockage [*Army*] (AABC)
SAS	Special Ammunition Storage (RDA)
SAS	Stability Augmentation System [*or Subsystem*] [*FAA*]
SAS	Staff Administrative Specialist [*Military*]
SAS	Statement of Auditing Standards
SAS	Station Air System [*Nuclear energy*] (NRCH)
SAS	Statistical Analysis System [*Programming language*] [*1966*]
SAS	Sterile Aqueous Suspension
SAS	Strategic Area Study (MCD)
SAS	Studia Academica Slovaca [*A publication*]
SAS	Sum of Adjacent Spans
SAS	Superior Atrial Septum [*Anatomy*]
SAS	Supersonic Attack Seaplane
SAS	Supravalvular Aortic Stenosis [*Cardiology*]
SAS	Surface Active Substances (IEEE)
SAS	Survival Avionics System [*Military*] (CAAL)
SAS	Suspended Aluminosilicate
SAS	Suspended Array System [*To detect submarines*]
SAS	Switched Access System [*Telecommunications*] (TEL)
SAS	System Acquisition School (MCD)
SAS	System Analysis Study
SAS	System Application Software [*Data processing*] (BUR)
SASA	Salta [*Argentina*] [*ICAO location identifier*] (ICLI)
SASA	Severe Accident Sequence Analysis [*Nuclear energy*] (NRCH)
SASA	Ski Area Suppliers Association (EA)
SASA	Small Arms Systems Agency [*Army*] (RDA)
SASA	South Asian Studies Association of Australia and New Zealand
SASA	Special Ammunition Supply Activity (MCD)
SASAE	Supplements. Annales. Service des Antiquites de l'Egypt [*Cairo*] [*A publication*]
SASAR	Segmented Aperture-Synthetic Aperture RADAR
SASAS	Southern Africa Society of Aquatic Scientists (EAIO)
SASAT	Shipboard Antisubmarine Attack Teacher [*Navy*]
SASB	Structural Analysis of Social Behavior
SASC	Salta [*Argentina*] [*ICAO location identifier*] (ICLI)
SASC	Sasco Cosmetics [*NASDAQ symbol*] (NQ)

SASC	Semiautomatic Stock Control
SASC	Senate Armed Services Committee
SASC	Senior Appointments Selection Committee [*British*]
SASC	Small Arms School Corps [*Military*] [*British*]
SASC	Subject Analysis Systems Collection [*University of Toronto*] [*Information service or system*] (IID)
SASC	Sydney Amateur Sailing Club [*Australia*]
SASC	Sydney Amateur Sport Club [*Australia*]
SASCA	South African Support Campaign Australia
SA Sch Post	South Australian School Post [*A publication*] (APTA)
SASCL	St. Ansgar's Scandinavian Catholic League (EA)
SASCOM	Southern Atlantic Satellite Communication
SASCOM	Special Ammunition Support Command [*Army*] (AABC)
SASCON	Southern African Solidarity Congress [*Zimbabwe*] [*Political party*] (PPW)
SASD	Static Adjustable Speed Drive
SASDT	Ships and Aircraft Supplemental Data Tables [*Navy*]
SASE	Self-Addressed Stamped Envelope
SASE	Small Arms Suppression Evaluation (MCD)
SASE	Space Adaptation Syndrome Experiment [*Pronounced "Sassy"*] [*Space shuttle experiment developed in Canada*]
SASF	SIDPERS [*Standard Installation/Division Personnel System*] Authorized Strength File [*Military*] (AABC)
SASFA	South Australian School Football Association
SASG	Security Assistance Steering Group [*Military*]
SASG	Smoke/Aerosol Steering Group [*DARCOM*] (RDA)
SASHA	Sanfujinka No Shimpo [*A publication*]
SASHEP	Study of Accreditation of Selected Health Educational Programs
SA Shipp News	South African Shipping News and Fishing Industry Review [*A publication*]
SASI	Ships and Air Systems Integration [*Navy*]
SASI	Shugart Associates Systems Interface
SASI	Society of Air Safety Investigators [*Later, ISASI*]
SASI	Southern Association of Science and Industry (EA)
SASI	Surface Air System Integration
SASI	System Automation Software, Incorporated
SASI	System on Automotive Safety Information [*General Motors Corp.*] [*Information service or system*]
S Asia R	South Asian Review [*A publication*]
SASIDS	Stochastic Adaptive Sequential Information Dissemination System
SASILO	Schriftenreihe. A. Stifer-Institut des Landes Oberoesterreich [*A publication*]
SASJ	Jujuy [*Argentina*] [*ICAO location identifier*] (ICLI)
SASJ	Self-Aligning Swivel Joint
SASK	Saskatchewan [*Canadian province*]
Sask	Saskatchewan Law Reports [*Canada*] [*A publication*] (DLA)
Saskatchewan Dept Nat Res Ann Rept Mineral Res Br Misc Paper	Saskatchewan. Department of Natural Resources. Annual Report. Mineral Resources Branch. Miscellaneous Paper [*A publication*]
Saskatchewan Geol Survey Rept	Saskatchewan Geological Survey. Report [*A publication*]
Saskatchewan L Rev	Saskatchewan Law Review [*A publication*]
Saskatch Med Quart	Saskatchewan Medical Quarterly [*A publication*]
Sask Bar Rev	Saskatchewan Bar Review [*A publication*]
Sask BR	Saskatchewan Bar Review [*A publication*]
Sask B Rev	Saskatchewan Bar Review [*A publication*]
Sask Bul	Saskatchewan Bulletin [*A publication*]
Sask Busn	Saskatchewan Business [*A publication*]
Sask Dep Miner Resour Geol Sci Br Precambrian Geol Div Rep	Saskatchewan. Department of Mineral Resources. Geological Sciences Branch. Precambrian Geology Division. Report [*A publication*]
Sask Dep Miner Resour Pet Natural Gas Reservoir Ann	Saskatchewan. Department of Mineral Resources. Petroleum and Natural Gas Reservoir. Annual [*A publication*]
Sask Dep Miner Resour Rep	Saskatchewan. Department of Mineral Resources. Report [*A publication*]
Sask Dep Nat Resour Fish Branch Fish Rep	Saskatchewan. Department of Natural Resources. Fisheries Branch. Fisheries Report [*A publication*]
Sask Dep Nat Resour Fish Wildl Branch Fish Rep	Saskatchewan. Department of Natural Resources. Fisheries and Wildlife Branch. Fisheries Report [*A publication*]
Sask Ed Admin	Saskatchewan Education Administrator [*A publication*]
Sask Gaz	Saskatchewan Gazette [*A publication*]
Sask Geol Soc Spec Publ	Saskatchewan Geological Society. Special Publication [*A publication*]
Sask Hist	Saskatchewan History [*A publication*]
Sask L	Saskatchewan Law [*A publication*] (DLA)
Sask Law Rev	Saskatchewan Law Review [*A publication*]
Sask Libr	Saskatchewan Library [*A publication*]
Sask LR	Saskatchewan Law Reports [*Canada*] [*A publication*] (DLA)
Sask LR	Saskatchewan Law Review [*A publication*]
Sask L Rev	Saskatchewan Law Review [*A publication*]
Sask (Prov) Dep Miner Resour Rep	Saskatchewan (Province). Department of Mineral Resources. Report [*A publication*]
Sask R	Saskatchewan Law Reports [*A publication*] (DLA)
Sask Res Counc Eng Div Rep	Saskatchewan Research Council. Engineering Division. Report [*A publication*]

Sask Res Counc Geol Div Rep ... Saskatchewan Research Council. Geology Division. Report [*A publication*]
Sask Res Counc Geol Div Rep G ... Saskatchewan Research Council. Geology Division. Report G [*A publication*]
Sask Rev Stat ... Saskatchewan Revised Statutes [*Canada*] [*A publication*] (DLA)
Sask Stat.... Saskatchewan Statutes [*Canada*] [*A publication*] (DLA)
SaskTel...... Saskatchewan Telecommunications [*Regina*] [*Information service or system*] (IID)
SASM........ Smithsonian Air and Space Museum
SASM........ Society for Automation in the Sciences and Mathematics
SASM....... South African Student Movement
SASM....... Special Assistant for Strategic Mobility [*Military*] (AFM)
SASMS..... Special Assistant for Surface Missile System
SASN........ Special Assistant to the Secretary of the Navy
SASNA..... South African Shipping News and Fishing Industry Review [*A publication*]
SASO........ Oran [*Algeria*] [*ICAO location identifier*] (ICLI)
SASO........ Sasol Ltd. [*NASDAQ symbol*] (NQ)
SASO........ Senior Air Staff Officer [*British*]
SASO........ Society of Australasian Specialists/Oceania (EA)
SASO........ South African Students' Organization (PD)
SASO........ Superintending Armament Supply Officer [*British military*] (DMA)
SASOC...... School Administrators and Supervisors Organizing Committee [*Later, AFSA*] (EA)
SASOP...... Sudan. Antiquities Service. Occasional Papers [*A publication*]
SASP........ Science and Application Space Platform (MCD)
SASP........ Shortest Activity from Shortest Project
SASP........ Single Advanced Signal Processor [*Military*] (CAAL)
SASP........ Site Activation and Support Plan (MCD)
SASP........ Society for the Advancement of Social Psychology (EA)
SASP........ Special Ammunition Supply Point [*Army*]
SASP........ Stand Alone Support Program
SASP........ State Agency for Surplus Property
SASP........ State Airport System Plan [*Department of Transportation*]
SASP........ Submarine Analytic Search Program [*Navy*] (CAAL)
SASPS...... SAMMS [*Standard Automated Materiel Management System*] Automated Small Purchase System
SASQ........ La Quiaca [*Argentina*] [*ICAO location identifier*] (ICLI)
SASq........ Strategic Aerospace Squadron [*Air Force*]
SASQUA... Southern African Society for Quaternary Research (EAIO)
SASR........ Rivadavia [*Argentina*] [*ICAO location identifier*] (ICLI)
SASR........ South Australian State Reports [*A publication*]
SASRAZ.... Sbornik Trudov Aspirantov i Molodykh Nauchnykh Sotrudnikov Vsesoyuznyi Nauchno-Issledovatel'skii Institut Rastenievodstva [*A publication*]
SASRS...... Satellite-Aided Search and Rescue System [*Telecommunications*]
SASS......... Saturn Automatic Software System [*NASA*]
SASS......... Schedules and Status Summary [*NASA*] (KSC)
SASS......... SEASAT [*Sea Satellite*]- A Scatterometer System [*NASA*]
SASS......... Small Airbreathing System Synthesis (MCD)
SASS......... Society for the Advancement of Scandinavian Study (EA)
SASS......... Society for Automation in the Social Sciences [*Later, SDE*]
SASS......... Source Assessment Sampling System [*Environmental Protection Agency*]
SASS......... South Australian Secrets Summary [*A publication*] (APTA)
SASS......... South Australian Social Science [*Information service or system*] [*A publication*] (APTA)
SASS......... Special Aircraft Service Shop (NG)
SASS......... SPEEDEX [*Systemwide Project for Electronic Equipment at Depots Extended*] Automatic Scheduling System [*Military*]
SASS......... Standard Army Supply System
SASS......... Strategic Airborne Surveillance System [*Military*]
SASS......... Strategic Alerting Sound System (AAG)
SASS......... Surveillance and Army Support Ship [*Australia*]
SASS......... Suspended Array Surveillance System [*To detect submarines*]
SASS......... Systems and Services Section [*Library Administration and Management Association*]
SASSAR.... Suid-Afrikaanse Spoorwee/South African Railways [*A publication*]
SASSC....... Senate Aeronautical and Space Sciences Committee (AAG)
SASSE....... Synchronous Altitude Spin-Stabilized Experiment
SASSI....... Synthetic Amorphous Silica and Silicates Industry Association (EA)
SASSIA..... Synthetic Amorphous Silica and Silicates Industry Association (EA)
SASSIF...... Self-Adjusting System of Scientific Information Flow
SASSTIXS ... Satellite Air, Surface, Subsurface Tactical Information Exchange System [*Navy*] (CAAL)
SASSY...... Small Angle Separator System [*Superheavy element research*]
SASSY...... Supported Activities Supply System [*Marine Corps*]
SAST........ Safety Standards
SAST........ Serum Aspartate Aminotransferase [*An enzyme*]
SAST........ Service Announcements in Science and Technology [*National Technical Information Service*] (EA)
SAST........ Single Asphalt Surface Treatment
SAST........ Society for the Advancement of Space Travel [*Defunct*] (MCD)

SAST........ Tartagal/Gral Mosconi [*Argentina*] [*ICAO location identifier*] (ICLI)
SASTA...... South Australian Secondary Teachers Association
SASTAJ.... SASTA [*South Australian Science Teachers Association*] Journal [*A publication*] (APTA)
SASTA Jl.. SASTA [*South Australian Science Teachers Association*] Journal [*A publication*]
SASTAR.... Support Activities Staffing Review (MCD)
SASTE...... Semiautomatic Shop Test Equipment (NG)
SA Storekeepers J ... South Australian Storekeepers and Grocers Journal [*A publication*] (APTA)
SASTP...... Stand-Alone Self-Test Program [*NASA*] (MCD)
SASTU...... Signal Amplitude Sampler and Totalizing Unit (IEEE)
SASU........ Saturn Apollo Systems Utilization [*NASA*]
SASUTA ... Southern African Society of University Teachers of Accounting (EAIO)
SASV........ Sisters of the Assumption of the Blessed Virgin [*Roman Catholic religious order*]
SASV........ Snap Action Spool Valve
SASWREC ... SACLANT [*Supreme Allied Commander, Atlantic*] Antisubmarine Warfare Research Center (NATG)
SAT........... Canadian Satellite Communications, Inc. [*Toronto Stock Exchange symbol*]
SAT........... Die Schriften des Alten Testaments in Auswahl Neu Uebersetzt und fuer die Gegenwart Erklaert [*Goettingen*] [*A publication*]
SAT........... Safe Arming Time
SAT........... Salamaua Aerial Transport [*Australia*]
SAT........... Sampler Address Translator
SAT........... San Antonio [*Texas*] [*Airport symbol*]
SAT........... Sang-Tuda [*USSR*] [*Seismograph station code, US Geological Survey*] [*Closed*] (SEIS)
SAT........... Satellite
Sat............. Satellite Science Fiction [*A publication*]
Sat............. Satirae [*or Sermones*] [*of Horace*] [*Classical studies*] (OCD)
SAT........... Satisfactory (AABC)
Sat............. Satura [*of Petronius*] [*Classical studies*] (OCD)
SAT........... Saturate (AAG)
SAT........... Saturatus [*Saturated*] [*Pharmacy*]
SAT........... Saturday (EY)
SAT........... Saturn [*Rocket*] (KSC)
Sat............. Saturn [*Record label*] [*France*]
SAT........... Saturn
Sat............. Saturnalia [*of Macrobius*] [*Classical studies*] (OCD)
SAT........... Schafer Value Trust, Inc. [*NYSE symbol*] (SPSG)
SAT........... Scholastic Aptitude Test [*Trademark of the College Entrance Examination Board*]
SAT........... School Ability Test [*Psychology*]
SAT........... School of Applied Tactics [*AAFSAT*]
SAT........... Scientific Advisory Team [*Navy*] (MCD)
SAT........... Scientific and Technical (MCD)
SAT...-- Security Alert Team [*Military*] (AFM)
SAT........... Security Assistance Team [*Military*] (AABC)
SAT........... Semiarid Tropics [*Geography*]
SAT........... Semiautomatic Test Equipment [*NASA*]
SAT........... Senior Apperception Technique [*Personality development test*] [*Psychology*]
SAT........... Senior Aptitude Tests [*Educational test*]
SAT........... Sennacieca Asocio Tutmonda [*Nationless Worldwide Association*] (EAIO)
SAT........... Service Acceptance Trials (NVT)
SAT........... Shakespearean Authorship Trust (EAIO)
SAT.... Ship Acceptance Test [*Navy*] (CAAL)
SAT........... Ship's Apparent Time [*Navigation*]
SATE........ Silicon Annular Transistor
SAT........... Sine Acido Thymonucleico [*Without Thymonucleic Acid*]
SAT........... Site Acceptance Test [*Military*] (AABC)
SAT........... Site Alteration Tests
SAT........... Site Assignment Time
SAT........... Sitting Atop [*Molecular configuration*]
SAT........... Small Angle Tagger (MCD)
SAT........... Snap Action Thermostat
SAT........... Societa Anonima Transadriatica [*Italy*]
SAT........... Sound-Apperception Test [*Psychology*]
SAT........... South Atlantic (AIA)
SAT........... Southern African Territories
SAT........... Southern Air Transport, Inc.
SAT........... Space Available Travel
SAT........... Speaker Authentication Technique
SAT........... Special Assistance Team [*Navy*] (NG)
SAT........... Specific Aptitude Test
SAT........... Specified Actions Table [*Military*]
SAT........... Spiral Aftereffect Test [*Psychology*]
SAT........... Stabilization Assurance Test (IEEE)
SAT........... Standard Area of Tinplate [*100,000 square inches*]
SAT........... Stanford Achievement Test [*Education*]
SAT........... Staphylococcus Adherence Test [*Clinical chemistry*]
SAT........... Static Air Temperature
SAT........... Stepped Atomic Time [*National Institute of Standards and Technology*]
SAT........... Strategic American Traveler

SAT............ Study of Appeal Tribunals [*British*]
SAT............ Subacute Thyroiditis [*Medicine*]
SAT............ Subassembly Template (MCD)
SAT............ Subscriber Access Terminal
SAT............ Subsumed Abilities Test [*Student attitudes test*]
SAT............ Successive Approximation Technique (NOAA)
SAT............ Support Analysis Test
SAT............ Surface Aerospace Technology
SAT............ Surface Antenna Terminal (MCD)
SAT............ Surveillance, Acquisition, and Tracking [*Military*] (RDA)
SAT............ Sustained Airborne Training [*Army*] (INF)
SAT............ System Access Technique [*Sperry UNIVAC*]
SAT............ System Alignment Test (NVT)
SAT............ Systematic Assertiveness Training
SAT............ Systems Acceptance Tests (KSC)
SAT............ Systems Approach to Training [*NASA*] (MCD)
SATA......... Die Schriften des Alten Testaments in Auswahl Neu Uebersetzt und fuer die Gegenwart Erklaert [*Goettingen*] [*A publication*]
SATA......... Safety and Arming Test Aid (MCD)
SATA......... Satellite Automatic Tracking Antenna (MCD)
SATA......... Sociedade Acoriana de Transportes Aereos Ltda. [*Airline*] [*Portugal*]
SATA......... Something about the Author [*A publication*]
SATA......... Student Air Travel Association
SATA......... Subsonic Aerodynamic Testing Association (MCD)
SATA......... Supervisory, Administrative, and Technical Association [*Union of Ship Distribution and Allied Workers*] [*British*] (DCTA)
SATAF...... Shuttle Activation Task Force [*NASA*] (NASA)
SATAF...... Site Activity [*or Alternation*] Task Force [*NASA*] (KSC)
SATAM..... Syndicat Autonome des Travailleurs de la Alimentation de Madagascar [*Autonomous Union of Food Workers of Madagascar*]
SATAN...... Satellite Active Nullifier [*Antisatellite weapon*]
SATAN...... Satellite Automatic Tracking Antenna
SATAN...... Sensor for Airborne Terrain Analysis
SATAN...... Strobes Against Troops at Night (MCD)
SATANAS ... Semiautomatic Analog Setting (IEEE)
SATANS .. Static and Transient Analysis, Nonlinear, Shells [*Computer program*] [*Navy*]
SATAR...... Satellite for Aerospace Research [*NASA*]
SA Tax Cas ... South African Tax Cases [*A publication*] (DLA)
SATB........ Simulated Air Training Bundle (MCD)
SATB........ Soprano, Alto, Tenor, Bass
SATB........ Specific Aptitude Test Battery
SATC........ Clorinda [*Argentina*] [*ICAO location identifier*] (ICLI)
SATC........ Ship Automatic Torpedo Countermeasures (MCD)
SATC........ South African Tax Cases [*A publication*] (DLA)
SATC........ Students Army Training Corps
SATC........ Suspended Acoustical-Tile Ceiling [*Technical drawings*]
SATCA...... Sino-American Technical Cooperation Association
SATCAMS ... Semiautomatic Tactical Control and Airspace Management System (MCD)
SATCC...... Southern Air Traffic Control Centre [*British*]
SATCH...... Salicylaldehyde Thiocarbohydrazone [*Organic chemistry*]
SATCHMO ... Satchel Mouth [*Nickname of late trumpeter Louis Armstrong*]
SATCO...... Senior Air Traffic Control Officer (NATG)
SATCO...... Signal Automatic Air Traffic Control System
SATCO...... South Australian Timber Corp.
SATCO...... Supervisory Air Traffic Control Organization [*FAA*]
SATCOM .. Satellite Command
SATCOM ... Satellite Communications [*Military*]
SATCOM ... Scientific and Technical Communication
SATCOMA ... Satellite Communications Agency [*AEC/DCA*]
SATCOM AGEN ... Satellite Communications Agency [*Army*]
SATCON... Satellite Condition [*Military*] (AABC)
SATCP ...... Sol-Air Tres Courte Portee [*Very Short Range Ground to Air*] [*Missile*] [*French*]
SATCRIS .. Semi-Arid Tropical Crops Information Service (IID)
SATCS....... Scandinavian Association for Thoracic and Cardiovascular Surgery (EA)
SATD........ El Dorado [*Argentina*] [*ICAO location identifier*] (ICLI)
SATD........ Saturated
SATD........ Seattle Army Terminal Detachment (AABC)
SATD........ Simulation and Training Device [*Army*]
SATD........ Strike Aircraft Test Directorate [*Military*] (CAAL)
SATDAT ... Satellite Data (MCD)
SATDB...... Sangyo To Denki [*A publication*]
SATDPI..... Salesmen's Association of the Textile Dyeing and Printing Industry (EA)
SATE......... Semiautomatic Test Equipment [*NASA*]
SATE......... Special Acceptance Test Equipment (MCD)
SATE......... Study of Army Test and Evaluation (MCD)
SATEA...... Soviet Atomic Energy [*English Translation*] [*A publication*]
SA Teachers J ... SA [*South Australia*] Teachers' Journal [*A publication*] (APTA)
SA Teach J ... South Australian Teachers' Journal [*A publication*] (APTA)
SATEC...... Semiautomatic Technical Control
SATEC...... Societe d'Aide Technique et de Cooperation [*An independent French company*]

SATELCO ... Satellite Telecommunications Company [*Japanese-American firm*]
SATELDATA ... Satellite Databank [*European Space Agency*] [*Database*]
Satel Dir..... Satellite Communications. Satellite Industry Directory [*A publication*]
Satell Commun ... Satellite Communications [*A publication*]
Satellite...... Satellite Communications [*A publication*]
SATELLITE ... Scientific and Technological Library Literature [*Conference*]
Satel News ... Satellite News [*A publication*]
SATENA ... Servicio de Aeronavegacion a Territorios Nacionales [*Colombian airline*]
Sat E P ...... Saturday Evening Post [*A publication*]
Sat Eve Post ... Saturday Evening Post [*A publication*]
SATF......... Shortest Access Time First
SATF......... Societe des Anciens Textes Francais [*A publication*]
SATF......... Substituted Anilines Task Force (EA)
SATFAL..... Satellite Data for Fallout (MCD)
SATFOR..... Special Air Task Force [*Navy*]
SATFY ...... Satisfactory (AFM)
SATG......... Goya [*Argentina*] [*ICAO location identifier*] (ICLI)
SATGA...... Societe Aerienne de Transport Guyane Antilles [*French Guiana Air Transport*]
SAT GCI.... Satellite Ground Controlled Interception (NATG)
SATH .... St. Thomas National Historic Site
SATH .... Society for the Advancement of Travel for the Handicapped (EA)
SATHA ...... Schweizer Archiv fuer Tierheilkunde [*A publication*]
SATI .... Bernardo De Irigoyen [*Argentina*] [*ICAO location identifier*] (ICLI)
SATI .... Satellite Information Systems Co. [*NASDAQ symbol*] (NQ)
SATI .... Society for the Advancement of the Tourism Industry
SATIF....... Scientific and Technical Information Facility [*NASA*]
SATIN .... SAC [*Strategic Air Command*] Automated Total Information Network (MCD)
SATIN .... SAGE [*Semiautomatic Ground Environment*] Air Traffic Integration
SATIN .... Satellite Inspector System (AAG)
SATIPS ..... Society of Assistants Training in Preparatory Schools [*British*]
SATIR .... System for Evaluation of Tactical Information on Missile Destroyers
SATIRE..... Scientific and Technical Information Reviewed and Exploited [*A publication*] (RDA)
SATIRE..... Semiautomatic Technical Information Retrieval
Satire N...... Satire Newsletter [*A publication*]
SatireNL.... Satire Newsletter [*A publication*]
SATIS........ Satisfactory (AAG)
SATISFN .. Satisfaction (ROG)
SATISFY.. Satisfactory (ROG)
SATIVA .... Society for Agricultural Training through Integrated Voluntary Activities (EA)
SATK........ Las Lomitas [*Argentina*] [*ICAO location identifier*] (ICLI)
SATK........ Strike Attack [*Military*]
SATKA...... Surveillance, Acquisition, Tracking, and Kill Assessment [*Section of SDI - Strategic Defense Initiative*]
SATKB...... Sanitarnaya Tekhnika [*A publication*]
SATL......... Satellite (AABC)
SATL......... Satellite Auction Network, Inc. [*Irving, TX*] [*NASDAQ symbol*] (NQ)
SATL......... Science and Advanced Technology Laboratory [*Army*] (RDA)
SATL........ South Atlantic
SATL........ Surgical Achilles Tendon Lengthening [*Medicine*]
S Atlan Bull ... South Atlantic Bulletin [*A publication*]
S Atlantic Q ... South Atlantic Quarterly [*A publication*]
SATLCONO ... Satellite Control Officer [*Air Force*]
S Atl Q .... South Atlantic Quarterly [*A publication*]
S Atl Quart ... South Atlantic Quarterly [*A publication*]
S Atl Rev.... South Atlantic Review [*A publication*]
SATM....... Mercedes [*Argentina*] [*ICAO location identifier*] (ICLI)
SAT-M ...... Scholastic Aptitude Test - Mathematics [*College Entrance Examination Board*]
SATM....... Sodium Aurothiomalate [*Organometallic chemistry*]
SATM....... Supply and Training Mission [*Military*] (CINC)
Sat Men .... Saturae Menippeae [*of Varro*] [*Classical studies*] (OCD)
SATMO..... Security Assistance Training Management Office [*Army*]
SATN........ Saturation
Sat N.......... Saturday Night [*A publication*]
SATN........ Saturn Energy & Resources Ltd. [*Vancouver, BC*] [*NASDAQ symbol*] (NQ)
SATNAV ... Satellite Navigation (AABC)
SATNET.... Satellite Data Broadcast Networks, Inc. [*New York, NY*] [*Telecommunications*] (TSSD)
Sat NL .... Satire Newsletter [*A publication*]
SATO .... Obera [*Argentina*] [*ICAO location identifier*] (ICLI)
SATO .... Scheduled Airlines Ticket Office
SATO .... Scheduled Airlines Traffic Office [*Military*]
SATO .... Self-Aligning Thick Oxide [*Process*]
SATO .... Shuttle Attached Teleoperator [*NASA*] (NASA)
SATO .... South American Travel Organization
SATO .... Station Airline Ticket Office (MCD)
SATO .... Supply and Transportation Operations [*NASA*] (NASA)
SATO .... Synthetic Aircraft Turbine Oil

SATODP...　Satellite Tracking Orbit Determination Program
Sat Oklahom ...　Saturday Oklahoman and Times [*A publication*]
SATON .....　Satisfaction　(ROG)
SATOUR...　South African Tourism Board　(EA)
SATP........　Security Assistance Training Program [*Military*]
SATP ....　Small Arms Target Practice [*Navy*]
SATP ....　Stabilization, Acquisition, Tracking, and Pointing
SATP ....　Supplier Assurance Test Procedures
SATPATT ...　Satellite Paper Tape Transfer
SATR........　Reconquista [*Argentina*] [*ICAO location identifier*]　(ICLI)
Sat R ....　Saturday Review [*A publication*]
SATR........　Scheduled Air Transport Rating
SATR........　So as to Reach [*Aviation*]　(FAAC)
SATRA......　Science and Technology Research Abstracts [*A publication*]
SATRA ......　Shoe and Allied Trades Research Association [*Later, Footwear Technology Centre*] [*British*]　(EA)
SATRA ......　Soviet-American Trade Association
SATRA Bull ...　SATRA [*Shoe and Allied Trades Research Association*] Bulletin [*A publication*]
SATRAC ...　Satellite Automatic Terminal Rendezvous and Coupling　(MCD)
SATRACK ...　Satellite Tracking　(MCD)
SATRAM ..　Systeme d'Atterrissage a Trajectoires Multiples [*Aviation*]
SATRAN...　Satellite Reconnaissance Advance Notice　(MCD)
Sat R Arts ..　Saturday Review of the Arts [*A publication*]
Sat R Ed....　Saturday Review of Education [*A publication*]
Sat Rev......　Saturday Review [*A publication*]
Sat R Lit....　Saturday Review of Literature [*A publication*]
SATROS ...　Science and Technology Regional Organizations [*British*]
Sat R Sci ...　Saturday Review of the Sciences [*A publication*]
Sat R Soc...　Saturday Review of Society [*A publication*]
Sat R/World ...　Saturday Review/World [*A publication*]
SATS ....　S. Allan Taylor Society　(EA)
SATS ....　Satellite Antenna Test System [*NASA*]
SATS ....　Short Airfield for Tactical Support [*Marine Corps*]
SATS ....　Shuttle Avionics Test System [*NASA*]　(NASA)
SATS ....　Simulated Airborne Transpondent System　(MCD)
SATS ....　Single Array Test System　(MCD)
SATS ....　Small Applications Technology Satellite　(MCD)
SATS ....　Small Arms Target System [*British military*]　(DMA)
SATS ....　Social and Technical Sciences
SATS ....　Surrogate Acquilla Training System [*Army*]
SATSA ......　Signal Aviation Test and Support Activity
SATSERV ...　Services by Satellite, Inc. [*Defunct*]
SATSF......　Special Assistance to Students Fund [*Australia*]
SATSIM...　Satellite Simulation [*Military*]　(CAAL)
SATSIM....　Saturation Countermeasures Simulator
SATSLAM ...　Satellite-Tracked Submarine-Launched Antimissile　(MCD)
SATT ....　Science, Applications, Technology Transfer, and Training [*System*] [*National Institutes of Health*]
SATT ....　Semiautomatic Transistor Tester [*NASA*]
SATT ....　Strowger Automatic Toll Ticketing [*Telecommunications*]
SATTDF....　Suid-Afrikaanse Tydskrif vir Natuurwetenskap en Tegnologie [*A publication*]
SATTR......　Satisfactory to Transfer　(NOAA)
SATU........　Curuzu Cuatia [*Argentina*] [*ICAO location identifier*]　(ICLI)
SATU........　Singapore Association of Trade Unions
SATU........　South African Typographical Union
SATUCC ...　Southern African Trade Union Coordination Council [*Gaborone, Botswana*]　(EAIO)
SATUD.....　South African Tunnelling [*A publication*]
SatUK.......　Satellite United Kingdom
SATUR......　Saturate　(AAG)
Saturday Rev ...　Saturday Review [*A publication*]
SAT-V........　Scholastic Aptitude Test - Verbal [*College Entrance Examination Board*]
SATW........　Society of American Travel Writers　(EA)
SATX ....　Satellite Express [*Telecommunications*]
Sau ....　All India Reporter, Saurashtra [*1950-57*] [*A publication*]　(DLA)
SAU ....　Saltair [*Utah*] [*Seismograph station code, US Geological Survey*]　(SEIS)
SAU ....　Samarkano Resources [*Vancouver Stock Exchange symbol*]
SAU ....　Saudi Arabia [*ANSI three-letter standard code*]　(CNC)
SAU ....　Saugeen Ontario Library Service [*UTLAS symbol*]
SAU ....　Sausalito, CA [*Location identifier*] [*FAA*]　(FAAL)
SAU ....　Sawu [*Indonesia*] [*Airport symbol*]　(OAG)
SAU ....　Scandinavian Association of Urology　(EA)
SAU ....　Scientific Arithmetic Unit
SAU ....　Search Attack Unit
SAU ....　Separate Administrative Unit [*Work Incentive Program*]
SAU ....　Signal Acquisition Unit　(NASA)
SAU ....　Smallest Addressable Unit
SAU ....　Social Affairs Unit [*British*]
SAU ....　Spectrum Analysis Unit
SAU ....　Sprawozdania Akademii Umiejetnosci [*A publication*]
SAU ....　Standard Advertising Unit [*System introduced to make national newspaper advertising pages uniform in size and format and to replace the agate line with the inch as a unit of measure*]
SAU ....　Statistical Analysis Unit

SAU ....　Strap-Around Unit [*NASA*]　(NASA)
SAU ....　Surface Attack Unit
SAU ....　System [*or Subsystem*] Availability Unit
SAUCB......　Soviet Automatic Control [*English Translation*] [*A publication*]
SAUCERS ...　Space and Unexplained Celestial Events Research Society　(EA)
Saudi Arabia Dir Gen Miner Resour Bull ...　Saudi Arabia. Directorate General of Mineral Resources. Bulletin [*A publication*]
Saudi Arabia Dir Gen Miner Resour Geol Map ...　Saudi Arabia. Directorate General of Mineral Resources. Geologic Map [*A publication*]
Saudi Arabia Dir Gen Miner Resour Miner Resour Rep Invest ...　Saudi Arabia. Directorate General of Mineral Resources. Mineral Resources Report of Investigations [*A publication*]
Saudi Arabia Dir Gen Miner Resour Miner Resour Res ...　Saudi Arabia. Directorate General of Mineral Resources. Mineral Resources Research [*A publication*]
SAUFI ....　Sindacato Autonomo Unificato Ferrovieri Italiani [*Autonomous Union of Italian Railroad Workers*]
SAU & G....　San Antonio, Uvalde & Gulf Railroad Co.
Saugar Univ J Part 2 ...　Saugar University. Journal. Part 2. Science [*A publication*]
Saugertierkd Mitt ...　Saugetierkundliche Mitteilungen [*A publication*]
Saugetierkundliche Mitt ...　Saugetierkundliche Mitteilungen [*A publication*]
SAUK ....　Scoliosis Association of the United Kingdom　(EAIO)
Sau LR ....　Saurastra Law Reports [*India*] [*A publication*]　(DLA)
Sauls ....　Reports Tempore Saulsbury [*5-6 Delaware*] [*A publication*]　(DLA)
Saund ....　Saunders' King's Bench Reports [*1666-73*] [*A publication*]　(DLA)
Saund & A ...　Saunders and Austin's Locus Standi Reports [*1895-1904*] [*A publication*]　(DLA)
Saund Ass ..　Saunders on Assault and Battery [*1842*] [*A publication*]　(DLA)
Saund & Aust ...　Saunders and Austin's Locus Standi Reports [*A publication*]　(DLA)
Saund & B ...　Saunders and Bidder's Locus Standi Reports [*England*] [*A publication*]　(DLA)
Saund Bast ...　Saunders on Affiliation and Bastardy [*11th ed.*] [*1915*] [*A publication*]　(DLA)
Saund & BC ...　Saunders and Cole's English Bail Court Reports [*1846-48*] [*A publication*]　(DLA)
Saund BC...　Saunders and Cole's English Bail Court Reports [*82 RR*] [*1846-48*] [*A publication*]　(DLA)
Saund & C ...　Saunders and Cole's English Bail Court Reports [*1846-48*] [*A publication*]　(DLA)
Saunders Monogr Clin Radiol ...　Saunders Monographs in Clinical Radiology [*A publication*]
Saund & M ...　Saunders and Macrae's English County Courts and Insolvency Cases [*County Courts Cases and Appeals, II-III*] [*A publication*]　(DLA)
Saund & Mac ...　Saunders and Macrae's English County Court Cases [*A publication*]　(DLA)
Saund Mag Pr ...　Saunders' Magistrates' Courts Practice [*6th ed.*] [*1902*] [*A publication*]　(DLA)
Saund Mil L ...　Saunders' Militia Law [*4th ed.*] [*1855*] [*A publication*]　(DLA)
Saund Mun Reg ...　Saunders' Municipal Registration [*2nd ed.*] [*1873*] [*A publication*]　(DLA)
Saund Neg ...　Saunders on Negligence [*2nd ed.*] [*1878*] [*A publication*]　(DLA)
Saund Pl & Ev ...　Saunders' Pleading and Evidence [*A publication*]　(DLA)
Saund Prec ...　Saunders' Precedents of Indictments [*3rd ed.*] [*1904*] [*A publication*]　(DLA)
Saund War ...　Saunders on Warranties and Representations [*1874*] [*A publication*]　(DLA)
SAUR ....　Small Auxin Up RNA [*Ribonucleic Acid*] [*Botany*]
SAUS........　Sausage　(DSUE)
SAUS.........　Soccer Association of the United States　(EA)
SAus..........　South Australia　(ADA)
Sau & Sc.....　Sausse and Scully's Irish Rolls Court Reports [*1837-40*] [*A publication*]　(DLA)
S Aus Nat Gal Bul ...　South Australia. National Gallery. Bulletin [*A publication*]
Sausse & Sc ...　Sausse and Scully's Irish Rolls Court Reports [*1837-40*] [*A publication*]　(DLA)
S Aust ....　South Australiana [*A publication*]　(APTA)
S Aust Clinics ...　South Australian Clinics [*A publication*]　(APTA)
S Aust Coal Abstr Bull ...　South Australian Coal Abstract Bulletin [*A publication*]　(APTA)
S Aust Dir Mines Gov Geol Annu Rep ...　South Australia. Director of Mines and Government Geologist. Annual Report [*A publication*]
S Aust Geol Atlas Ser ...　South Australia. Geological Survey. Atlas Series [*A publication*]　(APTA)
S Aust Geol Surv Bull ...　South Australia. Geological Survey. Bulletin [*A publication*]　(APTA)
S Aust Geol Surv 1:250000 Geol Ser ...　South Australia. Geological Survey. 1:250,000 Geological Series [*A publication*]　(APTA)
S Aust Geol Surv Q Geol Notes ...　South Australia. Geological Survey. Quarterly Geological Notes [*A publication*]
S Aust Geol Surv Rep Invest ...　South Australia. Geological Survey. Report of Investigations [*A publication*]　(APTA)
S Aust Indus R ...　South Australia Industrial Reports [*A publication*]　(DLA)
S Aust L......　South Australia Law [*A publication*]　(DLA)

S Austl .... South Australia State Reports [*A publication*] (DLA)
S Austl Acts ... South Australia Acts [*1866-1936*] [*A publication*] (DLA)
S Austl LR ... South Australian Law Reports [*A publication*]
S Aust LR .. South Australian Law Reports [*A publication*]
S Austl Stat ... South Australian Statutes [*1837-1975*] [*A publication*] (DLA)
S Austl St R ... South Australian State Reports [*A publication*] (DLA)
S Aust Miner Resour Rev ... South Australia Mineral Resources Review [*A publication*]
S Aust Nat ... South Australian Naturalist [*A publication*] (APTA)
S Aust Orn ... South Australian Ornithologist [*A publication*] (APTA)
S Aust Ornithol ... South Australian Ornithologist [*A publication*]
S Australia Geol Surv Rep Invest ... South Australia. Geological Survey. Report of Investigations [*A publication*]
S Australiana ... South Australiana [*A publication*] (APTA)
S Aust Rep Mus Board ... South Australia. Report of the Museum Board [*A publication*]
S Austr L .... South Australia Law [*A publication*] (DLA)
S Austrl LR ... South Australian Law Reports [*A publication*] (ILCA)
S Aust Teach J ... South Australian Teachers' Journal [*A publication*]
S Aust Wheatgr ... South Australian Wheatgrower [*A publication*]
SAUT .... Scottish Association of University Teachers [*A union*]
SAUZA ..... Stroitel'stvo i Arkhitektura Uzbekistana [*A publication*]
SaV .... Saguaro Cactus Virus
SAV .... Savannah [*Tasmania*] [*Seismograph station code, US Geological Survey*] (SEIS)
SAV .... Savannah [*Georgia*] [*Airport symbol*] (OAG)
SAV .... Savannah Electric & Power Co. [*NYSE symbol*] (SPSG)
SAV .... Saveloy (DSUE)
Sav .... Savile's English Common Pleas Reports [*A publication*] (DLA)
Sav .... Savings (DLA)
SAV .... Savior
Sav .... Savremenik [*A publication*]
SAV .... Schweizerisches Archiv fuer Volkskunde [*A publication*]
SAV .... Service Availability [*AT & T*]
SAV .... Slovenska Akademia Vied [*A publication*]
SAV .... Small Affluent Variable [*Moko disease of banana*] [*Plant pathology*]
SAV .... Society Against Vivisection (EA)
SAV .... Society of American Ventriloquists (EA)
SAV .... Spectra Ventures Ltd. [*Vancouver Stock Exchange symbol*]
SAV .... Standard Acceptance Value
SAV .... Statens Avtalsverk [*Sweden*]
SAV .... Stock at Valuation
SAV .... Strollad ar Vro [*Country Party*] [*France*] [*Political party*] (PPW)
SAV .... Student Alternatives to Violence [*Defunct*] (EA)
SAV .... Submerged Aquatic Vegetation
SAVA .... Piedra Del Aguila [*Argentina*] [*ICAO location identifier*] (ICLI)
SAVA .... Servicios do Aerotaxisa e Abastecimento do Vale Amazonica [*Airline*] [*Brazil*]
SAVA .... Sexual Abuse Victims Anonymous [*Canada*]
SAVAC ..... South Australian Visual Arts Committee
SAVAK ..... Sazemane Attalat Va Anmiyate Keshvar [*Iranian security and intelligence organization*]
SAVAS ...... Six-Factor Automated Vocational Assessment System [*Vocational guidance test*]
SAVASI ..... Simple [*or Simplified*] Abbreviated Visual Approach Slope Indicator [*FAA*]
SAVB .... El Bolson [*Argentina*] [*ICAO location identifier*] (ICLI)
Sav Bank J ... Savings Bank Journal [*A publication*]
SAVBOND ... War Savings Bond [*Allotment for purchase*] [*Navy*]
SAVC .... Air-Cushion Vehicle built by Sealand Air Cushion Vehicles [*US*] [*Usually used in combination with numerals*]
SAVC .... Comodoro Rivadavia/Gral Mosconi [*Argentina*] [*ICAO location identifier*] (ICLI)
SAVC .... Society for the Anthropology of Visual Communication (EA)
Sav Conf Law ... Savigny's Conflict of Laws [*2nd ed.*] [*1880*] [*A publication*] (DLA)
SAVD .... El Maiten [*Argentina*] [*ICAO location identifier*] (ICLI)
Sav Dr Rom ... Savigny's Droit Romain [*A publication*] (DLA)
SAVE .... Energy Resources of North Dakota, Inc. [*NASDAQ symbol*] (NQ)
SAVE .... Esquel [*Argentina*] [*ICAO location identifier*] (ICLI)
SAVE .... Self-Learning Audio Visual Education [*National Foundation for the Prevention of Oral Disease*]
SAVE .... Sensitive Activity Vulnerability Estimate
SAVE .... Service Activities of Voluntary Engineers
SAVE .... Shoppers Association for Value Economy (EA)
SAVE .... Shortages and Valuable Excesses [*Navy*] (NG)
SAVE .... Society of American Value Engineers (EA)
SAVE .... Society of American Vintage-Radio Enthusiasts
SAVE .... Society of Americans for Vashchenko Emigration (EA)
SAVE .... Stop Addiction through Voluntary Effort
SAVE .... Student Action Voters for Ecology
SAVE .... Students Against Volvo Exaggerations [*Student legal action organization*]
SAVE .... System for Automatic Value Exchange [*Data processing*]
SAVE .... System Availability Estimator
SAVE .... System Avionics Value Estimation

SAVE .... Systematic Alien Verification for Entitlements [*Immigration and Naturalization Service*]
SAVER ..... Shuttle Avionics Verification and Evaluation [*NASA*] (NASA)
SAVER ..... Stowable Aircrew Vehicle Escape Rotoseat (MCD)
SAVER ..... Study to Assess and Validate Essential Reports [*Military*] (AABC)
SAVES ...... Sizing Aerospace Vehicle Structures [*NASA*]
SAVES ...... South Australian Voluntary Euthanasia Society
SAVES ...... States Audiovisual Education Study
SAVF .... Comodoro Rivadavia [*Argentina*] [*ICAO location identifier*] (ICLI)
SAVH .... Las Heras [*Argentina*] [*ICAO location identifier*] (ICLI)
SAVICOM ... Society for the Anthropology of Visual Communication
Savigny Hist Rom Law ... Savigny's History of the Roman Law [*A publication*] (DLA)
Savigny System ... Savigny's System des Heutigen Roemischen Rechts [*A publication*] (DLA)
Savile .... Savile's English Common Pleas Reports [*123 English Reprint*] [*1580-94*] [*A publication*] (DLA)
SAVIM ...... Survivability and Vulnerability Improvement Modification [*Army*] (RDA)
Savings Bank J ... Savings Bank Journal [*A publication*]
Savings Banks Internat ... Savings Banks International [*A publication*]
SAVITAR ... Sanders Associates Video Input/Output Terminal Access Resource [*Data processing*] (IEEE)
SAVKWA ... Suider Afrikaanse Vereniging vir Kwarternavorsing [*Southern African Society for Quaternary Research*] (EAIO)
SAVL .... Studien zur Allgemeinen und Vergleichenden Literaturwissenschaft [*A publication*]
Sav & Loan N ... Savings and Loan News [*A publication*]
Sav Loan News ... Savings and Loan News [*A publication*]
SAVM .... Lago Musters [*Argentina*] [*ICAO location identifier*] (ICLI)
SAVMO ..... Service Audiovisual Management Office [*Army*]
Savng Inst ... Savings Institutions [*A publication*]
SAVO .... San Antonio Oeste [*Argentina*] [*ICAO location identifier*] (ICLI)
SAVO .... Schultz Sav-O Stores, Inc. [*NASDAQ symbol*] (CTT)
SAVOR ..... Single-Actuated Voice Recorder
SAVP .... Paso De Indios [*Argentina*] [*ICAO location identifier*] (ICLI)
Sav Pos ...... Savigny on Possessions [*6th ed.*] [*1848*] [*A publication*] (DLA)
Sav Priv ..... Trial of the Savannah Privateers [*A publication*] (DLA)
SAVQ .... Maquinchao [*Argentina*] [*ICAO location identifier*] (ICLI)
SAVR .... Alto Rio Senguerr [*Argentina*] [*ICAO location identifier*] (ICLI)
SAVR .... Savers', Inc. [*NASDAQ symbol*] (NQ)
Savremena Poljopr ... Savremena Poljoprivreda [*A publication*]
Savrem Med (Sofia) ... Savremenna Meditsina (Sofia) [*A publication*]
Savrem Poljoprivreda ... Savremena Poljoprivreda [*A publication*]
SAVS .... Safeguards Area Ventilation System [*Nuclear energy*] (NRCH)
SAVS .... Sierra Grande [*Argentina*] [*ICAO location identifier*] (ICLI)
SAVS .... Status and Verification System [*NASA*] (KSC)
SAVT .... Save Area Table [*Data processing*] (IBMDP)
SAVT .... Secondary Address Vector Table [*Data processing*] (IBMDP)
SAVT .... Trelew/Almirante Zar [*Argentina*] [*ICAO location identifier*] (ICLI)
SAVU .... Comodoro Rivadavia [*Argentina*] [*ICAO location identifier*] (ICLI)
SAVV .... Viedma/Gobernador Castello [*Argentina*] [*ICAO location identifier*] (ICLI)
Savv Kn ...... Savvina Kniga [*A publication*]
SAVY .... Puerto Madryn [*Argentina*] [*ICAO location identifier*] (ICLI)
Sav Zeitschr ... Zeitschrift der Savigny-Stiftung fuer Rechtsgeschichte. Romanistische Abteilung [*A publication*] (OCD)
SAW .... Gwinn, MI [*Location identifier*] [*FAA*] (FAAL)
SAW .... St. Andrews [*Washington*] [*Seismograph station code, US Geological Survey*] (SEIS)
SAW .... Sample Assignment Word
SAW .... Satellite Attack Warning
Saw .... Sawyer's United States Circuit Court Reports [*A publication*] (DLA)
SAW .... Scottish Association of Writers [*British*]
SAW .... Search-a-Word [*Neuropsychology test*]
SAW .... Seasonal Agricultural Worker
SAW .... Semiautomatic Weapons
SAW .... Signal Aircraft Warning
SAW .... Sitzungsberichte. Akademie der Wissenschaft in Wien [*A publication*]
SAW .... Small Arms Weapon
SAW .... Society of American Wars (EA)
SAW .... Solar Array Wing (MCD)
SAW .... South Albuquerque Works [*AEC*]
SAW .... Southern Army Worm [*Agronomy*]
SAW .... Sozialistische Arbeitswissenschaft [*A publication*]
SAW .... Special Agricultural Worker
SAW .... Special Air Warfare (AFM)
SAW .... Squad Automatic Weapon [*Army*]
SAW .... Strike Anywhere [*Match*]
SAW .... Subantarctic Water
SAW .... Submerged Arc Weld
SAW .... Surface Acoustic Wave [*Microwave system*]
SAWA .... Lago Argentino [*Argentina*] [*ICAO location identifier*] (ICLI)

SAWA .... Screen Advertising World Association [*London, England*]   (EAIO)
SAWA .... Society of Anaesthetists of West Africa [*Benin City, Nigeria*]   (EAIO)
SAWANS.. South African Women's Auxiliary Naval Service [*British military*]   (DMA)
SAWAS..... South African Women's Auxiliary Services
SA Waterabstr ... SA [*South African*] Waterabstracts [*A publication*]
SAWB....... Base Marambio [*Argentina*] [*ICAO location identifier*]   (ICLI)
SAWB....... Sitzungsberichte. Akademie der Wissenschaften zu Berlin [*A publication*]
SAWBET .. Supply Action Will Be Taken
SAWC....... Special Air Warfare Center
SAWD ...... Puerto Deseado [*Argentina*] [*ICAO location identifier*]   (ICLI)
SAWD ...... Solid Amine Water Desorbed   (NASA)
SAWE....... Rio Grande [*Argentina*] [*ICAO location identifier*]   (ICLI)
SAWE....... Simulated Area Weapons Effects
SAWE....... Society of Allied Weight Engineers   (EA)
SAWE-IF .. Simulated Area Weapons Effects - Indirect Fire
SAWEUNSW ... Shop Assistants and Warehouse Employees Union of New South Wales [*Australia*]
SAWF....... Special Air Warfare Forces   (AFM)
SAWG ...... Rio Gallegos [*Argentina*] [*ICAO location identifier*]   (ICLI)
SAWG ...... Schedule and Allocations Working Group [*NASA*]   (KSC)
SAWG ...... Special Advisory Working Group   (NATG)
SAWg .... Strategic Aerospace Wing [*Air Force*]   (AFM)
SAWGUS ... Standoff/Attack Weapons Guidance Utility Study   (MCD)
SAWH....... Ushuaia [*Argentina*] [*ICAO location identifier*]   (ICLI)
SAWI....... Society for Animal Welfare in Israel   (EAIO)
SAWIC...... South African Water Information Centre [*Information service or system*]   (IID)
SAWID...... Shipboard Acoustic Warfare Integrated Defense   (NVT)
SAWJ .... San Julian/Cap. D. J. D. Vasquez [*Argentina*] [*ICAO location identifier*]   (ICLI)
SAWLT ..... South African Written Language Test [*Educational test*]
SAWM ...... Rio Mayo [*Argentina*] [*ICAO location identifier*]   (ICLI)
SAWM ...... Sitzungsberichte. Akademie der Wissenschaften zu Muenchen [*A publication*]
SAWMA..... Soil and Water Management Association [*British*]
SAWMA.... Southern African Wildlife Management Association [*See also NVSA*] [*Pretoria, South Africa*]   (EAIO)
SAWMARCS ... Standard Aircraft Weapon Monitor and Release Control System   (NG)
SAWO .... Surface Acoustic Wave Oscillator [*Telecommunications*]   (TEL)
SAWP....... Perito Moreno [*Argentina*] [*ICAO location identifier*]   (ICLI)
SAWP....... Society of American Wood Preservers   (EA)
SAWPHK ... Saechsische Akademie der Wissenschaften zu Leipzig. Philologisch-Historische Klasse [*A publication*]
SAWR....... Gobernador Gregores [*Argentina*] [*ICAO location identifier*]   (ICLI)
SAWRS ..... Supplementary Aviation Weather Reporting Station [*National Weather Service*]   (FAAC)
SAWS....... Jose De San Martin [*Argentina*] [*ICAO location identifier*]   (ICLI)
SAWS....... Satellite Attack Warning System
SAWS....... Seventh-Day Adventist World Service [*Superseded by ADRA*]   (EA)
SAWS....... Small Arms Weapon Study [*Army*]
SAWS....... Small Arms Weapons System   (NATG)
SAWS....... Solar Array Wing Simulator   (MCD)
SAWS....... Special Airborne Weapon Subsystem   (MCD)
SAWS....... Squad Automatic Weapon System [*Army*]
SAWS....... Subacoustic Warfare System
SAWS....... Submarine Acoustic Warfare System [*Navy*]   (MCD)
SAWT....... Rio Turbio [*Argentina*] [*ICAO location identifier*]   (ICLI)
Sawtri Bull ... Sawtri Bulletin [*A publication*]
SAWU ...... Santa Cruz [*Argentina*] [*ICAO location identifier*]   (ICLI)
SAWW ...... Sitzungsberichte. Akademie der Wissenschaft in Wien [*A publication*]
Sawy.......... Sawyer's United States Circuit Court Reports [*A publication*]   (DLA)
Sawyer Circt ... Sawyer's United States Circuit Court Reports [*A publication*]   (DLA)
Sawyer's Gas Turbine Int ... Sawyer's Gas Turbine International [*A publication*]
Sawyer US Ct Rep ... Sawyer's United States Circuit Court Reports [*A publication*]   (DLA)
SAX.......... Sambu [*Panama*] [*Airport symbol*]   (OAG)
SAX.......... Saxon
Sax .... Saxony
SAX.......... Saxophone [*Music*]
Sax .... Saxton's New Jersey Chancery Reports [*A publication*]   (DLA)
SAX.......... Small-Angle X-ray [*Instrumentation*]
SAX.......... Small Automatic Exchange [*Telecommunications*]   (TEL)
SAX.......... Sparta, NJ [*Location identifier*] [*FAA*]   (FAAL)
SAX.......... States Exploration Ltd. [*Toronto Stock Exchange symbol*]
SAX.......... Strong Anion Exchanger [*Chemistry*]
SAXA........ Slotted Array X-Band Antenna
SAXD........ Small-Angle X-Ray Diffraction
SAXI .... Saxton Industries Ltd. [*NASDAQ symbol*]   (NQ)

SAXL........ Short-Arc Xenon Lamp
SAXLE ...... Single Cantilevered Axle
SAXO .... Saxon Oil Co. [*Dallas, TX*] [*NASDAQ symbol*]   (NQ)
SAXS......... Small-Angle X-Ray Scattering
Saxt.......... Saxton's New Jersey Chancery Reports [*A publication*]   (DLA)
Saxt Ch ...... Saxton's New Jersey Chancery Reports [*A publication*]   (DLA)
SAY.......... Salisbury [*Zimbabwe*] [*Airport symbol*] [*Obsolete*]   (OAG)
Say .... Sayer's English King's Bench Reports [*96 English Reprint*] [*A publication*]   (DLA)
SAY.......... Science Fiction Adventures Yearbook [*A publication*]
SAY.......... Severe Aster Yellows [*Plant pathology*]
SAY.......... Soccer Association for Youth   (EA)
SAY.......... Stanley Resources [*Vancouver Stock Exchange symbol*]
SAYE........ Save as You Earn [*National Savings Plan*] [*British*]
Sayer .... Sayer's English King's Bench Reports [*96 English Reprint*] [*1751-56*] [*A publication*]   (DLA)
Sayer (Eng) ... Sayer's English King's Bench Reports [*96 English Reprint*] [*A publication*]   (DLA)
SAYFC ...... Scottish Association of Young Farmers' Clubs   (EAIO)
SAYKA ...... Sovistva Atomnykh Yader [*A publication*]
Sayles' Ann Civ St ... Sayles' Annotated Civil Statutes [*Texas*] [*A publication*]   (DLA)
Sayles' Civ St ... Sayles' Revised Civil Statutes [*Texas*] [*A publication*]   (DLA)
Sayles' Rev Civ St ... Sayles' Revised Civil Statutes [*Texas*] [*A publication*]   (DLA)
Sayles' St ... Sayles' Revised Civil Statutes [*Texas*] [*A publication*]   (DLA)
Sayles' Supp ... Supplement to Sayles' Annotated Civil Statutes [*Texas*] [*A publication*]   (DLA)
SAYP........ SAY Packaging, Inc. [*NASDAQ symbol*]   (NQ)
Sayre Adm Cas ... Sayre's Cases on Admiralty [*A publication*]   (DLA)
SAZ........... Sasstown [*Liberia*] [*Airport symbol*]   (OAG)
SAZ........... Staples, MN [*Location identifier*] [*FAA*]   (FAAL)
SAZA........ Azul [*Argentina*] [*ICAO location identifier*]   (ICLI)
SAZB........ Bahia Blanca/Comdte. Espora [*Argentina*] [*ICAO location identifier*]   (ICLI)
SAZC......... Cnel. Suarez [*Argentina*] [*ICAO location identifier*]   (ICLI)
SAZD........ Dolores [*Argentina*] [*ICAO location identifier*]   (ICLI)
SAZE .... Pigue [*Argentina*] [*ICAO location identifier*]   (ICLI)
SAZF .... Olavarria [*Argentina*] [*ICAO location identifier*]   (ICLI)
SAZG........ General Pico [*Argentina*] [*ICAO location identifier*]   (ICLI)
SAZH .... Tres Arroyos [*Argentina*] [*ICAO location identifier*]   (ICLI)
SAZI .... Bolivar [*Argentina*] [*ICAO location identifier*]   (ICLI)
SAZJ .... Benito Juarez [*Argentina*] [*ICAO location identifier*]   (ICLI)
SAZK........ Cerro Catedral [*Argentina*] [*ICAO location identifier*]   (ICLI)
SAZL........ Santa Teresita [*Argentina*] [*ICAO location identifier*]   (ICLI)
SAZM........ Mar Del Plata [*Argentina*] [*ICAO location identifier*]   (ICLI)
SAZN .... Neuquen [*Argentina*] [*ICAO location identifier*]   (ICLI)
SAZO .... Necochea [*Argentina*] [*ICAO location identifier*]   (ICLI)
SAZO .... Seeker Azimuth Orientation [*Air Force*]
SAZP......... Pehuajo/Comodoro P. Zanni [*Argentina*] [*ICAO location identifier*]   (ICLI)
SAZQ........ Rio Colorado [*Argentina*] [*ICAO location identifier*]   (ICLI)
SAZR........ Santa Rosa [*Argentina*] [*ICAO location identifier*]   (ICLI)
SAZS .... San Carlos De Bariloche [*Argentina*] [*ICAO location identifier*]   (ICLI)
SAZT........ Tandil [*Argentina*] [*ICAO location identifier*]   (ICLI)
SAZU........ Puelches [*Argentina*] [*ICAO location identifier*]   (ICLI)
SAZV......... Villa Gesell [*Argentina*] [*ICAO location identifier*]   (ICLI)
SAZW....... Cutral-Co [*Argentina*] [*ICAO location identifier*]   (ICLI)
SAZX........ Nueve De Julio [*Argentina*] [*ICAO location identifier*]   (ICLI)
SAZY........ San Martin De Los Andes/Chapelco [*Argentina*] [*ICAO location identifier*]   (ICLI)
SAZZ........ Saztec International, Inc. [*NASDAQ symbol*]   (NQ)
SB .... Automotive Engine Rebuilders Association. Service Bulletin [*A publication*]   (EAAP)
SB .... Bachelor of Science
SB .... Beauval Public Library, Saskatchewan [*Library symbol*] [*National Library of Canada*]   (NLC)
SB .... International Standard Book Number [*Online database field identifier*]
SB .... La Sacra Bibbia [*Turin*] [*A publication*]   (BJA)
SB .... La Sainte Bible [*A publication*]   (BJA)
SB .... S-Band   (KSC)
SB .... SAAB-Scania AB [*Sweden*] [*ICAO aircraft manufacturer identifier*]   (ICAO)
SB .... Salary Band [*British*]   (DCTA)
SB .... Sales Book
SB .... Salomon, Inc. [*NYSE symbol*]   (SPSG)
SB .... Santa Barbara [*Television program*]
SB .... Sarah Bernhardt [*French actress, 1844-1923*]
S & B.......... Saunders and Bidder's Locus Standi Reports [*1905-19*] [*A publication*]   (DLA)
SB .... Save a Baby [*Later, LGM*]   (EA)
SB .... Savings Bank
SB .... Savings Bond [*Treasury Department security*]
SB .... Schistosoma Bovis [*Parasitic fluke*]
SB .... Schweizer Buch [*A publication*]
SB .... Science Books [*A publication*]
SB .... Science Books and Films [*A publication*]
SB .... Scoring Booklet   (MCD)

SB	Scouting-Bombing Plane [*When prefixed to Navy aircraft designation*]
SB	Scrieve Board
SB	Sea Base (MCD)
SB	Seaboard World Airlines, Inc. [*ICAO designator*]
SB	Secondary Battery [*Military*]
SB	Secondary Buffer [*Chemistry*]
SB	Section Base [*Military*]
SB	Securing Bands
SB	Selection Board [*Military*]
SB	Selective Bibliography (MCD)
SB	Selmer Bandwagon [*A publication*]
Sb	Senate Bill [*in state legislatures*]
SB	Senior Beadle [*Ancient Order of Foresters*]
SB	Separately Binned
SB	Serial Binary (CET)
SB	Serial Block (MSA)
SB	Serum Bilirubin [*Clinical chemistry*]
SB	Service Bulletin
SB	Serving Brother [*Church of England*]
SB	Shanti Bahini [*Peace Force*] [*Bangladesh*] [*Political party*]
SB	Shaper Block (MCD)
SB	Shipbuilding [*Navy*]
SB	Shipping Board
SB	Shoot Bud [*Botany*]
SB	Short Bill
SB	Shortness of Breath [*Cardiology*]
S/B	Should Be
SB	Shrunk Back-to-Back [*Packaging of volumes*] [*Publishing*]
SB	Sick Bay
SB	Sideband [*Radio frequency*] (AAG)
SB	Signal to Background
SB	Signal Battalion [*Army*]
SB	Signal Boatswain
SB	Signature Book (ROG)
SB	Silver Braze (MSA)
SB	Simultaneous Broadcast
SB	Single Blind [*Experimental condition*]
SB	Single Braid (CET)
SB	Single-Breasted
SB	Single Breath
SB	Single-Ended Boiler (DS)
SB	Sink Beater (ADA)
SB	Sinus Bradycardia [*Cardiology*]
SB	Sitzungsbericht [*Transaction*] [*German*]
SB	Skandinaviska Banken. Quarterly Review [*Later, Skandinaviska Enskilda Banken. Quarterly Review*] [*A publication*]
SB	Sleeve Bearing (KSC)
SB	Slow Burning
SB	Small Bonds
SB	Small Bore (ADA)
SB	Small Bowel
SB	Small Business
Sb	Small-Mouth Bass [*Ichthyology*]
S & B	Smith and Batty's Irish King's Bench Reports [*1824-25*] [*A publication*] (DLA)
SB	Smooth Bore [*Ballistics*]
SB	Social Biology Films [*National Science Foundation project*]
SB	Society for Biomaterials (EA)
SB	Sociologisch Bulletin [*A publication*]
SB	Sociologists in Business (EA)
SB	Sodium Bicarbonate [*Inorganic chemistry*]
SB	Sodium Bisulfite [*Inorganic chemistry*]
SB	Sodium Borate [*Inorganic chemistry*]
SB	Solid Base Bullet
SB	Solid Body [*Technical drawings*]
SB	Solomon Islands [*ANSI two-letter standard code*] (CNC)
s/b	Son Billet [*His Bill*] [*French*]
SB	Soncino Blaetter [*A publication*]
SB	Sonobuoy (NVT)
SB	Soot Blower (AAG)
SB	Sources Bibliques [*Paris*] [*A publication*]
SB	South Britain [*England and Wales*]
SB	South Buffalo Railway Co. [*AAR code*]
SB	Southbound
SB	Sovetskaya Bibliografia [*A publication*]
SB	Soviet Biotechnology [*A publication*]
SB	Space Base [*NASA*] (KSC)
SB	Special Bibliography
SB	Special Billing [*Telecommunications*] (TEL)
SB	Special Branch [*British police*]
SB	Special Bulletin. New York Department of Labor [*A publication*] (DLA)
SB	Speed Brake (MCD)
SB	Spin Block (MSA)
SB	Spina Bifida [*Medicine*]
SB	Splash Block
SB	Sports Bribery [*FBI standardized term*]
SB	Spring Back (ADA)
SB	Stabilized Breakdown
SB	Standard Babylonian (BJA)
SB	Standard Bead
SB	Standby
SB	Standby Base [*Air Force*] (AFM)
SB	Stanford-Binet [*Intelligence test*] [*Education*]
SB	Statement of Billing
SB	Statistical Bulletin
SB	Status Board [*Automated*] (MCD)
SB	Statute Book (ADA)
SB	Steamboat
S & B	Sterilization and Bath
SB	Sternal Border [*Anatomy*]
Sb	Stibium [*Antimony*] [*Chemical element*]
sb..............	Stilb [*Unit of luminance*]
SB	Stillborn [*Medicine*]
SB	Stockbroker
SB	Stolen Base [*Baseball*]
SB	Stove Bolt
Sb	Strabismus [*Medicine*]
SB	Straight Binary
SB	Stretcher-Bearer
SB	Studi Baltici [*A publication*]
SB	Studi Bizantini [*A publication*]
SB	Studies in Bibliography [*A publication*]
SB	Stuffing Box
SB	Sub Branch [*Banking*]
SB	Subbituminous
SB	Submarine Base [*Navy*]
SB	Submarine Boat [*British*] (ROG)
SB	Submarine Fog Bell [*Mechanical*] [*Maps and charts*]
SB	Substantive
SB	Supplementary Benefits
SB	Supply Bulletin [*Military*]
SB	Support Box
SB	Supreme Bench [*Legal term*] (DLA)
SB	Surface Binding [*Immunochemistry*]
SB	Surplus Budget
sb..............	Svalbard and Jan Mayen [*MARC country of publication code*] [*Library of Congress*] (LCCP)
SB	Switchboard
SB	Switchboard Operator [*Navy*]
SB	Symbiotic Bacteria [*Ecology*]
SB	Synchronization Base [*NASA*] (NASA)
SB	Synchronization Bit (MSA)
SBA............	Saabruecker Beitraege zur Altertumskunde [*Bonn*] [*A publication*] (BJA)
SBA............	Santa Barbara [*California*] [*Airport symbol*] (OAG)
SBA............	Satellite Broadcasters Association (EA)
SBA............	Sbarro, Inc. [*AMEX symbol*] (SPSG)
SBA............	Scott Base [*Antarctica*] [*Seismograph station code, US Geological Survey*] (SEIS)
SBA............	Scott Base [*Antarctica*] [*Geomagnetic observatory code*]
SBA............	Seat Back Assembly [*Aerospace*] (MCD)
SBA............	Second Bombardment Association (EA)
SBA............	Secondary Butyl Alcohol [*Organic chemistry*]
SBA............	Setback Axle [*Truck engineering*]
SBA............	Shaped Beam Antenna
SBA............	Shared Batch Area [*Data processing*] (IBMDP)
SBA............	Show Business Association [*New York, NY*] (EA)
SBA............	Siamese Breeders of America [*Later, GSCC*] (EA)
SBA............	Sick Bay Attendant [*Navy*]
SBA............	Sick Berth Attendant [*Australia*]
SBA............	Sitzungsberichte. Bayerische Akademie der Wissenschaften [*A publication*]
SBA............	Small Business Administration
SBA............	Small Businesses' Association [*British*] (DCTA)
SB of A.......	Smaller Business of America [*Defunct*] (EA)
SBA............	Social Behavior Assessment [*Social skills test*]
SBA............	Society of Batik Artists [*Inactive*] (EA)
SBA............	Soybean Agglutinin [*Immunology*]
SBA............	Spirit and Breath Association (EA)
SBA............	Standard Beam Approach [*British aircraft landing method*]
SBA............	Standard Chartered Review [*A publication*]
SBA............	Standing British Army
SBA............	Steroid-Binding Assay [*Clinical chemistry*]
SBA............	Structural Board Association (EA)
SBA............	Structure Borne Acoustics (KSC)
SBA............	Studies in Biblical Archaeology [*A publication*]
SBA............	Sun Basin Airlines [*Moses Lake, CA*] [*FAA designator*] (FAAC)
SBA............	Support Base Activation (AAG)
SBA............	Susan B. Anthony Dollar
SBA............	Sweet Bugger All [*An exclamation*] [*Slang*] [*British*] (DSUE)
SBA............	Systems Builders Association (EA)
SBAA.........	Conceicao Do Araguaia [*Brazil*] [*ICAO location identifier*] (ICLI)
SBAA.........	Ships-in-Bottles Association of America (EA)
SBAA.........	Spina Bifida Association of America (EA)
SBAAM.....	Small Business Association of Apparel Manufacturers (EA)
SBAC........	Small Business Assistance Center [*Worcester, MA*] (EA)
SBAC.........	Society of British Aerospace Companies (MCD)

SBAC......... Society of British Aircraft Constructors
SBAE......... Stabilized Bombing Approach Equipment [Navy]
SBAF......... Rio De Janeiro/Afonsos [Brazil] [ICAO location identifier] (ICLI)
SBAFWP... Standby Auxiliary Feed Water Pump (IEEE)
SBAG......... Schweizer Beitraege zur Allgemeinen Geschichte [A publication]
SBAH........ Sodium Bis(methoxyethoxy)aluminum Hydride [Organic chemistry]
S-Bahn....... Schnellbahn [High-Speed Railway] [German]
SbAk.......... Sbornik na Balgarskata Akademija na Naukite [A publication]
Sb Akad Nauk SSSR ... Sbornik Rabot Akademiya Nauk SSSR [A publication]
SBAkWissWien ... Sitzungsberichte der Oesterreichischen Akademie der Wissenschaften in Wien [A publication] (BJA)
SBAM........ Amapa [Brazil] [ICAO location identifier] (ICLI)
SBAM........ Space Based Antimissile
SBAMA...... San Bernardino Air Materiel Area
SBAMP..... Sea-Based Air Master Plan (MCD)
SBAN........ Anapolis (Base Aerea) [Brazil] [ICAO location identifier] (ICLI)
SBANE...... Smaller Business Association of New England [Waltham, MA] (EA)
SBAP......... Simple Bin Assignment Problem
SBAP......... Small Business Assistance Program
SBAP......... Society of Business Advisory Professions (EA)
SBAR........ Aracaju/Santa Maria [Brazil] [ICAO location identifier] (ICLI)
SBAR........ San/Bar Corp. [NASDAQ symbol] (NQ)
S Bar J....... State Bar Journal of California [A publication] (DLA)
SBARMO Bull ... SBARMO [Scientific Ballooning and Radiations Monitoring Organization] Bulletin [A publication]
SBAS......... S-Band Antenna Switch (MCD)
SBASI........ Single Bridgewire Apollo Standard Initiator [Explosive]
Sb Aspir Rab Kazan Gos Univ Estest Nauki ... Sbornik Aspirantskikh Rabot Kazanskii Gosudarstvennyi Universitet Estestvennye Nauki [A publication]
Sb Aspir Rab Kazan Gos Univ Estest Nauki Biol ... Sbornik Aspirantskikh Rabot Kazanskii Gosudarstvennyi Universitet Estestvennye Nauki Biologiya [A publication]
Sb Aspir Rab Kazan Gos Univ Tochn Nauki Mekh Fiz ... Sbornik Aspirantskikh Rabot Kazanskii Gosudarstvennyi Universitet Tochnye Nauki Mekhanika Fizika [A publication]
Sb Aspir Rab Kazan Khim Tekhnol Inst ... Sbornik Aspirantskikh Rabot Kazanskii Khimiko Tekhnologicheskii Institut [A publication]
Sb Aspir Rab Kazan Univ Estestv Nauk ... Sbornik Aspirantskikh Rabot Kazanskogo Universiteta Estestvennykh Nauk [A publication]
Sb Aspir Rab Ufim Neft Nauchno-Issled Inst ... Sbornik Aspirantskikh Rabot Ufimskii Neftyanoi Nauchno-Issledovatel'skii Institut [A publication]
Sb Aspir Rab Voronezh Lesotekh Inst ... Sbornik Aspirantskikh Rabot Voronezhskii Lesotekhnicheskii Institut [A publication]
Sb Aspir Rab Vses Nauchno Issled Inst Zhivotnovod ... Sbornik Aspirantskikh Rabot Vsesoyuznyi Nauchno Issledovatel'skii Institut Zhivotnovodstva [A publication]
SBAU......... Aracatuba [Brazil] [ICAO location identifier] (ICLI)
SBAV......... Teodoro Sampaio/Usina Porto Primavera [Brazil] [ICAO location identifier] (ICLI)
SBAW........ Sitzungsberichte. Bayerische Akademie der Wissenschaften [A publication]
SBAWSEF ... Susan B. Anthony Women's Spirituality Education Forum (EA)
SBAWW.... Sitzungsberichte. Akademie der Wissenschaft in Wien [A publication]
SBB........... Sabina Resources Ltd. [Vancouver Stock Exchange symbol]
SBB........... Saddle Back Butte [California] [Seismograph station code, US Geological Survey] (SEIS)
SBB........... Saudi-British Bank
SBB........... Schweizerische Bundesbahnen [Swiss Federal Railways]
SBB........... Self-Balancing Bridge
SBB........... Serikat Buruh Batik [Batik Workers' Union] [Indonesia]
SBB........... Single-Band Beaconry [RADAR]
SBB........... Soncino Books of the Bible [London] [A publication] (BJA)
SBB........... Studies in Bibliography and Booklore [A publication]
SBB........... Subtract with Borrow [Data processing] (PCM)
SBB........... System Building Block [Data processing]
SBBA........ Boca Do Acre [Brazil] [ICAO location identifier] (ICLI)
SBBA........ Spanish-Barb Breeders Association (EA)
Sb Bakteriofagiya ... Sbornik Bakteriofagiya [A publication]
SBBAW..... Sitzungsberichte. Bayerische Akademie der Wissenschaften [A publication]
SBBE......... Belem/Val-De-Caes [Brazil] [ICAO location identifier] (ICLI)
SB Berlin ... Sitzungsberichte. Deutsche Akademie der Wissenschaften zu Berlin. Klasse fuer Sprachen, Literatur, und Kunst [A publication]
SBBG......... Baje/Cmt. Gustavo Kraemer [Brazil] [ICAO location identifier] (ICLI)
SBBGA ...... Studia Universitatis Babes-Bolyai. Series Geologia-Geographia [A publication]

SBBH......... Belo Horizonte/Pampulha [Brazil] [ICAO location identifier] (ICLI)
SBBI .... Curitiba/Bacacheri [Brazil] [ICAO location identifier] (ICLI)
Sb Biokhim Zerna Akad Nauk SSSR Inst Biokhim A N Bakha ... Sbornik. Biokhimiya Zerna. Akademiya Nauk SSSR. Institut Biokhimii Imeni A. N. Bakha [A publication]
SBBKA ...... Seibutsu Butsuri Kagaku [A publication]
SBBL .... Belem [Brazil] [ICAO location identifier] (ICLI)
SBBN......... Standard Big Bang Nucleosynthesis [Cosmology]
Sb Bot Rab Beloruss Otd Vses Bot Ova ... Sbornik Botanicheskikh Rabot Belorusskoe Otdelenie Vsesoyuznogo Botanicheskogo Obshchestva [A publication]
Sb Bot Rabot Vses Bot Obshch Beloruss Otd ... Sbornik Botanicheskikh Rabot Vsesoyuznogo Botanicheskogo Obshchestva. Belorusskoe Otdelenie [A publication]
SBBPA ...... Studia Universitatis Babes-Bolyai. Series Physica [A publication]
SBBQ........ Barbacena [Brazil] [ICAO location identifier] (ICLI)
SBBR......... Brasilia/Internacional [Brazil] [ICAO location identifier] (ICLI)
SBBS .... Brasilia [Brazil] [ICAO location identifier] (ICLI)
SBBT .... Barretos [Brazil] [ICAO location identifier] (ICLI)
SBBT .... Short Basic Battery Test (NVT)
SBBU........ Bauru [Brazil] [ICAO location identifier] (ICLI)
SBBUD...... SBARMO [Scientific Ballooning and Radiations Monitoring Organization] Bulletin [A publication]
SBBV .... Boa Vista/Internacional [Brazil] [ICAO location identifier] (ICLI)
SBBW........ Barra Do Garcas [Brazil] [ICAO location identifier] (ICLI)
SBC........... Baptist College at Charleston, Charleston, SC [OCLC symbol] (OCLC)
SBC........... Ferrocarril Sonora Baja California SA de CV [AAR code]
SBC........... Saint Basil's College [Stamford, CT]
SBC........... Saint Benedict College [Indiana]
SBC........... Saint Bernard College [Alabama]
SBC........... Sam Browne's Cavalry [British military] (DMA)
SBC........... Santa Barbara [California] [Seismograph station code, US Geological Survey] (SEIS)
SBC........... Save the Battlefield Coalition (EA)
SBC........... Senate Budget Committee
SBC........... Service Bureau Corporation
SBC........... Sibasa [South Africa] [Airport symbol] (OAG)
SBC........... Simpson Bible College [Later, Simpson College] [California]
SBC........... Single Board Computer
SBC........... Single Burst Correcting
SBC........... Small Bayonet Cap
SBC........... Small Business Centre [British]
SBC........... Small Business Computer (BUR)
SBC........... Society of Business Communicators [Australia]
SBC........... Solid Bowl Centrifuge
SBC........... SONAR Breakout Cable
SBC........... Southeastern Bible College [Lakeland, FL]
SBC........... Southern Baptist College [Walnut Ridge, AR]
SBC........... Southern Baptist Convention
SBC........... Southwestern Bell Corporation [NYSE symbol] (SPSG)
SBC........... Spaceborne Computer
SBC........... Special Back Care [Medicine]
SBC........... Speed Brake Command (NASA)
SBC........... Standard Boundary Condition
SBC........... Standard Buried Collector [Circuit]
SBC........... Standing Balance: Eyes Closed [Test] [Occupational therapy]
SBC........... Start Breguet Cruise [SST]
SBC........... Statutes of British Columbia [British Columbia Attorney General's Ministry] [Information service or system] [A publication] (CRD)
SBC........... Strict Bed Confinement [Medicine]
SBC........... Studies in Browning and His Circle [A publication]
SBC........... Styrene Block Copolymer [Plastics technology]
SBC........... Sue Bennett College [London, KY]
SBC........... Summary Billing Card (AFM)
SBC........... Supplementary Benefits Commission [Department of Employment] [British]
SBC........... Surrogates by Choice (EA)
SBC........... Survey of Basic Competencies [Achievement test]
SBC........... Sweet Briar College [Virginia]
SBC........... Swiss Bank Corporation
SBC........... Swiss Broadcasting Corporation
SBCA........ Cascavel [Brazil] [ICAO location identifier] (ICLI)
SBCA........ Saint Bernard Club of America (EA)
SBCA........ Satellite Broadcasting and Communications Association (EA)
SBCA........ SBC [Swiss Bank Corporation] Australia
SBCA........ Seat Belt Control Apparatus
SBCA........ Sensor-Based Control Adapter
SBCA........ Small Business Council of America (EA)
SBCA........ Soybean Council of America [Defunct]
SBCABE.... Annual Symposium on Biomathematics and Computer Science in the Life Sciences. Abstracts [A publication]
SBCBA ...... Sounding Brass and the Conductor [A publication]
SBCC......... Cachimbo [Brazil] [ICAO location identifier] (ICLI)
SBCC........ St. Brendan Cup Committee in America [Defunct] (EA)
SBCC......... Senate Bonding and Currency Committee (OICC)

SBCC........	Separate Bias, Common Control
SBCC........	Southern Building Code Congress, International
SBCCA......	Still Bank Collectors Club of America (EA)
SBCCI.......	Southern Building Code Congress, International (EA)
SBCD........	Campo Grande [*Brazil*] [*ICAO location identifier*] (ICLI)
SBCD........	School-Based Curriculum Development (ADA)
SB/CD	Short Bed/Continuous Development [*Chamber for thin-layer chromatography*] [*Analytical biochemistry*]
SBCD........	Special Business and Contract Directories [*A publication*]
SBCD........	Subtract BCD [*Binary Coded Decimal*] Number [*Data processing*]
SBCE.........	Bachelor of Science in Civil Engineering
SBCE.........	Concordia [*Brazil*] [*ICAO location identifier*] (ICLI)
SBCED......	Scientific Bulletin. Canada Centre for Mineral and Energy Technology [*A publication*]
Sb Cesk Akad Zemed ...	Sbornik Ceskoslovenske Akademie Zemedelske [*A publication*]
Sb Cesk Akad Zemed Ved ...	Sbornik Ceskoslovenske Akademie Zemedelskych Ved [*A publication*]
Sb Cesk Akad Zemed Ved Lesn ...	Sbornik Ceskoslovenske Akademie Zemedelskych Ved. Lesnictvi [*A publication*]
Sb Cesk Akad Zemed Ved Rada A ...	Sbornik Ceskoslovenske Akademie Zemedelskych Ved. Rada A [*A publication*]
Sb Cesk Akad Zemed Ved Rada B ...	Sbornik Ceskoslovenske Akademie Zemedelskych Ved. Rada B [*A publication*]
Sb Cesk Akad Zemed Ved Rostl Vyr ...	Sbornik Ceskoslovenske Akademie Zemedelskych Ved. Rostlinna Vyroba [*A publication*]
Sb Cesk Akad Zemed Ved Rostl Vyroba ...	Sbornik Ceskoslovenske Akademie Zemedelskych Ved. Rostlinna Vyroba [*A publication*]
Sb Cesk Akad Zemed Ved Vet Med ...	Sbornik Ceskoslovenske Akademie Zemedelskych Ved. Veterinarni Medicina [*A publication*]
Sb Cesk Akad Zemed Ved Zivocisna Vyroba ...	Sbornik Ceskoslovenske Akademie Zemedelskych Ved. Zivocisna Vyroba [*A publication*]
SBCF	Belo Horizonte/Confins [*Brazil*] [*ICAO location identifier*] (ICLI)
SBCF	Seacoast Banking Corporation of Florida [*Stuart, FL*] [*NASDAQ symbol*] (NQ)
SBCF	Southern Baptist Convention Flyers [*Defunct*] (EA)
SBCG........	Campo Grande/Internacional [*Brazil*] [*ICAO location identifier*] (ICLI)
SBCH	Chapeco [*Brazil*] [*ICAO location identifier*] (ICLI)
SBCI	Carolina [*Brazil*] [*ICAO location identifier*] (ICLI)
SBCJ........	Maraba/Carajas [*Brazil*] [*ICAO location identifier*] (ICLI)
SBCJ.........	Store Block Control Journal [*Military*] (AABC)
SBCL	Cruz Alta/Carlos Ruhl [*Brazil*] [*ICAO location identifier*] (ICLI)
SBCLS......	South Bay Cooperative Library System [*Library network*]
SBCM........	Criciuma [*Brazil*] [*ICAO location identifier*] (ICLI)
SBCO........	Porto Alegre/Canoas [*Brazil*] [*ICAO location identifier*] (ICLI)
SBCO........	Shipbuilding Company
SBC/OC	Swiss Bank Corp./O'Connor & Associates Services (ECON)
SBCORP ...	Shipbuilding Corporation
SBCP	Campos/Bartolomeu Lisandro [*Brazil*] [*ICAO location identifier*] (ICLI)
SBCP	Spanish Base Construction Program
SBCPO......	Sick Bay Chief Petty Officer [*British military*] (DMA)
SBCR........	Corumba/Internacional [*Brazil*] [*ICAO location identifier*] (ICLI)
SBCR........	Stock Balance and Consumption Report (NASA)
SB & CR ...	Stock Balance and Consumption Report (AFM)
SBCS	Series Book Collectors' Society (EA)
SBCS	Shore-Based Correlation Subsystem [*Navy*] (CAAL)
SBCS	Steam Bypass Control System [*Nuclear energy*] (NRCH)
Sb Csl Akad Zemed Ved Rostlinna Vyroba ...	Sbornik Ceskoslovenske Akademie Zemedelskych Ved. Rada C. Rostlinna Vyroba [*A publication*]
Sb Csl Akad Zemed Ved Zemed Ekon ...	Sbornik Ceskoslovenske Akademie Zemedelskych Ved. Rada B. Zemedelska Ekonomika [*A publication*]
Sb Csl Akad Zemed Ved Ziv Vyroba ...	Sbornik Ceskoslovenske Akademie Zemedelskych Ved. Rada E. Zivocisna Vyroba [*A publication*]
SBCT	Curitiba/Afonso Pena [*Brazil*] [*ICAO location identifier*] (ICLI)
SBCU.........	Sensor-Based Control Unit [*Data processing*]
SBCV	Caravelas [*Brazil*] [*ICAO location identifier*] (ICLI)
SBCW........	Curitiba [*Brazil*] [*ICAO location identifier*] (ICLI)
SBCY.........	Cuiaba/Marechal Rondon [*Brazil*] [*ICAO location identifier*] (ICLI)
SBCZ.........	Cruzeiro Do Sul/Internacional [*Brazil*] [*ICAO location identifier*] (ICLI)
SBD	"Dauntless" Single-Engine Scout-Bomber [*Navy symbol*]
S-BD	S-Band (NASA)
SBD	San Bernardino, CA [*Location identifier*] [*FAA*] (FAAL)
SBD	San Bernardino Public Library, San Bernardino, CA [*OCLC symbol*] (OCLC)
SBD	Savings Bond Division [*Navy*]
SBD	Schematic Block Diagram [*NASA*] (NASA)
SBD	Schoolbestuur [*A publication*]
SBD	Schottky Barrier Diode [*Electronics*]
SBD	Space Business Daily [*A publication*]
SBD	Standard Bibliographic Description
SBD	Strawboard [*Shipping*]
SBD	Subcontractor Bid Document (MCD)
SBD	Sunbird Airlines, Inc. [*Maiden, NC*] [*FAA designator*] (FAAC)
SBD	Surface Barrier Detector
SBDAW.....	Sitzungsberichte. Deutsche Akademie der Wissenschaften zu Berlin. Klasse fuer Sprachen, Literatur, und Kunst [*A publication*]
SBDAWB ..	Sitzungsberichte. Deutsche Akademie der Wissenschaften zu Berlin. Klasse fuer Sprachen, Literatur, und Kunst [*A publication*]
SBDC.........	Shipbuilding and Drydock Company
SBDC.........	Small Business Development Center [*Lehigh University, University of Alabama in Birmingham*] [*Research center*]
SBDC.........	Small Business Development Corporation
SBDH	Sociedade Brasileira de Discos Historicos J. Leon [*Record label*] [*Brazil*]
SBDL.........	Solid Blank Delay Line
SBDM........	School-Based Decision Making (ADA)
SBDN	Presidente Prudente [*Brazil*] [*ICAO location identifier*] (ICLI)
SBDO	Space Business Development Operation (AAG)
Sb Dokl Gidrotekh Vses Nauchno Issled Inst Gidrotekh ...	Sbornik Dokladov po Gidrotekhnike. Vsesoyuznyi Nauchno-Issledovatel'skii Institut Gidrotekhniki [*A publication*]
Sb Dokl Nauchn Stud Ova Kalinin Gos Pedagog Inst ...	Sbornik Dokladov Nauchnogo Studencheskogo Obshchestva Kalininskii Gosudarstvennyi Pedagogicheskii Institut [*A publication*]
Sb Donetsk Nauchno Issled Ugoln Inst ...	Sbornik Donetskii Nauchno-Issledovatel'skii Ugol'nyi Institut [*A publication*]
SBDP.........	Serikat Buruh Djawatan Perindustrian [*Department of Industry Workers' Union*] [*Indonesia*]
SBDPU......	Serikat Buruh Djawantan Pekerdjaan Umun [*Public Works' Union*] [*Indonesia*]
SBDT.........	Surface Barrier Diffused Transistor
SBE............	S-Band Exciter [*System*] [*Also, SBES*]
SBE............	Sacred Books of the East [*A publication*] (BJA)
SBE............	Selebi-Pikwe [*Botswana*] [*Later, PKW*] [*Airport symbol*] (OAG)
SBE............	Self Breast Examination [*for cancer*]
SBE............	Semana Biblica Espanola [*A publication*]
SBE............	Shortness of Breath on Exertion [*Cardiology*]
SBE............	Simple Boolean Expression [*Mathematics*]
SBE............	Societe de Biologie Experimentale [*Society for Experimental Biology*] (EAIO)
SBE............	Society of Broadcast Engineers (EA)
SBE............	Society of Business Economists (EAIO)
SBE............	Society for Business Ethics [*Santa Clara, CA*] (EA)
SBE............	Solar Beam Experiment
SbE............	South by East
SBE............	Southwest Journal of Business and Economics [*A publication*]
SBE............	State Board of Education (OICC)
SBE............	Strategic Bomber Enhancement (MCD)
SBE............	Sub BIT [*Binary Digit*] Encoder (MCD)
SBE............	Subacute Bacterial Endocarditis [*Medicine*]
SBED.........	Serial BIT [*Binary Digit*] Error Detector
SBEE.........	Bachelor of Science in Electrical Engineering
SBEED	Storage Battery Electric Energy Demonstration
SBEG........	Manaus/Eduardo Gomes [*Brazil*] [*ICAO location identifier*] (ICLI)
SBEI	SBE, Incorporated [*NASDAQ symbol*] (NQ)
SBEK	Jacare-Acanga [*Brazil*] [*ICAO location identifier*] (ICLI)
SBelEx......	Bulletin. Societe Belge d'Etudes et d'Expansion [*A publication*]
S Bell..........	Bell's House of Lords Scotch Appeal Cases [*1842-50*] [*A publication*] (DLA)
SBEN	Campos/Plataforma SS-17 [*Brazil*] [*ICAO location identifier*] (ICLI)
Sb Ent Odd Nar Mus Praze ...	Sbornik Entomologickeho Oddeleni Narodniho Musea v Praze [*A publication*]
SBER	Eirunepe [*Brazil*] [*ICAO location identifier*] (ICLI)
SBER	Self-Balancing Electronics Recorder
Sber...........	Sitzungsbericht [*Transaction*] [*German*] (BJA)
SBER	Subbit Error Rate
Sber Bayer Akad Wiss ...	Sitzungsberichte. Bayerische Akademie der Wissenschaften zu Muenchen [*A publication*]
Sber Dt Akad Landwwiss Berl ...	Sitzungsberichte. Deutsche Akademie der Landwirtschaftswissenschaften zu Berlin [*A publication*]
Sber Ges Morph Physiol Muench ...	Sitzungsberichte. Gesellschaft fuer Morphologie und Physiologie in Muenchen [*A publication*]
Sber Ges Naturf Freunde Berl ...	Sitzungsberichte. Gesellschaft Naturforschender Freunde zu Berlin [*A publication*]
Sber K Boehm Ges Wiss ...	Sitzungsberichte der Koeniglich Boehmischen Gesellschaft der Wissenschaften [*A publication*]
Sber K Preuss Akad Wiss ...	Sitzungsberichte der Koeniglich Preussischen Akademie der Wissenschaften [*A publication*]
SBES	S-Band Exciter System [*Also, SBE*]
SBES	Sao Pedro Da Aldeia [*Brazil*] [*ICAO location identifier*] (ICLI)
SBET	Pedregulho/Estreito [*Brazil*] [*ICAO location identifier*] (ICLI)
SBET	Society of Biomedical Equipment Technicians (EA)
SBETC.......	Small Business Export Trade Corporation
SBEU.........	Singapore Bank Employees' Union

SBEUA...... Small Business and Economic Utilization Advisor [*Army*] (AABC)
SBF .... Salomon Brothers Fund [*NYSE symbol*] (SPSG)
SBF .... Salvo Buon Fine [*Under Usual Reserve*] [*Formula used in acknowledging receipt of checks*] [*Business term*] [*Italian*]
sbf.............. Sauf Bonne Fin [*Under Usual Reserve*] [*Formula used in acknowledging receipt of checks*] [*Business term*] [*French*]
SB & F ...... Science Books and Films [*A publication*]
SBF .... Science Books and Films [*A publication*]
SBF .... Scientific Balloon Facility
SBF .... Serologic Blocking Factor [*Cardiology*]
SBF .... Short Backfire [*Antenna*]
SBF .... Silicone Brake Fluid (MCD)
SBF .... Societe des Bourses Francaises [*France*] (ECON)
SBF .... Society of Business Folk [*Brown Deer, WI*] (EA)
SBF .... Southern Baptist Foundation (EA)
SBF .... Soy Base Formula [*Nutrition*]
SBF .... Splanchnic Blood Flow [*Physiology*]
SBF .... Standby Flying [*British military*] (DMA)
SBF .... Stonebridge, Inc. [*Toronto Stock Exchange symbol*]
SBF .... Studii Biblici Franciscani. Liber Annuus [*A publication*]
SBF .... Surface Burst Fuze
SBFA .... Set Back Front Axle [*Automotive engineering*]
SBFA .... Small Business Foundation of America [*Boston, MA*] (EA)
Sb Faun Praci Ent Odd Nar Mus Praze ... Sbornik Faunistickych Praci Entomologickeho Oddeleni Narodniho Musea v Praze [*A publication*]
SBFAW ..... Sitzungsberichte. Finnische Akademie der Wissenschaften [*A publication*]
SBFC .... Franca [*Brazil*] [*ICAO location identifier*] (ICLI)
SBFC .... Sawyer Brown Fan Club (EA)
SBFC .... Standby for Further Clearance [*Aviation*] (FAAC)
SBFI.......... Foz Do Iguacu/Cataratas [*Brazil*] [*ICAO location identifier*] (ICLI)
SBFI.......... Specialised Banking Furniture International [*Manufacturer*] [*British*]
SBFL.......... Florianopolis/Hercilioluz [*Brazil*] [*ICAO location identifier*] (ICLI)
SBFLA ...... Studii Biblici Franciscani. Liber Annuus [*A publication*] (BJA)
SBFM .... Silver-Band Frequency Modulation (IEEE)
SBFN .... Fernando De Noronha [*Brazil*] [*ICAO location identifier*] (ICLI)
SBFRA ...... Schriftenreihe. Bundesminister fuer Wissenschaftliche Forschung (Germany). Radionuklide [*A publication*]
SBFS.......... Southstate Bank for Savings [*NASDAQ symbol*] (NQ)
SBFSDH ... Synopses of the British Fauna. New Series [*A publication*]
SBFT .... Fronteira [*Brazil*] [*ICAO location identifier*] (ICLI)
SBFU .... Alpinopolis/Furnas [*Brazil*] [*ICAO location identifier*] (ICLI)
SBFU .... Standby Filter Unit (IEEE)
SBFZ .... Fortaleza/Pinto Martins [*Brazil*] [*ICAO location identifier*] (ICLI)
SBG........... School Board Gazette [*A publication*]
SBG........... Scottish Bus Group Ltd. (DCTA)
SBG........... Southern Business Group [*Commercial firm*] [*British*]
SBG........... Staatsbibliothek Preuss. Kulturbesitz - Gesamtkat. U. Dok., Berlin, Federal Republic of Germany [*OCLC symbol*] (OCLC)
SBG........... Standard Battery Grade
SBG........... Steinberg, Inc. [*Toronto Stock Exchange symbol*]
SBG........... Strategic Bomber Group
SBG........... Universite de Sherbrooke, Publications Officielles [*UTLAS symbol*]
SBGA........ Brasilia/Gama [*Brazil*] [*ICAO location identifier*] (ICLI)
SBGA........ Serum Beta-Glucuronidase Activity [*Serology*]
SBGDA...... Spisanie na Bulgarskoto Geologichesko Druzhestvo [*A publication*]
Sb Geol Ved Geol ... Sbornik Geologickych Ved. Geologie [*A publication*]
Sb Geol Ved Hydrogeol Inz Geol ... Sbornik Geologickych Ved. Hydrogeologie, Inzenyrska, Geologie [*A publication*]
Sb Geol Ved Loziskova Geol ... Sbornik Geologickych Ved. Loziskova Geologie [*Czechoslovakia*] [*A publication*]
Sb Geol Ved Loziskova Geol Mineral ... Sbornik Geologickych Ved. Loziskova Geologie. Mineralogie [*A publication*]
Sb Geol Ved Paleontol ... Sbornik Geologickych Ved. Paleontologie [*A publication*]
Sb Geol Ved Rada Loziskova Geol ... Sbornik Geologickych Ved. Rada Loziskova Geologie [*A publication*]
Sb Geol Ved Rada P Paleontol ... Sbornik Geologickych Ved. Rada P: Paleontologie [*A publication*]
Sb Geol Ved Rada Uzita Geofyz ... Sbornik Geologickych Ved. Rada Uzita Geofyzika [*A publication*]
Sb Geol Ved Technol Geochem ... Sbornik Geologickych Ved. Technologie, Geochemie [*A publication*]
Sb Geol Ved Uzita Geofyz ... Sbornik Geologickych Ved. Uzita Geofyzika [*Czechoslovakia*] [*A publication*]
SBGGAKOPR ... Sitzungsberichte. Gesellschaft fuer Geschichte und Altertumskunde der Ostseeprovinzen Russlands [*A publication*]
SBGGAKR ... Sitzungsberichte. Gesellschaft fuer Geschichte und Altertumskunde der Ostseeprovinzen Russlands [*A publication*]

SBGI .... Serikat Buruh Gelas Indonesia [*Glass Workers' Union of Indonesia*]
SBGKAT ... Godishnik na Sofiiskiya Universitet. Biologicheski Fakultet. Kniga 2. Botanika, Mikrobiologiya, Fiziologiya, i Biokhimiya Rasteniyata [*A publication*]
SBGL .... Rio De Janeiro/Internacional Galeao [*Brazil*] [*ICAO location identifier*] (ICLI)
SBGM........ Guajara-Mirim [*Brazil*] [*ICAO location identifier*] (ICLI)
SBGMA..... Sitzungsberichte. Gesellschaft zur Befoerderung der Gesamten Naturwissenschaften zu Marburg [*A publication*]
SBGMS ..... Shipbuilders', Boiler, and Gasometer Makers' Society [*A union*] [*British*]
SBGO .... Goiania/Santa Genoveva [*Brazil*] [*ICAO location identifier*] (ICLI)
SBGP......... Campos/Plataforma PNA-1 [*Brazil*] [*ICAO location identifier*] (ICLI)
SBGP......... Serikat Buruh Gula Proklamasi [*Sugar Workers' Union*] [*Indonesia*]
SBGP......... Strategic Bomber Group
SBGR......... Sao Paulo/Internacional Guarulhos [*Brazil*] [*ICAO location identifier*] (ICLI)
Sb Grozn Neft Inst ... Sbornik Groznenskii Neftyanoi Institut [*A publication*]
SBGS .... Ponta Grossa [*Brazil*] [*ICAO location identifier*] (ICLI)
SBGSN ...... Serikat Buruh Garam dan Soda Negeri [*Salt Workers' Association*] [*Indonesia*]
SBGTS....... Standby Gas Treatment System [*Nuclear energy*] (NRCH)
SBGW........ Guaratingueta [*Brazil*] [*ICAO location identifier*] (ICLI)
SBH .... St. Barthelemy [*Leeward Islands*] [*Airport symbol*] (OAG)
SBH .... Sea Blue Histiocytosis [*Medicine*]
SBH .... SmithKline Beecham PLC ADS [*NYSE symbol*] (SPSG)
SBH .... Sodium Borohydride [*Inorganic chemistry*]
SBH .... Southern Blot Hybridization [*Biochemistry*]
SBH .... State University of New York, Health Sciences Library, Buffalo, NY [*OCLC symbol*] (OCLC)
SBH .... Strip-Buried Heterostructure [*Telecommunications*] (TEL)
SBH .... Sumerisch-Babylonische Hymnen [*A publication*] (BJA)
SBH .... Supermassive Black Hole [*Cosmology*]
SBH .... Switch Busy Hour [*Telecommunications*] (IEEE)
SBHAD7 ... Social Biology and Human Affairs [*A publication*]
SBHAW ... Sitzungsberichte. Heidelberg Akademie der Wissenschaft [*A publication*]
SBHC ...... Society of the Bible in the Hands of Its Creators (EA)
SBHC ...... Speed Brake Hand Control (NASA)
SBHC ...... Studies in Browning and His Circle [*A publication*]
S B Heidelberg ... Sitzungsberichte. Heidelberg Akademie der Wissenschaften. Philosophisch-Historische Klasse [*A publication*]
SBHEU ..... Singapore Business Houses Employees' Union
SBHLA..... Schweizerische Blaetter fuer Heizung und Lueftung [*A publication*]
SBHRAL ... Biometrie Humaine [*A publication*]
SBHRG ..... Space-Based Hypervelocity Rail Gun [*Military*] (SDI)
SBHRT...... Serikat Buruh Hotel, Rumah-Makan dan Toko [*Hotel, Restaurant and Shops' Workers' Union*] [*Indonesia*]
SBHT........ Altamira [*Brazil*] [*ICAO location identifier*] (ICLI)
SBHT........ Studies in Burke and His Time [*A publication*]
SBI............ Columbia Bible College, Columbia, SC [*OCLC symbol*] (OCLC)
SBI............ Sabine Pass, TX [*Location identifier*] [*FAA*] (FAAL)
SBI............ Santa Barbara Island (MUGU)
SBI............ Scientific Bureau of Investigation [*In radio series "Armstrong of the SBI"*]
SBI............ Serikat Buruh Industri [*Industrial Workers' Union*] [*Indonesia*]
SB-I........... Service de Bibliographie sur l'Informatique [*Paris Gestion Informatique*] [*France*] [*Information service or system*] (CRD)
SBI............ Shares of Beneficial Interest [*Stock exchange term*]
SBI............ Shriners Burn Institute
SBI............ Single Byte Interleaved
SBI............ Small Business Institute [*Small Business Administration*]
SBI............ Soil Brightness Index
SBI............ Somerville Belkin Industries Ltd. [*Toronto Stock Exchange symbol*]
SBI............ Soviet Bureau of Information
SBI............ Soybean (Trypsin) Inhibitor [*Biochemistry*]
SBI............ Space-Based Interceptor [*Military*] (SDI)
SBI............ Special Background Investigation (NVT)
SBI............ Steel Boiler Institute [*Defunct*]
SBI............ Sun Belt Institute (EA)
SBI............ Synfuels Bibliography and Index [*A publication*]
SBIA .... Small Business Innovation Development Act [*1982*]
SBIA .... Spa Bath Industry of Australia
SBIBD .... Symmetrical Balanced Incomplete Block Designs (MCD)
SBIC .... Small Business Investment Company [*Generic term*]
SBICo .... Small Business Investment Company [*Generic term*]
SBIE .... Shared Bibliographic Input Experiment [*Special Libraries Association*]
SBIG......... [*The*] Seibels Bruce Group, Inc. [*NASDAQ symbol*] (NQ)
SBIL .... Ilheus [*Brazil*] [*ICAO location identifier*] (ICLI)
SBILS........ Scanning Beam Instrument Landing System (KSC)

SBIN.......... Fort Battleford National Historic Park, Parks Canada [*Parc Historique National Fort Battleford, Parcs Canada*] Battleford, Saskatchewan [*Library symbol*] [*National Library of Canada*] (NLC)

Sb Inf Obogashch Briket Uglei ... Sbornik Informatsii po Obogashcheniyu i Briketirovaniyu Uglei [*USSR*] [*A publication*]

Sb Inst Fiz Akad Nauk Gruz SSR ... Sbornik. Ordena Trudovogo Krasnogo Znameni Institut Fiziki. Akademiya Nauk Gruzinskoj SSR [*A publication*]

Sb Inst Neorg Khim Elektrokhim Akad Nauk Gruz SSR ... Sbornik Institut Neorganicheskoi Khimii i Elektrokhimii Akademiya Nauk Gruzinskoi SSR [*A publication*]

SBIO......... Synbiotics Corp. [*NASDAQ symbol*] (NQ)

SBIP.......... Ipatinga/Usiminas [*Brazil*] [*ICAO location identifier*] (ICLI)

SBIR.......... Small Business Innovation Research Program [*Small Business Administration*]

SBIR.......... Storage Bus in Register

SBIT.......... Itumbiara/Hidroelectrica [*Brazil*] [*ICAO location identifier*] (ICLI)

SBIZ.......... Hawkeye Entertainment, Inc. [*NASDAQ symbol*] (NQ)

SBIZ.......... Imperatriz [*Brazil*] [*ICAO location identifier*] (ICLI)

SBiz............ Studi Bizantini [*A publication*]

Sb "Izme Pochv Okul'turiv Klassifik Diagnostika" ... Sbornik "Izmenenie Pochv pri Okul'turivanii, Ikh Klassifikatsiya i Diagnostika" [*A publication*]

SBJ .... Journal. State Bar of California [*A publication*] (DLA)

SBJ .... Saul Bellow Journal [*A publication*]

SBJ .... Savings Bank Journal [*A publication*]

SBJ .... Schottky Barrier Junction [*Electronics*]

SBJ .... Solberg, NJ [*Location identifier*] [*FAA*] (FAAL)

SBJC......... Belem/Julio Cesar [*Brazil*] [*ICAO location identifier*] (ICLI)

SBJF......... Juiz De Fora/Francisco De Assis [*Brazil*] [*ICAO location identifier*] (ICLI)

Sb Jihoceskeho Muz Cesk Budejovicich Prir Vedy ... Sbornik Jihoceskeho Muzea v Ceskych Budejovicich Prirodni Vedy [*A publication*]

SBJP......... Joao Pessoa/Presidente Castro Pinto [*Brazil*] [*ICAO location identifier*] (ICLI)

SBJR......... Rio De Janeiro/Jacarepagua [*Brazil*] [*ICAO location identifier*] (ICLI)

SBJV......... Joinville [*Brazil*] [*ICAO location identifier*] (ICLI)

SBK........... St. Brieuc [*France*] [*Airport symbol*] (OAG)

SBK........... Serikat Buruh Kehutanan [*National Forestry Workers' Union*] [*Indonesia*]

SBK........... Serikat Buruh Kependjaaran [*Prisons Workers' Unions*] [*Indonesia*]

SBK........... Signet Banking Corp. [*NYSE symbol*] (SPSG)

SBK........... Single-Beam Klystron (MSA)

SBK........... Society for Behavioral Kinesiology

SBK........... Softwood Bleached Kraft [*Pulp and paper technology*]

SBK........... South Brooklyn Railway Co. [*AAR code*]

sbk............ Subangular Blocky Soil [*Agriculture*]

SBK........... Universite de Sherbrooke, Bibliotheque [*UTLAS symbol*]

Sb Karantinu Rast ... Sbornik po Karantinu Rastenii [*A publication*]

SBKAW..... Sitzungsberichte. Kaiserliche Akademie der Wissenschaften in Wien [*A publication*]

SBKAWW ... Sitzungsberichte. Kaiserliche Akademie der Wissenschaften in Wien [*A publication*]

SBKG........ Campina Grande/Joao Suassuna [*Brazil*] [*ICAO location identifier*] (ICLI)

SBKKV ..... Space-Based Kinetic Kill Vehicle [*Military*]

Sb Klubu Prirodoved Brno ... Sbornik Klubu Prirodovedeckeho v Brno [*A publication*]

SBKMAL .. Sbornik Trudov Byuro Glavnoi Sudebnomeditsinskoi Ekspertizy i Kafedry Sudebnoi Meditsiny Erevanskogo Meditsinskogo Instituta [*A publication*]

SBKP........ Sao Paulo (Campinas)/Viracopos [*Brazil*] [*ICAO location identifier*] (ICLI)

SBKP........ Serikat Buruh Kementerian Pertahanan [*Defense Ministry Union*] [*Indonesia*]

Sb Kratk Soobshch Fiz AN SSSR Fiz Inst P N Lebedeva ... Sbornik Kratkie Soobshcheniya po Fizike. Akademiya Nauk SSSR. Fizicheskii Institut Imeni P. N. Lebedeva [*A publication*]

Sb Kratk Soobshch Kazan Univ Bot Pochvoved ... Sbornik Kratkikh Soobshchenii Kazanskogo Universiteta Botanika i Pochvovedenie [*A publication*]

Sb Kratk Soobshch Kazan Univ Zool ... Sbornik Kratkikh Soobshchenii Kazanskogo Universiteta po Zoologii [*A publication*]

SBKS .... Suburban Bankshares, Inc. [*Lake Worth, FL*] [*NASDAQ symbol*] (NQ)

SBKU........ Cucui [*Brazil*] [*ICAO location identifier*] (ICLI)

s-bl--- .... Brazil [*MARC geographic area code*] [*Library of Congress*] (LCCP)

SBL........... Santa Ana [*Bolivia*] [*Airport symbol*] [*Obsolete*] (OAG)

SBL........... Schildersblad. Algemeen Vakblad voor het Schildersbedrijf en Afwerkingsbedrijf [*A publication*]

SBL........... Sealed Beam Lamp

SBL........... Serikat Buruh Logam [*Metal Workers' Union*] [*Indonesia*]

SBL........... Society of Biblical Literature (EA)

SBL........... Soybean Lecithin [*Biochemistry*]

SBL........... Space-Based LASER

SBL........... Sporadic Burkitt's Lymphoma [*Medicine*]

SBL........... Staphylococcal Bacteriophage Lysate

SBL........... State University of New York at Buffalo, Law Library, Buffalo, NY [*OCLC symbol*] (OCLC)

SBL........... Strong Black Liquor [*Pulp and paper technology*]

SBL........... Studies in Black Literature [*A publication*]

SBL........... Styrene-Butadiene Latexes [*Organic chemistry*]

SBLA......... Symbol Technologies, Inc. [*NYSE symbol*] (SPSG)

SBLA......... Small Business Loans Act [*Canada*]

SBLB .... Labrea [*Brazil*] [*ICAO location identifier*] (ICLI)

SBLC .... Shallow Bed Liquid Chromatography

SBLC .... Small Business Legislative Council [*Washington, DC*] (EA)

SBLC .... Standby Liquid Control [*Nuclear energy*] (NRCH)

SBLE .... Society of Biblical Literature and Exegesis [*Later, SBL*] (EA)

SBLEA ...... Sbornik Lekarsky [*A publication*]

SB (Leipzig) ... Sitzungsberichte. Saechsische Akademie der Wissenschaften (Leipzig) [*A publication*]

Sb Lek........ Sbornik Lekarsky [*A publication*]

Sb Lekar .... Sbornik Lekarsky [*A publication*]

Sb Leningr Elektro Mekh Inst ... Sbornik Leningradskogo Elektro-Mekhanicheskogo Instituta [*A publication*]

Sb Leningr Inst Inzh Zheleznodorozhn Transp ... Sbornik Leningradskogo Instituta Inzhenerov Zheleznodorozhnogo Transporta [*A publication*]

SBLI .... Savings Bank Life Insurance

SBLI .... Staff Builders, Inc. [*NASDAQ symbol*] (NQ)

SBLJ......... Lajes [*Brazil*] [*ICAO location identifier*] (ICLI)

SBLMC...... Styrene Butadiene Latex Manufacturers Council (EA)

SBLN........ Lins [*Brazil*] [*ICAO location identifier*] (ICLI)

SBLO........ Londrina [*Brazil*] [*ICAO location identifier*] (ICLI)

SBLO........ Strong Black Liquor Oxidation [*Pulp and paper technology*]

SBLOCA ... Small-Break Loss of Coolant Accident [*Nuclear energy*] (NRCH)

SBLP .... Bom Jesus Da Lapa [*Brazil*] [*ICAO location identifier*] (ICLI)

SBLP .... Simplified Bank Loan Participation Plan [*Small Business Administration*]

SBLS......... Lagoa Santa [*Brazil*] [*ICAO location identifier*] (ICLI)

SBLS......... Spaceborne LASER Ranging

SBLSA....... Small Business and Labor Surplus Advisor (AABC)

SBL Sem Pap ... Society of Biblical Literature. Seminar Papers [*A publication*]

SBM.......... College of Charleston, Charleston, SC [*OCLC symbol*] (OCLC)

SBM.......... St. Louis, Brownsville & Mexico [*AAR code*]

SBM.......... School in Basic Management [*LIMRA*]

SBM.......... Science-by-Mail (EA)

SBM.......... Sheboygan [*Wisconsin*] [*Airport symbol*] (OAG)

SBM.......... Sheboygan, WI [*Location identifier*] [*FAA*] (FAAL)

SBM.......... Single Black Male [*Classified advertising*]

SBM.......... Single-Buoy Mooring [*Oil tanker*]

SBM.......... Societe des Bains de Mer [*Monte Carlo*]

SBM.......... Society of Behavioral Medicine (EA)

SBM.......... Speed-O-Print Business Machines Corp. [*AMEX symbol*] (SPSG)

SBM.......... Stuttgarter Biblische Monographien [*Stuttgart*] [*A publication*]

SBM.......... Submerge [*or Submersible*] (KSC)

SBM.......... Submit (AABC)

SBM.......... System Balance Measure (BUR)

SBMA....... Maraba [*Brazil*] [*ICAO location identifier*] (ICLI)

SBMA....... Service Business Marketing Association (EA)

SBMA....... SINS [*Ship Inertial Navigational System*] Bedplate Mirror Assembly

SBMA....... Steel Bar Mills Association [*Later, SMA*] (EA)

Sb Masaryk Akad Pr ... Sbornik Masarykovy Akademie Prace [*A publication*]

Sb Mater Anapskoi Opytn Stn Nauchno Proizvodstvennoi Konf ... Sbornik Materialov Anapskoi Opytnoi Stantsii k Nauchno Proizvodstvennoi Konferentsii [*A publication*]

Sb Mater Avtom Proizvod Protsessov Dispetcher ... Sbornik Materialov po Avtomatizatsii Proizvodstvennykh Protsessov i Dispetcherizatsii [*A publication*]

Sb Mater Gorn Delu Obogashch Metall ... Sbornik Materialov po Gornomu Delu Obogashcheniyu i Metallurgii [*A publication*]

Sb Mater Vak Tekh ... Sbornik Materialov po Vakuumnoi Tekhnike [*A publication*]

SBMD........ Stochastic Boundary Molecular Dynamics [*Force energy simulation method*]

SBMDL..... Submodel

SBME........ Macae [*Brazil*] [*ICAO location identifier*] (ICLI)

SBME........ Society of Business Magazine Editors [*Later, ASBPE*]

SBMEA ..... Space Biology and Medicine [*English Translation*] [*A publication*]

SBMG........ Maringa [*Brazil*] [*ICAO location identifier*] (ICLI)

SBMI......... School Bus Manufacturers Institute (EA)

Sb Mikroelementy i Produktivn Rast ... Sbornik Mikroelementy i Produktivnost Rastenii [*A publication*]

SBMK........ Montes Claros [*Brazil*] [*ICAO location identifier*] (ICLI)

SBML........ Marilia [*Brazil*] [*ICAO location identifier*] (ICLI)

SBML........ Smooth Bore Muzzle Loading [*British military*] (DMA)

SBMMB.... Studia Universitatis Babes-Bolyai. Series Mathematica-Mechanica [*A publication*]

SBMN .... Manaus/Ponta Pelada [*Brazil*] [*ICAO location identifier*] (ICLI)

SBMO .... Maceio/Palmares [*Brazil*] [*ICAO location identifier*] (ICLI)

Sb Mosk Inst Stali Splavov ... Sbornik Moskovskii Institut Stali Splavov [*USSR*] [*A publication*]
SBMPL ..... Simultaneous Binaural Midplane Localization [*Audiometry*]
SBMQ .... Macapa/Internacional [*Brazil*] [*ICAO location identifier*] (ICLI)
SBMR .... Manoel Ribas [*Brazil*] [*ICAO location identifier*] (ICLI)
SBMS .... Mocoro/Dix-Sept Rosado [*Brazil*] [*ICAO location identifier*] (ICLI)
SBMSI .... Serikat Buruh Minjak Shell Indonesia [*Union of Oil Workers for Shell of Indonesia*]
SBMT .... Sao Paulo/Marte [*Brazil*] [*ICAO location identifier*] (ICLI)
SBMU .... Manaus [*Brazil*] [*ICAO location identifier*] (ICLI)
Sb Muz Antropol Etnogr ... Sbornik Muzeja Antropologii i Etnografii [*A publication*]
SBMV .... Southern Bean Mosaic Virus
SBMV-B .... Southern Bean Mosaic Virus - Strain B
SBMV-C .... Southern Bean Mosaic Virus - Cowpea Strain
SBMW .... Serikat Buruh Maclaine, Watson [*Maclaine Watson Company Workers' Union*] [*Indonesia*]
SBMY .... Manicore [*Brazil*] [*ICAO location identifier*] (ICLI)
SBMZ .... Porto De Moz [*Brazil*] [*ICAO location identifier*] (ICLI)
SBN .... Buffalo Narrows Public Library, Saskatchewan [*Library symbol*] [*National Library of Canada*] (NLC)
SBN .... Scrip. Leader in World Pharmaceutical News [*A publication*]
SBN .... Sheridan Broadcasting Network
SBN .... Sino Business Machine [*Vancouver Stock Exchange symbol*]
SBN .... Small Business Network [*Baltimore, MD*] (EA)
SBN .... South Bend [*Indiana*] [*Airport symbol*] (OAG)
SBN .... Spaceborne (KSC)
SBN .... Standard Book Number
SBN .... Strontium-Barium-Niobidium [*Inorganic chemistry*]
SBN .... Studi Bizantini e Neoellenici [*A publication*]
SBN .... Suburban Airlines [*Red Bank, NJ*] [*FAA designator*] (FAAC)
SBN₂ .... Sunbelt Nursery Group, Inc. [*AMEX symbol*] (SPSG)
SBN₂ .... Single Breath Nitrogen [*Test*] [*Medicine*]
Sb Nar Mus Praze Rada B Prir Vedy ... Sbornik Narodniho Muzea v Praze. Rada B: Prirodni Vedy [*A publication*]
Sb Nauchni Tr ... Sbornik Nauchni Trudove [*A publication*]
Sb Nauchno Issled Inst Gidrometeorol Priborostr ... Sbornik Nauchno-Issledovatel'skii Institut Gidrometeorologicheskogo Priborostroeniya [*A publication*]
Sb Nauchno Issled Inst Osn Podzemn Sooruzh ... Sbornik Nauchno-Issledovatel'skii Institut Osnovanii i Podzemnykh Sooruzhenii [*A publication*]
Sb Nauchno-Issled Rab Adygeisk Oblast Opyt Sta ... Sbornik Nauchno-Issledovatel'skikh Rabot Adygeikaya Oblast Opytnaya Stantsiya [*A publication*]
Sb Nauchno Issled Rab Aspir Altai Skh Inst ... Sbornik Nauchno-Issledovatel'skikh Rabot Aspirantov. Altaiskii Sel'skokhozyaistvennyi Institut [*A publication*]
Sb Nauchno-Issled Rab Aspir Molodykh Uch Altai Skh Inst ... Sbornik Nauchno-Issledovatel'skikh Rabot Aspirantov i Molodykh Uchenykh. Altaiskii Sel'skokhozyaistvennyi Institut [*A publication*]
Sb Nauchno-Issled Rab Azovo-Chernomorsk S-Kh Inst ... Sbornik Nauchno-Issledovatel'skikh Rabot Azovo-Chernomorskogo Sel'skokhozyaistvennogo Instituta [*A publication*]
Sb Nauchno-Issled Rab Gor'k Obl Opytn Stn Zhivotnovod ... Sbornik Nauchno-Issledovatel'skikh Rabot Gor'kovskoi Oblastnoi Opytnoi Stantsii Zhivotnovodstva [*A publication*]
Sb Nauchno-Issled Rab Orlov Gos Sel'-Khoz Opyt Sta ... Sbornik Nauchno-Issledovatel'skikh Rabot Orlovskoi Gosudarstvennoi Sel'skokhozyaistvennoi Opytnoi Stantsii [*A publication*]
Sb Nauchno-Issled Rab Pchel ... Sbornik Nauchno-Issledovatel'skikh Rabot po Pchelovodstvu [*A publication*]
Sb Nauchno Issled Rab Tashk Tekst Inst ... Sbornik Nauchno-Issledovatel'skikh Rabot Tashkentskogo Tekstil'nogo Instituta [*A publication*]
Sb Nauchno-Issled Rab Vses Nauchno-Issled Inst Tab Makhorki ... Sbornik Nauchno-Issledovatel'skikh Rabot Vsesoyuznogo Nauchno-Issledovatel'skogo Instituta Tabaka i Makhorki [*A publication*]
Sb Nauchno Issled Tr Mosk Tekst Inst ... Sbornik Nauchno-Issledovatel'skikh Trudov Moskovskii Tekstil'nyi Institut [*A publication*]
Sb Nauchn Rab Angar Nauchno-Issled Inst Gig Tr Prof Zabol ... Sbornik Nauchnykh Rabot Angarskogo Nauchno-Issledovatel'skogo Instituta Gigieny Truda i Professional'nykh Zabolevanii [*A publication*]
Sb Nauchn Rab Aspir Kabard Balkar Gos Univ ... Sbornik Nauchnykh Rabot Aspirantov Kabardino-Balkarskii Gosudarstvennyi Universitet [*A publication*]
Sb Nauchn Rab Aspir Voronezh Gos Univ ... Sbornik Nauchnykh Rabot Aspirantov Voronezhskogo Gosudarstvennogo Universiteta [*A publication*]
Sb Nauchn Rab Aspir Vses Nauchno Issled Inst Khlopkovod ... Sbornik Nauchnykh Rabot Aspirantov Vsesoyuznyi Nauchno-Issledovatel'skii Institut Khlopkovodstva [*A publication*]

Sb Nauchn Rab Beloruss Nauchno-Issled Kozhnovenerol Inst ... Sbornik Nauchnykh Rabot Belorusskogo Nauchno-Issledovatel'skogo Kozhnovenerologicheskogo Instituta [*A publication*]
Sb Nauchn Rab Beloruss Tekhnol Inst ... Sbornik Nauchnykh Rabot Belorusskii Tekhnologicheskii Institut [*A publication*]
Sb Nauchn Rab Checheno Ingush Nauchno Issled Vet Stn ... Sbornik Nauchnykh Rabot Checheno-Ingushskoi Nauchno-Issledovatel'skoi Veterinarnoi Stantsii [*A publication*]
Sb Nauchn Rab Dal'nevost Nauchno Issled Inst Stroit ... Sbornik Nauchnykh Rabot Dal'nevostochnyi Nauchno-Issledovatel'skii Institut po Stroitel'stvu [*A publication*]
Sb Nauchn Rab Dnepropetr Gos Med Inst ... Sbornik Nauchnykh Rabot Dnepropetrovskii Gosudarstvennyi Meditsinskii Institut [*A publication*]
Sb Nauchn Rab Inst Melior Vodn Bolotnogo Khoz Akad Nauk BSSR ... Sbornik Nauchnykh Rabot Instituta Melioratsii. Vodnogo i Bolotnogo Khozyaistva. Akademiya Nauk Belorusskoi SSR [*A publication*]
Sb Nauchn Rab Izhevsk Med Inst ... Sbornik Nauchnykh Rabot Izhevski Meditsinskii Institut [*A publication*]
Sb Nauchn Rab Kazan Gos Med Inst ... Sbornik Nauchnykh Rabot Kazanskogo Gosudarstvennogo Meditsinskogo Instituta [*A publication*]
Sb Nauchn Rab Khar'k Gos Med Inst ... Sbornik Nauchnykh Rabot Khar'kovskogo Gosudarstvennogo Meditsinskogo Instituta [*A publication*]
Sb Nauchn Rab Khar'k Inst Mekh Sots Sel'sk Khoz ... Sbornik Nauchnykh Rabot Khar'kovskii Institut Mekhanizatsii Sotsialisticheskogo Sel'skogo Khozyaistva [*A publication*]
Sb Nauchn Rab Khar'k Nauchno-Issled Inst Vaktsin Syvorot ... Sbornik Nauchnykh Rabot Khar'kovskogo Nauchno-Issledovatel'skogo Instituta Vaktsin i Syvorotok [*A publication*]
Sb Nauchn Rab Kiev Voen Gosp ... Sbornik Nauchnykh Rabot Kievskii Voennyi Gospital [*A publication*]
Sb Nauchn Rab Kirg Med Inst ... Sbornik Nauchnykh Rabot Kirgizskii Meditsinskii Institut [*A publication*]
Sb Nauchn Rab Kirg Nauchno Issled Inst Okhr Materin Det ... Sbornik Nauchnykh Rabot Kirgizskogo Nauchno-Issledovatel'skogo Instituta Okhrany Materinstva i Detstva [*A publication*]
Sb Nauchn Rab Kirg Nauchno-Issled Inst Tuberk ... Sbornik Nauchnykh Rabot Kirgizskogo Nauchno-Issledovatel'skogo Instituta Tuberkuleza [*A publication*]
Sb Nauchn Rab Krasnoyarsk Gos Med Inst ... Sbornik Nauchnykh Rabot Krasnoyarskogo Gosudarstvennogo Meditsinskogo Instituta [*A publication*]
Sb Nauchn Rab Kurgan Gos S-Kh Inst ... Sbornik Nauchnykh Rabot Kurganskii Gosudarstvennyi Sel'skokhozyaistvennyi Institut [*A publication*]
Sb Nauchn Rab Leningr Gos Inst Usoversh Vrachei ... Sbornik Nauchnykh Rabot Leningradskii Gosudarstvennyi Institut Usovershenstvovaniya Vrachei [*A publication*]
Sb Nauchn Rab Leningr Inst Sov Torg ... Sbornik Nauchnykh Rabot Leningradskii Institut Sovetskoi Torgovli [*A publication*]
Sb Nauchn Rab Leningr Khim-Farm Inst ... Sbornik Nauchnykh Rabot Leningradskogo Khimiko-Farmatsevticheskogo Instituta [*A publication*]
Sb Nauchn Rab Leningr Nauchno Issled Inst Antibiot ... Sbornik Nauchnykh Rabot Leningradskii Nauchno-Issledovatel'skii Institut Antibiotikov [*A publication*]
Sb Nauchn Rab Minsk Gos Med Inst ... Sbornik Nauchnykh Rabot Minskogo Gosudarstvennogo Meditsinskogo Instituta [*A publication*]
Sb Nauchn Rab Murm Olenevodcheskaya Opytn Stn ... Sbornik Nauchnykh Rabot Murmanskaya Olenevodcheskaya Opytnaya Stantsiya [*A publication*]
Sb Nauchn Rab Nauchno-Issled Inst Sadov Im I V Michurina ... Sbornik Nauchnykh Rabot Nauchno-Issledovatel'skogo Instituta Sadov Imeni I. V. Michurina [*A publication*]
Sb Nauchn Rab Novosib Nauchno Issled Vet Stn ... Sbornik Nauchnykh Rabot Novosibirskoi Nauchno-Issledovatel'skoi Veterinarnoi Stantsii [*A publication*]
Sb Nauchn Rab Rizh Med Inst ... Sbornik Nauchnykh Rabot Rizhskogo Meditsinskogo Instituta [*A publication*]
Sb Nauchn Rab Rostov Med Inst ... Sbornik Nauchnykh Rabot Rostovskogo Meditsinskogo Instituta [*A publication*]
Sb Nauchn Rab Ryazan S-Kh Inst ... Sbornik Nauchnykh Rabot Ryazanskii Sel'skokhozyaistvennyi Institut [*A publication*]
Sb Nauchn Rab Sarat Med Inst ... Sbornik Nauchnykh Rabot Saratovskii Meditsinskii Institut [*A publication*]
Sb Nauchn Rab Sib Zon Nauchno-Issled Vet Inst ... Sbornik Nauchnykh Rabot Sibirskogo Zonal'nogo Nauchno-Issledovatel'skogo Veterinarnogo Instituta [*A publication*]
Sb Nauchn Rab Stud Erevan Gos Univ ... Sbornik Nauchnykh Rabot Studentov Erevanskii Gosudarstvennyi Universitet [*A publication*]
Sb Nauchn Rab Stud Ivanov Gos Med Inst ... Sbornik Nauchnyk Rabot Studentov Ivanovskogo Gosudarstvennogo Meditsinskogo Instituta [*A publication*]

Sb Nauchn Rab Stud Karelo Fin Gos Univ ... Sbornik Nauchnykh Rabot Studentov Karelo-Finskogo Gosudarstvennogo Universiteta [*A publication*]

Sb Nauchn Rab Stud Kirg Gos Univ ... Sbornik Nauchnykh Rabot Studentov Kirgizskii Gosudarstvennyi Universitet [*A publication*]

Sb Nauchn Rab Stud Leningr Gorn Inst ... Sbornik Nauchnykh Rabot Studentov Leningradskogo Gornogo Instituta [*A publication*]

Sb Nauchn Rab Stud Petrozavodsk Gos Univ ... Sbornik Nauchnykh Rabot Studentov Petrozavodskogo Gosudarstvennogo Universiteta [*A publication*]

Sb Nauchn Rab Stud Sarat Zootekh Vet Inst ... Sbornik Nauchnykh Rabot Studentov Saratovskii Zootekhnichesko-Veterinarnyi Institut [*A publication*]

Sb Nauchn Rab Stud Stalingr S-Kh Inst ... Sbornik Nauchnykh Rabot Studentov Stalingradskogo Sel'skokhozyaistvennogo Instituta [*A publication*]

Sb Nauchn Rab Sverdl Med Inst ... Sbornik Nauchnykh Rabot Sverdlovskogo Meditsinskogo Instituta [*A publication*]

Sb Nauchn Rab Sverdl Otd Vses O-Va Anat Gistol Embriol ... Sbornik Nauchnykh Rabot Sverdlovskogo Otdeleniya Vsesoyuznogo Obshchestva Anatomov, Gistologov, i Embriologov [*A publication*]

Sb Nauchn Rab Tsentr Nauchno-Issled Lab Rostov Med Inst ... Sbornik Nauchnykh Rabot Tsentral'naya Nauchno-Issledovatel'skaya Laboratoriya Rostov'skogo Meditsinskogo Instituta [*A publication*]

Sb Nauchn Rab Ukr Nauchno Issled Inst Sadovod ... Sbornik Nauchnykh Rabot Ukrainskii Nauchno-Issledovatel'skii Institut Sadovodstva [*A publication*]

Sb Nauchn Rab Voen-Med Fak Kuibyshev Med Inst ... Sbornik Nauchnykh Rabot Voenno-Meditsinskogo Fakul'teta Kuibyshevskogo Meditsinskogo Instituta [*A publication*]

Sb Nauchn Rab Volgogr Gos Med Inst ... Sbornik Nauchnykh Rabot Volgogradskoi Gosudarstvennyi Meditsinskii Institut [*A publication*]

Sb Nauchn Rab Volgogr Med Inst ... Sbornik Nauchnykh Rabot Volgogradskogo Meditsinskogo Instituta [*A publication*]

Sb Nauchn Rab Volgogr Obl Klin Boln ... Sbornik Nauchnykh Rabot Volgogradskoi Oblastnoi Klinicheskoi Bol'nitsy [*A publication*]

Sb Nauchn Rab Volgogr Pedagog Inst ... Sbornik Nauchnykh Rabot Volgogradskogo Pedagogicheskogo Instituta [*A publication*]

Sb Nauchn Rab Vses Nauchno-Issled Inst Lek Rast ... Sbornik Nauchnykh Rabot Vsesoyuznyi Nauchno-Issledovatel'skii Institut Lekarstvennykh Rastenii [*A publication*]

Sb Nauchn Rab Vses Nauchno-Issled Inst Sadovod ... Sbornik Nauchnykh Rabot Vsesoyuznyi Nauchno-Issledovatel'skii Institut Sadovodstva [*A publication*]

Sb Nauchn Rab Vses Nauchno-Issled Inst Zhivotnovod ... Sbornik Nauchnykh Rabot Vsesoyuznyi Nauchno-Issledovatel'skii Institut Zhivotnovodstva [*A publication*]

Sb Nauchn Rab Yarosl Gorzdravotd ... Sbornik Nauchnykh Rabot Yaroslavskogo Gorzdravotdela [*A publication*]

Sb Nauchn Rab Yarosl Gorzdravotdela ... Sbornik Nauchnykh Rabot Yaroslavskogo Gorzdravotdela [*A publication*]

Sb Nauchn Rab Yarosl Med Inst ... Sbornik Nauchnykh Rabot Yaroslavskogo Meditsinskogo Instituta [*A publication*]

Sb Nauchn Rab Zaochn Inst Sov Torg ... Sbornik Nauchnykh Rabot Zaochnyi Institut Sovetskoi Torgovli [*A publication*]

Sb Nauchn Soobshch Dagest Gos Univ Kafedra Khim ... Sbornik Nauchnykh Soobshchenii Dagestanskii Gosudarstvennyi Universitet Kafedra Khimii [*A publication*]

Sb Nauchn Soobshch Dagest Otd Vses Bot Ova ... Sbornik Nauchnykh Soobshchenii Dagestanskogo Otdela Vsesoyuznogo Botanicheskogo Obshchestva [*A publication*]

Sb Nauchn Soobshch Estest Tekh Nauk Dagest Univ ... Sbornik Nauchnykh Soobshchenii Estestvennykh i Tekhnicheskikh Nauk Dagestanskogo Universitet [*A publication*]

Sb Nauchn Soobshch Kafedry Org Fizk Khim Dagest Gos Univ ... Sbornik Nauchnykh Soobshchenii Kafedry Organicheskoi i Fizkolloidnoi Khimii Dagestanskii Gosudarstvennyi Universitet [*A publication*]

Sb Nauchn Soobshch Kafedry Zool Biol Khim Dagest Univ ... Sbornik Nauchnykh Soobshchenii Kafedry Zoologii Biologii Khimii Dagestanskogo Universiteta [*A publication*]

Sb Nauchn Soobshch Sarat Avtomob Dorozhn Inst ... Sbornik Nauchnykh Soobshchenii Saratovskii Avtomobil'no Dorozhnyi Institut [*A publication*]

Sb Nauchn Statei Vinnitsk Gos Med Inst ... Sbornik Nauchnykh Statei Vinnitskogo Gosudarstvennogo Meditsinskogo Instituta [*A publication*]

Sb Nauchn Stud Ova Geol Fak Mosk Gos Univ ... Sbornik Nauchnogo Studencheskogo Obshchestva Geologicheskii Fakul'tet Moskovskii Gosudarstvennyi Universitet [*A publication*]

Sb Nauchn Stud Rab Omsk Gos Pedagog Inst ... Sbornik Nauchnykh Studencheskikh Rabot Omskii Gosudarstvennyi Pedagogicheskii Institut [*A publication*]

Sb Nauchn Stud Rab Sarat Zoovetinst ... Sbornik Nauchnykh Studencheskikh Rabot Saratovskogo Zoovetinstituta [*A publication*]

Sb Nauchn Tr Andizh Gos Med Inst ... Sbornik Nauchnykh Trudov Andizhanskii Gosudarstvennyi Meditsinskii Institut [*A publication*]

Sb Nauchn Tr Andizh Med Inst ... Sbornik Nauchnykh Trudov Andizhanskogo Meditsinskogo Instituta [*A publication*]

Sb Nauchn Tr Arm Gos Pedagog Inst Ser Fiz Mat ... Sbornik Nauchnykh Trudov Armyanskii Gosudarstvennyi Pedagogicheskii Institut. Seriya Fiziko-Matematicheskaya [*A publication*]

Sb Nauchn Tr Arm Gos Zaochn Pedagog Inst ... Sbornik Nauchnykh Trudov Gosudarstvennogo Zaochnogo Pedagogicheskogo Instituta [*A publication*]

Sb Nauchn Tr Arm Otd Vses Bot Ova ... Sbornik Nauchnykh Trudov Armyanskogo Otdelnykh Vsesoyuznogo Botanicheskoi Obshchestva [*A publication*]

Sb Nauchn Tr Arm S-Kh Inst ... Sbornik Nauchnykh Trudov Armyanskogo Sel'skokhozyaistvennogo Instituta [*A publication*]

Sb Nauchn Tr Azerb Nauchno Issled Inst Gematol Pereliv Krovi ... Sbornik Nauchnykh Trudov Azerbaidzhanskogo Nauchno-Issledovatel'skogo Instituta Gematologii i Perelivaniya Krovi [*A publication*]

Sb Nauchn Tr Azerb Nauchno-Issled Inst Pereliv Krovi ... Sbornik Nauchnykh Trudov Azerbaidzhanskogo Nauchno-Issledovatel'skogo Instituta Perelivaniya Krovi [*A publication*]

Sb Nauchn Tr Azerb Nauchno Issled Inst Perel Krovi ... Sbornik Nauchnykh Trudov Azerbaidzhanskogo Nauchno-Issledovatel'skogo Instituta Perelivaniya Krovi [*A publication*]

Sb Nauchn Tr Bashk Gos Med Inst ... Sbornik Nauchnykh Trudov Bashkirskogo Gosudarstvennogo Meditsinskogo Instituta [*A publication*]

Sb Nauchn Tr Bashk Med Inst ... Sbornik Nauchnykh Trudov Bashkirskogo Meditsinskogo Instituta [*A publication*]

Sb Nauchn Tr Bashk Nauchno-Issled Trakhomatoznogo Inst ... Sbornik Nauchnykh Trudov Bashkirskogo Nauchno-Issledovatel'skogo Trakhomatoznogo Instituta [*A publication*]

Sb Nauchn Tr Beloruss Inst Mekh Selsk Khoz ... Sbornik Nauchnykh Trudov Belorusskii Institut Mekhanizatsii Sel'skogo Khozyaistva [*A publication*]

Sb Nauchn Tr Beloruss Lesotekh Inst ... Sbornik Nauchnykh Trudov Belorusskogo Lesotekhnicheskogo Instituta [*A publication*]

Sb Nauchn Tr Beloruss Nauchno-Issled Inst Pochvoved Agrokhim ... Sbornik Nauchnykh Trudov Belorusskii Nauchno-Issledovatel'skii Institut Pochvovedeniya i Agrokhimii [*A publication*]

Sb Nauchn Tr Beloruss Nauchno-Issled Inst Zemled ... Sbornik Nauchnykh Trudov Belorusskii Nauchno-Issledovatel'skii Institut Zemledeliya [*A publication*]

Sb Nauchn Tr Beloruss Nauchno Issled Kozhno Venerol Inst ... Sbornik Nauchnykh Trudov Belorusskii Nauchno-Issledovatel'skii Kozhno-Venerologicheskii Institut [*A publication*]

Sb Nauchn Tr Beloruss Politekh Inst ... Sbornik Nauchnykh Trudov Belorusskii Politekhnicheskii Institut [*A publication*]

Sb Nauchn Tr Beloruss S-Kh Akad ... Sbornik Nauchnykh Trudov Belorusskoi Sel'skokhozyaistvennoi Akademii [*A publication*]

Sb Nauchn Tr Chelyab Nauchno Issled Inst Gorn Dela ... Sbornik Nauchnykh Trudov Chelyabinskii Nauchno-Issledovatel'skii Institut Gornogo Dela [*A publication*]

Sb Nauchn Tr Chelyab Politekh Inst ... Sbornik Nauchnykh Trudov Chelyabinskii Politekhnicheskii Institut [*USSR*] [*A publication*]

Sb Nauchn Tr Chit Gos Med Inst ... Sbornik Nauchnykh Trudov Chitinskii Gosudarstvennyi Meditsinskii Institut [*A publication*]

Sb Nauchn Tr Chuv Nauchno-Issled Trakhomatoznogo Inst ... Sbornik Nauchnykh Trudov Chuvashskogo Nauchno-Issledovatel'skogo Trakhomatoznogo Instituta [*A publication*]

Sb Nauchn Tr Dagest Gos Med Inst ... Sbornik Nauchnykh Trudov Dagestanskii Gosudarstvennyi Meditsinskii Institut [*A publication*]

Sb Nauchn Tr Dnepropetr Gos Med Inst ... Sbornik Nauchnykh Trudov Dnepropetrovskii Gosudarstvennyi Meditsinskii Institut [*A publication*]

Sb Nauchn Tr Dnepropetr Inzh Stroit Inst ... Sbornik Nauchnykh Trudov Dnepropetrovskii Inzhenerno-Stroitel'nyi Institut [*A publication*]

Sb Nauchn Tr Donskogo S-Kh Inst ... Sbornik Nauchnykh Trudov Donskogo Sel'skokhozyaistvennogo Instituta [*A publication*]

Sb Nauchn Tr Erevan Arm Gos Pedagog Inst Khim ... Sbornik Nauchnykh Trudov Erevanskii Armyanskii Gosudarstvennyi Pedagogicheskii Institut. Khimiya [*A publication*]

Sb Nauchn Tr Erevan Politekh Inst ... Sbornik Nauchnykh Trudov Erevanskii Politekhnicheskii Institut [*Armenian SSR*] [*A publication*]

Sb Nauchn Tr Est Nauchno-Issled Inst Zemled Melior ... Sbornik Nauchnykh Trudov Estonskogo Nauchno-Issledovatel'skogo Instituta Zemledeliya i Melioratsii [*A publication*]

Sb Nauchn Tr Est S-Kh Akad ... Sbornik Nauchnykh Trudov Estonskaya Sel'skokhozyaistvennaya Akademiya [*A publication*]

Sb Nauchn Tr Fiz Tekh Inst Akad Nauk B SSR ... Sbornik Nauchnykh Trudov Fiziko-Tekhnicheskii Institut Akademiya Nauk Belorusskoi SSR [*A publication*]

Sb Nauchn Tr Fiz Tekh Inst Nizk Temp Akad Nauk Ukr SSR ... Sbornik Nauchnykh Trudov Fiziko-Tekhnicheskii Institut Nizkikh Temperatur Akademiya Nauk Ukrainskoi SSR [*Ukrainian SSR*] [*A publication*]

Sb Nauchn Tr Gazov Khromatogr ... Sbornik Nauchnykh Trudov po Gazovoi Khromatografii [*A publication*]

Sb Nauchn Tr Glavgeologii Uzb SSR Tashk Politekh Inst ... Sbornik Nauchnykh Trudov Glavgeologii Uzbekskoi SSR i Tashkentskogo Politekhnicheskogo Instituta [*A publication*]

Sb Nauchn Tr Gos Nauchno Issled Inst Elektrodnoi Promsti ... Sbornik Nauchnykh Trudov Gosudarstvennyi Nauchno-Issledovatel'skii Institut Elektrodnoi Promyshlennosti [*A publication*]

Sb Nauchn Tr Gos Nauchno Issled Inst Keram Promsti ... Sbornik Nauchnykh Trudov Gosudarstvennyi Nauchno-Issledovatel'skii Institut Keramicheskoi Promyshlennosti [*A publication*]

Sb Nauchn Tr Gos Nauchno Issled Inst Keramzitu ... Sbornik Nauchnykh Trudov Gosudarstvennyi Nauchno-Issledovatel'skii Institut po Keramzitu [*A publication*]

Sb Nauchn Tr Gos Nauchno-Issled Inst Tsvetn Met ... Sbornik Nauchnykh Trudov Gosudarstvennogo Nauchno-Issledovatel'skogo Instituta Tsvetnykh Metallov [*A publication*]

Sb Nauchn Tr Gos Nauchno Issled Proektn Inst Metall Promsti ... Sbornik Nauchnykh Trudov Gosudarstvennyi Nauchno-Issledovatel'skii i Proektnyi Institut Metallurgicheskoi Promyshlennosti [*A publication*]

Sb Nauchn Tr Grodn Skh Inst ... Sbornik Nauchnykh Trudov Grodnenskii Sel'skokhozyaistvennyi Institut [*A publication*]

Sb Nauchn Tr Inst Biol Akad Nauk B SSR ... Sbornik Nauchnykh Trudov Institut Biologii Akademiya Nauk Belorusskoi SSR [*A publication*]

Sb Nauchn Tr Inst Geol Geofiz Akad Nauk Uzb SSR ... Sbornik Nauchnykh Trudov Instituta Geologii i Geofiziki Akademii Nauk Uzbekskoi SSR [*A publication*]

Sb Nauchn Tr Inst Melior Vodn Bolotnogo Khoz Akad Nauk BSSR ... Sbornik Nauchnykh Trudov Instituta Melioratsii Vodnogo i Bolotnogo Khozyaistva Akademiya Nauk Belorusskoi SSR [*A publication*]

Sb Nauchn Tr Inst Metallofiz Akad Ukr SSR ... Sbornik Nauchnykh Trudov Instituta Metallofiziki Akademiya Nauk Ukrainskoi SSR [*Ukrainian SSR*] [*A publication*]

Sb Nauchn Tr Inst Tsvetn Met ... Sbornik Nauchnykh Trudov Institut Tsvetnykh Metallov [*A publication*]

Sb Nauchn Tr Irkutsk Gos Nauchno-Issled Inst Redk Met ... Sbornik Nauchnykh Trudov Irkutskii Gosudarstvennyi Nauchno-Issledovatel'skii Institut Redkikh Metallov [*A publication*]

Sb Nauchn Tr Ivanov Energ Inst ... Sbornik Nauchnykh Trudov Ivanovskogo Energeticheskogo Instituta [*A publication*]

Sb Nauchn Tr Ivanov Gos Med Inst ... Sbornik Nauchnykh Trudov Ivanovskogo Gosudarstvennogo Meditsinskogo Instituta [*A publication*]

Sb Nauchn Tr Ivanov Med Inst ... Sbornik Nauchnykh Trudov Ivanovskogo Meditsinskogo Instituta [*A publication*]

Sb Nauchn Tr Ivanov S-Kh Inst ... Sbornik Nauchnykh Trudov Ivanovskogo Sel'skokhozyaistvennogo Instituta [*A publication*]

Sb Nauchn Tr Kalinin Gos Skh Opytn Stant ... Sbornik Nauchnykh Trudov Kalininskaya Gosudarstvennaya Sel'skokhozyaistvennaya Opytnaya Stantsiya [*A publication*]

Sb Nauchn Tr Kalinin Gos Skh Opytn Stn ... Sbornik Nauchnykh Trudov Kalininskaya Gosudarstvennaya Sel'skokhozyaistvennaya Opytnaya Stantsiya [*A publication*]

Sb Nauchn Tr Kamenets Podolsk Skh Inst ... Sbornik Nauchnykh Trudov Kamenets-Podol'skogo Sel'skokhozyaistvennogo Instituta [*A publication*]

Sb Nauchn Tr Kar'k Gos Med Inst ... Sbornik Nauchnykh Trudov Khar'kovskogo Gosudarstvennogo Meditsinskogo Instituta [*A publication*]

Sb Nauchn Tr Kaz Gorno-Metall Inst ... Sbornik Nauchnykh Trudov Kazakhskii Gorno-Metallurgicheskii Institut [*A publication*]

Sb Nauchn Tr Kaz Politekh Inst ... Sbornik Nauchnykh Trudov Kazakhskii Politekhnicheskii Institut [*A publication*]

Sb Nauchn Tr Khar'k Med Inst ... Sbornik Nauchnykh Trudov Khar'kovskogo Meditsinskogo Instituta [*A publication*]

Sb Nauchn Tr Khar'k Skh Inst Im V V Dokuchaeva ... Sbornik Nauchnykh Trudov Khar'kovskii Sel'skokhozyaistvennyi Institut Imeni V. V. Dokuchaeva [*A publication*]

Sb Nauchn Tr Kiev Inst Inzh Grazhd Aviats ... Sbornik Nauchnykh Trudov Kievskogo Instituta Inzhenerov Grazhdanskoi Aviatsii [*Ukrainian SSR*] [*A publication*]

Sb Nauchn Tr Kiev Inzh Stroit Inst ... Sbornik Nauchnykh Trudov Kievskogo Inzhenerno-Stroitel'nogo Instituta [*A publication*]

Sb Nauchn Tr Kirg Med Inst ... Sbornik Nauchnykh Trudov Kirkizskogo Meditsinskogo Instituta [*A publication*]

Sb Nauchn Tr Krasnoyarsk Gos Med Inst ... Sbornik Nauchnykh Trudov Krasnoyarskogo Gosudarstvennogo Meditsinskogo Instituta [*A publication*]

Sb Nauchn Tr Krivorozh Fil Inst Gorn Dela Akad Nauk Ukr SSR ... Sbornik Nauchnykh Trudov Krivorozhskii Filial Instituta Gornogo Dela Akademiya Nauk Ukrainskoi SSR [*A publication*]

Sb Nauchn Tr Krivorozh Gornorudn Inst ... Sbornik Nauchnykh Trudov Krivorozhskii Gornorudnyi Institut [*A publication*]

Sb Nauchn Tr Krym Gos Med Inst ... Sbornik Nauchnykh Trudov Krymskogo Gosudarstvennogo Meditsinskogo Instituta [*A publication*]

Sb Nauchn Tr Kuibyshev Ind Inst ... Sbornik Nauchnykh Trudov Kuibyshevskii Industrial'nyi Institut [*A publication*]

Sb Nauchn Tr Kuibyshev Inzh Stroit Inst ... Sbornik Nauchnykh Trudov Kuibyshevskii Inzhenerno-Stroitel'nyi Institut [*A publication*]

Sb Nauchn Tr Kuibyshev Nauchno Issled Inst Epidemiol Gig ... Sbornik Nauchnykh Trudov Kuibyshevskogo Nauchno-Issledovatel'skogo Instituta Epidemiologii i Gigieny [*A publication*]

Sb Nauchn Tr Kuibyshev Nauchno Issled Inst Gig ... Sbornik Nauchnykh Trudov Kuibyshevskii Nauchno-Issledovatel'skii Institut Gigieny [*A publication*]

Sb Nauchn Tr Kuibyshev Nauchno Issled Vet Stn ... Sbornik Nauchnykh Trudov Kuibyshevskoi Nauchno-Issledovatel'noi Veterinarnoi Stantsii [*A publication*]

Sb Nauchn Tr Kuzbasskii Politekh Inst ... Sbornik Nauchnykh Trudov Kuzbasskii Politekhnicheskii Institut [*A publication*]

Sb Nauchn Tr Lening Farm Inst ... Sbornik Nauchnykh Trudov Leningradskii Farmatsevticheskii Institut [*A publication*]

Sb Nauchn Tr Leningr Inst Sov Torg ... Sbornik Nauchnykh Trudov Leningradskii Institut Sovetskoi Torgovli [*A publication*]

Sb Nauchn Tr Leningr Inst Tochn Mekh Opt ... Sbornik Nauchnykh Trudov Leningradskii Institut Tochnoi Mekhaniki i Optiki [*A publication*]

Sb Nauchn Tr Leningr Inst Usoversh Vet Vrachei ... Sbornik Nauchnykh Trudov Leningradskogo Instituta Usovershenstvovaniya Veterinarnykh Vrachei [*A publication*]

Sb Nauchn Tr Leningr Inst Usoversh Vrachei ... Sbornik Nauchnykh Trudov Leningradskogo Instituta Usovershenstvovaniya Vrachei [*A publication*]

Sb Nauchn Tr Leningr Inzh-Stroit Inst ... Sbornik Nauchnykh Trudov Leningradskii Inzhenerno-Stroitel'nyi Institut [*A publication*]

Sb Nauchn Tr Leningr Khim Farm Inst ... Sbornik Nauchnykh Trudov Leningradskii Khimiko-Farmatsevticheskii Institut [*A publication*]

Sb Nauchn Tr Leningr Nauchno Issled Inst Antibiot ... Sbornik Nauchnykh Trudov Leningradskii Nauchno-Issledovatel'skii Institut Antibiotikov [*A publication*]

Sb Nauchn Tr Leningr Nauchno Issled Inst Lesn Khoz ... Sbornik Nauchnykh Trudov Leningradskii Nauchno-Issledovatel'skii Institut Lesnogo Khozyaistva [*A publication*]

Sb Nauchn Tr Leningr Nauchno-Issled Inst Pereliv Krovi ... Sbornik Nauchnykh Trudov Leningradskogo Nauchno-Issledovatel'skogo Instituta Perelivanya Krovi [*A publication*]

Sb Nauchn Tr Leningr Voen Mekh Inst ... Sbornik Nauchnykh Trudov Leningradskii Voenno-Mekhanicheskii Institut [*A publication*]

Sb Nauchn Tr Lugansk S-Kh Inst ... Sbornik Nauchnykh Trudov Luganskogo Sel'skokhozyaistvennogo Instituta [*A publication*]

Sb Nauchn Tr L'vov Nauchn Ovo Derm Venerol ... Sbornik Nauchnykh Trudov L'vovskoe Nauchnoe Obshchestvo Dermato-Venerologov [*A publication*]

Sb Nauchn Tr Magnitogorsk Gornometall Inst ... Sbornik Nauchnykh Trudov Magnitogorskii Gornometallurgicheskii Institut [*USSR*] [*A publication*]

Sb Nauchn Tr Minsk Gos Med Inst ... Sbornik Nauchnykh Trudov Minskii Gosudarstvennyi Meditsinskii Institut [*A publication*]

Sb Nauchn Tr Mogilev Obl Gos Skh Opytn Stn ... Sbornik Nauchnykh Trudov Mogilevskaya Oblastnaya Gosudarstvennaya Sel'skokhozyaistvennaya Opytnaya Stantsiya [*A publication*]

Sb Nauchn Tr Morfol Kafedry Bashk Med Inst ... Sbornik Nauchnykh Trudov Morfologicheskoi Kafedry Bashkirskogo Meditsinskogo Instituta [*A publication*]

Sb Nauchn Tr Mosk Gorn Inst ... Sbornik Nauchnykh Trudov Moskovskogo Gornogo Instituta [*A publication*]

Sb Nauchn Tr Mosk Inst Tsvetn Met Zolota ... Sbornik Nauchnykh Trudov Moskovskii Institut Tsvetnykh Metallov i Zolota [*A publication*]

Sb Nauchn Tr Mosk Nauchno Issled Inst Gig Im F F Erismana ... Sbornik Nauchnykh Trudov Moskovskii Nauchno-Issledovatel'skii Institut Gigieny Imeni F. F. Erismana [*A publication*]

Sb Nauchn Tr Mosk Poligr Inst ... Sbornik Nauchnykh Trudov Moskovskii Poligraficheskii Institut [*A publication*]

Sb Nauchn Tr Mosk Tekhnol Inst Pishch Promsti ... Sbornik Nauchnykh Trudov Moskovskii Tekhnologicheskii Institut Pishchevoi Promyshlennosti [*A publication*]

Sb Nauchn Tr Nauchno-Issled Inst Pereliv Krovi Arm SSR ... Sbornik Nauchnykh Trudov Nauchno-Issledovatel'skogo Instituta Gematologii i Perelivaniya Krovi Armyanskoi SSR [*A publication*]

Sb Nauchn Tr Nauchno-Issled Inst Zemled Echmiadzin (Arm SSR) ... Sbornik Nauchnykh Trudov Nauchno-Issledovatel'skii Institut Zemledeliya Echmiadzin (Armenian SSR) [*A publication*]

Sb Nauchn Tr Nauchno Issled Kozhno Venerol Inst (Minsk) ... Sbornik Nauchnykh Trudov Nauchno-Issledovatel'skii Kozhno-Venerologicheskii Institut (Minsk) [*A publication*]

Sb Nauchn Tr Permsk Gorn Inst ... Sbornik Nauchnykh Trudov Permskii Gornyi Institut [*A publication*]

Sb Nauchn Tr Permsk Gos Med Inst ... Sbornik Nauchnykh Trudov Permskii Gosudarstvennyi Meditsinskii Institut [*A publication*]

Sb Nauchn Tr Permsk Gos Skh Opytn Stn ... Sbornik Nauchnykh Trudov Permskaya Gosudarstvennaya Sel'skokhozyaistvennaya Opytnaya Stantsiya [*A publication*]

Sb Nauchn Tr Permsk Med Inst ... Sbornik Nauchnykh Trudov Permskogo Meditsinskogo Instituta [*A publication*]

Sb Nauchn Tr Permsk Politekh Inst ... Sbornik Nauchnykh Trudov Permskij Politekhnicheskij Institut [*A publication*]

Sb Nauchn Tr Primorsk S-Kh Inst ... Sbornik Nauchnykh Trudov Primorskogo Sel'skokhozyaistvennogo Instituta [*A publication*]

Sb Nauchn Tr Rostov Donu Gos Med Inst ... Sbornik Nauchnykh Trudov Rostovskogo-Na-Donu Gosudarstvennogo Meditsinskogo Instituta [*A publication*]

Sb Nauchn Tr Rostov Nauchno-Issled Inst Akad Kommunaln Khoz ... Sbornik Nauchnykh Trudov Rostovskii Nauchno-Issledovatel'skii Institut Akademii Kommunal'nogo Khozyaistva [*A publication*]

Sb Nauchn Tr Ryazan Med Inst ... Sbornik Nauchnykh Trudov Ryazanskogo Meditsinskogo Instituta [*A publication*]

Sb Nauchn Tr Ryazan S-Kh Inst ... Sbornik Nauchnykh Trudov Ryazanskogo Sel'skokhozyaistvennogo Instituta [*A publication*]

Sb Nauchn Tr Samark Gos Med Inst ... Sbornik Nauchnykh Trudov Samarkandskogo Gosudarstvennogo Meditsinskogo Instituta [*A publication*]

Sb Nauchn Tr Sanit Tekh ... Sbornik Nauchnykh Trudov po Sanitarnoi Tekhnike [*A publication*]

Sb Nauchn Tr Sev-Oset Gos Med Inst ... Sbornik Nauchnykh Trudov Severo-Osetinskii Gosudarstvennyi Meditsinskii Institut [*A publication*]

Sb Nauchn Tr Stalinskii Gos Med Inst ... Sbornik Nauchnykh Trudov Stalinskii Gosudarstvennyi Meditsinskii Institut [*A publication*]

Sb Nauchn Tr Sverdl Fil Mosk Inst Nar Khoz ... Sbornik Nauchnykh Trudov Sverdlovskii Filial Moskovskogo Instituta Narodnogo Khozyaistva [*A publication*]

Sb Nauchn Tr Tashk Gos Med Inst ... Sbornik Nauchnykh Trudov Tashkentskogo Gosudarstvennogo Meditsinskogo Instituta [*A publication*]

Sb Nauchn Tr Tashk Gos Univ ... Sbornik Nauchnykh Trudov Tashkentskiy Gosudarstvennyy Universitet [*A publication*]

Sb Nauchn Tr Teploobmenu Gidrodin ... Sbornik Nauchnykh Trudov po Teploobmenu i Gidrodinamike [*A publication*]

Sb Nauchn Tr Tomsk Inzh Stroit Inst ... Sbornik Nauchnykh Trudov Tomskii Inzhenerno-Stroitel'nyi Institut [*USSR*] [*A publication*]

Sb Nauchn Tr Tsentr Aptechn Nauchno-Issled Inst ... Sbornik Nauchnykh Trudov Tsentral'nogo Aptechnogo Nauchno-Issledovatel'skogo Instituta [*A publication*]

Sb Nauchn Tr Ukr Inst Usoversh Vrachei ... Sbornik Nauchnykh Trudov Ukrainskogo Instituta Usovershenstvovaniy Vrachei [*A publication*]

Sb Nauchn Tr Ukr Nauchno-Issled Inst Ogneuporov ... Sbornik Nauchnykh Trudov Ukrainskii Nauchno-Issledovatel'skii Institut Ogneuporov [*Ukrainian SSR*] [*A publication*]

Sb Nauchn Tr Ukr Nauchno Issled Inst Solyanoi Promsti ... Sbornik Nauchnykh Trudov Ukrainskii Nauchno-Issledovatel'skii Institut Solyanoi Promyshlennosti [*A publication*]

Sb Nauchn Tr Ukr Nauchno-Issled Uglekhim Inst ... Sbornik Nauchnykh Trudov Ukrainskii Nauchno-Issledovatel'skii Uglekhimcheskii I nstitut [*Ukrainian SSR*] [*A publication*]

Sb Nauchn Tr Vinnitsk Gos Med Inst ... Sbornik Nauchnykh Trudov Vinnitskogo Gosudarstvennogo Meditsinskogo Instituta [*A publication*]

Sb Nauchn Tr Vitebsk Gos Med Inst ... Sbornik Nauchnykh Trudov Vitebskogo Gosudarstvennogo Meditsinskogo Instituta [*A publication*]

Sb Nauchn Tr Vitebsk Med Inst ... Sbornik Nauchnykh Trudov Vitebskogo Meditsinskogo Instituta [*A publication*]

Sb Nauchn Tr Vladimir Vech Politekh Inst ... Sbornik Nauchnykh Trudov Vladimirskii Vechernii Politekhnicheskii Institut [*A publication*]

Sb Nauchn Tr Vladivost Med Inst ... Sbornik Nauchnykh Trudov Vladivostokskii Meditsinskii Institut [*A publication*]

Sb Nauchn Tr VNII Monokrist ... Sbornik Nauchnykh Trudov VNII [*Vsesoyuznyi Nauchno-Issledovatel'skii Institut*] Monokristallov [*A publication*]

Sb Nauchn Tr Voen Med Fak Sarat Medinst ... Sbornik Nauchnykh Trudov Voenno-Meditsinskii Fakul'tet Saratovskom Medinstitut [*A publication*]

Sb Nauchn Tr Voronezh Inzh Stroit Inst ... Sbornik Nauchnykh Trudov Voronezhskii Inzhenerno-Stroitel'nyi Institut [*A publication*]

Sb Nauchn Tr Vses Nauchno-Issled Gorno-Metall Inst Tsvet Met ... Sbornik Nauchnykh Trudov Vsesoyuznogo Nauchno-Issledovatel'skogo Gorno-Metallurgiceskogo Instituta Tsvetnykh Metallov [*USSR*] [*A publication*]

Sb Nauchn Tr Vses Nauchno Issled Gornometall Inst Tsvetn Met ... Sbornik Nauchnykh Trudov Vsesoyuznyi Nauchno-Issledovatel'skii Gornometallurgicheskii Institut Tsvetnykh Metallov [*A publication*]

Sb Nauchn Tr Vses Nauchno Issled Inst Gidrogeol Inzh Geol ... Sbornik Nauchnykh Trudov Vsesoyuznyi Nauchno-Issledovatel'skii Institut Gidrogeologii i Inzhenernoi Geologii [*A publication*]

Sb Nauchn Tr Vses Nauchno Issled Inst Metall Teplotekh ... Sbornik Nauchnykh Trudov Vsesoyuznyi Nauchno-Issledovatel'skii Institut Metallurgicheskoi Teplotekhniki [*A publication*]

Sb Nauchn Tr Vses Neftegazov Nauchno Issled Inst ... Sbornik Nauchnykh Trudov Vsesoyuznyi Neftegazovyi Nauchno-Issledovatel'skii Institut [*A publication*]

Sb Nauchn Tr Vses Sel Genet Inst ... Sbornik Nauchnykh Trudov Vsesoyuznogo Selektsionno-Geneticheskogo Instituta [*A publication*]

Sb Nauchn Tr Zaochn Inst Sov Torg ... Sbornik Nauchnykh Trudov Zaochnyi Institut Sovetskoi Torgovli [*A publication*]

Sb Nauchn Tr Zhdan Metall Inst ... Sbornik Nauchnykh Trudov Zhdanovskogo Metallurgicheskogo Instituta [*A publication*]

Sb Nauchn Tr Zootekh Fak Belotserk Skh Inst ... Sbornik Nauchnykh Trudov Zootekhnicheskogo Fakul'teta Belotserkovskii Sel'skokhozyaistvennyi Institut [*A publication*]

Sb Nauchn Voen-Med Fak Kuibyshev Med Inst ... Sbornik Nauchnykh Rabot Voenno-Meditsinskogo Fakul'teta Kuibyshevskogo Meditsinskogo Instituta [*USSR*] [*A publication*]

Sb Nauchn Vrachei Kabard Balkarii ... Sbornik Nauchnykh Vrachei Kabardino Balkarii [*A publication*]

Sb Nauch Tr Beloruss Nauch-Issled Inst Zemled ... Sbornik Nauchnykh Trudov Belorusskii Nauchno-Issledovatel'skii Institut Zemledeliya [*A publication*]

Sb Nauch Tr Eston Sel'skokhoz Akad ... Sbornik Nauchnykh Trudov Estonskoi Sel'skokhozyaistvennoi Akademii [*A publication*]

Sb Nauch Trud Eston Nauch Inst Zeml Melior ... Sbornik Nauchnykh Trudov Estonskogo Nauchnogo Instituta Zemledeliya i Melioratsii [*A publication*]

Sb Nauch Trud Eston Sel'khoz Akad ... Sbornik Nauchnykh Trudov Estonskoi Sel'skokhozyaistvennoi Akademii [*A publication*]

Sb Nauch Trud Leningr Inst Usoversh Vet Vrach ... Sbornik Nauchnykh Leningradskogo Instituta Usovershenstvovaniya Veterinarnykh Vrachei [*A publication*]

Sb Naucn Soobsc Dagestan Gos Univ ... Sbornik Naucnyh Soobscenii Dagestanskii Gosudarstvennyi Universitet Imeni V. I. Lenina [*A publication*]

Sb Nauc Trud Jaroslav Pedag Inst ... Sbornik Naucnyh Trudov Jaroslavskogo Pedagogiceskij Institut [*A publication*]

SBND .... Southbound (FAAC)

SBNF .... Navegantes [*Brazil*] [*ICAO location identifier*] (ICLI)

SBNH .... Society for the Bibliography of Natural History (EA)

SBNL .... Submarine Base, New London [*Connecticut*] [*Navy*]

SBNM .... Santo Angelo [*Brazil*] [*ICAO location identifier*] (ICLI)

SBNO .... Senior British Naval Officer

SBNOWA ... Senior British Naval Officer, Western Atlantic

SBNPB ...... Space-Based Neutral Particle Beam [*Military*] (SDI)

SBNS .... Society of British Neurological Surgeons

SBNT .... Natal/Augusto Severo [*Brazil*] [*ICAO location identifier*] (ICLI)

SBNT .... Single-Breath Nitrogen Test [*Physiology*]

SbNU .... Sbornik za Narodni Umotvorenija i Narodopis [*A publication*]

s-bo--- .... Bolivia [*MARC geographic area code*] [*Library of Congress*] (LCCP)

SBO .... Salina [*Utah*] [*Airport symbol*] (OAG)

SBO .... Showboat, Inc. [*NYSE symbol*] (SPSG)

SBO .... Silver Box Resources [*Vancouver Stock Exchange symbol*]

SBO .... Small Business Office

SBO .... Specific Behavioral Objectives [*Aviation*]

SBO .... Standing Balance: Eyes Open [*Test*] [*Occupational therapy*]

SBO .... Studia Biblica et Orientalia [*Rome*] [*A publication*] (BJA)

SBO .... Swainsboro, GA [*Location identifier*] [*FAA*] (FAAL)

SBOA .... Specialty Bakery Owners of America (EA)

SBOAA ...... Soobshcheniya Byurakanskoi Observatorii Akademiya Nauk Armyanskoi SSR [*A publication*]

SbOAW ..... Sitzungsberichte. Oesterreichische Akademie der Wissenschaften in Wien. Philosophisch-Historische Klasse [*A publication*]

SBoc .... Studi sul Boccaccio [*A publication*]

SBOI .... Oiapoque [*Brazil*] [*ICAO location identifier*] (ICLI)

SBol .... Strenna Bolognese [*A publication*]

SBOLS .... Shadow Box Optical Landing System

SBOM .... Soybean Oil Meal

SBON .... Siboney Corp. [*NASDAQ symbol*] (NQ)

SBOOM .... Sonic Boom [*Computer program*] [*NASA*]

Sbor Arch Praci ... Sbornik Archivnich Praci [*A publication*]

Sbor Narod Muz Praze ... Sbornik Narodniho Muzea v Praze [*Acta Musei Nationalis Pragae*]. Rada A: Historia [*A publication*]

SbornikP .... Sbornik Praci Filosoficke Fakulty Brnenske University [*A publication*]

Sbornik Praci Brnenske U Rada Hud ... Sbornik Praci Filosoficke Fakulty Brnenske University. Rada Hudebnevedna [*A publication*]

Sborn Rabot Lesn Hoz Vsesojuz Nauc-Issled Inst Lesovod ... Sbornik Rabot po Lesnomu Hozjajstvu. Vsesojuznyj Naucno-Issledovatel'skij Institut Lesovodstva i Mehanizacii Lesnogo Hozjajstva [*A publication*]

Sborn Rabot v Pam I M Sadovskago (S Peterburg) ... Sbornik Rabot v Pamiat Professora Ivana Mikhailovicha Sadovskago (S Peterburg) [*A publication*]

Sborn Ved Lesn Ust Vysoke Skoly Zemed ... Sbornik Vedeckeho Lesnickeho Ustavu Vysoke Skoly Zemedelske v Praze [*A publication*]

Sbor Praci Filos Fak ... Sbornik Praci Filosoficke Fakulty Brnenske University [*A publication*]

Sbor Vlast Prac Podblanicka ... Sbornik Vlastivednych Praci z Podblanicka [*A publication*]

SBOS .... Boston Bancorp [*Formerly, South Boston Savings Bank*] [*NASDAQ symbol*]   (NQ)

SBOSI .... Serikat Buruh Obat Seluruh Indonesia [*All Indonesian Medicinal Factory Workers' Union*]

SBOST ...... Slavonic Benevolent Order of the State of Texas [*Temple, TX*]   (EA)

SBOT .... Sacred Books of the Old Testament [*The "Rainbow Bible"*] [*A publication*]   (BJA)

SBOU .... Ourinhos [*Brazil*] [*ICAO location identifier*]   (ICLI)

SBP .... Etudes et Expansion [*A publication*]

SBP .... San Luis Obispo [*California*] [*Airport symbol*]   (OAG)

SBP .... Sec-Butyl Percarbonate [*Organic chemistry*]

SBP .... Serikat Buruh Pegadaian [*Pawnshop Workers' Union*] [*Indonesia*]

SBP .... Serikat Buruh Penerbangan [*Airways' Unions*] [*Indonesia*]

SBP .... Service Benefit Plan [*Military*]   (AABC)

SBP .... Shop Procedure Bulletin [*A publication*]   (EAAP)

SBP .... Societe Beneluxienne de Phlebologie [*Benelux Phlebology Society - BPS*]   (EA)

SBP .... Society for Behaviorial Pediatrics   (EA)

SBP .... Society of Biological Psychiatry   (EA)

SBP .... Sonic Boom Panel [*Aerospace*]   (MCD)

SBP .... Soziale Buergerpartei [*Social Citizen's Party*] [*Federal Republic of Germany*] [*Political party*]   (PPW)

SBP .... Spaceborne Programmer

SBP .... Special Block Purchase

SBP .... Special Businessowners Policy [*Insurance*]

SBP .... Spontaneous Bacterial Peritonitis [*Medicine*]

SBP .... Squalene-Binding Protein [*Biochemistry*]

SBP .... Standard Brands Paint Co. [*NYSE symbol*]   (SPSG)

SBP .... Standard Businessowners Policy [*Insurance*]

SBP .... Steroid-Binding Plasma Protein

SBP .... Subic Bay [*Philippines*] [*Seismograph station code, US Geological Survey*] [*Closed*]   (SEIS)

SBP .... Sumerian and Babylonian Psalms [*A publication*]   (BJA)

SBP .... Survivor Benefit Plan [*For survivors of retired military personnel*]

SBP .... Systolic Blood Pressure [*Medicine*]

SBPA .... Porto Alegre/Salgado Filho [*Brazil*] [*ICAO location identifier*]   (ICLI)

SBPA .... Southern Baptist Press Association   (EA)

Sb Pathofysiol Traveni Vyz ... Sbornik pro Pathofysiologii Traveni a Vyzivy [*A publication*]

SBPAW ..... Sitzungsberichte. Kaiserliche Preussische Akademie der Wissenschaften [*Berlin*] [*A publication*]

SBPAWB ... Sitzungsberichte. Kaiserliche Preussische Akademie der Wissenschaften (Berlin) [*A publication*]

SBPB .... Parnaiba [*Brazil*] [*ICAO location identifier*]   (ICLI)

SBPB .... Space-Based Particle Beam [*Military*]   (SDI)

SBPC .... Pocos De Caldas [*Brazil*] [*ICAO location identifier*]   (ICLI)

SBPD .... Society of Business Publication Designers [*Later, SPD*]   (EA)

Sb Pedagog Fak Plzni Ser Chem ... Sbornik Pedagogicke Fakulty v Plzni. Serie Chemie [*A publication*]

SBPF .... Passo Fundo/Lauro Kurtz [*Brazil*] [*ICAO location identifier*]   (ICLI)

SBPG .... Paranagua [*Brazil*] [*ICAO location identifier*]   (ICLI)

SBPG .... Serikat Buruh Perusahaan Gula [*Sugar Workers' Union*] [*Indonesia*]

SBPH .... Porto Velho [*Brazil*] [*ICAO location identifier*]   (ICLI)

SBPH .... Single Burst Probability of Hit [*Military*]   (AABC)

SBPI .... Petropolis/Pico do Couto [*Brazil*] [*ICAO location identifier*]   (ICLI)

SBPI .... Serikat Buruh Pelabuhan Indonesia [*Dockworkers' Union of Indonesia*]

SBPI .... Serikat Buruh Pendjahit Indonesia [*Tailors' Union of Indonesia*]

SBPI .... Southern Baptist Periodical Index [*A publication*]

SBPK .... Pelotas [*Brazil*] [*ICAO location identifier*]   (ICLI)

SBPKB .... Serikat Buruh Persuahaan Kaju and Bangunan [*Building, Road and Irrigation Workers' Union*] [*Indonesia*]

SBPL .... Petrolina [*Brazil*] [*ICAO location identifier*]   (ICLI)

SBPN .... Porto Nacional [*Brazil*] [*ICAO location identifier*]   (ICLI)

SBPO .... Sick Berth Petty Officer [*Australia*]

SBPP .... Ponta Pora/Internacional [*ICAO location identifier*]   (ICLI)

SBPP .... Serikat Buruh Pelabuhan dan Pelajaran [*Dockworkers' Union*] [*Indonesia*]

SBPPK ...... Serikat Buruh Pendidikan, Pengadjaran dan Kebudjaan [*Department of Education Workers' Union*] [*Indonesia*]

SBPR .... Piracaba [*Brazil*] [*ICAO location identifier*]   (ICLI)

SBPR .... Society for Back Pain Research [*British*]

Sb Prac Chem Fak SVST ... Sbornik Prac Chemickej Fakulty Slovenskej Vysokej Skoly Technickej [*A publication*]

Sb Praci Ped Fak v Ostrave Ser A ... Sbornik Praci Pedagogicke Fakulty v Ostrave. Seria A [*A publication*]

Sb Praci Prirodoved Fak Univ Palackeho v Olomouci ... Sbornik Praci Prirodovedecke Fakulty University Palackeho v Olomouci [*A publication*]

Sb Praci Prirodoved Fak Univ Palackeho v Olomouci Chem ... Sbornik Praci Prirodovedecke Fakulty University Palackeho v Olomouci. Obor Chemica [*A publication*]

Sb Praci Prirodoved Fak Univ Palackeho v Olomouci Fyz ... Sbornik Praci Prirodovedecke Fakulty University Palackeho v Olomouci. Obor Fyzika [*A publication*]

Sb Praci Prirodoved Fak Univ Palackeho v Olomouci Mat ... Sbornik Praci Prirodovedecke Fakulty University Palackeho v Olomouci. Obor Matematika [*A publication*]

Sb Prazhskogo Khim Tekhnol Inst Sekts Protsessy Appar ... Sbornik Prazhskogo Khimiko Tekhnologicheskogo Instituta Sektsiya. Protsessy i Apparaty [*A publication*]

SBPR Bol ... SBPR Boletin [*A publication*]

Sb Prednasek Prac Vyzk Ustavu Tepelne Tech ... Sbornik Prednasek Pracovniku Vyzkumneho Ustavu Tepelne Techniky [*A publication*]

Sb Pr Pedagog Fak Ostrave Rada A ... Sbornik Praci Pedagogicke Fakulty v Ostrave. Rada A. Matematika Fizika [*A publication*]

Sb Pr Pedagog Fak Ostrave Rada E ... Sbornik Praci Pedagogicke Fakulty v Ostrave. Rada E [*Czechoslovakia*] [*A publication*]

Sb Pr Pedagog Inst Ostrave Prir Vedy Mat ... Sbornik Praci Pedagogickeho Instituta i Ostrave Prirodni Vedy a Matematika [*A publication*]

Sb Pr Ustavu Vyzk Rud (Prague) ... Sbornik Praci Ustavu pro Vyzkum Rud (Prague) [*A publication*]

Sb Pr UVP ... Sbornik Praci UVP [*A publication*]

Sb Pr Vyzk Chem Vyuziti Uhli Dehtu Ropy ... Sbornik Praci z Vyzkumu Chemickeho Vyuziti Uhli. Dehtu a Ropy [*Czechoslovakia*] [*A publication*]

Sb Pr Vyzk Ustavu Zelezorudn Dolu Hrudkoven ... Sbornik Praci Vyzkumneho Ustavu Zelezorudnych Dolu a Hrudkoven [*A publication*]

SBPS .... Savings Bank of Puget Sound [*NASDAQ symbol*]   (NQ)

SBPT .... Serikat Buruh Perhubungan dan Transport [*Communications and Transportation Workers' Union*] [*Indonesia*]

SBPT .... Serikat Buruh Pertambangan Timah [*Tin Mine Labor Union*] [*Indonesia*]

SBPU .... Serikat Buruh Pekerdjaan Umum [*Public Workers' Ministry Union*] [*Indonesia*]

SBPV .... Porto Velho [*Brazil*] [*ICAO location identifier*]   (ICLI)

SBPW .... Pindamonhangaba/Visaba [*Brazil*] [*ICAO location identifier*]   (ICLI)

SBQ .... Grenada, MS [*Location identifier*] [*FAA*]   (FAAL)

SBQ .... Serikat Buruh Qantas [*Qantas Labor Union*] [*Indonesia*]

SBQV .... Vitoria Da Conquista [*Brazil*] [*ICAO location identifier*]   (ICLI)

SBR .... Saber Aviation, Inc. [*Charlotte, NC*] [*FAA designator*]   (FAAC)

SBR .... Sabine Royalty Trust [*NYSE symbol*]   (SPSG)

SBR .... Sale by Reference

SBR .... Seat Bucket Read   (NG)

SBR .... Segment Base Register   (BUR)

SBR .... Sequencing Batch Reactor [*Chemical engineering*]

SBR .... Service Billing Record

SBR .... Signal to Background Ratio [*Instrumentation*]

SBR .... Small Box-Respirator [*British military*]   (DMA)

SBR .... Small Business Report [*A publication*]

SBR .... Society of Bead Researchers   (EA)

SBR .... Society for Biological Rhythm

SBR .... Soviet Breeder Reactor

SBR .... Space-Based RADAR   (MCD)

SBR .... Standard Busy Rate   (NATG)

SBR .... Starburst Energy [*Vancouver Stock Exchange symbol*]

SBR .... Stimulus-Bound Repetition [*Medicine*]

SBR .... Storage Buffer Register

SBR .... Strict Bed Rest [*Medicine*]

SBR .... Styrene-Butadiene Rubber [*Also, GR-S*] [*Synthetic rubber*]

SBR .... Supplemental Budget Request

Sb Rab Agron Fiz ... Sbornik Rabot po Agronomicheskoi Fizike [*A publication*]

Sb Rab Ashkhab Gidrometeorol Obs ... Sbornik Rabot Ashkhabadskoi Gidrometeorologicheskoi Observatorii [*A publication*]

Sb Rab Aspir Krasnodar Gos Pedagog Inst ... Sbornik Rabot Aspirantov Krasnodarskogo Gosudarstvennogo Pedagogicheskogo Instituta [*A publication*]

Sb Rab Aspir Tadzh Gos Univ ... Sbornik Rabot Aspirantov Tadzhikskii Gosudarstvennyi Universitet [*A publication*]

Sb Rab Aspir Ukr Nauchno Issled Inst Fiziol Rast ... Sbornik Rabot Aspirantov Ukrainskii Nauchno-Issledovatel'skii Institut Fiziologii Rastenii [*A publication*]

Sb Rab Aspir Voronezh Gos Univ ... Sbornik Rabot Aspirantov Voronezhskogo Gosudarstvennogo Universiteta [*A publication*]

Sb Rab Basseinovoi Gidrometeorol Obs Chern Azovskogo Morei ... Sbornik Rabot Basseinovoi Gidrometeorologicheskoi Chernogo i Azovskogo Morei [*A publication*]

Sb Rab Beloruss Gos Med Inst ... Sbornik Rabot Belorusskii Gosudarstvennyi Meditsinskii Institut [*A publication*]

Sb Rab Biol Tekh Rybolov Tekhnol ... Sbornik Rabot po Biologii. Tekhnike Rybolovstva i Tekhnologii [*A publication*]

Sb Rab Buryat Otd Vses Nauchn Ova Anat Gistol Embriol ... Sbornik Rabot Buryatskogo Otdel'nogo Vsesoyuznogo Nauchnogo Obshchestva Anatomii, Gistologii, i Embriologii [*A publication*]

Sb Rab Chist Prikl Khim ... Sbornik Rabot po Chistoi i Prikladnoi Khimii [*A publication*]

Sb Rab Chuv Resp Vet Lab ... Sbornik Rabot Chuvashskoi Respublikanskoi Veterinarnoi Laboratorii [*A publication*]

Sb Rab Gidrol ... Sbornik Rabot po Gidrologii [*A publication*]

Sb Rab Gidrol Leningr Gos Gidrol Inst ... Sbornik Rabot po Gidrologii Leningradskogo Gosudarstvennogo Gidrologicheskogo Instituta [*A publication*]

Sb Rab Gor'k Volzh Rybinsk Gidrometeorol Obs ... Sbornik Rabot Gor'kovskoi Volzhskoi i Rybinskoi Gidrometeorologicheskikh Observatorii [*A publication*]

Sb Rab Gos Inst Prikl Khim ... Sbornik Rabot Gosudarstvennyi Institut Prikladnoi Khimii [*A publication*]

Sb Rab Ikhtiol Gidrobiol ... Sbornik Rabot po Ikhtiologii i Gidrobiologii [*A publication*]

Sb Rab Inst Prikl Zol Fitopatol ... Sbornik Rabot Instituta Prikladnoi Zoologii i Fitopatologii [*A publication*]

Sb Rab Inst Prikl Zool Fitopatol ... Sbornik Rabot Instituta Prikladnoi Zoologii i Fitopatologii [*A publication*]

Sb Rab Inst Tsitol Akad Nauk SSSR ... Sbornik Rabot Instituta Tsitologii Akademii Nauk SSSR [*A publication*]

Sb Rab Kafedry Fak Khir Sverdl Med ... Sbornik Rabot Kafedry i Fakul'tete Khirurgii Sverdlovskogo Meditsinskogo [*A publication*]

Sb Rab Kaz Resp Nauchn Ova Anat Gistol Embriol ... Sbornik Rabot Kazakhskogo Respublikanskogo Nauchnogo Obshchestva Anatomov, Gistologov, i Embriologov [*A publication*]

Sb Rab Khim Istochnikam Toka ... Sbornik Rabot po Khimicheskim Istochnikam Toka [*A publication*]

Sb Rab Kursk Gidrometeorol Obs ... Sbornik Rabot Kurskoi Gidrometeorologicheskoi Observatorii [*A publication*]

Sb Rab Lab Yuzhn Morei Gos Okeanogr Inst ... Sbornik Rabot Laboratoriya Yuzhnykh Morei Gosudarstvennyi Okeanograficheskii Institut [*A publication*]

Sb Rab Leningr Inst Sov Torg ... Sbornik Rabot Leningradskii Institut Sovetskoi Torgovli [*A publication*]

Sb Rab Leningr Vet Inst ... Sbornik Rabot Leningradskii Veterinarnyi Institut [*A publication*]

Sb Rab Lesn Khoz Mold Mold Lesn Opytn Stn ... Sbornik Rabot po Lesnomu Khozyaistva Moldavii Moldavskaya Lesnaya Opytnaya Stantsiya [*A publication*]

Sb Rab Maslichn Efiromaslichn Kul't ... Sbornik Rabot po Maslichnym i Efiromaslichnym Kul'turam [*A publication*]

Sb Rab Maslichn Kult ... Sbornik Rabot po Maslichnym Kul'turam [*A publication*]

Sb Rab Mezhdunar Geofiz Godu ... Sbornik Rabot po Mezhdunarodnomu Geofizicheskom Godu [*A publication*]

Sb Rab Mikol Algol Akad Kirg SSR ... Sbornik Rabot po Mikologii i Al'gologii Akademii Kirgizskoi SSR [*A publication*]

Sb Rab Mikol Al'gol Kirg SSR ... Sbornik Rabot po Mikologii i Al'gologii Akademii Kirgiszkoi SSR [*A publication*]

Sb Rab Minsk Med Inst ... Sbornik Rabot Minskogo Meditsinskogo Instituta [*A publication*]

Sb Rab Molodykh Uch Akad Nauk Mold SSR ... Sbornik Rabot Molodykh Uchenykh Akademii Nauk Moldavskoi SSR [*A publication*]

Sb Rab Molodykh Uch Gorskogo Skh Inst ... Sbornik Rabot Molodykh Uchenykh Gorskogo Sel'skokhozyaistvennogo Instituta [*A publication*]

Sb Rab Molodykh Vses Sel Genet Inst ... Sbornik Rabot Molodykh Vsesoyuznogo Selektsii Genetiki Instituta [*A publication*]

Sb Rab Mosk Lesotekh Inst ... Sbornik Rabot Moskovskii Lesotekhnicheskii Institut [*A publication*]

Sb Rab Nematodam Skh Rast ... Sbornik Rabot po Nematodam Sel'skokhozyaistvennykh Rastenii [*A publication*]

Sb Rabot Nauch Inst Udobr Insektofungits (Moscow) ... Sbornik Rabot Nauchnyi Institut po Udobreniyam i Insektofungitsidam (Moscow) [*A publication*]

Sb Rab Pozharno Ispyt Stn ... Sbornik Rabot Pozharno Ispytatel'nykh Stantsii [*A publication*]

Sb Rab Rostov Gidrometeorol Obs ... Sbornik Rabot Rostovskoi Gidrometeorologicheskoi Observatorii [*A publication*]

Sb Rab Rybinsk Gidrometeorol Obs ... Sbornik Rabot Rybinskoi Gidrometeorologicheskoi Observatorii [*A publication*]

Sb Rab Silikozu ... Sbornik Rabot po Silikozu [*A publication*]

Sb Rab Silikozu Ural Fil Akad Nauk SSSR ... Sbornik Rabot po Silikozu Ural'skii Filial Akademii Nauk SSSR [*A publication*]

Sb Rab Stud Nauchn Ova Leningr Inst Tochn Mekh Opt ... Sbornik Rabot Studencheskogo Nauchnogo Obshchestva. Leningradskii Institut Tochnoi Mekhaniki i Optiki [*A publication*]

Sb Rab Sverdl Gos Med Inst ... Sbornik Rabot Sverdlovskii Gosudarstvennyi Meditsinskii Institut [*A publication*]

Sb Rab Sverdl Med Inst ... Sbornik Rabot Sverdlovskogo Meditsinskogo Instituta [*A publication*]

Sb Rab Sverdl Nauchno Issled Kozhno Venerol Inst ... Sbornik Rabot Sverdlovskii Nauchno-Issledovatel'skii Kozhno Venerologicheskii Institut [*A publication*]

Sb Rab Tsentr Muz Pochvved Im V ... Sbornik Rabot Tsentral'nogo Muzeya Pochvvodeniya Imeni V. V. Dokuchaeva [*A publication*]

Sb Rab Tsentr Muz Pochvved Im V V Dokuchaeva ... Sbornik Rabot Tsentral'nogo Muzeya Pochvvodeniya Imeni V. V. Dokuchaeva [*A publication*]

Sb Rab Tsentr Nauchno Issled Inst Kozh Obuvn Promsti ... Sbornik Rabot Tsentral'nyi Nauchno-Issledovatel'skii Institut Kozhevenno Obuvnoi Promyshlennosti [*A publication*]

Sb Rab Tsiml Gidrometeorol Obs ... Sbornik Rabot Tsimlyanskoi Gidrometeorologicheskoi Observatorii [*A publication*]

Sb Rab Ukr Nauchno Issled Inst Ogneuporov ... Sbornik Rabot Ukrainskii Nauchno-Issledovatel'skii Institut Ogneuporov [*A publication*]

Sb Rab Vologod Nauchno-Issled Vet Opytn Stn ... Sbornik Rabot Vologodskoi Nauchno-Issledovat' Skoi Veterinarnoi Opytnoi Stantsii [*A publication*]

Sb Rab Vopr Proizvod Primen Biol Prep ... Sbornik Rabot Voprosov Proizvodstva i Primeneniya Biologicheskikh Preparatov [*A publication*]

Sb Rab Vses Nauchn Issled Inst Okhr Tr ... Sbornik Rabot Vsesoyuznyi Nauchno-Issledovatel'skii Institut Okhrany Truda [*A publication*]

Sb Rab Vses Zaochn Inst Pishch Promsti ... Sbornik Rabot Vsesoyuznyi Zaochnyi Institut Pishchevoi Promyshlennosti [*A publication*]

Sb Rab Vychisl Tsentra Mosk Gos Univ ... Sbornik Rabot Vychislitel'nogo Tsentral'nogo Moskovskogo Gosudarstvennogo Universiteta [*A publication*]

SBRB .... Rio Branco/Presidente Medici [*Brazil*] [*ICAO location identifier*]   (ICLI)

SBRC .... Santa Barbara Research Center [*Hughes Aircraft Co.*]

SBRC .... Southwest Border Regional Commission [*Department of Commerce*]

SBRE .... Recife [*Brazil*] [*ICAO location identifier*]   (ICLI)

SBRF .... Recife/Guararapes [*Brazil*] [*ICAO location identifier*]   (ICLI)

SBRG .... Seeburg Corp. [*NASDAQ symbol*]   (NQ)

SBRI .... Serikat Buruh Rokok Indonesia [*Cigarette Workers' Union of Indonesia*]

SBRI .... Southwest Biomedical Research Institute [*Arizona State University*] [*Research center*]   (RCD)

SBRI .... Space Biomedical Research Institute [*Houston, TX*] [*NASA*]

SBRIMCD ... Sun Bay Recovery - International Missing Children's Division   (EA)

SBRJ .... Rio De Janeiro/Santos Dumont [*Brazil*] [*ICAO location identifier*]   (ICLI)

SB-RK .... Bomber [*Russian aircraft symbol*]

Sb Rost Ustoichivost Rast Akad Nauk Ukr SSR Respub Mezhved ... Sbornik Rost i Ustoichivost' Rastenii Akademiya Nauk Ukrainskoi SSR Respublikanskii Mezhvedomstvennyi [*A publication*]

SBRP .... Ribeirao Preto/Leite Lopes [*Brazil*] [*ICAO location identifier*]   (ICLI)

SBRP .... Sonic Boom Research Program

SBRQ .... Sao Roque [*Brazil*] [*ICAO location identifier*]   (ICLI)

SBRRI .... Serikat Buruh Radio Republik Indonesia [*Broadcasting Workers' Association of Indonesia*]

SBRS .... Resende [*Brazil*] [*ICAO location identifier*]   (ICLI)

SBRS .... Social Behavior Rating Scale

SBRU .... Subaru of America, Inc. [*NASDAQ symbol*]   (NQ)

SBRV .... Small Ballistic Reentry Vehicle

SBS .... Salem Corp. [*AMEX symbol*]   (SPSG)

SBS .... Samuel Butler Society [*Defunct*]   (EA)

SBS .... Satellite Business Systems [*McLean, VA*] [*Telecommunications*]   (MCD)

SBS .... Scarborough Board of Education [*UTLAS symbol*]

SBS .... Semiconductor Bilateral Switch   (MSA)

SBS .... Sensor Based System   (BUR)

SBS .... Serially Balanced Sequence [*Statistics*]

SBS .... Sidi-Bou-Said [*Tunisia*] [*Seismograph station code, US Geological Survey*]   (SEIS)

SBS .... Silicon Bilateral Switch

SBS .... Singapore Bus Service   (DS)

SBS .... Single-Business Service

SBS .... Sisters of the Blessed Sacrament [*Roman Catholic religious order*]

SBS .... Small Business Sourcebook [*A publication*]

SBS .... Small Business Specialist [*DoD*]

SBS .... Small Business System   (ADA)

SBS .... Social Behavior Standards

SBS .... Soeurs de Bon Sauveur [*Caen, France*]   (EAIO)

SBS .... Solid Bleached Sulphate [*Fiber for paperboard packaging*]
SBS .... Southern Base Section [*England*]
SBS .... Spaniel Breeders Society   (EA)
SBS .... Spanish Benevolent Society "La Nacional"   (EA)
SBS .... Spanish Broadcasting System
SBS .... Special Block Sale
SBS .... Special Boat Section [*British military*]   (DMA)
SBS .... Special Boat Squadron [*British commando unit*]
SBS .... Standby Status   (AAG)
SBS .... Steamboat Springs [*Colorado*] [*Airport symbol*]   (OAG)
SBS .... Steel Building System
SBS .... Stimulated Brillouin Scattering   (IEEE)
SBS .... Straight Binary Second
SBS .... Strategic Balkan Services [*World War II*]
SBS .... Strategic Bombing Survey
SBS .... Strategic Business Segment
SBS .... Stuttgarter Bibelstudien [*A publication*]
SBS .... Stuttgarter Bibelstudien. Katholisches Bibelwerk [*Stuttgart*] [*A publication*]   (BJA)
SBS .... Styrene-Butadiene-Styrene [*Copolymer*]
SBS .... Subscript Character [*Data processing*]
SBS .... Superburn Systems Ltd. [*Vancouver Stock Exchange symbol*]
SBS .... Survey of Basic Skills [*Achievement test*]
SBS .... Swedish Behavioural Sciences [*Database*] [*National Library for Psychology and Education*] [*Information service or system*]   (CRD)
SBS .... Sweep Back Station   (MCD)
SBS .... Swiss Benevolent Society of New York   (EA)
SBS .... System Breakdown Structure [*Military*]   (AFIT)
SBSA .... Sao Carlos/Francisco Pereira Lopez [*Brazil*] [*ICAO location identifier*]   (ICLI)
SBSA .... Society of Basque Studies in America   (EA)
SBSanE ..... Bachelor of Science in Sanitary Engineering
SBSAW ..... Sitzungsberichte. Saechsische Akademie der Wissenschaften (Leipzig). Philologisch-Historische Klasse [*A publication*]
SBSAWL... Sitzungsberichte. Saechsische Akademie der Wissenschaften (Leipzig). Philologisch-Historische Klasse [*A publication*]
SBSB .... Small Business Service Bureau [*Worcester, MA*]   (EA)
SBSBA ...... Scottish Blackface Sheep Breeders Association   (EA)
SBSBDV... Symposium. British Society for Developmental Biology [*A publication*]
SBSBS ...... Smith Benevolent Sick and Burial Society [*British*]
SBSC .... Rio De Janeiro/Santa Cruz [*Brazil*] [*ICAO location identifier*]   (ICLI)
SBSC .... Saint Bernardine of Siena College [*New York*]
SBSC .... Saint Bernard's Seminary and College [*New York*]
SBSC .... Separate Bias, Single Control
SBSCA ...... Small Business Support Center Association [*Houston, TX*]   (EA)
SBSD .... Subside   (FAAC)
Sb Severocesk Mus Prir Vedy Sci Nat ... Sbornik Severoceskeho Musea Prirodni Vedy Scientiae Naturales [*A publication*]
SBSG .... Small Business Systems Group [*Westford, MA*] [*Telecommunications*]   (TSSD)
SBSI .... Seabrook Sea Island Cotton
SBSI .... Serikat Buruh Seluruh Indonesia [*All Indonesian Laborers' Union*]
SBSI .... Small Business Start-Up Index [*A publication*]
SBSJ .... Sao Jose Dos Campos [*Brazil*] [*ICAO location identifier*]   (ICLI)
SBSK .... Samodzielna Brygada Strzelcow Karpackich [*Poland*]
SBSKK...... Serikat Buruh Sepatu Keradjinan Kulit Karet [*Shoe Workers' Union*] [*Indonesia*]
SBSL .... Sao Luis/Marechal Cunha Machado [*Brazil*] [*ICAO location identifier*]   (ICLI)
SBSM .... Santa Maria [*Brazil*] [*ICAO location identifier*]   (ICLI)
SBSM .... Sisterhood of Black Single Mothers   (EA)
SBSN .... Santarem/Internacional [*Brazil*] [*ICAO location identifier*]   (ICLI)
SBSP .... Sao Paulo/Congonhas [*Brazil*] [*ICAO location identifier*]   (ICLI)
SBSP .... Single Base Solid Propellant   (MSA)
SB Sqn ...... Special Boat Squadron [*British commando unit*]   (DMA)
SBSR .... Sao Jose Do Rio Preto [*Brazil*] [*ICAO location identifier*]   (ICLI)
SBSS .... Space-Based Space Surveillance   (MCD)
SBSS .... Spare Band Surveillance System   (MCD)
SBSS .... Standard Base Supply System [*Military*]   (AFIT)
SBST .... Santos [*Brazil*] [*ICAO location identifier*]   (ICLI)
Sb Statei Aspir Kirg Gos Univ ... Sbornik Statei Aspirantov Kirgizskogo Gosudarstvennogo Universiteta [*A publication*]
Sb Statei Aspir Kirg Univ Fiz-Mat Estestv Nauk ... Sbornik Statei Aspirantov Kirgizskogo Universiteta Fiziko-Matematicheskikh Estestvennykh Nauk [*A publication*]
Sb Statei Erevan Gos Univ ... Sbornik Statei Erevanskii Gosudarstvennyi Universitet [*A publication*]
Sb Statei Geol Gidrogeol ... Sbornik Statei po Geologii i Gidrogeologii [*A publication*]
Sb Statei Gidrogeol Geoterm ... Sbornik Statei po Gidrogeologii i Geotermii [*A publication*]

Sb Statei Leningr Inst Tochn Mekh Opt ... Sbornik Statei Leningradskii Institut Tochnoi Mekhaniki i Optiki [*A publication*]
Sb Statei Leningr Tekhnol Inst Tsellyul Bum Promsti ... Sbornik Statei Leningradskogo Tekhnologicheskogo Instituta Tsellyulozno-Bumazhnoi Promyshlennosti [*A publication*]
Sb Statei Makeev Nauchno Issled Inst Bezop Rab Gorn Promsti ... Sbornik Statei Makeevskii Nauchno Issledovatel'skii Institut Bezopasnykh Rabot Gornoi Promyshlennosti [*A publication*]
Sb Statei Molodykh Nauchn Rab Leningr Inst Vodn Transp ... Sbornik Statei Molodykh Nauchnykh Rabotnikov Leningradskii Institut Vodnogo Transporta [*A publication*]
Sb Statei Mosk Inzh-Fiz Inst ... Sbornik Statei Moskovskii Inzhenerno-Fizicheskii Institut [*USSR*] [*A publication*]
Sb Statei Nauchno Issled Inst Org Poluprod Krasitelei ... Sbornik Statei Nauchno-Issledovatel'skii Institut Organicheskikh Poluproduktov i Krasitelei [*A publication*]
Sb Statei Rab Ukr Nauchno Issled Inst Maslozhir Promsti ... Sbornik Statei o Rabotakh Ukrainskogo Nauchno Issledovatel'skogo Instituta Maslozhirovoi Promyshlennosti [*A publication*]
Sb Statei Vses Nauchno Issled Inst Khim Reakt ... Sbornik Statei Vsesoyuznyi Nauchno-Issledovatel'skii Institut Khimicheskikh Reaktivov [*A publication*]
Sb Statniho Geol Ustavu Cesk Repub ... Sbornik Statniho Geologickeho Ustavu Ceskoslovenski Republiky [*A publication*]
Sb Statniho Vyzk Ustavu Tepelne Tech ... Sbornik Statniho Vyzkumneho Ustavu Tepelne Techniky [*A publication*]
Sb Stat Obsc Chim ... Sbornik Statej po Obscej Chimii [*A publication*]
SBStJ .... Serving Brother, Order of St. John of Jerusalem [*British*]
SBSTR....... Substrate [*Electronics*]
Sb Stud Nauchn Issled Rab Arkhang Lesotekh Inst ... Sbornik Studencheskikh Nauchno-Issledovatel'skikh Rabot Arkhangel'skii Lesotekhnicheskii Institut [*A publication*]
Sb Stud Nauchn Issled Rab Mosk Vet Akad ... Sbornik Studencheskikh Nauchno Issledovatel'skikh Rabot Moskovskaya Veterinarnaya Akademiya [*A publication*]
Sb Stud Nauchno-Issled Rab Kirg S-Kh Inst ... Sbornik Studencheskikh Nauchno-Issledovatel'skikh Rabot Kirgizskogo Sel'skokhozyaistvennogo Instituta [*A publication*]
Sb Stud Nauchn Rab Alma-At Zoovet Inst ... Sbornik Studencheskikh Nauchnykh Rabot Alma-Atinskogo Zooveterinarnogo Instituta [*A publication*]
Sb Stud Nauchn Rab Kabard Balkar Gos Univ ... Sbornik Studencheskikh Nauchnykh Rabot Kabardino Balkarskii Gosudarstvennyi Universitet [*A publication*]
Sb Stud Nauchn Rab Mosk Skh Akad ... Sbornik Studencheskikh Nauchnykh Rabot Moskovskaya Sel'skokhozyaistvennaya Akademiya [*A publication*]
Sb Stud Nauchn Rab Penz Skh Inst ... Sbornik Studencheskikh Nauchnykh Rabot Penzenskii Sel'skokhozyaistvennyi Institut [*A publication*]
Sb Stud Nauchn Rab Voronezh Gos Univ ... Sbornik Studencheskikh Nauchnykh Rabot Voronezhskii Gosudarstvennyi Universitet [*A publication*]
Sb Stud Nauchn Tr Erevan Gos Univ ... Sbornik Studencheskikh Nauchnykh Trudov Erevanskii Gosudarstvennyi Universitet [*A publication*]
Sb Stud Rab Krasnodar Gos Pedagog Inst ... Sbornik Studencheskikh Rabot Krasnodarskogo Gosudarstvennogo Pedagogicheskogo Instituta [*A publication*]
Sb Stud Rab Mosk Tekhnol Inst Myasn Molochn Promsti ... Sbornik Studencheskikh Rabot Moskovskogo Tekhnologicheskogo Instituta Myasnoi i Molochnoi Promyshlennosti [*A publication*]
Sb Stud Rab Rostov Gos Univ ... Sbornik Studencheskikh Rabot Rostovskogo Gosudarstvennogo Universiteta [*A publication*]
Sb Stud Rab Sredneaziat Gos Univ ... Sbornik Studencheskikh Rabot Sredneaziatskogo Gosudarstvennogo Universiteta [*A publication*]
Sb Stud Rab Uzb Gos Univ ... Sbornik Studencheskikh Rabot Uzbekskogo Gosudarstvennogo Universitet [*A publication*]
SBSUSA.... Sport Balloon Society of the United States of America   (EA)
SBSV .... Salvador/Dois de Julho [*Brazil*] [*ICAO location identifier*]   (ICLI)
SBSY .... Cristalandia/Santa Isabel do Morro [*Brazil*] [*ICAO location identifier*]   (ICLI)
SBT .... Salina Board of Trade   (EA)
SBT .... San Benito [*California*] [*Seismograph station code, US Geological Survey*]   (SEIS)
SBT .... San Bernardino, CA [*Location identifier*] [*FAA*]   (FAAL)
SBT .... Screening Breath Tester [*Drunken driving*]
SBT .... Seabright Resources, Inc. [*Toronto Stock Exchange symbol*]
SBT .... Segregated Ballast Tank [*Shipping construction*]
SBT .... Serikat Buruh Tambang [*Mine Workers' Union*] [*Indonesia*]
SBT .... Serikat Buruh Teknik [*Technicians' Union*] [*Indonesia*]
SBT .... Serikat Buruh Textil [*Textile Workers' Union*] [*Indonesia*]
SBT .... Serum Bactericidal Titer [*Clinical chemistry*]
SBT .... Shakespeare Birthplace Trust   (EA)
SBT .... Shanghai Book Traders
SBT .... Side Buoyancy Tank
SBT .... Simultaneous Baseband Transmission [*of information*]

SBT............ Six BIT [*Binary Digit*] Transcode   (CMD)
SBT............ Small Boat
SBT............ Sodium Bitartrate [*Inorganic chemistry*]
SBT............ Space-Based Tug [*NASA*]
SBT............ Studies in Biblical Theology [*A publication*]
SBT............ Submarine Bathythermograph
SBT............ Submarine Bubble Target [*British military*]   (DMA)
SBT............ Surface Barrier Transistor
SBT............ Svensk Botanisk Tidskrift [*A publication*]
SBT............ System Burning Time
SBTC......... SBT Corporation [*NASDAQ symbol*]   (NQ)
SBTC......... Sino-British Trade Council   (DS)
SBTC......... Speedbrake Thrust Control [*Aerospace*]   (MCD)
SBTC......... Tapuruquara [*Brazil*] [*ICAO location identifier*]   (ICLI)
SBTDA...... Sbornik Trudov Vsesoyuznogo Zaochnogo Politekhnicheskogo
        Instituta [*A publication*]
SBTE......... Teresina [*Brazil*] [*ICAO location identifier*]   (ICLI)
SBTF......... Tefe [*Brazil*] [*ICAO location identifier*]   (ICLI)
SBTG......... Sabotage   (AABC)
SBTI........... Soybean Trypsin Inhibitor
SBTK......... Tarauaca [*Brazil*] [*ICAO location identifier*]   (ICLI)
SBTOW..... Standby Towship [*Navy*]   (NVT)
SBTP........ Serikat Buruh Teknik dan Pelabuhan [*Technical and Harbour
        Workers' Union*] [*Indonesia*]
Sb Tr Agrofiz Nauchno Issled Inst ... Sbornik Trudov Agrofizicheskii
    Nauchno-Issledovatel'skii Institut [*A publication*]
Sb Tr Agron Fiz ... Sbornik Trudov po Agronomicheskoi Fizike [*A
    publication*]
Sb Tr Altai Gos Med Inst ... Sbornik Trudov Altaiskii Gosudarstvennyi
    Meditsinskii Institut [*A publication*]
Sb Tr Andizh Gos Med Inst ... Sbornik Trudov Andizhanskii
    Gosudarstvennyi Meditsinskii Institut [*A publication*]
Sb Tr Arkhang Gos Med Inst ... Sbornik Trudov Arkhangel'skii
    Gosudarstvennyi Meditsinskii Institut [*A publication*]
Sb Tr Arkhang Med Inst ... Sbornik Trudov Arkhangel'skogo Meditsinskogo
    Instituta [*A publication*]
Sb Tr Arm Nauchno-Issled Lesn Opytn Stn ... Sbornik Trudov Armyanskoi
    Nauchno-Issledovatel'skoi Lesnoi Opytnoi Stantsii [*A
    publication*]
Sb Tr Aspir Molodykh Nauchn Sotr Vses Inst Rastenievod ... Sbornik Trudov
    Aspirantov i Molodykh Nauchnykh Sotrudnikov
    Vsesoyuznyi Institut Rastenievodstva [*A publication*]
Sb Tr Aspir Tadzh Univ Estest Nauk ... Sbornik Trudov Aspirantov
    Tadzhikskogo Universiteta Estestvennykh Nauk [*A
    publication*]
Sb Tr Astrakh Gos S-Kh Opytn Stn ... Sbornik Trudov Astrakhanskoi
    Gosudarstvennoi Sel'skokhozyaistvennoi Opytnoi Stantsii
    [*A publication*]
Sb Tr Astrakh Protivochumn Stn ... Sbornik Trudov Astrakhanskoi
    Protivochumnoi Stantsii [*A publication*]
Sb Tr Azerb Gos Inst Usoversh Vrachei ... Sbornik Trudov Azerbaidzhanskii
    Gosudarstvennyi Institut Usovershenstvovaniya Vrachei
    [*A publication*]
Sb Tr Azerb Gos Med Inst ... Sbornik Trudov Azerbaidzhanskogo
    Gosudarstvennogo Meditsinskogo Instituta [*A publication*]
Sb Tr Azerb Nauchno-Issled Inst Kurortol Fiz Metod Lech ... Sbornik Trudov
    Azerbaidzhanskogo Nauchno-Issledovatel'skogo Instituta
    Kurortologii i Fizicheskikh Metodov Lecheniya [*A
    publication*]
Sb Tr Bashk Gos Zapov ... Sbornik Trudov Bashkirskogo Zapovednika [*A
    publication*]
Sb Tr Beloruss Gos Med Inst ... Sbornik Trudov Belorusskii Gosudarstvennyi
    Meditsinskii Institut [*A publication*]
Sb Tr Bryansk Inst Transp Mashinostr ... Sbornik Trudov Bryanskii Institut
    Transportnogo Mashinostroeniya [*A publication*]
Sb Tr Chelyab Elektrometall Komb ... Sbornik Trudov Chelyabinskogo
    Elektrometallurgicheskogo Kombinata [*A publication*]
Sb Tr Chelyabinsk Elektrometal Komb ... Sbornik Trudov Chelyabinskogo
    Elektrometallurgicheskogo Kombinata [*USSR*] [*A
    publication*]
Sb Tr Dal'nevost Nauchno-Issled Inst Lesn Khoz ... Sbornik Trudov
    Dal'nevostochnyi Nauchno-Issledovatel'skii Institut
    Lesnogo Khozyaistva [*A publication*]
Sb Tr Donetsk Nauchno-Issled Inst Cher Metall ... Sbornik Trudov Donetskii
    Nauchno-Issledovatel'skii Institut Chernoi Metallurgii [*A
    publication*]
Sb Tr Donets Nauchno-Issled Inst Chern Metall ... Sbornik Trudov Donetskii
    Nauchno-Issledovatel'skii Institut Chernoi Metallurgii
    [*USSR*] [*A publication*]
Sb Tr Geobot Eksped L'vov Univ ... Sbornik Trudov Geobotanicheskoi
    Ekspeditsii L'vovskogo Universiteta [*A publication*]
Sb Tr Glavniiproekt Energ Inst (USSR) ... Sbornik Trudov Glavniiproekt
    Energeticheskii Institut (USSR) [*A publication*]
Sb Tr Gor'k Skh Inst ... Sbornik Trudov Gor'kovskogo
    Sel'skokhozyaistvennogo Instituta [*A publication*]
Sb Tr Gos Inst Prikl Khim ... Sbornik Trudov Gosudarstvennogo Instituta
    Prikladnoi Khimii [*A publication*]
Sb Tr Gos Inst Proekt Zavodov Sanit Tekh Oborudovaniya ... Sbornik Trudov
    Gosudarstvennyi Institut po Proektirovaniyu Zavodov
    Sanitarno Tekhnicheskogo Oborudovaniya [*A publication*]

Sb Tr Gos Nauchno-Issled Energ Inst Im G M Krzhizhanovskogo ... Sbornik
    Trudov Gosudarstvennyi Nauchno-Issledovatel'skii
    Energeticheskii Institut Imeni G. M. Krzhizhanovskogo [*A
    publication*]
Sb Tr Gos Nauchno Issled Inst Rentgenol Radiol ... Sbornik Trudov
    Gosudarstvennyi Nauchno-Issledovatel'skii Institut
    Rentgenologii i Radiologii [*A publication*]
Sb Tr Gos Vses Nauchno-Issled Inst Stroit Mater Konstr ... Sbornik Trudov
    Gosudarstvennyi Vsesoyuznyi Nauchno-Issledovatel'skii
    Institut Stroitel'nykh Materialov i Konstruktsii [*A
    publication*]
Sb Tr Gruz Zootekh Vet Inst ... Sbornik Trudov Gruzinskii Zootekhnichesko
    Veterinarnyi Institut [*A publication*]
Sb Tr Gruz Zootekh-Vet Uchebn-Issled Inst ... Sbornik Trudov Gruzinskogo
    Zootekhnichesko-Veterinarnogo Uchebno-
    Issledovatel'skogo Instituta [*A publication*]
Sb Tr Inst Eksp Patol Ter Akad Med Nauk SSSR ... Sbornik Trudov Instituta
    Eksperimental'noi Patologii i Terapii Akademii
    Meditsinskikh Nauk SSSR [*A publication*]
Sb Tr Inst Elektrotekh Akad Nauk Ukr SSR ... Sbornik Trudov Instituta
    Elektrotekhniki Akademiya Nauk Ukrainskoi SSR [*A
    publication*]
Sb Tr Inst Epidemiol Gig Arm SSR ... Sbornik Trudov Instituta Epidemiologii
    i Gigieny Armyanskoi SSR [*A publication*]
Sb Tr Inst Gorn Dela Akad Nauk Ukr SSR ... Sbornik Trudov Instituta
    Gornogo Dela Akademiya Nauk Ukrainskoi SSR [*A
    publication*]
Sb Tr Inst Kurortol Fizioter Yerevan ... Sbornik Trudov Instituta Kurortologii
    i Fizioterapii Yerevan [*A publication*]
Sb Tr Inst Mashinoved Avtom Akad Nauk B SSR ... Sbornik Trudov Institut
    Mashinovedeniya i Avtomatizats Akademii Nauk
    Belorusskoi SSR [*A publication*]
Sb Tr Inst Neftekhim Protsessov Akad Nauk Az SSR ... Sbornik Trudov
    Institut Neftekhimicheskikh Protsessov Akademiya Nauk
    Azerbaidzhanskoi SSR [*A publication*]
Sb Tr Inst Stroit Mekh Seismostoikosti Akad Nauk Gruz SSR ... Sbornik
    Trudov Institut Stroitel'noi Mekhaniki i Seismostoikosti
    Akademiya Nauk Gruzinskoi SSR [*A publication*]
Sb Tr Inst Urol Akad Med Nauk SSSR ... Sbornik Trudov Instituta Urologii
    Akademii Meditsinskikh Nauk SSSR [*A publication*]
Sb Tr Inst Urol Gruz SSR ... Sbornik Trudov Instituta Urologii Gruzinskoi
    SSR [*A publication*]
Sb Tr Ivanov Med Inst ... Sbornik Trudov Ivanovskogo Meditsinskogo
    Instituta [*A publication*]
Sb Tr Izhevsk Med Inst ... Sbornik Trudov Izhevskogo Meditsinskogo
    Instituta [*A publication*]
Sb Tr Kafedry Mikrobiol Orenb Med Inst ... Sbornik Trudov Kafedry
    Mikrobiologii Orenburgskogo Meditsinskogo Instituta [*A
    publication*]
Sb Tr Kazan Gos Med Inst ... Sbornik Trudov Kazanskii Gosudarstvennyi
    Meditsinskii Institut [*A publication*]
Sb Tr Khar'k Avtomob Dorozhn Inst ... Sbornik Trudov Khar'kovskogo
    Avtomobil'no Dorozhnogo Instituta [*A publication*]
Sb Tr Khar'k Gidrometeorol Inst ... Sbornik Trudov Khar'kovskii
    Gidrometeorologicheskii Institut [*A publication*]
Sb Tr Khark Vet Inst ... Sbornik Trudov Khar'kovskogo Veterinarnogo
    Instituta [*A publication*]
Sb Tr Kiev Inzh Stroit Inst ... Sbornik Trudov Kievskii Inzhenerno-
    Stroitel'nyi Institut [*A publication*]
Sb Tr Kiev Stroit Inst ... Sbornik Trudov Kievskii Stroitel'nyi Institut [*A
    publication*]
Sb Tr Kirg Nauchno-Issled Inst Epidemiol Mikrobiol Gig ... Sbornik Trudov
    Kirgizskii Nauchno-Issledovatel'skii Institut Epidemiologii,
    Mikrobiologii, i Gigieny [*A publication*]
Sb Tr Klyuchevskogo Zavoda Ferrosplavov ... Sbornik Trudov Klyuchevskogo
    Zavoda Ferrosplavov [*A publication*]
Sb Tr Klyuchevsk Zavoda Ferrosplavov ... Sbornik Trudov Klyuchevskogo
    Zavoda Ferrosplavov [*USSR*] [*A publication*]
Sb Tr Krym Gos Med Inst ... Sbornik Trudov Krymskogo Gosudarstvennogo
    Meditsinskogo Instituta [*A publication*]
Sb Tr Krym Med Inst ... Sbornik Trudov Krymskogo Meditsinskogo Instituta
    [*A publication*]
Sb Tr Kursk Gos Med Inst ... Sbornik Trudov Kurskii Gosudarstvennyi
    Meditsinskii Institut [*A publication*]
Sb Tr Kursk Med Inst ... Sbornik Trudov Kurskogo Meditsinskogo Instituta
    [*A publication*]
Sb Tr Latv Fil Vses Ova Pochvovedov ... Sbornik Trudov Latviiskii Filial
    Vsesoyuznogo Obshchestva Pochvovedov [*A publication*]
Sb Tr Lening Gos Inst Usoversh Vrachei ... Sbornik Trudov Leningradskii
    Gosudarstvennyi Institut Usovershenstvaniya Vrachei [*A
    publication*]
Sb Tr Leningr Inst Inzh Zheleznodorozhn Transp ... Sbornik Trudov
    Leningradskii Institut Inzhenerov Zheleznodorozhnogo
    Transporta [*A publication*]
Sb Tr Leningr Inst Sov Torg ... Sbornik Trudov Leningradskii Institut
    Sovetskoi Torgovli [*A publication*]
Sb Tr Leningr Inst Usoversh Vrachei Im S M Kirova ... Sbornik Trudov
    Leningradskii Institut Usovershenstvovaniya Vrachei
    Imeni S. M. Kirova [*A publication*]
Sb Tr Leningr Inzh-Stroit Inst ... Sbornik Trudov Leningradskii Inzhenerno-
    Stroitel'nyi Institut [*A publication*]

Sb Tr Leningr Mekh Inst ... Sbornik Trudov Leningradskii Mekhanicheskii Institut [*A publication*]

Sb Tr Leningr Nauchno-Issled Inst Gematol Pereliv Krovi ... Sbornik Trudov Leningradskogo Nauchno-Issledovatel'skogo Instituta Gematologii i Perelivaniya Krovi [*A publication*]

Sb Tr Leningr Nauchn Issled Inst Vaktsin Syvorotok ... Sbornik Trudov Leningradskii Nauchno-Issledovatel'skii Institut Vaktsin i Syvorotok [*A publication*]

Sb Tr Leningr Nauchn O-Va Nevropatol Psikhiatr ... Sbornik Trudov Leningradskogo Nauchnogo Obshchestva Nevropatologov i Psikhiatrov [*A publication*]

Sb Tr Leningr Nauchn Ova Nevropatol Psikhiatrov ... Sbornik Trudov Leningradskogo Nauchnogo Obshchestva Nevropatologov i Psikhiatrov [*A publication*]

Sb Tr Lesn Khoz (Kazan) ... Sbornik Trudov po Lesnomu Khozyaistvu (Kazan) [*A publication*]

Sb Tr Med Uchrezhd Mosk Oksko Volzh Vozdravotdela ... Sbornik Trudov Meditsinskikh Uchrezhdenii Moskovsko-Oksko-Volzhskogo Vozdravotdela [*A publication*]

Sb Tr Mold Nauchno Issled Inst Epidemiol Mikrobiol Gig ... Sbornik Trudov Moldavskii Nauchno-Issledovatel'skii Institut Epidemiologii, Mikrobiologii, i Gigieny [*A publication*]

Sb Tr Mold Stn Vses Inst Zashch Rast ... Sbornik Trudov Moldavskoi Stantsii Vsesoyuznogo Instituta Zashchity Rastenii [*A publication*]

Sb Tr Molodykh Nauchn Rab Inst Bot Akad Nauk Gruz SSR ... Sbornik Trudov Molodykh Nauchnykh Rabotnikov Institut Botaniki Akademiya Nauk Gruzinskoi SSR [*A publication*]

Sb Tr Molodykh Uch Kirg Nauchno Issled Inst Zemled ... Sbornik Trudov Molodykh Uchenykh Kirgizskii Nauchno-Issledovatel'skii Institut Zemledeliya [*A publication*]

Sb Tr Molodykh Uch Tselinogr Med Inst ... Sbornik Trudov Molodykh Uchenykh Tselinogradskogo Meditsinskogo Instituta [*A publication*]

Sb Tr Mosk Inzh-Stroitel Inst Im V V Kuibysheva ... Sbornik Trudov Moskovskii Inzhenerno-Stroitel'nyi Institut Imeni V. V. Kuibysheva [*USSR*] [*A publication*]

Sb Tr Mosk Inzh Stroit Inst ... Sbornik Trudov Moskovskii Inzhenerno-Stroitel'nyi Institut [*A publication*]

Sb Tr Mosk Nauchno Issled Inst Kosmetol ... Sbornik Trudov Moskovskogo Nauchno-Issledovatel'skogo Instituta Kosmetologii [*A publication*]

Sb Tr Mosk Poligr Inst ... Sbornik Trudov Moskovskii Poligraficheskii Institut [*A publication*]

Sb Tr Mosk Tekhnol Inst ... Sbornik Trudov Moskovskii Tekhnologicheskii Institut [*A publication*]

Sb Tr Mosk Vech Metall Inst ... Sbornik Trudov Moskovskii Vechernii Metallurgicheskii Institut [*USSR*] [*A publication*]

Sb Tr Mosk Zaochn Poligr Inst ... Sbornik Trudov Moskovskii Zaochnyi Poligraficheskii Institut [*A publication*]

Sb Tr MVTU ... Sbornik Trudov MVTU [*A publication*]

Sb Tr Nauchn Issled Inst Kurortol Fizioter (Tiflis) ... Sbornik Trudov Nauchno-Issledovatel'skii Institut Kurortologii i Fizioterapii (Tiflis) [*A publication*]

Sb Tr Nauchn Issled Inst Probl Kursk Magn Anomalii ... Sbornik Trudov Nauchno-Issledovatel'skii Institut po Probleman Kurskoi Magnitnoi Anomalii [*A publication*]

Sb Tr Nauchno Issled Inst Akush Ginekol (Tbilisi) ... Sbornik Trudov Nauchno-Issledovatel'skii Institut Akusherstva i Ginekologii (Tbilisi) [*A publication*]

Sb Tr Nauchno-Issled Inst Eksp Klin Ter ... Sbornik Trudov Nauchno-Issledovatel'skii Institut Eksperimental'noi i Klinicheskoi Terapii [*A publication*]

Sb Tr Nauchno-Issled Inst Eksp Klin Ter Gruz SSR ... Sbornik Trudov Nauchno-Issledovatel'skii Instituta Eksperimental'noi Klinicheskoi Terapii Gruzinskoi SSR [*A publication*]

Sb Tr Nauchno Issled Inst Epidemiol Mikrobiol Gig ... Sbornik Trudov Nauchno-Issledovatel'skii Institut Epidemiologii, Mikrobiologii, i Gigieny [*A publication*]

Sb Tr Nauchno-Issled Inst Gematol Pereliv Krovi Gruz SSR ... Sbornik Trudov Nauchno-Issledovatel'skogo Instituta Gematologii i Perelivaniya Krovi Gruzinskoi SSR [*A publication*]

Sb Tr Nauchno Issled Inst Gematol Pereliv Krovi (Tiflis) ... Sbornik Trudov Nauchno-Issledovatel'skii Institut Gematologii i Perelivaniya Krovi (Tiflis) [*A publication*]

Sb Tr Nauchno-Issled Inst Gig Tr Profzabol Gruz SSR ... Sbornik Trudov Nauchno-Issledovatel'skii Institut Gigieny Truda i Profzabolevanii Gruzinskoi SSR [*A publication*]

Sb Tr Nauchno Issled Inst Gig Tr Profzabol (Tiflis) ... Sbornik Trudov Nauchno-Issledovatel'skii Institut Gigieny Truda i Profzabolevanii (Tiflis) [*A publication*]

Sb Tr Nauchno Issled Inst Kurortol Fizioter Abkhazskii Fil ... Sbornik Trudov Nauchno-Issledovatel'skii Institut Kurortologii i Fizioterapii Abkhazskii Filial [*A publication*]

Sb Tr Nauchno Issled Inst Med Parazitol Trop Med Gruz SSR ... Sbornik Trudov Nauchno-Issledovatel'skogo Instituta Meditsinskoi Parazitologii i Tropicheskoi Meditsiny Gruzinskoi SSR [*A publication*]

Sb Tr Nauchno Issled Inst Prom Stroit Ufa ... Sbornik Trudov Nauchno-Issledovatel'skii Institut Promyshlennogo Stroitel'stva Ufa [*A publication*]

Sb Tr Nauchno-Issled Inst Rentgenol Med Radiol Gruz SSR ... Sbornik Trudov Nauchno-Issledovatel'skogo Instituta Rentgenologii i Meditsinskoi Radiologii Gruzinskoi SSR [*A publication*]

Sb Tr Nauchno Issled Inst Rentgenol Med Radiol (Tiflis) ... Sbornik Trudov Nauchno-Issledovatel'skii Institut Rentgenologii i Meditsinskoi Radiologii (Tiflis) [*A publication*]

Sb Tr Nauchno-Issled Inst Sanit Gig Gruz SSR ... Sbornik Trudov Nauchno-Issledovatel'skogo Instituta Sanitarii i Gigieny Gruzinskoi SSR [*A publication*]

Sb Tr Nauchno-Issled Inst Sanit Tekh ... Sbornik Trudov Nauchno-Issledovatel'skii Institut Sanitarnoi Tekhniki [*A publication*]

Sb Tr Nauchno-Issled Inst Travmatol Ortoped Gruz SSR ... Sbornik Trudov Nauchno-Issledovatel'skogo Instituta Travmatologii i Ortopedii Gruzinskoi SSR [*A publication*]

Sb Tr Nauchno Issled Inst Travmatol Ortop Gruz SSR ... Sbornik Trudov Nauchno-Issledovatel'skogo Instituta Travmatologii i Ortopedii Gruzinskoi SSR [*A publication*]

Sb Tr Nauchno Issled Inst Zashch Rast Arm SSR ... Sbornik Trudov Nauchno-Issledovatel'skogo Institut Zashchity Rastenii Armyanskoi SSR [*A publication*]

Sb Tr Nauchno Issled Khozhno Venerol Inst Gruz SSR ... Sbornik Trudov Nauchno-Issledovatel'skogo Khozhno-Venerologicheskogo Instituta Gruzinskoi SSR [*A publication*]

Sb Tr Nauchnoizsled Inst Tr Khig Prof Bol ... Sbornik Trudov na Nauchnoizsledovatelskiya Instituta po Trudova-Khigienna i Professionalni Bolesti [*A publication*]

Sb Tr Nauchno Izsled Onkol Inst (Sofia) ... Sbornik Trudov Nauchno-Izsledovatelski Onkologichen Institut (Sofia) [*A publication*]

Sb Tr Nauchnoizsled Proekt Inst Rudodobiv Obogat Obogat ... Sbornik ot Trudov na Nauchnoizsledovatelskiya i Proektantski Institut za Rudodobiv i Obogatyavane. Obogatyavane [*A publication*]

Sb Tr Novosb Vseross O-Va Otolaringol ... Sbornik Trudov Novosibirskogo Otdeleniya Vserossiiskogo Obshchestva Otolaringologov [*A publication*]

Sb Tr Novosib Otd Vseross Ova Otolaringol ... Sbornik Trudov Novosibirskogo Otdeleniya Vserossiiskogo Obshchestva Otolaringologov [*A publication*]

Sb Tr Obshchetekh Kafedr Leningr Tekhnol Inst Kholod Promsti ... Sbornik Trudov Obshchetekhnicheskikh Kafedr Leningradskii Tekhnologicheskii Institut Kholodil'noi Promyshlennosti [*A publication*]

Sb Tr Odess Inzh Stroit Inst ... Sbornik Trudov Odesskii Inzhenerno-Stroitel'nyi Institut [*A publication*]

Sb Tr Odess Med Inst ... Sbornik Trudov Odesskii Meditsinskii Institut [*A publication*]

Sb Tr Osvo Terskokumskikh Peskov ... Sbornik Trudov Osvoeniyu Terskokumskikh Peskov [*A publication*]

Sb Tr Permsk Gor Psikhiatr Boln ... Sbornik Trudov Permskoi Gorodskoi Psikhiatricheskoi Bol'nitsy [*A publication*]

Sb Tr Povolzh Lesotekh Inst ... Sbornik Trudov Povolzhskogo Lesotekhnicheskogo Instituta [*A publication*]

Sb Tr Proektn Nauchno-Issled Inst Ural Promstroiniiproekt ... Sbornik Trudov Proektnyi i Nauchno-Issledovatel'skii Institut "Ural'skii Promstroiniiproekt" [*A publication*]

Sb Tr Rentgenol ... Sbornik Trudov po Rentgenologii [*A publication*]

Sb Tr Resp Kostno Tuberk Bol'n Im Lenina ... Sbornik Trudov Respubliki Kostno Tuberkuleznaya Bol'nitsa Imeni Lenina [*A publication*]

Sb Tr Resp Nauchno-Issled Inst Mestnykh Stroit Mater ... Sbornik Trudov Respublikanski Nauchno-Issledovatel'skii Institut Mestnykh Stroitel'nykh Materialov [*A publication*]

Sb Tr Resp Nauchno-Issled Inst Okhr Materin Det ... Sbornik Trudov Respublikanskii Nauchno-Issledovatel'skii Institut Okhrany Materinstva Detstva [*A publication*]

Sb Tr Samark Med Inst ... Sbornik Trudov Samarkandskogo Meditsinskogo Instituta [*A publication*]

Sb Tr Sekt Radiobiol Akad Nauk Arm SSR ... Sbornik Trudov Sektor Radiobiologii Akademiya Nauk Armyanskoi SSR [*A publication*]

Sb Tr Sev Nauchno-Issled Inst Promsti ... Sbornik Trudov Severnyi Nauchno-Issledovatel'skii Institut Promyshlennosti [*A publication*]

Sb Tr Stalingr Inst Inzh Gor Khoz ... Sbornik Trudov Stalingradskii Institut Inzhenerov Gorodskogo Khozyaistva [*A publication*]

Sb Tr Stalingr Opytno Melior Stn ... Sbornik Trudov Stalingradskaya Opytno-Meliorativnaya Stantsiya [*A publication*]

Sb Tr Stavrop Gos Pedagog Inst ... Sbornik Trudov Stavropol'skii Gosudarstvennyi Pedagogicheskii Institut [*A publication*]

Sb Tr Sud Med Sud Khim ... Sbornik Trudov po Sudebnoi Meditsine i Sudebnoi Khimii [*A publication*]

Sb Tr Sverdl Gor Klin Bol'n No 1 ... Sbornik Trudov Sverdlovskoi Gorodskoi Klinicheskoi Bol'nitsy No. 1 [*A publication*]

Sb Tr Sverdl Nauchno Issled Inst Pererab Drev ... Sbornik Trudov Sverdlovskii Nauchno-Issledovatel'skii Institut Pererabotki Drevesiny [*A publication*]

Sb Tr Sverdl Nauchno-Issled Inst Stroit ... Sbornik Trudov Sverdlovskii Nauchno-Issledovatel'skii Institut po Stroitel'stvu [*A publication*]

Sb Tr Tadzh Nauchno-Issled Inst Zemled ... Sbornik Trudov Tadzhikskogo Nauchno-Issledovatel'skogo Instituta Zemledeliya [*A publication*]

Sb Tr Tbilis Gos Nauchno Issled Inst Stroit Mater ... Sbornik Trudov Tbilisskii Gosudarstvennyi Nauchno-Issledovatel'skii Institut Stroitel'nykh Materialov [*A publication*]

Sb Tr Tbilis Inst Usoversh Vrachei ... Sbornik Trudov Tbilisskogo Instituta Usovershenstvovaniya Vrachei [*A publication*]

Sb Tr Tsent Nauchno-Issled Inst Chern Metall ... Sbornik Trudov Tsentral'nogo Nauchno-Issledovatel'skogo Instituta Chernoj Metallurgii [*USSR*] [*A publication*]

Sb Tr Tsentr Muz Pochvoved ... Sbornik Trudov Tsentral'nyi Muzei Pochvovedeniya [*A publication*]

Sb Tr Tsentr Nauchno Issled Inst Bum ... Sbornik Trudov Tsentral'nogo Nauchno-Issledovatel'skogo Instituta Bumagi [*A publication*]

Sb Tr Tsentr Nauchno-Issled Inst Chern Metall ... Sbornik Trudov Tsentral'nogo Nauchno-Issledovatel'skogo Instituta Chernoj Metallurgii [*A publication*]

Sb Tr Tsentr Nauchno-Issled Inst Olovyannoi Promsti ... Sbornik Trudov Tsentral'nyi Nauchno-Issledovatel'skii Institut Olovyannoi Promyshlennosti [*A publication*]

Sb Tr Tsentr Nauchno Issled Proektn Inst Lesokhim Promsti ... Sbornik Trudov Tsentral'nyi Nauchno-Issledovatel'skii Proektnyi Institut Lesokhiimicheskoi Promyshlennosti [*A publication*]

Sb Tr Tskhaltub Fil Nauchno Issled Inst Kurortol Fizioter ... Sbornik Trudov Tskhaltubskii Filial Nauchno-Issledovatel'skii Institut Kurortoloogii i Fizioterapii [*A publication*]

Sb Trud Agron Fiz ... Sbornik Trudov po Agronomicheskoi Fizike [*A publication*]

Sb Trud Moskov Obl Pedag Inst ... Sbornik Trudov Moskovskogo Oblastskogo Pedagogiceskij Institut [*A publication*]

Sb Trud Nauc-Issled Inst Hudoz Promys ... Sbornik Trudov Nauchno-Issledovatel'skogo Instituta Hudozestvennoj Promyshlennosti [*A publication*]

Sb Trudov Inst Problem Upravlen ... Sbornik Trudov Institut Problem Upravlenina [*A publication*]

Sb Trudov Odess Elektrotehn Inst Svjazi ... Sbornik Trudov Odesskogo Elektrotehniceskogo Instituta Svjazi Imeni A. S. Popova [*A publication*]

Sb Trudov Vsesojuz Zaocn Politehn Inst ... Sbornik Trudov Vsesojuznogo Zaocnogo Politehniceskogo Instituta [*A publication*]

Sb Trud Vopros Zool Kazansk Gos Pedagog Inst ... Sbornik Trudov Vopros Zool Kazanskii Gosudarstvennyi Pedagogicheskii Institut [*A publication*]

Sb Trud Zool Muz ... Sbornik Trudov Zoologicheskogo Muzeya [*A publication*]

Sb Tr Ufim Neft Inst ... Sbornik Trudov Ufimskogo Neftyanogo Instituta [*A publication*]

Sb Tr Ukr Nauchno-Issled Inst Met ... Sbornik Trudov Ukrainskij Nauchno-Issledovatel'skij Institut Metallov [*A publication*]

Sb Tr Ukr Nauchno Issled Inst Pishch Promsti ... Sbornik Trudov Ukrainskii Nauchno-Issledovatel'skii Institut Pishchevoi Promyshlennosti [*A publication*]

Sb Tr Ukr Nauchno Issled Inst Poligr Promsti ... Sbornik Trudov Ukrainskogo Nauchno-Issledovatel'skogo Instituta Poligraficheskoi Promyshlennosti [*A publication*]

Sb Tr Ukr Nauchno Issled Inst Tsellyul Bum Promsti ... Sbornik Trudov Ukrainskogo Nauchno-Issledovatel'skogo Instituta Tsellyulozno-Bumazhnoi Promyshlennosti [*A publication*]

Sb Tr Ukr Tsentr Nauchno-Issled Inst Ortop Travmatol ... Sbornik Trudov Ukrainskogo Tsentral'nogo Nauchno-Issledovatel'skogo Instituta Ortopedii i Travmatologii [*A publication*]

Sb Tr Ural Lesotekh Inst ... Sbornik Trudov Ural'skii Lesotekhnicheskii Institut [*A publication*]

Sb Tr Vil'nyus Gos Nauchno Issled Inst Stroit Mater ... Sbornik Trudov Vil'nyusskogo Gosudarstvennogo Nauchno-Issledovatel'skogo Instituta Stroitel'nykh Materialov [*A publication*]

Sb Tr Vladivost Nauchno Issled Inst Epidemiol Mikrobiol Gig ... Sbornik Trudov Vladivostokskogo Nauchno-Issledovatel'skogo Instituta Epidemiologii, Mikrobiologii, i Gigieny [*A publication*]

Sb Tr VNIIB ... Sbornik Trudov VNIIB [*A publication*]

Sb Tr Voronezh Inzh Stroit Inst ... Sbornik Trudov Voronezhskogo Inzhenerno-Stroitel'nogo Instituta [*A publication*]

Sb Tr Voronezh Otd Vses Khim Ova ... Sbornik Trudov Voronezhskogo Otdeleniya Vsesoyuznogo Khimicheskogo Obshchestva [*A publication*]

Sb Tr Voronezh S-Kh ... Sbornik Trudov Voronezhskogo Sel'skokhozyaistvennogo Instituta [*A publication*]

Sb Tr Voronezh S-Kh Inst ... Sbornik Trudov Voronezhskogo Sel'skokhozyaistvennogo Instituta [*A publication*]

Sb Tr Vrachei Dorogi ... Sbornik Trudov Vrachei Dorogi [*A publication*]

Sb Tr Vrachei Pribalt Zhelezn ... Sbornik Trudov Vrachei Pribaltiiskogo Zheleznodorozhiya [*A publication*]

Sb Tr Vses Inst Rastenievod ... Sbornik Trudov Vsesoyuznyi Institut Rastenievodstva [*A publication*]

Sb Tr Vses Nauchno-Issled Eksp-Konstr Inst Tary Upakovki ... Sbornik Trudov Vsesoyuznyi Nauchno-Issledovatel'skii i Eksperimental'no-Konstruktorskii Institut Tary i Upakovki [*A publication*]

Sb Tr Vses Nauchno-Issled Inst Bolezn Ptits ... Sbornik Trudov Vsesoyuznogo Nauchno-Issledovatel'skogo Instituta po Boleznyam Ptits [*A publication*]

Sb Tr Vses Nauchno-Issled Inst Derevoobrab Promsti ... Sbornik Trudov Vsesoyuznyi Nauchno-Issledovatel'skii Institut Derevoobrabatyvayuushchei Promyshlennosti [*A publication*]

Sb Tr Vses Nauchno-Issled Inst Gidroliza Rastit Mater ... Sbornik Trudov Vsesoyuznyi Nauchno-Issledovatel'skii Institut Gidroliza Rastitel'nykh Materialov [*USSR*] [*A publication*]

Sb Tr Vses Nauchno Issled Inst "Goznaka" ... Sbornik Trudov Vsesoyuznyi Nauchno-Issledovatel'skii Institut "Goznaka" [*A publication*]

Sb Tr Vses Nauchno-Issled Inst Nov Stroit Mater ... Sbornik Trudov Vsesoyuznyi Nauchno-Issledovatel'skii Institut Novykh Stroitel'nykh Materialov [*USSR*] [*A publication*]

Sb Tr Vses Nauchno-Issled Inst Stroit Mater Konstr ... Sbornik Trudov Vsesoyuznyi Nauchno-Issledovatel'skii Institut Stroitel'nykh Materialov i Konstruktsii [*A publication*]

Sb Tr Vses Nauchno-Issled Inst Tsellyul Bum Promsti ... Sbornik Trudov Vsesoyuznogo Nauchno-Issledovatel'skogo Instituta Tsellyulozno- Bumazhnoi Promyshlennosti [*A publication*]

Sb Tr Vses Nauchno Issled Inst Tverd Splavov ... Sbornik Trudov Vsesoyuznyi Nauchno-Issledovatel'skii Institut Tverdykh Splavov [*A publication*]

Sb Tr Vses Nauchno Issled Khim Farm Inst ... Sbornik Trudov Vsesoyuznogo Nauchno-Issledovatel'skogo Khimiko-Farmatsevticheskogo Instituta [*A publication*]

Sb Tr Vses Nauchno-Issled Proekt Inst Titana ... Sbornik Trudov Vsesoyuznyi Nauchno-Issledovatel'skii i Proektnyi Institut Titana [*USSR*] [*A publication*]

Sb Tr Vses Nauchno-Issled Proektn Inst Teplotekh Sooruzh ... Sbornik Trudov Vsesoyuznyi Nauchno-Issledovatel'skii i Proektnyi Institut po Teplotekhnicheskim Sooruzheniyam [*A publication*]

Sb Tr Vses Nauchno Issled Proektn Inst Titana ... Sbornik Trudov Vsesoyuznyi Nauchno-Issledovatel'skii i Proektnyi Institut Titana [*A publication*]

Sb Tr Vses Zaochn Inzh Stroit Inst ... Sbornik Trudov Vsesoyuznyi Zaochnyi Inzhenerno-Stroitel'nyi Institut [*A publication*]

Sb Tr Vses Zaochn Politekh Inst ... Sbornik Trudov Vsesoyuznogo Zaochnogo Politekhnicheskogo Instituta [*A publication*]

Sb Tr Yuzhn Nauchno Issled Inst Prom Stroit ... Sbornik Trudov Yuzknyi Nauchno-Issledovatel'skii Institut Promyshlennogo Stroitel'stva [*A publication*]

Sb Tr Zool Muz Mosk Univ ... Sbornik Trudov Zoologicheskogo Muzeya Moskovskogo Universiteta [*A publication*]

SBTS .... Shore-Based Tracking System

SBTS .... Stretch Block Template Set (MCD)

Sb Tsentr Nauchno Issled Inst Tekhnol Mashinostr ... Sbornik Tsentral'nyi Nauchno-Issledovatel'skii Institut Tekhnologii i Mashinostroeniya [*A publication*]

SBTT .... Serikat Buruh Tambang Timah [*Tin Mine Laborers' Union*] [*Indonesia*]

SBTT .... Southern Bell Telephone & Telegraph Co. (KSC)

SBTT .... Tabatinga/Internacional [*Brazil*] [*ICAO location identifier*] (ICLI)

SBTU .... Serikat Buruh Teknik Umum [*Indonesia*]

SBTU .... Tucurui [*Brazil*] [*ICAO location identifier*] (ICLI)

SBU .... Blue Earth, MN [*Location identifier*] [*FAA*] (FAAL)

SBU .... Mois Economique et Financier [*A publication*]

SBU .... Saint Bonaventure University [*New York*]

SBU .... Scottish Badminton Union (EAIO)

SBU .... Secondary Building Unit [*Physical chemistry*]

SBU .... Silver Brazing Union (MSA)

SBU .... Small Base Unit [*Telecommunications*]

SBU .... Small Battle Unit [*Navy*] (NVT)

SBU .... Small Business United [*Later, NSBU*] (EA)

SBU .... Special Business Unit

SBU .... Springbok [*South Africa*] [*Airport symbol*] (OAG)

SBU .... Stansbury Island [*Utah*] [*Seismograph station code, US Geological Survey*] [*Closed*] (SEIS)

SBU .... Station Buffer Unit [*Data processing*]

SBU .... Strategic Business Unit

SBU .... Svensk Biblisk Uppslagverk [*A publication*] (BJA)

SBU .... Symbolae Biblicae Upsalienses [*A publication*]

SBUA .... Sao Gabriel Da Cachoeira [*Brazil*] [*ICAO location identifier*] (ICLI)

Sb Uch Zap Aspir Latv Nauchno Issled Inst Zemled ... Sbornik Uchenykh Zapisok Aspirantov. Latviiskii Nauchno-Issledovatel'skii Institut Zemledeliya [*A publication*]

SBUE .... Switch-Backup Entry [*NASA*] (KSC)

SBUF .... Paulo Afonso [*Brazil*] [*ICAO location identifier*] (ICLI)

SBUG .... Uruguaiana/Rubem Berta [*Brazil*] [*ICAO location identifier*] (ICLI)

SBUI .... Carauari [*Brazil*] [*ICAO location identifier*] (ICLI)

SBUL .... Uberlandia [*Brazil*] [*ICAO location identifier*] (ICLI)

SBUP......... Castilho/Urubupunga [*Brazil*] [*ICAO location identifier*] (ICLI)
SBUPAC ... Symbolae Botanicae Upsalienses [*A publication*]
SBUR........ Uberaba [*Brazil*] [*ICAO location identifier*] (ICLI)
SBURCS.... Six-BIT [*Binary Digit*] Universal Random Character Set [*Data processing*]
Sb Ustavu Nerostych Surovin Kutne Hore ... Sbornik Ustavu Nerostych Surovin v Kutne Hore [*A publication*]
Sb Ustavu Vyzk Vyz Lidu Praze ... Sbornik Ustavu pro Vyzkum Vyzivy Lidu v Praze [*A publication*]
Sb Ustav Vedeckotech Inf Genet Slechteni ... Sbornik Ustav Vedeckotechnickych Informaci Genetika a Slechteni [*A publication*]
Sb Ustav Vedeckotech Inf Melior ... Sbornik Ustav Vedeckotechnickych Informaci. Rada Meliorace [*A publication*]
Sb Ustav Vedeckotech Inf Zemed Genet Slechteni ... Sbornik Ustav Vedeckotechnickych Informaci pro Zemedelstvi, Genetika, a Slechteni [*A publication*]
Sb Ustav Vedeckotech Inf Zemed Melior ... Sbornik Ustav Vedeckotechnickych Informaci pro Zemedelstvi Rada Meliorace [*A publication*]
Sb Ustred Ustavu Geol ... Sbornik Ustredniho Ustavu Geologickeho [*A publication*]
Sb Ustred Ustavu Geol Oddil Geol ... Sbornik Ustredniho Ustavu Geologickeho. Oddil Geologicky [*A publication*]
SBUV......... Solar Backscatter Ultraviolet [*Ozone measurement*]
SBUV......... Solar and Backscatter Ultraviolet Spectrometer (MCD)
Sb UVTI Genet Slechteni ... Sbornik UVTI [*Ustav Vedeckotechnickych Informaci*] Genetika a Slechteni [*A publication*]
Sb UVTI Melior ... Sbornik UVTI [*Ustav Vedeckotechnickych Informaci*] Meliorace [*A publication*]
Sb UVTI Ochr Rostl ... Sbornik UVTI [*Ustav Vedeckotechnickych Informaci*] Ochrana Rostlin [*A publication*]
Sb UVTI (Ustav Vedeckotech Inf) Zahradnictvi ... Sbornik UVTI (Ustav Vedeckotechnickych Informaci) Zahradnictvi [*A publication*]
Sb UVTIZ (Ustav Vedeckotech Inf Zemed) Ochr Rostl ... Sbornik UVTIZ (Ustav Vedeckotechnickych Informaci pro Zemedelstvi) Ochrana Rostlin [*A publication*]
SBUV/TOMS ... Solar and Backscattered Ultraviolet and Total Ozone Mapping System
SBV............ Sabah [*Papua New Guinea*] [*Airport symbol*] (OAG)
SBV............ Semiautomatic Bleeder Valve
SBV............ Single Binocular Vision
SBV............ South Boston, VA [*Location identifier*] [*FAA*] (FAAL)
SBV............ State Bank of Victoria [*Australia*]
SBVC......... San Bernardino Valley College [*California*]
SBVE......... State Board of Vocational Education [*State Board of Education*] (OICC)
Sb Ved Lesn Ustav Vys Sk Zemed Praze ... Sbornik Vedeckeho Lesnickeho Ustavu Vysoke Skoly Zemedelske v Praze [*A publication*]
Sb Ved Praci Ustred Statniho Ust Praze ... Sbornik Vedeckych Praci Ustredniho Statniho Ustavu v Praze [*A publication*]
Sb Ved Praci Vyzk Ustav Vyz Zvirat ... Sbornik Vedeckych Praci-Vyzkumny Ustav Vyzivy Zvirat [*A publication*]
Sb Ved Pr Lek Fak Karlovy Univ Hradci Kralove ... Sbornik Vedeckych Praci Lekarske Fakulty Karlovy University v Hradci Kralove [*A publication*]
Sb Ved Pr Lek Fak Karlovy Univ Hradci Kralove Suppl ... Sbornik Vedeckych Praci Lekarske Fakulty Karlovy University v Hradci Kralove. Supplementum [*A publication*]
Sb Ved Pr Lek Fak Univ Karlovy Hradci Kralove ... Sbornik Vedeckych Praci Lekarske Fakulty Karlovy University v Hradci Kralove [*A publication*]
Sb Ved Pr VLVDU Hradci Kralove ... Sbornik Vedeckych Praci VLVDU [*Vojenskeho Lekarskeho Vyzkumneho a Doskolovaciho Ustavu*] v Hradci Kralove [*A publication*]
Sb Ved Pr Vys Banske Ostrave Rada Hutn ... Sbornik Vedeckych Praci Vysoke Skoly Banske v Ostrave. Rada Hutnicka [*A publication*]
Sb Ved Pr Vys Sk Banske Ostrave Rada Horn-Geol ... Sbornik Vedeckych Praci Vysoke Skoly Banske v Ostrave. Rada Hornicko-Geologicka [*Czechoslovakia*] [*A publication*]
Sb Ved Pr Vys Sk Banske Ostrave Rada Hutn ... Sbornik Vedeckych Praci Vysoke Skoly Banske v Ostrave. Rada Hutnicka [*A publication*]
Sb Ved Pr Vys Sk Bransk Ostrave ... Sbornik Vedeckych Praci Vysoke Skoly Banske v Ostrave [*A publication*]
Sb Ved Pr Vys Sk Chem-Technol (Pardubice) ... Sbornik Vedeckych Praci. Vysoka Skola Chemickotechnologicka (Pardubice) [*A publication*]
SBVG......... Varginha/Jam Brigadeiro Trompowsky [*Brazil*] [*ICAO location identifier*] (ICLI)
SBVH .... Schwaebische Blaetter fuer Volksbildung und Heimatpflege [*A publication*]
SBVH .... Vilhena [*Brazil*] [*ICAO location identifier*] (ICLI)
Sb "Vop Issled Izpol'z Pochv Moldavii" ... Sbornik "Voprosy Issledovaniya i Izpol'zovaniya Pochv Moldavii" [*A publication*]
SBVS .... Saga-Book. Viking Society for Northern Research [*A publication*]
SBVS .... Shield Building Ventilation System [*Nuclear energy*] (NRCH)

Sb Vses Inst Zashch Rast ... Sbornik Vsesoyuznogo Instituta Zashchity Rastenii [*A publication*]
Sb Vses Sov Nauchno-Tekh Obshchestv Kom Korroz Zashch Met ... Sbornik Vsesoyuznyi Sovet Nauchno-Tekhnickeskikh Obshchestv. Komitet po Korrozi i Zashchite Metallov [*A publication*]
SBVT .... Vitoria/Goiabeira [*Brazil*] [*ICAO location identifier*] (ICLI)
Sb Vynalezu ... Sbirka Vynalezu [*A publication*]
Sb Vys Chem Technol Praze Ekon Rizeni Chem Prum ... Sbornik Vysoke Skoly Chemicko-Technologicke v Praze. Ekonomika a Rizeni Chemickeho Prumyslu [*A publication*]
Sb Vysk Pr Odboru Celul Pap ... Sbornik Vyskumnych Prac z Odboru Celulozy a Papiera [*A publication*]
Sb Vysk Sk Chem-Technol Praze (Oddil) Chem Inz ... Sbornik Vysoke Skoly Chemicko-Technologicke v Praze (Oddil). Chemicke Inzenyrstvi [*A publication*]
Sb Vysk Sk Chem-Technol Praze (Oddil) Chem Inz Autom ... Sbornik Vysoke Skoly Chemicko-Technologicke v Praze (Oddil). Chemicke Inzenyrstvi a Automatizace [*A publication*]
Sb Vysk Sk Chem Technol Praze (Oddil) K ... Sbornik Vysoke Skoly Chemicko-Technologicke v Praze (Oddil). K [*A publication*]
Sb Vysoke Uceni Tech v Brne ... Sbornik Vysokeho Uceni Technickeho v Brne [*A publication*]
Sb Vys Sk Chem-Technol Praze ... Sbornik Vysoke Skoly Chemicko-Technologicke v Praze [*A publication*]
Sb Vys Sk Chem Technol Praze Anal Chem ... Sbornik Vysoke Skoly Chemicko-Technologicke v Praze. Analyticka Chemie [*A publication*]
Sb Vys Sk Chem Technol Praze Anorg Chem Technol ... Sbornik Vysoke Skoly Chemicko-Technologicke v Praze. Anorganicka Chemie a Technologie [*A publication*]
Sb Vys Sk Chem Technol Praze Anorg Org Technol ... Sbornik Vysoke Skoly Chemicko-Technologicke v Praze. Anorganicka a Organicka Technologie [*A publication*]
Sb Vys Sk Chem Technol Praze Anorg Technol ... Sbornik Vysoke Skoly Chemicko-Technologicke v Praze. Anorganicka Technologie [*A publication*]
Sb Vys Sk Chem Technol Praze Chem Inz Autom ... Sbornik Vysoke Skoly Chemicko-Technologicke v Praze. Chemicke Inzenyrstvi a Automatizace [*A publication*]
Sb Vys Sk Chem Technol Praze Chem Technol Silik ... Sbornik Vysoke Skoly Chemicko-Technologicke v Praze. Chemie a Technologie Silikatu [*A publication*]
Sb Vys Sk Chem Technol Praze F Technol Vody Prostredi ... Sbornik Vysoke Skoly Chemicko-Technologicke v Praze. Rada F. Technologie Vody a Prostredi [*A publication*]
Sb Vys Sk Chem Technol Praze Mineral ... Sbornik Vysoke Skoly Chemicko-Technologicke v Praze. Mineralogie [*A publication*]
Sb Vys Sk Chem Technol Praze (Oddil) Fak Anorg Technol ... Sbornik Vysoke Skoly Chemicko-Technologicke v Praze (Oddil). Fakulty Anorganicke a Organicke Technologie [*A publication*]
Sb Vys Sk Chem Technol Praze (Oddil) Fak Potravin Technol ... Sbornik Vysoke Skoly Chemicko-Technologicke v Praze (Oddil). Fakulty Poetravinarske Technologie [*A publication*]
Sb Vys Sk Chem-Technol Praze (Oddil) Fak Technol Paliv Vody ... Sbornik Vysoke Skoly Chemicko-Technologicke v Praze (Oddil). Fakulty Technologie Paliv a Vody [*A publication*]
Sb Vys Sk Chem Technol Praze Org Chem Technol ... Sbornik Vysoke Skoly Chemicko-Technologicke v Praze. Organicka Chemie a Technologie [*A publication*]
Sb Vys Sk Chem-Technol Praze Rada B ... Sbornik Vysoke Skoly Chemicko-Technologicke v Praze. Rada B. Anorganicka Chemie a Technologie [*A publication*]
Sb Vys Sk Chem Technol Praze Rada H ... Sbornik Vysoke Skoly Chemicko-Technologicke v Praze. Rada H [*A publication*]
Sb Vys Sk Chem Technol Praze Technol Paliv ... Sbornik Vysoke Skoly Chemicko-Technologicke v Praze. Technologie Paliv [*Czechoslovakia*] [*A publication*]
Sb Vys Sk Chem-Technol Praze Technol Vody ... Sbornik Vysoke Skoly Chemicko-Technologicke v Praze. Technologie Vody [*A publication*]
Sb Vys Sk Chem-Technol Pr Potraviny ... Sbornik Vysoke Skoly Chemicko-Technologicke v Praze. Potraviny [*A publication*]
Sb Vys Skola Chem-Technol Fak Potrav Technol ... Sbornik Vysoka Skola Chemicko-Technologicka. Fakulta Potravinarske Technologie [*A publication*]
Sb Vys Skoly Polnohospod Nitre Prevadzkovo-Ekon Fak ... Sbornik Vysokej Skoly Polnohospodarskej v Nitre Prevadzkovo-Ekonomicka Fakulta [*A publication*]
Sb Vys Skoly Zemed Brne Rada A ... Sbornik Vysoke Skoly Zemedelske v Brne. Rada A [*A publication*]
Sb Vys Skoly Zemed Brne Rada B ... Sbornik Vysoke Skoly Zemedelske v Brne. Rada B [*A publication*]
Sb Vys Skoly Zemed Praze ... Sbornik Vysoke Skoly Zemedelske v Praze [*A publication*]
Sb Vys Sk Zemed Brne ... Sbornik Vysoke Skoly Zemedelske v Brne [*A publication*]
Sb Vys Sk Zemed v Brne A ... Sbornik Vysoke Skoly Zemedelske v Brne. Rada A [*A publication*]

Sb Vys Sk Zemed Brne Rada A ... Sbornik Vysoke Skoly Zemedelske v Brne. Rada A. Spisy Fakulty Agronomicke [*A publication*]
Sb Vys Sk Zemed Brne Rada C ... Sbornik Vysoke Skoly Zemedelske v Brne. Rada C. Spisy Fakulty Lesnicke [*A publication*]
Sb Vys Sk Zemed Brne Rada C Spisy Fak Lesn ... Sbornik Vysoke Skoly Zemedelske v Brne. Rada C. Spisy Fakulty Lesnicke [*A publication*]
Sb Vys Sk Zemed Lesn Fak Brne Rada C Spisy ... Sbornik Vysoke Skoly Zemedelske a Lesnicke Fakulty v Brne. Rada C. Spisy Fakulty Lesnicke [*A publication*]
Sb Vys Sk Zemed Lesn Fak Brne Rada C Spisy Fak Lesn ... Sbornik Vysoke Skoly Zemedelske a Lesnicke Fakulty v Brne. Rada C. Spisy Fakulty Lesnicke [*A publication*]
Sb Vys Sk Zemed Praze ... Sbornik Vysoke Skoly Zemedelske v Praze [*A publication*]
Sb Vys Sk Zemed Praze Fak Agron Rada A ... Sbornik Vysoke Skoly Zemedelske v Praze. Fakulta Agronomicka. Rada A. Rostlinna Vyroba [*A publication*]
Sb Vys Uceni Tech Brne ... Sbornik Vysokeho Uceni Technickeho v Brne [*A publication*]
Sb Vys Zemed Lesn Fak Brne B Spisy Fak Vet ... Sbornik Vysoke Skoly Zemedelske a Lesnicke Fakulty v Brne. Rada B. Spisy Fakulty Veterinarni [*A publication*]
Sb VZPI..... Sbornik Statej Vsesojuznogo Zaocnogo Politechniceskogo Instituta [*A publication*]
SBW.......... Shebandowan Resources [*Vancouver Stock Exchange symbol*]
SBW.......... Sibu [*Malaysia*] [*Airport symbol*]   (OAG)
SbW.......... South by West
SBW.......... Spectral Bandwidth
SBW.......... Spruce Budworm
SBW.......... Steel Basement Window
SBW.......... Submarine Warfare   (MCD)
SBWA....... 2nd Bomb Wing Association   (EA)
SbWAk...... Sitzungsberichte. Wiener Akademie [*A publication*]
SBWFA ..... Schriftenreihe. Bundesminister fuer Wissenschaftliche Forschung (Germany). Strahlenschutz [*A publication*]
SBWG........ Strategic Bomb Wing [*Military*]
S B Wien.... Sitzungsberichte. Oesterreichische Akademie der Wissenschaften in Wien [*A publication*]
SBWMV.... Soilborne Wheat Mosaic Virus
SBWR........ Simplified Boiling Water Reactor [*Developed by General Electric Co.*] [*Nuclear energy*]
SBWU .... Singapore Bus Workers' Union
SBWX........ Seaboard World Airlines, Inc. [*Air carrier designation symbol*]
SBX.......... S-Band Transponder
SBX.......... Seabright Explorations, Inc. [*Toronto Stock Exchange symbol*]
SBX.......... Shelby, MT [*Location identifier*] [*FAA*]   (FAAL)
SBX.......... Student Book Exchange
SBX.......... Subsea Beacon/Transponder
SBXG........ Barra Do Garcas/Xingu [*Brazil*] [*ICAO location identifier*]   (ICLI)
SBXV........ Xavantina [*Brazil*] [*ICAO location identifier*]   (ICLI)
SBY.......... Salisbury [*Maryland*] [*Airport symbol*]   (OAG)
SBY.......... Salisbury, MD [*Location identifier*] [*FAA*]   (FAAL)
SBY.......... Sand Bay [*Alaska*] [*Seismograph station code, US Geological Survey*] [*Closed*]   (SEIS)
SBY.......... Shapiro, Barney, Newark NJ [*STAC*]
SBY.......... Standby [*Airlines*]
SBYA........ Iauarete [*Brazil*] [*ICAO location identifier*]   (ICLI)
SBYS .... Piracununga/Campo Fontenelle [*Brazil*] [*ICAO location identifier*]   (ICLI)
SBZ.......... Sibiu [*Romania*] [*Airport symbol*]   (OAG)
SBZ.......... Sowjetische Besatzungszone [*Soviet Occupation Zone*] [*East Germany*]
SBZ Sanit Heiz Klimatech ... SBZ Sanitaer-, Heizungs-, und Klimatechnik [*West Germany*] [*A publication*]
SC .... All India Reporter, Supreme Court Reports [*A publication*]   (DLA)
SC .... Cape Of Good Hope Reports [*South Africa*] [*A publication*]   (DLA)
SC .... Catalan Solidarity [*Political party*]   (PPW)
SC .... Christian Scientist
SC .... Congregation of the Servants of Christ [*Anglican religious community*]
SC .... Court of Session Cases [*Scotland*] [*A publication*]   (DLA)
SC .... Cruiser Submarine [*Navy symbol*] [*Obsolete*]
SC .... Juta's Supreme Court Reports [*1880-1910*] [*Cape Of Good Hope, South Africa*] [*A publication*]   (DLA)
SC .... Manetti Roberts [*Italy*] [*Research code symbol*]
Sc .... Nederlandse Staatscourant [*A publication*]
SC .... Quebec Official Reports, Superior Court [*A publication*]   (DLA)
SC .... Sabra Connection [*An association*]   (EA)
SC .... Saccharomyces Cerevisiae [*Bacterium*]
SC .... Sacra Congregatio [*Sacred Congregation*] [*Latin*]
SC .... Sacrococcygeal [*Anatomy*]
SC .... Sacrosanctam Concilium [*Constitution on the Sacred Liturgy*] [*Vatican II document*]
SC .... Sad Case [*An unpopular person*] [*Teen slang*]
SC .... Safe Custody [*Banking*]
SC .... Saffery Champness International [*British accounting firm*]
S/C............ Sales Code

SC .... Sales Costs
SC .... Salesianorum Congregatio [*Congregation of St. Francis of Sales*] [*Salesian Fathers*] [*Roman Catholic religious order*]
SC .... Salmagundi Club   (EA)
SC .... Salvage Charges
SC .... Same Case [*Law*]
SC .... Same Coupling [*Music*]
SC .... Sandia Corporation
SC .... Sanitary Corps
SC .... Satellite Communications [*Military*]
SC .... Satellite Computer
SC .... Saturable Core   (MSA)
S & C........ Saunders and Cole's English Bail Court Reports [*A publication*]   (DLA)
Sc .... Scaccaria [*Exchequer*] [*Latin*]   (DLA)
SC .... Scale
Sc .... Scammon's Reports [*2-5 Illinois*] [*A publication*]   (DLA)
SC .... Scandinavian
Sc .... Scandium [*Chemical element*]
SC .... Scapula
SC .... Scarce [*Bookselling*]   (ROG)
SC .... Scavenge   (AAG)
SC .... Scene
SC .... Scented Cape [*Tea trade*]   (ROG)
SC .... Schilling [*Monetary unit*]   (ROG)
S/C............ Schmidt-Cassegrain [*Telescope*]
Sc .... Schmidt Number [*IUPAC*]
SC .... School Certificate
SC .... School Construction   (OICC)
SC .... Schools Council [*British*]
SC .... Schooner   (ROG)
SC .... Schwann Cell [*Biology*]
Sc .... Science [*A publication*]
SC .... Science
SC .... Science and Culture [*A publication*]
Sc .... Scientia [*A publication*]
Sc .... Scientia. Organo Internazionale di Sintesi Scientifica [*A publication*]
SC .... Scilicet [*Namely*] [*Legal term*] [*Latin*]
SC .... Scintillation Counter [*Instrumentation*]
SC .... Scope Change   (MCD)
SC .... Score   (AABC)
Sc .... Scoriae [*Quality of the bottom*] [*Nautical charts*]
SC .... Scoring Criteria   (MCD)
SC .... Scots
SC .... Scotsman [*A publication*]
SC .... Scottish Aviation Ltd. [*ICAO aircraft manufacturer identifier*]   (ICAO)
SC .... Scottish Constitution   (ADA)
Sc .... Scott's English Common Pleas Reports [*A publication*]   (DLA)
SC .... Scrap Carriage [*British military*]   (DMA)
SC .... Screen Coordinator [*Military*]   (CAAL)
SC .... Screen Flag [*Navy*] [*British*]
SC .... Screw
S/C............ Screwed and Coupled
SC .... Script [*Films, television, etc.*]
Sc .... Scriptorium [*A publication*]
SC .... Scruple
SC .... Sculpsit [*He, or She, Engraved It*] [*Latin*]
SC .... Sculptor
SC .... Sculpture Center   (EA)
SC .... Scuola Cattolica [*A publication*]
Sc .... Scutum [*of Hesiod*] [*Classical studies*]   (OCD)
SC .... [*The*] Seal Cylinders of Western Asia [*A publication*]   (BJA)
SC .... Seamen's Center [*Later, Seamen and International House*]   (EA)
S & C........ Search and Clear [*Military*]
SC .... Search Control   (IEEE)
SC .... Searchlight Carrier [*British*]
SC .... Searle [*G. D.*] & Co. [*Research code symbol*]
SC .... Seat Cabs
SC .... Seco-Cemp Ltd. [*Toronto Stock Exchange symbol*]
SC .... Secondary Code
SC .... Secondary Confinement [*or Containment*] [*Nuclear energy*]   (IEEE)
S-C............ Secret and Confidential Files [*Navy*]
SC .... Secretory Component [*Supersedes SP, TP*] [*Immunology*]
SC .... Secular College
SC .... Security Call [*Economics*]
SC .... Security Council of the United Nations
SC .... See Comments [*Routing slip*]
SC .... See Copy
SC .... Seed Coat [*Botany*]
SC .... Select Cases [*Oudh, India*] [*A publication*]   (DLA)
SC .... Select Committee
SC .... Selector Channel
SC .... Self-Care [*Medicine*]
SC .... Self-Check   (AAG)
SC .... Self-Closing
SC .... Self Compatible
SC .... Self-Contained

S/C	Self-Contained [*Housing*] [*British*]
SC	Semicactus [*Horticulture*]
SC	Semiclosed [*Anatomy*]
SC	Semiconductor
SC	Senatus Consulto [*By the Decree of the Senate*] [*Latin*]
SC	Senatus Consultum [*Classical studies*] (OCD)
SC	Sending Complete [*Telecommunications*] (TEL)
SC	Senior Cameraman
SC	Senior Counsel [*Ireland*]
S/C	Sensor Controller (MCD)
SC	Separate Cover
SC	Sequence Charts (AAG)
SC	Sequence Controller
SC	Sequence Counter
SC	Servants of Charity [*Roman Catholic men's religious order*]
S/C	Service Ceiling
SC	Service Center [*IRS*]
SC	Service Certificate [*Military*] [*British*]
SC	Service Change
SC	Service Charge [*Banking*]
SC	Service Club [*Military enlisted men's club*]
SC	Service Code [*Telecommunications*] (TEL)
SC	Service Command [*Marine Corps*]
SC	Service Connected [*Medicine*]
SC	Servicos Aereos Cruzeiro do Sul SA [*Brazil*] [*ICAO designator*] (FAAC)
SC	Session Cases [*Legal term*] [*British*]
SC	Session Control [*Data processing*] (IBMDP)
SC	Set/Clear [*Flip-flop*] [*Data processing*]
SC	Set Clock
S/C	Set Course [*Navigation*]
sc	Seul Cours [*Sole Quotation*] [*Stock exchange*] [*French*]
SC	Severest Critic [*Initialism used by E. B. White to describe his wife*]
SC	Sex Change [*Biology*]
SC	Seychelles [*ANSI two-letter standard code*] (CNC)
SC	Shaft Center (MSA)
SC	Shakespearean Criticism [*A publication*]
SC	Shaped Charge [*of explosive*]
SC	Sharp Cash [*Prompt payment*]
SC	Shell Transport & Trading Company Ltd. [*NYSE symbol*] (SPSG)
SC	Shift Control Counter [*Data processing*] (MDG)
SC	Ship Casualty Library [*Maritime Data Network, Inc.*] [*Information service or system*] (CRD)
S & C	Shipper and Carrier [*Business term*]
SC	Shipping Container
SC	Shipping Contract (MCD)
SC	Ship's Cook [*Navy*]
SC	Shire Council [*Australia*] (ADA)
SC	Shop Call (MCD)
SC	Shop Carpenter
SC	Shopping Concourses [*Public-performance tariff class*] [*British*]
SC	Short Circuit
SC	Short Course [*of instruction*]
SC	Should Cost (MCD)
SC	Sickle Cell [*Medicine*]
SC	Side Cabin
SC	Side Contact [*Valves*] (DEN)
SC	Sierra Club (EA)
SC	Signal Comparator
SC	Signal Conditioner
S & C	Signal and Conditioning (KSC)
SC	Signal Corps [*Later, Communications and Electronics Command*] [*Army*]
SC	Significant Characteristics (MCD)
SC	Silicone Coated
SC	Silver Certificate
SC	Silvered Copper [*Wire*] (IEEE)
SC	Simulation Coordinator
SC	Simulator Control (MCD)
SC	Sine Correction [*Without lenses*] [*Ophthalmology*]
SC	Sine-Cosine
S & C	Singh & Choudry [*Publisher*] [*British*]
SC	Single Case
SC	Single Cell
SC	Single Circuit [*Electricity*]
SC	Single Column
SC	Single Comb
SC	Single Contact [*Switch*]
SC	Single Counter
SC	Single Crochet
SC	Single Crystal
SC	Sinusoidal Collagen [*Anatomy*]
SC	Sisters of Charity [*Roman Catholic religious order*]
SC	Sisters of Charity [*Anglican religious community*]
SC	Sisters of Charity of Saint Vincent de Paul (EA)
SC	Site Contingency [*Nuclear energy*] (NRCH)
SC	Sized and Calendered [*Paper*]
S & C	Sized and Calendered [*Paper*]
SC	Skill Component

SC	Skin Conductance
SC	Slip Coupling (DS)
SC	Slow Component
SC	Slow Curing [*Asphalt grade*]
SC	Small Capitals [*Typography*]
SC	Small Compact [*Car size*]
SC	Small Craft
SC	Smooth Contour [*Technical drawings*]
SC	Snow Cover [*Meteorology*]
SC	So-Called
SC	Soccer Club [*Australia*]
SC	Social Casework [*A publication*]
SC	Social Compass [*A publication*]
SC	Social Credit Party [*British*]
SC	Socialist Commentary [*A publication*]
S en C	Sociedad en Comandita [*Limited partnership company*] [*Spanish*]
SC	Societas Fratrum Sacris Cordis [*Brothers of the Sacred Heart*] [*Roman Catholic religious order*]
SC	Societe Cooperative [*Cooperative*] [*French*] (IMH)
SC	Society of the Cincinnati (EA)
SC	Society for Cryobiology (EA)
S/C	Software Contractor [*NASA*] (NASA)
SC	Soil Characteristics
SC	Soil Conservation [*A publication*]
SC	Solar Cell
SC	Soldier Capabilities
SC	Sole Charge [*Ecclesiastical*] [*British*] (ROG)
SC	Solid Core [*Technical drawings*]
SC	Solid-State Circuit (MCD)
S/C	Son Compte [*His, or Her, Account*] [*French*]
SC	SONAR Channel [*Navy*] (CAAL)
SC	Soncino Chumash [*A publication*] (BJA)
SC	Songwriters Club [*Later, SLC*] (EA)
SC	Sons of Charity [*Paris, France*] (EAIO)
SC	Sound Channel [*Navy*] (CAAL)
SC	Source Code
SC	Sources Chretiennes [*Paris*] [*A publication*]
s/c	Sous le Couvert [*Under Cover*] [*French*]
SC	South Carolina [*Postal code*]
SC	South Carolina Musician [*A publication*]
SC	South Carolina Reports [*A publication*] (DLA)
Sc	South Carolina State Library, Columbia, SC [*Library symbol*] [*Library of Congress*] (LCLS)
SC	Southern California
SC	Southern Classification
SC	Southern Command [*British military*] (DMA)
SC	Southern Conference (EA)
SC	Southwark College [*London, England*]
SC	Spacecraft (MCD)
S/C	Spacecraft/Capsule
SC	Spark Control [*Automotive engineering*]
SC	Special Access, Compartmented (MCD)
SC	Special Care [*Medicine*]
SC	Special Circuit
SC	Special Circular
S/C	Special Conditions (MCD)
SC	Special Constable
SC	Specialty Code
SC	Specific Cueing
SC	Specification Change
SC	Speed Controller [*Nuclear energy*] (NRCH)
SC	Spermatocyte
SC	Spiroplasmavirus citri [*Bacteriology*]
S/C	Splitter/Combiner (NASA)
SC	Sports Council [*British*] (EAIO)
SC	Sporulation Capacity [*of fungi*]
SC	Spot Check (AAG)
SC	Spread Correlation
SC	Spreading Coefficient
SC	Spring Conditions [*Skiing*]
SC	Squamous Cell Carcinoma [*Also, SCC*] [*Medicine*]
S & C	Stabilization and Control [*Aerospace*] (KSC)
SC	Stack (Pipe) Cut [*Sanitation*] [*British*] (ROG)
SC	Staff Captain [*Military*] [*British*]
SC	Staff Car [*British*]
SC	Staff College [*Military*]
SC	Staff Corps
SC	Stage Center [*A stage direction*]
SC	Standard Candle [*Power*]
SC	Standard Conditions
S & C	Standards and Control
SC	Standing Committee (ADA)
SC	Standing Crop
SC	Star of Courage [*Award*] [*British*]
SC	Start Computer
SC	Start Conversion [*Data processing*]
sC	Statcoulomb [*Also, Fr, statC*] [*Unit of electric charge*]
SC	Statement of Capability [*NASA*]
S/C	Statement of Charges [*Army*]
SC	Statement of Compatibility [*NASA*] (MCD)

SC	Statistical Control
SC	Statistics Canada
SC	Status Statement [*Online database field identifier*]
SC	Statutes of Canada
S of C.........	Statutes of Canada [*A publication*] (DLA)
SC	Steel Casting
SC	Steel Cored [*Conductors*]
SC	Steering Committee (NATG)
Sc	Stellacyanin
SC	Stellar Camera
SC	Stendhal Club [*A publication*]
SC	Stepped Care [*Medicine*]
SC	Sternoclavicular [*Joint*] [*Anatomy*]
SC	Stock Certificate [*Investment term*]
Sc	Stonecat [*Ichthyology*]
SC	Stop-Continue (DEN)
SC	Stopcock
SC	Storage Capacity (AAG)
SC	Stored Command
S/C.............	Stowage Container
S & C.........	Strategic and Critical Raw Material [*Military*]
SC	Stratocumulus [*Cloud*] [*Meteorology*]
SC	Stress Cracking [*Metallurgy*]
SC	Strike Command [*Military*]
S/C.............	Strip Chart [*Recorder*] [*NASA*] (NASA)
SC	Stronnictwo Chlopskie [*Peasants' Party*] [*Poland*] [*Political party*] (PPE)
SC	Studi Colombiani [*A publication*]
SC	Studia Catholica [*A publication*]
SC	Studia Celtica [*A publication*]
SC	Su Cargo [*Your Debit*] [*Business term*] [*Spanish*]
SC	Su Cuenta [*Your Account*] [*Business term*] [*Spanish*]
s/c	Sua Carta [*Your Letter*] [*Portuguese*]
s/c	Sua Conta [*Your Account*] [*Business term*] [*Portuguese*]
S/C.............	Subcable (KSC)
S/C.............	Subcarrier (AAG)
SC	Subcommittee
SC	Subcontractor (NATG)
SC	Subcours
SC	Subcutaneous [*Beneath the Skin*] [*Medicine*]
SC	Subject Classification [*Library science*]
SC	Submarine Chaser [*110 foot*]
S/C.............	Submarine Coxswain [*British military*] (DMA)
SC	Sudden Commencement
SC	Suffolk and Cambridgeshire Regiment [*British military*] (DMA)
SC	Sugar-Coated [*Pharmacy*]
SC	Suisse Contemporaine [*A publication*]
SC	Summary Court [*Navy*]
SC	Sumter & Choctaw Railway Co. [*AAR code*]
SC	Supercalendered [*Paper*]
S/C.............	Superconducting Magnetic (MCD)
SC	Supercritical Chromatography
SC	Superimposed Coding [*Data processing*] (DIT)
SC	Superimposed Current
SC	Superintending Cartographer [*Navy*] [*British*]
SC	Superior Colliculus [*Brain anatomy*]
SC	Superior Court (DLA)
SC	Supervisor's Console
SC	Supervisory Control
SC	Supplemental Contract (AAG)
SC	Supplementary Information [*Telecommunications*] (TEL)
SC	Supply Catalog [*Military*] (AABC)
SC	Supply Control [*Military*]
SC	Supply Corps
SC	Support Chief
SC	Support Command [*Army*]
SC	Support Concept Manual [*Marine Corps*]
SC	Support Contractor (MCD)
SC	Support Controller [*NASA*] (KSC)
SC	Support Coordinator (AAG)
SC	Supporting Cells [*Zoology*]
SC	Suppressed Carrier (IEEE)
SC	Supreme Council [*Freemasonry*] (ROG)
SC	Supreme Court
SC	Supreme Court Reporter [*National Reporter System*] [*A publication*] (DLA)
SC	Surface Combustion [*Reducing gas process*]
SC	Surface Command [*NASA*] (MCD)
SC	Surgeon-Captain [*British military*]
SC	Surgeon-Commander [*British military*]
SC	Surgical Capsule [*of prostate gland*]
SC	Surrogates by Choice (EA)
SC	Surveillance Compliance [*Nuclear energy*] (NRCH)
S & C.........	Swan and Critchfield's Revised Statutes [*Ohio*] [*A publication*] (DLA)
SC	Swimmer-Canoeist [*British military*] (DMA)
SC	Swimming Club
SC	Switching Cell (IEEE)
SC	Symbolic Code (AAG)
SC	Synanon Church (EA)

SC	Synaptonemal Complex [*Botanical cytology*]
SC	Synchro-Cyclotron
SC	Synchrocyclotron [*Particle physics*]
SC	Synchronization Coefficient
SC	Synclinal [*Geology*]
SC	System Capability
SC	System Controller [*Military*] (CAAL)
SC	Systems Command [*Air Force*]
SC	Systolic Click [*Cardiology*]
S1C	Seaman, First Class [*Navy*]
SCA.............	Air Weather Service, Technical Library, Scott AFB, IL [*OCLC symbol*] (OCLC)
SCA.............	Archibald Library, Caronport, Saskatchewan [*Library symbol*] [*National Library of Canada*] (NLC)
SCA.............	SAAB Club of North America [*Acronym is based on former name, SAAB Clubs of America*] (EA)
SCA.............	Saluki Club of America (EA)
SCA.............	Samoyed Club of America (EA)
SCA.............	Santa Cruz [*Argentina*] [*Seismograph station code, US Geological Survey*] [*Closed*] (SEIS)
SCA.............	Satellite Committee Agency [*Army*] (MCD)
SCA.............	Satellite Communications Agency [*Army*]
SCA.............	Save the Children Alliance [*Gentofte, Denmark*] (EAIO)
Sca.............	Scala [*Record label*]
Sca.............	Scandinavia [*A publication*]
SCA.............	Scarborough Public Library [*UTLAS symbol*]
SCA.............	Schedule Change Authorization [*NASA*] (NASA)
SCA.............	Schipperke Club of America (EA)
SCA.............	School and College Ability [*Test*] [*of ETS*]
SCA.............	Science Clubs of America (EA)
SCA.............	Science Fiction Classics Annual [*A publication*]
SCA.............	Scientific Computing and Automation
SCA.............	Scottish Courts Administration (ILCA)
SCA.............	Screen Composers of America (EA)
SCA.............	Sea Cadet Association (EAIO)
SCA.............	Sebright Club of America (EA)
SCA.............	Secondary Communications Authorization (IEEE)
SCA.............	Secondary Control Assembly [*Nuclear energy*] (NRCH)
SCA.............	Selectivity Clear Accumulator
SCA.............	Senior Citizens of America [*Defunct*] (EA)
SCA.............	Sequence Control Area [*NASA*] (KSC)
SCA.............	Sequencer Control Assembly
SCA.............	Service Cinematographique des Armees [*France*]
SCA.............	Service and Compliance Administration [*US wage/price controls agency*]
SCA.............	Service Contract Act [*1965*]
SCA.............	Service Cryptologic Agencies [*Military*]
SCA.............	Servo Corporation of America [*AMEX symbol*] (SPSG)
SCA.............	Sex Chromosome Abnormality
SCA.............	Shareholder Credit Accounting
SCA.............	Shields Class Association (EA)
SCA.............	Ship Constructive Association [*A union*] [*British*]
SCA.............	Ship Cost Adjustment [*Navy*]
SCA.............	Shipbuilders Council of America (EA)
SCA.............	Shipping Control Authority (NVT)
SCA.............	Shooters Club of America [*Defunct*]
SCA.............	Should Cost Analysis (MCD)
SCA.............	Shuttle Carrier Aircraft [*NASA*] (NASA)
SCA.............	Sickle Cell Anemia [*Medicine*]
SCA.............	Signal Conditioning Assembly [*NASA*] (KSC)
SCA.............	Simulated Core Assembly [*Nuclear energy*] (NRCH)
SCA.............	Simulation Control Area [*NASA*] (MCD)
SCA.............	Simulation Conversion Assembly [*Deep Space Instrumentation Facility, NASA*]
SCA.............	Single Channel Analyzer
SCA.............	Ski Council of America [*Defunct*] (EA)
SCA.............	Small-Caliber Ammunition (MSA)
SCA.............	Smithsonian Contributions to Anthropology [*A publication*]
SCA.............	Smithsonian Contributions to Astrophysics [*A publication*]
SCA.............	Smoke Control Association (EA)
SCA.............	Sneak Circuit Analysis [*NASA*] (NASA)
SCA.............	Societe Canadienne des Anesthesistes [*Canadian Anaesthetists' Society*] (EAIO)
SCA.............	Societe Canadienne d'Astronomie
SCA.............	Society of Canadian Artists [*Formerly, Society of Co-Operative Artists*]
SCA.............	Society of Cardiovascular Anesthesiologists (EA)
SCA.............	Society for Commercial Archeology (EA)
SCA.............	Society for Coptic Archaeology (EA)
SCA.............	Society for Creative Anachronism (EA)
SCA.............	Society for Cultural Anthropology (EA)
SCA.............	Software Control Authorization [*NASA*] (KSC)
SCA.............	Soldiers Christian Association [*British military*] (DMA)
SCA.............	Sonar Class Association
S Ca.............	South Carolina Reports [*A publication*] (DLA)
SCA.............	South Central Air, Inc. [*Kenai, AK*] [*FAA designator*] (FAAC)
SCA.............	Southern Communications Area [*Military*]
SCA.............	Southern Cotton Association (EA)
SCA.............	Soybean Council of America [*Defunct*] (EA)
SCA.............	Spacecraft Adapter [*NASA*] (KSC)

SCA............ SPALTRA [*Special Projects Alterations, Training*] Control Activity
SCA............ Specific Combining Ability
SCA............ Specification Compliance Agreement (MCD)
SCA............ Speech Communication Association (EA)
SCA............ Speed Coaches Association (EA)
SCA............ Sperm-Coating Antigen
SCA............ Spinach Carbonic Anhydrase [*An enzyme*]
SCA............ Standard Consolidated Area [*Bureau of Census*]
SCA............ Steel-Cored-Aluminium
SCA............ Sterba Curtain Antenna
SCA............ Stevengraph Collectors' Association (EA)
SCA............ Stock Company Association [*Defunct*] (EA)
SCA............ Stock Control Activity (AFIT)
SCA............ Student Conservation Association (EA)
SCA............ Subcarrier Authorization (MSA)
SCA............ Subcarrier Channel [*Telecommunications*]
SCA............ Subchannel Adapter
SCA............ Subcontract Authorization (AAG)
SCA............ Subcritical Assembly (DEN)
SCA............ Subsequent Coupons Attached
SCA............ Subsidiary Communications Authorization [*Facilities used to transmit background music to subscribing customers*]
SCA............ Summary Cost Account [*Military*] (AABC)
SCA............ Superior Cerebellar Artery [*Anatomy*]
SCA............ Support Centers of America [*An association*] (EA)
SCA............ Supreme Court Appeals [*India*] [*A publication*] (ILCA)
SCA............ Supreme and Exchequer Courts Act [*Canada*] (ILCA)
SCA............ Surface Coatings Abstracts [*Paint Research Association of Great Britain*] [*Bibliographic database*]
SCA............ Survey of Current Business [*Washington, DC*] [*A publication*]
SCA............ Swedish Council of America (EA)
SCA............ Switch Control Assembly
SCA............ Switzerland Cheese Association (EA)
SCA............ Sydney College of the Arts [*Australia*]
SCA............ Sydney Cricket Association [*Australia*]
SCA............ Synagogue Council of America (EA)
SCA............ Synchronous Communications Adapter
SCA............ System Comparison Analysis [*Bell System*]
SCA............ System Control Area
SCAA......... Skin Care Association of America (EA)
SCAA......... Specialty Coffee Association of America (EA)
SCAA......... Spill Control Association of America (EA)
SCAA......... Superconductor Applications Association (EA)
SCAA......... Sussex Cattle Association of America (EA)
SCAAN...... System for Computerized Application Analysis [*Automotive engineering*]
SCAAP...... Special Commonwealth African Assistance Plan
SCAAS...... Strategic Communication and Alerting System
SCAB......... Streptozocin, CCNU [*Lomustine*], Adriamycin, Bleomycin [*Antineoplastic drug regimen*]
SCABG...... Single Coronary Artery Bypass Graft [*Cardiology*]
SCAC......... Ancud/Pupelde [*Chile*] [*ICAO location identifier*] (ICLI)
Scac........... Scaccaria Curia [*Court of Exchequer*] [*Latin*] (DLA)
SCAC......... School and College Advisory Center [*Later, EGASCAC*] (EA)
SCAC......... Self-Cleaning Air Cleaner
SCAC......... Standard Carriers Alpha Code (MCD)
SC Acad Sci Bull ... South Carolina Academy of Science. Bulletin [*A publication*]
SC (ACT)... Supreme Court (Australian Capital Territory) (DLA)
SC Acts...... Acts and Joint Resolutions of the State of South Carolina [*A publication*] (DLA)
SCAD........ Savannah College of Art and Design [*Georgia*]
SCAD........ Scan Converter and Display [*Systems*]
SCAD........ Schenectady Army Depot (AABC)
SCAD........ Small Current Amplifying Device
SCAD........ Societe Canadienne pour l'Analyse de Documents [*Indexing and Abstracting Society of Canada*]
SCAD........ State Commission Against Discrimination
SCAD........ Strategic Bomber Penetration Decoy [*Air Force*]
SCAD........ Subsonic Cruise Armed Decoy [*Air Force*]
SCADA...... Student Coalition Against Drug Abuse
SCADA...... Supervisory Control and Data Acquisition (IEEE)
SCADAR... Scatter Detection and Ranging
SCADC...... Standard Central Air Data Computer
SCADEU... Scottish Adult Basic Education Unit
SCADS ..... SAS Census Access and Display System [*Information service or system*] (IID)
SCADS ..... Scanning Celestial Attitude Determination System
SCADS ..... Shipborne Containerized Air Defense System
SCADS ..... Simulation of Combined Analog Digital Systems [*Data processing*] (IEEE)
SCADS ..... Sioux City Air Defense Sector [*ADC*]
Sc Advocate ... Science Advocate [*A publication*]
SCAE........ Scottish Center for Agricultural Engineering
SCAE........ Scottish Centre of Agricultural Engineering [*United Kingdom*] (IRUK)
SCAE........ Society for Computer-Aided Engineering (EA)
SCAEC...... Submarine Contact Analysis and Evaluation Center (NVT)
SCAEF....... Supreme Commander, Allied Expeditionary Force [*World War II*]

Scaen Rom Frag ... Scaenicorum Romanorum Fragmenta [*A publication*] (OCD)
SCAEPA.... Society for Computer Applications in Engineering, Planning, and Architecture [*Later, CEPA*] (EA)
SCAF........ Self-Centered-Altruism Fad
SCAF........ Supersonic Cruise Attack Fighter (MCD)
SCAF........ Suppressor Cell Activating Factor [*Biochemistry*]
SCAF........ Supreme Commander of Allied Forces (ADA)
SCAF........ Surgical Care Affiliates, Inc. [*Nashville, TN*] [*NASDAQ symbol*] (NQ)
SCAFB...... Schilling Air Force Base (AAG)
SCAFEDS ... Space Construction Automated Fabrication Experiment Definition Study (MCD)
SCAG........ Saigon Civil Assistance Group [*Vietnam*]
SCAG........ Sandoz Clinical Assessment of Geriatrics [*Psychometrics*]
SCAG........ Southern California Association of Governments
SCAG........ Special COMSEC Advisory Group [*US Army Communications Command*] (MCD)
SCAG........ Standing Committee of Attorneys-General [*Australia*]
SC Ag Dept ... South Carolina. Department of Agriculture, Commerce, and Industries. Publications [*A publication*]
SC Ag Exp ... South Carolina. Agricultural Experiment Station. Publications [*A publication*]
SC Agric Exp Stn Bull ... South Carolina. Agricultural Experiment Station. Bulletin [*A publication*]
SC Agric Exp Stn Circ ... South Carolina. Agricultural Experiment Station. Circular [*A publication*]
SC Agric Exp Stn Tech Bull ... South Carolina. Agricultural Experiment Station. Technical Bulletin [*A publication*]
SC Agr Res ... South Carolina Agricultural Research [*A publication*]
SCAHR...... School of Community and Allied Health Resources
ScAi .... Aiken-Bamberg-Barnwell-Edgefield Regional Library, Aiken, SC [*Library symbol*] [*Library of Congress*] (LCLS)
SCAI......... Societe des Comptables en Administration Industrielle du Canada
SCA & I.... Society for Cardiac Angiography and Interventions (EA)
ScAiD .... E. I. Du Pont de Nemours & Co., Aiken, SC [*Library symbol*] [*Library of Congress*] (LCLS)
SCAIF........ Sertoli-Cell Androgenic Inhibitory Factor [*Endocrinology*]
SCAJAP.... Shipping Control Administrator Japan
SCAL........ Silver City Airways Limited
SCAL........ Skin Diver Contact Air Lenses
SCAL........ STAR [*Self Testing and Reporting*] Computer Assembly Language
SCALA ...... Society of Chief Architects of Local Authorities [*British*]
S Cal Ac Sc B ... Southern California Academy of Sciences. Bulletin [*A publication*]
SCALD...... Structural Computer-Aided Logic Design
SCALE ...... Scales of Creativity and Learning Environment [*Educational test*]
SCALE ...... Space Checkout and Launch Equipment
SCALE ...... Supreme Court Almanac [*India*] [*A publication*]
SCALER.... Statistical Calculation and Analysis of Engine Removal [*Navy*]
S Calif Law Rev ... Southern California Law Review [*A publication*]
S Cal Law R ... Southern California Law Review [*A publication*]
S Cal L Rev ... Southern California Law Review [*A publication*]
SCALO...... Scanning Local Oscillator (NG)
SCALP....... Students Concerned about Legal Prices [*Student legal action organization*]
S CA LR..... Southern California Law Review [*A publication*]
SCALRA ... Scottish Adult Literacy Resource Agency
Scam .... Scammon's Reports [*2-5 Illinois*] [*A publication*] (DLA)
Sc Am .... Scientific American [*A publication*]
SCAM........ Selection Classification Age Maturity Program [*Medical screening procedure for athletes*]
SCAM........ Soil Classification and Mapping Branch [*Department of Agriculture*] (IID)
SCAM........ Spectrum Characteristics Analysis and Measurement [*FAA*]
SCAM........ Standing Conference for Amateur Music [*British*]
SCAM........ Station Control and Monitoring
SCAM........ Strike Camera (MCD)
SCAM........ Study Course in Agency Management [*LIMRA*]
SCAM........ Subsonic Cruise Armed Missile/Decoy [*Air Force*] (MCD)
SCAM........ Synchronous Communications Access Method
SCAMA..... Scientific American [*A publication*]
SCAMA..... Service Central des Approvisionements et Materiels Americains [*Central Office of American Supplies and Equipment*] [*World War II*]
SCAMA..... Skewed Circular Arc Method of Analysis
SCAMA..... Station Conferencing and Monitoring Arrangement [*NASA*]
SCAMA..... Switching, Conferencing, and Monitoring Arrangement [*NASA*]
SCAMC..... Symposium on Computer Applications in Medical Care [*Baltimore, MD*]
SCAM/D... Subsonic Cruise Armed Missile/Decoy [*Air Force*]
SCAMP..... Sectionalized Carrier and Multipurpose Vehicle [*Military*]
SCAMP..... Self-Contained Airborne Multipurpose Pod (MCD)
SCAMP..... Self-Contained Ancillary Modular Platform [*Woods Hole Oceanographic Institution*]
SCAMP..... Self-Propelled Crane for Aircraft Maintenance and Positioning (MCD)
SCAMP..... Sensor Control and Management Platoon [*Marine Corps*]

SCAMP..... Signal Conditioning Amplifier
SCAMP..... Single Channel Amplitude Monopulse Processing
SCAMP..... Small-Caliber Ammunition Modernization Program
    [*Army*] (RDA)
SCAMP..... Space-Controlled Army Measurements Probe
SCAMP..... Sperry Computer-Aided Message Processor [*British*]
SCAMP..... Standard Configuration and Modification Program [*Military*]
SCAMP..... Succinyl CAMP [*Biochemistry*]
SCAMP..... Summer Campus, Advanced Mathematics Program [*Institute*
    for Defense Analysis]
SCAMPERS ... Standard Corps-Army-MACOM [*Major Army Command*]
    Personnel System (AABC)
SCAMPS... Small Computer Analytical and Mathematical Programming
    System (IEEE)
SCAMPTME ... Succinyl CAMP Tyrosine Methyl Ester [*Biochemistry*]
SCAMS..... Scanning Microwave Spectrometer
Sc Am Sup ... Scientific American. Supplement [*A publication*]
ScAn........... Anderson County Library, Anderson, SC [*Library symbol*]
    [*Library of Congress*] (LCLS)
SCAN .... Satellite Cable Audio Networks [*Cable-television service*]
SCAN .... Savings Comparative Analysis [*Federal Home Loan Bank*
    Board] [*Database*]
SCAN .... Scandinavian
Scan .... Scandinavian Studies [*A publication*]
Scan .... Scandinavica [*A publication*]
SCAN .... Scanfile [*Database*] [*Australia*] (ADA)
SCAN .... Scanner Association of North America (EA)
SCAN .... Scintiscan [*Medicine*]
SCAN .... Screening Test for Identifying Central Auditory Disorders
SCAN .... Seismic Computerized Alert Network [*For warning of an*
    earthquake]
SCAN .... Selected Current Aerospace Notices [*NASA*]
SCAN .... Self-Correcting Automatic Navigator
SCAN .... Seniors Cooperative Alert Network [*An association*] (EA)
SCAN .... Service Center Advantage Network [*Federal-Mogul Corp.*]
SCAN .... Service Center for Aging Information [*Department of Health*
    and Human Services] [*Information service or*
    system] (IID)
SCAN .... Short Current Abstracts and Notes (DIT)
SCAN .... Signal Corps Administrative Network [*Obsolete*] [*Army*]
SCAN .... Silent Communication Alarm Network [*NASA*]
SCAN .... Small Computers in the Arts Network (EA)
SCAN .... Southern California Answering Network [*Los Angeles Public*
    Library] [*Information service or system*]
SCAN .... Spares Change Advance Notice (MCD)
SCAN .... State of California Answering Network [*Information service or*
    system] (EISS)
SCAN .... Stock Control and Analysis (BUR)
SCAN .... Stock Market Computer Answering Network [*British*]
SCAN .... Student Career Automated Network (IEEE)
SCAN .... Sufferers of Compulsive Anxiety Neurosis [*Australia*]
SCAN .... Suspected Child Abuse and Neglect
SCAN .... Switched Circuit Automatic Network [*Army*]
SCAN .... System for Collection and Analysis of Near-Collision
    Reports (AAG)
SCANA...... Self-Contained Adverse-Weather Night Attack
SCAND ..... Scandinavia
Scand .... Scandinavica [*A publication*]
SCAND ..... Single Crystal Automatic Neutron Diffractometer
Scand Actuar J ... Scandinavian Actuarial Journal [*A publication*]
SCANDAL ... Select Committee to Arrange a New Deal to Avoid Litigation
    [*Toledo, OH, group formed in 1973 to humorously protest*
    results of the Michigan-Toledo "War of 1835"] [*See also*
    FAT CHANCE]
Scand Audiol ... Scandinavian Audiology [*A publication*]
Scand Audiol Suppl ... Scandinavian Audiology. Supplement [*A publication*]
Scand Ec Hist Rev ... Scandinavian Economic History Review [*A publication*]
Scand Econ Hist Rev ... Scandinavian Economic History Review [*A*
    publication]
SCANDEFA ... Scandinavian Dental Fair [*Danish Dental*
    Association] (TSPED)
SCANDI.... Surveillance Control and Driver Information [*Traffic system*]
Scandinavian Econ Hist R ... Scandinavian Economic History Review [*A*
    publication]
Scandinavian Publ Libr Q ... Scandinavian Public Library Quarterly [*A*
    publication]
Scandinavian R ... Scandinavian Review [*A publication*]
Scandinav J Clin Lab Invest ... Scandinavian Journal of Clinical and
    Laboratory Investigation [*A publication*]
Scandinav J Econ ... Scandinavian Journal of Economics [*A publication*]
Scandinav J Gastroent ... Scandinavian Journal of Gastroenterology [*A*
    publication]
Scandinav J Haemat ... Scandinavian Journal of Haematology [*A publication*]
Scandinav J Resp Dis ... Scandinavian Journal of Respiratory Diseases [*A*
    publication]
Scand J Behav Ther ... Scandinavian Journal of Behaviour Therapy [*A*
    publication]
Scand J Clin Lab Inv ... Scandinavian Journal of Clinical and Laboratory
    Investigation [*A publication*]
Scand J Clin Lab Invest ... Scandinavian Journal of Clinical and Laboratory
    Investigation [*A publication*]

Scand J Clin Lab Invest Suppl ... Scandinavian Journal of Clinical and
    Laboratory Investigation. Supplement [*A publication*]
Scand J Dent Res ... Scandinavian Journal of Dental Research [*A publication*]
Scand J Econ ... Scandinavian Journal of Economics [*A publication*]
Scand J For Res ... Scandinavian Journal of Forest Research [*A publication*]
Scand J Gastroenterol ... Scandinavian Journal of Gastroenterology [*A*
    publication]
Scand J Gastroenterol Suppl ... Scandinavian Journal of Gastroenterology.
    Supplement [*A publication*]
Scand J Haematol ... Scandinavian Journal of Haematology [*A publication*]
Scand J Haematol Suppl ... Scandinavian Journal of Haematology.
    Supplement [*A publication*]
Scand J Haematol Suppl Ser Haematol ... Scandinavian Journal of
    Haematology. Supplement. Series Haematological [*A*
    publication]
Scand J Immunol ... Scandinavian Journal of Immunology [*A publication*]
Scand J Immunol Suppl ... Scandinavian Journal of Immunology. Supplement
    [*A publication*]
Scand J Infect Dis ... Scandinavian Journal of Infectious Diseases [*A*
    publication]
Scand J Infect Dis Suppl ... Scandinavian Journal of Infectious Diseases.
    Supplement [*A publication*]
Scand J Metall ... Scandinavian Journal of Metallurgy [*A publication*]
Scand J Plast Reconstr Surg ... Scandinavian Journal of Plastic and
    Reconstructive Surgery [*A publication*]
Scand J Plast Reconstr Surg Suppl ... Scandinavian Journal of Plastic and
    Reconstructive Surgery. Supplement [*A publication*]
Scand J Plast Recon Surg ... Scandinavian Journal of Plastic and
    Reconstructive Surgery [*A publication*]
Scand J Prim Health Care ... Scandinavian Journal of Primary Health Care [*A*
    publication]
Scand J Psychol ... Scandinavian Journal of Psychology [*A publication*]
Scand J Rehabil Med ... Scandinavian Journal of Rehabilitation Medicine [*A*
    publication]
Scand J Rehabil Med Suppl ... Scandinavian Journal of Rehabilitation
    Medicine. Supplement [*A publication*]
Scand J Rehab Med ... Scandinavian Journal of Rehabilitation Medicine [*A*
    publication]
Scand J Respir Dis ... Scandinavian Journal of Respiratory Diseases [*A*
    publication]
Scand J Respir Dis Suppl ... Scandinavian Journal of Respiratory Diseases.
    Supplement [*A publication*]
Scand J Rheumatol ... Scandinavian Journal of Rheumatology [*A publication*]
Scand J Rheumatol Suppl ... Scandinavian Journal of Rheumatology.
    Supplement [*A publication*]
Scand J Soc Med ... Scandinavian Journal of Social Medicine [*A publication*]
Scand J Soc Med Suppl ... Scandinavian Journal of Social Medicine.
    Supplement [*A publication*]
Scand J St ... Scandinavian Journal of Statistics [*A publication*]
Scand J Statist ... Scandinavian Journal of Statistics. Theory and Applications
    [*A publication*]
Scand J Stat Theory and Appl ... Scandinavian Journal of Statistics. Theory
    and Applications [*A publication*]
Scand J Thorac Cardiovasc Surg ... Scandinavian Journal of Thoracic and
    Cardiovascular Surgery [*A publication*]
Scand J Thorac Cardiovasc Surg Suppl ... Scandinavian Journal of Thoracic
    and Cardiovascular Surgery. Supplement
Scand J Urol Nephrol ... Scandinavian Journal of Urology and Nephrology [*A*
    publication]
Scand J Urol Nephrol Suppl ... Scandinavian Journal of Urology and
    Nephrology. Supplement [*A publication*]
Scand J Work Envir Hlth ... Scandinavian Journal of Work Environment and
    Health [*A publication*]
Scand J Work Environ Health ... Scandinavian Journal of Work Environment
    and Health [*A publication*]
SCANDOC ... Scandinavian Documentation Center [*Washington, DC*]
Scand Oil-Gas Mag ... Scandinavian Oil-Gas Magazine [*A publication*]
Scand Paint Printing Ink Res Inst Rept ... Scandinavian Paint and Printing
    Ink Research Institute. Reports [*A publication*]
Scand Polit St ... Scandinavian Political Studies [*A publication*]
Scand Pol Stud ... Scandinavian Political Studies [*A publication*]
Scand Public Lib Q ... Scandinavian Public Library Quarterly [*A publication*]
Scand Publ Libr Q ... Scandinavian Public Library Quarterly [*A publication*]
Scand R...... Scandinavian Review [*A publication*]
Scand Refrig ... Scandinavian Refrigeration [*Norway*] [*A publication*]
Scand Stud ... Scandinavian Studies [*A publication*]
Scand Stud Criminol ... Scandinavian Studies in Criminology [*A*
    publication] (DLA)
Scand Stud in L ... Scandinavian Studies in Law [*A publication*]
Scand Stud Law ... Scandinavian Studies in Law [*A publication*]
Scand Stud No ... Scandinavian Studies and Notes [*A publication*]
Scand Yb.... Scandinavian Yearbook [*A publication*]
Scan Electron Microsc ... Scanning Electron Microscopy [*A publication*]
SCANIIR... Surface Composition by Analysis of Neutral and Ion Impact
    Radiation [*Qualitative analysis*]
Scan J Sports Sci ... Scandinavian Journal of Sports Sciences [*A publication*]
Scan J Stat ... Scandinavian Journal of Statistics. Theory and Applications [*A*
    publication]
SCanL........ Studies in Canadian Literature [*A publication*]
SCAN MAG ... Scandalum Magnatum [*Defamation of Dignity*]
    [*Latin*] (ROG)

Scanning Electron Microsc ... Scanning Electron Microscopy [*A publication*]
SCANO ..... Automatic Scanning Unit Inoperative [*Aviation*] (FAAC)
SCANP ...... Scandinavian Periodicals Index in Economics and Business [*Helsinki School of Economics Library*] [*Information service or system*]
Scan R .... Scandinavian Review [*A publication*]
SCANS ...... Scheduling and Control by Automated Network System
SCANS ...... System Checkout Automatic Network Simulator
SCANSAR ... Scanning Synthetic Aperture RADAR
Scan Soc Forensic Odontol Newsl ... Scandinavian Society of Forensic Odontology. Newsletter [*A publication*]
SCAN-Test ... Scandinavian Pulp, Paper, and Board Testing Committee (EAIO)
SCAO .... Senior Civil Affairs Officer
SCAO .... Standing Committee on Army Organization [*British*]
SCAO .... Standing Conference of Atlantic Organisations [*London, England*] (EAIO)
SCAOK ...... Automatic Scanning Unit Operative [*Aviation*] (FAAC)
SCAO(P) ... Senior Civil Affairs Office, Police [*British*]
SCAP .... Alto Palena/Alto Palena [*Chile*] [*ICAO location identifier*] (ICLI)
SCAP .... Service Center Audit Program [*IRS*]
SCAP .... Silent Compact Auxiliary Power
SCAP .... Silicon Capacitance Absolute Pressure Sensor
SCAP .... Slow Component Axonal Particulate [*Neurology*]
SCAP .... Small Communications Augmentation Package (MCD)
SCAP .... Space Charge Atomizing Precipitaters (KSC)
SCAP .... Supreme Commander, Allied Powers [*World War II*] (MUGU)
SCAP .... Svenska Cellulosa Aktiebolaget [*Sundsvall, Sweden*] [*NASDAQ symbol*] (NQ)
SCAP .... Systems Concepts and Procedures
SCAPA ...... Society for Checking the Abuses of Public Advertising [*British*]
SCAPE ...... Self-Contained Atmospheric Personnel [*or Protective*] Ensemble [*Suit*] [*Aerospace*]
SCAPE ...... System Compatibility and Performance Evaluation [*Military*] (CAAL)
SCAPS ...... Small Capitals [*Typography*]
SCAR .... Arica/Internacional Chacalluta [*Chile*] [*ICAO location identifier*] (ICLI)
SCAR .... Satellite Capture and Retrieval (AFM)
SCAR .... Scandinavian Council for Applied Research
SCAR .... Scandinavian Review [*A publication*]
scar .... Scarlet [*Philately*]
SCAR .... Scientific Committee on Antarctic Research [*ICSU*] [*Cambridge, England*] (EAIO)
SCAR .... Signal Conditioner Assembly Request (MCD)
S Car .... South Carolina Reports [*A publication*] (DLA)
SCAR .... Spacecraft Assessment Report [*NASA*] (KSC)
SCAR .... Special Committee on Antarctic Research [*Australia*]
SCAR .... Special Committee on Atlantic Research
SCAR .... Special Committee on Atomic Research [*Pugwash Conference*]
SCAR .... Special International Committee on Antarctic Research
SCAR .... Status Control Alert and Reporting (MCD)
SCAR .... Strike Control and Reconnaissance [*Aircraft*]
SCAR .... Structure-Carcinogenic Activity Relationship [*Biochemistry*]
SCAR .... Subcaliber Aircraft Rocket
SCAR .... Submarine Celestial Altitude Recorder [*Navy*]
SCAR .... Subsequent Contrast Application Review (MCD)
SCAR .... Supersonic Cruise Aircraft [*or Airplane*] Research [*NASA*]
SCAR .... Supplier Corrective Action Request
SCARA ...... Selective Compliance Assembly Robot Arm [*IBM Corp.*]
SCARAB ... Submersible Craft Assisting Repair and Burial [*Autonomous underwater vehicle*]
Scarabot ...... [*Arnaldus*] Scaraboti [*Flourished, 1310-35*] [*Authority cited in pre-1607 legal work*] (DSA)
Scarborough Dist Archaeol Soc Res Rep ... Scarborough District Archaeological Society. Research Reports [*A publication*]
SCARDE ... Study Committee on Analysis of Research, Development, and Engineering
SCARE ...... Structural Ceramic Analysis and Reliability Evaluation [*NASA*]
SCAReU .... Stanford Community Against Reagan University [*Group opposed to proposed Ronald Reagan presidential library at Stanford University*]
SCARF ...... Santa Cruz Acoustic Range Facility [*Navy*]
SCARF ...... Self-Contained Automated Robotic Factory
SCARF ...... Side-Looking Coherent All-Range Focused
SCARF ...... Special Committee on the Adequacy of Range Facilities (MUGU)
SCARF ...... Survey of Change and Residential Finance [*Census Bureau*]
SCARF ...... System Control Audit Review File [*Data processing*]
SCARP ...... Society for Comic Art Research and Preservation
S Car R ...... South Carolina Law Reports [*A publication*] (DLA)
SCARS ...... SACEUR [*Supreme Allied Commander, Europe*] Command Alerting Reporting System [*Army*]
SCARS ...... Serialized Control and Record [*or Reporting*] System (NASA)
SCARS ...... Software Configuration Accounting and Reporting System
SCARS ...... Southern's Computer-Assisted Retrieval Service [*University of Southern Mississippi*] (OLDSS)
SCARS ...... Status Control Alert Reporting System (NATG)
SCARS ...... System Control and Receiving Station [*Air Force*]
SCART ...... Sperry Continuity and Resistance Tester

SCARWAF ... Special Category Army with Air Force
SCAS .... Signal Corps Aviation School [*Obsolete*] [*Army*]
SCAS .... Society for Companion Animal Studies (EAIO)
SCAS .... Southwest Center for Advanced Studies [*Later, University of Texas at Dallas*]
SCAS .... Stability Control Augmentation System (NVT)
SCAS .... State Cost Accounting System (OICC)
SCAS .... Subsystem Computer Application Software (MCD)
SCASG ...... SONAR Calibration and Alignment Steering Group
SCASH ...... Scottish Committee Action on Smoking and Health (EAIO)
SCASS ...... Signal Corps Aircraft Signal Service [*Obsolete*] [*Army*]
Sc As Trinidad Pr ... Scientific Association of Trinidad. Proceedings [*A publication*]
SCAT .... Scat Hovercraft, Inc. [*Miami, FL*] [*NASDAQ symbol*] (NQ)
SCAT .... Scatterometer
SCAT .... Scatula [*Package*] [*Pharmacy*]
SCAT .... School and College Ability Test [*of ETS*]
SCAT .... Schottky Cell Array Technology
SCAT .... Scout-Attack [*Helicopter*] (MCD)
SCAT .... Security Control of Air Traffic [*FAA*]
SCAT .... Selected Calibration and Alignment Test (MCD)
SCAT .... Self-Contained Automatic Transmitter (MCD)
SCAT .... Sequential Component Automatic Testing (MSA)
SCAT .... Service Code Automatic Tester [*Automotive engineering*]
SCAT .... Service Command Air Transportation
SCAT .... Share Compiler-Assembler, Translator
SCAT .... Sheep Cell Agglutination Test
SCAT .... Small Car Automatic Transit [*System*]
SCAT .... Solid Catalysts (KSC)
SCAT .... Solution to Customer Aircraft Troubles (MCD)
SCAT .... South Pacific Combat Air Transport [*World War II*]
SCAT .... Space Communications and Tracking
SCAT .... Special Advisory Committee on Telecommunications
SCAT .... Speed Command Attitude/Target [*FAA*]
SCAT .... Speed Control Approach/Takeoff
SCAT .... Sperry Canada Automatic Tester
SCAT .... State Change Algorithm Translator
SCAT .... Storage, Checkout, and Transportation [*Rack*] [*Aerospace*]
SCAT .... Submarine Classification and Tracking
SCAT .... Supersonic Commercial Air Transport [*NASA*]
SCAT .... Surface-Controlled Avalanche Transistor
SCAT .... Systems Consolidation of Accessions and Trainees [*Military*] (AABC)
SCATA ...... Survival Sited Casualty Treatment Assemblage (AFM)
SCATANA ... Security Control of Air Traffic and Air Navigation Aids [*FAA*]
SCATE ...... Self-Checking Automatic Testing Equipment
SCATE ...... Space Chamber Analyzer - Thermal Environment [*NASA*]
SCATE ...... Stromberg-Carlson Automatic Test Equipment
SCATER .... Security Control of Air Traffic and Electromagnetic Radiations [*During an air defense emergency*] [*FAA*]
Scates' Comp St ... Treat, Scates, and Blackwell's Compiled Illinois Statutes [*A publication*] (DLA)
SCATHA .... Spacecraft Charging at High Altitudes [*Satellite*]
SCathol ...... Studia Catholica [*A publication*]
SCAT ORIG ... Scatula Originalis [*Original Package*] [*Pharmacy*]
SCATS ...... Scheduling and Tracking System (MCD)
SCATS ...... Self-Contained Automatic Test System
SCATS ...... Sequentially Controlled Automatic Transmitter Start
SCATS ...... Simulation, Checkout, and Training System
SCATS ...... Simulation Control and Training System (NASA)
SCATT ...... Scientific Communication and Technology Transfer [*System*] [*University of Pennsylvania*]
SCATT ...... Shared Catalog Accessed Through Terminals [*Data processing system*]
SCAUA ...... Scientific Australian [*A publication*]
SCauc .... Studia Caucasica [*A publication*]
SCAUL ...... Standing Conference of African University Libraries [*Lagos, Nigeria*]
SCAULWA ... Standing Conference of African University Libraries (EAIO)
SCA(UN)... Department of Security Council Affairs of the United Nations
Scaur .... Pro Scauro [*of Cicero*] [*Classical studies*] (OCD)
SCAV .... Scavenge (AAG)
SCAW .... Scientists' Center for Animal Welfare (EA)
SCAW .... Subcommittee on Animal Welfare [*Animal Health Committee*] [*Australia*]
SCAW .... Supreme Camp of the American Woodmen (EA)
SCAWD ..... Scottish Churches Action for World Development (EAIO)
SCAWH-SAWRH ... Signal Company Aircraft Warning Hawaii - Signal Aircraft Warning Regiment Hawaii Association (EA)
SCAWNA ... Self-Contained Adverse-Weather Night Attack (MCD)
SCAWU ..... Singapore Clerical and Administrative Workers' Union
Sc Azione ... Scuola in Azione [*A publication*]
Sc B .... Bachelor of Science
ScB .... Beaufort County Library, Beaufort, SC [*Library symbol*] [*Library of Congress*] (LCLS)
SCB .... Sample Collection Bag [*NASA*]
SCB .... Scarborough [*Ontario*] [*Seismograph station code, US Geological Survey*] [*Closed*] (SEIS)
SCB .... Schedule Change Board [*NASA*] (NASA)
SCB .... Scholarly Book Center [*ACCORD*] [*UTLAS symbol*]
SCB .... School of Classical Ballet [*American Ballet Theater Foundation*

Sc B............ Scientiae Baccalaureus [*Bachelor of Science*] [*Latin*]
SCB............ Scorpion Resources [*Vancouver Stock Exchange symbol*]
SCB............ Scribner, NE [*Location identifier*] [*FAA*]   (FAAL)
SCB............ Secondary Carpet Backing
SCB............ Segment Control BIT [*Binary Digit*]
SCB............ Selection Control Board [*NASA*]   (NASA)
SCB............ Selector Control Box [*Aerospace*]   (MCD)
SCB............ Session Control Block [*Data processing*]   (BUR)
SCB............ Ship Characteristics Board
SCB............ Shipowners Claims Bureau [*New York, NY*]   (EA)
SCB............ Ships Characteristics Board
SCB............ Ship's Cook, Butcher [*Navy*]
SCB............ Silicon Cell Bridge
SCB............ Silicon Circuit Board
SCB............ Silver Cadmium Battery
SCB............ Society for Conservation Biology   (EA)
SCB............ Soeurs de la Charite de Besancon [*Sisters of Charity*]   (EAIO)
SCB............ Software Control Board [*Apollo*] [*NASA*]
SCB............ South Central Bulletin [*A publication*]
SCB............ South China Block [*Geology*]
SCB............ Specification Control Board [*NASA*]   (NASA)
SCB............ Stack Control Block
SCB............ Station Control Block [*Data processing*]   (IBMDP)
SCB............ Statistiska Centralbyran [*Statistics Sweden*] [*Stockholm*] [*Information service or system*]   (IID)
SCB............ Strictly Confined to Bed [*Medicine*]
SCB............ Studii si Cercetari de Bibliologie [*A publication*]
SCB............ Survey of Current Business [*United States*] [*A publication*]
SCBA......... Balmaceda/Balmaceda [*Chile*] [*ICAO location identifier*]   (ICLI)
ScBa........... Lexington County Circulating Library, Batesburg, SC [*Library symbol*] [*Library of Congress*]   (LCLS)
SCBA......... Self-Contained Breathing Apparatus
SCBA......... Supreme Circle Brotherhood of America   (EA)
SCBAL...... Standard Chartered Bank Australia Ltd.   (ADA)
Sc BAM.... Bachelor of Science in Applied Mathematics
SC in Banco ... Supreme Court in Banco [*Canada*] [*A publication*]   (DLA)
S & C Bank ... Standard and Chartered Review [*Formerly, Standard Bank Review*] [*Later, Standard Chartered Review*] [*A publication*]
Sc BC .... Bachelor of Science in Chemistry
SCBCA...... Small Claims Board of Contract Appeals
SCBD......... Scan Conversion and Bright Display
SCBD......... Seller's Approved Configuration Baseline Document [*NASA*]   (NASA)
Sc BE .... Bachelor of Science in Engineering
SCBE......... Societe Canadienne des Brevets et d'Exploitation
SCBF .... Sacred Cat of Burma Fanciers   (EA)
SCBF .... Spinal Cord Blood Flow
SCBL .... Quilpue/Mil el Belloto [*Chile*] [*ICAO location identifier*]   (ICLI)
SCBL .... Scotts Bluff and Agate Fossil Beds National Monuments
SCBNP...... Society for the Collection of Brand-Name Pencils [*Inactive*]   (EA)
SCBOA...... Studii si Cercetari de Biologie. Seria Botanica [*A publication*]
Sc BP .... Bachelor of Science in Physics
SCBQ......... Santiago/Mil el Bosque [*Chile*] [*ICAO location identifier*]   (ICLI)
SCBR........ Serum Cholesterol-Binding Reserve [*Medicine*]
SCBR......... Stationary Catalytic Basket Reactor [*Chemical engineering*]
SCBR......... Steam-Cooled Breeder Reactor [*Nuclear energy*]
SCBS .... Saint Charles Borromeo Seminary [*Pennsylvania*]
SCBS .... Society for the Conservation of Bighorn Sheep   (EA)
SC/BSE ..... Scientific Co-Operation Bureau for the European and North American Region [*United Nations*]   (EA)
SCBT .... Society of Computed Body Tomography   (EA)
SCBU......... Special Care Baby Unit [*Medicine*]
SCBUB...... Sierra Club. Bulletin [*A publication*]
SCBUB8 .... Sierra Club. Bulletin [*A publication*]
SCBW .... Society of Children's Book Writers   (EA)
SCBZA ...... Studii si Cercetari de Biologie. Seria Zoologie [*A publication*]
SCC............ Cameron's Supreme Court Cases [*Canada*] [*A publication*]   (DLA)
ScC............ Charleston Library Society, Charleston, SC [*Library symbol*] [*Library of Congress*]   (LCLS)
SCC............ Deadhorse [*Alaska*] [*Airport symbol*]   (OAG)
SCC............ Deadhorse, AK [*Location identifier*] [*FAA*]   (FAAL)
SCC............ Sacra Congregatio Concilii [*Sacred Congregation of the Council*] [*Latin*]
SCC............ Safety Control Center   (NASA)
SCC............ SAGE [*Semiautomatic Ground Environment*] Control Center
SCC............ Salivary Caffeine Clearance [*Physiology*]
SCC............ Santa Cruz [*California*] [*Seismograph station code, US Geological Survey*] [*Closed*]   (SEIS)
SCC............ Satellite Communication Concentrator
SCC............ Satellite Communications Controller
SCC............ Satellite Control Center
SCC............ Satellite-Controlled Clock
SCC............ Scandinavian Collectors Club   (EA)
SCC............ Scarborough Campus, University of Toronto [*UTLAS symbol*]
SCC............ Schools Councils Classics Committee [*British*]

SCC............ Science Council of Canada
SCC............ Science Fiction Chronicle [*A publication*]
SCC............ Sea Cadet Corps [*Navy*] [*British*]
SCC............ Sears Canada, Inc. [*Toronto Stock Exchange symbol*]
SCC............ Secondary Containment Cooling   (IEEE)
SCC............ Security Capital Corporation [*AMEX symbol*]   (SPSG)
SCC............ Security Commodity Code   (AAG)
SCC............ Security Control Center [*NASA*]   (KSC)
SCC............ Security Coordination Committee   (NATG)
SCC............ Select Cases in Chancery [*Legal*] [*British*]
SCC............ Select Cases in Chancery Tempore King, Edited by Macnaghten [*England*] [*A publication*]   (DLA)
SCC............ Self-Contained Canister   (MCD)
SCC............ Senate Children's Caucus   (EA)
SCC............ Senate Copper Caucus   (EA)
SCC............ Senior Command Course [*British military*]   (DMA)
SCC............ Sequence Control Chart
SCC............ Sequential Control Counter [*Data processing*]   (BUR)
scc .... Serbo-Croatian (Cyrillic) [*MARC language code*] [*Library of Congress*]   (LCCP)
SCC............ Serial Communications Controller
SCC............ Service Change Committee [*Military*]
SCC............ Services for Crippled Children
SCC............ Servo Control Cabinet [*Military*]   (CAAL)
SCC............ Set Conditionally [*Data processing*]
SCC............ Sexual Concerns Checklist [*Premarital and marital relations test*]
SCC............ Ship Control Center
SCC............ Short-Circuit Current
SCC............ Short-Course Chemotherapy [*Medicine*]
SCC............ Signaling Conversion Circuit [*Telecommunications*]   (TEL)
SCC............ Simplified Computer Code
SCC............ Simulation Control Center [*NASA*]   (KSC)
SCC............ Single Conductor Cable   (MSA)
SCC............ Single Copy Complexity [*Genetics*]
SCC............ Single Cotton-Covered [*Wire insulation*]
SCC............ Slidell Computer Complex [*NASA*] [*Slidell, LA*]
SCC............ Small Cause Court [*India*]   (DLA)
SCC............ Small Cell Cancer [*Oncology*]
SCC............ Small Center Contact
SCC............ Small Compressor Colorimeter   (MCD)
SCC............ Societe Canadienne de Cardiologie [*Canadian Cardiovascular Society*]   (EAIO)
SCC............ Societe Canadienne de Criminologie
SCC............ Societe Chimique des Charbonnages [*France*]
SCC............ Society for Children with Craniosynostosis   (EA)
SCC............ Society for the Christian Commonwealth
SCC............ Society of Cosmetic Chemists   (EA)
SCC............ Soeurs de la Croix de Chavanod [*Sisters of the Cross of Chavanod*] [*Chavanod, France*]   (EAIO)
SCC............ Software Checkout Console [*Army*]
SCC............ Source Classification Code [*Environmental Protection Agency*]
SCC............ Southern Connecticut State College, Division of Library Science, New Haven, CT [*OCLC symbol*]   (OCLC)
SCC............ Spacecraft Control Center [*NASA*]   (KSC)
SCC............ Spanish Chamber of Commerce   (DS)
SCC............ Spark Control Computer [*Automotive engineering*]
SCC............ Special Coordinating Committee [*National Security Council*] [*Terminated, 1981*]
SCC............ Specialized Common Carrier [*Telecommunications*]   (NRCH)
SCC............ Specific Clauses and Conditions   (NATG)
SCC............ Splenium of the Corpus Callosum [*Anatomy*]
SCC............ Squadron Control Center   (AAG)
SCC............ Squamous Cell Carcinoma [*Also, SC*] [*Medicine*]
SCC............ Standard Commodity Classification [*Military*]
SCC............ Standard Commodity Codes   (MCD)
SCC............ Standard Consultative Commission [*for resolving compliance disputes arising from SALT 1 accord*]
SCC............ Standard Cubic Centimeter   (KSC)
SCC............ Standardized Cost Categories
SCC............ Standards Council of Canada [*See also CCNO*]
SCC............ Standing Consultative Commission [*SALT agreements*] [*US/USSR*]
SCC............ Standing Interdepartmental Committee on Censorship [*War Cabinet*] [*British*]
SCC............ Starcraft Campers Club   (EA)
SCC............ State Coordination Committee [*Responsible for administering the Work Incentive Program at the state level*]
SCC............ State Corporation Commission
SCC............ Steel Carriers Conference [*Later, RDCC*] [*An association*]   (EA)
SCC............ Stock Clearing Corporation [*NYSE*]
SCC............ Stock Control Center [*Army*]
SCC............ Storage Connecting Circuit [*Teletype*]
SCC............ Strategic Communications Command [*Army*]   (MCD)
SCC............ Stress Corrosion Cracking [*Metals*]
SCC............ Student of Codrington College [*Barbados*]
SCC............ Studies in Comparative Communism [*A publication*]
SCC............ Studio Collector's Club   (EA)
SC(C).......... Submarine Chaser (Control) [*110 foot*] [*Obsolete*]
SCC............ Submission Control Code   (MCD)

SCC............ Sunbeam Car Club (EA)
SCC............ Suore della Carita Cristiana [*Sisters of Christian Charity*] [*Rome, Italy*] (EAIO)
SCC............ Supervisor Control Console
SCC............ Supervisory Control Conference (KSC)
SCC............ Supply Control Center [*Military*]
SCC............ Supreme Court of Canada
SCC............ Supreme Court Cases [*India*] [*A publication*] (DLA)
SCC............ Supreme Court Circular [*Ceylon*] [*A publication*] (ILCA)
SCCO............ Surveillance Coordination Center (NATG)
SCC............ Switching Control Center [*Bell System*]
SCC............ Synchronous Communications Controller
SCC............ Syndicat des Communications Canada
SCC............ System Command Center (FAAC)
SCC............ System Communication Controller
SCC............ System Coordinate Center [*Military*] (CAAL)
SCC............ Systems Control Center
SCCA......... Single Cell Cytotoxicity Assay [*Clinical chemistry*]
SCCA......... Society of Canadian Cine Amateurs
SCCA......... Society of Company and Commercial Accountants [*Edgbaston, Birmingham, England*] (EAIO)
SCCA......... Southeastern Cottonseed Crushers Association (EA)
SCCA......... Specification Compliance Concept Agreements (MCD)
SCCA......... Sports Car Club of America (EA)
SCCA......... Subcontract Change Authorization (AAG)
SCCAC...... Society for Conceptual and Content Analysis by Computer (EA)
SCC-ACO ... Strategic Communications Command Advanced Concepts Office [*Army*]
SC Cas ...... Supreme Court Cases [*A publication*] (DLA)
ScCatt .... Scuola Cattolica [*A publication*]
ScCB.......... Baptist College at Charleston, Charleston, SC [*Library symbol*] [*Library of Congress*] (LCLS)
SCCB......... Safety Change Control Board (MCD)
SCCB......... Site Configuration Control Board [*NASA*] (NASA)
SCCB......... Software Configuration Control Board (KSC)
SCCBS....... Science Council of Canada. Background Study [*A publication*]
SCCC......... Chile Chico/Chile Chico [*Chile*] [*ICAO location identifier*] (ICLI)
ScCC......... College of Charleston, Charleston, SC [*Library symbol*] [*Library of Congress*] (LCLS)
SCCC......... Satellite Communications Control Centre [*British*]
SCCC......... System Casualty Control Console [*Military*] (CAAL)
SCCCE....... Society of Certified Consumer Credit Executives (EA)
ScCCit....... Citadel, Charleston, SC [*Library symbol*] [*Library of Congress*] (LCLS)
SCCD......... Iquique/Los Condores [*Chile*] [*ICAO location identifier*] (ICLI)
ScCDHHi .. Dalcho Historical Society of the Episcopal Diocese of South Carolina, Charleston, SC [*Library symbol*] [*Library of Congress*] (LCLS)
SCCE......... Satellite Configuration Control Element (MCD)
SCCE......... School and College Conference on English
SCCE......... Scottish Council for Community Education
SCCE......... Society of Certified Credit Executives [*St. Louis, MO*] (EA)
SCCEA...... Strategic Communications Command Equipment Applications Directorate [*Army*]
SCCF......... Calama/El Loa [*Chile*] [*ICAO location identifier*] (ICLI)
ScCF.......... Charleston County Library, Charleston, SC [*Library symbol*] [*Library of Congress*] (LCLS)
SCCF......... Satellite Communication Control Facility
SCCF......... Security Clearance Case Files [*Military*] (AABC)
SCCF......... Service Center Control File [*IRS*]
SCCG......... Station Communications Control Group [*Ground Communications Facility, NASA*]
SCCH........ Chillan/Gral, Bernardo O'Higgins [*Chile*] [*ICAO location identifier*] (ICLI)
SCCH........ Society of Cinema Collectors and Historians (EA)
SCCH........ Standard Cubic Centimeters per Hour (MCD)
ScChwC ..... Chesterfield-Marlboro Technical College, Cheraw, SC [*Library symbol*] [*Library of Congress*] (LCLS)
SCCI.......... Punta Arenas/Internacional Carlos Ibanez Del Campo [*Chile*] [*ICAO location identifier*] (ICLI)
SCCI.......... Smurf Collectors' Club International (EA)
SCC(I)........ Special Coordination Committee (Intelligence) (MCD)
SCCJ.......... Supreme Court of Canada Judgements [*Canada Department of Justice*] [*Information service or system*] (CRD)
SCCL......... Small Cell (Anaplastic) Carcinoma of the Lung [*Oncology*]
SCCL......... Supply Catalog Components List [*Military*]
ScCleU....... Clemson University, Clemson, SC [*Library symbol*] [*Library of Congress*] (LCLS)
ScCliJ .... Jacobs Library, Clinton, SC [*Library symbol*] [*Library of Congress*] [*Obsolete*] (LCLS)
ScCIP......... Presbyterian College, Clinton, SC [*Library symbol*] [*Library of Congress*] (LCLS)
ScClTO...... Thornwell Orphanage, Clinton, SC [*Library symbol*] [*Library of Congress*] (LCLS)
ScCM......... Medical University of South Carolina, Charleston, SC [*Library symbol*] [*Library of Congress*] (LCLS)
SCCM........ Sertoli-Cell Culture Medium [*Clinical chemistry*]
SCCM........ Single Chamber Controllable Motor (MCD)

SCCM........ Society of Critical Care Medicine (EA)
SCCM........ Standard Cubic Centimeters per Minute (NASA)
SCCM........ Standing Commission on Church Music (EA)
ScCMP ...... Middleton Place, Charleston, SC [*Library symbol*] [*Library of Congress*] (LCLS)
ScCMu....... Charleston Museum Library, Charleston, SC [*Library symbol*] [*Library of Congress*] (LCLS)
SCCN........ Subcontract [*or Subcontractor*] Change Notice (KSC)
SCCNC...... Society of Critical Care Nurses of Canada
SCCO........ Security Classification Control Officer [*Military*]
ScCoAH..... South Carolina Department of Archives and History, Columbia, SC [*Library symbol*] [*Library of Congress*] (LCLS)
ScCoB .... Benedict College, Columbia, SC [*Library symbol*] [*Library of Congress*] (LCLS)
ScCoB .... Columbia Bible College, Columbia, SC [*Library symbol*] [*Library of Congress*] (LCLS)
ScCoC .... Columbia College, Columbia, SC [*Library symbol*] [*Library of Congress*] (LCLS)
SC Code ..... Code of Laws of South Carolina [*A publication*] (DLA)
SC Code Ann ... Code of Laws of South Carolina, Annotated [*A publication*] (DLA)
ScCoGS...... Church of Jesus Christ of Latter-Day Saints, Genealogical Society Library, Columbia Branch, Columbia, SC [*Library symbol*] [*Library of Congress*] (LCLS)
ScCon......... Horry County Memorial Library, Conway, SC [*Library symbol*] [*Library of Congress*] (LCLS)
Sc Conspectus ... Science Conspectus [*A publication*]
ScCoR .... Richland County Library, Columbia, SC [*Library symbol*] [*Library of Congress*] (LCLS)
Sc Costs ..... Scott's ABC Guide to Costs [*2nd ed.*] [*1910*] [*A publication*] (DLA)
ScCoT .... Lutheran Theological Southern Seminary, Columbia, SC [*Library symbol*] [*Library of Congress*] (LCLS)
ScCoV .... United States Veterans Administration Hospital, Columbia, SC [*Library symbol*] [*Library of Congress*] (LCLS)
SCCP .... Sabah Chinese Consolidated Party [*Political party*] [*Malaysia*] (FEA)
SCCP .... Signaling Connection Control Part [*Telecommunications*]
SCCP .... Systems Change Control Procedure [*Social Security Administration*]
SCCPG ...... Satellite Communications Contingency Planning Group (NATG)
SCCR .... Science Council of Canada. Report [*A publication*]
SCCR .... Society for Cross-Cultural Research (EA)
SCCR .... Stanford Center for Chicano Research [*Stanford University*] [*Research center*] (RCD)
SCCR .... Subcontractor Change Request (MCD)
ScCRC .... Charleston Diocesan Archives, Roman Catholic Church, Charleston, SC [*Library symbol*] [*Library of Congress*] (LCLS)
SCCRI .... Swedish Cement and Concrete Research Institute (MCD)
SCCS .... Satellite Communications Control System (MCD)
SCCS .... Secondary Chemical Control System [*Nuclear energy*] (NRCH)
SCCS .... Sodium Chemistry Control System [*Westinghouse Corp.*] (IEEE)
SCCS .... Source Code Control System [*Data processing*]
SCCS .... Souvenir Card Collectors Society (EA)
SCCS .... Souvenir China Collectors Society (EA)
SCCS .... Special Consultative Committee on Security [*OAS*]
SCCS .... Standard Commodity Classification System (NG)
SCCS .... Standard Cubic Centimeters per Second (NASA)
SCCS .... Standby Core Cooling System [*Nuclear energy*] (NRCH)
SCCS .... STRICOM [*Strike Command*] Command and Control System [*Army*] (AABC)
SCCS .... Switching Control Center System [*Telecommunications*] (TEL)
SCCSA .... Sports Car Collectors Society of America (EA)
ScCSM ...... Old Slave Mart Museum, Charleston, SC [*Library symbol*] [*Library of Congress*] (LCLS)
SCC Spec ... Soap/Cosmetics/Chemical Specialties [*A publication*]
SCCSS....... Science Council of Canada. Special Study [*A publication*]
ScCT .... Trident Technical College, Palmer Campus, Charleston, SC [*Library symbol*] [*Library of Congress*] (LCLS)
SCC-TED .. Strategic Communications Command - Test and Evaluation Directorate [*Army*]
SCCTR ...... Standing Committee for Controlled Thermonuclear Research [*Terminated, 1973*] [*AEC*] (EGAO)
SCCTSD .... Society of Catholic College Teachers of Sacred Doctrine [*Later, CTS*] (EA)
SCCU......... Single Channel Control Unit
SCCU......... Spacecraft Command Control Unit (KSC)
SCCU......... Specialist Claims Control Unit [*British*]
SCCUK...... Swedish Chamber of Commerce for the United Kingdom (DS)
SCCUS ...... Swedish Chamber of Commerce of the United States [*Later, Swedish-American Chamber of Commerce*]
ScCV .... United States Veterans Administration Hospital, Charleston, SC [*Library symbol*] [*Library of Congress*] (LCLS)
SCCW........ Scarritt College for Christian Workers [*Tennessee*]
SCCWRP... Southern California Coastal Water Research Project (NOAA)
SCCWRP TR ... SCCWRP (Southern California Coastal Water Research Project). TR [*A publication*]

SCCY.........	Coyhaique/Teniente Vidal [*Chile*] [*ICAO location identifier*] (ICLI)
SCCZ.........	Punta Arenas [*Chile*] [*ICAO location identifier*] (ICLI)
SCD	Darlington County Library, Darlington, SC [*OCLC symbol*] (OCLC)
SCD	Doctor of Commercial Science
Sc D...........	Doctor of Science
SCD	S-Band Cassegrain Diplexer
SCD	Satellite Control Department
SCD	Schedule (AABC)
SCD	Schneider Corp. [*Toronto Stock Exchange symbol*]
SCD	Science Communication Division [*George Washington University Medical Center*] [*Information service or system*] (IID)
Sc D...........	Scientiae Doctor [*Doctor of Science*] [*Latin*]
SCD	Scientific Computer Division [*Army Tank-Automotive Command*]
ScD	Scintillation Detector (IEEE)
SCD	Screen Door
SCD	Screwed (MDG)
SCD	Secondary Current Distribution [*Electroplating*]
SCD	Security Coding Device (NATG)
SCD	Senile Cognitive Decline [*Medicine*]
SCD	Senior Citizen Discount
SCD	Service Computation Date [*Military*] (AFM)
SCD	Service Control Drawing
SCD	Servo Chart Drive
SCD	Ship's Center Display [*Navy*] (NVT)
SCD	Sickle Cell Disease [*Medicine*]
SCD	Signal Canceling Device
SCD	Significant Construction Deficiency [*Nuclear energy*] (NRCH)
SCD	Simulated Communications Deception [*Army*] (INF)
SCD	Society of Craft Designers (EA)
SCD	Software Conceptual Design [*Data processing*]
SCD	Soil Conservation District [*Agriculture*]
SCD	Source Control Document (NASA)
SCD	Source Control Drawing
SCD	Space Control Document [*NASA*] (KSC)
SCD	Specification Control Document [*or Drawing*] [*NASA*] (NASA)
SCD	Spreading Cortical Depression
SCD	State Civil Defense
SCD	Static Column Decode [*Data processing*]
SCD	Sterile Connection Device [*Medicine*]
SC & D......	Stock Control and Distribution (AFM)
SCD	Strategic Communications Division [*Military*]
SCD	Streaming Current Detector
SCD	Structure-Chart Diagramer [*Data processing*]
SCD	Subacute Combined Degeneration [*of spinal cord*] [*Medicine*]
SCD	Subcarrier Discriminator
SCD	Subcontract Deviation
SCD	Subject Captain's Discretion [*Aviation*] (FAAC)
SCD	Sudden Cardiac Death [*Medicine*]
SCD	Sulfur Chemiluminescence Detector
SCD	Supply, Commissary, and Disbursing [*Navy*]
SCD	Surrey Commercial Dock [*British*]
SCD	Surveillance Criticality Designator [*DoD*]
SCD	Sylacauga, AL [*Location identifier*] [*FAA*] (FAAL)
SCD	System Coordination Document
SCD	Systems, Components, and Displays
ScDa..........	Darlington County Library, Darlington, SC [*Library symbol*] [*Library of Congress*] (LCLS)
SCDA........	Iquique/Gral Diego Aracena [*Chile*] [*ICAO location identifier*] (ICLI)
SCDA........	Safing, Cool Down, and Decontamination Area [*NASA*] (NASA)
SCDA........	SEATO [*Southeast Asia Treaty Organization*] Central Distribution Agency (NATG)
SCDA........	Situational Control of Daily Activities
SCDAP......	Severe Core Damage Analysis Package [*Nuclear energy*] (NRCH)
SCDC........	Scottish Cooperative Development Committee
SCDC........	Service Coding and Data Collection (AAG)
SCDC........	Societe des Comptables de Direction au Canada [*Society of Management Accountants of Canada - SMAC*]
SCDC........	Source Coding and Data Collection
SCDC........	Strategic Concepts Development Center [*National Defense University*]
SCDC........	Supreme Court Reports, District of Columbia [*A publication*] (DLA)
SCDCNS ...	Supreme Court Reports, District of Columbia, New Series [*A publication*] (DLA)
SCDCU......	Section Chief, Display Control Unit [*Army*]
SC/DDS	Sensor Control/Data Display Set (MCD)
Sc D in Ed ...	Doctor of Science in Education
SC Dent J ..	South Carolina Dental Journal [*A publication*]
ScDeV........	Voorhees College, Denmark, SC [*Library symbol*] [*Library of Congress*] (LCLS)
SCDFGNY ...	Sickle Cell Disease Foundation of Greater New York (EA)
Sc D Govt...	Doctor of Science in Government
Sc D in Hyg ...	Doctor of Science in Hygiene

SCDI.........	Science Dimension [*A publication*]
SCDI.........	Short Children's Depression Inventory [*Psychology*]
SCDIA	Science Digest [*Chicago*] [*A publication*]
SC Dig........	Cassel's Supreme Court Digest [*Canada*] [*A publication*] (DLA)
Sc Dimension ...	Science Dimension [*A publication*]
Sc & Div	Law Reports, Scotch and Divorce Appeals [*A publication*] (DLA)
Sc & Div App ...	Scotch and Divorce Appeals [*English Law Reports*] [*A publication*] (DLA)
SC Div Bad ...	Second Class Diver Badge [*Military decoration*]
SC Div Geol Geol Notes ...	South Carolina. Division of Geology. Geologic Notes [*A publication*]
SC Div Geol Miner Resour Ser ...	South Carolina. Division of Geology. Mineral Resources Series [*A publication*]
SC Div Geol Misc Rep ...	South Carolina. Division of Geology. Miscellaneous Report [*A publication*]
SC Div Geology Mineral Industries Lab Monthly Bull ...	South Carolina. Division of Geology. Mineral Industries Laboratory. Monthly Bulletin [*A publication*]
SCDL.........	Saturated Current Demand Logic
SCDL.........	Ship Configuration Detail List [*Navy*]
SCDL.........	Stabilized Carbon Dioxide LASER
SCDL.........	Surveillance and Control Data Link [*Military*]
Sc D (Med) ...	Doctor of Medical Science
SCDMR.....	Steam-Cooled Deuteriated Water-Moderated Reactor [*Nuclear energy*]
SCD OCSA ...	Staff Communications Division, Office, Chief of Staff, Army (AABC)
SCD OC of SA ...	Staff Communications Division, Office, Chief of Staff, Army (AABC)
Sc DP........	Right Scapuloposterior Position [*of the fetus*] [*Obstetrics*]
SCDP.........	Sedimentary Chlorophyll Degradation Product [*Paleontology*]
SCDP.........	Simulation Control Data Package [*NASA*] (NASA)
SCDP........	Society of Certified Data Processors [*Superseded by AICCP*] (EA)
SCDP........	Southern Cooperative Development Program [*Sponsored by Southern Consumers Education Foundation*]
SCDP........	Steel Cadmium Plated
SCDR........	Screwdriver (MSA)
SCDR........	Seller Critical Design Review [*NASA*] (NASA)
SCDR........	Shuttle Critical Design Review [*NASA*] (NASA)
SCDR........	Software Critical Design Review [*NASA*] (NASA)
SCDR........	Subcontractor Critical Design Review [*NASA*]
SCDR........	Subsystem Controller Definition Record [*Data processing*] (IBMDP)
SCDS	Scan Converter Display System (MCD)
SCDS	Sensor Communication and Display System (MCD)
SCDS	Shipboard Chaff Decoy System [*Navy*]
SCDS	Signal Circuits Design Section
SCDS	Staff of Chief of Defence Staff [*British*]
SCDSB	Suppressed-Carrier Double Sideband
SCDSD	Scientific Clearinghouse and Documentation Services Division [*National Science and Technology Authority*] [*Information service or system*] (IID)
SCD (St V) ...	Supreme Court Decisions (St. Vincent) [*1928-36*] [*A publication*] (DLA)
SCDU	Signal Conditioning and Display Unit [*NASA*] (NASA)
S & CDU....	Switch and Cable Distribution Unit (AAG)
ScDwE	Erskine College, Due West, SC [*Library symbol*] [*Library of Congress*] (LCLS)
ScDwE-T ...	Erskine College, Erskine Theological Seminary, Due West, SC [*Library symbol*] [*Library of Congress*] (LCLS)
ScE............	Edgefield County Library, Edgefield, SC [*Library symbol*] [*Library of Congress*] (LCLS)
SCE............	Saturated Calomel Electrode [*Electrochemistry*]
Sce..............	[*Quintus Mucius*] Scaevola [*Flourished, 1st century*] [*Authority cited in pre-1607 legal work*] (DSA)
SCE............	Scan Conversion Equipment [*Television*]
SCE............	SCEcorp. [*Formerly, Southern California Edison Co.*] [*NYSE symbol*] (SPSG)
SCE............	Schedule Compliance-Evaluation [*Polaris*]
SCE............	Schellex Gold [*Vancouver Stock Exchange symbol*]
SCE............	Schlegeis [*Austria*] [*Seismograph station code, US Geological Survey*] (SEIS)
ScE............	Sciences Ecclesiastiques [*Montreal-Brussels*] [*A publication*]
SCE............	Scottish Certificate of Education
SCE............	Scribe Ezra [*Freemasonry*]
SCE............	Secretory Carcinoma of Endometrium
SCE............	Select Cases Relating to Evidence (Strange) [*A publication*] (DLA)
SCE............	Selection Control Element
SCE............	Separated Career Employee
SCE............	Service Cryptologic Elements [*Army*]
SCE............	Signal Conditioning Equipment
SCE............	Signal Conversion Equipment [*Telecommunications*]
SCE............	Significant Combat Equipment [*Army*]
SCE............	Single Cotton-Covered Enameled [*Wire insulation*] (DEN)
SCE............	Single Cycle Execute
SCE............	Sister Chromatid Exchange [*Cytology*]
SCE............	Situationally Caused Error

SCE........... Small Current Element
SCE........... Societe Canadienne d'Esthetique [*Canadian Society for Aesthetics - CSAC*]
SCE........... Society of Carbide Engineers [*Later, SCTE*]   (EA)
SCE........... Society of Christian Engineers   (EA)
SCE........... Society of Christian Ethics   (EA)
SCE........... Society for Clinical Ecology [*Later, AAEM*]   (EA)
SCE........... Society for Creative Ethics [*Later, SPC*]   (EA)
SCE........... Solar Corona Explorer [*Project*] [*NASA*]
SCE........... Solder Circuit Etch
SCE........... Source   (MSA)
SCE........... Space Cabin Environment [*Skylab*] [*NASA*]
SCE........... Spacecraft Command Encoder   (MCD)
SCE........... Special Conditioning Equipment
SCE........... Spectrum Communications & Electronics Corp. [*Telecommunications service*]   (TSSD)
SCE........... Stabilization Control Electronics
SCE........... Standard Calomel Electrode
SCE........... State College [*Pennsylvania*] [*Airport symbol*]   (OAG)
SCENA........ State College, PA [*Location identifier*] [*FAA*]   (FAAL)
SCE........... Stored Controlled Energy
SCE........... Stratified-Charge Engine [*Auto engine*]
SCE........... Strukturen Christlicher Existenz [*A publication*]
SCE........... Supercritical Extract [*Separation technology*]
SCE........... Superintending Civil Engineer [*British*]
SCE........... United States Air Force, Armament Laboratory, Technical Library, Eglin AFB, FL [*OCLC symbol*]   (OCLC)
ScEA.......... John R. Abney Collection, Edgefield County Library, Edgefield, SC [*Library symbol*] [*Library of Congress*]   (LCLS)
ScEa.......... Pickens County Library, Easley, SC [*Library symbol*] [*Library of Congress*]   (LCLS)
SCEA........ Service Children's Education Authority [*Ministry of Defence*] [*British*]
SCEA........ Signal Conditioning Electronics Assembly
SCEA........ Society of Communications Engineers and Analysts
SCEA........ Society of Cost Estimating and Analysis   (EA)
SCEAB...... Studii si Cercetari de Astronomie [*A publication*]
SCEAR...... Scientific Committee on the Effects of Atomic Radiation
SCEB........ SHAPE [*Supreme Headquarters Allied Powers Europe*] Communications Electronics Board [*NATO*]   (NATG)
SCEB........ Societe Canadienne des Etudes Bibliques [*Canadian Society of Biblical Studies - CSBS*]
SCEB........ Syndicat Canadien des Employes de Bureau [*Canadian Office Employees Union - COEU*]
SCEC........ Secondary Computer Education Committee [*Victoria, Australia*]
SCEC........ Societe Canadienne des Eleveurs de Chevres
SCEC........ Societe Canadienne des Etudes Classiques [*Classical Association of Canada - CAC*]
SCEC........ Spaceborne Computer Engineering Conference   (MCD)
SCECA...... Studii si Cercetari de Chimie [*A publication*]
SCECC...... Societe Canadienne pour l'Etude Comparee des Civilisations [*Canadian Society for the Comparative Study of Civilizations - CSCSC*]
ScEccl........ Sciences Ecclesiastiques [*A publication*]
SCECI........ Societe Canadienne d'Education Comparee et Internationale
SCEDA....... Studii si Cercetari de Endocrinologie [*A publication*]
Sc Ed D...... Doctor of Science in Education
SCEDSIP Bull ... SCEDSIP [*Standing Conference on Educational Development Services in Polytechnics*] Bulletin [*A publication*]
SCEE........ Societe Canadienne pour l'Etude de l'Education [*Canadian Society for the Study of Education - CSSE*]
SCEE........ Southern Coalition for Educational Equity   (EA)
SCEE........ Student Committee for Economic Education   (EA)
SCEEA...... Studii si Cercetari de Energetica si Electrotehnica [*A publication*]
SCEEB...... Scottish Certificate of Education Examination Board
SCEEE....... Southeastern Center for Electrical Engineering Education [*Air Force*]
SCEERR.... Sacra Congregatio Episcoporum et Regularium [*Sacred Congregation of Bishops and Regulars*] [*Latin*]
SCEES....... Service Central des Enquetes et Etudes Statistiques [*Central Service for Statistical Inquiries and Studies*] [*Ministry of Agriculture*] [*Paris, France*]
SCEES....... Societe Canadienne pour l'Etude de l'Enseignement Superieur [*Canadian Society for the Study of Higher Education - CSSHE*]
SCEET....... Support Concept Economic Evaluation Technique   (MCD)
SCEF........ Isla Rey Jorge/Centro Meteorologico Antartico Presidente Frei [*Chile*] [*ICAO location identifier*]   (ICLI)
SCEF........ Southern Conference Educational Fund   (EA)
SCEFA...... Studii si Cercetari de Fizica [*A publication*]
SCEH........ Society for Clinical and Experimental Hypnosis   (EA)
SCEI........ Safe Car Educational Institute
SCEI........ Societe Canadienne pour les Etudes Italiennes [*Canadian Society for Italian Studies - CSIS*]
SCEI........ Special Committee on Environmental Information [*Special Libraries Association*]
SCEIBF..... Standing Conference for Europe of the International Basketball Federation   (EAIO)

SCEIL....... Service Ceiling
SCEIO....... Societe Canadienne pour Etudes d'Intelligence par Ordinateur
SCEKS...... Spectrum Clear Except Known Signals   (MUGU)
SCEL......... Santiago/Internacional Arturo Merino Benitez [*Chile*] [*ICAO location identifier*]   (ICLI)
scel .... Scellino [*Shilling*] [*Monetary unit*] [*Italian*]
SCEL........ Signal Corps Engineering Laboratories [*Obsolete*] [*Army*]
SCEL........ Small Components Evaluation Loop [*Nuclear energy*]   (NRCH)
SCEL........ Standing Committee on Education in Librarianship
SCELBAL ... Scientific Elementary Basic Language [*1963*] [*Data processing*]   (CSR)
SCEM....... Santiago/Arturo Merino Benitez (Edificio Direccion Meteorologica) [*Chile*] [*ICAO location identifier*]   (ICLI)
SCEN........ Santiago/Edificio Navegacion Aerea Arturo Merino Benitez [*Chile*] [*ICAO location identifier*]   (ICLI)
Scen........... Scenario [*A publication*]
SCEN........ Societe Canadienne pour l'Etude des Noms [*Canadian Society for the Study of Names - CSSN*]
SCEN........ South Central
SCENA...... Science and Engineering [*A publication*]
SCENE...... Studies of Coastal and Estuarine Environments [*National Oceanic and Atmospheric Administration*]   (MSC)
SCENIC .... Scientific Engineering Information Center   (KSC)
Scenic Trips Geol Past ... Scenic Trips to the Geologic Past [*A publication*]
SCEO........ Senior Chief Executive Officer [*Civil Service*] [*British*]
SCEO........ Station Construction Engineering Officer
SCEP .... Secure Communications Equipment Program [*Air Force*]   (CET)
SCEP .... Significant Criminal Enforcement Project [*Bureau of Alcohol, Tobacco, and Firearms*]
SCEP .... Societe Canadienne d'Enseignement Postscolaire
SCEP .... Study of Critical Environmental Problems [*MIT*]
SCEPC...... Senior Civil Emergency Planning Committee [*NATO*]   (NATG)
SCEPS...... Solar Cell Electric Power System   (RDA)
SCEPS...... Stored Chemical Energy Propulsion System
SCEPTR.... Suitcase Emergency Procedures Trainer   (MCD)
SCEPTRE ... System for Circuit Evaluation and Prediction of Transient Radiation Effect   (MCD)
SCEPTRE ... System Computerized for Economical Performance, Tracking, Recording and Evaluation [*North Central Airlines*]
SCEPTRE ... System for Constant Elevation Precipitation Transmission and Recording
SCEPTRON ... Spectral Comparative Pattern Recognizer
SC Eq......... South Carolina Equity Reports [*A publication*]   (DLA)
SCER........ Quintero [*Chile*] [*ICAO location identifier*]   (ICLI)
SCER........ Sheffield Centre for Environmental Research [*British*]   (CB)
SCER........ Societe Canadienne pour l'Etude de la Religion [*Canadian Society for the Study of Religion - CSSR*]
SCER........ Societe Canadienne d'Etudes de la Renaissance [*Canadian Society for Renaissance Studies - CSRS*]
SCER........ Standing Commission on Ecumenical Relations of the Episcopal Church   (EA)
SCERGA ... Societe Canadienne d'Economie Rurale et Gestion Agricole [*Canadian Agricultural Economics and Farm Management Society - CAEFMS*]
SCERT ...... System and Computer Evaluation Revision Technique
SCERT ...... Systems and Computers Evaluation and Review Technique [*Data processing*]
ScEs .... Science et Esprit [*A publication*]
SCES .... State Cooperative Extension Service
SCESBH ... Smithsonian Contributions to the Earth Sciences [*A publication*]
SCESOM .. Service Canadien pour les Etudiants et les Stagiaires d'Outre-Mer
SCESWUN ... Standing Committee on the Economic and Social Work of the United Nations
SCET .... Scottish Council for Educational Technology   (EISS)
SCET .... Spacecraft Event Time
SCETA ...... Societe de Controle et d'Exploitation de Transports Auxiliaires [*France*]
SCETV ...... South Carolina Educational Television [*Columbia*] [*Telecommunications*]   (TSSD)
SCEU........ Selector Channel Emulation Unit
SCEWA .... Society for Citizen Education in World Affairs [*Later, CEA*]
SCEZ........ Santiago [*Chile*] [*ICAO location identifier*]   (ICLI)
SCF........... Florence County Library, Florence, SC [*OCLC symbol*]   (OCLC)
SCF........... Phoenix [*Arizona*] Scottsdale [*Airport symbol*]   (OAG)
SCF........... S-Band Composite Feed
SCF........... Samoth Capital Corp. [*Toronto Stock Exchange symbol*]
SCF........... Sampled Channel Filter
SCF........... Satellite Control Facility [*Sunnyvale, CA*] [*NASA*]
SCF........... Save the Children Federation   (EA)
SCF........... Scandinavia Co. [*Formerly, Scandinavia Fund, Inc.*] [*AMEX symbol*]   (SPSG)
SCF........... Schedule Control File
SCF........... Schematic Concept Formation
SCF........... Science Fantasy [*A publication*]
SCF........... Scientific Computing Facility
SCF........... Secondary Checkpoint File
SCF........... Sectional Center Facility [*Air Force*]   (AFM)

SCF .... Sectional Center Facility [*First three digits of the ZIP code*] [*US Postal Service*]
SCF .... Self-Consistent Field [*Quantum mechanics*]
SCF .... Senior Chaplain to the Forces [*British*]
SCF .... Sequential Compatibility Firing [*Aerospace*]
SCF .... Single Catastrophic Failure   (AAG)
SCF .... Single Cost Factor
SCF .... Single Crystal Filament
SCF .... Skin Cancer Foundation   (EA)
SCF .... Slovak Catholic Federation   (EA)
SCF .... Small Company Fund [*Phillips and Drew Fund Management*] [*British*]
SCF .... SNAP [*Systems for Nuclear Auxiliary Power*] Critical Facility   (NRCH)
SCF .... Sociedad Centroamericana de Farmacologia [*Central American Society of Pharmacology - CASP*]   (EAIO)
SCF .... Society of the Compassionate Friends [*Later, TCF*]   (EA)
SCF .... Sodium Cleaning Facility [*Nuclear energy*]   (NRCH)
SCF .... Spacecraft Checkout Facility
SCF .... Spacecraft Control Facility [*NASA*]   (MCD)
SCF .... Spherical Cavity Flow
SCF .... Spinning Continuous Filament
SCF .... Spinning Crucible Furnace
SCF .... Standard Charge Factor   (NASA)
SCF .... Standard Cubic Foot
SCF .... Station Code File
SCF .... Statistical Collection File   (NASA)
SCF .... Steinbeck Center Foundation   (EA)
SCF .... Stress Concentration Factor   (MCD)
SCF .... Subchorionic Fibrin [*Obstetrics*]
SCF .... Sunnyvale Control Facility [*California*] [*NASA*]   (NASA)
SCF .... Supercritical Fluid
SCF .... Support Carrier Force
SCFA .... Antofagasta/Internacional Cerro Moreno [*Chile*] [*ICAO location identifier*]   (ICLI)
SCFA .... Segmented Continuous Flow Analysis [*Analytical chemistry*]
SCFA .... Short-Chain Fatty Acids [*Biochemistry*]
SCFA .... Slovak Catholic Federation of America [*Later, SCF*]   (EA)
SCFB .... South Carolina Federal Corp. [*NASDAQ symbol*]   (NQ)
SCFB .... Swirling Circulating Fluidized Bed
SCFBC .... Staged-Cascade Fluidized Bed Combustion
SCFBR .... Steam-Cooled Fast Breeder Reactor [*Nuclear energy*]
SCFC .... Scientific Communications, Inc. [*Garland, TX*] [*NASDAQ symbol*]   (NQ)
SCFC .... Southern California Film Circuit [*Library network*]
SCFC .... Steve Cochran Fan Club   (EA)
SCFD .... Standard Cubic Feet per Day
SC & FE ..... Sierra Club and Friends of the Earth [*Marine science*]   (MSC)
SCFE .... Supercritical Fluid Extraction [*Also, SFE*] [*Chemical engineering*]
SCFEL .... Standard COMSEC [*Communications Security*] Facility Equipment List
SCFF .... Scotopic Critical Flicker Frequency [*Magnetic environment*]
SCFGVPT ... Southern California Figure-Ground Visual Perception Test
SCFH .... Standard Cubic Feet per Hour   (AAG)
SCFI .... Streptococcal Chemotactic Factor Inhibitor [*Immunochemistry*]
ScFl .... Florence County Library, Florence, SC [*Library symbol*] [*Library of Congress*]   (LCLS)
ScFlM .... Francis Marion College, Florence, SC [*Library symbol*] [*Library of Congress*]   (LCLS)
ScFlT .... Florence-Darlington Technical College Library, Florence, SC [*Library symbol*] [*Library of Congress*]   (LCLS)
SCFM .... Porvenir/Capitan Fuentes Martinez [*Chile*] [*ICAO location identifier*]   (ICLI)
SCFM .... Scanforms, Inc. [*NASDAQ symbol*]   (NQ)
SCFM .... Standard Cubic Feet per Minute
SCFM .... Subcarrier Frequency Modulation [*Telecommunications*]   (TEL)
SCFMA ..... Summer and Casual Furniture Manufacturers Association   (EA)
SCFO .... Science Forum [*A publication*]
SCFOA ...... Schiffbauforschung [*A publication*]
SCFOB ...... Science Forum [*A publication*]
SCFP .... Science Career Facilitation Project [*National Science Foundation*]
SCFP .... Syndicat Canadien de la Fonction Publique [*Canadian Union of Public Employees - CUPE*]
SCFPA .... Structural Cement-Fiber Products Association   (EA)
SCFS .... S-Band Composite Feed System
SCFS .... Slip-Cast-Fused Silica   (RDA)
SCFS .... Standard Cubic Feet per Second   (AAG)
SCFSEC .... Standing Committee of French-Speaking Ethnical Communities   (EA)
SCFT .... Futaleufu/Futaleufu [*Chile*] [*ICAO location identifier*]   (ICLI)
SCFZ .... Antofagasta [*Chile*] [*ICAO location identifier*]   (ICLI)
SCFZA ...... Studii si Cercetari de Fiziologie [*A publication*]
SCG .... Air Force Geophysics Laboratory Research Library, Hanscom AFB, MA [*OCLC symbol*]   (OCLC)
ScG .... Greenville County Library, Greenville, SC [*Library symbol*] [*Library of Congress*]   (LCLS)

SCG .... St. Claude [*Guadeloupe*] [*Seismograph station code, US Geological Survey*]   (SEIS)
SCG .... SCANA Corp. [*NYSE symbol*]   (SPSG)
Sc G............ Science Gossip [*A publication*]
SCG .... Scientific Computing Group [*University of Toronto*] [*Research center*]   (RCD)
SCG .... Scoring   (ADA)
SCG .... Screen Cartoonists Guild [*Defunct*]   (EA)
SCG .... Search for Common Ground   (EA)
SCG .... Security Classification Guide   (AFM)
SCG .... Self Changing Gear   (DCTA)
SCG .... SEMMS [*Solar Electric Multiple-Mission Spacecraft*] Coordinating Group [*NASA*]
SCG .... Sequential Control Guidance   (KSC)
SCG .... Shipcraft Guild   (EA)
SCG .... Sigma Science [*Vancouver Stock Exchange symbol*]
SCG .... Sliding-Coil Gauge   (RDA)
SCG .... Social Credit Group [*British*]   (DAS)
SCG .... Societe Canadienne de Geotechnique [*Canadian Geotechnical Society*]   (EAIO)
SCG .... Society of the Classic Guitar   (EA)
SCG .... Sodium Cromoglycate [*Pharmacology*]
SCG .... Solution Crystal Growth
SCG .... Southern Cross Group [*Australia*]
SCG .... Space Charge Grid
SCG .... Space and Communications Group [*of General Motors Corp.*]
SCG .... Special Consultative Group [*NATO*]
SCG .... Steel Carriers Group [*Later, RDCC*]   (EA)
SCG .... Stored Cold Gas
SCG .... Supercritical Gas Extraction
SCG .... Superior Cervical Ganglion [*Anatomy*]
ScGa......... Cherokee County Public Library, Gaffney, SC [*Library symbol*] [*Library of Congress*]   (LCLS)
SCGA........ Sodium-Cooled Graphite Assembly [*Nuclear energy*]
SCGA........ Southern Cotton Ginners Association   (EA)
SCGA........ Synergistic Communications Group, Inc. [*NASDAQ symbol*]   (NQ)
ScGaL....... Limestone College, Gaffney, SC [*Library symbol*] [*Library of Congress*]   (LCLS)
ScGBJ........ Bob Jones University, Greenville, SC [*Library symbol*] [*Library of Congress*]   (LCLS)
SCGC........ Societe Canadienne de Genie Civil
SCGC........ Society of Carnival Glass Collectors
SCGCh....... Societe Canadienne du Genie Chimique
SCGD .... Specification Control Group Directive   (KSC)
SCGDL....... Signal Corps Group General Development Laboratory [*Obsolete*] [*Army*]
SCGE......... Sioux City Grain Exchange   (EA)
SCGE......... Societe Canadienne de Genie Electrique
ScGeo......... Georgetown County Memorial Library, Georgetown SC [*Library symbol*] [*Library of Congress*]   (LCLS)
ScGF .... Furman University, Greenville, SC [*Library symbol*] [*Library of Congress*]   (LCLS)
SCGGA...... Sonoma County Grape Growers Association   (EA)
SCGGA...... Studii si Cercetari de Geologie, Geofizica, si Geografie. Seria Geologie [*A publication*]
SCGI .... Small College Goals Inventory [*Test*]
SCGI .... Starstream Communications Group, Inc. [*NASDAQ symbol*]   (NQ)
SCGM ...... Senior Cook General Mess [*British military*]   (DMA)
SCGM ...... Societe Canadienne de Genie Mecanique
SCGMB...... Societe Canadienne de Genie Medical et Biologique
SCGP........ Scrabble Crossword Game Players [*Later, NSA*]   (EA)
SCGP........ Self-Contained Guidance Package   (AAG)
SCGR........ Societe Canadienne du Genie Rural
ScGrw....... Abbeville-Greenwood Regional Library, Greenwood, SC [*Library symbol*] [*Library of Congress*]   (LCLS)
ScGrwL...... Lander College, Greenwood, SC [*Library symbol*] [*Library of Congress*]   (LCLS)
ScGrwP...... Piedmont Technical College, Greenwood, SC [*Library symbol*] [*Library of Congress*]   (LCLS)
SCGSS...... Signal Corps Ground Signal Service [*Obsolete*] [*Army*]
SCGSS...... Super-Critical Gas Storage System [*NASA*]   (KSC)
SCGT........ Stanford's Compendium of Geography and Travel [*A publication*]
SCGZ......... Puerto Williams/Guardia-Marina Zanartu [*Chile*] [*ICAO location identifier*]   (ICLI)
SCH .... AFSC Technical Information Center, Washington, DC [*OCLC symbol*]   (OCLC)
SCH .... Schedule   (AAG)
SCH .... Schefferville [*Quebec*] [*Seismograph station code, US Geological Survey*]   (SEIS)
SCH .... Scheme   (ADA)
SCH .... Schenectady, NY [*Location identifier*] [*FAA*]   (FAAL)
SCH .... Schering [*Italy*] [*Research code symbol*]
SCH .... Schering-Plough Corp. [*Research code symbol*]
SCH .... Scherl and Roth Orchestra News [*A publication*]
SCH .... Schiller [*German poet, 1759-1805*]   (ROG)
SCH.......... Schilling [*Monetary unit*] [*Austria*]
Sch .... Schist [*Quality of the bottom*] [*Nautical charts*]
SCH .... Schoenaur Rifle

SCH .... Scholar
SCH .... Scholarship
Sch .... Scholastik [*A publication*]
SCH .... Scholium [*Note*] [*Latin*]
Sch .... School [*Toronto*] [*A publication*]
SCH .... School (AFM)
SCH .... Schooner
SCH .... Schreiber Resources Ltd. [*Vancouver Stock Exchange symbol*]
Sch .... Schultz Number
SCH .... Schwab [*Charles*] Corp. [*NYSE symbol*] (SPSG)
SCH .... Search (MCD)
SCH .... Seizures per Circuit per Hour [*Telecommunications*] (TEL)
SCH .... Sequencer Chassis
SCH .... Shelter Complex Headquarters [*Civil Defense*]
SCH .... Sisters of Charity of St. Vincent de Paul, Halifax [*Roman Catholic religious order*]
SCH .... Societe Canadienne d'Hermeneutique [*Canadian Society for Hermeneutics - CSH*]
SCH .... Society for Calligraphy and Handwriting (EA)
SCh .... Society of Christ [*Roman Catholic men's religious order*]
SCH .... Society for Colonial History [*Defunct*] (EA)
SCH .... Socket Head (AAG)
SCH .... Sole Community Hospital
SCh .... Sources Chretiennes [*A publication*]
SCH .... Square Cartridge Heater
SCH .... Student Credit Hours
SCH .... Studia ad Corpus Hellenisticum Novi Testamenti (BJA)
SCH .... Studies in Church History [*A publication*]
SCh .... Succinylcholine [*Biochemistry*]
SCH .... Supporting Checkout
SCHA .... Copiapo/Chamonate [*Chile*] [*ICAO location identifier*] (ICLI)
Scha .... [*Simon*] Schardius [*Deceased, 1573*] [*Authority cited in pre-1607 legal work*] (DSA)
ScHaC .... Coker College, Hartsville, SC [*Library symbol*] [*Library of Congress*] (LCLS)
Sch Activities ... School Activities [*A publication*]
Schalk .... Schalk's Jamaica Reports [*A publication*] (DLA)
Sch Aq R ... Schultes' Aquatic Rights [*1811*] [*A publication*] (DLA)
Sch Arts ..... School Arts Magazine [*A publication*]
Sch Arts M ... School Arts Magazine [*A publication*]
SCHASE ... Steeplechase
Schatzkammer ... Schatzkammer der Deutschen Sprachlehre. Dichtung und Geschichte [*A publication*]
SCHAVMED ... School of Aviation Medicine [*Later, School of Aerospace Medicine*] (MCD)
SChB .... Small Chemical Businesses [*American Chemical Society*]
Sch Bailm ... Schouler on Bailments [*A publication*] (DLA)
Sch Bell ...... School Bell [*A publication*] (APTA)
SCHC .... Scherer [*R. P.*] Corporation [*NASDAQ symbol*] (NQ)
SCHC .... Society of the Companions of the Holy Cross (EA)
Sch Coach .. Scholastic Coach [*A publication*]
Sch & Com ... School and Community [*A publication*]
Sch Community News ... School and Community News [*A publication*] (APTA)
Sch Counsel ... School Counselor [*A publication*]
SCHCR ...... Stanford Center for Health Care Research [*Closed, 1978*]
SCHD .... Scheduling
Sch Days ... School Days [*A publication*] (APTA)
Sch Dent Serv Gaz (NZ) ... School Dental Services Gazette (Wellington, New Zealand) [*A publication*]
Sch Dom Rel ... Schouler on Domestic Relations [*A publication*] (DLA)
SCHE .... Scheme (ROG)
SChE .... Serum Cholinesterase [*An enzyme*]
SCHE .... Societe Canadienne de l'Histoire de l'Eglise [*Canadian Society of Church History - CSCH*]
SCHEC ...... Societe Canadienne de l'Histoire de l'Eglise Catholique [*Canadian Catholic History Association - CCHA*]
SCHED ..... Schedule (KSC)
Sch Ed .... School and Home Education [*Illinois*] [*A publication*]
Sched Discounts Differentials Serv Charges Applying Wheat ... Schedule of Discounts, Differentials, and Service Charges Applying to Wheat [*A publication*]
SCHEDE... Schedule (ROG)
Scheif Pr .... Scheiffer's Practice [*A publication*] (DLA)
Sch (El Ed) ... School (Toronto) (Elementary Edition) [*A publication*]
SCHEM ...... Schematic
Sch Eng Bull NC State Univ ... School of Engineering. Bulletin. North Carolina State University [*A publication*]
Scher .... Scherer's New York Miscellaneous Reports [*22-47*] [*A publication*] (DLA)
SCHERZ ... Scherzando [*Playful*] [*Music*]
Sch Exec ... School Executive [*A publication*]
Sch Executives M ... School Executives Magazine [*A publication*]
SchF .... Schultexte aus Fara [*A publication*]
Sch Foodserv Res Rev ... School Foodservice Research Review [*A publication*]
SchG .... Schiedsgericht [*Arbitration Court*] [*German*] (ILCA)
SCHG .... Supercharge
SCHGM .... South Carolina Historical and Genealogical Magazine [*A publication*]
Sch Guidance W ... School Guidance Worker [*A publication*]
SChH .... Studies in Church History [*A publication*]

SCHHA ..... Schiff und Hafen [*A publication*]
Sch Health Rev ... School Health Review [*A publication*]
Sch and Home ... School and Home [*A publication*]
Sch H & W ... Schouler on Husband and Wife [*A publication*] (DLA)
ScHi .... South Carolina Historical Society, Charleston, SC [*Library symbol*] [*Library of Congress*] (LCLS)
Schiffstechnik ... Schiffstechnik. Forschungshefte fuer Schiffbau und Schiffsmaschinenbau [*A publication*]
Schild Steier ... Schild von Steier. Beitraege zur Steierischen Vor- und Fruehgeschichte und Muenzkunde [*A publication*]
SC His M... South Carolina Historical and Genealogical Magazine [*A publication*]
SC Hist Assn Proc ... South Carolina Historical Association. Proceedings [*A publication*]
SC Hist Mag ... South Carolina Historical Magazine [*A publication*]
SCHIZ .... Schizophrenia [*Medicine*]
schizo .... Schizophrenia [*Psychology*]
Schizophr Bull ... Schizophrenia Bulletin [*A publication*]
Schizophr Syndr ... Schizophrenic Syndrome [*A publication*]
Schizophr Syndr Annu Rev ... Schizophrenic Syndrome: An Annual Review [*A publication*]
SCHJ .... Societe Canadienne de l'Histoire Juive [*Canadian Jewish Historical Association - CJHS*]
SCHL .... Court of Session Cases, House of Lords [*Scotland*] [*A publication*] (DLA)
SC(HL) ...... Sessions Cases (House of Lords) [*Legal*] [*British*]
SCHL .... Societe Canadienne d'Hypotheques et de Logement [*Central Mortgage and Housing Corporation - CMHC*]
SCHLA ...... School for Latin America [*Military*] (AFM)
Schlachtofwes Lebensmittelueberwach ... Schlachtofwesen Lebensmittelueberwachung [*A publication*]
Sch L Bull .. School Law Bulletin [*A publication*]
Sch & Lef ... Schoales and Lefroy's Irish Chancery Reports [*A publication*] (DLA)
Sch Leg Rec ... Schuylkill's Pennsylvania Legal Record [*A publication*] (DLA)
Schleif Polier Oberflaechentech ... Schleif-, Polier-, und Oberflaechentechnik [*A publication*]
Schleif Poliertech (Hoya Weser Ger) ... Schleif- und Poliertechnik (Hoya-Weser, Germany) [*A publication*]
Schles Ges Jber ... Schlesische Gesellschaft fuer Vaterlaendische Kultur. Jahres-Bericht [*A publication*]
Schlesw-Holst Bienenztg ... Schleswig-Holsteinisches Bienenzeitung [*A publication*]
Schleswig Holsteinisches Aerztebl ... Schleswig-Holsteinisches Aerzteblatt [*A publication*]
Sch Lib ...... School Librarian [*A publication*]
Sch Lib .... School Libraries [*A publication*]
Sch Lib Assn Calif Bul ... School Library Association of California. Bulletin [*A publication*]
Sch Lib Can ... School Libraries in Canada [*A publication*]
Sch Lib J.... School Library Journal [*A publication*]
Sch Lib Med N ... School Library-Media News [*A publication*]
Sch Libn ..... School Librarian [*A publication*]
Sch Libr ..... School Libraries [*A publication*]
Sch Lib R ... School Library Review and Educational Record [*A publication*]
Sch Libr Bull ... School Library Bulletin [*A publication*] (APTA)
Sch Librn ... School Librarian and School Library Review [*Later, School Librarian*] [*A publication*]
Schlief-Poliertech ... Schlief- und Poliertechnik [*West Germany*] [*A publication*]
Sch Life ...... School Life [*A publication*]
Sch LR .... Schuylkill's Pennsylvania Legal Record [*A publication*] (DLA)
SCHLS ...... Schluszsatz [*Finale*] [*Music*]
SCHLSHIP ... Schoolship [*Navy*] (NVT)
SCHLSHP ... Scholarship
SCHLT ...... Searchlight (MSA)
SCHM .... Schematic (AAG)
Schm .... Schoolmaster [*Navy*] [*British*]
Sch M .... Schweizer Monatshefte [*A publication*]
SCHM .... Societe Canadienne d'Histoire de la Medecine [*Canadian Society for the History of Medicine - CSHM*]
SCHM .... South Carolina Historical and Genealogical Magazine [*A publication*]
Sch Manag ... School Management [*A publication*]
Sch Manage ... School Management Bulletin [*A publication*] (APTA)
Sch Management ... School Management [*A publication*] (APTA)
Sch Management Bul ... School Management Bulletin [*A publication*] (APTA)
Schm Civil Law ... Schmidt's Civil Law of Spain and Mexico [*A publication*] (DLA)
Sch Media Q ... School Media Quarterly [*A publication*]
Schmerz Narkose Anaesth ... Schmerz. Narkose-Anaesthesie [*A publication*]
Schm Exp ... Schmitthoff. Export Trade [*A publication*] (ILCA)
Sch Mgt ..... School Management [*A publication*]
Schmidt Civ Law ... Schmidt's Civil Law of Spain and Mexico [*A publication*] (DLA)
Schmierstoffe Schmierungstech ... Schmierstoffe und Schmierungstechnik [*East Germany*] [*A publication*]
Schmierst Schmierungstech ... Schmierstoffe und Schmierungstechnik [*A publication*]

Schmiertech Tribol ... Schmiertechnik und Tribologie [*A publication*]
SCHMILSCIO ... School of Military Sciences Officer [*Air Force*]
Sch Mines Q ... School of Mines Quarterly [*A publication*]
Schm LJ..... Schmidt's Law Journal [*New Orleans*] [*A publication*]   (DLA)
Schmollers Jahrb ... Schmollers Jahrbuch fuer Gesetzgebung, Verwaltung und Volkswirtschaft im Deutschen Reiche [*A publication*]
SCHMOO ... Space Cargo Handler and Manipulator for Orbital Operations
SCHMR .... Schoolmaster   (ROG)
Sch Mus..... School Music [*A publication*]
Sch Mus B ... Bachelor of School Music
Sch MZ...... Schweizerische Musikzeitung [*A publication*]
Schn .... [*Johannes*] Schneidewein [*Deceased, 1568*] [*Authority cited in pre-1607 legal work*]   (DSA)
SCHND..... Soon Chun Hyang Taehak Nonmunjip [*A publication*]
Schneeberger Hb ... Schneeberger Heimatbuechlein [*A publication*]
Schneid ...... [*Johannes*] Schneidewein [*Deceased, 1568*] [*Authority cited in pre-1607 legal work*]   (DSA)
Schnell Inf Hydraul & Pneum ... Schnell Informationen Hydraulik und Pneumatik [*A publication*]
Schnurpfeils Rev Glass Works ... Schnurpfeil's Review for Glass Works [*A publication*]
SCHO....... Scholar [*or Scholarship*]   (ROG)
SCHO....... Societe Canadienne d'Histoire Orale [*Canadian Oral History Association - COHA*]
SCHO....... Standard Controlled Heteroydne Oscillator
Schoales & L ... Schoales and Lefroy's Irish Chancery Reports [*A publication*]   (DLA)
Schoenberg Inst ... Arnold Schoenberg Institute. Journal [*A publication*]
Schol .... Scholar
SCHOL .... Scholarship
Schol .... Scholastik. Vierteljahresschrift fuer Theologie und Philosophie [*A publication*]
Schol .... Scholia [*Classical studies*]   (OCD)
Schol .... Scholiast [*Classical studies*]   (OCD)
SCHOL ..... Scholium [*Note*] [*Latin*]   (ROG)
SCHOLAR ... Schering-Oriented Literature Analysis and Retrieval System [*Schering-Plough Corp.*] [*Information service or system*]   (IID)
Scholarly Pub ... Scholarly Publishing [*A publication*]
Scholar Pub ... Scholarly Publishing [*A publication*]
Scholastic... Senior Scholastic [*Teacher Edition*] [*A publication*]
Scholastic D ... Scholastic Debater [*A publication*]
Schol Bern ... Scholia Bernensia ad Vergilii Bucolica et Georgica [*A publication*]   (OCD)
Schol Bob... Scholia Bobiensia [*Classical studies*]   (OCD)
Schol Coach ... Scholastic Coach [*A publication*]
Schol Cruq ... Scholia Cruquiana [*Classical studies*]   (OCD)
Schol Flor Callim ... Scholia Florentina in Callimachum [*Classical studies*]   (OCD)
Schol S....... Scholia Satyrica [*A publication*]
Schol Teach ... Scholastic Teacher [*A publication*]
Schol Teach JH/SH Ed ... Scholastic Teacher. Junior/Senior High Teacher's Edition [*A publication*]
Schomberg Mar Laws Rhodes ... Schomberg's Treatise on the Maritime Laws of Rhodes [*A publication*]   (DLA)
School of Advanced Studies Rev ... School of Advanced International Studies. Review [*A publication*]   (DLA)
School Arts M ... School Arts Magazine [*A publication*]
School & Col ... School and College [*A publication*]
School Fam ... School Family [*A publication*]   (APTA)
School Law Bul (Univ NC) ... School Law Bulletin (University of North Carolina) [*A publication*]
School Lib ... School Libraries [*A publication*]
School Libs Aust ... School Libraries in Australia [*A publication*]
School of LR ... School of Law. Review. Toronto University [*Canada*] [*A publication*]   (DLA)
School L Rep (Nat'l Org on Legal Probs in Educ) ... School Law Reporter. National Organization on Legal Problems in Education [*A publication*]   (DLA)
School L Rep Natl Org on Legal Probs in Educ ... School Law Reporter. National Organization on Legal Problems in Education [*A publication*]
Schoolmens W Univ PA Proc ... Schoolmen's Week. University of Pennsylvania. Proceedings [*A publication*]
School Mus ... School Musician [*A publication*]
School Rev ... School Review. A Journal of Secondary Education [*A publication*]
School and Soc ... School and Society [*A publication*]
Schopenhauer-Jahr ... Schopenhauer-Jahrbuch [*A publication*]
Schopenhauer-Jahrb ... Schopenhauer-Jahrbuch [*A publication*]
Schott Inf ... Schott Information [*A publication*]
Schouler Bailm ... Schouler on Bailments [*A publication*]   (DLA)
Schouler Dom Rel ... Schouler on Domestic Relations [*A publication*]   (DLA)
Schouler Pers Prop ... Schouler on the Law of Personal Property [*A publication*]   (DLA)
Schouler US Hist ... Schouler's History of the United States under the Constitution [*A publication*]   (DLA)
SchP.......... Ordo Clericorum Regularum Pauperum Matris Dei Scholarum Piarum [*Roman Catholic men's religious order*]
SchP.......... Scholarly Publishing [*A publication*]
Sch & Parent ... School and Parent [*A publication*]   (APTA)

SCHPB...... Bulletin et Memoires. Societe des Chirurgiens de Paris [*A publication*]
Sch Per Prop ... Schouler on the Law of Personal Property [*A publication*]   (DLA)
Sch Pharm Bull Univ Wis Ext Div ... School of Pharmacy. Bulletin. University of Wisconsin. Extension Division [*A publication*]
SCHPM..... Societe Canadienne d'Histoire et de Philosophie des Mathematiques [*Canadian Society for the History and Philosophy of Mathematics - CSHPM*]
SCHPS ...... Societe Canadienne d'Histoire et de Philosophie des Sciences [*Canadian Society for the History and Philosophy of Science - CSHPS*]
Sch Psychol R ... School Psychology Review [*A publication*]
SCHR .... Cochrane/Cochrane [*Chile*] [*ICAO location identifier*]   (ICLI)
SCHR .... Scherer Healthcare, Inc. [*NASDAQ symbol*]   (CTT)
Sch R.......... School Review [*A publication*]
SCHR .... Schooner
SchR........... Schweizerische Rundschau [*A publication*]
SCHR........... Societe Canadienne d'Histoire de la Rhetorique [*See also CSHR*] [*Canada*]
SCHR .... Supervisory Change Relations Test
Schrad........ [*Ludolphus*] Schrader [*Deceased, 1589*] [*Authority cited in pre-1607 legal work*]   (DSA)
Sch Reg...... Schuylkill's Pennsylvania Register [*A publication*]   (DLA)
Sch Rev ...... School Review [*A publication*]
Schr Geb Brennst Geol ... Schriften aus dem Gebiet der Brennstoff-Geologie [*A publication*]
Schriften Aerztl Fortbild ... Schriftenreihe der Aerztlichen Fortbildung [*A publication*]
Schriftenr Agrarwiss Fak Univ Kiel ... Schriftenreihe. Agrarwissenschaftliche Fakultaet. Universitaet Kiel [*A publication*]
Schriftenr Bauforsch Tech Organ ... Schriftenreihen der Bauforschung. Reihe Technik und Organisation [*A publication*]
Schriftenr Bayer Landesamt Wasserwirt ... Schriftenreihe. Bayerisches Landesamt fuer Wasserwirtschaft [*A publication*]
Schriftenr Bundesminist Wiss Forsch Forsch Bild ... Schriftenreihe. Bundesminister fuer Wissenschaftliche Forschung. Forschung und Bildung [*West Germany*] [*A publication*]
Schriftenr Bundesminist Wiss Forsch (Ger) Radionuklide ... Schriftenreihe. Bundesminister fuer Wissenschaftliche Forschung (West Germany). Radionuklide [*A publication*]
Schriftenr Bundesminist Wiss Forsch (Ger) Strahlenschutz ... Schriftenreihe. Bundesminister fuer Wissenschaftliche Forschung (West Germany). Strahlenschutz [*A publication*]
Schriftenr Bundesminist Wiss Forsch Kernenergierecht ... Schriftenreihe. Bundesminister fuer Wissenschaftliche Forschung. Kernenergierecht [*West Germany*] [*A publication*]
Schriftenr Bundesminist Wiss Forsch Strahlenschutz ... Schriftenreihe. Bundesminister fuer Wissenschaftliche Forschung. Strahlenschutz [*A publication*]
Schriften Bundesverb Dtsch Kalkind ... Schriftenreihe. Bundesverband der Deutschen Kalkindustrie [*A publication*]
Schriften Dtsch Atomforums ... Schriftenreihe des Deutschen Atomforums [*A publication*]
Schriftenreihe Didaktik Math ... Schriftenreihe Didaktik der Mathematik [*A publication*]
Schriftenreihe Landwirt Fak Univ Kiel ... Schriftenreihe der Landwirtschaftlichen Fakultaet der Universitaet Kiel [*A publication*]
Schriftenreihe Math ... Schriftenreihe fuer Mathematik [*A publication*]
Schriftenreihe Math Inst Univ Muenster ... Schriftenreihe. Mathematisches Institut. Universitaet Muenster [*A publication*]
Schriftenreihe Rechenzentrum Univ Koeln ... Schriftenreihe des Rechenzentrums. Universitaet zu Koeln [*A publication*]
Schriftenreihe Zentralinst Math Mech ... Schriftenreihe. Zentralinstitut fuer Mathematik und Mechanik [*A publication*]
Schriftenr Forschungsgem Schweiz Lackfabr ... Schriftenreihe. Forschungsgemeinschaft Schweizerischer Lackfabrikanten [*A publication*]
Schriftenr Forstl Fak Univ Goettingen ... Schriftenreihe. Forstliche Fakultaet. Universitaet Goettingen und Mitteilungen. Niedersaechsische Forstliche Versuchsanstalt [*A publication*]
Schriftenr Geb Off Gesundheitswes ... Schriftenreihe aus dem Gebiete des Oeffentlichen Gesundheitswesens [*A publication*]
Schriftenr Intensivmed Notfallmed Anaesthesiol ... Schriftenreihe Intensivmedizin, Notfallmedizin, Anaesthesiologie [*A publication*]
Schriftenr Int Ges Nahr Vitalst Forsch eV ... Schriftenreihe. Internationale Gesellschaft fuer Nahrungs- und Vitalstoff-Forschung eV [*A publication*]
Schriftenr Landesanst Immissionsschutz ... Schriftenreihe. Landesanstalt fuer Immissionsschutz [*West Germany*] [*A publication*]
Schriftenr Landschaftspflege Naturschutz ... Schriftenreihe fuer Landschaftspflege und Naturschutz [*A publication*]
Schriftenr Lebensmittelchem Lebensmittelqual ... Schriftenreihe. Lebensmittelchemie, Lebensmittelqualitaet [*A publication*]
Schriftenr Neurol ... Schriftenreihe Neurologie [*A publication*]
Schriftenr Neurol-Neurol Ser ... Schriftenreihe Neurologie-Neurology Series [*A publication*]

Schriftenr Oesterr Wasserwirtschaftsverb ... Schriftenreihe. Oesterreichischer Wasserwirtschaftsverband [*A publication*]
Schriftenr Otto Graf Inst Univ Stuttgart ... Schriftenreihe. Otto-Graf-Institut. Universitaet Stuttgart [*A publication*]
Schriftenr Schweissen Schneiden Ber ... Schriftenreihe Schweissen Schneiden. Bericht [*A publication*]
Schriftenr Theor Prax Med Psychol ... Schriftenreihe zur Theorie und Praxis der Medizinischen Psychologie [*A publication*]
Schriftenr Vegetationskd ... Schriftenreihe fuer Vegetationskunde [*A publication*]
Schriftenr Versuchstierkd ... Schriftenreihe Versuchstierkunde [*A publication*]
Schriftenr Ver Wasser Boden Lufthyg ... Schriftenreihe. Verein fuer Wasser, Boden, und Lufthygiene [*A publication*]
Schriftenr Zementind ... Schriftenreihe der Zementindustrie [*A publication*]
Schriftenr Zentralbl Arbeitsmed Arbeitsschtz Prophyl ... Schriftenreihe. Zentralblatt fuer Arbeitsmedizin, Arbeitsschutz, und Prophylaxe [*A publication*]
Schriften Wirtschaftwiss Forsch ... Schriften zur Wirtschaftwissenschaftlichen Forschung [*A publication*]
Schrift Naturf Gesellsch Kopenhagen ... Schriften. Naturforschende Gesellschaft zu Kopenhagen [*A publication*]
Schrifttum Agrarwirt ... Schriftum der Agrarwirtschaft [*A publication*]
Schr Math Inst Univ Muenster 2 ... Schriftenreihe. Mathematisches Institut. Universitaet Muenster. 2 Serie [*A publication*]
Schr Math Inst Univ Munster ... Schriftenreihe. Mathematisches Institut. Universitaet Muenster [*A publication*]
Schr Naturwiss Ver Schleswig-Holstein ... Schriften. Naturwissenschaftlicher Verein fuer Schleswig-Holstein [*A publication*]
Schrreihe Forstl Fak Univ Goettingen ... Schriftenreihe. Forstliche Fakultaet. Universitaet Goettingen [*A publication*]
SCHRUB... Schmidt Rubin Rifle
Schr Ver Verbr Naturwiss Kennt Wien ... Schriften. Verein zur Verbreitung Naturwissenschaftlicher Kenntnisse in Wien [*A publication*]
SCHS........ Scottish Church History Society   (EAIO)
SCHS........ Small Component Handling System [*Nuclear energy*]   (NRCH)
SCHS........ Supreme Court Historical Society   (EA)
SCHSA...... Soap and Chemical Specialties [*Later, Soap/Cosmetics/Chemical Specialties*] [*A publication*]
Sch Sci & Math ... School Science and Mathematics [*A publication*]
Sch Sci Rev ... School Science Review [*England*] [*A publication*]
Sch (Sec Ed) ... School (Toronto) (Secondary Edition) [*A publication*]
Sch Shop ... School Shop [*A publication*]
Sch & Soc ... School and Society [*A publication*]
Sch Trust ... School Trustee [*A publication*]
Schupo .... Schutzpolizist [*Policeman*] [*German*]
Schuy Leg Rec (PA) ... Schuylkill's Pennsylvania Legal Record [*A publication*]   (DLA)
Schuyl Legal Rec ... Schuylkill's Pennsylvania Legal Record [*A publication*]   (DLA)
Schuyl Leg Rec ... Schuylkill's Pennsylvania Legal Record [*A publication*]   (DLA)
Schuyl Leg Reg ... Schuylkill's Legal Register [*Pennsylvania*] [*A publication*]   (ILCA)
Schuy Reg (PA) ... Schuylkill's Pennsylvania Register [*A publication*]   (DLA)
SCHVD ..... Sachverhalte [*A publication*]
SCHWA .... Schweisstechnik Soudure [*A publication*]
Schwaeb Imkerkal ... Schwaebischer Imkerkalender [*A publication*]
Schw A Neur ... Schweizer Archiv fuer Neurologie, Neurochirurgie, und Psychiatrie [*A publication*]
SchwArchV ... Schweizerisches Archiv fuer Volkskunde [*A publication*]
Schwarz Int L ... Schwarzenberger's Manual of International Law [*A publication*]   (DLA)
Schwarz Man Int L ... Schwarzenberger's Manual of International Law [*A publication*]   (ILCA)
Schweisstech Soudure (Zurich) ... Schweisstechnik Soudure (Zurich) [*A publication*]
Schweiz Aerztztg ... Schweizerische Aerztezeitung [*A publication*]
Schweiz Alum Rundsch ... Schweizer Aluminium Rundschau [*A publication*]
Schweiz Anst Forstl Versuchswes Mitt ... Schweizerische Anstalt fuer das Forstliche Versuchswesen. Mitteilungen [*A publication*]
Schweiz Apoth Ztg ... Schweizerische Apotheker-Zeitung [*A publication*]
Schweiz Arch ... Schweizer Archiv [*A publication*]
Schweiz Arch Angew Wiss Tech ... Schweizer Archiv fuer Angewandte Wissenschaft und Technik [*A publication*]
Schweiz Archiv f Volksk ... Schweizerisches Archiv fuer Volkskunde [*A publication*]
Schweiz Arch Neurol Neurochir Psychiatr ... Schweizer Archiv fuer Neurologie, Neurochirurgie, und Psychiatrie [*A publication*]
Schweiz Arch Neurol Psychiatr ... Schweizer Archiv fuer Neurologie und Psychiatrie [*A publication*]
Schweiz Arch Tierh ... Schweizer Archiv fuer Tierheilkunde [*A publication*]
Schweiz Arch Tierh (Bern) ... Schweizerisches Archiv fuer Tierheilkunde und Tierzucht (Bern) [*A publication*]
Schweiz Arch Tierheilkd ... Schweizer Archiv fuer Tierheilkunde [*A publication*]
Schweiz Arch Verkehrswiss und Verkehrspol ... Schweizerisches Archiv fuer Verkehrswissenschaft und Verkehrspolitik [*A publication*]
Schweiz Bauztg ... Schweizerische Bauzeitung [*A publication*]

Schweiz Beitr Dendrol ... Schweizerische Beitrage zur Dendrologie [*A publication*]
Schweiz Bienen-Ztg ... Schweizerische Bienen-Zeitung [*A publication*]
Schweiz Bl Heiz Lueft ... Schweizerische Blaetter fuer Heizung und Lueftung [*Switzerland*] [*A publication*]
Schweiz Brau-Rundsch ... Schweizerische Brauerei-Rundschau [*A publication*]
Schweiz Chem Ztg ... Schweizerische Chemiker-Zeitung [*A publication*]
Schweiz Chem Ztg Tech Ind ... Schweizer Chemiker-Zeitung Technik-Industrie [*A publication*]
Schweiz Elektrotech Z ... Schweizerische Elektrotechnische Zeitschrift [*A publication*]
Schweizer Archiv Verkehrswiss u -Polit ... Schweizerisches Archiv fuer Verkehrswissenschaft und Verkehrspolitik [*A publication*]
Schweizer Arch Tierheilk ... Schweizer Archiv fuer Tierheilkunde [*A publication*]
Schweizer Arch Volksk ... Schweizer Archiv fuer Volkskunde [*A publication*]
Schweizer Mineralog u Petrog Mitt ... Schweizerische Mineralogische und Petrographische Mitteilungen [*A publication*]
Schweizer Natschutz ... Schweizer Naturschutz [*A publication*]
Schweizer Palaeont Abh Mem Suisses Paleontologie ... Schweizerische Palaeontologische Abhandlungen. Memoires Suisses de Palaeontologie [*A publication*]
Schweizer Z Soziol ... Schweizerische Zeitschrift fuer Soziologie [*A publication*]
Schweizer Z Volkswirtsch u Statist ... Schweizerische Zeitschrift fuer Volkswirtschaft und Statistik [*A publication*]
Schweiz Gaertnerztg ... Schweizerische Gaertnerzeitung [*A publication*]
Schweiz Ing & Archit ... Schweizer Ingenieur und Architekt [*A publication*]
Schweiz Jb f Internat Recht ... Schweizerisches Jahrbuch fuer Internationales Recht/Annuaire Suisse de Droit International [*Zurich, Switzerland*] [*A publication*]   (DLA)
Schweiz Landtech ... Schweizer Landtechnik [*A publication*]
Schweiz Landw Forsch ... Schweizerische Landwirtschaftliche Forschung [*A publication*]
Schweiz Landwirtsch Forsch Rech Agron Suisse ... Schweizerische Landwirtschaftliche Forschung/La Recherche Agronomique en Suisse [*A publication*]
Schweiz Landwirtsch Monatsh ... Schweizerische Landwirtschaftliche Monatshefte [*A publication*]
Schweiz Landw Mh ... Schweizerische Landwirtschaftliche Monatshefte [*A publication*]
Schweiz Med Wochenschr ... Schweizerische Medizinische Wochenschrift [*A publication*]
Schweiz Med Wochenschr Suppl ... Schweizerische Medizinische Wochenschrift. Supplementum [*A publication*]
Schweiz Med Wschr ... Schweizerische Medizinische Wochenschrift [*A publication*]
Schweiz Mh ... Schweizer Monatshefte [*A publication*]
Schweiz Mhefte Pol Wirt Kultur ... Schweizer Monatshefte. Zeitschrift fuer Politik, Wirtschaft, Kultur [*A publication*]
Schweiz Milchwirtsch Forsch ... Schweizerische Milchwirtschaftliche Forschung [*A publication*]
Schweiz Milchztg ... Schweizerische Milchzeitung [*A publication*]
Schweiz Mineral Petrogr Mitt ... Schweizerische Mineralogische und Petrographische Mitteilungen [*A publication*]
Schweiz Monatsschr Zahnheilkd ... Schweizerische Monatsschrift fuer Zahnheilkunde [*A publication*]
Schweiz Monatsschr Zahnmed ... Schweizerische Monatsschrift fuer Zahnmedizin [*A publication*]
Schweiz Muenzbl ... Schweizer Muenzblaetter [*Switzerland*] [*A publication*]
Schweiz Mus ... Schweizerische Musikzeitung [*A publication*]
Schweiz Naturf Ges Verh ... Schweizerische Naturforschende Gesellschaft. Verhandlungen [*A publication*]
Schweiz Naturschutz Prot Nat ... Schweizer Naturschutz. Protection de la Nature [*A publication*]
Schweiz Palaeontol Abh ... Schweizerische Palaeontologische Abhandlungen [*A publication*]
Schweiz Palaeontol Abh-Mem Suisse Palaeontol ... Schweizerische Palaeontologische Abhandlungen. Memoires Suisses de Palaeontologie [*A publication*]
Schweiz Photorundsch ... Schweizerische Photorundschau [*A publication*]
Schweiz Photo Ztg ... Schweizerische Photo-Zeitung [*A publication*]
Schweiz Rdsch ... Schweizerische Rundschau [*A publication*]
Schweiz Rundsch Med Prax ... Schweizerische Rundschau fuer Medizin Praxis [*A publication*]
Schweiz Strahler ... Schweizerische Strahler [*A publication*]
Schweiz Tech ... Schweizerische Technikerzeitung [*Switzerland*] [*A publication*]
Schweiz Tech Z ... Schweizerische Technische Zeitschrift [*Switzerland*] [*A publication*]
Schweiz Ver Atomenerg Bull ... Schweizerische Vereinigung fuer Atomenergie. Bulletin [*A publication*]
Schweiz Ver Gas-Wasserfachmaennern Monatsbull ... Schweizerische Verein von Gas- und Wasserfachmaennern. Monatsbulletin [*Switzerland*] [*A publication*]
Schweiz Ver Lack Farbenchem Bull ... Schweizerische Vereinigung der Lack- und Farbenchemiker. Bulletin [*A publication*]
Schweiz Volkskd ... Schweizer Volkskunde [*A publication*]
Schweiz Wochenschr Chem Pharm ... Schweizerische Wochenschrift fuer Chemie und Pharmacie [*A publication*]

Schweiz Wochenschr Pharm ... Schweizerische Wochenschrift fuer Pharmacie [*A publication*]
Schweiz Wohnschr Chem u Pharm ... Schweizerische Wochenschrift fuer Chemie und Pharmacie [*A publication*]
Schweiz Z Allg Path Bakt ... Schweizerische Zeitschrift fuer Allgemeine Pathologie und Bakteriologie [*A publication*]
Schweiz Z Allg Pathol Bakterol ... Schweizerische Zeitschrift fuer Allgemeine Pathologie und Bakteriologie [*A publication*]
Schweiz Z Biochem ... Schweizerische Zeitschrift fuer Biochemie [*A publication*]
Schweiz Z Forstwes ... Schweizerische Zeitschrift fuer Forstwesen [*A publication*]
Schweiz Z Gesch ... Schweizerische Zeitschrift fuer Geschichte [*A publication*]
Schweiz Z Gynaekol Geburtshilfe ... Schweizerische Zeitschrift fuer Gynaekologie und Geburtshilfe [*A publication*]
Schweiz Z Gynaekol Geburtshilfe Suppl ... Schweizerische Zeitschrift fuer Gynaekologie und Geburtshilfe. Supplementum [*A publication*]
Schweiz Z Hydrol ... Schweizerische Zeitschrift fuer Hydrologie [*A publication*]
Schweiz Z Obst-u Weinb ... Schweizerische Zeitschrift fuer Obst- und Weinbau [*A publication*]
Schweiz Z Obst-Weinbau ... Schweizerische Zeitschrift fuer Obst- und Weinbau [*A publication*]
Schweiz Z Pathol Bakteriol ... Schweizerische Zeitschrift fuer Pathologie und Bakteriologie [*A publication*]
Schweiz Z Pharm ... Schweizerische Zeitschrift fuer Pharmacie [*A publication*]
Schweiz Z Pilzkd ... Schweizerische Zeitschrift fuer Pilzkunde [*A publication*]
Schweiz Z Pilzkd Bull Suisse Mycol ... Schweizerische Zeitschrift fuer Pilzkunde. Bulletin Suisse de Mycologie [*A publication*]
Schweiz Z Psychol Anwend ... Schweizerische Zeitschrift fuer Psychologie und Ihre Anwendungen [*A publication*]
Schweiz Z Sozialversicherung ... Schweizerische Zeitschrift fuer Sozialversicherung [*A publication*]
Schweiz Z Sportmed ... Schweizerische Zeitschrift fuer Sportmedizin [*A publication*]
Schweiz Z f Strafrecht ... Schweizerische Zeitschrift fuer Strafrecht/Revue Penale Suisse [*Berne, Switzerland*] [*A publication*]   (DLA)
Schweiz Z Tuberk Pneumonol ... Schweizerische Zeitschrift fuer Tuberkulose und Pneumonologie [*A publication*]
Schweiz Z Verkehrswirt ... Schweizerische Zeitschrift fuer Verkehrswirtschaft [*A publication*]
Schweiz Z Vermess Photogramm Kulturtech ... Schweizerische Zeitschrift fuer Vermessung, Photogrammetrie, und Kulturtechnik [*A publication*]
Schweiz Z Volkswirt und Statis ... Schweizerische Zeitschrift fuer Volkswirtschaft und Statistik [*A publication*]
Schwenk..... Schwenckfeldiana [*A publication*]
Schwest Rev ... Schwestern Revue [*A publication*]
Schwiez Z Path Bakt ... Schweizerische Zeitschrift fuer Pathologie und Bakteriologie [*A publication*]
SchwKiZ .... Schweizerische Kirchenzeitung [*Lucerne*] [*A publication*]
SchwKZ ..... Schweizerische Kirchenzeitung [*Lucerne*] [*A publication*]
SchwM....... Schweizer Monatshefte [*A publication*]
Schw Mbl... Schweizer Muenzblaetter [*A publication*]
Schw Med Wo ... Schweizerische Medizinische Wochenschrift [*A publication*]
SchwMH ... Schweizer Monatshefte [*Zurich*] [*A publication*]
Schw Musikz ... Schweizerische Musikzeitung/Revue Musicale Suisse [*A publication*]
Schw NR .... Schweizerische Numismatische Rundschau [*A publication*]
SCHWR .... Steam-Cooled Heavy-Water Reactor
SchwRundschau ... Schweizerische Rundschau [*A publication*]
SchwV .... Schweizer Volkskunde [*A publication*]
Schw Z Gesc ... Schweizerische Zeitschrift fuer Geschichte [*A publication*]
Schw Z Hydrol ... Schweizerische Zeitschrift fuer Hydrologie [*A publication*]
Schw Z Pilzk ... Schweizerische Zeitschrift fuer Pilzkunde [*A publication*]
Schw Z Psyc ... Schweizerische Zeitschrift fuer Psychologie und Ihre Anwendungen [*A publication*]
Schw Z Psychol ... Schweizerische Zeitschrift fuer Psychologie und Ihre Anwendungen [*A publication*]
Schw Zs f G ... Schweizerische Zeitschrift fuer Geschichte [*A publication*]
Schw Z Soz ... Schweizerische Zeitschrift fuer Sozialversicherung [*A publication*]
Schw Z Sportmed ... Schweizerische Zeitschrift fuer Sportmedizin [*A publication*]
Schw Zs Tbk ... Schweizerische Zeitschrift fuer Tuberkulose [*A publication*]
Schw Zs Vermess ... Schweizerische Zeitschrift fuer Vermessungswesen [*A publication*]
Schw ZV St ... Schweizerische Zeitschrift fuer Volkswirtschaft und Statistik [*A publication*]
SCI............ Council for the Securities Industry [*Levy*] [*British*]
SCI............ Sacra Congregatio Indicis [*Sacred Congregation of the Index*] [*Latin*]
SCI............ Safari Club International   (EA)
SCI............ San Clemente Island
SCI............ San Clemente Island [*California*] [*Seismograph station code, US Geological Survey*]   (SEIS)
SCI............ Santa Cruz Island   (MUGU)
SCI............ Savio Club International   (EA)
SCI............ Scaleable Coherent Interface [*Data processing*]

SCI............ Schedule-Cost Index   (MCD)
SCI............ SCI Satellite Conferencing International Corp. [*Formerly, Valclair Resources, Ltd.*] [*Vancouver Stock Exchange symbol*]
SCI............ Science   (AFM)
SCI............ Science [*A publication*]
SCI............ Science Citation Index [*A publication*]
SCI............ Science of Creative Intelligence [*Transcendental meditation*]
SCI............ Science Curriculum Improvement [*Study*] [*Education*]
Sci............. Scientia. Revista Internazionale di Sintesi Scientifica [*A publication*]
Sci............. Scientia. Rivista de Tecnica y Cultura [*A publication*]
SCI............ Scientific Computers, Incorporated   (MCD)
SCI............ Scripta Classica Israelica [*A publication*]
ScI............ Scripta Islandica [*A publication*]
SCI............ Seabee Club International   (EA)
SCI............ Sealable Coherent Interface [*Data processing*]
SCI............ Seamen's Church Institute of New York/New Jersey   (EA)
SCI............ Security Container Institute [*Inactive*]   (EA)
SCI............ Selected Configured Item   (MCD)
SCI............ Seminar Clearinghouse International, Inc. [*Information service or system*]   (IID)
SCI............ Sensitive Compartmented Information [*Military*]
SCI............ Sequential Comparison Index [*Measures effect of chemical pollution in lakes and streams*]
SCI............ Serial Communication Interface [*Data processing*]
SCI............ Service Change Information   (MCD)
SCI............ Service Civil International [*International Voluntary Service*] [*Bangalore, India*]
SCI............ Sexual Communications Inventory [*Marital relations test*] [*Psychology*]
SCI............ Ship Controlled Intercept [*RADAR*] [*Navy*]
SCI............ Shipping Container Institute
SCI............ Shipping Corporation of India Ltd.
SCI............ Ship's Capability Impaired [*Navy*]
SCI............ Short Circuit
SCI............ Signal Corps Item [*Obsolete*] [*Army*]   (NATG)
SCI............ Simulation Councils, Incorporated
SCI............ Single-Channel Interface [*Data processing*]
SCI............ Single Column Inch   (ADA)
SCI............ Sister Cities International   (EA)
SCI............ Slot Cell Inserter
SCI............ Small Craft Instructor [*Red Cross*]
SCI............ Smoke Curtain Installation [*British military*]   (DMA)
SCI............ Societe de Chimie Industrielle   (EA)
SCI............ Society of Chemical Industry   (EA)
SCI............ Society of Composers   (EA)
SCI............ Soft Cast Iron
SCI............ Software Configuration Item [*Data processing*]
SCI............ Source Code Indicator   (MCD)
SCI............ Special Customs Invoice
SCI............ Spinal Cord Injury [*Medicine*]
SCI............ Sponge and Chamois Institute   (EA)
SCI............ Staging Connections, Inc. [*Telecommunications service*]   (TSSD)
SCI............ Stampe Club International   (EA)
SCI............ Steel Construction Institute [*British*]   (IRUK)
SCI............ Stein Collectors International   (EA)
SCI............ Stratospheric Circulation Index [*Geophysics*]
SCI............ Stroke Club International   (EA)
SCI............ Structured Clinical Interview
SCI............ Supervisory Cost Inspector [*Navy*]
SCI............ Switch Closure In   (MCD)
SCI............ System Control Interface
SciA .... Scientific American [*A publication*]
SCIA .... Signal Corps Intelligence Agency [*Obsolete*] [*Army*]
SCIA .... Smart Card Industry Association   (EA)
SCIA .... Social Competence Inventory for Adults [*Psychology*]
SCIA .... Studii si Cercetari de Istoria Artei. Seria Arta Plastica [*A publication*]
SCIA .... Systems Change Impact Analysis [*Social Security Administration*]
SciAb .... Science Abstracts [*A publication*]
Sci Abstr .... Science Abstracts [*A publication*]
Sci Abstr Ch ... Science Abstracts of China [*A publication*]
Sci Abstr China Biol Sci ... Science Abstracts of China. Biological Sciences [*A publication*]
Sci Abstr China Chem Chem Technol ... Science Abstracts of China. Chemistry and Chemical Technology [*A publication*]
Sci Abstr China Math Phys Sci ... Science Abstracts of China. Mathematical and Physical Sciences [*A publication*]
Sci Abstr China Med ... Science Abstracts of China. Medicine [*A publication*]
Sci Abstr China Tech Sci ... Science Abstracts of China. Technical Sciences [*A publication*]
SCIADJ..... Centro Internacional de Agricultura Tropical [*CIAT*]. Series Seminars [*A publication*]
Sci Adv Mater Process Eng Proc ... Science of Advanced Materials and Process Engineering. Proceedings [*A publication*]
Sci Adv Mater Process Eng Q ... Science of Advanced Materials and Process Engineering. Quarterly [*United States*] [*A publication*]
Sci Aer Aerotech ... Science Aerienne et l'Aerotechnique [*A publication*]

Sci Ag......... Scientific Agriculture [*A publication*]
Sci Agr .... Scientific Agriculture [*A publication*]
Sci Agric ...... Science in Agriculture [*A publication*]
Sci Agric Bohemoslov ... Scientia Agriculturae Bohemoslovaca [*A publication*]
Sci Agric PA State Univ Agric Exp Stn ... Science in Agriculture. Pennsylvania State University. Agricultural Experiment Station [*A publication*]
Sci Agron Rennes ... Sciences Agronomiques Rennes [*A publication*]
Sci Alaska Proc Alaskan Sci Conf ... Science in Alaska. Proceedings. Alaskan Science Conference [*A publication*]
Sci Aliment ... Scienza dell'Alimentazione [*A publication*]
Sci Aliments ... Sciences des Aliments [*A publication*]
Sci Am........ Scientific American [*A publication*]
Sci Amer ...... Scientific American [*A publication*]
Sci Am Monthly ... Scientific American Monthly [*A publication*]
Sci Am S .... Scientific American. Supplement [*A publication*]
Sci Ann Fac Phys Math Aristotelian Univ Thessalonian ... Scientific Annals. Faculty of Physics and Mathematics. Aristotelian University of Thessaloniki [*A publication*]
Sci Appliance ... Science and Appliance [*A publication*]
SCIAPS..... Senate Comprehensive Integrated Automated Printing System
SciArch....... Science and Archaeology [*A publication*]
Sci & Archaeol ... Science and Archaeology [*A publication*]
Sci Art Min ... Science and Art of Mining [*A publication*]
SCIAS........ Society of Chemical Industry, American Section   (EA)
SCIAS........ Supreme Council of the Independent Associated Spiritualists   (EA)
Sci Atmos Sin ... Scientia Atmospherica Sinica [*A publication*]
SCIATS..... Small Craft Instruction and Training School [*Navy*]
Sci Aust ...... Scientific Australian [*A publication*]   (APTA)
Sci & Aust Technol ... Science and Australian Technology [*A publication*]   (APTA)
Sci Aust Technol ... Science and Australian Technology [*A publication*]   (APTA)
Sci Av........ Sciences et Avenir [*A publication*]
Sci Avenir .. Sciences et Avenir [*France*] [*A publication*]
SCIB .... Significant Counterintelligence Briefs   (AFM)
SCIBA .... Studii si Cercetari de Inframicrobiologie [*A publication*]
Sci Basis Med ... Scientific Basis of Medicine [*A publication*]
Sci Basis Psychiatr ... Scientific Basis of Psychiatry [*A publication*]
Sci Bas Med Ann Rev ... Scientific Basis of Medicine. Annual Review [*A publication*]
Sci Biol J ... Science of Biology Journal [*A publication*]
Sci Biol Ser ... Science of Biology Series [*A publication*]
Sci Bk........ Science Books and Films [*A publication*]
Sci Bks...... Science Books [*A publication*]
Sci Bks & Films ... Science Books and Films [*A publication*]
SCIBP........ Special Committee for the International Biological Program [*National Research Council*]
Sci Bul........ Science Bulletin for Teachers in Secondary Schools [*A publication*]   (APTA)
Sci Bull Academ Min Metall (Krakow) Geol ... Scientific Bulletins. Academy of Mining and Metallurgy (Krakow). Geology [*A publication*]
Sci Bull Acad Min Metall (Krakow) Ceram ... Scientific Bulletins. Academy of Mining and Metallurgy (Krakow). Ceramics [*A publication*]
Sci Bull Acad Min Metall (Krakow) Electrif Mech Min Metall ... Scientific Bulletins. Academy of Mining and Metallurgy (Krakow). Electrification and Mechanization in Mining and Metallurgy [*A publication*]
Sci Bull Acad Min Metall (Krakow) Math Phys Chem ... Scientific Bulletins. Academy of Mining and Metallurgy (Krakow). Mathematics, Physics, Chemistry [*A publication*]
Sci Bull Acad Min Metall (Krakow) Metall Foundry Pract ... Scientific Bulletins. Academy of Mining and Metallurgy (Krakow). Metallurgy and Foundry Practice [*A publication*]
Sci Bull Acad Min Metall (Krakow) Min ... Scientific Bulletins. Academy of Mining and Metallurgy (Krakow). Mining [*A publication*]
Sci Bull Acad Min Metall (Krakow) Spec Ser ... Scientific Bulletins. Academy of Mining and Metallurgy (Krakow). Special Series [*A publication*]
Sci Bull At Energy New Energ Organ ... Scientific Bulletin. Atomic Energy and New Energies Organization [*A publication*]
Sci Bull Can Cent Miner Energy Technol ... Scientific Bulletin. Canada Centre for Mineral and Energy Technology [*A publication*]
Sci Bull Coll Agric Univ Ryukyus Okinawa ... Science Bulletin. College of Agriculture. University of Ryukyus. Okinawa [*A publication*]
Sci Bull Cotton Res Inst Sindos ... Science Bulletin. Cotton Research Institute. Sindos [*A publication*]
Sci Bull Dep Agric For Un S Afr ... Science Bulletin. Department of Agriculture and Forestry. Union of South Africa [*A publication*]
Sci Bull Dep Agric NSW ... Science Bulletin. Department of Agriculture. New South Wales [*A publication*]   (APTA)
Sci Bull Dept Agr NSW ... Science Bulletin. Department of Agriculture. New South Wales [*A publication*]
Sci Bull Dept Agr S Afr ... Science Bulletin. Department of Agriculture. South Africa [*A publication*]

Sci Bull Des Bot Gard Ariz ... Science Bulletin. Desert Botanical Garden of Arizona [*A publication*]
Sci Bull Fac Agric Kyushu Univ ... Science Bulletin. Faculty of Agriculture. Kyushu University [*A publication*]
Sci Bull Fac Agr Kyushu Univ ... Science Bulletin. Faculty of Agriculture. Kyushu University [*A publication*]
Sci Bull Fac Ed Nagasaki Univ ... Science Bulletin. Faculty of Education. Nagasaki University [*A publication*]
Sci Bull Fac Educ Nagasaki Univ ... Science Bulletin. Faculty of Education. Nagasaki University [*A publication*]
Sci Bull Repub S Afr Dept Agr Tech Serv ... Science Bulletin. Republic of South Africa. Department of Agricultural Technical Services [*A publication*]
Sci Bull Sci Found Philipp ... Science Bulletin. Science Foundation of the Philippines [*A publication*]
Sci Bull Stanislaw Staszic Univ Min Metall Ceram ... Scientific Bulletins. Stanislaw Staszic University of Mining and Metallurgy. Ceramics [*A publication*]
Sci Bull Stanislaw Staszic Univ Min Metall Geol ... Scientific Bulletins. Stanislaw Staszic University of Mining and Metallurgy. Geology [*A publication*]
Sci Bull Stanislaw Staszic Univ Min Metall Math Phys Chem ... Scientific Bulletins. Stanislaw Staszic University of Mining and Metallurgy. Mathematics, Physics, Chemistry [*A publication*]
Sci Bull Stanislaw Staszic Univ Min Metall Min ... Scientific Bulletins. Stanislaw Staszic University of Mining and Metallurgy. Mining [*A publication*]
Sci Bull Stanislaw Staszic Univ Min Metall Sozol Sozotech ... Scientific Bulletins. Stanislaw Staszic University of Mining and Metallurgy. Sozology and Sozotechnics [*A publication*]
Sci Bull Stanislaw Staszic Univ Min Metall Spec Ser ... Scientific Bulletins. Stanislaw Staszic University of Mining and Metallurgy. Special Series [*A publication*]
Sci Bull Univ Kans ... Science Bulletin. University of Kansas [*A publication*]
Sci Bull Univ Kansas ... Science Bulletin. Kansas University [*A publication*]
SCIC .... Curico/General Freire [*Chile*] [*ICAO location identifier*]   (ICLI)
SCIC .... Secretariat des Conferences Intergouvernementales Canadiennes
SCIC .... Semiconductor Integrated Circuit
SCIC .... Single-Column Ion Chromatography
SCICC ...... Service Center Internal Computer Code [*Data processing*]
Sci Ceram... Science of Ceramics [*England*] [*A publication*]
SCICF....... Safari Club International Conservation Fund   (EA)
SCICFNDT ... Standing Committee for International Cooperation within the Field of Non-Destructive Testing   (EA)
Sci & Child ... Science and Children [*A publication*]
Sci China Ser A ... Science in China. Series A. Mathematics, Physics, Astronomy, and Technological Sciences [*A publication*]
Sci Chron (Karachi) ... Science Chronicle (Karachi) [*A publication*]
Sci Cit Ind ... Science Citation Index [*A publication*]
SCICLOPS ... Systems Control, Incorporated Computerized Library Operations [*Information service or system*]   (IID)
Sci Comput Program ... Science of Computer Programming [*A publication*]
Sci Comput Programming ... Science of Computer Programming [*A publication*]
Sci Conf Ges Dtsch Naturforsch Aerzte ... Scientific Conference. Gesellschaft Deutscher Naturforscher und Aerzte [*A publication*]
Sci Counc Afr South Sahara Publ ... Scientific Council for Africa South of the Sahara. Publication [*A publication*]
Sci Counc Jap Annu Rep ... Science Council of Japan. Annual Report [*A publication*]
Sci Couns ... Science Counselor [*A publication*]
SCICS........ Spinal Cord Injury Care System [*University of Alabama in Birmingham*] [*Research center*]   (RCD)
Sci and Cult ... Science and Culture [*A publication*]
Sci Cult ...... Science and Culture [*A publication*]
Sci Cult (New Delhi) ... Science and Culture (New Delhi) [*A publication*]
Sci D .... Doctor of Science
SCID......... Severe Combined Immune Deficiency [*Immunology*]
SCID......... Small Column Insulated Delays   (MCD)
SCID......... Subcommutator Identification [*NASA*]
SCID-A...... Studies in Comparative International Development [*A publication*]
SCIDE .... Servicio Cooperativo Interamericano de Educacion
Sci Dep Bull United Plant Assoc South India ... Scientific Department Bulletin. United Planters' Association of Southern India [*A publication*]
Sci Dig ...... Science Digest [*A publication*]
Sci Digest... Science Digest [*A publication*]
Sci Diliman ... Science Diliman [*A publication*]
Sci Dimens ... Science Dimension [*A publication*]
Sci Dimension ... Science Dimension [*A publication*]
SCIDNT ..... System Control Incorporated Identification Program [*Navy*]
SCIE .... Concepcion/Carriel Sur [*Chile*] [*ICAO location identifier*]   (ICLI)
SCIE .... Scicom Data Services Ltd. [*Formerly, Scientific Computers*] [*NASDAQ symbol*]   (NQ)
SCIE .... Stolen Children Information Exchange   (EA)
SCIEA .... Science [*A publication*]

Sci Ed......... Science Education [*A publication*]
Sci Ed News ... Science Education Newsletter [*A publication*] (APTA)
Sci Educ..... Science Education [*A publication*]
Sci Educ Adm Agric Rev Man ARM-NE ... Science and Education Administration. Agricultural Reviews and Manuals. ARM-NE [*A publication*]
Sci Educ Adm Agric Rev Man ARM-W ... Science and Education Administration. Agricultural Reviews and Manuals. ARM-W [*A publication*]
Sci Educ Adm North Cent Reg Publ ... Science and Education Administration. North Central Region Publication [*A publication*]
Sci 80 (Eighty) ... Science 80 (Eighty) [*A publication*]
Sci Elec.... Scientia Electrica [*A publication*]
Sci Electr.... Scientia Electrica [*A publication*]
Science....... Science for People [*A publication*]
SCIENCE ... Stimulation des Cooperations Internationaux et des Echanges Necessaires aux Chercheurs Europeennes [*Stimulation of International Cooperation and the Necessary Exchanges of European Scientists*] [*EEC*]
Science Ed ... Science Education [*A publication*]
Science et Industrie Phot ... Science et Industries Photographiques [*A publication*]
Science N L ... Science News Letter [*A publication*]
Science Prog ... Science Progress [*A publication*]
Sciences Assoc Fr Av Sci ... Sciences. Association Francaise pour l'Avancement des Sciences [*A publication*]
Sciences NY Acad Sci ... Sciences. New York Academy of Sciences [*A publication*]
Sciences Pol ... Sciences Politiques [*A publication*]
Science and Tech Libs ... Science and Technology Libraries [*A publication*]
Sciencia Med ... Sciencia Medica [*A publication*]
Sci Eng...... Science and Engineering [*A publication*]
Sci and Eng Rep Def Acad ... Scientific and Engineering Reports. Defense Academy [*A publication*]
Sci and Eng Rep Natl Def Acad (Jpn) ... Scientific and Engineering Reports. National Defense Academy (Japanese) [*A publication*]
Sci & Eng Rep Saitama Univ C ... Science and Engineering Reports. Saitama University. Series C [*A publication*]
Sci and Eng Rep Saitama Univ Ser C ... Science and Engineering Reports. Saitama University. Series C [*A publication*]
Sci Eng Rev Doshisha Univ ... Science and Engineering Review. Doshisha University [*A publication*]
Sci Enseign Sci ... Sciences et l'Enseignement des Sciences [*A publication*]
SCIENT .... Scientific
Scient Agric ... Scientific Agriculture [*A publication*]
Scient Am .. Scientific American [*A publication*]
Scient Amer ... Scientific American [*A publication*]
Scient Am Suppl ... Scientific American. Supplement [*A publication*]
Scient Film Rev ... Scientific Film Review [*A publication*]
Scient Hort ... Scientific Horticulture [*A publication*]
Scientia Genet ... Scientia Genetica [*A publication*]
Scientiarum Hist ... Scientiarum Historia [*A publication*]
Scient Instrum ... Scientific Instruments [*A publication*]
Scient Mon ... Scientific Monthly [*A publication*]
Scient Month ... Scientific Monthly [*A publication*]
Scient Pap Coll Gen Educ Tokyo ... Scientific Papers. College of General Education. University of Tokyo [*A publication*]
Scient Papers Civil Vet Dept (Madras) ... Scientific Papers. Civil Veterinary Department (Madras) [*A publication*]
Scient Proc R Dubl Soc ... Scientific Proceedings. Royal Dublin Society [*A publication*]
Scient Rep Fac Agric Okayama Univ ... Scientific Reports. Faculty of Agriculture. Okayama University [*A publication*]
Scient Rep Govt Inst Infect Dis Tokyo Imp Univ ... Scientific Reports. Government Institute for Infectious Diseases. Tokyo Imperial University [*A publication*]
Scient Rep Kyoto Prefect Univ Agric ... Scientific Reports. Kyoto Prefectural University. Agriculture [*A publication*]
Scient Res (Bangladesh) ... Scientific Researches (Bangladesh) [*A publication*]
Scient Trans Dubl Soc ... Scientific Transactions. Royal Dublin Society [*A publication*]
Scient Work ... Scientific Worker [*A publication*]
Sci Environ ... Science and Environment [*A publication*]
Scienza Aliment ... Scienza dell'Alimentazione [*A publication*]
Scienza Tecnol Aliment ... Scienza e Tecnologia degli Alimenti [*A publication*]
Sci Espr...... Science et Esprit [*A publication*]
Sci Esprit ... Science et Esprit [*A publication*]
Sci Exploration ... Science Exploration [*Changsha*] [*A publication*]
SCIF .... Daughters of the Sacred Heart of Jesus [*Bethlehemite Sisters*] [*Roman Catholic religious order*]
SCIF .... Science Forum [*A publication*]
SCIF .... Special Compartmented Intelligence Facility [*DoD*]
SCIF .... Static Column Isoelectric Focusing [*Materials processing*]
SCIF .... Systems Certification and Integration Facility
SCI FA....... Scire Facias [*Please make known*] [*A writ to enforce, annul, or vacate a judgment, patent, charter or other matter of record*] [*Legal term*] [*Latin*]
Sci Fa ad Dis Deb ... Scire Facias ad Disprobandum Debitum [*Latin*] (DLA)
Sci Farm..... Science for the Farmer [*A publication*]
Sci Farm..... Scienza del Farmaco [*A publication*]
Sci Farmer ... Science for the Farmer [*A publication*]

SCIFC........ Sandy Croft International Fan Club (EA)
SCI-FI........ Science Fiction [*Also, SF*]
Sci Fiction Bk Rev Ind ... Science Fiction Book Review Index [*A publication*]
Sci Fict St... Science Fiction Studies [*A publication*]
Sci For........ Science Forum [*A publication*]
Sci Forum ... Science Forum [*A publication*]
Sci Freedom ... Science and Freedom [*A publication*]
SCIGA .... Society of Chemical Industry (London). Monograph [*A publication*]
SCIGB .... Sicherheitsingenieur [*A publication*]
Sci Genet.... Scientia Genetica [*A publication*]
Sci Geol Bull ... Sciences Geologiques. Bulletin [*A publication*]
Sci Geol Bull Inst Geol Univ Louis Pasteur Strasbourg ... Sciences Geologiques. Bulletin. Institut de Geologie. Universite Louis Pasteur de Strasbourg [*France*] [*A publication*]
Sci Geol Mem ... Sciences Geologiques. Memoires [*A publication*]
Sci Geol S .. Scientia Geologica Sinica [*A publication*]
Sci Geol Sin ... Scientia Geologica Sinica [*A publication*]
Sci Gov Rep ... Science and Government Report [*United States*] [*A publication*]
Sci Govt Rep ... Science and Government Report [*A publication*]
SCIGY .... Special Committee for the International Geophysical Year
SCIH......... Societe Canadienne d'Ingenierie Hospitaliere
Sci Hist ...... Scientiarum Historia [*A publication*]
Sci Hort...... Scientific Horticulture [*A publication*]
Sci Hortic... Scientia Horticulturae [*A publication*]
Sci Hortic (Amst) ... Scientia Horticulturae (Amsterdam) [*A publication*]
Sci Hortic (Canterbury) ... Scientific Horticulture (Canterbury) [*A publication*]
Sci Hum Life ... Science of Human Life [*A publication*]
SCII .... Science in Iceland [*A publication*]
SCII .... Southland Communication, Inc. [*NASDAQ symbol*] (NQ)
SCII .... Strong-Campbell Interest Inventory [*Vocational guidance*]
Sci Icel ...... Science in Iceland [*A publication*]
Sci Ilus ...... Science Illustrated [*A publication*]
Sci Ind....... Science et Industrie [*A publication*]
Sci Ind....... Science and Industry [*A publication*]
Sci Ind Ed Constr Trav Publics ... Science et Industrie. Edition Construction et Travaux Publics [*A publication*]
Sci Ind Ed Metall Constr Mec Energ ... Science et Industrie. Edition Metallurgie. Construction, Mecaniques, Energie [*A publication*]
Sci Ind Equip Bull ... Scientific and Industrial Equipment Bulletin [*A publication*] (APTA)
Sci Ind (Karachi) ... Science and Industry (Karachi) [*A publication*]
Sci in Ind (Lond) ... Science in Industry (London) [*A publication*]
Sci Ind (Melbourne) ... Science and Industry (Melbourne) [*A publication*]
Sci Ind (Philips) ... Science and Industry (Philips) [*The Netherlands*] [*A publication*]
Sci Ind Phot ... Science et Industries Photographiques [*A publication*]
Sci Ind Photogr ... Science et Industries Photographiques [*A publication*]
Sci Ind Spat ... Sciences et Industries Spatiales [*Switzerland*] [*A publication*]
Sci Ind Spatiales Space Res Eng Weltraumforsch Ind ... Sciences et Industries Spatiales, Space Research and Engineering, Weltraumforschung und Industrie [*A publication*]
Sci Inf News ... Science Informations News. National Science Foundation [*A publication*]
Sci Inf Notes ... Scientific Information Notes [*A publication*]
Sci Info N... Scientific Information Notes [*A publication*]
Sci Ins Contr ... Scientific Insect Control [*A publication*]
Sci Insect Control (Kyoto) ... Scientific Insect Control (Kyoto) [*A publication*]
Sci Instr ...... Scientific Instruments [*A publication*]
Sci Instr J Phys E ... Scientific Instruments. Journal of Physics. E [*A publication*]
Sci Instrum ... Journal of Physics. E: Scientific Instruments [*A publication*]
Sci Invest Freshwater Salmon Fish Res Scott Home Dep ... Scientific Investigations. Freshwater and Salmon Fisheries Research. Scottish Home Department [*A publication*]
Sci Invest Freshw Salmon Fish Res Scott Home Dep ... Scientific Investigations. Freshwater and Salmon Fisheries Research. Scottish Home Department [*A publication*]
Sci Island ... Scientia Islandica [*A publication*]
SCI-IVS..... SCI-International Voluntary Service (EA)
Sci J .... Science Journal [*A publication*]
Sci J (Lond) ... Science Journal (London) [*A publication*]
Sci Jour...... Science Journal [*A publication*]
Sci J R Coll Sci ... Scientific Journal. Royal College of Science [*A publication*]
Sci J Shivaji Univ ... Science Journal. Shivaji University [*A publication*]
SCIL .... Scilicet [*Namely*] [*Legal term*] [*Latin*]
SCIL .... Ship's Construction Item List (MCD)
SCIL .... Small Computers in Libraries [*A publication*]
SCIL .... Soft Consumable Item List
SCIL .... Support Center International Logistics [*Army*]
Sciland .... Scienceland [*A publication*]
Sci Leafl..... Science Leaflet [*A publication*]
SCILF........ Studii si Cercetari de Istorie Literara si Folclor [*A publication*]
Sci Life....... Science and Life [*A publication*]
Sci Light .... Science of Light [*A publication*]
SCILL........ Southern California Interlibrary Loan Project [*Library network*]
Sci Lubr ..... Scientific Lubrication [*A publication*]
Sci Lubr Liq Fuel ... Scientific Lubrication and Liquid Fuel [*A publication*]

SCIM......... Congregation des Soeurs Servantes du Coeur Immaculae de Marie [*Servants of the Immaculate Heart of Mary*] [*Good Shepherd Sisters*] [*Roman Catholic religious order*]
SCIM......... Savage's Cognitive Impairment Model
SCIM......... Selected Categories in Microfiche [*National Technical Information Service*]
SCIM......... Speech Communications Index Meter
SCIM......... Standard Cubic Inches per Minute   (AAG)
SCIM......... Subject Codes for Intelligence Management   (MCD)
Sci Mac..... Science of Machine [*Japan*] [*A publication*]
Sci Man...... Science of Man and Australasian Anthropological Journal [*A publication*]
Sci March .. Science on the March [*A publication*]
Sci Mat .... Scienze Matematiche [*A publication*]
Sci Mech... Science and Mechanics [*A publication*]
Sci Med..... Sciences Medicales [*A publication*]
Sci Med Ital ... Scientia Medica Italica [*A publication*]
Sci Med Ital (Engl Ed) ... Scientia Medica Italica (English Edition) [*A publication*]
Sci Med Man ... Science, Medicine, and Man [*A publication*]
Sci Meet.... Scientific Meetings [*A publication*]
SCIMITAR ... System for Countering Interdiction Missiles and Targets RADARs   (MCD)
Sci Mo........ Scientific Monthly [*A publication*]
Sci Monogr Univ Wyo Agric Exp Stn ... Science Monograph. University of Wyoming. Agricultural Experiment Station [*A publication*]
Sci Monogr Wyo Expl Stn ... Science Monograph. Wyoming Experimental Station [*A publication*]
SCIMP ...... Selective Cooperative Indexing of Management Periodicals [*Database*] [*European Business School Librarians Group*] [*Information service or system*]   (CRD)
SCIMP ...... Self-Contained Imaging Micro-Profiler [*Instrumentation*]
SCIMPEX ... Syndicat des Commercants Importateurs et Exportateurs de l'Ouest African [*Union of Commercial Importers and Exporters of West Africa*]
Sci Mus Minn Monogr ... Science Museum of Minnesota. Monograph [*A publication*]
Sci N .... Science News [*A publication*]
SCIN........... Self-Canceling Installment Note
SCINA...... Science and Culture [*A publication*]
Sci Nat ...... Science et Nature [*A publication*]
Sci New Guinea ... Science in New Guinea [*A publication*]
Sci News .... Science News [*A publication*]
Sci News (Harmondsworth) ... Science News (Harmondsworth) [*A publication*]
Sci News Lett ... Science News Letter [*United States*] [*A publication*]
Sci NL....... Science News Letter [*A publication*]
Sci Nourishment ... Science of Nourishment [*A publication*]
SCINT....... Scintillator [*Nucleonics*]
Sci Nuncius Radiophonicus ... Scientiarum Nuncius Radiophonicus [*A publication*]
SCIO.......... Staff Counterintelligence Officer [*Military*]   (NVT)
SCIOP....... Social Competence Inventory for Older Persons [*Psychology*]
Sci Opin .... Scientific Opinion [*A publication*]
Sci Orient.... Scientia Orientalis [*A publication*]
SCIP .... Isla De Pascua/Mataveri [*Easter Island*] [*Chile*] [*ICAO location identifier*]   (ICLI)
SCIP .... Scanning for Information Parameters
SCIP .... School Curriculum Industry Partnership [*British*]   (ECON)
SCIP .... Sea Counterinfiltration Patrol   (CINC)
SCIP .... Self-Contained Instrument Package   (KSC)
SCIP .... Ship's Capability Impaired for Lack of Parts [*Navy*]
SCIP .... Society of Competitor Intelligence Professionals   (EA)
SCIP .... Solid Cast Iron Propeller   (DS)
SCIP .... Special Crisis Intervention Program   (OICC)
SCIP .... Stanford Center for Information Processing [*Stanford University*] [*Later, CIT*]
SCIP .... Student Community Involvement Program [*Australia*]
Sci Paed Ex ... Scientia Paedagogica Experimentalis [*A publication*]
Sci Paed Exp ... Scientia Paedagogica Experimentalis [*A publication*]
Sci Pap Coll Ed ... Scientific Papers. College of General Education [*A publication*]
Sci Pap Coll Gen Educ Univ Tokyo ... Scientific Papers. College of General Education. University of Tokyo [*A publication*]
Sci Pap Coll Gen Educ Univ Tokyo (Biol Part) ... Scientific Papers. College of General Education. University of Tokyo (Biological Part) [*A publication*]
Sci Paperbacks ... Science Paperbacks [*A publication*]
Sci Papers College Gen Ed Univ Tokyo ... Scientific Papers. College of General Education. University of Tokyo [*A publication*]
Sci Papers Prague ICT C ... Scientific Papers. Prague Institute of Chemical Technology. Part C. Organic Chemistry and Technology [*A publication*]
Sci Pap Fac Eng Tokushima Univ ... Scientific Papers. Faculty of Engineering. Tokushima University [*A publication*]
Sci Pap Imp Fuel Res Inst (Jpn) ... Scientific Papers. Imperial Fuel Research Institute (Japan) [*A publication*]
Sci Pap Inst Algol Res Fac Sci Hokkaido Univ ... Scientific Papers. Institute of Algological Research. Faculty of Science. Hokkaido University [*A publication*]

Sci Pap Inst Chem Technol (Prague) Chem Eng Autom ... Scientific Papers. Institute of Chemical Technology (Prague). Chemical Engineering and Automation [*A publication*]
Sci Pap Inst Phys and Chem Res ... Scientific Papers. Institute of Physical and Chemical Research [*A publication*]
Sci Pap Inst Phys Chem Res (Jpn) ... Scientific Papers. Institute of Physical and Chemical Research (Japan) [*A publication*]
Sci Pap Inst Phys Chem Res (Tokyo) ... Scientific Papers. Institute of Physical and Chemical Research (Tokyo) [*A publication*]
Sci Pap Osaka Univ ... Scientific Papers. Osaka University [*A publication*]
Sci Pap Prague Inst Chem Technol Sect Chem Eng ... Scientific Papers. Prague Institute of Chemical Technology. Section: Chemical Engineering [*A publication*]
Sci Peche.... Science et Peche [*A publication*]
Sci Peo ...... Science for People [*A publication*]
Sci Peopl ... Science for People [*A publication*]
Sci Pest Contr ... Scientific Pest Control [*A publication*]
Sci Pest Control ... Scientific Pest Control [*A publication*]
Sci Pharm .. Scientia Pharmaceutica [*A publication*]
Sci Pharm Biol Lorraine ... Sciences Pharmaceutiques et Biologiques de Lorraine [*A publication*]
Sci Pict....... Science Pictorial [*People's Republic of China*] [*A publication*]
SCIPIO...... Sales Catalog Index Project Input On-Line [*Cleveland Museum of Art*] [*Information service or system*]   (IID)
SCIPMIS .. Standard Civilian Personnel Management Information System [*Army*]
SCIPP....... Santa Cruz Institute for Particle Physics [*University of California, Santa Cruz*] [*Research center*]   (RCD)
Sci Pro....... Science Progress [*A publication*]
Sci Pro........ Scientific Progress [*London*] [*A publication*]
Sci Proc Cardiff Med Soc ... Scientific Proceedings. Cardiff Medical Society [*A publication*]
Sci Proc Dublin Soc ... Scientific Proceedings. Royal Dublin Society [*A publication*]
Sci Proc R Dublin Soc ... Scientific Proceedings. Royal Dublin Society [*A publication*]
Sci Proc R Dublin Soc A ... Scientific Proceedings. Royal Dublin Society. Series A [*A publication*]
Sci Proc R Dublin Soc New Ser ... Scientific Proceedings. Royal Dublin Society. New Series [*A publication*]
Sci Proc R Dublin Soc Ser A ... Scientific Proceedings. Royal Dublin Society. Series A [*A publication*]
Sci Proc R Dublin Soc Ser B ... Scientific Proceedings. Royal Dublin Society. Series B [*A publication*]
Sci Proc Roy Dublin Soc Ser B ... Scientific Proceedings. Royal Dublin Society. Series B [*A publication*]
Sci Prog...... Science Progress [*A publication*]
Sci Prog Decouverte ... Science Progres Decouverte [*A publication*]
Sci Prog (Lond) ... Science Progress (London) [*A publication*]
Sci Prog (London) ... Science Progress (London) [*A publication*]
Sci Prog Nat ... Science, Progres, la Nature [*A publication*]
Sci Prog Nat (Paris) ... Science, Progres, la Natur (Paris) [*A publication*]
Sci Prog (New Haven) ... Science in Progress (New Haven) [*A publication*]
Sci Prog (Oxf) ... Science Progress (Oxford) [*A publication*]
Sci Progr...... Science Progress [*A publication*]
Sci Progr Decouverte ... Science Progres Decouverte [*A publication*]
Sci Psychoanal ... Science and Psychoanalysis [*A publication*]
Sci Publ Af ... Science and Public Affairs. Bulletin of the Atomic Scientists [*A publication*]
Sci Publ For Timber Ind ... Scientific Publications of Forestry and Timber Industry [*A publication*]
Sci Publ Fuji Photo Film C ... Scientific Publications. Fuji Photo Film Company Ltd. [*A publication*]
Sci Publ Fuji Photo Film Co Ltd ... Scientific Publications. Fuji Photo Film Company Limited [*Japan*] [*A publication*]
Sci Public Aff Bull At Sci ... Science and Public Affairs. Bulletin of the Atomic Scientists [*A publication*]
Sci Public Policy ... Science and Public Policy [*A publication*]
Sci Publ Pol ... Science and Public Policy [*A publication*]
Sci Publ Res Inst Radiol Radiat Hyg ... Scientific Publications. Research Institute of Radiology and Radiation Hygiene [*Bulgaria*] [*A publication*]
Sci Publ Sci Mus Minn ... Scientific Publications. Science Museum of Minnesota [*A publication*]
Sci Publ Sci Mus (St Paul) ... Scientific Publications. Science Museum of Minnesota (St. Paul) [*A publication*]
Sci Pub Pol ... Science and Public Policy [*A publication*]
Sci Q Natl Univ Peking ... Science Quarterly. National University of Peking [*A publication*]
Sci R........... Science Review [*Manila*] [*A publication*]
SCIR .... Society of Cardiovascular and Interventional Radiology   (EA)
SCIR .... Subsystem Capability Impact Reporting [*Military*]   (NVT)
SCIRA ...... Science Review [*Manila*] [*A publication*]
SCIRA ...... Snipe Class International Racing Association   (EA)
SCIRA .... Stable Carbon Isotope Ratio Analysis [*For determining material source*]
SCIRA ...... State Central Information Reception Agency
SCIRC....... Spinal Cord Injury Research Center [*Ohio State University*] [*Research center*]   (RCD)
S Circular... South Circular [*A publication*]
Sci Rec .... Science Record [*A publication*]

Sci Rec (Chin Ed) ... Science Record (Chinese Edition) [*People's Republic of China*] [*A publication*]

Sci Rec (Peking) ... Science Record (Peking) [*A publication*]

Sci Rec S M Kirov Kaz State Univ ... Scientific Records. S. M. Kirov Kazakh State University [*A publication*]

Sci Rep Agric Coll Norway ... Scientific Reports. Agricultural College of Norway [*A publication*]

Sci Rep Agric Col Norw ... Scientific Reports. Agricultural College of Norway [*A publication*]

Sci Rep Br Antarct Surv ... Scientific Reports. British Antarctic Survey [*A publication*]

Sci Rep Cent Res Inst Kasauli ... Scientific Report. Central Research Institute. Kasauli [*A publication*]

Sci Rep College Gen Ed Osaka Univ ... Science Reports. College of General Education. Osaka University [*A publication*]

Sci Rep Coll Gen Educ Osaka Univ ... Science Reports. College of General Education. Osaka University [*Japan*] [*A publication*]

Sci Rep Ehime Agric Coll ... Scientific Reports. Ehime Agricultural College [*A publication*]

Sci Rep Fac Agr Ibaraki Univ ... Scientific Report. Faculty of Agriculture. Ibaraki University [*A publication*]

Sci Rep Fac Agric Ibaraki Univ ... Scientific Reports. Faculty of Agriculture. Ibaraki University [*A publication*]

Sci Rep Fac Agric Kobe Univ ... Science Reports. Faculty of Agriculture. Kobe University [*A publication*]

Sci Rep Fac Agric Meijo Univ ... Scientific Reports. Faculty of Agriculture. Meijo University [*A publication*]

Sci Rep Fac Agr Okayama Univ ... Scientific Report. Faculty of Agriculture. Okayama University [*A publication*]

Sci Rep Fac Ed Gifu Univ Natur Sci ... Science Reports. Faculty of Education. Gifu University. Natural Science [*A publication*]

Sci Rep Fac Educ Fukushima Univ ... Science Reports. Faculty of Education. Fukushima University [*Japan*] [*A publication*]

Sci Rep Fac Educ Gunma Univ ... Science Reports. Faculty of Education. Gunma University [*A publication*]

Sci Rep Fac Liberal Art Educ Gifu Univ Natur Sci ... Science Report. Faculty of Liberal Arts and Education. Gifu University. Natural Science [*A publication*]

Sci Rep Fac Sci Ege Univ ... Scientific Reports. Faculty of Science. Ege University [*A publication*]

Sci Rep Fac Sci Kyushu Univ Geol ... Science Reports. Faculty of Science. Kyushu University. Geology [*Japan*] [*A publication*]

Sci Rep Gov Inst Infect Dis Tokyo Imp Univ ... Scientific Reports. Government Institute for Infectious Diseases. Tokyo Imperial University [*A publication*]

Sci Rep Hirosaki Univ ... Science Reports. Hirosaki University [*A publication*]

Sci Rep Hokkaido Fish Exp Stn ... Scientific Reports. Hokkaido Fisheries Experimental Station [*A publication*]

Sci Rep Hokkaido Salmon Hatchery ... Scientific Reports. Hokkaido Salmon Hatchery [*A publication*]

Sci Rep Hoyo Univ Agr ... Scientific Report. Hoyo University of Agriculture [*A publication*]

Sci Rep Hyogo Univ Agr Fac Agr Kobe Univ ... Science Reports. Hyogo University of Agriculture and Faculty of Agriculture. Kobe University [*A publication*]

Sci Rep Hyogo Univ Agric ... Science Reports. Hyogo University of Agriculture [*A publication*]

Sci Rep Hyogo Univ Agric Ser Agric ... Science Reports. Hyogo University of Agriculture. Series Agriculture [*A publication*]

Sci Rep Hyogo Univ Agric Ser Agric Chem ... Science Reports. Hyogo University of Agriculture. Series Agricultural Chemistry [*A publication*]

Sci Rep Hyogo Univ Agric Ser Agric Hortic ... Science Reports. Hyogo University of Agriculture. Series Agriculture and Horticulture [*A publication*]

Sci Rep Hyogo Univ Agric Ser Agric Technol ... Science Reports. Hyogo University of Agriculture. Series Agriculture Technology [*A publication*]

Sci Rep Hyogo Univ Agric Ser Nat Sci ... Science Reports. Hyogo University of Agriculture. Series Natural Science [*A publication*]

Sci Rep Hyogo Univ Agric Ser Plant Prot ... Science Reports. Hyogo University of Agriculture. Series Plant Protection [*A publication*]

Sci Rep Hyogo Univ Agric Ser Zootech Sci ... Science Reports. Hyogo University of Agriculture. Series Zootechnical Science [*A publication*]

Sci Rep (India) ... Science Reporter (India) [*A publication*]

Sci Rep Indian Agric Res Inst ... Scientific Reports. Indian Agricultural Research Institute [*A publication*]

Sci Rep Inter-Union Comm Geodyn ... Scientific Report. Inter-Union Commission on Geodynamics [*A publication*]

Sci Rep Ist Super Sanita ... Scientific Reports. Istituto Superiore di Sanita [*A publication*]

Sci Rep Kagawa Prefect Fish Exp Stn ... Scientific Reports. Kagawa Prefectural Fisheries Experimental Station [*A publication*]

Sci Rep Kagoshima Univ ... Science Reports. Kagoshima University [*A publication*]

Sci Rep Kanazawa Univ ... Science Reports. Kanazawa University [*A publication*]

Sci Rep Kanazawa Univ Part II Biol Geol ... Science Reports. Kanazawa University. Part II. Biology and Geology [*A publication*]

Sci Rep Kyoto Prefect Univ Agric ... Scientific Reports. Kyoto Prefectural University. Agriculture [*A publication*]

Sci Rep Kyoto Prefect Univ Nat Sci Life Sci ... Scientific Reports. Kyoto Prefectural University. Natural Science and Life Science [*Japan*] [*A publication*]

Sci Rep Kyoto Prefect Univ Nat Sci Living Sci Welfare Sci ... Scientific Reports. Kyoto Prefectural University. Natural Science, Living Science, and Welfare Science [*Japan*] [*A publication*]

Sci Rep Kyoto Prefect Univ Natur Sci Living Sci ... Kyoto Prefectural University. Scientific Reports. Natural Science and Living Science [*A publication*]

Sci Rep Kyoto Pref Univ ... Scientific Report. Kyoto Prefectural University [*A publication*]

Sci Rep Kyoto Pref Univ Natur Sci Living Sci ... Kyoto Prefectural University. Scientific Reports. Natural Science and Living Science [*A publication*]

Sci Rep Lab Amphib Biol Hiroshima Univ ... Scientific Report. Laboratory for Amphibian Biology. Hiroshima University [*A publication*]

Sci Rep Matsuyama Agric Coll ... Scientific Reports. Matsuyama Agricultural College [*A publication*]

Sci Rep Meiji Seika Kaisha ... Scientific Reports. Meiji Seika Kaisha [*A publication*]

Sci Rep Miyagi Agr Coll ... Scientific Report. Miyagi Agricultural College [*A publication*]

Sci Rep Natl Tsing Hua Univ Ser A ... Science Reports. National Tsing Hua University. Series A. Mathematical, Physical, and Engineering Sciences [*A publication*]

Sci Rep Natl Tsing Hua Univ Ser C ... Science Reports. National Tsing Hua University. Series C. Geological, Geographical, and Meteorological Sciences [*A publication*]

Sci Rep Natl Univ Peking ... Science Reports. National University of Peking [*A publication*]

Sci Rep Niigata Univ Ser A ... Science Reports. Niigata University. Series A. Mathematics [*A publication*]

Sci Rep Niigata Univ Ser B ... Science Reports. Niigata University. Series B. Physics [*A publication*]

Sci Rep Niigata Univ Ser C ... Science Reports. Niigata University. Series C. Chemistry [*A publication*]

Sci Rep Niigata Univ Ser D Biol ... Science Reports. Niigata University. Series D. Biology [*A publication*]

Sci Rep Niigata Univ Ser E ... Science Reports. Niigata University. Series E. Geology and Mineralogy [*A publication*]

Sci Rep Niigata Univ Ser F Geol Mineral ... Science Reports. Niigata University. Series F. Geology and Mineralogy [*A publication*]

Sci Rep Osaka Univ ... Science Reports. Osaka University [*A publication*]

Sci Rep Res Inst Engrg Kanagawa Univ ... Science Reports. Kanagawa University. Research Institute for Engineering [*A publication*]

Sci Rep Res Inst Theor Phys Hiroshima Univ ... Scientific Reports. Research Institute for Theoretical Physics. Hiroshima University [*Japan*] [*A publication*]

Sci Rep Res Inst Tohoku Univ ... Science Reports. Research Institutes. Tohoku University [*A publication*]

Sci Rep Res Inst Tohoku Univ A ... Science Reports. Research Institutes. Tohoku University. Series A. Physics, Chemistry, and Metallurgy [*A publication*]

Sci Rep Res Inst Tohoku Univ Med ... Science Reports. Research Institutes. Tohoku University. Series C. Medicine [*A publication*]

Sci Rep Res Inst Tohoku Univ Ser A ... Science Reports. Research Institutes. Tohoku University. Series A. Physics, Chemistry, and Metallurgy [*A publication*]

Sci Rep Res Inst Tohoku Univ Ser B ... Science Reports. Research Institutes. Tohoku University. Series B. Technology [*A publication*]

Sci Rep Res Inst Tohoku Univ Ser C ... Science Reports. Research Institutes. Tohoku University. Series C. Medicine [*A publication*]

Sci Rep Res Inst Tohoku Univ Ser C Med ... Science Reports. Research Institutes. Tohoku University. Series C. Medicine [*A publication*]

Sci Rep Res Inst Tohoku Univ Ser D ... Science Reports. Research Institutes. Tohoku University. Series D [*A publication*]

Sci Rep Res Inst Tohoku Univ Ser D Agric ... Science Reports. Research Institutes. Tohoku University. Series D. Agriculture [*A publication*]

Sci Rep Saitama Univ Ser A ... Science Reports. Saitama University. Series A. Mathematics, Physics, and Chemistry [*A publication*]

Sci Rep Saitama Univ Ser B Biol Earth Sci ... Science Reports. Saitama University. Series B. Biology and Earth Sciences [*A publication*]

Sci Rep Shiga Pref Jr Coll ... Scientific Report. Shiga Prefectural Junior College [*A publication*]

Sci Rep Shima Marinel ... Science Report. Shima Marineland [*A publication*]

Sci Rep Soc Res Phys Chem ... Science Reports. Society for the Research of Physics Chemistry [*A publication*]

Sci Rep Tohoku Imp Univ Ser 1 ... Science Reports. Tohoku Imperial University. Series 1. Mathematics, Physics, Chemistry [*A publication*]

Sci Rep Tohoku Imp Univ Ser 3 ... Science Reports. Tohoku Imperial University. Series 3. Mineralogy, Petrology, Economic Geology [*A publication*]
Sci Rep Tohoku Imp Univ Ser 4 ... Science Reports. Tohoku Imperial University. Series 4. Biology [*A publication*]
Sci Rep Tohoku Univ ... Science Reports. Tohoku University [*A publication*]
Sci Rep Tohoku Univ A ... Science Reports. Tohoku University. Series A [*A publication*]
Sci Rep Tohoku Univ Eighth Ser Phys and Astron ... Science Reports. Tohoku University. Eighth Series. Physics and Astronomy [*A publication*]
Sci Rep Tohoku Univ Fifth Ser ... Science Reports. Tohoku University. Fifth Series [*A publication*]
Sci Rep Tohoku Univ Fifth Ser Geophys ... Science Reports. Tohoku University. Fifth Series. Geophysics [*A publication*]
Sci Rep Tohoku Univ First Ser ... Science Reports. Tohoku University. First Series [*Japan*] [*A publication*]
Sci Rep Tohoku Univ Fourth Ser (Biol) ... Science Reports. Tohoku University. Fourth Series. Biology [*A publication*]
Sci Rep Tohoku Univ I ... Science Reports. Tohoku University. First Series [*A publication*]
Sci Rep Tohoku Univ Second Ser (Geol) ... Science Reports. Tohoku University. Second Series. Geology [*A publication*]
Sci Rep Tohoku Univ Ser 5 ... Science Reports. Tohoku University. Fifth Series. Geophysics [*Japan*] [*A publication*]
Sci Rep Tohoku Univ Ser IV ... Scientific Report. Tohoku University. Series IV. Biology [*A publication*]
Sci Rep Tohoku Univ Seventh Ser ... Science Reports. Tohoku University. Seventh Series [*Japan*] [*A publication*]
Sci Rep Tohoku Univ Third Ser ... Science Reports. Tohoku University. Third Series. Mineralogy, Petrology, and Economic Geology [*Japan*] [*A publication*]
Sci Rep Tohoku Univ 8th Series ... Science Reports. Tohoku University. Eighth Series [*A publication*]
Sci Rep Tokyo Bunrika Daigaku Sect A ... Science Reports. Tokyo Bunrika Daigaku. Section A. Mathematics, Physics, Chemistry [*A publication*]
Sci Rep Tokyo Bunrika Daigaku Sect B ... Science Reports. Tokyo Bunrika Daigaku. Section B [*A publication*]
Sci Rep Tokyo Bunrika Daigaku Sect C ... Science Reports. Tokyo Bunrika Daigaku. Section C [*A publication*]
Sci Rep Tokyo Kyoiku Daigaku Sect A ... Science Reports. Tokyo Kyoiku Daigaku. Section A [*A publication*]
Sci Rep Tokyo Kyoiku Daigaku Sect B ... Science Reports. Tokyo Kyoiku Daigaku. Section B [*A publication*]
Sci Rep Tokyo Kyoiku Daigaku Sect C ... Science Reports. Tokyo Kyoiku Daigaku. Section C [*A publication*]
Sci Rep Tokyo Woman's Christian College ... Science Reports. Tokyo Woman's Christian College [*A publication*]
Sci Rep Tokyo Woman's Christian Univ ... Tokyo Woman's Christian University. Science Reports [*A publication*]
Sci Rep Univ Chekiang ... Science Reports. University of Chekiang [*A publication*]
Sci Rep Whales Res Inst (Tokyo) ... Scientific Reports. Whales Research Institute (Tokyo) [*A publication*]
Sci Rep Yamaguchi Univ ... Science Reports. Yamaguchi University [*A publication*]
Sci Rep Yokohama Natl Univ I ... Science Reports. Yokohama National University. Section I. Mathematics, Physics, and Chemistry [*A publication*]
Sci Rep Yokohama Natl Univ Sect I ... Science Reports. Yokohama National University. Section I. Mathematics, Physics, and Chemistry [*A publication*]
Sci Rep Yokohama Natl Univ Sect II Biol Geol ... Science Reports. Yokohama National University. Section II. Biology and Geology [*A publication*]
Sci Rep Yokohama Natl Univ Sect II Biol Geol Sci ... Science Reports. Yokohama National University. Section II. Biological and Geological Sciences [*A publication*]
Sci Rep Yokohama Nat Univ Sect 2 ... Science Reports. Yokohama National University. Section 2. Biological and Geological Sciences [*A publication*]
Sci Rep Yokohama Nat Univ Sect I ... Science Reports. Yokohama National University. Section I. Mathematics and Physics [*A publication*]
Sci Rep Yokosuka City Mus ... Science Report. Yokosuka City Museum [*A publication*]
Sci Rep Yokosuka Cy Mus ... Science Report. Yokosuka City Museum [*A publication*]
Sci Res ... Scientific Researches [*A publication*]
Sci Res Abstr ... Science Research Abstracts [*A publication*]
Sci Res Abstr A ... Science Research Abstracts. Part A. Superconductivity, Magnetohydrodynamics, and Plasmas. Theoretical Physics [*A publication*]
Sci Res Abstr J B ... Science Research Abstracts Journal. Part B. Laser and Electro-Optic Reviews, Quantum Electronics, and Unconventional Energy Sources [*A publication*]
Sci Res Br Univ Coll ... Scientific Research in British Universities and Colleges [*A publication*]
Sci Res Counc Jam J ... Scientific Research Council of Jamaica. Journal [*A publication*]

Sci Res (Dacca) ... Scientific Research (Dacca) [*Pakistan*] [*A publication*]
Sci Res (Dacca, Bangladesh) ... Scientific Researches (Dacca, Bangladesh) [*A publication*]
Sci Res Natl Sci Ed ... Scientific Research. Natural Science Edition [*People's Republic of China*] [*A publication*]
Sci Res News ... Science Research News [*A publication*]
Sci Res News (Kanpur) ... Science Research News (Kanpur) [*A publication*]
Sci Res (NY) ... Scientific Research (New York) [*A publication*]
Sci Resour Lett ... Science Resource Letter [*A publication*]
Sci Rev ...... Scienca Revuo [*A publication*]
Sci Rev ...... Science Review [*A publication*]
Sci Rev (Belgrade) ... Scienca Revuo (Belgrade) [*A publication*]
Sci Rev Int Sci Asoc Esperantista ... Scienca Revuo. Internacia Scienca Asocio Esperantista [*A publication*]
Sci Rev (Manila) ... Science Review (Manila) [*A publication*]
Sci Rev (Neth) ... Scienca Revuo (Netherlands) [*A publication*]
Sci Rondo ... Scienca Rondo [*A publication*]
Sci R Toh A ... Science Reports. Research Institutes. Tohoku University. Series A. Physics, Chemistry, and Metallurgy [*A publication*]
SCIS .... Safety Containment Isolation System (IEEE)
SCIS .... SCI Systems, Inc. [*NASDAQ symbol*] (NQ)
SCIS .... Science Curriculum Improvement Study [*Education*]
SC Is .... Selected Judgments of the Supreme Court of Israel [*A publication*] (DLA)
SCIS .... Social Change in Sweden [*A publication*]
SCIS .... Spacecraft Interface Specification (MCD)
SCIS .... Spinal Cord Injury Service [*Medicine*]
SCIS .... Standard Cubic Inches per Second (NASA)
SCIS .... Survivable Communications Integration System
Sci S Afr ... Scientific South Africa [*A publication*]
Sci & Scty ... Science and Society [*A publication*]
SCISEARCH ... Science Citation Index Search [*Institute for Scientific Information*] [*Philadelphia, PA*] [*Bibliographic database*]
Sci Ser Inland Waters Dir (Can) ... Scientific Series. Inland Waters Directorate (Canada) [*A publication*]
Sci Ser Inland Waters Lands Dir (Can) ... Scientific Series. Inland Waters/Lands Directorate (Canada) [*A publication*]
Sci Serves Farm ... Science Serves Your Farm [*A publication*]
Sci Silvae ... Scientia Silvae [*A publication*]
Sci Sin .... Scientia Sinica [*A publication*]
Sci Sin B .... Scientia Sinica. Series B. Chemical, Biological, Agricultural, Medical, and Earth Sciences [*A publication*]
Sci Sinica ... Scientia Sinica [*A publication*]
Sci Sinica Ser A ... Scientia Sinica. Series A. Mathematical, Physical, Astronomical, and Technical Sciences [*A publication*]
Sci Sinica Ser B ... Scientia Sinica. Series B. Chemical, Biological, Agricultural, Medical, and Earth Sciences [*A publication*]
Sci Sinica Suppl ... Scientia Sinica. Supplement [*A publication*]
Sci Sin Ser B (Engl Ed) ... Scientia Sinica. Series B. Chemical, Biological, Agricultural, Medical, and Earth Sciences (English Edition) [*A publication*]
Sci Sinter ... Science of Sintering [*A publication*]
Sci Sintering ... Science of Sintering [*A publication*]
SCISO ...... Supreme Court, Individual Slip Opinions
Sci Soc .... Science and Society [*A publication*]
Sci & Soc ... Science and Society [*A publication*]
Sci Soc .... Sciences Sociales [*A publication*]
Sci Sol .... Science du Sol [*A publication*]
SCISOR ...... System for Conceptual Information Summarization, Organization, and Retrieval [*Software package*] (IT)
SCI/SR ...... Shakaichosa-Kenkyusho Consumer Index Summary Report [*Marketing Intelligence Corp.*] [*Japan*] [*Information service or system*] (CRD)
SCISRS ..... Sigma Center Information Storage and Retrieval System
Sci Stud ...... Science Studies [*A publication*]
Sci Stud St Bonaventure Univ ... Science Studies. St. Bonaventure University [*A publication*]
SCIT .... Science Teacher [*A publication*]
SCIT .... Scientific, Inc. [*NASDAQ symbol*] (NQ)
SCIT .... Small Craft Instructor Trainer [*Red Cross*]
SCIT .... Smaller Companies International Trust [*British*]
SCIT .... Special Commissions of Income Tax [*British*]
SCIT .... Standard Change Integration and Tracking (NASA)
SCIT .... Subcommittee on Interzonal Trade [*Allied German Occupation Forces*]
Sci Teach ... Science Teacher [*A publication*]
Sci Teach (New Delhi) ... Science Teacher (New Delhi) [*A publication*]
Sci Teach News ... Science Teachers News [*A publication*] (APTA)
SCITEC ..... [*The*] Association of the Scientific, Engineering, and Technological Community of Canada
Sci Tec .... Scienza e Tecnica [*A publication*]
Sci Tech ..... Science and Australian Technology [*A publication*] (APTA)
Sci Tech ..... Science and Technology [*A publication*]
Sci & Tech ... Science and Technology [*A publication*]
Sci Tech Aerosp Rep ... Scientific and Technical Aerospace Reports [*NASA*] [*A publication*]
Sci & Tech Aerosp Reports ... Scientific and Technical Aerospace Reports [*NASA*] [*A publication*]
Sci Tech Armement ... Sciences et Techniques de l'Armement [*A publication*]
Sci Tech Eau ... Sciences et Techniques de l'Eau [*A publication*]

Sci Tech Human Values ... Science, Technology, and Human Values [*A publication*]
Sci Tech Inf Process ... Scientific and Technical Information Processing [*A publication*]
Sci Tech Inf Process (Engl Transl) ... Scientific and Technical Information Processing (English Translation) [*A publication*]
Sci Tech Inf Process (Eng Transl Nauchno-Tekh Inf Ser I) ... Scientific and Technical Information Processing (English Translation of Nauchno-Tekhnicheskaya Informatsiya Seriya I) [*A publication*]
Sci Techn Aerospace Rep ... Scientific and Technical Aerospace Reports [*NASA*] [*A publication*]
Sci Tech News ... Science and Technology News [*A publication*]
Sci Technol ... Science and Technology [*A publication*]
Sci Technol ... Sciences and Technologies. Korea University [*Republic of Korea*] [*A publication*]
Sci Technol Aliment ... Science et Technologie Alimentaire [*People's Republic of China*] [*A publication*]
Sci Technol China ... Science and Technology in China [*A publication*]
Sci Technol Jpn ... Science and Technology of Japan [*A publication*]
Sci Technol Korea Univ ... Sciences and Technologies. Korea University [*A publication*]
Sci Technol Libr ... Science and Technology Libraries [*A publication*]
Sci Technol Ser ... Science Technology Series [*United States*] [*A publication*]
Sci Technol (Surrey Hills Aust) ... Science and Technology (Surrey Hills, Australia) [*A publication*]
Sci Tech (Paris) ... Sciences et Techniques (Paris) [*A publication*]
Sci Tech Pharm ... Sciences et Techniques Pharmaceutiques [*A publication*]
Sci Tec Latt-Casearia ... Scienza e Tecnica Lattiero-Casearia [*A publication*]
Sci Tecnol Alimenti ... Scienza e Tecnologia degli Alimenti [*A publication*]
SCITEC-PAC ... Science and Technology Political Action Committee   (EA)
SCITEF ..... Software and Interoperability Test Facility [*Fort Huachuca, AZ*] [*United States Army Electronic Proving Ground*]   (GRD)
Sci Terre .... Sciences de la Terre [*A publication*]
Sci Terre Inf Geol ... Sciences de la Terre. Informatique Geologique [*A publication*]
Sci Terre Mem ... Sciences de la Terre. Memoires [*A publication*]
Sci Today (Bombay) ... Science Today (Bombay) [*A publication*]
Sci Tools .... Science Tools [*A publication*]
Sci Total Environ ... Science of the Total Environment [*A publication*]
Sci Tree Top ... Scientific Tree Topics [*A publication*]
SCIU .... Selector Control Interface Unit   (MCD)
SCIU .... Spacecraft Interface Unit   (NASA)
SCI-USA ... Service Civil International - United States of America   (EA)
SCIV .... Studii si Cercetari de Istorie Veche [*Later, Studii si Cercetari de Istorie Veche si Arheologie*] [*A publication*]
SCIV .... Subclavian Intravenous Injection [*Medicine*]
SCIVA .... Studii si Cercetari de Istorie Veche si Arheologie [*A publication*]
Sci Vie .... Science et Vie [*A publication*]
SCIWE ...... Synthesis Center of the Institute for Wholistic Education   (EA)
Sci Works For Res Inst (Zvolen) ... Scientific Works. Forest Research Institute (Zvolen) [*A publication*]
Sci Works High Med Inst Pleven ... Scientific Works. Higher Medical Institute of Pleven [*A publication*]
Sci Works Poult Sci Poult Res Inst ... Scientific Works. Poultry Science. Poultry Research Institute [*A publication*]
Sci Works Res Inst Anim Prod Nitra ... Scientific Works. Research Institute of Animal Production at Nitra [*A publication*]
Sci Works Res Inst Epidemiol Microbiol (Sofia) ... Scientific Works. Research Institute of Epidemiology and Microbiology (Sofia) [*A publication*]
Sci World ... Scholastic Science World [*A publication*]
Sci World ... Scientific World [*England*] [*A publication*]
SCIX .... Scitex Corp. Ltd. [*NASDAQ symbol*]   (NQ)
Sci Yearb Vet Fac (Thessalonica) ... Scientific Yearbook. Veterinary Faculty (Thessalonica) [*A publication*]
SCIZ .... Isla De Pascua [*Easter Island*] [*Chile*] [*ICAO location identifier*]   (ICLI)
SCJ .... Congregatio Sacerdotum a Corde Jesu [*Congregation of the Priests of the Sacred Heart of Jesus*] [*Roman Catholic religious order*]
SC J .... Court of Justiciary Cases [*Scotland*]   (DLA)
SC J .... Nebraska Supreme Court Journal [*A publication*]   (DLA)
SCJ .... Science Council of Japan   (MCD)
SCJ .... Section of Criminal Justice [*American Bar Association*]   (EA)
SC(J) .... Sessions Cases (Judiciary Reports) [*Legal*] [*British*]
SCJ .... Siberian Chemistry Journal [*A publication*]
SC & J .... Signal Collection and Jamming
SCJ .... Sisters of the Child Jesus [*Roman Catholic religious order*]
SCJ .... Sixteenth Century Journal [*A publication*]
SCJ .... Society for Collegiate Journalists   (EA)
SCJ .... Spertus College of Judaica [*Chicago, IL*]   (BJA)
SCJ .... Standing Committee on Japan [*Australia*]
SCJ .... Stretch Chuck Jaws   (MCD)
SCJ .... Super Cobra Jet [*Automotive engineering*]
SC J .... Supreme Court Journal [*India*] [*A publication*]   (DLA)
SCJ .... Supreme Court of Justice [*British*]   (ROG)
SCJ .... Sydney Cinema Journal [*A publication*]   (APTA)
SCJA .... Senior Conformation Judges Association   (EA)
SCJAEF ..... Senior Conformation Judges Association Education Fund   (EA)
S C Jap ...... Studia Celtica Japonica [*A publication*]

SCJB .... Jamaica Supreme Court Judgment Books [*A publication*]   (DLA)
SCJC .... Saint Catharine Junior College [*Kentucky*]
Sc J Cl Inv ... Scandinavian Journal of Clinical and Laboratory Investigation [*A publication*]
Sc J Dent R ... Scandinavian Journal of Dental Research [*A publication*]
Sc J Gastr .. Scandinavian Journal of Gastroenterology [*A publication*]
Sc J Haemat ... Scandinavian Journal of Haematology [*A publication*]
Sc J Hist .... Scandinavian Journal of History [*A publication*]
Sc J Immun ... Scandinavian Journal of Immunology [*A publication*]
Sc J In Dis ... Scandinavian Journal of Infectious Diseases [*A publication*]
SCJM .... Sisters of Charity of Jesus and Mary [*See also ZLJM*] [*Brussels, Belgium*]   (EAIO)
SCJO .... Osborno/Canal Bajo [*Chile*] [*ICAO location identifier*]   (ICLI)
Sc J Plast ... Scandinavian Journal of Plastic and Reconstructive Surgery [*A publication*]
Sc J Psycho ... Scandinavian Journal of Psychology [*A publication*]
Sc J Re Med ... Scandinavian Journal of Rehabilitation Medicine [*A publication*]
Sc J Resp D ... Scandinavian Journal of Respiratory Diseases [*A publication*]
Sc J Rheum ... Scandinavian Journal of Rheumatology [*A publication*]
SCJS .... Seminary College of Jewish Studies   (BJA)
Sc J S Med ... Scandinavian Journal of Social Medicine [*A publication*]
ScJTh .... Scottish Journal of Theology [*Edinburgh*] [*A publication*]
Sc J Thor C ... Scandinavian Journal of Thoracic and Cardiovascular Surgery [*A publication*]
SCJUA ...... Science Journal Incorporating Discovery [*A publication*]
Sc Jur .... Scottish Jurist [*A publication*]   (DLA)
Sc J Urol N ... Scandinavian Journal of Urology and Nephrology [*A publication*]
SCK .... Air Force Weapons Laboratory, Kirtland AFB, NM [*OCLC symbol*]   (OCLC)
s-ck--- .... Colombia [*MARC geographic area code*] [*Library of Congress*]   (LCCP)
SCK .... Serum Creatine Kinase [*An enzyme*]
SCK .... Sisters of Christ the King [*Roman Catholic religious order*]
SCK .... SS Airways, Inc. [*Mission, KS*] [*FAA designator*]   (FAAC)
SCK .... Stockton [*California*] [*Airport symbol*]   (OAG)
SCK .... Stockton, CA [*Location identifier*] [*FAA*]   (FAAL)
SCK .... Studiecentrum voor Kernenergie [*Also, CEEN, NERC*] [*Nuclear energy*] [*Belgium*]   (NRCH)
SCKD .... Society of Certified Kitchen Designers   (EA)
SCKLS .... South Central Kansas Library System [*Library network*]
SCKSJ .... Supreme Commandery Knights of St. John   (EA)
SCKTPT .... Southern California Kinesthesia and Tactile Perception Tests
ScKW .... Williamsburg Technical College, Kingstree, SC [*Library symbol*] [*Library of Congress*]   (LCLS)
s-cl--- .... Chile [*MARC geographic area code*] [*Library of Congress*]   (LCCP)
SCL .... Great Falls, MT [*Location identifier*] [*FAA*]   (FAAL)
SCL .... Santa Clara Lawyer [*A publication*]
SCL .... Santa Clara - Ricard [*California*] [*Seismograph station code, US Geological Survey*] [*Closed*]   (SEIS)
SCL .... Santiago [*Chile*] [*Airport symbol*]   (OAG)
SCL .... Save a Cat League   (EA)
SCL .... Scale
SCL .... Scarlet   (ROG)
SCL .... Scrap Classification List [*DoD*]
Scl .... Sculptor [*Constellation*]
SCL .... Seaboard Coast Line Railroad Co. [*Subsidiary of Seaboard Coast Line Industries*] [*Later, CSX Corp.*] [*AAR code*]
SCL .... Secondary Coolant Line [*or Loop*] [*NASA*]   (NASA)
SCL .... Select Cases in Chancery Tempore King [*25 English Reprint*] [*1724-33*] [*A publication*]   (DLA)
SCL .... Selectively Cross Linked
SCL .... Senior Citizens League [*Defunct*]   (EA)
SCL .... Sequential Control Logic
SCL .... Service Control Layer [*Data processing*]
SCL .... Shaped Charge Liner
SCL .... Shaw Cablesystems Ltd. [*Toronto Stock Exchange symbol*]
SCL .... Ship Configuration List [*Navy*]   (CAAL)
SCL .... Signal Corps Laboratory [*Obsolete*] [*Army*]
SCL .... Signal Corps Letter   (MCD)
SCL .... Simmons College, Boston, MA [*OCLC symbol*]   (OCLC)
SCL .... Single Composition Lathe-Cut [*Dental alloy*]
SCL .... Sinus Cycle Length [*Cardiology*]
SCL .... Sisters of Charity (of Leavenworth) [*Roman Catholic religious order*]
SCL .... Site Concurrence Letter   (AFM)
SCL .... Skin Conductance Level [*Physiology*]
SCL .... Society for Caribbean Linguistics [*St. Augustine, Trinidad*]   (EAIO)
SCL .... Society for Computers and Law [*Abingdon, Oxfordshire, England*]   (EAIO)
SCL .... Society of County Librarians [*British*]
SCL .... Sofati Container Line [*Shipping line*]
SCL .... Soft Contact Lens
SCL .... Software Career Link [*Database producer*] [*Burlington, MA*]
SCL .... South Carolina Law Reports [*Pre-1868*] [*A publication*]   (DLA)
SCL .... South Central Regional Library System [*UTLAS symbol*]
SCL .... Southeastern Composers' League   (EA)

SCL...........	Southern California Law Review [*A publication*]
SCL...........	Space Charge Limited
SCL...........	Specification Change Log [*NASA*] (NASA)
SCL...........	Spontaneous Cycle Length
SCL...........	Standard Classification List [*Military*]
SCL...........	Standard Conventional Load
SCL...........	Stendhal Club [*A publication*]
SCL...........	Stepan Co. [*AMEX symbol*] (SPSG)
SCL...........	Stock Corporation Law [*A publication*] (DLA)
SCL...........	String Control Language [*Data processing*]
SCL...........	Student of the Civil Law
SCL...........	Studies in Canadian Literature [*A publication*]
SCL...........	Studii si Cercetari Lingvistice [*A publication*]
SCL...........	Super Chevys Limited (EA)
SCL...........	Symbolic Correction Loader
SCL...........	Symmetric Clipper
SCL...........	Symphony Command Language [*Data processing*]
SCL...........	System Command Language [*Data processing*]
SCL...........	Systems Component List (KSC)
SCL...........	Systems Control Language [*Data processing*]
Sc LA	Left Scapuloanterior Position [*of the fetus*] [*Obstetrics*]
ScLangU	United Merchants Research Center, Langley, SC [*Library symbol*] [*Library of Congress*] (LCLS)
Sc La R......	Scottish Land Court Reports [*Supplement to Scottish Law Review*] [*A publication*] (DLA)
Sc La Rep...	Report by the Scottish Land Court [*A publication*] (DLA)
Sc La Rep Ap ...	Appendices to the Report of the Scottish Land Court [*A publication*] (DLA)
Sc La Rep App ...	Appendices to the Report of the Scottish Land Court [*A publication*] (DLA)
SClas.........	Studii Clasice [*A publication*]
ScLau	Laurens County Library, Laurens, SC [*Library symbol*] [*Library of Congress*] (LCLS)
SCLAV	Sclavonic [*Language, etc.*] (ROG)
SCLC	Small-Cell Lung Cancer [*Oncology*]
SCLC	South Coast Labour Council [*Australia*]
SCLC	Southern Christian Leadership Conference (EA)
SCLC	Space-Charge-Limited Current
SCLCS.......	Ship Command-Launch Control Subsystem [*Navy*] (CAAL)
SCLDF	Sierra Club Legal Defense Fund (EA)
SCLE	Santiago/Los Leones [*Chile*] [*ICAO location identifier*] (ICLI)
SCLE	Society and Leisure [*Czechoslovakia*] [*A publication*]
SCLE	Subacute Cutaneous Lupus Erythematosus [*Medicine*]
SCLEC.......	Signal Corps Logistics Evaluation Committee [*Obsolete*] [*Army*] (KSC)
SCLER......	Scleroscope
SCLER......	Sclerosis [*Medicine*]
SCLERA....	Santa Catalina Laboratory for Experimental Relativity by Astrometry [*University of Arizona*] [*Research center*] (RCD)
SCLERO ...	Scleroderma [*Medicine*]
SCLI	Somerset and Cornwall Light Infantry [*British military*] (DMA)
SC Libn......	South Carolina Librarian [*A publication*]
SCLing......	Siouan and Caddoan Linguistics [*A publication*]
S Clin North America ...	Surgical Clinics of North America [*A publication*]
Sc LJ	Scottish Law Journal and Sheriff Court Record [*A publication*] (DLA)
Sc L J	Scottish Literary Journal [*A publication*]
SCLJ.........	South Carolina Law Journal [*A publication*] (DLA)
SCLK	Ship's Clerk
SCLL	Sandia Corporation, Livermore Laboratory
SCLL	Supreme Committee for the Liberation of Lithuania (EA)
SCLL	Vallenar/Vallenar [*Chile*] [*ICAO location identifier*] (ICLI)
Scl & Lbr Bul ...	Social and Labour Bulletin [*A publication*]
SC LM	Scottish Law Magazine and Sheriff Court Reporter [*A publication*] (DLA)
SCLM........	Stability, Control, and Load Maneuvers [*Aerospace*] (MCD)
SCLN........	Semicolon (FAAC)
SCLO........	Self-Consistent Local Orbital [*Method*] [*Mathematics*]
SCLO........	Statistical Clearance Liaison Officer [*Army*] (AABC)
SCLOG......	Security Log [*Telecommunications*] (TEL)
Sc LP........	Left Scapuloposterior Position [*of the fetus*] [*Obstetrics*]
SCLP	Santiago/Lo Prado [*Chile*] [*ICAO location identifier*] (ICLI)
Scl Problems ...	Social Problems [*A publication*]
SC L Q	South Carolina Law Quarterly [*A publication*]
SCLR	Santa Clara Law Review [*A publication*] (ILCA)
Sc LR	Scottish Law Reporter [*A publication*] (DLA)
Sc LR	Scottish Law Review and Sheriff Court Reports [*A publication*] (DLA)
SC LR	South Carolina Law Review [*A publication*]
SCLRA	School Review [*A publication*]
Sc L Rep....	Scottish Law Reporter [*Edinburgh*] [*A publication*] (DLA)
Sc L Rev....	South Carolina Law Review [*A publication*]
SCLS	Serra Cooperative Library System [*Library network*]
SCLS........	South Central Library System [*Library network*]
SCLS.........	Star Classics, Inc. [*NASDAQ symbol*] (NQ)
SCLSA....	Scandinavian Journal of Clinical and Laboratory Investigation. Supplement [*A publication*]
Scl Sci Q	Social Science Quarterly [*A publication*]
Scl Sec Bul ...	Social Security Bulletin [*A publication*]

Sc LT	Scots Law Times [*A publication*] (DLA)
SCLV.........	Subclavian Vein [*Anatomy*]
SCLY.........	Scullery (MSA)
Sc M	Master of Science
SCM	S-Band Cassegrain Monopulse
SCM	Sacra Caesarea Majestas [*Sacred Imperial Majesty*] [*Latin*]
SCM	Samarium Cobalt Magnet
SCM	Sanctae Memoriae [*Of Holy Memory*] [*Latin*]
SCM	Scammon Bay [*Alaska*] [*Airport symbol*] (OAG)
SCM	Scammon Bay, AK [*Location identifier*] [*FAA*] (FAAL)
SCM	School Musician. Director and Teacher [*A publication*]
SCM	SCM Corp. [*Formerly, Smith-Corona Marchant, Inc.*] [*NYSE symbol*] (SPSG)
SCM	Selective Complement Accumulator
SCM	Self-Contained Munitions
SCM	Sender's Composition Message [*Cable*]
SCM	Service Command Module [*Aerospace*] (MCD)
SCM	Sheep Creek Mountain [*Alaska*] [*Seismograph station code, US Geological Survey*] (SEIS)
SCM	Signal Conditioning Module
SCM	Simulated Core Mock-Up [*or Model*] [*Nuclear energy*] (NRCH)
SCM	Single-Channel MODEM [*Telecommunications*] (TEL)
SCM	Single Crystal Meteorite
SCM	Siscoe Callahan [*Vancouver Stock Exchange symbol*]
SCM	Site Configuration Message [*NASA*]
SCM	Small-Core Memory [*Data processing*]
SCM	Society of Community Medicine [*Later, SPH*] (EAIO)
SCM	Society for Computer Medicine [*Later, AMIA*] (EA)
SCM	Software Configuration Management (IEEE)
SCM	Solar Cell Module
SCM	Soluble Cytotoxic Mediator [*Immunology*]
SCM	Spares Calculation Model
SCM	Special Court-Martial
SCM	Specification Change Memorandum
SCM	Spleen Concanavalin A Medium [*Immunoassay*]
SCM	Squadron Corporal-Major [*British military*] (DMA)
SCM	Stamp Cancelling Machine (DCTA)
SCM	Standard Cubic Meter
SCM	State-Certified Midwife [*British*]
SCM	Steam Condensing Mode [*Nuclear energy*] (NRCH)
SCM	Sternocleidomastoid [*Anatomy*]
SCM	Stillman College, Tuscaloosa, AL [*OCLC symbol*] (OCLC)
S & CM	Strategic and Critical Materials [*Military*]
SCM	Strategic Cruise Missile (MCD)
SCM	Streamline Curvature Method [*Computer program*]
SCM	Streptococcal Cell Membrane [*Microbiology*]
SCM	Strouds Creek & Muddtley Railroad [*AAR code*]
SCM	Student Christian Movement [*British*]
SCM	Subscribers' Concentration Module [*Telecommunications*] (TEL)
SCM	Subsystem Configuration Management [*or Monitoring*] [*NASA*] (NASA)
SCM	Summary Court-Martial [*Army*]
SCM	Superconducting Magnet (IEEE)
SCM	Supervision Control Module [*Telecommunications*] (TEL)
SCM	Supply Categories of Material (MCD)
SCM	Suppressed-Carrier Modulation
SCM	Sussex County Magazine [*A publication*]
SCM	Sustained Competitive Motivation
SCM	System Control and Monitor [*Telecommunications*] (TSSD)
SCM	Systems Control Microprocessor
SCMA........	Silk Commission Manufacturers Association [*Defunct*] (EA)
SCMA........	Southern Cypress Manufacturers Association (EA)
SCMAA......	Studii si Cercetari de Mecanica Aplicata [*A publication*]
SCMAI......	Staff Committee on Mediation, Arbitration, and Inquiry [*American Library Association*]
SC Mar Resour Cent Tech Rep ...	South Carolina. Marine Resources Center. Technical Report [*A publication*]
SCMAT......	Southern California Motor Accuracy Test
SCMB........	Seaby's Coin and Medal Bulletin [*A publication*]
SCMB........	Standard Chartered Merchant Bank [*Singapore*]
SCMC........	S-Carboxymethylcysteine [*An amino acid*]
SCMC........	Sisters of Charity of Our Lady, Mother of the Church [*Roman Catholic religious order*]
SCMC........	Societe de Construction des Musees du Canada
SCMC........	Sodium(carboxymethyl)cellulose [*Organic chemistry*]
SCMC........	Strategic Cruise Missile Carrier
SCMD	Santiago/Ministerio de Defensa Nacional [*Chile*] [*ICAO location identifier*] (ICLI)
SCMD	Selectively Conductive Molding Device
SCME........	American Federation of State, County, and Municipal Employees
SCME........	Service Center Math Error [*IRS*]
SCME........	Society of Clinical and Medical Electrologists (EA)
SCMF........	Single Contact Midge Flange
SCMF........	Societe Canadienne de Musique Folklorique
Sc M in Hyg ...	Master of Science in Hygiene
SCMI.........	Society to Conquer Mental Illness [*Defunct*] (EA)
SCMM	Selections from China Mainland Magazines [*US Consulate, Hongkong*] [*A publication*]

SCMM ...... Sisters of Charity of Our Lady, Mother of Mercy [*Roman Catholic religious order*]
SCMM ...... Society of Catholic Medical Missionaries, Inc. [*Medical Mission Sisters*] [*Roman Catholic religious order*]
SCMO .... Senior Clinical Medical Officer [*British*]
SCMO .... Societe Canadienne de Meteorologie et d'Oceanographie [*Canadian Meteorological and Oceanographic Society - CMOS*]
SCMO .... Societe pour une Confederation au Moyen-Orient [*Society for Middle East Confederation - SMEC*] (EAIO)
SCMO .... Studie- en Informatiecentrum TNO voor Milieu-Onderzoek [*TNO Study and Information Center on Environmental Research*] [*Information service or system*] (IID)
SCMO .... Subsidiary Communications Multiplex Operation [*FM radio frequency unused portion*]
SCMO .... Summary Court-Martial Order [*Army*]
SCMOD .... Scale Model
SCMP........ Second-Class Mail Publications [*Later, ASCMP*] (EA)
SCMP........ Service Craft Modernization Program [*Navy*] (CAAL)
SCMP........ Society of Company Meeting Planners (EA)
SCMP........ South China Morning Post [*A publication*]
SCMP........ Sulfonated Chemimechanical Pulp [*Pulp and paper technology*]
SCMP........ Support Center Management Plan (AAG)
SCMP........ System Contractor Management Plan [*NASA*] (NASA)
SCMPBN .. South China Morning Post (Business News) [*A publication*]
SCMPT ...... Sperm Cervical Mucus Penetration Test [*Clinical chemistry*]
SCMR .... Secretary's Committee on Mental Retardation [*Department of Health and Human Services*]
SCMR .... South Canterbury Mounted Rifles [*British military*] (DMA)
SCMR .... Special Committee on Migration and Resettlement [*Department of State*] [*World War II*]
SCMR........ Surface Composition Mapping Radiometer [*NASA*]
SCMS .... Scientific Measurement Systems, Inc. [*Austin, TX*] [*NASDAQ symbol*] (NQ)
SCMS .... Serial Copy Management System [*for digital audio tape recording machines*]
SCMS .... Signal Command Management System [*Military*] (AABC)
SCMS .... Somali Current Monitoring System [*Marine science*] (MSC)
SCMS .... Standard Configuration Management Systems [*Military*] (AFIT)
SCMT........ Single-Cause Mortality Tape [*National Center for Health Statistics databank*]
Sc Mun App Rep ... Scotch Munitions Appeals Reports [*Edinburgh and Glasgow*] [*A publication*] (DLA)
SCMV........ Santa Cruz Mountain Vintners (EA)
SCMV........ Sugar Cane Mosaic Virus
SCN .... Citadel, Daniel Library, Charleston, SC [*OCLC symbol*] (OCLC)
SCN .... Saarbrucken [*West Germany*] [*Airport symbol*] (OAG)
SCN .... Satellite Communications Network, Inc. [*Edison, NJ*] [*Telecommunications*]
SCN .... Satellite Conference Network, Inc. [*New York, NY*] [*NYSE symbol*] [*Telecommunications service*] (TSSD)
SCN .... Satellite Control Network
SCN .... Scanner [*Data processing*]
SCN .... Schematic Change Notice
SCN .... Screen [*Technical drawings*]
SCN .... Scribe Nehemiah [*Freemasonry*]
SCN .... Search Control Number (MCD)
SCN .... Secretary's Commission on Nursing [*Department of Health and Human Services*]
SCN .... Securities Communications Network, Inc. [*Englewood, CO*] (TSSD)
SCN .... Self-Checking Number
SCN .... Self-Compensating Network [*Telecommunications*] (TEL)
SCN .... Self-Contained Navigation [*NASA*]
SCN .... Sensitive Command Network
SCN .... Seventeenth-Century News [*A publication*]
SCN .... Shipbuilding and Conversion, Navy
SCN .... Ships Construction, Navy [*Funding*]
SCN .... Shortest Connected Network
SCN .... Show Cause Notice
SCN .... Silent Canyon Resources Ltd. [*Vancouver Stock Exchange symbol*]
SCN .... Single Crystal Needle
SCN .... Sisters of Charity (of Nazareth) [*Roman Catholic religious order*]
SCN .... Sorting Code Number (DCTA)
SCN .... Soybean Cyst Nematode [*Botany*]
SCN .... Special Care Nursery
SCN .... Special Change Notice (KSC)
SCN .... Specific Control Number
SCN .... Specification Change Notice [*NASA*]
SCN .... Stock Control Number
SCN .... Studii si Cercetari de Numismatica [*A publication*]
SCN .... Summary and Charge Number
SCN .... Sunset Crater National Monument [*Arizona*] [*Seismograph station code, US Geological Survey*] (SEIS)
SCN .... Supply Corps, Navy
SCN .... Suprachiasmatic Nucleus [*or Nuclei*] [*of the hypothalamus*] [*Anatomy*]

SCN .... Sylvania-Corning Nuclear Corp.
SCN .... System Change Notice
SCN .... System Control Number
SCNA .... Self-Contained Night Attack (MCD)
SCNA .... Sikh Council of North America (EA)
SCNA .... Sudden Cosmic-Noise Absorption
SCNAWAF ... Special Category Navy with Air Force
SCNB......... Societe Nationale des Chemins de Fer Belges [*Belgian National Railways*]
ScNC.......... Newberry College, Newberry, SC [*Library symbol*] [*Library of Congress*] (LCLS)
SCNC......... South Carolina National Corporation [*NASDAQ symbol*] (NQ)
SCNCA...... Sciences [*New York*] [*A publication*]
SCND .... Scientific Industries, Inc. [*NASDAQ symbol*] (NQ)
SCND .... Second (FAAC)
scnDNA ..... Deoxyribonucleic Acid, Single Copy Nuclear [*Biochemistry, genetics*]
SCNEB...... Science News [*Washington, DC*] [*A publication*]
SCNG .... Scan-Graphics, Inc. [*NASDAQ symbol*] (NQ)
SCNG .... Scanning (MSA)
SCNI .... Select Committee on Nationalised Industries [*British*]
SC (Nig)..... Judgments of the Supreme Court of Nigeria [*A publication*] (DLA)
SCNN .... Scan-Tron Corp. [*NASDAQ symbol*] (NQ)
SCNO .... Savio Club National Office (EA)
SCNO .... Senior Canadian Naval Officer [*British military*] (DMA)
ScNoaSH... North Augusta Senior High School, North Augusta, SC [*Library symbol*] [*Library of Congress*] (LCLS)
SCNPWC .. Standing Committee for Nobel Prize Winners' Congresses (EA)
SCNR........ Scanner (MSA)
SCNR........ Scientific Committee of National Representatives [*NATO*]
Sc NR........ Scott's New English Common Pleas Reports [*A publication*] (DLA)
SCNR........ Sequence Control Number Register [*Data processing*]
SCNR........ Solid-Core Nuclear Rocket [*NASA*]
SCNR........ Supreme Council for National Reconstruction [*South Korea*]
SCNS......... Self-Contained Navigation System [*NASA*]
SCNS......... Subcutaneous Nerve Stimulation [*For treatment of pain*]
SCN/SIN... Sensitive Command Network/Sensitive Information Network (CET)
SCNTN...... Self-Contained
SCNUL...... Standing Conference on National and University Libraries [*British*]
SC Nurs ..... South Carolina Nursing [*A publication*]
SCO .... Converse College, Spartanburg, SC [*OCLC symbol*] (OCLC)
SCO .... Manetti Roberts [*Italy*] [*Research code symbol*]
SCO .... Sales Contracting Officer [*Army*]
SCO .... Sarawak Communist Organization [*Malaya*]
ScO .... Scientific Officer [*Also, SO*] [*Ministry of Agriculture, Fisheries, and Food*] [*British*]
SCO .... Scobey, MT [*Location identifier*] [*FAA*] (FAAL)
SCO .... Score Resources [*Vancouver Stock Exchange symbol*]
SCO .... Scoresbysund [*Greenland*] [*Seismograph station code, US Geological Survey*] [*Closed*] (SEIS)
Sco............. Scorpius [*Constellation*]
SCO .... Scottish (ROG)
Sco............. Scott's English Common Pleas Reports [*A publication*] (DLA)
SCO .... Selective Conscientious Objection
SCO .... Senior Chief Officer [*British military*] (DMA)
SCO .... Service Cryptologic Organizations (MCD)
SCO .... Single Crystal Orthoferrites
SCO .... Sisters of Charity of Ottawa [*Grey Nuns of the Cross*] [*Roman Catholic religious order*]
SCO .... Smith Corona Corp. [*NYSE symbol*] (SPSG)
SCO .... Society of Commissioned Officers (EA)
SCO .... Southern College of Optometry [*Tennessee*]
S/CO......... Spacecraft Observer (KSC)
SCO .... Spacecraft Operations [*NASA*] (KSC)
SCO .... Squadron Command Officer (AAG)
SCO .... Squadron Constructor Officer [*Navy*] [*British*]
SCO .... Staff Communications Office [*Army*]
SCO .... Start Checkout [*NASA*] (NASA)
SCO .... State Coordinating Officer [*Federal disaster planning*]
SCO .... Statistical Control Office [*or Officer*] [*Military*]
SCO .... Studi Classici e Orientali [*A publication*]
SCO .... Subcarrier Oscillator
SCO .... Subcommissural Organ [*Neuroanatomy*]
SCO .... Subcontract Consignment Order
SCO .... Successor Contracting Officer (MCD)
SCO .... Supercritical Oxygen (MCD)
SCO .... Switch Closure Out (MCD)
SCO .... Synthetic Crude Oil [*Fuel technology*]
SCO .... System Counterpart Officer [*Military*] (AFIT)
SCOA .... Saluki Club of America (EA)
SCOA .... Sample Cave Operating Area [*Nuclear energy*] (NRCH)
SCOA .... SCOA Industries, Inc. [*Canton, MA*] [*NASDAQ symbol*] (NQ)
SCOA .... Supreme Council Order of the Amaranth (EA)
SCOBA...... Standing Conference of the Canonical Orthodox Bishops in the Americas (EA)

SCOBBS.... School of Combined Operations, Beach and Boat Section [*Military*] [*British*]
SCOBO ..... Satellite Collection Buoy Observations
SCOBOL... Structured COBOL
SCOC........ Sediment Community Oxygen Consumption [*Marine biology*]
SCOC........ Short-Circuit Output Current
SCOC........ Societe Canadienne d'Orientation et de Consultation
SCOC........ Support Command Operations Center [*Military*]
SCOCE...... Special Committee on Compromising Emanations [*Military*] (AABC)
SCOCLIS.. Standing Conference of Co-Operative Library and Information Services [*British*]
Sco Costs.... Scott's Costs in the High Court [*4th ed.*] [*1880*] [*A publication*] (DLA)
SCOD .... Societe Cooperative Oecumenique de Developpement [*Ecumenical Development Cooperative Society - EDCS*] (EAIO)
SCOD .... South Coast One Design [*Cruising boat*]
SCOD .... Specific Chemical Oxygen Demand Value [*for Complete Oxidation*]
SCODA ..... Scan Coherent Doppler Attachment
SCODL...... Scan Conversion Object Description Language [*Data processing*] (PCM)
SCODS...... Study Commission on Ocean Data Stations [*Marine science*] (MSC)
SCOE........ Special Checkout Equipment [*NASA*] (NASA)
SCOEG...... Standing Conference of Employers of Graduates [*British*]
SCOFA...... Shipping Control Office, Forward Area [*Navy*]
SCOFOR... Scottish Forces [*World War II*]
SCOFOR... Scouting Force [*Navy*]
ScoGaelS ... Scottish Gaelic Studies [*A publication*]
ScoGS .... Scottish Gaelic Studies [*A publication*]
S and COH ... Son and Coheir [*Genealogy*]
SCOH........ Staff Corporal of Horse [*British military*] (DMA)
SCOHR ...... Students Committee on Human Rights
Sco Int........ Scott's Intestate Laws [*A publication*] (DLA)
Sco & J Tel ... Scott and Jarnigan on the Law of Telegraphs [*A publication*] (DLA)
SCOL........ School (NVT)
SCOLA...... Second Consortium of Local Authorities
SCOLAG Bull ... Scottish Legal Action Group. Bulletin [*A publication*] (DLA)
Scol Anon... Scolia Anonyma [*Classical studies*] (OCD)
SCOLAR... Standard Costing of Laboratory Resources
Scol Att ...... Scolia Attica [*Classical studies*] (OCD)
SCOLAVNMED ... School of Aviation Medicine [*Later, School of Aerospace Medicine*]
SCOLCAP ... Scottish Libraries Cooperative Automation Project
SCOLE...... Standing Committee on Library Education [*American Library Association*]
SCOLMA ... Standing Conference on Library Materials on Africa [*British*]
SCOLSHIP ... Schoolship [*Navy*] (NVT)
SCOM .... Scientific Committee [*NATO*] (NATG)
SCOM .... SCS/Compute, Inc. [*St. Louis, MO*] [*NASDAQ symbol*] (NQ)
SCOM .... Site Cutover Manager [*Telecommunications*] (TEL)
SCOM .... Spacecraft Communicator
SCOM ...... Supervisory Communication Relations Test
SCOMA ...... Shipping Control Office, Marianas [*Navy*]
SCOMO ... Satellite Collection of Meteorological Observations
S/COMPT ... Side Compartment [*Automotive engineering*]
SCON .... Quellon/Ad Quellon [*Chile*] [*ICAO location identifier*] (ICLI)
SCON .... Santiago/Quinta Normal [*Chile*] [*ICAO location identifier*] (ICLI)
SCON .... Syscon Corp. [*NASDAQ symbol*] (NQ)
Scone & Upper Hunter Hist Soc J ... Scone and Upper Hunter Historical Society. Journal [*A publication*] (APTA)
Sco NR....... Scott's New English Common Pleas Reports [*A publication*] (DLA)
SCONRES ... Senate Concurrent Resolution (AFIT)
SCONS...... Shipment Control System [*Military*]
SCONT...... Ship Control
SCONUL... Standing Conference on National and University Libraries [*British*]
SCOOP...... Scientific Computation of Optimal Programs (IEEE)
SCOOP...... Scientific Computation of Optimum Procurement [*Air Force*]
SCOOP...... Strategic Confirmation of Optical Phenomenology
SCOOP...... Support Plan to Continuity of Operations Plan [*Military*]
SCOP........ Ferrocarril del Sureste [*AAR code*]
SCOP........ Scopolamine [*Anticholinergic compound*]
SCOP........ Single Copy Order Plan [*Later, STOP*] [*Bookselling*]
SCOP........ Steering Committee on Pilotage (DS)
SCOPE...... Schedule-Cost-Performance (IEEE)
SCOPE...... Scientific Committee on Problems of the Environment [*ICSU*] (EA)
SCOPE...... Scripps Cooperative Oceanic Productivity Expedition [*1956*]
SCOPE...... Senior Citizens' Opportunities for Personal Enrichment [*Federal antipoverty program*]
SCOPE...... Sequential Customer Order Processing Electronically
SCOPE...... Service Center of Private Enterprise
SCOPE...... Simple Checkout-Oriented Program Language

SCOPE...... Simple Communications Programming Environment [*Data processing*]
SCOPE...... Southern Coastal Plains Expedition [*National Oceanic and Atmospheric Administration*] (MSC)
SCOPE...... Special Committee on Paperless Entries [*California interbank group*]
SCOPE...... Special Committee on Problems of the Environment [*of International Council of Scientific Unions*]
SCOPE...... Stromberg Central Operations Panel - Electric
SCOPE...... Student Council on Pollution and the Environment [*Association conceived in late 1969 by then Secretary of the Interior Walter J. Hickel*]
SCOPE...... Subsystem for the Control of Operations and Plan Evaluation
SCOPE...... Summer Community Organization and Political Education Program
SCOPE...... Supervisory Control of Program Execution (MCD)
SCOPE...... Supportive Council on Preventive Effort [*Ohio*]
SCOPE...... System to Coordinate the Operation of Peripheral Equipment
SCOPES.... Squad Combat Operations Exercise, Simulation [*Military*]
SCOPP..... School-College Orientation Program of Pittsburgh
SCOPS ...... Select Committee on Ocean Policy Study [*Federal Council for Science and Technology*]
SCOR........ Scientific Committee on Oceanic Research [*ICSU*] [*Halifax, NS*] (EAIO)
Scor .... Scorpius [*Constellation*]
SCOR........ Self-Calibrating Omnirange
SCOR........ Small Cycle Observation Recording
SCOR........ Special Center of Research [*HEW*]
SCOR........ Special Committee on Oceanographic Research
SCOR........ Specialized Center of Research in Atherosclerosis [*University of Chicago*] [*Research center*] (RCD)
SCOR........ Specialized Center of Research in Ischemic Heart Disease [*University of Alabama at Birmingham*] [*Research center*] (RCD)
SCOR........ Status Control of Rejections (MCD)
SCOR........ Syncor International Corp. [*NASDAQ symbol*] (NQ)
SCORAN... Scorer and Analyzer [*Computerized educational testing*]
ScOrC....... Claflin College, Orangeburg, SC [*Library symbol*] [*Library of Congress*] (LCLS)
SCORDES .. Sferics Correlation Detection System
SCORE...... Satellite Computer-Operated Readiness Equipment [*SSD*]
SCORE...... Scientific Cooperative Operational Research Expedition [*National Oceanic and Atmospheric Administration*] (MSC)
SCORE...... Selection Copy and Reporting (IEEE)
SCORE...... Selective Conversion and Retention [*Navy*]
SCORE...... Service Corps of Retired Employees [*Australia*]
SCORE...... Service Corps of Retired Executives Association [*Washington, DC*] (EA)
SCORE...... Short Course Off-Road Event [*Off-road vehicle racing*]
SCORE...... Signal Communication by Orbiting Relay Equipment [*Radio*]
Score .... Simulated Combat Operations Range Equipment (MCD)
SCORE...... Solving Community Obstacles and Restoring Employment [*Occupational therapy*]
SCORE...... Space Communications for Orbiting Relay Equipment (MCD)
SCORE...... Special Claim on Residual Equity
SCORE...... Spectral Combinations for Reconnaissance Exploitation [*Photography*]
SCORE...... Standing Committee on Regulatory Effectiveness [*Nuclear Regulatory Commission*] (NRCH)
SCORE...... Stratified Charge, Omnivorous Rotary Engine [*Automotive engineering*]
SCORE...... Street Corner Offense Reduction Experiment
SCORE...... Student Competitions on Relevant Engineering
SCORE...... Subsystem Control of Required Equipment (MCD)
SCORE...... Supervisory Coaching Relations Test
SCORE...... System for Computerized Olympic Results and Events [*Texas Instruments, Inc.*]
SCORE...... System Cost and Operational Resource Evaluation (MCD)
SCORE...... Systematic Communications of Range Effectiveness (MUGU)
SCORE...... Systems Coordinative Reporting (MCD)
SCORES.... Scenario-Oriented Evaluation System
SCORES.... Scenario-Oriented Recurring Evaluation System [*Military*]
SCORES.... Standard Combat Oriented Recurring Evaluation System [*Military*]
SCORN ..... Special Committee Opposing Resurgent Nazism
SCORON .. Scouting Squadron
SCOROR.. Secretary's Committee on Research on Reorganization [*Navy*]
S/Corp .... Staff Corporal [*British military*] (DMA)
SCORP...... Statewide Comprehensive Outdoor Recreation Plan
SCORPIO ... Subject-Content-Oriented Retriever for Processing Information On-Line [*Congressional Research Service*]
ScOrS .... South Carolina State College, Orangeburg, SC [*Library symbol*] [*Library of Congress*] (LCLS)
SCORU ..... Statistical Control and Operations Records Unit [*Air Force*]
SCOS......... Scottish Certificate in Office Studies
ScoS .... Scottish Studies [*A publication*]
SCOS .... Small Computer and Office Systems [*Honeywell, Inc.*]
SCOS........ Subsystem Computer Operating System [*NASA*] (NASA)
SCOSA...... Sadtler Commercial Spectra [*A publication*]

SCOSE ...... Standing Committee on Submarine Escape [*British military*] (DMA)
SCOST ...... Special Committee on Space Technology (KSC)
SCOSTEP ... Scientific Committee on Solar Terrestrial Physics (EA)
SCOT........ Satellite Communication Terminal [*Navy*] [*British*] (MCD)
SCOT........ Satellite Communications Overseas Transmission
SCOT........ Scotland [*or Scottish*] (EY)
SCOT........ Scott & Stringfellow Financial, Inc. [*Richmond, VA*] [*NASDAQ symbol*] (NQ)
SCOT........ Scottish [*or Scotsman*] (ROG)
SCOT........ Shell Claus Offgas Treating [*Chemical engineering*]
SCOT........ Shipborne SATCOM Terminal [*British*]
SCOT........ Shippers for Competitive Ocean Transportation [*Washington, DC*] (EA)
SCOT........ Standby Compatible One-Tape [*System*]
SCOT........ Standing Committee on Technology [*Australian Book Trade Committee*]
SCOT........ Steel Car of Tomorrow
SCOT........ Supplementary Checkout Trailer
SCOT........ Support-Coated Open-Tubular [*Column*] [*Chromatography*]
SCOTAC ... Speech-Compatible Tactile Communicant (MCD)
Scot A Forum ... Scottish Archaeological Forum [*A publication*]
Scot Agr ..... Scottish Agriculture [*A publication*]
Scot AL...... Scottish Art and Letters [*A publication*]
SCOTAPLL ... Standing Conference on Theological and Philosophical Libraries in London
Scot App Rep ... Scottish Appeal Reports [*A publication*] (DLA)
Scot Archaeol Forum ... Scottish Archaeological Forum [*A publication*]
Scot Art R .. Scottish Art Review [*A publication*]
Scot Art Rev ... Scottish Art Review [*A publication*]
SCOTBEC ... Scottish Business Education Council (DCTA)
SCOTBUILD ... Scottish Building and Public Works Exhibition [*Scottish Exhibitions Ltd.*] (TSPED)
SCOTCH... Summer Cultural Opportunities for Teams and Children [*National music program*]
SCOTEC ... Scottish Technical Education Council [*British*]
Scot Edu St ... Scottish Educational Studies [*A publication*]
SCOTENG ... Scottish Engineering Exhibition for Design, Production, and Automation [*Scottish Exhibitions Ltd.*] (TSPED)
Scot Geog M ... Scottish Geographical Magazine [*A publication*]
Scot Geogr Mag ... Scottish Geographical Magazine [*A publication*]
Scot GM..... Scottish Geographical Magazine [*A publication*]
Scot Hist R ... Scottish Historical Review [*A publication*]
Scot Hist Riv ... Scottish Historical Review [*A publication*]
SCOTHOT ... Scottish Hotel, Catering, and Licensed Trade Exhibition [*Scottish Exhibitions Ltd.*] (TSPED)
SCOTICE ... Scotland to Iceland Submarine Cable System [*Telecommunications*] (TEL)
Scot J Geol ... Scottish Journal of Geology [*A publication*]
Scot J PE ... Scottish Journal of Physical Education [*A publication*]
Scot J Pol Econ ... Scottish Journal of Political Economy [*A publication*]
Scot J Poli ... Scottish Journal of Political Economy [*A publication*]
Scot J Rel ... Scottish Journal of Religious Studies [*A publication*]
Scot J Rel St ... Scottish Journal of Religious Studies [*A publication*]
ScotJt........ Scottish Journal of Theology [*A publication*]
Scot J Th... Scottish Journal of Theology [*A publication*]
Scot J Theo ... Scottish Journal of Theology [*A publication*]
Scot Jur...... Scottish Jurist [*A publication*] (DLA)
SCOTL........ Scotland (ROG)
ScotL........ Scottish Language [*A publication*]
Scot Law J ... Scottish Law Journal [*Glasgow*] [*A publication*] (DLA)
Scotl Dep Agric Fish Mar Res ... Scotland Department of Agriculture and Fisheries. Marine Research [*A publication*]
Scotl Dep Agric Fish Tech Bull ... Scotland Department of Agriculture and Fisheries. Technical Bulletin [*A publication*]
Scot Lit J ... Scottish Literary Journal [*A publication*]
Scot LJ....... Scottish Law Journal and Sheriff Court Record [*A publication*] (DLA)
Scot LM..... Scottish Law Magazine and Sheriff Court Reporter [*A publication*] (DLA)
Scot L Mag ... Scottish Law Magazine [*Edinburgh, Scotland*] [*A publication*] (DLA)
Scot LR ...... Scottish Law Reporter [*A publication*] (DLA)
Scot LR ...... Scottish Law Review [*A publication*]
Scot L Rep ... Scottish Law Reporter [*A publication*] (DLA)
Scot L Rev ... Scottish Law Review [*A publication*]
Scot LT ...... Scots Law Times [*A publication*] (DLA)
Scot Med J ... Scottish Medical Journal [*A publication*]
SCOTMET ... Scottish Metropolitan [*Property developer*]
ScotNAE.... Scottish National Antarctic Expedition [*1902-04*]
SCOTNATS ... Scottish Nationalists
Scot Parl Acts ... Acts of the Parliaments of Scotland (DLA)
Scot R......... Scottish Review [*A publication*]
SCOTRACEN ... Scouting Training Center [*Navy*]
SCOTS ...... Surveillance and Control of Transmission Systems [*Bell Laboratories*]
SCOTS ...... System Checkout Test Set (MCD)
Scots LTR ... Scots Law Times Reports [*A publication*] (DLA)
Scots Mag ... Scots Magazine [*A publication*]
Scotsman Mag ... Scotsman Magazine [*A publication*]
Scots RR .... Scots Revised Reports [*1707-1873*] [*A publication*] (DLA)

Scot Stud.... Scottish Studies [*A publication*]
Scott........... Scott's English Common Pleas Reports [*A publication*] (DLA)
Scott........... Scott's Reports [*25, 26 New York Civil Procedure*] [*A publication*] (DLA)
SCOTT ...... Single Channel Objective Tactical Terminal [*Army*] (RDA)
SCOTT ...... Synchronous Continuous Orbital Three-Dimensional Tracking
Scott Agric ... Scottish Agriculture [*A publication*]
Scott Art Rev ... Scottish Art Review [*A publication*]
Scott Australas ... Scottish Australasian [*A publication*] (APTA)
Scott Bankers Mag ... Scottish Bankers Magazine [*A publication*]
Scott Bee J ... Scottish Bee Journal [*A publication*]
Scott Beekeep ... Scottish Beekeeper [*A publication*]
Scott Beekpr ... Scottish Beekeeper [*A publication*]
Scott Birds ... Scottish Birds [*A publication*]
Scott Birds J Scott Ornithol Club ... Scottish Birds. Journal. Scottish Ornithologists' Club [*A publication*]
Scott Econ Bull ... Scottish Economic Bulletin [*A publication*]
Scott Econ Soc Hist ... Scottish Economic and Social History [*A publication*]
Scott Educ Rev ... Scottish Educational Review [*A publication*]
Scott Elect Engr ... Scottish Electrical Engineer [*A publication*]
Scott (Eng) ... Scott's English Common Pleas Reports [*A publication*] (DLA)
Scott Field ... Scottish Field [*A publication*]
Scott Fish Bull ... Scottish Fisheries Bulletin [*A publication*]
Scott Fish Res Rep ... Scottish Fisheries Research Report [*A publication*]
Scott Fmr ... Scottish Farmer and Farming World [*A publication*]
Scott For ... Scottish Forestry [*A publication*]
Scott For J ... Scottish Forestry Journal [*A publication*]
Scott Genealog ... Scottish Genealogist [*A publication*]
Scott Geogr Mag ... Scottish Geographical Magazine [*A publication*]
Scott Hist Rev ... Scottish Historical Review [*A publication*]
Scott Ind Hist ... Scottish Industrial History [*A publication*]
Scottish Art R ... Scottish Art Review [*A publication*]
Scottish Bankers M ... Scottish Bankers Magazine [*A publication*]
Scottish Econ Bul ... Scottish Economic Bulletin [*A publication*]
Scottish Ednl J ... Scottish Educational Journal [*A publication*]
Scottish Ednl Studies ... Scottish Educational Studies [*A publication*]
Scottish Geog Mag ... Scottish Geographical Magazine [*A publication*]
Scottish Georgian Soc Bull ... Scottish Georgian Society. Bulletin [*A publication*]
Scottish J Pol Economy ... Scottish Journal of Political Economy [*A publication*]
Scottish Mus ... Scottish Music and Drama [*A publication*]
Scott J .... Reporter, English Common Bench Reports [*A publication*] (DLA)
Scott J Adult Educ ... Scottish Journal of Adult Education [*A publication*] ·
Scott J Agric ... Scottish Journal of Agriculture [*A publication*]
Scott J Geol ... Scottish Journal of Geology [*A publication*]
Scott J Polit Econ ... Scottish Journal of Political Economy [*A publication*]
Scott J Theology ... Scottish Journal of Theology [*A publication*]
Scott Jur .... Scottish Jurist [*A publication*]
Scott Labour Hist Soc J ... Scottish Labour History Society Journal [*A publication*]
Scott Lang ... Scottish Language [*A publication*]
Scott Life-Boat ... Scottish Life-Boat [*A publication*]
Scott Lit J .. Scottish Literary Journal [*A publication*]
Scott Mar Biol Assoc Annu Rep ... Scottish Marine Biological Association. Annual Report [*A publication*]
Scott Marxist ... Scottish Marxist [*A publication*]
Scott Med J ... Scottish Medical Journal [*A publication*]
Scott Mountaineering Club J ... Scottish Mountaineering Club Journal [*A publication*]
Scott Nat ... Scottish Naturalist [*A publication*]
Scott NR .... Scott's New English Common Pleas Reports [*A publication*] (DLA)
Scott R .... Scottish Review [*A publication*]
SCOTT-R ... Super-Critical, Once-Thru Tube Reactor [*Experiment*] [*General Electric Co.*]
Scott Rep.... Scott Report [*A publication*]
Scott Rev.... Scottish Review [*A publication*]
Scott S....... Scottish Studies [*A publication*]
Scott Stud... Scottish Studies [*A publication*]
Scotts Turfgrass Res Conf Proc ... Scotts Turfgrass Research Conference. Proceedings [*A publication*]
Scott Trade Union Rev ... Scottish Trade Union Review [*A publication*]
Scott Tradit ... Scottish Tradition [*A publication*]
Scott Wildl ... Scottish Wildlife [*A publication*]
SCOU ...... Ship Course
SC Oudh ..... Oudh Select Cases [*India*] [*A publication*] (DLA)
SCOUS..... Spectrum Clear of Unknown Signals (MUGU)
SCOUT...... Surface-Controlled Oxide Unipolar Transistor
Scouting in NSW ... Scouting in New South Wales [*A publication*] (APTA)
SCOWAH ... Schmulowitz Collection of Wit and Humor [*San Francisco Public Library*]
SCOWR..... Special Committee on Water Research [*International Council of Scientific Unions*]
SCP........... Brotherhood of Sleeping Car Porters [*Later, BRAC*] (EA)
SCP........... SAGE [*Semiautomatic Ground Environment*] Computer Program
SCP........... St. Catharines Public Library [*UTLAS symbol*]
SCP........... Satellite Cloud Photograph
SCP........... Satin Chrome Plated

SCP........... Scanner Control Power   (MCD)
SCP........... Scanning Phased Array
SCP........... Schematic Change Proposal
SCP........... Scoops [*A publication*]
SCP........... Scope Industries [*AMEX symbol*]   (SPSG)
SCP........... Scottish Conservative Party [*Political party*]
SCP........... Scrip   (ROG)
SCP........... Script [*Films, television, etc.*]
SCP........... Secondary Control Point
SCP........... Sector Command Post [*Military*]
SCP........... Secure Conferencing Project
SCP........... Security Classification Procedure [*Military*]
SCP........... Self-Consistent Phonon
SCP........... Senior Companion Program   (EA)
SCP........... Sertoli-Cell Protein [*Immunology*]
SCP........... Service Control Point [*DoD*]   (AFIT)
SCP........... Servo-Controlled Positioner
SCP........... Sheep Choroid Plexus
SCP........... Short-Circuit Protection
SCP........... Silver Cup Resources Ltd. [*Vancouver Stock Exchange symbol*]
SCP........... Simplified Clearance Procedure [*Customs*]   (DS)
SCP........... Simulation Control Program [*Military*]   (CAAL)
SCP........... Simulator Control Panel [*NASA*]
SCP........... Single-Cell Protein
SCP........... Single Component Peak [*Spectra*]
SCP........... Small Cardioactive Peptide [*Biochemistry*]
SCP........... Smaller Communities Program [*Department of Labor*]
SCP........... Social Credit Party of Canada [*Parti Credit Social du Canada*]   (PPW)
SCP........... Societe Canadienne de Pedatrie [*Canadian Paediatric Society*]   (EAIO)
SCP........... Societe Canadienne de la Population [*Canadian Population Society - CPS*]
SCP........... Societe Culinaire Philanthropique [*New York, NY*]   (EA)
SCP........... Society of California Pioneers   (EA)
SCP........... Society of Christian Philosophers   (EA)
SCP........... Society for Czechoslovak Philately   (EA)
SCP........... Sodium Cellulose Phosphate [*Kidney-stone drug*]
SCP........... Software Change Proposal   (MCD)
SCP........... Solar Cell Panel
SCP........... Sonobuoy Control Panel
SCP........... Spacecraft Platform [*NASA*]
SCP........... Spanish Communist Party
SCP........... Special Category Patient [*Aeromedical evacuation*]
SCP........... Specific Candlepower   (NASA)
SCP........... Specific Cleavage Product [*Biochemistry*]
SCP........... Spherical Candlepower
SCP........... Spiritual Counterfeits Project   (EA)
SCP........... Standardized Care Plans [*for hospitals*]
SCP........... Standing Committee on Packaging [*Australia*]
SCP........... State College [*Pennsylvania*] [*Seismograph station code, US Geological Survey*]   (SEIS)
SCP........... Station Communications Processor
SCP........... Sterol Carrier Protein
SCP........... Storage Control Processor   (NOAA)
SCP........... Stromberg-Carlson Practices [*Telecommunications*]   (TEL)
SCP........... Structural Ceramic Panel
SCP........... Subcontract Proposal   (AAG)
SCP........... Sudanese Communist Party [*Political party*]   (PD)
SCP........... Sulfachloropyridazine [*Antibacterial*]
SCP........... Supervisor's Control Panel
SCP........... Supervisory Control Program [*Burroughs Corp.*]
SCP........... Supplier's Contract Property   (MCD)
SCP........... Supply Cataloging Program
SCP........... Supply Control Plan [*World War II*]
SCP........... Survey Control Point [*Military*]
SCP........... Symbolic Conversion Program   (BUR)
SCP........... Synthetic Fuels Commercialization Program [*Also, SFCP*] [*Energy Resources Council*]
SCP........... Syrian Communist Party [*Political party*]   (PPW)
SCP........... System Change Package
SCP........... System Communication Pamphlet   (IEEE)
SCP........... System Concept Paper [*Army*]   (RDA)
SCP........... System Control Processor [*Honeywell, Inc.*]
SCP........... System Control Programming [*Data processing*]
SCP........... Systems Change Proposal   (AFM)
sCP........... Without Chest Pain [*Medicine*]
SCPA......... Solar Cell Panel Assembly
SCPA......... Southern Coal Producers Association [*Defunct*]   (EA)
SCPA......... Spacecraft Payload Adapter   (MCD)
Sc Paed...... Scientia Paedagogica [*A publication*]
Sc Parliament ... Science in Parliament [*A publication*]
SCPC......... Signal Corps Pictorial Center [*Obsolete*] [*Army*]
SCPC......... Single-Channel-per-Carrier [*Telecommunications*]
SCPCE....... Societe Canadienne pour la Prevention de Cruaute aux Enfants
SCPCU....... Society of Chartered Property and Casualty Underwriters   (EA)
SCPD........ Scratch Pad [*Data processing*]
Sc-PD........ Silicon Photodiode
SCPD........ Staff Civilian Personnel Division [*Army*]
S & CP Dec ... Ohio Decisions [*A publication*]   (DLA)

SCPD OC of SA ... Staff Civilian Personnel Division, Office, Chief of Staff, Army   (AABC)
SCPD OCSA ... Staff Civilian Personnel Division, Office, Chief of Staff, Army   (AABC)
SCPE......... Scope, Inc. [*NASDAQ symbol*]   (NQ)
SCPE......... Specialized Customer Premises Equipment [*for the handicapped*]
Sc for People ... Science for People [*A publication*]
SCPF......... Sacra Congregatio de Propaganda Fide [*Sacred Congregation for the Propagation of the Faith*] [*Latin*]
SCPGB....... Revista. Sociedad Cientifica del Paraguay [*A publication*]
SCPH........ Societe Canadienne des Pharmaciens d'Hopitaux [*Canadian Society of Hospital Pharmacists*]   (EAIO)
SCPI......... Scientists' Committee for Public Information [*Defunct*]
SCPI......... Small Computer Program Index [*No longer published*] [*ALLM Books*]   (IID)
SCPI......... Structural Clay Products Institute [*Later, BIA*]   (EA)
SCPL......... Senior Commercial Pilot's Licence [*British*]   (DBQ)
SCPL......... Signal Corps Photographic Laboratory [*Obsolete*] [*Army*]
SCPL......... Staff of Chief of Personnel and Logistics [*British military*]   (DMA)
S/Cpl........ Staff Corporal [*British military*]   (DMA)
SCPL/H .... Senior Commercial Pilot's Licence/Helicopters [*British*]   (AIA)
SCPM........ Sample Collection and Preparation Module [*X-ray spectrometry*]
SCPM........ Semiautomatic Circuit Performance Monitor [*Navy*]   (MCD)
SCPM........ Silwood Centre for Pest Management [*Imperial College*] [*British*]   (CB)
SCPMT ..... Southern California Perceptual Motor Tests
SCPN........ Scorpion Technologies, Inc. [*NASDAQ symbol*]   (NQ)
SCPNT...... Southern California Postrotary Nystagmus Test
SCPO........ Second-Class Post Office
SCPO........ Senior Chief Petty Officer [*Navy rating*]
SCPP......... Sierra Cooperative Pilot Project [*Department of the Interior*]
SCPP......... Sovereign Chemical & Petroleum Products, Inc. [*Chicago, IL*] [*NASDAQ symbol*]   (NQ)
SCPP......... Supreme Court, Preliminary Prints
SCPP......... Surveyor Command Preparation Program [*Aerospace*]
SCPPS...... Secondary Containment Purge and Pressure Control System [*Nuclear energy*]   (NRCH)
SCPR........ Semiconductor Parameter Retrieval [*Information Handling Services*] [*Database*]
SCPR......... Sri Chinmoy Oneness-Home Peace Run [*An association*]   (EA)
SCPR......... Standard Cardiopulmonary Resuscitation
SCPRA...... Science Progress [*Oxford*] [*A publication*]
SCPRF...... Structural Clay Products Research Foundation [*Absorbed by BIA*]   (EA)
SCPS........ [*The*] Scopas Technology Co., Inc. [*NASDAQ symbol*]   (NQ)
SCPS........ Servo-Controlled Positioning System
SCPS........ Society of Civil and Public Servants [*A union*] [*British*]   (DCTA)
SCP(S)....... Subscribers' Call Processing (Subsystem) [*Telecommunications*]   (TEL)
SCPS........ Survivable Collective Projected System
SCPSC...... South Carolina Public Service Commission Reports [*A publication*]   (DLA)
SCPT......... SAGE [*Semiautomatic Ground Environment*] Computer Programming Training
SCPT......... Script Systems, Inc. [*Hackensack, NJ*] [*NASDAQ symbol*]   (NQ)
SCPT......... Security Control Point [*Military*]   (MUGU)
SCPT......... Self-Consistent Perturbation Theory [*Physics*]
SCPTR...... Standing Committee on Personnel Training and Readiness [*Navy*]
SCPYB...... Social Policy [*A publication*]
SCQ .... Hanscom Air Force Base, Base Library, Hanscom AFB, MA [*OCLC symbol*]   (OCLC)
SCQ .... Saco Resources [*Vancouver Stock Exchange symbol*]
SCQ .... Santiago De Compostela [*Spain*] [*Airport symbol*]   (OAG)
SCQ .... Sisters of Charity of Quebec [*Grey Nuns*] [*Roman Catholic religious order*]
SCQC........ Scout Crew Qualification Course [*Army*]
SCQE........ Squad Combat Qualification Exercise [*Army*]   (INF)
SCR........... Canada. Supreme Court Reports [*A publication*]
SCR........... Cape Colony Supreme Court Reports [*A publication*]   (DLA)
SCR........... Chinook Regional Library, Swift Current, Saskatchewan [*Library symbol*] [*National Library of Canada*]   (NLC)
SCR........... Juta's Supreme Court Cases [*1880-1910*] [*Cape Of Good Hope, South Africa*] [*A publication*]   (DLA)
SCR........... Law Reports of Supreme Court of Sarawak, North Borneo, and Brunei [*A publication*]   (DLA)
SCR........... San Cristobal [*Chile*] [*Seismograph station code, US Geological Survey*] [*Closed*]   (SEIS)
SCR........... Scanning Control Register
SCR........... Schedule Change Request [*NASA*]   (NASA)
SCR........... Score   (ROG)
SCR........... Scourer[*s*] [*or Scouring*] [*Freight*]
SCR........... Scranton Public Library, Scranton, PA [*OCLC symbol*]   (OCLC)
Scr............ Scrapie [*Animal pathology*]
SCR........... Scratch

SCR............ Screw (AAG)
scr.............. Scribe [*MARC relator code*] [*Library of Congress*] (LCCP)
Scr............. Scrinium [*A publication*]
SCR............ Scrip (ADA)
Scr............. Scripture (BJA)
SCR............ Scruple
SCR............ Scrutiny [*A publication*]
SCR............ Scurry-Rainbow Oil Ltd. [*Toronto Stock Exchange symbol*]
SCR............ Sea Containers Ltd. [*NYSE symbol*] (SPSG)
SCR............ Section Cross Reference (MCD)
SCR............ Security Airways & Freight Express, Inc. [*Glen Burnie, MD*]
                [*FAA designator*] (FAAC)
SCR............ Selective Catalytic Reduction
SCR............ Selective Chopper Radiometer
SCR............ Selenium Control Rectifier [*Nuclear energy*] (NRCH)
SCR............ Semiconductor
SCR............ Semiconductor-Controlled Rectifier
SCR............ Senior Common Room [*in British colleges and public schools*]
SCR............ Senior Contractor Representative
SCR............ Sequence Checking Routine
scr.............. Serbo-Croatian (Roman) [*MARC language code*] [*Library of
                Congress*] (LCCP)
SCR............ Series Control Relay
SCr............ Serum Creatinine [*Hematology*]
SCR............ Set Complete Radio
SCR............ Shift Count Register
SCR............ Ship to Component Record [*Navy*]
SCR............ Short-Circuit Ratio
SCR............ Signal Conditioning Rack
SCR............ Signal Conversion Relay [*Telecommunications*] (TEL)
SCR............ Signal Corps Radio [*Followed by model number*] [*Obsolete*]
                [*Army*]
SCR............ Silicon-Controlled Rectifier [*Electronics*]
SCR............ Single-Channel Reception (DEN)
SCR............ Single Character Recognition
SCR............ Skin Conductance Response
SCR............ Sneak Circuit Report [*NASA*] (NASA)
SCR............ Society of Cardiovascular Radiology [*Later, SCVIR*] (EA)
SCR............ Society for Cultural Relations between the Peoples of the British
                Commonwealth and the USSR
SCR............ Sodium-Cooled Reactor [*Nuclear energy*]
SCR............ Software Change Request [*NASA*]
SCR............ Software Correction Report (CAAL)
SCR............ Software Cost Reduction [*Data processing*]
SCR............ Solar Cosmic Radiation [*or Ray*]
SCR............ [*Department of*] Soldiers' Civil Reestablishment [*Canada*]
SCR............ SONAR Control Room
SCR............ South Carolina Reports [*A publication*] (DLA)
SCR............ South Carolina Review [*A publication*]
SCR............ Soviet Cybernetics Review [*A publication*]
SCR............ Spacecraft Received Time
SCR............ Spanish Communication Region [*Air Force*] (MCD)
SCR............ Special Certification Roster
SCR............ Specific Commodity Rates (DS)
SCR............ Specification Clarification Request (MCD)
SCR............ Speed Change Rate
SCR............ Static Card Reader
SCR............ Strip Chart Recorder [*NASA*]
SCr............ Strumenti Critica [*A publication*]
S Cr............ Strumenti Critici [*A publication*]
SCR............ Studies in Comparative Religion [*A publication*]
SCR............ Sub-Chief Ranger [*Ancient Order of Foresters*]
SCR............ Summary Control Report [*Planning and Production*] [*Navy*]
SCR............ Supersonic Combustion Ramjet
SCR............ Support Control Room [*NASA*] (KSC)
SCR............ Supreme Court Reports [*India*] [*A publication*] (DLA)
SCR............ Supreme Court Reports [*New South Wales, Australia*] [*A
                publication*] (DLA)
SCR............ Supreme Court Reports [*1928-41, 1946-51*] [*Sarawak*] [*A
                publication*] (DLA)
SCR............ Supreme Court Reports [*Canada Department of Justice*]
                [*Information service or system*] (CRD)
SCR............ Surface-Contour RADAR
SCR............ Syrene-Chloroprene Rubber
SCR............ System Change Request
SCR............ System Control Registers [*Data processing*]
SCR............ System Control Routine
SCRA........ Single Channel Radio Access Subsystem (MCD)
SC & RA .... Specialized Carriers and Rigging Association (EA)
SCRA........ Stanford Center for RADAR Astronomy
SCRA........ Steel Can Recycling Association (EA)
SCRA........ Supreme Council of the Royal Arcanum [*Boston, MA*] (EA)
SCRAC...... Standing Conference of Regional Advisory Councils for Further
                Education
SCRAG...... Senior Civilian Representative, Attorney General [*Department
                of Justice civil disturbance unit*]
SCRAM..... Safety Control Rod Axe Man [*Nuclear energy*] (IEEE)
SCRAM..... Scottish Campaign to Resist the Atomic Menace
SCRAM..... Selective Combat Range Artillery Missile
SCRAM..... Self-Corrected Remedial Aid and Media [*Teaching method*]
SCRAM..... Service Change Release and Manufacture (MCD)

SCRAM..... Several Compilers Reworked and Modified
SCRAM..... Short-Range Attack Missile
SCRAM..... Space Capsule Regulator and Monitor
SCRAM..... Spares Components Reidentification and Modification
                [*Program*] [*DoD*]
SCRAM..... Spares Control, Release, and Monitoring
SCRAM..... Special Criteria for Retrograde of Army Materiel (AABC)
SCRAM..... Supersonic Combustion Ramjet Missile
SCRAM..... Synanon Committee for Responsible American Media [*Later,
                SCRAP*]
SCRAM Energy Bull ... SCRAM [*Scottish Campaign to Resist the Atomic
                Menace*] Energy Bulletin [*A publication*]
SCRAMJET ... Supersonic Combustion Ramjet
SCRAMM ... System Calibration, Repair, and Maintenance Model
                [*Military*] (CAAL)
SCraneN .... Stephen Crane Newsletter [*A publication*]
SCRAP ...... Selective Curtailment of Reports and Paperwork [*Navy*]
SCRAP ...... Series Computation of Reliability and Probability [*Data
                processing*]
SCRAP ...... Simple Complex Reaction-Time Apparatus
SCRAP ...... Society for Completely Removing All Parking Meters
SCRAP ...... Students Challenging Regulatory Agency Proceedings [*Student
                legal action organization*]
SCRAP ...... Super-Caliber Rocket-Assisted Projectile (IEEE)
SCRAP ...... Synanon Committee for a Responsible American Press (EA)
SCRAPE...... Screening Country Requirements Against Plus Excess [*DoD*]
SCRATA ... Steel Castings Research and Trade Association [*Sheffield,
                England*] (EAIO)
Scrat Bdg Soc ... Scratchley's Building Societies [*5th ed.*] [*1883*] [*A
                publication*] (DLA)
Scrat & Bra ... Scratchley and Brabook's Building Societies [*2nd ed.*] [*1882*]
                [*A publication*] (DLA)
SCRATCHPAD ... [*A*] programming language (CSR)
Scrat Life Ass ... Scratchley's Life Assurance [*13th ed.*] [*1887*] [*A
                publication*] (DLA)
SCRB........ Software Configuration Review Board (CAAL)
SCRB........ Structured Case Review Blank
SCRBA...... Student Committee for the Right to Bear Arms [*Defunct*] (EA)
Scr Bull .... Scripture Bulletin [*A publication*]
SCRD......... Scientific Radio Systems, Inc. [*NASDAQ symbol*] (NQ)
SCRD......... Secondary Control Rod Driveline [*Nuclear energy*] (NRCH)
SCRD......... Student Coalition for the Right to Drink [*Defunct*] (EA)
SCRD......... Vina Del Mar/Rodelillo [*Chile*] [*ICAO location
                identifier*] (ICLI)
SCRDB...... Screwed Bonnet
SCRDE...... Stores and Clothing Research and Development Establishment
                [*British*]
Scr Demolinguist ... Scritti Demolinguistici [*A publication*]
SCRDM..... Secondary Control Rod Drive Mechanism [*Nuclear
                energy*] (NRCH)
SCRDN...... Screw Down
SCRE........ Scandinavian Review [*A publication*]
SCRE......... Scottish Council for Research in Education [*British*]
SCRE......... Supreme Cossack Representation in Exile (EA)
SCREB...... Scientific Research [*A publication*]
Screen Ed ... Screen Education [*A publication*]
Screen Ed Notes ... Screen Education Notes [*A publication*]
SCREENEX ... Screening Exercise [*Military*] (NVT)
SC Rep .... Juta's Supreme Court Cases [*1880-1910*] [*Cape Of Good Hope,
                South Africa*] [*A publication*] (DLA)
SC Res .... Senate Concurrent Resolution (DLA)
SC Research Plan Devel Board Bull ... South Carolina Research Planning and
                Development Board. Bulletin [*A publication*]
SC Resour Cent Tech Rep ... South Carolina Marine Resources Center.
                Technical Report [*A publication*]
Sc Rev Rept ... Scots Revised Reports [*A publication*] (DLA)
S & C Rev St ... Swan and Critchfield's Revised Statutes [*Ohio*] [*A
                publication*] (DLA)
SCREWS... Solar Cosmic Ray Early Warning System (MUGU)
SCRF .... Small Craft Repair Facility [*Navy*] (NVT)
Scr Fac Sci Nat Univ Purkynianae Bru Biol ... Scripta Facultatis Scientiarum
                Naturalium Universita J. E. Purkyne Brunensis. Biiologia
                [*A publication*]
Scr Fac Sci Nat Univ Purkynianae Brun ... Scripta Facultatis Scientiarum
                Naturalium Universitatis Purkynianae Brunensis [*A
                publication*]
Scr Fac Sci Nat Univ Purkynianae Brunensis Geol ... Scripta Facultatis
                Scientiarum Naturalium Universitatis Purkynianae
                Brunensis. Geologia [*A publication*]
Scr Fac Sci Nat Univ Purkynianae Brunensis Phys ... Scripta Facultatis
                Scientiarum Naturalium Universitatis Purkynianae
                Brunensis. Physica [*A publication*]
SCRG......... Rancagua/De La Independencia [*Chile*] [*ICAO location
                identifier*] (ICLI)
SCRG......... Societe Canadienne de Recherche en Geriatrie
SCRG......... Stationary Cosmic Ray Gas
SCRG......... System Change Review Group [*George C. Marshall Space Flight
                Center*] (NASA)
Scr Geobot ... Scripta Geobotanica [*A publication*]
Scr Geogr ... Scripta Geographica [*A publication*]
Scr Geol (Leiden) ... Scripta Geologica (Leiden) [*A publication*]

ScrH.......... Scripta Hierosolymitana [*A publication*]
ScrHier ...... Scripta Hierosolymitana [*Jerusalem*] [*A publication*]
Scr Hieros ... Scripta Hierosolymitana. Publications of the Hebrew University. Jerusalem [*A publication*]
ScrHierosol ... Scripta Hierosolymitana [*Jerusalem*] [*A publication*]
Scr Hierosolymitana ... Scripta Hierosolymitana [*A publication*]
Scr Hierosolymitana Publ Heb Univ (Jerus) ... Scripta Hierosolymitana. Publications of the Hebrew University (Jerusalem) [*A publication*]
ScRhW....... Winthrop College, Rock Hill, SC [*Library symbol*] [*Library of Congress*] (LCLS)
SCRI .... Science Court and Research Institute (EA)
SCRI .... Scientists' Committee for Radiation Information (EA)
SCRI .... Scottish Crop Research Institute [*Research center*] (IRC)
SCRI .... South Central Reservoir Investigation [*Department of the Interior*] (GRD)
SCRI .... Southern Center for Research and Innovation, Inc. [*University of Southern Mississippi*] [*Research center*] (RCD)
SCRI .... Supercomputer Computations Research Institute [*Florida State University*] [*Research center*] (RCD)
Scrib.......... Scribner's Monthly [*A publication*]
Scrib Com .. Scribner's Commentator [*A publication*]
Scrib Dow .. Scribner on the Law of Dower [*A publication*] (DLA)
SCRIBE..... System for Correspondence Recording and Interrogation by EDP [*Electronic Data Processing*]
Scrib M ...... Scribner's Magazine [*A publication*]
Scribn Mag ... Scribner's Magazine [*A publication*]
Scr I Donn ... Scripta Instituti Donneriana Aboensis [*A publication*]
Scri Geol .... Scripta Geologica [*A publication*]
SCRIM ...... Sideway Force Coefficient Routine Investigating Machine [*Department of Transport*] [*British*]
SCRIM ...... Supersonic Cruise Intermediate Range Missile (MCD)
SCRIMP.... Save Cash, Reduce Immediately Meat Prices [*Boston, MA, group protesting high cost of food, 1973*]
Scrinia Flor Sel ... Scrinia Florae Selectae [*A publication*]
Scrin Theol ... Scrinium Theologicum. Contributi di Scienze Religiose [*A publication*]
Scrip.......... Scriptorium [*A publication*]
SCRIP....... Scriptum [*Something Written*] [*Latin*] (ROG)
SCRIP........ Scripture
SCRIP........ Statine Congener of Renin Inhibitory Peptide [*Biochemistry*]
SCRIP........ System for Controlling Returns in Inventory and Production Data [*IRS*]
Scrip Metal ... Scripta Metallurgica [*A publication*]
Scripps Inst Oceanogr Contrib ... Scripps Institution of Oceanography. Contributions [*A publication*]
SCRIPT..... Scientific and Commercial Subroutine Interpreter and Program Translator
Script .... Scriptorium [*A publication*]
Script .... Scripture [*A publication*]
SCRIPT...... Scripture
SCRIPT..... System Controlling Research Image Processing Tasks (MCD)
Scripta Fac Sci Natur UJEP Brunensis Biol ... Scripta Facultatis Scientiarum Naturalium Universita J. E. Purkyne Brunensis. Biologia [*A publication*]
Scripta Fac Sci Natur UJEP Brunensis Chem ... Scripta Facultatis Scientiarum Naturalium Universita J. E. Purkyne Brunensis. Chemia [*A publication*]
Scripta Fac Sci Natur UJEP Brunensis Geol ... Scripta Facultatis Scientiarum Naturalium Universita J. E. Purkyne Brunensis. Geologia [*A publication*]
Scripta Fac Sci Natur UJEP Brunensis Math ... Scripta Facultatis Scientiarum Naturalium Universita J. E. Purkyne Brunensis. Mathematica [*A publication*]
Scripta Fac Sci Natur UJEP Brunensis Phys ... Scripta Facultatis Scientiarum Naturalium Universita J. E. Purkyne Brunensis. Physica [*A publication*]
Scripta Math ... Scripta Mathematica [*A publication*]
Script B ...... Scripture Bulletin [*A publication*]
Script Eccl Hisp Lat ... Scriptores Ecclesiastici Hispano-Latini Veteris et Medii Aevi [*A publication*]
Script Lat Hib ... Scriptores Latini Hiberniae [*A publication*]
SCRIS........ Southern California Regional Information Study [*Bureau of Census*]
Scriv Cop.... Scriven on the Law of Copyholds [*7th ed.*] [*1896*] [*A publication*] (DLA)
Scriven .... Scriven on the Law of Copyholds [*A publication*] (DLA)
SCRJ .... Supersonic Combustion Ramjet
ScrJud........ Scripta Judaica [*Oxford*] [*A publication*]
SCRL........ Sensory Communication Research Laboratory [*Gallaudet College*] [*Research center*] (RCD)
SCRL .... Signal Corps RADAR Laboratory [*Obsolete*] [*Army*]
SCRL .... Skill Components Research Laboratory [*Air Force*] (MCD)
SCRL .... Station Configuration Requirement List [*NASA*] (MCD)
SCR (L)...... Supreme Court Reports (Law) [*New South Wales*] [*A publication*] (APTA)
SCRLC ...... South Central Research Library Council [*Library network*] (IID)
Scr LT........ Scranton Law Times [*Pennsylvania*] [*A publication*] (DLA)
SCRLV ...... Subterranean Clover Red Leaf Virus

SCRM........ Isla Rey Jorge/Base Aerea Teniente R. Marsh Martin [*Chile*] [*ICAO location identifier*] (ICLI)
SCRM........ Secondary Certified Reference Material [*Nuclear energy*] (NRCH)
Scr Med (Brno) ... Scripta Medica (Brno) [*A publication*]
Scr Med Fac Med Univ Brun Olomuc ... Scripta Medica. Facultatum Medicinae. Universitatum Brunensis et Olomucencis [*Czechoslovakia*] [*A publication*]
Scr Met ...... Scripta Metallurgica [*A publication*]
Scr Metall ... Scripta Metallurgica [*A publication*]
Scr Minora ... Scripta Minora-Regiae Societatis Humaniorum Litterarum Lundensis [*A publication*]
SCRN........ Screen[*s*] [*or Screening*] [*Freight*]
scRNP........ Ribonucleoprotein, Small Cytoplasmic
SCR (NS) (NSW) ... Supreme Court Reports (New Series) (New South Wales) [*A publication*] (APTA)
SCRNSW .. New South Wales Supreme Court Reports [*A publication*] (DLA)
SCR (NSW) ... Supreme Court Reports (New South Wales) [*A publication*] (APTA)
SCR (NSW) Eq ... Supreme Court Reports (Equity) (New South Wales) [*A publication*] (APTA)
SCRO........ Scottish Criminal Records Office [*Office of Population Census and Surveys*] [*British*]
SCRO........ Societe Canadienne de la Recherche Operationnelle
SCROLL ... String and Character Recording Oriented Logogrammatic Language [*1970*] [*Data processing*] (CSR)
SCROOGE ... Society to Curtail Ridiculous, Outrageous, and Ostentatious Gift Exchange (EA)
SC/ROSTENA ... Bureau Regional de Science et de Technologie pour l'Europe et l'Amerique du Nord [*Regional Office for Science and Technology for Europe and North America*] (EAIO)
SCRP .... Scripps-Howard Broadcasting Co. [*NASDAQ symbol*] (NQ)
SCRP .... Societe Canadienne des Relations Publiques
SCRP .... Supplemental Conventional Reading Program [*Education*]
SCRPA ...... Science Reporter [*New Delhi*] [*A publication*]
SCR (Q) ...... Queensland. Supreme Court. Reports [*A publication*] (APTA)
Sc RR .... Scotch Revised Reports [*A publication*] (DLA)
SCRS .... Secondary Control Rod System [*Nuclear energy*] (NRCH)
SCRS .... Self-Control Rating Scale
SCRS .... Service Center Replacement System [*Data processing*]
SCRS .... Society of Collision Repair Specialists (EA)
SCRS .... Strip Chart Recorder System [*NASA*]
Scr Sci Med Annu Sci Pap ... Scripta Scientifica Medica. Annual Scientific Papers [*A publication*]
SCRT .... Sealed Cathode Ray Tube
SCRT .... Subscribers' Circuit Routine Tester [*Telecommunications*] (TEL)
SCRTA ...... Steel Castings Research and Trade Association [*British*]
SCRTC ...... Signal Corps Replacement Training Center [*Obsolete*] [*Army*]
SCRTERM ... Screw Terminal
ScrTheol .... Scripta Theologica [*Pamplona*] [*A publication*]
SCRTY .... Security
SCRUMPie ... Socially Concerned Upwardly Mobile Professional [*Lifestyle classification*]
Scrut Charter ... Scrutton on Charter-Parties [*18th ed.*] [*1974*] [*A publication*] (DLA)
Scrutton ..... Scrutton on Charter-Parties [*16 eds.*] [*1886-1955*] [*A publication*] (DLA)
SCRWC ..... Sierra Club Radioactive Waste Campaign [*Later, RWC*] (EA)
ScS .... Reflected S Wave [*Earthquakes*]
SCS .... Safety Control Switch
SCS .... Saint Charles Seminary [*Later, SCBS*] [*Pennsylvania*]
SCS .... Santa Clara Systems, Inc. [*San Jose, CA*] [*Telecommunications service*] (TSSD)
SCS .... Satellite Control Satellite [*Telecommunications*] (TEL)
SCS .... Satellite Test Center Communications Subsystem (MCD)
SCS .... Scan Converter [*or Counter*] System
ScS .... Scandinavian Studies and Notes [*A publication*]
SCS .... Scientific Civil Service [*British*]
SCS .... Scientific Control Systems (DIT)
ScS .... Scottish Studies [*A publication*]
SCS .... Screening and Costing Staff [*NATO*] (NATG)
SCS .... Sea Control Ship [*Navy*] (NVT)
SCS .... Secondary Control Ship [*Navy*] (NVT)
SCS .... Secondary Control System (MCD)
SCS .... Secondary Coolant System [*Nuclear energy*] (NRCH)
SCS .... Secret Control Station [*NASA*] (KSC)
SCS .... Secret Cover Sheet (AAG)
SCS .... Section Control Station [*RADAR*]
SCS .... Secure Communications System [*Military*] (CAAL)
SCS .... Security Container System [*Army*] (AABC)
SCS .... Semiconductor Controlled Switch (MSA)
SCS .... Senior Citizen's Services [*A publication*]
SCS .... Septuagint and Cognate Studies (BJA)
SCS .... Sequence Control System (KSC)
SCS .... Sequencing and Command Systems Specialist [*NASA*]
SCS .... Ship Control Station [*Navy*] (CAAL)
SCS .... Short-Circuit-Stable
SCS .... Shutdown Cooling System [*Nuclear energy*] (NRCH)

SCS............ Sicasica [*Bolivia*] [*Seismograph station code, US Geological Survey*] [*Closed*] (SEIS)

SCS............ Sigmacom Systems [*Vancouver Stock Exchange symbol*]

SCS............ Signal Center and School [*Army*] (MCD)

SCS............ Signal Communications System [*Air Force*]

SCS............ Signal Conditioning System (KSC)

SCS............ Silicon-Controlled Switch

SCS............ Simulation Control Subsystem (KSC)

SCS............ Singapore Cosmos Shipping Co. Pty. Ltd. (DS)

SCS............ Single Channel Simplex

SCS............ Single Composition Spherical [*Dental alloy*]

SCS............ Single Control Support (BUR)

SCS............ Slovak Catholic Sokol (EA)

SCS............ Slow Code Scanner

SCS............ Small Components Structural

SCS............ Small Computer System

SCS............ Social Competence Scale

SCS............ Societe en Commandite Simple [*Simple Partnership*] [*Belgium*]

SCS............ Society for Carribean Studies (EAIO)

SCS............ Society for Ch'ing Studies (EA)

SCS............ Society for Cinema Studies (EA)

SCS............ Society of Civil Servants [*British*]

SCS............ Society of Clinical Surgery [*Defunct*] (EA)

SCS............ Society for Computer Simulation [*Later, SCSI*] (EA)

SCS............ Society for Conservative Studies [*Later, YAF*] (EA)

SCS............ Society of Construction Superintendents (EA)

SCS............ Society of Cosmetic Scientists (EAIO)

SCS............ Society of County Secretaries [*British*]

SCS............ Sodium Cellulose Sulfate [*Organic chemistry*]

SCS............ Sodium Characterization System [*Nuclear energy*] (NRCH)

SCS............ Software Communications Service

SCS............ Soil Conservation Service [*Department of Agriculture*]

SCS............ Solar Collector Subassembly (MCD)

SCS............ Solent Container Service [*British*] (DS)

SCS............ SONAR Calibration Set

SCS............ SONAR Communications Set

SCS............ Space Cabin Simulator (IEEE)

SCS............ Space Command Station (AAG)

SCS............ Spacecraft Control System (NASA)

SCS............ Spacecraft System [*NASA*] (KSC)

SCS............ Spanish Colonial Style [*Cigars*]

SCS............ Special Communications System (MCD)

SCS............ Special Contingency Stockpile [*Military*] (AABC)

SCS............ Speed Class Sequencing

SCS............ Spinal Cord Society (EA)

SCS............ Stabilization and Control System [*or Subsystem*] [*NASA*]

SCS............ Standard Coordinate System (KSC)

SCS............ Stationing Capability System [*Army*] (AABC)

SCS............ Statistical Control System

SCS............ Stiffened Cylindrical Shell

SCS............ Stimulated Compton Scattering [*Spectroscopy*]

SCS............ Stop Control Braking System [*Lucas Girling*]

SC & S .... Strapped, Corded, and Sealed [*As, of a package or bale*]

SCS............ Student's Confidential Statement [*Education*]

SCS............ Suit Communication System [*for spacesuits*] [*NASA*]

SCS............ Superintendent of Car Service

SCS............ Supervisory Control System (MCD)

SCS............ Supply Control Study

SCS............ Surface Composition Strengthened

SCS............ Suspect Chemicals Sourcebook [*Roytech Publications*] [*Information service or system*] (CRD)

SCS............ Sussex Cattle Society (EAIO)

SCS............ Swedish Colonial Society (EA)

SCS............ Sweeping Current Supply

SCS............ Sweetens Computer Services [*British*]

SCS............ University of South California, School of Library Science, Los Angeles, CA [*OCLC symbol*] (OCLC)

SCSA .... Ship Constructive and Shipwrights' Association [*A union*] [*British*]

SCSA .... Siamese Cat Society of America (EA)

SCSA .... Soil Conservation Society of America (EA)

SCSA .... Sports Car Collectors Society of America [*Later, SCCSA*] (EA)

SCSA .... Standard Consolidated Statistical Area [*Census Bureau*]

SCSA .... Steering Committee for Sustainable Agriculture [*Later, CSA*] (EA)

SCSA .... Supreme Council for Sport in Africa [*See also CSSA*] [*Yaounde, Cameroon*] (EAIO)

SCSB .... Standard Capital Superannuation Benefit [*British*]

SCSBCVG ... Suore di Carita delle Sante Bartolomea Capitanio e Vincenza Gerosa [*Sisters of Charity of Saints Bartholomew Capitanio and Vincent Gerosa*] [*Milan, Italy*] (EAIO)

SCSBM ..... Society for Computer Science in Biology and Medicine

SCSC .... Santiago/Ciudad [*Chile*] [*ICAO location identifier*] (ICLI)

SCSC .... Secondary Curriculum Study Center [*of NASSP*]

SCSC .... Sorores a Caritate Sanctae Crucis [*Sisters of Mercy of the Holy Cross*] [*Roman Catholic religious order*]

SCSC .... South Carolina State College

Sc-SC .... South Carolina Supreme Court, Columbia, SC [*Library symbol*] [*Library of Congress*] (LCLS)

SCSC .... Southern Connecticut State College [*New Haven*]

SCSC .... Standing Committee on Soil Conservation [*Australia*]

SCSC .... Strategic Conventional Standoff Capability (MCD)

SCSC .... Summer Computer Simulation Conference

SCSCA ...... Schweissen und Schneiden [*A publication*]

SCSCB...... Sisters of Charity of St. Charles Borromeo [*See also LCB*] (EAIO)

SCSCCL .... Sellin Center for Studies in Criminology and Criminal Law (EA)

SCSCD7 .... Smithsonian Contributions to the Marine Sciences [*A publication*]

SCSCLC .... Single-Carrier Space-Charge-Limited Current

SCSCO ...... Secure Submarine Communications (KSC)

SC (Scot).... Scottish Court of Session Cases, New Series [*A publication*] (DLA)

Sc SD .... Doctor of Social Sciences

SCSD......... School Construction Systems Development [*Project*] [*of Educational Facilities Laboratories*]

SCSD......... Simulation and Control Systems Division [*General Electric Co.*] (MCD)

SCSE .... La Serena/La Florida [*Chile*] [*ICAO location identifier*] (ICLI)

SCSE .... Smooth Curve - Smooth Earth

SCSE .... State Commission for Space Exploration [*USSR*]

SCSEP...... Senior Community Service Employment Program (EA)

Sc Sess Cas ... Scotch Court of Session Cases [*A publication*] (DLA)

SCSFI........ Studii si Cercetari Stiintifice. Filologie (Iasi) [*A publication*]

SCSG .... Signal Conditioning Subsystem Group (MCD)

SCSG .... Superior Cervical Sympathetic Ganglia [*Anatomy*]

SCSGIG..... Supreme Council Sovereign Grand Inspectors General [*Freemasonry*]

SCSH......... Sisters of Charity of St. Hyacinthe [*Grey Nuns*] [*Roman Catholic religious order*]

SCSH......... Structural Carbon Steel Hard

SCSH......... Survey of the Chronic Sick and Handicapped [*British*]

SCSHX...... Shutdown Cooling System Heat Exchange [*Nuclear energy*] (NRCH)

SCSI .... Sensors and Control Systems Institute [*Beltsville, MD*] [*Department of Agriculture*] (GRD)

SCSI .... Small Computer System Interface [*Pronounced "scuzzy"*]

SCSI .... Societe Canadienne de la Surete Industrielle

SCSI .... Society for Computer Simulation International (EA)

SCSIT....... Southern California Sensory Integration Test [*Ayres*] [*Education*]

SCSJAT .... Sisters of Charity of St. Jeanne Antide Thouret [*Rome, Italy*] (EAIO)

SCSL......... Sandia Corporation, Sandia Laboratory (AABC)

ScSl........... Scandoslavica [*A publication*]

SCSL......... Sisters of Charity of St. Louis [*Roman Catholic religious order*]

SCSL......... Standing Lenticular Stratocumulus [*Meteorology*] (FAAC)

SCSL......... Suncoast Savings & Loan Association [*Hollywood, FL*] [*NASDAQ symbol*] (NQ)

SCSLA....... Science du Sol [*A publication*]

SCSLP....... Smithsonian Center for Short-Lived Phenomena

SCSM .... Structural Carbon Steel Medium

SCSMHPS ... Special Constituency Section for Mental Health and Psychiatric Services (EA)

SCSN......... Santo Domingo/Santo Domingo [*Chile*] [*ICAO location identifier*] (ICLI)

SCSN......... Standard Computer Software Number

ScSo .... Science and Society [*A publication*]

SCSO........ Space Communications Station Operation

SCSO........ Superconducting Cavity Stabilized Oscillator [*For clocks*]

ScSocD...... Doctor of Social Science

ScSocL....... Licence in Social Science [*British*]

Sc Soc San Antonio B ... Scientific Society of San Antonio. Bulletin [*A publication*]

SCSP......... Secretariat of the Council for Scientific Policy [*British*]

SCSP......... Serum Cancer-Suppressive Peptide [*Oncology*]

SCSP......... Smaller Communities Services Program [*Department of Labor*]

SCSP......... Solid Cast Steel Propeller (DS)

ScSp .... Spartanburg County Public Library, Spartanburg, SC [*Library symbol*] [*Library of Congress*] (LCLS)

SC/SP........ Supracondylar/Suprapatellar [*Prosthesis*]

SCSP......... System Calibration Support Plan [*Air Force*] (CET)

ScSpC .... Converse College, Spartanburg, SC [*Library symbol*] [*Library of Congress*] (LCLS)

S & C Spec ... Soap/Cosmetics/Chemical Specialties [*A publication*]

ScSpM .... Milliken Research Corp., Research Library, Spartanburg, SC [*Library symbol*] [*Library of Congress*] (LCLS)

ScSpW .... Wofford College, Spartanburg, SC [*Library symbol*] [*Library of Congress*] (LCLS)

ScSpW-MHi ... Methodist Historical Society, South Carolina Conference of the Methodist Church, Wofford College, Spartanburg, SC [*Library symbol*] [*Library of Congress*] (LCLS)

SCSR .... Segundo Corral/Segundo Corral Alto [*Chile*] [*ICAO location identifier*] (ICLI)

SCSR .... Self-Contained Self-Rescuer [*Breathing device*]

SCSR .... Ship Construction Subsidy Regulations [*Canada*]

SCSRS....... Shoe Cove Satellite Receiving Station [*Canada*]

SCSRS-S ... Standard Command Supply Review System - SAILS

SCSS......... Satellite Communications System Control (NATG)

SCSS......... School Child Stress Scale [*Child development test*] [*Psychology*]

SCSS......... Self-Contained Starting System [*NASA*]

SCSS......... Sequence Coding and Search System
SCSS......... State Controller and System Services [*NASA*]
SCSS......... Structural Carbon Steel Soft
SCSST....... Standing Conference on School Science and Technology [*British*]
SCST .... Castro/Gamboa [*Chile*] [*ICAO location identifier*]   (ICLI)
SCST .... Scan Converter Storage Tube
ScSt.......... Scandinavian Studies [*A publication*]
SCST .... Society of Commercial Seed Technologists   (EA)
SC State Devel Board Div Geology Bull Geol Notes ... South Carolina State Development Board. Division of Geology. Bulletin. Geologic Notes [*A publication*]
SCSTC....... Senior Citizen Ski Touring Committee   (EA)
Sc St Crim ... Scandinavian Studies in Criminology [*1965*] [*A publication*]   (DLA)
SC St I .... Studii si Cercetari Stiintifice [*A publication*]
Sc St L....... Scandinavian Studies in Law [*A publication*]   (DLA)
Sc St N....... Scandinavian Studies and Notes [*A publication*]
Sc Stud ...... Scandinavian Studies [*A publication*]
Sc Stud Criminol ... Scandinavian Studies in Criminology [*1965*] [*A publication*]   (DLA)
Sc Stud L.... Scandinavian Studies in Law [*A publication*]
Sc Stud Law ... Scandinavian Studies in Law [*A publication*]
SCSU......... St. Cloud State University
ScSu.......... Sumter County Library, Sumter, SC [*Library symbol*] [*Library of Congress*]   (LCLS)
ScSuM .... Morris College, Sumter, SC [*Library symbol*] [*Library of Congress*]   (LCLS)
ScSum .... Timrod Library, Summerville, SC [*Library symbol*] [*Library of Congress*]   (LCLS)
SCSW .... Super-Chilled Seawater
SCSZ .... Sbornik Ceskoslovenske Spolecnosti Zemepisne [*A publication*]
SCT........... Air Force Institute of Technology, Wright-Patterson AFB, OH [*OCLC symbol*]   (OCLC)
SCT........... S-Band Cassegrain Transmit
SCT........... Sacrococcygeal Teratoma [*Oncology*]
S-C-T .... Salinity-Conductivity-Temperature
SCT........... Salmon Calcitonin [*Endocrinology*]
SCT........... Sample Control Tape [*Data processing*]
SCT........... Satellite Communication Terminal   (MCD)
SCT........... Scan Conversion Tube
SCT........... Scanning Telescope   (KSC)
SCT........... Scattered
SCT........... Schottky Clamped Transistor
SCT........... Scintrex Ltd. [*Toronto Stock Exchange symbol*]
SCT........... Scorpion Toxin [*Immunology*]
SCT........... Scotsman Industries, Inc. [*NYSE symbol*]   (SPSG)
SCT........... Scotty Lake [*Alaska*] [*Seismograph station code, US Geological Survey*]   (SEIS)
SCT........... Scout   (AABC)
SCT........... Screen Capture Test [*Data processing*]
Sct .... Scutum [*Constellation*]
SCT........... Semiconductor Curve Tracer
SCT........... Sentence Completion Technique [*or Test*]
SCT........... Sequence Checking Tape
SCT........... Service Counter Terminal [*Banking*]
SCT........... Single-Cell Test   (MCD)
SCT........... Single Channel Transponder   (MCD)
SCT........... Sioux City Terminal Railway [*AAR code*]
SCT........... Skylab Communication Terminal [*NASA*]   (KSC)
SCT........... Societe Canadienne de Theologie [*Canadian Theological Society - CTS*]
SCT........... Society of Cardiological Technicians [*British*]
SCTTB....... Society of Cleaning Technicians   (EA)
SCT........... Society for Clinical Trials   (EA)
SCT........... Society of Commercial Teachers   (EAIO)
SCT........... Society of County Treasurers [*British*]
SCT........... SONAR Certification Test
SCT........... Sous-Commission des Cartes Tectoniques [*Subcommittee for Tectonic Maps of the Commission for the Geological Map of the World - STMCGMW*]   (EAIO)
SCT........... South Central Air Transport, Inc. [*Natchez, MS*] [*FAA designator*]   (FAAC)
SCT........... Special Characters Table [*Data processing*]   (IBMDP)
SCT........... Spectral Control Technique
SCT........... Spectrographic Telescope
SCT........... Step Control Table   (CMD)
SCT........... Structural Clay Tile [*Technical drawings*]
SCT........... Student Coalition for Truth   (EA)
SCT........... Subroutine Call Table [*Data processing*]
SCT........... Subscriber Carrier Terminal [*Telecommunications*]   (TEL)
SCT........... Sugar-Coated Tablet
S Ct .... Supreme Court Reporter [*A publication*]   (DLA)
SCt........... Supreme Court Reports
SCT........... Swap Control Table [*Data processing*]   (BYTE)
SCT........... System Circuit Test
SCT........... System Compatibility Tests
SCTA........ Secondary Container Transfer Area [*Nuclear energy*]   (NRCH)
SCTA........ Ships' Clerk Trade Association [*A union*] [*British*]
SCTA........ Southern California Timing Association   (EA)
SCTA........ Steel Carriers Tariff Association, Inc. [*Riverdale, MD*]

SCTA........ Stone Carvers Trade Association [*A union*] [*British*]
s/cta .... Su Cuenta [*Your Account*] [*Business term*] [*Spanish*]
SCTB .... Santa Cruz Test Base   (MCD)
SCTB .... Santiago/Eulogio Sanchez [*Chile*] [*ICAO location identifier*]   (ICLI)
ScTB .... Scottish Tourist Board   (DCTA)
S Ct Bull (CCH) ... United States Supreme Court Bulletin (Commerce Clearing House) [*A publication*]   (DLA)
SCTC .... Small Craft Training Center
SCTC .... Submarine Chaser Training Center [*Navy*]
SCTC......... Systems & Computer Technology Corporation [*NASDAQ symbol*]   (NQ)
SCTC .... Temuco/Maquehue [*Chile*] [*ICAO location identifier*]   (ICLI)
SC (T & C) ... Thompson and Cook's New York Supreme Court Reports [*A publication*]   (DLA)
SCTCA ...... Schweisstechnik [*Berlin*] [*A publication*]
SCTD......... Scattered
SCTD......... Scottish Centre for the Tuition of the Disabled [*Queen Margaret College*]   (CB)
SCTD......... Subcaliber Training Device [*Military*]   (AABC)
SCTE .... Puerto Montt/Internacional El Tepual [*Chile*] [*ICAO location identifier*]   (ICLI)
SCTE .... Science of the Total Environment [*A publication*]
SCTE .... Society of Cable Television Engineers   (EA)
SCTE .... Society of Carbide and Tool Engineers   (EA)
SCTE .... Spacecraft Central Timing Equipment [*NASA*]
SCTF .... SHAPE [*Supreme Headquarters Allied Powers Europe*] Centralized Training Facility [*NATO*]   (NATG)
SCTF .... Sodium Chemical Technology Facility [*Nuclear energy*]   (NRCH)
SCTH .... Service Center for Teachers of History   (EA)
SCTHA...... Ssu Ch'uan Ta Hsueh Hsueh Pao - Tzu Jan K'o Hsueh [*A publication*]
SCTI .... Santiago/Internacional Los Cerillos [*Chile*] [*ICAO location identifier*]   (ICLI)
SCTI .... Scott Instruments Corp. [*NASDAQ symbol*]   (NQ)
SCTI .... Sodium Components Test Installation [*Nuclear energy*]
SCTI .... Solid Carbide Tool Institute   (EA)
SCTI .... University of Southern California Tax Institute   (DLA)
SCTL .... Short-Circuited Transmission Line
SCTL .... Small Components Test Loop [*Nuclear energy*]
SCTL .... Societe Canadienne des Technologistes de Laboratoire [*Canadian Society of Laboratory Technologists*]   (EAIO)
SCTN........ Chaiten/Chaiten [*Chile*] [*ICAO location identifier*]   (ICLI)
SCTN........ Service Center Taxpayer Notice [*IRS*]
SCTO......... Societe Canadienne des Technologistes en Orthopedie [*Canadian Society of Orthopaedic Technologists*]   (EAIO)
SCTOA...... Science Tools [*A publication*]
SCTOC...... Satellite Communications Test Operations Center
Sc Total Env ... Science of the Total Environment [*A publication*]
SCTP .... Ship Construction Test Plan [*Navy*]   (CAAL)
SCTP .... Straight Channel Tape Print [*Data processing*]   (KSC)
SCTP .... Syndicat Canadien des Travailleurs du Papier [*Canadian Paperworkers Union - CPU*]
SCTPP....... Straight Channel Tape Print Program [*Data processing*]   (KSC)
SCTR........ Scooter   (AAG)
SCTR........ Sector   (MSA)
SCTR......... Signal Corps Technical Requirements   (MCD)
SCTRACEN ... Submarine Chaser Training Center [*Navy*]
S Ct Rev .... Supreme Court Review [*A publication*]
SCTS .... SFOF [*Space Flight Operations Facility*] Communications Terminal Subsystem [*NASA*]
SCTS .... System Components Test Station   (MCD)
SCTTB....... Schmiertechnik und Tribologie [*A publication*]
SCTTU ...... Scottish Council of Textile Trade Unions   (DCTA)
SCTV .... Second City Television [*Television program, the title of which was later changed to its initialism*]
SCTV .... Standing Conference on Television Viewing [*British*]
SCTV-GDHS ... Spacecraft Television - Ground Data Handling System [*NASA*]
S Ct Vict..... Reports of Cases in the Supreme Court of Victoria [*1861-69*] [*Australia*] [*A publication*]   (DLA)
SCTY .... Security   (AFM)
SCTYB ...... Science Today (Bombay) [*A publication*]
SCTYPOLICESq ... Security Police Squadron [*Air Force*]
SCTYSERSCH ... Security Service School [*Air Force*]
SCTYSq..... Security Squadron [*Air Force*]
SCTZ .... Puerto Montt [*Chile*] [*ICAO location identifier*]   (ICLI)
SCU .... 6585th Test Group Technical Information Center, Holloman AFB, NM [*OCLC symbol*]   (OCLC)
SCU .... S-Band Cassegrain Ultra
SCU .... Santiago [*Cuba*] [*Airport symbol*]   (OAG)
SCU .... Scanner Control Unit
SCU .... Schweizer Buchhandel [*A publication*]
SCU .... Scottish Church Union
SCU .... Secondary Control Unit [*Aerospace*]   (AAG)
SCU .... Selector Checkout Unit
SCU .... Sensor Control Unit   (MCD)
SCU .... Sequence Control Unit [*Aerospace*]   (KSC)
SCU .... Service Command Unit
SCU .... Service and Cooling Umbilical [*Aerospace*]   (MCD)

SCU .... Servicing Control Unit [*Telecommunications*]   (TEL)
SCU .... Sheep Canyon [*Utah*] [*Seismograph station code, US Geological Survey*] [*Closed*]   (SEIS)
SCU .... Signal Conditioning Unit   (NASA)
SCU .... Signal Control Unit   (NASA)
SCU .... Single Conditioning Unit
scu .... South Carolina [*MARC country of publication code*] [*Library of Congress*]   (LCCP)
SCU .... Special Care Unit
SCU .... Static Checkout Unit   (KSC)
SCU .... Station Control Unit
SCU .... Statistical Control Unit [*Military*]
SCU .... Storage Control Unit
SCU .... Subscribers' Concentrator Unit [*Telecommunications*]   (TEL)
SCU .... Sulfur-Coated Urea [*Chemical technology*]
SCU .... Surface Control Unit
SCU .... Switch Control Unit   (MCD)
SCU .... Synchronous Controller Unit
SCU .... System Control Unit
ScU .... University of South Carolina, Columbia, SC [*Library symbol*] [*Library of Congress*]   (LCLS)
SCUA .... Suez Canal Users Association   (NATG)
SCUAE..... State Committee on the Utilization of Atomic Energy [*USSR*]
SCUAS...... Standing Conference of University Appointments Services [*British*]
ScUB.......... Scandinavian University Books [*A publication*]
SCUBA...... Self-Contained Underwater Breathing Apparatus
SCUC........ Satellite Communications Users Conference [*Convention*]   (TSSD)
SCUCC Dec ... South Carolina Unemployment Compensation Commission Decisions [*A publication*]   (DLA)
SCUCCR ... South Carolina Unemployment Compensation Commission Reports of Hearings [*A publication*]   (DLA)
Scu Citta .... Scuola e Citta [*A publication*]
SCUD .... Scunner [*Missile*]
SCUD .... Subsonic Cruise Unarmed Decoy [*Air Force*]   (MCD)
SCUDS...... Simplification, Clarification, Unification, Decimalization, Standardization
SCUIO....... Standing Conference of University Information Officers [*British*]
Scul .... Sculptor [*Constellation*]
SCUL......... Simulation of the Columbia University Libraries [*Data processing research*]
SCUL......... Soundings. University of California. Library [*Santa Barbara*] [*A publication*]
ScU-L........ University of South Carolina, Law School, Columbia, SC [*Library symbol*] [*Library of Congress*]   (LCLS)
SCULL...... Serial Communication Unit for Long Links
SCULP...... Sculpsit [*He, or She, Engraved It*] [*Latin*]
SCULP...... Sculptor
SCULP...... Sculpture   (ROG)
Sculp Int .... Sculpture International [*A publication*]
SCULPS.... Sculpsit [*He, or She, Engraved It*] [*Latin*]
SCULPT.... Sculptor [*or Sculpture*]
Sculpt Hellenist Age ... Sculpture of the Hellenistic Age [*A publication*]   (OCD)
Sculpt R .... Sculpture Review [*A publication*]
SCUM .... Society for Cutting Up Men
ScU-M .... University of South Carolina, School of Medicine, Columbia, SC [*Library symbol*] [*Library of Congress*]   (LCLS)
SCUMRA ... Societe Central de l'Uranium et des Minerals et Metaux Radioactifs [*France*]
SC(UN)...... Security Council of the United Nations
SC Univ Pubs Phys Sci Bull ... South Carolina University. Publications. Physical Sciences Bulletin [*A publication*]
Scuola Dir ... Scuola e Diritto [*A publication*]
Scuola Pos ... Scuola Positiva. Rivista di Criminologia e Diritto Criminale [*A publication*]
Scuol C....... Scuola Cattolica. Rivista di Scienze Religiose [*A publication*]
SCUP........ School Computer Use Plan   (IEEE)
SCUP........ Scupper
SCUP........ Service Center Unpostable [*IRS*]
SCUP........ Society for College and University Planning   (EA)
SCUPA...... Single-Chain Urokinase-Like Plasminogen Activator [*Anticlotting agent*]
SCUPU...... Self-Contained Underwater Pinger Unit [*SONAR*]
SCUS........ Supreme Court of the United States
ScU-S......... University of South Carolina, Science Library, Columbia, SC [*Library symbol*] [*Library of Congress*]   (LCLS)
SCUSA...... Student Conference on United States Affairs
Scu Salern ... Scuola Salernitana [*A publication*]
SCUSE ...... Special Committee for United States Exports [*Washington, DC*]   (EA)
ScU-Su....... University of South Carolina at Sumter, Sumter, SC [*Library symbol*] [*Library of Congress*]   (LCLS)
Scut .... Scutum [*of Hesiod*] [*Classical studies*]   (OCD)
Scut .... Scutum [*Constellation*]
SCUU .... Southern College University Union
SCV........... Eglin Regional Hospital Library, Eglin AFB, FL [*OCLC symbol*]   (OCLC)

SCV............ St. Croix [*Virgin Islands*] [*Seismograph station code, US Geological Survey*]   (SEIS)
SCV............ Seaclutter Visibility [*Navy*]   (CAAL)
SCV............ Side Control Valves
SCV............ Simultaneous Chest Compression and Ventilation [*Medicine*]
SCV............ Smooth, Capsulated, Virulent [*Bacteriology*]
SCV............ Solar Constant Variations
SCV............ Sons of Confederate Veterans   (EA)
SCV............ South Atlantic Ltd. [*Vancouver Stock Exchange symbol*]
SCV............ Speed Control Valve
SCV............ Steel Containment Vessel [*Nuclear energy*]   (NRCH)
SCV............ Stock Change Voucher [*Military*]   (AFIT)
SCV............ Strip Chart Viewer
SCV............ Sub Center Visibility   (MCD)
SCV............ Sub Clutter Visibility
SCV............ Suceava [*Romania*] [*Airport symbol*]   (OAG)
SCV............ Supersonic Cruise Missile
SCV............ System Compatibility Vehicle
SCVD......... System Component Verification
SCVD......... Valdivia/Pichoy [*Chile*] [*ICAO location identifier*]   (ICLI)
SCVIA .... Science et Vie [*A publication*]
SCVIR .... Society of Cardiovascular and Interventional Radiology   (EA)
SCVPH..... Sub-Committee on Veterinary Public Health [*Australia*]
SCVTR ...... Scan Converting Video Tape Recorder   (MCD)
SCW .... AFWAL [*Air Force Wright Aeronautical Laboratories*] Technical Information Center, Wright-Patterson AFB, OH [*OCLC symbol*]   (OCLC)
SCW .... St. Clair Paint & Wallpaper Corp. [*Toronto Stock Exchange symbol*]
SCW .... Schoenwereld. Vakblad voor de Schoenlederbranche [*A publication*]
SCW .... Sherman Crater - Mount Baker [*Washington*] [*Seismograph station code, US Geological Survey*] [*Closed*]   (SEIS)
SCW .... Silicone Carbide Whisker
SCW .... Society of Colonial Wars
SCW .... State College of Washington
SCW .... Super-Critical Wing
SCW .... Supercritical Water
SCW .... Superintendent of Contract Work [*Navy*]
SC (WA) .... Supreme Court (Western Australia)   (DLA)
ScWal .... Oconee County Library, Walhalla, SC [*Library symbol*] [*Library of Congress*]   (LCLS)
SC Water Resour Comm Rep ... South Carolina. Water Resources Commission. Report [*A publication*]
SCWC........ Special Commission on Weather Modification
SCWCU..... Supreme Council of the Western Catholic Union [*Later, Western Catholic Union*]   (EA)
SCWDS ..... Southeastern Cooperative Wildlife Disease Study [*University of Georgia*] [*Research center*]   (RCD)
SCWEP .... Spinnable Cotton Waste Equalization Program
SCWFA ..... Schip en Werf [*A publication*]
SCWG....... Satellite Communications Working Group [*NATO*]   (NATG)
SCWGA..... Sonoma County Wineries Association [*Acronym is based on former name, Sonoma County Wine Growers Association*]   (EA)
SCWIA ..... South Carolina Wildlife [*A publication*]
SC Wildl ..... South Carolina Wildlife [*A publication*]
ScWL......... Single-Comb White Leghorn [*Poultry*]
SCWO .... Supercritical Water Oxidation [*Waste disposal technology*]
SCWPH..... Students Concerned with Public Health [*Defunct*]   (EA)
SCWPLR... Special Committee for Workplace Product Liability Reform   (EA)
SCWR....... Supercritical Water Reactor
SCWS .... Scottish Co-Operative Wholesale Society
SCWSL ..... Small Caliber Weapon Systems Laboratory   (MCD)
SCWT....... System Cold Wire Tests
SCX........... Oneida, TN [*Location identifier*] [*FAA*]   (FAAL)
SCX........... Single-Charge Exchange
SCX........... Solar Coronal X-Ray
SCX........... Starrett [*L. S.*] Company [*NYSE symbol*]   (SPSG)
SCX........... Strong Cation Exchanger [*Chemistry*]
SCY........... Scan Converter Yoke
SCY........... Scurry, TX [*Location identifier*] [*FAA*]   (FAAL)
SCYL......... Single-Cylinder
SCZ........... Santa Cruz [*Solomon Islands*] [*Airport symbol*]   (OAG)
SCZ........... Schwitzer, Inc. [*NYSE symbol*]   (SPSG)
SCZ........... State Coastal Zone   (NOAA)
SCZFA ...... Schweizerische Zeitschrift fuer Forstwesen [*A publication*]
SD .... Decisions of the Sadr Court [*1845-62*] [*Bengal, India*] [*A publication*]   (DLA)
SD .... Diamant [*France*] [*Research code symbol*]
SD .... Sadr Diwani Adalat Court [*Bengal, India*]   (DLA)
SD .... Safe Deposit [*Business term*]
SD .... Safety Destructor   (NG)
SD .... Said   (ROG)
SD .... Sailed
S/D .... Sailing Date   (DS)
SD .... Sailing Directions [*British*]
S/D .... Salaried Direct [*Ratio*]
SD .... Salt Depletion
SD .... Salutem Dicit [*Sends Greetings*] [*Latin*]

SD	Same Day
SD	Sammlung Dieterich [*A publication*]
SD	Sample Data (NG)
SD	Sample Delay
SD	Sans Date [*No Date*] [*French*]
SD	Sash Door
SD	Saturation Deficit
SD	Scaling and Display (NASA)
SD	Scandinavian Delegation [*British*]
SD	Scanning Densitometer [*Instrumentation*]
SD	Schematic Diagram
SD	Scientiae Doctor [*Doctor of Science*] (ADA)
SD	Scientific Design [*Group*]
SD	Scientific Detective Monthly [*A publication*]
SD	Scottish District [*Council*]
SD	Scram Discharge [*Nuclear energy*] (NRCH)
SD	Sea Damaged
S/D	Seadrome
SD	Search Depth [*Navy*] (NVT)
S & D	Search and Destroy [*Army*] (AABC)
SD	Seasonal Derating (IEEE)
SD	Second Defense [*Men's lacrosse position*]
SD	Secondary Distribution [*Investment term*]
SD	Secretary of Defense
SD	Segregation Distorter [*Genetics*]
SD	Seismic Detector (MCD)
SD	Seize Detector
SD	Selenium Diode
SD	Self-Destroying [*Projectile*]
SD	Self-Destruct
SD	Semantic Differential
SD	Semidetached (ADA)
SD	Semidiameter
SD	Seminars Directory [*A publication*]
SD	Senate Document
SD	Senatus Decreto [*By Decree of the Senate*] [*Latin*]
SD	Send Data [*Data processing*]
SD	Send Digits [*Telecommunications*] (TEL)
SD	Senile Dementia [*Medicine*]
SD	Senior Deacon [*Freemasonry*]
SD	Senior Director [*FAA*] (FAAC)
SD	Septal Defect [*Medicine*]
SD	Serializer/Deserializer
SD	Serine Dehydratase [*An enzyme*]
SD	Serologically Defined [*Immunology*]
SD	Serologically Determined [*Medicine*]
SD	Service Dated (ROG)
SD	Service Dress
SD	Servicing Diagram
SD	Servus Dei [*Servant of God*] [*Latin*]
SD	Several Dates
SD	Severe Duty [*Truck*]
SD	Severely Diabetic
SD	Sewed
SD	Sewer Drain
SD	Shakedown [*Nuclear energy*] (NRCH)
S & D	Shaw, Dunlop, and Bell's Scotch Court of Session Reports, First Series [*1821-38*] [*A publication*] (DLA)
SD	Shell-Destroying [*Device*]
SD	Shield of David (BJA)
SD	Ship Destination Test [*Intelligence test*]
SD	Shop Drawing (AAG)
SD	Short Day [*Botany*]
SD	Short Delay
SD	Short Delivery
SD	Short Duration
SD	Shoulder Dislocation
SD	Shower Drain (AAG)
S/D	Shut Down
SD	Sicherheitsdienst [*Police Duty*] [*NAZI Germany*]
S-D	Sickle Cell Hemoglobin D [*Disease*] [*Medicine*]
SD	Side Deck
SD	Side Door
SD	Side Drum
SD	Siegfried AG [*Switzerland*] [*Research code symbol*]
SD	Sight Draft [*Business term*]
SD	Signals Division [*British military*] (DMA)
SD	Significant Digit [*Mathematics*]
SD	Simple Design
SD	Sine Dato [*Undated book*] [*Latin*]
SD	Sine Die [*Without Day*] [*Latin*]
SD	Single Deck [*Navigation*]
SD	Single Determination
SD	Single Distilled
SD	Single Domain [*Grains in rocks*] [*Geophysics*]
S & D	Single and Double [*Reduction gears*]
SD	Site Defense [*Military*] (AABC)
SD	Situation Display
SD	Skid
SD	Skin Destruction [*Medicine*]
SD	Skin Dose
SD	Sliding Door
SD	Slope Difference [*Statistics*]
SD	Slowdown
s/d	Small Damage (DS)
SD	Small-Scale Disturbance Field
SD	Smoke Detector (NASA)
SD	Social Democratic Party [*Federal Republic of Germany*]
SD	Socialdemokratiet i Danmark [*Social Democratic Party of Denmark*] [*Political party*] (PPE)
SD	Societas Docta (EA)
SD	Soft Drawn
SD	Software Dynamics [*Buena Park, CA*] (TSSD)
SD	Solicitation Document
SD	Solid Drawn
S & D	Song and Dance Act [*Slang*]
SD	Sort File Description [*Data processing*]
SD	Sorties per Day [*Air Force*] (AFIT)
SD	Sound [*Films, television, etc.*]
SD	Sound [*Board on Geographic Names*]
SD	Sounding Doubtful [*Nautical charts*]
SD	Source/Destination [*Inspection/Acceptance Point*] (MCD)
SD	Source Document [*Data processing*]
SD	South Dakota [*Postal code*]
SD	South Dakota Compiled Laws, Annotated [*A publication*] (DLA)
SD	South Dakota Musician [*A publication*]
SD	South Dakota Reports [*A publication*] (DLA)
Sd	South Dakota State Library Commission, Pierre, SD [*Library symbol*] [*Library of Congress*] (LCLS)
SD	South Division (ROG)
SD	Southern District (DLA)
SD	Space Digest [*A publication*]
SD	Space Division [*Air Force*] [*Los Angeles, CA*]
SD	Spare Disposition (MCD)
SD	Special Delivery
SD	Special Document
SD	Special Duties [*Military*] [*British*]
s/d	Special Duty [*Military*]
SD	Specially Denatured
SD	Specification for Design
SD	Specification Document [*NASA*] (NASA)
SD	Spectacle Dispenser [*Navy technician*]
SD	Spectral Distribution
SD	Speed Disk [*Computer program*] (PCM)
SD	Spin Device
SD	Splice Donor [*Genetics*]
SD	Spontaneous Delivery [*Obstetrics*]
Sd	Sprachdienst [*A publication*]
SD	Sprache und Dichtung [*A publication*]
SD	Staff Development (ADA)
SD	Staff Duties [*Military*] [*British*]
SD	Stage Direction
SD	Stage Door [*Theatrical slang*]
SD	Stamp Duty
SD	Standard Decision (MCD)
SD	Standard Deduction
SD	Standard Design [*of a vessel*] (DS)
SD	Standard Deviation [*Also, s*]
SD	Standard Dress [*Military*] [*British*]
SD	Standard Oil Co. of California [*NYSE symbol*] [*Delisted*] [*Vancouver Stock Exchange symbol*] (SPSG)
SD	Standardization Data
SD	Standardization Directory
SD	Standards Development (IEEE)
SD	Stands Detached [*Freight*]
SD	Stars of David (EA)
SD	State Department
SD	State Director
S/D	Statement of Differences
SD	Station Director [*Deep Space Instrumentation Facility, NASA*]
SD	Statutory Declaration
SD	Steel Deck (ADA)
SD	Stein & Day [*Publishers*]
SD	Stereo Directional
SD	Stern Discharge
SD	Steward [*Navy rating*]
SD	Stock Dividend [*Investment term*]
SD	Stone Disintegration [*Urology*]
S/D	Storage or Distribution
S & D	Storage and Distribution
SD	Stores Depot [*British military*] (DMA)
SD	Storm Data [*A publication*]
SD	Storm Detection [*RADAR*]
SD	Storm Drain [*Technical drawings*]
SD	Stowage Drawer
SD	Straight Duty
SD	Strength Differential [*Steel*]
SD	Strength-Duration (Curve) [*Prosthesis*]
SD	Streptodornase [*An enzyme*]
SD	Stronnictwo Demokratyczne [*Democratic Party*] [*Poland*] [*Political party*] (PPE)

SD	Structural Detail (AAG)
SD	Structural Dynamics (KSC)
SD	Studi Danteschi [*A publication*]
SD	Studia Delitschiana [*A publication*]
SD	Studia et Documenta ad Iura Orientis Antiqui Pertinenta [*Leiden*] [*A publication*] (BJA)
SD	Study Director (MCD)
SD	Subcontractor Data
SD	Subdural [*Anatomy*]
SD	Submarine Detector (ADA)
SD	Sudan [*ANSI two-letter standard code*] (CNC)
SD	Sudan Airways [*ICAO designator*] (FAAC)
S-D	Sudden Death [*Tiebreaking in sports*]
SD	Sudden Death [*Medicine*]
SD	Sugar Determination
SD	Sun's Declensions [*Astronomy*] (ROG)
SD	Super Duty [*Automotive engineering*]
SD	Superintendent of Documents [*US Government Printing Office*]
SD	Supplier Documentation (NASA)
SD	Supply Department [*Navy*]
SD	Supply Depot
SD	Supply Detachment [*British military*] (DMA)
SD	Supply Duct [*Nuclear energy*] (NRCH)
SD	Support Directive (KSC)
SD	Support [*or Supporting*] Document (KSC)
SD	Surface Duct [*Navy*] (CAAL)
SD	Surridge Dawson [*Commercial firm*] [*British*]
SD	Surveillance Drone [*Air Force*]
SD	Survival Dose
Sd	Suspended [*Regulation or order suspended*] [*Used in Shepard's Citations*] [*Legal term*] (DLA)
SD	Swaziland
SD	Sweep Driver
SD	Switch Driver
SD	Syllable Duration [*Entomology*]
SD	Synthetic Dextrose [*Biochemistry*]
SD	System Demonstration [*Military*]
SDA	System Description
SD	System Designator (AFIT)
SD	System Drawer
SD	Systems Designers [*Software manufacturer*] [*British*]
SD	Systems Development (MCD)
SD	Systems Directorate [*Army*] (RDA)
SD	Systems Division [*Department of Commerce*] [*Information service or system*] (IID)
SD	Systolic Discharge [*Cardiology*]
SD1	Steward, First Class [*Navy rating*]
S 2d	New York Supplement, Second Series [*A publication*] (DLA)
SD2	Steward, Second Class [*Navy rating*]
SD3	Steward, Third Class [*Navy rating*]
SDA	Augustana College, Sioux Falls, SD [*OCLC symbol*] (OCLC)
SDA	Baghdad-Saddam [*Iraq*] [*Airport symbol*] (OAG)
SDA	Sacrodextra Anterior [*A fetal position*] [*Obstetrics*]
SDA	Sadr Diwani Adalat Reports [*India*] [*A publication*] (DLA)
SD & A	San Diego & Arizona Railway
SDA	Scottish Development Agency (DS)
SDA	Scottish Diploma in Agriculture
SDA	Screw Displacement Axis
SDA	Section Department Authority
SDA	Seismic Data Analysis
SDA	Semidehydroascorbate [*Biochemistry*]
SDA	Sequential Degradation Analysis
SDA	Service Delivery Area [*Job Training and Partnership Act*] (OICC)
SDA	Seventh-Day Adventist
SDA	Sex Discrimination Act [*1975*] [*British*] (DCTA)
SDA	Shaft Drive Axis [*Aerospace*] (KSC)
SDA	Shenandoah, IA [*Location identifier*] [*FAA*] (FAAL)
SDA	Ship's Destination Authority (NVT)
SDA	Shoulder Disarticulation [*Medicine*]
SDA	Significant Digit Arithmetic
SDA	Simple Doublet Antenna
SDA	Sleeve Dipole Antenna
SDA	Slowdown Area
SDA	Soap and Detergent Association (EA)
SDA	Social Democratic Alliance [*British*]
SDA	Solvent Deasphalting
SDA	Source Data Acquisition (BUR)
SDA	Source Data Automation [*Military*]
SDA	Special Disbursing Agent, Bureau of Indian Affairs [*United States*] (DLA)
SDA	Special Duty Assignment (AFM)
SDA	Specially Denatured Alcohol
SDA	Specific Dynamic Action [*of foods*] [*Physiology*]
SDA	Spectral Distribution Analyzer
SDA	Spontaneous Divergent Academic [*Test*] [*Education*]
SDA	Stacked Dipole Array
SDA	Standard Gold Mines Ltd. [*Vancouver Stock Exchange symbol*]
SDA	Statistical Distribution Analyzer
SDA	Step Down Amplifier

SDA	Stepwise Discriminant Analysis
SDA	Stereo Dimensional Array
SDA	Steroid-Dependent Asthmatic [*Medicine*]
SDA	Stevens-Duryea Associates (EA)
SDA	Stirrer Drive Assembly
SDA	Students for Democratic Action
SDA	Subcarrier Demodulator Assembly [*Deep Space Instrumentation Facility, NASA*]
SDA	Succinic Dehydrogenase Activity
SDA	Sulfadiazine [*Antibiotic*]
SDA	Superficial Distal Axillary [*Lymph node*]
SDA	Supplier Data Approval [*Nuclear energy*] (NRCH)
SDA	Supporting Data Analysis
SDA	Surface Design Association (EA)
SDA	Sweet Damn All [*Nothing At All*] [*Slang*]
SDA	Symbolic Device Address
SDA	Symbolic Disk Address (AFM)
SDA	Symbols-Digits-Alphabetics
SDA	System Design Agency [*Bell Telephone Laboratory*] (MCD)
SDA	Systems Data Analysis
SDA	Systems Dynamic Analyzer
SDAA	Salt Distributors Association of America (EA)
SDAA	Servicemen's Dependents Allowance Act
SDAA	Skein Dyers Association of America [*Later, SRPDAA*] (EA)
SDAA	Stacked Dipole Aerial Array
SdAbA	Alexander Mitchell Library, Aberdeen, SD [*Library symbol*] [*Library of Congress*] (LCLS)
SdAbN	Northern State College, Aberdeen, SD [*Library symbol*] [*Library of Congress*] (LCLS)
SdAbP	Presentation College, Aberdeen, SD [*Library symbol*] [*Library of Congress*] (LCLS)
SDAC	Seismic Data Analysis Center
SDAC	Shelby Dodge Automobile Club [*Inactive*] (EA)
SDAC	Shipping Defence Advisory Committee [*General Council of British Shipping*] (DS)
SDACMG	Seventh-Day Adventist Church Musicians Guild (EA)
SDAD	Satellite Digital and Analog Display
SDAD	Special Domestically Available Documents [*NASA*] (KSC)
SDADA	Seventh-Day Adventist Dietetic Association (EA)
SD Admin R	Administrative Rules of South Dakota [*A publication*] (DLA)
SD Admin Reg	South Dakota Register [*A publication*] (DLA)
SDADS	Satellite Digital and Display System
SDAE	San Diego & Arizona Eastern Railway Co. [*AAR code*]
SDAE	Source Data Automation Equipment
SDAF	Solid-Rocket Booster Disassembly Facility [*NASA*] (NASA)
SDAF	Special Defense Acquisition Fund [*Military*]
SD Ag Exp	South Dakota. Agricultural Experiment Station. Publications [*A publication*]
SD Agric Exp Stn Bull	South Dakota. Agricultural Experiment Station. Bulletin [*A publication*]
SD Agric Exp Stn Circ	South Dakota. Agricultural Experiment Station. Circular [*A publication*]
SD Agric Exp Stn Tech Bull	South Dakota. Agricultural Experiment Station. Technical Bulletin [*A publication*]
S DAK	South Dakota
S Dak	South Dakota Reports [*A publication*] (DLA)
S Dak Acad Sci Proc	South Dakota Academy of Science. Proceedings [*A publication*]
S Dak Agr Expt Sta Tech Bull	South Dakota. Agricultural Experiment Station. Technical Bulletin [*A publication*]
S Dak Bus R	South Dakota Business Review [*A publication*]
SDAKC	Seventh-Day Adventist Kinship Canada (EAIO)
S Dak Farm Home Res	South Dakota Farm and Home Research [*A publication*]
S Dak Geol Surv Bull	South Dakota. Geological Survey. Bulletin [*A publication*]
S Dak Geol Surv Circ	South Dakota. Geological Survey. Circular [*A publication*]
S Dak Geol Survey Oil and Gas Inv Map Rept Inv	South Dakota. Geological Survey. Oil and Gas Investigations Map. Report of Investigation [*A publication*]
S Dak His R	South Dakota Historical Review [*A publication*]
S Dak His S	South Dakota State Historical Society. Collections [*A publication*]
S Dak HR	South Dakota Historical Review [*A publication*]
SDAKI	Seventh Day Adventist Kinship International (EA)
S Dak J Med	South Dakota Journal of Medicine [*A publication*]
S Dak J Med Pharm	South Dakota Journal of Medicine and Pharmacy [*A publication*]
S Dak Lib Bull	South Dakota Library Bulletin [*A publication*]
S Dak Libr Bull	South Dakota Library Bulletin [*A publication*]
S Dak Rev	South Dakota Review [*A publication*]
S Dak Sch Mines B	South Dakota. School of Mines. Bulletin [*A publication*]
S Dak State Geologist Bienn Rept	South Dakota State Geologist. Biennial Report [*A publication*]
S Dak State Univ Coop Ext Serv	South Dakota State University. Cooperative Extension Service [*A publication*]
SdAl	Alcester Public Library, Alcester, SD [*Library symbol*] [*Library of Congress*] (LCLS)
SDAL	Switched Data Access Line

SD Ala .... United States District Court for the Southern District of Alabama (DLA)
SdAle .... Alexandria Public Library, Alexandria, SD [*Library symbol*] [*Library of Congress*] (LCLS)
SDAM ...... Standard Deviation above the Mean [*Statistics*]
SDA Mad .. Madras Sadr Diwani Adalat Reports [*India*] [*A publication*] (DLA)
SDAML ..... Send by Airmail (NOAA)
SDANA ...... Shrine Directors Association of North America (EA)
SDAP .... Sociaal-Democratische Arbeiders Partij [*Social Democratic Workers' Party*] [*Netherlands*] [*Political party*] (PPE)
SDAP .... Special Duty Assignment Pay [*Army*] (INF)
SDAP .... System Development and Performance
SDAP .... Systems Development and Acquisition Plan (MCD)
SDAP .... Systems Development Analysis Program
SDAPP ..... Special Duty Assignment Proficiency Pay [*Air Force*]
SdAr .... Arlington Public Library, Arlington, SD [*Library symbol*] [*Library of Congress*] (LCLS)
SdArm .... Armour Public Library, Armour, SD [*Library symbol*] [*Library of Congress*] (LCLS)
SDAS .... Scientific Data Automation System (IEEE)
SDAS .... Shared Demand Assignment Signaling (MCD)
SDAS .... Simplified Directional Approach System [*Aviation*]
SDAS .... Source Data Automation System [*Military*] (AABC)
SDAS .... Systems Data Analysis Section
SDAT .... Safe Driver Attitude Test [*Educational test*]
SDAT .... Senile Dementia of the Alzheimer Type [*Medicine*]
SDAT .... Spacecraft Data Analysis Team [*NASA*]
SDAT .... Stanford Diagnostic Arithmetic Test
SDAT .... Stationary Digital Audio Tape
SDAU .... Subscriber Digital Access Unit [*Telecommunications*]
SDAUG ..... SDA [*Software Design Associates*] Users' Groups [*Later, IUG*] (EA)
SDAW .... Sitzungsberichte. Deutsche Akademie der Wissenschaften zu Berlin [*A publication*]
SDAWB ..... Sitzungsberichte. Deutsche Akademie der Wissenschaften zu Berlin [*A publication*]
SDB .... Sa Da Bandeira [*Angola*] [*Seismograph station code, US Geological Survey*] (SEIS)
SDB .... Salesians of Don Bosco [*Roman Catholic men's religious order*]
SDB .... Sandberg, CA [*Location identifier*] [*FAA*] (FAAL)
SDB .... Seaward Defence Boat [*British military*] (DMA)
SDB .... Securities Data Base System [*Information service or system*] (IID)
SDB .... Segment Descriptor Block
SDB .... Sex Discrimination Board [*South Australia*]
SDB .... Shakespeare Data Bank, Inc. [*Information service or system*] (IID)
SDB .... Shallow Draft Barge (MCD)
SDB .... Shallow Draft Board (NASA)
SD & B .... Shaw, Dunlop, and Bell's Scotch Court of Session Reports, First Series [*1821-38*] [*A publication*] (DLA)
SDB .... Skill Development Base [*Army*] (AABC)
SDB .... Small Disadvantaged Business [*Department of Commerce*]
SDB .... Sociaal-Democratische Bond [*Social Democratic League*] [*Netherlands*] [*Political party*] (PPE)
SDB .... Society for Developmental Biology (EA)
SDB .... South Dakota Business Review [*A publication*]
SdB .... South Dakota State University, Brookings, SD [*Library symbol*] [*Library of Congress*] (LCLS)
SDB .... South Dakota State University, Brookings, SD [*OCLC symbol*] (OCLC)
SDB .... Spacecraft Design Book
SDB .... Special District Bond
SDB .... Square Die Bushing
SDB .... Storage Data Bus
SDB .... Strength and Dynamics Branch [*Air Force*]
SDB .... Supplement au Dictionnaire de la Bible [*A publication*]
sdb .... Symbolic Debugger [*Also, SOLD, SYMDEB*] [*Data processing*] (BYTE)
SDB .... System Data Buffer (MCD)
SDB .... System Database
SDBCS ...... Steam Dump Bypass Control System [*Nuclear energy*] (NRCH)
SdBer .... Beresford Public Library, Beresford, SD [*Library symbol*] [*Library of Congress*] (LCLS)
SdBf .... Belle Fourche Public Library, Belle Fourche, SD [*Library symbol*] [*Library of Congress*] (LCLS)
SDBF .... System Development Breadboard Facility
SDBGC ...... Seventh Day Baptist General Conference (EA)
SDBHS ...... Seventh Day Baptist Historical Society (EA)
SD Bird Notes ... South Dakota Bird Notes [*A publication*]
SDB Jo .... South Dakota Bar Journal [*A publication*] (DLA)
SDBL .... Sight Draft Bill of Lading Attached [*Business term*]
SdB-M .... South Dakota State University, Minuteman Graduate Center Library, Ellsworth AFB, Rapid City, SD [*Library symbol*] [*Library of Congress*] (LCLS)
SDBMS ..... Seventh Day Baptist Missionary Society (EA)
SdBo .... Bonesteel Public Library, Bonesteel, SD [*Library symbol*] [*Library of Congress*] (LCLS)
SDBO .... Societe de Banque Occidentale [*France*] (EY)
SDBP .... Supine Diastolic Blood Pressure [*Medicine*]

Sd-BPH ..... South Dakota State Library for the Handicapped, Pierre, SD [*Library symbol*] [*Library of Congress*] (LCLS)
SdBro .... Brookings Public Library, Brookings, SD [*Library symbol*] [*Library of Congress*] (LCLS)
SdBrS .... Bristol Independent School District Library, Bristol, SD [*Library symbol*] [*Library of Congress*] (LCLS)
SDBS .... Sodium Dodecylbenzene Sulfonate [*Organic chemistry*]
SD & B Sup ... Shaw, Dunlop, and Bell's Supplement, Containing House of Lords Decisions [*A publication*] (DLA)
SD & B Supp ... Shaw, Dunlop, and Bell's Supplement, Containing House of Lords Decisions [*Scotland*] [*A publication*] (DLA)
SdBu .... Burke Public Library, Burke, SD [*Library symbol*] [*Library of Congress*] (LCLS)
SDBU/CR ... [*Office of*] Small and Disadvantaged Business Utilization and Civil Rights [*See also OSDBU*] [*Federal government*] (NRCH)
SDBWF ...... Seventh Day Baptist World Federation (EA)
SDBY .... Standby
SDC .... Chief Steward [*Later, MSC*] [*Navy rating*]
SDC .... Salivary Duct Carcinoma [*Oncology*]
SDC .... Salt Data Centre [*British*]
SDC .... Same Distribution Center Service Area [*US Postal Service*]
SDC .... Sample Data Collection
SDC .... San Diego - Robinson [*California*] [*Seismograph station code, US Geological Survey*] [*Closed*] (SEIS)
SDC .... Sands Minerals [*Vancouver Stock Exchange symbol*]
SDC .... Scientific Data Center (MCD)
SDC .... Scientific Documentation Center Ltd. [*Dunfermline, Fife, Scotland*]
SDC .... Seaward Defense Craft (NATG)
SDC .... Secondary Distribution Center (AAG)
SDC .... Secretarial Diploma College [*Australia*]
SDC .... Secure Data Cartridge (BYTE)
SDC .... Seismological Data Center [*Environmental Science Services Administration*]
SDC .... Seize Detector Control
SDC .... Self-Defense Corps [*Vietnam*]
SDC .... September Days Club (EA)
SDC .... Serum Digoxin Concentration [*Clinical chemistry*]
SDC .... Several Dancers Core [*Houston, TX and Atlanta, GA*]
SDC .... Shaft-Driven Counter
SDC .... Shield Design Code [*Nuclear energy*] (NRCH)
SDC .... Shipment Detail Card [*Military*]
SDC .... Shutdown Cooling [*Nuclear energy*] (NRCH)
SDC .... Signal Data Converter
SDC .... Single Drift Correction
SDC .... Situation Display Converter
SDC .... Society of Daily Communicants [*Defunct*] (EA)
SDC .... Society of the Divine Compassion [*Anglican religious community*]
SDC .... Society of Dyers and Colourists (EAIO)
SDC .... Sodium Deoxycholate [*Organic chemistry*]
SDC .... Software Development Computer [*NASA*] (NASA)
SDC .... Solid Dielectric Cable
SDC .... SONAR Data Computer [*Navy*] (CAAL)
SDC .... Southern Defense Command [*Army*]
SDC .... Space Data Corporation
SDC .... Space Defense Center [*Military*] (MCD)
SDC .... Space Defense Corporation (MCD)
SDC .... Space Development Corporation
SDC .... Spacecraft Data Simulator [*NASA*] (KSC)
SDC .... Spares Disposition Code [*NASA*] (NASA)
SDC .... Special Day Class [*Education*]
SDC .... Special Devices Center [*Navy*]
SDC .... Specific Damping Capacity [*Metals*]
SDC .... Stabilization Data Computer
SDC .... Standard Data Chain
SDC .... State Defense Council
SDC .... Static Dielectric Constant
SDC .... Strategic Defense Command [*Military*] (SDI)
SDC .... Structural Design Criteria [*Nuclear energy*]
SDC .... Studebaker Driver's Club (EA)
SDC .... Subcontractor's Data Catalog (MCD)
SDC .... Submersible Decompression Chamber [*Underwater tank*]
SDC .... Submersible Diving Capsule [*Oceanography*]
SDC .... Sundance Airways, Inc. [*San Antonio, TX*] [*FAA designator*] (FAAC)
SDC .... Supply Distribution Center [*Military*] (AFIT)
SDC .... Support Design Change
SDC .... Sydney Dance Company [*Australia*]
SDC .... System for Data Calculation [*Information retrieval*]
SDC .... System Design Confirmation
SDC .... System Designator Code (AFM)
SDC .... System Development Corporation [*Information service or system*] (IID)
SDC .... Systems Development District (AAG)
SDC .... Yankton College, Yankton, SD [*OCLC symbol*] (OCLC)
SdCa .... Canton Carnegie Public Library, Canton, SD [*Library symbol*] [*Library of Congress*] (LCLS)
SDCA .... Scottish Deerhound Club of America (EA)

SD Cal .... United States District Court for the Southern District of California (DLA)
SdCan .... Canova Public Library, Canova, SD [Library symbol] [Library of Congress] (LCLS)
SdCar......... Carthage Public Library, Carthage, SD [Library symbol] [Library of Congress] (LCLS)
SDCC......... Simulation Data Conversion Center [Space Flight Operations Facility, NASA]
SDCC......... Small-Diameter Component Cask [Nuclear energy] (NRCH)
SDCC......... Society of the Descendants of the Colonial Clergy (EA)
SDCD .... [Adjusted] Sea Duty Commencement Date
SDCE........ Scientific Data Collection Exercise
SDCE........ Society of Die Casting Engineers (EA)
SDCF........ Sampled Data Channel Filter
SdCh .... Chamberlain Public Library, Chamberlain, SD [Library symbol] [Library of Congress] (LCLS)
SDCH .... Society of Descendants of Colonial Hispanics (EA)
SDCIS ...... Supplier Data Control Information System (MCD)
SdCl .... Clark Public Library, Clark, SD [Library symbol] [Library of Congress] (LCLS)
SDCL........ South Dakota Codified Laws [A publication]
SDCL........ Supplier Documentation Checklist (NASA)
SdCla .... Claremont Public Library, Claremont, SD [Library symbol] [Library of Congress] (LCLS)
SDCM .... Master Chief Steward [Later, MSCM] [Navy rating]
SDC Mag.. Systems Development Corporation Magazine [A publication]
SdCo .... Colome Public Library, Colome, SD [Library symbol] [Library of Congress] (LCLS)
SD Codified Laws ... South Dakota Codified Laws [A publication] (DLA)
SD Codified Laws Ann ... South Dakota Codified Laws, Annotated [A publication] (DLA)
SD Comm... Doctor of Science in Commerce
SD Compiled Laws Ann ... South Dakota Compiled Laws, Annotated [A publication] (DLA)
SD Comp Laws Ann ... South Dakota Comp Laws, Annotated [A publication] (DLA)
SDCP........ Summary Development Cost Plan [NASA] (NASA)
SDCP........ Supply Demand Control Point [Military]
SDCR........ Source Data Communication Retrieval
SDCS........ SAIL [Shuttle Avionics Integration Laboratory] Data Communications System [NASA] (NASA)
SDCS .... Sample Data Control System (MCD)
SDCS .... Science Data Conditioning System
SDCS .... Senior Chief Steward [Navy rating] [Later, MSCS]
SDCS .... Shutdown Cooling System [Nuclear energy] (NRCH)
SDCS .... Simulation Data Conversion System [Space Flight Operations Facility, NASA]
SDCS .... Single Differential Cross Section
SDCT........ Slosson Drawing Coordination Test
SdCu .... Custer County Library, Custer, SD [Library symbol] [Library of Congress] (LCLS)
SDCW .... San Diego College for Women [California]
SDD .... Lubango [Angola] [Airport symbol] (OAG)
SDD .... Santo Domingo [Ciudad Trujillo] [Dominican Republic] [Seismograph station code, US Geological Survey] (SEIS)
SDD Cal .... Scottish Development Department (DCTA)
SDD .... Scottish Diploma in Dairying
SDD .... Second Development Decade [United Nations]
SDD .... Selected Dissemination of Documents
SD/D .... Service Deputy/Director (MUGU)
SDESG ...... Shuttle Design Directive [NASA] (NASA)
SDD .... Sierra Nevada Gold [Vancouver Stock Exchange symbol]
SDD .... Signal Data Demodulator
SDD .... Silicon Disk Drive [Data processing]
SDD .... Sioux Falls Public Library, Sioux Falls, SD [OCLC symbol] (OCLC)
SDD .... Slowdown Density
SDD .... Sodium Dimethyldithiocarbamate [Also, SDDC] [Organic chemistry]
SDD .... Software Description Document [NASA] (NASA)
SDD .... Software Design Description [Data processing] (IEEE)
SDD .... Software Design Document [NASA] (NASA)
SDD .... Specially Designated Distributor [Liquor]
SDD .... Stacy Design and Development, Inc. [Telecommunications service] (TSSD)
SDD .... Standard Delivery Date [Military]
SDD .... Store Door Delivery
SDD .... Stored Data Description
SDD .... Stress Degree Day [Crop inventory]
SDD .... Subchannel Data Distributor (KSC)
SDD .... Subsystem Design Description (MCD)
SDD .... System Design Description [Nuclear energy] (NRCH)
SDD .... System Design Document [NASA] (MCD)
SDD .... Systems Definition Directive [Military] (AFM)
SDD .... Systems Development Department [David W. Taylor Naval Ship Research and Development Center]
SDDC .... Self Determination for DC [District of Columbia] (EA)
SDDC .... Silver Diethyldithiocarbamate [Organic chemistry]
SDDC .... Sodium Dimethyldithiocarbamate [Organic chemistry] [Also, SDD]
SDDC .... Sterile Disposable Device Committee [Defunct]

SDDD .... Software Detailed Design Document [Army]
SDDE .... Surface Demand Diving Equipment
SDDE .... System Design and Development Environment
SdDel .... Dell Rapids Carnegie Public Library, Dell Rapids, SD [Library symbol] [Library of Congress] (LCLS)
SDDIDP .... Survey of Digestive Diseases [A publication]
SDDL........ Stored Data Definition Language
SDDM .... Secretary of Defense Decision Memorandum
SDD-NU... Summaries of Doctoral Dissertations. Northwestern University [A publication]
SDDP........ Sight Draft Documents Against Payment [Business term]
SdDr.......... Draper Public Library, Draper, SD [Library symbol] [Library of Congress] (LCLS)
SDDRA...... Showa Densen Denran Rebyu [A publication]
SdDs .... De Smet Public Library, De Smet, SD [Library symbol] [Library of Congress] (LCLS)
SDDS........ Satellite Data Distribution System
SDDS........ Secondary Data Display System (MCD)
SDDS........ Signal Data Demodulator Set [or System]
SD/DS........ Synchro-Digital/Digital-Synchro (CAAL)
SDDTTG... Stored Data Definition and Translation Task Group
SDDU .... Simplex Data Distribution Unit
SDDUW .... Summaries of Doctoral Dissertations. University of Wisconsin [A publication]
SDE .... Santiago Del Estero [Argentina] [Airport symbol] (OAG)
SDE .... Self-Disinfecting Elastomer
SDE .... Simple Designational Expression
SDE .... Simultaneous Distillation-Extraction [Chemical engineering]
SDE .... Societe de Droits d'Execution du Canada [Performing Rights Organization of Canada - PROC]
SDE .... Society of Data Educators (EA)
SDE .... Software Development Environment [NCR Corp.]
SDE .... Source Data Entry
SDE .... Space Division Evaluator [NASA] (NASA)
SDE .... Specific Dynamic Effect [Medicine]
SDE .... Standard Data Element [Army] (AABC)
SDE .... Standard Etac Corp. [Toronto Stock Exchange symbol]
SDE .... Steam Distillation Extracton
SDE .... Students for Data Education (IEEE)
SDE .... Support Data Engineering (MCD)
SDEC........ Sequential Detection of Emerging Competitive Target
SDE & C .. Standard Data Element and Codes [Air Force]
SDECE...... Service de Documentation Exterieure et de Contre-Espionnage [Pronounced "suh-deck"] [Intelligence organization] [France] [Later, DGSE]
SdEd .... Edgemont Public Library, Edgemont, SD [Library symbol] [Library of Congress] (LCLS)
SdEdH ...... Edgemont High School, Edgemont, SD [Library symbol] [Library of Congress] (LCLS)
S/DEFL..... Stone Deflector [Automotive engineering]
SDEG........ Special Doctrine Equipment Group [Army]
SDE/GWIS ... Sigma Delta Epsilon, Graduate Women in Science (EA)
SdEl .... Elkton Public Library, Elkton, SD [Library symbol] [Library of Congress] (LCLS)
Sdelovaci Tech ... Sdelovaci Technika [A publication]
SDEO .... Second Division of Executive Officers [A union] [British]
SDERDN... Seminars in Dermatology [A publication]
SdEs.......... Estelline Public Library, Estelline, SD [Library symbol] [Library of Congress] (LCLS)
SDES .... Submarine Data Extraction System [Navy] (CAAL)
SDESG ...... Strapdown Electrically Suspended Gyro (KSC)
SdEu .... Eureka Public Library, Eureka, SD [Library symbol] [Library of Congress] (LCLS)
SDEV........ [The] Software Developer's Co., Inc. [NASDAQ symbol] (NQ)
SDF............ Louisville [Kentucky] [Airport symbol] (OAG)
SDF............ Safing and Deservicing Facility [NASA] (NASA)
SDF............ Sanatana Dharma Foundation (EA)
SDF............ Satellite Distribution Frame [Telecommunications] (TEL)
SDF............ Screen Definition Facility [Data processing]
SdF............ Seasonal Derating Factor (IEEE)
SdF............ Self-Defense Force [Japan]
SDF............ Simplified Directional Facility [Aviation]
SDF............ Single Defruit [Aviation] (FAAC)
SDF............ Single Degree of Freedom [Also, SDOF] [Acoustics]
SDF............ Sioux Falls College, Sioux Falls, SD [OCLC symbol] (OCLC)
SDF............ Slow Death Factor [Medicine]
SDF............ Social Democratic Federation [Iceland] [Political party] (PPW)
SDF............ Social Democratic Federation [Shaminren] [Japan] [Political party] (PPW)
SDF............ Social Democratic Federation [Later, SDP] [Early British political party, members of which were sometimes referred to as "Silly Damn Fools"]
SDF............ Social Democratic Front [Ghana] [Political party] (PPW)
SDF............ Software Development Facility [Military] (CAAL)
SDF............ Software Development File
SDF............ Sonic Depth Finder
SDF............ Source Development Fund [Supply and Services Canada]
SDF............ Source Document Folders [IRS]
SDF............ Southern Development Foundation (EA)
SDF............ Special Denatured Formula [Applied to alcohol]
SDF............ Spectral Density Function

SDF............ Standard Distribution Format [*Data processing*]
SDF............ Standard Drug File [*Derwent Publications Ltd.*] [*Database*]
SDF............ Static Direction Finder
SDF............ Stopping Distance Factor   (MCD)
SDF............ Stowe-Day Foundation   (EA)
SDF............ Strategic Defensive Forces [*Army*]   (AABC)
SDF............ Structural Dynamics Malfunction
SDF............ Student Description Form [*Psychology*]
SDF............ Sudan Defence Force [*British*]
SDF............ Sundorph Aeronautical Corp. [*Cleveland, OH*] [*FAA designator*]   (FAAC)
SDF............ Supergroup Distribution Frame [*Telecommunications*]   (TEL)
SDF............ Surface Direct Fire [*Navy*]   (CAAL)
SDF............ Swedish Defense Forces
SDF............ System Data Format [*Data processing*]
SDF............ System Development Facility [*NASA*]   (KSC)
SD Farm Home Res ... South Dakota Farm and Home Research [*A publication*]
SD Farm Home Res SD Agric Exp Stn ... South Dakota Farm and Home Research. South Dakota Agricultural Experiment Station [*A publication*]
SDFAUS ... State Defense Force Association of the United States   (EA)
SDFC......... Space Disturbance Forecast Center [*Environmental Science Services Administration*]   (IEEE)
SDFC........ Standardized Discriminant Function Coefficient
SDFL......... Schottky Diode FET [*Field Effect Transistor*] Logic
SD Fla........ United States District Court for the Southern District of Florida   (DLA)
SDFN........ SONAR Dome Flow Noise
SdFr........... Freeman Public Library, Freeman, SD [*Library symbol*] [*Library of Congress*]   (LCLS)
SDFRA ...... Reports. Faculty of Science. Shizuoka University [*A publication*]
SDFS .... Same-Day Funds Settlement [*Securities and Exchange Commission*]
SDFS .... Standard Disk Filing System
SDFSNM .. Sons and Daughters of the First Settlers of Newbury, Massachusetts   (EA)
SDFTN...... Soda Fountain
SDG .... Sacred Dance Guild   (EA)
SDG .... Scan Display Generator
SDG .... Schriften. Droste-Gesellschaft [*A publication*]
SDG .... Screen Directors' Guild of America [*Later, DGA*]
SDG .... Siding   (AAG)
SDG .... Signed, Directed Graph [*Mathematics*]
SDG .... Simulated Data Generator
SDG .... Situation Display Generator
SDG .... Soli Deo Gloria [*Glory to God Alone*] [*Latin*]
SDG .... Special Development Groups [*Navy*]
SDG .... Stormont, Dundas and Glengarry Highlanders [*British military*]   (DMA)
SdG .... Studii de Gramatica [*A publication*]
SDG .... Subminiature Displacement Gyroscope
SDG .... Sucrose Density Gradients
SDG .... Sundance Gold Mining Ltd. [*Vancouver Stock Exchange symbol*]
SDG .... Supplier Documentation Group [*NASA*]   (NASA)
SDG .... System Design Group   (MCD)
SDGA .... Single Degaussing Cable
SDGA .... Sucrose Density Gradient Analysis [*Clinical chemistry*]
SD GA .... United States District Court for the Southern District of Georgia   (DLA)
SDGC .... Simulated Distillation Gas Chromatography
SDGC .... Sun-Diamond Growers of California   (EA)
SDGE .... Situation Display Generator Element
SdGe .... Sully-Potter County Library, Gettysburg, SD [*Library symbol*] [*Library of Congress*]   (LCLS)
SD Geol Surv Bull ... South Dakota. Geological Survey. Bulletin [*A publication*]
SD Geol Surv Misc Invest ... South Dakota. Geological Survey. Miscellaneous Investigations [*A publication*]
SD Geol Surv Rep Invest ... South Dakota. Geological Survey. Report of Investigations [*A publication*]
SD Geol Surv Spec Rep ... South Dakota. Geological Survey. Special Report [*A publication*]
SDGH........ Sweet Dough
SDGRA...... Report of Investigations. South Dakota Geological Survey [*A publication*]
SDGW .... Structural Design Gross Weight
SDH.......... Scottish Diploma in Horticulture
SDH.......... Seasonal Derated Hours   (IEEE)
SDH.......... Single Dad's Hotline   (EA)
SDH.......... Slavistische Drukken en Herdrukken [*A publication*]
SDH.......... Software Development Handbook [*NASA*]   (NASA)
SDH.......... Sorbitol Dehydrogenase [*Also, Sorb D*] [*An enzyme*]
SDH.......... South Dakota Historical Resource Center, Pierre, SD [*OCLC symbol*]   (OCLC)
SDH.......... Spinal Dorsal Horn [*Anatomy*]
SDH......... Structured Document Handbook [*Data processing*]
SDH......... Styling Data Handling
SDH.......... Subdural Hematoma [*Medicine*]

SDH.......... Succinic Dehydrogenase [*An enzyme*]
SDH.......... Support Dogs for the Handicapped   (EA)
SDH.......... System Development Handbook [*NASA*]   (NASA)
SDHD....... Society of Daughters of Holland Dames   (EA)
SDHD....... Sudden-Death Heart Disease [*Medicine*]
SDHE .... Spacecraft Data Handling Equipment
SdHi.......... South Dakota Department of Cultural Affairs, Historical Resources Center, Pierre, SD [*Library symbol*] [*Library of Congress*]   (LCLS)
SDHI........ Studia et Documenta Historiae et Iuris [*A publication*]
SdHig........ Hyde County Library, Highmore, SD [*Library symbol*] [*Library of Congress*]   (LCLS)
SDHIRS .... Subdistrict Headquarters Induction and Recruiting Station [*Navy*]
SdHM........ Minnehaha County Rural Library, Hartford, SD [*Library symbol*] [*Library of Congress*]   (LCLS)
SdHow....... Howard Public Library, Howard, SD [*Library symbol*] [*Library of Congress*]   (LCLS)
SDHP .... Sosyal Demokrasi Halkci Partisi [*Social Democratic Populist Party*] [*Turkey*] [*Political party*]   (MENA)
SDHR .... South Dakota Historical Review [*A publication*]
SDHS .... Satellite Data Handling System
SDHS .... Society of Dance History Scholars   (EA)
SdHsV .... United States Veterans Administration Center, Hot Springs, SD [*Library symbol*] [*Library of Congress*]   (LCLS)
SDHT .... Selectively Doped Heterostructure Transistor
SdHuro ...... Huron Public Library, Huron, SD [*Library symbol*] [*Library of Congress*]   (LCLS)
SdHuroC.... Huron College, Huron, SD [*Library symbol*] [*Library of Congress*]   (LCLS)
SDI............ Saidor [*Papua New Guinea*] [*Airport symbol*]   (OAG)
SDI............ Saudi Arabian
SDI............ Saudi Arabian Airlines
SDI............ Selected Descriptive Item
SDI............ Selective Dissemination of Information [*System*] [*Data processing*]
SDI............ Self-Description Inventory [*Vocational guidance test*]
SDI............ Serial Dilution Indicator [*Clinical chemistry*]
SDI............ [*Family Planning Program*] Service Delivery Improvement Research [*Department of Health and Human Services*] [*Washington, DC*]
SDI............ Service de Documentation Interministerielle [*Interministerial Documentation Service*] [*National Telecommunications Research Center*] [*Information service or system*]   (IID)
SDi............ Slovenske. Revue Dramatickych Umeni [*A publication*]
SDI............ Society of Designers in Ireland   (EAIO)
SDI............ Source Data Information
SDI............ Standard Data Interface [*Data processing*]
SDI............ Standard Deviation Interval [*Medicine*]
SDI............ Standardized Discharge Instructions [*for hospital patients*]
SDI............ State Disability Insurance
SDI............ Steel Deck Institute   (EA)
SDI............ Steel Door Institute   (EA)
SDI............ Strategic Defense Initiative [*Commonly known as "Starwars"*] [*Facetiously translated as "Silly Damn Idea"*]
SDI............ Subcontractor Data Item
SDI............ Submarine Detector Instructor [*British military*]   (DMA)
SDI............ Supplier Data Item   (MCD)
SDI............ Support Directive Instruction   (KSC)
SDI............ Symbolic Displays, Incorporated   (MCD)
SD & I .... System Development and Integration   (MCD)
SDI............ Systems Designers International PLC [*British*]   (IRUK)
SDIA.......... Small Defense Industries Association [*Later, Strategic Industries Association*]
SDIAC....... Strategic Defense Initiative Advisory Council [*Military*]   (SDI)
SDICC .... Societe de Developpement de l'Industrie Cinematographique Canadienne [*Canadian Film Development Corporation - CFDC*]
SDID......... Supplier Data Item Description   (MCD)
SDIE......... Special Defense Intelligence Estimate   (MCD)
SDIF .... Schistosome-Derived Immunosuppressive Factor [*Immunology*]
SDIF .... Software Development and Integration Facility [*NASA*]   (NASA)
SDIG......... Screen Directors International Guild [*Absorbed by Directors Guild of America*]
SDIHD ...... Sudden-Death Ischemic Heart Disease [*Medicine*]
SDII .... Strategic Defense Initiative Institute [*Military*]   (SDI)
SDILINE... Selective Dissemination of Information Online [*National Library of Medicine*] [*Bethesda, MD*] [*Bibliographic database*]
SD Ill .... United States District Court for the Southern District of Illinois   (DLA)
SDIM......... System for Documentation and Information in Metallurgy [*Fachinformationszentrum Werkstoffe e V*] [*Information service or system*]   (IID)
SDIN .... Special Defence Intelligence Notice   (MCD)
SD Ind........ United States District Court for the Southern District of Indiana   (DLA)
SDIO .... Serial Digit Input/Output [*Data processing*]

SDIO .... Strategic Defense Initiative Organization [*Washington, DC*] [*DoD*]　(GRD)
SDIOA .... Studia et Documenta ad Iura Orientis Antiqui Pertinenta [*A publication*]
SDIOAP .... Studia et Documenta ad Iura Orientis Antiqui Pertinenta [*A publication*]
SD Iowa ..... United States District Court for the Southern District of Iowa　(DLA)
SDIP .... Specifically Designated Intelligence Position　(AFM)
SDIP .... Strengthening Developing Institutions Program [*HEW*]
SDIP .... System Description and Implementation Plan [*Navy*]
SDIS .... Ship Distance
SDIS .... Ship Draft Indicating System　(MSA)
SDISDC .... Sexuality and Disability [*A publication*]
SDISM ...... Strategic Defense Initiative System Effectiveness Model [*Military*]
SDIT .... Service de Documentation et d'Information Techniques de l'Aeronautique
SDIT .... Ship Draft Indicator Transmitter　(MSA)
SDI/UC .... State Disability Insurance - Unemployment Compensation
SDIZ.......... Submarine Defense Identification Zone
SDJ .... Greensboro, NC [*Location identifier*] [*FAA*]　(FAAL)
SDJ .... Sanada [*Japan*] [*Seismograph station code, US Geological Survey*]　(SEIS)
SDJ .... Sendai [*Japan*] [*Airport symbol*]　(OAG)
SDJ .... Senn d'Or [*Vancouver Stock Exchange symbol*]
SDJ .... Society of the Devotees of Jerusalem　(EA)
SD J Med .. South Dakota Journal of Medicine [*A publication*]
SD J Med Pharm ... South Dakota Journal of Medicine and Pharmacy [*A publication*]
S & DJR..... Somerset & Dorset Joint Railway [*British*]
SDK .... Sandakan [*Malaysia*] [*Airport symbol*]　(OAG)
SDK .... Seljacko-Demokratska Koalicija [*Peasant-Democratic Coalition*] [*Yugoslavia*] [*Political party*]　(PPE)
SDK .... Shelter Deck
SDK .... Si De Ka Quarterly [*Ann Arbor, MI*] [*A publication*]　(DLA)
SDK .... Sigma Delta Kappa [*Fraternity*]
SDK .... Software Developer's Kit [*Data processing*]　(BYTE)
SDK .... Studebaker's Resource Development Ltd. [*Formerly, Rio Blanco Resources Ltd.*] [*Vancouver Stock Exchange symbol*]
SDK .... System Design Kit
SdKJ .... Jackson-Washabaugh County Library, Kadoka, SD [*Library symbol*] [*Library of Congress*]　(LCLS)
SDKK........ Studia z Dziejow Kosciola Katolickiego [*A publication*]
SDKOD ..... Saitama Daigaku Kiyo. Kogakubu [*A publication*]
SDKSB ..... Saitama Daigaku Kiyo. Shizenkagaku-Hen [*A publication*]
SdL............ Hearst Free Library, Lead, SD [*Library symbol*] [*Library of Congress*]　(LCLS)
SDL............ National Council, Sons and Daughters of Liberty　(EA)
SDL............ Saddle　(MSA)
SDL............ Scenario Development Language [*Military*]　(CAAL)
SDL............ Scientific DataLink [*Comtex Scientific Corp.*] [*Information service or system*]　(IID)
SDL............ Scottie Gold Mines Ltd. [*Vancouver Stock Exchange symbol*]
SDL............ Scottsdale, AZ [*Location identifier*] [*FAA*]　(FAAL)
SDL............ Self-Directed Learning　(ADA)
SDL............ Semiconductor Diode LASER [*Also, TDL*]
SDL............ Sensory Distal Latency [*Medicine*]
SDL............ Shaft Driver, Left
SDL............ Simulation Data Language
SDL............ Single Driver's License [*Law*]
SDL............ Slowdown Length
SDL............ Software Design Language
SDL............ Software Development Laboratory [*NASA*]　(NASA)
SDL............ Software Development Language [*Burroughs Corp.*]
SDL............ Software Development Library
SDL............ Sonic Delay Line
SDL............ Space Dynamics Laboratories [*Utah State University*] [*Research center*]　(RCD)
SDL............ Specification and Description Language [*Telecommunications*]　(TEL)
SDL............ Standard Deviation of the Logarithm [*Statistics*]
SDL............ Standard Distribution List [*NASA*]
SDL............ Stark County District Library, Canton, OH [*OCLC symbol*]　(OCLC)
SDL............ State-Dependent Learning [*Psychology*]
SDL............ Strip Delay Line
SDL............ Sundsvall [*Sweden*] [*Airport symbol*]　(OAG)
SDL............ Supporting Document List
SDL............ Surplus Distribution List　(AAG)
SDL............ System Descriptive Language [*Data processing*]　(IEEE)
SDL............ System Design Language
SDL............ System Development Language [*1971*] [*Data processing*]　(CSR)
SDL............ System Directory List [*Data processing*]　(BUR)
SDL............ Systematic Design Language [*Data processing*]
SDL............ Systems Development Laboratories　(MCD)
SDLC......... Synchronous Data-Link Control [*Telecommunications*]
SDLC......... System Data Link Control [*Telecommunications*]
SDLC......... System Development Life Cycle

SdLeH....... Lennox High School Library, Lennox, SD [*Library symbol*] [*Library of Congress*]　(LCLS)
SdLem....... Lemmon Public Library, Lemmon, SD [*Library symbol*] [*Library of Congress*]　(LCLS)
SdLemH .... Lemmon High School Library, Lemmon, SD [*Library symbol*] [*Library of Congress*]　(LCLS)
SDLM....... Scheduled Depot Level Maintenance [*Navy*]
SDLM....... Special Depot Level Maintenance
SDLM....... Standard Depot Level Maintenance　(MCD)
SDLO .... State, Defense Liaison Office [*Federal government*]　(AABC)
SDLP .... Social Democratic and Labour Party [*Northern Ireland*] [*Political party*]　(PPW)
SDLP .... Social Democratic and Liberal Party [*British*] [*Political party*]
SDLP .... Societe de Developpement du Livre et du Periodique [*Society for the Development of Books and Periodicals*] [*Canada*]
SD LR....... South Dakota Law Review [*A publication*]
SD L Rev.... South Dakota Law Review [*A publication*]
SdM .... Mitchell Public Library, Mitchell, SD [*Library symbol*] [*Library of Congress*]　(LCLS)
SDM .... National Association of Special Delivery Messengers [*Later, APWU*] [*AFL-CIO*]
SDM .... Samsonov Density Meter [*Gravimetrics*]
SDM .... San Diego, CA [*Location identifier*] [*FAA*]　(FAAL)
SDM .... Santiago De Maria [*El Salvador*] [*Seismograph station code, US Geological Survey*]　(SEIS)
SDM .... School in District Management [*LIMRA*]
SDM .... Selective Dissemination of Microfiche
SDM .... Semiconductor Disk Memory
SDM .... Sensory Detection Method [*for measuring blood pressure*]
SDM .... Sequency-Division Multiplexing　(IEEE)
SDM .... Ship Design Manager
SDM .... Short-Delay Monostable [*Circuitry*]
SDM .... Shutdown Margin [*Nuclear energy*]　(NRCH)
SDM .... Shutdown Mode　(IEEE)
SDM .... Shuttle Data Management [*NASA*]　(MCD)
SdM .... Siglo de las Misiones [*A publication*]
SDM .... Simulated Dynamic Missile [*Military*]　(CAAL)
SDM .... Site Defense of Minuteman [*Missiles*]　(MCD)
SDM .... Site-Directed Mutagenesis [*Biochemistry*]
SDM .... Slowdown Model
SDM .... Soma Dendrite Membrane
SDM .... Sons and Daughters of Malta　(EA)
SDM .... Space Division Multiplexing [*Physics*]
SDM .... Spares Determination Method [*Bell System*]
SDM .... Specially Designated Merchant [*Liquor sales*]
SDM .... Standardization Design Memoranda　(IEEE)
SDM .... STARAN Debug Module
SDM .... Statistical Delta Modulation
SDM .... Statistical-Dynamical Model
SDM .... Structural Development Model
SDM .... Structural Dynamics Modification
SDM .... Structures, Structural Dynamics, and Materials　(MCD)
SDM .... Subdivision Manager
SDM .... Subsystem Design Manual [*NASA*]　(MCD)
SDM .... Sugar Cane Downy Mildew [*Plant pathology*]
SDM .... Synchronous Digital Machine
SDM .... System Definition Manual [*NASA*]　(NASA)
SdMa .... Bennett County Library, Martin, SD [*Library symbol*] [*Library of Congress*]　(LCLS)
SDMA .... Sam Davis Memorial Association　(EA)
SDMA .... Shared Direct Memory Access [*Sperry UNIVAC*]
SDMA .... Sodium Dihydrobis(methoxyethoxy)aluminate [*Organic chemistry*]
SDMA .... Space Division Multiple Access
SDMAA ..... Stroitel'nye i Dorozhnye Mashiny [*A publication*]
SdMadT.... Dakota State College, Madison, SD [*Library symbol*] [*Library of Congress*]　(LCLS)
SdMar....... Dakota Wowapipahi Library, Marty, SD [*Library symbol*] [*Library of Congress*]　(LCLS)
SDME........ Synchronous Data Modern Equipment
SDMEA..... South Dakota Journal of Medicine [*A publication*]
SdMeS....... Menno Public School Library, Menno, SD [*Library symbol*] [*Library of Congress*]　(LCLS)
SD (Met).... Doctor of Science in Metallurgy
SDMH....... Shoalhaven District Memorial Hospital [*Australia*]
SDMH....... Symmetrical-Dimthylhydrazine [*Organic chemistry*]
SdMi .... Hand County Library, Miller, SD [*Library symbol*] [*Library of Congress*]　(LCLS)
S-DMICC ... State-Defense Military Information Control Committee　(AFM)
SdMil........ Milbank Carnegie Library, Milbank, SD [*Library symbol*] [*Library of Congress*]　(LCLS)
SDMIS ...... Standardization Data Management Information System
SD Miss..... United States District Court for the Southern District of Mississippi　(DLA)
SDMIX...... South Dakota Medical Information Exchange [*University of South Dakota*] [*Sioux Falls*] [*Telecommunications*]　(TSSD)
SDMJ........ September, December, March, and June [*Denotes quarterly payments of interest or dividends in these months*] [*Business term*]

SdMo .... A. H. Brown Public Library, Mobridge, SD [*Library symbol*] [*Library of Congress*] (LCLS)
SDMO ...... Specifications and Data Management Office [*Military*]
SDMO ...... Subcommand Data Management Office [*Military*] (AFIT)
SDMS .... Shipboard Data Multiplex System (MCD)
SDMS .... Society of Diagnostic Medical Sonographers (EA)
SDMS .... Spatial Data Management System (MCD)
SDMS .... Supplier Data Management System (MCD)
SDMT ...... Stanford Diagnostic Mathematics Test [*Education*]
SDMT ...... Stress and Degraded Mode Test (CAAL)
SdMW ...... Dakota Wesleyan University, Mitchell, SD [*Library symbol*] [*Library of Congress*] (LCLS)
SDN .... North American Baptist Seminary, Sioux Falls, SD [*OCLC symbol*] (OCLC)
SDN .... Sandane [*Norway*] [*Airport symbol*] (OAG)
SDN .... Satellite Data Network [*AgriData Resources, Inc.*] [*Telecommunications service*] [*Defunct*] (TSSD)
SDN .... Secret Document Number
SDN .... Sendirian [*Private Business Company*] [*Malaysian*]
SDN .... Separation Designation Number
SDN .... Service Dealer's Newsletter [*Lynott Associates*] [*A publication*] (IID)
SDN .... Sexually Dimorphic Nucleus [*Brain anatomy*]
SDN .... Societe Demographique Nordique [*Nordic Demographic Society - NDS*] (EAIO)
SDN .... Societe des Nations [*League of Nations*]
SDN .... Sodisco, Inc. [*Toronto Stock Exchange symbol*]
SDN .... Software Defined Network [*Telecommunications*]
SDN .... Software Development Note [*NASA*] (NASA)
SDN .... Subdeacon
SDN .... Subscriber's Directory Number [*Telecommunications*] (TEL)
SDN .... Sudan [*ANSI three-letter standard code*] (CNC)
SDN .... Swindon [*British depot code*]
SDN .... Synchronized Digital Network [*Telecommunications*] (TEL)
SDN .... System Development Notification
SDNB .... SDNB Financial Corp. [*NASDAQ symbol*] (NQ)
Sdn Bhd .... Sendirian Berhad [*Private Limited Company*] [*Malaysian*]
SDNCO ..... Staff Duty Noncommissioned Officer [*Army*]
SdNe .... Newell Public Library, Newell, SD [*Library symbol*] [*Library of Congress*] (LCLS)
SdNeu .... New Underwood Public Library, New Underwood, SD [*Library symbol*] [*Library of Congress*] (LCLS)
SDNIA ...... Saga Daigaku Nogaku Iho [*A publication*]
SDNID7 .... Bulletin. Faculty of Agriculture. Saga University [*A publication*]
SDNR .... Screw Down Non-Return Valve (DS)
SDNRIU.... Secure Digital Net Radio Interface Unit [*Army*] (RDA)
SDNS .... Secure Data Network System [*Data processing*]
SDN & SU ... Step-Down and Step-Up (MSA)
SDNT .... Student
SD Nurse ... South Dakota Nurse [*A publication*]
SDNY .... United States District Court for the Southern District of New York (DLA)
SDO .... Oglala Sioux Community College, Learning Resources Center, Pine Ridge, SD [*OCLC symbol*] (OCLC)
SdO .... Onida Public Library, Onida, SD [*Library symbol*] [*Library of Congress*] (LCLS)
SDO .... Salado [*Chile*] [*Seismograph station code, US Geological Survey*] [*Closed*] (SEIS)
SDO .... San Diego Gas & Electric Co. [*NYSE symbol*] (SPSG)
SDO .... Schedules Duty Officer (KSC)
SDO .... Senior Duty Officer [*Air Force*] [*British*]
SDO .... Serra Dor [*A publication*]
SDO .... Shielded Diatomic Orbitals [*Atomic physics*]
SDO .... Ship Development Objective [*Navy*]
SDO .... Shipboard Distribution Only [*Navy*] (CAAL)
SDO .... Signal Distribution Officer [*British military*] (DMA)
SDO .... Sod House, NV [*Location identifier*] [*FAA*] (FAAL)
SDO .... SONAR Detection Opportunity [*Navy*] (CAAL)
SDO .... Source Data Operation (MDG)
SDO .... Special Duty Officer (MCD)
SDO .... Special Duty Only [*Military*]
SDO .... Specialist Duty Only [*Navy personnel designation*]
SDO .... Squadron Duty Officer [*Navy*] (NVT)
SDO .... Staff Duty Officer [*Army*]
SDO .... Station Duty Officer [*Navy*]
SDO .... Synthetic Drying Oil
SDO .... Systems Development Office [*National Weather Service*]
SDOB .... Scaled Depth of Burst (MCD)
S Doc .... Senate Document (DLA)
SDOC .... Specific Direct Operating Costs
SDOE .... State Department of Education (OICC)
SDOF .... Single Degree of Freedom [*Also, SDF*] [*Acoustics*]
SDOG .... Sendschrift. Deutsche Orient-Gesellschaft [*Leipzig*] [*A publication*]
SD Ohio ..... United States District Court for the Southern District of Ohio (DLA)
SDOM ...... Society of Dirty Old Men (EA)
SDOM ...... Standard Deviation of Means [*Statistics*]
SDOP .... Sons and Daughters of Oregon Pioneers (EA)
SDOPR...... Sound Operator [*Navy*]
SDOSD...... Standard Deviation of Standard Deviation [*Statistics*]

SDP .... National Society of Sons and Daughters of the Pilgrims (EA)
SDP .... Sacrodextra Posterior [*A fetal position*] [*Obstetrics*]
SDP .... Sand Point [*Alaska*] [*Airport symbol*] (OAG)
SDP .... Sand Point, AK [*Location identifier*] [*FAA*] (FAAL)
SDP .... Scottish Diploma in Poultry Husbandry
SDP .... Sea Duty Pay [*Navy*]
SDP .... Sentry Dog Patrol (AFM)
SDP .... Set-Down Pool [*Nuclear energy*] (NRCH)
SDP .... Seychelles Democratic Party
SDP .... Shelf Dynamics Program [*CUE*] (MSC)
SDP .... Ship Development Plan [*Navy*]
SDP .... Short-Day Plant [*Botany*]
SDP .... Shuttle Data Processor [*NASA*] (MCD)
SDP .... Signal Data Processor
SDP .... Signal Dispatch Point [*Telecommunications*] (TEL)
SDP .... Silicon Diode Pellet
SDP .... Singapore Democratic Party [*Political party*] (PPW)
SDP .... Single Department Purchasing [*Agency*] [*Military*]
SDP .... Sirotherm Demineralization Process
SDP .... Sisters of Divine Providence [*Munster, Federal Republic of Germany*] (EAIO)
SDP .... Site Data Processor
SDP .... Site Development and Facilities Utilization Plan [*Oak Ridge National Laboratory*]
SDP .... Slowdown Power
SDP .... Small Distribution Phenomena
SDP .... Smoke Dispersion Pod
SDP .... Social Democratic Party [*Althyduflokkurinn*] [*Iceland*] [*Political party*] (PPW)
SDP .... Social Democratic Party [*Australia*] [*Political party*]
SDP .... Social Democratic Party [*Trinidad and Tobago*] [*Political party*] (PPW)
SDP .... Social Democratic Party [*Sangkhom Prachatipatai*] [*Thailand*] [*Political party*] (PPW)
SDP .... Social Democratic Party [*Federal Republic of Germany*] [*Political party*]
SDP .... Social Democratic Party [*Philippines*] [*Political party*] (PPW)
SDP .... Social Democratic Party [*Nigeria*] [*Political party*]
SDP .... Social Democratic Party [*British*] [*Political party*]
SDP .... Software Development Plan [*NASA*] (NASA)
SDP .... Solar Desalination Plant
SDP .... Source Data Processing
SDP .... Sozial Demokratesch Partei [*Social Democratic Party*] [*Luxembourg*] [*Political party*] (PPE)
SDP .... Spectral Dependence Photocurrent
SDP .... State Data Program [*Information service or system*] (IID)
SDP .... Station Data Processing
SDP .... Steyr-Daimler-Puch [*Manufacturing firm*] [*Automotive engineering*]
SDP .... Storage and Distribution Point [*Military*] (AFM)
SDP .... Stornaway Central Development [*Vancouver Stock Exchange symbol*]
SDP .... Stratospheric Dust Particle
SdP .... Sudetendeutsche Partei [*Sudeten German Party*] [*Czechoslovakia*] [*Political party*] (PPE)
SDP .... Sulfonyldiphenol [*Organic chemistry*]
SDP .... Sun Distributors LP Class A [*NYSE symbol*] (SPSG)
SDP .... Suomen Sosialidemokraattinen Puolue [*Finnish Social Democratic Party*] [*Political party*] (EAIO)
SDP .... Supervision Development Project [*Australia*]
SDP .... Supplier Data Package (NASA)
SDP .... Supply Distribution Point
SDP .... Surface Deformation Pattern
SDP .... Survey Data Processing
Sdp .... Suspended in Part [*Regulation or order suspended in part*] [*Legal term*] (DLA)
SDP .... Swaziland Democratic Party
SDP .... System Design Proposal [*Navy*]
SDP .... Systems Development Package [*or Plan*] [*Military*] (NG)
SdPa .... Parker Public Library, Parker, SD [*Library symbol*] [*Library of Congress*] (LCLS)
SDPA........ Small Defense Plants Administration [*Terminated, 1953*]
SDPC......... Shuttle Data Processing Complex [*NASA*] (MCD)
SDPC......... Social Democratic Party of Canada
SDPD........ Special Defense Projects Department
SDPDA..... Special Defense Property Disposal Account [*DoD*]
SdPEC .... South Dakota Department of Education and Cultural Affairs, Historical Resources Center, Pierre, SD [*Library symbol*] [*Library of Congress*] (LCLS)
SDPF .... Sensor Data Processing Facility (MCD)
SDPF .... Social-Democratic Party of Finland
SDPH .... Social Democratic Party of Hungary [*Political party*] (EAIO)
SdPiO .... Oglala Sioux Community College, Pine Ridge, SD [*Library symbol*] [*Library of Congress*] (LCLS)
SdPl .... Plankinton City Library, Plankinton, SD [*Library symbol*] [*Library of Congress*] (LCLS)
SDPL .... Safeguard Data Processing Laboratory [*Army*] (AABC)
SDPL .... Sensor Data Processing Laboratory (MCD)
SDPL......... Servomechanisms and Data Processing Laboratory [*Massachusetts Institute of Technology*] (MCD)
SDPO .... Site Defense Project Office [*Military*] (AABC)

SDPO	Space Defense Project Office [*AMC*]
SDPP	Social Democracy Popularist Party [*Turkey*] [*Political party*]
SdPr	Presho Public Library, Presho, SD [*Library symbol*] [*Library of Congress*] (LCLS)
SDPR	Sons and Daughters of Pioneer Rivermen (EA)
SDPR	System Design and Performance Requirements
SDPS	Signal Data Processing System
SDPT	Structured Doll Play Test [*Psychology*]
SDQ	Santo Domingo [*Dominican Republic*] [*Airport symbol*] (OAG)
SDQ	Self-Description Questionnaire
SDQ	Student Description Questionnaire
SDQFC	Sir Douglas Quintet Fan Club (EA)
SDR	New York State Department Reports [*A publication*] (DLA)
SdR	Rapid City Public Library, Rapid City, SD [*Library symbol*] [*Library of Congress*] (LCLS)
SDR	Santander [*Spain*] [*Airport symbol*] (OAG)
SDR	Schlumberger-Doll Research Center, Ridgefield, CT [*OCLC symbol*] (OCLC)
SDR	Scientific Data Recorder
SDR	Search Decision Rule [*Data processing*]
SDR	Seismic Detection and Ranging
SDR	Self-Decoding Readout
SDR	Sender (KSC)
SDR	Sensor Data Record [*For spacecraft*]
SDR	Service Difficulty Report (MCD)
SDR	Sezione Demografia e Razza [*A publication*]
SDR	Shaft Driver, Right
SDR	Sheffield District Railway (ROG)
SDR	Ship Destination Room (NATG)
SDR	Ship Diversion Room (NATG)
SDR	Shipment Document Release [*Military*] (AFIT)
SDR	Signal Data Recorder [*or Reproducer*] (MCD)
SDR	Signal Distribution Room [*NASA*] (KSC)
SDR	Significant Deficiency Report [*Nuclear energy*] (IEEE)
SDR	Simple Detection Response
SDR	Single-Drift Region (IEEE)
SDR	Sisters of the Divine Redeemer [*Roman Catholic religious order*]
SDR	Sloane, Donald R., New York NY [*STAC*]
SDR	Small Development Requirement [*Military*]
SDR	SNAP [*Systems for Nuclear Auxiliary Power*] Development Reactor
SDR	Snyder, TX [*Location identifier*] [*FAA*] (FAAL)
SDR	Society for Drug Research (EAIO)
SDR	Sodium Deuterium Reactor
SDR	Software Design Requirement [*NASA*] (NASA)
SDR	Software Design Review [*NASA*] (MCD)
SDR	Solution Development Record
S & DR	Somerset & Dorset Joint Railway [*British*] (ROG)
SDR	SONAR Data Recorder
SDR	Sophisticated Data Research, Inc. [*Information service or system*] (IID)
SDR	Sounder (MSA)
SDR	South Dakota Review [*A publication*]
SDR	South Devon Railway (ROG)
SDR	Space Division Regulation [*NASA*] (NASA)
SDR	Spacelab Disposition Record [*NASA*] (NASA)
SDPr	Special Dispatch Rider
SDR	Special Drawing Rights [*International Monetary Fund*]
SDR	Spin Dependent Resonance [*Physics*]
SDR	Splash Detection RADAR [*Military*]
SDR	Standard Deviation of the Regression [*Statistics*]
SDR	State-Dependent Retrieval [*Psychology*]
SDR	Statistical Data Recorder [*Data processing*] (MDG)
SDR	Storage Data Register (MCD)
SDR	Strip Domain Resonance
SDR	Stroud Resources Ltd. [*Toronto Stock Exchange symbol*]
SDR	Succession Duties Reports [*A publication*] (ILCA)
SDR	Successive Discrimination Reversal
SDR	Sueddeutscher Rundfunk [*South German Radio Network*]
SDR	Survey of Doctorate Recipients [*National Research Council*] [*Database*]
SDR	System Data Record
SDR	System for Data Retrieval [*Information retrieval*]
SDR	System Definition Record [*Data processing*] (IBMDP)
SDR	System Definition Requirements
SDR	System Design Report [*NATO*] (NATG)
SDR	System Design Review [*NASA*] (NASA)
SDR	System Development Requirement [*Air Force*]
SDR	System Discrepancy Report
S DRAKE ..	Second Dynamic Response and Kinematics Experiment [*Marine science*] (MSC)
SDRB	Software Design Review Board [*NASA*] (NASA)
SDRB	Supplier Documentation Review Board [*NASA*] (NASA)
SDR & C	Shipment Document Release and Control [*Military*] (AFIT)
SDRC	Structural Dynamics Research Corp. [*NASDAQ symbol*] (NQ)
SDRC Ops ...	South Dakota Board of Railroad Commissioners Opinions [*A publication*] (DLA)
SDRD	Supplier Data Requirements Description (NASA)
SDRD	Supplier Documentation Review Data (NASA)
SDRDDC...	Survey of Drug Research in Immunologic Disease [*A publication*]
SdRe	Redfield Carnegie Library, Redfield, SD [*Library symbol*] [*Library of Congress*] (LCLS)
SDRL	Subcontractor Data Requirements List
SDRL	Supplier Data Requirements List (NASA)
SDRM	San Diego Railroad Museum (EA)
SdRM	South Dakota School of Mines and Technology, Rapid City, SD [*Library symbol*] [*Library of Congress*] (LCLS)
SdRN	National College of Business, Rapid City, SD [*Library symbol*] [*Library of Congress*] (LCLS)
SDRNG	Sound Ranging (MUGU)
SDRP	Simulated Data Reduction Program
SdRS	Saint Martins Academy, Rapid City, SD [*Library symbol*] [*Library of Congress*] (LCLS)
SDRS	Signal Data Recording Set (MCD)
SDRS	Splash Detection RADAR System (MCD)
SDRSA	Shimane Daigaku Ronshu: Shizen Kagaku [*A publication*]
SDRT	Spadafore Diagnostic Reading Test [*Educational test*]
SDRT	Stanford Diagnostic Reading Test [*Education*]
SD Rulings ...	Stamp Duties Rulings [*Australia*] [*A publication*]
SDRW	SONAR Dome Rubber Window (NVT)
S-DRY	Surfaced Dry [*Lumber*]
SDS	Safety Data Sheet (KSC)
SDS	St. David's Society of the State of New York (EA)
SDS	Same Day Surgery [*Medicine*]
SDS	Samostalna Demokratska Stranka [*Independent Democratic Party*] [*Yugoslavia*] [*Political party*] (PPE)
SDS	Sample Display Service [*Department of Commerce*]
SDS	Sanatorio Duran [*Costa Rica*] [*Seismograph station code, US Geological Survey*] (SEIS)
SDS	Satellite Data System [*Air Force*]
SDS	School Dental Service
SDS	Scientific Data System [*Later, XDS*]
SDS	Self-Directed Search
SDS	Self-Rating Depression Scale [*Psychology*]
SDS	Sensory Deprivation Syndrome [*Medicine*]
SDS	Servo Drive System
SDS	Sexual Differentiation Scale [*Psychometrics*]
SDS	Ship Defense System
SDS	Shop Distribution Standards (KSC)
SDS	Short Distance Swimmer
SDS	Shuttle Dynamic Simulation [*NASA*] (NASA)
SDS	Sign-Digit Subtractor
SDS	Signal Distribution System
SDS	Simulating Digital Systems
SDS	Simulation Data Subsystem (KSC)
SDS	Sisters of the Divine Saviour [*Roman Catholic religious order*]
SDS	Smoke Destruction System
SDS	Sodium Dodecyl Sulfate [*Also, SLS*] [*Organic chemistry*]
SDS	Software Design Specification [*NASA*] (NASA)
SDS	Software Development System
SDS	Solar Disk Simulator
SDS	Sons and Daughters of the Soddies (EA)
SDS	South Dakota State Library Commission, Pierre, SD [*OCLC symbol*] (OCLC)
SDS	Sozialistischer Deutscher Studentenbund [*Student political organization*] [*Germany*]
SDS	Space Defense System (AAG)
SDS	Space Division Switching [*Telecommunications*]
SDS	Space Documentation Service [*NASA/ESRO*] (DIT)
SDS	Spacecraft Design Specification
SDS	Special Distress Signal (DEN)
SDS	Special Docking Simulator [*NASA*] (KSC)
SDS	Spectrometer Digital System
SDS	Splash Detection System
SDS	Standard Depot System [*Army*]
SDS	Status Display Support (MCD)
SDS	Steam Dump System [*Nuclear energy*] (NRCH)
SDS	Steering Damping System [*Aerospace*] (MCD)
SDS	Stimulator of DNA Synthesis [*Immunochemistry*]
SDS	Strategic Defense System [*DoD*]
SDS	Students for a Democratic Society (EA)
SDS	Submerged Demineralizer System [*Water purification*]
SDS	Subvent Datenbank Systeme [*Innovationstechnik GmbH & Co.*] [*Hamburg, Federal Republic of Germany*] [*Information service or system*] (IID)
SDS	Sudden Death Syndrome [*in children*] [*Medicine*]
SDS	Sudden Drowning Syndrome
SDS	Supplemental Data Sheet
SDS	Supplier Data Sheet
SDS	Supplier Delivery Schedules [*Chrysler Corp.*]
SDS	Sweet Dough Stabilizer [*Brand of bakery product from H. C. Brill Co., Inc.*]
SDS	Swimmer Distress Signal [*Navy*] (CAAL)
SDS	Sydsvenska Dagbladet Snaellposten [*A publication*]
SDS	Synchronous Data Set (NOAA)
SDS	System Data Synthesizer (KSC)
SDS	System Design Specification
SDS	Systematic Design Language [*Data processing*]

SDSAM..... Specifically Designated Special Air Mission [*Aircraft*] [*Air Force*]
SDSB........ [*The*] Southold Savings Bank [*NASDAQ symbol*]   (NQ)
SDSBE...... San Diego Symposium for Biomedical Engineering
SDSC........ San Diego State College [*California*]
SDSC........ San Diego Supercomputer Center [*California*] [*National Science Foundation*]
Sd-SC........ South Dakota Supreme Court Library, Pierre, SD [*Library symbol*] [*Library of Congress*]   (LCLS)
SD Sch Mines Bull ... South Dakota. School of Mines. Bulletin [*A publication*]
SDSD........ Saco Defense Systems Division [*Maremont Corp.*]   (RDA)
SDSD........ Satellite Data Services Division [*National Oceanic and Atmospheric Administration*] [*Information service or system*]   (IID)
SDSD........ Single Disk Storage Device [*Data processing*]   (BUR)
SDSD........ Studi e Documenti di Storia e Diritto [*A publication*]
SDSE........ Society of the Descendants of the Schwenkfeldian Exiles   (EA)
SD Sess Laws ... South Dakota Session Laws [*A publication*]   (DLA)
SDSH .... Society Devoted to the Sacred Heart [*Roman Catholic women's religious order*]
SDSI......... Shared Data Set Integrity
SdSi........... Sisseton Library, Sisseton, SD [*Library symbol*] [*Library of Congress*]   (LCLS)
SdSif......... Sioux Falls Carnegie Free Public Library, Sioux Falls, SD [*Library symbol*] [*Library of Congress*]   (LCLS)
SdSifA .... Augustana College, Sioux Falls, SD [*Library symbol*] [*Library of Congress*]   (LCLS)
SdSifB........ North American Baptist Seminary, Sioux Falls, SD [*Library symbol*] [*Library of Congress*]   (LCLS)
SdSifC........ Sioux Falls College, Sioux Falls, SD [*Library symbol*] [*Library of Congress*]   (LCLS)
SdSifH........ Coolidge High School Library, Sioux Falls, SD [*Library symbol*] [*Library of Congress*]   (LCLS)
SdSifV........ United States Veterans Administration Center, Sioux Falls, SD [*Library symbol*] [*Library of Congress*]   (LCLS)
SDSL......... Sail Dynamics Simulation Laboratory   (MCD)
SDSL......... Subject Directory of Special Libraries and Information Centers [*A publication*]
SD SMS CLSD ... Side Seams Closed [*Freight*]
SdSpe......... Grace Balloch Memorial Library, Spearfish, SD [*Library symbol*] [*Library of Congress*]   (LCLS)
SdSpen....... Hanson-McCook County Regional Library, Spencer, SD [*Library symbol*] [*Library of Congress*]   (LCLS)
SdSpeT ...... Black Hills State College, Spearfish, SD [*Library symbol*] [*Library of Congress*]   (LCLS)
SdSpU........ University of South Dakota at Springfield, Springfield, SD [*Library symbol*] [*Library of Congress*]   (LCLS)
SDS & RU ... Soil Data Storage and Retrieval Unit [*Department of Agriculture*]   (IID)
SDSS .... San Diego Shrinkers Society   (EA)
SDSS .... Satellite Data System Spacecraft [*Air Force*]
SDSS .... Self-Deploying Space Station
SDSS .... Single and Double Simultaneous Stimulation [*Neuropsychology test*]
SDSS .... Space Division Shuttle Simulator [*NASA*]   (NASA)
SDSSE...... Science Data System Support Equipment
SDSST....... Single and Double Simultaneous Stimulation Test [*Neuropsychology test*]
SdSt .... Sturgis Public Library, Sturgis, SD [*Library symbol*] [*Library of Congress*]   (LCLS)
SD St BJ .... South Dakota State Bar Journal [*A publication*]   (DLA)
SDSU........ San Diego State University [*California*]
SDSU........ South Dakota State University [*Brookings, SD*]
SDSVF...... State Dependent State Variable Feedback [*Rocket engine*] [*NASA*]
SDSW........ Sense Device Status Word
SDT .... National College Library, Rapid City, SD [*OCLC symbol*]   (OCLC)
SDT .... Sacrodextra Transversa [*A fetal position*] [*Obstetrics*]
SDT .... Saidu Sharif [*Pakistan*] [*Airport symbol*]   (OAG)
SDT .... Sanderson Tech, Inc. [*Vancouver Stock Exchange symbol*]
SDT .... Saturated Discharge Temperature [*Refrigeration*]
SDT .... Scaling and Display Task   (NASA)
SDT .... Science Data Team
SDT .... Scientific Distribution Technique
SDT .... Sea Depth Transducer
SDT .... Second Destination Transportation   (MCD)
SDT .... Serial Data Transmission
SDT .... Serum Dilution Test [*Clinical chemistry*]
SDT .... Shell-Destroying Tracer [*Ammunition*]
SDT .... Shipboard Data Terminal   (MCD)
SDT .... Shuttle Data Tape [*NASA*]
SDT .... Side Tank [*on a ship*]   (DS)
SDt .... Sifre on Deuteronomy [*A publication*]   (BJA)
SDT .... Signal Detection Theory
SDT .... Simplified Drive Train [*Navistar International Corp.*] [*Truck engineering*]
SDT .... Simulated Data Tape
SDT .... Simulated Dynamic Target [*Military*]   (CAAL)
SDT .... Skylab Data Task [*NASA*]

SDT .... Society of Dairy Technology [*British*]
SDT .... Soldier Data Tag
SDT .... Source Distribution Technique
SDT .... Speedy Drill Template   (MCD)
SD & T ..... Staff Duties and Training [*British military*]   (DMA)
SDT .... Start-Data-Traffic [*Data processing*]   (IBMDP)
SDT .... Steered Directional Transmission   (MCD)
SDT .... Step-Down Transformer
SDT .... Stromberg Dexterity Test [*Education*]
SDT .... Structural Dynamic Test [*NASA*]   (NASA)
SD/T......... Surface Detector/Tracker [*Navy*]   (CAAL)
SDT .... Surveillance Data Transmission
SDT .... System Dynamic Tester
SDTA....... Scottish Dance Teacher's Alliance [*Glasgow, Scotland*]   (EAIO)
SDTA........ Stewardsman Apprentice, Steward, Striker [*Navy rating*]
SDTA........ Structural Dynamic Test Article [*NASA*]   (NASA)
SD Tex...... United States District Court for the Southern District of Texas   (DLA)
SDTGA..... Staedtetag [*A publication*]
SDTI......... Selective Dissemination of Technical Information [*Data processing*]
SDTI......... Student Developmental Task Inventory [*Educational test*]
SDTIM...... Society for the Development of Techniques in Industrial Marketing [*British*]
SDTK....... Supported Drift Tube Klystron
SDTN .... Stewardsman, Steward, Striker [*Navy rating*]
SDTP........ Startover Data Transfer and Processing [*Program*]
SDTP PROGRM ... Startover Data Transfer and Processing Program
SDTR........ Serial Data Transmitter/Receiver [*Telecommunications*]   (TEL)
SDTS .... Satellite Data Transmission System   (DIT)
SDTT........ Silicon Diode Target Tube
SDU .... Huron College, Huron, SD [*OCLC symbol*]   (OCLC)
SDU .... Memphis, TN [*Location identifier*] [*FAA*]   (FAAL)
SDU .... Rio De Janeiro-Dumont [*Brazil*] [*Airport symbol*]   (OAG)
SDU .... Self-Destruct Unit
SDU .... Shelter Decontamination Unit
SDU .... Signal Distribution Unit   (AAG)
SDU .... Source Data Utility
sdu............. South Dakota [*MARC country of publication code*] [*Library of Congress*]   (LCCP)
SDU .... Soziale Demokratische Union [*Social Democratic Union*] [*Federal Republic of Germany*] [*Political party*]   (PPW)
SDU .... Spectrum Display Unit
SDU .... Station Display Unit
SDU .... Students for a Democratic University [*Canada*]
SDU .... Subcarrier Delay Unit
SDU .... Surface Drone Unit [*Navy*]   (CAAL)
SdU .... University of South Dakota, Vermillion, SD [*Library symbol*] [*Library of Congress*]   (LCLS)
SDUK .... Society for the Diffusion of Useful Knowledge
SdU-L........ University of South Dakota, Law Library, Vermillion, SD [*Library symbol*] [*Library of Congress*]   (LCLS)
SdU-M....... University of South Dakota, Medical School, Vermillion, SD [*Library symbol*] [*Library of Congress*]   (LCLS)
SDUN........ Standun, Inc. [*NASDAQ symbol*]   (NQ)
SD Uniform Prob Code ... South Dakota Uniform Probate Code [*A publication*]   (DLA)
SDUSA...... Social Democrats, USA   (EA)
SDV .... Santo Domingo [*Venezuela*] [*Seismograph station code, US Geological Survey*]   (SEIS)
SDV .... Scram Discharge Volume [*Nuclear energy*]   (NRCH)
SDV .... Shuttle Derived Vehicle   (MCD)
SDV .... Slowed-Down Video [*RADAR*]
SDV .... Society of Divine Vocations [*Vocationist Fathers*] [*Roman Catholic religious order*]
SDV .... Solar Daily Variation
SDV .... Soybean Dwarf Virus
SDV .... Spark Delay Valve [*Automotive engineering*]
SDV .... Specific Desensitizing Vaccine [*Medicine*]   (ADA)
S Dv .... Sprache und Datenverarbeitung [*A publication*]
SDV .... Swimmer Delivery Vehicle [*Navy symbol*] [*Obsolete*]   (MCD)
SDV .... Tel Aviv/Yafo [*Israel*] [*Airport symbol*]   (OAG)
SdV .... Vermillion Public Library, Vermillion, SD [*Library symbol*] [*Library of Congress*]   (LCLS)
S-DVB ...... Styrene-Divinylbenzene [*Organic chemistry*]
SDVF........ Software Development and Verification Facilities [*NASA*]   (NASA)
SDVI......... Service Disabled Veterans Insurance
SDW .... Dakota Wesleyan University, Layne Library, Mitchell, SD [*OCLC symbol*]   (OCLC)
SDW .... S. D. Warren [*Paper manufacturer*]
SDW .... Segment Descriptor Word
SDW .... Side Wheel   (DS)
SDW .... Six-Day War [*Arab-Israeli War, 1967*]   (BJA)
SDW .... Southdown, Inc. [*NYSE symbol*]   (SPSG)
SDW .... Spin-Density Wave [*Physics*]
SDW .... Standing Detonation Wave
SDW .... Sterile Distilled Water
SDW .... Swept Delta Wing

SdW	Watertown Regional Library, Watertown, SD [*Library symbol*] [*Library of Congress*] (LCLS)
SDWA	Safe Drinking Water Act [*1974*]
SdWa	Wagner Public Library, Wagner, SD [*Library symbol*] [*Library of Congress*] (LCLS)
SD Water Resour Comm Rep Invest ...	South Dakota. Water Resources Commission. Report of Investigations [*A publication*]
SdWau	Waubay Public Library, Waubay, SD [*Library symbol*] [*Library of Congress*] (LCLS)
SdWe	Webster Public Library, Webster, SD [*Library symbol*] [*Library of Congress*] (LCLS)
SdWes........	Wessington Springs Carnegie Public Library, Wessington Springs, SD [*Library symbol*] [*Library of Congress*] (LCLS)
SdWinT	Tripp County Library, Winner, SD [*Library symbol*] [*Library of Congress*] (LCLS)
SDWRF	Stochastic Dominance with Respect to Function [*Statistics*]
SD W Va....	United States District Court for the Southern District of West Virginia (DLA)
SDX	Satellite Data Exchange
SDX	Sedona [*Arizona*] [*Airport symbol*] (OAG)
S + DX......	Speech with Duplex Telegraph
SDXKDT...	Shanxi University Journal. Natural Science Edition [*A publication*]
SDY	Mount Marty College, Yankton, SD [*OCLC symbol*] (OCLC)
SDY	Sandy Corp. [*AMEX symbol*] (SPSG)
SDY	Sidney [*Montana*] [*Airport symbol*] (OAG)
SDY	Sidney, MT [*Location identifier*] [*FAA*] (FAAL)
SdY	Yankton Community Library, Yankton, SD [*Library symbol*] [*Library of Congress*] (LCLS)
SdYC.........	Yankton College, Yankton, SD [*Library symbol*] [*Library of Congress*] (LCLS)
SdYM	Mount Marty College, Yankton, SD [*Library symbol*] [*Library of Congress*] (LCLS)
SDYN	Staodyn, Inc. [*NASDAQ symbol*] (NQ)
SDZ	Southern Pines, NC [*Location identifier*] [*FAA*] (FAAL)
SDZ	Srpski Dijalektoloski Zbornik [*A publication*]
SDZ	Stardust Ventures [*Vancouver Stock Exchange symbol*]
SDZ	Stimmen der Zeit (BJA)
SD Zb........	Srpski Dijalektoloski Zbornik [*A publication*]
SE	British Charter [*United Kingdom*] [*ICAO designator*] (ICDA)
SE	Ferrocarriles Unidos del Sureste, SA de CV [*AAR code*]
SE	Sacris Erudiri. Jaarboek voor Godsdienstwetenschappen [*A publication*]
SE	Safety Equipment [*British military*] (DMA)
SE	Safety Evaluation (NRCH)
S & E.........	Salaries and Expenses
SE	Sales Engineer
SE	Saline Enema [*Medicine*]
SE	Sanford & Eastern Railroad [*AAR code*] [*Terminated*]
SE	Sanitary Engineer [*Academic degree*]
SE	Santos Dumont Experimental [*British military*] (DMA)
SE	Saorstat Eireann [*Irish Free State*]
SE	Saponification Equivalent [*Analytical chemistry*]
SE	Schleicher-Bruns [*Federal Republic of Germany*] [*ICAO aircraft manufacturer identifier*] (ICAO)
SE	School of Engineering (MCD)
SE	Sciences Ecclesiastiques [*A publication*]
S & E.........	Scientific and Engineering
S & E.........	Scientists and Engineers (RDA)
SE	Scouting Experimental [*British*] (DMA)
SE	Sea [*Maps and charts*]
SE	Second Entrance [*Theatrical slang*]
SE	Secretarial, Word Processing, and/or Medical Office Assistant Programs [*Association of Independent Colleges and Schools specialization code*]
SE	Securities Transaction [*Banking*]
SE	Seeing Eye [*An association*] (EA)
SE	Selenium [*Chemical element*]
SE	Seleucid Era (BJA)
SE	Self Employment [*Social Security Administration*] (OICC)
SE	Self-Evident Statement [*Used in correcting manuscripts, etc.*]
Se	Semeia [*A publication*]
Se	Semiotica [*A publication*]
SE	Senegal [*IYRU nationality code*] (IYR)
SE	Senior Editor [*Publishing*]
SE	September (ADA)
SE	Sequence of Events
SE	Series
SE	Series Statement [*Online database field identifier*]
SE	Service Engineer
SE	Service Equipment (AAG)
S & E.........	Services and Equipment
SE	Set
se	Seychelles [*bi (British Indian Ocean Territory) used in records cataloged before January 1978*] [*MARC country of publication code*] [*Library of Congress*] (LCCP)
SE	Shareholders' Equity [*Business term*]
SE	Sherritt Gordon Mines Ltd. [*Toronto Stock Exchange symbol*]
SE	Shielding Effectiveness (IEEE)
SE	Shift Engineer (NRCH)
SE	Shoot Emergence [*Botany*]
SE	Signal Excess (NVT)
SE	Single End
SE	Single-Ended, Cylindrical Boiler [*Navy*]
SE	Single Engine
SE	Single Entry [*Bookkeeping*]
SE	Slovenski Etnograf [*A publication*]
SE	Smoke Extract
SE	Social Education [*A publication*]
SE	Social Emotional
SE	Society of Engineers
SE	Society of Ethnobiology (EA)
SE	Socioeconomic
SE	Software Engineering (MCD)
SE	Soil Extract
SE	Solanaceae Enthusiasts (EA)
SE	Solar Ecliptic
SE	Solar Explorer [*NASA*]
SE	Solid Extract [*Pharmacy*]
SE	Solidaridad Espanola [*Spanish Solidarity*] [*Political party*] (PPW)
SE	Sonic Extract [*Cytology*]
SE	Southeast
SE	Southeastern Reporter [*National Reporter System*] [*A publication*] (DLA)
SE	Southern Europe (NATG)
SE	Sovetskaja Estonija [*A publication*]
SE	Sovetskaja Etnografija [*A publication*]
SE	Space Exploration (AAG)
SE	Spatial Emotional (Stimuli)
SE	Special Edition [*Car model designation*]
SE	Special Equipment
SE	Specialized Exhibition (IMH)
SE	Spectral Edge [*Cardiology*]
SE	Sphenoethmoidal [*Suture*] [*Medicine*]
SE	Spherical Equivalent
SE	Spin-Echo Scan [*Roentgenology*]
SE	Split End [*Football*]
SE	Stable Element
SE	Staff Engineer [*Navy*] [*British*] (ROG)
SE	Stage of Exhaustion [*of gas*] [*Medicine*]
SE	Stamped Envelope
SE	Standard English
SE	Standard Error
S/E	Standardization/Evaluation (AFM)
SE	Starch Equivalent
SE	Starter Electrode
SE	Stationary Eddy
SE	Status Enquiry [*British*]
SE	Status Epilepticus [*Medicine*]
SE	Steam Emulsion
SE	Stock Exchange
SE	Straight Edge [*Philately*]
SE	Studi Etruschi [*A publication*]
SE	Studia Estetyczne [*A publication*]
SE	Studia Evangelica [*A publication*]
SE	Studies in English [*A publication*]
SE	Subcontract Engineers (MCD)
SE	Subcritical Experiment [*Nuclear energy*]
se	Sugary Enhancer [*A gene in sweet corn*]
SE	Summer Emergency [*Vessel load line mark*]
SE	Sun Electric Corp. [*NYSE symbol*] (SPSG)
SE	Sunday Express [*United Kingdom*] [*A publication*]
SE	Superintending Engineer (ADA)
S & E.........	Supplies and Equipage [*Military*] (CINC)
SE	Support Equipment (AFM)
S & E.........	Surveillance and Entry
SE	Sustainer Engine (AAG)
SE	Sustaining Engineering
SE	Sweden [*Aircraft nationality and registration mark*] (FAAC)
SE	Sweden [*ANSI two-letter standard code*] (CNC)
SE	System Effectiveness [*Army*] (AABC)
SE	System Element (NASA)
SE	System Expansion [*In "Macintosh SE"*] [*Apple Computer, Inc.*]
SE	Systems Engineer [*or Engineering*] [*Data processing*]
S1E	Surfaced One Edge [*Technical drawings*]
SE2	Scientists and Engineers for Secure Energy (EA)
SEA...........	Clemson University, Clemson, SC [*OCLC symbol*] (OCLC)
SEA...........	Marine Manufacturers Safety Equipment Association (EA)
SEA...........	Safety Engineering Analysis (AFM)
SEA...........	Sailing Education Association
Sea	Sankt Eriks Arsbok [*A publication*]
SEA...........	Scandinavian Endodontic Association (EAIO)
SEA...........	Scanning Electrostatic Analysis (NASA)
SEA...........	Science and Education Administration [*Department of Agriculture*]
SEA...........	Scientific Exchange Agreement
SEA...........	Sea Echelon Area [*Navy*] (NVT)
SEA...........	Sea Education Association (EA)
SEA...........	Seashore Environmental Alliance
SEA...........	Seasonal Employees in Agriculture

SEA............ Seattle [*Washington*] [*Seismograph station code, US Geological Survey*] [*Closed*] (SEIS)
SEA............ Seattle/Tacoma [*Washington*] [*Airport symbol*] (OAG)
SEA............ Secondary Education Authority of Western Australia
SEA............ Securities Exchange Act [*1934*]
SEA............ Senior Enlisted Academy [*Navy*]
SEA............ Senior Enlisted Advisor [*Navy*]
SEA............ Senior Executives Association (EA)
SEA............ Service Educational Activities [*Military*] (AABC)
SEA............ Service Employers Association (EA)
SEA............ Sheep Erythrocyte Agglutination [*Test*]
SEA............ Sheltered Employment Allowance [*Australia*]
SEA............ Ship/Equipment/Alterations [*Navy*] (NG)
SEA............ Ships Editorial Association [*Navy*]
SEA............ Silicon Elastimeter Ablator (NASA)
SEA............ Sindicato de Escritores y Artistas [*Ecuador*]
SEA............ Single European Act [*EEC*]
SEA............ Socialist Educational Association [*British*]
SEA............ Societe d'Electronique et d'Automatique [*Became part of Compagnie Internationale d'Informatique*]
SEA............ Society for Education through Art [*British*]
SEA............ Society for the Elimination of Acronyms
SEA............ Society of Evangelical Agnostics (EA)
SEA............ Sociology of Education Association (EA)
SEA............ SONAR Evaluation and Assistance [*Teams*]
SEA............ Southeast Air, Inc. [*New Bedford, MA*] [*FAA designator*] (FAAC)
SEA............ Southeast Asia
SEA............ Southern Economic Association (EA)
SEA............ SPALT [*Special Projects Alterations*] Evaluation Area
SEA............ Special Equipment Authorization (AAG)
SEA............ Specific Energy Absorption
SEA............ Spherical Electrostatic Analyzer
SEA............ Standard Electronic Assembly
SEA............ Staphylococcal Enterotoxin A [*Medicine*]
SEA............ State Economic Area [*Bureau of Economic Analysis*] [*Department of Commerce*]
SEA............ State Education Agency [*Department of Education*]
SEA............ Static Error Analysis
SEA............ Statistical Energy Analysis [*or Approach*] [*Vibration analysis*]
SEA............ Students for Ecological Action
SEA............ Studies in Economic Analysis [*A publication*]
SEA............ Studies in Educational Administration [*A publication*] (APTA)
SEA............ Studies in English and American [*A publication*]
SEA............ Styrene and Ethylbenzene Association (EA)
SEA............ Subterranean Exploration Agency
SEAIC........ Sudden Enhancement of Atmospherics [*NASA*]
SEA............ Sulphur Extended Asphalt [*Paving material*]
SEA............ Survival Education Association (EA)
SEA............ Susquehanna Environmental Advocates (NRCH)
SEA............ Svensk Exegetisk Arsbok [*A publication*]
SEA............ System Engineering Analysis
SEA............ System Error Analysis
SEA............ Systems Effectiveness Analyzer (IEEE)
SEAA.......... Social Education Association of Australia
SEAAC........ Southeast Asian Art and Culture [*Foundation*]
SEAADSA ... Sea Automated Data Systems Activity [*Navy*]
SEAB.......... Seaboard Savings & Loan Association [*Virginia Beach, VA*] [*NASDAQ symbol*] (NQ)
SEABASS ... Ships Emergency Automatic Buoyancy and Stability System [*Seabass Ltd.*]
SEABEE.... Construction Battalion [*CB*] [*Acronym is a phonetic reference to a member of this Naval unit*]
SEABT ...... SEABEE Team [*Navy*] (NVT)
SEABU...... Southeast Asia Buildup (CINC)
Seab Vend ... Seaborne on Vendors and Purchasers [*9th ed.*] [*1926*] [*A publication*] (DLA)
Seabys Coin Bull ... Seaby's Coin and Medal Bulletin [*A publication*]
SEAC........ Seacoast
SEAC........ Social and Economic Archive Centre [*British*]
SEAC........ Society for Economic, Social, Cultural Study and Expansion in Central Africa
SEAC........ Society for Electroanalytical Chemistry
SEAC........ Southeast Archeological Center [*US Department of the Interior*] [*Research center*] (RCD)
SEAC........ Southeast Asia Center (EA)
SEAC........ Southeast Asia Command
SEAC........ Specialized Employability Assistance to Claimants (OICC)
SEAC........ Standards Eastern [*or Electronic*] Automatic Computer [*National Institute of Standards and Technology*]
SEAC........ Submarine Exercise Area Coordinator [*Navy*] (NVT)
SEACAD .. Sea Cadet Cruise [*Navy*] (NVT)
SEACDT ... Southeast Asia Collective Defense Treaty (AABC)
SEACE ...... Systeme Europeen d'Assurance-Credit a l'Exportation [*European System of Assurance Credit for Export*] [*Belgium*]
SEACF....... Support Equipment Assembly and Checkout Facility [*NASA*] (NASA)
SEACOM ... Southeast Asia Commonwealth
SEACOM ... Southeast Asia Communications (MCD)
SEACON... Seafloor Construction Experiment [*Navy*]

SEACOORD ... Southeast Asia Coordination Council [*Military*]
SEACOP ... Strategic Sealift Contingency Planning System [*Army*] (AABC)
SEACORE ... Southeast Asia Communications Research (MCD)
SEACS....... Search of Enemy Air Defense (MCD)
SEACS....... Ship Equipment Accounting System (MCD)
SE/ACT..... Southern Europe - ACTISUD [*Authority for the Coordination of Inland Transport in Southern Europe*] [*NATO*] (NATG)
SEAD........ Scottish Education and Action for Development (EAIO)
SEAD........ Seneca Army Depot [*New York*] (AABC)
SEAD........ Suppression of Enemy Air Defenses (AABC)
SEAD........ Survivable Electronic Air Defense
SEADAB.... Southeast Asia DataBase (MCD)
SEADAC... Seakeeping Data Analysis Center [*Navy*]
SEADAG... Southeast Asia Development Advisory Group [*Department of State*]
SEADCUG ... NAVSEA Data Communications Users Group [*Navy*]
SEADD...... South-East Asia Development Division [*Overseas Development Administration*] [*British*] (DS)
SEADEX ... Seaward Defense Exercise [*NATO*] (NATG)
SEADROP ... Small Expendable Air-Dropped Remote Ocean Platform [*Marine science*] (MSC)
SEADS ...... Shuttle Entry Air Data Sensor [*NASA*] (MCD)
SEADS ...... Shuttle Entry Air Data System [*or Subsystem*] (NASA)
SEADS ...... Survivable and Effective Airbreathing Defense [*Study*] (MCD)
SEADU...... Sea Duty
SEA-EX..... Sealift Express [*Military*]
SEAF .... Seafoods from Alaska, Inc. [*NASDAQ symbol*] (NQ)
SEAFAR.... Search and Automatic Track Fixed Array RADAR
SEAFDC.... South East Asian Fisheries Development Centre (EAIO)
SEAFDEC ... South East Asian Fisheries Development Centre
Sea Fish Res Stn (Haifa) Bull ... Sea Fisheries Research Station (Haifa). Bulletin [*A publication*]
Seafood Bus ... Seafood Business [*A publication*]
Seafood Export J ... Seafood Export Journal [*A publication*]
Seafood Merch ... Seafood Merchandising [*A publication*]
SEAFRON ... Sea Frontier
Sea Front ... Sea Frontiers [*A publication*]
SEAG........ Sea Galley Stores, Inc. [*NASDAQ symbol*] (NQ)
Seag Parl Reg ... Seager on Parliamentary Registration [*A publication*] (DLA)
Sea Grant Coll Tech Rep Univ Wis ... Sea Grant College Technical Report. University of Wisconsin [*A publication*]
Sea Grant LJ ... Sea Grant Law Journal [*A publication*] (DLA)
Sea Grant L & Pol'y J ... Sea Grant Law and Policy Journal [*A publication*] (DLA)
SEAGS ...... Southeast Asian Geotechnical Society (EAIO)
SEAIC .... Southeast Asia Information Center (NG)
SEAID .... Support Equipment Abbreviated Items Description [*NASA*] (NASA)
SEAIG .... Southeast Asia Information Group (AFM)
SEAIMP.... Solar Eclipse Atmospheric and Ionospheric Measurements Project (IEEE)
SEAISI ...... South East Asia Iron and Steel Institute (EA)
SEAITACS ... Southeast Asia Integrated Tactical Air Control System (CINC)
SEAJS .... Southeast Asian Journal of Sociology [*Singapore*] [*A publication*]
SEAJT....... South East Asia Journal of Theology [*A publication*]
SEAK........ Seahawk Oil International, Inc. [*NASDAQ symbol*] (NQ)
SEAL........ Los Alamos [*Ecuador*] [*ICAO location identifier*] (ICLI)
SEAL........ Sea, Air, and Land
SEAL........ Sea, Air, and Land Team [*Refers to Navy personnel trained in unconventional warfare*]
SEAL........ Seal Fleet, Inc. [*NASDAQ symbol*] (NQ)
SEAL........ Ship's Electronics Allowance List [*Navy*]
SEAL........ Signal Evaluation Airborne Laboratory [*FAA*]
SEAL........ Solar Energy Applications Laboratory [*Colorado State University*] [*Research center*] (RCD)
SEAL........ Standard Electronic Accounting Language [*Data processing*] (BUR)
SEAL........ Subsea Equipment Associates Limited [*Bermuda*]
SEALAB... Sea Laboratory
SEALF...... Semiempirical Absorption Loss Formula [*Radio*]
SEALF...... Southeast Asia Land Forces [*British*]
SEALITE .. Systematic Evaluation and Analysis of a LASER in a Test Environment (MCD)
SEALLINC ... Southeast Louisiana Library Network Cooperative [*Library network*]
SEALOB ... Sealift Obligation Report [*Army*]
SEALOCK ... Search, Locate, Communications, or Kill (MCD)
SEALR ...... Southeast Asia Logistic Requirement (AFM)
SEALS ...... Severe Environmental Air Launch Study (KSC)
SEALS....... Stored Energy Actuated Lift System
SEAM........ Ambato [*Ecuador*] [*ICAO location identifier*] (ICLI)
SEAM........ Seaman Furniture Co., Inc. [*Uniondale, NY*] [*NASDAQ symbol*] (NQ)
SEAM........ Sidewinder Expanded Acquisition Mode (MCD)
SEAM........ Society for the Emancipation of the American Male
SEAM........ Sociology and Economic Aspects of Medicine [*American Medical Association*] [*Information service or system*] (CRD)
SEAM........ Software Engineering and Management

SEAM........ Software Enhancement and Maintenance [*Contract*]
SEAM........ Southeast Asia Microfilm Project [*Library network*]
SEAM........ Subset Extraction and Association Measurement
SEAM........ Surface Environment and Mining Program
SEAMAP .. Systematic Exploration and Mapping Program [*National Oceanic and Atmospheric Administration*] (MSC)
SeaMARCI ... Sea Mapping and Remote Characterization I [*Oceanography*]
SEAMARF ... Southeast Asia Military Air Reservation Facility (CINC)
SEAMEC .. Southeast Asian Ministers of Education Council
Seamens J ... Seamen's Journal [*A publication*] (APTA)
SEAMES... Southeast Asian Ministers of Education Organization (EAIO)
SEAMES... Southeast Asian Ministers of Education Secretariat [*Thailand*]
SEAMEX .. Seamanship Exercise (NVT)
SEAMIC ... Southeast Asia Management Information Center [*Navy*]
SEAMINFO ... Surface Mining and Environment Information System [*University of Arizona*] (IID)
SEAMIST ... Seavan Management Information System
SEAMO..... South-East Asian Ministers of Education Organization
SEAMORE ... Southeast Asia Mohawk Revision Program [*Army aviation*]
SEAMS ..... Southeast Asian Mathematical Society [*Singapore, Singapore*]
SEAMS ..... System Effectiveness Assurance Management System (MCD)
SEAMUS .. Society for Electro-Acoustic Music in the United States (EA)
SEAN........ Ana Maria [*Ecuador*] [*ICAO location identifier*] (ICLI)
SEAN........ Scientific Event Alert Network [*Smithsonian Institution*] [*Washington, DC*] (MCD)
SEAN........ Strapdown Electrically Suspended Gyro Aerospace Navigation [*System*]
SEAN........ Syndicat des Enseignants Africains du Niger [*African Union of Teachers of Niger*]
Seanad Deb ... Seanad Debates [*Ireland*] [*A publication*]
SEAN Bull ... SEAN [*Scientific Event Alert Network*] Bulletin [*Washington, DC*] [*A publication*]
SEANC...... Southeast Asia NOTAM [*Notice to Airmen*] Center [*Military*]
Seance Pub Ann Acad Pharm ... Seance Publique Annuelle. Academie de Pharmacie [*A publication*]
Seanc Soc Belge Biol ... Seances. Societe Belge de Biologie [*A publication*]
Seanc Soc Fr Phys ... Seances. Societe Francaise de Physique [*A publication*]
SEANITEOPS ... Southeast Asia Night Operations [*Army*]
Sean O Cas ... Sean O'Casey Review [*A publication*]
SEAOC...... Structural Engineers Association of California (EA)
SEAOPSS ... Southeast Asia Operational Sensor System (MCD)
SEAOR...... Southeast Asia Operational Requirements (MCD)
SEAP........ Arapicos [*Ecuador*] [*ICAO location identifier*] (ICLI)
SEAP........ SEATO [*Southeast Asia Treaty Organization*] Administrative Publication
SEAP........ Securities and Exchange Authority of Pakistan (IMH)
SEAP........ Social Environment Assessment Policy [*Australia*]
SEAP........ Southeast Asia Program [*Cornell University*] [*Research center*] (RCD)
SEAP........ Special Economic Acquisition Provision [*Procurement*]
SEAPA ...... Society of Petroleum Engineers. American Institute of Mining, Metallurgical, and Petroleum Engineers. Papers [*A publication*]
SEAPA ...... Spectrothermal Emission Aerosol Particle Analyzer
SEAPAC... Sea Activated Parachute Automatic Crew Release (MCD)
SEAPADS ... Sea Planning Automated Data System
SEAPEX.... Southeast Asia Petroleum Exploration Society
SEAPG...... Support Equipment Acquisition Planning Group [*NASA*] (NASA)
SEAPRO ... Southeast Asia Programs Directorate
SEAPT ...... Seaport
Sea Pwr A .. Almanac of Seapower [*A publication*]
SeAQ .... Southeast Asia Quarterly [*A publication*]
SEAQ......... Stock Exchange Automated Quotation System [*London, England*]
SEAR........ Arajuno [*Ecuador*] [*ICAO location identifier*] (ICLI)
SEAR........ Safeguard Emergency Action Report [*Army*] (AABC)
SEAR........ Safety Evaluation Audit Report [*Nuclear energy*] (NRCH)
SEAR........ Summary Engineering Assessment Report (MCD)
SEAR........ System Engineering Analysis Report
SEAR........ Systematic Effort to Analyze Results
SEARA ...... Stockpile Evaluation and Reliability Assessment Program
SEARAM .. Semiactive RADAR Missile
Seara Med ... Seara Medica [*A publication*]
Seara Med Neurocir ... Seara Medica Neurocirurgica [*A publication*]
SEA RARE ... Sea Reinforcement and Resupply of Europe (MCD)
SEARC ...... Southeast Asia Regional Council
SEARCA ... SEAMEO Regional Center for Graduate Study and Research in Agriculture [*Research center*] [*Philippines*] (IRC)
SEARCA ... Southeast Asian Regional Center for Graduate Study and Research in Agriculture [*Information service or system*] [*Philippines*] (IID)
SEARCC .... SouthEast Asia Regional Computer Confederation (EA)
SEARCH... Science, Engineering, and Related Career Hints [*A publication*] [*Scientific Manpower Commission*]
SEARCH... Scientific Evaluation and Research of Charismatic Healing [*An association*] (EA)
SearcH....... Siberian Husky Eye Anomaly Research Committee (EA)
SEARCH... System for Electronic Analysis and Retrieval of Criminal Histories [*Project succeeded by National Crime Information Center*] [*Department of Justice*]

SEARCH... System Evaluation and Reliability Checker
SEARCH... System for Exploring Alternative Resource Commitments in Higher Education [*Data processing*]
SEARCH... System to Select Entries and Report to Customs Houses [*Australia*]
Search Agric Ent (Ithaca NY) ... Search Agriculture. Entomology (Ithaca, New York) [*A publication*]
Search Agric (Geneva NY) ... Search Agriculture (Geneva, New York) [*A publication*]
Search Agric NY State Agric Exp Stn (Ithaca) ... Search Agriculture. New York State Agricultural Experiment Station (Ithaca) [*A publication*]
SEARCHEX ... Sea/Air Search Exercise [*NATO*] (NATG)
SEARCHS ... Shuttle Engineering Approach/Rollout Control Hybrid Simulation (NASA)
Search & Seizure Bull ... Search and Seizure Bulletin [*A publication*] (DLA)
Search and Seizure L Rep ... Search and Seizure Law Report [*A publication*]
Search Together ... Searching Together [*A publication*]
SEAREQ ... Sea Requirement [*Canadian Navy*]
SEAREX..... Sea/Air Chemical Exchange [*Marine science*] (MSC)
SEARFS .... South East Asia Regional Feeder Service (DS)
Searle .... Searle's Supreme Court Reports [*1850-67*] [*Cape Colony*] [*A publication*] (DLA)
Searle Dig .. Searle's Minnesota Digest [*A publication*] (DLA)
Searle Sm... Searle and Smith's English Probate and Divorce Reports [*A publication*] (DLA)
Searle & Sm ... Searle and Smith's English Probate and Divorce Reports [*1859-60*] [*A publication*] (DLA)
Sears Found Marine Research Mem ... Sears Foundation for Marine Research. Memoir [*A publication*]
SEAS .... Ascazubi [*Ecuador*] [*ICAO location identifier*] (ICLI)
SEAS .... Centre of South-East Asian Studies [*University of Hull*] [*British*] (CB)
SEAS .... Science Accessories Corp. [*NASDAQ symbol*] (NQ)
SEAS .... Sea School [*Marine Corps*]
SEAS .... Seasons. Federation of Ontario Naturalists [*A publication*]
SEAS .... Selected Effects Armament Subsystem [*Army*] (RDA)
SEAS .... Ship/Equipment/Alterations Summary [*Navy*] (NG)
SEAS .... Shipboard Environmental Data Acquisition System [*National Oceanic and Atmospheric Administration*] (MSC)
SEAS .... Strategic Environmental Assessment System [*Environmental Protection Agency*]
SEAS .... Support Equipment Avionics System
SEAS .... Surveillance Environmental Acoustic Support [*Military*] (CAAL)
SEAS .... System Enhancement and Support [*Military*] (CAAL)
Se As Aff.... Southeast Asian Affairs [*Singapore*] [*A publication*]
SEASAME ... Southeast Asian Science and Mathematics Experiment [*RECSAM*]
SEASAR ... Sea Synthetic Aperture RADAR
SEASAT .... Sea Satellite [*NASA*]
SEASC...... Scientific Exploration of the Atlantic Shelf Committee
Se As Chron ... Southeast Asia Chronicle [*A publication*]
SEASCO ... Southeast Asia Science Cooperation Office
SEASET .... Separate Effects and Systems Effects Tests [*Nuclear energy*] (NRCH)
SEASIA ..... Southeast Asia (NG)
SE Asia ..... Southeast Asia Chronicle [*A publication*]
SE Asia J Th ... Southeast Asia Journal of Theology [*A publication*]
Se As Iron Steel Inst Q ... Southeast Asia Iron and Steel Institute Quarterly [*Singapore*] [*A publication*]
Se As J Soc Sci ... Southeast Asian Journal of Social Science [*Singapore*] [*A publication*]
Se As J Theo ... South East Asia Journal of Theology [*Singapore*] [*A publication*]
Sea & Sm ... Searle and Smith's English Probate and Divorce Reports [*A publication*] (DLA)
S E As R..... South East Asian Review [*India*] [*A publication*]
S E As Stud ... South East Asian Studies [*Kyoto*] [*A publication*]
SEASTAG ... Southeast Asia Treaty Organization Standardization Agreement
SEAT .... Atacames [*Ecuador*] [*ICAO location identifier*] (ICLI)
SEAT .... Sociedad Espanol de Automoviles de Turismo [*Spanish automobile manufacturer; acronym used as name of its cars*]
SEAT .... Standardization and Evaluation Assistance Team [*Military*]
SEATA ...... Sea Technology [*A publication*]
SEATAC ... Southeast Asian Agency for Regional Transport and Communications Development (EAIO)
SEATAF.... Southern European Atomic Task Force [*Military*]
SEATAR ... Search and Automatic Track Array RADAR
SEATAR ... Studies on East Asia Tectonics and Resources [*Marine science*] (MSC)
SEATEC ... Sea Test and Evaluation Capability [*Navy*] (CAAL)
SEATEC ... South East Asia Technology Co. Ltd. [*Thailand*] (DS)
Sea Technol ... Sea Technology [*A publication*]
SEATELCOM ... Southeast Asia Telecommunications System [*Military*] (AABC)
Seat F Ch ... Seaton's Forms in Chancery [*A publication*] (DLA)
SEATIC..... Southeast Asia Translation and Interrogation Center [*Navy*]
SEATO...... Southeast Asia Treaty Organization (DS)

SEATO Med Res Monogr ... Southeast Asia Treaty Organization. Medical Research Monograph [*A publication*]
Seatrade BR ... Seatrade Business Review [*A publication*]
Seatrade S ... Fuel Economy. A Seatrade Study [*A publication*]
Seatrade We ... Seatrade Week [*A publication*]
SEATS....... Shubert Entertainment and Arts Ticketing System [*National computerized theatre-ticket selling system*]
SEATS....... Special Education Administration Task Simulation Game
SEATS....... Stock Exchange Automated Trading System [*Australia*]
Seattl Bsn... Seattle Business [*A publication*]
(Seattle) Q ... Quarterly Review (Seattle) [*A publication*]
Seattle Sym ... Seattle Symphony Orchestra. Program Notes [*A publication*]
Seattle T.... Seattle Times [*A publication*]
Sea Vend.... Seaborne on Vendors and Purchasers [*9th ed.*] [*1926*] [*A publication*]   (DLA)
Sea View Hosp Bull ... Sea View Hospital. Bulletin [*A publication*]
SEAWARS ... Seawater Activated Release System [*Navy*]   (CAAL)
Seaway Rev ... Seaway Review [*A publication*]
SEAWBS... Southeast Asia Wideband System [*Military*]
SEAWEA .. Sea and Weather Observations [*Navy*]   (NVT)
SEA/W/O MEPS ... South Eastern Alaska/Washington/Oregon Minimum Earned Premium Scale [*Aviation*]   (AIA)
SEAX........ Seaxe Energy Corp. [*Jackson, MS*] [*NASDAQ symbol*]   (NQ)
SEAX........ Span East Airlines, Inc. [*Air carrier designation symbol*]
Sea Yrbk .... Seatrade North American Yearbook [*A publication*]
SEB............ Scientific Equipment Bay [*NASA*]   (KSC)
SEB............ Scottish Examining Board   (DCTA)
SEB............ Seaboard Corp. [*AMEX symbol*]   (SPSG)
SEB............ Sebenico [*Yugoslavia*] [*Seismograph station code, US Geological Survey*] [*Closed*]   (SEIS)
SEB............ Sebha [*Libya*] [*Airport symbol*]   (OAG)
Seb .... Sebir [*or Sebirin*]   (BJA)
SEB............ Secondary Education Board
SEB............ Selective Enlistment Bonus [*Navy*]   (NVT)
SEB............ Single-Ended Boiler   (DS)
SEB............ Skandinaviska Enskilda Banken [*Sweden*]
SEB............ Social and Emotional Behavior
SEB............ Societe des Etudes Bloyennes   (EAIO)
SEB............ Society for Economic Botany   (EA)
SEB............ Society for Experimental Biology   (EAIO)
SEB............ Socio-Economic Benefit
SEB............ Software Engineering Bibliographic Database [*Air Force Systems Command*] [*Information service or system*]   (CRD)
SEB............ Source Evaluation Board [*NASA*]
SEB............ South Equatorial Belt [*Planet Jupiter*]
SEB............ Special Enlistment Bonus   (MCD)
SEB............ Staphylococcal Enterotoxin B [*Medicine*]
SEB............ Statistische Studien (Brussels) [*A publication*]
SEB............ Strip Electron Beam
SEB............ Support Equipment Building [*NASA*]   (NASA)
SEB............ Support Equipment Bulletin   (MCD)
SEB............ System Error Bridge
SEB............ Systems Engineering Branch [*NASA*]   (NASA)
SEBA........ Babahoyo [*Ecuador*] [*ICAO location identifier*]   (ICLI)
SEBA........ Staphylococcal Enterotoxin B Antisera [*Medicine*]
SEBAC...... State Ethnic Broadcasting Advisory Council [*Australia*]
SEBAn....... Societe d'Emulation de Bruges. Annales [*A publication*]
Sebast Med ... Sebastianus Medices [*Flourished, 16th century*] [*Authority cited in pre-1607 legal work*]   (DSA)
Sebast Sap ... Sebastianus Sapia [*Deceased, 1523*] [*Authority cited in pre-1607 legal work*]   (DSA)
Sebast Vant ... Sebastianus Vantius [*Flourished, 16th century*] [*Authority cited in pre-1607 legal work*]   (DSA)
SEBBETSI ... Serikat Buruh Beras dan Seluruh Indonesia [*Rice and Tapioca Workers' Union of Indonesia*]
SEBC......... Bahia De Caraquez [*Ecuador*] [*ICAO location identifier*]   (ICLI)
SEBC......... South-Eastern Bible College [*Florida*]
SEBD........ Bola De Oro [*Ecuador*] [*ICAO location identifier*]   (ICLI)
SEBD........ Software Engineering Bibliographic Data Base [*Data and Analysis Center for Software*] [*Information service or system*]
SEBDA...... Serikat Buruh Daerah Autonoom [*Civil Servants' Union*] [*Indonesia*]
SEBE......... La Beata [*Ecuador*] [*ICAO location identifier*]   (ICLI)
SEbE......... Southeast by East
SEB/EB..... Economic Botany. New York Botanical Garden for the Society for Economic Botany [*A publication*]
SEBH........ Balao Chico [*Ecuador*] [*ICAO location identifier*]   (ICLI)
SEBI .... Boliche [*Ecuador*] [*ICAO location identifier*]   (ICLI)
SEBIC....... Sustained Electron Bombardment-Induced Conductivity
SEBL .... Self-Emptying Blind Loop [*Gastroenterology*]
SEBM........ Society for Experimental Biology and Medicine   (EA)
SEBQ........ Senior Enlisted Bachelor Quarters [*Army*]   (AABC)
SEBS .... Single-Ended Boiler Survey   (DS)
SEbS......... Southeast by South
SEBS .... Submarine Emergency Buoyancy System
Seb Sapi..... Sebastianus Sapia [*Deceased, 1523*] [*Authority cited in pre-1607 legal work*]   (DSA)
SEB Symp ... Symposia. Society for Experimental Biology [*A publication*]

SEBT .... El Batan [*Ecuador*] [*ICAO location identifier*]   (ICLI)
Seb Trade-Marks ... Sebastian on Trade-Marks [*A publication*]   (DLA)
Seb Tr M ... Sebastian on Trade-Marks [*5th ed.*] [*1911*] [*A publication*]   (DLA)
SEBUA...... Seibutsu Butsuri [*A publication*]
SEBUMI ... Serikat Buruh Minjak, Stanvac [*Oil Workers' Union, Stanvac*] [*Indonesia*]
SEBV .... Solder End Ball Valve
Seb Vant .... Sebastianus Vantius [*Flourished, 16th century*] [*Authority cited in pre-1607 legal work*]   (DSA)
s-ec--- .... Ecuador [*MARC geographic area code*] [*Library of Congress*]   (LCCP)
SEC............ Safeguards Equipment Cabinet   (IEEE)
SEC............ Sanitary Engineering Center
SEC............ Scandinavian Episcopal Conference   (EAIO)
S & EC .... Science & Engineering Consultants [*Reston, VA*]   (TSSD)
SEC............ Scientific and Engineering Computation
SEC............ Scientific Estimates Committee [*Military*]   (AABC)
SeC............ Scuola e Cultura del Mondo [*A publication*]
SEC............ SEC: Bi-Monthly Magazine for Employees of the State Electricity Commission of Victoria [*A publication*]   (APTA)
SEC............ Secant
SEC............ Second   (AFM)
Se C............ Second Coming [*A publication*]
Sec............. Secondary [*Chemistry*]
SEC............ Secondary
SEC............ Secondary Electron Conduction [*Television camera system*]
SEC............ Secondary Emission Conductivity
SEC............ Secret   (AFM)
SEC............ Secretariat
SEC............ Secretary [*A publication*]
SEC............ Secretary   (EY)
SEC............ Section
SEC............ Sector
SEC............ Secular
SEC............ Secundum [*According To*] [*Latin*]
SEC............ Secure   (KSC)
S & EC .... Securities and Exchange Commission
S & EC .... Securities and Exchange Commission
SEC............ Securities and Exchange Commission Decisions and Reports [*A publication*]   (DLA)
SEC............ Securities and Exchange Commission, Washington, DC [*OCLC symbol*]   (OCLC)
SEC............ Security   (AAG)
Sec............. Secus [*Otherwise*] [*Latin*]   (ILCA)
SEC............ Sensormatic Canada Ltd. [*Toronto Stock Exchange symbol*]
SEC............ Sequential Events Controller [*NASA*]   (NASA)
SEC............ Shaftless Expander-Compressor
SEC............ Simple Electronic Computer [*Birkbeck College*] [*London, England*]   (DEN)
SEC............ Single Error Correcting
SEC............ Size Exclusion Chromatography
SEC............ Social Economic Council [*Sociaal Economische Raad*] [*Netherlands*]
SEC............ Societe de l'Ecole des Chartes [*A publication*]
SEC............ Societe des Ecrivains Canadiens [*Society of Canadian Writers*]
SEC............ Societe Europeenne de Culture [*European Society of Culture - ESC*]   (EAIO)
SEC............ Society for Educative Communication   (EA)
SEC............ Society of Exchange Counselors   (EA)
SEC............ Soft Elastic Capsule [*Pharmacy*]
SEC............ Solar Energy Collector
SEC............ Solar Energy Concentrator
SEC............ Solid Electrolyte Capacitor
SEC............ Source Evaluation Committee [*NASA*]   (NASA)
SEC............ South Equatorial Current [*Oceanography*]   (MSC)
SEC............ Southeastern Command
SEC............ Southeastern Commuter Airlines [*Auburn, AL*] [*FAA designator*]   (FAAC)
SEC............ Southeastern Conference   (EA)
SEC............ Space Environmental Chamber   (AAG)
SEC............ Special Emergency Campaign [*Red Cross fund-raising*]
SEC............ Spectroelectrochemistry
SEC............ Staff Evaluation Coordinators   (MCD)
SEC............ Standard Error of Calibration
SEC............ Standards and Ethics Commission [*American Occupational Therapy Association*]
SEC............ Standing with Eyes Closed [*Equilibrium test*]
SEC............ State Electoral Council [*Australia*]
SEC............ Sterling Electronics Corporation [*AMEX symbol*]   (SPSG)
SEC............ Stevens Creek [*California*] [*Seismograph station code, US Geological Survey*]   (SEIS)
SEC............ Stock Exchange Council [*British*]
SEC............ Structural Engineers Councils   (KSC)
SEC............ Submarine Element Coordinator   (NVT)
SEC............ Sulphur Export Corporation [*An association*]   (EA)
SEC............ Supply Executive Committee [*NATO*]   (NATG)
SEC............ Support Equipment Change   (MCD)
SEC............ Switch Element Controller [*Telecommunications*]

SEC........... Switching Equipment Congestion [*Telecommunications*] (TEL)
SECA........ Catarama [*Ecuador*] [*ICAO location identifier*] (ICLI)
SECA........ Self-Employment Contributions Act of 1954 [*under which self-employed persons contribute to OASDI coverage for themselves*]
SECA........ Shiatsu Education Center of America [*Later, Ohashi Institute - OI*] (EA)
SECA........ Solar Energy Construction Association (EA)
SECA........ Southern Educational Communications Authority [*Television network*] [*Obsolete*]
SECA........ Sportbike Enthusiast Club of America (EA)
SECAB...... Secretaria Ejecutiva Permanente del Convenio Andres Bello [*Permanent Executive Secretariat of the Andres Bello Convention*] (EAIO)
SECAC...... Sectional Aeronautical Chart
SEC Accounting R CCH ... SEC [*Securities and Exchange Commission*] Accounting Rules. Commerce Clearing House [*A publication*]
SECAD...... Support Equipment Concept Approval Data
SECAL...... Sectoral Adjustment Loan [*World Bank*]
SECAL...... Selected Calling System [*Military*] (AFM)
SECAM..... Sequence Electronique Couleur avec Memoire [*Color Sequence with Memory*] [*French color television system*]
SECAM..... Systeme Electronique Couleur avec Memoire [*French broadcast color standard*]
SECAN...... Standing Group Communication Security and Evaluation Agency Washington
SECANT ... Separation and Control of Aircraft Using Nonsynchronous Techniques [*Collision avoidance*] [*RCA*]
SECAP ...... Systems Experiment Correlation and Analysis Program (MCD)
SECAR ...... Secondary RADAR (IEEE)
SECARMY ... Secretary of the Army
SEC ART... Secundum Artem [*According to the Art*] [*Latin*]
SECAS....... Ship Equipment Configuration Accounting System (NVT)
SECB........ Security Bancorp, Inc. [*NASDAQ symbol*] (NQ)
Sec Bk Judg ... Second Book of Judgments (Huxley) [*England*] [*A publication*] (DLA)
SECC......... Condorcocha [*Ecuador*] [*ICAO location identifier*] (ICLI)
SECC......... Safe Energy Communication Council (EA)
SECC......... Scientific and Engineering Computing Council (MCD)
SECC......... South Equatorial Countercurrent [*Oceanography*] (MSC)
SECC......... Studies in Eighteenth-Century Culture [*A publication*]
SECC......... Sun Equities Corporation [*NASDAQ symbol*] (NQ)
SECC......... Survivable Enduring Command and Control
SECCA ...... Southeastern Center for Contemporary Art [*North Carolina*]
Sec City...... Second City [*A publication*]
SEC Compl (P-H) ... Securities and Exchange Commission Compliance (Prentice-Hall, Inc.) [*A publication*] (DLA)
SECD........ Secondary (AABC)
SECD........ Secured (ROG)
SECDA...... Southeastern Community Development Association (EA)
SECDED ... Single-BIT [*Binary Digit*] Error Correction and Double-BIT [*Binary Digit*] Error Detection
SECDEF.... Secretary of Defense
Sec D & M ... Security Distributing and Marketing [*A publication*]
SEC Docket ... Securities and Exchange Commission Docket [*A publication*] (DLA)
Secd Pt Edw III ... Year Books, Part III [*England*] [*A publication*] (DLA)
Secd Pt H VI ... Year Books, Part VIII [*England*] [*A publication*] (DLA)
SECDY...... Secondary
SECE........ Santa Cecilia [*Ecuador*] [*ICAO location identifier*] (ICLI)
SECE......... Selfhelp of Emigres from Central Europe (EA)
Sec Ed .... Secondary Education [*A publication*]
SECED...... Society for Earthquake and Civil Engineering Dynamics [*British*]
SECEM ..... Support Equipment Cost Effectiveness Model (MCD)
Sec & Ex C ... Securities and Exchange Commission (DLA)
Sec & Fed Corp L Rep ... Securities and Federal Corporate Law Report [*A publication*]
SECFLT .... Second Fleet [*Atlantic*] [*Navy*]
SECG........ Silver Eureka Corporation [*NASDAQ symbol*] (NQ)
SECGRUHQ ... Security Group Headquarters
SECH .... Chone [*Ecuador*] [*ICAO location identifier*] (ICLI)
SECH .... Secant, Hyperbolic
Sechenov Physiol J USSR ... Sechenov. Physiological Journal of the USSR [*A publication*]
SECHT...... Scoping Emergency Cooling Heat Transfer [*Nuclear energy*] (KSC)
Sec Ind Digest ... Secondary Industries Digest [*A publication*] (APTA)
Sec Ind R.... Securities Industry Review [*Singapore*] [*A publication*]
SECINSP .. Security Inspection [*Military*] (NVT)
Sec Int........ Secretary of the Interior (DLA)
SECIR .... Semiautomatic Encoding of Chemistry for Information Retrieval (DIT)
SECIT........ Syndicat des Employes Indigenes du Commerce du Togo [*Union of Indigenous Employees of Commerce of Togo*]
SECJA....... Southern Economic Journal [*United States*] [*A publication*]
SEC Jud Dec ... Securities and Exchange Commission Judicial Decisions [*A publication*] (DLA)
SECL .... Chiles [*Ecuador*] [*ICAO location identifier*] (ICLI)

SECLA ...... Southeastern Connecticut Library Association [*Library network*]
SEC LEG... Secundum Legem [*According to Law*] [*Latin*]
Sec L Rev ... Securities Law Review [*A publication*]
SECLT....... Second Lieutenant [*Army*]
SECM........ Clementina [*Ecuador*] [*ICAO location identifier*] (ICLI)
SECM........ School of English Church Music [*Later, RSCM*]
SECM........ Secom General Corp. [*NASDAQ symbol*] (NQ)
SEC Mag ... SEC Magazine: Journal of the State Electricity Commission of Victoria [*A publication*] (APTA)
SECMem ... Societe d'Emulation de Cambrai. Memoires [*A publication*]
Sec Mgmt... Security Management [*A publication*]
Sec Mgt...... Security Management [*A publication*]
SECMR ..... Sector Manager [*Aviation*] (FAAC)
SECN........ Section (ROG)
SECN........ Sex Education Coalition News [*A publication*]
SECN......... Supplements to Electroencephalography and Clinical Neurophysiology [*Elsevier Book Series*] [*A publication*]
SECNA...... Secretary of the Navy (NOAA)
SEC NAT .. Secundum Naturam [*According to Nature*] [*Latin*]
SECNAV ... Secretary of the Navy
SECNAVINST ... Secretary of the Navy Instruction
SEC News ... SEC [*US Securities and Exchange Commission*] News Digest [*A publication*]
SECNY...... Sales Executives Club of New York (EA)
SECO......... Coca [*Ecuador*] [*ICAO location identifier*] (ICLI)
SECO........ Securities and Exchange Commission
SECO........ Securities and Exchange Commission Organization
SECO........ Self-Regulating Error-Correct Coder-Decoder
SECO........ Sequential Coding
SECO........ Sequential Control [*Teletype*] [*Data processing*]
SECO........ Station Engineering Control Office [*Telecommunications*] (TEL)
SECO........ Steam and Electric Cogeneration [*Power source*]
SECO........ Sustainer-Engine Cutoff [*Aerospace*]
SECOBI .... Servicio de Consulta a Bancos de Informacion [*Database Consultation Service*] [*Information service or system*] [*Mexico*] (IID)
SECOFF.... Section Office
SECOIN.... Security Consultants International
SECOL...... Southeastern Conference on Linguistics
SECOLAS ... Southeastern Conference on Latin American Studies [*United States*]
SECOLAS A ... SECOLAS [*Southeastern Conference on Latin American Studies*] Annals [*A publication*]
SECOLAS/SELA ... South Eastern Latin Americanist. Southeastern Conference on Latin American Studies [*A publication*]
SECOLR ... SECOL [*Southeastern Conference on Linguistics*] Review [*A publication*]
SECOM..... School Emergency Communication
SECOM..... Secretaria de Comercio [*Secretariat of Commerce*] [*Spanish*]
SECOMO ... Software Engineering Cost Model
SECON..... Secondary Electron Conduction [*Television camera system*]
Secondary Teach ... Secondary Teacher [*A publication*] (APTA)
Second Cent ... Second Century [*A publication*]
Second Ed .. Secondary Education [*A publication*]
Second Opin Health Care Issues ... Second Opinions of Health Care Issues [*A publication*]
Second Teach ... Secondary Teacher [*A publication*]
S Econ J ..... Southern Economic Journal [*A publication*]
SECOR...... Sequential Collation [*or Collection*] of Ranges [*Army*]
SECOR...... Sequential Correlation
SECOR...... Sequential Cosine Ranging [*System*] (MUGU)
SECORD... Secure Voice Cord Board [*Telecommunications*] (TEL)
SECP .... [*Division of*] Shore Establishment and Civilian Personnel [*Navy*]
SECP .... State Energy Conservation Program
SecPac..... Security Pacific [*Bank*] (ECON)
SECPR...... Standard External Cardiopulmonary Resuscitation
SECPS...... Secondary Propulsion System [*NASA*] (KSC)
SECR........ Curaray [*Ecuador*] [*ICAO location identifier*] (ICLI)
SECR........ Secor Bank, Federal Savings Bank [*NASDAQ symbol*] (NQ)
SECR........ Secretariat
SE & CR ... Southeastern & Chatham Railway [*Nickname: Seldom Ever Caught Running*]
SECRA ...... Secondary RADAR [*RADAR beacon*]
SEC REG... Secundum Regulam [*According to Rule*] [*Latin*]
Sec Reg Guide ... Securities Regulation Guide [*Prentice-Hall, Inc.*] [*A publication*] (DLA)
Sec Reg Guide P-H ... Securities Regulation Guide. Prentice-Hall [*A publication*]
Sec Reg LJ ... Securities Regulation Law Journal [*A publication*]
Sec Reg & L Rep ... Securities Regulation and Law Reports [*Bureau of National Affairs*] [*A publication*]
Sec Reg & L Rep BNA ... Securities Regulation and Law Report. Bureau of National Affairs [*A publication*]
Sec Reg & Trans ... Securities Regulations and Transfer Report [*A publication*]
SECREP.... Regional Representative of the Secretary of Transportation
SECRG ...... Securing
SECRL....... Secretarial

Secr Pap Int Wheat Counc ... Secretariat Papers. International Wheat Council [*A publication*]
SECS .... Seagrass Ecosystems Component Study [*Marine science*] (MSC)
SECS .... Selective Electron-Capture Sensitization [*Analytical chemistry*]
SECS .... Sequential Events Control System [*NASA*] (KSC)
SECS .... Shuttle Events Control Subsystem [*NASA*] (NASA)
SECS .... Simulation and Evaluation of Chemical Synthesis [*Data processing*]
SECS .... Solar Electric Communication Satellite
SECS .... Space Environmental Control System (AAG)
SECSTA ...... Stem Elevated Camera System
SECSTA ...... Naval Security Station
SECSW ..... Science and Engineering Committee for a Secure World (EA)
SECSY .... Spin-Echo Correlated Spectroscopy
SECT .... Secretariat
SECT .... Section (KSC)
SECT .... Submarine Emergency Communications Transmitter
SECTAM .. Sterile Environmental Control Technology Applications to Medicine
SECTASKFLT ... Second Task Fleet
SECTBASE ... Section Base [*Navy*]
SECTDQ ... Centro Internacional de Agricultura Tropical [*CIAT*]. Series EE [*A publication*]
Sec Teach ... Secondary Teacher [*A publication*] (APTA)
Sec Teacher ... Secondary Teacher [*A publication*] (APTA)
SECTL .... Secretarial
SECTLZD ... Sectionalized
SECTY .... Secretary
SECU .... Cuenca [*Ecuador*] [*ICAO location identifier*] (ICLI)
SECU .... Slave Emulator Control Unit
SEC(UN) ... Secretariat of the United Nations
SECURE ... Systems Evaluation Code Under Radiation Environment
Security Surv ... Security Surveyor [*A publication*]
Secur Manage ... Security Management [*A publication*]
Secur Med Trav ... Securite et Medecine du Travail [*A publication*]
Secur R Law ... Securities Regulation Law Journal [*A publication*]
SECUS ...... Supreme Emblem Club of the United States (EA)
SECWAR .. Secretary of War [*Obsolete*]
Sec Wave ... Second Wave [*A publication*]
SECWG ..... South Eastern Conservation Working Group [*Australia*]
Sec World .. Security World [*A publication*]
SECX .... Southern Electronics Corporation [*Tucker, GA*] [*NASDAQ symbol*] (NQ)
SECY .... Secretary
SECY .... Security
SED .... Sale/Engineering/Development [*Honda*] [*Automotive engineering*]
SED .... Sanitary Engineering Division [*MIT*] (MCD)
SED .... Saturn Electrostatic Discharges [*Planetary science*]
SED .... Scarborough Board of Education [*Professional Education Library*] [*UTLAS symbol*]
SED .... Scottish Education Department
SED .... Sedan (AAG)
SED .... Sedative [*Medicine*] (ROG)
SED .... Seddin [*German Democratic Republic*] [*Later, NGK*] [*Geomagnetic observatory code*]
Sed .... Sedes [*A Stool*] [*Medicine*]
SED .... Sediment
SED .... Sedition [*FBI standardized term*]
SED .... Sedona Air Center [*West Sedona, AZ*] [*FAA designator*] (FAAC)
SED .... Segmented Expanding Die (MCD)
SED .... Semiequilibrium Dialysis [*Physical chemistry*]
SED .... Sensor Evolutionary Development (MCD)
SED .... Seriously [*or Severely*] Emotionally Disturbed
SED .... Shipper's Export Declaration [*Customs Service*]
SED .... Shore Establishments Division [*Navy*]
SED .... Skin Erythema Dose [*Medicine*]
SED .... Software Engineering Data [*Data and Analysis Center for Software*] [*Information service or system*]
SED .... Solar Energy Density
SED .... Sound Energy Density
SED .... Sozialistische Einheitspartei Deutschlands [*Socialist Unity Party of Germany*] [*German Democratic Republic*] [*Political party*] (PPW)
SED .... Space Environment Division [*NASA*]
SED .... Special Electrical Devices (AABC)
SED ...... Spectral Energy Distribution
SED .... Spondyloepiphysial Dysplasia [*Medicine*]
SED .... Staphylococcal Enterotoxin D [*Medicine*]
SED .... State Executive Director
SED .... Status Entry Device [*Telecommunications*] (TEL)
SED .... Stray Energy Detector
SED .... Students for Economic Democracy (EA)
SED .... Sun Entertainment [*Vancouver Stock Exchange symbol*]
SED .... Survey of English Dialects [*A publication*]
SED .... Swansea East Dock [*Welsh depot code*]
SED .... System Engineering Division [*Apollo Spacecraft Program Office*]
Secd .... System Entry Date [*Military*] (AFIT)

SED .... Systems Effectiveness Demonstration (NG)
SE 2d .... Southeastern Reporter, Second Series [*A publication*] (DLA)
SEDA .... Safety Equipment Distributors Association (EA)
SEDA .... Side Effects of Drugs. Annual [*Elsevier Book Series*] [*A publication*]
SEDA .... State Emergency Defense Airlift
SEDA .... Structured Exploratory Data Analysis
Sedalia N H Soc B ... Sedalia Natural History Society. Bulletin [*A publication*]
SEDAM ..... Societe d'Etudes et de Development des Aeroglisseurs Marins Terrestres et Amphibies [*French*] (MCD)
SEDAR ...... Shipborne Electronic Deflection Array RADAR (MCD)
SEDAS ...... Spurious Emission Detection Acquisition System (MCD)
SEDB .... Singapore Economic Development Board (DS)
SEDC .... Society for Emotional Development in Children [*Canada*]
SEDC .... Steam Engine Direct Connected (MSA)
SEDCOR .. Specialty Electronics Development Corporation
SEDD .... Systems Evaluation and Development Division [*NASA*]
SEDES ...... Societe d'Editions d'Enseignement Superieur [*A publication*]
SEDES ...... Societe d'Etudes pour le Developpement Economique et Social [*Society for the Study of Economic and Social Development*] [*Information service or system*] (IID)
SEDFC ...... Steve Earle and Dukes Fan Organization (EA)
SEDFRE .... Scholarship, Education, and Defense Fund for Racial Equality
Sedg Dam .. Sedgwick on the Measure of Damage [*A publication*] (DLA)
Sed Geol .... Sedimentary Geology [*A publication*]
Sedg L Cas ... Sedgwick's Leading Cases on Damages [*A publication*] (DLA)
Sedg L Cas ... Sedgwick's Leading Cases on Real Property [*A publication*] (DLA)
Sedg Stat Law ... Sedgwick on Statutory and Constitutional Law [*A publication*] (DLA)
Sedg St & Const Law ... Sedgwick on Statutory and Constitutional Law [*A publication*] (DLA)
Sedg & W Tit ... Sedgwick and Wait on the Trial of Title to Land [*A publication*] (DLA)
Sedg & W Tr Title Land ... Sedgwick and Wait on the Trial of Title to Land [*A publication*] (DLA)
SEDIC .... Sociedad Espanola de Documentacion e Informacion Cientifica [*Spanish Society for Documentation and Information Sciences*] [*Information service or system*] (IID)
Sediment Ge ... Sedimentary Geology [*A publication*]
Sediment Geol ... Sedimentary Geology [*A publication*]
Sedimentol ... Sedimentology [*A publication*]
SEDIS .... Service Information-Diffusion [*Information Dissemination Office*] [*National Institute for Research in Informatics and Automation*] [*Information service or system*] (IID)
SEDIS .... Surface Emitter Detection, Identification System [*Navy*]
SEDIT .... Sophisticated String Editor (IEEE)
SEDL .... Southwest Educational Development Laboratory (EA)
SEDM .... Society for Experimental and Descriptive Malacology (EA)
SEDM .... Status Entry Device Multiplexer [*Telecommunications*] (TEL)
SEDME ...... Survey Electronics Distance Measuring Equipment
SEDME ...... Surveying Equipment Distance Measuring Electronic (MCD)
SEDOR ...... Spin Echo Double Resonance [*Physics*]
SEDP .... Support for Engineer Development Priorities (MCD)
SEDPC .... Scientific and Engineering Data Processing Center
SEDR .... Science Education Development and Research Division [*National Science Foundation*] (GRD)
SEDR .... Supplementary Experiment Data Record [*Aerospace*]
SEDR .... System Effective Data Rate (BUR)
SEDR .... Systems Engineering Department Report (IEEE)
SEDS .... Social and Economic Development Strategy
SEDS .... Social-Emotional Dimension Scale [*Behavior problems test*]
SEDS .... Society for Educational Data Systems [*Later, SDE*]
SEDS .... Space Electronics Detection System (KSC)
SEDS .... State Energy Data System [*Department of Energy*] [*Database*]
SEDS .... Students for the Exploration and Development of Space (EA)
SEDS .... Support Equipment Data System
SEDS .... System Effectiveness Data System [*Air Force*]
SEDSCAF ... Standard ELINT Data System Codes and Format (NVT)
SEE .... San Diego/Santee, CA [*Location identifier*] [*FAA*] (FAAL)
SEE .... Sealed Air Corp. [*NYSE symbol*] (SPSG)
SEE .... Secondary Electron Emission
SEE .... Seeing Essential English [*Sign language system for the hearing impaired*]
SEE .... Senior Environmental Employment Program [*Environmental Protection Agency*]
SEE .... Signals Experimental Establishment [*British military*] (DMA)
SEE .... Signing Exact English [*Sign language system for the hearing impaired*]
SEE .... Small Emplacement Excavations [*or Excavator*] [*Army*]
SEE .... Societe d'Etudes et d'Expansion [*Studies and Expansion Society - SES*] [*Later, Et Ex*] (EAIO)
SEE .... Societie pour l'Expansion des Exportations [*Export Development Corp.*] [*Canada*]
SEE .... Society of Earthbound Extraterrestrials (EA)
SEE .... Society of Environmental Engineers [*Later, Institute of Environmental Sciences*]
SEE .... Society of Explosives Engineers (EA)
SEE .... Southeastern Electric Exchange
SEE .... Special Purpose End Effector (MCD)
SEE .... Standard End Effector (NASA)

SEE.......... Standard Error of Estimate
SEE.......... Staphylococcal Enterotoxin E [*Medicine*]
SEE.......... State Economic Enterprise [*Turkey*]   (ECON)
SEE.......... Studies in Educational Evaluation [*A publication*]
SEE.......... Sun Earth Explorer [*Satellite*] [*NASA*]
SEE.......... Survival, Evasion, and Escape [*Military*]
SE & E .... Survival, Evasion, and Escape [*Military*]   (AABC)
SEE.......... Systems Effectiveness Engineering   (MCD)
SEE.......... Systems Effectiveness Evaluation   (NG)
SEE.......... Systems Efficiency Expert
SEE.......... Systems Equipment Engineer [*Telecommunications*]   (TEL)
SEEA........ Societe Europeenne d'Energie Atomique
SEEA........ Software Error Effects Analysis
SEEAPAC ... Shore Electronic Engineering Activity, Pacific
SEEB......... Seeburg Industries, Inc. [*NASDAQ symbol*]
SEECA ..... Solar Energy and Energy Conservation Act of 1980
SEECA ..... State Environmental Education Coordinators Association   (EA)
SEECCIASDI ... Standing EEC [*European Economic Community*] Committee of the International Association of the Soap and Detergent Industry [*See also CPCEAISD*] [*Brussels, Belgium*]   (EAIO)
SEECL....... Solar Energy and Energy Conversion Laboratory [*University of Florida*] [*Research center*]   (RCD)
SEED......... DEKALB Genetics Corp. [*NASDAQ symbol*]   (NQ)
SEED......... Safe Eye Exposure Distance [*Air Force*]
SEED........ Scientists and Engineers in Economic Development [*National Science Foundation*]
SEED......... Self Electrooptic Effect Device [*Optical analog of a transistor*]
SEED......... Sewall Early Education Developmental Profiles
SEED......... Skill Escalation Employment Development   (EA)
SEED .... Special Elementary Education for the Disadvantaged
SEED......... Supply of Essential Engineering Data
Seed Bull.... Seed Bulletin [*A publication*]
Seed Gard Merch ... Seed and Garden Merchandising [*A publication*]
SEEDIS..... Socio-Economic Demographic Information System [*Lawrence Berkeley Laboratory*] [*Database*]
Seed and Nursery Tr ... Seed and Nursery Trader [*A publication*]   (APTA)
Seed Res (New Delhi) ... Seed Research (New Delhi) [*A publication*]
SEEDS ...... Space Exposed Experiment Developed for Students
Seed Sci Techn ... Seed Science and Technology [*A publication*]
Seed Sci Technol ... Seed Science and Technology [*A publication*]
Seed Trade Rev ... Seed Trade Review [*A publication*]
SEEE .... Studies in Electrical and Electronic Engineering [*Elsevier Book Series*] [*A publication*]
SEEF .... Scientists and Engineers Emigrant Fund
SEEHRL ... Sanitary Engineering and Environmental Health Research Laboratory [*Research center*]   (RCD)
SEEI .... Selected Essays. English Institute [*A publication*]
SEEI .... Special Essential Elements of Information   (MCD)
SEE-IN ...... Significant Events Evaluation and Information Network
SEEJ .... Slavic and East European Journal [*A publication*]
SEEK .... Search for Education, Elevation, and Knowledge [*Program*]
SEEK .... Survival, Escape, and Evasion Kit [*Navy*]   (NG)
SEEK .... Systems Evaluation and Exchange of Knowledge [*Data processing*]
SEEN........ Syndicat d'Etudes de l'Energie Nucleaire [*Belgium*]
SEEO......... Salvis Erroribus et Omissis [*Errors and Omissions Excepted*] [*Latin*]
SEEO........ Shore Electronic Engineering Office [*Navy*]
SEEP .... Sex Equity in Education Program   (EA)
SEEP .... Shelf Edge Exchange Processes [*Oceanography*]   (NOAA)
SEEP .... Sixth Fleet Escort Evaluation Program [*Navy*]
SEEP .... Stimulated Emission of Energetic Particles [*Experiment for study of radio waves*]
SEEQ......... SEEQ Technology, Inc. [*NASDAQ symbol*]   (NQ)
SEEQ........ Side-Effects Expectancy Questionnaire [*Psychology*]
SEER .... Seasonal Energy-Efficiency Ratio [*of heat pumps, air conditioners, etc.*]
SEER .... Sensor Experimental Evaluation and Review [*Strategic Defense Initiative*]
SEER .... Service des Etudes Ecologiques Regionales [*Canada*]
SEER .... Slavonic and East European Review [*A publication*]
SEER .... Student Exposition on Energy Resources [*Project*]
SEER .... Submarine Explosive Echo Ranging
SEER .... Supervisory Electronic Engineer [*Radio*]
SEER .... Surveillance, Epidemiology, and End-Results [*Program*] [*National Cancer Institute*]
SEER .... Sustainable Equilibrium Exchange Rate [*Economics*]
SEER .... System for Electronic Evaluation and Retrieval [*Data processing*]
SEER .... Systems Engineering, Evaluation, and Research   (MCD)
SEERB ..... South African Engineer and Electrical Review [*A publication*]
SEEREP ... Ships' Essential Equipment Requisition Expediting Program [*Navy*]   (NVT)
SEERS...... Senior Enlisted Evaluation Reports [*Military*]   (INF)
SEES .... Esmeraldas/General Rivadeneira [*Ecuador*] [*ICAO location identifier*]   (ICLI)
SEES .... Slavic and East European Section [*Association of College and Research Libraries*]
SEES .... Slavic and East European Studies [*A publication*]
SEES .... Standard Entry/Exit System [*Army*]

SEES .... System Effectiveness Engineering Section
SEET .... Science End-to-End Test [*Space*]
SEET .... Scottish, English, and European Textiles [*Commercial firm*]
SEETB...... South East England Tourist Board   (DCTA)
SE Eur ...... Southeastern Europe [*A publication*]
SEEX .... Systems Evaluation Experiment   (MCD)
SEF .... SALT Education Fund [*Defunct*]   (EA)
SEF .... Sebring, FL [*Location identifier*] [*FAA*]   (FAAL)
Sef .... Sefarad [*A publication*]
SEF .... Self-Extinguishing Fiber [*Monsanto Co. trademark*]
SEF .... Sequential Excitation Fluorescence [*Aviation*] [*Navy*]
SEF .... Shielding Effectiveness Factor
SEF .... Simple Environment Factor
SEF .... Simulated Engine Failure   (ADA)
SEF .... Small-End Forward [*of command module*]
SEF .... Software Engineering Facility
SEF .... Solar Energy Flux
SEF .... Somatically Evoked Field [*Neurophysiology*]
SEF .... Sound Energy Flux
SEF .... Southern Education Foundation   (EA)
SEF .... Space Education Foundation [*Later, AEF*]
SEF .... Special Entry Flying List [*Navy*] [*British*]
SEF .... Standard External File
SEF .... Staphylococcus Aureus Enterotoxin F [*Toxic shock toxin*]
SEF .... Supermarketing [*A publication*]
SEF .... Surface Effect Ship
SEF .... Systems Engineering Facility [*Defense Communications Agency*]   (RDA)
SE/FAC..... Support Equipment/Facility [*NASA*]   (NASA)
SEFACAN ... Segregator, Facer, Canceller Machine
SEFAR ...... Sonic End Fire for Azimuth and Range
SE & FBR .. Science Fiction and Fantasy Book Review [*A publication*]
SEFC .... Southeast Fisheries Center [*Miami, FL*] [*National Marine Fisheries Service*]   (MSC)
SEFCL....... Southeastern Fish Control Station [*Department of the Interior*]   (GRD)
SEFD .... Seafood, Inc. [*NASDAQ symbol*]   (NQ)
SEFD .... Solar Energy Flux Density
SEFDAO ... Side Effects of Drugs [*A publication*]
SEFE .... Standardization Evaluation Flight Examiner
SEFEL....... Secretariat Europeen des Fabricants d'Emballages Metalliques Legers [*European Secretariat of Manufacturers of Light Metal Packages*]   (EA)
SEFES ...... Southeastern Forest Experiment Station [*Department of Agriculture*] [*Asheville, NC*]   (GRD)
SEFI.......... Sequential Electric Fuel Injection [*Automotive engineering*]
SEFI.......... Societe Europeenne pour la Formation des Ingenieurs [*European Society for Engineering Education*]   (EA)
SEFIC....... Seventh Fleet Intelligence Center [*Navy*]
SEFIP .... Statistical Estimation Fault Isolation Procedure   (MCD)
SEFLO ...... Sequence Flow [*Tracing technique*]
SEFM .... Support Equipment Field Modification   (AAG)
SEFOR ..... Southwest Experimental Fast Oxide Reactor [*Nuclear energy*]
SEFR .... Shielding Experiment Facility Reactor [*Nuclear energy*]
SEFR .... System Effectiveness Forecast Report
SEFRL....... Southeastern Field Research Laboratory [*Pennsylvania State University*]
SEFS........ Special Elite Forces Society   (EA)
SefT .... Sefer Torah. Post-Talmudic Tractate   (BJA)
SEFT .... Single Engine Flight Training
SEFT .... Society for Education in Film and Television [*British*]
SEG............ Saturday Evening Girls [*Decorators of Arts and Crafts pottery*]
SEG............ Screen Extras Guild   (EA)
SEG............ Sealing
Seg .... Segismundo [*A publication*]
SEG............ Segment   (AAG)
SEG............ Segno [*Sign*] [*Music*]
SEG............ Segue [*Follows*] [*Music*]
SEG............ Selinsgrove, PA [*Location identifier*] [*FAA*]   (FAAL)
SEG............ Sequence of Events Generator
SEG............ Side Entry Goniometer
SEG............ Sliding Electron Gun
SEG............ Society of Economic Geologists   (EA)
SEG............ Society of Exploration Geophysicists   (EA)
SEG............ Special Effect Generator [*Video technology*]
SEG............ Standardization Evaluation Group   (AFM)
SEG............ Subesophageal Ganglion [*Anatomy*]
SEG............ Supplementum Epigraphicum Graecum [*A publication*]
SEG............ System Engineering Groundrule [*NASA*]   (NASA)
SEG............ Systems Engineering Group [*Air Force*]
SEG............ Systems Evaluation Group
SEGBA ...... Servicios Electricos del Gran Buenos Aires, SA [*Electrical utility*] [*Argentina*]
SEGD....... Society of Environmental Graphics Designers   (EA)
SEGE........ Guale [*Ecuador*] [*ICAO location identifier*]   (ICLI)
SEGEA ..... Orthopaedic Surgery [*A publication*]
SEGH .... Society for Environmental Geochemistry and Health   (EA)
SEGI........ Sports/Entertainment Group, Inc. [*NASDAQ symbol*]   (NQ)
SEGL........ Gul [*Ecuador*] [*ICAO location identifier*]   (ICLI)
SEGM....... Segment
SEGR......... Guarumal [*Ecuador*] [*ICAO location identifier*]   (ICLI)

SEG/R & T ... Systems Engineering Group/Research and Technology [*Air Force*]
SEGS .... Galapagos (Baltra) [*Ecuador*] [*ICAO location identifier*]　(ICLI)
SEGU .... Guayaquil/Simon Bolivar [*Ecuador*] [*ICAO location identifier*]　(ICLI)
Segu .... [*Didacus de*] Segura [*Flourished, 16th century*] [*Authority cited in pre-1607 legal work*]　(DSA)
Seguranca Desenvolv ... Seguranca e Desenvolvimento. ADESG [*Revista da Associacao dos Diplomados da Escola Superior de Guerra*] [*Brazil*] [*A publication*]
SEGZ .... Gualaquiza [*Ecuador*] [*ICAO location identifier*]　(ICLI)
SEH .... Sehore [*India*] [*Seismograph station code, US Geological Survey*]　(SEIS)
SEH .... Shuttle Electronic Hardware [*NASA*]
SEH .... Single-Engined Helicopter　(MCD)
SEH .... Societe Europeenne d'Hematologie
SEH .... Solar Equivalent Hours
SEH .... Southern Economic Journal [*A publication*]
SEH .... Spartech Corp. [*AMEX symbol*]　(SPSG)
SEH .... Star/Earth Horizon Sightings
SEH .... Strobel, E. H., Saint Louis MO [*STAC*]
SEH .... Subependymal Hemorrhage [*Medicine*]
SEHAB ..... Sea Rehabilitation [*Navy*]　(NVT)
SEHI .... Cotacachi [*Ecuador*] [*ICAO location identifier*]　(ICLI)
SE-HPLC .. Size Exclusion-High Performance Liquid Chromatography
SEHR .... Scandinavian Economic History Review [*A publication*]
SEHT .... Hacienda Taura [*Ecuador*] [*ICAO location identifier*]　(ICLI)
SEI .... Safety Equipment Institute　(EA)
SEI .... Seitel, Inc. [*AMEX symbol*]　(SPSG)
SEI .... Self Employment Income [*Social Security Administration*]　(OICC)
SEI .... Senhor Do Bonfim [*Brazil*] [*Airport symbol*]　(OAG)
SEI .... Shane Resources [*Vancouver Stock Exchange symbol*]
SEI .... Societa Editrice Internazionale [*Italy*] [*Publisher*]
SEI .... Societas Ergophthalmologica Internationalis [*International Ergophthalmological Society*] [*Stockholm, Sweden*]　(EAIO)
SEI .... Society of Engineering Illustrators　(EA)
SEI .... Software Engineering Institute [*DoD*]
SEI .... Solid Electrolyte Interphase [*Battery technology*]
SEI .... Special Engineering Investigation　(MCD)
SEI .... Special Equipment Item　(MCD)
SEI .... Special Experience Identifier [*Military*]
SEI .... Statistical Engineering Institute　(MCD)
SEI .... Stern Environment Indexes [*Psychology*]
SEI .... Stockpile Entry Inspection [*Navy*]　(NG)
SEI .... Stray Energy Indicator
SEI .... Stress Evaluation Inventory [*Test*]
SEI .... Support Equipment Installation [*NASA*]　(NASA)
SEI .... System Engineering Instrumentation　(NASA)
SEI .... System/Equipment Inventory
SE & I .... Systems Engineering and Integration
SEIA .... Security Equipment Industry Association　(EA)
SEIA .... Solar Energy Industries Association　(EA)
SEIA .... Solar Energy Institute of America [*Later, SEINAM*]　(MCD)
SEIAC ...... Science Education Information Analysis Center [*ERIC*]
SEIB .... Ibarra [*Ecuador*] [*ICAO location identifier*]　(ICLI)
SEIB .... Service des Etudes et Inventaires Bio-Physiques [*Quebec*]
SEIB .... Statistical and Economic Information Bulletin for Africa [*A publication*]
SEIC .... SEI Corporation [*NASDAQ symbol*]　(NQ)
SEIC .... Solar Energy Information Center
SEIC .... Syndicat de l'Emploi et de l'Immigration du Canada
SEIC .... System Effectiveness Information Central
SEICO ...... Science and Engineering Information Center Co.　(EISS)
SEICO ...... Support Equipment Installation and Checkout [*NASA*]　(NASA)
SEIDB ...... Solar Energy Information Data Bank [*Department of Energy*]
SEIE .... Solvent Extraction and Ion Exchange [*A publication*]
SEIE .... Submarine Escape Immersion Equipment
Seifen Fachbl ... Seifen Fachblatt [*A publication*]
Seifen Ole .. Seifen, Oele, Fette, Waechse [*A publication*]
Seifensieder Ztg ... Seifensieder-Zeitung [*A publication*]
Seifensieder Ztg Allg Oel Fett Ztg ... Seifensieder-Zeitung in Gemeinschaft auf Kriegsdauer mit Allgemeine Oel- und Fett-Zeitung [*A publication*]
Seifens Zt ... Seifensieder-Zeitung [*A publication*]
SEIG .... Intag [*Ecuador*] [*ICAO location identifier*]　(ICLI)
SEIGA .... Seishin Igaku [*A publication*]
Seign Rep ... Lower Canada Seignorial Questions Reports [*A publication*]　(DLA)
SEIJAN ..... Congenital Anomalies [*A publication*]
SEIJD .... Seijinbyo [*A publication*]
Seikag .... Seikagaku [*Journal of the Japanese Biochemical Society*] [*A publication*]
Sei-i-Kai Med J ... Sei-i-Kwai Medical Journal [*A publication*]
Seik Ziho ... Seiken Ziho. Report of the Kihara Institute for Biological Research [*A publication*]
SEIL .... Science Experiments Integration Laboratories
SEIL .... Southeastern Educational Improvement Laboratory [*Research Triangle Park, NC*] [*Department of Education*]　(GRD)

SEIM .... Isla San Miguel [*Ecuador*] [*ICAO location identifier*]　(ICLI)
SEIMC ...... Special Education Instructional Materials Centers [*Office of Education*] [*Database producer*]　(IID)
SEIMS .... State Economic Information Management System [*State Department*] [*Database*]
SEINAM ... Solar Energy Institute of North America　(EA)
SEIOD .... Spogli Elettronici dell'Italiano delle Origini e del Duecento [*A lexical, morphological, and syntactical inventory of Old Italian texts*]
SEIP .... System Engineering Implementation Plan
SEIR .... Solar Energy Intelligence Report [*Business Publishers Inc.*] [*No longer available online*] [*Information service or system*]　(CRD)
SEIR .... Southeast Indian Ridge [*Antarctica*] [*Geology*]
SEIR .... Susceptible, Exposed, Infected or Immune, Recovered [*Epidemiological model*]
SEIRS .... Suppliers and Equipment Information Retrieval System [*International Civil Aviation Organization*] [*Databank*] [*Information service or system*]　(IID)
SEIS .... Seitel, Inc. [*NASDAQ symbol*]　(NQ)
SEIS .... Solar Energy Information Services　(IID)
SEIS .... Submarine Emergency Identification Signal　(NG)
SEIS .... Supplemental Environmental Impact Statement [*Department of Agriculture*]
SEISA .... South Eastern Intercollegiate Sailing Association
Seish Iga .... Seishin Igaku [*A publication*]
Seish Shink Zass ... Seishin Shinkeigaku Zasshi [*A publication*]
Seism Instrum ... Seismic Instruments [*A publication*]
SEISMOG ... Seismographic
SEISMOL ... Seismologic
Seismol Bull ... Seismological Bulletin [*A publication*]
Seismol and Geol ... Seismology and Geology [*A publication*]
Seismol Invest ... Seismological Investigations. British Association for the Advancement of Science [*A publication*]
Seismolog Soc Am Bull ... Seismology Society of America. Bulletin [*A publication*]
Seismol Ser Earth Phys Branch ... Seismological Series of the Earth Physics Branch [*A publication*]
Seismol Ser Geol Surv (S Afr) ... Seismologic Series. Geological Survey (South Africa) [*A publication*]
Seismol Serv Can Seismol Ser ... Seismological Service of Canada. Seismological Series [*A publication*]
Seismol Soc Am Bul ... Seismological Society of America. Bulletin [*A publication*]
Seismostoikost Sooruzh ... Seismostoikost Sooruzhenii [*USSR*] [*A publication*]
Seism Prib Instrum Sredstva Seism Nabl ... Seismichiskie Pribory. Instrumental'naye Sredstva Seismicheskikh Nablyudenii [*A publication*]
SEIT .... Satellite Educational and Informational Television
SEIT .... Supervisory Electronic Installation Technician
SEIT .... System Evaluation, Integration, and Test　(MCD)
SEITA Ann Dir Etud Equip Sect 2 ... SEITA [*Service d'Exploitation Industrielle des Tabacs et des Allumettes*] Annales de la Direction des Etudes de l'Equipement. Section 2 [*A publication*]
SEITA Annls ... Service d'Exploitation Industrielle des Tabacs et des Allumettes. Annales de la Direction des Etudes et de l'Equipement [*A publication*]
SEIU .... Service Employees International Union　(EA)
SEIWG ...... Security Equipment Integration Working Group
SE/IWT ..... Southern Europe - Inland Waterways Transport [*NATO*]　(NATG)
SEJ .... Australian Stock Exchange Journal [*A publication*]　(APTA)
SEJ .... Security Pacific National Bank. Quarterly Economic Report [*A publication*]
SEJ .... Sliding Expansion Joint [*Technical drawings*]
SEJ .... Southern Economic Journal [*A publication*]
SEJA .... Jaramillo [*Ecuador*] [*ICAO location identifier*]　(ICLI)
SEJCR .... Societe Europeenne des Jeunes de la Croix-Bleue [*European Society for Blue Cross Youth - ESBCY*]　(EAIO)
SEJG .... Sacris Erudiri. Jaarboek voor Godsdienstwetenschappen [*A publication*]
SEJI .... Jipijapa [*Ecuador*] [*ICAO location identifier*]　(ICLI)
SEK .... Synomospondia Ergaton Kyprou [*Cyprus Workers' Confederation*] [*"Free Labour Syndicats"*]
SEKE .... Sosialistikon Ergatikon Komma tis Elladas [*Socialist Labor Party of Greece*] [*Forerunner of Greek Communist Party (KKE)*]　(PPE)
SEKF .... Sister Elizabeth Kenny Foundation [*Later, SKI*]
SEKLS .... Southeast Kansas Library System [*Library network*]
SEKRLC .... Southeastern Kentucky Regional Library Cooperative [*Library network*]
Sek San Fuji Sor ... Sekai San Fujinka Soran. Survey of World Obstetrics and Gynaecology [*A publication*]
Sel .... Ducret-Thomson [*Formerly, Ducret Selmer*] [*Record label*] [*France*]
SEL .... Safety Engineering Laboratory [*British*]　(IRUK)
SEL .... Satellite Experiment Laboratory [*National Oceanic and Atmospheric Administration*]　(GRD)
SEL .... School of Electric Light [*British military*]　(DMA)

SEL............ Scouts' Esperanto League   (EA)
SEL............ Select [or Selection]   (AAG)
SEL............ Selected Equipment List   (NVT)
sel.............. Selection [Literature]
Sel .... Seleucid Era   (BJA)
SEL............ Seligman Select Municipal Fund [NYSE symbol]   (SPSG)
SEL............ Selkirk College Library [UTLAS symbol]
sel.............. Selkup [MARC language code] [Library of Congress]   (LCCP)
SEL............ Semi-Effective List [British military]   (DMA)
SEL............ Semlyachik [USSR] [Seismograph station code, US Geological Survey]   (SEIS)
SEL............ Seoul [South Korea] [Airport symbol]   (OAG)
SEL............ Seton Co. [AMEX symbol]   (SPSG)
SEL............ Signal Engineering Laboratories   (AAG)
SEL............ Single Engine Land [Pilot rating]   (AIA)
SEL............ Skolta Esperanto-Ligo [Scouts' Esperanto League]   (EAIO)
SEL............ Socialist Electoral League [Norway]   (PPW)
SEL............ Solar Environmental Laboratory [National Oceanic and Atmospheric Administration]
SEL............ Southeastern Educational Laboratory
SEL............ Space Environment Laboratory [Department of Commerce] [National Oceanic and Atmospheric Administration] [Boulder, CO]
SEL............ Spontaneously Emitted Light
SEL............ Standard Elektrik Lorenz AG [Germany]
SEL............ Stanford Electronics Laboratory [Stanford University] [Research center]   (MCD)
SEL............ Star/Earth Landmark Sightings
SEL............ Studies in English Literature [A publication]
SEL............ Super Einspritz Lang [Fuel-injection, long wheelbase] [As in 450 SEL, the model number of a Mercedes-Benz automobile]
SEL............ Support Equipment List [Navy]
SEL............ Surface Emitting LASER
SEL............ System Electronics Laboratory
SEL............ System Engineering Laboratories   (MCD)
SELA......... Lago Agrio [Ecuador] [ICAO location identifier]   (ICLI)
SELA......... Sistema Economico Latinoamericano [Latin American Economic System]   (EAIO)
SELA......... Systeme Economique Latino-Americain [Latin American Economic System - LAES] [French]
SELACJ .... Secretariado Latinoamericano de la Compania de Jesus [Latin American Bureau of Society of Jesus]   (EAIO)
Sel Annu Rev Anal Sci ... Selected Annual Reviews of the Analytical Sciences [A publication]
Sel App Beng ... Selected Appeals, Sadr Diwani Adalat [Bengal, India] [A publication]   (DLA)
SELAVIP .. Servicio Latinoamericano y Asiatico de Vivienda Popular [Latin American and Asian Low Income Housing Service]   (EAIO)
SelBab........ Babylonian Seleucid Era   (BJA)
Sel Bibliogr Algae ... Selected Bibliography on Algae [A publication]
Sel Bibliogr Middle East Geol ... Selected Bibliography of Middle East Geology [A publication]
SELC .... La Cecilia [Ecuador] [ICAO location identifier]   (ICLI)
SELC .... South East London College [London, England]
SELCAL.... Selective Calling [Radio]
Sel Cancer Ther ... Selective Cancer Therapeutics [A publication]
Sel Cas....... Select Cases, Central Provinces [India] [A publication]   (DLA)
Sel Cas Ch ... Select Cases in Chancery [England] [A publication]   (DLA)
Sel Cas Ch (T King) ... Select Cases in Chancery Tempore King [25 English Reprint] [1724-33] [A publication]   (DLA)
Sel Cas DA ... Select Cases, Sadr Diwani Adalat [India] [A publication]   (DLA)
Sel Cas Ev ... Select Cases in Evidence (Strange) [England] [A publication]   (DLA)
Sel Cas KB Edw I ... Select Cases in King's Bench under Edward I (Sayles) [England] [A publication]   (DLA)
Sel Cas NF ... Select Cases, Newfoundland [A publication]   (DLA)
Sel Cas NWP ... Select Cases, Northwest Provinces [India] [A publication]   (DLA)
Sel Cas NY ... Yate's Select Cases [1809] [New York] [A publication]   (DLA)
Sel Cas with Opin ... Select Cases with Opinions by a Solicitor [A publication]   (DLA)
Sel Cas SDA ... Select Cases, Sadr Diwani Adalat [Bengal, Bombay, India] [A publication]   (DLA)
Sel Cas T Br ... [Charles Purton] Cooper's Select Cases Tempore Brougham [A publication]   (DLA)
Sel Cas T King ... Select Cases in Chancery Tempore King [England] [A publication]   (DLA)
Sel Cas T Nap ... Select Cases Tempore Napier [Ireland] [A publication]   (DLA)
Sel Ca T King ... Select Cases in Chancery Tempore King [25 English Reprint] [1724-33] [A publication]   (DLA)
Sel Ch Cas ... Select Cases in Chancery Tempore King, Edited by Macnaghten [England] [A publication]   (DLA)
Sel Col Cas ... Select Collection of Cases [England] [A publication]   (DLA)
SELCOM.. Select Committee [Army Materiel Command]
SELCTV... Selected Television [Commercial firm] [British]
Seld.......... Selden's New York Reports [5-10 New York] [A publication]   (DLA)

SELDADS ... Space Environment Laboratory Data Acquisition and Display System [National Oceanic and Atmospheric Administration]
Sel Dec Bomb ... Select Cases, Sadr Diwani Adalat [Bombay, India] [A publication]   (DLA)
SEL DECK ... Select Decking [Lumber]
Sel Dec Madr ... Select Decrees, Sadr Adalat [Madras, India] [A publication]   (DLA)
Selden .... Selden's New York Court of Appeals Reports [A publication]   (DLA)
Selden Notes ... Selden's New York Court of Appeals Notes of Cases [1st ed.] [1853] [A publication]   (DLA)
Seld Fl....... Selden's Dissertatio ad Fletam [A publication]   (ILCA)
Seld J .... Selden's Jani Anglorum [A publication]   (ILCA)
Seld JP....... Selden's Judicature in Parliaments [1681] [A publication]   (DLA)
Seld Mar Cl ... Selden's Mare Clausum [A publication]   (ILCA)
Seld Mare Claus ... Selden's Mare Clausum [A publication]   (DLA)
Seld Notes ... Selden's New York Court of Appeals Notes [A publication]   (DLA)
Seld Off Ch ... Selden's Office of Lord Chancellor [1671] [A publication]   (DLA)
Seld R........ Selden's New York Court of Appeals Reports [A publication]   (DLA)
Seld Soc ..... Selden Society   (DLA)
Seld Soc Yrbk ... Selden Society Yearbook [United States] [A publication]   (DLA)
Seld Tit Hon ... Selden's Titles of Honor [A publication]   (DLA)
SELE .... SelecTronics, Inc. [NASDAQ symbol]   (NQ)
SELEC....... Select   (ROG)
SELEC....... Superelastic LASER Energy Conversion   (MCD)
Selec Ed R ... Selections from the Edinburgh Review [A publication]
Selecta Math Soviet ... Selecta Mathematica Sovietica [A publication]
Selecta Statist Canadiana ... Selecta Statistica Canadiana [A publication]
Selected Reports ... Selected Reports in Ethnomusicology [A publication]
Selected Water Resources Abstr ... Selected Water Resources Abstracts [A publication]
Select J....... Select Journal [A publication]
Selec Water Resources Abstr ... Selected Water Resources Abstracts [A publication]
Selek Semenovod ... Selektsiya i Semenovodstvo [A publication]
Selekts Semenov ... Selektsiya i Semenovodstvo [A publication]
SelEnv....... Selected References on Environmental Quality [A publication]
Selez Tec Molit ... Selezione di Tecnica Molitoria [A publication]
SELF.......... National Citizens Committee to Save Education and Library Funds
SELF.......... Self-Eject Launch Facility [NASA]   (MCD)
SELF.......... Short Expeditious Landing Field   (CINC)
SELF.......... Simplicity, Efficiency, Lower Rates, and Fairness Tax Plan
SELF.......... Societe des Ecrivains Luxembourgeois de Langue Francaise
SELF.......... Student Education Loan Fund [Minnesota]
Self Rel ...... Self-Reliance [A publication]
SELFTAV ... Self-Conducted Tender Availability [Navy]   (NVT)
Self Tr........ Selfridge's Trial [A publication]   (DLA)
SELGEM .. Self-Generating Master [Information management system] [Data processing]
SELI .... Limoncocha [Ecuador] [ICAO location identifier]   (ICLI)
SE Libn ...... Southeastern Librarian [A publication]
SELID .... Serials Librarian [A publication]
SELit.......... Studies in English Literature [Japan] [A publication]
SELJ.......... La Julia [Ecuador] [ICAO location identifier]   (ICLI)
SELJ.......... Studies in English Literature (Japan) [A publication]
SELK .... Selkirkshire [County in Scotland]
Sel'Khoz Beloruss ... Sel'skoe Khozyaistvo Belorussii [A publication]
Sel'-Khoz Biol ... Sel'skokhozyaistvennaya Biologiya [A publication]
Sel Khoz Kazakh ... Sel'skoe Khozyaisto Kazakstana [A publication]
Sel'Khoz Kirgizii ... Sel'skoe Khozyaistvo Kirgizii [A publication]
Sel'Khoz Povol ... Sel'skoe Khozyaistvo Povolzh'ya [A publication]
Sel'Khoz Sev Kavkaz ... Sel'skoe Khozyaisto Severnogo Kavkaza [A publication]
Sel'Khoz Sev-Zapad Zony ... Sel'skoe Khozyaisto Severo-Zapadnoi Zony [A publication]
Sel Khoz Sev Zap Zony ... Sel'skoe Khozyaisto Severo-Zapadnoi Zony [A publication]
Sel'Khoz Sib ... Sel'skoe Khozyaistvo Sibiri [A publication]
Sel Khoz Tadzhik ... Sel'skoe Khozyaistvo Tadzhikistana [A publication]
Sel'Khoz Tadzhikistana ... Sel'skoe Khozyaistvo Tadzhikistana [A publication]
Sel Khoz Tatarii ... Sel'skoe Khozyaistvo Tatarii [A publication]
Sel Khoz Turkmen ... Sel'skoe Khozyaistvo Turkmenistana [A publication]
SELL .... Llurimaguas [Ecuador] [ICAO location identifier]   (ICLI)
SELL .... Sales Environment Learning Laboratory [Computer-based marketing game]
SELL .... Studies in English Literature and Language [Japan] [A publication]
SELL .... Suomi, Eesti, Latvija, Lietuva [Finland, Estonia, Latvia, Lithuania]
Sel L Cas.... Select Law Cases [England] [A publication]   (DLA)
Sell Pr .... Sellon's Practice in the King's Bench [A publication]   (DLA)
Sell Prac..... Sellon's Practice in the King's Bench [A publication]   (DLA)
SELM .... Loma Larga [Ecuador] [ICAO location identifier]   (ICLI)

SE/LM ...... Systems Engineering/Logistics Management (MCD)
SelMac......... Macedonian Seleucid Era (BJA)
Sel Math Sov ... Selecta Mathematica Sovietica [A publication]
Sel Med...... Selecciones Medicas [A publication]
SEL MERC ... Select Merchantable [Lumber]
SELMOUS ... Special English Language Materials for Overseas University
    Students
SELN......... Limon [Ecuador] [ICAO location identifier] (ICLI)
SELN......... Selection (AAG)
Sel NP......... Selwyn's Law of Nisi Prius [A publication] (DLA)
SELO......... Loja (La Toma) [Ecuador] [ICAO location identifier] (ICLI)
Sel Odontol (Sao Paulo) ... Selecoes Odontologicas (Sao Paulo) [A
    publication]
Sel Off Ch ... Selden's Office of Lord Chancellor [1671] [A
    publication] (DLA)
SELOR...... Ship Emitter Location Report [Navy] (CAAL)
Sel Org Transform ... Selective Organic Transformations [A publication]
Sel Pap Environ Isr ... Selected Papers on the Environment in Israel [A
    publication]
Sel Pr .... Sellon's Practice [A publication] (DLA)
Sel PRC Mag ... Selections from People's Republic of China Magazines [Hong
    Kong] [A publication]
SELR......... Saturn Engineering Liaison Request [NASA] (KSC)
SELR......... Selector (AAG)
Sel Rand Abstr ... Selected Rand Abstracts [A publication]
SELREC.... Shore Electronics Reconnaissance System
SELREFTRA ... Selected Refresher Training [Navy] (NVT)
SELRES.... Selected Reserve [Military]
SELRFT....... Selected Refresher Training [Navy] (NVT)
SELS......... Selective Service
SELS......... Severe Local Storm [National Weather Service]
SELS......... Space Environment Laboratory Simulation [NASA]
SELSA...... Southeast Library Service Area [Library network]
Sel Sci Pap Ist Super Sanita ... Selected Scientific Papers. Istituto Superiore di
    Sanita [A publication]
Sel Semenovod (Kiev) ... Selektsiya i Semenovodstvo (Kiev) [A publication]
Sel Semenovod (Mosc) ... Selektsiya i Semenovodstvo (Moscow) [A
    publication]
Sel Semenovod Resp Mezhved Temat Sb ... Selektsiya i Semenovodstvo
    Respublikanskii Mezhvedomstvennyi Tematicheskii
    Sborrnik [A publication]
Sel Serv L Rep ... Selective Service Law Reporter [A publication] (DLA)
Sel Serv L Rptr ... Selective Service Law Reporter [A publication] (DLA)
Sel'sk Khoz ... Sel'skoe Khozyaistvo [A publication]
Sel'sk Khoz Kaz ... Sel'skoe Khozyaistvo Kazakhstana [A publication]
Sel'sk Khoz Kirg ... Sel'skoe Khozyaistvo Kirgizii [A publication]
Sel'sk Khoz Mold ... Sel'skoe Khozyaistvo Moldavii [A publication]
Sel'sk Khoz Podmoskov'ya ... Sel'skoe Khozyaistvo Podmoskov'ya [A
    publication]
Sel'sk Khoz Povolzh'ya ... Sel'skoe Khozyaistvo Povolzh'ya [A publication]
Sel'sk Khoz Rubezhom Rastenievod ... Sel'skoe Khozyaistvo za Rubezhom.
    Rastenievodstvo [A publication]
Sel'sk Khoz Sev Zapadn Zony ... Sel'skoe Khozyaistvo Severo-Zapadnoi Zony
    [A publication]
Sel'sk Khoz Tadzh ... Sel'skoe Khozyaistvo Tadzhikistana [A publication]
Sel'sk Khoz Tatar ... Sel'skoe Khozyaistvo Tatarii [A publication]
Sel'sk Khoz Tatarii ... Sel'skoe Khozyaistvo Tatarii [A publication]
Sel'sk Khoz Turkm ... Sel'skoe Khozyaistvo Turkmenistana [A publication]
Sel'skokhoz Biol ... Sel'skokhozyaistvennaya Biologiya [A publication]
Sel'skokhoz Proizv Nechernozem Zony ... Sel'skokhozyaistvennoe
    Proizvodstvo Nechernozemnoi Zony [A publication]
Sel'skokhoz Proizv Povol ... Sel'skokhozyaistvennoe Proizvodstvo Povolzh'ya
    [A publication]
Sel'skokhoz Proizv Sev Kavkaza TSCHO ... Sel'skokhozyaistvennoe
    Proizvodstvo Severnogo Kavkaza i TSCHO [A
    publication]
Sel'skokhoz Proizv Sib Dal'nego Vostoka ... Sel'skokhozyaistvennoe
    Proizvodstvo Sibiri i Dal'nego Vostoka [A publication]
Sel'skokhoz Proizv Urala ... Sel'skokhozyaistvennoe Proizvodstvo Urala [A
    publication]
Selskostop Misul ... Selskostopanska Misul [A publication]
Selskostop Nauka ... Selskostopanska Nauka [A publication]
Selskostop Tekh ... Selskostopanska Tekhnika [A publication]
Sel Sortoizuch Agrotekh Plodovykh Yagodnykh Kul't ... Selektsiya,
    Sortoizuchenie, Agrotekhnika Plodovykh i Yagodnykh
    Kul'tur [A publication]
SEL STR ... Select Structural [Lumber]
SELSW...... Selector Switch (MCD)
SELSYN.... Self-Synchronous [Trade name] [Motor]
SELT .... Latacunga [Ecuador] [ICAO location identifier] (ICLI)
SELT .... SAGE [Semiautomatic Ground Environment] Evaluation
    Library Tape
SELT .... Select Information Systems [NASDAQ symbol] (NQ)
SELT .... Self-Eject Launch Technique [NASA] (KSC)
SELT .... Sheet Explosive Loading Technique
Sel Teol ...... Selecciones de Teologia [A publication]
Sel Top Mod Phys ... Selected Topics in Modern Physics [A publication]
Sel Top Solid State Phys ... Selected Topics in Solid State Physics [A
    publication]

Sel Vet Ist Zooprofil Sper Lomb Emilia ... Selezione Veterinaria-Istituto
    Zooprofilattico Sperimentale della Lombardia e dell'Emilia
    [A publication]
SELW........ Selwyn College [Cambridge] [British] (ROG)
Selw........... Selwyn's Law of Nisi Prius [England] [A publication] (DLA)
Sel Water Res Abstr ... Selected Water Resources Abstracts [A publication]
Selw & Barn ... Barnewall and Alderson's English King's Bench Reports [1st
    part] [A publication] (DLA)
Selw NP ..... Selwyn's Law of Nisi Prius [England] [A publication] (DLA)
SELY .... Southeasterly [Meteorology] (FAAC)
SEM......... Scanning Electron Microscope [or Microscopy]
SEM........... Scanning Electron Microscopy [An association] [Later,
    SMI] (EA)
SEM......... Schedule Evaluation Model
SEM......... Secondary Electron Multiplier [Detector]
SEM......... Secondary Emission Microscope
SEM......... Secondary Emission Monitor
SEM......... Secondary Enrichment Medium [Microbiology]
SEM......... Security Environmental Systems, Inc. [Vancouver Stock
    Exchange symbol]
SEM......... Security Management [A publication]
SEM......... Seller's Engineering Memo [NASA] (NASA)
SEM......... Selma, AL [Location identifier] [FAA] (FAAL)
Sem......... Semahoth (BJA)
Sem .... Semana [A publication]
SEM......... Semaphore
SEM......... Semble [It Seems]
SEM......... Semel [Once]
SEM......... Semi [One-Half] [Pharmacy]
SEM......... Semicolon
SEM......... Semienriched Minimal [Agar]
Sem .... Seminar [A publication]
Sem .... Seminario Conciliar [A publication]
SEM......... Seminary
SEM......... Semipalatinsk [USSR] [Seismograph station code, US
    Geological Survey] (SEIS)
SEM......... Semitic [Language, etc.]
sem .... Semitic [MARC language code] [Library of Congress] (LCCP)
Sem .... Semitica [Paris] [A publication]
SEM......... Semo Aviation, Inc. [Malden, MO] [FAA designator] (FAAC)
SEM......... Sempre [Throughout] [Music]
SEM......... Shared Equity Mortgage
SEM......... Singularity Expansion Method (IEEE)
SEM......... Society of Engineers and Machinists [A union] [British]
SEM......... Society for Ethnomusicology (EA)
SEM......... Society for Experimental Mechanics (EA)
SEM......... Solar Environment Monitor
SEM......... Sortie Effectiveness Model [NASA] (MCD)
SEM......... Southeast Missouri State University, Cape Girardeau, MO
    [OCLC symbol] (OCLC)
SEM......... Southern Illinois University at Carbondale Center for Electron
    Microscopy [Research center] (RCD)
SEM......... Space Environment Monitor [NASA]
SEM......... Special Electric Motors [Manufacturing company] [British]
SEM......... Standard Electronic Module (CAAL)
SEM......... Standard Error of the Mean
SEM......... Standard Error of Measurement [Testing]
SEM......... Standard Estimating Module (IEEE)
SEM......... State-Event Matrix [Data processing]
SEM......... Station Engineering Manual [Telecommunications] (TEL)
SEM......... Stereoscan Electron Microscope
SEM......... Stray Energy Monitor
SEM......... Structural Econometric Model [Statistics]
SEM......... Subarray Electronics Module [Data processing]
SEM......... Subcontractor Engineering Memorandum (MCD)
S-EM .... Suck-Egg Mule [A publication]
SEM......... System Effectiveness Model (CAAL)
SEM......... System Engineering Management [NASA]
SEM........... Systems Engineering & Manufacturing Corp. [AMEX
    symbol] (SPSG)
S-E-M........ Systems/Equipment/Munitions [Army] (AFIT)
SEM......... Systolic Ejection Murmur [Cardiology]
SEMA....... Macara [Ecuador] [ICAO location identifier] (ICLI)
SEMA....... Semiotic Abstracts [A publication]
SEMA....... Societe d'Etudes de Mathematiques Appliquees [France]
SEMA....... Special Electronic Mission Aircraft (RDA)
SEMA....... Specialty Equipment Market Association [Later, SFI] (EA)
SEMAA...... Safety Equipment Manufacturers Agents Association (EA)
Semaine Med ... Semaine Medicale [A publication]
Semaine Vet ... Semaine Veterinaire [A publication]
Sem Anal ... Seminaire d'Analyse [A publication]
Sem Anal Moderne ... Seminaire d'Analyse Moderne [A publication]
Semana Med ... Semana Medica [A publication]
Semanario ... Semanario Judicial de la Federacion [Mexico] [A publication]
Sem Arth Rh ... Seminars in Arthritis and Rheumatism [A publication]
SEMATECH ... Semiconductor Manufacturing Technology Consortium
SemBEsp ... Semana Biblica Espanola [Madrid] [A publication]
Sem Bibl Esp ... Semana Biblica Espanola [A publication]
SEMC........ Macas [Ecuador] [ICAO location identifier] (ICLI)
SEMCC ..... Southeastern Massachusetts Health Sciences Libraries
    Consortium [Library network]

SEMCIP.... Shipboard Electromagnetic Capability Improvement Program [*Navy*] (NVT)
SEMCOG ... Southeast Michigan Council of Governments [*Detroit, MI*]
SEMCOR ... Semantic Correlation [*Machine-aided indexing*]
SEMD........ Stray Energy Monitor Device
SEM/E...... Ethnos. Statens Etnografiska Museum [*A publication*]
SEME........ Semicon, Inc. [*NASDAQ symbol*] (NQ)
SEMEL in D ... Semel in Die [*Once a Day*] [*Pharmacy*]
Semen Elette ... Sementi Elette [*A publication*]
SEMET..... Self-Evident Meteorological Code (NATG)
SEMG....... Scanning Electron Micrograph
SEMH .... Machala [*Ecuador*] [*ICAO location identifier*] (ICLI)
SEMH .... Service Engineering Man-Hours
Sem Hematol ... Seminars in Hematology [*A publication*]
SEMHI...... Southeastern Manufactured Housing Institute [*Later, Manufactured Housing Institute*] (EA)
Sem Hop .... Semaine des Hopitaux [*A publication*]
Sem Hop Inf ... Semaine des Hopitaux. Informations [*A publication*]
Sem Hop Paris ... Semaine des Hopitaux de Paris [*A publication*]
Sem Hop Paris Suppl Sem Med Prof Med Soc ... Semaine des Hopitaux de Paris. Supplement: Semaine Medicale Professionnelle et Medico-Sociale [*A publication*]
Sem Hop-The ... Semaine des Hopitaux-Therapeutique [*A publication*]
SEMI........ All American Semiconductor, Inc. [*NASDAQ symbol*] (NQ)
SEMI........ Self-Evacuating Multilayer Insulation [*System*]
SEMI........ Semiconductor Equipment and Materials Institute (EA)
SEMI........ Shipboard Electromagnetic Interference [*Navy*] (CAAL)
SEMI........ Societe d'Etudes de Marche et d'Informatique [*Society for the Study of Marketing and Informatics*] [*Information service or system*] [*Defunct*] (IID)
SEMI........ Special Electromagnetic Interference (MCD)
SEMICOND ... Semiconductor
Semicond and Insul ... Semiconductors and Insulators [*A publication*]
Semicond Insul ... Semiconductors and Insulators [*A publication*]
Semicond Int ... Semiconductor International [*A publication*]
Semicond Prod ... Semiconductor Production [*A publication*]
Semicond Prod ... Semiconductor Products [*A publication*]
Semicond Prod and Solid State Technol ... Semiconductor Products and Solid State Technology [*Later, Solid State Technology*] [*A publication*]
Semicond Semimet ... Semiconductors and Semimetals [*A publication*]
SEMIDR ... Semidrachma [*Half a Drachma*] [*Pharmacy*]
SEMIH...... Semihora [*Half an Hour*] [*Pharmacy*]
SEMIKON ... Seminare/Konferenzen [*Seminars/Conferences*] [*Society for Business Information*] [*Information service or system*] [*Defunct*] (IID)
Semin Arthritis Rheum ... Seminars in Arthritis and Rheumatism [*A publication*]
Semin Biomass Energy City Farm Ind ... Seminar on Biomass Energy for City, Farm, and Industry [*A publication*]
Semin Chim Etat Solide ... Seminaires de Chimie de l'Etat Solide [*A publication*]
Semin Dermatol ... Seminars in Dermatology [*A publication*]
Semin Drug Treat ... Seminars in Drug Treatment [*A publication*]
Semin Estratigrafia ... Seminarios de Estratigrafia [*Madrid*] [*A publication*]
SEMINEX ... Seminary in Exile [*Liberal-oriented Lutheran seminary*]
Semin Fam Med ... Seminars in Family Medicine [*A publication*]
Semin Hear ... Seminars in Hearing [*A publication*]
Semin Hematol ... Seminars in Hematology [*A publication*]
Semin Infect Dis ... Seminars in Infectious Disease [*A publication*]
Semin Interventional Radiol ... Seminars in Interventional Radiology [*A publication*]
Semin Liver Dis ... Seminars in Liver Diseases [*A publication*]
Semin Med ... Seminario Medico [*A publication*]
Semin Migr Relat Soc Health Probl Pap ... Seminar on Migration and Related Social and Health Problems in New Zealand and the Pacific. Papers [*A publication*]
Semin Neurol ... Seminars in Neurology [*A publication*]
Semin Nucl Med ... Seminars in Nuclear Medicine [*A publication*]
Semin Oncol ... Seminars in Oncology [*A publication*]
Semin Oncol Nurs ... Seminars in Oncology Nursing [*A publication*]
Semin Perinatol ... Seminars in Perinatology [*A publication*]
Semin Perinatol (NY) ... Seminars in Perinatology (New York) [*A publication*]
Semin Psychiatry ... Seminars in Psychiatry [*A publication*]
Semin Reprod Endocrinol ... Seminars in Reproductive Endocrinology [*A publication*]
Semin Respir Med ... Seminars in Respiratory Medicine [*A publication*]
Semin Roentgenol ... Seminars in Roentgenology [*A publication*]
Semin Speech Lang ... Seminars in Speech and Language [*A publication*]
Sem Inst Prikl Mat Annotac Dokladov ... Seminar Instituta Prikladnoi Matematiki. Annotacii Dokladov [*A publication*]
Semin Surg Oncol ... Seminars in Surgical Oncology [*A publication*]
Semin Technol INSERM ... Seminaire Technologique. INSERM [*Institut National de la Sante et de la Recherche Medicale*] [*A publication*]
Semin Thromb Hemostas ... Seminars in Thrombosis and Hemostasis [*A publication*]
Semin Thromb Hemostasis ... Seminars in Thrombosis and Hemostasis [*A publication*]
Semin Ultrasound ... Seminars in Ultrasound [*Later, Seminars in Ultrasound, CT, and MR*] [*A publication*]

Semin Ultrasound CT MR ... Seminars in Ultrasound, CT, and MR [*A publication*]
Semin Urol ... Seminars in Urology [*A publication*]
SEMIRAD ... Secondary Electron-Mixed Radiation Dosimeter (IEEE)
SEMIS...... Solar Energy Monitor in Space [*NASA*] (MCD)
SEMIS...... State Extension Management Information System [*Department of Agriculture*]
Sem'ja Sk... Sem'ja Skola [*A publication*]
Sem Judiciaire ... La Semaine Judiciaire [*A publication*] (DLA)
Sem Jur ... Semaine Juridique [*A publication*]
SEMKA ... Semento Kogyo [*A publication*]
Sem Kond... Seminarium Kondakovianum [*A publication*]
SEML........ Manglaralto [*Ecuador*] [*ICAO location identifier*] (ICLI)
SEMLAM ... Semiconductor LASER Amplifier
SEMLAT... Semiconductor LASER Array Techniques
SEMM...... Smoke Effectiveness Manual Model (MCD)
SEMM...... Solar Electric Multiple-Mission (MCD)
Sem Math ... Seminars in Mathematics [*A publication*]
Sem Math Sci ... Seminar on Mathematical Sciences [*Yokohama*] [*A publication*]
Sem Math Sup ... Seminaire de Mathematiques Superieures [*A publication*]
Sem Math Superieures ... Seminaire de Mathematiques Superieures [*Montreal*] [*A publication*]
Sem Math V A Steklov ... Seminars in Mathematics. V. A. Steklov Mathematical Institute [*Leningrad*] [*A publication*]
Sem Med.... Semaine Medicale [*A publication*]
Sem Med.... Semana Medica [*A publication*]
Sem Med Esp ... Semana Medica Espanola [*A publication*]
Sem Med Mex ... Semana Medica de Mexico [*A publication*]
Sem Med Prof Med Soc ... Semaine Medicale Professionnelle et Medico-Sociale [*A publication*]
SEMMS...... Solar Electric Multiple-Mission Spacecraft
SEMN .... Slow Extension Motoneuron [*Neurology*]
SEMN .... Superficial Extensor Motoneuron [*Neurology*]
Sem Nephrol ... Seminars in Nephrology [*A publication*]
Sem Nota ... Seminaro Nota [*A publication*]
SEMO .... Montalvo [*Ecuador*] [*ICAO location identifier*] (ICLI)
SEMO .... State Emergency Management Organisation [*New South Wales, Australia*]
SEMO ...... Systems Engineering and Management Operations [*Military*]
Semon .... Semonides [*Seventh century BC*] [*Classical studies*] (OCD)
SEMOPS .. Sequential Multiobjective Problem Solving
SEMP....... Mopa [*Ecuador*] [*ICAO location identifier*] (ICLI)
SEMP .... Sempre [*Throughout*] [*Music*]
SEMP .... Simplified Early Maturities Participation Plan [*Small Business Administration*]
SEMP .... Societe d'Editions Medico-Pharmaceutiques [*Medical-Pharmaceutical Publishing Co.*] [*Information service or system*] [*France*] (IID)
SEMP .... Socioeconomic Military Program (CINC)
SEMP .... Standard Electronics Module Program (MCD)
SEMP .... System Engineering Management Plan
SEMPA ..... Scanning Electron Microscope and Particle Analyzer
SEMPA ..... Scanning Electron Microscopy with Polarization Analysis
SEMPB ..... Schiffli Embroidery Manufacturers Promotion Board (EA)
SEMRE ..... SPRINT Electromagnetic Radiation Evaluation [*Army*] (AABC)
SEMRFL... Michigan Regional Libraries Film Program at Monroe [*Library network*]
Sem Roentg ... Seminars in Roentgenology [*A publication*]
SEMS........ Monjas Sur [*Ecuador*] [*ICAO location identifier*] (ICLI)
Sem S .... Semiotic Scene [*A publication*]
SEMS .... Severe Environment Memory Series [*or System*] [*Data processing*]
SEMS .... Space Environment Monitor System [*NASA*] (NASA)
SEMS .... Steam Engine Makers' Society [*A union*] [*British*]
SEMS .... Stray Energy Monitor System
SEMS .... Support Engineering Manhour Summary (MCD)
SEMS .... System Engineering Management Standard
SEMT .... Manta [*Ecuador*] [*ICAO location identifier*] (ICLI)
SEMT........ Science, Engineering, Medicine, and Technology [*A publication*]
SEMTD8... Special Topics in Endocrinology and Metabolism [*A publication*]
SEMTEC... Southeastern Marine Trades Exhibit and Conference [*National Marine Manufacturers Association*] (TSPED)
Sem Ther ... Semaine Therapeutique [*France*] [*A publication*]
SEMTR ..... SPRINT Early Missile Test RADAR [*Army*] (AABC)
SEMTR ..... Supervisory Electronic Maintenance Technician [*Relief*]
SEMTSA... Structural Econometric Modeling Time Series Analysis [*Statistics*]
Se Mulli (New Phys) ... Se Mulli (New Physics) [*A publication*]
Sem Vitivinic ... Semana Vitivinicola [*Spain*] [*A publication*]
SEMY........ Seminary
Sen .... De Senectute [*of Cicero*] [*Classical studies*] (OCD)
SEN .... Lexington, KY [*Location identifier*] [*FAA*] (FAAL)
SEN .... Science Engineering News [*National Oceanic and Atmospheric Administration*]
SeN .... Seara Nova [*A publication*]
SEN .... Semienclosed
SEN .... Senate

SEN .... Senator
SEN .... Sendai [*Mukaiyama*] [*Japan*] [*Seismograph station code, US Geological Survey*]   (SEIS)
Sen .... Seneca [*the Elder*] [*First century BC*] [*Classical studies*]   (OCD)
Sen .... Seneca [*the Younger*] [*First century AD*] [*Classical studies*]   (OCD)
SEN .... Senegal [*ANSI three-letter standard code*]   (CNC)
SEN .... Senior   (EY)
SEN .... Senlac Resources, Inc. [*Toronto Stock Exchange symbol*]
SEN .... Sennae [*Of Senna*] [*Pharmacy*]   (ROG)
SEN .... Sensitive
SEN .... Sensor   (AAG)
SEN .... Senza [*Without*] [*Music*]
SEN .... Single Edge Notched
SEN .... Societe Europeenne de Neuroscience [*European Neuroscience Association - ENA*]   (EA)
SEN .... Software Error Notification [*Data processing*]
SEN .... Sports Exchange Network [*Cable TV programming service*]
SEN .... State Enrolled Nurse [*British*]
SEN .... Steam Emulsion Number
SEN .... Strike Energy, Inc. [*Vancouver Stock Exchange symbol*]
SEN .... System Error Notification [*Data processing*]
SEN .... Systems Engineering Notice
SENA........ Nor Antizana [*Ecuador*] [*ICAO location identifier*]   (ICLI)
SENA........ Seaport Navigation Co. [*AAR code*] [*Later, SNCO*]
SENA........ Societe d'Energie Nucleaire Franco-Belge des Ardennes [*Belgian-French power consortium*]
SENA........ Sympathetic Efferent Nerve Activity
SENAAL... Agricultural Science [*Sofia*] [*A publication*]
SENAV...... Senior Naval Aviator   (NVT)
SENAVAV ... Senior Naval Aviator
SENAVOMAC ... Senior Naval Officer, Military Airlift Command   (MCD)
SENB........ Single Edge Notched Beam [*Materials science and technology*]
SENC........ Nor Cayambe [*Ecuador*] [*ICAO location identifier*]   (ICLI)
SenCh .... Senior Chaplain [*Navy*] [*British*]
Senckenb Biol ... Senckenbergiana Biologica [*A publication*]
Senckenberg Biol ... Senckenbergiana Biologica [*A publication*]
Senckenbergische Nat Ges Frankfurt Ber ... Senckenbergische Naturforschende Gesellschaft in Frankfurt Am Main. Bericht [*A publication*]
Senckenbergischen Naturf Gesell Senckenberg-Buch ... Senckenbergischen Naturforschenden Gesellschaft Senckenberg-Buch [*A publication*]
Senckenberg Marit ... Senckenbergiana Maritima [*A publication*]
Senckenb Lethaea ... Senckenbergiana Lethaea [*A publication*]
Senckenb Marit ... Senckenbergiana Maritima [*A publication*]
Senckenb Naturforsch Ges Abh ... Senckenbergische Naturforschende Gesellschaft. Abhandlungen [*A publication*]
SEND .... Scientists and Engineers for National Development [*Scholarship program*]
SEND .... Securities and Exchange Commission News Digest [*A publication*]
SEND .... Sentry Data, Inc. [*NASDAQ symbol*]   (NQ)
SEND .... Shared Equipment Need Date   (NASA)
SEND .... Southend [*County borough in England*]
Sendai Astron Rap ... Sendai Astronomiaj Raportoj [*A publication*]
Sen Doc...... Senate Document   (DLA)
SENE........ Seneca Foods Corp. [*NASDAQ symbol*]   (NQ)
Seneg......... Senegal
Senegal Cent Rech Oceanogr Dakar-Thiaroye Arch ... Senegal. Centre de Recherches Oceanographiques de Dakar-Thiaroye. Archive [*A publication*]
Senegal Cent Rech Oceanogr Dakar-Thiaroye Doc Sci ... Senegal. Centre de Recherches Oceanographiques de Dakar-Thiaroye. Document Scientifique [*A publication*]
Senegal Dir Mines Geol Bull ... Senegal. Direction des Mines et de la Geologie. Bulletin [*A publication*]
SENEGAMBIA ... Senegal and Gambia
SENEL...... Single Noise Exposure Level
SENET...... Scientific and Engineering Computer Network   (MCD)
SENG .... Single Engine
S in Eng..... Studies in English [*A publication*]
SEngFInstSMM ... Qualified Sales Engineer of the Institute of Sales and Marketing Management [*British*]   (DBQ)
SEngL........ Studies in English Literature [*The Hague*] [*A publication*]
SENI......... Nor Iliniza [*Ecuador*] [*ICAO location identifier*]   (ICLI)
Sen J .... Senate Journal [*A publication*]   (DLA)
Sen Jo .... Senate Journal [*A publication*]   (DLA)
SENL........ Standard Equipment Nomenclature List [*Military*]
SENLOG... Sentinel Logistics Command
SEN(M)..... State Enrolled Nurse (Mental Nursing) [*British*]   (DBQ)
SEN(MS) .. State Enrolled Nurse (Mental Subnormal Nursing) [*British*]   (DBQ)
Senn .... Sennaherib   (BJA)
SE'NNIGHT ... Seven Nights [*A week*]   (ROG)
SENO .... Steam Emulsion Number
SENPD...... Senpaku [*A publication*]
SENPO...... Sentinel Project Office [*Army*]   (MCD)
Sen R......... Seneca Review [*A publication*]
SENR........ Senior
SENR........ Senior Service Corp. [*Wilton, CT*] [*NASDAQ symbol*]   (NQ)

SENRAC... South Australian State Energy Research Advisory Committee
Sen Rep...... Senate Report [*A publication*]   (DLA)
Sen Rep...... United States Senate Committee Report [*A publication*]   (DLA)
Sens........... De Sensu [*of Aristotle*] [*Classical studies*]   (OCD)
SENS........ Sensitive   (MSA)
SENS........ Sensory
SENS........ Sentex Sensing Technology, Inc. [*Ridgefield, NJ*] [*NASDAQ symbol*]   (NQ)
SENS........ Social England Series [*A publication*]
Sens and Actuators ... Sensors and Actuators [*A publication*]
SENSB...... Sense Processes [*A publication*]
Sen Schol ... Senior Scholastic [*A publication*]
SENSCOM ... Sentinel Systems Command [*Army*]   (MCD)
SENSD...... Studies in Environmental Science [*A publication*]
SENSEA.... Sentinel System Evaluation Agency [*DoD*]
Sensibilizirovannaya Fluorests Smesej Parov Met ... Sensibilizirovannaya Fluorestsentsiya Smesej Parov Metallov [*A publication*]
SENSIM ... Sensor System Simulation
Sensing....... Remote Sensing [*A publication*]
SENSO...... Sensor Operator   (MCD)
SENSO...... Sentinel Systems Office [*Military*]
SENSOR... Sentinel Event Notification System for Occupational Risks [*Medicine*]
Sensor Rev ... Sensor Review [*A publication*]
Sens Process ... Sensory Processes [*A publication*]
SENT........ Sentence   (AABC)
Sent........... Sentenza [*Decision, Judgment*] [*Italian*]   (ILCA)
SENTA...... Societe d'Etudes Nucleaires et de Techniques Avancees [*France*]
SENTAC ... Society for Ear, Nose, and Throat Advances in Children   (EA)
SenTechWeldI ... Senior Technician of the Welding Institute [*British*]   (DBQ)
SENTOS ... Sentinel Operating System   (IEEE)
SENTRAB ... Syndicat des Travailleurs des Entreprises, Privees, Travaux Publics et Batiments [*Union of Workers of Private Enterprises, Public Works and Buildings*] [*Togo*]
SENTRE ... Sensor of Tail Region Emitters   (MCD)
SENTRY... Survey Entry
SENU .... Neuvo Rocafuerte [*Ecuador*] [*ICAO location identifier*]   (ICLI)
SENU .... Spectrum Efficient Network Unit   (MCD)
SENV........ Security Environmental Systems, Inc. [*NASDAQ symbol*]   (NQ)
SENYLRC ... Southeastern New York Library Resources Council [*Highland, NY*] [*Library network*]
SEO .... Salvage Engineering Order   (MCD)
SEO .... Salvo Erro ou Omissao [*Errors and Omissions Excepted*] [*Portuguese*]
SEO .... Satellite for Earth Observation
SEO .... Seaport Corp. [*AMEX symbol*]   (SPSG)
SEO .... Seguela [*Ivory Coast*] [*Airport symbol*]   (OAG)
SEO .... Senior Engineer Officer [*Navy*]
SEO .... Senior Executive Officer [*Civil Service*] [*British*]
SEO .... Senior Experimental Officer [*Also, SExO, SXO*] [*Ministry of Agriculture, Fisheries, and Food*] [*British*]
SEO .... Seoul [*Keizyo*] [*South Korea*] [*Seismograph station code, US Geological Survey*]   (SEIS)
SEO .... Serial Engineering Order   (MCD)
SEO .... Shoulder-Elbow Orthosis [*Medicine*]
SEO .... Sin Errores y Omisiones [*Errors and Omissions Excepted*] [*Business term*] [*Spanish*]
SEO .... Society of Education Officers [*British*]
SEO .... Special Engineering Order [*NASA*]   (NASA)
SEO .... State Electoral Office [*Australia*]
SEO .... State Energy Office
SEO .... Synchronous Equatorial Orbit [*or Orbiter*] [*NASA*]   (KSC)
SEOA .... Pasochoa [*Ecuador*] [*ICAO location identifier*]   (ICLI)
SEOC........ Submarine Extended Operating Cycle   (NVT)
SEOCS...... Sun-Earth Observatory and Climatology Satellite
SEODSE ... Special Explosive Ordnance Disposal Supplies and Equipment [*Army*]   (AABC)
SEOG .... Supplemental Educational Opportunity Grant [*Department of Education*]
SEOL........ Olmedo [*Ecuador*] [*ICAO location identifier*]   (ICLI)
SEON .... Solar Electro-Optical Network   (MCD)
SEOO .... Sauf Erreur ou Omission [*Errors and Omissions Excepted*] [*French*]
SEOO .... State Economic Opportunity Office
SEOP........ SHAPE [*Supreme Headquarters Allied Powers Europe*] Emergency Operating Procedures [*NATO*]   (NATG)
SEOP........ Siecor Electro-Optic Products [*Research Triangle Park, NC*]   (TSSD)
SEOP........ System Employment and Organizational Plan [*Army*]
SEOPSN... Select-Operate-Sense
SEOR........ Oro [*Ecuador*] [*ICAO location identifier*]   (ICLI)
SEOS........ SIGINT Equipment Operator Simulator [*Military*]
S/EOS .... Standard Earth Observation Satellite   (MCD)
SEOS........ Symmetric Exchange of Symmetry [*Spectrometry*]
SEOS........ Synchronous Earth Observatory Satellite [*NASA*]
SEOSS...... Slewable Electro-Optical Sensor System
Seoul J Med ... Seoul Journal of Medicine [*A publication*]
Seoul LJ..... Seoul Law Journal [*A publication*]   (DLA)

Seoul Natl Univ Coll Agric Bull ... Seoul National University. College of Agriculture. Bulletin [*A publication*]
Seoul Natl Univ Eng Rep ... Seoul National University. Engineering Reports [*A publication*]
Seoul Nat Univ Econ R ... Seoul National University. Economic Review [*A publication*]
Seoul Nat Univ Fac Pap Bio Agric Ser ... Seoul National University. Faculty Papers. Biology and Agriculture Series [*A publication*]
Seoul Nat Univ Fac Pap Med Pharm Ser ... Seoul National University. Faculty Papers. Medicine and Pharmacy Series [*A publication*]
Seoul Nat Univ Fac Pap Sci Technol Ser ... Seoul National University. Faculty Papers. Science and Technology Series [*A publication*]
Seoul Nat Univ J Agric Sci ... Seoul National University. Journal of Agricultural Sciences [*A publication*]
Seoul University J Pharm Sci ... Seoul University. Journal of Pharmaceutical Sciences [*A publication*]
Seoul Univ Fac Pap Ser C ... Seoul University. Faculty Papers. Series C. Science and Technology [*A publication*]
Seoul Univ Fac Pap Ser D ... Seoul University. Faculty Papers. Series D. Medicine and Pharmacy [*A publication*]
Seoul Univ Fac Pap Ser E ... Seoul University. Faculty Papers. Series E. Biology and Agriculture [*A publication*]
Seoul Univ J Biol Agric Ser B ... Seoul University. Journal. Series B. Biology and Agriculture [*A publication*]
Seoul Univ J Biol Agr Ser B ... Seoul University. Journal. Series B. Biology and Agriculture [*A publication*]
Seoul Univ J Med Pharm Ser C ... Seoul University. Journal. Series C. Medicine and Pharmacy [*A publication*]
Seoul Univ J Nat Sci Ser A ... Seoul University. Journal. Series A. Natural Science [*A publication*]
Seoul Univ J Nat Sci Ser B ... Seoul University. Journal. Series B. Natural Science [*A publication*]
Seoul Univ J Nat Sci Ser C ... Seoul University. Journal. Series C. Natural Science [*A publication*]
Seoul Univ J Pharm Sci ... Seoul University. Journal of Pharmaceutical Sciences [*A publication*]
Seoul Univ J Sci Technol Ser A ... Seoul University. Journal. Series A. Science and Technology [*A publication*]
SEOW .... Society of Engineering Office Workers   (EA)
SEP .... Salmonid Enhancement Program [*Canada*]
SEP .... Samenwerkende Elektriciteit Produktie Bedrijven [*Electric utility*] [*Netherlands*]
SEP .... Saturday Evening Post [*A publication*]
SEP .... Scientific and Engineering Personnel [*Military*]
SEP .... Secretaria de Educacion Publica [*Mexico*] [*A publication*]
SE(P) .... Security Executive, Control at Ports [*British*] [*World War II*]
SEP .... Selective Employment Payments [*British*]
SEP .... Self-Elevating Platform
SEP .... Self-Employed Pension [*British*]
SEP .... Sensory Evoked Potential [*Neurophysiology*]
SEP .... Separate   (AFM)
SEP .... Separation Parameter
SEP .... Sepia [*Stamp collecting*]   (ROG)
SEP .... September   (AFM)
SEP .... Septuagint [*Version of the Bible*]
SEP .... Sepultus [*Buried*] [*Latin*]
SEP .... Serial Entry Printer
SEP .... Shepherd Products Ltd. [*Toronto Stock Exchange symbol*]
SEP .... Simplified Employee Pension
SEP .... Site Emergency Plan [*Nuclear energy*]   (NRCH)
SEP .... Slow Electrical Process [*Human brain*]
SEP .... Slug Ejector Punch
SEP .... Society of Engineering Psychologists [*Later, DAEEP*]   (EA)
SEP .... Society for Exact Philosophy   (EA)
SEP .... Society of Experimental Psychologists   (EA)
SEP .... Software End Product [*Army*]
SEP .... Software Enhancement Proposal
SEP .... Solar Electric Power [*or Propulsion*]
SEP .... Solid Electrolyte Potentiometry
SEP .... Somatically Evoked Potential [*Neurophysiology*]
SEP .... SOSUS Estimated Position   (NVT)
SEP .... Source Evaluation Panel [*NASA*]   (NASA)
SEP .... Southern Education Program [*Defunct*]   (EA)
SEP .... Space Electronic Package
SEP .... Special Education Programs [*Department of Education*] [*Formerly, BEH*]
SEP .... Special Emphasis Program [*DoD*]
SEP .... Specific Excess Power   (MCD)
SEP .... Sperm Entry Point [*into egg*]
SEP .... Spherical Error Precision [*or Probability*]
SEP .... Stable Element Panel
SEP .... Standard Electronic Package
SEP .... Standard Engineering Practice   (AAG)
SEP .... Standard Error of Prediction
SEP .... Star Epitaxial Planar   (MSA)
SEP .... Stephenville, TX [*Location identifier*] [*FAA*]   (FAAL)
SEP .... Strong Equivalence Principle [*Thermodynamics*]
SEP .... Student Expense Program [*Civil Defense*]
SEP .... Studiegroup voor Europese Politiek   (EA)
SEP .... Supervisor Executive Program [*NASA*]   (KSC)

SEP .... Support Equipment Package [*NASA*]   (NASA)
SEP .... Surface Electrical Property [*Apollo*] [*NASA*]
SEP .... Surface Experiments [*NASA*]
SEP .... Surrendered Enemy Personnel
SEP .... Survey of Eastern Palestine [*A publication*]   (BJA)
SEP .... Symfonia Emboriou kai Pliromon [*Commerce and Payments Agreement*] [*Greek*]
SEP .... Systematic Evaluation Program [*Nuclear Regulatory Commission*]
SEP .... Systems Effectiveness Plan
SEP .... Systems Engineering Process
SEP .... Systems Extension Plan
SEP .... Systolic Ejection Period [*Cardiology*]
SEPA .... Pastaza [*Ecuador*] [*ICAO location identifier*]   (ICLI)
SEPA .... Soft Enhancement of Percutaneous Absorption [*Pharmacy*]
SEPA .... Southeast Pacific Area
SEPA .... Southeastern Power Administration [*Department of Energy*]
SEPA .... Southeastern Psychological Association   (MCD)
SEPA .... Soviet Extended Planning Annex   (MCD)
SEPA .... Spanish Evangelical Publishers Association   (EA)
SEP & A ..... Special Equipment Parts and Assemblies Section   (AAG)
SEPA .... System Evaluation Planning and Assessment Model   (MCD)
SEPAC ..... Space Experiments with Particle Accelerators [*Spacelab mission*]
SEPACFOR ... Southeast Pacific Force [*later, Command*] [*Navy*]
SEPAK ...... Suspension of Expendable Penetration Aids by Kite [*Military*]
SEPAP ...... Shuttle Electrical Power Analysis Program [*NASA*]
SEPAR ...... Shuttle Electrical Power Analysis Report [*NASA*]   (NASA)
Separation Sci Tech ... Separation Science and Technology [*A publication*]
SEPARON ... Separation   (ROG)
Separ Sci .... Separation Science [*Later, Separation Science and Technology*] [*A publication*]
SEPAWG .. Save EPA [*Environmental Protection Agency*] Working Group   (EA)
SE/PB .... Southern Europe - Ports and Beaches [*NATO*]   (NATG)
SEPC .... Space Exploration Program Council [*NASA*]
SEPCEN .... Separation Center [*Navy*]
SEPCOR ... Separate Correspondence   (MCD)
SEPD .... Scottish Economic Planning Department [*British*]
SEPD .... Separated
SEPD .... Special-Environment Powder Diffractometer [*Crystallography*]
SEPD .... State Emergency Planning Director [*Civil Defense*]
SEPE .... Pechichal [*Ecuador*] [*ICAO location identifier*]   (ICLI)
SEPE .... Seattle Port of Embarkation
SEPE .... Separate   (ROG)
SEPE .... Societe d'Edition et de Publications en Exlusivite
SEPEA ...... Societe Europeene de Psychiatrie de l'Enfant et de l'Adolescent [*European Society of Child and Adolescent Psychiatry - ESCAP*]   (EAIO)
SEPEL ...... Southeastern Plant Environment Laboratories [*Duke University and North Carolina State University*]
SEPEMIAG ... Societe d'Etudes pour l'Equipement Miniere, Agricole, et Industrial du Gabon [*Gabon Society for Study of Mining, Agricultural, and Industrial Equipment*]
SEPG .... Separating
SEPGA ...... Southeastern Pecan Growers Association   (EA)
Seph .... Sephardic [*Jews from Spain, Portugal, North Africa, and the Mediterranean*]   (BJA)
SEPI .... Pichincha [*Ecuador*] [*ICAO location identifier*]   (ICLI)
SEPI .... Silicon Electro-Physics, Incorporated [*NASDAQ symbol*]   (NQ)
SEPI .... Society for the Exploration of Psychotherapy Integration   (EA)
SEPI .... Sylvania Electric Products, Incorporated   (KSC)
SEPIL .... Selective Excitation of Probe Ion Luminescence [*Analytical chemistry*]
SEPL .... Playas [*Ecuador*] [*ICAO location identifier*]   (ICLI)
SEPL .... South European Pipeline [*Oil*]
SEPM .... Society for Sedimentary Geology [*Formerly, Society of Economic Paleontologists and Mineralogists*]   (EA)
SEPM Core Workshop ... Society of Economic Paleontologists and Mineralogists. Core Workshop [*A publication*]
SEPM (Soc Econ Paleontol Miner) Field Trip Guideb ... SEPM (Society of Economic Paleontologists and Mineralogists) Field Trip Guidebook [*A publication*]
SEPN .... Separation   (AAG)
SEPO .... Posorja [*Ecuador*] [*ICAO location identifier*]   (ICLI)
SEPO .... Space Electric Power Office [*AEC*]
SEPOL ...... Settlement Problem-Oriented Language [*Data processing*]   (IEEE)
SEPOL ...... Soil Engineering Problem-Oriented Language [*Data processing*]
SEPORT ... Supply and Equipment Report [*Army*]   (AABC)
SEPOS ...... Selected Enlisted Personnel for Overseas Service [*Military*]   (AABC)
SEPP .... Seppyo. Journal. Japanese Society of Snow and Ice [*A publication*]
SEPP .... Simplified Employee Pension Plan
Sep Purif M ... Separation and Purification Methods [*A publication*]
Sep Purif Methods ... Separation and Purification Methods [*A publication*]
SEPRD ...... Sensory Processes [*A publication*]
SEPRL ...... Southeast Poultry Research Laboratory [*University of Georgia*] [*Research center*]   (RCD)

SEPROS....   Separation Processing [*Military*]
SEPS......... Pasaje [*Ecuador*] [*ICAO location identifier*]   (ICLI)
SEPS......... Service Module Electrical Power System [*NASA*]   (KSC)
SEPS......... Severe Environment Power System   (IEEE)
SEPS......... Smithsonian Earth Physics Satellite
SEPS......... Socio-Economic Planning Sciences [*A publication*]
SEPS......... Solar Electric Propulsion System [*NASA*]
SEPS......... System/Equipment Population Summary
SEPSA......   Society of Educational Programmers and Systems Analysts
              [*Later, SDE*]
SEPS-B......   Socio-Economic Planning Sciences [*A publication*]
Sep Sci ...... Separation Science [*Later, Separation Science and Technology*]
              [*A publication*]
Sep Sci Technol ... Separation Science and Technology [*A publication*]
SEPSME...   Social Economic and Political Studies of the Middle East [*A
              publication*]   (BJA)
SEPST........ Solar Electric Propulsion System Technology
SEPT ....   Putumayo [*Ecuador*] [*ICAO location identifier*]   (ICLI)
SEPT ....   Separate
Sept........... Septem Contra Thebas [*of Aeschylus*] [*Classical
              studies*]   (OCD)
SEPT ....   September   (EY)
Sept........... Septuagint [*Version of the Bible*]   (BJA)
SEPTA .....   Southeastern Pennsylvania Transportation Authority
SEPTAR.....   Seaborne Powered Target [*Navy*]   (NVT)
SEPTD......   Separated
SEPTEL ....   Separate Telegram
Septent........ Septentrion. Revue Archeologique Trimestrielle [*A publication*]
SEPTG ......   Separating
SEPTLA....   Southeastern Pennsylvania Theological Library Association
              [*Library network*]
SEPTR......   Separator
SEPTR......   September   (ROG)
SEPU........   Puna [*Ecuador*] [*ICAO location identifier*]   (ICLI)
SEPULT.....   Sepultus [*Buried*] [*Latin*]   (ROG)
SEPV ....   Portoviejo [*Ecuador*] [*ICAO location identifier*]   (ICLI)
SEPY ....   Puyo [*Ecuador*] [*ICAO location identifier*]   (ICLI)
SEQ ....   Scientific Equipment   (KSC)
SEQ ....   Seguin, TX [*Location identifier*] [*FAA*]   (FAAL)
SEQ ....   Self-Esteem Questionnaire [*Personality development test*]
              [*Psychology*]
SEQ ....   Sequel
SEQ ....   Sequence   (AABC)
SEQ ....   Sequente [*And in What Follows*] [*Latin*]
SEQ ....   Sequential Pulse Counting [*Spectrometry*]
SEQ ....   Sequestrum [*Medicine*]
SEQ ....   Sequitur [*It Follows*] [*Latin*]
SEQ ....   Storage Equities, Inc. [*NYSE symbol*]   (SPSG)
SEQ ....   String Education Quarterly [*A publication*]
SEQE........   Quevedo [*Ecuador*] [*ICAO location identifier*]   (ICLI)
SEQI........   Storage Equities, Inc. [*NASDAQ symbol*]   (NQ)
SEQL........   Sequel Corp. [*Englewood, CO*] [*NASDAQ symbol*]   (NQ)
SEQ LUCE ... Sequenti Luce [*The Following Day*] [*Latin*]   (ADA)
SEQN .... Quininde [*Ecuador*] [*ICAO location identifier*]   (ICLI)
SEQOPT....   Sequential Optimization   (MCD)
SEQP........   Supreme Equipment & Systems Corp. [*NASDAQ
              symbol*]   (NQ)
SEQQ ......   Sequentes [*or Sequentia*] [*The Following*] [*Plural form*] [*Latin*]
SEQQ ....   Sequentibus [*In the Following Places*] [*Latin*]   (ADA)
SEQR........   Sequencer   (AAG)
SEQREC....   Sequence Recall [*Neuropsychology test*]
SEQS........   Simultaneous Equation Solver [*Computer program*]
SEQU .... Quito/Mariscal Sucre [*Ecudaor*] [*ICAO location
              identifier*]   (ICLI)
SEQU ....   Sequoia and Kings Canyon National Parks
SEQUAL....   Seasonal Equatorial Atlantic Experiment
SEQUEL...   Structured English Query Language [*1974*] [*Data
              processing*]   (CSR)
SEQUIN....   Sequential Quadrature Inband [*Television system*]   (DEN)
SEQUIP ...   Study of Environmental Quality Information Programs   (KSC)
SEQUR......   Safety Equipment Requirements
SER........... Cataloging Services Department, OCLC [*Online Computer
              Library Center*], Inc., Columbus, OH [*OCLC
              symbol*]   (OCLC)
SER.MAMI...   Safety Evaluation Report [*Nuclear energy*]   (NRCH)
SER........... Sandia Engineering Reactor [*Nuclear energy*]
SER........... Seder Eliyahu Rabbah   (BJA)
SER........... Selective Early Retirement [*Army*]
SER........... Sequential Events Recorder
SER........... Serial   (AFM)
SER........... Series   (AAG)
Ser............ Serine [*Also, S*] [*An amino acid*]
SER........... Sermon
Ser............ Serpens [*Constellation*]
SER........... Servant
Ser............ Service [*A publication*]
SER........... Service   (NATG)
SER........... Service, Employment, Redevelopment [*Operation for Mexican-
              Americans*] [*Later, SER - Jobs for Progress*]
SeR........... Sewanee Review [*A publication*]
SER........... Seymour, IN [*Location identifier*] [*FAA*]   (FAAL)

SER........... Shore Establishment Realignment [*Navy*]   (NVT)
SER........... Sierracin Corp. [*AMEX symbol*]   (SPSG)
SER........... Significant Event Report   (IEEE)
SER........... Sikorsky Engineering Report
SER........... Silver Eagle Resources [*Vancouver Stock Exchange symbol*]
SER........... Simultaneous Evoked [*Cortical*] Response [*Neurophysiology*]
SER........... Site Evaluation Report   (MCD)
SER........... Smooth [*Surfaced*] Endoplasmic Reticulum [*Cytology*]
SER........... SNAP [*Systems for Nuclear Auxiliary Power*] Experimental
              Reactor
SER........... Sociedad Espanola de Radiodifusion [*Broadcasting
              organization*]
SER........... Society for Ecological Restoration   (EA)
SER........... Society for Educational Reconstruction   (EA)
SER........... Society for Epidemiologic Research   (EA)
SER........... Somatosensory Evoked Response [*Neurophysiology*]
SER........... South-Eastern Railway [*British*]
SER........... Stem End Rot [*Plant pathology*]
SeR........... Studi e Ricerche [*A publication*]
SER........... Sua Eccellenza Reverendissima [*His Eminence*]   (EY)
SER........... Support Equipment Requirement
SER........... Surface Electrical Resistivity
SER........... System Environment Recording   (BUR)
SERA........   Sierra Railroad Co. [*AAR code*]
SERA........   Society for Entrepreneurship Research and Application
              [*Defunct*]   (EA)
SERA........   Stop Equal Rights Amendment [*An association*]
              [*Inactive*]   (EA)
SERAA .....   Seramikkusu [*A publication*]
SERAC......   Southeastern Regional Arts Council
SERANAK ...   Serge and Natalie Koussevitzky [*Acronym was name of
              summer home of Boston Symphony Orchestra conductor
              and his first wife*]
SERANDA ...   Service Record, Health Record, Pay Account, and Personal
              Effects [*Military*]
SERAPE....   Simulator Equipment Requirements for Accelerating
              Procedural Evolution
SERAPHIM ... Systems Engineering Respecting Acquisition and Propagation
              of Heuristic Instructional Materials [*Chemistry*]
Ser Astron Uniw Adama Mickiewicza Poznaniu ... Seria Astronomia.
              Uniwersytet Imeni Adama Mickiewicza w Poznaniu [*A
              publication*]
SERB........   Riobamba [*Ecuador*] [*ICAO location identifier*]   (ICLI)
SERB........   Selective Early Retirement Board [*Army*]   (INF)
SERB........   Serbia
SERB........   Shuttle Engineering Review Board [*NASA*]   (NASA)
SERB........   Societe Europeene de Radiobiologie [*European Society for
              Radiation Biology - ESRB*]   (EAIO)
SERB........   Study of the Enhanced Radiation Belt [*NASA*]
SERB........   Systems Engineering Review Board [*NASA*]   (NASA)
Serb Acad Sci Arts Bull ... Serbian Academy of Sciences and Arts. Bulletin [*A
              publication*]
Serb Acad Sci Arts Glas ... Serbian Academy of Sciences and Arts. Glas [*A
              publication*]
Serb Acad Sci Arts Monogr Dep Sci ... Serbian Academy of Sciences and Arts.
              Monographs. Department of Sciences [*A publication*]
Serb Acad Sci Arts Sep Ed Dep Nat Math Sci ... Serbian Academy of Sciences
              and Arts. Separate Editions. Department of Natural and
              Mathematical Sciences [*A publication*]
Serb Arch Gen Med ... Serbian Archives of General Medicine [*A publication*]
SERBAUD ...   Serikat Buruh Angkutan Udara [*Airways' Union*] [*Indonesia*]
Serbian Acad Sci and Arts Monogr Dep Tech Sci ... Serbian Academy of
              Sciences and Arts. Monographs. Department of Technical
              Sciences [*A publication*]
Ser Bibliogr INTA (Pergamino) ... Serie Bibliografica. Instituto Nacional de
              Tecnologia Agropecuaria (Pergamino, Argentina) [*A
              publication*]
Ser Biol Uniw Adama Mickiewicza Poznaniu ... Seria Biologia. Uniwersytet
              Imeni Adama Mickiewicza w Poznaniu [*A publication*]
SERBIUM ...   Serikat Buruh Industri dan Umum [*Industrial and General
              Workers' Union*] [*Indonesia*]
SERBU .....   Serikat Buruh Umum [*General Workers' Union*] [*Indonesia*]
SERBUHI ...   Serikat Buruh Harian Indonesia [*Newspaper Employees' Union
              of Indonesia*]
SERBUMAMI ... Serikat Buruh Makanan dan Minuman [*Food Workers'
              Union*] [*Indonesia*]
SERBUMIKSI ... Serikat Buruh Minjak Kelapa Seluruh [*Coconut Oil
              Workers' Union*] [*Indonesia*]
SERBUMIT ...   Serikat Buruh Minjak dan Tambang [*Oil and Minerals
              Workers' Union*] [*Indonesia*]
SERBUMUSI ... Serikat Buruh Muslimin Indonesia [*Moslem Workers'
              Union of Indonesia*]
SERBUNI ...   Serikat Buruh Unilever Indonesia [*Unilever Employees' Union
              of Indonesia*]
SERBUPI ...   Serikat Buruh Perkebunan Indonesia [*Plantation Workers'
              Union of Indonesia*]
SERBUPRI ...   Serikat Buruh Pertambangan Indonesia [*Mining Workers'
              Union of Indonesia*]
SERC......... Industry/University Cooperative Research Center for Software
              Engineering [*University of Florida, Purdue University*]
              [*Research center*]   (RCD)

SERC .... Science and Engineering Research Council [*British*]
SERC .... Smithsonian Environmental Research Center
SERC .... Southeastern Electric Reliability Council [*Regional power council*]
SERC .... Sussex European Research Centre [*Research center*] [*British*]   (IRC)
Ser Cana Azucar ... Serie Cana de Azucar [*A publication*]
Ser Chem Uniw Adama Mickiewicza Poznaniu ... Seria Chemia. Uniwersytet Imeni Adama Mickiewicza w Poznaniu [*A publication*]
Ser Conf Union Math Internat ... Serie des Conferences. Union Mathematique Internationale [*A publication*]
SERD .... Stored Energy Rotary Drive
SERD .... Support Equipment Recommendation Data [*NASA*]   (KSC)
SERD .... Support Equipment Requirements Data
SERDA ...... Signals and Electronic Warfare Research and Development Act
Ser Defects Cryst Solids ... Series Defects in Crystalline Solids [*A publication*]
SERDES .... Serializer/Deserializer
Ser Didact Univ Nac Tucuman Fac Agronom Zooteh ... Serie Didactica. Universidad Nacional de Tucuman. Facultad de Agronomia y Zootecnia [*A publication*]
Ser Div Ind Chem CSIRO ... Serial. Division of Industrial Chemistry. Commonwealth Scientific and Industrial Research Organisation [*A publication*]   (APTA)
Ser Divulg Agron Angolana ... Serie Divulgacao. Agronomia Angolana [*A publication*]
Ser Divulg Projeto Desenvolvimento Pesqui Florestal ... Serie Divulgacao. Projeto de Desenvolvimento e Pesquisa Florestal [*A publication*]
SERE .... Services Electronic Research Establishment [*British*]   (DEN)
SERE .... Survival, Evasion, Resistance, and Escape [*Military*]   (AFM)
Ser Emp ..... Service Employee [*A publication*]
SERENDIP ... Search for Extraterrestrial Radio Emission from Nearby Developed Intelligent Populations
Serengeti Res Inst Annu Rep ... Serengeti Research Institute. Annual Report [*A publication*]
Ser Entomol (The Hague) ... Series Entomologica (The Hague) [*A publication*]
SEREP .... System Environment Recording, Editing, and Printing [*Data processing*]
SEREP .... System Error Record Editing Program [*Data processing*]
SERF .... Sandia Engineering Reactor Facility [*Nuclear energy*]
SERF .... Service Fracturing Co. [*NASDAQ symbol*]   (NQ)
SERF .... Solar and Energy Research Facility [*University of Arizona*] [*Research center*]   (RCD)
SERF .... Space Environmental Research Facility
SERF .... Special Emergency Reaction Team Facility
SERF .... Special Environmental Radiometallurgy Facility [*Nuclear energy*]   (NRCH)
SERFE ...... Selection of Exempt Organization Returns for Examination [*IRS*]
SERFORSOPACSUBCOM ... Service Force, South Pacific, Subordinate Command
SERG .... Sergeant
SERG .... Serving   (MSA)
Serg Att ..... Sergeant on Attachment [*A publication*]   (DLA)
Serg Const L ... Sergeant's Constitutional Law [*A publication*]   (DLA)
SERGE ...... Socially and Ecologically Responsible Geographers [*Defunct*]   (EA)
Ser Geol Econ (Braz) Sup Desenvolvimento Nordeste Div Geol ... Serie Geologia Economica (Brazil). Superintendencia do Desenvolvimento do Nordeste. Divisao de Geologia [*A publication*]
Serg Land Laws PA ... Sergeant on the Land Laws of Pennsylvania [*A publication*]   (DLA)
Serg LL ...... Sergeant's Land Laws of Pennsylvania [*A publication*]   (DLA)
Serg & Lowb ... English Common Law Reports, Edited by Sergeant and Lowber [*A publication*]   (DLA)
Serg & Lowb Rep ... English Common Law Reports, Edited by Sergeant and Lowber [*A publication*]   (DLA)
Serg Mech L ... Sergeant on Mechanics' Lien Law [*A publication*]   (DLA)
Serg & R ..... Sergeant and Rawle's Pennsylvania Reports [*A publication*]   (DLA)
Serg & Raw ... Sergeant and Rawle's Pennsylvania Reports [*A publication*]   (DLA)
Serg & Rawl ... Sergeant and Rawle's Pennsylvania Supreme Court Reports [*1814-28*] [*A publication*]   (DLA)
SERGT ...... Sergeant
SERH .... Secretaria de Estado de Recursos Hidricos [*Argentina*]
Ser Haematol ... Series Haematologica [*A publication*]
SERI .... Aguarico [*Ecuador*] [*ICAO location identifier*]   (ICLI)
SERI .... Society for the Encouragement of Research and Invention   (EA)
SERI .... Solar Energy Research Institute [*Department of Energy*] [*Golden, CO*]
Serials BLL ... Serials in the British Lending Library [*A publication*]
Serials Libn ... Serials Librarian [*A publication*]
Serials Libr ... Serials Librarian [*A publication*]
Serials R .... Serials Review [*A publication*]
Sericult Res ... Sericultural Research [*Japan*] [*A publication*]
Serie Bibliogr Temat ... Serie Bibliografia Tematica [*A publication*]
Ser Inf Conf Cursos Reun Interam Inst Agric Sci ... Serie Informes de Conferencias. Cursos y Reuniones-Inter-American Institute of Agricultural Sciences [*A publication*]

SER-IV ..... Supination, External Rotation - Type IV Fracture
SERIX .... Swedish Environmental Research Index [*Swedish National Environmental Protection Board*] [*Database*]   (IID)
SERJ .... Serjeant [*Military*] [*British*]   (ROG)
SERJ .... Space Electric Ramjet [*Air Force*]
SERJ .... Supercharged Ejector Ramjet [*Aircraft engine*]
Serjt .... Serjeant [*Military*] [*British*]   (DMA)
SERJT-MAJ ... Serjeant-Major [*Military*] [*British*]   (ROG)
SERL .... Sanitary Engineering Research Laboratory [*University of California*]   (MCD)
Ser L .... Serie Linguistica [*A publication*]
SERL .... Services Electronic Research Laboratory [*British*]
SERLANT ... Service Forces, Atlantic [*Navy*]
Ser Lib ...... Serials Librarian [*A publication*]
Ser Libr ..... Serials Librarian [*A publication*]
SERLINE ... Serials On-Line [*National Library of Medicine*] [*Bethesda, MD*] [*Database*]
SERM .... Sermon   (ROG)
SERM .... Society of Early Recorded Music   (EA)
SERM .... Solar and Earth Radiation Monitor   (NOAA)
SERM .... Syncrude Environmental Research Monograph [*A publication*]
Ser Mat Fis ... Serie di Matematica e Fisica [*A publication*]
SERMCE .. Amalgamated Association of Street, Electric Railway, and Motor Coach Employees of America [*Later, ATU*]
SERME ...... Sign Error Root Modulus Error
SERMLP ... Southeastern Regional Medical Library Program [*Emory University*] [*Library network*]   (IID)
Ser Monogr Inst Zootec ... Serie Monografias. Instituto de Zootecnia [*A publication*]
SERN .... Southeastern [*Meteorology*]   (FAAC)
SERNO ..... Serial Number
SERNO ..... Service Number [*Military*]
SERO .... Santa Rosa [*Ecuador*] [*ICAO location identifier*]   (ICLI)
SERO .... Service Employment Redevelopment Operation   (OICC)
SERO .... System Engineering Release Order   (MCD)
SERODS .... Surface-Enhanced Raman Optical Data Storage Technology [*Developed at Oak Ridge National Laboratory*]
Serol Mus Bull ... Serological Museum Bulletin [*A publication*]
SERON ..... Service Squadron [*Navy*]
Serono Symp Proc ... Serono Symposia. Proceedings [*A publication*]
Serono Symp Publ Raven Press ... Serono Symposia Publications from Raven Press [*A publication*]
SERP .... Self-Employed Retirement Plan [*Keogh plan*]
Serp .... Serpens [*Constellation*]
SERP .... Simulated Ejector Ready Panel
SERP .... Software Engineering Research Projects [*Data and Analysis Center for Software*] [*Database*]
SERP .... Standardization/Evaluation Review Panel   (AFIT)
SERPA ...... Southeastern Resource Policy Association   (EA)
SERPAC .... Service Forces, Pacific [*Navy*]
Ser Paedopsychiatr ... Series Paedopsychiatrica [*A publication*]
SERPIN .... Serine Proteinase Inhibitor [*Biochemistry*]
Ser Piper .... Serie Piper [*A publication*]
Ser Poeyana Inst Biol Acad Cienc Cuba ... Serie Poeyana. Instituto de Biologia. Academia de Ciencias de Cuba [*A publication*]
Ser Poeyana Inst Zool Acad Cienc Cuba ... Serie Poeyana. Instituto de Zoologia. Academia de Ciencias de Cuba [*A publication*]
SERPS ...... Service Propulsion System [*or Subsystem*] [*NASA*]   (KSC)
SERPS ...... State Earnings-Related Pension Scheme [*British*]
Ser Publ US Northeast Reg Plant Introd Stn ... Serial Publication. United States Northeast Regional Plant Introduction Station [*A publication*]
Ser R .... Serials Review [*A publication*]
SERR .... Serrate   (MSA)
SerrC .... Serraika Chronika [*A publication*]
SERRON ..... Service Squadron [*Navy*]
SERRS ...... Surface-Enhanced Resonance Raman Scattering [*Spectroscopy*]
SE/RRT ..... Southern Europe - Railroad Transport [*NATO*]   (NATG)
SERS .... Rio Saloya [*Ecuador*] [*ICAO location identifier*]   (ICLI)
SERS .... Seaborne Environmental Reporting System
SERS .... Shuttle Equipment Record System [*NASA*]   (NASA)
SERS .... Southern Education Reporting Service
SERS .... State Employees Retirement System
SERS .... Support Equipment Requirements Sheet
SERS .... Surface-Enhanced Raman Scattering [*Spectroscopy*]
Ser Sl .... Serial Slants [*A publication*]
Sert .... Sertorius [*of Plutarch*] [*Classical studies*]   (OCD)
SERT .... Shipboard Electronic Readiness Team [*Navy*]   (CAAL)
SERT .... Single-Electron Rise Time [*Scintillation counting*]   (IEEE)
SE/RT ...... Southern Europe - Road Transport [*NATO*]   (NATG)
SERT .... Space Electric [*or Electronic*] Rocket Test
SERT .... Special Education Resource Teacher
SERT .... Special Education Review Team
SERT .... Special Emergency Reaction Team
SERT .... Spinning Satellite for Electric Rocket Test
SERT .... Sustained Ethanol Release Tube [*Pharmacology*]
SERTH ...... Satisfactory Evidence Received This Headquarters
SERT J ...... SERT [*Society of Electronic and Radio Technicians*] Journal [*A publication*]
SERTOMA ... Service to Mankind [*Meaning of name of Sertoma International Organization*]

SERUG...... SII [*Systems Integrators, Incorporated*] Eastern Regional Users Group   (EA)
Ser Universitaria ... Serie Universitaria [*A publication*]
SERV........ Servant
SERV........ Servian   (ROG)
SERV........ Service   (AAG)
Serv .... Service: A Review of Agricultural and Chemical Progress [*A publication*]
SERV........ Single-Stage Earth-Orbital Reusable Vehicle   (MCD)
SERV........ Space Emergency Reentry Vehicle [*NASA*]
SERV........ Surface Effect Rescue Vessel [*Coast Guard*]
Serv Can Faune Cah Biol ... Service Canadien de la Faune. Cahiers de Biologie [*A publication*]
Serv Cent Prot Rayonnem Ionis (Fr) Rapp Act ... Service Central de Protection Contre les Rayonnements Ionisants (France). Rapport d'Activite [*A publication*]
SERVCOMFMFPAC ... Service Command, Fleet Marine Force, Pacific
SERVDIV ... Service Division [*Navy*]
SERVE ...... Serve and Enrich Retirement by Volunteer Experience [*Staten Island, NY, project*]
SERVE ...... Service   (ROG)
Serv Esp Saude Publica Rev (Brazil) ... Servico Especial de Saude Publica. Revista (Brazil) [*A publication*]
Serv Farm Ranch Home ... Serving Farm, Ranch, and Home. Quarterly. University of Nebraska. College of Agriculture and Home Economics. Agricultural Experiment Station [*A publication*]
SERVFOR ... Service Force [*Navy*]
Serv Geol Bolivia Bol ... Servicio Geologico de Bolivia. Boletin [*A publication*]
Serv Geol Ital Mem Descr Carta Geol Ital ... Servizio Geologico d'Italia Memorie Descrittive della Carta Geologica d'Italia [*A publication*]
Serv Geol Port Mem ... Servicos Geologics de Portugal. Memoria [*A publication*]
SERVHEL ... Service Record and Health Record [*Military*]
Service Soc ... Service Social [*A publication*]
Servico Soc de Comer Bol Bibl ... Servico Social de Comercio. Boletim Bibliografico [*A publication*]
Servico Soc e Soc ... Servico Social e Sociedade [*A publication*]
SERVLANT ... Service Force, Atlantic Fleet
SERVLANTSUBORDCOMD ... Service Force, Atlantic Fleet, Subordinate Command
SERVMART ... Service Mart
Serv Nac Min Geol (Argent) Rev ... Servicio Nacional Minero Geologico (Argentina). Revista [*A publication*]
SERVNO... Service Number [*Navy*]
SERVO ...... Service Office
SERVO...... Servomechanism
SERVON... Service Squadron [*Navy*]
SERVPA... Service Record and Pay Record [*Military*]
SERVPAC ... Service Force, Pacific Fleet
SERVPAHEL ... Service Record, Pay Record, and Health Record [*Military*]
SERVREC ... Service Record
SERVS.......... Spanish/English Reading and Vocabulary Screening Test
SERVSCOLCOM ... Service School Command [*Navy*]
Serv Shell Agric Ser A ... Servicio Shell para el Agricultor. Serie A [*A publication*]
Serv Shell Agr Ser A ... Servicio Shell para el Agricultor. Serie A. Informe [*A publication*]
Serv Soc (Bruxelles) ... Service Social (Bruxelles) [*A publication*]
Serv Soc Monde ... Service Social dans le Monde [*A publication*]
Serv Soc (Quebec) ... Service Social (Quebec) [*A publication*]
SERVSOWESPAC ... Service Force, Southwest Pacific Fleet
SERVT ...... Servant
Serv World ... Service World International [*A publication*]
SERY .... Sarayacu [*Ecuador*] [*ICAO location identifier*]   (ICLI)
SES .... Group Psychotherapy Suitability Evaluation Scale [*Psychology*]
SES .... Samarbetsorganisationen for Emballagefragor i Skandinavien [*Scandinavian Packaging Association*]   (EA)
SES .... Satellite Earth Station
SES .... Schriften far Ekonomik un Statistik [*A publication*]
SES .... Science Ethic Society   (EA)
SES .... Scientific Exploration Society   (EA)
SES .... Scottish Economic Society [*British*]
SES .... Seafarers Education Service [*British*]
SES .... Seagrass Ecosystem Study [*Marine science*]   (MSC)
SES .... Secondary Electron Scattering
SES .... Section d'Eclaireurs-Skieurs [*of Chasseurs Alpins, French Army*]
SES .... Seismic Electric Signal
SES .... Senior Executive Service [*Civil Service*]
SES .... Sequential Environmental Stress
SES .... Service Evaluation System [*Telecommunications*]   (TEL)
SES .... Sesone [*Herbicide*] [*Trademark of Union Carbide Corp.*]
SES .... Ship Earth Station [*INMARSAT*]
SES .... Shuttle Engineering Simulation [*NASA*]   (NASA)
SES .... Sight Erection Support
SES .... Signal Enhancement Seismograph
SES .... Signals Exploitation Space   (MCD)
SES .... Single Engine Sea [*Pilot rating*]   (AIA)

SES .... Small Edison Screw
SES .... Social and Economic Studies [*A publication*]
SES .... Societe des Etudes Socialistes [*Society for Socialist Studies - SSS*]
SES .... Societe Europeenne des Satellites [*Luxembourg*]
SES .... Society of Educators and Scholars   (EA)
SES .... Society of Engineering Science   (EA)
SES .... Society for Environmental Stabilization [*Defunct*]   (EA)
SES .... Society of Eye Surgeons   (EA)
SES .... Socioeconomic Status [*or Strata*]
SES .... Soil Erosion Service [*Became Soil Conservation Service, 1935*]
SES .... Solar Eclipse Sensor   (MCD)
SES .... Solar Energy Society [*Later, International Solar Energy Society*]   (EA)
SES .... Solar Environment Simulator
SES .... SONAR Echo Simulator
SES .... Sophia English Studies [*A publication*]
SES .... Space Environment Simulator [*NASA*]
SES .... Space Erectable Structure
SES .... Special Emphasis Study   (NASA)
SES .... Special Exchange Service [*Telecommunications*]   (TEL)
SES .... SPRINT Engagement Simulation [*Missile system evaluation*] [*Army*]   (RDA)
SES .... Standards Engineering Society   (EA)
SES .... State Experiment Stations Division [*of ARS, Department of Agriculture*]
SES .... Stationary Engine Society   (EA)
SES .... Steam Electric Station [*Nuclear energy*]   (NRCH)
SES .... Steam Engine Systems Corp.
SES .... Stock Exchange of Singapore
SES .... Story of Exploration Series [*A publication*]
SES .... Strategic Engineering Survey [*Navy*]
SES .... Student Evaluation Scale [*Student attitudes test*]
SES .... Studies in Environmental Science [*Elsevier Book Series*] [*A publication*]
SES .... Studies and Expansion Society [*See also SEE*]   (EAIO)
SES .... Study of Education at Stanford [*Stanford University*]
SES .... Suffield [*Alberta*] [*Seismograph station code, US Geological Survey*]   (SEIS)
SES .... Supervisory Electronics Specialist
SES .... Surface Effects Ship [*Navy symbol*]
SES .... Sustaining Engineering Services
SES .... Synergist Erection System [*Medicine*]
SES .... System External Storage
SESA .... Salinas [*Ecuador*] [*ICAO location identifier*]   (ICLI)
SESA .... Seasons Savings Bank [*NASDAQ symbol*]   (NQ)
SESA .... Signal Equipment Support Agency
SESA .... Social and Economic Statistics Administration [*Terminated, 1975*] [*Department of Commerce*]
SESA .... Society for Experimental Stress Analysis [*Later, SEM*]   (EA)
SESA .... Solar Energy Society of America   (EA)
SESA .... Standard Electrica, Sociedad Anonima [*Brazilian affiliate of ITT*]
SESA .... State Employment Security Agency
SESA .... Story of the Empire Series [*A publication*]
SESAC...... Society of European Stage Authors and Composers
SESAC...... Space and Earth Science Advisory Committee [*NASA*]
SESAME... Search for Excellence in Science and Mathematics Education [*Graduate program at University of California at Berkeley*]
SESAME... Service, Sort and Merge [*Data processing*]
SESAME... Severe Environmental Storms and Mesoscale Experiment [*National Science Foundation/National Oceanic and Atmospheric Administration*]
SESAME... Systems Engineering Study on Atmospheric Measurements and Equipment   (NOAA)
SESA Pap ... SESA [*Society for Experimental Stress Analysis*] Papers [*A publication*]
SESAT...... Stanford Early School Achievement Test [*Educational test*]
SESB .... Sibambe [*Ecuador*] [*ICAO location identifier*]   (ICLI)
SESC .... Selective Elution Solvent Chromatography
SESC .... Sequential Elution Solvent Chromatography
SESC .... Shuttle Events Sequential Control [*NASA*]   (MCD)
SESC .... South Eastern State College [*Oklahoma*]
SESC .... Space Environment Services Center [*National Oceanic and Atmospheric Administration*] [*Boulder, CO*]   (KSC)
SESC .... Sucua [*Ecuador*] [*ICAO location identifier*]   (ICLI)
SESC .... Surface Environmental Sample Container [*Apollo*] [*NASA*]
SESCI .... Solar Energy Society of Canada, Incorporated [*Societe d'Energie Solaire du Canada*]
SESCO ...... Secure Submarine Communications
SESD .... Santo Domingo De Los Colorados [*Ecuador*] [*ICAO location identifier*]   (ICLI)
SESDA ...... Serikat Sekerdja Departemen Agama [*Brotherhood of Employees of Department of Religious Affairs*] [*Indonesia*]
SESDA ...... Small Engine Servicing Dealers Association   (EA)
SESDAQ ... Stock Exchange of Singapore Dealing and Automated Quotation System
SESE .... Secadal [*Educador*] [*ICAO location identifier*]   (ICLI)
SESE .... Secure Echo-Sounding Equipment [*SONAR*] [*Navy*]
SESE .... Shuttle Experiment Support Equipment

SE/SE........ Single Entry/Single Exit
SESE........ Space Electronics Support Equipment (MCD)
SESEF...... Ship Electronics System Evaluation Facility [*Navy*] (CAAL)
SESG........ Sangay [*Ecuador*] [*ICAO location identifier*] (ICLI)
SESG........ Southern Europe Shipping Group [*NATO*] (NATG)
SESH........ San Honorato [*Ecuador*] [*ICAO location identifier*] (ICLI)
SESI......... Sur Iliniza [*Ecuador*] [*ICAO location identifier*] (ICLI)
SE/SI........ Systems Engineering/Systems Integration (SDI)
SESJ......... San Jose [*Ecuador*] [*ICAO location identifier*] (ICLI)
SESK........ Silok [*Ecuador*] [*ICAO location identifier*] (ICLI)
SESL........ San Lorenzo [*Ecuador*] [*ICAO location identifier*] (ICLI)
SESL........ Self-Erecting Space Laboratory (AAG)
SESL........ Southeastern Savings Bank, Inc. [*NASDAQ symbol*] (NQ)
SESL........ Space Environment Simulation Laboratory [*NASA*]
SeSL......... Studi e Saggi Linguistici [*A publication*]
SESLP...... Sequential Explicit Stochastic Linear Programming [*Data processing*]
SESM........ Samborondon [*Ecuador*] [*ICAO location identifier*] (ICLI)
SESMD..... Sudan Stock Exchange and Securities Market Developments
SESMI...... Systems Engineering Support and Management Integration (MCD)
SESN........ San Carlos [*Ecuador*] [*ICAO location identifier*] (ICLI)
SESO......... La Estrella [*Ecuador*] [*ICAO location identifier*] (ICLI)
SESO......... Senior Equipment Staff Officer [*Air Force*] [*British*]
SESOC...... Surface Effect Ship for Ocean Commerce
SESOME .. Service, Sort, and Merge [*Data processing*] (IEEE)
SESP........ Society of Experimental Social Psychology (EA)
SESP........ Space Experiment Support Program (MCD)
SESPA....... Scientists and Engineers for Social and Political Action [*Later, SFTP*] (EA)
SESPENDO ... Serikat Buruh Pegawai Negeri dan Daeran Otonom [*Civil Servants Workers' Union*] [*Indonesia*]
SESPO ...... Surface Effect Ships Project Office [*Navy*]
SESQUIH ... Sesquihora [*An Hour and a Half*] [*Pharmacy*] (ROG)
SESQUIHOR ... Sesquihora [*An Hour and a Half*] [*Pharmacy*]
SESR .... San Rafael [*Ecuador*] [*ICAO location identifier*] (ICLI)
SESR .... Selected Equipment Status Report [*Navy*] (NG)
SESR .... Societe Europeenne de Sociologie Rurale [*European Society for Rural Sociology*]
SESR .... Special Environmental Storage Requirements (MCD)
SES Rep CSIRO Sol Energy Stud ... SES Report. Solar Energy Studies Unit. Commonwealth Scientific and Industrial Research Organisation [*A publication*] (APTA)
SESRTCIC ... Statistical, Economic, and Social Research and Training Center for Islamic Countries [*Research center*] [*Turkey*] (IRC)
SESS......... Session
SESS......... Society of Ethnic and Special Studies (EA)
SESS......... Space Environmental Support System
SESS......... Summer Employment for Science Students
Sess Ca..... Scotch Court of Session Cases [*A publication*] (DLA)
Sess Ca..... Sessions Cases, King's Bench [*1710-48*] [*England*] [*A publication*] (DLA)
Sess Cas.... Scotch Court of Session Cases [*A publication*] (DLA)
Sess Cas.... Session Cases. Court of Session [*Scotland*] [*A publication*]
Sess Cas.... Session Cases, High Court of Justiciary Section [*1906-16*] [*Scotland*] [*A publication*] (DLA)
Sess Cas.... Sessions Cases, King's Bench [*England*] [*A publication*] (DLA)
Sess Cas J ... Session Cases. High Court of Justiciary [*Scotland*] [*A publication*]
Sess Cas KB ... Sessions Settlement Cases, King's Bench [*England*] [*A publication*] (DLA)
Sess Cas Sc ... Scotch Court of Session Cases [*A publication*] (DLA)
Sess N .... Session Notes [*Scotland*] [*A publication*] (DLA)
Sess Pap CC ... Central Criminal Court Cases, Sessions Papers [*1834-1913*] [*England*] [*A publication*] (ILCA)
Sess Pap CCC ... Central Criminal Court Cases, Sessions Papers [*1834-1913*] [*England*] [*A publication*] (DLA)
Sess Pap OB ... Old Bailey's Sessions Papers [*A publication*] (DLA)
Sest .... Pro Sestio [*of Cicero*] [*Classical studies*] (OCD)
SEST .... San Cristobal (Galapagos) [*ICAO location identifier*] (ICLI)
SESTICON ... South Eastern Scientific and Technical Information Consortium [*Australia*]
SESTM...... Societe Europeenne de la Science et de la Technologie des Membranes [*European Society of Membrane Science and Technology - ESMST*] (EA)
SESUNC ... Sesuncia [*An Ounce and a Half*] [*Pharmacy*] (ROG)
SESY .... Sur Cayambe [*Ecuador*] [*ICAO location identifier*] (ICLI)
SESZ .... Sur Antizana [*Ecuador*] [*ICAO location identifier*] (ICLI)
Set .... English Settlement and Removal Cases [*Burrow's Settlement Cases*] [*A publication*] (DLA)
SET........... Safety Education and Training
SET........... Satellite Experimental Terminal (NATG)
SET........... Scientists, Engineers, Technicians
SET........... Securities Exchange of Thailand
SET........... Security Escort Team [*Military*]
SET........... Selective Electronic Training [*Navy*] (NG)
SET........... Selective Employment Tax [*British*]
SET........... Self-Employment Tax [*IRS*]
SET........... Self-Extending Translator (IEEE)
SET........... Senior Electronic Technician [*National Weather Service*]
SET........... Sensory Evaluation Test [*Army*]

SET........... Service Evaluation Telemetry (AAG)
SET........... Setif [*Algeria*] [*Seismograph station code, US Geological Survey*] (SEIS)
SET........... Setting (MSA)
SET........... Settlement (ROG)
SET........... Settling
SET........... Sheraton Executive Traveler [*Sheraton Corp.*]
SET........... Siemont Resources, Inc. [*Vancouver Stock Exchange symbol*]
SET........... Simplified Engineering Technique
SET........... Simulated Emergency Test
SET........... Single-Electron-Transfer [*Organic chemistry*]
SET........... Single Escape Tower
SET........... Society for Environmental Therapy [*British*]
SET........... Society for the Eradication of Television (EA)
SET........... Software Engineering Technology
SET........... Software Engineering Terminology [*Data processing*] (IEEE)
SET........... Solar Energy Thermionic [*Program*] [*NASA*]
SET........... Source Evaluation Team [*Army*]
SET........... South East Trawl [*Australia*]
SET........... Space Electronics and Telemetry (MCD)
SET........... Spacecraft Elapsed Time
SET........... Sports Emotion Test [*Research test*] [*Psychology*]
SET........... Stack Entry Time [*Aviation*] (FAAC)
SET........... Standard d'Exchange et de Transfert [*Computer graphics*] [*French*]
SET........... Stepped Electrode Transistor
SET........... Student Empowerment Training Project (EA)
SeT........... Studi e Testi [*Rome*] [*A publication*]
SET........... Studies in English (University of Texas) [*A publication*]
SET........... Submarine Engineering Technical
SET........... Suitability Evaluation Team (MCD)
SE & T ..... Supplies, Equipment, and Training [*Civil Defense*]
SET........... Symbol Elaboration Test [*Psychology*]
SET........... Synchro Error Tester
SET........... Syndicat des Enseignants du Togo [*Union of Togolese Teachers*]
SET........... System Extension Test
SET........... Systems Engineering Test (CET)
SETA........ Satellite Electrostatic Triaxial Accelerometer
SETA .... Simplified Electronic Tracking Apparatus [*Air Force*]
SETA .... Systems Engineering and Technical Assistance (MCD)
SETA .... Taura [*Ecuador*] [*ICAO location identifier*] (ICLI)
Seta Artif .. Seta Artificiale [*A publication*]
SETAB ...... Sets Tabular Material [*Phototypesetting computer*]
SETAC ...... Sector TACAN [*Tactical Air Navigation*] System
SETAC ...... Society of Environmental Toxicology and Chemistry (EA)
SETAC ...... Specially Equipped Traffic Accident Car [*British police*]
SETAD...... Secure Encryption of Tactical Analog Data
SETAD...... Secure Transmission of Acoustic Data (NVT)
SETAF...... Southern European Task Force [*NATO*]
SETAR ...... Serial Event Timer and Recorder
SETA-UITA ... Syndicat Europeen des Travailleurs de l'Alimentation, de l'Hotellerie, et des Branches Connexes dans l'UITA [*European Committee of Food, Catering, and Allied Workers' Unions within the IUF - ECF-IUF*] (EAIO)
SETB .... Secondary Education Text-Books [*A publication*]
SETB .... Set Theoretic Language - BALM [*1973*] [*Data processing*] (CSR)
SETB .... Sierra Real Estate Equity Trust '83 [*San Francisco, CA*] [*NASDAQ symbol*] (NQ)
SETB .... Timbre [*Ecuador*] [*ICAO location identifier*] (ICLI)
SETBGT.... Set Ballistic Gain Table
SETC .... Sierra Real Estate Equity Trust '84 Co. [*NASDAQ symbol*] (NQ)
SETC .... Solid Electrolyte Tantalum Capacitor
SETC .... Southeastern Theatre Conference (EA)
SETC .... Submarine Escape Training Centre [*British military*] (DMA)
SETD........ Sledborne Event Time Digitizer
SETD........ Space Environment Test Division [*NASA*]
SE & TD .... Systems Engineering and Technical Direction (AAG)
SETE .... Secretariat for Electronic Test Equipment [*DoD*]
SETE .... Status of Electronic Test Equipment (MCD)
SETE .... Support and Electronic Test Equipment
SETE .... System Evaluation Test Equipment [*Military*] (CAAL)
SETE .... Tena [*Ecuador*] [*ICAO location identifier*] (ICLI)
SETEL....... Societe Europeenne de Teleguidage [*Five European firms organized in 1958 under French law to act as European prime contractor for production of HAWK missiles*] [*NATO*]
SETEP....... Science and Engineering Technician Education Program [*National Science Foundation*]
SETF .... SNAP [*Systems for Nuclear Auxiliary Power*] Experimental Test Facility
SETF .... STARAN Evaluation and Training Facility
SETG........ Tenguel [*Ecuador*] [*ICAO location identifier*] (ICLI)
SET-GO .... Support and Encouragement for Talent - Gateway to Opportunity [*Project*] (EA)
SETH........ Taisha [*Ecudaor*] [*ICAO location identifier*] (ICLI)
Set Hall Leg J ... Seton Hall Legislative Journal [*A publication*]
Set H LR.... Seton Hall Law Review [*A publication*]
SETI .... Search for Extraterrestrial Intelligence

SETI .... Societe Europeenne pour le Traitement de l'Information [*European Society for the Processing of Information*]
SETI .... Tiputini [*Ecuador*] [*ICAO location identifier*] (ICLI)
SETINA .... Southeast Texas Information Network Association
SETIS .... Societe Europeenne pour l'Etude et l'Integration des Systemes Spatiaux
SETL .... Science Experiment Test Laboratory [*NASA*]
SETL .... Set Theoretic Language [*1971*] [*Data processing*] (CSR)
SETLG ...... Settling (MSA)
SETM .... Societe d'Etudes et de Travaux Mecanographiques
SET Manpower Comments ... Scientific Engineering. Technical Manpower Comments [*A publication*]
SETO .... Pacto [*Ecuador*] [*ICAO location identifier*] (ICLI)
SETOLS.... Surface Effect Takeoff and Land System [*Naval aviation*]
Seto Mar Biol Lab Publ ... Seto Marine Biological Laboratory. Publications [*A publication*]
Seton .... Seton's Forms of Decrees, Judgments, and Orders in Equity [*7 eds.*] [*1830-1912*] [*A publication*] (DLA)
Seton Dec.. Seton's Forms of Decrees, Judgments, and Orders in Equity [*7th ed.*] [*1912*] [*A publication*] (DLA)
Seton Hall Leg J ... Seton Hall Legislative Journal [*A publication*]
Seton Hall L Rev ... Seton Hall Law Review [*A publication*]
SETP .... Society of Experimental Test Pilots (EA)
SETP .... Tandapi [*Ecuador*] [*ICAO location identifier*] (ICLI)
SETR .... Setter (MSA)
SETR .... Tarapoa [*Ecuador*] [*ICAO location identifier*] (ICLI)
SETS .... Scottish Electrical Training Scheme Ltd. [*British*]
SETS .... Seeker Evaluation Test System [*Military*]
SETS .... Set Equation Transformation System [*1970*] [*Data processing*] (CSR)
SETS .... Skylab End-to-End Test System [*NASA*]
SETS .... Solar Electric Test Satellite
SETS .... Solar Energy Thermionic Conversion System [*NASA*]
SETS .... Special Electron Tube Section
SETS .... Standardized Environmental Technical Specifications [*Nuclear energy*] (NRCH)
Sett............ Settlement Cases [*A publication*] (DLA)
SETT .... Submarine Escape Training Tank
SETT .... Teniente Ortiz [*Ecuador*] [*ICAO location identifier*] (ICLI)
SETTA ...... Southeastern Test and Training Area [*Military*] (MCD)
Sett Cas..... Burrow's English Settlement Cases [*A publication*] (DLA)
Sett Cas...... Settlement and Removal Cases in English King's Bench [*A publication*] (DLA)
Settim Med ... Settimana Medica [*Italy*] [*A publication*]
Settim Osp ... Settimana Ospitaliera [*A publication*]
SETTL....... Settler [*Genealogy*]
SETTLET ... Settlement (ROG)
Sett & Rem ... Settlement and Removal Cases in English King's Bench [*A publication*] (DLA)
SETTT....... Settlement (ROG)
SETU .... Tulcan [*Ecuador*] [*ICAO location identifier*] (ICLI)
SEU .... Dynamik im Handel [*A publication*]
SEU .... Saint Edward's University [*Texas*]
SEU .... Sales Education Units
SEU .... Solar Energy Update [*A publication*]
SEU .... Source Entry Utility
SEU .... Southeastern University [*Washington, DC*]
SEU .... Spiral Optics [*Vancouver Stock Exchange symbol*]
SEU .... Subjective Expected Utility [*Concept*] [*Theory used for decision making*]
SEUG .... Screaming Eagles Users Group (EA)
SEUL......... Support Equipment Utilization List (NASA)
SEURE...... Systems Evaluation Code Under Radiation Environment (IEEE)
SEUS .... Single Event Upsets [*Astronautics*]
SEUS .... Southeastern United States
SEUSSN... Southeastern United States Seismic Network (NRCH)
SEUY......... Chanduy [*Ecuador*] [*ICAO location identifier*] (ICLI)
SEV .... Scout Evaluation Vehicle
SEV .... Sensor Equivalent Visibility
SEV........... Service City, AK [*Location identifier*] [*FAA*] (FAAL)
SEV........... Sevastopol [*USSR*] [*Seismograph station code, US Geological Survey*] [*Closed*] (SEIS)
SEV .... Seven
SEV........... Several
SEV........... Severe [*Used to qualify weather phenomena*]
SEV........... Severed
Sev........... Severus [*of Scriptores Historiae Augustae*] [*Classical studies*] (OCD)
SEV........... Sevres [*China*] (ROG)
SEV........... Ship Exercise Vehicle
SEV........... Simcoe Erie Investors Ltd. [*Toronto Stock Exchange symbol*]
SEV........... Small Earlywood Vessel [*Tree-ring property*]
SEV........... Societe d'Ethologie Veterinaire [*Society for Veterinary Ethology - SVE*] [*Edinburgh, Scotland*] (EAIO)
SEV........... Special Equipment Vehicle [*Military*]
SEVY......... Split End Vector [*System for plant cell transformation*]
SEV........... State Equalized Value [*Real estate*]
SEV........... Stockpile Emergency Verification [*DoD*]
SEV........... Surface Effects Vehicle [*Military*]
SEVA......... Skylab Extravehicular Visor Assembly [*NASA*]

SEVA........ Standup Extravehicular Activity [*Aerospace*]
SEVA........ Surface Extravehicular Activity [*Lunar exploration*]
SEVA........ Valdez [*Ecuador*] [*ICAO location identifier*] (ICLI)
SEVAC..... Secure Voice Access Console [*Army*] (AABC)
SEVAL ..... Senior Evaluator (MCD)
Sev App Cas ... Sevestre's Bengal High Court Appeal Cases [*1864-68*] [*India*] [*A publication*] (DLA)
SEVAS ..... Secure Voice Access Systems [*Army*] (AABC)
Sev Cent N ... Seventeenth-Century News [*A publication*]
SEVEC ...... Society for Educational Visits and Exchanges in Canada [*Societe Educative de Visites et d'Echanges au Canada*]
Seven Ct N ... Seventeenth-Century News [*A publication*]
SEVENTHFLT ... Seventh Fleet [*Navy*]
Severni Morava ... Severni Morava Vastivedny Sbornik [*A publication*]
Sevestre... Calcutta Reports of Cases in Appeal [*A publication*] (DLA)
SEVFLT .... Seventh Fleet [*Pacific*] [*Navy*]
Sev HC....... Sevestre's Bengal High Court Reports [*India*] [*A publication*] (DLA)
SEVI .... Villano [*Ecuador*] [*ICAO location identifier*] (ICLI)
SEVL .... Several (ROG)
SEVN......... Sevenson Environmental Services, Inc. [*NASDAQ symbol*] (NQ)
SEVN......... Vinces [*Ecuador*] [*ICAO location identifier*] (ICLI)
SEVOCOM ... Secure Voice Communications (AFM)
Sev-Oset Gos Pedagog Inst Uch Zap ... Severo-Osetinskii Gosudarstvennyi Pedagogicheskii Institut. Uchenye Zapiski [*A publication*]
SEVP .... Severance Pay [*Military*]
SEVPEN ... Service d'Edition et de Vente des Publications de l'Education Nationale [*A publication*]
Sev SDA..... Sevestre's Sadr Diwani Adalat Reports [*Bengal, India*] [*A publication*] (DLA)
SEVT .... Ventanas [*Ecuador*] [*ICAO location identifier*] (ICLI)
Sev-Vost Kompleks Nauch-Issled Inst Akad Nauk SSSR Sib Otd ... Severo-Vostochnyy Kompleksnyy Nauchno-Issledovatel'skiy Institut Akademiya Nauk SSSR Sibirskoye Otdeleniye [*A publication*]
Sev Zapad Evr Chasti SSSR ... Severo-Zapad Evropeiskoi Chasti SSSR [*A publication*]
Sev Zapadn Zaochn Politekh Inst Tr ... Severo-Zapadnyi Zaochnyi Politekhnicheskii Institut Trudy [*A publication*]
SEW........... Sewage [*or Sewer*] (AAG)
Sew............ Sewanee Review [*A publication*]
SEW........... Seward [*Alaska*] [*Seismograph station code, US Geological Survey*] (SEIS)
SEW........... Shipboard Electronics Warfare [*Navy*]
SEW........... Silicon Epitaxial Wafer
SEW........... SONAR Early Warning
SEW........... Sozialistische Einheitspartei Westberlins [*Socialist Unity Party of West Berlin*] [*Federal Republic of Germany*] [*Political party*] (PPW)
SE & W ...... Start Early and Walk [*Fictitious railroad initialism used to indicate one of the most reliable modes of rural transportation*]
SEW........... Surface Electromagnetic Wave
SEWACO ... Sensor Weapons Control and Command
Sewage Ind Waste Eng ... Sewage and Industrial Waste Engineering [*A publication*]
Sewage Ind Wastes ... Sewage and Industrial Wastes [*A publication*]
Sewage Purif Land Drain Water River Eng ... Sewage Purification. Land Drainage. Water and River Engineering [*A publication*]
Sewage Works Eng Munic Sanit ... Sewage Works Engineering and Municipal Sanitation [*A publication*]
Sewage Works J ... Sewage Works Journal [*A publication*]
Sewanee R ... Sewanee Review [*A publication*]
Sewanee Rev ... Sewanee Review [*A publication*]
Sewan R ..... Sewanee Review [*A publication*]
SEWC........ SIGINT/Electronic Warfare Coordination Element (MCD)
S/EWCC ... Signal Intelligence/Electronic Warfare Coordination Center (NVT)
Sew Cor...... Sewell on Coroners [*1843*] [*A publication*] (DLA)
Sewell Sheriffs ... Sewell on the Law of Sheriffs [*A publication*] (DLA)
SEWHO ..... Shoulder-Elbow-Wrist-Hand Orthosis [*Medicine*]
SEWL........ Southeast Water Laboratory [*Environmental Protection Agency*]
SEWMRPG ... Southern European Western Mediterranean Regional Planning Group [*NATO*] (NATG)
SEWO .... Shoulder-Elbow-Wrist Orthosis [*Medicine*]
SEWPS...... Safety Weather Probability Study (MCD)
Sew R .... Sewanee Review [*A publication*]
Sew Rev..... Sewanee Review [*A publication*]
SEWS .... Satellite Early Warning System
SEWS .... Sun-End Work Station [*NASA*] (KSC)
SEWS .... Surface Electromagnetic Wave Spectroscopy
Sew Sh .... Sewell on the Law of Sheriffs [*1842*] [*A publication*] (DLA)
SEWT........ Simulated Electronic Warfare Training [*Army*]
SEWT........ Simulator for Electronic Warfare Training
SEWY......... Seaway Food Town, Inc. [*NASDAQ symbol*] (NQ)
Sex .... Sextans [*Constellation*]
SEX........... Shipment Exception Code [*Military*] (AFIT)
SEX........... Summer Experiment Group [*Summer work for engineering undergraduates*]

SEXAFS	Surface-Extended X-Ray Absorption Fine Structure
SEXC........	Sierra Exploration Company [*NASDAQ symbol*] (NQ)
Sex Disabil ..	Sexuality and Disability [*A publication*]
S Exec Doc ...	Senate Executive Document [*A publication*] (DLA)
S Exec Rep ...	Senate Executive Report [*A publication*] (DLA)
S/EXH........	Single Exhaust [*Automotive engineering*]
SEXLF......	States Exploration Limited [*NASDAQ symbol*] (NQ)
Sex LR	Sexual Law Reporter [*A publication*] (DLA)
Sex L Rep ..	Sexual Law Reporter [*A publication*] (DLA)
SExO	Senior Experimental Officer [*Also, SEO, SXO*] [*Ministry of Agriculture, Fisheries, and Food*] [*British*]
Sex Pomp...	Sextus Pomponius [*Flourished, 2nd century*] [*Authority cited in pre-1607 legal work*] (DSA)
Sex Prob Ct Dig ...	Sex Problems Court Digest [*A publication*] (DLA)
SEXR........	Shoulder External Rotation [*Sports medicine*]
SEXRAT....	Sex Ratio [*Biology*]
Sex Scien ...	Working Papers on Sex, Science, and Culture [*A publication*]
Sext	Liber Sextus Decretalium [*A publication*] (DSA)
Sext	Sextans [*Constellation*]
SEXT	Shoulder Extension [*Sports medicine*]
Sext Emp ...	Sextus Empiricus [*Third century AD*] [*Classical studies*] (OCD)
Sex Transm Dis ...	Sexually-Transmitted Diseases [*A publication*]
SEY..........	Block Island, RI [*Location identifier*] [*FAA*] (FAAL)
SEY..........	Secondary Electron Yield
SEY..........	Selibaby [*Mauritania*] [*Airport symbol*] (OAG)
SEY..........	Seymchan [*USSR*] [*Seismograph station code, US Geological Survey*] (SEIS)
SEY..........	Southeastern Yiddish (BJA)
SEY..........	Starlight Energy [*Vancouver Stock Exchange symbol*]
SEY..........	Summer Employment Youth [*DoD*]
SEYA........	Yaupi [*Ecuador*] [*ICAO location identifier*] (ICLI)
Seybold Rep Off Systems ...	Seybold Report on Office Systems [*A publication*]
Seychelles Dep Agric Annu Rep ...	Seychelles Department of Agriculture. Annual Report [*A publication*]
Seych LR ...	Seychelles Law Reports [*A publication*] (DLA)
SEYF	Scottish Episcopal Youth Fellowship
SEYM.......	Secondary Electron Yield Measurement
Sey Merch Sh ...	Seymour's Merchant Shipping Acts [*2nd ed.*] [*1857*] [*A publication*] (DLA)
SEYMS	Secondary Electron Yield Measurement System
SEYS	Secondary Electron Yield System
Seysell........	[*Claudius de*] Seysellis [*Deceased, 1520*] [*Authority cited in pre-1607 legal work*] (DSA)
SEZ..........	Mahe Island [*Seychelles Islands*] [*Airport symbol*] (OAG)
SEZ..........	Sedona, AZ [*Location identifier*] [*FAA*] (FAAL)
SEZ..........	Seifen, Oele, Fette, Waechse. Die Internationale Fachzeitschrift [*A publication*]
Sez...........	Sezione [*Division*] [*Italian*] (ILCA)
SEZ..........	Special Economic Zone
SEZA........	Zamora [*Ecuador*] [*ICAO location identifier*] (ICLI)
SEzik........	Sapostavitelno Ezikoznanie [*A publication*]
SEZP	Zumba-Pucupamba [*Ecuador*] [*ICAO location identifier*] (ICLI)
SF.............	E. R. Squibb & Sons [*Research code symbol*]
SF.............	Fleet Submarine [*Navy symbol*] [*Obsolete*]
SF.............	Meiji Seika Kaisha Ltd. [*Japan*] [*Research code symbol*]
SF.............	Provisional Sinn Fein [*Northern Ireland*] [*Political party*] (PPW)
SF.............	Royal Scots Fusiliers [*Military unit*] (DMA)
SF.............	Sabre Foundation (EA)
SF.............	Sacrifice Fly [*Baseball*]
SF.............	Safe (NASA)
SF.............	Safety Factor
SF.............	Safety, Reliability, and Quality Assurance, and Protective Services [*Kennedy Space Center*] [*NASA*] (NASA)
SF.............	Salt Free [*Diet*]
SF.............	Sampled Filter (IEEE)
SF.............	San Francisco [*California*]
SF.............	Sans Frais [*Without Cost*] [*French*]
sf...............	Sao Tome and Principe [*MARC country of publication code*] [*Library of Congress*] (LCCP)
SF.............	Satiety Factor [*Physiology*]
SF.............	Saw Fixture (MCD)
SF.............	Sbornik Filologicky [*A publication*]
SF.............	Scale Factor
SF.............	Scarlet Fever [*Medicine*]
SF.............	Scheduling Forecast
SF.............	Scheibe-Flugzeugbau GmbH [*Federal Republic of Germany*] [*ICAO aircraft manufacturer identifier*] (ICAO)
SF.............	School of Chiropody Full Time [*British*]
SF.............	Science Fiction [*A publication*]
SF.............	Science Fiction [*Also, SCI-FI*]
SF.............	Science Frontiers [*An association*] (EA)
SF.............	Scleroderma Federation (EA)
SF.............	Scouting Force [*Navy*]
SF.............	Sea Flood
SF.............	Seasonal Food [*Department of Employment*] [*British*]
SF.............	Secondary Failure [*NASA*] (KSC)
SF.............	Secure Facility (MCD)
S & F	Security and Facilities [*DoD*]

SF.............	Security Forces [*Japanese army*]
SF.............	Security Forecast [*Control Risks Information Services - CRIS*] [*London, England*] [*Information service or system*] (IID)
Sf..............	Sefire Inscriptions (BJA)
SF.............	Select Frequency
SF.............	Selection Filter (MCD)
SF.............	Selous Foundation (EA)
SF.............	Semifinished [*Steel or other material*]
SF.............	Semifixed [*Ammunition*] (NATG)
SF.............	Seminal Fluid [*Medicine*]
SF.............	Senate File (OICC)
SF.............	Senior Fellow
SF.............	Separation Factor [*Chemical analysis*]
SF.............	Service Factor (MSA)
SF.............	Servicing Flight [*British military*] (DMA)
SF.............	Seva Foundation (EA)
SF.............	Sexagesimo-quarto [*Book up to 7-1/2 centimeters in height*] [*Bibliography*]
Sf..............	Sforzando [*With Additional Accent*] [*Music*]
SF.............	Sherwood Foresters [*Military unit*] [*British*]
SF.............	Shift Forward
SF.............	Shipfitter [*Navy*]
SF.............	Short Format
SF.............	Shortening Fraction [*Cardiology*]
SF.............	Side Frequency (DEN)
SF.............	Signal Frequency
SF.............	Silicia Fume [*Inorganic chemistry*]
S/F	Single Face
SF.............	Single Feeder
S/F	Single Flow (NASA)
SF.............	Single Frequency [*Telecommunications*]
SF.............	Single-Fronted (ADA)
SF.............	Sinking Fund [*Finance*]
SF.............	Sinn Fein [*Political front of the Irish Republican Army*]
SF.............	Skin Fibroblast [*Clinical chemistry*]
SF.............	Skip Flag [*Data processing*] (MDG)
SF.............	Sliding Filter (NASA)
SF.............	Slip Fit (MSA)
SF.............	Slot Format [*Microfiltration*]
SF.............	Slow Fire [*Military*]
SF.............	Social Forces [*A publication*]
SF.............	Socialisticki Front [*A publication*]
SF.............	Societe Aerienne Francaise d'Affretements [*France*] [*ICAO designator*] (FAAC)
SF.............	Society Farsarotul (EA)
SF.............	Soft [*Horse racing*]
SF.............	Soils and Fertilizers [*A publication*]
SF.............	Solar Flare [*Astronomy*]
SF.............	Soldiers of Freedom (EA)
SF.............	Solid Fuel (ADA)
SF.............	SONAR Frequency [*Military*] (CAAL)
SF.............	Sons of the Holy Family [*Roman Catholic men's religious order*]
SF.............	Sosialistisk Folkepartiet [*Socialist People's Party*] [*Norway*] [*Political party*] (PPE)
SF.............	Sound and Flash [*Military*]
S & F	Sound and Flash [*Military*]
SF.............	Source Factor [*Nuclear energy*] (NRCH)
SF.............	Source and Fissionable [*Material*] [*Obsolete; see SS*] [*Nuclear energy*]
SF.............	South Following [*Astronomy*]
SF.............	Southern Forest Products Association
SF.............	Space Filler [*Philately*]
SF.............	Space Flight [*A publication*]
SF.............	Spacial Factor
SF.............	Sparing Fitting [*Cargo battens*] [*Shipping*] (DS)
SF.............	Special Facilities
SF.............	Special Fixtures (MCD)
SF.............	Special Forces [*Military*]
SF.............	Spent Fuel [*Nuclear energy*] (NRCH)
SF.............	Spinal Fluid [*Medicine*]
SF.............	Spiritus Frumenti [*Whisky*] [*Pharmacy*] (ROG)
SF.............	Spontaneous Fission [*Radioactivity*]
SF.............	Sports Foundation (EA)
SF.............	Spot Face
Sf..............	Sprachforum [*A publication*]
SF.............	Spruce-Fast [*Forestry*]
SF.............	Squadron or Flotilla Flag [*Navy*] [*British*]
SF.............	Square Foot
S & F	Staff and Faculty
SF.............	Stainless Steel Fastenings
SF.............	Standard Form
SF.............	Standard Frequency
S/F	Stanton Foundation [*Later, KCSF*] (EA)
SF.............	Star Field (MCD)
SF.............	Starlight Foundation (EA)
SF.............	Startled Falcon [*Book written by Thomas Dunn English (1844)*]
SF.............	Statement of Functions (NATG)
sF	Statfarad [*Also, statF*] [*Unit of capacitance*]
SF.............	Static Firing [*NASA*] (NASA)
S/F	Statute of Frauds [*Business term*]

SF.............. Sterile Females [Genetics]
SF.............. Stifel Financial Corp. [NYSE symbol]   (SPSG)
S & F .... Stock and Fixtures
SF.............. Stock Fund   (AFM)
SF.............. Stopped-Flow [Spectroscopy]
S/F .... Store-and-Forward [Data communications]
SF.............. Stowage Factor [Shipping]
SF.............. Streptococcus faecilis [Microbiology]
SF.............. Stress Formula
SF.............. Structure Function
SF.............. Studi Francesi [A publication]
SF.............. Studia Fennica [A publication]
SF.............. Studia Filozoficzne [A publication]
SF.............. Su Favor [Your Favor] [Spanish]
SF.............. Sub Finem [Near the End] [Latin]
SF.............. Subcontractor Furnished [NASA]   (NASA)
SF.............. Subframe
SF.............. Success Factor
SF.............. Successful Flight   (MCD)
SF.............. Sufficient Funding   (MCD)
SF.............. Sugar Flotation [Soil testing]
SF.............. Sugar-Free [Pharmacy]
SF.............. Sulfation Factor [of blood serum]
SF.............. Sun Factor   (ADA)
SF.............. Sunk Face [Construction]
SF.............. Sunshine Foundation   (EA)
SF.............. Supply Fan   (AAG)
SF.............. Surface Foot
SF.............. Surfrider Foundation   (EA)
SF.............. Sustaining Fiber
SF.............. Swedenborg Foundation   (EA)
SF.............. Swiss Franc [Monetary unit]
SF.............. Symbral Foundation   (EA)
SF.............. Syndicat des Fonctionnaires [Lao Civil Servants' Union]
SF.............. Synovial Fluid [Medicine]
SF1............. Shipfitter, First Class [Navy]
SF2............. Shipfitter, Second Class [Navy]
SF3............. Shipfitter, Third Class [Navy]
SF3............. Society for the Furtherance and Study of Fantasy and Science
               Fiction   (EA)
SF-4 .... Shipping Fever [An influenza serotype]
SF6............. Sulfur Hexafluoride
SFA............ Sachs/Freeman Associates, Inc. [Telecommunications
               service]   (TSSD)
SFA............ Sadr Foujdaree Adalat Reports [India] [A publication]   (DLA)
SFA............ Saks Fifth Avenue [Retail department store]
SFA............ Scandinavian Fraternity of America   (EA)
SFA............ Science Fiction Adventures [1952-1954] [A publication]
SFA............ Scientific-Atlanta, Inc. [NYSE symbol]   (SPSG)
SFA............ Screw Focusing Adjustment [Optical]   (ROG)
SFA............ Segment Frequency Algorithm
SFA............ Segmented Flow Analysis
SFA............ Selected Financial Assistance [British]   (DCTA)
SFA............ Sempervivum Fanciers Association   (EA)
SFA............ Service-Factor Amperes   (MSA)
SFA............ Seven Falls [Quebec] [Seismograph station code, US Geological
               Survey] [Closed]   (SEIS)
SFA............ Sfax [Tunisia] [Airport symbol]   (OAG)
S & FA .... Shipping and Forwarding Agent
SFA............ Short Field Aircraft
SFA............ Show Folks of America   (EA)
SFA............ Sigmund Freud Archives   (EA)
SFA............ Simulated Flight - Automatic
SFA............ Single Failure Analysis [Nuclear energy]   (NRCH)
SFA............ Single-Frequency Approach [Aviation]   (FAAC)
SFA............ Slide Fastener Association   (EA)
SFA............ Slow Flying Aircraft
SFA............ Snack Food Association   (EA)
SFA............ Societe Francaise d'Acoustique [French Society of Acoustics -
               FSA]   (EAIO)
SFA............ Society of Filipino Accountants   (EA)
SFA............ Soil-Derived Fulvic Acid
SFA............ Solid Fuels Administration [Terminated, 1954]
SFA............ Soroptimist Federation of the Americas [Later, Soroptimist
               International of the Americas]   (EA)
SFA............ Southeastern Fabric Association   (EA)
SFA............ Southeastern Fisheries Association   (EA)
SFA............ Southern Freight Association
SFA............ Spatial Frequency Analyzer
SFA............ Special Forces Association   (EA)
SFA............ Special Forces Auxiliary [Military]
SFA............ Special Foreign Activities [Military]   (AABC)
SFA............ Speech Foundation of America   (EA)
SFA............ Standard Fuel Assembly [Nuclear energy]   (NRCH)
SFA............ Stopped-Flow Analyzer [Chemical analysis]
SFA............ Students for America   (EA)
SFA............ Subcommittee on Frequency Allocations
SFA............ Sun Finder Assembly [NASA]
SFA............ Superficial Femoral Artery [Anatomy]
SFA............ Supplementary Failure Analysis [NASA]   (KSC)
SFA............ Support Facility Annex [Army]

SFA............ Surface Fibroblast Antigen [Cytochemistry]
SFA............ Surface Force Apparatus [Physical chemistry]
SFA............ Surface Forces Apparatus [For study of bilayers] [Physical
               chemistry]
SFA............ Symphony Foundation of America   (EA)
SFAA.......... Society for Applied Anthropology   (EA)
SFAA.......... Society for French-American Affairs   (EA)
SFAAP .... Sunflower Army Ammunition Plant   (AABC)
SFAAW ...... Stove, Furnace, and Allied Appliance Workers International
               Union of North America [AFL-CIO]
SFAB .... Science Fiction Adventures [1958-1963] [A publication]
SFAC......... Science Fiction Adventure Classics [A publication]
SFAC......... Statement of Financial Accounting Concepts
SFACA....... Solid Fuel Advisory Council of America   (EA)
SFACI....... Software Flight Article Configuration Inspection
               [NASA]   (NASA)
SFAD......... Science Fiction Adventures [1956-1958] [A publication]
SFAD......... Society of Federal Artists and Designers [Later, FDC]   (EA)
SFADS ...... San Francisco Air Defense Sector [ADC]
SFAF .... San Francisco AIDS Foundation   (EA)
SFAHD...... Society of the Friends of Ancient and Historical
               Dubrovnik   (EAIO)
SFAL .... Samuel Feltman Ammunition Laboratory [Army]
SFAL .... Stanley Airport [Falkland Islands] [ICAO location
               identifier]   (ICLI)
SFANA2.... Sheepfarming Annual [A publication]
SFAOD...... Superficial-Femoral Artery Occlusive Disease [Medicine]
SFAP .... Society for Folk Arts Preservation   (EA)
SFAPS ...... Space Flight Acceleration Profile Simulator [NASA]
SFAR........ Sound Fixing and Ranging
SFAR........ Special Federal Aviation Regulation [FAA]
SFAR........ System Failure Analysis Report   (IEEE)
SFARG ..... SIOP [Single Integrated Operations Plan] Force Application
               Review Group   (CINC)
SFAS .... Safety Features Actuation Signal [Nuclear energy]   (NRCH)
SFAS .... Statement of Financial Accounting Standards
SFAV .... Surrogate Fast Attack Vehicle [Two-passenger wheeled
               vehicle]   (INF)
SFAW .... Solid Fuel Administration for War [World War II]
               [Terminated, 1947]
SFAW .... Stove, Furnace, and Allied Appliance Workers International
               Union of North America [AFL-CIO]
SFB .... San Francisco [California] [Seismograph station code, US
               Geological Survey] [Closed]   (SEIS)
SFB .... San Francisco Ballet
SFB .... Sanford, FL [Location identifier] [FAA]   (FAAL)
SFB .... Sbornik Filosoficke Fakulty v Bratislave [A publication]
SFB .... Science Fantasy [A publication]
SFB .... Semiconductor Functional Block   (IEEE)
SFB .... Sender Freies Berlin [Radio network] [West Germany]
SFB .... Sir Francis Bacon
SFB .... Society of Friendly Boilermakers [A union] [British]
SFB .... Solid Fiberboard
SFB .... Southwestern Freight Bureau, St. Louis MO [STAC]
SFB .... Spinning Form Block   (MCD)
SFB .... Standard Federal Bank [NYSE symbol]   (SPSG)
SFB .... Structural Feedback
SFB .... Sugarcane Farmers Bulletin [Quezon City] [A publication]
SFBA .... Steamship Freight Brokers Association
SFBARTD ... San Francisco Bay Area Rapid Transit District
SF Bay .... San Francisco Bay Guardian [A publication]
SF Bay Gdn ... San Francisco Bay Guardian [A publication]
SFBC .... San Francisco Bancorp [NASDAQ symbol]   (NQ)
SFBCS ...... Special Forces Burst Communications Systems [Army]   (RDA)
SFBI......... Spent Fuel Building Isolation [Nuclear energy]   (NRCH)
SFBL........ Self-Filling Blind Loop [Gastroenterology]
SFBM .... Security Federal Savings Bank [Billings, MT] [NASDAQ
               symbol]   (NQ)
SFBNS....... San Francisco Bay Naval Shipyard
SFBRI....... Science Fiction Book Review Index 1923-1973 [A publication]
SFC........... Chief Shipfitter [Navy rating]
SFC........... Colorado Springs, CO [Location identifier] [FAA]   (FAAL)
SFC........... S-Band Frequency Converter
SFC........... St. Francis Center   (EA)
SFC........... Saint Francis College [Indiana; Maine; New York;
               Pennsylvania; Wisconsin]
SFC........... San Francisco [California] [Seismograph station code, US
               Geological Survey]   (SEIS)
SFC........... San Francisco Examiner and Chronicle [This World Section] [A
               publication]
SFC........... School Facilities Council of Architecture, Education, and
               Industry [Later, ASBO]   (EA)
SFC........... School Furniture Complex [Department of Education, New
               South Wales] [Australia]
SFC........... Science Fiction Adventure Classics [A publication]
SFC........... Scottish Film Council
SFC........... Sectored File Controller
SFC........... Securities and Futures Commission [Hong Kong]   (ECON)
SFC........... Selection Filter Control   (MCD)
SFC........... Selector File Channel
SFC........... Sergeant First Class

SFC............	Serial Frame Camera (CAAL)
SFC............	SF Commentary [*A publication*]
SFC............	Ship Fire Control (AAG)
SFC............	Shipborne Fighter Control [*Navy*] (CAAL)
SFC............	Shoes Fan Club (EA)
SFC............	Sight Fire Control
SFC............	Sioux Falls College [*South Dakota*]
SFC............	Sis Fan Club [*Later, RFC*] (EA)
SFC............	Societe Francaise de Chimie [*French Chemical Society - FCS*] (EAIO)
SFC............	Societe Frederic Chopin [*International Frederic Chopin Foundation*] (EAIO)
SfC............	Society for Calligraphy (EA)
SFC............	Society of Flavor Chemists (EA)
SFC............	Solar Forecast Center [*Air Force*] (IEEE)
SFC............	Solid Fat Content [*Food analysis*]
SFC............	Soluble Fibrin-Fibrinogen Complex [*Hematology*]
SFC............	Space Flight Center [*NASA*]
SFC............	Special Flight Charts [*Air Force*]
SFC............	Special Foreign Currency [*US counterpart funds*]
SFC............	Specific Fuel Consumption
SFC............	Spinal Fluid Count [*Medicine*]
SFC............	Sports Fans Connection [*A publication*]
SFC............	Sports Federation of Canada (EAIO)
SFC............	Star Field Camera [*NASA*]
SFC............	Starfleet Command (EA)
SFC............	State Fund Chairmen [*Red Cross*]
SFC............	Subcritical Fluid Chromatography
SFC............	Supercritical Fluid Chromatography
SFC............	Superior Fine Cognac
SFC............	Surefire Fan Club [*Inactive*] (EA)
SFC............	Surface (AFM)
SFC............	Sweden Now [*A publication*]
SFC............	Switching Filter Connector
SFC............	Sylvia Fan Club (EA)
SFC............	Synchronized Framing Camera
SFC............	Synthetic Fuels Corporation [*Sponsored by the federal government*]
SFCB.........	Services de Formation et de Consultation aux Bandes [*Department of Indian and Inuit Affairs*] [*Canada*]
SFCB.........	Shipfitter, Construction Battalion [*Navy*]
SFCBB.......	Shipfitter, Construction Battalion, Blacksmith [*Navy*]
SFCBM......	Shipfitter, Construction Battalion, Mechanical Draftsman [*Navy*]
SFCBP.......	Shipfitter, Construction Battalion, Pipe Fitter and Plumber [*Navy*]
SFCBR.......	Shipfitter, Construction Battalion, Rigger [*Navy*]
SFCBS.......	Shipfitter, Construction Battalion, Steelworker [*Navy*]
SFCBW.....	Shipfitter, Construction Battalion, Welder [*Navy*]
SFCC.........	Sisters for a Christian Community
SFCD.........	Stopped-Flow Circular Dichroism [*Spectroscopy*]
SFCE.........	Surface
SFCH.........	Society of Freight Car Historians (EA)
SFCHD......	Solid Fuel Chemistry [*English Translation*] [*A publication*]
SFCI.........	Spirit of the Future Creative Institute [*Commercial firm*] (EA)
SFCM........	Master Chief Shipfitter [*Later, HTCM*] [*Navy rating*]
SFCMP......	Self-Rising Flour and Corn Meal Program [*Later, HBA*] (EA)
SFCO.........	Special Forces Company [*Military*] (CINC)
SFCP.........	Shore Fire Control Party [*Military*]
SFCP.........	Special Foreign Currency Program [*National Institute of Standards and Technology*]
SFCP.........	Suffield Financial Corp. [*NASDAQ symbol*] (NQ)
SFCP.........	Synthetic Fuels Commercialization Program [*Also, SCP*] [*Energy Resources Council*]
SFCPTNG ...	Shore Fire Control Party Training [*Navy*] (NVT)
SFCR.........	Storage Facility Control Room [*Nuclear energy*] (NRCH)
SFCRAO ...	Collection of Papers Presented at the Annual Symposium on Fundamental Cancer Research [*A publication*]
SFCRS.......	State-Federal Crop Reporting Service
SFCS.........	Saint Fidelis College and Seminary [*Pennsylvania*]
SFCS.........	Secondary Flow Control System [*Nuclear energy*] (NRCH)
SFCS.........	Senior Chief Shipfitter [*Later, HTCS*] [*Navy rating*]
SFCS.........	Spent Fuel Cooling System [*Nuclear energy*] (NRCH)
SFCS.........	Surveyor Flight Control Section
SFCS.........	Survivable Flight Control System [*Military*]
SFCSI........	Special Foreign Currency Science Information [*Program*] [*National Science Foundation*]
SFCSIP......	Special Foreign Currency Science Information Program [*National Science Foundation*]
SFCSR.......	Storage Facility Cable Spreading Room [*Nuclear energy*] (NRCH)
SFCTDX....	Centro Internacional de Agricultura Tropical [*CIAT*]. Series FE [*A publication*]
SFCW.......	San Francisco College for Women [*California*]
SFCW.......	Search for Critical Weakness [*Aerospace*] (AAG)
SFCW.......	Sweep Frequency, Continuous Wave
SFD...........	Florence-Darlington Technical College Library, Florence, SC [*OCLC symbol*] (OCLC)
SFD...........	San Fernando [*Venezuela*] [*Airport symbol*] (OAG)
SFD...........	Science Fiction Digest [*A publication*]
SFD...........	Signal Flow Diagram (MCD)

SFD...........	Single Family Dwelling [*Economics*]
SFD...........	Smith's Food & Drug Class B [*NYSE symbol*] (SPSG)
SFD...........	Society of Film Distributors [*British*]
SFD...........	Solar Flux Density
SFD...........	Sound and Vibration [*A publication*]
SFD...........	Source-to-Film Distance [*Radiology*]
SFD...........	Sudden Frequency Deviation
SFD...........	Suore Francescane di Dillingen [*Sisters of St. Francis of Dillingen - SSFD*] [*Rome, Italy*] (EAIO)
SFD...........	Supercritical Fluid Desorption [*Chemical engineering*]
SFD...........	Sympathetic Firing Device [*Military*] (CAAL)
SFD...........	System Function Description (IEEE)
SFD...........	System Functional Diagram [*or Drawing*] (KSC)
SFD...........	Systems Flexowriter Double Case
SFDA........	Sale of Food and Drugs Act [*British*]
SFDA........	Shakey's Franchised Dealers Association (EA)
SFDA........	Special Forces Direct Action [*Army*]
SFDE........	Staff and Faculty Development Elements
SFDH.......	Schriften des Freien Deutschen Hochstifts [*A publication*]
SFDI.........	Solar Facility Design Integration (MCD)
SFDP........	Societe Francophone de Primatologie [*Francophone Primatological Society - FPS*] [*Plelan Le Grand, France*] (EAIO)
SFDR........	Single-Feeder
SFDR........	Standard Flight Data Recorder
SFDS........	Smithfield Foods, Inc. [*NASDAQ symbol*] (NQ)
SFDS........	Standby Fighter Director Ship [*Navy*]
SFDS........	Strike Force Data System (NVT)
SFDS........	System Functional Design Specification (MCD)
SFDT........	Signal Format Development Team [*France*]
SFDT........	Site Format Dump Tape (MCD)
SFDW.......	Special Friends of Dottie West (EA)
SFE..........	Safeguard Scientifics, Inc. [*NYSE symbol*] (SPSG)
SFE..........	Scale Factor Error (KSC)
SFE..........	Seismic Feature Extraction (MCD)
SFE..........	Seller-Furnished Equipment (MCD)
SFE..........	Smart Front End
SFE..........	Societe Financiere Europeenne
SFE..........	Society of Financial Examiners (EA)
SFE..........	Society of Fire Engineers
SFE..........	Solar Flare Effect [*Physics*]
SFE..........	Solid Fuel Engine
SFE..........	Soviet Far East (FEA)
SFE..........	Special Furnished Equipment (MCD)
SFE..........	Stacking Fault Energy [*Alloy*]
SFE..........	Student-Faculty Evaluation
SFE..........	Students in Free Enterprise (EA)
SFE..........	Studies in Financial Economics [*Elsevier Book Series*] [*A publication*]
SFE..........	Supercritical Fluid Extraction [*Also, SCFE*] [*Chemical engineering*]
SFE..........	Surf Inlet Mines [*Vancouver Stock Exchange symbol*]
SFE..........	Surface-Free Energy
SFE..........	Sydney Futures Exchange [*Australia*] (ADA)
SFE..........	Synthetic Fermented Egg [*Animal repellent*]
SFEA........	Scottish Further Education Association [*British*]
SFEA........	Squib Fuse Electrical Assembly (KSC)
SFEA........	Survival [*formerly, Space*] and Flight Equipment Association [*Later, SAFE Association*]
SFEC........	Standard Facility Equipment Card [*Electronics*]
SFEL........	Standard Facility Equipment List [*Electronics*]
SFELT.......	Societe Francaise d'Editions Litteraires et Techniques [*A publication*]
SFEM........	Second-Tiered Foreign Exchange Market
SFEM........	Segner's Fortified Edd Meat [*Growth medium for phage*]
SFEM........	SFE Technologies [*NASDAQ symbol*] (NQ)
SFEM........	Southern Farm Equipment Manufacturers (EA)
SFEMG.....	Single Fiber Electromyography [*Neurophysiology*]
SFen..........	Studia Fennica [*A publication*]
SFENA......	Societe Francaise d'Equipements pour la Navigation Aerienne (MCD)
SFER........	Siata/Fiat 8V Register (EA)
SFERC.......	San Francisco Energy Research Center [*Energy Research and Development Administration*]
SFERICS...	Atmospherics (FAAC)
SFERT.......	Systeme Fundamental Europeen de Reference pour la Transmission Telephonique [*European master telephone reference system*] (DEN)
SFEX........	Solar Flare X-Ray Polarimeter (NASA)
SF Examiner ...	San Francisco Examiner [*A publication*]
SF/F..........	Science Fiction and Fantasy [*Literary genre*]
SFF...........	Science Fiction Foundation (EA)
SFF...........	Sea Frontier Force [*Navy*]
SFF...........	Self-Forging Fragment [*Warhead*] (MCD)
SFF...........	Sheffield [*Tasmania*] [*Seismograph station code, US Geological Survey*] (SEIS)
SFF...........	Site Field Force [*Army*] (AABC)
SFF...........	Slocan Forest Products Ltd. [*Toronto Stock Exchange symbol*] [*Vancouver Stock Exchange symbol*]
SFF...........	Slovene Franciscan Fathers (EA)
SFF...........	Solar Forecast Facility [*Air Force*] (MCD)

SFF .... Spiritual Frontiers Fellowship [*Later, SFFI*] (EA)
SFF .... Spokane, WA [*Location identifier*] [*FAA*] (FAAL)
SFF .... Standard File Format
SFF .... Step Family Foundation (EA)
SFF .... Supplementary Financing Facility [*International Monetary Fund*]
SFFA .... Fireman Apprentice, Shipfitter [*Navy rating*]
SFFAAM... Fauna Fennica [*A publication*]
SFFBU...... Sbornik Praci Filosoficke Fakulty Brnenske University [*A publication*]
SFFD .... SFFed Corp. [*Formerly, San Francisco Federal Savings & Loan Association*] [*NASDAQ symbol*] (SPSG)
SFFF .... Scandinavian Association of Zone-Therapeutists (EAIO)
SFFF .... Sedimentation Field Flow Fractionation [*For separation of colloids*]
SFFF .... Societas pro Fauna et Flora Fennica [*A publication*]
SFFF .... Summary Format of Family Functioning
SFFFM...... Societas pro Fauna et Flora Fennica. Memoranda [*A publication*]
SFFI.......... Spiritual Frontiers Fellowship International (EA)
SF/FIA ..... Stock Fund/Financial Inventory Accounting
SFFMP...... State/Federal Fisheries Management Program [*National Marine Fisheries Service*]
SFFN .... Fireman, Shipfitter, Striker [*Navy rating*]
SFFNC ...... Society of the Founders and Friends of Norwich, Connecticut (EA)
SFFS .... Satellite Frost Forecast System [*Department of Agriculture*]
SFFS .... Save the Flags of Fort Sumter (EA)
SFFUK ...... Sbornik Filozofickej Fakulty Univerzity Komenskeho. Philologica [*A publication*]
SFFUP...... Sbornik Filozofickej Fakulty Univerzity P. J. Safarika v Presove [*A publication*]
SFFUR ..... Safety and Flight Failure/Unsatisfactory Report
SFFV .... Spleen Focus Formation Virus
s-fg--- .... French Guiana [*MARC geographic area code*] [*Library of Congress*] (LCCP)
SFG .... St. Maarten [*Netherlands Antilles*] [*Airport symbol*] (OAG)
SFG .... Serial Publications of Foreign Governments [*A bibliographic publication*]
SFG .... SF Greats [*A publication*]
SFG .... Signal Flow Graph
SFG .... South Pacific Gold [*Vancouver Stock Exchange symbol*]
SFG .... Spanische Forschungen. Gorresgesellschaft [*A publication*]
SFG .... Special Forces Group [*Military*]
SFG .... Staircase Function Generator
SFG .... Sum Frequency Generation
SFGA .... Steel Fork Grinders' Association [*A union*] [*British*]
SFGD .... Safeguard (AABC)
SFGD .... Safeguard Health Enterprises, Inc. [*NASDAQ symbol*] (NQ)
SFGD .... Shell Flue Gas Desulfurization [*Air pollution control*]
SFGE .... San Francisco Grain Exchange [*Defunct*] (EA)
SFGEP...... Space Flight Ground Environment Panel [*NASA*] (KSC)
SFGF .... Shope Fibroma Growth Factor [*Biochemistry*]
SFGI .... Security Financial Group, Inc. [*NASDAQ symbol*] (NQ)
SFGL .... Safety Glass [*Technical drawings*]
SFGS .... Southwestern Federation of Geological Societies
SFH .... SF Horizons [*A publication*]
SFH .... Simulated Flight Hour (MCD)
SFH .... Slow Frequency Hopping (MCD)
SFH .... Standard Fading Hour [*National Institute of Standards and Technology*]
SFH .... Super Flux Harness
SFHb .... Stroma-Free Hemoglobin [*Hematology*]
SFHC........ Society of Folk Harpers and Craftsmen (EA)
SFHF .... Society of the Friends of the Holy Father
SFH-P....... Stroma-Free Hemoglobin Pyridoxylated [*Clinical chemistry*]
SFHS .... Society for French Historical Studies (EA)
SFI .... Sequential Fuel Injection [*Automotive engineering*]
SFI .... SF Impulse [*A publication*]
SFI .... SFI Foundation (EA)
SFI .... Sindacato Ferrovieri Italiani [*Union of Italian Railroad Workers*]
SFI .... Small Flow Indicator
SFI .... Societe Financiere Internationale [*International Finance Society*]
SFI .... Society of Friends of Icons (EAIO)
SFI .... Solid Fat Index [*Food analysis*]
SFI .... Southern Forest Institute [*Defunct*] (EA)
SFI .... Space Flight Instrumentation (AAG)
SFI .... Spendthrift Farm, Incorporated [*AMEX symbol*] (SPSG)
SFI .... Sport Fishing Institute (EA)
SFI .... Starfire Resources Ltd. [*Vancouver Stock Exchange symbol*]
SFI .... Statistiques Financieres Internationales [*A publication*]
SFI .... Step Function Input
SFI .... Strategic Facilities Initiative [*Oak Ridge National Laboratory*]
SFI .... Studi di Filogia Italiana [*A publication*]
SFIA .... School Fees Insurance Agency Ltd. [*British*]
SFIA .... Sea Fish Industry Authority [*British*]
SFIB.......... SFI [*Sport Fishing Institute*] Bulletin [*A publication*]
SFIB.......... Southern Freight Inspection Bureau
SFIC .... San Francisco Information Center [*Army Air Warning Service*]

SFic........... Science Fiction [*A publication*]
SFIC .... Societe et Federation Internationale de Cardiologie [*International Society and Federation of Cardiology*] (EAIO)
SFICEC .... State-Federal Information Clearinghouse for Exceptional Children
S Fict R ..... Science Fiction Review [*A publication*]
SFID .... Section Francaise de l'Internationale Ouvriere [*French Section of the Workers International*]
SFil .... Studime Filologjike [*A publication*]
SFIMR ...... Stock Fund Inventory Management Record [*Military*] (AFIT)
S-FIN........ Semi-Finished [*Automotive engineering*]
SFIN......... Southland Financial Corp. [*NASDAQ symbol*] (NQ)
SFInstE..... Senior Fellow of the Institute of Energy [*British*] (DBQ)
SFIO .... Section Francaise de l'Internationale Ouvriere [*French Socialist Party*]
SFIQ .... Science Fiction Quarterly [*1951-1958*] [*A publication*]
SFIR .... Specific Force Integrating Receiver [*Air Force*]
SFIREG..... State FIFRA [*Federal Insecticide, Fungicide, and Rodenticide Act*] Issues Research and Evaluation Group [*Environmental Protection Agency*] (EGAO)
SFIS .... Selective Fisheries Information Service (EISS)
SFIS.......... Stanford French and Italian Studies [*A publication*]
SFIT.......... Simplified Fault Isolation Test (MCD)
SFIT.......... Standard Family Interaction Test [*Psychology*]
SFJ .... Sondre Stromfjord [*Greenland*] [*Airport symbol*] (OAG)
SFJ .... Swept Frequency Jamming
SFK .... Periodiekenparade [*A publication*]
SFK .... Special Function Key [*Calculators*]
SFK .... Stonyfork, PA [*Location identifier*] [*FAA*] (FAAL)
SFKGA ..... Sprechsaal fuer Keramik, Glas, Email, Silikate [*A publication*]
SFL .... Salt Flat, TX [*Location identifier*] [*FAA*] (FAAL)
SFL .... San Felipe [*California*] [*Seismograph station code, US Geological Survey*] (SEIS)
SFL .... Santa Fe Pacific Pipeline LP [*NYSE symbol*] (SPSG)
SFL .... Sao Filipe [*Cape Verde Islands*] [*Airport symbol*] (OAG)
SFL .... Scholarships, Fellowships, and Loans [*A publication*]
SFL .... Secondary Freon Loop (NASA)
SFL .... Sequence Flash Lights [*FAA*]
SFL .... Sexual Freedom League (EA)
SFL .... Short Flashing Light [*Navigation signal*]
SFL .... Silver Falls Resources [*Vancouver Stock Exchange symbol*]
SFL .... Society of Federal Linguists (EA)
SFL .... Studies in French Literature [*A publication*]
SFL .... Substrate Fed Logic
SFL .... Surinam Florin [*Monetary unit in Surinam*]
SFLC .... San Francisco Laser Center [*Research center*] (RCD)
SFLD .... Sheffield Exploration Co., Inc. [*Denver, CO*] [*NASDAQ symbol*] (NQ)
SFLIS .... Sloga Fraternal Life Insurance Society [*Milwaukee, WI*] (EA)
SFLJ .... San Francisco Law Journal [*A publication*] (DLA)
SFLM .... Southern Film Extruders, Inc. [*NASDAQ symbol*] (NQ)
SFLR .... University of San Francisco. Law Review [*A publication*]
SFLRP...... Society of Federal Labor Relations Professionals (EA)
SFLS .... Semiflush
SFLX .... Shoulder Flexion [*Sports medicine*]
SFM .... Francis Marion College, Florence, SC [*OCLC symbol*] (OCLC)
SFM .... San Francisco - Josephine D. Randall Junior Museum [*California*] [*Seismograph station code, US Geological Survey*] (SEIS)
SFM .... San Francisco Movers Tariff Bureau, San Francisco CA [*STAC*]
SFM .... Sanford, ME [*Location identifier*] [*FAA*] (FAAL)
SFM .... Science Fiction Monthly [*A publication*]
SFM .... Serum Free Medium
SFM .... SFM Corp. [*AMEX symbol*] (SPSG)
SFM .... Shepherds Fold Ministries (EA)
SFM .... Shipfitter, Metalsmith [*Navy*]
SFM .... Simulated Flight - Manual
SFM .... Simulated Flow Method
SFM .... Sinai Field Mission [*US government*]
SFM .... Sinusoidal Frequency Modulation [*Physics*]
SFM .... Ski-Free Marine [*Vancouver Stock Exchange symbol*]
SFM .... Society for the Family of Man (EA)
SFM .... Society for Foodservice Management (EA)
SFM .... Spectrophotofluorometer
SFM .... Storage Facility Manual (MCD)
SFM .... Surface Feet per Minute
SFM .... Swept Frequency Modulation
SFM .... Switching Mode Frequency Multipliers
SFM .... Symposia. Fondation Merieux [*Elsevier Book Series*] [*A publication*]
SFMA .... Soda Fountain Manufacturers Association
SFMA .... Southern Furniture Manufacturers Association [*Later, AFMA*] (EA)
SFMA .... Steel Fork Makers' Association [*A union*] [*British*]
SFMA .... Subscription Fulfillment Managers Association [*Later, FMA*] (EA)
SFME .... Storable Fluid Management Experiment (NASA)
SFMF .... Student Foreign Missions Fellowship [*Later, IVMF*] (EA)
SFMG....... Franciscan Missionary Sisters of Assisi [*Roman Catholic religious order*]

SFMI	Soft Fibre Manufacturers' Institute [*Defunct*] (EA)
SFMJF	Satoko and Franz M. Joseph Foundation (EA)
S 8 Fmkr	Super 8 Filmaker [*A publication*]
SFML	Standard Facility Material List [*Electronics*]
SFMN	Slow Flexor Motoneuron [*Neurology*]
SFMN	Superficial Flexor Motoneuron [*Neurology*]
SFMP	Surplus Facilities Management Program [*Department of Energy*]
SFMR	Stepped-Frequency Microwave Radiometer [*For measuring rain rate and wind speed*]
SF-MX	Stopped-Flow Multimixing Spectroflourimeter
SFN............	San Francisco Naval Shipyard
SFN............	Santa Fe [*Argentina*] [*Airport symbol*] (OAG)
SFN............	Seattle First National Bank, Seattle, WA [*OCLC symbol*] (OCLC)
SFN............	See Footnote (ROG)
SFN............	SFRA Newsletter [*A publication*]
SFN............	Ships and Facilities, Navy (NG)
SFN............	Stefan Resources, Inc. [*Vancouver Stock Exchange symbol*]
SFNA........	Stabilized Fuming Nitric Acid
SFNC........	Simmons First National Corporation [*Pine Bluff, AK*] [*NASDAQ symbol*] (NQ)
SFNC........	Society of the Founders of Norwich, Connecticut (EA)
SFNCTU ...	Swiss Federation of National-Christian Trade Unions
SFNFC	Sally Field National Fan Club (EA)
SFNL	Shakespeare on Film Newsletter [*A publication*]
SFNS.........	Spear Financial Services, Inc. [*NASDAQ symbol*] (NQ)
SFNSY	San Francisco Naval Shipyard
SFNYA	Southern Florist and Nurseryman [*United States*] [*A publication*]
SFO............	Defense Solid Fuels Order [*United States*] [*A publication*] (DLA)
SFO............	San Fernando Observatory [*Research center*] (RCD)
SFO............	San Francisco [*California*] [*Airport symbol*]
SFO............	San Francisco/Oakland [*California*] [*Airport symbol*] (OAG)
SFO............	Santa Fe Opera [*New Mexico*]
SFO............	Sector Field Office [*Aviation*] (FAAC)
SFO............	Sector Frequency Only [*Military*] (CAAL)
SFO............	Secular Franciscan Order [*Roman Catholic religious order*] [*Formerly, TOSF*]
SFO............	Senior Flag Officer [*British military*] (DMA)
SFO............	Serious Fraud Office [*Proposed*] [*British government*]
SFO............	Service Fuel Oil
SFO............	SFO [*San Francisco and Oakland*] Helicopter Airlines, Inc. [*Air carrier designation symbol*]
SFO............	Simulated Flame Out [*Aviation*]
SFO............	Single-Frequency Outlet
SFO............	Space Flight Operations [*NASA*]
SFO............	Spot Face Other Side [*Technical drawings*] (MSA)
SFO............	Sterling Forest [*New York*] [*Seismograph station code, US Geological Survey*] (SEIS)
SFO............	Strathfield Oil & Gas Ltd. [*Toronto Stock Exchange symbol*]
SFO............	Subfornical Organ [*Brain anatomy*]
SFO............	Submarine Fog Oscillator [*Maps and charts*]
SFO............	Superannuation Funds Office [*Inland Revenue*] [*British*]
S & FO	Supply and Fiscal Officer
SFOB.........	Special Forces Operational Base [*Army*]
SFOBB	San Francisco-Oakland Bay Bridge
SFOC........	Space Flight Operations Complex [*NASA*]
SFOD........	San Francisco Ordnance District [*Military*]
SFOD........	Space Flight Operations Director [*NASA*]
SFOD........	Special Forces Operational Detachment [*Army*] (AABC)
SFOD-D	[*First*] Special Forces Operational Detachment - Delta [*Military*] (INF)
SFOF.........	Space Flight Operations Facility [*NASA*]
SFOG........	South Fork Oil & Gas [*NASDAQ symbol*] (NQ)
SFOK........	Sooner Federal Savings & Loan Association [*NASDAQ symbol*] (NQ)
SFOM........	Shuttle Flight Operations Manual [*NASA*] (MCD)
SFOM........	Space Flight Operations Memorandum [*NASA*]
SFOM.......	Stabilized Flight Operations Manual
SFOMS	Ships Force Overhaul Management Systems [*Navy*]
SFOO	San Francisco Operations Office [*Energy Research and Development Administration*]
SFOP.........	Safety Operating Procedure [*Kennedy Space Center*] [*NASA*] (NASA)
SFOP.........	Space Flight Operations Plan [*NASA*]
SFORD......	Sozialistische Forstwirtschaft [*A publication*]
Sforz..........	Sforzando [*With Additional Accent*] [*Music*]
SFP	Franciscan Sisters of the Poor [*Roman Catholic religious order*]
SFP	San Felipe [*Mexico*] [*Seismograph station code, US Geological Survey*] (SEIS)
SFP	Santa Fe Energy Partnership LP [*NYSE symbol*] (SPSG)
SFP	Santa Fe Public Library, Santa Fe, NM [*OCLC symbol*] (OCLC)
SFP	Science Fiction Plus [*A publication*]
SfP	Science for People [*A publication*]
SFP	Security Filter Processor
SFP	Sforzato Piano [*Sudden change from forte to piano*] [*Music*] (ROG)
SFP	Shipfitter, Pipefitter [*Navy*]
SFP	Shungwayah Freedom Party [*Kenya*]
SFP	Simultaneous Foveal Perception [*Ophthalmology*]
SFP	Single Failure Point [*NASA*] (MCD)
SFP	Sintered Ferrous Part
SFP	Skeleton Flight Plan
SFP	Slack Frame Program
SFP	Solar Flare Proton
SFP	Spartan-Furnished Property [*Missiles*] (MCD)
SFP	Special Film Project
SFP	Special Furnished Property (MCD)
SFP	Spent Fuel Pit [*Nuclear energy*] (NRCH)
SFP	Spent Fuel Pool [*Nuclear energy*] (NRCH)
SFP	Spinal Fluid Pressure [*Medicine*]
SFP	Stopped Flow Pressure
SFP	Straight Fixed Price
SFP	Strike for Peace [*Later, WDFP*] (EA)
SFP	Students for Peace (EA)
SFP	Summary Financial Program
SFP	Summary Flight Plan (MCD)
SFP	Super Flat Pack
SFP	Sustainer Firing Package
SFP	Svenska Folkpartiet [*Swedish People's Party*] [*Finland*] [*Political party*] (PPE)
SFPA	Science Fiction Poetry Association (EA)
SFPA	Single Failure Point Analysis [*NASA*] (KSC)
SFPA	Southern Forest Products Association (EA)
SFPA	Structural Fire Protection Association [*British*]
SFP-ANGS ...	Standardization Field Panel for Artillery and Naval Gunfire Support [*Army*] (AABC)
SFPAVS	Spent Fuel Pool Area Ventilation System [*Nuclear energy*] (NRCH)
SFPCCS	Spent Fuel Pool Cooling and Cleanup System [*Nuclear energy*] (NRCH)
SFPCS.......	Spent Fuel Pool Cooling System [*Nuclear energy*] (NRCH)
SFPE........	San Francisco Port of Embarkation [*Military*]
SFPE........	Society of Fire Protection Engineers (EA)
SFPE Technol Rep ...	SFPE [*Society of Fire Protection Engineers*] Technology Report [*A publication*]
SFPL........	San Francisco Public Library [*California*]
SFPM	Surface Feet per Minute
SFPOE	San Francisco Port of Embarkation [*Military*]
SFPOMMPAB ...	Society for the Prevention of Married Men Posing as Bachelors
SFPP.........	Spruce Fall Power & Paper [*AAR code*]
SFPPC	Science Fiction Pen Pal Club (EA)
SFPPL.......	Short Form Provisioning Parts List [*NASA*] (NASA)
SFPPS	Shore Facilities Planning and Programming System [*Navy*]
SFPRF	Semifireproof (MSA)
SFPRL.......	Spartan-Furnished Property Request List [*Missiles*] (MCD)
SFPS.........	Single Failure Point Summary [*NASA*] (NASA)
SFPS.........	Studia z Filologii Polskiej i Slowianskiej [*A publication*]
SFPT........	Society of Fire Protection Technicians (EA)
SFPTU	Swiss Federation of Protestant Trade Unions
SFQ............	Science Fiction Quarterly [*1940-1943*] [*A publication*]
SFQ............	Southern Folklore Quarterly [*A publication*]
SFQ............	Suffolk, VA [*Location identifier*] [*FAA*] (FAAL)
SFR............	Safety of Flight Requirements (AFM)
SFR............	San Fernando, CA [*Location identifier*] [*FAA*] (FAAL)
SFR............	San Francisco Review [*A publication*]
SFR............	San Francisco - Rincon [*California*] [*Seismograph station code, US Geological Survey*] (SEIS)
SFR............	Santa Fe Energy Resources [*NYSE symbol*] (SPSG)
SFR............	Santa Fe Regional Library [*Gainsville Public Library*] [*UTLAS symbol*]
SF & R	Scholars' Facsimiles and Reprints [*A publication*]
SfR............	Scholars' Facsimiles & Reprints, Inc., Delmar, NY [*Library symbol*] [*Library of Congress*] (LCLS)
sFr.............	Schweizer Frank [*Swiss Franc*] [*Monetary unit*]
SFR............	Science Fiction Review [*A publication*]
SFR............	Selective File Retrieval
SFR............	Semi-Fire-Resistive Construction
SFR............	Sequenced Flashing Lights
SFR............	Simon Fraser Resources [*Vancouver Stock Exchange symbol*]
SFR............	Small Fluidal Round Colonies [*Moko disease of Banana*] [*Plant pathology*]
SFR............	Solar Flare Radiation
SFR............	Sotto Fascia Raccomandata [*Registered Printed Matter*] [*Italian*]
SFR............	Space Frame RADOME
SFR............	Special Federal Responsibilities (OICC)
SFR............	Special Forces Reconnaissance [*Army*]
SFR............	Spin Flip Raman [*LASER*]
SFR............	Stanford French Review [*A publication*]
SFR............	Star Formation Rate [*Astronomy*]
S Fr	Studi Francesi [*A publication*]
SFR............	Submarine Fleet Reactor
S FR	Swiss Franc [*Monetary unit*]
SFRA.........	Science Fiction Research Association (EA)
SFRA	System Fielding Readiness Analysis [*Army*]
SFRA	System Fielding Readiness Assessment [*Army*]
S and FRAN ...	San Francisco [*California*] [*Navy*]

SFran .... Studi Francescani [*A publication*]
SFRB .... [*The*] Atchison, Topeka & Santa Fe Railway Co. - DF Loaders [*AAR code*]
SFRB .... San Francisco Review of Books [*A publication*]
SFRC .... Soya Food Research Council
SFRCS .... Steam and Feedwater Line Rupture Control System [*Nuclear energy*] (NRCH)
SFRD .... [*The*] Atchison, Topeka & Santa Fe Railway Co. - Refrigerator Cars [*AAR code*]
SFRD .... Safe Functional Requirements Document (MCD)
SFRD .... Secret Formerly Restricted
SF Rev Bks ... San Francisco Review of Books [*A publication*]
SFRF .... Sport Fishery Research Foundation [*Later, SFRP*] (EA)
SFRJ .... Solid Fuel Ramjet
SFrL .... Studies in French Literature [*A publication*]
SFRM .... Science Fiction Review. Monthly [*A publication*]
SFRP .... Sport Fishery Research Program (EA)
SFrQ .... San Francisco Quarterly [*A publication*]
SFRS .... Search for Random Success [*Aerospace*] (AAG)
SFRS .... Swept Frequency Radiometer System
SFRSAY ...... Food Research Institute. Studies [*Stanford*] [*A publication*]
SFRT .... Science Fiction and Fantasy RoundTable [*GE Information Services*] [*Information service or system*] (CRD)
SFRY .... Socialist Federal Republic of Yugoslavia
SFS .... S-Band Feed System
SFS .... Saint Francis Seminary [*Wisconsin*]
SFS .... San Fernando [*Spain*] [*Geomagnetic observatory code*]
SFS .... San Fernando [*Spain*] [*Seismograph station code, US Geological Survey*] (SEIS)
SFs .... Saybolt Furol Seconds [*Oil viscosity*]
SFS .... School of Field Studies [*Beverly, MA*]
SFS .... Science Fiction Stories [*A publication*]
SFS .... Science Fiction Studies [*A publication*]
SFS .... Science for Schools [*Manila*] [*A publication*]
SFS .... Seamen's and Firemen's Society [*A union*] [*British*]
SFS .... Sektion fuer Systementwicklung [*GID*] [*Information retrieval*]
SFS .... Senior Flight Surgeon [*Army*] (AABC)
SFS .... Serial Focal Seizures [*Medicine*]
SFS .... Shakespeare for Students [*A publication*]
SFS .... Shuttle Flight Status [*NASA*] (MCD)
SFS .... Simplified Firing System
SFS .... Sine Fraude Sua [*Without Fraud on His Part*] [*Latin*] (DLA)
SFS .... Small Firms Service [*British*]
SFS .... Smith's Flight System [*Aviation*] (AIA)
SFS .... Society for Foodservice Systems (EA)
SFS .... Society for Freedom in Science
SFS .... Society for French Studies [*British*]
SFS .... Sodium Formaldehyde Sulfoxylate [*Organic chemistry*]
SFS .... Software Facilities and Standards [*Data processing*] (TEL)
SFS .... Solicitors' Financial Services [*British*]
SFS .... Sonic Frequency System
SFS .... Sotto Fascia Semplice [*Unregistered Printed Matter*] [*Italian*]
SFS .... South San Francisco, CA [*Location identifier*] [*FAA*] (FAAL)
SFS .... Space Futures Society (EA)
SFS .... Star Field Sensor
SFS .... Steam and Feedwater System [*Nuclear energy*] (NRCH)
SFS .... Suomen Standardisoimisliitto [*Finnish Standards Association*] [*Information service or system*] (IID)
SFS .... Super Food Services, Inc. [*NYSE symbol*] (SPSG)
SF & S .... Supporting Facilities and Services
SFS .... Surfaced Four Sides [*Technical drawings*]
SFS .... Symbolic File Support
SFS .... System Failure Summaries [*NASA*] (KSC)
SFSA .... Scottish Field Studies Association [*British*]
SFSA .... Steel Founders' Society of America (EA)
SFSAFBI ... Society of Former Special Agents of the Federal Bureau of Investigation (EA)
SFSAS .... Standard Fuel Savings Advisor System
SFSC .... San Francisco State College [*Later, California State University*]
SFSCL .... Shunt Feedback Schottky Clamped [*Electronics*]
SFSCPD .... San Francisco Signal Corps Procurement District
SFSCT .... Smooth-Face Structural Clay Tile [*Technical drawings*]
S & FSD ...... Sea and Foreign Service Duty [*A Navy pay status*]
SFSD .... Star Field Scanning Device
S & FSD(A) ... Sea and Foreign Service Duty (Aviation) [*A Navy pay status*]
S & FSD(S) ... Sea and Foreign Service Duty (Submarine) [*A Navy pay status*]
SFSE .... San Francisco Stock Exchange
SFSI .... Sunwest Financial Services, Incorporated [*NASDAQ symbol*] (NQ)
SFSL .... Science Fiction. Review of Speculative Literature [*A publication*]
SFSL .... Security Federal Savings & Loan Association of Cleveland [*NASDAQ symbol*] (NQ)
SFSLA .... Sbornik Trudov po Agronomicheskoi Fizike [*A publication*]
SFSMD ..... Studia Fransisci Scholten Memorial Dicata (BJA)
SFSN .... Society of French-Speaking Neurosurgeons (EA)
SFSO .... San Francisco Symphony Orchestra
SFSP .... Spent Fuel Storage Pool [*Nuclear energy*] (NRCH)
SFSR .... Shipfitter, Ship Repair [*Navy*]
SFSRC .... Shipfitter, Ship Repair, Chipper-Caulker [*Navy*]
SFSRD .... Shipfitter, Ship Repair, Diver [*Navy*]

SFSRF ...... Shipfitter, Ship Repair, Steelworker-Anglesmith [*Navy*]
SFSRL ...... Shipfitter, Ship Repair, Driller-Reamer [*Navy*]
SFSRP ...... Shipfitter, Ship Repair, Pipe Fitter-Plumber [*Navy*]
SFSRR ...... Shipfitter, Ship Repair, Riveter [*Navy*]
SFSRS ...... Shipfitter, Ship Repair, Shipfitter [*Navy*]
SFSRW ..... Shipfitter, Ship Repair, Welder [*Navy*]
SFSS .... Satellite Field Services Stations [*National Weather Service*]
SFSS .... Svenska Fornskriftsaellskapets Skrifter [*A publication*]
SFST .... Scherenfernrohrstand [*Emplacement of battery commander's telescope*] [*German military - World War II*]
SFST .... Science Fiction Studies [*A publication*]
SFSt .... Swiss-French Studies [*Etudes Romandes*] [*A publication*]
SFSU .... San Francisco State University
SFSU .... Singapore Federation of Services' Unions
SFSU .... Single Frequency Signaling Unit
SFSU-35 ... San Francisco State University Videotex Cable Service [*Telecommunications service*] (TSSD)
SFSUA ..... Studia Forestalia Suecica [*A publication*]
SFSV .... Svenska Forfattare Utgivna av Svenska Vitterhetssamfundet [*A publication*]
SF Sym ..... San Francisco Symphony. Program Notes [*A publication*]
SF & T ...... Sawyer, Finn & Thatcher [*Advertising agency*]
SFT .... Shaft (MSA)
SFT .... Sheffield Morning Telegraph [*A publication*]
SFT .... Shift
SFT .... Simulated Flight Tests
SFT .... Skelleftea [*Sweden*] [*Airport symbol*] (OAG)
SFT .... Skinfold Thickness [*Medicine*]
SFT .... Skyfreight, Inc. [*Seattle, WA*] [*FAA designator*] (FAAC)
sft .... Soft [*Quality of the bottom*] [*Nautical charts*]
SFT .... Soviet and Eastern European Foreign Trade [*A publication*]
SFT .... Special Flight Test
SFT .... Specific Financial Transactions
SFT .... Spiral Fin Tubing
SFT .... Squeeze Film Test
SFT .... Stacking Fault Tetrahedra [*Metals*]
SFT .... Stanford [*California*] [*Seismograph station code, US Geological Survey*] (SEIS)
SFT .... Static Firing Test [*NASA*] (NASA)
SFT .... Stockpile Flight Tests
SFT .... Stop for Tea [*British*]
SFT .... Structural Firing Test [*Military*] (CAAL)
SFT .... Studi di Filologia Todeska [*A publication*]
SFT .... Sufficient Feasibility Test
SFT .... Superfast Train
SFT .... Supplemental Flight Test
SFT .... Swift Independent Corp. [*AMEX symbol*] (SPSG)
SFT .... System Fault Tolerant [*Novell, Inc.*] [*Orem, UT*] [*Telecommunications*]
SFTA .... Spent Fuel Transportation Accident [*Nuclear energy*] (NRCH)
SFTA .... Structural Fatigue Test Article [*NASA*] (NASA)
SFTB .... Science Fiction Times [*A publication*]
SFTB .... Southern Freight Tariff Bureau
SFTC .... Sherman Fairchild Technology Center (MCD)
SFTC .... Standard Freight Trade Classification [*Council for Mutual Economic Assistance*] (DS)
SFTCD ...... Senior Fellow, Trinity College, Dublin (ROG)
SFTE .... Society of Flight Test Engineers (EA)
SFTF .... Static Firing Test Facility [*NASA*] (NASA)
SFTFC ...... Search for Tomorrow Fan Club (EA)
SFTG .... Softguard Systems, Inc. [*Santa Clara, CA*] [*NASDAQ symbol*] (NQ)
SFTI.......... Special Flight Test Instrumentation (MCD)
SFTIP .... Special Flight Test Instrumentation Pool (NG)
SFTL .... Sonic Fatigue Test Laboratory (AAG)
SFTO .... San Diego Field Test Operations [*Aerospace*] (AAG)
SFTP .... Science for the People (EA)
SFTR .... Shipfitter (AAG)
SFTR .... Summary Flight Test Report (MCD)
SFTS .... San Francisco Theological Seminary [*San Anselmo, CA*]
SFTS .... Scale Factor Temperature Sensitivity
SFTS .... Service Flying Training School [*British*]
SFTS .... Sickle Forgers' Trade Society [*A union*] [*British*]
SFTS .... Space Flight Test System (MCD)
SFTS .... Standard Frequency and Time Signals (IEEE)
SFTS .... Synthetic Flight Training Simulator
SFTS .... Synthetic Flight Training System [*Army*]
SFTT .... Spent Fuel Transfer Tubes [*Nuclear energy*] (NRCH)
SFTW .... Stamps for the Wounded (EA)
SFTWE ..... Software (NASA)
SFTWR ..... Software [*Data processing*] (MCD)
SFTY .... Safety
SFU .... Furman University, Greenville, SC [*OCLC symbol*] (OCLC)
SFU .... Safia [*Papua New Guinea*] [*Airport symbol*] (OAG)
SFU .... Sector Field Unit [*Aviation*] (FAAC)
SFU .... Signals Flying Unit [*British*]
SFU .... Simon Fraser University [*Canada*]
SFU .... Simon Fraser University Library [*UTLAS symbol*]
SFU.......... Societe de Fluoration de l'Uranium [*An international nuclear fuel company*]
SFU.......... Special Function Unit

SFU............	Standard Firing Unit [*NASA*]　(NASA)
SFU............	Status Fill-In Unit [*Telecommunications*]　(TEL)
SFU............	Suriname Freedom Union　(EA)
SFU............	Synthetic Fuels Update [*A publication*]
SFUGE......	Singapore Federation of Unions of Government Employees
SF/UIS......	Space Frame and Unit Integrating System
SFUJA......	Steam and Fuel Users' Journal [*A publication*]
SFUK........	Sbornik Filozofickej Fakulty Univerzity Komenskeho [*A publication*]
SFUPD	Synthetic Fuels Update [*A publication*]
SFUS	Sbornik Filozofickej Fakulty Univerzity P. J. Safarika [*A publication*]
SFUS	Sovetskoe Finno-Ugrovedenie/Soviet Fenno-Ugric Studies [*A publication*]
SF/USA	Stopped-Flow/Unsegmented Storage Analyzer [*Chemical analysis*]
SFV............	Semliki Forest Virus
SFV............	Sight Feed Valve
SFV............	Simian Foamy Virus
SFVC.........	State Fund Vice Chairmen [*Red Cross*]
SFVCS	San Francisco Vocational Competency Scale
SFVK........	Svenska Folkskolans Vaenner. Kalender [*A publication*]
SFW..........	Sante Fe [*Panama*] [*Airport symbol*]　(OAG)
SFW..........	Sensor Fuzed Weapon
SFW..........	Shell Fragment Wound [*Medicine*]
SFW..........	Software　(NASA)
SFW..........	Special Filter Wheel [*Military*]　(CAAL)
SFW..........	Williston, ND [*Location identifier*] [*FAA*]　(FAAL)
SFWA........	Science Fiction Writers of America　(EA)
SFWA........	Sierra Foothill Winery Association　(EA)
SFWB	Single Fronted Weatherboard　(ADA)
SFWC	Supreme Forest Woodmen Circle [*Later, Woodmen of the World Life Insurance Society*]　(EA)
SFWEM	Static Feed Water Electrolysis Module [*NASA*]
SFWLI.......	Ship's Force Worklist Instruction
SFWM	Swiss Federation of Watch Manufacturers　(EA)
SFWR.......	Stewardesses for Women's Rights
SFWS	Stopped-Flow Wavelength Scanning [*Spectrometry*]
SFX..........	St. Francis Xavier University Library [*UTLAS symbol*]
SFX..........	Santa Fe Pacific Corp. [*NYSE symbol*]　(SPSG)
SFX..........	Sound Effects [*Script code*]
SFXD........	Semifixed
SFXR	Super Flash X-Ray　(MCD)
SFY	Savanna, IL [*Location identifier*] [*FAA*]　(FAAL)
SFY	Science Fiction Yearbook [*A publication*]
SFY	Standard Facility Years [*FAA*]
SFY	Swift Energy Company [*AMEX symbol*]　(SPSG)
SFZ	Pawtucket, RI [*Location identifier*] [*FAA*]　(FAAL)
Sfz	Sforzando [*With Additional Accent*] [*Music*]
SG	Command Surgeon [*AFSC*]
SG	Royal South Gloucestershire Light Infantry Militia [*British military*]　(DMA)
SG	Sa Grace [*His or Her Grace*] [*French*]
SG	Sa Grandeur [*His or Her Highness*] [*French*]
SG	Sabah Air [*Malaysia*] [*ICAO designator*]　(FAAC)
SG	Sachs-Georgi [*Test for syphilis*] [*Also, S-GT*] [*Obsolete*]
SG	Safety Guide　(NRCH)
SG	Salisbury Group　(EAIO)
SG	Salutis Gratia [*For the Sake of Safety*] [*Latin*]
SG	Sample Gas
SG	Sawtooth Generator
SG	Scanning Gate
SG	Schedule Generator
SG	School for Girls　(ADA)
S of G	School of Gunnery [*British military*]　(DMA)
SG	Schutzgemeinschaft Gegen Meinungsterror [*Guard Society Against Opinion Terror*] [*Germany*]
SG	Scots Guards [*Military unit*] [*British*]
SG	Screen Grid [*Electrode or vacuum tube*]
SG	Sculptors Guild　(EA)
SG	Sea Grant
SG	Seabird Group　(EAIO)
SG	Seaman Gunner [*British*] [*Obsolete*]
SG	Secretary-General [*United Nations*]
SG	Selling [*Exchange rate marking*] [*British*]
sg	Senegal [*MARC country of publication code*] [*Library of Congress*]　(LCCP)
SG	Senior Gleaners　(EA)
SG	Senior Grade
SG	Service Group　(MUGU)
SG	Set Gate
SG	Shell Gland
SG	Shell Gun
SG	Sheller-Globe Corp.
SG	Sherrgold, Inc. [*Toronto Stock Exchange symbol*]
SG	Ship and Goods [*British*]　(ROG)
SG	Shipcraft Guild　(EA)
SG	Siculorum Gymnasium [*A publication*]
SG	Siebelwerke ATG GmbH [*Federal Republic of Germany*] [*ICAO aircraft manufacturer identifier*]　(ICAO)
SG	Signal Generator

SG	Signal Ground　(BUR)
SG	Silica Gel [*Analytical chemistry*]
SG	Singapore [*ANSI two-letter standard code*]　(CNC)
SG	Singing
SG	Single Gourmet　(EA)
SG	Single Groove [*Insulators*]
Sg	Singular　(BJA)
SG	Sinte Geertruydtsbronne [*A publication*]
SG	Skin Graft [*Medicine*]
S/G	Slaved Gyro　(MCD)
S & G	Smale and Giffard's English Vice-Chancery Reports [*A publication*]　(DLA)
S/G	Smith/Greenland [*Advertising agency*]
SG	Smoke Generator
SG	Snow Grains [*Meteorology*]　(FAAC)
SG	Socialistische Gids [*A publication*]
SG	Society of Genealogists　(EA)
SG	Society of Gilders　(EA)
SG	Soft Gelatin [*Pharmacy*]
SG	Sol-Gel [*Materials science*]
SG	Solicitor General
SG	Soluble Gelatin
Sg	Song of Songs [*Old Testament book*] [*Roman Catholic canon*]　(BJA)
SG	Sort Generator　(BUR)
SG	Sound Generation　(MCD)
SG	South Georgia Railway Co. [*AAR code*] [*Terminated*]
SG	Sozialgericht [*Social Security Court*] [*German*]　(ILCA)
SG	Spark Gap　(DEN)
SG	Special Group [*NATO*]
SG	Specific Gravity [*Also, SPG, SPGR*]
SG	Spheroidal Graphite [*Ductile iron*]
SG	Sprach der Gegenwart [*A publication*]
SG	Stacking Gel [*Biochemistry*]
SG	Stained Glass
SG	Standardization Group [*Air Force*]　(AFM)
SG	Standing Group
SG	Steam Generator　(NRCH)
SG	Steel Girder [*Bridges*]
SG	Steering Group　(MCD)
SG	Stellate Ganglion [*Neuroanatomy*]
S & G	Stone and Graham's Court of Referees Reports [*England*] [*A publication*]　(DLA)
S & G	Stone and Graham's Private Bills Reports [*England*] [*A publication*]　(DLA)
SG	Stotler Group, Inc. [*AMEX symbol*]　(SPSG)
SG	Strain Gauge　(KSC)
SG	Structural Gene
SG	Structural Glass
SG	Student Guide
SG	Studi Genuensi [*A publication*]
SG	Studi Germanici [*A publication*]
SG	Studi Goriziani [*A publication*]
SG	Studium Generale [*A publication*]
S/G	Su Giro [*Your Draft*] [*Spanish*] [*Business term*]
SG	Substantia Gelatinosa [*Anatomy*]
SG	Summation Gallop [*Cardiology*]
SG	Sun Gate
SG	Sunkist Growers　(EA)
SG	Sunset Gun [*Military ceremonial*]
SG	Sunsweet Growers　(EA)
SG	Super Group　(NATG)
SG	Super Guppy　(KSC)
Sg	Supplementing [*New matter added to an existing regulation or order*] [*Used in Shepard's Citations*] [*Legal term*]　(DLA)
SG	Surgeon
SG	[*The*] Surgeon General [*Army, Air Force*]
SG	Swamp Glider
SG	Sweep Generator
SG	Sydney Gazette [*A publication*]　(APTA)
SG	Symbol Generator
SG	System Gain
1SG	First Sergeant [*Army*]
SGA	Saga Resources [*Vancouver Stock Exchange symbol*]
SGA	Savoonga, AK [*Location identifier*] [*FAA*]　(FAAL)
SGA	Scientific Glass Apparatus Co., Inc.
SGA	Screened Granulated Aluminate [*Inorganic chemistry*]
SGA	Sea Grant Association　(EA)
SG & A	Selling, General, and Administrative Expenses
SGA	Shirtsleeve Garment Assembly [*NASA*]
SGA	Sickle Grinders' Association [*A union*] [*British*]
SGA	Sigma Security, Inc. [*Vancouver Stock Exchange symbol*]
SGA	Single-Monitor Graphic Adaptor [*Computer graphics*]
SGA	Slave Gyro Assembly
SGA	Slavic Gospel Association　(EA)
SGA	Small for Gestational Age [*Pediatrics*]
SGA	Societe de Geologie Appliquee aux Gites Mineraux [*Society for Geology Applied to Mineral Deposits*] [*ICSU*]　(EAIO)
SGA	Society of Gastrointestinal Assistants [*Later, SGNA*]　(EA)
SGA	Society for Geology Applied to Mineral Deposits　(EAIO)

SGA .... Society of Governmental Appraisers [*Later, Association of Governmental Appraisers*] (EA)
SGA .... Society of Graphic Art [*British*]
SGA .... Solar Greenhouse Association (EA)
SGA .... Songwriters Guild of America (EA)
SGA .... Soybean Growers of America (EA)
SGA .... Spectrometric Gas Analysis
SGA .... Split Group Aperture
SGA .... Spouses of Gays Association (EA)
SGA .... Standards of Grade Authorization [*Military*]
SGA .... Stephens Glacier [*Alaska*] [*Seismograph station code, US Geological Survey*] [*Closed*] (SEIS)
SGA .... Substantial Gainful Activity [*Social Security Administration*] (OICC)
SGA .... Superior Geniculate Artery [*Anatomy*]
SGA .... Switch Group Assembly
SGAA .... Sporting Goods Agents Association (EA)
SGAA .... Stained Glass Association of America (EA)
SGAC........ Silvermine Guild Arts Center (EA)
SGAC........ State Governmental Affairs Council (EA)
SGACC...... Secretariat General de l'Aviation Civile et Commerciale [*France*]
SGAD .... Safeguard Army Depot (AABC)
SGAE......... Studiengesellschaft fuer Atomenergie [*Implements Austria's nuclear program*] (NRCH)
SGAHRS... Steam Generator Auxiliary Heat Removal System [*Nuclear energy*] (NRCH)
SGAIG...... Scholars Group Against the Invasion of Grenada (EA)
SGA J .... SGA [*Society of Gastrointestinal Assistants*] Journal [*A publication*]
SGAK........ Studien zur Germanistik, Anglistik und Komparatistik [*A publication*]
SGAL......... Sage-Allen & Co., Inc. [*NASDAQ symbol*] (NQ)
SGA of M-A ... Sod Growers Association of Mid-America (EA)
SGAOR ..... Sitzungsberichte. Gesellschaft fuer Geschichte und Altertumskunde der Ostseeprovinzen Russlands [*A publication*]
SGAS......... Asuncion/Presidente General Stroessner [*Paraguay*] [*ICAO location identifier*] (ICLI)
SGAS......... Society for German-American Studies (EA)
SGAS......... Space Geodesy Altimetry Study [*Raytheon Co.*]
SGAS......... Steam Generator Available Signal [*Nuclear energy*] (NRCH)
SGAT......... Seagate Technology, Inc. [*NASDAQ symbol*] (NQ)
SGAUA ..... Scitex Graphic Arts Users Association (EA)
SGAUG ..... Scitex Graphic Arts Users Group [*Later, SGAUA*] (EA)
SGAUSA ... St. George Association of the USA (EA)
sGAW .... Specific Airway Conductance
SGAW .... Subgroup on Assessment of Weapons [*NATO*] (NATG)
SGAY........ Ayolas [*Paraguay*] [*ICAO location identifier*] (ICLI)
SGB........... Santa Fe, NM [*Location identifier*] [*FAA*] (FAAL)
SGB........... Schlesische Geschichtsblaetter (Breslau) [*A publication*]
SGB........... Schweizerischer Gewerkschaftsbund [*Swiss Federation of Trade Unions*]
SGB........... Societe Generale de Banque [*Bank Society*] [*Information service or system*] (IID)
SGB........... Southern Gas Basin [*British*]
SGB........... Steam Generator Blowdown [*Nuclear energy*] (NRCH)
SGB........... Steam Generator Building [*Nuclear energy*] (NRCH)
SGB........... Steam Gunboat [*British military*] (DMA)
SGB........... Stellate Ganglion Blockade [*Anesthesiology*]
SGB........... Strain Gauge Bridge
SGB........... Studien und Mitteilungen zur Geschichte des Benediktiner-Ordens [*A publication*]
SGB........... Switchgear Block (MSA)
SGBD........ Steam Generator Blowdown [*Nuclear energy*] (NRCH)
SGBI......... Santa Gertrudis Breeders International (EA)
SGBIA .... Symposia Genetica et Biologica Italica [*A publication*]
SGBIP .... Subject Guide to Books in Print [*A publication*]
SGBPS....... Steam Generator Blowdown Processing System [*Nuclear energy*] (NRCH)
SGBS......... Steam Generator Blowdown System [*Nuclear energy*] (NRCH)
SGBV........ Bella Vista [*Paraguay*] [*ICAO location identifier*] (ICLI)
SGC .... Saint Gregory College [*Oklahoma*]
SGC .... Salivary Gland Choristoma [*Medicine*]
SGC .... Screen Grid Current
SGC .... Simulated Generation Control
SGC .... Solicitor General Canada
SGC .... South Georgia College [*Douglas*]
SGC .... Southern Governors Conference
SGC .... Space General Corporation (MCD)
SGC .... Spartan Guidance Computer [*Missiles*] (AABC)
SGC .... Spherical Gear Coupling
SGC .... Stabilized Ground Cloud [*NASA*] (MCD)
SGC .... Stabilizer Gyro Circuit
SGC .... Standard Geographical Classification [*Canada*]
SGC .... Strata Energy Corporation [*Vancouver Stock Exchange symbol*]
SGC .... Students Guide to Childcare [*British*]
SGC .... Supergroup Connector [*Telecommunications*] (TEL)
SGC .... Superior Geocentric Conjunction
SGC .... Superior Surgical Manufacturing Company, Inc. [*AMEX symbol*] (SPSG)

Sg C............ Surgeon-Captain [*British military*] (DMA)
SGC .... Washington, DC [*Location identifier*] [*FAA*] (FAAL)
SGCA .... Silvermine Guild Center for the Arts [*Later, SGAC*] (EA)
SGCC........ Safety Glazing Certification Council (EA)
SGCD .... Society of Glass and Ceramic Decorators (EA)
SGCE........ Ship Gyrocompass Equipment [*Navy*] (CAAL)
SGCEC ..... Standing Group Communications-Electronics Committee [*Later, MCEWG*] [*NATO*] (NATG)
SGCF .... SNAP [*Systems for Nuclear Auxiliary Power*] Generalized Critical Facility
SGCL......... Studies in General and Comparative Literature [*A publication*]
SGCMG..... Single Gimbal Control Moment Gyro [*Navigation*]
SGCO .... Concepcion [*Paraguay*] [*ICAO location identifier*] (ICLI)
SGCO .... Schacher, Greentree & Company, Inc. [*New York, NY*] [*NASDAQ symbol*] (NQ)
Sg Cr .... Surgeon-Commander [*British military*] (DMA)
SGCS......... Silicon Gate-Controlled Switch
SGCS......... Slave Gyro Control System
SGD .... Napa, CA [*Location identifier*] [*FAA*] (FAAL)
SGD .... Seafloor Geosciences Division (EA)
SGD .... Self-Generating Dictionary
SGD .... Senior Grand Deacon [*Freemasonry*]
SGD .... Shogun Developments Corp. [*Vancouver Stock Exchange symbol*]
SGD .... Signaling Ground [*Telecommunications*] (TEL)
SGD .... Signed
SGD .... Sliding Glass Door (ADA)
SGD .... Society of Geniuses of Distinction (EA)
SGD .... Society of Glass Decorators [*Later, SGCD*] (EA)
SGD .... Solar-Geophysical Data [*A publication*]
SGD .... Sonderborg [*Denmark*] [*Airport symbol*] (OAG)
SGD .... Sui Generis Degree
SGDCTO... Sangre de Cristo [*FAA*] (FAAC)
SGDE........ Steering Gear Dual Emergency (MSA)
SGDE........ System Ground Data Equipment [*RADAR*]
SGDF........ Supergroup Distribution Frame [*Telecommunications*] (TEL)
SGDG .... Sans Garantie du Gouvernement [*Without Government Guarantee*] [*French*] (ROG)
SGDHF ..... Sodium Glycodihydrofusidate [*Hemolytic*]
SGDI .... Swaging Die [*Tool*]
SGDI......... Switched Ground Discrete Input (MCD)
SGDN........ Surgidyne, Inc. [*NASDAQ symbol*] (NQ)
SGDO........ Switched Ground Discrete Output (MCD)
SGDPS....... Second Generation Data Processing System (MCD)
Sge .... Sagitta [*Constellation*]
SGE........... Secondary Grid Emission
SGE........... Severable Government Equipment
SGE........... Sigma Gamma Epsilon [*Society*]
SGE........... Society of Government Economists (EA)
SGE........... Subscriber Group Equipment [*Telecommunications*]
SGE........... Super-Critical Gas Extraction [*Chemical engineering*]
SGEG........ Syndicat General de l'Education en Guadeloupe (PD)
SGEGA...... Studia Geophysica et Geodaetica [*A publication*]
SGEM........ Study Group on Environmental Monitoring [*National Research Council*]
SGEMP ..... System-Generated Electromagnetic Pulse [*Army*]
SGEN .... Encarnacion [*Paraguay*] [*ICAO location identifier*] (ICLI)
SGen .... Studium Generale [*A publication*]
SGEP .... Socialist Group in the European Parliament [*See also GSPE*] (EAIO)
SGer .... Studia Germanica [*A publication*]
S Ger S ...... Stanford German Studies [*A publication*]
SGES .... Society of Grain Elevator Superintendents [*Later, GEAPS*]
SGET .... Spacecraft Ground Elapsed Time
SGEU .... Singapore General Employees' Union
SGF........... Sample Gas Flow
SGF........... Sarcoma Growth Factor
SGF........... Singapore Fund [*NYSE symbol*] (SPSG)
SGF........... Skeletal Growth Factor [*Genetics*]
SGF........... Small Gene Fragment [*Genetics*]
SGF........... Southern Group of Forces [*USSR*] (NATG)
SGF........... Spermiogenesis Growth Factor [*Biochemistry*]
SGF........... Springfield [*Missouri*] [*Airport symbol*] (OAG)
SGF........... Springfield, MO [*Location identifier*] [*FAA*] (FAAL)
SGF........... Stockholmer Germanistische Forschungen [*A publication*]
SGFA......... Asuncion [*Paraguay*] [*ICAO location identifier*] (ICLI)
SGFC......... Sharon Gless Fan Club (EA)
SGFI .... Filadelfia [*Paraguay*] [*ICAO location identifier*] (ICLI)
SGFID .... Seventh Generation Fund for Indian Development (EA)
SGFMV ..... Sammendrag af Groenlands Fangstilister MV [*A publication*]
SGFNT ..... Significant (FAAC)
SGFP .... Steam Generator Feed Pump (IEEE)
SGF Publ ... SGF [*Sveriges Gummitekniska Foerening*] Publicerande [*A publication*]
SGG .... Saint George Island, AK [*Location identifier*] [*FAA*] (FAAL)
SGG .... St. George Minerals [*Vancouver Stock Exchange symbol*]
SGG .... South Georgia [*United Kingdom*] [*Geomagnetic observatory code*]
SGG .... Studia Germanica Gandensia [*A publication*]
SGG .... Sustainer Gas Generator

SGGAOPR ... Sitzungsberichte. Gesellschaft fuer Geschichte und Altertumskunde der Ostseeprovinzen Russlands [*A publication*]
SGGP .... Seller's Guide to Government Purchasing [*A publication*]
SGGR .... Guaira [*Paraguay*] [*ICAO location identifier*]   (ICLI)
SGH .... Generale Maatschappij van Belgie. Informatieblad [*A publication*]
SGH .... Serum Growth Hormone [*Endocrinology*]
SGH .... Seth G. Huntington [*Designer's mark on US bicentennial half dollar*]
SGH .... Signal Hill Energy Corp. [*Vancouver Stock Exchange symbol*]
SGH .... Springfield, OH [*Location identifier*] [*FAA*]   (FAAL)
SGh .... Studia Ghisleriana [*Pavia*] [*A publication*]
SGH .... Sud-Ghoubbet [*Djibouti*] [*Seismograph station code, US Geological Survey*]   (SEIS)
SGH .... Surgical Hospital [*Medicine*]
SGHB .... Sag Harbor Savings Bank [*NASDAQ symbol*]   (NQ)
SGHI .... Silk Greenhouse, Inc. [*NASDAQ symbol*]   (NQ)
SGHLA ..... Stadt- und Gebaeudetechnik [*A publication*]
SGHW .... Steam-Generating, Heavy-Water [*Reactor*] [*British*] [*Nuclear energy*]   (NRCH)
SGHWR .... Steam-Generating, Heavy-Water Reactor [*British*] [*Nuclear energy*]   (NRCH)
SGI .... Sea Grant Institute [*University of Wisconsin*] [*Research center*]   (RCD)
SGI .... Search Group, Incorporated [*An association*]   (EA)
SGI .... Servicio Geodesico Interamericano [*Inter-American Geodetic Survey - IAGS*] [*United States*]
SGI .... Silicon Graphics [*NYSE symbol*]   (SPSG)
SGI .... Small Group Instructor [*Army*]   (INF)
SGI .... Society for Gynecologic Investigation   (EA)
SGI .... Specific Gravity Indicator
SGI .... Spring Garden Institute
SGI .... Standard Graphic Interface [*XOR Systems*]
SGI .... Studi di Grammatica Italiana [*A publication*]
SGI .... Systems Group, Inc. [*Telecommunications service*]   (TSSD)
SGIA .... Sun Glass Institute of America [*Defunct*]   (EA)
SGIB .... Itaipu [*Paraguay*] [*ICAO location identifier*]   (ICLI)
SGIB .... Slattery Group, Inc. [*NASDAQ symbol*]   (NQ)
SGIG .... Sovereign Grand Inspector-General [*Freemasonry*]   (ROG)
SGII .... SGI International [*NASDAQ symbol*]   (NQ)
SGIM .... Society of General Internal Medicine   (EA)
SGINDEX ... System Generation Cross-Reference Index [*NASA*]
SGIS .... Safeguards Initiation Signal [*Nuclear energy*]   (NRCH)
SGIS .... Steam Generator Isolation Signal   (IEEE)
SGIS .... Student Government Information Service   (EA)
SGIT .... Special Group Inclusive Tour [*Airline fare*]
SGJ .... Sagarai [*Papua New Guinea*] [*Airport symbol*]   (OAG)
SGJ .... St. Augustine, FL [*Location identifier*] [*FAA*]   (FAAL)
SGJ .... Supersonic Gas Jet
SGJA .... Sporting Goods Jobbers Association [*Later, NASGW*]
SGJKT ...... Society of Goldsmiths, Jewellers, and Kindred Trades [*A union*] [*British*]
SGJN .... San Juan Nepomuceno [*Paraguay*] [*ICAO location identifier*]   (ICLI)
SGJP .... Satellite Graphic Job Processor [*Data processing*]
SGK .... Hsinkong [*Republic of China*] [*Also, HSI*] [*Seismograph station code, US Geological Survey*]   (SEIS)
SGK .... Knoxville, TN [*Location identifier*] [*FAA*]   (FAAL)
SGKA .... Studien zur Geschichte und Kultur des Alterums [*A publication*]   (BJA)
SGKF .... Susan G. Komen Foundation   (EA)
SGL .... Mount Signal [*California*] [*Seismograph station code, US Geological Survey*]   (SEIS)
SGL .... Signal
SGL .... Single   (MSA)
SGL .... Sleeping Gold Ltd. [*Vancouver Stock Exchange symbol*]
SGL .... Society of Gas Lighting   (EA)
SGL .... South State Cooperative Library System, Los Angeles, CA [*OCLC symbol*]   (OCLC)
SGL .... Space-Ground Link   (MCD)
SGL .... Spiegel [*Hamburg*] [*A publication*]
SGL .... Studies in German Literature [*A publication*]
SGl .... Sumerisches Glossar [*A publication*]   (BJA)
SGL .... Sunglasses
SGL .... Supermarkets General Corp. [*NYSE symbol*]   (SPSG)
S GLAM ..... South Glamorgan [*County in Wales*]
SGL/B .... Boletin. Sociedad Geografica de Lima [*A publication*]
SGLC .... Strain Gauge Load Cell
Sg L Cr ...... Surgeon Lieutenant-Commander [*British military*]   (DMA)
SGLE .... Single   (AAG)
SGLF .... Scottish Grand Lodge of Freemasons
SGLF .... Symposia. Giovanni Lorenzini Foundation [*Elsevier Book Series*] [*A publication*]
SGLI .... Servicemen's Group Life Insurance [*Military*]
SGLI .... Slave Gyro Leveling Integrator
SGLI .... Societe Geographique de Liege. Bulletin [*Belgium*] [*A publication*]
SGLIC .... Steam Generator Level Instrumentation Cabinet [*Nuclear energy*]   (NRCH)

SGLL .... Studies in the Germanic Languages and Literatures [*A publication*]
SGLLI .... Section on Gay and Lesbian Legal Issues [*Association of American Law Schools*]   (EA)
SGLO .... Lobrego, Fortin [*Paraguay*] [*ICAO location identifier*]   (ICLI)
SGLO .... Standing Group Liaison Officer to the North Atlantic Council
SGLP .... Standing Group Representative Liaison Paper to the International Staff [*Obsolete*] [*NATO*]   (NATG)
SGLS .... Satellite Grand Link System   (NATG)
SGLS .... Space-Ground Link Station [*NASA*]   (NASA)
SGLS .... Space-to-Ground Link Subsystem [*NASA*]
SGLSA ...... Stomatoloski Glasnik Srbije [*A publication*]
SGLV .... La Victoria (Ex Casado) [*Paraguay*] [*ICAO location identifier*]   (ICLI)
SGLWCH ... Study Group on Labor and Working Class History   (EA)
SGM .... College Mathieu, Gravelbourg, Saskatchewan [*Library symbol*] [*National Library of Canada*]   (NLC)
SGM .... Scottish Geographical Magazine [*A publication*]
SGM .... Screen Grid Modulation
SGM .... Sea Gallantry Medal [*Navy*] [*British*]
SGM .... Sergeant Major   (AABC)
SGM .... Silver Gate [*Montana*] [*Seismograph station code, US Geological Survey*]   (SEIS)
SGM .... Society for General Microbiology [*British*]
SGM .... Society for General Music   (EA)
SGM .... Soeurs Grises de Montreal [*Sisters of Charity, Grey Nuns of Montreal*] [*Roman Catholic religious order*]
SGM .... Spark Gap Modulation
SGM .... Standing Group Memorandum [*Obsolete*] [*NATO*]   (NATG)
SGM .... Strategic Guidance Memo [*Navy*]
SGMA ...... Sigmaform Corp. [*NASDAQ symbol*]   (NQ)
SGMA ...... Sporting Goods Manufacturers Association [*North Palm Beach, FL*]   (EA)
SGMAA .... Sporting Goods Manufacturers Agents Association [*Later, SGRA*]
SGMC .... Standing Group Meteorological Committee [*Obsolete*] [*NATO*]   (NATG)
SGMCI ...... Sporting Goods Manufacturers' Credit Interchange [*Buffalo, NY*]   (EA)
SGMD .... Swaging Mandel
SGME .... Mariscal Estigarribia [*Paraguay*] [*ICAO location identifier*]   (ICLI)
SGME .... Service Generale des Moyens de l'Enseignement [*Canada*]
SGMH .... Study Group. Institute for Research into Mental and Multiple Handicap [*Elsevier Book Series*] [*A publication*]
SGMI .... S-G Metals Industries, Inc. [*NASDAQ symbol*]   (NQ)
SGML .... Standard Generalized Markup Language [*Also, GSML*] [*International Standards Organization*]
SGML .... Study Group for Mathematical Learning   (EA)
SGMN .... Signalman [*Military*] [*British*]
SGMP .... Society of Government Meeting Planners   (EA)
SGMS .... Shipboard Gravity Measuring System
SGMSR .... Steam Generator Maximum Steam Rate [*Nuclear energy*]   (NRCH)
SGMT .... Simulated Greenwich Mean Time   (MCD)
SGMT .... Subgroup Modern Terminal
SGM/USA ... Scripture Gift Mission/USA   (EA)
SGN .... Ho Chi Minh [*Vietnam*] [*Airport symbol*]   (OAG)
SGN .... Saigon [*Vietnam*]
SGN .... Sartigan Granite [*Vancouver Stock Exchange symbol*]
SGN .... Scan Gate Number
SGN .... Seamless Garment Network   (EA)
SGN .... Self-Generated Noise [*Oceanography*]
SGN .... Service Geologique National [*National Geological Survey*] [*Bureau of Geological and Mining Research*] [*Information service or system*]   (IID)
sgn .... Signer [*MARC relator code*] [*Library of Congress*]   (LCCP)
SGN .... Simulation Gaming News [*A publication*]
SGN .... Standing Group, North Atlantic Treaty Organization
SGN .... Surgeon [*Military*] [*British*]
SGN .... Surgeon General of the Navy
SGNA .... Nueva Asuncion [*Paraguay*] [*ICAO location identifier*]   (ICLI)
SGNA .... Society of Gastroenterology Nurses and Associates   (EA)
SGNAD ..... Shoni Geka Naika [*A publication*]
SGNET ...... Sea Grant Network [*National Oceanic and Atmospheric Administration*] [*Information service or system*]   (IID)
SGNLD ...... Signalled   (ROG)
SGNLS ...... Sequential Generalized Nonlinear Least Squares [*Statistics*]
SGNMOS ... Screen-Grid N-Channel Metal Oxide Semiconductor
SGNR .... Signature   (AABC)
SGNRA ..... Surgical Neurology [*Tryon, NC*] [*A publication*]
SGO .... Saint George [*Australia*] [*Airport symbol*]   (OAG)
SGO .... Sea Gold Oil Corp. [*Vancouver Stock Exchange symbol*]
SGO .... Seagull Energy Corp. [*NYSE symbol*]   (SPSG)
SGO .... Society of Geriatric Ophthalmology   (EA)
SGO .... Society of Gynecologic Oncologists   (EA)
SGO .... Squadron Gunnery Officer
SGO .... Stained Glass Overlay [*Commercial firm*] [*British*]
SGo .... Studi Goriziani [*A publication*]
SGO .... Subgenual Organ [*Entomology*]
SGO .... Surgeon General's Office

SGO	Sydney Godolphin Osborne [*Literary signature of 19th-century British writer*]
SGOBA......	Surgery, Gynecology, and Obstetrics [*A publication*]
SGOG	Steam Generators Owners Group [*Nuclear energy*] (NRCH)
SGOG	Suppressor Grid Orbitron Gauge
SGOL	Olimpo [*Paraguay*] [*ICAO location identifier*] (ICLI)
SGOL	St. Helena Gold Mines Ltd. [*NASDAQ symbol*] (NQ)
SGoldoniani ...	Studi Goldoniani [*A publication*]
SGOP	Seagull Energy Corp. [*NASDAQ symbol*] (NQ)
SGOR	Solution Gas-Oil Ratio
SGor	Studi Goriziani [*A publication*]
SGOS........	Shuttle Ground Operations Simulator [*NASA*] (NASA)
SGOT	Serum Glutamic Oxaloacetic Transaminase [*An enzyme*]
SGP............	San Gregorio [*Peru*] [*Seismograph station code, US Geological Survey*] [*Closed*] (SEIS)
SGP............	Schering-Plough Corp. [*NYSE symbol*] (SPSG)
SGP............	Secondary Gun Pointer [*Navy*]
SGP............	Seminiferous Growth Factor [*Biochemistry*]
SGP............	Singapore [*ANSI three-letter standard code*] (CNC)
SGP............	Single Ground Point [*NASA*] (MCD)
SGP............	Society of General Physiologists (EA)
SGP............	Society of Ghana Philatelists [*Defunct*] (EA)
SGP............	Solicitor General, Prairies [*UTLAS symbol*]
SGP............	South Galactic Pole
SGP............	Southern Galactic Pole
SGP............	Specialty Glass Products, Inc.
SGP............	Staatkundig Gereformeerde Partij [*Political Reformed Party*] [*Netherlands*] [*Political party*] (PPE)
SGP............	Stabilized Gyro Platform
SGP............	Standard Guidance Package
SGP............	Stephen Greene Press
SGP............	Sudeten German Party
SGP............	Sulfated Glycoprotein [*Biochemistry*]
SGPA........	Stained Glass Professionals Association [*Inactive*] (EA)
SGPB........	Southern Growth Policies Board
SGPC........	Soviet Government Purchasing Commission [*World War II*]
SGPI.........	Pilar [*Paraguay*] [*ICAO location identifier*] (ICLI)
SGPI.........	Superintendent of Government Printing, India (ROG)
SGPM.......	Saint-Gobain-Pont-A-Mousson [*French industrial giant*]
SgpNL	National Library, Singapore, Singapore [*Library symbol*] [*Library of Congress*] (LCLS)
SgpNU.......	Nangang University, Singapore, Singapore [*Library symbol*] [*Library of Congress*] (LCLS)
SGPO	Puerto Pinasco [*Paraguay*] [*ICAO location identifier*] (ICLI)
SGPO	Standing Group Representative Communication to the Private Office of the NATO Secretary General [*Obsolete*] (NATG)
SGPS	Ciudad Presidente Stroessner [*Paraguay*] [*ICAO location identifier*] (ICLI)
SGPT	Serum Glutamic-Pyruvic Transaminase [*An enzyme*]
SgpU	University of Singapore, Singapore, Singapore [*Library symbol*] [*Library of Congress*] (LCLS)
SGR	Greenville County Library, Greenville, SC [*OCLC symbol*] (OCLC)
SGR	Houston, TX [*Location identifier*] [*FAA*] (FAAL)
Sgr	Sagittarius [*Constellation*]
SGR	Saturn Energy & Resources Ltd. [*Vancouver Stock Exchange symbol*]
SGR	School of General Reconnaissance [*Air Force*] [*British*]
SGR	Science and Government Report [*A publication*]
SGR	Seismic Group Recorder [*Geophysics*]
SGR	Self-Generation Reactor [*Nuclear energy*] (NRCH)
SGR	Seminal Groove
SGR	Set Graphics Rendition [*Data processing*] (PCM)
SGR	Singer [*Music*]
SGR	Sodium Graphite Reactor [*Nuclear energy*]
SGR	Soft Gamma-Ray Repeater [*Astrophysics*]
SGR	Stack Gas Reheat [*Air pollution control*]
SGR	Steam Gas Recycle [*Shale oil process*]
S/GR	Steering Gear [*Automotive engineering*]
SGr	Studii de Gramatica [*A publication*]
SGR	Submandibular Gland Renin [*Endocrinology*]
SGR	Sugar Land [*Texas*] [*Airport symbol*] (OAG)
SGRA........	Sporting Goods Representatives Association [*of SIRA*] [*Later, SGAA*] (EA)
Sg RA........	Surgeon Rear-Admiral [*British military*] (DMA)
SGRAC......	Supreme Grand Royal Arch Chapter [*Freemasonry*] (ROG)
SGRAE......	Scientists' Group for Reform of Animal Experimentation (EA)
SGram.......	Studii de Gramatica [*A publication*]
SGRCA......	Sodium Graphite Reactor Critical Assembly (IEEE)
SGRD	Signal Ground (AAG)
SGRD	State Government Research Directory [*A publication*]
SGREP	Standing Group Representative [*NASA*]
S-GRN	Surfaced Green [*Lumber*]
SGRO	Rosario [*Paraguay*] [*ICAO location identifier*] (ICLI)
SGRS........	Stockton Geriatric Rating Scale [*Psychology*]
SGRT........	Soviet Geography. Review and Translations [*A publication*]
SGRU	Sawyers' General Representative Union [*British*]
SGS...........	Sage Resources Ltd. [*Vancouver Stock Exchange symbol*]
SGS...........	St. George [*South Carolina*] [*Seismograph station code, US Geological Survey*] (SEIS)
SGS...........	Scottish Gaelic Studies [*A publication*]

SGS...........	Scottish Guild of Servers [*Episcopalian*]
SGS...........	Secondary Grammar School (ADA)
SGS...........	Secretary of the General Staff [*Army*]
SGS...........	Segmented Gamma Scanner [*Nuclear energy*] (NRCH)
SGS...........	Signal Generating Station (CET)
SGS...........	Single Green Silk-Covered [*Wire insulation*]
SGS...........	Sisters of the Good Samaritan (ADA)
SGS...........	Society of the Golden Section [*Inactive*] (EA)
SGS...........	Society of the Good Shepherd [*Anglican religious community*]
SGS...........	Solution Gas Drive [*Petroleum engineering*]
SGS...........	Statistics Gathering System [*NASA*]
SGS...........	Steam Generator System [*Nuclear energy*] (NRCH)
SGS...........	Steep Glide Slope (NASA)
SGS...........	Strategy Gaming Society (EA)
SGS...........	Stream Generation Statement [*Data processing*]
SGS...........	Stretch Glass Society (EA)
SGS...........	Swiveling Gunner's Station
SGS...........	Symbol Generation and Storage [*Data processing*]
SGSC........	Samuel Gompers Stamp Club (EA)
SGSC........	Standing Group Security Committee [*Obsolete*] [*NATO*] (NATG)
SGSC........	Strain Gauge Signal Conditioner [*NASA*] (MCD)
SGSE........	Standard Ground Support Equipment
SGSFU......	Salt-Glazed Structural Facing Units [*Technical drawings*]
SGSHA......	Shigen Gijutsu Shikenjo Hokoku [*A publication*]
SGSI.........	Sage Software, Incorporated [*Rockville, MD*] [*NASDAQ symbol*] (NQ)
SGSI.........	Stabilized Glide Slope Indicator (NVT)
SGSN........	Skylab Ground Support Network [*NASA*]
SGSNY......	St. George's Society of New York (EA)
SGSO........	Space Ground Support Operations [*NASA*] (KSC)
SGSP........	Salt Gradient Solar Ponds [*Energy source*]
SGSP	Single Groove, Single Petticoat [*Insulators*]
SGSP	Society for Glass Science and Practices (EA)
SGSR........	Society for General Systems Research (EA)
SGSRDC.....	Selye's Guide to Stress Research [*A publication*]
SGSS	Study Group on Social Security [*Defunct*] (EA)
SGSUB......	Salt-Glazed Structural Unit Base [*Technical drawings*]
SGSVDV.....	Steam Generator Stop Valve Dump Valve (IEEE)
SGSYB......	Stadler Genetics Symposia [*A publication*]
S-GT	Sachs-Georgi Test [*for syphilis*] [*Also, SG*] [*Obsolete*]
SGT............	Satellite Ground Terminal
SGT............	Schriften. Gesellschaft fuer Theatergeschichte [*A publication*]
SGT............	Seagram's Gin and Tonic
SGT............	Segment Table [*Data processing*] (IBMDP)
SGT............	Sergeant (AABC)
SGT............	Small Gas Turbine
SGT............	Small Group Therapy
SGT............	Society of Glass Technology (EAIO)
SGT............	Special Gas Taper [*Thread*]
SGT............	Stuttgart, AR [*Location identifier*] [*FAA*] (FAAL)
SGT............	Subsystem Ground Test (MCD)
SGTA........	Servo Gear Train Assembly
SGTADY...	University of Southern California. Institute for Marine and Coastal Studies. Sea Grant Technical Report Series [*A publication*]
Sgte	Sagitta [*Constellation*]
SGTF	Steam Generator Test Facility [*Nuclear energy*] (NRCH)
SGTIA	Standing Group Technical Intelligence Agency [*NATO*] (NATG)
SGTI.......	Sawyer's Gas Turbine International [*A publication*]
Sgtl...........	Sightlines [*A publication*]
SGTM.......	Strain Gauge Thrust Meter
SGTM.......	Titanium Dioxide Manufacturers Sector Group (EAIO)
SGTMAJ...	Sergeant Major
SGTPA......	Sbornik Trudov Nauchno-Issledovatel'skii Institut Gigieny Truda i Profzabolevanii Imeni N. I. Makhviladze [*A publication*]
SGTPS......	Saw Grinders' Trade Protective Society [*A union*] [*British*]
Sgtr	Sagittarius [*Constellation*]
SGTR........	Standard Government Travel Request
SGTR........	Standardized Government Travel Regulations
SGTR........	Steam Generator Test Rig [*Nuclear energy*] (NRCH)
SGTR........	Steam Generator Tube Rupture [*Nuclear energy*] (NRCH)
SGTS	Satellite Ground Terminal System
SGTS	Standby Gas Treatment System [*Nuclear energy*] (NRCH)
SGTS	Swing Grip Thermal Stripper
SGU	Saint George [*Utah*] [*Airport symbol*] (OAG)
SGU	Saint George, UT [*Location identifier*] [*FAA*] (FAAL)
SGU	Sammelbuch Griechischer Urkunden aus Aegypten [*A publication*] (BJA)
SGU	Sidewinder Generator Unit (NG)
SGU	Single Gun Unit [*British military*] (DMA)
SGU	Studia Germanistica Upsaliensia [*A publication*]
SGU	Sveriges Geologiska Undersokning [*Geological Survey of Sweden*] [*Uppsala*] [*Information service or system*] (IID)
SGULF.......	Seagull Resources [*NASDAQ symbol*] (NQ)
S-G(UN).....	Secretary-General of the United Nations
SGUS........	Slovak Gymnastic Union Sokol of the USA (EA)
SGV	Saint Genevieve Resources Ltd. [*Toronto Stock Exchange symbol*]

SGV	Salivary Gland Virus
SGV	Sierra Grande [*Argentina*] [*Airport symbol*] (OAG)
SGV	Small Granular Vesicle [*Cytology*]
SGV	Summlung Gemeinverstaendlicher Vortraege und Schriften aus dem Gebiet der Theologie und Religionsgeschichte [*Tuebingen*] [*A publication*]
Sg VA........	Surgeon Vice-Admiral [*British military*] (DMA)
SGVGA.....	Sbornik Geologickych Ved. Geologie [*A publication*]
SGVLA.....	Sbornik Geologickych Ved. Loziskova Geologie [*A publication*]
SGVS.........	Summlung Gemeinverstaendlicher Vortraege und Schriften aus dem Gebiet der Theologie und Religionsgeschichte [*Tuebingen*] [*A publication*]
SGVUA	Sbornik Geologickych Ved. Uzita Geofyzika [*A publication*]
SGW	Salt-Glazed Ware
SGW	Security Guard Window (AAG)
SGW	Senior Grand Warden [*Freemasonry*]
SGW	South Carolina State College, Orangeburg, SC [*OCLC symbol*] (OCLC)
SGW	Stone Groundwood [*Pulp and paper technology*]
SGWLC	Steam Generator Water Level Control [*Nuclear energy*] (NRCH)
SGWM	Standing Group Working Memorandum [*NATO*] (NATG)
SGWS........	Shared Graphics Work Space
SGWS........	Stove Grate Workers' Society [*A union*] [*British*]
SGX	Selector Group Matrix [*Telecommunications*] (TEL)
SGX	Songea [*Tanzania*] [*Airport symbol*] (OAG)
SGX	Synergistics Industries Ltd. [*Toronto Stock Exchange symbol*]
s-gy---	Guyana [*MARC geographic area code*] [*Library of Congress*] (LCCP)
SGY	Skagway [*Alaska*] [*Airport symbol*] (OAG)
SGY	Skagway, AK [*Location identifier*] [*FAA*] (FAAL)
SGY	Sooner Energy Corp. [*Vancouver Stock Exchange symbol*]
SGym	Siculorum Gymnasium [*A publication*]
SGYR........	Yasyreta [*Paraguay*] [*ICAO location identifier*] (ICLI)
SGZ	Green Bay, WI [*Location identifier*] [*FAA*] (FAAL)
SGZ	Signet Resources, Inc. [*Vancouver Stock Exchange symbol*]
SGZ	Surface Ground Zero
SGZAB......	Sanyo Gijutsu Zasshi [*A publication*]
SH..............	Air-Cushion Vehicle built by Sealand Hovercraft [*England*] [*Usually used in combination with numerals*]
SH..............	Sa Hautesse [*His, or Her, Highness*] [*French*]
SH..............	Sacred Heart (ROG)
SH..............	Sacrifice Hit [*Baseball*]
SH..............	St. Helena [*ANSI two-letter standard code*] (CNC)
SH..............	Samaritan Free Hospital [*British*] (ROG)
S/H............	Sample and Hold (IEEE)
SH..............	Schering AG [*Germany*] [*Research code symbol*]
SH..............	Schistosoma Hematobium [*A parasitic fluke*]
SH..............	Schoolhouse
SH..............	Scinde Horse [*British military*] (DMA)
SH..............	Scleroscope Hardness
SH..............	Scottish Horse [*British military*] (DMA)
SH..............	Scratch Hardness [*Aerospace*]
SH..............	Scripophila Helvetica (EA)
SH..............	Scripta Hierosolymitana (BJA)
SH..............	Second Harvest, the National Food Bank Network (EA)
SH..............	Secondhand (ADA)
SH..............	Section Heading Code [*Online database field identifier*]
SH..............	Sefer ha-Shanah (BJA)
SH..............	Sekira Hodshit [*Tel Aviv*] (BJA)
SH..............	Semester Hour
SH..............	Send Hub [*Telegraphy*] (TEL)
SH..............	Sequence History
SH..............	Serum Hepatitis [*Medicine*]
SH..............	Service Hours [*Electronics*] (IEEE)
SH..............	Servicio Aereo de Honduras, Sociedad Anonima [*ICAO designator*] (FAAC)
SH..............	Session Handler
SH..............	Severely Handicapped
SH..............	Severn House [*Publisher*] [*Great Britain*]
SH..............	Sexual Harassment
SH..............	Shackle (AAG)
Sh..............	Shadforth's Reserved Judgements [*A publication*] (APTA)
Sh..............	Shale [*Lithology*]
SH..............	Shall
Sh..............	Shallow
Sh..............	Shand's Reports [*11-41 South Carolina*] [*A publication*] (DLA)
SH..............	Shanghai
SH..............	Share
Sh..............	Shauri (BJA)
Sh..............	[*W. G.*] Shaw's Reports [*30-35 Vermont*] [*A publication*] (DLA)
Sh..............	[*G. B.*] Shaw's Reports [*10, 11 Vermont*] [*A publication*] (DLA)
Sh..............	Shaw's Scotch Appeal Cases [*A publication*] (DLA)
Sh..............	Shaw's Scotch Justiciary Cases [*A publication*] (DLA)
Sh..............	Shaw's Scotch Session Cases [*A publication*] (DLA)
Sh..............	Shaw's Scotch Teind [*Tithe*] Court Reports [*A publication*] (DLA)
SH..............	Sheathing [*Technical drawings*]
SH..............	Sheep (ROG)

SH..............	Sheep Skin [*Bookbinding*] (ROG)
SH..............	Sheet
Sh..............	Sheldon's Superior Court Reports [*Buffalo, New York*] [*A publication*] (DLA)
SH..............	Shelf [*Technical drawings*]
SH..............	Shell Development Co. [*Research code symbol*]
sh..............	Shells [*Quality of the bottom*] [*Nautical charts*]
Sh..............	Shepherd's Alabama Reports [*A publication*] (DLA)
Sh..............	Shepley's Reports [*13-18, 21-30 Maine*] [*A publication*] (DLA)
Sh..............	Sheriff (DLA)
S & H	Sherratt & Hughes [*Commercial firm*] [*British*]
Sh..............	Sherwood Number
SH..............	Shield (MSA)
Sh..............	Shiel's Cape Times Law Reports [*South Africa*] [*A publication*] (DLA)
SH..............	Shilling [*Obsolete*] [*Monetary unit in Britain*]
SH..............	Ship
S & H	Shipping and Handling
Sh..............	Shipp's Reports [*66-67 North Carolina*] [*A publication*] (DLA)
SH..............	Ship's Head [*Heading*] [*Navigation*]
SH..............	Ship's Serviceman [*Navy rating*]
SH..............	Shipwright
Sh..............	Shire
Sh..............	Shirley's Reports [*49-55 New Hampshire*] [*A publication*] (DLA)
SH..............	Shoal (ROG)
SH..............	Shooting [*FBI standardized term*]
SH..............	Short (ROG)
SH..............	Short Brothers & Harland Ltd. [*ICAO aircraft manufacturer identifier*] (ICAO)
S/H............	Shorthand
sh..............	Shoulder
SH..............	Showers (AAG)
Sh..............	Shower's English King's Bench Reports [*A publication*] (DLA)
Sh..............	Shower's English Parliamentary Cases [*A publication*] (DLA)
SH..............	Shunt [*Electricity*]
SH..............	Shuttle (MCD)
SH..............	Sick in Hospital
SH..............	Single Heterostructure (MCD)
SH..............	Sinus Histiocytosis [*Medicine*]
S H	Slovenska Hudba [*A publication*]
SH..............	Small Heavy Seeds [*Botany*]
SH..............	Social History
SH..............	Socially Housed [*Experimental animals*]
SH..............	Society for HematoPathology (EA)
SH..............	Society for the Humanities (EA)
S/H............	Software/Hardware [*Cost*]
SH..............	Soldiers' Home [*Later, US Soldiers' and Airmen's Home*] [*Government agency*]
SH..............	Somatotrophic [*Growth*] Hormone [*Also, GH, STH*] [*Endocrinology*]
S and H	Son and Heir [*Genealogy*]
SH..............	Source Handshake
SH..............	Southern Hemisphere
SH..............	Southland Hussars [*British military*] (DMA)
SH..............	Southlife Holding Co. [*AMEX symbol*] (SPSG)
SH..............	Spanish Heritage (EA)
sh..............	Spanish Territories in Northern Morocco [*Spanish North Africa*] [*MARC country of publication code*] [*Library of Congress*] (LCCP)
SH..............	Special Hazards
SH..............	Special Honor
SH..............	Specified Hours
SH..............	Specified Hours of Operation [*Broadcasting term*]
S & H	Speech and Hearing [*Medicine*]
SH..............	Speighel Historiael van de Bond van Gentse Germanisten [*A publication*]
S & H	Sperry & Hutchinson Co.
SH..............	Spontaneously Hypertensive [*Medicine*]
sH..............	Stathenry [*Also, statH*] [*Unit of inductance*]
SH..............	Station Hospital [*Military*]
SH..............	Station House
SH..............	Stationary High-Power [*Reactor*] (NRCH)
SH..............	Steel Heads
SH..............	Steelton & Highspire Railroad Co. [*AAR code*]
S & H	Steering and Hydroplane [*British*]
SH..............	Stockholder
SH..............	Stored Heading (MCD)
SH..............	Stoy Hayward [*Venture capital group*] [*British*]
SH..............	Studia Hellenistica [*A publication*]
SH..............	Studia Hibernica [*Dublin*] [*A publication*]
SH..............	Sulfhydryl [*Chemistry*]
SH..............	Sun-Herald [*A publication*] (APTA)
S & H	Sundays and Holidays
SH..............	Super-High-Frequency [*Radio wave*] (NG)
SH..............	Superstructure Heater (DS)
SH..............	Surgical History [*Medicine*]
SH..............	Switch Handler [*Telecommunications*] (TEL)
SH..............	Sydney Herald [*A publication*] (APTA)
SH1............	Ship's Serviceman, First Class [*Navy rating*]
SH2............	Ship's Serviceman, Second Class [*Navy rating*]

sh₂ .... Shrunken-2 Gene [*In sweet corn*]
SH₂ .... Supercritical Hydrogen [*NASA*] (NASA)
SH3 .... Ship's Serviceman, Third Class [*Navy rating*]
S2H2 .... Short, Straight Hollow Hosel [*Golf clubs*]
SHA .... Ozark, AL [*Location identifier*] [*FAA*] (FAAL)
SHA .... Safety Hazard Analysis (MCD)
SHA .... Sailplane Homebuilders Association (EA)
SHA .... Sample and Hold Amplifier
SHA .... Scriptores Historiae Augustae [*Classical studies*] (OCD)
SHA .... Secretariat for Hispanic Affairs (National Conference of
        Catholic Bishops) (EA)
SHA .... Shakwak Exploration Co. [*Vancouver Stock Exchange symbol*]
SHA .... Shanghai [*China*] [*Airport symbol*] (OAG)
ShA .... Shulhan 'Arukh (BJA)
SHA .... Sidereal Hour Angle
SHA .... Sitzungsberichte. Heidelberg Akademie der Wissenschaft [*A
        publication*]
SHA .... Smith-Hurd's Illinois Annotated Statutes [*A
        publication*] (DLA)
SHA .... Societe Historique Acadienne [*Acadian Historical
        Society*] (EA)
SHA .... Society for Historical Archaeology (EA)
SHA .... Society for Humane Abortion (EA)
SHA .... Society for Humanistic Anthropology (EA)
SHA .... Sodium Hydroxide Addition [*Nuclear energy*] (NRCH)
SHA .... Solid Homogeneous Assembly [*Nuclear energy*]
SHA .... Southern Historical Association (EA)
SHA .... Special Health Authority [*Government body*] [*British*]
SHA .... Spherical Harmonic Analysis [*Geophysics*]
SHA .... Spring Hill [*Alabama*] [*Seismograph station code, US
        Geological Survey*] (SEIS)
SHA .... Station Housing Allowance [*Military*] (MCD)
SHa .... Sulgi Hymn A (BJA)
SHA .... Sun-Herald (Australia) [*A publication*]
SHA .... Support Harness Assembly
SHA .... System Hazard Analyses [*NASA*] (NASA)
SHAA .... Schaak Electronics, Inc. [*NASDAQ symbol*] (NQ)
SHAA .... Sealed Head Access Area [*Nuclear energy*] (NRCH)
SHAA .... Serum Hepatitis Associated Antigen [*Hematology*]
SHAA .... Society of Hearing Aid Audiologists [*Later, NHAS*] (EA)
SHAA-Ab ... Serum Hepatitis Associated Antigen-Antibody [*Hematology*]
SHA-Ab..... Serum Hepatitis Associated Antibody [*Hematology*]
Shab .... Shabbath (BJA)
SHABS..... Shock Absorber
SHAC .... Society for the History of Alchemy and Chemistry (EA)
SHAC .... Solar Heating and Air Conditioning
Sh Acc....... Hale's Sheriff's Account [*A publication*] (DLA)
SHACC..... Servicing Hotels and the Caribbean Community
SHACO ..... Shorthand Coding
SHACOB .. Solar Heating and Cooling of Buildings [*Energy Research and
        Development Administration*]
SHACV ..... Second Harmonic AC [*Alternating Current*] Voltammetry
        [*Instrumentation*]
Shad .... Shadforth's Reports [*Australia*] [*A publication*] (DLA)
SHAD .... Shallow Habitat Air Dive [*Navy*]
SHAD .... Sharpe Army Depot [*California*]
SHAD .... Shipboard Hazards Appraisal and Defense (CINC)
SHADCOM ... Shipping Advisory Committee [*NATO*]
SHADE ..... Shielded Hot-Air-Drum Evaporator [*Concentrator for
        hazardous wastes*]
SHADO..... Supreme Headquarters, Alien Defense Organization [*in
        television program "UFO"*]
SHADRAC ... Shelter Housed Automatic Digital Random Access [*Data
        processing*]
SHAEF...... Supreme Headquarters, Allied Expeditionary Force [*Europe*]
        [*World War II*]
SH-AF ...... Shelter-Afrique (EAIO)
SHAF........ Staying Healthy after Fifty [*Project*] [*AARP*]
SHAFB..... Sheppard Air Force Base [*Texas*] (AAG)
SHAFR...... Society for Historians of American Foreign Relations (EA)
SHAFT...... Second Home All-Inclusive First Trust [*Real estate*]
SHAFT..... Shaftsbury [*England*]
SHAG....... Simplified High-Accuracy Guidance [*NASA*] (NASA)
SHAGAn .. Societe d'Histoire et d'Archeologie de Gand. Annales [*A
        publication*]
SHAGBull ... Societe d'Histoire et d'Archeologie de Gand. Bulletin [*A
        publication*]
SHAH....... Shire National Corp. [*NASDAQ symbol*] (NQ)
SHAK .... Shakespeare
Shakes Jah ... Shakespeare-Jahrbuch [*A publication*]
Shakespeare-Jahrb ... Shakespeare-Jahrbuch [*A publication*]
Shakespeare Q ... Shakespeare Quarterly [*A publication*]
Shakespeare S ... Shakespeare Survey [*A publication*]
Shakes Q ... Shakespeare Quarterly [*A publication*]
Shakes Surv ... Shakespeare Survey [*A publication*]
Shakhtnoe Stroit ... Shakhtnoe Stroitel'stvo [*USSR*] [*A publication*]
Shak-Jahrb ... Shakespeare-Jahrbuch [*A publication*]
ShakS .... Shakespeare Studies [*A publication*]
SHAL .... Subject Heading Authority List [*Data processing*]
Shale .... Decrees and Judgments in Federal Anti-Trust Cases [*United
        States*] [*A publication*] (DLA)

Shale Ctry ... Shale Country [*A publication*]
Shale Rev ... Shale Review [*A publication*]
Shalm........ Shalmaneser (BJA)
SHALOM ... Synchronous Halo Monitor [*NASA*]
SHALPub ... Societe Historique et Archeologique dans le Duche de Limbourg.
        Publications [*A publication*]
SHAM .... Salicylhydroxamic Acid [*Chelating agent*]
SHAME .... Save, Help Animals Man Exploits [*Connecticut organization*]
SHAME .... Society to Humiliate, Aggravate, Mortify, and Embarrass
        Smokers
SHAMYR ... Shomrei Mitzvot Yotzei Russia (BJA)
SHAN........ Shannon Oil & Gas [*NASDAQ symbol*] (NQ)
Shan........... Shannon's Unreported Tennessee Cases [*A publication*] (DLA)
Shan Cas.... Shannon's Tennessee Cases [*A publication*] (DLA)
Shand........ Shand's Reports [*11-41 South Carolina*] [*A publication*] (DLA)
Shand Pr .... Shand's Practice, Scotch Court of Sessions [*A
        publication*] (DLA)
SHANE ..... Steerable Hydrophone Array, Nonlinear Element
Shanghai Iron Steel Res Inst Tech Rep ... Shanghai Iron and Steel Research
        Institute. Technical Report [*China*] [*A publication*]
SHANICLE ... Short-Range Navigation Vehicle [*System*] [*Air Force*]
Shankland's St ... Shankland's Tennessee Public Statutes [*A
        publication*] (DLA)
Shannon Cas (Tenn) ... Shannon's Unreported Tennessee Cases [*A
        publication*] (DLA)
Shannon's Code ... Shannon's Tennessee Annotated Code [*A
        publication*] (DLA)
SHANT ..... Shantung [*Province in China*] (ROG)
Shantung Med J ... Shantung Medical Journal [*People's Republic of China*]
        [*A publication*]
Shanxi Univ J Nat Sci Ed ... Shanxi University. Journal. Natural Science
        Edition [*A publication*]
SHAP .... Ship Acquisition Plan [*Navy*] (CAAL)
SHAPA..... Solids Handling and Processing Association (EAIO)
SHAPE...... Simulated Hospital Administration and Planning Exercise
SHAPE...... Supersonic High-Altitude Parachute Experiment [*NASA*]
SHAPE...... Supreme Headquarters, Allied Powers Europe [*NATO*]
SHAPEX... SHAPE [*Supreme Headquarters Allied Powers Europe*] Annual
        Command Exercise [*NATO*] (NATG)
SHAPM..... Ship Acquisition Project Manager [*Navy*]
Sh App .... Shaw's Scotch Appeal Cases, House of Lords [*A
        publication*] (DLA)
ShAr........... Shulhan 'Arukh (BJA)
SHAR .... Simplified Hourly Absence Reporting (MCD)
SHAR .... Sriharikota Island Launch Complex [*India*]
SHARE...... SHARE Foundation (EA)
SHARE...... Share Happily and Reap Endlessly [*Hollywood women's charity
        organization*]
SHARE...... Shared Area Resources Exchange [*Library network*]
SHaRE....... Shared Research Equipment Collaborative Research Program
        [*Oak Ridge, TN*] [*Oak Ridge National Laboratory*]
        [*Department of Energy*] (GRD)
SHARE...... So Handicapped All Read Easily
SHARE...... Society to Help Avoid Redundant Effort [*in data processing*]
SHARE...... Soldier Housing and Retirement Equity
SHARE...... Systems for Heat and Radiation Energy [*Nuclear energy*]
SHAREM ... Ship ASW [*Antisubmarine Warfare*] Readiness Effectiveness
        Measuring Program
SHARES...... Shared Acquisitions and Retention System
Shark Elec ... Sharkey's Practice of Election Committees [*2nd ed.*] [*1866*] [*A
        publication*] (DLA)
SHARNB .. Sharnbrook [*England*]
SHARP...... School Health Additional Referral Program [*Public Health
        Service*]
SHARP...... Senior High Assessment of Reading Performance [*Educational
        test*]
SHARP...... Ships Analysis and Retrieval Program [*Navy*]
SHARP...... Stationary [*or Strategic*] High-Altitude Relay Platform
        [*Microwave airplane*] [*Canada*]
SHARP...... Strategic High Altitude Relay Platform [*Aviation*]
Sharp Cong Ct ... Sharp on Congregational Courts [*A publication*] (DLA)
Sharpe........ Calendar of Coroners Rolls of the City of London [*A
        publication*] (DLA)
Sharpe........ Sharpe's London Magazine [*A publication*]
SHARPE .. Symbolic Hierarchical Automated Reliability and Performance
        Evaluator
Sharp Ins Dig ... Sharpstein's Insurance Digest [*A publication*] (DLA)
SHARPS ... Ship/Helicopter Acoustic Range-Prediction System
        [*Navy*] (NVT)
SHARPS ... Sonic High-Accuracy Ranging and Positioning System
Shars Black ... Sharswood's Edition of Blackstone's Commentaries [*A
        publication*] (DLA)
Shars Bl Comm ... Sharswood's Edition of Blackstone's Commentaries [*A
        publication*] (DLA)
Shars & B Lead Cas Real Prop ... Sharswood and Budd's Leading Cases on
        Real Property [*A publication*] (DLA)
Shars Comm L ... Sharswood's Commercial Law [*A publication*] (DLA)
Shars Law Lec ... Sharswood's Lectures on the Profession of the Law [*A
        publication*] (DLA)
Shars Leg Eth ... Sharswood's Legal Ethics [*A publication*] (DLA)

Shars Tab Ca ... Sharswood's Table of Cases, Connecticut [*A publication*] (DLA)

SHAS........ Shared Hospital Accounting System [*Data processing*]

SHaS........ Shishah Sedarim (BJA)

SHAT .... Shatterproof Glass Corp. [*NASDAQ symbol*] (NQ)

SHATAn .... Societe Historique et Archeologique de Tournai. Annales [*A publication*]

SHATC...... SHAPE [*Supreme Headquarters Allied Powers Europe*] Technical Center [*Formerly, SADTC*] [*NATO*] (NATG)

SHATCPS ... St. Helena, Ascension, and Tristan da Cunha Philatelic Society (EA)

SHAVE...... Sugar Hotel Alpha Victor Echo [*Apollo 10 astronauts' code for shaving operation*]

Shaw .... [*W. G.*] Shaw's Reports [*30-35 Vermont*] [*A publication*] (DLA)

Shaw .... [*G. B.*] Shaw's Reports [*10, 11 Vermont*] [*A publication*] (DLA)

Shaw .... Shaw's Scotch Appeal Cases [*A publication*] (DLA)

Shaw .... Shaw's Scotch Court of Session Cases, First Series [*A publication*] (DLA)

Shaw .... Shaw's Scotch Justiciary Cases [*A publication*] (DLA)

Shaw .... Shaw's Scotch Teind [*Tithe*] Court Reports [*A publication*] (DLA)

SHAW .... Shaw's Supermarkets, Inc. [*East Bridgewater, MA*] [*NASDAQ symbol*] (NQ)

SHAW .... Sitzungsberichte. Heidelberg Akademie der Wissenschaft [*A publication*]

Shaw App.... Shaw's Scotch Appeal Cases, English House of Lords [*A publication*] (DLA)

ShawB....... Shaw Bulletin [*A publication*]

SHAWCO ... Students' Health and Welfare Centers Organization

Shaw Crim Cas ... Shaw's Criminal Cases, Scotch Justiciary Court [*A publication*] (DLA)

Shaw & D... Shaw and Dunlop's Scotch Court of Session Reports, First Series [*A publication*] (DLA)

Shaw D & B ... Shaw, Dunlop, and Bell's Scotch Court of Session Reports, First Series [*A publication*] (DLA)

Shaw D & B Supp ... Shaw, Dunlop, and Bell's Supplement, Containing House of Lords Decisions [*Scotland*] [*A publication*] (DLA)

Shaw Dec ... Shaw's Decisions in Scotch Court of Sessions, First Series [*A publication*] (DLA)

Shaw Dig.... Shaw's Digest of Decisions [*Scotland*] [*A publication*] (DLA)

Shaw & Dunl ... Shaw and Dunlop's Scotch Court of Session Reports, First Series [*A publication*] (DLA)

Shaw Dunl & B ... Shaw, Dunlop, and Bell's Scotch Court of Session Cases, First Series [*1821-38*] [*A publication*] (DLA)

Shaw (G B) ... [*G. B.*] Shaw's Reports [*10, 11 Vermont*] [*A publication*] (DLA)

Shaw HL.... Shaw's Scotch Appeal Cases, House of Lords [*1821-24*] [*A publication*] (DLA)

Shaw J .... John Shaw's Justiciary Cases [*1848-52*] [*Scotland*] [*A publication*] (DLA)

Shaw Jus.... [*John*] Shaw's Justiciary Cases [*1848-52*] [*Scotland*] [*A publication*] (DLA)

SHAWL..... Special Hard-Target Assault Weapon LAW (RDA)

Shaw & M ... Shaw and Maclean's Scotch Appeal Cases [*A publication*] (DLA)

Shaw & Macl ... Shaw and Maclean's Scotch Appeal Cases [*A publication*] (DLA)

Shaw & M Sc App Cas ... Shaw and Maclean's Scotch Appeal Cases [*1835-38*] [*A publication*] (DLA)

Shaw P....... Patrick Shaw's Justiciary Cases [*1819-31*] [*Scotland*] [*A publication*] (DLA)

Shaw PL..... Shaw's Parish Law [*A publication*] (DLA)

Shaw R....... Shaw Review [*A publication*]

Shaw Rev ... Shaw Review [*A publication*]

Shaw Sc App Cas ... Shaw's Scotch Appeal Cases, House of Lords [*1821-24*] [*A publication*] (DLA)

Shaw TC .... Shaw's Scotch Teind [*Tithe*] Cases [*1821-31*] [*A publication*] (DLA)

Shaw T Cas ... Shaw's Scotch Teind [*Tithe*] Court Reports [*A publication*] (DLA)

Shaw Teind ... Shaw's Scotch Teind [*Tithe*] Court Decisions [*1821-31*] [*A publication*] (DLA)

Shaw (VT) ... [*G. B.*] Shaw's Reports [*10, 11 Vermont*] [*A publication*] (DLA)

Shaw (VT) ... [*W. G.*] Shaw's Reports [*30, 35 Vermont*] [*A publication*] (DLA)

Shaw W & C ... Shaw, Wilson, and Courtenay's Scotch Appeals Reports, House of Lords [*A publication*] (DLA)

Shaw (W G) ... [*W. G.*] Shaw's Reports [*30-35 Vermont*] [*A publication*] (DLA)

SHAZ .... Spirohydantoin Aziridine [*Biochemistry*]

SHAZAM ... [*Grace of*] Selena, [*Strength of*] Hippolyta, [*Skill of*] Ariadne, [*Fleetness of*] Zephyrus, [*Beauty of*] Aurora, [*Wisdom of*] Minerva [*Word used to change Mary Batson into Mary Marvel in the comic book series*]

SHAZAM ... [*Wisdom of*] Solomon, [*Strength of*] Hercules, [*Stamina of*] Atlas, [*Power of*] Zeus, [*Courage of*] Achilles, [*Speed of*] Mercury [*Word used to change Billy Batson into Captain Marvel in the comic book series*]

SHB........... Nakashibetsu [*Japan*] [*Airport symbol*] (OAG)

SHB........... Scotty's, Inc. [*NYSE symbol*] (SPSG)

SHB........... Second-Harmonic Band

SHB........... Shelbyville, IN [*Location identifier*] [*FAA*] (FAAL)

SHB........... Silhouette Harness Board (MCD)

SHB........... Sodium Hydroxybutyrate [*Organic chemistry*]

SHB........... Subacute Hepatitis with Bridging [*Medicine*]

SHBD .... Serum Hydroxybutyrate Dehydrogenase [*An enzyme*]

SHBG .... Sex-Hormone-Binding Globulin [*Endocrinology*]

SHBLDR... Shipbuilder (MSA)

SHBS........ ShareBase Corp. [*NASDAQ symbol*] (NQ)

S and H Bull ... Smoking and Health Bulletin [*A publication*]

SHBZ........ ShowBiz Pizza Time, Inc. [*NASDAQ symbol*] (CTT)

SHC........... Chief Ship's Serviceman [*Navy rating*]

SHC........... Mount St. Helena [*California*] [*Seismograph station code, US Geological Survey*] (SEIS)

SHC........... Sacred Heart College [*Cullman, AL*]

SHC........... Schult Homes Corp. [*AMEX symbol*] (SPSG)

SHC........... Self-Help Crafts [*An association*] (EA)

SHC........... Seton Hill College [*Greensburg, PA*]

SHC........... Shaklee Corporation [*NYSE symbol*] (SPSG)

SHC........... Shape and Hamiltonian Consistent [*Physics*]

SHC........... Shell Canada Ltd. [*Toronto Stock Exchange symbol*] [*Vancouver Stock Exchange symbol*]

SHC........... Shipping Coordinating Committee [*Coast Guard*]

SHC........... Shire Indaselassie [*Ethiopia*] [*Airport symbol*] (OAG)

SHC........... Siena Heights College [*Adrian, MI*]

SHC........... Silicones Health Council (EA)

SHC........... Sky Harbor Air Service, Inc. [*Cheyenne, WY*] [*FAA designator*] (FAAC)

SHC........... Societe Historique du Canada [*Canadian Historical Association - CHA*]

SHC........... Sodium Hypochlorite [*Inorganic chemistry*]

SHC........... Southern Humanities Conference (EA)

SHC........... Special Handling Code

SHC........... Spherical Harmonic Coefficient [*Geophysics*]

SHC........... Spring Hill College [*Mobile, AL*]

SHC........... Stanford Humanities Center [*Stanford University*] [*Research center*] (RCD)

SHC........... Superheat Control [*Boilers*]

SHC........... Superhybrid Composite [*Laminate*]

SHC........... Superior Heliocentric Conjunction

SHC........... Surveillance Helicopter Company [*Army*] (AABC)

SHCA .... Safety Helmet Council of America (EA)

SHCA .... Siberian Husky Club of America (EA)

SHCA .... Solid Homogeneous Critical Assembly [*Nuclear reactor*] [*Japan*]

SHC-BRC ... Small Homes Council-Building Research Council [*University of Illinois*] [*Research center*] (RCD)

SHCC .... Statewide Health Coordinating Council

SHCC .... Susan Hayward Collectors Club (EA)

SHCGSAS ... Shrimp Harvesters Coalition of the Gulf and South Atlantic States (EA)

Shchorichnyk Ukrayins'ke Bot Tov ... Shchorichnyk Ukrayins'ke Botanichne Tovarystvo [*A publication*]

SHCI.......... Salick Health Care, Incorporated [*Beverly Hills, CA*] [*NASDAQ symbol*] (NQ)

SHCJ........ Society for the History of Czechoslovak Jews (EA)

SHCJ........ Society of the Holy Child Jesus [*Roman Catholic women's religious order*]

SHCM...... Master Chief Ship's Serviceman [*Navy rating*]

SHCOS...... Supreme Headquarters, Chief of Staff [*World War II*]

SHCPP...... Sanitation Handbook of Consumer Protection Programs

SHCR .... Shipping Container

SHCR .... Skyline Hikers of the Canadian Rockies (EA)

Sh Crim Cas ... Shaw's Justiciary Court, Criminal Cases [*Scotland*] [*A publication*] (DLA)

SHCRT...... Short Circuit (AAG)

SHCS........ Senior Chief Ship's Serviceman [*Navy rating*]

SHCS........ Springer Series on Health Care and Society [*A publication*]

SHCSR...... Spicilegium Historicum Congregationis Smi Redemptoris [*A publication*]

SHCS USAF ... School of Health Care Sciences, United States Air Force (AFM)

SHCT .... Sheriff Court [*Legal*] [*British*]

SHCT .... Studies in the History of Christian Thought [*A publication*] (BJA)

Sh Ct Rep... Sheriff Court Reports [*Scotland*] [*A publication*] (DLA)

Sh Ct of Sess ... Shaw's Scotch Court of Session Cases [*A publication*] (DLA)

SHCW ...... Scottish History from Contemporary Writers [*A publication*]

SHD........... Sandhill Decline [*Citrus blight*]

SHD........... Scottish Home Department (ILCA)

SHD........... Shade

SHD........... Shahrud [*Iran*] [*Seismograph station code, US Geological Survey*] (SEIS)

SHD........... Sherwood Group, Inc. [*AMEX symbol*] (SPSG)

SHD........... Shield Development [*Vancouver Stock Exchange symbol*]

SHD........... Ship's Diver [*Navy*] [*British*]

SHD........... Shode

SHD........... Should (ROG)

SHD........... Shroud (AAG)

SHD.......... Silo Hardsite Defense
SHD.......... Society for the History of Discoveries   (EA)
SHD.......... Special Handling Designator   (MCD)
SHD.......... Staunton [*Virginia*] [*Airport symbol*]   (OAG)
SHD.......... Staunton/Waynesboro/Harrisonburg, VA [*Location identifier*] [*FAA*]   (FAAL)
SHd.......... Sulgi Hymn D   (BJA)
SHDA........ Selenaheptadecanoic Acid [*Organic chemistry*]
SHDC........ Sacred Heart Dominican College [*Texas*]
SHDC........ Subject Headings Used in the Dictionary Catalog [*Later, LCSH*] [*A publication*]
SHDI......... Supraoptic-Hypophyseal Diabetes Insipidus [*Endocrinology*]
Sh Dig........ Shaw's Digest of Decisions [*Scotland*] [*A publication*]   (DLA)
SHDN........ Shutdown   (NASA)
SHDPS...... St. Helena and Dependencies Philatelic Society   (EA)
SHDR........ Service and Hardware Difficulty Reports   (MCD)
SHDS........ Safety and Health Data Sheet [*Army*]
SHDS........ Second-Harmonic Discrimination System   (MCD)
Sh & Dunl .. Shaw and Dunlop's Scotch Court of Session Reports, First Series [*A publication*]   (DLA)
SHE........... Scrutineers for Honest Elections [*Australia*]
SHE........... Securities Hazards Expert [*In film title*]
SHE........... Self-Help Enterprises   (EA)
SHE........... Semihomogeneous Experiment [*Nuclear energy*]
SHE........... Sheba Copper Mines [*Vancouver Stock Exchange symbol*]
SHE........... Shemkha [*USSR*] [*Seismograph station code, US Geological Survey*]   (SEIS)
SHE........... Shenyang [*China*] [*Airport symbol*]   (OAG)
SHE........... Siderphile Superheavy Element [*Physics*]
SHE........... Signal Handling Equipment   (AAG)
SHE........... Society for the Health Education [*British*]
SHE........... Society for History Education   (EA)
SHE........... Sodium Heat Engine
SHE........... Spares Handling Expense
SHE........... Special Handling Equipment
SHE........... Standard Hydrogen Electrode [*Electrochemistry*]
SHE........... Subject Headings for Engineering [*A publication*]
S/HE......... Sundays and Holidays Excepted
SHE........... Supercritical Helium   (KSC)
SHE........... Superheavy Element [*Nuclear physics*]
SHE........... Syrian Hamster Embryonic [*Cells*]
SHEAR...... Society for Historians of the Early American Republic   (EA)
Shear Bar Ex ... Shearwood's Bar Examinations [*A publication*]   (DLA)
Shear Cont ... Shearwood on Contract [*1897*] [*A publication*]   (DLA)
Shearm & Red Neg ... Shearman and Redfield on the Law of Negligence [*A publication*]   (DLA)
Shear Pers Pr ... Shearwood on Personal Property [*1882*] [*A publication*]   (DLA)
Shear & R Neg ... Shearman and Redfield on the Law of Negligence [*A publication*]   (DLA)
Shear R Pr ... Shearwood on Real Property [*3rd ed.*] [*1885*] [*A publication*]   (DLA)
SHEB........ Shebear [*England*]
Sheb.......... Shebi'it   (BJA)
Shebi......... Shebi'it   (BJA)
Shebu........ Shebu'oth   (BJA)
SHECD ..... Solar Heating and Cooling [*A publication*]
SHED .... Sealed Housing for Evaporative Determinations [*EPA engine test*]
SHED .... Settlement Houses Employment Development [*Large group of settlement houses*]
SHEDS...... Ship Helicopter Extended Delivery System [*Navy*]   (NVT)
SHEEO ..... State Higher Education Executive Officers Association   (EA)
Sheep Beef Farm Surv ... Sheep and Beef Farm Survey [*A publication*]
Sheepfarm Annu ... Sheepfarming Annual [*A publication*]
Sheepfarming Annu ... Sheepfarming Annual [*A publication*]
Sheepfarming Annu Massey Agr Coll ... Sheepfarming Annual. Massey Agricultural College [*A publication*]
Sheep Goat Handb ... Sheep and Goat Handbook [*A publication*]
Sheet Met Ind ... Sheet Metal Industries [*A publication*]
Sheet Met Platework News ... Sheet Metal and Plateworking News [*A publication*]
SHEF........ Sandwich Chef, Inc. [*NASDAQ symbol*]   (NQ)
SHEFD..... Sheffield [*England*]
SHEFF ..... Shefford [*England*]
Sheffield Univ Geol Soc J ... Sheffield University. Geological Society. Journal [*A publication*]
SHEH........ Stanford Honors Essays in the Humanities [*A publication*]
SHEIA....... Steric Hindrance Enzyme Immunoassay [*Clinical chemistry*]
Sheil Ir Bar ... Sheil's Sketches of the Irish Bar [*A publication*]   (DLA)
SHEK .... Schweizer Hilfswerk fuer Emigrationskinder   (BJA)
Shek.......... Shekalim   (BJA)
SHEL........ Sheldahl, Inc. [*NASDAQ symbol*]   (NQ)
SHEL........ Shore ELINT [*Electromagnetic Intelligence*] System [*Navy*]   (NG)
Shel Bank .. Shelford's Bankrupt and Insolvency Law [*3rd ed.*] [*1862*] [*A publication*]   (DLA)
Shel Ca....... Shelley's Cases in Vol. 1 of Coke's Reports [*A publication*]   (DLA)
Sheld.......... Sheldon's Superior Court Reports [*Buffalo, New York*] [*A publication*]   (DLA)

Sheldon...... Sheldon's Superior Court Reports [*Buffalo, New York*] [*A publication*]   (DLA)
Sheld Subr ... Sheldon on Subrogation [*A publication*]   (DLA)
SHELF ...... Super-Hard Extremely-Low Frequency   (MCD)
Shelf J St Cos ... Shelford on Joint-Stock Companies [*A publication*]   (DLA)
Shelf Lun ... Shelford on Lunacy [*A publication*]   (DLA)
Shelf Mar & Div ... Shelford on Marriage and Divorce [*A publication*]   (DLA)
Shel High... Shelford on Highways [*4th ed.*] [*1869*] [*A publication*]   (DLA)
Shel J St Com ... Shelford on Joint Stock Companies [*2nd ed.*] [*1870*] [*A publication*]   (DLA)
Shell Agric ... Shell in Agriculture [*A publication*]
Shell Aviat News ... Shell Aviation News [*A publication*]
Shell Bitum Rev ... Shell Bitumin Review [*A publication*]
Shell Devel Co Explor and Production Research Div Pub ... Shell Development Company. Exploration and Production Research Division. Publication [*A publication*]
Shellfish..... Shellfish. Market Review and Outlook [*A publication*]
Shell House J ... Shell House Journal [*A publication*]   (APTA)
Shell J........ Shell Journal [*A publication*]   (APTA)
Shell Mag .. Shell Magazine [*England*] [*A publication*]
Shell Polym ... Shell Polymers [*A publication*]
SHELLREP ... Shelling Report [*Military*]   (NATG)
Shel Lun..... Shelford on Lunacy [*2nd ed.*] [*1847*] [*A publication*]   (DLA)
Shel M & D ... Shelford on Marriage and Divorce [*1841*] [*A publication*]   (DLA)
Shel Mort... Shelford on Mortmain and Charitable Uses [*1836*] [*A publication*]   (DLA)
Shel Prob ... Shelford on Probate, Legacy, Etc. [*2nd ed.*] [*1861*] [*A publication*]   (DLA)
SHELREP ... Shelling Report [*Military*]
SHELREPT ... Shelling Report [*Military*]   (MUGU)
Shel R Pr St ... Sheldon's Real Property Statutes [*9th ed.*] [*1893*] [*A publication*]   (DLA)
Shel Ry....... Shelford on Railways [*4th ed.*] [*1869*] [*A publication*]   (DLA)
Shelter........ Shelterforce [*A publication*]
Shel Will..... Shelford on Wills [*1838*] [*A publication*]   (DLA)
Shel Wills .. Shelford on Wills [*A publication*]   (DLA)
SHEMA .... Steam Heating Equipment Manufacturers Association [*Defunct*]   (EA)
S-HEMP ... System - Hydraulic, Electrical, Mechanical, Pneumatic
Shen .... Shenandoah [*A publication*]
SHEN .... Shenandoah National Park
Shep .... Select Cases [*37-39 Alabama*] [*A publication*]   (DLA)
Shep .... Shepherd's Alabama Reports [*A publication*]   (DLA)
Shep .... Shepley's Reports [*13-18, 21-30 Maine*] [*A publication*]   (DLA)
SHEP........ Shock Hydrodynamic Elastic Plastic   (MCD)
SHEP........ Solar High-Energy Particles
Shep Abr .... Sheppard's Abridgment [*A publication*]   (DLA)
Shep Act .... Sheppard's Action on the Case [*A publication*]   (DLA)
Shep Cas .... Sheppard's Cases of Slander, Etc. [*A publication*]   (DLA)
Shepherd.... Shepherd's Reports [*19-21, 24-41, 60, 63, 64 Alabama*] [*A publication*]   (DLA)
Sheph Sel Cas ... Shepherd's Select Cases [*Alabama*] [*A publication*]   (DLA)
Shepley...... Shepley's Reports [*13-18, 21-30 Maine*] [*A publication*]   (DLA)
Shep Prec... Sheppard's Precedent of Precedents [*9th ed.*] [*1825*] [*A publication*]   (DLA)
Shep Sel Cas ... Shepherd's Select Cases [*Alabama*] [*A publication*]   (DLA)
SHER .... Scottish Heritable, Inc. [*NASDAQ symbol*]   (SPSG)
SHERB...... Sandia Human Error Rate Bank [*NASA*]   (NASA)
SHERB...... Sherborne [*Urban district in England*]
Sher Ct Rep ... Sheriff Court Reports [*Scotland*] [*A publication*]   (DLA)
SHERK...... [*The*] New Schaff-Herzog Encyclopaedia of Religious Knowledge [*A publication*]   (BJA)
SHERLOC ... Something to Help Everyone Reduce Load on Computers [*Army*]
Sher Mar Ins ... Sherman's Marine Insurance [*A publication*]   (DLA)
Sher Pr....... Sheridan's Practice, King's Bench [*A publication*]   (DLA)
Sherst Delo ... Sherstyanoe Delo [*A publication*]
SHERVICK ... Sherman Tanks Converted into Tractors by Vickers Armstrong
Shev .... Shevi'it   (BJA)
Shevu .... Shevu'ot   (BJA)
SHEX .... Sundays and Holidays Excepted [*Business term*]
S & H/exct ... Sundays and Holidays Excepted in Lay Days   (DS)
SHF .... Schiffner Oilfield & Technology Corp. [*Vancouver Stock Exchange symbol*]
SHF .... Sea Heritage Foundation   (EA)
SHF .... Self Help Foundation   (EA)
SHF .... Shawinigan Falls [*Quebec*] [*Seismograph station code, US Geological Survey*] [*Closed*]   (SEIS)
SHF .... Shift   (MSA)
SHF .... Sisters of the Holy Faith [*Roman Catholic religious order*]
SHF .... Sisters of the Holy Family [*Roman Catholic religious order*]
SHF .... Societe de l'Histoire de France [*A publication*]
SHF .... Soil and Health Foundation [*Later, RI*]   (EA)
SHF .... Storage-Handling Facility [*Nuclear energy*]   (NRCH)
SHF .... Structures Heating Facility
SHF .... Super-High-Frequency [*Radio wave*]
SHF .... University of Sheffield, Postgraduate School of Librarianship, Sheffield, England [*OCLC symbol*]   (OCLC)
SHFA........ Single Conductor, Heat and Flame Resistant, Armor [*Cable*]

SHFABull ... Societe de l'Histoire de France. Annuaire Bulletin [*A publication*]
SHFCC ...... Shriners Hospitals for Crippled Children (EA)
SHF/EHF ... Super-High Frequency/Extremely-High Frequency (MCD)
SHFF .... Societe Historique et Folklorique Francaise (EA)
SHFG .... Society for History in the Federal Government (EA)
SHF-GMFSC ... Super-High-Frequency - Ground Mobile Forces Satellite Communications (MCD)
SHFL .... Shoulder Horizontal Flexion [*Sports medicine*]
SHFS .... Superhyperfine Structure
SHFT .... Shift (FAAC)
SHF-TDMA-MODEM ... Super-High-Frequency - Time Division Multiple Access - MODEM (MCD)
SHFTG ...... Shafting [*Freight*]
SHFTGR ... Shaft Gear
SHFX .... Shadowfax Resources Ltd. [*NASDAQ symbol*] (NQ)
SHG .... Second-Harmonic Generation [*LASER*]
SHG .... Selected Honor Guards (MCD)
SHG .... Sharpe Energy and Resources Ltd. [*Vancouver Stock Exchange symbol*]
SHG .... Shirttail Gulch [*California*] [*Seismograph station code, US Geological Survey*] (SEIS)
SHG .... Short-Handed Goal [*Hockey*]
SHG .... Shorthand Typist (Higher Grade) [*British military*] (DMA)
SHG .... Shungnak [*Alaska*] [*Airport symbol*] (OAG)
SHG .... Shungnak, AK [*Location identifier*] [*FAA*] (FAAL)
SHG .... Sister Servants of the Holy Ghost and Mary Immaculate [*Roman Catholic religious order*]
SHG .... Special High Grade [*Zinc metal*]
SHGAB8 ... Siriraj Hospital Gazette [*A publication*]
SHGED ..... Shoni Geka [*A publication*]
SHGM .... Shungum Corp. [*Livingston, NJ*] [*NASDAQ symbol*] (NQ)
SHGM .... Society for the History of the Germans in Maryland (EA)
SHGNA ..... Shigen [*A publication*]
SHGO .... Shop & Go, Inc. [*NASDAQ symbol*] (NQ)
SHH .... Shenandoah Resources Ltd. [*Vancouver Stock Exchange symbol*]
SHH .... Shishmaref [*Alaska*] [*Airport symbol*] (OAG)
SHH .... Shishmaref, AK [*Location identifier*] [*FAA*] (FAAL)
SHH .... Sociedad Honoraria Hispanica (EA)
SHHD .... Scottish Home and Health Department (ILCA)
SHHH .... Self-Help for Hard of Hearing People (EA)
SHHPB ...... Shu-Hsueh Hsueh-Pao [*A publication*]
SHHV .... Society for Health and Human Values (EA)
SHI .... Scenic Hudson (EA)
SHI .... Sheet Iron
SHI .... Shimojishima [*Japan*] [*Airport symbol*] (OAG)
SHI .... Shiraz [*Iran*] [*Seismograph station code, US Geological Survey*] (SEIS)
S-HI .... System-Human Interaction
SHib .... Studia Hibernica [*A publication*]
SHID .... Spartan Hardware Inspection Discrepancy [*Missiles*] (MCD)
SHIEF ...... Shared Information Elicitation Facility [*Data processing*]
Shiel .... Cape Times Law Reports, Edited by Shiel [*A publication*] (DLA)
Shiel .... Shiel's Cape Colony Reports [*A publication*] (DLA)
Shield .... Shield Civil Service News [*A publication*]
SHIELD .... Supreme Headquarters, International Espionage Law-Enforcement Division [*Organization in comic book "Nick Fury, Agent of SHIELD"*]
SHIELD .... Sylvania High-Intelligence Electronic Defense (MCD)
Shig .... Shigella [*Bacteriology*]
SHIGD4 .... Japanese Journal of Psychosomatic Medicine [*A publication*]
Shikoku Acta Med ... Shikoku Acta Medica [*A publication*]
Shikoku Agr Res ... Shikoku Agricultural Research [*A publication*]
SHIL .... Shillelagh [*Army surface-to-surface missile*] (AABC)
SHIL .... Shiloh National Military Park
Shill WC ... Shillman's Workmen's Compensation Cases [*Ireland*] [*A publication*] (DLA)
Shimadzu Rev ... Shimadzu Review [*A publication*]
Shimane J Med Sci ... Shimane Journal of Medical Science [*A publication*]
Shinagawa Tech Rep ... Shinagawa Technical Report [*A publication*]
SHIN BET ... Israel General Security Service [*Acronym represents Hebrew phrase*]
SHINC ...... Sundays and Holidays Included [*Business term*]
SHINCOM ... Ship Integrated Communications System [*Canadian Navy*]
Shingle .... [*The*] Shingle. Philadelphia Bar Association [*A publication*] (DLA)
Shinko Electr J ... Shinko Electric Journal [*A publication*]
SHINMACS ... Shipborne Integrated Machinery Control System [*Canadian Navy*]
Shinn Repl ... Shinn's Treatise on American Law of Replevin [*A publication*] (DLA)
Shinshu Med J ... Shinshu Medical Journal [*Japan*] [*A publication*]
Shinshu Univ Fac Sci J ... Shinshu University. Faculty of Science. Journal [*A publication*]
SHIO .... Sveriges Hantverks- och Industriorganisation-Familjefoeretagen [*Federation of Trades, Industries, and Family Enterprises*] [*Sweden*] (EY)
SHIOER .... Statistical Historical Input/Output Error Rate Utility [*Sperry UNIVAC*]

SHIP .... Regency Cruises, Inc. [*New York, NY*] [*NASDAQ symbol*] (NQ)
SHIP .... Self-Help Improvement Program
SHIP .... Self-Help Issue Point [*Army*]
SHIP .... Separator for Heavy Ion Reaction Products
SHIP .... Shipment
SHIP .... Slater Hall Information Products [*Database producer*] (IID)
SHIP .... Special Handling Inventory Procedure (MCD)
SHIP .... Standard Hardware Interface Program
SHIPACS ... Ship Acquisition Study [*Navy*]
SHIPALT ... Ship Alteration [*Navy*]
Shipbldg Mar Engng Int ... Shipbuilding and Marine Engineering International [*A publication*]
Shipbldg Shipp Rec ... Shipbuilding and Shipping Record [*A publication*]
Ship Boat ... Ship and Boat [*A publication*]
Ship and Boat ... Ship and Boat International [*A publication*]
Ship & Boat Int ... Ship and Boat International [*A publication*]
Shipbuild Mar Engine Build ... Shipbuilder and Marine Engine Builder [*England*] [*A publication*]
Shipbuild Mar Eng Int ... Shipbuilding and Marine Engineering International [*A publication*]
Shipbuild & Mar Engng Int ... Shipbuilding and Marine Engineering International [*A publication*]
Shipcare Marit Manage ... Shipcare and Maritime Management [*A publication*]
Ship Com Aviation ... Shipping, Commerce, and Aviation of Australia [*A publication*] (APTA)
SHIPCON ... Shipping Control [*NATO*] (NATG)
SHIPDA .... Shipping Data [*Military*]
SHIPDAFOL ... Shipping Data Follows
SHIPDAT ... Shipping Date
SHIPDTO ... Ship on Depot Transfer Order [*Military*]
Ship Gaz .... Shipping Gazette [*London*] [*A publication*] (DLA)
SHIPGO.... Shipping Order [*Military*]
SHIPIM .... Ship Immediately [*Military*]
Shipp.......... Shipp's Reports [*66-67 North Carolina*] [*A publication*] (DLA)
Shipping Reg P & F ... Shipping Regulation. Pike and Fischer [*A publication*]
Shipping Statis ... Shipping Statistics [*A publication*]
Shipping Statis and Econ ... Shipping Statistics and Economics [*A publication*]
Shipp Weekly ... Shipping Weekly [*A publication*]
Shipp Wld Shipbldr ... Shipping World and Shipbuilder [*A publication*]
Shipp World & Shipb ... Shipping World and Shipbuilder [*A publication*]
Shipp World & Shipbuild ... Shipping World and Shipbuilder [*A publication*]
SHIPREQ ... Ship to Apply on Requisition [*Military*]
SHIPS .... Satellite Housing Integrated Programmed Support [*Australia*]
SHIPS .... Shipment Planning System [*Military*]
SHIPSUM ... Shipping Summary
SHIPSYSCOM ... Ship Systems Command [*Navy*]
SHIPT .... Shipment
SHIR.......... Ship History and Inventory Record [*Navy*] (NG)
SHIRAN.... S-Band High-Accuracy Ranging and Navigation
Shir Cr L.... Shirley's Sketch of the Criminal Law [*2nd ed.*] [*1889*] [*A publication*] (DLA)
Shir DC Ca ... Shirley's Dartmouth College Case [*A publication*] (DLA)
Shire & Munic R ... Shire and Municipal Record [*A publication*] (APTA)
Shire & Munic Rec ... Shire and Municipal Record [*A publication*] (APTA)
Shire Munic Rec ... Shire and Municipal Record [*A publication*]
Shirl .... Shirley's Reports [*49-55 New Hampshire*] [*A publication*] (DLA)
Shirley .... Shirley's Reports [*49-55 New Hampshire*] [*A publication*] (DLA)
Shirley Inst Bull ... Shirley Institute. Bulletin [*A publication*]
Shirley Inst Mem ... Shirley Institute. Memoirs [*A publication*]
Shirl LC ..... Shirley's Leading Crown Cases [*England*] [*A publication*] (DLA)
Shir Mag L ... Shirley on Magisterial Law [*2nd ed.*] [*1896*] [*A publication*] (DLA)
SHIRTDIF ... Storage, Handling, and Retrieval of Technical Data in Image Formation [*Data processing*] (IEEE)
SHIRTS..... Smith-Houghton Infrared Temperature Sounder (NOAA)
SHIRW...... Shirwell [*England*]
SHIU .... Steering Hover Indicator Unit (MCD)
SHIVA....... Super-High-Intensity Vulnerability Assessor
Shivaji Univ J ... Shivaji University. Journal [*A publication*]
Shivaji Univ Sci J ... Shivaji University. Science Journal [*A publication*]
Shizenshi-Kenkyu Occas Pap Osaka Mus Nat Hist ... Shizenshi-Kenkyu Occasional Papers. Osaka Museum of Natural History [*A publication*]
Shizuoka Univ Fac Sci Rep ... Skizuoka University Faculty of Science. Reports [*A publication*]
Sh-J .... Shakespeare-Jahrbuch [*A publication*]
SHJ........... Shamrock Resources, Inc. [*Vancouver Stock Exchange symbol*]
SHJ........... Sharjah [*United Arab Emirates*] [*Airport symbol*] (OAG)
SHJ........... Shionomisaki [*Japan*] [*Seismograph station code, US Geological Survey*] (SEIS)
SHJ........... Society for Humanistic Judaism (EA)
Sh-Jb .... Shakespeare-Jahrbuch [*A publication*]
SHJC........ Sacred Heart Junior College [*North Carolina; Pennsylvania*]
SHJM....... Sisters of the Sacred Hearts of Jesus and Mary [*Roman Catholic religious order*]

SHJMD..... Soon Chun Hyang Journal of Medicine [*A publication*]
SHJP......... [*A*] History of the Jewish People in the Time of Jesus Christ [*Emil Schurer*] [*A publication*]   (BJA)
SHJR........ Senate-House Joint Reports [*A publication*]   (DLA)
Sh Jus .... Shaw's Scotch Justiciary Cases [*A publication*]   (DLA)
Sh Just....... [*P.*] Shaw's Justiciary Decisions [*Scotland*] [*A publication*]   (DLA)
SHK.......... Sehonghong [*Lesotho*] [*Airport symbol*]   (OAG)
SHK.......... Shank   (AAG)
Shk............ Shikimic Acid [*Biochemistry*]
SHK.......... Shiraki [*Japan*] [*Seismograph station code, US Geological Survey*]   (SEIS)
SHK.......... SHL Systemhouse, Inc. [*Toronto Stock Exchange symbol*]
SHK.......... Shock [*A publication*]
SHK.......... Shock   (MSA)
SHK.......... Speaker of the House of Keys [*British*]   (ROG)
SHK.......... Sun Hung Kai Securities [*Hong Kong*]
SHK.......... Systems Housekeeping
SHKBDX... Saito Ho-On Kai Museum of Natural History. Research Bulletin [*A publication*]
SHKDN..... Shakedown   (AABC)
SHKEA5.... Japanese Journal of Psychology [*A publication*]
SHKI .... SHL Systemhouse, Incorporated [*Ottawa, ON*] [*NASDAQ symbol*]   (NQ)
SHKKA ..... Shika Kiso Igakkai Zasshi [*A publication*]
SHL .... Amsterdam Studies in the Theory and History of Linguistic Science [*A publication*]
SHL .... Sacred Heart League   (EA)
SHL .... Sensorineural Hearing Loss [*Medicine*]
SHL .... Shaw Industries Ltd. [*Toronto Stock Exchange symbol*]
SHL .... Sheldon, IA [*Location identifier*] [*FAA*]   (FAAL)
SHL .... Shell   (AAG)
SHL .... Shell Canada Limited [*UTLAS symbol*]
SHL .... Shellac   (MSA)
SHL .... Shillong [*India*] [*Seismograph station code, US Geological Survey*]   (SEIS)
SHL .... Shillong [*India*] [*Geomagnetic observatory code*]
Sh L.......... Shipwright Lieutenant [*British military*]   (DMA)
SHL .... Shoal
SHL .... Southall [*British depot code*]
SHL .... Southern Hockey League
SHL .... Student Homophile League [*Superseded by Gay People at Columbia*]   (EA)
SHL-3........ Amsterdam Studies in the Theory and History of Linguistic Science. Series III. Studies in the History of Linguistics [*A publication*]
SHLB........ Shelby Federal Savings Bank [*Indianapolis, IN*] [*NASDAQ symbol*]   (NQ)
SHLB........ Simulation Hardware Load Boxes   (NASA)
SHLD .... Shield   (AAG)
SHLD .... Shoulder   (AAG)
SHLDR...... Shoulder   (MSA)
ShLH .... Shne Luhot Ha-Berit   (BJA)
Sh Lit .... Shortt on Works of Literature [*2nd ed.*] [*1884*] [*A publication*]   (DLA)
Sh Litt .... Shortt on Works of Literature [*2nd ed.*] [*1884*] [*A publication*]   (DLA)
SHLM .... Schulman [*A.*], Inc. [*NASDAQ symbol*]   (NQ)
SHLMA .... Southern Hardwood Lumber Manufacturers Association [*Later, HMA*]   (EA)
SHLN .... Shoreline   (MSA)
SHLS........ Shawnee Library System [*Library network*]
SHLS........ Shoals   (MCD)
SHLW ...... Shallow   (FAAC)
SHLW ...... Simulated High-Level Waste [*Nuclear engineering*]
SHLY....... Shelly Associates, Inc. [*Tustin, CA*] [*NASDAQ symbol*]   (NQ)
SHM.......... Nanki Shirahama [*Japan*] [*Airport symbol*]   (OAG)
SHM.......... Security Home Mortgage Investment Corp. [*Toronto Stock Exchange symbol*]
SHM.......... Shimizu [*Japan*] [*Seismograph station code, US Geological Survey*]   (SEIS)
SHM.......... Ship Heading Marker [*Navigation*]
SHM.......... Simple Harmonic Motion
SHM.......... Sinusoidal Hydrodynamic Modulation [*Electrochemistry*]
SHM.......... Stage Handling Manual [*NASA*]   (KSC)
Sh & Macl ... Shaw and Maclean's Scotch Appeal Cases [*A publication*]   (DLA)
SHMD....... Shore Manning Document [*Navy*]   (NVT)
SHMED .... State Hazardous Materials Enforcement Development [*Nuclear energy*]   (NRCH)
Sh Metal Inds ... Sheet Metal Industries [*A publication*]
SHMI .... Saddlery Hardware Manufacturers Institute [*Defunct*]   (EA)
SHMIS....... Society of Headmasters of Independent Schools [*British*]
SHMKR...... Shoemaker   (MSA)
SHMN....... Subacute Hepatitis with Multilobular Necrosis [*Medicine*]
SHMO....... Senior Hospital Medical Officer [*British*]
SHMO....... Shadow Mountain National Recreation Area
SHMO....... Social/Health Maintenance Organization [*Department of Health and Human Services*]
SHMP .... Sodium Hexametaphosphate [*Inorganic chemistry*]
SHMRD .... Shire and Municipal Record [*A publication*]

SHN.......... St. Helena [*ANSI three-letter standard code*]   (CNC)
SHN.......... Sclerosing Hyaline Necrosis [*Medicine*]
ShN.......... Shakespeare Newsletter [*A publication*]
shn............ Shan [*MARC language code*] [*Library of Congress*]   (LCCP)
SHN.......... Shandon Resources, Inc. [*Vancouver Stock Exchange symbol*]
SHN.......... Shelton, WA [*Location identifier*] [*FAA*]   (FAAL)
SHN.......... Shimonoseki [*Japan*] [*Seismograph station code, US Geological Survey*]   (SEIS)
SHN.......... Shoney's, Inc. [*NYSE symbol*]   (SPSG)
SHN.......... Shorthand Note
SHN.......... Shown   (AAG)
SHN.......... Spontaneous Hemorrhagic Necrosis [*Medicine*]
SHNA........ SHARAF Name Authority [*UTLAS symbol*]
SHNA........ Shawmut Corp. [*NASDAQ symbol*]   (NQ)
SHNAD..... Shoni Naika [*A publication*]
SHNC........ Scottish Higher National Certificate
SHND........ Scottish Higher National Diploma
SHNG........ Shingle
S/HNP........ Skagit/Hanford Nuclear Project   (NRCH)
SHNS........ Shoney's South, Inc. [*NASDAQ symbol*]   (NQ)
SHNS........ Society of Head and Neck Surgeons   (EA)
SHO.......... Schedule Order   (MCD)
SHO.......... Secondary Hypertrophic Osteoarthropathy [*Medicine*]
SHO.......... Senate Historical Office
SHO.......... Senior House Officer [*British*]
SHO.......... Shikotan [*USSR*] [*Seismograph station code, US Geological Survey*]   (SEIS)
sho............ Shona [*MARC language code*] [*Library of Congress*]   (LCCP)
SHO.......... Shore
SHO.......... Showing [*Technical drawings*]
SHO.......... Shutout [*Sports*]
SHO.......... Starrett Housing Corp. [*AMEX symbol*]   (SPSG)
SHO.......... Student Health Organizations [*Defunct*]
SHO.......... Super High Output [*Model of Ford automobile*]
SHOA........ Superannuation, Home, and Overseas Allowances [*Civil Service*] [*British*]
SHOB........ Shore-Based   (CINC)
SHOBOM ... Shore Bombardment [*Navy*]   (NVT)
SHOBOMTNG ... Shore Bombardment Training [*Navy*]   (NVT)
SHOC........ SHAPE [*Supreme Headquarters Allied Powers Europe*] Operations Center [*NATO*]   (NATG)
SHOC........ Software/Hardware Operational Control
SHOCK ..... Students Hot on Conserving Kilowatts [*Student legal action organization*]
Shock Cir Homeostasis Trans Conf ... Shock and Circulatory Homeostasis. Transactions of the Conference [*A publication*]
Shock Vib Bull ... Shock and Vibration Bulletin [*A publication*]
Shock Vib Dig ... Shock and Vibration Digest [*A publication*]
SHODOP.. Short-Range Doppler
SHOE........ Shoe City Corp. [*Montgomery, AL*] [*NASDAQ symbol*]   (NQ)
Shoe Leather Rep ... Shoe and Leather Reporter [*A publication*]
Shokubai Suppl ... Shokubai. Supplement [*Japan*] [*A publication*]
Shokubutsu Boeki Plant Prot ... Shokubutsu Boeki/Plant Protection [*A publication*]
SHOMADS ... Short-to-Medium-Range Air Defense System [*Army*]   (RDA)
Shome LR .. Shome's Law Reporter [*India*] [*A publication*]   (DLA)
SHOND..... Shoni No Noshinkei [*A publication*]
S'HONG.... Souchong [*Tea trade*]   (ROG)
SHOP........ Shell Higher Olefin Process [*Petrochemistry*]
SHOP........ Shopsmith, Inc. [*NASDAQ symbol*]   (NQ)
SHOPAIR ... Short Path Infrared   (MCD)
SHOPAT.... Shore Patrol [*Navy*]   (NVT)
ShopTV..... Shopping by Television [*British Telecom*]
SHOR....... Shorewood Packaging Corp. [*NASDAQ symbol*]   (NQ)
SHORAD... Short-Range Air Defense [*Army*]   (NATG)
SHORAD C² ... Short-Range Air Defense Command and Control
SHORADS ... Short-Range Air Defense System [*Army*]   (RDA)
SHORAN ... Short-Range Navigation
SHORDU ... Shore Duty [*Navy*]
SHOREALT ... Shore Alteration
SHOROC.. Shore-Required Operational Capability [*Navy*]
SHOROUTPUBINST ... Shore Duty Beyond the Seas Is Required by the Public Interest [*Navy*]
SHORPUBINT ... Shore Duty Is Required by the Public Interest [*Navy*]
SHORSTAMPS ... Shore Requirements, Standards, and Manpower Planning System [*Navy*]
SHORTD... Shortened   (ROG)
Short Rep Rhod Geol Surv ... Short Report. Rhodesia Geological Survey [*A publication*]
Shortt Inf ... Shortt on Informations, Criminal, Quo Warranto, Mandamus, and Prohibition [*1887*] [*A publication*]   (DLA)
Shortt Inform ... Shortt on Informations, Criminal, Quo Warranto, Mandamus, and Prohibition [*A publication*]   (DLA)
Shortt Lit ... Shortt on Literature and Art [*2nd ed.*] [*1884*] [*A publication*]   (DLA)
Short Wave Mag ... Short Wave Magazine [*A publication*]
SHORVEY ... Shore Duty Survey
SHOS .... Southern Hospitality Corp. [*NASDAQ symbol*]   (NQ)
SHOSJ...... Sovereign Hospitaller Order of St. John   (EA)
SHOT .... Shooting, Hunting, Outdoor Trade Show
SHOT .... Society for the History of Technology   (EA)

Show .... Shower's English King's Bench Reports [*A publication*]   (DLA)
Show .... Shower's English Parliamentary Cases [*A publication*]   (DLA)
SHOW...... Showscan Corp. [*NASDAQ symbol*]   (NQ)
Showa Wire and Cable Rev ... Showa Wire and Cable Review [*A publication*]
Showa Wire Cable Rev ... Showa Wire and Cable Review [*Japan*] [*A publication*]
Shower KB ... Shower's English King's Bench Reports [*89 English Reprint*] [*1678-95*] [*A publication*]   (DLA)
Shower KB (Eng) ... Shower's English King's Bench Reports [*89 English Reprint*] [*A publication*]   (DLA)
Shower PC (Eng) ... Shower's English Parliamentary Cases [*1 English Reprint*] [*A publication*]   (DLA)
Show KB ... Shower's English King's Bench Reports [*A publication*]   (DLA)
Show-Me ... Show-Me News and Views [*Missouri*] [*A publication*]
Show Me Lib ... Show-Me Libraries [*A publication*]
Show Parl Cas ... Shower's English Parliamentary Cases [*1 English Reprint*] [*A publication*]   (DLA)
Show PC .... Shower's English Parliamentary Cases [*1 English Reprint*] [*A publication*]   (DLA)
SHP .... Santa Helena [*Peru*] [*Seismograph station code, US Geological Survey*] [*Closed*]   (SEIS)
SHP .... Securities Shipped as Instructed
SHP .... Seeker Head Position
SHP .... Shaft Horsepower
SHP .... Shaker Heights Public Library, Shaker Heights, OH [*OCLC symbol*]   (OCLC)
ShP .... Shakespeare Pictorial [*A publication*]
SHP .... Shape   (MSA)
SHP .... Shearon Harris Plant [*Nuclear energy*]   (NRCH)
SHP .... Shoal Petroleum [*Vancouver Stock Exchange symbol*]
SHP .... Single Highest Peak [*Aerospace*]
SHP .... Society for Hospital Planning of the American Hospital Association [*Later, SHPM*]   (EA)
SHP .... Society for Hungarian Philately   (EA)
SHP .... Sosyal Demokrasi Halkci Partisi [*Social Democratic Populist Party*] [*Turkey*] [*Political party*]   (EAIO)
SHP .... Southern Hardwood Producers [*Later, HMA*]
ShP .... Southern Historical Press, Easley, SC [*Library symbol*] [*Library of Congress*]   (LCLS)
SHP .... Special Humanitarian Programme [*Australia*]
SHP .... Standard Hardware Program [*Military*]
SHP .... Standard Holding Pattern [*Aviation*]
SHP .... Standard Holding Procedure [*Aviation*]
Shp .... Starship. The Magazine about Science Fiction [*A publication*]
SHP .... State Health Plan [*Generic term*]   (DHSM)
SHP .... [*The*] Stop & Shop Companies, Inc. [*NYSE symbol*]   (SPSG)
SHP .... Wichita Falls, TX [*Location identifier*] [*FAA*]   (FAAL)
SHPA .... Prairie Agricultural Machinery Institute, Humboldt, Saskatchewan [*Library symbol*] [*National Library of Canada*]   (NLC)
SHPA .... Shelf Paper. Alaska Outer Continental Shelf Office [*A publication*]
SHPBD...... Shipboard   (MSA)
SHPC........ Scenic Hudson Preservation Conference [*Later, SHI*]   (EA)
SHPCL...... Ship Class
SHPD .... Seeker Head Position Display [*Military*]   (CAAL)
SHPD .... Super High-Performance Diesel [*Fuel*]
SHPDA ..... State Health Planning and Development Agency
SHPE .... Society of Hispanic Professional Engineers   (EA)
SHPG .... Shipping
SHPHG..... Shipment of Household Goods   (NOAA)
SHPHUJ... Scripta Hierosolymitana. Publications of the Hebrew University (Jerusalem) [*A publication*]
SHPM .... Society for Hospital Planning and Marketing of the American Hospital Association   (EA)
SHPMT..... Shipment   (AABC)
SHPNG ..... Shipping
SHPO .... State Historic Preservation Office
SHPR........ Shipper
SHPRF ...... Shakeproof   (MSA)
SHPS........ Seahead Pressure Simulator
SHPS........ Sodium Hydroxide Purge System   (IEEE)
SHPSD...... Shipside   (AABC)
SHPT........ Shipment   (AAG)
SHPTARBY ... Ship to Arrive By _____ [*Military*]
Sh Q........... Shakespeare Quarterly [*A publication*]
SHQ........... Shasper Industries Ltd. [*Toronto Stock Exchange symbol*]
SHQ........... Southwestern Historical Quarterly [*A publication*]
SHQ........... Squadron Headquarters [*British military*]   (DMA)
SHQ........... Station Headquarters
SHQ........... Supreme Headquarters
SHR........... Hotel Revue. Wochenzeitung fuer Hotellerie und Tourismus [*A publication*]
SHR........... Scottish Historical Review [*A publication*]
ShR........... Shakespeare Review [*A publication*]
SHR........... Share [*Stock exchange term*]
SHR........... Shepard Insurance Group [*Vancouver Stock Exchange symbol*]
SHR........... Sheridan [*Wyoming*] [*Airport symbol*]   (OAG)
SHR........... Sheridan, WY [*Location identifier*] [*FAA*]   (FAAL)
SHR........... Shirakawa [*Japan*] [*Seismograph station code, US Geological Survey*]   (SEIS)

SHR........... Shore   (MCD)
SHR........... Shower
SHR........... Single High-Resolution File [*Data processing*]
SHR........... Sisters of the Holy Redeemer [*Roman Catholic religious order*]
SHR........... Society for Historical Research   (EA)
SHR........... Solar Heat Reflecting   (KSC)
SHR........... Southern Humanities Review [*A publication*]
SHR........... Spontaneously Hypertensive Rats
SHR........... Step-Height Ratio [*Crystallography*]
SHR........... Supervisory Human Relations Test
Shr .... [*The*] Taming of the Shrew [*Shakespearean work*]
SHRAM .... Short-Range Air-to-Surface Missile
SHRAP...... Shrapnel
SHRC .... Safety and Health Regulations for Construction [*Bureau of Reclamation*]
SHRC .... Shared Housing Resource Center [*Later, NSHRC*]   (EA)
SHRD........ ShareData, Inc. [*NASDAQ symbol*]   (NQ)
SHRD........ Shredded [*Freight*]
SHRD........ Shroud [*Engineering*]
SHRD........ Supplemental Heat Rejection Devices   (NASA)
SHRDF...... Shroud Fin [*Engineering*]
SHRDR ..... Shredder   (MSA)
SHRE .... Sahara Resorts [*Las Vegas, NV*] [*NASDAQ symbol*]   (NQ)
SHRF........ Ship Regular Freight [*Military*]   (AABC)
SHRI.......... Sciences and Humanities Research Institute [*Iowa State University*] [*Research center*]   (RCD)
SHRIMP ... Super-High Resolution Ion Microprobe [*Analytical chemistry*]
SHRIV....... Shrivenham [*England*]
SHRM....... SAB Harmon Industries, Inc. [*NASDAQ symbol*]   (NQ)
SHRM....... Society for Human Resource Management   (EA)
Sh & R Neg ... Shearman and Redfield on the Law of Negligence [*A publication*]   (DLA)
SHRNG..... Shearing   (MSA)
SHROPS... Shropshire [*County in England*]
SHRP........ Sharpener   (MSA)
SHRP........ Sharper Image Corp. [*NASDAQ symbol*]   (NQ)
SHRP........ Society for History, Research, and Preservation   (EA)
SHRS........ Shores   (MCD)
SHRS........ Shutdown Heat Removal System [*Nuclear energy*]   (NRCH)
SHRS........ Supplementary Heat Removal System   (IEEE)
SHRSDV ... Scottish Historic and Research Society of Delaware Valley   (EA)
Shr Sui ...... Shrady on Suicide and Intemperance in Life Insurance [*A publication*]   (DLA)
SHRT .... [*The*] Shirt Shed, Inc. [*NASDAQ symbol*]   (NQ)
SHRT .... Short   (FAAC)
SHRTA ...... Scientia Horticulturae (Amsterdam) [*A publication*]
SHRTG ..... Shortage   (AABC)
SHRTWV ... Short Wave   (FAAC)
SHRW....... Sherwood Corp. [*NASDAQ symbol*]   (NQ)
SHS .... Galveston, TX [*Location identifier*] [*FAA*]   (FAAL)
SHS .... Sacred Heart Seminary [*Detroit, MI*]
SHS .... Sample Handling System [*Chemistry*]
SHS .... Sayer Head Sling [*Medicine*]
SHS .... Scandinavian Herpetological Society   (EAIO)
SHS .... Scottish History Society   (EA)
SHS .... Self-Propagating High-Temperature Synthesis [*Ceramic technolgy*]
SHS .... Senior High School
SHS .... Shaer Shoe Corp. [*AMEX symbol*]   (SPSG)
ShS........... Shakespeare Survey [*A publication*]
SHS .... Shares [*Stock exchange term*]
SHS .... Shashi [*China*] [*Airport symbol*]   (OAG)
SHS .... Shasta Dam [*California*] [*Seismograph station code, US Geological Survey*] [*Closed*]   (SEIS)
SHS .... Sheep Hemolyzate Supernatant
SHS .... Ship's Heading Servo
SHS .... Shop Television Network [*Vancouver Stock Exchange symbol*]
SHS .... Simulation Hardware System [*NASA*]   (MCD)
SHS .... Small Hydro Society   (EA)
SHS .... Social History Society of the United Kingdom
SHS .... Societas Heraldica Scandinavica   (EAIO)
SHS .... Societatis Historiae Socius [*Fellow of the Historical Society*] [*Latin*]
SHS .... Sod House Society   (EA)
SHS .... Sodium Hexadecyl Sulfate [*Organic chemistry*]
SHS .... Soil and Health Society [*Later, RI*]   (EA)
SHS .... Soviet Hydrometeorological Service
SHS .... Spartan Homing Sensor [*Missiles*]
SHS .... Sports Hall of Shame   (EA)
SHS .... Square Hollow Section [*Metal industry*]
SHS .... Standard Heavy Spanwire [*Military*]   (CAAL)
SHS .... Superheated Steam
SHS .... Surveyors Historical Society   (EA)
SHS .... Systemhouse Ltd. [*Toronto Stock Exchange symbol*]
SHS .... University of Sheffield, Postgraduate Librarianship, Sheffield, England [*OCLC symbol*]   (OCLC)
SHSA........ Saint Hubert Society of America   (EA)
SHSA........ Scottish Harp Society of America   (EA)
SHSA........ Seaman Apprentice, Ship's Serviceman, Striker [*Navy rating*]
SHSA........ Southern Hardwood Square Association   (EA)

SHSAC...... Supreme Headquarters, Supreme Allied Commander [*World War II*]
SHSB......... Southern Home Savings Bank [*Pensacola, FL*] [*NASDAQ symbol*]　(NQ)
Sh Sc App .. Shaw's Scotch Appeal Cases, House of Lords [*A publication*]　(DLA)
SHSD .... Shiseido Co. [*NASDAQ symbol*]　(NQ)
SHSGS...... Supreme Headquarters, Secretary General Staff [*World War II*]
ShSh .... Shomer Shabbat　(BJA)
SHSLB ...... Street and Highway Safety Lighting Bureau [*Defunct*]　(EA)
SHSLC ...... Siouxland Health Sciences Consortium [*Library network*]
SHSN .... Seaman, Ship's Serviceman, Striker [*Navy rating*]
SHSN .... Sod House Society of Nebraska [*Later, SHS*]　(EA)
SHSPB ...... Soviet Hydrology. Selected Papers [*A publication*]
SHSR......... Society for Humanity and Social Reform [*British*]
SHSS .... Stanford Hypnotic Susceptibility Scale [*Psychology*]
SHSTF ...... Scout Helicopter Special Task Force　(MCD)
SHSTS ...... Ship Status
ShStud ...... Shakespeare Studies [*Tokyo*] [*A publication*]
SHSV......... Superstructure Heater Safety Valve　(DS)
SHSWD..... Society for Hospital Social Work Directors　(EA)
SHT .... Recycling [*Dusseldorf*] [*A publication*]
SHT .... Sheet　(AAG)
SHT .... Shetland Times [*A publication*]
SHT .... Sholia Resources Ltd. [*Vancouver Stock Exchange symbol*]
SHT .... Short　(MSA)
SH & T...... Shower and Toilet　(AAG)
SHT .... Sidi Hakoma Tuff [*Geology*]
SHT .... Simple Hypocalcemic Tetany [*Medicine*]
SHT .... Society for the History of Technology　(EA)
SHT .... Society of the Most Holy Trinity [*Anglican religious community*]
SHT .... Space Hand Tool [*NASA*]
SHT .... Svensk Humanistisk Tidsskrift [*A publication*]
SHT .... Swansea Harbour Trust [*Wales*]
SHTC .... Short Time Constant　(MSA)
SHTDN ..... Shutdown　(FAAC)
Sh Teind Ct ... Shaw's Scotch Teind [*Tithe*] Court Decisions [*A publication*]　(DLA)
SHTG .... Sheeting [*Freight*]
SHTG .... Shortage　(AFM)
SHTHG..... Sheathing　(MSA)
SHT IRN ... Sheet Iron [*Freight*]
SHT IRN STL ... Sheet Iron or Steel [*Freight*]
SHTL......... Shuttle　(MSA)
SHTL......... Small Heat-Transfer Loop [*Nuclear energy*]　(NRCH)
SHT MTL ... Sheet Metal [*Freight*]
SHTN .... Short Ton [*2000 lbs.*]
SHTPB ..... Saturated Hydroxy-Terminated Polybutadiene
SHTR .... Shutter　(AAG)
SHTSD...... Short Side
SHT STL WRE ... Sheet Steel Ware [*Freight*]
SHTT........ Sequential Headturn Test
SHU.......... Sacred Heart University, Library, Bridgeport, CT [*OCLC symbol*]　(OCLC)
SHU.......... Seton Hall University [*South Orange, NJ*]
SHU.......... Shoe-Town, Inc. [*NYSE symbol*]　(SPSG)
SHU.......... Shuyak Island [*Alaska*] [*Seismograph station code, US Geological Survey*]　(SEIS)
SHU.......... Skyhigh Resources Ltd. [*Vancouver Stock Exchange symbol*]
SHUJA...... Shujutsu [*A publication*]
SHum........ Studies in the Humanities [*A publication*]
S Hum Rev ... Southern Humanities Review [*A publication*]
SHUR....... Selected History Update and Reporting　(MCD)
SHUR....... System for Hospital Uniform Reporting
SHURE ..... Save the Hawkesbury's Unique River Environment [*Australia*]
SHUSA...... Scottish Heritage USA　(EA)
SHUTDN .. Shutdown　(NASA)
Shuttle........ Shuttle, Spindle, and Dyepot [*A publication*]
Shuttle Spin and Dye ... Shuttle, Spindle, and Dyepot [*A publication*]
SHV .... Shavano Air, Inc. [*Poncha Springs, CO*] [*FAA designator*]　(FAAC)
SHV .... Sheave　(MSA)
SHV .... Shreveport [*Louisiana*] [*Airport symbol*]　(OAG)
SHV .... Shreveport, LA [*Location identifier*] [*FAA*]　(FAAL)
SHV .... Solenoid Hydraulic Valve
SHV .... Standard Havens, Inc. [*AMEX symbol*]　(SPSG)
SHV .... Sub Hoc Voce [*Under This Word*] [*Latin*]
SHVE .... Sammelblatt der Historischer Verein Eichstatt [*A publication*]
SHVF .... Sammelblatt der Historischer Verein Freising [*A publication*]
SHVG .... Shaving [*Freight*]
SHVHS ..... Sandy Hook Veterans Historical Society　(EA)
SHVI .... Sammelblatt der Historischer Verein Ingolstadt [*A publication*]
SHVSCE ... Shuttle Versus Current Expendable Launch Vehicle [*NASA*]　(KSC)
SHVSNE... Shuttle Versus New Expendable Launch Vehicle [*NASA*]　(KSC)
SHW.......... Mount St. Helens [*Washington*] [*Seismograph station code, US Geological Survey*]　(SEIS)
SHW.......... Shararah [*Saudi Arabia*] [*Airport symbol*]　(OAG)
SHW.......... Sherwin-Williams Co. [*NYSE symbol*]　(SPSG)

Sh W & C... Shaw, Wilson, and Courtenay's Scotch Appeals Reports [*Wilson and Shaw's Reports*] [*A publication*]　(DLA)
SHWPA..... Sheng Wu Hua Hsueh Yu Sheng Wu Wu Li Hsueh Pao [*A publication*]
SHWR....... Shower　(FAAC)
SHWS........ Shoppers World Stores, Inc. [*San Antonio, TX*] [*NASDAQ symbol*]　(NQ)
shwy .... Showy [*Horticulture*]
SHWY .... Super Highway　(TEL)
SHX .... Shageluk [*Alaska*]　(OAG)
SHX .... Shageluk, AK [*Location identifier*] [*FAA*]　(FAAL)
SHX .... Shaw Industries, Inc. [*NYSE symbol*]　(SPSG)
SHY .... Kaiser, MO [*Location identifier*] [*FAA*]　(FAAL)
SHY .... Sharon Energy Ltd. [*Vancouver Stock Exchange symbol*]
SHY .... Shinyanga [*Tanzania*] [*Airport symbol*]　(OAG)
SHY .... Syllable Hyphen Character [*Data processing*]
SHYD .... Sharon Energy Ltd. [*NASDAQ symbol*]　(NQ)
SHZ.......... Seshute's [*Lesotho*] [*Airport symbol*]　(OAG)
SHZ.......... Shizuoka [*Japan*] [*Seismograph station code, US Geological Survey*]　(SEIS)
SHZ.......... Steelhead Resources Ltd. [*Vancouver Stock Exchange symbol*]
SHZAA ..... Shoyakugaku Zasshi [*A publication*]
SHZAAY.. Japanese Journal of Pharmacognosy [*A publication*]
SHZD .... Steelhead Resources Ltd. [*NASDAQ symbol*]　(NQ)
SI............... ACM Government Spectrum Fund [*NYSE symbol*]　(SPSG)
SI............... Arab Wings Co. [*ICAO designator*]　(FAAC)
SI............... Sacroiliac [*Medicine*]
SI............... Safety Injection [*Nuclear energy*]　(NRCH)
SI............... Safety Inspection　(IEEE)
SI............... Sailmakers Institute　(EA)
SI............... Saintpaulia International　(EA)
SI............... Saline Injection [*Abortion technique*]
SI............... Salinity Indicator
SI............... Salmon Institute [*Formerly, CSI*]　(EA)
SI............... Salt Institute　(EA)
SI............... Sample Interval
SI............... Sandwich Islands
SI............... Sanitary Inspector [*British*]　(ROG)
si............... Sans Interet [*Ex-Dividend*] [*Stock exchange*] [*French*]
SI............... Saturation Index [*Chemistry*]
SI............... Saturday Inspection [*Slang*]
SI............... Save It [*Energy-saving campaign*] [*British*]
SI............... Savings Institutions [*A publication*]
S of I......... School of Infantry [*British military*]　(DMA)
SI............... School Inventory [*Psychology*]
SI............... Scientific Instrument　(NASA)
SI............... Screen Grid Input
SI............... Scuola Italiana [*A publication*]
SI............... Secondary Item [*Army*]
SI............... Security Identity
SI............... Seine Island [*Island off the coast of France*]　(ROG)
SI............... Selected Item　(MCD)
SI............... Selective Identification
SI............... Self Incompatible
SI............... Semi-Insulating
S-I............. Sensation-Intuition [*Jungian psychology*]
SI............... Sensitive Information　(MCD)
SI............... Sensory Integration
SI............... Septic Inflammation [*Medicine*]
SI............... Sergeant Instructor [*Military*] [*British*]
SI............... Serial Input
SI............... Seriously Ill [*Military*]　(AABC)
SI............... Serra International　(EA)
SI............... Sertoma International　(EA)
SI............... Serum Iron [*Serology*]
SI............... Servas International　(EA)
SI............... Service Indicator [*Telecommunications*]　(TEL)
SI............... Service Instruction
SI............... Service Interruption
SI............... Sex Inventory [*Psychology*]
SI............... Sexual Intercourse　(ADA)
SI............... Shetland Isles
SI............... Shift-In Character [*Keyboard*] [*Data processing*]
SI............... Ship Item　(MCD)
SI............... Shipping Instructions　(AFM)
SI............... Ship's Installation [*Navy*]
SI............... Short Interest [*Brokerage*]
SI............... Signal Intelligence　(MCD)
SI............... Signal Interface
S/I............. Signal-to-Interference
SI............... Signal-to-Intermodulation [*Ratio*]
SI............... Silence [*Navigation*]
Si............... Silicon [*Chemical element*]
Si............... Silty Soil [*Agronomy*]
SI............... Silver Institute　(EA)
SI............... Similarity Index
Si............... Simon de Bisignano [*Flourished, 1174-79*] [*Authority cited in pre-1607 legal work*]　(DSA)
SI............... Simple Interest [*Banking*]
SI............... Simulator Initiation　(MCD)

SI................	Sinai (BJA)
SI................	Sing Out [A publication]
si................	Singapore [MARC country of publication code] [Library of Congress] (LCCP)
SI................	Single Instruction
SI................	Single Silk [Wire insulation] (AAG)
SI................	Sinus Iridum [Bay of Rainbows] [Lunar area]
SI................	Sirach [Ecclesiasticus] [Old Testament book]
Si................	Sistema [A publication]
SI................	Site, Incorporated (EA)
SI................	Slaved Illuminator [Military] (CAAL)
SI................	Small Inclusions [Diamond clarity grade]
SI................	Small Intestine [Anatomy]
S/I............	Smectite-Illite [Clay mineral]
SI................	Smithsonian Institution
SI................	Socialist International [Political party] [London, England] (EAIO)
SI................	Society of Illustrators (EA)
SI................	Society of Indexers (EAIO)
SI................	Solar Inertial (MCD)
SI................	Solidarity International (EA)
SI................	Solubility Index [Water]
SI................	Soluble Insulin
SI................	Soroptimist International [Cambridge, England] (EAIO)
SI................	Source Impedance
SI................	Southeast Institute for Group and Family Therapy (EA)
SI................	Southpaw's International (EA)
SI................	Space Institute [University of Tennessee] [Research center] (RCD)
SI................	Space Intelligence [Parapsychology]
SI................	Spark Ignition
SI................	Speaker Intercom
SI................	Special Inquiry [Classification system used by doctors on Ellis Island to detain, re-examine, and possibly deny entry to certain immigrants]
SI................	Special Inspection (MCD)
SI................	Special Instruction
SI................	Special Intelligence [Army] (AABC)
SI................	Special Intervention [Medicine]
SI................	Specialist Insectivore
SI................	Spectrum Index
SI................	Speech Interpolation [Telecommunications] (TEL)
SI................	Spettatore Italiano [A publication]
SI................	Spokane International Railroad Co. [AAR code]
SI................	Sponsor Identification [Television]
SI................	Sports Illustrated [A publication]
SI................	Spot Inspection [Military] (AFM)
SI................	Spot Inventory
S und I........	Sprache und Information [A publication]
SI................	Spratly Islands [ANSI two-letter standard code] (CNC)
SI................	Square Inch (MCD)
SI................	Staff Inspector
SI................	Standardization and Interoperability
SI................	Standards Institution [Telecommunications]
SI................	Standing Instruction (MSA)
SI................	Star of India
SI................	Staten Island
SI................	Station Identification
si................	Statutory Instruments [Ireland] [A publication]
SI................	Steer, Inc. [An association] (EA)
SI................	Steering Intelligence (MCD)
SI................	Stimulation Index [Cytochemistry]
S & I..........	Stocked and Issued (AFM)
SI................	Storage Immediate
SI................	Straight-In Approach [Aviation]
SI................	Straight, Incorporated (EA)
SI................	Strathclyde Institute [Glasgow, Scotland]
SI................	Stretch-Inactivated Ion Channel
SI................	Stretch Inhibitor
S/I............	Strike/Interdiction (MCD)
SI................	Structure-of-Intellect [Model]
SI................	Student Investigator (KSC)
SI................	Studia Islamica [A publication]
SI................	Studii Italiene [A publication]
S/I............	Subject Issue
SI................	Subscription Item
SI................	Sulphur Institute (EA)
SI................	Sundance Institute (EA)
SI................	Superimpose (MDG)
S of I..........	Superintendent of Instruction [British military] (DMA)
SI................	Supply Instruction [Marine Corps]
SI................	Support Installation (MCD)
SI................	Surface Integrity
SI................	Surface Ionization [Physics]
S & I..........	Surveillance and Inspection (AAG)
SI................	Surveillance Inspection [Nuclear energy] (NRCH)
S & I..........	Surveys and Investigation
SI................	Survival International [London, England] (EAIO)
SI................	Suspect Index [British]
SI................	Svizzera Italiana [A publication]
SI................	Swap-In [Data processing]
SI................	Symbolic Input [Data processing]
SI................	System Information [Data processing] (PCM)
SI................	System Integration
SI................	Systeme International d'Unites [International System of Units] [Also, SIU]
SIA............	Sailing Industry Association (EA)
SIA............	San Francisco, CA [Location identifier] [FAA] (FAAL)
SIA............	Sanitary Institute of America [Later, IAWCM]
SIA............	Sasquatch Investigations of Mid-America (EA)
SIA............	Scaffold Industry Association (EA)
SIA............	Science Information Association
SIA............	Scottish Island Area [Council]
SIA............	Securities Industry Association (EA)
SIA............	Self-Insurers Association
SIA............	Self-Interstitial Atom
SIA............	Semiconductor Industry Association (EA)
SIA............	Sensor Interface Assembly
SIA............	Serial Input Adapter
SIA............	Service in Information and Analysis [Host] [British] (BUR)
SIA............	Shelter Oil & Gas Ltd. [Toronto Stock Exchange symbol]
SIA............	Shuttle Induced Atmosphere (NASA)
SIA............	Sialic Acid [Biochemistry]
SIA............	Sian [Republic of China] [Seismograph station code, US Geological Survey] [Closed] (SEIS)
SIA............	Sigma Immunoassay [Test for rubella]
SIA............	Signal Apparel Co., Inc. [NYSE symbol] (SPSG)
SIA............	Singapore Airlines
SIA............	Singles in Agriculture [An association] (EA)
SIA............	Ski Industries America (EA)
SIA............	Societa Italiana di Agopuntura [Italy]
SIA............	Societe Internationale d'Acupuncture [International Society of Acupuncture]
SIA............	Societe Internationale Arthurienne, [International Arthurian Society] North American Branch (EA)
SIA............	Society of Industrial Accountants of Canada
SIA............	Society for Industrial Archeology (EA)
SIA............	Society of Insurance Accountants [Crozet, VA] (EA)
SIA............	Software Impact Assessment [NASA] (NASA)
SIA............	Software Institute of America [Andover, MA] [Telecommunications] (TSSD)
SIA............	Solar Inertial Attitude (NASA)
SIA............	Soroptimist International of the Americas (EA)
SIA............	Speaker Intercom Assembly [NASA]
SIA............	Special Investor Account [Stock purchasing]
SIA............	Spinal Injuries Association [British]
SIA............	Sprinkler Irrigation Association [Later, IA] (EA)
SIA............	Standard Instrument Approach [RADAR] [Aviation]
SIA............	Standard Interface Adapter
SIA............	Station of Initial Assignment
SIA............	Steel Industry Authority [Australia]
SIA............	Storage Instantaneous Audimeter [Measures television viewing]
SIA............	Strategic Industries Association (EA)
SIA............	Stress-Induced Analgesia [Medicine]
SIA............	Structural Inventory and Appraisal [Of roads and bridges]
SIA............	Subminiature Integrated Antenna
SIA............	Survivors of Incest Anonymous (EA)
SIA............	Synalbumin-Insulin Antagonism [Medicine]
SIA............	System Integration Area (MCD)
SIA............	Xian [China] [Airport symbol] (OAG)
SIABA......	Sindacato Italiano Artisti Belle Arti [Italian Union of Fine Arts]
SIABC......	Sociedad Iberoamericana de Biologia Celular [Ibero-American Society for Cell Biology - IASCB] (EAIO)
SIAC..........	Secretariat International des Artistes Catholiques
SIAC..........	Securities Industry Automation Corporation [NYSE/ASE] [New York, NY]
SIAC..........	Societe Internationale des Artistes Chretiens [International Society for Christian Artists] [Lydiate, Merseyside, England] (EAIO)
SIAC..........	Southeastern Intercollegiate Athletic Association (MCD)
SIAC..........	Special Interest Auto Club (EA)
SIAC..........	State Industry Advisory Committee [Civil Defense]
SIAC..........	Studies in Automation and Control [Elsevier Book Series] [A publication]
SIAC..........	Submarine Integrated Attack Center (MCD)
SIAD..........	Chartered Society of Designers (EAIO)
SIAD..........	Sierra Army Depot [California] (AABC)
SIADH......	Syndrome of Inappropriate Antidiuretic Hormone [Endocrinology]
SIADS......	Sensor Integration and Display Sharing [Military] (CAAL)
SIAE..........	Scottish Institute of Agricultural Engineering [Research center] (IRC)
SIAF..........	Service Indicator Associated Field [Telecommunications] (TEL)
SIAF..........	Small Independent Action Force [Military]
SIAGL......	Survey Instrument, Azimuth Gyroscope, Lightweight (MCD)
SIA J..........	SIA [Societe des Ingenieurs de l'Automobile] Journal [France] [A publication]
SIAJ..........	SIAJ: Singapore Institute of Architects. Journal [A publication]
SIAL..........	Salon International de l'Alimentation [World Food Fair]
SIAL..........	Sialagogue [Promoting Flow of Saliva] [Medicine] (ROG)
SIAL..........	Sigma-Aldrich Corp. [NASDAQ symbol] (NQ)

SIAL......... Southeast Iowa Academic Libraries [*Library network*]
SIALON.... Silicon, Aluminum, Oxygen, and Nitrogen [*A ceramic*]
SIAM........ Self-Initiating Antiaircraft Munition [*ARPA*]
SIAM........ Separate Index Access Method [*Data processing*]   (BUR)
SIAM........ Signal Information and Monitoring Service [*American radio
            monitoring service*]
SIAM........ Society for Industrial and Applied Mathematics   (EA)
SIAM........ Strategic Impact and Assumptions Identification Method
SIAMA...... Society for Interests of Active Missionaries in Asia, Africa, and
            America   (EAIO)
SIAM J Algebraic Discrete Methods ... SIAM [*Society for Industrial and
            Applied Mathematics*] Journal on Algebraic and Discrete
            Methods [*A publication*]
SIAM J Algebraic and Discrete Methods ... SIAM [*Society for Industrial and
            Applied Mathematics*] Journal on Algebraic and Discrete
            Methods [*A publication*]
SIAM J A Ma ... SIAM [*Society for Industrial and Applied Mathematics*]
            Journal on Applied Mathematics [*A publication*]
SIAM J Appl Math ... SIAM [*Society for Industrial and Applied
            Mathematics*] Journal on Applied Mathematics [*A
            publication*]
SIAM J App Math ... SIAM [*Society for Industrial and Applied
            Mathematics*] Journal on Applied Mathematics [*A
            publication*]
SIAM J Comput ... SIAM [*Society for Industrial and Applied Mathematics*]
            Journal on Computing [*A publication*]
SIAM J Cont ... SIAM [*Society for Industrial and Applied Mathematics*]
            Journal on Control [*A publication*]
SIAM J Control ... SIAM [*Society for Industrial and Applied Mathematics*]
            Journal on Control [*A publication*]
SIAM J Control Optim ... SIAM [*Society for Industrial and Applied
            Mathematics*] Journal on Control and Optimization [*A
            publication*]
SIAM J Control and Optimiz ... SIAM [*Society for Industrial and Applied
            Mathematics*] Journal on Control and Optimization [*A
            publication*]
SIAM J Control Optimization ... SIAM [*Society for Industrial and Applied
            Mathematics*] Journal on Control and Optimization [*A
            publication*]
SIAM J Math ... SIAM [*Society for Industrial and Applied Mathematics*]
            Journal on Mathematical Analysis [*A publication*]
SIAM J Math Anal ... SIAM [*Society for Industrial and Applied
            Mathematics*] Journal on Mathematical Analysis [*A
            publication*]
SIAM J Num ... SIAM [*Society for Industrial and Applied Mathematics*]
            Journal on Numerical Analysis [*A publication*]
SIAM J Numer Anal ... SIAM [*Society for Industrial and Applied
            Mathematics*] Journal on Numerical Analysis [*A
            publication*]
SIAM J Sci and Stat Comput ... SIAM [*Society for Industrial and Applied
            Mathematics*] Journal on Scientific and Statistical
            Computing [*A publication*]
SIAM J Sci Stat Comput ... SIAM [*Society for Industrial and Applied
            Mathematics*] Journal on Scientific and Statistical
            Computing [*A publication*]
SIAM J Sci Statist Comput ... SIAM [*Society for Industrial and Applied
            Mathematics*] Journal on Scientific and Statistical
            Computing [*A publication*]
SIAM R ..... SIAM [*Society for Industrial and Applied Mathematics*] Review
            [*A publication*]
SIAM Rev ... SIAM [*Society for Industrial and Applied Mathematics*] Review
            [*A publication*]
SIAM (Soc Ind Appl Math) SIMS (SIAM Inst Math Soc) Conf Ser ... SIAM
            (Society for Industrial and Applied Mathematics) SIMS
            (SIAM Institute for Mathematics and Society) Conference
            Series [*A publication*]
SIAM Stud Appl Math ... SIAM [*Society for Industrial and Applied
            Mathematics*] Studies in Applied Mathematics [*A
            publication*]
SIAM Studies in Appl Math ... SIAM [*Society for Industrial and Applied
            Mathematics*] Studies in Applied Mathematics [*A
            publication*]
SIAN......... Societe Industrielle et Agriculturelle du Niari [*Industrial and
            Agricultural Society of Niari*]
SIANM...... Special Inspection, Army Nuclear Matters   (MCD)
SI/AO........ Smithsonian Institution/Astrophysical Observatory   (KSC)
SIAP .... SIAP. Revista de la Sociedad Interamericana de Planificacion
            [*Colombia*] [*A publication*]
SIAP .... Sociedad Interamericana de Planeficacion [*Inter-American
            Planning Society*] [*Mexico*]
SIAP .... Standard Instrument Approach Procedure [*Aviation*]
SIAP .... Standard-Italo Americana Petroli
SIAP .... Straight-In Approach [*Aviation*]
SIAR .... Small, Irregular, Agglutinated Rooms [*Architecture*]
SIAS .... Safety Injection Actuation Signal [*Nuclear energy*]   (NRCH)
SIAS .... Scandinavian Institute of Asian Studies [*See also CINA*] [*Later,
            NIAS*]   (EAIO)
SIAS .... Signals Intelligence Analysis System   (MCD)
SIAS .... Submarine Integrated Antenna System   (MCD)
SIASP....... Society for Italian-American Scientists and Physicians   (EA)
SIAT .... Single Integrated Attack Team

SIAT .... Societa Italiana Assicurazioni Trasporti [*Italy*]   (EY)
SIAT .... Synthesis of Impact Acceleration Technology   (MCD)
SIAU......... Seminario Internacional de Administracao Universitaria
SIAWS ...... Satellite-Interrogated Automatic Weather Station   (NOAA)
SIB............ Satellite Integrated Buoy
SIB............ Satellite Ionospheric Beacons [*Military*]
SIB............ Saudi International Bank
SIB............ Scale plus Index plus Base
SIB............ Scales of Independent Behavior [*Occupational therapy*]
SIB............ Screen Image Buffer [*Data processing*]
SIB............ Securities and Investments Board [*Great Britain*]
SIB............ Selection Interview Blueprint [*LIMRA*]
SIB............ Self-Injurious Behavior [*Abnormal psychology*]
SIB............ Serial Interface Board
SIB............ Ship Information Booklet [*Navy*]
SIB............ Shipbuilding Industry Board [*British*]
SIB............ Siberia
SIB............ Sibiti [*Congo*] [*Airport symbol*]   (OAG)
Sib............ Sibling
SIB............ Sibola Mines Ltd. [*Vancouver Stock Exchange symbol*]
Sib............ Sibyllines   (BJA)
SIB............ SIDPERS [*Standard Installation/Division Personnel System*]
            Interface Branch [*Military*]   (INF)
SIB............ Sistema de Informacion Bursatil [*Stock Exchange Information
            System*] [*Madrid Stock Exchange*] [*Information service or
            system*]   (IID)
SIB............ Societe Internationale de Biometeorologie [*International
            Society of Biometeorology*]   (EAIO)
SIB............ Special Investigation Branch [*Army*] [*British*]
SIB............ Standard Iron Bar   (MSA)
SIB............ Subject Interface Box   (KSC)
SIB............ System Interconnect Bus [*Data processing*]
SIB............ Systems Information Bulletin [*Data processing*]
SIBA .... Small Independent Brewers' Association [*British*]   (ECON)
SIBC .... Saudi Investment Banking Corporation
SIBC .... Societe Internationale de Biologie Clinique [*World Association
            of Anatomic and Clinical Pathology Societies*]
Sib Chem J ... Siberian Chemistry Journal [*A publication*]
SIBE .... Studies in Bayesian Econometrics [*Elsevier Book Series*] [*A
            publication*]
Sibelius ...... Sibelius-Mitteilungen [*A publication*]
Siberian Math J ... Siberian Mathematical Journal [*A publication*]
SIBEX........ Second International BIOMASS Experiment
SIBEX........ Singapore International Building Exhibition   (TSPED)
Sib Geogr Sb ... Sibirskii Geograficheskii Sbornik [*A publication*]
SIBH.......... Salicylideniminobenzohydroxamic Acid [*Biochemistry*]
SIBIL......... Systeme Integre pour les Bibliotheques Universitaires de
            Lausanne [*Integrated System for the University of
            Lausanne Libraries*] [*Switzerland*]   (IID)
Sibirsk Mat Z ... Sibirskii Matematiceskii Zurnal [*A publication*]
Sibirsk Mat Zh ... Akademiya Nauk SSSR. Sibirskoe Otdelenie. Sibirskii
            Matematicheskii Zhurnal [*A publication*]
Sibirsk Vrach Viedom ... Sibirskiia Vrachebnyia Viedomosti [*A publication*]
SIBIS......... Self-Injurious Behavior Inhibiting System [*Psychology*]
SIBIS......... Smithsonian Institution Bibliographic Information System
SIBL .... Separate Infantry Brigade Light   (INF)
SIBM......... Societe Internationale de Biologie Mathematique [*International
            Society of Mathematical Biology*]   (EAIO)
SIBMAS.... Societe Internationale des Bibliotheques et Musees des Arts du
            Spectacle [*International Association of Libraries and
            Museums of the Performing Arts*]   (EAIO)
Sib Math J ... Siberian Mathematical Journal [*A publication*]
Sib Mat Zh ... Sibirskij Matematicheskij Zhurnal [*A publication*]
SIB-MIBOC ... Securities and Investments Board and the Marketing of
            Investments Board Organisation Commission [*London,
            England*]
SibOr .... Sibylline Oracles   (BJA)
SIBOR....... Singapore Interbank Offered Rate
SIBR......... Sybra, Inc. [*Atlanta, GA*] [*NASDAQ symbol*]   (NQ)
SI/BRC..... Strategic Intelligence/Business Research Corporation
Sibri .... Sibrium. Collana di Studi e Documentazioni [*A publication*]
SIBS.......... Salk Institute for Biological Studies
SIBS.......... Semiconductor Industry & Business Survey [*Database*] [*HTE
            Management Resources*] [*Information service or
            system*]   (CRD)
SIBS.......... Stellar Inertial Bombing System
SIBTN .... Something Is Better than Nothing
Sib Vest Sel'Khoz Nauki ... Siberskii Vestnik Sel'skokhozyaistvennoi Nauki
            [*A publication*]
SIC............ Covington/Cincinnati, OH [*Location identifier*]
            [*FAA*]   (FAAL)
SIC............ High School Student Information Center   (EA)
SIC............ Safety Information Center [*National Safety Council*]   (IID)
SIC............ Sakharov International Committee   (EA)
SIC............ Science Information Council [*National Science Foundation*]
SIC............ Scientific Information Center
SIC............ Second Pilot in Command [*Aviation*]   (FAAC)
SIC............ Security Intelligence Centre [*British*] [*World War II*]
SIC............ Security Intelligence Corps
SIC............ Semiconductor Integrated Circuit

SIC............. Sept-Iles [*Quebec*] [*Seismograph station code, US Geological Survey*]   (SEIS)
SIC............. Serial Interface Chip
SIC............. Service, Inc., Omaha NE [*STAC*]
SIC............. Servicio Informativo Continental [*Press agency*] [*Argentina*]
SIC............. Siccus [*Dry*] [*Latin*]   (ADA)
SIC............. Sicily
SIC............. Sico, Inc. [*Toronto Stock Exchange symbol*]
SIC............. Silicon-Insulating Compound
SIC............. Silicon Integrated Circuit
SIC............. Simulated Interface Calibration
SIC............. Skills Inventory Coordinator
SIC............. Social Interaction Code
SIC............. Societa Italiana Cauzioni [*Italy*]   (EY)
SIC............. Societe Internationale de Cardiologie [*International Society of Cardiology*]
SIC............. Societe Internationale de Chirurgie [*International Society of Surgery - ISS*] [*Basel, Switzerland*]   (EA)
SIC............. Societe Internationale de Criminologie [*International Society of Criminology*]   (EA)
SIC............. Society of Inkwell Collectors   (EA)
SIC............. SONAR Information Center   (NVT)
SIC............. Sorties per Inspection Cycle [*Air Force*]   (AFIT)
SICSA......... Special Information Center   (MCD)
SIC............. Special Interest Committee
SIC............. Specific Inductive Capacity
SIC............. Split Investment Company [*Generic term*]
SIC............. Standard Industrial Classification [*File indexing code*] [*Also, an information service or system*]
SIC............. Standard Inspection Criteria
SIC............. States Information Center [*Council of State Governments*]   (IID)
SIC............. Status of Implementation Chart
SIC............. Structural Influence Coefficient
SIC............. Studies in Inorganic Chemistry [*Elsevier Book Series*] [*A publication*]
SIC............. Supervisory Inventory on Communication [*Test*]
SIC............. Survey Information Center [*Military*]
SIC............. Systeme Informatique pour la Conjoncture [*Information System for the Economy*] [*INSEE*] [*France*] [*Information service or system*]   (IID)
SIC............. Systems Integration Contractor
SICA.......... Secondary Inventory Control Activity   (MCD)
Sic A.......... Sicilia Archeologica [*A publication*]
SICA.......... Soccer Industry Council of America   (EA)
SICA.......... Society of Industrial and Cost Accountants of Canada
SICA.......... Subud International Cultural Association   (EA)
SICAB....... Sichere Arbeit [*A publication*]
SICAC....... Society of Inter-Celtic Arts and Culture   (EA)
SICAM...... Sex Information Council of America [*Later, CSIE*]   (EA)
SICBM...... Small Intercontinental Ballistic Missile   (MCD)
SICC.......... Safeguard Inventory Control Center [*Army*]   (AABC)
SICC.......... Service Inventory Control Center [*DoD*]
SICCS........ Social Interaction and Creativity in Communication System [*Educational test*]
SICDOC.... Special Interest Committee on Program Documentation [*Association for Computing Machinery*]
SICEA....... Steel Industry Compliance Extension Act of 1981
SICF......... Societe des Ingenieurs Civils de France
SicG .... Siculorum Gymnasium [*A publication*]
Sic Gymn .. Siculorum Gymnasium [*A publication*]
Sich Arb..... Sichere Arbeit [*Austria*] [*A publication*]
SICHD...... Sicherheit [*A publication*]
SICHEJ...... Studies in Inorganic Chemistry [*A publication*]
Sicherheit... Wirtschaftsschutz und Sicherheitstechnik [*A publication*]
Sicherheit Chem Umwelt ... Sicherheit in Chemie und Umwelt [*A publication*]
Sicherheitspol Heute ... Sicherheitspolitik Heute [*A publication*]
Sicilia Arch ... Sicilia Archaeologica. Rassegna Periodica di Studi, Notizie e Documentazione [*A publication*]
SICJA........ Siberian Chemistry Journal [*English Translation*] [*A publication*]
Sick .... Sickels' Reports [*46-85 New York*] [*A publication*]   (DLA)
Sick .... Single Income, Couple of Kids [*Lifestyle classification*]
Sick Min Dec ... Sickels' United States Mining Laws and Decisions [*A publication*]   (DLA)
Sick Op ...... Sickels' Opinions of the New York Attorneys-General [*A publication*]   (DLA)
SICL .... Sampling Inspection Checklist
SICL .... Selected Item Configuration Log
SICL .... Self-Interview Checklist [*Navy*]   (NVT)
SICM........ Scanning Ion-Conductance Microscope
SICM........ Scheduled Input Control Method   (MCD)
SICM........ Small Intercontinental Ballistic Missile   (MCD)
SICM........ Soybean Integrated Crop Management Model
SICMAU... International Congress for Microbiology. Symposia [*A publication*]
SICO......... Signal Control   (DEN)
SICO......... Switched in for Checkout [*NASA*]   (KSC)
SICO......... Systems Integration and Checkout

SICOB....... Salon International de l'Informatique, de la Communication, et de l'Organisation du Bureau [*Business equipment exhibition*]
SICOM...... Securities Industry Communication [*Western Union Corp.*] [*Information service or system*]
SI COMMS ... Special Intelligence Communications   (MCD)
S Icon......... Studies in Iconography [*A publication*]
SICOT .... Societe Internationale de Chirurgie Orthopedique et de Traumatologie [*International Society of Orthopaedic Surgery and Traumatology*] [*Brussels, Belgium*]   (EAIO)
SICOVAM ... Societe Interprofessionnelle pour la Compensation des Valeurs Mobilieres [*French depository body*]
SICP .... Selected Ion Current Profile [*Spectrometry*]
SICP .... Society of Indochina Philatelists   (EA)
SICPS....... Standardized Integrated Command Post System [*Army*]   (INF)
SICR .... Selected Item Configuration Record   (MCD)
SICR .... Specific Intelligence Collection Requirements [*Military*]   (AFM)
SICR .... Supply Item Change Record
SICRI........ Substances Immunologically Cross-Reactive with Insulin
SICS .... Safety Injection Control System [*Nuclear energy*]   (NRCH)
SICS .... Secondary Infrared Calibration System
SICS .... Ships Integrated Communications System   (MCD)
SICSA....... Sicher Ist Sicher [*A publication*]
SI & CTF .. Scottish Industry and Commerce Trade Fair   (ITD)
SICTLM.... Solomon Islands Cultural Traditional Leaders Movement
Sicu .... [*Abbas*] Siculus [*Deceased, 1445*] [*Authority cited in pre-1607 legal work*]   (DSA)
SICU......... Surgical Intensive Care Unit [*Medicine*]
Sicu Ab....... Abbas Siculus [*Deceased, 1445*] [*Authority cited in pre-1607 legal work*]   (DSA)
SID............. Doctor of Industrial Science
SID............. ICP [*International Computer Programs, Inc.*] Software Information Database [*Information service or system*]   (CRD)
SID............. Sal Island [*Cape Verde Islands*] [*Airport symbol*]   (OAG)
SID............. Scheduled Issue Date [*Telecommunications*]   (TEL)
SID............. Seal-In Device   (MSA)
SID............. Security and Intelligence Service [*Army*]
SID............. Seismic Intrusion Detector [*Army*]
sid............. Semel in Die [*Once a Day*] [*Pharmacy*]
SID............. Sequence Information Data
SID............. Serial Input Data [*Data processing*]
SID............. Servizio Informazioni Difesa [*Defense Intelligence Service*] [*Italy*]
SID............. Shuttle Integration Device [*NASA*]   (NASA)
SID............. Sida [*Iceland*] [*Seismograph station code, US Geological Survey*]   (SEIS)
sid............. Sidamo [*MARC language code*] [*Library of Congress*]   (LCCP)
SID............. Side-Impact Dummy [*Collision testing device*]
Sid .... Siderfin's King's Bench Reports [*82 English Reprint*] [*A publication*]   (DLA)
SID............. Silicon Imaging Device   (IEEE)
SID............. Silver Iodine Generator
SID............. Simulator Interface Device   (MCD)
SID............. Situation Display
SID............. Situation Information Display
SID............. Skin Inserted Detonator   (MCD)
SID............. Slew-Induced Distortion
SID............. Society for Information Display   (EA)
SID............. Society for International Development   (EA)
SID............. Society for Investigative Dermatology   (EA)
SID............. Sodium Ionization Detector [*Nuclear energy*]   (NRCH)
SID............. Software Interface Document   (MCD)
SID............. Sound Ideas, Inc. [*Vancouver Stock Exchange symbol*]
SID............. Sound Interface Device [*Computer chip*]
SID............. Source Image Distortion
SID............. Space and Information Systems Division [*NASA*]
SID............. Space Intruder Detector [*Burglar alarm*]
SID............. Special Intelligence Detachment [*Military*]   (CINC)
SID............. Specific Infrared Detector
SID............. Specification Interpretation Documentation   (MCD)
SID............. Spiritus in Deo [*Spirit Rests in God*] [*Latin*]
SID............. Sports Information Director
SID............. Standard Instrument Departure [*RADAR*] [*Aviation*]
SID............. Standard Interface Document   (NASA)
SID............. Strategic Intelligence Digests [*Military*]   (AABC)
SID............. Subcontract Item Definition
SID............. Subject Identification Module [*NASA*]
SID............. Subscriber Identification   (CAAL)
SID............. Sudden Infant Death [*Syndrome*] [*Medicine*]
SID............. Sudden Ionospheric Disturbance [*Geophysics*]
SID............. Surface-Induced Dissociation [*Physics*]
SID............. Surface Ionization Detector [*Instrumentation*]
S & ID........ Surveillance and Identification
SID............. SWIFT [*Society for Worldwide Interbank Financial Telecommunications*] Interface Device
SID............. Syntax Improving Device   (IEEE)
SID............. System Interface Document [*NASA*]   (NASA)
SID............. Systems Integration Demonstrator [*Aircraft*]

SID............ Systems Integration and Deployment [*Program*] [*Department of Transportation*]
SIDA.......... 7th Infantry Division Association   (EA)
SIDA.......... Societa Italiana di Assicurazioni SpA [*Italy*]   (EY)
SIDA.......... Societe Internationale Fernand de Vischer pour l'Histoire des Droits de l'Antiquite   (EA)
SIDA.......... Sudden Infant Death Association [*Australia*]
SIDA.......... Swedish International Development Agency
SIDAC .... Single Integrated Damage Anaysis Capability   (MCD)
Sida Contrib Bot ... Sida Contributions to Botany [*A publication*]
Sid Apoll .... Sidonius Apollinaris [*Fifth century AD*] [*Classical studies*]   (OCD)
SIDAR....... Selective Information Dissemination and Retrieval [*Data processing*]   (DIT)
SIDAR....... Symposium on Image Display and Recording
SIDASE..... Significant Data Selection
SIDC.......... Slaved Illuminator Data Converter [*Military*]   (CAAL)
SIDC.......... Supply Item Design Change [*Navy*]   (NG)
SIDC.......... Support Issue Development Committee [*Military*]   (CAAL)
SIDC.......... Systems Identification Data Cost
SIDC-PAV ... Special Interdepartmental Committee on Protection Against Violence [*Australia*]
SIDD.......... Scientific Information and Documentation Division [*Later, ESIC*]
SIDE.......... Suprathermal-Ion-Detector Experiment [*Apollo*] [*NASA*]
SIDEC .... Stanford International Development Education Center [*Stanford University*]
Side Eff Drugs ... Side Effects of Drugs [*A publication*]
Side Eff Drugs Annu ... Side Effects of Drugs. Annual [*A publication*]
SIDEFCOOP ... Sociedad Interamericana de Desarrollo de Financiamiento Cooperativo [*Inter-American Society for the Development of Cooperative Financing*] [*Buenos Aires, Argentina*]   (EAIO)
Sid (Eng).... Siderfin's King's Bench Reports [*82 English Reprint*] [*A publication*]   (DLA)
Sider Latinoam ... Siderurgia Latinoamericana [*A publication*]
SIDES........ Source Input Data Edit System
SIDF.......... Sinusoidal Input Describing Function [*Data processing*]
SIDFA....... Senior Industrial Development Field Adviser [*United Nations*]
Sid Gov ...... Sidney on Government [*A publication*]   (DLA)
SID J......... SID [*Society for Information Display*] Journal [*A publication*]
SIDL.......... System Identification Data List [*Navy*]   (NG)
SIDLOB..... Side Lobe [*Entomology*]
SIDM........ Shipboard Identification Demolition Model [*Navy*]
SIDM......... Syndicat International des Debardeurs et Magasiniers [*International Longshoremen's and Warehousemen's Union - ILWU*] [*Canada*]
Sid Mess .... Sidereal Messenger [*A publication*]
SIDN .... Small Industry Development Network [*Georgia Institute of Technology*]
SIDO .... Societe Internationale pour le Developpement des Organisations [*International Society for the Development of Organizations*]   (EAIO)
SIDOR....... Siderurgica del Orinoco [*Government steel company*] [*Venezuela*]
SIDP.......... Seed Industry Development Program [*UN Food and Agriculture Organization*]
SIDP.......... Sheep Industry Development Program   (EA)
SIDPERS .. Standard Installation/Division Personnel System [*Military*]   (AABC)
SIDRF .... Sudden Infant Death Research Foundation [*Australia*]
SIDS .... Satellite Imagery Dissemination System   (MCD)
SIDS .... Sensor Interface Data System [*Military*]   (CAAL)
SIDS .... Ships Integrated Defense System
SIDS .... Shrike Improved Display System [*Military*]   (NVT)
SIDS .... Societe Internationale de Defense Sociale [*International Society for Social Defence - ISSD*] [*Paris, France*]   (EAIO)
SIDS .... Societe Internationale de Droit Sociale
SIDS .... Space Investigations Documentation System [*NASA*]
SIDS .... Spares Integrated Data System   (MCD)
SIDS .... Specification Interpretation Documents   (MCD)
SIDS .... Standard Information Display System [*Military*]   (CAAL)
SIDS .... Stellar Inertial Doppler System
SIDS .... Sudden Infant Death Syndrome [*Medicine*]
SIDS .... Support Integrated Data System   (MCD)
SIDSA .... Sudden Infant Death Syndrome Act of 1974
SIDTC .... Single Integrated Development Test Cycle
SIDTEC..... Single Integrated Development Test Cycle   (MCD)
SIDTS....... Single Integrated Development Test System
SIDY .... Science Dynamics Corp. [*NASDAQ symbol*]   (NQ)
SIDZD....... Saitama Ika Daigaku Zasshi [*A publication*]
SIE............ Science Information Exchange [*Later, SSIE*] [*Smithsonian Institution*]
SIE............ Sea Isle, NJ [*Location identifier*] [*FAA*]   (FAAL)
SIE............ Select Information Exchange [*Information service or system*]   (IID)
SIE............ Selected Inertial Equipment
SIE............ Selected Item Exchange   (MCD)
SIE............ Serum Immunoreative Erythropoietin [*Immunochemistry*]
SIE............ Servizio Informazioni Esercito [*Italy*] [*Forces Intelligence Service*]

SIE............ Shanell International Energy Corp. [*Vancouver Stock Exchange symbol*]
SIE............ Shuttle Interface Equipment [*NASA*]   (NASA)
Sie .... Siemens [*Unit of electric conductance*]
SIE............ Siena [*Italy*] [*Seismograph station code, US Geological Survey*]   (SEIS)
SIE............ Sierra Express [*Reno, NV*] [*FAA designator*]   (FAAC)
SIE............ Sierra Health Services, Inc. [*AMEX symbol*]   (SPSG)
SIE............ Single Instruction Execute
SIE............ Societe Internationale d'Electrochimie [*International Society of Electrochemistry*]
SIE............ Society of Industrial Engineers [*Later, SAM*]
SIE............ Soroptimist International d'Europe [*Soroptimist International of Europe*]   (EAIO)
SIE............ Special Inspection Equipment
SIE............ Studies in International Economics [*Elsevier Book Series*] [*A publication*]
SIE............ Suicide Information and Education [*Suicide Information and Education Center*] [*Canada*] [*Information service or system*]   (CRD)
SIE............ Surface Ionization Engine
SIE............ System Integration Equipment   (KSC)
SIE............ System Investigation Equipment   (KSC)
SIEA .... Sensor Interface Electronics Assembly   (MCD)
SIEB .... Satellite-Interrogated Environmental Buoy
SIEBA7 ..... Sieboldia Acta Biologica [*A publication*]
SIEC .... Societe Internationale pour l'Enseignement Commercial [*International Society for Business Education*] [*Lausanne, Switzerland*]   (EAIO)
SIEC .... Suicide Information and Education Centre [*Canadian Mental Health Association*] [*Information service or system*]   (IID)
SIECCAN ... Sex Information and Education Council of Canada
SIECD .... Societe Internationale d'Education Continue en Dentisterie [*International Society of Continuing Education in Dentistry - ISCED*] [*Brussels, Belgium*]   (EAIO)
SIECOP..... Scientific Information and Education Council of Physicians   (EA)
SIECUS..... Sex Information and Education Council of the US   (EA)
SIED.......... Supplier Item Engineering Order   (MCD)
SIEDS....... Societe Internationale d'Etude du Dix-Huitieme Siecle [*International Society for Eighteenth-Century Studies - ISECS*]   (EAIO)
SIEF.......... Societe Internationale d'Ethnographie et de Folklore [*International Society for Ethnology and Folklore*]
SIEFA........ Source Inventory and Emission Factor Analysis [*Environmental Protection Agency*]
SIEGE .... Simulated EMP [*Electromagnetic Pulse*] Ground Environment [*Air Force*]
Siego .... Single, Intelligent, and Educated and Growing Old [*Lifestyle classification*]
Siemens-Albis Ber ... Siemens-Albis Berichte [*A publication*]
Siemens Components (Engl Ed) ... Siemens Components (English Edition) [*A publication*]
Siemens Electron Components Bull ... Siemens Electronic Components Bulletin [*A publication*]
Siemens Energietech ... Siemens Energietechnik [*West Germany*] [*A publication*]
Siemens Forsch Entwickl ... Siemens Forschungs- und Entwicklungsberichte. Research and Development Reports [*A publication*]
Siemens Forsch Entwicklungsber ... Siemens Forschungs- und Entwicklungsberichte [*A publication*]
Siemens Forsch- und Entwicklungsber ... Siemens Forschungs- und Entwicklungsberichte [*A publication*]
Siemens Forsch Entwicklungsber Res Dev Rep ... Siemens Forschungs- und Entwicklungsberichte. Research and Development Reports [*A publication*]
Siemens Power Eng ... Siemens Power Engineering [*West Germany*] [*A publication*]
Siemens Rev ... Siemens Review [*A publication*]
Siemens-Z ... Siemens-Zeitschrift [*A publication*]
sien............ Sienna [*Philately*]
SIEND....... Saiensu [*A publication*]
SIEP .... Screening Inspection for Electronic Parts [*NASA*]
SIEPM ...... Societe Internationale pour l'Etude de la Philosophie Medievale [*International Society for the Study of Medieval Philosophy*]   (EAIO)
SIER .... Sierra On-Line, Inc. [*NASDAQ symbol*]   (CTT)
SIERNEV ... Sierra Nevada [*FAA*]   (FAAC)
Sierra .... Sierra Club. Bulletin [*A publication*]
Sierra Club B ... Sierra Club. Bulletin [*A publication*]
Sierra Club Bull ... Sierra Club. Bulletin [*A publication*]
Sierra Ed News ... Sierra Educational News [*A publication*]
Sierra Leone Agric Div Minist Agric Nat Resour Rep ... Sierra Leone Agricultural Division. Ministry of Agriculture and Natural Resources. Report [*A publication*]
Sierra Leone Fish Div Tech Pap ... Sierra Leone Fisheries Division. Technical Paper [*A publication*]
Sierra Leone LR ... Law Reports, Sierra Leone Series [*A publication*]   (ILCA)
Sierra Leone L Rec ... Law Recorder (Sierra Leone) [*A publication*]   (ILCA)
Sierra Leone Rep Geol Surv Div ... Sierra Leone. Report on the Geological Survey Division [*A publication*]

SIES.......... Ship Integrated Electronic System
SIES.......... Sobek's International Explorer's Society [*Commercial firm*] (EA)
SIES.......... Society of the Incarnation of the Eternal Son [*Anglican religious community*]
SIES.......... Supervision, Inspection, Engineering, and Services (NASA)
SIESC........ Secretariat International des Enseignants Secondaires Catholiques [*International Secretariat of Catholic Secondary School Teachers*] [*Acronym used in association name, SIESC Pax Romana*] [*Nijmegen, Netherlands*] (EAIO)
SIESTA ..... Silent Energy Sources for Tactical Applications (MCD)
SIETAR/INTL ... International Society for Intercultural Education, Training, and Research (EA)
SIEUSE..... Secretariat International de l'Enseignement Universitaire des Sciences de l'Education
SI/EW .... Special Intelligence/Electronic Warfare (MCD)
Siex .... Superintendencia de Inversiones Extranjeras [*Supervisory Authority for Foreign Investments*] [*Venezuela*] (GEA)
SIF .... Reidsville, NC [*Location identifier*] [*FAA*] (FAAL)
SIF .... Salvo in Flight [*Military*] (CAAL)
SIF .... Science Information Facility [*FDA*]
SIF .... Scleroderma International Foundation (EA)
SIF .... Scotch-Irish Foundation (EA)
SIF .... Scott Industrial Foam
SIF .... Secure Identification Feature
SIF .... Security and Intelligence Foundation [*Later, CIS*] (EA)
SIF .... Selective Identification Feature [*Military decoder modification*]
SIF .... Service Incroyance et Foi [*Canadian Catholic Conference*]
SIF .... Short-Intrusion Fuze (RDA)
SIF .... SIFCO Industries, Inc. [*AMEX symbol*] (SPSG)
SIF .... Signaling Information Field [*Telecommunications*] (TEL)
SIF .... Simra [*Nepal*] [*Airport symbol*] (OAG)
SIF .... Single Face
SIF .... Small Intensely Fluorescent [*Cytology*]
SIF .... Social Investment Forum
SIF .... Sociedad Iberoamericana de Filosofia (EAIO)
SIF .... Society of International Friendship (EA)
SIF .... Sound Intermediate Frequency
SIF .... Storage Interface Facility
SIF .... Studi Internazionali di Filosofia [*A publication*]
SIF .... Switched In-Flight (KSC)
SIF .... Synthetic Interstitial Fluid [*Biochemistry*]
SIFA .... Society of Independent Financial Advisors [*Englewood, CO*] (EA)
SIFAD ...... Separate Ion Formation and Drift
SIFAR....... Surveillance Imagery Fast Access Recording (MCD)
SIFAT....... Servants in Faith and Technology (EA)
SIFC .... Saskatchewan Indian Federated College [*University of Regina*]
SIFC .... Sparks International Official Fan Club (EAIO)
SIFC .... Studi Italiani di Filologia Classica [*A publication*]
SIFCC....... Senate Interstate and Foreign Commerce Committee
SIFCS....... Sideband Intermediate Frequency Communications System (AAG)
SifDeut..... Sifrei Deuteronomy (BJA)
SIFE.......... Sanitation Inspection Fish Establishment [*National Marine Fisheries Service*] (NOAA)
SIFE.......... Students in Free Enterprise [*Bolivar, MO*] (EA)
SIFEA....... Silva Fennica [*A publication*]
SIFF.......... Stock Index Futures Fund
SIF/IFF ..... Selective Identification Feature/Identification Friend or Foe [*Military*] (AFM)
SIFJ .... Saskatchewan Indian Federated College. Journal [*A publication*]
SifNum..... Sifrei Numbers (BJA)
SIFO .... Societa Italiana di Farmacia Ospedaliera [*Italy*]
SIFO .... Svenska Institutet foer Opinionsundersoekningar
Si-Fo-An-Di ... Silica-Forsterite-Anorthite-Diopside [*Lunar geology*]
Si-Fo-Di ... Silica-Forsterite-Diopside [*Lunar geology*]
SIFR .... Simulated Instrument Flight Rules (AAG)
SIFR .... Sun-Improved Frequency Response
SIFT.......... Selected-Ion Flow Tube [*Instrumentation*]
SIFT.......... Share Internal FORTRAN Translator [*Data processing*] (IEEE)
SIFT.......... Simplified Input for Toss [*Data processing*]
SIFT.......... Software Implemented Fault Tolerance [*NASA*]
SIFT.......... Summary of Information on Film and Television [*British*]
SIFTOR..... Sifting of Information for Technology of Reactors [*MIT-AEC study*]
SIFX .... Simulated Installation Fixture (AAG)
SifZut........ Sifrei Zuta (BJA)
SIG........... San Juan-Isla Grande [*Puerto Rico*] [*Airport symbol*] (OAG)
SIG........... San Juan, PR [*Location identifier*] [*FAA*] (FAAL)
SIg........... Secretory Immunoglobin [*Immunology*]
SIG........... Senior Interagency Group [*Federal government*]
SIG........... Senior Interdepartmental Group [*Department of State*]
SIG........... Serum Immune Globulin [*Immunochemistry*]
SIG........... Ship Improvement Guide
Sig........... Sigma. Revue du Centre d'Etudes Linguistiques d'Aix Montpellier [*A publication*]
SIG........... Signa [*Write*] [*Pharmacy*]

SIG............ Signal
SIG............ Signalman [*Navy rating*] [*British*]
SIG............ Signature (AFM)
SIG............ Signetur [*Let It Be Labelled*] [*Pharmacy*]
sig............ Significant
SIG............ Signifying (ROG)
SIG............ Signore [*or Signora*] (EY)
SIG............ Silicon-Insulated Gate
SIG............ Silver-Intensified Gold [*Biological stain*]
SIG............ Silver Ridge Resources, Inc. [*Vancouver Stock Exchange symbol*]
SIG............ Simplicity Is Greatness [*See also GIS*]
SIG............ Simplified Inertial Guidance
SIG............ Society for Integrative Graphology [*Inactive*] (EA)
SIG............ South Ingalls [*Colorado*] [*Seismograph station code, US Geological Survey*] [*Closed*] (SEIS)
SIG............ Southern Indiana Gas & Electric Co. [*NYSE symbol*] (SPSG)
SIG............ Special Interest Group
SIG............ Special Investigative Group [*DoD*]
SIG............ Starfield Image Generator
SIG............ State Implementation Grant
SIG............ Stellar Inertial Guidance Signal
SIg............ Strapdown Inertial Guidance
sIg............ Surface Immunoglobulin [*Immunochemistry*]
SIG............ Sylloge Inscriptionum Graecarum [*A publication*]
SIG............ Three Sigma Market Newspaper Audiences [*Three Sigma Research Center, Inc.*] [*Information service or system*] (CRD)
S-IgA........ Secretory Immunoglobulin A [*Immunology*]
Siga .... Signora [*Madam*] [*Italian*]
SIGAB....... Saigai Igaku [*A publication*]
SIGACT .... Special Interest Group on Automata and Computability Theory (EA)
SIGADA.... Special Interest Group on Ada (EA)
SIG/AH..... Special Interest Group/Arts and Humanities [*of the American Society for Information Science*]
SIG/ALP... Special Interest Group/Automated Language Processing [*American Society for Information Science*]
SIGAP .... Surrey Investigation Group into Aerial Phenomena [*British*]
SIGAPL..... Special Interest Group on APL Programming Language (EA)
SIGARCH ... Special Interest Group for Architecture of Computer Systems (EA)
SIGART .... Special Interest Group on Artificial Intelligence (EA)
SIGBAT .... Signal Battalion [*Army*]
SIG/BC...... Special Interest Group/Biological and Chemical Information Systems [*of the American Society for Information Science*]
SIGBDP .... Special Interest Group for Business Data Processing and Management (EA)
SIGBI .... Soroptimist International of Great Britain and Ireland (EAIO)
SIGBIO ..... Special Interest Group on Biomedical Computing (EA)
SIG/BSS.... Special Interest Group/Behavioral and Social Sciences [*of the American Society for Information Science*]
SIGC.......... Signal Corps [*Later, Communications and Electronics Command*] [*Army*]
SIGCAPH ... Special Interest Group for Computers and the Physically Handicapped (EA)
SIGCAS..... Special Interest Group for Computers and Society (EA)
SIG/CBE... Special Interest Group/Costs, Budgeting, and Economics [*of the American Society for Information Science*]
SIGCEN .... Signal Center [*Military*] (AABC)
SIGCHI ..... Special Interest Group on Computer and Human Interaction (EA)
SIGCLD .... Significant Clouds [*Aviation*] (FAAC)
SIGCOMM ... Special Interest Group on Data Communication (EA)
SIGCONDR ... Signal Conditioner (MCD)
SIGCOR..... Signal Corps [*Later, Communications and Electronics Command*] [*Army*]
SIGCOSIM ... Special Interest Group on Computer Systems, Installation Management [*Association for Computing Machinery*]
SIGCPR..... Special Interest Group for Computer Personnel Research (EA)
SIG/CR ..... Special Interest Group/Classification Research [*of the American Society for Information Science*]
SIGCS........ Special Interest Group for Computers and Society [*Association for Computing Machinery*] (EA)
SIG CSE .... Special Interest Group for Computer Science Education (EA)
SIGCUE .... Special Interest Group for Computer Uses in Education (EA)
SIG-D........ Simplified Inertial Guidance-Demonstration [*Army*] (RDA)
SIGDA....... Special Interest Group for Design Automation (EA)
SIGDIV ..... Signal Division [*SHAPE*] (NATG)
SIGDOC.... Special Interest Group for Systems Documentation (EA)
SIGE.......... Silicon Germanium
SIGE.......... Societe Internationale de Gastro-Enterologie
SIGEA .... Silvae Genetica [*A publication*]
SIG/ES ...... Special Interest Group/Education for Information Science [*of the American Society for Information Science*]
SIGEX .... Signal Exercise (NATG)
SIGFIDET ... Special Interest Group on File Description and Translation [*Association for Computing Machinery*] [*Later, Special Interest Group on the Management of Data*]

SIG/FIS..... Special Interest Group/Foundations of Information Science [*of the American Society for Information Science*]
SIGGEN.... Signal Generator (IEEE)
SIGGRAPH ... Special Interest Group on Computer Graphics (EA)
Sight & S.... Sight and Sound [*A publication*]
Sight-Sav R ... Sight-Saving Review [*A publication*]
Sight-Sav Rev ... Sight-Saving Review [*A publication*]
SIGI.......... Selective Insurance Group, Incorporated [*Branchville, NJ*] [*NASDAQ symbol*] (NQ)
SIGI .... System for Interactive Guidance and Information [*Computerized career-counseling service offered by the Educational Testing Service*] [*Princeton, NJ*]
SIG/IAC.... Special Interest Group/Information Analysis Centers [*of the American Society for Information Science*]
SIGINT ..... Signal Intelligence [*Military*] (AABC)
SIGIR .... Special Interest Group on Information Retrieval (EA)
SIGIRD ..... Systeme Integre de Gestion Informatise des Ressources Documentaires [*Integrated System for the Management of Documentary Resources*] [*University of Quebec, Montreal*] [*Information service or system*] (IID)
SIG/ISE .... Special Interest Group/Information Services to Education [*of the American Society for Information Science*]
Sig L.......... Signal Lieutenant [*British military*] (DMA)
SIG/LA...... Special Interest Group/Library Automation and Networks [*of the American Society for Information Science*]
SIGLASH ... Special Interest Group on Language Analysis and Studies in the Humanities [*Association for Computing Machinery*]
SIGLE .... System for Information on Grey Literature in Europe [*European Association for Grey Literature Exploitation*] [*Commission of the European Communities*] [*Information service or system*] (IID)
SIGLEX..... Special Interest Group on Lexicography [*National Security Agency*]
SIGLINT... Signal Intelligence [*US surveillance satellite*]
Siglo Med .. Siglo Medico [*A publication*]
SIGM......... Sigma Designs, Inc. [*Fremont, CA*] [*NASDAQ symbol*] (NQ)
SIGM......... Syndicat International des Gens de Mer du Canada
SIGMA...... Sealed Insulating Glass Manufacturers Association (EA)
SIGMA...... Site Information Generation and Material Accountability Plan [*Army*] (AABC)
SIGMA...... Society of In-Plant Graphics Management Associations
SIGMA...... Society of Independent Gasoline Marketers of America [*Washington, DC*] (EA)
SIGMA...... Society of Inventors of Games and Mathematical Attractions [*British*]
SIGMA...... Standardized Inertial Guidance Multiple Application
SIGMALOG ... Simulation and Gaming Method for Analysis of Logistics [*Army*]
SIGMAP ... Special Interest Group for Mathematical Programming (EA)
SIGMAS ... Signal Measurement and Analysis System
Sigma Ser Pure Math ... Sigma Series in Pure Mathematics [*A publication*]
SIGMET ... Significant Meteorological Information [*Aviation*] (FAAC)
SIGMETRICS ... Special Interest Group on Measurement and Evaluation (EA)
SIGMICRO ... Special Interest Group on Microprogramming and Microarchitecture (EA)
SIGMINI .. Special Interest Group on Minicomputers [*Later, SIGSMALL*] [*Association for Computing Machinery*] (CSR)
SIGMN...... Signalman
sigmo.......... Sigmoidoscopy [*Medicine*]
SIGMOD .. Special Interest Group on Management of Data (EA)
SIGN .... Plasti-Line, Inc. [*NASDAQ symbol*] (NQ)
SIGN .... Signa [*Label*] [*Pharmacy*] (ROG)
SIGN .... Strapdown Inertial Guidance and Navigation (MCD)
SIGNA...... Signora [*Madam*] [*Italian*] (ROG)
Signa........ Signorina [*Miss*] [*Italian*]
SIGNA...... Species Iris Group of North America (EA)
Signalmans J ... Signalman's Journal [*A publication*]
Signal Process ... Signal Processing [*A publication*]
SIGNCE.... Significance (ROG)
SIGNE...... Signature
SIGNET ... Signal Network
SIGNF ...... Signify (ROG)
Sign Lang Stud ... Sign Language Studies [*A publication*]
SIGN N P .. Signetur Nomine Proprio [*Let It Be Written Upon with the Proper Name*] [*Pharmacy*] (ROG)
Signor de Homod ... Signorolus de Homodeis de Mediolano [*Flourished, 14th-15th century*] [*Authority cited in pre-1607 legal work*] (DSA)
SIG/NPM ... Special Interest Group/Nonprint Media [*of the American Society for Information Science*]
SIGNRE.... Signature (ROG)
Signs J Women Cult Soc ... Signs; Journal of Women in Culture and Society [*A publication*]
SIGNUM .. Special Interest Group on Numerical Control [*Military*]
SIGNUM .. Special Interest Group on Numerical Mathematics (EA)
SIGO .... Signal Officer
Sigo .... Signorolus de Homodeis de Mediolano [*Flourished, 14th-15th century*] [*Authority cited in pre-1607 legal work*] (DSA)
SIGOA....... Special Interest Group on Office Automation [*Later, SIGOIS*]
SIGOIS...... Special Interest Group on Office Information Systems (EA)

SIGOP....... Signal Optimization Program [*Federal Highway Administration*]
SIGOPS.... Special Interest Group on Operating Systems (EA)
SIGP.......... Bicoastal Corp. [*NASDAQ symbol*] (NQ)
SIGPC .... Special Interest Group on Personal Computing [*Association for Computing Machinery*]
SIGPLAN ... Special Interest Group on Programming Languages (EA)
SIGPRAD ... Special Interest Group on Phobias and Related Anxiety Disorders (EA)
SIGR.......... Sigma Research, Inc. [*NASDAQ symbol*] (NQ)
SIGRAM ... Sound Intensity Diagram (MCD)
SIGREAL ... Special Interest Group on Real Time Processing [*Association for Computing Machinery*]
SIG/RT...... Special Interest Group/Reprographic Technology [*of the American Society for Information Science*]
SIGS .... Sandia Interactive Graphics System
SIGS .... Simplified Inertial Guidance System (MCD)
SIGS .... Stellar Inertial Guidance System [*Air Force*] (AAG)
SIGSAC.... Special Interest Group on Security, Audit, and Control (EA)
SIGSAM ... Special Interest Group for Symbolic and Algebraic Manipulation (EA)
SIGSCSA .. Special Interest Group on Small Computing Systems and Applications [*Later, SIGSMALL*] [*Association for Computing Machinery*] (EA)
SIG/SDI .... Special Interest Group/Selective Dissemination of Information [*American Society for Information Science*]
SIGSEC..... Signal Security [*Military*] (AABC)
SIGSIM.... Special Interest Group on Simulation (EA)
SIGSMALL ... Special Interest Group on Small Computing Systems and Applications [*Formerly, SIGSCSA*] [*Association for Computing Machinery*] (EA)
SIGSOC .... Special Interest Group on Social and Behavioral Science Computing [*Association for Computing Machinery*]
SIGSOFT .. Special Interest Group on Software Engineering (EA)
SIGSOP..... Signals Operator (ADA)
SIGSPAC.. Special Interest Group on Urban Data Systems, Planning, Architecture, and Civil Engineering [*Association for Computing Machinery*]
SIGSPACE ... Senior Interagency Group (Space)
SIGSPCSA ... Special Interest Group on Small and Personal Computing Systems Applications (EA)
Sig Sta........ Signal Station [*Nautical charts*]
SIGSTN ... Signal Station [*Navigation*]
SIGTRAN ... Special Interest Group on Translation [*National Security Agency*]
SIGTTO .... Society of International Gas Tanker and Terminal Operators [*London, England*] (EAIO)
SIGUCCS ... Special Interest Group for University and College Computing Services (EA)
Sigurnost Rudn ... Sigurnost u Rudnicima [*A publication*]
SIGVOICE... Special Interest Group on Voice [*National Security Agency*]
SIGZA .... Showa Igakkai Zasshi [*A publication*]
SIH .... Schweizerisches Institut fuer Hauswirtschaft
SIH .... Scinde Irregular Horse [*British military*] (DMA)
SIH .... Seafarers and International House (EA)
SIH .... Silgarhi Doti [*Nepal*] [*Airport symbol*] (OAG)
SIH .... Societe Internationale d'Hematologie [*International Society of Hematology - ISH*] [*Buenos Aires, Argentina*] (EA)
SIH .... Society for Italic Handwriting (EA)
SIH .... South Irish Horse [*British military*] (DMA)
SIH .... Studies in the Humanities [*A publication*]
SIH .... Sun Ice Ltd. [*Toronto Stock Exchange symbol*]
SIH .... Superstar Ice Hockey [*Computer game*]
SIHAG ...... Experimental Farm, Agriculture Canada [*Ferme Experimentale, Agriculture Canada*], Indian Head, Saskatchewan [*Library symbol*] [*National Library of Canada*] (BIB)
SIHED....... Sanitaer-Installateur und Heizungsbauer [*A publication*]
SIHR.......... Supervisory Inventory on Human Relations [*Test*]
SIHS.......... SI Handling Systems, Inc. [*NASDAQ symbol*] (NQ)
SIHS.......... Society for Italian Historical Studies (EA)
SIHT.......... Space Impact Hand Tool [*NASA*]
SIHW .... Society for Italic Handwriting (EA)
SII .... School Interest Inventory [*Psychology*]
SII .... Security-Insecurity Inventory [*Psychology*]
SII .... Self-Interview Inventory [*Psychology*]
SII .... Short Interval Identification
SII .... Sitkinak Island [*Alaska*] [*Seismograph station code, US Geological Survey*] (SEIS)
SII .... Smith International, Incorporated [*NYSE symbol*] (SPSG)
SII .... Space Industries, Incorporated
SII .... Special Interest Items (MCD)
SII .... Standard Identification for Individuals [*Social security*] [*American National Standards Institute*]
SII .... Statement of Intelligence Interest [*Army*] (RDA)
SII .... Structural Impediments Initiative [*US-Japan trade negotiations*]
SII .... Sugar Information, Incorporated [*Defunct*] (EA)
SII .... Supervisory Immigrant Inspector [*Immigration and Naturalization Service*]
SIIA .... Self-Insurance Institute of America (EA)

SIIAEC...... Secretariat International des Ingenieurs, des Agronomes, et des Cadres Economiques Catholiques [*International Secretariat of Catholic Technologists, Agriculturists, and Economists*] [*Paris, France*]   (EAIO)
SIIC .... Secretariat International des Groupements Professionnels des Industries Chimiques des Pays de la CEE
SIIC .... Smith International, Inc. [*NASDAQ symbol*]   (NQ)
SIIC .... Special Interest Item Code [*Military*]   (AABC)
SIIFT........ Sociedad Internacional de Ingenieros Forestales Tropicales [*International Society of Tropical Foresters*]   (EAIO)
SIINA .... Silicates Industriels [*Belgium*] [*A publication*]
SIINC .... Scientific Instrumentation Information Network and Curricula [*National Science Foundation*]
SIIR .... Spares Item Inventory Record   (MCD)
SIIRS........ Smithsonian Institution Information Retrieval System   (DIT)
SIJ .... Minneapolis, MN [*Location identifier*] [*FAA*]   (FAAL)
SIJ .... Sacroiliac Joint
SIJ .... Siglufjordur [*Iceland*] [*Airport symbol*]   (OAG)
SIJ .... Small Industry Journal [*Quezon City*] [*A publication*]
SIJADEP .. International Secretariat of Jurists for an Amnesty and Democracy in Paraguay [*Paris, France*]   (EAIO)
SIK .... Sikeston, MO [*Location identifier*] [*FAA*]   (FAAL)
SIK............ Silknit Ltd. [*Toronto Stock Exchange symbol*]
SiK............ Single Income, Kids [*Lifestyle classification*]
SIK............ Studi Italici (Kyoto) [*A publication*]
SiK .... Sztuka i Krytyka [*A publication*]
Sikh R .... Sikh Review [*Calcutta*] [*A publication*]
SIKTA .... Silikaty [*A publication*]
SIL............ Ile a la Crosse Public Library, Saskatchewan [*Library symbol*] [*National Library of Canada*]   (NLC)
SIL............ Safety Information Letter   (IEEE)
SIL............ Scanner Input Language
SIL............ Schedule Interface Log
SIL............ Schools/Industry Link [*Australia*]
SIL............ SCN [*Stock Control Number*] Index and Log
SIL............ Selected Item List
SIL............ Semiconductor Injector LASER
SIL............ Seriously Ill List [*Military*]
SIL............ Service Information Letter
SIL............ Silcorp Ltd. [*Toronto Stock Exchange symbol*]
SIL............ Silence   (MSA)
SIL............ Silicate
SIL............ Silicon Systems, Inc. [*NYSE symbol*]   (SPSG)
Sil............. Silius Italicus [*First century AD*] [*Classical studies*]   (OCD)
SIL............ Sillimanite [*Mineralogy*]
SIL............ Silurian [*Period, era, or system*] [*Geology*]
SIL............ Silver   (AAG)
Sil............. Silver Tax Division (Internal Revenue Bulletin) [*A publication*]   (DLA)
Sil............. Silvester Godinho [*Deceased, 1244*] [*Authority cited in pre-1607 legal work*]   (DSA)
SIL............ Singapore Islands Line   (DS)
SIL............ Slidel, LA [*Location identifier*] [*FAA*]   (FAAL)
SIL............ Smithsonian Institution Information Leaflets
SIL............ Smithsonian Institution Libraries
SIL............ SNOBOL Implementation Language Reimplemented [*1974*] [*Data processing*]   (CSR)
SIL............ Societas Internationalis Limnologiae Theoreticae et Applicae [*International Association of Theoretical and Applied Limnology*]
SIL............ Societe Internationale de la Lepre [*International Leprosy Association*]
SIL............ Society for Individual Liberty   (EA)
SIL............ Sound Intensity Level
SIL............ Sound Interference Level [*NASA*]   (NASA)
SIL............ Special Import License [*Sri Lanka*]   (IMH)
SIL............ Special Interest Launch [*Military*]   (AFIT)
SIL............ Specific Individual Licence [*Importing*] [*British*]   (DS)
SIL............ Speech Interference Level
SIL............ Squamous Intraepithelial Lesion [*Medicine*]
SIL............ Steam Isolation Line   (IEEE)
SIL............ Store Interface Link
SIL............ Studies in Linguistics [*A publication*]
SIL............ Summer Institute of Linguistics
SIL............ Supply Information Letter   (MCD)
SIL............ Support Items List   (MCD)
SIL............ Surge Impedance Loading
SIL............ System Implementation Language [*Data processing*]
SIL............ Systems Integration Laboratory [*NASA*]   (MCD)
SILA.......... Scientific Laboratories, Inc. [*NASDAQ symbol*]   (NQ)
SILAD .... Siderurgia Latinoamericana [*A publication*]
SILAF........ Sindacato Italiano Lavoratori Appalti Ferroviari [*Italian Union of Railroad Contract Workers*]
SILAP........ Sindacato Nazionale Dipendenti Ministero del Lavori Pubblici [*National Union of Employees in the Ministry of Public Welfare*] [*Italy*]
SILAT........ Society for Iberian and Latin American Thought   (EA)
SILAT........ Subionospheric Latitude
SILCA .... Sindacato Italiano Lavoratori Cappellai ed Affini [*Italian Federation of Hat and Allied Workers*]

Sil (Ct of Ap) ... Silvernail's New York Court of Appeals Reports [*A publication*]   (DLA)
Silent Pic.... Silent Picture [*A publication*]
SILF.......... Societe Internationale de Linguistique Fonctionelle [*International Society of Functional Linguistics*]   (EAIO)
SILG .... Silencing   (MSA)
SILI .... Siliconix, Inc. [*NASDAQ symbol*]   (NQ)
SILI .... Sindacato Nazionale Lavoratori Italcable [*National Union of Cable Workers*] [*Italy*]
SILI .... Standard Item Location Index
SILICA...... System for International Literature Information on Ceramics and Glass [*Fachinformationszentrum Werkstoffe*] [*Database*]
Silicates Indus ... Silicates Industriels [*A publication*]
Silik.......... Silikaty [*A publication*]
SILK .... Silk, Silk, Silk International, Inc. [*NASDAQ symbol*]   (NQ)
Silk Rayon Ind India ... Silk and Rayon Industries of India [*A publication*]
Silkworm Inf Bull ... Silkworm Information Bulletin [*A publication*]
Sill Comp ... Sill on Composition in Bankruptcy [*A publication*]   (DLA)
Silliman J .. Silliman Journal [*A publication*]
S Ill ULJ.... Southern Illinois University. Law Journal [*A publication*]
SILM .... Single In-Line Module [*Data processing*]
SILMOD... Silhouette Model [*Military*]   (INF)
SILN .... Silicon General, Inc. [*NASDAQ symbol*]   (NQ)
SILO .... Security Intelligence Liaison Office [*Central Mediterranean Forces*] [*Navy*]
SILON...... Subionospheric Longitude
SILOP .... Studies in Linguistics. Occasional Papers [*A publication*]
SILP.......... Section of International Law and Practice   (EA)
SILP.......... Sindacato Italiano Lavoratori del Petrolio [*Italian Union of Oil Workers*]
SILP.......... Sindacato Italiano Lavoratori Postelegrafonici [*Italian Union of Postal and Telegraph Workers*]
SILPWS .... Sheet Iron and Light Plate Workers' Society [*A union*] [*British*]
SILS.......... Shipboard Impact Locator System
SILS.......... Shipley-Institute of Living Scale for Measuring Intellectual Impairment [*Psychology*]
SILS.......... Silver Solder
SILSP .... Safeguard Integrated Logistics Support Plan [*Army*]   (AABC)
Sil (Sup Ct) ... Silvernail's New York Supreme Court Reports [*A publication*]   (DLA)
SILT .... Stored Information Loss Tree
SILTA........ Studi Italiani di Linguistica Teorica ed Applicata [*A publication*]
SILTE....... Sindacato Italiano Lavoratori Telecomunicazioni [*Italian Union of Telecommunications Workers*]
SILTF .... System Integration Laboratory and Test Facility
SILTS .... Shuttle Infrared Leeside Temperature Sensing [*NASA*]   (NASA)
SILTS .... Sindacato Italiano Lavoratori Telefoni di Stato [*Italian Union of Government Telephone Workers*]
SILULAP .. Sindacato Italiano Lavoratori Uffici Locali ed Agenzie Postelegrafonici [*Italian Union of Local Post and Telegraph Office Workers*]
Silv .... Silvae [*of Statius*] [*Classical studies*]   (OCD)
SILV .... Silver   (ROG)
SILV .... Silver King Mines, Inc. [*NASDAQ symbol*]   (NQ)
Silv .... Silvernail's New York Criminal Reports [*9-14 New York*] [*A publication*]   (DLA)
Silv .... Silvernail's New York Reports [*1886-92*] [*A publication*]   (DLA)
Silv .... Silvernail's New York Supreme Court Reports [*1889-90*] [*A publication*]   (DLA)
Silv A .... Silvernail's New York Court of Appeals Reports [*A publication*]   (DLA)
Silvaecult Trop Subtrop ... Silvaecultura Tropica et Subtropica [*A publication*]
Silvae Genet ... Silvae Genetica [*A publication*]
Silva Fenn ... Silva Fennica [*A publication*]
Silv App ..... Silvernail's New York Court of Appeals Reports [*A publication*]   (DLA)
Silv Cit .... Silvernail's New York Citations [*A publication*]   (DLA)
Silv Ct App ... Silvernail's New York Court of Appeals Reports [*A publication*]   (DLA)
Silv Ct App (NY) ... Silvernail's New York Court of Appeals Reports [*A publication*]   (DLA)
Silve .... Silvester Godinho [*Deceased, 1244*] [*Authority cited in pre-1607 legal work*]   (DSA)
Silver Inst Lett ... Silver Institute Letter [*A publication*]
Silvernail's NY Rep ... Silvernail's New York Court of Appeals Reports [*A publication*]   (DLA)
SILVIC...... Silviculture
Silvic Sao Paulo ... Silvicultura em Sao Paulo [*A publication*]
Silv Notes Ont Dep Lds For ... Silvicultural Notes. Ontario Department of Lands and Forests [*A publication*]
Silvr........... Silvester Godinho [*Deceased, 1244*] [*Authority cited in pre-1607 legal work*]   (DSA)
Silv Res Note (Tanz) ... Silviculture Research Note (Tanzania) [*A publication*]
Silv Sup...... Silvernail's New York Supreme Court Reports [*A publication*]   (DLA)
Silv (Sup Ct) ... Silvernail's New York Supreme Court Reports [*A publication*]   (DLA)
Silv Unrep ... Silvernail's New York Unreported Cases [*A publication*]   (DLA)

SIM............ SACLANT [Supreme Allied Commander, Atlantic] Staff Instruction Manual　(NATG)
SIM............ Scanning Ion Microscope
SIM............ School of Industrial Management [MIT]　(MCD)
SIM............ Scientific Instrument Module [NASA]
SIM............ Sclerite-Inducing Membrane [Entomology]
SIM............ Selected Inventory Management [Military]　(CAAL)
SIM............ Selected Ion Monitoring [Chromatography]
SIM............ Selected Item Management
SIM............ Sequential Inference Machine [Data processing]
SIM............ Sergeant Instructor of Musketry
SIM............ Service Instructions Message [Telecommunications]　(TEL)
SIM............ Service International de Microfilm, Paris, France [Library symbol] [Library of Congress]　(LCLS)
SIM............ Servicio Intelligencia Militar [Military Intelligence Service] [Dominican Republic]
SIM............ Servizio Informazioni Militare [Military Intelligence Service] [Italy]
SIM............ Set Interrupt Mask [Data processing]
SIM............ Shima Resources [Vancouver Stock Exchange symbol]
SIMD......... Ship Instrumentation Manager
SIM............ Simbai [Papua New Guinea] [Airport symbol]　(OAG)
SIM............ Simferopol [USSR] [Seismograph station code, US Geological Survey]　(SEIS)
SIM............ Similar　(AAG)
SIM............ Simile [In a Similar Manner] [Music]
Sim............ Simmons' Reports [95-97, 99 Wisconsin] [A publication]
Sim............ Simons' English Chancery Reports [57-60 English Reprint] [1826-50] [A publication]　(DLA)
SIM............ Simplex
SIM............ Simposio Internacional de Macromoleculas [International Symposium on Macromolecules]
SIM............ Simulated [or Simulation]　(AABC)
SIM............ Simulator [Data processing]
SIM............ Small Intestine Metaplasia [Medicine]
SIM............ Societa Italiana di Metapsichica [Italy]
SIM............ Societe Internationale de la Moselle [International Moselle Company]
SIM............ Societe Internationale de Musicologie [International Musicological Society]
SIM............ Society for Industrial Microbiology　(EA)
SIM............ Society for Information Management [Chicago, IL]　(EA)
SIM............ Solar Interplanetary Model
SIM............ Somali Islamic Movement [Political party]
SIM............ Space Interceptor Missile　(MCD)
SIM............ Stage Inert Mass
SIM............ Standard Injection Method [Laboratory science]
SIM............ Steatite Insulation Material
SIMCOR...... Stellar Image Monitor
SIM............ Student Interracial Ministry [Defunct]
SIM............ Submarine Intended Movement　(NVT)
SIM............ Subsystem Interface Module
SIML......... Subtotal Integration Mode
SIM............ Sucrose-Isomaltose Deficiency [Medicine]
SIM............ Sudan Interior Mission
SIM............ Sulfide Production, Indole Production, and Motility [Growth medium]
SIM............ Surveillance Intelligence and Reconnaissance Mission [Military]　(CAAL)
SIM............ Synchronous Interface Module
SIM............ Systems Integration Model　(MCD)
SIMA........ Salon International de la Machine Agricole
SIMA........ Scientific Instrument Manufacturers' Association [British]
SIMA........ Shore Intermediate Maintenance Activity [Navy]　(NVT)
SIMA........ Steel Industry Management Association [Trade union] [British]
SIMA........ Studies in Mediterranean Archaeology [A publication]
SIMAC...... Sonic Instrument Measurement and Control　(AAG)
SIMAJ....... Scientific Instrument Manufacturers' Association of Japan
SIMArsbok ... Svenska Israels-Missionens Arsbok [Stockholm] [A publication]
SIMAS ...... Shuttle Information Management Accountability System [NASA]　(NASA)
SIMAS ...... SONAR In-Situ Mode Assessment System　(MSC)
SIMATS.... Supplementary Interim Medium Antitank System [Army]　(INF)
SIMBAD ... Simulation as a Basis for Social Agents' Decisions [Data processing]
SIMBAY ... Scientific Instrumentation Module Bay [NASA]　(KSC)
SIMC........ Silicon Integrated Monolithic Circuit
Sim & C...... Simmons and Conover's Reports [99-100 Wisconsin] [A publication]　(DLA)
SIMC........ Societe Internationale de Medecine de Catastrophe [International Society for Disaster Medicine - ISDM]　(EA)
SIMC........ Societe Internationale de Medecine Cybernetique [International Society of Cybernetic Medicine]
SIMC........ Societe Internationale pour la Musique Contemporaine [International Society for Contemporary Music]
SIMC........ Syndicat International des Marins Canadiens [Seafarers' International Union of Canada - SIU]

SIMCA...... Societe Industrielle de Mecanique et de Carrosserie Automobile [French automobile manufacturer; acronym used as name of its cars]
SIMCA...... Soft Independent Modeling of Class Analogy [Analytical chemistry technique]
SIMCANSOC ... Simulated Canadian Society [Simulation game]
SIMCAP.... Simulation, Corps Automated Procedures　(MCD)
SIMCE ...... Simulation Communications Electronics [Group of computer programs] [Army]
SIMCEN ... Simulation Center [Deep Space Network, NASA]
SIMCERT ... Simulator Certification
SIMCHE... Simulation and Checkout Equipment [NASA]　(KSC)
SIMCO...... Sea Ice Microbial Colony
SIMCOM ... Simulation Complex　(NASA)
SIMCOM ... Simulation and Computer [Data processing]
SIMCOM ... Simulator Compiler [Computer]
SIMCON... Scientific Inventory Management and Control
SIMCON... Simplified Control
SIMCON... Simulation Controller
Sim Ct M ... Simmons on Courts-Martial [A publication]　(DLA)
SIMD........ Single Instruction, Multiple Data　(IEEE)
SIMDEP... Simulation Development Program [DASA]
Sim Des Pat ... Simonds' Law of Design Patents [A publication]　(DLA)
Sim Dig ...... Simmons' Wisconsin Digest [A publication]　(DLA)
Sim Dig Pat Dec ... Simonds' Digest of Patent Office Decisions [United States] [A publication]　(DLA)
SIME........ Security Intelligence, Middle East [Navy]
SIME........ Studies in Mechanical Engineering [Elsevier Book Series] [A publication]
Sim Elect.... Simeon on Elections [A publication]　(DLA)
Sim (Eng)... Simons' English Chancery Reports [57-60 English Reprint] [A publication]　(DLA)
Simes & S Future Interests ... Simes and Smith on the Law of Future Interests [A publication]　(DLA)
SIMEX ...... Secondary Item Materiel Excess [DoD]
SIMEX ...... Singapore International Monetary Exchange
SIMFAC.... Simulation Facility [NASA]
SIMFAR.... Simulated Frequency Analysis and Recording　(MCD)
SIMFIRE .. Simulated Fire
SIMFIRE... Simulated Mission Firing
SIMG........ Sammelbaende. Internationale Musik Gesellschaft [A publication]
SIMG........ Societas Internationalis Medicinae Generalis [International Society of General Practice] [Klagenfurt, Austria]　(EAIO)
SIMGCA.... Similarity Graft Clustering Analysis [Plant phylogeny]
SIMHA ..... Societe Internationale de Mycologie Humaine et Animale [International Society for Human and Animal Mycology - ISHAM] [London, England]　(EA)
SIMI......... Scientific Imaging Instruments, Inc. [NASDAQ symbol]　(NQ)
SIMICOR ... Simultaneous Multiple Image Correlation
SIMILE..... Simulator of Immediate Memory in Learning Experiments
Sim Int ...... Simons' Law of Interpleader [A publication]　(DLA)
SIMJA....... Singapore Medical Journal [A publication]
SIML........ Similar　(AAG)
Simla......... All India Reporter, Simla [1951] [A publication]　(DLA)
SIMLR...... Similar　(ROG)
SIMM........ Simmons Airlines, Inc. [Chicago, IL] [NASDAQ symbol]　(NQ)
SIMM........ Single In-Line Memory Module [Data processing]
SIMM........ Studies in Indo-Muslim Mysticism [A publication]
SIMM........ Symbolic Integrated Maintenance Manual　(MCD)
SIMNET.... Simulation Network
Sim NS...... Simons' English Vice-Chancery Reports, New Series [61 English Reprint] [A publication]　(DLA)
SIMNS ...... Simulated Navigation Systems
Sim NS (Eng) ... Simons' English Vice-Chancery Reports, New Series [61 English Reprint] [A publication]　(DLA)
Simo.......... [Jacobus] Simonetta [Deceased, 1539] [Authority cited in pre-1607 legal work]　(DSA)
SIMO .... Simultaneously　(NASA)
SIMO .... Special Items Management Office
SIMOBS.... Simultaneous Observations [RADAR and optical]
SIMOC...... Simulated Occupant [People Machine] [Office of Civil Defense]
Simon....... [Jacobus] Simonetta [Deceased, 1539] [Authority cited in pre-1607 legal work]　(DSA)
Simon........ Simonides [Fifth century BC] [Classical studies]　(OCD)
Simon's TC ... Simon's Tax Cases [United Kingdom] [A publication]　(DLA)
Simon's Town Hist Soc ... Simon's Town Historical Society [A publication]
SIMOP...... Simultaneous Operation
SIMOS...... Space Imbalanced Military Occupational Specialty
SIMOX...... Separation by Implantation of Oxygen [Semiconductor technology]
SIMP........ Satellite Information Message Protocol
SIMP........ Shipboard Integrated Maintenance Program [Navy]　(NG)
SIMP........ Simpleton　(DSUE)
Simp.......... Single Income, Money Problems [Lifestyle classification]
SIMP........ Societa Italiana di Medicina Psicosomatica [Italy]
SIMP........ Specific Impulse　(MSA)
SIMPA ...... Rendiconti. Societa Italiana di Mineralogia e Petrologia [A publication]
SIMPAC..... Simplified Programming for Acquisition and Control　(IEEE)

SIMPAC.... Simulation Package [*Data processing*]
Sim Pat L... Simond's Patent Law [*A publication*]   (DLA)
Simp Inf...... Simpson on Infants [*4th ed.*] [*1926*] [*A publication*]   (DLA)
SIMPL...... Simulation Implementation Machine Programming
Languages   (KSC)
SIMPL/1... Simulation Language Based on Programming Language,
Version One
SIMPLAN ... Simple Modeling and Planning [*SIMPLAN Users Group*] [*New
York, NY*]   (CSR)
SIMPLAN ... Simplified Modeling and Planning [*Programming language*]
[*1973*]   (CSR)
SIMPLE.... Semi-Implicit Pressure-Linked Equation [*Algorithm*]
SIMPLE.... Simulation of Industrial Management Problems [*Program*]
[*1958*] [*Data processing*]   (CSR)
SIMPLE.... Solver for Implicit Equations [*Computer language*]
SIMPLE.... System for Integrated Maintenance and Program Language
Extension
SIMPO...... Simulation of Personnel Operations [*Army Research Institute
for the Behavioral and Social Sciences*]   (RDA)
Simp Otlalennoi Gibrid Rast ... Simpozium po Otlalennoi Gibridizatsii
Rastenii [*A publication*]
SIMPP...... Simple Image-Processing Package   (BYTE)
SIMPP....... Society of Independent Motion Picture Producers
SIMPU ...... Simulation Punch
SIMR......... Schenley Instant Market Reports
SIMR .... Simulator   (AAG)
SIMR .... Societe Internationale de Mecanique des Roches [*International
Society for Rock Mechanics - ISRM*]   (EAIO)
SIMR .... Systems Integration Management Review [*NASA*]   (MCD)
SIMRAND ... Simulation of Research and Development
SIMRDU... Survey of Immunologic Research [*A publication*]
Sim Ry Acc ... Simon's Law Relating to Railway Accidents [*1862*] [*A
publication*]   (DLA)
SIMS .... Scandinavian Simulation Society [*Also, SSS*]   (EAIO)
SIMS .... Secondary Ion Mass Spectrometry [*or Spectroscopy*]
SIMS .... Sedna Information Management System [*Sedna Corp.*]
[*Information service or system*]   (IID)
SIMS .... Selected Item Management System [*Military*]   (AABC)
SIMS .... Selective Interference Modulation Spectrometer
SIMS .... Shuttle Imaging Microwave System [*NASA*]   (NASA)
SIMS .... Shuttle Inventory Management System [*NASA*]   (NASA)
SIMS .... SIAM [*Society for Industrial and Applied Mathematics*]
Institute for Mathematics and Society
Sim & S...... Simons and Stuart's English Chancery Reports [*57 English
Reprint*] [*A publication*]   (DLA)
SIMS .... Single Item, Multisource   (IEEE)
SIMS .... Skandinaviska Simuleringssaellskapet [*Scandinavian
Simulation Society*]   (EA)
SIMS .... Societal Institute of the Mathematical Sciences [*Research
center*]   (RCD)
SIMS .... Stable Isotope Mass Spectrometer
SIMS .... Stellar Inertial Measurement System [*NASA*]
SIMS .... Strategic Integrated Management System [*American
Occupational Therapy Association*]
SIMS .... Students' International Meditation Society
SiMS......... Studier i Modern Sprakvetenskap [*A publication*]
SIMS .... Symbolic Integrated Maintenance System
SIMSA ...... Savings Institutions Marketing Society of America
SIMSCRIPT ... [*A*] simulation programming language [*1963*] [*Data
processing*]
SIMSEP .... Simulation of Solar Electric Propulsion [*NASA*]
SIMSI....... Selective Inventory Management of Secondary Items [*Navy*]
SIMSIN..... Simulated Strapdown Inertial Navigation   (MCD)
SIMSLIN .. Safety in Mines Scattered Light Instrument   (ADA)
SIMSOC ... Simulated Society
Sim & St..... Simons and Stuart's English Chancery Reports [*57 English
Reprint*] [*A publication*]   (DLA)
SIMSTF .... Societe Internationale de Mecanique des Sols et de Travaux de
Fondations [*International Society for Soil Mechanics and
Foundation Engineering - ISSMFE*]
Sim & Stu... Simons and Stuart's English Vice-Chancery Reports [*57 English
Reprint*] [*A publication*]   (DLA)
Sim & Stu (Eng) ... Simons and Stuart's English Chancery Reports [*57 English
Reprint*] [*A publication*]   (DLA)
SIMSUP.... Simulation Supervisor
SIMS-X ..... Selected Items Management System - Expanded   (MCD)
SIMSYS ... Simulated System   (CAAL)
SIMTOS ... Simulated Tactical Operations Systems [*Army*]   (RDA)
SIMTRACC ... Simulator Trainer Command and Control
SIMTS....... Scientific Instrument Makers Trade Society [*A union*] [*British*]
SIMU...... Simulated Inertial Measurement Unit   (NASA)
SIMUA...... Simulation [*A publication*]
SIMUL...... Simultaneous   (AABC)
SIMULA ... Simulation Language [*1964*] [*Data processing*]
Simulat Gam ... Simulation and Games [*A publication*]
Simulat & Games ... Simulation and Games [*A publication*]
Simulations Councils Proc ... Simulations Councils. Proceedings [*A
publication*]
Simul Counc Proc Ser ... Simulation Councils. Proceedings Series [*A
publication*]
Simul and Games ... Simulation and Games [*A publication*]

Simul Games Learn ... Simulation/Games for Learning [*A publication*]
SIMUPOL ... Simulative Procedure Oriented Language   (MCD)
SIN .... Salpingitis Isthmica Nodosum
SIN .... Scientific Information Notes [*A publication*]
SIN .... Security Information Network
SIN .... Sensitive Information Network
SIN .... Simultaneous Interpenetrating Networks [*Organic chemistry*]
SiN............ Sin Nombre [*A publication*]
SIN .... Sinagawa [*Japan*] [*Seismograph station code, US Geological
Survey*] [*Closed*]   (SEIS)
SIN .... Sinclair Community College, Dayton, OH [*OCLC
symbol*]   (OCLC)
SIN .... Sine [*Mathematics*]
SIN .... Sine [*Without*] [*Latin*]
SIN .... Sinecure   (ROG)
Sin............. Sinemurian [*Geology*]
SIN .... Singapore [*Singapore*] [*Airport symbol*]   (OAG)
SIN .... Single Identifying Number
SIN .... Sinistra [*Left Hand*] [*Music*]
Sin............. Sinter [*Record label*] [*Brazil*]
SIN .... Social Insurance Number [*Canada*]
SIN .... Society for International Numismatics   (EA)
SIN .... Spanish International Network [*Cable-television system*]
SIN .... Stop Inflation Now [*Variation on the anti-inflation WIN slogan
of President Gerald Ford*]
SIN .... Study Item Number [*Army*]   (AABC)
S IN............ Sub Initio [*Towards the Beginning*] [*Latin*]   (ROG)
SIN .... Subject Indication Number
SIN .... Support Information Network
SIN .... Symbolic Integrator
SIN .... Syngold Exploration, Inc. [*Toronto Stock Exchange symbol*]
SIN .... System Integrators, Inc. [*NYSE symbol*]   (SPSG)
SINA......... Scheduling Information Not Available   (KSC)
SINA......... Shellfish Institute of North America [*Also known as Oyster
Growers and Dealers Association of North America*]   (EA)
SINA......... Society for Indecency to Naked Animals [*A hoax association*]
SINACMA ... Sindacato Nazionale Dipendenti Corte dei Conti e Magistrature
Amministrative [*National Union of General Accounting
Office Employees*] [*Italy*]
SINAD...... Signal Plus Noise and Distortion
SINADIMID ... Sindacato Nazionale Dipendenti Ministero Difesa [*National
Union of Ministry of Defense Employees*] [*Italy*]
SINAF .... Sindacato Nazionale Dipendenti Ministero Agricoltura e
Foreste [*National Union of Ministry of Agriculture and
Forestry Employees*] [*Italy*]
Sinai Hosp J ... Sinai Hospital. Journal [*A publication*]
SINAMAI ... Sindacato Nazionale e Dipendenti Ministero Africa Italiana
[*National Union of Former Italian Employees of African
Ministry*] [*Italy*]
SINAMIL ... Sindacato Nazionale Dipendenti Ministero del Lavoro e
Previdenza Sociale [*National Union of Ministry of Labor
and Social Security Employees*] [*Italy*]
SINAMN... Sindacato Nazionale Dipendenti Marina Mercantile [*National
Union of Merchant Marine Workers*] [*Italy*]
SINAP....... Satellite Input to Numerical Analysis and Prediction [*National
Weather Service*]
SINAP....... Sinapis [*Mustard*] [*Pharmacology*]   (ROG)
SINAPI..... Sindacato Nazionale Ministero Pubblica Istruzione [*National
Union of Ministry of Public Instructors*] [*Italy*]
SINASCEL ... Sindacato Nazionale Scuola Elementare [*National Union of
Elementary School Teachers*] [*Italy*]
SINB......... Southern Interstate Nuclear Board
SINC......... Nicaraguan International Rescue from Communism   (PD)
SINC......... Seal, Incorporated [*NASDAQ symbol*]   (NQ)
SINCGARS ... Single-Channel Ground and Airborne Radio System [*or
Subsystem*]   (MCD)
SINCGARS-V ... Single-Channel Ground and Airborne Radio System, Very
High Frequency
Sinclair....... Sinclair's Manuscript Decisions, Scotch Session Cases [*A
publication*]   (DLA)
SINCOE.... Sindacato Nazionale Dipendenti Ministero Industria e
Commercio Estero [*National Union of Ministry of
Industry and Foreign Commerce Employees*] [*Italy*]
SINCTRAC ... Single Channel Tactical Radio Communications
[*Army*]   (RDA)
Sind............ All India Reporter, Sind [*1914-50*] [*A publication*]   (DLA)
Sind............ Indian Rulings, Sind Series [*A publication*]   (DLA)
SIND .... Saskatchewan Indian [*A publication*]
SIND .... Satellite Inertial Navigation Determination   (MCD)
SIND .... Southern Indiana Railway, Inc. [*AAR code*]
SIND .... Strobe Intersection Deghoster
SINDAF .... Sindacato Nazionale Dipendenti Amministrazioni Finanziarie
[*National Union of Financial Administration Employees*]
[*Italy*]
SINDB...... Science and Industry [*Karachi*] [*A publication*]
S Ind Stud .. Southern Indian Studies [*A publication*]
Sind Univ Res J Sci Ser ... Sind University Research Journal. Science Series
[*A publication*]
SINE......... Short Interspersed Nucleotide Element [*Genetics*]
Sinema .... Andere Sinema [*A publication*]
Sinet Ethiop J Sci ... Sinet: An Ethiopian Journal of Science [*A publication*]

SIN-ETH...   Swiss Institute of Nuclear Research - Eidgenoessische Technische Hochschule
SINEWS....   Ship Integrated Electronic Warfare System
SINF..........   Sinfonia [*Symphony*] [*Music*]
SINFDOK ..   Statens Rad for Vetenskaplig Information och Dokumentation [*Swedish Council for Scientific Information and Documentation*]   (IID)
SINFUB ....   Skrifter Utgitt. Instituttet foer Nordisk Filologi. Universitetet i Bergen [*A publication*]
SING ....   Singapore
SING ....   Singular
SING ....   Singulorum [*Of Each*] [*Pharmacy*]
SINGAN....   Singularity Analyzer [*Data processing*]
Singapore Bus ...   Singapore Business [*A publication*]
Singapore Dent J ...   Singapore Dental Journal [*A publication*]
Singapore J Phy ...   Singapore Journal of Physics [*A publication*]
Singapore J Primary Ind ...   Singapore Journal of Primary Industries [*A publication*]
Singapore J Trop Geogr ...   Singapore Journal of Tropical Geography [*A publication*]
Singapore Lib ...   Singapore Libraries [*A publication*]
Singapore L Rev ...   Singapore Law Review [*A publication*]
Singapore Med J ...   Singapore Medical Journal [*A publication*]
Singapore MJ ...   Singapore Medical Journal [*A publication*]
Singapore Natl Inst Chem Bull ...   Singapore National Institute of Chemistry. Bulletin [*A publication*]
Singapore Statist Bull ...   Singapore Statistical Bulletin [*A publication*]
Singer Prob Cas (PA) ...   Singer's Probate Cases [*Pennsylvania*] [*A publication*]   (DLA)
Singers ....   Singer's Probate Court [*Pennsylvania*] [*A publication*]   (DLA)
Sing Kir......   Singende Kirche [*A publication*]
Sing LR ......   Singapore Law Review [*A publication*]
Sing Pub Health B ...   Singapore Public Health Bulletin [*A publication*]
SINGR......   Singular
Sing Stat B ...   Singapore Statistical Bulletin [*A publication*]
SINH ....   Sine, Hyperbolic
SINIE ....   Sistema Nacional de Informacion Documental en Educacion [*National System of Documentary Information on Education*] [*Information service or system*]   (IID)
SINIST......   Sinister [*Left*] [*Latin*]
Sinister......   Sinister Wisdom [*A publication*]
Sink..........   Single Income, No Kids [*Lifestyle classification*]
Sin N ....   Sin Nombre [*A publication*]
SIN Newsl ...   SIN [*Schweizerisches Institut fuer Nuklearforschung*] Newsletter [*A publication*]
SIno.............   Thioinosine [*Also, Sno, M*] [*A nucleoside*]
Sino-Am Rels ...   Sino-American Relations [*Taiwan*] [*A publication*]
SINOCHEM ...   China National Chemicals Import & Export Corp. [*People's Republic of China*]   (IMH)
Sinop Odontol ...   Sinopse de Odontologia [*A publication*]
SINR.........   Shoulder Internal Rotation [*Sports medicine*]
SINR.........   Signal to Interference plus Noise Ratio   (MCD)
SINR.........   Swiss Institute for Nuclear Research
SINS ....   Satellite Interceptor Navigation System [*Navy*]   (CAAL)
SINS ....   Ship Inertial Navigational System
SINS ....   Sindacato Scuola non Statale [*Union of Private Schools' Employees*] [*Italy*]
SInstBB ....   Student of the Institute of British Bakers   (DBQ)
SInstPet ....   Student of the Institute of Petroleum [*British*]   (DBQ)
SINSU ....   Skrifter Utgivna. Institutionen foer Nordiska Sprak Vid. Uppsala Universitet [*A publication*]
SINSUU....   Skrifter Utgivna. Institutionen foer Nordiska Sprak Vid. Uppsala Universitet [*A publication*]
S INT ....   Senza Interruzione [*Without Interruption or Pause*] [*Music*]
Sint Almazy ...   Sinteticheskie Almazy [*A publication*]
Sint Anal Strukt Org Soedin ...   Sintez, Analiz, i Struktura Organicheskikh Soedinenii [*USSR*] [*A publication*]
S INTER....   Senza Interruzione [*Without Interruption or Pause*] [*Music*]   (ROG)
Sintesi Econ ...   Sintesi Economica [*A publication*]
Sint Fiz-Khim Polim ...   Sintez i Fiziko-Khimiya Polimerov [*A publication*]
Sint Org Soedin ...   Sintezy Organicheskikh Soedinenij [*A publication*]
SI N VAL...   Si Non Valeat [*If It Is Not Effective*] [*Pharmacy*]   (ROG)
SIO ....   Sacroiliac Orthosis [*Medicine*]
SIO ....   Scripps Institution of Oceanography [*La Jolla, CA*] [*Research center*]
SIO ....   Senior Information Officer   (DCTA)
SIO ....   Senior Intelligence Officer   (MCD)
SIO ....   Serial Input/Output   (MCD)
SIO ....   Ship's Information Officer [*Navy*]
SIO ....   Sindacato Italiano Ostetriche [*Italian Union of Midwives*]
sio..............   Siouan [*MARC language code*] [*Library of Congress*]   (LCCP)
SIO ....   Skidway Institute of Oceanography [*Georgia*]   (NOAA)
SIO ....   Smithton [*Australia*] [*Airport symbol*]   (OAG)
SIO ....   Sorting It Out   (EA)
SIO ....   Southern Union Resources [*Vancouver Stock Exchange symbol*]
SIO ....   Special Inquiry Officer
SIO ....   Special Intelligence Officer [*Military*]   (NVT)
SIO ....   Staged in Orbit
SIO-ETH...   Start Input/Output

SIO ....   Systems Integration Office [*NASA*]   (NASA)
SIOA....   System Input/Output Adapter   (CAAL)
SIOATH....   Source Identification and Ordering Authorization [*DoD*]
SIOBA.......   Sbornik Informatsii po Obogashcheniyu i Briketirovaniyu Uglei [*A publication*]
SIOC..........   Serial Input/Output Channel
SIOD ....   Sindacato Italiano Odonototecnici Diplomati [*Italian Union of Odontotechnicians*]
SIOE.........   Special Issue of Equipment
SIOFC ....   Sparks International Official Fan Club   (EA)
SIOG ....   Societe Internationale d'Ophtalmologie Geographique [*International Society of Geographic Opthalmology*]   (EAIO)
SIOH ....   Supervision, Inspection, and Overhead   (AFM)
SIOMS......   Surface Ionization Organic Mass Spectrometry
SIOP.........   Secure Identification Operating Procedure
SIOP.........   Selector Input/Output Processor [*Data processing*]   (IEEE)
SIOP.........   Single Integrated Operational [*or Operations*] Plan [*Military*]   (AFM)
SIOP.........   Societe Internationale d'Oncologie Pediatrique [*International Society of Pediatric Oncology*] [*Leeds, England*]   (EAIO)
SIOP.........   Strategic Integrated Operational Plan [*Nuclear warfare*]
SIOP-ESI..   Single Integrated Operational Plan - Extremely Sensitive Information [*Security level above Top Secret*]
SI OP SIT ...   Si Opus Sit [*If There Be Occasion*] [*Pharmacy*]   (ROG)
SIOR.........   Society of Industrial and Office Realtors   (EA)
SIOS.........   Spectrophotometer Input-Output System
SIOUX.......   Sequential and Iterative Operation Unit X   (IEEE)
SIP............   Safety Injection Pump   (IEEE)
SIP............   Safety Instrumentation Package   (MCD)
SIP............   Sampling Inspection Procedures
SIP............   Saskatchewan Institute of Pedology [*University of Saskatchewan*] [*Research center*]   (RCD)
SIP............   Satellite Information Processor
SIP............   Satellite Inspector Program   (AAG)
SIP............   Schedule-Induced Polydipsia [*Psychology*]
SIP............   Schedule of Investment Projects
SIP............   Scientific Information [*or Instruction*] Processor [*Honeywell, Inc.*]
SIP............   Scientific Instrument Package [*NASA*]   (KSC)
SIP............   Securities Investor Protection Corp.
SIP............   Selma [*Alabama*] Interreligious Project   (EA)
SIP............   Senior Intensified Program [*Education*]
SIP............   Separation Instrument Package [*NASA*]   (MCD)
SIP............   Sharebuilder Investment Plan [*Banking*]
SIP............   Shinkiari [*Pakistan*] [*Seismograph station code, US Geological Survey*]   (SEIS)
SIP............   Ship Improvement Program
SIP............   Ship in Production
SIP............   Short Interval Plan [*Management principles*]
SIP............   Short Irregular Pulses
SIP............   Sickness Impact Profile [*National Institutes of Health*]
SIP............   Simferopol [*USSR*] [*Airport symbol*]   (OAG)
SIP............   Simulated Input Processor [*Data processing*]
SIP............   Sindacato Italiano Pescatori [*Italian Union of Fishermen*]
SIP............   Single In-Line Package [*Data processing*]
SIP............   Single In-Line PIN [*Data processing*]   (PCM)
SIPA.........   Sipald Resources [*Vancouver Stock Exchange symbol*]
Sip............   Sipario [*A publication*]
SIP............   Sisterhood for International Peace [*Australia*]
SIP............   Skill Improvement Program [*Bureau of Apprenticeship and Training*] [*Department of Labor*]
SIP............   Slow Inhibitory Potential [*Electrophysiology*]
SIP............   Smithsonian Institution Press [*Publisher*]
SIP............   Sociedad Interamericana de Prensa [*Inter-American Press Association*]
SIP............   Sociedad Interamericana de Psicologia [*Interamerican Society of Psychology*]   (EAIO)
SIP............   Societa Italiana per l'Esercizio Telefonico [*Italian Society for Telephone Use*] [*Information service or system*]   (IID)
SIP............   Societe Genevoise d'Instruments de Physique [*Swiss*]
SIP............   Society of Indiana Pioneers   (EA)
SIP............   Society for Invertebrate Pathology   (EA)
SIP............   Society of Israel Philatelists   (EA)
SIP............   Sodium Iron Pyrophosphate [*Inorganic chemistry*]
SIP............   Software Instrumentation Package [*Sperry UNIVAC*] [*Data processing*]
SIP............   Software in Print [*Technique Learning*] [*Information service or system*]   (IID)
SIP............   Solar Instrument Probe   (MUGU)
SIP............   SPALT [*Special Projects Alterations*] Improvement Program
SIP............   Special Impact Program   (OICC)
SIP............   Standard Initial Provisioning System   (MCD)
SIP............   Standard Inspection Procedure [*Military*]
SIP............   Standard Interest Profile
SIP............   Standardization Instructor Pilot [*Military*]   (AABC)
SIP............   State Implementation Plan [*Environmental Protection Agency*]
SIP............   Step in Place
SIP............   Strain Isolator Pad [*Aerospace*]
SIP............   Student Insurance Producers Association   (EA)
SIP............   Studies in Process [*Jet Propulsion Laboratory, NASA*]

SIP	Subject Index to Periodicals [*A publication*]
SIP	Submerged Injection Process [*Steelmaking*]
SIP	Supermolecular Information Processor
SIP	Supersonic Infantry Projectile
SIP	Supplemental Income Plan
SIP	Supply Improvement Program
SIP	Symbolic Input Program [*Data processing*] (BUR)
SIP	Systems Implementation Plan [*Military*]
SIPA	Secondary Item Procurement Appropriation [*Army*]
SIPA	Securities Investor Protection Act [*1970*]
SIPAAP	Escuela Nacional de Agricultura [*Chapingo*]. Serie de Investigaciones [*A publication*]
SIPAG	Syndicat des Instituteurs, Professeurs, et Agents de la Guadeloupe (PD)
SIPAMA	Servico de Inspecao dos Produtos Agropecuarios e Materiais Agricolas [*Brazil*]
SIPB	Safety Injection Permissive Block (IEEE)
SIPC	Securities Investor Protection Corporation [*Government insurance agency for brokerage accounts*] [*Pronounced "sipic"*]
SIPC	Stationing and Installations Planning Committee [*Military*]
SIPCO	Signal Processor Checkout (CAAL)
SIPD	Supply Item Provisioning Document [*Navy*] (NG)
SIPE	Scientific Information Program on Eutrophication [*University of Wisconsin*]
SIPE	Societe Internationale de Psychopathologie de l'Expression [*International Society of Art and Psychopathology*]
SIPES	Society of Independent Professional Earth Scientists (EA)
SIPG	Societe Internationale de Pathologie Geographique [*International Society of Geographical Pathology*] [*Australia*] (EAIO)
SIPG	Special Intercept Priorities Group [*Armed Forces Security Agency*]
SIPH	Scandinavian International Property Holdings
SIPI	Scientists' Institute for Public Information (EA)
SIPI	Short Imaginal Process Inventory [*Personality development test*] [*Psychology*]
SIPI	Sisterhood Is Powerful Institute (EA)
SIPI	Southwestern Indian Polytechnic Institute [*New Mexico*]
SIPI	Supervisory Immigration Patrol Inspector [*Immigration and Naturalization Service*]
SIPL	Seeley's Illustrated Pocket Library [*A publication*]
SIPL	Studies in Philippine Linguistics [*A publication*]
SIPM	Star Identification Program, Mariner [*NASA*]
SIPN	Security Industry and Product News [*A publication*]
SIPN	Semi-Interpenetrating Polymer Network [*Organic chemistry*]
SIPO	Serial-In, Parallel-Out [*Telecommunications*] (TEL)
SIPO	Sicherheitspolizei [*Security Police*] [*NAZI*] (BJA)
SIPO	Soobshcheniia Imperatorskovo Pravoslavnovo Palestinskovo Obshchestva [*A publication*]
SIPO	Spacecraft Integration Project Office
SIPO	Swiss Intellectual Property Office [*Bern*] [*Information service or system*] (IID)
SIPOA	Servico de Inspecao de Produtos de Origem Animal [*Brazil*]
SIPOP	Satellite Information Processor Operational Program (AFM)
SIPOS	Semi-Insulating Polycrystalline Silicon [*Photovoltaic energy systems*]
SIPP	Sodium Iron Pyrophosphate [*Organic chemistry*]
SIPP	Standard Interline Passenger Procedures Manual [*Air Traffic Conference of America*] [*IATA*] (DS)
SIPP	Survey on Income and Program Participation [*Census Bureau, Department of Health and Human Services*]
SIPP	System Information Processing Program (MCD)
SIPPS	System of Information Processing for Professional Societies
Sippy	Senior Independent Pioneer [*Lifestyle classification*]
SIPR	Special In-Process Review (MCD)
SIPRA	Societa Italiana Pubblicita Per Azioni [*Italian radio and television advertising company*]
SIPRE	Snow, Ice, and Permafrost Research Establishment
SIPRI	Stockholm International Peace Research Institute [*Solna, Sweden*] (EAIO)
SIPROS	Simultaneous Processing Operation System [*Control Data Corp.*] [*Data processing*]
SIPRT	Societe Internationale pour les Plantes-Racines Tropicales
SIPS	Shipbuilding Industries Pension Scheme [*British*]
SIPS	Simulated Input Preparation System (IEEE)
SIPS	Small Instrument Pointing System (MCD)
SIPS	Societa Internazionale de Psicologia della Scrittura [*International Society of Psychology of Handwriting - ISPH*] (EAIO)
SIPS	Societe Internationale de Psychologie des Sports [*International Society of Sports Psychology*] (EAIO)
SIPS	Spartan Improved Performance Study [*Missiles*] (AABC)
SIPS	State Implementation Plan System [*Environmental Protection Agency*]
SIPS	Statistical Interactive Programming System
SIPSDE	Society of Independent and Private School Data Education [*Later, SDE*] (EA)
SIPT	Sensory Integration and Praxis Test [*Occupational therapy*]
SIPT	Simulating Part (AAG)
SIPTH	Serum Immunoreactive Parathyroid Hormone [*Endocrinology*]
SIPU	Selective Inactivation Photodynamic Unit
SIQ	Sick in Quarters
SIQ	Social Intelligence Quotient [*In book title*]
SIQ	Student Interests Quarterly [*A publication*]
SIQR	Studies: An Irish Quarterly Review of Letters, Philosophy, and Science [*A publication*]
SIR	Safari International Resources [*Vancouver Stock Exchange symbol*]
SIR	Safe Integral Reactor [*Nuclear energy*]
SIR	Safeguards Implementation Report [*Nuclear energy*] (NRCH)
SIR	Scientific Information Retrieval, Inc. [*Database management system*] [*Information service or system*] (IID)
SIR	Search, Inspection, and Recovery (NVT)
SIR	Secondary-Image-Registration [*Photography*]
SIR	Segment Identification Register
SIR	Selected Item Reporting
SIR	Selective Information Retrieval [*Data processing*]
SIR	Selective Ion Recording [*Spectrometry*]
SIR	Self-Indication Ratio
SIR	Self-Insured Retention [*Insurance*]
SIR	Semantic Information Retrieval [*Massachusetts Institute of Technology*] [*Data processing*] (DIT)
SIR	Semiannual Inventory Report [*Navy*] (NVT)
SIR	Serious Incident Report [*Military*] (AFM)
SIR	Service International de Recherches [*International Tracing Service*] [*Red Cross*]
SIR	Shipboard Intercept Receiver [*Navy*]
SIR	Shuttle Imaging RADAR [*of earth's surface*] [*NASA*]
SIR	Signal-to-Interference Ratio
SIR	Simultaneous Impact Rate (AFM)
SIR	Sinclair, WY [*Location identifier*] [*FAA*] (FAAL)
SIR	Single Imaging RADAR
SIR	Single Isomorphous Replacement [*Crystallography*]
SIR	Single Item Release
SIR	Sion [*Switzerland*] [*Airport symbol*]
Sir	Sirach [*Old Testament book*] [*Roman Catholic canon*]
SIR	Siria [*Venezuela*] [*Seismograph station code, US Geological Survey*] (SEIS)
Sir	Sirius [*Record label*] [*Sweden*]
SIR	Size Up, Interview, Rate [*Mnemonic used by Responsible Beverage Service in its bartender training program*]
SIR	Small Intestine Rinse [*Physiology*]
SIR	Snow and Ice on Runways [*Aviation*] (FAAC)
SIR	Societa Italiana Resine [*Italy*]
SIR	Societe Rorschach Internationale [*International Rorschach Society*] [*Originally, Societe Internationale du Test de Rorschach et Autres Methodes Projectives*]
SIR	Society for Individual Responsibility [*Defunct*] (EA)
SIR	Society of Industrial Realtors [*Association name and designation awarded by this group*] [*Washington, DC*] (EA)
SIR	Society of Insurance Research [*Appleton, WI*] (EA)
SIR	Software Incident Report (MCD)
SIR	Software Initiated Restart (NASA)
SIR	Sound Isolation Room
SIR	Spaceborne Imaging RADAR
SIR	Special Information Retrieval
SIR	Special Inspection Requirement
SIR	Special Investigative Requirement (AFM)
SIR	Specific Insulation Resistance
SIR	Specification Information Retrieval System [*Data processing*] (MCD)
SIR	Stable Isotopes Resource
SIR	Standarization, Interoperability, and Readiness [*NATO*] (MCD)
SIR	Staten Island Rapid Transit Railway Co. [*Later, SIRC*] [*AAR code*]
SIR	Statistical Information Retrieval
SIR	Statutory Invention Registration [*Patents*]
SIR	Stratified Indexing and Retrieval [*Japan*] [*Data processing*] (DIT)
SIR	Student Instructional Report [*Test of teacher performance*]
SIR	Studies in Romanticism [*A publication*]
SIR	Styrene-Isoprene Rubber
SIR	Subcontractor Information Request
SIR	Submarine Intermediate Reactor [*Nuclear energy*]
SIR	Subsurface Interface RADAR [*A trademark*]
SIR	Supersonic Infantry Rocket
SIR	Suppliers Information Request
SIR	Symbolic Input Routine [*Data processing*] (DIT)
SIR	Synthetic-Aperture Imaging RADAR [*System*]
SIR	System Initialization Routine
SIR	System Integration Receiver [*System*]
SIR	System Interface Requirements (NASA)
SIR	Systems Integration Review [*NASA*] (NASA)
SIRA	Safety Investigation Regulations (IEEE)
SIRA	Scientific Instrument Research Association [*British*]
SIRA	Social Issues Research Associates (EA)
SIRA	Sports Industries Representatives Association (EA)
SIRA	Stable Isotope Ratio Analysis
SIRA	Strapdown Inertial Reference Assembly (MCD)

SIRA .... Strategic Intelligence Research and Analysis
SIRA .... System for Instructional Response Analysis
Sirag........... Sirag. Amsagir Grakanut ean ew Aruesdi [*A publication*]
SIRAP .... System of Information Retrieval and Analysis, Planning [*Army*] [*Information service or system*] (IID)
SIRAS........ Single Isomorphous Replacement, Anomalous Scattering [*Crystallography*]
SIRB .... Sintered Iron Rotating Band
SIRC .... Science Information Resource Center [*Harper & Row*] [*Information service or system*]
SIRC .... Sirco International Corp. [*NASDAQ symbol*] (NQ)
SIRC .... Socialist International Research Council [*British*]
SIRC .... Spares Integrated Reporting and Control [*System*]
SIRC .... Sport Information Resource Centre [*Coaching Association of Canada*] [*Database*] (IID)
SIRC .... [*The*] Staten Island Railroad Corporation [*AAR code*]
SIRC .... Styrene Information and Research Center (EA)
SIR(CICR) ... Service International de Recherches (du Comite International de la Croix-Rouge) [*International Tracing Service of the International Committee of the Red Cross*]
SIRCS........ Shipboard Intermediate Range Combat System [*Navy*]
SIRCULS .. San Bernardino-Inyo-Riverside Counties United Library Services [*Library network*]
SIRCUS..... Standard Information Retrieval Capability for Users [*Army*]
SIRD.......... Shore-Based Interfare Requirement Date
SIRD.......... Support Instrumentation Requirements Document [*NASA*]
SIRE .... Satellite Infrared Experiment (MCD)
SIRE .... Society for the Investigation of Recurring Events (EA)
SIREA .... SIAM [*Society for Industrial and Applied Mathematics*] Review [*A publication*]
SIREMAR ... Sicilia Regionale Marittima SpA [*Italy*] (EY)
SIREN .... SIGSEC Resources and Equipment Needs (MCD)
SIREWS.... Shipboard Infrared Electronic Warfare System
SIRF .... System Information Reports Formatting (MCD)
SIRI .... Societe Internationale pour la Readaptation des Invalides
SIRIC........ Soybean Insect Research Information Center [*University of Illinois*] [*Champaign, IL*]
SIRIM .... Societe Internationale de Recherche Interdisciplinaire sur la Maladie
SIRIN .... Single Readiness Information System [*NORRS*]
Siriraj Hosp Gaz ... Siriraj Hospital Gazette [*A publication*]
SIRIS........ Sputter-Initiated Resonance Ionization Spectrometry
SIRIS........ Sylloge Inscriptionum Religionis Isiacae et Sarapiacae [*A publication*] (BJA)
SIRIVS...... Spaceborne Intensified Radiometer for Imaging Vetroviolet Spectroscopy (MCD)
Sir JS .... [*Sir John*] Strange's English Reports [*A publication*] (DLA)
SIRL .... Site Installation Requirements List (AAG)
SIRL .... Support Item Requirement List (MCD)
SIRLEJ ..... Societe Internationale de Recherche en Litterature d'Enfance et de Jeunesse [*International Research Society for Children's Literature - IRSCL*] (EA)
Sir L Jenk.. Wynne's Life of Sir Leoline Jenkins [*1724*] [*A publication*] (DLA)
SIRLS........ Information Retrieval System for the Sociology of Leisure and Sport [*University of Waterloo*] [*Information service or system*] (IID)
SIRLS........ Southwest Idaho Regional Library System [*Library network*]
SIRLS........ Specialized Information Retrieval and Library Services (EISS)
SIRM......... Saturation Isothermal Remanent Magnetization [*Paleomagnetics*]
SIRM......... Societe Internationale Robert Musil [*International Robert Musil Society - IRMS*] [*Saarbrucken, Federal Republic of Germany*] (EAIO)
SIRM......... Sterile Insect Release Method
SIRMA ...... Small Independent Record Manufacturers Association [*Stanford, CT*] (EA)
SIRMCE..... Societe Internationale pour la Recherche sur les Maladies de Civilisation et l'Environment [*International Society for Research on Civilization Diseases and Environment*] [*Brussels, Belgium*] (EAIO)
SIRMS ...... Stable Isotope Ratio Mass Spectrometer [*or Spectrometry*]
SIRO.......... CSIRO [*Commonwealth Scientific and Industrial Research Organisation*] Research in Progress [*Australia*] [*Information service or system*] (CRD)
SIROW...... Southwest Institute for Research on Women [*University of Arizona*] [*Research center*] (RCD)
SIRR .... Section on Individual Rights and Responsibilities (EA)
SIRR .... Software Integration Readiness Review [*NASA*] (NASA)
SIRR .... Southern Industrial Railroad, Inc. [*AAR code*]
SIRRBJ ..... Institutionen foer Skogsforyngring Rapporter och Uppsatser [*A publication*]
SIRS .... Salary Information Retrieval System (IEEE)
SIRS .... Satellite Infrared Spectrometer [*NASA*]
SIRS .... Saztec Information Retrieval Services [*Australia*]
SIRS .... Scheduled Issue Release System
SIRS .... Ship Installed RADIAC [*Radiation Detection, Indication, and Computation*] System (NATG)
SIRS .... Skills Inventory Retrieval System (MCD)
SIRS .... Small Independent Radio Stations [*An association*] [*British*]
SIRS .... Social Issues Resources Series [*A publication*]

SIRS .... Soils Information Retrieval Systems [*Database*] [*Army Corps of Engineers*]
SIRS .... Soluble Immune Response Suppressor [*Immunology*]
SIRS .... Special Issue Rating System [*Veterans Administration*]
SIRS .... Specification, Instrumentation, and Range Safety
SIRS .... Statewide Individual Referral System (OICC)
SIRS .... Supplemental Inflatable Restraint System [*Automotive engineering*]
SIRSA........ System Integration Receiver System (MCD)
SIRSA........ Special Industrial Radio Service Association (EA)
SIRT .... Signaling Information Receiver/Transmitter (MCD)
SIRT .... Staten Island Rapid Transit Railway Co. [*Later, SIRC*]
SIRTF........ Space [*formerly, Shuttle*] Infrared Telescope Facility [*NASA*]
Sir TJ......... [*Sir Thomas*] Jones' English King's Bench and Common Pleas Reports [*A publication*] (DLA)
Sir T Ray.... Sir T. Raymond's English King's Bench Reports [*A publication*] (DLA)
SIRU.......... Strapdown Inertial Reference Unit [*Navigation*]
SIRW......... Safety Injection and Refueling Water [*Nuclear energy*] (NRCH)
SIRWT ...... Safety Injection and Refueling Water Tank [*Nuclear energy*] (NRCH)
SIRWT ...... Safety Injection Reserve Water Tank (IEEE)
SIS .... Canadian Security and Intelligence Service [*UTLAS symbol*]
SIS .... Naval Intelligence Service [*Italy*]
SIS .... Safety Information System [*Department of Transportation*]
SIS .... Safety Injection System [*Nuclear energy*] (NRCH)
SIS .... SAGE [*Semiautomatic Ground Environment*] Interceptor Simulator
SIS .... SAIL [*Shuttle Avionics Integration Laboratory*] Interface System [*NASA*] (NASA)
SIS .... Satellite Infrared Spectrometer [*NASA*]
SIS .... Satellite Interceptor System [*Military*] (AFM)
SIS .... Savage Information Services (IID)
SIS .... Scale for the Identification of School Phobia [*Test*]
SIS .... Scanning Image Spectrometer
SIS .... Science Information Service (EA)
SIS .... Science Information Services [*Franklin Institute*]
SIS .... Scientific Instruction Set
SIS .... Scientific Instrument Society (EA)
SIS .... Scotch-Irish Society of the United States of America (EA)
SIs .... Scripta Islandica [*A publication*]
SIS .... Secondary Injection System
SIS .... Secret Intelligence Service [*British*]
SIS .... Semiautomatic Imagery Screening Subsystem (MCD)
SIS .... Semiconductor-Insulator-Semiconductor
SIS .... Seminar Information Service Database [*Seminar Information Service, Inc.*] [*Information service or system*] (CRD)
SIS .... Senior Intelligence Service [*CIA personnel*]
SIS .... Sensor Image Simulator (MCD)
SIS .... Serial Input System (MCD)
SIS .... Serving the Indigent Sick
SIS .... Share Information Service [*British*] (DCTA)
SIS .... Shared Information Service (CMD)
SIS .... Shipping Instruction Sheet
SIS .... Shock-Isolation Support
SIS .... Short Interval Scheduling [*Quality control*]
SIS .... Shut-In Society
SIS .... Shuttle Information System [*NASA*] (MCD)
SIS .... Shuttle Interface Simulator [*NASA*] (NASA)
SIS .... Signal Intelligence Service [*Later, Army Security Agency*]
SIS .... Signaling Interworking Subsystem [*Telecommunications*] (TEL)
SIS .... Silicon of Insulating Substrate (MCD)
SIS .... Silkridge Resources [*Vancouver Stock Exchange symbol*]
SIS .... Simian Sarcoma Virus [*Oncology*]
SIRSA........ Simulation Interface Subsystem (KSC)
SIS .... Single Item Squawk Sheet
SIS .... Singles in Service (EA)
SIS .... Sino-Indian Studies [*A publication*]
SIS .... Sion [*Switzerland*] [*Seismograph station code, US Geological Survey*] [*Closed*] (SEIS)
SIS .... Sishen [*South Africa*] [*Airport symbol*] (OAG)
SIS .... Sister
SIS .... Societa Internazionale Scotista [*International Scotist Society - ISS*] (EAIO)
SIS .... Society of International Secretaries
SIS .... Society for Iranian Studies (EA)
SIS .... Software Implementation Specifications [*NASA*] (NASA)
SIS .... Software Integrated Schedule [*NASA*] (NASA)
SIS .... Somatic Inkblot Series [*Personality development test*] [*Psychology*]
SIS .... Soviet Intelligence Services
SIS .... Space and Information System
SIS .... SPALT [*Special Projects Alterations*] Information Shut
SIS .... Spark Ignition System
SIS .... Speaker Intercom System (KSC)
SIS .... Special Industrial Services [*United Nations Industrial Development Organization*]
SIS .... Special Information System (MCD)
SIS .... Special Intelligence Service
SIS .... Special Interest Sessions

SIS .... Special Isotope Separation [*Physics*]
SIS .... Specification Information System
SIS .... Spectral Imaging Sensor
SIS .... Spectral Index of Sample [*Experimentation*]
SIS .... Spuria Iris Society   (EA)
SIS .... Stage Interface Substitute
SIS .... Stand-Alone Information System [*National Library of Medicine*]
SIS .... Standard Indexing System [*DoD*]
SIS .... Standard Instruction Set   (MSA)
SIS .... Standards Information Service [*National Institute of Standards and Technology*]   (IID)
SIS .... Standards Information Service [*Standards Council of Canada*] [*Information service or system*]   (IID)
SIS .... Station Identification Store [*Bell Laboratories*]
SIS .... Stator Interstage Seal
SIS .... STEP [*Scientific and Technical Exploitation Program*] Information Subsystem
SIS .... Sterile Injectable Suspension
SIS .... Strategic Intelligence School [*Military*]
SIS .... Strategic Intelligence Summary [*Military*]   (NATG)
SIS .... Strategic Intelligence Systems, Inc. [*Also, an information service or system*]   (IID)
SIS .... Student Instruction Sheet [*Military*]
SIS .... Student International Service [*Foundation*]
SIs .... Studi Ispanici [*A publication*]
SIS .... Styrene-Isoprene-Styrene [*Organic chemistry*]
SIS .... Submarine Integrated SONAR
SIS .... Superconductivity Information System [*Department of Energy*] [*Information service or system*]   (IID)
SIS .... Superconductor-Insulator-Superconductor [*Transistor technology*]
SIS .... Supervisory Inventory on Safety [*Test*]
SIS .... Supplier Identification System [*London Enterprise Agency*] [*Information service or system*]   (IID)
SIS .... Supply Item Status
SIS .... Surgical Infection Society   (EA)
S & IS .... Survey and Investigation Staff [*Navy*]   (NVT)
SIS .... Sveriges Standardiseringskommission [*Swedish Standards Institution*] [*Also, an information service or system*]   (IID)
SIS .... Swedish Standards Institution   (EISS)
SIS .... Synchronous Identification System   (MCD)
SIS .... System Integration Schedule [*NASA*]   (NASA)
SIS .... System Integration Support
SIS .... System Interrupt Supervisor
SISAC .... Serials Industry Systems Advisory Committee [*Book Industry Study Group*] [*Information service or system*]   (IID)
SISAM ...... Spectrometer with Interference Selective Amplitude Modulation [*Physics*]
SI/SAO ...... Special Intelligence/Special Activities Office   (MCD)
SISB .... SIS Corp. [*NASDAQ symbol*]   (NQ)
SISC .... Single Screw
SISC .... South India Shipping Corp. Ltd.   (DS)
SISC .... Statewide Information Steering Committee [*California*]
SISC .... Stewart Information Services Corporation [*NASDAQ symbol*]   (NQ)
SISCIS ...... Subject Index to Sources of Comparative International Statistics [*A publication*]
SISCO .... Special Inter-Departmental Selection Committee [*UN Food and Agriculture Organization*]
SISCON .... Science in Social Context
SISD .... Scientific Information Systems Department [*Information service or system*]   (IID)
SISD .... Single Instruction, Single Data   (IEEE)
SISEX .... Shuttle Imaging Spectrometer Experiment [*NASA*]
SISH .... Societe Internationale de la Science Horticole [*International Society for Horticultural Science - ISHS*]   (EAIG)
SISI .... Short Increment Sensitivity Index [*Medicine*]
SISI .... Surveillance and In-Service Inspection [*Nuclear energy*]   (NRCH)
SISIMS ..... Say It So It Makes Sense [*A publication*]
SISIR .... Singapore Institute of Standards and Industrial Research
SISKY .... Siskiyou [*FAA*]   (FAAC)
S Isl .... Sandwich Islands
SISL .... Sons of Italy Supreme Lodge   (EA)
SIsl .... Studia Islamica [*A publication*]
SISMS .... Standard Integrated Support Management System [*Joint Chiefs of Staff*]
SISO .... Science Information Services Organization [*Franklin Institute*]   (IID)
Si & So ...... Sight and Sound [*A publication*]
SISO .... Single-Input, Single-Output [*Process engineering*]
SISOR .... Supply Item Status Order Reporting [*Army*]
SISORS ..... Supply Item Status and Order Reporting System
SISP.......... Sudden Increase of Solar Particles
SISP.......... Surface Imaging and Sounding Package
SISPA .... Sequence-Independent Single Primer Amplification [*Genetics*]
SISR .... Selected Items Status Report [*Army*]   (AABC)
SISRBO ..... Institutionen foer Skogszoologi Rapporter och Uppsatser [*A publication*]

SISS .... Second International Science Study [*International Association for the Evaluation of Educational Achievement*]
SISS .... Semiconductor-Insulator-Semiconductor System
SISS .... Sensory Integration Special Interest Section [*American Occupational Therapy Association*]
SISS .... Single Item, Single Source   (IEEE)
SISS .... Societe Internationale de la Science du Sol
SISS .... Sources of Information on Social Security [*British*]
SISS .... Standoff Imaging Sensor System   (MCD)
SISS .... Submarine Integrated SONAR System
SISS .... Synchronous Identification System Study
SISS .... System Integration Support Service
SISSC .... Special Interest Sections Steering Committee [*American Occupational Therapy Association*]
SIST .... Self-Inflating Surface Target
SIST .... Sentence Imitation Screening Test [*Speech and language test*]
SIST .... Sister
Sist e Autom ... Sistemi e Automazione [*A publication*]
Sist Avtom Nauchn Issled ... Sistemy Avtomatisatsii Nauchnykh Issledovanii [*A publication*]
Sistema ...... Sistema Revista de Ciencias Sociales [*A publication*]
Sistem Metod Sovrem Nauka ... Sistemnyj Metod i Sovremennaja Nauka [*A publication*]
SISTER ..... Special Institution for Scientific and Technological Education and Research [*In proposal stage, 1964, in Great Britain*]
Sisters .... Sisters Today [*A publication*]
SISTM .... Simulation by Incremental Stochastic Transition Matrices   (MCD)
SISTMS ..... Standard Integrated Supply/Transportation Manifest System [*Military*]   (AABC)
Sist Nerv .... Sistema Nervoso [*A publication*]
Sistole Rev Urug Cardiol ... Sistole. Revista Uruguaya de Cardiologia [*A publication*]
SISTRAN ... System for Information Storage and Retrieval and Analysis
SISUSA ..... Scotch-Irish Society of the United States of America   (EA)
SiSV .... Simian Sarcoma Virus [*Also, SSV*]
SISWP .... Soroptimist International of the South West Pacific [*Sydney, NSW, Australia*]   (EAIO)
SIT .... Safety Injection Tank [*Nuclear energy*]   (NRCH)
SIT .... Safety Injection Transmitter [*Nuclear energy*]   (NRCH)
SIT .... Sensory Integration Training
SIT .... Separation-Initiated Timer
SIT .... Sequential Interval Timer
SIT .... Serum Inhibitory Titer [*Clinical chemistry*]
SIT .... Shorr Imagery Test [*Personality development test*] [*Psychology*]
SIT .... Shuttle Integrated Test [*NASA*]   (NASA)
SIT .... Shuttle Interface Test [*NASA*]   (NASA)
SIT .... Silicon Intensifier Target
SIT .... Silicon Intensifier Tube
SIT .... Simulation Input Tape
sit .... Sino-Tibetan [*MARC language code*] [*Library of Congress*]   (LCCP)
SIT .... Sitka [*Alaska*] [*Geomagnetic observatory code*]
SIT .... Sitka [*Alaska*] [*Seismograph station code, US Geological Survey*]   (SEIS)
SIT .... Sitka [*Alaska*] [*Airport symbol*]   (OAG)
SIT .... Sitka, AK [*Location identifier*] [*FAA*]   (FAAL)
SIT .... Situation   (AFM)
SIT .... Slosson Intelligence Test
SIT .... Social Intelligence Test [*Psychology*]
SIT .... Society of Industrial Tutors [*British*]
SIT .... Society of Instrument Technology [*British*]
SIT .... Society of International Treasurers   (EAIO)
SIT .... Software Integrated Test [*NASA*]   (KSC)
SIT .... Space Impact Tool [*NASA*]
SIT .... Spaceborne Infrared Tracker
SIT .... Special Information Tones [*Telecommunications*]
SIT .... Sperm Immobilization Test [*Clinical chemistry*]
SIT .... Spontaneous Ignition Temperature
SIT .... SSV [*Space Shuttle Vehicle*] Integrated Test [*NASA*]   (NASA)
SIT .... Statement of Inventory Transaction [*Military*]
SIT .... Static Induction Transistor [*Telecommunications*]   (TEL)
SIT .... Stevens Institute of Technology [*Hoboken, NJ*]
SIT .... Stop Immorality on Television [*An association*]
SIT .... Stopping in Transit
SIT .... Storage Inspection Test [*Navy*]   (NG)
SIT .... Storage in Transit
SIT .... Structurally Integrated Thruster   (MCD)
SIT .... Sugar Industry Technologists   (EA)
SIT .... System Integration Test
SIT .... Systems Interface Test   (NVT)
SI3T .... Association of French Telephone, Telegraph, and Related Telematics Industries [*Paris*] [*Telecommunications service*]   (TSSD)
SITA .... Sociedade Internacional de Trilogia Analitica [*International Society of Analytical Trilogy - ISAT*] [*Sao Paulo, Brazil*]   (EAIO)
SITA .... Societe Internationale des Telecommunications Aeronautiques [*International Society of Aeronautical Telecommunications*] [*London, England*]

SITA .... Students' International Travel Association
SITA .... System International Tinplate Area
SITAR ...... Societa Incremento Turismo Aereo [*Italy*]
SITB .... Shipbuilding Industrial Training Board [*British*]
SITC .... Satellite International Television Center
           [*Telecommunications*] (TEL)
SITC .... Single Integrated Test Cycle [*Army*]
SITC .... Standard Industrial Trade Classification [*United Nations*]
SITC .... Standard International Trade Classification
SITCA ...... Secretaria de Integracion Turistica Centroamericana
SITCEN ... Situation Center [*NATO*] (NATG)
SITCOM ... Situation Comedy [*Television*]
Sit-Comm.. Situation Commercial [*Advertisement imitating a TV sitcom*]
SITE .... Sample Instruction Test Exercise (MCD)
SITE .... Satellite Instructional Television Experiment [*NASA/Indian
           Space Research Organization, 1974*]
SITE .... Sculpture in the Environment [*In Best by SITE, Inc.*]
SITE .... Search Information Tape Equipment
SITE .... Shipboard Information, Training, and Education [*System*]
           [*Navy*] (NVT)
SITE .... Situate (ROG)
SITE .... Society of Incentive Travel Executives [*New York, NY*] (EA)
SITE .... Society of Insurance Trainers and Educators (EA)
SITE .... Spacecraft Instrumentation Test Equipment
SITE .... Suction Infusion Tissue Extractor [*Ophthalmology*]
SITE .... Superfund Innovative Technologies Evaluation Program
           [*Environmental Protection Agency*]
S-ITED ...... Superimposed Integrated Trajectory Error [*Aviation*]
SITEL .... Societe des Ingenieurs do Telecommunication
           [*Belgium*] (MCD)
SITES .... Smithsonian Institution Traveling Exhibition Service
Site Sel Hdbk ... Site Selection Handbook [*A publication*]
SITI .... Swiss Institute for Technical Information [*Information service
           or system*] (IID)
SITIM .... Societe Internationale des Techniques d'Imagerie Mentals
           [*International Society for Mental Imagery Techniques in
           Psychotherapy and Psychology*] [*Paris, France*] (EAIO)
SITK .... Sitka National Monument
SITKA ...... Silikattechnik [*East Germany*] [*A publication*]
SITL .... Southwestern Industrial Traffic League (EA)
SITMAP.... Situation Map (MCD)
SITN......... Situation (ROG)
SITOR....... Simplex TELEX over Radio
SITP .... Scheduled into Production
SITP .... Shipyard Installation Test Procedure [*or Program*]
SITP .... Site Inspection and Test Procedure [*Nuclear energy*] (NRCH)
SITP .... System Integration Test Program
SITP .... Systems Integrated Test Plan [*Military*] (CAAL)
SITPB....... System Integration Test Program Board
SITPRO..... Simplification of International Trade Procedures [*Committee or
           Board*] [*British*]
SITRAM ... Societe Ivoirienne de Transport Maritime [*The Ivorian national
           shipping industry*]
SITREP..... Situation Report
SITS......... IEEE Social Implications of Technology Society (EA)
SITS.......... SAGE [*Semiautomatic Ground Environment*] Intercept Target
           Simulation
SITS.......... Scientists in the Sea Program [*National Oceanic and
           Atmospheric Administration*] (MSC)
SITS.......... Secure Imagery Transmission System [*Military*] (CAAL)
SITS.......... Societe Internationale de Transfusion Sanguine [*International
           Society of Blood Transfusion - ISBT*] [*Paris, France*] (EA)
SITS.......... System Integration Test Service
SITS.......... System Integration Test Site [*Military*] (CAAL)
SITSUM.... Situation Summary [*Military*] (NVT)
SITTS........ Small-Inventory Top-Tier Site [*Industrial hazard designation*]
           [*British*]
SITU......... Society for the Investigation of the Unexplained (EA)
SITU......... South India Teachers' Union
SITU......... Surgical Intensive Therapy Unit
SITU......... Systeme d'Information des Trajets Urbains [*Computerized
           transit routing information service in Paris*]
SITV .... Southbrook International Television Co. PLC [*London,
           England*] [*NASDAQ symbol*] (NQ)
SITV .... System Integration Test Vehicle
SITVC .... Secondary Injection Thrust Vector Control
Sitz............ Sitzungsberichte [*Proceedings*] [*German*] (OCD)
Sitzungber Saechs Akad Wiss (Leipzig) Math-Natur Kl ... Sitzungsberichte.
           Saechsische Akademie der Wissenschaften (Leipzig).
           Mathematisch-Naturwissenschaftliche Klasse [*A
           publication*]
Sitzungsber d Akadem d Wiss ... Sitzungsberichte. Akademie der
           Wissenschaften [*A publication*]
Sitzungsber Akad Wiss DDR Math-Naturwiss-Tech Jahrgang 1977 ...
           Sitzungsberichte. Akademie der Wissenschaften der DDR.
           Mathematik-Naturwissenschaften-Technik. Jahrgang 1977
           [*A publication*]
Sitzungsber Akad Wiss DDR Math-Naturwiss Tech Jahrgang 1979 ...
           Sitzungsberichte. Akademie der Wissenschaften der DDR.
           Mathematik-Naturwissenschaften-Technik. Jahrgang 1979
           [*A publication*]

Sitzungsber Bayer Akad Wiss Math-Naturwiss Kl ... Sitzungsberichte.
           Bayerische Akademie der Wissenschaften. Mathematisch-
           Naturwissenschaftliche Klasse [*A publication*]
Sitzungsber Berl Ges Naturforsch Freunde ... Sitzungsberichte. Berlinische
           Gesellschaft Naturforschender Freunde [*A publication*]
Sitzungsber Deut Akad Landwirt Wiss Berlin ... Sitzungsberichte. Deutsche
           Akademie der Landwirtschaftswissenschaften zu Berlin [*A
           publication*]
Sitzungsber Deut Akad Wiss Berlin Kl Math Phys Tech ... Sitzungsberichte.
           Deutsche Akademie der Wissenschaften zu Berlin. Klasse
           fuer Mathematik, Physik, und Technik [*A publication*]
Sitzungsber Finn Akad Wiss ... Sitzungsberichte. Finnische Akademie der
           Wissenschaften [*A publication*]
Sitzungsber Ges Befoerd Ges Naturwiss Marburg ... Sitzungsberichte.
           Gesellschaft zur Befoerderung der Gesamten
           Naturwissenschaften zu Marburg [*West Germany*] [*A
           publication*]
Sitzungsber Ges Naturforsch Freunde Berlin ... Sitzungsberichte. Gesellschaft
           Naturforschender Freunde zu Berlin [*A publication*]
Sitzungsber Heidelb Akad Wiss Math-Natur Kl ... Sitzungsberichte.
           Heidelberg Akademie der Wissenschaften. Mathematisch-
           Naturwissenschaftliche Klasse [*A publication*]
Sitzungsber Heidelb Akad Wiss Math-Naturwiss Kl ... Sitzungsberichte.
           Heidelberg Akademie der Wissenschaften. Mathematisch-
           Naturwissenschaftliche Klasse [*A publication*]
Sitzungsber Mitt Braunschw Wiss Ges ... Sitzungsberichte und Mitteilungen
           der Braunschweigischen Wissenschaftlichen Gesellschaft [*A
           publication*]
Sitzungsber Oesterr Akad Wiss Math-Naturwiss Kl Abt II ...
           Sitzungsberichte. Oesterreichische Akademie der
           Wissenschaften. Mathematisch-Naturwissenschaftliche
           Klasse. Abteilung II. Mathematik, Astronomie, Physik,
           Meteorologie, und Technik [*A publication*]
Sitzungsber Preuss Akad Wiss ... Sitzungsberichte. Preussische Akademie der
           Wissenschaften [*A publication*]
Sitz Wien ... Sitzungsberichte der Akademie der Wissenschaften in Wien [*A
           publication*] (OCD)
SIU .... Saturn Instrumentation [*NASA*]
SIU .... Seafarers' International Union of North America [*AFL-CIO*]
SIU .... Sequence Initiate Update
SIU .... Shiloh Resources Ltd. [*Vancouver Stock Exchange symbol*]
SIU .... Signal Interface Unit (MCD)
SIU .... Simushir [*USSR*] [*Seismograph station code, US Geological
           Survey*] (SEIS)
SIU .... Slide-In Unit [*Telecommunications*] (TEL)
SIU .... Societe Internationale d'Urologie [*International Society of
           Urology - ISU*] [*Paris, France*] (EAIO)
SIU .... Sonobuoy Interface Unit [*Navy*] (CAAL)
SIU .... Southern Illinois University
SIU .... Special Investigation Unit [*Australia*]
SIU .... System [*or Subsystem*] Interface Unit
SIU .... Systeme International d'Unites [*International System of Units*]
           [*Also, SI*]
SIU-AGLI ... Seafarers' International Union of North America [*AFL-CIO*];
           Atlantic, Gulf, Lakes, and Inland Waters District
SIU-AGLIW ... Seafarers' International Union of North America [*AFL-CIO*];
           Atlantic, Gulf, Lakes, and Inland Waters District
SIUC......... Southern Illinois University, Carbondale
SIUCB....... Societa Italiana della Union Chimique Belge [*Italy*]
SIUFL........ Suspend Issue and Use of Following Lots
SIU-IUP ... Seafarers' International Union of North America [*AFL-CIO*];
           Inlandboatmen's Union of the Pacific
SIU-IUPW ... Seafarers' International Union of North America [*AFL-CIO*];
           International Union of Petroleum Workers
SIU-MCS .. Seafarers' International Union of North America [*AFL-CIO*];
           Marine Cooks and Stewards' Union
SIU-MFOW ... Seafarers' International Union of North America [*AFL-CIO*];
           Pacific Coast Marine Firemen, Oilers, Watertenders, and
           Wipers Association
SIUNA...... Seafarers' International Union of North America (EA)
SIUP.......... Southern Illinois University Press
SIUPA....... Solomon Islands United Party [*Political party*] (PPW)
SIUSA....... Survival International, USA (EA)
SIUSM...... Suspend from Issue and Use as Suspect Material
SIU-SUP ... Seafarers' International Union of North America [*AFL-CIO*];
           Sailors' Union of the Pacific
SIU-TSAW ... Seafarers' International Union of North America [*AFL-CIO*];
           Transporation Services and Allied Workers
SIV............. Sieve (NASA)
SIV............. Silicon Videcon [*TV system*]
SIV............. Silver Cloud Mines [*Vancouver Stock Exchange symbol*]
SIV............. Simian Immunodeficiency Virus
SIV............. Societa Italiana Vetro [*Glass manufacturer*] [*Italy*]
SIV............. Solar and Interplanetary Variability [*Meteorology*]
SIV............. Spectrum Identification Voltage [*Military*] (CAAL)
SIV............. Sullivan, IN [*Location identifier*] [*FAA*] (FAAL)
SIV............. Survey of Interpersonal Values [*Psychology*]
SIV............. Vierteljahrshefte zur Wirtschaftsforschung [*A publication*]
SIVB.......... Silicon Valley Bancshares [*NASDAQ symbol*] (NQ)
SIVD.......... Spacecraft Information Viewing Device
SIVE.......... Shuttle Interface Verification Equipment [*NASA*] (NASA)

SI VIR PERM ... Si Vires Permittant [*If the Strength Will Bear It*] [*Pharmacy*]   (ROG)
SIW............ Congregation of the Incarnate Word and the Blessed Sacrament [*Roman Catholic women's religious order*]
SIW............ Schmitt Industries, Inc. [*Vancouver Stock Exchange symbol*]
SIW............ Self-Inflicted Wound [*Military*]
SIW............ Serum Samples from Infertile Women [*Immunochemistry*]
SIW............ Socialist International Women   (EA)
SIW............ Strassburger Israelitisch Wochenschrift [*A publication*]   (BJA)
SIW............ Strategic Intelligence Wing   (MCD)
SIW............ Subpolar Intermediate Water [*Oceanography*]
SIWDR...... Sidewinder [*Naval ordnance*]
SIWL........ Single Isolated Wheel Load [*Aviation*]   (FAAC)
SIX............ Motel 6 LP [*NYSE symbol*]   (SPSG)
SIX............ Sigma [*A publication*]
SIX............ Singleton [*Australia*] [*Airport symbol*]   (OAG)
Six............ Sixties [*A publication*]
SIXATAF.. Sixth Allied Tactical Air Force, Southeastern Europe [*NATO*]   (NATG)
Six Cent J .. Sixteenth Century Journal [*A publication*]
Six Circ...... Cases on the Six Circuits [*1841-43*] [*Ireland*] [*A publication*]   (DLA)
Six Ct J...... Sixteenth Century Journal [*A publication*]
SIXEP........ Site Ion Exchange Effluent Plant [*Nuclear energy*]
SIXFLT ...... Sixth Fleet [*Atlantic*] [*Navy*]
SIXP .... Sixpenny [*England*]
SIXPAC..... System for Inertial Experiment Priority and Attitude Control   (MCD)
Sixteen Cent J ... Sixteenth Century Journal [*A publication*]
SIXTHFLT ... Sixth Fleet [*Atlantic*] [*Navy*]
SIY............ Montague, CA [*Location identifier*] [*FAA*]   (FAAL)
SIY............ Shropshire Imperial Yeomanry [*British military*]   (DMA)
SIY............ South of Ireland Yeomanry [*British military*]   (DMA)
SIY............ Staffordshire Imperial Yeomanry [*British military*]   (DMA)
SIY............ Sussex Imperial Yeomanry [*British military*]   (DMA)
SIZ............ Security Identification Zone
SIZ............ Sizeler Property Investors, Inc. [*NYSE symbol*]   (SPSG)
SiZ............ Studies in Zionism [*A publication*]
SIZSA........ Sapporo Igaku Zasshi [*A publication*]
SIZZ.......... Sizzler Restaurants International, Inc. [*NASDAQ symbol*]   (NQ)
SJ............ Saalburg-Jahrbuch [*A publication*]
SJ............ Sales Journal [*Accounting*]
SJ............ Samuel Johnson [*Initials used as pseudonym*]
SJ............ San Juan [*Puerto Rico*]
SJ............ Saxophone Journal [*A publication*]
SJ............ Schistosoma Japonicum [*Parasitic fluke*]
SJ............ Scottish Jurist [*1829-73*] [*A publication*]   (DLA)
SJ............ Service Junior
SJ............ Shakespeare-Jahrbuch [*A publication*]
SJ............ Side Judge [*Football*]
SJ............ Silliman Journal [*A publication*]
SJ............ Simulation Journal [*A publication*]
SJ............ Single Jewish [*Classified advertising*]
SJ............ SJ Huvudkontor [*Swedish State Railways*]   (DCTA)
sj............ Sjieling [*Shilling*] [*Monetary Unit*] [*Afrikaans*]
SJ............ Slip Joint [*Technical drawings*]
SJ............ Sloppy Joe [*Sandwich*]
SJ............ Slovensky Jazyk [*A publication*]
SJ............ Societas Jesu [*Society of Jesus*] [*Jesuits*] [*Roman Catholic men's religious order*]
SJ............ Solicitors' Journal [*A publication*] [*A publication*]   (DLA)
SJ............ Source Jamming
SJ............ Southern Air Transport, Inc. [*ICAO designator*]   (FAAC)
SJ............ Statens Jaernvaegar [*Sweden*]
SJ............ Sub Judice [*Under Consideration*] [*Latin*]
sj............ Sudan [*MARC country of publication code*] [*Library of Congress*]   (LCCP)
SJ............ Supersonic Jet [*Gas stream*]
SJ............ Svalbard and Jan Mayen Islands [*ANSI two-letter standard code*]   (CNC)
SJA............ San Juan Airlines [*Port Angeles, WA*] [*FAA designator*]   (FAAC)
SJA............ Service Job Analysis [*A publication*]
SJA............ Southwestern Journal of Anthropology [*A publication*]
SJA............ Staff Judge Advocate [*Military*]
SJAA........ Swedish Journalists Association of America   (EA)
SJAE........ Steam Jet Air Ejector [*Nuclear energy*]   (NRCH)
SJAEA...... Soviet Journal of Atomic Energy [*A publication*]
SJAnth....... Southwestern Journal of Anthropology [*A publication*]
SJART........ San Jacinto Army Terminal
SJB .... St. Joseph Belt Railway Co. [*AAR code*]
SJB .... Society of Jewish Bibliophiles   (EA)
SJB .... Society of Journeymen Brushmakers [*A union*] [*British*]
SJB .... Surinaams Juristenblad [*A publication*]
SJB .... Westfield, MA [*Location identifier*] [*FAA*]   (FAAL)
SJB .... Zeitschrift fuer Wirtschaftswissenschaften und Sozialwissenschaften [*A publication*]
SJBA .... Sephardic Jewish Brotherhood of America   (EA)
SJBC.......... Saint John the Baptist, Clewer

SJBCD5..... Soviet Journal of Bioorganic Chemistry [*English translation of Bioorganicheskaya Khimiya*] [*A publication*]
SJC .... Saint John's College [*California; Kansas; Maryland*]
SJC .... Saint Joseph College [*West Hartford, CT*]
SJC .... Saint Joseph's College [*California; Indiana; Maine; New Jersey; New York; Pennsylvania*]
SJC .... San Javier [*Chile*] [*Seismograph station code, US Geological Survey*] [*Closed*]   (SEIS)
SJC .... San Jose [*California*] [*Airport symbol*]   (OAG)
SJC .... San Jose, CA [*Location identifier*] [*FAA*]   (FAAL)
SJC .... Sayre Junior College [*Oklahoma*]
SJC .... Snead Junior College [*Boaz, AL*]
SJC .... Society of Jews and Christians
SJC .... Southerland, J. C., Dearborn MI [*STAC*]
SJC .... Standing Joint Committee
SJC .... Supreme Judicial Court
SJCC.......... Cayey [*Puerto Rico*] [*Seismograph station code, US Geological Survey*]   (SEIS)
SJCC.......... Saint John College of Cleveland [*Ohio*]
SJCC.......... San Jose City College [*California*]
SJCC.......... Scott Joplin Commemorative Committee   (EA)
SJCC.......... Spring Joint Computer Conference [*American Federation of Information Processing Societies*]
SJCCA........ Stroke [*A publication*]
SJCLA........ Scandinavian Journal of Clinical and Laboratory Investigation [*A publication*]
SJCOA ..... SIAM [*Society for Industrial and Applied Mathematics*] Journal on Control [*A publication*]
SJCOD ..... SIAM [*Society for Industrial and Applied Mathematics*] Journal on Control and Optimization [*A publication*]
SJCPS .... Society of Jewish Composers, Publishers, and Songwriters [*Defunct*]   (EA)
SJCS .... Secretary Joint Chiefs of Staff   (MCD)
SJCT.......... SJC Today. Sheldon Jackson College [*Sitka, AK*] [*A publication*]
SJCW .... Saint Joseph's College for Women [*Later, SJC*] [*New York*]
SJD............ Doctor of Juridical Science [*or Doctor of the Science of Jurisprudence or Doctor of the Science of Law*]
SJD............ Los Cabos [*Mexico*] [*Airport symbol*]   (OAG)
SJD............ St. Joseph's College, Philadelphia, PA [*OCLC symbol*]   (OCLC)
SJD............ Supervisory Job Discipline Test
SJDAOIIA ... Saint John of Damascus Association of Orthodox Iconographers, Iconologists, and Architects   (EA)
SJDBA ...... Soviet Journal of Developmental Biology [*A publication*]
SJDFC........ Spirit, John Denver Fan Club   (EA)
SJE .... St. Jude Express [*An association*]   (EA)
SJE .... San Jose Del Guaviaro [*Colombia*] [*Airport symbol*]   (OAG)
SJE .... Swedish Journal of Economics [*A publication*]
SJE .... Swiveling Jet Engine
SJECA........ Soviet Journal of Ecology [*English Translation*] [*A publication*]
SJER.......... Scandinavian Journal of Educational Research [*A publication*]
SJF............ Japanese Finance and Industry [*A publication*]
SJF............ Saint John [*Virgin Islands*] [*Airport symbol*]   (OAG)
SJF............ Shortest Job First [*Data processing*]
SJF............ Single Jewish Female [*Classified advertising*]
SJF............ Sonny James and Friends [*An association*]   (EA)
SJF............ Supersonic Jet Flow
SJFC.......... Saint John Fisher College [*Rochester, NY*]
SJFC.......... Skidrow Joe Fan Club   (EA)
SJFMA...... Soviet Journal of Non-Ferrous Metals [*English Translation*] [*A publication*]
SJFRE3...... Scandinavian Journal of Forest Research [*A publication*]
SJFT.......... Svenska Jerusalems-Foereningens Tidskrift [*A publication*]
SJFTD8..... Sudan Journal of Food Science and Technology [*A publication*]
SJG .... St. Joe Gold Corp. [*AMEX symbol*] [*Toronto Stock Exchange symbol*]   (SPSG)
SJG .... San Juan [*Puerto Rico*] [*Geomagnetic observatory code*]
SJG .... San Juan [*Puerto Rico*] [*Seismograph station code, US Geological Survey*]   (SEIS)
SJGE .... St. Joseph Grain Exchange   (EA)
SJGHA....... Sumitomo Jukikai Giho [*A publication*]
SJGRA .... Scandinavian Journal of Gastroenterology [*A publication*]
SJH............ St. Joseph Seminary [*California*] [*Seismograph station code, US Geological Survey*]   (SEIS)
SJH............ San Juan Del Cesar [*Colombia*] [*Airport symbol*]   (OAG)
SJH............ Shakespeare-Jahrbuch (Heidelberg) [*A publication*]
SJHAA....... Scandinavian Journal of Haematology [*A publication*]
SJI .... Mobile, AL [*Location identifier*] [*FAA*]   (FAAL)
SJI .... San Jose [*Philippines*] [*Airport symbol*]   (OAG)
SJI .... Society for Japanese Irises   (EA)
SJI .... South Jersey Industries, Inc. [*NYSE symbol*]   (SPSG)
SJI .... Steel Joist Institute   (EA)
SJI .... Supervisory Job Instruction Test
SJIA .... Saint Joan's International Alliance [*See also AIJA*]   (EAIO)
SJIFC......... Spike Jones International Fan Club   (EA)
SJIS........... State Judicial Information System   (OICC)
SJJ............ Sarajevo [*Yugoslavia*] [*Airport symbol*]   (OAG)
SJJC.......... Sheldon Jackson Junior College [*Sitka, AK*] [*Later, Sheldon Jackson College*]
SJJR.......... Societe Jean-Jacques Rousseau   (EAIO)
SJJR......... Standard Jack and Jennet Registry of America   (EA)

SJK............ Sao Jose Dos Campos [*Brazil*] [*Airport symbol*]   (OAG)
SJK............ Steam-Jacketed Kettle
SJL............ St. Jude League   (EA)
SJL............ San Joaquin Valley Library System, Fresno, CA [*OCLC symbol*]   (OCLC)
SJL............ Semitic Journal of Linguistics [*A publication*]
SJL............ Slovensky Jazyk a Literatura v Skole [*A publication*]
SJL............ Southwest Journal of Linguistics [*US*] [*A publication*]
SJLA........ Studies in Judaism in Late Antiquity [*A publication*]
SJLAC....... Soviet Jewry Legal Advocacy Center   (EA)
SJLB........ Selected Judgments, Lower Burma [*A publication*]   (DLA)
SJLC......... St. Johnsbury & Lamoille County R. R. [*AAR code*]
SJLC......... Single Junction Latching Circulator
SJLR........ St. John's Law Review [*A publication*]
SJM.......... San Jose De Maipo [*Chile*] [*Seismograph station code, US Geological Survey*] [*Closed*]   (SEIS)
SJM.......... Single Jewish Male [*Classified advertising*]
SJM.......... Smucker [*J. M.*] Co. [*NYSE symbol*]   (SPSG)
SJM.......... Special Joint Meeting
SJM.......... Svalbard and Jan Mayen Islands [*ANSI three-letter standard code*]   (CNC)
SJM.......... System Junction Module [*Deep Space Instrumentation Facility, NASA*]
SJMAA ..... SIAM [*Society for Industrial and Applied Mathematics*] Journal on Mathematical Analysis [*A publication*]
SJMC....... Signed Judgments of the Military Courts in the Administered Territories [*Israel*]   (BJA)
SJMED ..... South African Journal of Hospital Medicine [*A publication*]
SJMJ........ Societe de Jesus, Marie, et Joseph [*Society of Jesus, Mary, and Joseph*] [*Vught, Netherlands*]   (EAIO)
SJMS........ Speculum [*A publication*]
SJMSE7.... Suid-Afrikaanse Tydskrif vir Seewetenskap [*A publication*]
SJN.......... St. Johns, AZ [*Location identifier*] [*FAA*]   (FAAL)
SJN.......... San Juan [*Peru*] [*Seismograph station code, US Geological Survey*] [*Closed*]   (SEIS)
SJN.......... Supersonic Jet Noise
SJNAA ...... SIAM [*Society for Industrial and Applied Mathematics*] Journal on Numerical Analysis [*A publication*]
SJ24NACA ... San Juan 24 North American Class Association   (EA)
SJNB .... SJNB Financial Corp. [*San Jose, CA*] [*NASDAQ symbol*]   (NQ)
SJNCA ...... Soviet Journal of Nuclear Physics [*English Translation*] [*A publication*]
SJNTA ...... Soviet Journal of Nondestructive Testing [*English Translation*] [*A publication*]
SJO.......... Jahrbuch. Deutsche Shakespeare-Gesellschaft Ost [*A publication*]
SJO.......... San Jose [*Costa Rica*] [*Airport symbol*]   (OAG)
SJO.......... Service Junior - Oil-Resistant
SJOJ........ Savez Jevrejskih Opstina Jugoslavije   (BJA)
SJOTB....... Soviet Journal of Optical Technology [*English Translation*] [*A publication*]
SJP .... St. James Press [*Publisher*]
SJP .... St. Joe Paper Co. [*NYSE symbol*]   (SPSG)
SJP .... San Jose Public Library, San Jose, CA [*OCLC symbol*]   (OCLC)
SJP .... San Juan [*Puerto Rico*] [*Seismograph station code, US Geological Survey*] [*Closed*]   (SEIS)
SJP .... Sao Jose Do Rio Preto [*Brazil*] [*Airport symbol*]   (OAG)
SJP .... Scottish Journal of Political Economy [*A publication*]
SJP .... Serialized Job Processor
SJP .... Singapore Justice Party [*Political party*]   (PPW)
SJP .... Socialist Janata Party [*India*] [*Political party*]   (ECON)
SJP .... Southern Journal of Philosophy [*A publication*]
SJP .... Special Job Procedure [*Navy*]   (NG)
SJP .... Standard Jet Penetration [*Aviation*]
SJP .... Sun-Jupiter-Probe [*Angle*]
SJPC........ Standing Joint Pacifist Committee   (EAIO)
SJPE......... Scottish Journal of Political Economy [*A publication*]
S J Phil .... Southern Journal of Philosophy [*A publication*]
SJ Philos... Southern Journal of Philosophy [*A publication*]
SJPNA ...... Soviet Journal of Particles and Nuclei [*A publication*]
SJPRB....... Scandinavian Journal of Plastic and Reconstructive Surgery [*A publication*]
SJPS......... Saint John's Provincial Seminary [*Plymouth, MI*]
SJPSDL.... Suid-Afrikaanse Tydskrif vir Sielkunde [*A publication*]
SJPYA...... Scandinavian Journal of Psychology [*A publication*]
SJQ.......... San Joaquin Reservoir [*California*] [*Seismograph station code, US Geological Survey*] [*Closed*]   (SEIS)
SJR .... San Jose [*Costa Rica*] [*Seismograph station code, US Geological Survey*] [*Closed*]   (SEIS)
SJR .... San Juan Racing Association, Inc. [*NYSE symbol*]   (SPSG)
SJR .... Senate Joint Resolution
SJR .... Social Justice Review [*A publication*]
SJR .... Textile Month [*A publication*]
SJRB......... Soviet Jewry Research Bureau   (EA)
SJRDA ...... Scandinavian Journal of Respiratory Diseases [*A publication*]
SJRES ...... Senate Joint Resolution   (AFIT)
SJRF........ Scott Joplin Ragtime Festival   (EA)
SJRMF.... Senator Joseph R. McCarthy Foundation   (EA)
SJRT......... St. Johns River Terminal [*AAR code*]
SJS............ Saint John's Seminary [*Brighton, MA*]

SJS............ St. Johns Tracking Station [*Newfoundland*]
SJS............ Saint Joseph's Seminary [*Illinois; New York*]
SJS............ San Jose [*Costa Rica*] [*Seismograph station code, US Geological Survey*]   (SEIS)
SJS............ San Jose Studies [*A publication*]
SJS............ Search Jam System
SJS............ Secretary, Joint Staff [*Military*]   (CINC)
SJS............ Society of Jewish Science   (EA)
SJS............ Sunshine-Jr. Stores, Inc. [*AMEX symbol*]   (SPSG)
SJS............ Supervisory Job Safety Test
SJSC........ San Jose State College [*California*] [*Later, San Jose State University*]
SJSCDM... Shimane Journal of Medical Science [*A publication*]
SJSD........ Soviet Jewry Solidarity Day   (BJA)
SJSS........ Saint Joseph's Seraphic Seminary [*New York*]
SJSU .... San Jose State University [*California*]
SJSUD ..... Science Journal. Shivaji University [*A publication*]
SJT .... St. Joseph Terminal Railroad Co. [*AAR code*]
SJT .... San Angelo [*Texas*] [*Airport symbol*]   (OAG)
SJT .... San Angelo, TX [*Location identifier*] [*FAA*]   (FAAL)
SJT .... San Juan Basin Royalty Trust [*NYSE symbol*]   (SPSG)
SJT .... Scottish Journal of Theology [*A publication*]
Sjt .... Serjeant [*Military*] [*British*]   (DMA)
SJT .... Service Junior - Thermoplastic
SJT .... Southwestern Journal of Theology [*A publication*]
SJT .... Subsonic [*or Supersonic*] Jet Transport
SJTCA...... San Juan 21 Class Association   (EA)
SJTCA...... Scandinavian Journal of Thoracic and Cardiovascular Surgery [*A publication*]
SJTCC...... State Job Training Coordinating Council   (OICC)
SJTGD5 .... Singapore Journal of Tropical Geography [*A publication*]
SJTh .... Scottish Journal of Theology [*A publication*]   (BJA)
SJU .... St. John's University [*Minnesota; New York*]
SJU .... St. John's University, Division of Library and Information Science, Jamaica, NY [*OCLC symbol*]   (OCLC)
SJU .... San Juan [*Puerto Rico*] [*Airport symbol*]   (OAG)
SJUF .... Skandinavisk Jodisk Ungdomsforbund   (BJA)
SJUNA...... Scandinavian Journal of Urology and Nephrology [*A publication*]
S Jur.......... Sirey. Jurisprudence [*France*] [*A publication*]   (DLA)
S Jur I .... Sirey. Jurisprudence, Cour de Cassation [*France*] [*A publication*]   (DLA)
S Jur II....... Sirey. Jurisprudence, Other Courts [*France*] [*A publication*]   (DLA)
S Jur III ..... Sirey. Jurisprudence, Jurisprudence Administrative [*France*] [*A publication*]   (DLA)
S Just .... Shaw's Scotch Justiciary Cases [*A publication*]   (DLA)
SJV .... Kyoto University. Jimbun Kagaku Kenkyu-sho. Silver Jubilee Volume [*A publication*]
SJV .... St. John [*Virgin Islands*] [*Seismograph station code, US Geological Survey*]   (SEIS)
SJV .... Sharing Joint Venture
SjV .... Sirp ja Vasar [*A publication*]
SJV .... Societe Jules Verne   (EAIO)
SJVLS ...... San Joaquin Valley Library System [*Library network*]
SJVWGA .. San Joaquin Valley Wine Growers Association   (EA)
SJW .... St. Louis, MO [*Location identifier*] [*FAA*]   (FAAL)
SJW .... Shakespeare-Jahrbuch (Weimar) [*A publication*]
SJW .... Single Jewish Woman [*Classified advertising*]
SJWCP .... SJW Corp. [*AMEX symbol*]   (SPSG)
SJWCP...... Skid Jacket Water Cooling Pump [*Nuclear energy*]   (NRCH)
SJ(Weimar) ... Shakespeare-Jahrbuch (Weimar) [*A publication*]
SJWVUSA ... Sons of Jewish War Veterans of the United States of America   (EA)
SJX .... St. James, MI [*Location identifier*] [*FAA*]   (FAAL)
SJX .... Sartaneja [*Belize*] [*Airport symbol*]   (OAG)
SJY .... San Jacinto, CA [*Location identifier*] [*FAA*]   (FAAL)
SJZ .... Angola, IN [*Location identifier*] [*FAA*]   (FAAL)
SJZ .... Sao Jorge Island [*Azores*] [*Airport symbol*]   (OAG)
SJZ .... Schweizerische Juristen-Zeitung [*A publication*]
SJZ .... Selected Judgments, Zambia [*A publication*]   (DLA)
SJZ .... Sueddeutsche Juristenzeitung [*German*]   (ILCA)
SK .... Sack
SK .... Safekeeping
SK .... Safety-Kleen Corp. [*NYSE symbol*]   (SPSG)
SK .... Sanitaetskompanie [*Medical company*] [*German military - World War II*]
SK .... Santa Klaus   (ROG)
SK .... Saskatchewan [*Canadian province, postal code*]
SK .... Scandinavian Airlines System [*Sweden*] [*ICAO designator*]   (OAG)
SK .... Sealed Knot [*An association*]   (EAIO)
SK .... Seminarium Kondakovianum [*A publication*]
SK .... Service Kit
SK .... Sick
sk............... Sikkim [*ii (India) used in records cataloged after January 1978*] [*MARC country of publication code*] [*Library of Congress*]   (LCCP)
SK .... Sikorsky Aircraft Division [*United Aircraft Corp.*] [*ICAO aircraft manufacturer identifier*]   (ICAO)
SK .... Sinclair-Koppers Co. [*Later, Arco Polymers, Inc.*]

SK	Sink (AAG)
SK	Skein
SK	Skeletals (DCTA)
SK	Sketch (AAG)
S & K	Skills and Knowledges
SK	Skimmed
SK	Skinned (MSA)
SK	Skip
sk.	Skot [Unit of luminance]
SK	Smack (ROG)
SK	Socket (DEN)
SK	Sonic Key (MCD)
SK	South Kensington [District of London] (ROG)
SK	South Korea
SK	Sovetskii Kollektsioner [A publication]
SK	Sovetskyaya Kolonia [Soviet Colony]
SK	Station-Keeping
SK	Storekeeper [Navy rating]
SK	Streptokinase [An enzyme]
Sk.	Strike [or Stroke]
SK	Substance K [Biochemistry]
SK	Sumerische Kultlieder aus Altbabylonischer Zeit [A publication] (BJA)
SK1	Storekeeper, First Class [Navy rating]
SK2	Storekeeper, Second Class [Navy rating]
SK3	Storekeeper, Third Class [Navy rating]
SKA	Sikes Corp. Class A [AMEX symbol] (SPSG)
SKA	Skalstugan [Sweden] [Seismograph station code, US Geological Survey] (SEIS)
SKA	Skandinaviska Enskilda Banken. Quarterly Review [A publication]
SKA	Skill, Knowledge, and Ability [or Attitude] [Employment]
SKA	Spokane, WA [Location identifier] [FAA] (FAAL)
SKA	Station-Keeping Assistance (DS)
S/KA	Submarine Kit Allowance [British military] (DMA)
SKA	Switchblade Knife Act
s-ka akc.	Spolka Akcyjna [Joint Stock Company] [Polish]
SKAC	Sikes Corp. [NASDAQ symbol] (NQ)
SKAD	Survival Kit Air-Droppable [Military] [Canada]
SKAI	Skylink America, Inc. [NASDAQ symbol] (NQ)
SKAMP	Station-Keeping and Mobile Platform [Robot sailboat]
SKAN	Skaneateles Savings Bank [Skaneateles, NY] [NASDAQ symbol] (NQ)
Skand	Skandinavistik [A publication]
Skand Bank ...	Skandinaviska Enskilda Banken [A publication]
Skand Ensk Bank Quart R ...	Skandinaviska Enskilda Banken. Quarterly Review [A publication]
Skandia Int Symp ...	Skandia International Symposia [A publication]
Skandinavis ...	Skandinavistik [A publication]
Skandinaviska Enskilda Banken Q R ...	Skandinaviska Enskilda Banken. Quarterly Review [A publication]
Skand Numis ...	Skandinavisk Numismatik [A publication]
SKAND SF ...	Skandinaviska Seglarforbundet [Scandinavian Yachting Association - SYA] (EAIO)
Skand Vet Tidskr ...	Skandinavisk Veterinaertidskrift foer Bakteriologi, Patologi, samt Koettoch Mjoelkhygien [A publication]
SKAP	Armedia/El Elden [Colombia] [ICAO location identifier] (ICLI)
SKAP	Skills, Knowledge, Abilities, and Personnel [Attributes] (MCD)
SKAS	Puerto Asis [Colombia] [ICAO location identifier] (ICLI)
SKAT	Kommentar zum Alten Testament [A publication] (BJA)
SKAT	Sex Knowledge and Aptitude [Test]
SKATI	Skills, Knowledges, Aptitudes, Temperaments, Interests (OICC)
Skat Mag ...	Skating Magazine [A publication]
SKAWW....	Sitzungsberichte. Kaiserliche Akademie der Wissenschaften in Wien [A publication]
SKB	Saint Kitts [Leeward Islands] [Airport symbol] (OAG)
SKB	Skew Buffer
SKB	Skybridge International, Inc. [Vancouver Stock Exchange symbol]
SKB	SmithKline Beckman Corp. [Formerly, SKL] [NYSE symbol] (SPSG)
SKB	Wichita Falls, TX [Location identifier] [FAA] (FAAL)
SKBC	El Banco/Los Flores [Colombia] [ICAO location identifier] (ICLI)
SKBF	Schweizerische Koordinationsstelle fuer Bildungsforschung [Swiss Coordination Center for Research in Education] [Information service or system] (IID)
SKBG	Bucaramanga/Palo Negro Sur [Colombia] [ICAO location identifier] (ICLI)
SKBGD......	Sangyo Kogai Boshi Gijutsu [A publication]
SKBO	Bogota/Eldorado [Colombia] [ICAO location identifier] (ICLI)
SKBQ	Barranquilla/Ernesto Cortissoz [Colombia] [ICAO location identifier] (ICLI)
SKBS	Bahia Solano/Jose Celestino Mutis [Colombia] [ICAO location identifier] (ICLI)
SKBU	Buenaventura [Colombia] [ICAO location identifier] (ICLI)
SKC	Services Kinema Corporation [British military] (DMA)
SKC	Sky Clear [Meteorology] (FAAC)
SKC	Suki [Papua New Guinea] [Airport symbol] (OAG)

SKC	Waukesha, WI [Location identifier] [FAA] (FAAL)
SKCATL.....	South Korea Conventional Air Target List (MCD)
SKCB	Storekeeper, Construction Battalion, Stevedore [Navy rating]
SKCC	Cucuta/Camilo Daza [Colombia] [ICAO location identifier] (ICLI)
SKCD	Condoto/Mandinga [Colombia] [ICAO location identifier] (ICLI)
SKCG	Cartagena/Rafael Nunez [Colombia] [ICAO location identifier] (ICLI)
SKCH	Skyline Chili, Inc. [Cincinnati, OH] [NASDAQ symbol] (NQ)
SKCL	Cali/Alfonso Bonilla Aragon [Colombia] [ICAO location identifier] (ICLI)
SKCM	Master Chief Storekeeper [Navy rating]
SKCM	Society of King Charles the Martyr (EA)
SKCMA	Steel Kitchen Cabinet Manufacturers Association (EA)
SKCO	Tumaco/La Florida [Colombia] [ICAO location identifier] (ICLI)
SKCS	Senior Chief Storekeeper [Navy rating]
SKCZ	Corozal/Las Brujas [Colombia] [ICAO location identifier] (ICLI)
SKD	St. Katherine's Dock [Shipping] [British] (ROG)
SKD	Samarkand [USSR] [Airport symbol] (OAG)
SKD	Selve-Kornbegel-Dornheim [Name of a German small arms ammunition factory] [World War II]
SKD	Semi Knocked Down [Shipping]
SKD	Sitkalidak Island [Alaska] [Seismograph station code, US Geological Survey] (SEIS)
SKD	Skid
SKD	Skilled (MSA)
SKD	Skirted
SKD	Skyworld Resources & Development Ltd. [Vancouver Stock Exchange symbol]
SKD	Station-Keeping Distance [British military] (DMA)
SKD	Storekeeper, Disbursing [Navy rating]
SKD	Svenska Dagbladet [A publication]
SKDGQ	Sammlung Ausgewaehlter Kirchen- und Dogmengeschichtlichen Quellenschriften [A publication]
SKDH	Shikimate Dehydrogenase [An enzyme]
SKDL........	Suomen Kansan Demokraattinen Liitto [Finnish People's Democratic League] [Political party] (PPW)
SKDN	Shakedown [Navy] (NVT)
SKDNC......	Shakedown Cruise [Navy]
SKDNCRU ...	Shakedown Cruise [Navy] (NVT)
SKDP	Sambungan Komunikasi Data Packet [Indonesia] [Telecommunications service] (TSSD)
SKDU	Ship's Keyboard Display Unit
SKE	Belleville, IL [Location identifier] [FAA] (FAAL)
SKE	Skeena Resources Ltd. [Vancouver Stock Exchange symbol]
SKE	Skien [Norway] [Airport symbol] (OAG)
SKE	Sky Tours, Inc. [Port Clinton, OH] [FAA designator] (FAAC)
SKE	Station-Keeping Equipment
SKEC	Barranquilla [Colombia] [ICAO location identifier] (ICLI)
SKED........	Bogota [Colombia] [ICAO location identifier] (ICLI)
SKED........	Schedule (NG)
SKED........	Sort Key Edit [Library of Congress]
SKEDCON ...	Schedule Conference [Military] (NVT)
SKEIA	Sanshi Kagaku Kenkyusho Iho [A publication]
SKEJ..........	Barrancabermeja/Yariguis [Colombia] [ICAO location identifier] (ICLI)
SKEL	Skeletal (AAG)
Skeletal Radiol ...	Skeletal Radiology [A publication]
SKENAN...	Ecological Review [A publication]
Skene	[Sir John] Skene's De Verborum Significatione [Of the Signification of Words] [7 eds.] [1597-1683] [A publication] (DLA)
Skene De Verb Sign ...	Skene. De Verborum Significatione [Of the Signification of Words] [A publication] (DLA)
SKET	Skeleton Key (DSUE)
SKF	San Antonio, TX [Location identifier] [FAA] (FAAL)
SKF	Skycraft, Inc. [Seattle, WA] [FAA designator] (FAAC)
SKF	SmithKline Corp. [Formerly, Smith, Kline & French Co.] [Research code symbol]
SKF	Svenska Kullagerfabriken AB [Swedish manufacturer, especially of ball bearings; active in many countries]
SKFB	S & K Famous Brands, Inc. [NASDAQ symbol] (NQ)
SkFi	Skandinavskaga Filologija [A publication]
SKFL........	Florencia/Capitolio [Colombia] [ICAO location identifier] (ICLI)
SKF Psychiatr Rep ...	SK and F [Smith, Kline, and French] Psychiatric Reporter [A publication]
SKFR	SKF AB [Goteborg, Sweden] [NASDAQ symbol] (NQ)
SkFx	Skull Fracture [Medicine]
Skg............	Safekeeping
SKG	Schriften. Koenigsberger Gelehrten-Gesellschaft [A publication]
SKG	Sikaman Gold Resources Ltd. [Toronto Stock Exchange symbol]
SKG	Srpski Knjizevni Glasnik [A publication]
SKG	Thessaloniki [Greece] [Airport symbol] (OAG)
SKGG	Schriften. Koenigsberger Gelehrten-Gesellschaft [A publication]
SKGGD	Sammlung Kurzer Grammatiken Germanischer Dialekte [A publication]

SKGI......... Girardot/Santiago Vila [*Colombia*] [*ICAO location identifier*] (ICLI)
SKGND ..... Sanup Kwahak Gisul Yeonguso Nonmunjip [*Inha University*] [*A publication*]
SKGP........ Guapi [*Colombia*] [*ICAO location identifier*] (ICLI)
SKGSA ...... Sekiyu Gakkaishi [*A publication*]
SKH .... Selkirk Communications Ltd. [*Toronto Stock Exchange symbol*]
SKH .... Staatsblad van het Koninkrijk der Nederlanden [*A publication*]
SKH .... Surkhet [*Nepal*] [*Airport symbol*] (OAG)
S-Kh Biol ... Sel'skokhozyaistvennaya Biologiya [*A publication*]
S-Kh Proizvod Urala ... Sel'skokhozyaistvennoe Proizvodstvo Urala [*A publication*]
S-Kh Rub Rastenievod ... Sel'skokhozyaistvo za Rubezhom Rastenievodstvo [*A publication*]
SKHS........ Sri Kapila Humanitarian Society (EAIO)
SKHVL...... Skrifter Utgivna av Kungliga Humanistiska Vetenskapssamfundet i Lund [*A publication*]
SkHVSU ... Skrifter Utgivna. Humanistiska Vetenskapssamfundet i Uppsala [*A publication*]
SKI............ Sac City, IA [*Location identifier*] [*FAA*] (FAAL)
SKI............ St. Kitts [*St. Kitts*] [*Seismograph station code, US Geological Survey*] (SEIS)
SKI............ Sex Knowledge Inventory [*Premarital and marital relations test*]
SKI............ Sister Kenny Institute (EA)
SKI............ Sloan-Kettering Institute for Cancer Research
SKIB .... Ibague/Perales [*Colombia*] [*ICAO location identifier*] (ICLI)
Skid Min.... Skidmore's Mining Statutes [*A publication*] (DLA)
SKIF .... Social Security Number Key Index File [*IRS*]
SKIF .... Sotsyalistisher Kinder Farband (BJA)
SKII .... S-K-I Ltd. [*Killington, VT*] [*NASDAQ symbol*] (NQ)
SKIL .... Canterbury Educational Services, Inc. [*NASDAQ symbol*] (NQ)
SKIL .... Scanner Keyed Input Language
SKILA ...... Southern Korean Interim Legislative Assembly
SKILL........ Satellite Kill
Skillings' Min Rev ... Skillings' Mining Review [*A publication*]
Skill Pol Rep ... Skillman's New York Police Reports [*A publication*] (DLA)
Skil Mining ... Skillings' Mining Review [*A publication*]
Skin........... Skinner's English King's Bench Reports [*A publication*] (DLA)
Skin Diver Mag ... Skin Diver Magazine [*A publication*]
Skinker ...... Skinker's Reports [*65-79 Missouri*] [*A publication*] (DLA)
Skinner ...... Skinner's English King's Bench Reports [*90 English Reprint*] [*1681-98*] [*A publication*] (DLA)
Skinner (Eng) ... Skinner's English King's Bench Reports [*90 English Reprint*] [*A publication*] (DLA)
Skin Res..... Skin Research [*A publication*]
SKINS .... Supplemental Knowledge Incentive Notes [*Scrip offered to students for good performance*] [*Experimental learning program*]
SKIP .... Ipiales/San Luis [*Colombia*] [*ICAO location identifier*] (ICLI)
SKIP .... Sick Kids Need Involved People (EA)
SKIP .... Skinner Investigation Platform
SKIP .... Skipper's, Inc. [*NASDAQ symbol*] (NQ)
SKIPI........ Super Knowledge Information Processing Intelligence [*Data processing*]
SKIS .... St. Kilda Income Stretchers [*Australia*]
SKJ .... Sitkinak Island, AK [*Location identifier*] [*FAA*] (FAAL)
SKK........... Shaktoolik [*Alaska*] [*Airport symbol*] (OAG)
SKK........... Shaktoolik, AK [*Location identifier*] [*FAA*] (FAAL)
SKK........... Sikka [*USSR*] [*Seismograph station code, US Geological Survey*] [*Closed*] (SEIS)
SKK........... Sowjetische Kontrollkommission
SKK........... Sydslesvigsk Kirkekalender [*A publication*]
SKKCA ...... Supreme Knight of the Knights of Columbus of America
SKKEA ...... Sklar a Keramik [*A publication*]
SKKNAJ ... Annual Report. Sankyo Research Laboratories [*A publication*]
SKKOA...... Shin Kinzoku Kogyo [*A publication*]
SKL........... Isle Of Skye [*Scotland*] [*Airport symbol*] (OAG)
SKL........... Skilak [*Cooper Landing*] [*Alaska*] [*Seismograph station code, US Geological Survey*] (SEIS)
SKL........... Skill Level
SKL........... Skylight [*Technical drawings*]
SKL........... Stackpool Resources Ltd. [*Vancouver Stock Exchange symbol*]
SKL........... Suomen Kristillinen Liitto [*Finnish Christian League*] [*Political party*] (PPE)
SKLC .... Los Cedros/Uraba [*Colombia*] [*ICAO location identifier*] (ICLI)
SKLM........ La Mina/Riohacha [*Colombia*] [*ICAO location identifier*] (ICLI)
SKLT .... Leticia/Alfredo Vasquez Cobo [*Colombia*] [*ICAO location identifier*] (ICLI)
S Kl V .... Sammlung Klinischer Vortraege [*A publication*]
SKM .... Fayette Flying Service & Scheduled Skyways System [*Fayetteville, AR*] [*FAA designator*] (FAAC)
SKM .... Schuster-Kubelka-Munk [*Optics*]
SKM .... Schweizerische Kreditanstalt. Bulletin [*A publication*]
SKM .... Sine-Kosine Multiplier
SKMG .... Magangue/Baracoa [*Colombia*] [*ICAO location identifier*] (ICLI)

SkMg......... Sulfate of Potash Magnesia Export Association (EA)
SKMQ .... Mariquita/Mariquita [*Colombia*] [*ICAO location identifier*] (ICLI)
SKMR........ Monteria/Los Garzones [*Colombia*] [*ICAO location identifier*] (ICLI)
SKMRA.... Skillings' Mining Review [*A publication*]
SKMU .... Mitu/Mitu [*Colombia*] [*ICAO location identifier*] (ICLI)
SKMZ........ Manizales/La Nubia [*Colombia*] [*ICAO location identifier*] (ICLI)
SKN .... Skaneateles [*New York*] [*Seismograph station code, US Geological Survey*] (SEIS)
SKN .... Skein (ROG)
SKN .... Skolniks, Inc. [*AMEX symbol*] (SPSG)
SKN .... Skyline Aviation Service, Inc. [*Beaver Falls, PA*] [*FAA designator*] (FAAC)
SKN .... Smithville, TN [*Location identifier*] [*FAA*] (FAAL)
SKN .... Stokmarknes [*Norway*] [*Airport symbol*] (OAG)
SKNEA7.... Annual Report. Shionogi Research Laboratory [*A publication*]
SKNSAF.... Advances in Neurological Sciences [*A publication*]
SKNSB ...... Shokuhin Shosha [*A publication*]
SKNTO ..... St. Kitts-Nevis Tourist Office (EA)
S/KNU .... Steering Knuckle [*Automotive engineering*]
SKNV .... Neiva/La Manguila [*Colombia*] [*ICAO location identifier*] (ICLI)
SKO .... Deadhorse, AK [*Location identifier*] [*FAA*] (FAAL)
SKO .... Saskatchewan Oil & Gas Corp. [*Toronto Stock Exchange symbol*]
SKO .... Sets, Kits, and Outfits (MCD)
SKO .... Skopje [*Yugoslavia*] [*Seismograph station code, US Geological Survey*] (SEIS)
SKO .... Society of Kastorians "Omonoia" (EA)
SKO .... Sokoto [*Nigeria*] [*Airport symbol*] (OAG)
SKOC .... Ocana/Aguas Claras [*Colombia*] [*ICAO location identifier*] (ICLI)
Skoda Rev ... Skoda Review [*A publication*]
Skogshoegsk Inst Skogstek Rapp Uppsats Res Notes ... Skogshoegskolan, Institutionen foer Skogsteknik, Rapporter och Uppsatser. Research Notes [*Sweden*] [*A publication*]
Skogs-Lantbruksakad Tidskr ... Skogs- och Lantbruksakademiens Tidskrift [*A publication*]
Skogstradsforadling Inst Skogsforbattring ... Skogstradsforadling-Institutet foer Skogsforbattring [*A publication*]
SKOKAU .. Sbornik Nauchnykh Rabot Kafedry Otorinolaringologii Kishinevskogo Meditsinskogo Instituta Moldavskogo Nauchnogo Otorinolaringologicheskogo Obshchestva [*A publication*]
SKOLD...... Screening Kit of Language Development [*Child development test*]
SKOR .... Score Exploration Corp. [*NASDAQ symbol*] (NQ)
SKOT........ Otu/Otu [*Colombia*] [*ICAO location identifier*] (ICLI)
Skoteys ...... Spoiled Kids of the Eighties [*Lifestyle classification*] [*Offspring of the Yuppies*]
SKP............ Skip (BUR)
SKP............ Skopje [*Yugoslavia*] [*Airport symbol*] (OAG)
SKP............ Station-Keeping Position
SKP............ Suomen Kommunistinen Puolue [*Communist Party of Finland*] [*Political party*] (PPW)
SKP............ Sveriges Kommunistiska Partiet [*Communist Party of Sweden*] [*Political party*] (PPE)
S-K-P's...... Escapees, Inc. (EA)
SKPanKr.... Sprawozdania z Posiedzen Komisji Pan. Oddzial w Krakowie [*A publication*]
SKPB .... Puerto Bolivar/Riohacha [*Colombia*] [*ICAO location identifier*] (ICLI)
SKPC .... Puerto Carreno [*Colombia*] [*ICAO location identifier*] (ICLI)
SKPE .... Pereira/Matecana [*Colombia*] [*ICAO location identifier*] (ICLI)
SKPI .... Pitalito [*Colombia*] [*ICAO location identifier*] (ICLI)
SKPI .... Super Knowledge, Processing Interaction [*Concept advanced by Timothy Leary*]
SKPL .... Sketch Pad Layout (MCD)
SKPP .... Popayan/Guillermo Leon Valencia [*Colombia*] [*ICAO location identifier*] (ICLI)
SKPS .... Pasto/Antonio Narino [*Colombia*] [*ICAO location identifier*] (ICLI)
SKPTA ...... Skipsteknikk [*A publication*]
SKPV........ Providencia/Providencia [*Colombia*] [*ICAO location identifier*] (ICLI)
SKQ .... Sekakes [*Lesotho*] [*Airport symbol*] (OAG)
SKQ .... Sexual Knowledge Questionnaire
SKR........... Bedford, MA [*Location identifier*] [*FAA*] (FAAL)
SKR........... Sanskrit [*Language, etc.*]
SKR........... Saskatchewan Regional Libraries [*UTLAS symbol*]
SKR........... Saturn Kilometer-Wave Radiation [*Planetary science*]
SKR........... Sea King Replacement [*Naval aircraft*] [*British*]
SKR........... Separator-Key Generator-Recombiner (MCD)
SKR........... Severo-Kurilsk [*USSR*] [*Seismograph station code, US Geological Survey*] (SEIS)
SKR........... Shaker Heights City School District, Shaker Heights, OH [*OCLC symbol*] (OCLC)
Skr .... Skipper [*Navy*] [*British*]

SKR............	Skylark Resources Ltd. [*Vancouver Stock Exchange symbol*]
SKR............	South Korea Republic
SKR............	Station-Keeping RADAR
SKR............	Substance-K Receptor [*Biochemistry*]
S KR............	Swedish Krona [*Monetary unit*]
SKRAD....	Skeletal Radiology [*A publication*]
SKRG........	Rio Negro/Jose Maria Cordova [*Colombia*] [*ICAO location identifier*] (ICLI)
SKRH	Rio Hacha, Guajira [*Colombia*] [*ICAO location identifier*] (ICLI)
Skriftser Roskilde Universitetsbibl ...	Skriftserie. Roskilde Universitetsbibliotek [*A publication*]
Skr Lund	Skrifter Utgivna. Vetenskaps-Societeten i Lund [*A publication*]
Skr Mineral Paleontol Geol Inst ...	Skrifter fran Mineralogisk och Paleontologisk-Geologiska Institutionerna [*A publication*]
Skr Norske Vid-Akad Oslo I ...	Skrifter Utgitt. Norske Videnskaps-Akademi i Oslo. I. Matematisk-Naturvidenskapelig Klasse [*A publication*]
Skr Nor Vidensk-Akad Oslo I ...	Skrifter Utgitt. Norske Videnskaps-Akademi i Oslo. I. Matematisk-Naturvidenskapelig Klasse [*A publication*]
Skr Nor Vidensk-Akad Oslo I Mat-Naturvidensk Kl ...	Skrifter. Norske Videnskaps-Akademi i Oslo. I. Matematisk-Naturvidenskapelig Klasse [*A publication*]
Skr Szk Gl Gospod Wiejsk-Akad Roln Warszawie Ogrod ...	Skrypty Szkoly Glownej Gospodarstwa Wiejskiego-Akademii Rolniczej w Warszawie. Ogrodnictwo [*A publication*]
Skr Udgivet Univ Zool Mus (Kbh) ...	Skrifter Udgivet. Universitetets Zoologiske Museum (Kobenhavn) [*A publication*]
Skr Uppsala ...	Skrifter Utgivna av Kungliga Humanist. Vetenskaps-Samfundet i Uppsala [*A publication*]
SKS............	Career Development Center, Shaker Heights, OH [*OCLC symbol*] (OCLC)
SKS............	Savezna Komisija za Standardizacija [*Federal Commission for Standardization*] [*Yugoslavia*]
SKS............	Scanning Kinetic Spectroscopy
SKS............	Skrydstrup [*Denmark*] [*Airport symbol*] (OAG)
SKS............	Soren Kierkegaard Society [*Copenhagen, Denmark*] (EA)
SKS............	Sound Air Aviation [*Ronkonkoma, NY*] [*FAA designator*] (FAAC)
SKS............	Specialist Knowledge Services [*British organization for occult research*]
SKS............	Station-Keeping Ship
SKS............	Suomalainen Kirjallisuuden Seura [*A publication*]
SKSA........	Saravena/Saravena El Eden [*Colombia*] [*ICAO location identifier*] (ICLI)
SKSA........	Seaman Apprentice, Storekeeper, Striker [*Navy rating*]
SkSb..........	Skandinavskij Sbornik [*A publication*]
SKSD........	Streptokinase Streptodornase [*An enzyme mixture*] [*Medicine*]
SKSG........	Santagueda/Santagueda [*Colombia*] [*ICAO location identifier*] (ICLI)
SKSJ..........	San Jose Del Guaviare/S. J. Del Guaviore [*Colombia*] [*ICAO location identifier*] (ICLI)
SKSL........	Skaneateles Short Line Railroad Corp. [*Later, SSL*] [*AAR code*]
SKSM........	Santa Marta/Simon Bolivar [*Colombia*] [*ICAO location identifier*] (ICLI)
SKSN........	Seaman, Storekeeper, Striker [*Navy rating*]
SKSODV ...	Neurology. Series One. Neural Mechanisms of Movement [*A publication*]
SKSP	San Andres/Sesquicentenario, San Andres [*Colombia*] [*ICAO location identifier*] (ICLI)
SKSS........	Stoleczny Komitet Samopomocy Spolecznej [*Warsaw*] (BJA)
SKSV	San Vicente Del Caguan [*Colombia*] [*ICAO location identifier*] (ICLI)
SKT............	Sanskrit
SKT............	Saskatchewan Trust Co. [*Toronto Stock Exchange symbol*]
SKT............	Skill Knowledge Tests
SKT............	Skirt (MSA)
SKT............	Skwentna [*Alaska*] [*Seismograph station code, US Geological Survey*] (SEIS)
SKT............	Socket (MSA)
SKT............	Specialty Knowledge Test [*Military*] (AFM)
SKT............	Storekeeper, Technical [*Navy rating*]
SKT............	Svensk Kemisk Tidskrift [*A publication*]
SKT............	Tropical International, Inc. [*Miami, FL*] [*FAA designator*] (FAAC)
SKTD........	Trinidad [*Colombia*] [*ICAO location identifier*] (ICLI)
SKTEA	Sky and Telescope [*A publication*]
SKTF	Spring Knife Trade Federation [*A union*] [*British*]
SKTM........	Tame [*Colombia*] [*ICAO location identifier*] (ICLI)
SKTU........	Turbo, Gonzalo Mejia [*Colombia*] [*ICAO location identifier*] (ICLI)
SKU............	Newburgh, NY [*Location identifier*] [*FAA*] (FAAL)
SKU............	Sakura [*Japan*] [*Seismograph station code, US Geological Survey*] [*Closed*] (SEIS)
SKU............	Stock Keeping Unit [*Merchandising system*]
SKUC........	Arauca/Santiago Perez [*Colombia*] [*ICAO location identifier*] (ICLI)
SKUI..........	Quibdo/El Carano [*Colombia*] [*ICAO location identifier*] (ICLI)
SKV............	Santa Katarina [*Egypt*] [*Airport symbol*] (OAG)
SKV............	Skewing the Pitch Angle
SKV............	Skukum Gold [*Vancouver Stock Exchange symbol*]
SKV............	Storekeeper, Aviation [*Navy rating*]
SKVP........	Valledupar/Alfonso Lopez [*Colombia*] [*ICAO location identifier*] (ICLI)
SKVSAL....	Sbornik Trudov Khar'kovskogo Nauchno-Issledovatel'skogo Instituta Vaktsin i Syvorotok Imeni Mechnikov [*A publication*]
SKVV........	Schweizerischer Katholischer Volksverein
SKVV........	Villavicencio/Vanguardia [*Colombia*] [*ICAO location identifier*] (ICLI)
SKW	Shichikawa [*Japan*] [*Seismograph station code, US Geological Survey*] (SEIS)
SKW	Skwentna, AK [*Location identifier*] [*FAA*] (FAAL)
SKW	Sky West Aviation, Inc. [*St. George, UT*] [*FAA designator*] (FAAC)
SKW	Sueddeutsche Kalkstickstoffwerke [*AG*]
SKWKA.....	Sanop Kwa Kisul [*A publication*]
SKX............	Skyline Explorations Ltd. [*Vancouver Stock Exchange symbol*] [*Toronto Stock Exchange symbol*]
SKX............	Taos, NM [*Location identifier*] [*FAA*] (FAAL)
SKY............	Sandusky, OH [*Location identifier*] [*FAA*] (FAAL)
SKY............	Sky Flite, Inc. [*Tulsa, OK*] [*FAA designator*] (FAAC)
SKY............	Skyline Corp. [*NYSE symbol*] (SPSG)
SKY............	Skyrocket Exploration [*Vancouver Stock Exchange symbol*]
Sky............	Skywriting [*A publication*]
SKYBET....	Skylab Best Estimate of Trajectory [*NASA*]
SKYCAV ...	Sky Cavalry
SKYCOM ...	Skylab Communications Engineer [*NASA*]
SKYOA.....	Shikizai Kyokaishi [*A publication*]
SKYP........	Suomen Kansan Yhtenaeisyyden Puolue [*People's Unity Party*] [*Finland*] [*Political party*] (PPW)
SKYP........	Yopal/Yopal [*Colombia*] [*ICAO location identifier*] (ICLI)
Skyscraper Mgt ...	Skyscraper Management [*A publication*]
Sky & Tel...	Sky and Telescope [*A publication*]
Sky and Telesc ...	Sky and Telescope [*A publication*]
Sky Telesc ...	Sky and Telescope [*A publication*]
SKYW........	SkyWest, Inc. [*St. George, UT*] [*NASDAQ symbol*] (NQ)
SKYX........	Sky Express, Inc. [*Valley Stream, NY*] [*NASDAQ symbol*] (NQ)
SKZ............	Schweizerische Kirchenzeitung [*A publication*]
SKZ............	Sukkur [*Pakistan*] [*Airport symbol*] (OAG)
SL...............	Antares SpA [*ICAO designator*] (FAAC)
SL...............	Large-Scale Disturbance Field
SL...............	Lloydminster Public Library, Saskatchewan [*Library symbol*] [*National Library of Canada*] (NLC)
SL...............	Safe Locker (AAG)
SL...............	Safety Level [*Army*]
SL...............	Safety Limit [*Nuclear energy*] (NRCH)
S & L.........	Sale and Leaseback
SL...............	Sales Letter
SL...............	Salt Loading
SL...............	Salvage Loss
SL...............	Sample Laboratory (MCD)
SL...............	San Luis Obispo [*Mexican state; city and county in California*]
SL...............	Sand-Loaded [*Technical drawings*]
SL...............	Satellite-Like Virus
SL...............	Save Lebanon (EA)
S & L.........	Savings and Loan [*Association*]
SL...............	Savings and Loan [*Association*]
sl.................	Scale Leaf [*Botany*]
SL...............	Scanning Slit (MCD)
S & L.........	Schoales and Lefroy's Irish Chancery Reports [*1802-06*] [*A publication*] (DLA)
SL...............	School Leavers [*Department of Employment*] [*British*]
SL...............	Schutte Lanz [*World War I German aircraft designation*]
SL...............	Scientists for Life [*An association*] [*Defunct*] (EA)
SL...............	Scottish Liturgy [*Episcopalian*]
SL...............	Sea Level
SL...............	Seal (NASA)
SL...............	Searchlight
SL...............	Second Lieutenant
SL...............	Section Leader [*Nuclear energy*] (NRCH)
SL...............	Section List (MCD)
SL...............	Secundum Legem [*According to Law*] [*Latin*]
SL...............	Seditious Libeler
SL...............	Send Leg [*Telegraphy*] (TEL)
SL...............	Sendero Luminoso [*Shining Path*] [*Peru*] (PD)
SL...............	Sensation Level [*Audiometry*]
SL...............	Sensu Lato [*In a Broad Sense*] [*Latin*]
SL...............	Separate Lead [*Cables*]
SL...............	Sergeant-at-Law
SL...............	Service Letter (MCD)
SL...............	Servomechanisms Laboratory [*MIT*] (MCD)
SL...............	Session Laws (DLA)
SL...............	Shear Layer [*or Load*]
SL...............	Shelf Life (NASA)
SL...............	Shift Left
SL...............	Ship Library [*Maritime Data Network, Inc.*] [*Information service or system*] (CRD)
SL...............	Ship-of-the-Line

S-of-L	Ship-of-the-Line
SL	Shipowner's Liability [*Business term*]
S/L	Shops and Labs [*NASA*] (NASA)
SL	Short Landed [*Tea trade*] (ROG)
SL	Short Lengths [*Construction*]
SL	Short Letter (DCTA)
S-L	Short-Long [*as of a signal light's flash cycle*]
SL	Sick Leave (AFM)
SL	Side Load (AAG)
SL	Sidelobe (CAAL)
SL	Sierra Leone [*ANSI two-letter standard code*] (CNC)
sl	Sierra Leone [*MARC country of publication code*] [*Library of Congress*] (LCCP)
SL	Sigillo Locus [*Place for the Seal*] [*Latin*] (ROG)
SL	Signal Level
S & L	Signed and Limited Edition [*Publishing*]
SL	Significance Level
SL	Silicon Lacquer
SL	Silvaire [*ICAO aircraft manufacturer identifier*] (ICAO)
SL	Silver Library [*A publication*]
SL	Simulation Language [*Data processing*] (BUR)
SL	Sine Loco [*Without Place*] [*Latin*]
SL	Single Ledger [*Accounting*]
SL	Single Line
SL	Single-Locus [*Light flashes*]
SL	Sisters of Loretto at the Foot of the Cross [*Roman Catholic religious order*]
SL	Skill Level
SL	Skylab [*NASA*] (KSC)
SL	SL Industries, Inc. [*NYSE symbol*] (SPSG)
SL	Slain (ROG)
SL	Slate (AAG)
Sl	Slavia [*A publication*]
SL	Slavica [*A publication*]
SL	Sleeve [*Technical drawings*]
SL	Slesvigske Parti [*Schleswig Party*] [*Denmark*] [*Political party*] (PPE)
SL	Slide (AAG)
SL	Slightly
SL	Slip [*Knitting*]
SL	Slit Lamp [*Instrumentation*]
Sl	Slovo. Casopis Staroslavenskog Instituta [*A publication*]
SL	Slow [*Track condition*] [*Thoroughbred racing*]
SL	Small Light Seeds [*Botany*]
SL	Small Lymphocytes [*Hematology*]
SL	Salta Lymphoma [*Oncology*]
SL	Sociedad de Responsabilidad Limitada [*Private Limited Company*] [*Spanish*]
SL	Societas Liturgica (EA)
SL	Society of Limerents (EA)
SL	Sockellafette [*Pedestal mount*] [*German military - World War II*]
SL	Soft Landing (MCD)
SL	Soft LASER
SL	Solar Lobby [*An association*] (EA)
SL	Sold
SL	Solicitor-at-Law
SL	Sonic Log
SL	Sons of Liberty (EA)
SL	Sortie Lab [*NASA*]
SL	Sound Level (NASA)
SL	Sound Locator [*Military*]
S/L	Source Language [*Data processing*] (BUR)
SL	Source Level
SL	South Latitude
SL	Southeast Airlines, Inc. [*ICAO designator*] [*Obsolete*] (OAG)
SL	Southern Lumberman [*United States*] [*A publication*]
SL	Soviet Life [*A publication*]
SL	Soviet Literature [*A publication*]
S/L	Space Laboratory (KSC)
SL	Spacelab [*NASA*] (NASA)
SL	Spartacist League (EA)
SL	Special Layout (MCD)
SL	Special Libraries [*A publication*]
SL	Special Linear [*Group theory, mathematics*]
S/L	Speedletter
S/L	Split Level [*Home*] [*Classified advertising*]
SL	Spool
SL	Sprache und Literatur [*A publication*]
SL	Sprinkler Leakage [*Insurance*]
SL	Squadron-Leader [*Military*]
SL	Stage Left [*A stage direction*]
SL	Stagnation Line
SL	Standard Label [*Data processing*]
SL	Standard Length
SL	Standard of Living
SL	Standard Location [*Civil Defense*]
S & L	Standards and Limits
SL	Star Line
SL	Start Line
SL	Stationary Low-Power [*Reactor*] [*Dismantled*] (NRCH)
SL	Statistical List
S/L	Statute of Limitations (OICC)
SL	Stern Loading
SL	Stock Length [*Construction or manufacturing materials*]
SL	Stock Level (AFM)
SL	Stock List (MCD)
SL	Stomodeal Lip [*Endocrinology*]
SL	Storage Location
SL	Straight Line
SL	Streamline
SL	Streptolysin [*Hematology*]
SL	Stronnictwo Ludowe [*Peasant Party*] [*Poland*] [*Political party*] (PPE)
SL	Structures Laboratory [*Army*] (GRD)
SL	Studia Linguistica [*Lund*] [*A publication*]
SL	Studies in Linguistics [*A publication*]
SL	Studio Location
s/l	Sua Letra [*Your Letter*] [*Portuguese*]
SL	Sub-Lieutenant [*British military*]
SL	Suberin Lamella [*Botany*]
SL	Sublingual [*Medicine*]
SL	Submarine Lightwave Cable [*AT & T*] [*Telecommunications*]
SL	Submarine Qualification Lapsed [*Navy*]
SL	Subscriber's Loop [*Telecommunications*] (TEL)
SL	Sue and Labor Charges [*Insurance*]
SL	Sumarski List [*A publication*]
SL	Sumerian Laws (BJA)
SL	Sumerisches Lexikon [*Rome*] [*A publication*]
SL	Sunday League (EA)
SL	Superlattice [*Solid state physics*]
SL	Supplementary List [*Navy*] [*British*]
SL	Supplier Letter (MCD)
S & L	Supply and Logistics
SL	Support Line [*Military*]
SL	Surface Launch (MUGU)
SL	Surveillance Licence [*Importing*] [*British*] (DS)
SL	Svenska Landsmal och Svenskt Folkliv [*A publication*]
SL	Sydney & Louisburg Railway Co. [*AAR code*]
SL	Synchronous Line Medium Speed (BUR)
SL	Syria and Lebanon
SL	System Language
S & L	System and Logistics
SLA	La Ronge Public Library, Saskatchewan [*Library symbol*] [*National Library of Canada*] (NLC)
SLA	Left Sacroanterior Position [*of the fetus*] [*Obstetrics*]
SLA	Salta [*Argentina*] [*Airport symbol*] (OAG)
SLA	San Lorenzo [*Argentina*] [*Seismograph station code, US Geological Survey*] (SEIS)
SLA	Sandia Laboratories, Albuquerque (AABC)
SLA	Saturn LM [*Lunar Module*] Adapter [*NASA*]
SLA	School Lecturers' Association [*British*]
SLA	School Library Association
SLA	Scott Library [*A publication*]
SLA	Scottish Library Association
SLA	Sealed Lead Acid [*Battery*] [*Automotive engineering*]
SLA	Sequential Launch Adapter [*Missiles*] (RDA)
SLA	Shared Line Adapter
SLA	Short and Long Arm [*Automotive engineering*]
SLA	Showmen's League of America (EA)
SLA	Side-Looking LASER Altimeter (RDA)
SLA	Sierra Leone Airlines
SL & A	Sine Loco et Anno [*Without Place and Year*] [*Latin*]
SLA	Single-Line Approach
Sla	Slavia [*A publication*]
sla	Slavic [*MARC language code*] [*Library of Congress*] (LCCP)
SLA	Sleep-Learning Association (EA)
SLA	Slovak League of America (EA)
SLA	Society for Linguistic Anthropology (EA)
SLA	South Lebanon Army
SLA	Spacecraft LM [*Lunar Module*] Adapter [*NASA*]
SLA	Special Libraries Association (EA)
SLA	Specific Leaf Area [*Botany*]
SLA	Sports Lawyers Association (EA)
SLA	Square Loop Antenna
SLA	Standard Life Association (EA)
SLA	Standard Location Area [*Civil Defense*]
SLA	State Liquor Authority
SLA	Stereolithography [*Desktop manufacturing*]
SLA	Stored Logic Array
SLA	Stripline
SLA	Studies in Linguistic Analysis [*Elsevier Book Series*] [*A publication*]
SLA	Sulfur-Lead Analyzer
SLA	Supplies in Liberated Areas [*British*] [*World War II*]
SLA	Supply Loading Airfield
SLA	Support and Logistics Areas [*NASA*] (MCD)
SLA	Svenska Linne-Sallskapet Arsskrift [*A publication*]
SLA	Symbionese Liberation Army (EA)
SLA	Synchronous Line Adapter
SLAA	Sex and Love Addicts Anonymous (EA)
SLAA	Society for Latin American Anthropology (EA)

SLAA......... State and Local Assistance Act
SLA Adv & Mkt Div Bul ... Special Libraries Association. Advertising and Marketing Division. Bulletin [*A publication*]
SLA Alabama Chap Bul ... Special Libraries Association. Alabama Chapter. Bulletin [*A publication*]
SLAAP ...... St. Louis Army Ammunition Plant
SLAAS........ Supersonic Low-Altitude Attack Aircraft System (MCD)
SLAB........ Abopo [*Bolivia*] [*ICAO location identifier*] (ICLI)
SLAB........ Sage Laboratories, Inc. [*NASDAQ symbol*] (NQ)
SLAB........ Students for Labeling of Alcoholic Beverages [*Student legal action organization*]
SLABCON ... Slab Construction
SLA Biol Sci Div Reminder ... Special Libraries Association. Biological Sciences Division. Reminder [*A publication*]
Slaboproudy Obz ... Slaboproudy Obzor [*Czechoslovakia*] [*A publication*]
SLA Bus & Fin Div Bul ... Special Libraries Association. Business and Financial Division. Bulletin [*A publication*]
SLAC........ Special Committee on Latin American Coordination
SLAC........ Stanford Linear Accelerator Center [*Stanford, CA*] [*Department of Energy*]
SLAC........ Stowage Launch Adapter Container
SLAC........ Straight-Line (Linear) Accelerator [*Nuclear energy*]
SLAC........ Suburban Law Association Convention [*Victoria, Australia*]
SLAC........ Support List Allowance Card (MCD)
SLACS....... School Libraries and Computer Systems Group [*New South Wales Department of Education*] [*Australia*]
SLAD........ Salon Litteraire, Artistique, et Diplomatique
SLAD........ Shipboard Landing Assist Device
SLAD........ SONAR Locator, Altimeter, and Depthometer
SLAD........ System Logic and Algorithm Development
Slade .... Slade's Reports [*15 Vermont*] [*A publication*] (DLA)
SLADE...... Society of Lithographic Artists, Designers, and Engineers [*British*]
SLAE........ Standard Lightweight Avionics Equipment [*Army*] (RDA)
SLAET ...... Society of Licensed Aircraft Engineers and Technologists (EAIO)
SLA Fin Div Bul ... Special Libraries Association. Financial Division. Bulletin [*A publication*]
SLAFRS...... Southwestern Livestock and Forage Research Station [*Oklahoma State University*] [*Research center*] (RCD)
SLAG........ Monteagudo [*Bolivia*] [*ICAO location identifier*] (ICLI)
SLAG........ Safe Launch Angle Gate
SLAG........ Scottish Legal Action Group (ILCA)
SLAG........ Side-Looking Air-to-Ground [*RADAR*]
SLA GA Chap Bul ... Special Libraries Association. Georgia Chapter. Bulletin [*A publication*]
SLA Geog & Map Div Bul ... Special Libraries Association. Geography and Map Division. Bulletin [*A publication*]
SLA Geog and Map Div Bull ... Special Libraries Association. Geography and Map Division. Bulletin [*A publication*]
SLAHF...... Slovak League of America Heritage Foundation (EA)
SLAHTS ... Stowage List and Hardware Tracking System [*NASA*] (MCD)
SLA Ind Chap Slant ... Special Libraries Association. Indiana Chapter. Slant [*A publication*]
SLAIS........ School of Library, Archival, and Information Studies [*University of British Columbia, Vancouver*] [*Canada*]
SLAIT........ Study Group on Legal Aspects of Intermodal Transportation [*National Research Council*]
SLAK........ Spacelab Late Access Kit [*NASA*] (NASA)
SLAKSJ .... Supreme Ladies Auxiliary Knights of St. John (EA)
SLAL .... Stowage Launch Adapter, Lower
SLAM........ Samuel Lyman Atwood Marshall [*American general and author, 1900-1977*]
SLAM........ Scanning LASER Acoustic Microscope
SLAM........ Sea-Launched Air Missile (NVT)
SLAM........ Seeking, Locating, Annihilating, Monitoring [*Army project, Vietnam*]
SLAM........ Short LOFAR [*Low-Frequency Acquisition and Ranging*] Alerting Message (NVT)
SLAM........ Side Load Arresting Mechanism (KSC)
SLAM........ Sierra Leone Alliance Movement (PD)
SLAM........ Simulation Language for Alternative Modeling [*Data processing*] (CSR)
SLAM........ Society's League Against Molestation (EA)
SLAM........ Space-Launched Air Missile (MCD)
SLAM........ Spares Level Activity Model (MCD)
SLAM........ Standoff Land Attack Missile [*Military*]
SLAM........ Stowage Launch Adapter, Middle
SLAM........ Submarine-Launched Air Missile
SLAM........ Supersonic Low-Altitude Missile [*Later, LASV*] [*NATO*] (NATG)
SLAM........ Surface-Launched Air Missile
SLAM........ Surface Look-Alike Mine
SLAM........ Symbolic Language Adapted for Microcomputers
SLA Metals Div News ... Special Libraries Association. Metals Division. News [*A publication*]
SLAMEX .. Submarine-Launched Assault Missile Exercise (NVT)
SLA Mich Chap Bul ... Special Libraries Association. Michigan Chapter. Bulletin [*A publication*]
SLA Montreal Chap Bul ... Special Libraries Association. Montreal Chapter. Bulletin [*A publication*]

SLAMS ..... Simplified Language for Abstract Mathematical Structures [*Data processing*] (IEEE)
SLAMS ..... State and Local Air Monitoring Stations [*Environmental Protection Agency*]
SLAMS ..... Surface Look-Alike Mine System (MCD)
SLA Museum Div Bul ... Special Libraries Association. Museum Division. Bulletin [*A publication*]
SLAN........ Angora [*Bolivia*] [*ICAO location identifier*] (ICLI)
SLAN........ Shock Landing Analysis (MCD)
SLAN........ Sine Loco, Anno, vel Nomine [*Without Place, Year, or Name*] [*Latin*]
SLAN........ Slander [*or Slanderous*] [*FBI standardized term*]
SLA News ... SLA [*Scottish Library Association*] News [*A publication*]
S Lang........ Studies in Language [*A publication*]
SLANG...... Systems Language
SLANT ...... Simulator Landing Attachment for Night Landing Training
SlAnt.......... Slavia Antiqua [*A publication*]
Slants Khim Prom-St ... Slantsevaya i Khimicheskaya Promyshlennost [*Estonian SSR*] [*A publication*]
SLAO........ Committee on Supply Questions in Liberated Areas (Official) [*World War II*]
SLAP........ Apolo [*Bolivia*] [*ICAO location identifier*] (ICLI)
SLAP .... Office of State and Local Assistance Programs [*Department of Energy*]
SLAP .... Saboted Light Armor Penetrator [*Weaponry*] (MCD)
SLAP .... Sandia-Livermore Aeroheating Program
SLAP .... Service Life Assessment Program [*Military*]
SLAP .... Simplified Labor and Performance (MCD)
SLAP .... Symbolic Language Assembly Program [*Data processing*] (KSC)
SLAPC....... Studies in Latin American Popular Culture [*A publication*]
SLA Picture Div Picturescope ... Special Libraries Association. Picture Division. Picturescope [*A publication*]
SLA Pittsburgh Chap Bul ... Special Libraries Association. Pittsburgh Chapter. Bulletin [*A publication*]
SLAPN...... Succinyl-L-alanyl-L-alanyl-L-alanine-p-nitroanilide [*Biochemistry*]
SLAPP....... Strategic Lawsuit Against Public Participation [*Term coined by George Pring and Penelope Canan*]
SLAPS....... Subscriber Loop Analysis Program System [*Bell System*]
SLAQ........ Aiquile [*Bolivia*] [*ICAO location identifier*] (ICLI)
SLAR .... Select ADC [*Analog-to-Digital Converter*] Register [*Data processing*] (MDG)
SLAR .... Senior Logistics Aviation Representative (MCD)
SLAR .... Side-Looking Aerial [*or Airborne*] RADAR [*Military*]
SLAR .... Slant Range
SLAR .... Slargando [*Slackening*] [*Music*] (ROG)
SLAR .... Steerable LASER Radiometer (MCD)
SLARD ..... Saskatchewan Law Review [*A publication*]
SLARF ...... Slant Range Fuze (NG)
SLARG ...... Slargando [*Slackening*] [*Music*]
SLAS .... Ascencion De Guarayos [*Bolivia*] [*ICAO location identifier*] (ICLI)
SLAS .... Society for Latin American Studies [*British*]
SLAS .... State Library Agency Section [*Association of Specialized and Cooperative Library Agencies*]
SLASA....... School Library Association of South Australia
SLASC....... St. Louis Area Support Center [*Military*] (MCD)
SLA Sci-Tech News ... Special Libraries Association. Science-Technology Division. News [*A publication*]
SLASH ...... Second Edition List of Australian Subject Headings [*A publication*]
SLASH ...... Seiler Laboratory ALGOL Simulated Hybrid [*Data processing*]
SLASH ...... Small Light Antisubmarine Helicopter
Slaski Kwar Hist Sobotka ... Slaski Kwartalnik Historyczny Sobotka [*A publication*]
Slask STHT ... Slaskie Studia Historyczno-Teologiczne [*A publication*]
SLAST....... Submarine-Launched Antiship Torpedo
SLAT .... Sample Lot Acceptance Testing
SLAT .... Sindacato Lavoratori Amministrativi e Technichi [*Union of Administration and Technical Workers*] [*Somalia*]
SLAT .... Slater Electric, Inc. [*NASDAQ symbol*] (NQ)
SLAT .... South Latitude
SLAT .... Special Logistics Actions, Thailand (AABC)
SLAT .... Supersonic Low Activities Target (MCD)
SLAT .... Support List Allowance Tape (MCD)
SLAT .... Surface Launcher Air-Targeted [*Weapon*] (MCD)
SLATA....... Secondary Learning Assistance Teachers' Association. Newsletter [*A publication*]
SLATE ...... Organization of campus activists at the University of California, Berkeley [*Name, although capitalized, is not an acronym but is instead derived from the group's founding in 1958, when it ran a slate of candidates for student government*]
SLATE ...... Ship-Launched ASW [*Antisubmarine Warfare*] Two-Way Expendable [*Buoy*] [*Navy*] (CAAL)
SLATE ...... Small, Lightweight Altitude-Transmission Equipment [*FAA*]
SLATE ...... Stimulated Learning by Automated Typewriter Environment
SLA Texas Chap Bul ... Special Libraries Association. Texas Chapter. Bulletin [*A publication*]
SLATO...... Secretariado Latinamericano de Trotskismo Orthodoxo [*Peru*]

SLA Toronto Chap Bul ... Special Libraries Association. Toronto Chapter. Bulletin [*A publication*]
SLAU......... San Aurelio [*Bolivia*] [*ICAO location identifier*]　(ICLI)
SLAU......... Stowage Launch Adapter, Upper
SLAUGH .. Slaughter [*England*]
SLAV......... Avicaya [*Bolivia*] [*ICAO location identifier*]　(ICLI)
Slav .... Slavia [*A publication*]
SLAV .... Slavonic [*Language, etc.*]
SLAV .... Special Logistics Actions, South Vietnam　(CINC)
SlavA .... Slavia Antiqua [*A publication*]
SLAVCA ... Sindacato Nazionale Lavoratori Vetro e Ceramica [*National Union of Glass and Ceramics' Workers*] [*Italy*]
Slav East Eur Rev ... Slavonic and East European Review [*A publication*]
Slav E Eur ... Slavic and East European Journal [*A publication*]
SlavEnoch ... Slavic Book of Enoch　(BJA)
Slav Euro Educ Rev ... Slavic and European Education Review [*A publication*]
SlavF......... Slavjanskaja Filologija [*A publication*]
Slav Goth ... Slavica Gothoburgensia [*A publication*]
Slav Helv .. Slavica Helvetica [*A publication*]
Slavia Ant .. Slavia Antiqua [*A publication*]
Slavic E Eu ... Slavic and East European Journal [*A publication*]
Slavic & E Eur J ... Slavic and East European Journal [*A publication*]
Slavic R...... Slavic Review [*A publication*]
Slavic Rev .. Slavic Review [*A publication*]
Slav Lund... Slavica Lundensia [*A publication*]
SlavO......... Slavica Othiniensia [*A publication*]
Slav Occ..... Slavia Occidentalis [*A publication*]
Slavon E Eu ... Slavonic and East European Review [*A publication*]
Slavon & E Eur R ... Slavonic and East European Review [*A publication*]
Slavonic & E Eur R ... Slavonic and East European Review [*A publication*]
Slavonic R ... Slavonic Review [*A publication*]
Slav Or....... Slavia Orientalis [*A publication*]
SlavP......... Slavica Pragensia [*A publication*]
SlavR......... Slavic Review [*A publication*]
Slav R......... Slavische Rundschau [*A publication*]
SlavR......... Slavisticna Revija [*A publication*]
SLAVR ...... Slavonic Review [*A publication*]
SlavRev...... Slavisticna Revija [*A publication*]
SlavS......... Slavica Slovaca [*A publication*]
Slav S......... Slavisticki Studii [*A publication*]
SLAW........ Conference on the Sociology of the Languages of American Women [*1976*]
SLAW........ St. Lawrence Railroad [*Division of National Railway Utilization Corp.*] [*AAR code*]
SLAW........ School of Land Air Warfare [*Australia*]
SLA Western NY Chap Bul ... Special Libraries Association. Western New York Chapter. Bulletin [*A publication*]
SLAX......... Ay-Luri [*Bolivia*] [*ICAO location identifier*]　(ICLI)
SLB............ St. Louis Blueliners　(EA)
SLB............ Schaulade. Unabhaengiges Internationales Fachblatt fuer Porzellan, Keramik, Glas, Geschenkartikel, und Hausrat [*A publication*]
SLB............ Schlumberger Ltd. [*NYSE symbol*]　(SPSG)
SLB............ Self-Lubricating Bearing
SLB............ Short Leg Brace [*Medicine*]
SLB............ Side-Lobe Blanking [*RADAR*]
SLB............ Signal Light Bare　(MSA)
SLB............ Sintered Lead Bronze
SLB............ Solomon Islands [*ANSI three-letter standard code*]　(CNC)
SLB............ Southland Aviation, Inc. [*Destin, FL*] [*FAA designator*]　(FAAC)
SLB............ Steam Line Break　(NRCH)
SLB............ Storm Lake, IA [*Location identifier*] [*FAA*]　(FAAL)
SLB............ Studia ad Tabulas Cuneiformes Collectas a de Liagre Boehl Pertinentia [*A publication*]
SLB............ Superannuation Law Bulletin [*A publication*]
SLBC......... Boca Chapare [*Bolivia*] [*ICAO location identifier*]　(ICLI)
SLBEDP.... Suicide and Life-Threatening Behavior [*A publication*]
SLBF......... Blanca Flor [*Bolivia*] [*ICAO location identifier*]　(ICLI)
SLBH......... Buena Hora [*Bolivia*] [*ICAO location identifier*]　(ICLI)
SLBJ......... Bermejo [*Bolivia*] [*ICAO location identifier*]　(ICLI)
SLBL .... Soluble　(MSA)
SLBM......... Sea [*or Submarine or Surface*]-Launched Ballistic Missile [*Navy*]　(CAAL)
SLBMD & W ... Sea-Launched Ballistic Missile Detection and Warning
SLBMDWS ... Submarine-Launched Ballistic Missile Detection and Warning System　(IEEE)
SLBN......... Bella Union [*Bolivia*] [*ICAO location identifier*]　(ICLI)
SLBP .... Spring-Loaded Ball Plunger
SLBR .... Slaughter Brothers, Inc. [*NASDAQ symbol*]　(NQ)
SLBS......... Sierra Leone Broadcasting Service
SLBU......... Baures [*Bolivia*] [*ICAO location identifier*]　(ICLI)
SLBV .... Villa Vista [*Bolivia*] [*ICAO location identifier*]　(ICLI)
SLBW......... Buena Vista [*Bolivia*] [*ICAO location identifier*]　(ICLI)
SLBY......... Boyuibe [*Bolivia*] [*ICAO location identifier*]　(ICLI)
SLC............ Salt Lake City [*Utah*] [*Airport symbol*]　(OAG)
SLC............ Salt Lake City [*Utah*] [*Seismograph station code, US Geological Survey*]　(SEIS)
SLC............ Salt Lake City [*Utah*]
SLC............ Salt Lake City, UT [*Location identifier*] [*FAA*]　(FAAL)
SLC............ [*The*] San Luis Central Railroad Co. [*AAR code*]

SLC............ Sarah Lawrence College [*Bronxville, NY*]
SLC............ Satellite LASER Communication [*Military*]
SLC............ Scottish Land Court Reports [*A publication*]　(DLA)
SLC............ Scottish Leaving Certificate
SLC............ Sea-Level Canal Study　(IID)
SLC............ Searchlight Control [*Military*]
SLC............ Selector Channel
SLC............ Set Location Counter　(CMD)
SLC............ Shelf Life Code　(MCD)
SLC............ Shift Left and Count Instructions [*Data processing*]　(MDG)
SL & C .... Shipper's Load and Count [*Bills of lading*]
SLC............ Shuttle Launch Center [*Vandenberg Air Force Base, CA*] [*NASA*]
SLC............ Side-Lobe Cancellation [*RADAR*]
SLC............ Side-Lobe Clutter
SLC............ Simulated Linguistic Computer
SLC............ Single Launch Contractor　(KSC)
SLC............ Single Line Control　(BUR)
SLC............ Slice　(MSA)
SLC............ Small Library Computing, Inc. [*Information service or system*]　(IID)
SLC............ Smith's Leading Cases [*A publication*]　(DLA)
SLC............ Songwriters and Lyricists Club　(EA)
SLC............ Sonobuoy Launch Container　(NVT)
SLC............ South London College [*London, England*]
SLC............ Southland Corporation [*NYSE symbol*]　(SPSG)
SLC............ Space Launch Complex [*NASA*]
SLC............ Spanish Literature Committee　(EA)
SLC............ Special Libraries Cataloguing, Inc. [*Information service or system*]　(IID)
SLC............ Standard Launch Complex　(KSC)
SLC............ Standard Location Codes
SLC............ Standby Liquid Control [*Nuclear energy*]　(NRCH)
SLC............ Standing Liaison Committee
SLC............ Stanford Linear Collider [*High-energy physics*]
SLC............ State Legislative Committee
SLC............ State Library of Ohio, Catalog Center, Columbus, OH [*OCLC symbol*]　(OCLC)
SLC............ State Line Airport [*Leawood, KS*] [*FAA designator*]　(FAAC)
SLC............ Stockage List Code [*Military*]　(AABC)
SLC............ Straight-Line Capacitance [*or Capacity*]
SLC............ Strategic LASER Communications [*Military*]　(CAAL)
SLC............ Stuart's Lower Canada Appeal Cases [*1810-35*] [*A publication*]　(DLA)
SLC............ Sublingual Cleft [*Medicine*]
SLC............ Submarine LASER Communications
SLC............ Subscriber Loop Carrier [*Telecommunications*]　(TEL)
SLC............ Sue and Labor Clause [*Business term*]
SLC............ Surf Life Saving Club [*Australia*]
SLC............ Surgeon Lieutenant-Commander [*British military*]
SLC............ Susquehanna Library Cooperative [*Library network*]
SLC............ Sustained Load Crack [*Titanium alloy*]
SLC............ Synchro Loop Closure
SLC............ Synchronous Line Medium Speed with Clock　(BUR)
SLC............ System Life Cycle
SLCA......... Camiri [*Bolivia*] [*ICAO location identifier*]　(ICLI)
SLC App ...... Stuart's Lower Canada Appeal Cases [*A publication*]　(DLA)
SLCB .... Cochabamba/Jorge Wilsterman [*Bolivia*] [*ICAO location identifier*]　(ICLI)
SLCB .... Single-Line Color Bar　(IEEE)
SLCBMA .. Solid Leather Case and Bag Makers' Association [*A union*] [*British*]
SLCC......... Copacabana [*Bolivia*] [*ICAO location identifier*]　(ICLI)
SLCC .... Lincoln Cent Collectors Society　(EA)
SLCC .... Saturn Launch Control Computer [*NASA*]　(KSC)
SLCC .... Society of Local Council Clerks [*British*]
SLCD......... Surplus Land for Community Development
SLCG......... Charagua [*Bolivia*] [*ICAO location identifier*]　(ICLI)
SLCH......... Chapacura [*Bolivia*] [*ICAO location identifier*]　(ICLI)
SLCI......... Clara Rios [*Bolivia*] [*ICAO location identifier*]　(ICLI)
SLCJ......... Cavinas [*Bolivia*] [*ICAO location identifier*]　(ICLI)
SLCL......... Collpani [*Bolivia*] [*ICAO location identifier*]　(ICLI)
SLCL......... Shop/Lab Configuration Layout [*NASA*]　(MCD)
SLCL......... Sierra Leone Council of Labour
SLCL......... Small Lymphocyte Cell Lymphoma [*Oncology*]
SLCM......... Camiare [*Bolivia*] [*ICAO location identifier*]　(ICLI)
SLCM......... Sea-Launched Cruise Missile [*Pronounced "slick-em"*]　(AABC)
SLCM......... Ship Life-Cycle Management
SLCM......... Software Life Cycle Management
SLCM......... [*The*] Southland Corp. [*NASDAQ symbol*]　(NQ)
SLCM......... Structural Liquid Composite Molding [*Plastics technology*]
SLCM......... Submarine-Launched Cruise Missile　(IEEE)
SLCM......... Surface Launch Cruise Missile
SLCN......... Charana [*Bolivia*] [*ICAO location identifier*]　(ICLI)
SL Co .... Appendices of Proceedings of the Scottish Land Court [*A publication*]　(DLA)
SLCO......... Cobija [*Bolivia*] [*ICAO location identifier*]　(ICLI)
SL Co R...... Appendices of Proceedings of the Scottish Land Court [*A publication*]　(DLA)
SL Council Phila & Vicinity Bul ... Special Libraries Council of Philadelphia and Vicinity. Bulletin [*A publication*]

SLCP .... Concepcion [*Bolivia*] [*ICAO location identifier*]   (ICLI)
SLCP .... Ship's Loading Characteristics Pamphlet [*Navy*]   (NVT)
SLCP .... Standing Liaison Committee of Physiotherapists within the EEC [*European Economic Community*] [*See also CPLK*] [*Copenhagen, Denmark*]   (EAIO)
SLCQ .... Copaquilla [*Bolivia*] [*ICAO location identifier*]   (ICLI)
SLCR .... Comarapa [*Bolivia*] [*ICAO location identifier*]   (ICLI)
SLCR .... Salem Carpet Mills, Inc. [*NASDAQ symbol*]   (NQ)
SLCR .... Scottish Land Court Reports [*A publication*]   (DLA)
SLCRM ..... Ship Life-Cycle Reference Matrix [*Navy*]
SLCRS .... Supplementary Leak Collection and Release System [*Nuclear energy*]   (NRCH)
SLCS .... Cerdas [*Bolivia*] [*ICAO location identifier*]   (ICLI)
SLCS .... Standby Liquid Control System [*Nuclear energy*]   (NRCH)
SLCS .... Studies in Language. Companion Series [*A publication*]
SLCT .... Choreti [*Bolivia*] [*ICAO location identifier*]   (ICLI)
SLCT .... Select   (FAAC)
SLCU .... Standard Landing Craft Unit [*Military*]
SLCU .... Synchronous Line Control Unit
SLCV .... Cavinas [*Bolivia*] [*ICAO location identifier*]   (ICLI)
SLCV .... Squash Leaf Curl Virus
SLCY .... Collpa [*Bolivia*] [*ICAO location identifier*]   (ICLI)
SLCZ .... Santa Cruz/El Trompillo [*Bolivia*] [*ICAO location identifier*]   (ICLI)
SLD .... Sailed
SLD .... San Luis Dam [*California*] [*Seismograph station code, US Geological Survey*]   (SEIS)
SLD .... Sea Landing Division [*NATO*]
SLD .... Sealed
SLD .... Serum Lactate Dehydrogenase [*Also, SLDH*] [*An enzyme*]
SLD .... Shelf Life Data [*Army*]
SLD .... Shutdown Logic Diagram [*Nuclear energy*]   (NRCH)
SLD .... Simulated Launch Demonstration [*NASA*]   (KSC)
SLD .... Sliac [*Czechoslovakia*] [*Airport symbol*]   (OAG)
SLD .... Slide
SLet .... Sliding Door   (AAG)
SLD .... Slowdown   (AAG)
SLD .... Slumber Lodge Development Corp. Ltd. [*Vancouver Stock Exchange symbol*]
SLD .... Social and Liberal Democrats [*Great Britain*] [*Political party*]   (ECON)
SLD .... Society of Loyalist Descendants   (EA)
SLD .... Sold
SLD .... Solder
SLD .... Solid   (FAAC)
SLD .... Solid Logic Dense   (BUR)
SLD .... Sonic Layer Depth   (NVT)
SLD .... Source Language Debug [*Data processing*]   (IEEE)
SLD .... Source-Level Debugger [*Motorola, Inc.*]
SLD .... Specific Language [*or Learning*] Disability [*Education*]
SLD .... Square Law Detection
SLD .... Stiff-Leg Derrick   (NASA)
SLD .... Straight Line Depreciation [*Telecommunications*]   (TEL)
SLD .... Studia Litteraria (University of Debrecen) [*A publication*]
SLD .... Synchronous Line Driver
SLDAA ...... SACLANT [*Supreme Allied Commander, Atlantic*] Distributing and Accounting Agency   (NATG)
SLD CARB DI ... Solidified Carbon Dioxide [*Freight*]
SLDD .... Scientific Library and Documentation Division [*National Science and Technology Authority*] [*Philippines*] [*Information service or system*]   (IID)
SLDG .... Sliding
SLDH .... Serum Lactate Dehydrogenase [*Also, SLD*] [*An enzyme*]
SLDN .... El Desengano [*Bolivia*] [*ICAO location identifier*]   (ICLI)
SLDP .... Loma Del Porvenir [*Bolivia*] [*ICAO location identifier*]   (ICLI)
SLDPF .... Spacelab Data Processing Facility   (MCD)
SLDR .... Solder   (MSA)
SLDR .... Soldier
S/Ldr .... Squadron Leader [*British military*]   (DMA)
SLDR .... System Loader [*Data processing*]
SLDS .... Scanning LASER Doppler System [*NASA*]
SLDS .... Skylab Launch Data System [*NASA*]   (KSC)
SLDTF .... State and Local Documents Task Force [*Government Documents Round Table*] [*American Library Association*]
SLDTSS .... Single Language Dedicated Time-Sharing System
SLDVS ...... Scanning LASER Doppler Vortex System [*NASA*]
SLE .... St. Louis Encephalitis [*Medicine*]
SLE .... Salem [*Oregon*] [*Airport symbol*]   (OAG)
SLE .... Salem, OR [*Location identifier*] [*FAA*]   (FAAL)
SLE .... Sara Lee Corp. [*NYSE symbol*]   (SPSG)
SLE .... Service Life Evaluation
SLE .... Shuttle Transport [*New York, NY*] [*FAA designator*]   (FAAC)
SLE .... Sierra Leone [*ANSI three-letter standard code*]   (CNC)
SLE .... Small Lattice Experiment
SLE .... Small Local Exchange [*Telecommunications*]   (TEL)
SLE .... Smith, Leland C., Oakland CA [*STAC*]
SLE .... Societas Linguistica Europaea [*Linguistic Society of Europe*]   (EAIO)
SLE .... Society of Logistics Engineers   (MCD)
SLE .... Station Liaison Engineer [*NASA*]
SLE .... Stochastic Liouville Equation [*Statistical mechanics*]

SLE .... Student Letter Exchange   (EA)
SLE .... Studio Lighting Equipment
SLE .... Sulphurets Gold [*Vancouver Stock Exchange symbol*]
SLE .... Superheat Limit Explosion
SLE .... Systemic Lupus Erythematosus [*Medicine*]
SLEC .... El Cairo [*Bolivia*] [*ICAO location identifier*]   (ICLI)
SLEC .... Southland Energy Corporation [*NASDAQ symbol*]   (NQ)
SLED .... El Dorado [*Bolivia*] [*ICAO location identifier*]   (ICLI)
SLED .... State Level Electricity Demand [*Model*] [*Nuclear Regulatory Commission*]
SLED .... Surface Light Emitting Diode [*Electronics*]
SLEDGE ... Simulating Large Explosive Detonable Gas Experiments
SLEE .... Societe Lyonaise des Eaux et de l'Eclairage [*French*]
SLEEP .... Scanning Low-Energy Electron Probe   (IEEE)
SLEEP .... Silent, Lightweight, Electric Energy Plant   (RDA)
SLEEP .... Swedish Low-Energy Experimental Pile [*Nuclear energy*]
Sleep Sick Bureau Bull ... Sleeping Sickness Bureau. Bulletin [*A publication*]
SLEF .... El Triunfo [*Bolivia*] [*ICAO location identifier*]   (ICLI)
SLEICC ..... Statue of Liberty - Ellis Island Centennial Commission   (EA)
SLEIF .... Statue of Liberty - Ellis Island Foundation   (EA)
SLEJ .... El Jovi [*Bolivia*] [*ICAO location identifier*]   (ICLI)
SLEL .... El Roseda [*Bolivia*] [*ICAO location identifier*]   (ICLI)
SLEM .... Solution of Linearized Equations of Motion
SLEMA ..... Schiffli Lace and Embroidery Manufacturers Association   (EA)
SLEMU ..... Spacelab Engineering Model Unit [*NASA*]   (MCD)
SLENT .... Slentando [*Slackening*] [*Music*]   (ROG)
SLEO .... El Paraiso [*Bolivia*] [*ICAO location identifier*]   (ICLI)
SLEP .... El Peru [*Bolivia*] [*ICAO location identifier*]   (ICLI)
SLEP .... Second Large ESRO [*European Space Research Organization*] Project
SLEP .... Secondary Level English Proficiency Test
SLEP .... Service Life Extension Program [*Military*]   (MCD)
SLES .... Espiritu [*Bolivia*] [*ICAO location identifier*]   (ICLI)
SLESP .... Suplemento Literario do Estado de Sao Paulo [*A publication*]
Sleszky Num ... Sleszky Numismatik [*A publication*]
SLet .... Sestante Letterario [*A publication*]
SLEU .... Eucaliptos [*Bolivia*] [*ICAO location identifier*]   (ICLI)
SLEUTH ... UNIVAC 1108 Assembly Language
SLEV .... El Salvador [*Bolivia*] [*ICAO location identifier*]   (ICLI)
SLEV .... St. Louis Encephalitis Virus
SLEV .... Salaried Legal Expense Voucher
SLEVA ...... Slevarenstvi [*A publication*]
SLEW .... Static Load Error Washout
SLEZ .... La Esperanza [*Bolivia*] [*ICAO location identifier*]   (ICLI)
SLF .... Saturn Launch Facility [*NASA*]
SLF .... Savings and Loan Foundation [*Later, FSI*]   (EA)
SLF .... Scientific Laboratory Facility
SLF .... Shuttle Landing Facility [*NASA*]   (MCD)
SLF .... Skandinaviska Lackteknikers Forbund [*Federation of Scandinavian Paint and Varnish Technologists*] [*Finland*]
SLF .... Skrifter Utgivna av Svenska Litteratursaellskapet i Finland [*A publication*]
SLF .... Society of the Little Flower   (EA)
SLF .... South Luzon Force [*Army*] [*World War II*]
SLF .... Southwestern Legal Foundation   (DLA)
SLF .... Special Landing Forces [*Marine Corps*]
SLF .... Straight-Line Frequency
SLF .... Stress Loading Facility [*Fort Huachuca, AZ*] [*United States Army Electronic Proving Ground*]   (GRD)
SLF .... Suction Line Filter
SLF .... Super-Low-Frequency   (MCD)
SLF .... Svenska Litteratursaellskapet i Finland [*A publication*]
SLF .... System Library File [*Data processing*]   (BUR)
SLFA .... Fatima [*Bolivia*] [*ICAO location identifier*]   (ICLI)
SLFA .... Svensklaerarfoereningens Arsskrift [*A publication*]
SLFB .... Solid-Liquid Fluidized Bed [*Chemical engineering*]
SLFC .... Shoreline Financial Corp. [*NASDAQ symbol*]   (NQ)
SLFC .... Sierra Leone Full Court Reports [*A publication*]   (DLA)
SLFC .... Steve Long Fan Club   (EA)
SLFC .... Survivable Low-Frequency Communications [*Air Force*]
SLFCLN .... Self-Cleaning [*Engineering*]
SLFCS .... Survivable Low-Frequency Communications System [*Air Force*]
SLFD .... Steam Lava Flow Deflector   (MCD)
SLFGEN ... Self-Generating
SLFIA .... Substrate-Labeled Fluorescent Immunoassay
SLFIND ..... Self-Indicating
S-LFL .... Short-Long Flashing Light [*Navigation signal*]
SLFLKG .... Self-Locking [*Engineering*]
SLFOEAMTMTS ... St. Louis Field Office, Eastern Area, Military Traffic Management and Terminal Service [*Army*]   (AABC)
SLFP .... Sri Lanka Freedom Party [*Political party*]   (PPW)
SLFSE .... Self-Sealing [*Engineering*]
SLFTPG .... Self-Tapping [*Screw*] [*Design engineering*]
SLFU .... Skrifter Utgivna. Genom Landsmals-och Folk-Minnesarkivet i Uppsala [*A publication*]
SLFX .... Selfix, Inc. [*NASDAQ symbol*]   (CTT)
SLG .... Community of the Sisters of the Love of God [*Anglican religious community*]
SLG .... Lander College, Larry A. Jackson Library, Greenwood, SC [*OCLC symbol*]   (OCLC)

SLG........... Satellite Landing Ground [*British military*] (DMA)
SLG........... Scottish Law Gazette [*A publication*]
SLG........... Self-Launching Glider
SLG........... Seligman & Associates, Inc. [*AMEX symbol*] (SPSG)
SLG........... Shorthand Typist (Lower Grade) [*British military*] (DMA)
SLG........... Siloam Springs, AK [*Location identifier*] [*FAA*] (FAAL)
SLG........... Sludge (MSA)
SLG........... Slugger [*Percentage*] [*Baseball*]
SLG........... Soda Lime Glass
SLG........... Solid-Liquid-Gas [*Phase diagram line*]
SLG........... Southern Lights [*Vancouver Stock Exchange symbol*]
SLG........... State or Local Government
SLG........... Studia Linguistica Germanica [*A publication*]
SLG........... Synchronous Line Group (BUR)
SLGB........ Society of Local Government Barristers [*British*] (DLA)
SLGJ........ Guadalajara [*Bolivia*] [*ICAO location identifier*] (ICLI)
SLGM....... Surface-Launched Guided Missile
SLGP........ Student Loan Guaranty Program
SLGR........ Slinger
SLGT........ Slight (FAAC)
SLGW....... Salt Lake, Garfield & Western Railway Co. [*AAR code*]
SLGY........ Guayaramerin [*Bolivia*] [*ICAO location identifier*] (ICLI)
SLH .... Shearson Lehman Hutton [*NYSE symbol*] (SPSG)
SLH .... Sociedade Latinoamericana de Hepatologia [*Latin American Society of Hepatology - LASH*] (EAIO)
SLH .... Sola [*Vanuatu*] [*Airport symbol*] (OAG)
SLHA .... Small Luxury Hotel Association (EA)
SLHC........ Southlife Holding Company [*NASDAQ symbol*] (NQ)
SLHJ........ Huacaraje [*Bolivia*] [*ICAO location identifier*] (ICLI)
SLHN .... Chane Bedoya [*Bolivia*] [*ICAO location identifier*] (ICLI)
SLHR....... Society for Life History Research (EA)
SLHRC..... Sri Lankan Human Rights Campaign [*Australia*]
SLHRP ...... Society for Life History Research in Psychopathology [*Later, SLHR*] (EA)
SLHT........ Colquechaca [*Bolivia*] [*ICAO location identifier*] (ICLI)
SLHU .... Huachi [*Bolivia*] [*ICAO location identifier*] (ICLI)
SLHY....... Caquiaviri [*Bolivia*] [*ICAO location identifier*] (ICLI)
SLI .... Los Alamitos, CA [*Location identifier*] [*FAA*] (FAAL)
SLI .... St. Lucia [*St. Lucia*] [*Seismograph station code, US Geological Survey*] [*Closed*] (SEIS)
SLI .... Sea-Level Indicator (KSC)
SLI .... Seal and Label Institute
SLI .... Shelf Life Item [*Military*] (AABC)
SLI .... Shropshire Light Infantry [*British military*] (DMA)
SLI .... Signal Line Isolator
SLI .... Sikh Local Infantry [*British military*] (DMA)
SLI .... Silver Hill Mines [*Vancouver Stock Exchange symbol*]
SLI .... Slick Airways, Incorporated
SLI .... Slide Lobe Indicator
SLI .... Society for Louisiana Irises (EA)
SLI .... Somatostatin-Like Immunoreactivity
SLI .... Somerset Light Infantry [*Military unit*] [*British*]
SLI .... Sound Level Indicator
SLI .... Spacelab Integration (MCD)
SLI .... Special Libraries [*A publication*]
SLI .... Starting, Lighting, and Ignition [*Automobile system*]
SLI .... Steam Line Isolation [*Nuclear energy*] (NRCH)
SLI .... Studi Linguistici Italiani [*A publication*]
SLI .... Studies in the Literary Imagination [*A publication*]
SLI .... Suppress Length Indication (BUR)
SLI .... Synchronous Line Interface
SL & I ...... System Load and Initialization [*NASA*] (NASA)
SLIA .... Spiritual Life Institute of America (EA)
SLIAG ...... State Legalization Impact Assistance Grant [*Department of Health and Human Services*]
SLIB .... Source Library [*Data processing*]
SLIB .... Subsystem Library [*Data processing*] (IBMDP)
SLIC .... Coroico [*Bolivia*] [*ICAO location identifier*] (ICLI)
SLIC .... [*Federal*] Savings and Loan Insurance Corp. [*Functions transferred to SAIF, 1989*]
SLIC .... School Libraries in Canada [*A publication*]
SLIC .... Search of the Library Information Collection [*Search system*]
SLIC .... Second Life Insurance of Georgia [*NASDAQ symbol*] (NQ)
SLIC .... Selective Letters [*or Listing*] in Combination
SLIC .... Signature Library Intelligence Catalogue
SLIC .... Special Libraries in Civic [*Australia*]
SLIC .... Subscriber's Line Interface Circuit [*Telecommunications*] (TEL)
SLIC .... System Line Image Composer
SLICBM..... Sea-Launched Intercontinental Ballistic Missile (MUGU)
SLICE....... Source Label Indicating and Coding Equipment
SLICE....... Southwestern Library Interstate Cooperative Endeavor
SLICE....... Students Litigating Against Injurious Can Edges [*Student legal action organization*]
SLICE....... System Life Cycle Estimation
SLID .... Scanning Light Intensity Device
SLID .... Students League for Industrial Democracy [*Later, Students for a Democratic Society*]
SLIDE ...... [*A*] programming language (CSR)
SLif........... Slovjans'ke Literaturoznavstvo i Fol'klorystyka [*A publication*]
SLIG .... Inglaterra [*Bolivia*] [*ICAO location identifier*] (ICLI)

SLIG .... Sucker, Low-Brow, Idiot, Goodwill-Buster [*Acronym used as word meaning "act of discourtesy or stupid criticism"*] [*World War II*]
SLIGO ...... Sand Lake Irish Gatherings Organization
SLIH........ Samaihuate [*Bolivia*] [*ICAO location identifier*] (ICLI)
SLIH........ Second Level Interrupt Handler (CMD)
SLIJ .... Iniguazu [*Bolivia*] [*ICAO location identifier*] (ICLI)
SLIM .... Saint Louis Institute of Music
SLIM .... Side Line Indexing Method [*Spectrometry*]
SLIM .... Simplified Logistics and Improved Maintenance (MCD)
SLIM .... Slewed-Launch Interceptor Missile
SLIM .... Standards Laboratory Information Manual (NG)
SLIM .... Submarine-Launched Inertial Missile
SLIMS...... Supply Line Inventory Management System [*Bell System*]
SLIN........ Standard Library Identification Number
SLIN........ Standard Line Item Number [*Army*] (AABC)
SLIN........ Sub-Line Item Number (MCD)
SLIN........ System Line Item Number (MCD)
S Lincolnshire Archaeol ... South Lincolnshire Archaeology [*A publication*]
Slink........ Single, Lots of Income, No Kids [*Lifestyle classification*]
SLIP.......... Self Leisure Interest Profile
SLIP.......... Skills Level Improvement Program
SLIP.......... Symbolic List Processor
SLIP.......... Symmetric List Interpretive Program [*Data processing*]
SLIP.......... Symmetric List Processor [*FORTRAN extension*]
SLIPR....... Source Language Input Program
SLIQ........ Scott's Liquid Gold, Inc. [*NASDAQ symbol*] (NQ)
SLIQ........ Special Libraries in Queensland [*Australia*] [*A publication*]
SLIR .... Ibori [*Bolivia*] [*ICAO location identifier*] (ICLI)
SLIR .... School of Labor and Industrial Relations [*Michigan State University*] [*Research center*] (RCD)
SLIRBM.... Sea-Launched Intermediate-Range Ballistic Missile (MUGU)
SLIS .... School of Library and Information Studies [*Kuring-Gai College of Advanced Education*] [*Australia*]
SLIS .... Shared Laboratory Information System
SLIS .... Social Legislation Information Service (EA)
SLIS .... State Land Information System [*New South Wales, Australia*]
SLIT .... Itaguazurenda [*Bolivia*] [*ICAO location identifier*] (ICLI)
SLit .... Slovenska Literatura [*A publication*]
SLit .... Studies in Literature [*A publication*]
SLitI......... Studies in the Literary Imagination [*A publication*]
S Lit J ...... Southern Literary Journal [*A publication*]
SLIV .... Isla Verde [*Bolivia*] [*ICAO location identifier*] (ICLI)
S Liv .... Southern Living [*A publication*]
SLIV .... Steam Line Isolation Valve [*Nuclear energy*] (NRCH)
SLIX .... Ixiamas [*Bolivia*] [*ICAO location identifier*] (ICLI)
SLIZ .... Izozog [*Bolivia*] [*ICAO location identifier*] (ICLI)
SLJ .... Hattiesburg, MS [*Location identifier*] [*FAA*] (FAAL)
SLJ .... School Library Journal [*A publication*]
SLJ .... Scottish Law Journal [*Edinburgh*] [*A publication*] (DLA)
SLJ .... Silly Little Job (DSUE)
SLJ .... Southern Literary Journal [*A publication*]
SLJ .... Southwestern Law Journal [*A publication*]
SLJ .... Straits Law Journal [*1888-92*] [*Malasia*] [*A publication*] (DLA)
SLJD .... El Jordan [*Bolivia*] [*ICAO location identifier*] (ICLI)
SLJE........ San Jose [*Bolivia*] [*ICAO location identifier*] (ICLI)
SLJM....... San Juan De Fribal [*Bolivia*] [*ICAO location identifier*] (ICLI)
SLJN .... San Juan (Estancias) [*Bolivia*] [*ICAO location identifier*] (ICLI)
SLJO .... San Joaquin [*Bolivia*] [*ICAO location identifier*] (ICLI)
SLJR........ Sudan Law Journal and Reports [*A publication*] (DLA)
SLJT .... Santa Juanita [*Bolivia*] [*ICAO location identifier*] (ICLI)
SLJV........ San Javier [*Bolivia*] [*ICAO location identifier*] (ICLI)
SLK........... Atlanta Skylark Club, Inc. [*Atlanta, GA*] [*FAA designator*] (FAAC)
SLK........... Kitsaki School/Public Library, La Ronge, Saskatchewan [*Library symbol*] [*National Library of Canada*] (BIB)
SLK........... Saranac Lake [*New York*] [*Airport symbol*] (OAG)
SLK........... Saranac Lake, NY [*Location identifier*] [*FAA*] (FAAL)
SLK........... Schwerpunkte Linguistik und Kommunikationswissenschaft [*A publication*]
SLK........... Slick (MCD)
SLK........... Superior Limbic Keratoconjunctivitis [*Ophthalmology*]
SLk .... Surface Linking Number [*Genetics*]
SLKP .... Supreme Lodge Knights of Pythias (EA)
SLKPEN.... Slack and Penalty
SLKQ........ San Miguel [*Bolivia*] [*ICAO location identifier*] (ICLI)
SLKT........ Survivability, Lethality, and Key Technologies (SDI)
SLKW....... Schwerpunkte Linguistik und Kommunikationswissenschaft [*A publication*]
SLKY........ Puerto Yuca [*Bolivia*] [*ICAO location identifier*] (ICLI)
SLL........... La Loche Public Library, Saskatchewan [*Library symbol*] [*National Library of Canada*] (NLC)
SLL........... Salalah [*Oman*] [*Airport symbol*] (OAG)
SLL........... Sandia Laboratories, Livermore (AABC)
SLL........... Sandwell Swan Wooster, Inc. [*Toronto Stock Exchange symbol*]
SLL........... Shelf Life Limit (MCD)
SLL........... Signal Long Lines
SLL........... Skrifter Utgivna. Genom Landsmalsarkivet i Lund [*A publication*]
SLL........... Society for Libertarian Life (EA)

SLL............	Station List Publishing Company, St. Louis MO [*STAC*]
SLL............	Sterling Lord Literistic, Inc. [*Literary agency*] [*British*]
SLL............	Stollet [*Sweden*] [*Seismograph station code, US Geological Survey*] (SEIS)
SLL............	Studies in Language Learning [*A publication*]
SLL............	Suffolk University, Law Library, Boston, MA [*OCLC symbol*] (OCLC)
SLLA........	La Asunta [*Bolivia*] [*ICAO location identifier*] (ICLI)
SLLC........	La China [*Bolivia*] [*ICAO location identifier*] (ICLI)
SLLE	La Ele [*Bolivia*] [*ICAO location identifier*] (ICLI)
SLLI	La India [*Bolivia*] [*ICAO location identifier*] (ICLI)
SLLJ	Laja [*Bolivia*] [*ICAO location identifier*] (ICLI)
SLLL	Laguna Loa [*Bolivia*] [*ICAO location identifier*] (ICLI)
SLLL	Synchronous Line, Low, Load (BUR)
SLLP.........	La Paz/Kennedy Internacional [*Bolivia*] [*ICAO location identifier*] (ICLI)
SLLR	Sierra Leone Language Review [*A publication*]
SLLR	Sierra Leone Law Recorder [*A publication*] (DLA)
SLLS........	Snap Lock Limit Switch
SLLS........	Solid-State LASER Light Source
SLLT	Los Tajibos [*Bolivia*] [*ICAO location identifier*] (ICLI)
SLLU	San Lorenzo [*Cordillera*] [*ICAO location identifier*] (ICLI)
SLLV	La Selva [*Bolivia*] [*ICAO location identifier*] (ICLI)
SLLZ	San Lorenzo [*Bolivia*] [*ICAO location identifier*] (ICLI)
SLM...........	St. Louis [*Missouri*] [*Seismograph station code, US Geological Survey*] (SEIS)
SLM...........	Sales and Marketing Management [*A publication*]
SLM...........	School for Latin America [*Military*]
SLM...........	Sea-Launched Missile
SLM...........	Sealift Magazine [*A publication*]
SLM...........	Senior Level Management
SLM...........	Simulated Laboratory Module
SLM...........	Snow Lake Mines Ltd. [*Vancouver Stock Exchange symbol*]
SLM...........	Sound Level Meter
SLM...........	Southern Literary Messenger [*A publication*]
SLM...........	Spatial Light Modulator
SLM...........	Statistical Learning Model (IEEE)
SLM...........	Student Loan Marketing Association [*NYSE symbol*] (SPSG)
SLM...........	Submarine-Launched Missile
SLM...........	Subscriber Loop Multiplex [*Bell System*]
SLM...........	Supported Liquid Membrane [*Separation science and technology*]
SLM...........	Surface-Launched Missile [*Navy*] (CAAL)
SLM...........	Surrey Local Militia [*British military*] (DMA)
SLM...........	Synchronous Line Module
SLMA........	Shoe Lace Manufacturers Association [*Defunct*] (EA)
SLMA........	Southeastern Lumber Manufacturers Association (EA)
SLMA........	Student Loan Marketing Association [*Government-chartered private corporation*] [*Nickname: "Sallie Mae"*]
SLMA........	Student Loan Marketing Association [*NASDAQ symbol*] (NQ)
SLMAB	Single-Line Missile Assembly Building
SLMC........	School Library Media Centre [*Australia*]
SLMD........	Madidi [*Bolivia*] [*ICAO location identifier*] (ICLI)
SLMD(RA) ...	Searchlight Militia Depot (Royal Artillery) [*British military*] (DMA)
SLME........	Select Manual Entry Switch
SLMG........	Magdalena [*Bolivia*] [*ICAO location identifier*] (ICLI)
SLML	La Madre [*Bolivia*] [*ICAO location identifier*] (ICLI)
SLMM.......	Simultaneous Compass Locator at Middle Marker [*Aviation*] (FAAC)
SLMM.......	Submarine-Launched Mobile Mine (MCD)
SlMov	Sloc'jans'ke Movoznavstvo [*A publication*]
SLMP	Mapiri [*Bolivia*] [*ICAO location identifier*] (ICLI)
SLMP	School Library Manpower Project [*American Association of School Librarians*] (EA)
SLMQ.......	School Library Media Quarterly [*A publication*]
SLMR.......	Memore [*Bolivia*] [*ICAO location identifier*] (ICLI)
SLMR.......	Sailmaker [*Navy*] [*British*]
SLMS........	Scanning LASER Mass Spectrometry
SLMS........	Sound Level Measuring Set
SLMS	Surface-Launched Missile System
SLMSC......	South London (Volunteers) Medical Staff Corps [*British military*] (DMA)
SLMV	Monte Verde [*Bolivia*] [*ICAO location identifier*] (ICLI)
SLMW.......	Mategua [*Bolivia*] [*ICAO location identifier*] (ICLI)
SLMX.......	Monos Arana [*Bolivia*] [*ICAO location identifier*] (ICLI)
SLN	Salena Research Corp. [*Vancouver Stock Exchange symbol*]
SLN	Salina [*Kansas*] [*Airport symbol*] (OAG)
SLN	Salina, KS [*Location identifier*] [*FAA*] (FAAL)
SLN	Salinas [*Chile*] [*Seismograph station code, US Geological Survey*] (SEIS)
SLN	Santiago Library System, Orange, CA [*OCLC symbol*] (OCLC)
SLN	Secretariat Linguistiques Nordiques [*Nordic Language Secretariat - NLS*] [*Oslo, Norway*] (EAIO)
SLN	Section List Number (MCD)
SLN	Selena Research [*Vancouver Stock Exchange symbol*]
SLN	Sequence Line Number [*Army*]
SLN	Service Link Network [*Bell Laboratories*]
SLN	Sinclair Lewis Newsletter [*A publication*]
SLN	Solution
SLN	Southeastern Library Network [*Library network*]
SLN	Sri Lanka Navy
SLN	Statement of Logistical Needs [*Air Force*]
SLN	Superior Laryngeal Nerve [*Neuroanatomy*]
SLN/ALN ...	Archivos Latinoamericanos de Nutricion. Organo Oficial. Sociedad Latinoamericano de Nutricion [*A publication*]
SLND	Sine Loco Nec Data [*Without Place or Date of Printing*] [*Latin*]
SLNE	Nueva Era [*Bolivia*] [*ICAO location identifier*] (ICLI)
SLNK........	Satellink Corp. [*NASDAQ symbol*] (NQ)
SLNO	Nuevo Mundo [*Bolivia*] [*ICAO location identifier*] (ICLI)
SLNP........	Nueva Esperanza [*Bolivia*] [*ICAO location identifier*] (ICLI)
SLNQ	Nueva Esperanza (Marban) [*Bolivia*] [*ICAO location identifier*] (ICLI)
SLNS	Department of Northern Saskatchewan, La Ronge, Saskatchewan [*Library symbol*] [*National Library of Canada*] (NLC)
SLNV........	Nieve [*Bolivia*] [*ICAO location identifier*] (ICLI)
SLO	Salem, IL [*Location identifier*] [*FAA*] (FAAL)
SLO	Scanning LASER Ophthalmoscope
SLO	Searchlight Operator [*British military*] (DMA)
SLO	Segment Limits Origin
SLO	Shark Liver Oil
SLO	Ship Liaison Officer [*Navy*] (CAAL)
SLO	Single Loop Operation [*Nuclear energy*] (NRCH)
SLO	Slavia Orientalis [*A publication*]
SLO	Sligo [*County in Ireland*] (ROG)
SLO	Slocan Development [*Vancouver Stock Exchange symbol*]
SLO	Slocum Air, Inc. [*Miami, FL*] [*FAA designator*] (FAAC)
SLO	Slough [*British depot code*]
slo..............	Slovak [*MARC language code*] [*Library of Congress*] (LCCP)
SLO	Slow Lift-Off (MCD)
SLO	State Liaison Officer
SLO	State Library of Ohio
SLO	Stop-Limit Order [*Business term*]
SLO	Stop-Loss Order [*Business term*]
SLO	Streptolysin O [*Hematology*]
SLO	Submarine Liaison Officer [*Navy*] (NVT)
SLO	Swept Local Oscillator (IEEE)
Sloan	Sloan Management Review [*A publication*]
Sloan Leg Reg ...	Sloan's New York Legal Register [*A publication*] (DLA)
Sloan L & T ...	Sloan on Landlord and Tenant [*New York*] [*A publication*] (DLA)
Sloan Manag ...	Sloan Management Review [*A publication*]
Sloan Manage Rev ...	Sloan Management Review [*A publication*]
Sloan Mgmt Rev ...	Sloan Management Review [*A publication*]
Sloan Mgt R ...	Sloan Management Review [*A publication*]
SLOB........	Satellite Low-Orbit Bombardment
SLOB........	Strategic Low-Orbit Bomber (AAG)
SLOB........	Supplemental Layoff Benefits (MCD)
SLOB........	Supply Left of Baseline (MCD)
SLOC........	Sea Lines of Communication [*NATO*] (NATG)
SLOc........	Slavia Occidentalis [*A publication*]
SLOcc	Slavia Occidentalis [*A publication*]
SLOCOP ...	Specific Linear Optimal Control Program [*Hydrofoil*] [*Grumman Aerospace Corp.*]
SLOE........	Save Life on Earth (EA)
SLOE........	Special List of Equipment [*Air Force*]
SLOH	Skylab Operations Handbook [*NASA*] (MCD)
SLOI	Orialsa [*Bolivia*] [*ICAO location identifier*] (ICLI)
Slo L..........	Slovo Lektora [*A publication*]
SLOM	Simultaneous Compass Locator at Outer Marker [*Aviation*] (FAAC)
SLOMAR ...	Space Logistics, Maintenance, and Rescue
SLON	Sloan Technology Corp. [*NASDAQ symbol*] (NQ)
SLoP	Slovansky Prehled [*A publication*]
SLOPE	Study of Lunar Orbiter Photographic Evaluation (MCD)
SLOR........	Oruro [*Bolivia*] [*ICAO location identifier*] (ICLI)
SLOR........	Simultaneous Line Over-Relaxation [*Nuclear energy*]
SLOR........	Slavia Orientalis [*A publication*]
SLOR........	Swept Local Oscillator Receiver (NG)
SLORV	Structural Loads on Reentry Vehicles (MCD)
SLOS	Scanning Line of Sight (KSC)
SLOS	Secondary Line of Sight [*Sextants*]
SLOS	Sierra Leone Organization Society
SLOS	Star Line-of-Sight (MCD)
SLOS	Sun Line-of-Sight
SLOSH......	Sea, Lake, Overland Surge from Hurricanes [*National Oceanic and Atmospheric Administration*]
SLOSJ.......	State and Local Officials for Soviet Jews (EA)
SLO/SRI ...	Shift Left Out/Shift Right In
SLOT........	Sinaota [*Bolivia*] [*ICAO location identifier*] (ICLI)
SLOT........	Submarine-Launched One-Way Tactical [*Buoy*] (NVT)
SLOTH......	Suppressing Line Operands and Translating to Hexadecimal [*Telecommunications*] (TEL)
Slov	Slovenia
Slov A.........	Slovenska Archeologia [*A publication*]
Slov Akad Znan Umet Razred Prirodsl Vede Dela ...	Slovenska Akademija Znanosti in Umetnosti. Razred za Prirodoslovne Vede. Dela [*A publication*]
Slovak Mus ...	Slovak Musik [*A publication*]
Slov Arch ...	Slovenska Archeologia [*A publication*]
Slov Archeol ...	Slovenska Archeologia [*A publication*]

Slov Ceb	Slovenski Cebelar [*A publication*]
Slovenska Hud ...	Slovenska Hudba [*A publication*]
Slov Etnogr ...	Slovenski Etnograf [*A publication*]
Slov Hud	Slovenska Hudba [*A publication*]
Slov Lit......	Slovenska Literatura [*A publication*]
SlovN	Slovensky Narodopis [*A publication*]
Slov Num ...	Slovenska Numizmatika [*A publication*]
Slov Numiz ...	Slovenska Numizmatika [*A publication*]
SlovP..........	Slovensky Pohl'ady [*A publication*]
Slov Preh ..	Slovansky Prehled [*A publication*]
SlovS..........	Slovene Studies [*A publication*]
Slow Learn ...	Slow Learning Child [*A publication*]
Slow Learn Child ...	Slow Learning Child [*A publication*] (APTA)
SLOWPOKE ...	Safe Low-Power Critical Experiment [*Nuclear energy*]
SLOZA......	Slaboproudy Obzor [*A publication*]
SLP	Left Sacroposterior Position [*of the fetus*] [*Obstetrics*]
SLP	St. Lucie Plant [*Nuclear energy*] (NRCH)
SLP	School Lunch Program
SLP	Scintilore Explorations Ltd. [*Toronto Stock Exchange symbol*]
SLP	Scottish Labour Party [*Political party*] (PPW)
SLP	Scottish Liberal Party [*Political party*]
SLP	Scouting Landplane
SLP	Sea-Level Pressure
SLP	Secretary for Logistics Planning [*Air Force*]
SLP	Sectional Linear Programming [*Data processing*]
SLP	Segmented Level Programming [*Data processing*] (IEEE)
SLP	Serie Linguistica Peruana [*A publication*]
SLP	Sex-Limited Protein [*Immunology*]
SLP	Shelby, NC [*Location identifier*] [*FAA*] (FAAL)
SLP	Silicon Light Pulser
SLP	Sine Legitima Prole [*Without Lawful Issue*] [*Latin*]
SLP	Sleep
SLP	Slip (ADA)
SLP	Sloop
SLP	Slope (MSA)
SLP	Slovansky Prehled [*A publication*]
SLP	Slovensky Pohl'ady [*A publication*]
SLP	Slovensky Porocevalec [*A publication*]
SLP	Socialist Labor Party [*Egypt*] [*Political party*] (PPW)
SLP	Socialist Labor Party of America [*Political party*] (EA)
SLP	Soft Lander Probe [*Aerospace*]
SLP	Sound Level Plot [*Military*] (CAAL)
SLP	Source Language Processor [*Data processing*] (BUR)
SLP	Specific Line of Precipitin [*Immunology*]
SLP	Spring-Loaded Pulley
SLP	Stock List Price [*Military*] (AFIT)
S/LP	Stop Lamp [*Automotive engineering*]
SLP	Strategic Locations Planning [*Information service or system*] (IID)
SLP	Sun Energy Partners LP [*NYSE symbol*] (SPSG)
SLP	Super Long Play [*Video technology*]
SLP	Supersonic Local Pressure
SLP	Supplier Loaned Property (MCD)
SLP	Surface Launch Platform (NVT)
SLP	Systematic Layout Planning [*Industrial engineering*]
SLPA	Selected Legally Protected Animals [*Marine science*] (MSC)
SLPA	Silicon Light Pulser Array
SLPB	Spacelab Program Board [*NASA*] (NASA)
SLPC	St. Louis Production Center
SLPC	Socialist Labour Party of Canada
SLPC	Supported Liquid Phase Catalyst [*Chemical engineering*]
SLPD	Skylab Program Directive [*NASA*] (KSC)
SLPH........	Seat Lock Pin Handle
SLPHR	Sulphur
SLPL..........	St. Louis Public Library [*Missouri*]
SLPL..........	Sea Loading Pipe Line [*Technical drawings*]
SLPM	Palmira [*Bolivia*] [*ICAO location identifier*] (ICLI)
SLPM	Selected List of Published Material [*Her Majesty's Stationery Office*] [*British*]
SLPM	Silicon Light Pulser Matrix
SLPMS......	Single Level Power Management System
SLPO	Potosi [*Bolivia*] [*ICAO location identifier*] (ICLI)
SLPO	Skylab Program Office [*NASA*] (KSC)
SLPo	Slovensky Pohl'ady [*A publication*]
SLPoh	Slovensky Pohl'ady [*A publication*]
SLPP..........	Paraparau [*Bolivia*] [*ICAO location identifier*] (ICLI)
SLPP..........	Serum Lipophosphoprotein [*Serology*]
SLPP..........	Sierra Leone People's Party [*Political party*] (PD)
SLPP..........	Sri Lanka People's Party [*Political party*] (PPW)
SLPR	Puerto Rico [*Bolivia*] [*ICAO location identifier*] (ICLI)
SLPR	Sidelobe Pulse Rejection [*Military*] (CAAL)
SLPr..........	Slavica Pragensia [*A publication*]
SLPR	Slavistic Printings and Reprintings [*A publication*]
SLPR	Supplier Loaned Property Request (MCD)
SLPRB.......	Steroids and Lipids Research [*A publication*]
SLPRF.......	Northern Teacher Education Program, Inc., La Ronge, Saskatchewan [*Library symbol*] [*National Library of Canada*] (NLC)
SLPS..........	Puerto Suarez [*Bolivia*] [*ICAO location identifier*] (ICLI)
SLPS..........	Sonobuoy Launcher Pneumatic System
SLPS..........	State and Local Program Support [*Nuclear energy*] (NRCH)
SLPT	Peta [*Bolivia*] [*ICAO location identifier*] (ICLI)
SLPT	Scintilore Explorations Ltd. [*NASDAQ symbol*] (NQ)
SLPT	Socialist Labor Party of Turkey [*Turkiye Sosyalist Isci Partisi*] [*Political party*] (PPW)
SLPTC......	Solid-Liquid Phase-Transfer Catalysis
SLPU	Puchuni [*Bolivia*] [*ICAO location identifier*] (ICLI)
SLPV	Puerto Villa-Roel [*Bolivia*] [*ICAO location identifier*] (ICLI)
SLPW	Sloop-of-War
SLQ..........	Saint Louis Quarterly [*Baguio City*] [*A publication*]
SLQ..........	Sleetmute [*Alaska*] [*Airport symbol*] (OAG)
SLQ..........	Sleetmute, AK [*Location identifier*] [*FAA*] (FAAL)
SLQ..........	Surface Layer Quality
SLQY..........	Curichi [*Bolivia*] [*ICAO location identifier*] (ICLI)
SLR..........	Radcliffe College, Schlesinger Library, Cambridge, MA [*OCLC symbol*] (OCLC)
SLR..........	Sales Letter Report
SLR	Saskatchewan Law Reports [*A publication*] (DLA)
SLR	Satellite LASER Ranging [*for geodetic and geophysical measurements*]
SLR	Scottish Land Court Reports [*A publication*] (DLA)
SLR	Scottish Law Reporter [*Edinburgh*] [*A publication*] (DLA)
SLR	Scottish Law Review and Sheriff Court Reports [*1885-1963*] [*A publication*] (DLA)
SLR..........	Sealer
SLR	Self-Loading Rifle (MCD)
SLR	Sense Line Register
SLR	Service Level Reporter [*IBM Corp.*]
SLR	Seychelles Law Reports [*1921-23*] [*A publication*] (DLA)
SL & R	Shop Order Load Analysis and Reporting [*IBM Corp.*]
SLR	Side-Looking RADAR (AFM)
SLR	Simple Left to Right [*Data processing*]
SLR	Simple Linear Regression [*Statistics*]
SLR	Sind Law Reporter [*India*] [*A publication*] (DLA)
SLR	Singapore Law Reports [*1946-49, 1953-56*] [*A publication*] (DLA)
SLR	Single-Lens Reflex [*Camera*]
SLR	Skylab Rescue [*NASA*] (KSC)
SLR	Slager. Vakblad voor de Vleesspecialist [*A publication*]
SLR	Slavische Rundschau [*A publication*]
SLR	Slavisticna Revija [*A publication*]
SLR	Slavonic and East European Review [*A publication*]
SLR	Slush on Runway [*Aviation*] (FAAC)
SLR	Solar (AAG)
SLR	Sound Level Recorder
SLR	South Lancashire Regiment [*British*]
SLR	Southern Law Review [*St. Louis, MO*] [*A publication*] (DLA)
SLR	Special Leave Refused
SLR	Special Light Rifle (NATG)
SLR	Specific Lung Resistance
SLR	Spin Lattice Relaxation
SLR	Stabell Resources [*Vancouver Stock Exchange symbol*]
SLR	Stanford Law Review [*A publication*]
SLR	Static Line Regulation
SLR	Statute Law Revision [*A publication*] (DLA)
SLR	Storage Limits Register
SLR	Straight Leg Raising [*Medicine*]
SLR	Streptococcus lactis R Factor [*Biochemistry*]
SLR	Sulphur Springs, TX [*Location identifier*] [*FAA*] (FAAL)
SLR	Sydney Law Review [*A publication*] (APTA)
SLR	System Level Requirement [*Military*] (CAAL)
SLRA	San Ramon [*Bolivia*] [*ICAO location identifier*] (ICLI)
SLRA	Sierra Leone Royal Artillery [*British military*] (DMA)
SLRA	Soviet Long-Range Air (MCD)
SLRA	Suede and Leather Refinishers of America [*Defunct*] (EA)
SLRAAA ...	Sprache und Literatur. Regensburger Arbeiten zur Anglistik und Amerikanistik [*A publication*]
SLRAP	Standard Low-Frequency Range Approach
SLRB	Robore [*Bolivia*] [*ICAO location identifier*] (ICLI)
SLRB	State Labor Relations Board
SLRC........	San Luis Rey College [*California*]
SLRC	School Library Resource Centre [*Australia*]
SLRC/MILO ...	State Library Resource Center - Maryland Interlibrary Organization [*Library network*]
SLRD........	Searchlight RADAR
SLRE	El Remate [*Bolivia*] [*ICAO location identifier*] (ICLI)
SLRec	Slovenska Rec [*A publication*]
SL Rev	Scottish Law Review and Sheriff Court Reports [*A publication*] (DLA)
SLRev	Slavonic and East European Review [*A publication*]
SLRev	Slavonic Review [*A publication*]
SLRH........	Rancho Alegre [*Bolivia*] [*ICAO location identifier*] (ICLI)
SLRI	Riberalta [*Bolivia*] [*ICAO location identifier*] (ICLI)
SLRI	Shipboard Long-Range Input
SLRJ..........	St. Louis University. Research Journal. Graduate School of Arts and Sciences [*A publication*]
SLR Leic ...	Leicester's Straits Law Reports [*Malaya*] [*A publication*] (DLA)
SLR Leicester ...	Leicester's Straits Law Reports [*Malaya*] [*A publication*] (DLA)
SLRN........	Select Read Numerically
SLRN........	Solaron Corp. [*NASDAQ symbol*] (NQ)

SL RNG	Slope Range
SLRNS	Straits Law Reports, New Series [*Malasia*] [*A publication*]
SLRP	Rosapata [*Bolivia*] [*ICAO location identifier*] (ICLI)
SLRP	Society for Strategic and Long Range Planning [*Later, Strategic Planning Society - SP*] (EAIO)
SLRQ	Rurrenabaque [*Bolivia*] [*ICAO location identifier*] (ICLI)
SLRR	Retiro [*Bolivia*] [*ICAO location identifier*] (ICLI)
SLRRB	Senior Logistics Readiness Review Board [*Fort Lewis*] (MCD)
SLRS	Rio Seco [*Bolivia*] [*ICAO location identifier*] (ICLI)
SLRS	Satellite LASER Ranging System
SLRS	Sexual Law Reform Society [*British*]
SLRT	Santa Rita [*Bolivia*] [*ICAO location identifier*] (ICLI)
SLRT	Straight Leg Raising Test [*or Tenderness*] [*Medicine*]
SLRTB	Saskatchewan Department of Tourism and Small Business, La Ronge, Saskatchewan [*Library symbol*] [*National Library of Canada*] (NLC)
SlRund	Slavische Rundschau [*A publication*]
SLRV	Sellersville Savings & Loan Association [*NASDAQ symbol*] (NQ)
SLRV	Shuttle Launched Research Vehicle [*NASA*] (NASA)
SLRV	South London Regiment of Volunteers [*British military*] (DMA)
SLRV	Standard Light Rail Vehicle [*Mass transit*]
SLRV	Surveyor Lunar Roving Vehicle [*Aerospace*] (MCD)
SLRY	Reyes [*Bolivia*] [*ICAO location identifier*] (ICLI)
SLS	Saint Lawrence Seaway Development Corporation [*Department of Transportation*]
SLS	Saint Lawrence Seminary [*Wisconsin*]
SLS	Santiago Library System [*Library network*]
SLS	Sassafras Loamy Sand [*Type of soil*]
SLS	Saturn Longitude System [*Planetary science*]
SLS	School of Library Service [*Columbia University*] [*Defunct*]
SLS	School of Logistics Science [*Army*]
SLS	Sea-Land Service, Inc. [*AAR code*]
SLS	Sea Level, Standard Day
SLS	Sea-Level Static
SLS	Secondary Landing Site [*NASA*] (NASA)
SLS	Segment Long-Spacing Collagen Fiber
SLS	Selas Corp. of America [*AMEX symbol*] (SPSG)
SLS	Selective LASER [*Light Amplification by Stimulated Emission of Radiation*] Sintering [*Desktop manufacturing*]
SLS	Serra Cooperative Library System, San Diego, CA [*OCLC symbol*] (OCLC)
SLS	Shore Labourers Society [*A union*] [*British*]
SLS	Side-Lobe Suppression RADAR
SLS	Side-Looking SONAR
SLS	Sign Language Studies [*A publication*]
SLS	Signaling Link Selection [*Telecommunications*] (TEL)
SLS	Silicon Light Source
SLS	Silistra [*Bulgaria*] [*Airport symbol*] (OAG)
SLS	Sindacato Lavoratori della Somalia [*Workers Union of Somalia*]
SLS	Skylab Simulator [*NASA*] (KSC)
SLS	Slightly Soluble
SLS	Slovenska Ljudska Stranka [*Slovene People's Party*] [*Yugoslavia*] [*Political party*] (PPE)
SL'S	Slovenska L'Udova Strana [*Slovak People's Party*] [*Also, HSL'S*] [*Political party*] (PPE)
SLS	So-Luminaire Systems [*Vancouver Stock Exchange symbol*]
SLS	Society for Libyan Studies (EAIO)
SLS	Sodium Lauryl Sulfate [*Also, SDS*] [*Organic chemistry*]
SLS	Soengei Langka [*Sumatra*] [*Seismograph station code, US Geological Survey*] [*Closed*] (SEIS)
SLS	Sonobuoy Localization System (NVT)
SLS	Sortie Lab Simulator [*NASA*] (NASA)
SLS	Sound Learning Society [*British*]
SLS	Source Library System [*Data processing*]
SLS	Space Laboratory Simulator [*NASA*]
SLS	Space Launch System
SLS	Spacecraft Landing Strut
SLS	Specific Living Space (AAG)
SLS	Spoken Language Services, Inc.
SLS	Standard Light Spanwire [*Military*] (CAAL)
SLS	Statement Level Simulator [*NASA*] (NASA)
SLS	Stores Locator System (MCD)
SLS	Strained-Layer Superlattices [*Crystalline materials*]
SLS	Student Lesson Sheets
SLS	Students for a Libertarian Society (EA)
SLS	Styles of Leadership Survey [*Test*]
SLS	Suburban Library System [*Library network*]
SLS	Supplemental Loans for Students [*Department of Education*]
SLS	Surface Laboratory System [*NASA*] (KSC)
SLS	SWALCAP Library Services Ltd. [*Information service or system*] (IID)
SLSA	St. Lawrence Seaway Authority [*Canada*] [*See also AVMS*]
SLSA	Santa Ana De Yacuma [*Bolivia*] [*ICAO location identifier*] (ICLI)
SLSA	Seamen's Loyal Standard Association [*A union*] [*British*]
SLSA	Secondary Lead Smelters Association (EA)
SLSA	Shuttle Logistics Support Aircraft [*NASA*] (MCD)
SLSA	Slotting Saw
SLSA	Svenska Linne-Sallskapet Arsskrift [*Uppsala*] [*A publication*]
SLSAC	Saint Lawrence Seaway Authority of Canada
SLSADJ	Stores Locator System Adjustment (MCD)
SLSB	San Borja [*Bolivia*] [*ICAO location identifier*] (ICLI)
SlSb	Slezsky Sbornik [*A publication*]
SLSC	Santa Clara (Moxos) [*Bolivia*] [*ICAO location identifier*] (ICLI)
SLSc	Studies in the Linguistic Sciences [*A publication*]
SLSC	Surf Lifesaving Club [*Australia*]
SLSD	San Carlos Gutierrez [*Bolivia*] [*ICAO location identifier*] (ICLI)
SLSDC	Saint Lawrence Seaway Development Corporation [*Department of Transportation*]
SLSF	St. Louis-San Francisco Railway Co. [*AAR code*]
SLSF	San Francisco (Moxos) [*Bolivia*] [*ICAO location identifier*] (ICLI)
SLSF	Sodium Loop Safety Facility [*Nuclear energy*]
SLSF	Svenska Landsmal och Svenskt Folkliv [*Uppsala*] [*A publication*]
SLSG	S-Locus-Specific Glycoprotein [*Botany*]
SLSG	Sipuati [*Bolivia*] [*ICAO location identifier*] (ICLI)
SLSH	Santa Ana De Huachi [*Bolivia*] [*ICAO location identifier*] (ICLI)
SLSI	San Ignacio De Velasco [*Bolivia*] [*ICAO location identifier*] (ICLI)
SLSI	Super Large-Scale Integration
SLSJ	Salinas [*Bolivia*] [*ICAO location identifier*] (ICLI)
SLSK	Sauces [*Bolivia*] [*ICAO location identifier*] (ICLI)
SLSL	Santa Lucia (Cliza) [*Bolivia*] [*ICAO location identifier*] (ICLI)
SLSL	Statutory Long Service Leave (ADA)
SLSM	San Ignacio De Moxos [*Bolivia*] [*ICAO location identifier*] (ICLI)
SLSM	Silver Life-Saving Medal [*Military decoration*]
SLSMS	Spacelab Support Module Simulator [*NASA*] (MCD)
SLSN	Sanandita [*Bolivia*] [*ICAO location identifier*] (ICLI)
SLSO	Santa Barbara De Parra [*Bolivia*] [*ICAO location identifier*] (ICLI)
SLSO	Shipyard Labour Supply Officer [*British*]
SLSP	SACLANT Scheduled Program (MCD)
SLSp	Slovensky Spisovatel [*A publication*]
SLSP	Slow Speed
SLSQ	Saahaqui [*Bolivia*] [*ICAO location identifier*] (ICLI)
SLSR	Santa Rosa De Yacuma [*Bolivia*] [*ICAO location identifier*] (ICLI)
SLSS	Sasasama [*Bolivia*] [*ICAO location identifier*] (ICLI)
SLSS	Secondary Life Support System [*NASA*]
SLSS	Shuttle Launch Support System (MCD)
SL-SS	Spacelab Subsystem [*NASA*] (NASA)
SLSS	Swimmer Life Support System [*Navy*] (CAAL)
SLSS	Systems Library Subscription Service [*Data processing*] (IBMDP)
SLSSM	Submerged Launched Surface-to-Surface Missile (MCD)
SL-SSS	Spacelab Subsystem Segment [*NASA*] (NASA)
SLST	St. Louis, San Francisco & Texas Railway Co. [*AAR code*]
SLST	San Antonio [*Bolivia*] [*ICAO location identifier*] (ICLI)
Sl St	Slade's Compilation of the Statutes of Vermont [*A publication*] (DLA)
SLST	Slightly Staining
SLST	Slip Stitch [*Knitting*]
SLSU	Sucre [*Bolivia*] [*ICAO location identifier*] (ICLI)
SLSW	Santa Barbara (Versalles) [*Bolivia*] [*ICAO location identifier*] (ICLI)
SLSX	San Ramon De Senac [*Bolivia*] [*ICAO location identifier*] (ICLI)
SLT	Salant Corp. [*NYSE symbol*] (SPSG)
SLT	Salta [*Argentina*] [*Seismograph station code, US Geological Survey*] [*Closed*] (SEIS)
SLT	Scots Law Times [*A publication*]
SLT	Searchlight
SLT	Second Law of Thermodynamics
SLT	Self-Loading Tape (AFM)
SLT	Sellectek Industries, Inc. [*Vancouver Stock Exchange symbol*]
SLT	Shiga-Like Toxin [*Biochemistry*]
SLT	Ship Letter Telegram
SL & T	Shipper's Load and Tally [*Bills of lading*]
SLT	Shuttle Loop Transit [*NASA*]
SLT	Signaling Link Termination [*Telecommunications*]
SLT	Simulated Launch Test [*NASA*] (KSC)
SLT	Skylight (AAG)
SLT	Slate (MSA)
SLT	Slate Run, PA [*Location identifier*] [*FAA*] (FAAL)
SLT	Sleet [*Meteorology*] (FAAC)
SLT	Slit
SLT	Solid Logic Technique [*Data processing*] (IEEE)
SLT	Solid Logic Technology
SLT	Sonobuoy Launch Tube [*Navy*] (CAAL)
SLT	Special [*or Specific*] Launch Trajectory (AFM)
SLT	Spotlight (MSA)
SLT	Stockpile Laboratory Tests
SLT	Stress Limit Tests

SLT .... Structured Learning Therapy
S Lt .... Sub-Lieutenant [*British military*]   (DMA)
SLT .... Svensk Litteraturtidskrift [*A publication*]
SLT .... Switchman's Local Test [*Telecommunications*]   (TEL)
SLTB .... St. Lucia Tourist Board   (EA)
SLTB .... Society for Low Temperature Biology   (EA)
SLTC .... Siltec Corp. [*NASDAQ symbol*]   (NQ)
SLTC .... Society of Leather Technologists and Chemists [*British*]
SLTD .... Salted
SLTD .... Slotted   (MSA)
SLTDP .... Special LASER Technology Development Program
SLTE .... Teoponte [*Bolivia*] [*ICAO location identifier*]   (ICLI)
SLTEA ...... Sheffield Lighter Trades Employers' Association
               [*British*]   (DCTA)
SLTerm...... Slavjanska Lingvisticna Terminologija [*A publication*]
SLTF.......... San Telmo (Cordillera) [*Bolivia*] [*ICAO location
               identifier*]   (ICLI)
SLTF.......... Shortest Latency Time First
SLTF.......... Silo-Launch Test Facility
SLTG .... Santiago [*Bolivia*] [*ICAO location identifier*]   (ICLI)
SLTG .... Sterner Lighting Systems, Inc. [*NASDAQ symbol*]   (NQ)
SLTH......... Tumichucua [*Bolivia*] [*ICAO location identifier*]   (ICLI)
SLTI .... San Matias [*Bolivia*] [*ICAO location identifier*]   (ICLI)
SLTI .... Surgical Laser Technologies, Inc. [*NASDAQ symbol*]   (NQ)
SLTJ.......... Tarija [*Bolivia*] [*ICAO location identifier*]   (ICLI)
SLT (Lyon Ct) ... Scots Law Times (Lyon Court Reports) [*A
               publication*]   (DLA)
SLTM........ Selecterm, Inc. [*NASDAQ symbol*]   (NQ)
SLTM........ Standard Lap Turn Method   (NVT)
SLTM........ Storia delle Letteratura di Tutto il Mondo [*A publication*]
SLTM........ Structural Lander Test Model
SLTN........ Solectron Corp. [*NASDAQ symbol*]   (NQ)
SLT (Notes) ... Scots Law Times (Notes of Recent Decisions) [*A
               publication*]   (DLA)
SLTO......... Sea-Level Takeoff
SLTP .... Tipuani [*Bolivia*] [*ICAO location identifier*]   (ICLI)
SLTR .... Service Life Test Report   (AAG)
SLTR .... Trinidad [*Bolivia*] [*ICAO location identifier*]   (ICLI)
SLTS .... Todos Santos [*Bolivia*] [*ICAO location identifier*]   (ICLI)
SLT & SDL ... Searchlight and Sound Locator [*Navy*]
SLT (Sh Ct) ... Scots Law Times Sheriff Court Reports [*A
               publication*]   (DLA)
sLTSV....... Satellite Lucerne Transient Streak Virus
SLTT .... Total Bolivia [*Bolivia*] [*ICAO location identifier*]   (ICLI)
SLTU......... Tucavaca [*Bolivia*] [*ICAO location identifier*]   (ICLI)
SLTUF ...... Sri Lanka Trade Union Federation [*Sri Lanka Vurthiya Samithi
               Sammelanaya*]
SLTV .... St. Lucia Television Service
SLTX .... Sales Tax
SLTY .... Tiguipa [*Bolivia*] [*ICAO location identifier*]   (ICLI)
SLTZ .... Tupiza [*Bolivia*] [*ICAO location identifier*]   (ICLI)
SLU............ Pavlovsk [*USSR*] [*Later, LNN*] [*Geomagnetic observatory
               code*]
SLU............ Saint Lawrence University [*Canton, NY*]
SLU............ St. Louis University [*Missouri*]
SLU............ St. Louis University, Law Library, St. Louis, MO [*OCLC
               symbol*]   (OCLC)
SLU............ St. Lucia [*West Indies*] [*Airport symbol*]   (OAG)
SLU............ Secondary Logic Unit
SLU............ Serial Line Unit
Slu............. Slough [*Maps and charts*]
SLU............ Slutsk [*USSR*] [*Later, LNN*] [*Geomagnetic observatory code*]
SLU............ Source Library Update [*Data processing*]
SLU............ Southern Labor Union
SLU............ Special Liaison Unit [*Military intelligence*] [*World War II*]
SLU............ Spil. Een Progressief Onafhankelijk Maandblad voor
               Zelfstandigen en Werknemers in het Middenbedrijf en
               Kleinbedrijf [*A publication*]
SLU............ Studii de Literatura Universala [*Bucharest*] [*A publication*]
SLU............ Subscriber Line Use [*Telecommunications*]
SLU............ Svenska Litteratursaellskapet i Uppsala [*A publication*]
SLU............ Switching Logic Unit   (CAAL)
SLUC......... Standard Level User Charge
SLUC......... Uncia [*Bolivia*] [*ICAO location identifier*]   (ICLI)
Sludge Mag ... Sludge Magazine [*A publication*]
Sludge Manage Ser ... Sludge Management Series [*A publication*]
SLUF......... Short Little Ugly Feller [*Nickname for A-7 aircraft*]   (MCD)
SLUFAE.... Surface-Launched Unit, Fuel-Air Explosive Mine Neutralizer
               [*Army*]   (RDA)
SLUG......... Superconducting Low-Inductance Undulatory Galvanometer
SLULJ....... St. Louis University. Law Journal [*A publication*]
SLUMA..... Southern Lumberman [*United States*] [*A publication*]
SLURB ...... Slovenly Suburb
SLURJ....... St. Louis University. Research Journal [*Baguio City*] [*A
               publication*]
SLURP ...... Self Leveling Unit for Removing Pollution [*Marine
               science*]   (MSC)
SLURP ...... Spiny Lobster Undersea Research Project
SLURREX ... Slurry Reactor Experiment
SLUS .... Subscriber's Line Use System [*AT & T*]
               [*Telecommunications*]   (TEL)

SLUV......... Uvas Verdes [*Bolivia*] [*ICAO location identifier*]   (ICLI)
Sl UVAN ... Slavistica. Praci Institutu Slov'janoznavstva Ukrajins'koji
               Vil'noji Akademiji Nauk [*A publication*]
SLUY........ Uyuni [*Bolivia*] [*ICAO location identifier*]   (ICLI)
SLV............ El Salvador [*ANSI three-letter standard code*]   (CNC)
SLV............ Federal Carriers, Inc. [*White Lake, NY*] [*FAA
               designator*]   (FAAC)
SLV............ Salivate   (KSC)
SLV............ San Jose, CA [*Location identifier*] [*FAA*]   (FAAL)
SLV............ Satellite Launching Vehicle [*Air Force*]
SLV............ Satellite-Like Virus
SLV............ Saturn Launch Vehicle [*NASA*]   (KSC)
SLV............ Seldovia [*Alaska*] [*Seismograph station code, US Geological
               Survey*]   (SEIS)
SLv............ Sifra on Leviticus [*A publication*]   (BJA)
SLV............ Silver Lady Resources [*Vancouver Stock Exchange symbol*]
SLV............ Silvercrest Industries [*AMEX symbol*]   (SPSG)
SLV............ Simulated Launch Vehicle   (MCD)
SLV............ Sleeve   (AAG)
slv............. Slovenian [*MARC language code*] [*Library of
               Congress*]   (LCCP)
SLV............ Soft Landing Vehicle [*NASA*]
SLV............ Space Launch Vehicle [*NASA*]
SLV............ Space-Like Vector
SLV............ Standard Launch Vehicle
SLVA......... Villa Aroma [*Bolivia*] [*ICAO location identifier*]   (ICLI)
SLVC......... Selvac Corp. [*NASDAQ symbol*]   (NQ)
SLVD......... Covendo [*Bolivia*] [*ICAO location identifier*]   (ICLI)
SLVE......... Venecia [*Bolivia*] [*ICAO location identifier*]   (ICLI)
SLVG......... Sleeving [*Electricity*]
SLVG......... Special Launch Vehicle Group [*NASA*]   (KSC)
SLVG......... Valle Grande [*Bolivia*] [*ICAO location identifier*]   (ICLI)
SLVI.......... Caranavi [*Bolivia*] [*ICAO location identifier*]   (ICLI)
SLVM........ Villa Montes [*Bolivia*] [*ICAO location identifier*]   (ICLI)
SLVN......... Sylvan Learning Corp. [*Montgomery, AL*] [*NASDAQ
               symbol*]   (NQ)
SLVN......... Valencia [*Bolivia*] [*ICAO location identifier*]   (ICLI)
SLVR......... Silverado Mines Ltd. [*NASDAQ symbol*]   (NQ)
SLVR......... Viru Viru [*Bolivia*] [*ICAO location identifier*]   (ICLI)
SLVRJ....... Surface-Launched Low-Volume Ramjet
SLVT........ Solvent   (MSA)
SLVY........ Silvey Corp. [*NASDAQ symbol*]   (NQ)
SLW.......... Silversword Corp. [*Vancouver Stock Exchange symbol*]
SLW.......... Single Line Working [*Railway engineering term*]   (DCTA)
SLW.......... Sisters of the Living Word [*Roman Catholic religious order*]
SLW.......... Slow
SLW.......... Space-Based LASER Weapon   (MCD)
SLW.......... Specific Leaf Weight [*Botany*]
SLW.......... Spectral Line Width
SLW.......... Store Logical Word
SLW.......... Straight-Line Wavelength
SLW.......... Wooster, OH [*Location identifier*] [*FAA*]   (FAAL)
SLWA........ Santa Rosa De Abuna [*Bolivia*] [*ICAO location
               identifier*]   (ICLI)
SLWD........ Seis De Agosto [*Bolivia*] [*ICAO location identifier*]   (ICLI)
SLWFA ..... Schweizerische Landwirtschaftliche Forschung [*A publication*]
SLWL........ Straight-Line Wavelength   (MSA)
SLWMS .... Secondary Liquid Waste Management System [*Nuclear
               energy*]   (NRCH)
SL-Wola Ludu ... Stronnictwo Ludowe-Wola Ludu [*Peasant Party-People's
               Will*] [*Poland*] [*Political party*]   (PPE)
SLWT .... Side Loadable Warping Tug [*Navy*]   (CAAL)
SLX .... Salt Cay [*British West Indies*] [*Airport symbol*]   (OAG)
SLX .... Siltronics Ltd. [*Toronto Stock Exchange symbol*]
SLX .... Slate Creek, AK [*Location identifier*] [*FAA*]   (FAAL)
SLY .... Hayward, WI [*Location identifier*] [*FAA*]   (FAAL)
SLY .... Safety, Liquidity, Yield
SLY .... Skelly Resources Ltd. [*Vancouver Stock Exchange symbol*]
SLY .... Slijtersvakblad. Vakblad voor de Drankenbranche [*A
               publication*]
SLY .... Sloppy [*Horse racing*]
SLY .... Southerly
SLYA .... Yacuiba [*Bolivia*] [*ICAO location identifier*]   (ICLI)
SLYB .... El Bato [*Bolivia*] [*ICAO location identifier*]   (ICLI)
SLYI .... Yapacani [*Bolivia*] [*ICAO location identifier*]   (ICLI)
SLYP .... Muyupampa [*Bolivia*] [*ICAO location identifier*]   (ICLI)
SLYP .... Short Leaf Yellow Pine [*Lumber*]
SLYY .... San Yo Yo [*Bolivia*] [*ICAO location identifier*]   (ICLI)
SLZ .... Sao Luiz [*Brazil*] [*Airport symbol*]   (OAG)
SLZ .... Solidor Resources, Inc. [*Vancouver Stock Exchange symbol*]
SLZ .... Suppress Leading Zero [*Data processing*]
SLZA .... Scandinavian Lead Zinc Association [*Stockholm,
               Sweden*]   (EAIO)
SLZB .... San Pedro [*Bolivia*] [*ICAO location identifier*]   (ICLI)
SLZF......... San Francisco (Naciff) [*Bolivia*] [*ICAO location
               identifier*]   (ICLI)
SLZG .... San Agustin [*Bolivia*] [*ICAO location identifier*]   (ICLI)
SLZJ......... San Pedro (Richard) [*Bolivia*] [*ICAO location
               identifier*]   (ICLI)
SLZK........ San Lucas [*Bolivia*] [*ICAO location identifier*]   (ICLI)
SLZR .... San Rafael (Isidoro) [*Bolivia*] [*ICAO location identifier*]   (ICLI)

SLZX .... San Pedro (Salvatierra) [*Bolivia*] [*ICAO location identifier*] (ICLI)

SM .... Altair Linee Aeree SpA [*Italy*] [*ICAO designator*] (FAAC)

SM .... Dr. Schwarz Arzneimittelfabrik GmbH [*Germany*] [*Research code symbol*]

SM .... Master of Science

SM .... Medal of Service of the Order of Canada

SM .... Meteorological Aids Station [*ITU designation*]

SM .... Misericorde Sisters [*Roman Catholic religious order*]

SM .... Sa Majeste [*His or Her Majesty*] [*French*]

SM .... Sacred to the Memory of --- [*Epitaphs*] (ROG)

SM .... Sacred Music [*A publication*]

S & M .... Sadism and Masochism

SM .... St. Marys Railroad Co. [*AAR code*]

SM .... Sales Management [*Later, Sales and Marketing Management*] [*A publication*]

SM .... Sales Manager

SM .... Sales and Marketing Management [*A publication*]

SM .... Salvage Mechanic [*Navy*]

Sm .... Samarium [*See Sa*] [*Chemical element*]

SM .... Sammlung Metzler [*A publication*]

Sm .... Samuel [*Old Testament book*]

SM .... San Marco [*Satellite*] [*NASA/Italy*]

sm .... San Marino [*MARC country of publication code*] [*Library of Congress*] [*IYRU nationality code*] (LCCP)

SM .... San Marino [*ANSI two-letter standard code*] (CNC)

SM .... Sanctae Memoriae [*Of Holy Memory*] [*Latin*]

S & M .... Sappers and Miners [*British military*] (DMA)

SM .... Scheduled Maintenance (MCD)

SM .... Schistosoma Mansoni [*A parasitic fluke*]

S of M .... School of Musketry [*Military*] [*British*] (ROG)

S-M .... Schuetzenmine [*Antipersonnel mine*] [*German military - World War II*]

SM .... Schwarz/Mann [*Supply company in biochemistry and chemistry*]

SM .... Schweizer Muenzblaetter [*Gazette Numismatique Suisse*] [*A publication*]

SM .... Scientific Memorandum

SM .... Scientific Monthly [*A publication*]

Sm .... Sclerotinia minor [*A fungus*]

SM .... Seamen [*British military*] (DMA)

SM .... Seat Mile

SM .... Second Mortgage [*Banking*]

SM .... Secondary Market [*Investment term*]

SM .... Secondary Memory [*Data processing*] (BUR)

SM .... Secretary's Memorandum [*Military*]

SM .... Security Manual (AAG)

SM .... Security Monitor (AAG)

SM .... Seed Mass [*Botany*]

Sm .... Semahot (BJA)

SM .... Semiconductor Memory

SM .... Semimonthly

SM .... Senior Magistrate

S/M .... Sensory-to-Motor [*Ratio*]

SM .... Sentence Modifier [*Linguistics*]

S & M .... September and March [*Denotes semiannual payments of interest or dividends in these months*] [*Business term*]

SM .... Sequence Monitor

S & M .... Sequencer and Monitor (KSC)

SM .... Sergeant Major

SM .... Serious Music [*Canadian Broadcasting Corporation record series prefix*]

SM .... Serratia Marcescens [*Bacterium*]

S/M .... Service/Maintenance (NASA)

S & M .... Service and Maintenance

SM .... Service Manual

SM .... Service Mark [*Trademarks*]

SM .... Service Member [*Military*] (AABC)

SM .... Service Module [*NASA*]

SM .... Service Monitoring [*Telecommunications*] (TEL)

SM .... Set Mode (BUR)

SM .... Sewage Microparticulates [*Oceanography*]

SM .... Sewing Machine

S & M .... Sexton and Malone [*Comic book*] [*CBC TV series*]

SM .... Sexual Myths [*Scale*]

SM .... Shape Memory [*Metallurgy*]

SM .... Shared Memory [*Data processing*] (BUR)

S & M .... Shaw and Maclean's House of Lords Cases [*A publication*] (DLA)

SM .... Sheet Metal

SM .... Shell Model

SM .... Shelter Management [*Civil Defense*]

SM .... Ship Movement Library [*Maritime Data Network, Inc.*] [*Information service or system*] (CRD)

SM .... Shipment Memorandum [*Navy*]

SM .... Ship's Manifest (ADA)

SM .... Shock Mount

SM .... Shop Manual [*Air Force*] (AAG)

SM .... Short Meter [*Music*]

SM .... Short Module [*NASA*] (NASA)

SMX .... Shuttle Management [*Kennedy Space Center*] [*NASA*] (NASA)

SM .... SIAI-Marchetti SpA [*Italy*] [*ICAO aircraft manufacturer identifier*] (ICAO)

SM .... Siam

SM .... Signaling Module [*Telecommunications*] (TEL)

SM .... Signalman [*Navy rating*]

SM .... Silver Medalist

SM .... Silver Methenamine [*Biological stain*]

SM .... Silver Mica [*Capacitor*]

SM .... Simple Maintenance

SM .... Simple Mastectomy [*Medicine*]

SM .... Simulated Missile (AAG)

SM .... Simulators [*JETDS nomenclature*] [*Military*] (CET)

SM .... Single Manager [*Military*]

SM .... Sinistra Mano [*Left Hand*]

SM .... Sinus Medii [*Central Bay*] [*Lunar area*]

SM .... Sisters of Mercy [*Roman Catholic religious order*]

S de M .... Sisters Servants of Mary [*Roman Catholic religious order*]

SM .... Slow Moving

SM .... Small (AAG)

SM .... Small Pica

Sm .... Smectite [*Agronomy*]

S & M .... Smedes and Marshall's Mississippi Chancery Reports [*A publication*] (DLA)

S & M .... Smedes and Marshall's Mississippi Reports [*9-22 Mississippi*] [*1843-50*] [*A publication*] (DLA)

Sm .... Smena [*Moscow*] [*A publication*]

Sm .... Smith Antigen [*Immunology*]

Sm .... Smith Collection. British Museum [*London*] (BJA)

Sm .... Smithsonian [*A publication*]

SM .... SMM Enterprises Ltd. [*Vancouver Stock Exchange symbol*]

SM .... Smooth (MSA)

SM .... Sociaal Maandblad [*A publication*]

SM .... Socially Maladjusted

SM .... Societa Altair [*Italy*] [*ICAO designator*] (ICDA)

SM .... Societas Mariae [*Congregation of Mary*] [*Marists*] [*Roman Catholic religious order*]

SM .... Society of Medalists

S of M .... Society of Metaphysicians (EA)

SM .... Society of Miniaturists (EA)

SM .... Soft Manual (NASA)

SM .... Soil Mechanics

SM .... Solar Magnetic [*System*] [*NASA*]

SM .... Solar Magnetospheric

SM .... Soldier's Manual

SM .... Soldier's Medal [*Military decoration*]

SM .... Soldiers' Memorial Hospital [*Australia*]

SM .... Solicitor's Memorandum, United States Internal Revenue Bureau [*A publication*] (DLA)

SM .... Solid Measure (ROG)

SM .... Somatomedin [*Biochemistry*]

SM .... Song of Moses (BJA)

SM .... Sons of Malta

SM .... Sound Management [*Radio Advertising Bureau*] [*A publication*]

SM .... Southern Minnesota Railroad

SM .... Spanish Moss

SM .... Spawning Mark

SM .... Special Memorandum

SM .... Specification Memo (AAG)

SM .... Speculative Masonry [*Freemasonry*]

SM .... Speech Monographs [*A publication*]

SM .... SpenderMenders [*An association*] (EA)

SM .... Sphingomyelin [*Also, Sph*] [*Biochemistry*]

SM .... Sports Medicine [*A publication*]

SM .... Stabilized Member [*NASA*] (KSC)

SM .... Staff Manager [*Insurance*]

SM .... Staff Memorandum

SM .... Stage Manager

SM .... Standard Matched

SM .... Standard Memoranda (AAG)

SM .... Standard Methods

SM .... Standard Missile

SM .... Standards Manual

SM .... Staphylococcus Medium [*Microbiology*]

SM .... State Militia [*e.g., NJSM - New Jersey State Militia*]

SM .... Station Manager [*Deep Space Instrumentation Facility, NASA*]

SM .... Stationary Medium-Power [*Reactor*] [*Nuclear energy*]

SM .... Statistical Multiplexer (MCD)

SM .... Statistiske Meddelelser [*Denmark*]

SM .... Statute Mile

SM .... Stipendiary Magistrate

S & M .... Stock and Machinery

SM .... Stock Market

SM .... Strategic Missile (NATG)

SM .... Streptomycin [*An antibiotic*]

SM .... Stria Medullaris [*Neuroanatomy*]

SM .... Strip Mine

SM .... Structural Mechanical (MCD)

SM .... Structure Memory

S & M .... Structures and Materials (MCD)

SM .... Structures Memorandum

SM .... Student Manual [*Civil Defense*]
SM .... Studi Medievali [*A publication*]
S M .... Studia Musicologica. Academiae Scientiarum Hungaricae [*A publication*]
SM .... Studio SM [*Record label*] [*France*]
S/M .... Submarine [*British*]
SM .... [*Officer Qualified for*] Submarine Duties [*British*]
SM .... Submarine Flag [*Navy*] [*British*]
SM .... Submarine, Minelaying [*Obsolete*]
S/M .... Submarine Pay
sm .... Submetacentric [*Botany*]
SM .... Substitute Materials [*British*]
SM .... Suckling Mice
SM .... Sumerian Mythology [*S. N. Kramer*] [*A publication*] (BJA)
SM .... Summary Memorandum
SM .... Summer [*A publication*]
S & M .... Sun and Moon [*A publication*]
SM .... Super Maneuverable Aircraft
S/M .... Super Mare [*On Sea*] [*In place names*] [*Latin*] (ROG)
S & M .... Supply and Maintenance [*Army*] (AABC)
SM .... Supply Manual [*Military*]
SM .... Support Module [*NASA*] (NASA)
SM .... Surface Measure
SM .... Surface Missile (AAG)
S & M .... Surfaced and Matched [*Lumber*]
SM .... Surgeon Major
SM .... Suspended Matter [*Chemistry*]
SM .... Sustained Medication [*Pharmacology*]
SM .... Sydney Mail [*A publication*] (APTA)
SM .... Symbolic Manipulation [*Data processing*]
SM .... Synchronous MODEM
SM .... Synthetic Medium [*Microbiology*]
SM .... System Manager [*Military*] (AFM)
SM .... System Mechanics
SM .... System Monitor
SM .... Systema Malykh [*Small System*] [*Russian*] [*Data processing*]
SM .... Systemic Mastocytosis [*Medicine*]
SM .... Systems Management [*NASA*] (MCD)
SM .... Systems Memory [*Data processing*] (BUR)
SM .... Systolic Mean [*Cardiology*]
SM .... Systolic Murmur [*Cardiology*]
SM1 .... Signalman, First Class [*Navy rating*]
SM2 .... Signalman, Second Class [*Navy rating*]
SM3 .... Signalman, Third Class [*Navy rating*]
SMA .... Andreafsky/St. Marys, AK [*Location identifier*] [*FAA*] (FAAL)
SMA .... Sa Majeste Aulique [*His, or Her, Austrian Majesty*] [*French*] (ROG)
SMA .... Safe Manufacturers' Association
SMA .... Saigon Mission Association (EA)
SMA .... Salad Manufacturers Association (EA)
SMA .... Salt Manufacturing Association [*British*]
SMA .... San Manuel Arizona Railroad Co. [*AAR code*]
SMA .... Santa Maria [*Azores*] [*Airport symbol*] (OAG)
SMA .... Scale Manufacturers Association (EA)
SMA .... Scheduled Maintenance Action
SMA .... Screen Manufacturers Association (EA)
SMA .... Scythe Makers' Association [*A union*] [*British*]
SMA .... Semimajor Axis
SMA .... Senior Marine Advisor
SMA .... Senior Military Attache
SMA .... Sergeant Major Academy [*Army*]
SMA .... Sergeant Major of the Army (AABC)
SMA .... Service Merchandisers of America [*Later, NASM*] (EA)
SMA .... Shape Memory Alloy (RDA)
SMA .... Shelving Manufacturers Association (EA)
SMA .... Shielded Metal Arc [*Nickel and alloy welding*]
SMA .... Ship's Material Account
SMA .... Simultaneous Multiphasic Analysis [*Medicine*]
SMA .... Single Manager Approach
SMA .... Site Maintenance Area (AAG)
SMA .... Skymark Airlines (FAAC)
SMA .... Slave Manipulator Arm [*Astronautics*]
SMA .... Small Arms (NATG)
SMA .... Sociaal Maandblad Arbeid [*A publication*]
SMA .... Social Maturity Age
SMA .... Socialist Medical Association [*British*]
SMA .... Societe des Missionnaires d'Afrique [*Society of Missionaries of Africa*] (EA)
SMA .... Society of African Missions [*Roman Catholic men's religious order*]
SMA .... Society of Management Accountants
SMA .... Society of Manufacturer's Agents [*Later, SMR*] (EA)
SMA .... Society of Marine Artists [*British*]
SMA .... Society of Maritime Arbitrators (EA)
SMA .... Society of Medical Administrators (EA)
SMA .... Society for Medical Anthropology (EA)
SMA .... Society for Medieval Archaeology (EA)
SMA .... Society of Mineral Analysts (EA)
SMA .... Society of Municipal Arborists (EA)
SMA .... Software Maintenance Association (EA)
SMA .... Solar Maximum Analysis [*Meteorology*]

SMA .... Somatomedin A [*Biochemistry*]
SMA .... Southern Marketing Association. Proceedings [*A publication*]
SMA .... Southern Maryland Aviation, Inc. [*FAA designator*] (FAAC)
SMA .... Soviet Military Administration
SMA .... Special Miscellaneous Account
SMA .... Special Mission Alteration
SMA .... Spinal Muscular Atrophy [*Medicine*]
SMA .... Spiritual Ministry for Adults (EA)
SMA .... Spontaneous Motor Activity [*Neurophysiology*]
SMA .... Squadron Maintenance Area
SMA .... Stabilized Member Assembly [*NASA*]
SMA .... Stage Management Association [*British*]
SMA .... Standard Maintenance Allowance
SMA .... Standard Methods Agar [*Microbiology*]
SMA .... State Mutual Life Assurance Co. of America
SMA .... Steatite Manufacturers Association [*Later, DPCSMA*] (EA)
SMA .... Steel Manufacturers Association (EA)
SMA .... Stichting Mondiaal Alternatief [*Foundation for Ecological Development Alternatives*] (EAIO)
SMA .... Stoker Manufacturers Association (EA)
SMA .... Strategic Management Accounting (ADA)
SMA .... Strategic Mobility Analysis [*Military*]
SMA .... Stucco Manufacturers Association (EA)
S M (A) ...... Studies in Music (Australia) [*A publication*]
SMA .... Stylomastoid Artery [*Anatomy*]
SMA .... Styrene-Maleic Anhydride [*Organic chemistry*]
SMA .... Subject Matter Area (AFM)
SMA .... Submerged Metal Arc Welding
SMA .... Subsequent Maintenance Assessment
SMA .... Suggested for Mature Audiences [*Motion pictures*]
SMA .... Sukuma Exploration [*Vancouver Stock Exchange symbol*]
SMA .... Summerton [*South Carolina*] [*Seismograph station code, US Geological Survey*] [*Closed*] (SEIS)
SMA .... Superior Mesenteric Artery [*Anatomy*]
SMA .... Superplastic Metal Alloy
SMA .... Supplemental Maintenance Appraisal
SMA .... Supplementary Motor Area [*Anatomy*]
S & MA ...... Supply and Maintenance Agency [*System*] [*Army*]
SMA .... Support Management Area [*Mission Control Center*] [*NASA*]
SMA .... Surface Modulating Assembly [*Cytology*]
SMA .... Syrie et Monde Arabe [*Damascus*] [*A publication*]
SMAA .... Submarine Movement Advisory Authority (NVT)
SMAB .... Solid Motor Assembly Building [*for Missiles*]
SMAB .... Spartan Management Action Board [*Missiles*] (MCD)
SMAC .... Scene Matching Area Correlator [*Navy*] (MCD)
SMAC .... Science and Mathematics Analysis Center [*ERIC*]
SMAC .... Scientific Machine Automation Corporation
SMAC .... Senate Military Affairs Committee [*British*] (DAS)
SMAC .... Serial Memory Address Counter [*Computer*]
SMAC .... Shielded Metal Arc Cutting [*Welding*]
SMAC .... Simulation, Manual and Computerized
SMAC .... Single Manager for Ammunition, Conventional [*DoD*]
SMAC .... Society of Management Accountants of Canada
SMAC .... Special Mission Attack Computer
SMAC .... Striated Microtubule-Associated Components [*Botanical cytology*]
SMAC .... Submicron Aerosol Collector
SMAC .... System Management and Control
SMAC/CRC ... Surface Modification and Characterization Collaborative Research Center [*Oak Ridge, TN*] [*Oak Ridge National Laboratory*] [*Department of Energy*] (GRD)
SMACH .... Sounding Machine [*Engineering*]
SMACK ..... Society of Males Who Appreciate Cute Knees [*Group opposing below-the-knee fashions introduced in 1970*]
SMACNA ... Sheet Metal and Air Conditioning Contractors' National Association (EA)
SMACRATRACEN ... Small Craft Training Center
SMACS ..... Serialized Missile Accounting and Control System
SMACS ..... Simulated Message Analysis and Conversion Subsystem
Sm Act .... Smith's Action at Law [*12th ed.*] [*1876*] [*A publication*] (DLA)
SMAD .... Solvated Metal Atom Dispersion [*Chemistry*]
SMAD .... Sowjetische Militaeradministration
Sm Adm Pr ... Smith's Admiralty Practice [*4th ed.*] [*1892*] [*A publication*] (DLA)
SMAE .... Sbornik Muzeia Antropologii i Etnografii [*A publication*] (BJA)
SMAE .... Society of Model Aeronautical Engineers [*British*]
SMAE .... Superior Mesenteric Artery Embolus [*Medicine*]
SMAE .... System Management Application Entity
SMAF .... Afobaka [*Surinam*] [*ICAO location identifier*] (ICLI)
SMAF .... Smooth Muscle Activating Factor
SMAF .... Special Mission Aircraft Flights (NATG)
SMAF .... Specific Macrophage Arming Factor [*Hematology*]
SMAF .... Superior Mesenteric Artery Flow
SMAG .... Simulator Missile Airborne and Ground (MCD)
SMAG .... Star Magnitude (NASA)
SMAG .... Systems Management Analysis Group (MCD)
SMAGD .... Solaire 1 Magazine [*A publication*]
Sma & Giff ... Smale and Giffard's English Vice-Chancellors' Reports [*A publication*] (DLA)
SMAIL ...... Source Mail [*Electronic mail*]

SMAJ .... Sergeant Major
SMAL........ Single Mode Alignment　(CAAL)
SMAL........ Society for Musteline Arts and Literature　(EA)
SMAL........ Structural Macroassembly Language
SMAL........ System Material Analysis List
SMALC...... Sacramento Air Logistics Center　(MCD)
Smale & G ... Smale and Giffard's English Vice-Chancellors' Reports [*A publication*]　(DLA)
SMALGOL ... Small Computer Algorithmic Language
Small Bus... Small Business Reporter [*A publication*]
Small Bus Comp ... Small Business Computers Magazine [*A publication*]
Small Bus Comput ... Small Business Computers [*A publication*]
Small Bus Comput News ... Small Business Computer News [*A publication*]
Small Business ... Small Business Report [*A publication*]
Small Bus Reporter ... Small Business Reporter [*A publication*]
Small Bus Rt ... Small Business Report [*A publication*]
Small Comput Libr ... Small Computers in Libraries [*A publication*]
Small Gr B ... Small Group Behavior [*A publication*]
Small Group Behav ... Small Group Behavior [*A publication*]
Small Mamm Newsl ... Small Mammal Newsletters [*A publication*]
Small Pr..... Small Press Review [*A publication*]
Small Ruminant Res ... Small Ruminant Research [*A publication*]
Small-Scale Master Bldr ... Small-Scale Master Builder [*A publication*]
Small Stock Mag ... Small Stock Magazine [*A publication*]
Small Sys ... Small Systems World [*A publication*]
Small Sys Soft ... Small Systems Software [*A publication*]
Small Syst Software ... Small Systems Software [*A publication*]
Small Syst World ... Small Systems World [*A publication*]
SMALLTALK ... [*A*] programming language　(CSR)
SMAM ...... Amotopo [*Surinam*] [*ICAO location identifier*]　(ICLI)
SMAMA ..... Sacramento Air Materiel Area　(KSC)
SMAME...... Society of Marine Architects and Marine Engineers　(EA)
SMAN .... Standard Medium-Accuracy Navigator
SMANCS .. Styrene Maleic Acid Neocarzinostatin [*Antineoplastic drug*]
Smap.......... Surprised Middle-Aged Person [*Lifestyle classification*]
SMAP .... System Management Application Process
SMAP........ Systems Management Analysis Project　(MCD)
SMAR........ Sheet Metal Assembler Riveter　(MCD)
S & Mar ..... Smedes and Marshall's Mississippi Reports [*9-22 Mississippi*] [*A publication*]　(DLA)
SMARC..... Survivable-MOS [*Metal-Oxide Semiconductor*] Array Computer [*Air Force*]
SM Arch .... SM [*Solid Mechanics*] Archives [*A publication*]
S & Mar Ch ... Smedes and Marshall's Mississippi Chancery Reports [*A publication*]　(DLA)
SM Arch .... Solid Mechanics Archives [*A publication*]
SMART..... Salton's Magical Automatic Retriever of Texts [*Data processing*]
SMART..... Satellite Maintenance and Repair Techniques [*Air Force*]
SMART..... Scheduled Maintenance and Reliability Team　(MCD)
SMART..... Science, Mathematics, and Related Technologies
SMART..... Selected Methods for Attracting the Right Targets [*Bombing system*]　(AFM)
SMART..... Sensitive-Membrane-Antigen-Rapid-Test
SMART..... Sequential Mechanism for Automatic Recording and Testing
SMART..... Shuttle Meeting Action - Item Review Tracking [*NASA*]　(NASA)
SMART..... Socony Mobil Automatic Real Time　(DIT)
SMART..... Sort Merge and Reduction Tapes　(CAAL)
SMART..... Space Maintenance and Repair Techniques
SMART..... Space Management and Retail Tracking System [*Information Resources, Inc.*]
SMART..... Spacesaver Material Accounting Resource Terminal [*Spacesaver Corp.*]
SMART..... Specific, Measurable, Agreed-To, Reachable, Time-Specific [*Management technique*]
SMART..... Stop Merchandising Alcohol on Radio and Television
SMART..... Structural Maintenance and Repair Team　(MCD)
SMART..... Supersonic Military Air Research Track
SMART..... Supersonic Missile and Rocket Track
SMART..... Supply and Maintenance Assessment and Review Team [*Army*]
SMART..... System Malfunction Analysis Reinforcement Trainer
SMART..... System for Management and Allocation of Resources Technique [*Data processing*]
SMART..... System for Manipulation and Retrieval of Text
SMART..... System for the Mechanical Analysis and Retrieval of Text
SMART..... Systems Management Analysis, Research, and Testing　(MCD)
SMART..... Systems Managers Administrative Rating Test [*Simulation game*]
SMART..... University of Saskatchewan Libraries Machine-Assisted Reference Teleservices [*University of Saskatchewan Library*] [*Information service or system*]　(IID)
SMARTS... Selective Multiple Addresses Radio and Television Service [*A program delivery service introduced by RCA*]
SMARTS... Sport Management Art and Science Society [*Defunct*]　(EA)
SMARTS... Status Memory and Real Time System [*AT & T*]
SMARTS... Submarine Advanced Reactive Tactical Training System
SMAS....... Subcontract Material Availability Schedule
SMAS........ Submuscular Aponeurotic System [*Medicine*]
SMAS........ Superficial Musculoaponeurotic System [*Plastic surgery*]
SMAS........ Switched Maintenance Access System [*Bell System*]

SMASF...... Servicemen's Mutual Aid and Savings Fund [*South Vietnam*]
SMASH..... Southeast Asia Multisensor Armed Surveillance Helicopter
SMASH..... Step-by-Step Monitor and Selector Hold [*Telecommunications*]　(TEL)
SMASH..... Students Mobilizing on Auto Safety Hazards [*Student legal action organization*]　(EA)
SMASHEX ... Search for Simulated Submarine Casualty Exercise [*Navy*]　(NVT)
Smaskrift Landbruksdep Opplysningstjenesten ... Smaskrift-Norway. Landbruksdepartementet. Opplysningstjenesten [*A publication*]
SMAT........ School Motivation Analysis Test [*Personality development test*] [*Psychology*]
SMAT........ Superior Mesenteric Artery Thrombosis [*Medicine*]
SMATA..... Studia Mathematica [*A publication*]
SMATH ..... Satellite Materials Hardening　(MCD)
SMATS..... Speed-Modulated Augmented Thrust System　(NG)
SMATV..... Satellite Master Antenna Television
SMAW ...... Second Marine Aircraft Wing
SMAW ...... Shielded Metal Arc Welding
SMAW ...... Shoulder-Launched Multipurpose Assault Weapon　(MCD)
SMAW ...... Submerged Metal Arc Weld [*Nuclear energy*]　(NRCH)
SMAWT.... Short-Range Man-Portable Antitank Weapons Technology
SMB........... Bachelor of Sacred Music
SMB........... Sa Majeste Britannique [*His or Her Britannic Majesty*] [*French*]
SMB........... Samaipata [*Bolivia*] [*Seismograph station code, US Geological Survey*] [*Closed*]　(SEIS)
SMB........... Server Message Blocks　(PCM)
SMB........... Simba Resources, Inc. [*Vancouver Stock Exchange symbol*]
SMB........... Small and Medium-Sized Businesses
SMB........... Space Meteorology Branch [*NASA*]
SMB........... Standard Merchants Bank [*British*]
SMB........... Standard Mineral Base [*Medium*] [*Medicine*]
SMB........... Static Memory Board [*Data processing*]　(BYTE)
SMB........... Steve Miller Band [*Pop music group*]
SMB........... System Monitor Board
SMBA....... Scottish Marine Biological Association [*United Kingdom*]　(IRUK)
SMBA....... Slovenian Mutual Benefit Association [*Later, AMLA*]　(EA)
Sm & Bat.... Smith and Batty's Irish King's Bench Reports [*A publication*]　(DLA)
SMBC....... Santuario Madre del Buon Consiglio [*Pious Union of Our Mother of Good Counsel - PUMGC*] [*Genazzano, Italy*]　(EAIO)
SMBC....... Studien und Mitteilungen aus dem Benediktiner- und dem Cistercienser-Orden [*A publication*]
SMBCO..... Studien und Mitteilungen aus dem Benediktiner- und dem Cistercienser-Orden [*A publication*]
SMBCOZ.. Studien und Mitteilungen aus dem Benediktiner- und dem Cistercienser-Orden [*A publication*]
SMBD....... Stat'i Materialy po Bolgarskoj Dialektologii [*A publication*]
SMBDB..... Structural Margin Beyond Design Basis [*Nuclear energy*]　(NRCH)
SMBF....... Superior Mesenteric Blood Flow [*Physiology*]
SMBFT ..... Small Bowel Follow-Through [*Medicine*]
SMBG....... Bakhuys [*Surinam*] [*ICAO location identifier*]　(ICLI)
SMBG....... Self-Monitoring of Blood Glucose [*Medicine*]
SMBJ....... Style Manual for Biological Journals
SMBL....... Semimobile
SMBN....... Albina [*Surinam*] [*ICAO location identifier*]　(ICLI)
SMBO....... Botopasie [*Surinam*] [*ICAO location identifier*]　(ICLI)
Sm & BRR Cas ... Smith and Bates' American Railway Cases [*A publication*]　(DLA)
SMBS....... Safeguard Material Balance Simulator
SMBW....... Bronsweg [*Surinam*] [*ICAO location identifier*]　(ICLI)
SMBX....... Symbolics, Inc. [*NASDAQ symbol*]　(NQ)
SMC .... Chief Signalman [*Navy rating*]
SMC .... Medical University of South Carolina Library, Charleston, SC [*OCLC symbol*]　(OCLC)
SMC .... Sa Majeste Catholique [*His or Her Catholic Majesty*] [*of Spain*] [*French*]
SMC .... SAGE [*Semiautomatic Ground Environment*] Maintenance Control
SMC .... Saint Martin's College [*Washington*]
SMC .... Saint Mary's College [*Indiana; Kansas; Michigan; Minnesota*]
SMC .... Saint Michael's College [*Vermont*]
SMC .... Sales and Marketing Management in Canada [*A publication*]
SMC .... Save the Manatee Club　(EA)
SMC .... Scientific Manpower Commission　(EA)
SMC .... Segmented Maintenance Cask [*Nuclear energy*]　(NRCH)
SMC .... Senior Medical Consultant
SMC .... Senior Mission Controller　(MCD)
SMC .... Sequential Machine Controller [*Programming language*] [*1977-78*]　(CSR)
SMC .... Service Men's Center [*World War II*]
SMC .... Sheet Molding Compound [*Plastics technology*]
SMC .... Short-Run Marginal Cost Curve [*Economics*]
SMC .... Silicon Monolithic Circuit
SMC .... Silva Mind Control [*Psychic system*]
SMC .... Single Mothers by Choice　(EA)
SMC .... Small Magellanic Cloud [*Astronomy*]

SMC .... Smith [*A. O.*] Corporation [*AMEX symbol*]   (SPSG)
SMC .... Smithsonian Miscellaneous Collections [*A publication*]
SMC .... Smooth Muscle Cell [*Cytology*]
SMC .... Societe Mediterraneenne de Chimiotherapie [*Mediterranean Society of Chemotherapy - MSC*]   (EAIO)
SMC .... Society of Marine Consultants   (EA)
SMC .... Soil and Moisture Conservation
SMC .... Somatomedin C [*Biochemistry*]
SMC .... Somerset [*Colorado*] [*Seismograph station code, US Geological Survey*]   (SEIS)
SmC .... Southern Microfilm Corporation, Houston, TX [*Library symbol*] [*Library of Congress*]   (LCLS)
SMC .... Southern Missionary College [*Tennessee*]
SMC .... Southern Motor Carriers Rate Conference, Atlanta GA [*STAC*]
SMC .... Spanish Music Center [*Commercial firm*]   (EA)
SMC .... Special Mouth Care [*Medicine*]
S-M-C .... Sperm [*or Spore*] Mother-Cell
SMC .... Squared Multiple Correlation [*Psychology*]
SMC .... Squawk Mode Code   (FAAC)
SMC .... Staff Message Control [*Military*]
SMC .... Standard Mean Chord [*Aviation*]   (AIA)
SMC .... Standard-Modern Technologies Corp. [*Toronto Stock Exchange symbol*]
SMC .... Standard Molding Corporation
SMC .... Standard Motorists Centre [*Automotive sales and service chain*] [*British*]
SMC .... Station-Control and Monitor Console Subsystem [*Deep Space Instrumentation Facility, NASA*]
SMC .... Stepper Motor Control
SMC .... Storage Module Controller
SMC .... Student Mobilization Committee [*to End the War in Vietnam*] [*Defunct*]   (EA)
SMC .... Studies in Medieval Culture [*A publication*]
SMC .... Sub-Machine Carbine [*British military*]   (DMA)
SMC .... Sunnybrook Medical Centre, Toronto [*UTLAS symbol*]
SMC .... Super-Multi-Coating [*Camera lenses*]
SMC .... Supply and Maintenance Command [*Army*]
SMC .... Surface Movement Control [*Aviation*]
SMC .... Switch Maintenance Center [*Telecommunications*]   (TEL)
SMC .... Synchronized Maneuver Countermeasures Model   (MCD)
SMC .... System Monitor Console   (CAAL)
SMC .... Systems, Man, and Cybernetics   (MCD)
SMCA .... Cayana [*Surinam*] [*ICAO location identifier*]   (ICLI)
SMCA .... Single Manager for Conventional Ammunition [*DoD*]
SMCA .... Sodium Monochloroacetate [*Organic chemistry*]
SMCA .... Suckling Mouse Cataract Agent [*Microbiology*]
SMCAF ...... Society of Medical Consultants to the Armed Forces   (EA)
SMCC .... Saint Mary's College of California
SMCC .... Santa Monica City College [*California*]
SMCC .... Schield Management Company [*Denver, CO*] [*NASDAQ symbol*]   (NQ)
SMCC .... Shuttle Mission Control Center [*NASA*]   (NASA)
SMCC .... Simulation Monitor and Control Console   (KSC)
SMCC .... Society of Memorial Cancer Center
SMCC .... Sport Medicine Council of Canada
SMCC .... Standard Machinery Control Console [*Canadian Navy*]
SMCC .... State Manpower Coordinating Committee [*Department of Labor*]
SMCC .... Succinimidyl (Maleimidomethyl)cyclohexanecarboxylate [*Organic chemistry*]
SMC-CF .... Smooth Muscle Cell-Chemotactic Factor [*Oncology*]
Sm CCM .... Smith's Circuit Courts-Martial Reports [*Maine*] [*A publication*]   (DLA)
SMCD .... Supreme Military Council Decree [*Ghana*]   (DLA)
SMCE .... Master of Science in Civil Engineering
SMCE .... Sociedad Mexicana de Computacion Electronica [*Mexico*]
SMCG .... Stuart McGuire Co. [*NASDAQ symbol*]   (NQ)
SMCH ...... Service Merchandise Company, Inc. [*NASDAQ symbol*]   (NQ)
S & M Ch ... Smedes and Marshall's Mississippi Chancery Reports [*A publication*]   (DLA)
SMCH ...... Standard Mixed Cargo Harness   (NASA)
Sm Ch Pr ... Smith's Chancery Practice [*7th ed.*] [*1862*] [*A publication*]   (DLA)
S & M Ch R ... Smedes and Marshall's Mississippi Chancery Reports [*A publication*]   (DLA)
S & M Ch Rep ... Smedes and Marshall's Mississippi Chancery Reports [*A publication*]   (DLA)
S & M Chy ... Smedes and Marshall's Mississippi Chancery Reports [*A publication*]   (DLA)
SMCI .... Coeroeni [*Surinam*] [*ICAO location identifier*]   (ICLI)
SMCL .... Southeastern Massachusetts Cooperating Libraries [*Library network*]
SMCLN ..... Semicolon   (AABC)
SMCM ...... Master Chief Signalman [*Navy rating*]
SMCN ...... Selective Myocardial Cell Necrosis [*Cardiology*]
SMCO ...... Coronie [*Surinam*] [*ICAO location identifier*]   (ICLI)
SMCO ...... SAGE [*Semiautomatic Ground Environment*] Maintenance Control Office
Sm Com L .. Smith's Manual of Common Law [*12th ed.*] [*1905*] [*A publication*]   (DLA)
Sm Con....... Smith on Contracts [*8th ed.*] [*1885*] [*A publication*]   (DLA)

Sm Cond Ala ... Smith's Condensed Alabama Reports [*A publication*]   (DLA)
Sm Const Cons ... Smith on Constitutional and Statutory Construction [*A publication*]   (DLA)
Sm Conv..... Smith on Conveyancing [*A publication*]   (DLA)
SMCP....... San Marino Communist Party
SMCP....... Supply and Maintenance Control Point
SMCPA..... Simulation Councils. Proceedings Series [*A publication*]
SMCPCF... Fort Walsh National Historic Park, Parks Canada [*Parc Historique National Fort Walsh, Parcs Canada*] Maple Creek, Saskatchewan [*Library symbol*] [*National Library of Canada*]   (NLC)
SMCPSTC ... Supply and Maintenance Command Packaging Storage and Transportation Center [*Army*]
SMCR....... Selected Marine Corps Reserve
SMCR....... Society for Menstrual Cycle Research   (EA)
SMCR....... Summcorp [*Fort Wayne, IN*] [*NASDAQ symbol*]   (NQ)
SMCRA..... Surface Mining Control and Reclamation Act [*1977*]
SMCRC..... Southern Motor Carriers Rate Conference
SMCRD8.. Saunders Monographs in Clinical Radiology [*A publication*]
SMCS .... IEEE Systems, Man, and Cybernetics Society   (EA)
SMCS .... Senior Chief Signalman [*Navy rating*]
SMCS .... Separation Monitor and Control System [*NASA*]   (MCD)
SMCS .... Simulation Monitor and Control System   (CAAL)
SMCS .... Structural Mode Control System   (MCD)
SMCSG..... Special Military Construction Study Group   (AABC)
SMCT....... Cottica [*Surinam*] [*ICAO location identifier*]   (ICLI)
SMCU ...... Separation Monitoring Control Unit [*NASA*]   (MCD)
SMD .... Doctor of Sacred Music
SMD .... Fort Wayne, IN [*Location identifier*] [*FAA*]   (FAAL)
SMD .... Saint Michael's College, Library, Winooski, VT [*OCLC symbol*]   (OCLC)
SMD .... Sauter Mean Diameter   (KSC)
SMD .... Scheduling Management Display
SMD .... Scottish Malt Distillers [*British*]
SMD .... Senile Macular Degeneration [*Medicine*]
SMD .... Serum Malic Dehydrogenase [*An enzyme*]
SMD .... Ship Manning Document [*Navy*]
SMD .... Short Meter Double [*Music*]
SMD .... Silicon Multiplier Detector
SMD .... Singular Multinomial Distribution [*Statistics*]
SMD .... Society of Medical-Dental Management Consultants   (EA)
SMD .... Spacelab Mission Development [*NASA*]   (MCD)
SMD .... Special Measuring Device   (NASA)
SMD .... Statistical Methods Division [*Bureau of the Census*]   (OICC)
SMD .... Stop Motion Detector
SMD .... Storage Module Device [*Data processing*]
SMD .... Storage Module Drive
SMD .... Structures and Mechanics Division [*NASA*]
SMD .... Submanubrial Dullness [*Medicine*]
SMD .... Submarine Mine Depot
SMD .... Submersible Mining Device
SMD .... Surface Mounted Device [*Microelectronics*]
SMD .... Susceptor Meus Dominus [*God Is My Protector*] [*Latin*] [*Motto of Jacob, Margrave of Baden-Hochberg (1562-90); Georg Friedrich, Margrave of Baden-Hochberg (1573-1638)*]
SMD .... Symptom Medication Diary [*Medicine*]
SMD .... Synchronous Modulator-Demodulator   (MCD)
SMD .... System Management Directive [*AFM*]
SMD .... Systems Display [*Vancouver Stock Exchange symbol*]
SMD .... Systems Manufacturing Division [*IBM Corp.*]
SMD .... Systems Measuring Device   (KSC)
SMD .... Systems Monitor Display
SMDA ...... Drietabbetje [*Surinam*] [*ICAO location identifier*]   (ICLI)
SMDA ...... Second Marine Division Association   (EA)
SMDA ...... Sixth Marine Division Association [*Later, 6th MAR DIV*]   (EA)
SMDA ...... State Medicaid Directors Association   (EA)
SMDC ...... Saint Mary's Dominican College [*Louisiana*]
SMDC ...... Shielded Mild Detonating Cord
SMDC ...... Sisters of Mercy, Daughters of Christian Charity of St. Vincent de Paul [*Roman Catholic religious order*]
SMDC ...... Sodium Methyldithiocarbamate [*Fungicide*]
SMDC ...... Superconductive Materials Data Center   (KSC)
SMDE....... Static Mercury Drop Electrode [*Electrochemistry*]
SM Dendrol ... Master of Science in Dendrology
SMDF....... SCATS [*Simulation, Checkout, and Training System*] Main Distributing Frame
SMDI........ Surface Miss Distance Indicator [*Navy*]   (CAAL)
SMDJ........ Djoemoe [*Surinam*] [*ICAO location identifier*]   (ICLI)
SMDK....... Donderskamp [*Surinam*] [*ICAO location identifier*]   (ICLI)
SMDL....... Stoff- und Motivgeschichte der Deutschen Literatur [*A publication*]
SMDL....... Subminiature Microwave Delay Line
SMDMC ... Society of Medical-Dental Management Consultants   (EA)
SMDO .... Ladoeanie [*Surinam*] [*ICAO location identifier*]   (ICLI)
SMDO .... Special Microwave Devices Operation [*Raytheon Co.*]
SMD, OCOFS ... Staff Management Division, Office, Chief of Staff [*Army*]
SMD OCSA ... Staff Management Division, Office, Chief of Staff, Army   (AABC)
SMD OC of SA ... Staff Management Division, Office, Chief of Staff, Army   (AABC)

SMDPL..... Supply Management Date and Price List [*Navy*]
SMDPS..... Service Module Deluge Purge System [*NASA*] (KSC)
SMDR .... Selected Management Data Report [*DoD*]
SMDR .... Station Message Detail Recording [*Formerly, MDR*] [*Telecommunications*]
SMDR .... Summary Management Data Report [*DoD*]
SMDT....... Shore Mode Data Transmitter (MCD)
SMDTB..... School Musician. Director and Teacher [*A publication*]
SME........... Sales and Marketing Executives-International (EA)
SME........... Sancta Mater Ecclesia [*Holy Mother Church*] [*Latin*]
SME........... Scale Model Engineering [*Initialism is brand name of tone arm*]
SME........... School of Military Engineering
SME........... Semiconductor Manufacturing Equipment [*Sumitomo Metals*]
SME........... Service Merchandise Co., Inc. [*NYSE symbol*] (SPSG)
SME........... Shape Memory Effect [*Metal alloy property*]
SME........... Sheet Metal Enclosure
SME........... Shell Metal Extractant
SME........... Shipbuilding and Marine Engineering [*Department of Employment*] [*British*]
SME........... SHOWME [*VERALEX, Inc.*] [*Information service or system*] (CRD)
SME........... Singleton Materials Engineering Laboratories [*Tennessee Valley Authority*] (GRD)
SME........... Small and Medium-Size Enterprises
SME........... Societa Meridionale Finanziaria SpA [*Italian*]
SME........... Society of Manufacturing Engineers (EA)
SME........... Society of Military Engineers (KSC)
SME........... Society for Mining, Metallurgy, and Exploration, Inc. [*In association name, SME, Inc.*] (EA)
SME........... Soil Mechanics Experiment [*NASA*]
SME........... Solar Mesosphere Explorer (MCD)
SME........... Somerset, KY [*Location identifier*] [*FAA*] (FAAL)
SME........... Spartan Missile Equipment [*Missiles*] (MCD)
SME........... Squadron Medical Element
SME........... Stalk Median Eminence [*Anatomy*]
SME........... Standard Medical Examination [*Military*]
SME........... Stellar Mass Ejection
SMe .... Studi Medievali [*A publication*]
SME........... Studies in Monetary Economics [*Elsevier Book Series*] [*A publication*]
SME........... Subject Matter Expert (NVT)
SME........... Surface Measuring Equipment
SME........... Surface Movement Element (AFIT)
SMEA....... Studi Micenei ed Egeo-Anatolici [*A publication*]
SMEA....... Sun Marine Employees Association (EA)
SMEAC..... Science, Mathematics, and Environmental Education Information Analysis Center
SMEADO ... Selected Major Exploratory Advanced Development Objective (MCD)
SMEAG..... Research Station, Agriculture Canada [*Station de Recherches, Agriculture Canada*], Melfort, Saskatchewan [*Library symbol*] [*National Library of Canada*] (BIB)
SME of AIME ... Society of Mining Engineers of American Institute of Mining, Metallurgical, and Petroleum Engineers [*Later, SME, Inc.*] (EA)
SMEAT..... Skylab Medical Experiments Altitude Test [*NASA*]
SMEC....... Society for Middle East Confederation (EAIO)
SMEC....... Strategic Missile Evaluation Committee [*Air Force*]
Sm Ecc Cts ... Smith on Ecclesiastical Courts [*7th ed.*] [*1920*] [*A publication*] (DLA)
SMEC Mag ... SMEC [*Snowy Mountains Engineering Corporation*] Magazine [*A publication*] (APTA)
SME Collect Pap ... Society of Manufacturing Engineers. Collective Papers [*A publication*]
SME Creative Mfg Semin Tech Pap ... Society of Manufacturing Engineers. Creative Manufacturing Seminars. Technical Papers [*A publication*]
SMECTYMNUS ... Steven Marshall, Edward Calamy, Thomas Young, Matthew Newcomen, William Spurstow [*Collective author of 17th-century antiepiscopal tract*]
SMED....... Shared Medical Systems Corp. [*NASDAQ symbol*] (NQ)
Sm Ed........ Smith's Education for the English Bar [*A publication*] (DLA)
Sm E D....... [*E. D.*] Smith's New York Common Pleas Reports [*A publication*] (DLA)
SMed .... Studi Medievali [*A publication*]
Smedes and Marshall's Chy Repts ... Smedes and Marshall's Mississippi Chancery Reports [*A publication*] (DLA)
Smedes & M Ch ... Smedes and Marshall's Mississippi Chancery Reports [*A publication*] (DLA)
Smedes & M (Miss) ... Smedes and Marshall's Mississippi Reports [*A publication*] (DLA)
Smed & M ... Smedes and Marshall's Mississippi Reports [*A publication*] (DLA)
Smed & M Ch ... Smedes and Marshall's Mississippi Chancery Reports [*A publication*] (DLA)
Smee........... Collection of Abstracts of Acts of Parliament [*A publication*]
SMEE....... Master of Science in Electrical Engineering
SMEF....... Smooth Muscle-Derived Elastogenic Factor [*Biochemistry*]
SME-I........ Sales and Marketing Executives-International [*Cleveland, OH*] (EA)

SMEK........ Summary Message Enable Keyboard
Sm El........ Smith's Elements of Law [*A publication*] (DLA)
SMEMA.... Surface Mount Equipment Manufacturers Association (EA)
Sm Eng...... Smith's English King's Bench Reports [*A publication*] (DLA)
SMEP....... Society of Multivariate Experimental Psychology (EA)
Sm Eq........ [*J. W.*] Smith's Manual of Equity [*A publication*] (DLA)
Sm Eq........ Smith's Principles of Equity [*A publication*] (DLA)
SMER........ Skylab Mission Evaluation Report [*NASA*] (MCD)
SM-ER ..... Surface Missile, Extended Range
SMERC..... San Mateo Educational Resources Center [*San Mateo County Office of Education*] [*Information service or system*] (IID)
SMERE..... SPRINT Missile Electromagnetic Radiation Evaluation [*Army*] (AABC)
SMERF..... Social, Military, Ethnic, Religious, and Fraternal Groups [*Market segment*]
SMERSH .. Smert' Shpionam [*Russian phrase meaning "Death to the Spies," and name of a special division of USSR state security organizations charged with elimination of internal opposition to the regime from 1942 into postwar years*] [*Best known outside of USSR for role of its agents in the popular James Bond series of espionage stories*]
SMES .... Shuttle Mission Engineering Simulator [*NASA*] (NASA)
SMES .... Shuttle Mission Evaluation Simulation [*NASA*] (NASA)
SMES .... Superconducting Magnetic Energy Storage (NASA)
SME/SC ..... SPRINT Missile Engineering/Service Course [*Army*] (AABC)
SMET........ SiMETCO, Inc. [*NASDAQ symbol*] (CTT)
SMET........ Simulated Mission Endurance Test (MCD)
SMET........ Spacecraft Maneuver Engine Transients [*Apollo program*] [*NASA*]
SMETC ..... Swiss Mouse Embryo Tissue Culture
SMETDS... Standard Message Trunk Design System [*Telecommunications*] (TEL)
SME Tech Pap ... Society of Manufacturing Engineers. Technical Paper [*A publication*]
SME Tech Pap Ser AD ... SME [*Society of Manufacturing Engineers*] Technical Paper. Series AD. Assembly Division [*A publication*]
SME Tech Pap Ser EE ... Society of Manufacturing Engineers. Technical Paper. Series EE (Electrical Engineering) [*A publication*]
SME Tech Pap Ser EM ... Society of Manufacturing Engineers. Technical Paper. Series EM (Engineering Materials) [*A publication*]
SME Tech Pap Ser FC ... Society of Manufacturing Engineers. Technical Paper. Series FC (Finishing and Coating) [*A publication*]
SME Tech Pap Ser MF ... Society of Manufacturing Engineers. Technical Paper. Series MF (Material Forming) [*A publication*]
SME Tech Pap Ser MR ... Society of Manufacturing Engineers. Technical Paper. Series MR (Material Removal) [*A publication*]
Smeth LS ... Smethurst on Locus Standi [*1867*] [*A publication*] (DLA)
SMETO....... Staff Meteorological Officer [*NATO*] (NATG)
SME West Metal Tool Expos Conf Tech Pap ... Society of Manufacturing Engineers. Western Metal and Tool Exposition and Conference. Technical Papers [*A publication*]
Sm Ex Int... Smith on Executory Interest [*A publication*] (DLA)
SMF........... S-Band Multifrequency
SMF........... S & M Photolabels, Inc. [*Toronto Stock Exchange symbol*]
SMF........... Sacramento [*California*] [*Airport symbol*] (OAG)
SMF........... Sacramento, CA [*Location identifier*] [*FAA*] (FAAL)
SMF........... Sales Manpower Foundation (EA)
SMF........... Saticon Mixed-Field [*Video technology*]
SMF........... Saw Machine Fixture (MCD)
SMF........... Schumann Memorial Foundation [*Defunct*] (EA)
SMF........... Scientific Marriage Foundation (EA)
SMF........... Screw Machine Feeder
SMF........... Senior Management Forum [*Information Industry Association*]
SMF........... Service to Military Families [*Red Cross*]
SMF........... Shaker Museum Foundation (EA)
SMF........... Signal De Mont [*France*] [*Seismograph station code, US Geological Survey*] (SEIS)
SMF........... [*The*] Singer Co. [*NYSE symbol*] (SPSG)
SMF........... Site Modification Facility
SMF........... Skrifter Utgivna. Modernsmalslararnas Forening [*A publication*]
Sm F........... Small Farm [*A publication*]
SMF........... Snell Memorial Foundation, Inc.
SMF........... Societe Mathematique de France
SMF........... Society for the Maintenance of the Faith [*British*]
SMF........... Software Maintenance Function [*Data processing*] (TEL)
SMF........... Solar Magnetic Field
SMF........... Space Manufacturing Facility
SMF........... Spar Material Factor [*Yacht racing regulation*]
SMF........... Special Modifying Factor (DEN)
SMF........... Spectral Multilayer Filter
SMF........... Stable Matrix Form
SMF........... Standard MIDI [*Musical Instrument Digital Interface*] File
SMF........... Static Magnetic Field
SMF........... Streptozocin, Mitomycin C, Fluorouracil [*Antineoplastic drug regimen*]
SMF........... Student Missions Fellowship [*Later, IVMF*] (EA)
SMF........... Swift Museum Foundation (EA)
SMF........... Switchable Matched Filter

SMF........... System Management Facility [*IBM Corp.*]
SMF........... System Measurement Facility [*Data processing*] (IEEE)
SMFA......... Simplified Modular Frame Assignment System
　　　　　　[*Telecommunications*] (TEL)
SMFAS...... Simplified Mainframe Administration System (MCD)
SMFAS...... Simplified Modular Frame Assignment System [*Bell System*]
SMFC......... Shellee Morris Fan Club (EA)
SMFG........ Stearns Manufacturing Co. [*NASDAQ symbol*] (NQ)
SMFL......... Science, Mathematics, Foreign Languages
SmFlts........ Small Faults [*Philately*]
SMFMA..... Sprayed Mineral Fiber Manufacturers Association (EA)
Sm For Med ... Smith on Forensic Medicine [*10th ed.*] [*1955*] [*A
　　　　　　publication*] (DLA)
Sm Forms... Smith's Forms of Procedure [*A publication*] (DLA)
SMFP........ State Medical Facilities Plan [*Generic term*] (DHSM)
SMFP........ Systems Maintenance Field Party [*Aviation*] (FAAC)
SMFR........ Service to Military Families Representative [*Red Cross*]
SMFT........ Semitrailer-Mounted Fabric Tank [*for water distribution*]
　　　　　　[*Army*]
SMFW....... Society of Medical Friends of Wine (EA)
SMG.......... Megilot Genuzot [*E. L. Sukenik*] [*A publication*] (BJA)
SMG.......... San Miguel [*Portugal*] [*Geomagnetic observatory code*]
SMG.......... School of Military Government [*World War II*]
SMG.......... Schweizerische Musikforschende Gesellschaft. Mitteilungsblatt
　　　　　　[*A publication*]
SMG.......... Science Management Corp. [*AMEX symbol*] (SPSG)
SMG.......... Seismocardiogram
SMG.......... Sisters Poor Servants of the Mother of God [*Roman Catholic
　　　　　　religious order*]
Sm & G ...... Smale and Giffard's English Vice-Chancery Reports [*A
　　　　　　publication*] (DLA)
Sm & G ...... Smith and Guthrie's Missouri Appeal Reports [*81-101
　　　　　　Missouri*] [*A publication*] (DLA)
SMG.......... Software Message Generator [*Data processing*] (TEL)
SMG.......... Solids Moisture Gauge
SMG.......... Space Missions Group [*Ford Aerospace & Communications
　　　　　　Corp.*] [*Detroit, MI*] [*Telecommunications
　　　　　　service*] (TSSD)
SMG.......... Spacecraft Meteorology Group (KSC)
SMG.......... Spaceflight Meteorology Group [*NASA*] (NASA)
SMG.......... Speed Made Good [*Navy*] (NVT)
SMG.......... Submachine Gun
SMGB........ Studien und Mitteilungen zur Geschichte des Benediktiner-
　　　　　　Ordens und Seiner Zweige [*A publication*]
SMGBOZ ... Studien und Mitteilungen zur Geschichte des Benediktiner-
　　　　　　Ordens und Seiner Zweige [*Salzburg*] [*A publication*]
SMGC....... Sun-Maid Growers of California (EA)
SMGD....... Supply Management Grouping Designator [*Navy*] (NG)
SM Geol.... Master of Science in Geology
SMGO....... Senior Military Government Officer [*World War II*]
SMGP........ Strategic Missile Group [*Air Force*]
SMGS........ Southeastern Michigan Gas Enterprises, Inc. [*NASDAQ
　　　　　　symbol*] (NQ)
SMH.......... St. Michael's Hospital, Toronto [*UTLAS symbol*]
SMH.......... Scheduled Man-Hours (MCD)
SMH.......... Section for Metropolitan Hospitals (EA)
SMH.......... Semtech Corp. [*AMEX symbol*] (SPSG)
SMH.......... Speelgoed en Hobby. Vakblad voor de Speelgoedbranche [*A
　　　　　　publication*]
SMH.......... Standard Mirror Hybrid (MCD)
SMH.......... Sydney Morning Herald [*A publication*] (APTA)
SMHA........ Southern Mutual Help Association (EA)
SMHC....... Sarcomeric Myosin Heavy Chain [*Muscle physiology*]
SMHE....... Selected Material Handling Equipment [*Army*] (RDA)
SMH (Newspr) (NSW) ... Sydney Morning Herald Reports (Newspaper) (New
　　　　　　South Wales) [*A publication*] (APTA)
Sm Homest ... Smyth on the Law of Homesteads and Exemptions [*A
　　　　　　publication*] (DLA)
SMHR....... Smoking and Health Reporter [*A publication*]
SMHS....... Superstition Mountain Historical Society (EA)
SM in Hyg ... Master of Science in Hygiene
SMI........... Sa Majeste Imperiale [*His or Her Imperial Majesty*] [*French*]
SMI........... Sales Method Index [*LIMRA*]
SMI........... Samos Island [*Greece*] [*Airport symbol*] (OAG)
SMI........... Scanning Microscopy International (EA)
SMI........... Secondary Metal Institute (EA)
SMI........... Self-Metering Instrumentation
SMI........... Senior Medical Investigator
SMI........... Sergeant-Major Instructor [*British military*] (DMA)
SMI........... Service at Military Installations [*Red Cross*]
SMI........... Shelter Management Instructor [*Civil Defense*]
SMI........... Ship Missile Interface
SMI........... Simla [*India*] [*Seismograph station code, US Geological
　　　　　　Survey*] [*Closed*] (SEIS)
SMI........... Simulation of Machine Indexing
SMI........... Smithsonian Institution, Washington, DC [*OCLC
　　　　　　symbol*] (OCLC)
SMI........... Society for Machine Intelligence (EA)
SMI........... Soldier-Machine Interface [*Army*] (RDA)
SMI........... Sorptive Minerals Institute (EA)
SMI........... Special Manufacturing Instruction

SMI........... Special Multiperil Insurance
SMI........... Spectrametrics, Incorporated
SMI........... SpenderMenders International [*Inactive*] (EA)
SMI .. Spring Manufacturers Institute (EA)
SMI........... Springs Industries, Incorporated [*Formerly, Springs Mills,
　　　　　　Incorporated*] [*NYSE symbol*] (SPSG)
SMI........... Standard Measuring Instrument
SMI........... Static Memory Interface [*Data processing*] (MDG)
SMI........... Statute Miles
SMI........... Style of Mind Inventory [*Psychology*]
SMI........... Styles of Management Inventory [*Test*]
SMI........... Success Motivation Institute
SMI........... Super Market Institute [*Later, FMI*] (EA)
SMI........... Supplementary Medical Insurance
SMI........... Supply Management Inspection (NVT)
SMI........... Sustained Maximal Inspiration [*Physiology*]
SMI........... System Memory Interface [*Data processing*]
SMI........... Systems Measurement Instrument [*Data processing*]
SMIA........ Serial Multiplexer Interface Adapter (NASA)
SMIA........ Social Marketing International Association [*Queretaro,
　　　　　　Mexico*] (EAIO)
SMIA........ Steel Management in Action [*Bethlehem Steel Co.*]
SMIA........ Studies in Mathematics and Its Applications [*Elsevier Book
　　　　　　Series*] [*A publication*]
SMIAC...... Soil Mechanics Information Analysis Center [*Army Corps of
　　　　　　Engineers*] (IID)
SMIAT...... Special Military Intelligence Activities Team (CINC)
Smi & Bat... Smith and Batty's Irish King's Bench Reports [*A
　　　　　　publication*] (DLA)
SMIC........ Missionary Sisters of the Immaculate Conception of the Mother
　　　　　　of God [*Roman Catholic religious order*]
SMIC........ Sorghum and Millets Information Center [*ICRISAT*] [*India*]
SMIC........ Special Material Identification Code
SMIC........ Study of Man's Impact on Climate
SMIC........ Superior Manufacturing & Instrument Corporation [*NASDAQ
　　　　　　symbol*] (NQ)
SMIC........ Supply Management Information Center [*Military*] (CAAL)
SMICBM .. Semimobile Intercontinental Ballistic Missile
SMID........ Semiconductor Memory Integrated Device (MCD)
SMIDA...... Small Business Innovation Development Act [*1982*]
SMIEEE.... Senior Member of Institute of Electrical and Electronic
　　　　　　Engineers
SMIER ...... Societe Medicale Internationale d'Endoscopie et de
　　　　　　Radiocinematographie [*International Medical Society for
　　　　　　Endoscopy and Radiocinematography*]
SMIG........ Sergeant-Major Instructor of Gunnery [*British
　　　　　　military*] (DMA)
SmIg.......... Surface Membrane Immunoglobulin [*Immunochemistry*]
SMIIS....... Solar Microwave Interferometer Imaging System
SMIJA...... South African Mining and Engineering Journal [*A publication*]
SMIL........ Solidaritet med Israel
SMIL......... Statistical Methods in Linguistics [*A publication*]
SMIL......... Statistics and Market Intelligence Library [*Department of
　　　　　　Trade*] [*British*] (DCTA)
SMILE...... Safe Military Infrared LASER Equipment
SMILE...... Ship's Master Index Listing of Equipment (MCD)
SMILE...... Significant Milestone Integration Lateral Evaluation [*Data
　　　　　　processing*]
SMILE...... South Central Minnesota Interlibrary Exchange [*Library
　　　　　　network*]
SMILE...... Surface Mixed Layer Experiment (NOAA)
SMI²LE..... Space Migration, Intelligence Increase, Life Extension [*Idea
　　　　　　advanced by Timothy Leary, 1960's counterculture figure*]
SMILES .... Simplified Molecular Input Line Editor [*or Entry*] System [*Data
　　　　　　processing*]
SMILS...... Sonobuoy Missile Impact Location System [*Navy*] (CAAL)
SM/IM...... System Manager or Item Manager (AFIT)
SMIN .... Southern Mineral Corp. [*NASDAQ symbol*] (NQ)
Sm Ind....... Smith's Reports [*1-4 Indiana*] [*A publication*] (DLA)
SMIO........ Spares Multiple Item Order (AAG)
SMIP........ Ship's 3-M Improvement Plan [*Navy*] (NVT)
SMIP........ Structure Memory Information Processor
SMIPP...... Sheet Metal Industry Promotion Plan (EA)
SMIPS...... Small Interactive Image Processing System [*NASA*]
SMIRE ...... Senior Member of the Institution of Radio Engineers
SMIRR ...... Shuttle Multispectral Infrared Radiometer [*NASA*]
SMIRS...... School Management Information Retrieval Service [*University
　　　　　　of Oregon*] [*Eugene, OR*]
SMIS........ Safeguard Management Information System [*Army*] (AABC)
SMIS........ School of Management Information Systems [*Army*]
SMIS........ Ship Management Information System (MCD)
SMIS........ Society for Management Information Systems (EA)
SMIS........ Supply Management Information System
SMIS........ Survey Methodology Information System [*Inter-University
　　　　　　Consortium for Political & Social Research*] [*Database*]
SMIS........ Symbolic Matrix Interpretation System
SMIS INC ... Societe de Microelectronique Industrielle de Sherbrooke, Inc.
　　　　　　[*University of Sherbrooke*] [*Canada*] [*Research
　　　　　　center*] (RCD)
SMISOP.... Safeguard Management Information System Operating Program
　　　　　　[*Army*] (AABC)

SMiss.........	Studia Missionalia [*A publication*]
SMIT........	Sherman Mental Impairment Test [*Psychology*]
SMIT........	Simulated Midcourse Interaction Test [*NASA*]
SMIT........	Spin Motor Interruption Technique
SMIT........	Submit (ROG)
SMITE......	Simulated Mechanical Impact Test Equipment (MCD)
SMITE......	Simulation Model of Interceptor Terminal Effectiveness
Smith	Smith on English Registration [*A publication*] (DLA)
Smith	Smith, Reporter (7, 12 Heiskell's Tennessee Reports) [*A publication*] (DLA)
Smith	[*E. H.*] Smith's Court of Appeals Reports [*147-162 New York*] [*A publication*] (DLA)
Smith	[*E. P.*] Smith's Court of Appeals Reports [*15-27 New York*] [*A publication*] (DLA)
Smith	[*J. P.*] Smith's English King's Bench Reports [*A publication*] (DLA)
Smith	Smith's Indiana Reports [*A publication*] (DLA)
Smith	Smith's New Hampshire Reports [*A publication*] (DLA)
Smith	[*E. D.*] Smith's New York Common Pleas Reports [*A publication*] (DLA)
Smith	[*P. F.*] Smith's Pennsylvania State Reports [*A publication*] (DLA)
Smith	[*C. L.*] Smith's Registration Cases [*1895-1914*] [*A publication*] (DLA)
Smith	Smith's Reports [*2-4 South Dakota*] [*A publication*] (DLA)
Smith	Smith's Reports [*1-11 Wisconsin*] [*A publication*] (DLA)
Smith	Smith's Reports [*81-83 Missouri Appeals*] [*A publication*] (DLA)
Smith	[*E. B.*] Smith's Reports [*21-47 Illinois Appeals*] [*A publication*] (DLA)
Smith	Smith's Reports [*61-84 Maine*] [*A publication*] (DLA)
Smith	Smith's Reports [*54-62 California*] [*A publication*] (DLA)
Smith	Smithsonian [*A publication*]
Smith Act...	Smith's Actions at Law [*A publication*] (DLA)
Smith & B .	Smith and Bates' American Railway Cases [*A publication*] (DLA)
Smith & B ..	Smith and Batty's Irish King's Bench Reports [*A publication*] (DLA)
Smith & Bat ...	Smith and Batty's Irish King's Bench Reports [*A publication*] (DLA)
Smith & BRRC ...	Smith and Bates' American Railway Cases [*A publication*] (DLA)
Smith CCM ...	Smith's Circuit Courts-Martial Reports [*Maine*] [*A publication*] (DLA)
Smith Ch Pr ...	Smith's Chancery Practice [*A publication*] (DLA)
Smith Coll ...	Smith College. Studies in Social Work [*A publication*]
Smith Coll Mus Bul ...	Smith College. Museum of Art. Bulletin [*A publication*]
Smith Coll Stud Social Work ...	Smith College. Studies in Social Work [*A publication*]
Smith Com Law ...	Smith's Manual of Common Law [*A publication*] (DLA)
Smith Cond ...	Smith's Condensed Alabama Reports [*A publication*] (DLA)
Smith Cond Rep ...	Smith's Condensed Alabama Reports [*A publication*] (DLA)
Smith Cong Election Cases ...	Smith's Election Cases [*United States*] [*A publication*] (DLA)
Smith Cont ...	Smith on Contracts [*A publication*] (DLA)
Smith CP ...	[*E. D.*] Smith's New York Common Pleas Reports [*A publication*] (DLA)
Smith Ct App ...	[*E. P.*] Smith's Court of Appeals Reports [*15-27 New York*] [*A publication*] (DLA)
Smith De Rep Angl ...	[*Sir Thomas*] Smith. De Republica Anglica [*The Commonwealth of England and the Manner of Government Thereof*] [*1621*] [*A publication*] (DLA)
Smith Dict Antiq ...	Smith's Dictionary of Greek and Roman Antiquities [*A publication*] (DLA)
Smith E D ..	[*E. D.*] Smith's New York Common Pleas Reports [*1850-58*] [*A publication*] (DLA)
Smith E H ...	[*E. H.*] Smith's Court of Appeals Reports [*147-162 New York*] [*A publication*] (DLA)
Smith E P...	[*E. P.*] Smith's Court of Appeals Reports [*15-27 New York*] [*A publication*] (DLA)
Smith Ext Int ...	Smith on Executory Interest [*A publication*] (DLA)
Smith & G ...	Smith and Guthrie's Missouri Appeal Reports [*81-101 Missouri*] [*A publication*] (DLA)
Smith & H ...	Smith and Heiskell [*Tennessee*] [*A publication*] (DLA)
Smith-Hurd ...	Smith-Hurd's Illinois Annotated Statutes [*A publication*] (DLA)
Smith-Hurd Ann St ...	Smith-Hurd's Illinois Annotated Statutes [*A publication*] (DLA)
Smith Ind ...	Smith's Indiana Reports [*A publication*] (DLA)
Smith J P ...	[*J. P.*] Smith's English King's Bench Reports [*A publication*] (DLA)
Smith KB ...	Smith's English King's Bench Reports [*A publication*] (DLA)
Smith Laws PA ...	Smith's Laws of Pennsylvania [*A publication*] (DLA)
Smith LC ...	Smith's Leading Cases [*A publication*] (DLA)
Smith Lead Cas ...	Smith's Leading Cases [*A publication*] (DLA)
Smith LJ ...	Smith's Law Journal [*A publication*] (DLA)
Smith Man Eq Jur ...	Smith's Manual of Equity Jurisprudence [*A publication*] (DLA)
Smith ME ..	Smith's Reports [*61-84 Maine*] [*A publication*] (DLA)
Smith Merc Law ...	Smith on Mercantile Law [*A publication*] (DLA)
Smith NH ..	Smith's New Hampshire Reports [*A publication*] (DLA)
Smith NY...	Smith's Court of Appeals Reports [*15-27, 147-162 New York*] [*A publication*] (DLA)
Smith PA ...	[*P. F.*] Smith's Pennsylvania State Reports [*A publication*] (DLA)
Smith P F...	[*P. F.*] Smith's Pennsylvania State Reports [*A publication*] (DLA)
Smith Rec ..	Smith's Law of Receivers [*A publication*] (DLA)
Smith Reg ..	[*C. L.*] Smith's Registration Cases [*England*] [*A publication*] (DLA)
Smith Reg Cas ...	[*C. L.*] Smith's Registration Cases [*England*] [*A publication*] (DLA)
Smith Repar ...	Smith's Law of Reparation [*A publication*] (DLA)
Smith Rules ...	Smith's Chancery Rules [*A publication*] (DLA)
Smith's (Ind) R ...	Smith's Indiana Reports [*A publication*] (DLA)
Smith's Laws ...	Smith's Laws of Pennsylvania [*A publication*] (DLA)
Smith's Lead Cas ...	Smith's Leading Cases [*A publication*] (DLA)
Smithson Ann Flight ...	Smithsonian Annals of Flight [*A publication*]
Smithson Contr Bot ...	Smithsonian Contributions to Botany [*A publication*]
Smithson Contrib Anthropol ...	Smithsonian Contributions to Anthropology [*A publication*]
Smithson Contrib Astrophys ...	Smithsonian Contributions to Astrophysics [*A publication*]
Smithson Contrib Bot ...	Smithsonian Contributions to Botany [*A publication*]
Smithson Contrib Earth Sci ...	Smithsonian Contributions to the Earth Sciences [*A publication*]
Smithson Contrib Earth Sciences ...	Smithsonian Contributions to the Earth Sciences [*A publication*]
Smithson Contrib Mar Sci ...	Smithsonian Contributions to the Marine Sciences [*A publication*]
Smithson Contrib Paleobiol ...	Smithsonian Contributions to Paleobiology [*A publication*]
Smithson Contrib Zool ...	Smithsonian Contributions to Zoology [*A publication*]
Smithson Contr Zool ...	Smithsonian Contributions to Zoology [*A publication*]
Smithson Inst Annu Rep ...	Smithsonian Institution. Annual Report [*A publication*]
Smithson Inst Cent Short-Lived Phenom Annu Rep Rev Events ...	Smithsonian Institution. Center for Short-Lived Phenomena. Annual Report and Review of Events [*A publication*]
Smithson Misc Colins ...	Smithsonian Miscellaneous Collections [*A publication*]
Smithson Misc Collect ...	Smithsonian Miscellaneous Collections [*A publication*]
Smithson Rep ...	Smithsonian Institution. Annual Report [*A publication*]
Smithson Rept ...	Smithsonian Institution. Reports [*A publication*]
Smithson Year ...	Smithsonian Year [*A publication*]
Smith's R ...	Smith's Indiana Reports [*A publication*] (DLA)
Smith Wealth Nat ...	Smith's Inquiry into the Nature and Causes of the Wealth of Nations [*A publication*] (DLA)
Smith Wis ...	Smith's Reports [*1-11 Wisconsin*] [*A publication*] (DLA)
SMIU.........	Stove Mounters International Union of North America [*Later, Stove, Furnace, Allied Appliance Workers International Union of North America*]
SMIU.........	Studies by Members of the Istanbul University English Department [*A publication*]
SMIZD......	Sei Marianna Ika Daigaku Zasshi [*A publication*]
SMJ	Moose Jaw Public Library, Saskatchewan [*Library symbol*] [*National Library of Canada*] (NLC)
SMJ	Santa Marina Gold [*Vancouver Stock Exchange symbol*]
SMJ	Sarawak Museum. Journal [*A publication*]
SMJ	Services Missionnaires des Jeunes [*Canada*]
SMJ	Siberian Mathematical Journal [*A publication*]
SMJ	Sim [*Papua New Guinea*] [*Airport symbol*] (OAG)
SMJ	Society of Malawi. Journal [*A publication*]
SMJ	Society of Medical Jurisprudence (EA)
SMJ	Strategic Management Journal [*A publication*]
SMJAEM ...	Saskatchewan Department of Advanced Education and Manpower, Moose Jaw, Saskatchewan [*Library symbol*] [*National Library of Canada*] (NLC)
SMJC	Saint Mary's Junior College [*Minnesota; Missouri; North Carolina*]
SMJC	Service Module Jettison Controller [*NASA*] (MCD)
SM-JDCC ...	Sunshine Music - Jan and Dean Collectors Club (EA)
SMJK	Njoeng Jakob Kondre [*Surinam*] [*ICAO location identifier*] (ICLI)
SMJMA	SIAM [*Society for Industrial and Applied Mathematics*] Journal on Applied Mathematics [*A publication*]
SMJOA	Southern Medical Journal [*United States*] [*A publication*]
SMJP	Palliser Regional Library, Moose Jaw, Saskatchewan [*Library symbol*] [*National Library of Canada*] (NLC)
Sm J St Comp ...	Smith on Joint-Stock Companies [*A publication*] (DLA)
SMJT	Saskatchewan Technical Institute, Moose Jaw, Saskatchewan [*Library symbol*] [*National Library of Canada*] (NLC)
SMK	St. Michael [*Alaska*] [*Airport symbol*] (OAG)
SMK	St. Michael, AK [*Location identifier*] [*FAA*] (FAAL)
SMK	Sanmark-Stardust, Inc. [*AMEX symbol*] (SPSG)

SMK .... Smack [*Ship*]
SMK .... Smoke (AAG)
SMKA........ Kabalebo [*Surinam*] [*ICAO location identifier*] (ICLI)
Sm KB....... Smith's English King's Bench Reports [*A publication*] (DLA)
SMKE........ Kayser [*Surinam*] [*ICAO location identifier*] (ICLI)
SMKHDI... Science Report. Shima Marineland [*A publication*]
SMKLS ..... Smokeless (AAG)
SMKR....... Sim-Kar Lighting Fixture Co., Inc. [*NASDAQ symbol*] (NQ)
SMKRA...... Stroitel'naya Mekhanika i Raschet Sooruzheniy [*A publication*]
SMKSTK... Smokestack[*s*] [*Freight*]
SMKW ...... Paramaribo/Kwatta [*Surinam*] [*ICAO location identifier*] (ICLI)
SML.......... CV Sportsmark International, Inc. [*Vancouver Stock Exchange symbol*]
SML.......... Montreal Lake Library, Saskatchewan [*Library symbol*] [*National Library of Canada*] (NLC)
SML.......... Saluda Motor Lines [*AAR code*]
SML.......... Sawmill [*Alaska*] [*Seismograph station code, US Geological Survey*] (SEIS)
SMLC........ Search Mode Logic
SML.......... Security Market Line
SML.......... Semantic-Meta-Language
SML.......... Serials Master List
SML.......... Simulator Load
SML.......... Skylab Mobile Laboratory [*NASA*] (KSC)
SML.......... Small (FAAC)
SML.......... Software Master Library [*Data processing*] (TEL)
SML.......... Southern Maine Library District, Portland, ME [*OCLC symbol*] (OCLC)
SML.......... Spartan Material List [*Missiles*] (MCD)
SML.......... Spectrum Management Licence [*Telecommunications*] [*British*]
SML.......... Spool Multileaving [*Data processing*] (IBMDP)
SML.......... Standard Markup Language [*Data processing*]
SML.......... States Marine Lines
SML.......... Statistical Methods in Linguistics [*Stockholm*] [*A publication*]
SML.......... Stella Maris [*Bahamas*] [*Airport symbol*] (OAG)
SML.......... Stimmen aus Maria-Laach [*A publication*]
SML.......... Structure Mold Line (MCD)
SML.......... Subacute Myeloid Leukemia [*Oncology*]
SML.......... Support Material List
SML.......... Symbolic Machine Language [*Data processing*]
SMLA....... Kamala Soela [*Surinam*] [*ICAO location identifier*] (ICLI)
SMLAA..... Smokeless Air [*England*] [*A publication*]
Sm Lawy ... Smith's Lawyer and His Profession [*A publication*] (DLA)
SMLB....... Smith Laboratories, Inc. [*NASDAQ symbol*] (NQ)
Sm LC .... Smith's Leading Cases [*A publication*] (DLA)
SMLC....... Southwest Michigan Library Cooperative [*Library network*]
Sm L Cas Com L ... Smith's Leading Cases on Commercial Law [*A publication*] (DLA)
SMLD....... Suckling Mouse Mean Lethal Dose [*Microbiology*]
SMLE....... Short Magazine Lee-Enfield Rifle
SMLE....... Small-Medium Local Exchange [*Telecommunications*] (TEL)
SMLF....... Skrifter Utgivna. Modernsmalslararnas Forening [*A publication*]
SMLI........ Space Microwave Laboratories, Incorporated [*NASDAQ symbol*] (NQ)
SM Lit ...... Studies in Mystical Literature [*A publication*]
Sm LJ .... Law Journal (Smith) [*England*] [*A publication*] (DLA)
SMLJ .... St. Mary's Law Journal [*A publication*]
SMLM....... Simple-Minded Learning Machine (IEEE)
SMLM...... Soviet Military Liaison Mission [*Army*]
SMLO ...... Senior Military Liaison Officer
SMLR....... Stepwise Multiple Linear Regression [*Mathematics*]
SMLS .... Saint Mary of the Lake Seminary [*Mundelein, IL*]
SMLS .... Scimed Life Systems, Inc. [*NASDAQ symbol*] (NQ)
SMLS .... Sea-Based Mobile Logistics Supply [*Navy*] (CAAL)
SMLS .... Seamless (AAG)
SMLS .... Small and Medium-Sized Libraries Section [*Public Library Association*]
SMLT .... Langatabbetje [*Surinam*] [*ICAO location identifier*] (ICLI)
Sm L & T ... Smith's Landlord and Tenant [*A publication*] (DLA)
SMLV .... Studi Mediolatini e Volgari [*A publication*]
SMM .... Master of Sacred Music (BJA)
SMM .... Safeguards and Materials Management [*AEC*]
SMM .... Saigon Military Mission [*Vietnam*]
SMM .... Sancta Mater Maria [*Holy Mother Mary*] [*Latin*]
SMM .... Scanning Multichannel Microwave
SMM .... Scattering Matrix Method [*Materials research*]
SMM .... Secondary Mortgage Market (ADA)
SMM .... Semiconductor Memory Module
SMM .... Semporna [*Malaysia*] [*Airport symbol*] (OAG)
SMM .... Shared Multiport Memory
SMM .... Ship, Machinery, Marine Technology International Exhibition (TSPED)
Sm & M ..... Smedes and Marshall's Mississippi Reports [*9-22 Mississippi*] [*A publication*] (DLA)
SMM .... Societas Mariae Montfortana [*Missionaries of the Company of Mary*] [*Montfort Fathers*] [*Roman Catholic religious order*]
SMM .... Solar Maximum Mission [*NASA*] (MCD)

SMM .... Specially Meritorious Medal
SMM .... Spectral Matrix Method (KSC)
SMM .... Standard Method of Measurement (IEEE)
SMM .... Start of Manual Message (BUR)
SMM .... Stress Memo Manual
SMM .... Study of Media & Markets [*Simmons Market Research Bureau, Inc.*] [*Information service or system*] (CRD)
SMM .... Submarine Miners [*British military*] (DMA)
SMM .... Subsystem Measurement Management [*NASA*] (NASA)
SMM .... Summit Airlines [*Philadelphia, PA*] [*FAA designator*] (FAAC)
SMM .... Supervisory Middle Management
SMM .... Supplemental Minimal Medium [*Microbiology*]
SMM .... System Maintenance Manual
SMM .... Systems Maintenance Management [*Data processing*]
SMMA ...... Small Motor Manufacturers Association [*Libertyville, IL*] (EA)
Sm Man Eq ... [*J. W.*] Smith's Manual of Equity [*A publication*] (DLA)
SMMART ... Society for Mass Media and Resource Technology. Journal [*A publication*] (APTA)
SMMB...... Stores Management Multiplex Bus [*Data processing*] (MCD)
SMMC ...... System Maintenance Monitor Console [*FAA*]
Sm & M Ch ... Smedes and Marshall's Mississippi Reports [*9-22 Mississippi*] [*A publication*] (DLA)
SMMD ...... Specimen Mass Measurement Device [*NASA*] (KSC)
SMMDA .... Smaller Manufacturers Medical Device Association [*Inactive*] (EA)
Sm ME....... Smith's Reports [*61-84 Maine*] [*A publication*] (DLA)
SMME....... Society for Mining, Metallurgy, and Exploration [*In association name, SMME, Inc.*] (EA)
SMME....... Studies in Mathematical and Managerial Economics [*Elsevier Book Series*] [*A publication*]
Sm Merc L ... Smith on Mercantile Law [*13th ed.*] [*1931*] [*A publication*] (DLA)
SMMH...... Scheduled Maintenance Man-Hours (MCD)
SMMI........ El Senoussi Multiphasic Marital Inventory [*Psychology*]
SMMI........ Salesian Missionaries of Mary Immaculate [*See also SSMMI*] [*Gentilly, France*] (EAIO)
S & MMIS ... Supply and Maintenance Management Information System [*Army*]
SMMO....... Moengo [*Surinam*] [*ICAO location identifier*] (ICLI)
SMMP....... Screw Machine Metal Part
SMMP....... Standard Methods of Measuring Performance (IEEE)
SMMP....... System MANPRINT [*Manpower and Personnel Integration*] Management Plan [*Army*]
SMMR ...... Scanning Multichannel [*or Multifrequency or Multispectral*] Microwave Radiometer
SMMR ...... Simmons Major Market Research, Inc. [*New York, NY*] [*Information service or system*] (IID)
SMMR ...... Specific Mobilization Material Requirement [*Military*] (AFIT)
SM-MR ..... Surface Missile, Medium Range
SMMRT Journal ... Society for Mass Media and Resource Technology. Journal [*A publication*] (APTA)
SMMS....... Shipbuilding Material Management Systems [*Navy*] (NG)
Sm M & S .. Smith on Master and Servant [*8th ed.*] [*1931*] [*A publication*] (DLA)
SMMS....... Standard Maintenance Management System [*Military*] (CAAL)
SMMS...... Support Maintenance Management System [*Army*]
SMMT....... Society of Motor Manufacturers and Traders [*Defunct*] (EA)
SMMT....... Strategic Missiles Materials Technology (MCD)
SMMT....... Summit Savings Association [*NASDAQ symbol*] (NQ)
SMN......... Nuzi Texts in the Semitic Museum [*Harvard*] (BJA)
SMN .... Salmon, ID [*Location identifier*] [*FAA*] (FAAL)
SMN .... Seaman [*Military*] [*British*]
SMN .... Seamen's Corp. [*AMEX symbol*] (SPSG)
SMN .... Sleeping Mountain [*Nevada*] [*Seismograph station code, US Geological Survey*] [*Closed*] (SEIS)
SMN .... Studia Musicologica Norvegica [*A publication*]
SMNA ...... Safe Manufacturers' National Association (EA)
SMNA ...... Samna Corp. [*NASDAQ symbol*] (NQ)
SMNC ...... Splenic Mononuclear Cell [*Cytology*]
Sm Neg ...... Smith on Negligence [*2nd ed.*] [*1884*] [*A publication*] (DLA)
SMNI .... New Nickerie/Nickerie [*Surinam*] [*ICAO location identifier*] (ICLI)
SMNI .... Satellite Music Network, Incorporated [*Dallas, TX*] [*NASDAQ symbol*] (NQ)
SMNK ...... Smooth Neck
SMNO....... Singapore Malays National Organization [*Pertubohan Kebangsaan Melayu Singapore*] [*Political party*] (PPW)
SMNRY.... Seminary
SMNSA..... Soviet Mining Science [*English Translation*] [*A publication*]
SMO .... Santa Maria Resources Ltd. [*Toronto Stock Exchange symbol*]
SMO .... Santa Monica, CA [*Location identifier*] [*FAA*] (FAAL)
SMO .... Sea Airmotive, Inc. [*Anchorage, AK*] [*FAA designator*] (FAAC)
SMO .... Secondary Market Operation
SMO .... Senior Medical Officer [*Military*]
SMO .... Service Module Oxidizer [*NASA*]
SMO .... Small Magnetospheric Observatory [*Satellite*] [*NASA*]
SMO .... Smoke
SMO .... So Much Of
SMO .... Society of Military Ophthalmologists (EA)
SMO .... Society of Military Otolaryngologists [*Later, SMO-HNS*] (EA)

SMO.........	Sovereign Military Order [*British*]	
SMO.........	Special Military Operation	
SMO.........	Squadron Medical Officer	
SMO.........	Stabilized Master Oscillator	
SMO.........	State Maintenance Office [*or Officer*] [*Military*]	
SMO.........	Statistical Model of Overlap	
SMO.........	Supermassive Object [*Cosmology*]	
SMO.........	Supplementary Meteorological Office (FAAC)	
SMO.........	Supply Management Office [*Air Force*] (AFM)	
SMO.........	Surface Mining Office [*Department of the Interior*] (OICC)	
SMO.........	Survivability Management Office [*Adelphi, MD*] [*Army*]	
SMO.........	System Management Office (AFIT)	
SMO.........	Systems Methodology Office	
SMOA.......	Ships Material Office, Atlantic	
SMOA.......	Single-Manager Operating Agency [*Military*]	
SMOA.......	Superfund Memorandum of Agreement [*Environmental Protection Agency*]	
SMOBSMOD ...	Strategic Mobility Simulation Model	
SMOC.......	Simulation Mission Operation Computer [*NASA*] (MCD)	
SMOC.......	Submodule and Operator Controller [*For sequence of telephonic operations*]	
SM-OCIC ...	Service Missionnaire de l'Organisation Catholique Internationale du Cinema [*Missionary Service of the International Catholic Organization for Cinema and Audiovisual*] [*Vatican City, Vatican City State*] (EAIO)	
SMOG.......	Sales Management Organization Game	
SMOG.......	Save Me, Oh God	
SMOG.......	Smelost', Mysl', Obraz, Glubina [*Boldness, Thought, Image, Depth*] or Samoye Molodoye Obyedinenie Geniev [*Youngest Federation of Geniuses*] [*Clandestine group of writers in Moscow, USSR*]	
SMOG.......	Smoke and Fog	
SMOG.......	Special Monitor Output Generator (IEEE)	
SMOG.......	Sprite-Midget Owners Group (EA)	
SMOG.......	Structural Modeling Oriented Graphics [*Module*]	
SMOH.......	Society of Medical Officers of Health [*British*]	
SMOHI.....	Sheet Metal Occupational Health Institute (EA)	
SMO-HNS ...	Society of Military Otolaryngologists - Head and Neck Surgeons (EA)	
SMOKE.....	Surface Magnetooptic Kerr Effect [*Surface analysis*]	
SMOL.......	Oelemari [*Surinam*] [*ICAO location identifier*] (ICLI)	
SMOLANT ...	Ships Material Office, Atlantic (MCD)	
Smolensk Gos Ped Inst Ucen Zap ...	Smolenskii Gosudarstvennyi Pedagogiceskii Institut. Ucenye Zapiski [*A publication*]	
SMOM......	Sovereign Military Order of Malta (EA)	
SMon........	Studia Monastica [*A publication*]	
SMON.......	Subacute Myelo-Optic Neuropathy [*Medicine*]	
SMON......	Subacute Myelooptic Neuropathy [*Medicine*]	
SMOP	Ships Material Office, Pacific	
SMOP	So Much of Paragraph	
SMOPAC ...	Ships Material Office, Pacific (MCD)	
SMOPS.....	School of Maritime Operations [*British*]	
SMORG	Senior Marketing Officers Research Group [*LIMRA*]	
SMORZ.....	Smorzando [*Slower and Softer*] [*Music*]	
SMOS.......	Secondary Military Occupational Specialty	
SMOS.......	Senior Marketing Officers Seminar [*LIMRA*]	
SMOS.......	Society of Military Orthopaedic Surgeons (EA)	
SMOSC.....	Secondary Military Occupational Specialty Code (AABC)	
SMOT	Free Interprofessional Association of Soviet Workers (PD)	
SMOTE.....	Simulation of Turbofan Engine [*Air Force*]	
Smoult........	Notes of Cases in Smoult's Collection of Orders [*Calcutta, India*] [*A publication*] (DLA)	
SMOW	Standard Mean Ocean Water	
SMP.........	Sacred Music Press (BJA)	
SMP..........	St. Martin's Press	
SMP..........	Saint Mary's Press [*Record label*] [*New York*]	
SMP..........	Sampler (DEN)	
SMP..........	Santa Monica Public Library, Santa Monica, CA [*OCLC symbol*] (OCLC)	
SMP..........	Scanning and Measuring Projector	
SMP..........	Scheduled Maintenance Program (MCD)	
SMP..........	School Mathematics Project [*British*]	
SMP..........	See Me Please	
SMP..........	Self-Maintenance Period [*British military*] (DMA)	
SMP..........	Sensitized Material Print (MSA)	
SMP..........	Servo Meter Panel (AAG)	
SMP..........	Ship's Mission Profile [*Navy*] (CAAL)	
SMP..........	Simplon Resources Ltd. [*Vancouver Stock Exchange symbol*]	
SMP..........	Simultaneous Macular Perception [*Ophthalmology*]	
SMP..........	Simultaneous Membership Program [*Military*]	
SMP..........	Sine Mascula Prole [*Without Male Issue*] [*Latin*]	
SMP..........	Sisters of St. Mary of the Presentation [*Roman Catholic religious order*]	
SMP..........	Skimmed Milk Powder (ADA)	
SMP..........	Slow-Moving Protease	
SMP..........	Smudge Pot	
SMP..........	Social Marginal Productivity	
SMP..........	Society of Miniature Painters [*British*] (ROG)	
SMP..........	Sodium Mercaptopyruvate [*Organic chemistry*]	
SMP..........	Software Management Plan [*NASA*] (MCD)	

SMP..........	Somplago [*Italy*] [*Seismograph station code, US Geological Survey*] [*Closed*] (SEIS)	
SMP..........	Sound Motion Picture Technician [*Navy*]	
SMP..........	Special Maintenance Project [*FAA*]	
SMP..........	Special Manufacturing Procedure	
SMP..........	Special Marketing Program [*Business*]	
SMP..........	Special Multiperil [*Insurance*]	
SMP..........	Stampede Pass, WA [*Location identifier*] [*FAA*] (FAAL)	
SMP..........	Standard Maintenance Procedure	
SMP..........	Standard Motor Products, Inc. [*NYSE symbol*] (SPSG)	
SMP..........	Standard Motor Pump	
SMP..........	Standards, Methods, and Planning	
SMP..........	Statutory Maternity Pay [*British*]	
SMP..........	Stores Management Process (MCD)	
SMP..........	Submitochondrial Particle [*Cytology*]	
SMP..........	Sulfamethoxypyridazine [*Antimicrobial compound*]	
SMP..........	Summary Maneuver Plan	
SMP..........	Suomen Maaseudun Puolue [*Finnish Rural Party*] [*Political party*] (PPW)	
SMP..........	Supply Master Plan	
SMP..........	Symbolic Mathematics Program	
SMP..........	Symmetric Multiprocessing	
SMP..........	Syrtis Major Plantia [*A filamentary mark on Mars*]	
SMP..........	System Mechanical Performance	
SMP..........	System Modification Program [*Data processing*]	
SMP..........	Systems Maintenance Procedure (MCD)	
SMP..........	Systems Modernization Plan [*Social Security Administration*]	
SMP..........	Systems Monitoring Panel (NVT)	
SMPA.......	Paloemeu/Vincent Fajks [*Surinam*] [*ICAO location identifier*] (ICLI)	
SMPA.......	Solid Motor Processing Area [*NASA*] (KSC)	
SMPAD.....	Society of Motion Picture Art Directors [*Later, SMPTAD*] (EA)	
Sm Pat	Smith on Patents [*2nd ed.*] [*1854*] [*A publication*] (DLA)	
SMPB.......	Paramaribo [*Surinam*] [*ICAO location identifier*] (ICLI)	
SMPC.......	Saint Mary of the Plains College [*Dodge City, KS*]	
SMPC........	Simplified Model Predictive Control [*Chemical engineering*] [*Data processing*]	
SMPD.......	Ship Maintenance Planning Data (MCD)	
Sm Pd........	Small Pond [*A publication*]	
SMPD.......	Surface Missile Processing Description (MCD)	
SMPE.......	Society of Marine Port Engineers (EA)	
SMPF.......	Scientific & Medical Publications of France, Inc.	
SMPG........	Poesoegroenoe [*Surinam*] [*ICAO location identifier*] (ICLI)	
SMPG........	Small Magazine Publishers Group (EA)	
SMPG........	Standardization Management Policy Group	
SMPG........	Successful Magazine Publishers Group (EA)	
SMPI........	Surface Missile Proficiency Inspection (MCD)	
SMPKA.....	Sempaku [*A publication*]	
SMPL.......	Sample	
Sm Pl........	Somersetshire Pleas (Civil and Criminal), Edited by Chadwyck-Healey and Landon [*Somerset Record Society Publications, Vols. 11, 36, 41, 44*] [*A publication*] (DLA)	
SMPLG......	Sampling (MSA)	
SMPM.......	Paramaribo [*Surinam*] [*ICAO location identifier*] (ICLI)	
SMPM......	Structural Materials Property Manual [*NASA*] (NASA)	
SM/PM.....	System Management/Performance Monitor [*NASA*] (NASA)	
SMPO	SEATO [*Southeast Asia Treaty Organization*] Military Planning Office (CINC)	
SMPO.......	Sound Motion Picture Operator [*Navy*]	
Sm Poor L ...	Smith's Scotch Poor Law [*A publication*] (DLA)	
S-MPR......	Semimonthly Progress Reports [*Navy*]	
SMPR........	Supply and Maintenance Plan and Report [*Army*] (AABC)	
Sm Pr Eq...	Smith's Principles of Equity [*A publication*] (DLA)	
Sm Prob L ...	Smith's Probate Law and Practice [*A publication*] (DLA)	
Sm Pr R......	Small Press Review [*A publication*]	
SMPS	Simplified Message Processing Simulation (IEEE)	
SMPS	Simpson Industries, Inc. [*NASDAQ symbol*] (NQ)	
SMPS	Society for Marketing Professional Services [*Alexandria, VA*] (EA)	
SMPS	Special Mobile Provost Section [*British military*] (DMA)	
SMPSA......	Solid Motor Processing and Storage Car	
SMPT	Apentina [*Surinam*] [*ICAO location identifier*] (ICLI)	
SMPTA	Schweizerische Mineralogische und Petrographische Mitteilungen [*A publication*]	
SMPTAD ..	Society of Motion Picture and Television Art Directors (EA)	
SMPTE	Society of Motion Picture and Television Engineers (EA)	
SMPTE J ..	Society of Motion Picture and Television Engineers. Journal [*A publication*]	
SMPTRB..	Shuttle Main Propulsion Test Requirement Board [*NASA*] (MCD)	
SMPVS.....	Central Resource Centre, Prairie View School Division No. 74, Milestone, Saskatchewan [*Library symbol*] [*National Library of Canada*] (NLC)	
SMQ	School Media Quarterly [*A publication*]	
SMQ	Silvermaque Mining Ltd. [*Toronto Stock Exchange symbol*]	
SMQ	Social Maturity Quotient	
SMQ	Structure Module Qualification Test (MCD)	
SMQ	Surface Metastable Quenching [*Surface analysis*]	
SMR	Great Falls, MT [*Location identifier*] [*FAA*] (FAAL)	

SMR .... Midrash Rabbah [*H. Freedman and Maurice Simon*] [*A publication*]   (BJA)
SMR .... Sa Majeste Royale [*His, or Her, Royal Majesty*] [*French*]
SMR .... San Marino [*ANSI three-letter standard code*]   (CNC)
SMR .... Santa Marta [*Colombia*] [*Airport symbol*]   (OAG)
SMR .... Saskatchewan Mounted Rifles   (DMA)
SMR .... Scheduled Maintenance Replacement
SMR .... School of Materiel Readiness [*Formerly, SAM*] [*Army*]   (RDA)
SMR .... Secret Marriage Rite   (BJA)
SMR .... Semeru [*Java*] [*Seismograph station code, US Geological Survey*] [*Closed*]   (SEIS)
SMR .... Seminarians for Ministerial Renewal [*Later, NFCS*]   (EA)
SMR .... Senior Maintenance Rating [*British military*]   (DMA)
SMR .... Sensorimotor Rhythm [*Neurophysiology*]
SMR .... Series Mode Rejection
SMR .... Severely Mentally Retarded
SMR .... Shared Mobile Radio [*Telecommunications*]
SMR .... Sheffield and Midland Railway [*British*]   (ROG)
SMR .... Shield Mock-Up Reactor
S & MR ...... Shire and Municipal Record [*A publication*]   (APTA)
SMR .... Side-Looking Mapping RADAR
SMR .... Skeletal Muscle Relaxant [*Drug*]
SMR .... Sloan Management Review [*A publication*]
SMR .... Small Missile Range   (MCD)
SMR .... Society of Manufacturers' Representatives   (EA)
SMR .... Society of Mary Reparatrix [*Roman Catholic women's religious order*]
SMR .... Solid Moderated Reactor [*Nuclear energy*]
SMR .... Somnolent Metabolic Rate [*Medicine*]
SM & R .... Source, Maintenance, and Recoverability   (NG)
SMR .... Source, Maintenance, and Recoverability   (MCD)
SMR .... Spanish Mustang Registry   (EA)
SMR .... Special Money Requisition [*Military*]
SMR .... Specialized Mobile Radio
SMR .... St Mark's Review [*A publication*]   (APTA)
SMR .... Standard Malaysian Rubber [*Grade of natural rubber*]
SMR .... Standard Mortality Rate
SMR .... Standardized Mortality Ratio
SMR .... Stanmar Resources Ltd. [*Vancouver Stock Exchange symbol*]
SMR .... Statement of Material Requirements
SMR .... Status Monitoring Routine
SMR .... Statute Mile Radius   (FAAC)
SMR .... Steam-Methane Reforming [*Chemical engineering*]
SMR .... Stock Management Report [*Military*]
Smr............ Streptomycin Resistance [*Genetics*]
SMR .... Submucous Resection [*Medicine*]
SMR .... Super-Metal Rich [*Astronomy*]
SMR .... Supplemental Medical Report
SMR .... Supply Management Report
SMR .... Surface Movement RADAR
SMR .... Switching Mode Regulator
SMR .... System Malfunction Report
SMRA....... Raleighvallen [*Surinam*] [*ICAO location identifier*]   (ICLI)
SMRA....... Simultaneous Multicomponent Rank Annihilation [*Mathematics*]
SMRAS .... Safeguard Maintenance and Reporting Analysis System [*Army*]   (AABC)
SMRB....... Simmons Market Research Bureau, Inc. [*New York, NY*] [*Database producer*]
SMRC....... Silver Marten Rabbit Club   (EA)
SMRC....... Society of Miniature Rifle Clubs [*British*]   (ROG)
SMRCS .... Service Module Reaction Control System [*NASA*]   (KSC)
SMRD ...... Spin Motor Rotation [*or Running*] Detector   (MCD)
SMRD ...... Spin Motor Run Discrete   (NASA)
SMRE....... Safety in Mines Research Establishment [*British*]
SMRE....... Societe de Marie Reine d'Ecosse [*Mary Queen of Scots Society*]   (EAIO)
SMRE....... Submerged Repeater Monitoring Equipment [*RADAR*]
S & M Record ... Shire and Municipal Record [*A publication*]   (APTA)
SMRF....... Salvadoran Medical Relief Fund   (EA)
SMRF....... Small Materials Recovery Facility [*for recycling of glass, plastics, etc.*]
SMRGC.... Sun-Maid Raisin Growers of California   (EA)
SMRI....... Society for Magnetic Resonance Imaging   (EA)
SMRI....... Solution Mining Research Institute   (EA)
SMRIS ..... Soviet Missile Range Instrumented Ship   (CINC)
SMRL....... Stanford Magnetic Resonance Laboratory [*Stanford University*] [*Research center*]   (RCD)
SMRL....... Submarine Medical Research Laboratory
SMRLA..... Southern Maryland Regional Library Resource Center [*Library network*]
SMRLH..... Soldier's Mail, Rush Like Hell [*On correspondence*]
SMRM ..... Solar Maximum Repair Mission [*NASA*]   (NASA)
SMR/MIS ... Supply, Maintenance and Readiness Management Information System [*Logistics Management Information System*] [*Military*]   (AABC)
SMRP....... Society for Medieval and Renaissance Philosophy   (EA)
SMRP....... Strategic Mobilization Requirements and Program   (MCD)
Sm R & P Prop ... Smith on the Law of Real and Personal Property [*A publication*]   (DLA)
SMRR....... Supplier Material Review Record   (MCD)

SMRRA..... Report. Saskatchewan Department of Mineral Resources [*A publication*]
SMRS....... Specialized Mobile Radio System
SMRS....... Specific Mobilization Reserve Stock [*Military*]   (AFIT)
SM/RSF.... Ammunition Stores Management and Remote Set Fuzing   (MCD)
SMRT....... Scheduled Maintenance Replacement Time
SMRT....... Single Message Rate Timing
SMRT....... SmartCard International, Inc. [*New York, NY*] [*NASDAQ symbol*]   (NQ)
SMRU ...... Sea Mammal Research Unit [*British*]   (ARC)
SMRV....... South Middlesex Rifle Volunteers [*British military*]   (DMA)
SMRV....... Squirrel Monkey Retravirus
SMRVA..... Sloan Management Review [*A publication*]
SMRVS .... Small Modular Recovery Vehicle System [*Nuclear energy*]
SMRX....... Summa RX Laboratories, Inc. [*NASDAQ symbol*]   (NQ)
SMRY....... Summary   (FAAC)
SMS......... Marine Service Squadron
SMS......... Sa Majeste Suedoise [*His, or Her, Swedish Majesty*] [*French*]   (ROG)
SMS......... Safety Manual Supplement
SMS......... Saint Marie [*Madagascar*] [*Airport symbol*]   (OAG)
SMS......... Saint Mary's Seminary [*Connecticut; Missouri; Ohio; Vermont*]
SMS......... Sales Motivation Survey [*Test*]
SMS......... Samos [*Greece*] [*Seismograph station code, US Geological Survey*] [*Closed*]   (SEIS)
SMS......... Sample Management System [*Laboratory science*]
SMS......... Satellite Motion Simulator
SMS......... Scandinavian Migraine Society   (EA)
SMS......... Scientific Mission Support
SMS......... Screen Management System [*Computer technology*]
SMS......... Semiconductor-Metal-Semiconductor
SMS......... Sensor Monitoring Set   (MCD)
SMS......... Separation Mechanism Subsystem [*NASA*]   (NASA)
SMS......... Sequence Milestone System
SMS......... Serial Motor Seizures [*Medicine*]
SMS......... Service Management System [*Telecommunications*]
SMS......... Shared Mass Storage
SMS......... Ship Motion Simulator
SMS......... Ship's Missile System   (MCD)
SMS......... Shuttle Mission Simulator [*NASA*]   (NASA)
SMS......... Signal Messenger Service   (NATG)
SMS......... Signal Missile Support [*Air Force*]   (MUGU)
SMS......... Silane to Molten Silane [*Photovoltaic energy systems*]
SMS......... Silico-Manganese Steel
SMS......... Sinatra Music Society   (EAIO)
SMS......... Skandinavisk Migraeneselskab [*Scandinavian Migraine Society*]   (EAIO)
SMS......... Small Magnetospheric Satellite [*NASA*]
Sm & S .... Smith and Sager's Drainage Cases [*Canada*] [*A publication*]   (DLA)
SMS......... Solar Maximum Satellite [*NASA*]   (MCD)
SMS......... Spanish Market Selection [*Cigars*]
SMS......... Spares Management System
SMS......... Special Mint Set [*Numismatics*]
SMS......... Spectronics Micro Sytems [*Data processing*]
SMS......... Spin Motor Supply
SMS......... Standard Material Specification   (MCD)
SMS......... Standard Modular System
SMS......... Standard Molecular System
SMS......... Startling Mystery Stories [*A publication*]
SMS......... State Mutual Securities Trust [*NYSE symbol*]   (SPSG)
SMS......... Stationary Meteorological Satellite [*NASA*]
SMS......... Stores Management Sea [*Navy*]
SMS......... Stores Management System   (MCD)
SMS......... Strategic Management Society [*British*]
SMS......... Strategic Missile Squadron [*Air Force*]
SMS......... Structures and Mechanical System [*Skylab*] [*NASA*]
SMS......... Student Monitoring System [*Vocational guidance*]
SMS......... Studier i Modern Sprakvetenskap [*A publication*]
SMS......... Subject Matter Specialist
SMS......... Sumter, SC [*Location identifier*] [*FAA*]   (FAAL)
SMS......... Surface Missile Ship   (MUGU)
SMS......... Surface Missile System [*NASA*]
SMS......... SURTASS Measurement System [*Navy*]   (CAAL)
SMS......... Suspended Maneuvering System [*McDonnell Douglas Corp.*]   (MCD)
SMS......... Switching and Maintenance Set
SMS......... Synchronous Meteorological Satellite [*NASA*]
SMS......... Synoptic Meteorological Sounding
SMS......... Syro-Mesopotamian Studies [*Malibu, CA*] [*A publication*]   (BJA)
SMS......... System Migration Section [*Social Security Administration*]
SMS......... Systems Maintenance Sector [*Electronics*]   (FAAC)
SMS......... Systems Maintenance Service   (MCD)
SM & S .... Systems Management and Sequencing   (NASA)
SMSA....... Seaman Apprentice, Signalman, Striker [*Navy rating*]
SMSA....... Shop Missile Assembly and Maintenance
SMSA....... Signal Missile Support Agency [*Air Force*]   (AAG)
SMSA....... Standard Metropolitan Statistical Area [*Later, MSA*] [*Census Bureau*]

SMSA........	Super-Cooled Infrared Multispectral Survey and Analysis [*Traces mineral deposits*]
SMSAE	Surface Missile System Availability Evaluation [*NASA*] (KSC)
SMSanE	Master of Science in Sanitary Engineering
SMSB	Strategic Missile Support Base [*Air Force*] (AFM)
SMSC	Service Module Sequence Controller [*NASA*]
SMSC	Southeastern Missouri State College
SMSC	Standard Microsystems Corporation [*NASDAQ symbol*] (NQ)
SMSC	Standard Modular System Card [*Data processing*] (BUR)
SMSC	State Manpower Service Council [*Department of Labor*]
SMSCC	Shuttle Mission Simulator Computer Complex [*NASA*] (MCD)
SMSD	Ship Magnetic Submarine Detector
SMSE	Systems Maintenance Sector Electronics (FAAC)
SMSF	Special Maintenance Support Facility (MCD)
SMSG	School Management Study Group (EA)
SMSG	Self-Mutilators Support Group (EA)
SMSGT	Senior Master Sergeant
SMSH	Sisters of Sainte Marthe [*of St. Hyacinthe*] [*Roman Catholic religious order*]
SMSI	Scientific Micro Systems, Incorporated [*Mountain View, CA*] [*NASDAQ symbol*] (NQ)
SMSI	Sipaliwini [*Surinam*] [*ICAO location identifier*] (ICLI)
SMSI	Standard Manned Space Flight Initiator [*Later, NSI-I*] [*NASA*] (NASA)
SMSI	State Microscopical Society of Illinois (EA)
SMSI	Strong Metal-Support Interaction [*Catalysis*]
SMSIP......	Space Mission Survivability Implementation Plan
SMSIP......	Surface Missile Ship Improvement Program (MCD)
SMSJ	Scott's Monthly Stamp Journal [*A publication*]
SMSM	Kwamalasoemoetoe [*Surinam*] [*ICAO location identifier*] (ICLI)
SMSM	Soeurs Missionnaires de la Societe de Marie [*Missionary Sisters of the Society of Mary*] (EAIO)
SMSMS	Strategic Missile Squadron Munitions Section [*Air Force*] (AAG)
SMSN.......	Seaman, Signalman, Striker [*Navy rating*]
SMSNA.....	Smithsonian [*A publication*]
SMSO.......	Subcontract Material Sales Order
Sm & Sod L & T ...	Smith and Soden on Landlord and Tenant [*2nd ed.*] [*1878*] [*A publication*] (DLA)
SMSP	St. Peter's Abbey and College, Muenster, Saskatchewan [*Library symbol*] [*National Library of Canada*] (NLC)
SMSP	Security Military Space Program (MUGU)
SMSP	Soil Moisture Strength Prediction [*Army*]
SMSpr	Studier i Modern Sprakvetenskap [*A publication*]
SMSq.......	Strategic Missile Squadron [*Air Force*]
SMSR	Studi e Materiali di Storia della Religioni [*A publication*]
SMSRAH ...	Institutionen foer Skoglig Matematisk Statistik Rapporter och Uppsatser [*A publication*]
SMS Report ...	Socioeconomic Monitoring System Report [*A publication*]
SMSRL......	Sarah Mellon Scaife Radiation Laboratory [*University of Pittsburgh*] (MCD)
SMSRS.....	Shipboard Meteorological Satellite Readout Station
SMSS	School of Management and Strategic Studies [*Founded 1982 by Richard Farson, offers a two-year management program through GTE Telenet*]
SMSS	Studies in Management Science and Systems [*Elsevier Book Series*] [*A publication*]
SMST	Stoelmanseiland [*Surinam*] [*ICAO location identifier*] (ICLI)
Sm Stat Law ...	Smith's Statute Law [*A publication*] (DLA)
SMSV	San Miguel Sea Lion Virus
SMT..........	S-Band Megawatt Transmit
SMT..........	Sacred Marriage Texts (BJA)
SMT..........	Sample Mix Table [*Musical instrument digital interface*]
SMT..........	Samuel Manu-Tech, Inc. [*Toronto Stock Exchange symbol*]
SMT..........	Saturn Missile Test [*NASA*]
SMT..........	Segmented Mirror Telescope [*Astronomy*]
SMT..........	Selective Message Transaction (NASA)
SMT..........	Senior Medical Technician
SMT..........	Service Module Technician [*NASA*] (KSC)
SMT..........	Sexual Medicine Today [*A publication*]
SMT..........	Shelter Management Training [*Civil Defense*]
SMT..........	Ship Maintenance Test
SMT..........	Shipboard Marriage Test
SMT..........	Ship's Mean Time [*Navigation*]
SMT..........	Shop Mechanic's Test
SMT..........	Small Missile Telecamera
SMT..........	Society of Metropolitan Treasurers [*British*]
SMT..........	South Dakota School of Mines and Technology, Rapid City, SD [*OCLC symbol*] (OCLC)
SMT..........	Square Mesh Tracking [*Air Force*]
SMT..........	Stabilized March Technique
SMT..........	Standard Measurement Technique [*Navy*]
SMT..........	Station Management
SMT..........	Studies in Modern Thermodynamics [*Elsevier Book Series*] [*A publication*]
SMT..........	Submit (FAAC)
SMT..........	Successful Meetings [*A publication*]
SMT..........	Sultan-Mazar [*USSR*] [*Seismograph station code, US Geological Survey*] [*Closed*] (SEIS)
SMT..........	Summit (MCD)
SMT..........	Supermedial Thigh [*Flap for plastic surgery*]
SMT..........	Supplementary Monophonic Transmission (ADA)
SMT..........	Supply, Maintenance, and Transportation [*Directorate*] [*Army*] (RDA)
SMT..........	Surface Missile Test [*Navy*] (CAAL)
SMT..........	Surface-Mount Technology [*Electronics*]
SMT..........	System Maintenance Test
SMT..........	System Maintenance Trainer (MCD)
SMT..........	System Modulation Transfer [*Acutance*] [*Photography*]
SMT..........	Systems Manufacturing Technology [*San Marcos, CA*]
SMTA.......	Sewing Machine Trade Association (EA)
SMTA.......	Surface Mount Technology Association (EA)
SMTA.......	Tabiki [*Surinam*] [*ICAO location identifier*] (ICLI)
SMTAS	Shuttle Model Test and Analysis System [*NASA*] (NASA)
SMTB	Tafelberg/Rudi Kappel [*Surinam*] [*ICAO location identifier*] (ICLI)
SMTC	Sa Majeste Tres Chretienne [*His, or Her, Most Christian Majesty*] [*French*]
SMTD.......	Short Take-Off and Landing and Maneuvering Technology Demonstrator [*Air Force*]
SMTE	Society for Music Teacher Education (EA)
SMTEBI...	Entomologische Abhandlungen [*Dresden*] [*A publication*]
SMTF	Sa Majeste Tres Fidele [*His, or Her, Most Faithful Majesty*] [*French*]
SMTF	Spacecraft Magnetic Test Facility [*Goddard Space Flight Center*] [*NASA*]
SMTFBL...	Faunistische Abhandlungen [*Dresden*] [*A publication*]
SMTG.......	Solid-State and Molecular Theory Group [*MIT*] (MCD)
SMTH	Smooth (FAAC)
SMTI	Selective Moving Target Indicator (IEEE)
SMTI	Sodium Mechanisms Test Installation [*Nuclear energy*] (NRCH)
SMTI	Southeastern Massachusetts Technological Institute [*Later, Southeastern Massachusetts University*]
SMTI	Tibiti [*Surinam*] [*ICAO location identifier*] (ICLI)
SMTK.......	Sump Tank
SMTLB	Strength of Materials [*English Translation*] [*A publication*]
SMTM.......	Sometime (FAAC)
SMTN.......	Smoky Mound R. R. [*AAR code*]
SMTO	St. Maarten Tourist Office (EA)
SMTO	Senior Mechanical Transport Officer [*British military*] (DMA)
SMTP.......	Simple Mail Transfer Protocol [*Data processing*] (PCM)
SMTP.......	Tepoe [*Surinam*] [*ICAO location identifier*] (ICLI)
SMTRB	Ship and Marine Technology Requirements Board [*British*]
SMTS	Simulated Maintenance Training System [*Air Force*]
SMTS	Southern Manufacturing Technology Show and Conference (ITD)
SMTS	Synchronous Meteorological Test Satellite [*NASA*]
SMTSDS...	Annual Research Reviews. Somatostatin [*A publication*]
SMTS Journal ...	Saskatchewan Mathematics Teachers' Society. Journal [*A publication*]
SMTT	Small Bowel Transit Time [*Gastroenterology*]
SMU	St. Mary's University Library [*UTLAS symbol*]
SMU	Scottish Mothers' Union [*Episcopalian*]
SMU	Secondary Multiplexing Unit
SMU	Self-Maneuvering Unit [*Air Force*]
SMU	Sheep Mountain, AK [*Location identifier*] [*FAA*] (FAAL)
SMU	Single Motor Unit
SMU	Soft Mock-Up [*NASA*] (MCD)
SMU	Southeastern Massachusetts University [*North Dartmouth*]
SMU	Southeastern Massachusetts University, North Dartmouth, MA [*OCLC symbol*] (OCLC)
SMU	Southern Methodist University [*Texas*]
SMU	Spectrum Monitoring Unit
SMU	Store Monitor Unit
SMU	Sunnyside Mine [*Utah*] [*Seismograph station code, US Geological Survey*] [*Closed*] (SEIS)
SMU	Super-Module Unit [*Telecommunications*] (TEL)
SMU	System Maintenance Unit [*Data processing*]
SMU	System Monitoring Unit
SMUAP.....	Simple Motor Unit Action Potential [*Medicine*]
SMUC	Societe de Musique des Universites Canadiennes [*Canadian University Music Society - CUMS*]
SMUD	Sacramento Municipal Utility District [*Photovoltaic energy systems*]
SMUG	Smuggling [*FBI standardized term*]
SMus	Studia Musicologica [*Budapest*] [*A publication*]
S Mus D.....	Doctor of Sacred Music
SMUSE	Socialist Movement for the United States of Europe
SMUT	Shrink Mock-Up Template (MSA)
SMUT	Special Mission Utility Transport [*Aviation*]
SMV	Samovar Hills, AK [*Location identifier*] [*FAA*] (FAAL)
SMV	Samsville [*Illinois*] [*Seismograph station code, US Geological Survey*] (SEIS)
SMV	Santa Maria Valley Railroad Co. [*AAR code*]
SMV	Santa Monica Bank Voting Trust Certificates [*AMEX symbol*] (SPSG)
SMV	Satellite Mutual Visibility
SMV	Short Market Value [*Investment term*]
SMV	Sinusoidal Membrane Vesicle [*Anatomy*]
SMV	Skeletal Muscle Ventricle [*Medicine*]

SMV	Slow Moving Vehicle [*Emblem to prevent rear-end collisions*]
SMV	Soybean Mosaic Virus
SM/V	Squared-Mean to Variance
SMV	Studi Mediolatini e Volgari [*A publication*]
SMV	Superior Mesenteric Vein [*Anatomy*]
SMVH	Service in Military and Veterans Hospitals [*Red Cross*]
SMVMA....	Sbornik Trudov Moskovskii Vechernii Metallurgicheskii Institut [*A publication*]
SMVO	Avanavero [*Surinam*] [*ICAO location identifier*] (ICLI)
SMVP	Shuttle Master Verification Plan [*NASA*] (NASA)
SMVRD.....	Shuttle Master Verification Requirements Document [*NASA*] (NASA)
SMW	Second Main Watch
SMW	Sheet Metal Workers' International Association (EA)
SMW	Simpatico Wines [*Vancouver Stock Exchange symbol*]
SMW	Slotted Metal Window
SMW	Smara [*Morocco*] [*Airport symbol*] (OAG)
SMW	Society of Magazine Writers [*Later, ASJA*] (EA)
SMW	Society of Military Widows (EA)
SMW	South Mountain [*Washington*] [*Seismograph station code, US Geological Survey*] (SEIS)
SMW	Standard Materials Worksheet [*NASA*] (NASA)
SMW	Strategic Missile Wing [*Air Force*]
S Mw.........	Studien zur Musikwissenschaft [*A publication*]
SMWA	Wageningen [*Surinam*] [*ICAO location identifier*] (ICLI)
SMWC	Saint Mary-Of-The-Woods College [*Indiana*]
SMWDSEP ...	Single, Married, Widowed, Divorced, Separated
SMWG	Strategic Missile Wing [*Air Force*]
SMWIA	Sheet Metal Workers' International Association (EA)
SMWOA	Schweizerische Medizinische Wochenschrift [*A publication*]
SMWP.......	Strategic Mobility Work Project [*Army*] (AABC)
SMWS	Washabo [*Surinam*] [*ICAO location identifier*] (ICLI)
SMX	Santa Maria [*California*] [*Airport symbol*] (OAG)
SMX	Santa Maria, CA [*Location identifier*] [*FAA*] (FAAL)
SMX	Semi-Micro Xerography
SMX	Submultiplexer Unit
SMX	Sulfamethoxazole [*Also, S, SMZ*] [*Antibacterial compound*]
SMX	Systems Center, Inc. [*NYSE symbol*] (SPSG)
SMY	Ark Valley Airways [*Arkansas City, KS*] [*FAA designator*] (FAAC)
SMY	Marianna, FL [*Location identifier*] [*FAA*] (FAAL)
SMY	Scientist-Man Year
SMY	Shemya [*Alaska*] [*Seismograph station code, US Geological Survey*] (SEIS)
SMY	Simenti [*Senegal*] [*Airport symbol*] (OAG)
SMY	Smyrna Public Library, Smyrna, DE [*OCLC symbol*] (OCLC)
Smy	Smythe's Irish Common Pleas Reports [*1839-40*] [*A publication*] (DLA)
SMY	Solar Maximum Year [*August, 1979-February, 1981*]
SMy	Studia Mystica [*A publication*]
SMY	Summary (MSA)
Smy & B.....	Smythe and Bourke's Irish Marriage Cases [*1842*] [*A publication*] (DLA)
Smy Home ...	Smyth on the Law of Homestead and Exemptions [*A publication*] (DLA)
SMYRAD ...	Smithsonian Year [*A publication*]
SMYS.......	Specified Minimum Yield Strength
Smythe.......	Smythe's Irish Common Pleas Reports [*1839-40*] [*A publication*] (DLA)
S Mz...........	Schweizerische Musikzeitung/Revue Musicale Suisse [*A publication*]
SMZ	Stoelmanseiland [*Suriname*] [*Airport symbol*] (OAG)
SMZ	Sulfamethoxazole [*Also, S, SMX*] [*Antibacterial compound*]
SMZHA	Sibirskii Matematiceskii Zurnal [*A publication*]
SMZO	Paramaribo/Zorg en Hoop [*Surinam*] [*ICAO location identifier*] (ICLI)
SMZY.......	Paramaribo/Zandery [*Surinam*] [*ICAO location identifier*] (ICLI)
sn-----	Andean Area [*MARC geographic area code*] [*Library of Congress*] (LCCP)
SN	Parke, Davis & Co. [*Research code symbol*]
SN	Sacramento Northern Railway [*AAR code*]
SN	Safety Notice (MCD)
SN	Sample Name
SN	SAN [*Societe Aeronautique Normande*] [*France*] [*ICAO aircraft manufacturer identifier*] (ICAO)
SN	Santa [*Saint*] [*Italian*]
SN	Santo
SN	Saponification Number [*Analytical chemistry*]
SN	Saturday Night [*A publication*]
SN	Science News [*A publication*]
SN	Scientific Note
S & N	Scottish & Newcastle Breweries [*Commercial firm*] [*British*]
SN	Seaman [*Navy rating*]
SN	Secretary of the Navy
SN	Sector Number (MUGU)
SN	Secundum Naturam [*According to Nature*] [*Latin*]
SN	See Note (ROG)
SN	Semiconductor Network (IEEE)
SN	Senegal [*ANSI two-letter standard code*] (CNC)
SN	Senior Navigator [*Air Force*]
S/N	Sequence Number
SN	Sergeant Navigator [*British*]
SN	Serial Number
SN	Serum Neutralization Test
SN	Service Note (MSA)
SN	Service Number [*Military*]
SN	Session Notes [*Scotland*] [*A publication*] (DLA)
SN	Shakespeare Newsletter [*A publication*]
SN	Shalom Network (EA)
SN	Shaping Network (MCD)
Sn	Shingle [*Quality of the bottom*] [*Nautical charts*]
SN	Shipping Note [*Business term*]
S/N	Shipping Number
SN	Side Note
SN	Sigma Nu [*A national fraternity*]
SN	Sign (BUR)
SN	Signal Node
S/N	Signal to Noise Ratio [*Unweighted*] (CMD)
SN	Sine [*Without*] [*Latin*]
SN	Sine of the Amplitude (IEEE)
SN	Sinoatrial Node [*Medicine*]
SN	Siren
SN	Slovensky Narodopis [*A publication*]
sn.	Small Nuclear
SN	Small-Probe Nephelometer [*NASA*]
SN	Snellen [*Test types*] [*Ophthalmology*]
SN	Snow [*Meteorology*] (FAAC)
S/n	Sobre Nosotros [*On Us*] [*Business term*] [*Spanish*]
SN	Societe Anonyme Belge d'Exploitation de la Navigation Aerienne [*Sabena Belgian World Airlines*] [*ICAO designator*] (FAAC)
SN	Society for Neuroscience (EA)
SN	Solid Neutral
S/N	Sons of Norway (EA)
SN	Sovetskaja Nauka [*A publication*]
SN	Special Nuclear [*Material*]
S/N	Speech/Noise [*Ratio*] [*Electronics*]
SN	Sponsoring Agency [*Online database field identifier*]
SN	Sporting News [*A publication*]
SN	Standard Nomenclature
SN	Standard Oil Co. (Indiana) [*NYSE symbol*] [*Toronto Stock Exchange symbol*] (SPSG)
Sn	Stannum [*Tin*] [*Chemical element*]
S & N	Statesman and Nation [*A publication*]
SN	Stationing Flag [*Navy*] [*British*]
SN	Statutes of Newfoundland [*A publication*] (ILCA)
SN	Steam Navigation
sn.	Stereospecifically Numbered [*Biochemistry*]
SN	Sterling Nuclear Plant (NRCH)
sn.	Sthene [*Absolute unit of force*]
SN	Stock Number (MCD)
SN	Story of the Nations [*A publication*]
S-N............	Stress Number (NASA)
SN	Stronnictwo Narodowe [*Nationalist Party*] [*Poland*] [*Political party*] (PPE)
SN	Strouhal Number [*Sound*]
SN	Student Nurse
SN	Studia Neophilologica [*A publication*]
SN	Subnormal
SN	Substantia Nigra [*Brain anatomy*]
SN	Sunday Nation [*A publication*]
SN	Supernatant [*Chemistry*]
SN	Supernova
SN	Suprasternal Notch [*Anatomy*]
SN	Survey Number
SN	Syllable Number [*Entomology*]
SN	Synchronizers [*JETDS nomenclature*] [*Military*] (CET)
SN	Systems/Strategic Navigation [*Aviation*] (FAAC)
S-N (Plane) ...	Sella Turcica-Nasion [*Plane that passes through these points*] [*Cephalometrics*]
SNA	Orange County [*California*] [*Airport symbol*] (OAG)
SNA	Sadr Nizamut Adalat Reports [*India*] [*A publication*] (DLA)
SNA	Sanae [*Antarctica*] [*Geomagnetic observatory code*]
SNA	Sanae [*Antarctica*] [*Seismograph station code, US Geological Survey*] (SEIS)
SNA	Santa Ana, CA [*Location identifier*] [*FAA*] (FAAL)
SNA	Santana Petroleum [*Vancouver Stock Exchange symbol*]
SNA	Satellite Networking Associates, Inc. [*New York, NY*] [*Telecommunications*] (TSSD)
SNA	Saudi News Agency (BJA)
SNA	Scandinavian Neurological Association (EA)
SNA	Schlaraffia Nordamerika (EA)
SNA	Sella, Nasion, A [*Anthropometric landmark*]
SNA	Shakespeariana [*A publication*]
SNA	Snap-On Tools Corp. [*NYSE symbol*] (SPSG)
SNa	Sot la Nape [*A publication*]
SNA	Soviet Naval Aviation
SNA	Student Naval Aviator
SNA	Suburban Newspapers of America (EA)
SNA	Sudan News Agency (BJA)
SNA	Syrian News Agency (BJA)

SNA .... System of National Accounts [*United Nations*]
SNA .... Systems Network Architecture [*IBM Corp.*] [*Data processing*]
SNAA .... Syndicat National des Travailleurs de l'Amiante d'Asbestos [*Canada*]
SNAB........ Stock Number Action Bulletin
SNA Beng ... Sadr Nizamut Adalat Reports [*India*] [*A publication*]   (DLA)
SNA Beng (NS) ... Sadr Nizamut Adalat Reports, New Series [*1851-59*] [*Bengal, India*] [*A publication*]   (DLA)
SNACC...... Society of Neurosurgical Anesthesia and Critical Care   (EA)
SNACMA ... Snack, Nut, and Crisp Manufacturers' Association [*British*]
SNACS ...... Share News on Automatic Coding Systems [*Data processing*]
SNACS ...... Single Nuclear Attack Case Study [*DoD*]
SNACS ...... Stock Number Assignment Control System [*Air Force*]   (AFM)
SNADIGC ... Sindacato Nazionale Dipendenti Ministero Grazia e Giustizia [*National Union of Ministry of Justice Employees*] [*Italy*]
SNAF........ Soviet Naval Air Force
SNAFU...... Situation Normal, All Fouled Up [*Military slang*] [*Bowdlerized version*]
SNAG .... Short Notes on Alaskan Geology. Alaska Department of Natural Resources. Geologic Report [*A publication*]
SNAG .... Society of North American Goldsmiths   (EA)
SNagg........ Serum Normal Agglutinator [*Hematology*]
SNAIAS .... Ship's Navigation and Aircraft Inertial Alignment System [*Navy*]   (NG)
SNAKE...... Stochastic Network Adaptive Kinematics Evaluator
SNAKE...... Super-Normal Attitude Kinetic Enhancement [*Later, Enhanced Fighter Maneuverability*] [*X-31 experimental aircraft under development by Rockwell International Corp. and Messerschmitt-Boelkow-Blohm GmbH*]
SNAME..... Society of Naval Architects and Marine Engineers   (EA)
SNaN........ Signaling Not a Number [*Computer programming*]   (BYTE)
SNANSC... Society of Neurosurgical Anesthesia and Neurological Supportive Care [*Later, SNACC*]   (EA)
SNA Nursery Res J South Nurserymen's Assoc ... SNA Nursery Research Journal. Southern Nurserymen's Association [*A publication*]
SNAP........ Sarawak National Party [*Malaysia*] [*Political party*]   (PPW)
SNAP........ Satellite Nuclear Auxiliary Power [*Military*]   (CAAL)
SNAP........ Selective Niobium Anodization Process [*Semiconductor technology*]
SNAP........ Senior Naval Aviator Present
SNAP........ Sensory Nerve Action Potential [*Neurophysiology*]
SNAP........ Sharp National Account Program [*Sharp Electronics Corp.*]
SNAP........ Shelter Neighborhood Action Project
SNAP........ Shielded Neutron Assay Probe [*Nuclear energy*]   (NRCH)
SNAP........ Shipboard Nontactical ADP [*Automatic Data Processing*] Program [*Navy*]   (CAAL)
SNAP........ Short Notice Annual Practice [*Military*]
SNAP........ Simplified Needs Assessment Profile System [*Developed by Texas Instruments, Inc.*]
SNAP........ Simplified Numerical Automatic Programmer [*Data processing*]
SNAP........ Single Number Access Plan [*Telecommunications*]   (TEL)
SNAP........ Six Node Averaging Program [*Data processing*]
SNAP........ Small Nuclear Adapted Power Source
SNAP........ Small Nuclear Auxiliary Power
snap........... Snapdragon [*Horticulture*]
SNAP........ Society of National Association Publications   (EA)
SNAP........ Soviet Nuclear Artillery Projectile   (MCD)
SNAP........ Space Nuclear Auxiliary Power
SNAP........ Special Needs Access Project [*Australia*]
SNAP........ Special Night Answer Position [*Telecommunications*]
SNAP........ Specifications for Non-Heat-Set Advertising Printing
SNAP........ Staffing Needs Assessment Process
SNAP........ Standard Navy Accounting Procedures
SNAP........ Standard Network Access Protocol [*Data processing*]
SNAP........ Static Nibble Access Path [*Data processing*]
SNAP........ Steerable Null Antenna Processor   (RDA)
SNAP........ Sterile Nitrogen Atmosphere Processing
SNAP........ Structural Network Analysis Program
SNAP........ Student Naval Aviation Pilot
SNAP........ Summary of Navy Approved Programs
SNAP........ Supersonic Nonequilibrium Analysis Program   (MCD)
SNAP........ Switching Network Analysis Program [*Bell System*]
SNAP........ System Network Activity Program [*Sperry UNIVAC*]
SNAP........ Systematic National Acquisitions Programme [*Public Archives of Canada*]
SNAP........ Systems for Nuclear Auxiliary Power
SNAP(G)... Student Naval Aviation Pilot (Glider)
SNCLAR... Standard Notes and Parts Selection   (TEL)
SNAPS ...... State and National Apprenticeship Program Statistics [*Bureau of Apprenticeship and Training*] [*Department of Labor*]
SNAPS ...... Switching Node and Processing Sites [*ITT*]   (TEL)
SNAPTRAN ... Systems for Nuclear Auxiliary Power Transient
SNARE...... Sandia Nuclear Assembly for Reactor Experiments
SNARL...... Suggested No Adverse Risk Levels [*Environmental Protection Agency*]
SNAS........ Student Need Analysis System
SNASE...... Sindacato Nazionale Autonomo Scuola Elementare [*Primary teachers association*] [*Italy*]   (EY)

SNASOR... Static Nonlinear Analysis of Shells of Revolution [*Computer program*]
SNAT........ Serotonin N-Acetyltransferase [*An enzyme*]
SNAT........ Southern National Corp. [*NASDAQ symbol*]   (NQ)
SNAV .... Sindacato Nazionale Attrazionisti Viaggianti [*National Union of Traveling Entertainers*] [*Italy*]
SNB .... Lakeland Library Region, North Battleford, Saskatchewan [*Library symbol*] [*National Library of Canada*]   (NLC)
SNB .... Scalene Node Biopsy [*Medicine*]
SNB .... Sella, Nasion, B [*Anthropometric landmark*]
SNB .... Sierra Nevada Batholith [*Geology*]
SNB .... Snake Bay [*Australia*] [*Airport symbol*]   (OAG)
SNB .... Soviet News Bureau
SNB .... Spinal Nucleus of the Bulbocavernosus [*Neuroanatomy*]
SNB .... Statutes of New Brunswick [*Database*] [*Department of Justice*] [*Information service or system*]   (CRD)
SNB .... Sunbird, Inc. D/B/A Sunbird Airlines, Inc. [*Murray, KY*] [*FAA designator*]   (FAAC)
SNB .... Swiss National Bank
SNBH .... Battleford Union Hospital Memorial Library, North Battleford, Saskatchewan [*Library symbol*] [*National Library of Canada*]   (BIB)
SNBK........ Summit National Bank [*NASDAQ symbol*]   (NQ)
SNBL........ Sioux City & New Orleans Barge Line [*AAR code*]
SNBNK .... Snowbank   (FAAC)
SNBR........ Snubber [*Mechanical engineering*]
SNBRTU... Screw, Nut, Bolt, and Rivet Trade Union [*British*]
SNBS .... Slovene National Benefit Society   (EA)
SNBU .... Switched Network Backup [*Data processing*]   (IBMDP)
SNC .... Apollo Airways, Inc. D/B/A Pacific Coast Airlines [*Goleta, CA*] [*FAA designator*]   (FAAC)
SNC .... Saint Norbert College [*Wisconsin*]
SNC .... San Antonio College, San Antonio, TX [*OCLC symbol*]   (OCLC)
SNC .... San Nicolas Island [*California*] [*Seismograph station code, US Geological Survey*] [*Closed*]   (SEIS)
SNC .... Sanitary Corps [*Army*]
snc .... Saskatchewan [*MARC country of publication code*] [*Library of Congress*]   (LCCP)
SNC .... Satellite News Channel [*Cable-television system*] [*Went off the air October, 1983*]
S/NC........ Satisfactory/No Credit [*University grading system*]
SNC .... School of Naval Co-Operation [*Air Force*] [*British*]
SNC .... Scottish National Certificate
SNC .... Shawmut National Corp. [*NYSE symbol*]   (SPSG)
SNC .... Shergotty [*India*], Nakhla [*Egypt*], and Chassigny [*French*] [*Pronounced "snick"*] [*Classification for a group of meteorites recovered from these sites*]
SNC .... Shipped Not Credited [*Military*]   (AFIT)
SNC .... Skilled Nursing Care
SNC .... Standard Navigation Computer
SNC .... Submarine Net Controller   (MCD)
SNC .... Sunatco Development Corp. [*Vancouver Stock Exchange symbol*]
SNC .... Supreme National Council [*Cambodia*]   (ECON)
SNC .... Swiss Nonvaleurs Club [*Later, Scripophila Helvetica - SH*]   (EAIO)
SNC .... Syndicat National du Cinema [*National Syndicate of Motion Pictures*]
SNCA .... Seneca Oil Co. [*NASDAQ symbol*]   (NQ)
SNCC........ Student National Coordinating Committee [*Pronounced "snick"*]   (EA)
SNCC........ System Network Computer Center [*Louisiana State University*] [*Research center*]   (RCD)
SNCCDIPP ... Selected Non-Communist Countries Defense Intelligence Projection for Planning   (MCD)
S$NCD ...... Singapore Dollar Negotiable Certificate of Deposit
SNCF........ Societe Nationale des Chemins de Fer Francais [*French National Railways*]
SNCFA ...... Societe Nationale des Chemins de Fer Algeriens [*Algerian Railways*]
SNCI......... Societe Nationale de Credit a l'Industrie [*National Industrial Credit Society*] [*Belgium*]   (GEA)
SNCI......... Societe Nationale de Credit et d'Investissement [*Credit institution*] [*Luxembourg*]   (EY)
SN-CIE...... Statement of Need - Clothing and Individual Equipment [*Military*]
SNCL........ Serial Number Configuration List   (MCD)
SNCL........ Serial Number Conversion List
SNCLAR... University of Santa Clara School of Law   (DLA)
SNCLF ...... Societe de Neuro-Chirurgie de Langue Francaise [*Society of French-Speaking Neurosurgeons - SFSN*]   (EA)
SNCM .... Second Nicaraguan Campaign Medal
SNCO .... Seaport Navigation Co. [*AAR code*]
SNCO .... Senior Noncommissioned Officer
SNCO .... Sensor Control Corp. [*NASDAQ symbol*]   (NQ)
SNCO .... Staff Noncommissioned Officer [*Military*]
SNCOC ...... Senior Noncommissioned Officer Course
SNCP........ Salem National Corporation [*NASDAQ symbol*]   (NQ)
SNCP........ Special Navy Control Program   (MCD)
SNCR........ Selective Noncatalytic Reduction [*Combustion technology*]

SND........... San Diego - College [*California*] [*Seismograph station code, US Geological Survey*] (SEIS)
SND........... Sand (FAAC)
SND........... Sanford, FL [*Location identifier*] [*FAA*] (FAAL)
SND........... Sanfred Resources [*Vancouver Stock Exchange symbol*]
SND........... Sap No Defect
SND........... Scottish National Dictionary [*A publication*]
SND........... Scottish National Diploma
SND........... Second Class Passengers [*Shipping*] [*British*]
SND........... Selected Natural Diamond
SND........... Self-Powered Neutron Detector
SND........... Semiconductor Neutron Dosimeter
snd............. Sindhi [*MARC language code*] [*Library of Congress*] (LCCP)
SND........... Sisters of Notre Dame [*Roman Catholic religious order*]
SND........... Sisters of Notre Dame de Namur [*Roman Catholic religious order*]
SND........... Society of Newspaper Design (EA)
SND........... Sound (AAG)
SND........... Standardized Normal Distribution
SND........... Static No Delivery
SNDA........ Scottish National Dictionary Association
SNDA........ Student National Dental Association (EA)
SNDC........ Sand Technology Systems International, Inc. [*NASDAQ symbol*] (NQ)
SNDC........ Serbian National Defense Council (EA)
SNDG........ Sending (MSA)
SNDG........ Sounding (MSA)
SNDL........ Sandale R. R. [*AAR code*]
SNDL........ Standard Navy Distribution List
SNDL........ Studienausgaben zur Neueren Deutschen Literatur [*A publication*]
SNDLF...... Societe de Nutrition et de Dietetique de Langue Francaise [*French-Language Society of Nutrition and Dietetics - FLSND*] (EAIO)
SND-MB ... Selected Natural Diamond - Metal Bond
SNDN........ Sisters of Notre Dame de Namur [*Roman Catholic religious order*] [*Rome, Italy*] (EAIO)
SNDO........ Standard Nomenclature of Diseases and Operations [*Medicine*]
SNDPRF ... Soundproof (MSA)
SNDR........ Shimane Daigaku Ronshu: Jinbun Kagaku [*Journal of the Shimane University: Humanistic Sciences*] [*A publication*]
SNDS......... [*The*] Sands Regent [*Reno, NV*] [*NASDAQ symbol*] (NQ)
SNDS......... Stock Number Data Section (MCD)
SNDSB....... Sonderschule [*A publication*]
SNDT........ Shreemati Nathibai Domodar Thackersey Women's University [*India*]
SNDT........ Society for Nondestructive Testing [*Later, ASNT*] (KSC)
SNDT........ SunGard Data Systems, Inc. [*Wayne, PA*] [*NASDAQ symbol*] (NQ)
SNDV........ Strategic Nuclear Delivery Vehicle [*Army*] (AABC)
SNE........... Santa Elena, TX [*Location identifier*] [*FAA*] (FAAL)
SNE........... Sao Nicolau [*Cape Verde Islands*] [*Airport symbol*] (OAG)
SNE........... Severe Noise Environment
SNE........... Shawnee Airlines [*Orlando, FL*] [*FAA designator*] (FAAC)
SNE........... Society for Nutrition Education (EA)
SNE........... Sony Corp. America [*NYSE symbol*] [*Toronto Stock Exchange symbol*] [*Vancouver Stock Exchange symbol*] (SPSG)
SNE........... Spatial Nonemotional (Stimuli)
SNE........... Subacute Necrotizing Encephalomyelopathy [*Medicine*]
SNE........... Syndicat National de l'Edition [*French publishers' association*]
SNEA........ Societe Nationale ELF Aquitaine [*National ELF Aquitaine Company*] [*Information service or system*] (IID)
SNEA........ Student National Education Association (EA)
SNEC......... Saxton Nuclear Engineering Corporation
SNECI....... Sindicato Nacional dos Empregados do Comercio e da Industria da Provincia de Mocambique [*National Union of Commercial and Industrial Workers of Mozambique*]
SNECIPA ... Sindicato Nacional dos Empregados do Comercio e da Industria da Provincia de Angola [*National Syndicate of Workers of Commerce and Industry of the Province of Angola*]
SNECMA ... Societe Nationale d'Etude et de Construction de Moteurs d'Avion [*France*] (EY)
Sneed.......... Sneed's Kentucky Decisions [*2 Kentucky*] [*A publication*] (DLA)
Sneed.......... Sneed's Tennessee Reports [*33-37 Tennessee*] [*A publication*] (DLA)
Sneed Dec .. Sneed's Kentucky Decisions [*2 Kentucky*] [*A publication*] (DLA)
Sneed Tenn ... Sneed's Tennessee Reports [*A publication*] (DLA)
Sneed (Tenn) Rep ... Sneed's Tennessee Reports [*A publication*] (DLA)
SNEFU...... Situation Normal - Everything Fouled Up [*Bowdlerized version*] [*Obsolete*] (DSUE)
SNEG .... Syndicat National des Enseignants de Guinee [*National Union of Guinean Teachers*]
SNEI......... Societe Nouvelle d'Editions pour l'Industrie [*Industrial News Publishing Company*] (IID)
SNEIA....... Sbornik Nauchnykh Trudov Ivanovskogo Energeticheskogo Instituta [*A publication*]
SNEIL .... Secretariat for the Nordic Energy Information Libraries (EISS)
SNEL......... Snelling and Snelling, Inc. [*NASDAQ symbol*] (NQ)
SNEL......... Societe Nationale d'Electricite

SNEL......... Special Nuclear Effects Laboratory
Snell Eq..... Snell's Principles in Equity [*A publication*] (DLA)
SNELPIF .. Sindacato Nazionale Esperti Laureati Propagandisti Industrie Farmaceutiche [*National Union of University Graduated Experts for Propaganda in Pharmaceutical Industries*] [*Italy*]
SNEMSA .. Southern New England Marine Sciences Association
SNEPT ...... Space Nuclear Electric Propulsion Test
SNERA...... Statistica Neerlandica [*A publication*]
SNES......... Syndicat National de l'Enseignement Secondaire [*National Union of Secondary Schoolteachers*] [*France*]
SNET......... Southern New England Telecommunications Corp. [*New Haven, CT*] (TSSD)
SNET......... Syndicat National de l'Enseignement Technique [*National Union of Technical School Teachers*] [*France*]
S New........ Sidney Newsletter [*A publication*]
SNF........... Secret - No Foreigners [*Security classification*]
SNF........... Selskab foer Nordisk Filologi Arsberetning [*A publication*]
SNF........... Serb National Federation (EA)
SNF........... Short-Range Nuclear Forces
SNF........... Silicon Nitride Film
SNF........... Skilled Nursing Facility
SNF........... Solids Not Fat
SNF........... Spain Fund [*NYSE symbol*] (SPSG)
SNF........... Spent Nuclear Fuel
SNF........... Spot Noise Figure
SNF........... Sudanese National Front [*Political party*] (PD)
SNF........... System Noise Figure
SNFCC...... Shippers National Freight Claim Council [*Later, TCPC*] (EA)
SNFL......... Standing Naval Force, Atlantic (MCD)
SNFLD...... Secret - Limited Distribution - Not Releasable to Foreigners [*Security classification*]
SNFLK...... Snowflake (FAAC)
SNFO .... Student Naval Flight Officer
SNFPP...... Syndicat National de la Fonction Publique Provinciale [*National Union of Provincial Government Employees - NUPGE*] [*Canada*]
SNFR......... Small-Probe Net Flux Radiometer [*NASA*]
SNFRC...... Seattle National Fisheries Research Center [*Seattle, WA*] [*Department of the Interior*] (GRD)
SNFS......... Second National Federal Savings Bank [*NASDAQ symbol*] (NQ)
SNFS......... Student Naval Flight Surgeon
SNFU......... Scottish National Farmers' Union
SNG .... San Ignacio De Velasco [*Bolivia*] [*Airport symbol*] (OAG)
SNG .... Sans Notre Garantie [*Without Our Guarantee*] [*French*] [*Business term*]
SNG .... Solidified Nitroglycerol [*or Nitroglycerin*] [*Explosive*]
SNG .... Songkhla [*Thailand*] [*Seismograph station code, US Geological Survey*] (SEIS)
SNG .... Southern New England Telecommunications Corp. [*NYSE symbol*] (SPSG)
SNG .... Stabilization Network Group
SNG .... Sterling Energy Corp. [*Vancouver Stock Exchange symbol*]
SNG .... Substitute [*or Synthetic*] Natural Gas
Sng .... Synagogue (BJA)
SNG .... Synthetic Natural Gas (IEEE)
SNGA .... Sodium N-Glycoloylarsanilic [*or N-Glycolylarsanilic*] Acid [*Pharmacology*]
SNGFR...... Single Nephron Glomerular Filtration Rate
SNGL......... Single
SNGN........ Segmental Necrotizing Glomerulonephritis [*Medicine*]
SNGOD..... Special NGO [*Nongovernmental Organization*] Committee on Disarmament (EA)
SNGRA ..... Sangre [*A publication*]
SNGS......... Salem Nuclear Generating Station (NRCH)
SNH......... Savannah, TN [*Location identifier*] [*FAA*] (FAAL)
SNH......... Signtech, Inc. [*Toronto Stock Exchange symbol*]
snh............. Sinhalese [*MARC language code*] [*Library of Congress*] (LCCP)
SNH......... Skilled Nursing Home
SNH......... Snatch [*Block*] [*Design engineering*]
SNH......... Society for Nursing History (EA)
SNH......... South Nottinghamshire Hussars [*British military*] (DMA)
SNH......... Sunshine Point [*Alaska*] [*Seismograph station code, US Geological Survey*] (SEIS)
SNHA........ Shenandoah Natural History Association (EA)
SNI .... National Intelligence Service [*Zaire*] (PD)
SNI .... San Nicolas Island
SNI .... Selective Notification of Information
SNI .... Sequence Number Indicator
SNI .... Signal-to-Noise Improvement [*Data transmission*] (IEEE)
SNI .... Sinoe [*Liberia*] [*Airport symbol*] (OAG)
SNI .... Sistema Nacional de Informacion [*National Information System*] [*Colombia*] (IID)
SNI .... Sonor Investments Ltd. [*Toronto Stock Exchange symbol*]
SNI .... Sports Network, Incorporated [*Later, HSN*]
SNI .... Staatsblad Nederlands-Indie [*A publication*]
SNI .... Standard Network Interconnection [*Telecommunications*]
SNI .... Sun City Industries, Inc. [*AMEX symbol*] (SPSG)

SNI .... Syndicat National des Instituteurs [*National Union of Teachers*] [*France*]
SNIACE .... Sociedad Nacional Industrias Aplicaciones Celulosa Espanola SA [*Spanish*]
SNIA VISCOSA ... Societa Nazionale Industria Applicazioni Viscosa SpA [*Spanish*]
SNIC .... Sigmatron Nova, Inc. [*NASDAQ symbol*]   (NQ)
SNIC Bull ... SNIC [*Singapore National Institute of Chemistry*] Bulletin [*A publication*]
SNIE .... Sindacato Nazionale Insegnanti Elementari [*National Union of Elementary Teachers*] [*Italy*]
SNIE's .... Special National Intelligence Estimates [*Summaries of foreign policy information and advice prepared for the president*] [*Known informally as "sneeze"*]
SNIF .... Short-Term Note-Issuance Facility [*Banking*]
SNIF .... Site-Specific Natural Isotope Fractionation [*Analytical chemistry*]
SNIF .... Standby Note Issuance Facility [*Finance*]
SNIF .... Syndicated Note-Issuance Facility [*Banking*]   (ADA)
SNIFFEX .. Sniffer [*Exhaust trail indicator*] Exercise [*Military*]   (NVT)
SNIFTIRS ... Subtractively Normalized Interfacial FTIR [*Fourier Transform Infrared*] Spectroscopy
SNIMOG .. Sustained Noninflationary Market-Oriented Growth
SNIP .... Single Net Information and Position [*Reporting procedures*] [*Navy*]   (NVT)
SNIP .... Single Net Integrated Procedure [*Military*]   (CAAL)
SNIPE .... SDI [*Strategic Defense Initiative*] Network Interface Processor Engine   (SDI)
SNIPE .... Soviet Naval Interdiction Possibilities, Europe
SNIR .... Signal-to-Noise Plus Interference Ratio
SNIRD ...... Supposedly Noiseless Infrared Detector
SNIT .... Stock Number Identification Table
SNIVT .... Society of Non-Invasive Vascular Technology   (EA)
SNJ .... Everett, WA [*Location identifier*] [*FAA*]   (FAAL)
SNJ .... Sinj [*Yugoslavia*] [*Seismograph station code, US Geological Survey*] [*Closed*]   (SEIS)
SNJM .... Sisters of the Holy Names of Jesus and Mary [*Roman Catholic religious order*]
SNK .... Shannock Corp. [*Vancouver Stock Exchange symbol*]
SNK .... Snyder, TX [*Location identifier*] [*FAA*]   (FAAL)
SNK .... Student-Newman-Keuls [*Statistical procedure*]
SNK .... Swank, Inc. [*NYSE symbol*]   (SPSG)
SNKI .... Swank, Inc. [*NASDAQ symbol*]   (NQ)
SNKL........ Snorkel   (MSA)
SNKORL... Subject to No Known or Reported Losses [*Insurance*]   (AIA)
SNL .... Department of State. Newsletter [*A publication*]
SNL .... Sample Noise Level
SNL .... Sandia National Laboratories [*Department of Energy*] [*Albuquerque, NM*]   (GRD)
SNL .... Satire Newsletter [*A publication*]
SNL .... Saturday Night Live [*Television program*]
SNL .... Selected Nodes List [*Telecommunications*]   (TEL)
SNL .... Seminole Resources, Inc. [*Vancouver Stock Exchange symbol*]
SNL .... Sevenhill [*Australia*] [*Seismograph station code, US Geological Survey*] [*Closed*]   (SEIS)
SNL .... Shakespeare Newsletter [*A publication*]
SNL .... Shawnee, OK [*Location identifier*] [*FAA*]   (FAAL)
SNL .... Snout Length [*Pisciculture*]
SNL .... Somali National League
SNL .... Soonair Lines, Inc. [*Tulsa, OK*] [*FAA designator*]   (FAAC)
SNL .... Spore Newsletter [*A publication*]
SNL .... Standard Name Line [*Military*]
SNL .... Standard Nomenclature List [*Military*]
SNL .... State Narcotic Law
SNL .... Stock Not Listed   (AAG)
SNLA .... Sandia National Laboratory (Albuquerque)
SNLC........ Senior NATO Logistician Conference   (NATG)
SNLC........ Service National des Liberations Conditionnelles [*Canada*]
SNLF........ SNL Financial Corp. [*NASDAQ symbol*]   (NQ)
SNLG........ Signaling   (MSA)
SNLN .... Saskatchewan Native Library Services Newsletter [*A publication*]
SNLR........ Services No Longer Required
SNLS .... Society for New Language Study   (EA)
SNLT........ Sunlite, Inc. [*NASDAQ symbol*]   (NQ)
SNLV........ Strategic Nuclear Launch Vehicle
SNM .... Saint Mary's University, San Antonio, TX [*OCLC symbol*]   (OCLC)
SNM .... Satellite Navigation Map
SNM .... Sbornik Narodniho Muzea [*A publication*]
SNM .... Senior Naval Member
SNM .... Signal-to-Noise Merit
SNM .... Sindacato Nazionale Medici [*Doctors association*] [*Italy*]   (EY)
SNM .... Society of Nuclear Medicine   (EA)
SNM .... Socorro [*New Mexico*] [*Seismograph station code, US Geological Survey*]   (SEIS)
SNM .... Somali National Movement [*Political party*]   (PD)
SNM .... Special Nuclear Material
SNM .... Spent Nuclear Material   (IEEE)
SNM .... Square Nautical Mile   (NVT)
SNM .... Subject Named Member   (NVT)

SNM .... Sulfanilamide [*Antimicrobial compound*]
SNM .... Sunmask Petroleum [*Vancouver Stock Exchange symbol*]
SNMA .... Sonoma Vineyards [*NASDAQ symbol*]   (NQ)
SNMA .... Student National Medical Association   (EA)
SNMAD .... Southwest Bulletin [*A publication*]
SNMCB..... Scheduled Not Mission Capable Both [*Maintenance and supply*]   (MCD)
SNMCM ... Scheduled Not Mission Capable Maintenance   (MCD)
SNMD .... Sunrise Medical, Inc. [*NASDAQ symbol*]   (NQ)
SNMDCS ... Standard Navy Maintenance Data Collection System
SNMMMIS ... Standard Navy Maintenance and Material Management Information System
SNMMMS ... Standard Navy Maintenance and Material Management System
SNMP....... Simple Network Management Protocol [*Data processing*]
SNMP....... Spent Nuclear Material Pool   (IEEE)
SNMPAM ... Acta Musei Nationalis Pragae. Series B. Historia Naturalis [*A publication*]
SNMS........ Secondary Neutrals Mass Spectrometry
SNMS........ Sputtered Neutral Mass Spectrometry [*Surface analysis*]
SNMT .... Society of Nuclear Medical Technologists [*Defunct*]   (EA)
SNN .... Sha Na Na   (EA)
SNN .... Shannon [*Ireland*] [*Airport symbol*]   (OAG)
SNN .... Shared Nearest Neighbor   (MCD)
SNN .... Sienna Resources Ltd. [*Toronto Stock Exchange symbol*]
SNN .... Sining [*Republic of China*] [*Seismograph station code, US Geological Survey*]   (SEIS)
SNN .... Smith College, Northampton, MA [*OCLC symbol*]   (OCLC)
SNN .... Structure-Nomenclature Notation [*Chemistry*]
SNNG .... Schakels Nederlands Nieuw Guinea [*A publication*]
SNNSB3... Food Irradiation [*Japan*] [*A publication*]
SNNTS ...... Studies in the Novel. North Texas State University [*A publication*]
SNO .... Polaris Industries Partners LP [*AMEX symbol*]   (SPSG)
SNO .... Semiempirical Natural Orbital [*Physical chemistry*]
SNO .... Senior Naval Officer
SNO .... Senior Navigation Officer [*Air Force*] [*British*]
SNO .... Senior Nursing Officer [*British*]
SNO .... Serial Number   (MDG)
SNO .... Special Naval Operations   (NVT)
SNO .... Stock Number   (MSA)
SNO .... Sudbury Neutrino Observatory [*Proposed joint US-Canadian project*]
Sno .... Thioinosine [*Also, SIno, M*] [*A nucleoside*]
SNOAD ..... Senior Naval Officer Adriatic [*British*]
SNOB .... Senior Naval Officer on Board
S Nob .... Sine Nobilitate [*Without Nobility*] [*Notation used at Oxford University to indicate that a student was untitled. This abbreviation is claimed to have acquired its present connotation when commoners at the university put on more airs than did their titled counterparts*] [*Latin*]
SNOBOL... String-Oriented Symbolic Language [*1963*] [*Data processing*]
SNODO..... Standard Nomenclature of Diseases and Operations [*Medicine*]   (DHSM)
SNOE .... Smart Noise Equipment [*RADAR jammer*] [*Air Force*]
SNoF......... Studier i Nordisk Filologi [*A publication*]
SNOINCR ... Snow Depth Increase in Past Hour [*Meteorology*]   (FAAC)
SNOK .... Secondary Next of Kin [*Army*]   (AABC)
SNOL .... Senior Naval Officer, Landings [*British*]
SNOMed ... Systematized Nomenclature of Medicine
SNOO .... Small Nonoverlapping Offset [*Oceanography*]
SNOOP ..... Students Naturally Opposed to Outrageous Prying [*Student legal action organization*]   (EA)
SNOOPE... System for Nuclear Observation of Possible Explosives [*Science Applications International Corp.*] [*Aviation*]
SNOOPI.... System Network Online Operations Information [*Suggested name for the Library of Congress computer system*]
SNOP .... Senior Naval Officer Present
SNOP .... Standard Nomenclature of Pathology [*College of American Pathologists*]
SNOP .... Systematized Nomenclature of Pathology [*NCI*]
SNOPG ..... Senior Naval Officer, Persian Gulf [*British military*]   (DMA)
SNORE ..... Self-Noise Reduction
SNORE ..... Signal-to-Noise Ratio Estimator
SNORKEX ... Snorkel Detection Exercise [*Military*]   (NVT)
SNORT ..... Supersonic Naval Ordnance Research Track [*China Lake, CA*]
SNOS .... Scottish National Orchestra Society
SNOTEL... Snow Survey Telemetry Network [*Department of Agriculture*]
SNov .... Seara Nova [*A publication*]
S Nov .... Studi Novecenteschi [*A publication*]
SNovel ...... Studies in the Novel [*A publication*]
Snow.......... Snow's Reports [*3 Utah*] [*A publication*]   (DLA)
SNOW....... Standard Normal Ocean Water
SNOWCAT ... Support of Nuclear Operations with Conventional Air Tactics   (NATG)
SNOWFLEX ... Field Exercise under Snow Conditions [*Military*]   (NVT)
SNOWI ..... Senior Naval Officer, West Indies [*British*]
Snow Revel .. Snow Revelry [*A publication*]   (APTA)
SNOW TIME ... SAC-NORAD [*Strategic Air Command - North American Air Defense*] Operational Weapons Test Involving Military Electronics

SNP .... St. Paul Island [*Alaska*] [*Airport symbol*] (OAG)
SNP .... St. Paul Island, AK [*Location identifier*] [*FAA*] (FAAL)
S-N-P........ Salt and Pepa [*Rap recording group*]
SNP .... Samnordisk Planteforedling [*Internordic plant breeding*] [*An association*] (EAIO)
SNP .... School Nurse Practitioner
SNP .... Scottish National Party [*Political party*] (PPW)
SNP .... Skagit Nuclear Project (NRCH)
SNP .... Society for Natural Philosophy (EA)
SNP .... Sodium Nitroprusside [*A vasodilator*]
SNP .... Soluble Nucleoprotein
SNP .... Sonepat [*India*] [*Seismograph station code, US Geological Survey*] [*Closed*] (SEIS)
SNP .... Space Nuclear Propulsion
SNP .... Statistical Network Processor
SNP .... Studia Neophilologica [*A publication*]
SNP .... Suspected, Not Proved
SNP .... Synchro Null Pulse
SNP .... Synchronous Network Processor
SNP .... System Network Processor
SNPA .... Southern Newspaper Publishers Association
SNPh .... Studia Neophilologica [*A publication*]
SNPJ .... Slovene National Benefit Society (EA)
SNPM....... Standard and Nuclear Propulsion Module
SNPMA..... Student National Podiatric Medical Association (EA)
SNPO .... Society for Nonprofit Organizations (EA)
SNPO .... Space Nuclear Propulsion Office [*Later, Division of Space Nuclear Systems, of Energy Research and Development Administration*] [*AEC-NASA*]
SNPOA ..... Space Nuclear Propulsion Office, Albuquerque [*See SNPO*]
SNPOC..... Space Nuclear Propulsion Office, Cleveland [*See SNPO*]
SNPON ..... Space Nuclear Propulsion Office, Nevada [*See SNPO*]
SNPP .... Sequoyah Nuclear Power Plant (NRCH)
SNPR........ Screen Print (AAG)
SNPRI ...... Selected Nonpriority List Item [*Military*]
SNPS .... Shoreham Nuclear Power Station (NRCH)
SNPX........ SynOptics Communications, Inc. [*NASDAQ symbol*] (CTT)
SNQ.......... Scottish Notes and Queries [*A publication*]
SNQ.......... Sea-1 Aquafarms Ltd. [*Vancouver Stock Exchange symbol*]
SNQ.......... Sussex Notes and Queries [*A publication*]
SNR .... Saint Nazaire [*France*] [*Airport symbol*] (OAG)
SNR .... Schaffner Ranch [*California*] [*Seismograph station code, US Geological Survey*] (SEIS)
SNR .... Schenectady Naval Reactors Office [*Energy Research and Development Administration*]
SNR .... Schweizerische Numismatische Rundschau [*A publication*]
SNR .... Selective Noncatalytic Reduction [*Combustion technology*]
SNR .... Senior
SNR .... Senior National Representatives SONAR [*Four Power Army*] (MCD)
SNR .... Senor [*Mister*] [*Spanish*]
SNR .... Service Not Required
SNR .... Signal-to-Noise Ratio
SNR .... Slow Neutron Reactor [*Nuclear energy*] (NRCH)
SNR .... SONAR
SNr .... Substantia Nigra Pars Reticulata [*Brain anatomy*]
SNR .... Sudan Notes and Records [*A publication*]
SNR .... Supernova Remnant [*Astronomy*]
SNR .... Supplier Nonconformance Report [*Nuclear energy*] (NRCH)
SNRA .... Sawtooth National Recreation Area [*Idaho*]
SNRA .... Senora [*Mrs.*] [*Spanish*]
SNRAFU... Situation Normal, Really All Fouled Up [*Military slang*] [*Bowdlerized version*]
SNRC........ Sudanese National Research Council
SNRG .... Scientific NRG, Inc. [*NASDAQ symbol*] (NQ)
SNRLTCS ... Skilled Nursing and Related Long Term Care Services (EA)
snRNA ...... Ribonucleic Acid, Small Nuclear [*Biochemistry, genetics*]
snRNP ...... Ribonucleoprotein, Small Nuclear [*Biochemistry*]
SNRS........ Sunrise [*Meteorology*] (FAAC)
SNRS........ Sunrise Technologies, Inc. [*NASDAQ symbol*] (NQ)
SNRSA ...... Sunrise Savings & Loan Association of Florida Cl A [*NASDAQ symbol*] (NQ)
SNRT........ Sinus Node Recovery Time [*Cardiology*]
SNRTC...... Sinus Node Recovery Time Corrected [*Cardiology*]
SNRU .... Sunair Electronics, Inc. [*Fort Lauderdale, FL*] [*NASDAQ symbol*] (NQ)
SNS........... Salinas, CA [*Location identifier*] [*FAA*] (FAAL)
SNS.......... Samarbeidsnemden for Nordisk Skogforskning [*Nordic Forest Research Cooperation Committee - NFRCC*] (EAIO)
SNS........... San Onofre [*California*] [*Seismograph station code, US Geological Survey*] (SEIS)
SNS........... Scandinavian Neurosurgical Society (EA)
SNS........... Seabrook Nuclear Station (NRCH)
SNS........... Senior Nursing Sister [*Navy*] [*British*]
SNS........... Sensorstat System [*Vancouver Stock Exchange symbol*]
SNS........... Service National des Sauveteurs [*Canada*]
SNS........... Simulated Network Simulations (KSC)
SNS........... Skyline Network Service [*Satellite Business Systems*] [*McLean, VA*] [*Telecommunications*] (TSSD)
SNS........... Slovo na Storozi [*A publication*]
SNS........... Small Nuclear Stage (KSC)

SNS........... Society of Neurological Surgeons (EA)
SNS........... Somatic Nervous System
SNS........... Space Nuclear System
SNS........... Spallation Neutron Source
SNS........... Spanish Economic News Service [*A publication*]
SNS........... Special Night Squads [*Palestine*] (BJA)
SNS........... Stabilized Night Sight
SNS........... Sundstrand Corp. [*NYSE symbol*] (SPSG)
SN/SC ...... Sympathetic Nervous System [*Physiology*]
SN/SC ...... Stock Number Source Code (MCD)
SNSCNY .. St. Nicholas Society of the City of New York (EA)
SNSE .... Society of Nuclear Scientists and Engineers [*Defunct*]
SNSH .... Snow Showers [*Meteorology*]
SNSL .... Standard Navy Stock List
SNSL .... Stock Number Sequence Listing (MSA)
SNSM........ Sindacato Nazionale Scuola Media [*National Union of Intermediate School Teachers*] [*Italy*]
SNSN........ Standard Navy Stock Number
SNSO .... Space Nuclear Systems Office [*AEC/NASA*]
SNSO .... Superintending Naval Stores Officer [*British military*] (DMA)
SNSR........ Sensor (AAG)
SNSR........ Sensormatic Electronics Corp. [*NASDAQ symbol*] (NQ)
SNSS .... School Natural Science Society [*British*]
SNSS .... Skrifter Utgivna. Namnden foer Svensk Sprakvard [*A publication*]
SNST .... Sonesta International Hotels Corp. [*NASDAQ symbol*] (NQ)
SNST .... Sunset [*Meteorology*] (FAAC)
SNT .... Saint
SNT .... [*The*] Scrolls and the New Testament [*K. Stendahl*] [*A publication*] (BJA)
SNT .... Sealant [*Technical drawings*]
SNT .... Sears Point [*California*] [*Seismograph station code, US Geological Survey*] (SEIS)
SNT .... Selective Nuclear Transfer
SNT .... Silicon Needle Transducer
SNT .... Sindacato Nazionale Tabacchine [*National Union of Women Tobacco Workers*] [*Italy*]
SNT .... Single Negotiating Text [*UN Law of the Sea Conference*]
SNT .... Society for Nondestructive Testing [*Later, ASNT*] (EA)
SNT .... Sonat, Inc. [*NYSE symbol*] (SPSG)
SNT .... Supplements. Novum Testamentum [*Leiden*] [*A publication*]
SNT .... System Noise Temperature
SNTA........ Sodium Nitrilotriacetate
SNTA........ Syndicat National des Transporteurs Aeriens [*Airlines association*] [*France*] (EY)
SNTC........ Syndicat National des Transporteurs de Cameroun [*National Union of Cameroonese Transportation Workers*]
SNTC........ Syndicat National des Travailleurs Congolais [*National Union of Congolese Workers*] [*Leopoldville*]
SNTC........ Synetic, Inc. [*NASDAQ symbol*] (NQ)
SNTCC....... Simplified Neutron Transport Computer Code
SNTCDL... INTA [*Instituto Nacional de Tecnologia Agropecuaria*] Estacion Experimental Agropecuaria Concordia. Serie Notas Tecnicas [*A publication*]
SNTE........ Santec Corp. [*NASDAQ symbol*] (NQ)
SNTF........ Special Navy Task Force (MUGU)
SNTFC ...... Special Navy Task Force Commander
SNTF(SMS) ... Special Navy Task Force for Surface Missile Systems (MUGU)
SNTK........ Senetek PLC [*NASDAQ symbol*] (NQ)
SNTO .... Swiss National Tourist Office (EA)
SNTPC...... Scottish National Town Planning Council (DAS)
SNTR........ Sinter [*Metallurgy*]
SNTS .... Short-Length, Nonbuoyant Torpedo System
SNTS .... Society for New Testament Study [*Exeter, Devonshire, England*] (EA)
SNTSB ...... Studiorum Novi Testamenti Societas. Bulletin [*A publication*]
SNTSMS... Studiorum Novi Testamenti Societas. Monograph Series [*A publication*]
SNTZD...... Sensitized (MSA)
SNTZG...... Sensitizing (MSA)
SNu.......... Sifre on Numbers (BJA)
SNU.......... SNC Group, Inc. [*Toronto Stock Exchange symbol*]
SNU.......... Solar Neutrino Unit [*Astrophysics*]
SNU.......... Somali National Union
SNUB .... Show Nothing Unless Bad
SNUCD...... Software Newsletter [*A publication*]
SNUD....... Stock Number User Directory [*Air Force*] (AFM)
SNUJ........ Singapore National Union of Journalists
SNUPPS... Standardized Nuclear Unit Power Plant System [*Nuclear reactor combine*]
SNUR .... Significant New Use Rules [*Environmental Protection Agency*]
SNURP..... Small Nuclear Ribonucleoprotein Particle [*Genetics*]
SNV .... Santa Elena [*Venezuela*] [*Airport symbol*] (OAG)
SNV .... Spleen Necrosis Virus
SNV .... Statens Naturvardsverk [*National Environmental Protection Board*] [*Information service or system*] (IID)
SNV .... Suneva Resources [*Vancouver Stock Exchange symbol*]
SNV .... Synovus Financial Corp. [*NYSE symbol*] (SPSG)
SNV .... Systema Nervosum Vegetativo [*Obsolete term for the autonomic nervous system*] [*Medicine*]

SNVAO	Skrifter Utgitt. Det Norske Videnskaps-Akademi i Oslo [*A publication*]
SNVB	Society for Northwestern Vertebrate Biology (EA)
SNVKB	Sbornik Nauchnykh Rabot Voenno-Meditsinskogo Fakul'teta Kuibyshevskogo Meditsinskogo Instituta [*A publication*]
SNVO	Skrifter. Norske Videnskaps-Akademi i Oslo [*A publication*]
SNVPP	Simulated Night Vertical Pinpoint
SNVT	Short No-Voltage Tester [*Ground surveillance RADAR system*] (MCD)
SNW	Sandoway [*Burma*] [*Airport symbol*] (OAG)
SNW	Schip en Werf. Tijdschrift Gewijd aan Scheepsbouw en Werktuigbouw, Elektrotechniek, Scheepvaart, en Aanverwante Vakken [*A publication*]
S/Nw	Signal-to-Noise, Weighted
SNW	Snow [*Meteorology*] (FAAC)
SNW	Snowwater Resources Ltd. [*Vancouver Stock Exchange symbol*]
SNW	Stanwood Corp. [*AMEX symbol*] (SPSG)
SNW	Strategic Nuclear Weapon
SNW	Sun West Airlines [*Scottsdale, AZ*] [*FAA designator*] (FAAC)
Sn & W Ch ...	Snow and Winstanley's Chancery Practice [*A publication*] (DLA)
SNWFL	Snowfall (FAAC)
SNWS	Shipboard Nuclear Weapon Security [*Navy*] (CAAL)
SNWT	Snowshoe. Newsletter. NWT [*Northwest Territories, Canada*] Library Association [*A publication*]
SNWTH	Sources for NWT [*Northwest Territory*] History. Prince of Wales Northern Heritage Centre [*Canada*] [*A publication*]
SNX	Sunburst Exploration Ltd. [*Toronto Stock Exchange symbol*]
SNY	Sidney [*Nebraska*] [*Airport symbol*] (OAG)
SNY	Snyder Oil Corp. [*NYSE symbol*] (SPSG)
SNY	Southern New York Railway [*AAR code*]
SNY	Spanish Navy
SNY	Sunny (MSA)
SNYC	South Nottinghamshire Yeomanry Cavalry [*British military*] (DMA)
Snyder Mines ...	Snyder on Mines and Mining [*A publication*] (DLA)
SNYK	Security New York State Corp. [*NASDAQ symbol*] (NQ)
Sny Not Man ...	Snyder's Notaries' and Commissioners' Manual [*A publication*] (DLA)
Sny Rel Corp ...	Snyder on Religious Corporations [*A publication*] (DLA)
SNZ	Senzan [*Japan*] [*Seismograph station code, US Geological Survey*] (SEIS)
SNZ	Shipping Corporation of New Zealand (CDA) [*Toronto Stock Exchange symbol*]
SNZO	South Karori [*New Zealand*] [*Seismograph station code, US Geological Survey*] (SEIS)
SO	Austrian Air Services [*Austria*] [*ICAO designator*] (ICDA)
SO	SAI Ambrosini SpA [*Italy*] [*ICAO aircraft manufacturer identifier*] (ICAO)
SO	Sail Only (CINC)
SO	Sales Order
SO	Salpingo-Oophorectomy [*Medicine*]
SO	Salvis Omissis [*Omissions Excepted*] [*Latin*]
SO	Saturdays Only [*British railroad term*]
SO	Saturn Orbiter [*NASA*]
so	Sauf Omission [*Omissions Excepted*] [*French*]
SO	Schenectady Operation [*Energy Research and Development Administration*] (MCD)
SO	Scientific Officer [*Ministry of Agriculture, Fisheries, and Food*] [*Also, ScO*] [*British*]
SO	Scottish [*Communion*] Office [*Episcopalian*]
SO	Scouting-Observation Plane [*When prefixed to Navy aircraft designation*]
S(O)	Seaman (Operator) [*British military*] (DMA)
SO	Second Class Open [*Train ticket*] (DCTA)
SO	Second Opinion [*An association*] [*Defunct*] (EA)
SO	Secretary's Office [*Navy*]
SO	Secretary's Order
SO	Section Officer [*British military*] (DMA)
SO	Secure Operations (MCD)
SO	Security Office
SO	Seder 'Olam (BJA)
SO	Sell-Off (AAG)
SO	Seller's Option [*Stock exchange term*]
SO	Send Only
SO	Senior Officer [*Military, police*]
SO	Serial Output
SO	Service Order
SO2	Sex Offender
SO	Sheriff's Office [*or Officer*] (ROG)
SO	Shift-Out Character [*Keyboard*] [*Data processing*]
SO	Shipment [*or Shipping*] Order
SO	Ship's Option
SO	Ships-on-Order Library [*Maritime Data Network, Inc.*] [*Information service or system*] (CRD)
SO	Shop Order
SO	Shot
S-O	Shut-Off (AAG)
SO	Shutout [*Sports*]
SO	Sibirskie Ogni [*A publication*]
S/O	Sign Off
SO	Signal Officer
SO	Significant Other [*Term for members of unmarried couples*]
SO	Silvered Optics
SO	Slavia Occidentalis [*A publication*]
SO	Sleepout (ADA)
SO	Slope Occurrence
SO	Slow Operate [*Relay*]
SO	Slow Oxidative [*Fibers*] [*Neuroanatomy*]
SO	Small Oocyte
So	Societa [*A publication*]
SO	Society (ROG)
So	Sojourner [*A publication*]
So	Sokrates [*A publication*]
SO	Sold Out (ADA)
SO	Solicitor's Opinion [*Legal term*] (DLA)
so	Somalia [*MARC country of publication code*] [*Library of Congress*] (LCCP)
SO	Somalia [*ANSI two-letter standard code*] (CNC)
S/O	Son Of [*Genealogy*]
s/o	Son Ordre [*His Order*] [*French*] [*Business term*]
SO	SONARman [*Navy*]
So	Sophia: Studies in Western Civilization and the Cultural Interaction of East and West [*Tokyo*] [*A publication*]
SO	Sorrel Resources Ltd. [*Toronto Stock Exchange symbol*]
SO	Sorting Office [*British*] (ROG)
S/O	Sound Off
So	Soundings [*A publication*]
SO	Source [*Online database field identifier*]
SO	South [*or Southern*]
SO	Southern Airways [*ICAO designator*]
SO	Southern Co. [*NYSE symbol*] (SPSG)
SO	Southern Oscillation [*Meteorology*]
So	Southern Reporter [*National Reporter System*] [*A publication*] (DLA)
SO	Special Olympics [*Later, SOI*] (EA)
SO	Special Operations
SO	Special Orders [*Military*]
SO	Spheno-Occipital [*Synchondrosis*] [*Medicine*]
SO	Spiracular Organ [*Fish anatomy*]
SO	Spring Opening
SO	Staff Officer
SO	Stamp Office [*British*] (ROG)
SO	Standing Order
SO	Station Officer [*British police*]
SO	Stationery Office [*British*]
SO	Statutes of Ontario [*QL Systems Ltd.*] [*Information service or system*] (CRD)
SO	Stay Out [*Official leave from Eton College*] [*British*]
SO	Stock Option [*Investment term*]
SO	Stock Order (AAG)
SO	Stock Outboard [*Powerboat*]
SO	Stockage Objectives [*Military*]
SO	Stop Order (MCD)
SO	Stopover [*Slang*]
SO	Stores Officer [*British military*] (DMA)
SO	Strategic Outline Chart [*Air Force*]
SO	Strikeouts [*Baseball*]
SO	Studia Oliveriana [*A publication*]
SO	Studia Orientalia [*A publication*]
s/o	Sua Ordem [*Your Order*] [*Portuguese*] [*Business term*]
SO	Submarine Oscillator (DEN)
SO	Suboffice
S/O	Substance Of
SO	Superior Oblique [*Muscle*] [*Anatomy*]
SO	Superior Old [*Spirits*]
SO	Supply Officer
SO	Support Operations
SO	Surface Operations [*Navy*] (CAAL)
SO	Surveillance Officer
SO	Switching Oscilloscope
SO	Switchover
SO	Symbolae Osloenses [*A publication*]
SO	Symbolic Output [*Data processing*]
SO	Sympathetic Ophthalmia [*Medicine*]
SO	Symphony Orchestra
SO	System Override (AAG)
SO	Systems Orientation
SO1	SONARman First Class [*Navy*]
SO2	SONARman Second Class [*Navy*]
SO3	SONARman Third Class [*Navy*]
SO4	Science on 4 [*Radio program*] [*British*]
SOA	Safe Operating Area (IEEE)
SOA	Sales Order Authority (AAG)
SOA	Scandinavian Orthopaedic Association (EA)
SOA	School of the Air [*Army*] (TSSD)
SOA	Self-Optimizing and Adaptive
SOA	Senate Operating Agency (MCD)
SOA	Separate Operating Agency [*Air Force*] (AFM)
SOA	Serial Output Adapter
SOA	Shelby Owners of America (EA)
SOA	Ship Operating Automation

SOA .... Shipyard Overhaul Availability
SOA .... Shuttle Orbital Application [*NASA*]
SOA .... Smithsonian Office of Anthropology
SOA .... Society of Actuaries (EA)
SOA .... Society of Authors [*British*] (EAIO)
SOA .... Sonora, TX [*Location identifier*] [*FAA*] (FAAL)
SOA .... Sorata Development, Inc. [*Vancouver Stock Exchange symbol*]
SOA .... Soundness of Approach (MCD)
SOA .... Source of Assignment (MCD)
SOA .... Southern Airways (MCD)
SOA .... Special Open Allotment [*Military*] (AABC)
SOA .... Special Operating Agency [*Military*] (AABC)
SOA .... Speed of Advance [*Military*]
SOA .... Speed of Approach
SOA .... Spirit of Adventure (EA)
SOA .... Staff Officer, Administration [*British military*] (DMA)
SOA .... Standardbred Owners Association (EA)
SOA .... Start of Address
SOA .... State of the Art
SOA .... Statement of Assurance
SOA .... Stimulus Onset Asynchrony [*Psychology*]
SOA .... Student Orientation Assistant
SOA .... Superoxide Anion [*Chemistry*]
SOA .... Switch Off Assembly (MCD)
SOA .... Sydsvenska Ortnamns-Saellskapets Arsskrift [*A publication*]
SOAA .... Signed Out Against Advice [*Medicine*]
SOAA .... Staff Officers Association of America (EA)
SoAB .... South Atlantic Bulletin [*A publication*]
SOAC .... State-of-the-Art Car [*Transit*] [*Department of Transportation*]
SOAD .... Staff Officer, Air Defence [*British military*] (DMA)
SOAF .... South Atlantic Financial Corp. [*NASDAQ symbol*] (NQ)
SoAF .... Soviet Air Force
SOAF .... Sultanate of Oman Air Force
So Africa .... Southern Africa [*A publication*]
So African L ... South African Law Reports [*A publication*]
So African LJ ... South African Law Journal [*A publication*]
So Afr LJ ... South African Law Journal [*A publication*]
So Afr LR ... South African Law Reports [*A publication*]
So Afr LT ... South African Law Times [*A publication*] (DLA)
So Afr Prize Cas ... South African Prize Cases (Juta) [*A publication*] (DLA)
SoAfrStJ .... South African Statistical Journal [*A publication*]
SOAGD ..... Solar Age [*A publication*]
SOAI .... Service des Organisations Aeronautiques Internationales
                [*France*]
SOAIAG .... Annales Medicinae Militaris Fenniae [*A publication*]
SOAL .... Search Optical Augmentation LASER (MCD)
SOAMB ..... Soviet Applied Mechanics [*English Translation*] [*A publication*]
SOAMUS ... Study of One-Atmosphere Manned Underwater Structures
SoANGr ..... Soobscenija Akademiji Nauk Gruzinskoj SSR [*A publication*]
SOAP .... Pioneer Communications Network, Inc. [*Rocky Hill, CT*]
                [*NASDAQ symbol*] (NQ)
SOAP .... Sarnia Olefins and Aromatics Project [*Canadian ethylene
                project*]
SOAP .... Self-Optimizing Automatic Pilot
SOAP .... Ship Overhaul Assistance Program (MCD)
SOAP .... Simplify Obscure ALGOL [*Algorithmic Language*]
                Programs (MCD)
SOAP .... Society of Airway Pioneers (EA)
SOAP .... Society for Obstetric Anesthesia and Perinatology (EA)
SOAP .... Society of Office Automation Professionals [*Later, AMS*]
                [*Telecommunications service*] [*Willow Grove,
                PA*] (TSSD)
SOAP .... Spectrochemical [*or Spectrographic, Spectrometric, or
                Spectroscopic*] Oil Analysis Program [*Air Force*]
SOAP .... Standing Order Advance Payment
SOAP .... Students Opposed to Advertised Pollutants [*Student legal action
                organization*]
SOAP .... Subjective, Objective, Assessment, and Plan [*Medicine*]
SOAP .... Supply Operations Assistance Program [*Military*]
SOAP .... Symbolic Optimum Assembly Programming [*IBM Corp.*] [*Data
                processing*]
SOAP .... Symptoms, Observations, Assessment, Plan
SOAP .... Systems Operational Analysis Plan
Soap & Chem Spec ... Soap and Chemical Specialties [*Later, Soap/Cosmetics/
                Chemical Specialties*] [*A publication*]
Soap Chem Spec ... Soap and Chemical Specialties [*Later, Soap/Cosmetics/
                Chemical Specialties*] [*A publication*]
Soap Cosmet ... Soap/Cosmetics/Chemical Specialties [*A publication*]
Soap/Cosmet/Chem Spec ... Soap/Cosmetics/Chemical Specialities [*A
                publication*]
SOAPD ...... Southern Air Procurement District
Soap Perfum Cosmet ... Soap, Perfumery, and Cosmetics [*A publication*]
Soap Prf Cos ... Soap, Perfumery, and Cosmetics [*A publication*]
Soap & San Chem ... Soap and Sanitary Chemicals [*A publication*]
SOAR .... Safe Operating Area
SOAR .... Save Our American Resources [*Boy Scout project*]
SOAR .... Seminars on Aeroanxiety Relief
SOAR .... Shuttle Orbital Applications and Requirements [*NASA*]
SOAR .... Simulation of Airlift Resources [*Air Force*]
SOAR .... Simulation of Apollo Reliability [*NASA*] (KSC)
SOAR .... Staff Organization and Regulation

SOAR .... State-of-the-Art Report [*Navy*]
SOAR .... State Operator and Result [*Computer program*]
SOAR .... Stress on Analytical Reasoning
SOARS ...... Second Order Attitude Reference Set (MCD)
SOARS ...... Shuttle Operations Automated Reporting System
                [*NASA*] (NASA)
SOAS .... School of Oriental and African Studies [*University of London*]
So AS .... Somersetshire Archaeological and Natural History Society.
                Proceedings [*Later, Somerset Archaeology and Natural
                History*] [*A publication*]
SOASC(I) ... Senior Officer Assault Ships and Craft (India) [*British*]
SOase......... Sulfite Oxidase [*An enzyme*]
SOAS JLCR ... School of Oriental and African Studies. Jordan Lectures in
                Comparative Religion [*A publication*]
So Assn Q .. Southern Association Quarterly [*A publication*]
SOAS ULLOS ... School of Oriental and African Studies. University of
                London. London. Oriental Series [*A publication*]
So Atlan Bul ... South Atlantic Bulletin [*A publication*]
So Atlan Q ... South Atlantic Quarterly [*A publication*]
So Atl Quar ... South Atlantic Quarterly [*A publication*]
SOATS ...... Support Operations Automated Training System
                [*NASA*] (NASA)
So Aus Bul ... National Gallery of South Australia. Bulletin [*A publication*]
So Aus LR ... South Australian Law Reports [*A publication*] (APTA)
So Aust LR ... South Australian Law Reports [*A publication*]
So Austr L ... South Australian Law Reports [*A publication*]
So Austr St ... South Australian State Reports [*A publication*]
SOAW .... Sitzungsberichte. Oesterreichische Akademie der
                Wissenschaften in Wien. Philosophisch-Historische Klasse
                [*A publication*]
Sob .... De Sobrietate [*of Philo*] (BJA)
SOB .... Second Overtone Band
SOB .... Senate Office Building
SOB .... Service Observance Bureau [*A telephone-monitoring section of
                the Bell System*]
SOB .... Shipped on Board a Specified Vessel (DS)
SOB .... Shortness of Breath [*Cardiology*]
SOB .... Silly Old Bugger [*Officer over the age of 39*] [*British*] (DSUE)
SOB .... Son of a Bitch
SOB .... Souls on Board [*Aviation slang*] (FAAC)
SOB .... Space Orbital Bomber (AAG)
SOB .... Start of Block
SOB .... Sub-Occipito Bregma [*Medicine*] (ROG)
SOB .... Sudost-Bahn [*Swiss Southeastern Railway*]
SOB .... Sulfur Oxidizing Bacteria
SOB .... Superior Official Bureaucrat [*Satirical bureaucracy term*]
SOB's........ Sons of Bosses International [*An association*] [*Later,
                NFBC*] (EA)
SOB's......... South of Broad Street [*Reference is to residents of the historic
                and aristocratic section of Charleston, South Carolina*]
SOBA .... 605th Ordnance Battalion Association (EA)
SOBASSPIFTAGE ... Society of Beer and Sordid Sex Professional
                Invitational Fishing Tournament and Gastronomical
                Extravaganza
SOBC......... Save Our Barns Committee (EA)
SOBECOV ... Societe de Stockage et de Commercialisation des Produits
                Vivriers [*Development organization*] [*Burundi*] (EY)
SOBELAIR ... Societe Belge de Transports Pan Air [*Airline*] [*Belgium*]
SOBEP ...... Scale of Beliefs in Extraordinary Phenomena [*Research test*]
                [*Psychology*]
SOBIA .... Social Biology [*A publication*]
SOBIGM... Sign Off Brother, I've Got Mine [*Remark used by seamen who
                avoided risky assignments during World War II*] [*Also
                used as hoax by National Maritime Union for name of
                organization issuing pamphlet about low state of merchant
                marine service*]
So Biv........ Southern Bivouac [*A publication*]
SOBK......... Southern Bankshares, Inc. [*Beckley, WV*] [*NASDAQ
                symbol*] (NQ)
SOBLIN .... Self-Organizing Binary Logical Network [*OTS*]
So Bod....... Sounding Board [*A publication*]
SOBP......... Sentral Organisasi Buruh Pantjasila [*Central Organization of
                Pantjasila Labor*] [*Indonesia*]
Sobre Deriv Cana Azucar ... Sobre los Derivados de la Cana de Azucar [*Cuba*]
                [*A publication*]
SOBS......... Scanning Ocean Bottom SONAR
SOBS......... Society for Office-Based Surgery [*Later, ASOS*] (EA)
SOBU .... Student Organization for Black Unity
SOC .... Chief SONARman [*Navy rating*] [*Obsolete*]
SOC .... Saint Olaf College [*Northfield, MN*]
SOC .... Satellite Operations Center [*Cape Kennedy*]
SOC .... Satellite Orbit Control
SOC .... Scene of Crime
SOC .... Schedule of Organizational Change [*Air Force*] (AFM)
SOC .... Scottish Ornithologists' Club [*British*]
SOC .... Sector Operations Center [*Air Force*]
SOC .... Self-Organizing Control
SOC .... Separated Orbit Cyclotron (IEEE)
SOC .... Service and Overhaul Change (MSA)
SOC .... Servicemen's Opportunity College [*DoD*]
SOC .... Set Overrides Clear (IEEE)

SOC .... Shop Order Control
SO-in-C ..... Signal Officer-in-Chief [*British military*] (DMA)
SOC .... Silicon on Ceramic [*Technique for producing solar cells*]
SOC .... Simulated Operational Computer (KSC)
SOC .... Simulation Operations Center [*NASA*] (KSC)
SOC .... Singer Owners Club (EA)
SOC .... Single Orbit Computation
SOC .... Soap, Perfumery, and Cosmetics [*A publication*]
SOC .... Sochi [*USSR*] [*Seismograph station code, US Geological Survey*] (SEIS)
SOC .... Social
SOC .... Socialist (EY)
Soc............. Sociedad [*Society, Company*] [*Spanish*] [*Business term*]
Soc............. Sociedade [*Society, Company*] [*Portuguese*] [*Business term*]
Soc............. Societas [*A publication*]
SOC .... Society
Soc............. Society [*A publication*]
SOC .... Society of Cinematologists [*Later, SCS*] (EA)
SOC .... Sociology
SOC .... Socket (AAG)
SOC .... Socrates [*Greek philosopher, 470-399BC*] (ROG)
SOC .... Solo [*Indonesia*] [*Airport symbol*] (OAG)
SOC .... Somerset County College, Somerville, NJ [*OCLC symbol*] (OCLC)
So C............ South Carolina Reports [*A publication*] (DLA)
SOC .... South Coast Airways [*Nederland, TX*] [*FAA designator*] (FAAC)
SOC .... Southern Oregon College
SOC .... Space Operations Center
SOC .... Space Operations Controller
SOC .... Special Operations Command [*Military*] (AABC)
SOC .. Specialized Oceanographic Center [*National Oceanic and Atmospheric Administration*] (MSC)
SOC .... Specific Optimal Control
SOC .... Spouse Observation Checklist
SOC .... Squadron Operations Center [*Air Force*]
SOC .... Standard Occupational Classifications (OICC)
SOC .... Standard Oil Company
SOC .... Standards of Official Conduct [*A publication*] (DLA)
SOC .... Standing Order Confirmation [*Publishing*]
SOC .... Standing Orders Committee [*British*] (DCTA)
SOC .... Start of Construction [*Military*] (AFIT)
SOC .... Start of Conversion [*Navy*]
SOC .... State of Charge
SoC............ State of Consciousness
SOC .... State-Operated Contracts
SOC .... Statement of Capability (MCD)
SOC .... Statement of Conditions
SOC .... Station Operations Console (MCD)
SOC .... Strike Operations Coordinator [*Navy*] (NVT)
SOC .... Strike Options Comparison (MCD)
SOC .... Struck off Charge [*British military*] (DMA)
SOC .... Studies in Organic Chemistry [*Elsevier Book Series*] [*A publication*]
SOC .... Superior Oil Company [*Nevada*] [*NYSE symbol*] [*Delisted*] [*Toronto Stock Exchange symbol*] (SPSG)
SOC .... Superposition of Configuration [*Atomic physics*]
SOC .... Supply Overhaul Coordinator (MCD)
SOC .... Support Operations Center
SOC .... Suspended Organic Carbon [*Chemistry*]
SOC .... Synthetic Organic Chemical
SOC .... System Operational Concept
SOC .... System Option Controller [*NASA*] (NASA)
SOC .... Systems Operation Center
SOCA .... Cayenne/Rochambeau [*French Guiana*] [*ICAO location identifier*] (ICLI)
Soc A .... Sociological Abstracts [*A publication*]
SOCA .... Soul and Calypso [*Music*]
SOCA .... Staff Officer for Civil Affairs [*British*] [*World War II*]
SocAb........ Sociological Abstracts [*A publication*]
SOCABU.... Societe du Caoutchouc Butyl [*France*]
Soc Act...... Social Action [*A publication*]
Soc Action & L ... Social Action and the Law [*A publication*] (DLA)
Soc Act & L ... Social Action and the Law [*A publication*]
Soc Actuar Trans ... Society of Actuaries. Transactions [*A publication*]
SOCAD ..... Serviceman's Opportunity for College Associate Degree [*Military*] (MCD)
Soc Adv Electrochem Sci Technol Trans ... Society for the Advancement of Electrochemical Science and Technology. Transactions [*A publication*]
Soc African J ... Societe des Africanistes. Journal [*A publication*]
Soc Agric Alger Bull ... Societe des Agricultures d'Algerie. Bulletin [*Algeria*] [*A publication*]
SOCAL ...... Southern California [*Military*] (NVT)
SOCAL...... Standard Oil Co. of California
So Cal Bsn ... Southern California Business [*A publication*]
So Calif L Rev ... Southern California Law Review [*A publication*]
So Calif Q .. Southern California Quarterly [*A publication*]
So Calif Quar ... Southern California Quarterly [*A publication*]
So Calif Tax Inst ... University of Southern California School of Law Tax Institute (DLA)

So Cal LR .. Southern California Law Review [*A publication*]
Soc Alp Giulie Comm Grotte Eugenio Boegan Atti Mem ... Societa Alpina delle Giulie. Club Alpino Italiano. Sezione di Trieste. Commissione Grotte "Eugenio Boegan." Atti e Memorie [*A publication*]
SOCALSEC ... Southern California Sector, Western Sea Frontier
Soc Alt .... Social Alternatives [*A publication*]
Soc Altern .. Social Alternatives [*A publication*] (APTA)
Soc Alternatives ... Social Alternatives [*Australia*] [*A publication*]
Soc d Americanistes J ... Societe des Americanistes de Paris. Journal [*A publication*]
Soc Amer J ... Societe des Americanistes de Paris. Journal [*A publication*]
Soc Am For ... Society of American Foresters. Proceedings [*A publication*]
Soc Anal...... Sociological Analysis [*A publication*]
Soc Anarc.. Social Anarchism [*A publication*]
Soc Ane ...... Societe Anonyme [*Stock Company*] [*French*] [*Business term*] (GPO)
Soc Anthropol Paris Bull Mem ... Societe d'Anthropologie de Paris. Bulletins et Memoires [*A publication*]
SOCAP...... Society of Consumer Affairs Professionals in Business [*Alexandria, VA*] (EA)
Soc Appl Bacteriol Symp Ser ... Society for Applied Bacteriology. Symposium Series [*A publication*]
Soc Appl Bacteriol Tech Ser ... Society for Applied Bacteriology. Technical Series [*A publication*]
SOCAR..... Shuttle Operational Capability Assessment Report [*NASA*] (MCD)
So Car .... South Carolina Reports [*A publication*] (DLA)
So Ca R ...... South Carolina Review [*A publication*]
SOCAR..... Statement of Condition and Recommendation [*Military*] (AABC)
SOCAR...... Systems Operational Compatibility Assessment Review [*NASA*]
So Car BA Rep ... South Carolina Bar Association Reports [*A publication*] (DLA)
So Car BJ... South Carolina Business Journal [*A publication*]
Soc Archeol & Hist Limousin Bul ... Societe Archeologique et Historique du Limousin. Bulletin [*A publication*]
Soc Arch Hist J ... Society of Architectural Historians. Journal [*A publication*]
Soc Arch Hist Poitou Arch ... Societe des Archives Historiques du Poitou. Archives [*A publication*]
Soc Archit Hist J ... Society of Architectural Historians. Journal [*A publication*]
Soc Archtl Historians Jnl ... Society of Architectural Historians. Journal [*A publication*]
Soc of Archtl Historians Newsletter ... Society of Architectural Historians. Newsletter [*A publication*]
Soc of Archtl Historians Newsletter ... Society of Architectural Historians. Newsletter [*A publication*]
So Car Const ... South Carolina Constitutional Reports (Treadway, Mill, or Harper) [*A publication*] (DLA)
Soc Argent Cancerol Bol Trab ... Sociedad Argentina de Cancerologia. Boletines y Trabajos [*A publication*]
Soc Argent Cir Jornadas Quir ... Sociedad Argentina de Cirujanos Jornadas Quirurgicas [*A publication*]
So Car Hist Assoc Proc ... South Carolina Historical Association. Proceedings [*A publication*]
So Car Hist Mag ... South Carolina Historical and Genealogical Magazine [*A publication*]
So Car LJ... South Carolina Law Journal [*Columbia*] [*A publication*] (DLA)
So Car LQ ... South Carolina Law Quarterly [*A publication*]
So Car L Rev ... South Carolina Law Review [*A publication*]
Soc Army Hist Research Jour ... Society for Army Historical Research. Journal [*London*] [*A publication*]
So Car R..... South Carolina Law Reports [*A publication*] (DLA)
Soc Arts J .. Society of Arts. Journal [*A publication*]
SOCAS...... Subcommittee on Chemical Abstracts Service [*American Chemical Society*]
Soc Astron Ital Mem ... Societa Astronomica Italiana. Memorie [*A publication*]
SOCAT...... Student Occupational Competency Achievement Testing [*Educational test*]
SOCATS ... Scenario Oriented Corps Area Training System (MCD)
Soc Auto Eng J ... Society of Automotive Engineers. Journal [*A publication*]
SOCB......... Shop Order Control Board
SoCB.......... South Central Bulletin [*A publication*]
Soc Banque Suisse Bul ... Societe de Banque Suisse. Bulletin [*A publication*]
Soc Behav Pers ... Social Behavior and Personality [*A publication*]
Soc Beh Per ... Social Behavior and Personality [*A publication*]
Soc Belge d'Etudes Geog Bull ... Societe Belge d'Etudes Geographiques. Bulletin [*A publication*]
Soc Belge G B ... Societe Belge de Geologie. Bulletin [*A publication*]
Soc Belge Geol Bull ... Societe Belge de Geologie. Bulletin [*A publication*]
Soc Biol...... Social Biology [*A publication*]
Soc Biol Hum Aff ... Social Biology and Human Affairs [*A publication*]
Soc Bot France B ... Societe Botanique de France. Bulletin [*A publication*]
Soc Bras Nematol Publ ... Sociedade Brasileira de Nematologia. Publicacao [*A publication*]
Soc Brotheriana Bol ... Sociedade Brotheriana. Boletim [*A publication*]

SOCC......... Salvage Operational Control Center [*On submarine rescue ship during salvage operation*]
SOCC......... Satellite Oceanic Control Center
SOCC......... Satellite Operations Control Center [*NASA*]　(NASA)
SOCC......... Spacecraft Operations Control Center
SOCC......... Special Opportunities Counties and Cities Program [*Tennessee Valley Authority*]
SOCC......... Submarine Operations Control Center [*Navy*]　(CAAL)
SOCC......... Subordinate Operations Control Center
Soc Casework ... Social Casework [*A publication*]
SOCCER ... SMART's Own Concordance Constructor, Extremely Rapid [*Cornell University*] [*Data processing*]
Soccer J...... Soccer Journal [*A publication*]
Soc Chem Ind J ... Society of Chemical Industry. Journal [*A publication*]
Soc Chem Ind (Lond) Monogr ... Society of Chemical Industry (London). Monograph [*A publication*]
Soc Chem Ind Victoria Proc ... Society of Chemical Industry of Victoria. Proceedings [*A publication*]
Soc Cient Ant Alz Mem ... Sociedad Cientifica "Antonio Alzate." Memorias y Revista [*A publication*]
Soc Cient Parag Rev ... Sociedad Cientifica del Paraguay. Revista [*A publication*]
Soc Cognit ... Social Cognition [*A publication*]
SOC Coll.... Studia Orientalia Christiana. Collectanea [*A publication*]
Soc Comp... Social Compass [*A publication*]
Soc Compass ... Social Compass [*A publication*]
Soc Con ...... Social Concept [*A publication*]
SOCCS ...... Summary of Component Control Status [*Nuclear energy*]　(NRCH)
Soc Cubana Historia Nat Mem ... Sociedad Cubana de Historia Natural. Memorias [*A publication*]
Soc Cubana Ingenieros Rev ... Sociedad Cubana de Ingenieros. Revista [*A publication*]
Soc Cubana Ing Rv ... Sociedad Cubana de Ingenieros. Revista [*A publication*]
Socd........... Sociedad [*Society, Company*] [*Spanish*] [*Business term*]
SOCD .... Source Control Drawing
Soc Def .... Social Defence [*New Delhi*] [*A publication*]
SOCDS ...... Source Codes　(MCD)
Soc Dyers & Col J ... Society of Dyers and Colourists. Journal [*A publication*]
Soc Dyn....... Social Dynamics [*A publication*]
SOCE......... Staff Officer Construction Engineering
Soc Econ .... Social Economist [*A publication*]
Soc Econ Admin ... Social and Economic Administration [*A publication*]
Soc Econ Paleontol Mineral Pac Sect Guideb ... Society of Economic Paleontologists and Mineralogists. Pacific Section. Guidebooks [*A publication*]
Soc Econ Paleontol Mineral Paleontol Monogr ... Society of Economic Paleontologists and Mineralogists. Paleontological Monograph [*A publication*]
Soc Econ Paleontol Mineral Permian Basin Sect Publ ... Society of Economic Paleontologists and Mineralogists. Permian Basin Section. Publication [*A publication*]
Soc Econ Paleontol Mineral Repr Ser ... Society of Economic Paleontologists and Mineralogists. Reprint Series [*A publication*]
Soc Econ Paleontol Mineral Spec Publ ... Society of Economic Paleontologists and Mineralogists. Special Publication [*A publication*]
Soc Econ Paleontologists and Mineralogists Special Pub ... Society of Economic Paleontologists and Mineralogists. Special Publication [*A publication*]
Soc Econ Paleontologists and Mineralogists Spec Pub ... Society of Economic Paleontologists and Mineralogists. Special Publication [*A publication*]
Soc-Econ Plan Sci ... Socio-Economic Planning Sciences [*A publication*]
Soc Econ Stud ... Social and Economic Studies [*A publication*]
Soc & Econ Stud ... Social and Economic Studies [*A publication*]
Soc Econ Wetgeving ... Social Economisch Wetgeving. Tijdschrift voor Europees en Economisch Recht [*A publication*]　(DLA)
Soc Ed .... Social Education [*A publication*]
Soc Educ .... Social Education [*A publication*]
Soc Ekon Integrace ... Socialisticka Ekonomicka Integrace [*Czechoslovakia*] [*A publication*]
SOCELEX ... Society Against Elephant Exploitation　(EA)
Soc Eng (London) J ... Society of Engineers (London). Journal [*A publication*]
Soc Espan Hist Nat Bol Secc Geol ... Sociedad Espanola de Historia Natural. Boletin. Seccion Geologica [*A publication*]
Soc Espanola H N An ... Sociedad Espanola de Historia Natural. Anales [*A publication*]
Soc d'Etudes Sc d'Angers B ... Societe d'Etudes Scientifiques d'Angers. Bulletin [*A publication*]
Soc Etud et Expansion R ... Societe d'Etudes et d'Expansion. Revue [*A publication*]
Soc Etud Indochinoises Bul ... Societe des Etudes Indochinoises. Bulletin [*A publication*]
Soc Exp Biol Semin Ser ... Society for Experimental Biology. Seminar Series [*A publication*]
Soc Explor Geophys Annu Int Meet Abstr ... Society of Exploration Geophysicists. Annual International Meeting. Abstracts [*A publication*]
Soc Exp Stress Anal Pap ... Society for Experimental Stress Analysis. Papers [*A publication*]
SOCF......... Spacecraft Operations and Checkout Facility　(AAG)

Soc Fauna Flora Fenn Flora Fenn ... Societas pro Fauna et Flora Fennica. Flora Fennica [*A publication*]
Soc Fauna Flora Fenn Memo ... Societatis pro Fauna et Flora Fennica. Memoranda [*A publication*]
Soc Forces ... Social Forces [*A publication*]
Soc Francaise Mineralogie et Cristallographie Bull ... Societe Francaise de Mineralogie et de Cristallographie. Bulletin [*A publication*]
Soc Franc Miner B ... Societe Francaise de Mineralogie. Bulletin [*A publication*]
Soc Fr Dermatol Syphiligr Bull ... Societe Francaise de Dermatologie et de Syphiligraphie. Bulletin [*A publication*]
Soc Fr Gynecol C R ... Societe Francaise de Gynecologie. Comptes Rendus [*A publication*]
Soc Fribourgeoise Sc Nat B Mem ... Societe Fribourgeoise des Sciences Naturelles. Bulletin. Memoires [*A publication*]
Soc Fr Mineral Cristallogr Bull ... Societe Francaise de Mineralogie et de Cristallographie. Bulletin [*A publication*]
Soc F TV Arts J ... Society of Film and Television Arts. Journal [*A publication*]
Soc G Belgique An ... Societe Geologique de Belgique. Annales [*A publication*]
Soc Gen Physiol Ser ... Society of General Physiologists. Series [*A publication*]
Soc Geo A Oran ... Bulletin Trimestriel. Societe de Geographie et d'Archeologie de la Province d'Oran [*A publication*]
Soc Geog Fenniae Acta Geog ... Societas Geographica Fenniae. Acta Geographica [*A publication*]
Soc Geog Liege Bul ... Societe Geographique de Liege. Bulletin [*A publication*]
Soc Geog Lima Bol ... Sociedad Geografica de Lima. Boletin [*A publication*]
Soc Geog Mex B ... Sociedad de Geografia y Estadistica de la Republica Mexicana. Boletin [*A publication*]
Soc Geog (Paris) B ... Societe de Geographie (Paris). Bulletin [*A publication*]
Soc Geog Que B ... Societe de Geographie de Quebec. Bulletin [*A publication*]
Soc Geogr Bol (Madrid) ... Sociedad Geografica. Boletin (Madrid) [*A publication*]
Soc Geol Belg Ann ... Societe Geologique de Belgique. Annales [*A publication*]
Soc Geol Belgique Annales ... Societe Geologique de Belgique. Annales [*A publication*]
Soc Geol France Bull ... Societe Geologique de France. Bulletin [*A publication*]
Soc Geol Fr Bull ... Societe Geologique de France. Bulletin [*A publication*]
Soc Geol Fr Mem ... Societe Geologique de France. Memoires [*A publication*]
Soc Geol Fr Mem Hors Ser ... Societe Geologique de France. Memoire Hors Serie [*A publication*]
Soc Geol Ital Mem ... Societa Geologica Italiana. Memorie [*A publication*]
Soc Geol Mex Bol ... Sociedad Geologica Mexicana. Boletin [*A publication*]
Soc Geol Mexicana Bol ... Sociedad Geologica Mexicana. Boletin [*A publication*]
Soc Geol Mineral Bretagne Bull ... Societe Geologique et Mineralogique de Bretagne. Bulletin [*A publication*]
Soc Geol et Mineralog Bretagne Bull ... Societe Geologique et Mineralogique de Bretagne. Bulletin [*A publication*]
Soc Geol Nord Ann ... Societe Geologique du Nord. Annales [*A publication*]
Soc Geol Normandie Bull ... Societe Geologique de Normandie. Bulletin [*A publication*]
Soc Geol Peru Bol ... Sociedad Geologica del Peru. Boletin [*A publication*]
Soc Geol Port Bol ... Sociedade Geologica de Portugal. Boletim [*A publication*]
Soc G France B Mem ... Societe Geologique de France. Bulletin. Memoires [*A publication*]
Soc G Italiana B ... Societa Geologica Italiana. Bollettino [*A publication*]
Soc Glass Technology Jour ... Society of Glass Technology. Journal [*A publication*]
Soc G Mex B ... Sociedad Geologica Mexicana. Boletin [*A publication*]
Soc G Nord An Mem ... Societe Geologique du Nord. Annales. Memoires [*A publication*]
Soc G Normandie B ... Societe Geologique de Normandie. Bulletin [*A publication*]
SOCH........ Spacelab Orbiter Common Hardware [*NASA*]　(MCD)
Soc Haitienne Histoire Geographie Geologie Revue ... Societe Haitienne d'Histoire de Geographie et de Geologie. Revue [*A publication*]
SOCHINAFOR ... South China Force [*World War II*]
Soc Hist ..... Social History [*A publication*]
Soc Hist/Hist Soc ... Social History/Histoire Sociale [*A publication*]
So C Hist Mag ... South Carolina Historical Magazine [*A publication*]
Soc Hist Nat Toulouse Bull ... Societe d'Histoire Naturelle de Toulouse. Bulletin [*A publication*]
Soc Hongroise Geog Abrege B ... Societe Hongroise de Geographie. Abrege du Bulletin [*A publication*]
Soc Hygiene ... Social Hygiene [*A publication*]
SOCI......... Society Corp. [*NASDAQ symbol*]　(NQ)
Soci .... [*Marianus*] Socinus [*Authority cited in pre-1607 legal work*]　(DSA)
Social Biol ... Social Biology [*A publication*]
Social Case ... Social Casework [*A publication*]
Social Comp ... Social Compass [*A publication*]
Social en Democr ... Socialisme en Democratie [*A publication*]
Social Ec A ... Social and Economic Administration [*A publication*]
Social Econ ... Social and Economic Studies [*A publication*]
Social and Econ Admin ... Social and Economic Administration [*A publication*]
Social & Econ Stud ... Social and Economic Studies [*A publication*]

Social Educ ... Social Education [*A publication*]
Social Forc ... Social Forces [*A publication*]
Social Ind... Social Indicators Research [*A publication*]
Social Indicators Res ... Social Indicators Research [*A publication*]
Socialist Wkr ... Socialist Worker [*A publication*]
Social Pol... Social Policy [*A publication*]
Social Policy Admin ... Social Policy and Administration [*A publication*]
Social Prax ... Social Praxis [*A publication*]
Social Prob ... Social Problems [*A publication*]
Social Psy ... Social Psychiatry [*A publication*]
Social Psychol Q ... Social Psychology Quarterly [*A publication*]
Social Res .. Social Research [*A publication*]
Social Revol ... Socialist Revolution [*A publication*]
Social Sci ... Social Science Quarterly [*A publication*]
Social Scie ... Social Science [*A publication*]
Social Science J (Fort Collins) ... Social Science Journal (Fort Collins) [*A publication*]
Social Science Q ... Social Science Quarterly [*A publication*]
Social Sci Inf ... Social Science Information [*A publication*]
Social Sci Q ... Social Science Quarterly [*A publication*]
SOCIAL SCISEARCH ... Social Science Citation Index Search [*Database*]
Social Sc M ... Social Science and Medicine [*A publication*]
Social Sec... Social Security Bulletin [*US*] [*A publication*]
Social Security Bul ... Social Security Bulletin [*A publication*]
Social Se R ... Social Service Review [*A publication*]
Social Service R ... Social Service Review [*A publication*]
Social Services Abs ... Social Services Abstracts [*A publication*]
Social Services J ... Social Services Journal [*A publication*]   (APTA)
Social St S ... Social Studies of Science [*A publication*]
Social Stud ... Social Studies [*A publication*]
Social Theor Pract ... Social Theory and Practice [*A publication*]
Social Trud ... Socialisticeskij Trud [*A publication*]
Social Wk Today ... Social Work Today [*A publication*]
Societe d'Etudes et d'Expansion Revue ... Societe d'Etudes et d'Expansion. Revue [*A publication*]
SOCIM...... Society of Connoisseurs in Murder   (EA)
Soc Imp Nat Moscou B ... Societe Imperiale des Naturalistes de Moscou. Bulletin [*A publication*]
Soc Indep Prof Earth Sci Bull ... Society of Independent Professional Earth Scientists. Bulletin [*A publication*]
Soc Indicators Res ... Social Indicators Research [*A publication*]
Soc Indic Res ... Social Indicators Research [*A publication*]
Soc Ind Min B C R Men ... Societe de l'Industrie Minerale. Bulletin. Comptes Rendus Mensuels des Reunions [*A publication*]
Soc Ind Res ... Social Indicators Research [*A publication*]
Soc l'Industrie Minerale Cong Cent ... Societe de l'Industrie Minerale. Congres du Centenaire [*A publication*]
Soc Ing Civils France Mem ... Societe des Ingenieurs Civils de France. Memoires [*A publication*]
Soc Insects ... Social Insects [*A publication*]
Socin Sen ... Marianus Socinus, the Elder [*Deceased, 1467*] [*Authority cited in pre-1607 legal work*]   (DSA)
Soc Int Pedod J ... Societe Internationale de Pedodontie. Journal [*A publication*]
Socio-Econ ... Socio-Economic Planning Sciences [*A publication*]
Socioecon Issues Health ... Socioeconomic Issues of Health [*A publication*]
Socioecon Newsletter ... Socioeconomic Newsletter [*A publication*]
Socio-Econ Planning Sciences ... Socio-Economic Planning Sciences [*A publication*]
Socio-Econ Plann Sci ... Socio-Economic Planning Sciences [*A publication*]
Socioecon Rep ... Socioeconomic Report. California Medical Association [*A publication*]
Sociol .... Sociologus [*Berlin*] [*A publication*]
SOCIOL.... Sociology
Sociol .... Sociology [*A publication*]
Sociol Anal ... Sociological Analysis [*A publication*]
Sociol Anal Theory ... Sociological Analysis and Theory [*A publication*]
Sociol B...... Sociological Bulletin (New Delhi) [*A publication*]
Sociol B (Bombay) ... Sociological Bulletin (Bombay) [*A publication*]
Sociol Bull ... Sociological Bulletin [*A publication*]
Sociol Cas .. Sociologicky Casopis [*A publication*]
Sociol Contemp ... Sociologie Contemporaine [*A publication*]
Sociol of Ed ... Sociology of Education [*A publication*]
Sociol Educ ... Sociology of Education [*A publication*]
Sociol Educ Abstr ... Sociology of Education Abstracts [*A publication*]
Sociol Focu ... Sociological Focus [*A publication*]
Sociol Fors ... Sociologisk Forskning [*A publication*]
Sociol Gids ... Sociologische Gids [*A publication*]
Sociol Health Illn ... Sociology of Health and Illness [*A publication*]
Sociol Health Illness ... Sociology of Health and Illness [*A publication*]
Sociol Inq ... Sociological Inquiry [*A publication*]
Sociol Inquiry ... Sociological Inquiry [*A publication*]
Sociol Int (Berlin) ... Sociologia Internationalis (Berlin) [*A publication*]
Sociol Issled (Moskva) ... Sociologiceskie Issledovanija (Moskva) [*A publication*]
Sociol Issled (Sverdlovsk) ... Sociologiceskie Issledovanija (Sverdlovsk) [*A publication*]
Sociol Lav .. Sociologia del Lavoro [*A publication*]
Sociol Law ... Sociology of Law [*A publication*]
Sociol Meddel ... Sociologiske Meddelelser [*A publication*]
Sociol Meth ... Sociological Methods and Research [*A publication*]

Sociol Methods & Res ... Sociological Methods and Research [*A publication*]
Sociol Neer ... Sociologia Neerlandica [*A publication*]
Sociological R ... Sociological Review [*A publication*]
Sociologus ... Sociologus Zeitschrift fuer Empirische Soziologie, Sozialpsychologische, und Ethnologische Forschung [*A publication*]
Sociol Org ... Sociologia dell'Organizzazione [*A publication*]
Sociol Q ..... Sociological Quarterly [*A publication*]
Sociol Quart ... Sociological Quarterly [*A publication*]
Sociol R... Sociological Review [*A publication*]
Sociol Rev .. Sociological Review [*A publication*]
Sociol Rev Monogr ... Sociological Review. Monograph [*A publication*]
Sociol R Mg ... Sociological Review. Monograph [*A publication*]
Sociol R NS ... Sociological Review. New Series [*A publication*]
Sociol Rur .. Sociologia Ruralis [*A publication*]
Sociol Ruralis ... Sociologia Ruralis [*A publication*]
Sociol Rural Life Minn Univ Agric Ext Serv ... Sociology of Rural Life. Minnesota University. Agricultural Extension Service [*A publication*]
Sociol Sela ... Sociologija Sela [*A publication*]
Sociol et Soc ... Sociologie et Societes [*A publication*]
Sociol Soc... Sociology and Social Research [*A publication*]
Sociol Soci ... Sociologie et Societes [*A publication*]
Sociol & Social Res ... Sociology and Social Research [*A publication*]
Sociol & Soc Res ... Sociology and Social Research [*A publication*]
Sociol Symp ... Sociological Symposium [*A publication*]
Sociol Theory ... Sociological Theory [*A publication*]
Sociol Trav ... Sociologie du Travail [*A publication*]
Sociol Wk Occupat ... Sociology of Work and Occupations [*A publication*]
Sociol W Oc ... Sociology of Work and Occupations [*A publication*]
Sociol Yb Relig Britain ... Sociological Yearbook of Religion in Britain [*A publication*]
Sociom .... Sociometry [*A publication*]
Socio Meth ... Sociological Methodology [*A publication*]
Socio R....... Sociological Review [*A publication*]
Socio-Tech B ... Social-Technological Bulletin [*Quezon City*] [*A publication*]
Soc Isl .... Society Islands
SO Cist ...... Sacer Ordo Cisterciensis [*Order of Cistercians*] [*Roman Catholic men's religious order*]
Soc Italiana Sc Nat Milano Atti ... Societa Italiana di Scienze Naturali in Milano. Atti [*A publication*]
Soc Ital Sci Farm Doc ... Societa Italiana di Scienze Farmaceutiche Documento [*A publication*]
Soc Ital Sci Nat Mus Civ Stor Nat Milano Atti ... Societa Italiana di Scienze Naturali e Museo Civico di Storia Naturale di Milano. Atti [*A publication*]
Soc J........... Soccer Journal [*A publication*]
Soc Jus R ... Social Justice Review [*A publication*]
SocJust ...... Social Justice Review [*A publication*]
Socker Handli ... Socker Handlingar [*A publication*]
SOCL......... Social
Soc Lab Bull ... Social and Labour Bulletin [*A publication*]   (ILCA)
Soc Labour Bull ... Social and Labour Bulletin [*A publication*]
Soc Languedoc Geogr ... Societe Languedocienne de Geographie [*A publication*]
Soc Languedocienne Geogr Bull ... Societe Languedocienne de Geographie. Bulletin [*A publication*]
SOCLD...... Solar Cells [*A publication*]
Soc and Leisure ... Society and Leisure [*A publication*]
SOCLGY ... Sociology
Soc Ligustica Sc Nat Geog Atti ... Societa Ligustica di Scienze Naturali e Geografiche. Atti [*A publication*]
Soc Linn Bord Bull ... Societe Linneenne de Bordeaux. Bulletin [*A publication*]
Soc Linneenne Normandie Bull ... Societe Linneenne de Normandie. Bulletin [*A publication*]
Soc Linn Lyon Bull ... Societe Linneenne de Lyon. Bulletin Mensuel [*A publication*]
SOCM .... Master Chief SONARman [*Navy rating*]
SOCM .... Shanley Oil Company [*NASDAQ symbol*]   (NQ)
SOCM .... Standoff Cluster Munitions
SOCMA ..... Scottish Operative Coach Makers' Association [*A union*]
SOCMA ..... Synthetic Organic Chemical Manufacturers Association   (EA)
Soc Maandbl Arb ... Sociaal Maandblad Arbeid [*A publication*]
Soc Malac Belgique An ... Societe Malacologique de Belgique. Annales [*A publication*]
Soc Malacologica Rev ... Sociedad Malacologica. Revista [*A publication*]
Soc Malawi J ... Society of Malawi. Journal [*A publication*]
Soc Manuf Eng Tech Pap Ser AD ... Society of Manufacturing Engineers. Technical Paper. Series AD (Assembly Division) [*A publication*]
Soc Manuf Eng Tech Pap Ser EE ... Society of Manufacturing Engineers. Technical Paper. Series EE (Electrical Engineering) [*A publication*]
Soc Manuf Eng Tech Pap Ser EM ... Society of Manufacturing Engineers. Technical Paper. Series EM (Engineering Materials) [*A publication*]
Soc Manuf Eng Tech Pap Ser FC ... Society of Manufacturing Engineers. Technical Paper. Series FC (Finishing and Coating) [*A publication*]

Soc Manuf Eng Tech Pap Ser IQ ... Society of Manufacturing Engineers. Technical Paper. Series IQ (Inspection and Quality) [*A publication*]

Soc Manuf Eng Tech Pap Ser MF ... Society of Manufacturing Engineers. Technical Paper. Series MF (Material Forming) [*A publication*]

Soc Manuf Eng Tech Pap Ser MR ... Society of Manufacturing Engineers. Technical Paper. Series MR (Material Removal) [*A publication*]

Soc Manuf Eng Tech Pap Ser MS ... Society of Manufacturing Engineers. Technical Paper. Series MS [*A publication*]

Soc Mass Media Resour Technol J ... Society for Mass Media and Resource Technology. Journal [*A publication*]   (APTA)

SOCMC..... Special Order of the Commandant of the Marine Corps

Soc Mean Leg Con ... Social Meaning of Legal Concepts [*A publication*]   (ILCA)

Soc Med-Chir Hop Form Sanit Armees ... Societe Medico-Chirurgicale des Hopitaux et Formations Sanitaires des Armees [*A publication*]

Soc Med Mil Franc Bull ... Societe de Medecine Militaire Francaise. Bulletin [*A publication*]

Soc Med Tidskr ... Social-Medicinsk Tidskrift [*A publication*]

Soc Mex Geog Estadistica B ... Sociedad Mexicana de Geografia y Estadistica. Boletin [*A publication*]

Soc Mexicana Geografia y Estadistica Bol ... Sociedad Mexicana de Geografia y Estadistica. Boletin [*A publication*]

Soc Mexicana Historia Nat Rev ... Sociedad Mexicana de Historia Natural. Revista [*A publication*]

Soc Micros Can Bull ... Societe de Microscopie du Canada. Bulletin [*A publication*]

Soc Min Eng AIME Trans ... Society of Mining Engineers of AIME [*American Institute of Mining, Metallurgical, and Petroleum Engineers*]. Transactions [*A publication*]

Soc Miner France ... Societe Mineralogique de France. Bulletin [*A publication*]

Soc Mining Engineers AIME Trans ... Society of Mining Engineers of AIME [*American Institute of Mining, Metallurgical, and Petroleum Engineers*]. Transactions [*A publication*]

SocN .... Sociolinguistics Newsletter [*A publication*]

SOCN .... Source Control Number

Soc Nat Luxemb Bull ... Societe des Naturalistes Luxembourgeois. Bulletin [*A publication*]

Soc Nat Pet Aquitaine Bull Cent Rech Pau ... Societe Nationale des Petroles d'Aquitaine. Bulletin de Centres de Recherches de Pau [*A publication*]

Soc Nat Resour ... Society and Natural Resources [*A publication*]

Soc Nav Architects Mar Eng Tech Res Bull ... Society of Naval Architects and Marine Engineers. Technical and Research Bulletin [*New York*] [*A publication*]

Soc Nav Architects Mar Eng Trans ... Society of Naval Architects and Marine Engineers of New York. Transactions [*A publication*]

Soc Nav Archit Mar Eng Trans ... Society of Naval Architects and Marine Engineers. Transactions [*United States*] [*A publication*]

Soc Nematol Spec Publ ... Society of Nematologists. Special Publication [*A publication*]

Soc Neuchatel Geogr Bull ... Societe Neuchateloise de Geographie. Bulletin [*A publication*]

Soc Neurosci Abstr ... Society for Neuroscience Abstracts [*A publication*]

Soc Neurosci Symp ... Society for Neuroscience. Symposia [*A publication*]

Soc Nucl Med Southeast Chapter Contin Educ Lect ... Society of Nuclear Medicine. Southeastern Chapter. Continuing Education Lectures [*A publication*]

Soc Num Mexico Bol ... Sociedad Numismatica de Mexico. Boletin [*A publication*]

Soc Nurs Hist Gaz ... Society for Nursing History. Gazette [*A publication*]

SOCO .... Scenes-of-the-Crime Officer [*Scotland Yard*]

SOCO .... Standard Oil Company of California

SOCO .... Summit Oilfield Corporation [*NASDAQ symbol*]   (NQ)

SOCO .... Switched out for Checkout [*NASA*]   (KSC)

Soc Occup Medicine J ... Society of Occupational Medicine. Journal [*A publication*]

Soc Ocean J ... Societe des Oceanistes. Journal [*A publication*]

SOCOEE... Social Cognition [*A publication*]

SOCOM .... Society and Commerce Publications

SOCOM .... Solar Communications

SOCOM .... Southern Command   (MCD)

SOCOM .... Special Operations Command [*Military*]

SOCONY .. Standard Oil Company of New York [*Socony Mobil is now official name of firm*]

SOCORICO ... Society of Costa Rica Collectors   (EA)

SOCPAC ... Special Operations Center, Pacific Command   (CINC)

Soc Paleontol Ital Boll ... Societa Paleontologica Italiana. Bollettino [*A publication*]

Soc Perspect ... Social Perspectives [*A publication*]

Soc Pet E J ... Society of Petroleum Engineers. American Institute of Mining, Metallurgical, and Petroleum Engineers. Journal [*A publication*]

Soc Pet Eng AIME Improv Oil Recovery Field Rep ... Society of Petroleum Engineers. American Institute of Mining, Metallurgical, and Petroleum Engineers. Improved Oil Recovery Field Reports [*A publication*]

Soc Pet Eng AIME J ... Society of Petroleum Engineers. American Institute of Mining, Metallurgical, and Petroleum Engineers. Journal [*A publication*]

Soc Pet Eng AIME Pap ... Society of Petroleum Engineers. American Institute of Mining, Metallurgical, and Petroleum Engineers. Papers [*A publication*]

Soc Pet Eng AIME Trans ... Society of Petroleum Engineers. American Institute of Mining, Metallurgical, and Petroleum Engineers. Transactions [*A publication*]

Soc Pet Eng J ... Society of Petroleum Engineers. American Institute of Mining, Metallurgical, and Petroleum Engineers. Journal [*A publication*]

Soc Pet Engr J ... Society of Petroleum Engineers. American Institute of Mining, Metallurgical, and Petroleum Engineers. Journal [*A publication*]

Soc Pet Engrs J ... Society of Petroleum Engineers. American Institute of Mining, Metallurgical, and Petroleum Engineers. Journal [*A publication*]

Soc Petrol Eng J ... Society of Petroleum Engineers. American Institute of Mining, Metallurgical, and Petroleum Engineers. Journal [*A publication*]

Soc Petrol Eng Trans ... Society of Petroleum Engineers. American Institute of Mining, Metallurgical, and Petroleum Engineers. Transactions [*A publication*]

Soc Petroleum Engineers AIME Trans ... Society of Petroleum Engineers. American Institute of Mining, Metallurgical, and Petroleum Engineers. Transactions [*A publication*]

Soc Petroleum Engineers Jour ... Society of Petroleum Engineers. American Institute of Mining, Metallurgical, and Petroleum Engineers. Journal [*A publication*]

Soc Petroleum Engrs Jol ... Society of Petroleum Engineers. Journal [*A publication*]

Soc Phot Instr Eng Newsletter ... Society of Photographic Instrumentation Engineers. Newsletter [*A publication*]

Soc Photo-Opt Instrum Eng Proc ... Society of Photo-Optical Instrumentation Engineers. Proceedings [*United States*] [*A publication*]

Soc Physique et Histoire Nat Geneve Compte Rendu ... Societe de Physique et d'Histoire Naturelle de Geneve. Compte Rendu des Seances [*A publication*]

Soc Plant Prot North Jpn Spec Rep ... Society of Plant Protection of North Japan. Special Report [*A publication*]

Soc Plast Eng Div Tech Conf Tech Pap ... Society of Plastics Engineers. Divisional Technical Conference. Technical Papers [*A publication*]

Soc Plast Ind Struct Foam Conf Proc ... Society of the Plastics Industry. Structural Foam Conference. Proceedings [*A publication*]

SOCPO ...... Society of Chief Personnel Officers [*British*]

Soc Pol .... Social Policy [*A publication*]

Soc Policy .. Social Policy [*A publication*]

Soc-Polit Soc-Ekon Probl Razvit Social Obsc ... Social'no-Politiceskie i Social'no-Ekonomiceskie Problemy Razvitogo Socialisticeskogo Obscestva [*A publication*]

Soc Pr........ Social Progress [*A publication*]

Soc Prax.... Social Praxis [*A publication*]

Soc Prehist Francais Bull ... Societe Prehistorique Francaise. Bulletin [*A publication*]

Soc Prehist Francaise Bul ... Societe Prehistorique Francaise. Bulletin [*A publication*]

Soc Prehist Fr Bull ... Societe Prehistorique Francaise. Bulletin [*A publication*]

Soc Prob..... Social Problems [*A publication*]

Soc Probl.... Social Problems [*A publication*]

Soc Probl Nauc-Tehn Revol ... Social'nye Problemy Naucno-Tehniceskogo Revoljucii [*A publication*]

Soc Promotion Agr Sc Pr ... Society for the Promotion of Agricultural Science. Proceedings of the Annual Meeting [*A publication*]

Soc Psichol Filos ... Social'naja Psichologija i Filosofija [*A publication*]

Soc Psychiatry ... Social Psychiatry [*A publication*]

Soc Psychol ... Social Psychology [*A publication*]

Soc Psychol Q ... Social Psychology Quarterly [*A publication*]

Soc Psych Res Proc ... Society for Psychical Research. Proceedings [*A publication*]

SOCQ .... Stages of Concern Questionnaire [*Educational test*]

Soc Que Prot Plant Rapp ... Societe de Quebec pour la Protection des Plantes. Rapport [*A publication*]

Soc Quim Mexico Rev ... Sociedad Quimica de Mexico. Revista [*A publication*]

SOCR......... Scan-Optics, Inc. [*NASDAQ symbol*]   (NQ)

Soc R .... Social Research [*A publication*]

Soc R .... Socialist Review [*A publication*]

Soc R .... Sociological Review [*A publication*]

SoCR......... South Carolina Review [*A publication*]

SOCR........ Special Operational Contract Requirements   (AAG)

SOCR........ Sustained Operations Control Room [*NASA*]   (KSC)

SOCR........ Synchronous Orbit Communication Relay   (MCD)

Soc Radiol Prot J ... Society for Radiological Protection. Journal [*A publication*]

SOCRATES ... Service Order, Customer Records, and Terminal Entry System

SOCRATES ... System for Organizing Content to Review and Teach Educational Subjects

SOCRATES ... System for Organizing Current Reports to Aid Technology and Science
SOCRED... Social Credit Party [*British*]
Soc Regis.... Socialist Register [*A publication*]
Soc Rehabil Rec ... Social and Rehabilitation Record [*A publication*]
Soc Res...... Social Research [*A publication*]
Soc Res...... Social Reserve [*A publication*]
Soc Res Child Devel Monogr ... Society for Research in Child Development. Monographs [*A publication*]
Soc Research Administrators J ... Journal. Society of Research Administrators [*A publication*]
Soc Resp .... Social Responsibility [*A publication*]
Soc Rev ...... Socialist Review [*A publication*]
Soc Revol ... Socialist Revolution [*A publication*]
Soc R di Nap Accad di Archeol Atti ... Societa Reale di Napoli. Accademia di Archeologia, Lettere, e Belle Arti. Atti [*A publication*]
Soc R di Nap Accad di Sci Mor e Pol Atti ... Societa Reale di Napoli. Accademia di Scienze Morali e Politiche. Atti [*A publication*]
Soc R di Napoli Accad di Archeol Atti ... Societa Reale di Napoli. Accademia di Archeologia, Lettere, e Belle Arti. Atti [*A publication*]
Soc R di Napoli Accad d Sci Fis e Mat Atti ... Societa Reale di Napoli. Accademia delle Scienze, Fisiche, e Matematiche. Atti [*A publication*]
SOC ROS.. Societas Rosicruciana [*Freemasonry*]
Soc Royale Econ Pol Belgique Seance ... Societe Royale d'Economie Politique de Belgique. Seances [*A publication*]
Soc Roy Belge de Geog B ... Societe Royale Belge de Geographie. Bulletin [*A publication*]
SOCS........ Senior Chief SONARman [*Navy rating*]
SOCS........ Society for Savings Bancorp, Inc. [*NASDAQ symbol*]   (NQ)
SOCS........ Spacecraft-Orientation-Control System
SOCS........ Subsystem Operating and Checkout System [*NASA*]   (MCD)
Soc Sci....... Social Sciences [*A publication*]
Soc Scientist ... Social Scientist [*A publication*]
Soc Sci Fenn Arsb-Vuosik ... Societas Scientiarum Fennicae. Arsbok-Vuosikirja [*A publication*]
Soc Sci Fenn Commentat Biol ... Societas Scientiarum Fennica. Commentationes Biologicae [*A publication*]
Soc Sci Fenn Commentat Phys-Math ... Societas Scientiarum Fennica. Commentationes Physico-Mathematicae [*A publication*]
Soc Sci Fenn Comment Phys-Math ... Societas Scientiarum Fennica. Commentationes Physico-Mathematicae [*A publication*]
Soc Sci Fennica Arsb ... Societas Scientiarum Fennica. Arsbok [*A publication*]
Soc Sci Fennica Commentationes Phys-Math ... Societas Scientiarum Fennica. Commentationes Physico-Mathematicae [*A publication*]
Soc Sci Ind ... Social Sciences Index [*A publication*]
Soc Sci Inf ... Social Science Information [*A publication*]
Soc Sci Inform ... Social Science Information [*A publication*]
Soc Sci Inf Stud ... Social Science Information Studies [*A publication*]
Soc Sci J ... Social Science Journal [*A publication*]
Soc Sci Lettres & Arts Pau Bul ... Societe des Sciences, Lettres, et Arts. Pau Bulletin [*A publication*]
Soc Sci Lodz Acta Chim ... Societatis Scientiarum Lodziensis. Acta Chimica [*A publication*]
Soc Sci Med ... Social Science and Medicine [*A publication*]
Soc Sci and Med ... Social Science and Medicine [*A publication*]
Soc Sci Med A ... Social Science and Medicine. Part A. Medical Sociology [*A publication*]
Soc Sci Med B ... Social Science and Medicine. Part B. Medical Anthropology [*A publication*]
Soc Sci Med C ... Social Science and Medicine. Part C. Medical Economics [*A publication*]
Soc Sci Med D ... Social Science and Medicine. Part D. Medical Geography [*A publication*]
Soc Sci Medic ... Social Science and Medicine [*A publication*]
Soc Sci Med (Med Anthropol) ... Social Science and Medicine (Medical Anthropology) [*A publication*]
Soc Sci Med Med Econ ... Social Science and Medicine. Part C. Medical Economics [*A publication*]
Soc Sci Med (Med Geogr) ... Social Science and Medicine (Medical Geography) [*A publication*]
Soc Sci Med (Med Psychol Med Sociol) ... Social Science and Medicine (Medical Psychology and Medical Sociology) [*A publication*]
Soc Sci & Med Part A Med Psychol & Med Sociol ... Social Science and Medicine. Part A. Medical Psychology and Medical Sociology [*A publication*]
Soc Sci & Med Part A Med Sociol ... Social Science and Medicine. Part A. Medical Sociology [*A publication*]
Soc Sci & Med Part B Med Anthropol ... Social Science and Medicine. Part B. Medical Anthropology [*A publication*]
Soc Sci & Med Part C Med Econ ... Social Science and Medicine. Part C. Medical Economics [*A publication*]
Soc Sci & Med Part D Med Geogr ... Social Science and Medicine. Part D. Medical Geography [*A publication*]
Soc Sci & Med Part E Med Psychol ... Social Science and Medicine. Part E. Medical Psychology [*A publication*]
Soc Sci & Med Part F Med & Soc Ethics ... Social Science and Medicine. Part F. Medical and Social Ethics [*A publication*]
Soc Sci Monographs ... Social Science Monographs [*A publication*]   (APTA)

Soc Sci Nat Ouest Fr Bull ... Societe des Sciences Naturelles de l'Ouest de la France. Bulletin [*A publication*]
Soc Sci Nat Phys Maroc C R Seances Mens ... Societe des Sciences Naturelles et Physiques du Maroc. Comptes Rendus des Seances Mensuelles [*A publication*]
Soc Sci NL ... Social Science Newsletter [*A publication*]
Soc Sci Q.... Social Science Quarterly [*A publication*]
Soc Sci R.... Social Science Review [*Bangkok*] [*A publication*]
Soc Sci Res ... Social Science Research [*A publication*]
Soc Sci Res Council Bull ... Social Science Research Council. Bulletin [*A publication*]
Soc Sci (Winfield) ... Social Science (Winfield) [*A publication*]
Soc & Scl Res ... Sociology and Social Research [*A publication*]
Soc Sc Nat Neuchatel B ... Societe des Sciences Naturelles de Neuchatel. Bulletin [*A publication*]
Soc Sec Bull ... Social Security Bulletin [*US*] [*A publication*]
Soc Sec J.... Social Security Journal [*A publication*]
Soc Sec Q... Social Security Quarterly [*A publication*]
Soc Sec Rep ... Social Security Reporter [*A publication*]   (APTA)
Soc Secur Bull ... Social Security Bulletin [*A publication*]
Soc Secur Bull Annu Stat Suppl ... Social Security Bulletin. Annual Statistical Supplement [*US*] [*A publication*]
Soc Serbe Geographie Mem ... Societe Serbe de Geographie. Memoires [*A publication*]
Soc Ser Rev ... Social Service Review [*A publication*]
Soc Serv ..... Social Service [*A publication*]   (APTA)
Soc Services Rev ... Social Services Review [*A publication*]
Soc Serv J .. Social Services Journal [*A publication*]   (APTA)
Soc Serv Q ... Social Service Quarterly [*A publication*]
Soc Serv R ... Social Service Review [*A publication*]
Soc Serv Rev ... Social Service Review [*A publication*]
Soc Soc Hist Med Bull ... Society for the Social History of Medicine. Bulletin [*A publication*]
Soc Soc Res ... Sociology and Social Research [*A publication*]
Soc Sport J ... Sociology of Sport Journal [*A publication*]
Soc St .... Social Studies [*A publication*]
Soc de Statist de Paris J ... Societe de Statistique de Paris. Journal [*A publication*]
Soc Statist Paris J ... Societe de Statistique de Paris. Journal [*A publication*]
Soc Stud ..... Social Studies [*A publication*]
Soc Studies ... Social Studies [*A publication*]
Soc Stud Sci ... Social Studies of Science [*United Kingdom*] [*A publication*]
Soc Study Amphib Reptiles Herpetol Circ ... Society for the Study of Amphibians and Reptiles. Herpetological Circular [*A publication*]
Soc Study Inborn Errors Metab Proc Symp ... Society for the Study of Inborn Errors of Metabolism. Proceedings of the Symposium [*A publication*]
Soc Sur .... Social Survey [*A publication*]   (APTA)
Soc Surv ..... Social Survey [*A publication*]   (APTA)
Soc Survey ... Social Survey [*A publication*]   (APTA)
SOCTAP ... Sulfur Oxide Control Technology Assessment Panel [*Federal interagency committee*]
Soc Theory & Pract ... Social Theory and Practice [*A publication*]
Soc Thought ... Social Thought [*A publication*]
Soc Thr ...... Socialist Theory and Practice [*A publication*]
Soc Toscana Sci Nat Atti Mem Ser A ... Societa Toscana di Scienze Naturali. Atti. Memorie. Serie A [*A publication*]
Soc Tr........ Socialisticeskij Trud [*A publication*]
Soc Trav..... Sociologie du Travail [*A publication*]
Soc Travail ... Sociologie du Travail [*A publication*]
Soc Trends ... Social Trends [*A publication*]
Soc Tss....... Social Tidsskrift [*A publication*]
Soc Vac Coaters Proc Annu Conf ... Society of Vacuum Coaters. Proceedings. Annual Conference [*A publication*]
Soc Vaudoise Sci Nat Bull ... Societe Vaudoise des Sciences Naturelles. Bulletin [*A publication*]
Soc Venez Cienc Nat Bol ... Sociedad Venezolana de Ciencias Naturales. Boletin [*A publication*]
Soc Venezolana Ciencias Natur Bol ... Sociedad Venezolana de Ciencias Naturales. Boletin [*A publication*]
Soc Ven Sci Nat Lav ... Societa Veneziana di Scienze Naturali Lavori [*A publication*]
Soc W......... Social Work [*A publication*]
Soc Welfare ... Social Welfare [*A publication*]
Soc Wetensch ... Sociale Wetenschappen [*A publication*]
Soc Wk (Albany) ... Social Work (Albany) [*A publication*]
Soc Work ... Social Work [*A publication*]
Soc Work Health Care ... Social Work in Health Care [*A publication*]
Soc Work Lect ... Social Work Lectures [*New Zealand*] [*A publication*]
Soc Workr ... Socialist Worker [*A publication*]
Soc Work Res Abstr ... Social Work Research and Abstracts [*A publication*]
Soc Work Today ... Social Work Today [*A publication*]
SOCY........ Society   (ROG)
SOCY........ Sociology   (ROG)
SOCYA...... Society [*A publication*]
Soc Zemed ... Socialisticke Zemedelstvi [*A publication*]
Soc Zemes Ukis ... Socialistinis Zemes Ukis [*A publication*]
Soc Zemjod ... Socijalisticko Zemjodelstvo [*A publication*]
Soc Zool France B ... Societe Zoologique de France. Bulletin [*A publication*]
Soc Zool Fr Bull ... Societe Zoologique de France. Bulletin [*A publication*]

SOD	Sediment Oxygen Demand [*of water bodies*]
SOD	Sell-Off Date (AAG)
SOD	Seller's Option to Double [*Stock exchange term*]
SOD	Serial Output Data [*Data processing*]
SOD	Shorter Oxford Dictionary [*A publication*]
SOD	Shuttle Operational Data (MCD)
SOD	Small Object Detector
SOD	Socialisme en Democratie [*A publication*]
SOD	Society of Dismas (EA)
SOD	Sodalite [*A zeolite*]
SOD	Sodankyla [*Finland*] [*Geomagnetic observatory code*]
SOD	Sodankyla [*Finland*] [*Seismograph station code, US Geological Survey*] (SEIS)
SOD	Sodium (DHSM)
Sod	Sodobnost [*A publication*]
SOD	Sodomy [*FBI standardized term*]
SOD	Soldier Orientation and Development (MCD)
SOD	Solitron Devices, Inc. [*NYSE symbol*] (SPSG)
SOD	Sons of the Desert (EA)
SOD	Sound-on-Disk (DEN)
SOD	Special Operations Detachment [*Military*] (AABC)
SOD	Special Operations Division [*Office of Preparedness, General Services Administration*]
SOD	Special Order Discharge
SOD	Staff Operations Division [*NASA*] (MCD)
SOD	Superintendent of Documents [*US Government Printing Office*]
SOD	Superoxide Dismutase [*Also, SODI*] [*An enzyme*]
SOD	Surgical Operations Database [*Medicine*]
SOD	Sustained Operational Date (AFM)
SOD	Systems Operational Description [*or Design*]
So 2d	Southern Reporter, Second Series [*A publication*] (DLA)
SODA	A & W Brands, Inc. [*NASDAQ symbol*] (NQ)
SODA	Source Oriented Data Acquisition
SODA	Stamp Out Drug Addiction
SODAA	Solnechnye Dannye [*A publication*]
SODAC	Source Data Collection
So Dak B Jo	South Dakota Bar Journal [*A publication*] (DLA)
So Dak Hist	South Dakota History [*A publication*]
So Dak Hist Coll	South Dakota Historical Collections [*A publication*]
So Dak L Rev	South Dakota Law Review [*A publication*]
So Dakota Lib Bul	South Dakota Library Bulletin [*A publication*]
So Dak R	South Dakota Review [*A publication*]
SODAR	Sound Detecting and Ranging
SODAS	Sandia Optical Disk Archival System [*Online map database*] [*Developed by Sandia National Laboratories for the USGS*]
SODAS	Structure-Oriented Description and Simulation (IEEE)
SODAS	Synoptic Oceanographic Data Acquisition System [*Marine science*] (MSC)
SODB	Science Organization Development Board [*National Academy of Sciences*]
SODB	Shuttle [*or Spacecraft*] Operational Data Book [*NASA*]
SODB	Sodbury [*England*]
SODB	Start of Data Block (MCD)
SODC	Siblings of Disabled Children (EA)
Sodep	Social Democratic Party [*Turkey*] [*Political party*] (PPW)
SODEPALM	Societe pour le Developpement et l'Exploitation du Palmier a Huile [*Ivory Coast*]
SODEPAX	Committee on Society, Development, and Peace [*of the Roman Catholic Church and the World Council of Churches*] [*Defunct*] (EA)
SODEX	Social Data Exchange Association [*Council for Community Services*] [*Information service or system*] (IID)
SODI	Superoxide Dismutase [*Absorbed by SOD*] [*An enzyme*]
SODPAL	Social Democrat Party and Liberal [*British*]
SODRE	Servicio Oficial de Difusion Radio Electrica [*Radio and television network*] [*Uruguay*]
SODRS	Synchronous Orbit Data Relay Satellite
SODS	Saturn Operational Display System [*NASA*]
SODS	Shuttle Operational Data System [*NASA*] (MCD)
SODS	Skylab Orbit-Deorbit System [*NASA*] (MCD)
SODS	Subordinate Operations Data System (NVT)
SODT	Scope Octal Debugging Tape
SODTICIOAP	Special Ordnance Depot Tool Identification, Classification, Inventory, and Obsolescence Analysis Program [*Popularly called "Soda Cap"*]
SODU	Screen Oriented Disk Utility [*Data processing*]
SOE	Senior Officer Escort [*British military*] (DMA)
SOE	Sequence of Events
SOE	Short of Exchange [*Economics*]
SOE	Significant Operating Experience (IEEE)
SOE	Silver Oxide Electrode
SOE	Skylab Operational Environment [*NASA*]
SOE	Slater Orbital Exponents [*Atomic physics*]
SOE	Socio-Economic Planning Sciences [*A publication*]
SOE	Soft Drinks Trade Journal [*A publication*]
SOE	Souanke [*Congo*] [*Airport symbol*] (OAG)
SOE	Special Operations Executive [*British research unit corresponding to OSS*] [*World War II*]
SOE	Stage Operations Engineer
SOE	Start of Entry [*Data processing*]
SOE	State-Owned Enterprise
SOE	Status of Equipment [*Army*] (AABC)
SOE	Summary of Engagements (MCD)
SOE	Super Orbit Entry
SOEAP	Summary of Effective Allowance Parts List [*Navy*]
SOEASTPAC	Southeast Pacific Command [*Navy*]
So East Rep	Southeastern Reporter [*A publication*] (DLA)
SOEBT	Stationery and Office Equipment Board of Trade (EA)
SOEC	Statistical Office of the European Communities (DCTA)
SOECA	Soviet Electrochemistry [*English Translation*] [*A publication*]
So Econ J	Southern Economic Journal [*A publication*]
SOED	Shorter Oxford English Dictionary [*A publication*]
SOED	Southern Educators Life Insurance Co. [*NASDAQ symbol*] (NQ)
So Educ Report	Southern Education Report [*A publication*]
SOEEA	Soviet Electrical Engineering [*English Translation*] [*A publication*]
SOEH	Society for Occupational and Environmental Health (EA)
SOEMC	Senior Officer Executive Management Course [*Naval War College*]
SOEMD	Solar Energy Materials [*A publication*]
SOEND	Solar Engineering [*A publication*]
SOEP	Solar-Oriented Experimental Package [*NASA*]
SOER	Significant Operating Event Report (IEEE)
SOERO	Small Orbiting Earth Resources Observatory (IEEE)
SOES	Station Operations and Engineering Squadron [*Marine Corps*]
SOE/SO	Special Operations Executive, Special Operations [*British*] [*World War II*]
Soester Z	Soester Zeitschrift [*A publication*]
So Expose	Southern Exposure [*A publication*]
SOF	Safety of Flight [*NASA*] (NASA)
SoF	Samtid och Framtid [*A publication*]
SOF	Satisfactory Operation Factor [*Telecommunications*] (TEL)
SOF	Secretary's Open Forum (EA)
SOF	Shortest Operation First
Sof	Soferim (BJA)
SOF	Sofia [*Bulgaria*] [*Airport symbol*] (OAG)
SOF	Sofia [*Bulgaria*] [*Seismograph station code, US Geological Survey*] (SEIS)
SOF	Soldier of Fortune [*A publication*]
SOF	Soluble Organic Fraction [*Environmental chemistry*]
SOF	Sound on Film
SOF	Special Operations Force [*Military*]
SOF	Spillover Factor
SOF	Spreading Ocean Floor
SOF	Start-of-Format Control [*Data processing*]
SOF	Start of Frame
SOF	Status of Forces
SOF	Storage Oscilloscope Fragments
SOF	Strategic Offensive Forces [*Army*] (AABC)
SOF	Sub-Occipito Frontal [*Medicine*] (ROG)
SOF	Suedost-Forschungen [*A publication*]
SOF	Superior Orbital Fissure [*Eye anatomy*]
SOF	Supervisor of Flying (MCD)
SOFA	Bench Craft, Inc. [*NASDAQ symbol*] (NQ)
SOFA	Status of Forces Agreement [*International treaty*]
SOFA	Student Overseas Flights for Americans
SOFAR	Sound Fixing and Ranging [*Navy underground sound system*]
SOFAR	Sound Fusing and Ranging
SOFAS	Suitable Occupation for a Sloane [*British*] [*Slang*]
SOFAS	Survivable Optical Forward Acquisition Sensor
SOFAS	Survivable Optical Forward Acquisition System (MCD)
SOFC	Saturn Operational Flight Control [*NASA*]
SOFC	Solid Oxide Fuel Cell [*Energy source*]
SOFCS	Self-Organizing Flight Control System
SofD	Sons of David (BJA)
SOFE	Society of Financial Examiners (EA)
SOFE	Swedish Options and Futures Exchange
SOFEX	Southern Ocean Float Experiment [*Marine science*] (MSC)
S/OFF	Sign Off [*Data processing*] (MDG)
SOFFEX	Swiss Options and Financial Futures Exchange
SOFI	Spray-On Foam Insulation (NASA)
SOFIA	Stratospheric Observatory for Infrared Astronomy [*NASA*]
Sofia Univ Geol-Geogr Fak God Kn 2 Geogr	Sofia Universitet. Geologo-Geografski Fakultet. Godishnik. Kniga 2. Geografiya [*A publication*]
Sofia Univ Geol-Geogr Fak God Kniga 1 Geol	Sofia Universitet. Geologo-Geografski Fakultet. Godishnik. Kniga 1. Geologiya [*A publication*]
Sofia Vissh Minno Geol Inst God	Sofia Vissh Minno-Geolozhki Institut. Godishnik [*A publication*]
SOFIE	Sources de Financement des Entreprises [*CCMC Informatique de Gestion*] [*Database*]
SOFINA	Societe Financiere de Transports et d'Entreprises Industrielles [*French*]
SOFIX	Software Fix [*NASA*]
So Fla BJ	South Florida Business Journal [*A publication*]
SOFMA	Soviet Fluid Mechanics [*English Translation*] [*A publication*]
SOFNET	Solar Observing and Forecasting Network [*Air Force*]
SOFOA	Social Forces [*A publication*]

So Folklore Q ... Southern Folklore Quarterly [*A publication*]
SOFPAC ... Special Operating Forces, Pacific [*Military*]
SOFRECOM ... Societe Francaise d'Etudes et de Realisations d'Equipements de Telecommunications [*French communications engineering company*] [*Telecommunications*] (TEL)
SOFRES.... Societe Francaise d'Enquetes par Sondages [*French opinion-polling organization*]
SOFT........ Australian Software Locator [*John Fairfax & Sons Ltd.*] [*Information service or system*] (CRD)
SOFT........ Simple Output Format Translator (IEEE)
SOFT........ Society of Forensic Toxicologists (EA)
SOFT........ SofTech, Inc. [*NASDAQ symbol*] (NQ)
SOFT........ Software [*Data processing*]
SOFT........ Software Locator [*Database*] [*Australia*]
SOFT........ Space Operations and Flight Techniques [*NASA*] (NASA)
SOFT........ Special Operational Forces Taiwan (CINC)
SOFT........ Status of Forces Treaty
SOFT 18/13 ... Support Organization for Trisomy 18/13 (EA)
SOFTA...... Shippers Oil Field Traffic Association (EA)
SOFTCON ... Software Conference [*Trademark*]
Soft Eng ..... IEEE. Transactions on Software Engineering [*A publication*]
Soft Eng Notes ... Software Engineering Notes [*A publication*]
Soft News... Software News [*A publication*]
Software..... Software: Practice and Experience [*A publication*]
Software N ... Software News [*A publication*]
Software Pract Exper ... Software: Practice and Experience [*A publication*]
Software Pract and Exper ... Software: Practice and Experience [*A publication*]
Software Pub Rep ... Software Publishing Report [*A publication*]
Software Rev ... Software Review [*A publication*]
Software Tools Commun ... Software Tools Communications [*A publication*]
Softw Healthc ... Software in Healthcare [*A publication*]
Softw Newsl ... Software Newsletter [*A publication*]
Soft World ... Software World [*A publication*]
SOFTY...... Southern Federation of Temple Youth
Sof Vr......... Sofijskij Vremennik [*A publication*]
SOG.......... Same Output Gate [*Data processing*] (AAG)
SOG.......... Seat of Government [*Washington, DC*]
SOG.......... Second-Order Gradient
sog............. Sogdian [*MARC language code*] [*Library of Congress*] (LCCP)
SOG.......... Sogenannt [*So-Called*] [*German*]
SOG.......... Sogndal [*Norway*] [*Airport symbol*] (OAG)
SOG.......... Special Operations Group [*Navy*]
SOG........ Speed Made Good Over the Ground (NATG)
SOG........ Straits Oil & Gas [*Vancouver Stock Exchange symbol*]
SOG........ Studies and Observations Group [*Military*]
SOG........ Supraoesophageal Ganglion [*Invertebrate nuerology*]
SOGA........ Spouses of Gays Association (EA)
SOGAT...... Society of Graphical and Allied Trades [*British*]
SOGCC..... Sydney Olympic Games Citizens' Council [*Australia*]
SOGEA...... Southeastern Geology [*United States*] [*A publication*]
SOGEB...... Soviet Genetics [*English Translation*] [*A publication*]
Sog Iga....... Sogo Igaku [*A publication*]
SOGLF...... Shelter Oil & Gas Ltd. [*NASDAQ symbol*] (NQ)
Sogo Hog ... Sogo Hogaku [*A publication*]
Sogo Ky Kenk Kiyo ... Sogo Kyodo Kenkyusho Kiyo [*A publication*]
SOGp......... Special Operations Group [*Air Force*] (AFM)
Sog Rinsho... Sogo Rinsho [*A publication*]
SOGS........ Science Operations Ground System [*Space telescope software*]
Sog Shik Nenpo ... Sogo Shikensho Nenpo [*A publication*]
SOGWPIP ... Silly Old Grandmother with Pictures in Purse
SOH.......... Skylab Operations Handbook [*NASA*]
SOH.......... Southern Ohio Aviation Sales Co. [*West Carrollton, OH*] [*FAA designator*] (FAAC)
SOH.......... Standard Oil Co. (Ohio) [*NYSE symbol*] (SPSG)
SOH.......... Start of Header [*or Heading*] [*Transmission control character*] [*Data processing*]
SOH.......... Supply Overhaul (MCD)
SOHAM..... Southampton [*City in England*] (ROG)
SOHC........ Single Overhead Camshaft [*Automotive engineering*]
SOHED..... Sowjetunion Heute [*A publication*]
SOHF........ Sense of Humor Failure [*British*] [*Slang*]
SOHI......... Sponsors of Open Housing Investment [*Later, Fund for an Open Society*] (EA)
SOHIC...... Stress-Oriented Hydrogen-Induced Cracking [*Metallurgy*]
SOHID...... Sohioan [*A publication*]
SOHIO...... Standard Oil Co. (Ohio)
So His S..... Southern Historical Society [*A publication*]
So Hist Pap ... Southern Historical Society. Papers [*A publication*]
SOHO........ Solar and Heliospheric Observatory [*European Space Agency*]
SoHo.......... South of Houston Street [*See also NoHo, SoSo, TriBeCa*] [*Artists' colony in New York City*]
SOHR........ Solar Hydrogen Rocket Engine
SoHR........ Southern Humanities Review [*A publication*]
SOI........... Scientific and Optical Instruments
SOI........... Security and Operational Inspection [*Army*]
SOI........... Shoshoni Gold [*Vancouver Stock Exchange symbol*]
SOI........... Signal Operation Instructions
SOI........... Silicon-on-Insulator
SOI........... Solar Oscillations Imager [*Instrumentation*]
SOI........... South Molle Island [*Australia*] [*Airport symbol*] (OAG)

SOI........... Southern Illinois University at Carbondale, Carbondale, IL [*OCLC symbol*] (OCLC)
SOI........... Southern Indiana Railway, Inc. [*Later, SIND*] [*AAR code*]
SOI........... Southern Oscillation Index
SOI........... Space Object Identification (AFM)
SOI........... Special Olympics International (EA)
SOI........... Specific Operating Instruction (AFM)
SOI........... Sphere of Influence
SOI........... Standard Operating Instruction (KSC)
SOI........... State of Stimulus Overinclusion [*Schizophrenia*]
SOI........... Statistics of Income [*IRS*]
SOI........... Stimulus Onset Interval
SOI........... Surety and Operational Inspection [*Military*] (AFIT)
SOIC......... Small Outline Integrated Circuit [*Data processing*]
SOIC......... Supply Officer-in-Command [*Military*]
SOICAS .... Space Object Identification Central Analysis System
SOICC...... State Occupational Information Coordinating Committee
SOICS .... Summary of Installation Control Status [*Nuclear energy*] (NRCH)
SOID .... Shipboard Ordnance Infrared Decoy (MCD)
SOIFA .... Soils and Fertilizers [*A publication*]
SOIG .... Special Operations Industry Group [*Army*]
Soil Assoc Inf Bull Advis Serv ... Soil Association. Information Bulletin and Advisory Service [*England*] [*A publication*]
Soil Biochem ... Soil Biochemistry [*A publication*]
Soil Biol B ... Soil Biology and Biochemistry [*A publication*]
Soil Biol Biochem ... Soil Biology and Biochemistry [*A publication*]
Soil Biol and Biochem ... Soil Biology and Biochemistry [*A publication*]
Soil Biol Microbiol ... Soil Biology and Microbiology [*A publication*]
Soil Cons.... Soil Conservation [*A publication*]
Soil Conser ... Soil Conservation [*A publication*]
Soil Conserv ... Soil Conservation [*A publication*]
Soil Conserv US Soil Conserv Serv ... Soil Conservation. United States Soil Conservation Service [*A publication*]
Soil Cons Serv NSW J ... Soil Conservation Service of New South Wales. Journal [*A publication*] (APTA)
Soil Crop Sci Soc Fla Proc ... Soil and Crop Science Society of Florida. Proceedings [*A publication*]
Soil Fert ..... Soils and Fertilizers [*A publication*]
Soil Fertil... Soils and Fertilizers [*A publication*]
Soil Fert Taiwan ... Soils and Fertilizers in Taiwan [*A publication*]
Soil Ld-Use Surv Br Caribb ... Soil and Land-Use Surveys of the British Caribbean [*A publication*]
So Ill LJ ..... Southern Illinois University. Law Journal [*A publication*]
So Ill ULJ ... Southern Illinois University. Law Journal [*A publication*]
Soil Mech Found Eng ... Soil Mechanics and Foundation Engineering [*A publication*]
Soil Mech Found Engng ... Soil Mechanics and Foundation Engineering [*A publication*]
Soil Mech Found Eng Reg Conf Afr Proc ... Soil Mechanics and Foundation Engineering. Regional Conference for Africa. Proceedings [*A publication*]
Soil Publ .... Soil Publication. Commonwealth Scientific and Industrial Research Organisation [*Australia*] [*A publication*] (APTA)
Soil Publ CSIRO ... Soil Publication. Commonwealth Scientific and Industrial Research Organisation [*Australia*] [*A publication*] (APTA)
Soils Bull FAO ... Soils Bulletin. Food and Agriculture Organization [*A publication*]
Soil Sci....... Soil Science [*A publication*]
Soil Sci Agrochem ... Soil Science and Agrochemistry [*A publication*]
Soil Sci Agrochem Plant Prot ... Soil Science, Agrochemistry, and Plant Protection [*A publication*]
Soil Sci Agron ... Soil Science and Agronomy [*A publication*]
Soil Sci Plant Nutr ... Soil Science and Plant Nutrition [*A publication*]
Soil Sci Plant Nutr (Tokyo) ... Soil Science and Plant Nutrition (Tokyo) [*A publication*]
Soil Sci Pl Nutr ... Soil Science and Plant Nutrition [*A publication*]
Soil Sci So ... Soil Science Society of America. Proceedings [*A publication*]
Soil Sci Soc Am Book Ser ... Soil Science Society of America. Book Series [*A publication*]
Soil Sci Soc America Proc ... Soil Science Society of America. Proceedings [*A publication*]
Soil Sci Soc Am J ... Soil Science Society of America. Journal [*A publication*]
Soil Sci Soc Am Proc ... Soil Science Society of America. Proceedings [*A publication*]
Soil Sci Soc Fla Proc ... Soil Science Society of Florida. Proceedings [*A publication*]
Soil Ser Dep Soil Sci Minnesota Univ ... Minnesota. University. Department of Soil Science. Soil Series [*A publication*]
Soil Ser Minn Univ Agr Ext Serv ... Soil Series. Minnesota University. Agriculture Extension Service [*A publication*]
Soils Fert.... Soils and Fertilizers [*England*] [*A publication*]
Soils Fertil... Soils and Fertilizers [*A publication*]
Soils Fertil Taiwan ... Soils and Fertilizers in Taiwan [*A publication*]
Soils Found ... Soils and Foundations [*A publication*]
Soils Land Use Ser Div Soils CSIRO ... Soils and Land Use Series. Division of Soils. Commonwealth Scientific and Industrial Research Organisation [*A publication*] (APTA)

Soils Ld Use Ser Div Soils CSIRO ... Soils and Land Use Series. Division of Soils. Commonwealth Scientific and Industrial Research Organisation [*A publication*] (APTA)
Soils Rep Manitoba Soil Surv ... Soils Report. Manitoba Soil Survey [*A publication*]
Soil Surv Bull Samaru ... Soil Survey Bulletin. Samaru Institute for Agricultural Research [*A publication*]
Soil Surv Invest Rep ... Soil Survey Investigations. Report [*A publication*]
Soil Surv Pap Neth Soil Surv Inst ... Soil Survey Papers. Netherlands Soil Survey Institute [*A publication*]
Soil Tillage Res ... Soil and Tillage Research [*A publication*]
Soil Use Manage ... Soil Use and Management [*A publication*]
Soil and Water Conser News ... Soil and Water Conservation News [*A publication*]
Soil and Water Conserv Jour ... Soil and Water Conservation Journal [*A publication*]
SOINC....... Supply Officer-in-Charge [*Navy*]
Soins Chir ... Soins. Chirurgie [*A publication*]
Soins Gynecol Obst Pueric ... Soins. Gynecologie, Obstetrique, Puericulture [*A publication*]
Soins Pathol Trop ... Soins. Pathologie Tropicale [*A publication*]
SOIP.......... Sell-Off Impact Prognosticator [*Aerospace*] (AAG)
SOIP.......... Ship Overhaul Improvement Program [*Navy*]
SOIP.......... Sphere of Influence People
SOIS.......... Space Object Identification System
SOIS.......... Spacelab/Orbiter Interface Simulator [*NASA*] (NASA)
SOISCUM ... Space Object Identification Summary (MCD)
SOIVRE .... Servicio Oficial de Inspeccion, Vigilancia, y Regulacion de las Exportaciones [*Spain*] (IMH)
SOJ............ Sea of Japan (NVT)
SOJ............ Sorkjosen [*Norway*] [*Airport symbol*] (OAG)
SOJ............ Standoff Jammer (NVT)
SoJA.......... Soviet Jewish Affairs [*A publication*]
SO Jb......... Suedosteuropa-Jahrbuch [*A publication*]
So Jersey LS Dictum ... South Jersey Law School Dictum [*A publication*] (DLA)
SOJS .... Standoff Jammer Suppression (MCD)
SOJT........ Structured On-the-Job Training (MCD)
SOJT........ Supervised On-the-Job Training
SOJTA ...... State On-the-Job Training Agencies [*Department of Labor*]
Sojuzot Zdruzenijata Farm Farm Teh SR Maked Bilt ... Sojuzot na Zdruzenijata na Farmacevtite i Farmacevtskite Tehnicari na SR Makedonija. Bilten [*A publication*]
SOK.......... American Sokol Educational and Physical Culture Organization
SOK.......... Semongkong [*Lesotho*] [*Airport symbol*] [*Obsolete*] (OAG)
Sok............ Sokrates [*A publication*]
SOK.......... South Kauai, HI [*Location identifier*] [*FAA*] (FAAL)
SOK.......... Sprog og Kultur [*A publication*]
SOK.......... Suomen Osuuskauppojen Keskuskunta [*Co-Operative Wholesale Society*] [*Finland*] (EY)
SOK.......... Supply OK [*i.e., Authorized*]
SOKAB..... Sosei To Kako [*A publication*]
SOKS........ Sport of Kings Society (EA)
SOKSI ...... Sentral Organisasi Karyawan Sosialis Indonesia [*Central Organization of Indonesian Socialist Workers*]
SOL .... Safe Operating Limit
SOL .... Sasko Oil & Gas Ltd. [*Toronto Stock Exchange symbol*] [*Vancouver Stock Exchange symbol*]
SOL .... Saturation Output Level [*Recording tapes*]
SOL .... School of Living (EA)
SOL .... Second Order Logic
SOL .... Secretary of Labor (OICC)
SOL .... Senior Operator License [*Nuclear energy*] (NRCH)
SOL .... Shipowner's Liability [*Business term*]
SOL .... Short of Luck (DSUE)
SOL .... Simulation Oriented Language [*Data processing*]
SOL .... Sisters of Our Lady [*Roman Catholic religious order*]
SOL .... Social Organisation Limited
SOL .... Solar (AAG)
SOL .... Solder
sol............. Soldier
SOL .... Soldier out of Luck [*Military slang*]
SOL .... Solenoid (AAG)
SOL .... Soleus Muscle [*Anatomy*]
SOL .... Soliciting [*FBI standardized term*]
Sol .... Solicitor [*A publication*]
SOL .... Solicitor
SOL .... Solicitor of Labor [*Department of Labor*]
SOL .... Solid (MSA)
Sol .... Solidarity [*Manila*] [*A publication*]
SOL .... Solitaire [*Jewelry*] (ROG)
Sol .... Soloman's Court of Request Appeals [*Ceylon*] [*A publication*] (DLA)
SOL .... Solomon [*Biblical king*] (ROG)
SOL .... Solomon, AK [*Location identifier*] [*FAA*] (FAAL)
Sol .... Solon [*of Plutarch*] [*Classical studies*] (OCD)
SOL .... Solubilis [*Soluble*] [*Pharmacy*]
SOL .... Soluble
SOL .... Solutio [*Solution*] [*Pharmacy*]
SOL .... Solution
SOL .... Solve [*or Solutus*] [*Dissolve or Dissolved*] [*Pharmacy*] (ROG)

SOL .... Southern Illinois University, School of Law Library, Carbondale, IL [*OCLC symbol*] (OCLC)
So L............ Sowjetliteratur. Eine Monatsschrift [*A publication*]
SOL .... Space-Occupying Lesion [*Medicine*]
SOL .... Standard of Living
SOL .... Substitute Optical Landing System (NG)
SOL .... Sure out of Luck [*Bowdlerized version*]
SOL .... System Oriented Language
SOLA........ Selected Objects for Living Actively [*Commercial firm specializing in home furnishings for the elderly*]
SOLA........ Student Organization for Latin America [*University of Notre Dame*] [*Research center*] (RCD)
Sol Act ...... Solar Activity [*A publication*]
Sol Age...... Solar Age [*A publication*]
SOLAIR .... Solomon Islands Airways Ltd. (FEA)
Solaire 1 Mag ... Solaire 1 Magazine [*France*] [*A publication*]
SOLAN ..... Solid Angles
SOLANT.... South Atlantic Force [*Later, Command*] [*Navy*] [*World War II*]
SOLANTFOR ... South Atlantic Force [*Later, Command*] [*Navy*] [*World War II*]
SOLAR...... Sandel On-Line Automated Reference [*Information service or system*]
SOLAR..... Semantically Oriented Lexical Archive
SOLAR..... Serialized On-Line Automatic Recording [*Data processing*] (IEEE)
SOLAR...... Shop Operations Load Analysis Reporting
SOLAR..... Society of Loose Actors Revolving [*SOLAR Theater, Inc.*]
Solar 1985 ... Solar Energy Employment and Requirements, 1978-1985 [*A publication*]
Solar E D ... Solar Energy Digest [*A publication*]
Solar En D ... Solar Energy Digest [*A publication*]
Solar Energ ... Solar Energy [*A publication*]
Solar Intel ... Solar Energy Intelligence Report [*A publication*]
SOLARIS ... Submerged Object Locating and Retrieving Identification System
Solar L Rep ... Solar Law Reporter [*A publication*]
Solar Mag ... Solar Magazine [*A publication*]
SOLAR MAX ... Solar Maximum Mission Satellite
Solar Phys ... Solar Physics [*A publication*]
Solar Syst Res ... Solar System Research [*A publication*]
SOLAS ...... Safety of Life at Sea Conference [*Intergovernmental Maritime Consultative Organization*] (MSC)
SOLAT...... Style of Learning and Thinking [*Occupational therapy*]
So Law...... Southern Lawyer [*A publication*] (DLA)
So Law T.... Southern Law Times [*A publication*] (DLA)
SOLB........ Start of Line Block (CET)
Sol Cells ... Solar Cells [*A publication*]
SOLCGS ... Sisters of Our Lady of Charity of the Good Shepherd [*Roman Catholic religious order*] [*Rome, Italy*] (EAIO)
SOLCHEM ... Solar-Chemical [*Energy conversion process*]
Sol Cl Gaz ... Solicitors' Clerks' Gazette [*1921-40*] [*A publication*] (DLA)
SOLCR...... Solicitor
SOLD .... Simulation of Logic Design
SOLD .... Soldering
SOLD .... Symbolic Debugger [*Also, sdb, SYMDEB*] [*Data processing*]
SOLE......... Society of Logistics Engineers (EA)
SOLEC...... Stand on Leg, Eyes Closed [*Equilibrium test*]
Sol Energy ... Solar Energy [*A publication*]
Sol Energy Intell Rep ... Solar Energy Intelligence Report [*A publication*]
Sol Energy Mater ... Solar Energy Materials [*Netherlands*] [*A publication*]
Sol Energy Prog Aust NZ ... Solar Energy Progress in Australia and New Zealand [*A publication*] (APTA)
Sol Energy R & D Eur Community Ser E Energy Biomass ... Solar Energy R and D [*Research and Development*] in the European Community. Series E. Energy from Biomass [*A publication*]
Sol Energy Res Dev Rep ... Solar Energy Research and Development Report [*A publication*]
Sol Energy Res Rep Univ Queensl ... Solar Energy Research Report. University of Queensland [*A publication*] (APTA)
Sol Energy Update ... Solar Energy Update [*A publication*]
Sol Eng...... Solar Engineering [*A publication*]
Sol Eng Mag ... Solar Engineering Magazine [*A publication*]
SOLF......... Southern Oregon Library Federation [*Library network*]
SOLFEAS ... Solar Energy System Economic Feasibility Program [*Army*] (RDA)
Sol G.......... Solicitor General [*Legal term*] (DLA)
Sol-Gel...... Solution-Gelatin (SDI)
Sol Gen ...... Solicitor General [*Legal term*] (DLA)
Sol Heat Cool ... Solar Heating and Cooling [*A publication*]
SOLI.......... Solitec, Inc. [*NASDAQ symbol*] (NQ)
SOLI.......... Soviet Life [*A publication*]
SOLI.......... Symphony Orchestra Library Information [*Sinfonia Software*] [*Piedmont, CA*]
Solic .... Solicitor [*A publication*]
SOLIC .... Special Operations/Low Intensity Conflict [*Army*]
Solicitors' J ... Solicitors' Journal [*A publication*]
Solic J .... Solicitors' Journal [*A publication*]
SOLICO .... Sorenson Lighted Controls, Inc.
Solic Q .... Solicitor's Quarterly [*A publication*]

SOLID .... Self-Organizing Large Information Dissemination System (IEEE)
SOLID .... Simulation of Life Insurance Decisions [*Game*]
SOLID .... Solar Life [*A publication*]
Solid Fuel Chem ... Solid Fuel Chemistry [*English Translation of Khimiya Tverdogo Topliva*] [*A publication*]
Solid Fuel Chem (Engl Transl) ... Solid Fuel Chemistry (English Translation) [*A publication*]
Solid Mech Arch ... Solid Mechanics Archives [*A publication*]
Solid St Abstr ... Solid State Abstracts [*A publication*]
Solid Stat ... Solid State Technology [*A publication*]
Solid State Commun ... Solid State Communications [*A publication*]
Solid-State Electron ... Solid-State Electronics [*A publication*]
Solid State J ... Solid State Journal [*A publication*]
Solid State Phys ... Solid State Physics [*A publication*]
Solid State Phys Chem ... Solid State Physics and Chemistry [*Japan*] [*A publication*]
Solid State Phys (New York) ... Solid State Physics. Advances in Research and Applications (New York) [*A publication*]
Solid State Technol ... Solid State Technology [*A publication*]
Solid St Commun ... Solid State Communications [*A publication*]
Solid Waste Bull ... Solid Waste Bulletin [*A publication*]
Solid Wastes Manage ... Solid Wastes Management [*Later, World Wastes*] [*England*] [*A publication*]
Solid Wastes Manage Refuse Removal J ... Solid Wastes Management/Refuse Removal Journal [*Later, World Wastes*] [*A publication*]
Solid Wastes Mgmt ... Solid Wastes Management [*Later, World Wastes*] [*A publication*]
Solid Waste Syst ... Solid Waste Systems [*A publication*]
Solid WM .. Solid Wastes Management [*Later, World Wastes*] [*A publication*]
SOLINET ... Southeastern Library Network [*Atlanta, GA*] [*Library network*]
SOLINEWS ... Southeastern Library Network. Newsletter [*A publication*]
SOLION .... Solution of Ions [*Office of Naval Research*]
SOLIS .... Sozialwissenschaftliches LiteraturInformationssystem [*Database*] [*Informationszentrum Sozialwissenschaften*] [*Social Sciences Literature Information System*] [*German*] [*Information service or system*] (CRD)
SOLIS .... Symbionics On-Line Information System [*Data processing*]
SOLISTRON ... Solid-State Klystron
So Lit J ...... Southern Literary Journal [*A publication*]
SOliv .... Studia Oliveriana [*A publication*]
Sol J .... Solicitors' Journal [*A publication*]
So LJ .... Southern Law Journal and Reporter [*A publication*] (DLA)
SoLJ .... Southern Literary Journal [*A publication*]
Sol Jo (Eng) ... Solicitors' Journal (England) [*A publication*]
Sol J & R .... Solicitors' Journal and Reporter [*A publication*] (DLA)
Sol Law Rep ... Solar Law Reporter [*A publication*]
Sol Life .... Solar Life [*A publication*]
SOLM .... Sisters of Our Lady of Mercy [*Mercedarians*] [*Roman Catholic religious order*]
SOLM .... Soldier's Medal [*Military decoration*]
Sol Man Cl Gaz ... Solicitor's Managing Clerks' Gazette [*1941-62*] [*A publication*] (DLA)
SOLMD .... Solar Magazine [*A publication*]
SOLN .... Solution
Soln Akt ...... Solnechnaya Aktivnost [*A publication*]
Soln Dannye ... Solnechnye Dannye [*USSR*] [*A publication*]
Sol News Int ... Solar News International [*West Germany*] [*A publication*]
SOLO .... Selective Optical Lock-On [*Sighting device*]
SOLO .... Senior Officer Legal Orientation (MCD)
SOLO .... Southeastern Ohio Library Organization [*Library network*]
SOLO .... Status of Logistics Offensive [*Military*] (AABC)
SOLO .... Supply On-Line Option [*IMS America Ltd.*] [*Database*]
SOLO .... System for Ordinary Life Operations [*Insurance*]
SOLOC .... Southern Line of Communications [*World War II*]
Solo Cent Acad "Luiz De Queiroz" Univ Sao Paulo ... Solo Centro Academico "Luiz De Queiroz." Universidade de Sao Paulo [*A publication*]
SOLOG ..... Standardization of Certain Aspects of Operations and Logistics [*Military*]
SOLOMON ... Simultaneous Operation Linked Ordinal Modular Network
Sol Op .... Solicitor's Opinion [*Especially of Internal Revenue Bureau*] [*United States*] (DLA)
Sol Phys ..... Solar Physics [*A publication*]
Sol Q .... Solicitor Quarterly [*1962-65*] [*A publication*] (DLA)
Sol Q .... Solicitor's Quarterly [*A publication*]
So LQ .... Southern Law Quarterly [*A publication*] (DLA)
SOLQA ...... Sociological Quarterly [*A publication*]
SOLR .... Applied Solar Energy Corp. [*NASDAQ symbol*] (NQ)
SOLR .... Sidetone Objective Loudness Rating [*of telephone connections*] (IEEE)
SOLR .... Solicitor
So LR .... Southern Law Review [*Nashville, TN*] [*A publication*] (DLA)
SOLRAD ... Solar Radiation [*Satellite system*] [*Navy*]
SOLRAD-HI ... Solar Radiation - High-Altitude [*Satellite system*] [*Navy*]
SOL Rev .... School of Law. Review [*Canada*] [*A publication*] (DLA)
So L Rev ..... Southern Law Review [*A publication*] (DLA)
So L Rev NS ... Southern Law Review, New Series [*St. Louis, MO*] [*A publication*] (DLA)

So LRNS .... Southern Law Review, New Series [*St. Louis, MO*] [*A publication*] (DLA)
Sols Afr ...... Sols Africains [*A publication*]
SOL-SAL .. Solar Scientific Airlock
Sol St Comm ... Solid State Communications [*A publication*]
Sol-St Elec ... Solid-State Electronics [*A publication*]
Sol St Tech ... Solid State Technology [*A publication*]
Sol Syst Res ... Solar System Research [*A publication*]
So LT .... Southern Law Times [*A publication*] (DLA)
SOLTA ...... Sotsialisticheskiy Trud [*A publication*]
Sol Terr Environ Res Jpn ... Solar Terrestrial Environmental Research in Japan [*A publication*]
Sol Therm Components ... Solar Thermal Components [*A publication*]
Sol Therm Energy Util ... Solar Thermal Energy Utilization [*A publication*]
Sol Therm Heat Cool ... Solar Thermal Heating and Cooling [*A publication*]
Sol Therm Power Gener ... Solar Thermal Power Generation [*A publication*]
Sol Therm Rep ... Solar Thermal Report [*A publication*]
Sol Times ... Solar Times [*A publication*]
SOLTRAN ... Solar Spectrum and Transmittance [*Solar energy research*]
SOLUB ...... Aqueous Solubility Database [*Chemical Information Systems, Inc.*] [*Information service or system*] (CRD)
SOL U/T ... Solicitor's Undertaking (DCTA)
SOLUT ...... Solutus [*Dissolved*] [*Pharmacy*] (ROG)
SOLV .... Solenoid Valve [*Mechanical engineering*]
SOLV .... Solv-Ex Corp. [*NASDAQ symbol*] (NQ)
SOLV .... Solve [*Dissolve*] [*Pharmacy*]
SOLV .... Solvent
SOLV .... Super-Open-Frame Low Voltage (IEEE)
SOLVE C CAL ... Solve Cum Calore [*Dissolve by Heating*] [*Pharmacy*]
Solvent Ext ... Solvent Extraction and Ion Exchange [*A publication*]
Solvent Extr Ion Exch ... Solvent Extraction and Ion Exchange [*A publication*]
Solvent Extr Rev ... Solvent Extraction Reviews [*A publication*]
SOLW .... Society of Our Lady of the Way (EA)
SOLY .... Solubility
Som .... De Somniis [*of Philo*] (BJA)
SOM .... SACLANT [*Supreme Allied Commander, Atlantic*] Staff Organization Manual (NATG)
SOM .... San Tome [*Venezuela*] [*Airport symbol*] (OAG)
SOM .... Scanning Optical Microscope
SOM .... Securities Order Matching [*Data processing*]
SOM .... See Our Message
SOM .... Self-Organizing Machine
SOM .... Sensitivity-of-Method [*FDA*]
SOM .... Serous Otitis Media [*Ear inflammation*]
SOM .... Share of Market [*Advertising*]
SOM .... Share of Market [*Lundberg Survey, Inc.*] [*Information service or system*] (CRD)
SOM .... Shift Operations Manager (NRCH)
SOM .... Ship Operations Manager [*NASA*] (KSC)
SOM .... Skidmore, Owings & Merrill [*Architectural firm*]
SOM .... Small Office Microfilm
SOM .... Sociaal Maandblad Arbeid. Tijdschrift voor Sociaal Recht en Sociaal Geleid [*A publication*]
SOM .... Society of Medalists (EA)
SOM .... Society of Occupational Medicine [*British*]
SOM .... Somalia [*ANSI three-letter standard code*] (CNC)
som .... Somalia [*MARC language code*] [*Library of Congress*] (LCCP)
SOM .... Somatostatin [*Biochemistry*]
SOM .... Somatotrophin [*Endocrinology*]
SOM .... Sombrero [*Chile*] [*Seismograph station code, US Geological Survey*] (SEIS)
SOM .... Somerset [*County in England*]
SOM .... Somerset County Library, Bridgewater, NJ [*OCLC symbol*] (OCLC)
Som .... Somerset Legal Journal [*Pennsylvania*] [*A publication*] (DLA)
SOM .... Somersetshire [*County in England*]
SOM .... Somnus [*Sleep*] [*Latin*] (ROG)
SOM .... SONARman [*Navy*]
SOM .... Sound of Music [*Dolls by Alexander*] [*Doll collecting*]
So M .... Southern Magazine [*A publication*]
So M .... Sovetskaja Muzyka [*A publication*]
SOM .... Spacecraft Operations Manual
SOM .... Spares Optimization Model [*NASA*] (NASA)
SOM .... Stage Operating Manual [*NASA*] (KSC)
SOM .... Standard Operating Manual [*NASA*] (NASA)
SOM .... Standoff Missile (MCD)
SOM .... Start-of-Message
SOM .... Strap-On Motor
SOM .... Superior Oblique Muscle [*Eye anatomy*]
SOM .... Superior Old Marsala
SOM .... Survivability Optimization Model (MCD)
SOM .... Sustained Operations Manual
SOM .... Sustained Operations Model
SOM .... System Operator Manual [*Military*] (CAAL)
SOMA .... Services to Ongoing Mature Aging [*Counseling group*]
SOMA .... Sharing of Missionaries Abroad [*Church of England*]
SOMA .... Signed Out Against Medical Advice
SOMA .... Soobscenija Otdela Machanizacii i Avtomatizacii Informacionnych Rabot [*A publication*]
SoMa .... South of Market [*District of San Francisco*]
SOMA .... Student Osteopathic Medical Association (EA)

SOMADA ... Self-Organizing Multiple-Access Discrete Address [*Data processing*] (IEEE)
Som A Natur Hist ... Somerset Archaeology and Natural History [*A publication*]
Somatic Cell Genet ... Somatic Cell Genetics [*A publication*]
Somatic Cell Mol Genet ... Somatic Cell and Molecular Genetics [*A publication*]
Somatosens Mot Res ... Somatosensory and Motor Research [*A publication*]
Somatosens Res ... Somatosensory Research [*A publication*]
SOMB .... Somerset Bancorp, Inc. [*Somerville, NJ*] [*NASDAQ symbol*] (NQ)
SOMBA..... Southern Medical Bulletin [*United States*] [*A publication*]
Som Cell G ... Somatic Cell Genetics [*A publication*]
SOMDA .... Southwestern Medicine [*United States*] [*A publication*]
SOME .... Secretary's Office, Management Engineer [*Navy*]
SOME .... Senior Ordnance Mechanical Engineer [*British military*] (DMA)
SOME .... State-o-Maine, Inc. [*New York, NY*] [*NASDAQ symbol*] (NQ)
SOMEA..... Sovetskaya Meditsina [*A publication*]
SOMEG to ADV ... Something to Advantage [*Legal term*] [*Advertising*]
Somerset Archaeol Natur Hist ... Somerset Archaeology and Natural History [*A publication*]
Somerset Arch Nat Hist ... Somerset Archaeology and Natural History [*A publication*]
Somerset Industrial Archaeology Soc Jnl ... Somerset Industrial Archaeology Society. Journal [*A publication*]
Somerset Levels Pap ... Somerset Levels Papers [*A publication*]
Somerset LJ ... Somerset Legal Journal [*A publication*] (DLA)
SOMET.... Sometimes
SOMF........ SIDPERS [*Standard Installation/Division Personnel System*] Organization Master File [*Military*] (AABC)
SOMF........ Start of Minor Frame (MCD)
SOMH....... SONARman Harbor Defense [*Navy*]
SOM-H ..... Start-of-Message - High Precedence (CET)
SOMI .... Sternal-Occipital-Mandibular Immobilization [*Medicine*]
SOMIA8.... Sbornik Nauchnykh Rabot Moldavskogo Otdeleniya Vsesoyuznogo Nauchnogo Obshchestva Mikrobiologov, Epidemiologov, i Infektsionistov [*A publication*]
SOMIEX ... Societe Malienne d'Importation et d'Exportation [*Malian Import Export Co.*]
SOMISA .... Sociedad Mixta Siderurgia Argentina [*Steel producer in Argentina*]
SOMISS.... Study of Management Information Systems Support [*Army*]
SOM-L ...... Start-of-Message - Low Precedence (CET)
Som Leg J (PA) ... Somerset Legal Journal [*Pennsylvania*] [*A publication*] (DLA)
SOM-LI..... Somatostatin-Like Immunoreactivity
Som LJ....... Somerset Legal Journal [*Pennsylvania*] [*A publication*] (DLA)
Som LR ...... Somalia Law Reports [*A publication*] (DLA)
Somm .... Sommaires [*Summaries, Digests*] [*French*] (ILCA)
Somn on Gav ... Somner on Gavelkind [*A publication*] (DLA)
SOMO....... Semioccupied Molecular Orbital [*Physical chemistry*]
SOMO....... Senior Officer Management Office [*Army*] (INF)
Somogyi Muesz Sz ... Somogyi Mueszaki Szemle [*Hungary*] [*A publication*]
SOM-P .... Start-of-Message - Priority
SOMP .... Sydney Ocean Meeting Point [*Navy*]
SOMPA..... System of Multicultural Pluralistic Assessment [*Psychological and educational testing*]
Som Pl........ Somersetshire Pleas (Civil and Criminal), Edited by Chadwyck-Healey and Landon [*Somerset Record Society Publications, Vols. 11, 36, 41, 44*] [*A publication*] (DLA)
SOMR .... [*The*] Somerset Group, Inc. [*Indianapolis, IN*] [*NASDAQ symbol*] (NQ)
SOMRB..... Senior Officers Materiel Review Board [*Army*] (AABC)
SOMS........ Senior Officer, Minesweepers [*British military*] (DMA)
SOMS........ Service Order Mechanization [*or Mechanized*] System [*AT & T*]
SOMS....... Shuttle Orbiter Medical System [*NASA*] (MCD)
SOmS....... Synchronous, Operational Meteorological Satellite
SOMSA...... Soviet Materials Science [*English Translation*] [*A publication*]
SOMST ..... Somersetshire [*County in England*] (ROG)
SOMT .... Soldier Operator Maintainer Testing (MCD)
SOMTO .... Subversive Operations, Mediterranean Theatre of Operations [*World War II*]
SOMTS ..... Division of Ship Operations and Marine Technical Support [*Research center*] (RCD)
SoMV .... Sowbane Mosaic Virus
SON.......... Espiritu Santo [*Vanuatu*] [*Airport symbol*] (OAG)
S/ON......... Sign On [*Data processing*] (MDG)
SON.......... Slovenske Odborne Nazvoslovie [*A publication*]
SON.......... Society of Nematologists (EA)
son............. Songhai [*MARC language code*] [*Library of Congress*] (LCCP)
SON.......... Sonneberg [*Federal Republic of Germany*] [*Seismograph station code, US Geological Survey*] [*Closed*] (SEIS)
Son .... Sonnets [*Shakespearean work*]
Son .... Sonora [*Record label*] [*Sweden*]
SON.......... Sonora Gold Corp. [*Toronto Stock Exchange symbol*] [*Vancouver Stock Exchange symbol*]
SON.......... Statement of Operational Need
SON.......... Support of Other Nations [*Military support furnished certain nations and funded by the Air Force*]

SON.......... Supraoptic Nucleus [*Brain anatomy*]
SONA....... School of Naval Administration, Leland Stanford University
SonA........ Stratford-on-Avon [*Great Britain*]
SONAC..... SONAR Nacelle [*Sonacelle*]
SONAD..... Sonic Azimuth Detector (MCD)
SONAD..... Speech-Operated Noise Adjusting Device [*Telecommunications*] (TEL)
SONAR ..... Sonic Azimuth and Ranging [*British military*] (DMA)
SONAR ..... Sound Navigation and Ranging
SONARRAY ... SONAR Array [*Sounding system*] [*Navy*]
SONATRACH ... Societe Nationale de Transport et de Commercialisation des Hydrocarbures
SONB .... Sonobuoy
Sonc .... Soncino (BJA)
SoncinoB.... [*The*] Soncino Books of the Bible (Bornemouth) [*A publication*] (BJA)
SONCM..... SONAR Countermeasures and Deception [*Military*]
SONCR ..... SONAR Control Room (MSA)
SOND........ Secretary's Office, Navy Department
Sonderb Naturwiss Ver Hamb ... Sonderbaende des Naturwissenschaftlichen Vereins in Hamburg [*A publication*]
Sonderdr Internist Welt ... Sonderdruck aus Internistische Welt [*West Germany*] [*A publication*]
Sonderh Bayer Landw Jb ... Sonderhefte. Bayerisches Landwirtschaftliches Jahrbuch [*A publication*]
Sonderhefte zum Allgemein Statist Arch ... Sonderhefte zum Allgemeinen Statistischen Archiv [*A publication*]
Sonderh Landw Forsch ... Sonderheft zur Zeitschrift "Landwirtschaftliche Forschung" [*A publication*]
Sonderh Z PflKrankh PflPath PflSchutz ... Sonderheft. Zeitschrift fuer Pflanzenkrankheiten, Pflanzenpathologie, und Pflanzenschutz [*A publication*]
Sonderjydsk M-Skr ... Sonderjydsk Manedsskrift [*A publication*]
Sonenergie ... Sonnenenergie und Waermepumpe [*A publication*]
SONET..... Synchronous Optical Network [*Data processing*]
SONG........ Seeking of Noetic Goals Test [*Personality development test*] [*Psychology*]
Song .... Song of Songs [*Old Testament book*] [*Roman Catholic canon*]
SongCh ...... Song of the Three Children [*Old Testament book*] [*Apocrypha*] (BJA)
Song 3 Childr ... Song of the Three Children [*Old Testament book*] [*Apocrypha*]
Song Hits Mag ... Song Hits Magazine [*A publication*]
Songklanakarin J Sci Technol ... Songklanakarin Journal of Science and Technology [*A publication*]
SongR .... Song of Songs Rabbah (BJA)
SONGS..... San Onofre Nuclear Generating Station (NRCH)
Song Sol ...... Song of Solomon [*Old Testament book*]
Song of Three Childr ... [*The*] Song of the Three Holy Children [*Apocrypha*]
Songwriter ... Songwriter Magazine [*A publication*]
Songwriters R ... Songwriter's Review [*A publication*]
SONIC....... SPAN [*Space Physics Analysis Network*] Ocean Network Information Center [*Database*]
SONIC....... System-Wide On-Line Network for Information Control [*Data processing*]
SONKA ..... Shonika [*A publication*]
SONM........ Sonoma International [*NASDAQ symbol*] (NQ)
SONN........ Sonning [*England*]
SONN........ Sonora Gold Corp. [*NASDAQ symbol*] (NQ)
SONNA..... Somali National News Agency
Sonnenenerg ... Sonnenenergie [*A publication*]
Sonnenenerg Waermepumpe ... Sonnenenergie und Waermepumpe [*A publication*]
SONO........ Satellite Object Number (MUGU)
SONO........ Sonobuoy
SONO........ Sonoco Products Co. [*NASDAQ symbol*] (NQ)
SONO........ Sonogram [*Medicine*] (DHSM)
SONOAN ... Sonic Noise Analyzer
SOnoM ...... Studia Ononmastica Monacensia [*A publication*]
SONOSW ... Sonoswitch
SONP .... Solid Organs Not Palpable [*Medicine*]
So NQ .... Somerset Notes and Queries [*A publication*]
SONRD ...... Secretary's Office, Office of Research and Development [*Navy*]
SONRES ... Saturated Optical Nonresonant Emission Spectroscopy
SONS .... Seek Out New Suppliers
SONS .... Society of Non-Smokers (EA)
SONS .... Statistics of Naval Shipyards
Sonsbec ...... [*Franciscus*] Sonsbeccius [*Flourished, 16th century*] [*Authority cited in pre-1607 legal work*] (DSA)
Son Spec .... Sonorum Speculum [*A publication*]
SONWD..... Sonnenenergie und Waermepumpe [*A publication*]
SONX .... Sonex Research, Inc. [*Annapolis, MD*] [*NASDAQ symbol*] (NQ)
SOO .... Sault Meadows Energy [*Vancouver Stock Exchange symbol*]
SOO .... Schenectady Operations Office [*Energy Research and Development Administration*]
SOO .... Songo [*Mozambique*] [*Airport symbol*] (OAG)
SOO .... Soo Line Corp. [*NYSE symbol and AAR code*] (SPSG)
SOO.......... Staff Officer Operations [*British*]
Soob A N Gruz SSR ... Soobshcheniia Akademii Nauk Gruzinskoi SSR [*A publication*]

Soob Ermit ... Soobscenija Gosudarstvennogo Ordena Lenina Ermitaza [*A publication*]

Soob G Ermitazh ... Soobshcheniia Gosudarstvennogo Ermitazha [*A publication*]

Soob G Muz Izob Isk Pushkin ... Soobshcheniia Gosudarstvennyi Muzei Izobrazitel'nykh Iskusstv Imeni A. S. Pushkina [*A publication*]

Soob Kherson Muz ... Soobshcheniia Khersonnesskogo Muzeia [*Sebastopol*] [*A publication*]

Soobscenija Akad Nauk Gruz SSR ... Soobscenija Akademiji Nauk Gruzinskoj SSR [*A publication*]

Soobsc Gosud Russk Muz ... Soobscenija Gosudarstvennogo Russkogo Muzeja [*A publication*]

Soobsc Muz Isk Nar Vostoka ... Soobscenija Muzeja Iskusstva Narodov Vostoka [*A publication*]

Soobsc Vycisl Mat ... Soobscenija po Vychislitel noi Matematike [*A publication*]

Soobshch Akad Nauk Gruzin SSR ... Soobshcheniya Akademiya Nauk Gruzinskoi SSR [*A publication*]

Soobshch Akad Nauk Gruz SSSR ... Soobshcheniya Akademiya Nauk Gruzinskoi SSSR [*A publication*]

Soobshch Byurakan Obs Akad Nauk Arm SSR ... Soobshcheniya Byurakanskoi Observatorii Akademiya Nauk Armyanskoi SSR [*A publication*]

Soobshch Chuv Zon Agrokhim Lab ... Soobshcheniya Chuvashskoi Zonal'noi Agrokhimicheskoi Laboratorii [*A publication*]

Soobshch Dal'Nevost Fil Sib Otd Aka Nauk SSSR ... Soobshcheniya Dal'Nevostochnogo Filiala Sibirskogo Otdla Akademii Nauk SSSR [*A publication*]

Soobshch Inst Agrokhim Probl Gidroponiki Akad Nauk Arm SSR ... Soobshcheniya Instituta Agrokhimicheskikh Problem i Gidroponiki Akademiya Nauk Armyanskoi SSR [*Armenian SSR*] [*A publication*]

Soobshch Inst Lesa Akad Nauk SSSR ... Soobshcheniya Instituta Lesa Akademii Nauk SSSR [*A publication*]

SoobshchIPPO ... Soobshcheniya Imperialnovo Pravoslavnovo Palestinskavo Obshchestva [*A publication*]

Soobshch Mosk Otd Vses Bot Ova ... Soobshcheniya Moskovskogo Otdeleniya Vsesoyuznogo Botanicheskogo Obshchestva [*A publication*]

Soobshch Nauchno Issled Rab Kiev Politekh Inst ... Soobshcheniya o Nauchno-Issledovatel'skoi Rabote Kievskii Politekhnicheskii Institut [*A publication*]

Soobshch Ob'edin Inst Yad Issled (Dubna) ... Soobshcheniya Ob'edinennogo Instituta Yadernykh Issledovanii (Dubna) [*A publication*]

Soobshch Obshch Lab Agrokhim Akad Nauk Armyan SSR ... Soobshcheniya Obshchestvoi Laboratorii Agrokhimii Akademii Nauk Armyanskoi SSR [*A publication*]

Soobshch Sakhalin Fil Akad Nauk SSSR ... Soobshcheniya Sakhalinskogo Filiala Akademii Nauk SSSR [*A publication*]

Soobshch Shemakhinskoi Astrofiz Obs Akad Nauk Azerb SSR ... Soobshcheskoi Shemakhinskoi Astrofizicheskoi Observatorii Akademiya Nauk Azerbaidzhan SSR [*Azerbaidzhan SSR*] [*A publication*]

Soochow J Hum ... Soochow Journal of Humanities [*Taipei*] [*A publication*]

Soochow J Lit Soc Stud ... Soochow Journal of Literature and Social Studies [*Taipei*] [*A publication*]

Soochow J Math ... Soochow Journal of Mathematics [*Taipei*] [*A publication*]

Soochow J Math Natur Sci ... Soochow Journal of Mathematical and Natural Sciences [*Later, Soochow Journal of Mathematics*] [*A publication*]

SOOG .... Saint-Georges-De-L'Oyapock [*French Guiana*] [*ICAO location identifier*] (ICLI)

SOOM .... Saigon Officers Open Mess [*Vietnam*]

SOOM .... Saint-Laurent du Maroni [*French Guiana*] [*ICAO location identifier*] (ICLI)

SOON .... Sequence for Opportunities and Negatives [*Rand Corp.*]

SOON .... Solar Observing Optical Network [*Air Force*]

SOON .... Sooner Defense of Florida, Inc. [*NASDAQ symbol*] (NQ)

Soon Chun Hyang J Med ... Soon Chun Hyang Journal of Medicine [*Republic of Korea*] [*A publication*]

SOOP .... Special Old Oil Price

SOOP .... Submarine Oceanographic Observation Program

SOOR .... Regina [*French Guiana*] [*ICAO location identifier*] (ICLI)

SOOS .... Saul [*French Guiana*] [*ICAO location identifier*] (ICLI)

SOOY .... Sinnamary [*French Guiana*] [*ICAO location identifier*] (ICLI)

SOP .... Pinehurst [*North Carolina*] [*Airport symbol*] (OAG)

SOP .... Safety Operating Plan

SOP .... Saturn Orbiter Probe [*NASA*]

SOP .... Scavenging, Oil Pump (MSA)

SOP .... Scented Orange Pekoe [*Tea trade*] (ROG)

SOP .... Seat of the Pants

SOP .... Second Opinion Program [*Later, NSOP*] (EA)

SOP .... Secondary Operation

SOP .... Secondary Oxygen Pack [*NASA*]

SOP .... Semiopen Position [*Dancing*]

SOP .... Semiorganic Polymer

SOP .... Senior Officer Present

SOP .... Ship's Operational Program [*Navy*] (NVT)

SOP .... Shop Overload Parts (AAG)

SOP .... Simulated Output Program [*Data processing*]

SOP .... Simulation Operations Plan [*NASA*] (KSC)

SOP .... Sleeping-Out Pass [*British armed forces*]

SOP .... Soprano

SOP .... Sopron [*Hungary*] [*Seismograph station code, US Geological Survey*] (SEIS)

SOP .... Southern Pines, NC [*Location identifier*] [*FAA*] (FAAL)

So P .... Sovjetskaja Pecat' [*A publication*]

SOP .... Spacelab Opportunity Payload [*NASA*] (MCD)

SOP .... Spares Order Processing (MCD)

SOP .... Special Operating Procedure (IEEE)

SOP .... Special Order Price

SOP .... Staff Officer of Pensioners [*Army*] [*British*] (ROG)

SOP .... Standard Operating Plan (OICC)

SOP .... Standard [*or Standing*] Operating Procedure

SOP .... Statement of Policy [*SEC*]

SOP .... Statewide Operating Plan

SOP .... Station Operating Plan (AAG)

SOP .... Stock Option Plan

SOP .... Strategic Objectives Plan

SOP .... Strategic Orbit Point (KSC)

SOP .... Study Organization Plan (BUR)

SOP .... Subsystem Operating Program (NASA)

SOP .... Subsystems Operating Procedure [*NASA*] (NASA)

SOP .... Successive Organization of Perception [*Pilot behavior*]

SOP .... Sulfate of Potash [*Fertilizer*]

SOP .... Supplemental Oxygen Package (MCD)

SOP .... Supplier Operating Procedure (MCD)

SOP .... Surface Oil Pickup

SOP .... Surgical Outpatient [*Medicine*]

SOP .... Symbolic Optimum Program

SOP .... Systems Operation Plan [*NASA*] (KSC)

SOPA .... Senior Officer Present Afloat [*Navy*]

SOP(A) ...... Senior Officer Present (Ashore) [*Navy*]

SOPA .... Society of Professional Archeologists (EA)

SOPA .... Standoff Precision Attack [*Military*] (CAAL)

SOPAA ...... Soviet Physics. Acoustics [*English Translation*] [*A publication*]

SOPAC ...... Joint CCOP/IOC Program of Research on the South Pacific [*Marine science*] (MSC)

SOPAC ...... South Pacific Command [*Navy*]

SOPAC ...... Southern Pacific Railroad Co.

SOPACBACOM ... South Pacific Base Command [*Navy*] [*World War II*]

SOPACCOMS ... South Pacific Communications [*Navy*]

SOPAD ...... SOPA [*Senior Officer Present Afloat*] Administrative Duties [*Military*] (NVT)

SOPAD ...... Summary of Proceedings and Debate [*of House of Representatives*]

SOPAG ...... Societe des Participations Gardinier [*French fertilizer firm*]

SOPAT ...... South China Patrol [*Navy*] [*World War II*]

SOPC .... Sales Operations Planning and Control [*Management*]

SOPC .... Shuttle Operations and Planning Center [*NASA*] (MCD)

SOPC .... Shuttle Operations Planning Complex (NASA)

SOPDOSS ... Submersible Oriented Platform for Deep Ocean Sediment Studies [*Marine science*] (MSC)

SOPE .... Simulated Off-the-Pad Ejection [*NASA*]

SO-PE .... Sodium Pentathol [*Nickname*]

Soph .... Sopherim (BJA)

Soph .... Sophia [*A publication*]

Soph .... Sophista [*of Plato*] [*A publication*] (OCD)

SOPH .... Sophister [*British*] (ROG)

SOPH .... Sophocles [*Greek poet, 496-406BC*] [*Classical studies*] (ROG)

SOPH .... Sophomore

Soph .... Sophonias [*Old Testament book*] [*Douay version*]

SOPH .... Starboard Out, Port Home [*Variation of POSH*]

SOPHE ...... Society for Public Health Education (EA)

Soph El ...... Sophistici Elenchi [*of Aristotle*] [*Classical studies*] (OCD)

Sophia Econ R ... Sophia Economic Review [*Tokyo*] [*A publication*]

Sophia:T .... Sophia: Studies in Western Civilization and the Cultural Interaction of East and West (Tokyo) [*A publication*]

SOPI .... Superintendent of Public Instruction (OICC)

SOPJA ...... Soviet Physics Journal [*English Translation*] [*A publication*]

SOPLA ...... Soviet Plastics [*English Translation*] [*A publication*]

SOPLASCO ... Southern Plastics Company

SOPLC ...... Senior Officer Preventive Logistics Course (MCD)

SOPM ...... Standard Orbital Parameter Message [*NASA*] (KSC)

SOPMET .. Standing Operating Procedure - Meteorological Plan (NATG)

SOPO .... Society of Oral Physiology and Occlusion

SOPODA .. Social Planning, Policy & Development Abstracts [*Sociological Abstracts, Inc.*] [*Database*]

SOPONATA ... Sociedade Portuguesa de Navios Tanques [*Shipping company*] [*Portugal*] (EY)

SOPP .... Sodium Ortho-Phenylphenoxide [*Organic chemistry*]

SOPP .... Special Order Perfect Price [*for undamaged merchandise*]

SOPP .... Statement of Provisioning Policy [*Military*] (AFIT)

SOPPA ...... Soviet Plant Physiology [*English Translation*] [*A publication*]

SOPPC ...... Special Operations Photo Processing Cell (MCD)

SOPR .... South Pierce Railroad [*AAR code*]

SOPR .... Spanish Open Pool Reactor

SOPR .... Special Officer Personnel Requirements [*Military*]

SOPR .... Standing Operating Procedure Regulation [*Navy*] (MCD)

SOPS .... Shot Noise Optical Optimization Communication System with Stops [*NASA*]

S Op S........	Si Opus Sit [*If Needed*] [*Pharmacy*]
SOPS........	Spacecraft Operations Planning Section
SOPSA......	Shuttle Orbit-Injection Propulsion System Analysis [*NASA*]
SOPT........	Science Operations Planning Team
SOPUA......	Soviet Physics. Uspekhi [*English Translation*] [*A publication*]
SOPUS......	Senior Officer Present, United States Navy
SOQ..........	Senior Officers' Quarters
SOQ..........	Sick Officer Quarters
Soq...........	Soqotri (BJA)
SOQ..........	Sorong [*Indonesia*] [*Airport symbol*] (OAG)
So Q	Southern Quarterly Review [*A publication*]
SOQ..........	Star One Resources, Inc. [*Vancouver Stock Exchange symbol*]
SOQ..........	System Optical Quality (MCD)
SOQAS......	Statement of Quality and Support (MCD)
SOQUEM ...	Societe Quebecoise d'Exploration Miniere [*Quebec Mining Exploration Co.*]
SOQUIJ	Societe Quebecoise d'Information Juridique [*Quebec Society for Legal Information*] [*Information service or system*] (IID)
SOR	Sale or Return [*Business term*] (ADA)
SOR	Sampling Oscilloscope Recorder
SOR	Saxon Owners Registry (EA)
SOR	Seder 'Olam Rabbah (BJA)
SOR	Sensor Operation Room (AFM)
SOR	Serie Orientale Roma [*A publication*]
SOR	Service Operational Requirement
SOR	Single Order Release (MCD)
SOR	Society of Rheology (EA)
SOR	Sonor Petroleum Corp. [*Toronto Stock Exchange symbol*]
Sor.............	Soria [*Record label*]
SOR	Soroa [*Cuba*] [*Seismograph station code, US Geological Survey*] (SEIS)
SOR	Source Capital, Inc. [*NYSE symbol*] (SPSG)
SOR	Source of Repair (MCD)
So R...........	Southern Review [*US*] [*A publication*]
SoR	Southern Review: An Australian Journal of Literary Studies [*A publication*]
SOR	Specific Operational Requirement [*Military*]
SOR	Spilled Oil Research Team [*National Oceanic and Atmospheric Administration*] (MSC)
SOR	Squadron Operational Report
SOR	Stable-Orbit Rendezvous [*NASA*]
SOR	Standard Operating Report
SOR	Standard Operating Rules
SOR	Standoff Range (MCD)
sor	Starboard (DS)
SOR	Start of Record (MUGU)
SORE........	State of Readiness (MCD)
SOR	Statement of Requirement [*Military*] (AFIT)
SOR	Status or Operating Resources (MCD)
SOR	Statutory Orders and Regulations of Canada [*Canada Department of Justice*] [*Information service or system*]
SOR	Stearic/Oleic Acid Ratio [*Clinical chemistry*]
SOR	Stephens Owners Registry [*Inactive*] (EA)
S-O-R........	Stimulus-Organism-Response
SOR	Stockholder of Record
SOR	Students for Origins Research (EA)
S Or	Studia Orientalia [*A publication*]
SOR	Subcarrier Oscillator Rack
SOR	Successive Overrelaxation
SOR	Synchrotron Orbital Radiation [*High-energy physics*]
SOR	Systems Operational Requirement
SOR	Winfield/Arkansas City, KS [*Location identifier*] [*FAA*] (FAAL)
S Or A........	Sammlung Orientalistischer Arbeiten [*A publication*]
SORA	Secretary's Office, Records Administration [*Navy*]
SORA	Sorgento Rapido [*Reactor*] (NRCH)
SoRA.........	Southern Review (Adelaide, Australia) [*A publication*]
So R A........	Southern Review: An Australian Journal of Literary Studies [*A publication*]
SORAD	Sonic Ranging and Detection (KSC)
SORAFOM ...	Societe de Radiodiffusion de la France d'Outre-Mer [*Society for Radio Broadcasting of Overseas France*]
SORAP......	Signature Overlap Range Prediction
SORAP......	Standard Omnirange Approach
SORAT......	Submarine Operational Readiness Assessment and Training
SORB........	Subsistence Operations Review Board [*Military*] (AABC)
Sorb D........	Sorbitol Dehydrogenase [*Also, SDH*] [*An enzyme*]
SORC........	Signal Officers' Reserve Corps
SORC........	Sound Ranging Control
SORC........	Southern Ocean Racing Conference
SORC........	Station Operations Review Committee [*Nuclear energy*] (NRCH)
SORCS	Shipboard Ordnance Requirement Computer System [*Navy*]
SORD	Society of Record Dealers of America
SORD	Southwestern Order Retrieval and Distribution [*Southwest Bell Telephone Co.*]
SORD	Submerged Object Recovery Device
SORD	Systematic Organizational Design
SORDC......	Southwest Ohio Regional Data Center [*University of Cincinnati*] [*Research center*] (RCD)

SORE.........	Stamp Out Regulatory Excesses [*An association*] (EA)
SOREL.....	Sun-Orbiting Relativity Experiment Satellite
SOREM.....	Sleep-Onset REM [*Rapid Eye Movement*]
SOREMA ...	Societe de Reassurance des Assurances Mutuelles Agricoles [*France*] (EY)
So Rep......	Southern Reporter [*A publication*] (DLA)
So Repr	Southern Reporter [*A publication*] (DLA)
S O Rev......	Sean O'Casey Review [*A publication*]
SORG	Sorg Printing Co. [*NASDAQ symbol*] (NQ)
SORG	Submarine Operations Research Group [*Navy*]
SORI..........	Southern Research Institute (AAG)
SORIN......	Societa Ricerche Impianti Nucleari [*Italy*]
SORM	Set-Oriented Retrieval Module
SORNE(I) ...	Senior Officer, Royal Naval Establishment (India) [*British*] [*World War II*]
SORNG	Sound Ranging
SORO	Scan on Receive Only (MCD)
SORO	Special Operations Research Office
SORP........	Signature Overlay Range Prediction (MCD)
SORP........	Statement of Recommended Practice [*Accounting*] [*British*]
SORPTR ...	South Repeater [*NASA*] (MCD)
SORR	SIGINT [*Signal Intelligence*] Operations Readiness Review [*Military*] (AABC)
SORR	Submarine Operations Research Report [*Navy*]
SORRAT ...	Society for Research on Rapport and Telekinesis (EA)
SORS........	Shipboard Operational Readiness System [*Navy*] (CAAL)
SORS........	Spacecraft Oscillograph Recording System
SORSI.......	Sacro Occipital Research Society International (EA)
SORT........	Self-Observation and Report Technique
SORT........	Senior Officer Refresher Training
SORT........	Shippers of Recycled Textiles [*An association*] (EA)
SORT........	Ship's Operational Readiness Test
SORT........	Simulated Optical Range Target (MCD)
SORT........	Slosson Oral Reading Tests
SORT........	Special Operations Response Team [*Prison management*]
SORT........	Spilled Oil Response Team [*Marine science*] (MSC)
SORT........	Staff Organizations Round Table [*American Library Association*]
SORT........	Structured-Objective Rorschach Test [*Psychology*]
SORT........	Structures for Orbiting Radio Telescope (MCD)
SORT........	System Operational Readiness Test (MCD)
SORTE......	Summary of Radiation Tolerant Electronics
SORTEC...	Synchrotron Orbital Radiation Technology [*High-energy physics*]
SORTI	Satellite Orbital Track and Intercept [*ARPA*]
SORTI	Star-Oriented Real-Time Teaching Instrument (AAG)
SORTIE	Simulation of Reentry Target Interceptor Endgame (MCD)
SORTIE	Super-Orbital Reentry Test Integrated Environment (MUGU)
SORTS	Shipboard Organizational Troubleshooting System (MCD)
SORTS	Status of Resources and Training System Report [*Military*]
SORWUC ...	Service, Office, and Retail Workers Union of Canada
SOS...........	Coalition to Protect Social Security (EA)
SOS...........	Congress of Scientists on Survival [*Inactive*]
SOS...........	Safety Observation Station
SOS...........	Safety on the Streets [*Project of National Safety Council*]
SoS...........	Saga och Sed [*A publication*]
SOS...........	Same Old Sludge [*Slang phrase used to describe television programming*]
SOS...........	Same Old Stew [*Military slang*] [*Bowdlerized version*]
SOS...........	Same Old Stuff [*Reference to the weather*]
SOS...........	Same Only Softer [*Band leader's signal*] [*Slang*]
SOS...........	Sanity on Sex [*Group opposing sex education in schools*]
SOS...........	Satellite Observation System
SOS...........	Save Our Schools (EA)
SOS...........	Save Our Security (EA)
SOS...........	Save Our Ship [*or Souls*] [*Popular explanation of Morse code letters used as a signal for extreme distress*]
SOS...........	Save Our Shores (EA)
SOS...........	Save Our Sons [*Cancer information service*] [*British*]
SOS...........	Save Our Stages [*Australia*]
SOS...........	Save Our Strays (EA)
SOS...........	[*Anatoly*] Scharansky, [*Yuri*] Orlov, and [*Andrei*] Sakharov [*Organization named after dissident Soviet scientists*] (EA)
SOS...........	Scheduled Oil Sampling [*Automotive engineering*]
SOS...........	Science of Survival
SOS...........	Scientists for Sakharov, Orlov, and Shcharansky (EA)
SO & S	Scouting, Observation, and Sniping [*British military*] (DMA)
SOS...........	Secretary of State
SOS...........	Secular Organizations for Sobriety (EA)
SOS...........	Self-Opening Sack [*Paper bag*]
SOS...........	Self-Organizing System
SOS...........	Semitic and Oriental Studies [*A publication*]
SOS...........	Send Out Succor
SOS...........	Senior Opportunities and Services [*OEO*]
SOS...........	Sentinel on Station
SOS...........	Serial Output Special (MCD)
SOS...........	Service Order System [*Telecommunications*] (TEL)
SOS...........	Service of Supply [*Later, ASF*] [*Army*]
SOS...........	Shakespeare Oxford Society (EA)
SOS...........	Share Operating System [*Data processing*]

SOS............	Share Our Strength (EA)
SOS............	Ships Operational Safety [*A publication*]
SOS............	Ships Ordnance Summary
SOS............	Si Opus Sit [*If Needed*] [*Pharmacy*]
sos	Sien Ommesyde [*Please Turn Over*] [*Afrikaans*] [*Correspondence*]
SOS............	Signed-Off Sick
SOS............	Silicon-on-Sapphire [*Integrated circuit*]
SOS............	Simultaneous Oral Spelling [*Gillingham method*] [*Education*]
SOS............	Sisters of Service [*Roman Catholic religious order*]
SOS............	Slip on Show [*Indicates a woman's slip is showing*] (DSUE)
SOS............	Slum on a Shingle [*Army breakfast dish*] [*Bowdlerized version*]
SOS............	Sniping, Observation, and Scouting [*Course*] [*Military*] [*British*] [*World War I*]
SOS............	Society for Occlusal Studies (EA)
SOS............	Society of Operative Stonemasons [*A union*] [*British*]
SOS............	Society of Scribes (EA)
SOS............	Society of Separationists (EA)
SOS............	Society of Shuttlemakers [*A union*] [*British*]
SOS............	Society of Signalmen (EA)
SoS............	Song of Songs [*Old Testament book*] [*Roman Catholic canon*] (BJA)
SOS............	Sophisticated Operating System [*Apple III microcomputer*] [*Data processing*]
SOS............	Sostenuto [*Sustained*] [*Music*]
SOS............	Source of Supply
SOS............	Soviet Oceanographic Surveillance (MCD)
SOS............	Space Ordnance Systems, Inc. (MCD)
SOS............	Spare Operation Support
SOS............	Special Organizational Services [*An association*] (EA)
SOS............	Speed of Service [*Telecommunications*] (TEL)
SOS............	Speed of Sound
SOS............	SPRINT Operations Shelter [*Army*]
SOS............	Squadron Officers School [*Air Force*]
SOS............	Squadron Operational Support [*Military*] (AFIT)
SOS............	Stabilized Optical Sight
SOS............	Stamp Out Stupidity [*Student group opposing drug abuse*]
SOS............	Start of Significance [*Data processing*] (BUR)
SOS............	Statement of Service [*Military*]
SOS............	Station Operating Supervisor (IEEE)
SOS............	Stock Order Shipment
SOS............	Storage-on-Site [*Grolier Electronic Publishing, Inc.*]
SOS............	Store Overstocked [*Inventory*]
SOS............	Strategic Orbital System (AAG)
SOS............	Struck off Strength [*British military*] (DMA)
SOS............	Student Orientations Survey [*Student attitudes test*]
SOS............	Student-Originated Studies [*National Science Foundation*]
SOS............	Studies on Smoking, Inc. [*Research center*] (RCD)
SOS............	Suborbital Sequence [*NASA*]
SOS............	Sum-of-the-Squares
SOS............	Supervisor of Shipbuilding [*Navy*]
SOS............	Supplemental Oxygen System (MCD)
SOS............	Supplementary Ophthalmic Service [*Medicine*]
SOS............	Support Our Soldiers [*Network of antiwar-oriented coffee houses located near military bases*] (EA)
SOS............	Supporters of Silkwood [*Inactive*] (EA)
SOS............	Survivors of Sacrifice (EA)
SOS............	Survivors of Suicide
SOS............	Suspend Other Service [*Business term*]
SOS............	Suspension of Service [*Pilots' strike*]
SOS............	Symbolic Operating System [*Data processing*]
SOS............	Symmetry, Orbitals, and Spectra [*Atomic physics*]
SoS............	Syn og Segn [*A publication*]
SOS............	Synchronous Orbit Satellite (AAG)
SOS............	System Operational Specification [*Military*] (CAAL)
SOS............	Systems, Objectives, Solutions [*A publication*]
SOSA.........	Sell Overseas America, the Association of American Export [*Redondo Beach, CA*] (EA)
SOSA.........	Somerset Bankshares, Inc. [*NASDAQ symbol*] (NQ)
SOSA.........	Sustained Operations Support Area [*NASA*] (KSC)
Sos Aikakausk ...	Sosiaalinen Aikakauskirja [*A publication*]
SOSAL......	School of Systems and Logistics [*Military*]
SOSAT......	Submarine One-Way Satellite [*Navy*] (CAAL)
SOSC.........	Safety Observation Station Display Console
SOSC.........	Smithsonian Oceanographic Sorting Center
SOSC.........	Source of Supply Code
So School News ...	Southern School News [*A publication*]
SOSCU......	Stamps on Stamps - Centenary Unit (EA)
SOSD.........	Spatial Operational Sequence Diagram
SOSE.........	Science Operations Support Equipment
SOSE.........	Silicon-on-Something-Else [*Telecommunications*] (TEL)
SOSEC......	Satellite Ocean Surveillance Evaluation Center
SOSED......	Secretary's Office, Shore Establishments Division [*Incorporated into SECP, 1944*] [*Navy*]
SOSH........	Search for the Odd Shape [*Neuropsychology test*]
SO SH	Somali Shilling [*Monetary unit*]
Sosh..........	Soshioloji [*A publication*]
SOS:HRG ...	SOS: Human Rights for Guyana (EA)
SOSI.........	Shift In, Shift Out (IEEE)
SOSI.........	Sippican, Incorporated [*Formerly, Sippican Ocean Systems*] [*NASDAQ symbol*] (NQ)

SOS Intl.....	Society of Saunterers, International (EA)
SOSK.......	Squadron Operational Support Kit (MCD)
SO/SL	Saturn Orbiter Satellite Lander [*NASA*]
S Osl	Symbolae Osloenses [*A publication*]
SOSM.......	Ship Overhaul Schedule Milestone [*Navy*]
SOSM.......	Source of Supply Modifier
SOSO	Safety and Operating Systems Office [*NASA*]
SoSo	South of SoHo [*See also NoHo, SoHo, TriBeCa*] [*Artists' colony in New York City*]
SOSO	Synchronous Orbiting Solar Observatory
SOSP.......	Squadron Operational Support Package [*Military*] (AFIT)
SOSQ........	Special Operations Squadron
SOSR.......	Spin on Straight Rail
SOSS	Satellite Ocean Surveillance System
SOSS	Satellite Optical Surveillance Station (MCD)
SOSS	Shipboard Oceanographic Survey System
SOSS	SONAR Schoolship [*Navy*] (NVT)
SOSS	Sound Search Station
SOSS	Soviet Ocean Surveillance System (MCD)
SOSS	Strategic Orbital System Study (AAG)
SOSS	Structurally Oriented Simulation System [*NASA*]
SOSSI.......	Scouts on Stamps Society International (EA)
SOSSI.......	SOS Sahel International [*London, England*] (EAIO)
SOSSPA ...	Service of Supply, South Pacific Area [*Navy*] [*World War II*]
SOSSUS...	Study on Surgical Services in the United States [*Medicine*]
SOST........	Sostenuto [*Sustained*] [*Music*]
So St..........	Southern Studies [*A publication*]
SOST........	Special Operator Service Traffic [*Telecommunications*] (TEL)
SOSTEL....	Solid-State Electric Logic (NG)
SOSTEN ...	Sostenuto [*Sustained*] [*Music*]
SOSU.......	Scout Observation Service Unit [*Navy*]
SOSU.......	Ships on Stamps Unit (EA)
SOSUMO ...	Societe Sucriere du Moso [*Development organization*] [*Burundi*] (EY)
SOSUS	SONAR Surveillance System [*Military*]
SOSUS	Sound Surveillance System (MSA)
SOSUS	Sound Surveillance Undersea (MCD)
SOSUS	Sound Surveillance Underwater System [*Navy*]
SOSVS	Sound Surveillance System
SOT	Same Old Thing [*Slang*]
SOT	Secretary of Transportation (NATG)
SOT	Sensation of Transcendence
SOT	Shower over Tub [*Real estate*]
SoT...........	Sloejd och Ton [*A publication*]
SOT	Snowbird, TN [*Location identifier*] [*FAA*] (FAAL)
SOT	Society of Ornamental Turners (EA)
SOT	Society of Toxicology (EA)
SOT	Solar Optical Telescope
SOT	Son of Temperance [*A heavy drinker*] [*Slang*]
Sot.............	Sotah (BJA)
SOT	Sound on Tape [*Videotape*]
SOT	Sounds of Our Times, Cook Studio [*Record label*]
SOT	South Omaha Terminal Railway Co. [*AAR code*]
SOT	Soviet Orientation Team (MCD)
SOT	Spatial Orientation Trainer [*Air Force*]
SOT	Special Operations Team (ADA)
SOT	SRO Entertainment [*Vancouver Stock Exchange symbol*]
SOT	Start of Tape
SOT	Start of Text
SOT	State of Termination [*Telecommunications*] (TEL)
S-O-T.......	Stoke-On-Trent [*City in England*]
SOT	Strap-On Tank [*NASA*] (NASA)
SOT	Subscriber Originating Trunk [*Telecommunications*] (TEL)
SOT	Syntax-Oriented Translator (IEEE)
SOT	Systems Operating Test
SOTA	State of the Art
SOTA	Students Older than Average
SOTAC......	State-of-the-Art Car [*Transit*] [*Department of Transportation*]
SOTACA...	State-of-the-Art Contingency Analysis System [*Science Applications International Corp.*]
SOTAP......	Sophisticated Training Program
SOTARSS ...	Standoff Target Acquisition Reconnaissance Surveillance System (MCD)
SOTAS	Standoff Target Acquisition/Attack System
SOTASS....	Standoff Target Acquisition and Surveillance System [*Army*]
SOTB........	Secretary's Office, Transportation Branch [*Navy*]
SOTCA.....	Soudage et Techniques Connexes [*A publication*]
SOTDAT...	Source Test Data System [*Environmental Protection Agency*]
SOTE........	Standard Optical Test Equipment
So Tex LJ ..	Southern Texas Law Journal [*A publication*] (DLA)
SOTFE......	Special Operations Task Force, Europe [*Military*]
SOTG	Sales Other than Gasoline [*Business term*]
SOTI.........	[*A*] Survey of Old Testament Introductions [*Gleason L. Archer*] [*A publication*] (BJA)
SOTIB......	Sotsialisticheskaya Industriya [*A publication*]
SOTID......	Solar Times [*A publication*]
Sotilaslaak Aikak ...	Sotilaslaaketieteellinen Aikakauslehti [*A publication*]
SOTIM......	Sonic Observation of the Trajectory and Impact of Missiles
SOTK........	Sono-Tek Corp. [*NASDAQ symbol*] (NQ)
SOTP........	Ship Overhaul Test Program
SOTP........	Shipyard Overhaul Test Program

SOTP........ System Overhaul Test Program
SOTR........ SouthTrust Corp. [*NASDAQ symbol*]   (NQ)
SOTS........ Suborbital Tank Separation [*NASA*]   (MCD)
SOTS........ Synchronous Orbiting Tracking Stations   (MCD)
Sots Pollum ... Sotsialistik Pollumajandus [*A publication*]
Sots Sel'Khoz Azerb ... Sotsialisticheskoe Sel'skoe Khozyaistvo
            Azerbaidzhana [*A publication*]
Sots Sel'Khoz Uzbek ... Sotsialisticheskoe Sel'skoe Khozyaistvo Uzbekistana
            [*A publication*]
Sots Sel'sk Khoz Azerb ... Sotsialisticheskoe Sel'skoe Khozyaistvo
            Azerbaidzhana [*A publication*]
Sots Sel'sk Khoz Uzb ... Sotsialistichne Sel'skoe Khozyaistvo Uzbekistana
            [*A publication*]
Sots Trud ... Sotsialisticheskiy Trud [*USSR*] [*A publication*]
Sots Tvarinnit ... Sotsialistichne Tvarinnitstvo [*A publication*]
Sots Tvarynnytstvo ... Sotsialistychne Tvarynnytstvo [*A publication*]
SOTT........ Second-Order Transition Temperature
SOTT........ Synthetic Medium Old Tuberculin Trichloroacetic Acid
            Precipitated [*Later, PPD, Purified Protein Derivative*]
            [*Immunology*]
SOTUS...... Sequentially Operated Teletypewriter Universal Selector
SOU.......... Scandinavian Ornithological Union [*Lund, Sweden*]   (EAIO)
SOU.......... Souchong [*Tea trade*]   (ROG)
SOU.......... Sources Public Library [*UTLAS symbol*]
SOU.......... South   (ROG)
SOU.......... South. The Third World Magazine [*A publication*]
SOU.......... Southampton [*England*] [*Airport symbol*]   (OAG)
SOU.......... Southern Airways [*Air carrier designation symbol*]
SOU.......... Southern California Gas Co. [*AMEX symbol*]   (SPSG)
SOU.......... Southern Petroleum Corp. [*Vancouver Stock Exchange symbol*]
SOU.......... Southern Railway System [*AAR code*]
SOU.......... Statens Offentliga Utredningar [*Sweden*]
Sou Aus LR ... South Australian Law Reports [*A publication*]
Soudage Tech Connexes ... Soudage et Techniques Connexes [*A publication*]
Soud Lek.... Soudni Lekarstvi [*A publication*]
SOUL .... Studies of Ocean Upper Layers   (MSC)
Soule Syn ... Soule's Dictionary of English Synonymes [*A
            publication*]   (DLA)
Soul Il........ Soul Illustrated [*A publication*]
So U LR ..... Southern University Law Review [*A publication*]
So U L Rev ... Southern University Law Review [*A publication*]
Soun .... Soundings [*A publication*]
Sound .... Soundings [*A publication*]
Sound Brass ... Sounding Brass and the Conductor [*A publication*]
Sound (Can) ... Sound (Canada) [*A publication*]
Sound Vib .. Sound and Vibration [*A publication*]
Sound & Vib ... Sound and Vibration [*A publication*]
Sound Vis Broadc ... Sound and Vision Broadcasting [*A publication*]
So Univ L Rev ... Southern University Law Review [*A publication*]
SOUP .... Solar Optical Universal Polarimeter
SOUP .... Students Opposed to Unfair Practices [*in advertising*] [*Student
            legal action organization*]
SOUP .... Submarine Operational Update Program [*Canadian Navy*]
SOUQAR .. Section d'Oceanographie d'Universite de Quebec a Rimouski
            [*Canada*]   (MSC)
SOUR .... Sourdough Journal. Alaska Library Association [*A publication*]
SouR .... Southern Review [*US*] [*A publication*]
SOURCE... Simulation of Utilization, Resources, Cost, and Efficiency
Sources Chr ... Sources Chretiennes [*A publication*]
Sources Hist Math Phys Sci ... Sources in the History of Mathematics and
            Physical Sciences [*A publication*]
Sources in Hist of Math and Phys Sci ... Sources in the History of
            Mathematics and Physical Sciences [*A publication*]
Sources Sci ... Sources of Science [*A publication*]
Sources and Stud Hist Arabic-Islamic Sci Hist of Math Ser ... Sources and
            Studies in the History of Arabic-Islamic Science. History of
            Mathematics Series [*A publication*]
Sources Stud Hist Arabic-Islamic Sci Hist of Tech Ser ... Sources and Studies
            in the History of Arabic-Islamic Science. History of
            Technology Series [*A publication*]
Sources Stud Hist Arabic Math ... Sources and Studies in the History of
            Arabic Mathematics [*A publication*]
SOURS...... Subcommittee on Use of Radioactivity Standards [*National
            Research Council*]
SOUSAFE ... Status of United States Air Force Equipment
SOUSSA ... Steady, Oscillatory, and Unsteady, Subsonic, and Supersonic
            Aerodynamics [*NASA*]
SOUT .... SouthernNet, Inc. [*NASDAQ symbol*]   (NQ)
SOUT .... Swap-Out [*Data processing*]
SOUTB..... Statens Offentliga Utredningar [*A publication*]
SOUTC...... Satellite Operators and Users Technical Committee   (EA)
South.......... Southern Reporter [*National Reporter System*] [*A
            publication*]   (DLA)
South Afr Archaeol B ... South African Archaeological Bulletin [*A
            publication*]
South Afr Arch B ... South African Archaeological Bulletin [*A publication*]
South Afr Geogr J ... South African Geographical Journal [*A publication*]
South African J African Affairs ... South African Journal of African Affairs [*A
            publication*]
South African J Econ ... South African Journal of Economics [*Suid-Afrikaanse
            Tydskrif vir Ekonomie*] [*A publication*]

South African Labour Bul ... South African Labour Bulletin [*A publication*]
South African Med J ... South African Medical Journal [*A publication*]
South African Med Rec ... South African Medical Record [*A publication*]
South African Min Eng Jour ... South African Mining and Engineering Journal
            [*A publication*]
South African MJ ... South African Medical Journal [*A publication*]
South African Statist J ... South African Statistical Journal [*A publication*]
South Afr Int Quart ... South Africa International Quarterly [*A publication*]
South Afr J Afr Aff ... South African Journal of African Affairs [*A
            publication*]
South Afr J Econ ... South African Journal of Economics [*Suid-Afrikaanse
            Tydskrif vir Ekonomie*] [*A publication*]
South Afr J Sci ... South African Journal of Science [*A publication*]
South Afr J Surg ... South African Journal of Surgery [*A publication*]
South Afr Law J ... South African Law Journal [*A publication*]
South Afr LJ ... South African Law Journal [*A publication*]
South Afr Text ... Southern Africa Textiles [*A publication*]
South Am J Bio-Sci ... South American Journal of Bio-Sciences [*A
            publication*]
South Am J Med ... South American Journal of Medicine [*A publication*]
Southard .... Southard's New Jersey Law Reports [*4-5 New Jersey*] [*A
            publication*]   (DLA)
South Ariz Guideb ... Southern Arizona Guidebook [*A publication*]
South As Dig Reg Writ ... South Asian Digest of Regional Writing
            [*Heidelberg*] [*A publication*]
South Asian R ... South Asian Review [*A publication*]
South Asian Stud ... South Asian Studies [*A publication*]
South As Stud ... South Asian Studies [*Jaipur*] [*A publication*]
South As Surv ... South Asian Survey [*New Delhi*] [*A publication*]
South Atlan Q ... South Atlantic Quarterly [*A publication*]
South Atl Bull ... South Atlantic Bulletin [*A publication*]
South Atl Q ... South Atlantic Quarterly [*A publication*]
South Aus LR ... South Australian Law Reports [*A publication*]
South Aust Dep Agric Fish Agron Branch Rep ... South Australia. Department
            of Agriculture and Fisheries. Agronomy Branch. Report [*A
            publication*]
South Aust Dep Agric Fish Agron Bran Rep ... South Australia. Department of
            Agriculture and Fisheries. Agronomy Branch. Report [*A
            publication*]   (APTA)
South Aust Dep Mines Miner Resour Rev ... South Australia. Department of
            Mines. Mineral Resources Review [*A publication*]   (APTA)
South Aust Geol Surv Bull ... South Australia. Geological Survey. Bulletin [*A
            publication*]   (APTA)
South Aust Geol Surv 1:250000 Geol Ser ... South Australia. Geological
            Survey. 1:250,000 Geological Series [*A
            publication*]   (APTA)
South Aust Geol Surv Q Geol Notes ... South Australia. Geological Survey.
            Quarterly Geological Notes [*A publication*]   (APTA)
South Aust Geol Surv Rep Invest ... South Australia. Geological Survey.
            Report of Investigations [*A publication*]   (APTA)
South Aust Mot ... South Australian Motor [*A publication*]   (APTA)
South Aust Nat ... South Australian Naturalist [*A publication*]   (APTA)
South Aust Orn ... South Australian Ornithologist [*A publication*]   (APTA)
South Aust Rep Mus Board ... South Australia. Report of the Museum Board
            [*A publication*]
South Birds ... Southern Birds [*A publication*]
South Bus... South Business [*A publication*]
South Calif Coastal Water Res Proj Annu Rep ... Southern California Coastal
            Water Research Project. Annual Report [*A publication*]
South Calif L Rev ... Southern California Law Review [*A publication*]
South Calif Q ... Southern California Quarterly [*A publication*]
South Cal Law Rev ... Southern California Law Review [*A publication*]
South Canner Packer ... Southern Canner and Packer [*A publication*]
South Cant J ... South Canterbury Journal [*A publication*]
South Car... South Carolina Reports [*A publication*]   (DLA)
South Carolina Acad Sci Bull ... South Carolina Academy of Science. Bulletin
            [*A publication*]
South Carolina Div Geology Geol Notes ... South Carolina. Division of
            Geology. Geologic Notes [*A publication*]
South Carolina Div Geology Misc Rept ... South Carolina. Division of
            Geology. Miscellaneous Report [*A publication*]
South Carolina L Rev ... South Carolina Law Review [*A publication*]
South Car R ... South Carolina Review [*A publication*]
South Chem ... Southern Chemist [*A publication*]
South Chem Ind ... Southern Chemical Industry [*A publication*]
SOUTHCOM ... Southern Command [*Military*]   (AFM)
South Conf Gerontol Rep ... Southern Conference on Gerontology. Report [*A
            publication*]
South Coop Ser Bull ... Southern Cooperative Series Bulletin [*A publication*]
South Corn Impr Conf Rep ... Southern Corn Improvement Conference.
            Report [*A publication*]
South Dairy Prod J ... Southern Dairy Products Journal [*A publication*]
South Dak L Rev ... South Dakota Law Review [*A publication*]
South Dakota Geol Survey Guidebook ... South Dakota. Geological Survey.
            Guidebook [*A publication*]
South Dakota Geol Survey Rept Inv ... South Dakota. Geological Survey.
            Report of Investigations [*A publication*]
South Dakota Geol Survey Spec Rept ... South Dakota. Geological Survey.
            Special Report [*A publication*]

South Dakota Geol Survey Water Resources Rept ... South Dakota Geological Survey and South Dakota Water Resources Commission. Water Resources Report [*A publication*]
South Dakota L Rev ... South Dakota Law Review [*A publication*]
SOUTHDOC ... Southern Region Document Service [*Australia*]
Southeast Asia Bldg Materials & Equipment ... Southeast Asia Building Materials and Equipment [*A publication*]
Southeast Asia J Theol ... Southeast Asia Journal of Theology [*A publication*]
Southeast Asian Conf Soil Eng Proc ... Southeast Asian Conference on Soil Engineering. Proceedings [*A publication*]
Southeast Asian J Soc Sci ... Southeast Asian Journal of Social Science [*A publication*]
Southeast Asian J Trop Med Public Health ... Southeast Asian Journal of Tropical Medicine and Public Health [*A publication*]
South East Asian Stud ... South East Asian Studies [*A publication*]
Southeast Asia Pet Explor Soc Proc ... Southeast Asia Petroleum Exploration Society. Proceedings [*A publication*]
Southeastcon Reg 3 (Three) Conf Proc ... Southeastcon Region 3 (Three) Conference Proceedings [*United States*] [*A publication*]
Southeastern Geology Spec Pub ... Southeastern Geology. Special Publication [*A publication*]
Southeastern Rep ... South Eastern Reporter [*A publication*]   (DLA)
Southeast Geogr ... Southeastern Geographer [*A publication*]
Southeast Geol ... Southeastern Geology [*A publication*]
Southeast Geol Soc Field Conf Guideb ... Southeastern Geological Society. Field Conference Guidebook [*A publication*]
Southeast Geol Spec Publ ... Southeastern Geology. Special Publication [*A publication*]
South Econ ... Southern Economist [*Bangalore*] [*A publication*]
South Econ J ... Southern Economic Journal [*A publication*]
South Econ Jour ... Southern Economic Journal [*A publication*]
Southern .... Southern Reporter [*A publication*]   (DLA)
Southern Calif Acad Sci Bull ... Southern California Academy of Sciences. Bulletin [*A publication*]
Southern Econ J ... Southern Economic Journal [*A publication*]
Southern Folklore Q ... Southern Folklore Quarterly [*A publication*]
Southern H R ... Southern Humanities Review [*A publication*]
Southern Hum R ... Southern Humanities Review [*A publication*]
Southern J Med Phys Sc ... Southern Journal of the Medical and Physical Sciences [*A publication*]
Southern Lit J ... Southern Literary Journal [*A publication*]
Southern P R ... Southern Poetry Review [*A publication*]
Southern Pulp Paper Mfr ... Southern Pulp and Paper Manufacturer [*A publication*]
Southern R ... Southern Review [*A publication*]
Southern Rep ... Southern Reporter [*A publication*]   (DLA)
Southern Rev ... Southern Review [*A publication*]   (APTA)
South Exposure ... Southern Exposure [*United States*] [*A publication*]
South Fisherman ... Southern Fisherman [*A publication*]
South Florist Nurseryman ... Southern Florist and Nurseryman [*United States*] [*A publication*]
South Folkl Q ... Southern Folklore Quarterly [*A publication*]
South Folkl Quart ... Southern Folklore Quarterly [*A publication*]
South Folk Q ... Southern Folklore Quarterly [*A publication*]
South Food Process ... Southern Food Processor [*A publication*]
SOUTHFORNET ... Southern Forestry Information Network [*Forest Service*] [*IID*]
South Hist Assoc Publ ... Southern Historical Association. Publications [*A publication*]
South Hist Soc Papers ... Southern Historical Society. Papers [*A publication*]
South Hort ... Southern Horticulture [*New Zealand*] [*A publication*]
South Hortic ... Southern Horticulture [*A publication*]
South Hosp ... Southern Hospitals [*A publication*]
South Hum Rev ... Southern Humanities Review [*A publication*]
South Ill ULJ ... Southern Illinois University. Law Journal [*A publication*]
South Indian Hortic ... Southern Indian Horticulture [*A publication*]
South Ind St ... Southern Indian Studies [*United States*] [*A publication*]
South J Agric Econ ... Southern Journal of Agricultural Economics [*A publication*]
South J Appl For ... Southern Journal of Applied Forestry [*A publication*]
South Law J ... Southern Law Journal [*Tuscaloosa, AL*] [*A publication*]   (DLA)
South Law J & Rep ... Southern Law Journal and Reporter [*A publication*]   (DLA)
South Law Rev ... Southern Law Review [*A publication*]   (DLA)
South Law Rev NS ... Southern Law Review, New Series [*A publication*]   (DLA)
South Lit J ... Southern Literary Journal [*A publication*]
South Liv.... Southern Living [*A publication*]
South LJ.... Southern Law Journal [*A publication*]   (DLA)
South LJ & Rep ... Southern Law Journal and Reporter [*A publication*]   (DLA)
South L Rev ... Southern Law Review [*A publication*]   (DLA)
South L Rev NS ... Southern Law Review, New Series [*A publication*]   (DLA)
South Lumberman ... Southern Lumberman [*A publication*]
South M ..... South Magazine [*A publication*]
South Med ... Southern Medicine [*A publication*]
South Med Bull ... Southern Medical Bulletin [*A publication*]
South Med J ... Southern Medical Journal [*A publication*]
South Med Surg ... Southern Medicine and Surgery [*A publication*]

South Methodist Univ Inst Stud Earth Man Rep ... Southern Methodist University. Institute for the Study of Earth and Man. Reports of Investigations [*A publication*]
South MJ... Southern Medical Journal [*A publication*]
SOUTHN ... Southampton [*City in England*]   (ROG)
South Pac ... South Pacific [*A publication*]
South Pac Bull ... South Pacific Bulletin [*A publication*]
South Pac Comm Tech Pap ... Southern Pacific Commission. Technical Paper [*A publication*]
South Pacific B ... South Pacific Bulletin [*A publication*]
South Pacific Bul ... South Pacific Bulletin [*A publication*]   (APTA)
South Pacific J Ed ... South Pacific Journal of Education [*A publication*]   (APTA)
South Pac J Nat Sci ... South Pacific Journal of Natural Science [*A publication*]
South Pac J Teach Educ ... South Pacific Journal of Teacher Education [*A publication*]   (APTA)
South Pac Mar Geol Notes ... South Pacific Marine Geological Notes [*Suva*] [*A publication*]
South Pharm J ... Southern Pharmaceutical Journal [*A publication*]
South Plast Chem ... Southern Plastics and Chemicals [*A publication*]
South Power Ind ... Southern Power and Industry [*A publication*]
South Power J ... Southern Power Journal [*A publication*]
South Pract ... Southern Practitioner [*A publication*]
South Pulp Pap J ... Southern Pulp and Paper Journal [*A publication*]
South Pulp Pap Manuf ... Southern Pulp and Paper Manufacturer [*A publication*]
South Q...... Southern Quarterly [*A publication*]
South Quar ... Southern Quarterly Review [*A publication*]
South Quart ... Southern Quarterly [*A publication*]
South R ...... South Carolina Review [*A publication*]
South R ...... Southern Review [*A publication*]
South Rag .. Southern Rag [*A publication*]
South Res Inst Bull ... Southern Research Institute. Bulletin [*United States*] [*A publication*]
South Rhod Geol Surv Bull ... Southern Rhodesia. Geological Survey. Bulletin [*A publication*]
South Seedsman ... Southern Seedsman [*A publication*]
South Speech Comm J ... Southern Speech Communication Journal [*A publication*]
South Stars ... Southern Stars [*A publication*]
South Stud ... Southern Studies [*A publication*]
South Surg ... Southern Surgeon [*United States*] [*A publication*]
South Texas Geol Soc Bull ... South Texas Geological Society. Bulletin [*A publication*]
South Texas LJ ... South Texas Law Journal [*A publication*]
South Text Bull ... Southern Textile Bulletin [*A publication*]
South UL Rev ... Southern University Law Review [*A publication*]
SOUTHW ... Southwell [*City in England*]   (ROG)
Southwest Afr Ann ... Southwest Africa Annual [*A publication*]
Southwest Bull ... Southwest Bulletin [*United States*] [*A publication*]
Southwest Bus and Econ R ... Southwest Business and Economic Review [*United States*] [*A publication*]
Southwest Entomol ... Southwestern Entomologist [*A publication*]
Southwest Entomol Suppl ... Southwestern Entomologist. Supplement [*A publication*]
Southwestern As Petroleum G B ... Southwestern Association of Petroleum Geologists. Bulletin [*A publication*]
Southwestern LA Jour ... Southwestern Louisiana Journal [*A publication*]
Southwestern LJ ... Southwestern Law Journal [*A publication*]
Southwestern R Mgt and Econ ... Southwestern Review of Management and Economics [*United States*] [*A publication*]
Southwestern UL Rev ... Southwestern University. Law Review [*A publication*]
Southwestern Univ L Rev ... Southwestern University. Law Review [*A publication*]
Southwest Hist Q ... Southwestern Historical Quarterly [*A publication*]
Southwest J ... Southwest Journal [*A publication*]
Southwest J Anthropol ... Southwestern Journal of Anthropology [*A publication*]
Southwest Med ... Southwestern Medicine [*United States*] [*A publication*]
Southwest Miller ... Southwestern Miller [*A publication*]
Southwest Mus Paper ... Southwest Museum. Papers [*A publication*]
Southwest Nat ... Southwestern Naturalist [*A publication*]
Southwest Pet Short Course Proc Annu Meet ... Southwestern Petroleum Short Course. Proceedings of the Annual Meeting [*United States*] [*A publication*]
Southwest UL Rev ... Southwestern University. Law Review [*A publication*]
Southwest Vet ... Southwestern Veterinarian [*United States*] [*A publication*]
Southwest Water Works J ... Southwest Water Works Journal [*A publication*]
Southw His Q ... Southwestern Historical Quarterly [*A publication*]
Southw Hist Quar ... Southwestern Historical Quarterly [*A publication*]
Southw Hist Quart ... Southwestern Historical Quarterly [*United States*] [*A publication*]
Southw J Anthrop ... Southwestern Journal of Anthropology [*United States*] [*A publication*]
Southw Jnl Philos ... Southwestern Journal of Philosophy [*A publication*]
SouthWJTh ... Southwestern Journal of Theology [*Fort Worth, TX*] [*A publication*]
Southw LJ ... Southwestern Law Journal [*United States*] [*A publication*]
Southw LJ ... Southwestern Law Journal and Reporter [*A publication*]   (DLA)

Southw Lore ... Southwestern Lore [*A publication*]
Southw Pol Sci Quar ... Southwest Political Science Quarterly [*A publication*]
Southw Pol and Soc Sci Q ... Southwestern Political and Social Science Quarterly [*A publication*]
Southw Rev ... Southwest Review [*A publication*]
Southw Soc Sci Quar ... Southwestern Social Science Quarterly [*A publication*]
SOV .... Seldovia, AK [*Location identifier*] [*FAA*]   (FAAL)
SOV .... Sham Ovariectomy [*Endocrinology*]
SOV .... Share of Voice [*Advertising*]
SOV .... Shut-Off Valve
SOV .... Simulated Operational Vehicle   (MCD)
SOV .... Single-Occupancy Vehicle   (ECON)
SOV .... Solenoid-Operated Valve
SOV .... Somerset County Vocational and Technical School, Bridgewater, NJ [*OCLC symbol*]   (OCLC)
SOV .... Sovereign
SOV .... Soviet
SOV .... Sovran Financial Corp. [*NYSE symbol*]   (CTT)
SOV .... Study of Values
SOV .... Subjective Optical Vertical
SOVAC ...... Software Validation and Control System   (MCD)
SovAE .... Soviet Antarctic Expedition [*1955-*]
Sov Aeronaut ... Soviet Aeronautics [*English Translation of Izvestiya VUZ. Aviatsionnaya Teknika*] [*A publication*]
Sov Agron .. Sovetskaya Agronomiya [*A publication*]
Sov Antarct Exped Inf Bull ... Soviet Antarctic Expedition. Information Bulletin [*A publication*]
Sov Antarct Exped Inform Bull ... Soviet Antarctic Expedition. Information Bulletin [*A publication*]
Sov Antarkt Eksped Inform Byull ... Sovetskaya Antarkticheskaya Ekspeditsiya Informatsionnyy Byulletin [*A publication*]
Sov Anthr A ... Soviet Anthropology and Archeology [*A publication*]
Sov Anthro Arch ... Soviet Anthropology and Archeology [*New York*] [*A publication*]
Sov Appl Mech ... Soviet Applied Mechanics [*A publication*]
Sov Arch .... Sovetskaja Archeologija [*A publication*]
Sov Arh ...... Sovetskie Arhivi [*A publication*]
Sov Arkh .... Sovetskie Arkhivy [*A publication*]
Sov Arkheol ... Sovetskaya Arkheologiya [*A publication*]
Sov Astron ... Soviet Astronomy [*A publication*]
Sov Astron Lett ... Soviet Astronomy. Letters [*A publication*]
Sov Astron Lett (Engl Transl) ... Soviet Astronomy. Letters (English Translation) [*A publication*]
Sov At Energy ... Soviet Atomic Energy [*A publication*]
Sov At En R ... Soviet Atomic Energy (USSR) [*A publication*]
Sov Atom Energy ... Soviet Atomic Energy [*A publication*]
Sov Automat Contr ... Soviet Automatic Control [*A publication*]
Sov Autom Control ... Soviet Automatic Control [*A publication*]
Sov Bibliog ... Sovetskaya Bibliografia [*A publication*]
Sov Bibliotekov ... Sovetskaia Bibliotekovedenie [*A publication*]
Sov Bot ...... Sovetskaya Botanika [*A publication*]
Sov Chem Ind ... Soviet Chemical Industry [*A publication*]
Sov Cybern Rev ... Soviet Cybernetics Review [*A publication*]
SOVD .... Stabilized Optical Viewing Device
SOVEA ...... Southwestern Veterinarian [*United States*] [*A publication*]
Sov East Europ For Trade ... Soviet and Eastern European Foreign Trade [*A publication*]
Sov Educ .... Soviet Education [*A publication*]
Sov E E For ... Soviet and Eastern European Foreign Trade [*A publication*]
Sov & E Eur For Tr ... American Review of Soviet and Eastern European Foreign Trade [*A publication*]   (DLA)
Sov Elec Eng ... Soviet Electrical Engineering [*A publication*]
Sov Electr Eng ... Soviet Electrical Engineering [*English Translation of Elektrotekhnika*] [*A publication*]
Sov Electrochem ... Soviet Electrochemistry [*A publication*]
Sov Eng J ... Soviet Engineering Journal [*A publication*]
Sov Engng Res ... Soviet Engineering Research [*A publication*]
Sov Eng Res ... Soviet Engineering Research [*A publication*]
SovEt .... Sovetskaya Etnografija [*A publication*]
Sovet Geol ... Sovetskaya Geologiya [*A publication*]
Sovet Geologiya ... Sovetskaya Geologiya [*A publication*]
Sovet Muz ... Sovetskaya Muzyka [*A publication*]
SovEtn .... Sovetskaya Etnografija [*A publication*]
Sov Etnogr ... Sovetskaya Etnografija [*A publication*]
Sovetskaya M ... Sovetskaya Muzyka [*A publication*]
Sovetskoe Bibl ... Sovetskoe Bibliotekovedenie [*A publication*]
Sov Export ... Soviet Export [*A publication*]
Sov Farm .... Sovetskaya Farmatsiya [*A publication*]
Sov Film ..... Soviet Film [*A publication*]
Sov Finno-Ugroved ... Sovetskoje Finno-Ugrovedenie [*A publication*]
Sov Fluid Mech (Engl Transl) ... Soviet Fluid Mechanics (English Translation) [*A publication*]
Sov Foto ..... Sovetskoe Foto [*A publication*]
SovFU .... Sovetskoje Finno-Ugrovedenie [*A publication*]
Sov Genet ... Soviet Genetics [*A publication*]
Sov Genet (Engl Transl Genetika) ... Soviet Genetics (English Translation of Genetika) [*A publication*]
Sov Geogr ... Soviet Geography. Review and Translations [*A publication*]
Sov Geogr R ... Soviet Geography. Review and Translations [*A publication*]
Sov Geol ..... Sovetskaya Geologiya [*A publication*]

Sov Geol Geophys ... Soviet Geology and Geophysics [*A publication*]
Sov Geol and Geophys ... Soviet Geology and Geophysics [*A publication*]
Sov Geol Geophys (Engl Transl) ... Soviet Geology and Geophysics (English Translation) [*A publication*]
Sov Gos Pravo ... Sovetskoe Gosudarstvo i Pravo [*A publication*]
SovH .... Sovetish Heymland [*A publication*]
Sov Hydrol ... Soviet Hydrology. Selected Papers [*A publication*]
Sov Hydrol Sel Pap ... Soviet Hydrology. Selected Papers [*A publication*]
SOVIA .... Sound and Vibration [*A publication*]
Soviet Aeronaut ... Soviet Aeronautics [*A publication*]
Soviet Agric Sci ... Soviet Agricultural Science [*A publication*]
Soviet Appl Mech ... Soviet Applied Mechanics [*A publication*]
Soviet Astronom ... Soviet Astronomy [*A publication*]
Soviet Automat Control ... Soviet Automatic Control [*A publication*]
Soviet Chem Ind ... Soviet Chemical Industry [*A publication*]
Soviet and Eastern Eur For Trade ... Soviet and Eastern European Foreign Trade [*A publication*]
Soviet Ed .... Soviet Education [*A publication*]
Soviet F ...... Soviet Film [*A publication*]
Soviet Genet ... Soviet Genetics [*A publication*]
Soviet J Contemporary Math Anal ... Soviet Journal of Contemporary Mathematical Analysis [*A publication*]
Soviet J Ecol ... Soviet Journal of Ecology [*A publication*]
Soviet Jewry L Rev ... Soviet Jewry Law Review [*A publication*]   (DLA)
Soviet J Nuclear Phys ... American Institute of Physics. Soviet Journal of Nuclear Physics [*A publication*]
Soviet J Particles and Nuclei ... Soviet Journal of Particles and Nuclei [*A publication*]
Soviet Law and Govt ... Soviet Law and Government [*A publication*]
Soviet L & Govt ... Soviet Law and Government [*A publication*]
Soviet Lit .... Soviet Literature [*A publication*]
Soviet Math Dokl ... Soviet Mathematics. Doklady [*A publication*]
Soviet Math (Iz VUZ) ... Soviet Mathematics (Izvestija Vyssih Ucebnyh Zavedenii. Matematika) [*A publication*]
Soviet Phys Acoust ... Soviet Physics. Acoustics [*A publication*]
Soviet Phys Collection ... Soviet Physics. Collection [*English Translation*] [*A publication*]
Soviet Phys Cryst ... Soviet Physics. Crystallography [*A publication*]
Soviet Physics Acoust ... Soviet Physics. Acoustics [*A publication*]
Soviet Physics Dokl ... Soviet Physics. Doklady [*A publication*]
Soviet Physics J ... Soviet Physics Journal [*A publication*]
Soviet Phys J ... Soviet Physics Journal [*A publication*]
Soviet Phys JETP ... Soviet Physics. JETP [*Journal of Experimental and Theoretical Physics of the Academy of Sciences of the USSR*] [*A publication*]
Soviet Phys Uspekhi ... Soviet Physics. Uspekhi [*A publication*]
Soviet Plant Physiol ... Soviet Plant Physiology [*A publication*]
Soviet Pl Physiol ... Soviet Plant Physiology [*A publication*]
Soviet Sci Rev Sect C Math Phys Rev ... Soviet Scientific Reviews. Section C. Mathematical Physics Reviews [*A publication*]
Soviet Sociol ... Soviet Sociology [*A publication*]
Soviet Soil Sci ... Soviet Soil Science [*A publication*]
Soviet Stat & Dec ... Soviet Statutes and Decisions [*A publication*]   (DLA)
Soviet Stud ... Soviet Studies [*A publication*]
Soviet Stud Phil ... Soviet Studies in Philosophy [*A publication*]
Soviet YB Int'l L ... Soviet Year-Book of International Law [*A publication*]   (DLA)
SOVIN .... Samenwerkingsverband voor Opleiding en Vorming op het Terrein van de Informatieverzorging via Netwerken [*Collective for Training and Education in Connection with Information Provision via Networks*] [*Netherlands*] [*Information service or system*] [*Ceased operation*]   (IID)
Sov Instrum & Control J ... Soviet Journal of Instrumentation and Control [*A publication*]
Sovistva At Yader ... Sovistva Atomnykh Yader [*USSR*] [*A publication*]
SovJa .... Sovetska Jazykoveda [*A publication*]
Sov J At ..... Soviet Journal of Atomic Energy [*A publication*]
Sov J Bioorganic Chem ... Soviet Journal of Bioorganic Chemistry [*A publication*]
Sov J Bioorg Chem (Engl Transl Bioorg Khim) ... Soviet Journal of Bioorganic Chemistry (English Translation of Bioorganicheskaya Khimiya) [*A publication*]
Sov J Coord Chem (Engl Transl) ... Soviet Journal of Coordination Chemistry (English Translation) [*A publication*]
Sov J Coord Chem (Engl Transl Koord Khim) ... Soviet Journal of Coordination Chemistry (English Translation of Koordinatsionnaya Khimiya) [*A publication*]
Sov J Dev Biol (Engl Transl Ontogenez) ... Soviet Journal of Developmental Biology (English Translation of Ontogenez) [*A publication*]
Sov J Ecol .. Soviet Journal of Ecology [*A publication*]
Sov J Ecol (Engl Transl Ekologiya) ... Soviet Journal of Ecology (English Translation of Ekologiya) [*A publication*]
Sov Jew Aff ... Soviet Jewish Affairs [*A publication*]
Sov J Glass Phys Chem ... Soviet Journal of Glass Physics and Chemistry [*A publication*]
Sov J Glass Phys and Chem ... Soviet Journal of Glass Physics and Chemistry [*A publication*]
Sov J Glass Phys Chem (Engl Transl) ... Soviet Journal of Glass Physics and Chemistry (English Translation) [*A publication*]
Sov J Instrum Control ... Soviet Journal of Instrumentation and Control [*A publication*]

Sov J Low Temp Phys ... Soviet Journal of Low Temperature Physics [*A publication*]
Sov J Low Temp Phys (Engl Transl) ... Soviet Journal of Low Temperature Physics (English Translation) [*A publication*]
Sov J Mar Biol ... Soviet Journal of Marine Biology [*A publication*]
Sov J Mar Biol (Engl Transl) ... Soviet Journal of Marine Biology (English Translation) [*A publication*]
Sov J Mar Biol (Engl Transl Biol Morya) ... Soviet Journal of Marine Biology (English Translation of Biologiya Morya) [*A publication*]
Sov J Nondestr Test ... Soviet Journal of Nondestructive Testing [*A publication*]
Sov J Nondestruct Test ... Soviet Journal of Nondestructive Testing [*A publication*]
Sov J Non-Ferrous Met ... Soviet Journal of Non-Ferrous Metals [*A publication*]
Sov J Nucl Phys ... Soviet Journal of Nuclear Physics [*A publication*]
Sov J Nuc R ... Soviet Journal of Nuclear Physics (USSR) [*A publication*]
Sov J Opt Technol ... Soviet Journal of Optical Technology [*A publication*]
Sov J Part Nucl ... Soviet Journal of Particles and Nuclei [*A publication*]
Sov J Plasma Phys ... Soviet Journal of Plasma Physics [*A publication*]
Sov J Quant Electron ... Soviet Journal of Quantum Electronics [*A publication*]
Sov J Quantum Electron ... Soviet Journal of Quantum Electronics [*A publication*]
Sov Khlopok ... Sovetskii Khlopok [*A publication*]
Sov Kino Fotopromst ... Sovetskaya Kino-Fotopromyshlennost [*A publication*]
SovKniga.... Sovetskaya Kniga [*A publication*]
Sov Krasnyi Krest ... Soveti Krasnyi Krest [*USSR*] [*A publication*]
SovL........... Soviet Literature [*A publication*]
SOVLA...... Sovetskaya Latvia [*A publication*]
Sov Law Gov ... Soviet Law and Government [*A publication*]
Sov Law & Govt ... Soviet Law and Government [*A publication*]
Sov Lit........ Soviet Literature [*A publication*]
Sov M.......... Sovetskaya Muzyka [*A publication*]
Sov Mater Sci ... Soviet Materials Science [*A publication*]
Sov Mater Sci (Engl Transl) ... Soviet Materials Science (English Translation of Fiziko-Khimicheskaya Mekhanika Materialov) [*A publication*]
Sov Math ... Soviet Mathematics [*A publication*]
Sov Med..... Sovetskaya Meditsina [*A publication*]
SOVMEDRON ... Soviet Mediterranean Squadron [*NATO*]   (NATG)
Sovmestnaya Sov-Mong Nauchno-Issled Geol Eksped ... Sovmestnaya Sovetsko-Mongol'skaya Nauchno-Issledovatel'skaya Geologicheskaya Ekspeditsiya [*A publication*]
Sovmestnaya Sov-Mong Nauchno-Issled Geol Eksped Tr ... Sovmestnaya Sovetsko-Mongol'skaya Nauchno-Issledovatel'skaya Geologicheskaya Ekspeditsiya Trudy [*A publication*]
Sov Metall ... Sovetskaya Metallurgiya [*A publication*]
Sov Meteorol Hydrol ... Soviet Meteorology and Hydrology [*English translation of Meteorologiya i Gidrologiya*] [*A publication*]
Sov Meteorol and Hydrol ... Soviet Meteorology and Hydrology [*English translation of Meteorologiya i Gidrologiya*] [*A publication*]
Sov Meteorol Hydrol (Engl Transl) ... Soviet Meteorology and Hydrology (English Translation) [*A publication*]
Sov Microelectron ... Soviet Microelectronics [*A publication*]
Sov Min Sci ... Soviet Mining Science [*A publication*]
Sov Ml Rev ... Soviet Military Review [*A publication*]
Sov Nauka ... Sovetskaya Nauka [*A publication*]
Sov Neurol Psychiatry ... Soviet Neurology and Psychiatry [*A publication*]
Sov Neur R ... Soviet Neurology and Psychiatry (USSR) [*A publication*]
Sov Non-Ferrous Met Res ... Soviet Non-Ferrous Metals Research [*A publication*]
Sov Non-Ferrous Met Res (Engl Transl) ... Soviet Non-Ferrous Metals Research (English Translation) [*A publication*]
Sov Oceanogr ... Soviet Oceanography [*A publication*]
SOVOG ..... Sozialistiche Volksorganisation [*Socialist National Community*] [*Lithuania*] [*Political party*]   (PPE)
Sov Pedag .. Soviet Pedagogy [*A publication*]
Sov Ph Ac R ... Soviet Physics. Acoustics (USSR) [*A publication*]
Sov Ph Se R ... Soviet Physics. Semiconductors (USSR) [*A publication*]
Sov Phys Acoust ... Soviet Physics. Acoustics [*A publication*]
Sov Phys Collect ... Soviet Physics. Collection [*A publication*]
Sov Phys Coll (Engl Transl) ... Soviet Physics. Collection (English Translation) [*A publication*]
Sov Phys Cryst ... Soviet Physics. Crystallography [*A publication*]
Sov Phys Crystallogr ... Soviet Physics. Crystallography [*A publication*]
Sov Phys Dokl ... Soviet Physics. Doklady [*A publication*]
Sov Phys J ... Soviet Physics Journal [*A publication*]
Sov Phys JETP ... Soviet Physics. JETP [*Journal of Experimental and Theoretical Physics of the Academy of Sciences of the USSR*] [*A publication*]
Sov Phys Lebedev Inst Rep ... Soviet Physics. Lebedev Institute Reports [*English Translation of Sbornik Kratkie Soobshcheniya po Fizike*] [*A publication*]
Sov Phys Lebedev Inst Rep (Engl Transl) ... Soviet Physics. Lebedev Institute Reports (English Translation) [*A publication*]
Sov Phys Semicond ... Soviet Physics. Semiconductors [*A publication*]
Sov Phys Solid State ... Soviet Physics. Solid State [*English translation of Fizika Tverdogo Tela*] [*A publication*]
Sov Phys Sol St ... Soviet Physics. Solid State Physics [*A publication*]

Sov Phys Tech Phys ... Soviet Physics. Technical Physics [*A publication*]
Sov Phys Tech Phys Lett ... Soviet Physics. Technical Physics. Letters [*A publication*]
Sov Phys T P ... Soviet Physics. Technical Physics [*A publication*]
Sov Phys Usp ... Soviet Physics. Uspekhi [*A publication*]
Sov Phys Uspekhi ... Soviet Physics. Uspekhi [*A publication*]
Sov Plant Physiol ... Soviet Plant Physiology [*A publication*]
Sov Plant Physiol (Engl Transl Fiziol Rast) ... Soviet Plant Physiology (English Translation of Fiziologiya Rastenii) [*A publication*]
Sov Plast .... Soviet Plastics [*A publication*]
Sov Powder Metall and Met Ceram ... Soviet Powder Metallurgy and Metal Ceramics [*A publication*]
Sov Powder Metall Met Ceram ... Soviet Powder Metallurgy and Metal Ceramics [*A publication*]
Sov Powder Met Metal Ceram ... Soviet Powder Metallurgy and Metal Ceramics [*A publication*]
Sov Power Eng ... Soviet Power Engineering [*A publication*]
Sov Power Eng (Engl Transl) ... Soviet Power Engineering (English Translation of Elektricheskie Stantsii) [*A publication*]
Sov Prog Chem ... Soviet Progress in Chemistry [*A publication*]
Sov Psikhonevrol ... Sovetskaya Psikhonevrologiya [*A publication*]
Sov Psychol ... Soviet Psychology [*A publication*]
Sov Psyco R ... Soviet Psychology (USSR) [*A publication*]
Sov Public Health ... Soviet Public Health [*A publication*]
Sov Public Health (Engl Transl) ... Soviet Public Health (English Translation) [*A publication*]
SOVR .... Sovereign Corp. [*NASDAQ symbol*]   (NQ)
SovR........... Soviet Review [*A publication*]
Sov Radiochem ... Soviet Radiochemistry [*A publication*]
Sov Radio Eng ... Soviet Radio Engineering [*A publication*]
Sov Radiophys ... Soviet Radiophysics [*A publication*]
Sov Radiophys (Engl Transl) ... Soviet Radiophysics (English Translation of Izvestiya Vysshikh Uchebnykh Zavedenii Radiofizika) [*A publication*]
Sovrem Metody Issled ... Sovremennye Metody Issledovaniya [*A publication*]
Sovrem Probl Deyat Str Tsentr Nervn Sist ... Sovremennye Problemy Deyatel'nosti i Stroeniya Tsentral'noe Nervnoi Sistemy [*A publication*]
Sovrem Probl Fiz Khim ... Sovremennye Problemy Fizicheskoi Khimii [*A publication*]
Sovrem Probl Gastroenterol ... Sovremennye Problemy Gastroenterologii [*A publication*]
Sovrem Probl Gastroenterol Resp Mezhved Sb ... Sovremennye Problemy Gastroenterologii Respublikanskii Mezhvedomstvennyi-Sbornik [*A publication*]
Sovrem Probl Gematol Pereliv Krovi ... Sovremennye Problemy Gematologii i Perelivaniya Krovi [*A publication*]
Sovrem Probl Onkol ... Sovremennye Problemy Onkologii [*A publication*]
Sovrem Probl Org Khim ... Sovremennye Problemy Organicheskoi Khimii [*A publication*]
Sovrem Probl Otolaringol Resp Mezhved Sb ... Sovremennye Problemy Otolaringologii Respublikanskoi Mezhvedomstvennyi Sbornik [*A publication*]
Sovrem Probl Radiobiol ... Sovremennye Problemy Radiobiologii [*USSR*] [*A publication*]
Sovrem Psikhotropnye Sredstva ... Sovremennye Psikhotropnye Sredstva [*A publication*]
Sovrem Vopr Endokrinol ... Sovremennye Voprosy Endokrinologii [*A publication*]
Sovrem Vopr Sud Med Ekspertnoi Prak ... Sovremennye Voprosy Sudebnoi Meditsiny i Ekspertnoi Praktiki [*A publication*]
Sovrem Zadachi Tochn Naukakh ... Sovremennye Zadachi v Tochnykh Naukakh [*A publication*]
Sov Res Phys ... Soviet Research in Physics [*A publication*]
Sov Rubber Technol ... Soviet Rubber Technology [*A publication*]
SOVS .... Sovereigns [*Monetary unit*] [*Obsolete*] [*Great Britain*]
SovS .... Soviet Studies [*A publication*]
SovS .... Soviet Survey [*A publication*]
Sov Sakhar ... Sovetskii Sakhar [*A publication*]
Sov Sci ...... Soviet Science [*A publication*]
Sov Sci (Engl Transl) ... Soviet Science (English Translation) [*A publication*]
Sov Sci Rev ... Soviet Science Review [*England*] [*A publication*]
Sov Sci Rev Sect D Biol Rev ... Soviet Scientific Reviews. Section D. Biology Reviews [*A publication*]
Sov Shakhtior ... Sovetskii Shakhtior [*USSR*] [*A publication*]
SovSlav ...... Sovetskoe Slavjanovedenie [*A publication*]
Sov Soc....... Soviet Sociology [*A publication*]
Sov Sociol.... Soviet Sociology [*A publication*]
Sov Soil Sci ... Soviet Soil Science [*A publication*]
Sov Soil Sci (Engl Transl Pochvovedenie) ... Soviet Soil Science (English Translation of Pochvovedenie) [*A publication*]
Sov Soil Sci Suppl ... Soviet Soil Science. Supplement [*A publication*]
Sov Stat & Dec ... Soviet Statutes and Decisions [*A publication*]
Sov St Hist ... Soviet Studies in History [*A publication*]
Sov St Lit ... Soviet Studies in Literature [*A publication*]
Sov St Phil ... Soviet Studies in Philosophy [*A publication*]
Sov Stud..... Soviet Studies [*A publication*]
Sov Stud Hist ... Soviet Studies in History [*A publication*]
Sov Subtrop (Moscow) ... Sovetskie Subtropiki (Moscow) [*A publication*]

Sov Subtrop (Sukhumi USSR) ... Sovetskie Subtropiki (Sukhumi, USSR) [*A publication*]
SovT .... Sovetskaja Tjurkologija [*A publication*]
Sov Tech Phys Lett ... Soviet Technical Physics. Letters [*A publication*]
Sov Tech Phys Lett (Engl Transl) ... Soviet Technical Physics. Letters (English Translation) [*A publication*]
Sov Tjurkolog ... Sovetskaja Tjurkologija [*A publication*]
Sov T P Lett ... Soviet Technical Physics. Letters [*A publication*]
Sov Union .. Soviet Union [*A publication*]
Sov Veda Chem ... Sovetska Veda. Chemie [*A publication*]
SovVo .... Sovetskoje Vostokovedenije [*A publication*]
Sov Vrach Zh ... Sovetskii Vrachebnyi Zhurnal [*A publication*]
SOVX .... Sham Ovariectomized [*Endocrinology*]
Sov Zdravookhr ... Sovetskoe Zdravookhranenie [*A publication*]
Sov Zdravookhr Kirg ... Sovetskoe Zdravookhranenie Kirgizii [*A publication*]
Sov Zdravookhr Turkm ... Sovetskoe Zdravookhranenie Turkmenii [*A publication*]
Sov Zootekh ... Sovetskaya Zootekhniya [*A publication*]
SOW .... Scope of Work   (MCD)
SOW .... Show Low [*Arizona*] [*Airport symbol*] [*Obsolete*]   (OAG)
SOW .... Skylab Orbital Workshop [*NASA*]
SOW .... Special Operations Wing [*Military*]   (MCD)
SOW .... Standoff Weapons   (MCD)
SOW .... Start of Word
SOW .... Start of Work
SOW .... Statement of Work   (MCD)
SOW .... Subdivision of Work [*NASA*]   (NASA)
SOW .... Sunflower Ordnance Works [*Military*]
SOW .... Synthetic Ocean Water
SOWA ...... Stock Option Writers Association   (EA)
SOWC ...... Senior Officers' War Course [*British*]
SOWESPAC ... Southwest Pacific Command [*Navy*]
SOWESSEAFRON ... Southwest Sea Frontier [*Navy*]
SOWESTDIVDOCKS ... Southwest Division, Bureau of Yards and Docks [*Navy*]   (MUGU)
So West LJ ... Southwestern Law Journal [*A publication*]
So West Rep ... South Western Reporter [*A publication*]   (DLA)
SOWETO ... Southwestern Townships [*South Africa*]
SOWg .... Special Operations Wing [*Air Force*]   (AFM)
SOWIDOK ... Sozialwissenschaftliche Dokumentation [*Social Sciences Documentation Center*] [*Vienna Chamber of Labor*] [*Information service or system*]   (IID)
SOWIL ...... Status of Women in Libraries Special Interest Group [*Library Association of Australia*]
Sowjetw Ges ... Sowjetwissenschaft Gesellschaft [*A publication*]
Sowjetwiss ... Sowjetwissenschaft [*A publication*]
SOWM ...... Special Ocean Wave Model
So Workm ... Southern Workman [*A publication*]
SOWP .... Society of Wireless Pioneers   (EA)
SOWRBALL ... Southwest RADAR Balloon [*for illegal drug interdiction*]
SoWS .... Southern Writers Series [*A publication*]
SOW/S & D ... Statement of Work/Specifications and Design
SOX .... Sentry Resources Corp. [*Formerly, Sentry Oil & Gas*] [*Vancouver Stock Exchange symbol*]
SOX .... Solid Oxygen
SOX .... Sulfur Oxide
SOX .... Supercritical Oxygen [*NASA*]   (KSC)
SOXP .... Southeast Explorations Corp. [*NASDAQ symbol*]   (NQ)
SOY .... Sioux Center, IA [*Location identifier*] [*FAA*]   (FAAL)
SOY .... SO Resources [*Vancouver Stock Exchange symbol*]
SOY .... Stronsay [*Scotland*] [*Airport symbol*]   (OAG)
Soybean Dig ... Soybean Digest [*A publication*]
SOYD .... Sum of the Years' Digits Method [*Finance*]
SOYO .... Society of Orthodox Youth Organizations   (EA)
SOZ .... Seder 'Olam Zuta   (BJA)
SOZ .... Solo International Resources Limited [*Vancouver Stock Exchange symbol*]
SOZ .... Somerset, PA [*Location identifier*] [*FAA*]   (FAAL)
SOZ .... Soviet Occupied Zone   (NATG)
SoZ .... Sovremennye Zapiski [*A publication*]
Soz Arbeit .. Soziale Arbeit [*A publication*]
SOZDA ..... Sovetskoe Zdravookhranenie [*A publication*]
Soz Forstwirtsch ... Sozialistische Forstwirtschaft [*A publication*]
Soz Fortschritt ... Sozialer Fortschritt [*A publication*]
Sozialdemokr Pressedienst ... Sozialdemokratische Pressedienst [*A publication*]
Sozial Forstw ... Sozialistische Forstwirtschaft [*A publication*]
Sozialistische Arbeitswiss ... Sozialistische Arbeitswissenschaft [*A publication*]
Sozialistische Finwirt ... Sozialistische Finanzwirtschaft [*A publication*]
Sozialmed Paedagog Jugendkd ... Sozialmedizinische und Paedagogische Jugendkunde [*A publication*]
Sozial Polit ... Sozialistische Politik [*A publication*]
Soz Kommun ... Sozialisation und Kommunikation [*A publication*]
Soz- Praeventivmed ... Sozial- und Praeventivmedizin [*A publication*]
Soz Sicherheit ... Soziale Sicherheit [*A publication*]
Soz Welt ..... Soziale Welt [*A publication*]
Soz und Wirtpol MSpiegel ... Sozial- und Wirtschaftspolitischer Monatsspiegel aus Zeitungen und Zeitschriften [*A publication*]

Soz Wiss Jb Polit ... Sozialwissenschaftliches Jahrbuch fuer Politik [*A publication*]
Sp .... Biblioteca Nacional, Madrid, Spain [*Library symbol*] [*Library of Congress*]   (LCLS)
SP .... Error in Spelling [*Used in correcting manuscripts, etc.*]
SP .... International Society of Philology
sp---- .... La Plata River and Basin [*MARC geographic area code*] [*Library of Congress*]   (LCCP)
SP .... Motor Patrol Boat [*Navy symbol*] [*Obsolete*]
Sp .... [*The*] New Testament of Our Lord and Saviour Jesus Christ (1937) (Francis Aloysius Spencer) [*A publication*]   (BJA)
SP .... Office of State Programs [*Nuclear energy*]   (NRCH)
SP .... Poland [*Aircraft nationality and registration mark*]   (FAAC)
SP .... Sacra Pagina [*Paris-Gembloux*] [*A publication*]   (BJA)
S & P .... Salt and Pepper
SP .... Same Point   (ILCA)
SP .... Same Principle   (ILCA)
SP .... Sample Part
SP .... Sampling Point   (NRCH)
SP .... San Pedro [*California*]
SP .... Sanctissime Pater [*Most Holy Father*] [*Latin*]
sp .... Sans Prix [*Without Price*] [*French*] [*Business term*]
SP .... Satellite Processor [*Data transmission*]
S & P .... Save & Prosper [*Financial services group*] [*British*]
SP .... Schering-Plough Corp. [*Commercial firm*]
SP .... Scholarly Publishing [*A publication*]
SP .... Schools of Philosophy [*A publication*]
SP .... Science Pilot
SP .... Science Press [*Information service or system*]   (IID)
SP .... Scientific Paper
SP .... Scientific Processor   (BUR)
S/P .... Scientific Products
SP .... Scottish Peer   (ROG)
SP .... Scratch Pad [*Data processing*]
S/P .... Seaplane
SP .... Sea Platform   (MCD)
SP .... Secretory Piece [*Superseded by SC, Secretory Component*] [*Immunology*]
SP .... Secretory Protein [*Endocrinology*]
SP .... Section Patrol [*Navy*]
SP .... Security Police [*Air Force*]   (AFM)
SP .... Security Procedure   (NRCH)
SP .... Security Publication [*Navy*]
SP .... Seed Production [*Agriculture*]
SP .... Seeing Problems [*Research test*] [*Psychology*]
SP .... Selective Purchases
SP .... Self Potential [*Log*]
SP .... Self-Powered [*Gun*]   (MCD)
SP .... Self-Propelled [*Military*]
SP .... Selling Price
SP .... Seminar Press
SP .... Semipostal
S/P .... Semiprivate [*Room*]
SP .... Semipublic [*Telecommunications*]   (TEL)
SP .... Send Processor
SP .... Senile Plaque [*Neurology*]
SP .... Senior Partner
SP .... Senior Pilot [*Air Force*]
SP .... Sensor Processor   (BUR)
Sp .... Senterpartiet [*Center Party*] [*Norway*] [*Political party*]   (PPE)
SP .... Senza Pedale [*Without Pedals*] [*Music*]
SP .... Septum Pellucidum [*Brain anatomy*]
SP .... Sequence Programmer [*Data processing*]   (AAG)
S-P .... Sequential-Phase   (CET)
SP .... Sequential Processor
S/P .... Serial to Parallel   (KSC)
SP .... Servants of the Holy Paraclete [*Roman Catholic men's religious order*]
SP .... Service Panel
SP .... Service Phase   (MCD)
SP .... Service Police [*British military*]   (DMA)
SP .... Service Processor   (IEEE)
SP .... Service Publications   (AAG)
SP .... Serving Point [*Telecommunications*]
SP .... Session of Peace [*Legal*] [*British*]   (ROG)
SP .... Set Point
SP .... Severely, Profoundly Handicapped   (OICC)
SP .... Sewer Pipe [*Telecommunications*]   (TEL)
SP .... Shanti Project   (EA)
SP .... Shear Plate [*Technical drawings*]
SP .... Shift Pulses
SP .... Shipping Port
SP .... Shore Party [*Navy*]
SP .... Shore Patrol [*Navy*]
SP .... Shore Police [*Navy*]
SP .... Shoreline Protection [*Type of water project*]
SP .... Short Page
SP .... Short Perforation [*Philately*]
SP .... Short Period
SP .... Short Persistence
SP .... Short Position [*Investment term*]

SP..............	Short Pulse
SP..............	Shortest Path
SP..............	Shoulder Pitch (MCD)
SP..............	Shuttle Projects Office [*Kennedy Space Center*] [*NASA*] (NASA)
SP..............	Sic Porro [*So Forth*] [*Latin*]
SP..............	Sieve Pore [*Botany*]
SP..............	Sign Post
S/P.............	Signal Processor (NASA)
SP..............	Signal Publication [*British*]
SP..............	Signaling Projector [*British*]
SP..............	Signed Photograph
SP..............	Sikkim Parishad [*India*] [*Political party*] (PPW)
SP..............	Silver Plate
SP..............	Silver Protein [*An antiseptic*]
SP..............	Simple Printing
SP..............	Sine Prole [*Died Without Issue*] [*Latin*]
SP..............	Singing Point [*Telecommunications*] (TEL)
SP..............	Single Particle
SP..............	Single Payment (ILCA)
SP..............	Single-Phase
SP..............	Single-Pole [*Switch*]
SP..............	Single Precision (NASA)
SP..............	Single Programmer
SP..............	Single Purpose
SP..............	Sisters of the Presentation of Mary [*Roman Catholic religious order*]
SP..............	Sisters of Providence [*Roman Catholic religious order*]
SP..............	Skin Painting [*Method of administering experimental chemicals*]
SP..............	Skin Prick [*Immunology*]
SP..............	Sloop (ROG)
SP..............	Slovansky Prehled [*A publication*]
SP..............	Slugging Percentage [*Baseball*]
SP..............	Small Packet
SP..............	Small Paper [*Printing*]
SP..............	Small Pica
SP..............	Small Plaque
SP..............	Small Premises [*Hairdressers, doctors, dentists, etc.*] [*Public-performance tariff class*] [*British*]
SP..............	Smith Predictor [*Process control*]
SP..............	Smokeless Powder
SP..............	Smokeless Propellant (NATG)
SP..............	Smoki People (EA)
SP..............	Sniper's Post [*British military*] (DMA)
SP..............	Snow Pellets [*Meteorology*] (FAAC)
SP..............	Socialismo y Participacion [*A publication*]
SP..............	Socialist Party
SP..............	Socialistische Partij [*Socialist Party*] [*Belgium*] [*Political party*] (PPW)
SP..............	Sociedade Acoriana de Transportes Aereos Ltda. [*Portugal*] (FAAC)
SP..............	Society of Philaticians (EA)
SP..............	Society of Protozoologists (EA)
SP..............	Sociolinguistics Program (EA)
SP..............	Soil Pipe
SP..............	Soil Pit
SP..............	Soil Psychrometer
SP..............	Solar Panel
SP..............	Solar Physics (NASA)
SP..............	Soldiers for Peace (EA)
SP..............	Solid Propellant
S of P........	Sons of Phoenix [*Freemasonry*] (ROG)
S/P.............	Sotto Protesto [*Under Protest*] [*Italian*]
SP..............	Sound Powered (CAAL)
SP..............	Soundproof [*Technical drawings*]
SP..............	South Pacific
SP..............	South Pole [*Also, PS*]
SP..............	South Proceeding [*Astronomy*]
SP..............	Southern Pacific Transportation Co. [*AAR code*]
SP..............	Southern Pine [*Utility pole*] [*Telecommunications*] (TEL)
sp..............	Space [*Crocheting*]
SP..............	Space Character [*Keyboard*] (AAG)
SP..............	Space Patrol (AAG)
SP..............	Space and Power
SP..............	Space Propulsion [*A publication*]
Sp..............	Spacers [*Electron transfer*]
SP..............	Spain
sp..............	Spain [*MARC country of publication code*] [*Library of Congress*] (LCCP)
Sp..............	Spalte [*Column*] [*German*] (ILCA)
SP..............	Spanish (ROG)
SP..............	Spare (AAG)
SP..............	Spare Part
SP..............	Spares Planning (AAG)
SP..............	Spark (AAG)
SP..............	Sparkasse [*Savings Bank*] [*German*] [*Business term*]
SP..............	Spartan Program [*Missiles*] (MCD)
Sp..............	Spear's South Carolina Law Reports [*1842-44*] [*A publication*] (DLA)
SP..............	Special (AFM)

Sp..............	Special Branch [*Navy*] [*British*]
SP..............	Special Paper
SP..............	Special Performance
SP..............	Special Planning (AAG)
SP..............	Special Product (MCD)
SP..............	Special Proficiency [*British military*] (DMA)
SP..............	Special Progress [*Program*] [*Education*]
SP..............	Special Projects
SP..............	Special Propellants
SP..............	Special Publication
SP..............	Special Purchase (ADA)
SP..............	Special Purpose
SP..............	Specialist (ADA)
SP..............	Species [*Also, sp*]
SP..............	Specific (AAG)
SP..............	Specific Power
SP..............	Specimen
Sp..............	Spectator [*A publication*]
SP..............	Spectral Pitch [*Neurophysiology*]
Sp..............	Speculum [*A publication*]
SP..............	Speech Pathologist
SP..............	Speed (MSA)
SP..............	Spelling
SP..............	Spelling Entertainment [*AMEX symbol*] (SPSG)
SP..............	Spherical [*Buoy*]
SP..............	Spherical Polar
sp..............	Spherical Tank [*Liquid gas carriers*]
Sp..............	[*Jacobus*] Spiegelius [*Flourished, 1483-1547*] [*Authority cited in pre-1607 legal work*] (DSA)
S/P.............	Spikes Plant [*Wheat*]
SP..............	Spin Polarized [*Physics*]
SP..............	Spine [*or Spinal*]
SP..............	Spine Point Bullet
sp..............	Spinel [*CIPW classification*] [*Geology*]
Sp..............	Spinks' English Admiralty Prize Cases [*164 English Reprint*] [*1854-56*] [*A publication*] (DLA)
Sp..............	Spinks' English Ecclesiastical and Admiralty Reports [*A publication*] (DLA)
SP..............	Spirit
SP..............	Spirometry
SP..............	Spitze [*Point*] [*Music*]
SP..............	Splash Plate
SP..............	Splashproof (MSA)
SP..............	Splinting [*Dentistry*]
SP..............	Splitting [*Electronics*]
Sp..............	Spontaneous
SP..............	Spontaneous Potential [*Log*]
SP..............	Spool (MSA)
SP..............	Spore Plasma [*Botany*]
SP..............	Sport
SP..............	Sportavia Puetzer GmbH & Co. KG [*Federal Republic of Germany*] [*ICAO aircraft manufacturer identifier*] (ICAO)
SP..............	Sports for the People (EA)
SP..............	Spot Price [*Investment term*]
SP..............	Sprague-Dawley [*Rat variety*]
SP..............	Spray Pressure [*Agriculture*]
SP..............	Spring [*A publication*]
Sp..............	Spring Tide
Sp..............	Sputnik [*Moscow*] [*A publication*]
SP..............	Square Planar [*Organic chemistry*]
SP..............	Square Punch
SP..............	Stable Platform
SP..............	Stack Pointer [*Data processing*]
SP..............	Staff Paymaster [*Navy*] [*British*] (ROG)
SP..............	Stained Pollen [*Botany*]
S & P.........	Stake and Platform [*Technical drawings*]
SP..............	Standard Holding Pattern [*Aviation*]
SP..............	Standard or Peculiar (NASA)
SP..............	Standard Pile [*Nuclear reactor*]
SP..............	Standard Play [*Video technology*]
S & P.........	Standard & Poor's Corp.
SP..............	Standard Practice [*or Procedure*]
SP..............	Standard Price
SP..............	Standard Program [*Data processing*] (BUR)
SP..............	Standing Procedure (NATG)
SP..............	Standpipe (MSA)
SP..............	Start Permission (KSC)
SP..............	Starting Point
SP..............	Starting Price
SP..............	State Plan (OICC)
SP..............	Static Pointer [*Data processing*]
SP..............	Static Pressure
SP..............	Station Police [*British military*] (DMA)
SP..............	Station Pressure [*Meteorology*] (FAAC)
SP..............	Status Panel (CAAL)
S/P.............	Status Post [*Medicine*]
SP..............	Stern Post
SP..............	Stipule [*Botany*]
SP..............	Stirrup Pump
SP..............	Stool Preservative [*Medicine*]

SP.............	Stop Payment [*Banking*]
SP.............	Stop Press (ADA)
SP.............	Storage Protein [*Food industry*]
SP.............	Straight Partners (EA)
SP.............	Strategic Planning Chart [*Air Force*]
SP.............	Strategic Planning Society [*See also SPS*] [*London, England*] (EAIO)
S & P........	Strategy and Policy Group [*War Department*] [*World War II*]
SP.............	Street Price (ROG)
SP.............	Stretcher Party
SP.............	Structured Programming [*Data processing*] (BUR)
SP.............	Studia Papyrologica [*A publication*]
SP.............	Studia Patristica [*A publication*]
SP.............	Studies in Philology [*A publication*]
SP.............	Study Plan
SP.............	Subject-Predicate
SP.............	Subliminal Perception
SP.............	Submarine Patrol [*Navy*]
S/P............	Submarine Pay [*British military*] (DMA)
SP.............	Subplate [*Neurology*]
SP.............	Subprofessional [*Civil Service employees designation*]
SP.............	Substance P [*A peptide*] [*Biochemistry*]
SP.............	Successive Planometric [*A discrimination task*]
SP.............	Sugar Phosphate [*Biochemistry*]
SP.............	Suisse Primitive [*A publication*]
SP.............	Sumatra Post [*A publication*]
SP.............	Sumerian Proverbs (BJA)
SP.............	Summary Plotter [*RADAR*]
SP.............	Summating Potential [*Hearing*]
SP.............	Summus Pontifex [*Supreme Pontiff, Pope*] [*Latin*]
SP.............	Sunlit Period
SP.............	Sun's Parallax [*Astronomy*] (ROG)
SP.............	Superficial Pineal Organ [*Neuroanatomy*]
SP.............	Superparamagnetic [*Fraction in rock*] [*Geophysics*]
SP.............	Superseded in Part [*New matter substituted for part of an existing regulation or order*] [*Used in Shepard's Citations*] [*Legal term*] (DLA)
SP.............	Supervisory Process [*Telecommunications*] (TEL)
SP.............	Supplement
SP.............	Supply Point [*Military*] (NATG)
SP.............	Support
SP.............	Support Plan (MCD)
SP.............	Support Publications (AAG)
SP.............	Supraprotest
SP.............	Suprapubic [*Medicine*]
SP.............	Surveillance Procedure (NRCH)
SP.............	Surviving Propagules [*Botany*]
SP.............	Suspicious Person
SP.............	Sustainer Pitch (AAG)
SP.............	Swelling Power [*Food technology*]
SP.............	Switch Panel
SP.............	Switch Port [*Telecommunications*]
SP.............	Syllable Period [*Entomology*]
SP.............	Symbol Programmer (MUGU)
SP.............	Symphysis Pubica [*Anatomy*]
SP.............	Synperiplanar [*Chemistry*]
SP.............	System Parameter (KSC)
SP.............	System Processor (IEEE)
S-P............	Systems and Procedures
SP.............	Systolic Pressure [*Cardiology*]
SP4............	Specialist 4 [*Army*]
SP5............	Specialist 5 [*Obsolete*] [*Army*]
SP6............	Specialist 6 [*Obsolete*] [*Army*]
SP7............	Specialist 7 [*Army*]
SP8............	Specialist 8 [*Obsolete*] [*Army*]
SP9............	Specialist 9 [*Obsolete*] [*Army*]
SPA............	Dagblad Scheepvaart [*A publication*]
SPA............	Greenville/Spartanburg [*South Carolina*] Downtown [*Airport symbol*] (OAG)
SPA............	S-Band Power Amplifier
SPA............	Sacrum Palatium Apostolicum [*Sacred Apostolic Palace, Vatican, Quirinal*] [*Latin*]
SPA............	Salt-Poor Albumin [*Medicine*]
SPA............	Salt Producers Association [*Later, SI*] (EA)
SPA............	Sample Preparation Accessory [*Laboratory analysis*]
SPA............	Satellite Personnel Activity [*Military*]
SPA............	Saudi Press Agency
SPA............	Scandinavian Packaging Association (EAIO)
SPA............	Scatter Propagation Antenna
SPA............	Science and Public Affairs. Bulletin of the Atomic Scientists [*A publication*]
SPA............	Scintillation Proximity Assay [*Analytical biochemistry*]
SPA............	Scottish Paraplegic (Spinal Injury) Association [*British*]
SPA............	Screen Printing Association [*Australia*]
SPA............	Sea Photo Analysis [*Navy*]
SPA............	Seaplane Pilots Association (EA)
SPA............	Self-Phasing Array
SPA............	Semipermanently Associated [*Telecommunications*] (TEL)
SPA............	Service Pay and Allowances [*Military*] [*British*]
SPA............	Servo Power Amplifier (NASA)
SPA............	Servo Power Assembly (MCD)
SPA............	Servo Preamplifier
SPA............	Shared Peripheral Area (NASA)
SPA............	Sierra Pacific Airlines [*North Hollywood, CA*] [*FAA designator*] (FAAC)
SPA............	Signal Processor Assembly [*NASA*]
SPA............	Silicon Pulser Array
SPA............	Singapore People's Alliance
SPA............	Single Parameter Analysis
SPA............	Single Photon Absorptiometry [*Analytical chemistry*]
SPA............	Single Position Automatic [*Tester*]
SPA............	Sitzungsberichte. Preussische Akademie der Wissenschaften [*A publication*]
SPA............	Skill Performance Aid [*Army*] (RDA)
SPA............	Small-Particle Aerosol
SPA............	Socialist Party of Australia [*Political party*]
SpA............	Societa per Azioni [*Corporation*] [*Italian*] [*Business term*]
SPA............	Society of Participating Artists [*Record label*]
SPA............	Society for Personality Assessment (EA)
SPA............	Society for Personnel Administration [*Later, IPMA*] (EA)
SPA............	Society of Philatelic Americans [*Defunct*] (EA)
SPA............	Society of Philosophers in America (EA)
SPA............	Society of Professional Assessors [*Address unknown*]
SPA............	Society for Psychological Anthropology (EA)
SPA............	Society for Public Administration
SPA............	Sociological Practice Association (EA)
SPA............	Sodium Polyacrylate [*Organic chemistry*]
SPA............	Software Publishers Association (EA)
SPA............	Solar Power Array
SPA............	Songwriters Protective Association [*Later, AGAC*]
SPA............	SOSUS Probability Area (NVT)
SPA............	South Pacific Area [*World War II*]
SPA............	South Pole [*Antarctica*] [*Seismograph station code, US Geological Survey*] (SEIS)
SPA............	Southeastern Peanut Association (EA)
SPA............	Southern Pine Association [*Later, SFPA*] (EA)
SPA............	Southwestern Power Administration [*Department of Energy*]
SPA............	Space Processing Applications [*Program*] [*NASA*]
SPA............	Spade [*Freight*]
spa............	Spanish [*MARC language code*] [*Library of Congress*] (LCCP)
SPA............	Spanish
SPA............	Spartanburg, SC [*Location identifier*] [*FAA*] (FAAL)
SPA............	Sparton Corp. [*NYSE symbol*] (SPSG)
SPA............	Special Project Activities (MCD)
SPA............	Special Public Assistance
SPA............	Special-Purpose Aircraft [*Drone vehicle*] [*Military*]
SPA............	Special Purpose Alteration (MCD)
SPA............	Specialist, Physical Training Instructor [*Navy rating*]
SPA............	Spectair Industry [*Vancouver Stock Exchange symbol*]
SPA............	Spectrum Analyzer
SPA............	Splice Plug Assembly
SPA............	Sportsman Pilots Association
SPA............	Standard Practice Amendment (AAG)
SPA............	Staphylococcal Protein A [*Immunochemistry*]
SPA............	State Planning Agency [*Department of Justice*]
SPA............	Sterile Preparation Area (MCD)
SPA............	Stimulation-Produced Analgesia
SPA............	Strategic Planning Associates [*Singapore*]
SPA............	Strategic Posture Analysis [*Army*] (AABC)
SPA............	Subject to Particular Average [*Insurance*]
SPA............	Submarine Patrol Area [*Navy*] (NVT)
SPA............	Subpoena [*Legal term*]
SPA............	Substance P Antagonist [*Biochemistry*]
SPA............	Substitute Part Authorization (AAG)
SPA............	Sudden Phase Anomaly [*Radio engineering*]
SPA............	Sundry Persons' Account [*Banking*]
SPA............	Superphosphoric Acid [*Fertilizer*]
SPA............	Supervisory Performance Appraisal [*Civil Service*]
SPA............	Suprapubic Aspiration [*Medicine*]
SPA............	Supreme People's Assembly [*Political party*] [*Democratic People's Republic of Korea*] (FEA)
SPA............	Surface Vehicle Power Adapter
SPA............	SURTASS Probability Area [*Navy*] (CAAL)
SPA............	Survey of Personal Attitude [*Psychology*]
SPA............	System Performance Analyzer [*Motorola, Inc.*]
SPA............	Systems and Procedures Association [*Later, ASM*] (EA)
SPAA..........	Caraz [*Peru*] [*ICAO location identifier*] (ICLI)
SPAA..........	Sage Public Administration Abstracts [*A publication*]
SPAA........	Screen Producers' Association of Australia
SPAA..........	Spacecraft Performance Analysis Area
SPAAAX ..	Memoires Suisses de Paleontologie [*A publication*]
SPAAAX ..	Memorie Svizzere di Paleontologia [*A publication*]
SPAAC	Syndicat du Personnel Africain de l'Aeronautique Civile [*African Union for Civil Aviation Employees*]
SPAALAL ...	Society for the Promotion of African, Asian, and Latin American Literature [*See also GFLAAL*] (EAIO)
SPAAMFAA ...	Society for the Preservation and Appreciation of Antique Motor Fire Apparatus in America (EA)
SPAAN......	Societe Protectrice des Animaux en Afrique du Nord [*Society for the Protection of Animals in North Africa - SPANA*] [*London, England*] (EAIO)

SPAASS.... Synod Office, Diocese of Saskatchewan, Angelican Church of Canada, Prince Albert, Saskatchewan [*Library symbol*] [*National Library of Canada*] (NLC)
SPAB........ Huancabamba [*Peru*] [*ICAO location identifier*] (ICLI)
SPAB........ Society for the Protection of Ancient Buildings (EA)
SPAB........ Society of Psychologists in Addictive Behaviors [*Later, PAB*] (EA)
SPAB........ Supply, Priorities, and Allocations Board [*World War II*]
SPABH...... Society for the Preservation of American Business History (EA)
SPAC........ Ciro Alegria [*Peru*] [*ICAO location identifier*] (ICLI)
SPAC........ Saratoga Performing Arts Center [*Summer home of NYCB*] [*Saratoga Springs, NY*]
SPAC........ Secretary's Pesticide Advisory Committee [*HEW*]
SPAC........ Signal Programmer and Conditioner [*Air Force Eastern Test Range*]
S Pac......... South Pacific [*A publication*] (APTA)
SPAC........ Space Program Advisory Council [*Terminated, 1977*] [*NASA*]
SPAC........ Spacecraft Performance Analysis and Command [*NASA*]
SPAC........ Spacious (ADA)
SPAC........ Spatial Computer
SPACA ...... Spectrochimica Acta [*A publication*]
SPACCS.... Space Command and Control System
SPACD8.... Israel. Agricultural Research Organization. Special Publication [*A publication*]
SPACDocRap ... Societe Paleontologique et Archeologique de l'Arrondissement Judiciaire de Charleroi. Documents et Rapports [*A publication*]
SPACE...... Council of AFL-CIO Unions for Scientific, Professional, and Cultural Employees [*Later, Department for Professional Employees, AFL-CIO*]
SPACE ...... Sales Profitability and Contribution Evaluator [*Data processing*]
SPACE ...... Satellite Precipitation and Cloud Experiment [*National Oceanic and Atmospheric Administration*]
SPACE ...... Self-Programming Automatic Circuit Evaluator
SPACE ...... Sequential Position and Covariance Estimation (IEEE)
SPACE ...... Sidereal Polar Axis Celestial Equipment
SPACE ...... Society for Private and Commercial Earth Stations [*Telecommunications*] [*Information service or system*] (EA)
SPACE ...... Space Program American Citizens' Effort
SPACE ...... Spacecraft Prelaunch Automatic Checkout Equipment [*NASA*]
SPACE ...... Special Political Agricultural Community Education [*Milk cooperative trust fund*]
SPACE ...... Sperry Program for Advancing Careers through Education
SPACE ...... Support Package for Aerospace Computer Emulation (MCD)
SPACE ...... Symbolic Programming Anyone Can Enjoy
Space/Aeronaut ... Space/Aeronautics [*A publication*]
Space Biol Med (Engl Transl) ... Space Biology and Medicine (English Translation) [*A publication*]
Space Cit.... Space City News [*A publication*]
SPACECOM ... Space Command [*Military*]
SPACECOM ... Space Communications
Space Comm ... Space Commerce Bulletin [*A publication*]
Space Congr Proc ... Space Congress. Proceedings [*United States*] [*A publication*]
Space Life Sci ... Space Life Sciences [*A publication*]
Space Marke ... Space Markets [*A publication*]
Space Res... Space Research [*A publication*]
Space Res Bulg ... Space Research in Bulgaria [*A publication*]
SPACES.... Saving and Preserving Arts and Cultural Environments (EA)
Space Sci Instrum ... Space Science Instrumentation [*A publication*]
Space Sci R ... Space Science Reviews [*A publication*]
Space Sci Rev ... Space Science Reviews [*A publication*]
Space Sol Power Rev ... Space Solar Power Review [*A publication*]
SPACETAC ... Space and Tactical System Corporation (MCD)
SPACETRACK ... Space Tracking System [*Air Force*] (MCD)
SPACG...... Syndicat du Personnel de l'Aeronautique Civile du Gabon [*Union of Civil Aviation Employees of Gabon*]
S Pacific..... South Pacific [*A publication*] (APTA)
S Pacific Bull ... South Pacific Bulletin [*A publication*] (APTA)
SPACLALS ... South Pacific Association for Commonwealth Literature and Language Studies (EAIO)
S Pac LR.... South Pacific Law Review [*Australia*] [*A publication*] (DLA)
SPACON... Space Control
SPACS....... Sodium Purification and Characterization System [*Nuclear energy*] (NRCH)
SPAD........ Satellite Position Prediction and Display
SPAD........ Satellite Protection for Area Defense [*ARPA*]
SPAD........ Scratch Pad Memory [*Data processing*]
SPAD........ Seaway Port Authority of Duluth
SPAD........ Shuttle Payload Accommodation Document [*NASA*] (MCD)
SPAD........ Societe pour Aviation et ses Derives [*France*] [*World War I airplane*]
SPAD........ Space Patrol Active Defense
SPAD........ Space Patrol for Air Defense
SPAD........ Space Principles, Applications, and Doctrine [*Air Force Systems Command*]
SPAD........ SPRINT Air-Directed Defense [*Army*]
SPAD........ Submarine Patrol Area Definition (MCD)

SPAD........ Subsystem Postioning Aid Device (NASA)
SPADATS ... Space Detection and Tracking System [*Military*]
SPADATSC ... Space Detection and Tracking System Center [*Air Force*]
SPADATSS ... Space Detection and Tracking System Sensors [*Air Force*]
SPADCCS ... Space Defense Command and Control System (MCD)
SPADE...... Signal Processing and Display Equipment
SPADE...... Single-Channel-per-Carrier, Pulse-Code-Modulation, Multiple-Access, Demand-Assignment Equipment [*Telecommunications*]
SPADE...... Small Portable Analysis and Diagnostic Equipment [*Aircraft maintenance*]
SPADE...... Spare Parts Analysis, Documentation, and Evaluation
SPADE...... Sparta Acquisition Digital Equipment (MCD)
SPADE...... Sperry Air Data Equipment
SPADE...... Strike Planning and Damage Estimator [*Military*]
SPADES...... Solar Perturbation and Atmospheric Density Measurement Satellite
SPADETS ... Space Detection Network [*Military*]
SPADL...... Spare Parts Application Data List
SPADNS... (Sulfophenylazo)dihydroxynaphthalene-disulfonate [*Organic chemistry*]
SPADOC... Space Defense Operations Center [*DoD*]
SPADS ...... Satellite Position and Display System
SPADS ...... Shuttle Problem Action [*or Analysis*] Data System [*NASA*] (NASA)
SPADS ...... SPRINT Air-Directed Defense System [*Army*] (AABC)
SPADS ...... STRATCOM Program Automated Data System [*Army*]
SPA DT ...... Subpoena Duces Tecum [*Legal*] [*Latin*] (ROG)
SPAE .... Societe Planetaire pour l'Assainissement de l'Energie [*Planetary Association for Clean Energy*] (EAIO)
SPAEA ...... Space/Aeronautics [*A publication*]
SPAEF....... Societe des Petroles d'Afrique Equatoriale Francaise [*French Equatorial African Petroleum Co.*]
SPAEF....... Southern Public Administration Education Foundation (EA)
SPAF .... Forestry Branch, Saskatchewan Department of Natural Resources, Prince Albert, Saskatchewan [*Library symbol*] [*National Library of Canada*] (NLC)
SP-AF .... Shuttle Projects - Air Force Liaison Office [*Kennedy Space Center*] [*NASA*] (NASA)
SPAF .... Simulation Processor and Formatter (MCD)
SPAFA ...... SEAMEO Regional Centre for Archaeology and Fine Arts (EAIO)
SPAFA ...... Sports Afield [*A publication*]
SPAG........ South Plains Association of Governments
SPAG........ Space Radiation Analysis Group [*NASA*]
SPAG........ Spaghetti (DSUE)
SPAG........ Special Program/Analysis Guidance [*DoD*]
SPAG........ Standards Promotion Application Group [*Telecommunications*]
SPAH .... Society for the Preservation and Advancement of the Harmonica (EA)
SPAH .... Spacelab Payload Accommodations Handbook [*NASA*] (MCD)
SPAI .... Screen Printing Association International (EA)
SPAI .... Strategic Planning Associates, Incorporated [*Washington, DC*] [*NASDAQ symbol*] (NQ)
SPAIN .... Indian and Northern Affairs Canada [*Affaires Indiennes et du Nord Canada*] Prince Albert, Saskatchewan [*Library symbol*] [*National Library of Canada*] (NLC)
Spain Estac Cent Ecol Bol ... Spain. Estacion Centro de Ecologia. Boletin [*A publication*]
Spain Inst Geol Min Bol Geol Min ... Spain. Instituto Geologico y Minero. Boletin Geologico y Minero [*A publication*]
Spain Inst Geol Min Mem ... Spain. Instituto Geologico y Minero. Memorias [*A publication*]
Spain Junta Energ Nucl Rep ... Spain. Junta de Energia Nuclear. Report [*A publication*]
SPA Jnl ..... School of Planning and Architecture. Journal [*A publication*]
SpAk .... Spisanie na Bulgarskata Akademiya na Naukite [*A publication*]
SPAL .... Simulator, Projectile, Airburst, Liquid [*Chemical defense device*] [*Military*] (RDA)
SPAL .... Stabilized Platform Airborne LASER (RDA)
SPAL .... Succinyl-poly-DL-alanine Poly-L-lysine [*Biochemical analysis*]
S & P (Ala) Rep ... Stewart and Porter's Alabama Reports [*A publication*] (DLA)
Spald Cop .. Spalding on Copyright [*A publication*] (DLA)
SPALT....... Single-Point Articulated Loading Tower [*Engineering*]
SPALT....... Special Projects Alterations [*Navy*]
SPALTRA ... Special Projects Alterations, Training [*Navy*]
SPAM........ Camana [*Peru*] [*ICAO location identifier*] (ICLI)
SPAM........ S-Parameter Acquisition and Manipulation [*Computer software program*] [*General Motors Corp.*]
SPAM........ Satellite Processor Access Method
SPAM........ Scanning Photoacoustic Microscopy
SPAM........ Search Pattern Assessment Model [*Military*] (CAAL)
SPAM........ Ship Position and Attitude Measurement (IEEE)
SPAM........ Shipment Planning and Movement [*Army*]
SPAM........ Shop Portable Aircraft Maintenance [*Army*]
SPAM........ Society for the Publication of American Music [*Record label*]
SPAM........ Soil-Plant-Atmosphere [*Computer simulation model*]
SPAM........ Sonobuoy Placement Assortment Model (MCD)

SPAM....... Special Aeronautical Material [*Navy*] (NG)
SPAM....... Spiced Ham [*Hormel (George A.) & Co.*]
SPAMA..... Spanish Air Materiel Area
SPAMAG ... Space Medicine Advisory Group (MCD)
SPAMF ..... Seychelles Popular Anti-Marxist Front [*Political party*] (PD)
SPAMMER ... Space Hammer
SPAMS ..... Ship Position and Altitude Measurement System (MCD)
SPAN........ Social Policy and Administration Network [*A publication*]
SPAN........ Society of Philatelists and Numismatists (EA)
SPAN........ Solar Particle Alert Network [*National Oceanic and Atmospheric Administration*]
SPAN........ Solar Proton Alert Network
SPAN........ South Pacific Action Network
SPAN........ South Pacific Association for Commonwealth Literature and Language Studies. Newsletter [*A publication*]
SPAN........ Space Communications Network
SPAN........ Space Navigation
SPAN........ Space Physics Analysis Network [*Database*]
SPAN........ Space Plasma Analysis Network [*NASA*]
SPAN........ Spacecraft Analysis (KSC)
SPAN........ Span-America Medical Systems, Inc. [*NASDAQ symbol*] (NQ)
SPAN........ SPAN. Shell Public Health and Agricultural News [*A publication*]
SPAN........ SPAN: State Planning Authority News [*A publication*] (APTA)
SPAN........ Spaniard (ROG)
SPAN........ Spanish
SPAN........ Statistical Processing and Analysis [*Data processing*]
SPAN........ Storage Planning and Allocation [*Data processing*]
SPAN........ Stored Program Alphanumerics [*FAA*]
SPAN........ Submarine Piloting and Navigation [*Navy*]
SPAN........ Successive, Proportionate, Additive Numeration [*Decision making*]
SPAN........ Sullana [*Peru*] [*ICAO location identifier*] (ICLI)
SPAN........ System for Projection and Analysis
SPANA...... Society for the Protection of Animals in North Africa [*See also SPAAN*] [*London, England*] (EAIO)
SPANAT ... Systems Planning Approach - North Atlantic [*FAA*]
SPANC...... Wapiti Regional Library, Prince Albert, Saskatchewan [*Library symbol*] [*National Library of Canada*] (NLC)
SPAND...... Solar Proton Albedo Neutron Decay
SPANDAR ... Space and Range RADAR [*NASA*]
SPANGLISH ... Spanish and English
SPANI .... Northern Institute of Technology, Prince Albert, Saskatchewan [*Library symbol*] [*National Library of Canada*] (NLC)
SPANNER ... Special Analysis of Net Radio [*Study*]
SPAN Prog Agric ... SPAN [*Shell Public Health and Agricultural News*] Progress in Agriculture [*A publication*]
SPANRAD ... Superimposed Panoramic RADAR Display
SPANS ...... Sealift Procurement and National Security [*Study*]
SPAO......... San Juan Aposento [*Peru*] [*ICAO location identifier*] (ICLI)
SPAOPSUP ... Space Operations Support (NVT)
SPAP .... Picota [*Peru*] [*ICAO location identifier*] (ICLI)
SPAP .... Serum Prostatic Acid Phosphatase [*An enzyme*]
SPAP .... Special Package Auto Policy [*Insurance*]
SPap.......... Studia Papyrologica [*A publication*]
SPAQUA... Sealed Package Quality Assurance (IEEE)
SPAR........ Alerta [*Peru*] [*ICAO location identifier*] (ICLI)
SPAR........ SAC [*Strategic Air Command*] Peacetime Airborne Reconnaissance
SPAR........ Seagoing Platform for Acoustic Research [*NOL*]
SPAR........ Semper Paratus [*Always Ready*] [*Coast Guard motto*]
SPAR........ Sensitivity Prediction from the Acoustic Reflex [*Audiometry*]
SPAR........ Society of Photographers and Artist Representatives (EA)
SPAR........ Soil-Plant-Atmosphere-Research [*Agriculture*]
SPAR........ Space Precision Altitude Reference System (MCD)
SPAR........ Space Processing Applications Rocket [*NASA*]
SPAR........ SPALT [*Special Projects Alterations*] Planning and Authorization Report
Spar........... Spartan
SPAR........ Spartan Motors, Inc. [*Charlotte, MI*] [*NASDAQ symbol*] (NQ)
SPAR........ Special Prelaunch Analysis Request [*NASA*] (KSC)
SPAR........ Special Progressive Aircraft Rework
SPAR........ Spelling and Reading Tests
SPAR........ Staff Procurement Activity Requirement [*Military*]
SPAR........ Student Profile and Assessment Record [*Student attitudes test*]
SPAR........ Submersible Pipe Alignment Rig [*Deep-sea diving*]
SPAR........ Super-Precision Approach RADAR
SPAR........ Surveillance and Precision Approach RADAR (NATG)
SPAR........ Symbolic Program Assembly Routine [*Data processing*]
SPAR........ Synchronous Position Altitude Recorder
SPAR........ System Program Assessment Review [*Air Force*]
SPARC...... Scaleable Processor Architecture [*Data processing*]
SPARC...... Shore-Establishment Planning Analysis and Review Cooperation [*or Coordination*] [*Navy*] (NG)
SPARC...... Short Planning Analysis and Review Cooperation
SPARC...... Slab Penetration and Reflection Calculation
SPARC...... Space Air Relay Communications (MCD)
SPARC...... Space Program Analysis and Review Council [*Air Force*]
SPARC...... Space Research Capsule [*or Conic*] [*NASA*]
SPARC...... Spare Parts Provisioning for Combat
SPARC....... Spectral Analysis and Recognition Computer [*NASA*]

SPARC ..... Standards Planning and Requirements Committee [*ANSI*]
SPARC ...... Steam Plant Automation and Results Computer
SPARC ...... Support Planning Analysis Reporting and Control [*Navy*] (NG)
SPARC ...... Sustainability Predictions for Army Spare Component Requirements for Combat (RDA)
SPARC ...... System Parametric Allocation of Resources and Cost (MCD)
SPARCS.... Solar Pointing Aerobee Rocket Control System
SPARCS.... Statewide Planning and Research Cooperative System [*New York State Department of Health*] [*Albany*] [*Information service or system*] (IID)
SPARD ...... Sparkasse [*A publication*]
SPARE ...... Save Pound Animals from Research Experiments (EA)
SPARE ...... System for Projecting Ammunition Repairable End Items [*Military*]
SPARES .... Space Radiation Evaluation System [*NASA*] (KSC)
SPAREX.... Canada Regional Industrial Expansion [*Expansion Industrielle Regionale*], Prince Albert, Saskatchewan [*Library symbol*] [*National Library of Canada*] (BIB)
SPARK ...... Saboteurs for a Philistine America Redeemed from Kultur [*From book, "Bringing Down the House," by Richard P. Brickner*]
SPARK ...... Screen Pattern Analyzer and Rescreening Key [*Printing process*]
SPARK ...... Seminars on Practical Applications of Research Knowledge [*Advertising Research Foundation*]
SPARK ...... Solid Propellant Advanced Ramjet Kinetic Energy (MCD)
SPARK ...... Systematic Pulmono/Cardiac Anaphylaxis Resusitation Kit (MCD)
Sparkasse .. Zeitschrift des Deutschen Sparkassen [*A publication*]
Sparks........ Sparks' Reports [*British Burma*] [*A publication*] (DLA)
Spark's Am Biog ... Spark's Library of American Biography [*A publication*]
SPARM ..... Solid-Propellant Augmented Rocket Motor [*Navy*]
SPARM ..... Sparrow Antiradiation Missile (MCD)
SPARMIS ... Standard Police Automated Resource Management Information System
SPARMO ... Solar Particles and Radiations Monitoring Organization
SPARMO Bull ... SPARMO [*Solar Particles and Radiation Monitoring Organization*] Bulletin [*A publication*]
SPARPS .... Spares and Repair Parts Support [*Navy*] (NG)
SPARS....... Semper Paratus [*US Coast Guard Women's Auxiliary; name taken from Coast Guard motto*]
SPARS....... Site Production and Reduction System
SPARS....... Society of Professional Audio Recording Services (EA)
SPARS....... Space Precision Altitude [*or Attitude*] Reference System
SPARSA.... Sferics, Position [*or Pulse*], Azimuth, Rate, and Spectrum Analyzer
SPARSIM ... Spartan Simulation [*Missile system evaluation*] (RDA)
SPART ...... Space Research and Technology [*Report*] [*NASA*] (KSC)
SPART ...... Sunny Point Army Terminal
SPARTA.... Sequential Programmed Automatic Recording Transistor Analyzer
SPARTA.... Special Antimissile Research Tests in Australia
SPARTAN ... Shuttle-Pointed Autonomous Research Tool for Astronomy [*NASA*]
SPARTAN ... Special Proficiency at Rugged Training and Nation Building [*Training program for Green Berets*] [*Army*]
SPARTAN ... System for Personnel Automated Reports, Transactions, and Notices [*Census Bureau, NASA*]
SPARTECA ... South Pacific Area Regional Trade and Cooperation Agreement (ADA)
SPAS .... Shipboard Pollution Abatement System [*Navy*] (CAAL)
SPAS .... Shuttle Pallet Satellite [*NASA*]
SPAS .... Skill Performance Aids
SPAS .... Social Service Department, Prince Albert, Saskatchewan [*Library symbol*] [*National Library of Canada*] (NLC)
SPA-S .... Societa Prodotti Antibiotici [*Italy*] [*Research code symbol*]
SPAS .... Societatis Philosophicae Americanae Socius [*Member of the American Philosophical Society*]
SPAS .... Solar Proton Alpha Spectrometer
SPASCOMT ... Space Assignment Committee
SPASE....... South Pole Air Shower Experiment [*Astronomy*]
SPASEP .... Secretaria Permanente del Acuerdo Sudamericano de Estupefacientes y Psicotropicos [*Permanent Secretariat of the South American Agreement on Narcotic Drugs and Psychotropic Substances - PSSAANDPS*] (EAIO)
SPASM ..... Self-Propelled Air-to-Surface Missile (MCD)
SPASM ..... Smithsonian Package for Algebra and Symbolic Mathematics (MCD)
SPASM ..... Space Propulsion Automated Synthesis Modeling [*Program*]
SPASM ..... System Performance and Activity Software Monitor [*Data processing*] (IEEE)
SPAST....... Special Assistant [*Navy*]
SPASUR.... Space Surveillance System [*Navy*]
SPASYN.... Space-Syncromesh
SPAT......... Aguas Calientes [*Peru*] [*ICAO location identifier*] (ICLI)
SPAT......... Self-Propelled Antitank Gun (MCD)
SPAT......... Silicon Precision Alloy Transistor
SPAT......... Spleen Antigen [*Complement Fixation*] Test [*Immunology*]
SPat .... Studia Patavina [*A publication*]
SPAT......... Systems Programming Aptitude Test
SPATA ...... Society of Polish-American Travel Agents (EA)

SPATE ...... Sergeant Production Automatic Test Equipment
SPATE ...... South Pacific Association for Teacher Education [*Later, ATEA*]   (EA)
SPATE ...... Student Personnel Association for Teacher Education [*Later, AHEAD*]   (EA)
SPA ad TEST ... Subpoena ad Testificandum [*Subpoena to Testify*] [*Latin*]   (ROG)
S Patriot..... Southern Patriot [*A publication*]
SPATS....... Sound Preservation and Technical Services [*National Library of Australia*]
SPATS....... South Pacific Air Transportation Service [*Navy*]
Spat Vision ... Spatial Vision [*A publication*]
SPAU......... Signal Processing [*or Processor*] Arithmetic Unit [*Navy*]
SPAU......... Stable Platform Alignment Unit
Spaulding... Spaulding's Reports [*71-73 Maine*] [*A publication*]   (DLA)
SPAW........ Learning Resource Centre, Woodland Campus, Saskatchewan Institute of Applied Science and Technology, Prince Albert, Saskatchewan [*Library symbol*] [*National Library of Canada*]   (BIB)
SPAW........ Sitzungsberichte. Preussische Akademie der Wissenschaften [*A publication*]
Spawanie Ciecie Met ... Spawanie i Ciecie Metali [*A publication*]
SPAWAR .. Space and Naval Warfare Systems Command [*Washington, DC*] [*Navy*]   (GRD)
SPAWG...... Special Activity Wing   (MUGU)
SPAWN...... Salmon Protection Association of Western Newfoundland [*Canada*]   (ASF)
SPAYZ ...... Spatial Property Analyzer
SPAZD9 .... Agronomy Society of New Zealand. Special Publication [*A publication*]
SPB........... St. Thomas [*Virgin Islands*] Seaplane Base [*Airport symbol*]   (OAG)
SPB........... Scottish Prayer Book [*Episcopalian*]
SPB........... Seaplane Base
SPB........... Ship's Plotting Board
SPB........... Silver-Plated Bronze
SPB........... Society of the Precious Blood [*Anglican religious community*]
SPB........... Solar Particle Beams
SPB........... Sotheby Parke Bernet [*Formerly, PB*] [*Manhattan art auction house*]
SPB........... Special Pathogens Branch [*Centers for Disease Control*]
SPB........... Spindle Pole Body [*Cell biology*]
SpB........... Sprakliga Bidrag [*Lund*] [*A publication*]
SPB........... Springboard Resources Ltd. [*Vancouver Stock Exchange symbol*]
SPB........... Standard Practice Bulletin   (MCD)
SPB........... Standardized Performance Battery [*Acoustics*]
SPB........... Stored Program Buffer
SPB........... Studia Post-Biblica [*Leiden*] [*A publication*]
SPB........... Surplus Property Board
SPBA .... Society of Professional Benefit Administrators [*Washington, DC*]   (EA)
SPBA .... Specialty Paper and Board Affiliates [*Later, API*]   (EA)
SpBA......... Spisanie na Bulgarskata Akademiya na Naukite [*A publication*]
SPBAA ...... Spisanie na Bulgarskata Akademiya na Naukite [*A publication*]
SpBAkN .... Spisanie na Bulgarskata Akademiya na Naukite [*A publication*]
SpBAN ...... Spisanie na Bulgarskata Akademiya na Naukite [*A publication*]
SpBaU .... Universidad de Barcelona, Biblioteca Universitaria y Provincal, Barcelona, Spain [*Library symbol*] [*Library of Congress*]   (LCLS)
SPBB .... Moyobamba [*Peru*] [*ICAO location identifier*]   (ICLI)
SPBC .... Caballococha [*Peru*] [*ICAO location identifier*]   (ICLI)
SPBC .... St. Paul Bancorp, Inc. [*NASDAQ symbol*]   (NQ)
SPBC .... Saint Paul Bible College [*Saint Bonifacius, MN*]
SPBC .... Society of Professional Business Consultants [*Chicago, IL*]   (EA)
SPBC .... South Pacific Base Command [*Navy*] [*World War II*]
SPBD........ Springboard   (NVT)
SPBD........ Springboard Software, Inc. [*Minneapolis, MN*] [*NASDAQ symbol*]   (NQ)
SPBE .... Service de Presse Baptiste Europeen [*European Baptist Press Service - EBPS*]   (EAIO)
SPBE .... Society of Parrot Breeders and Exhibitors   (EA)
SPBEC....... South Pacific Bureau for Economic Cooperation in Developing Uniform Maritime Standards for the Pacific Area [*Suva, Fiji*]   (EAIO)
SPBI .... Serikat Buruh Pertjetakan Indonesia [*Printing Workers' Union of Indonesia*]
SPBI .... Society for Proclaiming Britain in Israel
SPBK .... Speed Brake   (NASA)
SPBL .... Bellavista/Huallaga [*Peru*] [*ICAO location identifier*]   (ICLI)
SPBM....... Single Point Buoy Mooring [*Oil platform*]
SPBOT ...... Stationers and Publishers Board of Trade [*Later, Stationery and Office Equipment Board of Trade*]
SPBP .... Society for the Preservation of Birds of Prey   (EA)
SPBR .... Iberia [*Peru*] [*ICAO location identifier*]   (ICLI)
SPBR .... Speed Brake   (MCD)
SPBS.......... Jeberos/Bellavista [*Peru*] [*ICAO location identifier*]   (ICLI)
SPBS.......... Schweizerische Partei der Behinderten und Sozialbenachteiligten [*Swiss Party of the Handicapped and Socially Disadvantaged*] [*Political party*]   (PPW)

SPBS.......... Standard Property Book System [*Army*]
SPBSES..... Special Publications Series. British Ecological Society [*A publication*]
SPBS-R...... Standard Army Property Book System - Redesign
SPBT .... Obenteni [*Peru*] [*ICAO location identifier*]   (ICLI)
SPBU .... Vista Breau [*Peru*] [*ICAO location identifier*]   (ICLI)
SPBUA ...... SPARMO [*Solid Particles and Radiation Monitoring Organization*] Bulletin [*A publication*]
Sp na Bulg Akad na Naukite ... Spisanie na Bulgarskata Akademiya na Naukite [*A publication*]
Sp na Bulg Geol D-Vo ... Spisanie na Bulgarskoto Geologichesko Druzhestvo [*A publication*]
Sp Bulg Geol D-Vo ... Spisanie na Bulgarskoto Geologichesko Druzhestvo [*A publication*]
SPBW .... Society for the Preservation of Beers from the Wood [*London, England*]   (EAIO)
SPC........... IEEE. Spectrum [*A publication*]
SPC........... Institute for Studies of Destructive Behaviors and the Suicide Prevention Center of Los Angeles [*California*]   (EA)
SPC........... Political Committee at Senior Level [*NATO*]   (NATG)
SPC........... St. Paul's Cathedral [*London, England*]
SPC........... Saint Paul's College [*Missouri; Virginia; Washington, DC*]
SPC........... Saint Paul's College, Lawrenceville, VA [*OCLC symbol*]   (OCLC)
SPC........... Saint Peter College [*Maryland; New Jersey*]
SPC........... Saint Procopius College [*Illinois*]
SPC........... Salicylamide, Phenacetin [*Acetophenetidin*], and Caffeine [*Pharmacy*]
SPC........... Santa Cruz La Palma [*Canary Islands*] [*Airport symbol*]   (OAG)
SPC........... Saratoga Processing Co. Ltd. [*Vancouver Stock Exchange symbol*]
SPC........... Satellite Processing Center [*Military*]
SPC........... Seattle Pacific College [*Washington*]
SPC........... Security Pacific Corporation [*NYSE symbol*]   (SPSG)
SPC........... Self-Polishing Copolymer [*Anti-fouling paint*]   (DS)
SPC........... Self-Programming Compiler [*Software*] [*Data processing*]
SPC........... Set Point Controller
SPC........... Shepparton Fruit Preserving Company Ltd. [*Australia*]
SPC........... Shipping and Packing Cost   (NASA)
SPC........... Shuttle Pin Clutch
SPC........... Shuttle Processing Contractor [*NASA*]
SPC........... Silver-Plated Copper
SPC........... Simultaneous Prism and Cover (Test) [*Ophthalmology*]
SPC........... Single Prime Contractor [*Weapon system procurement*] [*Air Force*]   (AAG)
SPC........... Site Programmer Course
SPC........... Size-Press Coated [*Publishing*]
SPC........... Skalnate-Pleso [*Czechoslovakia*] [*Seismograph station code, US Geological Survey*]   (SEIS)
SPC........... Small Peripheral Controller
SPC........... Soap Perfumery and Cosmetics [*A publication*]
SPC........... Socialist Party of Canada [*Political party*]
SPC........... Socialist Party of Chile
SPC........... Socialist Party of Cyprus [*Political party*]   (EAIO)
SPC........... Society for Philosophy of Creativity   (EA)
SPC........... Society for the Prevention of Crime   (EA)
SPC........... Solar Pointing Control
SPC........... Solid-Propellant Combustion
SPC........... Solid-Propellant Conference
S/P/C........ Sotto Protesto per Mettere in Conto [*Under Protest to Place to Account*] [*Italian*]
SPC........... South Pacific Commission [*See also CPS*]   (EAIO)
SPC........... South Pacific Island Airways, Inc. [*Pago Pago, American Samoa*]   (FAAC)
SPC........... South Polar Cap [*A filamentary mark on Mars*]
SPC........... Southern Pacific Communications Corp.
SPC........... Southern Ports Foreign Committee, Chicago IL [*STAC*]
SPC........... Soy Protein Council   (EA)
SPC........... Space Development Conference
SPC........... Space Projects Center [*NASA*]
SPC........... Spacer [*Technical drawings*]
SpC........... Spanish Columbia, San Sebastian [*Record label*] [*Spain*]
SPC........... Spare Parts Catalog
SPC........... Special Code
Sp C .... Special Commissioner   (DLA)
SPC........... Special Common [*Projectile*]
SPC........... Special Program Code [*Navy*]
SPC........... Special Project Code [*IRS*]
SPC........... Special Purpose Chaff [*Navy*]   (CAAL)
SPC........... Specialist, Classification Interviewer [*Navy rating*]
SPC........... Specific Propellant Consumption
SPC........... Standard Plate Count [*Microbiology*]
SPC........... Standard Products Committee [*Navy*]
SPC........... Standby Pressure Control [*Nuclear energy*]   (NRCH)
SPC........... Starting Point Code   (NASA)
SPC........... Static Power Conservers   (MCD)
SPC........... Static Pressure Compensation
SPC........... Station Program Cooperative [*Public television*]
SPC........... Statistical Process Control
SPC........... Sterilizable Potting Compound

SPC............ Stigmastanyl(phosphorylcholine) [*Biochemistry*]
SPC............ Stockage Priority Code [*Military*] (AFIT)
SPC............ Storage Planning Centre [*Shipping*]
SPC............ Stored Program Command [*or Control*] [*Data processing*]
SPC............ Strategy and Planning Committee [*Military*]
SPC............ Subcontract Plans Committee
SPC............ Sucrose-Phosphate-Citrate [*A culture medium*]
SPC............ Sugar Packet Club (EA)
SPC............ Supplemental Planning Card (AAG)
SPC............ Suspended Plaster Ceiling [*Technical drawings*]
SPC............ Switching and Processing Center [*EFTS*] [*Banking*]
SPC............ Syndicat des Postiers du Canada [*Canadian Union of Postal Workers - CUPW*]
SPC............ Synoptic Properties Code (MCD)
SPCA......... Barraca [*Peru*] [*ICAO location identifier*] (ICLI)
SPCA......... School Projectionist Club of America (EA)
SPCA......... Serum Prothrombin Conversion Accelerator [*Factor VII*] [*Also, PPCA*] [*Hematology*]
SPCA......... Society for the Prevention of Cruelty to Animals
SPCA......... Southern Pulpwood Conservation Association [*Later, SFI*] (EA)
SPCA......... Spark Plug Collectors of America (EA)
SPCA......... Special-Purpose Cable Assembly
SPCAP....... Society of Professors of Child and Adolescent Psychiatry (EA)
SPCAT....... Special Category (MSA)
SPCB......... Aguas Blancas [*Peru*] [*ICAO location identifier*] (ICLI)
SPCC......... Servo Pressure Control Console
SPCC......... Ship's Parts Control Center
SPCC......... Society for the Prevention of Cruelty to Children
SPCC......... Southern Pacific Communications Corporation
SPCC......... Space Parts Control Center (MUGU)
SPCC......... Spill Prevention Control and Countermeasure [*Petroleum industry*]
SPCC......... Staggered Phase Carrier Cancellation
SPCC......... Standardization, Policy, and Coordination Committee [*NATO*] (NATG)
SPCC......... Stored Program CAMAC [*Computer-Aided Measurement and Control*] Channel [*Data processing*]
SPCC......... Strength Power and Communications Cable
SPCC......... Study Planning and Coordinating Committee [*Army*]
SPCC......... Sugar Packet Collectors Club (EA)
SPCC......... Super-Packed Capillary Column [*Spectroscopy*]
SPCCS....... Spill Prevention Control and Countermeasure System [*Environmental Protection Agency*] [*Information service or system*] [*No longer exists*] (IID)
SPCDS....... Small Permanent Communications and Display Segment (MCD)
SPCEC....... Stereo Photographers, Collectors, and Enthusiasts Club (EA)
SPCF......... Special Project Control File [*IRS*]
Sp Ch .... Spears' South Carolina Chancery Reports [*A publication*] (DLA)
SPCH......... Speech
SPCH......... Tocache [*Peru*] [*ICAO location identifier*] (ICLI)
SPCHB...... Soviet Progress in Chemistry [*English Translation*] [*A publication*]
SPCHDX... Carnegie Museum of Natural History. Special Publication [*A publication*]
SPCHG...... Supercharge
SPCHGR... Supercharger (AAG)
SPCK......... Society for Promoting Christian Knowledge [*Publisher*] [*British*]
SPCL......... Pucallpa [*Peru*] [*ICAO location identifier*] (ICLI)
SPCL......... Special (MSA)
SPCL......... Spectrum Information Technologies, Inc. [*NASDAQ symbol*] (NQ)
SPCLASGN ... Special Assignment [*Military*] (NVT)
SPCLN ...... Special Cleaning
SPCLY...... Especially (FAAC)
SPCM........ Contamana [*Peru*] [*ICAO location identifier*] (ICLI)
SPCM........ Master Chief Steam Propulsionman [*Navy rating*]
SPCM........ Spanish Campaign Medal
SPCM........ Special Court-Martial
SPCM........ Specialty Composites Corp. [*NASDAQ symbol*] (NQ)
SPCMO..... Special Court-Martial Order
SPCMWOMJ ... Special Court-Martial without a Military Judge (AFM)
SPCN........ Stored Program Controlled Network [*Telecommunications*]
SPCNI...... Society for Pacific Coast Native Irises (EA)
SPCO......... Software Publishing Corporation [*Mountain View, CA*] [*NASDAQ symbol*] (NQ)
SPCO......... Southern Pacific Company
SPCOA...... Spark Plug Collectors of America (EA)
SPCONV... Speed Converter
SPCP......... Pucacaca [*Peru*] [*ICAO location identifier*] (ICLI)
SPCP......... Single Prime Contractor Policy [*Air Force*] (AAG)
SPCP......... Society of Professors of Child Psychiatry [*Later, SPCAP*] (EA)
SPCPB...... Space Congress. Proceedings [*A publication*]
SPCQB...... SPC [*South Pacific Commission*] Quarterly Bulletin [*A publication*]
SPC Quart Bull ... SPC [*South Pacific Commission*] Quarterly Bulletin [*A publication*]
SPCR......... Spacer

SPCR......... Spare Parts Change Request
Spcr............ Spectinomycin Resistance
Sp Cr Ct ... Special Criminal Court (DLA)
SPCS......... Schedule Planning and Control System (MCD)
SPCS......... Selective Paging Communications System
S & PCS ..... Silver and Pewter Collectors Society (EA)
SPCS......... Standard & Poor's COMPUSTAT Services, Inc. [*Also, an information service or system*] (IID)
SPCS......... Static Power Conversion System
SPCS......... Statistical Process Control Society (EA)
SPCS......... Storage and Processing Control System
SPCS......... Surgical Postcaval Shunt [*Medicine*]
SPCSDW... Commonwealth Bureau of Soils. Special Publication [*A publication*]
SPC/SQC .. Statistical Process/Statistical Quality Control
SPCT........ Chota [*Peru*] [*ICAO location identifier*] (ICLI)
SPCT........ Spectra Pharmaceutical Services, Inc. [*Hanover, MA*] [*NASDAQ symbol*] (NQ)
SPCT........ Studi e Problemi di Critica Testuale [*A publication*]
SPCTG....... Spherical Cartridge
Sp Ct RRRA ... Special Court Regional Railroad Reorganization Act [*A publication*] (DLA)
SPCTYS .... Society for the Prevention of Cruelty to Young Singers
SPCU........ Simulation Process Control Unit (MCD)
SPCU........ Skylab Process Control Unit [*NASA*]
SPCUS ..... Sweet Potato Council of the United States (EA)
SPCW....... Specialist, Chemical Warfare [*Navy rating*]
SPCW....... Stored Program Command Word [*Data processing*] (NASA)
SPD........... Doctor of Political Science
SPD........... S-Band Polarization Diversity
SPD........... Safety Program Directive [*NASA*]
SPD........... Saidpur [*Bangladesh*] [*Airport symbol*] (OAG)
SPD........... St. Peter's Dome Lookout [*New Mexico*] [*Seismograph station code, US Geological Survey*] (SEIS)
SPD........... Salutem Plurimam Dicit [*He Wishes Much Health*] [*Latin*]
SPD........... Sample Preparation and DNA [*Deoxyribonucleic Acid*] Probe
SPD........... Sampled [*Tea trade*] (ROG)
SPD........... Scientific Passenger Pod (MCD)
SPD........... Seaplane Depot Ship
SPD........... Sedona Industries Ltd. [*Toronto Stock Exchange symbol*]
SPD........... Semipermeable Dressing [*Medicine*]
SPD........... Separation Program Designator [*Military*] (AABC)
SPD........... Service Project Drawing
SPD........... Shearing, Piling, and Disking [*Forest management*]
SPD........... Ship Performance Department [*David W. Taylor Naval Ship Research and Development Center*]
SPD........... Ship Project Directive [*Navy*]
SPD........... Sigma Phi Delta (EA)
SPD........... Silicon Photodiode
SPD........... Single Path Doppler [*RADAR*] (AAG)
SPD........... Situation Projected Display
SPD........... Skylab Program Directive [*NASA*] (KSC)
SPD........... Society for Pediatric Dermatology (EA)
SPD........... Society of Professional Drivers (EA)
SPD........... Society of Publication Designers (EA)
SPD........... South Pacific Division [*Army*] [*World War II*]
SPD........... South Polar Distance
SPD........... Southern Procurement Division [*Navy*]
SPD........... Sozialdemokratische Partei Deutschlands [*Social Democratic Party of Germany*] [*West Germany*]
SpD........... Spanish Decca, San Sebastian [*Record label*] [*Spain*]
SPD........... Spectral Power Distribution (MCD)
SPD........... Speech Processing Device
SPD........... Speed (AABC)
Spd............ Spermidine [*Biochemistry*]
SPD........... Standard Periodical Database [*Oxbridge Communications, Inc.*] [*Information service or system*] (CRD)
SPD........... Standard Periodical Directory [*A publication*]
SPD........... Standard Practice Directive [*NASA*] (NASA)
SPD........... Standard Products Co. [*NYSE symbol*] (SPSG)
SPD........... Static Pressure Distribution
SPD........... Statistical Policy Division [*Office of Management and Budget*]
SPD........... Steamer Pays Dues [*Shipping*]
SPD........... Stick Positioning Device (MCD)
SPD........... Storage Pool Disease
SPD........... Stored Program Decoder [*or Decommutation*]
SPD........... Strategic Posture Display (MCD)
SPD........... Subjective Probability Distribution
SPD........... Supplemental Program Directive (AFIT)
SPD........... Supplementary Petroleum Duty [*Tax*] [*British*]
SPD........... Surge Protective Device (MCD)
SPD........... Suspended-Particle Display [*Glazing technology*]
SPD........... Synchronized Parallel Displacement [*Automotive engineering*]
SPD........... Synchronizer for Peripheral Devices
SPD........... Synchronous Phase Demodulator
SPD........... System Program Directive (AFIT)
SPD........... System Program Director [*Air Force*] (MCD)
SPD........... Systems Parameters Document (AAG)
SPD........... Systems Program Documentation
SPDA........ Single-Premium Deferred Annuity [*Insurance*]
SPDB......... Subsystem Power Distribution Box (MCD)

SPDBK	Speed Brake (MCD)
SPDC	S-P Drug Company [*NASDAQ symbol*] (NQ)
SPDC	Spare Parts Distributing Center [*Navy*]
SPDCI	Standard Payload Display and Control Interface (NASA)
SPDCU	Subsurface Probe Data and Control Unit
SPDF	Special Projects Data Facility
SPDF	Swedish Post Defense Forces
SPDG	Spectrum Digital Corp. [*Herndon, VA*] [*NASDAQ symbol*] (NQ)
SPDG	Spiral Point Drill Geometry
SPDHF	Special Pay for Duty Subject to Hostile Fire [*Military*]
SPDI	Special Discriminant (CAAL)
SPDL	Spin-Dependent Luminescence [*Physics*]
SPDL	Spindle (MSA)
SPDLTR....	Speedletter
SPDM.........	Special Purpose Dexterous Manipulator
SPDM.........	Subprocessor with Dynamic Microprogramming
SPDO	Mollendo [*Peru*] [*ICAO location identifier*] (ICLI)
SPDOM	Speedometer (MSA)
SPDP	Stored Program Data Processor (KSC)
SPDP	Succinimidyl(pyridyldithio)propionate [*Organic chemistry*]
SPDR.........	Software Preliminary Design Review [*NASA*] (NASA)
SPDR.........	Special Drill [*Tool*] (AAG)
SPDR.........	Spider [*Engineering acoustics*]
SP/DR	Systems Performance/Design Requirements
SPDRAB ...	Society for the Prevention of Disparaging Remarks about Brooklyn
SPDS	Safe-Practice Data Sheet (MSA)
SPDS	Safety Parameter Display System [*Instrumentation*]
SPDS	Sequential Payload Delivery System (MCD)
SPDS	Suggestion Program Data System [*Military*]
SPDT	Single-Pole, Double-Throw [*Switch*]
SPDTDB ...	Single-Pole, Double-Throw, Double-Break [*Switch*]
SPDTNCDB ...	Single-Pole, Double-Throw, Normally-Closed, Double-Break [*Switch*]
SPDTNO...	Single-Pole, Double-Throw, Normally-Open [*Switch*]
SPDTNODB ...	Single-Pole, Double-Throw, Normally-Open, Double-Break [*Switch*]
SPDTSW...	Single-Pole, Double-Throw Switch
SPDVB	Science Progres Decouverte [*A publication*]
SPDW........	South Pacific Deep Water
SPDWY.....	Speedway
SPDY	Spectradyne, Inc. [*NASDAQ symbol*] (NQ)
Spe	Durandi. Speculum Judiciale [*A publication*] (DSA)
s-pe---	Peru [*MARC geographic area code*] [*Library of Congress*] (LCCP)
SPE............	Senior Project Engineer
SPE............	Serum Protein Electrophoresis
SPE............	Shaft Position Encoder
SPE............	Sian [*Republic of China*] [*Seismograph station code, US Geological Survey*] (SEIS)
SPE............	Signal Processing Element [*Navy*]
SPE............	Sliding Padeye (MCD)
SPE............	Small Processing Element [*Data processing*]
SPE............	Society of Petroleum Engineers (EA)
SPE............	Society for Photographic Education (EA)
SPE............	Society of Plastics Engineers (EA)
SPE............	Society of Professors of Education (EA)
SPE............	Society for Pure English
SPE............	Solar Proton Event [*Geophysics*]
SPE............	Solid-Phase Extraction
SPE............	Solid Polymer Electrolyte
SPE............	Space Processing Equipment [*Astronautics*]
SPE............	Special-Purpose Equipment
SPE............	Specialty Equipment Companies [*NYSE symbol*] (SPSG)
SPE............	Sperry UNIVAC Information Center, Blue Bell, PA [*OCLC symbol*] (OCLC)
SPe............	Spettatore Italiano [*A publication*]
SPE............	Spherical Probable Error
SPE............	Static Phase Error [*NASA*]
SPE............	Station Project Engineer [*NASA*]
SPE............	Stepped Potential Electrode [*Electrode chemistry*]
SPE............	Stop Project ELF [*Extremely Low Frequency system*] (EA)
SPE............	Stored Program Element
SPE............	Studies in Public Economics [*Elsevier Book Series*] [*A publication*]
SPE............	Subport of Embarkation
SPE............	Sucrose Polyester [*Pharmacology*]
SPE............	Sun-Planet-Earth [*Astronomy*]
SPE............	Suriname Post [*A publication*]
SPE............	Symvoulion Proothiseos Exagogon [*Exports Promotion Council*] [*Greek*]
SPE............	System Performance Evaluation (KSC)
SPE............	Systems Performance Effectiveness
SPE............	Unilabo [*France*] [*Research code symbol*]
SPEA	Sales Promotion Executives Association [*Later, MCEI*] (EA)
SPEA	Scottish Physical Education Association [*British*]
SPEA	Southeastern Poultry and Egg Association (EA)
SPEAC	Selma Project Education Alternatives Center [*Alabama*] (EA)
SPEAC	Solar Photovoltaic Energy Advisory Committee [*Terminated, 1986*] (EGAO)

SPEAHR ...	Society for the Protection of East Asians' Human Rights/ USA (EA)
SPE of AIME ...	Society of Petroleum Engineers of American Institute of Mining, Metallurgical, and Petroleum Engineers (EA)
SPEAK	Society for Promoting and Encouraging the Arts and Knowledge of the Church (EA)
SPEAKEASY ...	[*An*] information retrieval system
SPEAL.......	Special-Purpose Engineering Analysis Language (MCD)
SPEAR	Signal Processing, Evaluation, Alert, and Report [*Navy*] (NVT)
SPEAR	SLAC Positron-Electron Asymmetric Ring
SPEAR	Small Payload Ejection and Recovery for the Space Shuttle [*NASA*] (MCD)
SPEAR	Source Performance Evaluation and Reporting
SPEAR	Spaceborne Earth Applications Ranging System (MCD)
Spear	Spears' South Carolina Law Reports [*1842-44*] [*A publication*] (DLA)
SPEAR	Squadron Performance Effectiveness Analysis Representation (MCD)
SPEAR	Stanford Positron-Electron Axisymmetric Ring
SPEAR	Statistical Property Estimation and Regeneration (MCD)
SPEAR	Supplier Performance Evaluation and Reporting [*or Review*] [*General Motors quality award*]
Spear Ch	Spears' South Carolina Chancery Reports [*A publication*] (DLA)
Spear Eq ...	Spears' South Carolina Equity Reports [*A publication*] (DLA)
Spear Ext ...	Spear's Law of Extradition [*A publication*] (DLA)
Spear High ...	Spearman on Highways [*1881*] [*A publication*] (DLA)
SPEARS ...	Satellite Photoelectric Analog Rectification System
SPEARS	Spaceborne Earth Applications Ranging System [*NASA*]
Spears	Spears' South Carolina Equity Reports [*1842-44*] [*A publication*] (DLA)
Spears	Spears' South Carolina Law Reports [*A publication*] (DLA)
Spears Eq...	Spears' South Carolina Equity Reports [*A publication*] (DLA)
SPEB	Pebas [*Peru*] [*ICAO location identifier*] (ICLI)
SPEBSQSA ...	Society for the Preservation and Encouragement of Barber Shop Quartet Singing in America (EA)
Spec............	De Specialibus Legibus [*of Philo*] (BJA)
SPEC	Scientific Pollution and Environmental Control Society
SPEC	Simulation of Propulsion Engine Cycle [*NASA*]
SPEC	Society of Philippine Electrical Contractors (DS)
SPEC	Society of Professional Engineering Checkers
SPEC	South Pacific Bureau for Economic Cooperation [*Fiji*] (ADA)
SPEC	South Pacific Education Centre [*Australia*]
SPEC	Special [*or Specialist*] (KSC)
SPEC	Specific
SPEC	Specification (AFM)
SPEC	Specimen (AAG)
Spec............	Spectator [*A publication*]
Spec............	Spectrum [*A publication*]
SPEC	Spectrum
SPEC	Spectrum Control, Inc. [*NASDAQ symbol*] (NQ)
Spec............	Speculation [*A publication*]
Spec............	Speculator [*Guillelmus Durandi*] [*Deceased, 1296*] [*Authority cited in pre-1607 legal work*] (DSA)
Spec............	Speculum [*A publication*]
SPEC	Speech Predictive Encoded Communications [*Telephone channels*]
SPEC	Staff of the Production Executive Committee [*of the WPB*] [*Obsolete*]
SPEC	Stored Program Educational Computer
SPEC	Studies in the Political Economy of Canada [*Society*]
SPEC	Systems and Procedures Exchange Center [*Association of Research Libraries*]
SPECA	Society for the Preservation and Enjoyment of Carriages in America (EA)
SPECA	Spectrum [*Oxford*] [*A publication*]
SPECAN ...	Spectral Analysis
SPECAT....	Special Category (AABC)
Spec Bull Coll Agric Utsunomiya Univ ...	Special Bulletin. College of Agriculture. Utsunomiya University [*A publication*]
Spec Bull Coll Agr Utsunomiya Univ ...	Special Bulletin. College of Agriculture. Utsunomiya University [*A publication*]
Spec Bull Dep Agric S Aust ...	Special Bulletin. Department of Agriculture. South Australia [*A publication*] (APTA)
Spec Bull Dep Agric South Aust ...	Special Bulletin. Department of Agriculture. South Australia [*A publication*] (APTA)
Spec Bull First Agron Div Tokai-Kinki Natl Agric Exp Stn ...	Special Bulletin. First Agronomy Division. Tokai-Kinki National Agricultural Experiment Station [*A publication*]
Spec Bull Mich Agric Exp Stn ...	Special Bulletin. Michigan Agricultural Experiment Station [*A publication*]
Spec Bull Mich State Univ Agr Exp Sta ...	Special Bulletin. Michigan State University. Agricultural Experiment Station [*A publication*]
Spec Bull Okayama Agr Exp Sta ...	Special Bulletin. Okayama Agricultural Experiment Station [*A publication*]
Spec Bull Rehovot Nat Univ Inst Agr ...	Special Bulletin. Rehovot. National and University Institute of Agriculture [*A publication*]
Spec Bull Taiwan For Res Inst ...	Special Bulletin. Taiwan Forestry Research Institute [*A publication*]

Spec Bull Tottori Agric Exp Stn ... Special Bulletin. Tottori Agricultural Experiment Station [*A publication*]
Sp Ecc & Ad ... Spinks' English Ecclesiastical and Admiralty Reports [*164 English Reprint*] [*1853-55*] [*A publication*]   (DLA)
Spec Care Dentist ... Special Care in Dentistry [*A publication*]
Spec Ceram ... Special Ceramics [*A publication*]
Spec Circ Mass Ext Serv ... Special Circular. Massachusetts Extension Service [*A publication*]
Spec Circ Ohio Agr Exp Sta ... Special Circular. Ohio Agricultural Experiment Station [*A publication*]
Spec Circ Ohio Agric Res Dev Cent ... Special Circular. Ohio Agricultural Research and Development Center [*A publication*]
Spec Circ PA State Univ Coll-Agric Ext Serv ... Special Circular. Pennsylvania State University. College of Agriculture. Extension Service [*A publication*]
Spec Circ Univ Wis Coll Agr Ext Serv ... Special Circular. University of Wisconsin. College of Agriculture. Extension Service [*A publication*]
Spec Collect ... Special Collections [*A publication*]
Spec Conf Atmos Deposition Proc ... Specialty Conference on Atmospheric Deposition. Proceedings [*A publication*]
Spec Contrib Geophys Inst Kyoto Univ ... Special Contributions. Geophysical Institute. Kyoto University [*Japan*] [*A publication*]
Spec Contrib Inst Geophys Natl Cent Univ (Miaoli Taiwan) ... Special Contributions. Institute of Geophysics. National Central University (Miaoli, Taiwan) [*A publication*]
Spec Courses Fd Ind ... Specialist Courses for the Food Industry [*A publication*]   (APTA)
Spec Courses Food Ind ... Specialist Courses for the Food Industry [*Food Industry News*] [*A publication*]   (APTA)
SPECD ...... Specification Data Base
SPECD ...... Spectrum [*Berlin*] [*A publication*]
SPECDEVCEN ... Special Devices Center [*Navy*]
Spec Discuss Faraday Soc ... Special Discussions. Faraday Society [*A publication*]
Spec Ed Counc News ... Special Education Council. Newsletter [*A publication*]
Spec Educ .. Special Education [*A publication*]
Spec Educ .. Special Education. Forward Trends [*A publication*]
Spec Educ Bull ... Special Education Bulletin [*A publication*]   (APTA)
Spec Educ Can ... Special Education in Canada [*A publication*]
Spec Educ Forward Trends ... Special Education. Forward Trends [*A publication*]
Spec Eng .... Specifying Engineer [*A publication*]
SPECHNDLG ... Special Handling   (MCD)
SPECI .... Specimen   (DSUE)
Special Bull Univ Minnesota Agric Exten Div ... Special Bulletin. University of Minnesota. Agricultural Extension Division [*A publication*]
Special Ed ... Special Education [*A publication*]
Special Ed ... Special Education in Canada [*A publication*]
Specialised Nat Councils' M (Egypt) ... Specialised National Councils' Magazine (Egypt) [*A publication*]
Speciality Chem ... Speciality Chemicals [*A publication*]
Special Lib ... Special Libraries [*A publication*]
Special Rep Ser Med Research Com (London) ... Special Report Series. Medical Research Committee (London) [*A publication*]
Special Sch Bul (NT) ... Special Schools Bulletin (Northern Territory) [*A publication*]   (APTA)
Special Sch Bul (Qld) ... Special Schools Bulletin (Queensland Department of Education) [*A publication*]   (APTA)
SPECIFD .. Specified   (ROG)
Specif Eng ... Specifying Engineer [*A publication*]
Specif Engr ... Specifying Engineer [*A publication*]
SPECIFN .. Specification   (ROG)
Spec Int .... Specialties International [*A publication*]
SPECINVESDIST ... Special Investigations District [*Air Force*]
Spec Issue Plant Cell Physiol ... Special Issue of Plant and Cell Physiology [*A publication*]
SPECL .... Special   (ROG)
SPECL .... Specialize
Spec Law Dig Health Care Mon ... Specialty Law Digest. Health Care Monthly [*A publication*]
Spec Liaison Rep Commonw Geol Liaison Off ... Special Liaison Report. Commonwealth Geological Liaison Office [*London*] [*A publication*]
Spec Libr .... Special Libraries [*A publication*]
Spec Libr Ass Toronto Chapter Bull ... Special Libraries Association. Toronto Chapter. Bulletin [*A publication*]
SPECLST ... Specialist
SPECMAP ... Spectral Mapping
SPECO ...... Steel Products Engineering Company
SPECOL .... Special Customer-Oriented Language
SPECOM .. Special Command
SPECOMALT ... Special Communications Alteration
SPECOMME ... Specified Command Middle East [*Military*]
SPECON ... Systems Performance Effectiveness Conference
SPECOPNSSq ... Special Operations Squadron [*Air Force*]
SPECOPS ... Special Operations [*Navy*]   (NVT)
SPECOR ... Spectral Correlation RADAR   (MCD)

Spec Pap Cent Precambrian Res Univ Adelaide ... Special Paper. Centre for Precambrian Research. University of Adelaide [*A publication*]
Spec Pap Dep Nat Resour (Qd) ... Special Papers. Department of Natural Resources (Queensland) [*A publication*]
Spec Pap Geol Ass Can ... Special Paper. Geological Association of Canada [*A publication*]
Spec Pap Palaeontol ... Special Papers in Palaeontology [*A publication*]
Spec Pap Univ Adelaide Cent Precambrian Res ... Special Paper. University of Adelaide. Centre for Precambrian Research [*A publication*]
Spec Period Rep Alicyclic Chem ... Specialist Periodical Reports. Alicyclic Chemistry [*A publication*]
Spec Period Rep Aliphatic Chem ... Specialist Periodical Reports. Aliphatic Chemistry [*A publication*]
Spec Period Rep Aliphatic Relat Nat Prod Chem ... Specialist Periodical Reports. Aliphatic and Related Natural Product Chemistry [*A publication*]
Spec Period Rep Alkaloids ... Specialist Periodical Reports. Alkaloids [*A publication*]
Spec Period Rep Amino-Acids Peptides Proteins ... Specialist Periodical Reports. Amino-Acids, Peptides, and Proteins [*A publication*]
Spec Period Rep Amino-Acids Pept Proteins ... Specialist Periodical Reports. Amino-Acids, Peptides, and Proteins [*A publication*]
Spec Period Rep Biosynth ... Specialist Periodical Reports. Biosynthesis [*A publication*]
Spec Period Rep Carbohydr Chem ... Specialist Periodical Reports. Carbohydrate Chemistry [*A publication*]
Spec Period Rep Catal ... Specialist Periodical Reports. Catalysis [*A publication*]
Spec Period Rep Electrochem ... Specialist Periodical Reports. Electrochemistry [*A publication*]
Spec Period Rep Electron Spin Reson ... Specialist Periodical Reports. Electron Spin Resonance [*A publication*]
Spec Period Rep Environ Chem ... Specialist Periodical Reports. Environmental Chemistry [*A publication*]
Spec Period Rep Foreign Compd Metab Mamm ... Specialist Periodical Reports. Foreign Compound Metabolism in Mammals [*A publication*]
Spec Period Rep Gas Kinet Energy Transfer ... Specialist Periodical Reports. Gas Kinetics and Energy Transfer [*A publication*]
Spec Period Rep Gen Synth Methods ... Specialist Periodical Reports. General and Synthetic Methods [*A publication*]
Spec Period Rep Heterocycl Chem ... Specialist Periodical Reports. Heterocyclic Chemistry [*A publication*]
Spec Period Rep Inorg Biochem ... Specialist Periodical Reports. Inorganic Biochemistry [*A publication*]
Spec Period Rep Inorg Chem Transition Elem ... Specialist Periodical Reports. Inorganic Chemistry of the Transition Elements [*A publication*]
Spec Period Rep Inorg React Mech ... Specialist Periodical Reports. Inorganic Reaction Mechanisms [*A publication*]
Spec Period Rep Macromol Chem ... Specialist Periodical Reports. Macromolecular Chemistry [*A publication*]
Spec Period Rep Mass Spectrom ... Specialist Periodical Reports. Mass Spectrometry [*A publication*]
Spec Period Rep Mol Struct Diffr Methods ... Specialist Periodical Reports. Molecular Structure by Diffraction Methods [*A publication*]
Spec Period Rep Nucl Magn Resonance ... Specialist Periodical Reports. Nuclear Magnetic Resonance [*A publication*]
Spec Period Rep Organomet Chem ... Specialist Periodical Reports. Organometallic Chemistry [*A publication*]
Spec Period Rep Organophosphorus Chem ... Specialist Periodical Reports. Organophosphorus Chemistry [*A publication*]
Spec Period Rep Org Compd Sulphur Selenium Tellurium ... Specialist Periodical Reports. Organic Compounds of Sulphur, Selenium, and Tellurium [*A publication*]
Spec Period Rep Photochem ... Specialist Periodical Reports. Photochemistry [*A publication*]
Spec Period Rep React Kinet ... Specialist Periodical Reports. Reaction Kinetics [*A publication*]
Spec Period Rep Spectrosc Prop Inorg Organomet Compd ... Specialist Periodical Reports. Spectroscopic Properties of Inorganic and Organometallic Compounds [*A publication*]
Spec Period Rep Terpenoids Steroids ... Specialist Periodical Reports. Terpenoids and Steroids [*A publication*]
Spec Period Rep Theor Chem ... Specialist Periodical Reports. Theoretical Chemistry [*A publication*]
Spec Prog News ... Special Programmes News [*A publication*]
Spec Pub Agric Res Org ... Special Publication. Agricultural Research Organization [*A publication*]
Spec Publ Acad Nat Sci Phila ... Special Publication. Academy of Natural Sciences. Philadelphia [*A publication*]
Spec Publ Am Littoral Soc ... Special Publication. American Littoral Society [*A publication*]
Spec Publ Am Soc Agron ... Special Publication. American Society of Agronomy [*A publication*]
Spec Publ Am Soc Mammal ... Special Publication. American Society of Mammalogists [*A publication*]

Spec Publ Aust Conserv Fdn ... Special Publication. Australian Conservation Foundation [*A publication*]   (APTA)

Spec Publ Aust Conserv Found ... Special Publication. Australian Conservation Foundation [*A publication*]   (APTA)

Spec Publ Br Ceram Res Assoc ... Special Publication. British Ceramics Research Association [*A publication*]

Spec Publ Br Ecol Soc ... Special Publication. British Ecological Society [*A publication*]

Spec Publ Chicago Acad Sci ... Special Publications. Chicago Academy of Science [*A publication*]

Spec Publ Coll Agric Natl Taiwan Univ ... Special Publication. College of Agriculture. National Taiwan University [*A publication*]

Spec Publ Coll Agr Nat Taiwan U ... Special Publications. College of Agriculture. National Taiwan University [*A publication*]

Spec Publ Colorado Geol Surv ... Special Publication. Colorado Geological Survey [*A publication*]

Spec Publ Commonw Bur Soils ... Special Publication. Commonwealth Bureau of Soils [*A publication*]

Spec Publ Entomol Soc Am ... Special Publication. Entomological Society of America [*A publication*]

Spec Publ Geol Soc Aust ... Special Publication. Geological Society of Australia [*A publication*]   (APTA)

Spec Publ Geol Soc London ... Special Publication. Geological Society of London [*A publication*]

Spec Publ Geol Soc Zimbabwe ... Special Publication. Geological Society of Zimbabwe [*A publication*]

Spec Publ Geol Surv S Afr ... Special Publications. Geological Survey of South Africa [*A publication*]

Spec Publ (Isr) Agric Res Org ... Special Publication (Israel). Agricultural Research Organization [*A publication*]

Spec Publ KY Geol Surv ... Special Publication. Kentucky Geological Survey [*A publication*]

Spec Publ Montana Bur Mines Geol ... Special Publication. Montana Bureau of Mines and Geology [*A publication*]

Spec Publ Natl Bur Stand US ... Special Publication. United States National Bureau of Standards [*A publication*]

Spec Publ NM Geol Soc ... Special Publication. New Mexico Geological Society [*A publication*]

Spec Publ Sado Mar Biol Stn Niigata Univ ... Special Publication. Sado Marine Biological Station. Niigata University [*A publication*]

Spec Publ S Afr Assoc Adv Sci ... Special Publication. South African Association for the Advancement of Science [*A publication*]

Spec Publs Am Ass Econ Ent ... Special Publications. American Association of Economic Entomology [*A publication*]

Spec Publ Ser Br Ecol Soc ... Special Publications Series. British Ecological Society [*A publication*]

Spec Publ Ser Int Atl Salmon Found ... Special Publication Series. International Atlantic Salmon Foundation [*A publication*]

Spec Publ Ser Soil Sci Soc Amer ... Special Publication Series. Soil Science Society of America [*A publication*]

Spec Publ Seto Mar Biol Lab Ser IV ... Special Publications. Seto Marine Biological Laboratory. Series IV [*A publication*]

Spec Publ Soc Gen Microbiol ... Special Publications. Society for General Microbiology [*A publication*]

Spec Publ South Aust Dep Mines Energy ... Special Publication. South Australia Department of Mines and Energy [*A publication*]

Spec Publ US Bur Mines ... Special Publications. United States Bureau of Mines [*A publication*]

Spec Publ US Natn Bur Stand ... Special Publications. United States National Bureau of Standards [*A publication*]

Spec Publ West Aust Mus ... Special Publication. Western Australian Museum [*A publication*]   (APTA)

Spec Pub R Soc Tasm ... Royal Society of Tasmania. Special Publications [*A publication*]   (APTA)

Spec Rep Agric Exp Stn Coop Ext Serv Univ Arkansas ... Special Report. Agricultural Experiment Station. Cooperative Extension Service. University of Arkansas [*A publication*]

Spec Rep Agric Exp Stn Oreg State Univ ... Special Report. Agricultural Experiment Station. Oregon State University [*A publication*]

Spec Rep Arctic Inst N Am ... Special Report. Arctic Institute of North America [*A publication*]

Spec Rep Ark Agr Exp Sta ... Special Report. Arkansas Agricultural Experiment Station [*A publication*]

Spec Rep Ark Agric Exp Stn ... Special Report. Arkansas Agricultural Experiment Station [*A publication*]

Spec Rep Colo Dep Game Fish Parks ... Special Report. Colorado Department of Game, Fish, and Parks [*A publication*]

Spec Rep Colo Div Game Fish Parks ... Special Report. Colorado Division of Game, Fish, and Parks [*A publication*]

Spec Rep Colo Div Wildl ... Special Report. Colorado Division of Wildlife [*A publication*]

Spec Rep Commonw Exp Bldg Stn ... Special Report. Commonwealth Experimental Building Station [*A publication*]   (APTA)

Spec Rep Electr Power Res Inst EPRI ER (Palo Alto, Calif) ... Special Report. Electric Power Research Institute. EPRI ER (Palo Alto, California) [*A publication*]

Spec Rep Electr Power Res Inst EPRI FP (Palo Alto, Calif) ... Special Report. Electric Power Research Institute. EPRI FP (Palo Alto, California) [*A publication*]

Spec Rep EPRI SR Electr Power Res Inst (Palo Alto Calif) ... Special Report. Electric Power Research Institute. EPRI SR (Palo Alto, Califor nia) [*A publication*]

Spec Rep GB For Prod Res ... Special Report. Great Britain Forest Products Research [*A publication*]

Spec Rep Geol Soc Lond ... Special Reports. Geological Society of London [*A publication*]

Spec Rep ICSU Comm Data Sci Technol ... Special Report. International Council of Scientific Unions. Committee on Data for Science and Technology [*A publication*]

Spec Rep Indiana Geol Surv ... Special Report. Indiana Geological Survey [*A publication*]

Spec Rep Iowa State Univ Coop Ext Serv ... Special Report. Iowa State University. Cooperative Extension Service [*A publication*]

Spec Rep Johns Hopkins Univ Appl Phys Lab ... Special Report. Johns Hopkins University. Applied Physics Laboratory [*A publication*]

Spec Rep Natl Inst Anim Ind ... Special Report. National Institute of Animal Industry [*A publication*]

Spec Rep Nebr Agr Exp Sta ... Special Report. Nebraska Agricultural Experiment Station [*A publication*]

Spec Rep NY State Agric Exp Stn (Geneva) ... Special Report. New York State Agricultural Experiment Station (Geneva) [*A publication*]

Spec Rep (Oregon) Agric Exp Stn ... Special Report (Oregon). Agricultural Experiment Station [*A publication*]

Spec Rep Oreg State Coll Agr Exp Sta ... Special Report. Oregon State College Agricultural Experiment Station [*A publication*]

Spec Rep Robert Wood Johnson Foundation ... Special Report. Robert Wood Johnson Foundation [*A publication*]

Spec Rep Ser Indian Counc Med Res ... Special Report Series. Indian Council of Medical Research [*A publication*]

Spec Rep Ser Med Res Counc (UK) ... Special Report Series. Medical Research Council (United Kingdom) [*A publication*]

Spec Rep Soc Plant Prot North Jpn ... Special Report. Society of Plant Protection of North Japan [*A publication*]

Spec Rep Univ Ill Urbana Champaign Water Resour Cent ... Special Report. University of Illinois at Urbana-Champaign. Water Resources Center [*A publication*]

Spec Rep Univ Minn Agr Ext Serv ... Special Report. University of Minnesota. Agricultural Extension Service [*A publication*]

Spec Rep Univ MO Coll Agr Exp Sta ... Special Report. University of Missouri. College of Agriculture. Experiment Station [*A publication*]

Spec Rep Univ MO Columbia Agric Exp Stn ... Special Report. University of Missouri, Columbia. Agricultural Experiment Station [*A publication*]

Spec Rep Wood Res Lab VA Polyt Inst ... Special Report. Wood Research Laboratory. Virginia Polytechnic Institute [*A publication*]

SPECS .... Spectacles   (ROG)

Spec Sci Rep FL Dep Nat Resour Mar Res Lab ... Special Scientific Report. Florida Department of Natural Resources. Marine Research Laboratory [*A publication*]

Spec Sci Rep Wildlife US Fish Wildlife Serv ... Special Scientific Report. Wildlife. United States Fish and Wildlife Service [*A publication*]

Spec Ser Fla Dep Agric ... Special Series. Florida Department of Agriculture [*A publication*]

Spec Steel ... Special Steel [*Japan*] [*A publication*]

Spec Steels Rev ... Special Steels Review [*A publication*]

Spec Steels Tech Rev (Sheffield) ... Special Steels Technical Review (Sheffield) [*A publication*]

Spec Stud Utah Geol Miner Surv ... Special Studies. Utah Geological and Mineral Survey [*A publication*]

SPECT .... Single Photon Emission Computed Tomography

Spect .... Spectacula [*of Martial*] [*Classical studies*]   (OCD)

Spect .... Spectator [*A publication*]

SPECT .... Spectrograph

SPECT .... Spectrometer   (NASA)

Spect Act A ... Spectrochimica Acta. Part A. Molecular Spectroscopy [*A publication*]

Spect Act B ... Spectrochimica Acta. Part B. Atomic Spectroscopy [*A publication*]

Spec Tech Assoc Publ ... Special Technical Association. Publication [*A publication*]

Spec Tech Publs Am Soc Test Mater ... Special Technical Publications. American Society for Testing Materials [*A publication*]

Spect Lett ... Spectroscopy Letters [*A publication*]

SPECTNG ... Specialist Training [*Navy*]   (NVT)

Spec Top Endocrinol Metab ... Special Topics in Endocrinology and Metabolism [*A publication*]

Spec Transp Plann Practice ... Specialized Transportation Planning and Practice [*A publication*]

SPECTRE ... Special Executive for Counterintelligence, Terrorism, Revenge, and Extortion [*Fictitious organization whose agents were characters in the late Ian Fleming's "James Bond" mysteries*]

Spectrochim Acta ... Spectrochimica Acta [*A publication*]

Spectrochim Acta A ... Spectrochimica Acta. Part A. Molecular Spectroscopy [*A publication*]
Spectrochim Acta B ... Spectrochimica Acta. Part B. Atomic Spectroscopy [*A publication*]
Spectrochim Acta Part A ... Spectrochimica Acta. Part A. Molecular Spectroscopy [*A publication*]
Spectrochim Acta Part A Mol Spectrosc ... Spectrochimica Acta. Part A. Molecular Spectroscopy [*A publication*]
Spectrochim Acta Part B ... Spectrochimica Acta. Part B. Atomic Spectroscopy [*A publication*]
Spectrochim Acta Part B At Spectrosc ... Spectrochimica Acta. Part B. Atomic Spectroscopy [*A publication*]
SPECTROL ... Scheduling, Planning, Evaluation, and Cost Control [*Air Force*]
Spectrosc Lett ... Spectroscopy Letters [*A publication*]
Spectrosc Mol ... Spectroscopia Molecular [*A publication*]
Spectros Prop Inorg Organomet Compd ... Spectroscopic Properties of Inorganic and Organometallic Compounds [*A publication*]
Spectrum Int ... Spectrum International [*A publication*]
Specu .... Speculator [*Guillelmus Durandi*] [*Deceased, 1296*] [*Authority cited in pre-1607 legal work*]   (DSA)
Specu .... Speculum [*A publication*]
Specula .... Speculator [*Guillelmus Durandi*] [*Deceased, 1296*] [*Authority cited in pre-1607 legal work*]   (DSA)
Speculations Sci and Technol ... Speculations in Science and Technology [*A publication*]
Speculations Sci Technol ... Speculations in Science and Technology (Complete Edition) [*A publication*]
Specul Sci Technol ... Speculations in Science and Technology [*Switzerland*] [*A publication*]
SPECVER ... Specification Verification [*Data processing*]   (IEEE)
SPED .... Sir Speedy Printing Centres [*NASDAQ symbol*]   (NQ)
SPED .... Special Education Director
Sp Ed .... Specialist in Education [*Academic degree*]
SPED .... Sulfur, Phosphorus, Emission Detector [*Chromatograph accessory*]
SPED .... Supersonic Planetary Entry Decelerator   (KSC)
SPEDA ...... Special Education [*A publication*]
SPEDAC ... Solid-State, Parallel, Expandable, Differential Analyzer Computer
SPEDCO ... Southeastern Pennsylvania Development Corporation
SPEDE ...... System for Processing Educational Data Electronically
SPEDIAT ... Special Diary Transcript [*Military*]
SPEDTAC ... Stored Program Educational Transistorized Automatic Computer
SPEDY ...... Summer Program for Economically Disadvantaged Youth [*Department of Labor*]
SPEE .... Society for the Promotion of Engineering Education [*Later, ASEE*]
SPEE .... Special Purpose End Effector   (MCD)
SPEE .... Studies in Production and Engineering Economics [*Elsevier Book Series*] [*A publication*]
SPEECH ... Society to Promote Essential Education for Children with Communications Handicaps [*Australia*]
Speech Commun ... Speech Communication [*A publication*]
Speech Found Am Publ ... Speech Foundation of America. Publication [*A publication*]
Speech Mon ... Speech Monographs [*A publication*]
Speech Monogr ... Speech Monographs [*A publication*]
Speech Pathol Ther ... Speech Pathology and Therapy [*A publication*]
Speech Teac ... Speech Teacher [*A publication*]
Speech Technol ... Speech Technology [*A publication*]
SPEED ...... Scheduled Procurement of Essential Equipment Deliveries [*US Postal Service*]
SPEED ...... Self-Programmed Electronic Equation Delineator
SPEED ...... Signal Processing in Evacuated Electronic Devices
SPEED ...... Single-Point Emergency Equipment Divestment
SPEED ...... Special Procedures for Expediting Equipment Development   (MCD)
SPEED ...... Study and Performance Efficiency in Entry Design
SPEED ...... Subsistence Preparation by Electronic Energy Diffusion
SPEED ...... Systematic Plotting and Evaluation of Enumerated Data [*National Institute of Standards and Technology*] [*Data processing*]
SPEED ...... Systems Planning and Effectiveness Evaluation Device   (MCD)
SPEED ...... Systemwide Project for Electronic Equipment at Depots [*Military*]   (AABC)
SPEEDEX ... Systemwide Project for Electronic Equipment at Depots Extended [*Military*]   (AABC)
SPEEDO ... Speedometer [*Automotive engineering*]
SPEEDX ... Society to Preserve the Engrossing Enjoyment of DXing   (EA)
SPEEL .... Shore Plant Electronic Equipment List   (MUGU)
SPEER .... Scientists and Professional Engineers Employment Registry [*Career Technologies Corp. - CTC*] [*Andover, MA*] [*Information service or system*]   (IID)
Speers .... Speers' [*or Spears'*] South Carolina Law Reports [*A publication*]   (DLA)
Speers Eq ... Speers' [*or Spears'*] South Carolina Equity Reports [*A publication*]   (DLA)
Speers Eq (SC) ... Speers' [*or Spears'*] South Carolina Equity Reports [*A publication*]   (DLA)

Speers L (SC) ... Speers' [*or Spears'*] South Carolina Law Reports [*A publication*]   (DLA)
SPEF .... Single Program Element Funding [*Military*]   (AABC)
SPEF .... Student Performance Evaluation Form
SPEG .... Serum Protein Electrophoretogram [*Clinical chemistry*]
SPEG .... Spencerville & Elgin Railroad Co. [*AAR code*]
SPEG .... Staff Planning Evaluation Group   (AAG)
SPEJ .... Society of Petroleum Engineers. American Institute of Mining, Metallurgical, and Petroleum Engineers. Journal [*A publication*]
SPE J .... SPE [*Society of Plastics Engineers*] Journal [*A publication*]
SPEJA .... SPE [*Society of Plastics Engineers*] Journal [*A publication*]
SPEJ Soc Pet Eng J ... SPEJ. Society of Petroleum Engineers [*of AIME*] Journal [*United States*] [*A publication*]
SPEK .... Spec's Music, Inc. [*Miami, FL*] [*NASDAQ symbol*]   (NQ)
Spektrum Wiss ... Spektrum der Wissenschaft [*German Federal Republic*] [*A publication*]
SPELD ...... Specific Learning Disability   (ADA)
SPELD Info ... SPELD [*Societe de Promotion a l'Etranger du Livre de Droit*] Information [*A publication*]
SPELEOL ... Speleological
Speleol Abstr ... Speleological Abstracts [*A publication*]
Speleol Biul Speleoklubu Warsz ... Speleologia Biuletyn Speleoklubu Warszawskiego [*A publication*]
Spel Feuds ... Spelman on Feuds [*A publication*]   (DLA)
Spel Gl .... Spelman's Glossarium Archaiologicum [*A publication*]   (DLA)
SPELL .... Society for the Preservation of English Language and Literature   (EA)
Spell Extr Rel ... Spelling on Extraordinary Relief in Equity and in Law [*A publication*]   (DLA)
Spell Extr Rem ... Spelling's Treatise on Injunctions and Other Extraordinary Remedies [*A publication*]   (DLA)
Spel LT ...... Spelman's Law Tracts [*A publication*]   (DLA)
Spelm .... Spelman's Glossarium Archaiologicum [*3 eds.*] [*1626-87*] [*A publication*]   (DLA)
Spelman ..... Spelman's Glossarium Archaiologicum [*3 eds.*] [*1626-87*] [*A publication*]   (DLA)
SPELPAT ... Spelling Patterns
Spel Rep ..... Spelman's Reports, Manuscript, English King's Bench [*A publication*]   (DLA)
SPEM .... Sindacato Petrolieri e Methanieri [*Union of Oil and Methane Gas Workers*] [*Italy*]
SPEMS ...... Self-Propelled Elevated Maintenance Stand   (MCD)
SPEMU ...... Stable-Price Economic and Monetary Union [*Europe*]   (ECON)
SPEN .... Iscozacin [*Peru*] [*ICAO location identifier*]   (ICLI)
SPENAVO ... Special Naval Observer
Spenc .... Spencer's Law Reports [*20 New Jersey*] [*A publication*]   (DLA)
Spenc .... Spencer's Reports [*10-20 Minnesota*] [*A publication*]   (DLA)
Spence Ch .. Spence's Equitable Jurisdiction of the Court of Chancery [*A publication*]   (DLA)
Spence Cop ... Spence on Copyright of Designs [*A publication*]   (DLA)
Spence Eq Jur ... Spence's Equitable Jurisdiction of the Court of Chancery [*A publication*]   (DLA)
Spence Or L ... Spence's Origin of Laws [*A publication*]   (DLA)
Spence Pat Inv ... Spence on Patentable Inventions [*1851*] [*A publication*]   (DLA)
Spencer ...... Spencer's Law Reports [*20 New Jersey*] [*A publication*]   (DLA)
Spencer ...... Spencer's Reports [*10-20 Minnesota*] [*A publication*]   (DLA)
SPEND ...... Specifying Engineer [*A publication*]
Spen (NJ) .. Spencer's Law Reports [*20 New Jersey*] [*A publication*]   (DLA)
Spenser St ... Spenser Studies [*A publication*]
Spens Sel Cas ... Spens' Select Cases [*Bombay, India*] [*A publication*]   (DLA)
SPEO .... Chimbote [*Peru*] [*ICAO location identifier*]   (ICLI)
SPEOPT .... Special Optical Tracking System [*NASA*]
SPEP .... Puerto Esperanza [*Peru*] [*ICAO location identifier*]   (ICLI)
SPEP .... Serum Protein Electrophoresis [*Clinical chemistry*]
SPEP .... Society for Phenomenology and Existential Philosophy   (EA)
SPEPD ...... Space Power and Electric Propulsion Division [*Formerly, Nuclear Systems and Space Power Division*] [*NASA*]
SPEPOS .... Society of Petroleum Engineers Production Operations Symposium and Exhibition   (ITD)
SPEPS .... Specialist, Motion Picture Service - Booker [*Navy rating*]
SPEQ .... Moquegua [*Peru*] [*ICAO location identifier*]   (ICLI)
Sp Eq .... Spears' South Carolina Equity Reports [*A publication*]   (DLA)
SPEQ .... Special Equipment   (AAG)
SPER .... Sperti Drug Products, Inc. [*NASDAQ symbol*]   (NQ)
SPERA ...... Sperimentale [*A publication*]
Sper Arch Biol Norm Patol ... Sperimentale. Archivio di Biologia Normale e Patologica [*A publication*]
SPERDVAC ... Society to Preserve and Encourage Radio Drama, Variety, and Comedy   (EA)
SPERE6 ...... Sbornik Provozne Ekonomicke Fakulty v Ceskych Budejovich. Zootechnicka Rada [*A publication*]
SPE Reg Tech Conf Tech Pap ... SPE [*Society of Plastics Engineers*] Regional Technical Conference. Technical Papers [*A publication*]
SPE Repr Ser ... Society of Petroleum Engineers. American Institute of Mining, Metallurgical, and Petroleum Engineers. Reprint Series [*United States*] [*A publication*]
Spe Rep Ser Ohio Agr Exp Sta ... Special Report Series. Ohio Agricultural Experiment Station [*A publication*]

Sperimentale Arch Biol Norm e Patol ... Sperimentale. Archivio di Biologia Normale e Patologica [*A publication*]
Sperimentale Sez Chim Biol ... Sperimentale. Sezione di Chimica Biologica [*A publication*]
SPERM ..... Secret Paper Reconstitution Mechanism [*Device to reclaim documents that have been inadvertently shredded*]
SPERMFLOW ... Society for the Preservation and Enhancement of the Recognition of Millard Fillmore, Last of the Whigs   (EA)
Sperry Technol ... Sperry Technology [*A publication*]
SPERT ...... Schedule Performance Evaluation and Review Technique
SPERT ...... Short Pulse Experimental RADAR Techniques   (MCD)
SPERT ...... Simplified Program Evaluation and Review Technique [*Trademark*]
SPERT ...... Special Power Excursion Reactor Test [*US reactor facilities*]
SPERTTT ... Society for Promotion of Educational Reform through Teacher Training [*British*]
SPERW ..... Specialist, Recreation and Welfare Assistant [*Navy rating*]
SPES .... Servico de Propaganda e Educacao Sanitaria [*Brazil*]
SPES .... Stored Program Element System [*Data processing*]   (IEEE)
SPE Soc Pet Eng AIME Publ ... SPE. Society of Petroleum Engineers of AIME [*American Institute of Mining, Metallurgical, and Petroleum Engineers*] Publications [*A publication*]
SPESS .... Stored Program Electronic Switching System [*Telecommunications*]   (TEL)
SPET .... Single Photon Emission Tomography
SPET .... Solid-Propellant Electric Thruster [*Aerospace*]
SPET .... Super Power Electron Tube
SPETE ...... Special Purpose Electronic Test Equipment [*Military*]   (CAAL)
SPETERL ... Ship Portable Electrical/Electronic Test Equipment Requirement List [*Navy*]   (CAAL)
SPetr .... Studi Petrarcheschi [*A publication*]
Spets Stali Splavy ... Spetsial'nye Stali Splavy [*USSR*] [*A publication*]
Spettatore Int ... Spettatore Internazionale [*A publication*]
Spettatore M ... Spettatore Musicale [*A publication*]
SPEX .... Small and Specialists Publishers Exhibition
SPEX .... Sozialwissenschaftliche Experten und Gutachter [*Social Science Experts*] [*NOMOS Datapool*] [*Database*]   (IID)
SPEX .... Special Exercise [*Navy*]   (NVT)
SPEX .... Spex Group, Inc. [*NASDAQ symbol*]   (NQ)
SPEZ .... Puerto Bermudez [*Peru*] [*ICAO location identifier*]   (ICLI)
SPF .... St. Paul-En-Foret [*France*] [*Seismograph station code, US Geological Survey*]   (SEIS)
SPF .... St. Photios Foundation   (EA)
SPF .... Science Policy Foundation [*Later, ISPF*] [*British*]
SPF .... Scottish Pharmaceutical Federation [*British*]
SPF .... Service Publication Form   (AAG)
SPF .... SIDPERS [*Standard Installation/Division Personnel System*] Personnel File [*Military*]   (AABC)
SPF .... Single Point Failure   (NASA)
SPF .... Single Project Funding   (MCD)
SPF .... Site Population Factor [*Nuclear energy*]   (NRCH)
SPF .... Skin Protection Factor [*Medicine*]
SPF .... Society for the Propagation of the Faith   (EA)
SPF .... Software Production Facility [*NASA*]   (NASA)
SPF .... Soy Protein Flour [*Food technology*]
SPF .... Space Power Facility
SPF .... Space Science Fiction Magazine [*A publication*]
SPF .... Spacelab Processing Facility [*NASA*]   (NASA)
SPF .... Spearfish, SD [*Location identifier*] [*FAA*]   (FAAL)
SPF .... Special Purpose Force   (MCD)
SPF .... Specialist, Firefighter [*Navy rating*]
SPF .... Specific-Pathogen Free [*Medicine*]
SPF .... Spectrophotofluorometer
SPF .... Spinning Form   (MCD)
Spf .... Sprachforum [*A publication*]
SPF .... Springfield Resources [*Vancouver Stock Exchange symbol*]
SPF .... Standard-Pacific Corp. [*NYSE symbol*]   (SPSG)
SPF .... Standard Pesticide File [*Derwent Publications Ltd.*] [*Database*]
SPF .... Standard Project Flood [*Nuclear energy*]   (NRCH)
SPF .... Strategic Protection Force
SPF .... Stressed Panel Fasteners
SPF .... Structured Programming Facility [*Data processing*]
SPF .... Subscriber Plant Factor [*Telecommunications*]
SPF .... Sun-Protection Factor [*Cosmetics industry*]
SPF .... Surrogate Parent Foundation   (EA)
SPF .... Survival Probability Function
SPF .... Synthetic Phenolic Foam
SPF .... System Performance Factor [*Telecommunications*]   (TEL)
SPF .... System Productivity Facility [*Data processing*]
SPFA .... Bulletin. Societe des Professeurs Francais en Amerique [*A publication*]
SPFA .... Single-Point Failure Analysis   (KSC)
SPFA .... Societe des Professeurs Francais et Francophones en Amerique   (EA)
SPFA .... Steel Plate Fabricators Association   (EA)
SPFB .... Sbornik Pedagogicke Fakulty v Brne [*A publication*]
SPFB .... Sbornik Praci Filosoficke Fakulty Brnenske University [*A publication*]
SPFC .... Site Peculiar Facility Change   (AAG)
SPFC .... Society for the Parents of Fugitive Children [*Fictional organization in film "Taking Off"*]

SPFC .... Solid Polymer Fuel Cell [*Energy source*]
SPF/DB .... Superplastic Forming/Diffusion Bonding [*Materials science*]
Spfdr .... Springfielder [*A publication*]
SpFest .... Spanish Festival [*Record label*]
SPFFA .... South Pacific Forum Fisheries Agency [*Honiara, Solomon Islands*]   (EAIO)
SPFFBU .... Sbornik Praci Filosoficke Fakulty Brnenske University [*A publication*]
SPFFC ...... Southern Ports Foreign Freight Committee
SP-FGS ..... Shuttle Projects - Flight and Ground Systems Office [*Kennedy Space Center*] [*NASA*]   (NASA)
SPFL .... Southern Philippines Federation of Labor
SPFLA ...... Spaceflight [*A publication*]
SPFM .... Society for the Preservation of Film Music   (EA)
SPFM .... Society of Priests for a Free Ministry   (EA)
SPFM .... Spinning Form [*Tool*]   (AAG)
SPFMV ...... Sweet Potato Feather Mottle Virus
SPFO .... Sbornik Pedagogicke Fakulty (Ostrava) [*A publication*]
SPFOL ...... Sbornik Pedagogicke Fakulty (Olomouci) [*A publication*]
SPFP .... Single Pass Fit Program   (MCD)
SPFP .... Single-Point Failure Potential   (KSC)
SPFP .... Sudanese People's Federal Party [*Political party*] [*Sudan*]   (MENA)
SPFPAD .... Spacecraft Performance and Flight Path Analysis Directorate [*NASA*]
SPFS .... Soldier Physical Fitness School [*Army*]   (INF)
SPFT .... Single-Pedestal Flat-Top [*Desk*]
SPFW .... Single-Phase Full Wave
SPFX .... Special Effects [*Filmmaking*]
SPG .... Saint Paul Guild   (EA)
SPG .... St. Petersburg, FL [*Location identifier*] [*FAA*]   (FAAL)
SPG .... Salicyl Phenolic Glucuronide [*Organic chemistry*]
SPG .... Saxifrage Publications Group   (EA)
SPG .... Scan Pattern Generator
SPG .... Screen Producers Guild [*Later, PGA*]   (EA)
SPG .... Seed Pea Group [*Defunct*]   (EA)
SPG .... Self-Propelled Gun [*British military*]   (DMA)
SPG .... Shift Pattern Generator [*Automotive engineering*]
SPG .... Short Pulse Generator
SPG .... Signal Point Ground   (NASA)
SPG .... Silver Spring Mining [*Vancouver Stock Exchange symbol*]
SPG .... Simple Phrase Grammar
SPG .... Single-Point Ground   (MCD)
SPG .... Sinusoidal Pressure Generator
SPG .... Society for the Propagation of the Gospel [*Later, USPG*] [*British*]
SPG .... Sort Program Generator [*Data processing*]   (BUR)
SPG .... Source Power Gain
SPG .... Special Patrol Group [*of the London Metropolitan Police, providing protection for public figures*]
SPG .... Special Performance Group [*In automobile name SAAB 900 Turbo SPG*]
SPG .... Special Project Group [*DoD*]
SPG .... Specialist, Gunnery [*Navy rating*]
SPG .... Specific Gravity [*Also, SP, SPGR*]
SPG .... Spiroglycol [*Organic chemistry*]
Spg .... Sponge [*Quality of the bottom*] [*Nautical charts*]
SPG .... Spooling   (MSA)
SPG .... Sprague Technologies [*NYSE symbol*]   (SPSG)
SPG .... Spring   (AAG)
SPG .... Stereophotogrammetry [*Medicine*]
SPG .... Study Planning Guide   (MCD)
SPG .... Sucrose, Phosphate, Glutamate [*A culture medium*]
SPG .... System Phasing Group   (MCD)
SPGA .... Southeastern Pecan Growers Association
SPGA .... Southwestern Peanut Growers Association   (EA)
SPGB .... Socialist Party of Great Britain   (PPW)
SPGCA ...... Survey of Progress in Chemistry [*A publication*]
SPGCPS .... Senior Policy Group for Canadian Production Sharing
SPGD .... Self-Powered Gamma Detector [*Nuclear energy*]   (NRCH)
SPGFP .... Society for the Propagation of the Gospel in Foreign Parts [*British*]   (DAS)
SPGG .... Solid-Propellant Gas Generator   (AAG)
SPGH .... Society for the Preservation of the Greek Heritage   (EA)
SPGJ .... Society for the Propagation of the Gospel among the Jews [*British*]
SPGKA ...... Senpatsu Gijutsu Kenkyujo Hokoku [*A publication*]
SPGL .... Spiegel, Inc. [*NASDAQ symbol*]   (NQ)
SPGL .... Studien zur Poetik und Geschichte der Literatur [*A publication*]
Sp Glos ...... Spelman's Glossarium Archaiologicum [*A publication*]   (DLA)
SPGM .... Specialist, Gunnery, Aviation Free Gunnery Instructor [*Navy rating*]
SPGM .... Tingo Maria [*Peru*] [*ICAO location identifier*]   (ICLI)
SPGN .... Specialist, Gunnery, Antiaircraft Gunnery Instructor [*Navy rating*]
SPGN .... Sympathetic Post-Ganglionic Neurone [*Neurology*]
SPGPM ...... Shots per Gun per Minute [*Military*]   (NVT)
SPGR .... Specific Gravity [*Also, SG, SPG*]
SPGS .... Lagunas [*Peru*] [*ICAO location identifier*]   (ICLI)
SPGS .... Spare Guidance System
SPGS .... Springs   (MCD)

SPGT........	Puerto Victoria [*Peru*] [*ICAO location identifier*] (ICLI)
SPGT........	Springfield Terminal Railway Co. [*Later, ST*] [*AAR code*]
SPGU........	Bagua [*Peru*] [*ICAO location identifier*] (ICLI)
SPH	San Pedro Hill [*California*] [*Seismograph station code, US Geological Survey*] [*Closed*] (SEIS)
SPH	Scans per Hour [*Photocopying, Microfilming*]
SPH	Self-Propelled Howitzer (MCD)
SPH	Severely and Profoundly Handicapped
SPH	Smoothed-Particle Hydrodynamics [*Statistical mechanics*]
SPH	Social Process in Hawaii [*A publication*]
SPH	Society of Public Health (EAIO)
SPH	Soy Protein Hydrolyzate
SPH	Space Heater (KSC)
SPH	Special Psychiatric Hospital [*USSR*]
SPH	Spherical (ROG)
SPH	Spherical Lens [*Ophthalmology*]
Sph............	Sphingosine [*Also, SM*] [*Biochemistry*]
SPH	Springhill, LA [*Location identifier*] [*FAA*] (FAAL)
SPH	Stable Platform Housing
SPH	Statement of Personal History [*Military*]
SPh	Studiea Phonetica [*A publication*]
S in Ph	Studies in Philology [*A publication*]
SPh	Studies in Philology [*A publication*]
SPHA	Chincha [*Peru*] [*ICAO location identifier*] (ICLI)
SPHC........	Chala [*Peru*] [*ICAO location identifier*] (ICLI)
SPHC........	Southern Pacific Hotel Corp. [*Australia*]
SPHCA......	Soviet Physics. Crystallography [*English Translation*] [*A publication*]
SPHCT......	Simplified Perturbed Hard Chain Theory [*Equation of state*]
SPHD........	Special Pay for Hostile Duty [*Military*] (AFM)
SP/Hd........	Spool Piece Head [*Nuclear energy*] (NRCH)
SPHDA	Soviet Physics. Doklady [*English Translation*] [*A publication*]
SPHE........	Society of Packaging and Handling Engineers [*Later, IoPP*] (EA)
SPHER......	Small-Particle Heat-Exchange Receiver [*Solar energy technology*]
SPHER......	Spherical
SPHERE ...	Scientific Parameters for Health and the Environment, Retrieval and Estimation [*Environmental Protection Agency*] [*Washington, DC*] [*Database*]
SPHF........	Spin-Polarized Hartree-Fock [*Atomic wave-function*]
SPHF........	Spontaneous Hole Filling [*Spectrometry*]
SPHI..........	Chiclayo/Cap. Jose Abelardo Quinones Gonzalez [*Peru*] [*ICAO location identifier*] (ICLI)
SPHINX....	Space Plasma High-Voltage Interaction Experiment [*Spacecraft*] [*NASA*]
SPHINX....	Survival Probability Hazard in a Nuclear Exchange
SPHJA	Soviet Physics. JETP [*Journal of Experimental and Theoretical Physics of the Academy of Sciences of the USSR*] [*English Translation*] [*A publication*]
SPHL........	Self-Propelled Hyperbaric Lifeboat (DS)
SP-HL........	Sun Present - Horizon Lost
SPHN	Siphon (MSA)
SPhNC.......	Studies in Philology. University of North Carolina [*A publication*]
SPHO	Ayacucho/Coronel FAP Alfredo Mendivil Duarte [*Peru*] [*ICAO location identifier*] (ICLI)
SPhon	Studia Phonologica [*Kyoto*] [*A publication*]
SPhP..........	Symbolae Philologorum Posnaniensium [*A publication*]
SPHQ	Shore Patrol Headquarters
SPHQ	Swedish Pioneer Historical Quarterly [*A publication*]
SPHS........	Society for the Promotion of Hellenic Studies (EA)
SPHS........	Swedish Pioneer Historical Society (EA)
SP/HT	Specific Heat
SPHT........	Super Pressure - High Temperature
SPHU	Huancayo [*Peru*] [*ICAO location identifier*] (ICLI)
SPHV	Huanuco Viejo [*Peru*] [*ICAO location identifier*] (ICLI)
SPHW	Single-Phase Half Wave
SPHY........	Andahuaylas [*Peru*] [*ICAO location identifier*] (ICLI)
SPHZ........	Anta/Comdte. FAP German Arias Grazziani [*Peru*] [*ICAO location identifier*] (ICLI)
SPI............	Die Sprache der Palmyrenischen Inschriften [*Leipzig*] [*A publication*] (BJA)
SPI............	Illinois State Library, Springfield, IL [*OCLC symbol*] (OCLC)
SPI............	St. Paul Island [*Alaska*] [*Seismograph station code, US Geological Survey*] [*Closed*] (SEIS)
SPI............	Scanning Pulse Immobilization
SPI............	Schedule Performance Index (MCD)
SPI............	School Psychology International [*A publication*]
SPI............	Scottish Provident Institution [*Commercial firm*]
SPI............	Secretariats Professionnels Internationaux
SPI............	Self-Paced Instruction (IEEE)
SPI............	Self-Perception Inventory [*Personality development test*] [*Psychology*]
SPI............	Senior Patrol Inspection [*Immigration and Naturalization Service*]
SPI............	Septum-Equipped Programmable Injector [*Gas chromatography*]
SPI............	Sequence of Pulse Intervals
SPI............	Serum Precipitable Iodine [*Serology*]
SPI............	Service Pedalogique Interafricain

SPI............	Service Publication Instruction (AAG)
SPI............	Severely and Profoundly Impaired
SPI............	Share Price Index (ADA)
SPI............	Shared Peripheral Interface
SPI............	Ship's Plan Index
SPI............	Signal Presence Indicator (CAAL)
SPI............	Single Point Injection [*Automotive engineering*]
SPI............	Single Processor Interface
SPI............	Single Program Initiation [*Data processing*]
SPI............	Site Peculiar Interference (AAG)
SPI............	Site Population Index [*Nuclear energy*] (NRCH)
SPI............	Smoke Point Improvement [*Petroleum refining*]
SPI............	Smoking Policy Institute (EA)
SPI............	Societe pour l'Informatique [*Company for Informatics*] [*Information service or system*] [*Defunct*] (IID)
SPI............	Societe de Placements Internationaux [*French*]
SPI............	Society of Photographic Illustrators (EA)
SPI............	Society of the Plastics Industry (EA)
SPI............	Society of Professional Investigators (EA)
SPI............	Solid Propellant Information
SPI............	South Pacific Island Airways, Inc. [*Pago Pago, American Samoa*] [*FAA designator*] (FAAC)
SPI............	Southern Pacific Insurance [*Australia*]
SPI............	Soy Protein Isolate [*Food technology*]
SPI............	Spanish Paprika Institute (EA)
SPI............	Special Position Identification
SPI............	Specialist, Punched Card Accounting Machine Operator [*Navy rating*]
SPI............	Specific Productivity Index (IEEE)
SPI............	SPI Pharmaceuticals, Inc. [*AMEX symbol*] (SPSG)
Spi............	Spicules [*Quality of the bottom*] [*Nautical charts*]
Spi............	[*Jacobus*] Spiegelius [*Flourished, 1483-1547*] [*Authority cited in pre-1607 legal work*] (DSA)
SPI............	Sports Philatelists International (EA)
SPI............	Springfield [*Illinois*] [*Airport symbol*] (OAG)
SPI............	Standard Performance Indicator [*Army*]
SPI............	Standard Practice Instructions (MCD)
SPI............	Standard Protective Item
SPI............	Statement of Policy or Interpretation [*Food and Drug Administration*]
SPI............	Station Program Identification [*Telecommunications*] (TEL)
SPI............	Storage Protein Isolate [*Food industry*]
SPI............	Strategic Planning Institute [*Cambridge, MA*]
SPI............	Supervisory Practices Inventory [*Test*]
SPI............	Surface Position Indicator (NASA)
SPI............	Synergy Power Institute (EA)
SPI............	Synthetic Phase Isolation [*Telemetry*]
SPI............	System Performance Indicator
SPIA	Ica [*Peru*] [*ICAO location identifier*] (ICLI)
SPIA	Solid Propellant Information Agency [*Air Force*]
SPIAM	Sodium Purity In-Line Analytical Module [*Nuclear energy*] (NRCH)
SPIAP........	Shuttle/Payload Integration Activities Plan (NASA)
SPIB	Scripta Pontificii Instituti Biblici [*A publication*] (BJA)
SPIB	Shetland Pony Identification Bureau
SPIB	Social and Prevocational Information Battery
SPIB	Society of Power Industry Biologists (EA)
SPIB	Southern Pine Inspection Bureau (EA)
SPIBB........	Sbornik Pedagogickeho Institutu v Banskej Bystrici [*A publication*]
SPIBS........	Satellite Positive-Ion-Beam System [*Air Force*] (MCD)
SPIC	Ship Position Interpolation Computer
SPIC	Sisters of Providence and of the Immaculate Conception [*Roman Catholic religious order*]
SPIC	Society of the Plastics Industry of Canada
SPIC	Standard and Poor's Index - Composite [*Stock market*]
SPIC	Students for Promotion of Identity on Campus [*New York group promoting ethnic pride among Latin American students*]
SPIC	Summary Punch IBM [*International Business Machines*] Collector
SPICE........	Sales-Point Information Computing Equipment [*Merchandising*]
SPICE........	Solar Particle Intensity Composition Experiment [*NASA*]
SPICE........	Space Power Internal Combustion Engine (MCD)
SPICE........	Spacelab Payload Integration and Coordination in Europe [*NASA*] (NASA)
SPICE........	Special Programs Increasing Counseling Effectiveness [*Pennsylvania State Department of Public Instruction*]
SPICE........	Stanford Program on International and Cross Cultural Education [*Stanford University*] [*Research center*] (RCD)
SPICI........	SPI [*Society of the Plastics Industry*] Composites Institute (EA)
SPID	Standard Performance Indicator Dictionary [*Army*]
SPID	Submersible Portable Inflatable Dwelling
SPID	Sum of Pain Intensity Differences
SPIDAC	Specimen Input to Digital Automatic Computer
SPIDER.....	Smokeless Propellant in Demonstration Experimental Rocket (KSC)
SPIDER.....	Sonic Pulse-Echo Instrument Designed for Extreme Resolution (IEEE)

SPIDER..... Systematic Planning for the Integration of Defense Engineering and Research [*Program*]
SPIDF........ Support Planning Identification File [*NASA*]   (MCD)
SPIDO....... Shuttle Payload Integration and Development Program Office [*NASA*]
SPIDPO .... Shuttle Payload Integration and Development Program Office [*Johnson Space Center*]   (NASA)
SPIDR .... Society of Professionals in Dispute Resolution   (EA)
SPIE .... Scavenging-Precipitation-Ion Exchange   (IEEE)
SPIE .... Secretariat Professionnel International de l'Enseignement [*International Federation of Free Teachers' Unions - IFFTU*] [*Amsterdam, Netherlands*]   (EAIO)
SPIE .... Self-Programmed Individualized Education   (IEEE)
SPIE .... Ships Precise Identification Emitter   (MCD)
SPIE .... Simulated Problem Input Evaluation
SPIE .... Society of Political Item Enthusiasts   (EA)
SPIE .... Special Patrol Insertion/Extraction   (MCD)
SPIE .... SPIE - the International Society for Optical Engineering   (EA)
Spie .... [*Jacobus*] Spiegelius [*Flourished, 1483-1547*] [*Authority cited in pre-1607 legal work*]   (DSA)
SPIEC....... Proceedings. Society of Photo-Optical Instrumentation Engineers [*A publication*]
Spieg .... [*Jacobus*] Spiegelius [*Flourished, 1483-1547*] [*Authority cited in pre-1607 legal work*]   (DSA)
Spiegel Hist ... Spiegel Historical [*A publication*]
Spiegel Let ... Spiegel der Letteren [*A publication*]
SPIE J .... SPIE [*Society of Photo-Optical Instrumentation Engineers*] Journal [*Later, Optical Engineering*] [*A publication*]
SPIE Journal ... Society of Photographic Instrumentation Engineers. Journal [*A publication*]
SPIE Semin Proc ... SPIE [*Society of Photo-Optical Instrumentation Engineers*] Seminar Proceedings [*A publication*]
SPIE Vol.... SPIE [*Society of Photo-Optical Instrumentation Engineers*] Volume [*United States*] [*A publication*]
SPIF.......... School Practices Information File [*BRS Information Technologies*] [*Information service or system*] [*Defunct*]
SPIF.......... Sequential Prime Implicant Form
SPIF.......... Standard Payload Interface Facility [*NASA*]   (MCD)
SPIFC....... Southern Pacific International Fan Club   (EA)
SPIFDA..... South Pacific Islands Fisheries Development Agency [*Noumea, New Caledonia*]   (EAIO)
SPIFDN..... International Commission for the Northwest Atlantic Fisheries. Selected Papers [*A publication*]
SPIG .... Sbornik Praci Pedagogickeho Institutu v Gottwaldove [*A publication*]
SPII .... Shuttle Program Implementation Instruction [*NASA*]   (NASA)
SPII .... Standard and Poor's Index - Industrials [*Stock market*]
SPIIN .... Supplemental Procurement Instrument Identification Number [*DoD*]
Spike M & S ... Spike on Master and Servant [*3rd ed.*] [*1872*] [*A publication*]   (DLA)
SPIL.......... Quincemil [*Peru*] [*ICAO location identifier*]   (ICLI)
SPIL.......... Self-Rating Psychiatric Inventory List [*Personality development test*] [*Psychology*]
SPIL.......... Sensitive Projects and Installation List   (MCD)
SPIL.......... Ship's Parts Integration List
SPIL.......... SPI-Suspension & Parts Industries Limited [*New York, NY*] [*NASDAQ symbol*]   (NQ)
SPILA........ Sports Illustrated [*A publication*]
SPILB........ Spiegel [*A publication*]
SP-ILS....... Shuttle Projects - Integrated Logistics Support [*Kennedy Space Center*] [*NASA*]   (NASA)
SPIM .... Lima-Callao/Internacional Jorge Chavez [*Peru*] [*ICAO location identifier*]   (ICLI)
SPIM .... Service de Previsions Ionospherique Militaire
SPIMD...... Siauliu Pedagoginio Instituto Mokslo Darbai [*A publication*]
SPIMS....... Shuttle Program Information Management System [*NASA*]
SPIN......... Sbornik Pedagogickeho Institutu v Nitre [*A publication*]
SPIN......... School Practices Information Network [*Bibliographic Retrieval Services*] [*Information service or system*]   (IID)
SPIN......... Science Procurement Information Network [*Canada*]
SPIN......... Searchable Physics Information Notices [*American Institute of Physics*] [*New York, NY*] [*Bibliographic database*]
SPIN......... Service Parts Information Notice
SPIN......... Space Inspection
SPIN......... Special Inquiry [*FBI term*]
SPIN......... Spinster   (ADA)
SPIN......... Standard & Poor's 500 Index Subordinated Notes
SPIN......... Standard Procedure Instructions   (KSC)
SPIN......... Strategies and Policies for Informatics [*Intergovernmental Bureau for Informatics*]
SPIN......... Submarine Program Information Notebook
SPIN......... Superconductive Precision Inertial Navigation
SPINAL..... Stimulator, Planetary Instrument Alignment
SPINDEX ... Selective Permutation Indexing [*Library of Congress*]
SPINDEX ... Subject Profile Index [*Computer-based*]
SPINE .... Simulated Program for Investigation of Nuclear Effects
SPINE .... Space Informatics Network Experiment [*European Space Agency*]
SPINES..... Science and Technology Policies Information Exchange System [*UNESCO*] [*Bibliographic database*]   (IID)

Spinks........ Spinks' English Ecclesiastical and Admiralty Reports [*164 English Reprint*] [*A publication*]   (DLA)
Spinks Eccl & Adm (Eng) ... Spinks' English Ecclesiastical and Admiralty Reports [*164 English Reprint*] [*A publication*]   (DLA)
Spinks PC ... Spinks' English Admiralty Prize Cases [*A publication*]   (DLA)
Spinks Prize Cas ... Spinks' English Admiralty Prize Cases [*164 English Reprint*] [*A publication*]   (DLA)
Spinks Prize Cas (Eng) ... Spinks' English Admiralty Prize Cases [*164 English Reprint*] [*A publication*]   (DLA)
Spinner Weber Textilveredl ... Spinner, Weber, Textilveredlung [*A publication*]
SPINSTRE ... Spencer Information Storage and Retrieval System   (DIT)
SPINT .... Special Intelligence   (MCD)
SPINTAC ... Special Interest Aircraft   (NVT)
SPINTCOM ... Special Intelligence Communications [*Later, DIN/DSSCS*]
SPINTCOMM ... Special Intelligence Communications [*Later, DIN/DSSCS*]   (CET)
SPINVESWG ... Special Investigation Wing   (MUGU)
SPIO .... Sbornik Praci Pedagogickeho Institutu v Ostrave [*A publication*]
SPIO .... Systems Planning and Integration Office [*NASA*]
SPIOL....... Sbornik Pedagogickeho Institutu v Olomouci [*A publication*]
SPIP.......... Satipo [*Peru*] [*ICAO location identifier*]   (ICLI)
SPIP.......... Sbornik Pedagogickeho Institutu v Plzni [*A publication*]
SPIP.......... Special Position Identification Pulse   (CET)
SPIPA........ Scientific Papers. Institute of Physical and Chemical Research [*A publication*]
SPIPE....... Spin-Polarized Inverse Photoemission [*Physics*]
S'PIPE....... Standpipe
SPIPL....... Sbornik Pedagogickeho Institutu v Plzni [*A publication*]
SPIR .... Patria [*Peru*] [*ICAO location identifier*]   (ICLI)
SPIR .... Search Program for Infrared Spectra [*Canada Institute for Scientific and Technical Information*] [*Information service or system*]
SPIR .... Spiral
SPIR .... Spire Corp. [*NASDAQ symbol*]   (NQ)
SPIR .... Spiritoso [*With Animation*] [*Music*]
SPIR .... Spiritus [*Spirit*] [*Pharmacy*]
SPIR .... Standard and Poor's Index - Rails [*Stock market*]
SPIR .... Standardized Proportional Incidence Ratio [*Epidemiology*]
SPIR .... Student Project for International Responsibility
SPIRAL..... Sperry Inertial RADAR Altimeter
SPIRBM.... Solid-Propellant Intermediate Range Ballistic Missile   (AAG)
SPIRE....... Spatial Inertial Reference Equipment
SPIREP ..... Spot Intelligence Report [*Air Force*]
SPIRES ..... Standard Personnel Information Retrieval System [*Military*]
SPIRES ..... Stanford Public Information Retrieval System [*Stanford University Libraries*] [*Stanford, CA*] [*Bibliographic database management system*] [*Information service or system*]
SPIRIT ...... Sales Processing Interactive Real-Time Inventory Technique [*NCR Corp. trademark*]
SPIRIT ...... Sensible Policy in Information Resources and Information Technology [*Defunct*]   (EA)
Spirit......... Spirit That Moves Us [*A publication*]
SPIRIT ..... Spiritoso [*With Animation*] [*Music*]
SPIRIT ..... Spiritus [*Spirit*] [*Latin*]   (ROG)
Spirit Mis .. Spirit of Missions [*A publication*]
Spirit Pilg .. Spirit of the Pilgrims [*A publication*]
Spirit Verkauf ... Spirituosen-Verkauf [*A publication*]
Spir Life..... Spiritual Life [*A publication*]
SPIRO .... Students Protesting Illegal Real Estate Operators [*Student legal action organization*]   (EA)
SPIRT........ Short Path Infrared Tester   (KSC)
SPIRT....... Stock Point Interrogation/Requirements Technique
Spir Tod .... Spirituality Today [*A publication*]
Spirto Vodochn Promst ... Spirto-Vodochnaya Promyshlennost [*A publication*]
Spirt Prom-St' ... Spirtovaya Promyshlennost' [*A publication*]
SPIS.......... Pias [*Peru*] [*ICAO location identifier*]   (ICLI)
SPIS.......... Senate Permanent Investigating Subcommittee   (AAG)
SPIS.......... Space Philatelists International Society   (EA)
Spis Bulg Akad Nauk ... Spisanie na Bulgarskata Akademiya na Naukite [*Bulgaria*] [*A publication*]
Spis Bulg Geol Druzh ... Spisanie na Bulgarskoto Geologichesko Druzhestvo [*A publication*]
Spis Bulg Geol Druzhu ... Spisania na Bulgarsoto Geologichesko Druzhestvo [*A publication*]
SPISE........ Special Projects in Science Education
Spis Nauchno-Issled Inst Minist Zemed Gorite ... Spisanie na Nauchno-Issledovatelskite Instituti pri Ministerstvata na Zemedelie i Gorite [*A publication*]
Spis Nauchnoizsled Inst Minist Zemed (Bulg) ... Spisanie na Nauchnoizsledovatelskite Instituti pri Ministerstvoto na Zemedelieto (Bulgaria) [*A publication*]
SPISS .... Spissus [*Dried*] [*Pharmacy*]
SPI Struct Foam Conf Proc ... SPI [*Society of the Plastics Industry*] Structural Foam Conference. Proceedings [*A publication*]
Spisy Lek Fak Masaryk Univ (Brno) ... Spisy Lekarske Fakulty Mesarykovy University (Brno) [*A publication*]

Spisy Pedagog Fak Ostrave ... Spisy Pedagogicke Fakulty v Ostrave [*A publication*]
Spisy Prir Fak Univ Brne ... Spisy Prirodovedecke Fakulty Universita v Brne [*Czechoslovakia*] [*A publication*]
Spisy Prirodoved Fak Univ JE Purkyne Brne ... Spisy Prirodovedecke Fakulty University J. E. Purkyne v Brne [*A publication*]
Spisy Priroved Fak Univ J E Purkyne Brne ... Spisy Prirodovedecke Fakulty University J. E. Purkyne v Brne [*A publication*]
Spisy Vydavane Prirodoved Fak Massarykovy Univ ... Spisy Vydavane Prirodovedeckou Fakultou Massarykovy University [*A publication*]
SPIT .... Paita [*Peru*] [*ICAO location identifier*]   (ICLI)
SPIT .... Secondary Power Integration Test   (MCD)
SPIT .... Selective Printing of Items from Tape [*Data processing*]
SPITS .... Scan Platform Inertial Thermal Simulator
SPIU .... Sbornik Praci Pedagogickeho Institutu, Usti Nad Labem [*A publication*]
SPIU .... Ship Position Interpolation Unit
SPIU .... Standard and Poor's Index - Utilities [*Stock market*]
SPIW .... ESCAP [*Economic and Social Commssion for the Asia and Pacific*] Division for Shipping, Ports, and Inland Waterways   (EAIO)
SPIW .... Special-Purpose Individual Weapon [*A rifle that fires flechettes or darts*] [*Pronounced "spew"*]
Spixiana Z Zool ... Spixiana. Zeitschrift fuer Zoologie [*A publication*]
SPIY .... Yauri [*Peru*] [*ICAO location identifier*]   (ICLI)
SPIZ .... Uchiza [*Peru*] [*ICAO location identifier*]   (ICLI)
SPJ .... Austria [*Republic of*] Stock Index Growth Notes [*NYSE symbol*]   (SPSG)
SPJ .... Senior Puisne Judge [*British*]   (ILCA)
SPJ .... Socialist Party of Japan [*Nikon Shakaito*] [*Political party*]   (PPW)
SPJ .... Socijalisticka Partija Jugoslavije [*Socialist Party of Yugoslavia*] [*Political party*]   (PPE)
SPJ .... Sparta [*Greece*] [*Airport symbol*] [*Obsolete*]   (OAG)
SPJ .... Special Purpose Jammer [*Military*]   (CAAL)
SPJA .... Rioja [*Peru*] [*ICAO location identifier*]   (ICLI)
SPJB .... Cajabamba/Pampa Grande [*Peru*] [*ICAO location identifier*]   (ICLI)
SPJC .... St. Petersburg Junior College [*Clearwater, FL*]
SP-JFI .... School Principal Job Functions Inventory [*Test*]
SPJI .... Juanjui [*Peru*] [*ICAO location identifier*]   (ICLI)
SPJJ .... Jauja [*Peru*] [*ICAO location identifier*]   (ICLI)
SPJL .... Juliaca [*Peru*] [*ICAO location identifier*]   (ICLI)
SPJN .... San Juan [*Peru*] [*ICAO location identifier*]   (ICLI)
SPJR .... Cajamarca/Mayor General FAP Armando Revoredo Iglesias [*Peru*] [*ICAO location identifier*]   (ICLI)
SPJ SDX ... Society of Professional Journalists, Sigma Delta Chi   (EA)
SPJSEY ..... South Pacific Journal of Natural Science [*A publication*]
SPJUA2 .... Sechenov Physiological Journal of the USSR [*English translation of Fiziologicheskii Zhurnal SSSR Imeni I. M. Sechenova*] [*A publication*]
SPK .... Reno, NV [*Location identifier*] [*FAA*]   (FAAL)
SPK .... Saporamean Kampuchea News Agency [*Cambodia*]
SPK .... Sapporo [*Japan*] [*Airport symbol*]   (OAG)
SPK .... Scotts Peak [*Tasmania*] [*Seismograph station code, US Geological Survey*]   (SEIS)
SPK .... Silver Tusk Mines [*Vancouver Stock Exchange symbol*]
SPK .... Socialist Party of Kurdistan [*Iraq*] [*Political party*]   (MENA)
SPK .... Spare Parts Kit
SPK .... Spark   (MSA)
spk .... Speckled [*Quality of the bottom*] [*Nautical charts*]
SPK .... Spike   (MSA)
SPK .... Spinnbarkheit [*With reference to cervical mucus*] [*Medicine*]
SPK .... Superficial Punctate Keratitis [*Ophthalmology*]
SPKL .... Sprinkle   (FAAC)
SPKP .... Suomen Perustuslaillinen Kansanpuolue [*Finnish Constitutional People's Party*] [*Political party*]   (PPW)
SPKR .... Speaker   (AAG)
SPKR .... Spinnaker Software Corp. [*NASDAQ symbol*]   (NQ)
SPKT .... Sprocket
SPKYB ...... Shih P'in Kung Yeh [*A publication*]
SPL .... Airspur Helicopters, Inc. [*Huntington Beach, CA*] [*FAA designator*]   (FAAC)
SPL .... Saskatoon Public Library [*UTLAS symbol*]
SPL .... Scott Paper Ltd. [*Toronto Stock Exchange symbol*] [*Vancouver Stock Exchange symbol*]
SPL .... Scratch Pad Line [*NASA*]   (MCD)
SPL .... Self-Propelled Launcher [*British military*]   (DMA)
SPL .... Separate Parts List   (MSA)
SPL .... Serialized Parts List [*NASA*]   (MCD)
SPL .... Service Priority List   (BUR)
SPL .... Signal Processing Language [*Data processing*]   (CSR)
SPL .... Signature and Propagation Laboratory [*Army*]   (RDA)
SPL .... Simple Phrase Language [*Data processing*]
SPL .... Simple Programming Language [*Data processing*]
SPL .... Simulation Programming Language [*Data processing*]
SPL .... Sine Prole Legitima [*Without Legitimate Issue*] [*Latin*]
SPL .... Single Pet Lover
SPL .... Single-Premium Life [*Insurance*]
SPL .... Single-Premium Whole Life [*Insurance*]

SPL .... Single Propellant Loading   (AFM)
SPL .... Skin Potential Level
SPL .... Sloane Physics Laboratory [*Yale*]   (MCD)
SPL .... Software Parts List [*Data processing*]   (TEL)
SPL .... Software Programming Language [*Data processing*]   (IEEE)
SPL .... Sound Power Level [*Acoustics*]
SPL .... Sound Pressure Level [*Acoustics*]
SPL .... Source Program Library
SPL .... Space Physics Laboratory [*Aerospace corporation*]
SPL .... Space Programming Language [*Data processing*]
SPL .... Space Programs Laboratory [*Fort Belvoir, VA*] [*United States Army Engineer Topographic Laboratories*]   (GRD)
SPL .... Spare Parts List
SPL .... Spartanburg County Public Library, Spartanburg, SC [*OCLC symbol*]   (OCLC)
SPL .... Special   (AAG)
SPL .... Special-Purpose Language [*Data processing*]
SPL .... Speed Phase Lock
SpL .... Spermatophore Length
SpL .... Spiegel der Letteren [*A publication*]
SPL .... Spiral   (MSA)
SPL .... Spiridon Lake [*Alaska*] [*Seismograph station code, US Geological Survey*]   (SEIS)
SPL .... Splice [*Telecommunications*]   (TEL)
SPL .... Splice Junction Mutation [*Genetics*]
SPL .... Sporulation per Lesion [*Plant pathology*]
SPL .... Spritsail [*Ship's rigging*]   (ROG)
SPL .... Standard Pulse LASER
SPL .... Standards Parts Listing   (MCD)
SPL .... Staphylococcal Phage Lysate [*Biochemistry*]
SPL .... Student Pilot's Licence   (AIA)
SPL .... Studie a Prace Linguisticke [*A publication*]
SPL .... Succinyl-Poly-L-Lysine [*Biochemical analysis*]
SPL .... Summary Parts List
SPL .... Sun Pumped LASER   (MCD)
SPL .... Superior Parietal Lobule [*Neuroanatomy*]
Spl .... Supplement   (BJA)
SPL .... Supplementary Flight Plan Message [*Aviation code*]
SPL .... Support Platoon Leader [*Military*]   (INF)
SPL .... Swiss Party of Labour
SPL .... System Program Loader
SPL .... System Programming Language [*Data processing*]   (NASA)
SPLA .... Louisiana [*Peru*] [*ICAO location identifier*]   (ICLI)
SPLA .... Special-Purpose Lead Azide   (MCD)
SPLA .... Sudan People's Liberation Army
SPLAASH ... Spacecraft Protective Landing Area for the Advancement of Science and Humanities [*Landing zone for flying saucers near Mt. Rainier, WA*]
SPLAN ...... Support Plan   (MCD)
SPLANCH ... Split-Level Ranch [*House*]
SPLASH .... Shipboard Platforms for Landing and Servicing Helicopters
SPLASH .... Special Program to List Amplitudes of Surges from Hurricanes
SPLAT .... Simplified Programming Language for Artists [*1978*] [*Data processing*]   (CSR)
SPLAT .... Student Potential Life Achievement Test [*Parody of Scholastic Aptitude Test preparation books*]
Sp Laws ..... Spirit of the Laws (Montesquieu) [*A publication*]   (DLA)
SPLC .... Ship Program Life Cycle [*Navy*]
SPLC .... Southern Poverty Law Center   (EA)
SPLC .... Spare Parts List for Codification
SPLC .... Splice
SPLC .... Standard Point Location Code [*American Trucking Association and Association of American Railroads*]
SPLC .... Student Press Law Center   (EA)
SPLD .... Celendin [*Peru*] [*ICAO location identifier*]   (ICLI)
SPLEB .... Spectroscopy Letters [*A publication*]
SPLEE2 ..... Studies in Plant Ecology [*A publication*]
SPLF .... [*The*] Sporting Life, Inc. [*Alexandria, VA*] [*NASDAQ symbol*]   (NQ)
SPLHC ...... Sgt. Pepper's Lonely Hearts Club   (EA)
SPLI .... Lima [*Peru*] [*ICAO location identifier*]   (ICLI)
SPLI .... Spermatophore Length Index
SPLI .... Substance P-Like Immunoreactivity
Sp Lib .... Special Libraries [*A publication*]
SPLICE ..... Stock Point Logistics Integrated Communications Environment Project [*Navy*]
SPLID .... SpeciaList [*A publication*]
SPLIT .... Space Program Language Implementation Tool   (KSC)
SPLIT .... Sundstrand Processing Language Internally Translated
SPLK .... Jones Spacelink Ltd. [*NASDAQ symbol*]   (NQ)
SPLK .... Studie Prazskeho Linguistickeho Krouzku [*A publication*]
SPLL .... Self-Propelled Launcher Loader   (MCD)
SPLL .... Standard Phase-Locked Loop
SPLLG .... Stable Production Low Leach Glass [*For nuclear wastes*]
SPLM .... Space Programming Language Machine
SPLN .... Rodriguez de Mendoz/San Nicolas [*Peru*] [*ICAO location identifier*]   (ICLI)
SPLN .... Spline [*Engineering*]
SPLNS ...... South Plains [*FAA*]   (FAAC)
SPLO .... Ilo [*Peru*] [*ICAO location identifier*]   (ICLI)
SPLP .... Las Palmas [*Peru*] [*ICAO location identifier*]   (ICLI)

SPLS.........	Staples, Inc. [*NASDAQ symbol*] (NQ)
SPLS.........	Zorrillos [*Peru*] [*ICAO location identifier*] (ICLI)
SPLSA.......	Space Life Sciences [*A publication*]
SPLT	Lobitos [*Peru*] [*ICAO location identifier*] (ICLI)
SPLT	Specialist, Link Trainer Instructor [*Navy rating*]
SPLTR.......	Splitter
SPLTRK....	Special Tracker [*Military*] (CAAL)
SPLV	Lago Verde [*Peru*] [*ICAO location identifier*] (ICLI)
SPLV	Stable Plurilamellar Vesicle [*Pharmacology*]
SPLX	Simplex [*Mathematics*]
SPLY	Spa Lady Corp. [*NASDAQ symbol*] (NQ)
SPLY	Supply (MSA)
SPM.........	St. Philips Marsh [*Bristol*] [*British depot code*]
SPM.........	St. Pierre and Miquelon [*ANSI three-letter standard code*] (CNC)
SPM.........	Salud Publica de Mexico [*A publication*]
SPM.........	Scanning Photoemission Microscope
SPM.........	Scanning Photon Microscope
SPM.........	Scratch Pad Memory [*Data processing*] (BUR)
SPM.........	Scripture Press Ministries (EA)
SPM.........	Sedimentary Phosphate Method
SPM.........	Self-Propelled Mount [*Military*]
SPM.........	Semipermeable Membrane
SPM.........	Senior Project Manager
SPM.........	Sequential Processing Machine (DIT)
SPM.........	Short Particular Metre [*Music*]
SPM.........	Shots per Minute [*Military*] (RDA)
SPM.........	Significant Probability Mapping
SPM.........	Sine Prole Mascula [*Without Male Issue*] [*Latin*]
SPM.........	Single-Point Management
SPM.........	Single-Point Mooring [*Oil platform*]
SPMV........	Single Program Manager [*Air Force*]
SPM.........	Six Point Mooring [*Oil platform*]
SPM.........	Smaller Profit Margin
SPM.........	Societas Patrum Misericordiae [*Fathers of Mercy*] [*Roman Catholic religious order*]
SPM.........	Society for Policy Modeling (EA)
SPM.........	Society of Pragmatic Mysticism (EA)
SPM.........	Society of Prospective Medicine (EA)
SPM.........	Software Programmer's Manual
SPM.........	Solar Polar Mission (MCD)
SPM.........	Solar Power Module
SPM.........	Solar Proton Monitor
SPM.........	Sound-Powered Microphone
SPM.........	Source Program Maintenance [*IBM Corp.*]
SPM.........	South Pacific Mail [*A publication*]
SPM.........	Special-Purpose Materials (MCD)
SPM.........	Specialist, Mail Clerk [*Navy rating*]
SPM.........	Spectrophosphorimeter
SPM.........	Spectrum Industrial Resources [*Vancouver Stock Exchange symbol*]
Sp M	Spicilegio Moderno [*A publication*]
SpM	Spiriformis Medialis Nucleus [*Brain anatomy*]
SPM.........	Split Phase Motor
SPM.........	Standard Payload Module (MCD)
SPM.........	Standard Practice Memo (MCD)
SPM.........	Standard Procedure Manual (AAG)
SPM.........	Standard Process Manual
SPM.........	Static Presentation Mode
SPM.........	Stationary Plasma Motor
SPM.........	Strokes per Minute
SPM.........	Subscriber's Private Meter [*Telecommunications*] (TEL)
SPM.........	Subsystem Project Manager [*NASA*] (NASA)
SPM.........	Sun Probe-Mars [*NASA*]
SPM.........	Superparamagnetic [*Fraction in rock*] [*Geophysics*]
SPM.........	Supervisory Management [*A publication*]
SPM.........	Support Program Management
SPM.........	Surface Plasmon Microscopy [*Physics*]
SPM.........	Suspended Particulate Matter
SPM.........	Symbol Processing Machine (IEEE)
SPM.........	Synaptic Plasma Membrane [*Neurophysiology*]
SPM.........	Synaptosomal Plasma Membrane [*Neurobiology*]
SPM.........	Synthetic Plasma Membrane [*Biochemistry*]
SPM.........	Systems Program Manager
SPMA.......	Rio Maranon [*Peru*] [*ICAO location identifier*] (ICLI)
SPMA.......	Shoe Pattern Manufacturers Association [*Inactive*] (EA)
SPMA.......	Society for Post-Medieval Archaeology [*British*]
SPMA.......	Soda Pulp Manufacturers Association [*Defunct*] (EA)
SPMA.......	Southwest Parks and Monuments Association (EA)
SPMA.......	Sump Pump Manufacturers Association [*Later, SSPMA*] (EA)
SPMB.......	Strong Partial Maternal Behavior [*Psychology*]
SPMC.......	Shannon Park Marine Center [*West Washington University*] [*Anacortes, WA*]
SPMC.......	Society of Paper Money Collectors (EA)
SPMC.......	Society of Professional Management Consultants [*Association name and designation awarded by this group*] [*Englewood, NJ*] (EA)
SPMC.......	Special Machine [*Tool*] (AAG)
SPMCA.....	Soviet Powder Metallurgy and Metal Ceramics [*English Translation*] [*A publication*]
SPMD.......	Spectramed, Inc. [*NASDAQ symbol*] (NQ)

SPME.......	Tumbes/Pedro Canga [*Peru*] [*ICAO location identifier*] (ICLI)
SPMEA......	Sulfate of Potash Magnesia Export Association (EA)
SPMGA......	Speech Monographs [*A publication*]
SPML.......	Special Meal [*Diabetic, low-cholesterol, low-calorie, hypoglycemic, or gluten-free*] [*Airline notation*] (ADA)
SPML.......	Supermail International, Inc. [*NASDAQ symbol*] (NQ)
SPMLF......	Societe de la Psychologie Medicale de Langue Francaise [*French-Language Society of Medical Psychology - FLSMP*] (EA)
SPMM.......	Society for the Promotion of Mohammedan Missions [*Defunct*] (EA)
SPMO	SAMMS [*Standard Automated Materiel Management System*] Program Management Office [*DoD*]
SPMOL......	Source Program Maintenance Online
Sp Mon	Speech Monographs [*A publication*]
SPMP........	Special-Purpose Multiprocessor [*Data processing*]
SP-MPC	Shuttle Projects - Management Planning and Control Office [*Kennedy Space Center*] [*NASA*] (NASA)
SPMR.......	Southern Provinces Mounted Rifles [*British military*] (DMA)
SPMR.......	Sub Postmaster [*British*] (DCTA)
SPMRL......	Sulphite Pulp Manufacturers' Research League (EA)
SPMS	Sine Prole Mascula Superstite [*Without Surviving Male Issue*] [*Latin*] (ADA)
SPMS	Solar Particle Monitoring System [*NASA*] (KSC)
SPMS	Special-Purpose Manipulator System [*NASA*] (NASA)
SPMS	Special-Purpose Monitoring Station [*Environmental Protection Agency*]
SPMS	Suppression Pool Makeup System [*Nuclear energy*] (NRCH)
SPMS	Surveyor Payload Mechanism Section
SPMS	System Program Management Surveys [*Air Force*]
SPMS	Yurimaguas [*Peru*] [*ICAO location identifier*] (ICLI)
SPMV.......	Satellite Panicum Mosaic Virus
SPMXA.....	Salud Publica de Mexico [*A publication*]
SPMY.......	Dos De Mayo [*Peru*] [*ICAO location identifier*] (ICLI)
SPN	Cape Shipunski [*USSR*] [*Seismograph station code, US Geological Survey*] (SEIS)
SPN	Pelican Narrows Public Library, Saskatchewan [*Library symbol*] [*National Library of Canada*] (NLC)
SPN	Saipan [*Mariana Islands*] [*Airport symbol*] (OAG)
SPN	Satellite Programming Network [*Cable-television system*]
SPN	Savanna Pastoral Neolithic [*Archeology*]
SPN	School Product News [*A publication*]
SPN	Secretariato da Propaganda Nacional [*Portugal*]
SPN	Separation Program Number [*Military*]
SPN	Shipment/Performance Notification [*DoD*]
SPN	Shuttle Project Notice [*Kennedy Space Center*] [*NASA*] (NASA)
SPN	Sparton Resources, Inc. [*Toronto Stock Exchange symbol*]
SPN	Special Program Number (MUGU)
SPN	Sponsor Program Number [*Military*]
SPN	Standard Precision Navigator
SPN	Subscriber Premises Network [*Telecommunications*]
SPN	Sydney Press Network [*Australia*]
SPN	Sympathetic Preganglionic Neuron [*Anatomy*]
SPNA.......	Punta De Lomas [*Peru*] [*ICAO location identifier*] (ICLI)
SPNC.......	Huanuco/Alferez FAP David Figuerao Fernandini [*Peru*] [*ICAO location identifier*] (ICLI)
SPND	Self-Powered Neutron Detector [*Nuclear energy*] (NRCH)
SPND	Suspend (NASA)
SPNEA......	Society for the Preservation of New England Antiquities (EA)
SPNF	Shot Peening Fixture (MCD)
SPNFT	South Pacific Nuclear Free Treaty
SPNG.......	Society for Provincial Notaries General [*British*]
SPNG........	Sponge
SPN/GEANS ...	Standard Precision Navigator/Gimballed Electrostatic Aircraft Navigation System
SPNH	Laguna Choclococha [*Peru*] [*ICAO location identifier*] (ICLI)
SPNI.........	Societe pour la Protection de la Nature en Israel [*Society for the Protection of Nature in Israel*] [*Tel Aviv*] (EAIO)
S/PNL	Side Panel [*Automotive engineering*]
SPNM.......	Society for the Promotion of New Music [*British*]
SPNO	Ancon [*Peru*] [*ICAO location identifier*] (ICLI)
sp nov	Species Nova [*New Species*] [*Biology*]
SPNP	Puno [*Peru*] [*ICAO location identifier*] (ICLI)
SPNR........	Ricran [*Peru*] [*ICAO location identifier*] (ICLI)
SPNR........	Spanner (AAG)
SPNS	Spoons (ROG)
SPNS	Switched Private Network Service [*ITT service mark*]
SPNSN......	Suspension (MSA)
SPNT	Intuto [*Peru*] [*ICAO location identifier*] (ICLI)
SPNU	Manu [*Peru*] [*ICAO location identifier*] (ICLI)
SPNX.......	Sphinx Mining, Inc. [*NASDAQ symbol*] (NQ)
SPNZ.......	Santa Cruz [*Peru*] [*ICAO location identifier*] (ICLI)
SPNZ.......	Socialist Party of New Zealand [*Political party*] (PPW)
SPO	Denver, CO [*Location identifier*] [*FAA*] (FAAL)
SPO	Sacramento Peak Observatory
SPO	Salomon Phibro Oil Trust [*AMEX symbol*] (SPSG)
SPo	Sao Paulo. Revista do Arquivo Municipal [*A publication*]
SPO	Saturn Program Office [*NASA*] (KSC)
SPO	Sausages, Potatoes, and Onions [*Meaning a cheap restaurant that specializes in these*] [*British slang*]

SPO .... Sea Post Office
SPO .... Senate Post Office
SPO .... Separate Partition Option
SPO .... Shore Patrol Officer [*Navy*]
SPO .... Short Period Oscillation
SPO .... Shuttle Project Office [*NASA*] (KSC)
SPO .... Signal Property Office [*Military*]
SPO .... Single Pickle Ordinary [*Metal industry*]
SPO .... Slaving Pick-Off
SPO .... Society of Planning Officials
SPO .... Sozialdemokratische Partei Oesterreichs [*Social Democratic Party of Austria*] [*Political party*]
SPO .... Sozialistische Partei Oesterreichs [*Socialist Party of Austria*] [*Political party*] (PPW)
SPO .... Spacelab Program Office [*NASA*]
SPO .... Spare Parts Order [*NASA*] (NASA)
SPO .... Special Placement Officer (ADA)
SP & O .... Special Plans and Operation [*Military*]
SPO .... Special Projects Office [*Navy*]
SPO .... Specialist, Inspector of Naval Material [*Navy rating*]
SPO .... Spokane [*Washington*] [*Seismograph station code, US Geological Survey*] [*Closed*] (SEIS)
SPO .... Spooner Mines & Oils Ltd. [*Toronto Stock Exchange symbol*]
SPO .... Spotlight [*A publication*]
SPO .... State Planning Organization [*Turkey*] (ECON)
SPO .... Stoker Petty Officer [*Navy*] [*British*] (DSUE)
SPO .... Subpurchase Order (AAG)
SPO .... Supplemental Production Order (AAG)
SPO .... Surplus Property Office [*Transferred to War Assets Administration, 1947*]
SPO .... System Program [*or Project*] Office [*Military*]
SPOA .... Les Sagesses du Proche-Orient Ancien. Colloque de Strasbourg [*1962*]. Travaux du Centre d'Etudes Superieurs Specialise d'Histoire des Religions de Strasbourg [*Paris*] [*A publication*] (BJA)
SPOA .... Saposoa [*Peru*] [*ICAO location identifier*] (ICLI)
SPOA .... Soviet Panorama [*A publication*]
SPOAV ...... Specialist, Inspector of Aviation Material [*Navy rating*]
SPOBS ...... Special Observer [*US Army group in London*] [*World War II*]
SPOC .... Shuttle Payload Operations Contractor (NASA)
SPOC .... Shuttle Payload Opportunity Carrier
SPOC .... Shuttle Portable Onboard Computer [*NASA*]
SPOC .... Single-Point Orbit Calculator
SPOC .... Spacecraft Oceanography Project [*Navy*]
SPOC .... Special Projects Operations Center [*Allied Force Headquarters*] [*World War II*]
SPOC .... Systems Program Office Cadre (MCD)
SPOCK ..... Simulated Procedure for Obtaining Common Knowledge
SPOCK ..... Special Purpose Operational Computing Kernel [*Pilot training device developed at Georgia Institute of Technology*]
SPOCM ..... Society for the Preservation of Old Mills (EA)
SPOCN ..... Subpurchase Order Change Notice (AAG)
SPOD .... Seaports of Debarkation (MCD)
SpOd .... Spanish Odeon, Barcelona [*Record label*] [*Spain*]
SPODA ...... Society for the Prevention of Drug Addiction
SPODAC ... SITS [*SAGE Intercept Target Simulation*] Probability of Detection and Conversion (MCD)
SPODP ...... Single Precision Orbit Determination Program [*NASA*]
SPOE .... Seaports of Embarkation (MCD)
SPOE .... Society of Post Office Engineers [*Pronounced "spowee"*] [*British*] (DCTA)
SPOE .... Sozialistische Partei Oesterreichs [*Socialist Party of Austria*]
SPOEN ...... Specialist, Engineering Inspector [*Navy rating*]
SPOFOR ... Sportwissenschaftliche Forschungsprojekte [*Bundesinstitut fuer Sportwissenschaft*] [*Federal Republic of Germany*] [*Information service or system*] (CRD)
SPOG .... Sales of Products Other than Gasoline
Spokane Bs ... Spokane Business Examiner [*United States*] [*A publication*]
SPOL .... Collique [*Peru*] [*ICAO location identifier*] (ICLI)
SPol .... Storia e Politica [*A publication*]
Spold Kwartal Nauk ... Spoldzielczy Kwartalnik Naukomy [*A publication*]
Spolia Zeylan ... Spolia Zeylanica [*A publication*]
Spolia Zool Mus Haun ... Spolia Zoologica Musei Hauniensis [*A publication*]
SPOLIT ..... Sportliteratur [*Bundesinstitut fuer Sportwissenschaft*] [*Federal Republic of Germany*] [*Information service or system*] (CRD)
SPOM .... Society of Post Office Managers [*A union*] [*British*]
SPOM .... Suspended Particulate Organic Material [*Environmental chemistry*]
SPOMCUS ... Selective Prepositioning of Materiel Configured to Unit Sets [*Army*] (AABC)
S Pomp....... Sextus Pomponius [*Flourished, 2nd century*] [*Authority cited in pre-1607 legal work*] (DSA)
SpomSAN ... Spomenik Srpske Akademije Nauka [*A publication*]
SPON .... Sponsor (AFM)
SPON .... Statistical Profile of Old Norse
SPONT...... Spontaneous
SPOOF...... Society for the Protection of Old Fishes (EA)
SPOOF..... Structure and Parity Observing Output Function
SPOOFS.... Society for the Promotion of Otherwise Overlooked Football Scores

SPOOK..... Supervisor Program Over Other Kinds [*Data processing*]
SPOOL...... Simultaneous Peripheral Operation Online [*Data processing*] (MCD)
SPOOL..... Simultaneous Production Operation Online
SPOOM ... Society for the Preservation of Old Mills (EA)
Spoon........ Spooner's Reports [*12-15 Wisconsin*] [*A publication*] (DLA)
Spooner..... Spooner's Reports [*12-15 Wisconsin*] [*A publication*] (DLA)
SPOOR...... Specialist, Ordnance Inspector [*Navy rating*]
SPOP........ Poto [*Peru*] [*ICAO location identifier*] (ICLI)
SPOP........ Scan Platform Operations Program
SPOPE...... Specialist, Petroleum Technician [*Navy rating*]
SP-OPN..... Shuttle Projects - Operations Planning Office [*Kennedy Space Center*] [*NASA*] (NASA)
SPO-PO .... System Program Office/Project Office [*Air Force*] (AFIT)
SPOPS...... Special Operations
SPORS ..... Slosson Pre-Observational Record Screen [*Educational test*]
SPORT..... St. Petersburg [*Florida*] Olympic Regatta Training
SPORT..... Space Probe Optical Recording Telescope [*Army*]
SPORT..... Sporting (ROG)
Sportarzt Sportmed ... Sportarzt Sportmedizin [*A publication*]
SPORTFOR ... Support Force
Sport Leis .. Sport and Leisure [*A publication*]
Spor Tr....... Sporting Traditions [*A publication*]
Sport Rec ... Sport and Recreation [*A publication*]
Sports and Ath ... Sports and Athletes [*A publication*]
Sports Ill .... Sports Illustrated [*A publication*]
Sports Illus ... Sports Illustrated [*A publication*]
Sports Med ... Sports Medicine [*A publication*]
Sports Med (Auckland) ... Sports Medicine (Auckland) [*A publication*]
Sports 'n Spokes ... Sports 'n Spokes Magazine [*A publication*]
Sports Turf Bull ... Sports Turf Bulletin [*A publication*]
Sport es Testn ... Sport es Testneveles [*A publication*]
SPOS .... Strong Point/Obstacle System [*Military*] (NVT)
SPOS .... Zorritos [*Peru*] [*ICAO location identifier*] (ICLI)
Sposoby Zap Inf Besserebr Nositelyakh ... Sposoby Zapisi Informatsii na Besserebryanykh Nositelyakh [*A publication*]
SPOSS...... Society for the Promotion of Science and Scholarship (EA)
SPOT......... Satellite pour Observation de la Terre [*French*]
SPOT......... Satellite and Physicians Office Testing
SPOT......... Satellite Positioning and Tracking
SPOT......... Simulated Pave Penny Omnidirectional Target (MCD)
SPOT......... Skill in Personnel through On-Site Training [*Department of Labor*]
SPOT......... Smithsonian Precision Optical Tracking
Spot........... Spotlight [*Record label*] [*Australia*]
SPOT......... Symptom Pattern Observation Technique [*Aviation*]
SPOTREP ... Spot Report [*Military*] (NVT)
SPOTS ...... Sikorsky Program Operations Tracking System (MCD)
SPOTS ..... Slosson Post-Observational Testing Screen [*Educational test*]
Spott.......... Spottiswoode's Equity [*Scotland*] [*A publication*] (DLA)
Spott Eq Rep ... Spottiswoode's English Equity Reports [*A publication*] (DLA)
Spottis........ [*R.*] Spottiswoode's Scotch Court of Session Reports [*A publication*] (DLA)
Spottis CL & Eq Rep ... Common Law and Equity Reports, Published by Spottiswoode [*A publication*] (DLA)
Spottis Eq .. Spottiswoode's Equity [*Scotland*] [*A publication*] (DLA)
Spottis Pr ... Spottiswoode's Practices [*Scotland*] [*A publication*] (DLA)
Spottis St ... Spottiswoode's Styles [*Scotland*] [*A publication*] (DLA)
Spottisw ..... Spottiswoode's Equity [*Scotland*] [*A publication*] (DLA)
Spottisw Eq ... Spottiswoode's Equity [*Scotland*] [*A publication*] (DLA)
SPOTY...... Single Parent of the Year
SPOUT...... System Peripheral Output Utility [*Nuclear energy*] (NRCH)
SPOV......... Leon Velarde/Shiringayoc O Hda. Mejia [*Peru*] [*ICAO location identifier*] (ICLI)
SPOY........ Atico [*Peru*] [*ICAO location identifier*] (ICLI)
SPP........... Menongue [*Angola*] [*Airport symbol*] (OAG)
SPP........... New York Society for the Prevention of Pauperism
SPP........... Peace Corps School Partnership Program [*Later, PCPP*] (EA)
SPP........... Safe-Practice Procedure (MCD)
SPP........... St. Paul [*Alaska*] [*Seismograph station code, US Geological Survey*] [*Closed*] (SEIS)
SPP........... St. Paul Public Library, St. Paul, MN [*OCLC symbol*] (OCLC)
SPP........... St. Philips Resources [*Vancouver Stock Exchange symbol*]
SPP........... Scientific Passenger Pod [*NASA*]
SPP........... Sclerosing Papillomatous Pattern [*Medicine*]
SPP........... Scott Paper Co. [*NYSE symbol*] (SPSG)
SPP........... Secular Periodic Perturbation
SPP........... Severe Parental Punishment
SPP........... Sexuality Preference Profile
SPP........... Signal Processing Peripheral
SPP........... Signal Processing Program [*BV Engineering*] [*Data processing*]
SPP........... Simulation Planning Panel [*NASA*] (NASA)
SPP........... Society for Pediatric Psychology (EA)
SPP........... Society of Private Printers [*Middlesex, England*]
SPP........... Society of Professional Pilots (EA)
SPP........... Sodium Pentachlorophenoxide [*Insecticide*]
SPP........... Soeurs de la Providence de Portieux (EAIO)
SPP........... Solar Photometry Probe (AAG)
SPP........... Solar Physics Payload [*NASA*] (MCD)
SPP........... Soluble Protein Preparation [*Biochemistry*]

SPP............	Song Position Pointer [*Data processing*] (PCM)
SPP............	Southwest Power Pool [*Regional power council*]
SPP............	Spare Parts Provisioning
SPP............	Special Proficiency Pay [*British military*] (DMA)
SPP............	Special Purpose Processor
SPP............	Specialist, Photographic Specialist [*Navy rating*]
SPP............	Species [*Plural form*] [*Also, spp*]
SPP............	Sponsor Program Proposal (MCD)
SPP............	Spot Product Prices [*Database*] [*Petroleum Intelligence Weekly*] [*Information service or system*] (CRD)
SPP............	Standard Practice Procedures (MCD)
SPP............	Still Picture Projector (MSA)
SPP............	Stock Purchase Plan [*Offered by a company to its employees*]
SPP............	Straight Path Penetration
SPP............	Suprapubic Prostatectomy [*Medicine*]
SPP............	Surplus Personal Property
SPP............	Swaziland Progressive Party
SPP............	System Package Plan [*or Program*] [*Military*]
SPPA.........	Puerto Ocopa [*Peru*] [*ICAO location identifier*] (ICLI)
SPPA.........	Screen Process Printing Association [*Later, SPAI*] (EA)
SPPA.........	Society for Philosophy and Public Affairs (EA)
SPPA.........	Society for the Preservation of Poultry Antiquities (EA)
SPPAY......	Semipost-Pay, Pay-Station [*Telecommunications*] (TEL)
SP-PAY.....	Shuttle Projects - Payload Integration Office [*Kennedy Space Center*] [*NASA*] (NASA)
SPPB........	Sodium Pyrophosphate Buffer [*Analytical chemistry*]
SPPB........	Statens Psykologisk-Pedagogiska Bibliotek [*National Library for Psychology and Education*] [*Information service or system*] (IID)
SPPC........	Spare Parts Provisioning Card
SPPD........	Space Propulsion and Power Division [*NASA*]
SPPD........	Spin-Polarized Photoelectron Diffraction [*Physics*]
SPPF.........	Seychelles People's Progressive Front (PPW)
SPPF.........	Solid-Phase Pressure Forming [*Shell Chemical Co.*]
SPPG........	Paramonga [*Peru*] [*ICAO location identifier*] (ICLI)
SPPGA......	Society of Economic Paleontologists and Mineralogists. Pacific Section. Guidebooks [*A publication*]
SPPI.........	Southern Production Program, Incorporated
SPPI.........	Symposium on the Preventability of Perinatal Injury
SPPIL.......	Shuttle Preferred Pyrotechnic Items List [*NASA*] (NASA)
SPPK........	Studien zur Palaeographie und Papyruskunde [*C. Wessely*] [*A publication*] (BJA)
SPPL........	Spare Parts Provisioning List [*NASA*] (NASA)
SPPL........	Spark Plug
SPPL.........	Statewide Public Library Interlibrary Loan and Reference Network [*Library network*]
SPPLB......	Science and Public Policy [*A publication*]
SPPLB......	Specialist, Photographer, Laboratory [*Navy rating*]
SPPLITT...	Southern Pacific Pipelines and International Tank Terminals [*Two companies jointly building deepwater port to accommodate outsize oil carriers*]
SpPm........	Biblioteca Publica, Palma De Mallorca, Spain [*Library symbol*] [*Library of Congress*] (LCLS)
SPPM........	Pomacocha [*Peru*] [*ICAO location identifier*] (ICLI)
SPPMA.....	Southern Pulp and Paper Manufacturer [*United States*] [*A publication*]
SPPMP......	Specialist, Motion Picture Production [*Navy rating*]
SPPN.........	Society of Private and Pioneer Numismatics (EA)
SPPO........	Scheduled Program Printout (NATG)
SPPO.........	Spacelab Payload Project Office [*NASA*]
SPPO.........	Special Projects Program Order (AAG)
SPPP.........	Huanacopampa [*Peru*] [*ICAO location identifier*] (ICLI)
SPPP.........	Spacelab Payloads Processing Project (NASA)
SPPP.........	Superior Performance Proficiency Pay (MCD)
SPPPA......	Spartan Potential Production Problem Analysis [*Missiles*] (MCD)
SPPPA......	Spartan Production Program Producibility Analysis [*Missiles*] (MCD)
SPPPG......	Specialist, Photogrammetry [*Navy rating*]
SPPPM.....	Surveyor Project Policy and Procedure Manual [*NASA*]
SPPR........	Special Peacetime Program Requirements [*DoD*]
SPPR........	Specialist, Public Relations [*Coast Guard*]
Sp Pr Cas...	Spinks' English Admiralty Prize Cases [*1854-56*] [*A publication*] (DLA)
SPPS.........	Semipost-Pay, Pay-Station [*Telecommunications*] (TEL)
SPPS.........	Solid-Phase Peptide Synthesis [*Biochemistry*]
SPPS.........	Specialist, Port Security [*Coast Guard*]
SPPS.........	Stable Plasma Protein Solution [*Medicine*]
SPPS.........	Subsystem Program Preparation Support [*Programming language*] [*Data processing*]
SPPT........	Southern Pacific Petroleum NL [*NASDAQ symbol*] (NQ)
SPPVM.....	Specialist, V-Mail [*Navy rating*]
SPPY........	Chachapoyas [*Peru*] [*ICAO location identifier*] (ICLI)
SPQ............	Memphis, TN [*Location identifier*] [*FAA*] (FAAL)
SPQ............	San Pedro [*California*] [*Airport symbol*] [*Obsolete*] (OAG)
SPQ............	Sandpiper Oil & Gas [*Vancouver Stock Exchange symbol*]
SPQ............	Stanford Parent Questionnaire [*Psychology*]
SPQCR......	Specialist, Communications Specialist, Cryptographer [*Navy rating*]
SPQIN.......	Specialist, Communications Specialist, Radio Intelligence [*Navy rating*]
SPQJ.........	Jaqui [*Peru*] [*ICAO location identifier*] (ICLI)
SPQN........	Requena [*Peru*] [*ICAO location identifier*] (ICLI)
SPQR........	Selected Product Quality Review [*DoD*]
SPQR........	Senatus Populusque Romanus [*The Senate and People of Rome*] [*Latin*]
SPQR........	Small Profits, Quick Returns
SPQRP......	Specialist, Communications Specialist, Registered Publication Clerk [*Navy rating*]
SPQS........	Self Profile Q-Sort [*Child development test*]
SPQT.........	Iquitos/Coronel FAP Francisco Secada Vignetta [*Peru*] [*ICAO location identifier*] (ICLI)
SPQTE......	Specialist, Communications Specialist, Technician [*Navy rating*]
SPQU........	Arequipa/Rodriguez Ballon [*Peru*] [*ICAO location identifier*] (ICLI)
SPR............	Puerto Rico Reports, Spanish Edition [*A publication*] (DLA)
SPR............	S-Band Planetary RADAR
SPR............	St. Pierre [*Quebec*] [*Seismograph station code, US Geological Survey*] [*Closed*] (SEIS)
SPR............	Sampling with Partial Replacement
SPR............	San Pedro [*Belize*] [*Airport symbol*] (OAG)
SPR............	Sandia Pulsed Reactor [*Nuclear energy*]
SPR............	Sapper [*Military*]
SPR............	Satellite Parametric Reduction
SPR............	Scientific Process & Research, Inc. [*Information service or system*] (IID)
SPR............	Seal Pressure Ratio
SPR............	Seconds per Revolution [*or Rotation*] (NVT)
SPR............	Secretary of the Air Force Program Review (MCD)
SPR............	Semipermanent Repellent (ADA)
SPR............	Send Priority and Route Digit [*Telecommunications*] (TEL)
SPR............	Sense Printer
SPR............	Sequential Probability Ratio [*Statistics*]
SPR............	Serial Probe Recognition [*Psychometrics*]
SPR............	Shock Position Ratio
SPR............	Shortest Possible Route (MCD)
SPR............	Silicon Power Rectifier
SPR............	Simplified Practice Recommendation
SPR............	Single-Ply Roofing
SPR............	Single-Point Refueling (MCD)
SPR............	Skin Potential Response [*Physiology*]
SPR............	Slavistic Printings and Reprintings [*A publication*]
SPR............	Society of Patient Representatives [*Later, NSPR*] (EA)
SPR............	Society for Pediatric Radiology (EA)
SPR............	Society for Pediatric Research (EA)
SPR............	Society for Philosophy of Religion (EA)
SPR............	Society for Psychical Research [*British*]
SPR............	Society for Psychophysiological Research (EA)
SPR............	Society for Psychosomatic Research (EAIO)
SPR............	Software Problem Report [*NASA*] (NASA)
SPR............	Solid-Phase Reactor
SPR............	Solid Phase Receptacle [*Laboratory testing*]
SPR............	Solid-Propellant Rocket
SPR............	South Polar Region
SPR............	Southern Poetry Review [*A publication*]
SPR............	Spacer (AAG)
SPR............	Spare [*Telecommunications*] (TEL)
SPR............	Special Program Requirement (AFM)
SPR............	Special Program Review [*Army*] (RDA)
SPR............	Special Project Report
SPR............	Special-Purpose RADAR
SPR............	Special-Purpose Requirements [*Army*]
SPR............	Specialist, Recruiter [*Navy rating*]
SPR............	Specific Price Reduction
SPR............	Spinster
SPR............	Sponsor
Spr.............	Sprache [*A publication*]
Spr.............	Sprague's United States District Court (Admiralty) Decisions [*A publication*] (DLA)
SPR............	Spratly Islands [*ANSI three-letter standard code*] (CNC)
SPR............	Spring (MSA)
SPR............	Springer Resources [*Vancouver Stock Exchange symbol*]
SPR............	Sprinkler (AAG)
SPR............	Statement of Procedural Rules [*A publication*] (DLA)
SPR............	Sterling Capital Corp. [*AMEX symbol*] (SPSG)
SPR............	Storage Protection Register
SPR............	Strategic Petroleum Reserve [*Department of Energy*]
SPR............	Stroposcopic Pulse Radiolysis [*Physical chemistry*]
SPR............	Structure-Property Relationship [*Chemistry*]
SPR............	Sub Petito Remissionis [*With Request for Return*] [*Latin*]
SPR............	Subcontractor Performance Review [*NASA*] (NASA)
SPR............	Substance P Receptor [*Biochemistry*]
SPR............	Sudden Pressure Relay
SPR............	Sun Protection Required [*Identification system for heat-sensitive cargo*] [*Shipping*] (DCTA)
SPR............	Supplementary Progress Report
SPR............	Supply Performance Report (CINC)
SPR............	Support Plans and Requirements
SPR............	Surface Plasmon Resonance [*Physics*]
SPR............	System Parameter Record [*Data processing*] (IBMDP)
SPR............	System Performance Rating

SPR........... System Problem Report (MCD)
SPR........... System Program Review [*Military*] (AABC)
SPR's .... Small Parcels and Rolls [*Postal Service*]
SPRA........ Space Probe RADAR Altimeter (KSC)
SPRA........ Special-Purpose Reconnaissance Aircraft [*Navy*]
SPRACAY ... Society for Prevention of Rock and Roll and Corruption of
      American Youth [*Organization in 1956 movie "Shake,*
      Rattle and Roll"]
Sprache und Datenverarb ... Sprache und Datenverarbeitung [*A publication*]
Sprache Tech Zeit ... Sprache im Technischen Zeitalter [*A publication*]
SPRAG...... Spray Arrester Gear (MCD)
SPRAG...... STS Payload Requirements and Analysis Group
      [*NASA*] (NASA)
Sprague...... Sprague's United States District Court (Admiralty) Decisions [*A*
      publication] (DLA)
Sprague's J ME His ... Sprague's Journal of Maine History [*A publication*]
Sprakvetensk Sallsk i Uppsala Forhandl ... Sprakvetenskapliga Sallskapets i
      Uppsala Foerhandlingar [*A publication*]
SPRAM..... Sao Paulo. Revista do Arquivo Municipal [*A publication*]
SPRAT ...... Small Portable RADAR Torch
Spraw........ Sprawozdania [*A publication*]
Spraw A ..... Sprawozdania Archeologiczne [*A publication*]
Spraw Kom Jez AU ... Sprawozdania z Posiedzen Komisji Jezykowej
      Akademii Umietjetnosci [*A publication*]
Spraw Opolskie Tow Przyj Nauk Wydz Nauk Med ... Sprawozdania Opolskie
      Towarzystwo Przyjaciol Nauk. Wydzial Nauk Medycznych
      [*A publication*]
Sprawozdania Kom Nauk PAN ... Sprawozdania z Posiedzen Komisji
      Naukowych. Polskiej Akademii Nauk [*A publication*]
Spraw Posied Tow Nauk Warsz ... Sprawozdania z Posiedzen Towarzystwa
      Naukowego Warszawskiego [*A publication*]
Spraw Poznan Tow Przyj Nauk ... Sprawozdania Poznanskiego Towarzystwa
      Przyjaciol Nauk [*A publication*]
Spraw Pr Pol Tow Fiz ... Sprawozdania i Prace Polskiego Towarzystwa
      Fizycznego [*A publication*]
Spraw TNW ... Sprawozdania z Posiedzen Towarzystwa Naukowego
      Warszawskiego [*A publication*]
Spraw Tow Nauk Lwowie ... Sprawozdania Towarzystwa Naukowego we
      Lwowie [*A publication*]
Spraw Tow Nauk Toruniu ... Sprawozdania Towarzystwa Naukowego w
      Toruniu [*A publication*]
Spraw Wrocław Tow Nauk ... Sprawozdania Wroclawskiego Towarzystwa
      Naukowego [*A publication*]
Spraw Wrocław Tow Nauk Ser A ... Sprawozdania Wroclawskiego
      Towarzystwa Naukowego. Seria A [*A publication*]
Spraw Wrocław Tow Nauk Ser B ... Sprawozdania Wroclawskiego
      Towarzystwa Naukowego. Seria B [*A publication*]
SprB........... Sprakliga Bidrag [*A publication*]
SPR BOG .. Springender Bogen [*Bouncing Bow*] [*Music*]
SPRC......... Seafood Products Research Center [*Public Health*
      Service] (GRD)
SPRC......... Self-Propelled Robot Craft (IEEE)
SPRC......... Society of Public Relations Counsellors
SPRD......... Science Policy Research Division [*of Congressional Research*
      Service, Library of Congress]
SPRD......... Spread (FAAC)
SPRDNG.... Spreading [*Freight*]
SPRDR....... Spreader (MSA)
SPRDS ...... Steam Pipe Rupture Detector System (IEEE)
SPRE .... Society of Park and Recreation Educators (EA)
SPRE .... Solid-Propellant Rocket Engine
SPRE .... Special Prefix Code [*Northern Telecom*] [*Telecommunications*]
SPREAD ... Spring Evaluation Analysis and Design (MCD)
SPREAD ... Supercomputer Project Research Experiment in Advanced
      Development [*Lawrence Livermore Laboratory, Los*
      Alamos National Laboratory, and SRI]
SPREC....... Specular Reflection Computer Program (MCD)
Sprechsaal Keram Glas Silik ... Sprechsaal fuer Keramik, Glas, Email, Silikate
      [*A publication*]
SPREE....... Solid-Propellant Exhaust Effects (MCD)
SPREE....... Structure Preserving Estimation (ADA)
SPREG ...... Speed Regulator
SPREP....... South Pacific Regional Environment Programme [*of the South*
      Pacific Commission] [*New Caledonia*]
SPRES....... Star Present (NASA)
S & P RES DIS ... Severn and Potomac Reserve District [*Marine Corps*]
SPRF .... Sandia Pulsed Reactor Facility [*Nuclear energy*]
SPRF .... Societe de Publications Romanes et Francaises [*A publication*]
SPRF .... Space Propulsion Research Facility (AAG)
SPRF .... Special-Purpose Receiving Facility
SPRG .... San Regis [*Peru*] [*ICAO location identifier*] (ICLI)
SPRG........ Social Policy Research Group, Inc. [*Information service or*
      system] (IID)
SPRG........ Spring
SPRG........ Sprinkling (MSA)
SPRH......... Spearhead Industries, Inc. [*NASDAQ symbol*] (NQ)
SPRI .... Scott Polar Research Institute [*Cambridge, England*]
SPRI .... Single Ply Roofing Institute (EA)
SPRI .... Social Problems Research Institute [*University of South*
      Carolina at Columbia] [*Research center*] (RCD)
SPRI .... Social Process Research Institute [*Research center*] (RCD)

SPRI .... Social Psychiatry Research Institute (EA)
SPRI .... Sperm Reservoir Length Index
SPRI .... Sugar Processing Research, Incorporated
SPRIA .... Solid-Phase Radioimmunoassay [*or Radioimmunoprecipitation*
      Assay] [*Clinical medicine*]
Springer Proc Phys ... Springer Proceedings in Physics [*A publication*]
Springer Semin Immunopathol ... Springer Seminars in Immunopathology [*A*
      publication]
Springer Ser Chem Phys ... Springer Series in Chemical Physics [*A*
      publication]
Springer Ser Electrophys ... Springer Series in Electrophysics [*A publication*]
Springer Ser Health Care Soc ... Springer Series on Health Care and Society
      [*A publication*]
Springer Ser Inform Sci ... Springer Series in Information Sciences [*A*
      publication]
Springer Ser Optical Sci ... Springer Series in Optical Sciences [*A publication*]
Springer Ser Opt Sci ... Springer Series in Optical Sciences [*A publication*]
Springer Ser Solid-State Sci ... Springer Series in Solid-State Sciences [*A*
      publication]
Springer Ser Statist ... Springer Series in Statistics [*A publication*]
Springer Ser Synergetics ... Springer Series in Synergetics [*A publication*]
Springer Tracts Modern Phys ... Springer Tracts in Modern Physics [*A*
      publication]
Springer Tracts Mod Phys ... Springer Tracts in Modern Physics [*A*
      publication]
Springer Tracts Nat Philos ... Springer Tracts in Natural Philosophy [*A*
      publication]
SPRINT..... Selective Printing [*Data processing*]
SPRINT..... Solid-Propellant Rocket Intercept Missile [*ARPA/AMC*]
SPRINT..... Southern Pacific Communications' Switched Long Distance
      Service [*Telecommunications*] (TEL)
SPRINT..... Spare Parts Review Initiatives [*Army*] (RDA)
SPRINT..... Special Police Radio Inquiry Network [*New York City*]
SPRINT..... Strategic Programme for Innovation and Technology Transfer
      [*European Commission*]
SPRINTER ... Specification of Profits with Interaction under Trial and Error
      Response
Spr Int L .... Sprague on International Law [*A publication*] (DLA)
SPRITE..... Signal Processing in the Element (MCD)
SPRITE..... Solid-Propellant Rocket Ignition Test and Evaluation (KSC)
SPRITE..... Surveillance, Patrol, Reconnaissance, Intelligence Gathering,
      Target Designation, and Electronic Warfare [*Unmanned*
      aircraft] [*Military*]
SPRJ......... Self-Powered Reference Junction
SPRK........ Sparkman Producing Co. [*NASDAQ symbol*] (NQ)
SprKJ........ Sprawozdania z Posiedzen Komisji Jezykowej Towarzystwa
      Naukowego Warszawskiego [*A publication*]
SPRKLG.... Sprinkling [*Freight*]
SPRKT ...... Sprocket (MSA)
SprKUL..... Sprawozdania z Czynnosci Wydawniczej i Posiedzen
      Naukowych Oraz Kronika Towarzystwa Naukowego
      Katolockiego Uniwersytetu Lubelskiego [*A publication*]
SPRL .... Societe de Personnes a Responsabilite Limitee [*Private Limited*
      Company] [*French*] [*Business term*]
SPRL .... Space Physics Research Laboratory [*University of Michigan*]
      [*Research center*] (RCD)
SPRL .... Spiral (FAAC)
SprLTN ..... Sprawozdania z Czynnosci i Posiedzen Lodzkiego Towarzystwa
      Naukowego [*A publication*]
SPRM........ San Ramon/Capitan Alvarino [*Peru*] [*ICAO location*
      identifier] (ICLI)
SPRM........ Special Reamer [*Tool*] (AAG)
Spr Miedzyn ... Sprawy Miedzynarodowe [*A publication*]
Spr Miedzynar ... Sprawy Miedzynarodowe [*A publication*]
SPRO......... Services Public Relations Officer [*British military*] (DMA)
SPROE...... Software Protection [*A publication*]
S-P/ROM ... Slave Programmable Read-Only Memory
SPROM..... Switched Programmable Read-Only Memory
SPRON...... Specific Populations Recreation Officers' Network [*Australia*]
SprPAUm .. Sprawozdania z Czynnosci i Posiedzen Polskiej Akademii
      Umiejetnosci [*A publication*]
SprPTPN... Sprawozdania Poznanskiego Towarzystwa Przyjaciol Nauk [*A*
      publication]
SPRR .... Selective Paramagnetic Relaxation Reagent [*Chemistry*]
SPRR .... Self-Propelled Recoilless Rifle [*British military*] (DMA)
SPRRS...... Southern Plains Range Research Station [*Oklahoma State*
      University] [*Research center*] (RCD)
SPRS .... Single Passenger Reservation System [*DoD*]
SPRS .... Society for the Promotion of Roman Studies (EAIO)
SPRS .... Special-Purpose RADAR Set
SPRS .... Student Proficiency Rating Scale
SPRS .... Sublime Power of the Royal Secret [*Freemasonry*] (ROG)
SprSUF..... Sprakvetenskapliga Sallskapets i Uppsala Foerhandlingar [*A*
      publication]
SPRT .... Rio Tigre [*Peru*] [*ICAO location identifier*] (ICLI)
SPRT .... Sequential Probability Ratio Test [*Statistics*]
SPRT .... Sportecular, Inc. [*Penfield, NY*] [*NASDAQ symbol*] (NQ)
SPRT .... Standard Platinum Resistance Thermometer
SPRT .... Support (MSA)
SPRT .... System Performance and Repeatability Test [*Military*] (CAAL)

SprTNW	Sprawozdania z Posiedzen Towarzystwa Naukowego Warszawskiego [A publication]
SprTT	Sprawozdania Towarzystwa Naukowego w Toruniu [A publication]
SPRU	Science Policy Research Unit [United Kingdom] [Research center] (IRC)
SPRU	Trujillo/Capitan Carlos Martinez de Pinillos - Huanchaco [Peru] [ICAO location identifier] (ICLI)
SPRUCE ...	Special Programs and Rehabilitation under Unemployment Compensation [Department of Labor]
SprV	Sprachkunst (Vienna) [A publication]
SPS	St. Patrick's Missionary Society [Roman Catholic men's religious order]
SPS	Saint Patrick's Seminary [Menlo Park, CA]
SPS	Samples per Second
SPS	San Pedro De Poas [Costa Rica] [Seismograph station code, US Geological Survey] (SEIS)
SPS	Satellite and Production Services [Tallahassee, FL] [Telecommunications] (TSSD)
SPS	Satellite Program Services [Australia]
SPS	Saturn Parts Sales [NASA]
SPS	Saturn Propulsion System [NASA]
SPS	Scene per Second (MCD)
SPS	Schedule Promulgated Separately [Navy] (NVT)
SPS	School of Practical Science
SPS	Scientific Power Switching
SPS	Seamen's Protection Society [A union] [British]
SPS	Second Preferred Stock [Investment term]
SPS	Secondary Plant System [Nuclear energy] (NRCH)
SPS	Secondary Power Source
SPS	Secondary Power System [or Subsystem] (MCD)
SPS	Secondary Propulsion System [NASA]
SPS	Sekcja Pracy Spolecznej [A publication] (BJA)
SPS	Self Protection System (MCD)
SPS	Series-Parallel-Serial Configuration [Electronics] (MDG)
SPS	Service Propulsion System [or Subsystem] [NASA]
SPS	Servo Parameter Shift
SPS	Set Point Station
SpS	Sharpshooter [Military decoration] (AABC)
SPS	Ship Planning System
SPS	Ship Program Schedule
SPS	Shipping/Production Scheduling
SPS	Shuttle Procedures Simulator [NASA] (NASA)
SPS	Signal Processing System (KSC)
SPS	Silent Propulsion System (MCD)
SPS	Simple Phrase System
SPS	Simplified Processing Station (MCD)
SPS	Simulated Parts Sketch (MCD)
SPS	Simulator Panel Set (MCD)
SPS	Sine Prole Superstite [Without Surviving Issue] [Latin]
SPS	Single-Pole Switch
SPS	Social Problems Series [A publication]
SPS	Socialistische Partij Suriname [Surinam Socialist Party] [Political party] (PPW)
SPS	Society of Pelvic Surgeons (EA)
SPS	Society for Pentecostal Studies (EA)
SPS	Society of Physics Students (EA)
SPS	Sodium Polyanetholesulfonate [Analytical biochemistry]
SPS	Sodium Polystyrene Sulfonate [Organic chemistry]
SPS	Soft Particle Spectrometer [Geophysics]
SPS	Software Procurement Specification
SPS	Software Product Specification
SPS	Software Products Scheme [Data processing] (DCTA)
SPS	Solar Panel Substrate
SPS	Solar Power Satellite [NASA]
SPS	Solar Power System (MCD)
SPS	Solar Probe Spacecraft [Pioneer satellite]
SPS	Solid Phase Synthesis [Chemistry]
SPS	Soluble Polysaccharide of Soybean [Food technology]
SPS	SONAR Phase Shifter
SPS	South Pole Station [National Weather Service]
SPS	Southwestern Public Service Co. [NYSE symbol] (SPSG)
SPS	Sozialdemokratische Partei der Schweiz [Social Democratic Party of Switzerland] [Political party] (PPE)
SPS	Sozialdemokratische Partei Suedtirols [Social Democratic Party of South Tirol] [Political party] (PPE)
SPS	Space Power System (CET)
SPS	Space Stories [A publication]
SPS	Spacecraft Propulsion System (AAG)
SP & S	Special Processes and Sequencing (NASA)
SPS	Special-Purpose SONAR (MCD)
SPS	Special Services [Military]
SPS	Specialist, Personnel Supervisor [Women's Reserve] [Navy rating]
SPS	Specialist, Shore Patrol and Security [Navy rating]
SPS	Specimina Philologiae Slavicae [A publication]
SPS	Spectrum Planning Subcommittee [FCC]
SPS	Speed Switch (IEEE)
SPS	Spokane, Portland & Seattle Railway System [AAR code]
SPS	SPS Technologies, Inc. [Formerly, Standard Pressed Steel Co.] (MCD)
SPS	Stabilized Platform Subsystem (KSC)
SPS	Standard Pipe Size
SPS	Standard Port System (MCD)
SPS	Standard Positioning Service
SPS	Standard Process Specification (MCD)
SPS	Standard Project Storm [Nuclear energy] (NRCH)
SPS	Standby Power Source [Electronics]
SPS	Statement of Prior Submission (NASA)
SPS	Static Power System
SPS	Static Pressure System
SPS	Statistical Performance Standards [Navy] (NG)
SPS	Stator Pivot Seal
SPS	Status Projection System
SPS	Steady Potential Shift
SPS	Steampipe Survey
SPS	Stereo Photographic System
SPS	Stichting Plurale Samenlevingen [Foundation for the Study of Plural Societies - FSPS] (EAIO)
SPS	Stored Program Simulator
SPS	Strategic Planning Society [Formerly, Society for Strategic and Long Range Planning] (EA)
SPS	Strategic Planning Staff [Social Security Administration]
SPS	Strategical Planning Section [Joint Planning Staff] [World War II]
SPS	Stratford Papers on Shakespeare [A publication]
SPS	String Processing System [Word processing software]
SPS	Student Profile Section [of the American College Testing Test Battery]
SPS	Submarine Piping System
SPS	Submerged Production System [Deepwater platform] [Humble Oil]
SPS	Subsea Production System [Petroleum technology]
SPS	Sucrose-Phosphate Synthase [An enzyme]
SPS	Suicide Probability Scale [Personality development test] [Psychology]
SPS	Sulfite-Polymyxin-Sulfadiazine [Agar] [Microbiology]
SPS	Summit Power Station [Nuclear energy] (NRCH)
SPS	Super Proton Synchrotron [Particle physics]
SPS	Supplementary Protection System [Nuclear energy] (NRCH)
SPS	Supply Point Simulation (MCD)
SPS	Symbolic Programming System [Data processing]
SPS	Symbols per Second [Data processing]
SPS	System Performance Score [Telecommunications] (TEL)
SPS	Wichita Falls [Texas] [Airport symbol] (OAG)
SPSA	Casma [Peru] [ICAO location identifier] (ICLI)
SPSA	Senate Press Secretaries Association (EA)
SPSA	Society of Philippine Surgeons in America (EA)
SPSA	Special Projects School for Air
SpSAG	Archivo General de Indias [Archives of the Indies], Seville, Spain [Library symbol] [Library of Congress] (LCLS)
SpSAN	Spomenik Srpske Akademije Nauka [A publication]
SPSBDR	Special Publications. Seto Marine Biological Laboratory. Series IV [A publication]
SPSC	Saharan People's Support Committee (EA)
SPSC	Seventy Plus Ski Club (EA)
SP/SC	Shield Plug/Support Cylinder [Nuclear energy] (NRCH)
SPSC	Signal Processing and Spectral Control
SPSC	Space Power Systems Conference
SPSC	Standard Performance Summary Charts (AAG)
SPSCR	Special Screw
SPSD	Space Power Systems Division [NASA]
SPSDC	Surface and Defect Properties of Solids [A publication]
SP-SDF	Socialist Party - Social Democratic Federation [Later, Socialist Party of the United States of America] (EA)
SPSDM	Society for the Philosophical Study of Dialectical Materialism (EA)
SPSDS	Ship's Passive Surveillance and Detection System [Navy] (CAAL)
SPSE	Society of Photographic Scientists and Engineers (EA)
SPSE	Special Purpose Support Equipment
SPSEA	Soviet Physics. Semiconductors [English translation] [A publication]
SPSEE3	Special Publication. South Australia Department of Mines and Energy [A publication]
Sp & Sel Cas ...	Special and Selected Law Cases [1648] [England] [A publication] (DLA)
SPSF	Self-Propagating-Star Formation [Galactic science]
SPSF	Society of the President Street Fellows (EA)
SPSFM	St. Patrick's Society for the Foreign Missions [See also SSPME] [Kiltegan, County Wicklow, Republic of Ireland] (EAIO)
SP/SHLD ...	Splash Shield [Automotive engineering]
SPSHP	Special Shaped
SPSHS	Stanford Profile Scales of Hypnotic Susceptibility [Psychology]
SPSI	Serikat Pelajaran Seluruh Indonesia [Sailors' Union of Indonesia]
SPSI	Society for the Promotion of Scientific Industry [British]
SPSJ	San Jose De Sisa [Peru] [ICAO location identifier] (ICLI)
SPSL	Lamas [Peru] [ICAO location identifier] (ICLI)
SPSL	Socialist Party of Sri Lanka
SPSL	Society for the Philosophy of Sex and Love (EA)
SPSL	Society for the Protection of Science and Learning [British]

SPSL.........	Spare Parts Selection List
SPSLGI	Society for the Psychological Study of Lesbian and Gay Issues (EA)
SPSM	Society for the Philosophical Study of Marxism (EA)
SPSM	Supply Point Simulation Model (MCD)
SPSMDQ ..	Special Publications. Society for General Microbiology [A publication]
SPSME......	Spacelab Payload Standard Modular Electronics (MCD)
SPSN	Submitted Package Sequence Number (MCD)
SPSO	Pisco [Peru] [ICAO location identifier] (ICLI)
SPSO	Senior Personnel Staff Officer [Air Force] [British]
SPSO	Senior Principal Scientific Officer [Ministry of Agriculture, Fisheries, and Food] [British]
SPSP.........	St. Peter and St. Paul [The Papal seal]
SPSP.........	Solid-Propellant Surveillance Panel [Military]
SPSP.........	Spare Parts Support Package
SPsp.........	Sprachspiegel. Schweizerische Zeitschrift fuer die Deutsche Muttersprache [A publication]
SPSP-AGE ...	Spare Parts Support Package for Aerospace Ground Equipment
SPSPCY	Specialist Periodical Reports. Spectroscopic Properties of Inorganic and Organometallic Compounds [A publication]
SPSPS	Specialist, Personnel Supervisor, V-10 [Navy rating]
SPSQ	Satisfaction with Performance Scaled Questionnaire
SpsQualBad ...	Sharpshooter Qualification Badge [Military decoration] (AABC)
SPSRA.......	Space Science Reviews [A publication]
SPSS.........	Masisea [Peru] [ICAO location identifier] (ICLI)
SPSS.........	Shield Plug Storage Station [Nuclear energy] (NRCH)
SPSS.........	Single Pulse Selection System
SPSS.........	Society of the Priests of St. Sulpice [See also CPSS] [Paris, France] (EAIO)
SPSS.........	Statistical Package for the Social Sciences [Programming language] [1970]
SPS-SCWG ...	Spanish Philatelic Society Spanish Civil War Study Group [Defunct] (EA)
SPSSI	Society for the Psychological Study of Social Issues (EA)
Sp St..........	Private and Special Laws [A publication] (DLA)
SPST.........	Single-Pole, Single-Throw [Switch]
SPST.........	Symonds Picture-Story Test [Psychology]
SPST.........	Tarapoto [Peru] [ICAO location identifier] (ICLI)
SPSTNC.....	Single-Pole, Single-Throw, Normally-Closed [Switch]
SPSTNO	Single-Pole, Single-Throw, Normally-Open [Switch]
SPSTNODM ...	Single-Pole, Single-Throw, Normally-Open, Double-Make [Switch]
SPSTP........	Solid-Propellant Rocket Static Test Panel [Military]
SPSTSW	Single-Pole, Single-Throw Switch
SPSU	Studia Philologiae Scandinavicae Upsaliensia [A publication]
SPSW	Single-Pole Switch
S/PSWO	Service/Parts Sales Work Order
SPSWO	Spare Parts Sales Work Order
S Psy	Social Psychology Quarterly [A publication]
SPT...........	Albuquerque, NM [Location identifier] [FAA] (FAAL)
SPT...........	Openbaar Vervoer [A publication]
SPT...........	Piedmont Technical College, Greenwood, SC [OCLC symbol] (OCLC)
SPT...........	Scaled-Particle Theory
SPT...........	School of Physical Training [British]
SPT...........	Scientist-Pilot [NASA] (KSC)
SPT...........	Seaport
SPT...........	Sectors per Track
SPT...........	Septic [Classified advertising] (ADA)
SPT...........	Septuple (MSA)
SPT...........	Shaft Position Transducer
SPT...........	Ship Position Transmitter
SPT...........	Shipper Pays Taxes
SPT...........	Silicon Planar Transistor
SPT...........	Silicon-Powered Transistor
SPT...........	Skin Prick Test [Immunology]
SPT...........	Slowest Processing Time
SPT...........	Small Perturbation Theory
SPT...........	Socialist Party of Thailand [Political party] (FEA)
SPT...........	Society of Painters in Tempera (EA)
SPT...........	Society for Philosophy and Technology (EA)
SPT...........	Society of Photo-Technologists (EA)
SPT...........	Society of Projective Techniques [Later, SPA] (EA)
SPT...........	Sodium Pyridinethione [Organic chemistry]
SPT...........	Sogepet Ltd. [Toronto Stock Exchange symbol]
SPT...........	Sound-Powered Telephone
SPT...........	South Point [Hawaii] [Seismograph station code, US Geological Survey] (SEIS)
SPT...........	Space Power Tool
SPT...........	Space Travel [A publication]
SPT...........	Span East Airlines, Inc. [Miami, FL] [FAA designator] (FAAC)
SpT...........	Spanish Telefunken [Record label]
SPT...........	Spare Parts Transfer
SPT...........	Special Perishable Tool (MCD)
SPT...........	Special Purpose Test [Nuclear energy] (NRCH)
SP T..........	Special Term [Legal term] (DLA)
SPT...........	Specialist, Teacher [Navy rating]
SpT...........	Speech Teacher [A publication]
SPT...........	Spirit

SPT...........	Split (MSA)
SPT...........	Spraytight
Spt...........	Spritsail [Ship's rigging] (DS)
SPT...........	Sputum
SPT...........	Standard Penetration Test [Nuclear energy] (NRCH)
SPT...........	Static Pressure Transducer
SPT...........	Streptomycin Phosphotransferase [An enzyme]
SPT...........	Structural Programming Technique
SPT...........	Supervisory Potential Test
SPT...........	Support (AFM)
SPT...........	Symbolic Play Test [Child development test]
SPT...........	Symbolic Program Tape [Data processing] (IEEE)
SPT...........	Symbolic Program Translator [Data processing] (IEEE)
SPT...........	System Page Table [Telecommunications] (TEL)
SPT...........	System Parameter Table [Data processing] (IBMDP)
SPT...........	System Planning Team [Military] (AFIT)
SP3T........	Single-Pole, Triple-Throw [Switch] (IEEE)
SP4T........	Single-Pole, Quadruple-Throw [Switch] (IEEE)
SPTA	Nauta [Peru] [ICAO location identifier] (ICLI)
SPTA	Southern Paper Trade Association [Defunct] (EA)
SPTA	Southern Pressure Treaters Association (EA)
Sp Tax Rul ...	Special Tax Ruling [Internal Revenue Service] [United States] [A publication] (DLA)
SPTC	Share-Purchase Tax Credit [Canada]
SPTC	Specified Period of Time Contract
SPTC	Studies in Physical and Theoretical Chemistry [Elsevier Book Series] [A publication]
SPTCDZ....	Studies in Physical and Theoretical Chemistry [Elsevier Book Series] [A publication]
SPTCEN....	Support Center [Army]
SPTD........	Signal Processor Techniques Department
SPTD........	Supplemental Provisioning Technical Documentation [NASA] (NASA)
SPTE	Special Purpose Test Equipment (MCD)
SPTE	Teresita [Peru] [ICAO location identifier] (ICLI)
SPTEA	Single Persons for Tax Equality Association (EAIO)
SPTF.........	Screen Printing Technical Foundation (EA)
SPTF.........	Signal Processing Test Facility
SPTF.........	Social Progress Trust Fund [Inter-American Development Bank]
SPTF........	Sodium Pump Test Facility [Energy Research and Development Administration]
SPTH........	Systolic Threshold Pressure [Cardiology]
SPT-HP.....	Scholastic Proficiency Test - Higher Primary Level [Educational test] [South Africa]
SPTI	Puerto Inca [Peru] [ICAO location identifier] (ICLI)
SPTI	Senior Physical Training Instructor [British military] (DMA)
SPTL	Society of Public Teachers of Law [British] (DLA)
SPTL	Support Line [Military]
SPTM	Spectrum Laboratories, Inc. [NASDAQ symbol] (NQ)
SPTN	Spill Technology Newsletter [A publication]
SPTN	Tacna [Peru] [ICAO location identifier] (ICLI)
SPTO	Sporto Corp. [Boston, MA] [NASDAQ symbol] (NQ)
SPTP	Special-Purpose Test Program (MCD)
SPTP	Talara/El Pato [Peru] [ICAO location identifier] (ICLI)
SPT & PA ...	Society for Projective Techniques and Personality Assessment [Later, SPA]
SPTPA.......	Soviet Physics. Technical Physics [English Translation] [A publication]
SPTPN	Sprawozdania Poznanskiego Towarzystwa Przyjaciol Nauk [A publication]
SP(TR)......	Specialist (Transportation) [Coast Guard]
SPTR	SpecTran Corp. [NASDAQ symbol] (NQ)
SPTR	Tournavista [Peru] [ICAO location identifier] (ICLI)
SPTRJ	Self-Powered Thermocouple Reference Junction
SPTS.........	Spirits
SPTS.........	Sport's Restaurants [NASDAQ symbol] (NQ)
S & PTS	Standard & Poor's Trading Systems [Standard & Poor's Corp.] [Information service or system] (IID)
SPTS.........	Stock Positioning and Transportation Study [DoD]
SPTSq.......	Support Squadron [Air Force]
SPTT	Single-Pole, Triple-Throw [Switch] (CET)
SPTU	Puerto Maldonado/Padre Aldamiz [Peru] [ICAO location identifier] (ICLI)
SPTUF	South Pacific Trade Union Forum [14-nation group opposed to nuclear testing and dumping in the Pacific]
SPTW	Single-Pedestal Typewriter [Desk]
SPTWC	Salle Palasz and Tri-Weapon Club (EA)
SPU...........	Mount Spur [Alaska] [Seismograph station code, US Geological Survey] (SEIS)
SPU...........	S-Band Polar Ultra
SPU...........	Salinas Public Library, Salinas, CA [OCLC symbol] (OCLC)
SPU...........	School Personnel Utilization
SPU...........	Service Propulsion Unit
SPU...........	Signal Processing Unit
SPU...........	Slave Processing Unit
SPU...........	Smallest Publishable Unit
SPU...........	Society for Pediatric Urology (EA)
SPU...........	Southeast Airmotive Corp. [Charlotte, NC] [FAA designator] (FAAC)
SPU...........	Specialist, Utility [Women's Reserve] [Navy rating]

SPU............ Split [Yugoslavia] [Airport symbol]   (OAG)
SPU............ Statutes of Practical Utility [A publication]   (APTA)
SPU............ Student Peace Union [Defunct]   (EA)
SPU............ Subsurface Propulsion Unit
SPU............ Supertech Industries [Vancouver Stock Exchange symbol]
SPU............ System Partitioning Unit [Data processing]
SPUC......... Huamachuco [Peru] [ICAO location identifier]   (ICLI)
SPUC......... Society for the Protection of Unborn Children   (EA)
SPUD........ One Potato 2, Inc. [NASDAQ symbol]   (NQ)
SPUD........ St. Paul Union Depot Co. [AAR code]
SPUD......... Sniff, Paw, Urinate, and Defecate [Ungulate territorial marking procedure]
SPUD........ Society for Prevention of Unwholesome Diet [National Potato Council]
SPUD........ Solar Power Unit Demonstrator
Spud .... Spudasmata [A publication]
SPUD........ Stored Program Universal Demonstrator
SPUK........ Special Projects, United Kingdom
SPUMS..... South Pacific Underwater Medicine Society   (EAIO)
SPUN .... Society for the Protection of the Unborn through Nutrition   (EA)
SPUP .... Seychelles People's United Party [Political party]   (PPW)
SPUR......... Piura/Capitan Concha [Peru] [ICAO location identifier]   (ICLI)
SPUR......... San Francisco Planning and Urban Research Association [California] [Information service or system]   (IID)
SPUR......... Single Precision Unpacked Rounded [floating-point package] [Computer program system] [Sperry Rand Corp.]
SPUR......... Source Program Utility Routine
SPUR......... Space Power Unit Reactor [Air Force]
SPUR......... Special Purchase Office [DoD]
SPUR......... Support for Promoting the Utilization of Resources [Esso Education Foundation]
SPUR......... Symbolic Processing Using RISC [Reduced Instruction Set Computer]
SPURM..... Special Purpose Unilateral Repetitive Modulation   (IEEE)
SPURT...... Small Primate Unrestrained Test
SPURT...... Spinning Unguided Rocket Trajectory
SPURV..... Self-Propelled Underwater Research Vehicle
SP-USA.... Socialist Party of the United States of America   (EA)
SP-USA.... Student Pugwash (USA)   (EA)
SPUTA...... Scientific Papers. College of General Education. University of Tokyo [A publication]
SPV............ Sa-Pa [Vietnam] [Seismograph station code, US Geological Survey]   (SEIS)
SPV............ Sensor Payload Vehicle
SPV............ Shope Papilloma Virus
SPV............ Slow-Phase Velocity [Ophthalmology]
SPV............ Space Adventures [A publication]
SpV .... Spanish RCA Victor [Record label]
SPV............ Special-Purpose Vehicle [Military]
SPV............ Specialist, Transport Airman [Navy rating]
SPV............ Specification Performance Validation [Military]   (CAAL)
SPV............ Split-Product Vaccine [Immunology]
SPV............ STN Shop Television Network Ltd. [Vancouver Stock Exchange symbol]
SPV............ Storage Process Vent [Nuclear energy]   (NRCH)
SPV............ Storage Protect Violation   (CMD)
SPV............ Sulfophosphovanillin (Reaction) [Clinical chemistry]
SPV............ Sun Probe near Limb of Venus [Angle]
SPV............ Surface Photovoltage [Photovoltaic energy systems]
SPV............ Survey of Personal Values [Psychology]
SPVA........ Society for the Preservation of Variety Arts   (EA)
SPVEA ...... Superintendencia do Plano de Valorizacao Economica da Amazonia [Brazil]
SPVIEU..... Spatial Vision [A publication]
SPVL .... Caraveli [Peru] [ICAO location identifier]   (ICLI)
SPVLI........ Single Premium Variable Life Investment [Insurance]
SPVN........ Supervision   (MSA)
SPVOL...... Specific Volume   (DEN)
SPVPF...... Shuttle Payload Vertical Processing Facility [NASA]   (MCD)
SPVR......... Storage Process Vent Room [Nuclear energy]   (NRCH)
SPVR......... Vitor/San Isidro [Peru] [ICAO location identifier]   (ICLI)
Spvry Mgt ... Supervisory Management [A publication]
SPVS......... Supervisors Section [American Association of School Librarians]
Spvsr .... Supervisor
SPW.......... Self-Protection Weapon
SPW.......... Seward Park [Washington] [Seismograph station code, US Geological Survey]   (SEIS)
SPW.......... Shipment Planning Worksheet
SPW.......... Shipping World and Shipbuilder [A publication]
SPW.......... Spaceway Science Fiction [A publication]
SPW.......... Spare Parts Withdrawal   (MCD)
SPW.......... Special Warfare   (NVT)
SPW.......... Specialist, Chaplain's Assistant [Navy rating]
SPW.......... Spencer [Iowa] [Airport symbol]   (OAG)
SPW.......... SPX Corp. [Formerly, Sealed Power Corp.] [NYSE symbol]   (SPSG)
SPW.......... Wofford College, Spartanburg, SC [OCLC symbol]   (OCLC)
SPWA........ Southern Peanut Warehousemen's Association   (EA)
SPWA........ Steel Products Warehouse Association

SPWAO..... Small Press Writers and Artists Organization   (EA)
SPWAR..... Special Warfare
SPWC....... Society for the Punishment of War Criminals   (EA)
SPWG....... Space Parts Working Group
SPWL....... Single Premium Whole Life Insurance Policy
SPWLA...... Society of Professional Well Log Analysts   (EA)
SPWLA Logging Symp Trans ... SPWLA [Society of Professional Well Log Analysts] Logging Symposium. Transactions [A publication]
SPWM....... Single-Sided Pulse Width Modulation [Telecommunications]
SPWP .... Society of Prayer for World Peace   (EAIO)
SPWR....... Small Pressurized Water Reactor
SPWS .... Shipment Planning Worksheet   (MCD)
SPWSM.... Spanish War Service Medal
SPWVSRA ... Selected Papers. West Virginia Shakespeare and Renaissance Association [A publication]
SPWWIII .. Society for the Prevention of World War III [Defunct]
SPX........... League City, TX [Location identifier] [FAA]   (FAAL)
SPX........... Simplex Circuit
SPX........... Simplex Instrument [Telegraphy]
SPX........... Spirit Petroleum [Vancouver Stock Exchange symbol]
SPX........... Superheat Power Experiment [Nuclear energy]
SPXAC ...... Specialist, Archivist [Navy rating]
SPXAR ...... Specialist, Artist [Navy rating]
SPXBL....... Specialist, Ballistics [Navy rating]
SPXCC ...... Specialist, Cable Censor [Navy rating]
SPXCG ...... Specialist, Crystal Grinder [Navy rating]
SPXCT....... Specialist, Cartographer [Navy rating]
SPXDI .... Specialist, Discharge Interviewer [Navy rating]
SPXED ...... Specialist, Engineering Draftsman [Navy rating]
SPXFP ...... Specialist, Fingerprint Expert [Navy rating]
SPXGU...... Specialist, Gauge Specialist [Navy rating]
SPXID .... Specialist, Intelligence Duties [Navy rating]
SPXIR .... Specialist, Interpreter [Navy rating]
SPXJO....... Specialist, Journalist [Navy rating]
SPXKP....... Specialist, Key Punch Operator and Supervisor [Navy rating]
SPXNC...... Specialist, Naval Correspondent [Navy rating]
SPXOP...... Specialist, Special Project [Navy rating]
SPXPC...... Specialist, Position Classifier [Navy rating]
SPXPI .... Specialist, Pigeon Trainer [Navy rating]
SPXPL....... Specialist, Plastic Expert [Navy rating]
SPXPR....... Specialist, Public Information [Navy rating]
SPXQM.... Specialist, Operations - Plotting and Chart Work [Navy rating]
SPXRL....... Specialist, Research Laboratory [Navy rating]
SPXRS....... Specialist, Armed Forces Radio Service and Special Naval Radio Units [Navy rating]
SPXSB....... Specialist, Telephone Switchboard Operator and Supervisor [Navy rating]
SPXST ...... Specialist, Strategic Services [Navy rating]
SPXTD...... Specialist, Topographic Draftsman [Navy rating]
SPXTS....... Specialist, Air Stations Operations Desk - Time Shack [Navy rating]
SPXVA ...... Specialist, Visual Training Aids [Navy rating]
s-py---......... Paraguay [MARC geographic area code] [Library of Congress]   (LCCP)
SPY........... Saint Paul Island, AK [Location identifier] [FAA]   (FAAL)
SPY........... San Pedro [Ivory Coast] [Airport symbol]   (OAG)
SPY........... Spectra-Physics, Inc. [NYSE symbol]   (SPSG)
SPY........... Square Pyramidal [Organic chemistry]
SPYA........ Luya [Peru] [ICAO location identifier]   (ICLI)
SPYC........ Yarinacocha [Peru] [ICAO location identifier]   (ICLI)
SPYL .... Talara/Capitan Montes [Peru] [ICAO location identifier]   (ICLI)
SPYO........ Pacasmayo [Peru] [ICAO location identifier]   (ICLI)
SPYR........ Sprayer   (MSA)
SPYU........ Yauca [Peru] [ICAO location identifier]   (ICLI)
SPZ........... Spar Aerospace Ltd. [Toronto Stock Exchange symbol]
SPZ........... Springdale [Arkansas] [Airport symbol]   (OAG)
SPZ........... Submarine Patrol Zone [Navy]   (NVT)
SPZ........... Sulfinpyrazone [Uricosuric compound]
SPZA........ Nazca [Peru] [ICAO location identifier]   (ICLI)
SPZH........ Pachiza [Peru] [ICAO location identifier]   (ICLI)
SPZK........ Sotziki [Peru] [ICAO location identifier]   (ICLI)
SPZO........ Cuzco/Velazco Astete [Peru] [ICAO location identifier]   (ICLI)
sp z oo........ Spolka z Ogranizcena Odpowiedzialnoscia [Limited Company] [Polish] [Business term]
sp z op .... Spolka z Ogranizcna Poreka [Company with Limited Liability] [Polish] [Business term]
SPZT .... Chazuta [Peru] [ICAO location identifier]   (ICLI)
SQ.............. E. R. Squibb & Sons [Research code symbol]
SQ.............. Safety Quotient
SQ.............. Sequens [Following] [Latin]
SQ.............. Shakespeare Quarterly [A publication]
SQ.............. Sick Quarters [Navy] [British]
SQ.............. Singapore Airlines Ltd. [ICAO designator]   (FAAC)
SQ.............. Situation Questionnaire
SQ.............. Social Quotient [Psychology]
SQ.............. Southern Quarterly [A publication]
SQ.............. Specialist Qualifications [British military]   (DMA)
SQ.............. Squadron
SQ.............. Squall [Meteorology]

SQ .... Squamous [*Cell*] [*Oncology*]
SQ .... Square (EY)
sq .... Square Tank [*Liquid gas carriers*]
SQ .... Squeezed Files [*Data processing*]
SQ .... Staff Qualified [*Military*] [*British*]
SQ .... Stereoquadraphonic [*Record playing system*] [*CBS*]
S-Q .... Stock Quality [*Pisciculture*]
SQ .... Subcutaneous [*Beneath the Skin*] [*Medicine*]
SQ .... Superquick [*Fuse*]
SQ .... Survival Quotient (ADA)
sq .... Swaziland [*MARC country of publication code*] [*Library of Congress*] (LCCP)
SQA .... Sequa Corp. [*NYSE symbol*] (SPSG)
SQA .... Software Quality Assurance [*Data processing*] (IEEE)
SQA .... South Queensland Airways [*Australia*]
SQA .... Sparrevohn, AK [*Location identifier*] [*FAA*] (FAAL)
SQA .... Squaring Amplifier
SQA .... Stina Resources Ltd. [*Vancouver Stock Exchange symbol*]
SQA .... Supplier Quality Assurance
SQA .... Surveyor Quality Assurance
SQA .... System Queue Area [*Data processing*] (BUR)
SQAD .... Surveyor Quality Assurance Directive
SQAI......... Square Industries, Inc. [*NASDAQ symbol*] (NQ)
SQAL......... Squall [*Meteorology*] (FAAC)
SQAP........ Supplemental Quality Assurance Provision [*Military*]
SQAPP ..... Software Quality Assurance Program Plan [*Data processing*]
SQAR .... Supplier Quality Assurance Representative
SQAT........ Ship's Qualification Assistance Team [*Navy*]
SQAW .... Schriften und Quellen der Alten Welt [*A publication*]
SQB .... Space Qualified Booster
SQB .... Squibb Corp. [*NYSE symbol*] (SPSG)
SQBC......... Space Qualified Booster Charger
SQC .... Self-Quenching Control
SQC .... Sierra Madre Resources [*Vancouver Stock Exchange symbol*]
SQC .... Social Questions Committee [*Church of England in Australia, Melbourne Diocese*]
SQC .... Southern Cross [*Australia*] [*Airport symbol*] (OAG)
SQC .... Station Quality Control [*RADAR*]
SQC .... Statistical Quality Control
SQCG .... Squirrel Cage [*Electricity*]
SQCM .... Square Centimeter (MSA)
SQCP........ Statistical Quality Control Procedure
SQD .... Self-Quenching Detector
SQD .... Signal Quality Detector
SQD .... Social Questions of Today [*A publication*]
SQD .... Squad (AABC)
SQD .... Squadron (NVT)
SQD .... Square D Co. [*NYSE symbol*] (SPSG)
SQDC......... Special Quick Disconnect Coupling
SQDN......... Squadron (AAG)
Sqdn Ldr .... Squadron-Leader [*British military*] (DMA)
SQE .... Software Quality Evaluation
SQE .... Startec Marketing [*Vancouver Stock Exchange symbol*]
SQE .... Supplier Quality Engineering (MCD)
SQF............. Cleveland, OH [*Location identifier*] [*FAA*] (FAAL)
SQF............. Semiquantitative Fibrinogen [*Hematology*]
SQF............. Socialist Thought and Practice [*A publication*]
SQFT .... Square Foot (MSA)
SQG .... Small Quantity Generator [*Automotive engineering*] [*Environmental Protection Agency*]
SQH........... Ford-Aire [*Sidney, NY*] [*FAA designator*] (FAAC)
SQH........... Square Head [*Bolt*]
SQHA........ Standard Quarter Horse Association (EA)
SQI .... Skill Qualification Identifier [*Army*] (INF)
SQI .... Special Qualifications Identifiers [*Army*] (AABC)
SQI .... Sterling/Rock Falls [*Illinois*] [*Airport symbol*] (OAG)
SQIC........... Suppliers Quality Identification Classification
SQIN......... Square Inch (MSA)
SQKM .... Square Kilometer (MSA)
SQL............. San Carlos, CA [*Location identifier*] [*FAA*] (FAAL)
SQL............. School Quota Letter
SQL............. Space Qualified LASER
SQL............. Squelch
SQL............. Standard High-Level Query Language
SQL............. Standard Quantum Limit [*Physics*]
SQL............. Strand Resources [*Vancouver Stock Exchange symbol*]
SQL............. Structured Query Language [*IBM Corp.*]
SQL/DS .... Structured Query Language/Data System [*IBM Corp.*]
SQLN......... Squall Line [*Meteorology*] (FAAC)
SQLW........ Sinclair QL World [*A publication*]
SQM .... Level Island, AK [*Location identifier*] [*FAA*] (FAAL)
SQM .... Sao Miguel Do Araguaia [*Brazil*] [*Airport symbol*] (OAG)
SQM .... Square Meter
SQMC......... Squadron Quartermaster-Corporal [*British military*] (DMA)
SQMD .... Squadron Manning Document (NVT)
SQMS......... Squadron Quartermaster-Serjeant [*Military*] [*British*] (ROG)
SQMS......... Staff Quartermaster Sergeant
SQMV .... Squash Mosaic Virus
SQN........... Sanana [*Indonesia*] [*Airport symbol*] (OAG)
SQN........... School Quota Number
SQN........... Spin Quantum Number [*Atomic physics*]

SQN........... Squadron (NATG)
SQN........... Susquehanna Corp. [*AMEX symbol*] (SPSG)
SQNA .... Squadron Airfield (NATG)
Sqn Ldr ...... Squadron-Leader [*British military*] (DMA)
Sqn Obs .... Squadron Observer [*British military*] (DMA)
Sqn Offr .... Squadron-Officer [*British military*] (DMA)
SQNT .... Sequent Computer Systems, Inc. [*NASDAQ symbol*] (NQ)
SQO........... Senior Quarters Officer [*British military*] (DMA)
SQO........... Squadron Officer
SQP........... Secret Pass Mine [*Vancouver Stock Exchange symbol*]
SQP........... Shippensburg State College, Shippensburg, PA [*OCLC symbol*] (OCLC)
SQP........... Successive Quadratic Programming [*Algorithm*] [*Data processing*]
SQPD........ Super Quick Point Detonating
SQPN .... Staggered Quadriphase Pseudorandom Noise (MCD)
SQQ .... San Quentin Quail [*A minor female*] [*Slang*]
SQQ .... Sequentibus [*In the Following Places*] [*Latin*]
SQR .... Sequence Relay (KSC)
SQR .... Sequoia Resources Ltd. [*Vancouver Stock Exchange symbol*]
SQR .... Soroako [*Indonesia*] [*Airport symbol*] (OAG)
SQR .... Square
SQR .... Square Root [*Data processing*]
SQR .... State Reports (Queensland) [*A publication*]
SQR .... Supplier Quality Rating
SQR .... Supplier Quality Representative [*Nuclear energy*] (NRCH)
SQ3R .... Survey, Question, Read, Review, Recite [*Psychology*]
SQRT......... Seismic Qualification Review Team [*Nuclear energy*] (NRCH)
SQRT........ Square Root
SQS............. Skill Qualification Score [*Military*] (AABC)
SQS............. Statistische Quellenwerke der Schweiz [*Switzerland*]
SQS............. Stochastic Queuing System
SQS............. Stratford American Corp. [*Vancouver Stock Exchange symbol*]
SQS............. Superquick Sensor (MCD)
SQ/SD .... Special Qualifications/Special Designation (NVT)
SQSSE .... Supplier Quality System Survey Evaluations (MCD)
SQT .... Melbourne, FL [*Location identifier*] [*FAA*] (FAAL)
SQT .... Queensland State Reports [*A publication*] (DLA)
SQT .... Ship Qualification Test [*or Trial*] [*Navy*]
SQT .... Silverquest Resources [*Vancouver Stock Exchange symbol*]
SQT .... Skill Qualification Test [*Army*]
SQT .... Soldier Qualification Test (MCD)
SQT .... Sterilization Qualification Tests
SQT .... System Qualification Tests
SQTIPT..... Ship Qualification Trials in Port [*Navy*] (NVT)
SQTNG ...... Squadron Training (NVT)
SQTT......... Ship Qualification Trial Team [*Navy*] (NG)
SQU .... E. R. Squibb & Sons, Princeton, NJ [*OCLC symbol*] (OCLC)
Squ .... Square (BJA)
SQU .... Squaw Peak [*Utah*] [*Seismograph station code, US Geological Survey*] (SEIS)
SQUAD ..... Squadron
SQUADEX ... Squadron Exercises [*Canadian Navy*]
SQUAF...... Sonobuoy Qualification Facility [*Navy*] (CAAL)
SQUALL... Salary Quotient at Lower Limits [*Business term*]
SQUAP...... Supplementary Quality Assurance Provisions
SQUARE.... Specifying Queries as Relational Expressions [*Programming language*] [*1973*] [*Data processing*] (CSR)
S Quart ...... Southern Quarterly [*A publication*]
Squibb Abstr Bull ... Squibb Abstract Bulletin [*A publication*]
Squibb Auc ... Squibb on Auctioneers [*2nd ed.*] [*1891*] [*A publication*] (DLA)
SQUID ..... Sperry Quick Updating of Internal Documentation (IEEE)
SQUID ...... Submerged Quick Intervention Device [*Human-powered submarine*]
SQUID ...... Superconducting Quantum Interference Detector [*or Device*] [*For study of magnetic fields*]
SQUIRE .... Submarine Quickened Response
SQUO....... Squadron-Officer [*British military*] (DSUE)
SQUOD... Selected Quantile Output Device [*Electronics*]
SQUOFF... Squadron-Officer [*British military*] (DSUE)
SQW .... Squarewave (MSA)
SQWV ...... Squarewave
SQX .... Sulfaquinoxaline [*or (Sulfanilamido)quinoxaline*] [*Animal antibiotic*]
SQZGR...... Squeeze Grip
SR .... Air-Cushion Vehicle built by Saunders Roe [*England*] [*Usually used in combination with numerals*]
SR .... Air Search RADAR Receiver [*Shipborne*]
SR .... General Society, Sons of the Revolution (EA)
SR .... New South Wales State Reports [*A publication*]
SR .... New York State Reporter [*A publication*] (DLA)
SR .... Partiia Sotsialistov Revolyutsionerov [*Socialist Revolutionary Party*] [*Russian*] [*Political party*] (PPE)
SR .... Regina Public Library, Saskatchewan [*Library symbol*] [*National Library of Canada*] (NLC)
SR .... Saarlandischer Rundfunk [*Radio network*] [*West Germany*]
SR .... Safety Recommendation (AAG)
SR .... Safety Release [*Army*]
S/R............. Safety Relief Valve [*Nuclear energy*] (NRCH)
S/R............. Safety Representative [*Insurance*]
SR .... Safety Rod [*Nuclear energy*] (NRCH)

SR	Salva Ratificatione [*On Condition of Ratification*] [*Latin*]
SR	Sample Rate
SR	Sanctioned Ritual [*British*] [*Slang*]
SR	Sarcoplasmic Reticulum [*Anatomy*]
SR	Saturable Reactor
SR	Saturation Recovery [*NMR imaging*]
SR	Saturday Review [*A publication*]
SR	Saudi Riyal [*Monetary unit*] (BJA)
SR	Savannah River Test Pile [*Nuclear energy*] (NRCH)
SR	Sawyer Rifle
SR	Scan Radius
SR	Scan Rate
SR	Scan Ratio (MCD)
SR	Scanning Radiometer
SR	Schooner [*Shipping*] (ROG)
SR	Schumann Runge [*Spectral region*]
SR	Schweizerische Rundschau [*A publication*]
SR	Sciences Religieuses [*A publication*]
SR	Scientific Report
SR	Scientific Research
SR	Scoring Reliability (MCD)
SR	Scottish Regional [*Council*]
SR	Scottish Rifles [*Military unit*] [*British*]
SR	Scripture Reader (ROG)
SR	Seaman Recruit [*Navy*]
SR	Seaplane Reconnaissance Aircraft
SR	Search RADAR
SR	Search and Reconnaissance [*Air Force*]
SR	Search and Recovery [*Military*]
SR	Search and Rescue
SR	Second-Harmonic Resonance (MCD)
SR	Secretion Rate [*Endocrinology*]
SR	Section Report
SR	Sedimentation Rate
SR	Selective Ringing
SR	Selenium Rectifier [*Electronics*]
SR	Self-Rectifying
SR	Semantic Reaction
SR	Senate Recedes
SR	Senate Report
SR	Senate Resolution
SR	Send and Receive
SR	Senior
SR	Senior Registrar
SR	Senior Reviewer
SR	Senor [*Mister*] [*Spanish*]
SR	Sensitivity Ratio
SR	Sensitivity Response [*Cell*] [*Radiology*]
SR	Sensitization Response
SR	Sensory Rhodopsin [*Biochemistry*]
SR	Separate Rations [*Military*]
S & R	Sergeant and Rawle's Pennsylvania Reports [*1824-28*] [*A publication*] (DLA)
SR	Series Number [*Online database field identifier*]
SR	Service Record [*Military*]
SR	Service Report
SR	Service Rifle [*British military*] (DMA)
S-R	Set-Reset [*Flip-Flop*] [*Data processing*]
SR	Settlement Register [*Data processing*]
SR	Severe, Right-Moving [*Thunderstorm*]
SR	Sewanee Review [*A publication*]
SR	Sex Ratio [*Biology*]
SR	Shaft Rate (NVT)
SR	Sharpened Romberg [*Equilibrium*]
SR	Shift Register
SR	Shift Reverse
SR	Shift Right
SR	Ship Repair Ratings
SR	Ship-to-Shore RADAR [*or Radio*] (DEN)
SR	Shipment [*or Shipping*] Request
S/R	Shipper/Receiver [*Difference*]
SR	Shipping Receipt [*Business term*]
SR	Ships Records (MCD)
SR	Shock Related
SR	Shock Resistance
SR	Short Range
SR	Short Rate
SR	Short Run [*Economics*]
SR	Shutdown Request [*NASA*] (KSC)
SR	Side Rails [*On a bed*] [*Medicine*]
SR	Sigma Reaction
SR	Signor [*Mister*] [*Italian*]
SR	Silicon Rectifier
SR	Silicon Rubber
SR	Simian Rotavirus [*Pathology*]
SR	Simla Rifles [*British military*] (DMA)
SR	Simulation Report
SR	Single Reduction
SR	Sinus Rhythm [*Medicine*]
SR	Sinus Roris [*Bay of Dew*] [*Lunar area*]
SR	Sir

SR	Sister
SR	Skeleton Records [*Army*]
SR	Skywave Synchronization (DEN)
SR	Slant Range
SR	Slave River Journal [*Fort Smith, Northwest Territory*] [*A publication*]
SR	Slavic Review [*A publication*]
SR	Slavisticna Revija [*A publication*]
SR	Slavonic Review [*A publication*]
SR	Slew Rate
SR	Sling Ring
SR	Slip Ring [*Electricity*]
SR	Sloane Ranger [*Member of a British social set satirized in "The Official Sloane Ranger Handbook, The First Guide to What Really Matters in Life"*] [*Name is derived from Sloane Square in Chelsea*]
SR	Slovenska Rec [*A publication*]
SR	Slow Release [*Electronics*]
SR	Small Ring
SR	Social Register
SR	Social Research [*A publication*]
SR	Socialist Revolutionary [*USSR*]
SR	Society of Radiographers (EAIO)
SR	Society of Rheology [*Later, SoR*] (EA)
SR	Society of Rosicrucians (EA)
SR	Sociologia Religiosa [*A publication*]
SR	Solar Radiation
SR	Solar Reference
SR	Solicitor's Recommendation [*Internal Revenue Bureau*] [*United States*] [*A publication*] (DLA)
SR	Solid Rocket
SR	Soluble, Repository [*With reference to penicillin*]
SR	Songwriter's Review [*A publication*]
SR	Soror [*Sister*]
SR	Sorter Reader
SR	Sortie Rate (MCD)
SR	Sound Ranging
SR	Sound Rating (IEEE)
SR	Sound Recordings [*US Copyright Office class*]
SR	Sound Report
SR	Source Range [*Nuclear energy*] (NRCH)
SR	Southern Railway Co. [*NYSE symbol*] (SPSG)
SR	Southern Review [*US*] [*A publication*]
SR	Southern Rhodesia [*Later, Zimbabwe*]
SR	Southern Rhodesia High Court Reports [*A publication*] (DLA)
SR	Southwest Review [*A publication*]
SR	Sovjetskaja Rossija [*A publication*]
SR	Spares Requirement
SR	Special Register
SR	Special Regulations [*Military*]
SR	Special Report
SR	Special Reserve
SR	Specific Range
SR	Specification Requirement
SR	Spectral Recording
SR	Speech Recognition
SR	Speed Recorder (IEEE)
SR	Speed Regulator
SR	Spelling Reform (ADA)
SR	Split Ring [*Technical drawings*]
SR	Spontaneous Discharge Rate [*Audiology*]
S/R	Spotter Reconnaissance [*Air Force*] [*British*]
S-R	Spring Inflow-River Inflow [*Geology*]
SR	Square [*Ship's rigging*] (ROG)
SR	Stable Recipient [*Medicine*]
SR	Staff Report
SR	Stage of Resistance [*in General-Adaptation Syndrome*]
SR	Stage Right [*A stage direction*]
SR	Standard Range Approach [*Aviation*]
SR	Standard Repair (AAG)
SR	Standard Requirement
SR	Standardization Report
SR	Star Route [*A type of rural postal delivery route*]
SR	Starting Relay (DEN)
SR	State Register
SR	Statement of Requirements [*NASA*] (MCD)
SR	Stateroom (MSA)
SR	Station Radio [*British*]
SR	Station Regulation
SR	Stationery Request (MCD)
SR	Statistical Reporter [*Manila*] [*A publication*]
SR	Statstjanstemannens Riksforbund [*National Association of Salaried Employees in Government Service*] [*Sweden*]
SR	Status Register [*Data processing*]
SR	Status Report
SR	Status Review [*NASA*] (NASA)
SR	Statutes Revised [*A publication*] (DLA)
SR	Statutory Regulations [*New Zealand*] [*A publication*]
SR	Statutory Rule (ADA)
SR	Steep Rock Resources, Inc. [*Toronto Stock Exchange symbol*]
sr	Steradian [*Symbol*] [*SI unit of solid angle*]

SR	Stereo Review [*A publication*]
SR	Steroid Receptor [*Endocrinology*]
S-R	Stimulus-Response
SR	Stock Replacement (AAG)
SR	Stock Report
SR	Storage Rack
SR	Storage Register
SR	Storage and Repair (MCD)
S/R	Storage/Retrieval [*Data processing*]
S & R	Storage and Retrieval [*Data processing*]
S & R	Storage Room
SR	Stove or Range
S & R	Stowage and Repair
SR	Strategic Research (MCD)
SR	Stress-Rupture (MCD)
SR	Strike Rate (ADA)
SR	Stripe Rot [*Plant pathology*]
Sr	Strontium [*Chemical element*]
Sr	Strouhal Number [*IUPAC*]
SR	Studia Rosenthaliana [*Assen*] [*A publication*]
SR	Studies in Religion [*A publication*]
SR	Studies in the Renaissance [*A publication*]
SR	Studies and Reports. Ben-Zvi Institute [*Jerusalem*] [*A publication*]
SR	Studies in Romanticism [*A publication*]
SR	Study Regulation (MCD)
SR	Study Requirement [*Air Force*]
SR	Styrene Rubber
SR	Su Remesa [*Your Remittance*] [*Spanish*] [*Business term*]
SR	Subject Ratio
SR	Submarine Recorder [*British military*] (DMA)
SR	Subroutine [*Data processing*] (AAG)
SR	Subscriber Register
SR	Sugar Requirements and Quotas
SR	Sulfonamide-Resistant [*Microbiology*]
SR	Summary Report
SR	Sunrise [*Meteorology*] (FAAC)
SR	Supervisor (TEL)
SR	Supplemental Report
SR	Supplementary Regulation
SR	Supplementary Reserve [*British military*] (DMA)
SR	Supply Room
SR	Support Reaction Load (NRCH)
SR	Support Request [*or Requirement*] (KSC)
SR	Support Room (MCD)
SR	Supporting Research [*Military*]
SR	Suppressor Receptor [*Embryology*]
SR	Supreme Court of Quebec, Reports [*A publication*] (DLA)
SR	Surface Roughness
sr	Surinam [*MARC country of publication code*] [*Library of Congress*] (LCCP)
SR	Surinam [*ANSI two-letter standard code*] (CNC)
SR	Surveillance RADAR [*Air Force*]
SR	Surveying Recorder [*Navy rating*] [*British*]
SR	Surveyor [*British military*] (DMA)
SR	Sustained Release [*Pharmacy*]
SR	Sveriges Radio
SR	Swissair [*Airline*] [*ICAO designator*]
SR	Switch Register
SR	Synchrotron Radiation [*High-energy physics*]
SR	Systematische Sammlung des Bundesrechts [*Switzerland*] [*A publication*]
SR	Systems Review [*Medicine*]
SR	Union of Soviet Socialist Republics [*IYRU nationality code*] (IYR)
SR-11	Sapporo Rat (Virus)
SRA	Journal. Society of Research Administrators [*A publication*]
SRA	Sair Aviation [*Syracuse, NY*] [*FAA designator*] (FAAC)
SRA	San Ramon [*Costa Rica*] [*Seismograph station code, US Geological Survey*] (SEIS)
SRA	Saskatchewan Archives, Regina, Saskatchewan [*Library symbol*] [*National Library of Canada*] (NLC)
SRA	Saturday Review of the Arts [*A publication*]
SRA	Screw Research Association (EA)
SRA	Scuba Retailers Association (EA)
SRA	Seatrade [*A publication*]
SRA	Selective Restricted Availability (MCD)
SRA	Self-Regulatory Agency [*Securities*] [*British*]
SrA	Senior Airman
SRA	Senior Residential Appraiser [*Designation awarded by Society of Real Estate Appraisers*]
SRA	Service and Regulatory Announcement, Department of Agriculture [*A publication*] (DLA)
SRA	Servicemen's Readjustment Act
SRA	Ship Radio Authorization [*Army*] (AABC)
SRA	Ship Replaceable Assembly (MCD)
SRA	Shipyard Restricted Availability [*Navy*] (CAAL)
SRA	Shop-Replaceable Assembly [*NASA*]
SRA	Short-Range Acquisition (MCD)
SRA	Short Reflex Arc
SRA	Simultaneous Range Adcock Antenna [*Military RADAR*]
SRA	Small, Replaceable Assembly (RDA)
SRA	Smoker's Rights Alliance (EA)
SRA	Social Research and Applications [*Research center*] (RCD)
SRA	Social Research Association [*British*]
SRA	Social Responsibility Auditing (ADA)
SRA	Society of Research Administrators (EA)
SRA	Society of Residential Appraisers [*Later, AI*]
SRA	Society for Risk Analysis (EA)
SRA	Sociological Research Association (EA)
SRA	Southern Rhodesia Artillery [*British military*] (DMA)
SRA	Southern Rural Action, Inc.
SRA	Spanish Refugee Aid (EA)
SRA	Special Refractories Association [*Defunct*] (EA)
SRA	Special Repair Activity (MCD)
SRA	Special Rules Area
SRA	Specialized Repair Activity
SRA	Specular Reflectance Accessory [*Spectrophotometry*]
SRA	Spin Reference Axis (KSC)
SRA	Squash Rackets Association [*British*]
SRA	Standards of Readiness and Availability (NATG)
SRA	Station Representatives Association (EA)
SRA	Stearman Restorers Association (EA)
SRA	Stock Record Account (AFM)
SR & A	Strategy, Research & Action [*Commercial firm*] [*British*]
SRA	Stratus Computer, Inc. [*NYSE symbol*] (SPSG)
SRA	Structures Research Associates
SRA	Subminiature Rotary Actuator
SRA	Sugar Rationing Administration [*Department of Agriculture*] [*Ceased functions, 1948*]
SRA	Sulforicinoleic Acid [*Organic chemistry*]
SRA	Sun's Right Ascension [*Astrology*] (ROG)
SRA	Supplemental Retirement Annuities
SRA	Support Requirements Analysis [*NASA*] (NASA)
SRA	Surgeon Rear-Admiral [*British military*]
SRA	Surveillance RADAR Approach
SRA	Syria. Revue d'Art Oriental et d'Archeologie [*A publication*]
SRA	System Reaction Analysis [*Bell System*]
SRA	System Reliability Analysis
SRA	System Requirements Analysis
SRA	Systems Research and Applications Corp. [*Arlington, VA*] (TSSD)
SRAA	Scholastic Rowing Association of America (EA)
SRAA	Senior Army Advisor (AABC)
SRAAG	Senior Army Advisor, Army National Guard (AABC)
SRAAM	Short-Range Air-to-Air Missile (MCD)
SRAAR	Senior Army Advisor, Army Reserve (AABC)
SRAB	Allan Blair Memorial Clinic, Regina, Saskatchewan [*Library symbol*] [*National Library of Canada*] (NLC)
SRAC	Alcoholism Commission of Saskatchewan, Regina, Saskatchewan [*Library symbol*] [*National Library of Canada*] (NLC)
SRAC	Safe Return Amnesty Committee (EA)
SRAC	Sears Roebuck Acceptance Corporation
SRAC	Short Run Average Costs
SRAC	Societe Royale d'Astronomie du Canada
SrAcftCrmnBad	Senior Aircraft Crewman Badge [*Military decoration*] (AABC)
SR-ACK	Service Request Acknowledgment [*Air Force*] (CET)
SRACR	Southern Rhodesia Armoured Car Regiment [*British military*] (DMA)
SRAD	Solar Radiation (NOAA)
SR/AD	Supporting Research and Advanced Development
SRAE	Solar Radio Astronomy Experiment
SRAEL	Labour Market Planning and Information Resource Centre, Saskatchewan Department of Advanced Education and Manpower, Regina, Saskatchewan [*Library symbol*] [*National Library of Canada*] (NLC)
SRAEN	Systeme de Reference pour la Determination de l'Affaiblissement Equivalent pour la Nettete [*Master telephone transmission reference system*] (DEN)
SRAEW	Women's Services Branch, Saskatchewan Department of Advanced Education and Manpower, Regina, Saskatchewan [*Library symbol*] [*National Library of Canada*] (NLC)
SRAF	Archibald Foundation, Regina, Saskatchewan [*Library symbol*] [*National Library of Canada*] (NLC)
SRAF	Social Revolutionary Anarchist Federation (EA)
SRAF	Standby Reserve of the Armed Forces
SRAFO	Senior Royal Air Force Officer [*British military*] (DMA)
SRAG	Saskatchewan Department of Agriculture, Regina, Saskatchewan [*Library symbol*] [*National Library of Canada*] (NLC)
SRAG	Semiactive RADAR Antiair Guidance System
SRAG	Space Radiation Analysis Group [*NASA*] (NASA)
SRAGE	Shared Services, Agriculture Canada [*Services en Commun, Agriculture Canada*], Regina, Saskatchewan [*Library symbol*] [*National Library of Canada*] (NLC)
SRAGR	Research Station, Agriculture Canada [*Station de Recherches, Agriculture Canada*] Regina, Saskatchewan [*Library symbol*] [*National Library of Canada*] (NLC)

SRAI.......... Soybean Research Advisory Institute [*Terminated, 1984*] (EGAO)
SRAI.......... Supercat Race Association International (EA)
SRA-J Soc R ... SRA - Journal of the Society of Research Administrators [*A publication*]
SRAM....... Semirandom Access Memory
SRAM....... Short-Range Attack Missile [*Military*]
SRAM....... Skill Qualification Test Requirements Alert Message
SRAM....... Some Remarks on Abstract Machines [*Data processing*]
SRAM....... SQT [*Ship's Qualification Trial*] Requirments Alert Message
SRAM....... Static Random Access Memory [*Data processing*]
SRAMA..... Spring Research and Manufacturers' Association (EAIO)
SRAM(T) .. Short-Range Attack Missile (Tactical) [*Military*]
SRAN .... Short-Range Aids to Navigation [*Navy*]
SRAN .... Skill Qualification Test Requirements Alert Notice
SRAN .... Stock Record Account Number (AFM)
SRANA..... Shrine Recorders Association of North America (EA)
SRANC...... Southern Rhodesia African National Congress
SRAO .... Supplemental Recreational Activities Overseas [*Red Cross*]
SRAP........ Service Record and Allied Papers [*Military*]
SRAP........ Slow Response Action Potentials [*Neurophysiology*]
SRAP........ Standard Range Approach [*Aviation*]
SRARAV .. Senior Army Aviator (AABC)
SrArAvBad ... Senior Army Aviator Badge [*Military decoration*]
SRARM..... Short-Range Antiradiation Missile
SR Arts...... Saturday Review of the Arts [*A publication*]
SRAS........ Albert South Library, Regina, Saskatchewan [*Library symbol*] [*National Library of Canada*] (NLC)
SRAT........ Search RADAR Alignment Test [*Military*] (CAAL)
SRAT........ Short-Range Applied Technology
SRAT-B .... Self-Report Assertiveness Test for Boys
SRATC...... Short-Run Average Total Cost [*Economics*]
SRATS...... Solar Radiation and Thermospheric Structure [*Japanese satellite*]
SRATUC ... Southern Rhodesian African Trade Union Congress
Sr Autobahn ... Strasse und Autobahn [*A publication*]
SRAVC...... Short-Run Average Variable Cost [*Economics*]
SRAW....... Short-Range Antitank Weapon
SRaw.......... Specific Resistance, Airway [*Medicine*]
SRAX........ Southern Air Transport, Inc. [*Air carrier designation symbol*]
SRAZ........ Studia Romanica et Anglica Zagrabiensia [*A publication*]
SRB.......... Safety Review Board [*Nuclear energy*] (NRCH)
SRB.......... Schilpp, Reed B., Los Angeles CA [*STAC*]
SRB.......... Scurry-Rainbow Oil Ltd. [*AMEX symbol*] (SPSG)
SRB.......... Seaplane Repair Base
SRB.......... Selective Reenlistment Bonus [*Military*] (AABC)
SRB.......... Self-Retaining Bolt
SRB.......... Service Record Book [*Military*]
SRB.......... Service Request Block [*Data processing*] (BUR)
SRB.......... Sheftall Record Book [*A publication*] (BJA)
SRB.......... Sky Ranch for Boys (EA)
SRB.......... Solar Reflectory Beacon
SRB.......... Solid-Rocket Booster [*NASA*]
SRB.......... Sorter Reader Buffer
SRB.......... Sparta, TN [*Location identifier*] [*FAA*] (FAAL)
SRB.......... Special Review Board [*Military*] (INF)
SRB.......... Spherical Roller Bearing
SRB.......... State Research Bureau [*Secret police*] [*Uganda*]
SRB.......... Styrene Rubber Butadiene (NG)
SRB.......... Sulfate Reducing Bacteria
SRB.......... Support Research Branch [*Springfield Armory*]
SRB.......... System Review Board (MCD)
SRBA........ Statistical Record of Black America [*A publication*]
SRBA........ Students for the Right to Bear Arms (EA)
SRBAB...... Solid-Rocket Booster Assembly Building [*NASA*] (NASA)
SRBC........ Serum-Treated Red Blood Cell [*Clinical chemistry*]
SRBC........ Sheep Red Blood Cell[s] [*Also, SRC*]
SRBC........ Sunrise Bancorp [*NASDAQ symbol*] (NQ)
SRBC........ Susquehanna River Basin Commission [*Federal government*] (EGAO)
SRBC........ Susquehanna River Basin Compact [*Maryland, Pennsylvania, New York*]
SRBCSS .... Scales for Rating the Behavioral Characteristics of Superior Students [*Educational test*]
SRBDF ...... Solid-Rocket Booster Disassembly Facility [*NASA*] (NASA)
SRBDM..... Short-Range Bomber Defense Missile
SRBE........ Societe Royale Belge des Electriciens [*Belgium*] (MCD)
SRBM........ Short-Range Ballistic Missile
SRBMI ...... BMI Finance, Regina, Saskatchewan [*Library symbol*] [*National Library of Canada*] (NLC)
SRBOC...... Super Rapid Bloom Off Board Chaff [*Navy*] (NVT)
SRBPF....... Solid-Rocket Booster Processing Facility [*NASA*] (NASA)
SRBT........ Single-Rod Burst Test [*Nuclear energy*] (NRCH)
SRBUC..... Scientific Research in British Universities and Colleges [*Later, RBUPC*] [*British Library*]
SRBUD...... Space Research in Bulgaria [*A publication*]
SRC.......... AMF Sunfish Racing Class Association (EA)
SRC.......... Richland County Library, Columbia, SC [*OCLC symbol*] (OCLC)
SRC............ Sacra Rituum Congregatio [*Sacred Congregation of Rites*] [*Latin*]

SRC........... Safety Research Center [*Bureau of Mines*]
SRC........... Safety Review Committee [*Australian Nuclear Science and Technology Organisation*]
SRC........... Salinas Road [*California*] [*Seismograph station code, US Geological Survey*] (SEIS)
SRC........... Sample Recovery Container [*NASA*] (KSC)
SRC........... Sample Return Container [*NASA*] (NASA)
SRC........... Sample Rock Container [*NASA*]
SRC........... Sarcoma
SRC........... Saskatchewan Research Council [*University of Saskatchewan*] [*Research center*] (RCD)
SRC........... Saturable Reactor Coil
SRC........... Scheduled Removal Component (MCD)
SRC........... Science Research Council [*Later, SERC*] [*British*]
SRC........... Scleroderma Renal Crisis [*Medicine*]
SRC........... Scott's Hospitality, Inc. [*Toronto Stock Exchange symbol*]
SRC........... Se Ruega Contestacion [*The Favor of a Reply Is Requested*] [*Spanish*]
SRC........... Searcy, AR [*Location identifier*] [*FAA*] (FAAL)
SRC........... Secured Returns Code [*IRS*]
SRC........... Securities Research Company
SRC........... Semiconductor Research Cooperative
SRC........... Senate Rail Caucus (EA)
S/RC......... Send/Receive Center (FAAC)
SRC........... Send Register Control [*Data processing*]
SRC........... Servants of Our Lady Queen of the Clergy [*Roman Catholic women's religious order*]
SRC........... Sheep Red Cell[s] [*Also, SRBC*]
SRC........... Shutdown Reactor Cooling [*Nuclear energy*] (NRCH)
SRC........... Signal Reserve Corps
SRC........... Silicon Readout Cell
SRC........... Silicon Rectifier Column
SRC........... Single Round Container [*for toxic chemicals*] [*Army*]
SRC........... Ski Retailers Council [*Inactive*] (EA)
SRC........... Slow-Recovery Capsules [*Pharmacy*]
SRC........... Snyder Research Company [*Information service or system*] (EISS)
SRC........... Social Rehabilitation Clinic (EA)
SRC........... Societe Royale du Canada [*Royal Society of Canada - RSC*]
SRC........... Solvent-Refined Coal
SRC........... Sound Ranging Control
SRC........... Sound Recording Company [*Record label*]
SRC........... Source Range Channel (IEEE)
SRC........... Southeast Asia Resource Center (EA)
SRC........... Southern Regional Council (EA)
SRC........... Southwest Radio Church [*An association*]
SRC........... Southwest Research Corporation
SRC........... Space Research Council [*British*]
SRC........... Spares Receiving Checklist (NRCH)
SRC........... Special Regular Commissions [*Army*] [*British*]
SRC........... Specific Reactant Consumption [*Engine*]
SRC........... Speech Recognition Computer
SRC........... Standard Requirements Code [*Military*]
SRC........... Standards Review Committee [*American Occupational Therapy Association*]
SRC........... Station Reliability Coordinator
SRC........... Statuts Revises du Canada [*Revised Statutes of Canada*] [*Database*] [*Federal Department of Justice*] [*Information service or system*] (CRD)
SRC........... Sterility Research Center [*Public Health Service*] (GRD)
SRC........... Stock Record Card [*Military*]
SRC........... Strasburg Railroad Company [*AAR code*]
SRC........... Stray Radiation Chamber
SRC........... Stuart's Lower Canada Reports [*A publication*] (DLA)
SRC........... Student Reaction to College [*Student attitudes test*]
SRC........... Students' Representative Council [*British*]
SRC........... Studies in Religion: A Canadian Journal [*A publication*]
SRC........... Subject-Field Reference Code (ADA)
SRC........... Submarine Rescue Chamber (MCD)
SRC........... Support Review Code (MCD)
SRC........... Survey Research Center [*University of Kentucky*] [*Research center*] (RCD)
SRC........... Survey Research Center [*Oregon State University*] [*Research center*] (RCD)
SRC........... Sustained-Release Capsule [*Pharmacology*]
SRC........... Swan River Colony [*Australia*]
SRC........... Swiss Red Cross
SRC........... Synchronous Remote Control
SRC........... Synchrotron Radiation Center [*University of Wisconsin - Madison*] [*Research center*] (RCD)
SRC........... Syracuse Research Corporation [*New York*] [*Information service or system*] (IID)
SRC........... Systems Release Certification [*Social Security Administration*]
SRC........... Systems Research Configuration
SRCA......... Saskatchewan Department of Consumer Affairs, Regina, Saskatchewan [*Library symbol*] [*National Library of Canada*] (NLC)
SRCA......... Slovenian Research Center of America (EA)
SRCA........ Specific Red Cell Adherence [*Test*] [*Clinical chemistry*]
SRCAS ...... Safety-Related Control Air System [*Nuclear energy*] (NRCH)

SRCB .... Canadian Bible College, Regina, Saskatchewan [*Library symbol*] [*National Library of Canada*]   (NLC)
SRCB .... Software Requirements Change Board [*NASA*]   (NASA)
SRCB .... Software Requirements Control Board [*NASA*]   (NASA)
SRCBD ...... Software Requirements Change Board Directive [*NASA*]   (NASA)
SRCBD ...... Software Requirements Control Board Directive [*NASA*]   (NASA)
SRCC .... Scandinavian Research Council for Criminology [*See also NSfK*] [*Helsinki, Finland*]   (EAIO)
SRCC .... Senior Control Center [*Air Force*]
SRCC .... Sensor Referenced and Computer Controlled [*For remote manipulators*]
SRCC .... Simplex Remote Communications Central
SRCC .... Solar Rating and Certification Corporation   (EA)
SR & CC .... Strikes, Riots, and Civil Commotions [*Insurance*]
SRCC .... Strikes, Riots, and Civil Commotions [*Insurance*]
SRCD .... Set-Reset Clocked Data [*Data processing*]
SRCD .... Society for Research in Child Development   (EA)
SRCD .... Society of Richmond County Descendants   (EA)
SRCE .... First Source Corp. [*NASDAQ symbol*]   (NQ)
SR-CEF ..... Schmidt-Ruppin Chick Embryo Fibroblast[*s*]
SRCH .... Search   (AAG)
SRCH .... Search Natural Resources, Inc. [*NASDAQ symbol*]   (NQ)
SRCI .... Safety-Related Controls and Instrumentation [*Nuclear energy*]   (NRCH)
SRCI .... Survey Research Consultants International, Inc. [*Information service or system*]   (IID)
SRCL .... Security Requirements Check List   (MCD)
SRCM .... Savonius Rotor Current Meter
SRCM .... Sisters of Reparation of the Congregation of Mary [*Roman Catholic religious order*]
SRCMP ...... Southern Rhodesia Corps of Military Police [*British military*]   (DMA)
SRCNET ... Science and Engineering Research Council Network [*Later, SERCNET*]
SRCO .... Sealright Company, Inc. [*Kansas City, MO*] [*NASDAQ symbol*]   (NQ)
SRCP .... Short Range Construction Program [*Military*]
SRCP .... Society of Retired Catholic Persons   (EA)
SRCP .... Special Reserve Components Program [*Military*]
SRCR .... Saskatchewan Culture and Recreation, Regina, Saskatchewan [*Library symbol*] [*National Library of Canada*]   (NLC)
SRCR .... SONAR Control Room
SRCR .... Stability Regulated Controlled Rectifier
SRCR .... System Run Control Record
SRCRA ...... Shipowners Refrigerated Cargo Research Association [*British*]   (IRUK)
SRCRC ...... Snake River Conservation Research Center [*University of Idaho*] [*Research center*]   (RCD)
SRCS .... Sustancia. Revista de Cultura Superior [*A publication*]
SRCT .... Standard Recovery Completion Time
SRCU .... Credit Union Central, Regina, Saskatchewan [*Library symbol*] [*National Library of Canada*]   (NLC)
SRCU .... Secretary's Records Correspondence Unit [*Department of Labor*]
SRD .... Safety and Reliability Directorate [*England*]   (IID)
SRD .... San Andres [*Colombia*] [*Seismograph station code, US Geological Survey*]   (SEIS)
SRD .... Satellite Racing Development [*British*]
SRD .... Scheduled Release Date   (MCD)
S Rd .... Schweizerische Rundschau [*A publication*]
SRD .... Secret - Restricted Data [*Security classification*]
SRD .... Seldom Reaches Destination
SRD .... Selective Radiation Detector
SRD .... Self-Reading Dosimeter   (IEEE)
SRD .... Serous Retinal Detachment [*Ophthalmology*]
SRD .... Service Revealed Deficiency [*or Difficulty*]
SRD .... Service Rum Diluted [*British military*]   (DMA)
SRD .... Shift Register Drive
S-RD .... Shipper-Receiver Difference   (NRCH)
SRD .... Shuttle Requirements Definition [*NASA*]   (NASA)
SRD .... Shuttle Requirements Document [*NASA*]   (NASA)
SRD .... Silver Drake Resources [*Vancouver Stock Exchange symbol*]
SRD .... Single Radial Diffusion [*or Immunodiffusion*] [*Analytical biochemistry*]
SRD .... Small Rigid Dome
SRD .... Society for the Relief of Distress [*British*]
SRD .... Society for the Right to Die   (EA)
SRD .... Software Requirements Document [*Data processing*]
SRD .... Special Research Detachment [*Army*]
SRD .... Stafford Road [*Wolverhampton*] [*British depot code*]
SRD .... [*The*] Standard Oil Co. [*NYSE symbol*]   (SPSG)
SRD .... Standard Reference Data
SRD .... Standard Repair Design [*Navy*]   (MCD)
SRD .... Standard Reporting Designator   (MCD)
SRD .... State Registered Dietitian
SRD .... Statistical Research Division [*Census*]   (OICC)
SRD .... Step Recovery Diode
SRD .... Studio Reference Disc [*Prosonus*] [*Electronic music*]
SRD .... Sutherland Resources [*Vancouver Stock Exchange symbol*]

SRD .... Systems Requirements Document [*NASA*]
Srd. .... Thiouridine [*Also, S, SU*] [*A nucleoside*]
SRDA .... Dunlop Art Gallery, Regina, Saskatchewan [*Library symbol*] [*National Library of Canada*]   (NLC)
SRDA .... Search RADAR Designation Alignment   (MCD)
SRDA .... Sodium Removal Development Apparatus [*Nuclear energy*]   (NRCH)
SRDAS ..... Service Recording and Data Analysis System   (IEEE)
SRDB .... Scientific Research and Development Branch [*Home Office*] [*British*]   (IRUK)
SRDC .... Standard Reference Data Center
SRDDD ...... Solar Energy R and D in the European Community. Series D [*A publication*]
SRDE .... Signals Research and Development Establishment [*British*]
SRDE .... Smallest Replaceable Defective Element
SRDG .... Software Research and Development Group [*University of Calgary*] [*Research center*]   (RCD)
SRDH .... Subsystems Requirements Definition Handbook [*NASA*]   (NASA)
SRDI .... Safety-Related Display Instrumentation [*Nuclear energy*]   (NRCH)
SRDL .... Saskatchewan Department of Labour, Regina, Saskatchewan [*Library symbol*] [*National Library of Canada*]   (NLC)
SRDL .... Signals Research and Development Laboratory [*Army*] [*British*]
SRDM ...... Subrate Data Multiplexer [*Telecommunications*]   (TEL)
SRDRD ...... Solar Energy Research and Development Report [*A publication*]
SRDS .... Shop Repair Data Sheets
SRDS .... Single Requirements Determination System
SRDS .... Standard Rate and Data Service, Inc. [*Information service or system*]   (MCD)
SRDS .... Standard Reference Data System   (DIT)
SRDS .... Systems Research and Development Service [*FAA*]   (MCD)
SRDT .... Single Rotating Directional Transmission [*Military*]   (CAAL)
SRE .... Sancta Romana Ecclesia [*Most Holy Roman Church*] [*Latin*]
SRE .... Sanctae Romanae Ecclesiae [*Of the Most Holy Roman Church*] [*Latin*]
SRE .... Saskatchewan Department of the Environment, Regina, Saskatchewan [*Library symbol*] [*National Library of Canada*]   (NLC)
SRE .... Saturday Review of Education [*A publication*]
SRE .... Schedule of Recent Experience [*Psychometrics*]
SRe .... Science Review [*Manila*] [*A publication*]
SRE .... Seminole, OK [*Location identifier*] [*FAA*]   (FAAL)
SRE .... Send Reference Equivalent, Search RADAR [*Telecommunications*]   (TEL)
SRE .... Series Relay [*Electronics*]
SRE .... Serum Response Element [*Genetics*]
SRE .... Serum-Response Enhancer [*Genetics*]
SRE .... Shelby's Rabbit Eater [*In model name Omni SRE, proposed for Dodge car designed by Carroll Shelby*]
SRE .... Signaling Range Extender [*Telecommunications*]   (TEL)
SRE .... Single Region Execution
SRE .... Single Round Effectiveness   (NATG)
SRE .... Single Rural Eligible [*Classified advertising*]
SRE .... Site Resident Engineer [*Telecommunications*]   (TEL)
SRE .... Society of Recreation Executives   (EA)
SRE .... Society of Relay Engineers [*British*]
SRE .... Society of Reliability Engineers   (EA)
SRE .... Society of Reproduction Engineers [*Later, IAVCM*]   (EA)
SRE .... Society of Reproductive Endocrinologists   (EA)
SRE .... Society for Reproductive Surgeons   (EA)
SRE .... Sodium Reactor Experiment [*Nuclear energy*]
SRE .... Sound Reproduction Equipment   (DEN)
SRE .... Special Re-Education
SRE .... Srednekan [*USSR*] [*Later, MGD*] [*Geomagnetic observatory code*]
SRE .... Standard RADAR Environment
SRE .... Statistical Reporter [*A publication*]
SRE .... Stoneridge Resources, Inc. [*NYSE symbol*]   (SPSG)
SRE .... Stray Radiant Energy
SRE .... Sucre [*Bolivia*] [*Airport symbol*]   (OAG)
SRE .... Surveillance RADAR Element
SRE .... Surveillance RADAR Equipment
SREA .... Senior Real Estate Analyst [*Designation awarded by Society of Real Estate Appraisers*]
SREA .... Society of Real Estate Appraisers [*Later, AI*]   (EA)
SREA .... Street Rod Equipment Association   (EA)
SREAE ...... AES Regina Weather Office, Environment Canada [*Bureau Meteorologique du SEA de Regina, Environnement Canada*] Saskatchewan [*Library symbol*] [*National Library of Canada*]   (NLC)
SREB .... Southern Regional Educational Board
SREC .... Executive Council, Regina, Saskatchewan [*Library symbol*] [*National Library of Canada*]   (NLC)
SREC .... Southern Rice Export Corporation   (EA)
SRED .... Saskatchewan Department of Education, Regina, Saskatchewan [*Library symbol*] [*National Library of Canada*]   (NLC)
Sred Med Rab ... Sreden Medicinski Rabotnik [*A publication*]

SREEP.......	Environmental Protection Service, Environment Canada [*Service de la Protection de l'Environnement, Environnement Canada*] Regina, Saskatchewan [*Library symbol*] [*National Library of Canada*] (NLC)
SREG.........	[*The*] Standard Register Co. [*NASDAQ symbol*] (NQ)
SREG.........	Standing Register [*Civil Service*]
SREI	Student Role Expectation Inventory
SREIW	Inland Waters Directorate, Environment Canada [*Direction Generale des Eaux Interieures, Environnement Canada*] Regina, Saskatchewan [*Library symbol*] [*National Library of Canada*] (NLC)
SREL	Savannah River Ecology Laboratory [*Department of Energy*] [*Aiken, SC*]
SREL	Space Radiation Effects Laboratory [*Langley, VA*] [*NASA*]
S Rel Sc Rel ...	Studies in Religion/Sciences Religieuses [*A publication*]
SREM.......	Scanning Reflection Electron Microscopy
S-REM	Sleep with Rapid Eye Movement
SREM.......	Software Requirements Engineering Methodology
SREM.......	Sound Ranging Evaluation Model (MCD)
SRen..........	Studies in the Renaissance [*A publication*]
SREND7.....	Science Research News [*Kanpur*] [*A publication*]
S Rep	Senate Reports [*A publication*] (DLA)
S Rep.........	Southern Reporter [*A publication*] (DLA)
SREPT......	Senate Committee Report (AFIT)
SRES	Senate Resolution (AFIT)
SRES	Senores [*Sirs, Gentlemen*] [*Spanish*]
SRES	Sierra Resources [*NASDAQ symbol*] (NQ)
SRES	Southern Railway Employees' Sangh [*India*]
S Res	United States Senate Resolution [*A publication*] (DLA)
SRESB.......	State Rescue and Emergency Service Board [*New South Wales, Australia*]
SRET	Satellite de Recherches et d'Environment Technique [*Satellite for Environmental and Technical Research*] [*France*]
SRET	Scanning Reference Electrode [*Corrosion testing*]
SRev..........	Sayers Review [*A publication*]
SRev..........	School Review [*A publication*]
SRE(V)	Singapore Royal Engineers (Volunteers) [*British military*] (DMA)
SRev..........	Slavic Review [*A publication*]
SRev..........	Southwest Review [*A publication*]
S Rev (Adel) ...	Southern Review (Adelaide) [*A publication*]
S Rev (Baton) ...	Southern Review (Baton Rouge) [*A publication*]
S Rev Lit	Saturday Review of Literature [*A publication*]
S Rev Pub Adm ...	Southern Review of Public Administration [*A publication*]
SRF...........	S-Band Receiver Filter
SRF...........	Salmonellosis-Resistance Factor
SRF...........	Sam Rayburn Foundation
SRF...........	San Rafael, CA [*Location identifier*] [*FAA*] (FAAL)
SRF...........	Scleroderma Research Foundation (EA)
SRF...........	Seal Rescue Fund (EA)
SRF...........	Secure Reserve Forces [*Military*] (MCD)
SRF...........	Selected Reserve Force [*Units*] [*of Army National Guard*] [*Discontinued, 1969*]
SR & F	Selection, Referral, and Followup
SRF...........	Self-Realization Fellowship (EA)
SRF...........	Self-Referenced Fringe (MCD)
SRF...........	Self-Resonant Frequency
SRF...........	Semireinforcing Furnace [*Carbon black manufacture*]
SRF...........	Serum Response Factor [*Biochemistry*]
SRF...........	Ship Repair Facility [*Navy*] (NVT)
SRF...........	Shuttle Refurbish Facility [*NASA*] (NASA)
SRF...........	Sido, Robert F., Edwardsville IL [*STAC*]
SRF...........	Skin Reactive Factor [*Immunochemistry*]
SRF...........	Skin Respiratory Factor [*Physiology*]
SRF...........	Slovak Relief Fund
SRF...........	Snake Ranch Flats [*New Mexico*] [*Seismograph station code, US Geological Survey*] [*Closed*] (SEIS)
SRF...........	Software Recording Facility
SRF...........	Software Recovery Facility [*Data processing*] (IBMDP)
SRF...........	Solar Radiation Flux
SRF...........	Somatotrophin-Releasing Factor [*Endocrinology*]
SRF...........	Sorter Reader Flow
SRF...........	Space Requirement Forms (AAG)
SRF...........	Spacecraft Research Foundation [*Inactive*] (EA)
SRF...........	Special Reporting Facility [*Department of State*]
SRF...........	Stable Radio Frequency
SRF...........	Strategic Reserve Forces (MCD)
SRF...........	Strategic Retaliatory Forces (AAG)
SRF...........	Strategic Rocket Forces (MCD)
SRF...........	Submarine Range-Finder
SRF...........	Submarine Repair Facility
SRF...........	Sun River Gold Corp. [*Vancouver Stock Exchange symbol*]
SRF...........	Supported Ring Frame
SRF...........	Surface Roughness Factor [*Telecommunications*] (TEL)
SRF...........	Survival Research Foundation (EA)
SRF...........	System Recovery Factor
SRFB	Space Research Facilities Branch [*National Research Council of Canada*]
SRFC	Shotgun Red Fan Club (EA)
SRFCEE....	Fox Chase Cancer Center. Scientific Report [*A publication*]
SRFCS.......	Self-Repairing Flight Control System

SRFD.........	Society for the Rehabilitation of the Facially Disfigured [*Later, National Foundation for Facial Reconstruction*] (EA)
SRFF..........	Set-Reset Flip-Flop [*Data processing*]
SRFI	Self-Rising Flour Institute [*Later, HBA*]
SRFI	Sugar Research Foundation, Incorporated [*Later, ISRF*] (EA)
SRFI	Super Rite Foods, Incorporated [*NASDAQ symbol*] (NQ)
SrFltSurgBad ...	Senior Flight Surgeon Badge [*Military decoration*] (AABC)
SRFM........	Source Range Flux Monitoring [*Nuclear energy*] (NRCH)
SRFTL.......	Secure Resource Force Target List (MCD)
SRFU........	Seal Research and Fisheries Unit [*British*]
SRG	Regina General Hospital, Saskatchewan [*Library symbol*] [*National Library of Canada*] (NLC)
SRG	Santa Sarita Mining [*Vancouver Stock Exchange symbol*]
SRG	Schering-Plough Corp. [*Research code symbol*]
SRG	Schriften. Raabe-Gesellschaft [*A publication*]
SRG	Semarang [*Indonesia*] [*Airport symbol*] (OAG)
SRG	Servomotor Rate Generator
SRG	Short Range (FAAC)
SRG	Sine-Random Generator
SRG	Social Research Group [*George Washington University*] [*Research center*] (RCD)
SRG	Society of Remedial Gymnasts (EA)
SRG	Sorg, Inc. [*AMEX symbol*] (SPSG)
SRG	Sound Ranging
SRG	Statistical Research Group [*Princeton University*] (MCD)
SRG	Stimulated Raman Gain [*Spectroscopy*]
SRg	Studies in Religion [*A publication*]
SRG	Surge (MSA)
SRG	System Routing Guide [*Military*] (CAAL)
SRG	Systems Research Group (CINC)
SRGA........	Stable Reactor, General, Atomic
SRGD	Gabriel Dumont Institute, Regina, Saskatchewan [*Library symbol*] [*National Library of Canada*] (NLC)
SRGE........	Saskatchewan Government Employees Association, Regina, Saskatchewan [*Library symbol*] [*National Library of Canada*] (NLC)
SRGH	Pasqua Hospital, Regina, Saskatchewan [*Library symbol*] [*National Library of Canada*] (NLC)
SRGI.........	Saskatchewan Government Insurance, Regina, Saskatchewan [*Library symbol*] [*National Library of Canada*] (NLC)
SRGM	Super Rapid Gun Mounting [*Military*]
SRGMF.....	Santa Sarita Mining [*NASDAQ symbol*] (NQ)
SRGR.........	Short-Range Guided Rocket
SRGS	St. Rosalie Generating Station [*Nuclear energy*] (NRCH)
SRGS	Saskatchewan Genealogical Society, Regina, Saskatchewan [*Library symbol*] [*National Library of Canada*] (NLC)
SRGS	Survivable Radio Guidance System [*Military*]
SRGSC	Southern Rhodesia General Service Corps [*British military*] (DMA)
SRGY........	American Surgery Centers Corp. [*NASDAQ symbol*] (NQ)
SRH	Saskatchewan Housing Corp., Regina, Saskatchewan [*Library symbol*] [*National Library of Canada*] (BIB)
SRH	Secretaria de Recursos Hidraulicos [*Mexico*]
SRH	Sequential Rough Handling (MCD)
SRH	Single Radial Hemolysis [*Immunochemistry*]
SRHD........	Smith, R. H., Minneapolis MN [*STAC*]
SRH	[*A*] Social and Religious History of the Jews [*S. W. Baron*] [*A publication*] (BJA)
SRH	Spontaneously Responding Hyperthyroidism [*Endocrinology*]
SRH	Stigmata of Recent Hemorrhage [*Medicine*]
SRH	Strathcona Resources Industries Ltd. [*Toronto Stock Exchange symbol*]
SRH	Subsystems Requirements Handbook [*NASA*] (NASA)
SRH	Supply Railhead
SRH	Switchyard Relay House [*Nuclear energy*] (NRCH)
SRHB	Society for Research into Hydrocephalus and Spina Bifida (EA)
SRHC	Shutdown Reactor Head Cooling [*Nuclear energy*] (NRCH)
SR HCR.....	Southern Rhodesia High Court Reports [*1911-55*] [*A publication*] (DLA)
SRHE........	Society for Religion in Higher Education [*Later, SVHE*] (EA)
SRHE........	Society for Research into Higher Education [*Guildford, Surrey, England*] (EAIO)
SRHE Bull ...	Society for Research into Higher Education. Bulletin [*A publication*]
SRHE Newsl ...	Society for Research into Higher Education. Newsletter [*A publication*]
SRHIT.......	Small RADAR-Homing Interceptor Technology
SRHJ.........	[*A*] Social and Religious History of the Jews [*S. W. Baron*] [*A publication*] (BJA)
SRHL........	Southwestern Radiological Health Laboratory [*HEW*]
S Rhodesia Geol Surv Bull ...	Southern Rhodesia. Geological Survey. Bulletin [*A publication*]
SRHP........	Planning Branch, Saskatchewan Department of Highways and Transportation, Regina, Saskatchewan [*Library symbol*] [*National Library of Canada*] (NLC)
SRHP........	Section for Rehabilitation Hospitals and Programs [*American Hospital Association*]
SRHQ........	Subregional Headquarters [*Military*] [*British*]
SRHS........	Health Sciences Library, Plains Health Centre, Regina, Saskatchewan [*Library symbol*] [*National Library of Canada*] (NLC)

SRHSB...... Society for Research into Hydrocephalus and Spina Bifida (EA)
SRI............ British Steel [*A publication*]
SRI............ Sacrum Romanum Imperium [*The Holy Roman Empire*] [*Latin*]
SRI............ Samarinda [*Indonesia*] [*Airport symbol*] (OAG)
SRI............ Scholarly Resources, Incorporated, Wilmington, DE [*Library symbol*] [*Library of Congress*] (LCLS)
SRI............ Sefid-Roud [*Iran*] [*Seismograph station code, US Geological Survey*] (SEIS)
SRI............ Selective Retention Indicators (NVT)
SRI............ Senior Resident Inspector [*Nuclear energy*] (NRCH)
SRI............ Servo Repeater Indicator
SRI............ Severe Renal Insufficiency [*Medicine*]
SRI............ Signal Routing and Interface (MCD)
SRI............ Silicon Rubber Insulation
SRI............ Ski Retailers International (EA)
SRI............ Social Research Institute [*University of Utah*] [*Research center*] (RCD)
SRI............ Society for Rational Individualism [*Later, SIL*] (EA)
SRI............ Sorry [*Communications operator's procedural remark*]
SRI............ Southeastern Reservoir Investigation [*Department of the Interior*] (GRD)
SRI............ Southern Research Institute
SRI............ Southwest Research Institute
SRI............ Space Research Institute [*Defunct*] (EA)
SRI............ Spalling Resistance Index (IEEE)
SRI............ Special Recreation, Incorporated (EA)
SRI............ Spectrum Resolver Integrator
SRI............ Spectrum Resources, Incorporated [*St. Charles, MO*] [*Telecommunications*] (TSSD)
SRI............ Speech Rehabilitation Institute (EA)
SRI............ Spring Research Institute (EA)
SRI............ Standard Research Institute (MCD)
SRI............ Standby Request for Information [*Military*] (AABC)
SRI............ Standing Request for Information (MCD)
SRI............ Stanford Research Institute [*Later, SRI International*] [*Databank originator*]
SRI............ Stick to Rudder Interconnect (MCD)
SRI............ Supply Requisition Inquiry
SRI............ Surface Roughness Indicator
SRI............ Sveriges Runinskrifter [*A publication*]
SRI............ Swiss Radio International
SRI............ Syllable Repetition Interval [*Entomology*]
SRIA......... Saskatchewan Intergovernmental Affairs, Regina, Saskatchewan [*Library symbol*] [*National Library of Canada*] (NLC)
SRIA......... State and Regional Indicators Archive [*University of New Hampshire*] [*Information service or system*] (IID)
SRIAER..... Scientific Research Institute for Atomic Energy Reactors [*USSR*]
SRIB......... Strike Route Information Book [*Strategic Air Command*] (AABC)
SRIC......... Short-Run Incremental Cost (ADA)
SRIC......... Southwest Research and Information Center (EA)
SRIC......... SRI Corporation [*NASDAQ symbol*] (NQ)
SRICDS..... Inter-American Tropical Tuna Commission. Special Report [*A publication*]
SRID......... Search RADAR Input Device (MCD)
SRIELA..... Selected Reports: Publication of the Institute of Ethnomusicology of the University of California at Los Angeles [*A publication*]
SRIF......... Somatotrophin-Releasing Inhibiting Factor [*Also, GH-RIF, GH-RIH, GRIF, SS*] [*Endocrinology*]
SRIF......... Special Risk Insurance Fund [*Federal Housing Administration*]
SRIFC....... Saskatchewan Indian Federated College, Regina, Saskatchewan [*Library symbol*] [*National Library of Canada*] (NLC)
SRIH........ Somatostatin [*Biochemistry*]
SRIIA....... Silk and Rayon Industries of India [*A publication*]
SRI J......... SRI [*Stanford Research Institute*] Journal [*A publication*]
Sri Lan J Hum ... Sri Lanka Journal of Humanities [*Peradeniya*] [*A publication*]
Sri Lanka Assoc Adv Sci Proc Annu Sess ... Sri Lanka Association for the Advancement of Science. Proceedings of the Annual Session [*A publication*]
Sri Lanka For ... Sri Lanka Forester [*A publication*]
Sri Lanka Geol Surv Dep Econ Bull ... Sri Lanka. Geological Survey Department. Economic Bulletin [*A publication*]
Sri Lanka Lab Gaz ... Sri Lanka Labour Gazette [*A publication*]
SriLJH...... Sri Lanka Journal of the Humanities [*A publication*]
SRILTA..... Stanford Research Institute Lead Time Analysis
SR-IM........ Office of Strategic Research, Intelligence Memoranda [*CIA*]
SRIM........ Selected Research in Microfiche [*A publication*]
SRIM........ Short-Range Intercept Missile (MCD)
SRIM........ Standing Order Microfiche Service
SRIM........ Structural Reaction Injection Molding [*Plastics*]
SRIN.......... Indian and Northern Affairs Canada [*Affaires Indiennes et du Nord Canada*], Regina, Saskatchewan [*Library symbol*] [*National Library of Canada*] (BIB)
SRIP......... Selected Reserve Incentive Program [*Army*]
SRIP......... Ship Readiness Improvement Plan [*Navy*] (NG)
SRIP......... Short-Range Impact Point (MUGU)

SRIP......... Society for the Research and Investigation of Phenomena (EAIO)
SRIP......... Specification Review and Improvement Program [*Navy*] (NG)
SRI Pestic Res Bull ... SRI [*Stanford Research Institute*] Pesticide Research Bulletin [*A publication*]
SRIS......... Safety Recommendation Information System [*Database*]
SRIS......... Safety Research Information Service [*National Safety Council*] (IID)
SRIS......... Science Reference and Information Service (IID)
SRISP....... Interprovincial Steel & Pipe Corp. Ltd., (IPSCO), Regina, Saskatchewan [*Library symbol*] [*National Library of Canada*] (NLC)
SRISS....... Scientia. Rivista Internazionale di Sintesi Scientifica [*A publication*]
SRIT......... Service and Repair Identification Tag (MCD)
SRIY......... Sherwood Rangers Imperial Yeomanry [*British military*] (DMA)
SRJ............ San Borja [*Bolivia*] [*Airport symbol*] (OAG)
SRJ............ Scorcorp Industries, Inc. [*Vancouver Stock Exchange symbol*]
SRJ............ Self-Restraint Joint
SRJ............ Short Run Job (MCD)
SRJ............ Standard-Range Juno [*Survey meter for radiation*]
SRJ............ Static Round Jet
SRJC........ Communications Policy Branch, Saskatchewan Department of Justice, Regina, Saskatchewan [*Library symbol*] [*National Library of Canada*] (NLC)
SRJC......... Santa Rosa Junior College [*California*]
SRJKAK..... Annual Report. Sado Marine Biological Station. Niigata University [*A publication*]
SRK........... Soave-Redlich-Kwong [*Equation of state*]
SRK........... Spirit Lake, IA [*Location identifier*] [*FAA*] (FAAL)
SRK........... Sredniy Kalar [*USSR*] [*Seismograph station code, US Geological Survey*] (SEIS)
SRK........... Stralak Resources [*Vancouver Stock Exchange symbol*]
SRKN......... Single Rotating Knife
SRL............ HRIN [*Human Resource Information Network*] Special Reports Library [*Executive Telecom System, Inc.*] [*Information service or system*] (CRD)
SRL............ Legislative Library of Saskatchewan, Regina, Saskatchewan [*Library symbol*] [*National Library of Canada*] (NLC)
SRL............ Santa Rosalia [*Mexico*] [*Seismograph station code, US Geological Survey*] [*Closed*] (SEIS)
SRL............ Saturday Review of Literature [*A publication*]
SRL............ Savannah River Laboratory [*Department of Energy*] [*Aiken, SC*]
SRL............ Save-the-Redwoods League (EA)
SRL............ Sceptre Resources Ltd. [*AMEX symbol*] [*Toronto Stock Exchange symbol*] (SPSG)
SRL............ Scheme Representation Language [*Artificial intelligence*]
SRL............ Scientific Research Laboratory (AAG)
SRL............ Screwworm Research Laboratory [*Department of Agriculture*] (GRD)
SRL............ Securities Regulation Law Journal [*A publication*]
SRL............ Seiler Research Laboratory [*Air Force*] (MCD)
SRL............ Service Rights Layer [*Data processing*]
SRL............ Singing Return Loss [*Telecommunications*] (TEL)
SRL............ Skin Resistance Level [*Physiology*]
SRL............ Sociedad de Responsabilidad Limitada [*Private Limited Company*] [*Spanish*] [*Business term*]
S de RL...... Sociedad de Responsabilidad Limitada [*Private Limited Company*] [*Spanish*]
SRL............ Societa a Responsabilita Limitata [*Limited Liability Company*] [*Italian*] [*Business term*]
SRL............ Society of Romance Linguistics [*Nancy, France*] (EAIO)
SRL............ Sonobuoy Receiver Logic [*Navy*] (CAAL)
SRL............ Sound Reference Laboratory [*Orlando, FL*] [*Navy*]
SRL............ Sound Research Laboratories Ltd. [*British*] (IRUK)
SRL............ Spares Recommendation List (MCD)
SRL............ Stability Return Loss [*Telecommunications*] (TEL)
SRL............ Standard Reference Library
SRL............ Strangeways Research Laboratory [*British*] (IRUK)
SRL............ Stress Relieving Liner (KSC)
SRL............ Structural Return Loss [*Telecommunications*] (TEL)
SRL............ Student Religious Liberals [*Later, SRL, A Free Religious Fellowship*] [*Defunct*]
SRL............ Studies in Romance Languages [*A publication*]
SRL............ Study Reference List (AFM)
SRL............ Summary Requirements List (MCD)
SRL............ Support Requirements Letter (CET)
SRL............ Surveillance Research Laboratory [*Australia*]
SRL............ Survey Research Laboratory [*University of Illinois*] [*Information service or system*] (IID)
SRL............ Systems Research Laboratory
SRLC........ Luther College, Regina, Saskatchewan [*Library symbol*] [*National Library of Canada*] (NLC)
SRLD......... Small Rocket Lift Device
SRLF......... Saggi e Ricerche di Letteratura Francese [*A publication*]
SRLing......... Studia Romanica et Linguistica [*A publication*]
SRLP......... Leader-Post Ltd., Regina, Saskatchewan [*Library symbol*] [*National Library of Canada*] (NLC)

SRLP	Socialist and Revolutionary Labour Party [*Gambia*] [*Political party*] (PD)
SRLR	Securities Regulation and Law Reports [*Bureau of National Affairs*] [*A publication*]
SRLS	Law Society of Saskatchewan Libraries, Regina [*Library symbol*] [*National Library of Canada*] (BIB)
Sr LS..........	Senior Life Saving [*Red Cross*]
SRLS	Starved Rock Library System [*Library network*]
SRLUDT ...	Scientific Report. Laboratory for Amphibian Biology. Hiroshima University [*A publication*]
SRLY	Series Relay (IEEE)
SRM	Schedule Request Message (MCD)
SRM	Scrim-Reinforced Material [*Nonwoven sheets*]
SRM	Secretory Rate Maximum [*Physiology*]
SRM	Sensor Response Model
SRM	Service Repair Manual
SRM	Shared Resource Management [*Data processing*]
SRM	Shift Register Memory
SRM	Ship Repair and Maintenance [*National Shipping Authority*]
SRM	Short-Range Missile [*Projected; not to be confused with SRAM*]
SRM	Short-Range MODEM
SRM	Single Register Machine
SRM	Smokeless Rocket Motor (MCD)
SRM	Snowmelt-Runoff Model [*Hydrology*]
SRM	Society for Range Management (EA)
SRM	Socorro - La Joya [*New Mexico*] [*Seismograph station code, US Geological Survey*] [*Closed*] (SEIS)
SRM	Solid-Rocket Motor
SRM	Source-Range Monitor [*Nuclear energy*] (NRCH)
SRM	Specific Repair Methods [*Boeing*]
SRM	Specification Requirements Manual [*NASA*] (NASA)
SRM	Speed of Relative Movement
SRM	Spiritual Regeneration Movement [*Foundation of America*] (EA)
SRM	Square Root Mode [*Data processing*]
SRM	Standard Reference Material [*National Institute of Standards and Technology*]
SRM	Standard Reference Module
SRM	Standard Repair Manual (MCD)
SRM	Strategic Reconnaissance Missile
SRM	Structural Repair Manual
SRM	Superior Rectus Muscle [*Eye anatomy*]
SRM	System Resource Manager [*IBM Corp.*] (BUR)
SRM	System for Resources Management [*Jet Propulsion Laboratory, NASA*]
SRMA........	Silk and Rayon Manufacturers Association [*Defunct*] (EA)
SRMA........	Ski Resort Marketing Association (EA)
SRMBDB ..	Marine Sciences Research Center [*Stony Brook*]. Special Report [*A publication*]
SRMC........	Society of Risk Management Consultants [*Baton Rouge, LA*] (EA)
SRMC........	Specification Requirements Manual (MCD)
SRMC........	Stimulus/Response Measurements Catalog (NASA)
SRMCASE ...	Symmetry-Restricted-Multiconfiguration Annihilation of Single Excitations [*Physics*]
SRMD	Senior Resident Medical Doctor [*Australia*]
SRMD	Stress-Related Mucosal Damage [*Medicine*]
SRML........	Short-Range Missile Launcher
SRMP........	Supply Readiness Milestone Plan [*Military*] (CAAL)
SRMR........	Saskatchewan Department of Mineral Resources, Regina, Saskatchewan [*Library symbol*] [*National Library of Canada*] (NLC)
SRMS........	Ships Records Management System (MCD)
SRMS........	Structure Resonance Modulation Spectroscopy
SRMSDS...	Montana. Forest and Conservation Experiment Station. Study Report [*A publication*]
SRMT........	Southern Rock Mountain Trench [*Geology*]
SRN	Sabine River & Northern Railroad Co. [*AAR code*]
SRN	Saskatchewan Registered Nurses Association, Regina, Saskatchewan [*Library symbol*] [*National Library of Canada*] (NLC)
SRN	Saturn Science Fiction and Fantasy [*A publication*]
SRN	Serial Reference Number
SRN	Simulation Reference Number
SRN	Software Release Notice [*NASA*] (NASA)
SRN	Southern
SRN	Southern Air Transport, Inc.
SRN	Souvenir Nieuws [*A publication*]
SRN	Specification Revision Notice (MCD)
SRN	State Registered Nurse [*British*]
SRN	Strathearn House Group Ltd. [*Toronto Stock Exchange symbol*]
SRN	Stretch Receptor Neuron
sRNA	Ribonucleic Acid, Soluble [*Replaced by tRNA*] [*Biochemistry, genetics*]
SRNB........	Sociology. Reviews of New Books [*A publication*]
SRNC........	Severn River Naval Command
SRND	Surround (FAAC)
S & R Neg ..	Shearman and Redfield on the Law of Negligence [*A publication*] (DLA)
S & R on Neg ...	Shearman and Redfield on the Law of Negligence [*A publication*] (DLA)

SRNFC.......	Source Range Neutron Flux Channel (IEEE)
SRNG	Syringe
SRNLS	Northern Library Services, Saskatchewan Library, Regina, Saskatchewan [*Library symbol*] [*National Library of Canada*] (NLC)
SRNR........	Stock Request Number
SRNS........	Steroid-Responsive Nephrotic Syndrome [*Medicine*]
SRNS........	Surveyor Retro Nozzle Structure
SR (NSW) ...	State Reports (New South Wales) [*A publication*] (APTA)
SR (NSW) B & P ...	State Reports (New South Wales). Bankruptcy and Probate [*A publication*] (APTA)
SR (NSW) Eq ...	State Reports (New South Wales). Equity [*A publication*] (APTA)
Sr Nurse.....	Senior Nurse [*A publication*]
SRNV	Subretinal Neovascularization [*Ophthalmology*]
SRO	S-Band RADAR Operational
SRO	Safety Recall Order (MCD)
SRO	Sales Release Order
SRO	Saskatchewan Oil Co., Regina, Saskatchewan [*Library symbol*] [*National Library of Canada*] (NLC)
SRO	Savannah River Operation [*Office*] [*Energy Research and Development Administration*]
SRO	Scarboro Resources Ltd. [*Toronto Stock Exchange symbol*]
SRO	Scottish Record Office
SRO	Self-Regulatory Organisation [*Financial Services Act of 1986*] [*British*]
SRO	Senior Range Officer
SRO	Senior Reactor Operator [*Nuclear energy*] (NRCH)
SRO	Senior Research Officer [*Ministry of Agriculture, Fisheries, and Food*] [*British*]
SRO	Sex-Ratio Organism [*Entomology*]
SRO	Shakespearean Research Opportunities [*A publication*]
SRO	Shop Repair Order
SRO	Short-Range Order [*Solid state physics*]
SRO	Shrobarova [*Czechoslovakia*] [*Seismograph station code, US Geological Survey*] (SEIS)
SRO	Single-Room Occupancy [*Housing*]
SRO	Singly Resonant Oscillator (IEEE)
SRO	Society of Radio Operators
SRO	Solar Radio Observatory
SRO	Southern Airlines, Inc. [*West Palm Beach, FL*] [*FAA designator*] (FAAC)
SRO	Spares Requirement Order
SRO	Special Rate Order [*Business term*]
SRO	Special Regional Operations (NATG)
SRO	Specification Release Order [*Nuclear energy*] (NRCH)
SRO	Spolecnost s Rucenim Omezenym [*Company with Limited Liability*] [*Czechoslovakian*] [*Business term*]
SRO	Squadron Recreation Officer [*Navy*] [*British*]
SRO	Standing Room Only [*Theater*]
SRO	Standing Route Order [*Army*] (AABC)
SR & O......	Statutory Rules and Orders [*England*] [*A publication*] (DLA)
SRO	Statutory Rules and Orders
SRO	Steele-Richardson-Olszewski Syndrome [*Medicine*]
SRo	Studi Romani [*Rome*] [*A publication*]
SRo	Studia Rosenthaliana [*A publication*] (BJA)
SRO	Superintendent [*or Supervisor*] of Range Operations [*NASA*]
SRO	Supplementary Reserve of Officers [*Military*] [*British*]
SRO	System Readiness Objective
SRO	Systems Reproduction Order (MCD)
SROA	Safety-Related Operator Action [*Nuclear energy*] (NRCH)
SROA	Society for Radiation Oncology Administrators (EA)
SROB........	Short-Range Omnidirectional Beacon [*Aerospace*]
SROD	Stove Rod
SROE........	[*Shipboard*] Satellite Readout Equipment (MCD)
SROEQ......	Selected References on Environmental Quality as It Relates to Health [*A publication*]
SROF........	Self-Renewal Occupational Field
SROF........	Sustained Rate of Fire [*Military*] (INF)
SROH	Societe de Recherche en Orientation Humaine [*Canada*]
SROKA......	Second Republic of Korea Army
SRom	Studi Romani [*Rome*] [*A publication*]
SROP.........	Senior Registered Options Principal [*Investment term*]
SR & O and SI Rev ...	Statutory Rules and Orders and Statutory Instruments Revised [*England*] [*A publication*] (DLA)
SROTC.......	Senior Reserve Officers' Training Corps [*Military*] (AABC)
SROTS	Superficial Rays of the Sun [*In reference to suntanning, supposedly occuring before 10am and after 2pm*] [*See also BROTS*]
SROWW ...	Statistical Record of Women Worldwide [*A publication*]
SRP...........	Safeguard Readiness Posture [*Army*] (AABC)
SRP...........	Salary Reduction Plan [*Business term*]
SRP...........	Saskatchewan Library and Union Catalogue, Regina, Saskatchewan [*Library symbol*] [*National Library of Canada*] (NLC)
SRP...........	Saskatchewan Provincial Library [*UTLAS symbol*]
SRP...........	Savannah River Plant [*Department of Energy*]
SRP...........	Savings and Retirement Plan
SRP...........	Scientific Research Proposal (AAG)
SRP...........	Sealift Readiness Program [*Military*]
SRP...........	Seat Reference Point

SRP........... Seismic Reflection Profile [*Marine science*] (MSC)
SRP........... Selective Reenlistment Program [*Air Force*]
SRP........... Self-Recording Penetrometer
SRP........... Sensor Reporting Post
SRP........... Shags Rocks Passage [*Oceanography*]
SRP........... Ship's Repair Party [*Navy*] [*British*]
SRP........... Short Ragweed Pollen [*Immunology*]
SRP........... Sierra Pacific Resources [*NYSE symbol*] (SPSG)
SRP........... Signal Recognition Particle [*Biochemistry*]
SRP........... Small Rotating Plug [*Nuclear energy*] (NRCH)
SRP........... Socialist Revolution Party [*Sosyalist Devrim Partisi*] [*Turkey*] [*Political party*] (PPW)
SRP........... Socialist Revolutionary Party [*USSR*] [*Political party*]
SRP........... Socialist Revolutionary Party [*India*] [*Political party*] (PPW)
SRP........... Socialisticka Radnicka Partija Jugoslavije [*Socialist Workers' Party of Yugoslavia*] [*Political party*] (PPE)
SRP........... Society for Radiological Protection [*British*] (DEN)
SRP........... Solar Radiation Pressure
SRP........... Solicitation Review Panel [*Air Force*]
SRP........... Sonobuoy Referenced Position [*Navy*] (NG)
SRP........... Source Record Punch
SRP........... Sozialistische Reichspartei [*Socialist Reich Party*] [*Federal Republic of Germany*] [*Political party*] (PPE)
SRP........... Space Requirement Program (MCD)
S & RP .... Spares and Repair Parts [*Navy*]
SRP........... Spin Recovery Parachute
SRP........... Stabilization Reference Package
SRP........... Standard Relative Power
SRP........... Standard Repair Procedures
SRP........... Standard Review Plan [*Nuclear energy*] (NRCH)
SRP........... Start Rendezvous Point (MCD)
SRP........... State Registered Physiotherapist [*British*]
SRP........... Stratospheric Research Program
SRP........... Stray Radiant Power
SRP........... Studia Rossica Posnaniensia [*A publication*]
SRP........... Suggested Retail Price
SRP........... Supply Readiness Program [*Air Force*]
SRP........... Supply Refuelling Point [*Air Force*] [*British*]
SRP........... Traverse City, MI [*Location identifier*] [*FAA*] (FAAL)
SRPA .... Senior Real Property Appraiser [*Designation awarded by Society of Real Estate Appraisers*]
SRPA .... Spherical Retarding Potential Analyzer (MCD)
Srp Akad Nauka Umet Od Prir-Mat Nauka (Glas) ... Srpska Akademija Nauka i Umetnosti Odeljenje Prirodno-Matematickikh Nauka (Glas) [*A publication*]
Srp Akad Nauka Umet Posebna Izdan Od Prir Mat Nauka ... Srpska Akademija Nauka i Umetnosti Posebna Izdanja Odeljenje Prirodno-Matematickikh Nauka [*A publication*]
SRPARABAD ... Senior Parachutist Badge [*Military decoration*]
Srp Arh Celok Lek ... Srpski Arhiv za Celokupno Lekarstvo [*A publication*]
Srp Arkh Tselok Lek ... Srpski Arkhiv za Tselokupno Lekarstvo [*A publication*]
SRPB .... Scottish River Purification Board
SRPBA ...... Scottish River Purification Boards Association
SRPC .... SaskPower, Regina, Saskatchewan [*Library symbol*] [*National Library of Canada*] (NLC)
SRPC .... Sulphate Resisting Portland Cement
SRPCRD ... Research and Development Center Library, SaskPower, Regina, Saskatchewan [*Library symbol*] [*National Library of Canada*] (NLC)
SRPD........ System Research and Planning Division [*NASA*] (KSC)
SRPDAA ... Silk and Rayon Printers and Dyers Association of America (EA)
SRPG........ Scraping
SRPG........ Steel Reinforcement Promotion Group [*Cement and Concrete Association of Australia*]
SRPH........ Saskatchewan Department of Health, Regina, Saskatchewan [*Library symbol*] [*National Library of Canada*] (NLC)
SRPI .... Scrap Rubber and Plastics Institute (EA)
SRPI .... Silk and Rayon Print Institute [*Defunct*] (EA)
SRPIS........ Southern Regional Plant Introduction Station [*University of Georgia*] [*Research center*] (RCD)
SRPJ......... Self-Restraining Pipe Joint
SRPMME ... Society for Research in the Psychology of Music and Music Education [*British*]
SRPN........ Special Requisition Priority Number
SRPO........ Science Resources Planning Office [*National Science Foundation*]
SRPO........ Soobchtcheniia Russkago Palestinskago Obchtshestva [*A publication*]
SRPP .... Public Participation Library, Regina, Saskatchewan [*Library symbol*] [*National Library of Canada*] (BIB)
SRPP .... Skeletal Rod of Palp
SRPR .... Saskatchewan Parks and Renewable Resources, Regina, Saskatchewan [*Library symbol*] [*National Library of Canada*] (NLC)
SRPR......... Scraper
SRPR......... Stray Radiant Power Ratio
SRPR......... Surtsey Research Progress Report [*A publication*]
SrPrchtBad ... Senior Parachutist Badge [*Military decoration*]

SRPS .... Saskatchewan Public Service Commission, Regina, Saskatchewan [*Library symbol*] [*National Library of Canada*] (NLC)
SRPS .... Scientific Research Project Support [*National Science Foundation*]
SRPS .... Secure Record and Playback System (MCD)
SRPS .... Sensor-Referenced Positioning System
SR/PS .... Shipping Request/Packing Sheet (MCD)
Srpsko Hem Drus Bull ... Srpsko Hemiskog Drustvo. Bulletin [*A publication*]
SRPV........ Stationary Remotely Piloted Vehicle (MCD)
SRPW........ Savannah River Plant - Well DRB-10 [*South Carolina*] [*Seismograph station code, US Geological Survey*] (SEIS)
SR & Q..... Safety, Reliability, and Quality (NASA)
SRQ .... Sarasota/Bradenton [*Florida*] [*Airport symbol*]
SRQ .... Service Request
SRQ .... State Reports (Queensland) [*A publication*] (APTA)
SR & QA.... Safety, Reliability, and Quality Assurance (NASA)
SRR............ Central New York Library Resources Council, Syracuse, NY [*OCLC symbol*] (OCLC)
SRR............ Schuh Kurier. Das Wirtschaftmagazin der Schuhbranche [*A publication*]
SRR............ Scots Revised Reports [*A publication*] (DLA)
SRR............ Search and Range RADAR
SRR............ Search and Rescue Region [*Aviation*] (FAAC)
SRR............ Seastar Resource Corp. [*Vancouver Stock Exchange symbol*]
SRR............ Security Rules and Regulations
srr.............. Serer [*MARC language code*] [*Library of Congress*] (LCCP)
SRR............ Serially Reusable Resource [*Data processing*]
SRR............ Shift Register Recognizer (IEEE)
SRR............ Short-Range RADAR
SRR............ Short-Range Recovery (IEEE)
SRR............ Shuttle Requirements Review [*NASA*] (MCD)
SRR............ Site Readiness Review [*NASA*] (NASA)
SRR............ Skin Resistance Response [*Physiology*]
SRR............ Slow Rotation Room [*NASA*]
SRR............ Socialist Republic of Romania
SRR............ Society for Reformation Research (EA)
SRR............ Software Requirements Review [*NASA*] (NASA)
SRR............ Sound Recorder-Reproducer (MSA)
SRR............ Source-Receptor Relation [*Environmental chemistry*]
SRR............ Special Reimbursement Rate (AFM)
SRR............ Special Report Writer [*NASA*]
SRR............ Spurious Response Rejection
SRR............ Stain Release Rating [*Textile technology*]
SRR............ State Regulation Report: Toxics [*Business Publishers, Inc.*] [*Information service or system*] (CRD)
SRR............ Steering Reversal Rate
SRR............ Strategic Ready Reserve [*Military*]
SRR............ Stride Rite Corp. [*NYSE symbol*] (SPSG)
SRR............ Supplementary Reserve Regulations [*Army*] [*British*]
SRR............ Support Requirements Records [*Navy*] (NG)
SRR............ Survival, Recovery, and Reconstitution [*Military*] (AFM)
SRR............ System Readiness Review
SRR............ System Requirements Review [*NASA*]
SRRA......... Sage Race Relations Abstracts [*A publication*]
SRRB........ Search and Rescue Radio Beacon
SRRC........ Resource Centre, RCMP [*Royal Canadian Mounted Police*] Academy, Regina, Saskatchewan [*Library symbol*] [*National Library of Canada*] (NLC)
SRRC........ Scottish Reactor Research Centre (DEN)
SRRC........ Southern Regional Research Center [*Department of Agriculture*] [*New Orleans, LA*] (GRD)
SRRC........ Sperry Rand Research Center (MCD)
SRRC........ Standing Results Review Committee [*Nuclear energy*] (NRCH)
SRRCP ...... Petroleum Division, Saskatchewan Research Council, Regina [*Library symbol*] [*National Library of Canada*] (BIB)
SRRCS....... Surface Raid Reporting Control Ship [*Navy*] (NVT)
SRRE........ Prairie Farm Rehabilitation Administration, Agriculture Canada [*Administration du Retablissement Agricole des Prairies, Agriculture Canada*] Regina, Saskatchewan [*Library symbol*] [*National Library of Canada*] (NLC)
SRREEC.... Institute of Soil Science. Academia Sinica. Soil Research Report [*A publication*]
SRRI .... Wascana Campus, Saskatchewan Institute of Applied Science and Technology, Regina, Saskatchewan [*Library symbol*] [*National Library of Canada*] (NLC)
SRRS......... Social Readjustment Rating Scale [*Psychometrics*]
SR-RSV ..... Rous Sarcoma Virus, Schmidt-Ruppin Strain
SRRT .... Social Responsibilities Round Table [*American Library Association*] (EA)
SRS .... Sales Relations Survey [*Test*]
SRS .... Salzburg Renaissance Studies [*A publication*]
SRS .... Saskoil, Regina, Saskatchewan [*Library symbol*] [*National Library of Canada*] (NLC)
SRS........... Satellite RADAR Station (NATG)
SRS........... Satellite Readout Station (MCD)
SRS........... Satellite Receiving Station
SRS........... Scandinavian Radiological Society (EA)
SRS........... Science Requirements Strategy [*Viking lander mission*] [*NASA*]
SRS........... Scientific Reference Service [*HEW*]

SRS............	Scientific Research Society of America [*Later, Sigma XI, The Scientific Research Society of America*] (AAG)
SRS............	Scottish Record Society [*Glasgow*] (EA)
SRS............	Search and Rescue Ship (KSC)
SRS............	Second Readiness State (AAG)
SRS............	Secondary RADAR System
SRS............	Secondary Recovery Ships [*NASA*] (KSC)
SRS............	Secure Range Safety [*NASA*] (KSC)
SRS............	Segment Ready Storage
SRS............	Seismic Recording System
SRS............	Selenium Rectifier Stack
SRS............	Self-Rating Scale [*Psychology*]
SRS............	Senate Recording Studio
SRS............	Series [*Deltiology*]
SRS............	Shakespeare Recording Society [*Commercial firm*] (EA)
SRS............	Shipboard RADAR System
SRS............	Short-Range Search (MCD)
SRS............	Shorter Range Scheduling
SRS............	Side-Looking RADAR System
SRS............	Sight Restoration Society (EA)
SRS............	Silent Running Society (EA)
SRS............	Silver-Russell Syndrome [*Medicine*]
SRS............	Simple Random Sample [*Statistics*]
SRS............	Simulated Raman Scattering
SRS............	Simulated Remote Sites [*NASA*] (KSC)
SRS............	Simulated Remote Station [*NASA*]
SRS............	Slave Register Set
SRS............	Sleep Research Society (EA)
SRS............	Slippery Rock State College, Slippery Rock, PA [*OCLC symbol*] (OCLC)
SRS............	Slow-Reacting Substance [*of anaphylaxis*] [*Leukotriene C*] [*Immunology*]
SRS............	Small Research Satellite (KSC)
SRS............	Social and Rehabilitation Service [*Abolished, 1977*] [*HEW*]
SRS............	Social and Rehabilitation Service. Publications [*A publication*]
SRS............	Societatis Regiae Socius [*Fellow of the Royal Society*]
SRS............	Society for Romanian Studies (EA)
SRS............	Sodium Removal Station [*Nuclear energy*] (NRCH)
SRS............	Software Requirements Specification [*NASA*] (NASA)
SRS............	Solar Radiation Simulator
SRS............	Solid RADWASTE [*Radioactive Waste*] System [*Nuclear energy*] (NRCH)
SRS............	Songwriters Resources and Services [*Later, NAS*] (EA)
SRS............	Sonobuoy Reference System [*Navy*] (CAAL)
SRS............	Sound Ranging Set
SRS............	Sound Recordings Specialists [*Record label*]
SRS............	Sound Retrieval System [*Hughes Aircraft Co.*]
SRS............	Sounding Rocket System
SRS............	Southern Railway System (MCD)
SRS............	Space Recovery Systems (KSC)
SRS............	Spaceborne Reconnaissance System
SRS............	Spares Recommendation Sheet (MCD)
SRS............	Special Revenue Sharing (OICC)
SRS............	Specification Requirement Sheet (RDA)
SRS............	Specification Revision Sheet [*NASA*] (NASA)
SRS............	Speech Reinforcement System
SRS............	Splenorenal Shunt [*Medicine*]
SRS............	Squad Radio Set
SRS............	Srpska Radikalna Stranka [*Serbian Radical Party*] [*Yugoslavia*] [*Political party*] (PPE)
S/RS..........	Staff Returns [*Marine Corps*]
SRS............	Standard Reference Section
SRS............	Standard Repair Specification (MCD)
SRS............	State Revenue Society (EA)
SRS............	Statistical Reporting Service [*Later, ESCS*] [*Department of Agriculture*]
SRS............	Stimulated Raman Scattering [*Spectrometry*]
SRS............	Strange Stories [*A publication*]
SRS............	Strategic Reconnaissance Squadron (MCD)
SRS............	Strike Reporting System
SRS............	Structural Research Series
SRS............	Student Response System [*Automated group instruction*]
SRS............	Submarine Reactor Small
SRS............	Subscriber-Response System [*Study of cable television*] [*Hughes Aircraft Co.*]
SRS............	Substitute Route Structure
SRS............	Sunrise Metals [*Vancouver Stock Exchange symbol*]
SRS............	Supplemental Restraint System [*Automotive engineering*]
SRS............	Supply Response Section [*Navy*]
SRS............	Support Requirement System [*NASA*] (NASA)
SRS............	Surgical Research Society [*British*]
SRS............	Surtsey Research Society (EAIO)
SRS............	Surveillance RADAR Station
SRS............	Survey Research Service [*National Opinion Research Center, University of Chicago*] [*Research center*]
SRS............	Survey Research Singapore (Pte) Ltd. [*Information service or system*] (EISS)
SRS............	Synchronous Relay Satellite [*Telecommunications*] (TEL)
SRS............	Synchrotron Radiation Source [*High-energy physics*]
SRS............	System Requirements Specification (MCD)
SRSA.........	Saskatchewan Arts Board, Regina, Saskatchewan [*Library symbol*] [*National Library of Canada*] (NLC)
SRSA.........	Scientific Research Society of America [*Later, Sigma XI, The Scientific Research Society of America*]
SRS-A........	Slow-Reacting Substance of Anaphylaxis [*Immunology*]
SR SATSIM ...	Search RADAR Satellite Simulation [*Military*] (CAAL)
SRSC	Safety Railway Services Corporation [*NASDAQ symbol*] (NQ)
SRSC	Saturday Review of the Sciences [*A publication*]
SRSC	Slippery Rock State College [*Pennsylvania*]
SRSC	Space Remote Sensing Center
SRSC	Sul Ross State College [*Later, SRSU*] [*Texas*]
SRSC	System Centre, Saskatchewan Revenue Supply and Services, Regina, Saskatchewan [*Library symbol*] [*National Library of Canada*] (NLC)
SRSCC......	Simulated Remote Station Control Center
SRSCCD....	Saskatchewan Co-Operation and Co-Operative Development, Regina, Saskatchewan [*Library symbol*] [*National Library of Canada*] (NLC)
Sr Sch........	Senior Scholastic [*A publication*]
Sr Schol	Senior Scholastic [*A publication*]
SR-Sci........	Saturday Review of the Sciences [*A publication*]
Sr Sci.........	Senior Science [*A publication*]
SRSCU	Saskatchewan Computer Utility Corp. [*SaskComp*], Regina, Saskatchewan [*Library symbol*] [*National Library of Canada*] (NLC)
SRSD	Saturday Review of Society [*A publication*]
SRSEM	Saskatchewan Department of Energy and Mines, Regina, Saskatchewan [*Library symbol*] [*National Library of Canada*] (NLC)
SRSEMG ..	Geological Laboratory, Saskatchewan Department of Energy and Mines, Regina, Saskatchewan [*Library symbol*] [*National Library of Canada*] (NLC)
SRSF.........	Saskatchewan Finance, Regina, Saskatchewan [*Library symbol*] [*National Library of Canada*] (NLC)
SRSF.........	SRB [*Solid-Rocket Booster*] Receiving [*or Refurbishment*] and Subassembly Facility [*NASA*] (NASA)
SRSG	Search RADAR Simulation Group [*Military*] (CAAL)
SRSG	Subsurface Geological Laboratory, Regina, Saskatchewan [*Library symbol*] [*National Library of Canada*] (NLC)
SRSH	Wascana Hospital, Regina, Saskatchewan [*Library symbol*] [*National Library of Canada*] (NLC)
SRSI	Sikh Religious Studies Information [*A publication*]
SRSI	Specialty Retail Services, Inc. [*NASDAQ symbol*] (NQ)
SRSIB	Salt Research and Industry [*A publication*]
SRSK	Short-Range Station Keeping (NG)
SRSL	Sunrise Bancorp, Inc. [*NASDAQ symbol*] (NQ)
SRSNY	Stockholder Relations Society of New York (EA)
SRSO........	Saturday Review of Society [*A publication*]
SRSO........	Scoliosis Research Society (EA)
SR-Soc	Saturday Review of Society [*A publication*]
SRSP	Stockpile Reliability/Survivability Program
SRSPMC...	Saskatchewan Property Management Corp., Regina, Saskatchewan [*Library symbol*] [*National Library of Canada*] (NLC)
SR Sq	Strategic Reconnaissance Squadron
SRSR	Schedule and Resources Status Report [*NASA*] (NASA)
SRSRDL....	Soviet Scientific Reviews. Section D. Biology Reviews [*A publication*]
SRSS.........	Resource Centre, Saskatchewan Department of Social Services, Regina, Saskatchewan [*Library symbol*] [*National Library of Canada*] (NLC)
SRSS.........	Shuttle Range Safety System [*NASA*] (NASA)
SRSS.........	Simulated Remote Sites Subsystem [*NASA*] (KSC)
SRSS.........	Sociological Resources for Social Studies [*Project of American Sociological Association*]
SRSS.........	Solar Radiation Simulator System
SRSS.........	Square Root of the Sum of the Squares (NRCH)
SRST	SASK TEL Corporate Library, Regina, Saskatchewan [*Library symbol*] [*National Library of Canada*] (NLC)
SRST	Speed Reading Self-Taught [*Learning International*]
SRSTA.......	Society of Roller Skating Teachers of America (EA)
SRSU........	Sul Ross State University [*Texas*]
SRSUE	Studies in Regional Science and Urban Economics [*Elsevier Book Series*] [*A publication*]
SRT...........	S-Band Radio Transmitter
SRT...........	Sagittal Ray Trace
SRT...........	Sarafotoxin [*Biochemistry*]
SRT...........	Sarutani [*Japan*] [*Seismograph station code, US Geological Survey*] (SEIS)
SRT...........	Scarlet Energy, Inc. [*Vancouver Stock Exchange symbol*]
SRT...........	School Readiness Test [*Child development test*]
SRT...........	Science Recommendation Team
SRT...........	Science, Research, and Technology
SRT...........	Search RADAR Terminal
SRT...........	Security Response Team [*Military*]
SRT...........	Sedimentation Rate Test
SRT...........	Self-Repair Technique
SRT...........	Serials Round Table [*Later, RTSD*] [*American Library Association*]
SRT...........	Short-Range Transport [*Aircraft*] (NATG)
SRT...........	Shuttle Requirements Traceability [*NASA*] (MCD)

SRT............	Silica RADOME Technique
SRT............	Simple Reaction Time [*Psychometry*]
SRT............	Single Requesting Terminal [*Data processing*] (IBMDP)
SRT............	Slow-Run-Through Trials [*Navy*] (NG)
SRT............	Social Relations Test [*Psychology*]
SRT............	Solar Radiation Test
SRT............	Solar Radio Telescope
SRT............	Solids Retention Time [*Water pollution*]
SRT............	Soroti [*Uganda*] [*Airport symbol*] (OAG)
SRT............	Special Rated Thrust [*Aerospace*] (MCD)
SRT............	Special Real-Time Command (MCD)
SRT............	Special Review Team [*Nuclear energy*] (NRCH)
SRT............	Specification Requirements Table [*NASA*] (NASA)
SRT............	Speech Reception Thresholds [*Audiometry*]
SRT............	Spent Resin Tank [*Nuclear energy*] (NRCH)
SRT............	Spousal Remainder Trust [*Banking*]
SRT............	Standard Rate Turn (NVT)
SRT............	Standard Remote Terminal
SRT............	State Railway of Thailand (DS)
SRT............	Station Readiness Test
SRT............	Step Recovery Transistor
SRT............	Strategic Relocatable Target [*DoD*]
SRT............	Strategic Rocket Troops (NATG)
SRT............	Stress Relief Tool
SRT............	Subcaliber Rocket Trainer [*Army*] (INF)
SRT............	Supply Response Time
SR & T	Supporting Research and Technology
SRT............	Supporting Research and Technology (MCD)
SRT............	Surface Recording Terminal (MCD)
SRT............	Sustained Release Theophylline [*Medicine*]
SRT............	Synchro and Resolver Transmission
SRT............	System Reaction Time (KSC)
SRT............	System Reliability Test
SRT............	Systems Readiness Test (KSC)
SRTA	Senorita [*Miss*] [*Spanish*]
SRTC	Scientific Research Tax Credit [*Canada*]
SRTC	Search RADAR Terrain Clearance (NG)
SRTC	Society of Ration Token Collectors (EA)
SRTC	Southern Rhodesia Transport Corps [*British military*] (DMA)
SRTC	Special Real-Time Command (KSC)
SRTC	Stored Program Real-Time Commands (MCD)
SRTD	Sorted (MCD)
SRTF	Short-Range Task Force
SRTF	Shortest Remaining Time First [*Data processing*]
SRTG-A	Science Reports. Tohoku University. Seventh Series. Geography [*Japan*] [*A publication*]
SRTN	Solar Radio Telescope Network
SRTN	Special Representative for Trade Negotiations [*Later, USTR*] [*Executive Office of the President*]
SRTP	Sensitized Room Temperature Phosphorescence
SRTS	Scaled Range Target System (MCD)
SRTS	Science Research Temperament Scale [*Psychology*]
SRTS	Short-Range Thermal Sight [*Army*] (INF)
SRTS	Surveillance RADAR Test Set
SRTSB.......	Business Library, Saskatchewan Department of Tourism and Small Business, Regina, Saskatchewan [*Library symbol*] [*National Library of Canada*] (NLC)
SRTU........	Ship Repair Training Unit
SRTUAW ...	Acta Geologica Taiwanica [*A publication*]
SRTUC......	Southern Rhodesian Trade Unions Congress
SRTVM.....	Short-Range Track via Missile [*Military*] (CAAL)
SRU	Santa Cruz, CA [*Location identifier*] [*FAA*] (FAAL)
SRU	Scottish Rugby Union (DAS)
SRU	Seaplane Reconnaissance Unit
SRU	Secondary Replaceable Unit
SRU	Selective Reserve Unit [*Navy*] (NVT)
SRU	Sensor Readout Unit (MCD)
SRU	Servo Repeater Unit
SRU	Ship Repair Unit
SRU	Shop-Replaceable Unit [*NASA*] (NASA)
SRU	Signal Responder Unit (AAG)
SRU	Silver Recovery Unit
SRU	Societe de Raffinage d'Uranium [*France*]
SRU	Space Replaceable Unit (MCD)
SRU	Structural Repeating Unit [*Polymer nomenclature system*]
SRu	Studi Rumeni [*Rome*] [*A publication*]
SRU	Subassembly Repairable Unit (MCD)
SRU	Submarine Repair Unit
SRU	Sulfur Recovery Unit [*Chemical engineering*]
SRU	Support Resource Unit (MCD)
SRU	Suspension and Release Units (AFM)
SRU	System Replaceable Unit
SRU	University of Regina, Saskatchewan [*Library symbol*] [*National Library of Canada*] (NLC)
SRU	University of Scranton, Scranton, PA [*OCLC symbol*] (OCLC)
SRUA	Saskatchewan Urban Affairs, Regina, Saskatchewan [*Library symbol*] [*National Library of Canada*] (NLC)
SRUC........	Regina Campus, Campion College, University of Saskatchewan, Saskatchewan [*Library symbol*] [*Natianal Library of Canada*] (NLC)
SRUE.........	Education Library, University of Regina, Saskatchewan [*Library symbol*] [*National Library of Canada*] (BIB)
SRUEA.....	Structural Engineer [*A publication*]
SRUFA.....	Faculty of Fine Arts, University of Regina, Saskatchewan [*Library symbol*] [*National Library of Canada*] (NLC)
SRUG	Department of Geography, University of Regina, Saskatchewan [*Library symbol*] [*National Library of Canada*] (NLC)
SRUNM	Norman MacKenzie Art Gallery, University of Regina, Saskatchewan [*Library symbol*] [*National Library of Canada*] (NLC)
SRUTA......	Soviet Rubber Technology [*English Translation*] [*A publication*]
SRV...........	Executive Air Services, Inc. [*Jacksonville, FL*] [*FAA designator*] (FAAC)
SRV...........	Safety Relief Valve [*Nuclear energy*] (NRCH)
SRV...........	Saline Retention Value
SRV...........	Satellite Reentry Vehicle
SRV...........	Service Corp. International [*NYSE symbol*] (SPSG)
SRV...........	Short-Range Viewer
SRV...........	Sirius Resources [*Vancouver Stock Exchange symbol*]
SRV...........	Socialist Republic of Vietnam
SRV...........	Society of Russian Veterans of the World War (EA)
SRv...........	Southwest Review [*A publication*]
SRV...........	Space Recovery [*or Rescue*] Vehicle
SRV...........	Step Recovery Varactor
SRV...........	Stony River [*Alaska*] [*Airport symbol*] (OAG)
SRV...........	Submerged Research Vehicle
SRV...........	Surface Recombination Velocity (DEN)
SRV...........	Surface Roving Vehicle [*NASA*] (KSC)
SRV...........	Surrogate Research Vehicle [*Army Tank-Automotive Command*]
SRV...........	System Readiness Verification
Srvc	Service
SRVC........	Sine-Random Vibration Control
SRVCLG ...	Service Ceiling [*Aerospace engineering*]
SRVDL......	Safety/Relief Valve Discharge Line [*Nuclear energy*] (NRCH)
Srve	Service
SRVEILOPS ...	Surveillance Operations [*Military*] (NVT)
SRVI	Servico, Inc. [*NASDAQ symbol*] (NQ)
SRVL	Survival (MSA)
SRVLSCH ...	Survival School [*Air Force*]
SRVSB......	Saturday Review of the Sciences [*A publication*]
SRW	Salisbury, NC [*Location identifier*] [*FAA*] (FAAL)
SRW	Saskatchewan Wheat Pool, Regina, Saskatchewan [*Library symbol*] [*National Library of Canada*] (NLC)
SRW	Saturday Review/World [*A publication*]
SRW	Short Ragweed [*Immunology*]
SRW	Silenced Reconnaissance Weapon (MCD)
SRW	Strategic Reconnaissance Wing [*Air Force*] (MCD)
SR (WA)...	State Reports (Western Australia) [*A publication*] (APTA)
SRWA	Swiss Review of World Affairs [*A publication*]
SRWBR....	Short-Range Wideband Radio (MCD)
SRWD	South Saskatchewan Committee for World Development, Regina, Saskatchewan [*Library symbol*] [*National Library of Canada*] (NLC)
SRWg........	Strategic Reconnaissance Wing [*Air Force*] (AFM)
SRWL........	Speeded Reading of Word List [*Neuropsychology test*]
SRW Nachr ...	SRW [*Siemens-Reiniger-Werke*] Nachricht [*West Germany*] [*A publication*]
SR/World ..	Saturday Review/World [*A publication*]
SRWR........	Saskatchewan Water Resources Commission, Regina, Saskatchewan [*Library symbol*] [*National Library of Canada*] (NLC)
SRWS	Simplified and Regularized Writing System
SRWS	Solid Radioactive Waste System [*Nuclear energy*] (NRCH)
SRWS	Standard Reference Water Sample [*US Geological Survey*]
SRWSDA ..	World Fertility Survey. Scientific Reports [*A publication*]
SRWU	Sudan Railways Workers' [*Trade*] Union
SRX...........	Sert [*Libya*] [*Airport symbol*] [*Obsolete*] (OAG)
SRX...........	SR Telecom, Inc. [*Toronto Stock Exchange symbol*]
SRY...........	Sherwood Rangers Yeomanry [*Military unit*] [*British*]
SRY...........	Ship Repair Yard (CINC)
SRY...........	Shiroyama [*Japan*] [*Seismograph station code, US Geological Survey*] (SEIS)
SRY...........	Stryker Resources Ltd. [*Vancouver Stock Exchange symbol*]
SRZ...........	San Marcos, TX [*Location identifier*] [*FAA*] (FAAL)
SRZ...........	Santa Cruz [*Bolivia*] [*Airport symbol*] (OAG)
SRZ...........	Satz Rechen Zentrum [*Computer Composition Center*] [*Hartmann & Heenemann*] [*Information service or system*] (IID)
SRZ...........	Special Rules Zone
SRZ...........	Stratas Corp. [*Vancouver Stock Exchange symbol*]
SRZ...........	Studia Romanica Zagrabiensia [*A publication*]
SRZF........	Synchro Resolver Zeroing Fixture
SRZLO......	Supreme Royal Zuanna, Ladies of the Orient [*Defunct*] (EA)
SS..............	Aerolineas Dominicanas SA [*Dominican Republic*] [*ICAO designator*] (FAAC)
SS..............	Faulty Sentence Structure [*Used in correcting manuscripts, etc.*]
SS..............	Passing Stop Sign [*Traffic offense charge*]
SS..............	Royal Statistical Society [*British*]
SS..............	Sa Saintete [*His Holiness*] [*The Pope*] [*French*]

SS..............	Sa Seigneurie [*His Lordship*] [*French*]
SS..............	Saccharin Sodium [*Sweetening agent*]
SS..............	Sacred Scripture
SS..............	Safe Shutdown [*Nuclear energy*] (NRCH)
SS..............	Safer Sex
SS..............	Safety Services [*Red Cross*]
SS..............	Safety Supervisor (MUGU)
SS..............	Safety Supplements [*Air Force*]
SS..............	Sagittal Sinus [*Anatomy*]
SS..............	Saint-Sacrement [*Blessed Sacrament*] [*French*]
SS..............	Saints [*as in "SS Peter and Paul"*]
SS..............	Saline Soak
SS..............	Salmonella-Shigella [*Microbiology*]
SS..............	Salt-Sensitive
SS..............	Same Size [*Photography, publishing*]
SS..............	Sample Sink [*Nuclear energy*] (NRCH)
SS..............	Sample Station [*Nuclear energy*] (NRCH)
S/S..............	Samples per Second (KSC)
SS..............	Sampling System (NRCH)
SS..............	Sancti [*Saints*] [*Latin*]
SS..............	Sanctissimus [*Most Holy*] [*Latin*]
SS..............	Sanctum Sanctorum [*Holy of Holies*] [*Latin*] [*Freemasonry*]
SS..............	Sand Springs Railway Co. [*AAR code*]
SS..............	Sandstone [*Lithology*]
SS..............	Sartre Society (EA)
SS..............	Saskatoon Public Library, Saskatchewan [*Library symbol*] [*National Library of Canada*] (NLC)
SS..............	Satellite-Switched
SS..............	Satellite System
SS..............	Saturated Solution [*Pharmacy*]
S & S..........	Sausse and Scully's Irish Rolls Court Reports [*1837-40*] [*A publication*] (DLA)
SS..............	Sawin Society (EA)
SS..............	Scandinavian Seminar (EA)
SS..............	Scandinavian Studies [*A publication*]
SS..............	Scanning Slit
SS..............	Schempp-Hirth KG [*Federal Republic of Germany*] [*ICAO aircraft manufacturer identifier*] (ICAO)
S en S........	Schip en Schade [*A publication*]
S & S..........	Schleicher & Schuell [*Filter-paper company*]
SS..............	School and Society [*A publication*]
S & S..........	School and Society [*A publication*]
SS..............	Schutzstaffel [*Elite Guard*] [*NAZI Germany*]
SS..............	Schwab Safe Co. [*AMEX symbol*] (SPSG)
SS..............	Science Service
S & S..........	Science and Society [*A publication*]
SS..............	Science and Society [*A publication*]
SS..............	Scilicet [*Namely*] [*Legal term*] [*Latin*]
SS..............	Scintiscanning [*Medicine*]
SS..............	Sclerotinia sclerlatiorum (Causative Agent of Peanut Blight)
SS..............	Screw Steamer
SS..............	Sea Scout - Nonrigid Airship [*Royal Naval Air Service*] [*British*]
SS..............	Sea Service [*British military*] (DMA)
SS..............	Sea State
S & S..........	Searle and Smith's English Probate and Divorce Reports [*1859-60*] [*A publication*] (DLA)
SS..............	Second Stage
SS..............	Secondary School
SS..............	Secondary Sources
SS..............	Secret Service
SS..............	Secretary for Scotland
S of S........	Secretary of State
SS..............	Secretary of State
S of S........	Secretary of State for Defence [*British*] (RDA)
SS..............	Secretary of State Department [*Canada*]
SS..............	Sections (ADA)
SS..............	Security Service
SS..............	Security Systems, Inc. [*In TV series "Max Headroom"*]
SS..............	See a Solicitor [*British*]
SS..............	Seingalt Society (EA)
SS..............	Selden Society (EA)
SS..............	Select Standby
SS..............	Selective Service
SS..............	Selective Signaling
SS..............	Selector Switch (IEEE)
SS..............	Selling Short [*or Short Sale*] [*Investment term*]
SS..............	Semifinal Splice [*Telecommunications*] (TEL)
SS..............	Semis [*One-Half*] [*Pharmacy*]
SS..............	Semisteel
SS..............	Semisubmersible [*Drilling unit*]
SS..............	Sempervivium Society [*Burgess Hill, West Sussex, England*] (EAIO)
SS..............	Senior Scholars (EA)
SS..............	Senior Scholastic [*A publication*]
SS..............	Senior Security [*Investment term*]
S & S..........	Sense and Sensibility [*Novel by Jane Austen*]
SS..............	Sensor [*Genetics*]
SS..............	Sensor Supervisor [*Military*] (CAAL)
SS..............	Sensu Stricto [*In a Narrow Sense*] [*Latin*]
SS..............	Sentence Suspended
SS..............	Senza Sordini [*Without Mutes*] [*Music*]
SS..............	Sequentia [*What Follows*] [*Latin*] (ROG)
SS..............	Sequential Switch
SS..............	Serials Section [*Resources and Technical Services Division*] [*American Library Association*]
SS..............	Series Separate
Ss..............	Serum Serologic [*Immunochemistry*]
SS..............	Serum Sickness [*Medicine*]
SS..............	Service Sink (MSA)
SS..............	Service Squadron (AAG)
SS..............	Service Structure (KSC)
SS..............	Sessions
SS..............	Set Screw [*Technical drawings*]
SS..............	Set Steering
S & S..........	Sex and Shopping [*Themes of Judith Krantz's novels*]
SS..............	Sezary Syndrome [*Dermatology*]
SS..............	Shackamaxon Society (EA)
SS..............	Shakespeare Survey [*A publication*]
SS..............	Sharpshooter [*Marine Corps*]
SS..............	Shear Strength (AAG)
SS..............	Shelf Stock
SS..............	Shell Shock
SS..............	Shift Supervisor (IEEE)
SS..............	Shimmy Showing [*From one girl to another, in reference to dress disarrangement*]
SS..............	Ship Service
S/S..............	Ship-to-Shore (MUGU)
SS..............	Ship Station
SS..............	Ship System
SS..............	Shipmasters' Society [*A union*] [*British*]
SS..............	Shipping Situation [*British*]
S & S..........	Shipping and Storage
SS..............	Shipside
SS..............	Shomrim Society (EA)
SS..............	Shoot Tip Abscission Scar [*Botany*]
SS..............	Shop Steward
SS..............	Short Sight (ADA)
SS..............	Short Sleeves
SS..............	Shortstop
SS..............	Shosin Society (EA)
SS..............	Shrinking Stock [*Corporate investment*]
SS..............	Shuttle System [*NASA*] (MCD)
SS..............	Side Scatter
SS..............	Side Seam
SS..............	Side to Side
SS..............	Side by Side (AAG)
SS..............	Side Slip (MCD)
SS..............	Sidestream Smoke [*from cigarettes*]
SS..............	Sight and Sound [*A publication*]
S & S..........	Sight and Sound [*A publication*]
S/S..............	Sign Signature (AAG)
SS..............	Signal Selector (DEN)
SS..............	Signal Strength [*Broadcasting*] (KSC)
SS..............	Signaling System [*Telecommunications*] (TEL)
SS..............	Signed and Sealed
S & S..........	Signs and Symptoms [*Medicine*]
S/S..............	Silk Screen (ADA)
SS..............	Silver Spur Resources [*Vancouver Stock Exchange symbol*]
SS..............	Silver Standard [*Vancouver Stock Exchange symbol*]
SS..............	Silver Star [*Military decoration*]
SS..............	Silvernail's New York Supreme Court Reports [*A publication*] (DLA)
S & S..........	Simon & Schuster [*Publisher*]
S de S........	Simon de Southwell [*Flourished, 1184-1209*] [*Authority cited in pre-1607 legal work*] (DSA)
S & S..........	Simons and Stuart's English Vice-Chancellors' Reports [*1822-26*] [*A publication*] (DLA)
SS..............	Simple Spike
SS..............	Simplified Spelling
SS..............	Single Scan
SS..............	Single Seated
SS..............	Single Shot
SS..............	Single Sideband
SS..............	Single Signal
SS..............	Single Stout [*Beer*] (ROG)
SS..............	Single-Stranded [*or ss*] [*Genetics*]
SS..............	Single Strength [*Citrus juices*]
SS..............	Single String (MCD)
SS..............	Sinistral Sig (EA)
SS..............	Sinner Saved [*Pseudonym used by William Huntington*]
SS..............	Site Safety [*Nuclear energy*] (NRCH)
SS..............	Site Suitability [*Nuclear energy*] (NRCH)
SS..............	Sjoegren's Syndrome [*Medicine*]
SS..............	Skid Strip (KSC)
SS..............	Skinners' Society [*A union*] [*British*]
SS..............	Slaters' Society [*A union*] [*British*]
SS..............	Sliding Scale (AAG)
SS..............	Slocum Society (EA)
SS..............	Slop Sink
SS..............	Slovo a Slovesnost [*A publication*]
SS..............	Slow Setting [*Asphalt grade*]

SS..............	Small Signal
SS..............	Small Subcompact [*Car size*]
SS..............	Smallest Subunit [*Genetics*]
SS..............	Smoke Stand (MSA)
SS..............	Smokeshop [*A publication*]
SS..............	Soap Solution
SS..............	Soapsuds
SS..............	Social Science
SS..............	Social Security
SS..............	Social Service
SS..............	Social Shopper
SS..............	Social Studies [*A publication*]
SS..............	Social Surveys
SS..............	Society of St. Sulpice [*Sulpicians*] [*Roman Catholic men's religious order*]
SS..............	Society of Separationists (EA)
SS..............	Society of Shuttlemakers [*A union*] [*British*]
SS..............	Society of Signalmen (EA)
SS..............	Society of the Silurians (EA)
SS..............	Society for Strings (EA)
SS..............	Sociological Studies [*A publication*]
SS..............	Soft Sarcoma [*Oncology*]
SS..............	SoftSearch, Inc. [*Information service or system*] (IID)
SS..............	Software Systems
SS..............	Solid Shield (MCD)
SS..............	Solid State
SS..............	Soluble Solids [*Chemistry*]
SS..............	Somatics Society [*Commercial firm*] (EA)
SS..............	Somatostatin [*Also, GH-RIF, GH-RIH, GRIF, SRIF*] [*Endocrinology*]
S of S.........	Song of Solomon [*Old Testament book*]
SS..............	Song Sparrow [*Ornithology*]
SS..............	Songsmith Society (EA)
SS..............	Sonneck Society (EA)
SS..............	Soprano Saxophone
SS..............	Sound and Sense [*Baguio City*] [*A publication*]
SS..............	Sound System
SS..............	Source Selection (MCD)
S/S.............	Source/Sink [*Data processing*] (IBMDP)
SS..............	Source/Source [*Inspection/Acceptance point*] (MCD)
SS..............	Source and Special [*Material*] [*Nuclear energy*]
SS..............	Source of Supply (AFM)
SS..............	South Saxon (ROG)
SS..............	Souvenir Sheet [*Philately*]
SS..............	Space Shuttle [*NASA*] (KSC)
SS..............	Space Simulator (IEEE)
SS..............	Space Station (AAG)
SS..............	Space Switch [*Telecommunications*] (TEL)
ss	Spanish Sahara [*Western Sahara*] [*MARC country of publication code*] [*Library of Congress*] (LCCP)
SS..............	Sparingly Soluble
SS..............	Special Series
SS..............	Special Service [*Vessel load line mark*]
SS..............	Special Session
SS..............	Special Settlement [*Business term*]
SS..............	Special Source Materials [*Nuclear energy*] (NRCH)
SS..............	Special Staff
SS..............	Special Strike (NATG)
SS..............	Special Study
SS..............	Special Subjects
SS..............	Special Survey [*Lloyd's Register of Shipping*] (DS)
SS..............	Specification for Structure
S/S.............	Spectrum Signature (NG)
SS..............	Speed Sensor (NRCH)
SS..............	Spenser Society (EA)
SS..............	Spherical Symmetry
S & S.........	Spigot and Socket
SS..............	Spin-Stabilized [*Rockets*]
SS..............	Spiral to Spiral
SS..............	Spore Surface [*Immunology*]
S o S.........	Sprak och Stil [*A publication*]
SS..............	Spread Spectrum (CET)
SS..............	Squawk Sheet (KSC)
SS..............	Stabilization System (AAG)
SS..............	Stack Segment [*Data processing*]
SS..............	Staff Sergeant [*Military*] [*British*] (ROG)
SS..............	Staff Specialist [*Military*]
SS..............	Staff Surgeon
SS..............	Stainless Steel
SS..............	Standard Frequency Station [*ITU designation*]
SS..............	Standard Score [*Psychology*]
SS..............	Standard Size (ADA)
SS..............	Standardized Solution [*Pharmacy*]
SS..............	Starlight Scope
S & S.........	Stars & Stripes [*A publication*]
S/S.............	Start/Stop
SS..............	Startling Stories [*A publication*]
SS..............	State School (ADA)
SS..............	State Supervisor
S/S.............	Statement of Service [*Military*]
SS..............	Statesman Series [*A publication*]
SS..............	Static Stretching [*Medicine*]
SS..............	Station Set [*NASA*] (NASA)
S to S.........	Station to Station
SS..............	Station Supervision
SS..............	Statistical Standards
SS..............	Statistics Sources [*A publication*]
sS	Statsiemens [*Also, statS*] [*Unit of electric conductance, admittance, and susceptance*]
SS..............	Steady State
SS..............	Steamship
SS..............	Steel Sash
SS..............	Steering Safety
SS..............	Steering System
SS..............	Stereoscopic Society [*Chessington, Surrey, England*] (EAIO)
SS..............	Stereoscopic Society - American Branch (EA)
SS..............	Sterile Solution
SS..............	Steroid Score [*Immunology*]
SS..............	Stimulator Substance [*Liver regeneration*]
SS..............	Storage to Storage (MCD)
SS..............	Straight Shank [*Screw*]
SS..............	Straight Sided
SS..............	Straits Settlements [*in Malaya*]
SS..............	Strategic Study [*Military*]
Ss	Striped Shiner [*Ichthyology*]
SS..............	Strong Safety [*Football*]
SS..............	Structure-Superstructure [*Economics*]
SS..............	Student at Staff College [*Army*] [*British*] (ROG)
SS..............	Studi Sardi [*A publication*]
SS..............	Studi Semitici [*A publication*]
SS..............	Studi Storici [*A publication*]
SS..............	Studia Serdicensia [*A publication*]
SS..............	Stumpwork Society (EA)
SS..............	Style Sac
SS..............	Subject-Subject [*Education of the hearing-impaired*]
SS..............	Subliminal Self [*Psychical research*]
SS..............	Submarine [*Navy symbol*]
SS..............	Submarine Qualification [*Navy*]
SS..............	Submarine Scout
SS..............	Submarine Studies [*SORG*]
SS..............	Subsagittal [*Medicine*]
SS..............	Subscriber Switching [*Telecommunications*] (TEL)
SS..............	Subsolar [*NASA*] (KSC)
SS..............	Substitutes [*Sports*]
ss	Substructure [*Data processing*]
SS..............	Subsystem (AAG)
SS..............	Successive Stereometric [*A discrimination task*]
SS..............	Sugar Series [*Elsevier Book Series*] [*A publication*]
SS..............	Sum-of-the-Squares
SS..............	Summary Sheet
SS..............	Summation Sound
SS..............	Summing Selector (MSA)
SS..............	Summons (ROG)
SS..............	Sun Seeker (AAG)
SS..............	Sun Sensor
SS..............	Sun Simulator (MCD)
SS..............	Sunday School
SS..............	Sunday Sport [*A publication*]
SS..............	Sunset [*Meteorology*] (FAAC)
SS..............	Super Search (MCD)
SS..............	Super Speed
SS..............	Super Sport [*In automobile model name*]
SS..............	Super Symmetric [*Particle physics*]
SS..............	Superintending Scientist [*British*] (ADA)
SS..............	Superintending Sister [*Navy*] [*British*]
SS..............	Supersensitive (AAG)
SS..............	Supersonic
SS..............	Supervisors Section [*American Association of School Librarians*]
S & S.........	Supply and Service [*Army*] (AABC)
SS..............	Supply Ship (MCD)
SS..............	Support System [*Air Force*]
SS..............	Supportive Service (OICC)
SS..............	Supra Scriptum [*Written Above*] [*Latin*]
SS..............	Surface Ship
SS..............	Surface-Sized [*Paper*]
SS..............	Surface-to-Surface (NATG)
SS..............	Surratt Society (EA)
SS..............	Surveillance Station [*RADAR*]
SS..............	Suspended Sentence
SS..............	Suspended Solids [*Wastewater treatment*]
S & S.........	Swan and Sayler's Revised Statutes of Ohio [*A publication*] (DLA)
SS..............	Swedish Society, Discofil [*Record label*] [*Sweden*]
SS..............	Switch Selector (KSC)
S & S.........	Sword and Sorcery
SS..............	Sworn Statement
SS..............	Sympathetically Stimulated [*Physiology*]
SS..............	Syn og Segn [*A publication*]
SS..............	Synchro Standard
SS..............	Synergetic Society (EA)

SS	Synopsis Series of the United States Treasury Decisions [*A publication*] (DLA)
S & S	Syntax and Semantics [*A publication*]
SS	System Segment (MCD)
SS	System Sensitivity
SS	System Software [*NASA*] (MCD)
SS	System Summary [*NASA*] (MCD)
SS	System Supervisor
SS	Systems Specifications [*NASA*] (NG)
S1S	Surfaced or Dressed One Side [*Technical drawings*]
S2S	Surfaced or Dressed Two Sides [*Technical drawings*]
S4S	Surfaced or Dressed Four Sides [*Technical drawings*]
SSA	Associate in Secretarial Science
SSA	Cargo Submarine [*Navy symbol*] [*Obsolete*]
SSA	First Soprano, Second Soprano, and Alto [*in all-women choral groups*]
SSA	S-Band Single Access (MCD)
SSA	Salisbury Sound Association (EA)
SSA	Salsalate [*Anti-inflammatory drug*]
SSA	Salvador [*Brazil*] [*Airport symbol*] (OAG)
SSA	Saskatchewan Archives Office, Saskatoon, Saskatchewan [*Library symbol*] [*National Library of Canada*] (NLC)
SSA	Sauna Society of America (EA)
SSA	Scandinavian Society of Anaesthesiologists (EA)
SSA	Scandinavian Sociological Association (EA)
SSA	Schools Sailing Association [*British*]
SSA	Scottish Schoolmasters Association [*British*]
SSA	Scottish Shipmasters' Association [*A union*]
SSA	Secretary of State for Air [*British*]
SS of A	Secular Society of America [*Defunct*]
SSA	Security Support Activity
SSA	Security Supporting Assistance [*US government program for promoting economic and political stability in areas of strategic interest*]
SSA	Segment Search Argument [*Data processing*] (BUR)
SSA	Seismological Society of America (EA)
SSA	Selective Service Act
SSA	Semiotic Society of America (EA)
SSA	Senior Scientific Assistant [*Ministry of Agriculture, Fisheries, and Food*] [*British*]
SSA	Sensat Technologies Ltd. [*Vancouver Stock Exchange symbol*]
SSA	Sequential Spectrometer Accessory [*Instrumentation*]
SSA	Series of Standard Additions
SSA	Service Support Arrangement
SSA	Shakespeare Society of America (EA)
SSA	Shan State Army [*Burma*] (PD)
SSA	Shaw Society of America [*Defunct*] (EA)
SSA	Sheath of Skeletal Axis
SSA	Ship's Stores Ashore [*Navy*]
SSA	Shuttle Simulation Aircraft [*NASA*] (NASA)
SSA	Signal Security Agency [*Later, Army Security Agency*]
SSA	Signal Supply Agency
SSA	Simian Society of America (EA)
SSA	Simpler Spelling Association [*Later, PSC*] (EA)
SSA	Sinatra Society of America (EA)
SSA	Single Line Synchronous Adapter (MCD)
SSA	Sisters of St. Ann of Providence [*Roman Catholic religious order*]
SS-A	Sjogren's Syndrome A [*Medicine*]
SSA	Slaving Signal Amplifier
SSA	Sleeve Stub Antenna
SSA	Slovak Studies Association (EA)
SSA	Soaring Society of America (EA)
SSA	Social Science Abstracts [*A publication*]
SSA	Social Security Act [*1935*] [*Also, SSACT*]
SSA	Social Security Administration [*Department of Health and Human Services*]
SSA	Social Security Administration. Publications [*A publication*]
SSA	Society of Security Analysts
SSA	Society for the Study of Addiction to Alcohol and Other Drugs (EAIO)
SSA	Solid-State Abstracts
SSA	Solid-State Amorphization [*Metallurgy*]
SSA	Sommelier Society of America (EA)
SSA	Source Selection Activity [*or Authority*] [*Military*]
SSA	Space Suit Assembly (KSC)
SS & A	Space Systems and Applications [*NASA*] (NASA)
SSA	Spanish-Surnamed American
SSA	Spatial Sound Around [*Acoustics*]
SSA	Special Service Agreement [*UN Food and Agriculture Organization*]
SSA	Special Survey Automated Controls [*Lloyd's Register of Shipping*]
SSA	Sportswear Salesmen's Association (EA)
SSA	Staff Supply Assistant [*Military*] (AABC)
SSA	Staff Support Agencies [*Military*]
SSA	Staging and Support Area [*NASA*] (KSC)
SSA	Standard Single Account (INF)
SSA	Standard Spending Assessment [*Department of the Environment*] [*British*]
SSA	Standard System Applications [*Military*]
SSA	Stars of the Stage [*A publication*]
SSA	Steuben Society of America (EA)
SSA	Stratford Public Library, Stratford, CT [*OCLC symbol*] (OCLC)
SSA	Student Ski Association (EA)
SSA	Studio Suppliers Association (EA)
SSA	Style Sac Artery
ssa	Sub-Saharan African [*MARC language code*] [*Library of Congress*] (LCCP)
SSA	Sub-Saharan African Country
SSA	Subterranean Sociological Association (EA)
SSA	Sulfite Sensitive Asthmatic
SSA	Sulfosalicylic Acid [*Organic chemistry*]
SSA	Sumi-E Society of America (EA)
SSA	Supply Support Activity [*Military*] (AABC)
SSA	Supply Support Arrangements [*A bilateral agreement between the United States and a friendly foreign government*]
SSA	Support Services Alliance [*Schoharie, NY*] (EA)
SSA	Survey of School Attitudes [*Student attitudes test*]
SSA	Survival Surface-to-Air (MCD)
SSA	Suspension Specialists Association (EA)
SSA	Symbol Synchronizer Assembly [*NASA*]
SSA	Synchro Signal Amplifier
SSA	System Safety Assessment [*Army*]
SSAA	Salzburger Studien zur Anglistik und Amerikanistik [*A publication*]
SSAA	Saskatchewan Institute of Applied Arts, Saskatoon, Saskatchewan [*Library symbol*] [*National Library of Canada*] (NLC)
SSAA	Shoe Suppliers Association of America (EA)
SSAA	Skate Sailing Association of America (EA)
SSAA	Social Security Acts Amendments [*A publication*] (DLA)
SSAA	Space Science Analysis Area [*Space Flight Operations Facility, NASA*]
SSAAAK	Studi Sassaresi. Sezione 3. Annali della Facolta di Agraria dell'Universita di Sassari [*A publication*]
SSAAII	Ses Altesses Imperiales [*Their Imperial Highnesses*] [*French*] (ROG)
SSAAT	Sun Sensor Attitude Angle Transducer
SSAC	Armak Chemicals, Saskatoon, Saskatchewan [*Library symbol*] [*National Library of Canada*] (NLC)
SSAC	Australian State System of Accounting and Control of Nuclear Materials
SSAC	Secondary School Admissions Center [*Defunct*] (EA)
SSAC	Social Security Advisory Committee [*British*]
SSAC	Society for the Study of Architecture in Canada [*Established 1974*]
SSAC	Source Selection Advisory Council [*Military*] (AFM)
SSAC	Space Science Analysis and Command [*Team*] [*NASA*]
SSAC	Sponsors' Standards Advisory Committee [*American National Standards Institute*]
SSAC	Standing State Advisory Committee [*Terminated, 1977*] [*of Water Resources Council*] (EGAO)
SSAC	Sterling Savings Association [*NASDAQ symbol*] (NQ)
SSAC	Suprasellar Arachnoid Cyst [*Medicine*]
SSAC	Suspended Sprayed Acoustical Ceiling [*Technical drawings*]
SSACT	Social Security Act [*1935*] [*Also, SSA*]
SSADARS	Social Security Administration Data Acquisition and Response System
SSADC	Solid-State Air Data Computer (MCD)
SSADH	Succinate-Semialdehyde Dehydrogenase [*An enzyme*]
SSADM	Structured Systems Analysis and Design Method [*British*]
SSAE	Society of Senior Aerospace Executives (EA)
SSAEA	Safety Series. IAEA [*International Atomic Energy Agency*] [*A publication*]
SSAEC	Society for the Study of Alchemy and Early Chemistry [*British*]
SSAF	Standard Single Account File [*Number*] (MCD)
SSAFA	Soldiers, Sailors, and Airmen's Family Association [*British*]
SSAG	Single-Step Acidulation Granulation [*Fertilizer technology*]
SSAG	Strategic Studies Advisory Group [*Army*] (AABC)
SSAGA	Animal Pathology Laboratory, Food Production and Inspection Branch, Agriculture Canada [*Laboratoire de Pathologie Veterinaire, Direction Generale de la Production et de l'Inspection des Aliments, Agriculture Canada*], Saskatoon, Saskatchewan [*Library symbol*] [*National Library of Canada*] (BIB)
SSAGR	Research Station, Agriculture Canada [*Station de Recherches, Agriculture Canada*] Saskatoon, Saskatchewan [*Library symbol*] [*National Library of Canada*] (NLC)
SSAIS	Senior South African Individual Scale [*Intelligence test*]
SSAJ	Sweep Stop Alarm Jam (MCD)
SSAL	Scientific Serials in Australian Libraries [*A publication*] (APTA)
SSAL	Shelton Savings Bank [*NASDAQ symbol*] (NQ)
SSAL	Simplified Short Approach Light [*Aviation*]
S-SAL	Solar Scientific Airlock (MCD)
SSALF	Simplified Short ALS [*Approach Light System*] with Sequenced Flashers [*Aviation*]
SSALR	Simplified Short ALS [*Approach Light System*] with Runway Alignment Indicator Lights [*Aviation*]
SSALS	Simplified Short Approach Light System [*Aviation*]

SSALSR .... Simplified Short Approach Light System with Runway Alignment Indicator Lights [*Aviation*]
SSAL Suppt ... SSAL [*Scientific Serials in Australian Libraries*] Supplement [*A publication*] (APTA)
SSAMR ..... John Dolan Resource Library, Saskatchewan Association for the Mentally Retarded, Saskatoon, Saskatchewan [*Library symbol*] [*National Library of Canada*] (NLC)
SSAN........ Social Security Account Number
SSAO........ Semicarbazide-Sensitive Amine Oxidase [*Biochemistry*]
SSAO........ Solid-State Audio Oscillator
SSAOA...... Soobshcheniya Shemakhinskoi Astrofizicheskoi Observatorii Akademiya Nauk Azerbaidzhanskoi SSR [*A publication*]
SSAP .... Source Service Access Point
SSAP .... Statement of Standard Accounting Practice
SSAP .... Survival Stabilator Actuator Package [*Hydraulic power*]
SSAPD ...... Symposium on Salt. Proceedings [*A publication*]
SSAPEA .... Swedish Society Against Painful Experiments on Animals (EAIO)
S-SAR....... Secret - Special Access Required [*Security classification*] (MCD)
SSAR .... Site Safety Analysis Report [*Nuclear energy*] (NRCH)
SSAR .... Society for the Study of Amphibians and Reptiles (EA)
SSAR .... Spin-Stabilized Aircraft Rocket
SSAR .... Standard Safety Analysis Report [*Nuclear energy*] (NRCH)
SSAR .... Steady State Adiabatic Reactor [*Chemical engineering*]
SSar .... Studi Sardi [*A publication*]
SSARB...... Sassar [*A publication*]
SSARR ...... Streamflow Synthesis and Reservoir Regulation [*Data processing*]
SSAS........ Salzburg Seminar in American Studies (EA)
SSAS........ Searchless Self-Adjusting System
SSAS........ Signal Security Assessment System [*Military*] (CAAL)
SSAS........ Small Sample Assay System [*Nuclear energy*] (NRCH)
SSAS........ Small Self-Administered Scheme [*Pensions*] [*British*]
SSAS........ Society for South Asian Studies (EAIO)
SSAS.......... Special Signal Analysis System [*Electronic countermeasures system*]
SSAS........ Static Stability Augmentation System [*Aviation*]
SSAS........ Station Signaling and Announcement Subsystem [*Telecommunications*] (TEL)
SSASH ...... Studia Slavica. Academiae Scientiarum Hungaricae [*A publication*]
SSAT .... Screening Speech Articulation Test [*Educational test*]
SSAT .... Secondary School Admission Test Board (EA)
SSAT .... Shuttle Service and Access Tower [*NASA*] (NASA)
SSAT .... Society for Surgery of the Alimentary Tract (EA)
SSAT .... Space Shuttle Access Tower [*NASA*] (MCD)
SSAT .... Sweep Stop Alarm Target [*Military*] (CAAL)
SSATB...... Secondary School Admission Test Board (EA)
SSAU........ Submarine Search Attack Unit (NVT)
SSAV .... Shoreline Savings Bank [*NASDAQ symbol*] (NQ)
SSAV .... Simian Sarcoma Associated Virus
SSAW........ Saatchi & Saatchi Advertising Worldwide (ECON)
SSAWL ..... Sitzungsberichte. Saechsische Akademie der Wissenschaften (Leipzig). Philologisch-Historische Klasse [*A publication*]
SSAWV .... Sons of Spanish American War Veterans (EA)
SSAX........ System Software Associates, Inc. [*NASDAQ symbol*] (NQ)
SSB .... Cave Junction, OR [*Location identifier*] [*FAA*] (FAAL)
SSB .... Fleet Ballistic Submarine [*Navy symbol*]
SSB .... Reserve Bank of Australia. Statistical Bulletin [*A publication*]
SSB .... St. Croix [*Virgin Islands*] Seaplane Base [*Airport symbol*] (OAG)
SSB .... St. Sauveur Badole [*France*] [*Seismograph station code, US Geological Survey*] (SEIS)
SSB .... Scots Styles Book [*A publication*] (ILCA)
SSB .... Scottish Society of Boilermakers [*A union*]
SSB .... Security Screening Board [*Army*]
SSB .... Selective Service Board
SSB .... Single Sideband
SSB .... Single-Strand Break [*Genetics*]
SSB .... Single-Stranded DNA [*Deoxyribonucleic Acid*] Binding Protein [*Biochemistry*]
SSB .... Sino-Soviet Bloc
SS-B........... Sjogren's Syndrome B [*Medicine*]
SSb............ Skandinavskij Sbornik [*A publication*]
SSB .... Social Security Board [*Abolished, 1946*]
SSB .... Social Security Bulletin [*US*] [*A publication*]
SSB .... Society for the Study of Blood (EA)
SSB .... Source Selection Board [*NASA*]
SSB .... Space Science Board [*National Research Council*]
SSB .... Special Service Battalion [*British military*] (DMA)
SSB .... Special Studies Branch [*Supreme Headquarters Allied Powers Europe*] (NATG)
SSB .... Spontaneous Symmetry Breaking [*Physics*]
SSB .... Standard Software Base (MCD)
SSB .... Submarine, Ballistic Missile [*Diesel*] [*NATO*]
SSB .... Subscriber Busy [*Telecommunications*] (TEL)
SSB .... Swimmer Support Boat
SSBA .... Seacoast Savings Bank [*NASDAQ symbol*] (NQ)
SSBA .... Sons of Scotland Benevolent Association (EA)
SSBAM ..... Single Sideband Amplitude Modulation (KSC)

SSBB .... Southington Savings Bank [*Southington, CT*] [*NASDAQ symbol*] (NQ)
SSBC .... Shelton Bancorp, Inc. [*NASDAQ symbol*] (NQ)
SSBC .... Solar System Barycenter [*Astronomy*]
SSBC .... Stock Status Balance Card (NG)
SSBC .... Summary Sheet Bar Chart [*NASA*] (NASA)
SSBD .... Single-Sideboard (IEEE)
SSBD .... Society for the Study of Breast Disease (EA)
SSB/DPUT ... Serikat Sekerdja Biro/Dinas Pembangunan Usaha Tani [*Agricultural Development Service Workers' Union*] [*Indonesia*]
SSBE .... Saskatoon Board of Education, Saskatchewan [*Library symbol*] [*National Library of Canada*] (NLC)
SSBF .... Single Sideband Filter
SSBFH ...... Star-Spangled Banner Flag House Association (EA)
SSBFM...... Single Sideband Frequency Modulation (IEEE)
SSBG .... Sex Steroid Binding Globulin [*Endocrinology*]
SSBG .... Single Sideband Generator
SSBG .... Social Services Block Grant [*Department of Health and Human Services*]
SSBG .... Southern Starr Broadcasting Group, Inc. [*NASDAQ symbol*] (NQ)
SSB/GP..... Source Selection Board/General Procurement (MCD)
SSBK .... Suffield Savings Bank [*Suffield, CT*] [*NASDAQ symbol*] (NQ)
SSBKD ...... Serikat Sekerdja/Buruh Ketapradja Djakarta Raja [*General Union of Government Officials of Greater Djakarta*] [*Indonesia*]
SSBKTN.... Serikat Sekerdja Bank Koporasi, Tani dan Nelajan Disingkat [*Cooperative, Farmers and Fishers Bank Employees' Union*] [*Indonesia*]
SSB/L........ Steamship Bill of Lading [*Shipping*]
SSBLA .... Sel'skokhozyaistvennaya Biologiya [*A publication*]
SSBM .... Single Sideband Modulation
SSBMA ..... Students to Save Baltic and Mediterranean Avenues (EA)
SSBN .... Fleet Ballistic Missile Submarine (Nuclear powered) [*Navy symbol*]
SSBN .... Ships Submersible Ballistic Nuclear [*British military*] (DMA)
SSBO .... Single Swing Blocking Oscillator (MSA)
SSBPI .... Serikat Sekerdja Bank Pembangunan Indonesia [*Indonesian Development Bank Employees' Union*]
SSBPS .... Social Security Benefit Protection Service (EA)
SSBPT .... Serikat Sekerdja Balai Penelitian Tekstil [*Textile Research Institute Workers' Union*] [*Indonesia*]
SSBR .... Smooth-Surface Built-Up Roof [*Technical drawings*]
SSBR .... Solid Strand Burning Rate (KSC)
SSBS.......... Sisters Servants of the Blessed Sacrament [*Roman Catholic religious order*]
SSBSC .... Single Sideband Suppressed Carrier [*Telecommunications*]
SSBSCOM ... Single Sideband Suppressed Carrier Optical Modulator
SSBSEF..... Scientia Sinica. Series B. Chemical, Biological, Agricultural, Medical, and Earth Sciences [*A publication*]
SSBUS....... South Slavic Benevolent Union Sloga [*Later, Sloga Fraternal Life Insurance Society*] (EA)
SSBWM .... Society of Scale Beam and Weighing Machinists [*A union*] [*British*]
SSC .... Co-Operative College of Canada, Saskatoon, Saskatchewan [*Library symbol*] [*National Library of Canada*] (NLC)
SSC .... Cruiser Submarine [*Navy symbol*] [*Obsolete*]
SSC .... Missionary Sisters of St. Columban [*Roman Catholic religious order*]
SSC .... Naval Service School Command
SSC .... St. Sauveur De Carouges [*Seismograph station code, US Geological Survey*] (SEIS)
SSC .... Saline Sodium Citrate [*Clinical chemistry*]
SSC .... Salisbury State College, Salisbury, MD [*OCLC symbol*] (OCLC)
SS & C .... Same Sea and Country [*or Coast*] [*Shipping*] (DS)
SSC .... Sample Survey Centre [*University of Sydney*] [*Australia*] [*Information service or system*] (IID)
SSC .... Sandford's New York Superior Court Reports [*A publication*] (DLA)
SSC .... Sarawak Supreme Court Reports [*A publication*] (DLA)
SSC .... Satellite Systems Corporation [*Virginia Beach, VA*] [*Telecommunications*] (TSSD)
S & Sc .... Sausse and Scully's Irish Rolls Court Reports [*A publication*] (DLA)
SSC .... Savannah State College [*Georgia*]
SSC .... Scan-to-Scan Correlation
SSC .... Scotch Session Cases [*A publication*] (DLA)
SSC .... Sculptors Society of Canada
SSC .... Sea-State Correction [*Doppler navigation*] (DEN)
SSC .... Sea Systems Command [*Also, NSSC*] [*Navy*]
SSC .... Second-Stage Conduit
SSC .... Sector Switching Center [*Telecommunications*] (TEL)
SSC .... Secure Systems Corporation [*Manassas, VA*] [*Telecommunications*] [*Defunct*] (TSSD)
SSC .... Security Classification Code (MCD)
SSC .... Selector Subchannels
SSC............ Senate Staff Club (EA)
SSC .... Senate Steel Caucus (EA)
SSC............ Senior Service College [*Army*] (AABC)

SSC...........	Sensor Signal Conditioner
SSC...........	Sequential Subsystem Controllers (MCD)
SSC...........	Serendipitous Survey Catalog [*Infrared Astronomical Satellite*] [*Astronomy*]
SSC...........	Serial Shift Counter [*Data processing*]
SSC...........	Service Schools Command (MCD)
SSC...........	Seven Springs Center [*An association*] (EA)
SSC...........	Ship Structure Committee (EA)
SSC...........	Ship Systems Command [*Navy*]
SSC...........	Shipbuilding Stabilization Committee [*World War II*]
SSC...........	Ship's Speed Converter (MCD)
SSC...........	Short Segmented Cask [*Nuclear energy*] (NRCH)
SSC...........	Short Service Commissions [*Army*] [*British*]
SSC...........	Short Story Criticism [*A publication*]
SSC...........	Shuttle System Contractor [*NASA*] (NASA)
SSC...........	Siblings for Significant Change (EA)
SSC...........	Side-Stick Controller
SSC...........	Signaling and Supervisory Control
SSC...........	Silver Star Citation [*Military award*]
SSC...........	Simulated Spacecraft [*NASA*]
SSC...........	Singapore Sports Council (DS)
SSC...........	Single Silk-Covered [*Wire insulation*]
SSC...........	Single-Stage Command (NASA)
SSC...........	Sisters of St. Casimir [*Roman Catholic religious order*]
SSC...........	Site Selection Criteria (AAG)
S & SC	Sized and Supercalendered [*Paper*]
SSC.......	Skill Specialty Code (MCD)
SSC...........	Small Saver Certificate [*Banking*]
SSC...........	Social Sciences Center [*University of Nevada*] [*Research center*] (RCD)
SSC...........	Socialist Scholars Conference (EA)
SSC...........	Societas Sanctae Crucis [*Society of the Holy Cross*] [*Latin*]
SSC...........	Society of the Sacred Cross [*Anglican religious community*]
SSC...........	Society of Silver Collectors (EA)
SSC...........	Society for the Study of Caucasia (EA)
SSC...........	Sodium Chloride-Sodium Citrate [*Analytical chemistry*]
SSC...........	Software Support Center [*Army*] (RDA)
SSC...........	Solar Stabilization Computer
SSC...........	Soldier Support Center
SSC...........	Solicitor, Supreme Court
SSC...........	Solid-Solution CERMET [*NASA*] (NASA)
SSC...........	Solid-State Circuit
SSC...........	Solid-State Computer
SSC...........	Soluble Solids Content [*Analytical chemistry*]
SSC...........	Southeastern Simulation Council
SSC...........	Southeastern State College [*Later, Southeastern Oklahoma State University*]
SSC...........	Southern State College [*Arkansas; South Dakota*]
SSC...........	Space Science Committee [*Formerly, Provisional Space Science Advisory Board for Europe*] [*of the European Science Foundation*] (EA)
SSC...........	Space Suit Communicator [*Apollo*] [*NASA*]
SSch........	Space Systems Center
SSC...........	Spacecraft System Console
SSC...........	Spanish Shippers Council (DS)
SSC...........	Special Service Center [*Bell System*]
SSC...........	Special Service Clergyman [*Church of England*]
SSC...........	Speciality Shopping Centre [*British*]
SSC...........	Spectroscopy Society of Canada [*Societe de Spectroscopie du Canada*]
SSC...........	Spin Synchronous Clock
SSC...........	Squadron Supervisory Console [*Air Force*]
SSC...........	Squadron Support Center (AAG)
SSC...........	Squib Simulator Console
SSC...........	Staff Selection Committee [*UN Food and Agriculture Organization*]
SSC...........	Staff Service Center (MCD)
SSC...........	Standard Saline Citrate
SSC...........	Standardization Status Code [*DoD*]
SSC...........	Standards Steering Committee [*ANSI*]
SSC...........	State Sports Centre [*Australia*]
SSC...........	State Superfund Contract [*Environmental Protection Agency*]
SSC...........	Static Standby Computer [*Mission Control Center*] [*NASA*]
SSC...........	Station Selection Code [*Western Union*] (BUR)
SSC...........	Statistical Society of Canada [*Societe Statistique du Canada*]
SSC...........	Stepping Switch Counter (AAG)
SSC...........	Stores Stock Catalog
SSC...........	Structures, Systems, and Components [*Nuclear energy*] (NRCH)
SSC...........	Submarine Supply Center
SSC...........	Subsystem Computer (MCD)
SSC...........	Subsystem Sequence Controller [*NASA*] (NASA)
SSC...........	Sudden Storm Commencement [*Physics*]
SSC...........	Sumter, SC [*Location identifier*] [*FAA*] (FAAL)
SSC...........	Sunshine Mining Company [*NYSE symbol*] (SPSG)
SSC...........	Super Serial Card [*Apple Computer, Inc.*]
SSC...........	Super System Code (NRCH)
SSC...........	Superconducting Super Collider [*Particle accelerator*]
SS & C	Supersized and Calendered [*Paper*]
SSC...........	Supply and Services Canada
SSC...........	Supply Status Code [*Army*] (AABC)
SSC...........	Supply Support Center [*Navy*]
SSC...........	Supply System Command [*Navy*] (MCD)
SSC...........	Swedish Shippers Council (DS)
SSC...........	Swiss Shippers Council (DS)
SSC...........	Systems Science and Cybernetics (MCD)
SSC...........	Systems Support Center (BUR)
SSCA........	Scottish Stone Cutters' Association [*A union*]
SSCA........	Seven Seas Cruising Association (EA)
SSCA........	Southern Speech Communication Association (EA)
SSCA........	Spray System Compressed Air [*Nuclear energy*] (NRCH)
SSCA........	Standard Schnauzer Club of America (EA)
SSCA........	Stockholm Studies in Classical Archaeology [*A publication*]
SSCA........	Super Sunfish Class Association (EA)
SSCA........	Surface Sampler Control Assembly [*NASA*] (NASA)
SSCAG......	Research Station, Agriculture Canada [*Station de Recherches, Agriculture Canada*] Swift Current, Saskatchewan [*Library symbol*] [*National Library of Canada*] (NLC)
SSCATS....	Skylab Simulation, Checkout, and Training System [*NASA*]
SSCB........	SCB Restaurant Systems [*NASDAQ symbol*] (NQ)
SSCC........	Common Channel Signaling System [*Telecommunications*] (TEL)
SSCC........	Congregation of the Sacred Hearts of Jesus and Mary [*Rome, Italy*] (EAIO)
SSCC........	IEEE Solid-State Circuits Council (EA)
SSCC........	Salt Shaker Collectors Club [*Later, AAGSSCS*] (EA)
SSCC........	SATCOM System Control Center (KSC)
SSCC........	Scandinavian Society for Clinical Chemistry [*See also NFKK*] [*Helsinki, Finland*] (EAIO)
SSCC........	Sea Surface Chlorophyll Concentration
SSCC........	Second-Stage Conduit Container
SSCC........	Sound Surveillance System Control Center (MCD)
SSCC........	Space Surveillance Control Center
SSCC........	Spin-Scan Cloud Camera [*NASA*]
SSCC........	Support Services Control Center [*NASA*] (MCD)
SSCCB......	Safeguard System Configuration Control Board [*Army*] (AABC)
SSCCS......	Solid State Component Control System [*Nuclear energy*] (NRCH)
SSCD........	Society of Small Craft Designers (EA)
SSCD........	Start Sample Command Delayed
SSCD........	Superheated Superconducting Colloid Detector [*Particle physics*]
SSCD........	Support System Concept Document
SSCDS......	Small Ship Combat Data System
SSCE........	Silver/Silver Chloride Electrode
SSCE........	Sodium Chloride Calomel Electrode
SSCES......	Stanford Studies in the Civilizations of Eastern Asia [*A publication*]
SS/CF.......	Signal Strength, Center Frequency [*Broadcasting*]
SSCF........	Space Subsystem Control Facility (NATG)
SSCF........	Stress/Strain Controlled Fatigue (MCD)
SSCH........	Sisters of Ste. Chretienne [*Roman Catholic religious order*]
SSch.........	State School [*Australia*]
SSCHS.....	Space Shuttle Cargo Handling System [*NASA*] (NASA)
SSCI........	Sanitation Suppliers and Contractors Institute (EA)
SSCI.........	Saskatoon Collegiate Institute, Saskatchewan [*Library symbol*] [*National Library of Canada*] (NLC)
SSCI.........	Senate Select Committee on Intelligence (MCD)
SSCI.........	Social Sciences Citation Index [*Institute for Scientific Information*] [*Database*] [*A publication*]
SSCI.........	Solar Satellite Communications, Incorporated [*Denver, CO*] [*NASDAQ symbol*] (NQ)
SSCI.........	Steel Service Center Institute (EA)
SSCI.........	Steel Shipping Container Institute (EA)
SSCISAM ...	Settimane di Studio del Centro Italiano di Studi sull'Alto Medioevo [*A publication*]
SSCJ.........	Sorores a Sacro Corde Jesu [*Sisters of the Sacred Heart of Jesus*] [*Roman Catholic religious order*]
SSCJ.........	Southern Speech Communication Journal [*A publication*]
SSCK........	Sister Servants of Christ the King [*Roman Catholic religious order*]
SSCL........	Shuttle System Commonality List [*NASA*] (NASA)
SSCL.........	Social Science Computing Laboratory [*University of Western Ontario*] [*Information service or system*] (IID)
SSCL.........	Swire Straits Container Line (DS)
SSCM........	Servants of the Holy Heart of Mary [*Roman Catholic women's religious order*]
SSCM........	Sisters of Saints Cyril and Methodius [*Roman Catholic religious order*]
SSCMA.....	Special Supplementary Clothing Monetary Allowance [*Military*]
SSCN.........	Nuclear Cruise Missile Submarine (MCD)
SSCN.........	Scotts Seaboard Corporation [*NASDAQ symbol*] (NQ)
SSC-NCR ..	Soldier Support Center - National Capitol Region [*Army*]
SSCNS......	Ship's Self-Contained Navigation System
SSCO........	Shipper Service Control Office [*Military*] (AABC)
SSCO........	Sunstyle Corporation [*NASDAQ symbol*] (NQ)
SSCP........	School Science Curriculum Project
SSCP.........	Small Self-Contained Payload (NASA)
SSCP........	Standard Saline Citrate Phosphate [*A buffer*]
SSCP.........	State Service Center Program (OICC)
SSCP.........	System Services Control Point [*Data processing*]

SSCQT ...... Selective Service College Qualifying Test
SSCR .... Set Screw
SSCR .... Sind Sadr Court Reports [*India*] [*A publication*]   (DLA)
SSCR .... Spectral Shift Control Reactor [*Nuclear energy*]
SSCr .... Stainless Steel Crown [*Dentistry*]
SSCRA ...... School Science Review [*A publication*]
SSCRA ...... Soldiers' and Sailors' Civil Relief Act [*1940*]
SSCRI .... Social Science Computer Research Institute [*University of Pittsburgh*] [*Pennsylvania*] [*Information service or system*]   (IID)
SSCRN ...... Silkscreen   (MSA)
SSCS .... Sea Shepherd Conservation Society   (EA)
SSCS .... Shipboard Satellite Communications System
SS & CS .... Ship's Stores and Commissary Stores [*Navy*]
SSCS .... Side-Stick Control System
SSCS .... Single Sideband Communications System
SSCS .... Southern Signal Corps School
SSCS .... Space Suit Communications System   (MCD)
SSCS .... Standards and Security Compliance Section [*Social Security Administration*]
SSCS .... Steep-Spectrum Compact Sources [*of galactic radio waves*]
SSCS .... Submarine SONAR Calibration Set
SSCS .... Synchronous Satellite Communications System
SSCSDJ .... SIAM [*Society for Industrial and Applied Mathematics*] SIMS [*SIAM Institute for Mathematics and Society*] Conference Series [*A publication*]
SSCSP ...... Space Shuttle Crew Safety Panel [*NASA*]   (NASA)
SSCT .... Shipboard Communications Terminal
SSCT .... Solid-State Celestial Tracker
SSCT .... Solid-State Control Transformer
SSCU .... Soil Sampler Control Unit
SSCU .... Spacecraft Systems Controller Unit [*NASA*]   (KSC)
SSCU .... Special Signal Conditioning Unit
SSCU .... Store Station Control Unit   (MCD)
SSCV .... Semisubmersible Crane Vessel
SSCX .... Solid-State Control Transformer
SSD .... Doctor of Sacred Scripture
SSD .... Institute of the Sisters of St. Dorothy [*Roman Catholic religious order*]
SSD .... Safe Separation Device
SSD .... Sanctissimus Dominus [*Most Holy Lord*] [*Latin*]
SSD .... Scrap Salvage Division [*Navy*]
SSD .... SDC Sydney Development Corp. [*Toronto Stock Exchange symbol*] [*Vancouver Stock Exchange symbol*]
SSD .... Second-Degree Stochastic Dominance [*Statistics*]
SSD .... Security Support Detachment   (MCD)
SSD .... Seize Signal Detector
SSD .... Semiconductor Silicon Detector
SSD .... Separation Systems Division [*Energy Research and Development Administration*]
SSD .... Sequence Switch Driver
S & SD ...... Sewerage and Sewage Disposal   (DCTA)
SSD .... Signal Seeking Device
SSD .... Single-Station DOVAP [*Doppler, Velocity, and Position*]
SSD .... Smoothing by Spectral Dispersion [*LASER technology*]
SSD .... Social Security Disability
SSD .... Software System Design [*Data processing*]
SSD .... Soldiers Service Dress [*British military*]   (DMA)
SSD .... Solid-State Detector
SSD .... Solid State Disk [*Data processing*]
SSD .... Solid-State Dosimeter
SSD .... Solid-State Storage Device [*Data processing*]
SSD .... Source-to-Skin [*or -Surface*] Distance [*Radiology*]
SSD .... Space Sciences Division [*Jet Propulsion Laboratory*]
SSD .... Space Shuttle Display [*NASA*]
SSD .... Space Systems Division [*Air Force*]
SSD .... Spacecraft Software Division [*NASA*]   (NASA)
SSD .... Special Service Division [*Army Services Forces*] [*World War II*]
SSD .... Specialized Storage Depot
SSD .... Specialized Support Department [*Air Force*]   (AFM)
SSD .... Specialized Support Depot [*Army*]   (AABC)
SSD .... Split-Screen Display
SSD .... Split Stage Demonstrator   (MCD)
SSD .... Squared Successive Differences [*Data processing*]
SSD .... Staatssicherheitsdienst [*State Security Service*] [*German Democratic Republic*]
SSD .... Stabilized Ship Detector [*Navy*]
SSD .... Stock Split-Down [*Investment term*]
SSD .... Subsoil Drain [*Technical drawings*]
SSD .... Sun Shadow Device
SSD .... Support Software Documentation   (MCD)
SSD .... Surface Sampler Device [*NASA*]
SSD .... Surveillance Situation Display
SSD .... Survival Support Device   (NVT)
SS & D ...... Synchronization Separator and Digitizer
SSD .... System Status Display
SSD .... System Summary Display [*NASA*]   (MCD)
SSD .... Systems Support Division [*Air Force*]
SSDA .... Sequential Similarity Detection Algorithm
SSDA .... Service Station Dealers of America   (EA)

SSDA .... Social Science Data Archive [*University of Iowa*] [*Iowa City*] [*Information service or system*]   (IID)
SSDA .... Social Science Data Archive [*Carleton University*] [*Canada*] [*Information service or system*]   (IID)
SSDA .... Social Science Data Archives [*Australian National University*] [*Information service or system*]   (IID)
SSDA .... Synchronous Serial Data Adapter
SSDB .... Shore Station Development Board
SSDC .... Sclerosing Sweat Duct Carcinoma [*Oncology*]
SSDC .... Signal Source Distribution Center   (AAG)
SSDC .... Social Science Data Center [*University of Connecticut*] [*Research center*]   (IID)
SSDC .... Social Science Data Center [*University of Pennsylvania*] [*Philadelphia*] [*Information service or system*]   (IID)
SSDC .... Social Science Documentation Centre [*UNESCO*]   (IID)
SSDC .... Social Science Documentation Centre [*Indian Council of Social Science Research*] [*Information service or system*]   (IID)
SSDC .... Social Self-Defense Committee [*Poland*]   (PD)
SSDC .... Society of Stage Directors and Choreographers   (EA)
SSDC .... Space Science Data Center [*NASA*]   (MCD)
SSDC .... Synoptic-Scale Subprogramme Data Centre [*Marine science*]   (MSC)
SSDD .... Single-Sided, Double-Density Disk [*Magnetic disk*] [*Data processing*]
SSDD .... Software System Design Document   (MCD)
SSDG .... Ship Service Diesel Generator [*Navy*]   (CAAL)
SSDG .... Society for the Study of Development and Growth [*Later, SDB*]   (EA)
SSDH .... Subsystem Data Handbook [*NASA*]   (NASA)
SSDHPER ... Society of State Directors of Health, Physical Education, and Recreation   (EA)
SSDI .... Social Security Disability Insurance
SSDI .... Support System Design Integration   (AAG)
SSDK .... Savannah State Docks Railroad Co. [*AAR code*]
SSDL .... Secondary Standard Dosimetry Laboratory
SSDL .... Social Science Data Library [*University of North Carolina*] [*Chapel Hill*] [*Information service or system*]   (IID)
SSDL .... Society for the Study of Dictionaries and Lexicography [*Later, DSNA*]   (EA)
SSDM .... Shielding Standard Design Method   (MCD)
SSDMIC.... Secretariat State-Defense Military Information Control Committee
SSDN .... Sanctissimus Dominus Noster [*Our Most Holy Lord, Jesus Christ*] [*Latin*]
SSDN .... Solar Systems by Sun Dance, Inc. [*Hialeah Gardens, FL*] [*NASDAQ symbol*]   (NQ)
ssDNA .... Deoxyribonucleic Acid, Single-Stranded [*Biochemistry, genetics*]
SSDP .... Serikat Sekerdja Djawalan Padjak [*Brotherhood of Tax Office Employees*] [*Indonesia*]
SSDP .... Standard Source Data Package   (AFIT)
SSDP .... Suomen Sosialidemokraattinen Puolue [*Finnish Social Democratic Party*] [*Political party*]   (PPW)
SSDPA ...... Soft-Serv Dairy Products Association [*Later, NSSFFA*]   (EA)
SSDPE....... Society for the Systematic Documentation of Paranormal Experiments   (EA)
SSDPS....... Solar System Data Processing System
SSDR .... Satellite Situation Display Room
SSDR .... SIGINT/SIGSEC Facilities Data Reporting System   (MCD)
SSDR .... Species Specific Defense Reaction
SSDR .... Steady State Determining Routine
SSDR .... Subsystem Development Requirement   (AFM)
SSDR .... Supermarket Subsystem Definition Record [*Data processing*]   (IBMDP)
SSDRS....... Safeguard System Design Release Schedule [*Army*]   (AABC)
SSDS .... Small Ship Data System   (MUGU)
SSDS .... Space Shuttle Display and Simulation [*NASA*]
SSDS .... Space Station Data System   (NASA)
SSDS .... Surface-Supported Diving System   (CAAL)
SSDSA....... Solomon Schecter Day School Association   (EA)
SSDSG ...... Special State Defense Study Group [*Military*]
SSDT .... Society of Soft Drink Technologists   (EA)
SSDVOR ... Single Sideband Doppler Very-High-Frequency Omnidirectional Range [*FAA*]
SSE .... North-Holland Series in Systems Science and Engineering [*Elsevier Book Series*] [*A publication*]
SSE .... Safe Shutdown Earthquake [*Nuclear energy*]   (NRCH)
SSE .... Safety System Engineering   (MCD)
SSE .... Salvador Society of Engineers
SSE .... Satellite Systems Engineering, Inc. [*Bethesda, MD*] [*Information service or system*]   (TSSD)
SSE .... Scale of Socio-Egocentrism [*Psychology*]
SSE .... Schick Shaving Experience [*Advertising slogan*]
SSE .... Scuola de Sviluppo Economico [*Italy*]
SSE .... Sector Scan Engagement [*Military*]   (CAAL)
SSE .... Security and Safety Equipment   (IMH)
SSE .... Seed Savers Exchange   (EA)
SSE .... Self-Sustained Emission
SSE .... SIGINT Support Element   (MCD)
SSE .... Signal Security Element [*Military*]   (AABC)
SSE .... Single Sideband Exciter

SSE .... Single Silk Covering over Enamel Insulation [*Telecommunications*] (TEL)
SSE .... Sisters of St. Elizabeth [*Roman Catholic religious order*]
SSE .... Skin Self Examination [*Medicine*]
SSE .... Soap Suds Enema [*Medicine*]
SSE .... Society of St. Edmund [*Roman Catholic men's religious order*]
SSE .... Society for Scientific Exploration (EA)
SSE .... Society for the Study of Evolution (EA)
SSE .... Solid-State Electronics
SSE .... South-Southeast
SSE .... Southeastern Stock Exchange
SSE .... Southwest Semiconductor and Electronics Exposition (TSPED)
SSE .... Space Shuttle Engines [*NASA*] (MCD)
SSE .... Special Support Equipment
SSE .... Spokane Stock Exchange [*Washington*]
SSE .... Squared Sum of Errors [*Statistics*]
SSE .... Stage Systems Engineer
SSE .... Stateside Energy Corp. [*Vancouver Stock Exchange symbol*]
SSE .... Straight to Services Economy
SSE .... Strangest Stories Ever Told [*A publication*]
SSe .... Studi Secenteschi [*A publication*]
SSE .... Submarine Scout Experimental [*British military*] (DMA)
SSE .... Subsystem Element [*NASA*] (NASA)
SSE .... Subsystem Support Equipment [*NASA*] (MCD)
SSS .... Sum of Squared Errors [*Statistics*]
SSE .... Supplemental Support Evaluation
SSE .... Support System Evaluation
SSE .... Support Systems Engineering [*Boeing*]
SSE .... Surface Support Equipment
SSE .... Sydney Stock Exchange [*Australia*] (ADA)
SSE .... System Safety Engineering (AFM)
SSE .... System Status Evaluation [*Army*] (AABC)
SSE .... System Support Engineering
SSE .... System Support Equipment
S1S1E .... Surfaced or Dressed One Side and One Edge [*Technical drawings*]
SSEA .... Sentinel System Evaluation Agency [*DoD*]
SSEA .... Separate Sampling and Excitation Analysis [*Spectroscopy*]
SSEA .... Stage-Specific Embryonic Antigen [*Immunology*]
SSEA .... System Safety Engineering Analysis (MCD)
SSEAM ...... Ship Systems Equipment Acquisition Manual (MCD)
SSEAT .... Surveyor Scientific Evaluation Advisory Team [*NASA*]
SSEB .... Source Selection Evaluation Board [*Military*] (AFM)
SSEB .... South of Scotland Electricity Board (ECON)
SSEC .... Selective Sequence Electronic Calculator [*Data processing*]
SSEC .... Social Science Education Consortium (EA)
SSEC .... Society for the Study of Early China (EA)
SSEC .... Solar System Exploration Committee [*NASA*]
SSEC .... Solid-State Electronic Chronograph
SSEC .... Sound Surveillance Evaluation Center [*Navy*] (NVT)
SSEC .... Space Science and Engineering Center [*University of Wisconsin - Madison*] [*Research center*] (RCD)
SSEC .... Static Source Error Correction
SSECF .... Stateside Energy Corporation [*NASDAQ symbol*] (NQ)
SSECO ...... Second-Stage Engine Cutoff
SSECS .... Space Station Environmental Control System
SSECW ..... Prairie Migratory Bird Research Centre, Canadian Wildlife Service, Environment Canada [*Centre de Recherches sur les Oiseaux Migrateurs des Prairies, Service Canadien de la Faune, Environnement Canada*] Saskatoon, Saskatchewan [*Library symbol*] [*National Library of Canada*] (NLC)
SSEE .... Standing-Shock Equilibrium Expansion
S-SEED ..... Symmetric Self-Electro-Optic Effect Device
SSE/EWE ... SIGINT [*Signal Intelligence*] Support Element/Electronic Warfare Element [*Military*] (AABC)
SSEF .... Solid-State Electro-Optic Filter
SSEF .... Support Squadron Eastern Flank [*British military*] (DMA)
SSEG .... Ship System Engineering Group [*British*]
SSEG .... System-Segment [*Data processing*]
SSEH .... National Hydrology Rsearch Centre, Environment Canada [*Centre National de Recherche en Hydrologie, Environnement Canada*] Saskatoon, Saskatchewan [*Library symbol*] [*National Library of Canada*] (NLC)
SSEIP .... Special Stockpile Engineering Investigation Program (MCD)
SSEKP ...... Single Shot Engagement Kill Probability (MCD)
SSEL .... Solid-State Electronics Laboratory [*Stanford University*] (MCD)
SSEL .... Space Science and Engineering Laboratory [*Pennsylvania State University*]
SSEL .... Standard Statistical Establishment List [*Bureau of the Census*]
SSEL .... Stockholm Studies in English Literature [*A publication*]
SSELA .... Standing Committee on Social Sciences, Economic, and Legal Aspects [*Great Lakes Research Advisory Board*]
SSELER .... Salzburg Studies in English Literature. Elizabethan and Renaissance [*A publication*]
SSELRR .... Salzburg Studies in English Literature. Romantic Reassessment [*A publication*]
SSEM .... Solid State Extended Memory (MCD)
SSEM .... South Sea Evangelical Mission [*Australia*]
SSEM .... Space System Effectiveness Model
SSEM .... Supply Support Element Manager

SSEng .... Sydney Studies in English [*A publication*]
SSEO .... SEABEE Support and Equipment Office [*Navy*]
SSEOS ...... Space Shuttle Engineering and Operations Support [*NASA*] (MCD)
SSEP .... Somatosensory Evoked Potential [*Neurophysiology*]
SSEP .... Submarine Surveillance Equipment Program (NVT)
SSEP .... System Safety Engineering Plan (AFM)
SSEPA ...... Society of Spanish Engineers, Planners, and Architects (EA)
SSept .... Studia Septentrionalia [*A publication*]
SSER .... Site Safety Evaluation Report [*Nuclear energy*] (NRCH)
SSER .... Somatosensory Evoked Response [*Neurophysiology*]
SSER .... Supplement to Safety Evaluation Report [*Nuclear energy*] (NRCH)
SSERN ...... South-Southeastern [*Meteorology*] (FAAC)
SSES .... Ship Signals Exploitation Space [*Navy*] (CAAL)
SSES .... Shipboard Signal Exploration System (MCD)
SSES .... Single Strip Engine System
SSES .... Social Security Enquiry System [*Australia*]
SSES .... Special Signal Exploitation Spaces (NVT)
SSES .... Susquehanna Steam Electric Station [*Nuclear energy*] (NRCH)
SSESC .... College of Emmanuel and St. Chad, Saskatoon, Saskatchewan [*Library symbol*] [*National Library of Canada*] (NLC)
SSESI .... Statistical and Social Enqiry Society of Ireland
SSESM ...... Spent Stage Experimental Support Module (KSC)
SSESS .... Soviet Space Event Support Ships (CINC)
SSET .... State Science, Engineering, and Technology Program [*National Science Foundation*]
SSEU .... System Selector Extension Unit
SSEWD ..... South-Southeastward [*Meteorology*] (FAAC)
SSF .... Congregation of the Sisters of the Family [*Roman Catholic religious order*]
SSF .... Safe Shutdown Facility [*Nuclear energy*] (NRCH)
SSF .... Saint Saulge [*France*] [*Seismograph station code, US Geological Survey*] (SEIS)
SSF .... Samantha Smith Foundation (EA)
SSF .... San Antonio, TX [*Location identifier*] [*FAA*] (FAAL)
SSF .... Saybolt Seconds Furol [*Oil viscosity*]
SSF .... Scottish Spring Fair (ITD)
SSF .... Service Storage Facility [*Military*]
SSF .... Service Support Force [*Military*]
SSF .... Ship's Service Force [*Navy*]
SSF .... Simulated Spinal Fluid [*Medicine*]
SSF .... Single-Seated Fighter
SSF .... Single Sideband Filter
SSF .... Single Sided Frame [*Telecommunications*] (TEL)
SSF .... Single Solar Flare
SSF .... Single-Stage Fan
SSF .... Sjogren's Syndrome Foundation (EA)
SSF .... Society of St. Francis [*Anglican religious community*]
SSF .... Society for the Study of Fertility [*British*]
SSF .... Sodium Silicofluoride [*Inorganic chemistry*]
SSF .... Software Support Facility (MCD)
SSF .... Solid-State Fermentation
SSF .... Solid Substrate Fermentation
SSF .... Soluble Suppressor Factor [*Immunology*]
SSF .... Somali Salvation Front (PD)
SSF .... Sona Systems Ltd. (Canada) [*Vancouver Stock Exchange symbol*]
SSF .... Space Simulation Facility (AAG)
SSF .... Special Security Facility
SSF .... Special Service Force [*Canadian and US troops under combined command*] [*World War II*]
SSF .... Spin Stretch Factor [*Textile technology*]
SSF .... Spun Soy Fiber [*Food technology*]
SSF .... SRB [*Solid-Rocket Booster*] Storage Facility [*NASA*] (NASA)
SSF .... Stainless Steel Fiber
SSF .... Standard Saybolt Furol [*Oil viscosity*]
SSF .... Standby Shutdown Facility [*Nuclear energy*] (NRCH)
SSF .... Studies in Short Fiction [*A publication*]
SSF .... Style Sac Flap
SSF .... Super Science Fiction [*A publication*]
SSF .... Supply Status File (MCD)
SSF .... Symmetrical Switching Function
SSF .... System Support Facility
SSFC .... Sequential Single Frequency Code System [*Telecommunications*] (TEL)
SSFC .... Social Science Federation of Canada [*Research center*] (IRC)
SSFC .... Solid State Frequency Changer [*Military*] (CAAL)
SSFC .... Susanne Severeid Fan Club (EA)
SSF CHL ... Societas Scientiarum Fennicae. Commentationes Humanarum Litterarum [*A publication*]
SSFD .... Sisters of St. Francis of Dillingen [*See also SFD*] [*Rome, Italy*] (EAIO)
SSFE .... Scandinavian Society of Forest Economics (EAIO)
SSFF .... Scholastic Science Fiction Federation [*Defunct*] (EA)
SSFGSS..... Space Shuttle Flight and Ground System Specification [*NASA*] (NASA)
SSFI .... Scaffolding, Shoring, and Forming Institute (EA)
SSFL .... Santa Susana Field Laboratory [*NASA*] (NASA)
SSFL .... Steady-State Fermi Level

SSFLC.......	Surface Stabilized Ferroelectric Liquid Crystal [*Physical chemistry*]
SSFM	Scandinavian Society of Forensic Medicine (EA)
SSFM	Single Sideband Frequency Modulation
SSFN	Solidarity: A Socialist-Feminist Network (EA)
SSFO	Scandinavian Society of Forensic Odontology (EA)
SSFO	Simultaneous Single Frequency Outlet
SS & FO....	Specialized Safety and Flight Operations
SSFR.........	Safety Services Field Representative [*Red Cross*]
SSFS.........	Samlingar Utgivna av Svenska Fornskriftssallskapet (Stockholm) [*A publication*]
SSFS.........	Space Shuttle Functional Simulator [*NASA*] (KSC)
SSFS.........	Special Services Forecasting System [*Telecommunications*] (TEL)
SSFS.........	Steven Spielberg Film Society (EA)
SSFT.........	Scientific Software-Intercomp, Inc. [*NASDAQ symbol*] (NQ)
SSFT.........	Self-Sealing Fuel Tank
SSFU	Scottish Sea Fishers' Union
SSFVT......	Subsystems Functional Verification Test [*NASA*]
SSG...........	Guided Missile Submarine [*Navy symbol*]
SSG...........	Malabo [*Equatorial Guinea*] [*Airport symbol*] (OAG)
SSG...........	Safety Study Group (MCD)
SSG...........	Schriften. Theodor-Storm-Gesellschaft [*A publication*]
SSG...........	Science Steering Group [*NASA*]
SSG...........	Scleroderma Support Group (EA)
SSG...........	Search Signal Generator
SSG...........	Senior Savers Guide Publishing, Inc. [*Vancouver Stock Exchange symbol*]
SSG...........	Shuttle Support Group (MCD)
SSG...........	Single Sideband Generator
SSG...........	Small Signal Gain (IEEE)
SSG...........	Solution-Sol-Gel [*Materials science*]
SSG...........	Southern Society of Genealogists (EA)
SSG...........	Special Security Group (MCD)
SSG...........	Special Studies Group [*Joint Chiefs of Staff*] [*Military*]
SSG...........	Special Support Group [*FBI*] (CINC)
SSG...........	Staff Sergeant [*Army*] (AABC)
SSG...........	State Services Group [*Information service or system*] (IID)
SSG...........	Stonehenge Study Group (EA)
SSG...........	Supply Spectrum Generator
SSG...........	Sweep Signal Generator
SSG...........	Symbolic Stream Generator [*Data processing*]
SSG...........	System Safety Group [*Air Force*]
SSGA........	Scottish Salmon Growers' Association
SSGA........	Society of St. Gregory of America [*Later, CMAA*] (EA)
SSGA........	Sterling Silversmiths Guild of America (EA)
SSGA........	Swordsmen and Sorcerers' Guild of America (EA)
SSGB	Suore di San Giovanni Baptista [*Sisters of St. John the Baptist - SSJB*] [*Rome, Italy*] (EAIO)
SSGC........	Saskatoon Gallery and Conservatory, Saskatchewan [*Library symbol*] [*National Library of Canada*] (NLC)
SSGC........	Short System Ground Check
SSGD........	Smoke Screen Generative Device
SSGED......	Seikei-Saigai Geka [*A publication*]
SSGJ.........	Single Strength Grapefruit Juice
SSGJ.........	Supersonic Gas Jet
SSGL	Studies in Slavic and General Linguistics [*A publication*]
SSGM........	Service Station & Garage Management [*Canada*] [*A publication*]
SSGMB	Sbornik Nauchnogo Studencheskogo Obshchestva Geologicheskii Fakul'tet Moskovskii Gosudarstvennyi Universitet [*A publication*]
SSGN........	Guided Missile Submarine (Nuclear Propulsion) [*Navy symbol*]
SSGP	Spin Stabilized Guided Projectile (MCD)
SSGp........	System Safety Group [*Air Force*] (AFM)
SSG/RGI...	Rivista Geografica Italiana. Societa di Studi Geografici e Coloniali [*A publication*]
SSGS	Solid-State Gamma Switch
SSGS	Standard Space Guidance System
SSGS	Stanford Studies in Germanics and Slavics [*A publication*]
SSGT	Ship Service Gas Turbine [*Navy*] (CAAL)
SSGT	Small-Scale Gap Test [*Explosive*]
SSGT	Staff Sergeant [*Military*]
SSGT	Subsystem Ground Test (MCD)
SSGTG	Ship's Service Gas Turbine Generator [*Navy*] (NVT)
SSGW........	Sitzungsberichte. Saechsische Gesellschaft der Wissenschaften (Leipzig) [*A publication*]
SSGW........	Surface-to-Surface Guided Weapon (NATG)
SSH	Schwartz-Slawsky-Herzfeld [*Theory*] [*Chemical kinetics*]
SSH	Second-Stage Hydraulics
SSH	Sharm E Sheikh [*Israel*] [*Airport symbol*] (OAG)
SSH	Site Selection Handbook [*A publication*]
SSH	Skytteanska Samfundets Handlinger [*A publication*]
SSH	Small-Scale Hydroelectric Project
SSH	Snowshoe Hare
SSH	Social Sciences and Humanities Index [*A publication*]
SSH	Social Sciences and Humanities Research Council of Canada [*UTLAS symbol*]
SSH	Social Service Handbooks [*A publication*]
SSH	South Shore [*AAR code*]
SSH	Special Survey of the Hull [*Lloyd's Register of Shipping*] (DS)
SSH	Studia Slavica. Academiae Scientiarum Hungaricae [*A publication*]
SSH	Studies in Society and History [*A publication*]
SSH	Substantial Stockholder
SSH	Sunshine [*Alaska*] [*Seismograph station code, US Geological Survey*] (SEIS)
SSHA........	Subsystem Hazard Analysis
SSHA........	Survey of Study Habits and Attitudes [*Education*]
SSHB........	Society for the Study of Human Biology (EA)
SSHB........	Stainless Steel Helium Bottle
SSHB........	Station Set Handbook [*NASA*] (NASA)
SSHC........	Single-Stage Hydrocracker [*Chemical engineering*]
SSHCG......	Students' Series of Historical and Comparative Grammars [*A publication*]
SSHD	Single-Silo Hardsite Defense
SSHE.........	Scraped-Surface Heat Exchanger [*Process engineering*]
SSHJM	Sisters of the Sacred Hearts of Jesus and Mary [*Roman Catholic religious order*]
SSHJP.......	Servants of the Sacred Heart of Jesus and of the Poor [*Roman Catholic women's religious order*]
S/SHLD	Side Shield [*Automotive engineering*]
SSHM	Society for the Social History of Medicine [*Oxford, England*] (EAIO)
SSHMA.....	Senior Secondary Headmasters' Association [*British*]
SSHP........	Single-Shot Hit Probability
SSHR........	Social Systems and Human Resources [*National Science Foundation*] (MCD)
SSHR........	Spartan Safety Hazard Report [*Missiles*] (MCD)
SSHRC......	Social Sciences and Humanities Research Council of Canada
SSHRCC ...	Social Sciences and Humanities Research Council of Canada [*Pronounced "sherk"*] [*See also CRSHC*]
SSHS	Stainless Steel Helium Sphere
SSHSA	Steamship Historical Society of America (EA)
SSHum	Social Sciences and Humanities Index [*A publication*]
SSI	Brunswick, GA [*Location identifier*] [*FAA*] (FAAL)
SSI	Safe Shutdown Impoundment [*Nuclear energy*] (NRCH)
SSI	SafeCard Services, Inc. [*NYSE symbol*] (SPSG)
SSI	Safeway Stores, Incorporated
SSI	Satellite Services, Incorporated [*Houston, TX*] [*Telecommunications*] (TSSD)
SSI	Scaffolding and Shoring Institute [*Later, SSFI*] (EA)
SSI	Scientific Systems, Inc.
SSI	Second-Stage Ignition
SSI	Sector Scan Indicator
SSI	Security Systems, Incorporated [*In TV series "Max Headroom"*]
SSI	Security Systems Inspectorate [*Established in 1987*] [*British*]
SSI	Seismic Survival Indicator [*Earthquake analysis program*] [*Data processing*]
SSI	Semisopochnoi Island [*Alaska*] [*Seismograph station code, US Geological Survey*] [*Closed*] (SEIS)
SSI	Service Social International [*International Social Service - ISS*] [*Geneva, Switzerland*] (EAIO)
SSI	Shaft Speed Indicator
SSI	Short Story International [*A publication*]
SSI	Shoulder Sleeve Insignia [*Military*] (AABC)
SSI	Significant Structural Item (NASA)
SSI	Single Service Institute [*Later, FPI*] (EA)
SSI	Single System Image
SSI	Site of Special Scientific Interest [*Great Britain*]
SSI	Skill Speciality Identifier (MCD)
SSI	Sky Survey Instrument
SSI	Slater Industries, Inc. [*Toronto Stock Exchange symbol*]
SSI	Slater Steels Corp. [*Formerly, Slater Steel Industries*] [*Toronto Stock Exchange symbol*]
SSI	Small-Scale Integration
SSI	Smart Set International [*Program to discourage drug abuse*] [*Defunct*] (EA)
SSI	Social Science Information [*A publication*]
SSI	Social Science Institute [*Washington University*] [*Research center*] (RCD)
SSI	Social Security Information
SSI	Society of Saunterers, International (EA)
SSI	Society of Scribes and Illuminators (EA)
SSI	Society for Siberian Irises (EA)
SSI	Society for the Study of Internationalism (EA)
SSI	Solid-State Inverter
SSI	Space Studies Institute (EA)
SSI	Spacecraft System Integration
SSI	Spares Status Inquiry (AAG)
SSI	Special Subject for Inspection [*DoD*]
SSI	Special Surveillance Inspection (MCD)
SSI	Specialty Skill Identifier [*Military*] (AABC)
SSI	Specific Searching Image [*Tendency of birds to select prey of the color to which they have been accustomed*]
SSI	Staff Sergeant Instructor [*Military*] [*British*]
SSI	Standing Signal Instructions [*Military*]
SSI	Start Signal Indicator [*Telecommunications*] (TEL)
SSI	Steady-State Irradiation [*Nuclear energy*] (NRCH)
SSI	Stockpile Surveillance Inspection
SSI	Storage-to-Storage Instruction (IEEE)

SSI .... Strategic Studies Institute (MCD)
SSI .... Structural Significant Item (MCD)
SSI .... Student/Supervisor Instructions [*Army Training Extension Course*] (INF)
SSI .... Sucro-Sac-Ologists Society International [*Defunct*] (EA)
SSI .... Supplemental Security Income [*Social Security Administration*]
SSI .... Supplemental Security Insurance [*Program*]
SSI .... Supply Support Index (CAAL)
SSI .... Surprise Security Inspection [*Navy*] (NVT)
SSI .... Survey Sampling, Incorporated [*Information service or system*] (IID)
SSI .... Sustaining Support Increment [*Military*]
SSI .... Symptom Sign Inventory [*Psychology*]
SSI .... Synchronous Systems Interface
SSI .... System Science Institute [*IBM Corp.*]
SSI .... System Status Indicator [*Bell System*]
SSIA .... Scottish Society for Industrial Archaeology (EA)
SSIA .... Second Sydney International Airport Group [*Australia*]
SSIA .... Shiprepairers and Shipbuilders Independent Association [*United Kingdom*] (DS)
SSIA .... Shoe Service Institute of America (EA)
SSIA .... Specification Serial of Individual Assigned
SSIA .... Stockholder Systems, Incorporated [*Norcross, GA*] [*NASDAQ symbol*] (NQ)
SSIAM ...... Structured and Scaled Interview to Assess Maladjustment [*Psychometrics*]
SSIB.......... Shop Stock Items Bin (MCD)
SSIBD....... Shuttle System Interface Block Diagram [*NASA*] (NASA)
SSIC .... Saskatchewan Indian Cultural College, Saskatoon, Saskatchewan [*Library symbol*] [*National Library of Canada*] (NLC)
SSIC .... Small-Scale Integrated Circuit
SSIC .... Southern States Industrial Council [*Later, USIC*] (EA)
SSIC .... Standard Subject Identification Code (NVT)
SSID .... Ship Systems Integration Data (MCD)
SSID .... Shuttle Stowage Installation Drawing (NASA)
SSIDS........ Siblings of Sudden Infant Death Syndrome Victims [*Medicine*]
SSIE.......... Skylab Systems Integration Equipment [*NASA*] (MCD)
SSIE.......... Smithsonian Science Information Exchange [*National Technical Information Service*] [*Later, FEDRIP*]
SSIE.......... Solid Surface Interaction Experiment
SSIEM....... Society for the Study of Inborn Errors of Metabolism [*Middleway, England*] (EAIO)
SSIF.......... [*The*] Southeastern Savings Institutions Fund, Inc. [*NASDAQ symbol*] (NQ)
SSIFC .... Saskatoon Campus, Saskatchewan Indian Federated College, Saskatchewan [*Library symbol*] [*National Library of Canada*] (BIB)
SSIFC .... Sharon Smith International Fan Club (EA)
SSIG .... Single Signal (IEEE)
SSIG .... State Student Incentive Grant [*Department of Education*]
SSIGS....... Special Survey of Inert Gas System [*Lloyd's Register of Shipping*] (DS)
S Sig Sta .... Storm Signal Station [*Nautical charts*]
SSII .... Solid-State Image Intensifier
SSII.......... Specialized Systems, Incorporated [*NASDAQ symbol*] (NQ)
SSI/ISS ..... Social Science Information/Information sur les Sciences Sociales [*A publication*]
SSIL.......... Supply Significant Items List (MCD)
SSILS .... Solid State Instrument Landing System (MCD)
SSIM .... Scientific Systems, Incorporated [*Cambridge, MA*] [*NASDAQ symbol*] (NQ)
SSIM .... Static Secondary Ion Mass Spectroscopy
SSIM .... Statistical, Sampling Inventory Method [*Military*] (AABC)
SSINA .... Scientia Sinica [*English Edition*] [*A publication*]
SSIOD .... Solid State Ionics [*A publication*]
SSIP.......... Secondary Students Information Press [*A publication*] (APTA)
SSIP.......... Ship Support Improvement Program [*DoD*]
SSIP.......... Shuttle Student Involvement Project [*NASA*]
SSIP.......... Specific, Sincere, Immediate, Private, and Personal [*Management technique*]
SSIP.......... Standard Systems Improvement Program
SSIP.......... Subsystems Integration Program [*or Project*] [*NATO*] (NATG)
SSIP.......... System Setup Indicator Panel
SSIP.......... Systems Software Interface Processing [*NASA*] (MCD)
SSIPL........ Support and Sustaining Implications of Increased POMCUS Levels [*Military*]
SSIR .... Soil Survey Investigations Report
SSIR .... Special Security Investigation Requirement (AFM)
SSIS .... Society for South India Studies (EA)
SSIS.......... Space Station Information System (NASA)
SSIS.......... Spacecraft System Integration Support
SSISS .... Spacecraft System Integration Support Service
SSITP .... Shuttle System Integrated Test Plan [*NASA*] (NASA)
SSIU.......... Subsystem Interface Unit (MCD)
SSIUL....... Social Sciences Information Utilization Laboratory
SSIUS....... Specialty Steel Industry of the United States (EA)
SSIWA ...... Shipwrights' and Shipwrights Iron Workers' Association [*A union*] [*British*]
SSIX .... Scribe Systems, Inc. [*NASDAQ symbol*] (NQ)

SSIX .... Submarine Satellite Information Exchange [*Geosynchronous communications satellite*]
SSIXS........ Submarine Satellite Information Exchange System (MCD)
SSJ............ Sandnessjoen [*Norway*] [*Airport symbol*] (OAG)
SSJ............ Savez Sindikata Jugoslavije [*Yugoslavia Federation of Trade Unions*]
SSJ............ Self-Aligning Swivel Joint
SSJ............ Self-Screening Jammer (MCD)
SSJ............ Sequential Spot Jamming [*Military*] (CAAL)
SSJ............ Servo Summing Junction
SSJ............ Shinshu-Shinmachi [*Japan*] [*Seismograph station code, US Geological Survey*] (SEIS)
SSJ............ Side-Support Jack
SSJ............ Sinatra Society of Japan [*Tokyo*] (EAIO)
SSJ............ Single Subsonic Jet
SSJ............ Sisters of St. Joseph [*Roman Catholic religious order*]
SSJ............ Sisters of St. Joseph of the Third Order of St. Francis [*Roman Catholic religious order*]
SSJ............ Societas Sancti Joseph Sanctissimi Cordis [*St. Joseph's Society of the Sacred Heart*] [*Josephites*] [*Roman Catholic men's religious order*]
SSJ............ Socijalisticka Stranka Jugoslavije [*Yugoslav Socialist Party*] [*Spain*] [*Political party*] (EAIO)
SSJ............ Solid-State Jammer
SSJ............ Southern Speech Journal [*A publication*]
SSJB.......... Sisters of St. John the Baptist [*See also SSGB*] [*Roman Catholic religious order*] [*Rome, Italy*] (EAIO)
SSJC.......... Southern Seminary and Junior College [*Virginia*]
SSJD.......... Society of St. John the Divine [*Anglican religious community*]
SSJE.......... Society of St. John the Evangelist [*Anglican religious community*]
SS-JFI ...... School Superintendent Job Functions Inventory [*Test*]
SSJG.......... Sisters of St. John of God [*Wexford, Republic of Ireland*] (EAIO)
SSJM........ United States Embassy. Summary of Selected Japanese Magazines [*A publication*]
SSJSM ...... Sisters of St. Joseph of St. Mark [*Roman Catholic religious order*]
SSK............ Antisubmarine Submarine [*Navy symbol*]
SSK............ Keethanou School/Public Library, Stanley Mission, Saskatchewan [*Library symbol*] [*National Library of Canada*] (BIB)
SSK............ Service Sink [*Technical drawings*]
SSK............ Softkey Software Products, Inc. [*Toronto Stock Exchange symbol*]
SSK............ Soil Stack
SSKAT ...... Socio-Sexual Knowledge and Attitudes Test [*Psychology*]
SSKDN..... Serikat Sekerdja Kementerian Dalam Negeri [*Union of Workers in the Department of Interior*] [*Indonesia*]
SSKI......... Saturated Solution of Potassium Iodide [*Medicine*]
SSKIL........ Library Technician Program, Kelsey Institute of Applied Arts & Sciences, Saskatoon, Saskatchewan [*Library symbol*] [*National Library of Canada*] (NLC)
SSKP .... Serikat Sekerdja Kementerian Pertaganan [*Ministry of Defense Workers' Unions*] [*Indonesia*]
SSKP .... Single-Shot Kill Probability
SSKPS .... Solid-State Klystron Power Supply
SSKY .... Super Sky International, Inc. [*NASDAQ symbol*] (NQ)
SSL .... Licentiate of Sacred Scripture
SSL .... Safety Systems Laboratory [*Formerly, Office of Vehicle Systems Research*] [*Department of Transportation*]
SSL .... Scandoslavica [*Copenhagen*] [*A publication*]
SSL .... School of Systems and Logistics [*Military*]
SSL .... Scientific Subroutine Library
SSL .... Scientific Support Laboratory [*CDEC*] (MCD)
SSL .... Seattle, WA [*Location identifier*] [*FAA*] (FAAL)
SSL .... Seismograph Service Ltd. [*British*]
SSL .... Selected Source List (AAG)
SSL .... Service Security Layer [*Data processing*]
SSL .... Shift and Select [*Data processing*] (MDG)
SSL .... Ship Shortage Log (AAG)
SSL .... Shop Stock List (MCD)
SSL .... Skaneateles Short Line Railroad Corp. [*AAR code*]
SSL .... Skin Surface Lipid [*Physiology*]
SSL .... Social Security Administration Library, Baltimore, MD [*OCLC symbol*] (OCLC)
SSL .... Sociosystem Laboratory
SSL .... Sodium Stearoyl Lactylate
SSL .... Soeurs de Saint Louis [*Sisters of Saint Louis*] (EAIO)
SSL .... Software Sciences Limited [*British*]
SSL .... Software Slave Library [*Data processing*] (TEL)
SSL .... Software Specification Language
SSL .... Solid-State LASER
SSL .... Source Statement Library [*Data processing*]
SSL .... Southern Star Resources Limited [*Vancouver Stock Exchange symbol*]
SSL .... Space Sciences Laboratory [*University of California, Berkeley*] [*Research center*] [*NASA*] (MCD)
SSL .... Space Simulation Laboratory
SSL .... Special Sensor-Lightning
SSL .... Spent Sulfite Liquor [*Papermaking*]

SSL	Storage Structure Language
SSL	Studi e Saggi Linguistici [*A publication*]
SSL	Studies in Scottish Literature [*A publication*]
SSL	Studies in Semitic Languages and Linguistics [*A publication*]
SSL	Sunset Lake [*Pennsylvania*] [*Seismograph station code, US Geological Survey*] [*Closed*] (SEIS)
SSL	Support Status List (MCD)
SSL	System Software Loader (NASA)
SSL	System Specification Language
SSL	System Stock List (NATG)
SSLA	Star Savings & Loan Association [*Sayre, PA*] [*NASDAQ symbol*] (NQ)
SSlav	Studia Slavica. Academiae Scientiarum Hungaricae [*A publication*]
SSlav	Symbolae Slavicae [*A publication*]
SSLC	Ship System Life Cycle [*Navy*]
SSLC	Society of Savings and Loan Controllers [*Later, Financial Managers Society*] (EA)
SSLC	Synchronous Single-Line Controller
SSLE	Subacute Sclerosing Leukoencephalitis [*Medicine*]
SSLF	Skrifter Utgivna. Svenska Litteratursallskapet i Finland [*A publication*]
SSLF	Southern Sudan Liberation Front (BJA)
SSLH	Society for the Study of Labour History [*Sheffield, England*] (EA)
SSLI	Serum Sickness-Like Illness [*Medicine*]
SSLI	Society of School Librarians International (EA)
SSLI	Southern Security Life Insurance Co. [*NASDAQ symbol*] (NQ)
SSLI	Studies in Semitic Languages and Linguistics [*A publication*]
SS Lit	Soviet Studies in Literature [*A publication*]
SSLL	Stanford Studies in Language and Literature [*A publication*]
SSLM	Solid-Supported Liquid Membrane [*Chemical engineering*]
SSLN	Security Investments Group, Inc. [*NASDAQ symbol*] (NQ)
SSLO	Solid-State Local Oscillator
SSLORAN	Skywave Synchronized Long-Range Aid to Navigation
SSLP	Transport Submarine (MCD)
SSL-POW/MIA	Seaside Support League - POW/MIA [*Prisoner of War/Missing in Action*] (EA)
SSLPS	Solid-State Logic Protection System [*Nuclear energy*] (NRCH)
SSLR	Straits Settlements Law Reports [*A publication*] (DLA)
SSLR Supp	Straits Settlements Law Reports, Supplement [*1897-99*] [*Malasia*] [*A publication*] (DLA)
SSLS	Solid-State LASER System
SSLS	Standard Space Launch System [*BSD*]
SSLSM	Single Service Logistics Support Manager (MCD)
SSLSN	Skrifter Utgivna. Svenska Litteratursallskapet Studier i Nordisk Filologi [*A publication*]
SSLT	Solid-State Logic Timer
SSLT	Starboard Side Light (MCD)
SSLT	Stock Status Lag Time (AABC)
SSLV	Southern San Luis Valley Railroad Co. [*AAR code*]
SSLV	Standard Space Launch Vehicle
SSM	P. T. Susinma Line (DS)
SSM	St. Thomas More College, Saskatoon, Saskatchewan [*Library symbol*] [*National Library of Canada*] (NLC)
SSM	Satellite Stratospheric Monitor (NOAA)
SSM	Sault Ste. Marie [*Michigan*] [*Airport symbol*] (OAG)
SSM	School in Sales Management [*LIMRA*]
S & Sm	Searle and Smith's English Probate and Divorce Reports [*A publication*] (DLA)
SSM	Second-Stage Motor
SSM	Second Surface Mirror
SSM	Second-Tier Securities Market [*Investment term*]
SSM	Self-Sterilizing-Material [*Pharmacology*]
SSM	Semiconductor Storage Module
SSM	Seminaire St. Martial [*Haiti*] [*Seismograph station code, US Geological Survey*] [*Closed*] (SEIS)
SSM	Serum-Supplemented Medium [*Microbiology*]
SSM	Sesquiterpenoid Stress Metabolite [*Plant physiology*]
SSM	Ship Simulation Model [*Navy*]
SSM	Signal Strength Monitor [*Broadcasting*]
SSM	Silver Star Medal [*Military decoration*]
SSM	Single Sideband Modulation
SSM	Single Sideband Signal Multiplier [*Telecommunications*]
SSM	Sisters of St. Mary of the Third Order of St. Francis [*Roman Catholic religious order*]
SSM	Sisters of the Sorrowful Mother [*Third Order of St. Francis*] [*Roman Catholic religious order*]
SSM	Small Semiconductor Memory
SSM	Society of the Sacred Mission [*Anglican religious community*]
SSM	Society of St. Margaret [*Anglican religious community*]
SSM	Society of St. Monica (EA)
SSM	Society of the Servants of Mary [*Anglican religious community*]
SSM	Solar Simulation Module
SSM	Solar Stereoscopic Mission [*NASA*]
SSM	Solid-State Materials (CET)
SSM	Southlands Mining [*Vancouver Stock Exchange symbol*]
SSM	Space Science Fiction Magazine [*A publication*]
SSM	Space Station Module [*NASA*] (KSC)
SSM	Spacecraft Systems Monitor [*NASA*] (MCD)
SSM	Spark Source Mass Spectroscopy
SSM	Special Safeguarding Measures [*Telecommunications*] (TEL)
SSM	Special Survey of the Machinery [*Lloyd's Register of Shipping*] (DS)
SSM	Spread Spectrum Modulation (NATG)
SSM	Squadron Sergeant Major
SSM	SSMC, Inc. [*NYSE symbol*] (SPSG)
SSM	Staff Sergeant Major [*Military*]
SSM	Staff Squadron Major [*Military*] [*British*]
SSM	Standard Surfacing Mat [*Fiberglass*]
SSM	Studies in Statistical Mechanics [*Elsevier Book Series*] [*A publication*]
SSM	Subsynaptic Membrane [*Anatomy*]
SSM	Subsystem Manager [*NASA*] (NASA)
SSM	Superficial Spreading Melanoma [*Oncology*]
SSM	Supply Support Management
SSM	Support Systems Module [*NASA*]
SSM	Surface-to-Surface Missile
SSM	System Supply Manager
SSM	System Support Machine [*Telecommunications*]
SSM	System Support Management [*or Manager*] [*Military*] (AFM)
SSM	Systems Support Module [*NASA*] (MCD)
SSMA	School Science and Mathematics Association (EA)
SSMA	Soldiers, Sailors, Marines, and Airmen's Club [*Washington, DC*]
SSMA	Solid-State Microwave Amplifier
SSMA	Southwest Spanish Mustang Association (EA)
SSMA	Spread-Spectrum Multiple Access [*Satellite communications*]
SSMB	Ship's Serviceman, Barber [*Navy rating*]
SSMB	Space Shuttle Maintenance Baseline [*NASA*] (MCD)
SSMB	Special Services Management Bureau [*Telecommunications*] (TEL)
SSMC	Second-Stage Motor Container
SSMC	Ship's Serviceman, Cobbler [*Navy rating*]
SSMC	Silver State Mining Corporation [*NASDAQ symbol*] (NQ)
SSMCIS	Secondary School Mathematics Curriculum Improvement Study [*National Science Foundation*]
SSMCNP	Safeguard System Management Communications Network Program [*Army*] (AABC)
SSMCO	SPARTAN Santa Monica Checkout [*NASA*]
SSMCS	Synchronous Satellite Military Communication System
SSMD	Saskatchewan Mining Development Corp., Saskatoon, Saskatchewan [*Library symbol*] [*National Library of Canada*] (NLC)
SSMD	Silicon Stud-Mounted Diode
SSME	Satellite System Monitoring Equipment
SSME	Society for the Study of Medical Ethics [*British*]
SSME	Space Shuttle Main Engine [*NASA*]
SSME	Spread Spectrum Modulation Equipment [*NATO*] (MCD)
SSMEC	Space Shuttle Main Engine Controller [*NASA*] (MCD)
SSMECA	Space Shuttle Main Engine Controller Assembly [*NASA*] (NASA)
SSMF	Symbol Sink - Matched Filter
SSMG	Satellite Systems Monitoring Group [*INTELSAT*]
SSMG	Ship's Service Motor Generator [*Navy*] (NVT)
SSMH	Scottish Society for the Mentally Handicapped (EAIO)
SSMHA	Studia Scientiarum Mathematicarum Hungarica [*A publication*]
SSMHRC	Spanish Speaking Mental Health Research Center [*Public Health Service*] [*Research center*] (RCD)
SSM/I	Sensor System Microwave/Imager
SSMI	Sister Servants of Mary Immaculate [*Roman Catholic religious order*]
SSMIF & G	Squadron Sergeant-Major Instructor in Fencing and Gymnastics [*Military*] [*British*] (ROG)
SSM/IM	System Support Manager/Inventory Manager (MCD)
SSMIMA	Scissor, Shear, and Manicure Implement Manufacturers Association [*Later, National Association of Scissors and Shears Manufacturers*] (EA)
SSMIS	Support Services Management Information System [*Army*]
SSML	Shaped Substrata Meanderline (MCD)
SSML	Ship's Serviceman, Laundryman [*Navy rating*]
SSML	Society for the Study of Midwestern Literature (EA)
SSMLL	Society for the Study of Medieval Languages and Literature [*British*]
SSMLN	Society for the Study of Midwestern Literature. Newsletter [*A publication*]
SSMM	Space Station Mathematical Model
SSMMA	Staple and Stapling Machine Manufacturers Association [*Defunct*]
SSMMI	Soeurs Salesiennes Missionnaires de Marie Immaculee [*Salesian Missionaries of Mary Immaculate - SMMI*] [*Gentilly, France*] (EAIO)
SSMN	Sisters of St. Mary of Namur [*Roman Catholic religious order*]
SSMO	Sisters of St. Mary of Oregon [*Roman Catholic religious order*]
SSMO	Summary of Synoptic Meteorological Observations [*National Oceanic and Atmospheric Administration*] (MSC)
SSMOB	Surface-to-Surface Missile Order of Battle (MCD)
SSMP	Safeguard System Master Plan [*Army*] (AABC)
SSMP	Stockholm Studies in Modern Philology [*A publication*]
SSMP	Supply Support Management Plan [*Military*] (CAAL)
SSMPP	Society for the Study of Male Psychology and Physiology (EA)

SSMRP......	Seismic Safety Margins Research Program [*Nuclear Regulatory Commission*]
SSMS	Solid-State Mass Spectrometer
SSMS	Sons of Sherman's March to the Sea (EA)
SSMS	Spark Source Mass Spectroscopy
SSMS	Submarine Safety Monitoring System
SSMSDZ....	Social Science and Medicine. Part A. Medical Psychology and Medical Sociology [*A publication*]
SSMSN	Surface-to-Surface Mission [*Military*] (AABC)
S SMS N CLSD ...	Side Seams Not Closed [*Freight*]
SSMT	Salvage Sales Material Transfer
SSM/T	Sensor System Microwave/Temperature
SSMT	Ship's Serviceman, Tailor [*Navy rating*]
SSMT	Site Security Maintenance Team
SSMT	Society for the Study of Myth and Tradition (EA)
SSMTG	Solid-State and Molecular Theory Group [*MIT*] (MCD)
SSMTS.....	Spade and Shovel Makers' Trade Society [*A union*] [*British*]
SSMV	Single-Shot Multivibrator
SSN..........	Romulus, NY [*Location identifier*] [*FAA*] (FAAL)
SSN..........	Samson Gold Corp. [*Vancouver Stock Exchange symbol*]
SSN..........	San Juan Del Sur [*Nicaragua*] [*Seismograph station code, US Geological Survey*] (SEIS)
SSN..........	Scandinavian Studies and Notes [*A publication*]
SSN..........	Segment Stack Number
SSN..........	Senior Security Network (EA)
SSN..........	Severely Subnormal
SSN..........	Ship, Submersible (Nuclear-Powered)
SSN..........	Social Security Number (AABC)
SSN..........	Soviet Sciences in the News [*A publication*]
SSN..........	Space Surveillance Network
SSN..........	Specification Serial Number [*Military*]
SSN..........	Standard Serial Numbers (DIT)
SSN..........	Standard Study Number [*Military*]
SSN..........	Station Serial Number (CET)
SSN..........	Stock Segregation Notice [*DoD*]
SSN..........	Studia Semitica Neerlandica [*Assen*] [*A publication*]
SSN..........	Submarine (Nuclear-Powered) [*Navy symbol*] (NVT)
SSN..........	Switched Service Network [*Telecommunications*]
SSN..........	Sykepleiernes Samarbeid i Norden [*Northern Nurses Federation - NNF*] (EAIO)
SSNAP	Single Seat Night Attack Program (MCD)
SSNCHK...	Social Security Number Check
SSND........	Secondary Students for Nuclear Disarmament [*Australia*]
SSND........	Solid-State Neutral Dosimeter
SSN(DS)....	Submarine (Nuclear-Powered) in Direct Support [*Navy symbol*] (NVT)
SSNDT	Scottish School of Non-Destructive Testing [*United Kingdom*] (IRUK)
SSNF	Source Spot Noise Figure
SSNJ	Self-Screening Noise Jammer (MCD)
SSNLO	Shan State Nationalities Liberation Organization [*Burma*] (PD)
SSNM........	Strategic Special Nuclear Materials
SSNMH ...	Scipio Society of Naval and Military History (EA)
SSNP	Syrian Social Nationalist Party (BJA)
SSNPP.......	Small-Size Nuclear Power Plant
SSNS	Scottish Society for Northern Studies
SSNS	Standard Study Numbering System [*Military*] (AABC)
SSNW	Social Scientists Against Nuclear War (EA)
SSNY........	Swiss Society of New York (EA)
SSO..........	Safety/Security Officer [*Military*] (AABC)
SSO..........	Safety Significant Operation [*Aerospace*]
SSO..........	San Simon, AZ [*Location identifier*] [*FAA*] (FAAL)
SSO..........	Schweizerische Monatsschrift fuer Zahnheilkunde [*A publication*]
SSO..........	Security System Organization
SSO..........	Self-Sustained Outlet (FAAC)
SSO..........	Senior Safety Officer [*Navy*] (CAAL)
SSO..........	Senior Scientific Officer [*Ministry of Agriculture, Fisheries, and Food*] [*British*]
SSO..........	Senior Staff Officer [*Military*] [*British*]
SSO..........	Senior Supply Officer [*Military*] [*British*]
SSO..........	Ship Safety Officer
SSO..........	Simosato [*Japan*] [*Later, HTY*] [*Geomagnetic observatory code*]
SSO..........	Single Sweep Operation
SSO..........	Society of Surgical Oncology (EA)
SSO..........	Solid-State Oscillator
SSO..........	Source Selection Official (NASA)
sso	Southern Sotho [*MARC language code*] [*Library of Congress*] (LCCP)
SSO..........	Space Shuttle Orbiter [*NASA*] (RDA)
SSO..........	Spares Shipping Order
SSO..........	Special Security Office [*or Officer*] [*Military*] (CINC)
SSO..........	Special Service Officer [*Military*]
SSO..........	Squadron Signals Officer [*Navy*] [*British*]
SSO..........	Srednee Spetsial'noe Obrazovanie [*Moscow*] [*A publication*]
SSO..........	Staff Security Officer (AAG)
SSO..........	Staff Signals Officer [*British military*] (DMA)
SSO..........	Station Staff Officer [*British military*] (DMA)
SSO........	Statistical Service Office [*Military*]
SSO..........	Steady-State Oscillation
SSO..........	Studier fra Sprog- og Oldtidsforskning [*A publication*]
SSO..........	Submarine Oiler [*Navy ship symbol*]
SSO..........	Submarine Supply Office
SSO..........	Subsystem Operation [*in Spacelab*] [*NASA*] (MCD)
SSO..........	Sunflower Seed Oil
SSO..........	Support System for OEX [*Orbiter Experiments*] (NASA)
SSO..........	System Service Order [*Bell System*]
SSO..........	System Staff Office
SSOA........	Software Services of America, Inc. [*NASDAQ symbol*] (NQ)
SSOA........	Subsurface Ocean Area (NVT)
SSOB........	Senior Scientist on Board [*Navy*]
SSOC........	Southern Student Organizing Committee [*Defunct*]
SSOC........	Switching Service Operations Center [*Telecommunications*]
SSOCA	Senior Staff Officer for Civil Affairs [*British*] [*World War II*]
SSOD........	Solid-State Optical Detector
SSOD........	Special Session on Disarmament [*A special session of the UN General Assembly held from May 23 to June 28, 1978*]
SSODCM ...	Space Systems Operational Design Criteria Manual [*NASA*]
SSODIA	Special Security Office, Defense Intelligence Agency (CINC)
SSOE........	Special Subject Operational Evaluation
SSOEC	Ship Suppliers' Organization of the European Community [*Hague, Netherlands*] (EAIO)
SSOED3....	Southwestern Entomologist. Supplement [*A publication*]
SSOFS.......	Smiling Sons of the Friendly Shillelaghs
SSOG........	Satellite Systems Operations Guide [*INTELSAT*]
SSOG........	Scandinavian Association of Obstetricians and Gynaecologists (EA)
SSOG........	Spur Stepover Gear
SSOJ	Savez Socialisticke Omladine Jugoslavije [*League of Socialist Youth of Yugoslavia*] [*Political party*] (PPE)
SSOJ	Single Strength Orange Juice
S of Sol......	Song of Solomon [*Old Testament book*] (ROG)
SSOM........	Solid-State Optical MASER
SSOM........	[*The*] Space Shuttle Operator's Manual
SSOO	Satellite Supply Operations Officer [*Military*] (AFIT)
SSOP........	Satellite Systems Operations Plan [*INTELSAT*]
SSOP	Space Systems Operating Procedures [*NASA*] (MCD)
SSOR........	Ship Systems Operational Requirements
S SORD	Senza Sordini [*Without Mutes*] [*Music*]
SSORD.....	Software Review [*A publication*]
SSORM.....	Standard Ship's Organization and Regulations Manual [*Navy*] (NVT)
SSORT	Ship's Systems Operational Readiness Test (MCD)
SSORT	Ships Systems Operational Requirements
SSOS	One Sky, the Saskatchewan Cross Cultural Centre, Saskatoon, Saskatchewan [*Library symbol*] [*National Library of Canada*] (NLC)
SSOS	Single Source of Supply (MCD)
SSOSM	Studi Storici dell'Ordine dei Servi de Maria [*A publication*]
SSOSMFC ...	Simply Simon - The Official Simon MacCorkindale Fan Club (EA)
SSOT	Special Session of Oyer and Terminer [*Legal*] [*British*] (ROG)
SSOTC	Skinner's School Officers Training Corps [*British military*] (DMA)
SSOU1.......	System Output Unit 1 [*IBM Corp.*] (MDG)
SSOWSJ ...	Supreme Shrine of the Order of the White Shrine of Jerusalem (EA)
SSP	Association of the Sons of Poland (EA)
SSP	Petroleum Air Transport, Inc. [*Lafayette, LA*] [*FAA designator*] (FAAC)
SSP	Plant Biotechnology Institute, National Research Council Canada [*Institut de Biotechologie des Plantes, Conseil National de Recherches Canada*], Saskatoon, Saskatchewan [*Library symbol*] [*Obsolete*] [*National Library of Canada*] (NLC)
SSP	SACEUR [*Supreme Allied Commander, Europe*] Schedule Program [*Army*] (AABC)
SSP	Sagittal Sinus Pressure [*Medicine*]
SSP	St. Philip's College, San Antonio, TX [*OCLC symbol*] (OCLC)
SSP	Salt Soluble Protein [*Food industry*]
SSP	Scientific Services Program [*Army Research Office*] (RDA)
SSP	Scientific Software Products, Inc. [*Information service or system*] (IID)
SSP	Scientific Subroutine Package [*Data processing*]
SSP	Scouting Seaplane
SSP	Seguro Resources [*Vancouver Stock Exchange symbol*]
SSP	Seismic Section Profiler
SSP	Selected Topics in Solid State Physics [*Elsevier Book Series*] [*A publication*]
SSP	Semi-Annual Service Program [*Army*] (INF)
SSP	Sensor Select Panel (MCD)
SSP	Sentence Synthesizing Program
SS & P......	Service, Supply, and Procurement [*Military*]
SSP	Ship Speed
SSP	Ship's Stores Profit [*Navy*]
SSP	Shortage Specialty Pay [*Navy*] (NVT)
SSP	Shoshone Peak [*Nevada*] [*Seismograph station code, US Geological Survey*] (SEIS)
SSP	SIGINT Support Plan (MCD)
SSP	Simulation Support Processor

SSP .... Single-Shot Probability [*Military*]
SSP .... Single Stock Point [*Military*] (AFIT)
SSP .... Skylab Student Project [*NASA*]
SSP .... Small Sortie Payload [*NASA*] (NASA)
SSP .... Society of St. Paul for the Apostolate of Communications [*Pauline Fathers*] [*Roman Catholic religious order*]
SSP .... Society of Satellite Professionals [*Later, SSPI*] (EA)
SSP .... Society for Scholarly Publishing (EA)
SSP .... Sodium Sampling Package [*Nuclear energy*] (NRCH)
SSP .... Solid-State Photodiode
SSP .... Solid-State Pneumatic
SSP .... Solid-State Preamplifier
SSP .... SONAR Signal Processor
SSP .... Source Selection Plan
SSP .... South Simpson, AK [*Location identifier*] [*FAA*] (FAAL)
SSP .... Space Shuttle Program [*NASA*] (NASA)
SSP .... Special Services Protection [*Telecommunications*] (TEL)
SSP .... Special Session of Peace [*Legal*] [*British*] (ROG)
SSP .... Species Survival Plans [*Program sponsored by the American Association of Zoological Parks and Aquariums to protect certain endangered species*]
SSP .... Staff Site Position [*Nuclear energy*] (NRCH)
SSP .... Stainless Steel Propeller (DS)
SSP .... Standard Shop Practice (MCD)
SSP .... Standard Subroutine Package
SSP .... Standard Switch Panel (MCD)
SSP .... Standby Status Panel
SSP .... State Supplementary Payment [*Department of Health and Human Services*]
SSP .... Static Sodium Pot [*Nuclear energy*] (NRCH)
SSP .... Statutory Sick Pay [*British*]
SSP .... Steam Service Pressure
SSP .... Stores Stressed Platform [*Military*] [*British*]
SSP .... Strategic Systems Project [*Office*] [*Navy*]
SSP .... Submarine Scout Patrol (DMA)
SSP .... Submarine Transport [*Navy symbol*] [*Obsolete*]
SSP .... Subsatellite Point [*Telecommunications*] (TEL)
SSP .... Subsolar Point [*Aerospace*]
SSP .... Subspecies [*Also, ssp*]
S/SP .... Subsystem Software Program (MCD)
SSP .... Supersensitivity Perception
SSP .... Supervisory Surveillance Program [*DoD*]
SSP .... Supplemental Standard Practice (AAG)
SSP .... Support Software Package (MCD)
SSP .... Surgical Specialist
SSP .... Sustained Superior Performance [*Military*]
SSP .... System Safety Plan (MCD)
SSP .... System Status Panel
SSP .... System Support Program (AFM)
SSPA .... Senescent-Soybean-Pod Agar [*Microbiology*]
SSPA .... Social Security Pensions Act [*1975*] [*British*] (DCTA)
SSPA .... Society of St. Peter Apostle (EA)
SSPA .... Solid State Phased Array (MCD)
SSPA .... Southern Sudanese Political Association [*Political party*] [*Sudan*] (MENA)
SSPANC .... Society of St. Peter the Apostle for Native Clergy [*Later, SSPA*] (EA)
SSPB .... Socket Screw Products Bureau [*Defunct*] (EA)
SSPB .... Swedish State Power Board [*Nuclear energy*]
SSPC .... Solid-State Power Controller [*NASA*]
SSPC .... Spacelab Stored Program Command [*NASA*] (MCD)
SSPC .... Steel Structures Painting Council (EA)
SSPC .... Suore Missionarie di San Pietro Claver [*Missionary Sisters of St. Peter Claver*] (EAIO)
SSPCL .... System Software Package Component List (MCD)
SSPCL .... System Support Package Component List (MCD)
SSPCP .... Shipboard Signal Processing Control Program [*Navy*] (CAAL)
SSPCT .... Technical Library, Potash Corp. of Saskatchewan, Saskatoon, Saskatchewan [*Library symbol*] [*National Library of Canada*] (NLC)
SSPD .... Shuttle System Payload Data [*NASA*] (NASA)
SSPD .... Shuttle System Payload Definition Study [*NASA*] (NASA)
SSPD .... Shuttle System Payload Description [*NASA*] (NASA)
S/SPD .... Single Speed [*Automotive engineering*]
SSPDA ...... Space Shuttle Payload Data Activity [*NASA*] (NASA)
SSPDA ...... Surface Sampler Processing and Distribution Assembly
SSPDB .... Subsystem Power Distribution Box (MCD)
SSPDPT ..... Salzburg Studies. Poetic Drama and Poetic Theory [*A publication*]
SSPDS .... Space Shuttle Payload Data Study [*NASA*] (NASA)
SSPE .... Subacute Sclerosing Panencephalitis [*Medicine*]
SSPE .... Support System Project Engineer
S Speech Commun J ... Southern Speech Communication Journal [*A publication*]
SSPF .... Structured Soy Protein Fiber [*Food industry*]
SSPFC .... Stainless Steel Plumbing Fixture Council [*Defunct*] (EA)
SSPHA ...... Solid State Physics [*A publication*]
SSPHS ...... Society for Spanish and Portuguese Historical Studies (EA)
SSPI .... Sight System Passive Infrared [*Sensor*] [*Army*]
SSPI .... Society of Satellite Professionals International (TSSD)
SSpJ .... Southern Speech Journal [*A publication*]

SSPK .... Single Shot Probability of Kill [*Military*]
SSPL .... Saturation Sound Pressure Level
SSPL .... Solid-State Pneumatic Logic
SSPL .... Steady-State Power Level (IEEE)
SSPL .... System Support Package List (MCD)
SSPM .... Single Strokes per Minute (MSA)
SSPM .... Space Shuttle Program Manager [*NASA*] (NASA)
SSPMA ..... Sump and Sewage Pump Manufacturers Association (EA)
SSPME ...... Societa di San Patrizio per le Missioni Estere [*St. Patrick's Society for the Foreign Missions - SPSFM*] [*Kiltegan, County Wicklow, Republic of Ireland*] (EAIO)
SSPMO ..... SONAR Systems Project Management Office
SSPN .... Satellite System for Precise Navigation [*Air Force*]
SSPN .... Ship's Stores and Profit, Navy
SSPN .... System for Precise Navigation [*Later, DNSS*] (MCD)
ssp nov ..... Subspecies Nova [*New Subspecies*] [*Biology*]
SSPO .... Space Shuttle Program Office [*NASA*] (KSC)
SSPO .... Strategic Systems Project Office [*Navy*]
SSPP .... POS Pilot Plant Corp., University of Saskatchewan Campus, Saskatoon, Saskatchewan [*Library symbol*] [*National Library of Canada*] (NLC)
SSPP .... Sancti Patres [*Holy Fathers*] [*Latin*]
SSPP .... Scandinavian Society for Plant Physiology (EAIO)
SSPP .... Schedule Status Preprocessor (MCD)
SSPP .... Serikat Sekerdja Pamong Pradja [*Public Officials' Union*] [*Indonesia*]
SSPP .... Society for the Study of Process Philosophies (EA)
SSPP .... Solar Sea Power Plant [*NASA*]
SSPP .... Subspecies [*Plural form*] [*Also, sspp*]
SSPP .... Subsynaptic Plate Perforation [*Neurophysiology*]
SSPP .... System Safety Program Plan [*Navy*]
SSPPSG ..... Space Shuttle Payload Planning Steering Group [*NASA*] (NASA)
SSPR .... Subcontract Schedule and Procurement Request
SSPRO ...... Space Shuttle Program Resident Office [*NASA*] (NASA)
SSPS .... Satellite Solar Power Station [*or System*] [*NASA*]
SSPS .... Sheffield Sawmakers' Protection Society [*A union*] [*British*] (DCTA)
SSPS .... Silver/Somatostatin Positive Structure [*Anatomy*]
SSPS .... Solar-Based Solar Power Satellite
SSPS .... Solid-State Protection System [*Nuclear energy*] (IEEE)
SSPS .... Space Shuttle Program Schedule [*NASA*] (NASA)
SSPS .... Spacecraft Support Planning Section
SSPSF .... Stochastic Self-Propagating Star Formation
SSPSG .... Science and Public Policy Studies Group [*Newsletter*]
SSPSM ...... Serikat Sekerdja Pabrik Sendjata dan Mesiu [*Armaments' Union*] [*Indonesia*]
SSPTF .... Santa Susana Propulsion Test Facility [*NASA*] (NASA)
SSPTT .... Serikat Sekerdja Pos, Telegrap dan Telepon [*National Postal, Telegraph and Telephone Employees' Union*] [*Indonesia*]
SSPU .... Ship's Service Power Unit [*Navy*] (CAAL)
SSPW .... Sun Sportswear, Inc. [*NASDAQ symbol*] (NQ)
SSPWB ...... Studium Spraw Polskich (Wielka Brytania) [*Information Centre for Polish Affairs*] (EAIO)
SSPWR ...... Small-Size Pressurized Water Reactor [*Nuclear energy*]
SSQ .... Shell Lake, WI [*Location identifier*] [*FAA*] (FAAL)
SSQ .... Simple Sinusoidal Quantity
SSQ .... Social Science Quarterly [*A publication*]
SSQ .... Society for Software Quality (EA)
SSQ .... Station Sick Quarters
SSQTA ...... Social Science Quarterly [*A publication*]
SSR .... RADAR Picket Submarine [*Navy symbol*]
SSR .... SACEUR [*Supreme Allied Commander, Europe*] Strategic Reserve [*Army*] (NATG)
SSR .... Safe Secure Railcar [*Army*]
SSR .... Safety Services Representative [*Red Cross*]
SSR .... Saskatchewan Research Council, Saskatoon, Saskatchewan [*Library symbol*] [*National Library of Canada*] (NLC)
SSR .... Satellite Situation Report (AAG)
SSR .... Schedule Shipment Record (MCD)
SSR .... Seal Steam Regulator [*Nuclear energy*] (NRCH)
SSR .... Secondary Surveillance RADAR
SSR .... Security Services [*Vancouver Stock Exchange symbol*]
SSR .... Security Survey Report [*Nuclear energy*]
SSR .... Seek-Storm RADAR
SSR .... Selenium Stack Rectifier
SSR .... Self-Sufficiency Ratio [*Business term*]
SSR .... Separate Superheater Reactor [*Nuclear energy*]
SSR .... Shipbuilding and Ship Repair [*Department of Employment*] [*British*]
SSR .... Shop Support Request [*NASA*] (NASA)
SSR .... SIA [*Semiconductor Industry Association*] Statistical Review [*A publication*] (EAAP)
SSR .... Signal-Sequence Receptor [*Biochemistry*]
SSR .... Sink to Source Relation
SSR .... Sisters Island, AK [*Location identifier*] [*FAA*] (FAAL)
SSR .... Site Suitability Report [*Nuclear energy*] (NRCH)
SSR .... Slate-Shingle Roof [*Technical drawings*]
SSR .... Slow Strain Rate [*Tensile test*]
SSR .... Social Security Reporter [*Australia*] [*A publication*]
SSR .... Social Security Review [*Australia*]

SSR............ Social Security Rulings [*on Old Age, Survivors, and Disability Insurance*] [*US*] [*A publication*]

SSR .... Societe Suisse de Radiodiffusion et Television [*Radio and television network*] [*Switzerland*]

SSR .... Society for the Study of Reproduction   (EA)

SSR .... Sociology and Social Research [*A publication*]

SSR .... Solid State Relay   (IEEE)

SSR .... South Staffordshire Regiment [*Military unit*] [*British*]

SSR .... Soviet Socialist Republic

SSR .... Special Scientific Report

SSR .... Special Services Request [*Travel industry*]

SSR .... Special Survey of Refrigerated Machinery [*Lloyd's Register of Shipping*] (DS)

SSR .... Spin-Stabilized Rockets

SSR .... Spotted Swine Record [*Later, National Spotted Swine Record*] (EA)

SSR .... Staff Support Room [*NASA*]

SSR .... Static Shift Register

SSR .... Static Squelch Range

SSR .... Station Set Requirement [*NASA*]   (NASA)

SSR .... Statistical Summary Report   (AAG)

SSR .... Steady-State Rate [*of production*] [*Medicine*]

SSR .... Stock Status Report

SSR .... Students for Social Responsibility   (EA)

SSR .... Studi e Materiali di Storia della Religioni [*A publication*]

SSR .... Subsynchronous Resonance   (IEEE)

SSR .... Sum of the Squared Residuals [*Econometrics*]

SSR .... Summarized Spares Requirement

SSR .... Supplementary Statement Required [*Civil Service*]

SSR .... Supply Support Request [*or Requirement*] [*Military*]   (AFM)

SSR .... Surface Slip Resistance

s-sr--- .... Surinam [*MARC geographic area code*] [*Library of Congress*] (LCCP)

SSR .... Susara [*Romania*] [*Seismograph station code, US Geological Survey*] (SEIS)

SSR .... Synchronous Stable Relaying   (IEEE)

SSR .... System Status Report

SSR .... System Study Requirement   (AAG)

SSR .... System Support Record

SSRA .... Spread Spectrum Random Access System [*Telecommunications*] (TEL)

SSRA .... System Safety Risk Analysis [*Army*]

SSRB .... Sole Source Review Board   (MCD)

SSRC .... Social Science Research Center [*Mississippi State University*] [*Research center*] (RCD)

SSRC .... Social Science Research Council   (EA)

SSRC .... Social Systems Research Center [*California State University, Dominguez Hills*] [*Research center*]   (RCD)

SSRC .... Society for the Study of Religion and Communism   (EA)

SSRC .... Structural Stability Research Council   (EA)

SSRC .... Swedish Space Research Committee

SSRCA ...... Super Sunfish Racing Class Association   (EA)

SSRCC....... Social Sciences Research Council of Canada [*See also CCRSS*] [*Later, SSHRCC*]

SSRC Newsl ... SSRC [*Social Science Research Council*] Newsletter [*A publication*]

SSRCR....... Suggested State Regulations for the Control of Radiation [*Nuclear Regulatory Commission*]   (NRCH)

SSRD......... Station Set Requirements Document [*NASA*]   (NASA)

SSRE .... Society for Social Responsibility in Engineering [*Australia*]

SSREA ...... Sight-Saving Review [*A publication*]

SSREIU..... Shipbuilding, Ship Repairing, and Engineering Industrial Union [*British*]

SSREX....... Canada Department of Regional Industrial Expansion [*Ministere de l'Expansion Industrielle Regionale*] Saskatoon, Saskatchewan [*Library symbol*] [*National Library of Canada*]   (NLC)

SSRF......... Shell-Supported Ring Frame

SSRF......... Small-Scale Raiding Force [*Military*]

SSR-F .... Special Scientific Report - Fisheries

SSRFC....... Social Science Research Facilities Center [*University of Minnesota*] [*Research center*]   (RCD)

SSRG......... Selective Service Regulations

SSRG......... Simple Shift Register Generator

SSRH......... General Constituency Section for Small or Rural Hospitals   (EA)

SSRI .... Social Science Research Institute [*of CRESS*] [*University of Hawaii at Manoa*] [*Research center*]   (RDA)

SSRI .... Social Science Research Institute [*University of Maine at Orono*] [*Research center*]   (RCD)

SSRI .... Social Systems Research Institute [*University of Wisconsin - Madison*] [*Research center*]   (RCD)

SSRL .... Stanford Synchrotron Radiation Laboratory [*Stanford, CA*] [*Department of Energy*]

SSRL .... Stockholm Studies in Russian Literature [*A publication*]

SSRL .... Systems Simulation Research Laboratory

SSRM........ Second-Stage Rocket Motor

SSRN......... RADAR Picket Submarine (Nuclear Powered) [*Navy symbol*] [*Obsolete*]

SSRN......... Service Shop Requirement Notice

SSRN......... System Software Reference Number [*NASA*]   (NASA)

SSRNJ....... Socijalisticka Savez Radnog Naroda Jugoslavije [*Socialist Alliance of Working People of Yugoslavia - SAWPY*] [*Political party*] (PPE)

Ssro .... Spolecnost s Rucenim Omezenym [*Company with Limited Liability*] [*Czechoslovakian*] [*Business term*]

SSRP .... Single Shot Kill Probability   (MCD)

SSRP .... Social Security Rights Project [*Australia*]

SSRP .... Somali Socialist Revolutionary Party

SSRP .... Stanford Synchrotron Radiation Project

SSRR .... Social Service Reporting Requirements [*HEW*]

SSRR .... Station Set Requirements Review [*NASA*]   (NASA)

SSRS......... SIGINT Surveillance and Reporting System   (MCD)

SSRS......... Society for Social Responsibility in Science   (EA)

SSRS......... Start-Stop-Restart System [*NASA*]   (KSC)

SSRS......... Submarine Sand Recovery System

SSRSB....... Safety and Special Radio Services Bureau [*of FCC*]

SSRSJC..... Saudi-Sudanese Red Sea Joint Commission [*Commercial firm*] [*Jeddah, Saudi Arabia*]   (EAIO)

SSRT .... Subsystem Readiness Test   (KSC)

SSRTP........ Solid Substrate Room Temperature Phosphorescence

SS-RTP...... Solid-Surface, Room-Temperature Phosphorescence [*Physics*]

SSRWA ..... Soviet Science Review [*A publication*]

SSS .... MSA Realty Corp. [*AMEX symbol*]   (SPSG)

SSS .... Safeguard Spartan System [*Aerospace*]   (MCD)

SSS .... San Salvador [*El Salvador*] [*Seismograph station code, US Geological Survey*]   (SEIS)

SSS .... Satellite Syndicated Systems [*Douglasville, GA*] [*Cable TV programming service*] [*Telecommunications*]

SSS .... Sauna - Swimming Pool - Storage Area [*Key fitting those locks in apartment complex*]

SSS .... Scandinavian Surgical Society   (EAIO)

SSS .... Scene Storage System   (MCD)

SSS .... School of Social Studies [*British*]

SSS .... Scientific Subroutine System [*Data processing*]   (BUR)

SSS .... Secondary Sampling System [*Nuclear energy*]   (NRCH)

S/SS........... Sector/Subsector

SSS .... Selective Service System

SSS .... Self-Service Store

SSS .... Semitic Study Series [*A publication*]   (BJA)

SSS .... Senior Service School [*Military*]   (AFM)

SSS .... Sensitized Stainless Steel   (NRCH)

SSS .... Sentinel-Spartan System   (MCD)

SSS .... Shevchenko Scientific Society   (EA)

SSS .... Shield and Seismic Support [*Nuclear energy*]   (NRCH)

SSS .... Ship's Service Stores

SSS .... Shnat Sherut Scheme   (BJA)

SSS .... Shore Signal Service [*British Royal Navy*]

SSS .... Siassi [*Papua New Guinea*] [*Airport symbol*]   (OAG)

SSS .... Sick Sinus Syndrome [*Medicine*]

SSS .... Signal Switching System

SSS .... Signature Security Service [*DoD*]

SSS .... Silicon-Symmetrical Switch   (CET)

SSS .... Simplified Spelling Society   (EA)

SSS .... Simulation Study Series   (KSC)

SSS .... Single Screw Ship

SSS .... Single Signal Supersonic [*Heterodyne*]   (DEN)

SSS .... Sisters of Social Service [*Roman Catholic religious order*]

SSS .... Site Security Supervisor   (AFM)

SSS .... Skills Support System [*Education*]

SSS .... Small Scientific Satellite [*NASA*]

SSS .... Small Solar Satellite [*NASA*]

SSS .... Small Starlight Scope [*Light-intensifying device*]

SSS .... Small Structures Survey [*Civil Defense*]

SSS .... Social Science Series [*A publication*]

SSS .... Social Status Study [*Psychology*]

SSS .... Societas Sanctissimi Sacramenti [*Congregation of the Blessed Sacrament*] [*Roman Catholic men's religious order*]

SSS .... Societe Scandinave de Simulation [*Scandinavian Simulation Society*]   (EAIO)

SSS .... Society of St. Stephen   (EA)

SSS .... Society for the Second Self   (EA)

SSS .... Society for Slovene Studies   (EA)

SSS .... Society for Socialist Studies [*Canada*] [*See also SES*]

SSS .... Society for the Suppression of Speculative Stamps [*Defunct*]

SSS .... Software Service System [*Anti-piracy device invented by Ryoichi Mori of the Japan Electronics Industry Development Association*]   (BYTE)

SSS .... Software Staging Section [*Social Security Administration*]

SSS .... Solid-State Spectrometer

SSS .... Solid-State Switching   (NG)

SSS .... Solid-State System

SSS .... SONAR Signal Simulator

SSS .... Sortie Support System   (MCD)

SSS .... Sound Suppression System   (NASA)

SSS .... Southern Satellite Systems, Inc. [*Tulsa, OK*] [*Telecommunications*]   (TSSD)

SSS .... Space Settlers' Society   (EAIO)

SSS .... Space Shuttle Simulation [*NASA*]

SSS .... Space Shuttle System [*NASA*]   (KSC)

SSS .... Space Station Simulator

SSS .... Space Surveillance System [*Navy*]   (MCD)

SSS .... Spacecraft System Support
SSS .... Special Safeguards Study [*Nuclear energy*] (NRCH)
SSS .... Special Safety Safeguards (NRCH)
SSS .... Specific Soluble Substance [*Polysaccharide hapten*]
SSS .... Spin-Stabilized Spacecraft
SSS .... Spinning Space Station
SSS .... Stabilized Sighting System
SSS .... Staff Summary Sheet (MCD)
SSS .... Stage Separation Subsystem [*NASA*] (NASA)
SSS .... Stainless Steel Sink [*Classified advertising*] (ADA)
SSS .... Standard Scratch Score [*Golf*]
SSS .... Standard Seawater Service [*British*]
SSS .... Standard Supply System [*Army*] (AABC)
SSS .... Stanford Sleepiness Scale
SSS .... Station Set Specification [*NASA*] (NASA)
SSS .... Stepping Switch Scanner
SSS .... Sterile Saline Soak
SSS .... Stockholders Sovereignty Society [*Later, FFSR*] (EA)
SSS .... STOL Support Ship [*Navy*] (CAAL)
SSS .... Storage Serviceability Standard [*Army*]
SSS .... Strategic Satellite System (MCD)
SSS .... Strategic Support Squadron [*Air Force*]
SSS .... Stratum Super Stratum [*Layer Over Layer*] [*Latin*]
SSSN .... Strike Support Ship [*Navy*] (NVT)
SSS .... Strong Soap Solution
SSS .... Structures Subsystem (KSC)
SSS .... Study Skills Surveys [*Educational test*]
SSS .... Subject Specialists Section [*Association of College and Research Libraries*]
SSS .... Subjective Stress Scale
SSS .... Subscribers' Switching Subsystem [*Telecommunications*] (TEL)
SSS .... Substructure Search System [*Later, SANSS*] [*NIH/EPA*]
SSS .... Subsystem Segment [*NASA*] (NASA)
SSS .... Subsystem Support Service (BUR)
SSS .... Sunday Shakespeare Society [*British*]
SSS .... Super Science Stories [*A publication*]
SSS .... Superior Shore Systems [*An association*] (EA)
SSS .... Supply Screening Section [*Navy*]
SSS .... Survivable Satellite System (MCD)
SSS .... Symbolic Shorthand System
SSS .... System Safety Society (EA)
SSS .... Systems Science and Software (MCD)
SSS .... Trois Fois Salut [*Thrice Greeting*] [*French*] [*Freemasonry*] (ROG)
SSSA .... St. Andrew's College, Saskatoon, Saskatchewan [*Library symbol*] [*National Library of Canada*] (NLC)
SSSA .... Self-Service Storage Association [*Later, SSA*] (EA)
SSSA .... Soil Science Society of America (EA)
SSSA .... Submarine SONAR Subjective Analysis (NVT)
SSSAS .... Society of Spanish and Spanish-American Studies (EA)
SSSA Spec Publ ... SSSA [*Soil Science Society of America*] Special Publication [*A publication*]
SSSA Spec Publ Ser ... SSSA [*Soil Science Society of America*] Special Publication Series [*A publication*]
SSSB .... Society for the Study of Social Biology (EA)
SSSB .... System Source Selection Board [*Air Force*]
SSSBCR ...... Star, Starling, Stuart, and Briton Car Register (EA)
SSSBP .... System Source Selection Board Procedure [*Air Force*]
SSSC .... Self-Service Supply Center [*Military*] (AFIT)
SSSC .... Single Sideband Suppressed Carrier
SSSC .... Soft-Sized Super-Calendered [*Paper*]
SSSC .... Space Science Steering Committee
SSSC .... Special Spectrum Study Committee
SSSC .... Stainless Steel Sink Council [*Defunct*] (EA)
SSSC .... Studies in Surface Science and Catalysis [*Elsevier Book Series*] [*A publication*]
SSSC .... Surface/Subsurface Control [*Navy*] (CAAL)
SSSC .... Surface/Subsurface Surveillance Center [*Navy*] (NVT)
SSSC .... Surface/Subsurface Surveillance Coordinator [*Navy*]
SSSCA .... Soviet Soil Science [*English translation*] [*A publication*]
SSSCAE ...... Soviet Soil Science [*English translation of Pochvovedenie*] [*A publication*]
SSSCC .... Staff Suggestions Scheme Consultative Committee [*Australia*]
SSSCD .... Social Studies of Science [*A publication*]
SSSD .... Second-Stage Separation Device
SSSD .... Single-Sided, Single-Density Disk [*Magnetic disk*] [*Data processing*]
SSSD .... Solid-State Solenoid Driver
SSSD .... Space Shuttle Simulation Display [*NASA*]
SSSEAK ..... Studi Sassaresi. Sezione 2. Archivio Bimestrale di Scienze Mediche e Naturali [*A publication*]
SSSEDA .... Aerospace Products Division, SED Systems Ltd., Saskatoon, Saskatchewan [*Library symbol*] [*National Library of Canada*] (NLC)
SSSERC .... Scottish Schools Science Equipment Research Centre (CB)
SSSF .... Stationary Source Simulator Facility [*Environmental science*]
SSSG .... SLCM [*Sea-Launched Cruise Missile*] Survivability Steering Group [*Navy*] (CAAL)

SSSI .... Kelsey Institute of Applied Arts and Sciences, Saskatoon, Saskatchewan [*Library symbol*] [*National Library of Canada*] (NLC)
SSSI .... Servamatic Solar Systems [*NASDAQ symbol*] (NQ)
SSSI .... Site of Special Scientific Interest [*British*]
SSSI .... Society for the Study of Symbolic Interaction (EA)
SSSI .... Special Steel Summary Invoice [*International Trade Administration*]
SSSI .... Steel Scaffolding and Shoring Institute [*Later, SSFI*] (EA)
SSSJ .... Single Subsonic Jet
SSSJ .... Student Struggle for Soviet Jewry (EA)
SSSJD .... Soil Science Society of America. Journal [*A publication*]
SSS Journal ... State Shipping Service of Western Australia. Journal [*A publication*] (APTA)
SSSL.......... Society for the Study of Southern Literature (EA)
SSSL.......... Sun State Savings & Loan Association [*Phoenix, AZ*] [*NASDAQ symbol*] (NQ)
SSSL.......... Supersonic Split Line (KSC)
SSSLF .... South Slavonian Socialist Labor Federation [*Defunct*] (EA)
SSSM .... Site Space Surveillance Monitor (AFM)
SSSM .... South Street Seaport Museum (EA)
SSSM .... Subset-Specified Sequential Machine [*Air Force*]
SSSMP...... Surface Ship SONAR Modernization Program (MCD)
SSSN .... Satellite Syndicated Systems [*NASDAQ symbol*] (NQ)
SSSN .... Secondary Social Security Number
S/S/SN ..... System/Subsystem/Subject Number (MCD)
SSSO .... Specialized Satellite Service Operators [*British*]
SSSO .... Specialized Surplus Sales Office [*Military*]
SSSP......... Society for the Study of Social Problems (EA)
SSSP......... Space Settlement Studies Program (EA)
SSSP......... Space Shuttle Synthesis Program [*National Academy of Sciences*]
SSSP......... Station to Station Send Paid [*Telecommunications*] (TEL)
SSSP......... Stockholm Studies in Scandinavian Philology [*A publication*]
SSSP......... System Source Selection Procedure [*Air Force*]
SSSQ .... McCarron-Dial Street Survival Skills Questionnaire [*Occupational therapy*]
SSSQ .... Southwestern Social Science Quarterly [*A publication*]
SS/SR .... Safety Standdown/Safety Review (MCD)
SSSR........ SAGE [*Semiautomatic Ground Environment*] System Status Report
SSSR........ Smallest Set of Smallest Rings [*Organic chemistry*]
SSSR........ Social Sciences Services and Resources (EA)
SSSR........ Society for the Scientific Study of Religion (EA)
SSSR........ Southwestern Social Science Review [*A publication*]
SSSR........ Soyuz Sovetskikh Sotsialisticheskikh Respublik [*Union of Soviet Socialist Republics*]
SSSR........ Syracuse Scales of Social Relations [*Education*]
SSSS .... Shallow Spherical Sandwich Shell
SSSS .... Society for the Scientific Study of Sex (EA)
SSSS .... Space Shuttle System Segment (MCD)
SSSS .... Space Shuttle System Specification [*NASA*] (NASA)
SSSS .... Staphylococcal Scalded Skin Syndrome [*Medicine*]
SSSS .... Stewart & Stevenson Services, Inc. [*NASDAQ symbol*] (NQ)
SSSSC .... Surface/Subsurface Surveillance Coordinator [*Navy*] (CAAL)
SSSST .... Subscale Subsonic Targets (MCD)
SSST .... S-Band Spread Spectrum Transponder (MCD)
SSST .... Site Suitability Source Term [*Nuclear energy*] (NRCH)
SSST .... Solid-State Silicon Target
SSST.......... Spectroscopic Survey Telescope [*Proposed*] [*Joint project of the University of Texas and Pennsylvania State University*]
SSStJ........ Serving Sister, Order of St. John of Jerusalem [*British*]
SSSV......... Scientific Systems Services, Inc. [*NASDAQ symbol*] (NQ)
SSSW .... Surface/Subsurface Warfare [*Navy*] (CAAL)
SSSYDF .... Synergetics [*Berlin*] [*A publication*]
SST .... Safe Secure Trailer [*For transporting nuclear materials*]
SST .... Safe Separate/Timing (CINC)
SST .... Saskatchewan Teachers' Federation Saskatoon, Saskatchewan [*Library symbol*] [*National Library of Canada*] (NLC)
SST .... Satellite-to-Satellite Tracking
SST .... Saturated Suction Temperature [*Refrigeration*]
SST .... Saturn Systems Test [*NASA*]
SST .... Science Stories [*A publication*]
SST .... Sea Surface Temperature [*Oceanography*]
SST .... Seaplane Shuttle Transport [*New York-Philadelphia air-link*]
SST .... Secondary Surge Tank [*Nuclear energy*] (NRCH)
SST .... Semi-Submerged Trimaran [*Tri-hull ship design invented by Calvin Gongwer*]
SST .... Serviceability Self-Test (MCD)
SST .... Shakespeare Studies (Tokyo) [*A publication*]
SST .... Shelter Components Corp. [*AMEX symbol*] (SPSG)
SST .... Shipboard [*Weapon*] Suitability Test [*Navy*] (NG)
SST .... Ships Service Turbine (MCD)
SST .... Short Selection Test [*Australia*]
SST .... Sideways-Spinning Tube [*Spectrometry*]
SST .... Sight, Sound, and Touch [*Ways to identify proper belt tension*] [*Automotive engineering*]
SST .... Silver Sceptre Resources [*Vancouver Stock Exchange symbol*]
SST........... Simulated Structural Test (KSC)
SST .... Single Sideband Transmission [*Telecommunications*] (TEL)
SST .... Single Subscriber Terminal [*Army*] (RDA)

SST .... Single Systems Trainer [*NASA*] (MCD)
SST .... Slide, Script, and Tape
SST .... Social Security Tax Ruling [*Internal Revenue Bulletin*] [*A publication*] (DLA)
SST .... Society for the Study of Theology [*British*]
SST .... Society of Surveying Technicians (EAIO)
SST .... Solid-State Transmitter (MCD)
SST .... SONAR Signaling (NVT)
SST .... Soviet Science and Technology [*IFI/Plenum Data Corp.*] [*Information service or system*] (IID)
SSt .... Sowjet Studien [*A publication*]
SST .... Space Surveillance Technology
SST .... Spacecraft System Test [*NASA*]
SST .... Special Strike Teletype (NATG)
SST .... Spectroscopic Survey Telescope [*Proposed*] [*Joint project of the University of Texas and Pennsylvania State University*]
SSt .... Spenser Studies [*A publication*]
SST .... Split Second Timing
SST .... Stainless Steel
SST .... Station Service Transformer [*Nuclear energy*] (NRCH)
SS/T .... Steady-State/Transient Analysis [*Nuclear energy*] (NRCH)
SST .... Stiffened Super-Tough [*Polymer technology*]
SST .... Stream Support Team (MCD)
SST .... Structural Static Test [*NASA*] (NASA)
SST .... Student Science Training [*Program*] [*National Science Foundation*] [*Defunct*]
SST .... Subject Standardized Test
SST .... Submarine Scout Twin-Type [*British military*] (DMA)
SST .... Subscriber Transferred [*Telecommunications*] (TEL)
SST .... Subsystem Terminal on Spacelab [*NASA*] (MCD)
SST .... Subsystems Test (KSC)
SST .... Superficial Spreading Type (Melanoma) [*Oncology*]
SS/T .... Supersonic Telegraphy [*British military*] (DMA)
SST .... Supersonic Transport
SST .... Supplementary Service Tariff [*British*] (DCTA)
SST .... Susitna [*Alaska*] [*Seismograph station code, US Geological Survey*] [*Closed*] (SEIS)
SST .... Synchronous System Trap
SST .... System Segment Table
SST .... System Survey Team [*Military*] (AFIT)
SST .... Systems Support Tape
SST .... Target and Training Submarine [*Self-propelled*] [*Navy symbol*]
SSTA .... Secondary School Theatre Association [*Inactive*] (EA)
SSTA .... Support System Task Analysis (AAG)
SSTADS .... Small Ship Typhoon Air Defense System (MCD)
SSTAR ...... Society for Sex Therapy and Research (EA)
SSTC .... Secondary School Theatre Conference [*Later, SSTA*] (EA)
SSTC .... Ship System Test Contractor (MCD)
SSTC .... Single-Sideband Transmitted Carrier (IEEE)
SSTC .... Solid-State Timer-Controller
SSTC .... Space Shuttle Test Conductor [*NASA*] (NASA)
SSTC .... Spacecraft System Test Console [*NASA*]
SSTC .... Specialized System Test Contractor
SSTC .... Summary of Supplemental Type Certificates
SSTD .... Surface Ship Torpedo Defense [*Navy*] (CAAL)
SSTDC ...... Society of Stage Directors and Choreographers (EA)
SST-DMA .. Satellite Switched Time Division Multiple Access
SSTDMA .. Spacecraft Switched Time Division Multiple Access [*Telecommunications*]
SS/TDMA ... Spread Spectrum/Time Division Multiple Access (MCD)
SSTDS .... Small Ship Tactical Data System [*Navy*] (CAAL)
SSTEP .... System Support Test Evaluation Program
SSTF .... Saturn Static Test Facility [*NASA*]
SSTF .... Shortest Seek Time First
SSTF .... Space Shuttle Task Force [*NASA*]
SSTF .... Space Simulation Test Facility (AAG)
SSTF .... Space Station Task Force [*NASA*]
SSTG .... Ship Service Turbo Generator (MSA)
SSTG .... Space Shuttle Task Group [*NASA*] (KSC)
SSTG .... Special Service Training Group [*World War II*]
SSTI .... Serikat Sekerdja Topografi Indonesia [*Indonesian Topography Employees' Union*]
SSTIR .... Sea Surface Temperature Imaging Radiometer
SSTIXS ..... Small Ship Teletype Information Exchange System [*or Subsystem*] (MCD)
SSTJA .... Solid State Journal [*A publication*]
SSTL .... Solid State Track Link [*TOW*] (MCD)
SSTLA ...... Strip Shunt Transmission Line Antenna [*Aviation*] (AIA)
SSTM .... SAGE [*Semiautomatic Ground Environment*] System Training Mission
SSTM .... Single Service Training Manager (MCD)
SSTM .... System Support Technical Manager [*Navy*] (NG)
SSTMS ...... Standard Supply Transportation Manifest System
SSTO .... Single Stage to Orbit [*NASA*]
SSTO .... Superintending Sea Transport Officer [*British military*] (DMA)
SSTO .... Systonetics, Inc. [*Fullerton, CA*] [*NASDAQ symbol*] (NQ)
SSTP .... Student Science Training Program [*National Science Foundation*] [*Defunct*]
SSTP .... Subsystems Test Procedure (KSC)
SSTP .... Supersonic Transport Panel [*International Civil Aviation Organization*]

SSTR .... Senior Staff Technical Representative (MCD)
SSTRA ...... Successive Subtraction with Total Recognition Accuracy [*Algorithm*]
SSTRD ...... Special Steels Technical Review [*A publication*]
SSTS .... Signaling and Supervision Techniques Study
SSTS .... Space Surveillance and Tracking System [*Military*]
SST Sver Skogsvaardsforb Tidskr ... SST. Sveriges Skogsvaardsfoerbunds Tidskrift [*A publication*]
SST-T-T .... Sound, Sense, Today, Tomorrow, Thereafter [*Teacher's Guide, published by Department of Transportation, for promoting supersonic travel*]
SSTU .... SAGE [*Semiautomatic Ground Environment*] System Training Unit
SSTU .... Seamless Steel Tubing
SStud .... Shakespeare Studies [*A publication*]
SSTV .... Congregation of Sisters of St. Thomas of Villanova [*Roman Catholic religious order*]
SSTV .... Sea Skimming Test Vehicles
SSTV .... Slow-Scan Television
SSTV .... Submarine Shock Test Vehicle
SStW .... Synoptische Studien fuer A. Wikenhauser [*1953*] [*A publication*] (BJA)
SSU .... San Pedro Sula [*Honduras*] [*Seismograph station code, US Geological Survey*] (SEIS)
SSU .... Saybolt Seconds Universal [*Oil viscosity*]
SSU .... Self-Service Unit
SSU .... Semiconductor Storage Unit [*Data processing*]
SSU .... Sensor Simulator Unit
SSU .... Sight Survey Unit
SSU .... Single Signaling Unit [*Telecommunications*] (TEL)
SSU .... Solvent Service Unit
SSU .... Source Resources Ltd. [*Vancouver Stock Exchange symbol*]
SSU .... Spacecraft Support Unit
SSU .... Special Service Unit [*Military*]
SSU .... Squadron Service Unit [*Aircraft*]
SSU .... Stabilized Sight Unit (MCD)
SSU .... Standard Saybolt Universal [*Oil viscosity*]
SSU .... Statistical Service Unit [*Military*]
SSU .... Strategic Services Unit [*Formerly, OSS*]
SSU .... Stratospheric Sounding Unit [*Telecommunications*] (TEL)
SSU .... Subscriber Switching Unit [*Telecommunications*] (TEL)
SSU .... Subsequent Signal Unit [*Group of BITS*] [*Telecommunications*] (TEL)
SSU .... Sunday School Union
SSU .... Surface Screen Unit [*Navy*] (NVT)
SSU .... Switch Selector Update
SSU .... System Selector Unit
SSU .... System Support Unification (MCD)
SSU .... University of Saskatchewan, Saskatoon, Saskatchewan [*Library symbol*] [*National Library of Canada*] (NLC)
SSU .... White Sulphur Springs, WV [*Location identifier*] [*FAA*] (FAAL)
SSUEM ..... Uranerz Exploration & Mining Ltd., Saskatoon, Saskatchewan [*Library symbol*] [*National Library of Canada*] (NLC)
SSUF .... Sprakvetenskapliga Sallskapets i Uppsala Foerhandlingar [*A publication*]
SSUGP ...... Government Publications, University of Saskatchewan, Saskatoon, Saskatchewan [*Library symbol*] [*National Library of Canada*] (NLC)
SSUJD ...... [*The*] Right Honourable John G. Diefenbaker Centre, University of Saskatchewan, Saskatoon, Saskatchewan [*Library symbol*] [*National Library of Canada*] (NLC)
SSUL .... Law Library, University of Saskatchewan, Saskatoon, Saskatchewan [*Library symbol*] [*National Library of Canada*] (NLC)
SSULS ...... Lutheran Seminary, University of Saskatchewan, Saskatoon, Saskatchewan [*Library symbol*] [*National Library of Canada*] (NLC)
SSUM .... Medical Library, University of Saskatchewan, Saskatoon, Saskatchewan [*Library symbol*] [*National Library of Canada*] (NLC)
SSUMC ..... Ukrainian Museum of Canada, Saskatoon, Saskatchewan [*Library symbol*] [*National Library of Canada*] (NLC)
SSUR .... Springfield Sunday Union and Republican [*A publication*]
SSURADS ... Shipboard Surveillance RADAR System (MCD)
SSUS .... Spin-Stabilized Upper Stage [*NASA*] (NASA)
SSUS .... Spinning Solid Upper Stage (RDA)
SSUS .... System Support Unification Subsystem (MCD)
SSUSA ...... Special Staff, United States Army
SSUS-A .... Spinning Solid Upper Stage - Atlas Class Spacecraft (MCD)
SSUS-D .... Spinning Solid Upper Stage - Delta Class Spacecraft (MCD)
SSUSN ...... Society of Sponsors of the United States Navy (EA)
SSUSP ...... Spinning Solid Upper Stage Project (MCD)
SSUTC ...... Special Service Unit Training Center [*World War II*]
SSV .... Satellite Servicing Vehicle
SSV .... Seraphic Society for Vocations [*Defunct*] (EA)
SSV .... Sheep Seminal Vesicle
SSV .... Ship-to-Surface Vessel
SSV .... Simian Sarcoma Virus [*Also, SiSV*]
SSV .... Small Synaptic Vesicle [*Neurobiology*]
SSV .... Space Shuttle Vehicle [*NASA*]

SSV........... Spool Selector Valve
SSV........... Static Self-Verification
SSV........... Sub Signo Veneni [*Under a Poison Label*] [*Pharmacy*]
SSV........... Subjective Scale Value
SSV........... Sumac Ventures, Inc. [*Vancouver Stock Exchange symbol*]
SSV........... Supersatellite Vehicle
SSV........... Supersonic Test Vehicles
SSV........... Sydslesvigsk Vaelgerforening [*South Schleswig Voters' Association*] [*Also, SSW*] [*Federal Republic of Germany*] [*Political party*] (PPW)
SSVA........ Signal Susceptibility and Vulnerability Assessment [*Military*] (CAAL)
SSVB .... Security Savings Bank FSB [*NASDAQ symbol*] (NQ)
SSVC........ Selective Service [*Military*]
SSVC........ Services Sound and Video Corp. [*British*]
SSVE .... Subacute Spongiform Virus Encephalopathies [*Medicine*]
SSVF......... Straits Settlements Volunteer Force [*British military*] (DMA)
SSV/GC & N ... Space Shuttle Vehicle/Guidance, Control, and Navigation [*NASA*]
SSVM........ Self-Scaling Variable Metric [*Algorithms*] [*Data processing*]
SsvOA........ Sydsvenska Ortnamns-Saellskapets Arsskrift [*A publication*]
SSVP......... Society of St. Vincent De Paul [*Paris, France*] (EAIO)
SSVP .... Soviet Ship Vulnerability Program
SSVS......... Slow-Scan Video Simulator
SSV-SSAV ... Simian Sarcoma Virus-Simian Sarcoma Associated Virus [*Complex*]
SSW........... Safety Switch
SSW........... St. Louis Southwestern Railway Co. [*AAR code*]
SSW........... Save the Strippers Wells (EA)
SSW........... Secretary of State for War [*British*]
SSW........... Senior Social Worker (ADA)
SSW........... Sense Switch [*Military*] (AFIT)
SSW........... Siemens-Schuckert Werke [*Germany*]
SSW........... Solid-State Welding
SSW........... South-Southwest
SSW........... Space Switch [*Telecommunications*] (TEL)
SSW........... Staggered Spondaic Word
SSW........... Standby Service Water [*Nuclear energy*] (NRCH)
SSW........... Sterling Software, Inc. [*NYSE symbol*] (SPSG)
SSW........... Suedschleswigscher Waehlerverband [*South Schleswig Voter's League*] [*Also, SSV*] [*Federal Republic of Germany*] [*Political party*] (PPE)
SSW........... Surface Science Western [*University of Western Ontario*] [*Research center*] (RCD)
SSW........... Surface Strike Warfare [*Navy*] (CAAL)
SSW........... Swept Square Wave (MCD)
SSW........... Synchro Switch [*Electronics*]
SSW........... Systems West Consultants Ltd. [*Vancouver Stock Exchange symbol*]
SSW........... Wheatland Regional Library, Saskatoon, Saskatchewan [*Library symbol*] [*National Library of Canada*] (NLC)
SSWA........ Sanitary Supply Wholesalers Association (EA)
SSWC....... Surface/Subsurface Warfare Coordinator [*Navy*] (CAAL)
SSWD....... Single, Separated, Widowed, or Divorced
SSWD....... Western Development Museum, Saskatoon, Saskatchewan [*Library symbol*] [*National Library of Canada*] (NLC)
SSWF .... Sudden Shortwave Fade
SSWG .... System Safety Working Group
SSWLH..... Society for the Study of Women in Legal History (EA)
SSWM...... Standing Spin Wave Mode (MCD)
SSWM...... Superimposed Surface Wave Modes
SSWO...... Special Service Work Order [*Telecommunications*] (TEL)
SSWP .... Station Service Water Pump [*Nuclear energy*] (NRCH)
SSWRN..... South-Southwestern [*Meteorology*] (FAAC)
SSWS....... Standby Service Water System [*Nuclear energy*] (NRCH)
SSWU....... Singapore Sawmill Workers' Union
SSWWD.... South-Southwestward [*Meteorology*] (FAAC)
SSWWS..... Seismic Sea-Wave Warning System
SSX........... Samsun [*Turkey*] [*Airport symbol*] (OAG)
SSX........... Space Ship Experimental
SSX........... SS1 [*Nevada*] [*Seismograph station code, US Geological Survey*] [*Closed*] (SEIS)
SSX........... Submarines, Experimental
SSX........... Sulfisoxazole [*An antibiotic*]
SSXBT....... Submarine Expendable Bathythermograph [*Marine science*] (MSC)
S & Sx Yeo ... Surrey and Sussex Yeomanry [*British military*] (DMA)
SSY........... M'Banza Congo [*Angola*] [*Airport symbol*] (OAG)
SSY........... Sharpshooters Yeomanry [*British military*] (DMA)
SSY........... Silver Strike Resources [*Vancouver Stock Exchange symbol*]
SSY........... South Somerset Yeomanry [*British military*] (DMA)
SSYS......... Sterling Medical Systems, Inc. [*NASDAQ symbol*] (NQ)
S/SYS....... Subsystem (NASA)
SSZ........... Pocket Submarine (NATG)
SSZ........... Saigon Special Zone [*Military*]
SSZ........... Samos Resources, Inc. [*Vancouver Stock Exchange symbol*]
SSZ........... Sea Scout Zero - Nonrigid Airship [*Royal Naval Air Service*] [*British*]
SSZ........... Society of Systematic Zoology (EA)
SSZ........... Specified Strike Zone [*Army*] (AABC)

SSZBA....... Sbornik Vysoke Skoly Zemedelske v Brne. Rada B [*A publication*]
St................ C. H. Boehringer Sohn, Ingelheim [*Germany*] [*Research code symbol*]
St................ E. Merck AG [*Germany*] [*Research code symbol*]
ST .... Journal of Structural Engineering [*A publication*]
ST .... Missionarii Servi Sanctissimae Trinitatis [*Missionary Servants of the Most Holy Trinity*] [*Roman Catholic men's religious order*]
ST .... Saddle Tank [*Trains*] [*British*]
ST .... Safety Tool (MCD)
ST .... Saint (EY)
ST .... St. Lawrence Cement, Inc. [*Toronto Stock Exchange symbol*]
ST .... Sainte
ST .... Sales Tax
ST .... Sales Tax Branch, United States Internal Revenue Bureau (DLA)
ST .... Sales Tax Rulings, United States Internal Revenue Bureau [*A publication*] (DLA)
ST .... Sample Tube
ST .... Sanitary Towel [*British*] (DSUE)
ST .... Sao Tome and Principe [*ANSI two-letter standard code*] (CNC)
ST .... Save the Theaters (EA)
ST .... Sawtooth [*Architecture*]
ST .... Scalar Totalizer
ST .... Scalloped Tinned [*Configuration*] (MCD)
ST .... Schmitt Trigger [*Electronics*]
ST .... Schuler Tuning
S & T......... Science and Technology (NATG)
ST .... Sclerotherapy [*Medicine*]
ST .... Screw Terminal
ST .... Seaman Torpedoman [*Obsolete*] [*Navy*]
S/T............. Search/Track
ST .... Seat
ST .... Secretary/Treasurer [*or Secretary and Treasurer*]
ST .... Sedimentation Time
ST .... Self-Test
ST .... Self-Toning [*Paper*] [*Photography*] (ROG)
ST .... Semitendinosus [*Muscle*]
ST .... Senior Teacher (ADA)
ST .... Sensitivity Training
ST .... Senza Tempo [*Without Regard to Time*] [*Music*]
ST .... Sequence Timer
ST .... Service Tabulating (AAG)
ST .... Service Test [*Military*]
ST .... Service Tools (AAG)
ST .... Set Trigger
ST .... Shares Time With [*Broadcasting term*]
S/T............. Shelter Taxi [*NASA*] (KSC)
ST .... Ship Trial (MCD)
ST .... Shipping Ticket [*Military*]
ST .... Shock Tube
ST .... Shock Tunnel
ST .... Shoot Tip [*Botany*]
ST .... Short-Term Stay [*in hospital*] [*British*]
ST .... Short Ton [*2000 lbs.*]
ST .... Short Tour [*Military*]
ST .... Shorthand Writer [*British military*] (DMA)
ST .... Shrink Template
ST .... Side Tank [*on a ship*] (DS)
ST .... Sidetone [*Telecommunications*] (TEL)
ST .... Sigma Tau [*Later, Tau Beta Pi Association*]
ST .... Signes du Temps [*A publication*]
ST .... Silent [*Films, television, etc.*]
ST .... Silicon Tube
ST .... Silicotungstate [*Inorganic chemistry*]
ST .... Simhat Torah (BJA)
ST .... Simplification Task (MCD)
S & T......... Simulation and Training
ST .... Simulator Training
st................. Sine Tempore [*At the Time Announced*] [*Latin*]
ST .... Single Throw [*Switch*]
ST .... Single Tire
ST .... Single Turn (MSA)
ST .... Sinus Tachycardia [*Cardiology*]
ST .... Skill Technical (INF)
ST .... Skin Test
ST .... Skin Track (MUGU)
S & T......... Sky and Telescope [*A publication*]
ST .... Sleeping Time
ST .... Slide and Tape
ST .... Slight Trace
ST .... Slovo a Tvar [*A publication*]
ST .... Societe Theosophique [*Theosophical Society*]
ST .... Society for Theriogenology (EA)
ST .... Solar Thermal [*Energy source*]
ST .... SONAR Technician [*Navy rating*]
S/T............. Sonic Telegraphy
ST .... Sons of Temperance
S of T......... Sons of Temperance
ST .... Sounding Tube

ST	Space Telescope [*NASA*]
ST	Space-Time
ST	Spacelab Technology [*NASA*] (NASA)
ST	Spasmodic Torticollis [*Medicine*]
ST	Special Test
ST	Special Text [*Military*]
ST	Special Translation
ST	Speech Teacher [*A publication*]
ST	Speech Therapist
ST	Speed Transmitter (NRCH)
ST	Springfield Terminal Railway Co. [*AAR code*]
ST	SPS Technologies, Inc. [*Formerly, Standard Pressed Steel Co.*] [*NYSE symbol*] (SPSG)
ST	Stable
ST	Stage
St	Stair's Decisions, Scotch Court of Session [*A publication*] (DLA)
St	Stair's Institutes [*5th ed.*] [*1832*] [*A publication*] (DLA)
St	Stamen [*Botany*]
ST	Stamped [*Stock exchange term*] (SPSG)
ST	Standard
ST	Standard Time
ST	Standardized Test [*Psychology*]
ST	Standby Time (MCD)
St	Stanton Number [*IUPAC*]
ST	Stanza
St	Star [*Johannesburg*] [*A publication*]
ST	Star Tracker [*NASA*] (AAG)
ST	Starboard Flag [*Navy*] [*British*]
ST	Start
S/T	Start Tank (AAG)
ST	Start Timing
ST	Starter (MCD)
ST	State
ST	State Trials [*Legal*] [*British*]
ST	Static (KSC)
ST	Static Test
ST	Static Thrust
ST	Statim [*Immediately*] [*Latin*] (ROG)
ST	Station [*Medicine*]
ST	Statistisk Tabelvaerk [*Denmark*]
ST	Statsoekonomisk Tidsskrift [*A publication*]
ST	Statt [*Instead Of*] [*German*]
ST	Status
ST	Statute
ST	Steam (AAG)
ST	Steam Tanker
ST	Steam Trawler
ST	Steam Tug
ST	Steam Turbine (MCD)
ST	Steamer (ROG)
ST	Steel [*Technical drawings*]
ST	Steel Truss [*Bridges*]
ST	Stem [*Linguistics*] [*Botany*]
ST	Stencil
ST	Stenographer [*British military*] (DMA)
S & T	Stenographer and Typist [*Examination*] [*Civil Service Commission*]
st	Stere [*Metric measure of volume*]
ST	Stereo [*A publication*]
St	Stereo Review [*A publication*]
ST	Stereocilia [*Zoology*]
ST	Stern Thruster [*Type of ship*] (DS)
ST	Sternothyroid [*Anatomy*]
ST	Sternotomy [*Medicine*]
ST	Stet [*Let It Stand*] [*Latin*]
ST	Stichting Tool [*Tool Foundation - TF*] [*Amsterdam, Netherlands*] (EAIO)
ST	Sticky Type [*Bomb*]
ST	Stigma [*Botany*]
ST	Stimulus [*Medicine*]
ST	Stinson [*ICAO aircraft manufacturer identifier*] (ICAO)
ST	Stitch
ST	Stock Transfer
St	Stokes [*Unit of kinematic viscosity*]
ST	Stone [*Unit of weight*]
ST	Stone Roller [*Ichthyology*]
St	Stones [*Quality of the bottom*] [*Nautical charts*]
ST	Stony Soil [*Agronomy*]
ST	Stop Tap
ST	Stop-Transfer [*Genetics*]
ST	Storage Tube
ST	Store (AAG)
ST	Stored Time
S & T	Storm and Tempest (ADA)
ST	Story (ROG)
St	Story's United States Circuit Court Reports [*A publication*] (DLA)
ST	Stotinki [*Monetary unit*] [*Bulgaria*]
ST	Strad [*A publication*]
S/T	Straight Time

ST	Strait
St	Strannik: Dukhovnyi, Ucheno-Literaturnyi Zhurnal [*A publication*]
ST	Straps [*JETDS nomenclature*] [*Military*] (CET)
ST	Strategic Transport [*Aircraft*] [*Military*]
S & T	Strategy and Tactics [*A publication*]
St	Stratosphere
ST	Stratus [*Meteorology*]
ST	Street (EY)
ST	Stress Testing [*Medicine*]
S-T	Strict [*Medicine*]
S-T	Strip-Tin (MSA)
ST	Stroma [*Medicine*]
ST	Strophe [*Poetry*] (ROG)
ST	Structural (NASA)
ST	Structure Tee (AAG)
St	Stuart, Milne, and Peddie's Scotch Court of Session Cases [*A publication*] (DLA)
ST	Student's t-Test [*Statistical mathematics*]
ST	Studi Tassiani [*A publication*]
ST	Studi e Testi [*A publication*]
ST	Studia Taiwanica [*A publication*]
ST	Studia Theologica [*A publication*]
St	Studies [*A publication*]
ST	Studies in Theology [*A publication*]
St	Studium [*A publication*]
ST	Stumped [*Cricket*]
St	Styrene [*Also, Sty*] [*Organic chemistry*]
ST	Substitution Theorem [*Logic*]
st	Subtelocentric [*Botany*]
ST	Subtentacular [*Zoology*]
ST	Sudan [*Aircraft nationality and registration mark*] (FAAC)
ST	Sulfotransferase [*An enzyme*]
ST	Summer Time [*Daylight saving time*]
ST	Sunday Telegraph [*A publication*] (APTA)
ST	Sunday Times [*United Kingdom*] [*A publication*]
ST	Super Tampella [*Explosive*] (INF)
ST	Superintendent of Transportation
S of T	Superintendent of Transportation
ST	Supplementary Term [*Online database field identifier*]
S & T	Supply and Transport [*Military*]
S & T	Supply and Transport Corps [*British*] (DMA)
ST	Supporting Technologies [*Military*] (RDA)
ST	Surface Target [*Navy*] (CAAL)
ST	Surface Tension
ST	Surface Tracker [*Navy*] (CAAL)
ST	Surgical Technician
ST	Surveillance Test (NATG)
ST	Survival Time
ST	Svensk Tidskrift [*A publication*]
S & T	Swabey and Tristram's Probate and Divorce Reports [*1858-65*] [*A publication*] (DLA)
ST	Swept Tone
ST	Symmetrical TOKAMAK
ST	System Response Time [*Computer order entry*]
ST	System Test
ST	Szondi Test [*Psychology*]
ST	Tradewinds Pte. Ltd. [*Great Britain*] [*ICAO designator*] (FAAC)
St	United States Statutes at Large [*A publication*] (DLA)
ST1	SONAR Technician, First Class [*Navy rating*]
ST2	SONAR Technician, Second Class [*Navy rating*]
ST3	SONAR Technician, Third Class [*Navy rating*]
STA	S-Band Test Antenna
STA	Sail Training Association (EA)
STA	Sales Transaction Audit [*Test*]
STA	Santa [*Saint*] [*Italian*]
STA	Satara [*India*] [*Seismograph station code, US Geological Survey*] [*Closed*] (SEIS)
STA	Satellite Tracking Annex (MUGU)
STA	Science and Technology Agent (SDI)
STA	Securities Transfer Association (EA)
STA	Security Traders Association (EA)
STA	Serum Thrombotic Accelerator [*Serology*]
STA	Serum Thymic-Like Activity [*Biochemistry*]
STA	Servico des Transportes Aereos [*Portuguese West Africa*]
STA	Shift Technical Adviser [*Nuclear energy*] (NRCH)
STA	Shipboard Transmitting Antenna
STA	Shore-Based Transmitting Antenna
STA	Short-Term Arrangements [*Department of State*]
STA	Short-Term Averaging (CAAL)
STA	Short-Terms Abroad
STA	Shuttle Training Aircraft [*NASA*]
STA	Sialyltransferase Activity [*Medicine*]
STA	Single Target Attack
STA	Skills Training Agency [*British*]
STA	Slaving Torquer Amplifier
STA	Slurry Technology Association [*Later, CSTA*] (EA)
STA	Small Tactical Airlifter [*Military*] [*British*]
STA	Society of Typographic Arts [*Later, ACD*] (EA)
STA	Softening Temperature of Ash

STA............ Solution Treat and Age [Metals]
STA............ Southern Textile Association (EA)
STA............ Space Technology Applications
STA............ Special Temporary Authorization [FCC]
STA............ Stacia Ventures [Vancouver Stock Exchange symbol]
STA............ Staff Training Assistant [Army] (AABC)
STA............ Stagger Tuned Antenna
STA............ Staley Continental, Inc. [NYSE symbol] (SPSG)
STA............ Stamped
STA............ Star Aviation Corp. [Denver, CO] [FAA designator] (FAAC)
STA............ Stara Dala [Czechoslovakia] [Later, HRB] [Geomagnetic observatory code]
STA............ State Technical Assistance (OICC)
STA............ State Transit Authority [New South Wales, Australia]
Sta............ Statham's Abridgment [A publication] (DSA)
STA............ Static Test Article (NASA)
STA............ Station [Telecommunications]
STA............ Stationary (MSA)
STA............ Status [Online database field identifier] (AABC)
STA............ Stauning [Denmark] [Airport symbol] (OAG)
STA............ Steel Carriers Tariff Association, Inc., East Riverdale MD [STAC]
STA............ Steel Tape Armored [Cables]
STA............ Stock Transfer Association [New York, NY] (EA)
STA............ Store Accumulator
STA............ Straight-In Approach [Aviation] (FAAC)
STA............ Strange Adventures [A publication]
STA............ Structural Test Article (NASA)
StA............ Studi Anselmiana [A publication]
St A............ Studia Archaeologica [A publication]
STA............ Submarine Tender Availability
STA............ Sunday Telegraph (Australia) [A publication]
STA............ Superficial Temporal Artery [Anatomy]
STA............ Superior Temporal Artery [Anatomy]
STA............ Supersonic Tunnel Association (EA)
STA............ Survival in Target Area (MCD)
STA............ Swedish Telecommunications Administration [Telecommunications] (TSSD)
STA............ Swimming Teachers' Association [British]
STA............ Syrie et Monde Arabe. Etude Mensuelle Economique, Politique, et Statistique [A publication]
STA............ Systems Test Area
STA............ University of Santa Clara, Orradre Library, Santa Clara, CA [OCLC symbol] (OCLC)
STAA......... Soldiers Total Abstinence Association [British military] (DMA)
STAA......... Staar Surgical Co. [NASDAQ symbol] (NQ)
STAA......... Surface Transportation Assistance Act [1978]
STAACT J ... STAACT [Science Teachers Association of the Australian Capital Territory] Journal [A publication] (APTA)
STAAD...... Submarine Tender Availability Arrival/Departure [Obsolete]
STAAF....... Study to Align AMC [Now DAR COM] Functions (MCD)
STAAG...... Standard Tachymetric Anti-Aircraft Gun [British military] (DMA)
STAAS ...... Surveillance and Target Acquisition Aircraft System (AFM)
Staat u Recht ... Staat und Recht [A publication]
Staatsanz Baden-Wuerttemb ... Staatsanzeiger fuer Baden-Wuerttemberg [A publication]
Staatsanz Rheinl-Pfalz ... Staatsanzeiger fuer Rheinland-Pfalz [German Federal Republic] [A publication]
Staatsbl...... Belgisch Staatsblad [A publication]
Staatsblad K Ned ... Staatsblad van het Koninkrijk der Nederlanden [A publication]
Staatsbl Koninkrijk Ned ... Staatsblad van het Koninkrijk der Nederlanden [A publication]
Staatsbuerger-Beil Bayer Staatsztg ... Staatsbuerger-Beilage der Bayerischen Staatszeitung [A publication]
Staatsverw ... Roemische Staatsverwaltung [A publication] (OCD)
Staat und Wirt in Hessen ... Staat und Wirtschaft in Hessen [A publication]
STAB......... Space, Time, and Beyond [Dance work choreographed by Marie Chouinard]
STAB......... Squadron Tactical Analysis Board [Military] (CAAL)
STAB......... Stabilize [or Stabilizer] [Aviation] (AAG)
STAB......... Standby Advisory Board [Army] (INF)
St Ab......... Statham's Abridgment [A publication] (DLA)
STAB......... Strike Assault Boat [Navy symbol]
STAB......... Supersonic Tests of Aerodynamic Bombs (MUGU)
STAB......... Supersonic Transport Advisory Board
STABEX.... Stabilization of Export Earnings [Program of the EEC]
StAbs......... Status Absolutus
STABS....... Suinn Test Anxiety Behavior Scale [Psychology]
Sta Bull Oreg State Coll Agr Exp Sta ... Station Bulletin. Oregon State College. Agricultural Experiment Station [A publication]
Sta Bull Univ Minn Agr Exp Sta ... Station Bulletin. University of Minnesota. Agricultural Experiment Station [A publication]
STABY ...... Stability (MSA)
STAC........ Science and Technology Advisory Committee [NASA] (MCD)
STAC........ Software Timing and Control
STAC........ Southern Technology Applications Center [NASA] [University of Florida] [Gainesville] [Information service or system] (IID)

STAC......... Staccato [Detached, Distinct] [Music]
STAC......... Standard Tariff Agents Code
STAC......... Submarine-to-Aircraft Communications
STAC......... Surface Target Attack Comparison Model (MCD)
STACC ..... Staccato [Detached, Distinct] [Music]
Sta Circ Wash Agr Exp Sta ... Station Circular. Washington Agricultural Experiment Station [A publication]
STACO...... Standing Committee for the Study of Scientific Principles of Standardization [ISO]
STACOM ... Standard Army Commissary Operating Manual
STACOM ... State Criminal Justice Communications
STACRES ... Standing Committee on Research and Statistics [UN Food and Agriculture Organization]
STACS...... Subtropical Atlantic Climate Studies [National Oceanic and Atmospheric Administration]
STACWV .. Standing Technical Advisory Committee on Water Quality [Department of the Environment] [British]
STAD........ Start Address [Telecommunications] (TEL)
STAD........ Submarine Tender Availability Document
STADAC ... Station Data Acquisition and Control [NASA] (NASA)
STADACOL ... Statistical Data Collection Program
STADAD... Satellite Tracking and Data Acquisition Department
STADAN... Satellite Tracking and Data Acquisition Network [Later, STDN]
STADAN... Space Tracking and Data Acquisition Network
STADD...... Ship-Towed Acoustic Deception Device (MCD)
Staden-Jb.. Staden-Jahrbuch [A publication]
STADES.... Standard Army Data Elements Systems (MCD)
STADES.... Standard Data Elements System (MCD)
STADIN .... Standing Administrative Instruction for Army Attaches (AABC)
STADINAIR ... Standing Administrative Instruction for Air Attaches (AFM)
Stadler Genet Symp ... Stadler Genetics Symposia [A publication]
St Adm NS ... Stuart's Lower Canada Vice-Admiralty Reports, New Series [A publication] (DLA)
STADMR .... Station Administrator [Aviation] (FAAC)
Stadt- Gebaeudetech ... Stadt- und Gebaeudetechnik [German Democratic Republic] [A publication]
Stadt-LB ... Stadt- und Landesbibliothek [A publication]
Stadt (Wien) ... Informationsdienst der Stadt (Wien) [A publication]
STADU...... System Termination and Display Unit (MCD)
STA-DYNULSIMU ... Static-Dynamic Ullage Simulation Unit
Stad Z .... Stadion. Zeitschrift fuer Geschichte des Sports und der Koerperkultur [A publication]
STAE......... Second Time Around Echo
STAE......... Specify Task Asynchronous Exit [Data processing]
Staedel Jb .. Staedel-Jahrbuch [A publication]
St Aeg .... Studia Aegyptiaca [A publication]
STAEP ...... Scientific and Technical Assessment of Environmental Pollutants [Marine science] (MSC)
STAESA.... Society of Turkish Architects, Engineers, and Scientists in America (EA)
StAeVO ..... Steueraenderungsverordnung [Tax Amendment Decree] [German]
STAF .... St. Thomas Aquinas Foundation (EA)
STAF .... Science Team Analysis Facility [NASA]
STAF .... Scientific and Technical Application Forecasts
STAF .... Staff Builders, Inc. [NASDAQ symbol] (NQ)
STA/F........ Standard Access and Format [Reference Technology, Inc. software]
STAFDA ... Specialty Tools and Fasteners Distributors Association (EA)
STAFEX .... Staff Exercises [NATO] (NATG)
STAFF....... Smart Target-Activated Fire and Forget [Antitank weapon system] (RDA)
STAFF....... Staffordshire [County in England]
STAFF....... Stellar Acquisition Flight Feasibility
Staff J (University of Reading) ... Staff Journal (University of Reading) [A publication]
Stafford...... Stafford's Reports [69-71 Vermont] [A publication] (DLA)
Staffordshire Archaeol ... Staffordshire Archaeology [A publication]
Staff Pap .... Staff Papers [A publication]
Staff Pap P Minn Univ Dep Agric Appl Econ ... Staff Paper P. Minnesota University. Department of Agricultural and Applied Economics [A publication]
Staff Pap Univ Florida Food Resour Econ Dep ... Staff Paper. University of Florida. Food and Resources Economics Department [A publication]
STAFFS .... Staffordshire [County in England]
STAFS....... Sugar, Tobacco, Alcohol, Fat, and Salt
STAFT....... Steerable Antenna Focusing Technique
STAG........ Security Tag Systems, Inc. [NASDAQ symbol] (NQ)
STAG........ Shuttle Turnaround Analysis Group [NASA] (NASA)
STAG........ Skills Training Adjustment Group [Educational project sponsored by The Hartford]
STAG........ Special Task Air Group
STAG........ Standards Technical Advisory Group
STAG........ Steam and Gas [Turbine]
STAG........ Straight-Talking American Government [Comedian Pat Paulsen's political party]
STAG........ Strategy and Tactics Analysis Group [Later, Concepts Analysis Agency] [Army] (KSC)

STAG......... Student Agitation [*FBI*]
STAG......... Submarine-Rocket Technical Advisory Group
STAGD...... Syndicat des Travailleurs de l'Administration Generale du Dahomey [*Dahomean Union of General Administration Workers*]
STAGE...... Simulated Total Atomic Global Exchange [*DoD*]
STAGG...... Small-Turbine Advanced Gas Generator
STAG-MAG ... Stage Manager [*Theater term*] (DSUE)
STAGN...... Stagnation [*Meteorology*] (FAAC)
STAGS ...... Simulated Tank and Antiarmor Gunnery System (INF)
STAGS ...... Structural Analysis of General Shells
STAGS ...... Swedish Tank Agility/Survivability Test (MCD)
STAGS-D.. Simulated Tank Antiarmor Gunnery System - Dragon [*Army*] (INF)
St A H .... Studies in American Humor [*A publication*]
STAHA ..... Stahlbau [*A publication*]
Stahlbau Rundsch ... Stahlbau Rundschau [*Austria*] [*A publication*]
Stahlbau Tech ... Stahlbau-Technik [*A publication*]
Stahlia Misc Pap ... Stahlia Miscellaneous Papers [*A publication*]
STAI......... State-Trait Anxiety Inventory [*Psychology*]
STAI......... Subtask ABEND [*Abnormal End*] Intercept [*Data processing*] (BUR)
STAI......... Systems Technology Associates, Incorporated [*Sterling, VA*] [*NASDAQ symbol*] (NQ)
STAIC .... State-Trait Anxiety Inventory for Children [*Psychology*]
STAID....... Station Identification
Stainless Steel Ind ... Stainless Steel Industry [*A publication*]
Stainl Steel ... Stainless Steel [*South Africa*] [*A publication*]
Stain Tech ... Stain Technology [*A publication*]
Stain Technol ... Stain Technology [*A publication*]
Stair .... Stair's Decisions of the Lords of Council and Session [*1661-81*] [*Scotland*] [*A publication*] (DLA)
STAIR ...... Structural Analysis Interpretive Routine
Stair I........ Stair's Institutes [*5 eds.*] [*1681-1832*] [*A publication*] (DLA)
Stair Inst.... Stair's Institutes [*5 eds.*] [*1681-1832*] [*A publication*] (DLA)
Stair Prin ... Stair's Principles of the Laws of Scotland [*A publication*] (DLA)
Stair Rep.... Stair's Decisions, Scotch Court of Session [*A publication*] (DLA)
STAIRS..... Standard Advanced Infrared Sensor [*Military*]
STAIRS..... Storage and Information Retrieval System [*IBM Corp.*]
STAIRS/VS ... Storage and Information Retrieval System/Virtual Storage [*IBM Corp.*]
STAK........ Short Takes, Inc. [*NASDAQ symbol*] (NQ)
STAL......... Screening Test of Adolescent Language [*Educational test*]
STAL......... Stalactite/Stalagmite Formation (DSUE)
STALAG ... Stammlager [*Prisoner-of-war camp*] [*German*]
STALAGLUFT ... Stammlagerluft [*Prisoner-of-war camp for airmen*] [*German*]
STALAS ... Stationary LASER Site [*NASA*]
Stal Elect ... Stalman on Election and Satisfaction [*1827*] [*A publication*] (DLA)
Staleplavil'n Proizvod ... Staleplavil'noe Proizvodstvo [*A publication*]
Staleplavil'n Proizvod (Moscow) ... Staleplavil'noe Proizvodstvo (Moscow) [*A publication*]
Stal Nemet Vklyucheniya ... Stal'e Nemetallicheskie Vklyucheniya [*A publication*]
STALO...... Stabilized Local Oscillator [*RADAR*]
STALOG.... Study of Automation of the Logistic System [*Military*]
STALOS.... Stabilized Tunable Local Oscillator
STALPETH ... Steel, Aluminum, Polyethylene [*Components of a type of telecommunications cable*]
STAL Sci Tech Anim Lab ... STAL. Sciences et Techniques de l'Animal de Laboratoire [*A publication*]
St Altaeg Kul ... Studien zur Altaegyptischen Kultur [*A publication*]
STaM........ Sefer Torah. Tefillin. Mezuzah
STAM........ Shared Tape Allocation Manager
STAM........ Statistics in Medicine [*A publication*]
STAM........ Submarine Tactical Advanced Missile (MCD)
STAM........ Superintendent of Technical Applications of Metals [*Ministry of Supply*] [*British*] [*World War II*]
STAM........ Surface Target Acquisition Model (MCD)
STAM........ System Telecommunications Access Method [*NCR Corp.*]
STAMAT .. Schaie-Thurstone Adult Mental Abilities Test [*Intelligence test*] [*Psychology*]
STAMIC ... Set Theory Analysis and Measure of Information Characteristics
STAMINRQ ... Status During Minimize Required (MCD)
STAMIS.... Standard Army Management Information System
STAMM.... Systematic Teaching and Measuring Mathematics [*Education*]
STAMMIS ... Standard Army Multicommand Management Information System (MCD)
STAMNI ... Sonic True Airspeed and Mach Number Indicator
STAMO..... Stable Master Oscillator
STAMOS .. Sortie Turn Around Maintenance Operations Simulation [*NASA*] (KSC)
STAMP..... Satellite Telecommunications Analysis and Modeling Program
STAMP..... Small Tactical Aerial Mobility Platform [*Proposed*] [*Marine Corps*]
STAMP..... Space Technology Analysis and Mission Planning (MCD)
STAMP..... Standard Air Munitions Package

STAMP ..... Systems Tape Addition and Maintenance Program [*Data processing*] (IEEE)
STAMPED ... Size, Temperature, Application, Material, Pressure, Ends, and Delivery [*To aid selection of industrial hose*]
STAMPEX ... National Stamp Exhibition [*British*] (ITD)
STAMPS... Spectrophotometric Transient Analysis Method for Multiple Positions and Species
St Am Renaissance ... Studies in the American Renaissance [*A publication*]
STAN........ Selectable Two-Area Nozzle (MCD)
STAN........ Stanchion
STAN........ Stanline, Inc. [*Norwalk, CA*] [*NASDAQ symbol*] (NQ)
STAN........ Stanstead [*England*]
STAN........ Sum Total and Nosegear (MCD)
STANA ..... Statistics on the North Atlantic [*Fisheries*] [*UN Food and Agriculture Organization*]
STANAG... Standardization Agreement [*NATO*]
STANAVFORCHAN ... Standing Naval Force, Channel [*NATO*] (NATG)
STANAVFORLANT ... Standing Naval Force, Atlantic [*Activated 1968*] [*NATO*]
STANAVITO ... Syndicat des Travailleurs de Transport et de la Navigation du Togo [*Union of Transport and Navigation Workers of Togo*]
STANB...... Stanborough [*England*]
STANCAL ... Standard Oil Co. of California
STANCHART ... Standard Chartered [*International bank*] [*British*]
STANCIB ... State-Army-Navy Communications Intelligence Board [*Later, USCIB*]
STAND...... Standard
Standard Chartered R ... Standard Chartered Review [*A publication*]
Stand Ass Aust Aust Stand ... Standards Association of Australia. Australian Standard [*A publication*] (APTA)
Stand Ass Aust Commercial Stand ... Standards Association of Australia. Commercial Standard [*A publication*] (APTA)
Stand Ass Aust Miscell Pub ... Standards Association of Australia. Miscellaneous Publication [*A publication*] (APTA)
Stand Bank ... Standard Bank Review [*A publication*]
Stand Chart Rev ... Standard Chartered Review [*London*] [*A publication*]
Stand Ex Prof Tax Rep ... Standard Excess Profits Tax Reporter [*Commerce Clearing House*] [*A publication*]
Stand Fed Tax Rep ... Standard Federal Tax Reporter [*Commerce Clearing House*] [*A publication*] (DLA)
Stand Fed Tax Rep CCH ... Standard Federal Tax Reports. Commerce Clearing House [*A publication*]
Stand GA Prac ... Standard Georgia Practice [*A publication*] (DLA)
Stan Dig ..... Stanton's Kentucky Digest [*A publication*] (DLA)
Stand Kach ... Standarty i Kachestvo [*A publication*]
Stand Methods Clin Chem ... Standard Methods of Clinical Chemistry [*A publication*]
Stand News ... Standardization News [*A publication*]
Stand PA Prac ... Standard Pennsylvania Practice [*A publication*] (DLA)
Stand Philip Per Ind ... Standard Philippine Periodicals Index [*A publication*]
Stand Qual ... Standardisierung und Qualitaet [*German Democratic Republic*] [*A publication*]
St Andrew Univ Sociol R ... St. Andrew's University. Sociological Review [*A publication*]
Stan Env't Ann ... Stanford Environmental Law Annual [*A publication*]
STAN/EVAL ... Standardization/Evaluation
STANFINS ... Standard Financial System [*Military*] (AABC)
Stanf J Int ... Stanford Journal of International Studies [*A publication*]
Stanford ..... Stanford's English Pleas of the Crown [*A publication*] (DLA)
Stanford Fr ... Stanford French Review [*A publication*]
Stanford Ichthyol Bull ... Stanford Ichthyological Bulletin [*A publication*]
Stanford J Internat Law ... Stanford Journal of International Law [*A publication*]
Stanford J Internat Studies ... Stanford Journal of International Studies [*A publication*]
Stanford J Int'l Stud ... Stanford Journal of International Studies [*A publication*]
Stanford J Int Stud ... Stanford Journal of International Studies [*A publication*]
Stanford La ... Stanford Law Review [*A publication*]
Stanford Law R ... Stanford Law Review [*A publication*]
Stanford Law Rev ... Stanford Law Review [*A publication*]
Stanford L Rev ... Stanford Law Review [*A publication*]
Stanford M Bull ... Stanford Medical Bulletin [*A publication*]
Stanford Med Bull ... Stanford Medical Bulletin [*A publication*]
Stanford Research Inst Jour ... Stanford Research Institute. Journal [*A publication*]
Stanford Stud Med Sci ... Stanford Studies in Medical Sciences [*A publication*]
Stanford Stud Psychol ... Stanford Studies in Psychology [*A publication*]
Stanford Univ Dep Civ Eng Tech Rep ... Stanford University. Department of Civil Engineering. Technical Report [*A publication*]
Stanford Univ Dep Mech Eng Tech Rep ... Stanford University. Department of Mechanical Engineering. Technical Report [*A publication*]
Stanford Univ Publ Geol ... Stanford University Publications in the Geological Sciences [*A publication*]
Stanford Univ Publ Geol Sci ... Stanford University. Publications in the Geological Sciences [*A publication*]

Stanford Univ Publ Univ Ser Biol Sci ... Stanford University. Publications. University Series. Biological Sciences [*A publication*]
Stanford Univ Publ Univ Ser Eng ... Stanford University. Publications. University Series. Engineering [*A publication*]
Stanford Univ Publ Univ Ser Math Astron ... Stanford University. Publications. University Series. Mathematics and Astronomy [*A publication*]
Stanford Univ Publ Univ Ser Med Sci ... Stanford University. Publications. University Series. Medical Sciences [*A publication*]
STANINE ... Standard Nine Score [*Military*]
Stan J Intl L ... Stanford Journal of International Law [*A publication*]
Stan J Intl St ... Stanford Journal of International Studies [*A publication*]
Stan J Int'l Stud ... Stanford Journal of International Studies [*A publication*]
Stanki i Instrum ... Stanki i Instrument [*A publication*]
Stanki Rezhushchie Instrum ... Stanki i Rezhushchie Instrumenty [*A publication*]
STANLANCRU ... Standard Landing Craft Unit [*Military*]
Stan Law .... Stanford Lawyer [*A publication*]
Stan LR ...... Stanford Law Review [*A publication*]
Stan L Rev ... Stanford Law Review [*A publication*]
STANO ..... Surveillance, Target Acquisition, and Night Observation [*DoD*]
STANOC ... Surveillance, Target Acquisition, Night Observation, and Counter - Surveillance [*British*]   (MCD)
STANOLIND ... Standard Oil Co. (Indiana)
STANORD ... Standardization Order [*Navy*]   (NG)
Sta Note For Exp Sta (Idaho) ... Station Note. Forest, Wildlife, and Range Experiment Station (Moscow, Idaho) [*A publication*]
Stan PA Prac ... Standard Pennsylvania Practice [*A publication*]   (DLA)
STANS ...... Soviet Tactical Nuclear Study   (MCD)
STANS ...... Standard Aircraft Navigation System
STANS ...... Standard Army Nonappropriated System   (MCD)
StAns ...... Studia Anselmiana [*Rome*] [*A publication*]
STANSM .. STANO [*Surveillance, Target Acquisition, and Night Observation*] System Manager [*Army*]   (RDA)
StANT .... Studien zum Alten und Neuen Testament [*Munich*] [*A publication*]
STANTEC ... Standard Telephones Electronic Computer   (MCD)
St Anth ...... St. Anthony Messenger [*A publication*]
Stanton .... Stanton's Reports [*11-13 Ohio*] [*A publication*]   (DLA)
Stanton's Rev St ... Stanton's Revised Kentucky Statutes [*A publication*]   (DLA)
STANVAC ... Standard Vacuum Oil Co.
STANY ...... Security Traders Association of New York
STAP .... Scientific and Technical Analysis and Programs Directorate
STAP .... Screening Test for Auditory Perception
STAP .... Shipbuilding Temporary Assistance Program
STAP .... Special Technical Assistance Program   (EA)
STAP .... Stapleton [*England*]
STAP .... Staploe [*England*]
STAP .... Survivability Test Advisory Panel [*Military*]   (CAAL)
Sta Pap For Exp Sta (Idaho) ... Station Paper. Forest, Wildlife, and Range Experiment Station (Moscow, Idaho) [*A publication*]
Sta P C .... Staundeforde's Pleas of Crown [*A publication*]   (DSA)
STAPFUS ... Stable Axis Platform Follow-Up System
STAPH ...... Staphylococcus [*Medicine*]
STAPL .... SIGPLAN Technical Committee on APL [*A Programming Language*] [*Association for Computing Machinery*]   (CSR)
STAPLAN ... Status, Time, Attrition, Planning Methodology
STAPP ...... Simulation Tape Print Program
STAPP ...... Single-Thread All-Purpose Program
STAPPA .... State and Territorial Air Pollution Program Administrators   (EA)
Stapp Car Crash Conf Proc ... Stapp Car Crash Conference. Proceedings [*A publication*]
Sta Pr .... Staundeforde's Exposition of the King's Prerogative [*A publication*]   (DSA)
STAPRC .... Scientific and Technical Association of the People's Republic of China
STAQ .... Security Traders Automated Quotation [*System*]
STAQ .... Student Teachers' Attitude Questionnaire
STAQC ...... Statistical Quality Control System [*Military*]
STAR .... Safe Teenage Rocketry
St A R .... St. Andrews Review [*A publication*]
STAR .... San Clemente 3-D Acoustic Range   (MCD)
STAR .... Satellite Telecommunications Automatic Routing
STAR .... Satellite Transponder Addressable Receiver
STAR .... Satellites for Telecommunications, Applications, and Research [*Consortium*]
STAR .... Science Teaching Achievement Recognition
STAR .... Scientific and Technical Aerospace Reports [*NASA*] [*Information service or system*] [*A publication*]
STAR .... Score, Teach, and Record [*Teaching machine*]
STAR .... Screening Test of Academic Readiness [*Child development test*]
STAR .... Second Time Around Racers [*Car racing*]
STAR .... Selective Training and Retention [*Navy*]
STAR .... Self-Test Antenna Radiation [*Military*]   (CAAL)
STAR .... Self-Test Automatic Readout
STAR .... Self-Testing and Repairing [*Computer self-repair*]
STAR .... Self-Training and Assessment of Readiness
STAR .... Serials Titles Automated Records [*US National Agricultural Library*] [*Beltsville, MD*] [*A publication*]

STAR .... Shell Transient Asymmetric Response
STAR .... Shield Test Air Reactor [*Nuclear energy*]
STAR .... Ship-Tended Acoustic Relay [*Military*]
STAR .... Shipboard Tactical Airborne Remote Piloted Vehicle [*Navy*]   (CAAL)
STAR .... Shuttle Turnaround Analysis Report [*NASA*]   (NASA)
STAR .... Simple Test Approach for Readability [*General Electric*]
STAR .... Simulation of Tactical Alternative Responses   (MCD)
STAR .... Simultaneous Temperature Alarm Readout
STAR .... Simultaneous Transmission and Reception RADAR [*DoD*]   (ECON)
STAR .... Sled Towed Array   (MCD)
STAR .... Societe de Transport Aerien du Rwanda [*Airline*]   (FAAC)
STAR .... Society for Test Anxiety Research   (EA)
STAR .... Space Technology and Advanced Research
STAR .... Space Technology and Research Center [*Research center*]   (RCD)
STAR .... Space Thermionic Auxiliary Reactor [*Nuclear energy*]
STAR .... Space-Time Autoregressive [*Statistics*]
STAR .... Special Treatment and Review [*Navy*]   (NG)
STAR .... Special Tube Analyzing Recorder
STAR .... Specialized Training and Reassignment [*Military*]
STAR .... Spectral Technology and Applied Research
STAR .... Speed through Aerial Resupply [*Air Force*]
STAR .... Sport, Travel, Art, and Recreation
STAR .... Standard Instrument Arrival [*Aviation*]   (FAAC)
STAR .... Standard Telecommunications Automatic Recognizer [*Data processing*]
STAR .... Standard Tensioned Alongside Receiver [*Navy*]   (NVT)
STAR .... Standard Terminal Arrival Route [*Aviation*]
STAR .... Standard Test Authorization and Report System [*Navy*]
Star .... Starkie's English Nisi Prius Reports [*A publication*]   (DLA)
STAR .... Stars to Go, Inc. [*NASDAQ symbol*]   (NQ)
Star .... Starship. The Magazine about Science Fiction [*A publication*]
STAR .... Statistical Table Assembly and Retrieval System [*Proposed for Social Security Administration*]
STAR .... Statistical Treatment of Aircraft Returns   (MCD)
STAR .... Steerable Array RADAR
STAR .... Stellar Attitude Reference
STAR .... Steps to Abstract Reasoning
STAR .... Stock Technical Analysis Reports [*Innovest Systems, Inc.*] [*Database*]
STAR .... Stop the Arms Race [*Women's International League for Peace and Freedom*]
STAR .... Streamlined Acquisition Requirements System [*DoD*]
STAR .... Strike, Transfers, Acquisitions, or Removals [*Navy*]   (NG)
STAR .... String Array [*Computer system*]   (MCD)
STAR .... String Array Processor
STAR .... Structural Testing, Analysis, and Reporting
STAR .... Submarine Test and Research   (MCD)
STAR .... [*The*] Sunday Times Atlantic Riband [*Award offered by a London newspaper to any sailboat beating the 1905 record for a transatlantic crossing*]
STAR .... Supplier Transmittal and Approval Request   (MCD)
STAR .... Surface-to-Air Recovery
STAR .... Surveillance, Target Acquisition, and Reconnaissance
STAR .... Swedish Tactical Attack RADAR
STAR .... System for Telephone Administrative Response [*Data processing*]
STAR .... System for Time and Accomplishment Reporting   (MCD)
STAR .... System Training Application Requirements
STAR .... Systems Test Bed for Avionics Research
STARAD ... Starfish Radiation [*Satellite*] [*NASA*]
STARAN ... Stellar Attitude Reference and Navigation
STARC ...... Solar Thermal Advanced Research Center [*University of Houston*] [*Research center*]   (RCD)
STARC ...... State Area Commands   (MCD)
Star Ch Ca ... Star Chamber Cases [*1477-1648*] [*England*] [*A publication*]   (DLA)
Star Ch Cas ... Star Chamber Cases [*1477-1648*] [*England*] [*A publication*]   (DLA)
Starchroom Laundry J ... Starchroom Laundry Journal [*A publication*]
STARCIPS ... Standard Army Civilian Pay System
STARCOM ... Strategic Army Command Network
STARCOM ... Strategic Army Communications System
STARD ..... Starch/Staerke [*A publication*]
STARE ...... Scandinavian Twin Auroral RADAR Experiment [*Ionospheric science*]
STARE ...... Steerable Telemetry Antenna Receiving Equipment
STA Rept Abstr ... Scientific and Technical Aerospace Reports Abstract [*A publication*]
STARFIARS ... Standard Army Financial Inventory Accounting and Reporting System
STARFIRE ... System to Accumulate and Retrieve Financial Information with Random Extraction [*Data processing*]
STARIMAR ... Space-Time Autoregressive Integrated Moving Average [*Statistics*]
Stark .... Starkie's English Nisi Prius Reports [*1815-22*] [*A publication*]   (DLA)
Stark CL .... Starkie's Criminal Law [*A publication*]   (DLA)
Stark Cr Pl ... Starkie's Criminal Pleading [*A publication*]   (DLA)

Stark Ev ..... Starkie on Evidence [*A publication*] (DLA)
Starkie .... Starkie's English Nisi Prius Reports [*A publication*] (DLA)
Starkie (Eng) ... Starkie's English Nisi Prius Reports [*171 English Reprint*] [*A publication*] (DLA)
Starkie Ev .. Starkie on Evidence [*A publication*] (DLA)
Starkie's ..... English Nisi Prius Reports [*171 English Reprint*] [*A publication*] (DLA)
Starkie Sland & L ... Starkie on Slander and Libel [*A publication*] (DLA)
Stark Jury Tr ... Starkie on Trial by Jury [*A publication*] (DLA)
Stark Lib .... Starkie on Libel [*A publication*] (DLA)
Stark NP .... Starkie's English Nisi Prius Reports [*A publication*] (DLA)
Stark Sl & L ... Starkie on Slander and Libel [*A publication*] (DLA)
STARLAB ... Space Technology Applications and Research Laboratory [*NASA*]
Starl I Cr Law ... Starling's East India Criminal Law and Procedure [*A publication*] (DLA)
STARLO ... Special Test Army Reserve Limited Objective
St Arm Leg Pow ... St. Armand on the Legislative Power of England [*A publication*] (DLA)
STARP ...... Supplemental Training and Readiness Program
STARPUBS ... Standard Army Publications System
STARR ...... Schedule, Technical, and Resources Report [*NASA*] (NASA)
STARR ...... Scientific and Technical Annual Reference Review [*A publication*]
STARR ...... Staff Assessment of Readiness Report (MCD)
STARR ...... Study Techniques for Advanced RADAR Requirements
Starr & C Ann St ... Starr and Curtis' Annotated Statutes [*Illinois*] [*A publication*] (DLA)
STARS ...... Satellite Telemetry Automatic Reduction System [*NASA*]
STARS ...... Satellite Transmission and Reception Specialists [*Houston, TX*] [*Telecommunications*] (TSSD)
STARS ...... Seaborne Tracking and Ranging Station
STARS ...... Sealink Ticket and Reservation System [*Sealink UK Ltd.*] [*Information service or system*] (IID)
STARS ...... Shell Theory Automated for Rotational Structures
STARS ...... Short-Term Auction-Rate Stock [*Investment term*]
STARS ...... Short-Term Auditory Retrieval and Storage Test
STARS ...... Short Track Auto Racing Series [*Car racing*]
STARS ...... Silent Tactical Attack Reconnaissance System
STARS ...... Simmons Teen-Age Research Study [*Simmons Market Research Bureau, Inc.*] [*Information service or system*] (CRD)
STARS ...... Simulation and Training Advanced Research System [*Air Force*]
STARS ...... Software Technology for Adaptable, Reliable Systems [*Military*]
STAR(S) ... Specialized Training and Reassignment (Student) [*Military*]
STARS ...... Stabilized Twin-Gyro Attitude Reference System
STARS ...... Standard Terminal Arrival Routes [*Aviation*] (MCD)
STARS ...... Standard, TRADOC Automated Retrieval System (MCD)
STARS ...... Stationary Automotive Road Simulator
STARS ...... Stellar Tracking Attitude Reference System
STARS ...... Study of Tactical Airborne RADAR System
STARS ...... Support Tracking Analysis Reporting Systems (MCD)
STARS ...... Surface-to-Air Recovery System
STARS ...... Surveillance Target Attack RADAR System
STARS ...... Synchronized Time, Automated Reporting System
STARS ...... System Test and Astronaut Requirement Simulation
STARS ...... System Thermal Air Platform Reconnaissance Signature (MCD)
Star SC ...... Star Session Cases [*1824-25*] [*A publication*] (DLA)
STARS II ... Shell Theory Automated for Rotational Structures - II (MCD)
START ...... Safety Technology Applied to Rapid Transit [*Committee*] [*American Public Transit Association*]
START ...... Selection to Activate Random Testing [*Module*] [*NASA*]
START ...... Service Technician Advancement, Recruitment, and Training
START ...... Space Test and Reentry Technology
START ...... Space Transport and Reentry Tests
START ...... Spacecraft Technology and Advanced Reentry Tests [*Air Force*]
START ...... Special Treatment and Rehabilitative Training [*Prisons project*]
START ...... Sports Technique and Reaction Trainer [*Computerized training program for baseball and tennis*]
START ...... Story-Telling Automatic Reading Tutor
START ...... Strategic Arms Reduction Talks
START ...... Summary Tape Assistance, Research, and Training
START ...... System of Transportation Applying Rendezvous Technique (MCD)
START ...... Systematic Tabular Analysis of Requirements Technique (IEEE)
STARTEX ... Start of the Exercise (MCD)
STARTLE ... Surveillance and Target Acquisition RADAR for Tank Location and Engagement [*Army*] (MCD)
STARTTS ... Service for the Treatment and Rehabilitation of Torture and Trauma Survivors [*Australia*]
STARUTE ... Stable Parachute
STAS .... Safe-to-Arm Signal
STAS .... Safe-to-Arm System (MUGU)
STAS .... Short Term Analysis Services [*Scientific Services Program*] [*Army*] (RDA)
STAS .... Startel Corp. [*NASDAQ symbol*] (NQ)
STAS .... Statutes
STASA ...... State Transport Authority of South Australia
STASD ...... Stainless Steel [*A publication*]

STASH ...... Student Association for the Study of Hallucinogens [*Defunct*] (EA)
STASHIP ... Station Ship [*Navy*] (NVT)
Sta Sper Maiscolt (Bergamo) ... Stazione Sperimentale di Maiscoltura (Bergamo) [*A publication*]
STASS ...... Submarine Tactical Array SONAR System
STASS ...... Submarine-Towed Array Surveillance System (NVT)
STAT .... SEABEE Technical Assistance Team [*Navy*]
STAT .... Society of Teachers of the Alexander Technique (EAIO)
Stat .... Stat. Bulletin of the Wisconsin Nurses' Association [*A publication*]
STAT .... Static (AAG)
STAT .... Statim [*Immediately*] [*Latin*]
STAT .... Station
STAT .... Stationary [*Chemistry*]
STAT .... Stationery Office [*British*]
STAT .... Statistic (AFM)
Stat .... Statius [*First century AD*] [*Classical studies*] (OCD)
Stat .... Stative (BJA)
STAT .... Statuary
STAT .... Status (MSA)
STAT .... Statute
STAT .... Statutory Tenant (DSUE)
STAT .... Stop Teen-Age Addiction to Tobacco (EA)
Stat .... United States Statutes at Large [*A publication*]
STATA ...... Stata Corp. Cl A [*NASDAQ symbol*] (NQ)
statA .... Statampere [*Also, sA*] [*Unit of electric current*]
Stat Ab (NZ) ... Monthly Abstract of Statistics (New Zealand) [*A publication*]
Stat Abs ...... Statistical Abstract. United States [*A publication*]
STAT AN .. Statistical Annals (DLA)
Stat Bull ..... Statistical Bulletin. Metropolitan Life Insurance Company [*A publication*]
Stat Bull Metrop Life Found ... Statistical Bulletin. Metropolitan Life Foundation [*A publication*]
Stat Bull Metrop Life Insur Co ... Statistical Bulletin. Metropolitan Life Insurance Company [*A publication*]
Stat Bull Metropol Life Ins Co ... Statistical Bulletin. Metropolitan Life Insurance Company [*A publication*]
Stat Bull US Farm Credit Admin Econ Anal Div ... Statistical Bulletin. United States Farm Credit Administration. Economic Analysis Division [*A publication*]
statC .... Statcoulomb [*Also, sC*] [*Unit of electric charge*]
StatCan ...... Statistics Canada [*Statistics Canada Library*] [*Information service or system*]
StatConst ... Status Constructus (BJA)
Stat Dec ...... Statutory Declaration
Stat Def ...... Statutory Definition [*Legal term*] (DLA)
STATE ...... Simplified Tactical Approach and Terminal Equipment
STATE ...... Simulation for Tank/Antitank Evaluation (NATG)
State Agric Coll Oreg Eng Exp Stn Circ ... State Agricultural College of Oregon. Engineering Experiment Station. Circular [*A publication*]
State of the Art Rev Occup Med ... State of the Art Reviews. Occupational Medicine [*A publication*]
State Court J ... State Court Journal [*A publication*]
State Dept Bull ... United States State Department. Bulletin [*A publication*] (DLA)
State Fish Chief Secr Dep NSW Res Bull ... State Fisheries Chief. Secretary's Department. New South Wales. Research Bulletin [*A publication*]
State Geologists Jour ... State Geologists Journal [*A publication*]
State Gov ... State Government [*A publication*]
State Govt .. State Government [*A publication*]
State Govt News ... State Government News [*A publication*]
State Hortic Assoc PA Proc ... State Horticultural Association of Pennsylvania. Proceedings [*A publication*]
State Ill Div State Geol Surv Bull ... State of Illinois. Division of the State Geological Survey. Bulletin [*A publication*]
State Legis ... State Legislatures [*A publication*]
State Libn .. State Librarian [*A publication*]
State Libr ... State Librarian [*A publication*]
State and Local Govt R ... State and Local Government Review [*A publication*]
State Locl & Urb L Newsl ... State, Local, and Urban Law Newsletter [*A publication*]
State Loc and Urb L Newsl ... State, Local, and Urban Law Newsletter [*A publication*]
STATEM .. Shipment Status System [*Military*] (AABC)
State Miner Profiles US Bur Mines ... State Mineral Profiles. United States Bureau of Mines [*A publication*]
State Mot Carr Guide ... State Motor Carrier Guide [*Commerce Clearing House*] [*A publication*] (DLA)
Staten Island As Pr ... Staten Island Association of Arts and Sciences. Proceedings [*A publication*]
Staten Island Inst Arts Sci Proc ... Staten Island Institute of Arts and Sciences. Proceedings [*A publication*]
Statens Inst Byggnadsforsk Handl (Trans) ... Statens Institut foer Byggnadsforskning. Handlingar (Translations) [*A publication*]

Statens Inst Byggnadsforsk Natl Swedish Bldg Res Doc ... Statens Institut foer Byggnadsforskning. National Swedish Building Research Document [*A publication*]

Statens Lantbrukskem Kontrollanst Medd ... Statens Lantbrukskemiska Kontrollanstalt. Meddelande [*A publication*]

Statens Lantbrukskem Lab Medd ... Statens Lantbrukskemiska Laboratorium. Meddelande [*A publication*]

Statens Naturvetensk Forskningsrad Ekologikomm Bull ... Statens Naturvetenskapliga Forskningsrad Ekologikommitter Bulletin [*A publication*]

Statens Offentliga Utredn ... Statens Offentliga Utredningar [*A publication*]

Statens Provingsanst (Stockholm) Cirk ... Statens Provningsanstalt (Stockholm). Cirkulaer [*A publication*]

Statens Provingsanst (Stockholm) Medd ... Statens Provningsanstalt (Stockholm). Meddelande [*A publication*]

Statens Skadedyrlab Arsberet ... Statens Skadedyrlaboratorium Arsberetning [*A publication*]

Statens Vaeginst (Swed) Medd ... Statens Baeginstitut (Sweden). Meddelande [*A publication*]

Statens Vaeginst (Swed) Rapp ... Statens Vaeginstitut (Sweden). Rapport [*A publication*]

Statens Vaxtskyddsanst Medd ... Statens Vaxtskyddsanstalt Meddelanden [*A publication*]

State Nurse Legis Q ... State Nursing Legislation. Quarterly [*A publication*]

State Plann and Environ Comm Tech Bull ... State Planning and Environment Commission. Technical Bulletin [*A publication*]   (APTA)

State R .... New York State Reporter [*A publication*]   (DLA)

State Rep.... New York State Reporter [*A publication*]   (DLA)

State Res ... State Research [*A publication*]

states .... Statesman [*or Stateswoman*]

State Tax Cas Rep ... State Tax Cases Reporter [*Commerce Clearing House*] [*A publication*]   (DLA)

State Tax Guide CCH ... State Tax Guide. Commerce Clearing House [*A publication*]

State Tr ...... State Trials (Howell) [*England*] [*A publication*]   (DLA)

State Tr NS ... State Trials, New Series, Edited by Macdonell [*England*] [*A publication*]   (DLA)

State Univ Coll For Syracuse Univ Tech Publ ... State University College of Forestry. Syracuse University. Technical Publication [*A publication*]

State Univ NY Mar Sci Res Cent (Stony Brook) Tech Rep Ser ... State University of New York. Marine Sciences Research Center (Stony Brook). Technical Report Series [*A publication*]

State Vet J ... State Veterinary Journal [*A publication*]

State Wash Dep Fish Res Div Inf Bkl ... State of Washington. Department of Fisheries. Research Division. Information Booklet [*A publication*]

State Wash Dep Fish Res Div Inf Booklet ... State of Washington. Department of Fisheries. Research Division. Information Booklet [*A publication*]

statF .... Statfarad [*Also, sF*] [*Unit of capacitance*]

Stat Glo ...... Statute of Gloucester [*First statute to give costs in actions*] [*A publication*]   (DLA)

statH .... Stathenry [*Also, sH*] [*Unit of inductance*]

Stath Abr ... Statham's Abridgment [*A publication*]   (DLA)

STATIC..... Student Taskforce Against Telecommunication Information Concealment [*Student legal action organization*]

Stat ICJ ..... Statute of the International Court of Justice [*A publication*]   (DLA)

STATINDEX ... Stationery Industry Exhibition [*British*]   (ITD)

STATINF ... Statistical Information System [*Bundesamt fuer Statistik*] [*Switzerland*] [*Information service or system*]   (CRD)

Stat Inst ..... Statutory Instruments [*A publication*]   (DLA)

Stat Instrum (Lond) ... Statutory Instrument (London) [*A publication*]

STATIS ..... Statistics

Statis .... Statistiques [*A publication*]

Statis Affaires Socs ... Statistiques des Affaires Sociales [*A publication*]

Statis Agric ... Statistique Agricole [*A publication*]

Statis and Econ Info Bul Africa ... Statistical and Economic Information Bulletin for Africa [*A publication*]

Statis Enseignements ... Statistiques des Enseignements [*A publication*]

Statis et Etud Fins (Ser Bleue) ... Statistiques et Etudes Financieres (Serie Bleue) [*A publication*]

Statis et Etud Fins (Ser Orange) ... Statistiques et Etudes Financieres (Serie Orange) [*A publication*]

Statis et Etud Fins (Ser Rouge) ... Statistiques et Etudes Financieres (Serie Rouge) [*A publication*]

Statis et Etud Midi Pyrenees ... Statistiques et Etudes Midi-Pyrenees [*A publication*]

Statis Judiciaires ... Statistiques Judiciaires [*A publication*]

Statis Mhefte Rheinland-Pfalz ... Statistische Monatshefte Rheinland-Pfalz [*A publication*]

Statis Nachr (Austria) NF ... Statistische Nachrichten (Austria). Neue Folge [*A publication*]

Statis Neerl ... Statistica Neerlandica [*Netherlands*] [*A publication*]

Statis Reporter ... Statistical Reporter [*A publication*]

Statist Abstr US ... Statistical Abstract. United States [*A publication*]

Statist Anal Donnees ... Statistique et Analyse des Donnees. Bulletin de l'Association des Statisticiens Universitaires [*A publication*]

Statist Bull USDA ... Statistical Bulletin. United States Department of Agriculture [*A publication*]

Statist Canad Consumpt Prodn Invent Rubb ... Statistics Canada. Consumption. Production Inventories of Rubber and Other Selected Sections [*A publication*]

Statist Decisions Econom ... Statistique et Decisions Economiques [*Paris*] [*A publication*]

Statist et Develop Loire ... Statistique et Developpement Pays de la Loire [*A publication*]

Statist Distributions Sci Work ... Statistical Distributions in Scientific Work [*A publication*]

Statist Ecology Ser ... Statistical Ecology Series [*A publication*]

Statist Econ Normande ... Statistiques pour l'Economie Normande [*A publication*]

Statist i Elektron-Vycisl Tehn v Ekonom ... Statistika i Elektronno-Vycislitel'naja Tehnika v Ekonomike Naucno-Issledovatel'skii Institut po Proektirovanija Vycislitel'nyh Centrov i Sistem Ekonomiceskoi Informacii CSU SSSR [*A publication*]

Statist Et Finance Et Econ (Ser Orange) ... Statistiques et Etudes Financieres. Etudes Economiques (Serie Orange) [*A publication*]

Statist Et Financ (Ser Bleue) ... Statistiques et Etudes Financieres (Serie Bleue) [*A publication*]

Statist Et Financ (Ser Rouge) ... Statistiques et Etudes Financieres (Serie Rouge) [*A publication*]

Statist Et Midi-Pyrenees ... Statistiques et Etudes Midi-Pyrenees [*A publication*]

Statist Foreign Trade B ... Statistics of Foreign Trade. Series B. Annual. Tables by Reporting Countries [*A publication*]

Statist Hefte ... Statistische Hefte [*A publication*]

Statistical Register of SA ... Statistical Register of South Australia [*A publication*]   (APTA)

Statistical Register of WA ... Statistical Register of Western Australia [*A publication*]   (APTA)

Statist M L ... Statistical Methods in Linguistics [*A publication*]

Statist Neerlandica ... Statistica Neerlandica [*A publication*]

Statist Newslett Abstr ... Statistical Newsletter and Abstracts. Indian Council of Agricultural Research [*A publication*]

Statist Paper ... Statistics of Paper [*A publication*]

Statist Probab Lett ... Statistics and Probability Letters [*A publication*]

Statist R (Beograd) ... Statisticka Revija (Beograd) [*A publication*]

Statist Sect Pap For Comm (Lond) ... Statistics Section Paper. Forestry Commission (London) [*A publication*]

Statist Theory Method Abstracts ... Statistical Theory and Method Abstracts [*A publication*]

Statist Trav Suppl B Mens ... Statistiques du Travail. Supplement au Bulletin Mensuel [*A publication*]

Statiszt Szle ... Statisztikai Szemle [*A publication*]

Stat Jahr.... Statistisches Jahrbuch fuer die Bundesrepublik Deutschland [*A publication*]

Stat Japan ... Statistics on Japanese Industries 1982 [*A publication*]

Stat at L ..... United States Statutes at Large [*A publication*]   (DLA)

STATLIB .. Statistical Computing Library [*Bell System*]

Stat Local... Governments Statute of Local Governments [*A publication*]   (DLA)

Stat LR....... Statute Law Review [*A publication*]

Stat Marl .. Statute of Marlbridge [*A publication*]   (DLA)

Stat Mech .. Statistical Mechanics [*A publication*]

Stat Med ... Statistics in Medicine [*A publication*]

Stat Mer..... Statute of Merton [*A publication*]   (DLA)

Stat Mert ... Statute of Merton [*A publication*]   (DLA)

Stat Mod Lev Fin ... Statute Modus Levandi Fines [*A publication*]   (DLA)

STATNET ... Statistical Analysis of Network

STAT News ... Science Teachers Association of Tasmania. Newsletter [*A publication*]   (APTA)

Stat News Lett (New Delhi) ... Statistical News Letter (New Delhi) [*A publication*]

Statni Tech Knih Praze Vymena Zkusenosti ... Statni Technicka Knihovna v Praze. Vymena Zkusenosti [*A publication*]

Statni Vyzk Ustav Sklarsky Kradec Kralove Inf Prehl ... Statni Vyzkumny Ustav Sklarsky. Kradec Kralove. Informativni Prehled [*A publication*]

Stat Notes Health Plann ... Statistical Notes for Health Planners [*A publication*]

Stat NSW .. Statutes of New South Wales [*Australia*] [*A publication*]   (DLA)

Stat NZ ...... Statutes of New Zealand [*A publication*]   (DLA)

Stat O & R ... Statutory Orders and Regulations [*Canada*] [*A publication*]   (DLA)

Stato Soc.... Stato Sociale [*A publication*]

STATPAC ... Statistics Package [*Computer program*]   (IEEE)

STATRAFO ... Standard Transfer Order

Stat Realm ... Statutes of the Realm [*England*] [*A publication*]   (DLA)

Stat Reg NZ ... Statutory Regulations [*New Zealand*] [*A publication*]   (DLA)

STATREP ... Advise Present Grade, Status, Physical Condition, and Mailing Address of Following Named [*Military*]

Stat Rep ..... Statistical Reporter [*A publication*]

Stat Rep Pollen Mold Comm Am Acad Allergy ... Statistical Report. Pollen and Mold Committee. American Academy of Allergy [*A publication*]

Stat R & O ... Statutory Rules and Orders [*1890-1947*] [*England*] [*A publication*]   (DLA)

Stat R & ONI ... Statutory Rules and Orders of Northern Ireland [*A publication*]   (DLA)
Stat R & O N Ir ... Statutory Rules and Orders of Northern Ireland [*A publication*]
Stat R & O & Stat Inst Rev ... Statutory Rules and Orders and Statutory Instruments Revised [*England*] [*A publication*]   (DLA)
Stat Rptr .... Statistical Reporter [*A publication*]
STATS...... Stationary Tank Automatic Target System   (MCD)
statS........... Statsiemens [*Also, sS*] [*Unit of electric conductance, admittance, and susceptance*]
STATSBOBP ... Scale of Teacher Attitudes toward Selective Behavior of Boy Pupils [*Satirical*]
Stats Can ... Statistics Canada
STAT-SEL ... Status Select [*Army*]
STATSERVOFF ... Statistical Service Office [*Supreme Headquarters Allied Powers Europe*]   (NATG)
Statsokon Tss ... Statsoekonomisk Tidsskrift [*A publication*]
Statsvet Ts ... Statsvetenskaplig Tidsskrift [*A publication*]
STATSVS ... Statistical Services   (MUGU)
STATT ...... Statement
statT........... Stattesla [*Unit of magnetic flux density*]
Stat Textb Monogr ... Statistics Textbooks and Monographs [*A publication*]
Stat Theor Meth Abstr ... Statistical Theory and Method Abstracts [*A publication*]
Stat Tidskr ... Statistisk Tidskrift [*A publication*]
Stat Tidskrift ... Statistick Tidskrift [*A publication*]
STATTS.... Stationary Automatic Tank Target System   (MCD)
STATUS.... Statute Search [*Australia*]
Stat Use Radiat Jpn ... Statistics on the Use of Radiation in Japan [*A publication*]
Statute L Rev ... Statute Law Review [*A publication*]
statV........... Statvolt [*Also, sV*] [*Electrostatic unit of potential difference*]
statWb ... Statweber [*Unit of magnetic flux*]
Stat Westm ... Statute of Westminster [*A publication*]   (DLA)
Stat Winch ... Statute of Winchester [*A publication*]   (DLA)
STATY ...... Statutory   (ROG)
Staub J....... Staub Journal [*A publication*]
Staub-Reinhalt Luft ... Staub, Reinhaltung der Luft [*A publication*]
Staundef..... Staundeforde's Exposition of the King's Prerogative [*A publication*]   (DLA)
Staundef PC ... Staundeforde's Pleas of Crown [*A publication*]   (DLA)
Staundf Pl Cor ... Staundeforde's Placita Coronae [*Pleas of Crown*] [*A publication*]   (DLA)
Staundf Prerog ... Staundeforde's Exposition of the King's Prerogative [*A publication*]   (DLA)
Staund Pl ... Staundeforde's Pleas of Crown [*A publication*]   (DLA)
Staunf Pr.... Staundeforde's Exposition of the King's Prerogative [*A publication*]   (DLA)
St Autobahn ... Strasse und Autobahn [*A publication*]
STAVA...... Stavivo [*Czechoslovakia*] [*A publication*]
Stavby Jadrovej Energ ... Stavby Jadrovej Energetiky [*Supplement to Inzenyrske Stavby*] [*Czechoslovakia*] [*A publication*]
Stavebnicky Cas ... Stavebnicky Casopis [*A publication*]
STAVRA ... Supreme High Command of the Soviet Armed Forces [*Russian*]   (MCD)
STAX........ Sludge Tracking Acoustical Experiment [*Marine science*]   (MSC)
STB .... Bachelor of the Science of Theology
StB .... Kommentar zum Neuen Testament aus Talmud und Midrasch (H. L. Strack - F. Billerbeck) [*A publication*]   (BJA)
STB........... Sacrae Theologiae Baccalaureus [*Bachelor of Sacred Theology*]
STB........... St. Blazey [*British depot code*]
STB........... Santa Barbara [*Venezuela*] [*Airport symbol*]   (OAG)
STB........... Scan True Bearing   (NVT)
STB........... Scandinavian Tourist Boards   (EA)
STB........... Scottish Tourist Board   (EAIO)
STB........... Segment Tag BITS [*Binary Digits*]
STB........... September Resources Ltd. [*Vancouver Stock Exchange symbol*]
STB........... Shore Terminal Box   (MSA)
STB........... Signal Training Brigade   (MCD)
STB........... Soprano, Tenor, Bass
STB........... Southeast Banking Corp. [*NYSE symbol*]   (SPSG)
STB........... Southern Tourist Board [*British*]   (DCTA)
STB........... Special Tax Bond
Stb............. Staatsblad [*Official Bulletin*] [*Netherlands*]   (ILCA)
STB........... Stable   (MSA)
STB........... Staged Turbulent Bed Process [*Chevron Corp.*] [*Oil shale pyrolysis*]
STB........... Standard Torsion Bar   (MCD)
STB........... State Training Board [*Victoria, Australia*]
STB........... Steinbach [*Federal Republic of Germany*] [*Seismograph station code, US Geological Survey*]   (SEIS)
StB .... Stenografische Berichte. Fuenf Hauptversammlungen. Verband der Deutschen Juden [*A publication*]
Stb............. Steuerberater [*A publication*]
STB........... Stillborn [*Medicine*]
STB........... Stock-Tank Barrel [*Petroleum industry*]
STB........... Stourbridge [*British depot code*]
STB........... Streaming Tape Backup Unit
STB........... Stretch Block   (MCD)
StB .... Studi sul Boccaccio [*A publication*]

STB............ Sun's True Bearing [*Navigation*]
STB............ Supertropical Bleach [*Sanitizing agent*]
STB............ System [*or Subsystem*] Test Bed [*NASA*]   (KSC)
STB............ Systems Testing Branch [*Social Security Administration*]
STBA .... Selective Top-to-Bottom Algorithm   (DIT)
St Barbara Mus Nat Hist Contrib Sci ... Santa Barbara Museum of Natural History. Contributions in Science [*A publication*]
St Bar Rev ... State Bar Review [*A publication*]   (DLA)
STBC .... School Readiness Tests for Blind Children
STBD......... Standard-Bred Pacers & Trotters, Inc. [*NASDAQ symbol*]   (NQ)
STBD......... Starboard
St Ber G .... Steuerberatungsgesetz [*A publication*]
StBFranc.... Studii Biblici Franciscani [*Jerusalem*] [*A publication*]
StBFranc LA ... Studii Biblici Franciscani. Liber Annuus [*Jerusalem*] [*A publication*]
sTBG.......... Slow Thyroxine-Binding Globulin [*Endocrinology*]
STBGA...... Structure and Bonding [*Berlin*] [*A publication*]
STBIB....... Studia Biophysica [*A publication*]
St Bibl Theol ... Studies in Biblical Theology [*A publication*]
St Bi Franc ... Studium Biblicum Franciscanum Liber Annuus [*A publication*]
St Biophys ... Studia Biophysica [*A publication*]
StBiz .... Studi Bizantini e Neoellenici [*A publication*]
Stb Jb.......... Steuerberater-Jahrbuch [*A publication*]
STBK .... State Street Boston Corp. [*NASDAQ symbol*]   (NQ)
STBL .... Stable   (FAAC)
St Bl .... Steuer und Zollblatt fuer Berlin [*A publication*]
STBLN....... Stabilization   (MSA)
St Bl Nds.... Steuerblatt fuer das Land Niedersachsen [*A publication*]
St Bl Schl H ... Steuerblatt fuer das Land Schleswig-Holstein [*A publication*]
STBLZ....... Stabilize   (AABC)
StBM.......... Stuttgarter Biblische Monographien [*A publication*]
STBN......... Southern Bancorp, Inc. [*NASDAQ symbol*]   (NQ)
St Bonaventure Sci Stud ... St. Bonaventure Science Studies [*A publication*]
StBoT........ Studien zu den Bogazkoey-Texten [*Wiesbaden*] [*A publication*]
STBR .... Stater Brothers, Inc. [*NASDAQ symbol*]   (NQ)
St BRD........ Statistik der Bundesrepublik Deutschland [*A publication*]
STBRIAV ... Saint Briavels [*England*]
St Brown .... Stewart-Brown's Cases in the Court of the Star Chamber [*1455-1547*] [*A publication*]   (DLA)
STBSCP .... Stroboscope [*Engineering*]
StBSt.......... Stuttgarter Bibelstudien [*Stuttgart*] [*A publication*]
STBT .... Steamboat   (ADA)
STBT......... Straits Times. Business Times [*A publication*]
STBT......... Subcaliber Tracer Bullet Trainer [*Army*]   (INF)
STBU......... Statistical Bulletin
STBY .... Standby   (AAG)
STBY......... Stansbury Mining Corp. [*NASDAQ symbol*]   (NQ)
STC............ Chief SONAR Technician [*Navy rating*]
STC............ Sacramento Test Center   (MCD)
STC............ St. Cloud, MN [*Location identifier*] [*FAA*]   (FAAL)
STC............ Sales Tax Cases [*A publication*]   (APTA)
STC............ Samuel Taylor Coleridge [*Nineteenth-century British poet*]
STC............ Satellite Television Corporation [*Washington, DC*] [*Telecommunications*]   (TSSD)
STC............ Satellite Test Center [*Air Force*]
STC............ Satellite Tracking Center [*Sunnyvale, CA*]
STC............ Satellite Tracking Committee [*Military*]
STC............ Scandinavian Travel Commission [*Later, Scandinavian National Travel Offices*]   (EA)
STC............ Science and Technology Center [*National Science Foundation*]
STC............ Security Time Control
STC............ Security Training Center
STC............ Senate Tourism Caucus   (EA)
STC............ Senior Training Corps [*British*]
STC............ Sensitivity-Time Control [*RADAR*]
STC............ Serum Theophylline Concentration [*Clinical chemistry*]
STC............ Service to Chapters [*Red Cross*]
STC............ Service to Claimants [*Unemployment Insurance Service*] [*Department of Labor*]
STC............ Service Technology Corporation [*of Ling-Temco-Vought, Inc.*]
STC............ Serving Test Center [*Bell System*]
STC............ Set Carry
STC............ [*The*] Seven Tablets of Creation [*L. W. King*] [*A publication*]   (BJA)
STC............ SHAPE [*Supreme Headquarters Allied Powers Europe*] Technical Center [*Formerly, SADTC*] [*The Hague, Netherlands*] [*NATO*]
STC............ Short Time Constant
STC............ Short Title Catalog [*A publication*]
STC............ Signal Training Centre [*British military*]   (DMA)
STC............ Simon's Tax Cases [*United Kingdom*] [*A publication*]
STC............ Simulation Tape Conversion
STC............ Singapore Technology Corp.   (ECON)
STC............ Single-Trip Container
STC............ Ski Touring Council   (EA)
STC............ Slow Time Constant   (MCD)
STC............ Smokeless Tobacco Council   (EA)
STC............ Society for Technical Communication   (EA)
STC............ Society of Telecommunications Consultants   (EA)
STC............ Society of Theatrical Carpenters [*A union*] [*British*]

STC........... Soft Tissue Calcification [*Medicine*]
STC........... Sound Transmission Class [*Followed by number, indicates FHA rating of sound insulating quality of a partition construction*]
STC........... Source Telecomputing Corporation [*McLean, VA*] [*Telecommunications*]   (TSSD)
STC........... South Thames College [*London, England*]
STC........... Space Technology Center
STC........... Space Test Center [*Air Force*]
STC........... Space-Time Continuum
STC........... Spacecraft Test Conductor [*NASA*]   (KSC)
STC........... Specialists Training Center
STC........... Specific Taste Changes
STC........... Specific Thermal Capacity
STC........... Spectral Transfer Coefficient
STC........... Standard Telephone and Cable [*IT & T affiliate*] [*British*]
STC........... Standard Test Configuration [*NASA*]   (NASA)
STC........... Standard Transmission Code [*Data processing*]
STC........... Standing Technical Committee [*British*]   (DCTA)
STC........... State Tax Cases [*Commerce Clearing House*] [*A publication*]   (DLA)
STC........... State Teachers College
STC........... Station Technical Control [*Telecommunications*]   (TEL)
STC........... Station Test and Calibration
StC............ Status Constructus   (BJA)
STC........... Step Timing Control [*Truck engineering*]
STC........... Stepchild
St C .... Stephen's Commentaries on the Laws of England [*21st ed.*] [*1950*] [*A publication*]   (DLA)
STC........... Stereo Tape Club of America
STC........... Stern Telecommunications Corporation [*New York, NY*] [*Telecommunications*]   (TSSD)
STC........... Stewart, Tabori & Chang [*Publisher*]
STC........... Stock Trust Certificate [*Investment term*]
STC........... Stone Canyon Observatory [*California*] [*Seismograph station code, US Geological Survey*]   (SEIS)
STC........... Storage Container   (MCD)
STC........... Stored Time Command
STC........... Straight Cactus [*Horticulture*]
STC........... Streamtube Curvature
StC............ Studia Catholica [*A publication*]
StC............ Studia Celtica [*A publication*]
STC........... Subtropical Convergence [*Oceanography*]
STC........... Summit Technical Center [*Celanese Research Co.*]
STC........... Supplemental Type Certificate
STC........... Synthetic Turf Council   (EA)
STC........... System Technical Control
STC........... System Test Configuration
STC........... System Test Console
STC........... System Transfer Constant
STC........... Systems Test Complex [*NASA*]
STCA........ Scottish Terrier Club of America   (EA)
STCA........ Short Tests of Clerical Ability
STCA........ Silky Terrier Club of America   (EA)
STCA........ Skye Terrier Club of America   (EA)
STCA........ Sodium Trichloroacetate [*Organic chemistry*]
STCA........ Staffordshire Terrier Club of America   (EA)
STCA........ Stockbridge Capital Ltd. [*Dallas, TX*] [*NASDAQ symbol*]   (NQ)
St Can Lit... Studies in Canadian Literature [*A publication*]
St Cas........ Stillingfleet's English Ecclesiastical Cases [*A publication*]   (DLA)
StCath........ Studia Catholica [*Nijmegen*] [*A publication*]   (BJA)
StCau .... Studia Caucasica [*A publication*]
STCB .... Subtask Control Block [*Data processing*]   (IBMDP)
STCC .... Spacecraft Technical Control Center   (MDG)
STCC .... Springfield Technical Community College [*Massachusetts*]
STCC .... Standard Transportation Commodity Classification [*or Code*]
STCC .... Standards Council of Canada [*See also CCNO*]
STCC .... Syndicat des Travailleurs en Communication du Canada
STCC .... Syndicat des Travailleurs en Communication, Electronique, Electricite, Techniciens, et Salaries du Canada [*Communications, Electronic, Electrical, Technical, and Salaried Workers of Canada - CWC*]
STCDHS ... Spacecraft Telemetry Command Data Handling System
STCDS .... System Test Complex Data System
STCDSS .... Standing Technical Committee on Disposal of Sewage Sludge [*British*]   (DCTA)
STCE .... System Test Complex Equipment
St Cerc Mat Fiz ... Studii si Cercetari de Matematica si Fizica [*A publication*]
STCFEO.... Science and Technology Center, Far East Office [*Army*]   (AABC)
STCH .... Shared Technologies, Inc. [*NASDAQ symbol*]   (NQ)
STCH .... Stitch   (MSA)
St Ch Cas... Star Chamber Cases [*England*] [*A publication*]   (DLA)
STCI .... Siebert Telecommunications Consulting, Incorporated [*Cincinnati, OH*] [*Telecommunications*]   (TSSD)
STCICS ..... Strike Command Integrated Communications System [*British*]
StCILF....... Studii si Cercetari de Astorie Literara si Folclor [*A publication*]
St C Istor.... Studii si Cercetari de Istorie Veche si Arheologie [*A publication*]
STCL .... Source-Term Control Loop [*Nuclear energy*]   (NRCH)

StCL........... Studii si Cercetari Lingvistice [*A publication*]
St Class Or ... Studia Classica et Orientalia [*A publication*]
STCLB........ Start Climb [*Aviation*]   (FAAC)
St Clem ...... St. Clement's Church Case [*Philadelphia, PA*] [*A publication*]   (DLA)
StClOr .... Studi Classici e Orientali [*A publication*]
STCM........ Master Chief SONAR Technician [*Navy rating*]
St C Num ... Studi si Cercetari de Numismatica [*A publication*]
STCO........ StratAmerica Corp. [*NASDAQ symbol*]   (NQ)
STCO........ Supervisor Training Conference Outline [*Air Force*]   (MCD)
St Comp Int Devel ... Studies in Comparative International Development [*A publication*]
STCP .... Short-Term Cost Plan [*NASA*]   (NASA)
STCP .... Society of Tympanuchus Cupido Pinnatus   (EA)
STCR........ Solar Thermal Central Receiver
StCrN........ Stephen Crane Newsletter [*A publication*]
STCS .... Senior Chief SONAR Technician [*Navy rating*]
St CS .... Studies in Contemporary Satire [*A publication*]
STCS .... Surveyor Thermal Control Section
StCSF .... Studii si Cercetari Stiintifice. Filologie [*A publication*]
STCT .... Small Transportable Communications Terminal
St Ct J .... State Court Journal [*A publication*]
StCu .... Stratocumulus [*Cloud*] [*Meteorology*]   (AIA)
STCW........ Standard of Training, Certification, and Watchkeeping Convention   (DS)
STCW........ Stichting Technisch Centrum Waalsteen [*Research center*] [*Netherlands*]   (IRC)
STCW........ System Time Code Word
STCY......... Stacy Industries, Inc. [*Wood-Ridge, NJ*] [*NASDAQ symbol*]   (NQ)
STD .... Banco Santander [*NYSE symbol*]   (SPSG)
STD .... Doctor of the Science of Theology
STD .... Sacrae Theologiae Doctor [*Doctor of Sacred Theology*] [*Latin*]
STD .... Safety Topic Discussion   (AAG)
STD .... Salinity/Temperature/Density [*or Depth*] [*Oceanography*]
STD .... Schools of Theology in Dubuque [*Library network*]
STD .... Sea Transport Department [*British military*]   (DMA)
STD .... Servo Tape Display
STD .... Sexually Transmitted Disease [*Medicine*]
STD .... Ship Training Detachment
STD .... Short-Term Disability
STD .... Shuttle Test Director [*NASA*]   (MCD)
STD .... Skin Test Dose
STD .... Sledborne Time Digitizer
STD .... Society for Theological Discussion [*Defunct*]   (EA)
STD .... Spacecraft Technology Division [*NASA*]   (KSC)
STD .... Sports Trainers Digest [*A publication*]
STD .... Standaard. Dagblad voor Staatkundige, Matschappelijke, en Economische Belangen [*A publication*]
STD .... Standard   (AFM)
STD .... Standard Airways [*El Paso, TX*] [*FAA designator*]   (FAAC)
STD .... Standard Test Dose
STD .... Standard Trustco Ltd. [*Toronto Stock Exchange symbol*]
STD .... Standing   (AABC)
STD .... Started   (ADA)
STD .... State-Transition Diagram [*Data processing*]
STD .... Stepwise Thermal Desorption [*Surface analysis*]
STD .... Steward [*British*]
ST D.......... Stopped Diapason [*Organ stop*] [*Music*]
STD .... Storage Tube Display
STD .... Strain Gauge Transient Dosimetry
STD .... Stripline Tunnel Diode
StD............. Studi Danteschi [*A publication*]
StD............. Studies and Documents [*A publication*]
STD .... Subscriber Toll Dialing [*Telecommunications*]   (TSSD)
STD .... Subscriber Trunk Dialing [*Telephone communications*]
STD .... Supporting Technology Development   (KSC)
STD .... Synopsis Series of the United States Treasury Decisions [*A publication*]   (DLA)
STD .... System Technology Demonstration Program   (RDA)
S-TDA ...... Selenium-Tellurium Development Association   (EA)
STDA........ Steward's Assistant [*Navy*]
STDA........ Stripline Tunnel Diode Amplifier
STDB........ Steward's Branch [*Marine Corps*]
STDBY...... Standby   (NVT)
STDC........ Southern Travel Directors Council
STDC........ Standards Council of Canada [*See also CCNO*]
STD/DEV ... Standard Deviation   (MCD)
STDDS ..... Submarine Tactical Data Display Subsystem   (MCD)
STDE........ Standard Energy Corp. [*NASDAQ symbol*]   (NQ)
St Dem ...... Studia Demograficzne [*A publication*]
St Dept....... State Department Reports [*A publication*]   (DLA)
STDF......... Sodium Taurodihydrofusidate [*Organic chemistry*]
STDF......... Standoff
STDHA ..... Staedtehygiene [*A publication*]
ST DIAP.... Stopped Diapason [*Organ stop*] [*Music*]
STDJ......... Studies on the Texts of the Desert of Judah [*A publication*]
St DKG ..... Studien zur Deutschen Kunstgeschichte [*A publication*]
STDL........ Standard Distribution List [*NASA*]   (NASA)
STDL........ Standard Logic, Inc. [*NASDAQ symbol*]   (NQ)
STDL........ Submarine Tactical Data Link   (NVT)

STDM....... Statistical Time-Division Multiplexer [*or Multiplexing*]

STDM........ Synchronous Time-Division Multiplexing [*Data processing*] (MDG)

STDN .... Set the Date Now [*Association supporting the end of US military involvement in Indochina*] [*Defunct*] (EA)

STDN .... Space Flight Tracking and Data Network [*Formerly, STADAN*] [*NASA*]

STDN .... Standardization (AFM)

STDNA...... ASTM [*American Society for Testing and Materials*] Standardization News [*A publication*]

STDO .... Standard Oil & Exploration of Delaware, Inc. [*NASDAQ symbol*] (NQ)

Std Obraztsy Chern Metall ... Standartnye Obraztsy v Chernoi Metallurgii [*A publication*]

St Doc Hist Iur ... Studia et Documenta Historiae et Iuris [*A publication*]

STDP......... Short-Term Dynamic Psychotherapy

STDP......... Special Training Devices Program (AFM)

St DR .... Statistik des Deutschen Reichs [*A publication*]

STDS......... Snake Torpedo Destruction System

STDS......... Standards [*Timber measurement*] (EY)

STDS......... Submarine Tactical Data System (MCD)

STDS......... System for Thermal Diagnostic Studies

STDST ...... Start Descent [*Aviation*] (FAAC)

STDV........ Start Tank Discharge Valve (KSC)

STDVG...... Stern Diving

STDWN .... Stand Down (MCD)

STDY......... Saturday

STDY......... Steady (MSA)

St Dziej Kosc Kat ... Studia z Dziejow Kosciola Katolickiego [*A publication*]

STDZN...... Standardization (AABC)

STE .... Sainte [*Female Saint*] (EY)

STE............ Segment Table Entry [*Data processing*] (MDG)

STE............ Self-Trapped Exciton [*Physical chemistry*]

STE............ Shield Test Experiment [*Nuclear energy*] (NRCH)

STE............ Shift Technical Engineer [*Nuclear energy*] (NRCH)

STE............ [*The*] Simplified Test Equipment [*Army*] (INF)

Ste .... Societe [*Company*] [*French*] [*Business term*]

STE............ Society of Telecom Executives [*Trade union*] [*British*]

STE............ Society of Tractor Engineers [*Later, SAE*]

STE............ Spacecraft Test Engineering [*NASA*] (KSC)

STE............ Span Terminating Equipment [*Telecommunications*] (TEL)

STE............ Special Test Equipment

STE............ Special-Type Ellipsometer

STE............ Specific Temperature Excursion

STE............ Stahl und Eisen. Zeitschrift fuer Technik und Wissenschaft der Herstellung und Verarbeitung von Eisen und Stahl [*A publication*]

STE............ Star Tracker Electronics [*Apollo*] [*NASA*]

STE............ Station Test Equipment [*Deep Space Instrumentation Facility, NASA*]

STE............ Statute

Ste .... Steaua [*A publication*]

STE............ Stelco, Inc. [*Toronto Stock Exchange symbol*] [*Vancouver Stock Exchange symbol*]

STE............ Stepanavan [*USSR*] [*Seismograph station code, US Geological Survey*] [*Closed*] (SEIS)

Ste .... Stephanus Provincialis [*Flourished, 1290-97*] [*Authority cited in pre-1607 legal work*] (DSA)

Ste .... Stephanus Tornacensis [*Deceased, 1203*] [*Authority cited in pre-1607 legal work*] (DSA)

STE............ Stevens Point [*Wisconsin*] [*Airport symbol*] [*Obsolete*] (OAG)

STE............ Stockton Terminal & Eastern Railroad [*AAR code*]

St E .... Studienreihe Englisch [*A publication*]

STE............ Suitability Test Evaluation (AAG)

STE............ Supergroup Translation Equipment

STE............ Support Test Equipment (MCD)

STE............ Syrian Telecommunications Establishment [*Syrian Arab Republic*] (TSSD)

STE............ System Test Engineer [*NASA*] (NASA)

STEA......... Short-Term Emergency Assistance

STEA......... Surveyor Test Equipment Assembly

STEA......... System Test, Evaluation, and Assembly

STEADG.... Sciences et Techniques de l'Eau [*A publication*]

STEAG...... Steinkohlen-Elektrizitaet AG [*West Germany*]

STEAM...... Department of Science, Technology, Energy, and Materials [*Proposed Cabinet department*]

STEAM...... Sensor Technology as Applied to the Marine Corps

STEAM...... Standard Towing Equipment for Aircraft Maintenance (MCD)

STEAM...... Streptonigrin, Thioguanine, Endoxan [*Cyclophosphamide*], Actinomycin, Mitomycin C [*Antineoplastic drug regimen*]

Steam Eng ... Steam Engineer [*A publication*]

Steam Fuel Users J ... Steam and Fuel Users' Journal [*A publication*]

Steam and Heat Eng ... Steam and Heating Engineer [*A publication*]

Steam Heat Eng ... Steam and Heating Engineer [*A publication*]

Steam Heat Engr ... Steam and Heating Engineer [*A publication*]

Steam Plant Eng ... Steam Plant Engineering [*A publication*]

Steam Pwr ... Steam Power [*A publication*]

Steamusers Fuel Users J ... Steamusers' and Fuel Users' Journal [*A publication*]

STEAP ...... Simulated Trajectories Error Analysis Program [*NASA*]

Stearns RA ... Stearn's Real Actions [*A publication*] (DLA)

Stearns Real Act ... Stearn's Real Actions [*A publication*] (DLA)

St Ebla ... Studi Eblaiti [*A publication*]

STEC......... Serv-Tech, Inc. [*NASDAQ symbol*] (NQ)

STEC......... Solar Thermal Electric Conversation (MCD)

STEC......... Southern Tablelands Education Centre [*Australia*]

STEC......... Syndicat des Travailleurs de l'Energie et de la Chimie [*Energy and Chemical Workers Union - ECWU*] [*Canada*]

St Eccl Cas ... Stillingfleet's English Ecclesiastical Cases [*A publication*] (DLA)

Stecher Agency & Partnership ... Stecher's Cases on Agency and Partnership [*A publication*] (DLA)

Stechert-Hafner Bk News ... Stechert-Hafner Book News [*A publication*]

STECR ...... Ships Tactical Environmental Control Receiver

STECS....... Software Technology and Engineering Center Staff [*Social Security Administration*]

STED......... Science, Technology, and Economic Development

STED......... Standard Technical Equipment Development Division [*Obsolete*] [*National Security Agency*]

STEDA...... Steroids [*A publication*]

STEDBAC ... Stearyldimethylbenzylammonium Chloride [*Organic chemistry*]

STEDI .... Space Thrust Evolution and Disposal Investigation [*Air Force*]

STEDMIS ... Ships Technical Data Management Information System [*Navy*]

STEDMIS ... Standard Technical Data Management Information System (CAAL)

STEEG ...... Scanned Topographic Electroencephalograph

Steel Const ... Steel Construction [*A publication*] (APTA)

Steel Constr ... Steel Construction [*A publication*] (APTA)

Steel Fabric J ... Steel Fabrication Journal [*A publication*] (APTA)

Steel Fabr J ... Steel Fabrication Journal [*A publication*] (APTA)

STEELFACTS ... Materials Database Steel and Iron [*German Iron and Steel Engineers Association*] [*Information service or system*] [*Ceased operation*] (IID)

Steel Founders' Res J ... Steel Founders' Research Journal [*A publication*]

Steel Furn Mon ... Steel Furnace Monthly [*A publication*]

Steel Horiz ... Steel Horizons [*A publication*]

Steel Ind ..... World Steel Industry. Into and Out of the 1990's [*A publication*]

Steel Ind Jpn Annu ... Steel Industry of Japan Annual [*A publication*]

Steel Int ...... Steel International [*A publication*]

Steel Met Int ... Steels and Metals International [*A publication*]

Steel Process ... Steel Processing [*A publication*]

Steel Process Convers ... Steel Processing and Conversion [*A publication*]

Steel Rev .... Steel Review [*A publication*]

Steel Stat ... Steel Statistics for Europe [*A publication*]

Steel Stat Q ... Quarterly Bulletin of Steel Statistics for Europe [*A publication*]

Steel Times Int ... Steel Times International [*England*] [*A publication*]

Steenth....... Sixteenth [*Stock and commodity price quotes*]

STEEP....... Safety Training for the Execution of Emergency Procedures [*NASA*]

STEEP....... Shock Two-Dimensional Eulerian Elastic Plastic [*Computer code*]

STEEP....... Solution to Environmental and Economic Problems

Steer PL..... Steer on Parish Law [*6th ed.*] [*1899*] [*A publication*] (DLA)

STEG......... Staatliche Gesellschaft zur Erfassung von Ruestungsgut [*German Public Corporation for the Collection and Distribution of War Materials*]

STEG........ Supersonic Transport Evaluation Group

STEIA .... Stahl und Eisen [*A publication*]

STE/ICE ... Simplified Test Equipment for Internal Combustion Engines (RDA)

STE/ICEPM ... Simplified Test Equipment for Internal Combustion Engine Powered Material (MCD)

STEIN .... System Test Environment Input

Steinbeck M ... Steinbeck Monograph Series [*A publication*]

Steinbeck Q ... Steinbeck Quarterly [*A publication*]

SteinbQ....... Steinbeck Quarterly [*A publication*]

S Teind....... Shaw's Scotch Teind [*Tithe*] Cases [*A publication*] (DLA)

Steiner Tb .. Rudolf Steiner Taschenbuchausgaben [*A publication*]

Steinind Steinstrassenbau ... Steinindustrie und Steinstrassenbau [*A publication*]

Stein-Ind Strassenbau ... Stein-Industrie und -Strassenbau [*A publication*]

Steinkohlenbergbauver Kurznachr ... Steinkohlenbergbauverein Kurznachrichten [*A publication*]

SteiQ.......... Steinbeck Quarterly [*A publication*]

Steirische Beitr Hydrogeol ... Steirische Beitraege zur Hydrogeologie [*A publication*]

Steirisch Imkerbote ... Steirischer Imkerbote [*A publication*]

St Ek .... Studiea Ekonomiczne [*A publication*]

Steklo Keram ... Steklo i Keramika [*A publication*]

Steklo i Keram ... Steklo i Keramika [*A publication*]

Steklo Sitally Silik Mater ... Steklo, Sitally, i Silikatnye Materialy [*Belorussian SSR*] [*A publication*]

Stekolnaya Keram Promst ... Stekol'naya i Keramicheskaya Promyshlennost [*A publication*]

Stekol'naya Prom-St ... Stekol'naya Promyshlennost [*USSR*] [*A publication*]

STEL .... Satelco, Inc. [*NASDAQ symbol*] (NQ)

STEL .... Short-Term Exposure Limit [*Environmental chemistry*]

STEL .... Society of Telegraphic Engineers [*British*]

STEL .... Structure Tests, English Language [*Educational test*]

STEL .... Studenta Tutmonda Esperantista Liga [*World League of Esperanto-Speaking Students*]

STEL .... Sunday Telegraph [*United Kingdom*] [*A publication*]
STELB ...... Stereo Review [*A publication*]
STELCO .... Steel Company of Canada
STELDF .... Science and Technology Libraries [*A publication*]
STELLA .... Satellite Transmission Experiment Linking Laboratories [*European Space Agency*]
STELLA .... Structural Thinking Experiential Learning Laboratory with Animation [*Software*]
STELLAR ... Star Tracker for Economical Long Life Attitude Reference [*NASA*]
Stellenbosse Stud ... Stellenbosse Student [*A publication*]
STEM .... Scanning Transmission Electron Microscope
STEM .... Science and Technology Employment [*Longman Cartermill Ltd.*] [*Scotland*] [*Information service or system*] (CRD)
STEM .... SEABEE Tactical Equipment Management [*Navy*]
STEM .... Searching Together Educational Ministries (EA)
STEM .... Shaped Tube Electrolytic Machining [*GE*]
STEM .... Shoplifters Take Everybody's Money
STEM .... Society of Teachers of Emergency Medicine (EA)
STEM .... Socio-Technological-Economic-Military [*DoD*]
STEM .... Solar-Terrestrial Environment Model [*to predict the terrestrial effects of solar events*]
STEM .... Special Technical and Economic Mission
STEM .... Special Telemetry Equipped Missile
STEM .... Stay Time Extension Module [*NASA*]
STEM .... Stellar Tracker Evaluation Missile
STEM .... Storable Tubular Extendable Member
STEM .... System Test Equipment Mission [*NASA*] (KSC)
STEM .... Systems for Tools and Equipment Management [*Military*] (AFIT)
STEM .... Systems Training and Exercise Module (MCD)
STEMFAB ... Storable Tubular Extendable Member Fabrication
STEMS ...... Small Terminal Evasive Missile System (MCD)
STEMS ...... Society to Encourage Miniskirts [*New York group opposing below-the-knee fashions introduced in 1970*]
STEM-TEM ... Scanning Transmission Electron Microscopy - Transmission Electron Microscopy
STEN .... Sheppard-Turpin-England [*Machine carbine codesigned by Sheppard and Turpin*]
STEN .... Stencil
STEN .... Stenographer
St Enc .... Study Encounter [*A publication*]
STENCH ... Society to Exterminate Neo-Communist Harbingers
Stendhal Cl ... Stendhal Club [*A publication*]
ST-ENDOR ... Special Triple-Electron Nuclear Double Resonance [*Spectroscopy*]
St Engl Lit ... Studies in English Literature [*A publication*]
STENO ...... Stenographer (MUGU)
STENS ...... Standard Terrestrial Navigation System (MCD)
Stenton .... Stenton. Rolls of the Justices in Eyre [*A publication*] (ILCA)
Stenton G ... Rolls of the Justices in Eyre for Gloucestershire, Worcestershire, and Staffordshire [*A publication*] (ILCA)
Stenton Y ... Rolls of the Justices in Eyre in Yorkshire [*A publication*] (ILCA)
STEO .... Special Test Equipment Order (MCD)
STeol .... Studii Teologice [*A publication*]
STEP .... Safeguard Test and Evaluation Program [*Army*] (AABC)
STEP .... Safety Test Engineering Program [*AEC*]
STEP .... Sales Tax Exemption Processing System [*Software*]
STEP .... School to Employment Program
STEP .... Scientific and Technical Exploitation Program (AFM)
STEP .... Selective Traffic Enforcement Program [*Department of Transportation*]
STEP .... Self-Teaching Exportable Package
STEP .... Sensitivity Temperature Error Program (MCD)
STEP .... Sequential Tests of Educational Progress [*of ETS; given in 10th and 12th grades*]
STEP .... Sequentially Timed Events Plotting [*In publication title, "Investigating Accidents with STEP"*] [*Marcel Decker, Inc.*]
STEP .... Shell Technology Enterprise Programme [*British*]
STEP .... Ship Type Electronics Plan [*Navy*] (NG)
STEP .... Short Term Enrichment Program [*of US Information Agency*]
STEP .... Simple Transition to Economical Processing (IEEE)
STEP .... Simple Transition to Electronic Processing
STEP .... Software Test and Evaluation Process [*DoD*]
STEP .... Solutions to Employment Problems [*A program of National Association of Manufacturers*]
STEP .... Space Technology Experiments Platform
STEP .... Space Terminal Evaluation Program
STEP .... Special Training Enlistment Program
STEP .... Special Training Equipment Program Document (AFIT)
STEP .... Staff Training Extramural Programs [*National Institutes of Health*]
STEP .... Standard Tape Executive Package [*or Program*] [*NCR Corp.*]
STEP .... Standard Terminal Program [*Data processing*] (IEEE)
STEP .... Standard Test Equipment Procedure (NG)
STEP .... Statistical Trajectory Estimation Program [*NASA*]
STEP .... Stratosphere-Troposphere Exchange Project [*NASA*]
STEP .... Student Education Program

STEP .... Student Transfer Education Plan [*Defunct*] [*National Urban League*]
STEP .... Students toward Environmental Participation [*UNESCO and National Park Service*]
STEP .... Summer Training Employment Program (MCD)
STEP .... Supervisory Tape Executive Program [*Data processing*]
STEP .... Supplemental Training and Employment Program (OICC)
STEP .... System for Testing Evaluation of Potential [*Employee evaluation software*] [*London House, Inc.*]
STEP .... Systematic Training for Effective Parenting
Steph .... Stephanus Pragensis [*Flourished, 14th century*] [*Authority cited in pre-1607 legal work*] (DSA)
Steph .... Stephanus Tornacensis [*Deceased, 1203*] [*Authority cited in pre-1607 legal work*] (DSA)
Steph .... Stephens' Supreme Court Decisions [*1774-1923*] [*Jamaica*] [*A publication*] (DLA)
Stepha Bertrand ... Stephanus Bertrandus [*Flourished, 16th century*] [*Authority cited in pre-1607 legal work*] (DSA)
Steph Cl ..... Stephens on Clergy [*1848*] [*A publication*] (DLA)
Steph Com ... Stephen's Commentaries on the Laws of England [*A publication*] (DLA)
Steph Comm ... Stephen's Commentaries on the Laws of England [*A publication*] (DLA)
Steph Const ... Stephens on the English Constitution [*A publication*] (DLA)
Steph Cr ..... Stephen's Digest of the Criminal Law [*A publication*] (DLA)
Steph Crim Dig ... Stephen's Digest of the Criminal Law [*A publication*] (DLA)
Steph Cr L ... Stephen's General View of the Criminal Law [*9 eds.*] [*1877-1950*] [*A publication*] (DLA)
Steph Cr Law ... Stephen's General View of the Criminal Law [*A publication*] (DLA)
Steph Dig ... Stephen's Digest, New Brunswick Reports [*A publication*] (DLA)
Steph Dig Cr L ... Stephen's Digest of the Criminal Law [*A publication*] (DLA)
Steph Dig Cr Law ... Stephen's Digest of the Criminal Law [*A publication*] (DLA)
Steph Dig Ev ... Stephen's Digest of the Law of Evidence [*A publication*] (DLA)
Steph Elect ... Stephens on Elections [*1840*] [*A publication*] (DLA)
Stephen F Austin State Coll Sch For Bull ... Stephen F. Austin State College. School of Forestry. Bulletin [*A publication*]
Stephen HCL ... Stephen's History of Criminal Law [*A publication*] (DLA)
Stephens .... Supreme Court Decisions, by J. E. R. Stephens [*A publication*] (DLA)
Steph Ev ..... Stephen's Digest of the Law of Evidence [*A publication*] (DLA)
Steph Gen View ... Stephen's General View of the Criminal Law [*2nd ed.*] [*1890*] [*A publication*] (DLA)
Steph J St Comp ... Steph's Joint-Stock Companies in Canada [*A publication*] (DLA)
Steph Lect ... Stephen's Lectures on the History of France [*A publication*] (DLA)
Steph NP ... Stephen's Law of Nisi Prius [*A publication*] (DLA)
Steph Pl ..... Stephen on Pleading [*A publication*] (DLA)
Steph Proc ... Stephens on Procurations [*A publication*] (DLA)
Steph Slav ... Stephens on Slavery [*A publication*] (DLA)
STEPP .... Society of Teachers in Education of Professional Photography (EA)
STEPR ...... Saturation Transfer Electron Paramagnetic Resonance [*Physics*]
STEPS .... Science and Technology Evaluation and Prioritization System [*Program*] (RDA)
STEPS .... Ships Technical Publication System [*Navy*]
STEPS .... Solar Thermionic Electrical Power System
STEPS .... Stored Thermal Energy Propulsion System
STER .... Seater
STER .... Stereotype
STER .... Sterilize (AABC)
STER .... Sterling
STER .... Sterna [*A publication*]
STER .... Successively Truncated Expectation of the Reciprocal [*Statistics*]
STER .... System Training Equipment Requirement
Stereo .... Stereo Review [*A publication*]
STEREO ... Stereophonic (MSA)
STEREO ... Stereoscope [*or Stereoscopic*]
STEREO ... Stereotype [*Refers to old news*] [*Slang*] (DSUE)
Stereochem Fundam Methods ... Stereochemistry. Fundamentals and Methods [*A publication*]
Stereo R ..... Stereo Review [*A publication*]
Stereotactic Funct Neurosurg ... Stereotactic and Functional Neurosurgery [*A publication*]
STERF .... Special Test Equipment Repair Facility
STERL .... Sterling (ADA)
STERNUT ... Sternutamentum [*Snuff*] [*Pharmacy*]
Steroids Lipids Res ... Steroids and Lipids Research [*A publication*]
Steroids Suppl ... Steroids. Supplement [*A publication*]
STES .... Solar Thermal Energy System
STES Newsl ... STES [*Seasonal Thermal Energy Storage*] Newsletter [*United States*] [*A publication*]
STE-T .... Simplified Test Equipment - Transitional [*Army*]
STET .... Specialized Technique for Efficient Typesetting

STET .... Steward, Technical [*Marine Corps*]
STET .... System Test Experiments Tape
STETF ...... Solar Total Energy Test Facility [*Energy Research and Development Administration*]
StEtr .... Studi Etruschi [*A publication*]
STETS .... Solar-Terrestrial Energy Transfer Studies [*Meteorology*]
Stetson L Rev ... Stetson Law Review [*A publication*]
Stettin Ent Ztg ... Stettiner Entomologische Zeitung [*A publication*]
STEUA ...... Steuerungstechnik [*A publication*]
STEV .... Stevedore
STEV .... Stevia Co., Inc. [*Arlington Heights, IL*] [*NASDAQ symbol*] (NQ)
StEv .... Studia Evangelica [*Berlin*] [*A publication*]
Stev Arb ..... Stevens on Arbitration [*2nd ed.*] [*1835*] [*A publication*] (DLA)
Stev Av ..... Stevens on Average [*5th ed.*] [*1835*] [*A publication*] (DLA)
Stev & Ben Ins ... Stevens and Benecke on Insurance [*A publication*] (DLA)
Stev Dig ..... Stevens' New Brunswick Digest [*A publication*] (DLA)
STEVE ...... Space Tool for Extravehicular Emergencies
Stevens & G ... Stevens and Graham's Reports [*98-139 Georgia*] [*A publication*] (DLA)
Stevens Ind ... Stevens Indicator [*A publication*]
Stevens Inst Technol (Hoboken NJ) Davidson Lab Rep ... Stevens Institute of Technology (Hoboken, New Jersey). Davidson Laboratory. Report [*A publication*]
Stev & G ..... Stevens and Graham's Reports [*98-139 Georgia*] [*A publication*] (DLA)
STEVS ...... Spartan Tactical Equipment Verification Site [*Missiles*] (MCD)
STEW .... Stewart Sandwiches, Inc. [*NASDAQ symbol*] (NQ)
Stew............ Stewart's Alabama Reports [*1827-31*] [*A publication*] (DLA)
Stew............ Stewart's Equity Reports [*28-45 New Jersey*] [*A publication*] (DLA)
Stew............ Stewart's Nova Scotia Admiralty Reports [*A publication*] (DLA)
Stew............ Stewart's Reports [*1-10 South Dakota*] [*A publication*] (DLA)
Stew Adm... Stewart's Nova Scotia Vice-Admiralty Reports [*1803-13*] [*A publication*] (DLA)
Stew Admr ... Stewart's Nova Scotia Admiralty Reports [*A publication*] (DLA)
Stew (Ala).. Stewart's Alabama Reports [*A publication*] (DLA)
Stew Ans .... Stewart's Answers to Dirleton's Doubts [*2 eds.*] [*1715, 1762*] [*Scotland*] [*A publication*] (DLA)
Stewart....... Stewart's Alabama Reports [*1827-31*] [*A publication*] (DLA)
Stewart....... Stewart's Equity Reports [*28-45 New Jersey*] [*A publication*] (DLA)
Stewart....... Stewart's Nova Scotia Admiralty Reports [*A publication*] (DLA)
Stewart....... Stewart's Reports [*1-10 South Dakota*] [*A publication*] (DLA)
Stewart (Ala) ... Stewart's Alabama Reports [*A publication*] (DLA)
Stewart-Brown ... Stewart-Brown's Lancashire and Cheshire Cases in the Court of Star Chamber [*A publication*] (DLA)
Stewart R ... Stewart's Alabama Reports [*A publication*] (DLA)
Stew Dig..... Stewart's Digest of Decisions of Law and Equity [*New Jersey*] [*A publication*] (ILCA)
Stew Eq ...... Stewart's Equity Reports [*28-45 New Jersey*] [*A publication*] (DLA)
Stew N Sc... Stewart's Nova Scotia Admiralty Reports [*A publication*] (DLA)
Stew & P .... Stewart and Porter's Alabama Supreme Court Reports [*1831-34*] [*A publication*] (DLA)
Stew and Porter ... Stewart and Porter's Alabama Reports [*A publication*] (DLA)
Stew & P Rep ... Stewart and Porter's Alabama Reports [*A publication*] (DLA)
STEWS...... Shipboard Tactical Electronic Warfare System [*Navy*]
Stewt Rep... Stewart's Alabama Reports [*A publication*] (DLA)
Stew VA ..... Stewart's Nova Scotia Vice-Admiralty Reports [*A publication*] (DLA)
STE-X....... Simplified Test Equipment-Expandable [*Army*] (RDA)
STEX .... Statute Expired [*IRS*]
S Texas LJ ... South Texas Law Journal [*A publication*]
S Tex LJ .... South Texas Law Journal [*A publication*]
STeZ.......... South Temperate Zone
STF .... S-Band Temperature Fahrenheit
STF .... S-Band Transmit Filter
STF .... Safety Test Facility [*Nuclear energy*]
STF .... Satellite Tracking Facility [*Air Force*]
STF .... Service Tabulating Form (AAG)
STF .... Signal Tracking Filter
STF .... Software Test Facility [*NASA*] (MCD)
STF .... Soviet Studies. A Quarterly Journal on the USSR and Eastern Europe [*A publication*]
STF .... Space Track Facility
STF .... Spacecraft Test Facility
STF .... Special Task Force [*Army*]
STF .... Special Technical Factors (MCD)
STF .... Special Tube Feeding [*Medicine*]
STF .... Spin Test Facility [*NASA*]
STF .... Staff (AFM)
STF .... Standardized Test of Fitness [*Canadian Association of Sports Sciences*]
STF .... Stanford Resources Ltd. [*Toronto Stock Exchange symbol*]

St F............. Starch-Free [*Pharmacy*]
STF .... Starkville, MS [*Location identifier*] [*FAA*] (FAAL)
STF .... Static Test Facility (KSC)
stf .... Stiff [*Quality of the bottom*] [*Nautical charts*]
STF .... Strange Fantasy [*A publication*]
STF .... Stratiform [*Meteorology*] (FAAC)
STF .... Structural Fatigue Test (MCD)
STF .... Subject to Finance (ADA)
STF .... Subjective Transfer Function (MCD)
STF .... Supervisory Time Frame
STF .... System Test Facility
STF .... Systems Technology Forum [*Fairfax, VA*] [*Telecommunications*] (TSSD)
STFAS...... Support to Total Force Analysis [*TRADOC*] (MCD)
STFD........ Standard Federal Savings and Loan Association [*NASDAQ symbol*] (NQ)
STFF .... Safeguard Tactical Field Force [*Army*] (AABC)
STFG .... Staffing Guides [*Army*] (AABC)
STFG .... Stuffing (MSA)
StFil .... Studia Filozoficzne [*A publication*]
STFM .... Societe des Textes Francais Modernes [*A publication*]
STFM .... Society of Teachers of Family Medicine (EA)
STFM .... Stretcher Form [*Tool*] (AAG)
St Form Sp ... Studies in Formative Spirituality [*A publication*]
St For Note Calif Div For ... State Forest Notes. California Division of Forestry [*A publication*]
STFPA....... Strahlenschutz in Forschung und Praxis [*A publication*]
STFR .... Stratus Fractus [*Meteorology*] (FAAC)
StFr.......... Studi Francescani [*A publication*]
STFRM ..... Stratiform [*Meteorology*] (FAAC)
STFSGT ... Staff Sergeant [*Marine Corps*]
STFT .... Stray Field Test (NVT)
St Furrow ... Straight Furrow [*A publication*]
STG........... Saint George Island [*Alaska*] [*Airport symbol*] (OAG)
STG........... Satellite Terminal Guidance
Stg............. Sea-Tangle [*Nautical charts*]
STG........... Seating [*Technical drawings*]
STG........... Sedalia, Marshall, Boonville Stage Line, Inc. [*Des Moines, IA*] [*FAA designator*] (FAAC)
STG........... SONAR Technician, Ground [*Navy rating*]
STG........... Souther Gold Resources [*Vancouver Stock Exchange symbol*]
STG........... Space Task Group [*Later, Manned Spacecraft Center*] [*NASA*]
STG........... Space Telescope Guidance [*NASA*]
STG........... Special Technology Group [*National Technical Information Service*] (MCD)
STG........... Split Thickness Graft [*Medicine*]
STG........... Staging (AABC)
STG........... Standing [*Numismatics*]
STG........... Starting (MSA)
STG........... State Government [*A publication*]
STG........... Steego Corp. [*Formerly, Sterling Precision Corp.*] [*NYSE symbol*] (SPSG)
STG........... Steering Task Group
STG........... Sterling
STG........... Stomatogastric Ganglion [*Neuroanatomy*]
STG........... Storage
STG........... Storage Triacylglycerol [*Biochemistry*]
STG........... Strathgordon [*Tasmania*] [*Seismograph station code, US Geological Survey*] (SEIS)
STG........... Strong (FAAC)
StG............ Studi Germanici [*A publication*]
StG............ Studium Generale [*Heidelberg*] [*A publication*]
STG........... Study Group [*NATO*]
STG........... Sturmgewehr [*Storm Rifle*] [*German military - World War II*]
STG........... Sydney Tourist Guide [*A publication*] (APTA)
STGA........ Saratoga Standardbreds, Inc. [*North Salem, NY*] [*NASDAQ symbol*] (NQ)
STGAA...... Shade Tobacco Growers Agricultural Association (EA)
StGAK .... Studien zur Germanistik, Anglistik und Komparatistik [*A publication*]
STGAR...... Staging Area [*Military*]
STGB........ Staging Base [*Military*]
StGB......... Strafgesetzbuch [*Penal Code*] [*German*]
STGC........ Secure Task Group, Common (MCD)
STGE........ Storage
STGEA...... Studium Generale [*A publication*]
STGEN...... Steam Generator
St Genuensi ... Studi Genuensi [*A publication*]
St Ger D & S ... St. German's Doctor and Student [*A publication*] (DLA)
STGG........ Staging (AABC)
STGH........ Stang Hydronics [*NASDAQ symbol*] (NQ)
STGHT...... Straight
StGKA .... Studien zur Geschichte und Kultur des Altertums [*A publication*]
St Gloc .... Statute of Gloucester [*First statute to give costs in actions*] [*A publication*] (DLA)
STGM........ Status Game Corp. [*NASDAQ symbol*] (NQ)
STGO .... Star-Glo Industries [*NASDAQ symbol*] (NQ)
STGP........ Subcontract Task Group Procurement
STGR........ Steiger Tractor, Inc. [*NASDAQ symbol*] (NQ)
STGR........ Stringer (AAG)

Stgr .... Studia Grammatica [*A publication*]
St Gr I .... Studi di Grammatica Italiana [*A publication*]
STGS .... Strings Ltd. [*NASDAQ symbol*]   (NQ)
STG/STF .. Special Task Group/Special Task Force [*Army*]   (MCD)
STGT .... Secondary Target [*Military*]
StGThK .... Studien zur Geschichte der Theologie und der Kirche [*A publication*]
S Th .... Scholar in Theology [*British*]
STH .... Seton Hall University, South Orange, NJ [*OCLC symbol*]   (OCLC)
STH .... Somatotrophic [*Growth*] Hormone [*Also, GH, SH*] [*Endocrinology*]
STH .... South
STH .... Stanhome, Inc. [*NYSE symbol*]   (SPSG)
STH .... Stoney Hill [*Jamaica*] [*Seismograph station code, US Geological Survey*]   (SEIS)
STH .... Stray Horse Resources, Inc. [*Vancouver Stock Exchange symbol*]
STH .... Student in Theology [*British*]
STh .... Studia Theologica [*A publication*]
STh .... Subthalamus [*Anatomy*]
STH .... Subtotal Hysterectomy [*Medicine*]
STH .... Toronto School of Theology Library, University of Toronto [*UTLAS symbol*]
St & H Abor ... Storer and Heard on Criminal Abortion [*A publication*]   (DLA)
Sth Afr Rep ... South African Republic High Court Reports [*A publication*]   (DLA)
SThB .... Sacrae Theologiae Baccalaureus [*Bachelor of Sacred Theology*]
SThD .... Sacrae Theologiae Doctor [*Doctor of Sacred Theology*]
STHEA ..... Steam and Heating Engineer [*A publication*]
StHefte .... Statistische Hefte [*A publication*]
Sthen .... Stheneboea [*of Euripides*] [*Classical studies*]   (OCD)
STHEST .... Southeast
STHESTN ... Southeastern
STHF .... Stanley Interiors Corp. [*Stanleytown, VA*] [*NASDAQ symbol*]   (NQ)
S ThL .... Sacrae Theologiae Lecentiatus [*Licentiate in Sacred Theology*]
STHLY .... Southerly [*A publication*]
STHMPN ... Southampton [*England*]
STHN .... Southern
Sthn Afr Fam Pract ... Southern African Family Practice [*A publication*]
Sthn Afr Text ... Southern Africa Textiles [*A publication*]
Sthn Birds ... Southern Birds [*A publication*]
STHP .... Shih-Ta Hsueh-Pao [*Bulletin of Taiwan Normal University*] [*A publication*]
STHPD ...... Shih-Ta Hsueh-Pao [*Bulletin of Taiwan Normal University*] [*A publication*]
StHR .... Stress Hypertensive Rats
STHRD ..... Solar Thermal Report [*A publication*]
STHS .... Scottish Thoracic Society
SThU .... Schweizerische Theologische Umschau [*A publication*]
St Hum .... Studies in the Humanities [*A publication*]
STHV .... Science, Technology, and Human Values [*A publication*]
STHWST .. Southwest
STHWSTN ... Southwestern
SThZ .... Schweizerische Theologische Zeitschrift [*Zurich*] [*A publication*]
STI .... Mountain Home, ID [*Location identifier*] [*FAA*]   (FAAL)
STI .... St. Thomas Institute [*Research center*]   (RCD)
STI .... Santiago [*Dominican Republic*] [*Airport symbol*]   (OAG)
STI .... Saskatoon Technical Institute [*UTLAS symbol*]
STI .... Saxton Industries [*Vancouver Stock Exchange symbol*]
STI .... Scientific and Technical Information [*System*] [*Canada*]
STI .... Scientific and Technical Information [*Facility*] [*NASA*]
STI .... Screw Thread Insert
STI .... Serum Trypsin Inhibitor [*Serology*]
STI .... Server Technology, Incorporated [*Information service or system*]   (IID)
STI .... Service Tools Institute [*Later, HTI*]   (EA)
STI .... Short-Term Integration   (CAAL)
STI .... Silicon Target Intensifier
STI .... Single Tooth Indexer
Sti .... Sirketi [*Company*] [*See also Ltd Sti*] [*Turkish*]
STI .... Small Towns Institute   (EA)
STI .... Software Tool Information Database [*Air Force Systems Command*] [*Information service or system*]   (CRD)
STI .... Soybean Trypsin Inhibition [*Biochemistry*]
STI .... Space Technology, Incorporated   (MCD)
STI .... Specifications Technology, Incorporated
STI .... Speech Transmission Index
STI .... Star Valley [*Idaho*] [*Seismograph station code, US Geological Survey*]   (SEIS)
STI .... State Technical Institute
STI .... Steel Tank Institute   (EA)
STI .... Stem Tolerance Index [*Botany*]
STI .... Stilbite [*A zeolite*]
Sti .... Stinson [*Record label*]
StI .... Studi Ispanici [*A publication*]
StI .... Studi Italiani [*A publication*]
StI .... Studia Islandica [*A publication*]

StI .... Studies: An Irish Quarterly Review of Letters, Philosophy, and Science [*A publication*]
STI .... SunTrust Banks, Incorporated [*NYSE symbol*]   (SPSG)
STI .... Surface Targets of Interest   (MCD)
STI .... Survive Tomorrow, Incorporated [*Commercial firm*]   (EA)
STI .... Systolic Time Interval [*Cardiology*]
STIA .... Scientific, Technological, and International Affairs Directorate [*National Science Foundation*]
STIAP .... Standard Instrument Approach [*RADAR*] [*Aviation*]
STIB .... Stimulus Train-Induced Bursting [*Neuroscience*]
STIBOKA ... Stichting voor Bodemkartering [*Netherlands Soil Survey Institute*] [*Wageningen*] [*Information service or system*]   (IID)
STIC .... Science and Technology Information Center [*National Science Council*]   (IID)
STIC .... Scientific and Technical Intelligence Center [*DoD*]
STIC .... Solid-State Transducer Intercompartmental Catheter [*Instrumentation*]
STIC .... Space Technical Information Control   (MCD)
STIC .... Space Toy Information Center   (EA)
STICAP .... Stiff Circuit Analysis Program [*Data processing*]
STICEC .... Special Travel Industry Council on Energy Conservation
ST/ICERD ... Suntory Toyota International Centre for Economics and Related Disciplines [*London School of Economics and Political Science*] [*British*]   (CB)
Stich .... Stichus [*of Plautus*] [*Classical studies*]   (OCD)
Sticht Bosbouwproefsta "Dorschkamp" Ber ... Stichting Bosbouwproefstation "De Dorschkamp." Berichten [*A publication*]
Sticht Bosbouwproefsta "Dorschkamp" Korte Meded ... Stichting Bosbouwproefstation "De Dorschkamp." Korte Mededelingen [*A publication*]
Sticht Bosbouwproefsta "Dorschkamp" Uitv Versl ... Stichting Bosbouwproefstation "De Dorschkamp." Uitvoerige Verslagen [*A publication*]
Sticht Bosbouwproefstn "De Dorschkamp" Korte Meded ... Stichting Bosbouwproefstation "De Dorschkamp." Korte Mededeling [*A publication*]
Sticht Coord Cult Onderz Broodgraan Jaarb ... Stichting voor Coordinate van Cultuur en Onderzoek van Broodgraan Jaarboekje [*A publication*]
Sticht Energieonderz Cent Ned Rep ... Stichting Energieonderzoek Centrum Nederland. Report [*A publication*]
Sticht Fundam Onderz Mater Jaarb ... Stichting voor Fundamenteel Onderzoek der Materie. Jaarboek [*A publication*]
Sticht Inst Kernphys Onderz Jaarb ... Stichting Instituut voor Kernphysisch Onderzoek. Jaarboek [*A publication*]
Sticht Inst Pluimveeonderz Het Spelderholt Jaarversl ... Stichting Instituut voor Pluimveeonderzoek "Het Spelderholt" Jaarverslag [*A publication*]
Sticht Inst Pluimveeonderz Spelderholt Jaarversl ... Stichting Instituut voor Pluimveeonderzoek "Het Spelderholt" Jaarverslag [*A publication*]
STICTION ... Static Friction
STID .... Scientific and Technical Information Dissemination [*NASA*]
STID .... Scientific and Technical Information Division [*NASA*]   (IEEE)
STIDAS ..... Speech Transmission Index Device [*Using*] Artificial Signals
STIF .... Scientific and Technical Information Facility [*NASA*]
STIF .... Short-Term Irradiation Facility [*Nuclear energy*]   (NRCH)
STIF .... Spectral Transmission Interference Filter
STIF .... Stiffener [*Civil engineering*]
STIFC .... Space Track Interim Fire Control
STII .... Science and Technology Information Institute [*Information service or system*]   (EISS)
STII .... Stanford Telecommunications, Incorporated [*NASDAQ symbol*]   (NQ)
St I I .... Studien zur Indologie und Iranistik [*A publication*]
STIIBO ...... Sbornik Trudov Nauchno-Issledovatel'skogo Instituta Travmatologii i Ortopedii Gruzinskoi SSR [*A publication*]
Stiinta Sol .. Stiinta Solului [*A publication*]
STIL .... Short-Term Inhalation Limits [*of air pollutants*]
STILB .... Software Test and Integration Laboratory [*NASA*]   (NASA)
STIL .... Statistical Interpretive Language [*Data processing*]   (MDG)
Stil .... Stillingfleet's English Ecclesiastical Cases [*1702-04*] [*A publication*]   (DLA)
StIL .... Studi. Istituto Linguistico [*A publication*]
Stiles .... Stiles' Reports [*22-29 Iowa*] [*A publication*]   (DLA)
Stiles (IA) .. Stiles' Reports [*22-29 Iowa*] [*A publication*]   (DLA)
STILLAT .. Stillatim [*By Drops or In Small Quantities*] [*Pharmacy*]
STILLB ..... Stillborn [*Medicine*]
Still Ecc Law ... Stillingfleet's Discourse on Ecclesiastical Law [*A publication*]   (DLA)
Still Eccl Cas ... Stillingfleet's English Ecclesiastical Cases [*A publication*]   (DLA)
STILS .... Stinger Launch Simulator   (MCD)
STIM .... Sensitivity Training Impact Model
STIM .... Stimulant   (DSUE)
STIM .... Stimulating   (ROG)
stim .... Stimulus
S Times ...... Sunday Times [*A publication*]
Stim Gloss ... Stimson's Law Glossary [*A publication*]   (DLA)
Stim Law Gloss ... Stimson's Law Glossary [*A publication*]   (DLA)

Stim L Gl ... Stimson's Law Glossary [*A publication*] (DLA)
Stimm Zeit ... Stimmen der Zeit [*A publication*]
STIMS....... Scientific and Technical Information Modular System [*NASA*] (MCD)
Stimson...... Stimson's Law Glossary [*A publication*] (DLA)
STIMU...... Stimutech, Inc. Uts [*NASDAQ symbol*] (NQ)
Stimul Newsl ... Stimulation Newsletter [*A publication*]
STINA....... Stanki i Instrument [*A publication*]
STINA....... Steel Tube Institute of North America (EA)
Stiness........ Stiness' Reports [*20-34 Rhode Island*] [*A publication*] (DLA)
STINFO....... Scientific and Technical Information Office [*Army*]
STING....... Swift Target Identification Notification Grid (MCD)
STINGER ... SEABEE Tactically Installed, Navy Generated, Engineer Resources [*System*] [*Navy*] (NVT)
STINGS .... Stellar Inertial Guidance System [*Air Force*]
St Inst .... Stair's Institutes [*5th ed.*] [*1832*] [*A publication*] (ILCA)
STIO......... Scientific and Technical Information Office [*NASA*]
STIP .... Scientific and Technical Information Program (MCD)
STIP .... Skill Training Improvement Program [*Department of Labor*]
STIP .... Solar Technical Information Program [*Solar Energy Research Institute*] [*Information service or system*] (IID)
STIP .... Stipend [*or Stipendiary*]
STIP .... Stipulation (DAS)
STIP .... Study of Travelling Interplanetary Phenomena [*Meteorology*]
STIPE........ Stipendiary Magistrate [*British*] (DSUE)
STIPIS ...... Scientific, Technical, Intelligence, and Program Information System [*HEW*]
STIR .... Scientific and Technical Intelligence Register (AFM)
STIR .... Scientists and Technologists in Reserve [*Australia*]
STIR .... Separate Track and Illumination RADAR [*Military*] (CAAL)
STIR .... Shield Test and Irradiation Reactor [*Nuclear energy*]
STIR .... Signal Track and Illuminating RADAR [*Canadian Navy*]
STIR .... SNAP [*Systems for Nuclear Auxiliary Power*] Shield Test Irradiation Reactor
StIR.......... Stanford Italian Review [*A publication*]
STIR .... Surplus to Immediate Requirements (ADA)
STIRD .... SAIL [*Shuttle Avionics Integration Laboratory*] Test Implementation Requirements Document [*NASA*] (NASA)
Stirling E N ... Stirling Engine Newsletter [*A publication*]
STIRS ...... Self-Training Interpretive Retrieval System
STIS.......... Scientific & Technical Information Services, Inc. [*Information service or system*] (IID)
STIS.......... Silicon Target Image Sensor
STIS.......... Specialized Textile Information Service
STIS.......... Sumika Technical Information Service, Inc. [*Information service or system*] (IID)
STISA....... Sbornik Nauchnykh Trudov Tomskii Inzhenerno-Stroitel'nyi Institut [*A publication*]
STISEC ..... Scientific and Technological Information Services Enquiry Committee [*Australia*]
StIsl .... Studia Islandica [*A publication*]
StIslam ...... Studia Islamica [*Paris*] [*A publication*]
Sti Solului .. Stiinta Solului [*A publication*]
StIsp......... Studi Ispanici [*A publication*]
STIT .... Signal Technical Intelligence Team [*Army*] (AABC)
St It .... Studi Italiani di Filologia Classica [*A publication*]
StIt........... Studi Italici [*Kyoto*] [*A publication*]
STIT .... Sweet's Technical Information Test [*Vocational guidance test*]
St Ital .... Studi Italiani di Filologia Classica [*A publication*]
STIT-CONUS ... Scientific and Technical Information Team, Continental United States [*Army*] (AABC)
STIT-EUR ... Scientific and Technical Information Team, Europe [*Army*] (AABC)
STIT-FE.... Scientific and Technical Information Team, Far East [*Army*] (AABC)
STIV .... Silicon Target Intensifier Vidicon
STIZ .... Scientific Technologies, Inc. [*NASDAQ symbol*] (NQ)
StiZ........... Stimmen der Zeit [*A publication*] (BJA)
STIZ .... Submarine Transit Identification Zones (NVT)
STJ .... St. John's [*Newfoundland*] [*Geomagnetic observatory code*]
STJ .... St. John's [*Newfoundland*] [*Seismograph station code, US Geological Survey*] (SEIS)
STJ .... Saint Joseph College, West Hartford, CT [*OCLC symbol*] (OCLC)
STJ .... St. Joseph, MO [*Location identifier*] [*FAA*] (FAAL)
StJ .... St. Joseph Railway
STJ .... Series Tee Junction
STJ .... Severn Tunnel Junction [*British depot code*]
STJ .... Society of St. Teresa of Jesus [*EAIO*]
STJ .... Special Trial Judge [*US Tax Court*]
STJ .... Steel Today and Tomorrow [*A publication*]
STJ .... Subtropical Jet Stream (ADA)
STJA(NC) ... St. John Ambulance (Nursing Cadets) [*British*]
StJb.......... Stifter-Jahrbuch [*A publication*]
STJCA....... Strojnicky Casopis [*A publication*]
St J LR ..... St. John's Law Review [*A publication*]
STJM......... St. Jude Medical, Inc. [*NASDAQ symbol*] (NQ)
St J MO PUC ... St. Joseph, Missouri, Public Utilities Commission Reports [*A publication*] (DLA)

STJO .... St. Joseph Bancorporation, Inc. [*South Bend, IN*] [*NASDAQ symbol*] (NQ)
St John's L Rev ... St. John's Law Review [*A publication*]
STJU .... St. John's University [*Minnesota; New York*]
StJud.......... Studia Judaica. Forschungen zur Wissenschaft des Judentums [*Berlin*] [*A publication*]
STJVA....... Strojniski Vestnik [*A publication*]
STJW .... Stretcher Jaws [*Tool*] (AAG)
stk .... Scotland [*MARC country of publication code*] [*Library of Congress*] (LCCP)
STK......... Single Tone Keying
STK......... Situation Track Display
STK......... Soiuz Trudovogo Krest'ianstva [*Union of Working Peasantry*] [*Russian*]
STK......... Stack (MSA)
STK......... Stakes Race [*Horse racing*]
STK......... Standard Test Key [*Data processing*]
STK......... Stephens Creek [*Australia*] [*Seismograph station code, US Geological Survey*] (SEIS)
STK......... Sterling, CO [*Location identifier*] [*FAA*] (FAAL)
stk .... Sticky [*Quality of the bottom*] [*Nautical charts*]
STK......... Stock (AAG)
STK......... Storage Technology Corp. [*NYSE symbol*] (SPSG)
STK......... Strake [*Mining engineering*]
STK......... Sturmkanone [*Self-propelled assault gun*] [*German military - World War II*]
STK......... Svensk Teologisk Kvartalskrift [*A publication*]
STKAB...... Standarty i Kachestvo [*A publication*]
STKC......... [*The*] Stanwick Corporation [*NASDAQ symbol*] (NQ)
STKD......... Stockade (AABC)
STK EX .... Stock Exchange
STKF......... Stock Fund [*Military*]
STKFA...... Stock Fund Accounting [*Military*]
STKFS....... Stock Fund Statement [*Military*]
STKG......... Sturzkampfgeschwader [*Dive-bomber wing*] [*German military - World War II*]
STKL......... Stake Technology Limited [*Oakville, ON*] [*NASDAQ symbol*] (NQ)
STKM........ Storm King Mines [*NASDAQ symbol*] (NQ)
STKMBC .. Mammalogical Informations [*A publication*]
STKMBC .. Saugetierkundliche Mitteilungen [*A publication*]
STKN........ Stockton Savings & Loan Association [*Stockton, CA*] [*NASDAQ symbol*] (NQ)
St u Komm V ... Staats und Kommunalverwaltung [*A publication*]
STKR........ Stocker & Yale, Inc. [*NASDAQ symbol*] (NQ)
STKR........ Stockroom (AABC)
STKR........ Stoker [*Navy*] [*British*]
STKRA ..... Steklo i Keramika [*A publication*]
STKS .... Stakes (ROG)
STKv........ Svensk Teologisk Kvartalskrift [*A publication*]
STKY........ Stokely USA, Inc. [*Oconomowoc, WI*] [*NASDAQ symbol*] (NQ)
STL .... Bibliotheque Municipale de Saint-Laurent [*UTLAS symbol*]
STL.......... Sacrae Theologiae Lector [*Reader in Sacred Theology*] [*Latin*]
STL.......... Sacrae Theologiae Licentiatus [*Licentiate in Sacred Theology*] [*Latin*]
STL.......... Safe Tow Length
STL........... St. Louis [*Missouri*] [*Airport symbol*]
STL.......... Santa Lucia [*Chile*] [*Seismograph station code, US Geological Survey*] [*Closed*] (SEIS)
STL......... Satellite
STL.......... Schottky Transistor Logic (IEEE)
STL........... Seatrain Lines, Inc. [*AAR code*]
STL.......... Sequential Table Lookup
STL......... Short Term Leaflet. Ministry of Agriculture, Fisheries, and Food [*A publication*]
STL......... Short-Term Loan (ADA)
STL......... Simulated Tape Load
STL......... Site Team Leader [*Nuclear energy*] (NRCH)
STL......... Southern Traffic League
STL......... Southern Transportation League (EA)
STL......... Space Technology Laboratories [*of TRW Group*]
STL......... Special Tool List
STL......... Standard Telegraph Level [*Telecommunications*] (TEL)
STL......... Startling Stories [*A publication*]
STL......... Steel (KSC)
STL......... Step-Through Latencies
STL......... Sterling Bancorp [*NYSE symbol*] (SPSG)
STL......... Stockage List [*Military*]
STL......... STOL Air Commuter [*San Rafael, CA*] [*FAA designator*] (FAAC)
St L .... Student Lawyer [*A publication*]
StL .... Students'ki List [*A publication*]
StL .... Studia Linguistica [*A publication*]
StL .... Studies on the Left [*A publication*]
STL......... Studies in Logic and the Foundations of Mathematics [*Elsevier Book Series*] [*A publication*]
STL......... Studio-Transmitter Link
STL.......... Sunday Times (London) [*A publication*]
STL.......... Supersonic Transition Locus [*Galactic winds*]
STL........... Support Table Load

STL............ Suppressor T Lymphocyte [*Immunology*]
STL............ Swelling, Tenderness, Limitation of Movement [*Medicine*]
STL............ Synchronous Transistor Logic   (MDG)
STL............ System Test Loop   (IEEE)
STL............ Systems Techniques Laboratory [*Stanford University*]   (MCD)
STLA........ Strip Transmission Line Adapter [*or Assembly*]
StLAR....... St. Lawrence & Atlantic Railway
St at Large ... Statutes at Large [*A publication*]   (DLA)
St Law........ Loughborough's Digest of Statute Law [*Kentucky*] [*A publication*]   (DLA)
STLB & M ... St. Louis, Brownsville & Mexico [*Railway*]
STLC .... Sequence Thin-Layer Chromatography
STLC .... Short-Term Lethal Concentration [*of air pollutants*]
STLC .... Soluble Threshold Limit Concentration [*Environmental chemistry*]
STLDD...... Software Top Level Design Document [*Army*]
STLF......... Southern Troops and Landing Force
StLF......... Studi di Letteratura Francese [*A publication*]
STLI .... Statue of Liberty National Monument
STLI .... Stockage List Item [*Military*]
StLI......... Studi di Letteratura Ispano-Americana [*A publication*]
St Lim....... Statute of Limitations [*A publication*]   (DLA)
StLIM & S ... St. Louis, Iron Mountain & Southern Railway
StLing....... Studies in Linguistics [*A publication*]
St Lit........ Studia Liturgica [*A publication*]
S T L J ...... South Texas Law Journal [*A publication*]
STLJD...... South Texas Law Journal [*A publication*]
St L J Th... St. Luke's Journal of Theology [*A publication*]
STLL .... Submarine Tender Load List
STLM....... Safeguard Tactical Logistics Management
St L M....... Studien zur Literatur der Moderne [*A publication*]
St Lngst..... Statistical Methods in Linguistics [*A publication*]
STLO........ St. Louis Steel Casting [*NASDAQ symbol*]   (NQ)
STLO......... Scientific and Technical Liaison Office [*AFSC*]
StLo........ Studia Logica [*A publication*]
St & Loc Taxes (BNA) ... State and Local Taxes (Bureau of National Affairs) [*A publication*]   (DLA)
St & Loc Tax Serv (P-H) ... State and Local Tax Service (Prentice-Hall, Inc.) [*A publication*]   (DLA)
StLog......... Studia Logica [*A publication*]
StL & OR ... St. Louis & Ohio River Railroad
STLOS ...... Star Line-of-Sight   (KSC)
St Lou Com ... St. Louis Commerce [*United States*] [*A publication*]
St Louis B .. St. Louis Business Journal [*United States*] [*A publication*]
St Louis Commer ... St. Louis Commerce [*A publication*]
St Louis L Rev ... St. Louis Law Review [*A publication*]   (DLA)
St Louis Metropol Med ... St. Louis Metropolitan Medicine [*A publication*]
St Louis Mus Bul ... St. Louis City Art Museum. Bulletin [*A publication*]
St Louis U L J ... St. Louis University. Law Journal [*A publication*]
St Louis Univ B ... St. Louis University. Bulletin [*A publication*]
St Louis Univ Public Law Forum ... St. Louis University. Public Law Forum [*A publication*]
St Louis U Res J ... St. Louis University. Research Journal [*Baguio City*] [*A publication*]
St Lou Mgr ... St. Louis Manager [*United States*] [*A publication*]
St Lou Pos ... St. Louis Post-Dispatch [*United States*] [*A publication*]
St Lou ULJ ... St. Louis University. Law Journal [*A publication*]
St L P .... Studia Linguistica et Philologica [*A publication*]
STL-QPSR ... Speech Transmission Laboratory. Royal Institute of Technology. Stockholm. Quarterly Progress and Status Reports [*A publication*]
STLR .... Semitrailer
STLS......... South Texas Library System [*Library network*]
STLS......... Southern Tier Library System [*Library network*]
STLS......... Stinger Training Launch Simulator   (MCD)
STL-SF...... St. Louis-San Francisco Railway Co.
STL-SF & T ... St. Louis, San Francisco & Texas Railway Co.
STL STL and WD ... Steel or Steel and Wood [*Freight*]
StL & SW .. St. Louis & South Western Railway
STLSW of T ... St. Louis Southwestern Railway Co. of Texas
STLT .... Satellite   (FAAC)
STLT .... Small Transportable Link Terminal
STLT .... Stellite [*Metallurgy*]
STLT .... Stolt Tankers & Terminals (Holdings) SA [*NASDAQ symbol*]   (NQ)
STLT .... Studio-Transmitter Link-Television
STLTA ...... Steel Times [*A publication*]
STLU........ St. Louis University [*Missouri*]
St LU Intra L Rev ... St. Louis University. Intramural Law Review [*A publication*]   (DLA)
St Luke J ... St. Luke's Journal of Theology [*A publication*]
St Luke's Hosp Gaz ... St. Luke's Hospital Gazette [*A publication*]
St LU LJ.... St. Louis University. Law Journal [*A publication*]
STLV......... Simian T-Cell Lymphotropic Virus
STL WD .... Steel or Wood [*Freight*]
STL WI...... Steel or Wire [*Freight*]
STM.......... Groupement International d'Editeurs Scientifiques, Techniques, et Medicaux [*International Group of Scientific, Technical, and Medical Publishers*]   (EAIO)
STM.......... International Group of Scientific, Technical, and Medical Publishers   (EAIO)

STM.......... Master of Arts in Theology
STM.......... Master of the Science of Theology
STM.......... Sacrae Theologiae Magister [*Master of Sacred Theology*]
STM.......... Safety Test Missile   (MCD)
STM.......... St. Martin Hospitals Group [*British*]
STM.......... Santarem [*Brazil*] [*Airport symbol*]   (OAG)
STM.......... Satellite Technology Management, Inc. [*Torrance, CA*] [*Telecommunications*]   (TSSD)
STM.......... Save the Manatee Club   (EA)
STM.......... Scanning Tunneling Microscope
STM.......... Scientific, Technical, and Medical
STM.......... Screened through Matching [*Parapsychology*]
STM.......... Section Technical Manual [*Jet Propulsion Laboratory, NASA*]
STM.......... Send Test Message   (AAG)
STM.......... Service Technique Militaire [*Switzerland*]
STM.......... Service Test Model   (NG)
STM.......... Shielded Tunable Magnetron
STM.......... Short-Term Memory
STM.......... Signal Termination Module [*NASA*]   (NASA)
STM.......... Significant Technical Milestone   (SDI)
STM.......... Slate Mountain [*Nevada*] [*Seismograph station code, US Geological Survey*] [*Closed*]   (SEIS)
STM.......... Society for Traditional Music   (EA)
STM.......... Southam, Inc. [*Toronto Stock Exchange symbol*] [*Vancouver Stock Exchange symbol*]
STM.......... Special Test Missile
STM.......... Specialized Trade Mission [*Department of Commerce*]
STM.......... Specification Test Material   (MCD)
STM.......... Spin Tuned Magnetron
STM.......... Spore Tip Mucilage [*Mycology*]
STM.......... Standard Test Methods Bulletins [*A publication*]   (EAAP)
STM.......... Standard Type Material   (MCD)
STM.......... Standards Tool Master   (MCD)
STM.......... State Transition Matrix
STM.......... Static Test Model   (MCD)
STM.......... Statistical Multiplexing [*Telecommunications*]
STM.......... Statute Mile
STM.......... Steam
STM.......... Steward's Mate [*Navy rating*]
STM.......... Storm   (FAAC)
STM.......... Strategic Mortgage Investments, Inc. [*NYSE symbol*]   (SPSG)
STM.......... Stream [*Board on Geographic Names*]
STM.......... Structural Test Model
StM.......... Studi e Materiali di Storia delle Religioni [*A publication*]
StM.......... Studia Monastica [*A publication*]
StM.......... Studien zur Musikwissenschaft [*A publication*]
STM.......... Subject to Mortgage   (ADA)
STM.......... Supersonic Tactical Missile   (MCD)
STM.......... Supplementary Technical Manual [*Military*]
STM.......... Support Test Manager   (NASA)
STM.......... Surface-to-Target-to-Missile
STM.......... Synthetic Timing Mode
STM.......... System Training Mission   (AFM)
STMA........ Space-Time Moving Average [*Statistics*]
STMA........ Sports Turf Managers Association [*Defunct*]   (EA)
STMA........ Statistical Theory and Method Abstracts [*A publication*]
STMA........ Stuffed Toy Manufacturers Association
STMAF ..... Stampede International Resources Cl A [*NASDAQ symbol*]   (NQ)
St Magreb ... Studi Magrebini [*A publication*]
St Marianna Med J ... St. Marianna Medical Journal [*Japan*] [*A publication*]
St Mark ..... St. Mark's Church Case [*Philadelphia, PA*] [*A publication*]   (DLA)
St Mark R ... St. Mark's Review [*A publication*]
St Mark Rev ... St. Mark's Review [*A publication*]   (APTA)
St Marks R ... St. Mark's Review [*A publication*]   (APTA)
St Marks Rev ... St. Mark's Review [*A publication*]   (APTA)
St Marlb .... Statute of Marlbridge [*A publication*]   (DLA)
St Mary's L J ... St. Mary's Law Journal [*A publication*]
St e Mat ..... Studi e Materiali di Storia della Religioni [*A publication*]
StMBC...... Studien und Mitteilungen aus dem Benediktiner- und dem Cistercienser-Orden [*A publication*]
STMC........ Standard Metals Corp. [*NASDAQ symbol*]   (NQ)
STMCGMW ... Subcommission for Tectonic Maps of the Commission for the Geological Map of the World   (EAIO)
STME........ Stellar Television Monitor Equipment
St Med .... Studi Medievali [*A publication*]
StMed........ Studia Mediewistyczne [*A publication*]
St Mert....... Statute of Merton [*A publication*]   (DLA)
STMEV ..... Storm Evasion [*Navy*]   (NVT)
S T Mf........ Svensk Tidskrift foer Musikforskning [*A publication*]
STMG....... Steaming   (MSA)
STMGA....... Salmon and Trout Magazine [*A publication*]
STMGA3... Salmon and Trout Magazine [*A publication*]
StMGB ...... Studien und Mitteilungen zur Geschichte des Benediktiner-Ordens [*A publication*]
STMGR...... Station Manager [*Aviation*]   (FAAC)
St Mi.......... Statute Mile [*Nautical charts*]
St Mis .... Studia Missionalia [*A publication*]
STMIS....... System Test Manufacturing Information System   (IEEE)

St Misc....... Studi Miscellanei, Seminario di Archeologia e Storia dell'Arte Greca e Romana dell'Universita di Roma [*A publication*]
STML........ Sindicato de Trabajadores Mineros de Llallagua
STML........ Stimulate (MSA)
STMLA..... Stomatologia [*Bucharest*] [*A publication*]
St M LJ ..... St. Mary's Law Journal [*A publication*]
St Mod Lev Fin ... Statute Modus Levandi Fines [*A publication*]   (DLA)
StMon........ Studia Monastica [*A publication*]
St Mot Carr Guide (CCH) ... State Motor Carrier Guide (Commerce Clearing House) [*A publication*]   (DLA)
STMP........ Ship Test Management Plan [*Navy*] (CAAL)
STMP........ System Training Management Plan (MCD)
STMR........ Steamer
S/T-MR...... Surplus Termination Material Requisition (MCD)
STMS........ St. Thomas More Society (EA)
STMS........ Scottish Tramway Museum Society (DCTA)
STMS........ Spring Trap Makers' Society [*A union*] [*British*]
STMS........ State Tax Management System [*Price Waterhouse & Co.*] (PCM)
St MS........ Steinbeck Monograph Series [*A publication*]
StMSR....... Studi e Materiali di Storia delle Religioni [*Rome/Bologna*] [*A publication*]
STMT........ Statement (AFM)
STMTA..... Stomatologica [*Genoa*] [*A publication*]
STMT of SVC ... Statement of Service [*Military*]
STMU .... Special Test and Maintenance Unit
STMW....... Subtropical Mode Water [*Oceanography*]
STMYA...... Stomatologiya [*A publication*]
St Myst .... Studia Mystica [*A publication*]
STN .... SAC [*Strategic Air Command*] Telephone Net
St N .... St. Nicholas [*A publication*]
STN .... Satellite Television Network [*Telecommunications*] [*Defunct*] (TSSD)
STN .... Satellite Theater Network [*Falls Church, VA*] (TSSD)
STN .... Satellite Tracking Network (MCD)
STN .... Saturn Airways, Inc. (MCD)
STN .... Scientific and Technical Information Network
STN .... Seatoun [*New Zealand*] [*Seismograph station code, US Geological Survey*] [*Closed*] (SEIS)
STN .... Software Trouble Note [*NASA*] (NASA)
STN .... Solar Telescope Network
STN .... Solitary Tract Nucleus [*Also, NST*] [*Anatomy*]
STN .... Special Traffic Notice [*British*] (DCTA)
STN .... Specification Transmittal Notice (MCD)
STN .... Staff Papers [*A publication*]
STN .... Stain [*Deltiology*]
STN .... Stainless
STN .... Stansted [*England*] [*Airport symbol*] (OAG)
STN .... Statement of Technology Needs [*Air Force*]
STN .... Station
STN .... Stevens [*J. P.*] & Co., Inc. [*NYSE symbol*] (SPSG)
STN .... Stone [*Unit of weight*] (AAG)
StN............ Studia Neotestamentica [*Paris/Bruges*] [*A publication*]
STN .... Subthalamic Nucleus [*Neurobiology*]
STN .... Switched Telecommunications Network
STNA........ Sons of Temperance of North America (EA)
STNA........ Stanadyne, Inc. [*NASDAQ symbol*] (NQ)
Stn Biol Mar Grande Riviere Que Rapp Annu ... Station de Biologie Marine. Grande Riviere, Quebec. Rapport Annuel [*A publication*]
Stn Bull Agric Exp Stn Univ Minn ... Station Bulletin. Minnesota Agricultural Experiment Station [*A publication*]
Stn Bull Dep Agri Econ Agric Exp Stn Purdue Univ ... Station Bulletin. Department of Agricultural Economics. Agricultural Experiment Station. Purdue University [*A publication*]
Stn Bull New Hamps Agric Exp Stn ... Station Bulletin. Agricultural Experiment Station. University of New Hampshire [*A publication*]
Stn Bull Ore Agric Exp Stn ... Station Bulletin. Oregon Agricultural Experiment Station [*A publication*]
STnC......... Skeletal Troponin C [*Biochemistry*]
Stn Chim Agrar Sper Torino Annu ... Stazione Chimico-Agraria Sperimentale di Torino. Annuario [*A publication*]
Stn Circ Ore Agric Exp Stn ... Station Circular. Oregon Agricultural Experiment Station [*A publication*]
STNEA...... Sterne [*A publication*]
StNeerla..... Statistica Neerlandica [*A publication*]
St Neophil ... Studia Neophilologica [*A publication*]
StNF .... Studier i Nordisk Filologi [*A publication*]
Stn Fed Essais Agric (Lausanne) Publ ... Stations Federales d'Essais Agricoles (Lausanne). Publication [*A publication*]
STNG .... Sustaining
STNI.......... Stendig Industries, Inc. [*Fairfield, NJ*] [*NASDAQ symbol*] (NQ)
STNI......... Subtotal Nodal Irradiation [*Oncology*]
Stn L .... Stanford Law Review [*A publication*]
STNLB ...... Stimulation Newsletter [*A publication*]
STNLS ...... Stainless (MSA)
STNR........ Stationary
Stn Rep Hort Res Stn (Tatura) ... Station Report. Horticultural Research Station (Tatura) [*A publication*]
STNRY...... Stationary (FAAC)

Stns Circ Wash Agric Exp Stns ... Stations Circular. Washington Agricultural Experiment Stations [*A publication*]
Stn Sper Agrar Ital ... Stazione Sperimentali Agrarie Italiane [*A publication*]
Stn Sper Vitic Enol (Conegliano Italy) Annu ... Stazione Sperimentale di Viticoltura e di Enologia (Conegliano, Italy). Annuario [*A publication*]
STNT........ Sprawozdania Towarzystwa Naukowego w Toruniu [*A publication*]
StNT .... Studien zum Neuen Testament [*A publication*]
Stn Tech Bull Ore Agric Exp Stn ... Station Technical Bulletin. Oregon Agricultural Experiment Station [*A publication*]
STNV........ Satellite Tobacco Necrosis Virus
STNWA...... Sci-Tech News [*A publication*]
STNWRE.. Stoneware [*Freight*]
STNYA...... Science and Technology [*New York*] [*A publication*]
StO............ St. Olaf [*Record label*]
STO .... Science and Technology Objectives (MCD)
STO .... Sea Transport Officer
STO .... Segment Table Origin
STO .... Service du Travail Obligatoire [*French labor force*] [*World War II*]
STO .... Short Takeoff (MCD)
STO .... Short-Term Objective
STO .... Slater-Type Orbital [*Atomic structure*]
STO .... Small-Time Operator [*Slang*]
STO .... Sojourner Truth Organization (EA)
STO .... Standard Transfer Order
STO .... Standing Order [*Business term*] (DCTA)
STO .... Standing Tool Order (KSC)
StO............ Steuerordnung [*Tax Law*] [*German*] (ILCA)
StO............ Stimmen des Orients [*A publication*]
STO .... Stockholm [*Sweden*] [*Airport symbol*] (OAG)
STO .... Stoker [*Navy*] [*British*]
STO .... Stone Container Corp. [*NYSE symbol*] (SPSG)
STO .... Stonehill College, North Easton, MA [*OCLC symbol*] (OCLC)
STO .... Stonyhurst [*Blackburn*] [*England*] [*Seismograph station code, US Geological Survey*] [*Closed*] (SEIS)
STO .... Storage Processor
STO .... Storekeeper [*Coast Guard*]
Sto .... Storey's Delaware Reports [*A publication*] (DLA)
Sto .... Story's United States Circuit Court Reports [*A publication*] (DLA)
STO .... Stow (NASA)
STO .... Strategic Technology Office [*Arlington, VA*] [*DoD*] (GRD)
StO............ Studia Oliveriana [*A publication*]
STO .... Swedish Trade Office (EA)
STO .... System Test Objectives
STOAA...... Stomatologiya [*Moscow*] [*A publication*]
Sto Abr Const ... Story's Abridgment of the Constitution [*A publication*] (DLA)
STOAD ..... Scientific and Technical Organizations and Agencies Directory [*A publication*]
Sto Ag .... Story on Agency [*A publication*] (DLA)
STOAL...... Short Takeoff Arrested Landing (MCD)
Sto Att Lien ... Stokes on Lien of Attorneys and Solicitors [*1860*] [*A publication*] (DLA)
Sto Bailm ... Story on Bailments [*A publication*] (DLA)
Sto Bills ..... Story on Bills [*A publication*] (DLA)
STobRV..... Satellite Tobacco Ringspot Virus
STOC........ Standard Tactical Operating Condition
STOC........ Systems for Test Output Consolidation [*Data processing*]
STOCC...... Space Telescope Operations Control Center [*NASA*] (NASA)
Sto CC........ Story's United States Circuit Court Reports [*A publication*] (DLA)
STOCD...... Software Tools Communications [*A publication*]
Stochastic Processes Appl ... Stochastic Processes and Their Applications [*A publication*]
Stoch Processes Appl ... Stochastic Processes and Their Applications [*A publication*]
Stock .... Stockton's New Brunswick Vice-Admiralty Reports [*1879-91*] [*A publication*] (DLA)
Stock .... Stockton's New Jersey Equity Reports [*A publication*] (DLA)
Stock Adm ... Stockton's New Brunswick Vice-Admiralty Reports [*A publication*] (DLA)
Stockett...... Stockett's Reports [*27-53 Maryland*] [*A publication*] (DLA)
STOCKH... Stockholmia [*Stockholm*] [*Imprint*] (ROG)
Stockh Contrib Geol ... Stockholm Contributions in Geology [*A publication*]
Stockholm Contrib Geol ... Stockholm Contributions in Geology [*A publication*]
Stockholm Tek Hogsk Avh ... Stockholm. Tekniska Hogskolan. Avhandling [*A publication*]
Stockholm Tek Hogsk Handl ... Stockholm. Tekniska Hogskolan. Handlingar [*Transactions*] [*A publication*]
Stock Non Com ... Stock on Non Compotes Mentis [*A publication*] (DLA)
Stockt......... Stockton's New Jersey Equity Reports [*9-11 New Jersey*] [*A publication*] (DLA)
Stockt Ch ... Stockton's New Jersey Equity Reports [*9-11 New Jersey*] [*A publication*] (DLA)
Stockton..... Stockton's New Brunswick Vice-Admiralty Reports [*A publication*] (DLA)

Stockton Adm (New Br) ... Stockton's New Brunswick Vice-Admiralty Reports [*A publication*] (DLA)
Stockt Vice-Adm ... Stockton's New Brunswick Vice-Admiralty Reports [*A publication*] (DLA)
Sto Comm .. Story's Commentaries on the Constitution of the United States [*A publication*] (DLA)
Sto Con ...... Story on Contracts [*A publication*] (DLA)
Sto Conf Law ... Story on Conflict of Laws [*A publication*] (DLA)
Sto Const.... Story's Commentaries on the Constitution of the United States [*A publication*] (DLA)
Sto Const Cl B ... Story's Constitutional Class Book [*A publication*] (DLA)
Sto Cont ..... Story on Contracts [*A publication*] (DLA)
StocProc...... Stochastic Processes and Their Applications [*A publication*]
STOCS .... South Texas Outer Continental Shelf
STOD .... Stodden [*England*]
Sto Eq Jur ... Story on Equity Jurisprudence [*A publication*] (DLA)
Sto Eq Pl.... Story on Equity Pleadings [*A publication*] (DLA)
St Offenbach ... Studien und Forschungen. Stadt- und Landkreis Offenbach Am Main [*A publication*]
STOG .... Science and Technology Objectives Guide (MCD)
Sto & G ...... Stone and Graham's Private Bills Decisions [*1865*] [*A publication*] (DLA)
STOGW .... Short Takeoff Gross Weight [*Aviation*]
Sto & H Cr Ab ... Storer and Heard on Criminal Abortion [*A publication*] (DLA)
STOIAC .... Strategic Technology Office Information Analysis Center [*Battelle Memorial Institute*] (MCD)
STOIIP....... Stock Tank Oil Initially in Place [*Petroleum technology*]
Stokes L of Att ... Stokes on Liens of Attorneys [*A publication*] (DLA)
STOL........ Saturn Test Oriented Language [*NASA*]
STOL........ Short Takeoff and Landing [*Aviation*]
STOL........ Standing Operating and Landing
STOL........ Systems Test and Operation Language
Sto Laws .... Story's Laws of the United States [*A publication*] (DLA)
Stolport ...... Short Takeoff and Landing Airport [*London, England*]
STOM .... Safe Transport of Munitions (MCD)
STOM .... Stomachic [*To Strengthen the Stomach*] [*Medicine*] (ROG)
STOM .... System Test and Operations Manual
Stomach Intest ... Stomach and Intestine [*Japan*] [*A publication*]
S Tomas Nurs J ... Santo Tomas Nursing Journal [*A publication*]
Stomatol DDR ... Stomatologie der DDR [*East Germany*] [*A publication*]
Stomatol Glas Srb ... Stomatoloski Glasnik Srbije [*A publication*]
Stomatol Vjesn ... Stomatoloski Vjesnik [*Stomatological Review*] [*A publication*]
Stomatol Zpr ... Stomatologicke Zpracy [*A publication*]
Sto Miscel Writ ... Story's Miscellaneous Writings [*A publication*] (DLA)
STON .... Daylight Industries, Inc. [*NASDAQ symbol*] (NQ)
STON .... Short Ton [*2000 lbs.*] (AABC)
Stone .... Stone's Justices' Manual (Annual) [*A publication*] (DLA)
STONE4...... Strahlentherapie und Onkologie [*A publication*]
Stone Ben Bdg Soc ... Stone's Benefit Building Societies [*1851*] [*A publication*] (DLA)
Stone C....... Stone Country [*A publication*]
Stone D ...... Stone Drum [*A publication*]
STONEH .... Stonehouse [*England*]
Stone Ind.... Stone Industries [*A publication*]
Stone Just Man ... Stone's Justices' Manual (Annual) [*A publication*] (DLA)
Stony .... Stony Hills [*A publication*]
STOP........ Save the Oppressed People Committee [*Defunct*] (EA)
STOP........ Selected Test Optimization Program (MCD)
STOP........ Ship's Toxicological Protective System
STOP........ Single Title Order Plan [*Formerly, SCOP*] [*ABA*]
STOP........ Society that Opposes Pornography
STOP........ Software Theft Opposition Project [*Project STOP*] [*Information service or system*] (CRD)
STOP........ Stable Ocean Platform
STOP........ Start Tromping on Pedal [*Facetious interpretation of the traffic sign*]
STOP........ Stop forced busing; Teach children, not bus them; Operate neighborhood schools for those in the neighborhood wishing to attend them; Put an end to government interference in the parent-child relationship (EA)
STOP........ Stop the Ocean Pollution [*Australia*]
STOP........ Stop the Oil Profiteers [*Antioil price slogan*]
STOP........ Stop the Olympic Prison [*Lake Placid Olympics, 1980*] [*Opposed possible later use of an Olympic building as a prison*] [*Defunct*]
STOP........ Stop This Outrageous Purge [*Group opposed to extremist measures used by segregationists in Arkansas; opposed by CROSS*]
STOP........ Strategic Orbit Point (AFM)
STOP........ Strategic Talks on Prevention [*of accidental atomic war and nuclear weapons proliferation*] [*Proposed by Sen. Gary Hart, 1982*]
STOP........ Student/Teacher Organization to Prevent Nuclear War (EA)
STOP........ Supersonic Transport Optimization Program [*NASA*]
STOP ABC ... Stop Abuse by Counselors (EA)
Sto Part ...... Story on Partnership [*A publication*] (DLA)
Sto Pl .... Story's Civil Pleading [*A publication*] (DLA)
STOP-NSA ... Students to Oppose Participation in the National Student Association (EA)

STOPP ...... Society of Teachers Opposed to Physical Punishment
STOPP ...... Society of Teachers of Professional Photography [*Later, STEPP*] (EA)
Stop Pregl .. Stopanski Pregled [*A publication*]
STOPPS.... Standard Transportation Operations Personnel Property (MCD)
Sto Pr .... Story on Prize Courts [*A publication*] (DLA)
Sto Pr Notes ... Story on Promissory Notes [*A publication*] (DLA)
STOPS ...... Shipboard Toxicological Operational Protective System [*Navy*]
STOPS ...... Stability Operations
STOPS ...... Stabilized Terrain Optical Position Sensor [*Army*]
STOPS ...... Supreme Temple Order Pythian Sisters (EA)
STOQ .... Storage Queue
STOR........ Scripps Tuna Oceanographic Research
STOR........ Segment Table Origin Register [*Data processing*] (BUR)
STOR........ Storage (AFM)
St Or .... Studia Orientalia [*A publication*]
StOr .... Studia Orientalia. Edidit Societas Orientalis Fennica [*Helsinki*] [*A publication*]
STOR........ Summary Tape Operations Rental [*Bureau of the Census*]
STOR........ System Test and Operations Report
STORAD.... Stored Address [*Data processing*]
STORADS ... Site Tactical Optimized Range Air Defense System
Storage Handl Distrib ... Storage Handling Distribution [*A publication*]
Stor Art...... Storia dell'Arte [*A publication*]
Stor Arte ..... Storia dell'Arte [*A publication*]
STORC...... Self-Ferrying Trans-Ocean Rotary-Wing Crane [*Helicopter*]
StOrChrColl ... Studia Orientalia Christiana. Collectanea [*Cairo*] [*A publication*]
Stor Dict..... Stormouth's Dictionary of the English Language [*A publication*] (DLA)
STORE...... Storage Technology for Operational Readiness
STORE...... Students to Observe Retail Establishments [*Student legal action organization*] (EA)
Stor Ebr It ... Storia dell'Ebraismo in Italia. Sezione Toscana [*A publication*]
Storefront.... Storefront Classroom [*A publication*]
STORES..... Syntactic Tracer Organized Retrospective Enquiry System [*Instituut voor Wiskunde, Informatiewerk, en Statistiek*] [*Data processing*] [*Netherlands*]
STORET ... Storage and Retrieval [*Data processing*]
STORET ... Storage and Retrieval for Water Quality Data [*Environmental Protection Agency*] [*Databank*] (MSC)
Stor & H Abor ... Storer and Heard on Criminal Abortion [*A publication*] (DLA)
Storia e Polit ... Storia e Politica [*A publication*]
STORLAB ... Space Technology Operations and Research Laboratory (IEEE)
STORM..... Safe Transport of Munitions Project (MCD)
STORM..... Sensor, Tank, Off-Route Mine (MCD)
STORM.... Statistically Oriented Matrix Program (IEEE)
STORM..... Stormscale Operational and Research Meteorology [*National Oceanic and Atmospheric Administration*]
STORMS .. Standardized Operation Research Management System (MCD)
STORMSAT ... Storm Satellite (MCD)
STORS...... Sludge to Oil Reactor System [*Battelle Memorial Institute*]
STORW..... Storer Communications Wts [*NASDAQ symbol*] (NQ)
Story.......... Story on Equity Jurisprudence [*1836-1920*] [*A publication*] (DLA)
Story.......... Story's United States Circuit Court Reports [*A publication*] (DLA)
Story Ag..... Story on Agency [*A publication*] (DLA)
Story Bailm ... Story on Bailments [*A publication*] (DLA)
Story Comm Const ... Story's Commentaries on the Constitution of the United States [*A publication*] (DLA)
Story Confl Laws ... Story on Conflict of Laws [*A publication*] (DLA)
Story Const ... Story's Commentaries on the Constitution of the United States [*A publication*] (DLA)
Story Cont ... Story on Contracts [*A publication*] (DLA)
Story Eq Jur ... Story on Equity Jurisprudence [*A publication*] (DLA)
Story Eq Pl .... Story's Equity Planning [*A publication*] (DLA)
Story Laws ... Story's Laws of the United States [*A publication*] (DLA)
Story Merchants ... Abbott's Merchant Ships and Seamen, by Story [*A publication*] (DLA)
Story Partn ... Story on Partnership [*A publication*] (DLA)
Story Prom Notes ... Story on Promissory Notes [*A publication*] (DLA)
Story R....... Story's United States Circuit Court Reports [*First Circuit*] [*A publication*] (DLA)
Story Sales ... Story on Sales of Personal Property [*A publication*] (DLA)
Story's Circuit CR ... Story's United States Circuit Court Reports [*First Circuit*] [*A publication*] (DLA)
Story's Laws ... Story's United States Laws [*A publication*] (DLA)
Story's Rep ... Story's United States Circuit Court Reports [*A publication*] (DLA)
Story US Laws ... Story's Laws of the United States [*A publication*] (DLA)
STOS........ Santos Ltd. [*NASDAQ symbol*] (NQ)
STOS......... Space Test Operations Section
Sto Sales ..... Story on Sales of Personal Property [*A publication*] (DLA)
STOT........ Scheduled Time over Target (AFM)
STOT........ Stockpile-to-Target (AFM)
STOTINS ... Standoff Techniques for Parachute Insertion (MCD)
StOTPr...... Studies in Old Testament Prophecy Presented to T. H. Robinson [*A publication*] (BJA)

Stotz-Kontakt-Roemmler Nachr ... Stotz-Kontakt-Roemmler Nachrichten [*A publication*]
StOU......... Stimmen Orient und Uebersee [*A publication*] (BJA)
Sto US Laws ... Story's Laws of the United States [*A publication*] (DLA)
Stov Hors ... Stovins' Law Respecting Horses [*A publication*] (DLA)
STOVL...... Short Takeoff and Vertical Landing (MCD)
STOW .... Side Transfer Optimum Warehousing
STOW .... Stowage (AAG)
STOW .... Swim the Ontario Waterways [*Personal incentive program for fitness swimmers*] [*Ontario Masters Swimming Club*]
STOW .... System for Takeoff Weight
STP............ NAVAS [*Nederlandse Aannemersvereniging van Afbouwen Stukadoorswerken*] 77 [*A publication*]
STP............ North-Holland Studies in Theoretical Poetics [*Elsevier Book Series*] [*A publication*]
STP............ Sacrae [*or Sacrosanctae*] Theologiae Professor [*Professor of Sacred Theology*]
STP............ SAGE [*Semiautomatic Ground Environment*] System Training Program
STP............ St. Paul, MN [*Location identifier*] [*FAA*] (FAAL)
STP............ Saint Peter's College, Jersey City, NJ [*OCLC symbol*] (OCLC)
STP............ Sao Tome and Principe [*ANSI three-letter standard code*] (CNC)
STP............ Satellite Ticket Printer [*Travel industry*]
STP............ Satellite Tracking Program [*of the Smithsonian Institution's Astrophysical Observatory*]
STP............ Save the Tallgrass Prairie [*An association*] (EA)
STP............ Scientifically Treated Petroleum [*A motor fuel oil additive*] [*Initials reported, by extension of meaning, also to stand for a hallucinogenic drug, DOM*]
STP............ Sea Test Phase [*Navy*] (CAAL)
STP............ Seal to Parents [*Genealogy*] (PCM)
STP............ Selective Tape Print
STP............ Self-Test Program (MCD)
STP............ Sent to Printer [*Publishing*]
STP............ Sewage Treatment Plant
STP............ Short-Term Program [*Nuclear energy*] (NRCH)
STP............ Short Term Projections [*Townsend, Greenspan & Co., Inc.*] [*Information service or system*] [*No longer available online*]
STP............ Shuttle Technology Panel [*NASA*] (NASA)
STP............ Signal Transfer Point [*Telecommunications*] (TEL)
STP............ Simultaneous Test Procedure [*Statistics*]
STP............ Simultaneous Track Processor
STP............ Singing Tree Press [*Publisher's imprint*]
ST-P........... Small Transmitter Coated with Paraffin
STP............ Socialism: Theory and Practice [*A publication*]
STP............ Society of Telecommunications Professionals (TSSD)
STP............ Society of Television Pioneers (EA)
STP............ Society for Thai Philately (EA)
STP............ Society of Toxicologic Pathologists (EA)
STP............ Sodium Triphosphate [*or Sodium Tripolyphosphate*] [*Also, STPP*] [*Inorganic chemistry*]
STP............ Solar-Terrestrial Physics (IID)
STP............ Solar-Terrestrial Probe [*NASA*]
STP............ Soldier Training Publications [*Military*] (INF)
STP............ South Texas Project [*Nuclear energy*] (NRCH)
STP............ Space Technology Payload [*NASA*] (MCD)
STP............ Space Test Program [*Air Force*]
STP............ Special Technical Publication (MCD)
STP............ Special Tool Production
STP............ Spectrum of Time Project [*Astronomy*]
STP............ Stamp (MSA)
STP............ Standard Temperature and Pressure
STP............ Standard [*Normal*] Temperature and Pulse [*Medicine*]
STP............ Standard Test Procedure
STP............ Standard Type Process (MCD)
STP............ Standardized Test Program
St P............ State Papers [*A publication*] (DLA)
STP............ Sterilization Test Program
St & P......... Stewart and Porter's Alabama Reports [*A publication*] (DLA)
STP............ Stop Character [*Data processing*]
STP............ Stop the Pentagon/Serve the People (EA)
STP............ Stoppage (AABC)
STP............ Storage Tube Processor
STP............ Storm Track Prediction (MCD)
STP............ Strength, Toughness, Pride
STP............ Strip
StP............ Studi Petrarcheschi [*A publication*]
StP............ Studia Palmyrenskie [*Warsaw*] [*A publication*]
StP............ Studia Patristica [*A publication*]
St u P......... Studium und Praxis [*A publication*]
STP............ Subsystem Test Plan [*NASA*] (NASA)
STP............ Supracondylar Tibial Prosthesis [*Medicine*]
STP............ Sustainment Training Program [*Army*] (INF)
STP............ Sycamore Test Procedure [*Aerospace*] (AAG)
STP............ System Test Plan
STP............ System Test Program [*Navy*] (CAAL)
STP............ Systems Technology Program (MCD)
STP............ Systems Training Program [*RADAR*]
StPa .... Studia Patristica [*A publication*]

StPapyr...... Studia Papyrologica [*Barcelona*] [*A publication*]
StPatrist..... Studia Patristica [*Berlin-Ost*] [*A publication*]
St Paul Med J ... St. Paul Medical Journal [*A publication*]
StPB........... Studia Post-Biblica [*A publication*]
St P Brook ... Staff Papers. Brookings Institution [*A publication*]
StPCyRy.... St. Paul City Railway
StP & D..... St. Paul & Duluth Railroad
STPD......... Stamped (ROG)
STPD......... Standard Temperature and Pressure, Dry
STPD......... Stripped (MSA)
STPDN...... Stepdown
St Petersb Med Wchnschr ... St. Petersburger Medizinische Wochenschrift [*A publication*]
STPF......... Shield Test Pool Facility [*Nuclear energy*]
STPF......... Stabilized Temperature Platform Furnace
STPG .... Spare-Time Production for Gain [*FAO*]
STPG .... Stamping (ROG)
STPG .... Stepping (MSA)
STPGA ...... Steel Processing [*A publication*]
STPH......... Static Phase Error [*NASA*] (NASA)
STPHB ...... Springer Tracts in Modern Physics [*A publication*]
St Philon .... Studia Philonica [*A publication*]
STPI .... Science and Technology Policy Implementation [*Project*]
STPL .... [*The*] St. Paul Companies, Inc. [*NASDAQ symbol*] (NQ)
STPL .... Sidetone Path Loss [*Telecommunications*] (TEL)
STPL .... Steeple (DS)
STPL .... Stern Plane
St Pl Cr ...... Staundeforde's Pleas of Crown [*A publication*] (DLA)
STP-M .... Solar-Terrestrial Physics - Meteorology
STPM .... Syndicat Togolais du Personnel de la Meteorologie [*Togolese Union of Meteorological Personnel*]
StPM & M ... St. Paul, Minneapolis & Manitoba Railway
STPNG ...... Stopping (MSA)
STPO......... Science and Technology Policy Office [*Supersedes OST*] [*National Science Foundation*]
StPO .... Strafprozessordnung [*Code of Criminal Procedure*] [*German*] (ILCA)
St and Port ... Stewart and Porter's Alabama Reports [*A publication*] (DLA)
StP & P ...... St. Paul & Pacific Railroad
STPP .... Sodium Tripolyphosphate [*Also, STP*] [*Inorganic chemistry*]
STPP .... Student Teacher Performance Profile
STPR .... Semiannual Technical Progress Report
St Pr .... Staundeforde's Exposition of the King's Prerogative [*A publication*] (DLA)
STPR .... Stepper [*Motor*] [*Electronics*]
STPR .... Stripper
STPR .... Stumper [*Freight*]
St Pr Reg.... Style's Practical Register [*England*] [*A publication*] (DLA)
STPS......... Solar Thermal Power System
STPS......... Stern Teacher Preference Schedule
STPS......... Summary Task Planning Sheet
STPSA....... Studia Psychologica [*A publication*]
StP & SC... St. Paul & Sioux City Railroad
STPST........ Stop-Start [*Telecommunications*] (TEL)
STPT .... Society of Town Planning Technicians [*British*]
STPT .... Starpointe Savings Bank [*Plainfield, NJ*] [*NASDAQ symbol*] (NQ)
STPTC...... Standardization of Tar Products Test Committee
STPUB ...... Stem Pubescence [*Botany*]
StPUD .... St. Paul Union Depot
StPUSY.... St. Paul Union Stock Yards Co.
STPX .... Systems Training Program Exercise (AABC)
STQ .... Society of Translators of Quebec [*Canada*]
StQ............ Steinbeck Quarterly [*A publication*]
StQ............ Streator, IL [*Location identifier*] [*FAA*] (FAAL)
STR............ Questar Corp. [*NYSE symbol*] (SPSG)
STR............ Scientific Technical Report
STR............ Scientific and Technological Research (DEN)
STR............ Sea Test Range (MUGU)
STR............ Search and Track RADAR
STR............ Seater (ADA)
STR............ Segment Table Register
STR............ Senior Technical Representative
STR............ Service Test Review
STR............ Service Trouble Report
STR............ Short-Term Returns
STR............ Sidetone Reduction [*Telecommunications*] (TEL)
STR............ Society for Theatre Research (EA)
STR............ Society of Thoracic Radiology (EA)
STR............ Software Trouble Report (MCD)
STR............ Soul-Taehakkyo Ronmunjip. Inmun-Sahoe-Kwahak [*Seoul University Journal. Humanities and Social Sciences*] [*A publication*]
STR............ Spacecraft Telemetry Regenerator (MCD)
STR............ Special Theory of Relativity
STR............ Special Trade Representative
STR............ Speed Tolerant Recording [*Electronic Processors, Inc.*]
St u R .... Staat und Recht [*A publication*]
STR............ Staff Technical Representative
STR............ Standard Broadcasting Corp. Ltd. [*Toronto Stock Exchange symbol*]

STR........... Standard Taxiway Routing
STR........... Standard Tool Request
STR........... Standard Training Requirements [*Navy*]   (NVT)
STR........... Star Science Fiction [*A publication*]
STR........... Status Register [*Data processing*]
STR........... Steamer
STR........... Stereo Review [*A publication*]
STR........... Storage Rack   (MCD)
STR........... Store
STR........... Straight   (AAG)
STR........... Strainer   (AAG)
STR....... Strait [*Maps and charts*]
Str .... Strange's Cases of Evidence [*1698-1732*] [*England*] [*A publication*]   (DLA)
Str .... Strange's English King's Bench Reports [*1716-49*] [*A publication*]   (DLA)
STR........... Strasbourg [*France*] [*Seismograph station code, US Geological Survey*]   (SEIS)
STR........... Strasse [*Street*] [*German*]
Str .... Strategemata [*of Frontinus*] [*Classical studies*]   (OCD)
STR........... Strategic Training Range   (MCD)
STR........... Streak
str .... Streaky [*Quality of the bottom*] [*Nautical charts*]
STR........... Stream [*Maps and charts*]
STR........... Street
STR........... Streichinstrumente [*Stringed Instruments*] [*Music*]
STR........... Strength   (AFM)
STR........... Streptococcus [*Medicine*]
STR........... Stretch [*Horse racing*]
Str .... Striatum [*Brain anatomy*] [*Also, ST*]
STR........... String
STR........... Stringendo [*Hastening*] [*Music*]
STR........... Strings [*of an orchestra*]
STR........... Strip   (AAG)
STRC........ Stroke
STR........... Strophe [*Classical studies*]   (OCD)
STR........... Structural [*Lumber*]
St R .... Stuart's Lower Canada Appeal Cases [*Quebec*] [*A publication*]   (DLA)
StR .... Studi Religiosi [*A publication*]
StR .... Studi Romagnoli [*A publication*]
STr............ Studi Trentini [*A publication*]
STr............ Studi Trentini di Scienze Storiche [*A publication*]
StR .... Studia Romanica [*A publication*]
StR .... Studie o Rukopisech [*A publication*]
STR........... Stuttgart [*West Germany*] [*Airport symbol*]   (OAG)
STR........... Subject Terminal Control Release [*Aviation*]   (FAAC)
STR........... Submarine Test Reactor
STR........... Submarine Thermal Reactor [*Nuclear energy*]
STR........... Submersible Test Rack
STR........... Summary Technical Report
STR........... Super Transportable RADAR
STR........... Surplus to Requirements   (ADA)
STR........... Synchronous Transmitter Receiver [*Data processing*]
STR........... System Test Review [*NASA*]   (NASA)
STR........... Systems Technology RADAR   (MCD)
STRAW...... Supply and Training Mission [*Military*]   (CINC)
STRAA...... Strahlentherapie [*A publication*]
STRAAD... Special Techniques Repair Analysis Aircraft Damage [*Navy*]   (NVT)
STRAB ..... Strabismus [*Medicine*]
Strab .... Strabo [*First century BC*] [*Classical studies*]   (OCD)
STRAB ..... Strain [*A publication*]
STRABAD... Strategic Base Air Defense [*Military*]   (AABC)
STRAC...... Standards in Training Commission [*Army*]   (INF)
STRAC ..... Strategic Army Corps [*Acronym has come to mean "ordered" or "neat"*]
STRACOS ... Strategic Air Combat Operations Staff
STRACS.... Small Transportable Communications Stations
STRACS.... Surface Traffic Control System   (MCD)
STRAD...... Signal Transmission Reception and Distribution   (IEEE)
Strad .... Stradivari [*Record label*]
STRAD...... Stradivarius Violin [*Music*]   (DSUE)
STRAD...... Strategic Aerospace Division [*Air Force*]   (AFM)
STRAD...... Switching, Transmitting, Receiving, and Distribution
STRADAP ... Storm RADAR Data Processor [*ESD*]
STRAF ...... Special Therapeutic and Rehabilitation Activities Fund [*Department of Veterans Affairs*]
STRAF ...... Strategic Army Forces
STRAFE.... Students Resisting Aerosol Flurocarbon Emissions [*Student legal action organization*]   (EA)
Strafford .... Smith's New Hampshire Reports [*A publication*]   (DLA)
STRAFIP .. Strategic Army Forces Readiness Improvement Program   (AABC)
STRAFLO ... Straight-Flow [*Water turbine*]
STRAFPOA ... Strategic Air Force, Pacific Ocean Area
STRAG...... Straggler
STRAGL ... Straggler Line [*Military*]
Strahan ...... Strahan's Reports [*19 Oregon*] [*A publication*]   (DLA)
Strah Domat ... Strahan's Domat's Civil Law [*A publication*]   (DLA)

Strahlenschutz Forsch Prax ... Strahlenschutz in Forschung und Praxis [*West Germany*] [*A publication*]
Strahlenthe ... Strahlentherapie [*A publication*]
Strahlenther Sonderb ... Strahlentherapie. Sonderbaende [*A publication*]
STRAIN .... Structural Analytical Interpreter
STRAIRPOA ... Strategic Air Force, Pacific Ocean Area
Straits LJ & Rep ... Straits Law Journal and Reporter [*A publication*]   (DLA)
Straits Times A ... Straits Times Annual [*Singapore*] [*A publication*]
STRAM..... Synchronous Transmit Receive Access Method   (CMD)
Strand .... Strand Magazine [*A publication*]
Strand (Lond) ... Strand Magazine (London) [*A publication*]
Strand (NY) ... Strand Magazine (New York) [*A publication*]
STRANGE ... SAGE [*Semiautomatic Ground Environment*] Tracking and Guidance Evaluation System
Strange....... Strange's English Court Reports [*A publication*]   (DLA)
Strange (Eng) ... Strange's English Courts Reports [*93 English Reprint*] [*A publication*]
Strange Madras ... Strange's Notes of Cases, Madras [*A publication*]   (DLA)
STRAP ...... SCAR Team Report Analysis Program   (MCD)
STRAP ..... Simplified Transient Radiation Analysis Program   (MCD)
STRAP ...... Simultaneous Transmission and Recovery of Alternating Pictures [*TV system*]
STRAP ...... Sonobuoy Thinned Random Array Program [*Navy*]   (CAAL)
STRAP ...... Star [*or Stellar*] Tracking Rocket Attitude Positioning [*System*] [*NASA*]
STRAP ...... Stretch Assembly Program [*IBM Corp.*]
STRAP ...... Structural Analysis Package
STRAPP.... Standard Tanks, Racks, Adapter, and Pylon Packages   (MCD)
STRASB .... Strasbourg [*Imprint*]   (ROG)
Strasb Med ... Strasbourg Medical [*A publication*]
STRAT ...... Strategic   (AFM)
STRAT ...... Stratigraphic
STRAT ...... Stratton [*England*]
STRATAD ... Strategic Aerospace Division [*Air Force*]
STRATCOM ... Strategic Communications Command [*Army*]   (RDA)
STRATCOM ... Stratospheric Composition   (MCD)
Strateg Anal ... Strategic Analysis [*India*] [*A publication*]
Strategic Dig ... Strategic Digest [*A publication*]
Strategic R ... Strategic Review [*A publication*]
Strateg Manage J ... Strategic Management Journal [*A publication*]
STRATF.... Stratford [*England*]
Strathclyde Bioeng Semin ... Strathclyde Bioengineering Seminars [*A publication*]
STRATMAS ... Strategic Mobility [*Planning and*] Analysis System [*Military*]   (NVT)
STRATO ... Stratosphere   (AFM)
Strat R........ Strategic Review [*Washington, DC*] [*A publication*]
Strat Rev .... Strategic Review [*A publication*]
STRATSAT ... Strategic Satellite System [*Air Force*] [*Telecommunications*]   (TEL)
Strat Svy .... Strategic Survey [*A publication*]
Stratton...... Stratton's Reports [*12-14 Oregon*] [*A publication*]   (DLA)
STRATWARM ... Stratospheric Warming
Strauss .... Internationale Richard-Strauss-Gesellschaft. Mitteilungen [*A publication*]
Str Autobahn ... Strasse und Autobahn [*A publication*]
STRAW..... Simultaneous Tape Read and Write
STRB .... Strobe   (NASA)
STRB .... [*The*] Strober Organization, Inc. [*Brooklyn, NY*] [*NASDAQ symbol*]   (NQ)
STRBK ...... Strongback
STRC........ Science and Technology Research Center [*North Carolina*]   (MCD)
STRC........ Scientific and Technical Research Centres in Australia [*Information service or system*] [*A publication*]   (APTA)
STRC........ Scientific, Technical, and Research Commission   (EY)
STRC........ Society of Traditional Roman Catholics   (EA)
STRC........ Stratford American Corp. [*NASDAQ symbol*]   (CTT)
STRC........ Switch Tail Ring Counter
Str Cas Ev ... Strange's Cases of Evidence ("Octavo Strange") [*A publication*]   (DLA)
STRCH..... Stretch   (AAG)
STRC-IVS ... STRC [*Science and Technology Research Center*] Inverted File Search System [*Search system*]
STRD........ Short Tour Return Date [*Military*]
STRD........ Stored
STRD........ Strand [*Engineering*]
STRE .... Specialist Teams Royal Engineers [*Military*] [*British*]
STREAM .. Standard Tensioned Replenishment Alongside Method [*Military*]   (NVT)
S Treaty Doc ... Senate Treaty Documents [*A publication*]   (DLA)
Street Ry Rep ... Street Railway Reports [*A publication*]   (DLA)
StRel/ScRel ... Studies in Religion/Sciences Religieuses [*A publication*]
Strem Chem ... Strem Chemiker [*A publication*]
St Ren .... Studies in the Renaissance [*A publication*]
Streng and H ... Strength and Health [*A publication*]
STRENGTHD ... Strengthened   (ROG)
Strength Mater ... Strength of Materials [*A publication*]
Strenna Stor Bolognese ... Strenna Storica Bolognese [*A publication*]
STREP....... Ship's Test and Readiness Evaluation Procedure
STREP....... Space Trajectory Radiation Exposure Procedure

St Rep .... State Reporter [*A publication*]   (DLA)
St Rep .... State Reports [*A publication*]   (DLA)
STREP...... Status Report [*IRS*]
Strep........... Strepsiptera [*Entomology*]
STREP...... Streptococcus [*Medicine*]
STREP...... Systems Technology Reentry Experiment Program [*Military*]
St Rep (NSW) ... State Reports (New South Wales) [*A publication*]
St Rep Queensl (Austr) ... Queensland State Reports (Australia) [*A publication*]   (DLA)
STREPTO ... Streptomycin [*An antibiotic*]   (DSUE)
STRES....... Store Release Evaluation System   (MCD)
STRESS ...... Satellite Transmission Effects Simulation   (MCD)
STRESS .... Stop the Robberies, Enjoy Safe Streets [*Detroit police unit*] [*Disbanded*]
STRESS .... Structural Engineering Systems Solver [*Programming language*] [*1962*]
STRETCH ... [*An*] early large computer [*IBM 7030*]
STRETCH ... Space Technology Requirements Engineering Test of Component Hardware [*NASA*]   (KSC)
Str Ev .... Strange's Cases of Evidence [*1698-1732*] [*England*] [*A publication*]   (DLA)
STRF .... Sea Turtle Rescue Fund   (EA)
STRFLD.... Star Field   (MCD)
STRG......... Steering   (AAG)
STRG......... String   (NASA)
STRG......... Strong   (MSA)
STRG WND ... String or Wind [*Freight*]
STRHA....... Staub, Reinhaltung der Luft [*A publication*]
Str & HC.... Streets and Highways Code [*A publication*]   (DLA)
Str HL........ Strange's Hindoo Law [*A publication*]   (DLA)
STRI .... Smithsonian Tropical Research Institute [*Miami, FL*]
STRI .... Sports Turf Research Institute [*British*]   (IRUK)
STRI .... Stones River National Battlefield
Strick Ev .... Strickland on Evidence [*1830*] [*A publication*]   (DLA)
St Ric Lat... Studi e Ricerche. Istituto di Latino. Universita di Genova [*A publication*]
STRICOM ... Strike Command [*Military*]
STRIDE..... Standard Reactor Island Design [*Nuclear energy*]   (NRCH)
STRIDE..... System to Retrieve Information from Drug Evidence [*Drug Enforcement Administration*]
STRIKEOPS ... Strike Operations [*Military*]   (NVT)
STRIKEX.. Strike Exercise [*Navy*] [*NATO*]   (NATG)
STRIKFLTLANT ... Striking Fleet Atlantic [*Military*]
STRIKFORSOUTH ... Striking and Support Forces Southern Europe [*Navy*]
STRIKFTLANTREPEUR ... Striking Fleet Atlantic Representative in Europe [*NATO*]   (NATG)
STRING .... Stringendo [*Hastening*] [*Music*]
Stringf........ Stringfellow's Reports [*9-11 Missouri*] [*A publication*]   (DLA)
Stringfellow ... Stringfellow's Reports [*9-11 Missouri*] [*A publication*]   (DLA)
STRINO..... Stringendo [*Hastening*] [*Music*]   (ROG)
STRIP....... Specification Technical Review and Improvement Program [*Navy*]   (NG)
STRIP....... Standard Requisition and Issue Procedures [*Military*]   (CINC)
STRIP....... Standard Taped Routines for Image Processing [*National Institute of Standards and Technology*]
STRIP....... Stock Turn-In and Replenishment Invoicing Procedures
STRIP....... String Processing Language [*Data processing*]   (DIT)
STRIPE ..... Swap Transferring Risk with Participating Element [*Finance*]
STRIPS ..... Separate Trading of Registered Interest and Principal of Securities [*Investment term*]
STRIVE..... Standard Techniques for Reporting Information on Value Engineering
St Riv Wat Supply Comm Tech Bull ... Victoria. State Rivers and Water Supply Commission. Technical Bulletin [*A publication*]   (APTA)
STRJ......... Self-Powered Thermocouple Reference Junction
STRJA...... Strojirenstvi [*A publication*]
STRK........ Star Tracker   (NASA)
STRK........ Stroke   (MSA)
STRKA...... Staerke [*A publication*]
STRKR...... Striker [*Automotive engineering*]
STRL......... Sea Trials [*Navy*]   (NVT)
STRL......... Sterling, Inc. [*Akron, OH*] [*NASDAQ symbol*]   (NQ)
Str L .... Straight Line [*Freight*]
STRL .... Structural
STR LGTHS ... Straight Lengths [*Freight*]
STRLN...... Streamline   (MSA)
STRM....... Storeroom   (MSA)
Str M .... Strand Magazine [*A publication*]
STRM....... Stream
STRN........ Standard Technical Report Number
STRN........ Strength   (AAG)
STRN........ Sutron Corp. [*NASDAQ symbol*]   (NQ)
Str NC....... [*Sir T.*] Strange's Notes of Cases [*Madras*] [*A publication*]   (DLA)
STRND..... Sternenbote [*A publication*]
STRNG..... Steering
STRNR..... Strainer   (AAG)
STRO........ Scandinavian Tire and Rim Organization   (EA)
STRO........ Stereo Routes   (FAAC)
StRo .... Studi Romani [*Rome*] [*A publication*]

Strob .... Strobhart's South Carolina Law Reports [*1846-50*] [*A publication*]   (DLA)
Strob Ch..... Strobhart's South Carolina Equity Reports [*A publication*]   (DLA)
STROBE ... Satellite Tracking of Balloons and Emergencies
STROBE ... Stroboscopic   (MSA)
Strob Eq ..... Strobhart's South Carolina Equity Reports [*1846-50*] [*A publication*]   (DLA)
STROBES ... Shared-Time Repair of Big Electronic Systems [*Data processing*]
Strobh Eq (SC) ... Strobhart's South Carolina Equity Reports [*A publication*]   (DLA)
Strobh L (SC) ... Strobhart's South Carolina Law Reports [*A publication*]   (DLA)
Stroemungsmech Stroemungsmasch ... Stroemungsmechanik und Stroemungsmaschinen [*A publication*]
Stroezh Funkts Mozuka ... Stroezh i Funktsii na Mozuka [*A publication*]
STROFAC ... Stabilized Routing for Afloat Commands   (MCD)
STR OFF FIXT ... Store or Office Fixture[*s*] [*Freight*]
Stroit Alyum Konstr ... Stroitel'nye Alyuminievye Konstruktsii [*A publication*]
Stroit Arkhit Leningrada ... Stroitel'stvo i Arkhitektura Leningrada [*A publication*]
Stroit Arkhit Uzb ... Stroitel'stvo i Arkhitektura Uzbekistana [*A publication*]
Stroit Dorog ... Stroitel'stvo Dorog [*A publication*]
Stroit Dorozhn Mash ... Stroitel'nye i Dorozhnye Mashiny [*A publication*]
Stroit Keram ... Stroitel'naya Keramika [*A publication*]
Stroit Konstr ... Stroitel'nye Konstruktsii [*A publication*]
Stroit Konstr Alyum Splavov ... Stroitel'nye Konstruktsii iz Alyuminievkh Splavov [*A publication*]
Stroit Mater ... Stroitel'nye Materialy [*A publication*]
Stroit Mater (1929-32) ... Stroitel'nye Materialy (1929-32) [*A publication*]
Stroit Mater (1933-38) ... Stroitel'nye Materialy (1932-38) [*A publication*]
Stroit Mater Betony ... Stroitel'nye Materialy i Betony [*A publication*]
Stroit Mater Detali Izdeliya ... Stroitel'nye Materialy. Detali i Izdeliya [*A publication*]
Stroit Mater Izdeliya Konstr ... Stroitel'nye Materialy. Izdeliya i Konstruktsii [*A publication*]
Stroit Mater Konstr ... Stroitel'nye Materialy i Konstruktsii [*A publication*]
Stroit Mater Silik Prom-St ... Stroitelni Materiali i Silikatna Promishlenost [*Bulgaria*] [*A publication*]
Stroit Mekh Raschet Sooruz ... Stroitel'naya Mekhanika i Raschet Sooruzhenii [*USSR*] [*A publication*]
Stroit Predpr Neft Promsti ... Stroitel'stvo Predpriyatii Neftyanoi Promyshlennosti [*A publication*]
Stroit Promst ... Stroitel'naya Promyshlennost [*A publication*]
Stroit Truboprovodov ... Stroitel'stvo Truboprovodov [*USSR*] [*A publication*]
Strojir Vyroba ... Strojirenska Vyroba [*A publication*]
Strojnicky Cas ... Strojnicky Casopis [*Czechoslovakia*] [*A publication*]
Strojniski Vestn ... Strojniski Vestnik [*A publication*]
Stroj Vest ... Strojniski Vestnik [*A publication*]
Stroke Suppl ... Stroke. Supplement [*A publication*]
Strom .... Stromateis [*of Clemens Alexandrinus*] [*Classical studies*]   (OCD)
STROM..... Stromberg [*Automotive engineering*]
St Rom .... Studi Romani [*A publication*]
StRom .... Studia Romanica [*A publication*]
StRom .... Studies in Romanticism [*A publication*]
St Romagnoli ... Studi Romagnoli [*A publication*]
Stromprax ... Strompraxis [*A publication*]
Stroud Sl .... Stroud on Slavery [*A publication*]   (DLA)
STRP .... Strap
STRP .... Striker Petroleum Corp. [*NASDAQ symbol*]   (NQ)
St RQ (Q)..... Queensland State Reports [*Australia*] [*A publication*]   (DLA)
St R (Q)..... State Reports (Queensland) [*A publication*]   (APTA)
St R Qd ..... Queensland State Reports [*Australia*] [*A publication*]   (DLA)
St R (Qd)..... State Reports (Queensland) [*A publication*]   (APTA)
St R (Queensl) ... State Reports (Queensland) [*A publication*]
STRR........ Star Technologies, Inc. [*Sterling, VA*] [*NASDAQ symbol*]   (NQ)
STRS .... Sprouse-Reitz Stores, Inc. [*Portland, OR*] [*NASDAQ symbol*]   (NQ)
STRT .... [*The*] Stewartstown Railroad Co. [*AAR code*]
STRT .... Strait [*Board on Geographic Names*]
Str Tiefbau ... Strassen- und Tiefbau [*A publication*]
STRTL....... Structural
STRTR....... Starter [*Automotive engineering*]
STRU......... Structofab, Inc. [*NASDAQ symbol*]   (NQ)
STRU......... Styrelserepresentationsutredningen [*Sweden*]
STRUBAL ... Structured Basic Language [*Data processing*]   (CSR)
STRUC...... Structure   (AABC)
Struc Rev.... Structuralist Review [*A publication*]
STRUCT ... Structure   (AAG)
Struct Bonding ... Structure and Bonding [*A publication*]
Struct Concr ... Structural Concrete [*A publication*]
Struct Eng ... Structural Engineer [*A publication*]
Struct Eng ... Structural Engineer. Parts A and B [*A publication*]
Struct Engr ... Structural Engineer [*A publication*]
Struct Foam Conf Proc ... Structural Foam Conference. Proceedings [*A publication*]
Struct Funct Brain ... Structure and Functions of the Brain [*A publication*]

Struct Glass ... Structure of Glass [*A publication*]
Struct Mater Note Aust Aeronaut Res Lab ... Australia. Department of Supply. Aeronautical Research Laboratories. Structures and Materials Note [*A publication*]   (APTA)
Struct Mater Rep Aust Aeronaut Res Lab ... Australia. Aeronautical Research Laboratories. Structures and Materials Report [*A publication*]   (APTA)
Struct Note Aust Aeronaut Res Lab ... Australia. Aeronautical Research Laboratories. Structures Note [*A publication*]   (APTA)
Struct Rep ... Structure Reports [*A publication*]
Struct Rep Aust Aeronaut Res Lab ... Australia. Aeronautical Research Laboratories. Structures Report [*A publication*]   (APTA)
Struct Rep Dep Archit Sci Syd Univ ... Structures Report. Department of Architectural Science. University of Sydney [*A publication*]   (APTA)
Struct Saf ... Structural Safety [*A publication*]
Struct Surv ... Structural Survey [*A publication*]
STRUDL ... Structural Design Language [*Data processing*]   (MCD)
STRUFO ... Structural Formula [*Data processing*] [*Chemistry*]
Strukt Funkts Fermentov ... Struktura i Funktsiya Fermentov [*A publication*]
Strukt Modif Khlopk Tsellyul ... Struktura i Modifikatsiya Khlopkovoi Tsellyulozy [*A publication*]
Strukt Rol Vody Zhivom Org ... Struktura i Rol Vody v Zhivom Organizme [*A publication*]
Strukt Svoistva Krist ... Struktura i Svoistva Kristallov [*A publication*]
Strukt Svoistva Litykh Splavov ... Struktura i Svoistva Litykh Splavov [*A publication*]
Strukturn i Mat Lingvistika ... Strukturnaja i Matematiceskaja Lingvistika [*A publication*]
ST Rulings ... Sales Tax Rulings [*Australia*] [*A publication*]
Strum Crit ... Strumenti Critici [*A publication*]
Strum una Nuova Cultur Guida e Manual ... Strumenti per una Nuova Cultura. Guida e Manuali [*A publication*]
Struve ... Struve's Washington Territory Reports [*1854-88*] [*A publication*]   (DLA)
Str Verkehr ... Strasse und Verkehr [*A publication*]
STRW ... Strawbridge & Clothier [*NASDAQ symbol*]   (NQ)
STRX ... Syntrex, Inc. [*NASDAQ symbol*]   (NQ)
STRY ... Stryker Corp. [*NASDAQ symbol*]   (NQ)
STRYCH ... Strychnina [*Strychnine*] [*Pharmacy*]   (ROG)
St Ry Rep ... Street Railway Reports [*United States*] [*A publication*]   (DLA)
STrZ ... South Tropical Zone [*Planet Jupiter*]
STRZ ... Star Banc Corp. [*NASDAQ symbol*]   (NQ)
STS ... Office of State Technical Services [*Also, OSTS*] [*Abolished, 1970*] [*Department of Commerce*]
STS ... S-Band Transmitter System
STS ... Saint Thomas Seminary [*Colorado; Connecticut; Kentucky*]
STS ... Sale Technical School [*Australia*]
STS ... Santa Rosa [*California*] [*Airport symbol*]   (OAG)
STS ... Santiago [*Spain*] [*Seismograph station code, US Geological Survey*]   (SEIS)
STS ... Satellite-to-Satellite   (CET)
STS ... Satellite Tracking Station
STS ... Satellite Transmission Systems, Inc. [*Hauppauge, NY*] [*Telecommunications*]   (TSSD)
STS ... Scheduled Truck Service [*Army*]
STS ... School-to-School [*Red Cross Youth*]
STS ... School Television Service
STS ... Science Talent Search   (EA)
STS ... Science and Technology Section [*Association of College and Research Libraries*]
STS ... Science, Technology, and Society
STS ... Science of To-Day Series [*A publication*]
STS ... Scottish Tartans Society   (EA)
STS ... Scottish Text Society [*A publication*]
STS ... Sea Training Staff [*Canadian Navy*]
STS ... Security Termination Statement [*Military*]   (AFM)
STS ... Self-Test Select
STS ... Seminex [*Concordia Seminary in Exile*] Library, St. Louis, MO [*OCLC symbol*]   (OCLC)
STS ... Sequence-Tagged Site [*Genetics*]
STS ... Serological Test for Syphilis [*Medicine*]
STS ... Servo Test System
STS ... Sewage Treatment System [*Navy*]   (CAAL)
STS ... Shared Tenant Services [*Telecommunications*]   (TSSD)
STS ... Ship-to-Shore
STS ... Shuttle Test Station   (NASA)
STS ... Shuttle Transportation System   (MCD)
STS ... Siltstone [*Lithology*]
STS ... Simulator Test Set   (CAAL)
STS ... Skaggs Telecommunications Service [*Salt Lake City, UT*] [*Telecommunications*]   (TSSD)
STS ... Skylab Terminal System [*NASA*]
STS ... Society for Textual Scholarship   (EA)
STS ... Society of Thoracic Surgeons   (EA)
STS ... Socio-Technical Systems [*Management technique*]
STS ... Sodium Tetradecyl Sulfate [*Organic chemistry*]
STS ... Sodium Thiosulfate [*Inorganic chemistry, biochemistry*]
STS ... Soft Tissue Sarcoma [*Oncology*]
STS ... Solar Tracking System
STS ... SONAR Technician, Submarine [*Navy rating*]

STS ... SONAR Test System
STS ... Sonic Telex System [*Sonicair*] [*Phoenix, AZ*] [*Telecommunications*]   (TSSD)
STS ... Space-Time-Space [*Digital switching structure*] [*Telecommunications*]   (TEL)
STS ... Space Transportation System
STS ... Spacecraft Telecommunications System
STS ... Spacecraft Tracking Station [*NASA*]   (KSC)
STS ... Special Task Stores [*Military*] [*British*]
STS ... Special Test System [*Air Force*]   (AFM)
STS ... Special Training Standard [*Air Force*]   (AFM)
STS ... Special Treatment Steel
STS ... Specialty Training System
STS ... Specific Tensile Strength
STS ... Spring Trapmakers' Society [*British*]   (DCTA)
STS ... Stabilized Telescope System
StS ... Stamp Seal   (BJA)
STS ... Standard (Galilean) Telescopes [*Instrumentation*]
STS ... Standard Technical Specifications [*Nuclear energy*]   (NRCH)
STS ... Standard Test for Syphilis [*Medicine*]
STS ... Standard Threshold Shift
STS ... State Technical Services [*Abolished, 1970*]
STS ... Static Test Stand
STS ... Station to Station
STS ... Stationary Time Series
STS ... Sterol-sulphatase [*An enzyme*]
STS ... Stirring Science Stories [*A publication*]
STS ... Stock Trading System
STS ... Stockpile-to-Target Sequence [*Military*]
STS ... Stomatogastric Nervous System [*Neuroanatomy*]
STS ... Strategic Technical Service   (CINC)
STS ... Strategic Training Squadron   (MCD)
STS ... Structural Transition Section [*NASA*]   (MCD)
StS ... Studia Slavica [*A publication*]
STS ... Superior Temporal Sulcus [*Brain anatomy*]
STS ... Supersonic Target System
STS ... Supplementary Test Site [*Nuclear energy*]   (IID)
STS ... Surveillance Test Set   (MCD)
STS ... Survey Tabulation Services, Inc. [*Information service or system*]   (IID)
STS ... Synchronous Transport Signal [*Data processing*]
STS ... System Test Set
STS ... System Test Software   (CAAL)
STS ... System Trouble Shooting
STS ... System Trouble Survey   (CET)
STSA ... Seaman Apprentice, SONAR Technician, Striker [*Navy rating*]
STSA ... Southern Thoracic Surgical Association   (EA)
STSA ... State Technical Services Act
StSa ... Studi Salentini [*A publication*]
St Salent ... Studi Salentini [*A publication*]
STSALV ... Standby Salvage Ship [*Navy*]   (NVT)
St Sard ... Studi Sardi [*A publication*]
ST-SAS ... Septic Tank-Subsurface Absorption System
STSB ... Seattle Trust & Savings Bank [*NASDAQ symbol*]   (NQ)
STSBDL ... Studi Trentini di Scienze Naturali. Acta Biologica [*A publication*]
STSC ... Scientific Time Sharing Corporation [*Host*] [*Information service or system*]   (IID)
STSC ... Scottish Teachers Salaries Committee [*British*]
ST SCI ... Space Telescope Science Institute [*Johns Hopkins University*] [*Research center*]   (RCD)
STSCM ... Space Transportation System Cost Model [*NASA*]   (KSC)
STSD ... Society of Teachers of Speech and Drama [*British*]
StSec ... Studi Secenteschi [*A publication*]
StSem ... Studi Semitici [*A publication*]
StSemNeerl ... Studia Semitica Neerlandica [*Assen*] [*A publication*]
STSFSC ... Scarf Trailers Science Fiction Social Club [*Inactive*]   (EA)
STSG ... Shuttle Test Group [*NASA*]   (NASA)
STSG ... Space Topics Study Group   (EA)
STSG ... Split Thickness Skin Graft
STSGD2 ... Studi Trentini di Scienze Naturali. Acta Geologica [*A publication*]
STSH ... Stabilized Shunt [*Electricity*]
STSI ... Space Telescope Science Institute [*NASA*]
STSK ... Scandinavian Committee for Satellite Communications [*Telecommunications*]   (TEL)
StSl ... Studia Slavica [*A publication*]
StSLL ... Studies in Semitic Languages and Linguistics [*A publication*]
STSM ... Surface-to-Target-to-Surface-to-Missile
STSN ... Seaman, SONAR Technician, Striker [*Navy rating*]
STSN ... Set-and-Test-Sequence-Number [*Data processing*]   (IBMDP)
STSO ... Senior Technical Staff Officer [*British*]
STSODQ ... Annual Report. Natural Products Research Institute. Seoul National University [*A publication*]
STSOPO ... Shuttle Transportation Systems Operations Program Office [*Johnson Space Center*]   (NASA)
ST & SP ... Start and Stop
ST-SR ... Small Transmitter Coated with Silicon Rubber
STSR ... System Test Summary Report [*NASA*]   (NASA)
STSS ... Sensitive Thrust Stand System
STSS ... Society for Traumatic Stress Studies   (EA)

STSS.........	Star States Corp. [*NASDAQ symbol*] (NQ)
STSS.........	Studi Trentini di Scienze Storiche [*A publication*]
Ststcian......	Statistician [*A publication*]
St Stor Rel ...	Studi Storico-Religioso [*A publication*]
STT...........	Charlotte Amalie, VI [*Location identifier*] [*FAA*] (FAAL)
STT...........	Saigon Transportation Terminal Command [*Republic of Vietnam Armed Forces*]
STT...........	St. Thomas [*Virgin Islands*] [*Airport symbol*]
STT...........	Save the Theatres (EA)
STT...........	School of Tank Technology [*British military*] (DMA)
STT...........	School of Technical Training [*British military*] (DMA)
STT.........	Science Stories [*A publication*]
STT...........	Seattle - Marshall [*Washington*] [*Seismograph station code, US Geological Survey*] [*Closed*] (SEIS)
STT...........	Seek Time per Track
STT...........	Semitendinosus Tendon [*Anatomy*]
STT...........	Sensitization Test
STT...........	Sent to Typesetter [*Publishing*]
STT...........	Ship Turn Transmitter
STT...........	Shore Targeting Terminal [*Navy*] (CAAL)
STT...........	Short-Term Test [*Toxicology*]
STT...........	Signal Tracing Tester
STT...........	Single Target Track [*Navy*] (NG)
STT...........	Skid-to-Turn
STT...........	Skin Temperature Test [*Physiology*]
STT...........	Spacecraft Terminal Thrust
STT...........	Spacelab Transfer Tunnel (NASA)
STT...........	Spade Tongue Terminal
STT...........	Standard Triple Therapy [*For hypertension*]
STT...........	Stenographer, Medical [*Navy*]
STT...........	Strange Tales of Mystery and Terror [*A publication*]
StT...........	Studi Tassiani [*A publication*]
STT...........	Superior Teletec Corp. [*AMEX symbol*] (SPSG)
STT...........	Sutton Resources Ltd. [*Vancouver Stock Exchange symbol*]
STT...........	Svensk Traevaru- och Pappersmassetidning [*A publication*]
STT...........	Syndicat des Travailleurs en Telecommunications [*Telecommunications Workers Union - TWU*] [*Canada*]
St Tax Cas CCH ...	State Tax Cases. Commerce Clearing House [*A publication*]
St Tax Cas Rep (CCH) ...	State Tax Cases Reporter (Commerce Clearing House) [*A publication*] (DLA)
St Tax Cas Rep CCH ...	State Tax Cases Reports. Commerce Clearing House [*A publication*]
St Tax Rep (CCH) ...	State Tax Reporter (Commerce Clearing House) [*A publication*] (DLA)
St Tax Rep CCH ...	State Tax Reports. Commerce Clearing House [*A publication*]
STTBA	Strassen- und Tiefbau [*A publication*]
STTC.........	Scottish Textile and Technical Centre Ltd. [*United Kingdom*] (IRUK)
STTC.........	Sheppard Technical Training Center (AFM)
StTCL........	Studies in Twentieth-Century Literature [*A publication*]
StTDJ........	Studies on the Texts of the Desert of Judah [*J. Van Der Ploeg*] [*Leiden*] [*A publication*] (BJA)
ST & TE	Special Tools and Test Equipment (MCD)
STTE	Special Tools and Test Equipment
STTEA	Stain Technology [*A publication*]
StTeol.........	Studii Teologice [*Bucharest*] [*A publication*]
StTEstmatn ...	Statistical Theory of Estimation [*A publication*]
STTF	Sanskrittexte aus den Turfanfunden [*A publication*]
STTF	SONAR Test Tower Facility
STTF	Special Tank Task Force (MCD)
STTF	System Technology Test Facility (MCD)
STT-FNB ..	Suomen Tietotoimisto-Finska Notisbyran [*Press agency*] [*Finland*]
STTG.........	[*The*] Statesman Group, Inc. [*NASDAQ symbol*] (NQ)
StTh...........	Studia Theologica [*A publication*]
StTheol......	Studia Teologica [*A publication*]
StThL........	Studia Theologica Lundensia. Skrifter Utgivna av Teologiska Fakulteten i Lund [*A publication*]
StThVars ...	Studia Theologica Varsaviensia [*Warsaw*] [*A publication*]
S/TTL........	Schottky Transistor-Transistor Logic
STTL	Sit Tibi Terra Levis [*May the Earth Lie Light on Thee*] [*Letters found on Roman tombs*] [*Latin*]
STTM........	Stabilized Tracking Tripod Module (RDA)
STTNG......	Star Trek, the Next Generation [*Television program*]
STTO.........	Sawtooth Timing Oscillator (DEN)
STTO.........	Staking Tool (AAG)
StTO..........	Stueckgut-Transport-Ordnung [*Less than Carload (Freight) Transportation Regulations*] [*German*]
St Tomas J Med ...	Santo Tomas Journal of Medicine [*A publication*]
St Tomas Nurs J ...	Santo Tomas Nursing Journal [*A publication*]
STTOT......	Single Target Track on Target [*Navy*]
St Tr...........	Howell's English State Trials [*1163-1820*] [*A publication*] (DLA)
STTR.........	Stator
STTRA	Stroitel'stvo Truboprovodov [*A publication*]
St Tri.........	State Trials [*A publication*] (DLA)
St Tr NS	Macdonell's State Trials [*1820-58*] [*A publication*] (DLA)
STTS	S-Band Transponder Test Set (MCD)
STTS	Shipboard Target Tracking System
STTSRA	Scoot-Tours Touring Scooter Riders Association (EA)
STTT	Space Telescope Task Team [*NASA*]
St Twen Ct ...	Studies in Twentieth-Century Literature [*A publication*]
STTX	Steel Technologies, Inc. [*Louisville, KY*] [*NASDAQ symbol*] (NQ)
STU	Schweizerische Theologische Umschau [*A publication*]
STU	Secure Telephone Unit [*Data processing*]
STU	Seeker Test Unit (MCD)
STU	Service Trials Unit
STU	Servo Test Unit
STU	Short Ton Unit
STU	Signal Transfer Unit
STU	Skin Test Unit
STU	Space-Time Unit [*Computer*]
STU	Special Test Unit (CET)
STU	Special Training Unit
STU	Star Tracker Unit [*NASA*] (MCD)
STU	Static Test Unit (KSC)
STU	Step Up
STU	Stuart (ROG)
STU	Stuart [*D. A.*] Ltd. [*Toronto Stock Exchange symbol*]
STU	Student (AFM)
Stu.............	Studia [*A publication*]
STU	Studies on International Relations [*Warsaw*] [*A publication*]
Stu.............	Studium [*A publication*]
STU	Stuttgart [*Federal Republic of Germany*] [*Seismograph station code, US Geological Survey*] (SEIS)
STU	Styrelsen foer Teknisk Utveckling [*Swedish Board for Technical Development*]
STU	Submarine Test Unit
STU	Submersible Test Unit [*Navy*]
STU	Subscribers' Trunk Unit [*Telecommunications*] (TEL)
STU	System Timing Unit
STU	System Transition Unit [*Data processing*]
STU	Systems Test Unit (KSC)
STU	University of Steubenville, Steubenville, OH [*OCLC symbol*] (OCLC)
Stu Adm	Stuart's Lower Canada Vice-Admiralty Reports [*A publication*] (DLA)
Stu Adm NS ...	Stuart's Lower Canada Vice-Admiralty Reports, New Series [*A publication*] (DLA)
Stu Ap	Stuart's Lower Canada King's Bench Reports, Appeal Cases [*A publication*] (DLA)
Stuart	Stuart, Milne, and Peddie's Scotch Court of Session Cases [*A publication*] (DLA)
Stuart	Stuart's Lower Canada Reports [*A publication*] (DLA)
Stuart	Stuart's Lower Canada Vice-Admiralty Reports [*A publication*] (DLA)
Stuart Adm NS ...	Stuart's Lower Canada Vice-Admiralty Reports, New Series [*A publication*] (DLA)
Stuart Beng ...	Stuart's Select Cases [*1860*] [*Bengal, India*] [*A publication*] (DLA)
Stuart KB...	Stuart's Lower Canada King's Bench Reports [*1810-25*] [*Quebec*] [*A publication*] (DLA)
Stuart KB (Quebec) ...	Stuart's Lower Canada King's Bench Reports [*Quebec*] [*A publication*] (DLA)
Stuart LCKB ...	Stuart's Lower Canada King's Bench Reports [*A publication*] (DLA)
Stuart LCVA ...	Stuart's Lower Canada Vice-Admiralty Reports [*A publication*] (DLA)
Stuart M & P ...	Stuart, Milne, and Peddie's Scotch Court of Session Cases [*1851-53*] [*A publication*] (DLA)
Stuart & Por ...	Stuart [*or Stewart*] and Porter's Alabama Reports [*A publication*] (DLA)
Stuart & Porter ...	Stuart [*or Stewart*] and Porter's Alabama Reports [*A publication*] (DLA)
Stuart's Adm ...	Stuart's Lower Canada Vice-Admiralty Reports [*A publication*] (DLA)
Stuart's R ...	Stuart's Lower Canada King's Bench Reports, Appeal Cases [*Quebec*] [*A publication*] (DLA)
Stuart Vice-Adm ...	Stuart's Lower Canada Vice-Admiralty Reports [*A publication*] (DLA)
STUB.........	Stadt- und Universitaetsbibliothek Frankfurt [*Database producer*]
Stubbs CH ...	Stubb's Constitutional History [*A publication*] (DLA)
Stubbs Sel Ch ...	Stubb's Select Charters [*A publication*] (DLA)
STUC.........	Sarawak Trade Union Congress
STUC.........	Scottish Trades Union Congress
STUC.........	Singapore Trade Union Congress
Stu Cer Fiz ...	Studii si Cercetari de Fizica [*A publication*]
STUD	Standard Tractor, Universal with Dozer [*Army*]
STUD	Student
Stud..........	Studien [*A publication*]
STUD	Studies
Stud...........	Studies [*A publication*]
Stud...........	Studies: An Irish Quarterly Review of Letters, Philosophy, and Science [*A publication*]
Stud Account ...	Studies in Accountancy [*A publication*]
Stud Acta Orient ...	Studia et Acta Orientalia [*A publication*]
StudActOr ...	Studia et Acta Orientalia [*A publication*]
StudAeg	Studia Aegyptiaca [*Rome*] [*A publication*]

Stud Afr Linguist ... Studies in African Linguistics [*A publication*]
Stud Age Chaucer ... Studies in the Age of Chaucer [*A publication*]
Stud Ag Econ ... Stanford University Food Research Institute Studies in Agricultural Economics, Trade, and Development [*A publication*]
Stud Alb ..... Studia Albanica [*A publication*]
Stud Algebra Anwendungen ... Studien zur Algebra und Ihre Anwendungen [*A publication*]
Stud Aliment Apa ... Studii de Alimentari cu Apa [*A publication*]
Stud Am Fic ... Studies in American Fiction [*A publication*]
Stud Anc Technol ... Studies in Ancient Technology [*A publication*]   (OCD)
Stud Angew Wirtschaftsforsch Statist ... Studien zur Angewandten Wirtschaftsforschung und Statistik [*A publication*]
Stud Appl M ... Studies in Applied Mathematics [*A publication*]
Stud Appl Math ... Studies in Applied Mathematics [*A publication*]
Stud Appl Mech ... Studies in Applied Mechanics [*A publication*]
Stud Art Ed ... Studies in Art Education [*A publication*]
Stud Art Educ ... Studies in Art Education [*A publication*]
Stud Automat Control ... Studies in Automation and Control [*A publication*]
Stud Bank Fin ... Studies in Banking and Finance [*A publication*]
Stud Bayesian Econometrics ... Studies in Bayesian Econometrics [*A publication*]
Stud Bibliog ... Virginia University. Bibliographical Society. Studies in Bibliography [*A publication*]
Stud Bibliog & Bklore ... Studies in Bibliography and Booklore [*A publication*]
Stud Biol .... Studies in Biology [*A publication*]
Stud Biol Acad Sci Hung ... Studia Biologica. Academiae Scientiarum Hungaricae [*A publication*]
Stud Biol Hung ... Studia Biologica Hungarica [*A publication*]
Stud Biophy ... Studia Biophysica [*A publication*]
Stud Biophys ... Studia Biophysica [*A publication*]
Stud Black Lit ... Studies in Black Literature [*A publication*]
Stud Bot ..... Studia Botanica [*A publication*]
Stud Bot Cech ... Studia Botanica Cechoslavaca [*A publication*]
Stud Bot Hung ... Studia Botanica Hungarica [*A publication*]
Stud Brain Funct ... Studies in Brain Function [*A publication*]
Stud Br His ... Studies in British History and Culture [*A publication*]
Stud Broadcast ... Studies of Broadcasting [*A publication*]
Stud Brown ... Studies in Browning and His Circle [*A publication*]
StudBT .... Studia Biblica et Theologica [*New Haven, CT*] [*A publication*]
Stud Burke Time ... Studies in Burke and His Time [*A publication*]
Stud Can .... Studia Canonica [*A publication*]
StudCath .... Studia Catholica [*A publication*]
Stud Cerc Buzan ... Studii si Cercetari de Istorie Buzoiana [*A publication*]
Stud Cerc Docum ... Studii si Cercetari de Documentare [*A publication*]
Stud Cerc Econom ... Studii si Cercetari Economice [*A publication*]
Stud Cercet Agron Acad Rep Pop Romine Fil (Cluj) ... Studii si Cercetari de Agronomie. Academia Republicii Populare Romine Filiala (Cluj) [*A publication*]
Stud Cercet Antropol ... Studii si Cercetari de Antropologie [*A publication*]
Stud Cercetari Istoria Artei ... Studii si Cercetari de Istoria Artei [*A publication*]
Stud Cercet Astron ... Studii si Cercetari de Astronomie [*A publication*]
Stud Cercet Biochim ... Studii si Cercetari de Biochimie [*A publication*]
Stud Cercet Biol ... Studii si Cercetari de Biologie [*A publication*]
Stud Cercet Biol Acad Rep Pop Romine Fil (Cluj) ... Studii si Cercetari de Biologie. Academia Republicii Populare Romine Filiala (Cluj) [*A publication*]
Stud Cercet Biol Acad Rep Pop Romine Ser Biol Veg ... Studii si Cercetari de Biologie. Academia Republicii Populare Romine. Seria Biologi Vegetala [*A publication*]
Stud Cercet Biol Ser Biol Anim ... Studii si Cercetari de Biologie. Seria Biologie Animala [*A publication*]
Stud Cercet Biol Ser Bot ... Studii si Cercetari de Biologie. Seria Botanica [*A publication*]
Stud Cercet Biol Ser Zool ... Studii si Cercetari de Biologie. Seria Zoologie [*A publication*]
Stud & Cercet Calcul Econ & Cibern Econ ... Studii si Cercetari de Calcul Economic si Cibernetica Economica [*A publication*]
Stud Cercet Chim ... Studii si Cercetari de Chimie [*A publication*]
Stud & Cercet Doc ... Studii si Cercetari de Documentare [*A publication*]
Stud Cercet Embriol Citol Ser Embriol ... Studii si Cercetari de Embriologie si Citologie. Seria Embriologie [*Romania*] [*A publication*]
Stud Cercet Endocrinol ... Studii si Cercetari de Endocrinologie [*A publication*]
Stud Cercet Energ ... Studii si Cercetari de Energetica [*A publication*]
Stud Cercet Energ Electroteh ... Studii si Cercetari de Energetica si Electrotehnica [*A publication*]
Stud Cercet Energ Ser A ... Studii si Cercetari de Energetica. Seria A. Energetica Generala si Electroenergetica [*A publication*]
Stud Cercet Energ Ser B ... Studii si Cercetari de Energetica. Seria B. Termoenergetica si Utilizarea Energetica a Combustibililor [*A publication*]
Stud Cercet Fiz ... Studii si Cercetari de Fizica [*A publication*]
Stud Cercet Fiziol ... Studii si Cercetari de Fiziologie [*Romania*] [*A publication*]
Stud Cercet Geol Geofiz Geogr Ser Geofiz ... Studii si Cercetari de Geologie, Geofizica, si Geografie. Seria Geofizica [*A publication*]
Stud Cercet Geol Geofiz Geogr Ser Geogr ... Studii si Cercetari de Geologie, Geofizica, si Geografie. Seria Geografie [*A publication*]

Stud Cercet Geol Geofiz Geogr Ser Geol ... Studii si Cercetari de Geologie, Geofizica, si Geografie. Seria Geologie [*A publication*]
Stud Cercet Ig Sanat Publica ... Studii si Cercetari de Igiena si Sanatate Publica [*A publication*]
Stud Cercet Inframicrobiol ... Studii si Cercetari de Inframicrobiologie [*A publication*]
Stud Cercet Inframicrobiol Microbiol Parazitol ... Studii si Cercetari de Inframicrobiologie, Microbiologie, si Parazitologie [*A publication*]
Stud Cercet Inst Cercet Piscic ... Studii si Cercetari. Institutul de Cercetari Piscicole [*A publication*]
Stud Cercet Inst Cercet Proiect Piscic ... Studii si Cercetari. Institutul de Cercetari si Proiectari Piscicole [*A publication*]
Stud Cercet Inst Meteorol Hidrol Partea 1 ... Studii si Cercetari. Institutul de Meteorologie si Hidrologie. Partea 1. Meteorologie [*A publication*]
Stud Cercet Inst Meteorol Hidrol Partea 2 ... Studii si Cercetari. Institutul de Meteorologie si Hidrologie. Partea 2. Hidrologie [*A publication*]
Stud Cercet Mec Apl ... Studii si Cercetari de Mecanica Aplicata [*A publication*]
Stud Cercet Med (Cluj) ... Studii si Cercetari de Medicina (Cluj) [*A publication*]
Stud Cercet Med Interna ... Studii si Cercetari de Medicina Interna [*A publication*]
Stud Cercet Metal ... Studii si Cercetari de Metalurgie [*Romania*] [*A publication*]
Stud Cercet Metal Comun Stiint ... Studii si Cercetari de Metalurgie. Comunicari Stiintifice [*A publication*]
Stud Cercet Neurol ... Studii si Cercetari de Neurologie [*A publication*]
Stud Cercet Piscic Inst Cercet Proiect Aliment ... Studii si Cercetari Piscicole. Institutul de Cercetari si Proiectari Alimentare [*A publication*]
Stud Cercet Silvic ... Studii si Cercetari de Silvicultura [*A publication*]
Stud Cercet Silvic Inst Cercet Amenajari Silvice ... Studii si Cercetari de Silvicultura. Institutul de Cercetari si Amenajari Silvice [*A publication*]
Stud Cercet Virusol ... Studii si Cercetari de Virusologie [*A publication*]
Stud Cerc Fiz ... Studii si Cercetari de Fizica [*A publication*]
Stud Cerc Inst Cerc For (Industr Lemn) ... Studii si Cercetari. Institutul de Cercetari Forestiere (Industrializarea Lemnului) [*A publication*]
Stud Cerc Inst Cerc For (Mec Lucr For) ... Studii si Cercetari. Institutul de Cercetari Forestiere (Mecanizarea Lucrarilor Forestiere) [*A publication*]
Stud Cerc Inst Cerc For (Silv) ... Studii si Cercetari. Institutul de Cercetari Forestiere (Silvicultura) [*A publication*]
Stud Cerc Mat ... Studii si Cercetari Matematice [*A publication*]
Stud Cerc Mec Apl ... Studii si Cercetari de Mecanica Aplicata [*A publication*]
Stud Chemother Inst Med Res ... Studies. Chemotherapeutic Institute for Medical Research [*Japan*] [*A publication*]
Stud Ch G P ... Studies in Chinese Government and Politics [*A publication*]
Stud Church Hist ... Studies in Church History. American Society of Church History [*A publication*]
Stud Cl .... Studii Clasice [*A publication*]
StudClas .... Studii Clasice [*A publication*]
Stud Class ... Studies of Classical India [*A publication*]
Stud Com Co ... Studies in Comparative Communism [*A publication*]
Stud Com I D ... Studies in Comparative International Development [*A publication*]
Stud Com L G ... Studies in Comparative Local Government [*A publication*]
Stud Comm R ... Studies in Communism, Revisionism, and Revolution [*A publication*]
Stud Comp Com ... Studies in Comparative Communism [*Los Angeles*] [*A publication*]
Stud Comp Commun ... Studies in Comparative Communism [*A publication*]
Stud Comp Communism ... Studies in Comparative Communism [*A publication*]
Stud Comp Int Dev ... Studies in Comparative International Development [*New Jersey*] [*A publication*]
Stud Comp Int Develop ... Studies in Comparative International Development [*A publication*]
Stud in Comp Local Govt ... Studies in Comparative Local Government [*A publication*]
Stud Comp R ... Studies in Comparative Religion [*A publication*]
Stud Comp Relig ... Studies in Comparative Religion [*A publication*]
Stud Comun (Brukenthal) ... Studii si Comunicari (Brukenthal) [*A publication*]
Stud Comun (Pitesti) ... Studii si Comunicari (Pitesti) [*A publication*]
Stud Comun (Satu Mare) ... Studii si Comunicari (Satu Mare) [*A publication*]
Stud Conserv ... Studies in Conservation [*A publication*]
Stud Cont Ed ... Studies in Continuing Education [*A publication*]
Stud in Contin Educ ... Studies in Continuing Education [*A publication*]   (APTA)
Stud Cosmic Ray ... Studies of Cosmic Ray [*Japan*] [*A publication*]
Stud Demogr ... Studia Demograficzne [*A publication*]
Stud Design Educ Craft Technol ... Studies in Design Education, Craft, and Technology [*A publication*]
Stud Develop ... Middle East Technical University. Studies in Development [*A publication*]

Stud Develop Special Issue ... Studies in Development. Special Issue. Middle East Technical University [*A publication*]
Stud Dipl.... Studia Diplomatica [*Brussels*] [*A publication*]
Stud Diplom ... Studia Diplomatica [*A publication*]
Stud & Doc His Jur ... Studia et Documenta Historiae et Juris [*A publication*]
Stud Doc Hist Iur ... Studia et Documenta Historiae et Iuris [*Rome*] [*A publication*]   (OCD)
Stud Docum Asian Docum ... Studies and Documents. Asian Documentation and Research Center [*A publication*]
STUDE...... Studebaker [*Automotive engineering*]
Stud Ecol.... Studies in Ecology [*A publication*]
Stud Econ.... Studi Economici [*A publication*]
Stud Ed .... Studies in Education [*A publication*]
Stud Educ Adults ... Studies in the Education of Adults [*A publication*]
Stud Eight ... Studies in Eighteenth-Century Culture [*A publication*]
Stud Eighteenth-Century Cult ... Studies in Eighteenth-Century Culture [*A publication*]
Stud Engl L ... Studies in English Literature, 1500-1900 [*A publication*]
Stud Engl Lit ... Studies in English Literature [*A publication*]
Stud Engl Phil ... Studien zur Englischen Philologie [*A publication*]
Stud Engl (T) ... Studies in English Literature (Tokyo) [*A publication*]
Student Adv ... Student Advocate [*A publication*]
Studente Vet ... Studente Veterinario [*A publication*]
StudentIElecIE ... Student of the Institution of Electrical and Electronic Incorporated Engineers [*British*]   (DBQ)
StudentIWHTE ... Student of the Institution of Works and Highways Technician Engineers [*British*]   (DBQ)
Student Law ... Student Lawyer [*A publication*]
Student Law J ... Student Lawyer Journal [*A publication*]   (DLA)
Student L Rev ... Student Law Review [*A publication*]   (DLA)
Student Musicol ... Student Musicologists at Minnesota [*A publication*]
Stud Entomol ... Studia Entomologica [*A publication*]
Student Q J Instn Elec Engrs ... Institution of Electrical Engineers. Student Quarterly Journal [*A publication*]
Students'ky Nauk Pratsi Kyyv Derzh Unyv ... Students'ky Naukovi Pratsi Kyyivs'kyyi Derzhavnyyi Unyversytet [*A publication*]
Stud Epurarea Apelor ... Studii de Epurarea Apelor [*A publication*]
Stud Etr...... Studi Etruschi [*Firenze*] [*A publication*]   (OCD)
Stud Europ Soc ... Studies in European Society [*A publication*]
Stud Fam Pl ... Studies in Family Planning [*A publication*]
Stud Fam Plann ... Studies in Family Planning [*A publication*]
Stud Fauna Curacao Other Caribb Isl ... Studies on the Fauna of Curacao and Other Caribbean Islands [*A publication*]
Stud Fauna Suriname Other Guyanas ... Studies of the Fauna of Suriname and Other Guyanas [*A publication*]
Stud Fenn ... Studia Fennica [*A publication*]
Stud Filol ... Studime Filologjike [*A publication*]
Stud Finans ... Studia Finansowe [*A publication*]
Stud Form Spir ... Studies in Formative Spirituality [*A publication*]
Stud For Suec ... Studia Forestalia Suecica [*A publication*]
Stud For Suec (Skogshogsk) ... Studia Forestalia Suecica (Skogshogskolan) [*A publication*]
Stud Found Methodol Philos Sci ... Studies in the Foundations, Methodology, and Philosophy of Science [*A publication*]
Stud Fran ... Studi Francesi [*A publication*]
Stud Gen .... Studium Generale [*A publication*]
Stud Genet ... Studies in Genetics [*A publication*]
Stud Geogr Cesk Akad Ved Geogr Ustav (Brno) ... Studia Geographica. Ceskoslovenska Akademie Ved. Geograficky Ustav (Brno) [*A publication*]
Stud Geol Mineral Inst Tokyo Univ Educ ... Studies from the Geological and Mineralogical Institute. Tokyo University of Education [*A publication*]
Stud Geol Pol ... Studia Geologica Polonica [*A publication*]
Stud Geol Salamanca ... Studia Geologica. Universidad de Salamanca [*A publication*]
Stud Geol (Tulsa Okla) ... Studies in Geology (Tulsa, Oklahoma) [*A publication*]
Stud Geol Univ Salamanca ... Studia Geologica. Universidad de Salamanca [*A publication*]
Stud Geomorphol Carpatho-Balcanica ... Studia Geomorphologica Carpatho-Balcanica [*A publication*]
Stud Geoph ... Studia Geophysica et Geodaetica [*A publication*]
Stud Geophys Geod ... Studia Geophysica et Geodaetica [*A publication*]
Stud Geophys Geod (Cesk Akad Ved) ... Studia Geophysica et Geodaetica (Ceskosloven-Akademie Ved) [*A publication*]
Stud Geotech ... Studia Geotechnica. Politechnika Wroclawaka [*A publication*]
Stud Geotech Mech ... Studia Geotechnica et Mechanica [*A publication*]
Stud Geoteh Fund Constr Hidroteh ... Studii de Geotekhnica. Fundatii si Constructii Hidrotehnice [*A publication*]
Stud Gesch Akad Wiss DDR ... Studien zur Geschichte der Akademie der Wissenschaften der Deutsche Demokratische Republik [*A publication*]
Stud Gesch Kult Alt ... Studien zur Geschichte und Kultur des Altertums [*A publication*]   (OCD)
Stud Gr Rom Hist ... Studies in Greek and Roman History [*A publication*]   (OCD)
Stud H Art ... Studies in the History of Art [*A publication*]
Stud Helminthol ... Studia Helminthologica [*A publication*]
Stud Hib..... Studia Hibernica [*A publication*]

Stud High Educ ... Studies in Higher Education [*A publication*]
Stud High Temp Supercond ... Studies of High Temperature Superconductors. Advances in Research and Applications [*A publication*]
Stud Hist.... Studies in History, Economics, and Public Law [*A publication*]   (DLA)
Stud Hist.... Studime Historike [*A publication*]
Stud Hist Art ... Studies in the History of Art [*A publication*]
Stud Hist Biol ... Studies in History of Biology [*A publication*]
Stud Hist Math Phys Sci ... Studies in the History of Mathematics and Physical Sciences [*A publication*]
Stud Hist Med ... Studies in History of Medicine [*A publication*]
Stud Hist Modern Sci ... Studies in the History of Modern Science [*A publication*]
Stud Hist P ... Studies in History and Philosophy of Science [*A publication*]
Stud Hist Philos Sci ... Studies in History and Philosophy of Science [*A publication*]
Stud Hist & Soc ... Studies in History and Society [*A publication*]
Studia Alban ... Studia Albanica [*A publication*]
Studia Automat ... Studia z Automatiki [*A publication*]
Studia Can ... Studia Canonica [*A publication*]
Studia Ent ... Studia Entomologica [*A publication*]
Studia Forest Suecica ... Studia Forestalia Suecica [*A publication*]
Studia For Suec ... Studia Forestalia Suecica [*A publication*]
Studia Geotech Mech ... Studia Geotechnica et Mechanica [*A publication*]
Studia I ...... Studia Iranica [*A publication*]
Studia Leibnitiana Suppl ... Studia Leibnitiana. Supplementa [*A publication*]
Studia M .... Studia Missionalia [*A publication*]
Studia Math ... Studia Mathematica [*A publication*]
Studia Math/Math Lehrbuecher ... Studia Mathematica/Mathematische Lehrbuecher [*A publication*]
Studia Math/Math Lehrbuecher Taschenbuch ... Studia Mathematica/Mathematische Lehrbuecher. Taschenbuch [*A publication*]
Studia Mus ... Studia Musicologica [*A publication*]
Studia Mus Nor ... Studia Musicologica Norvegica [*A publication*]
Studia Neophil ... Studia Neophilologica [*A publication*]
Studia Sci Math Hungar ... Studia Scientiarum Mathematicarum Hungarica [*A publication*]
Studia Ser Math ... Studia. Series Mathematica [*A publication*]
Studia Univ Babes-Bolyai Math ... Universitatis Babes-Bolyai. Studia. Series Mathematica [*A publication*]
Studia Univ Babes-Bolyai Ser Math-Mech ... Studia Universitatis Babes-Bolyai. Series Mathematica-Mechanica [*A publication*]
Studia Univ Babes-Bolyai Ser Phys ... Studia Universitatis Babes-Bolyai. Series Physica [*A publication*]
Studia Zool R Scient Univ Hung Budapest ... Studia Zoologica Regiae Scientiarum Universitatis Hungaricae Budapestensis [*A publication*]
Studi Cl Orient ... Studi Classici e Orientali [*A publication*]
Studiecent TNO Scheepsbouw Navig Commun ... Studiecentrum TNO [*Toegepast Natuurwetenschappelijk Onderzoek*] voor Scheepsbouw en Navigatie. Communication [*A publication*]
Studiecent TNO Scheepsbouw Navig Rep ... Studiecentrum TNO [*Toegepast Natuurwetenschappelijk Onderzoek*] voor Scheepsbouw en Navigatie. Report [*A publication*]
Studi Econ (Cagliari) ... Studi di Economia (Cagliari) [*A publication*]
Studi Econ (Naples) ... Studi Economici (Naples) [*A publication*]
Studi Emigr ... Studi Emigrazione [*A publication*]
Studienb Naturwiss Tech ... Studienbuecher Naturwissenschaft und Technik [*A publication*]
Studien und Mitteilungen ... Studien und Mitteilungen aus dem Benediktiner- und dem Cistercienser-Orden [*A publication*]
Studienskripten zur Soziol ... Studienskripten zur Soziologie [*A publication*]
Studies .... Studies in Political Economy [*A publication*]
Studies Appl Math ... Studies in Applied Mathematics [*A publication*]
Studies App Math ... Studies in Applied Mathematics [*A publication*]
Studies in Art Ed ... Studies in Art Education [*A publication*]
Studies in Aust Bibliog ... Studies in Australian Bibliography [*A publication*]   (APTA)
Studies of Bcasting ... Studies of Broadcasting [*Japan*] [*A publication*]
Studies in Can Lit ... Studies in Canadian Literature [*A publication*]
Studies Conserv ... Studies in Conservation [*A publication*]
Studies Crim L ... Studies in Criminal Law and Procedure [*A publication*]   (DLA)
Studies Econ Analysis ... Studies in Economic Analysis [*A publication*]
Studies Hum ... Studies in the Humanities [*A publication*]
Studies Internat Relations (Warsaw) ... Studies on International Relations (Warsaw) [*A publication*]
Studies L & Econ Develop ... Studies in Law and Economic Development [*A publication*]
Studies Mus ... Studies in Music [*A publication*]
Studies Parasitol and Gen Zool ... Studies in Parasitology and General Zoology [*A publication*]
Studies Philol ... Studies in Philology [*A publication*]
Studies Pol Economy ... Studies in Political Economy [*A publication*]
Studies Zool Lab Univ Nebr ... Studies. Zoological Laboratory. University of Nebraska [*A publication*]
Studi Franc ... Studi Francesi [*A publication*]
Studii Cerc Biol ... Studii si Cercetari de Biologie [*A publication*]
Studii Cerc Biol Biol Anim ... Studii si Cercetari de Biologie. Seria Biologie Animala [*A publication*]

Studii Cerc Biol Zool ... Studii si Cercetari de Biologie. Seria Zoologie [*A publication*]
Studii Cercet Chim ... Studii si Cercetari de Chimie [*A publication*]
Studii Cercet Econ ... Studii si Cercetari Economice [*A publication*]
Studii Cerc Geol Geofiz Geogr ... Studii si Cercetari de Geologie, Geofizica, si Geografie. Seria Geografie [*A publication*]
Studii Cerc Stiint Iasi Biol Stiint Agric ... Studii si Cercetari Stiintifice. Filiala Iasi. Academia RPR. [*Republicii Populare Romine*]. Biologice si Stiinte Agricole [*A publication*]
Studi Ital Filol Cl ... Studi Italiani di Filologia Classica [*A publication*]
StudiItalFilol Class ... Studi Italiani di Filologia Classica [*Florence*] [*A publication*]
Studii Teh Econ Inst Geol Rom ... Studii Tehnice si Economice. Institutului Geologic al Romaniei. Stiinta Solului [*A publication*]
Studijni Inform Lesnictyi ... Studijni Informace. Lesnictyi [*A publication*]
Studi M ...... Studi Musicali [*A publication*]
StudIManf ... Student Member of the Institute of Manufacturing [*British*]   (DBQ)
StudIMS .... Student of the Institute of Management Specialists [*British*]   (DBQ)
Stud Indo-As Art Cult ... Studies in Indo-Asian Art and Culture [*New Delhi*] [*A publication*]
Stud Inorg Chem ... Studies in Inorganic Chemistry [*A publication*]
Stud In Relat ... Studies on International Relations [*A publication*]
StudInstBTM ... Student Member of the Institute of Business and Technical Management [*British*]   (DBQ)
Stud Inst Divi Thomae ... Studies. Institutum Divi Thomae [*A publication*]
Stud Inst Med Res (Malaya) ... Studies. Institute for Medical Research (Malaya) [*A publication*]
Stud Int ...... Studio International [*A publication*]
Stud Intellectual Precocity ... Studies of Intellectual Precocity [*A publication*]
Stud Intell Obs ... Student and Intellectual Observer [*A publication*]
Stud & Intel Obs ... Student and Intellectual Observer [*A publication*]
Stud Int'l Fiscal L ... Studies on International Fiscal Law [*A publication*]   (DLA)
Studio .... Studio International [*A publication*]
Studio Int ... Studio International [*A publication*]
Studio Intl ... Studio International [*A publication*]
Studi Sassaresi Sez 2 Arch Bimest Sci Med Nat ... Studi Sassaresi. Sezione 2. Archivio Bimestrale di Scienze Mediche e Naturali [*A publication*]
Studi Sassar Sez 2 ... Studi Sassaresi. Sezione 2. Archivio Bimestrale di Scienze Mediche e Naturali [*A publication*]
Studi Sassar Sez 3 ... Studi Sassaresi. Sezione 3. Annali della Facolta di Agraria dell Universita di Sassari [*A publication*]
Studi Sassar Sez III Ann Fac Agrar Univ Sassari ... Studi Sassaresi. Sezione III. Annali. Facolta di Agraria. Universita di Sassari [*A publication*]
Stud Islam ... Studia Islamica [*A publication*]
Studi Stor ... Studi Storici per l'Antichita Classica [*A publication*]   (OCD)
Studi Stor ... Studi Storici Instituto Gramisci Editor [*A publication*]
Stud It .... Studi Italiani di Filologia Classica [*A publication*]
Stud Ital ..... Studi Italiani di Filologia Classica [*A publication*]   (OCD)
Studi Teh Econ Inst Geol Rom ... Studii Tehnice si Economice. Institutului Geologic al Romaniei [*A publication*]
Studi Trentini Sci Nat ... Studi Trentini di Scienze Naturali [*A publication*]
Studi Trentini Sci Nat Acta Geol ... Studi Trentini di Scienze Naturali. Acta Geologica [*A publication*]
Studi Trentini Sci Nat Sez B Biol ... Studi Trentini di Scienze Naturali. Sezione B. Biologica [*A publication*]
Studi Urbinati Fac Farm ... Studi Urbinati. Facolta di Farmacia [*A publication*]
Stud J Inst Electron Telecommun Eng ... Students' Journal. Institution of Electronics and Telecommunication Engineers [*A publication*]
Stud J Inst Electron and Telecommun Eng ... Students' Journal. Institution of Electronics and Telecommunication Engineers [*A publication*]
Stud Jugendzahn A ... Student und Jugendzahnarzt [*A publication*]
Stud Kulturkunde ... Studien zur Kulturkunde [*A publication*]
Stud Laboris Salutis ... Studia Laboris et Salutis [*A publication*]
Stud Labour Hist ... Studies in Labour History [*A publication*]
Stud Lang ... Studies in Language. International Journal [*A publication*]
Stud Lang C ... Studies in Language. Companion Series [*A publication*]
Stud Law Lex ... Students' Pocket Law Lexicon [*A publication*]   (DLA)
Stud L & Econ Dev ... Studies in Law and Economic Development [*A publication*]   (DLA)
Stud Leibn ... Studia Leibnitiana [*A publication*]
Stud Leibnit ... Studia Leibnitiana [*A publication*]
Stud Leibnitiana ... Studia Leibnitiana [*A publication*]
Stud Ling ... Studia Linguistica [*A publication*]
Stud Ling ... Studies in Linguistics [*A publication*]
Stud Ling Friul ... Studi Linguistici Friulani [*A publication*]
Stud Ling Lang Learn ... Studies in Linguistics and Languages Learning
Stud Ling Sci ... Studies in the Linguistic Sciences [*Urbana*] [*A publication*]
Stud Lit ...... Studia Liturgica [*A publication*]
Stud Lit Im ... Studies in the Literary Imagination [*A publication*]
Stud Liturg ... Studia Liturgica [*A publication*]
Stud Log ..... Studia Logica [*A publication*]
Stud Logic Foundations Math ... Studies in Logic and the Foundations of Mathematics [*A publication*]

Stud M .... Studies in Music [*A publication*]
Stud Magr ... Studi Magrebini [*A publication*]
Stud Management Sci ... Studies in the Management Sciences [*A publication*]
Stud Management Sci Systems ... Studies in Management Science and Systems [*A publication*]
Stud Materialien Geschichte Philos ... Studien und Materialien zur Geschichte der Philosophie [*A publication*]
Stud Mater Weiterbild Med Tech Laborassistenten ... Studien-Material zur Weiterbildung Medizinisch-Technischer Laborassistenten [*A publication*]
Stud Math ... Studia Mathematica [*A publication*]
Stud Math Appl ... Studies in Mathematics and Its Applications [*A publication*]
Stud Math Managerial Econom ... Studies in Mathematical and Managerial Economics [*A publication*]
Stud Mat Ist Medie ... Studii si Materiale de Istorie Medie [*A publication*]
Stud Mat Muz Ist Mil ... Studii si Materiale de Muzeografie si Istorie Militara [*A publication*]
Stud Mat Muz (Tirgu Mures) ... Studii si Materiale Muzeul Judetean (Tirgu-Mures, Romania) [*A publication*]
Stud Mat Stor Rel ... Studi e Materiali di Storia della Religioni [*A publication*]
Stud Mat (Suceava) ... Studii si Materiale Muzeul Judetean (Suceava, Romania) [*A publication*]
Stud Med ... Student Medicine [*A publication*]
Stud Med Chir Sport ... Studi di Medicina e Chirurgia dello Sport [*A publication*]
Stud Med Geogr ... Studies in Medical Geography [*A publication*]
Stud Mediev ... Studies in Medieval Culture [*A publication*]
Stud Med Szeged ... Studia Medica Szegedinensia [*A publication*]
Stud Med Szegedinensia ... Studia Medica Szegedinensia [*A publication*]
Stud Microbiol ... Studia Microbiologica [*A publication*]
Stud Microbiol ... Studies in Microbiology [*A publication*]
Stud Miss ... Studia Missionalia [*A publication*]
Stud Mitt Bened Cisterc ... Studien und Mitteilungen aus dem Benediktiner- und dem Cistercienser-Orden [*A publication*]
Stud Mitt Gesch Benediktinerorden ... Studien und Mitteilungen zur Geschichte des Benediktiner-Ordens und Seiner Zweige [*A publication*]
Stud Modern Thermodynamics ... Studies in Modern Thermodynamics [*A publication*]
StudMon .... Studia Monastica [*A publication*]
Stud Musicol ... Studia Musicologica [*A publication*]
Stud Musicol Norvegica ... Studia Musicologica Norvegica [*A publication*]
Stud Muzicol ... Studii de Muzicologie [*A publication*]
Stud MW ... Studien zur Musikwissenschaft [*A publication*]
Stud Mycol ... Studies in Mycology [*A publication*]
Stud Myst .. Studia Mystica [*A publication*]
Stud Nakamura Gakuin Univ ... Studies. Nakamura Gakuin University [*A publication*]
Stud Nat Sci ... Studies in the Natural Sciences [*A publication*]
Stud Nat Sci (Portales NM) ... Studies in Natural Sciences (Portales, New Mexico) [*A publication*]
Stud Nauchno Issled Rab Sib Tekhnol Inst ... Studencheskie Nauchno-Issledovatel'skie Raboty. Sibirskii Tekhnologicheskii Institut [*A publication*]
Stud Nauchn Rab Univ Druzhby Nar ... Studencheskie Nauchnye Raboty. Universitet Druzhby Narodov [*A publication*]
Stud Nauk Polit ... Studia Nauk Politycznych [*A publication*]
Stud Nauk Pr Kiiv Derzh Univ ... Students'ki Naukovi Pratsi Kiivs'kii Derzhavnii Universitet [*A publication*]
Stud Neoph ... Studia Neophilologica [*A publication*]
Stud Neophilol ... Studia Neophilologica [*A publication*]
StudNeot .... Studia Neotestamentica [*Paris/Bruges*] [*A publication*]
Stud Neotrop Fauna ... Studies on the Neotropical Fauna [*Later, Studies on the Neotropical Fauna and Environment*] [*A publication*]
Stud Neotrop Fauna Environ ... Studies on the Neotropical Fauna and Environment [*A publication*]
Stud Neuro Anat ... Studies in Neuro-Anatomy [*A publication*]
Stud Niger Lang ... Studies in Nigerian Languages [*A publication*]
Stud No Phil ... Studies and Notes in Philology and Literature [*A publication*]
Stud Novel ... Studies in the Novel [*A publication*]
StudNT ...... Studien zum Neuen Testament [*Guetersloh*] [*A publication*]
StudOr ...... Studia Orientalia [*Helsinki*] [*A publication*]
Stud Orient ... Studia Orientalia [*Helsinki*] [*A publication*]
Stud Ov ...... Studium Ovetense [*A publication*]
Stud Pac Lang Cult ... Studies in Pacific Languages and Cultures in Honour of Bruce Biggs [*A publication*]
Stud Paint (Osaka) ... Studies in Paint (Osaka) [*Japan*] [*A publication*]
StudPal ...... Studien zur Palaeographie und Papyruskunde [*Leipzig*] [*A publication*]
StudPap ...... Studia Papyrologica [*A publication*]
Stud Papyrol ... Studia Papyrologica [*A publication*]
Stud Patr ...... Studia Patristica [*A publication*]
Stud (Pavia) ... Studi nelle Scienze Giuridiche e Sociali (Pavia) [*A publication*]
Stud Person Psychol ... Studies in Personnel Psychology [*A publication*]
Stud Pers P ... Studies in Personnel Psychology [*A publication*]
Stud Pers Psych ... Studies in Personnel Psychology [*A publication*]
Stud Phil ... Studia Philosophica [*A publication*]
Stud Phil .... Studies in Philology [*A publication*]
Stud Phil Christ ... Studia Philosophiae Christiane [*A publication*]
Stud Phil E ... Studies in Philosophy and Education [*A publication*]

Stud Phil & Ed ... Studies in Philosophy and Education [*A publication*]
Stud Phil H ... Studies in Philosophy and the History of Philosophy [*A publication*]
Stud Phil Hist Phil ... Studies in Philosophy and the History of Philosophy [*A publication*]
Stud Phil Ling ... Studies in Philippine Linguistics [*Manila*] [*A publication*]
Stud Philol ... Studies in Philology [*A publication*]
Stud Philos ... Studies in Philosophy [*The Hague*] [*A publication*]
Stud Philos & Educ ... Studies in Philosophy and Education [*A publication*]
Stud Philos Med ... Studies in Philosophy of Medicine [*A publication*]
Stud Phil (Switzerland) ... Studia Philosophica (Switzerland) [*A publication*]
Stud Phonet ... Studia Phonetica [*A publication*]
Stud Phonol ... Studia Phonologica [*A publication*]
Stud Phys Anthropol ... Studies in Physical Anthropology [*A publication*]
Stud Phys Theor Chem ... Studies in Physical and Theoretical Chemistry [*A publication*]
Stud Picena ... Studia Picena [*A publication*]
Stud Plant Ecol ... Studies in Plant Ecology [*A publication*]
Stud Pneumol Phtiseol Cech ... Studia Pneumologica et Phtiseologica Cechoslovaca [*A publication*]
Stud Prawno-Ekon ... Studia Prawno-Ekonomiczne [*A publication*]
Stud Pr Cr ... Studi e Problemi di Critica Testuale [*A publication*]
Stud Prot Epurarea Apelor ... Studii de Protectia si Epurarea Apelor [*A publication*]
Stud Psych ... Studia Psychologica [*A publication*]
Stud Psycho ... Studia Psychologica [*Bratislava*] [*A publication*]
Stud Psychol ... Studia Psychologiczne [*A publication*]
Stud Psychol (Bratisl) ... Studia Psychologica (Bratislava) [*A publication*]
Stud Psychol Psychiat Cath Univ Amer ... Studies in Psychology and Psychiatry. Catholic University of America [*A publication*]
Stud Q J Inst Electr Eng ... Students Quarterly Journal. Institution of Electrical Engineers [*England*] [*A publication*]
Stud QJ Inst El Eng ... Students Quarterly Journal. Institution of Electrical Engineers [*A publication*]
Stud Radiat Eff Solids ... Studies in Radiation Effects in Solids [*A publication*]
Stud Regional Sci Urban Econom ... Studies in Regional Science and Urban Economics [*A publication*]
Stud Rel ..... Studies in Religion [*Ontario*] [*A publication*]
Stud Relig .. Studies in Religion [*A publication*]
Stud Ren .... Studies in the Renaissance [*A publication*]
Stud Rep Hydrol IAHS - UNESCO ... Studies and Reports in Hydrology. International Association of Hydrological Sciences - United Nations Educational, Scientific, and Cultural Organization [*A publication*]
Stud Res Inst Meteorol Hydrol Part 2 ... Studies and Research. Institute of Meteorology and Hydrology. Part 2. Hydrology [*A publication*]
Stud Ric Div Geomineraria Com Naz Ric Nucl ... Studi e Ricerche. Divisione Geomineraria. Comitato Nazionale per le Ricerche Nucleari [*A publication*]
Stud Ric Ist Mineral Petrogr Univ Pavia ... Studi e Ricerche. Istituto di Mineralogia e Petrografia. Universita di Pavia [*A publication*]
StudRom .... Studi Romani [*Rome*] [*A publication*]
StudRom .... Studi Romanzi [*Padua*] [*A publication*]
Stud Romagn ... Studi Romagnoli [*A publication*]
Stud Roman ... Studies in Romanticism [*A publication*]
Stud Romant ... Studies in Romanticism [*A publication*]
Stud Romanticism ... Studies in Romanticism [*A publication*]
Stud Rsch... Studentische Rundschau [*A publication*]
StudSal ...... Studi Salentini [*A publication*]
StudSard .... Studi Sardi [*A publication*]
Stud Sassar Sez 1 ... Studi Sassaresi. Sezione 1 [*A publication*]
Stud Sci Educ ... Studies in Science Education [*A publication*]
Stud Sci Giur Soc ... Studi delle Scienze Giuridiche e Sociali [*A publication*]
Stud Sci Math Hung ... Studia Scientiarum Mathematicarum Hungarica [*Hungary*] [*A publication*]
Stud Sc Lit ... Studies in Scottish Literature [*A publication*]
Stud Scott Lit ... Studies in Scottish Literature [*A publication*]
StudSCP .... Student of the Society of Certified Professionals [*British*] (DBQ)
StudSE .... Student of the Society of Engineers [*British*] (DBQ)
StudSemNeerl ... Studia Semitica Neerlandica [*Assen*] [*A publication*]
Stud Sh Fic ... Studies in Short Fiction [*A publication*]
Stud Short Fict ... Studies in Short Fiction [*A publication*]
Stud Short Fiction ... Studies in Short Fiction [*A publication*]
StudSLAET ... Student of the Society of Licensed Aircraft Engineers and Technologists [*British*] (DBQ)
Stud Sociol ... Studi di Sociologia [*A publication*]
Stud Socjol ... Studia Socjologiczne [*A publication*]
Stud Soc Li ... Studies in Social Life [*A publication*]
Stud Soc Pol ... Studia Socjologiczno-Polityczne [*A publication*]
Stud Soc Sci Torun Sect A ... Studia Societatis Scientiarum Torunensis. Sectio A. Mathematica-Physica [*A publication*]
Stud Soc Sci Torun Sect B ... Studia Societatis Scientiarum Torunensis. Sectio B (Chemie) [*A publication*]
Stud Soc Sci Torun Sect C (Geogr Geol) ... Studia Societatis Scientiarum Torunensis. Sectio C (Geographia et Geologia) [*A publication*]
Stud Soc Sci Torun Sect D (Bot) ... Studia Societatis Scientiarum Torunensis. Sectio D (Botanica) [*A publication*]

Stud Soc Sci Torun Sect E (Zool) ... Studia Societatis Scientiarum Torunensis. Sectio E (Zoologia) [*A publication*]
Stud Soc Sci Torun Sect F ... Studia Societatis Scientiarum Torunensis. Sectio F (Astronomia) [*Poland*] [*A publication*]
Stud Soc Sci Torun Sect G (Physiol) ... Studia Societatis Scientiarum Torunensis. Sectio G (Physiologia) [*A publication*]
Stud Soc Wk ... Studies on Social Work [*A publication*]
Stud Solid Phys Chem ... Studies on Solid State Physics and Chemistry [*Japan*] [*A publication*]
Stud Sov Th ... Studies in Soviet Thought [*A publication*]
Stud Sov Thought ... Studies in Soviet Thought [*A publication*]
Stud Spelaeol ... Studies in Spelaeology [*A publication*]
Stud Speleol ... Studies in Speleology [*A publication*]
Stud Statist Mech ... Studies in Statistical Mechanics [*A publication*]
Stud Stat Mech ... Studies in Statistical Mechanics [*A publication*]
Stud Stn Fish Res Board Can ... Studies. Stations of the Fisheries Research Board of Canada [*A publication*]
Stud Storic ... Studi Storici [*A publication*]
Stud Surf Sci Catal ... Studies in Surface Science and Catalysis [*Netherlands*] [*Elsevier Book Series*] [*A publication*]
Stud TC ...... Studies in the Twentieth Century [*A publication*]
Stud Teh Econ Inst Geol (Rom) Ser A ... Studii Tehnice si Economice. Institutul Geologic (Romania). Seria A. Prospectiuni si Explorari Geologice [*A publication*]
Stud Teh Econ Inst Geol (Rom) Ser B ... Studii Tehnice si Economice. Institutul Geologic (Romania). Seria B. Chimie [*A publication*]
Stud Teh Econ Inst Geol (Rom) Ser C ... Studii Tehnice si Economice. Institutul Geologic (Romania). Seria C. Pedologie [*A publication*]
Stud Teh Econ Inst Geol (Rom) Ser D ... Studii Tehnice si Economice. Institutul Geologic (Romania). Seria D. Prospectiuni Geofizice [*A publication*]
Stud Teh Econ Inst Geol (Rom) Ser E ... Studii Tehnice si Economice. Institutul Geologic (Romania). Seria E. Hidrogeologie [*A publication*]
Stud Teh Econ Inst Geol (Rom) Ser F ... Studii Tehnice si Economice. Institutul Geologic (Romania). Seria F. Geologie Tehnice [*A publication*]
Stud Teh Econ Inst Geol Ser E ... Studii Tehnice si Economice. Institutul Geologic (Romania). Seria E. Hidrogeologie [*A publication*]
Stud Teh Econ Inst Geol Ser I ... Studii Tehnice si Economice. Institutul Geologic (Romania). Seria I. Mineralogie-Petrografie [*A publication*]
Stud Teh Econ Ser D Inst Geol Geofiz (Bucharest) ... Studii Tehnice si Economice. Seria D. Prospectiuni Geofizice. Institutul de Geologie si Geofizica (Bucharest) [*Romania*] [*A publication*]
Stud Teh Econ Ser E Inst Geol Geofiz ... Studii Tehnice si Economice. Seria E. Hidrogeologie. Institutul de Geologie si Geofizica [*A publication*]
Stud Th ...... Studia Theologica [*A publication*]
Stud Theol ... Studia Theologica [*A publication*]
Stud Third World Soc ... Studies in Third World Societies [*Williamsburg*] [*A publication*]
Stud Tokugawa Inst ... Studies. Tokugawa Institute [*A publication*]
Stud Tour Rep Dep Prim Ind (Queensl) ... Study Tour Report. Department of Primary Industries (Queensland) [*A publication*] (APTA)
Stud Trade Unionists ... Studies for Trade Unionists [*A publication*]
Stud Trop Oceanogr Inst Mar Sci Univ Miami ... Studies in Tropical Oceanography. Institute of Marine Science. University of Miami [*A publication*]
Stud Trop Oceanogr (Miami) ... Studies in Tropical Oceanography (Miami) [*A publication*]
Stud Uch Zap Erevan Gos Univ ... Studencheskie Uchenye Zapiski. Erevanskii Gosudarstvennyi Universitet [*A publication*]
Stud Univ Babes-Bolyai Biol ... Studia Universitatis Babes-Bolyai. Series Biologia [*A publication*]
Stud Univ Babes-Bolyai Chem ... Studia Universitatis Babes-Bolyai. Series Chemia [*A publication*]
Stud Univ Babes-Bolyai Geol-Geogr ... Studia Universitatis Babes-Bolyai. Series Geologia-Geographia [*A publication*]
Stud Univ Babes-Bolyai Math ... Studia Universitatis Babes-Bolyai. Series Mathematica [*A publication*]
Stud Univ Babes-Bolyai Phys ... Studia Universitatis Babes-Bolyai. Series Physica [*A publication*]
Stud Univ Babes-Bolyai Ser Biol ... Studia Universitatis Babes-Bolyai. Series Biologia [*A publication*]
Stud Univ Babes-Bolyai Ser Chem ... Studia Universitatis Babes-Bolyai. Series Chemia [*A publication*]
Stud Univ Babes-Bolyai Ser Geol-Minerol ... Studia Universitatis Babes-Bolyai. Series Geologia-Mineralogia [*A publication*]
Stud Univ Babes-Bolyai Ser Math-Phys ... Studia Universitatis Babes-Bolyai. Series Mathematica-Physica [*A publication*]
Stud Univ Babes-Bolyai Ser Phys ... Studia Universitatis Babes-Bolyai. Series Physica [*A publication*]
Stud Urb .... Studi di Urbanistica Antica [*A publication*] (OCD)
Stud Urb .... Studi Urbinati di Storia, Filosofia, e Letteratura [*A publication*]
Stud Urb (Ser A) ... Studi Urbinati di Scienze Giuridiche ed Economiche (Ser. A) [*A publication*]

Stud Urb St ... Studi Urbinati di Storia, Filosofia, e Letteratura [*A publication*]

Stud Venez ... Studi Veneziani [*A publication*]

Stud Voltaire ... Studies on Voltaire and the Eighteenth Century [*A publication*]

Stud Voltaire Eighteenth Century ... Studies on Voltaire and the Eighteenth Century [*A publication*]

Stud VT Geol ... Studies in Vermont Geology [*A publication*]

Stud W .... Student World [*A publication*]

Stud W Aust Hist ... Studies in Western Australian History [*A publication*]

StudWeldI ... Student of the Welding Institute [*British*]   (DBQ)

Study Elem Particles ... Study of Elementary Particles [*Japan*] [*A publication*]

Study of Soc ... Study of Society [*A publication*]   (APTA)

Study Tea ... Study of Tea [*A publication*]

Stud Zrodloznawcze ... Studia Zrodloznawcze. Commentationes [*A publication*]

StudzumAuNT ... Studien zum Alten und Neuen Testament [*Munich*] [*A publication*]

STUF .... Stuff Yer Face, Inc. [*NASDAQ symbol*]   (NQ)

STUFF .... System to Uncover Facts Fast

STUFT ...... Ships Taken Up from Trade

STUG .... Sturmgeschuetz [*Self-propelled assault gun*] [*German military - World War II*]

STUH .... Stuart Hall Co., Inc. [*NASDAQ symbol*]   (NQ)

STUK .... Sturmkanone [*Self-propelled assault gun*] [*German military - World War II*]

STUKA ...... Sturzkampfflugzeug [*Dive bomber*] [*German military - World War II*]

Stu KB .... Stuart's Lower Canada King's Bench Reports [*1810-35*] [*A publication*]   (DLA)

Stu LC .... Stuart's Lower Canada King's Bench Reports [*1810-35*] [*A publication*]   (DLA)

Stu Mil & Ped ... Stuart, Milne, and Peddie's Scotch Court of Sessions Reports [*A publication*]   (DLA)

Stu Mon ..... Studia Monastica [*A publication*]

Stu M & P ... Stuart, Milne, and Peddie's Scotch Court of Sessions Reports [*A publication*]   (DLA)

StUmwNT ... Studien zur Umwelt des Neuen Testament [*Goettingen*] [*A publication*]

St UNT ...... Studien zur Umwelt des Neuen Testament [*A publication*]

STUOA ...... Sbornik Nauchnykh Trudov Ukrainskii Nauchno-Issledovatel'skii Institut Ogneuporov [*A publication*]

STUP .... Spinning Tubular Projectile   (MCD)

Stu Pat ...... Studia Patavina [*A publication*]

STUPID .... Simulation of the Underlying Processes in Decisions   (MCD)

Stu Prob & St ... Studies in Probability and Statistics [*A publication*]

STURAA ... Surface Transportation and Uniform Relocation Assistance Act [*1987*]

S Turb .... Steam Turbine   (DS)

St Urbin ..... Studi Urbinati [*A publication*]

Sturg BL ..... Sturgeon. Bankrupt Acts [*A publication*]   (ILCA)

Sturg Ins D ... Sturgeon's Insolvent Debtors Act [*1842*] [*A publication*]   (DLA)

STURM ..... Sturminster [*England*]

Stu Ros .... Studia Rosenthaliana [*A publication*]

STURP ...... Shroud of Turin Research Project   (EA)

Stur & Porter ... Stuart [*or Stewart*] and Porter's Alabama Reports [*A publication*]   (DLA)

STUS .... Stuarts Department Stores, Inc. [*Hopkinton, MA*] [*NASDAQ symbol*]   (NQ)

StuSta .... Studia Staropolskie [*A publication*]

StuTC .... Studies in the Twentieth Century [*A publication*]

Stutt Beitr Naturk ... Stuttgarter Beitraege zur Naturkunde [*A publication*]

Stuttgarter Beitraege ... Stuttgarter Beitraege zur Geschichte und Politik [*A publication*]

Stuttg Beitr Naturkd ... Stuttgarter Beitraege zur Naturkunde [*A publication*]

Stuttg Beitr Naturkd Ser A (Biol) ... Stuttgarter Beitraege zur Naturkunde. Serie A (Biologie) [*A publication*]

Stuttg Beitr Naturkd Ser B (Geol Palaeontol) ... Stuttgarter Beitraege zur Naturkunde. Serie B (Geologie und Palaeontologie) [*A publication*]

Stuttg Beitr Naturk Ser C Allg Aufsaetze ... Stuttgarter Beitraege zur Naturkunde. Serie C. Allgemeinverstaendliche Aufsaetze [*A publication*]

Stuttg Geogr Stud ... Stuttgarter Geographische Studien [*A publication*]

Stu VA .... Stuart's Lower Canada Vice-Admiralty Reports [*A publication*]   (ILCA)

STUVAC ... Study Vacation [*Australian*] [*Slang*]   (DSUE)

STUWA ..... Sterne und Weltraum [*A publication*]

STV .... Santa Anna Di Valdieri [*Italy*] [*Seismograph station code, US Geological Survey*]   (SEIS)

STV .... Separation Test Vehicle

STV .... Short-Tube Vertical [*Evaporator*]

STV .... Single Transferable Vote

STV .... Small Test Vessel [*Nuclear energy*]   (NRCH)

STV .... Solar Thermal Vacuum

STV .... Solidaridad de Trabajadores Vascos [*Solidarity of Basque Workers*] [*In exile*] [*Spain*]

STV .... Space Test Vehicle [*NASA*]   (KSC)

STV .... Special Test Vehicle

STV .... Standard Test Vehicle

STV .... Stikine Silver [*Vancouver Stock Exchange symbol*]

STV .... Stonewall, TX [*Location identifier*] [*FAA*]   (FAAL)

STV .... Stove [*Classified advertising*]   (ADA)

STV .... Structural Test Vehicle [*NASA*]   (KSC)

StV .... Studies on Voltaire and the Eighteenth Century [*A publication*]

STV .... Submarine Target Vessel   (NVT)

STV .... Subscription Television

STV .... Supersonic Test Vehicle   (AAG)

STV .... Surveillance Television   (AFM)

STVA .... Self-Tuning Vibration Absorber [*Navy*]   (CAAL)

Stva .... Stvaranje [*A publication*]

STVA .... Subscription Television Association [*Defunct*]   (EA)

STV Bull .... STV [*Schweizerischer Technischer Verband*] Bulletin [*A publication*]

STVC .... Sumerian Texts of Varied Context [*E. Chiera*] [*A publication*]

STVCA ...... Stavebnicky Casopis [*A publication*]

STVD .... Spacecraft Television Video Data

stvdr .... Stevedore   (DS)

St Vd VUB ... Studies en Voordrachten. VUB [*Vrije Universiteit te Brussel*] [*A publication*]

STVE .... Steve's Homemade Ice Cream, Inc. [*Lindenhurst, NY*] [*NASDAQ symbol*]   (NQ)

STVFB ...... Samoletostroenie i Tekhnika Vozdushnogo Flota [*A publication*]

St VG .... Straphenverrkehrsgesetz [*A publication*]

STVI .... STV Engineers, Incorporated [*NASDAQ symbol*]   (NQ)

St Vj .... Statistische Vierteljahrsschrift [*A publication*]

St VK .... Studien und Voelkerkunde [*A publication*]

STVL .... Stereo Village, Inc. [*Decatur, GA*] [*NASDAQ symbol*]   (NQ)

StVladSemQ ... St. Vladimir's Seminary. Quarterly [*New York*] [*A publication*]

St Vl Th Q ... Saint Vladimir's Theological Quarterly [*A publication*]

STVM .... Semitrailer Van Mount

St VO .... Strafvollstreckungsordnung [*A publication*]

St VO .... Strassenverkehrsordnung [*A publication*]

St Vollstr O ... Strafvollstreckungsordnung [*A publication*]

STVP .... Short-Term Vehicle Park   (DS)

STVS .... Short-Term Visual Storage [*or Store*] [*Psychophysiology*]

STVS .... Surinaamse Televisie Sichtung [*Television network*] [*Surinam*]

STVT .... Sterivet Laboratories Ltd. [*NASDAQ symbol*]   (NQ)

St VZO ...... Strassenverkehrszulassungsordnung [*A publication*]

STW .... Save the Whales   (EA)

STW .... Southwest Tech [*Vancouver Stock Exchange symbol*]

STW .... Speed Made Good Through the Water   (NATG)

STW .... Standard Commercial Tobacco Co. [*NYSE symbol*]   (SPSG)

STW .... Star Trek Welcommittee   (EA)

STW .... Stern Wheel [*of a ship*]

St u W .... Steuer und Wirtschaft [*A publication*]

St W .... Steuer und Wirtschaft [*A publication*]

STW .... Stillwater, NJ [*Location identifier*] [*FAA*]   (FAAL)

STW .... Stillwater Public Library, Stillwater, OK [*OCLC symbol*]   (OCLC)

STW .... Storm Water

STW .... Striped Peak [*Washington*] [*Seismograph station code, US Geological Survey*]   (SEIS)

STW .... Subtropical Water

ST. WAPNIACL ... State, Treasury, War, Attorney General, Postmaster General, Navy, Interior, Agriculture, Commerce, Labor [*Pre-1947 mnemonic guide to names of the departments in the President's Cabinet, in order of creation*] [*Obsolete*]

STWB .... Statewide Bancorp [*NASDAQ symbol*]   (NQ)

STWBRD .. Strawboard [*Shipping*]

STWD .... Steward   (FAAC)

STWE .... Society of Technical Writers and Editors [*Later, STWP, STC*]

St Westm ..... Statute of Westminster [*A publication*]   (DLA)

STWG .... Stowage   (MSA)

St u Wi .... Steuer und Wirtschaft [*A publication*]

STWP .... Society of Technical Writers and Publishers [*Formerly, STWE*] [*Later, STC*]   (EA)

STWP .... Steam Working Pressure   (MSA)

STWS .... Stewardess   (FAAC)

STWY .... Stairway   (AAG)

STWY .... Stopway   (FAAC)

STX .... Christiansted, St. Croix, VI [*Location identifier*] [*FAA*]   (FAAL)

STX .... St. Croix [*Virgin Islands*] [*Airport symbol*]

STX .... Saxitoxin [*A neurotoxin*]

STX .... Situational Training Exercise [*Army*]   (INF)

STX .... Spherical Torus Experiment [*Oak Ridge National Laboratory*]

STX .... Starrex Mining Corp. Ltd. [*Toronto Stock Exchange symbol*]

STX .... Start of Text Character [*Keyboard*] [*Data processing*]

STX .... Station 2 [*Nevada*] [*Seismograph station code, US Geological Survey*] [*Closed*]   (SEIS)

STX .... Sterling Chemicals, Inc. [*NYSE symbol*]   (CTT)

STX .... Stewart-Warner Corp. [*NYSE symbol*]   (SPSG)

STXL .... Sports-Tech International, Inc. [*NASDAQ symbol*]   (NQ)

STXRF ...... Source-Tuned X-Ray Fluorescence [*Spectroscopy*]

STY .... Salto [*Uruguay*] [*Airport symbol*]   (OAG)

STY .... Space-Time Yield [*Chemical engineering*]

StY .... Standard Yiddish   (BJA)

STY .... Sterling Drug, Inc. [*NYSE symbol*]   (SPSG)

STY............ Stony River [*Alaska*] [*Seismograph station code, US Geological Survey*]   (SEIS)
Sty.............. Style's English King's Bench Reports [*1646-55*] [*A publication*]   (DLA)
Sty.............. Styrene [*Also, St*] [*Organic chemistry*]
Style........... Style's English King's Bench Reports [*A publication*]   (DLA)
Style Pr Reg ... Style's Practical Register [*A publication*]   (DLA)
STYP .... Styptic [*Stopping Bleeding*] [*Medicine*]   (ROG)
Sty Pr Reg ... Style's Practical Register [*1657-1710*] [*A publication*]   (DLA)
Styr Tek Utveckling Inf Energitek ... Styrelsen foer Teknisk Utveckling Informerar om Energiteknik [*Sweden*] [*A publication*]
STZ............ Santa Terezinha [*Brazil*] [*Airport symbol*]   (OAG)
STZ............ Schweizerische Technische Zeitschrift [*A publication*]
STZ............ Schweizerische Theologische Zeitschrift [*Zurich*] [*A publication*]   (BJA)
STZ............ Serum-Treated Zymosan [*Clinical chemistry*]
STZ............ Southern Transgressive Zone [*Geology*]
STZ............ Sprache im Technischen Zeitalter [*A publication*]
STZ............ Stallion Resources Ltd. [*Vancouver Stock Exchange symbol*]
STZ............ Stratford [*New Zealand*] [*Seismograph station code, US Geological Survey*] [*Closed*]   (SEIS)
STZ............ Streptozocin [*Antineoplastic drug*]
St ZA .... Steuer-Zentralarchiv [*A publication*]
STZED ...... Stimmen der Zeit [*A publication*]
SU .... AEROFLOT [*Aero Flotilla*] [*USSR*] [*ICAO designator*]   (FAAC)
Su .... Ciba-Geigy Corp. [*Research code symbol*]
SU .... Optical Device [*JETDS nomenclature*] [*Military*]   (CET)
SU .... Salicyluric Acid [*Also, SUA*] [*Biochemistry*]
SU .... Salmon Unlimited   (EA)
SU .... Samostijna Ukraina [*Independent Ukraine*] [*A publication*]
su .... Saudi Arabia [*MARC country of publication code*] [*Library of Congress*]   (LCCP)
SU .... Savings Unit
SU .... Schriften des Urchristentums [*A publication*]
SUAS.......... Scorable Unit
SU .... Scripture Union [*British*]
SU .... Seamen's Union [*British*]
SU .... Selectable Unit   (BUR)
SU .... Sensation Units
SU .... Separation Ullage
SU .... Service Unit [*Military*]
SU .... Set Up [*Freight*]
SU .... Shipment Unit [*Army*]
SU .... Siemens Unit
SU .... Sigma Units
SU .... Signaling Unit
SU .... Sindicato Unitario [*United Syndicate*] [*Trade union*] [*Spain*]   (EY)
SU .... Single Uptake [*Boilers*]
SU .... Single User [*The military activity that has the sole interest in an item of supply*] [*DoD*]
SU .... Society of the Sisters of St. Ursula of the Blessed Virgin [*Roman Catholic religious order*]
SU .... Somogyi Unit [*of amylase*] [*Clinical chemistry*]
SU .... Sonics and Ultrasonics   (MCD)
SU .... Soviet Union [*The USSR*]
SU .... Space Unit   (EA)
SU .... Special Unitary [*Algebra*]
SU .... Standard Upkeep
SU .... Stanford University [*California*]
SU .... Start Up [*of a relay, power switchgear*]   (IEEE)
S/U .... Startup [*Nuclear energy*]   (NRCH)
SU .... Storage Unit [*Data processing*]
SU .... Stripers Unlimited   (EA)
SU .... Strontium Units [*Nuclear energy*]
SU .... Student Union
SU .... Studi Urbinati [*A publication*]
SU .... Stunts Unlimited   (EA)
SU .... Subject [*Online database field identifier*]
SU .... Subscriber Unit [*RADA*] [*Army*]   (RDA)
Su .... Sufentanil [*or Sulfentanyl*] [*An analgesic*]
su .... Sugary [*A gene in sweet corn*]
Su .... Suite
SU .... Sukhoy [*Aircraft*]
Su .... Sulcus [*Brain anatomy*]
Su .... Sumarstvo [*A publication*]
Su .... Sumet [*Let Him, or Her, Take*] [*Pharmacy*]
SU .... Suncor, Inc. [*Toronto Stock Exchange symbol*]
SU .... Sunday
SU .... Super Unleaded (Gasoline)
Su .... Superb [*Philately*]
Su .... Superior Court   (DLA)
SU .... Supply [*Business term*]
SU .... Support Unit [*NASA*]   (NASA)
SU .... Suppressor [*Electronics*]   (MDG)
SU .... Switching Unit
SU .... Syracuse University [*New York*]
SU .... Thiouridine [*Two-letter symbol; see Srd*]
SU .... Union of Soviet Socialist Republics [*ANSI two-letter standard code*]   (CNC)

SU .... United Arab Republic [*Aircraft nationality and registration mark*]   (FAAC)
SUA .... Salicyluric Acid [*Also, SU*] [*Biochemistry*]
SUA .... Satellite Unfurlable Antenna
SUA .... Serum Uric Acid [*Clinical chemistry*]
SUA .... Silver Users Association   (EA)
SUA .... Small Unit Action [*Military*]   (CINC)
SUA .... Society for Urban Anthropology   (EA)
SUA .... Standard Unit of Accounting [*Data processing*]
SUA .... State Universities Association [*Later, NASULGC*]
SUA .... Stuart [*Florida*] [*Airport symbol*]   (OAG)
SUA .... Stuart, FL [*Location identifier*] [*FAA*]   (FAAL)
SUA .... Summit Tax Exempt Bond Fund LP [*AMEX symbol*]   (SPSG)
SUA .... Superior Acceptance Corp. Ltd. [*Toronto Stock Exchange symbol*]
SUA .... Supplemental Unemployment Assistance
SUA .... Susitna [*Alaska*] [*Seismograph station code, US Geological Survey*]   (SEIS)
SUA .... Sweetener Users Association   (EA)
SUAA .... Montevideo/Angel S. Adami [*Uruguay*] [*ICAO location identifier*]   (ICLI)
SUAB........ Svenska Utvecklingsaktiebolaget [*Swedish Corporation for Development*]
SUADPS ... Shipboard Uniform Automatic Data Processing System [*Navy*]
SUAEWICS ... Soviet Union Airborne Early Warning and Interceptor Control System   (MCD)
SUAG .... Artigas/Aeropuerto Deptal [*Uruguay*] [*ICAO location identifier*]   (ICLI)
SUAGDL.... Sulphur in Agriculture [*A publication*]
SUALM..... Submerged Anchor Leg Mooring [*Engineering*]
SUAR .... Start Unload Address Register
Suar............ [*Rodericus*] Suarez [*Flourished, 15th century*] [*Authority cited in pre-1607 legal work*]   (DSA)
Suara Ekon ... Suara Ekonomi [*Singapore*] [*A publication*]
Suas............ Suasoriae [*of Seneca the Elder*] [*Classical studies*]   (OCD)
SUAS.......... System for Upper Atmosphere Sounding   (MCD)
SUAWACS ... Soviet Union Airborne Warning and Control System   (MCD)
SUB .... Scandinavian University Books [*A publication*]
SUB .... Student Union Building [*Canada*]
SUB .... Subaltern
SUB .... Subaud [*Understand*] [*Latin*]
Sub .... Subcommittee   (DLA)
SUB .... Subeditor
SUB .... Subject
SUB .... Subjunctive [*Grammar*]
SUB .... Submarine   (AFM)
SUB .... Submerged
SUB .... Subordinate   (DSUE)
SUB .... Subroutine
Sub .... Subscriber [*Finance*]
SUB .... Subscription [*Finance*]
SUB .... Subsidiary [*Business term*]
SUB .... Substitute
SUB .... Substitute Character [*Keyboard*]   (AFM)
SUB .... Substratum
SUB .... Subtract
SUB .... Subtract Binary Number [*Data processing*]
SUB .... Suburban
SUB .... Subway   (AAG)
SUB .... Supplemental Unemployment Benefits
SUB .... Surabaya [*Indonesia*] [*Airport symbol*]   (OAG)
SUBACLANT ... Submarine Allied Command, Atlantic [*NATO*]   (NATG)
SUBACS ... Submarine Advanced Combat System
SUBAD...... Submarine Air Defense
SUBAD...... Submarine Force, Pacific Fleet Administration
SUBADMI ... Submarine Force, Pacific Fleet Administration, Mare Island
SUBASE.... Submarine Base [*Navy*]
SUBASELANT ... Submarine Bases, Atlantic [*Navy*]
SUBASEPAC ... Submarine Bases, Pacific [*Navy*]
SUBASSY ... Subassembly
SUBASWEX ... Submarine-Antisubmarine Warfare Exercise   (NVT)
SUBB........ Studia Universitatis Babes-Bolyai. Series Philologia [*A publication*]
SUBB........ Suburban Bancorp, Inc. [*Palatine, IL*] [*NASDAQ symbol*]   (NQ)
SUBBA..... Studia Universitatis Babes-Bolyai. Series Biologia [*A publication*]
SUB-BELL ... Submarine Fog Bell [*Mechanical*]
SUBBP ...... Studia Universitatis Babes-Bolyai. Series Philologia [*A publication*]
SUBC........ Subler, Carl, Agent, Versailles OH [*STAC*]
SUBCA...... Studia Universitatis Babes-Bolyai. Series Chemia [*A publication*]
SUBCAL ... Subcaliber
Sub-Cell Bi ... Sub-Cellular Biochemistry [*A publication*]
Sub-Cell Biochem ... Sub-Cellular Biochemistry [*A publication*]
SUBCOM ... Subcommittee
SUBCOM ... Subordinate Command, Service Force, Pacific Fleet
SUBCOMNELM ... Subordinate Command, [*US*] Naval Forces, Eastern Atlantic and Mediterranean
subcrep....... Subcrepitant [*Medicine*]

SUBCU...... Subcutaneous [*Beneath the Skin*] [*Medicine*]
subcut......... Subcutaneous [*Beneath the Skin*] [*Medicine*]
Subd.......... Subdivision (DLA)
SUBDEVGRUONE ... Submarine Development Group One [*San Diego*]
SUBDEVGRUTWO ... Submarine Development Group Two [*New York*]
SUBDIV.... Submarine Division [*Navy*]
SUBDIZ.... Submarine Defense Identification Zone
SUBEASTLANT ... Submarine Force, Eastern Atlantic [*NATO*]
SUBED...... Submarine Electromagnetic Deception System
SUBEX...... Submarine Exercise (NATG)
SUBFIN COCT ... Sub Finem Coctionis [*When the Boiling Is Nearly Finished*] (ROG)
SUBFIX..... We Forward Subject to Correction [*Code*] (FAAC)
SUBFLOT ... Submarine Flotilla [*Navy*]
subg......... Subgenus
SUBGEN... Subgenus
SUBGRU... Submarine Group
SUBH........ Scripta Universitatis atque Bibliotecae Hierosolymitanarum Jerusalem [*A publication*] (BJA)
SUBIC...... Submarine Integrated Control Systems
SUBINSURV ... Inspection and Survey Board Sub Board [*Navy*]
SUBJ......... Subject (AFM)
SUBJ......... Subjective (ROG)
SUBJ......... Subjunctive [*Grammar*]
Subj of Day ... Subject of the Day [*A publication*]
SUBK........ Suffolk Bancorp [*Riverhead, NY*] [*NASDAQ symbol*] (NQ)
SUBL........ Sublime [*or Subliming*]
SUBLANT ... Submarine Force, Atlantic Fleet
Sub Life...... Suburban Life [*A publication*]
subling....... Sublingual [*Medicine*]
Sub-Lt........ Sub-Lieutenant [*British military*] (DMA)
SUBM ...... Submerged
SUBM ...... Submission [*or Submit*] (AFM)
SUBMACOM ... Major Army Subcommand (AABC)
submand..... Submandibular [*Medicine*]
SUBMD .... Studia Universitatis Babes-Bolyai. Series Mathematica [*A publication*]
SUBMED ... Submarines Mediterranean [*NATO*] (NATG)
SUBMEDCEN ... Submarine Medical Center [*Navy*]
SUBMEDNOREAST ... Submarines Northeast Mediterranean [*NATO*] (NATG)
SUBMG .... Submerged (MSA)
SUBMIN.... Subminiature
SUBMISS ... Submarine Missing [*Navy*] (NVT)
SUBMIS/SUBSUNK ... Submarine Missing/Presumed Sunk [*Navy*]
SUBMON ... Submission (ROG)
Subm W ..... Submerged Well [*Nautical charts*]
SUBN .... [*The*] Summit Bancorporation [*NASDAQ symbol*] (NQ)
SUBNO...... Substitutes Not Desired [*Military*]
sub nom...... Sub Nomine [*Under the Name*] [*Latin*] (DLA)
SUBNOT.... Submarine Notice (MCD)
SUBNOTE ... Submarine Notice [*Navy*] (NVT)
Subnucl Ser ... Subnuclear Series [*A publication*]
SUBOK ..... Substitution Acceptable [*Military*]
SUBOPAUTH ... Submarine Operating Authority [*Navy*] (NVT)
SUBOR...... Subordinate (AFM)
SUBORCOM ... Subordinate Command
SUBORCOMSERVLANT ... Subordinate Command, Service Force, Atlantic Fleet
SUBORCOMSERVPAC ... Subordinate Command, Service Force, Pacific Fleet
SUBORD... Subordinate [*Linguistics*]
SUB-OSC ... Submarine Oscillator
SUBPA...... Antisubmarine Warfare Barrier Submarine Patrol Area [*Navy*] (NVT)
SUBPA...... Studia Universitatis Babes-Bolyai. Series Mathematica-Physica [*A publication*]
SUBPAC ... Submarine Force, Pacific Fleet
SUBPACAD ... Submarine Force, Pacific Fleet, Administrative Command
SUBPACSUBORDCOM ... Submarine Force, Pacific Fleet, Subordinate Command
Subpar........ Subparagraph (DLA)
SUBPARA ... Subparagraph
SUBPDJ.... Annual Research Reviews. Substance P [*A publication*]
SUBPZ...... Antisubmarine Warfare Barrier Submarine Patrol Zone [*Navy*] (NVT)
SUB Q .... Subcutaneous [*Beneath the Skin*] [*Medicine*]
SUBQ....... Subsequent (AABC)
SUBRAP ... Submarine Range Prediction System [*Navy*] (NVT)
SUBRO...... Subrogation
SUBROC... Submarine Rocket
SUBRON .. Submarine Squadron [*Navy*]
SUBRPIO ... Sub-Registered Publications Issuing Office
SUBRQMT ... Subrequirement
SUBRU..... Submarine Repair Unit
SUBS........ Salford University Business Services [*British*]
SUBS........ Subsidiary [*Business term*]
SUBS........ Subsistence (AABC)
SUBS........ Substantive [*Grammar*]
SUBS........ Substitute
SUBSAFE ... Submarine Safety [*Program*]

SUBSAFECEN ... Submarine Safety Center [*Navy*]
Subsc.......... Subscription (DLA)
SUBSCD ... Subscribed (ROG)
SUBSCOFOR ... Submarines Scouting Force [*Pacific Fleet*]
SUBSCR.... Subscription [*Finance*] (ROG)
SUBSCRON ... Subscription [*Finance*] (ROG)
SUBSEC.... Subsection
SUBSELS ... Subsisting Elsewhere
SUBSEQ ... Subsequent (ROG)
Subser Optical Sci Engrg ... Subseries on Optical Science and Engineering [*A publication*]
SUBSET.... Subscriber Set (CET)
SUBSID ... Subsidiary [*Business term*] (ROG)
Subsidia Med ... Subsidia Medica [*A publication*]
SUBSIS.... Subsistence (AFM)
SUBSLANT ... Submarines, Atlantic Fleet
SUBSLY.... Subsequently (ROG)
SUBSP...... Subspecies
SUBSPAC ... Submarines, Pacific Fleet
subspp........ Subspecies [*Plural form*]
SUBSQ...... Subsequently (ADA)
SUBSS...... Submarine Schoolship [*Navy*] (NVT)
SUBSSOWESPAC ... Submarines, Southwest Pacific Force
SUBST ...... Substance (ROG)
SUBST ...... Substantive (ROG)
SUBST ...... Substitute (AAG)
SUBSTA.... Substation
Subst Alcohol Actions Misuse ... Substance and Alcohol Actions/Misuse [*A publication*]
SUBSTD ... Substituted (ROG)
SUBSTG ... Substituting (AAG)
SUBSTN ... Substitution
SUBSTR.... Substructure (AAG)
SUBSTTD ... Substituted
SUBSUNK ... Submarine Sunk [*Navy*] (NVT)
SUBSYS.... Subsystem (AAG)
SUBTACGRU ... Submarine Tactical Group [*NATO*] (NATG)
SUBTAG.... Submarine Tactics Analysis Group
Sub Torg .... Sovetskaya Torgovlya [*A publication*]
SUBTR...... Subtraction (MSA)
SUBTRAFAC ... Submarine Training Facility
SUBTRAP ... Submersible Training Platform [*Marine science*] (MSC)
subtrop...... Subtropical
Subtrop Kul't ... Subtropicheskie Kul'tury [*A publication*]
Subtrop Kul't Min Sel'Khoz SSSR ... Subtropicheskie Kul'tury. Ministerstvo Sel'skogo Khozyaistva SSSR [*A publication*]
SUBV......... Subversion (AAC)
Sub Vol ...... Submarine Volcano [*Nautical charts*]
SUBWESTLANT ... Submarine Force, Western Atlantic Area [*NATO*] (NATG)
Suby .... Subsidiary [*Business term*]
SUC .... Saggi di Umanismo Cristiano [*A publication*]
SUC .... Society of University Cartographers [*British*]
SUC .... Southern Union College [*Wadley, AL*]
SUC .... Succeeding (MSA)
SUC .... Successor (ADA)
Suc .... Succinoyl [*Biochemistry*]
SUC .... Succus [*Juice*] [*Pharmacy*]
SUC .... Sucre [*Bolivia*] [*Seismograph station code, US Geological Survey*] [*Closed*] (SEIS)
SUC .... Sucrose [*Organic chemistry*]
SUC .... Suction (ADA)
Suc .... Sucursal [*Branch*] [*Spanish*] [*Business term*]
SUC .... Suncoast Petroleum [*Vancouver Stock Exchange symbol*]
SUC .... Sundance, WY [*Location identifier*] [*FAA*] (FAAL)
SUC .... University of South Carolina, Columbia, SC [*OCLC symbol*] (OCLC)
SUCA .... Colonia/Aeropuerto Deptal. [*Uruguay*] [*ICAO location identifier*] (ICLI)
SUCC........ State University Computation Center [*Iowa State University*] [*Research center*] (RCD)
SUCC........ Succentor [*Ecclesiastical*] (ROG)
SUCC........ Successor (ROG)
SUCC........ Succinate
SUCC........ Succinum [*Amber*] [*Latin*] (ROG)
Success Farming ... Successful Farming [*A publication*]
Success Farm South ... Successful Farming in the South [*A publication*]
Successful F ... Successful Farming [*A publication*]
Success Mtg ... Successful Meetings [*A publication*]
SUCCN...... Succession (ROG)
SUCCON .. Succession
SUCCR...... Successor
SUCEE...... Socialist Union of Central and Eastern Europe (PD)
Suc Farm .... Successful Farming [*A publication*]
SUCHTRANS ... Such Transportation as Command Indicated Designates
SUCHTRANSAVAIL ... Such Transportation as Available
SUCI......... Socialist Unity Center of India [*Political party*] (PPW)
SUCKER ... Society for Understanding Cats, Kangaroos, Elks, and Reptiles [*Slang*]
SUCL......... Set Up in Carloads [*Freight*]
SUCL......... Stetson University College of Law (DLA)

SUCO .... Service Universitaire Canadien Outre-Mer [*Canadian University Service Overseas - CUSO*]
SUCR........ Sunset Crater National Monument
Sucr Belg Sugar Ind Abstr ... Sucrerie Belge and Sugar Industry Abstracts [*A publication*]
SUCT........ Suction　(AAG)
Su Ct Rev ... Supreme Court Review [*A publication*]　(ILCA)
SuD .... Sprache und Dichtung [*A publication*]
SUD .... Stretched Upper Deck　(AIA)
SUD .... Stroud, OK [*Location identifier*] [*FAA*]　(FAAL)
SUD .... Sudbury [*Ontario*] [*Seismograph station code, US Geological Survey*]　(SEIS)
SUD .... Sudbury Board of Education [*UTLAS symbol*]
SUD .... Sudbury Contact Mines Ltd. [*Toronto Stock Exchange symbol*]
SUD .... Sudden Unexpected [*or Unexplained*] Death [*Medicine*]
SUD .... Sudestasie. Magazine d'Information [*A publication*]
SUD .... Sudorific [*Causing Sweat*] [*Pharmacy*]　(ROG)
SUDAER..... Stanford University, Department of Aeronautics and Astronautics　(MCD)
SUDAM .... Editorial Sudamericana, BA [*A publication*]
SUDAM .... Sunk or Damaged [*Navy*]
Sudan Eng Soc J ... Sudan Engineering Society. Journal [*A publication*]
Sudan Geol Surv Dep Bull ... Sudan. Geological Survey Department. Bulletin [*A publication*]
Sudan J Econ and Social Studies ... Sudan Journal of Economic and Social Studies [*A publication*]
Sudan J Food Sci Technol ... Sudan Journal of Food Science and Technology [*A publication*]
Sudan J Vet Sci Anim Husb ... Sudan Journal of Veterinary Science and Animal Husbandry [*A publication*]
Sudan LJ & Rep ... Sudan Law Journal and Reports [*Khartoum*] [*A publication*]　(DLA)
Sudan Notes ... Sudan Notes and Records [*A publication*]
Sudan Notes Rec ... Sudan Notes and Records [*A publication*]
Sudan Soc .. Sudan Society [*A publication*]
SUDAP...... Superintendencia da Agricultura e Producao [*Brazil*]
SUDBODEN ... Sueddeutsche Bodenkreditbank, Aktiengesellschaft [*South German Land Credit Bank Joint Stock Company*]
Sud Dew Ad ... Sudder Dewanny Adawlut [*or Sadr Diwani Adalat*] Reports [*India*] [*A publication*]　(DLA)
Sud Dew Rep ... Sudder Dewanny [*or Sadr Diwani*] Reports, Northwest Province [*India*] [*A publication*]　(DLA)
Sudebno-Med Ekspert ... Sudebno-Meditsinskaya Ekspertiza [*A publication*]
SUDEC...... Superintendencia do Desenvolvimento Economico e Cultural [*Brazil*]
SUDEL...... Groupe Regional pour la Coordination de la Production et du Transport de l'Energie Electrique entre l'Autriche, la Grece, l'Italie et la Yougoslavie　(EA)
SUDENE... Superintendencia do Desenvolvimento do Nordeste [*Brazil*]
SUDENE Bol Recur Nat ... SUDENE [*Superintendencia do Desenvolvimento do Nordeste*] Boletim do Recursos Naturais [*A publication*]
Sudhoffs Arch ... Sudhoffs Archiv. Zeitschrift fuer Wissenschaftsgeschichte [*A publication*]
SUDI .... State Unemployment Disability Insurance　(AAG)
SUDIC....... Sulfur Development Institute of Canada
SUDIC....... Sulphur Development Institute of Canada
Sud Inform Econ Provence-Cote D'Azur-Corse ... Sud. Information Economique Provence-Cote D'Azur-Corse [*A publication*]
Sud Med Chir ... Sud Medical et Chirurgical [*A publication*]
Sud-Med Ekspert ... Sudebno-Meditsinskaya Ekspertiza [*A publication*]
Sud Med Ekspert Krim Sluzhbe Sledstviya ... Sudebno-Meditsinskaya Ekspertiza i Kriminalistika na Sluzhbe Sledstviya [*A publication*]
Sud Med J ... Sudan Medical Journal [*A publication*]
Su Doc........ Superintendent of Documents, Government Printing Office　(DLA)
SUDOSAT ... Sudanian Satellite
SUDS......... Satellite Undetected Duds
SUDS......... Silhouetting Underwater Detecting System
SUDS........ Single-Use Diagnostic System [*Trademark of the Murex Corp.*]
SUDS........ Small Unit Delivery System　(MCD)
SUDS......... State's Urban Development Something-or-Other [*Slang for Urban Development Corporation, New York*]
SUDS......... Steps Up Developmental Screening Program [*Child development test*] [*Psychology*]
SUDS......... Subjective Units of Disturbance
SUDS......... Submarine Detecting System
SUDS........ Sudbury, Inc. [*NASDAQ symbol*]　(NQ)
SUDT........ Silicon Unilateral Diffused Transistor
SUDU .... Durazno/Santa Bernardina Internacional de Alternativa [*Uruguay*] [*ICAO location identifier*]　(ICLI)
SUDZUCKER ... Sueddeutsche Zucker-Aktiengesellschaft [*South German Sugar Joint Stock Company*]
SUE .... Sahara Upwelling Experiment [*US, Spain*]　(MSC)
SUE .... Seismic Underwater Explorer
SUE .... Servants' United Effort [*Lemonade*] [*Slang*] [*British*]　(DSUE)
SUE .... Shuttle Unique Equipment　(MCD)
SUE .... Signal Underwater Exploding [*British military*]　(DMA)
SUE .... Significantly Underutilized Employee Program [*DoD*]
SUE .... Skylab Upwelling Experiment [*Marine science*]　(MSC)

SUE .... Strontium Unit Equivalent
SUE .... Sturgeon Bay, WI [*Location identifier*] [*FAA*]　(FAAL)
SUE .... Sub-Unit Evaluation　(MCD)
SUE .... Sudden Expansion
SUE .... Suzie Mining Exploration [*Vancouver Stock Exchange symbol*]
SuedA....... Suedostdeutsches Archiv [*A publication*]
Sueddt Ap Zt ... Sueddeutsche Apothekerzeitung [*A publication*]
Sueddt Mh ... Sueddeutsche Monatshefte [*A publication*]
Sueddtsch Ztg ... Sueddeutsche Zeitung [*A publication*]
SUEDE...... Surface Evaluation and Definition
SuedoA....... Suedostdeutsches Archiv [*A publication*]
Suedost Eur Jb ... Suedosteuropa-Jahrbuch [*A publication*]
Suedosteur Mitt ... Suedosteuropa Mitteilungen [*A publication*]
Suedost F ... Suedost-Forschungen [*A publication*]
Suedost-Forsch ... Suedost-Forschungen. Internationale Zeitschrift fuer Geschichte, Kultur, und Landeskunde Sued-Osteuropas [*A publication*]
Suedwestdt Imker ... Suedwestdeutscher Imker [*A publication*]
SUEL........ Sperry Utah Engineering Laboratory　(MCD)
Suelos Ecuat ... Suelos Ecuatoriales [*A publication*]
SUEM .... Syndicat Unique des Enseignants de Mauritanie [*Unitary Union of Mauritanian Teachers*]
SUEO .... Montevideo [*Uruguay*] [*ICAO location identifier*]　(ICLI)
SUEOTU... Supreme Unsurpassable Engineers of the Universe [*Rank in Junior Woodchucks organization mentioned in Donald Duck comic by Carl Barks*]
SUERF ...... Societe Universitaire Europeenne de Recherches Financieres　(EAIO)
SUET........ Small Unit Evaluation and Training　(MCD)
Suet .... Suetonius [*First century AD*] [*Classical studies*]　(OCD)
SUF........... Lametia-Terme [*Italy*] [*Airport symbol*]　(OAG)
SUF........... Scottish Union of Fishermen
SuF........... Sinn und Form [*A publication*]
SUF........... Socialist Unity Front [*Romania*] [*Political party*]　(PPW)
SUF........... Southernera Resources Ltd. [*Toronto Stock Exchange symbol*]
SUF........... Sufficient　(AFM)
SUF........... Suffolk University, Boston, MA [*OCLC symbol*]　(OCLC)
SUF........... Swaziland United Front
SUFF .... Sufficient
SUFF .... Sufficit [*Suffices*] [*Latin*]
SUFF .... Suffix　(AAG)
SUFF .... Suffolk [*County in England*]
SUFF .... Suffragan [*Ecclesiastical*]　(ROG)
SUFFER.... Save Us from Formaldehyde Environmental Repercussions [*Later, CURE Formaldehyde Poisoning Association*]　(EA)
SUFFER.... System Utility Facility for Easy Recovery [*NASA*]
Suffolk Transnatl LJ ... Suffolk Transnational Law Journal [*A publication*]
Suffolk U L Rev ... Suffolk University. Law Review [*A publication*]
Suffolk Univ L Rev ... Suffolk University. Law Review [*A publication*]
SUFFT....... Sufficient
Suff Trans LJ ... Suffolk Transnational Law Journal [*A publication*]
SUFFTY... Sufficiently　(ROG)
Suff U LR... Suffolk University. Law Review [*A publication*]
SUFPAC.... Surface Force Pacific　(MCD)
SUFSW ..... Small Unit Fire Support Weapon　(MCD)
SUG........... Asheville, NC [*Location identifier*] [*FAA*]　(FAAL)
SUG........... Sell Under the Guise of Market Research [*Marketing*] [*British*]
SUG........... Smartmac User Group　(EA)
SUG .... Southern Union Co. [*Formerly, Southern Union Gas Co.*] [*NYSE symbol*]　(SPSG)
SuG........... Sprache und Gemeinschaft [*A publication*]
SUG .... Sugar
SUG .... Sugar Island [*Michigan*] [*Seismograph station code, US Geological Survey*] [*Closed*]　(SEIS)
SUG .... Suggest　(AFM)
SUG .... Surigao [*Philippines*] [*Airport symbol*]　(OAG)
Sugaku ...... Sugaku. Mathematical Society of Japan [*A publication*]
SUGAR ..... Software Users Guide to Available Resources [*Australia*] [*A publication*]
Sugar.......... Sugar y Azucar [*A publication*]
Sugarbeet Grow ... Sugarbeet Grower [*A publication*]
Sugar Beet J ... Sugar Beet Journal [*A publication*]
Sugar Bul ... Sugar Bulletin [*A publication*]
Sugar Bull ... Sugar Bulletin [*United States*] [*A publication*]
Sugarcane Breed Newsl ... Sugarcane Breeders' Newsletter [*A publication*]
Sugarcane Var Tests Fla ... Sugarcane Variety Tests in Florida [*A publication*]
Sugar Ind Abstr ... Sugar Industry Abstracts [*A publication*]
Sugar J....... Sugar Journal [*A publication*]
Sugar Mol ... Sugar Molecule [*A publication*]
Sugar Technol Rev ... Sugar Technology Reviews [*A publication*]
Sug Azuc .... Sugar y Azucar [*A publication*]
Sugd Powers ... Sugden on Powers [*A publication*]　(DLA)
Sugd Vend ... Sugden on Vendors and Purchasers [*A publication*]　(DLA)
SUGEND .. Sugendus [*To Be Sucked*] [*Pharmacy*]
Sug Est....... Sugden on the Law of Estates [*A publication*]　(DLA)
SUGG .... Suggestion　(ROG)
Sug Hd Bk ... Sugden's Hand-Book of Property Law [*A publication*]　(DLA)
SUGI........ SAS [*Statistical Analysis System*] Users Group International　(EA)
Sug J .... Sugar Journal [*A publication*]

SUGMAW ... Glas. Srpska Akademija Nauka i Umetnosti Odeljenje Medicinskih Nauka [*A publication*]
Sug Pow ..... Sugden on Powers [*8 eds.*] [*1808-61*] [*A publication*] (DLA)
Sug Pr .... Sugden on the Law of Property [*A publication*] (DLA)
Sug Prop .... Sugden on the Law of Property as Administered by the House of Lords [*A publication*] (DLA)
Sug Pr St.... Sugden on Property Statutes [*A publication*] (DLA)
SUGR .... Summagraphics Corp. [*NASDAQ symbol*] (NQ)
SUGS......... University of Sydney Students' Geological Society [*Australia*]
Sug Vend..... Sugden on Vendors and Purchasers [*A publication*] (DLA)
Sug V & P .. Sugden on Vendors and Purchasers [*14 eds.*] [*1805-62*] [*A publication*] (DLA)
SUH.......... Rockland, ME [*Location identifier*] [*FAA*] (FAAL)
SUHC........ Summit Holding Corporation [*Beckley, WV*] [*NASDAQ symbol*] (NQ)
SUHL .... Sylvania Ultrahigh-Level Logic (IEEE)
SUHR .... Society for Underwater Historical Research [*Australia*]
SUHS .... Susitna Hydro Studies [*A publication*]
SUI .... Safe Use Instructions [*General Motors Corp.*]
SUI .... Standard Universal Identifying Number
SUI .... Stanford University Institute for Plasma Research
SUI .... State University of Iowa [*Later, University of Iowa*]
SUI .... Suihwa [*Republic of China*] [*Seismograph station code, US Geological Survey*] (SEIS)
SUI .... Summit Resources Ltd. [*Toronto Stock Exchange symbol*]
SUIAP ...... Simplified Unit Invoice Accounting Plan
SUIC......... Salford University Industrial Centre Ltd. [*British*] (IRUK)
SUICA....... Soul Uitae Chapchi [*A publication*]
Suicide Life Threat Behav ... Suicide and Life-Threatening Behavior [*A publication*]
Suicide Life Threatening Behav ... Suicide and Life Threatening Behavior [*A publication*]
SUID .... Sudden Unexpected Infant Death [*Medicine*]
Suid-Afrikaanse Tydskr Natuurwetenskap Tegnol ... Suid-Afrikaanse Tydskrif vir Natuurwetenskap en Tegnologie [*A publication*]
Suid Afr Tyd Geneesk ... Suid-Afrikaanse Tydskrif vir Geneeskunde [*A publication*]
Suid-Afr Tydskr Geneesk ... Suid-Afrikaanse Tydskrif vir Geneeskunde [*A publication*]
Suid-Afr Tydskr Landbouwetenskap ... Suid-Afrikaanse Tydskrif vir Landbouwetenskap [*A publication*]
SUIP......... Support Unit Improvement Program (MCD)
SUIS......... Smoloskyp, Ukrainian Information Service (EA)
SUIT......... Sight Unit Infantry Trilux [*United Kingdom*]
SUIV......... Suivant [*Following*] [*French*]
SUJ........... Satu Mare [*Romania*] [*Airport symbol*] (OAG)
SUJ........... Side Upset Jaw (MSA)
SUJ........... Suntac Minerals [*Vancouver Stock Exchange symbol*]
SUJB .... Southern Universities Joint Board [*for school examinations*] [*British*] (DCTA)
SUK .... Suckling Hill [*Alaska*] [*Seismograph station code, US Geological Survey*] (SEIS)
Suk............ Sukkah (BJA)
suk............ Sukuma [*MARC language code*] [*Library of Congress*] (LCCP)
SUK .... Sumitomo Bank Review [*A publication*]
SUKGA ..... Sumitomo Kikai Giho [*A publication*]
SUKLO...... Senior United Kingdom Liaison Officer [*Later, BJSM*] [*British*]
SUKUA ..... Subtropicheskie Kul'tury [*A publication*]
SUL........... Per lo Studio e l'Uso del Latino [*A publication*]
SUL........... Simplified User Logistics [*Military*] (AABC)
SUL........... Singapore Union Line (DS)
SUL........... Small University Libraries
SUL........... Sophia University [*UTLAS symbol*]
SuL........... Sprache und Literatur [*A publication*]
SUL........... Standard User Labels [*Data processing*]
SUL........... State University of New York, Union List of Serials, Albany, NY [*OCLC symbol*] (OCLC)
SUL........... Sui [*Pakistan*] [*Airport symbol*] (OAG)
SUL........... Sulpetro Ltd. [*Toronto Stock Exchange symbol*]
SUL........... Sulphur Creek [*New Britain*] [*Seismograph station code, US Geological Survey*] (SEIS)
SULAAL ... Surinam Agriculture [*A publication*]
SULC......... Sulcus Computer Corp. [*Greensburg, PA*] [*NASDAQ symbol*] (NQ)
SULC......... Sydney University Liberal Club [*Australia*]
SULCL ...... Set Up in Less than Carloads [*Freight*]
SuLEXCo... Sulphur Export Corporation [*An association*] (EA)
SULF........ Southern United Life Insurance Co. [*NASDAQ symbol*] (NQ)
SULF .... Speedball Up-Range Launch Facility [*Army*] (AABC)
Sulfuric Acid Ind ... Sulfuric Acid and Industry [*Japan*] [*A publication*]
SULI .... Skrifter Utgivna av Litteraturvetenskapliga Institutionen Vid. Uppsala Universitet [*A publication*]
SULINAC ... Super Linear Accelerator [*Space flight simulator*]
SULIS........ Syracuse University Libraries Information System [*Syracuse University Libraries*][*New York*] [*Information service or system*] (IID)
Sull............ Pro Sulla [*of Cicero*] [*Classical studies*] (OCD)
Sull............ Sulla [*of Plutarch*] [*Classical studies*] (OCD)
Sullivan...... Smith's New Hampshire Reports [*A publication*] (DLA)
Sull Ld Tit ... Sullivan's Land Titles in Massachusetts [*A publication*] (DLA)

Sull Lect..... Sullivan's Lectures on Constitution and Laws of England [*A publication*] (DLA)
Sulphur Agric ... Sulphur in Agriculture [*A publication*]
Sulphur Inst J ... Sulphur Institute. Journal [*A publication*]
Su LR .... Suffolk University. Law Review [*A publication*]
SUL Rev .... Southern University Law Review [*A publication*]
SULS .... Maldonado/Base Aeronaval C/C Carlos A. Curbelo [*Uruguay*] [*ICAO location identifier*] (ICLI)
SULT........ Sultan
Sulzer Tech Rev ... Sulzer Technical Review [*A publication*]
Sulz Tech Rev ... Sulzer Technical Review [*A publication*]
Sum............ Hale's Summary of the Pleas of the Crown [*England*] [*A publication*] (DLA)
SUM .... Saturn Umbilical Maintenance [*NASA*]
SUM .... Save Uganda Movement
SUM .... Servicio Universitario Mundial [*World University Service*]
SUM .... Set-Up [*Control*] Module [*Telecommunications*] (TEL)
SUM .... Shallow Underwater Missile
SUM .... Socialist Unionist Movement [*Al Haraka at Tawhidiyya al Ishtirakiyya*] [*Syria*] [*Political party*] (PPW)
SUM .... Software User's Manual [*Army*]
SUM .... Solar Ultraviolet Monitor (MCD)
SUM .... Sullivan Mines, Inc. [*Toronto Stock Exchange symbol*]
Sum .... Sumatra
SUM .... Sume [*Take*] [*Pharmacy*]
Sum............ Sumer. A Journal of Archaeology and History in Iraq [*A publication*]
Sum........... Sumerian (BJA)
SUM .... Summary (AABC)
SUM .... Summer
SUM .... Summing
Sum............ Summit: Journal of the Liturgical Commission [*of the Archdiocese of Melbourne*] [*A publication*] (APTA)
SUM .... Summoned
Sum............ Sumner's United States Circuit Court Reports [*A publication*] (DLA)
SUM .... Sumoto [*Japan*] [*Seismograph station code, US Geological Survey*] (SEIS)
SUM .... Sumter [*South Carolina*] [*Airport symbol*] (OAG)
SUM .... Surface-to-Underwater Missile
SUM .... System Check and Utility Master (MCD)
SUM .... System Utilization Monitor [*Data processing*]
SUM .... Systems Unit Method [*Medical transcription*]
SUM .... University of South Carolina, School of Medicine, Columbia, SC [*OCLC symbol*] (OCLC)
SUMA .... Summa Medical Corp. [*NASDAQ symbol*] (NQ)
SUMAC.... Sheffield University Metals Advisory Centre [*British*] (IRUK)
Sumatra Res B ... Sumatra Research Bulletin [*A publication*]
SUMC .... Space Ultrareliable Modular Computer
SUMCA..... Summer & Company Cl A [*NASDAQ symbol*] (NQ)
SUMCM .... Summary Court-Martial
SUMCMO ... Summary Court-Martial Order
Sum Dec..... Summary Decisions [*Bengal, India*] [*A publication*] (DLA)
SUME .... Mercedes/Ricardo de Tomasi [*Uruguay*] [*ICAO location identifier*] (ICLI)
SUMED .... Suez-Mediterranean [*Pipeline*]
SUMEX..... Stanford University Medical Experimental Computer Project [*Stanford University*] [*Research center*] (RCD)
SUMH....... Summit Health Ltd. [*NASDAQ symbol*] (NQ)
SUMI........ Sumitomo Bank of California [*NASDAQ symbol*] (NQ)
SUMIT...... Standard Utility Means for Information Transformation [*Data processing*]
Sumitomo... Sumitomo Bank Review [*A publication*]
Sumitomo Bank R ... Sumitomo Bank Review [*A publication*]
Sumitomo Bull Ind Health ... Sumitomo Bulletin of Industrial Health [*A publication*]
Sumitomo Elec Tech Rev ... Sumitomo Electric Technical Review [*A publication*]
Sumitomo Electr Rev ... Sumitomo Electric Review [*Japan*] [*A publication*]
Sumitomo Electr Tech Rev ... Sumitomo Electric Technical Review [*A publication*]
Sumitomo Light Metal Tech Rep ... Sumitomo Light Metal Technical Reports [*A publication*]
Sumitomo Light Met Tech Rep ... Sumitomo Light Metal Technical Reports [*A publication*]
Sumitomo Mach ... Sumitomo Machinery [*Japan*] [*A publication*]
Sumitomo Met ... Sumitomo Metals [*A publication*]
Sumitomo Q ... Sumitomo Quarterly [*A publication*]
Sum Jur ..... Sumarios Juridicos. Compilacao de Doutrina e Jurisprudencia dos Tribunais Comuns e Especiais [*Lousa, Portugal*] [*A publication*] (DLA)
Sum List..... Sumarski List [*A publication*]
SUMM ...... Summary
SUMM ...... Summer
SUMM ...... Summitatis [*Summits or Tops*] [*Pharmacy*] (ROG)
SUMMA ... Superconducting Magnetic Mirror Apparatus
SUMMAC ... Stanford University Modified Markers and Cell Method
Summa Phytopathol ... Summa Phytopathologica [*A publication*]
SUMMCO ... Summary Court-Martial Order
Summ Dec ... Summary Decisions [*Bengal, India*] [*A publication*] (ILCA)

Summer Comput Simul Conf Proc ... Summer Computer Simulation Conference. Proceedings [*A publication*]
Summerfield ... Summerfield's Reports [*21 Nevada*] [*A publication*]   (DLA)
Summerfield S ... S. Summerfield's Reports [*21 Nevada*] [*A publication*]   (DLA)
Summer Inst Part Phys Proc ... Summer Institute on Particle Physics. Proceedings [*A publication*]
SUMMIT ... Sperry UNIVAC Minicomputer Management of Interactive Terminals
SUMMIT ... Supervisor of Multiprogramming, Multiprocessing, Interactive Time Sharing [*Data processing*]   (IEEE)
Summit Mag ... Summit Magazine [*A publication*]
Summ NP .. Summary of the Law of Nisi Prius [*A publication*]   (DLA)
Summ Proc Aust Conf Nucl Tech Anal ... Australian Conference on Nuclear Techniques of Analysis. Summary of Proceedings [*A publication*]   (APTA)
Summ Proc West Cotton Prod Conf ... Summary of Proceedings. Western Cotton Production Conference [*A publication*]
Summ Prog Geol Surv Div (Nigeria) ... Summary of Progress. Geological Survey Division (Nigeria) [*A publication*]
Summ Rep Electrotech Lab ... Summary Reports. Electrotechnical Laboratory [*Japan*] [*A publication*]
Summ World Broadcasts Part 1 ... Summary of World Broadcasts. Part 1. The USSR Weekly Economic Report [*A publication*]
Summ World Broadcasts Part 2 ... Summary of World Broadcasts. Part 2. Eastern Europe Weekly Economic Report [*A publication*]
Summ World Broadcasts Part 3 ... Summary of World Broadcasts. Part 3. The Middle East, Africa, and Latin America Weekly Economic Report [*A publication*]
Sumn .... Sumner's United States Circuit Court Reports [*A publication*]   (DLA)
Sumner .... Sumner's United States Circuit Court Reports [*A publication*]   (DLA)
SUMNS ..... Summons   (ROG)
Sumn Ves ... Sumner's Edition of Vesey's Reports [*A publication*]   (DLA)
SUMO .... Melo/Aeropuerto Deptal de Cerro Largo [*Uruguay*] [*ICAO location identifier*]   (ICLI)
SUMPAC .. Southampton University Man-Powered Aircraft [*British*]
SUMPM ...... Summary Performance Measure   (MCD)
Sum Proc Soil Sci Soc NC ... Summary of Proceedings. Soil Science Society of North Carolina [*A publication*]
Sum Rep ..... Sumner's United States Circuit Court Reports [*A publication*]   (DLA)
Sum Rep Electrotech Lab (Tokyo Japan) ... Summaries of Reports. Electrotechnical Laboratory (Tokyo, Japan) [*A publication*]
SUMS .... Shuttle Upper-Atmosphere Mass Spectrometer [*NASA*]   (MCD)
SUMS .... Specialized Unit Maintenance Support   (MCD)
SUMS .... Sperry UNIVAC Material System
SUMS .... Standard USAREUR Munitions System
SUMS .... Summons   (ROG)
SUMSTAT ... Summary Statistical Data [*Federal government*]
SUMT .... Sequential Unconstrained Minimization Technique
SUM TAL ... Sumat Talem [*Take One Like This*] [*Pharmacy*]
SUMU .... Montevideo/Carrasco Internacional [*Uruguay*] [*ICAO location identifier*]   (ICLI)
Sum UCCR ... Sumner's United States Circuit Court Reports [*A publication*]   (DLA)
Sum Ves ..... Sumner's Edition of Vesey's Reports [*A publication*]   (DLA)
SUN .... Hailey, ID [*Location identifier*] [*FAA*]   (FAAL)
SUN .... OPTEVFOR [*Operational Test and Evaluation Force*] Detachment, Sunnyvale, CA [*Navy*]   (CAAL)
SUN .... Serum Urea Nitrogen [*Clinical medicine*]
SUN .... Spanish Universal Network [*Cable-television system*]
SUN .... Spiritual Unity of Nations [*An association*]
SUN .... Standard Units and Nomenclature   (MCD)
SUN .... State University of Nebraska
SUN .... Sun Aire Lines [*Palm Springs, CA*] [*FAA designator*]   (FAAC)
SUN .... Sun Co., Inc. [*NYSE symbol*]   (SPSG)
SUN .... Sun Life Assurance Company of Canada [*UTLAS symbol*]
SUN .... Sun Valley [*Idaho*] [*Airport symbol*]   (OAG)
sun .... Sundanese [*MARC language code*] [*Library of Congress*]   (LCCP)
SUN .... Sunday   (AFM)
SUN .... Sundstrand-Turbo Division   (AAG)
SUN .... Sunnyside [*Utah*] [*Seismograph station code, US Geological Survey*] [*Closed*]   (SEIS)
SUN .... Sunset Railway Co. [*AAR code*]
SUN .... Suntec Ventures Ltd. [*Vancouver Stock Exchange symbol*]
SUN .... Suntech Library and Information Center, Marcus Hook, PA [*OCLC symbol*]   (OCLC)
SUN .... Switching Unit
SUN .... Symbols, Units, and Nomenclature [*Commission*] [*IUPAC*]
SUN .... Symphony for United Nations   (EA)
SUN .... Union of Soviet Socialist Republics [*ANSI three-letter standard code*]   (CNC)
SUNA .... Seafarers' International Union of North America [*AFL-CIO*]   (EA)
SUNA .... Sudan News Agency
SUNA .... Sunworld International Airways, Inc. [*Las Vegas, NV*] [*NASDAQ symbol*]   (NQ)

SUNA .... Switchmen's Union of North America [*Later, United Transportation Union*]
SUNAT ..... Scandinavian Union for Non-Alcoholic Traffic   (EA)
SUnBH ...... Scripta Universitatis atque Bibliotecae Hierosolymitanarum Jerusalem [*A publication*]   (BJA)
SUNCOR .. Sun Oil Company of Radnor [*Pennsylvania*]
SUND .... Sound Advice, Inc. [*NASDAQ symbol*]   (NQ)
SUND .... Sunday
SUND .... Sundries
SUNDAE .. Stanford University Division of Aero Engineering   (AAG)
Sunday M .. Sunday Magazine [*A publication*]
Sunday Rev ... Sunday Review [*A publication*]
Sun Demo & Ch ... Sunday Democrat and Chronicle [*A publication*]
Sund H .... Sunday Herald [*Melbourne*] [*A publication*]
Sund M ...... Sunday Magazine [*A publication*]
SUNDS ...... Sudden Unexpected Nocturnal Death Syndrome [*Medicine*]   (ECON)
SUNDS ...... Sundries   (ROG)
SUNF .... SUNF, Inc. [*NASDAQ symbol*]   (NQ)
SUNFED ... Special United Nations Fund for Economic Development
Sun Gaz-Ma ... Sunday Gazette-Mail [*A publication*]
Sung Kyun Kwan Univ J ... Sung Kyun Kwan University. Journal [*A publication*]
Sung Stud Newsl ... Sung Studies Newsletter [*A publication*]
SUNI .... Southern Universities Nuclear Institute
SUNI .... Sun Coast Plastics, Incorporated [*NASDAQ symbol*]   (NQ)
SUNIST .... Serveur Universitaire National de l'Information Scientifique et Technique [*Online service*]
Sunk .... Single, Unemployed, No Kids [*Lifestyle classification*]
Sun M .... Sun and Moon [*A publication*]
SUNN .... SunGroup, Inc. [*NASDAQ symbol*]   (NQ)
SUNO .... Southern University in New Orleans
SUNOCO ... Sun Oil Company [*Later, Sun Co., Inc.*]
Sun Oklahom ... Sunday Oklahoman [*A publication*]
SUNR .... Sunrise Preschools, Inc. [*NASDAQ symbol*]   (NQ)
SUNS .... Small Unit Navigation System
SUNS .... Sunshine Mining Co. [*NASDAQ symbol*]   (NQ)
SUNSAT ... Sun-Energy Collecting Satellite
Sunset Mag ... Sunset Magazine [*A publication*]
Sunshine St Agric Res Rep ... Sunshine State Agricultural Research Report [*A publication*]
Sunshine State Agric Res Rep ... Sunshine State Agricultural Research Report [*A publication*]
Sunshine State Agr Res Rep ... Sunshine State Agricultural Research Report. Florida University Agricultural Experiment Station [*A publication*]
SUNSPOT ... Study of Utilization Systems, Policies, and Techniques   (MCD)
SUNSTAR ... Stanford University Network for Space Telescience Applications Research [*Research center*]   (RCD)
SUNT .... Studien zur Umwelt des Neuen Testament [*Goettingen*] [*A publication*]
SunT .... Sunday Times [*A publication*]
SUNT .... Sunward Technologies, Inc. [*NASDAQ symbol*]   (SPSG)
Sun Times ... Sunday Times [*A publication*]
SUNW .... Sun Microsystems, Inc. [*Mountain View, CA*] [*NASDAQ symbol*]   (NQ)
SUNWACD ... Swaleureniddwharfeairecalderdon [*British town*]
Sun Wld ..... Sun World [*A publication*]
Sun Work Br ... Sun at Work in Britain [*A publication*]
SUNX .... Sunbelt Exploration [*NASDAQ symbol*]   (NQ)
SUNY .... State University of New York [*Computer retrieval and control projects*] [*Albany, NY*]
SUNYA ..... State University of New York at Albany
SUNYAB ... State University of New York at Buffalo
SUNY BCN ... State University of New York Biomedical Communication Network   (EA)
SUNY/OCLC ... State University of New York Online Computer Library Center [*Library network*]
SunyP .... State University of New York Press, Albany, NY [*Library symbol*] [*Library of Congress*]   (LCLS)
SUO .... Senior Under-Officer [*Royal Military Academy*] [*British*]   (ROG)
SUO .... Shell Oil Co. [*Toronto Stock Exchange symbol*]   (SPSG)
SUO .... Society of University Otolaryngologists [*Later, SOU-HNS*]   (EA)
SUO .... Sun River [*Oregon*] [*Airport symbol*] [*Obsolete*]   (OAG)
SUO-HNS ... Society of University Otolaryngologists - Head and Neck Surgeons   (EA)
Suom Elainlaakaril ... Suomen Elainlaakarilehti [*A publication*]
Suomen Elainlaakril Fin Veterinartidskr ... Suomen Elainlaakarilehti. Finsk Veterinartidskrift [*A publication*]
Suomen Kem A B ... Suomen Kemistilehti A, B [*A publication*]
Suomen Kemistil A ... Suomen Kemistilehti A [*A publication*]
Suomen Maataloust Seura Maataloust Aikakausk ... Suomen Maataloustieteellinen Seura. Maataloustieteellinen Aikakauskirj [*A publication*]
Suomen Maataloust Seuran Julk ... Suomen Maataloustieteellisen Seuran Julkaisuja [*A publication*]
Suomen M Vuosikirja ... Suomen Musukin Vuosikirja [*A publication*]
Suom Hammaslaak Toim ... Suomen Hammaslaakariseuran Toimituksia [*A publication*]

Suom Hammaslaak Toimi ... Suomen Hammaslaakariseuran Toimituksia [*A publication*]
Suom Hyonteistiet Aikak ... Suomen Hyonteistieteellinen Aikakauskirja [*A publication*]
Suom Kalatalous ... Suomen Kalatalous [*A publication*]
Suom Kemistil A ... Suomen Kemistilehti A [*A publication*]
Suom Kemistil B ... Suomen Kemistilehti B [*A publication*]
Suom Kemistiseuran Tied ... Suomen Kemistiseuran Tiedonantoja [*A publication*]
Suom Kemistis Tied ... Suomen Kemistiseuran Tiedonantoja [*A publication*]
Suom Maataloustiet Seuran Julk ... Suomen Maataloustieteellisen Seuran Julkaisuja [*A publication*]
Suom Maatal Seur Julk ... Suomen Maataloustieteellisen Seuran Julkaisuja [*A publication*]
Suom Naishammaslaak Julk ... Suomen Naishammaslaakarit Ryhma Julkaisu [*A publication*]
Suom Psykiatr ... Suomalaista Psykiatriaa [*A publication*]
SUOT .... Spacelab Ultraviolet Telescope
SUP .... ABC Airlines, Inc. [*DFW Airport*] [*Mesquite, TX*] [*FAA designator*]   (FAAC)
SUP .... Sabah United Party [*Political party*] [*Malaysia*]
SUP .... Sailors' Union of the Pacific   (EA)
SUP .... Single Unit Pack [*for vehicles*]
SUP .... Single Unit Package [*Pharmacy*]
SUP .... Single Unit Parameter
SUP .... Special Utility Program [*NASA*]   (KSC)
SUP .... Spisy University J. E. Purkyne [*A publication*]
SUP .... Standard Unit of Processing [*Data processing*]
SUP .... Statistical Utility Program
SUP .... Superfine
SUP .... Superior   (AFM)
SUP .... Superior Industries International, Inc. [*NYSE symbol*]   (SPSG)
SUP .... Superior Oil Co., Exploration Library, Houston, TX [*OCLC symbol*]   (OCLC)
SUP .... Superlative
SUP .... Supervision [*A publication*]
SUP .... Supine
SUP .... Supplement   (AFM)
SUP .... Supply [*Business term*]   (AFM)
SUP .... Support
SUP .... Suppress   (DEN)
SUP .... Supra [*Above*] [*Latin*]
Sup .... Supraphon [*Record label*] [*Czechoslovakia*]
SUP .... Supreme
SUP .... Supreme Resources, Inc. [*Vancouver Stock Exchange symbol*]
SUPLO ...... Sydney University Press [*Australia*]   (ADA)
SUP .... System Utilization Procedure
SUPA .... Society of University Patent Administrators   (EA)
SUPA .... Sydney University Pharmacy Association [*Australia*]
SUPAD ...... Supplementary Address   (MCD)
SUPADS .... Suppression of Air Defense System   (MCD)
SUPANX .... Supply Annex
SUPARCO ... Space and Upper Atmospheric Research Committee [*Pakistan*]
SUPARS ..... Supply Acquisition Regulation Supplement [*Navy*]
SUPCE ...... Syracuse University Publications in Continuing Education   (EA)
SUPCEN .... Supply Center
SUPCHG .... Supercharge   (FAAC)
SUPCOM ... Support Command [*Army*]
SUPCOM ... Supreme Command
SUPCON .... Superintending Constructor
SUPCOSTINS ... Supervisory Cost Inspector [*Navy*]
Sup Court Rep ... Supreme Court Reporter [*A publication*]   (DLA)
SUPCRIT ... Super Critical   (MCD)
Sup Ct .... Supreme Court   (DLA)
Sup Ct .... Supreme Court Reporter [*National Reporter System*] [*A publication*]   (DLA)
Sup Ct App ... Supreme Court Appeals [*India*] [*A publication*]   (DLA)
Sup Ct Hist Socy YB ... Supreme Court Historical Society. Yearbook [*US*] [*A publication*]
Sup Ct J ..... Supreme Court Journal [*India*] [*A publication*]   (DLA)
Sup Ct L Rev ... Supreme Court Law Review [*A publication*]
Sup Ct MR ... Supreme Court Monthly Review [*India*] [*A publication*]   (DLA)
Sup Ct Pr ... Supreme Court Practice [*A publication*]   (DLA)
Sup Ct R ..... Supreme Court Reports [*India*] [*A publication*]   (DLA)
Sup Ct R ..... United States Supreme Court Rule [*A publication*]   (DLA)
Sup Ct Rep ... Supreme Court Reporter [*A publication*]   (DLA)
Sup Ct Repr ... Supreme Court Reporter [*A publication*]   (DLA)
Sup Ct Rev ... Supreme Court Review [*A publication*]
Sup Ct R (NY) ... New York Supreme Court Reports [*A publication*]   (DLA)
SUPCUR ... Superimposed Current
SUPD .... Supradur Companies, Inc. [*NASDAQ symbol*]   (NQ)
SUPDEP .... Supply Depot
SUPDIV .... Supervisor of Diving [*Navy*]
SUPDT ...... Superintendent   (ADA)
SUPE .... Punta Del Este/Aeropuerto Deptal de Maldonado [*Uruguay*] [*ICAO location identifier*]   (ICLI)
SUPE .... [*The*] Superior Electric Co. [*NASDAQ symbol*]   (NQ)
SUPER ...... Superannuation Pension [*Australia*]   (DSUE)
SUPER ...... Superficial

SUPER ...... Superfine
SUPER ...... Superimpose
SUPER ...... Superintendent
SUPER ...... Superior
Super .... Superior Court   (DLA)
Super .... Superior Court Reports [*A publication*]   (DLA)
SUPER ...... Supernumerary
SUPER ...... Supersede   (MUGU)
SUPER ...... Supervisor   (DSUE)
Super Bsns ... Supermarket Business [*A publication*]
Super Ct ..... Superior Court   (DLA)
Super Ct App Div ... Superior Court, Appellate Division   (DLA)
Super Ct Ch Div ... Superior Court, Chancery Division   (DLA)
Super Ct Law Div ... Superior Court, Law Division   (DLA)
Super Ct Rep ... Superior Court Reports [*New York, Pennsylvania, etc.*] [*A publication*]   (DLA)
Super Ct (RI) ... Rhode Island Superior Court   (DLA)
SUPERFL ... Superficial   (ROG)
SUPERHET ... Superheterodyne
SUPERL .... Superlative
Superlatt M ... Superlattices and Microstructures [*A publication*]
Supermark Retail ... Supermarket and Retailer [*A publication*]
Super Mgt ... Supervisory Management [*A publication*]
Supermkt ... Supermarketing [*A publication*]
Supermkt Bus ... Supermarket Business [*A publication*]
Super News ... Supermarket News [*A publication*]
SUPERNOVA ... [*A*] NOVA Computer [*Data General Corp.*]
Superphosphat-Mitt ... Superphosphat-Mitteilungen [*A publication*]
SUPERSTR ... Superstructure
Superv Manage ... Supervisory Management [*A publication*]
Superv Nurse ... Supervisor Nurse [*A publication*]
Supery Manage ... Supervisory Management [*A publication*]
SUPF .... Superior Foods, Inc. [*NASDAQ symbol*]   (NQ)
SUPG .... System Utilization Procedural Guide
SUP GOSSYP ... Super Gossypium [*On Cotton Wool*] [*Pharmacy*]
SUPHTD ... Superheated   (AAG)
SUPHTR ... Superheater   (AAG)
SUPIER ..... Supply Pier [*Navy*]
SUPINSMAT ... Supervising Inspector of Naval Material
SUPINSP ... Supply Inspection [*Navy*]   (NVT)
SUPINTREP ... Supplementary Intelligence Report [*Military*]   (AABC)
SUPIR .... Supplementary Photographic Interpretation Report [*Military*]
Sup Jud Ct ... Supreme Judicial Court [*Massachusetts*]   (DLA)
Supl Antropol ... Suplemento Antropologico [*A publication*]
SUP LINT ... Super Linteum [*On Lint*] [*Pharmacy*]
SUPLO ...... Scottish Union of Power Loom Overlookers
SUPMG ..... Southern University Press Marketing Group [*Acronym is pronounced "soupmug"*]
SUPMTL ... Supplemental
SUPNZ ...... Socialist Unity Party of New Zealand
SUPO .... Super Power [*Water boiler*] [*Nuclear reactor*]
SUPO .... Supply Officer
SUPOHDU ... Supply from Stock on Hand or Due In
SUPOPS ... Supply Operations [*DoD*]
Supp .... New York Supplement Reports [*A publication*]   (DLA)
SUPP .... Sarawak United People's Party [*Malaysia*] [*Political party*]   (PPW)
SUPP .... Supplement   (KSC)
Supp .... Supplices [*of Euripides*] [*Classical studies*]   (OCD)
Supp .... Supplices Contra Thebas [*of Aeschylus*] [*Classical studies*]   (OCD)
SUPP .... Supply
SUPP .... Support   (AAG)
SUPP .... Suppositorium [*Suppository*] [*Pharmacy*]
supp .... Suppurative [*Medicine*]
SUPPACT ... Support Activity
Supp Aesch ... Supplementum Aeschyleum [*A publication*]   (OCD)
SUPPL ...... Supplement   (AABC)
Suppl .... Supplementary   (DLA)
Suppl Acta Agric Scand ... Acta Agriculturae Scandinavica. Supplementum [*A publication*]
Suppl Acta Univ Carol Biol ... Supplementum. Acta Universitatis Carolinae. Biologica [*A publication*]
Suppl Agrokem Talajt ... Supplementum. Agrokemia es Talajtan [*A publication*]
Suppl Annls Agric Fenn ... Annales Agriculturae Fenniae. Supplementum [*A publication*]
Suppl Annls Gembloux ... Supplement. Annales de Gembloux [*A publication*]
Suppl Annls Inst Pasteur (Paris) ... Supplement. Annales de l'Institut Pasteur (Paris) [*A publication*]
Suppl Certif Eng ... Supplement. Certificated Engineer [*A publication*]
Suppl Collect Sci Works Charles Univ Fac Med Hradec Kralove ... Supplement to Collection of Scientific Works. Charles University Faculty of Medicine. Hradec Kralove [*A publication*]
Suppl For Rep (Sixth) Discuss Meet (Edinb) ... Supplement to Forestry. Report of the Sixth Discussion Meeting (Edinburgh) [*A publication*]
Suppl Geophys ... Supplement. Geophysics [*A publication*]
Suppl Israel J Bot ... Supplement. Israel Journal of Botany [*A publication*]

Suppl J Phys Soc Jap ... Supplement. Journal of the Physical Society of Japan [*A publication*]
Suppl LC Subj Head ... Supplement. LC [*United States Library of Congress*] Subject Headings [*A publication*]
Suppl Nord Jordbrforsk ... Nordisk Jordbrugsforskning. Supplement [*A publication*]
SUPPLOT ... Supplemental Plot   (MCD)
Suppl Prog Theor Phys ... Supplement. Progress of Theoretical Physics [*A publication*]
Suppl Ric Biol Selvaggina ... Supplemento alle Ricerche di Biologia della Selvaggina [*A publication*]
Suppl Ric Sci ... Supplemento a la Ricerca Scientifica [*A publication*]
Suppl Sb Ved Pr Lek Fak Univ Karlovy (Hradci Kralove) ... Supplementum. Sborniku Vedeckych Praci Lekarske Fakulty University Karlovy (Hradci Kralove) [*A publication*]
Supplta Ent ... Supplementa Entomologica [*A publication*]
Sup Pop Sci Mo ... Supplement. Popular Science Monthly [*A publication*]
SUPPOS ... Suppository [*Pharmacy*]
Supp Pr T P ... Supplement. Progress of Theoretical Physics [*A publication*]
SUPPR ... Suppression   (MSA)
SUPPREP ... Supplemental Reporting Code
Supp Rev .... Supplement to the Revision [*A publication*]   (DLA)
Supp Rev St ... Supplement to the Revised Statutes [*A publication*]   (DLA)
SUPPS .... Regional Supplementary Procedures [*Aviation code*]
SUPPT ...... Supply Point [*Military*]
Supp Ves Jun ... Supplement to Vesey, Junior's, Reports [*A publication*]   (DLA)
SUPR .... Supercomputing Solutions, Inc. [*NASDAQ symbol*]   (NQ)
SUPR .... Superintendent   (ROG)
SUPR .... Superior   (AABC)
SUPR .... Supervisor
SUPR .... Suppress
SUPR .... Supreme
SUPRA ...... Suppression Pool Retention Analysis [*Nuclear energy*]
SUPRA ...... Sydney University Postgraduate Representative Association [*Australia*]
SUPRAD ... Supplementary Radio   (NG)
Supr Court ... Supreme Court Review [*A publication*]
Supr Ct .... Pennsylvania Superior Court Reports [*A publication*]   (DLA)
Supr Ct LR ... Supreme Court Law Review [*A publication*]
Supr Ct Rep ... Supreme Court Reporter [*A publication*]   (DLA)
Supreme Court LR ... Supreme Court Law Review [*A publication*]
Supreme Court Rev ... Supreme Court Review [*A publication*]
SUPRN ..... Suppression
SUPROX ... Successive Approximation   (IEEE)
SUPRSTR ... Superstructure   (AAG)
SUPS .... Seamen's United Protection Society [*A union*] [*British*]
SUPSAL ..... Supervisor of Salvage [*Navy*]
SUPSALV ... Supervisor of Salvage [*Navy*]
SUPSD .... Supersede   (AFM)
SUPSENS ... Supersensitive
SUPSGT .... Supply Sergeant [*Marine Corps*]
SUPSHIP ... Supervisor of Shipbuilding [*Navy*]
SUPSTARS ... Supply Selective Treatment and Review System
Sup Stud ... Superior Student [*A publication*]
SUPSYSCOM ... Supply System Command [*Navy*]
SUPT .... Specialized Undergraduate Pilot Training [*Air Force*]
SUPT .... Superintendent   (EY)
SUPT .... Support   (CINC)
SUPTG ...... Supporting   (AAG)
SUPTNAVOBSY ... Superintendent, Naval Observatory
SUPU .... Paysandu/Aeropuerto Deptal [*Uruguay*] [*ICAO location identifier*]   (ICLI)
SUPUSLL ... Stanford University. Publications. University Series. Languages and Literatures [*A publication*]
SUPV .... Supervisor   (AAG)
SUPVR ...... Supervisor   (AFM)
Supvry Mgmt ... Supervisory Management [*A publication*]
SUPVSN ... Supervision
SUPWB ..... Socialist Unity Party of West Berlin [*Germany*]
SUPX .... Supertex, Inc. [*NASDAQ symbol*]   (NQ)
SUPY .... Supervisory   (DEN)
Sur .... Revista Sur [*A publication*]
SUR .... SCOR US Corp. [*NYSE symbol*]   (SPSG)
SUR .... Seemingly Unrelated Regression [*Statistics*]
SUR .... Small Unit Radio [*Military*]   (INF)
SUR .... Speech Understanding Research
SUR .... Start-Up Rate   (NRCH)
SUR .... State University Railroad Co. [*AAR code*]
SUR .... Sul Ross State University, Library, Alpine, TX [*OCLC symbol*]   (OCLC)
SUR .... Supervisory Union Relations Test
Sur .... Sural Nerve
SUR .... Surcharge [*Business term*]   (ROG)
Sur .... Surety   (DLA)
SUR .... Surface   (AABC)
SUR .... Surgery
SUR .... Surinam [*ANSI three-letter standard code*]   (CNC)
SUR .... Surlari [*Romania*] [*Geomagnetic observatory code*]
SUR .... Surplus [*Business term*]
SUR .... Surround

SUR .... Survey of Current Affairs [*A publication*]
SUR .... Sutherland [*South Africa*] [*Seismograph station code, US Geological Survey*]   (SEIS)
SUR .... Sydney University Regiment [*Australia*]
Sur .... Thiouracil [*Also, SUra*] [*Biochemistry*]
SURA .... Shan United Revolutionary Army [*Burma*]   (PD)
SUra .... Thiouracil [*Also, Sur*] [*Biochemistry*]
SURAB ..... Surgery Annual [*A publication*]
SURANO .. Surface RADAR and Navigation Operation
SURBAT ... Simultaneous Unlimited Rigorous Block Analytical Triangulation [*Apollo program*] [*NASA*]
SURC .... Syracuse University Research Corporation
SURCAL ... Surveillance Calibration Satellite
SURCAP ... Surviving Capability Plan [*Military*]
SURCO ..... State University Research Center at Oswego [*State University College at Oswego*] [*Research center*]   (RCD)
Sur Ct .... Surrogate's Court   (DLA)
SURE .... Sensor Upgrade and Refurbishment Effort [*Marine Corps*]   (MCD)
SURE .... Shuttle Users Review and Evaluation [*NASA*]   (NASA)
SURE .... Simplicity, Useability, Reliability, Economy
SURE .... Subsystem Replacement
SURE .... Sulphate Regional Experiment [*Electric Power Research Institute*]
SURE .... Symbolic Utilities Revenue Environment [*IBM Corp.*]
SUREJ ...... Surface Ship Electromagnetic Jammer
SUREPI .... Surface Ship Electromagnetic Passive Intercept System
SUREQ ...... Submit Requisition   (NOAA)
SURF .... Antisubmarine Warfare Barrier Surface Patrol Ship [*Navy*]   (NVT)
SURF .... Single Unit Retrieval Format
SURF .... Standard UNREP [*Underway Replenishment*] Receiving Fixture [*Navy*]   (NVT)
SURF .... Support of User Records and Files [*Data processing*]
SURF .... Surface
surf .... Surfactant
SURF .... Synchrotron Ultraviolet Radiation Facility [*National Institute of Standards and Technology*]
SURFAC ... Surveillance Facility [*Navy*]
Surface Sci ... Surface Science [*A publication*]
Surface Techn ... Surface Technology [*A publication*]
Surfacing J ... Surfacing Journal [*United Kingdom*] [*A publication*]
Surfactant Sci Ser ... Surfactant Science Series [*A publication*]
Surf Coat ... Surface Coatings [*A publication*]
Surf Coat Aust ... Surface Coatings Australia [*A publication*]
Surf Colloid Sci ... Surface and Colloid Science [*A publication*]
Surf Defect Prop Solids ... Surface and Defect Properties of Solids [*A publication*]
SURF DET TRKR ... Surface Detector/Tracker [*Navy*]   (CAAL)
SUR/FIN ... American Electroplaters' and Surface Finishers Society Exposition   (ITD)
Surf and Interface Anal ... Surface and Interface Analysis [*A publication*]
Surf Interface Anal ... Surface and Interface Analysis [*A publication*]
Surf J ... Surfacing Journal [*A publication*]
Surf Min Reclam Symp ... Surface Mining and Reclamation Symposia [*A publication*]
SURFPA .... Antisubmarine Warfare Barrier Surface Patrol Area [*Navy*]   (NVT)
SURFPZ .... Antisubmarine Warfare Barrier Surface Patrol Zone [*Navy*]   (NVT)
Surf Sci ...... Surface Science [*A publication*]
Surf Sci R ... Surface Science Reports [*A publication*]
Surf Sci Rep ... Surface Science Reports [*A publication*]
SURFSIDE ... Small Unified Reactor Facility Systems for Isotopes, Desalting, and Electricity [*Nuclear energy*]
Surf Tech ... Surface Technology [*A publication*]
Surf Technol ... Surface Technology [*A publication*]
SURFWARDEVGRU ... Surface Warfare Development Group [*Also, SWDG*] [*Navy*]
Surf Warf ... Surface Warfare [*A publication*]
SURG .... International Surgical and Pharmaceutical Corp. [*NASDAQ symbol*]   (NQ)
SURG .... Surgeon [*or Surgery or Surgical*]   (AFM)
Surg Annu ... Surgery Annual [*A publication*]
SURGAZ ... Surgery [*Saint Louis*] [*A publication*]
Surg Bus ...... Surgical Business [*A publication*]
Surg Cdr ..... Surgeon-Commander [*British military*]
Surg Clin N Am ... Surgical Clinics of North America [*A publication*]
Surg Clin North Am ... Surgical Clinics of North America [*A publication*]
Surg Cl NA ... Surgical Clinics of North America [*A publication*]
SURGE ...... SEASAT Users Group of Europe   (MSC)
SURGE ...... Sorting, Updating, Report Generating, Etc. [*IBM Corp.*] [*Data processing*]
SURGEN ... [*The*] Surgeon General [*Army, Air Force*]
Surg Forum ... Surgical Forum [*A publication*]
Surg Gastroenterol ... Surgical Gastroenterology [*A publication*]
Surg Gynec and Obst ... Surgery, Gynecology, and Obstetrics [*A publication*]
Surg Gynecol Obstet ... Surgery, Gynecology, and Obstetrics [*A publication*]
Surg Gyn Ob ... Surgery, Gynecology, and Obstetrics [*A publication*]
Surgical ...... Surgical Business [*A publication*]
Surg Ital ..... Surgery in Italy [*A publication*]

Surg Lt .... Surgeon Lieutenant [*British military*]
Surg Lt Cdr ... Surgeon Lieutenant-Commander [*British military*]
SURGN ..... Surgeon
Surg Neurol ... Surgical Neurology [*A publication*]
Surg Radiol Anat ... Surgical and Radiologic Anatomy [*A publication*]
Surg Technol ... Surgical Technologist [*A publication*]
Surg Ther... Surgical Therapy [*Japan*] [*A publication*]
SURI.......... Syracuse University Research Institute   (MCD)
SURIC ...... Surface Ship Integrated Control System [*Obsolete*] [*Navy*]
Surinaam ... Surinaamse Landbouw [*A publication*]
Surinam Agric ... Surinam Agriculture [*A publication*]
SURISS ..... Sheffield Urban and Regional Instructional Simulation System
            [*British*]
SURMAC ... Surface Magnetic Confinement   (MCD)
SUROB...... Surf Observation Report [*Navy*]   (NVT)
Surowce Miner ... Surowce Mineralne [*A publication*]
SURP......... Submerged Unmanned Recovery Platform   (NVT)
SURPIC.... Surface Picture [*AMVER*] [*Coast Guard*]
Surps.......... Surplus
SURR........ Surrender   (AABC)
SURR........ Surrey [*County in England*]
SURR........ Surrogate
SURRC...... Scottish Universities Research and Reactor Centre [*Research
            center*]   (IRC)
Surr Ct Proc Act ... Surrogate's Court Procedure Act [*A publication*]   (DLA)
SURRD...... Surrendered   (ROG)
Surrey Archaeol Collect ... Surrey Archaeological Collections [*A publication*]
Surrey Arch Coll ... Surrey Archaeological Collections [*A publication*]
SURRO ... Surrogate   (ADA)
Surry A Coll ... Surrey Archaeological Collections [*A publication*]
SURS........ Standard Umbilical Retraction System   (NASA)
SURS........ Surface Export Cargo System [*Military*]   (AABC)
SURSAN ... Superintendencia de Urbanizacao e Saneamento [*Brazil*]
SURSAT ... Satellite Surveillance Program [*Canada*]   (MSC)
SURSAT ... Survey Satellite [*NASA*]
SURTAC ... NORAD Surveillance and Tactical Network   (MCD)
SURTASS ... Surveillance Towed Array SONAR System
SURTEMS ... Surface Temperature Measuring System
SURTOPS ... Surveillance Training and Operating Procedures
            Standardization [*Military*]   (CAAL)
Surtsey Res Prog Rep ... Surtsey Research Progress Report [*A publication*]
SURV........ Rivera/Aeropuerto Deptal [*Uruguay*] [*ICAO location
            identifier*]   (ICLI)
SURV........ Standard Underwater Research Vehicle
SURV........ Surveillance   (AAG)
SURV........ Survey   (AABC)
SURV........ Surveyor
Surv.......... Survival [*A publication*]
SURV........ Survival   (AFM)
SURV........ Survival Technology, Inc. [*NASDAQ symbol*]   (NQ)
SURV........ Surviving
Surv.......... Survivor
SURVAL... Simulator Universal Radio Variability Library
Surv Anesthesiol ... Survey of Anesthesiology [*A publication*]
Surv Biol Prog ... Survey of Biological Progress [*A publication*]
Surv Bus..... Survey of Business [*United States*] [*A publication*]
Surv Cur Bus ... Survey of Current Business [*A publication*]
Surv Curr Affairs ... Survey of Current Affairs [*London*] [*A publication*]
Surv Curr Bus ... Survey of Current Business [*A publication*]
Surv Curr Busin ... Survey of Current Business [*A publication*]
Surv Dig Dis ... Survey of Digestive Diseases [*A publication*]
Surv Drug Res Immunol Dis ... Survey of Drug Research in Immunologic
            Disease [*A publication*]
Survey Bus (Univ Tenn) ... Survey of Business (University of Tennessee) [*A
            publication*]
Survey Calif L ... Survey of California Law [*A publication*]   (DLA)
Survey Cur Bus ... Survey of Current Business [*A publication*]
Survey Current Bus ... Survey of Current Business [*A publication*]
Survey G .... Survey Graphic [*A publication*]
Surveying Tech ... Surveying Technician [*A publication*]
Survey Progr Chem ... Survey of Progress in Chemistry [*A publication*]
Surveys Reference Works Math ... Surveys and Reference Works in
            Mathematics [*A publication*]
Surv High Energy Phys ... Surveys in High Energy Physics [*Switzerland*] [*A
            publication*]
SURVI........ Surveillance
SURVIAC ... Survivability/Vulnerability Information Analysis Center [*DoD*]
            [*Wright-Patterson Air Force Base, OH*]   (MCD)
Surv Immunol Res ... Survey of Immunologic Research [*A publication*]
Surv Immun Res ... Survey of Immunologic Research [*A publication*]
SURVL....... Surveillance   (AFM)
Surv-Local Gov Technol ... Surveyor-Local Government Technology [*A
            publication*]
SURVM..... Surveillance and Maintenance [*Army*]   (AABC)
Surv & Map ... Surveying and Mapping [*A publication*]
Surv Mapp ... Surveying and Mapping [*A publication*]
Surv Munic Cty Eng ... Surveyor and Municipal and County Engineer [*A
            publication*]
Surv Notes Utah Geol Miner Surv ... Survey Notes. Utah Geological and
            Mineral Survey [*A publication*]
Surv Ophthalmol ... Survey of Ophthalmology [*A publication*]

SURVOPS ... Survey Operations [*Navy*]   (NVT)
SURVOR... Survivor
Surv Pap Horace Lamb Centre Oceanogr Res ... Survey Paper. Horace Lamb
            Centre for Oceanographical Research. Flinders University
            of South Australia [*A publication*]   (APTA)
Surv Prog Chem ... Survey of Progress in Chemistry [*A publication*]
SURVR...... Surveyor
SURVR...... Survivor   (AAG)
SURVRAP ... Surveillance Range Acoustics Prediction System   (MCD)
SURVSA ... Survivable Satellite Communications System   (MCD)
SURVSAT ... Survivable Satellite
SURVSATCOM ... Survivable Satellite Communications System
SURVSUM ... Surveillance Summary Reports   (NVT)
Surv Synth Pathol Res ... Survey and Synthesis of Pathology Research [*A
            publication*]
SURWAC ... Surface Water Automatic Computer   (AAG)
SUS............ St. Louis [*Missouri*] Spirit of St. Louis Airport [*Airport symbol*]
            [*Obsolete*]   (OAG)
SUS............ Samband Ungra Sjalfstaedismanna [*National Youth
            Organization of the Independence Party*] [*Iceland*]
            [*Political party*]   (EAIO)
SUS............ Saybolt Universal Seconds [*Oil viscosity*]
SUS............ Semiconductor Unilateral Switch   (MSA)
SUS............ Signal Underwater Sound
SUS............ Silicon Unilateral Switch
SUS............ Small Ultimate Size [*Telecommunications*]   (TEL)
SUS............ Society of University Surgeons   (EA)
SUS............ Society for Utopian Studies   (EA)
SUS............ Sound Underwater Source [*Navy*]   (CAAL)
SUS............ Speech Understanding System
SUS............ Startup System [*Nuclear energy*]   (NRCH)
SUS............ Stop Unnecessary Spending
SUS............ Studi Urbinati di Storia, Filosofia, e Letteratura [*A publication*]
SUS............ Suesswaren. Die Fachzeitschrift der Suesswaren Industrie.
            Produktion, Verpackung, Verkauf [*A publication*]
SUS............ Suit Umbilical System   (MCD)
SUS............ Sunshine Columbia [*Vancouver Stock Exchange symbol*]
SUS............ Sunstates Corp. [*AMEX symbol*]   (SPSG)
SUS............ Susaki [*Mitsui*] [*Japan*] [*Seismograph station code, US
            Geological Survey*] [*Closed*]   (SEIS)
Sus .... Susanna [*Apocrypha*]   (BJA)
SUS............ Suspect
SUS............ Suspended [*Technical drawings*]
SUS............ Suspense [*A publication*]
SUS............ Suspicion Law [*Statute permitting policemen to detain
            individuals suspected of criminal activity*] [*British*]
SUS............ Susquehanna University, Selinsgrove, PA [*OCLC
            symbol*]   (OCLC)
SUS............ Susquehanna University. Studies [*A publication*]
Sus .... Susreti [*A publication*]
SUS............ Sustainer   (AAG)
sus .... Susu [*MARC language code*] [*Library of Congress*]   (LCCP)
SUSA........ Sage Urban Studies Abstracts [*A publication*]
SUSA........ Seventh United States Army
SUSAFFS ... Society of United States Air Force Flight Surgeons
SUSAI ...... SIAMA [*Society for Interest of Active Missionaries Abroad*]
            USA, Inc.   (EA)
SUSAN...... System Utilizing Signal-Processing for Automatic
            Navigation   (MCD)
SUSAT ...... Sight Unit Small Arms Trilux [*United Kingdom*]
SUSC......... Religieuses de la Sainte-Union des Sacres-Coeurs de Jesus et
            Marie [*Religious of the Holy Union of the Sacred Hearts*]
            [*Roman Catholic women's religious order*]
SUScA ...... Sydney University Science Association [*Australia*]
SUS per COLL ... Suspensio per Collum [*Hanged by the Neck*] [*Latin*]
SUSD........ State University of South Dakota
SUS DUP .. Suspected Duplicate
SUSEME ... Superintendencia de Servicos Medicos [*Brazil*]
SUSF........ Samlingar Utgivna av Svenska Fornskriftssallskapet [*A
            publication*]
SUSF .... State University System of Florida   (NOAA)
SUSFL....... Studi Urbinati di Storia, Filosofia, e Letteratura [*A publication*]
SUSFU ...... Situation Unchanged, Still Fouled Up [*Military slang*]
            [*Bowdlerized version*]
SUSGA...... University of Sydney Students' Geological Society [*Australia*]
SUSGR...... Southwestern Union for the Study of Great Religions   (EA)
SUSH........ Set-Up Sheet   (AAG)
SUSIE .... Stock Updating Sales Invoicing Electronically   (IEEE)
SUSIM....... Solar Ultraviolet Spectral Irradiance Monitor   (MCD)
SUSIO....... State University System of Florida Institute of
            Oceanography   (NOAA)
SUSIS........ Sport und Sportwissenschaftliche Informationssystem [*Sport
            and Sports-Scientific Information System*] [*West
            Germany*]   (IID)
Sus Leg Chron ... Susquehanna Legal Chronicle [*Pennsylvania*] [*A
            publication*]   (DLA)
SUSLO...... Senior United States Liaison Officer [*National Security Agency*]
SUSM........ Scottish United Services Museum [*British military*]   (DMA)
SUSMOP.. Senior United States Military Observer Palestine

SUSNO ..... Senior United States Naval Officer
SUSO .... Salto/Aeropuerto Deptal [*Uruguay*] [*ICAO location identifier*] (ICLI)
SUSOPS.... Sustained Operations [*Study of soldier performance in extended combat situation*] [*Army*]
SUSP .... Suspected [*Passage or line of a work*] [*Literary criticism*] (ROG)
SUSP .... Suspend [*or Suspension*] (AFM)
SUSP .... Suspicion [*FBI standardized term*]
SUSPD ..... Suspended
SUSPDNG ... Suspending [*Freight*]
SUSP L ...... Suspecta Lectio [*Double Reading*] [*Latin*] (ROG)
SUSQ .... Susquehanna Bancshares, Inc. [*Lititz, PA*] [*NASDAQ symbol*] (NQ)
Susq LC ..... Susquehanna Leading Chronicle [*Pennsylvania*] [*A publication*] (DLA)
Susq L Chron ... Susquehanna Legal Chronicle [*Pennsylvania*] [*A publication*] (DLA)
Susq Legal Chron ... Susquehanna Legal Chronicle [*Pennsylvania*] [*A publication*] (DLA)
Susq Leg Chron ... Susquehanna Legal Chronicle [*Pennsylvania*] [*A publication*] (DLA)
Susquehanna Leg Chron (PA) ... Susquehanna Legal Chronicle [*Pennsylvania*] [*A publication*] (DLA)
SUSRA ...... Steel in the USSR [*A publication*]
SUSRD8.... Sbornik UVTIZ [*Ustav Vedeckotechnickych Informaci pro Zemedelstvi*] Ochrana Rostlin [*A publication*]
SUSREP.... Senior United States Representative to Defense Production Board [*NATO*] (NATG)
SUSS .... Signalmen's United and Sick Society [*A union*] [*British*]
SUSS .... Sound Underwater Signal Source (MCD)
SUSS .... Submarine Schoolship [*Navy*] (NVT)
SUSS .... Sussex [*County in England*]
Sussex A Coll ... Sussex Archaeological Collections [*A publication*]
Sussex Arch Coll ... Sussex Archaeological Collections Relating to the Antiquities of the County [*A publication*]
SUST .... Sustainer
SUSTD ...... Sustained [*Legal*] (ROG)
SUSTN ..... Sustain [*Legal*] (ROG)
SUSTN ..... Sustentation [*Ecclesiastical*] (ROG)
SuSu .... Suomalainen Suomi [*A publication*]
SuSuomi.... Suomalainen Suomi [*A publication*]
SuSuV .... Suomalainen Suomi. Kulttuuripolittinen Aikakauskirja/Valvoja [*A publication*]
SUSV .... Small Unit Support Vehicle [*Military*] (RDA)
SUSY's ..... Supersymmetric Theories [*Particle physics*]
SUT .... Satellite under Test
SUT .... Set-Up Time
SUT .... Small Unit Transceiver [*Military*] (INF)
SUT .... Society for Underwater Technology (EA)
SUT .... Southport, NC [*Location identifier*] [*FAA*] (FAAL)
SUT .... Start-Up Transformer (NRCH)
SUT .... State Unemployment Tax (MCD)
SUT .... Subunit Test
SUT .... Suttsu [*Japan*] [*Seismograph station code, US Geological Survey*] (SEIS)
SUT .... Syndicat Uni du Transport [*United Transportation Union - UTU*] [*Canada*]
SUT .... System under Test (AAG)
SUTAGS ... Shuttle Uplink Text and Graphics Scanner (NASA)
SUTARS ... Search Unit Tracing and Recording System
SUTB .... Tacuarembo [*Uruguay*] [*ICAO location identifier*] (ICLI)
SUTD .... Soviet Union Today [*A publication*]
SUTEC ...... Seneca Underwater Test and Evaluation Center
SUTH .... Sutherland [*County in Scotland*]
Suth.......... Sutherland's Calcutta Reports [*India*] [*A publication*] (DLA)
Suth App... Sutherland's Appeal Reports, Small Causes Court [*1861-65*] [*Bengal, India*] [*A publication*] (DLA)
Suth Bengal ... Sutherland's Bengal High Court Reports [*India*] [*A publication*] (DLA)
Suth Dam... Sutherland on the Law of Damages [*A publication*] (DLA)
Suth FBR... Sutherland's Bengal Full Bench Reports [*India*] [*A publication*] (DLA)
Suth Mis ... India Weekly Reporter, Miscellaneous Appeals [*A publication*] (DLA)
Suth PCA... Sutherland's Privy Council Appeals [*A publication*] (DLA)
Suth PCJ ... Sutherland's Privy Council Judgments [*A publication*] (DLA)
Suth Sp N .. Full Bench Rulings [*Calcutta*] [*A publication*] (DLA)
Suth Sp N .. Sutherland's Special Number of Weekly Reporter [*A publication*] (DLA)
Suth Stat Const ... Sutherland on Statutes and Statutory Construction [*A publication*] (DLA)
Suth St Const ... Sutherland on Statutes and Statutory Construction [*A publication*] (DLA)
Suth WR ... Sutherland's Weekly Reporter, Calcutta [*1864-76*] [*A publication*] (DLA)
Suth WR Mis ... Sutherland's Weekly Reports, Miscellaneous Appeals [*India*] [*A publication*] (DLA)
SUTR........ Treinta Y Tres [*Uruguay*] [*ICAO location identifier*] (ICLI)
SUTRASFCO ... Sindicato Unificado de Trabajadores de la Standard Fruit Company [*Honduras*]

SUTT......... Small Unit Training Team [*Military*]
Sutton......... Sutton on Personal Actions at Common Law [*A publication*] (DLA)
SUU .... Fairfield, CA [*Location identifier*] [*FAA*] (FAAL)
SUU .... Santaquin Canyon [*Utah*] [*Seismograph station code, US Geological Survey*] (SEIS)
SUU .... Society of University Urologists (EA)
SUU .... Suspension Unit (AFM)
SUUG .... Sbornik Ustredniho Ustavu Geologickeho [*A publication*]
SUV .... Small Unilamellar Vesicle [*Pharmacy*] [*Biochemistry*]
SUV .... Sociocated Unilamellar Vesicles
SUV .... Sport-Utility Vehicle [*Type of truck*]
SUV .... Sumpter Valley Railway [*AAR code*]
SUV .... Suva [*Fiji*] [*Seismograph station code, US Geological Survey*] (SEIS)
SUVAT...... Suva [*Fiji*] [*Airport symbol*] (OAG)
SUVAT...... Support Unit Vehicle Automatic Tester
SUVCW..... Sons of Union Veterans of the Civil War (EA)
SUVI........ Strong Ultraviolet Index
SUVO .... Student Voice [*A publication*]
Suvrem Med ... Suvremena Meditsina [*Bulgaria*] [*A publication*]
Suvrem Probl Endokrinol ... Suvremenni Problemi na Endokrinologiyata [*A publication*]
SUVSL...... Skrifter Utgivna. Vetenskaps-Societeten i Lund [*A publication*]
SUW .... Struthers Wells Corp. [*AMEX symbol*] (SPSG)
SUW .... Superior, WI [*Location identifier*] [*FAA*] (FAAL)
SUWC .... Surface Warfare (NVT)
SUWC .... Surface Warfare Coordinator [*Also, SWC*] (NVT)
SUWU .... Skilled and Unskilled Workers' Union - Somali Republic
SUX .... Sioux City [*Iowa*] [*Airport symbol*] (OAG)
sux............. Sumerian [*MARC language code*] [*Library of Congress*] (LCCP)
SUY .... State University Railroad Co. [*Later, SUR*] [*AAR code*]
SUY .... Sudureyri [*Iceland*] [*Airport symbol*] (OAG)
s-uy---........ Uruguay [*MARC geographic area code*] [*Library of Congress*] (LCCP)
SUYR........ Southampton University Yacht Research Group [*British*]
SUZ .... Suez Petroleum Corp. [*Vancouver Stock Exchange symbol*]
SUZ .... Suria [*Papua New Guinea*] [*Airport symbol*] (OAG)
SV .... El Salvador [*ANSI two-letter standard code*] (CNC)
SV .... Safety Valve (AAG)
SV .... Sailing Vessel
SV .... Sales Voucher [*Business term*] (DCTA)
SV .... Sancta Virgo [*Holy Virgin*] [*Latin*]
SV .... Sanctitas Vestra [*Your Holiness*] [*Latin*]
SV .... Saponification Value [*Organic analytical chemistry*]
SV .... Sapper Vehicle [*Military*]
SV .... Satellite Virus
SV .... Saudi Arabian Airlines [*ICAO designator*] (FAAC)
SV .... Saves [*Baseball*]
SV .... Savings Transfer [*Banking*]
SV .... Scalp Vein [*Medicine*]
SV .... Schedule Variance (MCD)
SV .... Schweizer Volkskunde [*A publication*]
SV .... Schweizerische Volkspartei [*Swiss People's Party*] [*Political party*]
SV .... Scuola e Vita [*A publication*]
SV .... Secondary Valve
SV .... Secular Variation [*Geophysics*]
SV .... Security Violation (AAG)
SV .... Selecta Vision [*RCA brand name for tape cartridges of TV programs*]
SV .... Selective Volunteer [*Navy*]
SV .... Selenoid Valve (MCD)
SV .... Self-Ventilated (MSA)
SV .... Self Verification
SV .... Seminal Vesicle [*Anatomy*]
SV .... Service
SV .... Set Value
S & V .... Shock and Vibration
SV .... Shuttle Vehicle [*NASA*] (NASA)
S de V........ Sicardus Fabri de Vauro [*Deceased, 1323*] [*Authority cited in pre-1607 legal work*] (DSA)
SV .... Side Valve [*Automotive engineering*]
SV .... Side View (MSA)
SV .... Sieve
Sv .... Sievert [*SI unit for radioactive dose equivalent*]
SV .... Silicone Varnish
SV .... Silvercraft SpA [*Italy*] [*ICAO aircraft manufacturer identifier*] (ICAO)
SV .... Simian Virus
SV .... Simulated Video (MCD)
SV .... Single Silk Varnish [*Wire insulation*] (AAG)
SV .... Single Value
SV .... Single Vibrations [*Half cycles*]
SV .... Sinus Venosus [*Anatomy*]
SV .... Siste, Viator [*Stop, Traveller*] [*Latin*] (ROG)
SV .... Slide Valve
SV .... Slovesna Veda [*A publication*]
SV .... Slowed-Down Video [*RADAR*] (CET)
SV .... Sluice [*or Stop*] Valve

SV	Snake Venom [*Medicine*]
SV	Sodium Vapor
SV	Soft Valve
SV	Solenoid Valve (KSC)
SV	Solicited Volunteer [*In drug studies*]
SV	Sons of Veterans
SV	Sophisticated Vocabulary (AAG)
SV	Sosialistisk Valgforbund [*Socialist Electoral Alliance*] [*Norway*] [*Political party*] (PPE)
SV	Sosialistisk Venstreparti [*Socialist Left Party*] [*Norway*] [*Political party*] (PPE)
SV	Sotto Voce [*In an Undertone*] [*Music*]
S/V	Sound and Vibration [*A publication*]
SV	Sovetskaia Vostokovedenie [*A publication*]
SV	Space Vehicle
SV	Space Velocity [*Chemical engineering*]
SV	Space Visualization [*Visual perception*]
SV	Specified Value (MCD)
SV	Spiritus Vinosus [*Ardent Spirit*] [*Pharmacy*] (ROG)
SV	Star of Valour [*British*] (ADA)
SV	State Vector (KSC)
SV	Status Valid
sV	Statvolt [*Also, stat V*] [*Electrostatic unit of potential difference*]
SV	Steam Valve
SV	Stimulation Value [*Psychology*]
SV	Storm Vulcan
SV	Stripping Voltammetry [*Electroanalytical chemistry*]
SV	Stroke Volume [*Physiology*]
SV	Study of Values [*Psychology*]
SV	Sub Verbo [*or Sub Voce*] [*Under the Word*] [*Latin*]
SV	Subclavian Vein [*Cardiology*]
SV	Subdivision Flag [*Navy*] [*British*]
SV	Subject-Verb [*Education of the hearing-impaired*]
SV	Subjective Vertical [*Neurology*]
S/V	Supply Valve (MCD)
SV	Support Vehicle [*British military*] (DMA)
SV	Supraventricular [*Cardiology*]
SV	Surface Vessel
S/V	Surface/Volume [*Ratio*]
S/V	Surrender Value [*Insurance*]
S/V	Survivability/Vulnerability [*Applied to ability of weapon systems to survive attacks*] [*Military*]
SV	Suvaguq. Pond Inlet [*A publication*]
sv	Swan Islands [*ho (Honduras) used in records cataloged after January 1978*] [*MARC country of publication code*] [*Library of Congress*] (LCCP)
SV	Swept Volume
SV	Symptomatic Volunteer [*In drug studies*]
SV	Synaptic Vesicle [*Neurobiology*]
SVA	Sample Valve Assembly
SVA	Savoonga [*Alaska*] [*Airport symbol*] (OAG)
SVA	School of Visual Arts [*New York, NY*]
SVA	SEABEE Veterans of America (EA)
SVA	Sectionalized Vertical Antenna
SVA	Security and Vulnerability Analysis (MCD)
SVA	Shared Virtual Area [*Data processing*]
SVA	Singapore Volunteer Artillery [*British military*] (DMA)
SVA	Single-Valve First-Actuation [*Nuclear energy*] (NRCH)
SVA	Singular-Value Analysis [*Industrial control*]
SVA	Society for Visual Anthropology (EA)
SVA	Solar Vane Actuators
SVA	Statistical Vibration Analysis
SVA	Stock Valuation Adjustment [*Business term*] (ADA)
SVA	Sun Valley Airlines (FAAC)
SVA	Suva [*Fiji*] [*Seismograph station code, US Geological Survey*] (SEIS)
SVAA	Super Vernier Auto Alert [*Military*] (CAAL)
SVAB	Shuttle Vehicle Assembly Building [*NASA*] (NASA)
SVABB	Schweizerische Vereinigung fuer Atomenergie. Bulletin [*A publication*]
SVAC	Acarigua, Portuguesa [*Venezuela*] [*ICAO location identifier*] (ICLI)
SVA & C	Shuttle Vehicle Assembly and Checkout [*NASA*] (NASA)
SVAC	Singapore Volunteer Artillery Corps [*British military*] (DMA)
SVACB	Sbornik Vysoke Skoly Chemicko-Technologicke v Praze. Anorganicka Chemie a Technologie [*A publication*]
SVAD	Savanna Army Depot [*Illinois*] (AABC)
SVADA	Savanna Army Depot Activity (AABC)
Sv Aeroplan Ab SAAB Tech Notes	Svenska Aeroplan Aktiebolaget [*Linkoping, Sweden*]. SAAB Technical Notes [*A publication*]
SVAFB	South Vandenberg Air Force Base [*California*] (NASA)
SVALC	Sangamon Valley Academic Library Consortium [*Library network*]
SVAN	Anaco, Anzoategui [*Venezuela*] [*ICAO location identifier*] (ICLI)
SVAN	Savannah Foods & Industries, Inc. [*NASDAQ symbol*] (NQ)
SVAO	Service at Veterans Administration Offices [*Red Cross*]
SVAPA	Svarochnoe Proizvodstvo [*A publication*]

SVAR	Stuart's Lower Canada Vice-Admiralty Reports [*A publication*] (DLA)
Svarka Vzryvom Svoistva Svarnykh Soedin	Svarka Vzryvom i Svoistva Svarnykh Soedinenii [*A publication*]
Svar Proizvod	Svarochnoe Proizvodstvo [*A publication*]
SVAT	San Fernando De Atabapo, T. F. Amazonas [*Venezuela*] [*ICAO location identifier*] (ICLI)
SVAT	Standard Version Acceptance Test (MCD)
SVB	Sambava [*Madagascar*] [*Airport symbol*] (OAG)
SVB	Savin Corp. [*NYSE symbol*] (SPSG)
SVB	Shuttle Vehicle Booster [*NASA*] (NASA)
SVB	Space Vehicle Booster [*NASA*] (MCD)
SVB	Sterivet Laboratories Ltd. [*Toronto Stock Exchange symbol*]
SV:B	Study of Values: British Edition [*Psychology*]
SVBC	Barcelona/Gral. Jose Antonio Anzoategui Internacional Anzoategui [*Venezuela*] [*ICAO location identifier*] (ICLI)
SVBEEQV	Si Vales, Bene Est; Ego Quoque Valeo [*I Hope You're Well; I Am*] [*Latin*]
SVBI	Barinas, Barinas [*Venezuela*] [*ICAO location identifier*] (ICLI)
SVBL	Maracay/El Libertador, Base Aerea Aragua [*Venezuela*] [*ICAO location identifier*] (ICLI)
SVBM	Barquisimeto/Internacional, Lara [*Venezuela*] [*ICAO location identifier*] (ICLI)
SVBP	Single-Variable Bypass Program [*DoD*]
SVBS	Maracay/Mariscal Sucre, Base Aerea Aragua [*Venezuela*] [*ICAO location identifier*] (ICLI)
SVBSA	Sivilt Beredskap [*A publication*]
SVBT	Space Vehicle Booster Test (AAG)
SVBUA	Shock and Vibration Bulletin [*A publication*]
SVBZ	Bruzual, Apure [*Venezuela*] [*ICAO location identifier*] (ICLI)
SVC	Saint Vincent College [*Latrobe, PA*]
SVC	Selective Venous Catheterization [*Cardiology*]
SVC	Service (AFM)
SVC	Service Command [*Army*]
SVC	Service Message [*Aviation code*]
SVC	Silver City [*New Mexico*] [*Airport symbol*] (OAG)
SVC	Silver Creek [*California*] [*Seismograph station code, US Geological Survey*] (SEIS)
SVC	Sine Vibration Control
SVC	Singapore Volunteer Corps [*British military*] (DMA)
SVC	Single Variable Control
SVC	Society of Vacuum Coaters (EA)
SVC	Space Vehicle Code
SVC	Spiroplasmavirus citri [*Bacteriology*]
SVC	Spring Viremia of Carp
SVC	Still Video Camera
SVC	Stokely-Van Camp, Inc. [*NYSE symbol*] (SPSG)
SVC	Superior Vena Cava [*Anatomy*]
SVC	Supervisor Call (NASA)
SVC	Switched Virtual Circuit
SVCA	Caracas Maiquetia Distrito Federal [*Venezuela*] [*ICAO location identifier*] (ICLI)
SVCAB	Saphenous Vein Coronary Artery Bypass [*Cardiology*]
SVCB	Ciudad Bolivar, Bolivar [*Venezuela*] [*ICAO location identifier*] (ICLI)
SVCBL	Serviceable
SVCC	Caracas Ciudad Distrito Federal [*Venezuela*] [*ICAO location identifier*] (ICLI)
SVCD	Caicara De Orinoco, Bolivar [*Venezuela*] [*ICAO location identifier*] (ICLI)
SVCE	Service
SVCG	Spatial Vectorcardiogram [*Cardiology*]
SVCH	Achaguas, Apure [*Venezuela*] [*ICAO location identifier*] (ICLI)
SVCI	Cachipo, Monagas [*Venezuela*] [*ICAO location identifier*] (ICLI)
SVCIA	Soviet Chemical Industry [*English Translation*] [*A publication*]
SVCJ	San Carlos, Cojedes [*Venezuela*] [*ICAO location identifier*] (ICLI)
SVCL	Calabozo, Guarico [*Venezuela*] [*ICAO location identifier*] (ICLI)
SVCMN	Service Man (NVT)
SVCN	Canaima, Bolivar [*Venezuela*] [*ICAO location identifier*] (ICLI)
SVCO	Carora, Lara [*Venezuela*] [*ICAO location identifier*] (ICLI)
SVCO	Shillelagh Ventures, Chartered [*NASDAQ symbol*] (NQ)
SVCP	Carupano/Gral. en Jefe Jose Francisco Bermudez, Sucre [*Venezuela*] [*ICAO location identifier*] (ICLI)
SVCP	Special Virus Cancer Program [*National Cancer Institute*]
SVCR	Coro/Internacional, Falcon [*Venezuela*] [*ICAO location identifier*] (ICLI)
SVCS	Caracas/Internacional del Centro Miranda [*Venezuela*] [*ICAO location identifier*] (ICLI)
SVCS	Superior Vena Caval Syndrome [*Medicine*]
SvcStrs	Service Stars [*Military decoration*]
SVCU	Cumana, Sucre [*Venezuela*] [*ICAO location identifier*] (ICLI)
SVCU	Space Visualization Contralateral Use [*Occupational therapy*]
SVD	St. Vincent [*Windward Islands*] [*Airport symbol*] (OAG)
SVD	Share Valuation Division [*Inland Revenue*] [*British*]
SVD	Silver Talon Mines Ltd. [*Vancouver Stock Exchange symbol*]
SVD	Simple Vertex Delivery [*Medicine*]

SVD .... Simplified Vapor Detector
SVD .... Simultaneous Voice/Data
SVD .... Singular Value Decomposition [*Mathematics*]
SVD .... Societas Verbi Divini [*Society of the Divine Word*] [*Roman Catholic men's religious order*]
SVD .... Soviet Export. Soviet Foreign Trade Bimonthly [*A publication*]
SVD .... Space Vehicles Division [*NASA*] (MCD)
SVD .... Spontaneous Vaginal Delivery [*Gynecology*]
SVD .... Surveyor Vehicle Department
SvD .... Svenska Dagbladet [*A publication*]
SVD .... Sverdlovsk [*USSR*] [*Geomagnetic observatory code*]
SVD .... Swine Vesicular Disease
SVDF .... Segmented Virtual Display File
SVDI .... Serie de Vocabularios y Diccionarios Indigenas [*A publication*]
SVDP .... La Divina Pastora, Bolivar [*Venezuela*] [*ICAO location identifier*] (ICLI)
SVDP .... Saint Vincent de Paul (ADA)
SVDP .... Skylab Video Documentation Project [*NASA*] (KSC)
SVDS .... Space Vehicle Dynamic Simulator [*NASA*] (NASA)
SVE .... Secure Voice Equipment (NATG)
SVE .... Seminal Vesicle Epithelium [*Anatomy*]
SVE .... Severide Resources, Inc. [*Vancouver Stock Exchange symbol*]
SVE .... Society for Vector Ecology (EA)
SVE .... Society for Veterinary Ethology [*See also SEV*] [*Edinburgh, Scotland*] (EAIO)
SVE .... Supraventricular Ectopic [*Beat*] [*Cardiology*]
SVE .... Susanville, CA [*Location identifier*] [*FAA*] (FAAL)
SVE .... Sverdlovsk [*Ekaterinburg*] [*USSR*] [*Seismograph station code, US Geological Survey*] (SEIS)
SVE .... Swept Volume Efficiency [*Air Force*]
SVE .... System Valve Engineering
s-ve--- .... Venezuela [*MARC geographic area code*] [*Library of Congress*] (LCCP)
SVEA .... Schweizerischer Verband Evangaelischer Arbeitnehmer [*A union*] [*Swiss*] (DCTA)
SVEA .... Supplemental Vocational Education Assistance (OICC)
SvEA .... Svensk Exegetisk Arsbok [*A publication*]
SVEAA ...... Schweizerischer Verband Evangelischer Arbeiter und Angestellter [*Swiss Federation of Protestant Trade Unions*]
SVEAD ...... State Variable Estimation and Accuracy Determination
SVEC .... Studies on Voltaire and the Eighteenth Century [*A publication*]
SVED .... El Dorado, Bolivar [*Venezuela*] [*ICAO location identifier*] (ICLI)
Sved Zemed ... Svedeniya po Zemedelieto [*A publication*]
SVEN .... Shipboard Voice-Enhanced Navigation System [*for blind sailors*]
Sven Bot Tidskr ... Svensk Botanisk Tidskrift [*A publication*]
Sven Bryggarefoeren Manadsbl ... Svenska Bryggarefoereningens Manadsblad [*A publication*]
Sven Bryggeritidskr ... Svensk Bryggeritidskrift [*A publication*]
Sven Faerg Tek Tidskr ... Svensk Faerg-Teknisk Tidskrift [*A publication*]
Sven Farm Tidskr ... Svensk Farmaceutisk Tidskrift [*A publication*]
Sven Farm Tidskr Sci Ed ... Svensk Farmaceutisk Tidskrift. Scientific Edition [*A publication*]
Sven Foerfattningssaml ... Svensk Foerfattningssamling [*A publication*]
Sven Forskningsinst Cem Betong K Tek Hoegsk Stockholm Handl ... Svenska Forskningsinstitutet foer Cement och Betong vid Kungliga Tekniska Hoegskolan i Stockholm. Handlingar [*A publication*]
Sven Forskningsinst Cem Betong K Tek Hoegsk Stockholm Medd ... Svenska Forskningsinstitutet foer Cement och Betong vid Kungliga Tekniska Hoegskolan i Stockholm. Meddelanden [*A publication*]
Sven Forskningsinst Cem Betong K Tek Hoegsk Stockholm Saertr ... Svenska Forskningsinstitutet foer Cement och Betong vid Kungliga Tekniska Hoegskolan i Stockholm. Saertryck [*A publication*]
Sven Forskningsinst Cem Betong K Tek Hoegsk Stockholm Utredn ... Svenska Forskningsinstitutet foer Cement och Betong vid Kungliga Tekniska Hoegskolan i Stockholm. Utredningar [*A publication*]
Sven Forskningsinst Cem Betong K Tek Hogsk ... Svenska Forskningsinstitutet foer Cement och Betong vid Kungliga i Stockholm. Meddelanden Tekniska Hoegskolan [*Sweden*] [*A publication*]
Sven Fotogr Tidskr ... Svensk Fotografisk Tidskrift [*A publication*]
Sven Frotidn ... Svensk Froetidning [*A publication*]
Sven Gasfoeren Manadsbl ... Svenska Gasfoereningens Manadsblad [*A publication*]
Sven Gasverksfoeren Aarsb ... Svenska Gasverksfoereningens Aarsbok [*A publication*]
Sven Hydrogr Biol Komm Skr Ny Ser Biol ... Svenska Hydrografisk-Biologiska Kommissionens Skrifter. Ny Serie. Biologi [*A publication*]
Sven Inst Konserveringsforsk Publ ... Svenska Institutet foer Konserveringsforskning. Publikation [*A publication*]
Sven Kem Tidskr ... Svensk Kemisk Tidskrift [*A publication*]
Sven Kraftverksfoeren Publ ... Svenska Kraftverksfoereningens Publikationer [*A publication*]
Sven Kraftverksfoeren Publ Medd ... Svenska Kraftverksfoereningens Publikationer Meddelande [*A publication*]

Sven Laekaresaellsk Foerh ... Svenska Laekaresaellskapets Foerhandlingar [*A publication*]
Sven Laekartidn ... Svenska Laekartidningen [*A publication*]
Sven Linne-SallskArsskr ... Svenska Linne-Sallskapet Arsskrift [*A publication*]
Sven Mejeriernas Riksfoeren Produkttek Avd Medd ... Svenska Mejeriernas Riksfoerening. Produkttekniska Avdelningen. Meddelande [*A publication*]
Sven Mejeritidn ... Svenska Mejeritidningen [*A publication*]
Sven Mosskulturfoeren Tidskr ... Svenska Mosskulturfoereningens Tidskrift [*A publication*]
Sven Naturvetensk ... Svensk Naturvetenskap [*A publication*]
Sven Papperfoeraedlingstidskr ... Svensk Pappersfoeraedlingstidskrift [*A publication*]
Sven Pappersmassetidn ... Svensk Pappersmassetidning [*A publication*]
Sven Papperstidn ... Svensk Papperstidning [*A publication*]
Svensk Bot Tidskr ... Svensk Botanisk Tidskrift [*A publication*]
Svensk Froetidn ... Svensk Froetidning [*A publication*]
Svensk Geog Arsbok ... Svensk Geografisk Arsbok [*A publication*]
Svensk Jur-Tidn ... Svensk Juristtidning [*Stockholm, Sweden*] [*A publication*] (DLA)
Svensk Kem Tidskr ... Svensk Kemisk Tidskrift [*A publication*]
Svensk Litt ... Svensk Litteraturtidskrift [*A publication*]
Sven Skogsvardsforen Tidskr ... Svenska Skogsvardsforeningens Tidskrift [*A publication*]
SvenskPapr ... Svensk Papperstidning [*A publication*]
Svensk Teol Kvartalskr ... Svensk Teologisk Kvartalskrift [*A publication*]
Svensk Tid ... Svensk Tidskrift foer Musikforskning [*A publication*]
Svenskt MHistoriskt ... Svenskt Musikhistoriskt Arkiv. Bulletin [*A publication*]
Svensk Travarutidn ... Svensk Traevaru- och Pappersmassetidning [*A publication*]
Svensk Vet-tidskr ... Svensk Veterinaertidskrift [*A publication*]
Svens Pap T ... Svensk Papperstidning Tidskrift [*A publication*]
Sven Tandlaek Tidskr ... Svensk Tandlaekare Tidskrift [*A publication*]
Sven Tandlakareforb Tidn ... Svensk Tandlaekareforbunds Tidning [*Sweden*] [*A publication*]
Sven Tandlak Tidskr ... Svensk Tandlaekare Tidskrift [*A publication*]
Sven Tids M ... Svensk Tidskrift foer Musikforskning [*A publication*]
Sven Traevaru-Tidn ... Svensk Traevaru-Tidning [*A publication*]
Sven Vall Mosskulturfoeren Medd ... Svenska Vall- och Mosskulturfoereningens Meddelanden [*A publication*]
Sven Vattenkraftfoeren Publ ... Svenska Vattenkraftforeningens Publikationer [*A publication*]
Sven Veterinartidn ... Svensk Veterinaertidning [*A publication*]
SVER .... State Veterans Employment Representative [*Department of Labor*]
Sverdlovsk God Ped Inst Naucn Trudy ... Sverdlovskii Gosudarstvennyi Pedagogiceskii Institut. Naucnyi Trudy [*A publication*]
Sverdlovsk Gos Ped Inst Ucen Zap ... Sverdlovskii Gosudarstvennyi Pedagogiceskii Institut. Ucenye Zapiski [*A publication*]
Sver Geol Unders Arsb ... Sveriges Geologiska Undersoekning. Arsbok [*A publication*]
Sver Geol Unders Arsb Ser C Avh Uppsatser ... Sveriges Geologiska Undersoekning. Arsbok. Serie C. Avhandlingar och Uppsatser [*A publication*]
Sver Gummitek Foren Publ ... Sveriges Gummitekniska Foerening. Publicerande [*A publication*]
Sveriges Geol Unders Ser C ... Sveriges Geologiska Undersoekning. Arsbok. Serie C. Avhandlingar och Uppsatser [*A publication*]
Sveriges Riksbank Q R ... Sveriges Riksbank. Quarterly Review [*A publication*]
Sveriges Skogsvforb Tidskr ... Sveriges Skogsvardsfoerbunds Tidskrift [*A publication*]
Sveriges Utsaedesfoer Tidskr ... Sveriges Utsaedesfoerenings Tidskrift [*A publication*]
Sver Lantbruksuniv Inst Biom Skogsindelning Rapp ... Sveriges Lantbruksuniversitet Institutionen foer Biometri och Skogsindelning. Rapport [*A publication*]
Sver Lantbruksuniv Inst Lantbrukets Byggnadstek Rapp ... Sveriges Lantbruksuniversitet Institutionen foer Lantbrukets Byggnadsteknik. Rapport [*A publication*]
Sver Lantbruksuniv Inst Mikrobiol Rapp ... Sveriges Lantbruksuniversitet Institutionen foer Mikrobiologi. Rapport [*A publication*]
Sver Lantbruksuniv Inst Tradgardsvetensk Rapp ... Sveriges Lantbruksuniversitet Institutionen foer Tradgardsvetenskap. Rapport [*A publication*]
Sver Lantbruksuniv Konsulentavd Rapp Landskap ... Sveriges Lantbruksuniversitet Konsulentavdelningens Rapporter Landskap [*A publication*]
Sver Lantbruksuniv Vaxtskyddsrapp Avh ... Sveriges Lantbruksuniversitet Vaxtskyddsrapporter Avhandlingar [*A publication*]
Sver Lantbruksuniv Vaxtskyddsrapp Tradg ... Sveriges Lantbruksuniversitet Vaxtskyddsrapporter Tradgard [*A publication*]
Sver Mekanforb Mekanresult ... Sveriges Mekanforbund, Mekanresultat [*A publication*]
Sver Nat ..... Sveriges Natur [*A publication*]
Sver Nat Arsb ... Sveriges Natur Arsbok [*A publication*]
Sver Off Stat Bergshantering ... Sveriges Officiella Statistik Bergshantering. Statistika Centralbyran [*Stockholm*] [*A publication*]

Sver Pomol Foeren Arsskr ... Sveriges Pomologiska Foerening Arsskrift [*A publication*]
Sver Skogsvardsfoerbunds Tidskr ... Sveriges Skogsvardsfoerbunds Tidskrift [*A publication*]
Sver Skogsvardsforb Tidskr ... Sveriges Skogsvardsfoerbunds Tidskrift [*A publication*]
SVERT ...... Subvert (ROG)
Svertyvayushchaya Sist Krovi Akush Ginekol ... Svertyvayushchaya Sistema Krovi v Akusherstve i Ginekologii [*A publication*]
Sver Utsadesforen Tidskr ... Sveriges Utsaedesfoerenings Tidskrift [*A publication*]
Sver Utsaedesfoer Tidskr ... Sveriges Utsaedesfoerenings Tidskrift [*A publication*]
Svetotekh ... Svetotekhnika [*A publication*]
Svetotekhnika Svetotekh Kom Akad Nauk SSSR ... Svetotekhnika. Svetotekhnicheskaya Komissiya Akademii Nauk SSSR [*A publication*]
Svetsaren Dtsch Ausg ... Svetsaren. Deutsche Ausgabe [*A publication*]
Svetsaren Ed Fr ... Svetsaren. Edition Francaise [*A publication*]
Svetsaren Weld Rev ... Svetsaren: A Welding Review [*A publication*]
SvExAb......... Svensk Exegetisk Arsbok [*A publication*]
SvExArsb...... Svensk Exegetisk Arsbok [*A publication*]
SVEZ.......... Elorza, Apure [*Venezuela*] [*ICAO location identifier*] (ICLI)
SVF............. Save [*Benin*] [*Airport symbol*] (OAG)
SVF............. Silverleaf Resources Ltd. [*Vancouver Stock Exchange symbol*]
SVF............. Standard Vented Furnace
SVF............. State Variable Filter
SVF............. Stoicorum Veterum Fragmenta [*A publication*] (OCD)
Sv Farm Tid ... Svensk Farmaceutisk Tidskrift [*A publication*]
SVF Fachorgan Textilveredl ... SVF [*Svetsteknika Foereningen*] Fachorgan fuer Textilveredlung [*A publication*]
SVFM........ Caracas/Generelisimo Francisco De Miranda Base Aerea La Carlota, Miranda [*Venezuela*] [*ICAO location identifier*] (ICLI)
SVFR......... Special Visual Flight Rules [*Aviation*]
SVG.......... Gids voor Personeelsbeleid. Arbeidsvraagstukken en Sociale Verzekering [*A publication*]
SVG.......... Saphenous Vein Graft [*Cardiology*]
SVG.......... Sauvagine [*A polypeptide*]
SVG.......... Servicing
SVG.......... Spiritus Vini Gallici [*Brandy*] [*Pharmacy*] (ROG)
SVG....... Stavanger [*Norway*] [*Airport symbol*] (OAG)
SVG.......... Stephens Graphics [*AMEX symbol*] (SPSG)
SVG.......... Sun Valley Gold Mines Ltd. [*Vancouver Stock Exchange symbol*]
SVGC........ Secure Voice and Graphic Conferencing (MCD)
SVGD........ Guasdualito, Apure [*Venezuela*] [*ICAO location identifier*] (ICLI)
SVGI......... Guiria, Sucre [*Venezuela*] [*ICAO location identifier*] (ICLI)
SVGI......... Silicon Valley Group, Incorporated [*NASDAQ symbol*] (NQ)
SVGLA...... Sovetskaya Geologiya [*A publication*]
SVGS......... Savings
SVGT........ Guasipati, Bolivar [*Venezuela*] [*ICAO location identifier*] (ICLI)
SVGU........ Guanare, Portuguesa [*Venezuela*] [*ICAO location identifier*] (ICLI)
SVGU........ Sveriges Geologiska Undersoekning [*A publication*]
SVH.......... Seven Mile High Resources, Inc. [*Vancouver Stock Exchange symbol*]
SVH.......... Severely Handicapped
SVH.......... Statesville, NC [*Location identifier*] [*FAA*] (FAAL)
SVHE........ Society for Values in Higher Education (EA)
SVHG........ Higuerote, Miranda [*Venezuela*] [*ICAO location identifier*] (ICLI)
SVHS........ Super Video Home System [*Japan Victor Co.*]
SVI............. St. Vincent [*St. Vincent*] [*Seismograph station code, US Geological Survey*] [*Closed*] (SEIS)
SVI............. San Vincente Del Caguan [*Colombia*] [*Airport symbol*] (OAG)
SVI............. Service Interception [*Telecommunications*] (TEL)
SVI............. Singapore Volunteer Infantry [*British military*] (DMA)
SVI............. Single Vendor Integrity (MCD)
SVI............. Single Vibrational Level [*Physics*]
SVI............. Sludge Volume Index [*Wastewater treatment*]
SVI............. Sound Velocity Indicator
SVI............. Spiritus Vini Industrialis [*Industrial Alcohol*] [*Pharmacy*]
SVI............. Stroke Volume Index [*Medicine*]
SVI............. Sveriges Riksbank. Quarterly Review [*A publication*]
SvI............. Svizzera Italiana [*A publication*]
SVI............. System Verification Installation
SVIA......... Specialty Vehicles Institute of America (EA)
SVIB......... Strong Vocational Interest Blank [*Psychology*]
SVIC......... Icabaru, Bolivar [*Venezuela*] [*ICAO location identifier*] (ICLI)
SVIC.......... Shock and Vibration Information Center [*Terminated*] [*Navy*] (MCD)
SVIC.......... Silicon Valley Information Center [*Database producer*] (IID)
SVIC.......... Sweet Victory, Incorporated [*New York, NY*] [*NASDAQ symbol*] (NQ)
SVICLC..... Shenandoah Valley Independent College Library Cooperative [*Library network*]
SVIE.......... Isla De Coche, Nueva Esparta [*Venezuela*] [*ICAO location identifier*] (ICLI)

SVIL.......... Seville Energy Corp. [*NASDAQ symbol*] (NQ)
SVIMS...... Short Vehicle Integrated Management System
Svinovod..... Svinovodstvo [*A publication*]
SVIO......... Superintending Veterinary Investigation Officer [*Ministry of Agriculture, Fisheries, and Food*] [*British*]
SVIP......... Secure Voice Improvement Program [*DoD*]
SVIPA....... Swiss Videotex Industry Association [*Information service or system*] (IID)
SVIPA....... Swiss Viewdata Information Providers Association [*Zurich*] [*Telecommunications*] (TSSD)
SVITA...... Spectravideo, Inc. Cl A [*NASDAQ symbol*] (NQ)
SVJ............ Lompoc, CA [*Location identifier*] [*FAA*] (FAAL)
SVJ............ Sovetska Veda. Jazykoveda [*A publication*]
SVJ............ Steed Ventures Corp. [*Formerly, Poney Explorations Ltd.*] [*Vancouver Stock Exchange symbol*]
SVJ............ Svolvaer [*Norway*] [*Airport symbol*] (OAG)
SVJC......... Paraguana/Josefa Camejo Internacional, Falcon [*Venezuela*] [*ICAO location identifier*] (ICLI)
SvJerTs...... Svenska Jerusalems-Foereningens Tidskrift [*Uppsala*] [*A publication*]
Sv JT......... Svensk Juristtidning [*Sweden*] [*A publication*] (DLA)
SVKA........ Kavanayen, Bolivar [*Venezuela*] [*ICAO location identifier*] (ICLI)
SVKM........ Kamarata, Bolivar [*Venezuela*] [*ICAO location identifier*] (ICLI)
Sv Kraftverksforen Publ ... Svenska Kraftverksfoereningens Publikationer [*A publication*]
SVKTA...... Strassenverkehrstechnik [*A publication*]
SVL........... Sapphire Vacuum Lens
SVL........... Savonlinna [*Finland*] [*Airport symbol*] (OAG)
SVL........... Scripps Visibility Laboratory
SVL........... Silver Lake Resources, Inc. [*Toronto Stock Exchange symbol*]
SVL........... Snout-to-Vent Length [*Biometry*]
SVL........... Star Valley Resources [*Vancouver Stock Exchange symbol*]
SVL........... Studien zur Vergleichenden Literaturgeschichte [*A publication*]
SVL........... Support Validation Laboratory [*Army*]
SVLA......... Steered Vertical Line Array [*Military*] (CAAL)
SVLAA...... Svenska Laekartidningen [*A publication*]
SVLB......... Sapphire Vacuum Lens Blank
SVLF......... La Fria, Tachira [*Venezuela*] [*ICAO location identifier*] (ICLI)
SVLF......... Shipboard Very Low Frequency [*Navy*] (NG)
SVLH......... Surma Valley Light Horse [*British military*] (DMA)
SVLKAO... Collection of Scientific Works. Faculty of Medicine. Charles University (Hradec Kralove) [*A publication*]
SVLL......... Short Vertical Lower Left
SvLm.......... Svenska Landsmal och Svenskt Folkliv [*A publication*]
SVLO......... La Orchila - Dependencia Federal [*Venezuela*] [*ICAO location identifier*] (ICLI)
SVLOG...... Servicing Log [*Telecommunications*] (TEL)
SVLP......... Special Virus Leukemia Program [*National Cancer Institute*]
SVLR......... Short Vertical Lower Right
SVLTE....... Services Valve Life Test Establishment [*British*] (MCD)
SVLW........ Sectoraal Verband Landbouwwetenschappen [*Committee on International Education in Agricultural Sciences*] [*Netherlands*] (EAIO)
SVM.......... Salem, MI [*Location identifier*] [*FAA*] (FAAL)
SVM.......... Seminal Vesicle Mesenchyme [*Anatomy*]
SVM.......... Seminal Vesicle Microsome [*Anatomy*]
SVM.......... Semitrailer Van Mount
SVM.......... Service Volontaire Mennonite [*Mennonite Voluntary Service*]
SVM.......... ServiceMaster Limited Partnership [*NYSE symbol*] (SPSG)
SVM.......... Ship Vulnerability Model (MCD)
SVM.......... Silicon Video Memory
SVM.......... Silver City [*New Mexico*] [*Seismograph station code, US Geological Survey*] (SEIS)
SVM.......... Silver Hart Mines Ltd. [*Vancouver Stock Exchange symbol*]
SVM.......... Sisters of the Visitation of the Congregation of the Immaculate Heart of Mary [*Roman Catholic religious order*]
SVM.......... Special Vehicle Management [*Automotive engineering*]
SVM.......... Spiritus Vini Methylatus [*Methylated Spirit*] [*Pharmacy*]
SVM.......... Stamp Vending Machine (DCTA)
SvM.......... Svensk Missionstidskrift [*A publication*]
SVM.......... System Validation Model (NVT)
SVMA........ Space Vehicle Mission Analysis
SVMC........ Maracaibo/La Chinita Internacional, Zulia [*Venezuela*] [*ICAO location identifier*] (ICLI)
SVMCD8.... Sciences Veterinaires Medecine Comparee [*A publication*]
SVMD........ Merida/Alberto Carnevalli, Merida [*Venezuela*] [*ICAO location identifier*] (ICLI)
SVMG....... Margarita/Internacional del Caribe Gral Santiago Marino, Neuva Esparta [*Venezuela*] [*ICAO location identifier*] (ICLI)
SVMH....... Silver Hart Mines Ltd. [*NASDAQ symbol*] (NQ)
SVMI......... Caracas/Simon Bolivar Internacional Maiquetia Distrito Federal [*Venezuela*] [*ICAO location identifier*] (ICLI)
SVMP........ Caracas/Metropolitano Internacional, Miranda [*Venezuela*] [*ICAO location identifier*] (ICLI)
SVMPCG .. Grasslands National Park, Parks Canada [*Parc National Grasslands, Parcs Canada*] Val Marie, Saskatchewan [*Library symbol*] [*National Library of Canada*] (NLC)

SVMR....... Maracay/Centro Nacional de Comunicaciones/Meteorologicos, Aragua [*Venezuela*] [*ICAO location identifier*]   (ICLI)
SVMT....... Maturin/Internacional, Monagas [*Venezuela*] [*ICAO location identifier*]   (ICLI)
SVMTR..... Servomotor [*Control systems*]
SVN .... Savannah, GA [*Location identifier*] [*FAA*]   (FAAL)
SVN .... South Vietnam   (CINC)
SVNAB.... Svensk Naturvetenskap [*A publication*]
SVNESE... South Vietnamese
SVNM ...... St. Vincent National Movement [*Political party*]   (PPW)
SVNRF ..... State of Vietnam Ribbon of Friendship [*Military decoration*]   (AABC)
SVNVAC... Sunny Von Bulow National Victim Advocacy Center [*Later, NVC*]   (EA)
SVO .... Moscow [*USSR*] Sheremetyevo Airport [*Airport symbol*]   (OAG)
SVO .... Senior Veterinary Officer [*British military*]   (DMA)
SVO .... Servo   (KSC)
SVO .... Space Vehicle Operations   (MCD)
SVO .... Special Vehicle Operation [*Ford Motor Co.*]
SVO .... Subject-Verb-Object [*Education of the hearing-impaired*]
SVOD .... Soviet Aircraft Navigation and Landing System   (MCD)
SVOIR....... Specification Verification Open Item Report
Svoista Veshchesty Str Mol ... Svoistva Veshchestv i Stroenie Molekul [*A publication*]
Svojstva At Yader ... Svojstva Atomnykh Yader [*A publication*]
SVP........... Bie [*Angola*] [*Airport symbol*]   (OAG)
SVP........... St. Louis Public Library, St. Louis, MO [*OCLC symbol*]   (OCLC)
SVP........... Security Vehicle Patrol [*Air Force*]   (AFM)
SVP........... Seminal Vesicle Protein [*Biochemistry*]
SVP........... Senior Vice President
SVP........... Service Processor   (BUR)
SVP........... Services Vegetable Production [*British military*]   (DMA)
SVP........... Sewer Vent Pipe
SVP........... S'il Vous Plait [*If You Please*] [*French*]
SVP........... Silver Princess Resources [*Vancouver Stock Exchange symbol*]
SVP........... Small Volume Parenteral [*Pharmacy*]
SVP........... Snake Venom Phosphodiesterase [*Also, SVPDE*] [*An enzyme*]
SVP........... Societe pour Vaincre la Pollution [*Canada*]
SVP........... Society of St. Vincent de Paul
SVP........... Society of Vertebrate Paleontology   (EA)
SVP........... Sound Velocity Profile
SVP........... Specific Vocational Preparation [*US Employment Service*] [*Department of Labor*]
SVP........... Steam Vacuum Pulse
SVP........... Sudtiroler Volkspartei [*South Tyrolean People's Party*] [*Italy*] [*Political party*]   (EAIO)
SVP........... Supplemental Vacation Plan
SVPA........ Puerto Ayacucho, T. F. Amazonas [*Venezuela*] [*ICAO location identifier*]   (ICLI)
SVPB .... Supraventricular Premature Beats [*Cardiology*]
SVPC .... Puerto Cabello/Gral. Bartolome Salom Internacional, Carabobo [*Venezuela*] [*ICAO location identifier*]   (ICLI)
SVPDE ...... Snake Venom Phosphodiesterase [*Also, SVP*] [*An enzyme*]
SVPIA ...... Surface and Vacuum Physics Index [*A publication*]
SVPM........ San Cristobal/Paramillo, Tachira [*Venezuela*] [*ICAO location identifier*]   (ICLI)
SVPM........ Small Vehicles, Program Manager
SVPP .... Schweizerische Vereinigung fuer Parapsychologie
SVPP/A..... Archivos Venezolanas de Puericultura y Pediatria. Sociedad Venezolana de Puericultura y Pediatria [*A publication*]
SVPR .... Guayana/Puerto Ordaz Internacional, Bolivar [*Venezuela*] [*ICAO location identifier*]   (ICLI)
SVPT .... Palmarito, Apure [*Venezuela*] [*ICAO location identifier*]   (ICLI)
SVPVA ...... Sbornik Vedeckych Praci. Vysoka Skola Chemickotechnologicka (Pardubice) [*A publication*]
SVQ .... Seville [*Spain*] [*Airport symbol*]   (OAG)
SVR........... Severe   (FAAC)
SVR........... Singapore Volunteer Rifles [*British military*]   (DMA)
SVR........... Slant Visual Range
SVR........... Society of Vietnamese Rangers   (EA)
SVR........... Spiritus Vini Rectificatus [*Rectified Spirit of Wine*] [*Pharmacy*]
SVR........... Super Video Recorder
SVR........... Supply-Voltage Rejection   (IEEE)
SVR........... Systemic Vascular Resistance [*Medicine*]
SVRA........ Sportscar Vintage Racing Association   (EA)
SVRA........ State Vehicular Recreation Area
SVRB........ Supervisor Request Block [*Data processing*]   (BUR)
SVRBAR ... Sbornik Vysoka Skola Zemedelska v Praze Provozne Ekonomicke Fakulty v Ceskych Budejovicich Biologicka Rada [*A publication*]
SVRD........ Silicon Voltage Reference Diode
SVRDA..... Soviet Radiochemistry [*English Translation*] [*A publication*]
SVREP ...... Southwest Voter Registration Education Project   (EA)
SVRI .... Systemic Vascular Resistance Index
SVRL........ Several   (FAAC)
SVRL........ Silvar-Lisco [*NASDAQ symbol*]   (NQ)
SVRN .... Sovereign Bancorp, Inc. [*NASDAQ symbol*]   (NQ)
SVRR........ Software Verification Readiness Review [*NASA*]   (NASA)

SVRS .... Los Roques, Dependencia Federal [*Venezuela*] [*ICAO location identifier*]   (ICLI)
SVS............ Eastern Commuter, Inc. [*Hasbrouck Heights, NJ*] [*FAA designator*]   (FAAC)
SVS............ Saga-Book. Viking Society for Northern Research [*A publication*]
SVS............ Schedule Visibility System   (AAG)
SVS............ Secure Voice Switch
SVS............ Secure Voice System [*Telecommunications*]
SVS............ Service School [*Military*]
SVS............ Silverside Resources, Inc. [*Toronto Stock Exchange symbol*]
SVS............ Single Virtual Storage [*IBM Corp.*] [*Data processing*]
SVS............ Slandsville [*South Carolina*] [*Seismograph station code, US Geological Survey*]   (SEIS)
SVS............ Society for Vascular Surgery   (EA)
SVS............ Sound Velocity Structure
SVS............ Space Vehicle Simulator   (AAG)
SVS............ Spectroradiometer Visible System
SVS............ Spinning Vehicle Simulator
SVS............ Stabilized Viewing System
SVS............ Statistica Neerlandica [*A publication*]
SVS............ Stevens Village [*Alaska*] [*Airport symbol*]   (OAG)
SVS............ Still-Camera Video System [*Canon, Inc.*]
SVS............ Suit Ventilation System [*Aerospace*]   (MCD)
SVS............ Synthetic Vision Systems, Inc.
SVSA .... San Antonio, Tachira [*Venezuela*] [*ICAO location identifier*]   (ICLI)
SVSB .... Santa Barbara De Barinas, Barinas [*Venezuela*] [*ICAO location identifier*]   (ICLI)
SVSC .... San Carlos De Rio Negro, T. F. Amazonas [*Venezuela*] [*ICAO location identifier*]   (ICLI)
SVSC .... Space Vehicle Sectoring Code
SVSE .... Santa Elena de Uairen, Bolivar [*Venezuela*] [*ICAO location identifier*]   (ICLI)
SVSHA ...... Sovetskii Shakhtior [*A publication*]
SVSHKG... Schriften. Verein fuer Schleswig-Holsteinische Kirchengeschichte [*A publication*]
SVSL .... Skrifter Utgivna. Vetenskaps-Societeten i Lund [*A publication*]
SVSO........ Santo Domingo/Mayor Buenaventura Vivas A. B., Tachira [*Venezuela*] [*ICAO location identifier*]   (ICLI)
SVSO........ Superintending Victualling Stores Officer [*British*]
S V Sound Vib ... S V. Sound and Vibration [*A publication*]
SVSP .... San Felipe/Subteniente Nestor Arias, Yaracuy [*Venezuela*] [*ICAO location identifier*]   (ICLI)
SVSP .... School Volunteer Services Program
SV-SP....... Spray Volume - Spray Pressure
SVSPO....... Sbornik Vysoke Skoly Pedagogicke v Olomouci [*A publication*]
SVSPO(JL) ... Sbornik Vysoke Skoly Pedagogicke v Olomouci. Jazyka a Literatura [*A publication*]
SVSPP....... Sbornik Vysoke Skoly Pedagogicke v Praze. Jazyka a Literatura [*A publication*]
SVSR .... San Fernando De Apure, Apure [*Venezuela*] [*ICAO location identifier*]   (ICLI)
SVSR .... Silverside Resources, Inc. [*NASDAQ symbol*]   (NQ)
SVSS.......... Sprague Voltage-Sensitive Switch
SVST .... San Tome, Anzoategui [*Venezuela*] [*ICAO location identifier*]   (ICLI)
SVSThR .... Sammlung Gemeinverstaendlicher Vortraege und Schriften aus dem Gebiet der Theologie und der Religionsgeschichte [*A publication*]
SVSZ .... Santa Barbara Del Zulia, Zulia [*Venezuela*] [*ICAO location identifier*]   (ICLI)
SVT............ St. Vincent [*St. Vincent*] [*Seismograph station code, US Geological Survey*]   (SEIS)
SVT............ Secure Voice Terminal   (MCD)
SVT............ Self Valuation Test [*Psychology*]
SVT............ Servotronics, Inc. [*AMEX symbol*]   (SPSG)
SVT............ Silicon Vidicon Target
SVT............ Silverton Resources Ltd. [*Toronto Stock Exchange symbol*]
SVT............ Solar Vacuum Telescope
SVT............ Space Vehicle Test
SVT............ Space Visualization Test
SVT............ Spiritus Vini Tenuis [*Proof Spirit of Wine*] [*Pharmacy*]
SVT............ Stray Voltage Tester
SVT............ Supplements. Vetus Testamentum [*Leiden*] [*A publication*]
SVT............ Supralaryngeal Vocal Tract [*Anatomy*]
SVT............ Supraventricular Tachycardia [*Cardiology*]
SvT............ Svenska Texter [*A publication*]
SVT............ System Validation Testing
SVTC......... Surrey Volunteer Training Corps [*British military*]   (DMA)
SVTC......... Tucupita, T. F. Delta Amacuro [*Venezuela*] [*ICAO location identifier*]   (ICLI)
SVTFDI..... Sugarcane Variety Tests in Florida [*A publication*]
SvTK......... Svensk Teologisk Kvartalskrift [*A publication*]
SvTKv....... Svensk Teologisk Kvartalskrift [*A publication*]
SVTL........ Semivital
SVTL........ Services Valve Test Laboratory [*British*]   (NATG)
SVTM........ Shielded Voltage Tunable Magnetron
SVTM........ Tumeremo, Bolivar [*Venezuela*] [*ICAO location identifier*]   (ICLI)
S/VTOL .... Short/Vertical Takeoff and Landing [*Aviation*]   (NATG)

SVTP.........	Sound, Velocity, Temperature, Pressure
SVTP.........	Studia in Veteris Testamenti Pseudepigrapha [*A publication*]
SVTQ.........	St. Vladimir's Theological Quarterly [*A publication*]
Sv Trav Pap ...	Svensk Traevaru- och Pappersmassetidning [*A publication*]
SVT(S)......	Space Vehicle Test (Supervisor)
SvTs...........	Svensk Tidskrift [*A publication*]
SVTT..........	Surface Vessel Torpedo Tube (NVT)
SVU	Savusavu [*Fiji*] [*Airport symbol*] (OAG)
S/VU.........	Sound/Video Unlimited
SVU	Spur Ventures [*Vancouver Stock Exchange symbol*]
SVU	Super Valu Stores, Inc. [*NYSE symbol*] (SPSG)
SVU	Surface Vehicular Unit
SVU	System Verification Unit
SVUL........	Short Vertical Upper Left
SVUL........	Suomen Valtakunnan Uhreiluliitto [*Finnish Central Sports Federation*]
SVUM	Uriman, Bolivar [*Venezuela*] [*ICAO location identifier*] (ICLI)
SVUOJ......	Sri Venkateswara University. Oriental Journal [*A publication*]
SVUQ	Uonquen, Bolivar [*Venezuela*] [*ICAO location identifier*] (ICLI)
SVUR.........	Short Vertical Upper Right
SVV............	Sit Venia Verbo [*Forgive the Expression*] [*Latin*]
SVVA.........	Valencia/Internacional, Carabobo [*Venezuela*] [*ICAO location identifier*] (ICLI)
SVVL.........	Valera/Dr. Antonio Nicolas Briceno, Trujillo [*Venezuela*] [*ICAO location identifier*] (ICLI)
SVVP.........	Valle De La Pascua, Guarico [*Venezuela*] [*ICAO location identifier*] (ICLI)
SVW	Silverhawk Resources [*Vancouver Stock Exchange symbol*]
SVW	Sparrevohn [*Alaska*] [*Seismograph station code, US Geological Survey*] (SEIS)
SVW	Sparrevohn, AK [*Location identifier*] [*FAA*] (FAAL)
SVX............	Socanav, Inc. [*Toronto Stock Exchange symbol*]
SVY...........	Survey
Svy Sports ...	Survey on Sports Attendance [*A publication*]
SVZ............	San Antonio [*Venezuela*] [*Airport symbol*] (OAG)
SVZ............	Sisters of Charity of St. Vincent de Paul [*Roman Catholic religious order*]
SVZM.......	Maiquetia [*Venezuela*] [*ICAO location identifier*] (ICLI)
SVZZ.........	Maiquetia [*Venezuela*] [*ICAO location identifier*] (ICLI)
SW	Methylphosphonous Dichloride [*Toxic compound*] [*Army symbol*]
SW	Namib Air (Pty) Ltd. [*South Africa*] [*ICAO designator*] (FAAC)
Sw..............	Royal Swedish Library (Kungl. Biblioteket), Stockholm, Sweden [*Library symbol*] [*Library of Congress*] (LCLS)
SW	Sadler's Wells Theatre [*London*]
SW	Salt Water
SW	Sandwich-Wound (DEN)
SW	Sapwood [*Botany*]
SW	Satan Worship
SW	Science Wonder Stories [*A publication*]
SW	Seaboard World Airlines, Inc.
SW	Seawater
S/W............	Seaworthy (ADA)
SW	Secret Writing [*Espionage*]
SW	Secretary of War [*Obsolete*]
SW	Security Watch
SW	Semiweekly
SW	Senior Warden [*Freemasonry*]
SW	Senior Wolf [*An accomplished philanderer*] [*Slang*]
SW	Senior Woodward [*Ancient Order of Foresters*]
SW	Sent Wrong [*i.e., misdirected*]
SW	Service Water [*Nuclear energy*] (NRCH)
SW	Sewing Machine Repair Program [*Association of Independent Colleges and Schools specialization code*]
SW	Shallow Water Attack Craft [*Navy symbol*]
SW	Shallow Water Diver [*British military*] (DMA)
SW	Shelter Warden [*British Home Defence*] [*World War II*]
SW	Shipper's Weights [*Bills of lading*]
SW	Ship's Warrant [*Marine Corps*]
SW	Shirl J. Winter [*Designer's mark when appearing on US coins*]
SW	Short Weight
SW	Shortwave [*Electronics*]
SW	Shotgun Wedding [*Forced marriage*] [*Slang*]
SW	Side Wheel
SW	Sidewinder
SW	Simple Wear
SW	Single Wall (AAG)
SW	Single Weight
SW	Slavic Word [*A publication*]
SW	Slow Wave [*Electroencephalograph*]
S & W........	Smith and Wesson (MCD)
SW	Smith's Weekly [*A publication*]
SW	Snow [*Ship's rigging*] (ROG)
SW	Snow Showers [*Meteorology*] (FAAC)
S & W........	Soap and Water [*Enema*] [*Medicine*]
SW	Social Work [*or Worker*]
SW	Socialist Worker [*A publication*] (APTA)
SW	Socket Weld
SW	Software [*Data processing*]

SW	Softwood
SW	Solar Wing (MCD)
SW	Solid Waste
SW	Son of a Witch (EA)
SW	Sound Whistle [*British railroad term*]
SW	South Wales
SW	South and West [*A publication*]
S & W........	South and West [*A publication*]
SW	South Western Reporter [*National Reporter System*] [*A publication*] (DLA)
SW	Southwest
SW	Southwest Africa (MCD)
SW	Southwestern Musician - Texas Music Educator [*A publication*]
SW	Special Warfare
SW	Special Weapon
SW	Specific Weight
SW	Sperm Whale
SW	Spontaneous Swallows [*Gastroenterology*]
SW	Spore Wall [*Botany*]
SW	Spores Injected into Wounded Kernels [*Plant pathology*]
SW	Spotweld [*Technical drawings*]
SW	Stall Warning System (MCD)
SW	Standard Winter
SW	Standby Service Water [*Nuclear energy*] (NRCH)
SW	Station Wagon [*Car*]
SW	Status of Women [*Canada*]
SW	Status Word
SW	Steam Wagon [*British*]
SW	Steelworker [*Navy rating*]
SW	Stenciled Weight
SW	Sterile Water
SW	Stewart-Warner Corp.
SW	Stock Width [*Construction or manufacturing materials*]
SW	Stone & Webster, Inc. [*NYSE symbol*] (SPSG)
SW	Strafwetboek [*A publication*]
SW	Strategic Warning (MCD)
SW	Strategic Wing [*Military*]
SW	Stud-Arc Welding
SW	Subjective Weakness [*Medicine*]
SW	Sueddeutsche Waehrung [*South German Currency*] [*German*]
SW	Surface Warfare (MCD)
Sw.............	Swabey's English Admiralty Reports [*A publication*] (DLA)
Sw.............	Swabey's English Ecclesiastical Reports [*1855-59*] [*A publication*] (DLA)
sw	Swamp [*Maps and charts*]
SW	Swamp (ROG)
Sw.............	Swann [*Blood group*]
Sw.............	Swan's Tennessee Reports [*31, 32 Tennessee*] [*A publication*] (DLA)
Sw.............	Swanston's English Chancery Reports [*A publication*] (DLA)
SW	Swash
SW	Swear
SW	Swearingen Aircraft [*ICAO aircraft manufacturer identifier*] (ICAO)
SW	Sweden
sw	Sweden [*MARC country of publication code*] [*Library of Congress*] (LCCP)
Sw.............	Sweeney's New York Superior Court Reports [*A publication*] (DLA)
SW	Swell Organ
Sw.............	Swinton's Scotch Justiciary Cases [*A publication*] (DLA)
SW	Swiss
SW	Switch (AAG)
SW	Switchband Wound [*Relay*]
SW	Switzerland
S1W	Security of the First World [*Rap music group*]
SW1	Steelworker, First Class [*Navy rating*]
SW2	Steelworker, Second Class [*Navy rating*]
SW3	Steelworker, Third Class [*Navy rating*]
SWA	Reports of the High Court of South-West Africa [*1920-46*] [*A publication*] (DLA)
SWA	Scheduler Work Area [*Data processing*] (IBMDP)
SWA	Scope of Word Addendum (MCD)
SWA	Seriously Wounded in Action [*Military*]
SWA	Shallow Water Acoustics
SWA	Shantou [*China*] [*Airport symbol*] (OAG)
SWA	Shayna International Industry [*Vancouver Stock Exchange symbol*]
SWA	Single Wire Armored [*Cables*]
SWA	Sitzungsberichte. Wiener Akademie [*A publication*]
SWA	Solo Wargamers Association (EAIO)
SWA	Southern Water Authority [*British*] (DCTA)
SWA	Southern Wholesalers Association [*Atlanta, GA*] (EA)
SWA	Southern Woodwork Association (EA)
SWA	Southwest Africa
SWA	Southwest Airlines Co. [*San Antonio, TX*] [*FAA designator*] (FAAC)
SWA	Southwest Art [*A publication*]
SWA	Southwest Asia
SWA	Specialty Wire Association [*Later, AWPA*]
SWA	Standing Wave Apparatus

SWA .... State Welfare Agency [*Social Security Administration*]   (OICC)
SWA .... Straight Wire Antenna
SWA .... Stunt Women of America [*Later, SAMP*]   (EA)
SWA .... Superwomen's Anonymous   (EA)
SWA .... Support Work Authorization [*NASA*]   (MCD)
swa .... Swahili [*MARC language code*] [*Library of Congress*]   (LCCP)
SWA .... Swan Island [*Swan Island*] [*Seismograph station code, US Geological Survey*] [*Closed*]   (SEIS)
SWA .... Swedish Warmblood Association   (EA)
SWA .... Swissair [*Airline*]   (MCD)
SWA .... System Work Area
SWAA .... Slovak Writers and Artists Association   (EA)
SWAA .... Society of Wildlife Artists of Australasia
SWAA .... Spacelab Window Adapter Assembly   (NASA)
Swab........... Swabey's English Ecclesiastical Reports [*1855-59*] [*A publication*]   (DLA)
Swab Admr ... Swabey's English Admiralty Reports [*166 English Reprint*] [*A publication*]   (DLA)
Swab Div.... Swabey on Divorce and Matrimonial Causes [*3rd ed.*] [*1859*] [*A publication*]   (DLA)
Swabey Adm ... Swabey's English Admiralty Reports [*166 English Reprint*] [*1855-59*] [*A publication*]   (DLA)
Swabey Adm (Eng) ... Swabey's English Admiralty Reports [*166 English Reprint*] [*A publication*]   (DLA)
Swabey & T (Eng) ... Swabey and Tristram's Probate and Divorce Reports [*164 English Reports*] [*A publication*]   (DLA)
Swab & T ... Swabey and Tristram's Probate and Divorce Reports [*164 English Reprint*] [*A publication*]   (DLA)
Swab & Tr ... Swabey and Tristram's Probate and Divorce Reports [*164 English Reprint*] [*A publication*]   (DLA)
SWAC........ Shallow Water Attack Craft, Light   (MCD)
SWAC........ Special Warhead Arming Control   (AFM)
SWAC........ Specification Writers Association of Canada
SWAC........ Spotweld Accessory [*Tool*]   (AAG)
SWAC........ Standards Western Automatic Computer [*National Institute of Standards and Technology*]
SWACHA ... Southwestern Automated Clearing House Association
SWACS ..... Space Warning and Control System [*NORAD*]
SWAD .... Special Warfare Aviation Detachment [*Army*]
SWAD .... Subdivision of Work Authorization Document [*NASA*]   (NASA)
SWADE..... Second Wives of America Demanding Equality
SWADS..... Scheduler Work Area Data Set [*IBM Corp.*]   (MCD)
SWAFAC .. Southwest Atlantic Fisheries Advisory Commission [*FAO*]
SWAG .... Scientific Wild Aim Guess [*Bowdlerized version*]
SWAG .... Standard Written Agreement [*Military*]
SWAGS..... Scientific Wild-Aim Guess System [*Bowdlerized version*]   (MCD)
SWAJB...... South and Western Australia Judgements Bulletin [*A publication*]
SWAK....... Sealed with a Kiss [*Correspondence*]
SWAK....... Spinners and Weavers Association of Korea [*Defunct*]   (EA)
SWAL........ Shallow Water Attack Craft, Light [*Navy symbol*]   (NVT)
SwAL........ Southwestern American Literature [*A publication*]
SWAL........ StatesWest Airlines, Inc. [*Phoenix, AZ*] [*NASDAQ symbol*]   (NQ)
SWALC .... Southwest Academic Library Consortium [*Library network*]   (IID)
SWALCAKWS ... Sealed with a Lick 'Cause a Kiss Won't Stick [*Correspondence*]   (DSUE)
SWALK..... Sealed with a Loving Kiss [*Correspondence*]
SWALM..... Switch Alarm   (AAG)
SWAM ...... Shallow Water Attack Craft, Medium [*Navy symbol*]   (NVT)
SWAM ...... Sine Wave Amplitude Modulation
SWAMI..... Software-Aided Multiform Input [*Software*] [*Data processing*]
SWAMI..... Speech with Alternating Masking Index [*Discrimination test*]
SWAMI..... Stall Warning and Margin Indicator
SWAMI..... Standing Wave Area Monitor Indicator   (MUGU)
SWAMI..... Stanford Worldwide Acquisition of Meteorological Information [*Weather prediction system*]
SWAN .... Second Wives Association of North America   (EA)
SWAN .... Severe Weather Avoidance Nationwide [*National Oceanic and Atmospheric Administration*]
SWAN .... Swan Resources Ltd. [*NASDAQ symbol*]   (NQ)
Swan........... Swan's Tennessee Supreme Court Reports [*1851-53*] [*A publication*]   (DLA)
Swan........... Swanston's English Chancery Reports [*A publication*]   (DLA)
Swan Ch..... Swanston's English Chancery Reports [*A publication*]   (DLA)
Swan & CR St ... Swan and Critchfield's Revised Statutes [*Ohio*] [*A publication*]   (DLA)
Swan Eccl C ... Swan's Ecclesiastical Courts [*1830*] [*A publication*]   (DLA)
Swan Just... Swan's Justice [*Ohio*] [*A publication*]   (DLA)
SWANK .... Sealed with a Nice Kiss [*Correspondence*]
Swank .... Single Woman and No Kids [*Lifestyle classification*]
Swan Pl & Pr ... Swan on Pleading and Practice [*Ohio*] [*A publication*]   (DLA)
Swan Pr..... Swan on Practice [*Ohio*] [*A publication*]   (DLA)
SWANS...... State Wildlife Advisory News Service [*A publication*]   (APTA)
Swan's........ Swan's Tennessee Reports [*A publication*]   (DLA)
Swans......... Swanston's English Chancery Reports [*A publication*]   (DLA)

Swansea Coll Fac Ed J ... University College of Swansea. Collegiate Faculty of Education. Journal [*A publication*]
Swan's R .... Swan's Tennessee Reports [*A publication*]   (DLA)
Swan & S St ... Swan and Sayler's Supplement to the Revised Statutes [*Ohio*] [*A publication*]   (DLA)
Swan's St ... Swan's Ohio Statutes [*A publication*]   (DLA)
Swanst........ Swanston's English Chancery Reports [*36 English Reprint*] [*A publication*]   (DLA)
Swanst (Eng) ... Swanston's English Chancery Reports [*36 English Reprint*] [*A publication*]   (DLA)
Swan Tr...... Swan's Ohio Treatise [*A publication*]   (DLA)
SWANU .... South West Africa National Union [*Namibia*] [*Political party*]   (PPW)
SWAP........ Section on Women and Psychology [*Canadian Psychology Association*]
SWAP........ Severe Weather Avoidance Plan   (FAAC)
SWAP........ Smith-Winnick-Abrams-Prausnitz [*Vapor pressure correlation equation*]
SWAP........ Society for Wang Applications and Programs   (CSR)
SWAP........ Standard Wafer Array Programming
SWAP........ Stress Wave Analyzing Program
SWAP........ Student Woodlawn Area Project [*Chicago, IL*]
SWAP........ SWAP [*Salesmen with a Purpose*] Club International [*Arvada, CO*]   (EA)
SWAP........ Systems Worthiness Analysis Program [*FAA*]
SWAPO....... South West Africa People's Organization [*Namibia*]   (PD)
SWAPS ..... Ship Workload and Priority Systems [*Navy*]
SWAPS ..... Special Wire Assembly Planning System   (MCD)
SWAR........ Schwartz Brothers, Inc. [*NASDAQ symbol*]   (NQ)
Swarajya A ... Swarajya. Annual Number [*Madras*] [*A publication*]
SWARC..... Sydney Women Against Rape Collective [*Australia*]
SWARK..... Southwark [*Borough of London*]   (ROG)
SWARM..... Southwestern and Rocky Mountain Division [*AAAS division*]
SWARMS ... Small Warhead and Reentry Multiple System
SWAS....... Slim Whitman Appreciation Society of the United States   (EA)
SWASG..... Submarine Sensor to Weapon Alignment Steering Group
SWASGB .. Slim Whitman Appreciation Society of Great Britain   (EAIO)
SWASS..... Screwworm Adult Suppression System [*Medicine*]
SWASS..... Slim Whitman Appreciation Society of Scotland   (EAIO)
SWAT........ Secure Wire Access Terminal   (MCD)
SWAT........ Service Weapons Acceptability Tests
SWAT........ Sidewinder Acquisition Track   (IEEE)
SWAT........ Sidewinder Angle Tracking [*Missiles*]   (NG)
SWAT........ Simultaneous Wide Area Telecommunications Service   (TSSD)
SWAT........ Sipay Word Analysis Test [*Educational test*]
SWAT........ Solid Waste Assessment Test
SWAT........ Special Warfare Armored Transporter [*A vehicle*]
SWAT........ Special Weapons and Tactics [*Police*]
SWAT........ Squad Weapon Analytical Trainer   (MCD)
SWAT........ Strengths, Weaknesses, Alternatives, Threats [*Analysis*]   (ADA)
SWAT........ Stress Wave Analysis Technique
SWATCH ... Swiss Watch
SWATF ..... South-West Africa Territory Force
SWATH ... Small Waterplane Area Twin Hull [*Ship*] [*Navy*]
SWATM..... Shallow Water Antitraffic Mine [*Military*]
SWATS ..... Shallow Water Acoustic Tracking System [*Navy*]   (CAAL)
SWATT ..... Simulator for Antitank Tactical Training [*Army*]   (INF)
SWAW ...... Sitzungsberichte. Wiener Akademie der Wissenschaften [*A publication*]
SWAX........ Southwest Airlines Co. [*Air carrier designation symbol*]
Swaziland Annu Rep Geol Surv Mines Dep ... Swaziland. Annual Report. Geological Survey and Mines Department [*A publication*]
Swaziland Geol Surv Mines Dep Annu Rep ... Swaziland. Geological Survey and Mines Department. Annual Report [*A publication*]
SWB........... Sandia Wind Balloon   (MUGU)
SWB........... Scheduled Weather Broadcast   (FAAC)
SWB........... Short Wheelbase
SWB........... Single with Bath [*Hotel room*]
SWB........... South Wales Borderers [*Military unit*] [*British*]
SWB........... South Westchester BOCES [*Boards of Cooperative Educational Services*] [*UTLAS symbol*]
SWB........... Southwest Bancorp [*AMEX symbol*]   (SPSG)
SWB........... Southwestern Motor Freight Bureau, Dallas TX [*STAC*]
SWB........... Stichting Weg. Bulletin [*A publication*]
SWB........... Summary of World Broadcasts [*British Broadcasting Corporation*]
SWB........... Switchboard   (NATG)
SWBAA ..... Schweizerische Bauzeitung [*A publication*]
SWBD....... Switchboard   (AAG)
SWBHD ...... Swash Bulkhead
SWB & IE ... South West Business and Industry Exhibition [*British*]   (ITD)
SWBP........ Service Water Booster Pump [*Nuclear energy*]   (IEEE)
SWBRD....... Sun at Work in Britain [*A publication*]
SWBS .... Ship Work Breakdown Structure [*Navy*]   (CAAL)
SWBS .... Software Work Breakdown Structure   (MCD)
SWBS .... Solid Waste Barrel Storage [*Nuclear energy*]   (NRCH)
SWbS........ Southwest by South
SWBS .... Subcontract Work Breakdown Structure   (MCD)
SWbW .... Southwest by West
SWC .... Chief Steelworker [*Navy rating*]
SWC .... Omaha, NE [*Location identifier*] [*FAA*]   (FAAL)

SWC	Safe Water Coalition (EA)
SWC	Saline Water Conversion (MCD)
SWC	Scanning with Compensation
SWC	Second Wives Coalition (EA)
SWC	Semi-Wadcutter [*Ammunition*]
SWC	Senate Wine Caucus (EA)
SWC	Share the Work Coalition (EA)
SWC	Ship Weapon Coordinator (NVT)
SWC	Shock Wave Control
SWC	Shortwave Converter
SWC	Signals Warfare Center [*Army*] [*Warrenton, VA*]
SWC	Simon Wiesenthal Center (EA)
SWC	Single Wire Connector
SWC	Skywave Correction [*Aircraft navigation*]
SWC	Slovak World Congress (EAIO)
SWC	Social Work and Christianity [*A publication*]
SWC	Soil and Water Conservation Research Division [*of ARS, Department of Agriculture*]
SWC	Solar Wind Compensator [*or Composition*] [*Apollo 11*] [*NASA*]
SWC	Solid Wastes Cask [*Nuclear energy*] (NRCH)
SWC	Southwest Conference [*College sports*]
SWC	Southwestern Connecticut Library Council, Bridgeport, CT [*OCLC symbol*] (OCLC)
SWC	Special Warfare Center [*Later, J. F. Kennedy Center for Special Warfare*] [*Army*]
SWC	Special Warfare Craft [*Navy*] (CAAL)
SWC	Special Weapons Center [*or Command*]
SWC	Stall Warning Computer (MCD)
SWC	Stawell [*Australia*] [*Airport symbol*] (OAG)
SWC	Submersible Work Chamber
SWC	Superior White Crystal [*Sugar*]
SWC	Supreme War Council [*World War II*]
SWC	Surewin Resources Corporation [*Vancouver Stock Exchange symbol*]
SWC	Surface Warfare Coordinator [*Also, SUWC*] (NVT)
SWC	Surface Weapons Control
SWC	Surface Weapons Coordinator [*Navy*] (CAAL)
SWC	Surge Withstand Capability (IEEE)
SWC	System Weapons Coordinator [*Navy*] (CAAL)
SWCA.......	Constructionman Apprentice, Steelworker, Striker [*Navy rating*]
SWCA.......	Silver Wyandotte Club of America (EA)
SWCB.......	[*The*] Sandwich Co-Operative Bank [*Sandwich, MA*] [*NASDAQ symbol*] (NQ)
SWCC.......	Southwest Capital Corporation [*Albuquerque, NM*] [*NASDAQ symbol*] (NQ)
SWCDEF ..	South West Corridor Development and Employment Association [*Australia*]
SWCEL	Southwestern Cooperative Educational Laboratory
SWCENT ..	Switching Central [*Telecommunications*] (AABC)
SWCH	Switch (MCD)
SWCL.......	Seawater Conversion Laboratory (KSC)
SWCL.......	Special Warfare Craft, Light [*Navy symbol*]
SWCL.......	State Worker's Compensation Law (OICC)
SWCLR	Southwest Council of La Raza [*Mexican-American organization*] (EA)
SWCM.......	Master Chief Steelworker [*Navy rating*]
SW/CM.....	Software Configuration Management (MCD)
SWCM.......	Special Warfare Craft, Medium [*Navy symbol*]
SWCN	Constructionman, Steelworker, Striker [*Navy rating*]
SWCP.......	Saline Water Conversion Program [*Department of the Interior*]
SWCP.......	Salt-Water Circulating Pump (MSA)
SWCP.......	Society of the War of 1812 in the Commonwealth of Pennsylvania (EA)
SWCPI	Solid Waste Council of the Paper Industry (EA)
SWCS	SAC Warning and Control System (MCD)
SWCS.......	Salt-Water Cooling System [*Nuclear energy*] (NRCH)
SWCS.......	Senior Chief Steelworker [*Navy rating*]
SWCST	Saturn Workshop Cockpit Simulation Trainer [*NASA*]
SWD	Self-Wiring Data [*Telecommunications*] (TEL)
SWD	Senior Weapon Director [*Air Force*]
SWD	Seward, AK [*Location identifier*] [*FAA*] (FAAL)
SWD	Sewed
SWD	Short-Wave Diathermy [*Medicine*]
SWD	Side Water Depth
SWD	Single Word Dump
SWD	Sliding Watertight Door
SWD	Smaller Word
SWD	Softwood
SWD	Southwestern Division [*Army Corps of Engineers*]
SWD	Special Water Dispenser [*British military*] (DMA)
SWD	Standing Wave Detector
SWD	Stormwater Drain
SWD	Submarine Wire Dispenser
SWD	Sun, Wind, Dust [*Goggles*] (MCD)
SWD	Surface Wave Dielectrometer
SWD	Swaziland [*Swaziland*] [*Seismograph station code, US Geological Survey*] (SEIS)
SWD	Synchronous Wave Device
SW 2d	South Western Reporter, Second Series [*A publication*] (DLA)

SWDA	Solid Waste Disposal Act [*1965*]
SWDA	Step-Wise Discriminant Analysis
SWDB.......	Special Weapons Development Board
SWDC.......	Shock Wave Data Center [*Lawrence Radiation Laboratory*]
SWDF........	South-West Forests Defence Foundation [*Australia*]
SWDG	Surface Warfare Development Group [*Also, SURFWARDEVGRU*] [*Navy*]
SWDL........	Safe Winter Driving League (EA)
SWDL........	Surface Wave Delay Line
SWDS.......	Scrolls from the Wilderness of the Dead Sea. Smithsonian Institution Exhibit Catalogue [*Washington, DC*] (BJA)
SWDS........	Software Development System (MCD)
SWDVS......	Software Development and Verification System [*NASA*]
SWDYN......	Single-Wheel Dynamometer
SWE..........	Scalar Wave Equation
SWE..........	Shift Word, Extracting
SWE..........	Simulated Work Experience
SWE..........	Society of Wine Educators (EA)
SWE..........	Society of Women Engineers (EA)
SWE..........	Solar Wind Experiment [*NASA*] (KSC)
SWE..........	Spherical Wave Expansion [*Telecommunications*] (TEL)
SWE..........	Status Word Enable
SWE..........	Steelworker Erector [*Navy rating*]
SWE..........	Stress Wave Emission
SWE..........	Sweden [*ANSI three-letter standard code*] (CNC)
swe	Swedish [*MARC language code*] [*Library of Congress*] (LCCP)
SWE..........	Swensen's, Inc. [*Vancouver Stock Exchange symbol*]
SWEA........	Swedish Women's Educational Association, International (EA)
SWECS	Small Wind Energy Conversion Systems
SWED.......	Sweden [*or Swedish*]
SWED.......	Swedlow, Inc. [*NASDAQ symbol*] (NQ)
SwedAE	Swedish Antarctic Expedition [*1901-04*]
Swed Am TN ...	Swedish American Trade News [*A publication*]
Swed Bud ...	Swedish Budget [*A publication*]
Swed Dent J ...	Swedish Dental Journal [*A publication*]
Swed Dent J (Suppl) ...	Swedish Dental Journal (Supplement) [*A publication*]
Swed Foersvarets Forskningsanst FOA Rep ...	Sweden. Foersvarets Forskningsanstalt. FOA Report [*A publication*]
Swed Geol Unders Ser Ae Geol Kartbl 1:50000 ...	Sweden. Geologiska Undersoekning. Serie Ae. Geologiska Kartblad i Skala 1:50,000 [*A publication*]
Swed Geol Unders Ser C ...	Sweden. Geologiska Undersoekning. Serie C [*A publication*]
Swed Geol Unders Ser Ca Avh Uppsatser ...	Sweden. Geologiska Undersoekning. Serie Ca. Avhandlingar och Uppsatser [*A publication*]
Swed Geotech Inst Proc ...	Swedish Geotechnical Institute. Proceedings [*A publication*]
Swed Geotech Inst Rep ...	Swedish Geotechnical Institute. Report [*A publication*]
Swed Inst Agric Eng Circ ...	Swedish Institute of Agricultural Engineering. Circular [*A publication*]
SWEDIS....	Swedish Drug Information System [*Swedish National Board of Health and Welfare*] [*Databank*] (IID)
Swedish Aust & Swedish NZ Trade J ...	Swedish-Australian and Swedish-New Zealand Trade Journal [*A publication*] (APTA)
Swedish Deep-Sea Expedition Repts ...	Swedish Deep-Sea Expedition. Reports [*A publication*]
Swedish Ec ...	Swedish Economy [*A publication*]
Swedish Econ ...	Swedish Economy [*A publication*]
Swedish Hist Soc Yearbook ...	Swedish Historical Society. Yearbook [*A publication*]
Swedish J Econ ...	Swedish Journal of Economics [*A publication*]
Swed J Agric Res ...	Swedish Journal of Agricultural Research [*A publication*]
Swed J Econ ...	Swedish Journal of Economics [*A publication*]
SWEDL.....	Southwest Educational Development Laboratory
Swed Pap J ...	Swedish Paper Journal [*A publication*]
Swed State Shipbuild Exp Tank Report ...	Swedish State Shipbuilding Experiment Tank. Report [*A publication*]
SWEDTEL ...	Swedish Telecoms International AB [*Telecommunications*] (TSSD)
Swed Univ Agric Sci Dep Agric Eng Rep ...	Swedish University of Agricultural Sciences. Department of Agricultural Engineering. Report [*A publication*]
Swed Univ Agric Sci Dep Farm Build Rep ...	Swedish University of Agricultural Sciences. Department of Farm Buildings. Report [*A publication*]
Swed Univ Agric Sci Dep Hortic Sci Rep ...	Swedish University of Agricultural Sciences. Department of Horticultural Science. Report [*A publication*]
Swed Univ Agric Sci Dep Microbiol Rep ...	Swedish University of Agricultural Sciences. Department of Microbiology. Report [*A publication*]
Swed Univ Agric Sci Dep Plant Husb Rep ...	Swedish University of Agricultural Sciences. Department of Plant Husbandry. Report [*A publication*]
Swed Univ Agric Sci Rep For Ecol For Soils ...	Swedish University of Agricultural Sciences. Reports in Forest Ecology and Forest Soils [*A publication*]
Swed Weed Conf Rep ...	Swedish Weed Conference. Reports [*A publication*]

Swed Wildl Res (Viltrevy) ... Swedish Wildlife Research (Viltrevy) [*A publication*]
SWEE........ Southwest Electronic Exhibit
Sween........ Sweeney's New York Superior Court Reports [*31-32 New York*] [*1869-70*] [*A publication*] (DLA)
Sweeney (NY) ... Sweeney's New York Superior Court Reports [*31-32 New York*] [*A publication*] (DLA)
Sweeny........ Sweeney's New York Superior Court Reports [*31-32 New York*] [*A publication*] (DLA)
SWEEP ..... Structures with Error Expurgation Program
SWEET ..... Stay at Work, Earn Extra Time [*United Auto Workers*]
Sweet........ Sweet on the Limited Liability Act [*A publication*] (DLA)
Sweet........ Sweet on Wills [*A publication*] (DLA)
Sweet........ Sweet's Law Dictionary [*A publication*] (DLA)
Sweet........ Sweet's Marriage Settlement Cases [*A publication*] (DLA)
Sweet........ Sweet's Precedents in Conveyancing [*A publication*] (DLA)
Sweet LD ... Sweet's Dictionary of English Law [*1882*] [*A publication*] (DLA)
Sweet LL.... Sweet on the Limited Liability Act [*A publication*] (DLA)
Sweet M Sett Cas ... Sweet's Marriage Settlement Cases [*England*] [*A publication*] (DLA)
Sweet Pr Conv ... Sweet's Precedents in Conveyancing [*4th ed.*] [*1886*] [*A publication*] (DLA)
SWEFCO .. Special Weapons Ferry Control Office [*or Officer*]
SWEHO....... Scandinavian Journal of Work Environment and Health [*A publication*]
SWEIA ...... Studies in Wind Engineering and Industrial Aerodynamics [*Elsevier Book Series*] [*A publication*]
SWEJDFC ... Sing with the Earth John Denver Fan Club (EA)
SWEL........ Southwestern Electric Service Co. [*NASDAQ symbol*] (NQ)
SWEL........ Special Weapons Equipment List
Swell .... Single Woman Earning Lots in London [*Lifestyle classification*]
SWELSTRA ... Special Weapons Equipment List Single Theater Requisitioning Agency
SWEMED ... Swedish Medical Literature [*Database*] [*Karolinska Institute Library and Information Center/Medical Information Center*] [*Information service or system*] (CRD)
Swen.......... Sweeney's New York Superior Court Reports [*31-32 New York*] [*A publication*] (DLA)
SWEN ...... Swensen's, Inc. [*NASDAQ symbol*] (NQ)
SW Entomol ... Southwestern Entomologist [*A publication*]
SWES........ Southwest Leasing Corp. [*NASDAQ symbol*] (NQ)
SWESS...... Special Weapons Emergency Separation System (AFM)
SWESSAR ... Stone and Webster Standard Safety Analysis Report [*Nuclear energy*] (NRCH)
SWest Entomologist ... Southwestern Entomologist [*A publication*]
SWest Nat ... Southwestern Naturalist [*A publication*]
SWET........ Simulated Water Entry Test [*Nuclear energy*]
SWETS...... Solid Waste Engineering Transfer System
SWETTU .. Special Weapons Experimental Tactical Test Unit
SWF.......... Newburgh [*New York*] [*Airport symbol*] (OAG)
SWF.......... Seawater Feed
SWF.......... Shortwave Fadeouts
SWF.......... Silver Wings Fraternity (EA)
SWF.......... Single White Female [*Classified advertising*]
SWF.......... Southwest Folklore [*A publication*]
SWF.......... Southwest Forest Industries, Inc. [*NYSE symbol*] (SPSG)
SWF.......... Special Warning Function (MCD)
SWF.......... Special Weapons Facility [*Navy*]
SWF.......... Steelworker Fabricator [*Navy rating*]
SWF.......... Stelway Food [*Vancouver Stock Exchange symbol*]
SWF.......... Still Waters Foundation (EA)
SWF.......... Sturge-Weber Foundation (EA)
SWF.......... Suedwestfunk [*Radio network*] [*West Germany*]
SWFB........ Southwestern Freight Bureau
SWFC........ Southwest Fisheries Center [*Department of Commerce*] [*La Jolla, CA*]
SWFC........ Surface Weapons Fire Control
SWFG........ Secondary Waveform Generator [*Telecommunications*] (TEL)
SWFPA ..... Structural Wood Fiber Products Association [*Later, SCFPA*] (EA)
SWFR........ Slow Write, Fast Read [*Data processing*] (IEEE)
SWFTU....... Sudan Workers Federation of Trade Unions
SWFX........ Spotweld Fixture [*Tool*]
SWG.......... Salam-Weinberg-Glashow [*One unified field theory in physics*]
SWG.......... Scientific Working Group [*EXAMETNET*]
SWG.......... Shock Wave Generator
SWG.......... Shuttle Working Group [*NASA*] (MCD)
SWG.......... Sine Wave Generator
SWG.......... Slotted Waveguide
SWG.......... Society of Woman Geographers (EA)
SWG.......... Software Working Group [*NASA*] (NASA)
SWG.......... Songwriters Guild of Great Britain
SWG.......... South-West Gold Corp. [*Vancouver Stock Exchange symbol*]
SWG.......... Special Wireless Group [*World War II*] [*British*]
SWG.......... Special Working Group
SWG.......... Squarewave Generator
SWG.......... Staff Working Group
SWG.......... Standard Wire Gauge [*Telecommunications*]
SWG.......... Standard/Working Group (MCD)
SWG.......... Stubs Wire Gauge

SWG.......... Swing (MSA)
SWGD....... Swinging Door
SWGH........ Schriften. Strassburger Wissenschaftliche Gesellschaft in Heidelberg [*A publication*]
SWGM...... Spanish World Gospel Mission (EA)
SWGR........ Switchgear
SwGU .... Goteborgs Universititsbibliotek, Goteborg, Sweden [*Library symbol*] [*Library of Congress*] (LCLS)
SWH.......... Scottish Women's Hospital [*British military*] (DMA)
SWH.......... Seaway Multi-Corp Ltd. [*Toronto Stock Exchange symbol*]
SWH.......... Significant Wave Height [*Oceanography*]
SWH.......... Sociale Wetenschappen [*A publication*]
SWH.......... Spaghetti Warehouse [*AMEX symbol*] (SPSG)
SWHA........ Social Welfare History Archives Center [*University of Minnesota*] [*Research center*] (RCD)
SWHC....... Social Work in Health Care [*A publication*]
SWHG........ Social Welfare History Group [*Western Michigan University*] [*Kalamazoo*] (EA)
SWHI .... Sound Warehouse, Incorporated [*Dallas, TX*] [*NASDAQ symbol*] (NQ)
SW Hist Q ... Southwestern Historical Quarterly [*A publication*]
SWHQ........ Southwestern Historical Quarterly [*A publication*]
SWHS........ Scissor Workboard Hands' Society [*A union*] [*British*]
SWI.......... Salt-Water Igniter
SWI.......... Scottish Woollen Industry
SWI.......... Sealant and Waterproofers Institute (EA)
SWI.......... Seawind Resources, Incorporated [*Vancouver Stock Exchange symbol*]
SWI.......... Seaworthiness Impairment (NVT)
SWI.......... Service World International [*A publication*]
SWI.......... Sherman [*Texas*] [*Airport symbol*] (OAG)
SWI.......... Shock Wave Interaction
SWI.......... Sine Wave Inverter
SWI.......... Software Interrupt [*Data processing*]
SWI.......... Special Weather Intelligence (MCD)
SWI.......... Special World Intervals
SWI.......... Stall Warning Indicator
SWI.......... Standing Wave Indicator
SWI.......... Steel Window Institute (EA)
SWI.......... Stroke Work Index [*Neurology*]
SWI.......... Sunworld International Airways, Inc. [*Las Vegas, NV*] [*FAA designator*] (FAAC)
SWICA ...... Self Winding Clock Association (EA)
SWID........ Southwest India Docks [*Shipping*] (ROG)
SWIDOC... Sociaal-Wetenschappelijk Informatie- en Documentatiecentrum [*Social Science Information and Documentation Center*] [*Netherlands*] [*Information service or system*] (IID)
SWIFT....... Significant Word in the Full Title [*Data processing*] (DIT)
SWIFT....... Society for Worldwide Interbank Financial Telecommunication [*Belgium*] [*Banking network*]
SWIFT....... Software Implemented Friden Translator [*Data processing*]
SWIFT....... Stored Wave Inverse Fourier Transform [*Spectrometry*]
SWIFT....... Strength of Wings Including Flutter
SWIFT....... System Workshops in Forecasting Techniques [*Bell System*]
SWIFT-ANSWER ... Special Word Indexed Full Text Alpha Numeric Storage with Easy Retrieval [*Software*]
Swift Dig.... Swift's Connecticut Digest [*A publication*] (DLA)
Swift Ev.... Swift on Evidence, and Bills and Notes [*A publication*] (DLA)
SWIFT LASS ... Signal Word Index of Field and Title - Literature Abstract Specialized Search (DIT)
SWIFT SIR ... Signal Word Index of Field and Title - Scientific Information Retrieval (DIT)
Swift Sys .... Swift's System of the Laws of Connecticut [*A publication*] (DLA)
SWIG........ Southwestern Irrigated Cotton Growers Association
SWIM........ San Juan Fiberglass Pools, Inc. [*NASDAQ symbol*] (NQ)
SWIM........ Sea Warfare Interim Model (CINC)
SWIM........ Sperm-Washing Insemination Method
SWIM........ Standard Wozniak Integrated Machine [*Data processing*]
SWIM........ Super Wozniak Integrated Machine [*Data processing*]
Swimm Tech ... Swimming Technique [*A publication*]
Swimm World Jun Swimm ... Swimming World and Junior Swimmer [*A publication*]
SWIMS ..... Serialized Weapons Information Management System [*Navy*]
Swim Wld .. Swimming World and Junior Swimmer [*A publication*]
Swin .... Swinburne on Wills [*10 eds.*] [*1590-1803*] [*A publication*] (DLA)
SWIN........ Swinehead [*England*]
Swin .... Swinton's Scotch Justiciary Reports [*1835-41*] [*A publication*] (DLA)
Swinb Desc ... Swinburne on Descents [*1825*] [*A publication*] (DLA)
Swinb Mar ... Swinburne on Married Women [*1846*] [*A publication*] (DLA)
Swinb Spo .. Swinburne on Spousals [*A publication*] (DLA)
Swinb Wills ... Swinburne on Wills [*A publication*] (DLA)
SWINE....... Students Wildly Indignant about Nearly Everything [*Group in "L'il Abner" comic strip*]
Swine Day Univ Calif ... Swine Day. University of California [*A publication*]
Swine Rep Univ Hawaii Coop Ext Serv ... Swine Report. University of Hawaii. Cooperative Extension Service [*A publication*]
SWINGR... Sweep Integrator (AAG)
Swin Jus Cas ... Swinton's Scotch Justiciary Cases [*A publication*] (DLA)

Swin Reg App ... Swinton's Scotch Registration Appeal Cases [*1835-41*] [*A publication*]   (DLA)
Swint .... Swinton's Scotch Justiciary Cases [*A publication*]   (DLA)
SWINTER ... Service Women in Non-Traditional Environmental Roles [*Canadian armed forces*]
SWIO .... SACLANT [*Supreme Allied Commander, Atlantic*] War Intelligence Organization   (NATG)
SWIP .... Secret Work in Process   (MCD)
SWIP .... Society for Women in Philosophy   (EA)
SWIP .... Soil-Wheel Interaction Performance
SWIP .... Standing Wave Impedance Probe [*Geophysical instrument*]
SWIP .... Super-Weight Improvement Program [*Navy*]   (NG)
SWIPMD .. Society for Women in Philosophy, Midwest Division   (EA)
SWIR .... Shortwave Infrared
SWIR .... Special Weapons Inspection Report
SWIRL ...... South Western Industrial Research Limited [*British*]   (ARC)
SWIRLS .... Southwest Regional Library System [*Library network*]
SWIRS .... Solid Waste Information Retrieval System [*Environmental Protection Agency*]
SWIS .... St. Ives Laboratories Corp. [*NASDAQ symbol*]   (NQ)
SWIS .... Satellite Weather Information System [*National Oceanic and Atmospheric Administration*]
SWIS .... Sensitive Wildlife Information System [*Army*]   (IID)
SWIS .... Swiss Wildlife Information Service [*Zurich*] [*Information service or system*]   (IID)
SWISSAIR ... Swiss Air Transport Co. Ltd.
Swiss Credit Bank Bul ... Swiss Credit Banking Bulletin [*A publication*]
Swiss J Hydrol ... Swiss Journal of Hydrology [*A publication*]
Swiss News ... Swiss Economic News [*A publication*]
Swiss R Wld Aff ... Swiss Review of World Affairs [*A publication*]
SWIT .... Switzerland
SWITL .... Southwestern Industrial Traffic League   (EA)
SWITT .... Surface Wave Independent Tap Transducer   (IEEE)
SWITZ ...... Switzerland
SWJ .... Single Wire Junction
SWJ .... Socket Wrench Joint
SW J Anthrop ... Southwestern Journal of Anthropology [*A publication*]
SW J Phil .. Southwestern Journal of Philosophy [*A publication*]
Sw J T .... Southwestern Journal of Theology [*A publication*]
SW J Th .... Southwestern Journal of Theology [*A publication*]
SWK .... Southwark [*England*]
SWK .... [*The*] Stanley Works [*NYSE symbol*]   (SPSG)
SWK .... Stewart Lake Resources, Inc. [*Toronto Stock Exchange symbol*]
SW KR ...... Swedish Krona [*Monetary unit*]
SWL .... Safe Working Load [*Shipping*]
SWL .... Short Wavelength LASER
SWL .... Short Wavelength Limit
SWL .... Shortwave Listener [*Radio*]
SWL .... Signals Warfare Laboratory [*Army*]   (RDA)
SWL .... Single-Wheel Loading [*Aviation*]
SWL .... Snow Hill, MD [*Location identifier*] [*FAA*]   (FAAL)
SWL .... Solid Waste Litter
SWL .... South West Air Ltd. [*Windsor, ON, Canada*] [*FAA designator*]   (FAAC)
SWL .... Southwest Realty [*AMEX symbol*]   (SPSG)
SWL .... Still Water Level
SWL .... Sulfite Waste Liquor
SWL .... Surface Wave Line
SWLA .... Southwestern Library Association
SW Law J .. Southwestern Law Journal [*A publication*]
SWLC .... South West London College [*London, England*]
SWLC .... Southwestern Connecticut Library Council [*Library network*]
SWLDG ..... Socket Welding
Sw Legal Found Inst on Oil and Gas L and Tax ... Southwestern Legal Foundation. Institution on Oil and Gas Law and Taxation [*United States*] [*A publication*]
SWLF .... Southwestern Legal Foundation   (EA)
SWLG .... Swelling   (FAAC)
SWLG .... SWLG Corp. [*NASDAQ symbol*]   (NQ)
SW L J ...... Southwestern Law Journal [*A publication*]
SWL Rev .... Southwestern Law Review [*A publication*]   (DLA)
SwLU .... Lunds Universitet [*University of Lund*], Lund, Sweden [*Library symbol*] [*Library of Congress*]   (LCLS)
SWLY .... Southwesterly [*Meteorology*]   (FAAC)
SWM .... Sawmill [*California*] [*Seismograph station code, US Geological Survey*] [*Closed*]   (SEIS)
SWM .... Serber-Wilson Method [*Nuclear energy*]   (NRCH)
SWM .... Shipboard Wave Meter
SWM .... Single White Male [*Classified advertising*]
SwM .... Southwest Microfilm, Inc., El Paso, TX [*Library symbol*] [*Library of Congress*]   (LCLS)
SWM .... Special Warfare Mission   (AABC)
SWM .... Spotweld Machine [*Tool*]
SWM .... Stan West Mining Corp. [*Toronto Stock Exchange symbol*]
SWM .... Suia-Missu [*Brazil*] [*Airport symbol*]   (OAG)
SWM .... Surface Wave Mode
SWMA ...... Society of Women in Military Aviation   (EA)
SWMA ...... Solid Waste Management Association
SWMA ...... Southwestern Monuments Association [*Later, SPMA*]   (EA)
SWMAT .... Switch Matrix   (MCD)
SWMC .... Stan West Mining Corp. [*NASDAQ symbol*]   (NQ)

SWMCA .... Schweizer Maschinenmarkt [*A publication*]
SWMCCS ... Standard Weather Messages Command and Control System   (MCD)
SWMF .... South Wales Miners' Federation   (DAS)
SWMFB .... Southwestern Motor Freight Bureau
SWMGA .... Solid Wastes Management [*Later, World Wastes*] [*A publication*]
SWMO ...... Solid Waste Management Office [*Later, Office of Solid Waste Management Programs*] [*Environmental Protection Agency*]
SWMS .... Solid Waste Management System [*Nuclear energy*]   (NRCH)
SW Musician ... Southwestern Musician [*A publication*]
SWN .... Leadville, CO [*Location identifier*] [*FAA*]   (FAAL)
SWN .... Notre Dame College, Wilcox, Saskatchewan [*Library symbol*] [*National Library of Canada*]   (NLC)
SWN .... Southwestern Energy Co. [*NYSE symbol*]   (SPSG)
SWN .... Sworn   (ROG)
SWNAA ..... Southwestern Naturalist [*United States*] [*A publication*]
SWNCC ..... State, War, Navy Coordinating Committee [*Later, SANAAC*]
SWND ...... Social Workers for Nuclear Disarmament   (EA)
SWNJ .... Southwest New Jersey Consortium for Health Information Services [*Library network*]
SWNS .... Sprawozdanie z Prac Naukowych Wydzialu Nauk Spolecznych Pan [*A publication*]
SWO .... Senior Watch Officer [*Navy*]   (NVT)
SWO .... Shallow Resources, Inc. [*Vancouver Stock Exchange symbol*]
SWO .... Solid Waste Office [*Later, Office of Solid Waste Management Programs*] [*Environmental Protection Agency*]
SWO .... Southwestern Oregon Community College, Coos Bay, OR [*OCLC symbol*]   (OCLC)
SWO .... Squadron Wireless Officer [*Navy*] [*British*]
SWO .... Squarewave Oscillator
SWO .... Staff Watch Officer   (NVT)
SWO .... Staff Weather Officer [*Military*]
SWO .... Station Warrant Officer [*Air Force*] [*British*]
SWO .... Stillwater [*Oklahoma*] [*Airport symbol*]   (OAG)
SWO .... Stop Work Order
SWO .... Stud Welding Outfit
SWO .... Support Work Order   (AAG)
SWO .... Surface Warfare Officer [*Navy*]   (NVT)
SW/O .... Switchover
SWOB ...... Salaries, Wages, Overhead, and Benefits   (NASA)
SWOB ...... Ship Waste Off-Loading Barge [*Navy*]   (CAAL)
SWOC .... Special Weapons Operation Center [*Army*]   (AABC)
SWOC .... Steel Workers Organizing Committee [*Became United Steelworkers of America*]
SWOC .... Subject Word out of Context [*Data processing*]   (DIT)
SWOD ...... Special Weapons Ordnance Devices
SWOG ...... Special Weapons Overflight Guide   (AFM)
SWOP .... Service Weapons Operational Procedures   (MCD)
SWOP .... Special Weapons Ordnance Publication [*Navy*]   (NVT)
SWOP .... Specifications for Web Offset Publications [*Printing technology*]
SWOP .... Stop without Pay
SWOP .... Structural Weight Optimization Program [*NASA*]   (KSC)
SWOP .... Switchboard Operator [*British military*]   (DMA)
SWOPS ..... Single Well Oil Production Ship [*British*]
SWOPSI .... Stanford Workshop on Political and Social Issues [*Stanford University*]
SWORD .... Separated, Widowed, or Divorced [*New York City association*]
SWORD .... Shallow Water Oceanographic Research Data [*System*] [*Naval Ordnance Laboratory and Naval Oceanographic Office*]
SWORD .... Small Wars Operational Research Division [*Military*]   (INF)
SWORDS ... Standard Work Ordering and Reporting Data System [*Army*]
SWORL ..... Southwestern Ohio Rural Libraries [*Library network*]
SwOrM ...... Regionsjukhuset, Medicinska Biblioteket [*Regional Hospital, Medical Library*], Orebro, Sweden [*Library symbol*] [*Library of Congress*]   (LCLS)
SWOS .... Surface Warfare Officer's School [*Navy*]   (NVT)
SWOSCOLCOM ... Surface Warfare Officer's School Command [*Navy*]   (NVT)
SWOT .... Strengths, Weaknesses, Opportunities, Threats [*Analysis for organizations*]
SWOV .... Switchover   (MSA)
SWP .... Safe Working Pressure
SWP .... Salt-Water Pump   (MSA)
SWP .... Science Working Panel [*NASA*]
SWP .... Scientific Word Processor [*Data processing*]
SWP .... Sector Working Party [*British*]   (DCTA)
SWP .... Semi-Tech Microelectronics, Inc. [*Toronto Stock Exchange symbol*]
SWP .... Service Water Pump [*Nuclear energy*]   (NRCH)
SWP .... Shock Wave Profile
SWP .... Short Wavelength Prime [*Camera for spectra*]
SWP .... Socialist Workers Party [*Political party*]   (EA)
SWP .... Socialist Workers' Party [*Great Britain*] [*Political party*]   (PPW)
SWP .... Society of Wireless Pioneers
SWP .... Society for Women in Plastics   (EA)
SWP .... Soil-Test Water Probe
SWP .... Solid Waste Packaging [*Nuclear energy*]   (NRCH)
SWP .... Solid Waste Processing [*Nuclear energy*]   (NRCH)
SWP .... Southwest Pacific

SWP..........	Space, Weight, and Power
SWP..........	Special Weapons Project [*Military*]
SWP..........	Special Working Party [*Military*]
SWP..........	Standby Warning Panel (MCD)
SWP..........	State Water Project [*California*] (ECON)
SWP..........	Stiftung Wissenschaft und Politik [*Foundation for Science and Politics*] [*Information service or system*] (IID)
SWP..........	Submersible Water Pump
SWP..........	Summer Work Program
SWP..........	Supply Working Party of Official Committee on Armistice Terms and Civil Administration [*World War II*]
SWP..........	Surface Warfare Plan [*Navy*] (CAAL)
SWP..........	Surface Wave Phenomena
SWP..........	Survey of Western Palestine [*C. R. Conder et al*] [*A publication*] (BJA)
SWP..........	Swamp (ADA)
SWP..........	Swamp Creek [*Montana*] [*Seismograph station code, US Geological Survey*] [*Closed*] (SEIS)
SWP..........	Sweep
SWP & A ...	Seamen's War Pensions and Allowances Act [*Australia*]
SWPA.......	Section for Women in Public Administration (EA)
SWPA........	Southwest National Corp. [*Greensburg, PA*] [*NASDAQ symbol*] (NQ)
SWPA.......	Southwest Pacific Area [*World War II*]
SWPA.......	Southwestern Power Administration [*Department of Energy*]
SWPA.......	Southwestern Psychological Association (MCD)
SWPA.......	Spotweld Pattern [*Tool*] (AAG)
SWPA.......	Submersible Wastewater Pump Association (EA)
SWPA.......	Surplus War Property Administration [*Terminated, 1944*]
SW Pacific ...	South West Pacific [*A publication*] (APTA)
SWPB.......	Surplus War Property Board [*Terminated, 1945*]
SWPC.......	Short Wing Piper Club (EA)
SWPC.......	Smaller War Plants Corporation [*World War II*]
SWPC.......	Southwest Pacific Command [*Navy*]
SWPCP	Prince Albert National Park, Parks Canada [*Parc National Prince Albert, Parcs Canada*] Waskesiu Lakes, Saskatchewan [*Library symbol*] [*National Library of Canada*] (NLC)
SWPF	Southwest Pacific Force [*Later, Southwest Pacific Command*] [*Navy*]
SW Phil Stud ...	Southwest Philosophical Studies [*United States*] [*A publication*]
SWPIA	Southwest Pacific Island Arc [*Oceanography*]
SWPJ	Study of Western Palestine: Jerusalem [*C. Warren and C. R. Conder*] [*A publication*] (BJA)
SWPM.......	Survey of Western Palestine: Memoirs [*C. R. Conder*] [*A publication*] (BJA)
SW Pol Sci Q ...	Southwestern Political Science Quarterly [*A publication*] (DLA)
SWPP	Service Water Pressurization Pump [*Nuclear energy*] (IEEE)
SWPP	Southwest Power Pool [*Regional power council*] (NRCH)
SWPPD	Society for Women in Philosophy, Pacific Division (EA)
SWPR.......	Swedish Polar Research [*A publication*]
SWP(S).....	Solid Waste Processing System [*Nuclear energy*] (NRCH)
SWPSA	Southwestern Peanut Shellers Association (EA)
SWPSD	Society for Women in Philosophy, Southwest Division (EA)
SWPSP......	Survey of Western Palestine: Special Papers [*A publication*] (BJA)
SWPT	Service Weapons Test (NVT)
SWR	Serum Wassermann Reaction [*Clinical chemistry*]
SWR	Service Water Reservoir [*Nuclear energy*] (NRCH)
SwR............	Sewanee Review [*A publication*]
SWR	Short Wavelength Radiation (KSC)
SWR	Shortwave Ratio (DEN)
SWR	Sine Wave Response
SWR	Siphon Withdrawal Response
SWR	Sodium-Water Reaction [*Nuclear energy*] (NRCH)
SWR	Sons of the Whiskey Rebellion (EA)
SWSR	South Western Reporter [*A publication*] (DLA)
SWR	Southwest Review [*A publication*]
SWR	Southwestern Railway [*British*] (ROG)
SWR	Special Warning Receiver (MCD)
SWR	Standing Wave Ratio [*Voltage*] [*Electronics*]
SWR	Steel Wire Rope
SWR	Stonewall Resources [*Vancouver Stock Exchange symbol*]
SWR	Stress Wave Riveter [*Metal forming*]
SWR	Submarine Water Reactor [*Nuclear energy*] (NRCH)
SWR	Switch Rails
SWRA........	Selected Water Resources Abstracts [*US Geological Survey*] [*Information service or system*] (CRD)
SWRA........	Social Work Research and Abstracts [*A publication*]
SWRB........	Sadler's Wells Royal Ballet [*British*]
SWRB........	Standing Wave Ratio Bridge [*Electronics*]
SW Rep	South Western Reporter [*A publication*] (DLA)
SW Repr ...	South Western Reporter [*A publication*] (DLA)
SWRF........	Sine Wave Response Filter [*Program*]
SWRHL....	Southwestern Radiological Health Laboratory [*HEW*]
SWRI.........	Southwestern Research Institute [*San Antonio, TX*] [*Research center*]
SWRJ	Split Wing Ramjet

SwRK.........	Schwingungsrisskorrosionsverhalten [*Fatigue Corrosion Behavior*] [*German*]
SWRL........	Southwest Regional Laboratory [*Research center*] (RCD)
SWRL........	Southwest Regional Laboratory for Educational Research and Development
SWRLSS ...	Southwest Regional Library Service System [*Library network*]
SWRM	Standing Wave Ratio Meter [*Electronics*]
SWRMPAC ...	Southwestern Regional Manpower Advisory Committee [*Terminated, 1974*] [*Department of Labor*] (EGAO)
SWRN	Southwestern [*Meteorology*] (FAAC)
SWROM ...	Standing Wave Read-Only Memory [*Data processing*]
SWROSS...	Southwest Regional Office for Spanish Speaking (EA)
SWRP	Satellite Wildlife Research Project
SWRP	Sectionalized Work Requirements Package (MCD)
SWRPRS...	Sodium-Water Reaction Pressure Relief Subsystem [*Nuclear energy*] (NRCH)
SWRSIC ...	Southern Water Resources Scientific Information Center [*Raleigh, NC*]
SWRVDT ..	Swedish Wildlife Research Viltrevy [*A publication*]
SWS	Saturn Workshop [*NASA*]
SWS	Seam Welding System
SWS	Service Water System [*Nuclear energy*] (NRCH)
SWS	Service-Wide Supply
SWS	Shallow Water SONAR
SWS	Shift Word, Substituting
SWS	Shock Wave Sensor (RDA)
SWS	Shore Wireless Service [*British military*] (DMA)
SWS	Single White Silk-Covered [*Wire insulation*]
SWS	Slow-Wave Sleep
SWS	Sniper Weapon Sight (INF)
SWS	Sociologists for Women in Society (EA)
SWS	Solar Wind Spectrometer
SWS	Solid Waste System [*Nuclear energy*] (NRCH)
SwS	Solidarity with Solidarity [*See also SzS*] [*London, England*] (EAIO)
SWS	Southwest Writers Series [*A publication*]
SWS	Southwestern Studies [*University of Texas, El Paso*] [*A publication*]
SWS	Space Weapon Systems [*Air Force*]
SWS	Special Weapon Systems [*Military*]
SWS	Standard Weapon Station [*Nuclear arms control*]
SWS	Static Water Supply (ADA)
SWS	Still Water Surface
SWS	Strategic Weapon System [*Military*] (CAAL)
SWS	Swansea [*Wales*] [*Airport symbol*] (OAG)
SWS	Swift Minerals Ltd. [*Vancouver Stock Exchange symbol*]
SWS	Switch Scan (MCD)
SWS	Switch Stand
SWSA	Systolic Wall Stress [*Cardiology*]
SWSA	Southern Wood Seasoning Association
SWSD	Special Weapons Supply Depot
SWSE	Southeast Regional Library, Weyburn, Saskatchewan [*Library symbol*] [*National Library of Canada*] (NLC)
SWSF	Society for a World Service Federation (EA)
SWSG	Security Window Screen and Guard
SWSI	Stanley Well Service [*NASDAQ symbol*] (NQ)
SWSJ........	Son of WSFA Journal [*A publication*]
SwSK	Kungliga Tekniska Hoegskolan [*Royal Institute of Technology*], Stockholm, Sweden [*Library symbol*] [*Library of Congress*] (LCLS)
SwSKB......	Kungliga Biblioteket, Bibliotheca Regia Holmiensis, Stockholm, Sweden [*Library symbol*] [*Library of Congress*] (LCLS)
SwSKM	Kungliga Karolinska Mediko-Kirurgiska Institutes, Stockholm, Sweden [*Library symbol*] [*Library of Congress*] (LCLS)
SwSL..........	Latinamerika-Institutet, Stockholm, Sweden [*Library symbol*] [*Library of Congress*] (LCLS)
SWSM.......	Special Weapons Supply Memorandum [*Army*] (AABC)
SW Social Sci Q ...	Southwestern Social Science Quarterly [*A publication*]
SWSR........	Solid Waste Shipping Room [*Nuclear energy*] (NRCH)
SWST	Service Water Storage Tank [*Nuclear energy*] (IEEE)
SWST	Society of Wood Science and Technology (EA)
SW St (UTEP) ...	Southwestern Studies (University of Texas, El Paso) [*A publication*]
SwSU	Stockholms Universitetsbiblioteket, Stockholm, Sweden [*Library symbol*] [*Library of Congress*] (LCLS)
SWSVC	Souris Valley Regional Care Center, Weyburn, Saskatchewan [*Library symbol*] [*National Library of Canada*] (NLC)
SW-SWIP ...	Society for Women in Philosophy, Southwestern Division (EA)
SWSWTU ...	Sheffield Wool Shear Workers' Trade Union [*British*] (DCTA)
SWT..........	Safe Women's Transport [*British*]
SWT..........	Scottish Wildlife Trust [*British*]
SWT..........	Search-while-Track (CAAL)
SWT..........	Seward, NE [*Location identifier*] [*FAA*] (FAAL)
SWT..........	Shortwave Transmitter
SWT..........	Silent Witness [*Vancouver Stock Exchange symbol*]
SWT..........	Single-Weight [*Paper*]
SWT..........	Special Weapons Test
SWT..........	Spiral Wrap Tubing
SWT..........	Spotweld Template (MCD)
SWT..........	Supersonic Wind Tunnel (MCD)
SWT..........	Sweat

SWT..........	Swept Frequency Transform (CAAL)
SWT..........	Swift Aire Lines, Inc. [*San Luis Obispo, CA*] [*FAA designator*] (FAAC)
SWT..........	Switch Ties
SWT..........	System Work Team (MCD)
SWTA........	Special Weapons Training Allowance
SWTC........	Special Weapon Technical Command [*Navy*] (MCD)
SWTC........	Stop War Toys Campaign (EA)
SWTED....	Solar Waerme Technik [*A publication*]
SWTI........	Special Weapons Technical Instructions [*Army*] (AABC)
SWTL........	Surface Wave Transmission Line
SWTN.......	Sprawozdania Wroclawskiego Towarzystwa Naukowego [*A publication*]
SWTN.......	Swanton Corp. [*NASDAQ symbol*] (NQ)
SWTP.......	School to Work Transition Program [*Australia*]
SWTR.......	Southern California Water Co. [*NASDAQ symbol*] (NQ)
Sw & Tr..	Swabey and Tristram's Probate and Divorce Reports [*164 English Reprint*] [*A publication*] (DLA)
SWTS.......	Secondary Waste Treatment System [*Nuclear energy*] (NRCH)
SWTT.......	Single-Well Tracer Test [*Petroleum technology*]
SWTTEU..	Special Weapons Test and Tactical Evaluation Unit
SWTX.......	Southwall Technologies, Inc. [*NASDAQ symbol*] (NQ)
SWTZ.......	Switzerland
SWU..........	Idaho Falls, ID [*Location identifier*] [*FAA*] (FAAL)
SWU..........	Sagami Women's University [*UTLAS symbol*]
SWU..........	Separative Work Unit [*Measure of uranium enrichment capability*]
SWU..........	Slovenian Women's Union (EA)
SWU..........	Steelhawk Resources Ltd. [*Vancouver Stock Exchange symbol*]
Sw U LR ...	Southwestern University. Law Review [*A publication*]
Sw U L Rev ...	Southwestern University. Law Review [*A publication*]
SwUmU....	Umea Universitetsbibliotek, Umea, Sweden [*Library symbol*] [*Library of Congress*] (LCLS)
SWUS.......	Southwest United States
SWUSL.......	Southwestern University School of Law (DLA)
SwUU	Universitet i Uppsala [*University of Uppsala*], Uppsala, Sweden [*Library symbol*] [*Library of Congress*] (LCLS)
SWV..........	Squarewave Voltammetry [*Electrochemistry*]
SWV..........	Suave Shoe Corp. [*NYSE symbol*] (SPSG)
SWV..........	Swan View [*Australia*] [*Seismograph station code, US Geological Survey*] (SEIS)
SWV..........	Swivel (AAG)
SWVA.......	Scottish War Veterans of America (EA)
SWVA.......	Shemya WWII Veterans Association (EA)
SWVA.......	Steel of West Virginia, Inc. [*NASDAQ symbol*] (NQ)
SWVB.......	Social Work Vocational Bureau (EA)
SWVL.......	Swivel (MSA)
SWW........	Hotels and Restaurants International [*A publication*]
SWW........	Severe Weather Warning (KSC)
SWW........	Stow Resources [*Vancouver Stock Exchange symbol*]
SWW........	Sweetwater, TX [*Location identifier*] [*FAA*] (FAAL)
SWW........	Winthrop College, Rock Hill, SC [*OCLC symbol*] (OCLC)
SWWA......	South-West Water Authority [*British*] (DCTA)
SWWBDS...	Software Work Breakdown Structure (MCD)
SWWBS....	Software Work Breakdown Structure
SWWC.......	Southwest Water Company [*La Puente, CA*] [*NASDAQ symbol*] (NQ)
SWWF.......	Speed-Welding Wire Feeder
SWWG......	Social Work with Groups [*A publication*]
SWWOAH ...	Society of World War One Aero Historians (EA)
SWWU	Singapore Wood Workers' Union
SWX.........	Southwest Gas Corp. [*NYSE symbol*] (SPSG)
SWXO	Staff Weather Officer [*NASA*] (KSC)
SWY.........	Albemarle, NC [*Location identifier*] [*FAA*] (FAAL)
SWY.........	Safeway, Inc. [*NYSE symbol*] (SPSG)
SWY.........	Stopway
SWY.........	Stornaway Resources Corp. [*Vancouver Stock Exchange symbol*]
SWY.........	Swedish Economy [*A publication*]
SWY.........	Swiss Yiddish (BJA)
SWZ..........	Smyrna, TN [*Location identifier*] [*FAA*] (FAAL)
SWZ........	Special Watch Zone [*Navy*] (NVT)
SWZ..........	Swaziland [*ANSI three-letter standard code*] (CNC)
SWZ..........	Swiss Helvetia Fund [*NYSE symbol*] (SPSG)
SWZBA	Schweizer Buch [*A publication*]
SX	Greece [*Aircraft nationality and registration mark*] (FAAC)
SX	Pia Societas Sancti Francisci Xaverii pro Exteris Missionibus [*St. Francis Xavier Foreign Mission Society*] [*Xaverian Missionary Fathers*] [*Roman Catholic religious order*]
SX	Sacks
SX	Sigma Xi [*Society*]
SX	Simplex [*Transmission direction*] (CET)
SX	Society of St. Francis Xavier for the Foreign Missions [*Also known as Xaverian Missionaries*] (EAIO)
SX	Solvent Extraction (DEN)
sx..............	South West Africa [*Namibia*] [*MARC country of publication code*] [*Library of Congress*] (LCCP)
SX	Stability Index [*Aviation*] (FAAC)
SX	Sterling Philippines Airways, Inc. [*ICAO designator*] (FAAC)
SX	Sussex [*County in England*]
SX	SXT Resources Ltd. [*Vancouver Stock Exchange symbol*]
SX	Union of Soviet Socialist Republics [*Later, FC*] [*License plate code assigned to foreign diplomats in the US*]
SX-1980	Model number used by U.S. Pioneer Electronic Corp. [*Name is derived from "S" in "stereo amplifier" and "X" in "TX tuner"*]
SXA...........	Stored Index to Address
SXAD.......	Sioux Army Depot
SXAPS.......	Soft X-Ray Appearance Potential Spectrometer [*or Spectroscopy*]
SXB...........	Strasbourg [*France*] [*Airport symbol*] (OAG)
SXBT	Shipboard Expendable Bathythermograph [*System*] [*Naval Oceanographic Office*]
SXC...........	Saint Xavier College [*Chicago, IL*]
SXC...........	Santa Catalina, CA [*Location identifier*] [*FAA*] (FAAL)
SXCO........	Switchco, Inc. [*NASDAQ symbol*] (NQ)
SXD...........	Notes et Etudes Documentaires [*A publication*]
SXD...........	Springfield, VT [*Location identifier*] [*FAA*] (FAAL)
SXE...........	Sale [*Australia*] [*Airport symbol*] (OAG)
SXE...........	Soft X-Ray Experiment [*Also, SXX*]
SXE...........	Spencer Explorations Ltd. [*Vancouver Stock Exchange symbol*]
SXEW........	Solvent Extraction and Electrowinning [*Metallurgy*]
SXF...........	Berlin [*East Germany*] [*Airport symbol*] (OAG)
SXF...........	Solvent Extraction Feed [*Nuclear energy*] (NRCH)
SXG...........	Senanga [*Zambia*] [*Airport symbol*] (OAG)
SXH	Sehulea [*Papua New Guinea*] [*Airport symbol*] (OAG)
SXI...........	Singapore Business [*A publication*]
SXI...........	Software Extraordinaire, Inc. [*Telecommunications service*] (TSSD)
SXI...........	Standex International Corp. [*NYSE symbol*] (SPSG)
SXI...........	Synex International, Inc. [*Toronto Stock Exchange symbol*]
SXIS.........	Scattered X-Ray Internal Standard [*for surface analysis*]
SXL...........	Sexless [*Connector*]
SXL...........	Short-Arc Xenon Lamp
SXL...........	Soft X-Ray LASER
SXL...........	Summersville, WV [*Location identifier*] [*FAA*] (FAAL)
SXM	St. Maarten [*Netherlands Antilles*] [*Airport symbol*]
SXM	Sphinx Mining Inc. [*Vancouver Stock Exchange symbol*]
SXML........	San Xavier Mining Laboratory [*University of Arizona*] [*Research center*] (RCD)
SXN	Sao Jose Do Xingu [*Brazil*] [*Airport symbol*] (OAG)
SXN	Section (MDG)
SXNP........	Saxton Products [*NASDAQ symbol*] (NQ)
SXO	Senior Experimental Officer [*Also, SEO, SExO*] [*Ministry of Agriculture, Fisheries, and Food*] [*British*]
SXP...........	Sheldon Point [*Alaska*] [*Airport symbol*] (OAG)
SXP...........	Sunnyvale Public Library, Sunnyvale, CA [*OCLC symbol*] (OCLC)
SXQ	Soldotna, AK [*Location identifier*] [*FAA*] (FAAL)
SXR...........	Soft X-Ray Region
SXR...........	Srinagar [*India*] [*Airport symbol*] (OAG)
SXRF	Synchrotron X-Ray Fluorescence [*Spectrometry*]
SXS...........	Sigma Xi Society
SXS...........	Stellar X-Ray Spectra
SxS...........	Step-by-Step Switching System [*Telecommunications*]
SXSKA	Sakura X-Rei Shashin Kenkyu [*A publication*]
SXT...........	Sextant (NASA)
SXT...........	Sexton Summit, OR [*Location identifier*] [*FAA*] (FAAL)
SXT...........	Sextuple (MSA)
SXT...........	Stable X-Ray Transmitter
SXTF	Satellite X-Ray Test Facility
SXTN........	Sextant (MSA)
SXX...........	Secolul XX [*A publication*]
SXX...........	Soft X-Ray Experiment [*Also, SXE*]
SXY...........	Sidney [*New York*] [*Airport symbol*] (OAG)
SY	Air Alsace [*France*] [*ICAO designator*] (FAAC)
SY	School Year (AABC)
SY	Security
SY	Sefer Yezirah (BJA)
SY	Seychelles
SY	Shelby Williams Industries, Inc. [*NYSE symbol*] (SPSG)
SY	Shipyard
SY	Shoulder Yaw (MCD)
SY	Shropshire Yeomanry [*British military*] (DMA)
SY	Sloppy [*Track condition*] [*Thoroughbred racing*]
SY	Southern Yiddish (BJA)
SY	Spring Yearling
SY	Square Yard
SY	Staff Years (OICC)
SY	Steam Yacht (ROG)
SY	Supply [*Business term*]
SY	Surrey [*County in England*]
SY	Survey
SY	Sussex Yeomanry [*British military*] (DMA)
SY	Sustainer Yaw (AAG)
Sy	Symmachus (BJA)
SY	Symposium [*A publication*]
Sy	Symptoms [*Medicine*]
SY	Synchronized (MDG)
Sy	Synchronous System [*on a ship*] (DS)
SY	Synthesis [*A publication*]
SY	Syphilis [*Medicine*]

SY	Syria [*or Syrian Arab Republic*] [*ANSI two-letter standard code*] (CNC)
sy	Syria [*MARC country of publication code*] [*Library of Congress*] (LCCP)
Sy	Syria. Revue d'Art Oriental et d'Archeologie [*A publication*]
SY	System
SYA	Save Your Afterdeck [*Bowdlerized version*]
SYA	Scandinavian Yachting Association [*See also SKAN SF*] (EAIO)
SYA	Shemya Island [*Alaska*] [*Airport symbol*] (OAG)
SYA	Subud Youth Association (EA)
SYAH	Aishalton [*Guyana*] [*ICAO location identifier*] (ICLI)
SYAN	Annai [*Guyana*] [*ICAO location identifier*] (ICLI)
SYAP	Apoteri [*Guyana*] [*ICAO location identifier*] (ICLI)
SYAW	Awaruwaunawa [*Guyana*] [*ICAO location identifier*] (ICLI)
SYB	Seal Bay [*Alaska*] [*Airport symbol*] (OAG)
SYB	Syracuse University, Syracuse, NY [*OCLC symbol*] (OCLC)
SYBEAUXARTS	Syndicat des Beaux Arts Africains [*Union of African Fine Arts*]
SYBF	Share Your Birthday Foundation (EA)
SYBR	Baramita [*Guyana*] [*ICAO location identifier*] (ICLI)
SYBT	Bartica [*Guyana*] [*ICAO location identifier*] (ICLI)
SyBU	Symbolae Biblicae Upsalienses [*A publication*]
SYC	Seychelles [*ANSI three-letter standard code*] (CNC)
SYC	Sycamore (AAG)
SYC	Synco Development [*Vancouver Stock Exchange symbol*]
SYCATE	Symptom-Cause-Test
SYCLOPS	SYFA Concurrent Logic Operating System
SYCOM	Synchronous Communications [*Satellite*] [*GSFC*]
SYCOM	Systems Command
SYCOSPARE	Shipyard Checkout Spare
SYCOT	Shipyard Checkout Test
SYCP	Syncom Corporation [*NASDAQ symbol*] (NQ)
SYD	Casper, WY [*Location identifier*] [*FAA*] (FAAL)
SYD	Scheer Energy Development Corp. [*Vancouver Stock Exchange symbol*]
SYD	Scotland Yard
SYD	Shipyard
SYD	South Yemen Dinar (BJA)
SYD	[*Release*] Subject Your Discretion (FAAC)
SYD	Sum of the Year's Digits [*Statistics*]
SYD	Sydney [*Australia*] [*Seismograph station code, US Geological Survey*] [*Closed*] (SEIS)
SYD	Sydney [*Australia*]
SYD	Sydney [*Australia*] [*Airport symbol*] (OAG)
Syd App	Sydney Appeals [*Australia*] [*A publication*] (DLA)
SYDAS	System Data Acquisition System
SYDEC	Selective Yield Delayed Coking [*Foster Wheeler USA Corp. process*]
SYDHARB	Sydney Harbour [*Measurement of water*] [*Australia*] (ADA)
SYDIA	System Developer Interface Activity [*Data processing*]
Syd Inst Crim Proc	University of Sydney Faculty of Law. Proceedings of the Institute of Criminology [*A publication*]
Syd Jaycee	Sydney Jaycee [*A publication*] (APTA)
Syd Jewish News	Sydney Jewish News [*A publication*] (APTA)
Syd Law R	Sydney Law Review [*A publication*] (APTA)
Syd LR	Sydney Law Review [*A publication*] (APTA)
Syd L Rev	Sydney Law Review [*A publication*] (APTA)
SYDMF	Scheer Energy Development Corp. [*NASDAQ symbol*] (NQ)
Syd Morning Her	Sydney Morning Herald [*A publication*]
Syd Morning Herald	Sydney Morning Herald [*A publication*] (APTA)
Sydney GCN	Sydney Gay Community News [*A publication*] (APTA)
Sydney Law R	Sydney Law Review [*A publication*] (APTA)
Sydney Law Rev	Sydney Law Review [*A publication*] (APTA)
Sydney L Rev	Sydney Law Review [*A publication*]
Sydney Q Mag	Sydney Quarterly Magazine [*A publication*] (APTA)
Sydney Univ Gaz	Sydney University. Gazette [*A publication*]
Sydney Univ Med J	Sydney University. Medical Journal [*A publication*] (APTA)
Sydney Univ Rev	Sydney University. Review [*A publication*]
Sydney Univ Sch Civ Eng Res Rep	Sydney University. School of Civil Engineering. Research Report [*A publication*] (APTA)
Sydney Water Bd J	Sydney Water Board. Journal [*A publication*] (APTA)
Sydowia Ann Mycol	Sydowia. Annales Mycologici [*A publication*]
Sydowia Ann Mycolog Beih	Sydowia. Annales Mycologici. Beihefte [*A publication*]
Syd R	Sydney Review [*A publication*]
SYDSTOCK	Sydney Stock Exchange Share Prices [*Database*] [*Sydney Stock Exchange*] [*Australia*] [*Information service or system*] (CRD)
Syd Stud	Sydney Studies in English [*A publication*] (APTA)
Sydsven Medicinhist	Sydsvenska Medicinhistoriska Saellskapets Arsskrift [*A publication*]
Sydsvenska Ortnamns-Sallsk Arsskr	Sydsvenska Ortnamns-Saellskapets Arsskrift [*A publication*]
Syd Univ Ag Economics Res Bul	University of Sydney. Department of Agricultural Economics. Research Bulletin [*A publication*] (APTA)
Syd Univ Civ Engng Schl Res Rep	University of Sydney. School of Civil Engineering. Research Report [*A publication*] (APTA)

Syd Univ Dep Agric Econ Mimeo Rep	University of Sydney. Department of Agricultural Economics. Mimeographed Report [*A publication*] (APTA)
Syd Univ Gaz	Sydney University. Gazette [*A publication*] (APTA)
Syd Univ Med J	Sydney University. Medical Journal [*A publication*] (APTA)
Syd Univ Post Grad Comm Med Bul	University of Sydney. Postgraduate Committee in Medicine. Bulletin [*A publication*] (APTA)
Syd Univ Post Grad Comm Med Oration	University of Sydney. Postgraduate Committee in Medicine. Annual Postgraduate Oration [*A publication*] (APTA)
Syd Univ Sch Agric Rep	University of Sydney. School of Agriculture. Report [*A publication*] (APTA)
Syd Wat Bd J	Sydney Water Board. Journal [*A publication*] (APTA)
Syd Water Bd J	Sydney Water Board. Journal [*A publication*] (APTA)
Syd Water Board J	Sydney Water Board. Journal [*A publication*] (APTA)
SYE	Sa'Dah [*Yemen Arab Republic*] [*Airport symbol*] (OAG)
SYEB	Ebini [*Guyana*] [*ICAO location identifier*] (ICLI)
SYENDM	Systematic Entomology [*A publication*]
SYEP	Summer Youth Employment Program [*Department of Labor*]
SYEP	Symmetrical Disubstituted Ethoxy Propane [*Organic chemistry*] (MCD)
SYES	Syesis [*A publication*]
SYF	St. Francis, KS [*Location identifier*] [*FAA*] (FAAL)
SYFA	System for Application [*Data processing*]
SYFANET	System for Access Network [*Wespac*] (TSSD)
SYG	Arcola, TX [*Location identifier*] [*FAA*] (FAAL)
SYG	Secretary-General (NATG)
SYG	Synergy International [*Vancouver Stock Exchange symbol*]
SYGA	Systems Gauge [*Tool*] (AAG)
SYGC	Georgetown [*Guyana*] [*ICAO location identifier*] (ICLI)
SYGH	Good Hope [*Guyana*] [*ICAO location identifier*] (ICLI)
SYGN	Synergen, Inc. [*Boulder, CO*] [*NASDAQ symbol*] (NQ)
SYGO	Ogle [*Guyana*] [*ICAO location identifier*] (ICLI)
SYGT	Georgetown [*Guyana*] [*ICAO location identifier*] (ICLI)
SYH	Scottish & York Holdings Ltd. [*Toronto Stock Exchange symbol*]
SYH	See You Home [*Teen slang*]
Syh	Syrohexapla (BJA)
SYHA	Scottish Youth Hostels Association
SYI	Shelbyville, TN [*Location identifier*] [*FAA*] (FAAL)
SYI	Symes Resources [*Vancouver Stock Exchange symbol*]
SYI	Systems Industries, Inc. [*AMEX symbol*] (CTT)
SYIB	Imbaimadai [*Guyana*] [*ICAO location identifier*] (ICLI)
Sy J Int L	Syracuse Journal of International Law and Commerce [*A publication*]
SYK	Skyhawk Resources, Inc. [*Vancouver Stock Exchange symbol*]
SYK	Stykkisholmur [*Iceland*] [*Airport symbol*] (OAG)
SYKA	Kaieteur [*Guyana*] [*ICAO location identifier*] (ICLI)
SYKE	Sykes Datatronics, Inc. [*NASDAQ symbol*] (NQ)
SYKI	Kaow Island [*Guyana*] [*ICAO location identifier*] (ICLI)
SYKK	Kurukabaru [*Guyana*] [*ICAO location identifier*] (ICLI)
SYKM	Kamarang [*Guyana*] [*ICAO location identifier*] (ICLI)
SYKR	Karanambo [*Guyana*] [*ICAO location identifier*] (ICLI)
SYKS	Karasabai [*Guyana*] [*ICAO location identifier*] (ICLI)
SYKT	Kato (Karto) [*Guyana*] [*ICAO location identifier*] (ICLI)
SYKW	Kwakwani [*Guyana*] [*ICAO location identifier*] (ICLI)
SYL	San Miguel, CA [*Location identifier*] [*FAA*] (FAAL)
SYL	Somali Youth League [*Political party*]
SYL	Spartacus Youth League (EA)
Syl	[*The*] Syllabi [*A publication*] (DLA)
SYL	Syllable (ADA)
Syl	Syllogos. Journal de la Societe Philologique Grecque de Constantinople [*A publication*]
SYLD	Linden [*Guyana*] [*ICAO location identifier*] (ICLI)
SY & LI	Sherwood Yeomanry and Light Infantry [*British military*] (DMA)
SYLK	Symbolic Link [*Data format*]
SYLL	Syllable
SYLL	Syllogeus [*A publication*]
SYLP	Lumid Pau [*Guyana*] [*ICAO location identifier*] (ICLI)
SYLP	Support Your Local Police
Sy LR	Syracuse Law Review [*A publication*]
SYLT	Lethem [*Guyana*] [*ICAO location identifier*] (ICLI)
Sylvatrop Philipp For Res J	Sylvatrop. The Philippine Forest Research Journal [*A publication*]
SYM	Salesian Youth Movement (EA)
SYM	Secondary Yield Measurement
SYM	Seymour Resources [*Vancouver Stock Exchange symbol*]
SYM	Simao [*China*] [*Airport symbol*] (OAG)
SYM	Simmons Aviation [*Negaunee, MI*] [*FAA designator*] (FAAC)
SYM	Symbiont
SYM	Symbol [*or Symbolic*] (AAG)
Sym	Symmachus' Greek Translation of the Bible [*A publication*] (BJA)
sym	Symmetrical [*Also, s*] [*Chemistry*]
SYM	Symmetry
SYM	Symphony
Sym	Symphony Recording Co. [*Record label*]
Sym	Symposium [*A publication*]
SYM	Syms Corp. [*NYSE symbol*] (SPSG)

SYM .... System (MDG)
SYMAN .... Symbol Manipulation [Data processing]
SYM/ANNOT ... Symbology Annotation (MCD)
SYMAP..... Synagraphic Mapping System [Computer-made maps]
SYMB....... Mabaruma [Guyana] [ICAO location identifier] (ICLI)
SYMB........ Symbion, Inc. [NASDAQ symbol] (NQ)
SYMB........ Symbol
SYMBA..... Symbioses [A publication]
SYMBAL .. Symbolic Algebraic Language [Data processing]
SYMBAS... Symbolization All Series (ADA)
SYMBOLANG ... Symbolic Manipulation Language [Data
            processing] (CSR)
SymbOsl ... Symbolae Osloenses [A publication]
Symb Oslo ... Symbolae Osloenses [A publication]
Symb Philol Danielsson ... Symbolae Philologicae [O. A.] Danielsson
            Octogenario Dicatae [Uppsala] [A publication] (OCD)
SYMC........ Symantec Corp. [NASDAQ symbol] (NQ)
SYMCA..... Symposium (International) on Combustion. Proceedings [A
            publication]
Sym Code... Syms' Code of English Law [1870] [A publication] (DLA)
SYMD .... Mahdia [Guyana] [ICAO location identifier] (ICLI)
SYMD .... Systemed, Inc. [Salt Lake City, UT] [NASDAQ symbol] (NQ)
SYMDEB .. Symbolic Debugger [Also, sdb, SOLD] [Data processing]
Syme .... Syme's Scotch Justiciary Reports [1826-30] [A
            publication] (DLA)
SYMED..... Synthetic Metals [A publication]
SYMEVETOPHARSA ... Syndicat des Medecins, Veterinaires, Pharmaciens,
            et Sages Femmes Africains du Mali [Union of African
            Doctors, Pharmacists, Midwives, and Veterinarians of the
            Mali Federation]
Symf.......... Symfoni & Artist [Record label] [Sweden]
SYMK........ Sym-Tek Systems, Inc. [NASDAQ symbol] (NQ)
SYMM ...... Monkey Mountain [Guyana] [ICAO location identifier] (ICLI)
SYMM ...... Symmetrical (MSA)
Sym Mag ... Symphony Magazine [A publication]
SYMMOD ... Symbolic Modeling [Data processing]
SYMMTRAC ... Sylvania Multimode Tracking [Aerospace] (MCD)
SYMN .... Manari [Guyana] [ICAO location identifier] (ICLI)
Sym News .. Symphony News [A publication]
SYMP........ Mountain Point [Guyana] [ICAO location identifier] (ICLI)
Symp.......... Symposium [of Plato] [Classical studies] (OCD)
SYMP........ Symposium (MSA)
Symp .... Symposium [of Lucian] [Classical studies] (OCD)
Symp .... Symposium [of Xenophon] [Classical studies] (OCD)
SYMPA..... Symposia on Theoretical Physics and Mathematics [A
            publication]
Symp Abnorm Subsurf Pressure Proc ... Symposium on Abnormal Subsurface
            Pressure. Proceedings [A publication]
SYMPAC .. Symbolic Program for Automatic Control
Symp Angiol Sanitoriana ... Symposia Angiologica Sanitoriana [A
            publication]
sympat........ Sympathetic [Neurology]
Symp Biol Hung ... Symposia Biologica Hungarica [A publication]
Symp Br Soc Dev Biol ... Symposium. British Society for Developmental
            Biology [A publication]
Symp Br Soc Parasitol ... Symposia. British Society for Parasitology [A
            publication]
Symp Cell Biol ... Symposia for Cell Biology [Japan] [A publication]
Symp Chem Nat Prod Symp Pap ... Symposium on the Chemistry of Natural
            Products. Symposium Papers [A publication]
Symp Coal Manag Tech Pap ... Symposium on Coal Management
            Techniques. Papers [A publication]
Symp Coal Mine Drain Res Pap ... Symposium on Coal Mine Drainage
            Research. Papers [A publication]
Symp Coal Prep Pap ... Symposium on Coal Preparation. Papers [A
            publication]
Symp Coal Util Pap ... Symposium on Coal Utilization. Papers [A
            publication]
Symp Ecol Res Humid Trop Vegtn ... Symposium on Ecological Research in
            Humid Tropics Vegetation [A publication]
Symp Eng Appl Mech ... Symposium on Engineering Applications of
            Mechanics [A publication]
Symp Eng Geol Soils Eng Proc ... Symposium on Engineering Geology and
            Soils Engineering. Proceedings [A publication]
Symp Faraday Soc ... Symposia. Faraday Society [A publication]
Symp Foods ... Symposium of Foods [A publication]
Symp Freq Control Proc ... Symposium on Frequency Control. Proceedings [A
            publication]
Symp Fundam Cancer Res ... Symposium on Fundamental Cancer Research
            [A publication]
Symp Fundam Cancer Res Collect Pap ... Symposium on Fundamental Cancer
            Research. Collections of Papers [A publication]
Symp Genet Biol Ital ... Symposia Genetica et Biologica Italica [A publication]
Symp Genet Breed Wheat Proc ... Symposium on Genetics and Breeding of
            Wheat. Proceedings [A publication]
SYMPH..... Symphony (ADA)
Symp (Int) Combust Proc ... Symposium (International) on Combustion.
            Proceedings [A publication]
Symp Int Soc Cell Biol ... Symposia. International Society for Cell Biology [A
            publication]

Symp Int Union Biol Sci Proc ... Symposium. International Union of
            Biological Sciences. Proceedings [A publication]
Symp Maize Prod Southeast Asia ... Symposium on Maize Production in
            Southeast Asia [A publication]
Symp Med Hoechst ... Symposia Medica Hoechst [A publication]
Symp Microb Drug Resist ... Symposium on Microbial Drug Resistance [A
            publication]
Symp Mine Prep Plant Refuse Disposal Pap ... Symposium on Mine and
            Preparation Plant Refuse Disposal. Papers [A publication]
Symp Moessbauer Eff Methodol Proc ... Symposium on Moessbauer Effect
            Methodology. Proceedings [A publication]
Symp Natl Phys Lab (UK) ... Symposium. National Physical Laboratory
            (United Kingdom) [A publication]
Symp Neurosci ... Symposia in Neuroscience [A publication]
Symp Ocul Ther ... Symposium on Ocular Therapy [A publication]
Symp Oral Sens Percept ... Symposium on Oral Sensation and Perception [A
            publication]
Symposium ... Symposium: A Quarterly Journal in Modern Foreign
            Literatures [A publication]
Sympos Math ... Symposia Mathematica [A publication]
Symposum Jun Bar ... Symposium. Association de Jeune Barreau de Montreal
            [A publication] (DLA)
Sympos Univ Upsaliensis Annum Quingentesimum Celebrantis ... Symposia
            Universitatis Upsaliensis Annum Quingentesimum
            Celebrantis [A publication]
Symp Pap Symp Chem Nat Prod ... Symposium Papers. Symposium on the
            Chemistry of Natural Products [A publication]
Symp Particleboard Proc ... Symposium on Particleboard. Proceedings [A
            publication]
Symp Pharmacol Ther Toxicol Group ... Symposium. Pharmacology,
            Therapeutics, and Toxicology Group. International
            Association for Dental Research [A publication]
Symp Priv Invest Abroad ... Symposium. Private Investors Abroad [A
            publication]
Symp Pyrrolizidine Senecio Alka ... Symposium on Pyrrolizidine Senecio
            Alkaloids. Toxicity [A publication]
Symp Regul Enzyme Act Synth Norm Neoplast Tissues Proc ... Symposium
            on Regulation of Enzyme Activity and Syntheses in Normal
            and Neoplastic Tissues. Proceedings [A publication]
Symp R Entomol Soc Lond ... Symposia. Royal Entomological Society of
            London [A publication]
Symp R Entomol Soc London ... Symposia. Royal Entomological Society of
            London [A publication]
Symp Salivary Gland ... Symposium for the Salivary Gland [A publication]
Symp Ser Australas Inst Min Metall ... Symposia Series. Australasian
            Institute of Mining and Metallurgy [A publication]
Symp Ser Immunobiol Stand ... Symposia Series in Immunobiological
            Standardization [A publication]
Symp Ser Inst Fuel (London) ... Symposium Series. Institute of Fuel (London)
            [A publication]
Symp Soc Dev Biol ... Symposia. Society for Developmental Biology [A
            publication]
Symp Soc Exp Biol ... Symposia. Society for Experimental Biology [A
            publication]
Symp Soc Gen Microbiol ... Symposium. Society for General Microbiology [A
            publication]
Symp Soc Study Dev Growth ... Symposium. Society for the Study of
            Development and Growth [A publication]
Symp Soc Study Hum Biol ... Symposia. Society for the Study of Human
            Biology [A publication]
Symp Soc Study Inborn Errors Metab ... Symposium. Society for the Study of
            Inborn Errors of Metabolism [A publication]
Symp Surf Min Reclam Pap ... Symposium on Surface Mining and
            Reclamation. Papers [A publication]
Symp Surf Phenom Enhanced Oil Recovery ... Symposium on Surface
            Phenomena in Enhanced Oil Recovery [A publication]
Symp Swed Nutr Found ... Symposia. Swedish Nutrition Foundation [A
            publication]
sympt .... Symptom [Medicine]
Symp Theor Phys Math ... Symposia on Theoretical Physics and Mathematics
            [United States] [A publication]
Symp Turbul Liq Proc ... Symposium on Turbulence in Liquids. Proceedings
            [A publication]
Symp Underground Min Pap ... Symposium on Underground Mining. Papers
            [A publication]
Symp Zool Soc Lond ... Symposia. Zoological Society of London [A
            publication]
SYMR........ Matthews Ridge [Guyana] [ICAO location identifier] (ICLI)
SYMRO..... System Management Research Operation (DIT)
SYMS........ Secondary Yield Measurement System
SYMT........ Symetrics Industries, Inc. [NASDAQ symbol] (NQ)
SYMW ...... Maruranawa [Guyana] [ICAO location identifier] (ICLI)
SYMWAR ... System for Estimating Wartime Attrition and Replacement
            Requirements (AABC)
SYN .... Stanton, MN [Location identifier] [FAA] (FAAL)
SYN .... Synagogue
SYN .... Synaptec, a Knowledge Engineering Corp. [Vancouver Stock
            Exchange symbol]
Syn............ Synbiotics Corp.
SYN .... Synchronous (AAG)

SYN .... Synchronous Idle [*Transmission control character*] [*Data processing*]
SYN .... Syndicate   (ROG)
SYN .... Synod
SYN .... Synonym
Syn .... Synopsis   (DLA)
syn.............. Synovial [*Fluid*] [*Medicine*]
syn.............. Synovitis [*Medicine*]
SYN .... Syntex Corp. [*NYSE symbol*]   (SPSG)
SYN .... Syntex Corp., Palo Alto, CA [*OCLC symbol*]   (OCLC)
Syn .... Syntheses [*A publication*]
SYN .... Synthesizer
SYN .... Synthetic   (AAG)
SYNA .... New Amsterdam [*Guyana*] [*ICAO location identifier*]   (ICLI)
SYNAC... Synthesis of Aircraft   (MCD)
SYNAPSE ... CUEA Synthesis and Publication Segment [*Marine science*]   (MSC)
SYNBAPS ... Synthetic Bathymetric Profiling System [*Naval Oceanographic Office*]
SYNC........ Synchromechanism
SYNC........ Synchronize   (AAG)
sync........ Synchrony
SYNCD...... Synchronized   (AAG)
SYNCELL ... Synthetic Cell [*Biological research*]
SYNCG....... Synchronizing   (AAG)
SYNCH ..... Synchronize
SYNCH ..... Synchronous Transmission [*Data processing*]   (TSSD)
SYNCOM ... Synchronous-Orbiting Communications Satellite [*GSFC*]
Syn Commun ... Synthetic Communications [*A publication*]
SYNCR....... Synchronizer   (AAG)
SYNCRO... Synchromesh [*Automotive engineering*]
SYNCRUDE ... Synthetic Crude
SYNCS ...... Synchronous   (AAG)
SYND .... Syndicate
synd........... Syndrome [*Medicine*]
SYNDARC ... Standard Format for Exchange of MAPMOPP Data among Data Centers   (MSC)
SYNDETS ... Synthetic Detergents
SYNDEX... Syndicated Exclusivity [*FCC*]
SYNE......... Syntech International, Inc. [*NASDAQ symbol*]   (NQ)
SYNED....... Synerjy [*A publication*]
SYNEE7.... Symposia in Neuroscience [*A publication*]
SYNESCI.. Syndicat National des Enseignants du Second Degre de Cote d'Ivoire
SYNFRQ... Synthesizer Frequency
SYNFUELS ... Synthetic Fuels
SYNG .... Synergetics International, Inc. [*NASDAQ symbol*]   (NQ)
SYNG .... Synergy. Syncrude Canada [*A publication*]
Syn Hist L ... Synthese Historical Library [*A publication*]
Syn Inorg Met-Org Chem ... Synthesis in Inorganic and Metal-Organic Chemistry [*Later, Synthesis and Reactivity in Inorganic and Metalorganic Chemistry*] [*A publication*]
SYNMAS.. Synchronous Missile Alarm System
SYNON..... Synonym   (ROG)
SYNOP...... Synopsis   (AABC)
Synop Br Fauna New Ser ... Synopses of the British Fauna. New Series [*A publication*]
Synopsis R ... Synopsis Revue [*A publication*]
Synopsis Swedish Bldg Res ... Synopsis of Swedish Building Research [*A publication*]
Syn Org...... Synthetische Methoden der Organischen Chemie [*Synthetic Methods of Organic Chemistry*] [*A publication*]
Synpt......... Synoptic [*or Synoptist*]   (BJA)
SYNR........ Synercom Technology, Inc. [*NASDAQ symbol*]   (NQ)
SYNRAMS ... Synoptic Random Access Measurement System   (NOAA)
Syn Reac In ... Synthesis and Reactivity in Inorganic and Metalorganic Chemistry [*A publication*]
Syn Reactiv Inorg Metal Org C ... Synthesis and Reactivity in Inorganic and Metalorganic Chemistry [*A publication*]
SYNROC... Synthetic Rock [*For storage of nuclear waste*]
SYNS........ Synopsis   (MSA)
SYNSCP.... Synchroscope   (KSC)
SYNSEM .. Syntax and Semantics   (IEEE)
Syn Ser....... Synopsis Series of the United States Treasury Decisions [*A publication*]   (DLA)
SYNSPADE ... Symposium on the Numerical Solution of Partial Differential Equations [*Book title, Academic Press*]
SYNT........ Syntro Corp. [*NASDAQ symbol*]   (NQ)
SYNTAC... Synthetic Tactics
SYNTEEDISETO ... Syndicat des Travailleurs de l'Energie Electrique et de Distribution d'Eau du Togo [*Union of Electrical and Water Distribution Workers of Togo*]
Synth.......... Syntheses. An International Quarterly for the Logical and Psychological Study of the Foundations of the Sciences [*A publication*]
SYNTH ..... Synthesizer
SYNTH ..... Synthetic
Synth Commun ... Synthetic Communications [*A publication*]
Synthesis (C) ... Synthesis (Cambridge) [*A publication*]
Synth Fuels ... Synthetic Fuels [*A publication*]
Synth Fuels Update ... Synthetic Fuels Update [*A publication*]

Synth Libr ... Synthese Library [*A publication*]
Synth Met ... Synthetic Metals [*Switzerland*] [*A publication*]
Synth Methods Org Chem Yearb ... Synthetic Methods of Organic Chemistry Yearbook [*A publication*]
Synth Pipeline Gas Symp Proc ... Synthetic Pipeline Gas Symposium. Proceedings [*A publication*]
Synth React Inorg Metorg Chem ... Synthesis and Reactivity in Inorganic and Metalorganic Chemistry [*A publication*]
Synth Rubber ... Synthetic Rubber [*A publication*]
Synth Rubber Ind (Lanzhou People's Repub China) ... Synthetic Rubber Industry (Lanzhou, People's Republic of China) [*A publication*]
SYNTI ...... Synchro Tie
SYNTIRT ... Syndicat des Travailleurs des Industries Reunies du Togo [*Union of Workers of United Industries of Togo*]
SYNTOL... Syntagmatic Organization Language [*Data processing*]
SYNTRAN ... Syntax Translation [*Data processing*]   (DIT)
SYNZYMES ... Synthetic Enzymes
SYO .... Sayre, OK [*Location identifier*] [*FAA*]   (FAAL)
SYO .... Skygold Resources [*Vancouver Stock Exchange symbol*]
SYO .... Synalloy Corp. [*AMEX symbol*]   (SPSG)
SYO .... Syowa [*Ongul*] [*Antarctica*] [*Seismograph station code, US Geological Survey*]   (SEIS)
SYO .... Syowa Base [*Antarctica*] [*Geomagnetic observatory code*]
SYOR .... Orinduik [*Guyana*] [*ICAO location identifier*]   (ICLI)
Syoyak Zass ... Syoyakugaku Zasshi. Japanese Journal of Pharmacognosy [*A publication*]
SYP........... Parkland Regional Library, Yorkton, Saskatchewan [*Library symbol*] [*National Library of Canada*]   (NLC)
SYP........... Santa Ynez Peak [*California*] [*Seismograph station code, US Geological Survey*]   (SEIS)
SYP........... Southern Yellow Pine
SYP........... Spiritualist Yoga Fellowship   (EAIO)
SYP........... Suomen Yksityisyrittaejaein Puoluejaerjesto [*Finnish Private Entrepreneurs' Party*] [*Political party*]   (PPE)
Syp .... Syropalaestinum   (BJA)
SYPH........ Syphilis   (DSUE)
Sy PO........ Supply Petty Officer [*British military*]   (DMA)
SYPR........ Paruima [*Guyana*] [*ICAO location identifier*]   (ICLI)
syr .... Sirop [*Syrup*] [*Pharmacy*]
SYR.......... Smyrna [*Washington*] [*Seismograph station code, US Geological Survey*]   (SEIS)
SYR.......... South Yorkshire Railway [*British*]   (ROG)
SYR........... Syracuse [*New York*] [*Airport symbol*]
SYR........... Syria [*or Syrian Arab Republic*] [*ANSI three-letter standard code*]   (CNC)
Syr .... Syria. Revue d'Art Oriental et d'Archeologie [*A publication*]
syr .... Syriac [*MARC language code*] [*Library of Congress*]   (LCCP)
SYR.......... Syrian [*Language, etc.*]   (ROG)
SYR.......... Syringe [*Medicine*]
SYR.......... Syrupus [*Syrup*] [*Pharmacy*]
SYRA........ Syracuse Supply Co. [*NASDAQ symbol*]   (NQ)
Syrac Law R ... Syracuse Law Review [*A publication*]
SYRACUSE ... System of Radio Communications Using a Satellite [*Telecommunications*]   (TSSD)
Syracuse HA ... Syracuse Herald-America and Post-Standard [*A publication*]
Syracuse HJ ... Syracuse Herald Journal [*A publication*]
Syracuse Int'l L & Com ... Syracuse Journal of International Law and Commerce [*A publication*]
Syracuse J Int'l L ... Syracuse Journal of International Law [*A publication*]   (DLA)
Syracuse L Rev ... Syracuse Law Review [*A publication*]
Syr D.......... De Syria Dea [*of Lucian*] [*Classical studies*]   (OCD)
SyrH .... Hexaplaric Syriac   (BJA)
Syrian J Stomatol ... Syrian Journal of Stomatology [*A publication*]
Syria R .... Syria. Revue d'Art Oriental et d'Archeologie [*A publication*]
Syr J Intl..... Syracuse Journal of International Law and Commerce [*A publication*]
Syr J Intl L & Com ... Syracuse Journal of International Law and Commerce [*A publication*]
Syr LR........ Syracuse Law Review [*A publication*]
Syr Mesop St ... Syro-Mesopotamian Studies [*A publication*]
SYRP........ Summer Youth Recreation Program
SYRUCL... Syracuse University College of Law   (DLA)
SyrW......... Syriac Version in Walton's Polyglot   (BJA)
SYS........... ISI Systems [*AMEX symbol*]   (SPSG)
SYS........... See Your Service   (FAAC)
SYS........... Sobeys Stores Ltd. [*Toronto Stock Exchange symbol*]
SYS........... Somerset, PA [*Location identifier*] [*FAA*]   (FAAL)
SYS........... Sweet Yet Simple [*Data processing*]
Sy S........... Syn og Segn. Norsk-Tidsskrift [*A publication*]
SYS........... System   (AFM)
SYSAD ...... Systems Adviser
SYSADMIN ... System Administrator [*Data processing*]
SYSCAP... System of Circuit Analysis Program
SYSCOM .. System Communications
SYSCOM .. Systems Command [*Navy*]
SYSCON ... Systems Control [*Military*]   (AABC)
SYSDEV... Systems Development   (NOAA)
SYSE .... Systems Equipment Corp. [*NASDAQ symbol*]   (NQ)
SYSEC....... System Synthesizer and Evaluation Center

SYSG .... Systematics General Corp. [*NASDAQ symbol*] (NQ)
SYSGEN ... Systems Generator [*or Generation*] [*Data processing*]
SYSIN .... System Input [*Data processing*] (MDG)
SYSLIB ...... System Library [*Data processing*] (MDG)
SYSLOG ... System Log [*Data processing*]
SYSOP .... System Operator [*Computer networking*]
SYSOUT ... System Output [*Data processing*] (IBMDP)
SYSP .... Sixth-Year Specialist Program [*Library science*]
SYSPLLTM ... System Purchase of Long Lead Time Material
SYSPM .... System Performance Measure (MCD)
SYSPOP .... System Programmed Operators [*Data processing*] (MDG)
Sys Proced ... Systems and Procedures [*A publication*]
SYSRES .... System Residence [*Data processing*]
Sys and Soft ... Systems and Software [*A publication*]
SYST .... System
SYST .... Systematics, Inc. [*NASDAQ symbol*] (NQ)
syst .... Systemic [*Medicine*]
Syst .... Systems [*A publication*]
syst .... Systolic [*Cardiology*]
Syst Appl Microbiol ... Systematic and Applied Microbiology [*A publication*]
Syst Assoc Publ ... Systematics Association. Publication [*A publication*]
Syst Assoc Spec Vol ... Systematics Association. Special Volume [*A publication*]
Syst Ass Spec Vol ... Systematics Association. Special Volume [*A publication*]
Syst Bot ...... Systematic Botany [*A publication*]
Syst-Comput-Controls ... Systems-Computers-Controls [*A publication*]
Syst & Control ... Systems and Control [*A publication*]
Syst and Control Lett ... Systems and Control Letters [*A publication*]
Systematics Assoc Pub ... Systematics Association. Publication [*A publication*]
Systems-Comput-Controls ... Systems-Computers-Controls [*A publication*]
Systems Control Lett ... Systems and Control Letters [*A publication*]
Systems & Proc J ... Systems and Procedures Journal [*A publication*]
Systems Sci ... Systems Science [*A publication*]
Systems Theory Res ... Systems Theory Research [*A publication*]
Syst Entomol ... Systematic Entomology [*A publication*]
SYSTEP .... Systems Test and Evaluation Plan [*Military*] (AABC)
Syst Int...... Systems International [*A publication*]
Syst Logiques ... Systemes Logiques [*A publication*]
SYSTO ...... System Staff Office [*or Officer*]
Syst Objectives Solutions ... Systems, Objectives, Solutions [*A publication*]
Syst Parasitol ... Systematic Parasitology [*A publication*]
SYSTRAN ... Systems Analysis Translator [*Data processing*]
Syst Sci ...... Systems Science [*A publication*]
Syst Technol ... Systems Technology [*A publication*]
Syst Theory Res ... Systems Theory Research [*A publication*]
Syst Zool ..... Systematic Zoology [*A publication*]
Sys User ..... Systems User [*A publication*]
SYSVER .... System Specification Verification (IEEE)
SYT........... Sweet Young Thing [*An attractive girl*] [*Slang*]
SYTA .... Sustained-Yield Tropical Agroecosystem
SYTM........ Georgetown/Timehri Internacional [*Guyana*] [*ICAO location identifier*] (ICLI)
SYU .... Sudanese Youth Union
SYU .... Synchronization Signal Unit [*Telecommunications*]
SYU .... Syuhurei [*South Korea*] [*Seismograph station code, US Geological Survey*] [*Closed*] (SEIS)
SYUBAT ... Science Reports. Yokohama National University. Section II. Biology and Geology [*A publication*]
SYUS........ Specialized Youth Units [*Canada*]
SYV........... Saynor Varah, Inc. [*Toronto Stock Exchange symbol*]
SYV........... Society for Young Victims [*Later, SYV/MCC*] (EA)
SYV........... Sylvester, GA [*Location identifier*] [*FAA*] (FAAL)
SYV.......... Syva Research Library, Palo Alto, CA [*OCLC symbol*] (OCLC)
SYV/MCC ... Society for Young Victims, Missing Children Center (EA)
Syvrem Med ... Syvremenna Meditsina [*A publication*]
SYVV .... Sowthistle Yellow Vein Virus
SYW .... Skyway Resources Ltd. [*Vancouver Stock Exchange symbol*]
SYWI........ Wichabai [*Guyana*] [*ICAO location identifier*] (ICLI)
SYWPP ..... South Yarra Work Preparation Program [*Australia*]
SYY.......... Stornoway [*Scotland*] [*Airport symbol*] (OAG)
SYY........... Sysco Corp. [*NYSE symbol*] (SPSG)
SYZ........... Shelbyville, IL [*Location identifier*] [*FAA*] (FAAL)
SYZ........... Shiraz [*Iran*] [*Airport symbol*] (OAG)
SZ .... Aerolineas de El Salvador [*ICAO designator*] (FAAC)
SZ .... Sceptre Investment Counsel Ltd. [*Toronto Stock Exchange symbol*]
sz .... Schizophrenia [*Psychology*]
Sz .... Schweizerische Landesbibliothek [*Swiss National Library*], Bern, Switzerland [*Library symbol*] [*Library of Congress*] (LCLS)
SZ .... Schweizerische Zeitschrift fuer Volkswirtschaft und Statistik [*A publication*]
SZ .... Secondary Zone
SZ .... Seizure [*Telecommunications*] (TEL)
sz .... Seizure [*Medicine*]
SZ .... Sekspirovskij Zbornik [*A publication*]
SZ .... Sha'arei Zedek (BJA)
SZ .... Shigaku Zasshi [*A publication*]
SZ .... Size (MDG)
SZ .... Sovremennye Zapiski [*A publication*]

SZ .... Splash Zone
SZ .... Stimmen der Zeit [*A publication*]
SZ .... Streptozocin [*Antineoplastic drug*]
SZ .... Sueddeutsche Zeitung [*A publication*]
SZ .... Surface Zero [*Navy*] (NVT)
SZ .... Swaziland [*ANSI two-letter standard code*] (CNC)
sz .... Switzerland [*MARC country of publication code*] [*Library of Congress*] (LCCP)
SZA............ Solar Zenith Angle [*Geophysics*]
SZA............ Soyo [*Angola*] [*Airport symbol*] (OAG)
Szakszerv Szle ... Szakszervezeti Szemle [*A publication*]
Szamki Koezlem ... Szamki Koezlemenyek [*A publication*]
Szamki Tanulmanyok ... Szamitogepalkalmazasi Kutato Intezet. Tanulmanyok [*A publication*]
Szamvit Uegyviteltech ... Szamvitel es Ugyviteltechnika [*A publication*]
SZB............ Silver-Zinc Battery
SZB............ Sintered Zinc Battery
SzBaL .... Lonza Aktiengesellschaft, Zentralbibliothek, Basel, Switzerland [*Library symbol*] [*Library of Congress*] (LCLS)
SzBaM....... Museum fur Volkerkunde und Schweizerisches Museum fur Volkskunde, Basel, Switzerland [*Library symbol*] [*Library of Congress*] (LCLS)
SzBaU........ Universitat Basel, Basel, Switzerland [*Library symbol*] [*Library of Congress*] (LCLS)
SzBaU-IO ... Institut fur Organische Chemie der Universitat Basel, Basel, Switzerland [*Library symbol*] [*Library of Congress*] (LCLS)
SZC............ Silver-Zinc Cell
SZC............ Studia Zrodloznawcze. Commentationes [*A publication*]
SZCSAV..... Annual Review of the Schizophrenic Syndrome [*A publication*]
SZD .... St. George, SC [*Location identifier*] [*FAA*] (FAAL)
SZD .... Sierra Capital Realty Trust IV Co. [*AMEX symbol*] (CTT)
SZD .... Sovetski Zhelezno-Dorozhni [*Soviet railways*] [*USSR*]
S Zd........... Sovetskoe Zdravoochranenie [*A publication*]
SZDKA...... Sovetskoe Zdravookhranenie Kirgizii [*A publication*]
SzDL......... Studien zur Deutschen Literatur [*A publication*]
SZE............ Szeged [*Hungary*] [*Seismograph station code, US Geological Survey*] [*Closed*] (SEIS)
SZEC .... Silver-Zinc Electrochemical Cell
SZECC ...... Silver-Zinc Electrochemical Cell
S Zek......... Sociale Zekerheidsgids [*A publication*]
SzEP .... Studien zur Englischen Philologie [*A publication*]
SZF .... Schweizerische Zeitschrift fuer Forstwesen [*A publication*]
SZF .... Sierra Capital Realty Trust VI Co. [*AMEX symbol*] (SPSG)
SZG .... Salzburg [*Austria*] [*Airport symbol*] (OAG)
SZG .... Schweizerische Zeitschrift fuer Geschichte [*A publication*]
SZG .... Sierra Capital Realty Trust VII Co. [*AMEX symbol*] (SPSG)
SZG .... Soviet Zone Germany (NATG)
SzGB.......... Bibliotheque Battelle, Centre de Recherche, Geneve, Switzerland [*Library symbol*] [*Library of Congress*] (LCLS)
SzGBNU.... Bibliotheque des Nations Unies, Geneve, Switzerland [*Library symbol*] [*Library of Congress*] (LCLS)
SzGE.......... Ecole de Chimie, Geneva, Switzerland [*Library symbol*] [*Library of Congress*] (LCLS)
SzGPAr...... Archives Jean Piaget, Geneve, Switzerland [*Library symbol*] [*Library of Congress*] (LCLS)
SzGSI......... Societe Generale pour l'Industrie, Geneve, Switzerland [*Library symbol*] [*Library of Congress*] (LCLS)
SZH .... Sierra Capital Realty Trust VIII Co. [*AMEX symbol*] (SPSG)
SZHYA...... Schweizerische Zeitschrift fuer Hydrologie [*A publication*]
SZI............. Seattle, WA [*Location identifier*] [*FAA*] (FAAL)
Szigma Mat-Koezgazdasagi Folyoirat ... Szigma. Matematikai-Koezgazdasagi Folyoirat [*A publication*]
SZJ .... Atlanta, GA [*Location identifier*] [*FAA*] (FAAL)
SZK .... Roanoke, VA [*Location identifier*] [*FAA*] (FAAL)
SZK............ Skukuza [*South Africa*] [*Airport symbol*] (OAG)
Szk Gl Gospod Wiejsk Akad Roln Warszawie Zesz Nauk Ogrod ... Szkola Glowna Gospodarstwa Wiejskiego - Akademia Rolnicza w Warszawie. Zeszyty Naukowe. Ogrodnictwo [*A publication*]
Szk Gl Gospod Wiejsk Akad Roln Warszawie Zesz Nauk Roln ... Szkola Glowna Gospodarstwa Wiejskiego - Akademia Rolnicza w Warszawie. Zeszyty Naukowe. Rolnictwo [*A publication*]
Szk Gl Gospod Wiejsk Akad Roln Warszawie Zesz Nauk Zootech ... Szkola Glowna Gospodarstwa Wiejskiego - Akademia Rolnicza w Warszawie. Zeszyty Naukowe. Zootechnika [*A publication*]
Szk Gl Gospod Wiejsk Akd Roln Warszawie Zesz Nauk Weter ... Szkola Glowna Gospodarstwa Wiejskiego - Akademia Rolnicza w Warszawie. Zeszyty Naukowe. Weterynaria [*A publication*]
SZKKB ...... Shimizu Kensetsu Kenkyusho-Ho [*A publication*]
Szklo i Ceram ... Szklo i Ceramika [*A publication*]
Szklo Ceram ... Szklo i Ceramika [*A publication*]
SZL............ Knob Noster, MO [*Location identifier*] [*FAA*] (FAAL)
SzL............ Schriften zur Literatur [*A publication*]
SZL............ Spielzeug. Internationales Fachblatt fuer Spielmittel, Hobby- und Modellbau-Artikel, Christbaumschmuck, Fest- und Scherzartikel, Rohstoffe, Halbteile, Werkzeuge, Maschinen, und Verpackung [*A publication*]
SZL............ SZL Sportsight [*Vancouver Stock Exchange symbol*]

SzLaCU ..... Bibliotheque Cantonal et Universitaire de Lausanne, Lausanne,
              Switzerland [*Library symbol*] [*Library of
              Congress*]   (LCLS)
SzLaS......... Station Federale d'Essais Agricoles, Lausanne, Switzerland
              [*Library symbol*] [*Library of Congress*]   (LCLS)
SZLGD...... Sozialgerichtsbarkeit [*A publication*]
SZM .... Stereo Zoom Microscope
SZM .... Synthetic Zeolite Molecule
SZN .... Santa Barbara, CA [*Location identifier*] [*FAA*]   (FAAL)
SzNU .... Sbornik za Narodni Umotvorenija [*A publication*]
SZO .... Student Zionist Organization [*Defunct*]   (EA)
SZOG .... Soviet Zone of Occupation of Germany   (NATG)
Szolesz Boraszat ... Szoleszet es Boraszat [*A publication*]
SZOR......... Sintered Zinc Oxide Resistor
SZOT......... Szakszervezetek Orszagos Tanacsa [*National Trade Union
              Council*] [*Hungary*]
SZP............ Santa Paula, CA [*Location identifier*] [*FAA*]   (FAAL)
SZP............ Surf Zone Process
SZP............ Synchro Zeroing Procedure
SZPAA ...... Schweizerische Zeitschrift fuer Psychologie und Ihre
              Anwendungen [*A publication*]
SZPMA ..... Sozial- und Praeventivmedizin [*A publication*]
SZPMAA .. Medecine Sociale et Preventive [*A publication*]
SZR........... Sintered Zinc Resistor
SZR............ Stargazer Resources Ltd. [*Vancouver Stock Exchange symbol*]
SZR............ University of South Carolina, Regional Campus Processing
              Center, Columbia, SC [*OCLC symbol*]   (OCLC)
SZS .... Schweizerische Zeitschrift fuer Sozialversicherung [*A
              publication*]
SzS .... Solidarnosc z Solidarnoscia [*Solidarity with Solidarity - SwS*]
              [*London, England*]   (EAIO)
SZS .... Srpska Zemljoradnicka Stranka [*Serbian Agrarian Party*]
              [*Yugoslavia*] [*Political party*]   (PPE)
SZS .... Staatliche Zentrale fuer Strahlenschutz Berlin [*East Germany*]
SZS .... Stewart Island [*New Zealand*] [*Airport symbol*]   (OAG)
SZSB .... Silver-Zinc Secondary [*or Storage*] Battery
SzStg......... Stadtbibliothek Vadiana, St. Gallen, Switzerland [*Library
              symbol*] [*Library of Congress*]   (LCLS)
SZ Str R..... Schweizerische Zeitschrift fuer Strafrecht [*A publication*]
SZT............ Sandpoint, ID [*Location identifier*] [*FAA*]   (FAAL)
SzT............ Schriften zur Theaterwissenschaft [*A publication*]
SZTZA ...... Schweizerische Technische Zeitschrift [*Switzerland*] [*A
              publication*]
SZutNu ...... Sifre Zuta on Numbers   (BJA)
SZVR........ Silicon Zener Voltage Regulator
SZY........... Selmer, TN [*Location identifier*] [*FAA*]   (FAAL)
SZZ............ Szczecin [*Poland*] [*Airport symbol*]   (OAG)
SzZ............ Zentralbibliothek Zurich, Zurich, Switzerland [*Library symbol*]
              [*Library of Congress*]   (LCLS)
SzZE .... Eidgenoessische Technische Hochschule, Zurich, Switzerland
              [*Library symbol*] [*Library of Congress*]   (LCLS)
SzZU.......... Universitat Zurich, Universitatsspital-Bibliothek,
              Kantonsspital, Zurich, Switzerland [*Library symbol*]
              [*Library of Congress*]   (LCLS)

T

T................	Absolute Temperature [*Symbol*] [*IUPAC*]
T................	Aerotec [*Sociedade Aerotec Ltda.*] [*Brazil*] [*ICAO aircraft manufacturer identifier*] (ICAO)
T................	Air Temperature Correction
T................	American Telephone & Telegraph Co. [*NYSE symbol*] [*Wall Street slang name: "Telephone"*] (SPSG)
t------..........	Antarctic [*MARC geographic area code*] [*Library of Congress*] (LCCP)
T................	Backhoe Trench [*Archaeology*]
t................	Celsius Temperature [*Symbol*] [*IUPAC*]
T................	Cleared Through for Landing and Takeoff [*Aviation*] (FAAC)
T................	Internal Transmittance [*Symbol*] [*IUPAC*]
T................	Kinetic Energy [*Symbol*] [*IUPAC*]
t................	Marginal Propensity to Tax [*Economics*]
T................	Meridian Angle
T................	Military Sealift Command Ship [*When precedes vessel classification*] [*Navy symbol*]
T................	Octodecimo [*Book from 12-1/2 to 15 centimeters in height*] [*Bibliography*]
T................	Ribothymidine [*One-letter symbol; see Thd*]
T................	Shape Descriptor [*T-bar and T-square, for example. The shape resembles the letter for which it is named*]
T................	Table
T................	Tablespoon [*Measure*]
T................	Tablet-Shaped [*As in "T-grains"*] [*Photography*]
T................	Tabulated [*or Charted*] LORAN [*Long-Range Aid to Navigation*] Reading
T................	Tace [*Be Silent*]
T................	Tackle [*Football*]
T................	Tactical Organization
T................	Tactual
T................	Taken
T................	Takeoff [*Aviation*] (FAAC)
T................	Tala [*Monetary unit in Western Samoa*]
T................	Talc
T................	Talk/Monitor (NASA)
T................	Talon [*Heel of the Bow*] [*Music*]
T................	Tamoxifen [*Antineoplastic drug*]
T................	Tan (FAAC)
T................	Tango [*Phonetic alphabet*] [*International*] (DSUE)
T................	Tanhuma (BJA)
T................	Tank [*Trains*] [*British*]
T................	Tanna (BJA)
T................	Taped Commentary [*On a bus tour*] [*British*]
T................	Taper
T................	Tapered Hatchway [*on a ship*] (DS)
T................	Tappan's Ohio Common Pleas Reports [*A publication*] (DLA)
T................	Tare [*Phonetic alphabet*] [*World War II*] (DSUE)
T................	Target
T................	Tasto [*Touch, Key, Fingerboard*] [*Music*]
T................	Taxation [*Economics*]
T................	Taxes (DLA)
T................	Teacher
T................	Tear [*Phonetic alphabet*] [*World War II*]
t................	Teaspoon [*Measure*]
T................	Teatar [*Sofia*] [*A publication*]
T................	Teatr [*A publication*]
T................	Technical [*or Technician*]
T................	Technical College [*British*]
T................	Technological Service [*Queen's Award*] [*British*]
T................	Tee [*Piping joint, etc.*] [*Technical drawings*]
T................	Teeth [*Technical drawings*]
T................	Teich [*Pond*] [*German military*]
T................	Telefunken [*Record label*] [*Germany, etc.*]
T................	Telegram (BJA)
T................	Telegraph (ROG)
T................	Telegrapher [*Navy*]
T................	Telephone
T................	Telephone Trunk Call [*British*] (ROG)
T................	Teletype
t................	Telocentric
T................	Temperance [*i.e., entitled to a daily rum ration but voluntarily not drawing it and receiving money instead*] [*See also G, UA*] [*Navy*] [*British*]
T................	Temperature
T................	Tempo
T................	Temporal
T................	Temporary
T................	Tempore [*In the Time of*] [*Latin*]
T................	Tender [*Horticulture*]
T................	Tendre [*Tender*] [*Music*]
T................	Tenero [*Tender*]
T................	Tennessee State Library and Archives, Nashville, TN [*Library symbol*] [*Library of Congress*] (LCLS)
T................	Tenor
T................	Tenor [*Genotype of Phlox paniculata*]
T................	Tense
T................	Tension
T................	Tensor
T................	Tentative Target
T................	Ter [*Three Times*] [*Pharmacy*]
T................	Tera [*A prefix meaning multiplied by 10¹² SI symbol*]
T................	Teracycle (BUR)
T................	Term [*Medicine*]
T................	Terminal
T................	Terminal Area Chart [*Followed by identification*] [*Aviation*]
T................	Termination
T................	Terminator [*Genetics*]
T................	Terminus [*Biochemistry*]
T................	Terrain
T................	Territory
T................	Tertiary
t................	Tertiary [*Also, tert*] [*Chemistry*]
T................	Tesla [*Symbol*] [*SI unit of flux density*]
T................	Test (MSA)
T................	Test Equipment (NG)
T................	Test Reactor
T................	Test Set
T................	Testament (ROG)
T................	Testator [*Legal term*]
T................	Tetracycline [*Antibiotic compound*]
T................	Teuthonista [*A publication*]
T................	Texana [*A publication*]
T................	Thaler [*or Talari*] [*Monetary unit*] [*Ethiopia*]
T................	Than
T................	That
T................	Theatres [*Public-performance tariff class*] [*British*]
T................	Theft
T................	Theology [*A publication*]
T................	Theophylline [*Pharmacology*]
T................	Thermodynamic Temperature [*Symbol*] [*IUPAC*]
T................	Thermometer
T................	Thermoplastic [*Also, TP*] [*Plastics technology*] (MSA)
T................	Thermostabilized (NASA)
T................	Thickness
T................	Thief
T................	Thioguanine [*Also, TG*] [*Antineoplastic drug*]
T................	Thiopental [*An anesthetic*]
T................	Third Word Designator [*Data processing*]
T................	Thomas Mieres [*Flourished, 1429-39*] [*Authority cited in pre-1607 legal work*] (DSA)
T................	Thoracic [*Anatomy*]
T................	Thread
T................	Threonine [*One-letter symbol; see Thr*] [*An amino acid*]
T................	Thromboxane [*Also, TA, Tx, TX*] [*Biochemistry*]
T................	Throttle Command (NASA)
T................	Thrust of Propeller [*Naval engineering*] (DAS)
T................	Thruster [*of a ship*] (DS)
T................	Thunderstorm [*Meteorology*]
T................	Thymine [*Also, Thy*] [*Biochemistry*]
T................	Thymus [*Medicine*]
T................	Thymus Derived [*Hematology*]

T...............	Thyroid [*Medicine*]
T...............	Tidal Gas [*Respiration*] [*Medicine*]
T...............	Tide Rips [*Navigation*]
T...............	Tie [*Sports*]
T...............	Tier [*Psychology*]
T...............	Tiler [*Freemasonry*]
T...............	Tilic Subgroup [*Ilmenite, titanite, perofskite, rutile*] [*CIPW classification*] [*Geology*]
T...............	Time
t...............	Time [*Symbol*] [*IUPAC*]
T...............	Time [*A publication*]
T...............	Time Consumed in Playing Game [*Baseball*]
T+............	Time Postintegration (NASA)
T-.............	Time Prior to Launch [*Usually followed by a number*] [*NASA*] (KSC)
T...............	Time-Reversal [*Atomic physics*]
t...............	Time in Seconds [*Aerospace*]
T...............	Time Trial
T...............	Timekeeper [*Sports*]
T...............	Times [*London*] [*A publication*]
T...............	Tip [*Switchboard plug*] [*Telecommunications*] (TEL)
T...............	Tipper [*Shipping*] (DS)
T...............	Tithing [*Geographical division*] [*British*]
T...............	Title [*Bibliography*]
t...............	Titre [*Security Stock*] [*French*] [*Business term*]
T...............	Toarcian [*Geology*]
T...............	Tobacco Tax Ruling, Internal Revenue Bureau [*United States*] [*A publication*] (DLA)
T...............	Toc [*Phonetic alphabet*] [*Pre-World War II*] (DSUE)
T...............	Tocopherol [*Biochemistry*]
T...............	Toe
T...............	Toilet (MSA)
T...............	Toll
T...............	Tome [*Volume*] [*French*] (ILCA)
T...............	Tommy [*Phonetic alphabet*] [*Royal Navy*] [*World War I*] (DSUE)
T...............	Tomo [*Volume*] [*Italian*] (ILCA)
T...............	Tomus [*Volume*]
T...............	Ton
T...............	Tonnage [*Shipping*]
t...............	Tonne [*Metric*]
T...............	Tooth
T...............	Top
t...............	Top [*or Truth*] (Quark) [*Atomic physics*]
T...............	Top Secret
T...............	Topical (ADA)
T...............	Toronto Stock Exchange
T...............	Torpedo [*Obsolete*] [*Navy*] [*British*] (ROG)
T...............	Torpedoman [*Navy*] [*British*]
T-0............	Torque
T...............	Tosefta (BJA)
T...............	Total
T...............	Tourist [*Rate*] [*Value of the English pound*]
T...............	Toward [*Altitude difference*]
T...............	Town
T...............	Township
T...............	Trace of Precipitation [*Less than 0.005 inch of rain or 0.05 inch of snow*]
T...............	Tracer [*Ammunition*] (NATG)
T...............	Trachea [*Anatomy*]
T₃..............	Track
T...............	Tracker [*British military*] (DMA)
T...............	Traded
T...............	Tradesman [*British military*] (DMA)
T...............	Traditio [*A publication*]
T...............	Traditional (BJA)
T...............	Trafalgar [*On army list*] [*British*] (ROG)
T...............	Traffic Cases [*A publication*] (DLA)
T...............	Traffic Headquarters
T-.............	Trainer [*Designation for all US military aircraft*]
T...............	Training (FAAC)
t...............	Trans [*Chemical conformation*]
T...............	Transaction
T...............	Transcription
T...............	Transducer
t...............	Transfer [*Genetics*]
T...............	Transferred [*Navy*]
T...............	Transferrin [*Also, TF, TRF*] [*Biochemistry*]
T...............	Transformation Rule [*Linguistics*]
T...............	Transformer
T...............	Transfusion [*Medicine*]
T...............	Transient [*Bureau of the Census*]
T...............	Transit
T...............	Transition
T...............	Transitive
T...............	Translated (ROG)
T...............	Translation
T...............	Translocation
T...............	Transmit [*or Transmitting*]
T...............	Transmitter
T...............	Transpiration [*Botany*]

T...............	Transport (NATG)
t...............	Transport Number [*Symbol*] [*Electrochemistry*]
T...............	Transvaal Provincial Division Reports [*South Africa*] [*A publication*] (DLA)
T...............	Transverse Tubule [*Muscle neurobiology*]
T...............	Trawling
T...............	Tread [*Stair details*] [*Technical drawings*]
T...............	Treasurer
T...............	Treasury [*As in T-Bill, T-Bond, T-Note*]
T...............	Treated
T...............	Treatment
T...............	Treble [*Music*] (ROG)
T...............	Triangle
T...............	Trichome [*Botany*]
T...............	Triggered [*Cardiology*]
T...............	Trillion [*10¹²*
T...............	Trillo [*Trill*] [*Music*]
T...............	Trimethoprim [*Also, TMP*] [*Antibacterial compound*]
T...............	Trinitas [*The Trinity*]
T...............	Triode
T...............	Triple
T...............	Tritium [*Also, H₃ Radioisotope of hydrogen*]
t...............	Triton [*A nuclear particle*]
T...............	Triton Industries, Inc. [*Toronto Stock Exchange symbol*]
T...............	Tropical [*Load line mark, or air mass*]
T...............	Trotter
T...............	Troy [*A system of weights for precious metals*]
T...............	Truce
T...............	True [*Direction*]
T...............	Truss (AAG)
T...............	Tubulin [*A protein*]
T...............	Tuesday
T...............	Tufa [*Quality of the bottom*] [*Nautical charts*]
T...............	Tug [*Navy*]
T...............	Tumor [*Oncology*]
T...............	Tun [*Unit of liquid capacity*]
T...............	Turbocharged [*Automotive engineering*]
T...............	Turin [*A publication*]
T...............	Turkish
T...............	Turn [*or Turning*]
T...............	Turner [*Navy rating*] [*British*]
T...............	Turnover Index [*Botany*]
T...............	Tutti [*Sing or Play Together*] [*Music*]
T...............	Twentyfourmo [*Book up to 15 centimeters in height*]
T...............	Twin Screw [*Shipping*] (DS)
T...............	Typed [*Manuscript descriptions*]
T...............	Typhlosole [*Biology*]
T...............	Typhoid
T...............	Wrong Tense of Verb [*Used in correcting manuscripts, etc.*]
T-0............	Time Zero (MCD)
T-1............	Carrier which identifies the all-digital communications links (TSSD)
T1..............	First Transcript [*Genetics*]
T₁..............	Tricuspid First Heart Sound [*Cardiology*]
T₂..............	Diiodothyronine [*Endocrinology*]
T2..............	Second Transcript [*Genetics*]
T2..............	Time of Flight to Intercept [*Military*] (CAAL)
T₂..............	Tricuspid Second Heart Sound [*Cardiology*]
T3..............	Tank Track Test [*Army*]
T-3............	Tocotrienol [*Biochemistry*]
T₃..............	Triiodothyronine [*Also, TITh*] [*Endocrinology*]
3T..............	Triple Throw [*Switch*]
T4..............	Thyroxine [*Also, Thx, Ty*] [*An amino acid*] [*Endocrinology*]
5T..............	Mauritania [*Aircraft nationality and registration mark*] (FAAC)
T/5............	Technician Fifth Grade [*Army*]
7T..............	Algeria [*Aircraft nationality and registration mark*] (FAAC)
T-10..........	Codename used by Ronald Reagan while serving as an FBI informant during his term as president of the Screen Actors Guild
T (Bird)......	Thunderbird [*Automobile*] (DSUE)
T (Colds)....	Toxic Colds [*Medicine*]
T (Day).......	Transition Day [*Based on the expected transition from a two-front to a one-front war*] [*World War II*]
T (Day).......	Truce Day
TA..............	Chinese Taipei [*IYRU nationality code*] (IYR)
Ta..............	Ta'anith (BJA)
TA..............	Table of Allowances (MCD)
TA..............	Tabled Agreement [*in labor relations*]
TA..............	Tablet (ADA)
TA..............	TACA International Airlines SA [*El Salvador*] [*ICAO designator*] (ICDA)
TA..............	TACAN [*Tactical Air Navigation*] Approach (FAAC)
TA..............	Tactical Air Missile
TA..............	Tactical Aircraft
T/A............	Tactical Airlift [*Tactical Air Command*]
TA..............	Tailhook Association (EA)
TA..............	Talanta [*A publication*]
TA..............	Talmudical Academy (BJA)
TA..............	Talmudische Archaeologie [*A publication*] (BJA)
TA..............	Tanabe Seiyaku Co. Ltd. [*Japan*] [*Research code symbol*]
TA..............	Tangible Asset

TA	Tank Army (MCD)
TA	Tank Tainers [*Shipping*] (DCTA)
TA	Tanker [*Shipping*] (DCTA)
Ta	Tantalum [*Chemical element*]
TA	Tape Adapter
TA	Tape Advance (AAG)
TA	Tape Armored [*Telecommunications*] (TEL)
TA	Target (DEN)
TA	Target Acquisition (MCD)
TA	Target Aircraft (MUGU)
TA	Target Area [*Military*] (AFM)
TA	Targeting Agent [*Medicine*]
TA	Tariff Act [*1930*]
TA	Tartana [*Ship's rigging*] (ROG)
TA	Task Analysis
TA	Task Assignment (AAG)
TA	Tax Abatement
TA	Tax Agent
TA	Tax Amortization [*Plan*]
TA	Tea Association of the USA (EA)
TA	Teaching Assistant [*in a university*]
TA	Technical Advisor (MCD)
TA	Technical Analysis (NG)
TA	Technical Assessor
TA	Technical Assistance [*or Assistant*]
TA	Technology Assessment Database [*Fachinformationszentrum Karlsruhe GmbH*] [*Federal Republic of Germany*] [*Information service or system*] (CRD)
TA	Technonet Asia (EA)
TA	Tel Aviv [*Israel*] (BJA)
TA	Telegraphic Address
TA	Telephone Apparatus [*JETDS nomenclature*] [*Military*] (CET)
TA	Telescope Assembly (KSC)
TA	Television Associates [*Mountain View, CA*] (TSSD)
TA	Television/Radio Age [*A publication*]
TA	Tell-Amarna [*Egypt*] (BJA)
TA	Tell Asmar [*Iraq*] (BJA)
TA	Telluride Association (EA)
TA	Temperature, Axillary
TA	Temple Autobiographies [*A publication*]
TA	Temporal Arteritis [*Medicine*]
TA	Tension by Applanation [*Ophthalmology*]
TA	Tension Arterielle [*Blood Pressure*] [*Medicine*]
TA	Tenuazonic Acid [*Biochemistry*]
TA	Teologinen Aikakauskirja [*Helsinki*] [*A publication*] (BJA)
TA	Terephthalic Acid [*Also, TPA*] [*Organic chemistry*]
TA	Terminal Adapter [*Telecommunications*]
T of A	Terms of Agreement (NATG)
TA	Terrain Avoidance [*Helicopter*]
TA	Terrarium Association (EA)
TA	Territorial Army
TA	Test Access [*Telecommunications*] (TEL)
TA	Test Accessory (AAG)
TA	Test Article (NASA)
TA	Testantibus Actis [*As the Records Show*] [*Latin*]
TA	Theater Army
TA	Theatre Annual [*A publication*]
TA	Theatre Arts [*A publication*]
TA	Theatre Authority (EA)
TA	Therapeutic Abortion [*Medicine*]
TA	Thermal Activation [*Physics*]
TA	Thermal Analysis
TA	Thermophilic Actinomyces [*Microbiology*]
TA	Third Attack [*Men's lacrosse position, until 1933*]
TA	Threat Analysis (MCD)
TA	Threat Axis [*Military*] (NVT)
TA	Thromboxane [*Also, T, Tx, TX*] [*Biochemistry*]
TA	Thromboxane A [*Also, TxA, TXA*] [*Biochemistry*]
TA	Thunderbirds of America (EA)
TA	Tibialis Anterior [*A muscle*]
TA	Time Actual (NASA)
T & A	Time and Allowance
T & A	Time and Attendance (AFM)
TA	Time and Attendance
TA	Tippers Anonymous (EA)
TA	Tithe Annuity
TA	Titratable Acid [*Clinical chemistry*]
TA	Titration Alkalinity [*Oceanography*]
TA	Tnu'at 'Aliyah (BJA)
TA	Tobacco Associates (EA)
T & A	Tonsillectomy and Adenoidectomy [*or Tonsils and Adenoids*] [*Medicine*]
TA	Tool Available
T & A	Tops and Accessories [*Show business slang*] [*Bowdlerized version*]
TA	Torah Atmosphere (BJA)
TA	Total Aboard [*Aviation*] (FAAC)
TA	Total Adenine [*Nucleotide pool*] [*Medicine*]
TA	Total Alkaloids [*Medicine*]
TA	Total Audience [*Television ratings*]
TA	Toward
TA	Toxin-Antitoxin [*Also, TAT*] [*Immunology*]
TA	Tracers Association [*A union*] [*British*]
TA	Track Accelerator [*Missile simulator*]
T/A	Trade Acceptance [*Business term*]
TA	Trade Agreements Act
TA	Trade Association (DCTA)
TA	Trading As
TA	Traduction Automatique [*A publication*]
TA	Traffic Agent [*or Auditor*]
T/A	Traffic Analysis [*National Security Agency*]
TA	Trained Aide [*Medicine*]
TA	Training Allowance [*British military*] (DMA)
T/A	Training As
TA	Transactional Analysis [*System of psychotherapy developed by Eric Berne, MD*]
TA	Transalta Resources Corp. [*Toronto Stock Exchange symbol*]
TA	Transamerica Corp. [*NYSE symbol*] (SPSG)
T/A	Transfer of Accountability
TA	Transfer Agent [*Business term*]
TA	Transfer Aisle (NRCH)
TA	Transfusion Associated
TA	Transient Alert (MCD)
TA	Transit Authority
TA	Transition Agreement
TA	Transition Allowance [*Australia*]
TA	Transition Altitude
TA	Transition Area [*For chart use only*] [*Aviation*]
TA	Transmission Authenticator [*Telecommunications*] (TEL)
TA	Transplantation Antigen [*Medicine*]
TA	Transportability Approval [*Army*]
TA	Transportation Agent
TA	Transportation Alternatives (EA)
TA	Transportation Authorization (AAG)
TA	Transverse Acoustic
TA	Travel Allowance
TA	Travel [*or Trip*] Authorization (MCD)
TA	Traveler's Advisory [*Weather information*]
TA	Triacetin [*Antifungal compound*] [*Organic chemistry*]
TA	Triamcinolone Acetonide [*Also, TAA*] [*Synthetic steroidal drug*]
TA	Tribunal Administratif [*Administrative Court*] [*French*] (ILCA)
TA	Tricuspid Atresia [*Cardiology*]
TA	Trierisches Archiv [*A publication*]
TA	Trinidad Artillery [*British military*] (DMA)
TA	Triple Antigen [*Medicine*]
TA	Triplex Annealed
TA	Trophoblast Antigen [*Immunochemistry*]
TA	Truck Assembly
TA	True Altitude [*Height*] [*Navigation*]
TA	True Anomaly
TA	Trunnion Angle (KSC)
TA	Trustee under Agreement [*Legal term*] (DLA)
TA	Truth in Advertising [*An association*] [*Defunct*] (EA)
TA	Tuberculin, Alkaline [*Medicine*]
TA	Tubular Atrophy [*Nephrology*]
T/A	Turboalternator
TA	Turbulence Amplifier
TA	Turkish Army (NATG)
T/A	Turnaround (NASA)
T & A	Turnbull & Asser [*Men's fashions*]
TA	Type Americain [*World War I troop train in France made according to US specifications*]
TA	Type Approval
TA	Type Availability
TA	VEB Fahlberg-List [*East Germany*] [*Research code symbol*]
TA1	Trophoblast Antigen One [*Immunochemistry*]
TAA	Tactical Air Army (NATG)
TAA	Tactical Army Automation (MCD)
TAA	Tactical Automation Appraisal (MCD)
TAA	Taiwanese Association of America (EA)
TAA	Tamburitza Association of America (EA)
TAA	Tannic Acid Agar [*Culture media*]
TAA	Technical Assistance Administration [*United Nations*]
TAA	Technical Assistance Agreement [*NASA*] (NASA)
TAA	Technology Assessment Annex (MCD)
TAA	Telephone Artifacts Association (EA)
TAA	Television Appliance Association
TAA	Temporary Access Authorization (NASA)
TAA	Terre Adelie [*Antarctica*] [*Seismograph station code, US Geological Survey*] [*Closed*] (SEIS)
TAA	Territorial Army Association [*British*]
TAA	Tertiary-Amyl Alcohol [*Organic chemistry*]
TAA	Texas Armadillo Association [*Commercial firm*] (EA)
TAA	Textbook Authors Association (EA)
TAA	Thioacetamide [*Organic chemistry*]
TAA	Thoracic Aortic Aneurysm [*Cardiology*]
TAA	Three-Axis Accelerometer
TAA	Ticket Agents' Association [*British*]
TAA	Tobacconists' Association of America (EA)
TAA	Total Aerospace Vehicle [*or Aircraft*] Authorization

TAA .... Total Army Analysis (AABC)
TAA .... Trade Adjustment Act
TAA .... Trade Adjustment Assistance [*Department of Commerce*]
TAA .... Trade Agreements Act
TAA .... Trans-American Airline
TAA .... Trans-Antarctic Association [*British*]
TAA .... Trans-Australia Airlines (ADA)
TAA .... Transactions and Proceedings. American Philological
              Association [*A publication*]
TAA .... Transcript of Absentee's Account
TAA .... Transferable Account Area [*Business term*] (DCTA)
TAA .... Transient Absorption Anisotropy [*Physics*]
TAA .... Transit Advertising Association [*Washington, DC*] (EA)
TAA .... Transportation Association of America
TAA .... Triamcinolone Acetonide [*Also, TA*] [*Synthetic steroidal drug*]
TAA .... Tumor-Associated Antigen [*Immunology*]
TAA .... Turbine Alternator Assembly
TAA .... Turkish-American Associations (EA)
TAAA .... Teen-Age Assembly of America (EA)
TAAA .... Thoracoabdominal Aortic Aneurysm [*Cardiology*]
TAAA .... Travelers Aid Association of America (EA)
TAABS ...... [*The*] Army Automated Budget System
TAAC .... Target Area Advisory Council (OICC)
TAAC .... Technology Assessment Advisory Council [*Washington,
              DC*] (EGAO)
TAAC .... Trade Adjustment Assistance Center [*Department of
              Commerce*]
TAAC .... Training Ammunition Authorization Committee (MCD)
TAAC .... Troubles d'Apprentissage - Association Canadienne [*Learning
              Disabilities Association of Canada*] (EAIO)
TAACOM ... Theater Army Area Command (AABC)
TAAD .... Task Assignment and Directive (MCD)
TAAD .... Terrain Avoidance Accessory Device
TAADC ..... Theater Army Air Defense Command (AABC)
TAADCOM ... Theater Army Air Defense Command (AABC)
TAADS ...... [*The*] Army Authorization Document System
TAAF........ Test, Analyze, and Fix Program [*Navy*] (MCD)
TAAF........ Thromboplastic Activity of Amniotic Fluid [*Medicine*]
TAAFA ...... Territorial Army and Air Force Association [*British
              military*] (DMA)
TAAFFEE ... Tactical Air Against First and Following Enemy
              Echelons (MCD)
TAAG .... Technical Analysis and Advisory Group [*Navy*] (MCD)
TAAG .... Tropical Africa Advisory Group [*British Overseas Trade
              Board*] (DS)
TAAGA ..... Transactions. American Association of Genito-Urinary
              Surgeons [*A publication*]
TAALODS ... [*The*] Army Automated Logistic Data System
TAALS ...... [*The*] American Association of Language Specialists (EA)
TAALS ...... [*The*] Judge Advocate General Automated Army Legal System
TAALS ...... Tactical Army Aircraft Landing Systems
TAAM .... Tomahawk Air Field Attack Missile (MCD)
TAAM .... Transportation Army Aviation Maintenance
Ta'an.......... Ta'anith (BJA)
TAAN .... Transworld Advertising Agency Network [*Englewood,
              CO*] (EA)
TAANA ..... [*The*] American Association of Nurse Attorneys (EA)
TAAOA ..... Transactions. American Academy of Ophthalmology and Oto-
              Laryngology [*A publication*]
TAAP........ Three-Axis Antenna Positioner
TAAP........ Trade Adjustment Assistance Program [*Department of
              Commerce*]
TAAP........ Transient Analysis Array Program
TAAPA...... Transactions. Association of American Physicians [*A
              publication*]
TAAR .... Target Area Analysis-RADAR
TAARS ...... [*The*] Army Ammunition Reporting System (AABC)
TAARSAN ... Trans-Australia Airlines Reservations System Automatic
              Network (ADA)
TAAS........ Tactical Air Armament Study (MCD)
TAAS........ Terminal Advanced Automation System [*Aviation*]
TAAS........ Thorotrast-Associated Angiosarcoma [*Oncology*]
TAAS........ Three-Axis Attitude Sensor (IEEE)
TAAS........ Traffic Account Analysis System [*Military*] [*British*]
TAASC ...... [*The*] Association of American Sword Collectors (EA)
TAASP ...... [*The*] Association for the Anthropological Study of Play (EA)
TAB .... Airborne Tanker, Boom (NVT)
TAB .... Tabaktueel Magazine [*A publication*]
TAB .... Tabella [*Tablet*] [*Pharmacy*]
TAB .... Table
Tab............. Tablet. A Weekly Newspaper and Review [*A publication*]
TAB............ Tabloncillo [*Race of maize*]
TAB .... Tabriz [*Iran*] [*Seismograph station code, US Geological
              Survey*] (SEIS)
TAB .... Tabular Language [*Data processing*] (IEEE)
TAB .... Tabulate (AAG)
TAB .... Tactical Air Base (AFM)
TAB .... Tamper Attempt Board
TAB .... Tape Automated Bonding [*Integrated circuit technology*]
TAB .... Target Acquisition Battalion [*Military*]
TAB .... Target Acquisition Battery (MCD)

TAB .... Tax Anticipation Bill [*Obligation*] [*Department of the
              Treasury*]
TAB .... Technical Abstract Bulletin [*ASTIA*] [*A publication*]
TAB .... Technical Activities Board (MCD)
TAB .... Technical Assistance Board [*United Nations*]
TAB .... Technology Assessment Board [*Washington, DC*] (EGAO)
TAB .... Telecommunications Advisory Board
TAB .... Temporarily Able-Bodied
TAB .... Testing, Adjusting, and Balancing [*Heating and cooling
              technology*]
TAB .... Tetraaminobiphenyl [*Organic chemistry*]
T-AB .... Thai-American Business [*A publication*] (IMH)
TAB .... Thiolacetoxybenzanilide [*Organic chemistry*]
TAB .... Title Announcement Bulletin
TAB .... Tobago [*Trinidad and Tobago*] [*Airport symbol*] (OAG)
TAB .... Total Abstinence Brotherhood
TAB .... Traffic Audit Bureau [*Later, TABMM*] (EA)
TAB .... Training Aid Bulletins [*Navy*]
TAB .... Transatlantic Broadcasting Company [*In TV series "W.E.B."*]
TAB .... Transports Aeriens du Benin [*Benin*] (EY)
TAB .... Typhoid, Paratyphoid A and B [*Vaccine*]
TABA........ [*The*] American Book Award [*Later, ABA*]
TABA........ Transcaribe [*Airline*] [*Colombia*]
TABA........ Transportes Aereos da Bacia Amazonica [*Airline*] [*Brazil*]
TABAMLN ... Tampa Bay Medical Library Network [*Library network*]
TABBSS...... Tactical Bare Base Support Study [*Air Force*]
TABC........ Total Aerobic Bacteria Counts
TABCASS ... Tactical Air Beacon Command and Surveillance
              System (MCD)
TAB-CD .... Tabulating Card
TABE........ Tests of Adult Basic Education [*Achievement test*]
TABEL ..... Tabella [*Tablet*] [*Pharmacy*] (ROG)
TABL........ Tropical Atlantic Biological Laboratory
TableR ...... La Table Ronde [*Paris*] [*A publication*]
TABMM ... Traffic Audit Bureau for Media Measurement (EA)
TABP......... Tetraaminobenzophenone [*Organic chemistry*]
TABPM...... Transportation Authorized in Accordance with BUPERS
              Manual, Article _____
TabR .... La Table Ronde [*Paris*] [*A publication*]
TABS .... Tabulator Stops (AAG)
TABS .... Tactical Airborne Beacon System (AFM)
TABS .... Tangential Bomb Suspension (MCD)
TABS .... Team Approach to Better Schools [*National Education
              Association program*]
TABS .... Technical and Business Service
TABS .... Telephone Area Billing System
TABS .... Terminal Access to Batch Service [*Data processing*] (BUR)
TABS .... Tests of Achievement in Basic Skills [*Educational test*]
TABS .... Theater Air Base Survivability [*Air Force*]
TABS .... Theological Abstracting and Bibliographical Services [*A
              publication*]
TABS .... Time Analysis and Billing System (BUR)
TABS .... Total Automatic Banking System [*Trademark of Diebold, Inc.*]
TABS .... Transatlantic Book Service [*British*]
TABS .... TRIS-Acetate-Buffered Saline [*Clinical chemistry*]
TABSIM ... Tabulator Simulator
TABSOL ... Tabular Systems-Oriented Language [*General Electric Co.*]
              [*British*]
TABSTONE ... Target and Background Signal-to-Noise Evaluation (MUGU)
TAB Tyres Access Batt ... TAB. Tyres, Accessories, Batteries [*A publication*]
TABU .... Typical Army Ball-Up [*Slang for a military muddle*]
Tabulae Biol ... Tabulae Biologicae [*A publication*]
Tabul Biol .. Tabulae Biologicae [*A publication*]
TABV .... Theater Air Base Vulnerability [*Air Force*] (AFM)
TAB VEE .. Theater Air Base Vulnerability [*Air Force*]
TABWAG ... Tank Battle War Game
TABWDS.. Tactical Air Base Weather Dissemination System [*Air Force*]
TABWE..... Tactical Air Base Weather Element [*Air Force*]
TABWS..... Tactical Airborne Weather Stations (MCD)
TABWX..... Tactical Air Base Weather
TAC .... [*The*] Aeroplane Collection [*British*]
TAC .... [*The*] Alien Critic [*A publication*]
TAC .... [*The*] Architects Collaborative [*Design firm*]
TAC .... [*The*] Athletics Congress [*Track*] [*An association*]
TAC .... Austin Community College, Austin, TX [*OCLC
              symbol*] (OCLC)
Tac .... Tacitus [*First century AD*] [*Classical studies*] (OCD)
TAC .... Tacloban [*Philippines*] [*Airport symbol*] (OAG)
TAC .... Tacon [*Flamenco dance term*]
TAC .... Tactical (AAG)
TAC .... Tactical Air Command [*Air Force*]
TAC .... Tactical Air Controller (NVT)
TAC .... Tactical Assignment Console
TAC .... Tactical Coordinator (NATG)
TAC .... Tacubaya [*Mexico*] [*Later, TEO*] [*Geomagnetic observatory
              code*]
TAC .... Tacubaya [*Mexico*] [*Seismograph station code, US Geological
              Survey*] (SEIS)
TAC .... Tamoxifen, Adriamycin, Cyclophosphamide [*Antineoplastic
              drug regimen*]
TAC .... Tandycrafts, Inc. [*NYSE symbol*] (SPSG)

TAC	Target Acquisition Center [*Army*]
TAC	Target Acquisition Console [*Military*] (CAAL)
TAC	Tasmanian Aboriginal Centre [*Australia*]
TAC	Tax Court of the United States Reports [*A publication*]
TAC	Team Activity Chart
TAC	Technical Advisory Center [*National Bureau of Standards*]
TAC	Technical Advisory Committee
TAC	Technical Applications Center [*Air Force*]
TAC	Technical Area Coordinator
TAC	Technical Assignment Control [*Nuclear energy*] (NRCH)
TAC	Technical Assistance Center [*Telecommunications*]
TAC	Technical Assistance Center [*State University College at Plattsburgh*] [*Research center*] (RCD)
TAC	Technical Assistance Committee [*of the Economic and Social Council of the United Nations*]
TAC	Technical Assistance Contract [*Nuclear energy*] (NRCH)
TAC	Technology Application Center [*University of New Mexico*] [*Albuquerque, NM*]
TAC	Teleconference Association of Canada [*Toronto, ON*] [*Information service or system*] (TSSD)
TAC	Telemetry and Command (MCD)
TAC	TELENET Access Controller
TAC	Television Advisory Committee [*British*] (DEN)
TAC	Temperature Altitude Chamber
TAC	Terminal Access Controller [*Advanced Research Projects Agency Network*] [*DoD*]
TAC	Terminal Area Chart [*FAA*] (FAAC)
TAC	Terrain Analysis Center [*Army*] (RDA)
TAC	Test Access Control [*Telecommunications*] (TEL)
TAC	Test Advisory Committee (MUGU)
TAC	Test of Auditory Comprehension
TAC	Thai Airways Company Ltd. [*Later, Thai Airways International*]
TAC	Theatres Advisory Committee [*British*]
TAC	Time Action Calendar [*Management*]
TAC	Time-to-Amplitude Converter
TAC	Time at Completion (MCD)
TAC	Tobacco Advisory Council [*British*]
TAC	Total Alkaloids of Cinchona [*Medicine*]
TAC	Total Allowable Catch [*Fishing regulation proposed by EEC*]
TAC	Total Annualized Cost
TAC	Total Average Cost (KSC)
TAC	Tracking Accuracy Control
TAC	Trade Agreements Committee [*An interagency committee of the executive branch of US government*] [*Terminated, 1963*]
TAC	Traders and Contacts
TAC	Trades Advisory Council [*British*]
TAC	Training Alarm Controller
TAC	Trans-Aminocrotonic Acid [*Also, TACA*] [*Organic chemistry*]
TAC	TRANSAC [*Transistorized Automatic Computer*] Assembler Compiler
TAC	Transformer Analog Computer
TAC	Transistor-Assisted Circuit (ADA)
TAC	Transistorized Automatic Control
TAC	Translations Activities Committee [*Special Libraries Association*]
TAC	Translator, Assembler, Compiler
TACO	Transonic Aerodynamic Characteristics
TAC	Transport Accident Commission [*Victoria, Australia*]
TAC	Transport Agencies Corp. [*Burma*] (DS)
TAC	Transportation Account Code [*Military*] (AFM)
TAC	Transportes, Aduanas, y Consignaciones SA [*Shipping company*] [*Spain*] (EY)
TAC	Trapped Air Cushion
TACL	Travel Air Club (EA)
TAC	Travelcraft Ambassadors Club (EA)
TAC	Trialkoxycitrate [*Organic chemistry*]
TAC	Triallyl Cyanurate [*Organic chemistry*]
TAC	Triamcinolone Cream [*Anti-inflammatory steroid*]
TAC	Trouble Analysis Chart
TAC	True Airspeed Computer
TAC	Turboalternator Compressor
TAC	Type of Activity Code [*Military*]
TAC	Types of Assistance Code [*Army*]
TACA	[*The*] Association of Comedy Artists (EA)
TAC(A)...	Tactical Air Coordinator (Airborne) [*Military*] (NVT)
TACA	Tactical Airborne Controller Aircraft [*Military*] (CAAL)
TACA	TELECOMS Authorities Cryptographic Algorithm [*Bell Telephone encryption chip*]
TACA	Test of Adult College Aptitude
TACA	Trans-Aminocrotonic Acid [*Also, TAC*] [*Organic chemistry*]
TACA	Tucker Automobile Club of America (EA)
TACAC......	Theater Army Civil Affairs Command (AABC)
TACAD	Tactical Advisory [*Military*] (CAAL)
TACAD	Traffic Alert and Collision Avoidance Detection [*Aviation*]
TACADE...	Teachers' Advisory Council on Alcohol and Drug Education [*British*]
TACADS...	Tactical Automated Data Processing System
TAC/AFSC ...	Tactical Air Command/Air Force Systems Command
TACAID....	Tactical Airborne Information Document (NVT)
TACAIR....	Tactical Air [*Military*] (AABC)
TACAIRLIFTSq ...	Tactical Airlift Squadron [*Air Force*]
TACAIRLIFTTNGSq ...	Tactical Airlift Training Squadron [*Air Force*]
TACAMO ...	Take Charge and Move Out Aircraft [*Military*]
TACAN	Tactical Air Navigation [*System*]
TACAN-DME ...	Tactical Air Navigation Distance Measuring Equipment
TACAP......	Tactical Air Command Aircraft Profiler Capability [*Air Force*]
TACAV......	Linea Aerea TACA de Venezuela
TACAV......	Tactical Aviation Model
TACBOMBSq ...	Tactical Bomb Squadron [*Air Force*]
TACC........	[*The*] Australian Comic Collector [*A publication*] (APTA)
TACC........	Tactical Air Command Center [*Air Force*] (NVT)
TACC........	Tactical Air Command and Control [*Air Force*]
TACC........	Tactical Air Control Center [*Air Force*]
TACC........	Tactical Air Coordination Center [*Military*] (CAAL)
TACC........	Thorotrast-Associated Cholangiocarcinoma [*Oncology*]
TACC........	Time Averaged Clutter Coherent (MCD)
TACC........	Total Army Career Counselor [*Inservice recruiter*] (INF)
TACCAR...	Time Averaged Clutter Coherent Airborne RADAR
TACCO	Tactical Air Control Coordinator
TACCO	Tactical Control Officer [*Army*] (AABC)
TACCOM ...	Tactical Communications (MCD)
TACCONSq ...	Tactical Control Squadron [*Air Force*]
TACCOPS ...	Tactical Air Control Center Operations (NVT)
TACCP......	Tactical Command Post [*Army*]
TACCS	Tactical Air Command Control System (MCD)
TACCS	Tactical Army Combat Service Support Computer System
TACCS-K..	Theater Automated Command and Control System - Korea
TACCTA ...	Tactical Commander's Terrain Analysis [*Military*] (AABC)
TAC-D......	Tactical Deception (MCD)
TACDA	[*The*] American Civil Defense Association (EA)
TACDACS ...	Target Acquisition and Data Collection System
TAC D & E...	Tactical Development and Evaluation [*Military*] (CAAL)
TACDEN ...	Tactical Data Entry Unit [*Army*]
TACDEW ...	Tactical Advanced Combat Direction and Electronic Warfare (MCD)
TACE........	Tactical Air Coordination Element
TAC-E	Tactical Emergency [*Army*]
TACE........	Talos Conversion Equipment (MCD)
TACE........	Tri-para-anisylchloroethylene [*Estrogen*]
TACED......	Tank Appended Crew Evaluation Device (MCD)
TACELIS..	Tactical Communications Emitter Location and Identification System [*Army*] (MCD)
TACEST....	Tactical Test [*Military*] (NVT)
TACEVAL ...	Tactical Evaluation (MCD)
TACFAX ...	Tactical Digital Facsimile Equipment (MCD)
TACFDC ...	Tactical Fire Direction Center [*Army*] (AABC)
TACFIRE ...	Tactical Fire [*Military*]
TACFO......	TASAMS [*The Army Supply and Maintenance System*] Coordination Field Office (AABC)
TACFTRRSq ...	Tactical Fighter Replacement Squadron [*Air Force*]
TACG	Tactical Air Control Group [*Military*]
TACGP......	Tactical Air Control Group [*Military*]
TACGRU...	Tactical Air Control Group [*Military*] (NVT)
TACH	Athens Community Hospital, Athens, TN [*Library symbol*] [*Library of Congress*] (LCLS)
TACH	Tachometer (AAG)
TACHA	Tennessee Automated Clearing House Association
TACHO.....	Tachometer (DSUE)
TACI	Test Access Control Interface [*Telecommunications*] (TEL)
TACINTEL ...	Tactical Intelligence Information Exchange System (NVT)
TACIT	Technical Advisory Committee on Inland Transport
TACIT	Time-Authenticated Cryptographic Identity Transmission [*Military*]
TACJAM ..	Tactical Jamming
TACL........	Tactical Air Command Letter [*Air Force*]
TACL........	Tank-Automotive Concepts Laboratory [*Army*] (RDA)
TACL........	Theater Authorized Consumption List [*Army*] (AABC)
TACL........	Time and Cycle Log [*NASA*] (KSC)
TACLAND ...	Tactical Instrument Landing (MCD)
TACLET....	Tactical Law Enforcement Teams [*Coast Guard*]
TACLO......	Tactical Air Command Liaison Officer [*Air Force*] (FAAC)
TACLOG...	Tactical-Logistical [*Army*] (AABC)
TACM	Tactical Air Command Manual [*Air Force*]
TACM	Transit Air Cargo Manifest
TACMAN ...	Tactical Manuals [*Aircraft*] (MCD)
TACMAR ...	Tactical Multifunction Array RADAR [*Air Force*]
TACMIS ...	Tactical Management Information System [*Army*] (RDA)
TACMS.....	Tactical Missile System [*Provisional*] [*Army*] (RDA)
TACNAV...	Tactical Navigation System
TACNAVMOD ...	Tactical/Navigational Modernization [*Navy*]
TACNOTE ...	Tactical Notice (NVT)
TACO	Good Taco Corp. [*NASDAQ symbol*] (NQ)
TACO	Tactical Coordinator (NG)
TACO	Tamoxifen, Adriamycin, Cyclophosphamide, Oncovin [*Vincristine*] [*Antineoplastic drug regimen*]
TACO	Test and Checkout Operations [*NASA*] (NASA)
TACOC	Tactical Air Control Operation Center
TACODA ..	Target Coordinate Data (IEEE)
TACOL......	Thinned Aperture Computed Lens (IEEE)
TACOM	Tactical Area Communications System (MCD)
TACOM	Tactical Communications (AFM)

TACOM .... Tank-Automotive Command [*Army*] [*Warren, MI*]   (MCD)
TACOMM ... Tactical Communications [*Military*]   (AABC)
TACOMPLAN ... Tactical Communications Plan [*NATO*]
TACOMSAT ... Tactical Communications Satellite [*Also, TACSAT*] [*DoD*]
TACON ..... Tactical Control [*Military*]   (CAAL)
TACOPNSSq ... Tactical Operations Squadron [*Air Force*]
TACOR ..... Threat Assessment and Control Receiver [*Air Force*]
TACOS ...... Tactical Air Combat Simulation   (NATG)
TACOS ...... Tactical Airborne Countermeasures or Strike [*Air Force*]
TACOS ...... Tactical Communications System
TACOS ...... Talos Adaptable Computer System [*Navy*]
TACOS ...... Tool for Automatic Conversion of Operational Software
TACOS ...... Travel Agents Computer Society   (EA)
TACOSS ... Tactical Container Shelter System [*Rockwell International Corp.*]
TACP .... Tactical Air Command Pamphlet [*Air Force*]
TACP .... Tactical Air Command Post [*Air Force*]   (MCD)
TACP .... Tactical Air Control Party [*Air Force*]
TACP .... Tactical Air Control Point
TACP .... Technical Analysis of Cost Proposals [*DoD*]
TACPACS ... Tactical Packet Switching System [*Army*]   (RDA)
TACPOL ... Tactical Procedure Oriented Language [*Data processing*]   (CSR)
TACPOL ... Tactile Procedure-Oriented Language   (CSR)
TACR .... TACAN [*Tactical Air Navigation*] Collocated with VOR [*Very-High-Frequency Omnidirectional Range*]   (FAAC)
TACR .... Tactical Air Command Regulation [*Air Force*]
TAC/R ...... Tactical Reconnaissance
TACR .... Time and Cycle Record [*NASA*]   (KSC)
TAC/RA ... TACAN [*Tactical Air Navigation*] RADAR Altimeter   (NASA)
TACRAC ... Tactical Warfare Research Advisory Committee [*Military*]   (RDA)
TACRAPS ... Tactical Range Prediction System
TACREACT ... Tactical Reconnaissance Reaction Aircraft   (MCD)
TAC RISE ... Tactical Reconnaissance Intelligence System Enhancement [*Air Force*]
TACRON .. Tactical Air Control Squadron [*Military*]
TACRV ...... Tracked Air-Cushion Research Vehicle [*DoD*]
TACS .... Tactical Air Control System [*Air Force*]
TACS .... Technical Assignment Control System [*Nuclear energy*]   (NRCH)
TACS .... Test Assembly Conditioning Station [*Nuclear energy*]   (NRCH)
TACS .... Theater Area Communications Systems [*Military*]
TACS .... Thruster Attitude Control System [*NASA*]
TACS .... Total Access Communications System [*Commercial firm*] [*British*]
TACSAT ... Tactical Communications Satellite [*Also, TACOMSAT*] [*DoD*]
TACSATCOM ... Tactical Satellite Communications [*Military*]
TACSI .... Tactical Air Communications [*or Control*] System Improvements [*Air Force*]   (MCD)
TACSOP ... Tactical Standing Operating Procedure [*Army*]   (INF)
TACSQ ...... Tactical Air Control Squadron [*Air Force*]
TACSS ...... Tactical Schoolship [*Navy*]   (NVT)
TACS/TADS ... Tactical Air Control System/Tactical Air Defense System
TACSYR ... Tactical Communications Systems Requirements   (MCD)
Tact .... Tactica [*of Arrian*] [*Classical studies*]   (OCD)
TACT .... Tactical Air Control Training
TACT .... Tactical Transport [*Aircraft*]
TACT .... Terminal Activated Channel Test
TACT .... Transact International, Inc. [*NASDAQ symbol*]   (NQ)
TACT .... Transactional Analysis Control Technique [*Training program*] [*American Airlines*]
TACT .... Transistor and Component Tester
TACT .... Transonic Aircraft Technology [*Program*] [*NASA and Air Force*]
TACT .... Truth about Civil Turmoil   (EA)
TAC/TADS ... Tactical Air Control/Tactical Air Defense System [*Military*]   (CAAL)
TACTAN ... Tactical Air Control and Navigation
TACTAS ... Tactical Towed Array Sensor [*Formerly, ETAS*] [*Navy*]
TACTASS ... Tactical Tone and Acoustic Surveillance System [*Military*]   (CAAL)
TACTEC ... Tactical Technology Information Analysis Center [*Columbus, OH*] [*DoD*]   (GRD)
TACTEC ... Totally Advanced Communications Technology
TACTECS ... Tables and Charts through Extended Character Sets [*Data processing*]
TACTIC .... Technical Advisory Committee to Influence Congress [*Federation of American Scientists*]
TACTICS .. Technical Assistance Consortium to Improve College Services [*Defunct*]   (EA)
TACTL ...... Tactical   (AAG)
TACTLASS ... Tactical Towed Array Surveillance System [*Military*]   (MCD)
TAC T MR ... Tactical Transport Medium Range [*Aircraft*]
TACTRUST ... [*The*] Athletics Congress/USA Trust Fund
TACTS ...... Tactical Aircrew Combat Training System   (NVT)
TACTS/ACMI ... Tactical Aircrew Combat Training System/Air Combat Maneuvering Instrumentation   (MCD)
TAC T SR ... Tactical Transport Short Range [*Aircraft*]
TACUDC ... Tests of Agrochemicals and Cultivars [*A publication*]
TAC/USA ... [*The*] Athletics Congress/USA   (EA)

TACV .... Tracked Air-Cushion Vehicle [*High-speed ground transportation*]
TACVA ...... Tactical Vulnerability Assessment [*Military*]   (MCD)
TACVA/CEWIS ... Tactical Communications Vulnerability Assessment of Combat Electronics Warfare Intelligence System   (MCD)
TACWE ...... Tactical Weather System   (MCD)
TAD .... Air Traffic Control Tower, Approach Control, and Departure Control Facility [*Aviation*]   (FAAC)
TAD .... Airborne Tanker, Drogue   (NVT)
TAD .... [*The*] Armchair Detective [*A publication*]
TAD .... Tactical Action Display [*SAGE*]
TAD .... Tactical Air Defense   (MCD)
TAD .... Tactical Air Direction [*Military*]
TAD .... Tactical Atomic Demolition [*Munitions*] [*Obsolete*] [*Military*]   (NG)
TAD .... Tadotu [*Japan*] [*Seismograph station code, US Geological Survey*] [*Closed*]   (SEIS)
TAD .... Target Acquisition Data
TAD .... Target Activation Date   (AAG)
TAD .... Target Area Designator [*Air Force*]
TAD .... Target Audience Description [*Army*]
TAD .... Task Assignment Directive   (KSC)
TAD .... Task Assignment Drawing   (MCD)
TAD .... Tax Advisor [*A publication*]
TAD .... Technical Acceptance Date   (AAG)
TAD .... Technical Analysis Division [*National Bureau of Standards*]
TAD .... Technical Approach Demonstration
TAD .... Technical Approval Demonstration   (AAG)
TAD .... Technology Area Description   (MCD)
TAD .... Telecommunications Automation Directorate [*Army*]   (RDA)
TAD .... Telemetry Analog to Digital [*Information converter*]
TAD .... Telephone Answering Device
TAD .... Television Advertising Duty
TAD .... Temperature and Dew Point   (NASA)
TAD .... Temporary Additional Duty [*Military*]
TAD .... Temporary Attached Duty
TAD .... Terminal Address Designator
TAD .... Test and Development   (MCD)
TAD .... Thermal Analysis Data
TAD .... Thioguanine, ara-C, Daunomycin [*Daunorubicin*] [*Antineoplastic drug regimen*]
TAD .... Thomas Aloysius Dorgan [*Satirical cartoonist*]
TAD .... Throw Away Detector [*Space shuttle*] [*NASA*]
TAD .... Thrust-Augmented Delta [*NASA*]
TAD .... Time Available for Delivery   (CET)
TAD .... Tobyhanna Army Depot, Library, Tobyhanna, PA [*OCLC symbol*]   (OCLC)
TAD .... Tooele Army Depot [*Utah*]
TAD .... Top Assembly Drawing
TAD .... Toward Affective Development [*Educational tool*]
TAD .... Traffic Accident Data [*Project*] [*National Safety Council*]
TAD .... Trailing-Arm-Drive
TAD .... Training Aids Division [*Navy*]
TAD .... Traitement Automatique des Donnees [*Automatic Data Processing*] [*French*]
TAD .... Transaction Application Drive [*Computer Technology, Inc.*]
TAD .... Traveling Around Drunk
TAD .... Trinidad [*Colorado*] [*Airport symbol*] [*Obsolete*]   (OAG)
TAD .... Trio Archean Developments [*Vancouver Stock Exchange symbol*]
TAD .... Turk Arkeoloji Dergisi [*Ankara*] [*A publication*]
TADA .... Tasmanian Aboriginal Descent Association [*Australia*]
TADAR ...... Tactical Area Defense Alerting RADAR   (MCD)
TADARS ... Target Acquisition/Designation Aerial Reconnaissance System   (MCD)
TADAS ...... Tactical Air Defense Alerting System [*Army*]
TADC .... Tactical Air Direction Center [*Military*]
TADC .... Training and Distribution Center [*Navy*]
TADD .... Tangential Abrasive Dehulling Device [*for grains*]
TADD .... Target Alert Data Display Set   (MCD)
TADD .... Termite and Ant Detection Dog [*In TADD Services Corp.*]
TADD .... Truckers Against Drunk Drivers   (EA)
TADDS ...... Target Alert Data Display Set   (RDA)
TADE .... Tetraaminodiphenylether [*Organic chemistry*]
TADF .... Thermally Activated Delayed Fluorescence [*Analytical chemistry*]
TADF .... Thomas A. Dooley Foundation [*Later, Dooley Foundation/Intermed-USA*]
TADGC ..... Tactical Air Designation Grid System [*Tactical Air Command*]
TADIC .... Telemetry Analog-Digital Information Converter
TADIL .... Tactical Data Information Link [*Tactical Air Command*]
TADILS ..... Tactical Automatic Data Information Links   (MCD)
TADIXS .... Tactical Data Information Exchange Subsystem
TAD J .... Technical Aid to the Disabled Journal [*A publication*]   (APTA)
TADJET ..... Transport Air Drop and Jettison Test [*Air Force, Army*]
TADLR ...... Tooling Automated Direct Labor Reporting   (MCD)
TADM .... Tactical Atomic Demolition Munitions [*Obsolete*] [*Military*]   (AABC)
TADO .... Tactical Airlift Duty Officer   (AFM)
TADOR ..... Table Data Organization and Reductions
TADP .... Tactical Air Direction Post [*Military*]

TAD/P	Terminal Area Distribution Processing
TADP	Toronto Anti-Draft Programme [*Defunct*] (EA)
TA3DPT	Twitchell-Allen Three-Dimensional Personality Test [*Psychology*]
TADR	Tabulated Drawing (MSA)
TADR	Test Answer Document Reader
TADREPS	Tactical Data Replay System (NVT)
TADRS	Target Acquisition/Designation Reconnaissance System (MCD)
TADS	Tactical Air Defense Systems (RDA)
TADS	Tactical Automatic Digital Switch [*Military*]
TADS	Target Acquisition and Designation System (MCD)
TADS	Target and Activity Display System [*Military*]
TADS	Technical Assistance Data
TADS	Teletypewriter Automatic Dispatch System
TADS	Thermal Analysis Data Station
TADS	Tracking and Display System
TADS	Type [*Command*] Automated Data System [*Navy*]
TADSO	Tactical Digital Systems Office [*Navy*] (MCD)
TADS/PNVS	Target Acquisition Designation System/Pilot Night Vision System [*Army*] (RDA)
TADSS	Tactical Automatic Digital Switching System
TADSYS	Turbine Automated Design System
TADYL	Tom Dooley Youth League [*Defunct*]
TadzhSSR	Tadzhik Soviet Socialist Republic
Tadzik Gos Univ Trudy Meh-Mat Fak	Tadzikskii Gosudarstvennyi Universitet Imeni V. I. Lenina. Trudy Mehaniko-Matematiceskogo Fakulteta [*A publication*]
Tadzik Gos Univ Ucen Zap	Tadzikskii Gosudarstvennyi Universitet Imeni V. I. Lenina. Ucenye Zapiski. Trudy Fiziko-Matematiceskogo Fakulteta. Serija Matematiceskaja [*A publication*]
Tadzik S-H Inst Trudy	Tadzikskii Sel'skohozjaistvennyi Institut i Tadzikskii Gosudarstvennyi Universitet. Trudy [*A publication*]
TAE	Tactical Aeromed Evacuation (CINC)
TAE	Taegu [*South Korea*] [*Seismograph station code, US Geological Survey*] [*Closed*] (SEIS)
TAE	Tannic Acid Equivalent [*Analytical chemistry*]
TAE	Tertiary Admissions Examination [*Australia*]
TAE	Test and Evaluation (MCD)
TAE	Textes Arameens d'Egypte [*A publication*] (BJA)
TAE	Transantarctic Expedition (ADA)
TAE	Transcatheter Arterial Embolization [*Medicine*]
TAE	Transoceanic Airborne Environment
TAE	Travelling Art Exhibition [*Australia*]
TAE	Tris-Acetate-EDTA [*Ethylenediaminetetraacetate*] [*Buffer*]
TAEA	Tangipahoa & Eastern [*AAR code*]
TAEAS	Tactical ASW [*Antisubmarine Warfare*] Environmental Acoustic Support [*Navy*] (CAAL)
TAeB	Tuebinger Aegyptologische Beitraege [*A publication*]
TAEC	Thailand Atomic Energy Commission for Peace
TAEC	Turkish Atomic Energy Commission
TAED	Tetraacetylethylenediamine [*Laundry bleaching agent*]
TAEDA Newsl	TAEDA [*Technology Assessment of Energy Development in Appalachia*] Newsletter [*United States*] [*A publication*]
TAEDP	Total Army Equipment Distribution Program (AABC)
TAEDS	Total Army Equipment Distribution System (MCD)
TAEG	Training Analysis and Evaluation Group [*Navy*]
TAEM	Terminal Area Energy Management [*NASA*] (NASA)
TAEMS	Transportable Automated Electromagnetic Measurement System (MCD)
TAEO	Test Article Engineering Order (MCD)
TAER	Time, Azimuth, Elevation, and Range [*Aerospace*]
TAERS	[*The*] Army Equipment Record System [*Later, TAMMS*]
TAES	Tactical Aeromedical Evacuation System
TAES	Texas Agricultural Experiment Station [*Texas A & M University*] [*Research center*] (RCD)
TAETGM	Test and Evaluation Task Group Manager (MCD)
TAF	Aerodrome Forecast [*Aviation*] (FAAC)
TAF	Arnold Engineering Development Center, Arnold Air Force Station, TN [*OCLC symbol*] (OCLC)
TAF	[*The*] Asia Foundation (EA)
TAF	Oran-Tafaraoui [*Algeria*] [*Airport symbol*] (OAG)
TAF	Stores Ship [*Military Sea Transportation Service*] (CINC)
TAF	Tactical Air Force
TAF	Tactical Area Files [*Military*] (CAAL)
TAF	Taforalt [*Morocco*] [*Seismograph station code, US Geological Survey*] (SEIS)
TAF	Task Analysis Form
TAF	Technology Access Fund [*Chrysler Corp.*]
TAF	Terminal Aerodrome Forecast [*Also, TAFOR*]
TAF	Test, Analyze, Fix (MCD)
TAF	Third Air Force
TAF	Top of Active Fuel [*Nuclear energy*] (NRCH)
TAF	Toxoid-Antitoxin Floccules [*Immunology*]
TAF	Traditional Acupuncture Foundation (EA)
TAF	Training Analysis and Feedback (MCD)
TAF	Transaction Facility
TAF	Trim after Forming (MSA)
TAF	Tumor-Angiogenesis Factor [*Medicine*]

TAF	Turkish Air Force (NATG)
TAFA	Territorial and Auxiliary Forces Association [*British military*] (DMA)
TAFAD	Task Force Air Defense (MUGU)
TAFB	Travis Air Force Base [*California*]
TAFB	Tyndall Air Force Base [*Florida*]
TAFCSD	Total Active Federal Commissioned Service to Date [*Military*]
TAFD	Test for Auditory Figure-Ground Discrimination
TAFDS	Tactical Airfield Fuel Dispensing System (NG)
TAFE	Transverse Alternating Field Electrophoresis
TAFEQ	TAFE [*New South Wales Department of Technical and Further Education*] Quarterly [*A publication*] (APTA)
TAFESA	Technical and Further Education Staff Association [*South Australia*]
TAFFE	Tactical Air Against First and Follow-On Eschelon (MCD)
Taffie	Technologically Advanced Family [*Lifestyle classification*]
TAFFS	[*The*] Army Functional Files System
TAFFTS	[*The*] Army Functional Files Test System (MCD)
TAFG	Two-Axis Free Gyro (AAG)
TAFHQ	Tactical Air Force Headquarters
TAFI	Technical Association of the Fur Industry
TAFI	Turnaround Fault Isolation [*Aviation*]
TAFIES	Tactical Air Forces Intelligence Exploitation System
TAFIIS	Tactical Air Force Integrated Information Systems (MCD)
TAFIN	Tactical Air Force Initiative (MCD)
TAFMM	Tactical Air Force Maintenance Management (MCD)
TAFMSD	Total Active Federal Military Service to Date
TAFNORNOR	Allied Tactical Air Force, Northern Norway [*NATO*]
TAFO	Theater Accounting and Finance Office [*Military*] (AFM)
TAFOR	Terminal Aerodrome Forecast [*Also, TAF*]
TAFR	Trouble and Failure Report [*Army*]
TAFROC	Tactical Air Force Required Operational Capability (MCD)
TAFS	Stores Ship
TAFS	Training Aid Feasibility Studies (AAG)
TAFSA	Transactions. American Fisheries Society [*A publication*]
TAFSD	Technical Report. AFWAL-TR. United States Air Force Wright Aeronautical Laboratories [*A publication*]
TAFSEA	Technical Applications for Southeast Asia [*Air Force*]
TAFSEG	Tactical Air Force Systems Engineering Group (MCD)
TAFSONOR	Allied Tactical Air Force, South Norway [*NATO*] (NATG)
TAFSUS	Turkish American Friendship Society of the United States (EA)
TAFT	Technical Assistance Field Team (MCD)
TAFUBAR	Things Are Fouled Up Beyond All Recognition [*Military slang*] [*Bowdlerized version*]
TAFVER	Terminal Aerodrome Forecast Verification
TAFX	Tapping Fixture
TAFY	American Theatre Arts for Youth (EA)
TAG	[*The*] Acronym Generator [*An RCA computer program*]
TAG	[*The*] Acrylonitrile Group (EA)
TAG	[*The*] Adjutant General [*Army*]
TAG	Airborne Tanker, General (NVT)
TAG	American Group of CPA Firms [*Lombard, IL*] (EA)
TAG	[*The*] Association for the Gifted (EA)
TAG	[*The*] Attorneys Group
TAG	[*The*] Audiotex Group [*Princeton, NJ*] [*Telecommunications service*] (TSSD)
TAG	Orion Air, Inc. [*Chapel Hill, NC*] [*FAA designator*] (FAAC)
TAG	Tactical Airlift Group (MCD)
TAG	Tactical Analysis Group [*Military*] (CAAL)
tag	Tagalog [*MARC language code*] [*Library of Congress*] (LCCP)
TAG	Tagbilaran [*Philippines*] [*Army*] (OAG)
Tag	Tagoro [*A publication*]
TAG	Target Attitude Group [*Advertising*]
TAG	Tavern and Guild Association [*Division of Homophile Effort for Legal Protection*] (EA)
TAG	Taxi Air Group, Inc.
TAG	Technical Air-to-Ground (NASA)
TAG	Technical Art Group
TAG	Technical Assessment Group [*Navy*]
TAG	Technical Assistance Grant
TAG	Technical Assistance Group [*NASA*] (KSC)
TAG	Technical Assistance Group [*An association*] (EA)
TAG	Technical Assistance Guides (OICC)
TAG	Technician Affiliate Group [*of American Chemical Society*]
TAG	Telecomputer Applications Group
TAG	Telegraphist Air Gunner [*British military*] (DMA)
TAG	Telemetry System Analysis Group
TAG	Tennessee, Alabama & Georgia Railway Co. [*AAR code*]
TAG	Terminal Applications Group, Inc.
TAG	Terminating and Grounding
TAG	Test Analysis Guide
TAG	Test Assembly Grapple [*Nuclear energy*] (NRCH)
TAG	Test Automation Growth
TAG	Texas A & M University at Galveston, Galveston, TX [*OCLC symbol*] (OCLC)
TAG	Thomson Advisory Group [*NYSE symbol*] (SPSG)
TAG	Tijdschrift Aardrijkskundig Genootschap [*A publication*]
TAG	Time Arrive Guarantee (AAG)
TAG	Time Automated Grid
TAG	Training Aids Guide [*Navy*]

TAG.......... Trans-Atlantic Geotraverse [*Project*] [*National Oceanic and Atmospheric Administration*]
TAG.......... Transient Analysis Generator
TAG.......... Transport Air Group [*Joint Army, Navy, and Marine Corps*]
TAG.......... Trauma Action Group (EA)
TAG.......... Triacylglycerol [*Food technology*]
TAGA....... Technical Association of the Graphic Arts (EA)
TAGA....... Telegraphist Air Gunner's Association [*Navy*] [*British*]
TAGA....... Trace Atmospheric Gas Analyser [*Instrument*]
TAGA....... Travel Agents Guild of America (EA)
TAGAMET ... Antagonist Cimetidine [*Ulcer medicine manufactured by SmithKline Beckman Corp.*]
Tagber Dt Akad Landw-Wiss Berl ... Tagungsberichte. Deutsche Akademie der Landwirtschaftswissenschaften zu Berlin [*A publication*]
TAGC....... Tripped Automatic Gain Control
TAGCEN... [*The*] Adjutant General Center [*Army*] (AABC)
TAGER..... [*The*] Association for Graduate Education and Research
TAGEX..... Travel at Government Expense [*Aviation*] (FAAC)
TAGI .... Terminal Applications Group, Incorporated [*NASDAQ symbol*] (NQ)
TAGIU ...... Tracking and Ground Instrumentation Unit [*NASA*]
TAGLA...... Tropical Agriculture [*A publication*]
TAGM....... Range Instrumentation Ship
TAGM....... Table and Art Glassware Manufacturers [*Defunct*] (EA)
Tag Muellerei-Technol Ber ... Tagung ueber die Muellerei-Technologie. Bericht [*A publication*]
TAGN....... Triaminoguanidine Nitrate [*Propellant ingredient*]
TAGO....... [*The*] Adjutant General's Office [*Army*]
TAGO....... Tago, Inc. [*NASDAQ symbol*] (NQ)
TAGRDCUSA ... [*The*] Adjutant General's Research and Development Command, United States Army
TAGS........ FBM [*Fleet Ballistic Missile*] Support Ship
TAGS........ Tactical Aircraft Guidance System [*Air Force*]
TAGS........ Teledyne Airborne Geophysical Services
TAGS........ Text and Graphics System [*or Subsystem*] (NASA)
TAGS........ Theater Air-Ground Warfare Simulation (MCD)
TAGSRWC ... [*The*] Andy Griffith Show Rerun Watchers Club (EA)
TAGSUSA ... [*The*] Adjutant General's School [*United States*], Army
TAGUA ..... Transactions. American Geophysical Union [*A publication*]
Tagungsber Akad Landwirtschaftswiss Dtsch Demokr Repub ... Tagungsbericht. Akademie der Landwirtschaftswissenschaften der Deutschen Demokratischen Republik [*A publication*]
Tagungsber Deut Akad Landwirt Wiss Berlin ... Tagungsberichte. Deutsche Akademie der Landwirtschaftswissenschaften zu Berlin [*A publication*]
Tagungsber Ges Inn Med DDR ... Tagungsbericht. Gesellschaft fuer Innere Medizin der DDR [*A publication*]
TAH.......... [*The*] American Hispanist [*A publication*]
TAH.......... Hospital Ship
Tah............ Taehti [*Record label*] [*Finland*]
TAH.......... Tahiti [*Society Islands*] [*Seismograph station code, US Geological Survey*] [*Closed*] (SEIS)
TAH.......... Tanna Island [*Vanuata*] [*Airport symbol*] (OAG)
TAH.......... Tell Abu Huwam (BJA)
TAH........ Total Abdominal Hysterectomy [*Medicine*]
TAH........ Total Artificial Heart
TAHA....... Tapered Aperture Horn Antenna
TAHCD.... Taehan Ankwa Hakhoe Chapchi [*A publication*]
TAHFDQ .. Allan Hancock Foundation. Technical Reports [*A publication*]
TAHOE..... TOW Against Helicopter Operational Equipment (RDA)
TAHOP..... Tank/Attack Helicopter Operational Performance (MCD)
TAHQ....... Theater Army Headquarters
TAI .... National Organization for Travelers Aid Societies [*Also known as Travelers Aid International*] (EA)
TAI .... T. A. Informations [*Formerly, Traduction Automatique*] [*A publication*]
TAI .... Tainan [*Republic of China*] [*Seismograph station code, US Geological Survey*] (SEIS)
TAI .... Taiz [*Yemen Arab Republic*] [*Airport symbol*] (OAG)
TAI .... Target Area of Interest [*Army intelligence matrix*] (INF)
TAI .... Tax Management International Journal [*A publication*]
TAI .... Teacher Attitude Inventory [*Teacher evaluation test*]
TAI .... Temps Atomique International [*International Atomic Time*] [*Telecommunications*] (TEL)
TAI .... Test Anxiety Inventory [*Educational test*]
TAI .... Thai Airways International (MCD)
TAI .... Therapy Attitude Inventory [*Test*] [*Psychology*]
TAI .... Time-to-Autoignition [*NASA*] (KSC)
TAI .... Total Active Inventory (MCD)
TAI .... Total Aircraft Inventory
TAI .... Traditionally Administered Instruction (BUR)
TAI .... Transamerica Income Shares, Inc. [*NYSE symbol*] (SPSG)
TAI .... Transports Aeriens Intercontinentaux [*Privately owned French airline*]
TAI .... Turnaround Index [*Data processing*]
TAI .... Tuskegee Airmen, Inc. (EA)
TAIC........ Technical Air Intelligence Center [*Navy*]
TAIC.......... Tokyo Atomic Industrial Consortium

TAIC.......... Triallylisocyanurate [*Organic chemistry*]
TAICH ...... Technical Assistance Information Clearing House [*of ACVAFS*] [*Information service or system*] (EA)
TAID .... Thrust-Augmented Improved Delta [*Launch vehicle*] [*NASA*]
TAID .... Thunderbird American Indian Dancers (EA)
TAIDB........ Tank-Automotive Integrated Database (MCD)
TAIDET .... Triple Axis Inertial Drift Erection Test
TAIDHS.... Tactical Air Intelligence Data Handling System (NATG)
TAik.......... Teologinen Aikakauskirja. Teologisk Tidskrift [*Helsinki*] [*A publication*]
Taikomoji Branduoline Fiz ... Taikomoji Branduoline Fizika [*A publication*]
TAILRATS ... Tail RADAR Acquisition and Tracking System (MCD)
TAILS....... Tactical Automatic Landing System [*Aviation*] (NG)
TA Inf .... Traduction Automatique Informations [*A publication*]
TAINS....... TERCOM [*Terrain Contour Mapping*]-Assisted Inertial Navigation System (MCD)
TAIP........ Terminal Area Impact Point (MUGU)
Taipower .... Taiwan Power Co. (ECON)
TAIR........ Terminal Area Instrumentation RADAR (MCD)
TAIR........ Test Assembly Inspection Record [*NASA*] (NASA)
TAIRCG ... Tactical Air Control Group [*Military*] (AFIT)
TAIS .... Tactical Air Intelligence System [*Military*] (MCD)
TAIS .... Telecom Australia Information Systems
TAISSA..... Travelers Aid - International Social Service of America [*Later, ISS/AB*]
Tait............ Tait's Edinburgh Magazine [*A publication*]
Tait............ Tait's Index to Morison's Dictionary [*Scotland*] [*A publication*] (DLA)
Tait............ Tait's Index to Scotch Session Cases [*1823*] [*A publication*] (DLA)
Tait............ Tait's Manuscript Decisions, Scotch Session Cases [*A publication*] (DLA)
Tait Ev ...... Tait on Evidence [*A publication*] (DLA)
Tait Ind ...... Tait's Index to Scotch Session Cases [*1823*] [*A publication*] (DLA)
Tait JP .... Tait's Justice of the Peace [*A publication*] (DLA)
TAIU .... Technical Aircraft Instrument Unit [*Navy*]
Taiwan Agric Bimon ... Taiwan Agriculture Bimonthly [*A publication*]
Taiwan Agr Res J ... Taiwan Agricultural Research Journal [*A publication*]
Taiwan Environ Sanit ... Taiwan Environmental Sanitation [*A publication*]
Taiwan Fish Res Inst Fish Cult Rep ... Taiwan. Fisheries Research Institute. Fish Culture. Report [*A publication*]
Taiwan Fish Res Inst Lab Biol Rep ... Taiwan. Fisheries Research Institute. Laboratory of Biology. Report [*A publication*]
Taiwan Fish Res Inst Lab Fish Biol Rep ... Taiwan. Fisheries Research Institute. Laboratory of Fishery Biology. Report [*A publication*]
Taiwan J Th ... Taiwan Journal of Theology [*A publication*]
Taiwan J Vet Med Anim Husb ... Taiwan Journal of Veterinary Medicine and Animal Husbandry [*A publication*]
Taiwan Sugar Exp Stn Annu Rep ... Taiwan. Sugar Experiment Station. Annual Report [*A publication*]
Taiwan Sugar Exp Stn Res Rep ... Taiwan. Sugar Experiment Station. Research Report [*A publication*]
Taiwan Sugar Res Inst Annu Rep ... Taiwan. Sugar Research Institute. Annual Report [*A publication*]
Taiwan Trade Mo ... Taiwan Trade Monthly [*A publication*]
Taiw Ind ...... Taiwan Industrial Panorama [*A publication*]
Taiw Stat .... Taiwan Statistical Data Book [*A publication*]
Taiw Svy .... Monthly Economic Survey. Taiwan [*A publication*]
TAJ .... Tadji [*Papua New Guinea*] [*Airport symbol*] (OAG)
taj .... Tajik [*MARC language code*] [*Library of Congress*] (LCCP)
TAJ .... Tanegashima [*Ryukyu Islands*] [*Seismograph station code, US Geological Survey*] (SEIS)
TAJ .... Thermal Arc Jet
TAJ .... Turbulent Air Jet
TAJA .... The Abibi Jazz Artists [*British*]
TAJAG ...... [*The*] Assistant Judge Advocate General [*Army*] (AABC)
TAK .... Cargo Ship [*Military Sea Transportation Service*] (CINC)
TAK .... Takaka [*New Zealand*] [*Seismograph station code, US Geological Survey*] [*Closed*] (SEIS)
TAK .... Takamatsu [*Japan*] [*Airport symbol*] (OAG)
TAK .... Taken
TAK .... Tonan Ajia Kenkyu [*Southeast Asia Studies*] [*A publication*]
TAK .... Trainer Appraisal Kit
TAK .... Transparent Armor Kit
TAKAAN .. Japanese Journal of Physical Fitness and Sports Medicine [*A publication*]
TAKC........ Taking Care. Newsletter of the Center for Consumer Health Education [*A publication*]
TAKC........ Theological Associate, King's College [*London*]
TAKEAZ ... Japanese Journal of Physical Education [*A publication*]
TAKEAZ ... Research Journal of Physical Education [*A publication*]
Takenaka Tech Res Rep ... Takenaka Technical Research Report [*A publication*]
TAKIS .... Tutmonda Asocio pri Kibernetiko, Informatiko, kaj Sistemiko [*World Association of Cybernetics, Computer Science, and System Theory*] (EAIO)
TAKIT .... Teaching Aids Kit [*Red Cross Youth*]
TAKR .... Vehicle Cargo Ship
TAKRX...... Fast Sealift Ship

TAKV	Cargo Ship and Aircraft Ferry [*Military Sea Transportation Service*] (CINC)
TAKX	Maritime Prepositioning Ship
TAL	[*The*] Apocryphal Literature: A Brief Introduction [*1945*] [*A publication*] (BJA)
Tal	Cases Tempore Talbot, English Chancery [*1734-38*] [*A publication*] (DLA)
TAL	Tailor (MSA)
TAL	Taiwan Industrial Panorama [*A publication*]
TAL	Talara [*Peru*] [*Seismograph station code, US Geological Survey*] (SEIS)
Tal	Talbot's Cases in Equity [*1734-38*] [*A publication*] (DLA)
TAL	Talcorp Ltd. [*Toronto Stock Exchange symbol*]
Tal	Taliesin [*England*] [*A publication*]
Tal	Talis [*Such*] [*Pharmacy*]
Tal	Talisman [*A publication*]
TAL	Talladega College, Talladega, AL [*OCLC symbol*] (OCLC)
TAL	Talley Industries, Inc. [*NYSE symbol*] (SPSG)
TAL	Talmud
TAL	Tanana [*Alaska*] [*Airport symbol*] (OAG)
TAL	Target Acquisition Laboratory
TAL	Taxation for Lawyers [*A publication*]
TAL	Technische Akademie der Luftwaffe [*Germany*] (MCD)
TAL	Telecommunications Access Language
TAL	TEPI [*Technical Equipment Planning Information*] Approved Letter
TAL	Terminal Application Language
TAL	Territory Airlines [*Australia*]
TAL	Tetraalkyllead [*Organic chemistry*]
TAL	Training Aids Library [*Navy*]
TAL	Transalpine [*Pipeline*] [*Western Europe*]
TAL	Transatlantic Landing
TAL	Transocean Air Lines
TAL	Transoceanic Abort Landing (NASA)
TAL	Transporter Air Lock [*Nuclear energy*] (NRCH)
TALA	Teacher Author League of America [*Formerly, TALNY*] (EA)
TALA	Textile Association of Los Angeles (EA)
TALAFIT	Tank, Laying, Aiming, and Firing Trainer (MCD)
TALAR	Tactical Approach and Landing RADAR [*NASA*]
TALAR	Talos Activity Report (MCD)
Talb	Cases Tempore Talbot, English Chancery [*1734-38*] [*A publication*] (DLA)
Talb	Talbot's Cases in Equity [*1734-38*] [*A publication*] (DLA)
TALBE	Talk and Listen Beacon [*Radio*]
TALC	Tactical Airlift Center (AFM)
TALC	Take-a-Look-See (MCD)
TALC	Tank-Automotive Logistics Command [*Army*]
TALCM	Tactical Air-Launched Cruise Missile (MCD)
TALDT	Total Administrative and Logistics Downtime (MCD)
TALF	Take a Look Foundation (EA)
TALFF	Total Allowable Level of Foreign Fishing
TALIA	Transactions. Association of Life Insurance Medical Directors of America [*A publication*]
TALIS	Topics in Australasian Library and Information Studies [*A publication*]
TALISMAN	Transfer Accounting, Lodging for Investments, and Stock Management for Jobbers [*Stock exchange term*] [*British*]
TALISSI	Tactical Light Shot Simulation (MCD)
TALK	Titles Alphabetically Listed by Keyword (KSC)
T-ALL	T-Cell Acute Lymphoblastic Leukemia [*Oncology*]
Tallin Polueteh Inst Toim	Tallinna Poluetehnilise Instituudi Toimetised [*A publication*]
Tall Timbers Res Stn Misc Publ	Tall Timbers Research Station. Miscellaneous Publication [*A publication*]
TALMIS	Technology-Assisted Learning Market Information Services [*Educational Programming Systems, Inc.*]
TALMS	Tangier American Legation Museum Society (EA)
TALMS	Tunable Atomic Line Molecular Spectroscopy
TALNY	Teacher Author League of New York [*Later, TALA*] (EA)
TALO	Tactical Air Liaison Officer [*Air Force*]
TALO	Time after Lift-Off
TALOG	Theater Army Logistical Command
TALON	South Central Regional Medical Library Program [*Library network*]
TALON	Tactical Air-Land Operations (MCD)
TALONS	Tactical Airborne LORAN Navigation System [*Model*] (MCD)
TALOP	Terminology, Administrative, Logistical, and Operational Procedures [*Military*]
TALPS	Transactional Analysis Life Position Survey [*Psychology*]
TAL QUAL	Talis Qualis [*Such As It Is*] [*Latin*] (ROG)
TALR	Law Reports of the District Court of Tel Aviv [*A publication*] (BJA)
TALS	[*The*] American Lupus Society (EA)
TALS	[*The*] Army Language School
TALS	Barge Cargo Ship
TALS	Transport Approach and Landing Simulator
TALT	Tracking Altitude
TALTC	Test Access Line Termination Circuit [*Telecommunications*] (TEL)
TALTT	Thrust Augmented Long Tank Thor (MCD)
TALUS	Transportation and Land Use Study [*Michigan*]

TAm	[*The*] Americas: A Quarterly Review of Inter-American Cultural History [*A publication*]
TAM	[*The*] Associated Missions (EA)
TAM	Tactical Air Missile
TAM	Tactical Air Mission [*Air Force*]
TAM	Tactical Airlift Modernization
TAM	Tamanrasset [*Algeria*] [*Seismograph station code, US Geological Survey*] (SEIS)
TAM	Tamanrasset [*Algeria*] [*Geomagnetic observatory code*]
TAM	Tamara Resources, Inc. [*Vancouver Stock Exchange symbol*]
TAM	Tamerton [*England*]
Tam	Tamid (BJA)
TAM	Tamil [*Language, etc.*] (ROG)
tam	Tamil [*MARC language code*] [*Library of Congress*] (LCCP)
Tam	Tamlyn's English Rolls Court Reports [*48 English Reprint*] [*A publication*] (DLA)
TAM	Tamoxifen [*Antineoplastic drug*]
TAM	Tampico [*Mexico*] [*Airport symbol*] (OAG)
TAM	Tangent Approximating Manifold
TAM	Tanque Argentino Mediano
TAM	Target Acquisition Model [*Military*]
TAM	Target Activated Munition [*Air-delivered land mines*]
TaM	Tarybine Mokykla [*A publication*]
TAM	Taxes. The Tax Magazine [*A publication*]
TAM	Technical Acknowledgment Message [*Aviation*]
TAM	Technical Ammunition
TAM	Technical Area Manager
TAM	Techniques of Alcohol Management [*Campaign, sponsored in part by the National Licensed Beverage Association, to prevent drunk driving*]
TAM	Telecommunications Access Method
TAM	Telephone Answering Machine (IEEE)
TAM	Television Audience Measurement
TAM	Teresian Apostolic Movement [*See also MTA*] [*Rome, Italy*] (EAIO)
TAM	Terminal Access Method
TAM	Terre, Air, Mer [*French*]
TAM	Test Access Multiplexer [*Telecommunications*] (TEL)
TAM	Texas A & M University [*College Station, TX*]
TAM	Theatre Arts Magazine [*A publication*]
TAM	Theatre Arts Monthly [*A publication*]
TAM	Thermal Analytical Model [*Apollo*] [*NASA*]
TAM	Throw Away Maintenance
TAM	Time and Materials (MCD)
TAM	Tituli Asiae Minoris [*Vienna*] [*A publication*] (OCD)
TAM	Total Active Motion [*Orthopedics*]
TAM	Toxoid-Antitoxin Mixture [*Immunology*]
TAM	Trajectory Application Method (MCD)
TAM	Transparent Anatomical Manikin [*An exhibit at the Chicago Museum of Science and Industry*]
TAM	Trialkylamine [*Organic chemistry*]
TAM	Triangle Amplitude Modulation
TAM	Tubos de Acero de Mexico SA [*AMEX symbol*] (SPSG)
TAM	Tumor-Associated Macrophages [*Immunology*]
TAM	Twentieth Anniversary Mobilization (EA)
TAM	Type-Approval Model
TAMA	Technical Assistance and Manufacturing Agreement
TAMA	Training Aids Management Agency [*Army*] (AABC)
TAMAC	Three-Axis Manual Attitude Controller
Tamarack R	Tamarack Review [*A publication*]
Tamb	Tambyah's Reports [*Ceylon*] [*A publication*] (DLA)
TamC	Tamil Culture [*A publication*]
TAMC	Tripler Army Medical Center (AABC)
TAMCO	Training Aid for MOBIDIC Console Operations
TAME	Tactical Air-to-Air Mission Evaluation (MCD)
TAME	Tactical Missile Encounter [*Air Force*] (KSC)
TAME	Tertiary-Amyl Methyl Ether [*Gasoline additive*]
TAME	Tosyl-L-arginine Methyl Ester [*Also, TosArgOMe*] [*Biochemical analysis*]
TAMED	Totally Automated Method Development [*High-performance liquid chromatography*]
TAMF	Tactical Automated Maintenance Facility
T Am Fish S	Transactions. American Fisheries Society [*A publication*]
T Am Geophy	Transactions. American Geophysical Union [*A publication*]
TAMI	Tanks and Mechanized Infantry Experiment (MCD)
TAMI	Tip Air Mass Injection [*Helicopter*]
Tamil Nadu J Coop	Tamil Nadu Journal of Co-operation [*A publication*]
TAMIRAD	Tactical Mid-Range Air Defense Program [*Army*] (AABC)
TAMIS	Telemetric Automated Microbial Identification System
TAMIS	Training Ammunition Management Information System (MCD)
Tamkang J Math	Tamkang Journal of Mathematics [*Taipei*] [*A publication*]
Tamkang R	Tamkang Review [*A publication*]
Tamkang Rev	Tamkang Review [*A publication*]
TamkR	Tamkang Review [*A publication*]
Taml	Tamlyn's English Rolls Court Reports [*48 English Reprint*] [*A publication*] (DLA)
TAML	Taunton Municipal Lighting Plant [*Nuclear energy*] (NRCH)
Taml Ev	Tamlyn's Evidence in Chancery [*2nd ed.*] [*1846*] [*A publication*] (DLA)

Taml TY .... Tamlyn's Terms of Years [*1825*] [*A publication*]   (DLA)
Tamlyn....... Tamlyn's English Rolls Court Reports [*48 English Reprint*] [*A publication*]   (DLA)
Tamlyn Ch ... Tamlyn's English Rolls Court Reports [*48 English Reprint*] [*A publication*]   (DLA)
Tamlyn (Eng) ... Tamlyn's English Rolls Court Reports [*A publication*]   (DLA)
TAMM ...... Tetrakis(acetoxymercuri)methane [*Organic chemistry*]
T Am Math S ... Transactions. American Mathematical Society [*A publication*]
TAMMC ... Theater Army Materiel Management Center
T Am Micros ... Transactions. American Microscopical Society [*A publication*]
TAMMIS-D ... Theater Army Medical Management Information System - Division
TAMMS.... [*The*] Army Maintenance Management System [*Formerly, TAERS*]   (AABC)
T Am Nucl S ... Transactions. American Nuclear Society [*A publication*]
TAMO....... Tooling Advance Material Order   (MCD)
TAMO....... Training Aids Management Office [*Army*]   (AABC)
TAMOS..... Terminal Automatic Monitoring System
TAMP....... Tactical Armament Master Plan   (MCD)
TAMP....... Tampering [*FBI standardized term*]
TAMP....... Tertiary-Amylphenol [*Disinfectant*]
TAMP....... Thailand Ammunition Manufacturing Plant   (CINC)
TAMP....... Tufts Assessment of Motor Performance [*Occupational therapy*]
Tampa Bay ... Tampa Bay Business [*A publication*]
Tampa Trib ... Tampa Tribune [*A publication*]
Tampa Tr & Ti ... Tampa Tribune and Times [*A publication*]
TAMPD..... TAPPI [*Technical Association of the Pulp and Paper Industry*] Annual Meeting. Proceedings [*United States*] [*A publication*]
TAMPER .. Tables for Approximation of Midpoints for Exponential Regression   (MCD)
T Am Phil S ... Transactions. American Philosophical Society [*A publication*]
TAMPS .... Teaming Analysis Model Personnel Selector   (MCD)
TamR .... Tamarack Review [*Toronto*] [*A publication*]
TAMR ...... Teen Association of Model Railroading   (EA)
TAMRA .... Technical and Miscellaneous Revenue Act of 1988
TAMS .... Tactical Avionics Maintenance Simulation   (KSC)
TAMS .... Tandem Accelerator Mass Spectrometry
TAMS .... Target Activated Munitions System
TA-MS ...... Thermal Analysis Mass Spectrometry
TAMS .... Thruster-Assisted Mooring System [*of a ship*]   (DS)
TAMS .... Token and Medal Society   (EA)
TAMS .... Total Active Military Service   (AFM)
TAMS .... Total Automotive Management Service
TAMS .... Training Ammunition Management Study [*Army*]   (MCD)
TAMSA .... Transactions. American Microscopical Society [*A publication*]
TAMSA .... Transportes Aereos Mexicano, Sociedad Anonima
T Am S Art ... Transactions. American Society for Artificial Internal Organs [*A publication*]
TAMSJ .... TAMS [*Token and Medal Society*] Journal [*A publication*]
Tamsui Oxford Coll Lecture Notes Ser ... Tamsui Oxford College. Lecture Notes Series [*A publication*]
TAMT ...... [*The*] American Mime Theatre   (EA)
TAMTA .... Transactions. American Mathematical Society [*A publication*]
TAMU ...... Texas A & M University
TAMVEC ... Texas A & M University Variable Energy Cyclotron
TAN .... Tactical Air Navigational Aid   (FAAC)
TAN .... Tananarive [*Madagascar*] [*Seismograph station code, US Geological Survey*]   (SEIS)
TAN .... Tananarive [*Madagascar*] [*Geomagnetic observatory code*]
Tan .... Tancredus [*Deceased circa 1236*] [*Authority cited in pre-1607 legal work*]   (DSA)
TAN .... Tandem   (AAG)
TAN .... Tandy Corp. [*NYSE symbol*]   (SPSG)
Tan .... Taney's United States Circuit Court Reports [*A publication*]   (DLA)
TAN .... Tangent [*Mathematics*]
TAN ...... Tangential Cell [*Neurology*]
TAN ...... Tanglewood Consolidated Resources, Inc. [*Toronto Stock Exchange symbol*]
Tan .... Tanhuma   (BJA)
TAN ...... Tanned   (MSA)
TAN .... Task Authorization Notice
TAN .... Taunton, MA [*Location identifier*] [*FAA*]   (FAAL)
TAN .... Tax Administrators News [*Federation of Tax Administrators*] [*A publication*]
TAN ...... Tax Anticipation Note [*Obligation*] [*State or local government*]
TAN ...... Technische Arbeitsnorm
TAN ...... Teletype Alert Network   (NVT)
TAN ...... Test Area North [*AEC*]
TAN .... Thiazolylazonaphthol [*An indicator*] [*Chemistry*]
TAN .... Title Analytic [*Bibliography*]
TAN ...... Total Acid Number [*Oil analysis*]
TAN ...... Total Adenine Nucleotide [*Medicine*]
TAN ...... Total Ammonia Nitrogen
TAN .... Trainable Adaptive Network
TAN .... Transall-Normen   (MCD)

TAN .... Transonic Aerodynamic Nozzle
TAN .... Transportes Aereos Nacionales, SA [*TAN Airlines*]
TAN .... Twilight All Night
TANAA ..... Transactions. American Neurological Association [*A publication*]
Tanc .... Tancredus [*Deceased circa 1236*] [*Authority cited in pre-1607 legal work*]   (DSA)
TANC .... Total Absorption Nuclear Cascade
TANCAV... Tactical Navigation and Collision Avoidance [*Military*]   (CAAL)
T Anc Monum ... Ancient Monuments Society. Transactions [*A publication*]
Tanc QW ... Tancred. Quo Warranto [*A publication*]   (ILCA)
Tancre........ Tancredus [*Deceased circa 1236*] [*Authority cited in pre-1607 legal work*]   (DSA)
Tancred ...... Tancredus [*Deceased circa 1236*] [*Authority cited in pre-1607 legal work*]   (DSA)
TAND .... Tandem   (FAAC)
TANDA ..... Time and Attendance Report   (FAAC)
TANDEM ... Tibi Aderit Numen Divinum, Expecta Modo [*God Will Help Thee - Only Wait*] [*Latin*] [*Motto of Elisabeth Ernestine Antonie, Duchess of Saxony (1681-1766)*]
TANDOC .. Tanzania National Documentation Centre [*National Central Library*] [*Information service or system*]   (IID)
TANE .... Transportes Aereos Nacionales Ecuatorianas [*Airline*] [*Ecuador*]
TANESCO ... Tanzania Electric Supply Company
Taney .... Taney's United States Circuit Court Reports [*A publication*]   (DLA)
TANEYCOMO ... Taney County, MO [*A lake at Branson, MO*]
Taney's CC Dec ... Taney's United States Circuit Court Reports [*A publication*]   (DLA)
Taney's Dec (USCC) ... Taney's United States Circuit Court Reports [*A publication*]   (DLA)
TANFL..... Tasmanian National Football League [*Australia*]
TANG....... Tangential   (AAG)
TANGLE.... Angle at Tip of Leaf [*Botany*]
TANH....... Tangent, Hyperbolic
Tanh........... Tanhuma   (BJA)
TANi.......... Recueil de Jurisprudence des Tribunaux de l'Arrondissement de Nivelles [*A publication*]
TANJUG... Telegrafska Agencija Nove Jugoslavije [*Press agency*] [*Yugoslavia*]
TANK .... Floatation Tank Association   (EA)
TANKBAT ... Tank Battalion [*Army*]
Tank Bulk Marit Manage ... Tanker and Bulker Maritime Management [*England*] [*A publication*]
Tanker Bulk Carr ... Tanker and Bulk Carrier [*A publication*]
Tanker Bulker Int ... Tanker and Bulker International [*England*] [*A publication*]
TANKEX... Tank Field Exercise   (NVT)
Tan Lect HV ... Tanner Lectures on Human Values [*A publication*]
Tan LR....... Tanganyika Territory Law Reports [*A publication*]   (DLA)
Tann........... Tanner's Reports [*8-14 Indiana*] [*A publication*]   (DLA)
Tann........... Tanner's Reports [*13-17 Utah*] [*A publication*]   (DLA)
TANN........ Taqrimiut Nipingat News [*Salluit, Quebec*] [*A publication*]
Tanner........ Tanner's Reports [*8-14 Indiana*] [*A publication*]   (DLA)
Tanner........ Tanner's Reports [*13-17 Utah*] [*A publication*]   (DLA)
TANO .... Tano Corp. [*NASDAQ symbol*]   (NQ)
TANO .... Triacetoneamine Nitroxide [*Organic chemistry*]
TANREM ... Tactical Nuclear Weapons Requirements Methodology
TANS........ Tactical Air Navigation System [*Helicopter*]
TANS........ Tax Anticipation Notes
TANS........ Terminal Area Navigation System
TANS........ Territorial Army Nursing Service [*British*]
TA-NS ...... Total Abstinence - No Smoking [*On social invitations*]
TANSA ...... Transactions. American Nuclear Society [*A publication*]
TANSTAAFL ... There Ain't No Such Thing As a Free Lunch [*Principle of economics indicating that one cannot get something for nothing*] [*See also TINSTAAFL*]
TANT .... Tennant Co. [*NASDAQ symbol*]   (NQ)
TANU........ Tanganyika African National Union [*Political party*]
Tanulmanyok Magy Tud Akad Szamitastech es Autom Kut Intez ... Tanulmanyok Magyar Tudomanyos Akademia Szamitastechnikai es Automatizalasi Kutato Intezet [*A publication*]
Tanulmanyok MTA Szamitastechn Automat Kutato Int (Budapest) ... Tanulmanyok. MTA [*Magyar Tudomanyos Akademia*] Szamitastechnikai es Automatizalasi Kutato Intezet (Budapest) [*A publication*]
TANWERE ... Tactical Nuclear Weapons Requirements   (CINC)
TANY .... Typographers Association of New York   (EA)
Tanz .... Tanzania
TAN-ZAM ... Tanzania-Zambia [*Railway*]
Tanzania Miner Resour Power Annu Rep Geol Surv Div ... Tanzania. Ministry of Industries. Mineral Resources and Power. Annual Report of the Geological Survey Division [*A publication*]
Tanzania Rec Geol Surv Tanganyika ... Tanzania. Records of the Geological Survey of Tanganyika [*A publication*]
Tanzania Silvic Res Note ... Tanzania Silviculture Research Note [*A publication*]

Tanzania Silvic Res Stn Tech Note (New Ser) ... Tanzania. Silviculture Research Station. Technical Note (New Series) [*A publication*]
TAO .... Auxiliary Oiler [*Military Sea Transportation Service*]
TAO .... Hammond, LA [*Location identifier*] [*FAA*]   (FAAL)
TAO .... Qingdao [*China*] [*Airport symbol*]   (OAG)
TAO .... TACAN [*Tactical Air Navigation*] Only (FAAC)
TAO .... Tactical Action Observer [*Military*]   (CAAL)
TAO .... Tactical Action Officer [*Navy*]   (NVT)
TAO .... Tactical Air Observation [*or Observer*]   (NATG)
TAO .... Tactical Air Officer   (NVT)
TAO .... Tactical Air Operations
TAO .... Technical Analysis Office   (MCD)
TAO .... Technical Analysis Order
TAO .... Technical Assistance Operations [*United Nations*]
TAO .... Technical Assistance Order   (KSC)
TAO .... Technology Applications Office [*NASA*]
TAO .... Technology Assistance Officer [*Small Business Administration*]
TAO .... Telephone Area Office [*British*]
TAO .... Terrain Avoidance Override   (MCD)
TAO .... Test Analysis Outline
TAO .... Thromboangitis Obliterans [*Cardiology*]
TAO .... Time and Altitude Over [*Aviation*]   (FAAC)
TAO .... Tokyo Astronomical Observatory
TAO .... Total Acid Output [*Clinical chemistry*]
TAO .... Transportation Applications Office [*Jet Propulsion Laboratory, NASA*]
TAO .... Troleandomycin [*Formerly, Triacetyloleandomycin*] [*Antibacterial compound*]
TAOBBATED ... [*The*] Adventures of Buckaroo Banzai across the Eighth Dimension [*1984 movie title*]
TAOC .... [*The*] Army Operations Center
TAOC .... Tactical Air Operations Center
TAOC .... Train Axis Optical Cube
TAOCC .... Tactical Air Operations Control Center   (NATG)
TAOG .... Gasoline Tanker [*Military Sea Transportation Service*]   (CINC)
TAOI .... Tactical Area of Interest [*Military*]
TAOO .... Tactical Air Operations Officer [*Tactical Air Command*]
TAOR .... Tactical Area of Responsibility [*Military*]   (AFM)
TAOS .... Thrust-Assisted Orbiter Shuttle [*NASA*]
TAOS .... Travel Allowance on Separation [*Military*]
TA/OSD .... Task Analysis/Operational Sequence Diagram
TAOT .... Transport Oiler Ship
TAP .... Amarillo Public Library, Amarillo, TX [*OCLC symbol*]   (OCLC)
TAP .... [*The*] Angel Planes   (EA)
TAP .... [*The*] Army Plan
TAP .... Onitap Resources, Inc. [*Toronto Stock Exchange symbol*]
TAP .... T-Cell-Activating Protein [*Biochemistry*]
TAP .... Tabaksplant. Maandblad voor de Sigaren, Sigaretten, en Tabakshandel en Industrie [*A publication*]
TAP .... Table of Authorized Personnel   (NATG)
TAP .... Tackled Attempting to Pass [*Football*]
TAP .... Tactical Action Programs
TAP .... Tactical Armament Plan   (MCD)
TAP .... Taipei [*Taihoku*] [*Taiwan*] [*Seismograph station code, US Geological Survey*]   (SEIS)
TAP .... Taipei [*Taiwan*] [*Later, LNP*] [*Geomagnetic observatory code*]
TAP .... Tapachula [*Mexico*] [*Airport symbol*]   (OAG)
TAP .... Tapestry   (ADA)
Tap .... Tappan's Ohio Common Pleas Reports [*A publication*]   (DLA)
TAP .... Target Aim Points
TAP .... Target Analysis and Planning [*Computer system*] [*Military*]
TAP .... Target Assignment Panel
TAP .... Task Area Plan
TAP .... Teacher's Aide Program
TAP .... Technical Achievement Plan [*NASA*]   (NASA)
TAP .... Technical Action Panel [*Department of Agriculture*]
TAP .... Technical Action Program   (OICC)
TAP .... Technical Advisory Panel [*United Nations*]
TAP .... Technical Area Plan [*Navy*]   (MCD)
TAP .... Technical Assistance Project   (EA)
TAP .... Technological Adjustment Pay
TAP .... Technological American Party   (EA)
TAP .... Technology Adaptation Program [*Massachusetts Institute of Technology*] [*Research center*]   (RCD)
TAP .... Technology Applications Program [*NASA*] [*University of Kentucky*] [*Lexington, KY*]
TAP .... Technology Assistance Program [*Army*]
TAP .... Telemetry Acceptance Pattern   (KSC)
TAP .... Telemetry Antenna Pedestal
TAP .... Temporal Analysis of Products [*System developed by Monsanto Chemical Co.*]
TAP .... Tension by Applanation [*Ophthalmology*]
TAP .... Terminal Access Processor
TAP .... Terminal Applications Package   (IEEE)
TAP .... Terrestrial Auxiliary Power
TAP .... Tertiary Awareness Program [*Australia*]
TAP .... Test Administration Plan   (NASA)
TAP .... Test Anxiety Profile [*Educational test*]
TAP .... Test Assistance Program [*Sperry UNIVAC*]

TAP .... Test of Auditory-Perceptual Skills
TAP .... Tests of Achievement and Proficiency [*Educational test*]
TAP .... Theater of All Possibilities [*International touring company of actor-authors*]
TAP .... Thermal Analysis Program [*Nuclear energy*]
TAP .... Thermosiphoning Air Pan
TAP .... Thermoviscoelastic Analysis Program   (MCD)
TAP .... Thesaurus at Play [*Acronym is trademark for word game*]
TAP .... Thiol Alkaline Phosphatase [*An enzyme*]
TAP .... Three-Axis Package
TAP .... Tibetan Aid Project   (EA)
TAP .... Time-Sharing Assembly Program [*Data processing*]   (DIT)
TAP .... Total Action Against Poverty [*A federal government program*]
TAP .... Total Air Pressure [*NASA*]
TAP .... Total Annualized Profit
TAP .... Toxicological Agent Protective Item   (MCD)
TAP .... Tracking Alarms Processor [*Space Flight Operations Facility, NASA*]
TAP .... Training for Aboriginals Program [*Australia*]
TAP .... Trajectory Analysis Program   (MCD)
TAP .... Trans-Alaska Pipeline
TAP .... Transaction Application Program [*Data processing*]
TAP .... Transcription Activating Protein [*Biochemistry*]
TAP .... Transferable Assets Program
TAP .... Transformation-Associated Protein [*Biochemistry*]
TAP .... Transponder Access Program [*Satellite Business Systems*] [*McLean, VA*] [*Telecommunications*]   (TSSD)
TAP .... Transport Ship [*Military Sea Transportation Service*]   (CINC)
TAP .... Transportes Aereos Portugueses, SARL [*Portuguese Air Transport*]
TAP .... Trend Analysis Program [*American Council of Life Insurance*] [*Washington, DC*] [*Information service or system*]   (IID)
TAP .... Triaminopyrimidine [*Organic chemistry*]
TAP .... Trickle Ammonia Process [*for drying grain feedstuffs*]
TAP .... Trimethylaminoethylpiperazine [*Organic chemistry*]
TAP .... Truck Assembly Plants
TAP .... Trustee, Administration, and Physician's Institute [*Seminar*]
TAP .... Tunis-Afrique Presse [*Press agency*] [*Tunisia*]
TAPA .... St. Johns/V. C. Bird [*Antigua Island*] [*ICAO location identifier*]   (ICLI)
TAPA .... (Tetranitrofluorylideneaminooxy)propionic Acid
TAPA .... Three-Dimensional Antenna Pattern Analyzer [*Air Force*]
TAPA .... Total Army Personnel Agency   (INF)
TAPA .... Transactions and Proceedings. American Philological Association [*A publication*]
TAPA .... Turkish American Physicians Association   (EA)
TAPAC ...... Tape Automatic Positioning and Control
TAPAC ...... Transportation Allocations, Priorities, and Controls Committee [*Military*]
TAPAK ...... Tape-Pack
TAPAT ...... Tape Programmed Automatic Tester
TAPATS .... Threat Artillery Preparation Against Thermal Sights   (MCD)
TAPCC ...... Technology and Pollution Control Committee [*Environmental Protection Agency*]
TAPCHAN ... Tapered Channel [*Wave power technology*]
Tap Chi Toan Hoc ... Tap Chi Toan Hoc. Progress of Mathematical Sciences [*A publication*]
Tap CM ..... Tapping's Copyholder's Manual [*A publication*]   (DLA)
TAPCO ...... Thompson Products, Inc. [*Later, Thompson Ramo Woolridge, Inc.*]
TAP-D .... Test of Articulation Performance - Diagnostic
TAPE .... Magnetech Corp. [*NASDAQ symbol*]   (NQ)
TAPE .... Tactical Air Power Evaluation [*Air Force*]
TAPE .... Tape Automatic Preparation Equipment
TAPE .... Target Profile Examination Technique [*RADAR analysis concept*] [*Air Force*]
TAPE .... Technical Advisory Panel for Electronics [*Air Force*]
TAPE .... Television Audience Program Evaluation
TAPE .... Tentative Annual Planning Estimate   (NVT)
TAPE .... Timed Access to Pertinent Excerpts
TAPE .... Total Application of Prerecorded Evidence
TAPE .... Totally Automated Programming Equipment
TAPER ...... [*The*] Army Plan for Equipment Records
TAPER ...... Temporary Appointment Pending Establishment of a Register [*Civil Service*]
TAPER ...... Theater Army Personnel   (MCD)
TAPER ...... Turbulent Air Pilot Environment Research [*NASA-FAA project*]
TAPFOR ... [*The*] Army Portion of Force Status and Identify Report [*Force Status Report*]   (AABC)
TAPH .... Codrington [*Barbuda Island*] [*ICAO location identifier*]   (ICLI)
TAPH .... Toluic Acid Phenylhydrazide [*Organic chemistry*]
TAPhA ...... Transactions and Proceedings. American Philological Association [*A publication*]
TAPIR .... Transition Automatique par Inertie et Radio [*French*]
TAPIT .... Tactical Photographic Image Transmission
TAPITS ..... Tactical Airborne Processing, Interpretation, and Transmission System [*Military*]
TAPITS ..... Tactical Photographic Image Transmission System
TAPLINE ... Trans-Alaska Pipeline
TAPLINE ... Trans-Arabian Pipeline

Tap Man	Tapping on the Writ of Mandamus [*1848*] [*A publication*] (DLA)
TAPO	Termination Accountable Property Officer
TAPO	Tris(l-aziridinyl) Phosphine Oxide [*Organic chemistry*]
Tapp...........	Tappan's Ohio Common Pleas Reports [*A publication*] (DLA)
TAPP	Total Assets Protection, Inc. [*Arlington, TX*] [*NASDAQ symbol*] (NQ)
TAPP........	Trade Association of Proprietary Plants (EA)
TAPP........	Tumor Acquisition, Processing, and Preservation [*Oncology*]
TAPP........	Two-Axis Pneumatic Pickup (IEEE)
Tappan.......	Tappan's Ohio Common Pleas Reports [*A publication*] (DLA)
Tappan (Ohio) ...	Tappan's Ohio Common Pleas Reports [*A publication*] (DLA)
Tappan's Ohio Rep ...	Tappan's Ohio Common Pleas Reports [*A publication*] (DLA)
Tappan's R ...	Tappan's Ohio Common Pleas Reports [*A publication*] (DLA)
TAPPI	TAPPI [*Technical Association of the Pulp and Paper Industry*] Journal [*A publication*]
TAPPI	Technical Association of the Pulp and Paper Industry (EA)
TAPPI Alkaline Pulping Conf Prepr ...	TAPPI [*Technical Association of the Pulp and Paper Industry*] Alkaline Pulping Conference Preprint [*A publication*]
TAPPI Annu Meet Prepr ...	TAPPI [*Technical Association of the Pulp and Paper Industry*] Annual Meeting. Preprint [*A publication*]
TAPPI Annu Meet Proc ...	TAPPI [*Technical Association of the Pulp and Paper Industry*] Annual Meeting. Proceedings [*A publication*]
TAPPI Bibl ...	TAPPI [*Technical Association of the Pulp and Paper Industry*] Bibliography of Pulp and Paper Manufacture [*A publication*]
TAPPI Coat Conf Prepr ...	TAPPI [*Technical Association of the Pulp and Paper Industry*] Coating Conference. Preprint [*A publication*]
TAPPI Environ Conf Proc ...	TAPPI [*Technical Association of the Pulp and Paper Industry*] Environmental Conference. Proceedings [*A publication*]
TAPPI For Biol Wood Chem Conf Conf Pap ...	TAPPI [*Technical Association of the Pulp and Paper Industry*] Forest Biology - Wood Chemistry Conference. Conference Papers [*A publication*]
TAPPI J Tech Assoc Pulp Paper Ind ...	TAPPI. Journal of the Technical Association of the Pulp and Paper Industry [*A publication*]
TAPPI Monogr Ser ...	TAPPI [*Technical Association of the Pulp and Paper Industry*] Monograph Series [*A publication*]
Tapping......	Tapping on the Writ of Mandamus [*A publication*] (DLA)
TAPPI Papermakers Conf Pap ...	TAPPI [*Technical Association of the Pulp and Paper Industry*] Papermakers Conference. Papers [*A publication*]
TAPPI Papermakers Conf Proc ...	TAPPI [*Technical Association of the Pulp and Paper Industry*] Papermakers Conference. Proceedings [*A publication*]
TAPPI Special Rept ...	TAPPI [*Technical Association of the Pulp and Paper Industry*] Special Reports [*A publication*]
TAPPI Spec Tech Assoc Publ ...	TAPPI [*Technical Association of the Pulp and Paper Industry*] Special Technical Association. Publication [*A publication*]
Tapp M & Ch ...	Tapp on Maintenance and Champerty [*1861*] [*A publication*] (ILCA)
TAPPS......	[*The*] Automated Procurement Planning System
TAPR........	Toxic Altitude Propulsion Research (MCD)
TAPRE	Tracking in an Active and Passive RADAR Environment
TAPS	Tactical Area Positioning System [*Military*]
TAPS	Tactical Protective Structures (MCD)
TAPS	Tarapur Atomic Power Station [*India*]
TAPS	Teachers Audio Placement System
TAPS	Telemetry Antenna Positions System [*Military*] (CAAL)
TAPS	TERCOM [*Terrain Contour Mapping*] Aircraft Positioning Systems [*Air Force*]
TAPS	Terminal Application Program System [*Data processing*]
TAPS	Terminal Area Positive Separation [*FAA*]
TAP-S........	Test of Articulation Performance - Screen
TAPS	Time Analysis of Program Status
TAPS	Total Atoll Production System (NOAA)
TAPS	Trajectory Accuracy Prediction System [*Air Force*]
TAPS	Trans-Alaska Pipeline System [*Department of Energy*]
TAPS	Transactions. American Philosophical Society [*A publication*]
TAPS	Tris(hydroxymethyl)methylamino Propanesulfonic Acid
TAPS	Turboalternator Power System (IEEE)
TAPS	Turret-Anchored Production System [*Petroleum engineering*]
TAPSC	Trans-Atlantic Passenger Steamship Conference [*Later, IPSA*] (EA)
TAPU	Tanganyika African Postal Union
TAPVC......	Total Anomalous Pulmonary Venous Connection [*Cardiology*]
TAPVR......	Total Anomalous Pulmonary Venous Return [*Cardiology*]
Taq............	Thermus Aquaticus [*Bacteria*]
TAQ..........	Trans Asian Resources [*Vancouver Stock Exchange symbol*]
TAQ..........	Transient Airman Quarters [*Air Force*] (AFM)
TAQK........	Taqralik [*A publication*]
TAQL	Taqralik [*Montreal*] [*A publication*]
TAQO.......	Tawow. Canadian Indian Cultural Magazine [*A publication*]
TAQT	Task Assignment Queue Table (MCD)
TAQTD	Task Assignment Queue Table Display (MCD)

TAQTU	Task Assignment Queue Table Update (MCD)
TAR	Tactical Air Reconnaissance (AFM)
TAR	Tactical Air Request (NVT)
TAR	Tactical Aircraft Recovery (CINC)
tar..............	Tadzhik Soviet Socialist Republic [*MARC country of publication code*] [*Library of Congress*] (LCCP)
TAR	Tansy Resources, Inc. [*Vancouver Stock Exchange symbol*]
TAR	Tara Exploration & Development Co. Ltd. [*Toronto Stock Exchange symbol*]
TAR	Tara. Schweizerische Fachzeitschrift fuer Moderne Verpackung [*A publication*]
TAR	Taranto [*Italy*] [*Seismograph station code, US Geological Survey*] (SEIS)
TAR	Target
tar..............	Tatar [*MARC language code*] [*Library of Congress*] (LCCP)
TAR	Tax Advance Rulings [*Database*] [*Taxation Canada*] [*Information service or system*] (CRD)
TAR	Technical Action Request [*Army*] (AABC)
TAR	Technical Analysis Request [*NASA*] (KSC)
TAR	Technical Assistance Request [*Nuclear energy*] (NRCH)
tar..............	Teen Alle Risiko [*Against All Risks*] [*Afrikaans*] [*Business term*]
TAR	Terminal Address Register
TAR	Terminal Area Surveillance RADAR
TAR	Terrain Avoidance RADAR
TAR	Territorial Army Regulations [*British military*] (DMA)
TAR	Test Action Requirement (NASA)
TAR	Test Agency Report (NASA)
TAR	Test Analysis Report
TAr	Theater Arts [*A publication*]
TAR	Threat Avoidance Receiver (MCD)
TAR	Thrombocytopenia with Absent Radii [*Medicine*]
TAR	Thrust-Augmented Rocket [*NASA*]
TAR	Total Assets Reporting (MCD)
TAR	Towed Array RADAR
TAR	Track Address Register
TAR	Training and Administration of the Reserve
TAR	Trajectory Analysis Room [*NASA*] (KSC)
TAR	Trans-Acting Responsive Sequence [*Genetics*]
TAR	Trans-Activator Response Element [*Genetics*]
TAR	Transportes Aereos Regionais [*Airline*] [*Brazil*]
TAR	Triannual Review (NATG)
TAR	Truck and Rail
TAR	Turnaround Ratio
TARA	Taurus Resources Ltd. [*NASDAQ symbol*] (NQ)
TARA	Technical Assistant, Royal Artillery [*British military*] (DMA)
TA/RA	Technical Availability/Restricted Availability [*Navy*] (NVT)
TARA	Territorial Army Rifle Association [*British military*] (DMA)
TARA	Total Articular Replacement Arthroplasty [*Orthopedics*]
TARA	Truck-Frame and Axle Repair Association (EA)
TARABS ...	Tactical Air Reconnaissance and Aerial Battlefield Surveillance System [*Military*]
TARADCOM ...	Tank-Automotive Research and Development Command [*Army*]
TARAN	Tactical Attack RADAR and Navigation
TARAN	Test and Repair [*or Replace*] as Necessary
Tarb	Tarbiz. Jerusalem (BJA)
Tar Bak Orm Gen Mud Yay ...	Tarim Bakanligi. Orman Genel Mudurlugu Yayinlarindan [*A publication*]
TARC.........	[*The*] Army Research Council
TARC.........	Tactical Air Reconnaissance Center [*Shaw Air Force Base*]
TARC.........	Television Allocation Research Committee [*or Council*]
TARC.........	Theater Army Replacement Command
TARC.........	Through Axis Rotational Control [*Aerospace*] (MCD)
TARC.........	Total Available Residual Chlorine [*Water quality*]
TARC.........	Toxics Testing and Assessment Research Committee [*Terminated, 1984*] [*Environmental Protection Agency*] (EGAO)
TARC.........	TransAtlantic Resources [*NASDAQ symbol*] (NQ)
TARCAP ..	Target Combat Air Patrol [*Navy*]
TARCOG ..	Top of Alabama Regional Council of Governments
TARCOM ...	Tank-Automotive Materiel Readiness Command [*Army*]
TARCOMSA ...	Tank-Automotive Materiel Readiness Command, Selfridge Activity (MCD)
TArDC.......	Arlington Development Center, Arlington, TN [*Library symbol*] [*Library of Congress*] (LCLS)
TARDIS	Time and Relative Dimensions in Space [*Acronym is name of spaceship in British TV series "Dr. Who"*]
TARDIS	Tropical Analysis and Real-Time Display [*National Oceanic and Atmospheric Administration*]
TARE........	Telegraphic Automatic Relay [*or Routing*] Equipment (NG)
TARE........	Telemetry Automatic Reduction Equipment
TARE........	Transistor Analysis Recording Equipment
TAREA......	Terminal Leaf Area [*Botany*]
TAREWS ..	Tactical Air Reconnaissance and Electronic Warfare Support (MCD)
TAREX	Target Exploitation [*Military*] (AABC)
TARF........	[*The*] Acid Rain Foundation (EA)
TARF........	Tracking and Reporting Format [*Military*] (CAAL)
TARFU......	Things Are Really Fouled Up [*Military slang*] [*Bowdlerized version*]

TARFX ...... Tracking and Reporting Format Extended [*Military*]   (CAAL)
Targ .... Targum   (BJA)
TARGA ..... Truevision Advanced Raster Graphics Adapter [*AT & T*]
TARGET ... Team to Advance Research for Gas Energy Transformation [*Group of US gas and gas-electric companies*]
TARGET ... Thermal Advanced Reactor, Gas-Cooled, Exploiting Thorium [*Nuclear energy*]
TARGET ... Transportability Analysis Reports Generator [*Military*]   (MCD)
TARGET ... Transportation Accident Research Graduate Education and Training
Targeted Diagn Ther Ser ... Targeted Diagnosis and Therapy Series [*A publication*]
Target Mark ... Target Marketing [*A publication*]
TargJer ...... [*The*] Jerusalem Targum of the Pentateuch   (BJA)
TargJon ..... Targum Jonathan   (BJA)
TargOnk ..... Targum Onkelos   (BJA)
TargYer ..... Targum Yerusahlmi   (BJA)
TARIC ...... Texas American Resources [*NASDAQ symbol*]   (NQ)
TARIF .... Telegraphic Automatic Routing in the Field   (MCD)
Tarl .... Tarleton Term Reports [*A publication*]   (APTA)
TARL .... Training Aids Research Laboratory [*Air Force*]   (MCD)
TARLOCS ... Target Locating System [*Military*]   (MCD)
Tarl Term R ... Tarleton Term Reports [*A publication*]   (APTA)
TARMAC ... Tar Macadam
TARMAC ... Terminal Area RADAR/Moving Aircraft   (KSC)
TARMOCS ... [*The*] Army Operations Center System
TArnA .... ARO, Inc., AEDC Library, Arnold Air Force Station, TN [*Library symbol*] [*Library of Congress*]   (LCLS)
TARND ..... Turnaround   (FAAC)
TARO .... Taro-Vit Industries Ltd. [*NASDAQ symbol*]   (NQ)
TARO .... Territorial Army Reserve of Officers [*British*]
TAROM ..... Transporturi Aeriene Romane [*Romanian Air Transport*]
TAROT ..... [*The*] Associated Readers of Tarot International   (EA)
TARP .... Tactical Airborne Reconnaissance Pod
TARP .... Tactical Airborne Recording Package
TARP .... Tarpaulin   (AAG)
TARP .... Test and Repair Processor [*Data processing*]
TARP .... Theater Army Repair Program
TARP .... Total Army Requirements Program
TARP .... Transient Acoustic Radiation Program
TARP .... Typical Airland Resupply Profile   (MCD)
TARPAC ... Television and Radio Political Action Committee [*National Association of Broadcasters*]
TARPS ...... Tactical Aerial Reconnaissance Pod System   (MCD)
TARPTOLA ... Theologiae Apud Remonstrantes Professorem, Tyrannidis Osorem, Limburgium Amstelodamensem [*Pseudonym used by John Locke*]
TARS .... Tactical Air Reconnaissance School [*Air Force*]
TARS .... Tactical Air Research and Survey Office [*Air Force*]
TARS .... Technical Assistance Recruitment Service [*United Nations*]
TARS .... Teen Age Republicans
TARS .... Terminal Automated RADAR Services [*Aviation*]   (FAAC)
TARS .... Terrain Analog RADAR Simulator
TARS .... Terrain Avoidance RADAR System   (MCD)
TARS .... Test and Repair Station
TARS .... Theater Army Replacement System   (AABC)
TARS .... Three-Axis Reference System [*Used in reference to Titan missile*]
TARS .... Training and Administrative Reserves [*on permanent active duty*]
TARS .... Transportation Aircraft Rebuild Shops [*National Guard*]   (MCD)
TARS .... Turnaround Ranging Station [*Telecommunications*]   (TEL)
TARS-75.... Tactical Reconnaissance and Surveillance - 1975 [*Army*]
TARSA ...... Transportes Aereos Ranquetes, Sociedad Anonima [*Argentina*]
Tarsad Szle ... Tarsadalmi Szemle [*A publication*]
Tarsadtud Kozl ... Tarsadalomtudomanyi Kozlemenyek [*A publication*]
TARSCC ... Three-Axis Reference System Checkout Console [*Used in reference to Titan missile*]
TARSD ...... Tropical Agriculture Research Series [*A publication*]
TARSLL.... Tender and Repair Ship Load List [*Navy*]   (NG)
TARS OCUL ... Tarsis Oculorum [*To the Eyelids*] [*Pharmacy*]
TART .... Tactical Antiradiation Tracker [*Military*]   (CAAL)
TART .... Tartarum [*Tartar*] [*Pharmacy*]   (ROG)
TART .... Tartrate
TART .... Task Analysis Reduction Technique [*Navy*]
TART .... Theodore Army Terminal
TART .... Transonic Armament Technology   (MCD)
TART .... Twin Accelerator Ring Transfer   (IEEE)
TARTA ...... Tactical RADAR Target Analysis [*Military*]   (CAAL)
TARTC ...... Theater Army Replacement and Training Command
TArts .... Theater Arts [*A publication*]
Tartu Riikl Ul Toimetised ... Tartu Riikliku Uelikooli Toimetised [*A publication*]
TARU Research Note ... New South Wales. Traffic Accident Research Unit. TARU Research Note [*A publication*]   (APTA)
TARVAN... Truck and Rail Van
TARWI...... Target Weather Information
TAS........... [*The*] Air Surgeon [*Army*]
TAS........... [*The*] Architectural Show [*Australia*]
TAS........... [*The*] Army Staff

TAS........... Tactical Advisory Service [*Department of Commerce*]
TAS........... Tactical Air Support [*Tactical Air Command*]
TAS........... Tactical Airlift Squadron [*Air Force*]
TAS........... Tactical Area Switching
TAS........... Tactical Automated System   (MCD)
TAS........... Tactical Automatic Switch [*Military*]   (AABC)
TAS........... Taiwanese-American Society   (EA)
TAS........... Tallow Alkyl Sulfate [*Surfactant*]
TAS........... Tampa Southern Railroad [*AAR code*]
TAS........... Taos, NM [*Location identifier*] [*FAA*]   (FAAL)
TAS........... Tape Alteration Subroutine
TAS........... Target Acquisition System
TAS........... Tashkent [*USSR*] [*Seismograph station code, US Geological Survey*]   (SEIS)
TAS........... Tashkent [*USSR*] [*Airport symbol*]   (OAG)
TAS........... Tasmania
TAS........... Tasu Resources Ltd. [*Vancouver Stock Exchange symbol*]
TAS........... Tax Administration System [*Internal Revenue Service*]
TAS........... Technical Advisory Services [*Army*]   (RDA)
TAS........... Telecommunications Authority Singapore   (TEL)
TAS........... Telemetry Antenna Subsystem   (NASA)
TAS........... Telephone Answering Service [*or System*]
TAS........... Telephone Area Staff [*British*]
TAS........... Temperature-Actuated Switch   (IEEE)
TAS........... Terminal Access System   (MCD)
TAS........... Terminal Address Selector
TAS........... Test Access Selector [*Telecommunications*]   (TEL)
TAS........... Test Answer Sheets
TAS........... Test Article Specification   (NASA)
TAS........... Test and Set [*Data processing*]
TAS........... Texture Analysis System [*Image analysis for biochemistry*]
TAS........... Theatre Arts Society [*British*]
TAS........... Three-Axis Stabilization   (AAG)
TAS........... Time Air Speed   (NATG)
TAS........... Torpedo and Antisubmarine [*Obsolete*] [*Navy*] [*British*]
TAS........... Towed Array SONAR
TAS........... Tracking Adjunct System [*I-HAWK*]   (MCD)
TAS........... Tracking Antenna System
TAS........... Traditional Acupuncture Society [*Stratford-Upon-Avon, Warwickshire, England*]   (EAIO)
TAS........... Traffic Analysis Survey   (MCD)
TAS........... Training Aids Section [*Navy*]
TAS........... Transportes Aereos Salvador [*Brazil*]
TAS........... Transverse Air Spring
TAS........... Tribunal Arbitral du Sport [*Court of Arbitration of Sport - CAS*] [*Lausanne, Switzerland*]   (EAIO)
TAS........... Troop Airlift Squadron   (CINC)
TAS........... True Airspeed
TAS........... Turk Anonim Sirketi [*Turkish Joint-Stock Company*]   (CED)
TAS........... Tychon's Assembler   (MCD)
TAS3.......... Transportation Aviation Supply Support System
TASA......... [*The*] Aircraft Service Association
TASA......... [*The*] Antique Stove Association   (EA)
TASA......... [*The*] Assistant Secretary of the Army
TASA......... Tactical Air Support Aircraft
TASA......... Task and Skill Analysis [*Military*]   (AABC)
TASA......... Teaching Atypical Students in Alberta [*A publication*]
TASA......... Technical Advisory Service for Attorneys [*Technical Advisory Service, Inc.*] [*Information service or system*]
TASA......... Television Audio Support Activity [*Army*]
TASA......... Test Area Support Assembly
TASA......... Tumor-Associated Surface Antigen [*Immunology*]
TasAC........ Tasmanian Aero Club [*Australia*]
TASAE....... Training and Audio-Visual Support Activity - Europe   (MCD)
T ASAE ...... Transactions. ASAE [*American Society of Agricultural Engineers*] [*A publication*]
TASAG...... TACOM [*Tank Automotive Command*] Scientific Advisory Group [*DoD*]   (EGAO)
TASAMS .. [*The*] Army Supply and Maintenance System   (AABC)
TASAP ...... [*The*] Army Scientific Advisory Panel
Tas Arch ... Tasmanian Architect [*A publication*]   (APTA)
Tas Architect ... Tasmanian Architect [*A publication*]   (APTA)
TASB......... Texas Archaeological Society. Bulletin [*A publication*]
Tas Bldg App R ... Tasmanian Building Appeal Reports [*A publication*]   (APTA)
Tas Build ... Tasmanian Builder [*A publication*]
Tas Build J ... Tasmanian Building Journal [*A publication*]
TASC......... [*The*] Analytic Sciences Corporation
TASC......... Tabular Sequence Control
TASC......... Tactical Air Support Center   (CINC)
TASC......... Target Area Sequential Correlator   (MCD)
TASC......... Teaching as a Career [*British*]
TASC......... Technical Activity Steering Committee [*Nuclear energy*]   (NRCH)
TASC......... Tehran Area Support Center [*Military*]   (MCD)
TASC......... Telecommunication Alarm Surveillance and Control [*AT & T*]
TASC......... Terminal Area Sequencing and Control
TASC......... Test Anxiety Scale for Children [*Psychology*]
TASC......... Total Absorption Shower Cascade
TASC......... Total Avionic Support Capability
TASC......... Training Aids Support Center [*Army*]

TASC......... Training and Audiovisual Support Center [*Army*]
TASC......... Treatment Alternatives to Street Crime [*Antidrug program*]
TASC......... True Airspeed Computer
TASCC...... Tactical Air Support Coordination Center   (MCD)
TASCC...... Test Access Signaling Conversion Circuit [*Telecommunications*]   (TEL)
Tasch Cr Acts ... Taschereau's Criminal Law Acts [*Canada*] [*A publication*]   (DLA)
TASCO...... Tactical Automatic Switch Control Office
TASCOM ... Theater Army Support Command [*Terminated, 1975*] [*West Germany*]   (AABC)
TASCOM ... University of Tasmania COM [*Computer Output Microform*] Catalogue [*Australia*]
TASCOM(S) ... Theater Army Support Command (Supply)
TASCON.. Television Automatic Sequence Control
TASD........ Tactical Action Situation Display
TASD........ Terminal Railway, Alabama State Docks [*AAR code*]
TASDA...... [*The*] American Safe Deposit Association   (EA)
TASDA...... Tactical Airborne SONAR Decision Aid
TASDC...... Tank-Automotive Systems Development Center [*Army*]
Tas Dep Agric Bull ... Bulletin. Department of Agriculture (Tasmania) [*A publication*]   (APTA)
Tas Div Bul ... Institution of Engineers of Australia. Tasmania Division. Bulletin [*A publication*]   (APTA)
TASE........ Tactical Air Support Element [*Military*]   (AABC)
TASE........ Tactical Support Equipment
TASE........ Tel Aviv Stock Exchange [*Israel*]   (IMH)
Tas Ed........ Tasmanian Education [*A publication*]   (APTA)
Tas Ed Gaz ... Tasmanian Education Gazette [*A publication*]   (APTA)
Tas Ed Rec ... Educational Record. Tasmania Education Department [*A publication*]   (APTA)
Tas Educ .... Tasmanian Education [*A publication*]   (APTA)
TASER...... Teleactive Shock Electronic Repulsion [*Nonlethal weapon*]
TASER...... Tom Swift and His Electric Rifle [*Electronic "stun gun"*] [*A trademark*]
TASES...... Tactical Airborne Signal Exploitation System   (MCD)
TASF........ Tactical Air Strike Force [*Air Force*]
Tas Fish..... Tasmanian Fisheries Research [*A publication*]   (APTA)
TASFMA .. Target Acquisition Systems Force Mix Analysis [*Military*]
Tas Fruitgrower and Farmer ... Tasmanian Fruitgrower and Farmer [*A publication*]   (APTA)
TASFUIRA ... Things Are So Fouled Up It's Really Amazing [*Military slang*] [*Bowdlerized version*]
TASG........ Tactical Air Support Group [*Air Force*]   (AFIT)
Tas Geol Surv Geol Atlas 1 Mile Ser ... Tasmanian Geological Survey. Geological Atlas. 1 Mile Series [*A publication*]   (APTA)
Tas Govt Gaz ... Tasmanian Government Gazette [*A publication*]   (APTA)
TASH .... [*The*] Association for the Severely Handicapped [*Later, TASH: the Association for Persons with Severe Handicaps*]   (EA)
Tas Hist Research Assoc Papers & Proc ... Tasmanian Historical Research Association. Papers and Proceedings [*A publication*]   (APTA)
Tas Hotel R ... Tasmanian Hotel Review [*A publication*]   (APTA)
TASI.......... Time Assignment Speech Interpolation [*Timesharing technique*] [*Telecommunications*]
TASI.......... Torpedo and Anti-Submarine Instructor [*British military*]   (DMA)
TASI.......... Transactional Analysis Systems Institute
Tas Ind....... Tasmanian Industry [*A publication*]   (APTA)
Tas Irreg Notes ... Tasmanian Irregular Notes [*A publication*]
TASIS........ [*The*] American School in Switzerland
TASJ .... Transactions. Asiatic Society of Japan [*A publication*]
Tas J Ag..... Tasmanian Journal of Agriculture [*A publication*]   (APTA)
Tas J Agric ... Tasmanian Journal of Agriculture [*A publication*]   (APTA)
Tas J Ed...... Tasmanian Journal of Education [*A publication*]   (APTA)
TASK........ Temporary Assigned Skeleton [*Data processing*]
Taskent Gos Ped Inst Ucen Zap ... Taskentskii Gosudarstvennyi Pedagogiceskii Institut Imeni Nizami Ucenye Zapiski [*A publication*]
Taskent Gos Univ Buharsk Ped Inst Naucn Trudy ... Taskentskii Gosudarstvennyi Universitet Buharskii Pedagogiceskii Institut Naucnye Trudy [*A publication*]
Taskent Gos Univ Naucn Trudy ... Taskentskii Gosudarstvennyi Universitet Imeni V. I. Lenina Naucnye Trudy [*A publication*]
Taskent Gos Univ Sb Naucn Trudov ... Taskentskii Gosudarstvennyi Universitet Sbornik Naucnyh Trudov [*A publication*]
Taskent Inst Inz Zeleznodoroz Transporta Trudy ... Taskentskii Institut Inzenerov Zeleznodoroznogo Transporta Trudy [*A publication*]
Taskent Inst Narod Hoz Naucn Zap ... Taskentskii Institut Narodnogo Hozjaistva Naucnye Zapiski [*A publication*]
Taskent Inst Narod Hoz Naucn Zap Mat v Prilozen ... Taskentskii Institut Narodnogo Hozjaistva Naucnye Zapiski. Matematika v Prilozenijah [*A publication*]
Taskent Politehn Inst Naucn Trudy ... Taskentskii Politehniceskii Institut Naucnye Trudy. Novaja Serija [*A publication*]
Taskent Politehn Inst Naucn Trudy NS ... Taskentskii Politehniceskii Institut Naucnye Trudy. Novaja Serija [*A publication*]
TASKFLOT ... Task Flotilla
TASKFORNON ... Allied Task Force, North Norway [*NATO*]   (NATG)
Tasks Veg Sci ... Tasks for Vegetation Science [*A publication*]

TASL......... Theater Authorized Stockage List [*Military*]   (AABC)
Tas Lab & Ind Bul ... Tasmania. Department of Labour and Industry. Bulletin [*A publication*]   (APTA)
Tas LN....... Tasmanian Law Newsletter [*A publication*]
Tas LR....... Tasmanian Law Reports [*A publication*]   (APTA)
Tas L Rev... University of Tasmania. Law Review [*A publication*]   (APTA)
TASM........ Tactical Air-to-Surface Missile   (NATG)
TASM........ Tasmania   (ROG)
Tasm .... Tasmanian State Reports [*A publication*]
TASM........ Tomahawk Antiship Missile   (MCD)
TASM........ Trialkylstannylmaleate [*Organic chemistry*]
TASM........ Turbo Assembler [*Data processing*]
Tasm Acts ... Tasmania Acts of Parliament [*A publication*]   (DLA)
Tasmania Build J ... Tasmanian Building Journal [*A publication*]   (APTA)
Tasmania Dep Agric Annu Rep ... Tasmania. Department of Agriculture. Annual Report [*A publication*]
Tasmania Dep Mines Geol Atlas 1:250000 Ser SK ... Tasmania. Department of Mines. Geological Atlas. 1:250,000 Series SK [*A publication*]
Tasmania Dep Mines Geol Surv Bull ... Tasmania. Department of Mines. Geological Survey. Bulletin [*A publication*]   (APTA)
Tasmania Dep Mines Geol Surv Rec ... Tasmania. Department of Mines. Geological Survey. Record [*A publication*]   (APTA)
Tasmania Dep Mines Geol Surv Rep ... Tasmania. Department of Mines. Geological Survey. Report [*A publication*]   (APTA)
Tasmania Dep Mines Tech Rep ... Tasmania. Department of Mines. Technical Report [*A publication*]   (APTA)
Tasmania Dep Mines Underground Water Supply Pap ... Tasmania. Department of Mines. Underground Water Supply Paper [*A publication*]   (APTA)
Tasmania For Comm Bull ... Tasmania. Forestry Commission. Bulletin [*A publication*]
Tasmania Geol Surv Bull ... Tasmania. Geological Survey. Bulletin [*A publication*]   (APTA)
Tasmania Geol Surv Explanatory Rep ... Tasmania. Geological Survey. Explanatory Report [*A publication*]
Tasmania Geol Surv Explan Rep Geol Atlas 1 Mile Ser ... Tasmania. Geological Survey. Explanatory Report. Geological Atlas. 1 Mile Series [*A publication*]
Tasmania Geol Surv Rec ... Tasmania. Geological Survey. Record [*A publication*]   (APTA)
Tasmania Geol Surv Rep ... Tasmania. Geological Survey. Report [*A publication*]   (APTA)
Tasmania Geol Surv Underground Water Supply Pap ... Tasmania. Geological Survey. Underground Water Supply Paper [*A publication*]   (APTA)
Tasmania Inland Fish Comm Rep ... Tasmania. Inland Fisheries Commission. Report [*A publication*]
Tasmania LR ... University of Tasmania. Law Review [*A publication*]   (DLA)
Tasmania Mines Dep Bull ... Tasmania. Department of Mines. Bulletin [*A publication*]   (APTA)
Tasmanian Dep Agric Insect Pest Surv ... Tasmanian Department of Agriculture. Insect Pest Survey [*A publication*]
Tasmanian Dep Agric Pamp ... Tasmanian Department of Agriculture. Pamphlet [*A publication*]
Tasmanian Fish Res ... Tasmanian Fisheries Research [*A publication*]
Tasmanian Fis Res ... Tasmanian Fisheries Research [*A publication*]
Tasmanian For Comm Bull ... Tasmanian Forestry Commission. Bulletin [*A publication*]
Tasmanian J Agr ... Tasmanian Journal of Agriculture [*A publication*]
Tasmanian J Agric ... Tasmanian Journal of Agriculture [*A publication*]
Tasmanian U L Rev ... Tasmanian University. Law Review [*A publication*]
Tasmanian Univ L Rev ... Tasmanian University. Law Review [*A publication*]
Tasmania Parl Dir Mines Annu Rep ... Tasmania. Parliament. Director of Mines. Annual Report [*A publication*]
Tasm Dep Agric Bull ... Tasmania. Department of Agriculture. Bulletin [*A publication*]   (APTA)
Tasm Dep Agric Res Bull ... Tasmania. Department of Agriculture. Research Bulletin [*A publication*]   (APTA)
TASME..... Tosyl-L-arginyl Sarcosine Methyl Ester [*Biochemistry*]
Tasm Fmr .. Tasmanian Farmer [*A publication*]   (APTA)
Tasm Fruitgr Fmr ... Tasmanian Fruitgrower and Farmer [*A publication*]   (APTA)
Tasm Fruitgrow Fmr ... Tasmanian Fruitgrower and Farmer [*A publication*]   (APTA)
Tasm Geol Surv Bull ... Tasmania. Geological Survey. Bulletin [*A publication*]   (APTA)
Tasm Geol Surv Geol Atlas 1 Mile Ser ... Tasmania. Geological Survey. Geological Atlas. 1 Mile Series [*A publication*]   (APTA)
Tasm Geol Surv Undergr Wat Supply Pap ... Tasmania. Geological Survey. Underground Water Supply Paper [*A publication*]   (APTA)
TASMGS .. Tomahawk Antiship Missile Guidance Set   (MCD)
Tasm Hist Res Ass Pap Proc ... Tasmanian Historical Research Association. Papers and Proceedings [*A publication*]   (APTA)
Tasm J Agr ... Tasmanian Journal of Agriculture [*A publication*]
Tasm J Agric ... Tasmanian Journal of Agriculture [*A publication*]
Tasm LR.... Tasmania Law Reports [*A publication*]   (DLA)
Tasm Nat... Tasmanian Naturalist [*A publication*]   (APTA)
TASMO..... Tactical Air Support for Maritime Operations [*Navy*]   (NVT)
TASMOL.. Tactical Aircraft Support Model   (MCD)

Tas Motor Trade & Transport J ... Tasmanian Motor Trade and Transport Journal [*A publication*]   (APTA)
Tasm SR .... Tasmanian State Reports [*A publication*]
Tasm Stat... Tasmanian Statutes [*A publication*]   (DLA)
Tasm Stat R ... Tasmanian Statutory Rules, with Tables [*A publication*]   (DLA)
Tasm St R .. Tasmanian State Reports [*A publication*]
Tasm UL Rev ... Tasmanian University. Law Review [*A publication*]
Tasm Univ Law Rev ... University of Tasmania. Law Review [*A publication*]   (APTA)
Tas Nat ...... Tasmanian Naturalist [*A publication*]   (APTA)
Tas News ... Tasmanian Motor News [*A publication*]   (APTA)
Tas News ... Tasmanian News Reports [*A publication*]   (APTA)
Tas Nurse .. Tasmanian Nurse [*A publication*]   (APTA)
TASO .... Television Allocations Study Organization [*Defunct*]
TASO .... Terminal Area Security Officer [*Military*]   (AABC)
TASO .... Training Aids Service Office [*Army*]   (AABC)
TASO .... Training and Audiovisual Support Officer [*Military*]
TASOS ..... Towed Array SONAR System
TASP .... [*The*] Army Studies Program   (AABC)
TASP .... Target Antisubmarine Patrol   (NVT)
TASP .... Telemetry Analysis and Simulation Program [*Spacecraft*] [*NASA*]
TASP .... Tentative Acceptance Sampling Procedure [*Army*]
TASP .... Texas Archaeological Society. Papers [*A publication*]
TASP .... Toll Alternatives Studies Program [*Telecommunications*]   (TEL)
TAS-PAC .. Total Analysis System for Production, Accounting, and Control [*Data processing*]
TASPR ...... Technical and Schedule Performance Report [*NASA*]   (NASA)
TASQ........ Tactical Airlift Squadron [*Air Force*]
Tas R.......... Tasmanian Reports [*A publication*]   (APTA)
Tas R.......... Tasmanian State Reports [*A publication*]
TASR........ Terminal Area Surveillance RADAR
TASR........ Torque Arm Speed Reducer
TASRA ..... Tabular System Reliability Analysis
TASRA ..... Thermal Activation-Strain Rate Analysis
TASROCO ... Tactical Aerial Surveillance and Reconnaissance Operational Capability Objectives [*1995*]   (MCD)
TASS .... [*The*] Army Study System
TASS .... Tactical Air Support Section [*Military*]
TASS .... Tactical Air Support Squadron [*Military*]
TASS .... Tactical Avionics System Simulator [*Army*]   (MCD)
TASS .... Tactical Signal Simulator [*Canadian Astronautics Ltd. RADAR threat simulation system*]
TASS .... Technical, Administrative, and Supervisory Section [*Amalgamated Union of Engineering Workers - Engineering Section*] [*British*]
TASS .... Technical Assembly System
TASS .... Telegraphnoye Agentstvo Sovyetskovo Soyuza [*Telegraph Agency of the Soviet Union*] [*News agency*]
TASS .... Terminal Application Support System   (MCD)
TASS .... Terrain Analyst's Synthesizer Station [*Army*]   (RDA)
TASS .... Towed Acoustic Surveillance System [*Marine science*]   (MSC)
TASS .... Towed Array SONAR System
TASS .... Towed Array Surveillance System [*Navy*]   (CAAL)
TASS .... Trouble Analysis System or Subsystem [*Telecommunications*]   (TEL)
TASSA ..... [*The*] Army Signal Supply Agency
TASSC...... [*The*] American Specialty Surety Council [*Later, ASA*]   (EA)
TasSchArt ... Tasmania School of Art [*Australia*]
TASSEL .... Three-Astronaut Space System Experimental Laboratory   (MCD)
TASSI....... Tactical Airborne SIGINT Support Improvement Acquisition Plan   (MCD)
TASSO ...... Tactical Special Security Office [*Army*]   (AABC)
TASSO ...... Transatlantic Air Safety Service Organization
TASSO ...... Two-Arm Spectrometer Solenoid   (MCD)
TASSq ...... Tactical Air Support Squadron [*Military*]   (AFM)
Tas S R ...... Tasmanian State Reports [*A publication*]   (APTA)
TASSRAP ... Towed Array Surveillance Range Prediction   (MCD)
TASST...... Tentative Airworthiness Standards for Supersonic Transports
TAST........ Tactical Assault Supply Transport   (MCD)
TAST........ Test Article Signal Translator   (MCD)
TAST........ Thermoacoustic Sensing Technique   (IEEE)
TASTA ...... [*The*] Administrative Support Theaters Army
TASTE ...... Thermal Accelerated Short Time Evaporator [*Facetious term used in orange juice industry*]
Tas Teach .. Tasmanian Teacher [*A publication*]   (APTA)
Tas Teacher ... Tasmanian Teacher [*A publication*]   (APTA)
TASTNGSq ... Tactical Air Support Training Squadron [*Air Force*]
Tas Trader ... Tasmanian Trader and Successful Independent [*A publication*]   (APTA)
Tas Tramp ... Tasmanian Tramp [*A publication*]   (APTA)
Tas Univ Gaz ... University of Tasmania. Gazette [*A publication*]   (APTA)
Tas Univ Law R ... University of Tasmania. Law Review [*A publication*]   (APTA)
Tas Univ Law Rev ... University of Tasmania. Law Review [*A publication*]   (APTA)
Tas Univ L Rev ... Tasmanian University. Law Review [*A publication*]

TASWD..... Torpedo, Anti-Submarine, and Mine Warfare Division [*British military*]   (DMA)
Tasw Lang Hist ... Taswell-Langmead's English Constitutional History [*10th ed.*] [*1946*] [*A publication*]   (DLA)
TASWM..... Test ASW [*Antisubmarine Warfare*] Missile [*Navy*]   (CAAL)
TAT .... [*The*] Absolute Truth [*In Julian Barnes' novel "Staring at the Sun"*]
TAT .... [*The*] Associated Turtles [*Defunct*]   (EA)
TAT .... Tactical Armament Turret   (NG)
T & AT ...... Tank and Antitank [*Artillery and ammunition*]   (NATG)
TAT .... Target Abilities Test [*Psychometrics*]
TAT .... Target Aircraft Transmitter
TAT .... Task Assignment Table   (MCD)
TAT .... Tateyama [*Japan*] [*Seismograph station code, US Geological Survey*]   (SEIS)
TAT .... Tatry/Poprad [*Czechoslovakia*] [*Airport symbol*]   (OAG)
TAT .... Technical Acceptance Team [*NASA*]   (AAG)
TAT .... Technical Approval Team
TAT .... Technical Assistance Team [*Air Force*]   (AFM)
TAT .... Technical Assistance and Training
TAT .... Technology Application Team [*NASA*]
TAT .... Television Awareness Training
TAT .... Temporary Ambulance Train [*British military*]   (DMA)
TAT .... Tensile Adhesion Test [*for coatings*]
TAT .... Terrorist Action Team [*Military*]   (MCD)
TAT .... Tetanus Antitoxin [*Medicine*]
TAT .... Thematic Apperception Test [*Psychology*]
TAT .... Thinned Aperture Telescope
TAT .... Thromboplastin Activation Test [*Clinical chemistry*]
TAT .... Thrust-Augmented Thor [*NASA*]
TAT .... To Accompany Troops
TAT .... Tochas Affen Tish [*In television production company name "TAT Productions." Words are Yiddish and translate figuratively as "Let's Be Honest"*]
TAT .... Torpedo Attack Teacher [*Navy*]
TAT .... Total Air Temperature   (NASA)
TAT .... Total Aircraft Time   (MCD)
TAT .... Total Alert Time
TAT .... Touraine Air Transport [*Private airline*] [*French*]   (EY)
TAT .... Toxin-Antitoxin [*Also, TA*] [*Immunology*]
TAT .... Trace Acceptance Tester
TAT .... Training and Technology
TAT .... Trans-Activator [*Genetics*]
TAT .... Trans Atlantic Resources, Inc. [*Vancouver Stock Exchange symbol*]
TAT .... Transatlantic Telephone [*Cable*]
TAT .... Transcontinental Air Transport
TAT .... Transportes Aeroside Timor [*Portuguese Timor*]
TAT .... Triamterene [*Diuretic*]
TAT .... True Air Temperature   (AFM)
TAT .... Turnaround Time
TAT .... Two-Axis Tracking
TAT .... Type-Approval Test
TAT .... Tyrosine Aminotransferase [*An enzyme*]
Tatabanyai Szenbanyak Musz Kozgazdasagi Kozl ... Tatabanyai Szenbanyak Muszaki Kozgazdasagi Kozlemenyei [*Hungary*] [*A publication*]
TATAC...... Temporary Air Transport Advisory Committee [*NATO*]   (NATG)
Tata Inst Fund Res Lectures on Math and Phys ... Tata Institute of Fundamental Research. Lectures on Mathematics and Physics [*A publication*]
Tata Inst Fund Res Studies in Math ... Tata Institute of Fundamental Research. Studies in Mathematics [*A publication*]
Tatar Neft ... Tatarskaya Neft [*A publication*]
TATAWS .. Tank, Antitank, and Assault Weapons Study [*or System*] [*Army*]
TATB......... Theater Air Transportation Board
TATB......... Triaminotrinitrobenzene [*Organic chemistry*]
TATC......... Tactical Air Traffic Control   (NVT)
TATC......... Terminal Air Traffic Control
TATC......... Transatlantic Telephone Cable   (IEEE)
TATCA...... Trialkoxytricarballylate [*Organic chemistry*]
TATCE ...... Terminal Air Traffic Control Element
TATCF ...... Terminal Air Traffic Control Facility
TATCO...... Tactical Automatic Telephone Central Office [*Military*]
TATCS ...... Terminal Air Traffic Control System
TATD......... Task Assignment Table Display   (MCD)
TATDL...... Tabulated Assembly Technical Data List
TATE......... Ashton-Tate Corp. [*NASDAQ symbol*]   (NQ)
TATE......... Tank Arrangement Thermal Efficiency [*Computer program*]   (KSC)
TATEJ....... Tasmanian Association for the Teaching of English. Journal [*A publication*]   (APTA)
TATER...... Talos-Terrier-Recruit [*Flight-test vehicle*]
Tate's Dig .. Tate's Digest of Laws [*Virginia*] [*A publication*]   (DLA)
TATG .... Tuned Anode Tuned Grid   (DEN)
TATHS..... Tool and Trades History Society   (EAIO)
TATI.......... Total Air Temperature Indicator
TATI.......... Tumor-Associated Trypsin Inhibitor [*Medicine*]

Tatigkeitsber Bundesanst Geowiss Rohst ... Taetigkeitsbericht. Bundesanstalt fuer Geowissenschaften und Rohstoffe [*A publication*]
Tatigkeitsber Geol Landsamt Nordrhein-Westfal ... Taetigkeitsbericht. Geologisches Landesamt Nordrhein-Westfalen [*A publication*]
Tatigkeitsber Niedersach Landsamt Bodenforsch ... Taetigkeitsbericht. Niedersachsisches Landesamt fuer Bodenforschung [*A publication*]
TATM .... Tatum Petroleum Corp. [*Downey, CA*] [*NASDAQ symbol*] (NQ)
TATO .... Taipei [*Taiwan*] [*Seismograph station code, US Geological Survey*] (SEIS)
TATP .... Two-Axis Tracking Pedestal
TATR .... Tactical Air Target Recommender
TATr .... Tyrosine Aminotransferase Regulator
TATRC ...... Type-Approval Test Review Committee
TATS .... Tactical Aerial Targets Squadron (MCD)
TATS .... Tactical Armament Turret System
TATS .... Tactical Transmission System Summary (KSC)
TATS .... Target Acquisition and Track System (MUGU)
TATS .... Technical Assistance and Training Survey [*Department of Labor*] (OICC)
TATS .... Test and Training Satellite [*Also, TETR, TTS*] [*NASA*]
TATSA ...... Transportation Aircraft Test and Support Activity [*Military*]
Tatslil .... Tatslil [*The Chord*]. Forum for Music Research and Bibliography [*A publication*]
Tatsuta Tech Rev ... Tatsuta Technical Review [*A publication*]
TATT .... Technical Assistance and Technology Transfer (NOAA)
TATTE ...... Talos [*Missile*] Tactical Test Equipment
TATU .... Technical Advanced Training for Units (MCD)
TAU .... Fort Meade, MD [*Location identifier*] [*FAA*] (FAAL)
TAU .... Tasmania University [*Tasmania*] [*Seismograph station code, US Geological Survey*] (SEIS)
Tau .... Taurus [*Constellation*]
TAU .... Technical Advisory Unit (OICC)
TAU .... Tel Aviv University [*Israel*]
TAU .... Temporary Authorization [*Personnel*] (OICC)
TAU .... Test Access Unit [*Telecommunications*] (TEL)
TAU .... Thousand Astronomical Units
TAU .... Transalta Utilities Corp. [*Toronto Stock Exchange symbol*]
TAU .... Triton Acid Urea
TAU .... Trunk Access Unit
TAU .... Twin Agent Unit [*Fire fighting*] (NVT)
TAUCH ..... Tauchnitz [*Bibliography*] (ROG)
TAUF .... Test Assembly Unloading Fixture [*Nuclear energy*] (NRCH)
TAUM .... Groupe de Recherches pour la Traduction Automatique [*Universite de Montreal*] [*Canada*] [*Research center*]
Taun .... Taunton's English Common Pleas Reports [*A publication*] (DLA)
TAUN .... Technical Assistance of the United Nations
Taunt (Eng) ... Taunton's English Common Pleas Reports [*127, 129 English Reprint*] [*A publication*] (DLA)
TAUPDJ ... Trends in Autonomic Pharmacology [*A publication*]
Taur .... Taurus [*Constellation*]
TAUR .... Taurus Petroleum, Inc. [*Denver, CO*] [*NASDAQ symbol*] (NQ)
TAUS .... Tobacco Association of United States (EA)
TAUSA ...... Trans-Atlantic Universities Speech Association
Taut .... Taunton's English Common Pleas Reports [*A publication*] (DLA)
TAUT .... Tautology (ADA)
TAUTDV .. Texas A & M University. Sea Grant College. TAMU-SG [*A publication*]
TAV .... Tau [*American Samoa*] [*Airport symbol*] (OAG)
TAV .... Tavern (ROG)
TAV .... Tavistock [*England*]
TAV .... Tavurvur [*New Britain*] [*Seismograph station code, US Geological Survey*] (SEIS)
TAV .... Technical Assistance Visit (MCD)
TAV .... Technical Availability [*Navy*] (NG)
TAV .... Tender Availability [*Navy*]
TAV .... Test and Validation (KSC)
TAV .... Tomato Aspermy Virus
TAV .... Transatmospheric Vehicle [*Proposed futuristic plane capable of flying at hypersonic speeds*]
TAVC .... Total Active Vitamin C [*Nutrition*]
TAVD .... Trans-Atlantic Video, Inc. [*NASDAQ symbol*] (NQ)
TAVE .... Average Temperature (NRCH)
TAVE .... Thor-Agena Vibration Experiment [*NASA*]
TAVET ...... Temperature Acceleration Vibration Environmental Tester
TAVI .... Thorn Apple Valley, Incorporated [*Southfield, MI*] [*NASDAQ symbol*] (NQ)
TAVIP .... Tahun Vivere Pericoloso [*The Year of Living Dangerously*] [*President Sukarno's national policy in 1964*] [*Indonesia*]
T & AVR ... Territorial and Army Volunteer Reserve [*British*]
TAVRA ...... Territorial Auxiliary and Volunteer Reserve Association [*British Armed Forces*]
TAVS .... Turbine Area Ventilation System [*Nuclear energy*] (NRCH)
TAW .... Tactical Air [*or Airlift*] Wing
TAW .... Tactical Assault Weapon

TAW .... Tawu [*Republic of China*] [*Seismograph station code, US Geological Survey*] (SEIS)
TAW .... Tennessee Wesleyan College, Athens, TN [*Library symbol*] [*Library of Congress*] (LCLS)
TAW .... Terrawest [*Vancouver Stock Exchange symbol*]
TAW .... Thrust-Augmented Wing [*NASA*] (MCD)
TAW .... [*The*] Toledo, Angola & Western Railway Co. [*AAR code*]
TAW .... Troop Airlift Wing (CINC)
TAW .... Twice a Week [*Advertising frequency*]
TAWACS .. Tactical Airborne Warning and Control System (AFM)
TAWAR ..... Tactical All Weather Attack Requirements [*Air Force*] (MCD)
TAWB .... Through Air Waybill [*Shipping*] (DS)
TAWC .... Tactical Air Warfare Center [*Air Force*]
TAWC .... Tactical Armored Weapons Carrier (MCD)
TAWCS ..... Tactical Air Weapons Control System
TAWDS ..... Target Acquisition Weapon Delivery System [*Air Force*] (MCD)
TAWDS ..... Terminal Area Weapon Delivery Simulator (MCD)
TAWG .... Tactical Air Warfare Group
TAWG .... Target Acquisition Working Group [*Air Force*]
TAWOG ..... Travel Arrangements without Government Expense (FAAC)
TAWRS ..... Tower Aviation Weather Reporting Station (NOAA)
TAWS .... Tactical Area Weather Sensor (MCD)
TAWS .... Tactical Automatic Weather Station [*Buoy*] (MSC)
TAWS .... Tactical Warfare Center [*Army*] (AABC)
TAWS .... Technical Analysis Work Sheet (AAG)
TAWS .... Terrain Analyst Work Station [*Army*] (RDA)
TAWS .... Total Airborne Weapon Systems (MUGU)
TAWS .... Total Armament Weapons System (MUGU)
TAWT .... Tawton [*England*]
TAWU .... Transport and Allied Workers' Union [*Rhodesia, Nyasaland, and Kenya*]
TAX .... Madison, WI [*Location identifier*] [*FAA*] (FAAL)
TAX .... Tactical Air Exercise (CINC)
TAX .... Tarxien International, Inc. [*Toronto Stock Exchange symbol*]
Tax .... Taxandria [*A publication*]
Tax .... Taxation [*A publication*]
TAX .... Taxation for Accountants [*A publication*]
TAX .... Taxiing [*Aviation*]
TAX .... Training Assessment Exercise
Tax ABC ... Canada Tax Appeal Board Cases [*A publication*] (DLA)
Tax Acct ..... Taxation for Accountants [*A publication*] (DLA)
Tax Ad .... Tax Advisor [*A publication*]
Tax Adm'rs News ... Tax Administrators News [*A publication*] (DLA)
Tax Adv ...... Tax Advisor [*A publication*]
Tax in Aust ... Taxation in Australia [*A publication*] (APTA)
Tax Aust ..... Taxation in Australia [*A publication*]
Tax Cas .... Tax Cases [*A publication*] (DLA)
Tax Conf .... Tax Conference [*A publication*]
Tax Coun Q ... Tax Counselor's Quarterly [*A publication*]
Tax Ct Mem Dec ... Tax Court Memorandum Decisions [*Commerce Clearing House*] [*A publication*] (DLA)
Tax Ct Mem Dec CCH ... Tax Court Memorandum Decisions. Commerce Clearing House [*A publication*]
Tax Ct Mem Dec P-H ... Tax Court Memorandum Decisions. Prentice-Hall [*A publication*]
Tax Ct Rep ... Tax Court Reporter [*Commerce Clearing House*] [*A publication*] (DLA)
Tax Ct Rep CCH ... Tax Court Reports. Commerce Clearing House [*A publication*]
Tax Ct Rep Dec ... Tax Court Reported Decisions [*Prentice-Hall, Inc.*] [*A publication*] (DLA)
Tax Ct Rep Dec P-H ... Tax Court Reported Decisions. Prentice-Hall [*A publication*]
Tax Ct Rep & Mem Dec (P-H) ... Tax Court Reported and Memorandum Decisions (Prentice-Hall, Inc.) [*A publication*] (DLA)
Taxes .... Tax Magazine [*A publication*] (DLA)
Tax Exec .... Tax Executive [*A publication*]
Tax-Exempt Org P-H ... Tax-Exempt Organizations. Prentice-Hall [*A publication*]
Tax Expend ... Tax Expenditures. Budget Control Options and 5-Year Projections for Fiscal Years 1983-1987 [*A publication*]
Tax Fin and Est Pl ... Tax, Financial, and Estate Planning for the Owner of a Closely Held Corporation [*A publication*]
TAXI .... Transparent Asynchronous Transceiver Interface
TAXIR .... Taxonomic Information Retrieval [*Data processing*] (DIT)
Tax Law ..... Tax Lawyer [*A publication*]
Tax for Law ... Taxation for Lawyers [*A publication*]
Tax Law R ... Tax Law Review [*A publication*]
Tax Law Rep ... Tax Law Reporter [*A publication*] (DLA)
TAXLE .... Tandem Cantilevered Axle
Tax LR .... Tax Law Reporter [*A publication*] (DLA)
Tax LR .... Tax Law Review [*A publication*]
Tax L Rep ... Tax Law Reporter [*A publication*] (DLA)
Tax L Rev .. Tax Law Review [*A publication*]
Tax Mag .... Tax Magazine [*A publication*] (DLA)
Tax Man .... Tax Management [*A publication*] (DLA)
Tax Management Int'l ... Tax Management International Journal [*A publication*]
Tax Mgmt (BNA) ... Tax Management (Bureau of National Affairs) [*A publication*] (DLA)

Tax Mgmt Int'l J ... Tax Management International Journal [*A publication*] (DLA)
Tax Mngm't ... Tax Management [*Bureau of National Affairs*] [*A publication*] (DLA)
Tax Mo (Manila) ... Tax Monthly (Manila) [*A publication*]
TAXN .... Taxation (ROG)
Taxn in Aust ... Taxation in Australia [*A publication*] (APTA)
TAXON ..... Taxonomy
Taxon Index ... Taxonomic Index [*A publication*]
Taxpayers Bul ... Taxpayers' Bulletin [*A publication*] (APTA)
Tax Pl Int ... Tax Planning International [*A publication*] (DLA)
Tax Pl Rev ... Tax Planning Review [*A publication*] (DLA)
Tax Pract Forum ... Tax Practitioners Forum [*A publication*] (DLA)
Tax R .... Tax Review [*A publication*]
Tax R .... Taxation Reports [*England*] [*A publication*] (DLA)
Tax Rev ...... Tax Review [*A publication*]
Tax & Rev ... Taxation and Revenue (DLA)
t-ay--- .... Antarctica [*MARC geographic area code*] [*Library of Congress*] (LCCP)
TAY .... Taylor, FL [*Location identifier*] [*FAA*] (FAAL)
Tay .... Taylor's North Carolina Reports [*1 North Carolina*] [*1798-1802*] [*A publication*] (DLA)
Tay .... Taylor's Supreme Court Reports [*1847-48*] [*Bengal, India*] [*A publication*] (DLA)
Tay .... Taylor's Upper Canada King's Bench Reports [*1823-1827*] [*A publication*] (DLA)
TAY .... Tule Lake Aster Yellows [*Plant pathology*]
Tay & B ...... Taylor and Bell's Bengal Reports [*India*] [*A publication*] (DLA)
Tay Bank L ... Taylor on the Bankruptcy Law [*A publication*] (DLA)
Tay Bk R .... Taylor's Book of Rights [*1833*] [*A publication*] (DLA)
Tay Civ L .... Taylor's Elements of Civil Law [*A publication*] (DLA)
TAYD .... Taylor Devices, Inc. [*NASDAQ symbol*] (NQ)
Tay Eq Jur ... Taylor on Equity Jurisprudence [*A publication*] (DLA)
Tay Ev .... Taylor on Evidence [*12th ed.*] [*1931*] [*A publication*] (DLA)
Tay Glos ..... Taylor's Law Glossary [*2nd ed.*] [*1823*] [*A publication*] (DLA)
Tay Gov ...... Taylor on Government [*A publication*] (DLA)
Tay J L .... [*J. L.*] Taylor's Reports [*1 North Carolina*] [*A publication*] (DLA)
Tayl Civil Law ... Taylor on Civil Law [*A publication*] (DLA)
Tayl Corp ... Taylor on Private Corporations [*A publication*] (DLA)
Tayl Ev .... Taylor on Evidence [*A publication*] (DLA)
Tay L Gl ...... Taylor's Law Glossary [*A publication*] (DLA)
Tayl Gloss ... Taylor's Law Glossary [*A publication*] (DLA)
Tayl Hist Gav ... [*Silas*] Taylor's History of Gavelkind [*A publication*] (DLA)
Tayl Landl & Ten ... Taylor's Landlord and Tenant [*A publication*] (DLA)
Tayl Med Jur ... Taylor's Medical Jurisprudence [*A publication*] (DLA)
Tayl NC ..... Taylor's North Carolina Reports [*1 North Carolina*] [*A publication*] (DLA)
Taylor .... Taylor's Customary Laws of Rembau [*1903-28*] [*Malaya*] [*A publication*] (DLA)
Taylor .... Taylor's North Carolina Reports [*1 North Carolina*] [*A publication*] (DLA)
Taylor .... Taylor's North Carolina Term Reports [*4 North Carolina*] [*A publication*] (DLA)
Taylor .... Taylor's Reports [*Bengal, India*] [*A publication*] (DLA)
Taylor .... Taylor's Upper Canada King's Bench Reports [*A publication*] (DLA)
Taylor KB (Can) ... Taylor's Upper Canada King's Bench Reports [*A publication*] (DLA)
Taylor (Malaya) ... Taylor's Customary Laws of Rembau [*1903-28*] [*Malaya*] [*A publication*] (DLA)
Taylor Soc Bul ... Taylor Society. Bulletin [*A publication*]
Taylor UC ... Taylor's Upper Canada King's Bench Reports [*A publication*]
Tayl Priv Corp ... Taylor on Private Corporations [*A publication*] (DLA)
Tayl St .... Taylor's Revised Statutes [*Wisconsin*] [*A publication*] (DLA)
Tay L & T .. Taylor's Landlord and Tenant [*A publication*] (DLA)
Tay Med Jur ... Taylor's Medical Jurisprudence [*12th ed.*] [*1966*] [*A publication*] (DLA)
TAYMEL .. Taylor Woodrow Management & Engineering Ltd. [*British*] (IRUK)
Tay NC ...... Taylor's North Carolina Reports [*1 North Carolina*] [*A publication*] (DLA)
Tay Poi .... Taylor on Poisons [*3rd ed.*] [*1875*] [*A publication*] (DLA)
Tay Rep ...... Taylor's North Carolina Reports [*1 North Carolina*] [*A publication*] (DLA)
TAYS .... Taylor [*S.*] Companies, Inc. [*Columbus, GA*] [*NASDAQ symbol*] (NQ)
Tay Tit .... Taylor on Tithe Commutation [*1876*] [*A publication*] (DLA)
Tay UC ...... Taylor's Upper Canada King's Bench Reports [*1 vol.*] [*1823-27*] [*A publication*] (DLA)
Tay Wills ... Taylor's Precedents of Wills [*A publication*] (DLA)
Tay Wis Stat ... Taylor's Wisconsin Statutes [*A publication*] (DLA)
TAZ .... Tabak Zeitung. Fachorgan der Tabakwirtschaft [*A publication*]
TAZ .... Tactical Alert Zone (NATG)
TAZ .... Taylorville, IL [*Location identifier*] [*FAA*] (FAAL)
TAZ .... Theater Administrative Zone [*Military*]
TAZ .... Triazolam [*Tranquilizer*]
TAZARA ... Tanzania-Zambia Railway

TAzerbPI ... Trudy Azerbaidzhanskogo Gosudarstvennogo Pedagogicheskogo Instituta [*A publication*]
TB .... Aerospatiale (SOCATA) Stark KG [*Federal Republic of Germany*] [*ICAO aircraft manufacturer identifier*] (ICAO)
TB .... Automotive Engine Rebuilders Association. Technical Bulletin [*A publication*] (EAAP)
Tb .... Body Temperature [*Medicine*]
TB .... Tabulation Block (MSA)
TB .... Tail Back [*Football*]
TB .... Talk Back [*NASA*] (KSC)
TB .... Talmud Bavli (BJA)
TB .... Tangential Bracket
TB .... Tank Battalion [*Army*]
TB .... Tape Backup Unit
TB .... Tapes for the Blind [*Defunct*] (EA)
TB .... Tariff Bureau
T & B .... Taylor and Bell's Calcutta Supreme Court Reports [*India*] [*A publication*] (DLA)
TB .... Techbyte, Inc. [*Vancouver Stock Exchange symbol*]
TB .... Technical Bulletin [*Military*]
TB .... Telegraph Bureau
TB .... Temple Biographies [*A publication*]
TB .... Tempo Brasileiro [*A publication*]
TB .... Temporary Buoy [*Nautical charts*]
Tb .... TeraBIT [*Binary Digit*] [*10¹² BITs*]
TB .... Terabyte [*10¹² bytes*]
Tb .... Terbium [*Chemical element*]
TB .... Terminal Base (MCD)
TB .... Terminal Block
TB .... Terminal Board
TB .... Test Bed (MCD)
TB .... Test Bulletin
TB .... Theologische Blaetter [*Leipzig*] [*A publication*]
TB .... Thermobarometer
TB .... Thoroughbred
TB .... Thrill Book [*A publication*]
TB .... Thromboxane B [*Also, TxB, TXB*] [*Biochemistry*]
T/B .... Thunderbird [*Automobile*]
TB .... Thymol Blue [*An indicator*]
TB .... Tile Base [*Technical drawings*]
T/B .... Tile Block [*Technical drawings*]
TB .... Time-Bandwidth
TB .... Time Base
TB .... Time Duration of Burn (MCD)
TB .... Time between Points [*Experimentation*]
TB .... Times at Bat [*Baseball*]
Tb .... Tobit [*Old Testament book*] [*Roman Catholic canon*]
TB .... Toggle Buffer (MCD)
TB .... Toluidine Blue [*Organic chemistry*]
TB .... Tone Burst
T & B .... Top and Bottom [*Technical drawings*]
T/B .... Top to Bottom
TB .... Top Boy [*British*] (DSUE)
TB .... Torch Bible Commentaries [*A publication*] (BJA)
TB .... Torch Brazing
TB .... Torpedo Boat [*Navy symbol*] [*Obsolete*]
TB .... Torpedo Bomber [*or Bombing*]
TB .... Total Bases
TB .... Total Bilirubin [*Clinical chemistry*]
TB .... Total Blank [*Entertainment slang for poor show town*]
TB .... Total Body [*Nuclear energy*] (NRCH)
TB .... Total Bouts [*Boxing*]
TB .... Total Burn
TB .... Towel Bar [*Technical drawings*]
TB .... Tracer Bullet
TB .... Tracheal-Bronchiolar [*Region*] [*Medicine*]
TB .... Tracheobronchitis [*Medicine*]
TB .... Tractor Biplane
TB .... Trading Bank
TB .... Trafalgar Brookmount [*British*]
TB .... Traffic Bureau
TB .... Training Back [*Main parachute*]
TB .... Training Battalion [*British military*] (DMA)
TB .... Tranquility Base [*Moon landing site*]
TB .... Transfer Building
TB .... Transmitter-Blocker (DEN)
TB .... Trapezoid Body [*Audiometry*]
TB .... Travelair [*Cargo*] BV [*Netherlands*] [*ICAO designator*] (FAAC)
TB .... Treasury Bill
TB .... Treasury Board Secretariat [*Canada*]
TB .... Trial Balance [*Bookkeeping*]
TB .... Trial Balloon
TB .... Triple-Braided (CET)
TB .... Troop Basis [*Military*]
T & B .... Truck and Bus
TB .... True Bearing [*Navigation*]
TB .... True Blue [*A fluorescent dye*]
TB .... Tryptone Broth [*Culture medium*]
TB .... Tubercle Bacillus [*Bacteriology*]

TB	Tuberculin [*or Tuberculosis*] (AABC)
TB	Tumor-Bearing [*Animal*]
TB	Tundra Biome [*Ecological biogeographic study*]
TB	Turbine Building [*Nuclear energy*] (NRCH)
T & B	Turn-and-Bank Indicators
T and B	Turned and Bored
TB	Tvorba [*A publication*]
TB	Twin Branch Railroad Co. [*AAR code*]
TB	Twirly Birds (EA)
TB	Two Beauts [*Slang*] [*Australian*] (DSUE)
TB	Tyndale Bulletin [*A publication*]
TBA	[*The*] Bettmann Archive [*A publication*]
TBA	Tabibuga [*Papua New Guinea*] [*Airport symbol*] (OAG)
TBA	Tables of Basic Allowances [*Previously, Basic Tables of Commissioning Allowances*] [*Navy*]
TBA	Task Budget Allocation (MCD)
TBA	Taurine Bibliophiles of America (EA)
TBA	Television Bureau of Advertising
TBA	Terminal Board Assembly (MSA)
TBA	Tertiary Butyl Acetate [*Organic chemistry*]
TBA	Tertiary Butyl Alcohol [*Gasoline additive*]
TBA	Tertiary-Butylarsine [*Organic chemistry*]
TBA	Test of Basic Assumptions [*Psychology*]
TBA	Test Bed Aircraft
TBA	Test Boring Association (EA)
TBA	Thiobarbituric Acid [*Organic chemistry*]
TBA	Tires, Batteries, and Accessories
TBA	To Be Activated [*Military*]
TBA	To Be Added (AAG)
TBA	To Be Agreed (AIA)
TBA	To Be Announced
TBA	To Be Assigned
TBA	To Be Avoided [*Slang*]
TBA	Torsional Braid Analysis [*Instrumentation*]
TBA	Towed Buoy Antenna
TBA	Tributylamine [*Organic chemistry*]
TBA	Trichlorobenzoic Acid [*Herbicide*] [*Organic chemistry*]
TBA	Tuba [*Music*]
TBA	Twin Bonanza Association (EA)
TBAB.........	Theosophical Book Association for the Blind (EA)
TBACC.....	Tetrabutylammonium Chlorochromate [*Organic chemistry*]
TBAC/FLM ...	Treasury Board Advisory Committee on Federal Land Management [*Canada*]
TBAD	To Be Advised (AIA)
TBAF........	Tetrabutylammonium Fluoride [*Organic chemistry*]
TBAG	To Be Agreed (AIA)
TBAH.......	Tetrabutylammonium Hydroxide [*Organic chemistry*]
TBAI	Temporary Base Activation Instruction (AAG)
TBAI........	Tidbit Alley, Incorporated [*New York, NY*] [*NASDAQ symbol*] (NQ)
TBAM	Tone Burst Amplitude Modulation
TBAN	To Be Announced [*Army*] (AABC)
TBAP........	Tetrabutylammoniumperchlorate [*Photovoltaic energy systems*]
TBARA......	Trakehner Breed Association and Registry of America [*Defunct*] (EA)
TBAS.........	[*The*] Band Appreciation Society (EAIO)
TBAT........	Tow/Bushmaster Armored Turret [*Military*]
TBAWRBA ...	Travel by Military Aircraft, Military and/or Naval Water Carrier, Commercial Rail and/or Bus Is Authorized [*Army*] (AABC)
TBAX........	Tube Axial
TBAZFCA ...	Toledo Bird Association, Zebra Finch Club of America (EA)
TBB...........	Columbus, MS [*Location identifier*] [*FAA*] (FAAL)
TBB...........	Die Tempel von Babylon und Borsippa [*A publication*] (BJA)
TBB...........	Temporal Bone Banks [*Otology*] (EA)
TBB...........	Tenor, Baritone, Bass
TBB...........	Tobex Resources Ltd. [*Vancouver Stock Exchange symbol*]
T & BB	Top and Bottom Bolt [*Technical drawings*]
TBB...........	Transbronchial Biopsy [*Medicine*]
TBB...........	Trolleybus Bulletin [*A publication*] (EAAP)
TB & B	Tuberculosis and Brucellosis [*Medicine*] (ADA)
TBBA.........	Terephthalyl Bis(butylaniline) [*Organic chemistry*]
TBBF.........	Top Baseband Frequency
TBBFA......	Trudy Buryatskogo Instituta Estestvennykh Nauk Buryatskii Filial Sibirskoe Otdelenie Akademiya Nauk SSSR [*A publication*]
TBBM.......	Total Body Bone Mineral
TBBPA	Tetrabromobisphenol-A [*Organic chemistry*]
TBBSA	Transactions. British Bryological Society [*A publication*]
TBC...........	Belmont College, Nashville, TN [*OCLC symbol*] (OCLC)
TBC...........	Confederation College of Applied Arts and Technology [*UTLAS symbol*]
TBC...........	Taiwan Base Command (CINC)
TBC...........	Tanker and Bulk Carrier
TBC...........	Tasty Baking Company [*AMEX symbol*] (SPSG)
TBC...........	Technology & Business Communications, Inc. [*Information service or system*] (IID)
TBC...........	Television Briefing Console
TBC...........	Tembec Inc. [*Toronto Stock Exchange symbol*]
TBC...........	Terminal Buffer Controller (NASA)
TBC...........	Theatre Ballet of Canada
TBC...........	Thermal Barrier Coating (RDA)
TBC...........	Thyroxine-Binding Capacity [*Biochemistry*]
TBC...........	Time Base Corrector [*Videotape recording element*] [*Early processing device*]
TBC...........	To Be Cooked [*Food*]
TBC...........	Token Bus Controller [*Motorola, Inc.*]
TBC...........	Torch Bible Commentaries [*New York/London*] [*A publication*] (BJA)
TBC...........	Torrey Botanical Club (EA)
TBC...........	Toss Bomb Computer
TBC...........	Total Body Calcium
TBC...........	Trinidad Base Command [*World War II*]
TBC...........	Trunk Block Connector
TBC...........	Tuba City, AZ [*Location identifier*] [*FAA*] (FAAL)
TBC...........	Tube Bending Chart
TBC...........	Tubercle Bacillus [*Bacteriology*]
TBC...........	Tuberculosis
TBC...........	Turbulent Bed Contactor [*Chemical engineering*]
TBCA........	Test Boring Contractors Association [*Later, TBA*] (EA)
TBCA........	Transportation Brokers Conference of America (EA)
TBCC........	TBC Corporation [*NASDAQ symbol*] (NQ)
TBCC........	Tom Baker Cancer Centre [*University of Calgary*] [*Formerly, Southern Alberta Cancer Centre*] [*Research center*] (RCD)
TBCCW.....	Turbine-Building Closed Cooling Water [*Nuclear energy*] (NRCH)
TBCR........	Times British Colonies Review [*London*] [*A publication*]
TBCX........	[*The*] Banking Center [*Waterbury, CT*] [*NASDAQ symbol*] (NQ)
TBD	Tactical Battle Drill [*Army*] (INF)
TBD	Target Bearing Designator [*Navy*]
TBD	Terminal Bomber Defense [*Army*] (AABC)
TBD	Thibodaux, LA [*Location identifier*] [*FAA*] (FAAL)
TBD	Thousand Barrels per Day [*Also, KBD*]
TBD	To Be Declassified (AAG)
TBD	To Be Defined
TBD	To Be Designated (MCD)
TBD	To Be Determined (AFM)
TBD	To Be Developed (NASA)
TBD	To Be Disbanded
TBD	To Be Done (AAG)
TBD	Too Badly Decomposed
TBD	Torpedo-Boat Destroyer [*Obsolete*]
TBD	Trans Border Energy [*Vancouver Stock Exchange symbol*]
TBD	Triazabicydo-decene [*Organic chemistry*]
TBD	Troubleshooting Block Diagram
TBD	Twin Boundary Diffusion
TBDF........	Transborder Data Flows [*Also, TDF*] [*Telecommunications*]
TBDL........	To Be Designated Later (CINC)
TBDL........	Total Bile-Duct Ligation [*Medicine*]
TBDMIM ...	Tertiary-Butyldimethylsilylimidazole [*Organic chemistry*]
TBDS........	Test Base Dispatch Service (AAG)
TBD/TDA ...	Too Badly Decomposed/Technician Destroyed Animal [*Laboratory testing*]
TBE...........	Federation Europeenne des Fabricants de Tuiles et de Briques [*European Association of Brick and Tile Manufacturers*] (EAIO)
TBE...........	Tetrabromoethane [*Microscopy*]
TBE...........	Texas Business Executive [*A publication*]
TBE...........	Thread Both Ends (MSA)
TBE...........	Tiber Energy Corp. [*Toronto Stock Exchange symbol*]
TBE...........	Tick-Borne Encephalitis
TBE...........	Time Base Error
TBE...........	To Be Evaluated (NASA)
TBE...........	To Be Expended (AAG)
TBE...........	Tobe, CO [*Location identifier*] [*FAA*] (FAAL)
TBE...........	Toronto Board of Education, Professional Library [*UTLAS symbol*]
TBE...........	Total Body Ergometer
TBE...........	Total Breech Extraction [*Gynecology*]
TBE...........	Trade Opportunities in Taiwan [*A publication*]
TBE...........	Transmitter Buffer Empty [*Data processing*]
TBE...........	Tris-Borate Buffer Electrophoresis
TBE...........	Tris-Borate-EDTA [*Ethylenediaminetetraacetate*] [*Buffer*]
TBE...........	Tuberculin Bacillen Emulsion [*Medicine*]
TBEA........	Truck Body and Equipment Association (EA)
TBE Class ...	Timber Bulletin for Europe. Classification and Definitions of Forest Products [*A publication*]
TBEM.......	Terminal-Based Electronic Mail
TBeP.........	Polk County High School, Benton, TN [*Library symbol*] [*Library of Congress*] (LCLS)
TBEP........	Tri(butoxyethyl) Phosphate [*Organic chemistry*]
TBESI.......	Turbine-Building Exhaust System Isolation [*Nuclear energy*] (NRCH)
T Best........	Tijdschrift voor Bestuurswetenschappen [*A publication*]
T Best Publ R ...	Tijdschrift voor Bestuurswetenschappen en Publiek Recht [*A publication*]
TBEX........	Tube Expander
TBF...........	Tabiteuea North [*Kiribati*] [*Airport symbol*] (OAG)
TBF...........	Tail Bomb Fuse (KSC)

TBF............	Test de Bon Fonctionnement [*Spacelab*]　(MCD)
TBF............	Testicular Blood Flow [*Physiology*]
TBF............	Tie Bus Fault
TBF............	Time between Failures [*Quality control*]　(AFIT)
TBF............	To Be Funded [*Contracting*] [*Military*]
TBF............	Torpedo Bomber Fighter　(NATG)
TBF............	Total Body Fat
TBF............	Tour Basing Fare [*Air travel term*]
TBF............	Tributyl Phosphate [*Organic chemistry*]
TBF............	Two-Body Force
TBFC.........	Teresa Brewer Fan Club　(EA)
TBFC.........	Tom Burford Fan Club　(EA)
TBFC.........	Tony Booth Fan Club　(EA)
TBFG.........	Tom Baker Friendship Group　(EAIO)
TBFSA.......	True Blue Floor Sanding Association [*Australia*]
TBFX.........	Tube Fixture [*Tool*]　(AAG)
TBG	Tabubil [*Papua New Guinea*] [*Airport symbol*]　(OAG)
TBG	Testosterone-Binding Globulin [*Endocrinology*]
TBG	Teubners Bibliotheca Scriptorum Graecorum et Romanorum　(BJA)
TBG	Thyroxine-Binding Globulin [*Biochemistry*]
TBG	Thyssen-Bornemisza Group NV [*Netherlands*]
TBG	Tijdschrift Bataviasch Genootschap [*A publication*]
TBG	Tipping Bucket Gauge　(NOAA)
TBG	Tubing　(MSA)
TBGAA.....	Travel by Government Automobile Authorized
TBGP........	Tactical Bomb Group [*Air Force*]
TBGP........	Total Blood Granulocyte Pool [*Hematology*]
TBGTA......	Travel by Government Transportation Authorized [*Military*]　(AABC)
TBGU	Trudy Belorusskogo Gosudarstvennogo Universiteta [*A publication*]
TBH..........	Tablas [*Philippines*] [*Airport symbol*]　(OAG)
TBH..........	Technical Benzene Hexachloride [*Organic chemistry*]
TBH..........	Test Bed Harness　(MCD)
TBH..........	Test Bench Harness　(NG)
TBH..........	TourBase Hotel-/Unterkunftsdaten [*Jaeger-Verlag GmbH*] [*Federal Republic of Germany*] [*Information service or system*]　(CRD)
TBH..........	Trinidad [*Brigand Hill*] [*Trinidad-Tobago*] [*Seismograph station code, US Geological Survey*]　(SEIS)
TBHBA	Tribromo(hydroxy)benzoic Acid [*Organic chemistry*]
TBHP	Tertiary-Butyl Hydroperoxide [*Organic chemistry*]
TBHP	Trihydroxybutyrophenone [*Antioxidant*] [*Organic chemistry*]
TBHQ........	Tertiary-Butylhydroquinone [*Also, MTBHQ*] [*Organic chemistry*]
TBI...........	Ink and Print [*A publication*]
TBI...........	Target Bearing Indicator [*Military*]
TBI...........	Telecom Broadcasting, Incorporated [*Oceanside, CA*] [*Telecommunications service*]　(TSSD)
TBI...........	Test Bed Installation　(MCD)
TBI...........	Test Bench Installation　(NG)
TBI...........	Thomson Business Information [*The Thomson Corp.*] [*Publishing*]
TBI...........	Threaded Blind Insert
TBI...........	Throttle Body Fuel Injection [*Automotive engineering*]
TBI...........	Through-Bulkhead Initiator [*Military*]　(MCD)
TBI...........	Time, Bulb, Instantaneous [*Initials on certain Kodak cameras*]
TBI...........	Time between Inspections [*Quality control*]
TBI...........	To Be Inactivated
TBI...........	To Be Indicated　(AIA)
TBI...........	Total Body Irradiation [*Medicine*]
TBI...........	Training [*A publication*]
TBI...........	Traumatic Brain Injury [*Medicine*]
TBI...........	Trinity Bible Institute, Ellendale, ND [*OCLC symbol*]　(OCLC)
TBI...........	Tromboni [*Trombones*]
TBI...........	Tubuai [*Tubuai Islands*] [*Seismograph station code, US Geological Survey*]　(SEIS)
TBIFC........	Thom Bierdz International Fan Club　(EA)
TbIG.........	Terbium Iron Garnet　(IEEE)
TBII..........	Thyrotropin-Binding Inhibitor Immunoglobulin
TBIL.........	Total Bilirubin [*Clinical chemistry*]
Tbilis Gos Univ Inst Prikl Mat Tr ... Tbilisskii Gosudarstvennyi Universitet Institut Prikladnoi Matematiki Trudy [*A publication*]
Tbilisis Univ Sromebi ... Stalinis Sacheolobis Tbilisis Universitatis Sromebi [*A publication*]
Tbiliss Gos Univ Inst Prikl Mat Trudy ... Tbilisskii Gosudarstvennyi Universitet Institut Prikladnoi Matematiki Trudy [*A publication*]
TBIS	Technology Base Investment Strategy [*Army*]
TBJ	Turbulent Bounded Jet
TBJT	Turbojet　(FAAC)
TBK	TEFLON Bonding Kit
TBK	Tolland Bank [*AMEX symbol*]　(SPSG)
TBK	Total Body Potassium [*Clinical chemistry*]
TBK	Toyo Bungaku Kenkyu [*Studies on Oriental Literature*] [*A publication*]
T/BKL	Turn Buckle [*Automotive engineering*]
TBKZA......	Trudy Instituta Botaniki Akademiya Nauk Kazakhskoi SSR [*A publication*]

TBL............	Tabele [*Papua New Guinea*] [*Seismograph station code, US Geological Survey*]　(SEIS)
TBL............	Table
TBL............	Tactical Bomb Line　(NVT)
TBL............	[*The*] Tamarind Book of Lithography
TBL............	Terminal Ballistics Laboratory [*Army*]
TBL............	Thin Base Laminate
TBL............	Thomas Branigan Memorial Library, Las Cruces, NM [*OCLC symbol*]　(OCLC)
TBL............	Through Back of Loop [*Knitting*]
TBL............	Through Bill of Lading [*Shipping*]
TBL............	Timberland Co. [*AMEX symbol*]　(SPSG)
TBL............	Tombill Mines Ltd. [*Toronto Stock Exchange symbol*]
TBL............	Tootal Broadhurst Lee [*Textile testing*] [*Obsolete*]
TBL............	Trouble [*Telecommunications*]　(TEL)
TBL............	True Blood Loss
TBL............	Turbulent Boundary Layer
TBLC.........	Term Birth, Living Child [*Medicine*]
TBLE.........	Top Blacks in Law Enforcement [*Later, BLE*]　(EA)
T/BLK	Terminal Block [*Automotive engineering*]
TBLN.........	Tracheobronchial Lymph Node [*Anatomy*]
TBLR.........	Tumbler　(MSA)
TBLS	Trail Blazer Library System [*Library network*]
TBLSP.......	Tablespoon
TBM	School of Aerospace Medicine, Brooks AFB, TX [*OCLC symbol*]　(OCLC)
TBM	Tactical Ballistic Missile [*Military*]　(CAAL)
TBM	Tax Board Memorandum [*Internal Revenue Bulletin*] [*United States*] [*A publication*]　(DLA)
TBM	TBM NT Corp. [*Toronto Stock Exchange symbol*]
TBM	Tell Beit Mirsim　(BJA)
TBM	Temporary Bench Mark
TBM	TeraBIT [*Binary Digit*] Memory [*Data processing*]
TBM	Theater Ballistic Missile
TBM	Theater Battle Model　(MCD)
TBM	Tijdschrift voor Milieu en Recht [*A publication*]
TBM	Tone Burst Modulation
TB & M......	Tracewell, Bowers, and Mitchell's United States Comptroller's Decisions [*A publication*]　(DLA)
TBM	Tuberculous Meningitis [*Medicine*]
TBM	Tubular Basement Membrane
TBM	Tunnel Boring Machine
TBMA	Textile Bag Manufacturers Association　(EA)
TBMAA.....	Travel by Military Aircraft Authorized
TBMAC.....	Tributylmethylammonium Chloride [*Organic chemistry*]
TBMC........	Test Bed Mode Control
TBMD	Terminal Ballistic Missile Defense [*Army*]　(AABC)
TBMO	Test Base Material Operation　(AAG)
T B Mon.....	T. B. Monroe's Kentucky Supreme Court Reports [*17-23 Kentucky*] [*1824-28*] [*A publication*]　(DLA)
T B Mon (KY) ... T. B. Monroe's Kentucky Reports [*17-23 Kentucky*] [*A publication*]　(DLA)
TBMOS.....	TeraBIT Memory Operating System　(NOAA)
TBMS........	Text-Based Management Systems [*Data processing*]
TBMSDT ..	Mississippi. Agricultural and Forestry Experiment Station. Technical Bulletin [*A publication*]
TBMT........	Transmitter Buffer Empty [*Data processing*]
TBMX........	Tactical Ballistic Missile Experiment
TBN	Fort Leonard Wood [*Missouri*] [*Airport symbol*]　(OAG)
TBN	Tertiary-Butylnaphthalene [*Organic chemistry*]
TBN	Tetrabenzonaphthalene [*Organic chemistry*]
TBN	Thailand Business [*A publication*]
TBN	Titratable Base Number [*Analytical chemistry*]
TBN	To Be Negotiated　(NASA)
TBN	To Be Nominated
TBN	Total Base Number [*Automotive engineering*]
TBN	Traveling Businesswomen's Network　(EA)
TBN	Trinity Broadcasting Network [*Cable-television system*]
TBNA	Treated but Not Admitted [*Medicine*]
TBNAA	Total Body Neutron Activation Analysis
TBNHL	Tippecanoe Battleground National Historical Landmark　(EA)
Tbnl...........	Tribunal
TBNNA	Trudy Bashkirskii Nauchno-Issledovatel'skii Institut po Pererabotke Nefti [*A publication*]
TBO	Tabora [*Tanzania*] [*Airport symbol*]　(OAG)
TBO	Tacoma Boatbuilding Co. [*NYSE symbol*]　(SPSG)
TBO	Thermal Bakeout
TBO	Time between Overhauls [*of engine, or other equipment*]
TBO	TourBase Ortsdaten [*Jaeger-Verlag GmbH*] [*Federal Republic of Germany*] [*Information service or system*]　(CRD)
TBO	Transactions by Others [*Military*]
TBOA	T-18 Builders and Owners Association　(EA)
TBOA	Tuna Boat Owners' Association [*Defunct*]　(EA)
t-Boc........	Butoxycarbonyl [*or t-BOC*] [*Biochemistry*]
t-BOC.......	tert-Butyloxycarbonyl [*Also, t-Boc*] [*Organic chemistry*]
TBOI........	Tentative Basis of Issue [*Army*]　(AABC)
TBOIP......	Tentative Basis of Issue Plan [*Army*]　(AABC)
TBolMH ...	Western Mental Health Institute, Boliver, TN [*Library symbol*] [*Library of Congress*]　(LCLS)
TBON	[*The*] Bank of Nashville [*NASDAQ symbol*]　(NQ)
TBOS.........	[*The*] Bank of Southington [*NASDAQ symbol*]　(NQ)

TBP	Tab Products Co. [AMEX symbol] (SPSG)
TbP	Tampa Blue Print Co., Tampa, FL [Library symbol] [Library of Congress] (LCLS)
TBP	Tau Beta Pi Association
TBP	Tertiary Butyl Phosphine [Organic chemistry]
TBP	Tethered Buoyed Platform [Petroleum engineering]
TBP	Tetraphenylboron [Analytical chemistry]
TBP	Thiobisdichlorophenol [Pharmacology]
TBP	Thyroxine-Binding Protein [Biochemistry]
TBP	Timing Belt Pulley
TBP	To Be Planned (MCD)
TBP	To Be Provided (NASA)
TBP	Trainable Bow Propeller
TBP	Tributyl Phosphate [Organic chemistry]
TBP	Tributyl Phosphine [Organic chemistry]
TBP	Trigonal Bipyramidal [Geometry of molecular structure]
TBP	True Boiling Point
TBP	Tumbes [Peru] [Airport symbol] (OAG)
TBP	Twisted Bonded Pair
TBP	Two-Body Problem
TBPA	Tetrabromophthalic Anhydride [Flame retardant] [Organic chemistry]
TBPA	Textile Bag and Packaging Association (EA)
TBPA	Thyroxine-Binding Prealbumin [Biochemistry]
TBPA	Transatlantic Brides and Parents Association (EA)
TBPB	Bridgetown/Grantley Adams Internacional [Barbados] [ICAO location identifier] (ICLI)
TBPC	Text-Books of Physical Chemistry [A publication]
TBPI	Thigh Brachial Pressure Index
TBPO	Bridgetown [Barbados] [ICAO location identifier] (ICLI)
TBPS	Tert-Butylbicyclophosphorothionate [Biochemistry]
TBPU	To Be Picked Up [Postal service marking] [British]
TBQ	Addison, TX [Location identifier] [FAA] (FAAL)
TBR	Advisory Tax Board Recommendation [Internal Revenue Bureau] [United States] [A publication] (DLA)
TBR	New York Times Book Review [A publication]
TBR	Statesboro, GA [Location identifier] [FAA] (FAAL)
TBR	T-Bar, Inc. [AMEX symbol] (SPSG)
TBR	Table Base Register
TBR	Table Rock [New York] [Seismograph station code, US Geological Survey] (SEIS)
TBR	Test of Behavioral Rigidity [Psychology]
TBR	Three Banks Review [A publication]
TBR	Tilt Board Reach [Test] [Occupational therapy]
TBR	Torpedo Bomber Reconnaissance Aircraft [Navy]
TBR	Training Base Review (MCD)
TBR	Trickle Bed Reactor [Chemical engineering]
TBR	Tumor-Bearing Rabbit Serum [Immunology]
TBR	Turbo Resources Ltd. [Toronto Stock Exchange symbol]
TBRC	Top-Blown Rotary Converter [Nonferrous metallurgy]
TBRD	Taxation Board of Review Decisions [A publication] (APTA)
TBRD	Taxation Board of Review Decisions. New Series [Australia] [A publication] (DLA)
TBRD (NS)	Taxation Board of Review Decisions (New Series) [A publication] (APTA)
TBRG	Thomson Book/Reference Group [The Thomson Corp.] [Publishing]
TBRI	Technical Book Review Index
TBriH	Bristol Memorial Hospital, Bristol, TN [Library symbol] [Library of Congress] (LCLS)
TBriK	King College, Bristol, TN [Library symbol] [Library of Congress] (LCLS)
T Br Mycol	Transactions. British Mycological Society [A publication]
TBroH	Haywood Park General Hospital, Brownsville, TN [Library symbol] [Library of Congress] (LCLS)
TBS	Sir Thomas Beecham Society (EA)
TBS	Tablespoon
TBS	Tactical Bomb Squadron [Air Force]
TBS	Talk-between-Ships [which are tactically maneuvering; also, the VHF radio equipment used for this purpose]
TBS	Tape and Buffer System [Data processing]
TBS	Task Breakdown Structure (NASA)
TBS	Tbilisi [USSR] [Airport symbol] (OAG)
TBS	Temple, Barker & Sloane, Inc. [Lexington, MA] [Telecommunications service] (TSSD)
TBS	Tertiary Butylphenyl Salicylate [Food packaging]
TBS	Test Bench Set (MCD)
TBS	Tetrapropylene Alkylbenesulfonate [Surfactant] [Organic chemistry]
TBS	Text-Books of Science [A publication]
TBS	Tight Building Syndrome [Air quality]
TBS	Tired Bureaucrat Syndrome
TBS	To Be Selected (KSC)
TBS	To Be Specified (NASA)
TBS	To Be Superseded (NASA)
TBS	To Be Supplied (KSC)
TBS	Tobacco Black-Shank Nematode [Plant pathology]
TBS	Tokyo Broadcasting System
TB & S	Top, Bottom, and Sides [Lumber]
TBS	Toronto Baptist Seminary
TBS	Toronto Board of Education, Secondary Schools [UTLAS symbol]
TBS	Total Body Solute [Biochemistry]
TBS	Total Body Surface [Medicine]
TBS	Training and Battle Simulation [SAGE]
TBS	Translator Bail Switch
TBS	Treasury Board Secretariat [Canada]
TBS	Tribromosalicylanilide [or Tribromsalan] [Organic chemistry]
TBS	Trinitarian Bible Society [British]
TBS	TRIS-Buffered Saline [Solution]
TBS	Tubeshaft (DS)
TBS	Turbine Bypass System [Nuclear energy] (NRCH)
TBS	Turner Broadcasting System, Inc. [AMEX symbol] (SPSG)
TBSA	Total Body Surface Area [Medicine]
TBSA	TRIS-Buffered Saline Azide [Culture media]
TBSCCW	Turbine Building Secondary Closed Cooling Water [Nuclear energy] (NRCH)
TBSG	Test Base Support Group (AAG)
TBSM	Tributylstannylmaleate [Organic chemistry]
TBSP	Tablespoon
TBST'G	Troubleshooting
TBSV	Time between Scheduled Visits (MCD)
TBSV	Tomato Bushy Stunt Virus
TBT	Mid American Baptist Theological Seminary, Memphis, TN [OCLC symbol] (OCLC)
TBT	Tabatinga [Brazil] [Airport symbol] (OAG)
TBT	Taburiente [Canary Islands] [Seismograph station code, US Geological Survey] (SEIS)
TBT	Target Bearing Transmitter
TBT	Terminal Ballistic Track
TBT	Tetrabutyl Titanate [Organic chemistry]
TBT	Thallium Beam Tube
TBT	Tilt Board Tip [Test] [Occupational therapy]
TBT	Trends in Biotechnology [A publication]
TBTF	Tributyltin Fluoride [Antimicrobial agent]
TBTH	Tributylin Hydride [Organic chemistry]
TBTI	Telebyte Technology, Incorporated [NASDAQ symbol] (NQ)
TBTO	Tributyltin Oxide [Organic chemistry]
TBTP	Tributyl Trithiophosphate [Defoliant] [Organic chemistry]
TBTS	Tributyltin Sulfide
TBTU	Tributylthiourea [Organic chemistry]
TBU	Hong Kong Enterprise [A publication]
TBU	Terminal Buffer Unit [Telecommunications] (TEL)
TBU	Test Before Using (MCD)
TBU	Time Base Unit
TBU	Tongatapu [Tonga Island] [Airport symbol] (OAG)
TBurNII	Trudy Burjatskogo Komplesnogo Naucno-Issledovatel'skogo Instituta [A publication]
TBV	Thermal Bypass Valve
TBV	Total Blood Volume [Physiology]
TBV	Trabecular Bone Volume
TBV	Tubercle Bacillus Vaccine [Medicine]
TBV	Turbine Building Ventilation [Nuclear energy] (NRCH)
TBVE	Two-Point Boundary Value Equation [Mathematics]
TBW	[The] Business World [A publication]
TBW	Tampa Bay-Ruskin, FL [Location identifier] [FAA] (FAAL)
TBW	That Bloody Woman [Nickname given to British Prime Minister Margaret Thatcher]
TBW	Titanium Butt Weld
TBW	To Be Withheld
TBW	Tobacco Bud Worm [Agronomy]
TBW	Total Bandwidth
TBW	Total Body Water [Man]
TBW	Total Body Weight [Medicine]
TBW	Tracking Band Width (MCD)
TBWCA	Texas Barbed Wire Collectors Association (EA)
TBWEP	Trial Boll Weevil Eradication Program [Department of Agriculture]
TBWG	Tactical Bomb Wing [Air Force]
TBWO	Tuned Backward Wave Oscillator
TBX	Tactical Ballistic Missile, Experimental
TBY	Oxford, CT [Location identifier] [FAA] (FAAL)
TBY	TCBY Enterprises, Inc. [NYSE symbol] (CTT)
TBY	Terrace Bay Resources [Vancouver Stock Exchange symbol]
TBZ	Istanbul [Trabzon] [Turkey] [Seismograph station code, US Geological Survey] (SEIS)
TBZ	Tabriz [Iran] [Airport symbol] (OAG)
TBZ	Tetrabenazine [Tranquilizer]
TBZ	Thiabendazole [or Thiazolyl] Benzimidazole [Pesticide]
TC	13 Coins Restaurants Ltd. [Vancouver Stock Exchange symbol]
TC	Air Tanzania [ICAO designator] (FAAC)
TC	All India Reporter, Travancore-Cochin [1950-57] [A publication] (DLA)
TC	Chattanooga-Hamilton County Bicentennial Library, Chattanooga, TN [Library symbol] [Library of Congress] (LCLS)
TC	Chronicle (Toowoomba) [A publication] (APTA)
TC	Cold Leg Temperature [Nuclear energy] (NRCH)
Tc	Core Temperature [Medicine]
TC	[The] Courier [Code name for Robert W. Owen, participant in the Iran-Contra affair during the Reagan Administration]

TC .... Journal of Technical Topics in Civil Engineering [*A publication*]
TC .... Order of the Trinity Cross [*Trinidad and Tobago*]
TC .... Reports of English Tax Cases [*A publication*] (DLA)
TC .... Reports of Tax Cases [*United Kingdom*] [*A publication*]
TC .... T-Carrier [*Telecommunications*] (TEL)
TC .... Table of Contents (IT)
TC .... Tablettes Cappadociennes [*Paris*] [*A publication*] (BJA)
TC .... Tabulating Card (AAG)
TC .... Tactical Command (NATG)
TC .... Tactical Computer (IEEE)
T/C .... Tactical Coordinator (NVT)
TC .... Tactile Communicator [*Device which aids the deaf by translating certain sounds into coded vibrations*]
TC .... Tail Clamp
TC .... Talk[*ing*] Club
TC .... Tamil Culture [*A publication*]
TC .... Tank Car
TC .... Tank Commander (RDA)
TC .... Tank Company [*Military*] (MCD)
TC .... Tank Corps
TC .... Tantalum Capacitor (IEEE)
TC .... Tape Command
TC .... Tape Core
TC .... Target Cell [*Immunology*]
TC .... Target Control (MCD)
TC .... Tariff Circular
TC .... Tariff Commission [*Later, International Trade Commission*]
TC .... Tax Cases [*Legal*] [*British*]
TC .... Tax Certificate
TC .... Tax Council (EA)
TC .... Tax Court [*of the United States*] [*Also, TCUS*] [*Later, United States Tax Court*]
TC .... Taxpayers' Committee (EA)
TC .... Taylorcraft [*ICAO aircraft manufacturer identifier*] (ICAO)
TC .... Tayu Center (EA)
TC .... Tea Council of the United States of America (EA)
TC .... Teacher's Certificate [*British*]
TC .... Teachers College
TC .... Teardown Compliance
Tc .... Technetium [*Chemical element*]
TC .... Technical Characteristics [*Military*] (AABC)
TC .... Technical Circular
TC .... Technical College
TC .... Technical Committee
TC .... Technical Communication
TC .... Technical Control (MSA)
TC .... Technical Cooperation
TC .... Technicolor (KSC)
T & C .... Technology and Culture [*A publication*]
TC .... Tekakwitha Conference National Center [*Later, TCNC*] (EA)
T/C .... Telecine
TC .... Telecommunications
TC .... Telecommunications Counselor [*Voice & Data Resources, Inc.*] [*Information service or system*] [*Defunct*] (IID)
TC .... TeleCommuting Report [*Electronic Services Unlimited*] [*Information service or system*] (CRD)
TC .... Temperament Comparator [*Psychology*]
TC .... Temperature Capability
TC .... Temperature Change [*Refrigeration*]
TC .... Temperature Coefficient
TC .... Temperature Compensating (MSA)
TC .... Temperature Control
TC .... Temperature Controller [*Nuclear energy*] (NRCH)
TC .... Temple Classics [*A publication*]
TC .... Temporary Chaplain [*British military*] (DMA)
TC .... Temporary Constable
T/C .... Temporary Correction
TC .... Tennessee Central Railway Co. [*AAR code*]
TC .... Tennis Club
TC .... Teracycle
TC .... Terciarios Capuchinos de Nostra Signora de los Dolores [*Tertiary Capuchins of Our Lady of Sorrows*] [*Rome, Italy*] (EAIO)
TC .... Terminal Computer (BUR)
TC .... Terminal Concentrator
TC .... Terminal Congestion [*Telecommunications*] (TEL)
TC .... Terminal Controller
T/C .... Termination Check [*NASA*] (NASA)
T/C .... Termination for Convenience [*DoD*]
T & C .... Terms and Conditions
TC .... Terra Cotta [*Technical drawings*]
TC .... Terrain Clearance [*Military*] (NG)
TC .... Terrain Correlation (MCD)
TC .... Test Chief
TC .... Test Collection [*Educational Testing Service*] [*Information service or system*] (IID)
TC .... Test Conductor (AAG)
TC .... Test Console
TC .... Test Controller
TC .... Test Coordinator

TC .... Testing Complete (CAAL)
TC .... Tetracycline [*Antibiotic compound*]
TC .... Tetrahedral Cubic [*Metallography*]
TC .... Texas Central Railroad Co.
TC .... Thai Capital Fund, Inc. [*NYSE symbol*] (SPSG)
TC .... Theory of Computation Series [*Elsevier Book Series*] [*A publication*]
TC .... Therapeutic Concentration [*Pharmacology*]
TC .... Thermal Conductivity
TC .... Thermal Control (KSC)
TC .... Thermal Cracker [*Chemical engineering*]
TC .... Thermal Cutting [*Welding*]
TC .... Thermocouple
TC .... Thermocurrent (IEEE)
TC .... Thickness Chord Wing [*Aviation*] (AIA)
TC .... Thinking Cap [*Layman's term for neocortex*]
TC .... Thomas C. Calvin [*Character in TV series "Magnum, P.I."*]
T & C .... Thompson and Cook's New York Supreme Court Reports [*A publication*] (DLA)
TC .... Thoracic Cage [*Medicine*]
TC .... Thread Cutting (MSA)
TC .... Throat Culture [*Clinical chemistry*]
TC .... Thrust Chamber [*Air Force, NASA*]
TC .... Tical [*Monetary unit in Thailand*]
TC .... Tidal Constants [*Marine science*] (MSC)
TC .... Tie Connector (MCD)
TC .... Tierce [*Unit of measurement*]
T/C .... Till Counterbalanced
TC .... Till Countermanded
TC .... Tilt Covered [*Truck*] (DCTA)
TC .... Time Certificate of Deposit [*Banking*]
T & C .... Time and Charges [*Telecommunications*] (TEL)
T/C .... Time Charter [*Shipping*]
TC .... Time Check
TC .... Time to Circular (MCD)
TC .... Time Clock
TC .... Time Closing (MSA)
TC .... Time Compensation
TC .... Time to Computation
TC .... Time Constant (MSA)
TC .... Timing Channel
TC .... Timing Cover Gasket [*Automotive engineering*]
TC .... Tinned Copper
TC .... Tissue Culture [*Microbiology*]
TC .... To Contain [*Pipet calibration*]
TC .... Tobramycin-Clindamycin [*Antibiotic compound*]
TC .... Togoland Congress [*Ghana*] [*Political party*]
TC .... Toilet Case (MSA)
TC .... Toll Center [*Telecommunications*]
TC .... Toll Completing [*Telecommunications*]
TC .... Toluene-Cellosolve [*Scintillation solvent*]
TC .... Top Carnivore
TC .... Top Cat [*Cartoon character*]
TC .... Top Center [*Valve position*]
TC .... Top Chord
TC .... Top of Column
TC .... Top Contact [*Valve*] (DEN)
TC .... Topographic Center [*Defense Mapping Agency*]
TC .... Torpedo Control [*British military*] (DMA)
TC .... Torpedo Coxswain [*British military*] (DMA)
TC .... Total Capacity [*Lung*]
TC .... Total Carbon
TC .... Total Chances
TC .... Total Cholesterol [*Medicine*]
TC .... Total Colonoscopy [*Proctoscopy*]
TC .... Total Cost
TC .... Touring Club
T of C .... Tournament of Champions
TC .... Town Clerk [*or Councillor*]
T & C .... Town & Country [*A publication*]
TC .... Traceability Code (NASA)
TC .... Track Circuit (DCTA)
TC .... Track Commander [*Army*] (INF)
TC .... Tracking Camera
TC .... Tracking Console
TC .... Trade Cases [*Commerce Clearing House*] [*A publication*] (DLA)
TC .... Traffic Collision
TC .... Traffic Commissioner [*or Consultant*]
TC .... Traffic Controller (CAAL)
TC .... Training Center [*Military*]
TC .... Training Chest [*Emergency parachute*]
TC .... Training Circular [*Military*]
TC .... Training Command (AAG)
TC .... Training Corps [*British military*] (DMA)
TC .... Transaction Code [*Military*]
TC .... Transceiver Code [*Navy*]
TC .... Transcobalamin [*Biochemistry*]
TC .... Transcutaneous
TC .... Transfer Canal [*Nuclear energy*] (NRCH)
TC .... Transfer Clerk

TC	Transistorized Carrier
TC	Transit Canal (NVT)
TC	Translation Controller
TC	Transmission Controller
TC	Transpersonal Consciousness [*Parapsychology*]
TC	Transponder Component (MCD)
TC	Transport Canada
TC	Transport Cargo (NATG)
TC	Transport Combine [*Combined Transport*] [*French*] [*Business term*]
TC	Transport Command [*British military*] (DMA)
TC	Transport and Communications [*Department of Employment*] [*British*]
TC	Transportation Corps [*Military*]
TC	Transporte Combinado [*Combined Transport*] [*Spanish*] [*Business term*]
TC	Transporto Combinato [*Combined Transport*] [*Italian*] [*Business term*]
TC	Transvaal Cadets [*British military*] (DMA)
TC	Travellers Cheque [*British*] (ADA)
TC	Tre Corde [*With Three Strings, or Release the Soft Pedal*] [*Music*]
TC	Treasury Circular
T/C	Treated Versus Cured [*Medicine*]
T/C	Treatment Charge [*Metallurgy*]
TC	Trial Counsel [*Military*]
TC	Tribology Centre [*British*]
TC	Tribunal des Conflits [*Tribunal of Conflicts*] [*French*] (ILCA)
TC	Tricuspid Closure [*Cardiology*]
TC	Tricycle Club [*British*]
TC	Triennial Cycle (BJA)
TC	Trierische Chronik [*A publication*]
TC	Trilateral Commission (EA)
TC	Trim Coil (AAG)
TC	[*Order of the*] Trinity Cross [*Trinidad and Tobago*]
TC	Trip Coil
TC	Triplet Connection (EA)
TC	Triton Corporation (EA)
TC	Troop Carrier [*Air Force*]
TC	Tropical Continental [*American air mass*]
TC	Tropical Cyclone (ADA)
TC	Truck Commander [*Military*] (INF)
T/C	True Complement
TC	True Course
TC	Truncated Cone [*Golf balls*]
TC	Trunk Control
TC	Trusteeship Council [*of the United Nations*]
TC	Tubing Connector [*Instrumentation*]
TC	Tubocurarine [*Muscle relaxant*]
TC	Turf Course [*Horse racing*]
TC	Turkey [*Aircraft nationality and registration mark*] (FAAC)
TC	Turkey Coryza [*Pathology*]
TC	Turks and Caicos Islands [*ANSI two-letter standard code*] (CNC)
tc..................	Turks and Caicos Islands [*MARC country of publication code*] [*Library of Congress*] (LCCP)
TC	Turn-Cock (ROG)
T & C..........	Turn and Cough [*Medicine*]
TC	Turnip Crinkle Virus
TC	Turret Captain [*Navy*]
TC	Twentieth Century [*A publication*]
TC	[*The*] Twentieth Century New Testament [*A publication*] (BJA)
TC	Two Cycle [*Mechanics*]
TC	Tworczosc [*A publication*]
TC	Type Certificate
TC	Type Classification
TC	Type and Crossmatch [*of blood*]
TC	United States Tax Court Cases [*A publication*] (DLA)
TC3	Telecommunications, Command, Control, and Computer System
T4C	Technology for Children [*Vocational program*]
TCA	Adventist Network of Georgia, Cumberland Elementary Library, Collegedale, TN [*OCLC symbol*] (OCLC)
TCA	[*The*] Canadian Amateur [*A publication*]
TCA	Tactical Combat Aircraft (IEEE)
TCA	Tactical Communications Area
TCA	Tandem Club of America (EA)
TCA	Tanner's Council of America [*Later, LIA*] (EA)
TCA	Tanzer 22 Class Association (EA)
TCA	Target Class Assignment
TCA	Tattoo Club of America (EA)
TCA	Taxe sur le Chiffre d'Affaires [*Business Turnover Tax*] [*French*] [*Business term*]
TCA	Teach Cable Assembly [*Robot technology*]
TCA	Teaching Curriculum Association [*A generic term; not the name of a specific organization*]
TCA	Technical Change Analysis (MCD)
TCA	Technical Contract Administrator
TCA	Technical Cooperation Administration [*Transferred to Foreign Operations Administration, 1953*]

TCA	Technician in Costing and Accounting [*British*] (DBQ)
TCA	Tele-Communications Association (EA)
TCA	Telemarketing Corporation of America [*Phoenix, AZ*] (TSSD)
TCA	Telemetering Control Assembly (AAG)
TCA	Telephone Consultants of America [*Bergenfield, NJ*] [*Telecommunications*] (TSSD)
TCA	Television Critics Association (EA)
TCA	Tempelhof Central Airport [*West Berlin*]
TCA	Temperature Control Assembly (KSC)
TCA	Temperature-Controlled Animal
TCA	Ten Class Association (EA)
TCA	Tennant Creek [*Australia*] [*Airport symbol*] (OAG)
TCA	Tennessee Code Annotated [*A publication*]
TCA	Terminal Cancer [*Medicine*]
TCA	Terminal Communication Adapter
TCA	Terminal Control Area [*Aviation*] (AFM)
TCA	Tetracyanoanthracene [*Organic chemistry*]
TCA	Textile Converters Association (EA)
TCA	Theater Commander's Approval [*Military*]
TCA	Therapeutic Communities of America (EA)
TCA	Thermal Critical Assembly [*Nuclear energy*]
TCA	Thermo Cardiosystems, Inc. [*AMEX symbol*] (SPSG)
TCA	Thermocentrifugometric Analysis [*Analytical chemistry*]
TCA	Thermochimica Acta [*A publication*]
TCA	Thiocarbanilide [*Organic chemistry*]
TCA	Thistle Class Association (EA)
TCA	Thoroughbred Club of America (EA)
TCA	Thrust Chamber Assembly [*Missile technology*]
TCA	Thyrocalcitonin [*Also, CT, TCT*] [*Endocrinology*]
TCA	Tiger Cat Association [*Defunct*] (EA)
TCA	Tile Council of America (EA)
TCA	Tilt-Up Concrete Association (EA)
TCA	Time of Closest Approach [*Aerospace*]
TCA	Tissue Culture Association (EA)
TCA	Tithe Commutation Act [*British*]
TCA	To Come Again [*in a given number of days*] [*Medicine*]
TCA	TOKAMAK [*Toroidal Kamera Magnetic*] Chauffage Alfven [*Plasma physics instrumentation*]
TCa	Total Calcium [*Clinical chemistry*]
TCA	Trace Contamination Analysis
TCA	Track Continuity Area (NATG)
TCA	Track Crossing Angle
TCA	Traffic Control Area [*Aviation*]
TCA	Trailer Coach Association [*Later, Manufactured Housing Institute*] (EA)
TCA	Train Collectors Association (EA)
TCA	Trans-Canada Airlines [*Facetious translation: "Two Crashes Apiece"*]
TCA	Translation Controller Assembly (NASA)
TCA	Travellers Cheque Association Ltd. [*British*]
TCA	Tricarboxylic Acid [*Cycle*] [*Biochemistry*]
TCA	Trichloroacetate [*Organic chemistry*]
TCA	Trichloroacetic Acid [*Also, TCAA*] [*Organic chemistry*]
TCA	Trichloroanisole [*Organic chemistry*]
TCA	Trichosanic Acid [*Biochemistry*]
TCA	Tricyclic Antidepressant [*Medicine*]
TCA	Turbulent Contacting Absorber
TCA	Turks and Caicos Islands [*ANSI three-letter standard code*] (CNC)
TCA	Two Hundred Contemporary Authors [*A publication*]
TCA	Typographic Communications Association (EA)
TCAA	Tile Contractors' Association of America (EA)
TCAA	Trichloroacetic Acid [*Also, TCA*] [*Organic chemistry*]
TCAAP	Twin Cities Army Ammunition Plant (AABC)
TCAAS	Transactions. Connecticut Academy of Arts and Sciences [*A publication*]
TCAB........	Temperature of Cabin [*Aerospace*] (MCD)
TCAB........	Tetrachloroazobenzene [*Organic chemistry*]
TCABG......	Triple Coronary Artery Bypass Graft [*Cardiology*]
TCAC........	Technical Control and Analysis Center
TC ACCIS ...	Transportation Coordination Automated Command and Control Information System [*Military*]
TCAC-D.....	Technical Control and Analysis Center - Division
TCAE........	Technical Control and Analysis Element (INF)
TCAF........	TEFLON-Coated Aluminum Foil
TCAI........	Tutorial Computer-Assisted Instruction (IEEE)
TCAL........	Total Calorimeter (KSC)
TCAM	Telecommunications Access Method [*IBM Corp.*] [*Data processing*]
TCAM	Thinking Creatively in Action and Movement [*Test*]
TCA Man ..	TCA [*Tissue Culture Association*] Manual [*A publication*]
TCaMH.....	Smith County Memorial Hospital, Carthage, TN [*Library symbol*] [*Library of Congress*] (LCLS)
TCANAQ ..	Commonwealth Bureau of Animal Nutrition. Technical Communication [*A publication*]
TCAOB......	Tetrachloroazoxybenzene [*Organic chemistry*]
TCAP........	Tactical Channel Assignment Panel [*Military radio*]
T/CAP.......	Thermal Capacitor (MCD)
TCAP........	Tricyanoaminopropene [*Organic chemistry*]
TCAP........	Trimethylcetylammonium Pentachlorphenate [*Organic chemistry*]

TCAPE...... Truck Computer Analysis of Performance and Economy
TCaS.......... Smith County High School Library, Carthage, TN [*Library symbol*] [*Library of Congress*] (LCLS)
TCAS........ T-Carrier Administration System [*Minicomputer*] [*Bell System*]
TCAS........ Technical Control and Analysis System (MCD)
TCAS........ Three Counties Agricultural Society [*British*]
TCAS........ Traffic Alert and Collision Avoidance System [*Aviation*]
TCASNY ... Turkish Cypriot Aid Society of New York (EA)
TCAT........ Tape-Controlled Automatic Testing
TCAT........ TCA Cable TV, Inc. [*NASDAQ symbol*] (NQ)
TCAT........ Test Coverage Analysis Tool (IEEE)
TCATA..... Textile Care Allied Trades Association (EA)
TCATA..... TRADOC Combined Arms Test Activity [*Army*] (MCD)
TCAus....... Twentieth Century (Australia) [*A publication*]
TCAX........ Trans Continental Air Transport [*Air carrier designation symbol*]
TCB............ [*The*] College Board (EA)
TCB............ [*The*] Conference Board (EA)
TCB............ Fort Worth, TX [*Location identifier*] [*FAA*] (FAAL)
TCB............ Take Care of Business [*Slang*]
TCB............ Taking Care of Business [*Brand name of Alberto-Culver Co.*]
TCB............ Tantalum Carbon Bond
TCB............ Task Control Block [*Data processing*]
TCB............ Task Force for Community Broadcasting (EA)
TCB............ Taylor-Carlisle Bookseller [*ACCORD*] [*UTLAS symbol*]
TCB............ TCF Financial Corp. [*NYSE symbol*] (SPSG)
TCB............ Technical Coordinator Bulletin [*NASA*] (KSC)
TCB............ TEN Private Cable Systems, Inc. [*Vancouver Stock Exchange symbol*]
TCB............ Tent City Bravo [*Area near Tan Son Nhut Air Base, formerly site of USAR headquarters*]
TCB............ Tetrachlorobiphenyl [*Organic chemistry*]
TCB............ Themes Concerning Blacks [*Personality development test*] [*Psychology*]
TCB............ Thermal Compression Bond
TCB............ Time Correlation Buffer (MCD)
TCB............ Title Certificate Book [*A publication*] (DLA)
TCB............ Trans-Continental Freight Bureau, Chicago IL [*STAC*]
TCB............ Transfer Control Block
TCB............ Treasure Cay [*Bahamas*] [*Airport symbol*] (OAG)
TCB............ Trusted Computing Base
TCB............ Tulare County Free Library System, Visalia, CA [*OCLC symbol*] (OCLC)
TCB............ Tumor Cell Burden [*Oncology*]
TCBA........ Tesla Coil Builders Association (EA)
T-CBA....... Transfluxor, Constant Board Assembly (AAG)
TCBAAQ... Commonwealth Bureau of Animal Breeding and Genetics. Technical Communication [*A publication*]
TCBC........ Trichlorobenzyl Chloride [*Organic chemistry*]
TCBC........ [*The*] TrustCompany Bancorporation [*Jersey City, NJ*] [*NASDAQ symbol*] (NQ)
TCBC........ Twin Cities Biomedical Consortium [*Library network*]
TCBCO...... Thallium Calcium Barium Copper Oxide [*Inorganic chemistry*]
TCBCS ..... Blue Cross and Blue Shield of Tennessee, Chattanooga, TN [*Library symbol*] [*Library of Congress*] (LCLS)
TCBE........ Thermocompression Bonding Equipment
TCBEFC... TCB [*Taking Care of Business*] for Elvis Fan Club (EA)
TCBG........ Training Centre Brigade of Gurkhas [*British military*] (DMA)
TCBHHA .. [*The*] Church of the Brethren Homes and Hospitals Association [*Later, BHOAM*] (EA)
TCBI........ Television Center for Business and Industry
TCBM....... Transcontinental Ballistic Missile [*Air Force*]
TCBO .... Trichlorobutylene Oxide [*Organic chemistry*]
TCBS........ Thiosulfate-Citrate-Bile Salt Sucrose [*Growth medium*]
TCBS........ Transactions. Cambridge Bibliographical Society [*A publication*]
TCBV....... Temperature Coefficient of Breakdown Voltage
TCBY....... [*The*] Country's Best Yogurt [*Store franchise*]
TCC .... [*The*] Cesarean Connection (EA)
TCC .... [*The*] Coin Coalition (EA)
TCC .... [*The*] Cola Clan [*Later, Coca-Cola Collectors Club International*] (EA)
TCC .... [*The*] Comedy Channel
TCC .... [*The*] Computer Company [*Information service or system*] (IID)
TCC .... [*The*] Conservative Caucus (EA)
TCC .... [*The*] Curwood Collector [*A publication*] (EA)
TCC .... New Mexico Institute of Mining and Technology Computer Center [*Research center*] (RCD)
TCC .... T-Cell Clone [*Cytology*]
TCC .... Tactical Command Control (MCD)
TCC .... Tactical Communications Center
TCC .... Tactical Control Center [*Military*]
TCC .... Tactical Control Computer (AAG)
TCC .... Tactical Control Console (NATG)
TCC .... Tag Closed Cup [*Flash point test*]
TCC .... Tagliabue Closed Cup [*Analytical chemistry*]
TCC .... Tara Collectors Club (EA)
TCC .... Task Control Character (CMD)
TCC .... Tasman Cable Co. [*Australia*]

TCC .... Teachers College of Connecticut
TCC .... Technical Change Centre [*British*] (CB)
TCC .... Technical Computing Center (IEEE)
TCC .... Technical Control Center
TCC .... Technology Commercialization Center [*Minority Business Development Administration*]
TCC .... Telecommunications Center (CET)
TCC .... Telecommunications Consumer Coalition (EA)
TCC .... Telecommunications Coordinating Committee [*Department of State*]
TCC .... Teleconcepts in Communications, Inc. [*New York, NY*] [*Telecommunications*] (TSSD)
TCC .... TeleConcepts Corporation [*AMEX symbol*] (SPSG)
TCC .... Television Control Center
TCC .... Temperature Coefficient of Capacitance
TCC .... Temperature Control Circuit
TCC .... Temporary Council Committee [*NATO*]
TCC .... Terminal Control Corridor [*Aviation*]
TCC .... Test Conductor Console (AAG)
TCC .... Test Control Center [*NASA*]
TCC .... Test Controller Computer (MCD)
TCC .... Test Controller Console (KSC)
TCC .... Test Coordinating Center [*Army*]
TCC .... Test Coordinator Console (CAAL)
TCC .... Tetrachlorocatechol [*Organic chemistry*]
TCC .... Theater Communications Center (MCD)
TCC .... Theater Communications Command (MCD)
TCC .... Thermal Control Coating
TCC .... Therefor Catalytic Cracking
TCC .... Thiamine Cobalt Chlorophyllin [*Antiulcer*]
TCC .... Thiokol Chemical Corporation [*Later, Thiokol Corp.*] (AAG)
TCC .... Third Continental Congress (EA)
TCC .... Thromboplastic Cell Component [*Hematology*]
TCC .... Through-Connected Circuit [*Telecommunications*] (TEL)
TCC .... Time Compression Coding
TCC .... Toroidal Combustion Chamber
TCC .... Torque Converter Clutch [*Automotive engineering*]
TCC .... TOS [*TIROS Operational Satellite*] Checkout Center [*Goddard Space Flight Center*] (NOAA)
TCC .... Total Car Coefficient [*Formula*] [*Automobile analysis*]
TCC .... Total Comparative Costs [*Army*]
TCC .... Tracking and Communication Component
TCC .... Tracking Computer Controls (MCD)
TCC .... Tracking and Control Center
TCC .... Traffic Control Center
TCC .... Transcontinental Corps [*Amateur radio*]
TCC .... Transfer Channel Control (IEEE)
TCC .... Transient Combustion Chamber [*Analysis*] (MCD)
TCC .... Transitional Cell Carcinoma
TCC .... Transmission Control Character [*Telecommunications*] (TEL)
TCC .... Transmit Carry and Clear
TCC .... Transport Control Center [*Air Force*]
TCC .... Transportation Commodity Classification Code
TCC .... Transportation Control Card [*Military*]
TCC .... Transportation Control Center
TCC .... Transportation Control Committee [*Navy*]
TCC .... Travel Classification Code
TCC .... Travel Correction Calculator (MSA)
TCC .... Travelers' Century Club (EA)
TCC .... Triactor Resources Corporation [*Vancouver Stock Exchange symbol*]
TCC .... Trichlorocarbanilide [*Organic chemistry*]
TCC .... Triclocarban [*Pharmacology*]
TCC .... Trilobita-Crustacea-Chelicerata [*Evolution history*]
TCC .... Triple Cotton-Covered [*Wire insulation*]
TCC .... Troop Carrier Command [*World War II*]
TCC .... Tucumcari, NM [*Location identifier*] [*FAA*] (FAAL)
TCC .... Turbine Close Coupled (MSA)
TCC .... Turnbull Canyon [*California*] [*Seismograph station code, US Geological Survey*] [*Closed*] (SEIS)
TCC .... Type of Changed Code [*Army*]
TCCA........ Teachers' Committee on Central America (EA)
TCCA........ Textile Color Card Association of the US [*Later, CAUS*]
TCCA........ Thermometer Collectors Club of America (EA)
TCCA........ Tin Container Collectors Association (EA)
TCCA........ Trichloroisocyanuric Acid [*Organic chemistry*]
T & CCA ... Turks and Caicos Canadian Association
TCCB........ Test and County Cricket Board [*British*]
TCCBL ...... Tons of Cubic Capacity Bale Space [*Shipping*]
TCCC........ Tower Control Computer Complex [*Aviation*]
TCC/CT .... Telecommunications/Communications Terminal (MCD)
TCCDC..... Chattem Drug and Chemical Co., Chattanooga, TN [*Library symbol*] [*Library of Congress*] (LCLS)
TCCF........ Tactical Communications Control Facility [*Air Force*] (MCD)
TCCFU...... Typical Coastal Command Foul Up [*RAF slang*] [*World War II*]
TCCH........ Tracer Control Chassis
TCCM........ Thermal Control Coating Material
TCCND5 ... Commonwealth Bureau of Nutrition. Technical Communication [*A publication*]

TCCO .... Technical Communications Corporation [*NASDAQ symbol*] (NQ)
TCCO .... Temperature-Compensated Crystal Oscillator (MCD)
TCCOB ...... Textile Chemist and Colorist [*A publication*]
T & CCP .... Telecommunications and Command and Control Program [*Air Force*] (AFIT)
TCCP .... Tissue Culture for Crops Project [*Colorado State University*] [*Research center*] (RCD)
TCCPSWG ... Tactical Command and Control Procedures Standardization Working Group [*Army*] (AABC)
TCCRAEF ... [*The*] Conservative Caucus Research, Analysis, and Education Foundation (EA)
TCCS .... Technical Committee on Communications Satellites
TCCS .... Tide Communication Control Ship (NATG)
TCCS .... Toyota's Computer-Controlled System (ADA)
TCCS .... Trace Contaminant Control System
TCCS .... Trans Caucasian Container Service (DS)
TCC/SCA .. Tai Chi Chuan/Shaolin Chuan Association (EA)
TCCT .... Tactical Communications Control Terminal (MCD)
TCD .... Chad [*ANSI three-letter standard code*] (CNC)
TCD .... Consolidated Companies [*AMEX symbol*] (SPSG)
TCD .... Department of Technical Cooperation for Development [*United Nations*]
TCD .... Tactical Communications Division [*Military*]
TCD .... Target Center Display
TCD .... Task Completion Date (AAG)
TCD .... Technical Contracts Department
TCD .... Telemetry and Command Data (KSC)
TCD .... Tentative Classification of Damage
TCD .... Tentative Classification of Defects (NG)
TCD .... Tentative Classification of Documents
TCD .... Terminal Countdown Demonstration
TCD .... Test Completion Date (NASA)
TCD .... Test Control Document [*NASA*] (MCD)
TCD .... Test Control Drawings (MCD)
TCD .... Thermal Conductivity Detector [*Analytical instrumentation*]
TCD .... Thermochemical Deposition
TCD .... Three-Channel Decoder
TCD .... Thyratron Core Driver
TCD .... Time Compliance Directive [*Air Force*] (MCD)
TCD .... Time Correlation Data
T & CD ...... Timing and Countdown [*NASA*] (NASA)
TCD .... Tor-Cal Resources Ltd. [*Toronto Stock Exchange symbol*]
TCD .... Total Cost Approach to Distribution
TCD .... Tour Completion Date
TCD .... TOXLINE Chemical Dictionary [*A publication*]
TCD .... Transistor Chopper Driver
TCD .... Transistor-Controlled Delay (MCD)
TCD .... Transportability Clearance Diagram (MCD)
TCD .... Trinity College, Dublin [*Ireland*]
TCD .... Tumor Control Dose [*Oncology*]
TCD .... Type Classification Date [*Army*]
TCD$_{50}$ ...... Tissue Culture Dose, 50% Infectivity
TC & DB .... Turn, Cough, and Deep Breathe [*Medicine*]
TCDC .... Taurochenodeoxycholate [*Biochemistry*]
TCDC .... Technical Cooperation among Developing Countries [*United Nations*]
TCDC .... Two Count Holding Co. [*NASDAQ symbol*] (NQ)
TCDC/INRES ... Information Referral System for Technical Co-operation among Developing Countries [*United Nations Development Programme*] [*Information service or system*] (IID)
TCDD .... Tetrachlorodibenzodioxin [*Organic chemistry*]
TCDF .... Temporary Container Discharge Facility
TCDF .... Tetrachlorodibenzofuran [*Organic chemistry*]
TCDF .... TIN [*Taxpayer Identification Number*] Control Number/DLN [*Document Locator Number*] File [*IRS*]
TCDMS ..... Telecommunication/Data Management System
TCDN .... Techdyne, Inc. [*Hialeah, FL*] [*NASDAQ symbol*] (NQ)
TCDP .... Transmitter Control and Display Panel
TCDR .... Cedar Income Fund 2, Ltd. [*NASDAQ symbol*] (NQ)
TCDS .... Tryptamine Chemical Delivery System [*Pharmacology*]
TCDU .... Transport Command Development Unit [*British military*] (DMA)
TCE .... 20th Century Energy [*Vancouver Stock Exchange symbol*]
TCE .... Taking Care of Elvis [*Motto of Elvis Presley fans*]
TCE .... Talker Commission Error (MUGU)
TCE .... Tax Counseling for the Elderly [*Internal Revenue Service*]
TCE .... Teachers' Centers Exchange (EA)
TCE .... Telemetry Checkout Equipment (KSC)
TCE .... Telephone Company Engineered [*Telecommunications*] (TEL)
TCE .... Temperature Coefficient of Expansion
TCE .... Terminal Control Element (CAAL)
TCE .... Terminal Cretaceous Event [*Geology*]
TCE .... Terrace (ROG)
TCE .... Tetrachloroethylene [*Also, P*] [*Organic chemistry*]
TCE .... Thermal Canister Experiment [*Space shuttle*] [*NASA*]
TCE .... Thermal Coefficient of Expansion
TCE .... Tons of Coal Equivalent
TCE .... Total Composite Error
TCE .... Total Concept Engineering

TCE .... TOW [*Tube-Launched, Optically Tracked, Wire-Guided Weapon*] Crew Evaluator [*Military*] (INF)
TCE .... Trans-Colorado Airlines, Inc. [*Gunnison, CO*] [*FAA designator*] (FAAC)
TCE .... Transportation-Communication Employees Union [*Later, TCIU*]
TCE .... Trichloroethanol [*Organic chemistry*]
TCE .... Trichloroethylene [*Also, TRI*] [*Organic chemistry*]
TCE .... Tubular Carbon Electrode
TCE .... Tulcea [*Romania*] [*Airport symbol*] (OAG)
TCEA .... Theoretical Chemical Engineering Abstracts [*A publication*]
TCEA .... Training Center for Experimental Aerodynamics [*NATO*]
TCEA .... Trichloroethane [*Organic chemistry*]
TCEBA ...... Tribune. CEBEDEAU [*Centre Belge d'Etude et de Documentation des Eaux et de l'Air*] [*A publication*]
TCEC .... Erlanger Medical Center, Medical Library, Chattanooga, TN [*Library symbol*] [*Library of Congress*] (LCLS)
TCEC-N .... Erlanger Medical Center, Nursing School, Chattanooga, TN [*Library symbol*] [*Library of Congress*] (LCLS)
TCEC-P .... Erlanger Medical Center, I. C., Thompson's Children's Pediatric Library, Chattanooga, TN [*Library symbol*] [*Library of Congress*] (LCLS)
TCED .... Thrust Control Exploratory Development (KSC)
TCEL .... T Cell Sciences, Inc. [*Cambridge, MA*] [*NASDAQ symbol*] (NQ)
TCEL .... Thought Currents in English Literature [*A publication*]
TCEO .... Theatre Committee for Eugene O'Neill (EA)
TCEP .... Tris(chloroethyl)phosphite [*Organic chemistry*]
TCEP .... Tris(cyanoethoxy)propane [*Organic chemistry*]
TCert .... Teacher's Certificate [*British*] (DBQ)
TCES .... [*Romberg*] Tiburon Center for Environmental Studies [*San Francisco State University*] [*Research center*]
TCES .... Transcutaneous Cranial Electrical Stimulation [*Medicine*]
TCESOM .. Trichlorethylene-Extracted Soybean Oil Meal
TCET .... Transcerebral Electrotherapy
TCF .... [*The*] Children's Foundation (EA)
TCF .... [*The*] Compassionate Friends (EA)
TCF .... T-Lymphocyte Chemotactic Factor
TCF .... Tactical Control Flight
TCF .... Tank Checkout Facility [*NASA*] (NASA)
TCF .... Technical Control Facility [*or Function*]
TCF .... Temporary Chaplain to the Forces [*British*]
TCF .... Terminal Communication Facility [*Telecommunications*] (TSSD)
TCF .... Terminal Configuration Facility [*Data processing*]
TCF .... Territorial Cadet Force [*British military*] (DMA)
TCF .... Test Control Fixture (MCD)
TCF .... Time Correction Factor (ADA)
TCF .... Toulx Ste. Croix [*France*] [*Seismograph station code, US Geological Survey*] (SEIS)
TCF .... Training Check Frame [*Data processing*]
TCF .... Transparent Computing Facility
TCF .... Travel Compensation Fund [*Australia*]
TCF .... Tres Cher Frere [*Dear Brother*] [*French*] [*Freemasonry*] (ROG)
TCF .... Trillion Cubic Feet
TCF .... Troop Carrier Forces [*Military*]
TCF .... Tunable Control Frequency
TCF .... Twentieth Century Fiction [*A publication*]
TCF .... Twentieth Century Fund (EA)
TCFB .... Trans-Continental Freight Bureau
TCFC .... [*The*] Cars Fan Club (EA)
TCFC .... Thom Christopher Fan Club (EA)
TCFC .... Tom Cruise Fan Club (EA)
TCFC .... Tommy Cash Fan Club (EA)
TCFC .... Turkish Children Foster Care (EA)
TCFIC .... Textile, Clothing, and Footwear Industries Committee [*British*] (DCTA)
TCFlt .... Tactical Control Flight
TCFM .... Teilhard Centre for the Future of Man (EAIO)
TCFM .... Temperature Control Flux Monitor [*NASA*]
TCFNO ..... [*The*] Common Fund for Nonprofit Organizations [*Ford Foundation*]
TCFS .... Turkish Cypriot Federated State
TCFU .... Tumor Colony-Forming Unit [*Oncology*]
TCG .... [*The*] Crimson Group [*Cambridge, MA*] [*Telecommunications*] (TSSD)
TCG .... Technical Coordination Group (MCD)
TCG .... Telecommunications Consulting Group, Inc. [*Washington, DC*] (TSSD)
TCG .... Telecommunications Group [*Range Commanders Council*] [*NASA*]
TCG .... Territorial College of Guam
TCG .... Test Call Generator [*Telecommunications*] (TEL)
TCG .... Test Control Group [*NASA*] (NASA)
TCG .... Theatre Communications Group (EA)
TCG .... Time Code Generator
TCG .... Time-Compensated Gain [*Cardiology*]
TCG .... Time Controlled Gain (AAG)
TCG .... Tooling Coordination Group (AAG)
TC/G .... Total Fielding Chances per Game [*Baseball*]

TCG .... Trans Canada Glass Ltd. [*Toronto Stock Exchange symbol*] [*Vancouver Stock Exchange symbol*]
TCG .... Transponder Control Group
TCG .... Tritocerebral Commissure, Giant [*Zoology*]
TCG .... Tucson, Cornelia & Gila Bend Railroad Co. [*AAR code*]
TCG .... Tune-Controlled Gain
TCGCB ...... Transactions. Caribbean Geological Conference [*A publication*]
TCGE........ Tool and Cutter Grinding Equipment   (MCD)
TCGE-G .... Technika Hronika (Greece) [*A publication*]
TCGF......... T-Cell Growth Factor [*Biochemistry*] [*See also IL-2*]
TCGF .... Thymus Cell Growth Factor [*Cytology*]
TCGH........ Downtown General Hospital, Chattanooga, TN [*Library symbol*] [*Library of Congress*]   (LCLS)
TCGp .... Tactical Control Group [*Air Force*]   (AFM)
TCGS........ Terak Corporation [*NASDAQ symbol*]   (NQ)
TCGT......... Georgia-Tennessee Regional Health Commission, Chattanooga, TN [*Library symbol*] [*Library of Congress*]   (LCLS)
TCGT........ Tool and Cutter Grinding Tool   (MCD)
TCGU .... Texaco Continuous Grease Unit
TCH........... Chattanooga-Hamilton County Bicentennial Library, Chattanooga, TX [*OCLC symbol*]   (OCLC)
TCH........... Compania de Telefonos de Chile SA ADS [*NYSE symbol*]   (SPSG)
TCH........... Tchibanga [*Gabon*] [*Airport symbol*]   (OAG)
TCH........... Tchimkent [*USSR*] [*Seismograph station code, US Geological Survey*] [*Closed*]   (SEIS)
TCH........... Tchoupitoulas [*Virus*]
TCH........... Tec Tech [*Vancouver Stock Exchange symbol*]
TCH........... TechAmerica Group, Inc. [*AMEX symbol*]   (SPSG)
TCH........... Technologie-Centrum Hannover GmbH [*Database producer*]   (IID)
TCH........... Technovation [*Netherlands*] [*A publication*]
TCh........... Temoignage Chretien [*A publication*]
TCH........... Temporary Construction Hole [*Technical drawings*]
TCH........... Tetrachlorohydroquinone [*Organic chemistry*]
TCH........... Thiocarbohydrazide [*Organic chemistry*]
TCH........... Threshold Crossing Height [*Aviation*]   (FAAC)
TCH........... Trade Channel [*A publication*]
TCH........... Trans-Canada Highway
TCH........... Transfer in Channel
TCH........... Trust Chamber [*NASA*]   (KSC)
TCH........... Turn, Cough, Hyperventilate [*Medicine*]
TCHCB..... Chattanooga-Hamilton County Bicentennial Library, Chattanooga, TN [*Library symbol*] [*Library of Congress*]   (LCLS)
TCHD....... Threshold Crossing Height Downwind [*Aviation*]   (FAAC)
TCHEP...... Technical Committee on High Energy Physics [*of the Federal Council for Science and Technology*]
TCHG........ Teaching
TCHHC.... Ti Ch'iu Hua Hsueh [*A publication*]
TCHHW.... Tropic Higher High Water [*Tides*]
TCHHWI.. Tropic Higher High-Water Interval [*Tides*]
TCHLW .... Tropic Higher Low Water [*Tides*]
TCHMA.... Technika v Chemii [*A publication*]
TCHNG.... Teaching
TChO........ Olin Corp., D. B. Beene Technical Information Center, Charleston, TN [*Library symbol*] [*Library of Congress*]   (LCLS)
TCHPAX... Acta Geologica Sinica [*A publication*]
TCHR....... Teacher
T Christ Wet ... Tydskrif vir Christelike Wetenskap [*A publication*]
TCHT........ Tanned-Cell Hemagglutination Test [*Immunology*]
TCHU........ Threshold Crossing Height Upwind [*Aviation*]   (FAAC)
TCI............. Tall Clubs International   (EA)
TCI............. Technical Component Industries [*Aerospace*] [*British*]
TCI............. Technical Critical Item   (NASA)
TCI............. Technology Catalysts, Incorporated [*Information service or system*]   (IID)
TCI............. Technology Communications, Incorporated
TCI............. Technology Concepts, Incorporated [*Sudbury, MA*] [*Telecommunications*]   (TSSD)
TCI............. Tele-Communications, Incorporated [*Brookpark, OH*]   (TSSD)
TCI............. Teleconferencing Systems International, Inc. [*Elk Grove Village, IL*] [*Telecommunications*]   (TSSD)
TCI............. Telemetry Components Information   (KSC)
TCI............. Telephone Collectors International   (EA)
TCI............. Temperature Control Instrument
TCI............. Temporary Customs Impost [*British*]
TCI............. Tenerife [*Canary Islands*] [*Airport symbol*]   (OAG)
TCI............. Terminal Communications Interface
TCI............. Terrain Clearance Indicator
TCI............. Test Control Instruction   (KSC)
TCI............. Theoretical Chemistry Institute [*University of Wisconsin - Madison*] [*Research center*]   (RCD)
TCI............. Thimble Collectors International   (EA)
TCI............. Time Change Item   (MCD)
TCI............. To Come In [*to hospital*] [*Medicine*]
TCI............. Total Cerebral Ischemia
TCI............. Traffic Clubs International   (EA)
TCI............. Transcontinental Realty Investors [*NYSE symbol*]   (SPSG)
TCI............. Transient Cerebral Ischemia [*Medicine*]

TCI............. Transportation Clubs International   (EA)
TCI............. Travel Consultants, Incorporated
TCI............. Trunk Cut-In
TCI............. Twentieth Century Interpretations [*A publication*]
TCIA......... Truck Cap Industry Association   (EA)
TCIC......... Technical Coatings, Incorporated [*Lubbock, TX*] [*NASDAQ symbol*]   (NQ)
TCIC......... Technical Committee on Industrial Classification [*Office of Management and Budget*] [*Washington, DC*]   (EGAO)
TCID......... Terminal Computer Identification   (KSC)
TCID......... Test Configuration Identifier   (NASA)
TCID......... Tissue Culture Infectious [*or Infective*] Dose
Tc-IDA...... Technetium Iminodiacetic Acid [*Clinical chemistry*]
TCIF .... Telecommunications Industry Forum   (EA)
TCII........... TCI International, Incorporated [*NASDAQ symbol*]   (NQ)
TCIN .... Tasmania Curriculum Information Network [*Australia*]
TCIR......... Technical Command Informal Reports [*Army*]   (MCD)
TCIS......... TELEX Computer Inquiry Service
TCITA ...... Transactions. Chalmers University of Technology [*Gothenburg, Sweden*] [*A publication*]
TCIU......... Transportation Communications International Union   (EA)
TCJ............. Tactical Communications Jamming [*Military*]   (CAAL)
TCJ............. Tarrant County Junior College, Hurst, TX [*OCLC symbol*]   (OCLC)
TCJ............. Thermocouple Junction
T & CJ ...... Town and Country Journal [*A publication*]   (APTA)
TCJ............. Town and Country Journal [*A publication*]   (APTA)
TCJ............. Turbulent Confined Jet
TCJAA ...... Telecommunication Journal of Australia [*A publication*]
TCJCC....... Trades Councils' Joint Consultative Committee [*British*]   (DCTA)
TCJOA ..... Telecommunication Journal [*A publication*]
TCK .... Thermochemical-Kinetic
TCK .... Tilletia controversa Kuehn [*Wheat fungus*]
TCK .... Track   (AAG)
TCK .... Two-Cavity Klystron
TCKHA ..... Ti Chih Ko Hsueh [*A publication*]
TCL............ Takeoff Cruise Landing [*Aviation*]
TCL............ Telecommunication Laboratories [*Taiwan*]
TCL............ Telephone Cables Limited [*British*]
TCL............ Terminal Command Language [*Applied Digital Data Systems*]
TCL............ Terminal Control Language
TCL............ Textes Cuneiformes. Departement des Antiquites Orientales. Musee du Louvre [*A publication*]   (BJA)
TCL............ Thin Charcoal Layer
TCL............ Time and Cycle Log [*NASA*]   (KSC)
TCL............ Toll Circuit Layout [*Telecommunications*]   (TEL)
TCL............ Tool Control List [*Military*]   (AFIT)
TCL............ Transcon, Inc. [*NYSE symbol*]   (SPSG)
TCL............ Transfer Chemical LASER   (IEEE)
TCL............ Transistor Contact Land
TCL............ Transistor Coupled Logic
TCL............ Transport Canada Library, Ottawa [*UTLAS symbol*]
TCL............ Transportable Calibration Laboratory
TCL............ Trap Control Line
TCL............ Trinity College, London
TCL............ Troposcatter Communications Link
TCL............ Tulane Computer Laboratory [*Tulane University*] [*Research center*]   (RCD)
TCL............ Tuscaloosa [*Alabama*] [*Airport symbol*]   (OAG)
TCL............ Tusculum College, Greenville, TN [*OCLC symbol*] [*Inactive*]   (OCLC)
TCL............ Twentieth Century Literature [*A publication*]
TClA .... Austin Peay State University, Clarksville, TN [*Library symbol*] [*Library of Congress*]   (LCLS)
TCLAS ...... Type Classification [*Military*]   (AABC)
TCLBRP.... Tank Cannon Launched Beam Rider Projectile   (MCD)
TCLBS...... Tropical Constant-Level Balloon System [*Meteorology*]
TCLC......... Travaux. Cercle Linguistique de Copenhague [*A publication*]
TCLC......... Tri-State College Library Cooperative [*Rosemont College Library*] [*Rosemont, PA*] [*Library network*]
TCLC......... Twentieth-Century Literary Criticism [*A publication*]
TC/LD....... Thermocouple/Lead Detector [*Nuclear energy*]   (NRCH)
TCle.......... Cleveland Public Library, Cleveland, TN [*Library symbol*] [*Library of Congress*]   (LCLS)
TCLE......... Thermal Coefficient of Linear Expansion [*Rocket motor stress*]
TCleB......... Bradley Memorial Hospital, Cleveland, TN [*Library symbol*] [*Library of Congress*]   (LCLS)
TCleC......... Cleveland State Community College, Cleveland, TN [*Library symbol*] [*Library of Congress*]   (LCLS)
TCleL......... Lee College, Cleveland, TN [*Library symbol*] [*Library of Congress*]   (LCLS)
TClH......... Clarksville Memorial Hospital, Clarksville, TN [*Library symbol*] [*Library of Congress*]   (LCLS)
TCLHW .... Tropic Lower High Water [*Tides*]
TCLL......... T-Cell Chronic Lymphocytic Leukemia [*Oncology*]
TCLLW ..... Tropic Lower Low Water [*Tides*]
TCLLWI... Tropic Lower Low-Water Interval [*Tides*]
TCLN........ Techniclone International Corp. [*NASDAQ symbol*]   (NQ)
TCLNA...... Tall Cedars of Lebanon of North America   (EA)

TCLP .... Toxicity Characteristic Leaching Procedure [*Environmental Protection Agency*]
TCLP .... Travaux. Cercle Linguistique de Prague [*A publication*]
TCLP .... Type Classification, Limited Procurement
TCLR .... Toll Circuit Layout Record [*Telecommunications*] (TEL)
TCLSC ...... Theater COMSEC [*Communications Security*] Logistic Support Center [*Army*] (AABC)
TCLSC-E... Theater COMSEC Logistics Support Center - Europe (MCD)
TCM .... T/SF Communications Corp. [*AMEX symbol*] (SPSG)
TCM .... Tacoma, WA [*Location identifier*] [*FAA*] (FAAL)
TCM .... Tactical Cruise Missile (MCD)
TCM .... Tax Court Memorandum Decisions [*Commerce Clearing House or Prentice-Hall, Inc.*] [*A publication*] (DLA)
TCM .... Teaching Career Month
TCM .... Technical Committee Minutes [*Military*] (AFIT)
TCM .... Technical Coordination Meeting (MCD)
TCM .... Telecommunications Monitor
TCM .... Teledyne Continental Motors [*Muskegon, MI*] [*FAA designator*] (FAAC)
TCM .... Telemetry Code Modulation
TC & M...... Telemetry Control and Monitoring
TCM .... Telephone Channel Monitor
TCM .... Temperature Control Model
TCM .... Teratogenesis, Carcinogenesis, and Mutagenesis [*A publication*]
TCM .... Terminal-to-Computer Multiplexer
TCM .... Termination of Centralized Management (MCD)
TCM .... Terrain Clearance Measurement
TCM .... Terrestrial Carbon Model [*Earth science*]
TCM .... Test Call Module [*Telecommunications*] (TEL)
TCM .... Tetrachloromercurate [*Inorganic chemistry*]
TCM .... Textil-Mitteilungen. Unabhangige Textil Zeitung fuer Handel und Industrie [*A publication*]
TCM .... Theater Combat Model (NATG)
TCM .... Thermal Conduction Module [*IBM Corp.*]
TCM .... Thermoplastic Cellular Molding [*Plastics technology*]
TCM .... Tissue Culture Medium
TCM .... Toroidal Carbohydrate Module [*i.e., doughnut*] [*Slang*]
TCM .... Torpedo Countermeasures (NVT)
TCM .... Total Downtime for Corrective Unscheduled Maintenance [*Quality control*] (MCD)
TCM .... Toxic Chemical Munitions [*Army*]
TCM .... Trade and Commerce [*A publication*]
TCM .... Trajectory Correction Maneuver
TCM .... Transcutaneous [*Oxygen*] Monitoring [*Medicine*]
TCM .... Transfluxor Constants Matrix (AAG)
TCM .... Translator Command Module [*Fluorescence technique*]
TCM .... Trellis-Coded Modulation [*Data transmission*] (BYTE)
TCM .... Troop Corporal-Major [*British military*] (DMA)
TCM .... Truck Components Marketing [*Eaton Corp.*]
TCM .... Tubing Connector Manifold [*Instrumentation*]
TCM .... Tucuman [*Argentina*] [*Seismograph station code, US Geological Survey*] [*Closed*] (SEIS)
TCM .... Twentieth Century Monthly [*A publication*]
TCM .... Twin-Cartridge Machine
TCMA .... Tabulating Card Manufacturers Association [*Later, IOSA*] (EA)
TCMA .... Textile Chemical Manufacturers Association [*Later, IOSA*] (EA)
TCMA .... Third Class Mail Association (EA)
TCMA .... Tooling Component Manufacturers Association (EA)
TCM/A...... Toxic Chemical Munitions/Agents (MCD)
TCMB........ Turkiye Cumhuriyet Merkez Bankasi [*The Central Bank of the Republic of Turkey*]
TCM (CCH) ... Tax Court Memorandum Decisions (Commerce Clearing House) [*A publication*] (DLA)
TCMD .... Transportation Cargo Manifest Document
TCMD .... Transportation Control and Movement Document [*Military*]
TCMDBN ... Handelinge van die Kollege van Geneeskunde van Suid-Afrika [*A publication*]
TC Memo... Tax Court Memorandum Decisions [*Commerce Clearing House or Prentice-Hall, Inc.*] [*A publication*] (DLA)
TCMF........ Touch Calling Multifrequency (IEEE)
TCMH....... Memorial Hospital, Chattanooga, TN [*Library symbol*] [*Library of Congress*] (LCLS)
TCMI......... Moccasin Bend Mental Health Institute, Chattanooga, TN [*Library symbol*] [*Library of Congress*] (LCLS)
T C MITS ... [*The*] Common Man in the Street [*The average man*] [*See also MITS*]
TCMP........ Taxpayer Compliance Measurement Program [*IRS*]
TCM (P-H) ... Tax Court Memorandum Decisions (Prentice-Hall, Inc.) [*A publication*] (DLA)
TCMS........ Technical Control and Management Subsystem (MCD)
TC-MS....... Thermal Chromatography/Mass Spectrometry
TCMS........ Toll Centering and Metropolitan Sectoring [*AT & T*] [*Telecommunications*] (TEL)
TCMS........ Training Certification Management System [*NASA*]
TCMTA..... Technometrics [*A publication*]
TCMUA..... Telecommunications [*English Translation*] [*A publication*]
TCMUD8 .. Teratogenesis, Carcinogenesis, and Mutagenesis [*A publication*]
TCMUE9 .. Topics in Chemical Mutagenesis [*A publication*]

TCN .... Carson-Newman College, Jefferson City, TN [*OCLC symbol*] (OCLC)
TCN .... Telecommunications Cooperative Network (EA)
TCN .... Teleconference Network [*University of Nebraska Medical Center*] [*Omaha, NE*] [*Telecommunications*] (TSSD)
TCN .... Territorial Command Net
TCN .... Test Change Notice [*NASA*] (MCD)
TCN .... Texcan Technology Corp. [*Vancouver Stock Exchange symbol*]
TCN .... Tobacco Cyst Nematode [*Plant pathology*]
TCN .... Toconce [*Chile*] [*Seismograph station code, US Geological Survey*] (SEIS)
TCN .... Tracing Change Notice
TCN .... Trade Commission of Norway (EA)
TCN .... Trans Continental Airlines [*Ypsilanti, MI*] [*FAA designator*] (FAAC)
TCN .... Transportation Control Number [*Air Force*] (AFM)
TCN .... Trolley Coach News [*A publication*] (EAAP)
TCNA .... Tube Council of North America (EA)
TCNB .... Tetracyanobenzene [*Organic chemistry*]
TC-NBT ..... Thiocarbamyl-nitro-blue Tetrazolium [*Organic chemistry*]
TCNC .... Tekakwitha Conference National Center (EA)
TCNCO ...... Test Control Noncommissioned Officer (AFM)
TCNE .... Tetracyanoethylene [*Organic chemistry*]
TCNEO ...... Tetracyanoethylene Oxide [*Organic chemistry*]
TCNJ .... Trust Co. of New Jersey [*NASDAQ symbol*] (NQ)
TCNM .... Trimethylcyclopropenyl(nitrophenyl)malononitrile [*Organic chemistry*]
TCNOA ...... Technology [*Sindri, India*] [*A publication*]
TCNPEX ... Bulletin. Taichung District Agricultural Improvement Station [*A publication*]
TCNQ .... Tetracyanoquinodimethane [*Organic chemistry*]
TCNRS...... Transactions. Canadian Numismatic Research Society [*A publication*]
TCNSB...... Technos [*A publication*]
TCNT .... Transpiration-Cooled Nose Tip
TCNTL...... Transcontinental (FAAC)
TCO .... Tactical Combat Operations
TCO .... Tactical Control Officer [*Army*]
TCO .... Taken Care Of (MCD)
TCO .... Technical Checkout [*Nuclear*] (MCD)
TCO .... Technical Contracting Office [*Navy*]
TCO .... Technical Cooperation Officer [*British*]
TCO .... Telecommunications Certifying Officer [*Air Force*] (AFIT)
TCO .... Telemetry and Command Subsystem [*Deep Space Instrumentation Facility, NASA*]
TCO .... Terminal Control Office [*or Officer*]
TCO .... Termination Contracting Officer [*Military*]
T & C/O.... Test and Checkout [*NASA*] (KSC)
TCO .... Test Control Officer [*Military*]
TCO .... Thrust Cutoff (NVT)
TCO .... Tillamook County Library, Tillamook, OR [*OCLC symbol*] (OCLC)
TCO .... Time and Charges, Operate
TCO .... Tjaenstemaennens Centralorganisation [*Central Organization of Salaried Employees*] [*Sweden*]
TCO .... Tool Change Order (MCD)
TCO .... Torpedo Control Officer [*British military*] (DMA)
TCO .... Train Conducting Officer [*British military*] (DMA)
TCO .... Trans Canada Options [*Stock exchange network of VSE, TSE, and MSE*]
TCO .... Trans-Canada Resources Ltd. [*Toronto Stock Exchange symbol*]
TCO .... Transparent Conductive Oxide [*Photovoltaic energy systems*]
TCO .... Transportation Company [*Army*]
TCO .... Transportation Control Officer [*Air Force*] (AFM)
TCO .... Trinity College, Oxford [*British*] (DAS)
TCO .... Trunk Cutoff
TCO .... Tumaco [*Colombia*] [*Airport symbol*] (OAG)
TCOA .... Telephone Contract Officers' Association [*A union*] [*British*]
TCOBS ...... Type Classification - Obsolete (MCD)
TCOC .... Transverse Cylindrical Orthomorphic Chart
TColISM... Southern Missionary College, Collegedale, TN [*Library symbol*] [*Library of Congress*] (LCLS)
TCOM .... Tele-Communications, Inc. [*NASDAQ symbol*] (NQ)
TCOM .... Terminal Communications (FAAC)
TCOM .... Terminal or Computer Originated Mail Systems, Inc. [*Washington, DC*] (TSSD)
TCOM .... Tethered Communications, Inc. [*Westinghouse subsidiary*]
TCOM .... Texas College of Osteopathic Medicine
T-Comm.... Terret Communications [*Whitehouse Station, NJ*] (TSSD)
TCOMP.... Tape Compare Processor [*Data processing*]
T/COMP... Trimmed Complete [*Automotive engineering*]
T/CONT... Throttle Control [*Automotive engineering*]
T/CONV... Torque Converter [*Automotive engineering*]
TCoo .... Putnam County Public Library, Cookeville, TN [*Library symbol*] [*Library of Congress*] (LCLS)
TCooH .... Cookeville General Hospital, Stephen Farr Health Sciences Library, Cookeville, TN [*Library symbol*] [*Library of Congress*] (LCLS)
TCooP........ Tennessee Technological University, Cookeville, TN [*Library symbol*] [*Library of Congress*] (LCLS)

TCOP	Test and Checkout Plan [*NASA*] (KSC)	
TCOR	Chrysler Town and Country Owners Registry (EA)	
TCOR	Tandon Corporation [*NASDAQ symbol*] (NQ)	
TCORA	Teacher's College Record [*A publication*]	
TCOS........	Trunk Class of Service [*Telecommunications*] (TEL)	
TCOT	Tension Control Optimisation Theory [*Tire manufacturing*]	
T-COUNT ...	Terminal Count [*Flight readiness count*] (MCD)	
TCovH	Tipton County Hospital, Covington, TN [*Library symbol*] [*Library of Congress*] (LCLS)	
TCP...........	Tactical Computer Processor	
TCP...........	Tactical Control Panel (MCD)	
TCP...........	Tactical Cryptologic Program [*DoD*]	
TCP...........	Tape Conversion Program [*Data processing*] (MDG)	
TCP...........	Task Change Proposal (AAG)	
TCP...........	Task Control Packet (NASA)	
TCP...........	Task Control Program	
TCP...........	Teachers College Press	
TCP...........	Technical Change Proposal	
TCP...........	Technical Coordination Program [*Military*] (AFIT)	
TCP...........	Technical Cost Proposal (AAG)	
TCP...........	Technology Coordinating Paper	
TCP...........	Telemetry and Command Processor Assembly [*Deep Space Instrumentation Facility, NASA*]	
TCP...........	Temple Cyclopaedic Primers [*A publication*]	
TCP...........	Temporary Change Procedure (AAG)	
TCP...........	Terminal Control Program	
TCP...........	Test Change Proposal (CAAL)	
TCP...........	Test Checkout Panel	
TCP...........	Test and Checkout Procedure [*NASA*] (KSC)	
TCP...........	Test Control Package (NASA)	
TCP...........	Test of Creative Potential	
TCP...........	Tetrachlorobiphenyl [*Organic chemistry*]	
TCP...........	Tetrachlorophenol [*Organic chemistry*]	
TCP...........	Tetracyanoplatinate [*Inorganic chemistry*]	
TCP...........	Tetracyanopyrazine [*Organic chemistry*]	
TCP...........	Thienyl(cyclohexyl)piperidine [*Biochemistry*]	
TCP...........	Thrust Chamber Pressure [*Aerospace*] (IEEE)	
TCP...........	Time, Cost, and Performance	
TCP...........	Time Limited Correlation Processing	
TCP...........	Timing and Control Panel	
TCP...........	Tocopilla [*Chile*] [*Seismograph station code, US Geological Survey*] [*Closed*] (SEIS)	
TCP...........	Tool Center Point [*Robotics*]	
TCP...........	Torpedo Certification Program [*Military*] (CAAL)	
TCP...........	Total Clottable Protein [*Clinical chemistry*]	
TC + P......	Total Colonoscopy plus Polypectomy [*Proctoscopy*]	
TCP...........	Town and Country Planning Act [*British*]	
TCP...........	Traffic Control Point [*or Post*] [*Military*]	
TCP...........	Trainer Change Proposal [*Military*] (AFIT)	
TCP...........	Training Controller Panel	
TCP...........	Transmission Control Program	
TCP...........	Transmission Control Protocol [*Advanced Research Projects Agency Network*] [*DoD*]	
TCP...........	Transparent Conducting Polymers [*Photovoltaic energy systems*]	
TCP...........	Transport Command Police [*British military*] (DMA)	
TCP...........	Transport Control Protocol [*Telecommunications*]	
TCP...........	Tricalcium Phosphate [*Inorganic chemistry*]	
TCP...........	Trichlorophenol [*Organic chemistry*]	
TCP...........	(Trichlorophenoxy)acetic Acid [*Also known as 2,4,5-T*] [*Herbicide*]	
TCP...........	Trichloropropane [*Organic chemistry*]	
TCP...........	Tricresyl Phosphate [*Organic chemistry*]	
TCP...........	Tropical Canine Pancytopenia (RDA)	
TCP...........	Trust Chamber Pressure [*Missile technology*] (KSC)	
TCPA........	Tetrachlorophthalic Anhydride [*Flame retardant*] [*Organic chemistry*]	
TCPA........	Time to Closest Point of Approach [*Navigation*]	
TCPA........	Town and Country Planning Association [*British*]	
T & CPA	Town and Country Planning Authority [*Australia*]	
TCPA........	Trichlorophenylacetic Acid [*Herbicide*] [*Organic chemistry*]	
TCPAM.....	Tentative CNO [*Chief of Naval Operations*] Program Analysis Memorandum (NVT)	
TCPC........	Tab Card Punch Control	
TCPC........	Transportation Claims and Prevention Council (EA)	
TCP(CC)R ...	Town and Country Planning (Compensation and Certificates) Regulations [*British*]	
TCP(CPRW)R ...	Town and Country Planning (Churches, Places of Religious Worship, and Burial Grounds) Regulations [*British*]	
T C Peirce ..	Transactions. Charles S. Peirce Society [*A publication*]	
TCPGR......	Town and Country Planning General Regulations [*British*]	
TCPH	Toluoyl Chloride Phenylhydrazine [*Drug for sheep*]	
TCPI	"To Complete" Performance Index (MCD)	
TCPI	Transportation Club of the Petroleum Industry (EA)	
TCP/IP......	Transmission Control Protocol and Internet Protocol (PCM)	
TCPL........	TransCanada Pipelines Ltd. [*Commercial firm*]	
TCPLA......	Town and Country Planning [*A publication*]	
TCP(M)R ..	Town and Country Planning (Minerals) Regulations [*British*]	
TCPO	bis(Trichlorophenyl) Oxalate [*Organic chemistry*]	
TCPO	Third-Class Post Office	
TCPP	(Tetrachlorophenyl)pyrrole [*Organic chemistry*]	

TCPPA	(Trichlorophenoxy)propionic Acid [*Plant hormone*] [*Herbicide*]	
TCPTF......	Target Cost plus Target Fee	
TC Pub......	Tariff Commission Publications [*A publication*] (DLA)	
TCpY	Transcarpathian Yiddish (BJA)	
TCQ	Tacna [*Peru*] [*Airport symbol*] (OAG)	
TCQ	Tax Counselor's Quarterly [*A publication*]	
TCQ	Trichlorobenzoquinoneimine [*Reagent*]	
TCQC	Tank Crew Qualification Course [*Army*]	
TCQM	[*The*] Chief Quartermaster [*Military*]	
TCR	Central Air Transport, Inc. [*Nashville, TN*] [*FAA designator*] (FAAC)	
TCR	T-Cell Reactivity	
TCR	T-Cell Receptor [*Immunology*]	
TCR	T-Cell Recovery Column [*Chromatography*]	
TCR	Tab Card Reader	
TCR	Tantalum-Controlled Rectifier	
TCR	Tape Cassette Recorder	
TCR	Task Change Request [*Army*]	
TCR	Taxe de Cooperation Regionale [*Regional Cooperation Tax*] [*French*]	
TCR	Teacher's College Record [*A publication*]	
TCR	Technical Change Request	
TCR	Technical Characteristics Review	
TCR	Technical Compliance Record	
TCR	Technology Review [*A publication*]	
TCR	Telemetry Compression Routine	
TCR	Temperature Coefficient of Resistance	
TCR	Temperature Control Reference	
TCR	Tentative Cancellation Request	
TCR	Terrain Clearance RADAR	
TCR	Test Compare Results (MCD)	
TCR	Test Condition Requirements [*Army*]	
TCR	Test Conductor (MCD)	
TCR	Test Constraints Review [*NASA*] (MCD)	
TCR	Tetrachlororesourcinol [*Organic chemistry*]	
TCR	Thalamocortical Relay [*Neurology*]	
TCR	Thermal Concept Review (NASA)	
TCR	Thermochemical Recuperator [*Proposed heat recovery system*]	
TCR	Thitec Recovery [*Vancouver Stock Exchange symbol*]	
TCR	Tie Control Relay (MCD)	
TCR	Time Code Reader	
TCR	Time Critical Requirements (MCD)	
TCR	Tonecraft Realty, Inc. [*Toronto Stock Exchange symbol*]	
TCR	Tool Completion Report	
TCR	Tooling Change Request	
TCR	Total Contractual Requirements (MCD)	
TCR	Total Control Racing [*Road-racing game*] [*Ideal Toy Corp.*]	
TCr............	Total Creatine [*Pool*]	
TCR	Tracer (AAG)	
TCR	Traffic Control RADAR	
TCR	Trainer Change Request [*Military*]	
TCR	Training/Conversion/Replacement (MCD)	
TCR	Trammell Crow Real Estate Investment [*NYSE symbol*] (SPSG)	
TCR	Transceiver (AABC)	
TCR	Transfer Control Register	
TCR	Transit Commission Reports [*New York*] [*A publication*] (DLA)	
TCR	Transmittal Control Record [*Data processing*]	
TCR	Transportation Corps Release [*Military*]	
TCR	Travaux. Centre de Recherche sur le Proche-Orient et la Grece Antiques. Universite de Sciences Humaines de Strasbourg [*A publication*] (BJA)	
TCR	Tubing Connector Reducer [*Instrumentation*]	
TCR	Two-Color Radiometer	
TCrA	Art Circle Public Library, Crossville, TN [*Library symbol*] [*Library of Congress*] (LCLS)	
TCRC........	Time and Cycle Record Card [*NASA*] (KSC)	
TCRD	Telecredit, Inc. [*NASDAQ symbol*] (NQ)	
TCRD	Test and Checkout Requirements Document [*NASA*] (KSC)	
TCRE........	Temperature-Compensated Reference Element	
TCREA......	Telecommunications and Radio Engineering [*English Translation*] [*A publication*]	
TCREC......	Transportation Research Command [*Army*] (MCD)	
T Crit	Texto Critico [*A publication*]	
TCRJ	Thermocouple Reference Junction	
TCRM	Thermochemical Remanent Magnetization	
TCRMG	Tripartite Commission for the Restitution of Monetary Gold (EAIO)	
TCRN	Temporary Chaplain to the Royal Navy [*British*]	
TCRP........	Tactical Command Readiness Program [*Army*]	
TCRPA......	Trans-Continental Railroad Passenger Association [*Defunct*] (EA)	
TCRPC......	Tri-County Regional Planning Commission [*Information service or system*] (IID)	
TCRSD......	Test and Checkout Requirements Specification Documentation [*NASA*] (KSC)	
TCRUA	Technische Rundschau [*A publication*]	
TCS...........	[*The*] Classification Society (EA)	
TCS...........	[*The*] Coastal Society (EA)	

TCS............	[The] Computer Store [NASDAQ symbol] (NQ)
TCS............	[The] Constant Society (EA)
TCS............	[The] Cousteau Society (EA)
TCS............	[The] Crustacean Society (EA)
TCS............	[The] Cybele Society (EA)
TCS............	Tactical Computer System [Army] (MCD)
TCS............	Tactical Control Squadron
TCS............	Tanking Control System (AAG)
TCS............	Target Control System
TCS............	Target Cost System
TCS............	TCS Enterprises, Inc. [AMEX symbol] (SPSG)
TCS............	Teacher Characteristics Schedule
TCS............	Technical Change Summary [NASA] (MCD)
TCS............	Technical Concurrence Sheets [NASA] (NASA)
TCS............	Technical Countdown Sequences (KSC)
TCS............	Telecommunications Consulting Services [Richard A. Eisner & Co.] [New York, NY] (TSSD)
TCS............	Telecommunications Control System [Toshiba Corp.] [Data processing]
TCS............	Telecommunications System
TCS............	Teleconference System [Memorial University of Newfoundland] [St. John's, NF] [Telecommunications] (TSSD)
TCS............	Telemetry and Command Station [Aerospace] (MCD)
TCS............	Telephone Conference Summary (NRCH)
TCS............	Television Camera System
TCS............	Television Control Set
TCSS..........	Temperature Control Subsystem (KSC)
TCS............	Temperature Controlled Storage and Distribution [A publication]
TCS............	Temporary Change of Station [Military]
TCS............	Temporary Conditioning Station [Nuclear energy] (NRCH)
TCS............	Temporary Correction Sheet (MCD)
TCS............	Terminal Communications Subsystem
TCS............	Terminal Computer System (BUR)
TCS............	Terminal Control System [Hewlett-Packard Co.]
TCS............	Terminal Countdown Sequencer [or Sequences] [NASA] (KSC)
TCS............	Ternary Compound Semiconductor
TCS............	Test of Cognitive Skills [Achievement test]
TCS............	Test Control Supervisor (NASA)
TCS............	Test Control System (NASA)
TCS............	Texas Centennial Society (EA)
TCS............	Texts from Cuneiform Sources [A publication] (BJA)
TCS............	Thermal Conditioning System (KSC)
TCS............	Thermal Control System [or Subsystem]
TCS............	Thermally Stimulated Charge [Analytical chemistry]
TCS............	Timing Cover and Seal Set [Automotive engineering]
TCS............	Tin Can Sailors (EA)
TCS............	Tool Clearance Slip (AAG)
TCS............	Tool Coordinate System
TCS............	Total Communication Systems [Pittsburgh, PA] [Telecommunications service] (TSSD)
TCS............	Trac Industries, Inc. [Toronto Stock Exchange symbol] [Vancouver Stock Exchange symbol]
TCS............	Tracheal Cellular Score [Medicine]
TCS............	Traction Control System [Alfred Teves GmbH] [Automotive engineering]
TCS............	Trade Commission of Spain (EA)
TCS............	Traffic Control Satellite
TCS............	Traffic Control Station
TCS............	Traffic Control System [Army]
TCS............	Transaction Control System [Hitachi Ltd.]
TCS............	TransCanada Telephone System [Later, Telecom Canada] (TSSD)
TCS............	Transcutaneous Stimulation
TCS............	Transducer Calibration System
TCS............	Transfer Carry Subtract
TCS............	Transmission Controlled Spark (MCD)
TCS............	Transportable Communications System
TCS............	Transportation and Communications Service [of GSA] [Abolished, 1972]
TCS............	Transportation Consulting & Service Corp., Chicago IL [STAC]
TCS............	Transportation Costing Service [Database] [A. T. Kearney, Inc.] [Information service or system] (CRD)
TCS............	Trichlorosilane [Inorganic chemistry]
TCS............	Trim Control System
TCS............	Troop Carrier Squadron [Military] (CINC)
TCS............	Troposcatter Communications System
TCS............	Truth or Consequences, NM [Location identifier] [FAA] (FAAL)
TCS............	Tube Cooling Supply
TCS............	Turbine Control System [Nuclear energy] (NRCH)
TCS............	Two-Photon Coherent States (MCD)
TCSA.........	Tetrachlorosalicylanilide [Organic chemistry]
TCSAA......	Twentieth Century Spanish Association of America (EA)
TCSC........	Time-Critical Shipment Committee [Defunct] (EA)
TCSC........	Toyota Celica Supra Club (EA)
TCSC........	Trainer Control and Simulation Computer
TCSC........	Two-Channel Scan Camera (NOAA)
TCSCLC....	Two-Carrier Space-Charge-Limited Current
TCSD.........	Telemetry and Communications Systems Division [Apollo] [NASA]
TCS & D	Temperature Controlled Storage and Distribution Exhibition [British] (ITD)
TCSE.........	TCS Enterprises, Inc. [NASDAQ symbol] (NQ)
T C Ser Soil Conserv Auth (Vic) ...	T C Series. Soil Conservation Authority (Victoria) [A publication] (APTA)
T C Ser Soil Conserv Auth (Vict) ...	T C Series. Soil Conservation Authority (Victoria) [A publication] (APTA)
TCSF	Thomson-CSF [France] [NASDAQ symbol] (NQ)
TCSF	Total Counts of Successive Fractions [Chromatography]
TCSG.........	[The] Center for Social Gerontology (EA)
TCSL	Tri-County Savings & Loan Association [NASDAQ symbol] (NQ)
TCSM.......	Test of Cognitive Style in Mathematics [Educational test]
TCSM.......	Transactions. Colonial Society of Massachusetts [A publication]
TCSMC	Transportation Corps Supply Maintenance Command [Army]
TCSP	Tactical Communications Satellite Program [DoD] (MCD)
TCSP	Tandem Cross-Section Program [Bell System]
TCSP	Test Checkout Support Plan (KSC)
TCSPr........	Second Presbyterian Church Library, Chattanooga, TN [Library symbol] [Library of Congress] (LCLS)
TCSq..........	Troop Carrier Squadron [Air Force] (AFM)
TCSR	Tri-Comp Sensors [NASDAQ symbol] (NQ)
TCSR	Typographic Council for Spelling Reform (EA)
TCSS	Tactical Control Surveillance System
TCSS	Tri-Cone Support Structure [NASA]
TCSSS	Thermal Control Subsystem Segment [NASA] (NASA)
TCST	Chattanooga State Technical Community College, Chattanooga, TN [Library symbol] [Library of Congress] (LCLS)
TCST	Telecast, Inc. [Fraser, MI] [NASDAQ symbol] (NQ)
TC STD	Type Classification - Standard (MCD)
TCSTE	Triangle Coalition for Science and Technology Education (EA)
TCSUH	Texas Center for Superconductivity, University of Houston [Research center] (RCD)
TCSW	Thinking Creatively with Sounds and Words [Educational test]
TCT............	Tactical Communications Terminal
TCT............	Tactical Computer Terminal [Army] (MCD)
TCT............	Takotna [Alaska] [Airport symbol] (OAG)
TCT............	Takotna, AK [Location identifier] [FAA] (FAAL)
T Ct............	Tax Court of the United States, Reports [A publication] (DLA)
TCT............	Taxe Conjecturelle Temporaire [Temporary Surtax] [French] (IMH)
TCT............	Telemetry-Computer Translator [Bell Laboratories]
TCT............	Tennessee Temple Schools, Chattanooga, TN [Library symbol] [Library of Congress] (LCLS)
TCT............	Tennessee Temple University, Chattanooga, TN [OCLC symbol] (OCLC)
TCT............	Terracotta Tile [Classified advertising] (ADA)
TCT............	Texas City Terminal Railway Co. [AAR code]
TCT............	Thrombin Clotting Time [Clinical chemistry]
TCT............	Thyrocalcitonin [Also, CT, TCA] [Endocrinology]
TCT............	Time Code Translator
TCT............	Tin Can Tourists of the World (EA)
TCT............	Toll Connecting Trunk [Telecommunications] (TEL)
TCT............	Tool Change Time
TCT............	Total Composite Tolerance
TCT............	Traffic Control Transponder
TCT............	Translator and Code Treatment Frame (IEEE)
TCT............	Tricentrol PLC [NYSE symbol] [Toronto Stock Exchange symbol] (SPSG)
TCT............	True Centerline Tested
TCT............	Two-Component TOKAMAK
TCTA........	Teaching Certificate for Teachers of Art [British]
T & CTB	Thames and Chilterns Tourist Board [British] (DCTA)
Tctbl..........	Tractatenblad [A publication]
TCTC........	Temperature-Controlled Test Chamber [EPA engine test]
TCTC........	Tompkins County Trust Company [Ithaca, NY] [NASDAQ symbol] (NQ)
TCTC........	Transportation Corps Technical Committee [Army]
TCTFE	Trichlorotrifluoroethane [Organic chemistry]
TCTI.........	Time Compliance Technical Instruction (NASA)
TCTL........	Tactical (AAG)
TCTL........	Tectel, Inc. [NASDAQ symbol] (NQ)
TCTM.......	Aircraft Time Compliance Technical Manuals
T Ct Mem ..	Tax Court of the United States, Memorandum [A publication] (DLA)
TCTNB......	Trichlorotrinitrobenzene [Organic chemistry]
TCTO	Technical Changes to Technical Orders
TCTO	Time Compliance Technical Order [NASA] (AAG)
TCTOA.....	Tectonophysics [A publication]
TCTP........	Tetrachlorothiophene [Organic chemistry]
TCTP	Tricapped Triangular Prism
TCTS	Tactical Communications Systems Technical Standards [Military]
TCTS	Tank Crew Turret Simulator (MCD)
TCTS	Trans-Canada Telephone System (MCD)
TCTU	Turkish Confederation of Trade Unions
TCTV........	Telemedia Communication Television [Cable-television system]
TCTV........	Today's Child, Tomorrow's Victim [Book title]

TCTVA...... Tennessee Valley Authority, Technical Library, Chattanooga, TN [*Library symbol*] [*Library of Congress*] (LCLS)
TCTY........ Twin City Barge, Inc. [*NASDAQ symbol*]   (NQ)
TCU .... Tactical Control Unit   (MCD)
TCU .... Taichung [*Taityu*] [*Republic of China*] [*Seismograph station code, US Geological Survey*]   (SEIS)
TCU .... Tape Control Unit
TCU .... Tecumseh, MI [*Location identifier*] [*FAA*]   (FAAL)
TCU .... Teletype Communications Unit   (NVT)
TCU .... Teletypewriter Control Unit   (CET)
TCU .... Temperature Control Unit
TCU .... Tentative Clean Up   (MCD)
TCU .... Terminal Cluster Unit
TCU .... Terminal Control Unit   (MCD)
TCU .... Test Computer Unit
TCU .... Test of Concept Utilization [*Psychometrics*]
TCU .... Test Control Unit
TCU .... Texas Christian University [*Fort Worth, TX*]
TCU .... Thermal Control Unit
TCU .... Threshold Control Unit   (CET)
TCU .... Thrust Control Unit
TCU .... Time Change Unit   (MCD)
TCU .... Timing Control Unit
TCU .... Topping Control Unit   (AAG)
TCU .... Torpedo Control Unit
TCU .... Towering Cumulus [*Meteorology*]
TCU .... Transmission Control Unit
TCU .... Transport Conversion Unit [*British military*]   (DMA)
TCU .... Transportation-Communication Employees Union [*Later, TCIU*]
TCU .... Transportation, Communications, and Utilities
TCU .... Tri-College University Library Consortium [*Library network*]
TCU .... Turbine Control Unit
TCU .... University of Tennessee at Chattanooga, Chattanooga, TN [*Library symbol*] [*Library of Congress*]   (LCLS)
TCUA .... [*The*] Committee to Unite America [*Inactive*]   (EA)
TCUA .... Time-Critical, Unspecified Area
TCUCC...... Texas Christian University Computer Center [*Research center*]   (RCD)
TCUL........ Tap Changing Under Load   (MSA)
TC(UN) ..... Trusteeship Council of the United Nations
TCUS........ Tax Court of the United States [*Also, TC*] [*Later, United States Tax Court*]
TCUSA...... Trans Am Club USA   (EA)
TCV .... Tank Cleaning Vessel   (ADA)
TCV .... Temperature Coefficient of Voltage
TCV .... Temperature Control Valve   (AAG)
TCV .... Terminal-Configured Vehicle [*NASA*]
TCV .... Thoracic Cage Volume [*Medicine*]
TCV .... Thrust Chamber Valve   (MCD)
TCV .... Thrust Control Valve
TCV .... TOKAMAK [*Toroidal Kamera Magnetic*] Chauffage Variable [*Plasma physics instrumentation*]
TCV .... Total Containment Vessel   (CAAL)
TCV .... Tracked Combat Vehicle   (MCD)
TCV .... Troop Carrying Vehicle
TCV .... Turbine Control Valve [*Nuclear energy*]   (NRCH)
TCV .... Turnip Crinkle Virus
TCV .... Twentieth Century Views [*A publication*]
TCVA........ Terminal-Configured Vehicles and Avionics [*Program*] [*NASA*]
TCVC........ Tape Control via Console
TCVD .... Technical Committee on Veterinary Drugs [*Australian Agricultural Council*]
TCVR........ Transceiver   (CET)
TCW .... Time Code Word
TCW .... Tinned Copper Weld
TCW .... Tocumwal [*Australia*] [*Airport symbol*]   (OAG)
TCW .... Today's Christian Woman [*A publication*]
TCW .... Track Confirmation Word [*Data processing*]
TCW .... Triple-Crown Resources [*Vancouver Stock Exchange symbol*]
TCW .... Troop Carrier Wing [*Military*]   (CINC)
TCWA .... Transactions. Cumberland and Westmorland Antiquarian and Archaeological Society [*A publication*]
TCWC........ Texas Cooperative Wildlife Collections [*Texas A & M University*] [*Research center*]   (RCD)
TCWG .... Telecommunication Working Group
TCWg .... Troop Carrier Wing [*Air Force*]   (AFM)
T-CW & IB ... Trans-Continental Weighing and Inspection Bureau
TCWSA ..... T'ai-Wan Huan Ching Wei Sheng [*A publication*]
TCX .... Transfer of Control Cancellation Message [*Aviation*]
TCXO .... Temperature-Compensated Crystal Oscillator
TCYC........ Tropical Cyclone   (FAAC)
TCZD .... Temperature-Compensated Zener Diode
TD .... Area Training Director [*Red Cross*]
TD .... Chad [*ANSI two-letter standard code*]   (CNC)
Td .... Dorsal Touch Neurons [*of a leech*]
Td .... T-Cell, Delayed Type [*Immunology*]
TD .... T-Dependent [*Immunology*]
TD .... Table of Distribution [*Military*]
TD .... Tabular Data   (BUR)
TD .... Tactical Division [*Air Force*]

TD .... Tank Destroyer [*Military*]
TD .... Tank Division   (MCD)
TD .... Tape Degausser
TD .... Tape Drive
TD .... Tardive Dyskinesia [*Medicine*]
TD .... Target Designator   (MCD)
TD .... Target Discrimination
TD .... Target Drone
TD .... Task Description   (AAG)
TD .... Task Directive   (AAG)
TD .... Teacher's Diploma [*British*]
TD .... Teachta Dala [*Member of Parliament*] [*Ireland*]
TD .... Tealto Dail [*Member of the Dail*] [*Irish*]   (ILCA)
TD .... Technical Data
TD .... Technical Demonstration   (AAG)
TD .... Technical Design   (AAG)
TD .... Technical Direction [*or Directive*]
TD .... Technical Director [*Television*]
TD .... Technical Division
TD .... Technical Drawing
TD .... Technological Dependence
TD .... Technology Document   (KSC)
TD .... Telegraph Department
TD .... Telegraphist Detector [*British military*]   (DMA)
TD .... Telemetry Data
TD .... Telephone Department
TD .... Telephone Directory
T/D .... Temperature Datum   (NG)
TD .... Temperature Differential   (MSA)
TD .... Temporarily Discontinued [*Fog signal*]
TD .... Temporary Disability
TD .... Temporary Duty
TD .... Ter in Die [*Three Times a Day*] [*Pharmacy*]
TD .... Terminal Device [*of a prosthesis*]
TD .... Terminal Digit [*Telecommunications*]   (TEL)
TD .... Terminal Display   (BUR)
TD .... Terminal Distributor   (KSC)
T (for) D .... Termination for Default   (MCD)
TD .... Territorial Decoration [*Military*] [*British*]
TD .... Test Data
TD .... Test Design Specification   (IEEE)
TD .... Test Directive   (AAG)
TD .... Test Director
TD .... Test Distributor [*Telecommunications*]   (TEL)
TD .... Test Drawing   (MCD)
TD .... Testing and Development Division [*Coast Guard*]
TD .... Testing Device   (MSA)
TD .... Tetanus and Diphtheria [*Toxoids*] [*Medicine*]
Td .... Tetrahedral [*Molecular geometry*]
TD .... Theatre Documentation [*A publication*]
TD .... Theology Digest [*St. Mary's, KS*] [*A publication*]
TD .... Theoretical Density [*Nuclear energy*]   (NRCH)
TD .... Therapy [*or Treatment*] Discontinued [*Medicine*]
TD .... Thermal Desorption [*from surfaces*]
TD .... Thermodilution
TD .... Thioredoxin [*Also, TR, Trx*] [*Biochemistry*]
TD .... Third Defense [*Men's lacrosse position, until 1933*]
TD .... Thor-Delta [*Satellite*]
TD .... Thoracic Duct [*Anatomy*]
TD .... Thoria Dispersed [*Nickel*]
TD .... Threat Determination   (MCD)
TD .... Threshold Detection
TD .... Threshold Dose [*Medicine*]
TD .... Thymus Dependent [*Cells*] [*Hematology*]
TD .... Tied
TD .... Tilbury Docks   (ROG)
TD .... Tile Drain [*Technical drawings*]
TD .... Time Delay
TD .... Time of Departure
TD .... Time Deposit [*Banking*]
TD .... Time Difference [*or Differential*]
TD .... Timed Disintegration [*Pharmacy*]
TD .... Timing Device
TD .... Tinned
TD .... To Deliver [*Pipet calibration*]
TD .... Tod [*Unit of weight*]
TD .... Tolerance Detector
TD .... Tons per Day
TD .... Tool Design
TD .... Tool Disposition
TD .... Tool Drawing   (MCD)
TD .... Top Down
TD .... Topographic Draftsman [*Navy*]
TD .... Toronto Dominion Bank [*Toronto Stock Exchange symbol*] [*Vancouver Stock Exchange symbol*]
TD .... Torpedo Dive Bomber Aircraft
T and D ..... [*Jayne*] Torvill and [*Christopher*] Dean [*British ice dancers*]
TD .... Total Damage [*Meteorology*]
TD .... Total Denier [*Textile technology*]
TD .... Total Depth
TD .... Total Dictatorship

TD............	Total Disability [*Medicine*]
TD............	Total Dose [*of radiation*]
TD............	Touchdown [*Football*]
T/D..........	Touchdown [*NASA*] (NASA)
TD............	Track Data
TD............	Track Display
TD............	Track Dog [*Dog show term*]
TD............	Tractor-Drawn
TD............	Trade Dispute (OICC)
TD............	Trade Division [*British military*] (DMA)
TD............	Tradesman [*British military*]
TD............	TRADEVMAN [*Training Devices Man*] [*Navy rating*]
TD............	Traffic Decisions [*Interstate Commerce Commission*]
TD............	Traffic Department [*Scotland Yard*]
TD............	Traffic Director
TD............	Training Detachment
T & D........	Training and Detention (ADA)
TD............	Training Developments
TD............	Training Device (MCD)
TD............	Training of Documentalists
TD............	Trajectory Diagram [*Army*] (MCD)
TD............	Transfer Dolly [*Bottom-loading transfer cask*] [*Nuclear energy*] (NRCH)
TD............	Transform Domain
TD............	Transient Detector
T & D........	Transmission and Distribution
TD............	Transmit Data (IEEE)
T-D..........	Transmitter-Distributor
TD............	Transport Driver (NOAA)
TD............	Transportation Department
TD............	Transportation and Docking (MCD)
TD............	Transporte Aereo de Cargo SA [*Venezuela*] [*ICAO designator*] (FAAC)
T & D........	Transposition and Docking [*NASA*] (KSC)
TD............	Transverse Diameter [*Of heart*] [*Anatomy*]
TD............	Transverse Direction
TD............	Transverse Division [*Cytology*]
TD............	Treasury Decision [*In references to rulings*]
TD............	Treasury Department
TD............	Treatment Day
T/D..........	Treatment Discontinued [*Medicine*]
TD............	Trinidad and Tobago
TD............	Tropical Depression [*Meteorology*]
TD............	Tropical Deterioration Committee Reports [*of NDRC*] [*World War II*]
TD............	Truck Driving Program [*Association of Independent Colleges and Schools specialization code*]
TD............	True Depth [*Diamond drilling*]
TD............	Trust Deed
TD............	Tuberoinfundibular Dopaminergic [*Neurons*] [*Neurology*]
TD............	Tundra Drums [*A publication*]
TD............	Tunnel Diode
TD............	Turbine Direct
TD............	Turbine Drive [*or Driven*]
TD............	Turbodiesel [*Automotive engineering*]
TD............	Turntable Desk (DEN)
TD............	Tyne Division [*British military*] (DMA)
TD............	Typographic Draftsman [*Navy*]
TD1..........	TRADEVMAN [*Training Devices Man*], First Class [*Navy rating*]
TD2..........	TRADEVMAN [*Training Devices Man*], Second Class [*Navy rating*]
TD3..........	TRADEVMAN [*Training Devices Man*], Third Class [*Navy rating*]
TDA..........	American Train Dispatchers Association
TDA..........	[*The*] Disposables Association
TDA..........	Table of Distribution and Allowances [*Military*] (AABC)
TDA..........	Table of Distribution-Augmentation [*Military*]
TDA..........	Tactical Decision Aid
TDA..........	Tactical Development Agent [*Military*] (CAAL)
TDA..........	Target Docking Adapter [*NASA*] (KSC)
TDA..........	Tasmanian Development Authority [*Australia*]
TDA..........	Tax Deferred Annuity [*Insurance*]
TDA..........	Taxpayer Delinquent Account [*IRS*]
TDA..........	Technical Directing Agency
TDA..........	Telecommunications Dealers Association (EA)
TDA..........	Telemetric Data Analyzer
TDA..........	Test Development Activity [*Army*]
TDA..........	Test Development Agent (CAAL)
TDA..........	Tetradecenyl Acetate [*Organic chemistry*]
TDA..........	Textile Distributors Association (EA)
TDA..........	Thermal Depolarization Analysis
TDA..........	Thermodifferential Analysis
TDA..........	Time Delay Amplifier
TDA..........	Titanium Development Association (EA)
TDA..........	Today (FAAC)
TDA..........	Toll Dial Assistance [*Telecommunications*] (TEL)
TDA..........	Toluenediamine [*Organic chemistry*]
TDA..........	Torpedo Danger Area (NVT)
TDA..........	Total Dissolved Arsenic
TDA..........	Town Development Act [*Town planning*] [*British*]

T & DA	Tracking and Data Acquisition (CET)
TDA..........	Tracking and Data Acquisition
TDA..........	Tracking Data Analysis
TDA..........	Training Development Advisors (MCD)
TDA..........	Training and Development Alert [*Advanced Personnel Systems*] [*Information service or system*] (CRD)
TDA..........	Transport Distribution Analysis (DCTA)
TDA..........	Transportation Development Agency [*British*]
TDA..........	Trigger Distribution Amplifier [*Aviation*] (FAAC)
TDA..........	Tundra Gold Mines [*Vancouver Stock Exchange symbol*]
TDA..........	Tuning Device Assembly
TDA..........	Tunnel-Diode Amplifier
TDA..........	Tyrosine-D-Arginine [*Biochemistry*]
TDAA........	Airman Apprentice, TRADEVMAN [*Training Devices Man*], Striker [*Navy rating*]
TDA/AE......	Tracking and Data Acquisition/Advanced Engineering
TDaB	William Jennings Bryan University, Dayton, TN [*Library symbol*] [*Library of Congress*] (LCLS)
TDA Bull ...	Timber Development Association. Bulletin [*A publication*]
TDAC	Training Data and Analysis Center
TDAC	Tropical Deterioration Administrative Committee [*of NDRC*] [*World War II*]
TDAC	Tumor-Derived Activated Cell [*Oncology*]
TDAD	Trade Development Assistance Division [*Bureau of East-West Trade*] [*USSR*] (IMH)
TDAE	Tactics Development and Evaluation [*Military*] (MCD)
TDAE	Test Design and Evaluation (MCD)
TDAFP	Turbine-Driven Auxiliary Feed Pump [*Nuclear energy*] (NRCH)
TDAFWP ..	Turbine-Driven Auxiliary Feedwater Pump [*Nuclear energy*] (NRCH)
TDAIR.......	Taxpayer Delinquent Account Information Record [*IRS*]
TDAL	Tetradecenal [*Biochemistry*]
TDAMM	Training Device Acquisition Management Model (MCD)
TDAMTB ...	Tables of Distribution and Allowances Mobilization Troop Basis [*Army*] (AABC)
TDAN........	Airman, TRADEVMAN [*Training Devices Man*], Striker [*Navy rating*]
TDANA	Time-Domain Automatic Network Analyzer [*National Institute of Standards and Technology*]
TDARA	Threat Determination and Resource Allocation (MCD)
TDAS........	Thermal Decomposition Analytical System [*For study of incineration*]
TDAS........	Thermocouple Data Acquisition System
TDAS........	Thickness Data Acquisition System [*Southwest Research Institute*]
TDAS........	Tracking and Data Acquisition System
TDAS........	Traffic Data Administration System [*Bell System*]
TDAS........	Training Device Acquisition Strategy
TDAS........	Tunnel-Diode Amplifier System
TDAT	Teradata Corp. [*NASDAQ symbol*] (NQ)
TDAZA	Tautsaimnieciba Derigie Augi [*A publication*]
TDB	Temporary Disability Benefits [*Insurance*]
TDB	Terminological Data Bank
TDB	Terrestrial Dust Belt
TDB	Test Documentation Booklet [*Navy*] (CAAL)
TDB	Tetebedi [*Papua New Guinea*] [*Airport symbol*] (OAG)
TDB	Top Drawing Breakdown (AAG)
TDB	Total Disability Benefit (DLA)
TDB	Toxicology Data Bank [*National Library of Medicine*] [*Information service or system*] (IID)
TDB	Trade Development Bank [*Subsidiary of American Express Bank*]
TDB	Trade and Development Board [*United Nations Conference on Trade and Development*]
TDB	Transportable Database [*Telecommunications*]
TDB	Turbine-Driven Blower
TdbE	Tanna di-be Eliahu (BJA)
TDBG	Training Depot Brigade of Gurkhas [*British military*] (DMA)
TDBI.........	Training Directory for Business and Industry [*A publication*]
TDBMS....	Tactical Database Management System
TDBP........	Tris(dibromopropyl) Phosphate [*Also, TDBPP, Tris, Tris-BP*] [*Flame retardant, mutagen*]
TDBPP	Tris(dibromopropyl) Phosphate [*Also, TDBP, Tris, Tris-BP*] [*Flame retardant, mutagen*]
TDC	Chief TRADEVMAN [*Training Devices Man*] [*Navy rating*]
TDC	Dallas Christian College, Dallas, TX [*OCLC symbol*] (OCLC)
TDC	[*The*] Developing Child [*A publication*] (APTA)
TDC	[*The*] Discovery Channel [*Television*]
TDC	Tactical Data Converter
TDC	Tactical Digital Computer (MCD)
TDC	Tactical Document Copier (MCD)
TDC	Taiwan Defense Command (MCD)
TDC	Tank Destroyer Center [*Army*]
TDC	Target Data Collection
TDC	Tarif Douanier Commun [*Common Customs Tariff*]
TDC	Taurodeoxycholate [*or Taurodeoxycholic*] Acid [*Biochemistry*]
TDC	Technical Data Center [*Department of Labor*] [*Information service or system*] (IID)
TDC	Technical Development Center
TDC..........	Technical Development Contractor

TDC	Technical Directive Compliance (MCD)
TDC	Technical Document Center
TDC	Technical Document Change (MCD)
TDC	TEFLON Dielectric Capacitor
TDC	Teledyne Canada Ltd. [*Toronto Stock Exchange symbol*]
TDC	Temperature Density Computer
TDC	Temporary Detective Constable [*Scotland Yard*]
TDC	Terminal Data Corporation [*Information service or system*] (IID)
TDC	Termination Design Change
TDC	Test Director Console
TDC	Thermal Diffusion Chamber
TDC	Thermal Diffusion Coefficient [*Nuclear energy*] (NRCH)
TDC	Through Deck Cruisers [*British*]
TDC	Time Data Card (AAG)
TDC	Time Delay Closing
TDC	Time Distribution Card (AAG)
TDC	Time-Domain Coding
TDC	Tooling Design Change
TDC	Top Dead Center
TDC	Torpedo Data Computer [*Navy*] (NVT)
TDC	Total Design Concept [*Sarcastic reference to a completely coordinated wardrobe, decorating scheme, etc.*] [*Slang*]
TDC	Total Distributed Control [*Data processing*]
TDC	Track Data Central
TDC	Track Data Corporation [*Software firm*] [*Information service or system*] (IID)
TDC	Trade Development Council [*Australia*]
TDC	Training Device Center
T & DC	Training and Distribution Center [*Navy*]
TDC	Transferable Development Credit
TDC	Transportation Development Center [*Cambridge, MA*] [*Department of Transportation*] [*Formerly, NASA Electronic Research Center*]
TDC	Transportation Development Centre [*Transport Canada*] [*Research center*] (RCD)
TDC	Transportation Development Centre Library [*UTLAS symbol*]
TDC	Treasury Department Circular [*A publication*] (DLA)
TDC	Tridecylcyclohexane [*Organic chemistry*]
TDC	Trinidad [*Colorado*] [*Seismograph station code, US Geological Survey*] [*Closed*] (SEIS)
TDC	Tube Deflection Coil
TDC	Type Directors Club (EA)
TDCC	Tactical Data Communications Center
TDCC	Transportation Data Coordinating Committee [*Later, EDIA*]
TDCC/EDIA ...	TDCC [*Transportation Data Coordinating Committee*]: the Electronic Data Interchange Association [*Telecommunications service*] (TSSD)
TDCE	Technical Direction Contract Effort
TDCF	Technical Directive Compliance Form (NVT)
TDCK	Technisch Documentatie Centrum voor der Krijgsmacht [*Netherland Armed Services Technical Documentation and Information Center*] (MCD)
TDCM	Master Chief TRADEVMAN [*Training Devices Man*] [*Navy rating*]
TDCM	Transistor Driver Core Memory
TD/CMS	Technical Data/Configuration Management System (MCD)
TDCN	Technical Data Change Notice (MCD)
TDCN	Time Delay Compression Network
TDCO	Test Director Console Operator [*Navy*] (CAAL)
TDCO	Thermal Dilution Cardiac Output
TDCO	Torpedo Data Computer Operator [*Navy*]
TDCR	Teacher's Diploma of the College of Radiographers [*British*] (DBQ)
TDCR	Technical Data Change Request [*NASA*] (KSC)
TDCR	Technical Data Contract Requirement (MCD)
TDCR	Test Deficiency Change Request [*Nuclear energy*] (NRCH)
TDCS	Senior Chief TRADEVMAN [*Training Devices Man*] [*Navy rating*]
TDCS	Tape Data Control Sheet [*Data processing*]
TDCS	Target Detection-Conversion Sensor
TDCS	Time-Division Circuit Switching [*Telecommunications*]
TDCS	Traffic Data Collection System (MCD)
TDCSP	Tactical Defense Communications Satellite Program (MCD)
TDCT	Time-Domain Coding Technique
TDCT	Tunnel-Diode Charge Transformer
TDCTL	Tunnel-Diode Charge-Transformer Logic
TDCU	Target Data Control Unit (AAG)
TDCU	Target Designator Control Unit (MCD)
TDCU	Threat Display Control Unit (MCD)
TDCU	Tinned Copper
TDCX	Technology Development Corp. [*NASDAQ symbol*] (NQ)
TDD	Tactical Data Display
TDD	Target Detecting Device
TDD	Task Description Document (NASA)
TDD	Teardown Deficiency (MCD)
TDD	Technical Data Digest [*Air Force*]
TDD	Technical Documents Division [*Naval Air Systems Command*]
TDD	Telecommunications Device for the Deaf
TDD	Telemetry Data Digitizer
TDD	Telephone Device for the Deaf

TDD	Test Definition Document
TDD	Test Design Description [*Nuclear energy*] (NRCH)
TDD	Test Development Director
TDD	Tetradecadiene [*Organic chemistry*]
TDD	Thedford, NE [*Location identifier*] [*FAA*] (FAAL)
TDD	Thoracic Duct Drainage [*Medicine*]
TDD	Three D Departments, Inc. [*AMEX symbol*] (SPSG)
TDD	Treasury Department Decision (AFIT)
TDD	Trinidad [*Bolivia*] [*Airport symbol*] (OAG)
TDD	Tuberculous Diseases Diploma [*British*]
TDDA	Tetradecadienyl Acetate [*Biochemistry*]
TDDL	Time-Division Data Link [*Radio*]
TDDM	Time Division Digital Multiplexer (MCD)
TDDM	Training Device Development Management [*Model*] (MCD)
TDDO	Time Delay Dropout [*Relay*] (AAG)
TDDR	Technical Data Department Report [*NASA*] (KSC)
TDDR	Transdermal Drug Delivery Research
TDDRS	Total Dose/Dose Rate Simulator
TDDS	Tactical Data Display System (MCD)
TDDS	Teacher Development in Desegregating Schools [*Office of Education*]
TDDS	Television Data Display System (KSC)
TDE	Tactical Deception Element (NVT)
TDE	Tactics Development Evaluation (MCD)
TDE	Technical Data Engineer (MCD)
TDE	Technical Data Evaluation
TD & E	Test Design and Evaluation
TDE	Testing Difficulty Estimator
TDE	Tetrachlorodiphenylethane [*Also, DDD*] [*Insecticide*]
TDE	Toluene-Dioxane-Ethanol [*Scintillation solvent*]
TDE	Total Data Entry
TDE	Total Differential Equation
TDE	Total Digestible Energy [*Nutrition*]
TDE	Trans-Dominion Energy Corp. [*Toronto Stock Exchange symbol*]
TDE	Transdermal Estradiol [*Pharmacology*]
TD & E	Transposition, Docking, and Ejection [*NASA*] (KSC)
TDE	Triethylene Glycol Diglycidyl Ether [*Medicine*]
TDE	Two-Dimensional Equilibrium
TDEC	Technical Development Evaluation Center
TDEC	Technical Division and Engineering Center [*FAA*] (MCD)
TDEC	Telephone Line Digital Error Checking
TDECC	Tactical Display Engagement Control Console [*Military*] (RDA)
TDED	Istanbul Universitesi Edegiyat Fakultesi Turk Dili ve Edebiyati Dergisi [*A publication*]
TDED	Trade Data Elements Directory (DS)
TDEFWP ..	Turbine-Driven Emergency Feedwater Pump [*Nuclear energy*] (NRCH)
TDEL	Time Delay (FAAC)
TDEN	Total Density [*Ecology*]
TDEP	Tracking Data Editing Program [*NASA*]
TDES	[*The*] Duke Ellington Society (EA)
TDF	Tactical Digital Facsimile (MCD)
TDF	Tape Data Family
TDF	Target Development Facility [*Proposed, 1986, for fusion research*]
TDF	Task Deletion Form [*Nuclear energy*] (NRCH)
TDF	Telediffusion de France [*Broadcasting agency*] [*French*]
TDF	Temporary Detention Facility
TDF	Testis-Determining Factor [*Genetics*]
TDF	Theatre Development Fund (EA)
TDF	Thin Dielectric Film
TDF	Time-Domain Filter
TDF	Time Dose Fractionation Factor [*Roentgenology*]
TDF	Tonga Defence Force [*British military*] (DMA)
TDF	Training Directors' Forum [*An association*] (EA)
TDF	Transborder Data Flows [*Also, TBDF*] [*Telecommunications*]
TDF	Trial-Dependent-Forgetting [*Process*] [*Psychology*]
TDF	Trim and Drill Fixture (MCD)
TDF	Trunk Distribution Frame (DEN)
TDF	Two Degrees of Freedom
TDFC	Thomas Dolby Fan Club (EA)
TDFCHB ..	Telemetry Data Format Control Handbook (KSC)
TDFS	Terminal Digit Fitting System [*Military*] (AABC)
TDG	Tactical Development Group [*Military*] (CAAL)
TDG	Tactical Drone Group (MCD)
TD & G	Tall, Dark, and Gruesome [*Slang*]
TDG	Talladega, AL [*Location identifier*] [*FAA*] (FAAL)
TDG	Tandag [*Philippines*] [*Airport symbol*] (OAG)
TDG	Technical Design Guide
TDG	Technical Developing Group [*of the Publishers' Association*] [*British*]
TDG	Telemetry Data Generation
TDG	Test Data Generator (BUR)
TDG	Test Display Generator
TDG	Test Documentation Group
TDG	Tetradecanylglutarate [*Biochemistry*]
TDG	Textile Designers Guild (EA)
TDG	Thio(deaza)guanine [*Antineoplastic drug*]
TDG	Thiodigalactoside [*Organic chemistry*]

TDG..........	Time Delay Generator
TDG..........	Timesharer Developers' Group [British]
TDG..........	Toodoggone Gold [Vancouver Stock Exchange symbol]
TDG..........	Top-Down Greedy
TDG..........	TOTAL Energold Corp. [Toronto Stock Exchange symbol]
TDG..........	Trading (DCTA)
TDG..........	Transport Development Group PLC [British]
TDG..........	Transportation of Dangerous Goods [International symposium]
TDG..........	Twist Drill Gauge
TD & GS....	Technical Documentation and Graphic Services
TDGS.......	Test Data Generation Section [Social Security Administration]
TD & H......	Tall, Dark, and Handsome [Slang]
TDH..........	Terre des Hommes [An international organization]
TDH..........	Total Dynamic Head (AAG)
TDH..........	Tracking Data Handling
TDH..........	Transport Disengaging Height [Fluidized beds of particles]
TDHGA.....	Travel of Dependents and Household Goods Authorized [Military] (AABC)
TDHL.......	Transdihydrolisuride [Biochemistry]
TDHS.......	Tape Data Handling System
TDHYA.....	Tohoku Daigaku Hisuiyoeki Kagaku Kenkyusho Hokoku [A publication]
TDI	[The] Democracy International (EA)
TDI	TACAN [Tactical Air Navigation] Distance Indicator
TDI	Target Data Inventory [Military] (AFM)
TDI	Target Doppler Indicator [RADAR]
TDI	Task Description Item (MCD)
TDI	Taxpayer Delinquent Investigation [IRS]
TDI	Teardown Inspection
TDI	Technical Data International [Information service or system] (IID)
TDI	Technology Dynamics Institute [Telecommunications service] (TSSD)
TDI	Telecommunications Data Interface
TDI	Telecommunications for the Deaf, Incorporated (EA)
TDI	Telegraphist Detector Instructor [British military] (DMA)
TDI	Teletec Development, Incorporated [Vancouver Stock Exchange symbol]
TDI	Temporary Disability Insurance [Unemployment]
TDI	Test Data Interpolation
TDI	Textile Dye Institute [Later, American Dye Manufacturers Institute]
TDI	Therapeutic Donor Insemination [Obstetrics]
TDI	Therapy Dogs International (EA)
TDI	Time Delay and Integration (MCD)
TDI	Toluene [or Tolylene] Diisocyanate [Organic chemistry]
TDI	Tool and Die Institute (KSC)
T & DI......	Tool and Die Institute (EA)
TDI	Total Domestic Incomes [Department of Employment] [British]
TDI	Trade Data Interchange (DS)
TDI	Training Developments Institute [Army]
TDI	TSH [Thyroid-Stimulating Hormone] Displacing Immunoglobulin [Endocrinology]
TDI	Turbine Disk Integrity [Nuclear energy] (NRCH)
TDI	Twin Disc, Inc. [NYSE symbol] (SPSG)
TDI	Tymnet DTS, Incorporated [San Jose, CA] [Telecommunications] (TSSD)
TDIC.........	Target Data Input Computer
TDIC.........	Total Dissolved Inorganic Carbon [Environmental chemistry]
TDIL.........	Target Detection, Identification, and Location
TDINF......	Taxpayer Delinquency Investigation Notice File [IRS]
TDIO........	Timing Data Input-Output
TDIP.........	Total Disability Income Provisions [Military] (AABC)
TDIPR......	Test Design In-Process Review (MCD)
TDIS.........	Technical Data Impact Summary (MCD)
TDIS.........	Terminal Data Input System (MCD)
TDIS.........	Thai Development Information Service (EAIO)
TDIS.........	Time Distance [Military] (AABC)
TDIS.........	Training Development Information System [Army]
TDIS.........	Travel Document and Issuance System [US passport] [Department of State]
TDISTR....	Tape Distributor (MSA)
TDIU	Target Data Input Unit
TDJ..........	Dallas County Community College District, Dallas, TX [OCLC symbol] (OCLC)
TDJ..........	Tadjoura [Djibouti] [Airport symbol] (OAG)
TDJ..........	Tadjoura [Djibouti] [Seismograph station code, US Geological Survey] (SEIS)
TDJ..........	Training and Development Journal [A publication]
TDJC........	Technical Data Justification Code [Army]
TDJKA.....	Tokyo Daigaku Jishin Kenkyusho Iho [A publication]
TDK..........	TDK Corp. [NYSE symbol] (SPSG)
TDK..........	Test of Diabetes Knowledge
TDK..........	Tokyo Denki Kagaku [Tokyo Electronics and Chemical Co.] [Initialism is now name of recording tape manufacturer and brand name of its products]
TDK..........	Toyo Daigaku Kiyo [Bulletin. Department of Liberal Arts. Tokyo University] [A publication]

TDKF........	Fahrzeugtestdatenbank [Dokumentation Kraftfahwesen eV] [Federal Republic of Germany] [Information service or system] (CRD)
TDKIB.......	Tokai Daigaku Kiyo Kogakubu [A publication]
TDKNAF...	Annual Report. Takeda Research Laboratories [A publication]
TDKP........	Turkish Revolutionary Communist Party [Political party] (PD)
TDL	David Lipscomb College, Nashville, TN [OCLC symbol] (OCLC)
TDL	Tactical Data Link
TDL	Tandil [Argentina] [Airport symbol] (OAG)
TDL	Tapped Delay Line
TDL	Target Development Laboratory [Eglin AFB] (AAG)
TDL	Task-Directed Learning
TDL	Technical Data Laboratory [National Weather Service]
TDL	Technical Document List
TDL	Test Description Log (MCD)
TDL	Test and Diagnostic Language (MCD)
TDL	Thoracic Duct Lymphocyte [Immunochemistry]
TDL	Threshold Damage Level
TDL	Threshold Detection Level
TDL	Thymus-Dependent Lymphocyte [Hematology]
TDL	Topographic Developments Laboratory [Fort Belvoir, VA] [United States Army Engineer Topographic Laboratories] (GRD)
TDL	Transaction Definition Language
TDL	Transformation Definition Language [Data processing] (IBMDP)
TDL	Translation Definition Language
TDL	Tunable Diode LASER [Also, SDL]
TDL	Tunnel-Diode Logic
TDLAS......	Tunable Diode LASER Absorption Spectrometry
TDLBAI	Deutsche Akademie der Landwirtschaftwissenschaften zu Berlin. Tagungsberichte [A publication]
TDLCA.....	Thoracic Duct Lining Cells Antigen [Immunology]
TDLOA	Training Device Letter of Agreement
TDLR........	Terminal Descent and Landing RADAR
TDLR........	Training Device Letter Requirement [Military]
TDLS........	Topographic Data Library System
TDLU	Terminal Duct Lobular Unit [Of mammary gland]
TDM..........	Mount Alvernia Friary, Wappingers Falls, NY [OCLC symbol] [Inactive] (OCLC)
TDM..........	Tandem (AAG)
TDM..........	Tandem Computers, Inc. [NYSE symbol] (SPSG)
TDM..........	Tandem Resources [Vancouver Stock Exchange symbol]
TDM..........	Tank Destroyer Armed with Missiles (INF)
TDM..........	Task Description Memo (MCD)
TDM..........	Technical Division Manager
TDM..........	Telecommunications Data-Link Monitor (CET)
TDM..........	Telemetric Data Monitor
TDM..........	Template Descriptor Memory
TDM..........	Ternary Delta Modulation
TDM..........	Test Data Memorandum (AAG)
TDM..........	Test Development Manager [Military] (CAAL)
TDM..........	Therapeutic Drug Monitoring
TDM..........	Thermal Development Model
TDM..........	Thermal Diffusion Method
TDM..........	Thermodynamic Molding
TDM..........	Time-Division Multiplexing [Telecommunications]
TDM..........	Time Duration Modulation (DEN)
TDM..........	Tire Degradation Monitor (MCD)
TDM..........	Tool Design Manual (MCD)
TDM..........	Torpedo Detection Modification [SONAR]
TDM..........	Total Dissolvable Manganese [Chemistry]
TDM..........	Trehalose Dimycolate [Biochemistry]
TDM..........	Trouble Detection and Monitoring
TDM..........	Tunnel-Diode Mixer
TDMA.......	Tape Direct Memory Access
TDMA.......	Time-Division [or Time-Domain] Multiple Access [Computer control system]
TDMA.......	Trophy Dealers and Manufacturers Association (EA)
TDMAC....	Tridodecylmethylammonium Chloride [Organic chemistry]
TDMC.......	Technical Data Management Center [Department of Energy] [Information service or system] [Defunct] (IID)
TDMD......	Time-Division Multiplex Device [Radio]
TDME......	Test, Diagnostic, and Measurement Equipment (MCD)
TDMG......	Telegraph and Data Message Generator (MCD)
TDMM......	International Union of Tool, Die, and Mold Makers
TDMO......	Technical Data Management Office [Navy]
TDMOD....	Therapeutic Drug Monitoring [A publication]
TDMP......	Technical Data Management Program [Navy]
TDMR......	Technical Division Memo Report [Army] [World War II]
TDMRA.....	Texas Delaine-Merino Record Association [Later, TDSA] (EA)
TDMS.......	Telegraph Distortion Measuring System
TDMS.......	Telemetry Data Monitor Set
TDMS.......	Thermal Desorption Mass Spectroscopy
TDMS.......	Time-Division Multiplex System [Radio] (MCD)
TDMS.......	Time-Shared/Data Management System
TDMS.......	Transmission Distortion Measuring Set
TDMTB.....	Tables of Distribution Mobilization Troop Basis [Army] (AABC)

TDM-VDMA ... Time-Division Multiplex - Variable Destination Multiple Access [*Telecommunications*]   (TEL)
TDN........... Target Doppler Nullifier [*RADAR*]
TDN........... Tendances de la Conjoncture. Graphiques Mensuels [*A publication*]
TdN........... Tijdschrift der Notarissen [*A publication*]
TDN........... Total Digestible Nutrients
TDN........... Touchdown [*Aviation*]   (FAAC)
TDN........... Travel as Directed Is Necessary in the Military Service   (MUGU)
T-DNA....... Transfer-Deoxyribonucleic Acid
TDNCA ..... Texas Date Nail Collectors Association   (EA)
TDNLA ..... Trudy Universiteta Druzhby Narodov [*A publication*]
TDNN .... Time Delay Neural Network [*Data processing*]
TDNS .... Total Data Network System   (TEL)
TDNT .... Theological Dictionary of the New Testament [*A publication*]   (BJA)
TDO........... Technical Development Objective
TDO........... Technical Directives Ordnance   (NG)
TDO........... Technical Divisions Office [*Jet Propulsion Laboratory, NASA*]
TDO........... Telegraph Delivery Order
TDO........... Time Delay Opening
TDO........... Toledo, WA [*Location identifier*] [*FAA*]   (FAAL)
TDO........... Tornado
TDO........... Training Development Office [*Army*]
TDO........... Training Development Officer [*British*]
TDO........... Treasury Department Order [*A publication*]   (DLA)
TDO........... Tuesday Downtown Operators and Observers [*An association*]   (EA)
TDOA....... Time Delay of Arrival   (MCD)
TDOA....... Time Deposit, Open Account [*Banking*]
TDOA....... Time Difference of Arrrival
TDOA/DD ... Time Difference of Arrival and Differential Doppler   (MCD)
TDOD....... Training and Development Organizations Directory [*A publication*]
TDOL........ Tetradecanol [*Organic chemistry*]
TDOP .... Time Dilution of Precision
TDOP .... Truck Design Optimization Project [*Railroads*]
TDOS .... Tape Disk Operating System [*Data processing*]
TDOT .... Thorndike Dimensions of Temperament [*Psychology*]
TDP .... Tank Development Program [*Military*]
TDP .... Target Data Processor   (NVT)
TDP .... Target Director Post [*RADAR*] [*Military*]
TDP .... Technical Data Package [*Military*]
TDP .... Technical Development Plan
TDP .... Technical Documentation for Provisioning [*Military*]   (AFIT)
TDP .... Teledata Processing
TDP .... Temperature Density Plotter
TDP .... Temperature and Dew Point   (KSC)
TDP .... Temporary Detention of Pay
TDP .... Test Design Plan [*Army*]
TDP .... Thermal Death-Point
TDP .... Thermistor Detector Package
TDP .... Thiamine Diphosphate [*Also, DPT, TPP*] [*Biochemistry*]
TDP .... Thiodiphenol [*Organic chemistry*]
TDP .... Thymidine Diphosphate [*Biochemistry*]
TDP .... Toluene Disproportionation Process [*Organic chemistry*]
TDP .... Total Development Plan
TDP .... Touchdown Protection [*Military*]   (MCD)
TDP .... Tracking Data Processor
TDP .... Tracking and Display Processor   (CAAL)
TDP .... Trade and Development Program [*US International Development Cooperation Agency*]
TDP .... Traffic Data Processing
TDP .... Traffic Demand Predictor [*Aviation*]
TDP .... Trainee Discharge Program [*Army*]
TDP .... Trim and Drain Pump [*Navy*]   (CAAL)
TDPA .... Textile Data Processing Association [*Later, ATMI*]   (EA)
TDPA .... Thiodipropionic Acid [*Organic chemistry*]
TDPAC...... Time Differential Perturbed Angular Correlation [*Physics*]
TDPB....... Tactical Display Plotting Board
TDPD .... Dominica/Melville Hall [*Dominica*] [*ICAO location identifier*]   (ICLI)
TDPF........ Tail Damping Power Factor [*Aviation*]
TDPFO...... Temporary Duty Pending Further Orders [*Military*]
TDPJ........ Truck Discharge Point Jet   (NATG)
TDPL........ Technical Data Package List [*Military*]   (AABC)
TDPL........ Top-Down Parsing Language
TDPM .... Truck Discharge Point Mogas   (NATG)
TDPP........ Traffic Data Processing Program   (MCD)
TDPR....... Roseau [*Dominica*] [*ICAO location identifier*]   (ICLI)
TDPRha .... Thymidine Diphosphorhamnose [*Biochemistry*]
TDPS........ Tracking Data Processor System   (MCD)
TDPSK....... Time Differential Phase-Shift Keying
TDPU....... Telemetry Data Processing Unit   (CAAL)
TDQP....... Trimethyldihydroquinoline Polymer [*Organic chemistry*]
TDR .... Drama Review [*Formerly, Tulane Drama Review*] [*A publication*]
TDR .... Tail Damping Ratio [*Aviation*]
TDR .... Talos Discrepancy Report   (MCD)
TDR .... Tape Data Register

TDR .... Target Detection and Recognition   (MCD)
TDR .... Target Discrimination RADAR   (IEEE)
TDR .... Teardown Deficiency Report
TDR .... Technical Data Relay   (IEEE)
TDR .... Technical Data Report
TDR .... Technical Data Requests
TDR .... Technical Deficiency Report
TDR .... Technical Design Review   (NASA)
TDR .... Technical Development Requirement
TDR .... Technical Directive Records   (NG)
TDR .... Technical Documentary Report
TDR .... Technology Review [*A publication*]
TDR .... Temperature-Dependent Resistor   (BYTE)
TDR .... Temperature Depth Recorder
TDR .... Temporarily Disconnected at Subscriber's Request [*Telecommunications*]   (TEL)
TDR .... Tender [*Navy*]   (NVT)
TDR .... Terminal Digit Requested [*Telecommunications*]   (TEL)
TDR .... Test Data Recorder
TDR .... Test Data Report   (AAG)
TDR .... Test Deficiency Report [*Nuclear energy*]   (NRCH)
TD/R .... Test Disable/Reset   (AAG)
TDR .... Test Discount Rate
TDR .... Test Discrepancy Report   (MCD)
TDR .... Thailand Development Report [*Bangkok*] [*A publication*]
TDR .... Threat Detection RADAR [*Military*]   (CAAL)
TDR .... Time Delay Relay
TDR .... Time-Domain Reflectometry
TDR .... Todoroki [*Japan*] [*Seismograph station code, US Geological Survey*] [*Closed*]   (SEIS)
TDR .... Tone Dial Receiver
TDR .... Tool Design Request   (KSC)
TDR .... Torque-Differential Receiver   (MUGU)
TDR .... Total Defect Rate
TDR .... Track Data Request   (CAAL)
TDR .... Tracking and Data Relay [*NASA*]
TDR .... Training Device Requirement [*Army*]   (AABC)
TDR .... Transferable Development Rights [*Community planning*]
TDR .... Transistorized Digital Readout
TDR .... Transmit Data Register [*Data processing*]   (MDG)
TDR .... Transnational Data and Communicative Report [*A publication*]   (TSSD)
TDR .... Trap Designator Register
TDR .... Treasury Deposit Receipt
TDR .... Triplet-Doublet Resonance [*Physics*]
TDR .... Tropical Disease Research [*WHO*]
TDR .... Tudor Corp. Ltd. [*Toronto Stock Exchange symbol*]
TD & RA ... Threat Determination and Resource Allocation
TDRC .... Total Diet Research Center [*Public Health Service*]   (GRD)
TDRCAH .. Contributions. Institute of Geology and Paleontology. Tohoku University [*A publication*]
TDRE .... Tracking and Data Relay Experiment [*Telecommunications*]   (TEL)
TDRF .... Target Doppler Reference Frequency
TDRI......... Tropical Development and Research Institute [*United Kingdom*] [*Research center*]   (IRC)
TDRL......... Temporary Disability Retired List [*Military*]
TDRL......... Tudor Corp. Ltd. [*NASDAQ symbol*]   (NQ)
T/DRLY ... Time Delay Relay
TDRM .... Time-Domain Reflectometry Microcomputer
TDRR .... Test Data Recording and Retrieval   (NASA)
TDRRB ...... Technical Data Requirement Review Board
TDRRC..... Training Device Requirements Review Committee [*Army*]
TDRS........ Technical Data Requirements Sheet
TDRS........ Telemetering Data Recording Set   (CAAL)
TDRS........ Telemetry Downlist Receiving Site   (NASA)
TDRS........ Tracking and Data Relay Satellite [*NASA*]
TDRS........ Traffic Data Recording System [*Bell System*]
TDRS........ Transnational Data Reporting Service, Inc. [*Springfield, VA*] [*Telecommunications service*]   (TSSD)
TDRSS ...... Tracking and Data Relay Satellite Services [*or System*] [*NASA*]
TDRTC..... Tank Destroyer Replacement Training Center
TDS .... 3-D Systems [*Vancouver Stock Exchange symbol*]
TDS .... Tactical Data System
TDS .... Tactical Display System   (CAAL)
TDS .... Tape Data Selector
TDS .... Tape Decal System
TDS .... Target Data Sheet   (MCD)
TDS .... Target Designation System [*Navy*]
TDS .... Technical Data Specialist
TDS .... Technical Data System   (KSC)
TDS .... Technical Database Services, Inc. [*Information service or system*]   (IID)
TDS .... Technical Description Sheet
TDS .... Technical Directive System   (MCD)
TDS .... Technology Demonstration Satellite [*NASA*]   (NASA)
TDS .... Teleflora Delivery Service   (EA)
TDS .... Telemetry Decommutation System
TDS .... Telephone & Data Systems, Inc. [*AMEX symbol*]   (SPSG)
TDS .... Temperature-Depth-Salinity [*Oceanography*]
TDS .... Temporary Duty Station [*Air Force*]   (AFM)

TDS	Ter in Die Sumendum [*To Be Taken Three Times a Day*] [*Pharmacy*]
TDS	Test Data Sheet (KSC)
TDS	Test Data System (NASA)
TDS	Thermal Degradation Sample [*Apollo*]
TDS	Thermal Desorption Spectroscopy
TDS	Time Delay Switch
TDS	Time, Distance, Speed
TDS	Time Distribution System (MCD)
TDS	Time-Division Switching [*Telecommunications*]
TDS	Time-Domain Spectroscopy (IEEE)
TDS	Tool Data Sheet (MCD)
TDS	Tool Design Service (MCD)
TDS	Tool Design Study (MCD)
TDS	Torpedo Deflection Sight
TDS	Torpedo Destruction System
TDS	Total Dissolved Solids
TDS	Track Data Simulator
TDS	Track Data Storage
TDS	Tracking and Data System [*NASA*]
T & DS......	Tracking and Data System [*NASA*]
TDS	Training Depot Station [*British military*] (DMA)
TDS	Training Developments Study
TDS	Training Directors Seminar [*LIMRA*]
TDS	[*Annual*] Training Duty Status [*Navy Reserve*]
TDS	Transaction Distribution System
TDS	Transaction Driven System [*Honeywell, Inc.*]
TDS	Transistor Display and Data-Handling System [*Data processing*] (MDG)
TDS	Translation and Docking Simulator [*Navy*] (KSC)
TDS	Trap Designator Set
TDS	Trash Disposal System
TDS	Traverse des Sioux Library System, Mankato MN [*OCLC symbol*] (OCLC)
TDS	[*US*] Treasury Daily Statement
TDS	Tunnel Destruct System
TDSA.......	Technical Data Status Accounting (MCD)
TDSA........	Telegraph and Data Signals Analyzer (MCD)
TD & SA....	Telephone, Data, and Special Audio (NASA)
TDSA........	Texas Delaine Sheep Association (EA)
TDSA.........	TRADEVMAN [*Training Devices Man*], Seaman Apprentice [*Navy rating*]
TDSC........	Tesdata Systems Corporation [*NASDAQ symbol*] (NQ)
TDSCC......	Tidbinbilla Deep Space Communications Complex
TDSDT......	Tactical Data System Development Testbed
TDSIC.......	Theatre/Drama, and Speech Information Center (IID)
TDSKB......	Reports. Research Institute for Strength and Fracture of Materials. Tohoku University [*A publication*]
TDSMO	Tactical Data Systems Management Office [*Army*] [*Fort Leavenworth*] (MCD)
TDSN	TRADEVMAN [*Training Devices Man*], Seaman [*Navy rating*]
TDSP........	Technical Data Support Package [*Navy*]
TDSQB......	Time Delay Squib [*Navy*]
TDSS	3-D Systems, Inc. [*NASDAQ symbol*] (NQ)
TDST........	Track Data Storage (MSA)
TDT	Tactical Data Terminal (MCD)
TDT	Target Designation Transmitter
TDT	Target Docking Trainer [*NASA*] (KSC)
TDT	Tavil-Dara [*USSR*] [*Seismograph station code, US Geological Survey*] [*Closed*] (SEIS)
TDT	Terminal Deoxynucleotidyl Transferase [*An enzyme*]
TDT	Test Direction Team
TDT	Test Dwell Time
TDT	Thermal Death Time [*Bacteriological testing*]
TDT	Thiodiethanethiol [*Organic chemistry*]
TDT	This Day Tonight (ADA)
TDT	Tidioute, PA [*Location identifier*] [*FAA*] (FAAL)
TDT	Tone Decay Test [*Audiometry*]
TDT	Toronto Dance Theatre
TDT	Total Delay Time
TDT	Translation and Docking Trainer
TDT	Transonic Dynamic Tunnel [*NASA*]
TDT	Tunnel-Diode Transducer
TDT	Turret Director Trainer [*British military*] (DMA)
TDTB........	Turk Dis Ticaret Bankasi [*Turkish Foreign Trade Bank*]
TDT and CU ...	Target Designation Transmitter and Control Unit
TD/TDNA ...	Tardive Dyskinesia/Tardive Dystonia National Association (EA)
TDT/FC	Tank Destroyer Tactical and Firing Center
TDTG	True Date-Time Group [*Military*]
TDTL........	Tunnel-Diode Transistor Logic
TDTS	Tactical Data Transfer System (NATG)
TDU	Tactical Deception Unit (NVT)
TDU	Tactical Display Unit (NVT)
TDU	Target Detection Unit
TDU	Teamsters for a Democratic Union (EA)
TDU	Threat Display Unit (MCD)
TDU	Time Display Unit (NASA)
TDU	Tondu [*British depot code*]
TDU	Towed Unit [*Aerial Target*] (CAAL)
TDU	Tracking Display Unit
TDU...........	Trigger Delay Unit
TDU...........	Tropendienstunfaehig [*Unfit for service in tropics*] [*German military - World War II*]
TDUKA	Tokyo Daigaku Uchu Koku Kenkyusho Hokoku [*A publication*]
TDUM.......	Tape Dump and Utility Monitor [*Data processing*]
TDUP	Technical Data Usage Program
TDV	Technology Development Vehicle (IEEE)
TDV	Terminal Delivered Vehicle [*Army*]
TDV	Test Data Van (NASA)
TDV	Touchdown Velocity [*Aviation*]
TDV	Tumbleweed Diagnostic Vehicle
TDVA	37th Division Veterans Association (EA)
TDW	Amarillo, TX [*Location identifier*] [*FAA*] (FAAL)
TDW	Tidewater, Inc. [*NYSE symbol*] (SPSG)
TDW	Tons Deadweight (DS)
TDW	Trunk Destination Words (CET)
TDWO	Test and Development Work Order
TDWT	Transonic Dynamic Wind Tunnel [*NASA*] (KSC)
TDWU.......	Transport and Dock Workers' Union [*India*]
TDX	Thermal Demand Transmitter (MSA)
TDX	Time-Division Exchange
TDX	Torque-Differential Transmitter (MUGU)
TDX	Transportation Data Xchange, Inc. (EISS)
TDX	Tridex Corp. [*AMEX symbol*] (SPSG)
TDY	Teledyne, Inc. [*NYSE symbol*] (SPSG)
TDY	Temporary Duty
TDY	Trading Bay, AK [*Location identifier*] [*FAA*] (FAAL)
TDYKA	Tokushima Daigaku Yakugaku Kenkyu Nempo [*A publication*]
TDYKA8 ...	Annual Reports. Faculty of Pharmaceutical Sciences. Tokushima University [*A publication*]
TDYN	Thermodynetics, Inc. [*NASDAQ symbol*] (NQ)
TDZ	Thioridazine [*Tranquilizer*]
TDZ	Toledo, OH [*Location identifier*] [*FAA*] (FAAL)
TDZ	Torpedo Danger Zone (NVT)
TDZ	Touchdown Zone [*Aviation*] (FAAC)
TDZ	Trade Development Zone (ADA)
TDZ	Transcontinental Dislocation Zone [*Geology*]
TDZ	Tridel Enterprises, Inc. [*Toronto Stock Exchange symbol*]
TDZL........	Touchdown Zone Lights [*Aviation*] (FAAC)
TE	Air New Zealand Ltd. [*International*] [*New Zealand*] [*ICAO designator*] (FAAC)
TE	[*The*] Engelettes [*An association*] (EA)
TE	Journal of Transportation Engineering [*A publication*]
TE	Light Temporarily Extinguished [*Navigation*]
TE	Ling-Temco-Vought [*LTV*] [*ICAO aircraft manufacturer identifier*] (ICAO)
TE	Table of Equipment [*Army*]
T/E.............	Tactical Emergency [*Army*]
TE	Tageseinfluesse [*Weather factors, a gunnery term*] [*German military - World War II*]
TE	Talmudic Encyclopedia [*A publication*] (BJA)
TE	Tamper Evident
TE	Tangent Elevation (MSA)
TE	Task Element
TE	Tatin Experimental [*British military*] (DMA)
TE	Teacher Education [*A publication*]
TE	Teacher of Electrotherapy [*British*]
Te	Teatr [*Moscow*] [*A publication*]
TE	Technical Engineer
TE	Technical Evaluation [*Army*]
TE	Technical Exchange
TE	Technician [*Communications*] [*Navy rating*]
TE	Technological Engineer [*A publication*]
TE	TECO Energy, Inc. [*NYSE symbol*] (SPSG)
TE	Tele-Engineering Corp. [*Telecommunications service*] (TSSD)
TE	Telecom Eireann [*Dublin, Ireland*] [*Telecommunications service*] (TSSD)
TE	Telegram
TE	Teleman [*Navy rating*] [*British*]
TE	Teller of the Exchequer [*British*] (ROG)
Te	Tellurium [*Chemical element*]
TE	Temperature Element [*Nuclear energy*] (NRCH)
Te	Tempo [*A publication*]
TE	Tenants by the Entirety [*Legal term*]
TE	Tension Equalizer [*Electrical*] Wave
TE	Teologia Espiritual [*A publication*]
TE	Terminal Equipment
TE	Terminal Exchange (MCD)
TE	Tertiary Entrance (ADA)
TE	Test and Engineering (MCD)
TE	Test Equipment
T & E..........	Test and Evaluation [*Navy*] (NG)
TE	Test Exception [*Nuclear energy*] (NRCH)
TE	Test Explicit
TE	Tetlit Tribune [*Fort McPherson*] [*A publication*]
TE	Tetracycline [*Antibiotic compound*]
TE	Text Editor [*Data processing*]
TE	Theatre in Education (EA)
TE	Theistic Evolutionist
TE	Theological Educator [*A publication*]

TE	Theological Examination
TE	Thermactor Emission [*Automotive engineering*]
TE	Thermal Efficiency
TE	Thermal Element (KSC)
TE	Thermal Expansion Load [*Nuclear energy*] (NRCH)
TE	Thermoelectric
TE	Threat Evaluation (NVT)
TE	Thromboembolic [*Medicine*]
TE	Throughput Efficiency (CAAL)
TE	Thunder Engines Corp. [*Vancouver Stock Exchange symbol*]
TE	Tiger's Eye [*A publication*]
TE	Tight End [*Football*]
Te	Tigre (BJA)
TE	Time Earliest/Expected (NASA)
TE	Time to Echo [*Medicine*]
TE	Time Error in Psychophysical Judgments [*Psychology*]
T & E	Time and Events (AAG)
T/E	Time Expired (ADA)
TE	Timing Electronics (KSC)
TE	Tocopherol Equivalent [*Nutrition*]
TE	Today's Education [*A publication*]
TE	Toluene-Ethanol [*Scintillation solvent*]
TE	Topographical Engineer
TE	Tornisterempfaenger [*Pack-type portable receiver*] [*German military - World War II*]
TE	Total Expenditure
TE	Totally Enclosed (MSA)
TE	Tracheary Element [*Botany*]
TE	Tracheoesophageal [*Also, TOE*] [*Medicine*]
TE	Tracking Enhancement (MCD)
TE	Traction Engine [*British*]
TE	Trade Expenses [*Business term*]
TE	Trailing Edge [*Aviation*]
T & E	Training and Education
TE	Training Equipment
TE	Training Establishment [*British military*] (DMA)
TE	Training and Evaluation (OICC)
TE	Trajectory Engineer
TE	Transequatorial [*Scatter*]
TE	Transient Eddy
TE	Transient Event [*Nuclear energy*] (NRCH)
TE	Transitional Engineering (MCD)
TE	Transport Empty
TE	Transportation Engineer Magazine [*A publication*] (EAAP)
T/E	Transporter-Erector [*NASA*] (KSC)
TE	Transposable Element [*Genetics*]
TE	Transverse Electric [*or Electrostatic*] [*Wave propagation mode*]
TE	Travaux. Musee d'Etat de l'Ermitage [*A publication*]
T & E	Travel and Entertainment [*IRS*]
T & E	Traverse and Elevation [*Weapons*] [*Army*] (INF)
TE	Trial and Error
TE	Triple Expansion (DS)
TE	Tuning Eye
TE	Turbine Electric Drive
TE	Twin Engine
TE	Type Equipment (MCD)
TE2	That's Entertainment, Part 2 [*Initialism is shortened form of movie title*]
TEA	T Early Alpha [*Genetics*]
TEA	Task Equipment Analysis
TEA	Tasman Empire Airways Ltd. [*Aerospace*]
Tea	Tea Boards of Kenya, Uganda, and Tanganyika. Journal [*A publication*]
TEA	Tea and Coffee Trade Journal [*A publication*]
TEA	Technical Engineers Association (EA)
TEA	Technical Exchange Agreement
TEA	Tegra Enterprises, Inc. [*Vancouver Stock Exchange symbol*]
TEA	Temporary Employment Assistance
TEA	Tensile Energy Absorption [*Physics*]
TEA	Territory Enterprise Award [*Northern Territory, Australia*]
TEA	Test Engineer's Assistant [*Computer-aided design tool*]
TEA	Test Equipment Accessory (MCD)
TEA	Test Equipment Analysis
TEA	Test and Evaluation Agency
TEA	Tetraethylammonium [*Organic chemistry*]
TEA	Textile Export Association of the US (EA)
TEA	Thai Exiles Association (CINC)
TEA	Theatre Equipment Association (EA)
TEA	Thermal Energy Analysis [*or Analyzer*]
TEA	Thiazoylethylamine [*Organic chemistry*]
TEA	Tiselius Electrophoresis Apparatus
TEA	Titanic Enthusiasts of America [*Later, THS*] (EA)
TEA	Trade Expansion Act [*1962*]
TEA	Training Effectiveness Analysis
TEA	Transferred Electron Amplifier
TEA	Transportability Engineering Analysis [*Army*]
TEA	Transversely Excited Atmospheric [*LASER*] (RDA)
TEA	Treasury Enforcement Agent
TEA	Triethanolamine [*Organic chemistry*]
TEA	Triethylaluminum [*Organic chemistry*]
TEA	Triethylamine [*Organic chemistry*]

TEA	Triethylammonium [*Organic chemistry*]
TEA	Tunnel-Emission Amplifier (IEEE)
TEAAC.......	Trade Expansion Act Advisory Committee [*Terminated, 1975*] (EGAO)
TEAB........	Tetraethylammonium Bromide [*Organic chemistry*]
TEAC........	Test and Evaluation Advisory Council [*Military*] (CAAL)
TEAC........	Tetraethylammonium Chloride [*Organic chemistry*]
TEAC........	Tokyo Electro Acoustical Company [*Acronym is now name of electronics company and brand name of its products*]
TEAC........	Turbine Engine Analysis Check (AABC)
TEAC........	Victorian Transition Education Advisory Committee [*Australia*]
Teach	Teacher [*A publication*]
TEACH	Teacher Equity and Choice Act [*Proposed*]
TEACH	Teaching Each Other about Conquering Handicaps (EA)
TEACH	Training and Education Activities Clearing House [*Military*]
Teach Adults ...	Teaching Adults [*A publication*]
Teach Aids News ...	Teaching Aids News [*A publication*] (APTA)
TEACHCERT ...	Teaching Certificate
Teach Coll Rec ...	Teacher's College Record [*A publication*]
Teach Col R ...	Teacher's College Record [*A publication*]
Teach Deaf ...	Teacher of the Deaf [*A publication*]
Teach Dist ...	Teaching at a Distance [*A publication*]
Teach Ed ...	Teacher Education [*A publication*]
Teach Educ ...	Teacher Education [*A publication*]
Teach Eng ...	Teaching of English [*A publication*] (APTA)
Teach Engl ...	Teaching of English [*A publication*] (APTA)
Teach Engl Deaf ...	Teaching English to the Deaf [*A publication*]
Teacher Ed ...	Teacher Education in New Countries [*A publication*]
Teacher Librn ...	Teacher-Librarian [*A publication*]
Teachers J ...	Teachers' Journal [*A publication*] (APTA)
Teach Excep Child ...	Teaching Exceptional Children [*A publication*]
Teach Feedback ...	Teacher Feedback [*A publication*] (APTA)
Teach Guild NSW Proc ...	Teachers Guild of New South Wales. Proceedings [*A publication*] (APTA)
Teach Hist ...	Teaching History [*A publication*] (APTA)
Teaching Engl ...	Teaching of English [*A publication*]
Teaching Polit Sci ...	Teaching Political Science [*A publication*]
Teach J ...	Teachers' Journal [*A publication*] (APTA)
Teach J and Abst ...	Teachers' Journal and Abstract [*A publication*]
Teach J Spec Educ ...	Teachers' Journal of Special Education [*A publication*] (APTA)
Teach J Vic ...	Teachers' Journal (Victorian Teachers Union) [*A publication*] (APTA)
Teach Lib...	Teacher-Librarian [*A publication*] (APTA)
Teach Lond Kids ...	Teaching London Kids [*A publication*]
Teach Math ...	Teaching Mathematics [*A publication*] (APTA)
Teach Meth Page ...	Teaching Methods Page [*A publication*]
Teach News Birm ...	Teaching News. University of Birmingham [*A publication*]
Teach Newsl ...	Teaching Newsletter [*A publication*]
Teach Phil ...	Teaching Philosophy [*A publication*]
Teach Pol S ...	Teaching Political Science [*A publication*]
Teach Pol Sci ...	Teaching Political Science [*A publication*]
Teach Socio ...	Teaching Sociology [*A publication*]
Teach Sociol ...	Teaching Sociology [*A publication*]
Teach Train ...	Teaching and Training [*A publication*]
Tea & Coff ...	Tea and Coffee Trade Journal [*A publication*]
TEAD	Tooele Army Depot [*Utah*] (AABC)
TE/AE	Tigers East/Alpines East (EA)
TEAE........	Triethylaminoethyl [*Organic chemistry*]
Tea East Afr ...	Tea in East Africa [*A publication*]
TEA-ER.....	Traffic Executives Association, Eastern Railroads [*Later, ERA*]
TEAF........	Total Environmental Action Foundation (EA)
TEAF........	Triethylammonium Formate [*Organic chemistry*]
TEAHA	Trans-East African Highway Authority (EA)
TEAL........	Tactics, Equipment, and Logistics Conference [*between US, Great Britain, Australia, and Canada*] [*Developed "duck" designations for Mallard and Gander military communications systems*]
TEAL........	Tasman Empire Airways Limited [*Australia*] (ADA)
TEAL........	Transversely Excited Atmospheric LASER (RDA)
Tea Lib........	Teacher-Librarian [*A publication*] (APTA)
TEAL Occ Pap ...	Teachers of English as an Additional Language. Occasional Papers [*A publication*]
TEALS	Triethanolamine Lauryl Sulfate [*Organic chemistry*]
TEAM	[*The*] European-Atlantic Movement [*London, England*]
TEAM	[*The*] Evangelical Alliance Mission (EA)
TEAM	National TechTeam, Inc. [*NASDAQ symbol*] (NQ)
TEAM	Teacher Education and Media [*Project*]
TEAM	Teamster Economic Action Mobilization
TEAM	Technical Engineer-Architect Management (MCD)
TEAM	Technique for Evaluation and Analysis of Maintainability
TEAM	Technology Evaluation and Acquisition Method
TEAM	Teleterminals Expandable Added Memory
TEAM	Terminology Evaluation and Acquisition Method
TEAM	Test and Evaluation of Air Mobility
TEAM	Test, Evaluation, Analysis, and Modeling [*Army*] (RDA)
TEAM	Top European Advertising Media
TEAM	Torpedo Evasive Maneuvering (MCD)

TEAM .... Total Exposure Assessment Methodology [or Monitoring] [Environmental chemistry]
TEAM .... Towards Excellent Australian Manufacturing
TEAM .... Training and Education in Adoption Methods [Conference sponsored by the North American Council on Adoptable Children]
TEAM .... Training/Employment of Automotive Mechanics [Project]
TEAM .... Training in Expanded Auxiliary Management
TEAM .... Trend Evaluation and Monitoring [Congressional Clearinghouse on the Future] (EA)
TEAM .... Truck Expense Analysis and Management [Data processing]
TEAM A... Theological Education Association of Mid-America, Library Section [Library network]
TEAMMATE ... Total Electronic Advanced Microprocessing Maneuvers and Tactics Equipment [A game]
TEAMS..... Test Evaluation and Monitoring System
TEAMS..... Tests of Engineering Aptitude, Mathematics, and Science
TEAMS..... Trend and Error Analysis Methodology System (MCD)
TEAM-UP ... Test, Evaluation, Analysis, and Management Uniformity Plan [or Procedure] [Army]
TEAO .... Teacher Education Advisory Office [New South Wales, Australia]
TEAP........ Tetraethylammonium Perchlorate [Organic chemistry]
TEAP........ Trajectory Error Analysis Program [NASA]
TEAP........ Transversely Excited Atmospheric Pressure
TEAP........ Triethylammonium Phosphate [Organic chemistry]
TEAPA...... Technikas Apskats [A publication]
TEAPA...... Triethanolamine Phosphoric Acid [Organic chemistry]
Tea Q .... Tea Quarterly [A publication]
TEAR........ [The] Evangelical Alliance Relief [of The TEAR Fund] (EA)
TEAR........ Time, Elevation, Azimuth, Range (MCD)
TEARA...... Terapevticheskii Arkhiv [A publication]
Tea Res Assoc Annu Sci Rep ... Tea Research Association. Annual Scientific Report [A publication]
Tea Res Inst Ceylon Annu Rep ... Tea Research Institute of Ceylon. Annual Report [A publication]
Tea Res Inst Sri Lanka Tech Rep ... Tea Research Institute of Sri Lanka. Technical Report [A publication]
Tea Res J ... Tea Research Journal [A publication]
TEARR...... Times, Elevations, Azimuths, Ranges, and Range Rates [Aerospace]
TEARS ...... [The] Exeter Abstract Reference System [Exeter University] [Information service or system] (IID)
TEAS........ Test and Evaluation, Aircraft Survivability
TEAS........ Threat Evaluation and Action Selection [Civilian defense program]
TEAS........ Twayne's English Author Series [A publication]
TEASE ...... Tracking Errors and Simulation Evaluation [RADAR]
TEASER..... Tunable Electron Amplifier for Stimulated Emission of Radiation (MCD)
teasp........... Teaspoonful
TEAT........ Obras de Teatro Estrenadas en Espana [Ministerio de Cultura] [Spain] [Information service or system] (CRD)
TEA-TOW ... Training Effectiveness Analysis - Tube-Launched Optically Tracked Wire-Guided (MCD)
TEB........... Tax-Exempt Bond [Investment term]
TEB........... Teterboro, NJ [Location identifier] [FAA] (FAAL)
TEB........... Textile Economics Bureau
TEB........... Tone Encoded Burst
TEB........... Triethylbenzene [Organic chemistry]
TEB........... Triethylborane [Organic chemistry]
TEB........... Tropical Experiment Board [of World Meteorological Organization and International Council on Scientific Unions]
TEB........... Turk Ekonomi Bankasi AS [Turkey]
TEBA......... Tutmonda Esperantista Biblioteka Asocio [International Association for Esperanto in Libraries - IAEL] (EAIO)
TEBAC...... Triethylbenylammonium Chloride [Organic chemistry]
TEBDA...... Truck Equipment and Body Distributor Association [Later, NTEA] (EA)
TeBG.......... Testosterone-Estradiol Binding Globulin [Endocrinology]
Tebiwa J Idaho Mus Nat Hist ... Tebiwa Journal. Idaho Museum of Natural History [A publication]
Tebiwa Misc Pap Idaho State Univ Mus Nat Hist ... Tebiwa Miscellaneous Papers. Idaho State University. Museum of Natural History [A publication]
TEBOL...... Terminal Business-Oriented Language
TEBPP....... Theoretical and Experimental Beam-Plasma Physics
TEBUTATE ... Tertiary Butyl Acetate [Organic chemistry] [USAN]
TEC........... Blacksburg, VA [Location identifier] [FAA] (FAAL)
TEC........... Department of Technical and Economic Cooperation [Thailand] (DS)
TEC........... [The] Electrification Council (EA)
TEC........... [The] Entertainment Channel [Pay-television network] [Obsolete]
TEC........... Tactical Electromagnetic Coordinator (IEEE)
TEC........... Tactical Exercise Controller [Marine Corps] (MCD)
TEC........... Target Engagement Console
TEC........... Target Entry Console
TEC........... Tarif Exterieur Commun [Common External Tariff] [for EEC countries]

TEC........... Technical
TEC........... Technical Education Center
TEC........... Technical Escort Center [Army] (RDA)
Tec .... Technischord [Record label]
TEC........... Technological Excellence Commission
TEC........... Technology for Energy Corporation (NRCH)
TEC........... Tele-Engineering Corporation [Framingham, MA] [Telecommunications] (TSSD)
TEC........... Telecommunications Policy [A publication]
TEC........... Telemetry and Command
TEC........... Telephone Engineering Center [Telecommunications] (TEL)
TEC........... Temporary Engineering Change (AAG)
TEC........... Temporary Extended Compensation [Labor]
TEC........... Ternary Eutectic Chloride [Fire extinguishing agent]
TEC........... Test Equipment Center [NASA] (NASA)
TEC........... Test Equipment Committee (AAG)
T & EC...... Test and Evaluation Command [Army]
TEC........... Thermal End Cover
TEC........... Thermal Expansion Coefficient
TEC........... Thermionic Energy Converter (RDA)
TEC........... Tlemcen [Algeria] [Seismograph station code, US Geological Survey] (SEIS)
TEC........... Tokyo Electronics Corp.
TEC........... Ton Equivalent of Coal
TEC........... TOS [TIROS Operational Satellite] Test Evaluation Center [Goddard Space Flight Center] (NOAA)
TEC........... Total Eosinophil Count [Hematology]
TEC........... Total Estimated Cost
TEC........... Tower En-Route Control [Aviation] (FAAC)
TEC........... Track Entry Console (MCD)
TEC........... Tract Evaluation Computer (NATG)
TEC........... Training and Enterprise Council [British]
TEC........... Training Evaluation and Control
TEC........... Training Exercise Coordinator [Military] (NVT)
TEC........... Training Extension Course [Army]
TEC........... Transearth Coast [AEC]
TEC........... Transient Early Curvature [Orthopedics]
TEC........... Transient Erythroblastopenia of Childhood [Hematology]
TEC........... Transport Environment Circulation [A publication]
T & EC...... Trauma and Emergency Center [Medicine]
TEC........... Tripartite Engineering Committee [Allied German Occupation Forces]
TEC........... Triple Erasure Correction
TEC........... Tropical Experiment Council [of World Meteorological Organization and International Council on Scientific Unions]
TEC........... Truck Electrical Center [Volvo White Truck Corp.]
TECA........ Tartan Educational and Cultural Association (EA)
TECA........ Technical Evaluation and Countermeasures Assignment
TECA........ Temporary Emergency Court of Appeals
TECA........ Totally Enclosed - Closed-Air Circuit
TECA........ Tower En-Route Control Area [Aviation] (FAAC)
TECAD..... Technical Advisory [Military] (CAAL)
TECADS..... Techniques to Counter Air Defense Suppression (MCD)
Tec Agr ..... Tecnica Agricola [A publication]
Tec Agric (Catania) ... Tecnica Agricola (Catania) [A publication]
Tec Autom ... Tecniche dell'Automazione [A publication]
TECC......... Technology Education for Children Council (EA)
TECC......... Texas Education Computer Cooperative [Houston] [Information service or system] (IID)
TECC......... Texas Educational Computer Courseware Database [Texas Education Computer Cooperative] [Information service or system] [Defunct] (CRD)
TECC......... Thermal Exploration Co. [NASDAQ symbol] (NQ)
TECCE ...... Tactical Exploitation Collection and Coordination Element (MCD)
TECD........ Tech Data Corp. [Clearwater, FL] [NASDAQ symbol] (NQ)
TECD........ Training Equipment Change Directives [Navy]
TECE......... Teleprinter Error Correction Equipment
TECED..... Techniques de l'Energie [A publication]
TECG........ Test and Evaluation Coordinating Group [Military] (CAAL)
TECH........ Teach Each Customer How [Tire repair training seminar] [Technical Rubber Co.]
TECH .... Technical (AAG)
TECH .... Technician
TECH .... Technique
TECH .... Technological Education Clearinghouse
TECH .... Technology (AAG)
Tech .... Technology [A publication] (APTA)
TECH .... Techtran Industries, Inc. [NASDAQ symbol] (NQ)
TECH .... Toxic, Explosive, Corrosive, Hazardous Cargo [Shipping] (DS)
Tech Abstr Bull ... Technical Abstract Bulletin [A publication]
TECHAD .. Technical Advisor [Navy]
Tech Adj ... Technical Adjutant [British military] (DMA)
Tech Adv Shikoku Agric ... Technical Advances in Shikoku Agriculture [A publication]
Tech Agri ... Technique Agricole [France] [A publication]
Tech Appl Pet ... Techniques et Applications du Petrole [France] [A publication]
Tech Apskats ... Technikas Apskats [United States] [A publication]
Tech Assn Pa ... Technical Association Papers [A publication]

TECHAV... Technical Availability [*Navy*] (NVT)

Tech Bau.... Technik am Bau [*West Germany*] [*A publication*]

Tech Belge Prothese Dent ... Technicien Belge en Prothese Dentaire [*A publication*]

Tech Ber Heinrich-Hertz Inst (Berlin-Charlottenburg) ... Technischer Bericht. Heinrich-Hertz Institut (Berlin-Charlottenburg) [*A publication*]

Tech Ber Sticht Nederl Graan-Cent ... Technisch Bericht. Stichting Nederlands Graan-Centrum [*A publication*]

Tech Bibliogr Birmingham Public Lib ... Technical Bibliographies. Birmingham Public Libraries [*A publication*]

Tech Bibliogr Ser Birmingham Cent Lib ... Technical Bibliographies Series. Birmingham Central Libraries [*A publication*]

Tech Biochem Biophys Morphol ... Techniques of Biochemical and Biophysical Morphology [*A publication*]

Tech Bul Dep Agric (Malaysia) ... Technical Bulletin. Department of Agriculture (Malaysia) [*A publication*]

Tech Bull Agric Exp Stn Ore St Univ ... Technical Bulletin. Agricultural Experiment Station. Oregon State University [*A publication*]

Tech Bull Agric Exp Stn Univ Ariz ... Technical Bulletin. Arizona Agricultural Experiment Station. University of Arizona [*A publication*]

Tech Bull Agric Exp Stn Wash St ... Technical Bulletin. Agricultural Experiment Station. Washington State Institute of Agricultural Sciences [*A publication*]

Tech Bull Agric Res Inst (Cyprus) ... Technical Bulletin. Agricultural Research Institute (Cyprus) [*A publication*]

Tech Bull Amersham Buchler ... Technisches Bulletin - Amerisham Buchler [*A publication*]

Tech Bull Anim Ind Agric Branch NT ... Technical Bulletin. Animal Industry and Agricultural Branch. Department of the Northern Territory [*A publication*] (APTA)

Tech Bull Anim Ind Agric Br NT ... Technical Bulletin. Animal Industry and Agriculture Branch. Northern Territory [*A publication*] (APTA)

Tech Bull Ariz Agr Exp Sta ... Technical Bulletin. Arizona Agricultural Experiment Station [*A publication*]

Tech Bull Ariz Agric Exp Stn ... Technical Bulletin. Arizona Agricultural Experiment Station [*A publication*]

Tech Bull At Energy Organ Iran ... Technical Bulletin. Atomic Energy Organization of Iran [*A publication*]

Tech Bull Banana Res Adv Comm ... Technical Bulletin. Banana Research Advisory Committee [*A publication*] (APTA)

Tech Bull Can Inland Waters Dir ... Technical Bulletin. Canada Inland Waters Directorate [*A publication*]

Tech Bull Colo Agric Exp Stn ... Technical Bulletin. Colorado Agricultural Experiment Station [*A publication*]

Tech Bull Colo State Univ Agr Exp Sta ... Technical Bulletin. Colorado State University. Agricultural Experiment Station [*A publication*]

Tech Bull Commonwealth Inst Biol Contr ... Technical Bulletin. Commonwealth Institute of Biological Control [*A publication*]

Tech Bull Commonw Inst Biol Control ... Technical Bulletin. Commonwealth Institute of Biological Control [*A publication*]

Tech Bull Cyprus Agr Res Inst ... Technical Bulletin. Cyprus Agricultural Research Institute [*A publication*]

Tech Bull Dep Agric NSW ... New South Wales. Department of Agriculture. Technical Bulletin [*A publication*] (APTA)

Tech Bull Dep Agric Vict ... Technical Bulletin. Department of Agriculture. Victoria [*A publication*] (APTA)

Tech Bull Dep Agric West Aust ... Technical Bulletin. Department of Agriculture. Western Australia [*A publication*] (APTA)

Tech Bull Exp For Taiwan Univ ... Technical Bulletin. Experimental Forest. National Taiwan University [*A publication*]

Tech Bull Fac Agric Kagawa Univ ... Technical Bulletin. Faculty of Agriculture. Kagawa University [*A publication*]

Tech Bull Fac Agr Kagawa Univ ... Technical Bulletin. Faculty of Agriculture. Kagawa University [*A publication*]

Tech Bull Fac Hort Chiba Univ ... Technical Bulletin. Faculty of Horticulture. Chiba University [*A publication*]

Tech Bull Fac Hortic Chiba Univ ... Technical Bulletin. Faculty of Horticulture. Chiba University [*A publication*]

Tech Bull Fla Agric Exp Stn ... Technical Bulletin. Florida Agricultural Experiment Station [*A publication*]

Tech Bull GA Agr Exp Sta ... Technical Bulletin. Georgia Agricultural Experiment Stations. University of Georgia. College of Agriculture [*A publication*]

Tech Bull Gt Brit Min Agr Fish Food ... Technical Bulletin. Great Britain Ministry of Agiculture, Fisheries, and Food [*A publication*]

Tech Bull Harper Adams Agr Coll ... Technical Bulletin. Harper Adams Agricultural College [*A publication*]

Tech Bull Hawaii Agric Exp Stn ... Technical Bulletin. Hawaii Agricultural Experiment Station [*A publication*]

Tech Bull Hokkaido Agric Exp Stn ... Technical Bulletin. Hokkaido Agricultural Experiment Station [*A publication*]

Tech Bull Inst Ld Wat Mgmt Res ... Technical Bulletin. Institute for Land and Water Management Research [*A publication*]

Tech Bull Kagawa Agr Coll ... Technical Bulletin. Kagawa Agricultural College [*A publication*]

Tech Bull Kans Agr Exp Sta ... Technical Bulletin. Kansas Agricultural Experiment Station [*A publication*]

Tech Bull Kans Agric Exp Stn ... Technical Bulletin. Kansas Agricultural Experiment Station [*A publication*]

Tech Bull Land Resour Div Dir Overseas Surv ... Technical Bulletin. Land Resources Division. Directorate of Overseas Surveys [*A publication*]

Tech Bull Life Sci Agric Exp Stn (Maine) ... Technical Bulletin. Life Sciences and Agriculture Experiment Station (Maine) [*A publication*]

Tech Bull Life Sci Agric Exp Stn Univ Maine ... Technical Bulletin. Life Sciences and Agriculture Experiment Station. University of Maine at Orono [*A publication*]

Tech Bull Mich State Univ Agr Exp Sta ... Technical Bulletin. Michigan State University. Agricultural Experiment Station [*A publication*]

Tech Bull Mich St Coll Agric Exp Stn ... Technical Bulletin. Michigan State College. Agricultural Experiment Station [*A publication*]

Tech Bull Minist Agric E Niger ... Technical Bulletin. Ministry of Agriculture of Eastern Nigeria [*A publication*]

Tech Bull Minist Agric Fish Fd ... Technical Bulletin. Ministry of Agriculture, Fisheries, and Food [*A publication*]

Tech Bull Minist Agric Fish Food (GB) ... Technical Bulletin. Ministry of Agriculture, Fisheries, and Food (Great Britain) [*A publication*]

Tech Bull Minn Agric Exp Sta ... Technical Bulletin. University of Minnesota. Agricultural Experiment Station [*A publication*]

Tech Bull Minn Agric Exp Stn ... Technical Bulletin. Minnesota Agricultural Experiment Station [*A publication*]

Tech Bull Miss Agr Exp Sta ... Technical Bulletin. Mississippi Agricultural Experiment Station [*A publication*]

Tech Bull Miss Agric For Exp Stn ... Technical Bulletin. Mississippi Agricultural and Forestry Experiment Station [*A publication*]

Tech Bull Miyagi Prefect Agr Exp Sta ... Technical Bulletin. Miyagi Prefectural Agricultural Experiment Station [*A publication*]

Tech Bull Mont Agr Exp Sta ... Technical Bulletin. Montana Agricultural Experiment Station [*A publication*]

Tech Bull NC Agr Exp Sta ... Technical Bulletin. North Carolina Agricultural Experiment Station [*A publication*]

Tech Bull NC Agric Exp Sta ... Technical Bulletin. North Carolina Agricultural Experiment Station [*A publication*]

Tech Bull N Carol Agric Exp Stn ... Technical Bulletin. North Carolina Agricultural Experiment Station [*A publication*]

Tech Bull N Carol St Coll Agric Exp Stn ... Technical Bulletin. North Carolina State College. Agricultural Experiment Station [*A publication*]

Tech Bull N Carol St Univ Agric Exp Stn ... Technical Bulletin. North Carolina State University. Agricultural Experiment Station [*A publication*]

Tech Bull Okla State Univ Agr Exp Sta ... Technical Bulletin. Oklahoma State University. Agricultural Experiment Station [*A publication*]

Tech Bull Ore Agric Exp Stn ... Technical Bulletin. Oregon Agricultural Experiment Station [*A publication*]

Tech Bull Oreg State Coll Agr Exp Sta ... Technical Bulletin. Oregon State College. Agricultural Experiment Station [*A publication*]

Tech Bull Regist Med Technol ... Technical Bulletin. Registry of Medical Technologists [*A publication*]

Tech Bull Rhodesia Agric J ... Technical Bulletin. Rhodesia Agricultural Journal [*A publication*]

Tech Bull SC Agric Exp Stn ... Technical Bulletin. South Carolina Agricultural Experiment Station [*A publication*]

Tech Bull S Dak Agr Exp Sta ... Technical Bulletin. South Dakota Agricultural Experiment Station [*A publication*]

Tech Bull Sug Manufact Ass ... Technical Bulletin. Sugar Manufacturers' Association [*A publication*]

Tech Bull Sulphur Inst ... Technical Bulletin. Sulphur Institute [*A publication*]

Tech Bull Taiwan Agric Res Inst ... Technical Bulletin. Taiwan Agricultural Research Institute [*A publication*]

Tech Bull Taiwan Fertil Co ... Technical Bulletin. Taiwan Fertilizer Company [*A publication*]

Tech Bull TARC (Trop Agric Res Cent) ... Technical Bulletin. TARC (Tropical Agriculture Research Center) [*A publication*]

Tech Bull Tex Eng Exp Stn ... Technical Bulletin. Texas Engineering Experiment Station [*A publication*]

Tech Bull Tokushima Bunri Univ ... Technical Bulletin. Tokushima Bunri University [*A publication*]

Tech Bull Trop Agric Res Cent ... Technical Bulletin. Tropical Agriculture Research Center [*A publication*]

Tech Bull UAR Minist Agric Agrar Reform ... Technical Bulletin. United Arab Republic Ministry of Agriculture and Agrarian Reform [*A publication*]

Tech Bull Univ Maine Life Sci Agric Exp Stn ... Technical Bulletin. University of Maine. Life Sciences and Agriculture Experiment Station [*A publication*]

Tech Bull Univ Minn Agr Exp Sta ... Technical Bulletin. University of Minnesota. Agricultural Experiment Station [*A publication*]

Tech Bull Univ Nev Agr Exp Sta ... Technical Bulletin. University of Nevada. Agricultural Experiment Station [*A publication*]

Tech Bull Univ Philippines Coll Agr ... Technical Bulletin. University of the Philippines. College of Agriculture [*A publication*]

Tech Bull USDA ... Technical Bulletin. United States Department of Agriculture [*A publication*]

Tech Bull US Dep Agric ... Technical Bulletin. United States Department of Agriculture [*A publication*]

Tech Bull US Dep Agric Agric Res Serv ... Technical Bulletin. United States Department of Agriculture. Agricultural Research Service [*A publication*]

Tech Bull US For Serv ... Technical Bulletin. United States Forest Service [*A publication*]

Tech Bull VA Agr Exp Sta ... Technical Bulletin. Virginia Agricultural Experiment Station [*A publication*]

Tech Bull Vic Ctry Rd Bd ... Technical Bulletin. Victoria Country Roads Board [*A publication*]　(APTA)

Tech Bull Wash Agr Exp Sta ... Technical Bulletin. Washington Agricultural Experiment Station [*A publication*]

Tech Bull Wash Agric Exp Stn ... Technical Bulletin. Washington Agricultural Experiment Station [*A publication*]

Tech Bull Wash State Univ Coll Agric Res Cent ... Technical Bulletin. Washington State University. College of Agriculture. Research Center [*A publication*]

Tech Bull West Aust Dep Agric ... Technical Bulletin. Western Australian Department of Agriculture [*A publication*]

Tech Bul VIUS Agric Exp Stn ... Technical Bulletin. Virgin Islands of the United States Agricultural Experiment Station [*A publication*]

Tech CEM ... Techniques CEM [*Compagnie Electro-Mecanique*] [*A publication*]

Tech Chem (Prague) ... Technika v Chemii (Prague) [*A publication*]

Tech Chron ... Technika Chronika [*A publication*]

Tech Circ Maurit Sug Ind Res Inst ... Technical Circular. Mauritius Sugar Industry Research Institute [*A publication*]

Tech Commun ... Technical Communications [*A publication*]

Tech Commun Bur Sugar Exp Sts (Queensl) ... Technical Communication. Bureau of Sugar Experiment Stations (Queensland) [*A publication*]　(APTA)

Tech Commun Bur Sug Exp Stns (Qd) ... Technical Communication. Bureau of Sugar Experiment Stations (Queensland) [*A publication*]　(APTA)

Tech Commun Central Inform Libr Edit Sect CSIRO ... Technical Communication. Central Information, Library, and Editorial Section. Commonwealth Scientific and Industrial Research Organisation [*A publication*]　(APTA)

Tech Commun CILES CSIRO ... Technical Communication. Central Information, Library, and Editorial Section. Commonwealth Scientific and Industrial Research Organisation [*A publication*]　(APTA)

Tech Commun CSIRO (Aust) ... Technical Communication. Minerals Research Laboratories. Commonwealth Scientific and Industrial Research Organisation (Australia) [*A publication*]

Tech Commun CSIRO Div Mineral ... Australia. Commonwealth Scientific and Industrial Research Organisation. Division of Mineralogy. Technical Communication [*A publication*]　(APTA)

Tech Commun CSIRO Div Miner Chem ... Australia. Commonwealth Scientific and Industrial Research Organisation. Division of Mineral Chemistry. Technical Communication [*A publication*]　(APTA)

Tech Commun CSIRO Inst Earth Resour ... CSIRO [*Commonwealth Scientific and Industrial Research Organisation*] Institute of Earth Resources. Technical Communication [*A publication*]　(APTA)

Tech Commun CSIRO Miner Res Lab ... CSIRO [*Commonwealth Scientific and Industrial Research Organisation*] Minerals Research Laboratories. Technical Communication [*A publication*]　(APTA)

Tech Commun Dept Agr Tech Serv Repub S Afr ... Technical Communication. Department of Agricultural Technical Services. Republic of South Africa [*A publication*]

Tech Commun Div Miner Chem CSIRO ... Technical Communication. Division of Mineral Chemistry. Commonwealth Scientific and Industrial Research Organisation [*A publication*]　(APTA)

Tech Commun Div Miner CSIRO ... Technical Communication. Division of Mineralogy. Commonwealth Scientific and Industrial Research Organisation [*A publication*]　(APTA)

Tech Commun For Bur (Oxf) ... Technical Communication. Commonwealth Forestry Bureau (Oxford) [*A publication*]

Tech Commun Miner Res Lab CSIRO ... Technical Communication. Minerals Research Laboratories. Commonwealth Scientific and Industrial Research Organisation [*A publication*]　(APTA)

Tech Commun R Sch Mines ... Technical Communications. Royal School of Mines [*A publication*]

Tech Commun S Afr Dep Agric Fish ... Technical Communication. South Africa Department of Agriculture and Fisheries [*A publication*]

Tech Commun S Afr Dep Agric Tech Serv ... Technical Communications. South Africa Department of Agricultural Technical Services [*A publication*]

Tech Commun Woodld Ecol Unit CSIRO ... Technical Communication. Woodland Ecology Unit. Commonwealth Scientific and Industrial Research Organisation [*A publication*]　(APTA)

Tech Conf Proc Irrig Assoc ... Technical Conference Proceedings. Irrigation Association [*A publication*]

Tech & Cult ... Technology and Culture [*A publication*]

Tech & Culture ... Technology and Culture [*A publication*]

Tech Cybern USSR ... Technical Cybernetics USSR [*A publication*]

TECHDATA ... Technical Data [*DoD*]

Tech Data Digest ... Technical Data Digest [*United States*] [*A publication*]

Tech Dig .... Technical Digest [*A publication*]

Tech Doc FAO Plant Prot Comm Southeast Asia Pac Reg ... Technical Document. Food and Agriculture Organization of the United Nations. Plant Protection Committee for the South East Asia and Pacific Region [*A publication*]

Tech Eau.... Technique de l'Eau et de l'Assainissement [*A publication*]

Tech Econ Publ Tatabanyai Szenbanyak ... Technical-Economical Publication. Tatabanyai Szenbanyak [*A publication*]

Tech Econ Stud Inst Geol Geophys Ser I ... Technical and Economical Studies. Institute of Geology and Geophysics. Series I. Mineralogy-Petrology [*A publication*]

Tech Educ.. Technical Education [*A publication*]

Tech Educ Abstr ... Technical Education Abstracts [*A publication*]

Tech Educ Yrbk ... Technician Education Yearbook [*A publication*]

Tech Electrochem ... Techniques of Electrochemistry [*A publication*]

Tech Electron Son Telev ... Techniques Electroniques - Son - Television [*A publication*]

Tech Energ ... Techniques de l'Energie [*France*] [*A publication*]

Tech Energie ... Techniques de l'Energie [*A publication*]

Tech Energ (Paris) ... Techniques de l'Energie (Paris) [*A publication*]

Tech Environ ... Technology and Environment [*A publication*]

TECHEVAL ... Technical Evaluation [*Navy*]　(NG)

Tech Fore ... Technology Forecasts and Technology Surveys [*A publication*]

Tech Forum Soc Vac Coaters ... Technical Forum. Society of Vacuum Coaters [*A publication*]

Tech Gem... Technische Gemeinschaft [*A publication*]

Tech Gemeindebl ... Technisches Gemeindeblatt [*West Germany*] [*A publication*]

TechGeol.... Technical Associate of the Geological Society [*British*]　(DBQ)

Tech Gesch ... Technik-Geschichte [*A publication*]

Tech Gids Ziekenhuis Instelling ... Technische Gids voor Ziekenhuis en Instelling [*A publication*]

TECHGL... Technological

Tech Gospod Morsk ... Technika i Gospodarka Morska [*Poland*] [*A publication*]

Tech Heute ... Technik Heute [*German Federal Republic*] [*A publication*]

Tech Hochsch Leipzig Wiss Z ... Technische Hochschule Leipzig. Wissenschaftliche Zeitschrift [*A publication*]

Tech Hogesch Delft Afd Werktuigbouwkd (Rep) WTHD ... Technische Hogeschool Delft. Afdeling der Werktuigbouwkunde (Report) WTHD [*A publication*]

Tech Illus... Technology Illustrated [*A publication*]

TECHIMPORT ... China National Technical Import Corp. [*People's Republic of China*]　(IMH)

Tech-Index Plasmaphys Forsch Fusionreakt ... Technik-Index ueber Plasmaphysikalische Forschung und Fusionsreaktoren [*West Germany*] [*A publication*]

Tech Inf Bull ... Technical Information Bulletin. National Information Service on Drug Abuse [*A publication*]

Tech Inf GRW ... Technische Information GRW [*Geraete- und Regler Werke*] [*East Germany*] [*A publication*]

TECHINFO ... Technical Information [*DoD*]

Tech Info Service ... Technical Information Service [*A publication*]

Tech Ing Genie Chim ... Techniques de l'Ingenieur. Genie Chimique [*A publication*]

TECHINT ... Technical Intelligence [*Spy satellites, etc.*]

Tech Jahrb ... Technica Jahrbuch [*A publication*]

Tech J Ankara Nucl Res Cent ... Technical Journal. Ankara Nuclear Research Center [*A publication*]

Tech J Ankara Nucl Res Train Cent ... Technical Journal. Ankara Nuclear Research and Training Center [*A publication*]

Tech J Jap Broadcast Corp ... Technical Journal. Japan Broadcasting Corporation [*A publication*]

Tech J Jpn Broadcast Corp ... Technical Journal. Japan Broadcasting Corporation [*A publication*]

Tech Knih .. Technicka Knihovna [*A publication*]

Tech Knihovna ... Technicka Knihovna [*A publication*]

Tech Kurir ... Technikai Kurir [*Hungary*] [*A publication*]

TECHL...... Technical

Tech Lab Cent Res Inst Electr Power Ind Rep ... Technical Laboratory. Central Research Institute of the Electrical Power Industry. Report [*Japan*] [*A publication*]

Tech Landwirt ... Technik und Landwirtschaft. Landtechnischer Ratgeber [*A publication*]

Tech Life Sci Biochem ... Techniques in the Life Sciences. Biochemistry [*A publication*]

Tech Lotnicza Astronaut ... Technika Lotnicza i Astronautyczna [*Poland*] [*A publication*]

Tech Manpower ... Technical Manpower [*A publication*]   (APTA)
Tech Meas Med ... Techniques of Measurement in Medicine [*A publication*]
Tech Mem Calif Inst Technol Jet Propul Lab ... Technical Memorandum.
  California Institute of Technology. Jet Propulsion
  Laboratory [*A publication*]
Tech Memo Daresbury Lab ... Technical Memorandum. Daresbury
  Laboratory [*A publication*]
Tech Memo Daresbury Nucl Phys Lab ... Technical Memorandum. Daresbury
  Nuclear Physics Laboratory [*A publication*]
Tech Memo Div Appl Geomech CSIRO ... Technical Memorandum. Division
  of Applied Geomechanics. Commonwealth Scientific and
  Industrial Research Organisation [*A publication*]   (APTA)
Tech Memo Div Land Use Res CSIRO ... Technical Memorandum. Division
  of Land Use Research. Commonwealth Scientific and
  Industrial Research Organisation [*A publication*]   (APTA)
Tech Memo Div Wildl Res CSIRO ... Technical Memorandum. Division of
  Wildlife Research. Commonwealth Scientific and Industrial
  Research Organisation [*A publication*]   (APTA)
Tech Memo Jet Propul Lab Calif Inst Technol ... Technical Memorandum. Jet
  Propulsion Laboratory. California Institute of Technology
  [*A publication*]
Tech Memor Plant Protection Ltd ... Technical Memoranda. Plant Protection
  Limited [*A publication*]
Tech Mess ATM ... Technisches Messen ATM [*Archiv fuer Technisches
  Messen*] [*A publication*]
Tech Mess-TM ... Techinsches Messen-TM [*A publication*]
Tech Methods Polym Eval ... Techniques and Methods of Polymer Evaluation
  [*A publication*]
Tech Meun ... Technique Meuniere [*A publication*]
Tech Mitt... Technische Mitteilungen [*A publication*]
Tech Mitt AEG-Telefunken ... Technische Mitteilungen AEG- [*Allgemeine
  Elektrizitaets-Gesellschaft*] Telefunken [*A publication*]
Tech Mitteil Krupp Forschungsber ... Technische Mitteilungen Krupp.
  Forschungsberichte [*A publication*]
Tech Mitteil Krupp Werksber ... Technische Mitteilungen Krupp.
  Werksberichte [*A publication*]
Tech Mitt (Essen) ... Technische Mitteilungen (Essen) [*A publication*]
Tech Mitt Krupp ... Technische Mitteilungen Krupp [*West Germany*] [*A
  publication*]
Tech Mitt Krupp Forschungsber ... Technische Mitteilungen Krupp.
  Forschungsberichte [*A publication*]
Tech Mitt Krupp Werksber ... Technische Mitteilungen Krupp. Werksberichte
  [*A publication*]
Tech Mitt PTT ... Technische Mitteilungen PTT [*A publication*]
Tech Mitt RFZ ... Technische Mitteilungen. RFZ [*Rundfunk- und
  Fernsehtechnisches Zentralamt*] [*A publication*]
Tech Mod... Technique Moderne [*A publication*]
TECHMOD ... Technology Modernization Program [*DoD*]
Tech Motoryzacyjna ... Technika Motoryzacyjna [*A publication*]
TECHN ..... Technical   (EY)
TECHN ..... Technician
TECHN ..... Technology
Techn Agric Int ... Technique Agricole Internationale [*A publication*]
Techn Archit ... Techniques et Architecture [*A publication*]
Techn Ber Lorenz ... Technische Berichte der C. Lorenz [*A publication*]
Techn Bull Reg Med Technol ... Technical Bulletin. Registry of Medical
  Technologists [*A publication*]
Techn Chron ... Technika Chronika [*A publication*]
Techn Cult ... Technology and Culture [*A publication*]
Techn Dict ... Crabb's Technological Dictionary [*A publication*]   (DLA)
Tech News ... Technical News [*A publication*]
Tech Newslett For Prod Res Inst (Ghana) ... Technical Newsletter. Forest
  Products Research Institute (Kumasi, Ghana) [*A
  publication*]
Tech News Serv Sarabhai M Chem ... Technical News Service. Sarabhai M.
  Chemicals [*A publication*]
Techn Hosp ... Techniques Hospitalieres, Medico-Sociales, et Sanitaires [*A
  publication*]
Technical J ... Technical Journal [*A publication*]
Technic Int ... Technic International [*West Germany*] [*A publication*]
Techn Ind Rd ... Technische und Industrielle Rundschau [*A publication*]
Technion Isr Inst Technol Dep Chem Eng Rep CE ... Technion-Israel Institute
  of Technology. Department of Chemical Engineering.
  Report CE [*A publication*]
Techniques Phys ... Techniques of Physics [*A publication*]
Techn Lab ... Techniques de Laboratoire [*A publication*]
Technmcs... Technometrics [*A publication*]
Techn Mitt Krupp ... Technische Mitteilungen Krupp [*A publication*]
Techn Mod ... Technique Moderne [*A publication*]
TECHNOL ... Technologic
Technol ...... Technology [*A publication*]   (APTA)
Technol Conserv ... Technology and Conservation [*A publication*]
Technol Cul ... Technology and Culture [*A publication*]
Technol Dev Rep EPS (Can Environ Prot Serv) ... Technology Development
  Report EPS (Canada Environmental Protection Service) [*A
  publication*]
Technol For ... Technological Forecasting and Social Change [*A publication*]
Technol Forecast ... Technological Forecasting [*Later, Technological
  Forecasting and Social Change*] [*A publication*]

Technol Forecasting ... Technological Forecasting [*Later, Technological
  Forecasting and Social Change*] [*United States*] [*A
  publication*]
Technol Forecasting Soc Change ... Technological Forecasting and Social
  Change [*A publication*]
Technol Forecast and Soc Change ... Technological Forecasting and Social
  Change [*A publication*]
Technol Index Plasmaphys Res Fusion React ... Technology Index for
  Plasmaphysics Research and Fusion Reactors [*West
  Germany*] [*A publication*]
Technol Inf (Sapporo) ... Technology and Information (Sapporo) [*A
  publication*]
Technol Ireland ... Technology Ireland [*A publication*]
Technol Japan ... Science and Technology of Japan [*A publication*]
Technol J Natl Sci Dev Board (Philip) ... Technology Journal. National
  Science Development Board (Philippines) [*A publication*]
Technol-Nachr Manage Inf ... Technologie-Nachrichten. Management-
  Informationen [*West Germany*] [*A publication*]
Technol-Nachr Programm-Inf ... Technologie-Nachrichten Programm-
  Informationen [*A publication*]
Technol-Nachr Sonderdienst-Programme ... Technologie-Nachrichten
  Sonderdienst-Programme [*German Federal Republic*] [*A
  publication*]
Technol News ... Technology News. Bureau of Mines [*United States*] [*A
  publication*]
Technol News Bur Mines ... Technology News. Bureau of Mines [*United
  States*] [*A publication*]
Technolog Pap Div Forest Prod CSIRO ... Technological Paper. Division of
  Forest Products. Commonwealth Scientific and Industrial
  Research Organisation [*A publication*]   (APTA)
Technol Pap Div Forest Prod CSIRO ... Technological Paper. Division of
  Forest Products. Commonwealth Scientific and Industrial
  Research Organisation [*A publication*]   (APTA)
Technol Pap Forest Prod Lab Div Appl Chem CSIRO ... Technological Paper.
  Forest Products Laboratory. Division of Applied
  Chemistry. Commonwealth Scientific and Industrial
  Research Organisation [*A publication*]
Technol Pap Forest Prod Lab Div Bldg Res CSIRO ... Technological Paper.
  Forest Products Laboratory. Division of Building Research.
  Commonwealth Scientific and Industrial Research
  Organisation [*A publication*]   (APTA)
Technol Pap For Prod Lab Div Appl Chem CSIRO ... Technological Paper.
  Forest Products Laboratory. Division of Applied
  Chemistry. Commonwealth Scientific and Industrial
  Research Organisation [*A publication*]   (APTA)
Technol Pap For Prod Lab Div Build Res CSIRO ... Technological Paper.
  Forest Products Laboratory. Division of Building Research.
  Commonwealth Scientific and Industrial Research
  Organisation [*A publication*]   (APTA)
Technol R... Technology Review [*Boston*] [*A publication*]
Technol Rep Iwate Univ ... Technology Reports. Iwate University [*A
  publication*]
Technol Rep Kansai Univ ... Technology Reports. Kansai University [*A
  publication*]
Technol Rep Kyushu Univ ... Technology Reports. Kyushu University [*A
  publication*]
Technol Rep Osaka Univ ... Technology Reports. Osaka University [*A
  publication*]
Technol Rep Seikei Univ ... Technology Reports. Seikei University [*A
  publication*]
Technol Rep Tohoku Univ ... Technology Reports. Tohoku University
  [*Sendaik, Japan*] [*A publication*]
Technol Rep Tohoku Univ (Jpn) ... Technology Reports. Tohoku University
  (Japan) [*A publication*]
Technol Rep Yamaguchi Univ ... Technology Reports. Yamaguchi University
  [*A publication*]
Technol Respir ... Technologie Respiratoire [*A publication*]
Technol Rev ... Technology Review [*A publication*]
Technol Rev Chonnam Natl Univ ... Technological Review. Chonnam
  National University [*Republic of Korea*] [*A publication*]
Technols .... Technologies
Technol Sci Chung Ang Univ ... Technologies and Sciences. Chung-Ang
  University [*A publication*]
Technol Soc ... Technology and Society [*A publication*]
Technol (Syd) ... Technology (Sydney) [*A publication*]   (APTA)
Technol Use Lignite ... Technology and Use of Lignite. Proceedings of a
  Symposium [*A publication*]
Technomet ... Technometrics [*A publication*]
Technop ..... Technopaegnion [*of Ausonius*] [*Classical studies*]   (OCD)
Tech Note Aust Def Stand Lab ... Technical Note. Australia Defence
  Standards Laboratories [*A publication*]
Tech Note Brick Manuf Assoc NSW ... Technical Note. Brick Manufacturers
  Association of New South Wales [*A publication*]   (APTA)
Tech Note Brick Mf Assoc NSW ... Technical Note. Brick Manufacturers
  Association of New South Wales [*A publication*]   (APTA)
Tech Note Charles Kolling Res Lab ... Technical Note. Charles Kolling
  Research Laboratory. Department of Mechanical
  Engineering. University of Sydney [*A publication*]   (APTA)
Tech Note Def Stand Lab Aust ... Australia. Defence Standards Laboratories.
  Technical Note [*A publication*]   (APTA)

Tech Note Dep For Res (Nigeria) ... Technical Note. Department of Forest Research (Nigeria) [*A publication*]
Tech Note E Afr Agric For Res Organ ... Technical Note. East African Agriculture and Forestry Research Organization [*A publication*]
Tech Note For Dep (Brit Solomon Islands Protect) ... Technical Note. Forestry Department (British Solomon Islands Protectorate) [*A publication*]
Tech Note For Dep (Kenya) ... Technical Note. Forest Department (Nairobi, Kenya) [*A publication*]
Tech Note For Dep (Uganda) ... Technical Note. Forest Department (Uganda) [*A publication*]
Tech Note For Prod Res Ind Dev Comm (Philipp) ... Technical Note. Forest Products Research and Industries Development Commission (Philippines) [*A publication*]
Tech Note For Prod Res Inst (Ghana) ... Technical Note. Forest Products Research Institute (Ghana) [*A publication*]
Tech Note For Timb Bur ... Technical Note. Bureau of Forestry and Timber [*A publication*]   (APTA)
Tech Note Harbour Tech Res Inst Minist Transp (Jpn) ... Technical Note. Port and Harbour Technical Research Institute. Ministry of Transportation (Japan) [*A publication*]
Tech Note Mater Res Lab Aust ... Australia. Materials Research Laboratories. Technical Note [*A publication*]   (APTA)
Tech Note Oji Inst For Tree Impr ... Technical Note. Oji Institute for Forest Tree Improvement [*A publication*]
Tech Note Quetico-Sup Wild Res Cent ... Technical Note. Quetico-Superior Wilderness Research Center [*A publication*]
Tech Note Res Inst Ind Saf ... Technical Note. Research Institute of Industrial Safety [*A publication*]
Tech Notes Clay Prod ... Technical Notes on Clay Products [*Brick Development Research Institute*] [*A publication*]   (APTA)
Tech Notes For Comm NSW ... Technical Notes. Forestry Commission of New South Wales [*A publication*]
Tech Notes NSW For Comm Div Wood Technol ... New South Wales. Forestry Commission. Division of Wood Technology. Technical Notes [*A publication*]   (APTA)
Tech Note Sol Energy Stud CSIRO ... Technical Note. Solar Energy Studies. Commonwealth Scientific and Industrial Research Organisation [*A publication*]   (APTA)
Tech Notes Rubber Ind ... Technical Notes for the Rubber Industry [*A publication*]
Tech Notes Rubb Ind ... Technical Notes for the Rubber Industry [*A publication*]
Techn Pharm ... Technique Pharmaceutique [*A publication*]
TECHNQ .. Technique
Techn Rd .... Technische Rundschau [*A publication*]
Techn Rep Brit El All Ind Res Ass ... Technical Report. British Electrical and Allied Industries Research Association [*A publication*]
Techn Rep Ser Wld Hlth Org ... Technical Report Series. World Health Organisation [*A publication*]
Techn Rep Tohoku ... Technology Reports. Tohoku Imperial University [*A publication*]
Techn Rundschau ... Technische Rundschau [*A publication*]
Techn Sci Munic ... Techniques et Sciences Municipales [*A publication*]
Techn Soc ... Technology and Society [*A publication*]
Techn Ueberw ... Technische Ueberwachung [*A publication*]
TECHOPEVAL ... Technical Operational Evaluation
Tech Pap Agric Exp Stn (P Rico) ... Technical Paper. Agricultural Experiment Station (Puerto Rico) [*A publication*]
Tech Pap Amer Pulpw Ass ... Technical Papers. American Pulpwood Association [*A publication*]
Tech Pap Anim Res Lab CSIRO ... Technical Paper. Animal Research Laboratories. Commonwealth Scientific and Industrial Research Organisation [*A publication*]   (APTA)
Tech Pap Anim Res Labs CSIRO ... Technical Paper. Animal Research Laboratories. Commonwealth Scientific and Industrial Research Organization [*A publication*]
Tech Pap (Aust) CSIRO Div Appl Geomech ... Technical Paper. (Australia) Commonwealth Scientific and Industrial Research Organisation. Division of Applied Geomechanics [*A publication*]
Tech Pap (Aust) CSIRO Div Mineragraphic Invest ... Technical Paper. (Australia) Commonwealth Scientific and Industrial Research Organisation. Division of Mineragraphic Investigation [*A publication*]
Tech Pap Aust Water Resour Coun ... Technical Paper. Australian Water Resources Council [*A publication*]   (APTA)
Tech Pap Aust Wat Resour Coun ... Technical Paper. Australian Water Resources Council [*A publication*]   (APTA)
Tech Pap Calif Dep Agric ... Technical Papers. California Department of Agriculture [*A publication*]
Tech Pap Canad Pulp Pap Ass ... Technical Paper. Canadian Pulp and Paper Association [*A publication*]
Tech Pap Dep For (Qd) ... Technical Paper. Department of Forestry (Queensland) [*A publication*]   (APTA)
Tech Pap Dep For (Queensl) ... Technical Paper. Department of Forestry (Queensland) [*A publication*]   (APTA)
Tech Pap Div Appl Chem CSIRO ... Technical Paper. Division of Applied Chemistry. Commonwealth Scientific and Industrial Research Organisation [*A publication*]   (APTA)

Tech Pap Div Appl Geomech CSIRO ... Technical Paper. Division of Applied Geomechanics. Commonwealth Scientific and Industrial Research Organisation [*A publication*]   (APTA)
Tech Pap Div Appl Miner CSIRO ... Technical Paper. Division of Applied Mineralogy. Commonwealth Scientific and Industrial Research Organisation [*A publication*]   (APTA)
Tech Pap Div Appl Org Chem CSIRO ... Technical Paper. Division of Applied Organic Chemistry. Commonwealth Scientific and Industrial Research Organisation [*A publication*]   (APTA)
Tech Pap Div Atmosph Phys CSIRO ... Technical Paper. Division of Atmospheric Physics. Commonwealth Scientific and Industrial Research Organisation [*A publication*]   (APTA)
Tech Pap Div Atmos Phys CSIRO ... Technical Paper. Division of Atmospheric Physics. Commonwealth Scientific and Industrial Research Organisation [*A publication*]   (APTA)
Tech Pap Div Bldg Res CSIRO ... Technical Paper. Division of Building Research. Commonwealth Scientific and Industrial Research Organisation [*A publication*]   (APTA)
Tech Pap Div Build Res CSIRO ... Technical Paper. Division of Building Research. Commonwealth Scientific and Industrial Research Organisation [*A publication*]   (APTA)
Tech Pap Div Chem Technol CSIRO ... Technical Paper. Division of Chemical Technology. Commonwealth Scientific and Industrial Research Organisation [*A publication*]   (APTA)
Tech Pap Div Ent CSIRO ... Technical Paper. Division of Entomology. Commonwealth Scientific and Industrial Research Organisation [*A publication*]   (APTA)
Tech Pap Div Fd Preserv CSIRO ... Technical Paper. Division of Food Preservation. Commonwealth Scientific and Industrial Research Organisation [*A publication*]   (APTA)
Tech Pap Div Fd Res CSIRO ... Technical Paper. Division of Food Research. Commonwealth Scientific and Industrial Research Organisation [*A publication*]   (APTA)
Tech Pap Div Fd Res CSIRO (Aust) ... Technical Paper. Division of Food Research. Commonwealth Scientific and Industrial Research Organisation (Australia) [*A publication*]
Tech Pap Div Fish Oceanogr CSIRO ... Technical Paper. Division of Fisheries and Oceanography. Commonwealth Scientific and Industrial Research Organisation [*A publication*]   (APTA)
Tech Pap Div Food Res CSIRO ... Technical Paper. Division of Food Research. Commonwealth Scientific and Industrial Research Organisation [*A publication*]   (APTA)
Tech Pap Div Land Resour Manage CSIRO ... Technical Paper. Division of Land Resources Management. Commonwealth Scientific and Industrial Research Organisation [*A publication*]   (APTA)
Tech Pap Div Land Use Res CSIRO ... Technical Paper. Division of Land Use Research. Commonwealth Scientific and Industrial Research Organisation [*A publication*]   (APTA)
Tech Pap Div Ld Res CSIRO ... Technical Paper. Division of Land Research. Commonwealth Scientific and Industrial Research Organisation [*A publication*]   (APTA)
Tech Pap Div Ld Res Reg Surv CSIRO (Aust) ... Technical Papers. Division of Land Research and Regional Survey. Commonwealth Scientific and Industrial Research Organisation (Australia) [*A publication*]
Tech Pap Div Ld Use Res CSIRO ... Technical Paper. Division of Land Use Research. Commonwealth Scientific and Industrial Research Organisation [*A publication*]   (APTA)
Tech Pap Div Math Stat CSIRO ... Technical Paper. Division of Mathematics and Statistics. Commonwealth Scientific and Industrial Research Organisation [*A publication*]   (APTA)
Tech Pap Div Math Statist CSIRO ... Technical Paper. Division of Mathematical Statistics. Commonwealth Scientific and Industrial Research Organisation [*A publication*]
Tech Pap Div Mat Statist CSIRO ... Technical Paper. Division of Mathematical Statistics. Commonwealth Scientific and Industrial Research Organisation [*A publication*]   (APTA)
Tech Pap Div Meteorol Phys CSIRO ... Technical Paper. Division of Meteorological Physics. Commonwealth Scientific and Industrial Research Organisation [*A publication*]   (APTA)
Tech Pap Div Met Phys CSIRO ... Technical Paper. Division of Meteorological Physics. Commonwealth Scientific and Industrial Research Organisation [*A publication*]   (APTA)
Tech Pap Div Plant Ind CSIRO ... Technical Paper. Division of Plant Industry. Commonwealth Scientific and Industrial Research Organisation [*A publication*]   (APTA)
Tech Pap Div Pl Ind CSIRO ... Technical Paper. Division of Plant Industry. Commonwealth Scientific and Industrial Research Organisation [*A publication*]   (APTA)
Tech Pap Div Pl Ind CSIRO (Aust) ... Technical Papers. Division of Plant Industry. Commonwealth Scientific and Industrial Research Organisation (Australia) [*A publication*]
Tech Pap Div Soil Mechanics CSIRO ... Technical Paper. Division of Soil Mechanics. Commonwealth Scientific and Industrial Research Organisation [*A publication*]   (APTA)
Tech Pap Div Soils CSIRO ... Technical Paper. Division of Soils. Commonwealth Scientific and Industrial Research Organisation [*A publication*]   (APTA)

Tech Pap Div Tech Conf Soc Plast Eng ... Technical Papers. Divisional Technical Conference. Society of Plastics Engineers [*A publication*]

Tech Pap Div Trop Agron CSIRO ... Technical Paper. Division of Tropical Agronomy. Commonwealth Scientific and Industrial Research Organisation [*A publication*]   (APTA)

Tech Pap Div Trop Crops Pastures CSIRO ... Technical Paper. Division of Tropical Crops and Pastures. Commonwealth Scientific and Industrial Research Organisation [*A publication*]   (APTA)

Tech Pap Div Trop Pastures CSIRO ... Technical Paper. Division of Tropical Pastures. Commonwealth Scientific and Industrial Research Organisation [*A publication*]   (APTA)

Tech Pap Div Wildl Res CSIRO ... Technical Paper. Division of Wildlife Research. Commonwealth Scientific and Industrial Research Organisation [*A publication*]   (APTA)

Tech Pap For Comm NSW ... Technical Paper. Forestry Commission of New South Wales [*A publication*]

Tech Pap For Res Inst NZ For Serv ... Technical Paper. Forest Research Institute. New Zealand Forest Service [*A publication*]

Tech Pap Hydrol ... Technical Papers in Hydrology [*A publication*]

Tech Pap Inst Pet ... Technical Papers. Institute of Petroleum [*London*] [*A publication*]

Tech Pap Intersoc Energy Convers Eng Conf ... Technical Papers. Intersociety Energy Conversion Engineering Conference [*A publication*]

Tech Pap Natl Meas Lab CSIRO ... Technical Paper. National Measurement Laboratory. Commonwealth Scientific and Industrial Research Organisation [*A publication*]   (APTA)

Tech Pap Natn Stand Lab CSIRO ... Technical Paper. National Standards Laboratory. Commonwealth Scientific and Industrial Research Organisation [*A publication*]   (APTA)

Tech Pap NY State Dep Environ Conserv ... Technical Paper. New York State Department of Environmental Conservation [*A publication*]

Tech Pap SME Ser EE ... Technical Paper. Society of Manufacturing Engineers. Series EE (Electrical Engineering) [*A publication*]

Tech Pap Soc Manuf Eng Ser AD ... Technical Paper. Society of Manufacturing Engineers. Series AD (Assembly Division) [*A publication*]

Tech Pap Soc Manuf Eng Ser EE ... Technical Paper. Society of Manufacturing Engineers. Series EE (Electrical Engineering) [*A publication*]

Tech Pap Soc Manuf Eng Ser EM ... Technical Paper. Society of Manufacturing Engineers. Series EM (Engineering Materials) [*A publication*]

Tech Pap Soc Manuf Eng Ser FC ... Technical Paper. Society of Manufacturing Engineers. Series FC (Finishing and Coating) [*A publication*]

Tech Pap Soc Manuf Eng Ser IQ ... Technical Paper. Society of Manufacturing Engineers. Series IQ (Inspection and Quality) [*A publication*]

Tech Pap Soc Manuf Eng Ser MF ... Technical Paper. Society of Manufacturing Engineers. Series MF (Material Forming) [*A publication*]

Tech Pap Soc Manuf Eng Ser MR ... Technical Paper. Society of Manufacturing Engineers. Series MR (Material Removal) [*A publication*]

Tech Pap Univ PR Agr Exp Sta ... Technical Paper. University of Puerto Rico. Agricultural Experiment Station [*A publication*]

Tech Pet..... Techniques du Petrole [*France*] [*A publication*]

Tech Phot... Technical Photography [*A publication*]

Tech-Phys Monogr ... Technisch-Physikalische Monographien [*A publication*]

Tech Phys Ser ... Techniques of Physics Series [*A publication*]

Tech Poszukiwan ... Technika Poszukiwan [*A publication*]

Tech Poszukiwan Geol ... Technika Poszukiwan Geologicznych [*A publication*]

Tech Poszukiwan Geol Geosynoptyka Geoterm ... Technika Poszukiwan Geologicznych, Geosynoptyka, i Geotermia [*A publication*]

Tech Pr ...... Technika Prace [*Czechoslovakia*] [*A publication*]

Tech Prat Agr ... Technique et Pratique Agricoles [*A publication*]

Tech Prepr Am Soc Lubr Eng ... Technical Preprints. American Society of Lubrication Engineers [*A publication*]

Tech Prog Rep US Bur Mines ... Technical Progress Report. United States Bureau of Mines [*A publication*]

Tech Progr Rep Hawaii Agr Exp Sta ... Technical Progress Report. Hawaii Agricultural Experiment Station. University of Hawaii [*A publication*]

Tech Publ Aust Soc Dairy Technol ... Australian Society of Dairy Technology. Technical Publication [*A publication*]   (APTA)

Tech Publ Div Wood Technol For Comm NSW ... Technical Publication. Division of Wood Technology. Forestry Commission of New South Wales [*A publication*]   (APTA)

Tech Publ NY St Coll For ... Technical Publication. New York State University. College of Forestry [*A publication*]

Tech Publs ... Technical Publications [*A publication*]

Tech Publs Aust Soc Dairy Technol ... Technical Publications. Australian Society of Dairy Technology [*A publication*]   (APTA)

Tech Publs Dep Agric (Vict) ... Technical Publications. Department of Agriculture (Victoria) [*A publication*]   (APTA)

Tech Publs Div Wood Technol NSW For Comm ... Technical Publications. Division of Wood Technology. New South Wales Forestry Commission [*A publication*]   (APTA)

Tech Publs NSW For Comm Div Wood Technol ... Technical Publications. New South Wales Forestry Commission. Division of Wood Technology [*A publication*]   (APTA)

Tech Publ State Biol Surv Kans ... Technical Publications. State Biological Survey of Kansas [*A publication*]

Tech Publ State Univ Coll For Syracuse Univ ... Technical Publication. State University College of Forestry. Syracuse University [*A publication*]

Tech Q .... Technology Quarterly and Proceedings. Society of Arts [*A publication*]

Tech Quart Master Brew Ass Amer ... Technical Quarterly. Master Brewers Association of America [*A publication*]

Tech R........ Technology Review [*A publication*]

Tech Radia & Telew ... Technika Radia i Telewizji [*A publication*]

Tech Rdsch (Bern) ... Technische Rundschau (Bern) [*Switzerland*] [*A publication*]

Tech Refrig Air Cond ... Technics of Refrigeration and Air Conditioning [*A publication*]

Tech Release Amer Pulpw Ass ... Technical Release. American Pulpwood Association [*A publication*]

TECHREP ... Technical Representative [*Military*]

Tech Rep AFAPL TR Air Force Aero Propul Lab (US) ... Technical Report. AFAPL-TR. Air Force Aero Propulsion Laboratory (United States) [*A publication*]

Tech Rep AFFDL TR Air Force Flight Dyn Lab (US) ... Technical Report. AFFDL-TR. Air Force Flight Dynamics Laboratory (United States) [*A publication*]

Tech Rep AFML TR Air Force Mater Lab (US) ... Technical Report. AFML-TR. Air Force Materials Laboratory (United States) [*A publication*]

Tech Rep AFWAL-TR US Air Force Wright Aeronaut Lab ... Technical Report. AFWAL-TR. United States Air Force Wright Aeronautical Laboratories [*A publication*]

Tech Rep Agric Chem Branch (Queensl) ... Technical Report. Agricultural Chemistry Branch (Queensland) [*A publication*]

Tech Rep Agric Eng Res Stn Min Agric For Ser F ... Technical Report. Agricultural Engineering Research Station. Ministry of Agriculture and Forestry. Series F. General [*Japan*] [*A publication*]

Tech Rep Agric Ld Serv Minist Agric Fish Fd ... Technical Report. Agricultural Land Service. Ministry of Agriculture, Fisheries, and Food [*A publication*]

Tech Rep Air Pollut Yokohama-Kawasaki Ind Area ... Technical Report on Air Pollution in Yokohama-Kawasaki Industrial Area [*Japan*] [*A publication*]

Tech Rep Aust Weapons Res Establ ... Technical Report. Australia Weapons Research Establishment [*A publication*]

Tech Rep Bur Met ... Technical Report. Bureau of Meteorology [*A publication*]   (APTA)

Tech Rep Bur Meteorol ... Technical Report. Bureau of Meteorology [*A publication*]   (APTA)

Tech Rep Cent Res Inst Electr Power Ind ... Technical Report. Central Research Institute of the Electrical Power Industry [*Japan*] [*A publication*]

Tech Rep Cent Res Water Resour Univ Tex Austin ... Technical Report. Center for Research in Water Resources. University of Texas at Austin [*A publication*]

Tech Rep Constr Eng Res Lab ... Technical Report. Construction Engineering Research Laboratory [*United States*] [*A publication*]

Tech Rep Dep Mines Tas ... Technical Report. Department of Mines. Tasmania [*A publication*]   (APTA)

Tech Rep Desert Locust Control Organ East Afr ... Technical Report. Desert Locust Control Organization for Eastern Africa [*A publication*]

Tech Rep Div Appl Geomech CSIRO ... Technical Report. Division of Applied Geomechanics. Commonwealth Scientific and Industrial Research Organisation [*A publication*]   (APTA)

Tech Rep Div Mech Eng CSIRO ... Technical Report. Division of Mechanical Engineering. Commonwealth Scientific and Industrial Research Organisation [*A publication*]   (APTA)

Tech Rep Div Mech Engng CSIRO ... Technical Report. Division of Mechanical Engineering. Commonwealth Scientific and Industrial Research Organisation [*A publication*]   (APTA)

Tech Rep Div Soil Mech CSIRO ... Technical Report. Division of Soil Mechanics. Commonwealth Scientific and Industrial Research Organisation [*A publication*]   (APTA)

Tech Rep Eng Res Inst Kyoto Univ ... Technical Reports. Engineering Research Institute. Kyoto University [*A publication*]

Tech Rep Fac For Univ Toronto ... Technical Report. Faculty of Forestry. University of Toronto [*A publication*]

Tech Rep Grassld Res Inst ... Technical Report. Grassland Research Institute [*A publication*]

Tech Rep Inst At Energy Kyoto Univ ... Technical Reports. Institute of Atomic Energy. Kyoto University [*A publication*]

Tech Rep Inst Atom Energy Kyoto Univ ... Technical Reports. Institute of Atomic Energy. Kyoto University [*A publication*]

Tech Rep Inst Printed Circuits ... Technical Report. Institute of Printed Circuits [*A publication*]

Tech Rep ISSP (Inst Solid State Phys) Ser A ... Technical Report. ISSP (Institute for Solid State Physics). Series A [*A publication*]
Tech Rep Jet Propul Lab Calif Inst Technol ... Technical Report. Jet Propulsion Laboratory. California Institute of Technology [*A publication*]
Tech Rep JSS Proj ... Technical Report. JSS [*Japanese, Swiss, Swedish*] Project [*A publication*]
Tech Rep Kansai Univ ... Technology Reports. Kansai University [*A publication*]
Tech Rep Nanyang Univ Coll Grad Stud Inst Nat Sci ... Technical Report. Nanyang University. College of Graduate Studies. Institute of Natural Sciences [*A publication*]
Tech Rep Natl Space Dev Agency Jpn ... Technical Report. National Space Development Agency of Japan [*A publication*]
Tech Rep Nisshin Steel Co Ltd ... Technical Report. Nisshin Steel Company Limited [*Japan*] [*A publication*]
Tech Rep Off Nav Res (USA) ... Technical Report. Office of Naval Research (USA) [*A publication*]
Tech Reports Osaka Univ ... Technology Reports. Osaka University [*A publication*]
Tech Rep Osaka Univ ... Technology Reports. Osaka University [*A publication*]
Tech Rep Reg Res Sta (Samaru) ... Technical Report. Regional Research Station (Samaru) [*A publication*]
Tech Repr Graver Water Cond Co ... Technical Reprint. Graver Water Conditioning Company [*A publication*]
Tech Rep Sch For Resour NC St Univ ... Technical Report. School of Forest Resources. North Carolina State University [*A publication*]
Tech Rep Ser ARL/TR Aust Radiat Lab ... Australia. Australian Radiation Laboratory. Technical Report Series ARL/TR [*A publication*] (APTA)
Tech Rep Ser Carcinog Nat Cancer Inst (US) ... Technical Report Series: Carcinogenesis. National Cancer Institute (United States) [*A publication*]
Tech Rep Ser Int Atom Energy Ag ... Technical Reports Series. International Atomic Energy Agency [*A publication*]
Tech Rep Ser Victoria Dep Agric ... Victoria. Department of Agriculture. Technical Report Series [*A publication*] (APTA)
Tech Rep Soil Res Inst Ghana Acad Sci ... Technical Report. Soil Research Institute. Ghana Academy of Sciences [*A publication*]
Tech Rep Syst Am Soc Met ... Technical Report System. American Society for Metals [*A publication*]
Tech Rep Syst ASM ... Technical Report System. American Society for Metals [*A publication*]
Tech Rep Tasmania Dep Mines ... Tasmania. Department of Mines. Technical Report [*A publication*] (APTA)
Tech Rep Tasm Dep Mines ... Technical Report. Tasmania Department of Mines [*A publication*] (APTA)
Tech Rep Tex For Serv ... Technical Report. Texas Forest Service [*A publication*]
Tech Rep Toyo Kohan Co Ltd ... Technical Reports. Toyo Kohan Company Limited [*Japan*] [*A publication*]
Tech Rep Univ Tex Austin Cent Res Water Resour ... Technical Report. University of Texas at Austin. Center for Research in Water Resources [*A publication*]
Tech Rep US Army Eng Waterw Exp Stn ... Technical Report. United States Army Engineers. Waterways Experiment Station [*A publication*]
Tech Rep Water Resour Res Cent Hawaii Univ ... Technical Report. Hawaii University. Water Resource Research Center [*A publication*]
Tech Rep Yale Sch For ... Technical Report. Yale University. School of Forestry [*A publication*]
Tech Res Cent Finland Electr and Nucl Technol Publ ... Technical Research Centre of Finland. Electrical and Nuclear Technology Publication [*A publication*]
Tech Res Cent Finland Mater and Process Technol Publ ... Technical Research Centre of Finland. Materials and Processing Technology Publication [*A publication*]
Tech Res Cent Finl Build Technol Community Dev Publ ... Technical Research Centre of Finland. Building Technology and Community Development Publication [*A publication*]
Tech Res Cent Finl Electr Nucl Technol Publ ... Technical Research Centre of Finland. Electrical and Nuclear Technology Publication [*A publication*]
Tech Res Cent Finl Gen Div Publ ... Technical Research Centre of Finland. General Division Publication [*A publication*]
Tech Res Cent Finl Mater Process Technol Publ ... Technical Research Centre of Finland. Materials and Processing Technology Publication [*A publication*]
Tech Res Cent Finl Publ ... Technical Research Centre of Finland. Publications [*A publication*]
Tech Res Cent Finl Res Rep ... Technical Research Centre of Finland. Research Reports [*A publication*]
Tech Rev .... Technology Review [*A publication*]
Tech Rev Mitsubishi Heavy-Ind (Jpn Ed) ... Technical Review. Mitsubishi Heavy-Industries (Japanese Edition) [*A publication*]
Tech Rev Sumitomo Heavy Ind Ltd ... Technical Review. Sumitomo Heavy Industries Limited [*A publication*]
TechRMS .. Technological Qualification in Microscopy, Royal Microscopical Society [*British*] (DBQ)

Tech Routiere ... Technique Routiere [*Belgium*] [*A publication*]
Tech Rundsch ... Technische Rundschau [*A publication*]
Tech Rundsch Sulzer ... Technische Rundschau Sulzer [*Switzerland*] [*A publication*]
TECHSAT ... Technology Satellite (MCD)
Tech Sci Aeronaut Spat ... Technique et Science Aeronautiques et Spatiales [*France*] [*A publication*]
Tech et Sci Inf ... Technique et Science Informatiques [*A publication*]
Tech Sci Munic ... Techniques et Sciences Municipales [*France*] [*A publication*]
Tech Sci Munic Eau ... Techniques et Sciences Municipales/l'Eau [*A publication*]
Tech Ser Bur Ent US ... Technical Series. Bureau of Entomology. United States Department of Agriculture [*A publication*]
Tech Ser Fla Dep Nat Resour Mar Res Lab ... Technical Series. Florida Department of Natural Resources. Marine Research Laboratory [*A publication*]
Tech Serv Newsl ... Technical Services Newsletter [*A publication*]
Tech Skoda ... Technika Skoda [*A publication*]
Tech Smarownicza ... Technika Smarownicza [*A publication*]
Tech Smarownicza Trybol ... Technika Smarownicza. Trybologia [*A publication*]
Tech Soc Pacific Coast Tr ... Technical Society of the Pacific Coast. Transactions [*A publication*]
Tech Stud Common Exp Bldg Stn ... Technical Studies. Commonwealth Experimental Building Station [*A publication*] (APTA)
Tech Stud Commonw Exp Bldg Stn ... Technical Studies. Commonwealth Experimental Building Station [*A publication*] (APTA)
TECHSVS ... Technical Services [*Army*]
TECHTAF ... Technical Training Air Force
Tech Teach ... Technical Teacher [*A publication*] (APTA)
Tech Timber Guide ... Technical Timber Guide [*A publication*] (APTA)
Tech Timb Guide ... Technical Timber Guide [*A publication*] (APTA)
Tech Times ... Technology Transfer Times [*A publication*]
TECHTNG ... Technical Training (NVT)
TECHTNGSq ... Technical Training Squadron [*Air Force*]
TECHTRA ... Air Technical Training [*Navy*]
Tech Trans Bull ... Technical Translation Bulletin [*A publication*]
Tech Trav... Techniques des Travaux [*Belgium*] [*A publication*]
Tech Trav (Liege) ... Techniques des Travaux (Liege) [*A publication*]
Tech Tworczego Myslenia ... Techniki Tworczego Myslenia [*A publication*]
Tech Ueberwach ... Technische Ueberwachung [*Technological Supervising*] [*A publication*]
Tech Umweltschutz ... Technik und Umweltschutz [*East Germany*] [*A publication*]
Tech Univ Muenchen Jahrb ... Technische Universitaet Muenchen. Jahrbuch [*A publication*]
Tech W ...... Technical World [*Chicago*] [*A publication*]
Tech W ...... Technology Week [*A publication*]
TechWeldI ... Technician of the Welding Institute [*British*] (DBQ)
Tech-Wiss Abh Osram-Ges ... Technisch-Wissenschaftliche Abhandlungen der Osram-Gesellschaft [*A publication*]
Tech Wk .... Technology Week [*A publication*]
Tech Wlok ... Technik Wlokienniczy [*A publication*]
Tech World ... Technical World Magazine [*A publication*]
Tech Zentralbl ... Technisches Zentralblatt [*A publication*]
Tech Zukunft ... Techniken der Zukunft [*A publication*]
TECIB .... Technic International [*A publication*]
Tec Ind (Madrid) ... Tecnica Industrial (Madrid) [*A publication*]
Tec Ital...... Tecnica Italiana [*A publication*]
TECL......... Test Equipment Configuration Log [*NASA*] (KSC)
TECL......... Transmission-Engine Communication Link [*Automotive engineering*]
TECLA...... Tecnica (Lisbon) [*A publication*]
TECM....... Test Equipment Commodity Manager
TECMA....... Technical Ceramics Manufacturers Association (EA)
Tec Metal... Tecnica Metalurgica [*Spain*] [*A publication*]
Tec Met (Barcelona) ... Tecnica Metalurgica (Barcelona) [*A publication*]
Tec Mit K F ... Technische Mitteilungen Krupp. Forschungsberichte [*A publication*]
Tec Mit K W ... Technische Mitteilungen Krupp. Werksberichte [*A publication*]
TECMOD ... Technology Modernization (MCD)
Tec Molit ... Tecnica Molitoria [*A publication*]
TECN .... Technalysis Corp. [*NASDAQ symbol*] (NQ)
TEC-NACS ... Teachers Educational Council - National Association Cosmetology Schools
Tecnica Ital ...... Tecnica Italiana [*A publication*]
Tecnica Lisb ... Tecnica. Rivista de Engenharia (Lisboa) [*A publication*]
Tecn Ital..... Tecnica Italiana [*A publication*]
Tecnol Aliment ... Tecnologia Alimentaria [*A publication*]
Tecnol Elettr ... Tecnologie Elettriche [*A publication*]
Tecnopolim Resine ... Tecnopolimeri e Resine [*A publication*]
TECO .... Technical Co-Operation Committee [*OECD*] (DS)
TECO .... Terra Cotta [*Pronounced "tee-ko"*] [*Type of American art pottery*]
TECO .... Tesco American, Inc. [*NASDAQ symbol*] (NQ)
TECO .... Trinity Engineering Company [*Huxley, IA*] [*Telecommunications service*] (TSSD)
TECO .... Turbine Engine Checkout

TECOM .... Test and Evaluation Command [*Army*] [*Aberdeen Proving Ground, MD*]
TECOMAP ... Technical Conference of the Observation and Measurement of Atmospheric Pollution [*Helsinki, 1973*]
TECP .... Training Equipment Checkout Procedure
TECPD ...... TAPPI [*Technical Association of the Pulp and Paper Industry*] Environmental Conference. Proceedings [*A publication*]
Tec Pecuar Mex ... Tecnica Pecuaria en Mexico [*A publication*]
Tec Pecu Mex ... Tecnica Pecuaria en Mexico [*A publication*]
TECR......... Technical Reason [*Aviation*]
TECR......... Technical Requirement (AABC)
Tec R......... Technology Review [*A publication*]
TECR......... Test Equipment Change Requirement (NATG)
TECRAS..... Technical Reconnaissance and Surveillance (MCD)
Tec Regul & Mando Autom ... Tecnica de la Regulacion y Mando Automatico [*A publication*]
TECS .... Television Confirming Sensor (MCD)
TECS .... Total Environmental Control System [*Army*] (RDA)
TECS .... Treasury Enforcement Communications System [*Customs Service*]
Tec Sint Spec Org ... Tecniche e Sintesi Speciali Organiche [*A publication*]
TECSTAR ... Technical Missions, Structures and Career Development [*Military*]
Tectonophys ... Tectonophysics [*A publication*]
TECTRA ... Technology Transfer Data Bank [*California State University*] [*Sacramento*] [*Information service or system*] (IID)
TECU .... Tecumseh Products Co. [*NASDAQ symbol*] (NQ)
TECU .... Thermoelectric Environmental Control Unit
TECU .... Transportation Employees' Canadian Union
TED .... Electrical Distributor [*A publication*] (EAAP)
TED .... International Association for Training and Education in Distribution
TED .... Tasks of Emotional Development Test [*Psychology*]
TeD .... Te Deum [*Music*]
TED .... Teacher Education Division [*Council for Exceptional Children*]
TeD .... Telefunken-Decca [*Video disk system*]
TED .... Tenders Electronic Daily [*Office for Official Publications of the European Communities*] [*Database*] [*Luxembourg*]
TED .... Terminal Editor (ADA)
TED .... Test Engineering Division [*Navy*]
TED .... Test Engineering Documentation (MCD)
TED .... Test, Evaluation, and Development (MUGU)
TED .... Test and Evaluation Division [*National Weather Service*]
T Ed .... Theological Educator [*A publication*]
TED .... Thermionic Emission Detector [*For gas chromatography*]
TED .... Thermoelectric Device
TED .... Thisted [*Denmark*] [*Airport symbol*] (OAG)
TED .... Thomas Edmund Dewey [*Republican candidate for President, 1948*]
TED .... Threshold Erythema Dose [*Medicine*]
TED .... Threshold Extension Demodulator
TED .... Thromboembolic Disease [*Medicine*]
TED .... Toledo Edison Co. [*NYSE symbol*] (SPSG)
TED .... Total Energy Detector
TED .... Trace Element Doping
TED .... Tracking Error Detector (MCD)
TED .... Trailing Edge Down [*Aviation*] (MCD)
TED .... Training Equipment Development [*Military*]
TED .... Traitement Electronique des Donnees [*Electronic Data Processing - EDP*] [*French*]
TED .... Transfer Effective Date [*Military*] (AFM)
TED .... Transferred Electron Device [*Air Force*]
TED .... Translation Error Detector (DIT)
TED .... Troop Exercise Director (CINC)
TED .... True Economic Depreciation
TED .... Trunk Encryption Device [*Telecommunications*] (TEL)
TED .... Turbine Electric Drive
Ted R.......... Turbine Engine Division [*Air Force*]
TED .... Turtle Exclusion Device [*Tool attached to shrimp boats in the Gulf of Mexico which allows the endangered Kemp's ridley turtle to escape the shrimp nets*] [*Facetious translations: "Trawler Extinction Device," "Trawling Efficiency Device"*]
TEDA ...... Theatre Equipment Dealers Association [*Later, TEA*] (EA)
TEDA .... Triethylenediamine [*Organic chemistry*]
TEDAR ...... Telemetered Data Reduction (AAG)
TEDC .... Technical Education Center
TEDC .... Tellurium Diethyldithiocarbamate [*Organic chemistry*]
TEDDS...... Tactical Environmental Dissemination and Display (MCD)
TEDE....... Temperature-Enhanced Displacement Effect
TEDES ..... Telemetry Data Evaluation System
TEDGA ..... Technical Digest [*A publication*]
TEDL....... Transferred-Electron-Device Logic (MSA)
TEDMA ..... Triethylene Dimethacrylate [*Organic chemistry*]
TEDP....... Tetraethyl Dithionopyrophosphate [*Organic chemistry*]
TEDPAS ... Technical Data Package Automated System
TEDS....... Tactical Expendable Drone System (MCD)
TEDS....... Target Effluent Detection System (MCD)
TEDS....... Teleteach Expanded Delivery System [*US Air Force*] [*Wright-Patterson AFB, OH*] [*Telecommunications*] (TSSD)

TEDSCO ... Test Equipment Documentation Scheduling Committee
TEE........... [*The*] Entrepreneurial Economy [*Corporation for Enterprise Development*] [*A publication*]
TEE........... Tape Editing Equipment
TEE........... Tbessa [*Algeria*] [*Airport symbol*] (OAG)
TEE........... Teeples Ranch [*Montana*] [*Seismograph station code, US Geological Survey*] [*Closed*] (SEIS)
TEE........... Teeshin Resources Ltd. [*Vancouver Stock Exchange symbol*]
TEE........... Telecommunications Engineering Establishment [*British*]
TEE........... Terminal Effects and Experimentation (MCD)
TEE........... Tertiary Entrance Examination [*Western Australia*]
TEE........... Test Equipment Engineering (AAG)
TEE........... Tex-Textilis. Technisch Wetenschappelijk Maandblad voor de Benelux Textielindustrie [*A publication*]
TEE........... Theological Education by Extension [*Church of England*]
TEE........... Torpedo Experimental Establishment [*British*]
TEE........... Total Effective Exposure [*Advertising*]
TEE........... Training Effectiveness Evaluation
TEE........... Trans-Europ-Express [*Continental high-speed train*]
TEE........... Transesophageal Echocardiography
TEE........... Trapeza Exagogon-Eisagogon [*Export-Import Bank*] [*Greek*]
TEE........... Triaxial Earth Ellipsoid
TEEF .... Tax-Exempt Equity Fund
TEEL .... Temporary Expedient Equipment List [*Army*] (AABC)
TEEM........ Test for Examining Expressive Morphology [*Educational test*]
TEEM........ Trans-Europ-Express-Marchandises [*Continental high-speed train*]
TEES .... Texas Engineering Experiment Station [*Texas A & M University*] [*Research center*]
TEESS....... Tank Engine Exhaust Smoke System (MCD)
TEES Tech Bull ... TEES [*Texas Engineering Experiment Station*] Technical Bulletin [*A publication*]
TEF........... [*The*] Eagle Foundation [*Defunct*] (EA)
TEF........... [*The*] Environmental Fund [*Later, PEB*] (EA)
TEF........... Tear Efficiency Factor [*Textiles*]
Tef........... Tefillin (BJA)
TEF........... Telefonica de Espana ADS [*NYSE symbol*] (SPSG)
TEF........... Telex Africa [*A publication*]
TEF........... Telfer [*Australia*] [*Airport symbol*] (OAG)
TEF........... Temperance Education Foundation [*Defunct*] (EA)
TEF........... Tracheoesophageal Fistula [*Medicine*]
TEF........... Transverse Electric Field
TEF........... Tunable Etalon Filter
TEF........... Turkey Embryo Fibroblast [*Biochemistry*]
TEFA .... Total Essential Fatty Acid [*of foodstuffs*]
TEFA .... Total Esterified Fatty Acid
TEFA .... Tube-Excited X-Ray Fluorescence Analyzer
TEFAP ...... Temporary Emergency Food Assistance Program [*Department of Agriculture*]
TEFC .... Totally Enclosed - Fan Cooled
TEFL .... Teaching English as a Foreign Language
TEFLON ... Tetrafluoroethylene Resin [*Du Pont*]
TEFL/TESL Newsl ... TEFL [*Teaching English as a Foreign Language*]/TESL [*Teaching English as a Second Language*] Newsletter [*A publication*] (APTA)
TEFO........ Technological Forecasting and Social Change [*A publication*]
TEFORS.... Technological Forecasting and Simulation for Program Selection (MCD)
TEFP........ Transportability Engineering Focal Point
TEFRA ...... Tax Equity and Fiscal Responsibility Act of 1982
TEG .... Tactical Employment Guide [*Military*] (CAAL)
Teg .... Tegula [*Entomology*]
TEG .... Templar Mining [*Vancouver Stock Exchange symbol*]
TEG .... Test Element Group
TEG .... Tetraethylene Glycol [*Organic chemistry*]
TEG .... Thermoelectric Generator
TEG .... Thromboelastogram [*or Thromboelastograph*] [*Medicine*]
TEG .... Tijdschrift voor Economische en Sociale Geografie [*A publication*]
TEG .... Top Edge Gilt [*Bookbinding*]
TEG .... Triethyl Gallium [*Organic chemistry*]
TEG .... Triethylene Glycol [*Organic chemistry*]
TEGAS ...... Test Generation and Simulation
TEGAS...... Time Generation and Simulation [*Telecommunications*] (TEL)
TEGD .... Technical Enforcement Guidance Document [*Environmental Protection Agency*]
TEGDME ... Tetraethylene Glycol Dimethyl Ether [*Organic chemistry*]
TEGDN ..... Triethylene Glycol Dinitrate [*An explosive*]
TEGG .... Thermogrip Electric Glue Gun
TEGMA ..... Terminal Elevator Grain Merchants Association (EA)
TEGMA .... Triethylene Glycol Dimethacrylate [*Organic chemistry*] (MCD)
Teg Meded S Afr Dep Landbou Viss ... Tegniese Mededeling. Suid Afrika Departement van Landbou en Visserye [*A publication*]
TEGNA ..... Tegnikon [*A publication*]
TEGO .... Taylor's Encyclopedia of Government Officials [*A publication*]
TEGTA...... Technische Gemeinschaft [*A publication*]
TEGWAR ... [*The*] Exciting Game Without Any Rules [*Card game*]
TEH........... Blare Lake, AK [*Location identifier*] [*FAA*] (FAAL)
Teh........... Tehillim (BJA)

TEH .... Tehran [*Iran*] [*Seismograph station code, US Geological Survey*] (SEIS)
TEH .... Tehran [*Iran*] [*Geomagnetic observatory code*]
TEH .... Tehua [*Race of maize*]
TEH .... Topics in Environmental Health [*Elsevier Book Series*] [*A publication*]
TEH .... Twin-Engined Helicopter (MCD)
TEHBA ..... Tehnika (Belgrade) [*A publication*]
Teh Fiz ...... Tehnicka Fizika [*A publication*]
Teh Hronika ... Tehnika Hronika [*A publication*]
TEHP .... Thermoelectric Heat Pump (MCD)
Teh Rud Geol Metal ... Tehnika Rudarstvo Geologiya i Metalurgija [*A publication*]
Teh Tootmine ... Tehnika ja Tootmine [*Estonian SSR*] [*A publication*]
TEI .... [*The*] Entrepreneurship Institute (EA)
TEI .... Tax Executives Institute (EA)
TEI .... Technical Engineering Item (MCD)
TE & I .... Technology Evaluation and Integration (MCD)
TEI .... Telecommunications Engineering, Incorporated [*Dallas, TX*] (TSSD)
TEI .... Temporary Engineering Instruction [*Navy*] (NG)
TEI .... Texas International Co. [*NYSE symbol*] [*Toronto Stock Exchange symbol*]
TEI .... Thorne Ecological Institute (EA)
TEI .... Trait Evaluation Index [*Psychology*]
TEI .... Transearth Injection [*AEC*]
TEI .... Transfer on Error Indication
TEI .... Trucking Employers, Incorporated [*Later, TMI*]
TEIC .... Tissue Equivalent Ionization Chamber
TEICA .... Transactions. Engineering Institute of Canada [*A publication*]
TEIGA ...... Teishin Igaku [*A publication*]
TEIGN....... Teignmouth [*Urban district in England*]
TEIGNBR ... Teignbridge [*England*]
Teilhard Rev ... Teilhard Review [*London*] [*A publication*]
Teilhard St ... Teilhard Studies [*A publication*]
TEIM .... Travel Economic Impact Model [*Department of Commerce*]
Teint Apprets ... Teinture et Apprets [*A publication*]
TEIP .... Tax-Exempt Investor Program [*Investment term*]
TEIR .... Thomas Edison Inns, Inc. [*NASDAQ symbol*] (NQ)
TEIRD .... Technology Ireland [*A publication*]
TEIRDC .... Tamil Eelam International Research and Documentation Centre [*Canada*]
Teiss .... Teissler's Court of Appeal, Parish of Orleans, Reports [*1903-17*] [*A publication*] (DLA)
Teissler ...... Teissler's Court of Appeal, Parish of Orleans, Reports [*1903-17*] [*A publication*] (DLA)
TEJ .... Emmanuel School of Religion, Johnson City, TN [*OCLC symbol*] (OCLC)
TEJ .... Transverse Expansion Joint [*Technical drawings*]
TEJA .... Tutmonda Esperantista Jurnalista Asocio [*World Association of Esperanto Journalists - WAEJ*] (EAIO)
TEJAC ...... Trade Effluent Joint Advisory Committee [*British*] (DCTA)
TEJIA....... Transport Engineer [*A publication*]
TEJO .... Tutmonda Esperantista Junulara Organizo [*World Organization of Young Esperantists*] (EAIO)
TEJPA...... Tejipar [*A publication*]
TEJS......... Tejas Gas Corp. [*NASDAQ symbol*] (NQ)
TEK .... Teck Corp. [*Toronto Stock Exchange symbol*] [*Vancouver Stock Exchange symbol*]
TEK .... Teekin [*Tonga*] [*Seismograph station code, US Geological Survey*] (SEIS)
TEK .... Tektronix, Inc. [*NYSE symbol*] (SPSG)
TEK .... Test Equipment Kit
TeK .... Text und Kontext [*A publication*]
TEK .... Truppenentgiftungskompanie [*Personnel decontamination company*] [*German military - World War II*]
Tek Aikak ... Teknillinen Aikakauslehti [*A publication*]
Tek Bul Petkim Petrokimya A S Arastirma Mudurlugu ... Teknik Bulten. Petkim Petrokimya A. S. Arastirma Mudurlugu [*A publication*]
TEKE......... Tau Kappa Epsilon [*Fraternity*] (EA)
Tek Forum ... Tekniskt Forum [*Finland*] [*A publication*]
TEKHA ..... Teoreticheskaya i Eksperimental'naya Khimiya [*A publication*]
Tekh Dokl Gidrol ... Tekhnicheskie Doklady po Gidrologii [*A publication*]
Tekh Ekon Izv Tatabanyai Szenbanyak ... Tekhnichesko Ekonomicheskie Izvestiya Tatabanyai Szenbanyak [*A publication*]
Tekh Estetika ... Tekhnicheskaya Estetika [*USSR*] [*A publication*]
Tekh Inf Sov Nar Khoz Kuibyshev Ekon Adm Raiona ... Tekhnicheskaya Informatsiya. Sovet Narodnogo Khozyaistva Kuibyshevskogo Ekonomicheskogo Administrativnogo Raiona [*A publication*]
Tekh Kibern ... Tekhnicheskaya Kibernetika [*A publication*]
Tekh Kino Telev ... Tekhnika Kino i Televideniya [*A publication*]
Tekh Kino i Telev ... Tekhnika Kino i Televideniya [*A publication*]
Tekh Mis'l ... Tekhnicheska Mis'l [*A publication*]
Tekh Misul ... Tekhnicheska Misul [*Bulgaria*] [*A publication*]
Tekh Molodezhi ... Tekhnika Molodezhi [*A publication*]
Tekhnol Legk Splavov ... Tekhnologiya Legkikh Splavov [*A publication*]
Tekhnol Mashinostr (Moscow) ... Tekhnologiya Mashinostroeniya (Moscow) [*A publication*]
Tekhnol Mater ... Tekhnologiya Materialov [*A publication*]

Tekhnol Neorg Veshchestv ... Tekhnologiya Neorganicheskikh Veshchestv [*A publication*]
Tekhnol Organ Mekh Liteinogo Proizvod ... Tekhnologiya, Organizatsiya, i Mekhanizatsiya Liteinogo Proizvodstva [*A publication*]
Tekhnol Organ Proizvod ... Tekhnologiya i Organizatsiya Proizvodstva [*A publication*]
Tekhnol Proizvod Sukhikh Diagn Pitatel'nykh Sred ... Tekhnologiya Proizvodstva Sukhikh Diagnosticheskikh Pitatel'nykh Sred [*A publication*]
Tekhnol Stroit Proizvod ... Tekhnologiya Stroitel'nogo Proizvodstva [*A publication*]
Tek Hoegsk Handl ... Tekniska Hoegskolan Handlingar [*A publication*]
Tek Hogsk Helsingfors Vetensk Publ ... Tekniska Hoegskolan i Helsingfors Vetenskapliga Publikationer [*A publication*]
Tekh Sel'Khoz ... Tekhnika v Sel'skom Khozyaistve [*A publication*]
Tekh Usloviya Metody Opred Vrednykh Veshchestv Vozdukhe ... Tekhnicheskie Usloviya na Metody Opredeleniya Vrednykh Veshchestv v Vozdukhe [*A publication*]
Tekh Vooruzhenie ... Tekhnika i Vooruzhenie [*USSR*] [*A publication*]
Tekh Vozdushn Flota ... Tekhnika Vozdushnogo Flota [*A publication*]
Tekh Zhelezn Dorog ... Tekhnika Zheleznykh Dorog [*A publication*]
Tek Inf .... Teknisk Information [*Sweden*] [*A publication*]
TEKKA...... Tekkokai [*A publication*]
Tek Kem Aikak ... Teknillisen Kemian Aikakauslehti [*Finland*] [*A publication*]
Tek Medd .. Tekniska Meddelanden [*Sweden*] [*A publication*]
Tekn Forsknstift Skogsarb ... Teknik Forskningsstiftelsen Skogsarbeten [*A publication*]
Tekn Kino Televid ... Tekhnika Kino i Televideniya [*A publication*]
Teknol Avtom Mashinostr ... Tekhnologiya i Avtomatizatsiya Mashinostroeniya [*A publication*]
TEKSA ...... Tekhnika (Sofia) [*A publication*]
Tek Samf Hand ... Tekniska Samfundets Handlingar [*A publication*]
TEKSIF..... Turkiye Tekstil ve Orme Sanayii Iscileri Sendikalari Federasyonu [*National Federation of Textile Unions*] [*Turkey*]
Tekstil Prom ... Tekstil'naya Promyshlennost [*A publication*]
Tekst Ind ... Tekstilna Industrija [*A publication*]
Tekst Prom (Moscow) ... Tekstil'naya Promyshlennost (Moscow) [*A publication*]
Tekst Prom (Sofia) ... Tekstilna Promishlennost (Sofia) [*A publication*]
Tekst Prom-St ... Tekstil'naya Promyshlennost [*A publication*]
TEKTA ...... Tekstil [*A publication*]
Tek Tidskr ... Teknisk Tidskrift [*A publication*]
Tek Tidsskr Text Beklaedning ... Teknisk Tidsskrift for Textil og Beklaedning [*A publication*]
Tektonika Sib ... Tektonika Sibiri [*A publication*]
Tek Ukebl ... Teknisk Ukeblad [*A publication*]
Tek Vetensk Forsk ... Teknisk Vetenskaplig Forskning [*Sweden*] [*A publication*]
Tek Yay Kavak Arast Enst (Izmit) ... Teknik Yayinlar. Kavakcihk Arastirma Enstitusu (Izmit, Turkey) [*A publication*]
TEL.......... Task Execution Language
TEL.......... Taxpayers Education Lobby (EA)
TEL.......... TeleCom Corp. [*NYSE symbol*] (SPSG)
TEL.......... Telecommunications (FAAC)
TEL.......... Telegraaf [*A publication*]
TEL.......... Telegram
TEL.......... Telegraph
TEL.......... Telemetry (KSC)
TEL.......... Telephone (AAG)
TEL.......... Telescope (AAG)
Tel........... Telescopium [*Constellation*]
TEL.......... Teletypewriter [*Telecommunications*] (NOAA)
TEL.......... Tell City, IN [*Location identifier*] [*FAA*] (FAAL)
tel .... Telugu [*MARC language code*] [*Library of Congress*] (LCCP)
TEL........... Tennis Electric Lines [*Australia*]
TEL.......... Terex Equipment Limited
TEL.......... Test of Economic Literacy [*Educational test*]
TEL.......... Test Log
TEL.......... Tests for Everyday Living [*Educational test*]
TEL.......... Tetraethyllead [*Organic chemistry*]
TEL.......... Thalner Electronic Laboratories, Inc. [*Ann Arbor, MI*] (TSSD)
TEL.......... Thomas Edward Lawrence [*Lawrence of Arabia*] [*British archaeologist, soldier, and writer, 1888-1935*]
TEL.......... Training Equipment List
TEL.......... Transporter-Erector-Launcher [*Air Force*]
Telan .... Telenoticiosa Americana [*Press agency*] [*Argentina*]
TELATS.... Tactical Electronic Locating and Targeting System (MCD)
Tel Aviv J Inst A ... Tel Aviv. Journal of the Tel Aviv University Institute of Archaeology [*A publication*]
Tel Aviv Univ Stud L ... Tel Aviv University Studies in Law [*Tel-Aviv, Israel*] [*A publication*] (DLA)
Tel-Aviv U Stud L ... Tel-Aviv University Studies in Law [*Tel-Aviv, Israel*] [*A publication*] (DLA)
TELB .... Telephone Booth
TELC........ Telco Systems, Inc. [*NASDAQ symbol*] (NQ)
TELC........ Teleglobe Canada
TELCAM .. Telecommunication Equipment Low-Cost Acquisition Method [*Navy*]

TELCO...... Telephone Operating Company [*Also, TELOP*]
TELCOM ... Telecommunications   (NASA)
Telcom Rep ... Telcom Report [*A publication*]
TELCON... Telephone Conference [*or Conversation*]   (AAG)
TELD........ Test of Early Language Development
TELE .... Telegram
TELE .... Telegraph
TELE .... Telephone
Tele .... Telescopium [*Constellation*]
TELE .... Television   (ADA)
TELE .... TPI Enterprises [*Formerly, Telecom Plus International*]
          [*NASDAQ symbol*]   (SPSG)
TELEA ...... Tetrahedron Letters [*A publication*]
TELEC ...... Telecommunication
TELEC ...... Teleglobe Canada
TELEC ...... Thermoelectronic LASER Energy Converter
TELECAMRA ... Television Camera   (MDG)
TELECAR ... Telemetry Carrier Acquisition and Recovery   (MCD)
TELECAST ... Television Broadcasting   (CET)
TELECC.... Telecommunication
Telecom...... Telecommunications [*A publication*]
TELECOM ... Telecommunications   (AFM)
Telecom Aust Res Q ... Telecom Australia Research Quarterly [*A
          publication*]   (APTA)
Telecom J... Telecommunication Journal of Australia [*A
          publication*]   (APTA)
Telecom J Aust ... Telecommunication Journal of Australia [*A
          publication*]   (APTA)
Telecomm... Telecommunications [*A publication*]
Telecomm J ... Telecommunication Journal [*A publication*]
Telecomm J Aust ... Telecommunication Journal of Australia [*A
          publication*]   (APTA)
Telecom ML ... Telecom Market Letter [*A publication*]
Telecomm Po ... Telecommunications Policy [*A publication*]
Telecomm Prod ... Telecommunication Products and Technology [*A
          publication*]
Telecomms ... Telecommunications [*International Edition*] [*A publication*]
Telecommun J ... Telecommunication Journal [*A publication*]
Telecommun J Aust ... Telecommunication Journal of Australia [*A
          publication*]
Telecommun J (Engl Ed) ... Telecommunication Journal (English Edition) [*A
          publication*]
Telecommun Policy ... Telecommunications Policy [*A publication*]
Telecommun Radio Eng ... Telecommunications and Radio Engineering [*A
          publication*]
Telecommun and Radio Eng Part 1 ... Telecommunications and Radio
          Engineering. Part 1. Telecommunications [*A publication*]
Telecommun and Radio Eng Part 2 ... Telecommunications and Radio
          Engineering. Part 2. Radio Engineering [*A publication*]
Telecommun Radio Eng (USSR) Part 1 ... Telecommunications and Radio
          Engineering. Part 1. Telecommunications (USSR) [*A
          publication*]
Telecommun Radio Eng (USSR) Part 2 ... Telecommunications and Radio
          Engineering (USSR). Part 2. Radio Engineering [*A
          publication*]
TELECOMS ... Telecommunications Authority of Singapore   (TSSD)
TELECON ... Telephone [*or Teletype*] Conference [*or Conversation*]   (AFM)
TELECONV ... Telephone Conversation
TELEDAC ... Telemetric Data Converter
TELEDAQ ... Television Data Acquisition System   (MCD)
TELEDIS .. Teletypewriter Distribution   (NATG)
Tele (Engl Ed) ... Tele (English Edition) [*A publication*]
TELEFLORA ... Telegraph Florists Delivery Service
Telefon Rep ... Telefon Report [*A publication*]
Telef Rep...... Telefon Report [*A publication*]
Telefunken-Ztg ... Telefunken-Zeitung [*West Germany*] [*A publication*]
TELEG ...... Telegram
TELEG ...... Telegraph
Telegr & Telef ... Telegraaf en Telefoon [*A publication*]
TELEMAN ... Telephone Management System
Telem Ant .. Telemetry Antenna
Telemktg.... Telemarketing [*A publication*]
TELENET ... Cooperative Extension Service Telephone Network [*University
          of Illinois at Champaign-Urbana*] [*Telecommunications
          service*]   (TSSD)
TELENET ... TELENET Communications Corp. [*GTE*]   (TEL)
Tele News .. Telephone News [*A publication*]
TELEPAK ... Telemetering Package
TELEPH ... Telephone
Teleph Eng & Manage ... Telephone Engineer and Management [*A
          publication*]
Telephone .. Telephone Engineer and Management [*A publication*]
TELER ...... Telecommunications Requirements   (MCD)
TELERAN ... Television and RADAR Navigation System   (MUGU)
TELESAT ... Telecommunications Satellite
TELESUN ... Telecommunications Software User's Network [*Telesun Corp.*]
          [*Englewood, OH*]   (TSSD)
Tele (Swed Ed) ... Tele (Swedish Edition) [*A publication*]
TELETECH ... National Telecommunications & Technology Fund, Inc. [*New
          York, NY*]   (TSSD)

Tele-Tech & Electronic Ind ... Tele-Tech and Electronic Industries [*A
          publication*]
Teleteknik Engl Ed ... Teleteknik. English Edition [*A publication*]
Telettra Rev ... Telettra Review [*A publication*]
TELETYPE ... Teletypewriter [*Telecommunications*]
Telev Eng... Television Engineering [*A publication*]
Televerket.. National Swedish Telecommunications Administration
          [*Stockholm*] [*Information service or system*]   (IID)
Television JR Telev Soc ... Television. Journal of the Royal Television Society
          [*A publication*]
Telev Quart ... Television Quarterly [*A publication*]
Telev/Radio Age ... Television/Radio Age [*A publication*]
TELEX ...... Automatic Teletypewriter Exchange Service [*of Western Union*]
TELF .... Tamil Eelam Liberation Front [*Sri Lanka*] [*Political
          party*]   (PPW)
TELFAD ... Telephone Executive Leader for a Day [*New England Telephone
          Co. program for high school students*]
TELG........ Telegram
Telhan Patrica Oilseeds J ... Telhan Patrica/Oilseeds Journal [*A publication*]
TELID ...... Teletypewriter Identification   (NOAA)
TELIDON ... [*A*] television terminal-based interactive information retrieval
          system
TELINT .... Telemetry Intelligence
TELISA..... Thermometric Enzyme-Linked Immunosorbent Assay
          [*Analytical biochemistry*]
TELIST ..... Telegraphist   (DSUE)
TELL .... [*The*] Excellent Lodge Leader [*Freemasonry*]
TELL .... Teleci, Inc. of Texas [*NASDAQ symbol*]   (NQ)
TELLA ...... Tellus [*Sweden*] [*A publication*]
TELL-A-GRAF ... [*A*] programming language [*1978*]   (CSR)
Tellus Ser A ... Tellus. Series A. Dynamic Meteorology and Oceanography [*A
          publication*]
Tellus Ser A Dyn Meteorol Oceanogr ... Tellus. Series A. Dynamic
          Meteorology and Oceanography [*A publication*]
Tellus Ser B ... Tellus. Series B. Chemical and Physical Meteorology [*A
          publication*]
Tellus Ser B Chem Phys Meteorol ... Tellus. Series B. Chemical and Physical
          Meteorology [*A publication*]
TELM........ Telegram   (ROG)
TELMTR .. Telemotor
TELNET ... Georgia Telecommunications Network [*Georgia Hospital
          Association*] [*Atlanta, GA*]
          [*Telecommunications*]   (TSSD)
TELO......... Tamil Eelam Liberation Organization [*Sri Lanka*] [*Political
          party*]
TELO........ Tel Offshore Trust [*NASDAQ symbol*]   (NQ)
Tel Off ...... Telegraph Office
TELOP....... Telephone Operating Co. [*Also, TELCO*]
TELOPS.... Telemetry Online Processing System [*Data processing*]
TELPAK.... Telephone Package
TelQ........... Tel Quel [*A publication*]
TELQ......... TeleQuest, Inc. [*San Diego, CA*] [*NASDAQ symbol*]   (NQ)
TELR......... Teleram Communications [*NASDAQ symbol*]   (NQ)
Tel Rad E R ... Telecommunications and Radio Engineering (USSR) [*A
          publication*]
TELRY ...... Telegraph Reply   (FAAC)
TELS .... TEL Electronics, Inc. [*American Fork, UT*] [*NASDAQ
          symbol*]   (NQ)
TELS .... Test of Early Learning Skills [*Child development test*]
TELS .... Turbine Engine Loads Simulator
TELSAM... Telephone Service Attitude Measurement [*Telephone
          interviews*] [*AT & T*]
TELSCAR ... Transmit Electronically Location Shippers' Car Advice Reports
TELSCOM ... Telemetry-Surveillance-Communications
TELSCPD ... Telescoped
TELSIM... Teletypewriter Simulation
TELSUN ... Television Series for United Nations [*A foundation formed to
          produce, and telecast on a commercial basis, dramatized
          descriptions of UN activities*]
TEL SUR... Telephone Survey   (MUGU)
TEL-SYS... Telephone System
TELT .... Teltronics, Inc. [*NASDAQ symbol*]   (NQ)
TELTA ...... Tethered Lighter-than-Air   (KSC)
TELUQ..... Tele-Universite [*University of Quebec*] [*Telecommunications
          service*]   (TSSD)
TELUQ...... Tele-Universite (University of Quebec) [*Quebec, PQ*]
          [*Telecommunications*]   (TSSD)
TELUS ...... Telemetric Universal Sensor
TELV........ TeleVideo Systems, Inc. [*NASDAQ symbol*]   (NQ)
Tel Vaani ... Telugu Vaani [*Hyderabad*] [*A publication*]
TEM .... Exporter. Malta's Monthly Export Journal [*A publication*]
TEM .... Memphis University School, Hyde Library, Memphis, TN
          [*OCLC symbol*]   (OCLC)
TeM .... O Tempo e o Modo [*A publication*]
TEM .... Officers for Temporary Service [*Navy*] [*British*]   (ROG)
TEM .... Roswell Park Memorial Institute [*Research code symbol*]
TEM .... Target Engagement Message   (NVT)
TEM .... Target Evaluation Maintenance   (MCD)
TEM .... Technical Error Message [*Aviation*]

TE & M...... Telephone Engineer and Management [*Harcourt Brace Jovanovich Publications, Inc.*] [*Geneva, IL*] [*Information service or system*] [*A publication*]
TEM .... Temco National Corp. [*AMEX symbol*] (SPSG)
TEM .... Temiskaming & Northern Ontario Railway [*AAR code*]
tem .... Temne [*MARC language code*] [*Library of Congress*] (LCCP)
TEM .... Temora [*Australia*] [*Airport symbol*] (OAG)
TEM .... Temperature (DEN)
TEM .... Tempered (DEN)
Tem............ [*The*] Templar [*1788-79*] [*London*] [*A publication*] (DLA)
TEM .... Template (DEN)
Tem............ Tempo [*Record label*] [*Germany*]
Tem............ Tempo [*Music*]
Tem............ Tempore [*In the Time Of*] [*Latin*] (DLA)
TEM .... Temuco [*Chile*] [*Seismograph station code, US Geological Survey*] [*Closed*] (SEIS)
TeM .... Tennessee Microfilms, Nashville, TN [*Library symbol*] [*Library of Congress*] (LCLS)
TEM .... Terramar Resources Corp. [*Toronto Stock Exchange symbol*] [*Vancouver Stock Exchange symbol*]
TEM .... Thailand Exhibitions and Management Co. Ltd. (DS)
TEM .... Thermoelectric Module
TEM .... Transmission Electron Micrograph
TEM .... Transmission Electron Microscope [*or Microscopy*]
TEM .... Transverse Electromagnetic [*Wave*] [*Radio*]
TEM .... Triethylenemelamine [*Organic chemistry*]
TEM .... Typical Egg Mass
TEMA .... Telecommunication Engineering and Manufacturing Association [*British*]
TEMA .... Test of Early Mathematics Ability
TEMA .... Trace Elements in Man and Animals [*An international symposium*]
TEMA .... Training, Education, and Mutual Assistance in the Marine Sciences [*IOC working committee*] (MSC)
TEMA .... Tubular Exchanger Manufacturers Association (EA)
TEMAC..... Temporary Active Duty
TEMACDIFOT ... Temporary Active Duty in a Flying Status Involving Operational or Training Flights [*Navy*]
TEMACDIFOTINS ... Temporary Active Duty under Instruction in a Flying Status Involving Operational or Training Flights [*Navy*]
TEMACDU ... Temporary Active Duty [*Navy*]
TEMACINS ... Temporary Active Duty under Instruction [*Navy*]
TEMADD ... Temporary Additional Duty [*Navy*]
TEMADDCON ... Temporary Additional Duty in Connection with [*Specified activity*] [*Navy*]
TEMADDINS ... Temporary Additional Duty under Instruction [*Navy*]
TEMARS .. Transportation Environmental Measurement and Recording System (MCD)
Temas Odontol ... Temas Odontologicos [*A publication*]
Temas Quim Bibliogr Quim Argent ... Temas de Quimica y Bibliografia Quimica Argentina [*A publication*]
Temas Socs ... Temas Sociales [*A publication*]
Temat Sb Inst Fiziol Biofiz Rast Akad Nauk Tadzh SSR ... Tematicheskii Sbornik Institut Fiziologii i Biofiziki Rastenii. Akademiya Nauk Tadzhikskoi SSR [*A publication*]
Temat Sb Nauc Trud Alma-Atin Semipalatin Zoovet Inst ... Tematicheskii Sbornik Nauchnykh Trudov Alma-Atinskogo i Semipalatinskogo Zooveterinarnykh Institutov [*A publication*]
Temat Sb Otd Fiziol Biofiz Rast Akad Nauk Tadzh SSR ... Tematicheskii Sbornik Otdel Fiziologii i Biofiziki Rastenii Akademiya Nauk Tadzhikskoi SSR [*A publication*]
Temat Sb Rab Gel'mintol Skh Zhivotn ... Tematicheskii Sbornik Rabot po Gel'mintologii Sel'skokhozyaistvennykh Zhivotnykh [*A publication*]
Temat Sb Vses Nauchno Issled Inst Gidrogeol Inzh Geol ... Tematicheskii Sbornik Vsesoyuznogo Nauchno-Issledovatel'skogo Instituta Gidrogeologii Inzhenerskoi Geologii [*A publication*]
Temat Sb Vses Neftegazov Nauchno Issled Inst ... Tematicheskii Sbornik Vsesoyuznyi Neftegazovyi Nauchno-Issledovatel'skii Institut [*A publication*]
TEMAW ... Tactical Effectiveness of Minefields in Antiarmor Warfare Systems [*Army*] (INF)
TEMAWS ... Tactical Effectiveness of Minefields in Antiarmor Warfare Systems [*Army*]
TEMC........ Temco Home Health Care Products, Inc. [*NASDAQ symbol*] (NQ)
TEMC........ Test and Evaluation Management Course (MCD)
TEMDIFOT ... Temporary Duty in a Flying Status Involving Operational or Training Flights [*Navy*]
TEMDIFOTINS ... Temporary Duty under Instruction in a Flying Status Involving Operational or Training Flights [*Navy*]
TEMDU .... Temporary Duty [*Navy*]
TEMDUCON ... Temporary Duty in Connection With [*Specified activity*] [*Navy*]
TEMDUINS ... Temporary Duty under Instruction [*Navy*]
TEMEC..... Translational Electromagnetic Environment Chamber (MCD)
TEMED..... Tetramethylethylenediamine [*Also, TMED, TMEDA*] [*Organic chemistry*]
TEMFLY... Temporary Duty Involving Flying [*Navy*]

TEMFLYINS ... Temporary Duty Involving Flying under Instruction [*Navy*]
TEMIA...... Technische Mitteilungen [*A publication*]
TEMIC...... Telecommunications Executive Management Institute of Canada (TSSD)
TEMINS ... Temporary Duty under Instruction [*Navy*]
TEMMF..... Tax-Exempt Money Market Fund [*Investment term*]
TEMO........ Test and Evaluation Management Office [*Army*] (RDA)
TEMOA .... Tecnica Molitoria [*Italy*] [*A publication*]
TEMOD .... Test, Measurement, and Diagnostic Equipment Modernization [*Military*] (RDA)
TEMP........ Electrical Resistance Temperature (MCD)
TEMP........ Tachyelectromagnetic Pulse
TEMP........ Taxation Employment Number [*Canada*]
TEMP........ Technique for Econometric Modeling Program (BUR)
TEMP........ Temp-Stik Corp. [*NASDAQ symbol*] (NQ)
TEMP........ Temperance (ADA)
TEMP........ Temperate Zone
TEMP........ Temperature (AAG)
TEMP........ Tempered (AAG)
TEMP........ Template (AAG)
TEMP........ Tempo [*Music*]
TEMP........ Temporal
TEMP........ Temporary
Temp......... Temporary Light [*Navigation signal*]
TEMP........ Temporary Worker
TEMP........ Test Evaluation Master Plan (MCD)
TEMP........ Texas Educational Microwave Project
TEMP........ Total Energy Management Professionals [*Defunct*] (EA)
Temp Bar ... Temple Bar [*A publication*]
TEMP DEXT ... Tempus Dextra [*Right Temple*] [*Medicine*]
Temp Emer Ct App ... Temporary Emergency Court of Appeals [*United States*] (DLA)
TEMPER .. Technological, Economic, Military, and Political Evaluation Routine [*Computer-based simulation model*]
TEMPER .. Tent, Extendable, Modular, Personnel [*DoD*]
Temp Geo II ... Cases in Chancery Tempore George II [*England*] [*A publication*] (DLA)
TEMPISTORS ... Temperature Compensating Resistors (NATG)
TEMPL ..... Template [*Engineering*]
Temple Dent Rev ... Temple Dental Review [*A publication*]
Temple Law ... Temple Law Quarterly [*A publication*]
Temple L Quart ... Temple Law Quarterly [*A publication*]
Temple & M ... Temple and Mew's English Crown Cases [*A publication*] (DLA)
Temple & M (Eng) ... Temple and Mew's English Crown Cases [*A publication*] (DLA)
Temp L Q... Temple Law Quarterly [*A publication*]
Temp & M ... Temple and Mew's English Crown Cases [*1848-51*] [*A publication*] (DLA)
TEMPO..... Tactical Electromagnetic Project Office [*Military*] (CAAL)
TEMPO..... Technical Electronic Management Planning Organization
TEMPO..... Technical Military Planning Operation (AAG)
TEMPO..... Technique for Extreme Point Optimization (BUR)
TEMPO..... Temporary (AAG)
TEMPO..... Tetramethylpiperidinol N-oxyl [*Organic chemistry*]
TEMPO..... Time and Effort Measurement through Periodic Observation (MCD)
TEMPO..... Total Evaluation of Management and Production Output
TEMPOS .. Timed Environment Multipartitioned Operating System
TEMP PRIM ... Tempo Primo [*Original Tempo*] [*Music*]
TEMPROX ... Temporary Duty Will Cover Approximately [*Navy*]
TEMPS ..... Transportable Electromagnetic Pulse Simulator (RDA)
TEMPSAL .. Temperature-Salinity Data [*Oceanography*] (MCD)
TEMP SINIST ... Tempori Sinistro [*To the Left Temple*] [*Pharmacy*] (ADA)
Temps Mod ... Temps Modernes [*A publication*]
Temp Univ LQ ... Temple University. Law Quarterly [*A publication*] (DLA)
Temp Wood ... Manitoba Reports Tempore Wood [*Canada*] [*A publication*] (DLA)
TEMPY ..... Temporary
TEMS........ Test Equipment Maintenance Set
TEMS........ Thermal Elastic Model Study
TEMS........ Toyota Electronically Modulated Suspension [*Automotive engineering*]
TEMS........ Transport Environment Monitoring System [*NASA*] (MCD)
TEMS........ Turbine Engine Monitoring System
TEMSEPRAD ... Temporary Duty Connection, Separation Processing. Upon Completion and When Directed Detach; Proceed Home for Release from Active Duty in Accordance with Instructions [*Navy*]
TEMSS...... Total Emergency Medical Services System
TEMWAIT ... Temporary Duty Awaiting [*Specified event*] [*Navy*]
TEN .... Canarias [*Formerly, Tenerife*] [*Spain*] [*Geomagnetic observatory code*]
Ten............ Littleton's Tenures [*A publication*] (DSA)
TEN .... Tee-Comm Electronics, Inc. [*Toronto Stock Exchange symbol*]
ten .... Tenacious [*Quality of the bottom*] [*Nautical charts*]
TEN .... Tenerife [*Canary Islands*] [*Seismograph station code, US Geological Survey*] (SEIS)
TEN .... Tennessee (ROG)
TEN .... Tennessee Airways [*Alcoa, TN*] [*FAA designator*] (FAAC)

Ten............ Tennessee Reports [*A publication*]   (ILCA)
TEN.......... Tenor
TEN.......... Tenuto [*Held, Sustained*] [*Music*]
TEN.......... Total Enteral Nutrition
TEN.......... Total Excreted [*or Excretory*] Nitrogen
TEN.......... Toxic Epidermal Necrolysis [*Medicine*]
Tenakh....... Torah, Veni'im, Ketubim   (BJA)
Ten App..... Tennessee Appeals Reports [*A publication*]   (DLA)
TENCA...... Traffic Engineering and Control [*England*] [*A publication*]
TENCAP.... Tactical Exploitation of National Space Capabilities
Ten Cas...... Shannon's Tennessee Cases [*A publication*]   (DLA)
Ten Cas...... Thompson's Unreported Tennessee Cases [*A publication*]   (DLA)
TENCATE ... Koninklijke Textielfabrieken Nijverdal-Ten Cate NV [*Netherlands*]
TENCY...... Tenancy   (ROG)
Tendances Conjonct ... Tendances de la Conjoncture [*A publication*]
Tendances Polit Act Dom ... Tendances et Politiques Actuelles dans le Domaine de l'Habitation de la Construction et de la Planification [*A publication*]
TENDR ..... Tendring [*England*]
TENEMT ... Tenement   (ROG)
TENES...... Teaching English to the Non-English Speaking
TEng.......... Teaching English [*A publication*]
TENG........ Technical Engineers Association
TEng.......... Technician Engineer [*British*]   (DBQ)
TEngAMIN ... Technician Engineer of the Institution of Metallurgists [*British*]   (DBQ)
TEngAMI-ProdE ... Associate Member of the Institution of Production Engineers [*British*]   (DBQ)
Ten Mag .... Tennis Magazine [*A publication*]
TENN........ Tennessee   (AAG)
TENN........ Tennessee Natural Resources [*NASDAQ symbol*]   (NQ)
TENN........ Tennessee Railway Co. [*AAR code*]
Tenn.......... Tennessee Supreme Court Reports [*A publication*]   (DLA)
Tenn Admin Comp ... Official Compilation of the Rules and Regulations of the State of Tennessee [*A publication*]   (DLA)
Tenn Admin Reg ... Tennessee Administrative Register [*A publication*]   (DLA)
Tenn Ag Exp ... Tennessee. Agricultural Experiment Station. Publications [*A publication*]
Tenn Agric Exp Stn Annu Rep ... Tennessee. Agricultural Experiment Station. Annual Report [*A publication*]
Tenn Agric Exp Stn Bull ... Tennessee. Agricultural Experiment Station. Bulletin [*A publication*]
Tenn Agric Exp Stn Farm Econ Bull ... Tennessee. Agricultural Experiment Station. Farm Economics Bulletin [*A publication*]
Tenn Apiculture ... Tennessee Apiculture [*A publication*]
Tenn App ... Tennessee Appeals Reports [*A publication*]   (DLA)
Tenn App ... Tennessee Appellate Bulletin [*A publication*]   (DLA)
Tenn App ... Tennessee Civil Appeals Reports [*A publication*]   (DLA)
Tenn App Bull ... Tennessee Appellate Bulletin [*A publication*]   (DLA)
Tenn Appeals ... Tennessee Appeals Reports [*A publication*]   (DLA)
Tenn App R ... Tennessee Appeals Reports [*A publication*]   (DLA)
Tenn Bar J ... Tennessee Bar Journal [*A publication*]
Tenn BJ ..... Tennessee Bar Journal [*A publication*]
Tenn Cas.... Shannon's Unreported Tennessee Cases [*1847-1894*] [*A publication*]   (DLA)
Tenn Cas (Shannon) ... [*R. T.*] Shannon's Tennessee Cases [*A publication*]   (DLA)
Tenn Cas (Shannon) ... Thompson's Unreported Tennessee Cases [*1847-69*] [*A publication*]   (DLA)
Tenn CCA ... Tennessee Court of Civil Appeals   (DLA)
Tenn CCA (Higgins) ... Higgins' Tennessee Court of Civil Appeals Reports [*A publication*]   (DLA)
Tenn Ch ..... Cooper's Tennessee Chancery Reports [*A publication*]   (DLA)
Tenn Ch A ... Tennessee Chancery Appeals [*A publication*]   (DLA)
Tenn Chancery ... Tennessee Chancery Reports (Cooper) [*A publication*]   (DLA)
Tenn Chancery App ... Tennessee Chancery Appeals Reports (Wright) [*A publication*]   (DLA)
Tenn Ch App ... Tennessee Chancery Appeals (Wright) [*A publication*]   (DLA)
Tenn Ch App Dec ... Tennessee Chancery Appeals Decisions [*1895-1907*] [*A publication*]   (DLA)
Tenn Ch Ap Reps ... Wright's Tennessee Chancery Appeals Reports [*A publication*]   (DLA)
Tenn Ch R ... Tennessee Chancery Reports (Cooper) [*A publication*]   (DLA)
Tenn Civ A ... Tennessee Civil Appeals [*A publication*]   (DLA)
Tenn Civ App ... Tennessee Civil Appeals [*A publication*]   (DLA)
Tenn Code Ann ... Tennessee Code, Annotated [*A publication*]   (DLA)
Tenn Conservationist ... Tennessee Conservationist [*A publication*]
Tenn Cr App ... Tennessee Criminal Appeals [*A publication*]   (DLA)
Tenn Crim App ... Tennessee Criminal Appeals Reports [*A publication*]   (DLA)
Tenn Dep Conserv Div Geol Bull ... Tennessee. Department of Conservation. Division of Geology. Bulletin [*A publication*]
Tenn Dep Conserv Div Geol Inf Circ ... Tennessee. Department of Conservation. Division of Geology. Information Circular [*A publication*]

Tenn Dept Labor Ann Rept ... Tennessee. Department of Labor. Annual Report [*A publication*]
Tenn Div Geol Bull ... Tennessee. Division of Geology. Bulletin [*A publication*]
Tenn Div Geol Environ Geol Ser ... Tennessee. Division of Geology. Environmental Geology Series [*A publication*]
Tenn Div Geol Inf Circ ... Tennessee. Division of Geology. Information Circular [*A publication*]
Tenn Div Geol Inform Circ ... Tennessee. Division of Geology. Information Circular [*A publication*]
Tenn Div Geol Rep Invest ... Tennessee. Division of Geology. Report of Investigations [*A publication*]
Tenn Div Water Resour Water Resour Ser ... Tennessee. Division of Water Resources. Water Resources Series [*A publication*]
Tenn Eng ... Tennessee Engineer [*A publication*]
Tennessee Acad Sci Jour ... Tennessee Academy of Science. Journal [*A publication*]
Tennessee Div Geology Geol Map ... Tennessee. Division of Geology. Geologic Map [*A publication*]
Tennessee Div Geology Rept Inv ... Tennessee. Division of Geology. Report of Investigations [*A publication*]
Tennessee R ... Tennessee Reports [*A publication*]   (DLA)
Tennessee Rep ... Tennessee Reports [*A publication*]   (DLA)
Tennessees Bus ... Tennessee's Business [*A publication*]
Tenn Farm & Home Sci ... Tennessee Farm and Home Science [*A publication*]
Tenn Farm Home Sci Progr Rep ... Tennessee Farm and Home Science. Progress Report. University of Tennessee. Agricultural Experiment Station [*A publication*]
Tenn Fm Home Sci Prog Rep ... Tennessee Farm and Home Science. Progress Report [*A publication*]
Tenn Folk S ... Tennessee Folklore Society. Bulletin [*A publication*]
Tenn G S Res Tenn B ... Tennessee State Geological Survey. Resources of Tennessee. Bulletin [*A publication*]
Tenn His M ... Tennessee Historical Magazine [*A publication*]
Tenn Hist Mag ... Tennessee Magazine of History [*A publication*]
Tenn Hist Q ... Tennessee Historical Quarterly [*A publication*]
Tenn Jur ... Tennessee Jurisprudence [*A publication*]   (DLA)
Tenn Juris ... Tennessee Jurisprudence [*A publication*]   (DLA)
Tenn Law ... Tennessee Lawyer [*A publication*]   (DLA)
Tenn Law Rev ... Tennessee Law Review [*A publication*]
Tenn Leg Rep ... Tennessee Legal Reporter [*A publication*]   (DLA)
Tenn Libn .. Tennessee Librarian [*A publication*]
Tenn Libr... Tennessee Librarian [*A publication*]
Tenn Librn ... Tennessee Librarian [*A publication*]
Tenn L R.... Tennessee Law Review [*A publication*]
Tenn L Rev ... Tennessee Law Review [*A publication*]
Tenn Mag .. Tennessee Magazine [*A publication*]
Tenn Priv Acts ... Private Acts of the State of Tennessee [*A publication*]   (DLA)
Tenn Pub Acts ... Public Acts of the State of Tennessee [*A publication*]   (DLA)
Tenn R .... Tennessee Reports [*A publication*]   (DLA)
Tenn Rep.... Tennessee Reports [*A publication*]   (DLA)
Tenn St Bd Health B Rp ... Tennessee State Board of Health. Bulletin. Report [*A publication*]
Tenn Surv Bus ... Tennessee Survey of Business [*A publication*]
TENN-TOM ... Tennessee-Tombigbee [*Proposed waterway*]
Tenn Univ Eng Exp Sta Bull ... Tennessee University. Engineering Experiment Station. Bulletin [*A publication*]
Tenn Univ Water Resour Res Cent Res Rep ... Tennessee University. Water Resources Research Center. Research Report [*A publication*]
Tenn Val Auth Chem Eng Bul ... Tennessee Valley Authority. Chemical Engineering Bulletin [*A publication*]
Tenn Val Auth Natl Fert Dev Cent Bull Y ... Tennessee Valley Authority. National Fertilizer Development Center. Bulletin Y [*A publication*]
Tenn Valley Perspect ... Tennessee Valley Perspective [*A publication*]
Tenn Wildl ... Tennessee Wildlife [*A publication*]
TENOC..... Ten-Year Oceanographic Program [*Navy*]
TENR .... Technically Enhanced Naturally Radioactive   (NRCH)
TENRAP... Technically Enhanced Naturally Radioactive Product   (NRCH)
TENS........ Tensile
TENS........ Tension   (AAG)
TENS........ Training Element Need Statement
TENS........ Transcutaneous Electrical Nerve Stimulation [*Also, TES, TNS*] [*A method of pain control*] [*Medicine*]
Tensai Kenkyu Hokoku Suppl ... Tensai Kenkyu Hokoku. Supplement [*Japan*] [*A publication*]
TENSEGRITY ... Tensional Integrity [*Construction principle named by Buckminster Fuller*]
Tenside ...... Tenside-Detergents [*A publication*]
Tenside-Deterg ... Tenside-Detergents [*A publication*]
TENT .... Tenant   (ROG)
TENT .... Tenement   (ROG)
TENT .... Tentative   (AAG)
TENV .... Totally Enclosed - Nonventilated
TEO .... Teal Industry Ltd. [*Vancouver Stock Exchange symbol*]
TEO .... Technical Electronic Office [*Data General Corp.*]
TEO .... Telephone Equipment Order [*Telecommunications*]   (TEL)
TEO .... Teoloyucan [*Mexico*] [*Geomagnetic observatory code*]
TEO .... Terapo [*Papua New Guinea*] [*Airport symbol*]   (OAG)

TEO .... Terato Resources Ltd. [*Toronto Stock Exchange symbol*]
TEO .... Test Equipment Operator
TEO .... To Expiry Only   (AIA)
TEO .... Total Extractable Organic [*Analytical chemistry*]
T & EO ..... Training and Evaluation Outline
TEO .... Transferred Electron Oscillator
TEO .... Transmittal Engineering Order
TEOA .... Test and Evaluation Objectives Annex   (MCD)
TEOA .... Triethanolamine [*Organic chemistry*]
TEOC .... Texas Eagle Oil Company [*NASDAQ symbol*]   (NQ)
TEOF .... Triethyl Orthoformate [*Organic chemistry*]
Teolisuuden Keskuslab Tied ... Teolisuuden Keskuslaboratorion Tiedonantoja [*A publication*]
Teollis Tiedottaa ... Teollisuuslitto Tiedottaa [*A publication*]
Teol Vida ... Teologia y Vida [*A publication*]
TEOM .... Tapered Element Oscillating Microbalance
TEOM .... Transformer Environment Overcurrent Monitor   (IEEE)
Teor Ehlektrotekh ... Teoreticheskaya Ehlektrotekhnika [*A publication*]
Teor Eksp Biofiz ... Teoreticheskaya i Eksperimental'naya Biofizica [*A publication*]
Teor & Eksp Khim ... Teoreticheskaya i Eksperimental'naya Khimiya [*A publication*]
Teoret Elektrotekhn ... L'vovskii Gosudarstvennyi Universitet. Teoreticheskaya Elektrotekhnika [*A publication*]
Teoret Mat Fiz ... Teoreticeskaja i Matematiceskaja Fizika [*A publication*]
Teoret i Prikladna Meh ... Teoreticna i Prikladna Mehanika Harkivs'kii Derzavnii Universitet Imeni O. M. Gor'kogo [*A publication*]
Teoret Prikl Mat ... Teoreticna i Prikladna Matematika [*A publication*]
Teoret i Prikl Mekh ... Belorusskii Politekhnicheski Institut. Teoreticheskaya i Prikladnaya Mekhanika [*A publication*]
Teoret Priloz Meh ... B'lgarska Akademija na Naukite. Teoreticna i Prilozna Mehanika [*A publication*]
Teoret i Priloz Meh ... Teoreticna i Prilozna Mehanika [*A publication*]
Teor Funktsii Funktsional Anal i Prilozhen ... Khar'kovskii Ordena Trudovogo Krasnogo Znameni Gosudarstvennyi Universitet Imeni A. M. Gor'kogo Teoriya Funktsii Funktsional'nyi Analiz i Ikh Prilozheniya [*A publication*]
Teor Konecn Avtomatov i Prilozen ... Institut Elektroniki i Vycislitel'noi Tehniki. Akademija Nauk Latviiskoi SSR. Teorija Konecnyh. Avtomatov i Ee Prilozenja [*A publication*]
Teor i Mat Fiz ... Teoreticheskaya i Matematicheskaya Fizika [*A publication*]
Teor Mat Fiz ... Teoreticheskaya i Matematicheskaya Fizika [*A publication*]
Teor Metod ... Teorie a Metoda [*A publication*]
Teor Osn Khim Tekhnol ... Teoreticheskie Osnovy Khimicheskoi Tekhnologii [*A publication*]
Teor Prakt ... Teoriya Praktika [*A publication*]
Teor Prakt Fiz Kul't ... Teoriya i Praktika Fizicheskoi Kul'tury [*A publication*]
Teor Prakt Metall ... Teoriya i Praktika Metallurgii (Chelyabinsk) [*USSR*] [*A publication*]
Teor Prakt Metall (Chelyabinsk) ... Teoriya i Praktika Metallurgii (Chelyabinsk) [*A publication*]
Teor Prakt Metall (Dnepropetrovsk) ... Teoriya i Praktika Metallurgii (Dnepropetrovsk) [*A publication*]
Teor Prakt Podgot Koksovaniya Uglei ... Teoriya i Praktika Podgotovki i Koksovaniya Uglei [*A publication*]
Teor Prakt Stomatol ... Teoriya i Praktika Stomatologii [*A publication*]
Teor Prakt Szhiganiya Gaza ... Teoriya i Praktika Szhiganiya Gaza [*USSR*] [*A publication*]
Teor Prakt Vopr Mikrobiol Epidemiol ... Teoreticheskie i Prakticheskie Voprosy Mikrobiologii i Epidemiologii [*A publication*]
Teor Prakt Vopr Mikrobiol Epidemiol Resp Mezhved Sb ... Teoreticheskie i Prakticheskie Voprosy Mikrobiologii i Epidemiologii Respublikanskii Mezhvedomstvennyi Sbornik [*A publication*]
Teor Prakt Vopr Vaktsinno Syvorot Dela ... Teoreticheskie i Prakticheskie Voprosy Vaktsinno Syvorotochnogo Dela [*A publication*]
Teor Prilozh Mekh ... Teoretichna i Prilozhna Mekhanika [*A publication*]
Teor Primen Meh ... Jugoslovensko Drustvo za Mehaniku. Teorijska i Primenjena Mehanika [*A publication*]
TEORS ...... Transient Electro-Optic Raman Scattering [*Physics*]
Teor Verojatn Mat Stat ... Teoriya Verojatnostej i Matematicheskaya Statistika [*A publication*]
Teor Verojatnost i Mat Statist ... Teorija Verojatnostei i Matematiceskaja Statistika [*A publication*]
Teor Veroya ... Teoriya Veroyatnostei i Ee Primeneniya [*A publication*]
Teor Veroyatn i Primen ... Teoriya Veroyatnostei i Ee Primeneniya [*A publication*]
Teor Veroyatn Primen ... Teoriya Veroyatnostei i Ee Primeneniya [*A publication*]
Teor Veroyat Primen ... Teoriya Veroyatnostei i Ee Primeneniya [*USSR*] [*A publication*]
Teor Vopr Obrab Pochv ... Teoreticheskie Voprosy Obrabotki Pochv [*A publication*]
TEOS .... Tetraethyl Orthosilicate [*Organic chemistry*]   (NASA)
TEOSS ...... Tactical Emitter Operational Support System   (MCD)
TEOTA ...... [*The*] Eyes of the Army   (AAG)
TEP .... Table Editing Process
TEP .... Tactical ELINT Processor   (MCD)
TEP .... Tape Edit Processor [*Data processing*]
TEP .... Tau Epsilon Phi [*Fraternity*]

TEP .... Technical Education Program   (OICC)
TEP .... Technical Evaluation Panel [*In various federal government agencies*]   (NASA)
TEP .... Tepecintle [*Race of maize*]
TEP .... Teptep [*Papua New Guinea*] [*Airport symbol*]   (OAG)
TEP .... Terminal Error Program
TEP .... Territory Enterprises Proprietary
TEP .... Test and Evaluation Plan [*Military*]   (CAAL)
TEP .... Tetraethoxypropane [*Organic chemistry*]
TEP .... Thermal Enzyme Probe
TEP .... Thermoelectric Power [*Thermodynamics*]
TEP .... Token Economy Program [*Psychiatry*]
TEP .... Tons Equivalent of Petroleum [*Fuel measure*]
TEP .... Total Extractable Protein [*Food technology*]
TEP .... Toxicant Extraction Procedure
TEP .... Trace Element Pattern   (KSC)
TEP .... Tracheo-Esophageal Puncture [*Medicine*]
TEP .... Transmitter Experiment Package
TEP .... Transparent Electrophotography [*Proposed archival storage medium*]
TEP .... Triethyl-Phosphine [*Organic chemistry*]
TEP .... Tube Evaluation Program
TEP .... Tucson Electric Power Co. [*NYSE symbol*]   (SPSG)
TEP .... Turbine Extreme Pressure   (MCD)
TEP .... Turkiye Emekci Partisi [*Workers' Party of Turkey*] [*Political party*]   (PPW)
TEP .... Tyrone Energy Park   (NRCH)
TEPA .... Roswell Park Memorial Institute [*Research code symbol*]
TEPA .... Tetraethylenepentamine [*Organic chemistry*]
TEPA .... Triethylenephosphoramide [*Also, APO*] [*Organic chemistry*]
TEPAC ...... Tube Engineering Panel Advisory Council   (EA)
TEPC .... Test and Evaluation Planning Committee [*Military*]   (CAAL)
TEPCO ...... Tokyo Electric Power Company
TEPD .... Trademark Examining Procedure Directives [*A publication*]
TEPE .... Target Engagement Proficiency Exercise [*Military*]
TEPG .... Test Evaluation Planning Group   (MCD)
TEPG .... Thermionic Electrical Power Generator   (IEEE)
TEPI .... Technical Equipment Planning Information
TEPI .... Terminal Phase Intercept
TEPI .... Training Equipment Planning Information [*Military*]   (AFM)
TEPI .... Triadal Equated Personality Inventory [*Psychology*]
TEPIAC ..... Thermophysical and Electronic Properties Information Analysis Center [*Later, HTMIAC*] [*Purdue University*]
TEPIC .... Tris(epoxypropyl)isocyanurate [*Organic chemistry*]
TEPID .... Tepidus [*Lukewarm*] [*Pharmacy*]   (ROG)
TEPIGEN ... Television Picture Generator   (MCD)
Tepl Naprazh Elem Konstr ... Teplovye Napryazheniya v Elementakh Konstruktsii [*A publication*]
Teploehnerg ... Teploehnergetika [*A publication*]
Teploenergetika Akad Nauk SSSR Energ Inst ... Teploenergetika Akademiya Nauk SSSR. Energeticheskii Institut [*A publication*]
Teplofiz Kharakt Veshchestv ... Teplofizicheskie Kharakteristiki Veshchestv [*USSR*] [*A publication*]
Teplofiz Optim Tepl Protsessov ... Teplofizika i Optimizatsiya Teplovykh Protsessov [*A publication*]
Teplofiz Svoistva Veshchestv ... Teplofizicheskie Svoistva Veshchestv [*A publication*]
Teplofiz Svoistva Veshchestv Mater ... Teplofizicheskie Svoistva Veshchestv i Materialov [*A publication*]
Teplofiz Teplotekh ... Teplofizika i Teplotekhnika [*A publication*]
Teplofiz Vys Temp ... Teplofizika Vysokikh Temperatur [*A publication*]
Teploprovodnost Diffuz ... Teploprovodnost i Diffuziya [*A publication*]
Teplosi Khoz ... Teplosilovoc Khozyaistvo [*A publication*]
Teplotekh Probl Pryamogo Preobraz Energ ... Teplotekhnicheskie Problemy Pryamogo Preobrazovaniya Energii [*Ukrainian SSR*] [*A publication*]
TEPOS ...... Test Program Operating System
TEPP .... Tetraethyl Pyrophosphate [*Insecticide*] [*Pharmacology*]
TEPPS .... Technique for Establishing Personnel Performance Standards [*Navy*]
TEPR .... Training Equipment Progress Report
TEPRSSC ... Technical Electronic Product Radiation Safety Standards Committee   (MCD)
TEPS .... National Commission on Teacher Education and Professional Standards [*Defunct*]
TEPSA ...... Trans European Policy Studies Association   (EA)
TEQ .... Trian Equities Ltd. [*Vancouver Stock Exchange symbol*]
TEQ .... Turner Equity Investors, Inc. [*AMEX symbol*]   (SPSG)
TEQ .... Twenty-Foot Equivalent [*Shipping*]
TEQE .... Trian Equities Ltd. [*NASDAQ symbol*]   (NQ)
TER .... Tau Epsilon Rho [*Fraternity*]
TeR .... Te Reo [*A publication*]
TER .... Technical Evaluation Report [*Nuclear energy*]   (NRCH)
TER .... Tera Mines Ltd. [*Toronto Stock Exchange symbol*]
TER .... Teradyne, Inc. [*NYSE symbol*]   (SPSG)
TER .... Terceira [*Azores*] [*Airport symbol*]   (OAG)
TER .... Tere [*Rub*] [*Pharmacy*]
Ter .... Terence [*Second century BC*] [*Classical studies*]   (OCD)
ter .... Tereno [*MARC language code*] [*Library of Congress*]   (LCCP)
TER .... Terra Mines Ltd. [*Toronto Stock Exchange symbol*] [*Vancouver Stock Exchange symbol*]

TER .... Terrace
TER .... Terranova [Guatemala] [Seismograph station code, US Geological Survey]   (SEIS)
TER .... Terrazzo
TER .... Territory
Ter............. Terry's Delaware Reports [A publication]   (DLA)
TER .... Tertiary   (KSC)
Ter........... Terumot   (BJA)
TER .... Test Effectiveness Ratio [Data processing]
TER .... Test Equipment Readiness [NASA]   (NASA)
TER .... Test Evaluation Report [NASA]   (KSC)
TER .... Thermal Enhancement Ratio
TE-R .... Thermostable E-Rosetting [Cells] [Medicine]
TER .... Time Estimating Relationship   (NASA)
TER .... Time and Event Recorder
TER .... Total Endoplasmic Reticulum [Cytology]
TER .... Total External Reflection
TE/R......... Trailing Edge Radius   (MSA)
TER .... Training Equipment Requirements Plan
TER .... Transcapillary Escape Rate
TER .... Transfer Effectiveness Ratio
TER .... Transmission Equivalent Resistance   (IEEE)
TER .... Triple Ejection Rack   (NVT)
TER .... True Height Above Aerodrome Level [Aviation]   (AIA)
TERA......... Teradyne, Inc. [NASDAQ symbol]   (NQ)
TERA......... Terminal Effects Research and Analysis Group [New Mexico Institute of Mining and Technology] [Research center]   (RCD)
TERA......... Test of Early Reading Ability
TERA......... Tradable Emission Reduction Assessments [Environmental Protection Agency]
TERA......... TSCA [Toxic Substances Control Act] Experimental Release Application [Environmental Protection Agency]
TERAA...... Terapia [A publication]
TERAC...... Tactical Electromagnetic Readiness Advisory Council   (MCD)
Ter Arkh .... Terapevticheskii Arkhiv [A publication]
TERAS ...... Tactical Energy Requirements and Supply System   (MCD)
TERAT...... Teratology   (ROG)
Teratog Carcinog Mutagen ... Teratogenesis, Carcinogenesis, and Mutagenesis [A publication]
Teratogenesis Carcinog Mutagen ... Teratogenesis, Carcinogenesis, and Mutagenesis [A publication]
TERB........ Terrazzo Base
TERC......... Technical Education Research Centers, Inc. [Cambridge, MA] [Research center]
TERCOM ... Terrain Contour Mapping   (MCD)
TERCOM ... Terrain Contour Matching [Navigation system] [Air Force]
TERCOM ... Terrain Correlation Method
TERD .... Turbine Electric Reduction Drive
TEREA ...... Technology Review [A publication]
TEREBINTH ... Terebinthinae Oleum [Oil of Turpentine] [Pharmacology]   (ROG)
TEREC ...... Tactical Electronic Reconnaissance [Aircraft]
Terent........ Terentius Clemens [Flourished, 2nd century] [Authority cited in pre-1607 legal work]   (DSA)
TERENVSVC ... Terrestrial Environmental Services [Army]   (AABC)
TERF......... Trudeau Early Retirement Fund [Defunct] [Established 1982 by Canadians who hoped that the money would persuade their prime minister to retire from office]
TERG........ Training Equipment Requirements Guide   (KSC)
TERI......... Torpedo Effective Range Indicator
TERL........ Test Engineer Readiness List [NASA]   (NASA)
TERL........ Test Equipment Readiness List [NASA]   (NASA)
TERLS...... Thumba Equatorial Launching Station [Indian rocket station]
TERM....... Temporary Equipment Recovery Mission   (CINC)
Term.......... Term Reports [North Carolina] [1816-18] [A publication]   (DLA)
Term........... Term Reports, English King's Bench (Durnford and East's Reports) [A publication]   (DLA)
TERM....... Terminal   (AAG)
TERM....... Terminal Data Corp. [NASDAQ symbol]   (NQ)
TERM....... Terminate   (AFM)
TERM....... Terminology
TERM....... Termite   (ADA)
TERMA..... Termotecnica [A publication]
Termeloeszoevet Tanacsadoja ... Termeloeszoevetkezetek Tanacsadoja [A publication]
Termes de la Ley ... Terms of the Common Laws and Statutes Expounded and Explained by John Rastell [1685] [A publication]   (DLA)
Termeszettud Koezloeny ... Termeszettudomanyi Koezloeny [A publication]
TERMIA ... Association Internationale de Terminologie [International Association of Terminology] [Quebec, PQ]   (EAIO)
TERMINACTRAORD ... Directed to Request Termination of Inactive Duty Training Orders [Navy]
TERMINON ... Termination   (ROG)
TERMINOQ ... Banque de Terminologie de Quebec [Terminology Bank of Quebec] [French Language Board] [Information service or system]
Term de la L ... Les Termes de la Ley [Terms of the Law] [A law French dictionary] [A publication]   (DLA)
TERMN .... Termination

Term NC.... Taylor's North Carolina Term Reports [A publication]   (DLA)
TERMNET ... International Network for Terminology [INFOTERM] [Vienna, Austria]
Term Obrab Fiz Met ... Termicheskaya Obrabotka i Fizika Metallov [A publication]
Termodin Fiz Kinet Strukturoobra Svoista Chuguna Stali ... Termodinamika i Fizicheskaya Kinetika Strukturoobrazovaniya i Svoistva Chuguna i Stali [A publication]
Termodin Fiz Kinet Strukturoobraz Stali Chugune ... Termodinamika i Fizicheskaya Kinetika Strukturoobrazovaniya v Stali i Chugune [A publication]
Termodin Fiz Kinet Strukturoobraz Svoistva Chuguna Stali ... Termodinamika i Fizicheskaya Kinetika Strukturoobrazovaniya i Svoistva Chuguna i Stali [A publication]
Termoprochn Mater Konstr Elem ... Termoprochnost Materialov i Konstruktivnykh Elementov [USSR] [A publication]
Termotecnica Suppl ... Termotecnica. Supplemento [Italy] [A publication]
TERM PWR ... Terminator Power [Data processing]
Term R .... Term Reports, English King's Bench (Durnford and East's Reports) [A publication]   (DLA)
Term Rep ... Term Reports, English King's Bench (Durnford and East's Reports) [England] [A publication]   (DLA)
Term Rep (NC) ... Taylor's North Carolina Term Reports [4 North Carolina] [A publication]   (DLA)
TERMS ..... Terminal Management System [Military]   (AABC)
TERMTRAN ... Terminal Translator   (KSC)
TERO .... Tribal Employment Rights Office
Ter Ortop Stomatol ... Terapevticheskaya i Ortopedicheskaya Stomatologiva [A publication]
TERP......... Terminal Equipment Replacement Program [Electronic communications system] [Department of State]
TERP......... Terminal Instrument Procedure [Aviation]
TERP......... Terrain Elevation Retrieval Program   (IEEE)
TERPACIS ... Trust Territory of the Pacific Islands
TERPE ...... Tactical Electronic Reconnaissance Processing and Evaluation [Air Force]   (MCD)
TERPES.... Tactical Electronic Reconnaissance Processing and Evaluation System   (MCD)
TERPS...... Terminal Enquiry/Response Programming System [British]
TERPS...... Terminal Instrument Procedures [Military]
TERPS...... Terminal Planning System [Military]
TERR........ Terrace
Terr .... Terrell's Reports [38-71 Texas] [A publication]   (DLA)
TERR....... Territory   (AFM)
Terr .... Terrorist [Slang term used by whites in Zimbabwe to refer to a black nationalist guerrilla]
TERRA...... Terricide-Escape by Rethinking, Research, Action [An association]
Terra Amer ... Terra America [A publication]
TERRAP ... TERRAP [Territorial Apprehensiveness] Programs [Commercial firm]   (EA)
Terra Trent ... Terra Trentina [A publication]
Terre Maroc ... Terre Marocaine [A publication]
TERRES.... Territorial Residents
Terre Vie Rev Ecol Appl ... Terre et la Vie. Revue d'Ecologie Appliquee [A publication]
Ter Rev Med ... Terapeutica. Revista de Medicina [A publication]
TERRHICO ... Territorial Rhine Coordination [NATO]   (NATG)
Territ......... Territorian [A publication]   (APTA)
TERRIT..... Territory
Terr L....... Territories Law [Northwest Territories] [A publication]   (DLA)
Terr L (Can) ... Territories Law Reports [1885-1907] [Canada] [A publication]   (DLA)
Terr LJ...... Territory Law Journal [A publication]   (APTA)
Terr LR ..... Territories Law Reports [1885-1907] [Canada] [A publication]   (DLA)
Terr Magn ... Terrestrial Magnetism and Atmospheric Electricity [A publication]
Terr Magn Atmos Electr ... Terrestrial Magnetism and Atmospheric Electricity [A publication]
Terror........ Terrorism [A publication]
Terrorilla ... Terrorism and Guerrilla Warfare [Israeli]
Terr & Wal ... Terrell and Walker's Reports [38-51 Texas] [A publication]   (DLA)
Terr & Walk ... Terrell and Walker's Reports [38-51 Texas] [A publication]   (DLA)
TERS .... Tactical Electronic Reconnaissance System   (IEEE)
TerS .... Terra Santa [Jerusalem]   (BJA)
TER SIM... Tere Simul [Rub Together] [Latin]   (ADA)
TERSSE.... Total Earth Resources System for the Shuttle Era [NASA]
Ter Stomatol ... Terapevticheskaya Stomatologiya [A publication]
TERT........ Tertiary [Period, era, or system] [Geology]
tert............. Tertiary [Also, t] [Chemistry]
TERT........ Tertius [Third] [Latin]
Tert .... Tertullian [160-240AD] [Classical studies]   (OCD)
TERT......... Tracking/Erosion Resistance Tester
Tertiary Res Spec Pap ... Tertiary Research Special Papers [A publication]
TERTM ...... Thermal Expansion Resin Transfer Molding
TERTSD ... Tertiary Sand [Agronomy]

Tertul .... Tertullianus [*Flourished, 2nd-3rd century*] [*Authority cited in pre-1607 legal work*] (DSA)
TERU .... Teruletrendezes [*Hungary*] [*A publication*]
Teruv .... Teruvenkatachariar's Railway Cases [*India*] [*A publication*] (DLA)
TERX........ Terex Corp. [*NASDAQ symbol*] (NQ)
TES............ [*The*] Engineers School (MCD)
TES............ Tactical Environment Simulator [*Navy*] (MCD)
TES............ Target Engagement Simulator [*Military*] (MCD)
TES............ Team Effectiveness Survey [*Test*]
TES............ Technical Engagement Simulation
TES............ Technical Enquiry Service [*British*] (DCTA)
TES............ Telemetry Evaluation Station
TES............ Temporary Employment Subsidy [*British*] (DCTA)
TES............ Terminal Encounter System
TeS............ Terre Sainte (BJA)
TES............ Territorial Experiment Stations Division [*of ARS, Department of Agriculture*]
Tes .... Tesaur [*A publication*]
TES............ Test and Evaluation Support
TES............ Test Squadron [*Air Force*]
TES............ Text Editing System
TES............ Textiles Suisses. Revue de l'Industrie Suisse des Textiles d'Habillement [*A publication*]
TES............ Theatre Education Society (EA)
TES............ Thermal Energy Storage
TES............ Thin Elastic Shell
TES............ Thymic Epithelial Supernatant [*Endocrinology*]
TES........... Tidal Electric Station
TES........... Time Encoded Speech [*Telecommunications*] (TEL)
TES........... Times Educational Supplement [*A publication*]
TES........... Training Equipment Summary (MCD)
TES............ Transcutaneous Electrical Stimulation [*Also, TENS, TNS*] [*A method of pain control*] [*Medicine*]
TES............ Transmural Electrical Stimulation
TES............ Transportable Earth Station [*British*]
TES............ Tris(hydroxymethyl)methylaminoethanesulfonic Acid [*A buffer*]
TES............ Tungsten Electron Snatcher
TES............ Twelve English Statesmen [*A publication*]
TESA .... Television and Electronics Service Association
TESAC ...... Temperature-Salinity-Currents [*Oceanography*] (IID)
TESCA ...... TAFE [*Technical and Further Education*] Educational Services Co-Ordinators' Association [*Australia*]
TESDA .... Tenside [*Later, Tenside-Detergents*] [*A publication*]
TESE .... Tactical Exercise Simulator and Evaluator (NVT)
TE(S)FC ..... Totally-Enclosed (Separately) Fan-Cooled [*Reactor*] (DEN)
TESG......... Target Echo Signature Generator [*SONAR*]
TESG......... Tijdschrift voor Economische en Sociale Geografie [*A publication*]
TESG-A ..... Tijdschrift voor Economische en Sociale Geografie [*Netherlands*] [*A publication*]
TESH........ Technical Shop (NASA)
TESI .... Thermal Energy Storage [*NASDAQ symbol*] (NQ)
TESI .... Transfer of Electrostatic Images [*Electrophotography*]
TESICO ..... Threshold Electron Secondary Ion Coincidence [*Spectroscopy*]
TESL .... Teaching English as a Second Language
TESLAC...... Testolactone [*Antineoplastic drug*]
Tesla Electron ... Tesla Electronics [*A publication*]
Tesla Electron Q Rev Czech Electron Telecommun ... Tesla Electronics. Quarterly Review of Czechoslovak Electronics and Telecommunications [*A publication*]
TESL Can J ... TESL [*Teaching English as a Second Language*] Canada Journal [*A publication*]
TESM........ Triethylstannylmaleate [*Organic chemistry*]
TESMA ..... Theatre Equipment and Supply Manufacturers Association [*Later, TEA*] (EA)
TESOB...... Terra e Sole [*A publication*]
TESOL ...... Teachers of English to Speakers of Other Languages (EA)
TESOLQ ... TESOL [*Teachers of English to Speakers of Other Languages*] Quarterly [*A publication*]
TESOL Quart ... TESOL [*Teachers of English to Speakers of Other Languages*] Quarterly [*A publication*]
Tesoro Sacro M ... Tesoro Sacro-Musical [*A publication*]
TESP .... Telephone Specialists, Inc. [*NASDAQ symbol*] (NQ)
TESR .... Tactical Environment Satellite Readout (MCD)
TESR .... Test Equipment Status Report
TESR .... Time of Sunrise
TESRP...... Test and Evaluation Support Resource Plan (MCD)
TESS .... Tactical Electromagnetic Systems Study (IEEE)
TESS .... Tactical Engagement Simulation System [*Developed by Sandia National Laboratories for the Defense Nuclear Agency*]
TESS .... Tactical and Environmental Support System [*Military*] (CAAL)
TESS .... Temporary Employment Subsidy Scheme [*Department of Employment*] [*British*]
TESS .... Time of Sunset
TESS .... Top Electronic Security Systems [*Commercial firm*] [*British*]
TESSA....... Tax-Exempt Special Savings Account [*British*]
TESSA...... Total Energy Suppression Shield Array [*Nuclear structure*]
Tessaur ...... [*Antonius*] Tessaurus [*Flourished, 17th century*] [*Authority cited in pre-1607 legal work*] (DSA)

TEST .... Tanner Eclectic Stuttering Therapy Program
TEST .... Teen-Age Employment Skills Training, Inc.
TEST .... Testament
Test .... Testamentary [*Legal term*] (DLA)
TEST .... Testator (ADA)
TEST .... Testimonial (ADA)
TEST .... Thesaurus of Engineering and Scientific Terms [*A publication*]
TEST .... Track Evaluation System [*Canadian National Railways*]
TEST .... Transamerica Electronic Scoring Technique [*Credit risk evaluation*]
TEST .... Two Element Synthesis Telescope (ADA)
testa........... Testamentaria [*Estate Of*] [*Spanish*]
TestAbr...... Testament of Abraham [*Pseudepigrapha*] (BJA)
TestAsh...... Testament of Asher [*Pseudepigrapha*] (BJA)
TestBen..... Testament of Benjamin [*Pseudepigrapha*] (BJA)
TESTCOMDNA ... Test Command Defense Nuclear Agency [*Military*] (AABC)
Test Eng Manage ... Test Engineering and Management [*A publication*]
TESTFAC ... Test Facility
Test Instrum Controls ... Testing, Instruments, and Controls [*Australia*] [*A publication*]
TestIss ...... Testament of Issachar [*Pseudepigrapha*] (BJA)
TestJos ...... Testament of Joseph [*Pseudepigrapha*] (BJA)
TestJud ..... Testament of Judah [*Pseudepigrapha*] (BJA)
TestLevi..... Testament of Levi [*Pseudepigrapha*] (BJA)
Test Memor Timb Res Developm Ass ... Test Memorandum. Timber Research and Development Association [*A publication*]
TestNaph.... Testament of Naphtali [*Pseudepigrapha*] (BJA)
TESTO...... Testigo [*Witness*] [*Latin*] (ADA)
TESTOR ... Testator (ROG)
Test Polym ... Testing of Polymers [*A publication*]
TESTRAN ... Test Translator [*Data processing*]
Test Rec Timb Res Developm Ass ... Test Record. Timber Research and Development Association [*A publication*]
TestReub.... Testament of Reuben [*Pseudepigrapha*] (BJA)
TESTRIX .. Testatrix (ROG)
TESTS....... Technical-Engineering-Science Training for Secretaries
TESTS...... Test Squadron (MCD)
Tests Agrochem Cultiv ... Tests of Agrochemicals and Cultivars [*A publication*]
TestSim...... Testament of Simeon [*Pseudepigrapha*] (BJA)
TESTT...... Testament
TestXII ..... Testaments of the Twelve Patriarchs [*Pseudepigrapha*] (BJA)
TESTY ...... Testamentary (ROG)
TestZeb..... Testament of Zebulun [*Pseudepigrapha*] (BJA)
TET........... East Tennessee State University, Johnson City, TN [*OCLC symbol*] (OCLC)
TeT .... Taal en Tongval [*Antwerpen*] [*A publication*]
TET............ Teacher Effectiveness Training [*A course of study*]
TET............ Teacher of Electrotherapy [*British*]
TET............ Technical Evaluation Team (MCD)
TET............ Telescope and Electron Telescope
TET............ Test Equipment Team (AAG)
TET............ Test Equipment Tool (AAG)
TET............ Test Evaluation Team [*NASA*] (KSC)
Tet............. Tetanus [*Medicine*]
TET............ Tete [*Mozambique*] [*Airport symbol*] (OAG)
TET............ Tete [*Mozambique*] [*Seismograph station code, US Geological Survey*] (SEIS)
TET............ Tetrachloride [*Chemistry*] (AAG)
Tet............. Tetracycline [*Antibiotic compound*]
TET............ Tetrahedron (FAAC)
Tet............. Tetralogy [*Medicine*]
TET............ Tetrode [*Electronics*]
TET............ Texas Eastern Corp. [*Formerly, Texas Eastern Transmission Corp.*] [*NYSE symbol*] [*Toronto Stock Exchange symbol*] (SPSG)
TET............ Thermionic Emission Technique
TET............ Thermometric Enthalpy Titration [*Analytical chemistry*]
TET............ Titanium Elevon Track
TET............ Total Elapsed Time (KSC)
TET............ Transistor Evaluation Test
TET............ Transportable Electronic Tower (MCD)
TET............ Troop Evaluation Tests [*Army*]
TET............ Turbine Entry Temperature [*Aviation*]
TET............ Turbo-Electric Tanker
TETA........ Test Equipment Technical Adviser
TETA........ Travelers Emergency Transportation Association [*Sought to pool transportation of salesmen traveling similar routes*] [*World War II*]
TETA........ Triethylenetetramine [*Organic chemistry*]
TETAM..... Tactical Effectiveness Testing of Antitank Missiles [*DoD*]
TETB........ Tetbury [*England*]
TETD........ Tetraethylthiuram Disulfide [*Also, TTD*] [*Organic chemistry*]
TETEP ...... Test for Entrance into Teacher Education Programs [*Achievement test*]
TETF .... Terminal Equipment Test Facility [*Army*] (RDA)
TETFLEYNE ... Tetrafluoroethylene [*Organic chemistry*]
T & ETGM ... Test and Evaluation Task Group Manager
TETHB...... Tethys [*A publication*]
Tethys Suppl ... Tethys. Supplement [*A publication*]

TETM....... Thermal Effects Tests Model
TETOC...... Council for Technical Education and Training for Overseas Countries [*British*]
TETR......... Test and Training Satellite [*Also, TATS, TTS*] [*NASA*]
TETR........ Tetragonal
TETRA...... Terminal Tracking Telescope
TETRA...... Tetrahedron [*A publication*]
tetra.......... Tetraploid [*Genetics*]
TETRAC ... Tension Truss Antenna Concept
Tetrahedr L ... Tetrahedron Letters [*A publication*]
Tetrahedron Lett ... Tetrahedron Letters [*A publication*]
Tetrahedron Suppl ... Tetrahedron. Supplement [*A publication*]
TETROON ... Tetrahedral Balloon [*Meteorology*]
Tetsu Hagan ... Tetsu To Hagane Journal. Iron and Steel Institute of Japan [*A publication*]
TEU .... Te Anau [*New Zealand*] [*Airport symbol*]   (OAG)
TEU .... Technical Escort Unit [*Army*]   (AABC)
TeU .... Tekst en Uitleg   (BJA)
TEU .... Telemetry Equipment Unit
TEU .... Temple University, Philadelphia, PA [*OCLC symbol*]   (OCLC)
TEU .... Ter Elfder Ure [*A publication*]
TEU .... Test of Economic Understanding
TEU .... Tetraethyl Urea [*Organic chemistry*]
TEU .... Transducer Excitation Unit
TEU .... Tropical Experimental Unit [*British military*]   (DMA)
TEU .... Twenty-Foot Equivalent Unit [*Used to compare capacity of containerships*]
Teubner Studienskr ... Teubner Studienskripten [*A publication*]
Teubner-Texte zur Math ... Teubner-Texte zur Mathematik [*A publication*]
TEUC .... Temporary Extended Unemployment Compensation [*Labor*]
TEUN .... Trust for Education on the United Nations   (EA)
Teut.......... Teuthonista [*A publication*]
TEUT........ Teuton
TEV .... Talipes Equinovarus [*Anatomy*]
T Ev.......... Taylor on Evidence [*12th ed.*] [*1931*] [*A publication*]   (DLA)
TEV .... Terminal Equipment Vehicle [*British military*]   (DMA)
TeV .... Tetra-Electron Volt
TEV .... Thermo Environmental [*AMEX symbol*]   (SPSG)
TEV .... Thermoelectric Voltage
TEV .... Thermostatic Expansion Valve [*Refrigeration*]
TEV .... Time Expanded Video
TEV .... Tobacco Etch Virus
TEV .... Today's English Version [*of the Bible*]
TEV .... Tomato Etch Virus
TEV .... Total Economic Value
TeV .... Trillion Electron Volts
TEV .... Turbo-Electric Vessel
TEV .... Victoria College, Victoria, TX [*OCLC symbol*]   (OCLC)
TEVA....... Tennessee Virginia Energy Corp. [*NASDAQ symbol*]   (NQ)
TEVA........ Tutmonda Esperantista Vegetara Asocio [*World Esperantist Vegetarian Association - WEVA*]   (EAIO)
TEVAL...... Target Engagement Evaluation [*Military*]
TEVI......... Teva Pharmaceutical Industries Ltd. [*NASDAQ symbol*]   (NQ)
TEVROC... Tailored Exhaust Velocity Rocket
TEW .... Tactical Early Warning
TEW .... Tactical Electronic Warfare [*Aircraft*]   (NATG)
TEW .... Total Equivalent Weight
TE/W........ Tractive Effort to Weight Ratio   (MCD)
TEWA .... Target Evaluation and Weapon Assignment   (MCD)
TEWA .... Threat Evaluation and Weapons Assignment   (NVT)
TEWC....... Totally-Enclosed Water-Cooled [*Reactor*]   (DEN)
TEWDS..... Tactical Electronic Warfare Deception System   (MCD)
TEWG ...... Test and Evaluation Work Group [*Military*]   (CAAL)
TEWGp ..... Tactical Electronic Warfare Group [*Air Force*]   (AFM)
TEWK....... Tewkesbury [*Municipal borough in England*]
TEWL........ Transepidermal Water Loss [*Physiology*]
TEWP........ Williams [*T. E.*] Pharmaceuticals, Inc. [*NASDAQ symbol*]   (NQ)
TEWS....... Tactical Effectiveness of Weapons Systems [*Army*]   (AABC)
TEWS....... Tactical Electronic Warfare Support   (MCD)
TEWS....... Threat Evaluation and Weapon Selection [*Military*]   (CAAL)
TEWSq...... Tactical Electronic Warfare Squadron [*Air Force*]
TEWT........ Tactical Exercise without Troops
TEW Tech Ber ... TEW [*Technische Edelstahlwerke*] Technische Berichte [*Later, Thyssen Edelstahl Technische Berichte*] [*A publication*]
TEX .... Air Texana [*Beaumont, TX*] [*FAA designator*]   (FAAC)
TEX .... Automatic Teleprinter Exchange Service [*of Western Union Corp.*]
TEX .... Revue Francaise des Telecommunications [*A publication*]
TEX .... Teletype Exchange
TEX .... TELEX
tex .... Tex [*Formerly, den*] [*Linear density*] [*SI unit*]
TEX .... Texas   (AAG)
TEX .... Texas Airlines, Inc. [*Galveston, TX*] [*FAA designator*]   (FAAC)
Tex .... Texas Supreme Court Reports [*A publication*]   (DLA)
TEX .... Textile   (AABC)
TEX .... Transaction Exception Code [*Military*]   (AFIT)
TEX .... Tumbling Explorer [*Aerospace*]
TEX .... University of Texas at Tyler, Tyler, TX [*OCLC symbol*]   (OCLC)

Tex A Civ... White and Wilson's [*or Willson's*] Civil Cases, Texas Court of Appeals [*A publication*]   (DLA)
Tex A Civ Cas ... White and Wilson's [*or Willson's*] Civil Cases, Texas Court of Appeals [*A publication*]   (DLA)
Tex A Civ Cas (Wilson) ... Texas Court of Appeal Civil Cases (Wilson) [*or Willson*] [*A publication*]   (DLA)
TEXACO... Texas Company
Tex Admin Code ... Texas Administrative Code [*A publication*]   (DLA)
Tex Ag Exp ... Texas. Agricultural Experiment Station. Publications [*A publication*]
Tex Agric Exp Stn Bull ... Texas. Agricultural Experiment Station. Bulletin [*A publication*]
Tex Agric Exp Stn Leafl ... Texas. Agricultural Experiment Station. Leaflet [*A publication*]
Tex Agric Exp Stn Misc Publ ... Texas. Agricultural Experiment Station. Miscellaneous Publication [*A publication*]
Tex Agric Exp Stn Prog Rep ... Texas. Agricultural Experiment Station. Progress Report [*A publication*]
Tex Agric Exp Stn Res Monogr ... Texas. Agricultural Experiment Station. Research Monograph [*A publication*]
Tex Agric Exp Stn Tech Monogr ... Texas. Agricultural Experiment Station. Technical Monograph [*A publication*]
Tex Agric Ext Serv Fish Dis Diagn Lab ... Texas. Agricultural Extension Service. Fish Disease Diagnostic Laboratory [*A publication*]
Tex Agric Prog ... Texas Agricultural Progress [*A publication*]
Tex Agric Prog Tex Agric Exp Stn ... Texas Agricultural Progress. Texas Agricultural Experiment Station [*A publication*]
Tex Agr Progr ... Texas Agricultural Progress [*A publication*]
Tex A & M Univ Dep Civ Eng Rep ... Texas A & M University. Department of Civil Engineering. Report [*A publication*]
Tex A M Univ Oceanogr Stud ... Texas A & M University. Oceanographic Studies [*A publication*]
Tex A & M Univ Sea Grant Coll TAMU-SG ... Texas A & M University Sea Grant College. TAMU-SG [*A publication*]
Tex A & M Univ Syst Tex Agric Ext Serv Fish Dis Diagn Lab ... Texas A & M University System. Texas Agricultural Extension Service. Fish Disease Diagnostic Laboratory [*A publication*]
Tex A M Univ Syst Tex Agric Ext Serv Fish Dis Diagn Lab FDDL ... Texas A & M University System. Texas Agricultural Extension Service. Fish Disease Diagnostic Laboratory. FDDL [*A publication*]
Tex A & M Univ Tex Eng Exp Stn Tech Bull ... Texas A & M University. Texas Engineering Experiment Station. Technical Bulletin [*A publication*]
Tex App ..... Texas Civil Appeals Cases [*A publication*]   (DLA)
Tex App ..... Texas Court of Appeals Reports (Criminal Cases) [*A publication*]   (DLA)
Tex App Civ Cas (Wilson) ... White and Wilson's [*or Willson's*] Civil Cases, Texas Court of Appeals [*A publication*]   (DLA)
TEXAS ...... Tactical Exchange Automation System   (MCD)
Texas Acad of Sci Trans ... Texas Academy of Sciences. Transactions [*A publication*]
Texas Archeol Paleont Soc Bull ... Texas Archeological and Paleontological Society. Bulletin [*A publication*]
Texas BJ.... Texas Bar Journal [*A publication*]
Texas Board of Water Engineers Bull ... Texas. Board of Water Engineers. Bulletin [*A publication*]
Texas Bus Rev ... Texas Business Review [*A publication*]
Texas Civ... Texas Civil Appeals Reports [*A publication*]   (DLA)
Texas Civ App ... Texas Civil Appeals Reports [*A publication*]   (DLA)
Texas Cour Rec Med ... Texas Courier Record of Medicine [*A publication*]
Texas Cr App ... Texas Court of Appeals Reports [*A publication*]   (DLA)
Texas Crim ... Texas Criminal Reports [*A publication*]   (DLA)
Texas Crim App ... Texas Criminal Appeals Reports [*A publication*]   (DLA)
Texas Crim Rep ... Texas Criminal Reports [*A publication*]   (DLA)
Texas Cr Rep ... Texas Criminal Reports [*A publication*]   (DLA)
Texas Ct of App ... Texas Court of Appeals Reports [*A publication*]   (DLA)
Texas Ct App ... Texas Court of Appeals Reports [*A publication*]   (DLA)
Texas Ct App Civ Cas ... Texas Civil Cases [*A publication*]   (DLA)
Texas Ct Rep ... Texas Court Reporter [*1900-1908*] [*A publication*]   (DLA)
Texas Dig... Texas Digest [*A publication*]   (DLA)
Texas Eng Expt Sta Research Rept ... Texas. Engineering Experiment Station. Research Report [*A publication*]
Texas Internat L Forum ... Texas International Law Forum [*A publication*]
Texas Internat LJ ... Texas International Law Journal [*A publication*]
Texas Int'l LF ... Texas International Law Forum [*A publication*]
Texas Int'l LJ ... Texas International Law Journal [*A publication*]
Texas Jour Sci ... Texas Journal of Science [*A publication*]
Texas J Sci ... Texas Journal of Science [*A publication*]
Texas L Rev ... Texas Law Review [*A publication*]
Texas Med ... Texas Medicine [*A publication*]
Texas Memorial Mus Pearce-Sellards Ser ... Texas Memorial Museum. Pearce-Sellards Series [*A publication*]
Texas MJ .. Texas Medical Journal [*A publication*]
Texas Mo... Texas Monthly [*A publication*]
Texas Nurs ... Texas Nursing [*A publication*]
Texas Oil Jour ... Texas Oil Journal [*A publication*]
Texas Petroleum Research Comm Bull ... Texas Petroleum Research Committee. Bulletin [*A publication*]
Texas R...... Texas Reports [*A publication*]   (DLA)

Texas Rep .. Texas Reports [*A publication*] (DLA)
Texas Rep Biol Med ... Texas Reports on Biology and Medicine [*A publication*]
Texas South UL Rev ... Texas Southern University. Law Review [*A publication*]
Texas Tech L Rev ... Texas Tech Law Review [*A publication*]
Texas Univ Austin Bur Econ Geology Geol Circ ... Texas University at Austin. Bureau of Economic Geology. Geological Circular [*A publication*]
Texas Univ Austin Bur Econ Geology Geol Quad Map ... University of Texas at Austin. Bureau of Economic Geology. Geologic Quadrangle Map [*A publication*]
Texas Univ Austin Bur Econ Geology Guidebook ... Texas University at Austin. Bureau of Economic Geology. Guidebook [*A publication*]
Texas Univ Austin Bur Econ Geology Rept Inv ... University of Texas at Austin. Bureau of Economic Geology. Report of Investigations [*A publication*]
Texas Univ Pub Bur Econ Geology Mineral Res Circ Rept Inv ... Texas University. Publication. Bureau of Economic Geology. Mineral Resource Circular. Report of Investigations [*A publication*]
Texas Water Devel Board Rept ... Texas. Water Development Board. Report [*A publication*]
Tex B J ...... Texas Bar Journal [*A publication*]
Tex Board Water Eng Bull ... Texas. Board of Water Engineers. Bulletin [*A publication*]
Tex Board Water Eng Chem Compos Tex Surf Waters ... Texas. Board of Water Engineers. Chemical Composition of Texas Surface Waters [*A publication*]
Tex Bus Corp Act Ann ... Texas Business Corporation Act, Annotated [*A publication*] (DLA)
Tex Bus Exec ... Texas Business Executive [*A publication*]
Tex Busin Rev ... Texas Business Review [*A publication*]
Tex Bus R .. Texas Business Review [*A publication*]
Tex Bus Rev ... Texas Business Review [*A publication*]
TEXC .... Texas Central Railroad Co. [*AAR code*]
Tex Civ App ... Texas Civil Appeals Reports [*A publication*] (DLA)
Tex Civ Cas ... Texas Court of Appeals Decisions, Civil Cases (White and Wilson) [*or Willson*] [*1876-92*] [*A publication*] (DLA)
Tex Civ Rep ... Texas Civil Appeals Reports [*A publication*] (DLA)
Tex Coach ... Texas Coach [*A publication*]
Tex Code Ann ... Texas Codes, Annotated [*A publication*] (DLA)
Tex Code Crim Proc Ann ... Texas Code of Criminal Procedure, Annotated [*A publication*] (DLA)
Tex Cr .... Texas Criminal [*A publication*] (DLA)
Tex Cr App ... Texas Criminal Appeals Reports [*A publication*] (DLA)
Tex Crim .... Texas Criminal Reports [*A publication*] (DLA)
Tex Crim Rep ... Texas Criminal Reports [*A publication*] (DLA)
Tex Cr R .... Texas Criminal Appeals Reports [*A publication*] (DLA)
Tex Cr Rpts ... Texas Criminal Reports [*A publication*] (DLA)
Tex Ct App ... Texas Court of Appeals Reports [*A publication*] (DLA)
Tex Ct App Civ ... Texas Civil Cases [*A publication*] (DLA)
Tex Ct App Dec Civ ... Texas Civil Cases [*A publication*] (DLA)
Tex Ct App R ... Texas Court of Appeals Reports [*A publication*] (DLA)
Tex Ct Rep ... Texas Court Reporter [*A publication*] (DLA)
TEXDEALAM ... Textile Dealers Association of America (EA)
Tex Dec ...... Texas Decisions [*A publication*] (DLA)
Tex Dent Assist Assoc Bull ... Texas Dental Assistants Association. Bulletin [*A publication*]
Tex Dent J ... Texas Dental Journal [*A publication*]
Tex Dig Op Att'y Gen ... Digest of Opinions of the Attorney General of Texas [*A publication*] (DLA)
Tex Elec Code Ann ... Texas Election Code, Annotated [*A publication*] (DLA)
Tex Energy ... Texas Energy [*A publication*]
Tex Energy Miner Resour ... Texas Energy and Mineral Resources [*A publication*]
Tex Eng Exp Stn Bull ... Texas. Engineering Experiment Station. Bulletin [*A publication*]
Tex Eng Exp Stn News ... Texas. Engineering Experiment Station. News [*A publication*]
Tex Eng Exp Stn Res Rep ... Texas. Engineering Experiment Station. Research Report [*A publication*]
TEXF .... TGIF Texas, Inc. [*NASDAQ symbol*] (NQ)
Tex For Pap ... Texas Forestry Paper [*A publication*]
Tex Gen Laws ... General and Special Laws of the State of Texas [*A publication*] (DLA)
Tex Geogr Mag ... Texas Geographic Magazine [*A publication*]
Tex G S Rp Prog ... Texas. Geological Survey. Report of Progress [*A publication*]
Tex Heart Inst J ... Texas Heart Institute. Journal [*A publication*]
Tex His Q .. Texas State Historical Association. Quarterly [*A publication*]
Tex Hist Assoc Q ... Texas State Historical Association. Quarterly [*A publication*]
Tex Hosp ... Texas Hospitals [*A publication*]
Tex Hospitals ... Texas Hospitals [*A publication*]
Tex Ins Code Ann ... Texas Insurance Code, Annotated [*A publication*] (DLA)
Tex Inst ...... Texas Institutes [*A publication*]
Tex Int L Forum ... Texas International Law Forum [*A publication*]

Tex Int L J ... Texas International Law Journal [*A publication*]
Tex Intl LJ ... Texas International Law Journal [*A publication*]
Tex J .... Texas Journal [*A publication*]
Tex J Pharm ... Texas Journal of Pharmacy [*A publication*]
Tex J Sci .... Texas Journal of Science [*A publication*]
Tex J Sci Spec Publ ... Texas Journal of Science. Special Publication [*A publication*]
Tex Jur ...... Texas Jurisprudence [*A publication*] (DLA)
Tex Jur 2d ... Texas Jurisprudence [*2nd ed.*] [*A publication*] (DLA)
Tex Law ...... Texas Lawman [*A publication*] (DLA)
Tex Law & Leg ... Texas Law and Legislation [*A publication*] (DLA)
Tex Law Rev ... Texas Law Review [*A publication*]
TexLex ...... Texas Lexicon [*Slang*]
Tex Lib ...... Texas Libraries [*A publication*]
Tex Lib J .... Texas Library Journal [*A publication*]
Tex Libr ..... Texas Libraries [*A publication*]
Tex LJ .... Texas Law Journal [*A publication*] (DLA)
Tex L R .... Texas Law Review [*A publication*]
Tex L Rep .. Texas Law Reporter [*1882-84*] [*A publication*] (DLA)
Tex L Rev ... Texas Law Review [*A publication*]
Tex Med .... Texas Medicine [*A publication*]
Tex Mem Mus Misc Pap ... Texas Memorial Museum. Miscellaneous Papers [*A publication*]
TEX MEX ... Texas Mexican Railway Co.
TexMex ..... Texas and Mexico [*Refers to fashion, food, language, or lifestyle that has characteristics of these two regions*]
Tex Mo ...... Texas Monthly [*A publication*]
Tex Nurs ... Texas Nursing [*A publication*]
Tex Nutr Conf Proc ... Texas Nutrition Conference. Proceedings [*A publication*]
Tex Outl ..... Texas Outlook [*A publication*]
TEXP .... Time Exposure [*Photography*]
Tex Parks Wildl ... Texas Parks Wildlife [*A publication*]
Tex Pharm ... Texas Pharmacy [*A publication*]
Tex Q .... Texas Quarterly [*A publication*]
Tex Rep Bio ... Texas Reports on Biology and Medicine [*A publication*]
Tex Rep Biol Med ... Texas Reports on Biology and Medicine [*A publication*]
Tex Res ...... Textile Research [*A publication*]
Tex Res J ... Textile Research Journal [*A publication*]
Tex Rev ...... Texas Review [*A publication*]
Tex Rev Civ Stat Ann (Vernon) ... Texas Revised Civil Statutes, Annotated (Vernon) [*A publication*] (DLA)
TEXS .... Tactical Explosive System [*Military*] (RDA)
Tex S .... Texas Supreme Court Reports, Supplement [*A publication*] (DLA)
Tex S Ct ..... Texas Supreme Court Reporter [*A publication*] (DLA)
Tex Sess Law Serv ... Texas Session Law Service (Vernon) [*A publication*] (DLA)
Tex So Intra L Rev ... Texas Southern Intramural Law Review [*A publication*] (DLA)
Tex So LR ... Texas Southern Law Review [*A publication*]
Tex So U L Rev ... Texas Southern University. Law Review [*A publication*]
Tex Stat Ann ... Texas Statutes, Annotated [*A publication*] (DLA)
Tex State Hist Assoc Quar ... Texas State Historical Association. Quarterly [*A publication*]
Tex State J Med ... Texas State Journal of Medicine [*A publication*]
Tex St Lit ... Texas Studies in Literature and Language [*A publication*]
Tex Stud Lit & Lang ... Texas Studies in Literature and Language [*A publication*]
Tex SUL Rev ... Texas Southern University. Law Review [*A publication*]
Tex Supp .... Texas Supplement [*A publication*] (DLA)
Tex Suppl ... Texas Supplement [*A publication*] (DLA)
TEXT .... Intex Software Systems International Ltd. [*New York, NY*] [*NASDAQ symbol*] (NQ)
TEXT .... Texas Experimental TOKAMAK [*Atomic physics*]
TEXT .... Textile
TEXTA ...... Technical Extracts of Traffic [*National Security Agency*] [*A publication*]
Text Abstr ... Textile Abstracts [*A publication*]
Text Age .... Textile Age [*A publication*]
Text Am ..... Textile American [*A publication*]
Text Argus ... Textile Argus [*A publication*]
Text Asia ... Textile Asia [*A publication*]
Tex Tax-Gen Ann ... Texas Tax-General, Annotated [*A publication*] (DLA)
Text Beklaedning ... Textil og Beklaedning [*A publication*]
Text Betr (Poessneck Ger) ... Textil-Betrich (Poessneck, Germany) [*A publication*]
Text Bull .... Textile Bulletin [*A publication*]
Text Chem Color ... Textile Chemist and Colorist [*A publication*]
Text Chim ... Textiles Chimiques [*A publication*]
Text Color ... Textile Colorist [*A publication*]
Text Color Converter ... Textile Colorist and Converter [*A publication*]
Text Cordage Q ... Textile and Cordage Quarterly [*A publication*]
Text Dyer Printer ... Textile Dyer and Printer [*A publication*]
Tex Tech LR ... Texas Tech Law Review [*A publication*]
Tex Tech L Rev ... Texas Tech Law Review [*A publication*]
Texte Kritisch Psych ... Texte zur Kritischen Psychologie [*A publication*]
TexteM ...... Texte Metzler [*A publication*]
Textes et Doc (Bruxelles) ... Textes et Documents (Bruxelles) [*A publication*]
Textes Math ... Textes Mathematiques [*A publication*]
Tex-Text .... Tex-Textilis [*A publication*]

Text Faerberei Ztg ... Textil und Faerberei-Zeitung [*A publication*]
Text Faserstofftech ... Textil und Faserstofftechnik [*A publication*]
Text Forsch ... Textil-Forschung [*A publication*]
Text Hist.... Textile History [*A publication*]
Text Horizons ... Textile Horizons [*A publication*]
Text I Ind... Textile Institute and Industry [*A publication*]
Textilchem Color ... Textilchemiker und Colorist [*A publication*]
Textile Ind ... Textile Industries [*A publication*]
Textile Inst ... Textile Institute and Industry [*A publication*]
Textile Inst Ind ... Textile Institute and Industry [*A publication*]
Textile J Aust ... Textile Journal of Australia [*A publication*]　(APTA)
Textile Jl.... Textile Research Journal [*A publication*]
Textile Mfr ... Textile Manufacturer [*A publication*]
Textile Progr ... Textile Progress [*A publication*]
Textile Res J ... Textile Research Journal [*A publication*]
Textile Technol Dig ... Textile Technology Digest [*A publication*]
Textil Ind... Textile Industries [*A publication*]
Textil Mnth ... Textile Month [*A publication*]
Textil Prax ... Textil Praxis International [*A publication*]
Textil Rent ... Textile Rental [*A publication*]
Textil Rep .. America's Textiles Reporter Bulletin [*A publication*]
Textilvered ... Textilveredelung [*A publication*]
Textil-W .... Textil-Wirtschaft [*A publication*]
Textil Wld ... Textile World [*A publication*]
Textil Wld ... Textile World Buyer's Guide/Fact File [*A publication*]
Text Ind ..... Textile Industries [*A publication*]
Text Ind Dyegest Sthn Afr ... Textile Industries Dyegest Southern Africa [*A publication*]
Text Ind Exporter ... Textile Industry and Exporter [*A publication*]
Text Ind (Moenchen Gladbach Ger) ... Textil-Industrie (Moenchen Gladbach, Germany) [*A publication*]
Text Ind (Munich) ... Textil-Industrie (Munich) [*A publication*]
Text Ind Sthn Afr ... Textile Industries Southern Africa [*A publication*]
Text Ind (Zurich) ... Textil-Industrie (Zurich) [*A publication*]
Text Inf Users Coun Proc Meet ... Textile Information Users Council. Proceedings of the Meeting [*A publication*]
Text Inst Ind ... Textile Institute and Industry [*A publication*]
TEXTIR..... Text Indexing and Retrieval [*Data processing*]
Text J Aust ... Textile Journal of Australia [*A publication*]
Text Konfekt ... Textil och Konfektion [*A publication*]
Text Krit .... Text und Kritik [*A publication*]
Text Mag ... Textile Magazine [*A publication*]
Text Manuf J ... Textile Manufacturer's Journal [*A publication*]
Text Mercury Int ... Textile Mercury International [*A publication*]
Text Metod Mat ... Textos de Metodos Matematicos [*A publication*]
Text Mfr .... Textile Manufacturer [*A publication*]
Text Mon... Textile Month [*A publication*]
TEXTOR... TOKAMAK [*Toroidal Kamera Magnetic*] Experiment for Technical Oriented Research [*Oak Ridge National Laboratory*]
Text-Prax .. Textil-Praxis [*Later, Textil Praxis International*] [*A publication*]
Text Prax Int ... Textil Praxis International [*A publication*]
Text Prog ... Textile Progress [*A publication*]
Text Q........ Textile Quarterly [*A publication*]
Tex Transp Res ... Texas Transportation Researcher [*A publication*]
Text Rec..... Textile Recorder [*A publication*]
TEXT REC ... Textus Receptus [*The Received Text*] [*Latin*]
Text Rent ... Textile Rental [*A publication*]
Text Res J ... Textile Research Journal [*A publication*]
Text Ring ... Textil-Ring [*A publication*]
Text Rundsch ... Textil-Rundschau [*A publication*]
Texts Monographs Phys ... Texts and Monographs in Physics [*A publication*]
Text Tech Dig ... Textile Technology Digest [*A publication*]
Texture Cryst Solids ... Texture of Crystalline Solids [*A publication*]
Textures and Microstruct ... Textures and Microstructures [*A publication*]
Textures Microstruct ... Textures and Microstructures [*A publication*]
Text Wkly ... Textile Weekly [*A publication*]
Text World ... Textile World [*A publication*]
Text World J ... Textile World Journal [*A publication*]
Text World R ... Textile World Record [*A publication*]
Tex Univ B Min S B ... Texas University. Bulletin. Mineral Survey Bulletin [*A publication*]
Tex Univ Bur Econ Geol Geol Circ ... Texas University. Bureau of Economic Geology. Geological Circular [*A publication*]
Tex Univ Bur Econ Geol Miner Resour Circ ... Texas University. Bureau of Economic Geology. Mineral Resource Circular [*A publication*]
Tex Univ Bur Econ Geol Publ ... Texas University. Bureau of Economic Geology. Publication [*A publication*]
Tex Univ Bur Econ Geol Rep Invest ... Texas University. Bureau of Economic Geology. Report of Investigations [*A publication*]
Tex Univ Bur Econ Geol Res Note ... Texas University. Bureau of Economic Geology. Research Note [*A publication*]
Tex Univ Bur Eng Res Circ ... Texas University. Bureau of Engineering Research. Circular [*A publication*]
Tex Univ Cent Res Water Resour Tech Rep ... Texas University. Center for Research in Water Resources. Technical Report [*A publication*]
Tex Univ Publ ... Texas University. Publication [*A publication*]
Tex Unrep Cas ... Posey's Unreported Cases [*Texas*] [*A publication*]　(DLA)

TE (XVIII) ... Textos y Estudios del Siglo XVIII [*A publication*]
Tex Water Comm Bull ... Texas Water Commission. Bulletin [*A publication*]
Tex Water Comm Circ ... Texas Water Commission. Circular [*A publication*]
Tex Water Comm Mem Rep ... Texas Water Commission. Memorandum Report [*A publication*]
Tex Water Dev Board Rep ... Texas. Water Development Board. Report [*A publication*]
TEY .... Thingeyri [*Iceland*] [*Airport symbol*]　(OAG)
TeZ .... Texte und Zeichen [*A publication*]
TEZ........... Tezpur [*India*] [*Airport symbol*]　(OAG)
Tez Doklad Nauch Konf Zootech Sek ... Tezisy Dokladov Nauchnoi Konferentsii. Zootekhnicheskaya Sektsiya [*A publication*]
TEZG........ Tribological Experiments in Zero Gravity
Tezhka Prom ... Tezhka Promishlenost [*A publication*]
Tezisy Dokl Vses Nauchno Metod Konf Vet Patoloanat ... Tezisy Dokladov Vsesoyuznoi Nauchno-Metodicheskoi Konferentsii Veterinarnykh Patologoanatomov [*A publication*]
TF .... [*The*] FORUM [*Foundation of Research for Understanding Man*]　(EA)
TF .... French Southern and Antarctic Lands [*ANSI two-letter standard code*]　(CNC)
TF .... Iceland [*Aircraft nationality and registration mark*]　(FAAC)
TF .... Tabulating Form　(AAG)
TF .... Tactical Fighter　(AFM)
TF .... Tactile Fremitus [*Medicine*]
TF .... Taeria Foundation　(EA)
Tf................ Tafel　(BJA)
TF .... Tallulah Falls Railway Co. [*AAR code*]
TF .... Tank Farm　(NATG)
TF .... Tape Feed
TF .... Target File　(MCD)
TF .... Task Force
TF .... Tax Foundation　(EA)
TF .... Tayu Fellowship　(EA)
TF .... Teaching Fellow
TF .... Tear Fund [*An association*]　(EA)
TF .... Teased Fibers [*Neurology*]
TF .... Technical File　(MCD)
TF .... Technological Forecasting
TF .... Telegram for Delivery by Telephone
TF .... Telegraph Form　(ROG)
TF .... Telephone　(NATG)
TF .... Temperature Factor
TF .... Temporary Fix　(AAG)
TF .... Terminal Forecast
TF .... Terminal Frame　(NATG)
TF .... Terrain-Following [*Helicopter*]
TF .... Territorial Force [*Military*] [*British*]
TF .... Test Facility [*NASA*]　(NASA)
TF .... Test Fixture　(KSC)
TF .... Test Flight [*Air Force*]
TF .... Test Frame [*Telecommunications*]　(TEL)
TF .... Tetralogy of Fallot [*Cardiology*]
TF .... Text-Fiche
TF .... THEOS [*They Help Each Other Spiritually*] Foundation　(EA)
TF .... Thin Film
TF .... Thoreau Fellowship　(EA)
TF .... Thread Forming　(MSA)
TF .... Thymidine Factor [*Endocrinology*]
TF .... Thymol Flocculation [*Clinical chemistry*]
TF .... Tibet Fund　(EA)
T & F.......... Ticknor & Fields [*Publisher*]
TF .... Tile Floor [*Technical drawings*]
TF .... Till Forbidden [*i.e., repeat until forbidden to do so*] [*Advertising*]
TF .... Time Factor　(CAAL)
T/F............. Time of Fail　(MSA)
TF .... Time of Flight [*Ballistics*]
TF .... Time Frame
TF .... Time to Function
TF .... Tissue Factor [*Clinical chemistry*]
TF .... To Fill
TF .... To Follow
TF .... Tolkien Fellowships　(EA)
TF .... Tolstoy Foundation　(EA)
TF .... Tool Foundation [*See also ST*] [*Amsterdam, Netherlands*]　(EAIO)
TF .... Toroidal Field　(MCD)
TF .... Torpedo Fighter Aircraft [*Navy*]
TF .... Total Flowers [*Plant pathology*]
TF .... Total Forfeiture [*of all pay and allowances*] [*Army*]　(AABC)
TF .... Toward Freedom　(EA)
TF .... Toxicology Forum　(EA)
TF .... Tracking Filter
TF .... Trailfinders [*Travel agency*] [*British*]
TF .... Trainer Fighter
TF .... Training Film [*Military*]
TF .... Training Flight [*British military*]　(DMA)
TF .... TransAfrica Forum　(EA)
TF .... Transcription Factor [*Genetics*]
TF .... Transfer Factor [*Immunochemistry*]

TF	Transfer Fee [*Banking*]
TF	Transfer Function (AAG)
T/F	Transfer of Function [*Military*] (AFM)
TF	Transferrin [*Also, T, TRF*] [*Biochemistry*]
TF	Transformation [*A publication*]
TF	Transformers [*JETDS nomenclature*] [*Military*] (CET)
TF	Transmitter Frequency
TF	Transportation Factor (MCD)
TF	Transportes Aereos Regionais (TAR) SA [*Brazil*] [*ICAO designator*] (ICDA)
TF	Travail Force [*Penal Servitude*] [*French*]
TF	Travellers Fare [*Train catering service*] [*British*]
TF	Trench Feet [*or Fever*]
TF	Trench Fighter [*British military*] (DMA)
TF	Trichloroethylene Finishing
TF	Triple Frequency
TF	Triple Fronted [*Classified advertising*] (ADA)
TF	Tropical Fresh Water [*Vessel load line mark*]
TF	Trunk Frame [*Telecommunications*] (TEL)
TF	Trust Fund
TF	Tuberculin Filtrate [*Medicine*]
TF	Turbofan [*Engine*]
TF	Twentieth Century-Fox Film Corp. [*NYSE symbol*] (SPSG)
TF	Twins Foundation (EA)
TF	Type of Foundation [*IRS*]
TF1	Channel One [*French television station*]
TFA	[*The*] Ferroalloys Association (EA)
TFA	Target Factor Analysis [*Statistical technique*]
TFA	Task Force A
TFA	Tax Free America (EA)
TFA	Taxation for Accountants [*A publication*]
TFA	Tie Fabrics Association [*Defunct*] (EA)
TFA	Timing Filter Analyzer
TFA	Top Farmers of America Association [*Milwaukee, WI*] (EA)
TFA	Total Fatty Acids
TFA	Transaction Flow Auditing (ADA)
TFA	Transfer Function Analyzer
TFA	Transistor Feedback Amplifier
TFA	Transverse Fascicular Area [*Neuroanatomy*]
TFA	Transverse Film Attenuator
TFA	Trifluoroacetic [*or Trifluoroacetyl*] Acid [*Organic chemistry*]
TFA	Trifluoroacetic Anhydride [*Organic chemistry*]
TFA	Tube Failure Alarm
TFA	Two-Way Finite Automata
TFA	United States Trout Farmers Association
TFAA	Track and Field Athletes of America
TFAA	Trifluoroacetic Anhydride [*Organic chemistry*]
TFAG	Tropical Forest Action Group (EA)
TFAI	Territoire Francaise des Afars et des Issas [*French Territory of the Afars and Issas*]
TFAI	Trifluoroacetylimidazole [*Organic chemistry*]
TFAIP	Task Force on Alternatives in Print (EA)
TFANP	Task Force Against Nuclear Pollution (EA)
TFAR	Tentative Findings and Recommendations
TFA/USA ...	Track and Field Association of the United States of America (EA)
TFB	Taft Broadcasting Co. [*NYSE symbol*] (SPSG)
TFB	Testing Facilities Branch [*Social Security Administration*]
TFB	Thin-Film Barrier
TFBA	Textile Fibers and By-Products Association [*Charlotte, NC*]
TFBPA	Textile Fibers and By-Products Association (EA)
TFC	[*The*] Felician College [*Chicago, IL*]
TFC	[*The*] Freedom Council (EA)
TFC	Tactical Fire Control (MCD)
TFC	Tactical Flag Commander (MCD)
TFC	Tactical Flight Control
TFC	Tactical Fusion Center (MCD)
TFC	Tank Fire Control
TFC	Tantalum Foil Capacitor
TFC	Terminal Flight Control (NATG)
TFC	Territorial Fund Campaign [*Red Cross*]
TFC	Thin-Film Capacitor
TFC	Thin-Film Cell
TFC	Thin-Film Circuit
TFC	Time from Cutoff [*NASA*] (NASA)
TFC	Time of First Call [*Navy*]
TFC	Toccoa Falls College [*Georgia*]
TFC	Top Flight Club [*Northwest Airlines' club for frequent flyers*] (EA)
TFC	Torpedo Fire Control
TFC	Total Fixed Cost
TFC	Total Flow Control [*Automotive engineering*]
TFC	Total Fuel Consumption (KSC)
TFC	Traffic
TFC	Traffic Control (NG)
TFC	Transcapital Financial Corp. [*NYSE symbol*] (SPSG)
TFC	Transfer Function Computer
TFC	Transfer Function, Cumulative
TFC	Transistorized Frequency Converter
TFC	Transmission Fault Control [*Telecommunications*] (TEL)
TFC	Transport for Christ International (EA)
TFC	Transportation Facilitation Center [*Department of Transportation*]
TFC	Trifluoromethyldichlorocarbanilide [*Organic chemistry*]
TFC	Trigonometric Function Computer
TFC	Trilon Financial Corp. [*Toronto Stock Exchange symbol*] [*Vancouver Stock Exchange symbol*]
TFC	Trustees for Conservation [*Defunct*] (EA)
TFC	Turret Fire Control
TFC	United States Overseas Tax Fairness Committee (EA)
TFC	US-Japan Trade Facilitation Committee (IMH)
TFCA	Thin-Film Cell Array
TF-CAS	Time Frequency Collision Avoidance System
TFCB	Thanks for Coming By [*Exxon slogan*]
TFCC	Tactical Flag Command Center [*Navy*]
TFCC	Tank Fire Combat Computer
TFCC	Triangular Fibrocartilage Complex [*Anatomy*]
TFCCS	Tactical Flag Command Center System [*Navy*]
TFCF	Twenty-First Century Foundation (EA)
TFCG	Thin Film Crystal Growth
TFCM	Three Factor Contribution Method [*Insurance*]
TFCNN	Task Force Commander, North Norway [*NATO*] (NATG)
TFCOS	Task Force on Children Out of School (EA)
TFCP	Technical Facility Change Procedure (AAG)
TFCS	Tank Fire Control System
TFCS	Task Force for Child Survival (EA)
TFCS	TFC Teleservices Corp. [*Fort Lauderdale, FL*] [*NASDAQ symbol*] (NQ)
TFCS	Torpedo Fire Control System
TFCS	Treasury Financial Communication System [*Department of the Treasury*]
TFCS	Triplex Flight Control System [*or Subsystem*] [*NASA*] (NASA)
TFCSD	Total Federal Commissioned Service to Date [*Military*]
TFCU	Transportable Field Calibration Unit
TFCX	TOKAMAK [*Toroidal Kamera Magnetic*] Fusion Core Experiment [*Plasma physics*]
TFCYC	Terry Fox Canadian Youth Centre
TFD	Tactical Fighter Dispenser (MCD)
TFD	Target-to-Film Distance [*X-Ray machine*] [*Navy*]
TFD	Television Feasibility Demonstration [*NASA*] (KSC)
TFD	Terrain-Following Display
TFD	Test Flow Diagram (MCD)
TFD	Thin-Film Distillation
TFD	Time Frequency Digitizer (MCD)
TF/D	Time-Frequency Dissemination (IEEE)
TFD	Total Frequency Deviation (AAG)
TFD	Tube Flood and Drain
TFD	Tube Form Die (MCD)
TFDA	Textile Fabric Distributors Association [*Later, TDA*] (EA)
TFDM	Tactical Fighter Dispensing Munition (AFM)
TFDM	Technical Feasibility Demonstration Model
TFDOP	Total Field Detection Only Processor (CAAL)
TFDRL	Trustees of the Franklin Delano Roosevelt Library [*Abolished, 1958*] [*Library is now operated by the General Services Administration*]
TFDS	Tactical Ferret Display System
TFDS	Tactical Fighter Display Systems [*Air Force*]
TFDS	Tactical Flag Data System (NG)
TFDS	Troms Fylkes Dampskipsselskap [*Shipping line*] [*Norway*]
TFDTB	Tactical Fighter Dispenser Test Bed
TFDU	Thin Film Deposition Unit
TFE	Orlando, FL [*Location identifier*] [*FAA*] (FAAL)
TFE	Terminal Flight Evaluation
TFE	Terrain-Following Evaluator
TFE	Tetrafluoroethylene [*Organic chemistry*]
TFE	Thermionic Fuel Element [*Nuclear energy*]
TFE	Thin-Film Electrode [*Electrochemistry*]
TFE	Time from Event [*NASA*] (KSC)
TFE	Total Fly-By Energy
TFE	Trainer Flight Equipment (MCD)
TFE	Transform Fault Effect [*Geology*]
TFE	Transportation Feasibility Estimator
TFE	Trifluoroethanol [*Organic chemistry*]
TFE	Turbofan Engine
TFE	Two-Fraction Fast Exchange [*Biophysics*]
TFECB	Task Force on Emphysema and Chronic Bronchitis [*Public Health Service and National Lung Association*] (EA)
TFECS	Theater Force Evaluation by Combat Simulation (MCD)
TFEDSA	Tetrafluoroethanedisulfonic Acid [*Organic chemistry*]
TFEL	Thin-Film Electroluminescence
TFEO	Tetrafluoroethylene-Epoxide [*Organic chemistry*]
TFEO	Tetrafluoroethylene Oxide [*Organic chemistry*]
TFER	Transfer
TFEWJ	Task Force on Equality of Women in Judaism (EA)
TFF	Fletcher School of Law and Diplomacy, Tufts University, Medford, MA [*OCLC symbol*] (OCLC)
TFF	Tactical Fighter Force (ADA)
TFF	Tangential Flow Filtration
TFF	Tefe [*Brazil*] [*Airport symbol*] (OAG)
TFF	Terrain-Following Flight
TFF	Time of Free Fall [*NASA*] (KSC)
TFF	Total Feedwater Flow

TFF	Transverse Flow Fan
TFF	Tuning Fork Filter
TFF	Turbine Flow Function
TFFA	Desirade/Grande-Anse, Guadeloupe [*French Antilles*] [*ICAO location identifier*] (ICLI)
TFFASF	Temporaries Food for All Seasons Foundation (EA)
TFFB	Basse-Terre/Baillif [*French Antilles*] [*ICAO location identifier*] (ICLI)
TFFC	[*The*] Fixx Fan Club (EA)
TFFC	Saint-Francois [*French Antilles*] [*ICAO location identifier*] (ICLI)
TFFC	Task Force on Families in Crisis (EA)
TFFC	Twenty-First Century Film Corp. [*NASDAQ symbol*] (NQ)
TFFD	Fort-De-France, Martinique [*French Antilles*] [*ICAO location identifier*] (ICLI)
TFFE	Terrain-Following Flight Evaluator
TFFF	Fort-De-France/Le Lamentin, Martinique [*French Antilles*] [*ICAO location identifier*] (ICLI)
TFFG	Saint-Martin/Grand'Case, Guadeloupe [*French Antilles*] [*ICAO location identifier*] (ICLI)
TFFJ	Saint-Barthelemy [*French Antilles*] [*ICAO location identifier*] (ICLI)
TFFLU	Trimmers, Firemen, and Foundry Labourers Union [*British*]
TFFM	Grand-Bourg/Marie-Galante [*French Antilles*] [*ICAO location identifier*] (ICLI)
TFFR	Pointe-A-Pitre/Le Raizet, Guadeloupe [*French Antilles*] [*ICAO location identifier*] (ICLI)
TFFS	Les Saintes/Terre-De-Haut [*French Antilles*] [*ICAO location identifier*] (ICLI)
TFFS	Thermoform, Fill, and Seal [*Pharmaceutical packaging*]
TFG	[*The*] Fashion Group (EA)
TFG	[*The*] Futures Group [*Commercial firm*] (EA)
TFG	Tactical Fighter Group [*Air Force*]
TFG	Tentative Fiscal Guidance (MCD)
TFG	Tentative Force Guidance (NG)
TFG	Terminal Facilities Guide [*DoD*]
TFG	Test File Generator [*Data processing*]
TFG	Textile Foremen's Guild
TFG	Transmit Format Generator
TFG	Typefounding (ADA)
TFGA	Tasmanian Farmers' and Graziers' Association [*Australia*]
TFGM	Tentative Fiscal Guidance Memorandum [*Military*] (AFIT)
TFGP	Tactical Fighter Group [*Air Force*]
TFH	Thick-Film Hybrid
TFH	Touch for Health Foundation (EA)
TFH	Transfer Function Hazard
TFH	Transit Financial Holdings, Inc. [*Toronto Stock Exchange symbol*]
TFH	Tufts University, Health Sciences Library, Boston, MA [*OCLC symbol*] (OCLC)
TFHSA	Tennessee Farm and Home Science [*A publication*]
TFI	Deutsches Teppich-Forschungsinstitut [*German Carpet Research Institute - GCRI*] (EAIO)
TFI	[*The*] Fertilizer Institute (EA)
TFI	Table Fashion Institute (EA)
TFI	Taurus Footwear, Inc. [*Toronto Stock Exchange symbol*]
TFI	Tax Foundation, Incorporated
TFI	Textile Foundation, Incorporated
TFI	Theatre for Ideas (EA)
TFI	Thick Film Ignition [*System*] [*Ford Motor Co.*] [*Automotive engineering*]
TFI	Time from Ignition [*Apollo*] [*NASA*]
tfi	Travel for Industry [*Commercial firm*] [*British*]
TFI	True Fibrous Involution [*Medicine*]
TFI	Tufi [*Papua New Guinea*] [*Airport symbol*] (OAG)
TFIB	Thin-Film Interface Barrier
TFIC	Times Fiber Communications [*NASDAQ symbol*] (NQ)
TFI-I	Thin Film Ignition [*Automotive engineering*]
TFIM	Tool Fabrication Instruction Manual (MCD)
TFIN	TecFin Corp. [*NASDAQ symbol*] (NQ)
TFIS	Theft from Interstate Shipment [*FBI standardized term*]
TFIT	To-Fitness, Inc. [*NASDAQ symbol*] (NQ)
TfK	Tidskrift foer Konstvetinskap [*A publication*]
TFKVA	Teplofizicheskie Kharakteristiki Veshchestv [*A publication*]
TFL	Tail-Flick Latency
TFL	Taiwan Federation of Labor [*Nationalist China*]
TFL	Tanganyika Federation of Labor
TFL	Telemetry Format Load (MCD)
TFL	Tensor Fascia Lata [*Anatomy*]
TFL	Through Flow Line
TFL	Time to Failure Location
TFL	Time from Launch [*NASA*]
TFL	Training for Life [*Young Men's Christian Association*] [*British*]
TFL	Transient Fault Locator
TFL	Trees for Life [*An association*] (EA)
TFLAC	Fellowship of Reconciliation Task Force on Latin America and Caribbean (EA)
TFLC	Tulane Factors of Liberalism-Conservatism [*Psychology*]
TFLX	Termiflex Corp. [*NASDAQ symbol*] (NQ)
TFM	Tactical Flight Management (MCD)
TFM	Tape File Management
TFM	Teaching Family Model [*Psychology*]
TFM	Telefomin [*Papua New Guinea*] [*Airport symbol*] (OAG)
TFM	Tentative Final Monograph [*Food and Drug Administration*]
TFM	Terminal Forecast Manual
TFM	Testators Family Maintenance [*Australia*]
TFM	Testicular Feminization [*Endocrinology*]
TFM	Textes Francais Modernes [*A publication*]
TFM	Thin-Film Microelectronics
TFM	Toronto International Furniture Market [*Canada*] (ITD)
TFM	Transmit Frame Memory
TFM	Transmitter Frequency Multiplier
TFM	Transportation Financial Management [*Army*]
TFM	Trifluoromethylnitrophenol [*Organic chemistry*]
TFM	Turbine Flow Meter (KSC)
TFM	Two-Fluid Manometer
TFMA	Technical Facility Modification Authorization (AAG)
TFME	Thin-Film Mercury Electrode [*Electrochemistry*]
TFMPP	Trifluoromethyl(phenyl)piperazine [*Organic chemistry*]
TFMRA	Top Fuel Motorcycle Riders Association (EA)
TFMRC	Thermo-Fluid Mechanics Research Centre [*University of Sussex*] [*British*] (CB)
TFMS	Tactical Frequency Management System (MCD)
TFMS	Text and File Management System
TFMS	Trunk and Facilities Maintenance System [*Telecommunications*] (TEL)
TFMSA	Trifluoromethanesulfonic Acid [*Organic chemistry*]
TFN	Tax File Number [*Australia*]
TFN	Till Further Notice
TFN	Total Fecal Nitrogen
TFN	Total Fruit Number [*Botany*]
TFN	Track File Number (CAAL)
TFNA	Tennis Foundation of North America [*Later, ATF*] (EA)
TFNG	Thirty-Five New Guys [*Group of new astronauts*] [*NASA*]
TFNS	Territorial Force Nursing Service
TFO	Telemedicine for Ontario [*Toronto, ON*] [*Telecommunications*] (TSSD)
TFO	Tiffany Resources, Inc. [*Vancouver Stock Exchange symbol*]
TFO	Tonto Forest Array [*Arizona*] [*Seismograph station code, US Geological Survey*] [*Closed*] (SEIS)
TFO	Transactions for Others [*Military*]
TFO	Tuning Fork Oscillator
TFOL	Tape File Octal Load
TFON	Telefonos de Mexico SA de CV [*NASDAQ symbol*] (NQ)
TFOPS	Task Force Operations [*Navy*] (NVT)
TFORA	Tekniskt Forum [*A publication*]
TFORMR	Transformer
TFOS	Total Federal Officer Service [*Military*] (AABC)
TFOTB	[*The*] Friends of Tom Baker (EA)
TFOUT	Thin-Film Oxygen Uptake Test
TFOV	Total Field of View (MCD)
TFP	American Society for the Defense of Tradition, Family and Property (EA)
TFP	[*The*] Feminist Press (EA)
TFP	[*The*] Friends Program (EA)
TFP	[*The*] Fund for Peace [*An association*] (EA)
TFP	Teachers Freedom Party (EA)
TFP	Teachers for Peace (EAIO)
TFP	Temporary Forfeiture of Pay
TFP	Test Facility Program [*NASA*] (KSC)
TFP	Total Factor Productivity [*Economics*]
TFP	Total Finish Positions [*Horse racing*]
TFP	Trans-Fiberoptic-Photographic [*Electron microscopy*]
TFP	Travaux. Faculte de Philosophie et Lettres. Universite Catholique de Louvain [*A publication*] (BJA)
TFP	Trifluoperazine [*Also, Trifluoroperazine*] [*Organic chemistry*]
TFP	Trifluoroperazine [*Also, Trifluoroperazine*] [*Organic chemistry*]
TFPA	Tubular Finishers and Processors Association (EA)
TFPC	Thin-Film Photovoltaic Cell
TFPCA	Thin-Film Photovoltaic Cell Array
TFPECTS	Thin-Film Personal Communications and Telemetry System (MCD)
TFPIA	Textile Fiber Products Identification Act [*1960*]
TFPL	Task Force Pro Libra Ltd. (EISS)
TFPL	Texas Forest Products Laboratory
TFPL	Training Film Production Laboratory [*Military*]
T and F Q Rev	Track and Field Quarterly Review [*A publication*]
TFR	Pueblo, CO [*Location identifier*] [*FAA*] (FAAL)
TFR	Tape-to-File Recorder
TFR	Technological Forecasting and Social Change. An International Journal [*A publication*]
TFR	Television Film Recorder
TFR	Terrain-Following RADAR
TFR	Territorial Force Reserve [*British*]
TFR	Test Failure Report (CAAL)
TFR	Theoretical Final Route [*Telecommunications*] (TEL)
TFR	Thin-Film Resist
TFR	TOKAMAK [*Toroidal Kamera Magnetic*] at Fontenay-aux-Roses
T/FR	Top of Frame (AAG)
TFR	Total Fertility Rate [*Medicine*]
TFR	Total Final Reports

TFR........... Trafalgar Resources, Inc. [*Vancouver Stock Exchange symbol*]
TFR........... Transaction Formatting Routines
TFR........... Transfer
TFR........... Transfer Function Response
TfR........... Transferrin Receptor [*Immunology*]
TFR........... Traveler/Failure Report [*Deep Space Instrumentation Facility, NASA*]
TFR........... Trouble and Failure Report [*NASA*]
TFR........... Tubular Flow Reactor
TFR........... Tunable Frequency Range
TFR/CAR ... Trouble and Failure Report/Corrective Action Report
TFRCD...... Traffic Received   (FAAC)
TFRD....... Test Facilities Requirements Document
TFRE......... International 800 Telecom Corp. [*NASDAQ symbol*]   (NQ)
TFS........... Tactical Fighter Squadron [*Air Force*]
TFS........... Tape File Supervisor
TFS........... Tax Free Shopping
TFS........... Tbilisi [*USSR*] [*Geomagnetic observatory code*]
TFS........... Technological Forecasting and Social Change [*A publication*]
TFS........... Telemetry Format Selection   (NASA)
TFS........... Tenerife-Reina Sofia [*Canary Islands*] [*Airport symbol*]   (OAG)
TFS........... Tennessee Folklore Society   (EA)
TFS........... Terrain-Following System
TFS........... Testicular Feminization Syndrome [*Endocrinology*]
TFS........... Theological Faculty, Sydney [*Australia*]
TFS........... Thomson Financial Services [*The Thomson Corp.*] [*Publishing*]
TFS........... Thrombus-Free Surface [*Hematology*]
TFS........... Time and Frequency Standard
TFS........... Tin-Free Steel
TFS........... Traffic Flow Security [*Telecommunications*]   (TEL)
TFS........... Traffic Forecasting System [*Telecommunications*]   (TEL)
TFS........... Transport Ferry Service [*English Channel*]
TFS........... Transverse Feed System
TFS........... Trim Fuel System   (MCD)
TFS........... Trunk Forecasting System [*Telecommunications*]   (TEL)
TFS........... Tuliptree Flower Spiroplasma [*Plant pathology*]
TFS........... Tunable Frequency Source
TFS........... Turbine First Stage [*Nuclear energy*]   (NRCH)
TFS........... Turbine Flow Sensor
TFS........... Type Finish Specification   (MCD)
TFSA........ 304th Fighter Squadron Association   (EA)
TFSA........ Thin-Film Spreading Agent [*For enhanced oil recovery*]
TFSB........ [*The*] Federal Savings Bank [*NASDAQ symbol*]   (NQ)
TFSB........ Tennessee Folklore Society. Bulletin [*A publication*]
TFSC........ [*From the Latin for*] Franciscan Tertiaries of the Holy Cross
TFSC........ Turkish Federated State of Cyprus
TFSCB...... Technological Forecasting and Social Change [*A publication*]
TFSO........ Tonto Forest Seismological Observatory [*Arizona*]
TFSOA...... Transactions. Faraday Society [*A publication*]
TFSOA4 .... Faraday Society. Transactions [*A publication*]
TFSP........ Task Force on Service to the Public [*Canada*]
TFSP........ Texas Folklore Society. Publications [*A publication*]
TFSQ........ Tactical Fighter Squadron [*Air Force*]
TFSS.......... Technical Facilities Subsystem [*Space Flight Operations Facility, NASA*]
TFST .... Thin Films Science and Technology [*Elsevier Book Series*] [*A publication*]
TFSUSS .... Task Force on Scientific Uses of the Space Station [*NASA*]
TFT........... Tabular Firing Table [*Military*]   (AABC)
TFT........... Tangential Flow Torch [*For plasma generation*]
TFT........... Technical Feasibility Testing [*Army*]
TF & T .... Theatre, Film, and Television Biographies Master Index [*A publication*]
TFT........... Thermal Fatigue Test
TFT........... Thin-Film Field-Effect Transistor
TFT........... Thin-Film Technique
TFT........... Thin-Film Technology
TFT........... Thin-Film Transducer
TFT........... Thin-Film Transistor
TFT........... Threshold Failure Temperatures
TFT........... Tight Fingertip [*Medicine*]
TFT........... Tit for Tat [*Slang*]
TFT........... Trifluorothymidine [*Pharmacology*]
TF/TA .... Terrain Following/Terrain Avoidance   (MCD)
TFTASq..... Tactical Fighter Training Aggressor Squadron [*Air Force*]
TFTB .... Taping for the Blind   (EA)
TF/TG .... Task Force/Task Group
TFTNGSq ... Tactical Fighter Training Squadron [*Air Force*]
TFTP .... Task Force on Teaching as a Profession [*Defunct*]   (EA)
TFTP .... Television Facility Test Position [*Telecommunications*]   (TEL)
TFTP .... Trivial File Transfer Protocol   (BYTE)
TFTR........ TOKAMAK [*Toroidal Kamera Magnetic*] Fusion Test Reactor [*Princeton, NJ*]
TFTS .... Tactical Fighter Training Squadron [*Air Force*]   (MCD)
TFTS .... TOW [*Tube-Launched, Optically Tracked, Wire-Guided Weapon*)] Field Test Set   (MCD)
TFTTA ...... Teplofizika i Teplotekhnika [*A publication*]
TFTW....... Tactical Fighter Training Wing [*Air Force*]   (MCD)
TFTY .... Thrifty Rent-a-Car System, Inc. [*NASDAQ symbol*]   (NQ)
TFU .... Tactical Forecast Unit

TFU .... Telecommunications Flying Unit [*British*]
TFU .... Test Facility Utilization [*NASA*]   (NASA)
TFU .... Theoretical First Unit [*Economics*]
TFV .... Twin Falls Victory [*Tracking ship*] [*NASA*]
TFW .... Tactical Fighter Wing [*Air Force*]
TFW .... Tethered Free-Floating Worker
TFW .... Thermoplastic Fan Wheel
TFW .... Tokyo Financial Wire [*COMLINE International Corp.*] [*Japan*] [*Information service or system*]   (CRD)
TFW .... Tropical Fresh Water
TFW .... Tufts University, Medford, MA [*OCLC symbol*]   (OCLC)
TFW .... Turbulent Far Wake
TFWBKEL ... Theologische Forschung Wissenschaftliche Beitraege zur Kirchlichevangelischen Lehre [*A publication*]
TFWC....... Tactical Fighter Weapons Center [*Air Force*]   (AFM)
TFWG....... Tactical Fighter Wing [*Air Force*]
TFWRR .... Task Force on Women's Rights and Responsibilities [*National Council on Family Relations*]   (EA)
TFWS .... Tactical Fighter Weapon School [*Air Force*]   (MCD)
TFWS .... Task Force on Women in Sports [*of NOW*]   (EA)
TFX .... Tactical Fighter Experimental [*Air Force*]
TFX .... Teleflex, Inc. [*AMEX symbol*]   (SPSG)
TFX .... Thymic Factor X [*Endocrinology*]
TFX .... Tri-Service Fighter, Experimental   (MCD)
TFX-N ...... Tactical Fighter Experimental - Navy
TFX-O ..... Tactical Fighter Experimental - Offensive
TFX-R....... Tactical Fighter Experimental - Reconnaissance
TFY .... Target Fiscal Year   (MCD)
TFYAP ..... Tobacco Free Young America Project   (EA)
TFYQA...... Think for Yourself and Question Authority [*Term coined by Dr. Timothy Leary*]
TFZ........... Tail Fuze   (MSA)
TFZ........... Traffic Zone   (FAAC)
TFZ........... Trifluroperazine [*Tranquilizer*]
TFZ........... Tropospheric Frontal Zone
Tg............. Glass Transition
TG............. Guatemala [*Aircraft nationality and registration mark*]   (FAAC)
TG............. Positioning Devices [*JETDS nomenclature*] [*Military*]   (CET)
TG............. Tail Gear
TG............. Tangent Group   (EA)
TG............. Tape Gauge
TG............. Target Gate   (CAAL)
TG............. Task Group [*Military*]
TG............. Task Guidance
TG............. Technology Gap
TG............. Telegram
TG............. Telegraph
TG............. Teleilaet Ghassul   (BJA)
TG............. Temporary Gentleman [*British slang term for officer for duration of the war*] [*World War I*]
TG............. Terminal Guidance
TG............. Terminator Group
TG............. Test Group
TG............. Test Guaranteed
TG............. Testamentsgesetz [*Law on Wills*] [*German*]   (ILCA)
TG............. Thai Airways International [*ICAO designator*]   (FAAC)
TG............. Theatre Guild   (EA)
TG............. Theologie und Glaube [*A publication*]
TG............. Therapeutic Gazette [*Philadelphia*] [*A publication*]
TG............. Thermogravimetry
TG............. Thioglucose [*Biochemistry*]
TG............. Thioglycolate [*Biochemistry*]
TG............. Thioguanine [*Also, T*] [*Antineoplastic drug*]
TG............. Third Generation   (EA)
TG............. Thoracic Ganglion [*Neuroanatomy*]
TG............. Thromboglobulin [*Clinical chemistry*]
TG............. Thyroglobulin [*Also, Thg*] [*Endocrinology*]
TG............. Tijdschrift voor Geschiedenis. Land en Volkenkunde [*A publication*]
TG............. Timing Gate   (AAG)
TG............. Tithing [*Church of England*]
TG............. Togo [*ANSI two-letter standard code*]   (CNC)
tg .... Togo [*MARC country of publication code*] [*Library of Congress*]   (LCCP)
TG............. Toho Gakuho [*A publication*]
TG............. Tollgate [*Maps and charts*]
T & G .... Tongue and Groove [*Lumber*]
TG............. Torpedo Group
T & G .... Touch and Go [*Landings*] [*Aviation*]   (MCD)
TG............. Track Geometry [*In TG-01, an Austrian built subway inspection car*]
TG............. Tracking and Guidance
TG............. Traders Group Ltd. [*Toronto Stock Exchange symbol*] [*Vancouver Stock Exchange symbol*]
TG............. Traffic Guidance [*Aviation*]
T-G........... Transformational-Generative [*Linguistics*]
TG............. Transgenic [*Genetics*]
TG............. Transglutaminase [*An enzyme*]
TG............. Transgranular [*Metallurgy*]
TG............. Transmissible Gastroenteritis [*Virus*]
TG............. Tredegar Industries, Inc. [*NYSE symbol*]   (SPSG)

TG............ Tribune de St. Gervais [*A publication*]
TG............ Trigeminal Ganglion [*Neuroanatomy*]
TG............. Triglyceride [*Biochemistry*]
TG.............. Tropical Gulf [*American air mass*]
TG............. Tuned Grid   (KSC)
TG............ Turbine Generator   (NRCH)
TG............ Turbogenerator
TG............ TV Guide [*A publication*]
TG............ Tying Goals [*Sports*]
TG............. Type Genus
T & G ...... Tyrwhitt and Granger's English Exchequer Reports [*1835-36*]
            [*A publication*]   (DLA)
T2G........... Technician, Second Grade [*Military*]
TGA........... Antibody Thyroglobulin [*Immunology*]
TGA........... [*The*] Generation After [*An association*]   (EA)
TGA........... [*The*] Glutamate Association - United States   (EA)
TGA........... Taurocholate-Gelatin Agar [*Microbiology*]
T/GA .... Temperature Gauge [*Automotive engineering*]
TGA........... Thermogravimetric [*or Thermogravimetry*] Analysis
            [*Instrumentation*]
TGA........... Thioglycolic Acid [*Organic chemistry*]
TGA......... Toilet Goods Association [*Later, CTFA*]   (EA)
TGA......... Tolmetin Glycine Amide [*Biochemistry*]
TGA......... Total Glycoalkaloids [*Analytical biochemistry*]
TGA......... Touristische Gemeinschaft der Alpenlander [*Alpine Tourist
            Commission - ATC*] [*Zurich, Switzerland*]   (EAIO)
TGA........... Trace Gas Analysis
TGA........... Trade with Greece (Athens) [*A publication*]
TGA........... Transient Global Amnesia [*Medicine*]
TGA......... Transposition of Great Arteries [*Cardiology*]
TGA......... Treasury General Account [*Department of the Treasury*]
TGA......... Triglycollamic Acid [*Organic chemistry*]
TGA........... Tropical Growers' Association   (EAIO)
TGA........... Tuebinger Germanistische Arbeiten [*A publication*]
TGA........... Turf Growers Association [*Australia*]
TGAb......... Thyroglobulin Antibody
TGAJA8 .... TGA [*Toilet Goods Association*] Cosmetic Journal [*A
            publication*]
T-GAM...... Training - Guided Air Missile   (MUGU)
TGANA ..... Tsitologiya i Genetika [*A publication*]
TGAOTU .. [*The*] Great Architect of the Universe [*Freemasonry*]
TGARQ ..... Telegraphic Approval Requested   (NOAA)
TGAS........ TACAN [*Tactical Air Navigation*] Guidance Augmentation
            System [*Military*]   (CAAL)
TGAS........ Trace Gas Acquisition System
TGA (Toilet Goods Assoc) Cosmet J ... TGA (Toilet Goods Association)
            Cosmetic Journal [*A publication*]
TG-ATS..... Theatre Guild-American Theatre Society   (EA)
TGaV .... Volunteer State Community College, Learning Resources
            Center, Gallatin, TN [*Library symbol*] [*Library of
            Congress*]   (LCLS)
TGB .... Tongued, Grooved, and Beaded [*Lumber*]
TGB .... Torpedo Gunboat   (ROG)
TGB .... Turbine Generator Building [*Nuclear energy*]   (NRCH)
TGB .... Twist-Grain-Boundary [*Liquid crystal science*]
TGBL........ Through Government Bill of Lading [*Military*]   (AABC)
Tgb-Nr...... Tagebuchnummer [*Day-Book Number*] [*German*] [*Business
            term*]
TGBR........ Trans-Global Resources NL [*NASDAQ symbol*]   (NQ)
TGC .... [*The*] Grantsmanship Center   (EA)
TGC .... Teleglobe Canada
TGC .... Theater Ground Command [*Military*]
TGC .... Thermocouple Gauge Control
TGC .... Throttle Governor Control
TGC .... Tobacco Growers' Council [*Australia*]
TGC .... Tomato Genetics Cooperative   (EA)
TGC .... Total Gas-Phase Carbon [*Environmental chemistry*]
TGC .... Tougaloo College, Tougaloo, MS [*OCLC symbol*]   (OCLC)
TGC .... Transfer Gear Case   (MCD)
TGC .... Transmit Gain Control   (MSA)
TGC .... Travel Group Charter [*Airline fare*]
TGC .... Trenton, TN [*Location identifier*] [*FAA*]   (FAAL)
TGCA .... Texas Gun Collectors Association
TGCA .... Transportable Group Control Approach   (NG)
TGCGA..... Transactions. Gulf Coast Association of Geological Societies [*A
            publication*]
TGCO .... Transidyne General Corporation [*NASDAQ symbol*]   (NQ)
TGCR .... Tactical Generic Cable Replacement
TGCS........ Transportable Ground Communications Station
TGD.......... Task Group Delta   (MCD)
TGD.......... Technical Guidance Directions
TGD........... Titograd [*Yugoslavia*] [*Airport symbol*]   (OAG)
TGD.......... Trajectory and Guidance Data
TGDDM..... Tetraglycidyl(diaminodiphenyl)methane [*Organic chemistry*]
TGDG....... TOTAL Energold Corp. [*NASDAQ symbol*]   (NQ)
TGDR........ Tokyo Gailkokugo Daigaku Ronshu [*Area and Cultural
            Studies*] [*A publication*]
TGE .... Transmissible Gastroenteritis [*Virus*]
TGE .... Traverse Gravimeter Experiment   (KSC)
TGE .... Trialkoxyglyceryl Ether [*Organic chemistry*]
TGE .... Tryptone Glucose Extract [*Cell growth medium*]

TGE .... Tuskegee, AL [*Location identifier*] [*FAA*]   (FAAL)
TGEEP....... Terminal Guidance Environmental Effects Program   (MCD)
T Geesteswet ... Tydskrif vir Geesteswetenskappe [*A publication*]
TGegw....... Theologie der Gegenwart [*A publication*]
TGEN .... Technology General Corp. [*NASDAQ symbol*]   (NQ)
TGEOD..... Technika Poszukiwan Geologicznych [*A publication*]
TGEP......... Turbine Generator Emergency Power [*Nuclear
            energy*]   (NRCH)
T Gesch...... Tijdschrift voor Geschiedenis [*A publication*]
TGET......... Target Ground Elapsed Time
TGF .... Therapeutic Gain Factor [*Medicine*]
TGF .... Through Group Filter [*Telecommunications*]   (TEL)
TGF .... Tijdschrift voor Geschiedenis en Folklore [*A publication*]
TGF .... Top Groove Fill [*Lubricating oil test*]
TGF .... Tragicorum Graecorum Fragmenta [*A publication*]   (OCD)
TGF .... Transforming Growth Factor
TGF .... Transonic Gasdynamics Facility [*Air Force*]
TGF .... Treasury Guard Force
TGF .... Triglycine Fluoberyllate [*Ferroelectrics*]
TGF .... Tumor Growth Factor [*Oncology*]
TGF-A....... Transforming Growth Factor - Alpha
TGFA......... Triglyceride Fatty Acid [*Biochemistry*]
TGFC........ Tammy Graham Fan Club   (EA)
TGFC........ Terri Gibbs Fan Club   (EA)
TGG .... Kuala Trengganu [*Malaysia*] [*Airport symbol*]   (OAG)
TGG .... Templeton Global Government Income Trust [*NYSE
            symbol*]   (CTT)
TGG .... Temporary Geographic Grid
TGG .... Third Generation Gyro   (MCD)
TGG .... Turkey Gamma G [*Immunology*]
TGGL-B ... Travaux Geographique de Liege (Belgium) [*A publication*]
TGH.......... Tongoa [*Vanuatu*] [*Airport symbol*]   (OAG)
TGI .... Instellingen [*A publication*]
TGI .... Tactics Guide Issued   (CAAL)
TGI .... Taghi Ghambar [*Iran*] [*Seismograph station code, US
            Geological Survey*]   (SEIS)
TGI .... Tangier, VA [*Location identifier*] [*FAA*]   (FAAL)
TGI .... Target Group Index [*British Market Research Bureau Ltd.*]
            [*Information service or system*]
TGI .... Target Intensifier
TGI .... Telco Group, Inc. [*Telecommunications service*]   (TSSD)
TGI .... Textbuch zur Geschichte Israels [*A publication*]   (BJA)
TGI .... TGI Friday's [*NYSE symbol*]   (SPSG)
TGI .... Tingo Maria [*Peru*] [*Airport symbol*]   (OAG)
TGI .... Tournament Golf International
TGIC........ Tobacco Growers' Information Committee   (EA)
TGIC........ Triglycidyl Isocyanurate [*Organic chemistry*]
TGID........ Trunk Group Identification [*Telecommunications*]   (TEL)
TGIF........ Terminal Guidance Indirect Fire   (MCD)
TGIF........ Thank God It's Friday [*Meaning work-week is nearly over*]
TGIF......... Toe Goes in First [*As in "You're so dumb you have 'TGIF' on
            your shoes"*]
TGIF......... Transportable Ground Intercept Facility
*TGIF-OTMWDUM ... Thank God It's Friday - Only Two More Work Days
            Until Monday [Pentagon saying]*
TGIM .... Trudy Gosudarstvennogo Istoriceskogo Muzeja [*A publication*]
TGIS .... Thank God It's Summer
TGJ........... Tiga [*Loyalty Islands*] [*Airport symbol*]   (OAG)
TGKHA..... Takenaka Gijutsu Kenkyu Hokoku [*A publication*]
TGKZA...... Trudy Instituta Geologicheskikh Nauk Akademiya Nauk
            Kazakhskoi SSR [*A publication*]
TGL .... Tagula [*Papua New Guinea*] [*Airport symbol*]   (OAG)
TGL .... Tangent Oil & Gas [*Vancouver Stock Exchange symbol*]
TGL .... Task Group Leader
TGL .... Technische Normen, Gutevorschriften, und Lieferbedingungen
            [*German*]
TGL .... Temperature Gradient Lamp [*Spectroscopy*]
T Gl........... Theologie und Glaube [*A publication*]
TGL .... Thin Glass Laminate
TGL .... Toggle   (AAG)
TGL .... Touch and Go Landings [*Aviation*]
TGL .... Treasury Gold License   (MCD)
TGL .... Triangular Guide Line
TGL .... Triglyceride Lipase [*Clinical chemistry*]
TGL .... Triglycerides [*Clinical chemistry*]
TGL .... Triton Group Limited [*NYSE symbol*]   (SPSG)
TGLC........ Total Gate Leakage Current
TGLM .... Task Group Lung Model [*ICRP*]
TG-LORAN ... Traffic-Guidance Long-Range Aid to Navigation   (DEN)
TGLS .... Tongueless
TGLV .... Tijdschrift voor Geschiedenis. Land en Volkenkunde [*A
            publication*]
TGLVQ...... Terminal Guidance for Lunar Vehicles [*Aerospace*]   (AAG)
TGM .... Tactical Generic Multiplex
TGM .... Task Group Manager   (CAAL)
TGM .... Telegram   (ROG)
TGM......... Theatre Guild Magazine [*A publication*]
TGM......... Tirgu Mures [*Romania*] [*Airport symbol*]   (OAG)
TGM......... Torpedo Gunner's Mate [*Obsolete*] [*Navy*] [*British*]
TGM......... Total Gaseous Mercury [*Environmental chemistry*]
TGM.......... Training Guided Missile [*Air Force*]

TGM..........	Transportability Guidance Manual
TGM..........	Trunk Group Multiplexer [*Telecommunications*] (TEL)
TGM..........	Turbine Generator Management
TGMA........	Tone Generator and Master Alarm (KSC)
TGMD........	Test of Gross Motor Development [*Sensorimotor skills test*]
TGMEA	Tropical and Geographical Medicine [*A publication*]
TG-MS.......	Thermogravimetry - Mass Spectrometry
TGMTS.....	Tank Gunnery and Missile Tracking System
TGMV........	Tomato Golden Mosaic Virus
TGN..........	Anchorage, AK [*Location identifier*] [*FAA*] (FAAL)
TGN..........	Tecogen, Inc. [*AMEX symbol*] (SPSG)
TGN..........	Tournigan Mining Explorations Ltd. [*Vancouver Stock Exchange symbol*]
TGN..........	Trans Golgi Network [*Cytology*]
TGN..........	Trigeminal Neuralgia [*Medicine*]
TGN..........	Trunk Group Number [*Telecommunications*] (TEL)
TGNMO....	Total Gaseous Non-Methane Organic [*Environmental chemistry*]
TGNR........	Tactics Guide Not Required (CAAL)
TGNU........	Transitional Government of National Unity [*South Africa*]
TGNX........	Tournigan Mining Explorations Ltd. [*NASDAQ symbol*] (NQ)
TGO..........	Time to Go [*Apollo*] [*NASA*]
TGO..........	Togo [*ANSI three-letter standard code*] (CNC)
TGO..........	Tongliao [*China*] [*Airport symbol*] (OAG)
TGO..........	Tuned Grid Oscillator
TGOPS......	Task Group Operations [*Navy*] (NVT)
TGorPI	Trudy Goriiskogo Gosudarstvennogo Pedagogicheskogo Instituta [*A publication*]
TGO Tijdschr Ther Geneesmiddel Onder ...	TGO. Tijdschrift voor Therapie, Geneesmiddel, en Onderzoek [*A publication*]
TGOWG....	Teleoperator Ground Operations Working Group [*NASA*] (NASA)
TGP..........	[*The*] Giraffe Project [*An association*] (EA)
TGP..........	Tasmanian Government Publications [*A publication*] (APTA)
TGP..........	Technigen Platinum Corp. [*Vancouver Stock Exchange symbol*]
TGP..........	Theft of Government Property [*FBI standardized term*]
TGP..........	Timothy Grass Pollen [*Immunology*]
TGP..........	Tobacco Glycoprotein [*Biochemistry*]
TGP..........	Tone Generator Panel
TGP..........	Transcontinental Gas Pipe Line Corp. [*NYSE symbol*] (SPSG)
TGPA........	Technigen Corp. [*NASDAQ symbol*] (NQ)
TGPG	St. Georges [*Grenada*] [*ICAO location identifier*] (ICLI)
TGPIA	Trudy Gruzinskii Politekhnicheskii Institut Imeni V. I. Lenina [*A publication*]
TGPSG......	Tactical Global Positioning System Guidance (MCD)
TGPWU	Transport, General and Port Workers' Union [*Aden*]
TGPY........	Point Saline [*Grenada*] [*ICAO location identifier*] (ICLI)
TGR..........	Tiger International, Inc. [*Formerly, FLY*] [*NYSE symbol*] (SPSG)
TGR	Tohoku Gakuin Daigaku Ronshu [*North Japan College Review: Essays and Studies in English Language and Literature*] [*A publication*]
TGR	Touggourt [*Algeria*] [*Airport symbol*] (OAG)
TGRLSS....	Two-Gas Regenerative Lift Support System
TGrT..........	Tusculum College, Greeneville, TN [*Library symbol*] [*Library of Congress*] (LCLS)
TGS...........	[*The*] Galactic Society (EA)
TGS...........	Gulf States Utilities Co., Beaumont, TX [*OCLC symbol*] (OCLC)
TGS...........	Target Generating System
TGS...........	Taxiing Guidance System [*Aviation*]
TGS...........	Telemetry Ground Station
TGS...........	Telemetry Ground System (NASA)
TGS...........	Telemetry Guidance System [*From computer game "Hacker II"*]
TGS...........	Terminal Guidance Sensor [*or System*]
TGS...........	Thermogravimetric [*or Thermogravimetry*] System [*Instrumentation*]
TGS...........	Tide Gauge System
TGS...........	Traite de Grammaire Syriaque [*A publication*] (BJA)
TGS...........	Transcontinental Geophysical Survey (NOAA)
TGS...........	Translator Generator System (IEEE)
TGS...........	Transportable Ground Station
TGS...........	Triglycine Sulfate [*Ferroelectrics*]
TGS...........	Turbine Generator System [*Nuclear energy*] (NRCH)
TGS...........	Turkish General Staff (NATG)
TGSDA......	Tulsa Geological Society. Digest [*A publication*]
TGSE........	Tactical Ground Support Equipment
TGSE........	Telemetry Ground Support Equipment [*NASA*] (KSC)
TGSG........	Transactions. Gaelic Society of Glasgow [*A publication*]
TGSI.........	Transactions. Gaelic Society of Inverness [*A publication*]
TGSIFC.....	T. G. Sheppard International Fan Club (EA)
TGSM.......	Terminally Guided Submissile (MCD)
TGSM.......	Terminally Guided Submunitions (MCD)
TGSR........	Triglyceride Secretion Rate [*Physiology*]
TGSS	Terminal Guidance Sensor System
TGSS	Turbine Gland Sealing System [*Nuclear energy*] (NRCH)
TGSSA	Transactions. Geological Society of South Africa [*A publication*]
TGSS/UGS ...	Tactical Ground Sensor System/Unattended Ground Sensor (MCD)

TGT	German Tribune [*A publication*]
TGT	Tail Gate
TGT	Tanga [*Tanzania*] [*Airport symbol*] (OAG)
TGT	Target (AAG)
TGT	Tenneco, Inc. [*Formerly, Tennessee Gas Transmission Co.*] [*NYSE symbol*] [*Toronto Stock Exchange symbol*] (SPSG)
TGT	Thermocouple Gauge Tube
TGT	Thromboplastin Generation Test [*Hematology*]
TGT	True Ground Track (MCD)
TGT	Turbine Gas Temperature (NATG)
TGTM	Transportability Guidance Technical Manual
TGTU	Tail-Gas Treating Unit [*Petroleum engineering*]
TGU	Technical Guidance Unit (NVT)
TGU	Tegucigalpa [*Honduras*] [*Airport symbol*] (OAG)
TGU	Templeton Global Utilities, Inc. [*AMEX symbol*] (SPSG)
TGU	Tri Gold Industry [*Vancouver Stock Exchange symbol*]
TGU	Triglycidylurazol [*Antineoplastic drug*]
TG or UA ..	Temperance, Grog, or Underage [*British military*]
TGUBA	Bulletin. Tokyo Gakugei University [*A publication*]
TGUOS	Transactions. Glasgow University Oriental Society [*A publication*]
TGURG	Telegraphic Authority Requested (NOAA)
TGV	Targovishte [*Bulgaria*] [*Airport symbol*] (OAG)
TGV	Thomson Gold Co. [*Vancouver Stock Exchange symbol*]
TGV	Train a [*or Tres*] Grande Vitesse [*High-Speed Train*]
TGV	Transposition of the Great Vessels [*Cardiology*]
TGV	Turbine Governor Valve [*Nuclear energy*] (NRCH)
TGV	Two Gentlemen of Verona [*Shakespearean work*]
TGW	Terminally Guided Warhead [*or Weapon*]
TGW	Theologie der Gegenwart [*A publication*]
TGW	Things Gone Wrong [*Measure of automobile customer satisfaction*]
TGWU	Transport and General Workers' Union [*British*]
TGX	Tube-Generated X-Ray
TGZ	Tuxtla Gutierrez [*Mexico*] [*Airport symbol*] (OAG)
TGZIA	Technische Gids voor Ziekenhuis en Instelling [*A publication*]
TGZM	Temperature-Gradient Zone-Melting [*Chemistry*]
Th..............	C. H. Boehringer Sohn, Ingelheim [*Germany*] [*Research code symbol*]
TH..............	Harriman Public Library, Harriman, TN [*Library symbol*] [*Library of Congress*] (LCLS)
TH..............	Hot Leg Temperature [*Nuclear energy*] (NRCH)
TH..............	Reports of the Witwatersrand High Court [*Transvaal, South Africa*] [*A publication*] (DLA)
Th..............	T-Cell, Helper Type [*Immunology*]
Th..............	T-Helper [*Immunology*]
T-H	Taft-Hartley [*Act*]
TH..............	Tally Ho [*Air Force*]
TH..............	Teacher of Hydrotherapy [*British*]
TH..............	Teaching History [*A publication*] (APTA)
TH..............	Teaching Hospital [*British*]
TH..............	Technische Hochschule [*Technical College*] [*German*]
TH..............	Teki Historyczne [*A publication*]
TH..............	Telegraph Apparatus [*JETDS nomenclature*] [*Military*] (CET)
TH..............	Tell Halaf (BJA)
TH..............	Temporary Hold
TH..............	Terrain Height (MCD)
TH..............	Territory of Hawaii [*to 1959*]
T & H	Test and Handling [*Equipment*] (NG)
TH..............	Thai Airways Co. Ltd. [*Later, TG*] [*ICAO designator*] (FAAC)
TH..............	Thailand [*ANSI two-letter standard code*] [*IYRU nationality code*] (CNC)
th	Thailand [*MARC country of publication code*] [*Library of Congress*] (LCCP)
T & H	Thames & Hudson [*Publisher*]
TH..............	Tharsis Region [*A filamentary mark on Mars*]
TH..............	Theatre (ROG)
TH..............	Their Highnesses (ADA)
Th..............	Themis. Verzameling van Bijdragen tot de Kennis van het Publiek- en Privaatrecht [*A publication*]
Th..............	Thenar [*Anatomy*]
th	Thenardite [*CIPW classification*] [*Geology*]
Th..............	Theodotion (BJA)
Th..............	Theogonia [*of Hesiod*] [*Classical studies*] (OCD)
Th..............	Theologia [*A publication*]
Th..............	Theology
Th..............	Theology [*A publication*]
TH..............	Theraplix [*France*] [*Research code symbol*]
TH..............	Therapy [*Medicine*] (DHSM)
TH..............	Thermal
T/H	Thermal and Hydraulic [*Nuclear energy*] (NRCH)
Th..............	Thessalonians [*New Testament book*] (BJA)
TH..............	Thick [*Automotive engineering*]
Th..............	Thin [*Philately*]
Th..............	Things [*A publication*]
TH..............	Thionine [*Organic chemistry*]
Th..............	Thiopental [*An anesthetic*]
Th..............	Thomas de Piperata [*Flourished, 1268-72*] [*Authority cited in pre-1607 legal work*] (DSA)
TH..............	Thoracic Surgery [*Medicine*]

Th.............	Thorium [*Chemical element*]
Th.............	Thought [*A publication*]
TH.............	Through-Hole [*Data processing*]
TH.............	Thunder
TH.............	Thursday
TH.............	Thyroid Hormone [*Thyroxine*] [*Endocrinology*]
TH.............	Today's Health [*A publication*]
TH.............	Toilet-Paper Holder
TH.............	Toluene-Hyamine [*Scintillation solvent*]
TH.............	Tommy Hilfiger [*Fashion designer*]
TH.............	Total Hysterectomy [*Medicine*]
TH.............	Town Hall (ROG)
TH.............	Tracing-Hold
T-H	Transhydro (AABC)
TH.............	Transient Hyperphosphatasemia [*Medicine*]
TH.............	Transmission Header [*Data processing*] (IBMDP)
TH.............	Transponder-Hopping
T/H	Transportation and Handling [*Army*]
TH.............	True Heading
TH.............	Trust House [*British*]
TH.............	Two Hands
TH.............	Tyrosine Hydroxylase [*An enzyme*]
TH.............	Tzivos Hashem (EA)
ThA...........	Associate in Theology (ADA)
THA..........	Taft-Hartley Act [*1947*]
T-HA	Terminal High Altitude
THA..........	Tetrahydroamino-Acridine [*Drug being tested for treatment of Alzheimer's disease*]
THA..........	Tetrahydroaminoacridine [*Pharmacology*]
tha	Thai [*MARC language code*] [*Library of Congress*] (LCCP)
THA..........	Thailand [*ANSI three-letter standard code*] (CNC)
THA..........	Thames Ontario Library Service Board [*UTLAS symbol*]
ThA...........	Theatre Annual [*A publication*]
ThA...........	Thoracic Aorta [*Medicine*]
THA..........	Thorcheron Hunter Association (EA)
THA..........	Total Hip Arthroplasty [*Orthopedics*]
THA..........	Total Hydrocarbon Analyzer
THA..........	Tower Hill School, Wilmington, DE [*OCLC symbol*] (OCLC)
THA..........	Transvaal Horse Artillery [*British military*] (DMA)
THA..........	Treasury Historical Association (EA)
THA..........	Tullahoma, TN [*Location identifier*] [*FAA*] (FAAL)
THA.......	Turk Haberler Ajansi [*Press agency*] [*Turkey*]
THAA........	Tourist House Association of America (EA)
THAB.......	Tetrahexylammonium Benzoate [*Organic chemistry*]
THABTS...	Thereabouts [*Legal term*] [*British*]
Thac Cr Cas ...	Thacher's Criminal Cases [*1823-42*] [*Massachusetts*] [*A publication*] (DLA)
Thach Cr....	Thacher's Criminal Cases [*Massachusetts*] [*A publication*] (DLA)
Thacher Cr ...	Thacher's Criminal Cases [*Massachusetts*] [*A publication*] (DLA)
Thacher Cr Cas ...	Thacher's Criminal Cases [*Massachusetts*] [*A publication*] (DLA)
Thacher Crim Cas (Mass) ...	Thacher's Criminal Cases [*Massachusetts*] [*A publication*] (DLA)
THAE........	Transcatheter Hepatic Artery Embolization [*Medicine*]
THAI........	Thai Airways International
(Thai) Bus R ...	Business Review (Thailand) [*A publication*]
Thai J Agric Sci ...	Thai Journal of Agricultural Science [*A publication*]
Thai J Dev Adm ...	Thai Journal of Development Administration [*Bangkok*] [*A publication*]
Thai J Nurs ...	Thai Journal of Nursing [*A publication*]
Thai J Surg ...	Thai Journal of Surgery [*A publication*]
Thailand Dep Miner Resour Ground Water Bull ...	Thailand. Department of Mineral Resources. Ground Water Bulletin [*A publication*]
Thailand Dep Miner Resour Rep Invest ...	Thailand. Department of Mineral Resources. Report of Investigation [*A publication*]
Thailheimer's Synth Methods of Org Chem Yearb ...	Thailheimer's Synthetic Methods of Organic Chemistry Yearbook [*A publication*]
Thail Plant Prot Serv Tech Bull ...	Thailand Plant Protection Service. Technical Bulletin [*A publication*]
Thai Natl Sci Pap Fauna Ser ...	Thai National Scientific Papers. Fauna Series [*A publication*]
Thai Nurses Assoc J ...	Thai Nurses Association Journal [*A publication*]
Thai Sci Bull ...	Thai Science Bulletin [*A publication*]
THAJ........	Tasmania House of Assembly - Journals [*A publication*]
Thal...........	Thalassemia [*Medicine*]
Thalassia Jugosl ...	Thalassia Jugoslavica [*A publication*]
THAM.......	Tris(hydroxymethyl)aminomethane [*Also, TRIS*] [*Biochemical analysis*]
THAMA....	Toxic and Hazardous Materials Agency [*Army*] (RDA)
THAP........	Tactical High-Altitude Penetration (MCD)
THAQ........	Tetrahydroanthraquinone [*Organic chemistry*]
Tharandter Forstl Jahrb ...	Tharandter Forstliches Jahrbuch [*A publication*]
Tharandt Forstl Jb ...	Tharandter Forstliches Jahrbuch [*A publication*]
Thar Forstl Jb ...	Tharandter Forstliches Jahrbuch [*A publication*]
THARIES ...	Total Hip Articular Replacement with Internal Eccentric Shells [*Orthopedics*]
THaroL......	Lincoln Memorial University, Harrogate, TN [*Library symbol*] [*Library of Congress*] (LCLS)
THART	Theodore Army Terminal
ThArts	Theatre Arts [*A publication*]
THAS........	Tumbleweed High-Altitude Samples (MUGU)
ThAT	Theologie des Alten Testaments [*A publication*] (BJA)
THAT........	Theologisches Handwoerterbuch zum Alten Testament [*A publication*]
THAT	Twenty-Four-Hour Automatic Teller [*Trademark for self-service banking display panel*]
Th Aust......	Theatre Australia [*A publication*] (APTA)
THAWS	Tactical Homing and Warning System
Thayer........	Thayer's Reports [*18 Oregon*] [*A publication*] (DLA)
Thayer Prelim Treatise Ev ...	Thayer's Preliminary Treatise on Evidence [*A publication*] (DLA)
THB..........	Thaba Tseka [*Lesotho*] [*Airport symbol*] (OAG)
Th B	Theologiae Baccalaureas [*Bachelor of Theology*]
ThB...........	Theologische Blaetter [*A publication*]
ThB...........	Theologische Buecherei. Neudrucke und Berichte aus dem 20 Jahrhundert [*Munich*] [*A publication*] (BJA)
THB..........	Third-Harmonic Band
THB..........	Today's Housing Briefs [*A publication*]
TH & B	[*The*] Toronto, Hamilton & Buffalo Railway Co. [*Nickname: To Hell and Back*]
THB..........	[*The*] Toronto, Hamilton & Buffalo Railway Co. [*AAR code*]
THB..........	Trierer Heimatbuch [*A publication*]
Th Ber........	Theologische Berichte [*A publication*]
THBF........	Total Hepatic Blood Flow
THBF........	Traditional Hi-Bye Function [*Army*]
THBI	Thyroid Hormone Binding Inhibitor [*Clinical chemistry*]
Thbilis Sahelmc Univ Gamoqeneb Math Inst Srom ...	Thbilisis Sahelmcipho Universiteti Gamoqenebithi Mathematikis Instituti. Sromebi [*A publication*]
Thbilis Univ Srom ...	Thbilisis Universitetis. Phizika-Mathematikisa de Sabunebismetqvelo Mecnierebani. Sromebi [*A publication*]
Thbilis Univ Srom A ...	Thbilisis Universitetis. Phizika-Mathematikisa de Sabunebismetqvelo Mecnierebani. Sromebi. A [*A publication*]
THbl	Trierische Heimatblaetter [*A publication*]
ThBNL	National Library, Bangkok, Thailand [*Library symbol*] [*Library of Congress*] (LCLS)
THBP........	Tetrahydrobenzopyrene [*Organic chemistry*]
Th Br.........	Thesaurus Brevium [*2 eds.*] [*1661, 1687*] [*A publication*] (DLA)
THBR........	Thoroughbred Half-Bred Registry (EA)
THBR........	Thyroid Hormone Binding Ratio [*Clinical chemistry*]
THBY........	Thereby
Th C	Candidate of Theology
THC..........	Houston Community College System, Learning Resource Center, Houston, TX [*OCLC symbol*] (OCLC)
THC..........	Hydraulic Company [*NYSE symbol*] (SPSG)
THC..........	Target Homing Correlator
THC..........	Tchien [*Liberia*] [*Airport symbol*] (OAG)
THC..........	Teachers Higher Certificate [*Australia*]
TH & C	Terpin Hydrate and Codeine [*Medicine*]
THC..........	Tetrahydrocannabinol [*Active principle of marijuana*]
THC..........	Tetrahydrocortisol
THC..........	Thermal Converter (MSA)
THC..........	Thiocarbanidin [*Pharmacology*]
Th & C	Thompson and Cook's New York Supreme Court Reports [*1873-75*] [*A publication*] (DLA)
THC..........	Thrust Hand Controller [*NASA*] (KSC)
THC..........	Topics in Health Care Financing [*A publication*]
THC..........	Total Hydrocarbon
THC..........	Translation Hand Controller [*NASA*]
THC..........	Tridont Health Care, Inc. [*Toronto Stock Exchange symbol*]
THC..........	Tube Humidity Control
T & HCA ...	Towboat and Harbor Carriers Association of New York and New Jersey (EA)
T-HCA.......	Trans-Hydroxycrotonic Acid [*Organic chemistry*]
THCA	Trihydroxycholestanoic Acid [*Biochemistry*]
THCA	Trihydroxycoprostanic Acid [*Biochemistry*]
Th Ca Const Law ...	Thomas' Leading Cases in Constitutional Law [*A publication*] (DLA)
Th CC	Thacher's Criminal Cases [*1823-42*] [*Massachusetts*] [*A publication*] (DLA)
THCC........	Tube Heating and Cooling Control
Th C Const Law ...	Thomas' Leading Cases on Constitutional Law [*A publication*] (DLA)
THCF........	Thompson-Huston Company of France
THCF........	Topics in Health Care Financing [*A publication*]
THCHDM ...	Specialist Periodical Reports. Theoretical Chemistry [*A publication*]
THCN........	Tetrahydrocorynantheine [*Biochemistry*]
THCO........	[*The*] Hammond Company [*NASDAQ symbol*] (NQ)
THCOL......	Thorn Color [*Botany*]
THCS	Temperature of Hot-Channel Sodium [*Nuclear energy*] (NRCH)
THCUR.....	Thorn Curvature [*Botany*]
ThD...........	Doctor of Thinkology [*Honorary degree awarded the scarecrow by the wizard in 1939 film "The Wizard of Oz"*]
Thd...........	Ribothymidine [*Also, T*] [*A nucleoside*]
THD..........	Testicular Hypothermia Device [*Medicine*]
Th D..........	Theologiae Doctor [*Doctor of Theology*]

ThD........... Theology Digest [*St. Mary's, KS*] [*A publication*]
THD........... Third Canadian General Investment Trust Ltd. [*Toronto Stock Exchange symbol*]
THD........... Thread (AAG)
THD........... Thunander Corp. [*AMEX symbol*] (SPSG)
THD........... Thunderhead (FAAC)
THD........... Total Harmonic Distortion [*Electronics*]
THD........... Tube Heat Dissipator
THD........... University of Houston, Downtown College, Houston, TX [*OCLC symbol*] (OCLC)
THDA........ Telluraheptadecanoic Acid [*Organic chemistry*]
THDA........ Thermal Hydrodealkylation [*Petroleum technology*]
THDA........ Toluene Hydrodealkylation [*Organic chemistry*]
THDC........ Technical Handbook Distribution Code (MCD)
THDI........ Thread Die
ThDig........ Theology Digest [*St. Mary's, KS*] [*A publication*]
ThDip........ Diploma in Theology (ADA)
THDNK..... Threaded Neck
THDOC..... Tetrahydrodeoxycorticosterone [*Biochemistry*]
THDPC..... Threadpiece
THDr......... Doctor of Theology
THDR........ Thunder (FAAC)
THDS........ Time Homogenous Data Set (MCD)
THE.......... T & H Resources Ltd. [*Toronto Stock Exchange symbol*]
THE.......... Tape-Handling Equipment
THE.......... Technical Help to Exporters [*British Standards Institution*]
THE.......... Teresina [*Brazil*] [*Airport symbol*] (OAG)
THE.......... Tetrahydrocortisone [*Endocrinology*]
ThE.......... Theologische Existenz Heute [*Munich*] [*A publication*] (BJA)
THE.......... Thomas Hewett Edward Cat [*In TV series "T.H.E. Cat"*]
THE.......... Total Height Expansion
THE.......... Transhepatic Embolization [*Medicine*]
THE.......... Transportable Helicopter Enclosure (RDA)
THE.......... Tube Heat Exchanger
THEA........ Theata [*A publication*]
THEAT..... Theatrical
Theat Ann ... Theatre Annual [*A publication*]
Theat C...... Theatre Crafts [*A publication*]
Theat Craft .. Theatre Crafts [*A publication*]
Theat Heute ... Theater Heute [*A publication*]
Theat J....... Theatre Journal [*A publication*]
Theat Note ... Theatre Notebook [*A publication*]
Theat Q...... Theatre Quarterly [*A publication*]
Theat Quart ... Theatre Quarterly [*A publication*]
Theatre Arts M ... Theatre Arts Magazine [*A publication*]
Theatre J ... Theatre Journal [*A publication*]
Theatre M ... Theatre Magazine [*A publication*]
Theatre Notebk ... Theatre Notebook [*A publication*]
Theatre Pol ... Theatre en Pologne - Theatre in Poland [*A publication*]
Theatre Q... Theatre Quarterly [*A publication*]
Theatre Res Int ... Theatre Research International [*A publication*]
Theatre S .. Theatre Studies [*A publication*]
Theatre S .. Theatre Survey [*A publication*]
Theat Res I ... Theatre Research International [*A publication*]
Theat Stud ... Theatre Studies [*A publication*]
Theat Surv ... Theatre Survey [*A publication*]
Theat Zeit .. Theater der Zeit [*A publication*]
Theb........... Thebais [*of Statius*] [*Classical studies*] (OCD)
THEBES ... [*The*] Electronic Banking Economics Society [*New York, NY*] (EA)
THECC...... Truck and Heavy Equipment Claims Council (EA)
Th Ed....... Theological Education [*A publication*]
T Heden Rom-Holl Reg ... Tydskrif vir Hedendaagse Romeins-Hollandse Reg [*A publication*]
Th Educ ... Theological Education [*A publication*]
THEED ..... Tetrahydroxyethylethylenediamine [*Organic chemistry*]
THEG........ [*The*] Group, Inc. [*NASDAQ symbol*] (SPSG)
THEI .... Today Home Entertainment, Inc. [*NASDAQ symbol*] (NQ)
THEIC....... Tris(hydroxyethyl)isocyanurate [*Organic chemistry*]
THE J....... THE [*Technological Horizons in Education*] Journal [*A publication*]
THE Jrnl ... THE [*Technological Horizons in Education*] Journal [*A publication*]
Thel........... Theloall's Le Digest des Briefs [*2 eds.*] [*1579, 1687*] [*A publication*] (DLA)
Them.......... American Themis [*A publication*] (DLA)
Them.......... La Themis [*A publication*] (DLA)
Them.......... Themelios [*A publication*]
Them.......... Themistocles [*of Plutarch*] [*Classical studies*] (OCD)
Themis....... Rechtsgeleerd Magazijn Themis [*A publication*]
Themis....... Revue Juridique Themis [*A publication*]
THEN........ Those Hags Encourage Neuterism [*Organization opposed to NOW (National Organization for Women)*]
THEO........ Theology
THEO........ Theophylline [*Pharmacology*]
THEO........ Theoretical
Theo Am A ... Theobald's Act for the Amendment of the Law [*A publication*] (DLA)
Theobald.... Theobald on Wills [*11 eds.*] [*1876-1954*] [*A publication*] (DLA)
Theoc .... Theocritus [*Third century BC*] [*Classical studies*] (OCD)

Theod .... Theodotion (BJA)
Theo Ecl..... Theological Eclectic [*A publication*]
Theog......... Theogonia [*of Hesiod*] [*Classical studies*] (OCD)
Theokr .... Theokratia [*Leiden/Cologne*] [*A publication*]
Theol......... Theologia [*A publication*]
THEOL...... Theological
Theol.......... Theology [*London*] [*A publication*]
Theol Akad ... Theologische Akademie [*A publication*]
TheolArb .... Theologische Arbeiten [*A publication*] (BJA)
Theol Dgst ... Theology Digest [*A publication*]
Theol Evang ... Theologia Evangelica [*A publication*]
Theol Geg .. Theologie der Gegenwart [*A publication*]
Theol Gl..... Theologie und Glaube [*A publication*]
Theo & Lit J ... Theological and Literary Journal [*A publication*]
Theol Jb..... Theologisches Jahrbuch [*A publication*]
Theol Lit Z ... Theologische Literaturzeitung [*A publication*]
Theol LZ.... Theologische Literaturzeitung [*A publication*]
THEOLOG ... Theology Student (DSUE)
Theol Phil .. Theologie und Philosophie [*A publication*]
Theol Pract ... Theologia Practica [*A publication*]
Theol Pr Q Schr ... Theologisch-Praktische Quartalschrift [*A publication*]
Theol Pr Qu Schr ... Theologisch-Praktische Quartalschrift [*A publication*]
Theol Quart ... Theologische Quartalschrift [*A publication*]
Theol Quart-Schrift ... Theologische Quartalschrift [*A publication*]
Theol R ..... Theologische Revue [*A publication*]
Theol & Rel Ind ... Theological and Religious Index [*A publication*]
Theol Ru .... Theologische Rundschau [*A publication*]
Theol St ..... Theological Studies [*A publication*]
Theol St ..... Theologische Studien [*A publication*]
Theol Stds ... Theological Studies [*A publication*]
Theol St Krit ... Theologische Studien und Kritiken [*A publication*]
Theol Stud .. Theological Studies [*A publication*]
Theol Today ... Theology Today [*A publication*]
Theol Via ... Theologia Viatorum [*A publication*]
Theol Zs..... Theologische Zeitschrift [*A publication*]
Theom L..... Theomonistic Licensee
Theo Mo .... Theological Monthly [*A publication*]
Theophil..... Theophilus [*Flourished, 6th century*] [*Authority cited in pre-1607 legal work*] (DSA)
Theophr..... Theophrastus [*Third century BC*] [*Classical studies*] (OCD)
Theopomp ... Theopompus Historicus [*Fourth century BC*] [*Classical studies*] (OCD)
Theo Pres Pr ... Theory of Presumptive Proof [*A publication*] (DLA)
Theo Pr & S ... Theobald's Principal and Surety [*1832*] [*A publication*] (DLA)
Theo R .... Theological Review [*A publication*]
THEOR..... Theorem (ROG)
THEOR..... Theoretical (AAG)
Theor A Gen ... Theoretical and Applied Genetics [*A publication*]
Theor Appl Genet ... Theoretical and Applied Genetics [*A publication*]
Theor Appl Mech (Sofia) ... Theoretical and Applied Mechanics (Sofia) [*A publication*]
Theor Chem ... Theoretical Chemistry [*A publication*]
Theor Chem Adv Perspect ... Theoretical Chemistry. Advances and Perspectives [*A publication*]
Theor Chem Engng Abstr ... Theoretical Chemical Engineering Abstracts [*A publication*]
Theor Chem (NY) ... Theoretical Chemistry (New York) [*A publication*]
Theor Chem Period Chem Biol ... Theoretical Chemistry. Periodicities in Chemistry and Biology [*A publication*]
Theor Chim ... Theoretica Chimica Acta [*A publication*]
Theor Chim Acta ... Theoretica Chimica Acta [*A publication*]
Theor Comput Sci ... Theoretical Computer Science [*A publication*]
Theor Decis ... Theory and Decision [*A publication*]
Theo Repos ... Theological Repository [*A publication*]
Theoret Appl Genet ... Theoretical and Applied Genetics [*A publication*]
Theoret Chim Acta ... Theoretica Chimica Acta [*A publication*]
Theoret Comput Sci ... Theoretical Computer Science [*A publication*]
Theoret Linguist ... Theoretical Linguistics [*A publication*]
Theoret and Math Phys ... Theoretical and Mathematical Physics [*A publication*]
Theoret Population Biol ... Theoretical Population Biology [*A publication*]
Theoret Population Biology ... Theoretical Population Biology [*A publication*]
Theor Exp Biol ... Theoretical and Experimental Biology [*A publication*]
Theor Exp Biophys ... Theoretical and Experimental Biophysics [*A publication*]
Theor Exp Chem ... Theoretical and Experimental Chemistry [*A publication*]
Theor Exper Chem ... Theoretical and Experimental Chemistry [*A publication*]
Theor Exp Methoden Regelunstech ... Theoretische und Experimentelle Methoden der Regelungstechnik [*A publication*]
Theor Foundations Chem Engng ... Theoretical Foundations of Chemical Engineering [*A publication*]
Theor Found Chem Eng ... Theoretical Foundations of Chemical Engineering [*A publication*]
Theorie et Polit ... Theorie et Politique [*A publication*]
Theor Klin Med Einzeldarst ... Theoretische und Klinische Medizin in Einzeldarstellungen [*A publication*]
Theor Klin Med Einzeldarstell ... Theoretische und Klinische Medizin in Einzeldarstellungen [*West Germany*] [*A publication*]
Theor Math ... Theoretical and Mathematical Physics [*A publication*]

Theor Math Phys ... Theoretical and Mathematical Physics [*A publication*]
Theor and Math Phys ... Theoretical and Mathematical Physics [*A publication*]
Theor Med ... Theoretical Medicine [*A publication*]
Theor Pop B ... Theoretical Population Biology [*A publication*]
Theor Popul Biol ... Theoretical Population Biology [*A publication*]
Theor Probability Appl ... Theory of Probability and Its Applications [*A publication*]
Theor Theor ... Theoria to Theory [*A publication*]
Theory Exp Exobiol ... Theory and Experiment in Exobiology [*A publication*]
Theory Probab and Appl ... Theory of Probability and Its Applications [*A publication*]
Theory Probab Appl ... Theory of Probability and Its Applications [*A publication*]
Theory Probability and Math Statist ... Theory of Probability and Mathematical Statistics [*A publication*]
Theory Probab Math Statist ... Theory of Probability and Mathematical Statistics [*A publication*]
Theory Sci Dev ... Theory of Science Development [*A publication*]
Theory and Soc ... Theory and Society [*A publication*]
Theory Soc ... Theory and Society [*A publication*]
THEOS ..... Theosophy
THEOS ..... They Help Each Other Spiritually [*Motto of THEOS Foundation*]
Theosophy in Aust ... Theosophy in Australia [*A publication*]   (APTA)
Theos Q ..... Theosophical Quarterly [*A publication*]
THEOS R ... Theosophical Review [*A publication*]   (ROG)
Theo Today ... Theology Today [*A publication*]
Theo Wills ... Theobald on Wills [*13th ed.*] [*1971*] [*A publication*]   (DLA)
THer .... Ladies Hermitage Association, Hermitage, TN [*Library symbol*] [*Library of Congress*]   (LCLS)
THER .... Therapeutic
Ther .... Theriaca [*of Nicander*] [*Classical studies*]   (OCD)
THERAP... Therapeutic
Therap .... Therapie [*A publication*]
Therapeutic Ed ... Therapeutic Education [*A publication*]
Therap Gegenw ... Therapie der Gegenwart [*A publication*]
Therap Halbmonatsh ... Therapeutische Halbmonatshefte [*A publication*]
Therap Hung ... Therapia Hungarica [*Hungarian Medical Journal*] [*A publication*]
Therapie Gegenw ... Therapie der Gegenwart [*A publication*]
Therap Monatsh Vet-Med ... Therapeutische Monatshefte fuer Veterinaermedizin [*A publication*]
Therap Umschau ... Therapeutische Umschau und Medizinische Bibliographie [*A publication*]
Ther Ber..... Therapeutische Berichte [*A publication*]
Ther Drug Monit ... Therapeutic Drug Monitoring [*A publication*]
THERE...... [*The*] Heterogeneous Environment for Remote Execution [*Data processing*]
The Rep...... [*The*] Reporter, Phi Alpha Delta [*A publication*]   (DLA)
The Rep...... [*The*] Reports, Coke's English King's Bench [*A publication*]   (DLA)
Ther Gaz.... Therapeutic Gazette [*A publication*]
Ther Ggw ... Therapie der Gegenwart [*A publication*]
Ther Halbmonatsh ... Therapeutische Halbmonatshefte [*A publication*]
Ther Hung ... Therapia Hungarica [*A publication*]
THERM .... Thermal   (DEN)
THERM .... Thermometer   (AAG)
Therm .... Thermonews [*A publication*]
THERM .... Thermostat   (DEN)
THERMA ... Transfer of Heat Reduced Magnetically
Therm Abstr ... Thermal Abstracts [*A publication*]
Therm Eng ... Thermal Engineering [*A publication*]
Therm Engng ... Thermal Engineering [*A publication*]
Therm Engr ... Thermal Engineering [*A publication*]
Therm Eng (USSR) ... Thermal Engineering (USSR) [*A publication*]
THERMISTOR ... Thermal Resistor
Therm Nucl Power ... Thermal and Nuclear Power [*Japan*] [*A publication*]
THERMO ... Thermal and Hydrodynamic Experiment Research Module in Orbit   (MCD)
THERMO ... Thermodynamic Property Values Database [*Chemical Information Systems, Inc.*] [*Information service or system*]   (CRD)
THERMO ... Thermostat   (AAG)
Thermoc Act ... Thermochimica Acta [*A publication*]
Thermochim Acta ... Thermochimica Acta [*A publication*]
THERMODYN ... Thermodynamics   (AAG)
Ther Monatsh ... Therapeutische Monatshefte [*A publication*]
Therm Power Conf Proc ... Thermal Power Conference. Proceedings [*United States*] [*A publication*]
Therm Power Gener ... Thermal Power Generation [*A publication*]
Ther Nervensys ... Therapie ueber das Nervensystem [*A publication*]
Ther Nervensyst ... Therapie ueber das Nervensystem [*A publication*]
THerP......... [*The*] Papers of Andrew Jackson, Hermitage, TN [*Library symbol*] [*Library of Congress*]   (LCLS)
THERP...... Technique for Human Error Rate Prediction
Ther Probl Today ... Therapeutic Problems of Today [*A publication*]
Ther Recreation J ... Therapeutic Recreation Journal [*A publication*]
Ther Recr J ... Therapeutic Recreation Journal [*A publication*]
Ther R J..... Therapeutic Recreation Journal [*A publication*]
Ther Sem Hop ... Therapeutique. Semaine des Hopitaux [*A publication*]

Ther Umsch ... Therapeutische Umschau [*A publication*]
Thes .... Thesaurus [*A publication*]
THES........ Theses of Economics and Business in Finland [*Helsinki School of Economics Library*] [*Information service or system*]   (CRD)
Thes .... Theseus [*of Plutarch*] [*Classical studies*]   (OCD)
THES........ Thesis   (ADA)
Thes .... Thessalonians [*New Testament book*]
THES........ Times Higher Education Supplement [*A publication*]
THESA N ... Teachers of Home Economics Specialist Association. Newsletter [*A publication*]
Thes Brev... Thesaurus Brevium [*A publication*]   (DLA)
Theses Cathol Med Coll ... Theses. Catholic Medical College [*A publication*]
Theses Cathol Med Coll (Seoul) ... Theses. Catholic Medical College (Seoul) [*A publication*]
Theses Collect Chonnam Univ Chonnam Univ ... Theses Collection of Chonnam University. Chonnam University [*A publication*]
Theses Collect Incheon Jr Coll ... Theses Collection. Incheon Junior College [*A publication*]
Theses Collect Kyungnam Ind Jr Coll ... Theses Collection. Kyungnam Industrial Junior College [*Republic of Korea*] [*A publication*]
Theses Collect Kyungnam Univ ... Theses Collection. Kyungnam University [*Republic of Korea*] [*A publication*]
Theses Collect Sookmyung Women's Univ ... Theses Collection. Sookmyung Women's University [*A publication*]
Theses Collect Yeungnam Univ ... Theses Collection. Yeungnam University [*Republic of Korea*] [*A publication*]
Theses Collect Yeungnam Univ Nat Sci ... Theses Collection. Yeungnam University. Natural Sciences [*Republic of Korea*] [*A publication*]
Theses Doct Ing Univ Dakar Ser Sci Nat ... Theses de Docteur-Ingenieur. Universite de Dakar. Serie Sciences Naturelles [*A publication*]
Theses Zool ... Theses Zoologicae [*A publication*]
Thesis .... Thesis Eleven [*A publication*]
Thesis Theo Cassettes ... Thesis Theological Cassettes [*A publication*]
THESLA ... Tennessee Health Science Library Association [*Library network*]
Thesm .... Thesmophoriazusae [*of Aristophanes*] [*Classical studies*]   (OCD)
Thess.......... Thessalonians [*New Testament book*]
THETA ..... [*The*] Handicapped and Elderly Travelers Association [*Defunct*]   (EA)
THETA ..... Teenage Health Education Teaching Assistants [*National Foundation for the Prevention of Oral Disease*]
THETA ..... Tunneling Hot-Electron Transfer Amplifier [*Semiconductor technology*]
Theta NR ... Theta News Release [*A publication*]
T Heth........ Text der Hethiter [*A publication*]
THEX .... [*The*] Hitech Engineering Co. [*McLean, VA*] [*NASDAQ symbol*]   (NQ)
Th Ex H..... Theologische Existenz Heute [*A publication*]
ThExNF .... Theologische Existenz Heute. Neue Folge [*A publication*]   (BJA)
THF .... Freelance Research Service, Houston, TX [*OCLC symbol*]   (OCLC)
THF .... Target Height Finding   (MCD)
THF .... Tetrahydrofluorenone [*Organic chemistry*]
THF .... Tetrahydrofolate [*Biochemistry*]
THF .... Tetrahydrofuran [*Organic chemistry*]
ThF .... Theologische Forschung [*Hamburg*] [*A publication*]
THF .... Thermal Hysteresis Factor
THF .... Thymic Humoral Factor [*Endocrinology*]
THF .... Thymic Hypocalcemic Factor [*Biochemistry*]
THF .... Tian Hua Fen [*Chinese herbal medicine*]
THF .... Tremendously High Frequency [*Telecommunications*]   (TEL)
THF .... Trust Houses Forte Ltd. [*Hotel empire*]
THFA .... Tetrahydrofolic Acid [*Biochemistry*]
THFA .... Tetrahydrofurfuryl Alcohol [*Organic chemistry*]
THFA .... Three-Conductor, Heat and Flame Resistant, Armor Cable
THFC .... Troy Hess Fan Club   (EA)
THFI......... Plymouth Five Cents Savings Bank [*Plymouth, MA*] [*NASDAQ symbol*]   (NQ)
Th F Jb ...... Tharandter Forstliches Jahrbuch [*A publication*]
THFM .... Therefrom [*Legal term*] [*British*]
THFOR ..... Therefor [*Legal term*] [*British*]   (ROG)
THFR .... Thetford Corp. [*NASDAQ symbol*]   (NQ)
THFR .... Three-Conductor, Heat and Flame Resistant, Radio Cable
THFROM ... Therefrom [*Legal term*] [*British*]   (ROG)
THG.......... Biloela [*Australia*] [*Airport symbol*]
ThG.......... Theologie der Gegenwart [*A publication*]
ThG.......... Theologie und Glaube [*A publication*]
Th G .... Therapie der Gegenwart [*A publication*]
Th d G........ Therapie der Gegenwart [*A publication*]
THG.......... Third-Harmonic Generation [*Physics*]
THG.......... Thomson, GA [*Location identifier*] [*FAA*]   (FAAL)
Thg............ Thyroglobulin [*Also, TG*] [*Endocrinology*]
THGA........ Thread Gauge
THGA........ Trihydroxyglutamic Acid [*Organic chemistry*]

THGA........ Trihydroxyglutaric Acid [*Organic chemistry*]
TH GAZ .... Therapeutic Gazette [*Philadelphia*] [*A publication*] (ROG)
THGEA ..... Therapie der Gegenwart [*A publication*]
ThGG........ Thueringer Gasgesellschaft [*Thuringian Gas Association*] [*Business term*] [*Federal Republic of Germany*]
THGG........ Transportable Horizontal Gravity Gradiometer
THHF........ Tetrahydrohomofolate [*Organic chemistry*]
ThHK........ Theologischer Hand-Kommentar zum Neuen Testament [*A publication*] (BJA)
THHN .... Thermoplastic, Heat-Resistant, High-Temperature, Nylon-Jacketed [*Electric cable*]
THHP........ Target Health Hazard Program [*Occupational Safety and Health Administration*]
THHP........ Tung-Hai Hsueh-Pao [*Tunghai Journal*] [*A publication*]
THI .... Telehop, Incorporated [*Fresno, CA*] [*Telecommunications*] (TSSD)
THI .... Temperature-Humidity Index
THi .... Tennessee Historical Society, Nashville, TN [*Library symbol*] [*Library of Congress*] (LCLS)
THI .... Terre Haute [*Indiana*] [*Seismograph station code, US Geological Survey*] (SEIS)
THI .... Texas Heart Institute [*University of Texas*] [*Research center*] (RCD)
THI .... Theodor Herzl Institute   (EA)
THI .... Thermo Instrument Systems, Inc. [*AMEX symbol*] (SPSG)
THI .... Thios Resources, Inc. [*Vancouver Stock Exchange symbol*]
THI .... Time Handed In [*Navy*]
THI .... Travelers Health Institute [*Later, ITHI*]
THI .... Trihydroxyindol [*Organic chemistry*]
THIEF....... [*The*] Human-Initiated Equipment Failures
Thiemig-Taschenb ... Thiemig-Taschenbuecher [*A publication*]
Thiemig Tb ... Thiemig-Taschenbuecher [*A publication*]
Thieraerzt Mitth (Carlsruhe) ... Thieraerztliche Mittheilungen (Carlsruhe) [*A publication*]
Thiermed Rundschau ... Thiermedicinische Rundschau [*A publication*]
THIJDO..... Texas Heart Institute. Journal [*A publication*]
THINGS.... Totally Hilarious Incredibly Neat Games of Skill [*Milton-Bradley product*]
Thin Sol Fi ... Thin Solid Films [*A publication*]
THIO........ Thiopental [*An anesthetic*]
THioTEPA ... Triethylenethiophosphoramide [*Also, TSPA*] [*Antineoplastic drug*]
THIP .... Tetrahydroisooxazolopyridineol [*Organic chemistry*]
THIR .... Temperature-Humidity Infrared Radiometer
TH-IR........ Tyrosine Hydroxylase-Immunoreactivity [*Physiology*]
Third Wld .. Third World Forum [*A publication*]
Third Wld Agric ... Third World Agriculture [*A publication*]
Third World Planning R ... Third World Planning Review [*A publication*]
Third World Q ... Third World Quarterly [*A publication*]
Third World Soc ... Third World Socialists [*A publication*]
Thirties Soc Jnl ... Thirties Society. Journal [*A publication*]
Thirty-3...... 33 Magazine [*A publication*]
Thirty-Three/33 Mag Met Prod Ind ... Thirty-Three/33. Magazine of the Metals Producing Industry [*A publication*]
THIS.......... [*The*] Hospitality and Information Service [*For diplomatic residents and families in Washington, DC*]
This Mag ... This Magazine Is about Schools [*Later, This Magazine: Education, Culture, Politics*] [*A publication*]
THIV .... History Institute, Victoria [*Australia*]
THJ .... Laurel, MS [*Location identifier*] [*FAA*] (FAAL)
ThJ .... Theologische Jahrbuecher [*A publication*]
Th Jb.......... Theologisches Jahrbuch [*A publication*]
THJCS ...... Tsing Hua Journal of Chinese Studies [*A publication*]
THJUA ..... Thalassia Jugoslavica [*A publication*]
THK.......... Taiheiyo Hoso Kyokai [*Pacific Broadcasting Association*] (EAIO)
THK.......... Thackeray Corp. [*NYSE symbol*] (SPSG)
THK.......... Thick [*or Thickness*] (AAG)
THKF .... Thick Film (MSA)
THKNS ..... Thickness
THKR .... Thicker (MSA)
THKSA...... Taiki Hoshano Kansoku Seiseki [*A publication*]
Th L .... Licentiate in Theology
'tHL .... 'T Heiling Land [*Nijmegen*] [*A publication*] (BJA)
THL.......... Tachilek [*Burma*] [*Airport symbol*] (OAG)
THL.......... Tally-Ho Explorations Ltd. [*Vancouver Stock Exchange symbol*]
ThL.......... Theologisches Literaturblatt [*Leipzig*] [*A publication*]
THL.......... Thermoluminescence [*Also, TL*]
THL.......... Thule [*Denmark*] [*Geomagnetic observatory code*]
THL.......... Transhybrid Loss [*Telecommunications*] (TEL)
THL.......... Tuned Hybrid Lattice
THL.......... University of Houston, Law Library, Main, Houston, TX [*OCLC symbol*] (OCLC)
ThLB.......... Theologisches Literaturblatt [*A publication*]
ThlBer........ Theologischer Literaturbericht [*A publication*] (BJA)
ThLBl........ Theologisches Literaturblatt [*Leipzig*] [*A publication*]
THLD........ Threshold
THLEN ..... Thorn Length [*Botany*]
Th Life ...... Theology and Life [*A publication*]
Th Lit .... Theologische Literaturzeitung [*A publication*]

Th Lit Z ..... Theologische Literaturzeitung [*A publication*]
ThLL.......... Thesaurus Linguae Latinae [*A publication*]
THLM .... Lehman [*T. H.*] & Co., Inc. [*New York, NY*] [*NASDAQ symbol*] (NQ)
Th (Lond)... Theology (London) [*A publication*]
THLR .... Thaler [*Numismatics*]
THLRA ...... Taft-Hartley Labor Relations Act   (OICC)
THLS........ Turret Head Limit Switch
ThLZ .... Theologische Literaturzeitung [*A publication*]
THM........ Tapia House Movement [*Trinidad and Tobago*] [*Political party*] (PPW)
THM.......... Textos Hispanicos Modernos [*A publication*]
Th M.......... Theologiae Magister [*Master of Theology*]
THM.......... Therm (MSA)
THM.......... Thermwood Corp. [*AMEX symbol*] (SPSG)
Thm............ Thomist [*A publication*]
THM.......... Thompson Falls, MT [*Location identifier*] [*FAA*] (FAAL)
THM.......... Thomson Newspapers Ltd. [*Toronto Stock Exchange symbol*]
THM.......... Tien Hsia Monthly [*A publication*]
THM.......... Topics in Health Care Materials Management [*A publication*]
THM.......... Traveling Heater Method
THM.......... Trihalomethane [*Organic chemistry*]
THM.......... TRIS, HEPES, Mannitol [*A buffer*]
THM.......... Trotting Horse Museum (EA)
THM.......... University of Tennessee at Martin, Martin, TN [*OCLC symbol*] (OCLC)
THMA....... Trailer Hitch Manufacturers Association (EA)
Th Markings ... Theological Markings [*A publication*]
THMFP..... Trihalomethane Formation Potential [*Environmental chemistry*]
THMF-TS-TGSE ... Teachers Have More Fun - They Should - They Get Stewed Enough [*Slogan*] [*Bowdlerized version*]
THMP .... Tetrahydromethanopterin [*Biochemistry*]
THMP .... Thermal Industries, Inc. [*NASDAQ symbol*] (NQ)
THMS .... Thermistor [*Electronics*]
Th M S ..... Thomas Mann-Studien [*A publication*]
THMTG .... Target Holding Mechanism, Tank Gunnery
THMZ...... Three Hundred Mile Zone
THN .... Thin (FAAC)
THN .... Trihydroxynaphthalene [*Organic chemistry*]
THN .... Trollhattan [*Sweden*] [*Airport symbol*] (OAG)
Th Nb........ Theatre Notebook. A Quarterly of Notes and Research [*A publication*]
THNR .... Thinner [*Freight*]
THNR T .... Thinner Than [*Freight*]
THO .... Thogoto Virus [*Virology*]
Tho .... Thomas Aquinas [*Deceased, 1274*] [*Authority cited in pre-1607 legal work*] (DSA)
Tho............ Thomas Mieres [*Flourished, 1429-39*] [*Authority cited in pre-1607 legal work*] (DSA)
Tho............ Thomas de Piperata [*Flourished, 1268-72*] [*Authority cited in pre-1607 legal work*] (DSA)
THO .... Thomsonite [*A zeolite*]
THO .... Thor Industries, Inc. [*NYSE symbol*] (SPSG)
THO .... Thorco Resources, Inc. [*Toronto Stock Exchange symbol*]
THO .... Thorshofn [*Iceland*] [*Airport symbol*] (OAG)
THO .... Though
Tho............ Thought. A Review of Culture and Idea [*A publication*]
THO .... Thursdays Only [*British railroad term*]
THO .... Tonto Hills Observatory [*Arizona*] [*Seismograph station code, US Geological Survey*] [*Closed*] (SEIS)
THOF....... Thereof
Tho de For ... Thomas de Formaginis [*Flourished, 1331-38*] [*Authority cited in pre-1607 legal work*] (DSA)
Tho For ...... Thomas de Formaginis [*Flourished, 1331-38*] [*Authority cited in pre-1607 legal work*] (DSA)
Tho Form ... Thomas de Formaginis [*Flourished, 1331-38*] (DSA)
Tho Foroli ... Thomas Foroliviensis [*Authority cited in pre-1607 legal work*] (DSA)
Tho Grama ... Thomas Grammaticus [*Flourished, 16th century*] [*Authority cited in pre-1607 legal work*] (DSA)
THOLD..... Threshold (NASA)
Thol Ed ..... Theological Educator [*A publication*]
Tho de Lya ... Thomas de Elya [*Authority cited in pre-1607 legal work*] (DSA)
Thom........ Thomas' Reports [*1 Wyoming*] [*A publication*] (DLA)
Thom........ Thomist [*A publication*]
Thom........ Thomson's Nova Scotia Reports [*A publication*] (DLA)
Thomas ...... Thomas' Reports [*1 Wyoming*] [*A publication*] (DLA)
Thomas Mortg ... Thomas on Mortgages [*A publication*] (DLA)
Thomas Negl ... Thomas on Negligence [*A publication*] (DLA)
Thomas Say Found ... Thomas Say Foundation [*A publication*]
Thomas Say Found Monogr ... Thomas Say Foundation. Monographs [*A publication*]
Thom BBS ... Thompson. Benefit Building Societies [*A publication*] (ILCA)
Thom Bills ... Thomson on Bills and Notes [*A publication*] (DLA)
Thom B & N ... Thomson on Bills and Notes [*A publication*] (DLA)
Thom Camp ... Thomas Campegius [*Deceased, 1564*] [*Authority cited in pre-1607 legal work*] (DSA)
THOMCAT ... Thomas Register Catalog File [*A publication*]

Thom Co Lit ... Thomas' Edition of Coke upon Littleton [*A publication*] (DLA)
Thom Co Litt ... Thomas' Edition of Coke upon Littleton [*A publication*] (DLA)
Thom Const L ... Thomas' Leading Cases on Constitutional Law [*A publication*] (DLA)
Thom Dec .. Thomson's Nova Scotia Reports [*1834-52*] [*A publication*] (DLA)
Thom & Fr ... Thomas and Franklin's Chancery Reports [*1 Maryland*] [*A publication*] (DLA)
THOMIS... Total Hospital Operating and Medical Information System
Thom LC.... Thomas' Leading Cases on Constitutional Law [*A publication*] (DLA)
Thom de Mar ... [*Johannes*] Thomas de Marinis [*Flourished, 16th century*] [*Authority cited in pre-1607 legal work*] (DSA)
Thom Mort ... Thomas on Mortgages [*A publication*] (DLA)
Thom N Sc ... Thomson's Nova Scotia Reports [*1834-51, 1856-59*] [*Canada*] [*A publication*] (DLA)
Thomp & C ... Thompson and Cook's New York Supreme Court Reports [*A publication*] (DLA)
Thomp Cal ... Thompson's Reports [*39, 40 California*] [*A publication*] (DLA)
Thomp Car ... Thompson on Carriers [*A publication*] (DLA)
Thomp Cas ... Thompson's Cases [*Tennessee*] [*A publication*] (DLA)
Thomp Ch Jur ... Thompson on Charging the Jury [*A publication*] (DLA)
Thomp Cit ... Thompson's Ohio Citations [*A publication*] (DLA)
Thomp & Cook ... Thompson and Cook's New York Supreme Court Reports [*A publication*] (DLA)
Thomp Corp ... Thompson's Commentaries on Law of Private Corporations [*A publication*] (DLA)
Thomp Dig ... Thompson's Digest of Laws [*Florida*] [*A publication*] (DLA)
Thomp Ent ... Thompson's Entries [*A publication*] (DLA)
Thomp Farm ... Thompson's Law of the Farm [*A publication*] (DLA)
Thomp H & Ex ... Thompson on Homesteads and Exemptions [*A publication*] (DLA)
Thomp High ... Thompson on the Law of Highways [*A publication*] (DLA)
Thomp Liab Off ... Thompson on Liability of Officers of Corporations [*A publication*] (DLA)
Thomp Liab St ... Thompson on Liability of Stockholders [*A publication*] (DLA)
Thomp Liab Stockh ... Thompson on Liability of Stockholders [*A publication*] (DLA)
Thomp & M Jur ... Thompson and Merriam on Juries [*A publication*] (DLA)
Thomp NB Cas ... Thompson's National Bank Cases [*A publication*] (DLA)
Thomp Neg ... Thompson's Cases on Negligence [*A publication*] (DLA)
Thomp Pat ... Thompson on Patent Laws of All Countries [*13th ed.*] [*1905*] [*A publication*] (DLA)
Thomp Prov Rem ... Thompson's Provisional Remedies [*A publication*] (DLA)
Thomps Cas ... Thompson's Tennessee Cases [*A publication*] (DLA)
Thompson.. Thompson's Reports [*39, 40 California*] [*A publication*] (DLA)
Thompson & C ... Thompson and Cook's New York Supreme Court Reports [*A publication*] (DLA)
Thompson's Fla Dig ... Thompson's Digest of Laws [*Florida*] [*A publication*] (DLA)
Thompson Unrep (PA) ... Thompson's Unreported Cases (Pennsylvania) [*A publication*] (DLA)
Thompson Yates and Johnston Lab Rep ... Thompson, Yates, and Johnston Laboratories Reports [*A publication*]
Thompson Yates Lab Rep ... Thompson-Yates Laboratories Reports [*A publication*]
Thomp & St ... Thompson and Steger's Code [*Tennessee*] [*A publication*] (DLA)
Thomp & St Code ... Thompson and Steger's Code [*Tennessee*] [*A publication*] (DLA)
Thomp Tenn Cas ... Thompson's Unreported Tennessee Cases [*A publication*] (DLA)
Thomp Trials ... Thompson on Trials [*A publication*] (DLA)
Thom Rep .. Thomson's Nova Scotia Reports [*A publication*] (DLA)
Thom Sc Acts ... Thomson's Scotch Acts [*A publication*] (DLA)
Thom Sel Dec ... Thomson's Nova Scotia Select Decisions [*A publication*] (DLA)
Thoms Jud Fac ... Thoms' Judicial Factors [*A publication*] (DLA)
Thomson's Process Chem Eng ... Thomson's Process and Chemical Engineering [*Australia*] [*A publication*]
Thom St Sum ... Thomas' Leading Statutes Summarized [*A publication*] (DLA)
Thom Un Jur ... Thomas' Universal Jurisprudence [*2nd ed.*] [*1829*] [*A publication*] (DLA)
THON .... Thereon [*Legal term*] [*British*]
Tho Parpal ... Thomas Parpalea [*Flourished, 16th century*] [*Authority cited in pre-1607 legal work*] (DSA)
THOPS...... Tape Handling Operational System [*Data processing*] (IEEE)
THOR....... Tape-Handling Optional Routines [*Honeywell, Inc.*]
THOR....... Thesaurus-Oriented Retrieval [*Information service or system*]
Thor .... Thorax [*British Medical Association*] [*A publication*]
Thor .... Thorington's Reports [*107 Alabama*] [*A publication*] (DLA)
THOR....... Thought Organizer [*Computer program produced by Fastware, Inc.*]
THOR....... Transistorized High-Speed Operations Recorder
THOR....... Tsing Hua Open-Pool Reactor [*Formosa*]
THORAC .. Thoraci [*To the Throat*] [*Pharmacy*]

Thorac Cardiovasc Surg ... Thoracic and Cardiovascular Surgeon [*A publication*]
THORAD ... Thor-Agena D [*Rocket*] [*NASA*]
Thorax Chir ... Thoraxchirurgie und Vaskulaere Chirurgie [*A publication*]
Thoraxchir Vask Chir ... Thoraxchirurgie und Vaskulaere Chirurgie [*A publication*]
Thor Bank ... Thorborn on Bankers' Law [*A publication*] (DLA)
Thoreau JQ ... Thoreau Journal Quarterly [*A publication*]
Thoreau Q ... Thoreau Quarterly [*A publication*]
Thorn .... Thornton's Notes of Ecclesiastical and Maritime Cases [*1841-50*] [*A publication*] (DLA)
THORNB ... Thornbury [*England*]
Thorn Conv ... Thornton's Conveyancing [*A publication*] (DLA)
Thornt & Bl Bldg & Loan Ass'ns ... Thornton and Blackledge's Law Relating to Building and Loan Associations [*A publication*] (DLA)
Thornton Gifts ... Thornton on Gifts and Advancements [*A publication*] (DLA)
Thoro .... Thoroughfare [*Maps and charts*]
Thoroton Soc Rec Ser ... Thoroton Society. Record Series [*A publication*]
THORP .... Thermal Oxide Reprocessing Plant [*Nuclear energy*]
Thorpe .... Thorpe's Annual Reports [*52 Louisiana*] [*A publication*] (DLA)
Thorpe Anc L ... Thorpe's Ancient Laws of England [*A publication*] (DLA)
THORS ..... Thermal-Hydraulic Out-of-Reactor Safety Facility [*Department of Energy*]
Thos Co Lit ... Thomas' Edition of Coke upon Littleton [*A publication*] (DLA)
THOT....... Thought
Thoth Res .. Thoth Research Journal [*A publication*]
THOU .... Thousand (AFM)
THOUS .... Thousand (NASA)
THP .... [*The*] Hunger Project (EA)
THP .... Terminal Handling Processor
TH & P ...... Terre Haute & Peoria Railroad [*Nickname: Take Hold and Push*]
THP .... Tetrahydropalmatine [*Organic chemistry*]
THP .... Tetrahydropapaveroline [*Biochemistry*]
thp .... Tetrahydropyranyl [*Organic chemistry*]
THP .... Tetrakis(hydroxymethyl)phosphonium [*Organic chemistry*]
THP .... Thermopolis, WY [*Location identifier*] [*FAA*] (FAAL)
THP .... Through Hole Probe
THP .... Thrust Horsepower [*Jet engines*]
T & HP ...... Transportation and Handling Procedure
THP .... Triangle Home Products, Inc. [*AMEX symbol*] (SPSG)
THP .... Trihydroxypropane [*Organic chemistry*]
THP .... (Trimethylhydrazinium) Propionate [*Biochemistry*]
THP .... Tris(hydroxymethyl)phosphine [*Organic chemistry*]
THPA .... Tetrahydrophthalic Anhydride [*Organic chemistry*]
THPC .... Tetrakis(hydroxymethyl)phosphonium Chloride [*Flame retardant*]
THPDX ..... Tetrahydropyranyldoxorubicin [*Antineoplastic drug*]
THPF........ Total Hepatic Plasma Flow [*Physiology*]
THPFB...... Treated Hard-Pressed Fiberboard [*Technical drawings*]
Th & Ph ..... Theologie und Philosophie [*A publication*]
THPO .... Tris(hydroxymethyl)phosphine Oxide [*Organic chemistry*]
Th P Q ...... Theologisch-Praktische Quartalschrift [*A publication*]
THPR .... Thermal Profiles, Inc. [*NASDAQ symbol*] (NQ)
T & H Prac ... Troubat and Haly's Pennsylvania Practice [*A publication*] (DLA)
Th Pract..... Theologia Practica [*A publication*]
ThPract..... Theologie en Practijk [*Rotterdam*] [*A publication*] (BJA)
ThPrM....... Theologisch-Praktische Monatsschrift [*A publication*] (BJA)
Th Pr Ma St ... Theory of Probability and Mathematical Statistics [*A publication*]
Th Prob Ap ... Theory of Probability and Its Applications [*A publication*]
ThPrQSchr ... Theologisch-Praktische Quartalschrift [*Linz, Austria*] [*A publication*]
THPS........ Tetrakis(hydroxymethyl)phosphonium Sulfate [*Flame retardant*] [*Organic chemistry*]
THQ .... Tennessee Historical Quarterly [*A publication*]
THQ .... Tetrahydroxyquinone [*Chemical indicator*]
THQ .... Theater Headquarters [*Military*]
ThQ............ Theatre Quarterly [*A publication*]
ThQ............ Theologische Quartalschrift [*A publication*]
THQ .... Troop Headquarters
ThQ............ Tuebinger Theologische Quartalschrift [*A publication*]
ThQR......... Theological Quarterly Review [*A publication*]
Th QS .... Theologische Quartalschrift [*A publication*]
THR........... Target Heart Rate [*Exercise*] (INF)
THR........... Tehran [*Iran*] [*Airport symbol*] (OAG)
ThR .... Theatre Research [*A publication*]
THR........... Their (ROG)
THR........... Their Royal Highnesses [*British*] (ROG)
ThR .... Theological Review [*Princeton, NJ*] [*A publication*]
ThR .... Theologische Revue [*A publication*]
ThR .... Theologische Rundschau [*A publication*]
THR........... There (ROG)
THR........... Thor Energy Resources, Inc. [*AMEX symbol*] (SPSG)
Thr .... Threni (BJA)
Thr .... Threonine [*Also, T*] [*An amino acid*]
THR.......... Threshold

THR.......... Through (ADA)
THR.......... Throughput Rate
THR.......... Thrust (AAG)
THR.......... Thrust. Journal for Employment and Training Professionals [*A publication*]
THR.......... Total Hip Replacement [*Medicine*]
THR.......... Total Hydrocarbon Reforming [*Hydrogen production*]
THR.......... Transmittal Header Record [*Data processing*]
THR.......... Transmitter Holding Register
THR.......... Travaux d'Humanisme et Renaissance [*A publication*]
THRA....... Theratech Corp. [*NASDAQ symbol*] (NQ)
THRABTS ... Thereabouts [*Legal term*] [*British*] (ROG)
THRAP ..... Tasmanian Historical Research Association. Papers and Proceedings [*A publication*] (ADA)
THRAR ..... Thereafter [*Legal term*] [*British*] (ROG)
THRAT .... Thereat [*Legal term*] [*British*] (ROG)
THRB .... Theodore Roosevelt Birthplace National Historic Site
Th Rd .... Theologische Rundschau [*A publication*]
THRD....... Thread
Th Rdschau ... Theologische Rundschau [*A publication*]
Three Bank ... Three Banks Review [*A publication*]
Three Banks R ... Three Banks Review [*A publication*]
Three Banks Rev ... Three Banks Review [*A publication*]
Three Forks ... Three Forks of Muddy Creek [*A publication*]
Three R Int ... Three R International [*West Germany*] [*A publication*]
TH Rep Eindhoven Univ Technol Dep Electr Eng ... TH-Report-Eindhoven University of Technology. Department of Electrical Engineering [*A publication*]
ThRev .... Theologische Revue [*A publication*]
THRF .... Thyrotrophic Hormone-Releasing Factor [*Endocrinology*]
THRFTR ... Thereafter (FAAC)
Thr Hist Tr ... Thrupp's Historical Law Tracts [*A publication*] (DLA)
THR-HR ... Tydskrif vir Hedendaagse Romeins-Hollandse Reg [*A publication*] (DLA)
Th RI .... Theatre Research International [*A publication*]
THRIC ...... Treasure Hunter Research and Information Center (EA)
THRILLO ... Transfer to Higher Rated Job in Lieu of Layoff (MCD)
THRIN ...... Therein
THRINAR ... Thereinafter [*Legal term*] [*British*] (ROG)
THRINBEFE ... Thereinbefore [*Legal term*] [*British*] (ROG)
Thring J St Com ... Thring on Joint Stock Companies [*5th ed.*] [*1889*] [*A publication*] (DLA)
Thring LD ... Thring on the Land Drainage Act [*1862*] [*A publication*] (DLA)
THRIP....... Thriplow [*England*]
Th Ri Po... Three Rivers Poetry Journal [*A publication*]
THRM....... Thermal (AAG)
THRMST ... Thermostat
THRMSTC ... Thermostatic (MSA)
ThRNF ...... Theologische Rundschau. Neue Folge [*Tuebingen*] [*A publication*]
THRO........ Theodore Roosevelt National Memorial Park
THRO........ Through
ThroBL...... Through Bill of Lading [*Shipping*]
THROF....... Thereof
Thromb Diat ... Thrombosis et Diathesis Haemorrhagica [*A publication*]
Thromb Diath Haemorrh ... Thrombosis et Diathesis Haemorrhagica [*A publication*]
Thromb Diath Haemorrh Suppl ... Thrombosis et Diathesis Haemorrhagica. Supplementum [*A publication*]
Thromb Haemost ... Thrombosis and Haemostasis [*A publication*]
Thromb Haemostas ... Thrombosis and Haemostasis [*A publication*]
Thromb Res ... Thrombosis Research [*A publication*]
Thromb Res Suppl ... Thrombosis Research. Supplement [*A publication*]
THRON..... Thereon [*Legal term*] [*British*] (ROG)
Throop Pub Off ... Throop's Treatise on Public Officers [*A publication*] (DLA)
THROT..... Throttle (AAG)
THROUT ... Thereout [*Legal term*] [*British*] (ROG)
THRP .... Therapist
THRPY...... Therapy
Th Rsch...... Theologische Rundschau [*A publication*]
THRSHL... Thrust Shell
THRSUM ... Threat Summary Message (MCD)
THRT .... Threat [*or Threatening*] [*FBI standardized term*]
THRT .... Throat
THRU........ I am connecting you to another switchboard [*Telecommunications*] (FAAC)
ThRu.......... Theologische Rundschau [*A publication*]
THRU....... Through (AAG)
THRU....... Thrust [*A publication*]
THRU........ Toxic Hazards Research Unit [*NASA*] (KSC)
THRUPON ... Thereupon [*Legal term*] [*British*] (ROG)
THRUSH.. Technological Hierarchy for the Removal of Undesirables and the Subjugation of Humanity [*Fictitious organization in "The Man from UNCLE" television series*]
THRUT ..... Throughout (FAAC)
Th Rv .... Theologische Revue [*A publication*]
Thr Verb Agr ... Throop on the Validity of Verbal Agreements [*A publication*] (DLA)
Thr Wld Q ... Third World Quarterly [*A publication*]
THRX........ Theragenics Corp. [*NASDAQ symbol*] (NQ)

THS .... [*The*] Hydrographic Society [*Dagenham, Essex, England*] (EAIO)
THS .... St. Thomas, PA [*Location identifier*] [*FAA*] (FAAL)
THS .... Target Homing System
THS .... Technical High School (ADA)
THS .... Tenement House Smell [*British*] (ROG)
THS Tetrahydro-11-Deoxycortisol
THS .... Textes pour l'Histoire Sacree [*A publication*]
THS .... Textile History Society [*Defunct*] (EA)
THS .... Theatre Historical Society (EA)
ThS .... Theatre Survey [*A publication*]
ThS .... Theological Studies [*A publication*]
ThS .... Theologische Studien und Kritiken [*A publication*]
THS .... Thermostat Switch
THS .... Thomas Hardy Society (EAIO)
THS .... Three-Stage Least Squares [*Econometrics*]
ThS .... Thymidylate Synthase [*Also, TS*] [*An enzyme*]
THS .... Times Health Supplement [*London*] [*A publication*]
THS .... Titanic Historical Society (EA)
THS .... Tourist Hospitality Service [*British*]
THS .... Transparent Hull Submersible [*Navy*]
THS .... Tube Heating Supply
THSA .... Thomas Hardy Society of America (EA)
THSA .... Traveling Hat Salesmen's Association [*Defunct*] (EA)
THSAM .... Topographie Historique de la Syrie Antique et Medievale [*A publication*] (BJA)
THSC .... Transactions. Honourable Society of Cymmrodorion [*A publication*]
THSD ...... Thousand (FAAC)
THSG .... Transactions. Historical Society of Ghana [*A publication*]
THSI......... Thermal Systems, Incorporated [*NASDAQ symbol*] (NQ)
ThSK........ Theologische Studien und Kritiken [*Hamburg/Berlin*] [*A publication*]
THSP........ Temporary-Help Supplier Personnel
THSP........ Thermal Spray [*Also, TS*] [*Coating technology*]
THSRB ..... Tufts Health Science Review [*A publication*]
ThSt .... Theological Studies [*A publication*]
Th St .... Theologische Studien [*A publication*]
Th St B....... Theologische Studien. Karl Barth [*A publication*]
ThStKr....... Theologische Studien und Kritiken [*Hamburg/Berlin*] [*A publication*]
ThSzemle.... Theologiai Szemle [*Budapest*] [*A publication*] (BJA)
THT.......... Papeete [*Orstom*] [*Society Islands*] [*Seismograph station code, US Geological Survey*] (SEIS)
THT.......... Teacher of Hydrotherapy [*British*]
THT.......... Tetrahydrothiophene [*Organic chemistry*]
Tht .... Theaetetus [*of Plato*] [*Classical studies*] (OCD)
ThT .... Theologisch Tijdschrift [*A publication*]
Th T .... Theology Today [*A publication*]
THT.......... Thrust Resources, Inc. [*Vancouver Stock Exchange symbol*]
THT.......... Total Homing Time
THTA .... Thread Tap
THTAD .... Thiemig-Taschenbuecher [*A publication*]
THTD....... Too Hard to Do (CAAL)
THTF....... Thermal Hydraulic Test Facility [*Nuclear energy*] (NRCH)
THTH........ Too Hot to Handle
THTMS..... Tetramethylthiuram Monosulfide [*Also, TMTD*] [*Organic chemistry*]
THTN........ Threaten (FAAC)
THTO....... Thereto
THTO....... Threading Tool (AAG)
Th Today ... Theology Today [*A publication*]
THTR .... Theater (AFM)
THTR .... Thorium High-Temperature Reactor [*Nuclear energy*]
THU .... Tetrhydrouridine [*Biochemistry*]
THU .... Thule [*Greenland*] [*Seismograph station code, US Geological Survey*] [*Closed*] (SEIS)
THU .... Thunder Explorations [*Vancouver Stock Exchange symbol*]
THU .... Thursday (AFM)
Thuc .... De Thucydide [*of Dionysius Halicarnassensis*] [*Classical studies*] (OCD)
THUC....... Thucydides [*Greek historian, c. 460-400BC*] [*Classical studies*] (ROG)
THUD ...... Thorium, Uranium, Deuterium
THUDD .... Thermal Uplink Data Display [*Data processing*]
ThuGl........ Theologie und Glaube [*A publication*]
Thule Int Symp ... Thule International Symposia [*A publication*]
THUMB.... Tiny Humans Underground Military Bureau [*Government organization in TV cartoon series "Tom of T.H.U.M.B."*]
THUMS .... Texaco, Humble, Union, Mobil, and Shell [*Petroleum companies*]
Thurg B...... Thurgauische Beitraege zur Vaterlaendischen Geschichte [*A publication*]
Thur Mar L Rev ... Thurgood Marshall Law Review [*A publication*] (DLA)
Thur Marsh LJ ... Thurgood Marshall Law Journal [*A publication*]
THURS ..... Thursday
THURST.. Thurstable [*England*]
THUT....... Thyroid Hormone Uptake Test [*Clinical chemistry*]
THV.......... Terminal Homing Vehicle
ThV........... Theologia Viatorum. Jahrbuch der Kirchlichen Hochschule [*Berlin*] [*A publication*]

THV...........	Thoracic Vertebra [*Medicine*]
THV...........	Tool Handling Vehicle (MCD)
THV...........	Total Heart Volume [*Physiology*]
THV...........	York, PA [*Location identifier*] [*FAA*] (FAAL)
ThViat.......	Theologia Viatorum. Jahrbuch der Kirchlichen Hochschule [*Berlin*] [*A publication*]
ThW...........	Theologisches Woerterbuch zum Neuen Testament [*A publication*] (BJA)
THW........	Therewith [*Legal term*] [*British*] (ROG)
THW........	Thermoplastic, Heat-Resistant, Wet-Location [*Electric cable*]
Thw...........	Thwartship (DS)
THW........	Torsion Head Wattmeter
ThWAT	Theologisches Woerterbuch zum Alten Testament [*A publication*] (BJA)
ThWB	Theologisches Woerterbuch zum Neuen Testament [*A publication*] (BJA)
ThWBNT ..	Theologisches Woerterbuch zum Neuen Testament [*A publication*] (BJA)
Th Wiss	Theologische Wissenschaft [*A publication*]
THWITH ..	Therewith [*Legal term*] [*British*] (ROG)
THWM.......	Trinity High-Water Mark
THWN.......	Thermoplastic, Heat-Resistant, Wet-Location, Nylon-Jacketed [*Electric cable*]
ThWNT	Theologisches Woerterbuch zum Neuen Testament [*A publication*] (BJA)
THWR.......	Thrower
THWT	Throwout [*Mechanical engineering*]
THX...........	Thor Explorations [*Vancouver Stock Exchange symbol*]
THX...........	Three Rivers, TX [*Location identifier*] [*FAA*] (FAAL)
THX...........	Thyroxine [*Also, T4, Ty*] [*An amino acid*] [*Endocrinology*]
THX...........	Tomlinson-Holman Cross-Over [*Motion picture theater sound system*]
THX...........	Total Hypophysectomy [*Medicine*]
THY...........	Thomas Hardy Yearbook [*A publication*]
Thy............	Thymine [*Also, T*] [*Biochemistry*]
THY...........	Thymocyte [*Clinical chemistry*]
THY...........	Turk Hava Yollari AO [*Turkish Airlines, Inc.*]
THYB	Tai Hei Yo Bashi [*Bridge over the Great Ocean*] (EA)
THYMD....	Thymus [*A publication*]
THYMOTRO ...	Thyratron Motor Control [*Electronics*] (MCD)
THYMOTROL ...	Thyratron Motor Control [*Electronics*]
THYP.......	Total Hydroxyproline [*Clinical chemistry*]
THYR........	Thyristor [*Electronics*]
Thyssen Edelstahl Tech Ber ...	Thyssen Edelstahl Technische Berichte [*A publication*]
Thyssen Forsch Ber Forsch Betr ...	Thyssen Forschung. Berichte aus Forschung und Betrieb [*A publication*]
Thyssen Tech Ber ...	Thyssen Technische Berichte [*A publication*]
THZ...........	Tahoua [*Niger*] [*Airport symbol*] (OAG)
THz...........	Terahertz
Th Z...........	Theater der Zeit [*A publication*]
ThZ...........	Theologische Zeitschrift [*A publication*]
THZOEN..	Theses Zoologicae [*A publication*]
TI	Costa Rica [*Aircraft nationality and registration mark*] (FAAC)
TI	Table Indicator [*Data processing*]
TI	Tamarind Institute (EA)
TI	Tamiment Institute (EA)
TI	Tape Inverter
TI	Target Identification
TI	Target Indicator
TI	Target Intelligence (MCD)
TI	Tariff Item
T & I........	Tax and Insurance Payment [*Banking*]
TI	Taxable Income
TI	Teardown Inspection
ti	Technical Indexes Ltd. [*Information service or system*] (IID)
TI	Technical Information (CINC)
TI	Technical Information for Industry [*A publication*]
TI	Technical Inspection [*Military*]
TI	Technical Institute
TI	Technical Instruction [*or Instructor*]
TI	Technical Integration [*NASA*] (NASA)
TI	Technical Intelligence [*Military*]
TI	Technical Interchange (KSC)
TI	Tehrik-i-Istiqlal [*Solidarity Party*] [*See also TIP*] [*Political party*] [*Pakistan*] (FEA)
TI	Telecommunication Industry
TI	Teleos Institute (EA)
TI	Temperature Indicator
Ti..............	Temperature of Injectate
TI	Temporary Instruction [*Nuclear energy*] (NRCH)
TI	Teresian Institute (EA)
TI	Terminal Interface
TI	Terminal Island [*San Pedro*] [*Navy base*]
TI	Termination Instruction
TI	Test Implicit
TI	Test Index (CAAL)
TI	Test Instruction (MCD)
TI	Test Instrumentation
TI	Texas Instruments, Inc.
TI	Textile Institute [*Manchester, England*] (EAIO)

TI	Thalassemia Intermedia [*Hematology*]
TI	Think Ink [*An association*] (EA)
TI	Thread Institute [*Defunct*] (EA)
TI	Thursday Island [*Australia*] (ADA)
TI	Thymidine-Labeling Index [*Biochemical analysis*]
TI	Thymus Independent [*Cells*] [*Hematology*]
TI	TI Travel International, Inc. [*Vancouver Stock Exchange symbol*]
TI	Tie In (MCD)
TI	Tiferet Israel (BJA)
TI	TII Industries, Inc. [*AMEX symbol*] (SPSG)
Ti	Timaeus [*of Plato*] [*Classical studies*] (OCD)
Ti	Timarit Pjooreknisfelags Islendinga 1957 [*A publication*]
TI	Timberman. An International Lumber Journal [*A publication*]
TI	Time Index
TI	Time Interval (IEEE)
TI	Tippers International (EA)
Ti	Titanium [*Chemical element*]
TI	Title [*Online database field identifier*] [*Data processing*]
TI	Title Information [*Publishing*]
Ti	Titus [*New Testament book*]
TI	Toastmasters International (EA)
TI	Tobacco Institute (EA)
TI	Tobacco Intelligence [*A publication*]
TI	Tobacco International [*A publication*]
TI	Together, Incorporated (EA)
TI	Together International/Anti-Soviet Research Center (EA)
TI	Tonic Immobility [*Neurophysiology*]
TI	Torpedo Instructor [*British military*] (DMA)
T/I..............	Torque/Inertia
TI	Total Immersion [*Language study*]
T/I..............	TPFDD Interface
TI	Track Identity
TI	Track Initiator
TI	Trade and Industry Index [*Information Access Corp.*] [*Information service or system*] (IID)
TI	Traditional Instruction
TI	Traffic Identification
TI	Training Instructor
TI	Training Integrator [*or Integration*] (MCD)
TI	Trajectory Integration (CAAL)
TI	Transaction Interpretation (MCD)
TI	Transfer Impedance (IEEE)
TI	Transfrigoroute International (EA)
TI	Transillumination
TI	Transmission Identification (NG)
TI	Transportation Institute [*Camp Springs, MD*] (EA)
TI	Transportes Aereos Internacionales, SA [*TAISA*] [*Peru*] [*ICAO designator*] (FAAC)
TI	Treasure Island [*San Francisco Bay*] [*Navy base*]
TI	Treasury Instruction (ADA)
TI	Trial Installation (MCD)
TI	Tricuspid Insufficiency [*Cardiology*]
TI	Troop Information
TI	True Independent [*Australia*]
TI	Trusteeship Institute (EA)
TI	Trypsin Inhibitor [*Food technology*]
TI	Tube Investments Ltd. [*British*]
Ti	Tumor-inducing [*Plasmids*] [*Plant cytology*]
TI	Tungsten Institute [*Defunct*] (EA)
TI	Tuning Indicator (DEN)
ti	Tunisia [*MARC country of publication code*] [*Library of Congress*] (LCCP)
TI	Turbine Intelligence [*A publication*]
TI	Turing Institute [*United Kingdom*] (IRUK)
TI	Type Item [*Military*]
T2000I	Transport 2000 International [*London, England*] (EAIO)
TIA	[*The*] International Alliance, an Association of Executive and Professional Women [*Baltimore, MD*] (EA)
TIA	Tactical Identification and Acquisition [*Navy*] (NG)
TIA	Taian [*Republic of China*] [*Seismograph station code, US Geological Survey*] (SEIS)
TIA	Task Item Authorization (MCD)
TIA	Tax Institute of America [*Later, NTA-TIA*] (EA)
TIA	Taxation in Australia [*A publication*] (APTA)
TIA	Taxation Institute of Australia
TIA	Teacher Investigator Awards
TIA	Telecommunications Industry Association (EA)
TIA	Test Interface Assembly
TIA	Thallium Acetate
TIA	Thin-Layer Immunoassay [*Analytical biochemistry*]
TIA	Tiaprofenic Acid
TIA	Tilapia International Association (EAIO)
TIA	Tin International [*London*] [*A publication*]
TIA	Tirana [*Albania*] [*Airport symbol*] (OAG)
TIA	Tobacco Institute of Australia
TIA	Tortilla Industry Association (EA)
TIA	Total Inactive Aerospace Vehicle [*or Aircraft*] Authorization
TIA	Trans International Airlines
TIA	Transient Ischemic Attack [*Medicine*]
TIA	Transimpedance Amplifier [*Instrumentation*]

TIA	Transportation Intelligence Agency (AAG)
TIA	Travel Industry Association of America (EA)
TIA	Treaties and Other International Acts
TIA	Trend Impact Analysis [*The Futures Group, Inc.*] [*Information service or system*] (IID)
TIA	Trends, Indicators, and Analyses [*on the Southeast Asia war*] [*Classified Air Force document*]
TIA	Tri-Basin Resources Ltd. [*Vancouver Stock Exchange symbol*]
TIA	Tricot Institute of America [*Defunct*]
TIA	Trouser Institute of America [*Absorbed by NOSA*] (EA)
TIA	Trypsin Inhibitor Activity [*Food technology*]
TIA	Tumor-Induced Angiogenesis [*Immunology*]
TIA	Turbidimetric Immunoassay [*Immunology*]
TIA	Typographers International Association (EA)
TIAA	Task Identification and Analysis (MCD)
TIAA	Teachers Insurance and Annuity Association [*New York, NY*] (EA)
TIAA	Timber Importers Association of America
TIAA	Travel Industry Association of America
TIAC	Technical Information Advisory Committee [*AEC*]
TIAC	Technical Information Analysis Centers
TIAC	Techniques and Instrumentation in Analytical Chemistry [*Elsevier Book Series*] [*A publication*]
TIAC	Texas Instruments Automatic Computer
TIAC	Tourism Industry Association of Canada
TIAC	Transport Industries Advisory Committee [*Australia*]
TIAC	Travel [*later, Tourism*] Industry Association of Canada
TIAFT	[*The*] International Association of Forensic Toxicologists [*Newmarket, Suffolk, England*] (EAIO)
TI Agree.....	Treaties and Other International Agreements of the United States of America [*A publication*] (DLA)
TIAH	Totally Implantable Artificial Heart
TIALD	Thermal Imaging, Airborne LASER Designator [*British Royal Air Force*] [*Air Force*] [*British*]
Tianjin J Oncol ...	Tianjin Journal of Oncology [*A publication*]
Tianjin Med J ...	Tianjin Medical Journal [*A publication*]
TIARA	Tactical Intelligence and Related Activity
TIARA	Target Illumination and Recovery Aid
TIARA	Telephone Installation and Requisition Application (MCD)
TIAS	Target Identification and Acquisition System
TIAS	Taxation Incentives for the Arts Scheme [*Australia*]
TIAS	Treaties and Other International Acts Series [*A publication*]
TIAVSC.....	[*The*] International Assets Valuation Standards Committee [*of the American Institute of Real Estate Appraisers*] [*London, England*] (EAIO)
TIAX	Trans International Airlines [*Air carrier designation symbol*]
TIB	Tasmanian Imperial Bushmen [*British military*] (DMA)
TIB	Technical Information Base (MCD)
TIB	Technical Information Branch [*US Public Health Service*] [*Information service or system*] (IID)
TIB	Technical Information Bulletin [*Cincinnati, OH*] (AAG)
TIB	Technical Information Bureau [*British*]
TIB	Technische Informationsbibliothek [*Technical Information Library*] [*Germany*]
TIB	Temporary Importation Bond (MCD)
TIB	This I Believe Test [*Education*]
Tib.	Tiberius [*of Suetonius*] [*Classical studies*] (OCD)
tib	Tibetan [*MARC language code*] [*Library of Congress*] (LCCP)
Tib.	Tibullus [*First century BC*] [*Classical studies*] (OCD)
TIB	Tourist Information Brussels [*Belgium*] (EY)
TIB	Training Improvement Board [*Military*] (CAAL)
TIB	Treasury Indexed Bond (ADA)
TIB	Triisopropylbenzene [*Also, TIPB*] [*Organic chemistry*]
TIB	Trimmed in Bunkers [*Shipping*] (DS)
TIBA	Triiodobenzoic Acid [*Plant growth regulator*]
TIBA	Triisobutylaluminum [*Organic chemistry*]
TIBA	Triisobutylamine [*Organic chemistry*]
TIBALD ...	Tibaldstone [*England*]
TIBC	[*The*] International Beverage Corp. [*NASDAQ symbol*] (NQ)
TIBC	Total Iron-Binding Capacity [*Hematology*]
Tibetan R ...	Tibetan Review [*New Delhi*] [*A publication*]
Tibet J.......	Tibet Journal [*Dharmasala*] [*A publication*]
Tibet Soc B ...	Tibet Society. Bulletin [*United States*] [*A publication*]
TIB and FIB ...	Tibia and Fibula (DSUE)
TIBI	[*The*] Image Bank, Inc. [*NASDAQ symbol*] (NQ)
TIBOE	Transmitting Information by Optical Electronics (KSC)
T I Br Geog ...	Transactions. Institution of British Geographers [*A publication*]
TIBS	Trends in Biochemical Sciences [*A publication*]
TIBTPG.....	Texas Instruments Bourdon Tube Pressure Gauge
TIC	[*The*] Interchurch Center (EA)
TIC	International Financial Law Review [*A publication*]
TIC	Tactical Intelligence Concepts (MCD)
TIC	Tactical Intercom Systems (MCD)
TIC	Taken into Consideration
TIC	Tantalum-Niobium International Study Center [*Formerly, Tantalum Producers International Study Center*] (EA)
TIC	Tantalum Producers International Study Center [*Later, Tantalum-Niobium International Study Center*] (EAIO)
TIC	Tape Identification Card
TIC	Tape Intersystem Connection [*Data processing*]
TIC	Target Integration Center (MCD)
TIC...........	Target Intercept Computer [*Military*]
TIC...........	Tasmanian Industrial Commission [*Australia*]
TIC...........	Teacher in Charge (ADA)
TIC...........	Teacher Information Center (EA)
TIC...........	Technical Information Capability
TIC...........	Technical Information Center [*Department of Energy*]
TIC...........	Technical Institute Council (EA)
TIC...........	Technical Instructors Course [*Air Force*] (AFM)
TIC...........	Technical Intelligence Center [*Navy*]
TIC...........	Technical Interface Concepts (RDA)
TIC...........	Technicon Integrator/Calculator
TIC...........	Technology Innovation Center [*University of Iowa*] [*Research center*] (RCD)
TIC...........	Technology and Innovation Council [*Information Industry Association*]
TIC...........	Telecommunications Information Center [*George Washington University*] [*Information service or system*] (IID)
TIC...........	Telemetry Instruction Conference (KSC)
TIC...........	Telemetry Instrumentation Controller
TIC...........	Temperature Indicator Controller
TIC...........	Terminal Identification Code
TIC...........	Textile Industries Corp. [*Burma*] (DS)
TIC...........	Thai Information Center (EA)
TIC...........	Thermionic Integrated Circuit [*Electronics*]
TIC...........	Thermostatic Ignition Control [*Automotive engineering*]
TIC...........	Time Interval Counter
TIC...........	Tinak [*Marshall Islands*] [*Airport symbol*] (OAG)
TIC...........	Tool Issue Center [*Military*] (AFIT)
TIC...........	Total Inorganic Carbon [*Chemistry*]
TIC...........	Total Installed Cost [*Engineering*]
TIC...........	Total Ion Chromatography
TIC...........	Total Ion Current [*Spectroscopy*]
TIC...........	Total Item Change (NASA)
TIC...........	Toumodi [*Ivory Coast*] [*Seismograph station code, US Geological Survey*] (SEIS)
TIC...........	Trade Information Committee [*Department of State*] (EA)
TIC...........	Transaction Identification Code [*Military*] (AFIT)
TIC...........	Transducer Information Center (MCD)
TIC...........	Transfer-In Channel (CMD)
TIC...........	Transport Industries Committee [*Trades Union Congress*] [*British*] (DCTA)
TIC...........	Transvaal Indian Congress [*South Africa*] (PD)
TIC...........	Travel Information Center [*An association*] (EA)
TIC...........	[*The*] Travelers Corporation [*NYSE symbol*] (SPSG)
TIC...........	Troops-in-Contact
TIC...........	True Interest Cost [*Finance*]
TIC...........	Trypsin Inhibitory Capacity [*Biochemistry*]
TIC...........	Tuned Integrated Circuit
TICA.........	[*The*] International Cat Association (EA)
TICA.........	Tactical Intercom Assembly [*Ground Communications Facility, NASA*]
TICA.........	Technical Information Center Administration [*Conference*]
TICA.........	Timpanogos Cave National Monument
TICACE	Technical Intelligence Center Allied Command Europe [*NATO*] (NATG)
TICAF	[*The*] Industrial College of the Armed Forces [*Later, UND*]
TICC.........	Technical Industrial Cooperation Contract
TICC.........	Technical Intelligence Coordination Center [*NATO*] (NATG)
TICCIH	[*The*] International Committee for the Conservation of the Industrial Heritage (EA)
TICCIT......	Time-Shared Interactive Computer-Controlled Information Television [*System*] [*Mitre Corp.*] [*Brigham Young University*] [*1971*]
TICE.........	Time Integral Cost Effectiveness
TICER.....	Temporary International Council for Educational Reconstruction (DLA)
TICF	Transient Installation Confinement Facility [*Military*] (AABC)
Tichb Tr....	Report of the Tichborne Trial [*London*] [*A publication*] (DLA)
T I Chem En ...	Transactions. Institution of Chemical Engineers and the Chemical Engineer [*A publication*]
TICI	TIC International Corp. [*NASDAQ symbol*] (NQ)
TICKS	Two Incomes, Kids [*Lifestyle classification*]
TICL.........	Topics in Culture Learning [*A publication*]
TICLER.....	Technical Input Checklist/Evaluation Report (MCD)
TICM........	Test Interface and Control Module (MCD)
TICM........	Thermal Imaging Common Modules
TICM........	Trust Investment Committee Memorandum [*A publication*] (DLA)
TICO	Transactions. International Congress of Orientalists [*A publication*] (BJA)
TICOA......	Testing, Instruments, and Controls [*A publication*]
TICODS	Time Compression Display System (NVT)
TICOJ	Transactions. International Conference of Orientalists in Japan [*A publication*]
TICOM	Texas Institute for Computational Mechanics [*University of Texas at Austin*] [*Research center*] (RCD)
TICOS	Truncated Icosahedra [*Crystallography*]
TICP.........	Theater Inventory Control Point [*Military*] (AABC)
TICP.........	Travaux. Institut Catholique de Paris [*A publication*] (BJA)
TICS	Teacher Interactive Computer System (IEEE)
TICS	Telecommunication Information Control System

TICS .... Turret Interaction Crew Simulator (MCD)
TICT .... Tactical Intelligence Collection Team [*Military*] (AFM)
TICT .... Twisted Intramolecular Charge Transfer [*Biochemistry*]
TICTAC .... Time Compression Tactical Communications
TICUS ...... Tidal and Current Survey (NOAA)
TICUS ...... Tidal Current Survey System [*National Oceanic and Atmospheric Administration*]
TICWAN... Trailerable Intracoastal Waterway Aids to Navigation [*Boat*]
TID .... Tactical Information Display
TID .... Tactical Intrusion Detectors (MCD)
TID .... Target Identification Device [*Military*] (CAAL)
TID .... Technical Information Division [*Romar Consultants, Inc.*] [*Information service or system*] (IID)
TID .... Technical Information Document [*A publication*]
TID .... Technology Information Division [*Department of Energy, Mines, and Resources*] (IID)
TID .... Telecommunications Interception Division [*Australian Federal Police*]
TID .... Ter in Die [*Three Times a Day*] [*Pharmacy*]
TID .... Test Identify (CAAL)
TID .... Thermal Imaging Devices (MCD)
TID .... Thermionic Ionization Detector [*Instrumentation*]
TID .... Ticket Information Data
TID .... Total Integrated Dose [*Nuclear energy*] (NRCH)
TID .... Touch Information Display
TID .... Traitement Integre des Donnees [*Integrated Data Processing - IDP*] [*French*]
TID .... Traveling Ionospheric Disturbance
TID .... Trifluoromethyl(iodophenyl)deazirine [*Biochemistry*]
TID .... Turn-In Document [*DoD*]
TIDA .... 30th Infantry Division Association (EA)
TIDA .... Technology and Industry Development Authority [*Western Australia*]
TIDAR...... Texas Instruments Digital Analog Readout
TIDAR...... Time Delay Array RADAR
Tidd........... Tidd's Costs [*A publication*] (DLA)
Tidd........... Tidd's Practice [*A publication*] (DLA)
TIDDAC.... Time in Deadband Digital Attitude Control
Tidd App.... Appendix to Tidd's Practice [*A publication*] (DLA)
Tidd Co ..... Tidd's Costs [*A publication*] (DLA)
Tid Dok...... Tidskrift foer Dokumentation [*A publication*]
Tidd Pr...... Tidd's Practice [*A publication*] (DLA)
Tidd Prac ... Tidd's Practice [*A publication*] (DLA)
Tidd's Pract ... Tidd's Practice [*A publication*] (DLA)
TIDE......... Tactical International Data Exchange (NG)
TIDE......... Tide West Oil Co. [*NASDAQ symbol*] (NQ)
TIDE......... Timer Demodulator
TIDE......... Travel Industry and Disabled Exchange (EA)
TIDES ...... Time-Division Electronics Switching System (KSC)
Tidewtr VA ... Tidewater Virginian [*A publication*]
TIDF......... Trunk Intermediate Distribution Frame [*Telecommunications*] (TEL)
TIDMA ..... Tape Interface Direct Memory Access
Tidn Byggnadskonst ... Tidning foer Byggnadskonst [*A publication*]
TIDOC ...... Technical Information Documentation Center [*Advisory Group for Aerospace Research and Development*] (NATG)
TIDOS...... Table and Item Documentation System
TIDP......... Technical Interface Design Plans
TIDP-TE ... Technical Interface Design Plan - Test Edition (RDA)
TIDS......... Tactical Information Distribution Systems [*Army*] (RDA)
TIDS......... Technical Information Distribution Service [*Publisher*]
Tidsk Dokum ... Tidskrift foer Dokumentation [*A publication*]
Tidskr Dok ... Tidskrift foer Dokumentation [*A publication*]
Tidskr Hushallningssaellsk Skogsvardsstyr Gaevleborgs Laen ... Tidskrift foer Hushallningssaellskapet och Skogsvardsstyrelsen i Gaevleborgs Laen [*A publication*]
Tidskr Lantmaen Andelsfolk ... Tidskrift foer Lantmaen och Andelsfolk [*A publication*]
Tidskr Lantm Andelsfolk ... Tidskrift foer Lantmaen och Andelsfolk [*A publication*]
Tidskr Mil Halsov ... Tidskrift i Militar Halsovard [*Sweden*] [*A publication*]
Tidskr Sjukvardspedagog ... Tidskrift foer Sjukvardspedagoger [*A publication*]
Tidskr Skogbruk ... Tidskrift foer Skogbruk [*A publication*]
Tidskr Skog Lantbruksakad ... Tidskrift. Skogs- och Lantbruksakademien [*A publication*]
Tidskr Sver Sjukskot ... Tidskrift foer Sveriges Sjukskoterskor [*A publication*]
Tidskr Sver Skogvardsforb ... Tidskrift Sveriges Skogsvardsforbund [*A publication*]
Tidskr Sver Utsadesforen ... Tidskrift. Sveriges Utsaedesfoereningen [*A publication*]
Tidskr Varme- Vent- Sanitetstek ... Tidskrift foer Varme-, Ventilations-, och Sanitetsteknik [*Sweden*] [*A publication*]
Tids Samfun ... Tidsskrift foer Samfunnsforskning [*A publication*]
Tidssk Kjemi Bergves Metall ... Tidsskrift foer Kjemi. Bergvesen og Metallurgi [*A publication*]
Tidsskr Biavl ... Tidsskrift foer Biavl [*A publication*]
Tidsskr Froavl ... Tidsskrift foer Froavl [*A publication*]
Tidsskr Hermetikind ... Tidsskrift foer Hermetikindustri [*A publication*]
Tidsskr Kemi ... Tidsskrift foer Kemi [*A publication*]

Tidsskr Kemi Farm Ter ... Tidsskrift foer Kemi. Farmaci og Terapi [*A publication*]
Tidsskr Kjemi Bergv ... Tidsskrift foer Kjemi og Bergvesen [*A publication*]
Tidsskr Kjemi Bergves ... Tidsskrift foer Kjemi og Bergvesen [*A publication*]
Tidsskr Kjemi Bergvesen Met ... Tidsskrift foer Kjemi. Bergvesen og Metallurgi [*A publication*]
Tidsskr Landokon ... Tidsskrift foer Landokonomi [*A publication*]
Tidsskr Nor Laegeforen ... Tidsskrift foer den Norske Laegeforening [*A publication*]
Tidsskr Nor Landbruk ... Tidsskrift foer det Norske Landbruk [*A publication*]
Tidsskr Norske Laegeforen ... Tidsskrift foer den Norske Laegeforening [*A publication*]
Tidsskr Norske Landbruk ... Tidsskrift foer det Norske Landbruk [*A publication*]
Tidsskr Papirind ... Tidsskrift foer Papirindustri [*A publication*]
Tidsskr Plant ... Tidsskrift foer Planteavl [*A publication*]
Tidsskr Planteavl ... Tidsskrift foer Planteavl [*A publication*]
Tidsskr Plavl ... Tidsskrift foer Planteavl [*A publication*]
Tidsskr Prakt Tandlaeg ... Tidsskrift foer Praktiserende Tandlaeger [*A publication*]
Tidsskr Samfunnsforskning ... Tidsskrift foer Samfunnsforskning [*A publication*]
Tidsskr Skogbr ... Tidsskrift foer Skogbruk [*A publication*]
Tidsskr Skogbruk ... Tidsskrift foer Skogbruk [*A publication*]
Tidsskr Textiltek ... Tidsskrift foer Textilteknik [*A publication*]
Tid Tann .... Tidens Tann [*A publication*]
TIDY......... Teletypewriter Integrated Display (NVT)
TIDY......... Track Identity
TIE........... [*The*] Information Exchange (EA)
TIE........... [*The*] Information Exchange on Young Adult Chronic Patients (EA)
TIE........... [*The*] Institute of Ecology [*Defunct*]
TIE........... [*The*] Issue Exchange (EA)
TIE........... Target Identification Equipment (MCD)
TIE........... Technical Idea Exchange (MCD)
TIE........... Technical Independent Evaluator [*Army*]
TIE........... Technical Information Exchange [*National Bureau of Standards*]
TIE........... Technical Integration and Evaluation [*Apollo*] [*NASA*]
TIE........... Technology Information Exchange (IID)
TIE........... Temporary/Intermittent Employee
TIE........... Terminal Interface Equipment
TIE........... Texas Information Exchange
TIE........... Texas Israel Exchange [*A trade and research venture*]
TIE........... TIE/Communications, Inc. [*AMEX symbol*] (SPSG)
TIE........... Tientsin [*Republic of China*] [*Seismograph station code, US Geological Survey*] (SEIS)
TIE........... Time Interval Error [*Telecommunications*] (TEL)
TIE........... Tippi [*Ethiopia*] [*Airport symbol*] (OAG)
TIE........... Toxicity Identification Evaluation
TIE........... Toyota Industrial Equipment
TIE........... Training ICON Environment
TIE........... Training Instrumentation Evaluation (MCD)
TIE........... Transient Ischemic Episode [*Medicine*]
TIE........... Travel Industry for the Environment
TI & E........ Troop Information and Education
TIEA......... Tax Information Exchange Agreement (ECON)
TIED......... Troop Information and Education Division
Tiedeman Real Prop ... Tiedeman on Real Property [*A publication*] (DLA)
Tied Lim Police Power ... Tiedeman's Treatise on the Limitations of Police Power in the United States [*A publication*] (DLA)
Tied Metsateho ... Tiedotus Metsateho [*A publication*]
Tied Mun Corp ... Tiedeman's Treatise on Municipal Corporations [*A publication*] (DLA)
Tied Valt Tekn Tutkimusl ... Tiedotus. Valtion Teknillinen Tutkimuslaitos [*A publication*]
Tied Valt Tek Tutkimuskeskus Poltto Voiteluainelab ... Tiedonanto-Valtion Teknillinen Tutkimuskeskus, Poltto-, ja Voiteluainelaboratorio [*Finland*] [*A publication*]
TIEED....... Transactions. Institute of Electronics and Communication Engineers of Japan. Section E (English) [*A publication*]
TIEG......... Teen International Entomology Group [*Later, YES*] (EA)
TIE-IN....... Technology Information Exchange-Innovation Network [*Ohio State Department of Development*] [*Information service or system*] (IID)
TIEO......... Toyota Industrial Engine Operations [*Torrance, CA*]
TIER......... Tierce [*Unit of measurement*] (ROG)
TIER......... [*The*] Tierco Group, Inc. [*NASDAQ symbol*] (NQ)
Tieraerztl Prax ... Tieraerztliche Praxis [*A publication*]
Tieraerztl Rd ... Tieraerztliche Rundschau [*A publication*]
Tieraerztl Rundsch ... Tieraerztliche Rundschau [*A publication*]
Tieraerztl Rundschau ... Tieraerztliche Rundschau [*A publication*]
Tieraerztl Umsch ... Tieraerztliche Umschau [*A publication*]
Tieraerztl Z ... Tieraerztliche Zeitschrift [*A publication*]
Tierernaehr Fuetter ... Tierernaehrung und Fuetterung [*A publication*]
Tier Erzeu .. Viehbestand und Tierische Erzeugung Land und Forstwirtschaft Fischerei [*A publication*]
Tierphysiol Tierernaehr Futtermittelk ... Tierphysiologie, Tierernaehrung, und Futtermittelkunde [*A publication*]
Tierra y Soc ... Tierra y Sociedad [*A publication*]

TIERS........ Title I Evaluation and Reporting System [*Department of Education*]
TIES .... Tactical Information Exchange System [*Navy*] (MCD)
TIES .... Technological Information Exchange System [*UNIDO*]
TIES .... Textbook Information and Exchange Service [*Regional clearinghouses for used textbooks*]
TIES .... Theater Information and Engagement System [*Military*] (MCD)
TIES .... Total Information for Educational Systems [*Saint Paul, MN*] (BUR)
TIES .... Total Integrated Engineering System
TIES .... Translators' and Interpreters' Educational Society (EA)
TIES .... Transmission and Information Exchange System
Tieteel Tutk ... Tietyeellisiae Tutkimuksia [*A publication*]
Tiet Julk Helsingin Tek Korkeakoulu ... Tieteellisia Julkaisuja. Helsingin Teknillinen Korkeakoulu [*A publication*]
TIEtn .... Trudy Instituta Etnografii Imeni N. N. Miklucho Maklaja Akademija Nauk SSSR [*A publication*]
TIEYACP ... [*The*] Information Exchange on Young Adult Chronic Patients (EA)
TIF............ [*The*] International Foundation (EA)
TIF............ Tagged Image File [*Data processing*] (PCM)
TIF............ Taif [*Saudi Arabia*] [*Airport symbol*] (OAG)
TIF............ Tape Inventory File (IEEE)
TIF............ Target Intelligence File (CINC)
TIF............ Task Initiation Force [*Nuclear energy*] (NRCH)
TIF............ Task Initiation Form [*Nuclear energy*] (NRCH)
TIF............ Tax Increment Financing
TIF............ Taxpayer Information File [*IRS*]
TIF............ Technical Information File
TIF............ Telecommunication Interference Filter [*Data processing*]
TIF............ Telephone Interference Factor (DEN)
TIF............ Terminal Independent Format
TIF............ Thin Iron Film
TIF............ Tiffany & Co. [*NYSE symbol*] (SPSG)
TIF............ Tiflis [*Tbilisi*] [*USSR*] [*Seismograph station code, US Geological Survey*] (SEIS)
TIF............ Tilapia International Foundation (EA)
TIF............ Tomato Intercellular Fluid
TIF............ Transport International par Fer [*International Transport of Goods by Railway*] [*French*]
TIF............ Treaties in Force [*A publication*] (DLA)
TIF............ True Involute Form
TIF............ Tumor-Inducing Factor [*Oncology*]
TIF............ Tumor-Infiltrating Lymphocyte [*Immunotherapy*]
TIF............ Tumor Inhibitory Factor [*Oncology*]
TIFA .... Tourist Information Facts and Abstracts [*Economic Documentation and Information Ltd.*] [*Ringmer Near Lewes, East Sussex, England*] [*Information service or system*] (IID)
Tif & Bul Tr ... Tiffany and Bullard on Trusts and Trustees [*A publication*] (DLA)
TIFF .... Tagged Image File Format [*Data processing*]
Tiff............ Tiffany's Reports [*28-39 New York Court of Appeals*] [*A publication*] (DLA)
TIFF .... Tokyo International Film Festival [*Japan*]
Tiffany .... Tiffany's Reports [*28-39 New York Court of Appeals*] [*A publication*] (DLA)
Tiffany Landlord & Ten ... Tiffany on Landlord and Tenant [*A publication*] (DLA)
Tiffany Landl & T ... Tiffany on Landlord and Tenant [*A publication*] (DLA)
Tiffany Real Prop ... Tiffany on Real Property [*A publication*] (DLA)
Tif Gov .... Tiffany on Government and Constitutional Law [*A publication*] (DLA)
TIFI .... Titus Foods, Incorporated [*NASDAQ symbol*] (NQ)
TIFO .... Technical Inspection Field Office, Office of the Inspector General
TIFO .... Technische Informationen [*A publication*]
TIFR .... Tata Institute for Fundamental Research [*British*]
TIFR .... Total Improved Frequency Response
TIFS.......... Total In-Flight Simulation [*or Simulator*] [*Air Force*]
Tif & Sm Pr ... Tiffany and Smith's New York Practice [*A publication*] (DLA)
TIG .... [*The*] Inspector General [*Army*]
TIG .... Target Image Generator
TIG .... Taxicab Industry Group (EA)
TIG .... Telegram Identification Group [*Telecommunications*] (TEL)
TIG .... Teletype Input Generator
TIG .... Tetanus Immune Globulin [*Immunology*]
tig .... Tigre [*MARC language code*] [*Library of Congress*] (LCCP)
TIG .... Tigris Minerals [*Vancouver Stock Exchange symbol*]
TIG .... Time in Grade [*Air Force*]
TIG .... Time of Ignition
TIG .... Tungsten-Inert-Gas
TIGA .... TI [*Texas Instruments, Inc.*] Graphics Architecture [*Data processing*]
TIGC.......... Topics in Inorganic and General Chemistry [*Elsevier Book Series*] [*A publication*]
TIGER .... Terrorist Intelligence Gathering Evaluation and Review [*British*]

TIGER .... Topologically Integrated Geographic Encoding and Referencing [*Bureau of the Census*]
TIGER .... Total Information Gathering and Executive Reporting [*International Computers Ltd.*]
TIGER .... Traveling Industrial Gaseous Emission Research [*Vehicle*] [*Exxon Corp.*]
TIG(H) ...... Tetanus Immune Globulin (Human) [*Immunology*]
TIGN .... Time of Ignition
TIGR......... Transmission Integrated Rotor
TIGR......... Treasury Investment Growth Receipts [*Merrill Lynch & Co.*] [*Finance*]
TIGR......... Turbine-Integrated Geared Rotor
Ti Gracch ... Tiberius Gracchus [*of Plutarch*] [*Classical studies*] (OCD)
TIGRB .... Technische Information GRW [*Geraete- und Regler Werke*] [*A publication*]
TIGRIS...... Televised Images of Gaseous Region in Interplanetary Space
TIGS .... Terminal Independent Graphics System
TIGS .... Transactions. Inverness Gaelic Society [*A publication*]
TIGT......... Turbine Inlet Gas Temperature [*Aviation*]
TIGZD....... Teikyo Igaku Zasshi
TIH .... Technical Information Handbook
TIH .... Their Imperial Highnesses
TIH .... Tikehau [*French Polynesia*] [*Airport symbol*] (OAG)
TIH .... Toromont Industries Ltd. [*Toronto Stock Exchange symbol*]
TIH .... Total Installed Horsepower
TIH .... Trinity International Holdings [*British*]
TIH .... Trunk Interface Handler
Tihanyi Biol Kutatointezetenek Evkoen ... Tihanyi Biologiai Kutatointezetenek Evkoenyve [*A publication*]
TIHP .... Total Installed Horsepower
TII............. European Association for the Transfer of Technologies, Innovation, and Industrial Information [*Information service or system*] (IID)
TII............. [*The*] Independent Institute [*An association*] (EA)
TII............. Talos Integration Investigation
TII............. Texas Instruments, Incorporated
TII............. Texas Instruments, Incorporated, IS & S Library, Dallas, TX [*OCLC symbol*] (OCLC)
TII............. Thomas Industries, Incorporated [*NYSE symbol*] (SPSG)
TII............. Tiffin, OH [*Location identifier*] [*FAA*] (FAAL)
TII............. Tooling Inspection Instrumentation (NASA)
TII............. Total Inactive Aerospace Vehicle [*or Aircraft*] Inventory
TII............. Trusteeship Institute, Incorporated (EA)
TIIAE .... Trudy Instituta Istorii, Archeologii, i Etnografii [*A publication*]
TIIAL .... [*The*] International Institute of Applied Linguistics
TIIC .... Technical Industrial Intelligence Committee [*US Military Government, Germany*]
TIID.......... Technical Industrial Intelligence Division [*Allied Board set up to send experts into Germany to ferret out Germany's war-developed scientific secrets*] [*Post-World War II*]
TIIF .... Tactical Imagery Interpretation Facility [*Military*]
TIIPS......... Technically Improved Interference Prediction System (IEEE)
TIJ .... Tijuana [*Mexico*] [*Airport symbol*] (OAG)
TIJa .... Trudy Instituta Jazykoznanija [*A publication*]
Tijd............ Onze Tijd [*A publication*]
Tijd Ec Soc ... Tijdschrift voor Economische en Sociale Geografie [*A publication*]
Tijd Ec Soc Geogr ... Tijdschrift voor Economische en Sociale Geografie [*A publication*]
Tijd Ent...... Tijdschrift voor Entomologie [*A publication*]
Tijd Filos.... Tijdschrift voor Filosofie [*A publication*]
Tijd Gesch ... Tijdschrift voor Geschiedenis [*A publication*]
Tijd Ind TLV ... Tijdschrift voor Indische Taal-, Land-, en Volkenkunde [*A publication*]
Tijd ITL ..... Tijdschrift van het Instituut voor Toegepaste Linguistiek [*A publication*]
Tijd Kindergeneeskd ... Tijdschrift voor Kindergeneeskunde [*A publication*]
Tijd Logop Audiol ... Tijdschrift voor Logopedie en Audiologie [*A publication*]
Tijd Ned T ... Tijdschrift voor Nederlandsche Taal- en Letterkunde [*A publication*]
Tijd Phil..... Tijdschrift voor Philosophie [*A publication*]
Tijd Psych ... Tijdschrift voor Psychiatrie [*A publication*]
Tijd R Gesch ... Tijdschrift voor Rechtsgeschiedenis [*A publication*]
Tijdschr Bestuursw ... Tijdschrift voor Bestuurswetenschappen [*A publication*]
Tijdschr Diergeneeskd ... Tijdschrift voor Diergeneeskunde [*A publication*]
Tijdschr Diergeneeskd Q Engl Issue ... Tijdschrift voor Diergeneeskunde. Quarterly English Issue [*A publication*]
Tijdschr Econ Soc Geogr ... Tijdschrift voor Economische en Sociale Geografie [*A publication*]
Tijdschr Ent ... Tijdschrift voor Entomologie [*A publication*]
Tijdschr Entomol ... Tijdschrift voor Entomologie [*A publication*]
Tijdschr Filosof ... Tijdschrift voor Filosofie [*A publication*]
Tijdschr Gastro-Enterol ... Tijdschrift voor Gastro-Enterologie [*A publication*]
Tijdschr Gemeent ... Tijdschrift voor Gemeenten [*A publication*]
Tijdschr Geneeskd ... Tijdschrift voor Geneeskunde [*A publication*]
Tijdschr Geschied Natuurwet Wiskd Tec ... Tijdschrift voor Geschiedenis Natuurwetenschap Wiskundig. Techniek [*A publication*]

Tijdschrift voor Econ en Soc Geog ... Tijdschrift voor Economische en Sociale Geografie [*A publication*]
Tijdschrift Taal & Lett ... Tijdschrift voor Taal en Letteren [*A publication*]
Tijdschr Ind Taal- Land- en Volkenkunde ... Tijdschrift voor Indische Taal-, Land-, en Volkenkunde [*A publication*]
Tijdschr Kindergeneeskd ... Tijdschrift voor Kindergeneeskunde [*A publication*]
Tijdschr K Ned Heidemaatsch ... Tijdschrift der Koninklijke Nederlandsche Heidemaatschappij [*A publication*]
Tijdschr d Ktg ... Tijdschrift der Kantongerechten [*A publication*]
Tijdschr Lev Talen ... Tijdschrift voor Levende Talen [*A publication*]
Tijdschr Ned Dierkd Ver ... Tijdschrift der Nederlandsche Dierkundige Vereniging [*A publication*]
Tijdschr Ned Elektron- & Radiogenoot ... Tijdschrift van het Nederlands Elektronica- en Radiogenootschap [*A publication*]
Tijdschr Ned Heidemaatsch ... Tijdschrift der Nederlandsche Heidemaatschappij [*A publication*]
Tijdschr Ned TL ... Tijdschrift voor Nederlandsche Taal- en Letterkunde [*A publication*]
Tijdschr Ned Ver Klin Chem ... Tijdschrift van de Nederlandse Vereniging voor Klinische Chemie [*A publication*]
Tijdschr Oppervlaktetech Mater ... Tijdschrift voor Oppervlaktetechnieken van Materialen [*A publication*]
Tijdschr Oppervlakte Tech Metal ... Tijdschrift voor Oppervlakte Technieken van Metalen [*A publication*]
Tijdschr Plantenz ... Tijdschrift voor Plantenziekten [*A publication*]
Tijdschr Plantenziekten ... Tijdschrift voor Plantenziekten [*A publication*]
Tijdschr Polit ... Tijdschrift voor Politicologie [*Netherlands*] [*A publication*]
Tijdschr Primaire Energ ... Tijdschrift Primaire Energie [*Belgium*] [*A publication*]
Tijdschr Soc Geneeskd ... Tijdschrift voor Sociale Geneeskunde [*A publication*]
Tijdschr Strafrecht ... Tijdschrift voor Strafrecht [*A publication*]
Tijdschr Stud Verlichting ... Tijdschrift voor Studie. Verlichting [*A publication*]
Tijdschr Ther Geneesmiddel Onderz ... Tijdschrift voor Therapie, Geneesmiddel, en Onderzoek [*A publication*]
Tijdschr Veeartsenijk ... Tijdschrift voor Veeartsenijkunde [*A publication*]
Tijdschr Veeartsenijk en Veeteelt ... Tijdschrift voor Veeartsenijkunde en Veeteelt [*A publication*]
Tijdschr Ziekenverpl ... Tijdschrift voor Ziekenverpleging [*A publication*]
Tijds Econ ... Tijdschrift voor Economie [*A publication*]
Tijds Gem Recht ... Tijdschrift voor Gemeenterecht [*A publication*]
Tijds Not ... Tijdschrift voor Notarissen [*A publication*]
Tijd Soc Wet ... Tijdschrift voor Sociale Wetenschappen [*A publication*]
Tijds Priv ... Tijdschrift voor Privaatrecht [*A publication*]
Tijds Soc Wetensch ... Tijdschrift voor Sociale Wetenschappen [*A publication*]
TIJI ... Tribune Internationale des Jeunes Interpretes [*International Rostrum of Young Performers - IRP*] (EAIO)
TIK ... Oklahoma City, OK [*Location identifier*] [*FAA*] (FAAL)
TIK ... Target Indicator Kit
TIK ... Tiara Enterprises Ltd. [*Vancouver Stock Exchange symbol*]
TIK ... Tiksi [*USSR*] [*Seismograph station code, US Geological Survey*] (SEIS)
TIK ... Tixie [*USSR*] [*Geomagnetic observatory code*]
TIKKB8 ... Trudy Nauchno-Issledovatel'skogo Instituta Kartofel'nogo Khozyaistva [*A publication*]
TIKP ... Turkiye Isci Koylu Partisi [*Worker-Peasant Party of Turkey*] [*Political party*] (PD)
TIL ... Taiwan International Line Ltd. (DS)
TIL ... Temperature Indicating Label
TIL ... Temporary Instructor Lieutenant [*Navy*] [*British*]
TIL ... Tilco Aviation Co., Inc. [*Baton Rouge, LA*] [*FAA designator*] (FAAC)
Til ... Tilskueren [*A publication*]
TIL ... Travaux. Institut de Linguistique [*A publication*]
TIL ... Tree Island Industries Ltd. [*Toronto Stock Exchange symbol*] [*Vancouver Stock Exchange symbol*]
TIL ... Tumor Infiltrating Lymphocyte [*Oncology*]
TIL ... Until (FAAC)
TILA ... Telemail International Licensees' Association (TSSD)
TILA ... Truth-in-Lending Act [*1968*]
TILAS ... Travaux. Institut d'Etudes Latino-Americaines. Universite de Strasbourg [*A publication*]
TILE ... Color Tile, Inc. [*NASDAQ symbol*] (NQ)
TILF ... Tactical Integrity Loss Factor
TILL ... Total Initial Lamp Lumens
Tillman ... Tillman's Reports [*68, 69, 71, 73, 75 Alabama*] [*A publication*] (DLA)
TILLO ... Transfer in Lieu of Layoff (MCD)
Till & Yates App ... Tillinghast and Yates on Appeals [*A publication*] (DLA)
TILMC ... Tobacco Industry Labor/Management Committee (EA)
TILO ... Technical Industrial Liaison Office
Til Prec ... Tillinghast's Precedents [*A publication*] (DLA)
TILRA ... Tribal Indian Land Rights Association (EA)
TILS ... Tactical Instrument Landing System
TILS ... Technical Information & Liaison Service [*Information service or system*] (EISS)
Til & Sh Pr ... Tillinghast and Shearman's New York Practice [*A publication*] (DLA)

TILSRA ... Truth-in-Lending Simplification and Reform Act [*1980*]
Tils St L ... Tilsley on Stamp Laws [*3rd ed.*] [*1871*] [*A publication*] (DLA)
TILT ... Taxpayer Inquiry Lookup Table [*IRS*]
TILT ... Transmission Intercept and Landing Terminated (MCD)
TIM ... Table Input to Memory
TIM ... Tangential Inlet Manifold
TIM ... Target Intelligence Material (MCD)
TIM ... Technical Information Manual
TIM ... Technical Information on Microfilm [*British*] (DIT)
TIM ... Technical Interchange Meeting (NASA)
TIM ... TEFLON Insulation Material
TIM ... Tembagapura [*Indonesia*] [*Airport symbol*] (OAG)
TIM ... Temperature Indicator Monitor
TIM ... Test Instrumented Missile [*Army*]
TIM ... Test Interface Module (CAAL)
TIM ... Test Item Malfunction (MCD)
TIM ... Texas Instruments, Inc., Central Library Services, Dallas, TX [*OCLC symbol*] (OCLC)
TIM ... Thailand Independence Movement [*Communist-directed activity outside Thailand*] [*Merged with TPF*]
TIM ... Ticket Issue Machines
TIM ... Time [*A publication*]
TIM ... Time Indicator, Miniature (MUGU)
TIM ... Time Interval Measurement
TIM ... Time Interval Meter
TIM ... Time Interval Monitor (NASA)
TIM ... Time Meter (AAG)
Tim. ... Timely [*Record label*]
TIM ... Timisoara [*Romania*] [*Seismograph station code, US Geological Survey*] (SEIS)
TIM ... Timminco Ltd. [*Toronto Stock Exchange symbol*]
Tim. ... Timoleon [*of Plutarch*] [*Classical studies*] (OCD)
Tim. ... Timon of Athens [*Shakespearean work*]
Tim. ... Timothy [*New Testament book*]
TIM ... Titanium Mesh [*Medicine*]
TIM ... Token/Net Interface Module [*Telecommunications*] (TSSD)
TIM ... Topic Indexing Matrix
TIM ... Total Ion Scanning Mode [*Spectroscopy*]
TIM ... Track Imitation (MSA)
TIM ... Track Initiator Monitor (CAAL)
TIM ... Tracking Information Memorandum
TIM ... Tracking Instruction Manual
TIM ... Tracking Instrument Mount (MUGU)
TIM ... Transient Intermodulation [*Distortion*]
TIM ... Transistor Information Microfile
TIM ... Trigger Inverter Module
TIM ... Triose Phosphate Isomerase [*An enzyme*]
TIMA ... Technical Illustrators Management Association [*Later, IG*]
TIMA ... Truth in Mileage Act of 1986
TIMAR ... Near-Term Improvement in Materiel Asset Reporting [*Military*] (AABC)
Timarit Hjukrunarfel Isl ... Timarit Hjukrunarfelags Islands [*Reykjavik*] [*A publication*]
Timarit Verkfraedingafelags Is ... Timarit Verkfraedingafelags Islands [*A publication*]
TIMATION ... Time Location System [*Navy*]
TIMB ... Timballes [*Kettle drum*]
TIMB ... Timber (ADA)
TIMB ... Timberland Industries, Inc. [*NASDAQ symbol*] (NQ)
Timb Bull Eur ... Timber Bulletin for Europe [*A publication*]
Timb Bull Europe FAO ... Timber Bulletin for Europe. Food and Agricultural Organization [*A publication*]
Timber B ... Timber Bulletin for Europe [*A publication*]
Timber BAR ... Timber Bulletin for Europe. Annual Forest Products Market Review [*A publication*]
Timber BFS ... Timber Bulletin for Europe. Forest Fire Statistics [*A publication*]
Timber B (Hu) ... Timber Bulletin for Europe. Forest and Forest Products Country Profile (Hungary) [*A publication*]
Timber B Pr ... Timber Bulletin for Europe. Monthly Prices for Forest Products. Supplement [*A publication*]
Timber BWP ... Timber Bulletin for Europe. Survey of the Wood-Based Panels Industries [*A publication*]
Timber Dev Assoc Inf Bull A/IB ... Timber Development Association. Information Bulletin A/IB [*A publication*]
Timber Dev Assoc Inf Bull B/IB ... Timber Development Association. Information Bulletin B/IB [*A publication*]
Timber Dev Assoc Inf Bull G/IB ... Timber Development Association. Information Bulletin G/IB [*A publication*]
Timber Dev Assoc Res Rep C/RR ... Timber Development Association. Research Report C/RR [*A publication*]
Timber Res Dev Assoc Res Rep C/RR ... Timber Research and Development Association. Research Report C/RR [*A publication*]
Timber Sit ... An Analysis of the Timber Situation in the United States 1952-2030 [*A publication*]
Timber Supp Rev ... Timber Supply Review [*A publication*] (APTA)
Timber Technol ... Timber Technology [*A publication*]
Timber Trades J ... Timber Trades Journal and Woodworking Machinery [*Later, Timber Trades Journal and Wood Processing*] [*A publication*]
Timb Grower ... Timber Grower [*A publication*]

Timb Leafl For Dep (Brit Solomon Islands Protect) ... Timber Leaflet. Forestry Department (British Solomon Islands Protectorate) [*A publication*]
Timb Leafl For Dep (Kenya) ... Timber Leaflet. Forest Department (Nairobi, Kenya) [*A publication*]
Timb Leafl For Dep (Uganda) ... Timber Leaflet. Forest Department (Uganda) [*A publication*]
Timb & Plyw Ann ... Timber and Plywood Annual [*A publication*]
Timb Pres Assoc Aust ... Timber Preservers' Association of Australia. Pamphlet [*A publication*]   (APTA)
Timb Trades J Wood Process ... Timber Trades Journal and Wood Processing [*A publication*]
Timb Tr J ... Timber Trades Journal [*A publication*]
TIM/DL .... Trunk Interface Module for Data Links [*Telecommunications*]
TIME .... Technique for Information Management and Employment
TIME .... Time Energy Systems [*NASDAQ symbol*]   (NQ)
Time A .... Time Australia [*A publication*]   (APTA)
TIMEA .... Transactions. Institute of Marine Engineers [*A publication*]
Time (Can) ... Time (Canada) [*A publication*]
Timely Turf Top ... Timely Turf Topics [*A publication*]
Time-Picay ... Times-Picayune [*A publication*]
Times Br Col R ... Times British Colonies Review [*A publication*]
Times Ednl Supp ... Times Educational Supplement [*A publication*]
Times Educ Supp ... Times Educational Supplement [*A publication*]
Times Higher Ed Supp ... Times Higher Education Supplement [*A publication*]
Times Higher Educ Supp ... Times Higher Education Supplement [*A publication*]
Times Higher Educ Suppl ... Times Higher Education Supplement [*A publication*]
Times Ind A ... Times of India Annual [*Bombay*] [*A publication*]
Times L .... Times Literary Supplement [*A publication*]
Times L (Eng) ... Times Law Reports [*England*] [*A publication*]   (DLA)
Times Lit Supp ... Times Literary Supplement [*A publication*]
Times Lit Suppl ... Times Literary Supplement [*A publication*]
Times (Lond) ... Times (London) [*A publication*]
Times LR ... Times Law Reports [*Ceylon*] [*A publication*]   (DLA)
Times LR ... Times Law Reports [*England*] [*A publication*]   (DLA)
Times L Rep ... Times Law Reports [*Ceylon*] [*A publication*]   (DLA)
Times L Rep ... Times Law Reports [*England*] [*A publication*]   (DLA)
Times Rev Ind ... Times Review of Industry [*A publication*]
Times R Ind ... Times Review of Industry [*A publication*]
Times R Ind & Tech ... Times Review of Industry and Technology [*A publication*]
Times Sci Rev ... Times Science Review [*A publication*]
Times Trib ... Times Tribune [*A publication*]
TIMFA ...... Transactions. Institute of Metal Finishing [*A publication*]
TIMI .... Technical Information Maintenance Instruction
TIMI .... Thrombolysis in Myocardial Infarction (Study) [*Medicine*]
TIMIG .... Time in Grade [*Army*]
TIMINT ..... Time Interval   (AABC)
Timisoara Inst Politeh Traian Vuia Bul Stiint Teh Ser Chim ... Timisoara. Institutul Politehnic "Traian Vuia." Buletinul Stiintific si Tehnic. Seria Chimie [*A publication*]
Timisoara Med ... Timisoara Medicala [*Romania*] [*A publication*]
TIMIX .... [*The*] International Microcomputer Information Exchange   (EA)
TiMixE ...... TI-MIX [*Texas Instruments Mini/Microcomputer Information Exchange*] Europe   (EA)
TIMM .... Thermionic Integrated Micromodule
TIMM .... Timberline Minerals, Inc. [*NASDAQ symbol*]   (NQ)
TIMMS ..... Total Integrated Manpower Management System
TIMP .... Tavistock Institute of Medical Psychology [*British*]
TIMP .... Texas Instructional Media Project [*Education*]
TIMP .... Timpani [*Kettle drum*]
TIMP .... Tissue Inhibitor of Metalloproteinases [*Biochemistry*]
TIMS .... [*The*] Institute of Management Sciences [*Providence, RI*]   (EA)
TIMS .... [*The*] International Molinological Society   (EA)
TIMS .... Tactical Incapacitating Munitions System   (MCD)
TIMS .... Technology Integration of Missile Subsystems   (MCD)
TIMS .... Telephone Information and Management Systems   (ADA)
TIMS .... Test Interactive Management System
TIMS .... Text Information and Management System [*Data processing*]
TIMS .... Thermal Infrared Multispectral Scanner [*Airborne instrument for geological applications*]
TIMS .... Thermal Ionization Mass Spectrometry
TIMS .... Time Sharing Resources, Inc. [*NASDAQ symbol*]   (NQ)
TIMS .... Total Ion Measurement Source
TIMS .... Transmission Impairment Measuring Set [*Telecommunications*]   (TEL)
TIN .... Ebanewsletter. Daily Economic and Political News Indicators from Turkey [*A publication*]
TIN .... Taro Industries Ltd. [*Toronto Stock Exchange symbol*]
TIN .... Task Implementation Notice
TIN .... Taxpayer Identification Number [*IRS*]
TIN .... Temperature Independent [*Ferrite computer memory core*]
TIN .... Temple-Inland, Inc. [*NYSE symbol*]   (SPSG)
TIN .... Temporary Identification Number [*Military*]
TIN .... Temporary Instruction Notice
TIN .... Ter in Nocte [*Three Times a Night*] [*Pharmacy*]

Tin .... [*Alfanus*] Tindarus [*Flourished, 15th century*] [*Authority cited in pre-1607 legal work*]   (DSA)
TIN .... Tindouf [*Algeria*] [*Airport symbol*]   (OAG)
TIN .... Tinemaha [*California*] [*Seismograph station code, US Geological Survey*]   (SEIS)
TIN .... Transaction Identification Number   (AFM)
TIN .... Tubulointerstitial Nephritis [*Nephrology*]
TINA .... There Is No Alternative [*Nickname given to British Prime Minister Margaret Thatcher because she so often uses this phrase to defend her government's economic policies*]
TINC .... Tincture   (ADA)
TINCT .... Tinctura [*Tincture*] [*Pharmacy*]
Tind .... [*Alfanus*] Tindarus [*Flourished, 15th century*] [*Authority cited in pre-1607 legal work*]   (DSA)
TINDECO ... Tin Decorating Company
TINDX ...... Texas Instruments Index Access Method
TINE .... There Is No Excuse   (ECON)
TI-NET .... Transparent Intelligent Network
TINET .... Travel Industry Network, Inc. [*Winter Springs, FL*] [*Telecommunications*]   (TSSD)
TINFO .... Tieteellisen Informoinnin Neuvosto [*Finnish Council for Scientific Information and Research Libraries*] [*Helsinki*] [*Information service or system*]   (IID)
TIN/FS ...... Taxpayer Identification Number/File Source [*IRS*]
Tingo Maria Peru Est Exp Agric Bol ... Tingo Maria, Peru. Estacion Experimental Agricola. Boletin [*A publication*]
Tin Int .... Tin International [*A publication*]
Tin Inter ...... Tin International [*A publication*]
Tin Intern ..... Tin International [*A publication*]
Tink .... Two Incomes, No Kids [*Lifestyle classification*]
TINKER .... Timber Information Keyword Retrieval [*Timber Research and Development Association*] [*Information service or system*]   (IID)
TINNER .... Tea and Dinner [*Slang*] [*British*]   (DSUE)
TINOP .... Transponder Inoperative [*Aviation*]   (FAAC)
Tin Print Box Mkr ... Tin-Printer and Box Maker [*A publication*]
TINR .... Target Identification Navigation RADAR
Tin Res Inst (Greenford Engl) Publ ... Tin Research Institute (Greenford, England). Publication [*A publication*]
TINS .... Thermal Imaging Navigation Set [*Hughes Aircraft Co.*] [*Navy*]   (ECON)
TINS .... Trends in Neurosciences [*A publication*]
Tinsley .... Tinsley's Magazine [*A publication*]
TINSTAAFL ... There Is No Such Thing as a Free Lunch [*Principle of economics indicating that one cannot get something for nothing*] [*See also TANSTAAFL*]
TINS Trends Neurosci ... TINS. Trends in Neurosciences [*A publication*]
TINSY .... Treasure Island Naval Shipyard [*San Francisco Bay*]
TINT .... Target Intercept Timer   (MCD)
TINTM .... Triisononyl Trimellitate [*Organic chemistry*]
TINTS .... Tactical Intelligence Transfer System
TINTS .... Turret Integrated Night Thermal Sight
Tin Uses ..... Tin and Its Uses [*A publication*]
Tinw .... Tinwald's Reports, Scotch Court of Session [*A publication*]   (DLA)
TIO .... Target Indication Officer [*Navy*]
TIO .... Technical Information Office
TIO .... Technology Integration Office [*Army*]   (RDA)
TIO .... Television Information Office [*Defunct*]   (EA)
TIO .... Test Input/Output [*Data processing*]
TIO .... Time Interval Optimization   (IEEE)
TIO .... Tiouine [*Morocco*] [*Seismograph station code, US Geological Survey*]   (SEIS)
TIO .... Transistorized Image Orthicon
TIO .... Troop Information Officer
TIOC .... Terminal Input/Output Coordinator [*Data processing*]   (IBMDP)
TIOC .... Triumph International Owners Club   (EA)
TIOF .... [*The*] International Osprey Foundation   (EA)
TIOH .... [*The*] Institute of Heraldry [*Military*]
TIOKA .... Trudy Instituta Okeanologii Akademiya Nauk SSSR [*A publication*]
TIOLR .... Texas Instruments Online Reporting System [*Data processing*]
TIOM .... Terminal Input/Output Module [*Data processing*]
TIOOA ...... Transactions. Indiana Academy of Ophthalmology and Otolaryngology [*A publication*]
TIOS .... Tactical Integrated Ocean Surveillance [*Military*]   (CAAL)
TIOT .... Task Input/Output Table [*Data processing*]   (BUR)
TIOTM ...... Triisooctyl Trimellitate [*Organic chemistry*]
TIOWQ ..... Terminal Input/Output Wait Queue [*Data processing*]
TIP .... [*The*] Information Partnership [*Information service or system*]   (IID)
TIP .... [*The*] Information Place [*Information service or system*]   (EISS)
TIP .... Tactical Improvement Program [*Military*]
TIP .... Tactile Information Presentation [*Biotechnology*]
TIP .... Target Identification Point   (NATG)
TIP .... Target Impact Point
TIP .... Target Industries Program [*Occupational Safety and Health Administration*]
TIP .... Target Input Panel

TIP...........	Target Intelligence Package (MCD)
TIP...........	Task Initiation and Prediction
TIP...........	Tax-Based Incomes Policy
TIP...........	Taxpayer Information Processing [*IRS*]
TIP...........	Teachers Instructional Plan
TIP...........	Technical Improvement Program
TIP...........	Technical Information Panel [*AEC*] [*Terminated, 1971*]
TIP...........	Technical Information Pilot [*A publication*] [*Obsolete*]
TIP...........	Technical Information Pool
TIP...........	Technical Information Processing (IEEE)
TIP...........	Technical Information Program
TIP...........	Technical Information Project [*MIT*]
TIP...........	Technology Internship Program [*Oak Ridge National Laboratory*]
TIP...........	Tehrik-i-Istiqlal [*Solidarity Party*] [*See also TI*] [*Political party*] [*Pakistan*] (FEA)
TIP...........	TELENET Interface Processor
TIP...........	Telephone Information Processing (MCD)
TIP...........	Teletype Input Processing
TIP...........	Temperature-Independent Paramagnetism
TIP...........	Terminal Impact Prediction
TIP...........	Terminal Interface Package [*Data processing*]
TIP...........	Terminal Interface [*Message*] Processor [*Data processing*] [*DoD*]
TIP...........	Tests in Print [*A publication*]
TIP...........	Theory into Practice [*A publication*]
TIP...........	Thrust Inlet Pressure (MCD)
TIP...........	Tiburon Petroleum [*Vancouver Stock Exchange symbol*]
TIP...........	Tilt Isolation Platform
TIP...........	Times of Increased Probability [*Earthquake prediction*]
TIP...........	TIROS [*Television and Infrared Observation Satellite*] Information Processor [*Telecommunications*]
TIP...........	To Insure Promptness
TIP...........	Tool Inventors Program [*Automobile tool design*]
TIP...........	Total Information Processing (BUR)
TIP...........	Total Isomerization Process [*Petroleum refining*]
TIP...........	Toxic Integration Program [*Environmental Protection Agency*]
TIP...........	Toxicology Information Program [*National Library of Medicine*] [*Bethesda, MD*]
TIP...........	Track Initiation and Prediction [*RADAR*]
TIP...........	Tracking Impact Prediction [*of satellites*]
TIP...........	Trans-Israel Pipeline
TIP...........	Transaction Interface Package [*Sperry UNIVAC*] [*Data processing*]
TIP...........	Transaction Interface Processor
TIP...........	Transient [*or Traveling or Traversing*] In-Core Probe [*Nuclear energy*] (NRCH)
TIP...........	Transit Improvement Program [*Satellite*] (MCD)
TIP...........	Translation Inhibitory Protein
TIP...........	Transponder Interrogator Processor
TIP...........	Transport Individuel Publique [*Also known as PROCOTIP*] [*French auto cooperative*]
TIP...........	Transportation Improvement Program
TIP...........	Tripoli [*Libya*] [*Airport symbol*] (OAG)
TIP...........	Troop Information Program
TIP...........	Truth in Press [*An association*] (EA)
TIP...........	Tumor-Inducing Principle [*Plant cytology*]
TIP...........	Tumor Inhibitory Principle [*Oncology*]
TIP...........	Turbine Inlet Pressure (MSA)
TIP...........	Turn In a Pusher [*Organization combating drug traffic*]
TIP...........	Until Past [*Followed by place*] (FAAC)
TIPA........	Triisopropanolamine [*Organic chemistry*]
TIPACS.....	Texas Instruments Planning and Control System
TIPAT	Technical Information on Patents [*Swiss Intellectual Property Office*] [*Bern*] [*Information service or system*] (IID)
TIPB........	Triisopropylbenzene [*Also, TIB*] [*Organic chemistry*]
TIPC.........	Texas Instruments Pressure Controller
TIPCC	TI [*Texas Instruments*] Programmable Calculator Club (EA)
TIPE.........	Transponder, Interrogator, Pinger, and Echo Sounder
Tip Fak Mecm ...	Tip Fakultesi Mecmuasi. Istanbul Universitesi [*A publication*]
TIPG.........	Thomson Information/Publishing Group [*The Thomson Corp.*]
TIPGA.......	Trudy Instituta Prikladnoi Geofiziki [*A publication*]
TIPI..........	Tactical Information Processing and Interpretation [*Military*] (AFM)
TIPI..........	Transportable Automated Intelligence Processing and Interpretation System (MCD)
TIPIC........	Turkish Investment Promotion and Information Center [*Subdivision of the Union of Chambers of Commerce, Industry, and Commodity Exchanges of Turkey*]
TIPITEF....	Tactical Information Processing and Interpretation Total Environment Facility (MCD)
TIPL.........	Tactical Imagery Processing Laboratory [*Army*] (MCD)
TIPL.........	Tactical Information Processing Laboratory [*Army*] (MCD)
TIPL.........	Teach Information Processing Language
TIPMG......	[*The*] International Project Management Group, Inc. [*Glyndon, MD*] [*Telecommunications*] (TSSD)
TIPN........	International Platinum Corp. [*NASDAQ symbol*] (NQ)
TIPP.........	Technology and Information Policy Program [*Syracuse University*] [*Research center*] (RCD)
TIPP.........	Time Phasing Program [*NASA*] (KSC)

TIPP	Tipperary [*County in Ireland*]
TIPPS.......	Tetraiodophenolphthalein Sodium [*Pharmacology*]
TIPPS.......	Total In-House Publication Production System (MCD)
TIPR........	Tactics Inspection Procedures Report
TIPR........	Tipperary Corp. [*NASDAQ symbol*] (NQ)
TIPRE.......	Tactical Inertial Performance Requirements (MCD)
TIPRO......	Texas Independent Producers and Royalty Owners Association (EA)
TIPRO Rep ...	TIPRO [*Texas Independent Producers and Royalty Owners Association*] Reporter [*A publication*]
TIPS	[*The*] Italia Philatelic Society (EA)
TIPS	Tactical Imagery Processing Set
TIPS	Tactical Information about Perilous Situations [*New York City Fire Department program*]
TIPS	Tactical Information Processing System [*Military*] (CAAL)
TIPS	Teaching Individual Protective Strategies and Teaching Individual Positive Solutions [*In association name TIPS Program*] (EA)
TIPS	Teaching Information Processing System
TIPS	Technical Information Periodicals Service [*General Electric Co.*]
TIPS	Technical Information Processing System [*Rockwell International Corp.*] [*Downey, CA*] (AFM)
TIPS	Technical Information for Product Safety [*Consumer Product Safety Commission*] (IID)
TIPS	Technical Information and Product Service
TIPS	Techniques in Product Selection [*National Association of Manufacturers*]
TIPS	Telemetry Impact Prediction System [*Air Force*]
TIPS	Telemetry Integrated Processing System [*Air Force*]
TIPS	Terminal Information Processing System [*Aviation*] (FAAC)
TIPS	Test Information Processing System [*Air Force*]
TIPS	Text Information Processing System
TIPS	Textile Industry Product Safety [*A publication*]
TIPS	Thermally Induced Phase Separation [*Chemistry*]
Tips	Tiny Income, Parents Supporting [*Lifestyle classification*]
TIPS	Total Information Processing System [*Veterans Administration*]
TIPS	Total Integrated Pneumatic System (MCD)
TIPS	Transistorized Inverter Power Supply
TIPS	Transportation Induced Pollution Surveillance [*Marine science*] (MSC)
TIPS	Trends in Pharmacological Sciences [*A publication*]
TIPS	Truevision Image Processing Software [*AT & T*]
TIPSY.......	Task Input Parameter Synthesizer
TIPT	Tipton Centers, Inc. [*St. Louis, MO*] [*NASDAQ symbol*] (NQ)
TIP/TAP ...	Target Input Panel and Target Assign Panel
TIPTOP....	Tape Input - Tape Output [*Honeywell, Inc.*] [*Data processing*]
TIP TOP....	Tax Information Plan and Total Owed Purchase Accounting
TIQ	Paris, TN [*Location identifier*] [*FAA*] (FAAL)
TIQ	Task Input Queue [*Data processing*] (IBMDP)
TIQ	Tetrahydroisoquinoline [*Biochemistry*]
TIQ	Tinian [*Mariana Islands*] [*Airport symbol*] (OAG)
TI/QC.......	Technical Inspection/Quality Control (MCD)
TIQRC.......	Toxicology Information Query Response Center [*National Library of Medicine*]
TIR...........	Target Illuminating RADAR [*Air Force*]
TIR...........	Target Indication Room [*Navy*]
TIR...........	Target Industries [*Industry segments which have been selected by the US Department of Commerce for special trade promotion emphasis*]
TIR...........	Target Instruction Register
TIR...........	Technical Information Release
TIR...........	Technical Information Report (IEEE)
TIR...........	Technical Intelligence Report
TIR...........	Telecommunications Industry Research [*British*] (ECON)
TIR...........	Terminal Imaging RADAR [*Military*] (RDA)
TIR...........	Terminal Innervation Ratio [*Psychiatry*]
TIR...........	Test Incidence and Reporting System
tir.............	Tigrina [*MARC language code*] [*Library of Congress*] (LCCP)
TIR...........	Time in Rate
TIR...........	Tirana [*Albania*] [*Seismograph station code, US Geological Survey*] (SEIS)
TIR...........	Tirupati [*India*] [*Airport symbol*] (OAG)
TIR...........	Tolerance in Radius
TIR...........	Tooling Investigation Report
TIR...........	Total Immunoreaction [*Immunochemistry*]
TIR...........	Total Indicated Runout
TIR...........	Total Indicator Reading
TIR...........	Total Internal Reflecting
TIR...........	Total Item Record (MCD)
TIR...........	Transaction Item Report [*Navy*] (NG)
TIR...........	Transmission Infrared [*Spectroscopy*]
TIR...........	Transport International Routier [*International Transport of Goods by Road*] [*French*]
TIRA........	Thrift Industry Recovery Act [*1987*]
TIRA........	Thrift Institutions Restructuring Act [*1982*]
TIRACS.....	Telecommanded Inertially Referenced Attitude Control System (MCD)
Tiraq	[*Andreas*] Tiraquellus [*Deceased, 1558*] [*Authority cited in pre-1607 legal work*] (DSA)

3406 Acronyms, Initialisms & Abbreviations Dictionary • 1992

Tiraquel ..... [*Andreas*] Tiraquellus [*Deceased, 1558*] [*Authority cited in pre-1607 legal work*]   (DSA)

TIRAS .... Technical Information Retrieval and Analysis System   (CAAL)

Tiraspol Gos Ped Inst Ucen Zap ... Tiraspol'skii Gosudarstvennyi Pedagogiceskii Institut Imeni T. G. Sevcenko. Ucenyi Zapiski [*A publication*]

TIRB .... Transportation Insurance Rating Bureau [*Later, AAIS*]   (EA)

TIRC .... T Tauri Infrared Companion [*Object believed to be first planet sighted that is not in our solar system*]

TIRC .... Tobacco Industry Research Committee   (EA)

TIRC .... Toxicology Information Research Center [*Department of Energy*] [*Oak Ridge National Laboratory*] [*Oak Ridge, TN*]

TIRC .... Toxicology Information Response Center [*Information service or system*]   (EISS)

TIRE .... One Liberty Firestone [*NASDAQ symbol*]   (NQ)

TIRE .... Tank Infrared Elbow [*Night vision device*] [*Army*]   (RDA)

TIRE .... Tires as Imaginative Recreation Equipment

TIREC .... TIROS [*Television and Infrared Observation Satellite*] Ice Reconnaissance [*NASA*]

Tire Dealr .. Modern Tire Dealer [*A publication*]

Tire Rev ..... Tire Review [*A publication*]

Tire Rev D ... Tire Review. 1986 Sourcebook and Directory [*A publication*]

Tire Sci Technol ... Tire Science and Technology [*A publication*]

TIRF .... Total Internal Reflection Fluorescence

TIRF .... Traffic Injury Research Foundation of Canada [*Research center*]   (RCD)

TIRH .... Theoretical Indoor Relative Humidity

TIRIS .... Traversing Infrared Inspection System   (MCD)

TIRJa .... Trudy Instituto Russkogo Jazyka [*A publication*]

TIRKS ...... Trunks Integrated Record Keeping System [*Bell System*]

TIRM .... Transparent Infrared Material

TIRMMS .. Technical Information Reports for Music-Media Specialists [*Music Library Association publication series*]

TIROD ...... Test Instruction Record of Discussion   (MCD)

T Iron St I ... Transactions. Iron and Steel Institute of Japan [*A publication*]

TIROS .... Television and Infrared Observation Satellite [*NASA*]

TIROS .... Topographical Infrared Operations Satellite   (NASA)

TIRP .... Total Internal Reflection Prism

TIRPF .... Total Integrated Radial Peaking Factor   (IEEE)

TIRR .... [*The*] Institute for Rehabilitation and Research [*Houston, TX*]

TIRR .... Tactics Inspection Results Report

TIRR .... Tradestar Corp. [*Formerly, Tierra Energy Corp.*] [*NASDAQ symbol*]   (NQ)

TIRS .... Tactical Information Recording System [*Military*]   (CAAL)

TIRS .... Thermal Infrared Scanner   (RDA)

TIRS .... Travaux. Institut de Recherches Sahariennes [*A publication*]

TIRT .... Tidelands Royalty Trust "B" [*NASDAQ symbol*]   (NQ)

TIRT .... Total Internal Reflection Technique

TIRU .... Service du Traitement Industriel des Residus Urbains [*France*]

TIRVB ...... Toronto University. Institute for Aerospace Studies. UTIAS Review [*A publication*]

TIS .... [*The*] Infantry School [*Army*]

TIS .... Tactical Intelligence Squadron   (MCD)

TIS .... Taft Information System [*Provides information on private foundations*]   (IID)

TIS .... Target Identification Software [*Military*]   (CAAL)

TIS .... Target Information Sheet [*Air Force*]

TIS .... Target Information System

TIS .... Technical Information Section [*Navy*]

TIS .... Technical Information Service [*American Institute of Aeronautics and Astronautics*]   (IID)

TIS .... Technical Information Service [*Caribbean Industrial Research Institute*] [*Trinidad*] [*Information service or system*]   (IID)

TIS .... Technical Information Services [*Acurex Corp.*]   (IID)

TIS .... Technical Information Systems [*Department of Agriculture*]

TIS .... Technical Interface Specification   (NATG)

TIS .... Technical Research Centre of Finland, Espoo, Finland [*OCLC symbol*]   (OCLC)

TIS .... Technology, Information, and Society

TIS .... Technology Information System [*Lawrence Livermore National Laboratory*] [*University of California*]   (IID)

TIS .... Telemetry Input System

TIS .... Telephone Information Services [*Commercial firm*] [*British*]

TIS .... Telephone Interpreter Service [*Australia*]

TIS .... Temperature Indicating Switch

TIS .... Terminal Interface Subsystem [*Telecommunications*]   (TEL)

TIS .... Terrain Information System

TIS .... Test Information Sheet   (MCD)

TIS .... Test Instrumentation System

TIS .... Test Interface Subsystem   (NASA)

TIS .... Test Interface Summary   (MCD)

TIS .... Test Item Simulator [*Fort Huachuca, AZ*] [*United States Army Electronic Proving Ground*]   (GRD)

TIS .... Tetracycline-Induced Steatosis [*Medicine*]

TIS .... Tetrahydroisoquinoline Sulfonamide [*A drug*]

TIS .... Theater Intelligence Section [*Navy*]

TIS .... Thermal Imaging Scanner

TIS .... Thermal Imaging Sight [*Artillery*] [*Army*]   (INF)

TIS .... Thermal Insulation System

TIS .... Thursday Island [*Australia*] [*Airport symbol*]   (OAG)

TIS .... Time Resources Corp. [*Vancouver Stock Exchange symbol*]

TIS .... Time in Service   (FAAC)

TIS .... Times [*London*] [*A publication*]

TIS .... TIS Mortgage Investment Co. [*NYSE symbol*]   (CTT)

TIS .... Tissue   (ADA)

TIS .... Tobacco Inspection Service [*Philippines*]

TIS .... Tops in Science Fiction [*A publication*]

TIS .... Total Information System [*Data processing*]

TIS .... Tracking and Injection Station

TIS .... Tracking Instrumentation Subsystem   (MCD)

TIS .... Trading Information System [*AutEx Systems*] [*Information service or system*]   (CRD)

TIS .... Traffic Information System

TIS .... Transponder Interrogation SONAR

TIS .... Travel Information Service   (EA)

TIS .... Travelers Information Service [*Oracle Corp.*] [*Information service or system*]   (IID)

TIS .... Triskaidekaphobia Illuminatus Society   (EA)

TIS .... Trypsin-Insoluble Segment [*Cytochemistry*]

TIS .... Tumor in Situ [*Oncology*]

TIS .... Two-Impinging-Stream Reactor [*Chemical engineering*]

TISA .... Technical Information Support Activities [*Army*]

TISA .... Technique for Interactive Systems Analysis   (NVT)

TISA .... Troop Issue Subsistence Activity [*Military*]   (AABC)

TISA .... Troop Issue Support Agency   (MCD)

TISAL .... Tactical Instrument Steep Approach and Landing System   (MCD)

TISAP .... Technical Information Support Activities Project [*Army*]   (DIT)

TISAP .... Totalized Interface Subroutine and Post Processor [*Data processing*]   (BUR)

TISC .... Technology Integration Steering Committee [*Army*]   (RDA)

TISC .... Tertiary Institutions Service Centre [*Australia*]

TISC .... Tire Industry Safety Council   (EA)

TISC .... Treasury Inter-Services Committee [*British military*]   (DMA)

TISCA .... Technical Information System for Carrier Aviation [*Navy*]   (MCD)

TISCO ...... TISCO [*Tata Iron & Steel Company*] Technical Journal [*A publication*]

TISCO Rev ... TISCO [*Tata Iron & Steel Company*] Review [*A publication*]

TISEO .... Target Identification System, Electro-Optical [*Air Force*]

TISHUG .... Texas Instruments Home Computer Users' Group [*Australia*]

TISI .... Tenet Information Services, Inc. [*NASDAQ symbol*]   (NQ)

TISI .... Thai Industrial Standards Institute   (DS)

TISL .... Telecommunications and Information Systems Laboratory [*University of Kansas*] [*Research center*]   (RCD)

TISL .... Thomson Information Services Ltd. [*The Thomson Corp.*] [*Publishing*]

TISO .... Threat Integrated Staff Officer [*Army*]

TISO .... Troop Issue Subsistence Officer [*Military*]   (AABC)

TISP .... Technical Information Support Personnel [*Department of Labor*]

TISP .... Thickness-Insensitive Solar Paint [*Coating technology*]

TISPOC ..... Trent Institute for the Study of Popular Culture [*Trent University*] [*Canada*] [*Research center*]   (RCD)

TISq .... Tactical Intelligence Squadron [*Air Force*]

TISS .... Troop Issue Support System [*Army*]

TISSG .... Travel Industry Systems Standards Group [*British*]

Tissue Anti ... Tissue Antigens [*A publication*]

Tissue React ... Tissue Reactions [*A publication*]

TIST .... St. Thomas/Harry S. Truman [*Virgin Islands*] [*ICAO location identifier*]   (ICLI)

TISTHR .... Tool Inspection Small Tools Historical Record   (MCD)

TISX .... St. Croix/Alexander Hamilton [*Virgin Islands*] [*ICAO location identifier*]   (ICLI)

Tit .... Divus Titus [*of Suetonius*] [*Classical studies*]   (OCD)

TIT .... Technician-in-Training   (ADA)

TIT .... Technology in Training [*DoD*]

TIT .... Terminal Interface Table   (MCD)

TIT .... Test Item Taker

TIT .... Thermal Inactivation Time

TIT .... Thermoisolation Technique

Tit .... Titan [*Record label*]

Tit .... Tithe   (ILCA)

TIT .... Title [*Bibliography*]

Tit .... Titus [*New Testament book*]

Tit .... Titus Andronicus [*Shakespearean work*]

TIT .... Total Insertion Time

TIT .... Treponema Immobilization Test [*Clinical chemistry*]

TIT .... Turbine Inlet Temperature

TIT .... Turbine Interstage Temperature

TITC .... Traction-Immune Track Circuits [*Railway signals system*] [*British*]

TITE .... Tijuana & Tecate Railway Co. [*Later, TTR*] [*AAR code*]

TI Tech Inf Ind ... TI. Technical Information for Industry [*South Africa*] [*A publication*]

TITh .... Triiodothyronine [*Also, T_3 Endocrinology*]

TIT J Lif .... TIT [*Tower International Technomedical*] Journal of Life Sciences [*A publication*]

TIT J Life Sci ... TIT [*Tower International Technomedical*] Journal of Life Sciences [*A publication*]
TITL .... Tijdschrift van het Institut voor Toegepaste Linguistiek [*Leuven*] [*A publication*]
TITLA ...... Tecnica Italiana [*A publication*]
TITLV ...... Tijdschrift voor Indische Taal-, Land-, en Volkenkunde [*A publication*]
TITO .... Troops In, Troops Out
TITPG .... Taft Institute for Two-Party Government [*Later, TTI*]   (EA)
titr .... Titrate [*Analytical chemistry*]
TI/TTR ...... Target Illumination/Target Tracking RADAR   (MCD)
TITUS .... Textile Information Treatment Users' Service [*French Textile Institute*] [*Bibliographic database*] [*Information service or system*]   (IID)
TIU .... Tape Identification Unit
TIU .... Target Indication Unit [*Navy*]
TIU .... Telecommunications International Union   (EA)
TIU .... Terminal Interface Unit [*Bell System*]
TIU .... Timaru [*New Zealand*] [*Airport symbol*]   (OAG)
TIU .... Time Isolation Unit
TIU .... Toxicologically Insignificant Usage
TIU .... Trigger Inverter Unit
TIU .... Trypsin Inhibitory Unit [*Food analysis*]
TIUC .... Textile Information Users Council   (EA)
TIUV .... Total Intrauterine Volume [*Gynecology*]
TIV .... Target Intensifier Vidicon
TIV .... Time in View
TIV .... Tivat [*Yugoslavia*] [*Airport symbol*]   (OAG)
TIV .... Tiverton [*Municipal borough in England*]
TIV .... Tiverton Petroleums Ltd. [*Toronto Stock Exchange symbol*]
TIV .... Tivoli Music Hall [*London*]   (DSUE)
TIW .... Tacoma, WA [*Location identifier*] [*FAA*]   (FAAL)
TIW .... Tamarind Institute Workshop [*Graphic arts school*] [*New Mexico*]
TIW .... TEFLON-Insulated Wire
tiw .... Three Times a Week [*Pharmacology*]
TIW .... Today's Insurance Woman [*National Association of Insurance Women (International)*] [*A publication*]
TIWG .... Terrorism Incident Working Group [*Bureau of Diplomatic Security*] [*Department of State*]   (EGAO)
TIWSS .... Theater Integrated Warfare Scenarios Study
TIX .... Timeplex, Inc. [*NYSE symbol*]   (SPSG)
TIX .... Titusville, FL [*Location identifier*] [*FAA*]   (FAAL)
TIXA .... Thioxanthone [*Organic chemistry*]
TIXI .... Turret Integrated Xenon Illuminator
TIY .... Tidjikja [*Mauritania*] [*Airport symbol*]   (OAG)
TIY .... Tir Systems Ltd. [*Vancouver Stock Exchange symbol*]
TIYADG .... Tianjin Medical Journal [*A publication*]
TIZ .... Tari [*Papua New Guinea*] [*Airport symbol*]   (OAG)
TIZ .... Tonindustrie-Zeitung und Keramische Rundschau. Zentralblatt fuer das Gesamtgebiet der Steine und Erden [*A publication*]
TIZZY .... Tinny and Buzzing [*Sounds*]
TJ .... Air Traffic GmbH [*ICAO designator*]   (FAAC)
TJ .... Cameroun [*Aircraft nationality and registration mark*]   (FAAC)
TJ .... East Germany [*License plate code assigned to foreign diplomats in the US*]
TJ .... Tait's Justice of the Peace [*A publication*]   (DLA)
TJ .... Talk Jockey [*Radio*]
TJ .... Talmud Jerushalmi   (BJA)
TJ .... Targum Jonathan   (BJA)
TJ .... Technical Journal   (MCD)
TJ .... Telephone Jack   (DEN)
TJ .... Temperature Junction   (MCD)
TJ .... Terajoule [*SI unit of energy*]
TJ .... Test Jack   (DEN)
TJ .... Theatre Journal [*A publication*]
TJ .... Thermal Junction   (KSC)
TJ .... Thomas Jefferson [*US president, 1743-1826*]
TJ .... Tijuana [*Mexico*]
TJ .... Today's Japan [*A publication*]
TJ .... Tolkien Journal [*A publication*]
TJ .... Tomato Juice
TJ .... Tommy John [*Baseball pitcher*]
TJ .... Trajectory   (AABC)
TJ .... Trans-Jordan   (BJA)
TJ .... Triceps Jerk
TJ .... Trinity Journal [*A publication*]
TJ .... Turbojet
TJA .... Focus Japan (Tokyo) [*A publication*]
TJA .... Tarija [*Bolivia*] [*Airport symbol*]   (OAG)
TJA .... Telecommunication Journal of Australia [*A publication*]   (APTA)
TJA .... Trial Judge Advocate [*Army*]
TJA .... Turbojet Aircraft
TJADA ...... Teratology [*A publication*]
TJADC ...... Theater Joint Air Defense Command [*Military*]   (AABC)
TJAETDS ... Turbine and Jet Aircraft Engine Type Designation System
TJAG .... [*The*] Judge Advocate General [*Army*]
TJAGC .... [*The*] Judge Advocate General's Corps [*Army*]

TJaGH ...... Jackson-Madison County General Hospital, Learning Center, Jackson, TN [*Library symbol*] [*Library of Congress*]   (LCLS)
TJAGSA.... [*The*] Judge Advocate General's School, Army
TJak .... Trudy Instituta Jazyka, Literatury, i Istorii [*A publication*]
TJaL .... Lane College, Jackson, TN [*Library symbol*] [*Library of Congress*]   (LCLS)
TJaLam ..... Lambuth College, Jackson, TN [*Library symbol*] [*Library of Congress*]   (LCLS)
TJaLaw ...... Tennessee State Law Library, Jackson, TN [*Library symbol*] [*Library of Congress*]   (LCLS)
T Jap I Met ... Transactions. Japan Institute of Metals [*A publication*]
TJAS .... Tom Jones Appreciation Society   (EAIO)
TJASA....... Transactions. Japan Society for Aeronautical and Space Sciences [*A publication*]
TJaU .... Union University, Jackson, TN [*Library symbol*] [*Library of Congress*]   (LCLS)
TJB .... Theologischer Jahresbericht [*A publication*]
TJB .... Tijuana Brass [*Musical group*]
TJB .... Tilting Journal Bearing
TJB .... Time-Sharing Job Control Block [*Data processing*]   (IBMDP)
TJB .... Trench Junction Box
TJBQ .... Aguadilla/Borinquen [*Puerto Rico*] [*ICAO location identifier*]   (ICLI)
T J Br Cer ... Transactions and Journal. British Ceramic Society [*A publication*]
TJC .... [*The*] Jockey Club   (EA)
TJC .... Targeted Jobs Credit [*Tax credit*]
TJC .... Temple Junior College [*Texas*]
TJC .... Thomas Jefferson Center   (EA)
TJC .... Thornton Junior College [*Illinois*]
TJC .... Trajectory Chart
TJC .... Trinidad [*Colorado*] [*Seismograph station code, US Geological Survey*]   (SEIS)
TJC .... Tyler Junior College [*Texas*]
TJC .... Vanderbilt University Library, Nashville, TN [*OCLC symbol*]   (OCLC)
TJCG .... Vieques/Camp Garcia Airstrip [*Puerto Rico*] [*ICAO location identifier*]   (ICLI)
TJCK .... Timberjack Corp. [*NASDAQ symbol*]   (NQ)
TJCO .... TJ International, Inc. [*NASDAQ symbol*]   (NQ)
TJCP .... Culebra [*Puerto Rico*] [*ICAO location identifier*]   (ICLI)
TJD .... Trajectory Diagram
TJE .... Trojan Energy Corp. [*Vancouver Stock Exchange symbol*]
TJE .... Turbojet Engine
TJEDS .... Trainer Jet Exhaust Decontamination System
TJefC .... Carson-Newman College, Jefferson City, TN [*Library symbol*] [*Library of Congress*]   (LCLS)
TJEMA ..... Tohoku Journal of Experimental Medicine [*A publication*]
TJEMD ..... Tokai Journal of Experimental and Clinical Medicine [*A publication*]
TJETS .... Thomas Jefferson Equal Tax Society   (EA)
TJF .... Time-to-Jitter Flag
TJFA .... Fajardo [*Puerto Rico*] [*ICAO location identifier*]   (ICLI)
TJFC........... [*The*] Johnsons Fan Club   (EA)
TJFC........... Tasmanian Junior Football Club [*Australia*]
TJFC........... Tex Jones Fan Club   (EA)
TJFC........... Tomy Jennings Fan Club   (EA)
TJFF .... Ramey [*Puerto Rico*] [*ICAO location identifier*]   (ICLI)
TJFF .... Trans-Jordan Frontier Force [*British military*]   (DMA)
TJFL .... Tasmanian Junior Football League [*Australia*]
TJFS .... T. J.'s [*Tom Jones'*] Fans of Soul   (EA)
TJG .... Tom Jones Gadabouts   (EA)
TJG .... Travel Journalists Guild   (EA)
TJGTOI ... [*The*] Judge GTO International   (EA)
TJHC .... Theology. Journal of Historic Christianity [*A publication*]
TJHPA .... T'u Jang Hsueh Pao [*A publication*]
TJHPAE ... Acta Pedologica Sinica [*A publication*]
TJI .... Tabak Journal International [*A publication*]
TJI .... Tex Johnston, Incorporated
TJI .... Trus-Joist I-Beam
TJID .... Terminal Job Identification   (BUR)
TJIDA .... Tokyo Jikeikai Ika Daigaku Zasshi [*A publication*]
TJIG .... San Juan/Isla Grande [*Puerto Rico*] [*ICAO location identifier*]   (ICLI)
TJISRF ...... Thomas Jefferson Institute for the Study of Religious Freedom   (EA)
TJIZA .... Tokyo Joshi Ika Daigaku Zasshi [*A publication*]
TJL .... [*The*] Jonxis Lectures [*Elsevier Book Series*] [*A publication*]
TJM .... Tower Jettison Motor
TJM .... Vanderbilt Medical Center, Nashville, TN [*OCLC symbol*]   (OCLC)
TJMZ .... Mayaguez [*Puerto Rico*] [*ICAO location identifier*]   (ICLI)
TJNR .... Roosevelt Roads Naval Air Station [*Puerto Rico*] [*ICAO location identifier*]   (ICLI)
T Jo .... T. Jones' English King's Bench Reports [*84 English Reprint*] [*A publication*]   (DLA)
TJOC .... Theater Joint Operations Center [*Military*]
TJoE .... Emmanuel School of Religion, Johnson City, TN [*Library symbol*] [*Library of Congress*]   (LCLS)

TJoMC ...... Johnson City Medical Center Hospital, Learning Resources Center, Johnson City, TN [Library symbol] [Library of Congress] (LCLS)

T Jones ...... T. Jones' English King's Bench Reports [84 English Reprint] [A publication] (DLA)

T Jones (Eng) ... T. Jones' English King's Bench Reports [84 English Reprint] [A publication] (DLA)

TJoS .... East Tennessee State University, Johnson City, TN [Library symbol] [Library of Congress] (LCLS)

TJoS-M ..... East Tennessee State University, Medical Library, Johnson City, TN [Library symbol] [Library of Congress] (LCLS)

TJoV .... United States Veterans Administration Center, Johnson City, TN [Library symbol] [Library of Congress] (LCLS)

TJP .... Tactical Jamming Pod [Military] (CAAL)

TJP .... Turbojet Propulsion

TJPDA ...... Turkish Journal of Pediatrics [A publication]

TJPOI ...... Twisted Jute Packing and Oakum Institute [Defunct] (EA)

TJPS......... Ponce/Mercedita [Puerto Rico] [ICAO location identifier] (ICLI)

TJQ .... Tanjung Pandan [Indonesia] [Airport symbol] (OAG)

TJQ .... Thoreau Journal Quarterly [A publication]

TJR .... Tactical Jammer [Military] (CAAL)

TJR .... Tajee Resources Ltd. [Vancouver Stock Exchange symbol]

TJR .... Tenri Journal of Religion [A publication]

TJR .... Trunk and Junction Routing [Telecommunications] (TEL)

TJRC .... Thomas Jefferson Research Center [Later, TJC] (EA)

TJS .... Tactical Jamming System

TJS .... Target Jamming System

TJS .... Tenajon Resources Corp. [Formerly, Tenajon Silver] [Vancouver Stock Exchange symbol]

TJS .... Terminal Junction System

TJS .... Timber Trades Journal and Woodworking Machinery [Later, Timber Trades Journal and Wood Processing] [London] [A publication]

TJS .... Transverse Junction Stripe (MCD)

TJSCA...... Texas Journal of Science [A publication]

TJSF........ Temperature Jump-Stopped Flow [Spectroscopy]

TJSJ .... San Juan/Puerto Rico International [Puerto Rico] [ICAO location identifier] (ICLI)

TJSUDJ .... Thai Journal of Surgery [A publication]

TJT .... Tactical Jamming Transmitter [Navy]

TJT .... Tough Jeans Territory [Sears, Roebuck & Co. advertising slogan]

TJTA .... Taylor-Johnson Temperament Analysis [Psychology]

TJTC .... Targeted Jobs Tax Credits [Federal program]

TJTCC....... Targeted Jobs Tax Credit Coalition (EA)

TJTTFC .... Tom Jones "Tom Terrific" Fan Club (EA)

Tju........... Tjuringa: an Australasian Benedictine Review [A publication] (APTA)

Tjumen Gos Ped Inst Ucen Zap ... Ministerstvo Prosvescenija RSFSR Tjumenskii Gosudarstvennyi Pedagogiceskii Institut. Ucenye Zapiski [A publication]

TJVQ........ Vieques [Puerto Rico] [ICAO location identifier] (ICLI)

TJW........... North Haven, ME [Location identifier] [FAA] (FAAL)

TJX.......... TJX Companies [NYSE symbol] (SPSG)

TJY.......... Tulsa, OK [Location identifier] [FAA] (FAAL)

TJZS......... San Juan [Puerto Rico] [ICAO location identifier] (ICLI)

Tk............. Milli Kutuphane [National Library], Ankara, Turkey [Library symbol] [Library of Congress] (LCLS)

Tk............. T-Cell, Killer Type [Immunology]

TK .... Tank (AAG)

TK .... Tanker

TK .... Tekawennake. Six Nations. New Credit Reporter [A publication]

TK .... Tetzugaku-Kenkyu [Tokyo] [A publication]

T und K ..... Text und Kontext [A publication]

TK .... Text und Kritik [A publication]

TK .... Thick (ROG)

TK .... Through Knee [Medicine]

TK .... Thymidine Kinase [An enzyme]

TK .... To Kum [i.e., To Come] [Publishing]

TK .... Tokelau Islands [ANSI two-letter standard code] (CNC)

TK .... Tool Kits [JETDS nomenclature] [Military] (CET)

TK .... Torath Kohanim (BJA)

TK .... Track

TK .... Transducer Kit (MCD)

TK .... Transketolase [An enzyme]

TK .... Truck (AAG)

TK .... Trunk Equipment [Telecommunications] (TEL)

TK .... Turk Hava Yollari AO [Turkish Airlines, Inc.] [ICAO designator] (FAAC)

TK .... Turkey [IYRU nationality code]

TK .... Tuskegee R. R. [AAR code]

TK .... Tyrosine Kinase Domain [Genetics]

TKA .... Talkeetna, AK [Location identifier] [FAA] (FAAL)

TKA .... Tanaka [New Britain] [Seismograph station code, US Geological Survey] (SEIS)

TKA .... Terminator Kit Assembly [Robot]

TKA .... Thermokinetic Analysis

TKA .... Tonka Corp. [NYSE symbol] (SPSG)

TKA .... Total Knee Arthroplasty [Medicine]

TKA .... Toy Knights of America (EA)

TKA .... Trudy Kierskoi Dukhovnoi Akademii [A publication]

TKAI........ Teknowledge, Incorporated [Palo Alto, CA] [NASDAQ symbol] (NQ)

TKAM .... Knoxville Academy of Medicine, Knoxville, TN [Library symbol] [Library of Congress] (LCLS)

TKar.......... Trudy Karel'skogo Filiala Akademii Nauk SSSR [A publication]

TKAT........ Technology 80, Inc. [Minneapolis, MN] [NASDAQ symbol] (NQ)

TKB .... Kingsville, TX [Location identifier] [FAA] (FAAL)

TKBD .... Tackboard [Technical drawings]

TKBN .... Tank Battalion [Marine Corps]

TKBRAS ... Transactions. Korean Branch. Royal Asiatic Society [A publication]

TKC .... Thiokol Corp. [NYSE symbol] (SPSG)

TKCS........ Knoxville City School, Knoxville, TN [Library symbol] [Library of Congress] (LCLS)

TKD .... Takada [Japan] [Seismograph station code, US Geological Survey] (SEIS)

TKD .... Tokodynamometer

TKD .... Top Kit Drawing

TKDE .... Tetrakis(dimethylamino)ethylene [Organic chemistry]

TKE .... Tau Kappa Epsilon [Fraternity] [Later, TEKE]

TKE .... Tenakee [Alaska] [Airport symbol] (OAG)

TKE .... Tenakee Springs, AK [Location identifier] [FAA] (FAAL)

TKE .... Total Kinetic Energy

TKE .... Track Angle Error

TKE .... Turbulent Kinetic Energy

TKEBH....... East Tennessee Baptist Hospital, Knoxville, TN [Library symbol] [Library of Congress] (LCLS)

TKESB ...... Tekhnicheskaya Estetika [A publication]

TKETHi ..... East Tennessee Historical Society, Knoxville, TN [Library symbol] [Library of Congress] (LCLS)

TKF........... Turkish Investment Fund [NYSE symbol] (SPSG)

TKFN........ Telkwa Foundation. Newsletter [Telkwa, British Columbia] [A publication]

TKFSM ...... Fort Sanders Regional Medical Center, Knoxville, TN [Library symbol] [Library of Congress] (LCLS)

TKG .... Bandar Lampung [Indonesia] [Airport symbol] (OAG)

TKG .... Capsule Technology Group, Inc. [Toronto Stock Exchange symbol]

TKG .... Tanking (AAG)

TKG .... Tokodynagraph

TKG .... Tongkang [Ship's rigging] (ROG)

TKGA .... [The] Knitting Guild of America (EA)

TKGJA ...... Taisei Kensetsu Gijutsu Kenkyusho-Ho [A publication]

TKGS........ Church of Jesus Christ of Latter-Day Saints, Genealogical Society Library, Knoxville Branch, Knoxville, TN [Library symbol] [Library of Congress] (LCLS)

TKH.......... Tikhaya Bay [USSR] [Later, HIS] [Geomagnetic observatory code]

TKi .... Kingsport Public Library, Kingsport, TN [Library symbol] [Library of Congress] (LCLS)

TKI........... McKinney, TX [Location identifier] [FAA] (FAAL)

TKI........... Trial Kit Installation (CAAL)

TKIF .... Training Name and Address Key Index File [IRS]

TKiH.......... Holston Valley Community Hospital, Health Science Library, Kingsport, TN [Library symbol] [Library of Congress] (LCLS)

TKimJ....... Johnson Bible College, Knoxville, TN [Library symbol] [Library of Congress] (LCLS)

TKIO .... [The] Tokio Marine & Fire Insurance Co. Ltd. [NASDAQ symbol] (NQ)

Tk J.......... Tamkang Journal [A publication]

TKJ........... Tok, AK [Location identifier] [FAA] (FAAL)

TKK .... Token Kenkyu Kai (EA)

TKK .... Toyo Kogyo Co. [Auto manufacturer]

TKK .... Truk [Caroline Islands] [Airport symbol] (OAG)

TKKSA ...... Trudy Khar'kovskogo Sel'skokhozyaistvennogo Instituta [A publication]

TKKTA...... Trudy po Khimii i Khimicheskoi Tekhnologii [A publication]

TKKTFSLB ... [The] Kandy-Kolored Tangerine-Flake Streamline Baby [Title of book by Tom Wolfe]

TKL.......... Knoxville-Knox County Public Library, Knoxville, TN [OCLC symbol] (OCLC)

TKL.......... Public Library of Knoxville and Knox County, Knoxville, TN [Library symbol] [Library of Congress] (LCLS)

TKL.......... Tackle [Mechanical engineering]

TKL.......... Taku Lodge, AK [Location identifier] [FAA] (FAAL)

TKL.......... Tanker Oil & Gas [Vancouver Stock Exchange symbol]

TKL.......... Tijdschrift voor Kadaster en Landmeetkunde [A publication]

TKL.......... Tokelau Islands [ANSI three-letter standard code] (CNC)

TKLaw .... Tennessee State Law Library, Knoxville, TN [Library symbol] [Library of Congress] (LCLS)

TKLC........ TEKELEC [Calabasas, CA] [NASDAQ symbol] (NQ)

TKLMI...... Lakeshore Mental Health Institute, Staff Library, Knoxville, TN [Library symbol] [Library of Congress] (LCLS)

TKLN .... Toklan Oil Corp. [NASDAQ symbol] (NQ)

TKM .... Takamatsu [Japan] [Seismograph station code, US Geological Survey] (SEIS)

TKM .... TRIS, Potassium Chloride, Magnesium Chloride [*A buffer*]
TKMEB ..... Theoretische und Klinische Medizin in Einzeldarstellungen [*A publication*]
TKMSB ..... Tekhnicheska Misul [*A publication*]
TKN .... Tek-Net International Ltd. (Canada) [*Vancouver Stock Exchange symbol*]
TKN .... Tokuno Shima [*Japan*] [*Airport symbol*]   (OAG)
TKN .... Total Kjeldahl Nitrogen [*Organic analysis*]
TKN .... Tractatenblad van het Koninkrijk der Nederlanden [*A publication*]
TKN .... University of Tennessee, Knoxville, TN [*OCLC symbol*]   (OCLC)
TKNA .... Tekna-Tool, Inc. [*NASDAQ symbol*]   (NQ)
TKNGMP ... Tijdschrift. Koninklijk Nederlandsch Genootschap voor Munt en Penningkunde [*A publication*]
TKNKB ..... Tekniikka [*A publication*]
TKO .... Mankato, KS [*Location identifier*] [*FAA*]   (FAAL)
TKO .... Taseko Mines Ltd. [*Vancouver Stock Exchange symbol*]
TKO .... Technical Knockout [*Boxing*]
TKO .... Technieuws Tokio. Korte Berichten op Technisch Wetenschappelijk Gebied [*A publication*]
TKO .... Technische Kontrollorganisation
TKO .... To Keep Open [*Medicine*]
TKO .... Trunk Offer [*Telecommunications*]   (TEL)
TKOF .... Takeoff [*Aviation*]
TKP .... [*The*] Knapp Press [*Book publisher*]
TKP .... Takapoto Island [*French Polynesia*] [*Airport symbol*]   (OAG)
TKP .... Theta Kappa Phi [*Fraternity*]
TKP .... Ton-Kilometer Performed
TKP .... Trans Korea Pipeline
TKP .... Turkiye Komunist Partisi
TKPH .... Park West Hospital, Knoxville, TN [*Library symbol*] [*Library of Congress*]   (LCLS)
TKPK .... Basseterre/Golden Rock [*St. Kitts Island*] [*ICAO location identifier*]   (ICLI)
TKP-ML.... People's Revolutionary Union - Marxist-Leninist [*Turkey*]   (PD)
TKPN .... Charlestown/Newcastle [*Nevis Island*] [*ICAO location identifier*]   (ICLI)
TKPS .... Tuvalu and Kiribati Philatelic Society   (EA)
TKQ .... Kigoma [*Tanzania*] [*Airport symbol*]   (OAG)
TKR .... [*Telephone*] Talker
TkR .... Tamkang Review [*A publication*]
TKR .... Tanker   (AAG)
TKR .... Terrestrial Kilometric Radiation [*Physics*]
TKR .... [*The*] Timken Co. [*Formerly, TDX*] [*NYSE symbol*]   (SPSG)
TKR .... Total Knee Replacement [*Medicine*]
tkr.............. Turkmen Soviet Socialist Republic [*MARC country of publication code*] [*Library of Congress*]   (LCCP)
TKRAS ..... Transactions. Korean Branch. Royal Asiatic Society [*A publication*]
TKrasPI..... Trudy Krasnodarskogo Gosudarstvennogo Pedagogicheskogo Instituta [*A publication*]
TKS .... Knoxville City School, Knoxville, TN [*OCLC symbol*]   (OCLC)
TKS .... Tackstrip [*Technical drawings*]
TKS .... Tamavack Resources, Inc. [*Vancouver Stock Exchange symbol*]
TKS .... Thanks   (ADA)
TKS .... Throttle Kicker Solenoid [*Automotive engineering*]
TKS .... Tokushima [*Japan*] [*Airport symbol*]   (OAG)
TKS .... Tokushima [*Japan*] [*Seismograph station code, US Geological Survey*]   (SEIS)
TKS .... Tokyo Kikai Seisakusho [*Japan*]
TKSBB ..... Tektonika Sibiri [*A publication*]
TK-SC .... Tennessee State Supreme Court Law Library, Knoxville, TN [*Library symbol*] [*Library of Congress*] [*Obsolete*]   (LCLS)
TKSGA ..... Trudy Koordinatsionnykh Soveshchanyi po Gidrotekhnike [*A publication*]
TKSGB ..... Tektonika i Stratigrafiya [*A publication*]
TKSMC ..... Saint Mary's Medical Center, Medical Library, Knoxville, TN [*Library symbol*] [*Library of Congress*]   (LCLS)
TKSMC-N ... Saint Mary's Medical Center, Nursing School Library, Knoxville, TN [*Library symbol*] [*Library of Congress*]   (LCLS)
TKST .... Tukisiviksat [*A publication*]
TK SUP ..... Track Supervisor   (CAAL)
TKT .... Tashkent [*USSR*] [*Geomagnetic observatory code*]
TKT .... Ticker Tape Resources Ltd. [*Vancouver Stock Exchange symbol*]
TKT .... Ticket
TKTEA ..... Tekhnika Kino i Televideniya [*A publication*]
TKTF .... Tanker Task Force
TKTRANSR ... Tank Transporter [*Military*]   (AABC)
TKTS .... Thermodynamic Kelvin Temperature Scale
TKTU .... Thymidine Kinase (Activity) Transforming Unit [*Biochemistry*]
TKTVA ...... Tennessee Valley Authority, Knoxville, TN [*Library symbol*] [*Library of Congress*]   (LCLS)
TKU .... Takayasuyama [*Japan*] [*Seismograph station code, US Geological Survey*]   (SEIS)
TKU .... Turku [*Finland*] [*Airport symbol*]   (OAG)
TKUAA ..... Trudy Kuibyshevskii Aviatsionnyi Institut [*A publication*]

TKUN .... TMK/United, Inc. [*Birmingham, AL*] [*NASDAQ symbol*]   (NQ)
TKutPI .... Trudy Kutaisskogo Gosudarstvennogo Pedagogiceskogo Instituta [*A publication*]
TKV .... Tatakoto [*French Polynesia*] [*Airport symbol*]   (OAG)
TKVD .... Techvend, Inc. [*NASDAQ symbol*]   (NQ)
TKW .... Thermal Kilowatts
TKX .... Kennett, MO [*Location identifier*] [*FAA*]   (FAAL)
TKY .... Takayama [*Japan*] [*Seismograph station code, US Geological Survey*]   (SEIS)
TKZRA ..... Taika Zairyo [*A publication*]
TL .... Central African Republic [*Aircraft nationality and registration mark*]   (FAAC)
Tl .... Lateral Touch Neuron [*of a leech*]
TL .... Reports of the Witwatersrand High Court [*Transvaal, South Africa*] [*A publication*]   (DLA)
TL .... Tackline [*British naval signaling*]
T/L............. Tactical Landing
TL .... Tail-Lift [*of trucks and vans*]   (DCTA)
T/L............. Talk/Listen   (NASA)
TL .... Tank Lease   (ADA)
TL .... Tape Library   (BUR)
TL .... Target Language
TL .... Task Leader   (NRCH)
T/L............. Task List   (KSC)
TL .... Team Leader   (AABC)
TL .... Technical Letter
TL .... Technical Library
TL .... Telegraphist-Lieutenant [*Navy*] [*British*]
T-L .... Tennessee State Law Library, Nashville, TN [*Library symbol*] [*Library of Congress*]   (LCLS)
TL .... Termes de la Ley [*Terms of the Law*] [*Law French dictionary*] [*A publication*]   (DLA)
TL .... Terminal Limen
TL .... Terra Lliure [*Free Land*] [*Spanish terrorist group*]
TL .... Test Laboratory   (AFM)
TL .... Test Link
TL .... Test Load
TL .... Test Log   (IEEE)
TL .... Testolactone [*Biochemistry*]
TL .... Texas League [*Baseball*]
Tl .... Thallium [*Chemical element*]
TL .... Theologische Literaturzeitung [*A publication*]
TL .... Theologisches Literaturblatt [*Leipzig*] [*A publication*]
TL .... Theoretical Linguistics [*Berlin*] [*A publication*]
TL .... Therapeutic Level [*Medicine*]
TL .... Thermal Liquefaction [*Chemical engineering*]
TL .... Thermoluminescence [*Also, THL*]
TL .... Thoreau Lyceum   (EA)
T & L........ Thrift & Loans [*Industrial loan company*]
TL .... Throws Left-Handed [*Baseball*]
TL .... Thrust Level   (NASA)
TL .... Thrust Line
TL .... Thymic Lymphoma [*Medicine*]
TL .... Thymus-Derived Lymphocyte [*Hematology*]
TL .... Thymus Leukemia [*Hematology*]
TL .... Ticket of Leave   (ADA)
TL .... Tie Line [*Communication channel*]
TL .... Time, Inc. [*NYSE symbol*] [*Later, TWX*]   (SPSG)
TL .... Time Latest   (NASA)
TL .... Time to Launch [*Navy*]   (CAAL)
TL .... Time Lengths
T-L .... Time-Life Books [*Publisher*]
TL .... Time Limit
T/L............. Time Loan [*Banking*]
TL .... Timeline   (MCD)
TL .... Title List
tl .... Tokelau Islands [*MARC country of publication code*] [*Library of Congress*]   (LCCP)
TL .... Ton Load
TL .... Tool Life
TL .... Tool List
TL .... Tools [*JETDS nomenclature*] [*Military*]   (CET)
TL .... Torpedo Lieutenant [*Navy*] [*British*]
TL .... Torus Longitudinalis [*Anatomy*]
TL .... Total
TL .... Total Body Length [*Of Crustacea*]
TL .... Total Length
TL .... Total Lipids [*Clinical chemistry*]
TL .... Total Load [*Engineering*]
TL .... Total Loss [*Insurance*]
TL .... Total Luminescence [*Spectroscopy*]
TL .... Tower of London
TL .... Tracker Lock [*NASA*]   (KSC)
TL .... Trade-Last
TL .... Trading Limit
T/L............. Training Literature
TL .... Trans Mediterranean Airlines [*Lebanon*] [*ICAO designator*]   (FAAC)
TL .... Transaction Language
TL .... Transaction Listing   (AFM)

TL	Transfer Line [*Manufacturing*]
T/L	Transformer Load (NASA)
TL	Transient Load (MCD)
TL	Translocation Defect [*Medicine*]
TL	Transmission Level [*or Line*]
TL	Transmittal Letter (AAG)
TL	Transmitter Location
T/L	Transporter/Launcher [*NASA*] (KSC)
T/L	Transporter/Loader (MCD)
TL	Trial
TL	Triboluminescence [*Atomic physics*]
TL	Triple-Layer [*Pharmacy*]
TL	Triple Lindy [*Dance step*]
TL	Truck Lock [*Nuclear energy*] (NRCH)
TL	Truckload [*24,000 pounds or more*]
T-i-L	Truth-in-Lending Act [*1968*]
TL	Trybuna Literacka [*A publication*]
TL	Tubal Ligation [*Medicine*]
TL	Turkish Lira (BJA)
TL	Turntable Ladder
T²L	Transistor-Transistor Logic [*Also, TTL*]
TLA	A-A-A Air Enterprises, Inc. [*Omaha, NE*] [*FAA designator*] (FAAC)
TLA	Tasmanian Logging Association [*Australia*]
TLA	Tatlar Resources Ltd. [*Vancouver Stock Exchange symbol*]
TLA	Tax Lawyer [*A publication*]
TLA	Teller [*Alaska*] [*Airport symbol*] (OAG)
TLA	Teller, AK [*Location identifier*] [*FAA*] (FAAL)
TLA	Temporary Lodging Allowance [*Military*]
TLA	Terminal Low Altitude
TLA	Textile Labor Association [*India*]
TLA	Theatre Library Association (EA)
TLA	Time Line Analysis
TLA	Toy Libraries Association [*British*]
TLa	Transition Layer
TLA	Translumbar Aortogram [*Medicine*]
TLA	Transmission Line Adapter [*or Assembly*]
TLA	Transportation Lawyers Association (EA)
TLA	Travel and Living Allowance [*Military*] (AABC)
TLA	Trunk Line Association
TLAB	Tellabs, Inc. [*NASDAQ symbol*] (NQ)
TLAB	Translation Lookaside Buffer [*Data processing*] (CMD)
TLAC	Test Listening Accuracy in Children [*Educational test*]
TLAC	Top Loading Air Cleaner (MCD)
TLACV	Track-Laying Air-Cushion Vehicle
TLAG	Tooheys Leaseholders Action Group [*Australia*]
TLAM	Tomahawk Land Attack Missile (MCD)
TLAM	Tony Lama Co., Inc. [*NASDAQ symbol*] (NQ)
TLAM-N ..	Tomahawk Land Attack Missile - Nuclear (MCD)
TLAP	Prace Komisji Jezykowej Polskiej Akademii Umiejetnosci. Travaux de la Commission Linguistique de l'Academie Polonaise des Sciences et des Lettres [*A publication*]
TLAR	Tele-Art, Inc. [*NASDAQ symbol*] (NQ)
TLAS	Tactical Logical and Air Simulation
TLAT	TOW [*Tube-Launched, Optically Tracked, Wire-Guided (Weapon)*] Light Antitank Battalion (MCD)
T Lawyr	Tax Lawyer [*A publication*] (ILCA)
TLAY	Tule Lake Aster Yellows [*Plant pathology*]
TLB	Temporary Lighted Buoy [*Maps and charts*]
TLB	Texas-Louisiana Freight Bureau, St. Louis MO [*STAC*]
TLB	Theologisches Literaturblatt [*A publication*]
TLB	Time-Life Books
TLB	Tractor/Loader/Backhoe
TLB	Translation Lookaside Buffer [*Data processing*] (BUR)
TLBAA	Texas Longhorn Breeders Association of America (EA)
TL/BBC	Tax Limitation/Balanced Budget Coalition (EA)
TLBID	TLB [*Translation - Lookaside - Buffers*] Identifier
TLBl	Theologisches Literaturblatt [*A publication*]
TLBR	Tactical LASER Beam Recorder (MCD)
TLC	[*The*] Learning Channel [*Cable-television system*]
TLC	Lee College, Cleveland, TN [*OCLC symbol*] (OCLC)
TLC	T-Lymphocyte Clones [*Immunology*]
TLC	Tactical Leadership Course [*Army*] (INF)
TLC	Tangent Latitude Computer
TLC	Tank Landing Craft [*Army*] [*British*]
TLC	Task Level Controller
TLC	Tele-Link, Inc. [*Miami, FL*] [*Telecommunications service*] (TSSD)
TLC	Telecommand (NASA)
TLC	Teletype, Line Printer, Card Reader Controller (NOAA)
TLC	Television Licensing Center (EA)
TLC	Tender Loving Care
TLC	Test of Language Competence [*Educational test*]
TLC	Texas Lutheran College
TLC	Textile Laundry Council (EA)
TLC	Thin-Layer Chromatography [*Analytical chemistry*]
TLC	Tillicum Industry [*Vancouver Stock Exchange symbol*]
TLC	Time-Lapse Cinematography
TLC	Time Line Controller
TLC	Tom's Love Connection (EA)
TLC	Total L-Chain Concentration

TLC	Total Load Control (MCD)
TLC	Total Lung Capacity [*Physiology*]
TLC	Total Lung Compliance [*Medicine*]
TLC	Total Lymphocyte Count [*Clinical chemistry*]
TLC	Touch and Learn Computer
TLC	Transient Late Curvature [*Orthopedics*]
TLC	Translunar Coast [*Aerospace*]
TLC	Tri-County Library Council, Inc. [*Library network*]
TLC	Trilateral Commission [*International study group*]
TLC	Truth and Liberation Concern [*Australia*]
TLC	Type and Learn Concept [*Minolta Corp. office system*]
TLCA	Tangent Latitude Computer Amplifier
TLCC	Telecalc, Inc. [*Bellevue, WA*] [*NASDAQ symbol*] (NQ)
TLCC	Thin-Line Communications Connectivity
TLC(C)	Trades and Labour Congress of Canada [*1883-1956*]
TLCCP	Total Life Cycle Competition Plan [*Army*]
TLCCS	Total Life Cycle Competition Strategy [*Army*]
TLCE	Transmission Line Conditioning Equipment (MCD)
TLCF	Tactical Link Control Facility [*Military*] (CAAL)
TLCI	Tea Leaf Club International (EA)
TLCI	Tender Loving Care Health Care, Incorporated [*NASDAQ symbol*] (NQ)
TLC/IR	Thin-Layer Chromatography/Infrared [*Analytical chemistry*]
TLCK	Tosyllysine Chloromethyl Ketone [*Biochemistry*]
T-LCL	T-Cell Lymphosarcoma Cell Leukemia [*Oncology*]
TLCN	Talcon LP [*NASDAQ symbol*] (NQ)
TLCO	Teleco Oilfield Service [*NASDAQ symbol*] (NQ)
TLCOA	Telecommunications [*Dedham, MA*] [*A publication*]
TLCPC	Trunk Line-Central Passenger Committee
TLCR	Telecrafter Corp. [*NASDAQ symbol*] (NQ)
TLCT	Total Life Cycle Time
TL-CTR	Trunk Line-Central Territory Railroad Tariff Bureau
TLD	[*The*] Living Daylights [*A publication*] (APTA)
TLD	Technical Logistics Data [*Army*] (AABC)
TLD	Thermoluminescent Device
TLD	Thermoluminescent Dosimeter [*or Dosimetry*]
TLD	Tiled [*Classified advertising*] (ADA)
TLD	Traffic Loading Device (CAAL)
TLDB	Transportation Legislative Data Base [*Department of Energy*] [*Battelle Memorial Institute*] [*Information service or system*] (IID)
TLDC	Taiwan Land Development Corporation
TLDF	Thomas Legal Defense Fund (EA)
TLDI	Technical Logistics Data and Information [*Army*] (AABC)
TLDIP	Technical Logistics Data Information Program
TLE	[*The*] Learning Exchange (EA)
TLE	Target Location Error [*Military*] (AABC)
TLE	Technical Liaison Engineer
TLE	Temperature-Limited Emission
TLE	Temporal Lobe Epilepsy [*Medicine*]
TLE	Thin-Layer Electrophoresis [*Analytical chemistry*]
TLE	Thin Leading Edge
TLE	Total Erickson Resources Ltd. [*Toronto Stock Exchange symbol*] [*Vancouver Stock Exchange symbol*]
TLE	Total Lipid Extract [*Biochemistry*]
TLE	Toward Liberal Education [*In book title*]
TLE	Tower Lighting Equipment
TLE	Tracking Light Electronics (KSC)
TLE	Traffic Law Enforcement
TLE	Transferline Heat Exchanger [*Chemical engineering*]
TLE	Tulear [*Madagascar*] [*Airport symbol*] (OAG)
TLebC	Cumberland College of Tennessee, Lebanon, TN [*Library symbol*] [*Library of Congress*] (LCLS)
TLEICS	Treasury Law Enforcement Information and Communications System
TLEPA	Trudy Laboratorii Elektromagnitnykh Polei Radiochastot Instituta Gigieny Truda i Professional'nykh Zabolevanii Akademii Meditsinskikh Nauk SSSR [*A publication*]
T Letterkd ...	Tydskrif vir Letterkunde [*A publication*]
TLEX	Total Erickson Resources Ltd. [*North Vancouver, BC*] [*NASDAQ symbol*] (NQ)
TLF	Temporary Loading Facilities (MCD)
TLF	Temporary Lodging Facility
TLF	Terminal Launch Facility
TLF	Textes Litteraires Francais [*A publication*]
TLF	Time Line Form
TLF	Trunk Link Frame [*Telecommunications*] (TEL)
TLFB	Texas-Louisiana Freight Bureau
TLFC	Terri LaVelle Fan Club (EA)
TLFC	Traci Lords Fan Club (EA)
TLFN	Tunison Laboratory of Fish Nutrition [*Department of the Interior*] [*Cortland, NY*] (GRD)
TLG	Consolidated Thompson-Lundmark Gold Mines Ltd. [*Toronto Stock Exchange symbol*]
TLG	Tail Landing Gear
TLG	Talgar [*Also, AAB*] [*Alma-Ata*] [*USSR*] [*Seismograph station code, US Geological Survey*] (SEIS)
TLG	Telegraph (AAG)
TLG	Tentative Logistics Guidance (MCD)
TLG	Thin-Layer Gel [*Filtration*] [*Analytical chemistry*]
TLG	Tilting

T Lg............	Travaux de Linguistique [*A publication*]
TLGB........	Tube-Launched Guided Projectiles (MCD)
TLH............	Tallahassee [*Florida*] [*Airport symbol*] (OAG)
TLH............	Tulloch Resources [*Vancouver Stock Exchange symbol*]
TLHT	Total Health Systems, Inc. [*Great Neck, NY*] [*NASDAQ symbol*] (NQ)
TLI.............	T-Logic, Incorporated [*Information service or system*] (IID)
TLI.............	Telephone Line Interface (IEEE)
TLI.............	Term Life Insurance
TLI.............	Theoretical Lethality Index (MCD)
TLI.............	Thymidine-Labeling Index [*Oncology*]
TLI.............	Time-Life International
tli...............	Tlingit [*MARC language code*] [*Library of Congress*] (LCCP)
TLI.............	Tolitoli [*Indonesia*] [*Airport symbol*] (OAG)
TLI.............	Total Lymphoid Irradiation
TLI.............	Translunar Injection [*Aerospace*]
TLI.............	Triangle Resources, Inc. [*Vancouver Stock Exchange symbol*]
TLI.............	Trinidad Light Infantry [*British military*] (DMA)
TLI.............	True Life Institute (EA)
TLIB.........	Tape Library [*National Center for Atmospheric Research*]
TLIB.........	Transportation Library [*National Academy of Sciences*] [*Information service or system*] (IID)
TLIEF........	Thin-Layer Isoelectric Focusing [*Analytical chemistry*]
TLIG.........	Tasmanian Legal Information Guide [*A publication*] (APTA)
TLII	Trans Leasing International, Incorporated [*Northbrook, IL*] [*NASDAQ symbol*] (NQ)
TLJ	Laredo Junior College, Laredo, TX [*OCLC symbol*] (OCLC)
TLJ	Tatalina [*Alaska*] [*Airport symbol*] (OAG)
TLJ	Tatalina, AK [*Location identifier*] [*FAA*] (FAAL)
TLJ	Transportation Law Journal [*A publication*]
TLJ	Travancore Law Journal [*India*] [*A publication*] (DLA)
TLK............	New York, NY [*Location identifier*] [*FAA*] (FAAL)
TLK............	Talkeetna Mountains [*Alaska*] [*Seismograph station code, US Geological Survey*] (SEIS)
TLK............	Talking [*Telecommunications*] (TEL)
TLK............	Teaching London Kids [*A publication*]
TLK............	Test Link (IEEE)
TLK............	University of Tennessee, Law Library, Knoxville, TN [*OCLC symbol*] (OCLC)
T-LL..........	T-Cell Lymphoblastic Lymphoma [*Oncology*]
TLL............	Tallinn [*USSR*] [*Airport symbol*] (OAG)
TLL............	Tank Lighter
TLL............	Television LASER Link
TLL............	Tender Load List
TLL............	Threshold Lactose Load [*Clinical chemistry*]
TLL............	Tololo Astronomical Observatory [*Chile*] [*Seismograph station code, US Geological Survey*] (SEIS)
TLL............	Tom's Look of Love (EA)
TLL............	Travaux de Linguistique et de Litterature [*Strasbourg*] [*A publication*]
TLLD........	Total Load
TLLM........	Temperature and Liquid Level Monitor [*Nuclear energy*] (NRCH)
TLLS	Tellus Industries, Inc. [*Sacramento, CA*] [*NASDAQ symbol*] (NQ)
TLLS	Travaux de Linguistique et de Litterature (Strasbourg) [*A publication*]
TLLW........	Tank Lighter (Medium Tank-Well Type)
TLM	Technical Liaison Memo
TLM	Telemeter [*or Telemetry*] (AAG)
TLM	Tilimsen [*Algeria*] [*Airport symbol*] (OAG)
TLM	Toledo-Lucas County Public Library, Toledo, OH [*OCLC symbol*] (OCLC)
TLM	Tolmezzo [*Italy*] [*Seismograph station code, US Geological Survey*] (SEIS)
TLM	Transmission Line Method [*Photovoltaic energy systems*]
TLM	Transmitted Light Microscope
TLM	Trillium Telephone Systems, Inc. [*Toronto Stock Exchange symbol*]
TLM	Tube-Launched Missile (MCD)
TLMA........	Trial Lawyers Marketing Association (EA)
TLMB........	Telemetry Data Buffer
TLMD	Telemundo Group, Inc. [*NASDAQ symbol*] (NQ)
TLMG	Telemetering (AAG)
TLMI........	Tag and Label Manufacturers Institute (EA)
TLMMDD ...	Malaysia. Ministry of Agriculture. Technical Leaflet [*A publication*]
TLMN	Talman Home Federal Savings & Loan Association of Illinois [*NASDAQ symbol*] (NQ)
TLMS	Tape Library Management System
TLMT........	Telemation, Inc. [*NASDAQ symbol*] (NQ)
TLMY........	Telemetry (MSA)
TLN	Talang [*Sumatra*] [*Seismograph station code, US Geological Survey*] [*Closed*] (SEIS)
TLN	Tasmanian Law Newsletter [*A publication*]
TLN	Thermolysin [*An enzyme*]
TLN	Title plus Last Name
TLN	Torque-Limiting Nut
TLN	Toulon/Hyeres [*France*] [*Airport symbol*] (OAG)
TLN	Transmittal Locator Number [*Data processing*]
TLN	Trunk Line Network

TLNDA	Telonde [*France*] [*A publication*]
TLO	[*The*] Last One [*A microcomputer program manufactured by DJ-AI*]
TLO	[*The*] Lifestyles Organization (EA)
TLO	Technical Liaison Office [*Military*]
TLO	Terminal Learning Objective
TLO	Tol [*Papua New Guinea*] [*Airport symbol*] (OAG)
TLO	Toledo [*Spain*] [*Seismograph station code, US Geological Survey*] (SEIS)
TLO	Total Loss Only
TLO	Tracking Local Oscillator
TLO	Training Liaison Officer [*Ministry of Agriculture, Fisheries, and Food*] [*British*]
TLOBS	Tailored List of Base Spares [*Military*] (AFIT)
TLOCC.....	Tomlinson Oil [*NASDAQ symbol*] (NQ)
TLOG	Transform Logic Corp. [*Scottsdale, AZ*] [*NASDAQ symbol*] (NQ)
TLOP........	[*The*] Language of Poetry [*A publication*]
TLOS........	Tailored List of Spares [*Military*] (AFIT)
TLOS........	Telos Corp. [*Santa Monica, CA*] [*NASDAQ symbol*] (NQ)
TLOS........	Troop List for Operations and Supply
TLO(S)	Turbine Lube Oil (System) [*Nuclear energy*] (NRCH)
TLOST	Turbine Lube Oil Storage Tank [*Nuclear energy*] (NRCH)
TLP...........	Tabular List of Parts (AAG)
TLP...........	Tactical Leadership Program [*Military*]
T/LP.........	Tail Lamp [*Automotive engineering*]
TLP...........	Tapered Link Pin
TLP...........	Target Letter Position [*Psychology*]
TLP...........	Telegraph Line Pair (BUR)
TLP...........	Telephone Line Patch
TLP...........	Tenera LP [*AMEX symbol*] (SPSG)
TLP...........	Tension-Leg Platform [*Oil exploration*]
TLP...........	Term-Limit Pricing [*Agreement*] [*Price Commission*]
TLP...........	Therapeutic Learning Program [*Psychology*]
TLP...........	Threshold Learning Process (IEEE)
TLP...........	Top Load Pad (NRCH)
TLP...........	Top Load Plane [*Nuclear energy*] (NRCH)
TLP...........	Torpedo Landplane [*Navy*]
TLP...........	Total Language Processor [*Data processing*] (IEEE)
TLP...........	Total Liquid Product [*Chemical engineering*]
TLP...........	Total Loss of Pay [*Court-martial sentence*] [*Military*]
TLP...........	Transient Lunar Phenomena
TLP...........	Transmission Level Point [*Telecommunications*]
TLP...........	Travaux Linguistiques de Prague [*A publication*]
TLP...........	Trouble Location Problem (AAG)
TLP...........	Truck Loading Point (NATG)
0TLP........	Zero Transmission Level Point (IEEE)
TLPC........	Castries/Vigie [*St. Lucia*] [*ICAO location identifier*] (ICLI)
TLPC........	Tailpiece
TLPJ........	Trial Lawyers for Public Justice (EA)
TLPL	Vieux-Fort/Hewanorra International [*St. Lucia*] [*ICAO location identifier*] (ICLI)
TLPR........	Terrestrial Low-Power Reactor
TLQ	Temple Law Quarterly [*A publication*]
TLQ	Travaux de Linguistique Quantitative [*A publication*]
TLQue........	Travaux de Linguistique Quebecoise [*A publication*]
TLR...........	Tailor
TLR...........	Tally Resources [*Vancouver Stock Exchange symbol*]
TLR...........	Tanganyika Law Reports [*1921-52*] [*A publication*] (DLA)
TLR...........	Tanzania Gazette Law Reports [*A publication*] (DLA)
TLR...........	Tape Loop Recorder
TLR...........	Tasmanian Law Reports [*A publication*] (APTA)
TLR...........	Tax Law Review [*A publication*]
TLR...........	Telerate, Inc. [*NYSE symbol*] (SPSG)
TLR...........	Teller
TLR...........	Tiler [*Freemasonry*]
TLR...........	Tiller (MSA)
TLR...........	Times Law Reports [*1884-1952*] [*England*] [*A publication*] (DLA)
TLR...........	Toll Line Release
TLR...........	Tool Liaison Request (AAG)
TLR...........	Top Level Requirements [*Navy*]
TLR...........	Topped Long Resid [*Petroleum technology*]
TLR...........	Trailer (AAG)
TLR...........	Travancore Law Reports [*India*] [*A publication*] (DLA)
TLR...........	Triangulation-Listening-Ranging [*SONAR*]
TLR...........	Tulane Law Review [*A publication*]
TLR...........	Tulare, CA [*Location identifier*] [*FAA*] (FAAL)
TLR...........	Twin Lens Reflex [*Camera*] (MCD)
TLRC........	Technology and Livelihood Resource Center [*Philippines*] [*Information service or system*] (IID)
TLRG........	Target List Review Group (CINC)
TLRMTD ..	Trailer Mounted
TLRNC.......	Tolerance (FAAC)
TLRP........	Track Last Reference Position
TLR (R)	Tanganyika Law Reports (Revised) [*1921-52*] [*A publication*] (DLA)
TLR/S........	Total Logistic Readiness/Sustainability Analysis [*Military*]
TLRS	Transportable LASER Ranging Station [*for measurement of earth movement*]
TLRT........	Telerent Leasing Corp. [*NASDAQ symbol*] (NQ)

TLRV........	Tracked Levitated Research Vehicle
TLS...........	Laredo State University, Laredo, TX [*OCLC symbol*] (OCLC)
TLS...........	Tactical Landing System
TLS...........	Talasea [*New Britain*] [*Seismograph station code, US Geological Survey*] (SEIS)
TLS...........	Tank LASER Sight (MCD)
TLS...........	Tape Librarian System
TLS...........	Target Location System
TLS...........	Technical Library Service (IID)
TLS...........	Telecommunication Liaison Staff (IEEE)
TLS...........	Telemetry Listing Submodule
TLS...........	Telescope (KSC)
TLS...........	Terminal Landing System (KSC)
TLS...........	Territorial Long Service Medal [*Military*] [*British*]
TLS...........	Testing the Limits for Sex [*Psychology*]
TLS...........	Theater Level Scenario [*Military*]
TLS...........	Thin Liquid Stillage [*Fermentation byproduct*]
TLS...........	Throttle Lever Setting (KSC)
TLS...........	Tifton Loamy Soil [*Agronomy*]
TLS...........	Time Limited Signal
TLS...........	Time Line Sheet [*NASA*]
TLS...........	Times Literary Supplement [*London*] [*A publication*]
TLS...........	Tool Lending Service [*Australia*]
TLS...........	Top Left Side (MCD)
TLS...........	Top Level Specification [*Military*] (CAAL)
TLS...........	Total Library System [*OCLC*]
TLS...........	Total Logic Solution
TLS...........	Total Luminescence Spectroscopy
TLS...........	Toulouse [*France*] [*Airport symbol*] (OAG)
TLS...........	Training Launch Station (MCD)
TLS...........	Two-Level System [*Physics*]
TLS...........	Typed Letter Signed
TLSA........	Torso Limb Suit Assembly (MCD)
TLSA........	Transparent Line Sharing Adapter
TLSAP.......	Wydawnictwa Slaskie Polskiej Akademii Umiejetnosci. Prace Jezykowe. Publications Silesiennes. Academie Polonaise des Sciences et des Lettres. Travaux Linguistiques [*A publication*]
TLSC........	Target Logistics Support Costs
TLSC........	TLS Company [*NASDAQ symbol*] (NQ)
TLSCP.......	Telescope (MSA)
TLSD........	Torque-Limiting Screwdriver
TLSFT.......	Tailshaft
TLSG........	Turret Lathe Stop Gauge
TLSGT.......	Tactical Landing System Guidance Techniques (MCD)
TLSM........	Talouselama [*A publication*]
TLSO........	Thoracolumbosacral Orthosis [*Medicine*]
TLSP........	Telecommunications Specialists, Inc. [*NASDAQ symbol*] (NQ)
TLSP........	Transponder Location by Surface Positioning [*RADAR*]
TLSS.........	Tactical Life Support System [*G-suit developed by Boeing Co.*]
TLSS.........	Technical Library Services Section
TLSS.........	Telesis Systems Corp. [*Chelmsford, MA*] [*NASDAQ symbol*] (NQ)
TLT...........	LeTourneau College, Longview, TX [*OCLC symbol*] (OCLC)
TLT...........	Teleprinter Load Tables (KSC)
TLT...........	Telstar Resource Corp. [*Vancouver Stock Exchange symbol*]
TLT...........	Toilet
TLT...........	Transportable Link Terminal [*AMC*]
TLT...........	Travancore Law Times [*India*] [*A publication*] (DLA)
TLT...........	Tuluksak [*Alaska*] [*Airport symbol*] (OAG)
TLT...........	Tuluksak, AK [*Location identifier*] [*FAA*] (FAAL)
TLTA........	Thin Line Towed Array [*Navy*] (CAAL)
TLTA........	Two-Loop Test Apparatus [*Nuclear energy*] (NRCH)
TLTB........	Trunk Line Tariff Bureau
TLTC........	Ta-Lu Tsa-Chih [*Continent Magazine*] [*Taiwan*] [*A publication*]
TLTK........	Teletek, Inc. [*NASDAQ symbol*] (NQ)
TLTK........	Tool Truck
TL to TL	Tangent Line to Tangent Line [*Engineering*]
TLTL........	Teaching Language through Literature [*A publication*]
TLTM........	Teletimer International, Inc. [*NASDAQ symbol*] (NQ)
TLTM........	Third Level Thermal Margin [*Nuclear energy*] (NRCH)
TLTP.........	Too Long to Print [*Strip marking*] [*Aviation*] (FAAC)
TLTP.........	Trunk Line Test Panel [*Telecommunications*] (TEL)
TLTR.........	Translator (AFM)
TLTS.........	Tracking Loop Test Set
TLU	Table Look Up [*Data processing*]
TLU	Terminal Logic Unit [*Telecommunications*] (TEL)
TLU	Threshold Logic Unit
TLU	Time of Last Update
TLU	Tolu [*Colombia*] [*Airport symbol*] (OAG)
TLU	Transportable LASER Unit
TLU	Tropical Livestock Unit [*Ratio of livestock to humans*]
TLV...........	Talemon Investments Ltd. [*Vancouver Stock Exchange symbol*]
TLV...........	Target Launch Vehicle [*NASA*]
TLV...........	Tel Aviv-Yafo [*Israel*] [*Airport symbol*] (OAG)
TLV...........	Threshold Limit Value [*Industrial hygiene*]
TLV...........	Total Lung Volume [*Physiology*]
TLV...........	Track Levitated Vehicle [*Department of Transportation*]
TLv...........	Transition Level
TLV...........	Transporter - Loader Vehicle [*NASA*] (NASA)
TLV...........	Two-Lung Ventilation [*Medicine*]
TLW..........	[*The*] Lighted Way [*An association*] (EA)
TLW..........	Test Load Wire
TLW	Torpedo Lieutenant's Writer [*British military*] (DMA)
TLWD........	Tail Wind (FAAC)
TLWM........	Trinity Low-Water Mark
TLWS........	Terrier Land Weapon System
T Lwyr	Tax Lawyer [*A publication*]
TLX...........	TELEX [*Automated Teletypewriter Exchange Service*] [*Western Union Corp.*]
TLX...........	Trans-Lux Corp. [*AMEX symbol*] (SPSG)
TLX...........	Transfer-Line Exchanger [*Manufacturing technology*]
TLX...........	Tri-Line Expressways Ltd. [*Toronto Stock Exchange symbol*]
TLX...........	Trophoblast/Lymphocyte Cross-Reactive (Antigens) [*Immunochemistry*]
TLXN	Telxon Corp. [*NASDAQ symbol*] (NQ)
TLY...........	Tally
TLYYA4	Co-Operative Bulletin. Taiwan Forestry Research Institute [*A publication*]
TLZ...........	Target Launch Zone
TLZ...........	Theologische Literaturzeitung [*A publication*]
TLZ...........	Titanium-Lead-Zinc
TLZ...........	Transfer on Less than Zero
TM............	Linhas Aereas de Mocambique [*LAM*] [*Mozambique*] [*ICAO designator*] (FAAC)
TM............	[*The*] Maccabees [*Southfield, MI*] (EA)
TM............	Memphis-Shelby County Public Library and Information Center, Memphis, TN [*Library symbol*] [*Library of Congress*] (LCLS)
TM............	National Income Tax Magazine [*A publication*] (DLA)
TM............	T-Cell Marker [*Biochemistry*]
TM............	Table Maintenance (NASA)
TM............	Tactical Manager [*Military*] (CAAL)
TM............	Tactical Missile [*Air Force*]
TM............	Tactical Monitor
TM............	Tailor-Made (DSUE)
TM............	Talking Machine
TM............	Tangent Mechanism
TM............	Tape Mark [*Data processing*] (BUR)
TM............	Tape Module (DEN)
TM............	Target Mechanism (MCD)
TM............	Taurine Mustard [*Antineoplastic drug*]
TM............	Tax Magazine [*A publication*] (DLA)
TM............	Tax Management [*A publication*] (DLA)
TM............	Tax Memo [*A publication*] (DLA)
TM............	Tax Module [*IRS*]
TM............	Team (AABC)
TM............	Team Member
TM............	Technical Manager
TM............	Technical Manual
TM............	Technical Memorandum
TM............	Technical Minutes
TM............	Technical Monograph
TM............	Tectorial Membrane [*of the cochlea*] [*Ear anatomy*]
TM............	Tele-Metropole, Inc. [*Toronto Stock Exchange symbol*]
TM............	Telegramme Multiple [*Telegram with Multiple Addresses*] [*French*] (ROG)
TM............	Telemetry
TM............	Telephone Museum (EA)
TM............	Temperature, Mean
TM............	Temperature Meter
TM............	Temperature Monitor (NRCH)
TM............	Temple Magazine [*A publication*] (ROG)
TM............	Temple of Man (EA)
T & M	Temple and Mew's English Criminal Appeal Cases [*A publication*] (DLA)
T & M	Temple and Mew's English Crown Cases [*1848-51*] [*A publication*] (DLA)
TM............	Temporomandibular [*Anatomy*]
TM............	Temps Modernes [*A publication*]
TM............	Tennessee Musician [*A publication*]
TM............	Tenu'at Ha-Moshavim (BJA)
TM............	Test Manual
T & M	Test and Measurement [*Quality control*]
TM............	Test Mode
TM............	Test Model [*NASA*]
T & M	Test and Monitor (CAAL)
TM............	Texas Mexican Railway Co. [*AAR code*]
TM............	Textus Minores [*A publication*]
TM............	Thalassemia Major [*Hematology*]
TM............	Thames Measurement [*Formula for rating yachts*] [*British*]
TM............	Theatre Magazine [*A publication*]
TM............	Their Majesties
TM............	Thematic Mapper [*Satellite technology*]
TM............	Thermal Mapper
TM............	Third Market [*Securities*]
TM............	Thompson Medical Co., Inc. [*NYSE symbol*] (SPSG)
Tm............	Thulium [*Chemical element*]
Tm............	Time [*A publication*]
TM............	Time Management (MCD)

T & M	Time and Materials
TM	Time, Mission
TM	Time Modulation
TM	Time Monitor
TM	Time Motion Technique
TM	Timing of Movements [*Physiology*]
Tm	Timothy [*New Testament book*]
TM	Titanium Chloride [*Inorganic chemistry*]
TM	Tlalocan: A Journal of Source Materials on the Native Cultures of Mexico [*A publication*]
TM	Tobramycin [*An antibiotic*]
TM	Toelichting-Meijers [*A publication*]
TM	Tolerant Majority　(EA)
TM	Ton-Miles
TM	Tone Modulation
TM	Tons per Minute
TM	Top Man
TM	Top Management
TM	Torpedoman's Mate [*Navy rating*]
T/M	Torque Meter　(NG)
TM	Torque Motor
TM	Tour du Monde [*World Tour*] [*French*]　(BJA)
TM	Tourism Management [*A publication*]
TM	Town Major [*British military*]　(DMA)
TM	Track Monitor　(CAAL)
TM	Tractor Monoplane
TM	Trade Mission
TM	Trademark
TM	Traffic Manager
TM	Traffic Model　(NASA)
TM	Trager's Medium [*Chemically defined culture medium*]
TM	Trained Man [*British military*]　(DMA)
TM	Training Manual [*Military*]
TM	Training Memorandum　(DAS)
TM	Training Missions [*Air Force*]
TM	Trainmaster [*Railroading*]
TM	Transantarctic Mountains
TM	Transcendental Meditation
TMaab	Transfer Memorandum
TM	Transition Management
TM	"Transitional" Mucosa [*Oncology*]
TM	Transmedullary [*Anatomy*]
TM	Transmembrane Domain [*Genetics*]
TM	Transmembrane Substitution Mutants [*Genetics*]
TM	Transmetatarsal [*Anatomy*]
TM	Transmission Matrix　(IEEE)
TM	Transmittal Memorandum　(MCD)
TM	Transport Mechanism [*Physiology*]
TM	Transverse Magnetic
TM	Travelwriter Marketletter [*Information service or system*]　(IID)
TM	Trench Mortar
TM	Trombone, Muted
TM	Tropical Maritime
TM	Tropical Medicine
TM	Tropomyosin [*Biochemistry*]
TM	True Mean
TM	True Motion [*RADAR*]　(DEN)
TM	Truncation Mutant
TM	Tuberal Magnocellular [*Nuclei, neuroanatomy*]
TM	Tunicamycin [*Biochemistry*]
TM	Tuning Meter　(DEN)
TM	Turing Machine [*Mathematical model*] [*Data processing*]
TM	Turkiyat Mecmuasi [*A publication*]
TM	Twisting Moment
TM	Tygodnik Morski [*A publication*]
TM1	Tympanic Membrane [*Anatomy*]
TM1	Torpedoman's Mate, First Class [*Navy rating*]
T/M²d	Metric Tons per Square Meter
TM2	Torpedoman's Mate, Second Class [*Navy rating*]
T/M³	Metric Tons per Cubic Meter
TM3	Torpedoman's Mate, Third Class [*Navy rating*]
TMA	Memphis Academy of Arts, Memphis, TN [*Library symbol*] [*Library of Congress*]　(LCLS)
TMA	Memphis State University, Memphis, TN [*OCLC symbol*]　(OCLC)
TMA	[*The*] Money Advocate [*A publication*]
TMA	[*The*] Mosquito Association　(EA)
TMA	Taiwan Maintenance Agency [*Military*]　(AABC)
TMA	Target Motion Analyzer
TMA	Telecommunications Managers Association [*Orpington, England*]　(TSSD)
TMA	TeleManagement Associates [*Telecommunications service*]　(TSSD)
TMA	Temperature Monitoring Apparatus
TMA	Tennis Manufacturers Association [*Later, ATF*]　(EA)
TMA	Terminal Control Area [*Aviation*]　(FAAC)
TMA	Terminal Maneuvering Area [*Aviation*]
TMA	Tetramethylammonium [*Organic chemistry*]
TMA	Theatrical Mutual Association　(EA)
TMA	Thermomagnetic Analysis [*Analytical chemistry*]
TMA	Thermomechanical Analysis [*or Analyzer*]
TMA	Thienylmalonic Acid [*Organic chemistry*]
TMA	Thiomalic Acid [*Organic chemistry*]
TMA	Thomas More Association　(EA)
TMA	Thomson McKinnon, Inc. [*NYSE symbol*]　(SPSG)
TMA	Thrombotic Microangiopathy [*Nephrology*]
TMA	Thyroid Microsomal Antibody [*Immunology*]
TMA	Tifton, GA [*Location identifier*] [*FAA*]　(FAAL)
TMA	Tile Manufacturers Association　(EA)
TMA	Time-Modulated Antenna
TMA	Tobacco Mechanics' Association [*A union*] [*British*]　(DCTA)
TMA	Tobacco Merchants Association of United States　(EA)
TMA	Toiletry Merchandising Association [*Later, NASM*]　(EA)
TMA	Tooling and Manufacturing Association
TMA	Top Management Abstracts [*A publication*]
TMA	Torpedo Main Assembly
TMA	Total Maintenance Actions　(MCD)
TMA	Total Materiel Assets [*Military*]
TMA	Toy Manufacturers of America　(EA)
TMA	Toyota Manufacturing Australia Ltd.
TMA	Trace Metals Analyzer
TMA	Traffic Management [*A publication*]
TMA	Traffic Management Agency　(CINC)
TMA	Trailer Manufacturers Association [*Later, NAMPS*]　(EA)
TMA	Training Media Association　(EA)
TMA	Trans-Mediterranean Airways　(BJA)
TMA	Trans Mo Airlines [*Jefferson City, MO*] [*FAA designator*]　(FAAC)
TMA	Transistor Magnetic-Pulse Amplifier
TMA	Transmetatarsal Amputation [*Medicine*]
TMA	Transport Museum Association　(EA)
TMA	Transportation Management Association
TMA	Trimac Ltd. [*Toronto Stock Exchange symbol*]
TMA	Trimellitic Anhydride [*Chemistry*]
TMA	Trimethyladenine [*Biochemistry*]
TMA	Trimethylaluminum [*Organic chemistry*]
TMA	Trimethylamine [*Organic chemistry*]
TMA	Trimethylammonium [*Organic chemistry*]
TMaab	Thyroid Microsomal Autoantibody [*Immunology*]
TMAB	Telecommunications Managers Association - Belgium　(TSSD)
TMAB	Temporary Missile Assembly Building　(AAG)
TMAB	Tetramethylammonium Borohydride [*Organic chemistry*]
TMA BITS	TMA [*Tobacco Merchants Association*] Bibliographic Index to the Tobacco Scene [*Database*]
TMAC	Agrico Chemical Co., Memphis, TN [*Library symbol*] [*Library of Congress*]　(LCLS)
TMAC	Telecommunication Management and Control [*AT & T*]
T-MAC	Test of Minimal Articulation Competence [*Speech evaluation test*]
TMACA	Telecommunications Managers Association of the Capital Area　(TSSD)
TMACS	Tone Multiplex Apollo Command System [*NASA*]　(KSC)
TMACS	Training Management Control System [*Army*]　(INF)
TMAD	Tank Main Armament Development　(MCD)
TMAD	Target Marker Air Droppable　(MCD)
TMAD	Target Marker and Dispenser　(MCD)
TMadH	Nashville Memorial Hospital, Madison, TN [*Library symbol*] [*Library of Congress*]　(LCLS)
TMadM	Madison Academy, Madison College, TN [*Library symbol*] [*Library of Congress*]　(LCLS)
TMAE	Tetrakis(dimethylamino)ethylene [*Organic chemistry*]
TMAG	Travel More Advantageous to the Government　(AAG)
TMAGD	Tennessee Magazine [*A publication*]
TMAH	Tetramethylammonium Hydroxide [*Organic chemistry*]
TMAI	Tetramethylammonium Iodide [*Organic chemistry*]
TMAIC	Trimethallyl Isocyanurate [*Organic chemistry*]
TMAM	Training and Doctrine Command Mission Area Manager [*Army*]
TMAMAP	Ezhegodnik Instituta Eksperimental'noi Meditsiny Akademii Meditsinskikh Nauk SSSR [*A publication*]
TMAN	Tel/Man, Inc. [*Greenville, SC*] [*NASDAQ symbol*]　(NQ)
TMAO	Trimethylamine Oxide [*Organic chemistry*]
TMAO	Troop Movement Action Officer
TMAO	Troop Movement Assignment Order
TMAP	Teleoperated Mobile Antiarmor Platform [*Army*]　(INF)
TMAP	Temporary Mortgage Assistance Payments Program [*HUD*]
TMAP	Textile Mills Association of the Philippines　(DS)
TMARS	Technical Manual Audit and Requirement Reporting System　(MCD)
TMaryB	Blount Memorial Hospital, Medical Library, Maryville, TN [*Library symbol*] [*Library of Congress*]　(LCLS)
TMaryC	Maryville College, Maryville, TN [*Library symbol*] [*Library of Congress*]　(LCLS)
TMAS	Tank Main Armament Systems　(RDA)
TMAS	Taylor Manifest Anxiety State [*Psychology*]
TMAS	TriMas Corp. [*NASDAQ symbol*]　(CTT)
TMATB	Technische Mitteilungen AEG- [*Allgemeine Elektrizitaets-Gesellschaft*] Telefunken [*A publication*]
TMaU	University of Tennessee at Martin, Martin, TN [*Library symbol*] [*Library of Congress*]　(LCLS)
TMAX	Maximum Time [*Telecommunications*]　(TEL)

TMAX	Telematics International, Inc. [*NASDAQ symbol*] (NQ)
TMB	David W. Taylor Model Basin [*Also, DATMOBAS, DTMB*] [*Later, DTNSRDC, NSRDC*]
TMB	Iemootsies [*A publication*]
TMB	Miami, FL [*Location identifier*] [*FAA*] (FAAL)
TMB	Tambrands, Inc. [*NYSE symbol*] (SPSG)
TMB	Task Maintenance Burden
TMB	Tetramethylbenzidine [*Organic chemistry*]
TMB	Textes Mathematiques Babyloniens [*A publication*] (BJA)
TMB	Thimble
TMB	Tide-Measuring Buoy
TMB	Time Maintenance Began [*Military*] (AFIT)
TMB	Transportation Management Bulletin [*NASA*] (NASA)
TMB	Trench Mortar Battery [*British military*] (DMA)
TMB	Trimethoxyboroxine [*Organic chemistry*]
TMB	Trimethylbenzene [*Organic chemistry*]
TMB	Tumble (MSA)
TMB	University of Texas, Medical Branch Library, Galveston, TX [*OCLC symbol*] (OCLC)
TMBA	Brooks Art Gallery, Memphis, TN [*Library symbol*] [*Library of Congress*] (LCLS)
TMBA	Tetramethylene-bis-Acetamide [*Biochemistry*]
TMBA	Trimethylbenzanthracene [*Carcinogen*]
TMBAC	Trimethylbenzylammonium Chloride [*Also, BTM*] [*Organic chemistry*]
TMBC	Buckeye Cellulose Corp., Technical Division Library, Memphis, TN [*Library symbol*] [*Library of Congress*] (LCLS)
TMBDA	Tetramethylbutanediamine [*Organic chemistry*]
TMBDB	Thermal Margin beyond Design Basis [*Nuclear energy*] (NRCH)
TMBH	Baptist Memorial Hospital, Memphis, TN [*Library symbol*] [*Library of Congress*] (LCLS)
TMBH-N	Baptist Memorial Hospital, School of Nursing, Memphis, TN [*Library symbol*] [*Library of Congress*] (LCLS)
TMBL	Buckman Laboratories, Inc., Memphis, TN [*Library symbol*] [*Library of Congress*] (LCLS)
TMBL	Tacoma Municipal Belt Line Railway [*AAR code*]
TMBO	Team Management by Objectives [*Management technique*] (ADA)
TMBP	(Tetramethylbutyl)phenol [*Organic chemistry*]
TMBR	Timber (AAG)
TMBR	Tom Brown, Inc. [*NASDAQ symbol*] (NQ)
TMBS	Timberline Software Corp. [*NASDAQ symbol*] (NQ)
TMBU	Table Maintenance Block Update (NASA)
TM Bull	Trade Mark Bulletin, New Series [*A publication*] (DLA)
TMC	Chief Torpedoman's Mate [*Navy rating*]
TMC	Houston Academy of Medicine for Texas Medical Center, Houston, TX [*OCLC symbol*] (OCLC)
TMC	Indo-Pacific International [*Tamuning, GU*] [*FAA designator*] (FAAC)
TMC	[*The*] Maintenance Council of the American Trucking Associations (EA)
TMC	[*The*] Mouse Club (EA)
TMC	[*The*] Movie Channel [*Cable-television system*]
TMC	Revue Tiers-Monde [*A publication*]
TMC	Table Mountain [*California*] [*Seismograph station code, US Geological Survey*] [*Closed*] (SEIS)
TMC	Tactical Medical Center
TMC	Tambolaka [*Indonesia*] [*Airport symbol*] (OAG)
TMC	Tape Management Catalog
TMC	Telamarketing Communications, Inc. [*Louisville, KY*] [*Telecommunications*] (TSSD)
TMC	Telecommunications Management Corporation [*Needham Heights, MA*] (TSSD)
TMC	Telecommunications Marketing Corporation [*Bay Shore, NY*] (TSSD)
TMC	Temporary Minor Change (MCD)
TMC	Terrestrial Microcosm Chamber [*For environmental studies*]
TMC	Test, Monitor, and Control [*Aviation*]
TMC	Test Monitoring Console (NASA)
TMC	Thermal Micrometeoroid Cover (MCD)
TMC	Thick Molding Compound [*Plastics technology*]
TM-C	Thomas Micro-Catalogs
TMC	Three-Mode Control (AAG)
TMC	Thrust Magnitude Control (KSC)
TMC	[*The*] Times Mirror Company [*NYSE symbol*] (SPSG)
TMC	Titan Missile Contractor (AAG)
TMC	Tool Management Culture
TMC	Total Market Coverage [*Advertising*]
TMC	Transition Metal Chemistry [*A publication*]
TMC	Transmedia Enterprises, Inc. [*Vancouver Stock Exchange symbol*]
TMC	Transmission Maintenance Center [*Telecommunications*] (TEL)
TMC	Transport Movement Control [*Military*] (AFM)
TMC	Transportation Materiel Command [*AMC - Mobility*]
TMC	Trinity Ministries Center (EA)
TMC	Triple Molecular Collision
TMC	Tube Moisture Control
TMCA	Thrust Management Control Analysis
TMCA	Titanium Metals Corporation of America

TMCA	Toxic Materials Control Activity [*General Motors Corp.*]
TMCBC	Christian Brothers College, Memphis, TN [*Library symbol*] [*Library of Congress*] (LCLS)
TMCC	Chapman Chemical Co., Memphis, TN [*Library symbol*] [*Library of Congress*] (LCLS)
TMCC	Theater Movement Control Center [*Military*] (AABC)
TMCC	Time-Multiplexer Communications Channels
TMCDT	Trimethylcyclododecatriene [*Organic chemistry*]
TMCF	Campbell Foundation, Memphis, TN [*Library symbol*] [*Library of Congress*] (LCLS)
TMCH	City of Memphis Hospital, Memphis, TN [*Library symbol*] [*Library of Congress*] (LCLS)
TMCHD	Transition Metal Chemistry [*A publication*]
TMCI	Telemetering Control Indicator
TMCI	TM Century [*NASDAQ symbol*] (NQ)
TMCIA	Temperature. Its Measurement and Control in Science and Industry [*A publication*]
TMckB	Bethel College, McKenzie, TN [*Library symbol*] [*Library of Congress*] (LCLS)
TMckB-C	Cumberland Presbyterian Theological Seminary, Bethel College, McKenzie, TN [*Library symbol*] [*Library of Congress*] (LCLS)
TMCL	Target Map Coordinate Locator [*Military*]
TMCM	Master Chief Torpedoman's Mate [*Navy rating*]
TMCO	Time Management Corp. [*NASDAQ symbol*] (NQ)
TMCOMP	Telemetry Computation
TMCOT	Tetramethylcyclooctatetraene [*Organic chemistry*]
TMCP	Trimethylcyclopentanone [*Organic chemistry*]
TMCR	Technical Manual Change Request [*or Requirement*]
TMCR	Technical Manual Contract Requirement
TMCRL	Tailored Master Cross Reference List [*Military*] (AABC)
TMCS	Memphis City Schools Professional Library, Memphis, TN [*Library symbol*] [*Library of Congress*] (LCLS)
TMCS	Senior Chief Torpedoman's Mate [*Navy rating*]
TMCS	Tactical Maintenance Control System
TMCS	Toshiba Minicomputer Complex System
TMCS	Trimethylchlorosilane [*Organic chemistry*]
TMD	Meharry Medical College, Nashville, TN [*OCLC symbol*] (OCLC)
TMD	Tactical Mission Data [*Military*] (AFM)
TMD	Tactical Munitions Dispenser (MCD)
TMD	Technical Manual Designation
TMD	Telemedia, Inc. [*Toronto Stock Exchange symbol*]
TMD	Telemetered Data (AAG)
TMD	Temperature of Maximum Density
TMD	Tetramethyldioxetane [*Organic chemistry*]
TMD	Theater Missile Defense
TMD	Theoretical Maximum Density
TMD	Thermedics, Inc. [*AMEX symbol*] (SPSG)
TMD	Timed (MSA)
TMD	Toluene-Methanol-Dioxane [*Scintillation solvent*]
TMD	Toxicology and Microbiology Division [*Cincinnati, OH*] [*Environmental Protection Agency*] (GRD)
TMD	Training Media Database [*Access Innovations, Inc.*] [*Information service or system*] (CRD)
TMD	Transient Mass Distribution Code [*Nuclear energy*] (NRCH)
TMD	Transmembrane Domain [*Genetics*]
TMDA	Training Media Distributors Association [*Later, TMA*] (EA)
TMDAG	This Mode of Transportation has been Determined to be More Advantageous to the Government
TMDC	Technical Manual Data Cards [*DoD*] (MCD)
TMDC	TIME-DC, Inc. [*NASDAQ symbol*] (NQ)
TMDC	Transportation Movement Document Control (MCD)
TM & DE	Test, Measuring, and Diagnostic Equipment [*Later, TMDE*] [*Army*] (AABC)
TMDE	Test, Measuring, and Diagnostic Equipment [*Formerly, TM & DE*] [*Army*] (AABC)
TMDESE	Test, Measurement, and Diagnostic Equipment Support Equipment [*Army*]
TMDESG	Test, Management, and Diagnostic Equipment Support Group [*Army*] (MCD)
TMDI	Transponder Miss Distance Indicator
TMDI	Trimethylhexamethylene Diisocyanate [*Organic chemistry*]
TMDI	United States Defense Industrial Plant Equipment Center, Memphis, TN [*Library symbol*] [*Library of Congress*] (LCLS)
TMDL	Technical Manual Data List [*DoD*]
TMDL	Total Maximum Daily Load [*Environmental Protection Agency*]
TMDO	Training Management Development Office [*Army*]
TMDP	Technetium Methylene Diphosphonate [*Organic chemistry*]
TMDR	Technical Manual Data Record [*DoD*] (MCD)
TMDS	Test, Measurement, and Diagnostic Systems [*Army*] (RDA)
TMDS	Tetramethyldisilazane [*Organic chemistry*]
TMDS	Trilineage Myelodysplasia Syndrome [*Medicine*]
TMDT	Total Mean Downtime
TMDT	Trace Metals Detection Technique
TMDT	Trimethyldodecatetraene [*Organic chemistry*]
TME	Eastwood Hospital, Memphis, TN [*Library symbol*] [*Library of Congress*] (LCLS)
TME	[*The*] Main Event [*A publication*]

TME	Tame [*Colombia*] [*Airport symbol*] (OAG)
TME	Teacher of Medical Electricity [*British*]
TME	Termex Resources, Inc. [*Vancouver Stock Exchange symbol*]
TME	Test Maintenance Equipment [*Data processing*]
TME	Test Marketing Exemption [*Environmental Protection Agency*]
TME	Test and Measurement Equipment (MCD)
TME	Tetramethylethylene [*Organic chemistry*]
TME	Theatre Mask Ensemble
TME	Thermal Marrow Expansion [*Roentgenology*]
TME	Thermal/Mechanical Enzyme [*Fermentation*]
TME	Thrust Monopropellant Engine
TME	TME Resources, Inc. [*Vancouver Stock Exchange symbol*]
TME	Torpedoman's Mate, Electrical [*Navy rating*]
TME	Total Market Estimate (ADA)
TME	Total Metabolizable Energy [*Nutrition*]
TME	Transmissible Mink Encephalopathy
TME	Transmural Enteritis [*Medicine*]
TME	Trimethylolethane [*Organic chemistry*]
TMEA	Typewriter Manufacturers Export Association [*Defunct*]
TMECO	Time of Main Engine Cutoff [*Aerospace*] (MCD)
TMED	Tetramethylethylenediamine [*Also, TEMED, TMEDA*] [*Organic chemistry*]
TMED	Trimedyne, Inc. [*NASDAQ symbol*] (NQ)
TMEDA	Tetramethylethylenediamine [*Also, TEMED, TMED*] [*Organic chemistry*]
TMEDA	Trimethylenediamine [*Organic chemistry*]
TME/FH...	Total Maintenance Effort per Flight Hour [*Navy*] (NG)
TMEL......	Tender Master Equipment List
TMEL......	Trimethylethyllead [*Organic chemistry*]
TM-ENG...	Technical Manual - Engineering [*Marine Corps*]
TMEP......	Trademark Manual of Examining Procedure [*A publication*] (DLA)
TMeP......	Trimethylpsoralen [*Photochemotherapeutic compound*]
TMEPS	Transverse-Mounted Engine Propulsion System
TMES.......	Tactical Missile Electrical Simulator [*Obsolete*]
TMESS......	Telemessage (DS)
TMETN.....	Trimethylolethane Trinitrate [*Organic chemistry*]
TMEV	Theiler's Murine Encephalitis Virus
TMEX......	Terra Mines Ltd. [*NASDAQ symbol*] (NQ)
TMF	Technical Transmitter Holding Future (MCD)
TMF	Telemetry Module Facility
TMF	Test Mode Fail [*Apollo*] [*NASA*]
TMF	Time Marker Frequency
TMF	Transaction Monitoring Facility [*Tandem Computers*]
TMF	Transfer Mold Forming (MCD)
TMF	Transporter Maintenance Facility [*NASA*] (NASA)
TMF	Trunk Maintenance Files [*Telecommunications*] (TEL)
TMFC......	Ted McGinley Fan Club (EA)
TMFL......	Time of Flight (MSA)
TMFZA	Teoreticheskaya i Matematicheskaya Fizika [*A publication*]
TMG.........	Goodwyn Institute, Memphis, TN [*Library symbol*] [*Library of Congress*] (LCLS)
TMG.........	Tactical Missile Group [*Air Force*]
TMG.........	Tetramethylguanidine [*Organic chemistry*]
TMG.........	Thermal Meteoroid [*or Micrometeoroid*] Garment [*NASA*] (KSC)
TMG.........	Thermomagnetometry [*Analytical chemistry*]
TMG.........	Thiomethylgalactoside [*Organic chemistry*]
TMG.........	Time Mark Generator
TMG.........	Timing
TMG.........	Tomanggong [*Malaysia*] [*Airport symbol*] (OAG)
TMG.........	Track Made Good [*Aviation*]
TMG.........	Trimethylgallium [*Organic chemistry*]
TMG.........	Trimethylguanosine [*Biochemistry*]
TMGA	Tetramethyleneglutaric Acid [*Organic chemistry*]
TMGC	W. R. Grace & Co., Agricultural Chemicals Group, Memphis, TN [*Library symbol*] [*Library of Congress*] (LCLS)
TMGD......	Timing Devices (MSA)
TMGE	Thermomagnetic-Galvanic Effect
TMGFC.....	[*The*] Mel Gibson Fan Club [*Defunct*] (EA)
TMGG	Goldsmith Civic Garden Center, Memphis, TN [*Library symbol*] [*Library of Congress*] (LCLS)
TMGRS.....	Trace Material Generation Rate Simulator
TMGS........	Church of Jesus Christ of Latter-Day Saints, Genealogical Society Library, Memphis Branch, Memphis, TN [*Library symbol*] [*Library of Congress*] (LCLS)
TMGS........	Terrestrial Magnetic Guidance System [*Aerospace*] (AAG)
TMH.........	Harding Graduate School of Religion, Memphis, TN [*Library symbol*] [*Library of Congress*] (LCLS)
TMH.........	Tanahmerah [*Indonesia*] [*Airport symbol*] (OAG)
TMH.........	Texas Military History [*A publication*]
TMH.........	Texte und Materialien der Frau Professor Hilprecht Collection of Babylonian Antiquities im Eigentum der Universitaet Jena (BJA)
TMH.........	Tomahawk Resources [*Vancouver Stock Exchange symbol*]
TMH.........	Tons per Man-Hour
TMH.........	Trainable Mentally Handicapped
TMH.........	Trimethylhexane [*Organic chemistry*]
TMH.........	Trolley-Mounted Hoist (NRCH)
TMHA.......	Memphis Housing Authority, Memphis, TN [*Library symbol*] [*Library of Congress*] (LCLS)

TMHA.......	[*The*] Military Housing Association
TMHB.......	Harland Bartholomew & Associates, Memphis, TN [*Library symbol*] [*Library of Congress*] (LCLS)
TMHI	Holiday Inns of America, Memphis, TN [*Library symbol*] [*Library of Congress*] (LCLS)
TMHI-U....	Holiday Inn University, Olive Branch, MS [*Library symbol*] [*Library of Congress*] (LCLS)
TMHL.......	Triplet Metastable Helium Level
TMI	International Harvester Co., Memphis, TN [*Library symbol*] [*Library of Congress*] (LCLS)
TMI	[*The*] Media Institute (EA)
TMI	Midwestern State University, George Moffett Library, Wichita Falls, TX [*OCLC symbol*] (OCLC)
TMI	[*The*] Monroe Institute (EA)
TMI	[*The*] Mortgage Index, Inc. [*Remote Computing Corp.*] [*Information service or system*] (IID)
TMI	Tax Management International Journal [*A publication*]
TMI	Taylor Mountain [*Idaho*] [*Seismograph station code, US Geological Survey*] (SEIS)
TMI	Team, Incorporated [*AMEX symbol*] (SPSG)
TMI	Technical Management Items (NASA)
TMI	Technical Manual Index [*Navy*]
TMI	Teen Missions International (EA)
TMI	Telecommunications Management, Incorporated [*Oakbrook, IL*] [*Telecommunications*] (TSSD)
TmI	Telematica, Inc. [*Telecommunications service*] (TSSD)
TMI	Thornicroft's Mounted Infantry [*Military*] [*British*] (ROG)
TMI	Three Mile Island [*Pennsylvania*] [*Site of nuclear reactor accident, 1979*]
TMI	Time Air Corp. [*Toronto Stock Exchange symbol*]
TMI	Time Manager International [*Commercial firm*] [*British*]
TMI	Tolyl(mono)isocyanate [*Organic chemistry*]
TMI	Tool Manufacturing Instruction (AAG)
TMI	Tracking Merit Interception
TMI	Trans-Mars Injection [*Aerospace*]
TMI	Transmural Myocardial Infarction [*Cardiology*]
TMI	Travel Managers International (EA)
TMI	Trucking Management, Incorporated (EA)
TMI	Tumlingtar [*Nepal*] [*Airport symbol*] (OAG)
TMI	Tune-Up Manufacturers Institute (EA)
TMIA........	Three Mile Island Alert (EA)
TMIC........	Thomas Marketing Information Center [*Thomas Publishing Co.*] [*Information service or system*] (IID)
TMIC........	Toxic Materials Information Center [*Oak Ridge National Laboratory*] (IID)
TMICP	Topographic Map Inventory Control Point [*Army*] (AABC)
TMIEB	Trudy Moskovskii Institut Elektronnogo Mashinostroeniya [*A publication*]
TMIF........	Tumor-Cell Migratory Inhibition Factor [*Immunology*]
TMIFC	Tom Mix International Fan Club (EA)
TMIG	[*The*] Marketing Information Guide [*A publication*]
TMIG	Time in Grade [*Navy*]
TMilM.......	Milligan College, Milligan College, TN [*Library symbol*] [*Library of Congress*] (LCLS)
TMIMIS ...	Technical Manual Integrated Management Information Systems [*DoD*]
TMIN	Minimum Time [*Telecommunications*] (TEL)
TMiNA......	United States Naval Air Station Library, Millington, TN [*Library symbol*] [*Library of Congress*] (LCLS)
TMiNH	United States Naval Hospital, Millington, TN [*Library symbol*] [*Library of Congress*] (LCLS)
TMINS......	Technical Manual Identification Numbering System (MCD)
TMINS......	Three Mile Island Nuclear Station (NRCH)
TMIP........	Training Management Instruction Packet
TMIS	Tank Management Information System (MCD)
TMIS	Technical Meetings Information Service
TMIS	Total Management Information System
TMIU	Teletype Modulator Interface Units (MCD)
TMJ..........	Temporomandibular Joint Disorder [*Medicine*]
TMJ..........	Trade Marks Journal [*A publication*]
TMJS	Temporomandibular Joint Syndrome [*Medicine*]
TMK	Kimberly-Clark Corp., Memphis, TN [*Library symbol*] [*Library of Congress*] (LCLS)
TMK	Timiskaming [*Quebec*] [*Seismograph station code, US Geological Survey*] [*Closed*] (SEIS)
TMK	Tiravita Munnerrat Kalam
TMK	Tomahawk Airways, Inc. [*Alcoa, TN*] [*FAA designator*] (FAAC)
TMK	Tomsk [*USSR*] [*Geomagnetic observatory code*]
TMK	Tonnage Mark [*Found on each side of the ship aft*] (DS)
TMK	Torchmark Corp. [*NYSE symbol*] (SPSG)
TMK	Transistor Mounting Kit
TMK	Trumark Resource Corp. [*Vancouver Stock Exchange symbol*]
TMKFA	Technische Mitteilungen Krupp. Forschungsberichte [*A publication*]
TMKT	Technology Marketing, Inc. [*NASDAQ symbol*] (NQ)
TMKWA ...	Technische Mitteilungen Krupp. Werksberichte [*A publication*]
TML	Lakeside Hospital, Memphis, TN [*Library symbol*] [*Library of Congress*] (LCLS)
TML	Tamale [*Ghana*] [*Airport symbol*] (OAG)
TML	Tandem Matching Loss [*Telecommunications*] (TEL)

TML .... Technical Manual List (MCD)
TML .... Terminal (AABC)
TML .... Terrestrial Microwave Link
TML .... Tetramethyl Lead (MCD)
TML .... Tetramethyllead [*Organic chemistry*]
TML .... Texas Tech University, School of Medicine at Lubbock, Library of the Health Science, Lubbock, TX [*OCLC symbol*] (OCLC)
TML .... Thermomechanical Loading
TML .... Three-Mile Limit
TML .... Titanium Metallurgical Laboratory (MCD)
TML .... Transmanche-Link [*Eurotunnel*] (ECON)
TML .... Transportable Moisture Limit [*Shipping*] (DS)
TMLBC ..... Le Bonheur Children's Medical Center, Health Sciences Library, Memphis, TN [*Library symbol*] [*Library of Congress*] (LCLS)
TMLE........ Transient-Mode Liquid Epitaxy
TMLG .... Memphis Light, Gas, and Water Division Library, Memphis, TN [*Library symbol*] [*Library of Congress*] (LCLS)
TMLJ .... Thurgood Marshall Law Journal [*A publication*] (DLA)
TMLO .... LeMoyne-Owen College, Memphis, TN [*Library symbol*] [*Library of Congress*] (LCLS)
TM/LP ...... Thermal Margin/Low Pressure [*Nuclear energy*] (NRCH)
TML Rev ... Thurgood Marshall Law Review [*A publication*] (DLA)
TMM......... Memphis State University, Memphis, TN [*Library symbol*] [*Library of Congress*] (LCLS)
TMM......... Tamatave [*Madagascar*] [*Airport symbol*] (OAG)
TMM...... Tank Master Mechanic (MCD)
TMM...... Tax Management Memorandum [*Bureau of National Affairs*] [*A publication*] (DLA)
TMM........ Technocrat. A Monthly Review of Japanese Technology and Industry [*A publication*]
TMM........ Technologico De Monterrey [*Mexico*] [*Seismograph station code, US Geological Survey*] (SEIS)
TMM........ Test Message Monitor
TMM........ Thermal Mathematical Model
TMM........ Too Many Metaphors [*Used in correcting manuscripts, etc.*]
TMM........ Trimethylenemethane [*Organic chemistry*]
TMM........ Trimethylolmelamine [*Organic chemistry*]
TMMAB ... Mid-America Baptist Theological Seminary, Memphis, TN [*Library symbol*] [*Library of Congress*] (LCLS)
TMM-B..... Memphis State University, Bureau of Business Research Library, Memphis, TN [*Library symbol*] [*Library of Congress*] (LCLS)
TMMB ...... Truck Mixer Manufacturers Bureau (EA)
TMMBC... Mid-South Bible College, Memphis, TN [*Library symbol*] [*Library of Congress*] (LCLS)
TMMC ..... Tetramethylammonium Manganese Chloride [*Organic chemistry*]
TMMC ..... Theater Materiel Management Center [*Military*] (AABC)
TMMD...... Tactical Moving Map Display (MCD)
TMM-E..... Memphis State University, Engineering Library, Memphis, TN [*Library symbol*] [*Library of Congress*] (LCLS)
TMMEE.... Memphis Eye and Ear Hospital, Memphis, TN [*Library symbol*] [*Library of Congress*] (LCLS)
TMMG ...... Teacher of Massage and Medical Gymnastics [*British*]
TMMH...... Methodist Hospital, Stratton Medical Library, Memphis, TN [*Library symbol*] [*Library of Congress*] (LCLS)
TMMH-P ... Methodist Hospital, Pathology Library, Memphis, TN [*Library symbol*] [*Library of Congress*] (LCLS)
TMM-L..... Memphis State University, School of Law, Memphis, TN [*Library symbol*] [*Library of Congress*] (LCLS)
TMMM..... Textes et Monuments Figures Relatifs aux Mysteres de Mithra [*A publication*] (BJA)
TMMP...... Technical Manual Management Program [*Navy*] (NVT)
TMM-SH ... Memphis State University, Speech and Hearing Center, Memphis, TN [*Library symbol*] [*Library of Congress*] (LCLS)
TMMT ...... Technical Manual Management Team [*DoD*]
TMN......... Charlotte Amalie, St. Thomas, VI [*Location identifier*] [*FAA*] (FAAL)
TMN......... Memphis and Shelby County Public Library and Information Center, Memphis, TN [*OCLC symbol*] (OCLC)
TMN......... National Cotton Council of America, Memphis, TN [*Library symbol*] [*Library of Congress*] (LCLS)
TMN......... Tamana [*Kiribati*] [*Airport symbol*] (OAG)
TMN......... Tax Matters Newsletter [*Australia*] [*A publication*]
TMN......... Technical and Management Note (IEEE)
TMN......... Timber Mountain [*Nevada*] [*Seismograph station code, US Geological Survey*] (SEIS)
TMN......... Transmission (AFM)
TMN......... Trigeminal Mesencephalic Nucleus [*Neuroanatomy*]
TMN......... True Mach Number
TMNC...... Thai Maritime Navigation Co. Ltd. (DS)
TMNI....... Transmedia Network, Incorporated [*New York, NY*] [*NASDAQ symbol*] (NQ)
TMNP ...... [*The*] Mystery Readers Newsletter [*A publication*]
TMNT .... Teen-Age Mutant Ninja Turtles [*Name of comic book and cartoon characters and line of toys by Playmates Toys*]
TMo .... O Tempo e o Modo [*A publication*]
TMO.......... Targets Management Office [*MIRCOM*] (RDA)

TMO......... Technology Management Office [*Army*]
TMO......... Telegraph Money Order
TMO......... Test Manufacturing Order (NASA)
TMO......... Thermo Electron Corp. [*NYSE symbol*] (SPSG)
TMO......... Time Out
TMO......... Tool Manufacturing Order [*NASA*] (NASA)
TMO......... Tooling Manufacturing Outline
TMO......... Total Materiel Objective [*Military*]
TMO......... Traffic Management Office [*or Officer*] [*Air Force*] (AFM)
TMO......... Trans MO Airlines [*Jefferson City, MO*] [*FAA designator*] (FAAC)
TMO......... Transportation Movements Office [*or Officer*] [*Military*]
TMO......... Treminco Resources Ltd. [*Toronto Stock Exchange symbol*] [*Vancouver Stock Exchange symbol*]
TMO......... Tumeremo [*Venezuela*] [*Airport symbol*] (OAG)
TMOB .... Trade Marks Opposition Board [*Information service or system*] (EISS)
TMOD....... TMDE [*Test, Measuring, and Diagnostic Equipment*] Modernization [*Army*] (RDA)
TMOR ...... Technical Manual Ordtask Requirement (MCD)
TMorM...... Morristown College, Morristown, TN [*Library symbol*] [*Library of Congress*] (LCLS)
TMorNII ... Trudy Mordovskogo Nauchno-Issledovatel'skogo Instituta Jazyka, Literatury, Istorii, i Ekonomiki [*A publication*]
TMorNR... Nolichucky Regional Library Center, Morristown, TN [*Library symbol*] [*Library of Congress*] (LCLS)
TMOS ...... Tetramethoxysilane [*Organic chemistry*]
TMOS ...... Thermosetting (MSA)
T-MOS...... Trench-Metal Oxide Silicon [*Transistor*]
TMOT .... Target [*or Total*] Maximum Operating Time
TMOTFSM ... [*The*] Master of the Free School, Margate [*Pseudonym used by Zachariah Cozens*]
TMP .... East Timor [*ISO three-letter standard code*] (CNC)
TMP .... [*The*] Madison Project (EA)
TMP .... [*The*] Management Processor (MCD)
TMP .... Tampere [*Finland*] [*Airport symbol*] (OAG)
TMP .... Target Materials Program [*DoD*]
TMP .... Technical Manual Parts [*Army*] (AABC)
TMP .... Technical Manual Plan [*DoD*]
TMP .... Teleprinter Message Pool
TMP .... Temazepam [*Tranquilizer*]
TMP .... Temperature (BUR)
Tmp........... [*The*] Tempest [*Shakespearean work*]
TMP .... Terminal Monitor Program [*Data processing*] (BUR)
TMP .... Terminal Panel (NASA)
TMP .... Test Maintenance Panel [*Data processing*]
TMP .... Test Methods and Procedures
TMP .... Theodolite Measuring Point (MUGU)
TMP .... Thermal Mass Penalty (KSC)
TMP .... Thermal Modeling Program
TMP .... Thermomechanical Processing
TMP .... Thermomechanical Pulps
TMP .... Thermomicrophotometry
TMP .... Thymidine Monophosphate [*Biochemistry*]
TMP .... Thymolphthalein Monophosphate [*Biochemistry*]
TMP .... Time Management Processor (NASA)
TMP .... Times Mirror Press
TMP .... Total Milk Proteinate [*Trademark of New Zealand Milk Products, Inc.*]
TMP .... Traditional Medical Practice
TMP .... Trans Mountain Pipe Line Co. Ltd. [*Toronto Stock Exchange symbol*] [*Vancouver Stock Exchange symbol*]
TMP .... Transistor Mounting Pad
TMP .... Transmembrane Potential [*Biochemistry*]
TMP .... Transmembrane Protein [*Biochemistry*]
TMP .... Transportable Measurement Package (MCD)
TMP .... Transportation Motor Pool [*Military*] (AABC)
TMP .... Transversely Magnetized Plasma
TMP .... Trimetaphosphate [*Organic chemistry*]
TMP .... Trimethoprim [*Also, T*] [*Antibacterial compound*]
TMP .... Trimethyl Phosphate [*Organic chemistry*]
TMP .... Trimethylolpropane [*Organic chemistry*]
TMP .... Trimethylpentane [*Organic chemistry*]
TMP .... Trimethylphosphine [*Organic chemistry*]
TMPA........ Transocean Marine Paint Association (EAIO)
TMPA........ Trimethylphosphoramide [*Organic chemistry*]
TMPC........ Memphis Planning Commission, Memphis, TN [*Library symbol*] [*Library of Congress*] (LCLS)
TMPD .... Tempered (MSA)
TMPD .... Tetramethyl-para-phenylenediamine [*Analytical chemistry*]
TMPD .... Trimethylpentanediol [*Organic chemistry*]
TMPI......... Plough, Inc., Memphis, TN [*Library symbol*] [*Library of Congress*] (LCLS)
TMPI......... Target Material Production Instruction [*Air Force*]
TMPN .... Tetramethylpiperidinol N-oxyl [*Organic chemistry*]
TMPO .... Total Materiel Procurement Objective [*Military*]
TMPO .... Traffic Management and Proceedings Office [*CONUS*] (MCD)
TMPRG..... Tempering
TMPRLY .. Temporarily (MDG)
TMPROC ... Telemetry Processing
TMPRY...... Temporary (AFM)

TMPS........	Temperature Monitoring Power Supply
TMPS........	Test Maintenance Panel Subassembly [*Data processing*]
TMPS........	Theater Mission Planning System [*Military*] (CAAL)
TMPS........	Tracking Modifier Power Supply
TMPS........	Trans-Mississippi Philatelic Society (EA)
TMPT........	Tactical Marine Petroleum Terminal (MCD)
TMPTA.....	Technische Mitteilungen PTT [*A publication*]
TMPTA.....	Trimethylolpropane Triacrylate [*Organic chemistry*]
TMPTMA ...	Trimethylolpropane Trimethacrylate [*Organic chemistry*]
TMPV.......	Torque Motor Pilot Valve (NASA)
TMPZ........	Tetramethylpyrazine [*Biochemistry*]
TMR.........	Tactical Microwave Radio
TMR.........	Tactical Missile Receiver
TMR.........	Tamanrasset [*Algeria*] [*Airport symbol*] (OAG)
TMR.........	Tandem Mirror Reactor (MCD)
TMR.........	Technical Memorandum Report
TMR.........	Technology Management Review [*Military*] (AFIT)
TMR.........	Telecommunications Marketing Resource Ltd. [*Telecommunications service*] (TSSD)
TMR.........	Telemanagement Resources, Inc. [*Charlotte, NC*] [*Telecommunications*] (TSSD)
TMR.........	Temo Resources Ltd. [*Vancouver Stock Exchange symbol*]
TMR.........	Terrestrial Myriametric Radiation [*Physics*]
TMR.........	Tetramethylrhodamine [*Fluorescent dye*]
TMR.........	Texas Meridian Resources [*AMEX symbol*] (SPSG)
TMR.........	Thermistor Micropower Resistor
TMR.........	Timber Management Research [*Department of Agriculture*] (GRD)
TMR.........	Time Meter Reading
TMR.........	Timer (AAG)
TMR.........	Tomakomai [*Japan*] [*Seismograph station code, US Geological Survey*] (SEIS)
TMR.........	Topical Magnetic Resonance [*Medical diagnostic technique*]
TMR.........	Total Materiel Requirement [*Military*] (AABC)
TMR.........	Total Metal Removed
TMR.........	Trade-Mark Reporter [*A publication*]
TMR.........	Trainable Mentally Retarded
TMR.........	Transportation Movements Release [*Military*] (AABC)
TMR.........	Transvaal Mounted Rifles [*British military*] (DMA)
Tmr	Trimmer [*British military*] (DMA)
TMR.........	Triple Modular Redundancy [*Data processing*]
TMR.........	True Money Rate [*Finance*]
TMRA	Texas Meridian Resources Ltd. [*NASDAQ symbol*] (NQ)
TMRAO ...	Table Mountain Radio Astronomy Observatory
TMRBM....	Transportable Medium-Range Ballistic Missile
TMRC	Technical Maintenance Repair Center (MCD)
TMRC	Theoretical Maximum Residue Contribution [*to acceptable daily intake*] [*Environmental Protection Agency*]
TMRD	Technical Management Requirements Document
TMRD	Transportation Movement Requirements Data (MCD)
TM Rec.....	Trade Mark Record [*United States*] [*A publication*] (DLA)
TM Rep	Trade-Mark Reporter [*A publication*]
TMRI........	RAMCON, Inc., Environmental Engineering Library, Memphis, TN [*Library symbol*] [*Library of Congress*] (LCLS)
TMRI........	Tetramethylrhodamine Isothiocyanate [*Analytical biochemistry*]
TMRK	Canadian Trade Marks [*Canada Systems Group*] [*Information service or system*] (IID)
TMRKH	Tromura. Tromsoe Museum Rapportserie. Kulturhistorie [*A publication*]
TMRN	[*The*] Mystery Readers Newsletter [*A publication*]
TMRNV	Tromura. Tromsoe Museum Rapportserie. Naturvitenskap [*A publication*]
TMRP.......	Technology Mobilization and Reemployment Program [*Department of Labor*]
TMR Prac ...	Trademark Rules of Practice [*A publication*] (DLA)
TMRS........	Traffic Measuring and Recording System [*Telecommunications*] (TEL)
TMRSDT ..	Tropical Medicine Research Studies Series [*A publication*]
TmRSV......	Tomato Ringspot Virus
TMRVDP ...	Terminal-Modified RADAR Video Data Processor [*Noise control*]
TMS...........	[*The*] Magnolia Society (EA)
TMS...........	[*The*] Masonry Society (EA)
TMS...........	Minerals, Metals, and Materials Society (EA)
TMS...........	Sao Tome Island [*Sao Tome Islands*] [*Airport symbol*] (OAG)
TMS...........	Siena College, Memphis, TN [*Library symbol*] [*Library of Congress*] (LCLS)
TMS...........	Southern Missionary College, Collegedale, TN [*OCLC symbol*] (OCLC)
TMS...........	Tactical Missile Squadron [*Air Force*]
TMS...........	Tape Management System (MCD)
TMS...........	Target Marking System
TMS...........	Target Materials Squadron (MCD)
TMS...........	Technisonic [*Record label*]
TMS...........	Technological Market Segmentation
TMS...........	Telecommunications Message Switcher
TMS...........	Telemetry Modulation System
TMS...........	Telemetry Multiplex System
TMS...........	Temperature Management Station

TMS...........	Temperature Measurement Society
TMS...........	Temporomandibular Syndrome [*Medicine*]
TMS...........	Temsco Helicopters, Inc. [*Ketchikan, AK*] [*FAA designator*] (FAAC)
TMS...........	Tesla Memorial Society (EA)
TMS...........	Test Monitor System
TMS...........	Test and Monitoring Station
TMS...........	Tetramethoxysilane [*Organic chemistry*]
TMS...........	Tetramethylsilane [*Organic chemistry*]
TMS...........	Textile Market Studies [*British*]
TMS...........	Thallium Myocardial Scintigraphy [*Cardiology*]
TMS...........	Thematic Mapper Simulator [*for aerial photography*]
TMS...........	Thermomechanical System [*Instrumentation*]
TMS...........	Thread Mate System [*Dentistry*]
TMS...........	Thrust Measuring System
TMS...........	Tight Model Series (MCD)
TMS...........	Time and Motion Study (NG)
TMS...........	Time Multiplexed Switching [*Telecommunications*]
TMS...........	Time-Shared Monitor System [*Data processing*] (IEEE)
TMS...........	Times Square Energy Resource Ltd. [*Vancouver Stock Exchange symbol*]
TMS...........	Tissu Musculaire Specifique [*Medicine*] [*France*]
TMS...........	Tlalocan: A Journal of Source Materials on the Native Cultures of Mexico [*A publication*]
TMS...........	Tomisaki [*Mera*] [*Japan*] [*Seismograph station code, US Geological Survey*] [*Closed*] (SEIS)
TMS...........	Top Management Simulation [*Game*]
TMS...........	TOW [*Tube-Launched, Optically Tracked, Wire-Guided (Weapon)*] Missile System (RDA)
TMS...........	Toyota Motor Sales, Inc.
TMS...........	Trademark Section, Official Gazette [*Federal government*]
TMS...........	Trademark Society (EA)
TMS...........	Traffic Measurement System
TM/S.........	Trained in Minesweeping [*British military*] (DMA)
TMS...........	Trainee Management System (MCD)
TMS...........	Training Material Support
TMS...........	Training Media Services
TMS...........	[*The*] Tramway Museum Society [*British*] (DCTA)
TMS...........	Transaction Management System (BUR)
TMS...........	Transmatic Money Service
TMS...........	Transmission Measuring Set [*Bell Laboratories*]
TMS...........	Transport Management Survey (MCD)
TMS...........	Transportation Management School [*Navy*]
TMS...........	Treasury Management Services [*British*]
TMS...........	Trimethylsilyl [*Organic chemistry*]
TMS...........	Turbine Management Station
TMS...........	Turbulence Measuring System
TMS...........	Type, Model, and Series
TMSA........	Technical Marketing Society of America (EA)
TMSA........	Telecommunications Marketing/Sales Association [*Defunct*] (EA)
TMSA........	Thomas More Society of America (EA)
TMSA........	Trimethylsilyl Azide [*Organic chemistry*]
TMSAA.....	Transactions. Metallurgical Society of AIME [*American Institute of Mining, Metallurgical, and Petroleum Engineers*] [*A publication*]
TMSAN.....	Trimethylsilylacetonitrile [*Organic chemistry*]
TMSB........	Memphis and Shelby County Bar Association, Memphis, TN [*Library symbol*] [*Library of Congress*] (LCLS)
TMSC........	Southwestern at Memphis, Memphis, TN [*Library symbol*] [*Library of Congress*] (LCLS)
TMSC........	Talcott Mountain Science Center for Student Involvement, Inc. [*Avon, CT*] [*Telecommunications service*] (TSSD)
TMSCH.....	Memphis and Shelby County Health Department, Memphis, TN [*Library symbol*] [*Library of Congress*] (LCLS)
TMSCJ......	Trade Movement Society of Carpenters and Joiners [*A union*] [*British*]
TMSCl.......	Trimethylsilyl Chloride [*Organic chemistry*]
TMSCN.....	Trimethylsilylcyanide [*Organic chemistry*]
TMS-CPG ...	Trimethylsilylated Controlled-Pore Glass [*Packing for chromatography*]
TMSCS	Memphis and Shelby County Safety Council, Memphis, TN [*Library symbol*] [*Library of Congress*] (LCLS)
TMSD........	Total Military Service to Date
TMSD........	Training Material Support Detachment [*Army*]
TMSDC.....	Thermomechanical Model Software Development Center [*Research center*] (RCD)
TMSDEA ..	Trimethylsilyldiethylamine [*Organic chemistry*]
TMSIM	(Trimethylsilyl)imidazole [*Also, TSIM*] [*Organic chemistry*]
TMSM.......	Shiloh Military Trail Library, Memphis, TN [*Library symbol*] [*Library of Congress*] (LCLS)
TMSM.......	Trimethylstannylmaleate [*Organic chemistry*]
TMSMC....	Semmes-Murphey Clinic, Memphis, TN [*Library symbol*] [*Library of Congress*] (LCLS)
TMSN	Tomsun Foods International [*Greenfield, MA*] [*NASDAQ symbol*] (NQ)
TMSO	Southern College of Optometry, Memphis, TN [*Library symbol*] [*Library of Congress*] (LCLS)
TMSq........	Tactical Missile Squadron [*Air Force*]
TMSR........	Technical Manual Status Report (MCD)

TMSS .... Shelby State Community College, Memphis, TN [*Library symbol*] [*Library of Congress*] (LCLS)
TMSS .... Technical Manual Specifications and Standards [*Military*] (AFIT)
TMSS .... Technical Munitions Safety Study [*Air Force*]
TMSS .... Tecmar Music Synthesis System
TMSS .... Towanda-Monroeton Shippers Lifeline, Inc. [*AAR code*]
TMST .... Thomaston Mills, Inc. [*NASDAQ symbol*] (NQ)
TMStF .... Saint Francis Hospital, Medical Library, Memphis, TN [*Library symbol*] [*Library of Congress*] (LCLS)
TMStJ .... Saint Jude Children's Research Hospital, Memphis, TN [*Library symbol*] [*Library of Congress*] (LCLS)
TMStJo ...... Saint Joseph Hospital, Memphis, TN [*Library symbol*] [*Library of Congress*] (LCLS)
TMSVCS... TOW [*Tube-Launched, Optically Tracked, Wire-Guided (Weapon)*] Missile Sight Video Camera System (MCD)
TMT .... Tactical Marine Terminal (MCD)
TMT .... Talcott Mountain [*Connecticut*] [*Seismograph station code, US Geological Survey*] [*Closed*] (SEIS)
TMT .... Temperature (MDG)
TMT .... Terminal Monitor Program [*Data processing*] (MDG)
TMT .... Testing Methods and Techniques [*Telecommunications*] (TEL)
TMT .... Tetramethylthiourea [*Also, TMTU*] [*Organic chemistry*]
TMT .... Thermal Measurement Treatment
TMT .... Thermomechanical Treatment
TMT .... Thousand Metric Tons (IMH)
TMT .... Tire Management Terminal [*Automotive engineering*]
TMT .... Total Maintenance Time (MCD)
TMT .... Total Mission Time
TMT .... TOW [*Tube-Launched, Optically Tracked, Wire-Guided (Weapon)*] Missile Transporter (MCD)
TMT .... Toxic Materials Transport [*Business Publishers, Inc.*] [*Information service or system*] (CRD)
TMT .... Trans Midwest Airlines, Inc. [*Columbus, GA*] [*FAA designator*] (FAAC)
TMT .... Transmit (FAAC)
TMT .... Transonic Model Tunnel [*NASA*]
TMT .... Transportation Motor Transport [*Military*] (AABC)
TMT .... Travail Mecanique de la Tole SA [*Belgium*]
TMT .... Treatment [*Medicine*]
TMT .... Troy Mineral & Tech [*Vancouver Stock Exchange symbol*]
TMT .... Tudomanyos es Muszaki Tajekoztatas [*A publication*]
TMT .... Turret Maintenance Trainer (MCD)
TMTBL ..... Transmittable (FAAC)
TMTC .... Thru-Mode [*or Tri-Mode*] Tape Converter
TMTD ...... Tetramethylthiuram Disulfide [*Also, THTMS, TMTDS*] [*Organic chemistry*]
TMTD ...... Transmitted (FAAC)
TMTDS ..... Tetramethylthiuram Disulfide [*Also, TMTD, THTMS*] [*Organic chemistry*]
TMTF .... Tile, Marble, and Terrazzo Finishers and Shopmen International Union
TMTG .... Transmitting (FAAC)
TMTI .... State Technical Institute at Memphis, Memphis, TN [*Library symbol*] [*Library of Congress*] (LCLS)
TMTN ...... Transmission (FAAC)
TMTNO.... No Transmitting Capability (FAAC)
TMTP .... Tennessee Psychiatric Hospital and Institute, Memphis, TN [*Library symbol*] [*Library of Congress*] (LCLS)
TMTR .... Thermistor (AAG)
TMTR .... Transmitter
TMTS .... Memphis Theological Seminary of the Cumberland Presbyterian Church, Memphis, TN [*Library symbol*] [*Library of Congress*] (LCLS)
TMTSF .... Tetramethyltetraselenafulvene [*Organic chemistry*]
TMTU ...... Tetramethylthiourea [*Also, TMT*] [*Organic chemistry*]
TMTX ...... Temtex Industries, Inc. [*NASDAQ symbol*] (NQ)
TMU .... Groton, CT [*Location identifier*] [*FAA*] (FAAL)
TMU .... Tactical Mobile Unit [*Police*]
TMU .... Temperature Measurement Unit (NASA)
TMU .... Temuco [*Chile*] [*Seismograph station code, US Geological Survey*] (SEIS)
TMU ...... Test Maintenance Unit [*Data processing*]
TMU .... Tetramethylurea [*Organic chemistry*]
TMU .... Thermal-Mechanical Unit
TMU .... Time Measurement Unit [*Industrial engineering*]
TMU .... Transmission Message Unit
TMU .... Turret Mock-Up (MCD)
TMUP .... Union Planters National Bank, Memphis, TN [*Library symbol*] [*Library of Congress*] (LCLS)
TMurH ..... Highland Rim Regional Library Center, Murfreesboro, TN [*Library symbol*] [*Library of Congress*] (LCLS)
TMurS .... Middle Tennessee State University, Murfreesboro, TN [*Library symbol*] [*Library of Congress*] (LCLS)
TMUS ...... Temporarily Mounted User Set [*Data processing*] (ADA)
TMUS ...... Toy Manufacturers of the United States
TMUSAE ... United States Army Engineers Library, Memphis, TN [*Library symbol*] [*Library of Congress*] (LCLS)
TMUSDC ... United States Department of Commerce, Memphis, TN [*Library symbol*] [*Library of Congress*] (LCLS)

TMV .... Tanker Motor Vessel [*Shipping*] (DS)
TMV .... Texas A & M University, Medical Sciences Library, College Station, TX [*OCLC symbol*] (OCLC)
TMV .... Tobacco Mosaic Virus
TMV .... Todd Memorial Volumes [*A publication*]
TMV .... Torpedoman's Mate, Aviation [*Navy rating*]
TMV .... True Mean Value
TMV .... Turnip Mosaic Virus
TMV .... United States Veterans Administration Hospital, Memphis, TN [*Library symbol*] [*Library of Congress*] (LCLS)
TMV-C ...... Turnip Mosaic Virus - Common
TMV-L ...... Turnip Mosaic Virus - Legume
TMVP........ Tobacco Mosaic Virus Protein
TMVS .... Times Mirror Videotex Services, Inc. [*Information service or system*] [*Inactive*] (IID)
TMW .... Tactical Missile Wing [*Air Force*]
TMW .... Tamworth [*Australia*] [*Airport symbol*] (OAG)
TMW .... Thermal Megawatt [*Also, Mwt*]
TMW .... Tijdschrift voor Maatschappelijk Werk [*A publication*]
TMW .... Tomorrow (FAAC)
TMW .... Toyota Motor Workers' Union
TMW .... Transverse Magnetic Wave [*Radio*]
TMW .... Welzijnsweekblad [*A publication*]
TMWR ...... Tax Management Weekly Report [*Bureau of National Affairs*] [*Information service or system*] (CRD)
TMWR ...... Technical Manual Work Requirement (MCD)
TMX .... Tandem Mirror Experiment [*Atomic fusion*]
TMX .... Telemeter Transmitter
TMXDI ..... Tetramethylxylene Diisocyanate [*Organic chemistry*]
TMXO ...... Tactical Miniature Crystal Oscillator
TMXRT .... Three-Mirror X-Ray Telescope [*NASA*]
TMZ .... Houston, TX [*Location identifier*] [*FAA*] (FAAL)
TMZ .... Textile Magazine. Vakblad voor de Handel in Textiel, Kleding, en Woningtextiel [*A publication*]
TN .... Congo (Brazzaville) [*Aircraft nationality and registration mark*] (FAAC)
TN .... [*The*] Navigators (EA)
TN .... Public Library of Nashville and Davidson County, Nashville, TN [*Library symbol*] [*Library of Congress*] (LCLS)
TN .... Stewardsman [*Nonrated enlisted man*] [*Navy*]
TN .... Tagesarbeitsnormen [*Workday Standards*] [*German*]
TN .... Talking Newspaper News [*A publication*]
T/N .... Tar and Nicotine [*In cigarettes*]
TN .... Tariff Number
TN .... Tarragon Oil & Gas Ltd. [*Toronto Stock Exchange symbol*]
TN .... Taunton [*British depot code*]
TN .... Team Nursing
TN .... Technical Note
TN .... Technology Needs (MCD)
TN .... Telephone (NATG)
TN .... Telephone Number
TN .... Tell en-Nasbeh (BJA)
TN .... Temperature Normal [*Medicine*]
TN .... Temple Name (BJA)
TN .... Tennessee [*Postal code*]
TN .... Tennessee Reports [*A publication*] (DLA)
TN .... Terminal Node
TN .... Test Narrative (CAAL)
TN .... Test Negative [*Clinical chemistry*]
TN .... Test Number (AAG)
TN .... Texas & Northern Railway Co. [*AAR code*]
TN .... Theatre Notebook [*A publication*]
TN .... Thermonuclear
TN .... Tin
tn .... Titanite [*CIPW classification*] [*Geology*]
TN .... Title News [*A publication*]
TN .... Ton
TN .... Tone (MSA)
TN .... Top of the News [*A publication*]
TN .... Total Nitrogen [*Analytical chemistry*]
TN .... Town
TN .... Track Number
TN .... Trade Name (DEN)
TN .... Train (AAG)
TN .... Trans-Australia Airlines [*ICAO designator*] (FAAC)
TN .... Transfer on Negative
TN .... Transferable Notice [*Business term*]
TN .... Transfield (NSW) Pty. Ltd. [*Transavia Division*] [*Australia*] [*ICAO aircraft manufacturer identifier*] (ICAO)
TN .... Translator's Note
TN .... Transport
TN .... Transportation
TN .... Transverse Nerve [*Neuroanatomy*]
TN .... Travel News [*A publication*]
TN .... Triafol
TN .... Troponin [*Biochemistry*]
T/N .... True Name
TN .... True Negative [*Medicine*]
TN .... True North
Tn .... Tukulti-Ninurta (BJA)
TN .... Tuning Units [*JETDS nomenclature*] [*Military*] (CET)

TN..............	Tunisia [*ANSI two-letter standard code*] [*IYRU nationality code*] (CNC)
TN..............	Twelfth Night [*Shakespearean work*]
TN..............	Twisted Nematic [*Telecommunications*] (TEL)
TN²	[*The*] News Is the News [*Television comedy program*]
TNA...........	Jinan [*China*] [*Airport symbol*] (OAG)
TNA...........	[*The*] National Alliance of Professional and Executive Women's Networks [*Later, TIA*] (EA)
TNA...........	[*The*] National Archives [*of the United States*]
TNA...........	Office of Terrorism and Narcotics Analysis [*Washington, DC*] [*Bureau of Intelligence and Research*] [*Department of State*] (GRD)
TNA...........	Telecommunications Network Architects [*Telecommunications service*] (TSSD)
TNA...........	Telocator Network of America (EA)
TN A.........	Tennessee Appeals Reports [*A publication*] (DLA)
TNA...........	Tetranitroadamantane [*Explosive*] [*Organic chemistry*]
TNA...........	Tetranitroaniline [*Organic chemistry*]
TNA...........	Thermal Neutron Analysis [*For detection of explosives*]
TNA...........	Thomas Nelson - Australia [*Publisher*]
TNA...........	Tidsskrift foer Norron Arkeologi [*A publication*]
Tna.............	Tigrinya (BJA)
TNA...........	Time of Nearest Approach
TNA...........	Tin City [*Alaska*] [*Seismograph station code, US Geological Survey*] (SEIS)
TNA...........	Total Nucleic Acid
TNA...........	Trans National Airlines [*South San Francisco, CA*] [*FAA designator*] (FAAC)
TNA...........	Transient Network Analyzer (IEEE)
TNA...........	Trinitroaniline [*Organic chemistry*]
TNA...........	Tropicana Development Corp. [*Vancouver Stock Exchange symbol*]
TNAE	United States Army Engineer District, Nashville, Nashville, TN [*Library symbol*] [*Library of Congress*] (LCLS)
TNAEA	Teplovye Napryazheniya v Elementakh Konstruktsii [*A publication*]
TNAF	Training Name and Address File [*IRS*]
TNAM.......	Theater Network Analysis Model [*Europe*] (MCD)
TNAN.......	Texas Numismatic Association. News [*A publication*]
TNAUK.......	Talking Newspaper Association, United Kingdom
TNB	Tanabu [*Japan*] [*Seismograph station code, US Geological Survey*] [*Closed*] (SEIS)
TNB	Technical News Bulletin [*National Bureau of Standards*]
TNB	Technion News Bulletin [*Haifa*] [*A publication*] (BJA)
TNB	Thio(nitro)benzoic Acid [*Analytical biochemistry*]
TNB	Thomas & Betts Corp. [*NYSE symbol*] (SPSG)
TNB	Transnasal Butorphanol [*Analgesic*]
TNB	Trinitrobenzene [*Explosive*]
TNBA	Tri-normal-butylamine [*Organic chemistry*]
TNBe	Belmont College, Nashville, TN [*Library symbol*] [*Library of Congress*] (LCLS)
TNBH	Baptist Hospital, Medical Library, Nashville, TN [*Library symbol*] [*Library of Congress*] (LCLS)
TNBMD	Bureau of Mines. Technology News [*United States*] [*A publication*]
TNBS........	Trinitrobenzenesulfonic Acid [*Biochemistry*]
TNBT	American Baptist Theological Seminary, Nashville, TN [*Library symbol*] [*Library of Congress*] (LCLS)
TNBT	Tetranitro Blue Tetrazolium [*A dye*] [*Organic chemistry*]
TNC...........	Country Music Foundation Library and Media Center, Nashville, TN [*Library symbol*] [*Library of Congress*] (LCLS)
TNC...........	[*The*] National Crossbowmen (EA)
TNC...........	[*The*] Nature Conservancy (EA)
TNC...........	[*The*] Nerve Center (EA)
TNC...........	Tail Number Change [*Air Force*] (AFIT)
TNC...........	Tekniska Nomenklaturcentralen [*Swedish Center for Technical Terminology*] [*Information service or system*] (IID)
TNC...........	Terminal Network Controller
TNC...........	Terminal Node Controller [*Data processing*]
TNC...........	Texas Nuclear Corporation (KSC)
TNC...........	Theater Naval Commander
TNC...........	Thymic Nurse Cell [*Cytology*]
TNC...........	Tide Net Controller (NATG)
TNC...........	Tin City [*Alaska*] [*Airport symbol*] (OAG)
TNC...........	Tin City, AK [*Location identifier*] [*FAA*] (FAAL)
TNC...........	Too Numerous to Count
TNC...........	Town & Country Corp. [*AMEX symbol*] (SPSG)
TNC...........	Track Navigation Computer
TNC...........	Track No Conversion
TNC...........	Trans-National Communications, Inc.
TNC...........	Transnational Corporation
TNC...........	Transport Network Controller
TNC...........	Trevecca Nazarene College [*Tennessee*]
TNC...........	Trinitrocellulose [*Organic chemistry*]
TNC...........	Trionics Technology Ltd. [*Vancouver Stock Exchange symbol*]
TNC...........	Tripartite Naval Commission [*Allied German Occupation Forces*]
TnC...........	Troponin C [*Biochemistry*]
TNCA	Oranjestad/Reina Beatrix, Aruba Island [*Netherlands Antilles*] [*ICAO location identifier*] (ICLI)
TNCA	Thionaphthenecarboxylic Acid [*Organic chemistry*]
TNCB	Kralendijk/Flamingo, Bonaire Island [*Netherlands Antilles*] [*ICAO location identifier*] (ICLI)
TNCC	Tripartite Nuclear Cross-Sections Committee [*British, Canadian, and US*]
TNCC	Willemstad/Hato, Curacao Island [*Netherlands Antilles*] [*ICAO location identifier*] (ICLI)
TNCD........	Ten Nation Committee on Disarmament [*Defunct, 1960*]
TNCE	Oranjestad/F. D. Roosevelt, Sint Eustatius Island [*Netherlands Antilles*] [*ICAO location identifier*] (ICLI)
TNCF	Curacao [*Netherlands Antilles*] [*ICAO location identifier*] (ICLI)
TNCL........	Tail Number Configuration List [*Navy*] (NG)
TNCM	Philipsburg/Prinses Juliana, Sint Maarten Island [*Netherlands Antilles*] [*ICAO location identifier*] (ICLI)
TN Cr........	Tennessee Criminal Appeals Reports [*A publication*] (DLA)
TNCS........	Saba/Yrausquin [*Netherlands Antilles*] [*ICAO location identifier*] (ICLI)
TNCSDT ...	North Carolina. Agricultural Research Service. Technical Bulletin [*A publication*]
TnCSI	Technician of the Construction Surveyor's Institute [*British*] (DBQ)
TNCSS	Temporary National Commission on Supplies and Shortages [*Initiated 1974*]
TND...........	Teachers for Nuclear Disarmament [*Australia*]
TND...........	Telecommunications Network for the Deaf
TND...........	Tinned
TND...........	Todwind Development Corp. [*Vancouver Stock Exchange symbol*]
TND...........	Trace Narcotics Detector
TND...........	Trade Names Database [*Information service or system*] (IID)
TND...........	Trade Names Dictionary [*Later, BTC*] [*A publication*]
TND...........	Transnational Data Report. Information Politics and Regulation [*A publication*]
TND...........	Turned (AAG)
TNDC........	Disciples of Christ Historical Society, Nashville, TN [*Library symbol*] [*Library of Congress*] (LCLS)
TNDC........	Thai National Documentation Center (IID)
TNDC........	Trade Negotiations among Developing Countries (IMH)
TND:CI	Trade Names Dictionary: Company Index [*Later, CTB*] [*A publication*]
TNDCY	Tendency (FAAC)
Tnd Hotel...	Trends in the Hotel-Motel Industry [*A publication*]
TNDNA.......	Tokyo Nogyo Daigaku Nogaku Shuho [*A publication*]
TNDNAG ...	Journal of Agricultural Science. Tokyo Nogyo Daigaku [*A publication*]
TNDP	Tetranitrodiphenyl [*Organic chemistry*]
TNDS	Tactical Navigational Display System
TNDS	Total Network Data System [*Bell System*]
TNDS	TS Industries, Inc. [*Huntington Beach, CA*] [*NASDAQ symbol*] (NQ)
TNDSA......	Trends [*A publication*]
TNDU........	Technodyne, Inc. [*NASDAQ symbol*] (NQ)
TNDZR	Tenderizer
TNE	Tanegashima [*Japan*] [*Airport symbol*] (OAG)
TNE	Terra Nova Energy [*Vancouver Stock Exchange symbol*]
TNE	TRIS, Sodium Chloride, EDTA [*A buffer*]
TNEC	Temporary National Economic Committee [*Congressional committee which studied the American economic system*] [*World War II*]
TNEF........	Trinitroethyl Formal [*An explosive*]
TNEL........	Nelson [*Thomas*], Inc. [*NASDAQ symbol*] (NQ)
TNEMBJ ..	Annals. Research Institute of Epidemiology and Microbiology [*A publication*]
TNEOC	Trinitroethyl Orthocarbonate [*An explosive*]
TNEOF	Trinitroethyl Orthoformate [*An explosive*]
TNET	Telenetics Corp. [*NASDAQ symbol*] (NQ)
TNF	Fisk University, Nashville, TN [*Library symbol*] [*Library of Congress*] (LCLS)
TNF	Tactical Nuclear Force (MCD)
TNF	Theater Nuclear Forces
TNF	Thin Nickel Film
TNF	Third Normal Form [*Databases*]
TNF	Timing Negative Film
TNF	Trainfire
TNF	Transfer on No Overflow
TNF	Trinitrofluorenone [*Organic chemistry*]
TNF	True North Film [*Vancouver Stock Exchange symbol*]
TNF	Tumor Necrosis Factor [*Antineoplastic drug*] [*Immunology*]
TNF-A	Tumor Necrosis Factor-Alpha
TNFB........	Free-Will Baptist Bible College, Nashville, TN [*Library symbol*] [*Library of Congress*] (LCLS)
TNFS........	Theater Nuclear Forces Survivability (MCD)
TNFSS.......	Theater Nuclear Forces Survivability and Security (MCD)
TNG...........	[*The*] Newspaper Guild (EA)
TNG...........	Tanger [*Morocco*] [*Airport symbol*] (OAG)
TNG...........	Tangerang [*Java*] [*Geomagnetic observatory code*]
TNG...........	Tangerang [*Java*] [*Seismograph station code, US Geological Survey*] (SEIS)
TNG...........	Territory of New Guinea
TNG...........	Tongue (MSA)

TNG.......... Training (AAG)
TNG.......... Transdermal Nitroglycerine Patch [Medicine]
TNG.......... Tungco Resources Corp. [Vancouver Stock Exchange symbol]
TNGANCH ... Training Anchorage [Navy] (NVT)
TNGE........ Tonnage [Shipping]
TNGLIT...... Training Literature [Military]
TngS......... Training Subject
TNGSUP... Training Support [Navy] (NVT)
TNGSVCS ... Training Services [Navy] (NVT)
TNGT........ Tonight (FAAC)
TNH .... Tampa-Hillsborough County Public Library, Tampa, FL
            [OCLC symbol] (OCLC)
TNH .... Tax Notes Highlights [Tax Analysts] [Information service or
            system] (CRD)
TNH .... Tienshui [Republic of China] [Seismograph station code, US
            Geological Survey] (SEIS)
TNHCA..... Hospital Corp. of America, Research/Information Services,
            Nashville, TN [Library symbol] [Library of
            Congress] (LCLS)
TNHCA..... Taehan Naekwa Hakhoe Chapchi [A publication]
TNHQ .... Theater Navy Headquarters
TNI .... [The] Network, Inc. [An association] (EA)
TNI .... [The] Networking Institute [Commercial firm] (EA)
TNI .... Peipeinimaru, TT [Location identifier] [FAA] (FAAL)
TNI .... Thin Nickel Iron
TNI .... Tin News. Accurate Information on World Tin Production,
            Prices, Marketing Developments, and New Uses and
            Applications [A publication]
TNI .... Total Nodal Irradiation [Oncology]
TNI .... Traffic Noise Index [Department of Transportation]
TNI .... Trans International Gold [Vancouver Stock Exchange symbol]
TNI .... Transcisco [AMEX symbol] (SPSG)
TnI .... Troponin I [Biochemistry]
TNIA .... [The] Network Incorporated of America [Information service or
            system] (IID)
TNIF......... Thin Nickel Iron Film
TNII.......... Telecommunications Network, Inc. [NASDAQ symbol] (NQ)
TnIMBM... Technician of the Institute of Municipal Building Management
            [British] (DBQ)
TNizam...... Trudy Instituta Literatury i Jazyka Imeni Nizami [A
            publication]
TNJ........... Joint University Libraries, Nashville, TN [Library symbol]
            [Library of Congress] (LCLS)
TNJ........... Tanjung Pinang [Indonesia] [Airport symbol] (OAG)
TNJ-L....... Joint University Libraries, Vanderbilt School of Law, Nashville,
            TN [Library symbol] [Library of Congress] (LCLS)
TNJ-M ...... Joint University Libraries, Vanderbilt Medical Center,
            Nashville, TN [Library symbol] [Library of
            Congress] (LCLS)
TNJ-P....... Joint University Libraries, George Peabody College for
            Teachers, Nashville, TN [Library symbol] [Library of
            Congress] (LCLS)
TNJ-R....... Joint University Libraries, Vanderbilt School of Religion,
            Nashville, TN [Library symbol] [Library of
            Congress] (LCLS)
TNJ-S....... Joint University Libraries, Scarritt College for Christian
            Workers, Nashville, TN [Library symbol] [Library of
            Congress] (LCLS)
TNK.......... Tank (AAG)
TNK.......... Tinkers Knob [California] [Seismograph station code, US
            Geological Survey] (SEIS)
TNK.......... Tunkwa Copper Mining [Vancouver Stock Exchange symbol]
TNK.......... Tununak [Alaska] [Airport symbol] (OAG)
TNK.......... [The] Two Noble Kinsmen [Shakespearean work]
TNKPB..... Trudy Nauchno-Issledovatel'skogo Instituta Kraevoi Patologii
            [Alma-Ata] [A publication]
TNKR .... Tanker (FAAC)
TNKUL ..... Towarzystwo Naukowe Katolickiego Uniwersytet Lubelskiego
            [A publication]
TNKULWP ... Towarzystwo Naukowe Katolickiego Uniwersytet Lubelskiego.
            Wyklady i Przemowienia [Lublin] [A publication]
TNL .... David Lipscomb College, Nashville, TN [Library symbol]
            [Library of Congress] (LCLS)
TNL .... Technical Newsletter
TNL .... Technitrol, Inc. [AMEX symbol] (SPSG)
TN L .... Tennessee Law Review [A publication]
TNL .... Terminal Net Loss
TNL .... Times Newspapers Limited [British]
TNL .... Tunnel (MSA)
TnL .... Tunnel Luminescence [Physics]
TNLAAH .. Tidsskrift foer den Norske Laegeforening [A publication]
TNLDIO.... Tunnel Diode [Electronics]
TNLG .... Technology, Inc. [NASDAQ symbol] (NQ)
TNLR .... Railroad Tunnel [Board on Geographic Names]
TN LR .... Tennessee Law Review [A publication]
TNLRA...... Tennessee Law Review [A publication]
TNLS........ Trans-National Leasing, Inc. [NASDAQ symbol] (NQ)
TNM.......... Meharry Medical College, Nashville, TN [Library symbol]
            [Library of Congress] (LCLS)
TNM.......... Tashota-Nipigon Mines [Vancouver Stock Exchange symbol]
TNM.......... Tetranitromethane [Organic chemistry]

TNM.......... Texas-New Mexico Railway Co. [AAR code]
TNM.......... Topical Nitrogen Mustard [Dermatology]
TNM.......... Tumor classification system derived from symbols: T for
            Primary Tumor; N for Regional Lymph Node Metastasis;
            M for Remote Metastasis [Medicine]
TNMH ...... Metro General Hospital, Nashville, TN [Library symbol]
            [Library of Congress] (LCLS)
TNMPH .... Methodist Publishing House Library, Nashville, TN [Library
            symbol] [Library of Congress] (LCLS)
TNMR....... Tritium Nuclear Magnetic Resonance [Spectrometry]
TNN.......... [The] Nashville Network [Cable-television system]
TNN.......... Nashville Public Library, Nashville, TN [OCLC
            symbol] (OCLC)
TNN.......... Tainan [Taiwan] [Airport symbol] (OAG)
TNN.......... Tanana [Alaska] [Seismograph station code, US Geological
            Survey] (SEIS)
TNN.......... Teleconnect Co. [NYSE symbol] (SPSG)
TNN.......... TermNet News [A publication]
TNNIA ...... Trudy Groznenskogo Neftyanogo Nauchno-Issledovatel'skogo
            Instituta [A publication]
TNO.......... Nederlandse Centrale Organisatie voor Toegepast
            Natuurwetenschappelijk Onderzoek [Netherlands Institute
            for Applied Scientific Research]
TNO.......... Tamarindo [Costa Rica] [Airport symbol] (OAG)
TNO.......... Tenore Oil & Gas [Vancouver Stock Exchange symbol]
TNO.......... Texas & New Orleans R. R. [AAR code]
TNO.......... Torino [Italy] [Seismograph station code, US Geological
            Survey] (SEIS)
TNOC....... Threads No Couplings
TNO Div Nutr Food Res TNO Rep ... TNO [Nederlands Centrale Organisatie
            voor Toegepast-Natuurwetenschappelijk Onderzoek]
            Division for Nutrition and Food Research TNO. Report [A
            publication]
TNOP........ Total Network Operations Plan [Telecommunications] (TEL)
TNO Proj... TNO [Nederlands Centrale Organisatie voor Toegepast-
            Natuurwetenschappelijk Onderzoek] Project [A
            publication]
TNOR........ Temiskaming & Northern Ontario Railway
TNOSA ...... Tunnels et Ouvrages Souterrains [A publication]
T vh Not ... Tijdschrift voor het Notarisambt [A publication]
T Not.......... Tijdschrift voor Notarissen [A publication]
TNOT........ Total Not Operating Time
TNP .... [The] New Party [Australia] [Political party]
TNP .... Thailand National Police (CINC)
TNP .... Theatre National Populaire [France]
TNP .... TNP Enterprises, Inc. [NYSE symbol] (SPSG)
TNP .... Tonopah [Nevada] [Seismograph station code, US Geological
            Survey] (SEIS)
TNP .... Trinitrophenol [or Trinitrophenyl] [Organic chemistry]
TNP .... Trojan Nuclear Plant (NRCH)
TNP .... Twentynine Palms [California] [Airport symbol] (OAG)
TNP .... Twentynine Palms, CA [Location identifier] [FAA] (FAAL)
TNPA .... Tri-normal-propylamine [Organic chemistry]
TNPF......... Tidewater Nicaragua Project Foundation (EA)
TNPG .... [The] Nuclear Power Group [British]
TNPH........ Tennessee Department of Public Health, Nashville, TN [Library
            symbol] [Library of Congress] (LCLS)
TNPK .... Turnpike
TNP-KLH ... Trinitrophenyl Keyhole Limpet Hemocyanin [Immunology]
Tn Plann Rev ... Town Planning Review [A publication]
TNPO .... Terminal Navy Post Office (AFM)
TNPP......... Planned Parenthood of Nashville, Nashville, TN [Library
            symbol] [Library of Congress] (LCLS)
TNPP......... Tris(nonylphenyl) Phosphite [Organic chemistry]
TNPWS...... Tasmania National Parks and Wildlife Service [Australia]
TNPZOW ... Towarzystwo Niesienia Pomocy Zydom Ofiarom Wojny [A
            publication] (BJA)
TNR .... Antananarivo [Madagascar] [Airport symbol] (OAG)
TNR .... [The] New Repertory
TNR .... [The] New Republic [A publication]
TNR .... Non-RADAR Transfer of Control Message
            [Communications] (FAAC)
TNR .... Tanganyika Notes and Records [A publication]
TNR .... Tanzania Notes and Records [A publication]
TNR .... Thinner
TNR .... Titan Resources Ltd. [Vancouver Stock Exchange symbol]
TNR .... Tone Not Relevant
TNR .... Tonic Neck Reflex [Physiology]
TNR .... Trainer (AAG)
TNR .... Transit Nuclear Radiation
TNRE .... Transit Nuclear Radiation Effect
TNRIS....... Texas Natural Resources Information System [Austin]
            [Information service or system] (IID)
TNRIS .... Transportation Noise Research Information Service
            [Department of Transportation]
TNRT .... TNR Technical, Inc. [Farmingdale, NY] [NASDAQ
            symbol] (NQ)
TNRY .... Tannery
TNS .... [The] Names Society (EA)
TNS .... [The] National Switchboard [Phoenix, AZ]
            [Telecommunications] (TSSD)

TNS .... [*The*] New Salesmanship [*Book by Steve Salerno*]
TNS .... [*The*] Next Step [*Physics*]
TNS .... Tank Nitrogen Supply   (AAG)
TNS .... Tanos Petroleum Corp. [*Vancouver Stock Exchange symbol*]
TNS .... Taunus [*Federal Republic of Germany*] [*Seismograph station code, US Geological Survey*]   (SEIS)
TNS .... Telecommunications Network Services [*Data Resources*] [*Information service or system*]   (CRD)
TNS .... Tennessee State Library and Archives, Nashville, TN [*OCLC symbol*]   (OCLC)
TNS .... Thames Navigation Service [*British*]   (DS)
TNS .... Thermal Night Site
TNS .... Thomas Nast Society   (EA)
TNS .... Timber Trade Review [*Kuala Lumpur*] [*A publication*]
TNS .... Toluidinylnaphthalene Sulfonate [*Organic chemistry*]
TNS .... Topical Numismatic Society   (EA)
TNS .... Toronto Normal School
TNS .... Transaction Network Service [*AT & T*]
TNS .... Transcutaneous Nerve Stimulation [*Also, TENS, TES*] [*A method of pain control*] [*Medicine*]
TNS .... Triple Nine Society   (EA)
TNS .... Tunable Noise Source
TNSA .... [*The*] National Spiritual Alliance of the United States of America
TNSA .... Technical Nuclear Safety   (MCD)
TNSB .... Southern Baptist Convention Historical Commission, Nashville, TN [*Library symbol*] [*Library of Congress*]   (LCLS)
TNSCDR ... TINS. Trends in Neurosciences [*A publication*]
TNSDUNSPHI ... [*The*] National Society to Discourage Use of the Name Smith for Purposes of Hypothetical Illustration
TNSI .... [*A*] Text-Book of North-Semitic Inscriptions [*A publication*]   (BJA)
TNSKA .... Tohoku Nogyo Shikenjo Kenkyu Hokoku [*A publication*]
TNSL .... Tensile
TNSL .... Tinsley Laboratories, Inc. [*NASDAQ symbol*]   (NQ)
TNSN .... Tension   (MSA)
TNSP .... Transportation   (CINC)
TNSRA ...... Tensor [*A publication*]
TNStT .... Saint Thomas Hospital, Health Sciences Library, Nashville, TN [*Library symbol*] [*Library of Congress*]   (LCLS)
TN Stud Lit ... Tennessee Studies in Literature [*A publication*]
TNSX .... Taniisix. Aleutian Regional School District [*A publication*]
TNT .... Miami, FL [*Location identifier*] [*FAA*]   (FAAL)
TNT .... Tapes 'n' Texts [*Australia*]
TNT .... Tax Notes Today [*Database*] [*Tax Analysts*] [*Information service or system*]   (CRD)
TNT .... Teleconference Network of Texas [*University of Texas*] [*San Antonio*] [*Telecommunications*]   (TSSD)
TNT .... Tinto Gold Corp. [*Vancouver Stock Exchange symbol*]
TNT .... Titles Now Troublesome [*School books*] [*American Library Association*]
TNT .... TNT Tariff Agents, Inc., New York NY [*STAC*]
TNT .... Tobramycin-Nafcillin-Ticarcillin [*Antibiotic combination*]
TNT .... Toronto [*Ontario*] [*Seismograph station code, US Geological Survey*] [*Closed*]   (SEIS)
TNT .... Torque, Nip, and Tension [*Winding technology*]
TNT .... Towarzystwo Naukowe w Toruniu [*A publication*]
TNT .... Transient Nuclear Test
TNT .... Transnational Terrorism   (ADA)
TNT .... Transportation News Ticker [*Knight-Ridder Business Information Services*] [*Information service or system*]   (CRD)
TNT .... Trim, Neat, and Terrific [*Slang*]
TNT .... Trinitrotoluene [*Explosive*]
TnT .... Troponin T [*Biochemistry*]
TNT .... Turner Network Television [*Cable-television system*]
TNTC .... Too Numerous to Count [*Microbiology*]
TNTC .... Tyndale New Testament Commentary [*A publication*]   (BJA)
TNTDL....... Tabulated Numerical Technical Data List
TNTDR ..... Thermonuclear TOKAMAK Demonstration Reactor [*Particle physics*]
TNT-FF ..... Towarzystwo Naukowe w Toruniu. Prace Wydziau Filologiczno-Filosoficznego [*A publication*]
TNTHA ..... Tennessee Hospital Association, Nashville, TN [*Library symbol*] [*Library of Congress*]   (LCLS)
TNTL........ Tijdschrift voor Nederlandsche Taal- en Letterkunde [*Leiden*] [*A publication*]
TNTN .... Trevecca Nazarene College, Nashville, TN [*Library symbol*] [*Library of Congress*]   (LCLS)
TNTO .... Tintoretto, Inc. [*New York, NY*] [*NASDAQ symbol*]   (NQ)
TNTU .... University of Tennessee, Nashville, TN [*Library symbol*] [*Library of Congress*]   (LCLS)
TNTV .... Tentative   (AFM)
TNU .... Newton, IA [*Location identifier*] [*FAA*]   (FAAL)
tnu .... Tennessee [*MARC country of publication code*] [*Library of Congress*]   (LCCP)
TNU .... Upper Room Devotional Library and Museum, Nashville, TN [*Library symbol*] [*Library of Congress*]   (LCLS)
TNUK........ Thomas Nelson - United Kingdom [*Publisher*]

TNUM....... United Methodist Publishing House, Nashville, TN [*Library symbol*] [*Library of Congress*]   (LCLS)
TNUVAN ... Trudy Novokuznetskogo Gosudarstvennogo Instituta Usovershenstvovaniya Vrachei [*A publication*]
TNV .... Navasota, TX [*Location identifier*] [*FAA*]   (FAAL)
TNV .... Tobacco Necrosis Virus
TNV .... Total Net Value
TNV .... Trinova Corp. [*NYSE symbol*]   (SPSG)
TNVS........ Thermal Night Vision System
TNW .... Tactical Nuclear Warfare   (MCD)
TNW .... Tactical Nuclear Weapon
TNW .... Talking Newspaper Week [*British*]
TNW .... Theater Nuclear Weapon
TNW .... Tijdschrift van den Nederlandschen Werkloosheidsraad [*A publication*]
TNW .... Towarzystwo Naukowe Warszawskie [*A publication*]
TNWRRI... Tennessee Water Resources Research Center [*Knoxville, TN*] [*Department of the Interior*]   (GRD)
TNX .... Thanks [*Communications operator's procedural remark*]
TNX .... Tonopah, NV [*Location identifier*] [*FAA*]   (FAAL)
TNX .... Trinitroxylene [*Organic chemistry*]
TNY .... Tenney Engineering, Inc. [*AMEX symbol*]   (SPSG)
TNY .... Trans New York [*New York, NY*] [*FAA designator*]   (FAAC)
TNY .... Trinity University, Library, San Antonio, TX [*OCLC symbol*]   (OCLC)
T NY Ac Sci ... Transactions. New York Academy of Sciences [*A publication*]
TNYTI....... [*The*] New York Times Index
TNZ .... Tarata [*New Zealand*] [*Seismograph station code, US Geological Survey*]   (SEIS)
TNZ .... Thermoneutral Zone
TNZ .... Transfer on Nonzero
TNZ .... Tranzonic Companies [*AMEX symbol*]   (SPSG)
TO .... Games Taken Out [*Baseball*]
TO .... [*The*] Medina Aviation Co. [*ICAO designator*]   (FAAC)
TO .... Oak Ridge Public Library, Oak Ridge, TN [*Library symbol*] [*Library of Congress*]   (LCLS)
TO .... People's Republic of South Yemen [*Aircraft nationality and registration mark*]   (FAAC)
TO .... Table of Organization
TO .... Tactical Observer
TO .... Tactical Officer [*Military*]   (RDA)
TO .... Take One [*A publication*]
T/O .... Take Over   (MCD)
T & O .... Taken and Offered [*Sporting*] [*British*]
TO .... Takeoff [*Aviation*]
TO .... Tandem Outlet
T/O .... Target of Opportunity
TO .... Targum Onkelos   (BJA)
TO .... Task Order   (MCD)
TO .... Tech/Ops Landauer [*AMEX symbol*]   (SPSG)
TO .... Technical Objective
TO .... Technical Observer
TO .... Technical Officer [*Military*] [*British*]
TO .... Technical Order
TO .... Telegraph Office
TO .... Telephone Office
TO .... Telephone Order [*Medicine*]
TO .... Tell el-Obed   (BJA)
TO .... Temperature, Oral [*Medicine*]
TO .... Test Operation   (AAG)
T & O .... Test and Operation [*NASA*]   (KSC)
TO .... Test Outline   (CAAL)
TO .... Theater of Operations [*Military*]
TO .... Theiler's Original [*Strain of mouse encephalitis virus*]
TO .... Thiazole Orange [*Organic chemistry*]
TO .... Through Ownership [*Shipping*]
TO .... Ticked Off [*Slang*]
T v O .... Tijdschrift voor Overheidsadministratie en Openbaar Bestuur [*A publication*]
T-O .... Time of Launch [*NASA*]   (KSC)
TO .... Time Opening
TO .... Time-Out
TO .... Tinctura Opii [*Tincture of Opium*]
T/O .... To Oblige   (AIA)
TO .... Tobacco Observer [*A publication*]
to .... Tonga [*MARC country of publication code*] [*Library of Congress*]   (LCCP)
TO .... Tonga [*ANSI two-letter standard code*]   (CNC)
TO .... Tonnage Opening   (DS)
TO .... Tool Order
TO .... Tops Order   (MCD)
TO .... Toronto
TO .... Torpedo Officer [*Obsolete*] [*Navy*] [*British*]
TO .... Township
TO .... Traded Options Market [*London Stock Exchange*]
TO .... Traditional Orthography [*Writing system*]
TO .... Traffic Officer
TO .... Trained Operator [*British military*]   (DMA)
T & O .... Training and Operations [*Military*]
TO .... Transfer Order
TO .... Transistor Outline   (IEEE)

TO............	Transmission Only [*Telecommunications*]
TO............	Transmitter Oscillator
TO............	Transportation Officer [*Military*]
TO............	Transverse Optic
TO............	Travel Order
TO............	Treasury Obligation [*Finance*]
TO............	Treasury Order [*British*] (ROG)
TO............	Tricuspid Valve Opening [*Cardiology*]
TO............	Troy Ounce
TO............	Tryptophan Oxygenase [*Also, TP, TPO*] [*An enzyme*]
TO............	Tuberculin Ober [*Supernatant portion*] [*Medicine*]
TO............	Tuberculin Old [*or Original*] [*Also, OT*] [*Medicine*]
TO............	Tuesdays Only [*British railroad term*]
TO............	[*A*] Turn Over [*A prospective customer who cannot be sold by one clerk and is turned over to another*] [*Merchandising slang*]
T/O..........	Turned Out [*for Examination*] [*Tea trade*] (ROG)
TO............	Turnout (AAG)
TO............	Turnover [*Number*] [*With reference to enzyme activity*]
TO............	Type of Organization Code [*IRS*]
TO............	Tyrosine Oxidase [*An enzyme*]
TOA.........	Table of Allowances
TOA.........	Table of Organization and Allowance
TOA.........	Terms of Agreement [*Army*] (AABC)
TOA.........	Theatre Owners of America [*Later, NATO*] (EA)
TOA.........	Thermal Optical Analysis
TOA.........	Tijdschrift voor Openbaar Bestuur [*A publication*]
TOA.........	Time of Arrival (AFM)
TOA.........	Time Out of Area (MCD)
TOA.........	Tolsona [*Alaska*] [*Seismograph station code, US Geological Survey*] (SEIS)
TOA.........	Top of the Atmosphere [*Meterology*]
TOA.........	Torrance, CA [*Location identifier*] [*FAA*] (FAAL)
TOA.........	Total Obligational Authority [*Military*]
TOA.........	Toyota Owners Association (EA)
TOA.........	Trade-Off Analysis [*Military*]
TOA.........	Trans Oceanic Airways Ltd. [*British*]
TOA.........	Transportation Operating Agencies (AFM)
TOA.........	Transportation Operations Authority (MCD)
TOA.........	Trim on Assembly (MCD)
TOA.........	Truck Operation Analysis
TOA.........	Tubo-Ovarian Abscess [*Medicine*]
TOAA.......	Total Overall Aerospace Vehicle [*or Aircraft*] Authorization
TOAC.......	Tool Accessory (AAG)
TOAD.......	Take Off and Die [*Surfers' slang for a very dangerous wave*]
TOAD.......	Tobyhanna Army Depot [*Pennsylvania*] (AABC)
TOAD.......	Towed Optical Assessment Device [*Marine science*] (MSC)
TOADS	Terminal-Oriented Administrative Data System
TOAI........	Total Overall Aerospace Vehicle [*or Aircraft*] Inventory
TOAL.......	Test of Adolescent Language
TOAL.......	Total Ordnance Alteration Application List [*Navy*]
TOAMAC ...	[*The*] Optimum Army Materiel Command (RDA)
TOAP.......	Prace Komisji Orientalistycznej Polskiej Akademii Umiejetnosci. Travaux de la Commission Orientaliste de l'Academie Polonaise des Sciences et des Lettres [*A publication*]
TOAP.......	Thioguanine, Oncovin [*Vincristine*], ara-C, Prednisone [*Antineoplastic drug regimen*]
TOB.........	Takeoff Boost [*Aviation*]
TOB.........	Telemetry Output Buffer [*Data processing*]
TOB.........	Tobacco (ADA)
Tob...........	Tobacco [*A publication*]
Tob...........	Tobacco Branch, Internal Revenue Bureau [*United States*] (DLA)
TOB.........	Tobias [*Old Testament book*] [*Douay version*]
TOB.........	Tobit [*Old Testament book*] [*Roman Catholic canon*] (ROG)
TOB.........	Toboggan
TOB.........	Tobruk [*Libya*] [*Airport symbol*] (OAG)
TOB.........	Tow Bar (MCD)
TOB.........	Tube over Bar [*Suspension*] (MCD)
TOBA.......	Theater Owners Booking Association [*Vaudeville*]
TOBA.......	Thoroughbred Owners and Breeders Association (EA)
TOBA.......	Tough on Black Actors [*Facetious translation of acronym for Theater Owners Booking Association*]
TOBAA8 ...	Tobacco [*New York*] [*A publication*]
Tob Abstracts ...	Tobacco Abstracts [*A publication*]
Tobacco....	Tobacco International [*A publication*]
Tobacco J..	Tobacco Journal [*A publication*] (APTA)
TOBE	Test of Basic Experiences [*Child development test*]
Tobey........	Tobey's Reports [*9, 10 Rhode Island*] [*A publication*] (DLA)
TOBI........	Test of Basic Information [*Education*]
TOBI.........	Toxicity Bibliography [*MEDLARS*]
Tob Int (NY) ...	Tobacco International (New York) [*A publication*]
Tob Leaf.....	Tobacco Leaf [*A publication*]
Tob Manuf Standing Comm Res Pap ...	Tobacco Manufacturers' Standing Committee. Research Papers [*A publication*]
Tob Res......	Tobacco Research [*A publication*]
Tob Res Board Rhod Bull ...	Tobacco Research Board of Rhodesia. Bulletin [*A publication*]
Tob Res Counc Res Pap ...	Tobacco Research Council. Research Paper [*England*] [*A publication*]

TobRV	Tobacco Ring Spot Virus
TOBS........	Telemetering Ocean Bottom Seismometer [*Marine science*] (MSC)
Tob Sci	Tobacco Science [*A publication*]
TOBWE.....	Tactical Observing Weather Element [*Air Force*]
TOC..........	[*The*] Operations Council of the American Trucking Associations (EA)
TOC..........	Table of Coincidences [*Telecommunications*] (TEL)
TOC..........	Table of Contents
TOC..........	Tactical Operations Center [*Military*]
TOC..........	Tag Open Cup [*Flash point test*]
TOC..........	Tagliabue Open Cup [*Analytical chemistry*]
TOC..........	Tanker Operational Circular
TOC..........	Task Order Contract
TOC..........	Task-Oriented Costing [*Telecommunications*] (TEL)
TOC..........	Tech/Ops Sevcon [*AMEX symbol*] (SPSG)
TOC..........	Technical Operating Center [*Telecommunications*] (TSSD)
TOC..........	Technical Order Compliance [*Military*]
TOC..........	Television Operating Center
TOC..........	Television Operators Caucus (EA)
TOC..........	Test of Cure [*Medicine*]
TOC..........	Test Operations Center [*NASA*] (NASA)
TOC..........	Test Operations Change [*NASA*] (NASA)
TOC..........	Theater of Operations Command [*Military*]
TOC..........	Tiers Ordre Carmelitaine [*Carmelite Third Order*] [*An association*] (EAIO)
TOC..........	Timber Operators Council (EA)
TOC..........	Time of Correlation (MCD)
TOC..........	Time Optimal Control (MCD)
TOC..........	Timing Operation Center
TOC..........	Tinctura Opii Camphorata [*Paregoric Elixir*] [*Pharmacy*] (ROG)
TOC..........	To Be Continued, Circuit Time Permitting (FAAC)
TOC..........	Toccoa, GA [*Location identifier*] [*FAA*] (FAAL)
TOC..........	Tocklai [*India*] [*Seismograph station code, US Geological Survey*] (SEIS)
TOC..........	Tooling Order Change
TOC..........	Top of Climb [*Aviation*]
TOC..........	TOS [*TIROS Operational Satellite*] Operations Center (NOAA)
TOC..........	Total Operational Cost [*Engineering*]
TOC..........	Total Organic Carbon
TOC..........	Traditional Organized Crime
TOC..........	Trans Ocean Containers Ltd.
TOC..........	Transfer of Control
TOC..........	Turn-On Command (KSC)
TOCA	[*The*] Order of the Crown in America (EA)
TOCAP......	Terminal Oriented Control Applications Program
TOCC	Technical and Operations Control Center [*INTELSAT*]
TOCC	Test Operations Control Center [*NASA*]
TOCC	Transfer of Control Card
TOCCA	TAFE [*Technical and Further Education*] Off-Campus Co-Ordinating Authority [*Australia*]
TOC/CP	Tactical Operations Center/Command Post [*Military*]
TOCCWE ...	Tactical Operations Control Center Weather Element [*Air Force*]
TOC/ECP ...	Technical Order Compliance/Engineering Change Proposal [*Military*] (AFIT)
TOCED	Table of Contents Editor Processor [*Data processing*]
Tocklai Exp Stn Advis Bull ...	Tocklai Experimental Station. Advisory Bulletin [*A publication*]
Tocklai Exp Stn Advis Leafl ...	Tocklai Experimental Station. Advisory Leaflet [*A publication*]
TOCl..........	Total Organic Chlorine [*Analytical chemistry*]
TOCM.......	Tocom, Inc. [*NASDAQ symbol*] (NQ)
TOCM.......	Trust Officers Committee Minutes [*A publication*] (DLA)
TOCN.......	Technical Order Change Notice [*Air Force*] (MCD)
Tocn i Nadezn Kibernet Sistem ...	Tocnost i Nadeznost Kiberneticeskih Sistem [*A publication*]
TOCOM.....	Tokyo Commodity Exchange for Industry [*Japan*] (ECON)
TOCP	Tri-ortho-cresyl Phosphate [*Organic chemistry*]
TOCR	Tocor, Inc. [*NASDAQ symbol*] (NQ)
TOCS........	Oriental Ceramic Society. Transactions [*A publication*]
TOCS........	Terminal Operations Control System
TOCS........	Terminal-Oriented Computer System
TOCS........	Textile Operational Control System [*Data processing*]
TOCS........	Tool Order Control System (MCD)
TOCSY......	Total Correlated Spectroscopy
TOCSY......	Total Correlation Spectroscopy
TOCU........	Tornado Operational Conversion Unit [*British military*] (DMA)
TOD..........	Technical Objective Directive [*or Document*] [*Air Force*] (MCD)
TOD..........	Technical Operations Department
TOD..........	Test Operations Directorate (RDA)
TOD..........	Theater-Oriented Depot [*Military*]
TOD..........	Theoretical Oxygen Demand [*Analytical biochemistry*]
TOD..........	Time of Day
TOD..........	Time of Delivery
TOD..........	Time of Departure (NVT)
TOD..........	Time of Despatch [*British*]
TOD..........	Tioman [*Malaysia*] [*Airport symbol*] (OAG)

TOD.......... Total Oxygen Demand [*Analytical chemistry*]
TOD.......... Tourist-Oriented-Directional [*Traffic sign*]
TOD.......... Trade-Off Determination [*Military*]   (AABC)
TOD.......... Turnover Device
TODA....... Takeoff Distance Available [*Aviation*]   (FAAC)
TODA....... Technical Order Distribution Activity
TODA....... Third-Octave Digital Analyzer
Toda Educ ... Today's Education [*A publication*]
TODARS... Terminal Oriented Data Analysis and Retrieval System
               [*National Institute of Standards and Technology*]
TODAS ..... Towed Oceanographic Data Acquisition System   (MSC)
TODAS ..... Typewriter-Oriented Documentation-Aid System
Today........ Today for Tomorrow [*A publication*]
Todays Chiro ... Today's Chiropractic [*A publication*]
Today's Ed ... Today's Education [*A publication*]
Todays Educ ... Today's Education [*A publication*]
Todays Exec ... Today's Executive [*A publication*]
Today's Fmkr ... Today's Filmmaker [*A publication*]
Todays Nurs Home ... Today's Nursing Home [*A publication*]
Today's Sec ... Today's Secretary [*A publication*]
Todays VD Vener Dis Control Probl ... Today's VD. Venereal Disease Control
               Problem [*A publication*]
Today Technol ... Today Technology [*A publication*]
Today & Tomorrow Educ ... Today and Tomorrow in Education [*A
               publication*]
TODC....... Technical Order Distribution Code [*Air Force*]
TODC....... Theater-Oriented Depot Complex [*Military*]   (AABC)
Tod Cath Teach ... Today's Catholic Teacher [*A publication*]
TODD....... [*The*] Todd-AO Corp. [*NASDAQ symbol*]   (NQ)
TODD-AO ... Todd-American Optical Co. [*Wide-screen system used by
               producer Michael Todd and the American Optical Co.*]
TODES...... Transcript of Data Extraction System   (MCD)
TODN....... Telephone Order Dispatch Notice
TODO....... Technical Order Distribution Office [*or Officer*]
Tod Parish ... Today's Parish [*A publication*]
TODR....... Takeoff Distance Required [*Aviation*]   (AIA)
TODrL...... Trudy Otdela Drevnerusskoj Literatury [*A publication*]
TODS........ Test-Oriented Disk System   (IEEE)
TODS........ Transactions on Database Systems
TODT........ Tool Detail   (AAG)
TOE.......... Epidermatophyton
TOE.......... Tables of Organization and Equipment [*Military*]
TO & E ..... Tables of Organization and Equipment [*Military*]   (AAG)
TOE.......... Talker Omission Error   (MUGU)
T & OE ...... Tentage and Organizational Equipment Branch [*US Army
               Natick Research, Development, and Engineering Center*]
TOE.......... Term of Enlistment [*Military*]
TOE.......... Texas, Oklahoma & Eastern Railroad Co. [*AAR code*]
TOE.......... Theory of Everything [*Cosmology*]
TOE.......... Thread One End   (MSA)
TOE.......... Time of Entry   (MCD)
TOE.......... Time of Event [*Military*]   (CAAL)
TOE.......... Tons of Oil Equivalent
TOE.......... Tony, Oscar, Emmy [*Refers to actors who have won these three
               major awards, for stage, film, and television work,
               respectively*]
TOE.......... Top of Edge   (AAG)
TOE.......... Total Operating Expense
TOE.......... Tozeur [*Tunisia*] [*Airport symbol*]   (OAG)
TOE.......... Tracheoesophageal [*Also, TE*] [*Medicine*]
TOE.......... Trainborne Operational Equipment
TOE.......... Tryout Employment [*Job Training and Partnership
               Act*]   (OICC)
TOE.......... United States Energy Research and Development
               Administration, Technical Information, Oak Ridge, TN
               [*Library symbol*] [*Library of Congress*]   (LCLS)
TOEFL...... Teaching of English as a Foreign Language
TOEFL...... Test of English as a Foreign Language
TOEIC...... Test of English for International Communication
TOEL....... Time Only Emitter Location System   (MCD)
TOELA...... Toute l'Electronique [*A publication*]
TOEMTB ... Tables of Organization and Equipment Mobilization Troop
               Basis [*Army*]   (AABC)
TOES........ Trade-Off Evaluation System
TOESD...... Test of Early Socioemotional Development [*Child development
               test*]
TOES-NA ... [*The*] Other Economic Summit of North America   (EA)
TOF.......... Beverly, MA [*Location identifier*] [*FAA*]   (FAAL)
TOF.......... [*The*] Obesity Foundation   (EA)
TOF.......... Tales of the Frightened [*A publication*]
TOF.......... Test Operations Facility [*NASA*]   (MCD)
TOF.......... Tetralogy of Fallot [*Cardiology*]
TOF.......... Time of Filing
TOF.......... Time of Fire [*Military*]   (CAAL)
TOF.......... Time of Flight
TOF.......... To Order From
TOF.......... Today's Office [*A publication*]
TOF.......... Tofutti Brands, Inc. [*AMEX symbol*]   (SPSG)
TOF.......... Tone Off [*Telecommunications*]   (TEL)
TOF.......... Top of File
TOF.......... Top of Form [*Data processing*]

TOF .... Transfer of Function   (MCD)
TOF .... Turnover Frequency [*Chemical engineering*]
TOFA....... Tall Oil Fatty Acids [*Organic chemistry*]
TOFABS ... Time-of-Flight Aerosol Beam Spectrometry
TOFC....... Tony Orlando Fan Club [*Defunct*]   (EA)
TOFC....... Trailer on Flatcar [*Railroad*]
TOFCN ..... Technical Order Field Change Notice [*Air Force*]   (MCD)
TOFDC..... Total Operational Flying Duty Credit [*Military*]   (AABC)
TOFI........ Time-of-Flight Isochronous Spectrometer
TOFL....... Takeoff Field Length [*Aviation*]
TOFM ...... Tooling Form   (AAG)
TOFMS..... Time-of-Flight Mass Spectrometer
To For .... Thomas de Formaginis [*Flourished, 1331-38*] [*Authority cited
               in pre-1607 legal work*]   (DSA)
To de For.... Thomas de Formaginis [*Flourished, 1331-38*] [*Authority cited
               in pre-1607 legal work*]   (DSA)
TOFS........ Time-of-Flight Spectrometer [*or Spectroscopy*]
TOFSARS ... Time-of-Flight Scattering and Recoiling Spectrometry
TOFSIMS ... Time-of-Flight Secondary Ion Mass Spectrometry
TOFU .... Tofu Time, Inc. [*NASDAQ symbol*]   (NQ)
TOG.......... Skyway of Ocala [*Ocala, FL*] [*FAA designator*]   (FAAC)
TOG.......... Takeoff Gross [*Weight*] [*Aviation*]
TOG.......... Target-Observer-Gun [*Method*] [*Army*]
TOG.......... Target Opportunity Generator   (KSC)
TOG.......... Technical Operations Group [*Air Force*]
TOG.......... Temagami Oil & Gas Ltd. [*Toronto Stock Exchange symbol*]
TOG.......... Togane [*Japan*] [*Seismograph station code, US Geological
               Survey*] [*Closed*]   (SEIS)
TOG.......... Together
TOG.......... Toggle
TOG.......... Togiak [*Alaska*] [*Airport symbol*]   (OAG)
TOG.......... Togiak Village, AK [*Location identifier*] [*FAA*]   (FAAL)
TOG.......... Top of Grade   (MCD)
TOG.......... Toronto Game [*Simulation game*]
TOGA....... Tooling Gauge   (AAG)
TOGA....... Tropical Oceans and Global Atmosphere Project [*World
               Meteorological Organization*]
TOGAD2... Topics in Gastroenterology [*A publication*]
Tog Cand ... Oratio in Senatu in Toga Candida [*of Cicero*] [*Classical
               studies*]   (OCD)
TOGI .... Target Oil & Gas, Incorporated [*NASDAQ symbol*]   (NQ)
TOGI .... Trans-Oceanic Geophysical Investigations [*Marine
               science*]   (MSC)
TOGLA ..... Tea Operators' and General Labourers' Association [*A union*]
               [*British*]
(Togo) Plan ... Fourth Plan of Economic and Social Development. Summary
               1981-1985 (Togo) [*A publication*]
TOGR........ Together   (ROG)
TOGW....... Takeoff Gross Weight [*Aviation*]
TOH .... Natchitoches, LA [*Location identifier*] [*FAA*]   (FAAL)
TOH .... Oak Ridge Hospital, Oak Ridge, TN [*Library symbol*] [*Library
               of Congress*]   (LCLS)
TOH .... Time Overhead   (NVT)
Toh............ Tohoroth [*or Toharoth*]   (BJA)
TOH .... Tyrosine Hydroxylase [*An enzyme*]
T & OHI .... Truck & Off-Highway Industries [*A publication*]
Toh J Ex Me ... Tohoku Journal of Experimental Medicine [*A publication*]
TOHM ...... Terohmmeter   (IEEE)
Toho.......... Tohoroth [*or Toharoth*]   (BJA)
Tohoku Agr Res ... Tohoku Agricultural Research [*A publication*]
Tohoku Geophys J Sci Rep Tohoku Univ Fifth Ser ... Tohoku Geophysical
               Journal. Science Reports of the Tohoku University. Fifth
               Series [*A publication*]
Tohoku Imp Univ Technol Rep ... Tohoku Imperial University Technology
               Reports [*Japan*] [*A publication*]
Tohoku J Agric Res ... Tohoku Journal of Agricultural Research [*A
               publication*]
Tohoku J Agr Res ... Tohoku Journal of Agricultural Research [*A publication*]
Tohoku J Exp Med ... Tohoku Journal of Experimental Medicine [*A
               publication*]
Tohoku Math ... Tohoku Mathematical Journal [*A publication*]
Tohoku Math J ... Tohoku Mathematical Journal [*A publication*]
Tohoku Math J 2 ... Tohoku Mathematical Journal. Second Series [*A
               publication*]
Tohoku Med J ... Tohoku Medical Journal [*A publication*]
Tohoku Psychol Folia ... Tohoku Psychologica Folia [*A publication*]
Tohoku Univ Inst Agric Res Rep ... Tohoku University. Institute for
               Agricultural Research. Reports [*A publication*]
Tohoku Univ Sci Rep Ser 2 ... Tohoku University. Science Reports. Series 2.
               Geology [*A publication*]
Tohoku Univ Sci Rep Ser 3 ... Tohoku University. Science Reports. Series 3.
               Mineralogy, Petrology, and Economic Geology [*A
               publication*]
Tohoku Univ Sci Rep Ser 5 ... Tohoku University. Science Reports. Series 5 [*A
               publication*]
Tohoku Univ Sci Repts Geology ... Tohoku University. Science Reports.
               Geology [*A publication*]
TOHP........ Takeoff Horsepower [*Aviation*]
TOI........... Target of Interest [*Military*]   (CAAL)
TOI........... Technical Operation Instruction   (KSC)
TOI........... Technical Operations, Incorporated   (MCD)

TOI .... Term of Induction [*Military*]
TOI .... Time of Intercept [*Military*]   (CAAL)
TOI .... Transfer Orbital Insertion [*NASA*]
TOI .... Troy, AL [*Location identifier*] [*FAA*]   (FAAL)
TOID .... Technical Order Identification   (MCD)
TOIL .... Time Off in Lieu
Toim Eesti NSV Tead Akad Fuus Mat ... Toimetised. Eesti NSV Teaduste
        Akadeemia. Fuusika. Matemaatika [*A publication*]
TOJ .... Track on Jamming
To Jo .... [*Sir Thomas*] Jones' English King's Bench Reports [*A
        publication*]   (DLA)
TOK .... Thrust Okay [*NASA*]   (KSC)
TOK .... Toeristenkampioen [*A publication*]
TOK .... Tokheim Corp. [*NYSE symbol*]   (SPSG)
TOK .... Tokyo [*Japan*] [*Later, KAK*] [*Geomagnetic observatory code*]
TOK .... Tokyo [*Japan*] [*Seismograph station code, US Geological
        Survey*]   (SEIS)
TOK .... Torokina [*Papua New Guinea*] [*Airport symbol*]   (OAG)
Tokai J Exp Clin Med ... Tokai Journal of Experimental and Clinical
        Medicine [*Japan*] [*A publication*]
Tokai-Kinki Natl Agric Exp Stn Res Prog Rep ... Tokai-Kinki National
        Agricultural Experiment Station. Research Progress Report
        [*A publication*]
Tokai Technol J ... Tokai Technological Journal [*Japan*] [*A publication*]
TOKAMAK ... Toroidal Kamera Magnetic [*Thermonuclear-fusion system*]
        [*Acronym formed from the Russian*]
Tokoginecol Prac ... Toko-Ginecologia Practica [*A publication*]
Toko-Ginecol Pract ... Toko-Ginecologia Practica [*A publication*]
TOKSA ...... Tokushuko [*A publication*]
Toksikol Nov Prom Khim Veshchestv ... Toksikologiya Novykh
        Promyshlennykh Khimicheskikh Veshchestv [*A
        publication*]
TOKTA ..... Teoreticheskie Osnovy Khimicheskoi Tekhnologii [*A
        publication*]
Tokushima J Exp Med ... Tokushima Journal of Experimental Medicine [*A
        publication*]
Tokyo Astron Bull ... Tokyo Astronomical Bulletin [*A publication*]
Tokyo Astron Bull Ser II ... Tokyo Astronomical Bulletin. Series II [*A
        publication*]
Tokyo Astron Obs Kiso Inf Bull ... Tokyo Astronomical Observatory. Kiso
        Information Bulletin [*A publication*]
Tokyo Astron Obs Rep ... Tokyo Astronomical Observatory. Report [*A
        publication*]
Tokyo Astron Obs Time and Latitude Bull ... Tokyo Astronomical
        Observatory. Time and Latitude Bulletins [*A publication*]
Tokyo Bk Dev Centre Newsl ... Tokyo Book Development Centre. Newsletter
        [*A publication*]
Tokyo Fin R ... Tokyo Financial Review [*A publication*]
Tokyo Inst Technol Bull ... Tokyo Institute of Technology. Bulletin [*A
        publication*]
Tokyo Jikeika Med J ... Tokyo Jikeika Medical Journal [*A publication*]
Tokyo J Math ... Tokyo Journal of Mathematics [*A publication*]
Tokyo J Med Sci ... Tokyo Journal of Medical Sciences [*A publication*]
Tokyo Kyoiku Daigaku Sci Rep Sec C ... Tokyo Kyoiku Daigaku. Science
        Reports. Section C. Geology, Mineralogy, and Geography
        [*A publication*]
Tokyo Metrop Isot Cent Annu Rep ... Tokyo Metropolitan Isotope Centre.
        Annual Report [*A publication*]
Tokyo Metrop Res Inst Environ Prot Annu Rep Engl Transl ... Tokyo
        Metropolitan Research Institute for Environmental
        Protection. Annual Report. English Translation [*A
        publication*]
Tokyo Metrop Univ Geogr Rep ... Tokyo Metropolitan University.
        Geographical Reports [*A publication*]
Tokyo Munic News ... Tokyo Municipal News [*A publication*]
Tokyo Natl Sci Mus Bull ... Tokyo National Science Museum. Bulletin [*A
        publication*]
Tokyo Tanabe Q ... Tokyo Tanabe Quarterly [*A publication*]
Tokyo Univ Coll Gen Educ Sci Pap ... Tokyo University. College of General
        Education. Scientific Papers [*A publication*]
Tokyo Univ Earthquake Research Inst Bull ... Tokyo University. Earthquake
        Research Institute. Bulletin [*A publication*]
Tokyo Univ Fac Eng J Ser B ... Tokyo University. Faculty of Engineering.
        Journal. Series B [*A publication*]
Tokyo Univ Faculty Sci Jour ... Tokyo University. Faculty of Science. Journal
        [*A publication*]
TOL .... Test-Oriented Language [*Data processing*]
TOL .... Ticket of Leave
TOL .... Toledo [*Ohio*] [*Airport symbol*]   (OAG)
TOL .... Toledo [*Spain*] [*Geomagnetic observatory code*]
TOL .... Toledo [*Spain*] [*Seismograph station code, US Geological
        Survey*]   (SEIS)
TOL .... Tolerance   (AAG)
TOL .... Toll Brothers, Inc. [*NYSE symbol*]   (SPSG)
TOL .... Tower of London
TOL .... Trial of Labor [*Gynecology*]
TOL .... Trucial Oman Levies [*British military*]   (DMA)
TOL .... University of Toledo, Toledo, OH [*OCLC symbol*]   (OCLC)
TOLA .... Takeoff and Landing Analysis [*Air Force*]
TOLA .... Theatre of Latin America   (EA)
TOLAR...... Terminal On-Line Availability Reporting

TOLCAT ... Takeoff and Landing Clear Air Turbulence [*Aviation*]
TOLCAT ... Takeoff and Landing Critical Atmosphere Turbulence
        [*Aviation*]   (MCD)
TOLD .... TELECOMS On-Line Data System
        [*Telecommunications*]   (TEL)
TOLD .... Test of Language Development [*Education*]
Toledo L Rev ... University of Toledo. Law Review [*A publication*]
Toledo Mus N ... Toledo Museum of Art. Museum News [*A publication*]
Toledo Univ Inst Silicate Research Inf Circ ... Toledo University. Institute of
        Silicate Research. Information Circular [*A publication*]
TOLEYIS ... Turkiye Otel, Lokanta ve Eglence Yerleri Isci Sendikalari
        Federasyonu [*National Federation of Hotel, Restaurant,
        and Amusement Places Workers' Unions*] [*Turkey*]
TOLIP .... Trajectory Optimization and Linearized Pitch [*Computer
        program*]
TOLL......... Tollerford [*England*]
Toller......... Toller on Executors [*A publication*]   (DLA)
Toll Ex .... Toller on Executors [*A publication*]   (ILCA)
Tol LR....... University of Toledo. Law Review [*A publication*]
TOLM .... Toledo Mining [*NASDAQ symbol*]   (NQ)
TOLO .... Tool and Operation Liaison Order   (AAG)
TOLO .... Tooling Layout   (AAG)
TOLP........ Test for Oral Language Production [*Educational test*]
TOLR .... Toll Restricted [*Telecommunications*]   (TEL)
TOLR .... Transmitting Objective Loudness Rating [*of telephone
        connections*]   (IEEE)
To LR .... University of Toledo. Law Review [*A publication*]
TOLS......... Times On-Line Services [*Information service or system*]   (EISS)
Tolst Div ..... Tolstoy on Divorce and Matrimonial Causes [*A
        publication*]   (DLA)
TOLT........ Towing Light   (AAG)
TOLTEP ... Teleprocessing On-Line Test Executive Program [*IBM Corp.*]
TOLTS ..... Total On-Line Testing System [*Honeywell, Inc.*]
Tolva .... Tolva. Revista del Trigo. Harina y del Pan [*A publication*]
Tolvmandsbl ... Tolvmandsbladet [*A publication*]
TOM.......... GMT [*Greenwich Mean Time*] of Orbital Midnight
TOM.......... [*The*] Old Man
TOM.......... Technical Operations Manager [*Navy*]
TOM.......... Terz'Ordine dei Minimi [*Third Order of Minimi*] [*Rome,
        Italy*]   (EAIO)
TOM.......... Texas College of Osteopathic Medicine, Fort Worth, TX [*OCLC
        symbol*]   (OCLC)
TOM.......... Text on Microform [*Information Access Co. - IAC*]
        [*Information service or system*]   (IID)
TOM.......... Third Order of Mary   (EA)
TOM.......... Thompson-Lundmark Gold Mines Ltd. [*Toronto Stock
        Exchange symbol*]
TOM.......... Tombouctou [*Mali*] [*Airport symbol*]   (OAG)
TOM.......... Tomie [*Japan*] [*Seismograph station code, US Geological
        Survey*] [*Closed*]   (SEIS)
TOM.......... Toronto, Ottawa, Montreal [*Derogatory reference to people in
        these cities; used by other Canadians who think people
        living in these cities "run things"*]
TOM.......... Totem Capital Corp. [*Vancouver Stock Exchange symbol*]
TOM.......... Tracking Operation Memorandum [*Obsolete*]
TOM.......... Translator Octal Mnemonic
TOM.......... Typical Ocean Model [*Oceanography*]
TOMA .... Technical Order Management Agency [*Military*]   (AFIT)
TOMA .... Test of Mathematical Abilities
TOMA .... Turn Off My Addiction [*Proposed clinic*]
TOMARA ... Texas Outlaw Midget Automobile Racing Association [*Car
        racing*]
TOMB .... Technical Organizational Memory Bank   (RDA)
TOMCAT ... Telemetry On-Line Monitoring Compression and Transmission
TOMCAT ... Teleoperator for Operations, Maintenance, and Construction
        Using Advanced Technology
TOMCAT ... Theater of Operations Missile Continuous-Wave Antitank
        Weapon
TOMH ...... Regional Mental Health Center of Oak Ridge, Oak Ridge, TN
        [*Library symbol*] [*Library of Congress*]   (LCLS)
Toming....... [*Jacobus*] Tomingius [*Deceased, 1576*] [*Authority cited in pre-
        1607 legal work*]   (DSA)
Tom Inst ..... Tomkins' Institutes of Roman Law [*A publication*]   (DLA)
Tom & J Comp ... Tomkins and Jenckens' Compendium of the Modern
        Roman Law [*A publication*]   (DLA)
TOMK ...... Tomkins PLC [*NASDAQ symbol*]   (NQ)
Tomkins & J Mod Rom Law ... Tomkins and Jencken's Compendium of the
        Modern Roman Law [*A publication*]   (DLA)
Toml.......... Tomlins' Election Cases [*1689-1795*] [*A publication*]   (DLA)
Toml Cas..... Tomlins' Election Cases [*1689-1795*] [*A publication*]   (DLA)
Toml Cr L .. Tomlin's Criminal Law [*A publication*]   (DLA)
Tom & Lem Gai ... Tomkins and Lemon's Translation of Gaius [*A
        publication*]   (DLA)
Tomlins...... Tomlins' Law Dictionary [*A publication*]   (DLA)
Toml Law Dict ... Tomlins' Law Dictionary [*A publication*]   (DLA)
Toml LD .... Tomlins' Law Dictionary [*A publication*]   (DLA)
Toml Supp Br ... Tomlins' Supplement to Brown's Parliamentary Cases [*A
        publication*]   (DLA)
TOMM...... Time-Oriented Metropolitan Model   (MCD)
TOMMS ... Terminal Operations and Movements Management
        System   (MCD)

TomNDV ...	Tomato Necrotic Dwarf Virus
TOMR	Tomorrow (ROG)
TomRSV	Tomato Ringspot Virus
TomRSV-S ...	Tomato Ringspot Virus - Seed Borne
TOMS	Torus Oxygen Monitoring System (IEEE)
TOMS	Total Ozone Mapping Spectrometer (MCD)
TOMS	Total Ozone Mapping System [*Meteorology*]
TOMS	Transactions on Mathematical Software
TOMSI	Transfer of Master Scheduled Item
Tomsk Gos Pedagog Inst Uch Zap ...	Tomskii Gosudarstvennyi Pedagogicheskii Institut. Uchenye Zapiski [*A publication*]
Tomsk Gos Univ Ucen Zap ...	Tomskii Gosudarstvennyi Universitet Imeni V. V. Kuibyseva. Ucenye Zapiski [*A publication*]
TOMSS	Theater of Operations Medical Support System [*Military*] (MCD)
TOMT	Target Organizational Maintenance Trainer (MCD)
TOMUS	[*The*] On-Line Multi-User System [*Carlyle Systems, Inc.*] [*Information service or system*] (IID)
TON	Threshold Odor Number [*Water analysis*]
TON	Tone On [*Telecommunications*] (TEL)
TON	Tonga [*ANSI three-letter standard code*] (CNC)
TON	Tongariro [*New Zealand*] [*Seismograph station code, US Geological Survey*] [*Closed*] (SEIS)
TON	Tonic [*Permanently Strengthening*] [*Pharmacy*] (ROG)
TON	Tonopah Resources, Inc. [*Vancouver Stock Exchange symbol*]
TON	Top of the News [*A publication*]
TONAC	Tyrone, PA [*Location identifier*] [*FAA*] (FAAL)
TONAC	Technical Order Notification and Completion System (AAG)
TONE	[*The*] One Bancorp [*Portland, ME*] [*NASDAQ symbol*] (NQ)
TON/FT²	Tons per Square Foot
TONGA	Trudy Nauchno-Issledovatel'skogo Instituta Onkologii Gruzinskoi SSR [*A publication*]
TONI	Test of Nonverbal Intelligence
Tonind Zeitung ...	Tonindustrie-Zeitung [*A publication*]
Tonind-Ztg Keram Rundsch ...	Tonindustrie-Zeitung und Keramische Rundschau [*A publication*]
TONL	Union Carbide Nuclear Co., Oak Ridge National Laboratories, Oak Ridge, TN [*Library symbol*] [*Library of Congress*] (LCLS)
TONLAR ..	Tone-Operated Net Loss Adjuster Receiving
TONL-B	Union Carbide Nuclear Co., Oak Ridge National Laboratories, Biology Library, Oak Ridge, TN [*Library symbol*] [*Library of Congress*] (LCLS)
TONL-T	Union Carbide Nuclear Co., Oak Ridge National Laboratories, Thermal-Nuclear Library, Oak Ridge, TN [*Library symbol*] [*Library of Congress*] (LCLS)
TONL-Y	Union Carbide Nuclear Co., Oak Ridge National Laboratories, Y-12 Technical Library, Oak Ridge, TN [*Library symbol*] [*Library of Congress*] (LCLS)
TONN	Tonnage [*Shipping*]
TONS	Tons of Toys, Inc. [*NASDAQ symbol*] (NQ)
TONS	Topical Numismatic Society (EA)
TONT	Tonto National Monument
TONT	Toronto Native Times [*A publication*]
TOO	2001 Resource Industries Ltd. [*Vancouver Stock Exchange symbol*]
TOO	La Tour de l'Orle d'Or [*A publication*]
TOO	Target of Opportunity [*Military*] (CAAL)
TOO	Test Operations Order [*NASA*]
TOO	Threshold of Odor (NASA)
TOO	Time of Origin [*Communications*]
TOO	Toolangi [*Australia*] [*Seismograph station code, US Geological Survey*] (SEIS)
TOO	Toolangi [*Australia*] [*Geomagnetic observatory code*]
TOOIS	Transactions on Office Information Systems [*A publication*]
TOOL	Easco Hand Tools, Inc. [*NASDAQ symbol*] (NQ)
TOOL	Teams of Our Lady [*See also END*] (EAIO)
TOOL	Test-Oriented Operated Language [*Programming language*] [*Data processing*]
Tool Die J ..	Tool and Die Journal [*A publication*]
Tool Eng	Tool Engineer [*A publication*]
Tooling P ...	Tooling and Production [*A publication*]
Tool Mfg Eng ...	Tool and Manufacturing Engineer [*A publication*]
Tool & Mfg Eng ...	Tool and Manufacturing Engineer [*A publication*]
Tool and Prod ...	Tooling and Production [*A publication*]
Tool Prod ...	Tooling and Production [*A publication*]
TOOS	Torque Overload Switch (NRCH)
TOOT	202 Data Systems. Inc. [*NASDAQ symbol*] (NQ)
TOOTJFC ...	[*The*] One and Only Tom Jones Fan Club (EA)
TOP	[*The*] Opportunity Prospector [*A publication*]
TOP	[*The*] Option Process [*HUD*]
TOP	Table of Output Products
TOP	Tactical Operations Plot [*Military*] (CAAL)
TOP	Target Occulting Processor (MCD)
TOP	Targeted Outreach Program [*Department of Labor*]
TOP	Tax-Offset Pension [*Account*]
TOP	Teacher Organizing Project (EA)
TOP	Technical, Office, and Professional Department [*UAW*]
TOP	Technical and Office Protocol [*Data communications standards*]
TOP	Technical Operating Procedure

TOP	Temple Opportunity Program [*Temple University*] (EA)
TOP	Temporarily Out of Print
TOP	Tertiary Operation
TOP	Test and Operations Plan
TOP	Test Outline Plan [*Army*] (AABC)
TOP	Topeka [*Kansas*] [*Airport symbol*] (OAG)
TOP	Topeka, KS [*Location identifier*] [*FAA*] (FAAL)
Top	Topic [*Record label*] [*Great Britain*]
Top	Topica [*of Aristotle*] [*Classical studies*] (OCD)
Top	Topica [*of Cicero*] [*Classical studies*] (OCD)
top	Topical
TOP	Topographic
TOP	Topoisomerase [*An enzyme*]
TOP	Topology
TOP	Topolovo [*USSR*] [*Seismograph station code, US Geological Survey*] (SEIS)
TOP	Toponymic [*Anatomy*]
TOP	Torque Oil Pressure [*Air Force*]
TOP	Total Obscuring Power [*Smoke cloud*]
TOP	Total Office Products Group [*Commercial firm*] [*British*]
TOP	Trade Opportunities Program [*Departments of State and Commerce*]
TOP	Training Operation Plan [*Military*] (CAAL)
TOP	Transient Overpower Accident [*Nuclear energy*]
TOP	Transovarial Passage [*Virology*]
TOP	Transverse Optical Pumping (MCD)
TOP	Trinity Occasional Papers [*A publication*]
TOP	Turn Out Perfection [*US Air Force Southern Command's acronym for the Zero Defects Program*]
TOP	Turn Over, Please [*Correspondence*] (ROG)
TOPA	Tooling Pattern
Top Allerg Clin Immun ...	Topics in Allergy and Clinical Immunology [*A publication*]
Top Antibiot Chem ...	Topics in Antibiotic Chemistry [*A publication*]
Top Appl Phys ...	Topics in Applied Physics [*A publication*]
Top Astrophys Space Phys ...	Topics in Astrophysics and Space Physics [*A publication*]
Top Autom Chem Anal ...	Topics in Automatic Chemical Analysis [*A publication*]
Top Bioelectrochem Bioenerg ...	Topics in Bioelectrochemistry and Bioenergetics [*A publication*]
TOPCAP ...	Total Objective Plan for Career Airmen Personnel [*Air Force*] (AFM)
Top Chem Mutagen ...	Topics in Chemical Mutagenesis [*A publication*]
Top Clin Nurs ...	Topics in Clinical Nursing [*A publication*]
Top Curr Chem ...	Topics in Current Chemistry [*A publication*]
Top Curr Phys ...	Topics in Current Physics [*A publication*]
Top Emerg Med ...	Topics in Emergency Medicine [*A publication*]
Top Environ Health ...	Topics in Environmental Health [*A publication*]
Top Enzyme Ferment Biotechnol ...	Topics in Enzyme and Fermentation Biotechnology [*A publication*]
TOPES	Telephone Office Planning and Engineering System [*Telecommunications*] (TEL)
TOPEX	Topographic Experiment [*Proposed oceanographic satellite*]
TOPEX	Typhoon Operational Experiment [*Meteorology*]
TOPF	Transplant Organ Procurement Foundation (EA)
TOPG	Topping (MSA)
Top Gastroenterol ...	Topics in Gastroenterology [*A publication*]
TOPHAT ..	Terrier Operation Proof High-Altitude Target (MUGU)
Top Health Care Financ ...	Topics in Health Care Financing [*A publication*]
Top Health Rec Manage ...	Topics in Health Record Management [*A publication*]
Top Horm Chem ...	Topics in Hormone Chemistry [*A publication*]
Top Hosp Pharm Manage ...	Topics in Hospital Pharmacy Management [*A publication*]
T Ophth Soc ...	Transactions. Ophthalmological Societies of the United Kingdom [*A publication*]
Top Hum Genet ...	Topics in Human Genetics [*A publication*]
TOPIC	[*The*] Objective Personnel Inventory - Civilian [*Air Force*]
TOPIC	Time-Ordered Programmer Integrated Circuit [*NASA*]
TOPICS	Test of Performance in Computational Skills [*Educational test*]
TOPICS	Total On-Line Program and Information Control System [*Japan*]
TOPICS	Traffic Operations to Increase Capacity and Safety [*Department of Transportation*]
TOPICS	Transcripts of Parlibs Information Classification System [*Queensland Parliamentary Library*] [*A publication*] (APTA)
Topics Appl Phys ...	Topics in Applied Physics [*A publication*]
Topics Clin Nurs ...	Topics in Clinical Nursing [*A publication*]
Topics Current Phys ...	Topics in Current Physics [*A publication*]
Top Infect Dis ...	Topics in Infectious Diseases [*A publication*]
TOPIX	Tokyo Stock Price Index [*Japan*] (ECON)
TOPLAS	Transactions on Programming Languages and Systems (MCD)
Top Lipid Chem ...	Topics in Lipid Chemistry [*A publication*]
TOPM	Top Air Manufacturing, Inc. [*NASDAQ symbol*] (NQ)
Top Manage Abstr ...	Top Management Abstracts [*A publication*]
Top Math Phys ...	Topics in Mathematical Physics [*A publication*]
Top Med Chem ...	Topics in Medicinal Chemistry [*A publication*]
Top Mol Struct Biol ...	Topics in Molecular and Structural Biology [*A publication*]

Top News...   Top of the News [*A publication*]
T of OPNS ...   Theater of Operations [*Military*]
TOPNS......   Theater of Operations [*Military*]
TOPO........   Test Operations and Policy Office [*TECOM*]   (RDA)
TOPO........   Topography   (AFM)
TOPO........   Tri-n-Octyl Phosphine Oxide [*Organic chemistry*]
TOPO........   Trioctylphosphine Oxide [*Organic chemistry*]
TOPOCOM ...   Topographic Command [*Army*]
TOPOENGR ...   Topographical Engineer
TOPOG.....   Topography
Topology Appl ...   Topology and Its Applications [*A publication*]
Topology Proc ...   Topology Proceedings [*A publication*]
TOPO-MIBK ...   Trioctylphosphorine Oxide/Methyl Isobutyl Keton [*Solvent mixture*]
TOPP........   [*The*] Organization of Plastics Processors   (EA)
TOPP........   Terminal-Operated Production Program   (BUR)
TOPP........   [*The*] Topps Company, Inc. [*NASDAQ symbol*]   (NQ)
Top Paediatr ...   Topics in Paediatrics [*A publication*]
TOPPER ...   Toy Press Publishers, Editors, and Reporters
Top Perinat Med ...   Topics in Perinatal Medicine [*A publication*]
Top Pharm Sci ...   Topics in Pharmaceutical Sciences [*A publication*]
Top Phosphorus Chem ...   Topics in Phosphorus Chemistry [*A publication*]
Top Photosynth ...   Topics in Photosynthesis [*A publication*]
Top Probl Psychiatry Neurol ...   Topical Problems in Psychiatry and Neurology [*A publication*]
Top Probl Psychother ...   Topical Problems of Psychotherapy [*A publication*]
TOPR ....   Taiwan Open Pool Reactor
TOPRA......   Tooling and Production [*A publication*]
TOPREP....   Total Objective Plan for Reserve Personnel [*Air Force*]   (AFM)
Top Rep NB Miner Resour Branch ...   Topical Report. New Brunswick Mineral Resources Branch [*A publication*]
Top Rev Haematol ...   Topical Reviews in Haematology [*A publication*]
TOPS.........   [*The*] Operational PERT System
TOPS.........   [*The*] Optimum Publishing System [*IBM Corp.*]
TOPS.........   Tactical Optical Projection System   (NVT)
TOPS.........   Tailored Owner Protection System [*Automotive optional warranty*]
TOPS........   Take Off Pounds Sensibly   (EA)
TOPS.........   Telemetry On-Line Processing System [*Data processing*]
TOPS.........   Telephone Order Personalities and Smiles [*Organization of chief telephone operators*]
TOPS........   Telephone Order Processing System
TOPS.........   Telephone Order Purchasing System   (MCD)
TOPS.........   Teleregister Omni Processing and Switching [*Data processing*]
TOPS.........   Teletype Optical Projection System   (IEEE)
TOPS.........   Terminal Oriented Planning System   (MCD)
TOPS.........   Test Operations Procedures [*Army*]   (RDA)
TOPS.........   Test of Problem Solving [*Intelligence test*]
TOPS.........   Tested Overhead Projection Series [*Education*]
TOPS........   Testing and Operating System
TOPS.........   Theatre Organ Preservation Society [*British*]
TOPS.........   Thermal Noise Optical Optimization Communication System [*NASA*]
TOPS.........   Thermoelectric Outer Planet Spacecraft [*NASA*]
TOPS.........   Time-Sharing Operating System
TOPS.........   Top One Percent Society   (EA)
TOPS........   Top Sound International, Inc. [*NASDAQ symbol*]   (NQ)
TOPS.........   Total Operations Processing System [*Data processing*]
TOPS.........   Total Organ Perfusion System
TOPS.........   Traffic Operator Position System [*Telecommunications*]   (TEL)
TOPS.........   Training Opportunities Schemes [*Department of Employment*] [*British*]
TOPS.........   Transcendental Network [*Centram Systems West, Inc.*] [*Berkeley, CA*] [*Telecommunications*]   (TSSD)
TOPS.........   Transistorized Operational Phone System   (MCD)
TOPS.........   Transportation Operational Personal Property System [*Army*]
TOPS.........   Truck Ordering and Pricing System
TOPS.........   United States Travelers' Overseas Personalized Service [*Also known as USTOPS*]
TOPSEC ...   Top Secret [*Security classification*]
TOPSEP....   Targeting/Optimization for Solar Electric Propulsion [*NASA*]
TOPSI ....   Topside Sounder, Ionosphere [*NASA*]
TOPSTAR ...   [*The*] Officer Personnel System, The Army Reserve   (AABC)
Top Stereochem ...   Topics in Stereochemistry [*A publication*]
Top Sulfur Chem ...   Topics in Sulfur Chemistry [*A publication*]
TOPSY ......   Test Operations Planning System
TOPSY ......   Thermally Operated Plasma System
TOPT........   Tele-Optic, Inc. [*NASDAQ symbol*]   (NQ)
Top Therap ...   Topics in Therapeutics [*A publication*]
TOPTS ......   Test-Oriented Paper-Tape System [*Data processing*]   (IEEE)
TOPV........   Trivalent Oral Poliomyelitis Vaccine [*Medicine*]
TOR..........   Tactical Operational Requirement [*Military*]   (CAAL)
TOR..........   Tactical Operations Room [*Air Force*]
TOR..........   Tall Oil Rosin [*Organic chemistry*]
TOR..........   Technical Operating Report
TOR..........   Technical Operations Research   (KSC)
TOR..........   Technical Override
TOR..........   Telegraph on Radio [*Telecommunications*]   (TEL)
TOR..........   Teleprinter on Radio [*Telecommunications*]   (TSSD)
TOR..........   Tentative Operational Requirement
Top News...   Terms of Reference [*Army*]   (AABC)

TOR..........   Test Operation Report   (KSC)
TOR..........   Third Order Regular of St. Francis [*Roman Catholic men's religious order*]
TOR..........   Time of Receipt [*Military*]   (AABC)
TOR..........   Time of Reception [*Communications*]
TOR..........   Time on Risk [*Insurance*]   (AIA)
TOR..........   Torhsen Energy Corp. [*Vancouver Stock Exchange symbol*]
TOR..........   Torishima [*Japan*] [*Seismograph station code, US Geological Survey*] [*Closed*]   (SEIS)
TOR..........   Toronto   (ROG)
TOR..........   Toronto Airways Ltd. [*Markom, ON*] [*FAA designator*]   (FAAC)
TOR..........   Torque   (AAG)
TOR..........   Torrance [*California*]
Tor ....   Torre [*A publication*]
TOR..........   Torrington, WY [*Location identifier*] [*FAA*]   (FAAL)
TOR..........   Totalizing Relay
TOR..........   Tournament of Roses Association   (EA)
TOR..........   Traffic on Request [*Aviation*]   (FAAC)
TOR..........   Turn-On Rate   (CAAL)
TORA ....   Takeoff Run Available [*Aviation*]   (FAAC)
TORAC .....   Torpedo Acquisition
TORAH....   Tough Orthodox Rabbis and Hassidim [*An association*]
TORC ....   Test of Reading Comprehension
TORC ....   Thai Oil Refinery Co. Ltd.   (DS)
TORC ....   Traffic Overload Reroute Control
TORCH.....   Toxoplasma, Other [*Viruses*], Rubella, Cytomegaloviruses, Herpes [*Virus*]
TOREA .....   Toshiba Review [*A publication*]
TOREADOR ...   Torero-Matador [*Said to have been coined by Georges Bizet for opera "Carmen"*]
TORF........   Time of Retrofire [*NASA*]   (KSC)
Torf Delo....   Torfyanoe Delo [*A publication*]
Torfnachrichten Forsch Werbestelle Torf ...   Torfnachrichten der Forschungs- und Werbestelle fuer Torf [*A publication*]
Torf Promst ...   Torfyanaya Promyshlennost [*A publication*]
Tori Bull Ornithol Soc Jpn ...   Tori. Bulletin of the Ornithological Society of Japan [*A publication*]
Torino Univ Ist Geol Pub ...   Torino Universita. Istituto Geologico. Pubblicazioni [*A publication*]
Tor Life ......   Toronto Life [*A publication*]
TORM ......   Torquemeter
TORNL ......   Torsional
Toronto U Faculty L Rev ...   Toronto University. Faculty Law Review [*Canada*] [*A publication*]   (DLA)
Toronto Univ Dep Mech Eng Tech Publ Ser ...   Toronto University. Department of Mechanical Engineering. Technical Publication Series [*A publication*]
Toronto Univ Inst Aerosp Stud UTIAS Rep ...   Toronto University. Institute for Aerospace Studies. UTIAS Report [*A publication*]
Toronto Univ Inst Aerosp Stud UTIAS Rev ...   Toronto University. Institute for Aerospace Studies. UTIAS Review [*A publication*]
Toronto Univ Inst Aerosp Stud UTIAS Tech Note ...   Toronto University. Institute for Aerospace Studies. UTIAS Technical Note [*A publication*]
Toronto Univ Studies G S ...   Toronto University Studies. Geological Series [*A publication*]
TORP ....   Test of Orientation for Rehabilitation Patients [*Occupational therapy*]
TORP ....   Torpedo   (AABC)
TORP ....   Total Ossicular Replacement Prosthesis
TORPA.....   Torfyanaya Promyshlennost [*A publication*]
TORPCM ...   Torpedo Countermeasures and Deception
TORPEX...   Torpedo Exercise   (NVT)
TORPRON ...   Torpedo Squadron
TORQ........   Torquay [*England*]
TORQ........   Torque [*Automotive engineering*]
TORQUE..   Tests of Reasonable Quantitative Understanding of the Environment [*Education*]
TORQUE..   Truck Operators Road Qualifying Exam [*National Highway Traffic Safety Administration*]
TORR ....   Takeoff Run Required [*Aviation*]   (AIA)
TORR ....   Torricelli [*Unit of pressure*]
TORR ....   Torrington [*England*]
Torreia Nueva Ser ...   Torreia Nueva Serie [*A publication*]
Torrey Bot Club Bull ...   Torrey Botanical Club. Bulletin [*A publication*]
Torry Res ...   Torry Research [*A publication*]
Torry Res Stn (Aberdeen Scotl) Annu Rep ...   Torry Research Station (Aberdeen, Scotland). Annual Report [*A publication*]
Torry Res Stn Annu Rep Handl Preserv Fish Fish Prod ...   Torry Research Station. Annual Report on the Handling and Preservation of Fish and Fish Products [*A publication*]
TORS........   Time-Ordered Reporting System   (MCD)
TORS........   Torsion [*Automotive engineering*]
TORS.........   Trade Opportunity Referral Service [*Department of Agriculture*] [*Information service or system*]   (IID)
TORSEN...   Torque Sensing Differential [*Audi*] [*Automotive engineering*]
TORT ....   Tactical Operational Readiness Trainer
TORT ....   Truck Operator Road Test [*Part of TORQUE*]
TOS ....   Tactical Offense Subsystem
TOS ....   Tactical Operation Simulator

TOS	Tactical Operations System [*ADSAF*]
TOS	Taken Out of Service [*Telecommunications*] (TEL)
TOS	Taken on Strength [*British military*] (DMA)
TOS	Tape Operating System [*IBM Corp.*] [*Data processing*]
TOS	Technical Operational Support
TOS	Technical Operations Squadron [*Air Force*]
TOS	Temporarily Out of Service (DEN)
TOS	Temporarily Out of Stock [*Business term*]
TOS	Term of Service [*Military*]
TOS	Terminal-Oriented Software [*Data processing*] (IEEE)
TOS	Terminal-Oriented System [*Data processing*] (IEEE)
TOS	Test Operating System (MCD)
TOS	Texas Ornithological Society. Bulletin [*A publication*]
TOS	Thermally and Oxidatively Stable
TOS	Thoracic Outlet Syndrome [*Medicine*]
TOS	Time-Ordered System (MCD)
TOS	Time-on-Station [*Military*] (INF)
TOS	TIROS [*Television and Infrared Observation Satellite*] Operational Satellite [*NASA*]
TOS	Top of Stack [*Data processing*]
TOS	Top of Steel [*Flooring*] (AAG)
TOS	Torque Overload Switch [*Nuclear energy*] (NRCH)
Tos	Tosafoth (BJA)
TOS	Tosco Corp. [*NYSE symbol*] (SPSG)
TOS	Tosco Corp., Los Angeles, CA [*OCLC symbol*] (OCLC)
Tos	Tosefta (BJA)
tos..............	Tosyl [*As substituent on nucleoside*] [*Biochemistry*]
Tos	Tosyl [*Also, Ts*] [*Organic chemistry*]
TOS	Toxic Oil Syndrome [*Medicine*]
TOS	Tramiel Operating System [*Atari, Inc.*]
TOS	Transfer Orbit Stage [*Satellite booster*]
TOS	Tromso [*Norway*] [*Airport symbol*] (OAG)
TOS	Trucial Oman Scouts [*British military*] (DMA)
TOS	Turkiye Ogretmenler Sendikasi
TOS2	Type of Shipment
TOS2	Tactical Operations System Operable Segment (MCD)
TOSA	Theatre Organ Society of Australia
Tosaf	Tosafoth (BJA)
TosArgOMe ...	Tosylarginine Methyl Ester [*Also, TAME*] [*Biochemistry*]
TOSBAC ...	Toshiba Scientific and Business Automatic Computer [*Toshiba Corp.*]
TOSC........	Tactical Ocean Surveillance Coordinator [*Military*] (CAAL)
TOSC........	To Other Service Center [*IRS*]
TOSC........	Touch-Operated Selector Control
TOSCA......	Test of Scholastic Abilities [*Achievement test*]
TOSCA......	Tobacco Science [*A publication*]
TOSCA......	Total On-Line Searching and Cataloging Activities [*Information service or system*]
TOSCA......	Toxic Substances Control Act [*1976*]
TOSCOM ...	TOS [*TIROS Operational Satellite*] Communications System (NOAA)
TOSD	Telephone Operations and Standards Division [*Rural Electrification Administration*] [*Telecommunications*] (TEL)
TOSD	Third Order of Saint Dominic [*Rome, Italy*] (EAIO)
TOSE........	Tooling Samples
Tosef	Tosefta (BJA)
Toseph	Tosephta (BJA)
TOSF........	Tertiary of Third Order of St. Francis [*Later, SFO*] [*Roman Catholic religious order*]
TOSF........	Test of Oral Structures and Functions [*Speech evaluation test*]
TOSHIBA ...	Tokyo Shibaura Electric Co. [*Computer manufacturer*] [*Japan*]
Toshiba Rev ...	Toshiba Review [*Japan*] [*A publication*]
Toshiba Rev (Int Ed) ...	Toshiba Review (International Edition) [*A publication*]
Tosh-Kai	Toshokan-Kai [*A publication*]
Tosh Kenk ...	Toshokan Kenkyu [*A publication*]
Tosh Zass ..	Toshokan Zasshi [*A publication*]
TOSL..........	Terminal-Oriented Service Language
TOSMIC ...	Toluenesulfonylmethyl Isocyanide [*or Tosylmethylisocyanide*] [*Organic chemistry*]
TOSMIC ...	Tosylmethyl Isocyanide [*Organic chemistry*]
TOS/OITDS ...	Tactical Operations System/Operations and Intelligence Tactical Data Systems [*Military*] (RDA)
TOSPDR ...	Technical Order System Publication Deficiency Report [*Military*] (AFIT)
TosPheCH₂Cl ...	Tosylphenylalanine Chloromethyl Ketone [*Biochemistry*]
TOSR........	Technical Order Status Report (MCD)
TOSR........	Thermally and Oxidatively Stable Resin
TOSS........	Tactical Operational Scoring System (MCD)
TOSS........	Tactical Operations Support System (MCD)
TOSS........	Television Ordnance Scoring System (MCD)
TOSS........	Terminal-Oriented Support System
TOSS........	Test Operation Support Segment
TOSS........	Tethered Orbiting Satellite Simulator
TOSS........	TIROS [*Television and Infrared Observation Satellite*] Operational Satellite System [*NASA*]
TOS-S........	Transfer Orbit Stage - Shortened Version [*Space technology*]
TOSS........	Transient and/or Steady State [*Nuclear energy*] (NRCH)
TOSS........	Turbine-Operated Suspension System [*NASA*]
TOSSA	Transient or Steady-State Analysis [*Data processing*]

Tosyl	Tolylsulfonyl [*Organic chemistry*]
TOT	Denver, CO [*Location identifier*] [*FAA*] (FAAL)
T/OT	Table of Organization (Tentative)
TOT..........	Takeoff Trim [*Aviation*] (MCD)
TOT..........	Tales of Tomorrow [*A publication*]
TOT..........	Task Oriented Training (MCD)
TOT..........	Telephone Organization of Thailand (DS)
TOT..........	Terms of Trade
TOT..........	Texaco Overseas Tankerships
TOT..........	Texas Opera Theatre
TOT..........	Theatrum Orbis Terrarum [*Dutch firm*]
TOT..........	Time of Takeoff [*Air Force*] (AFIT)
TOT..........	Time on Tape [*Military*]
TOT..........	Time on Target [*Artillery support*]
TOT..........	Time over Target [*Air support*]
TOT..........	Time on Track
TOT..........	Time of Transmission [*Communications*]
TOT..........	Time of Travel (MCD)
TOT..........	Tincture of Time [*Medical slang for treatment of problems that are better left alone*]
TOT..........	Tip-of-Tongue Phenomenon [*Medicine*]
TOT..........	Toe-Out-in-Turns [*Automotive engineering*]
TOT..........	Total (AAG)
TOT..........	Totem Industries [*Vancouver Stock Exchange symbol*]
Tot.............	Tothill's English Chancery Reports [*A publication*] (DLA)
Tot.............	Tothill's Transactions in Chancery [*21 English Reprint*] [*A publication*] (DLA)
TOT..........	Totnes [*Municipal borough in England*]
TOT..........	Tottori [*Japan*] [*Seismograph station code, US Geological Survey*] (SEIS)
TOT..........	Tourist Organization of Thailand (DS)
TOT..........	Trade-Off and Technology
TOT..........	Transfer of Technology [*Telecommunications*] (TEL)
TOT..........	Transfer-of-Training
TOT..........	Transovarial Transmission [*Virology*]
TOT..........	Transportation Office Will Furnish the Necessary Transportation [*Military*]
TOT..........	Tris-ortho-thymotide [*Organic chemistry*]
TOT..........	Turbine Outlet Temperature (NG)
TOT..........	Turn-On Time
TOT..........	Type of Transport [*Shipping*] (DS)
Total Inf.....	Total Information [*A publication*]
TOTE	Teleprocessing On-Line Test Executive [*Data processing*] (IBMDP)
TOTE	Test-Operator-Test-Exit [*Unit*] [*Psychology*]
TOTE	Time Out to Enjoy (EA)
TOTE	United Tote, Inc. [*Shepherd, MT*] [*NASDAQ symbol*] (NQ)
TOTEM ...	Theater Operations and Tactical Evaluation Model
TOTES......	Time-Ordered Techniques Experiment System
TOTFORF ...	Total Forfeiture [*of all pay and allowances*] [*Army*] (AABC)
TOTH........	Toth Aluminum Corp. [*NASDAQ symbol*] (NQ)
Toth...........	Tothill's English Chancery Reports [*A publication*] (DLA)
Toth...........	Tothill's Transactions in Chancery [*21 English Reprint*] [*A publication*] (DSA)
Tothill (Eng) ...	Tothill's English Chancery Reports [*A publication*] (DLA)
Tothill (Eng) ...	Tothill's Transactions in Chancery [*21 English Reprint*] [*A publication*] (DLA)
TOTJ........	Training on the Job
TOTL........	Test Operating Time Log
TOTL........	Total Research Corp. [*NASDAQ symbol*] (NQ)
TOTLZ......	Totalize
TOTM	Totalmed Associates [*NASDAQ symbol*] (NQ)
TOTM	Trioctyl Trimellitate [*Chemistry*]
TOTO........	Tongue of the Ocean [*Area of the Bahama Islands*] [*Navy*]
TOTO........	Totable Tornado Observatory [*National Oceanic and Atmospheric Administration*]
TOTP........	Tooling Template
TOTP........	Top of the Pops [*Television program*] [*British*]
TOTP........	Triorthotolylphosphate [*Organic chemistry*]
TOTPAR...	Total Pain Relief [*Medicine*]
TOTR	Test Observation and Training Room [*Military*] (CAAL)
TOTRAD ..	Tape Output Test Rack Autonetics Diode
TOTS........	Total Operating Traffic System [*Bell System*]
TOTS........	Turn Off Television Saturday [*of Action for Children's Television organization*]
TOU..........	Neah Bay, WA [*Location identifier*] [*FAA*] (FAAL)
TOU..........	Oak Ridge Associated Universities, Oak Ridge, TN [*Library symbol*] [*Library of Congress*] (LCLS)
TOU..........	Time of Use [*Utility rates*]
TOU..........	Touho [*New Caledonia*] [*Airport symbol*] (OAG)
TOU..........	Trace Operate Unit
Touch	Sheppard's Touchstone [*A publication*] (DLA)
Toull...........	Toullier's Droit Civil Francais [*A publication*] (DLA)
Toulouse Med ...	Toulouse Medical [*A publication*]
TOUR........	Tourist Class Passengers [*British*]
TOUR........	WorldGroup Companies, Inc. [*Evergreen, CO*] [*NASDAQ symbol*] (NQ)
Tourbe Philos ...	Tourbe Philosophique [*A publication*]
Tourg Dig...	Tourgee's North Carolina Digest [*A publication*] (DLA)
Tourism Aust ...	Tourism Australia [*A publication*] (APTA)
Tourism Engl ...	Tourism in England [*A publication*]

Tourism Intell Q ... Tourism Intelligence Quarterly [*A publication*]
TOURN..... Tournament
TOUS .... Test on Understanding Science
TOUS .... Transmission Oscillator Ultrasonic Spectrometer
Toute Electron ... Toute l'Electronique [*A publication*]
TOV.......... El Indio, TX [*Location identifier*] [*FAA*]   (FAAL)
TOV.......... El Tocuyo [*Venezuela*] [*Seismograph station code, US
          Geological Survey*]   (SEIS)
TOV.......... Telemetering Oscillator Voltage
TOV.......... Time out of View
TOV.......... Tooele Valley Railway Co. [*AAR code*]
Tov .... Tovaris [*A publication*]
TOVA .... [*The*] Other Victims of Alcoholism   (EA)
TOVALOP ... Tanker Owners Voluntary Agreement on Liability for Oil
          Pollution
Tovar Poshir Polit Nauk Znan Ukr SSR ... Tovaristvo dlya Poshirennya
          Politichnikh i Naukovikh Znan Ukrains'koi SSR [*A
          publication*]
TOVC .... Top of Overcast [*Aviation*]   (FAAC)
TOVD........ Transistor-Operated Voltage Divider
TOVR .... Turnover   (NVT)
TOVS......... TIROS [*Television and Infrared Observation Satellite*]
          Operational Vertical Sounder [*NASA*]
TOW.......... Cooperstown, ND [*Location identifier*] [*FAA*]   (FAAL)
TOW.......... Takeoff Weight [*Aviation*]
TOW.......... Tales of Wonder [*A publication*]
TOW......... Tank and Orbiter Weight [*NASA*]   (MCD)
TOW......... Target on Wire [*British military*]   (DMA)
TOW......... Towards   (ROG)
TOW......... Tube-Launched, Optically Tracked, Wire-Guided [*Weapon*]
TOWA ...... Terrain and Obstacle Warning and Avoidance
TOW CAP ... TOW [*Tube-Launched, Optically Tracked, Wire-Guided
          (Weapon)*] Cover Artillery Protection
TOWER .... Testing Orientation and Work Evaluation for Rehabilitation
Tower Hamlets Local Trade Dev ... Tower Hamlets Local Trade Development
          [*A publication*]
TO WHD.. Two Wheeled [*Freight*]
TOWL .... Test of Written Language
TOWL .... Towle Manufacturing Co. [*NASDAQ symbol*]   (NQ)
Towle Const ... Towle's Analysis of the United States Constitution [*A
          publication*]   (DLA)
TOWN....... Towne-Paulsen, Inc. [*NASDAQ symbol*]   (NQ)
Town Cntry Plann ... Town and Country Planning [*A publication*]
Town Co ... Townshend's Code [*A publication*]   (DLA)
Town Com Law ... Townsend on Commercial Law [*A publication*]   (DLA)
Town & Country Plan ... Town and Country Planning [*A publication*]
Town Ctry Plan ... Town and Country Planning [*A publication*]
Town Jud ... Townsend's Judgment [*A publication*]   (DLA)
Town Pl...... Townshend's Pleading [*A publication*]   (DLA)
Town Plan Inst J ... Town Planning Institute. Journal [*A publication*]
Town Planning R ... Town Planning Review [*United Kingdom*] [*A
          publication*]
Town Plann Inst J ... Town Planning Institute. Journal [*A publication*]
Town Plann Q ... Town Planning Quarterly [*New Zealand*] [*A publication*]
Town Plann Rev ... Town Planning Review [*A publication*]
Town Plann Today ... Town Planning Today [*A publication*]
Town Plan R ... Town Planning Review [*A publication*]
Town Pr...... Townshend's Practice [*A publication*]   (DLA)
Town Pr Pl ... Townshend's Precedents of Pleading [*A publication*]   (DLA)
Townsh Pl ... Townshend's Pleading [*A publication*]   (DLA)
Townsh Sland & L ... Townshend on Slander and Libel [*A
          publication*]   (DLA)
Town Sl & Lib ... Townshend on Slander and Libel [*A publication*]   (DLA)
Town St Tr ... Townsend's Modern State Trials [*1850*] [*A publication*]   (DLA)
Town Sum Proc ... Townshend's Summary Landlord and Tenant Process [*A
          publication*]   (DLA)
Townsville Nat ... Townsville Naturalist [*A publication*]   (APTA)
TOWPROS ... TOW [*Tube-Launched, Optically Tracked, Wire-Guided
          (Weapon)*] Protective Shelters   (MCD)
TOWR ...... Tower Federal Savings Bank [*NASDAQ symbol*]   (NQ)
TOX.......... Total Oxidants
TOX.......... Toxicology
Tox Appl Ph ... Toxicology and Applied Pharmacology [*A publication*]
TOXBACK ... TOXLINE Back-File
TOXBIB ... Toxicity Bibliography [*MEDLARS*]
TOXIA....... Toxicon [*A publication*]
Toxic Appl Pharmac ... Toxicology and Applied Pharmacology [*A
          publication*]
Toxic Hazard Waste Disposal ... Toxic and Hazardous Waste Disposal [*A
          publication*]
TOXICOL ... Toxicology
Toxicol Annu ... Toxicology Annual [*A publication*]
Toxicol Appl Pharmacol ... Toxicology and Applied Pharmacology [*A
          publication*]
Toxicol Appl Pharmacol Suppl ... Toxicology and Applied Pharmacology.
          Supplement [*A publication*]
Toxicol Environ Chem ... Toxicological and Environmental Chemistry [*A
          publication*]
Toxicol Environ Chem Rev ... Toxicological and Environmental Chemistry
          Reviews [*A publication*]
Toxicol Eur Res ... Toxicological European Research [*A publication*]

Toxicol Ind Health ... Toxicology and Industrial Health [*A publication*]
Toxicol Lett ... Toxicology Letters [*A publication*]
Toxicol Lett (Amst) ... Toxicology Letters (Amsterdam) [*A publication*]
Toxicol Pathol ... Toxicologic Pathology [*A publication*]
TOXICON ... Toxicology Information Conversational On-Line Network
          [*National Library of Medicine*] [*Later, TOXLINE*]
Toxic Subst J ... Toxic Substances Journal [*A publication*]
TOXLINE ... Toxicology Information On-Line [*National Library of
          Medicine*] [*Bethesda, MD*] [*Bibliographic database*]
TOXLIST ... Toxic Regulatory Listings [*American Petroleum Institute*]
          [*Information service or system*]   (CRD)
TOXNET... Toxicology Data Network [*National Library of Medicine*]
          [*Information service or system*]   (IID)
TOXO....... Toxoplasmosis [*Medicine*]
TOXREP... Toxic Incident Report
TOXREPT ... Toxic Incident Report   (MUGU)
TOXT .... Toxteth   (ROG)
TOXY .... Tri Coast Environmental Corp. [*NASDAQ symbol*]   (NQ)
TOY.......... Toyama [*Japan*] [*Seismograph station code, US Geological
          Survey*]   (SEIS)
TOY.......... Toys R Us, Inc. [*NYSE symbol*]   (SPSG)
TOY.......... Troy, IL [*Location identifier*] [*FAA*]   (FAAL)
TOYCOM ... [*A*] programming language [*1971*]   (CSR)
TOYM....... Ten Outstanding Young Men of America [*Jaycees' program*]
TOYO....... Toyota Motor Corp. [*NASDAQ symbol*]   (NQ)
Toyo Bunka Kenkyu Kiyo ... Toyo Bunka Kenkyusho Kiyo [*A publication*]
Toyo Junior Coll Food Technol Toyo Inst Food Technol Res Rep ... Toyo
          Junior College of Food Technology and Toyo Institute of
          Food Technology. Research Report [*Japan*] [*A publication*]
Toyo Ongaku ... Toyo Ongaku Kenkyu [*A publication*]
Toyota Eng ... Toyota Engineering [*Japan*] [*A publication*]
TOYS........ Toys Plus, Inc. [*St. Charles, MO*] [*NASDAQ symbol*]   (NQ)
TOZ.......... Harvard University, Tozzer Library, Cambridge, MA [*OCLC
          symbol*]   (OCLC)
TOZ.......... Touba [*Ivory Coast*] [*Airport symbol*]   (OAG)
TOZ.......... Towarzystwo Ochrony Zdrowia [*A publication*]   (BJA)
TP .... East Timor [*ISO two-letter standard code*]   (CNC)
TP .... Palestinian Talmud   (BJA)
TP .... [*The*] Prosperos   (EA)
T-P .... Tabloncillo Perla [*Race of maize*]
TP .... Tail-Pinch Stress
TP .... Tank Parliament [*British*]
TP .... Tank Piercing [*Ammunition*] [*Military*]
TP .... Tank Pressure   (DS)
TP .... Tape   (BUR)
TP .... Target Point
TP .... Target Population
TP .... Target Practice [*Military*]
TP .... Task Processor [*Telecommunications*]   (TSSD)
TP .... Tax Planning [*A publication*]   (DLA)
TP .... Taxpayer
TP .... Teaching Practice
TP .... Technical Pamphlet
TP .... Technical Paper
TP .... Technical Performance   (MCD)
TP .... Technical Problem
TP .... Technical Proposal
TP .... Technical Publication
TP .... Technographic Publication
TP .... Technology Parameter
TP .... Technophility Index [*Mining technology*]
TP .... Telemetry Processor
TP .... Telephone   (CET)
TP .... Teleprensa [*Press agency*] [*Colombia*]
TP .... Teleprinter
TP .... Teleprocessing [*Data processing*]   (MCD)
T/P............ Temperature to Precipitation Ratio [*Botany*]
TP .... Temperature and Pressure [*Medicine*]
TP .... Temperature Probe   (AAG)
T + P .... Temperature and Pulse [*Medicine*]
TP .... Tempo Presente [*A publication*]
TP .... Tempo Primo [*Original Tempo*] [*Music*]
TP .... Temporary Patient [*British*]
TP .... Tempore Paschale [*At Easter Time*] [*Latin*]
TP .... Tensile Properties   (MCD)
TP .... Tentative Pamphlet
TP .... Term Pass   (AAG)
TP .... Terminal Phalanx [*Anatomy*]
TP .... Terminal Point   (NATG)
TP .... Terminal Pole [*Telecommunications*]   (TEL)
TP .... Terminal Processor
TP .... Terrestrial Plants
TP .... Territorial Party [*Northern Marianas*]   (PPW)
TP .... Terzo Programma [*Roma*] [*A publication*]
T/P............ Test Panel   (AAG)
TP .... Test Plan
TP .... Test Point
TP .... Test Port   (KSC)
TP .... Test Position
TP .... Test Positive [*Clinical chemistry*]
TP .... Test Pressure [*Nuclear energy*]   (NRCH)

TP	Test Procedure (NATG)
TP	Testosterone Propionate [*Endocrinology*]
TP	[*The*] Texas & Pacific Railway Co. [*Absorbed into Missouri Pacific System*] [*AAR code*]
T and P.......	[*The*] Texas & Pacific Railway Co. [*Absorbed into Missouri Pacific System*]
TP	Text Processor
T and P.......	Theft and Pilferage
TP	Thermoplastic [*Also, T*] [*Plastics technology*]
TP	Thermosphere Probe
TP	Thiamphenicol [*Antimicrobial compound*]
TP	Thiopental [*An anesthetic*]
T/P.............	Third Party (ADA)
TP	Thomas Power ["*Tay Pay*"] O'Connor [*Irish journalist and politician, 1848-1929*]
TP	Thomson Press (India) Ltd. [*Publisher*]
TP	Thought Patterns [*A publication*]
TP	Thrombocytopenic Purpura [*Medicine*]
TP	Thrombophlebitis [*Medicine*]
TP	Throttle Positioner [*Automotive engineering*]
TP	Thymic Polypeptide [*Endocrinology*]
TP	Thymidine Phosphorylase [*An enzyme*]
TP	Thymopentin [*Biochemistry*]
TP	Thymopoietin
TP	Thymus Protein
TP	Tibialis Posterior [*Anatomy*]
TP	Tie Plate [*Technical drawings*]
TP	Tie Point
TP	Tijdschrift voor Philosophie [*A publication*]
TP	Tijdschrift voor de Politie [*A publication*]
T-P.............	Timbre Poste [*Postage Stamp*] [*French*]
TP	Time to Perigee (MCD)
TP	Time Pulse
TP	Timing Point (AFM)
TP	Timpano [*Music*]
TP	Tin Plate
TP	Title Page [*Bibliography*]
TP	To Pay (ADA)
TP	Toilet Paper [*Slang*] [*To be "TP'd" is to have your yard covertly decorated with unrolled toilet paper*]
TP	Toll Point [*Telecommunications*] (TEL)
TP	Toll Prefix [*Telecommunications*] (TEL)
TP	Toothpick
TP	Top
TP	Top Priority
TP	Topics in Photosynthesis [*Elsevier Book Series*] [*A publication*]
TP	Torpedo Part of Beam (MSA)
TP	Total Parts
TP	Total Phenolic Levels [*Chemistry*]
TP	Total Phosphorus [*Analytical chemistry*]
TP	Total Points
TP	Total Power
TP	Total Pressure
TP	Total Production [*or Product*] [*Ecology*]
TP	Total Protein
TP	Totally Positive
TP	Touchdowns Passing [*Football*]
TP	T'oung Pao [*A publication*]
TP	Township
TP	Toxic Pregnancy [*Gynecology*]
TP	Tracking Program (MUGU)
TP	Trade Protection Service [*or Society*] [*British*]
TP	Traffic Post
TP	Training Period [*Military*] (AFM)
TP	Training Plan (NASA)
TP	Training, Practicing [*Ammunition*]
TP	Transaction Processing [*Data processing*]
TP	Transaction Program [*Data processing*] (BYTE)
TP	Transannular Patch [*Cardiology*]
TP	Transfer on Positive
TP	Transforming Principle [*Bacteriology*]
TP	Transition Period (NASA)
TP	Transition Plans (MCD)
TP	Translucent Paper (ADA)
TP	Transnational Prospectives [*A publication*]
TP	Transplant
TP	Transport Pack
TP	Transport Pilot
TP	Transport Protein [*Superseded by SC, Secretory Component*] [*Immunology*]
TP	Transport Protocol [*Data processing*]
TP	Transportation Priority [*Military*] (AFM)
TP	Transporter (DCTA)
TP	Transportes Aereos Portugueses [*ICAO designator*] (FAAC)
TP	Transvaal Province [*Republic of South Africa*]
TP	Transvaal Supreme Court Reports [*South Africa*] [*A publication*] (DLA)
TP	Travaux Forces a Perpetuite [*Penal Servitude for Life*] [*French*]
TP	Travaux Publics [*Public Works*] [*French*]
TP	Travers Pensions [*Formerly, Naval Knights of Windsor*] [*Military*] [*British*] (ROG)

TP	Treaty Port
TP	Tree Project (EA)
TP	TreePeople (EA)
TP	Treponema Pallidum [*A spirochete*] [*Clinical chemistry*]
TP	Trigonometrischer Punkt [*Triangulation Point*] [*German military - World War II*]
TP	Triple Play [*Baseball*]
TP	Triple Pole [*Switch*]
TP	Troop
TP	Troop Program [*Military*] (AABC)
TP	Tropical Pacific [*American air mass*]
TP	True Position
TP	True Positive [*Medicine*]
TP	True Profile [*Technical drawings*]
TP	Trumpet
TP	Tryptophan Pyrrolase [*Also, TPO*] [*An enzyme*]
TP	Tuberculin Precipitation [*Medicine*]
TP	Tuned Plate (DEN)
TP	Turboprop (AAG)
TP	Turbopump (AAG)
T & P.........	Turner and Phillips' English Chancery Reports [*A publication*] (DLA)
TP	Turning Point
TP	Tyndale Paper [*A publication*] (APTA)
TP	Type (NASA)
TPA	Austin Peay State University, Clarksville, TN [*OCLC symbol*] (OCLC)
TPA	Taildragger Pilots Association (EA)
TPA	Tala Pozo [*Argentina*] [*Seismograph station code, US Geological Survey*] [*Closed*] (SEIS)
TPA	Tallgrass Prairie Alliance (EA)
TPA	Tampa Air Center [*Tampa, FL*] [*FAA designator*] (FAAC)
TPA	Tampa/St. Petersburg/Clearwater [*Florida*] [*Airport symbol*]
TPA	Tannic Acid, Phosphomolybdic Acid, Amido Acid Black [*A staining technique*]
TPA	Tantalum Producers Association (EA)
TPA	Tape Pulse Amplifier
TPA	Target Position Analyzer [*Military*] (CAAL)
TPA	Tariff Programs and Appraisals [*Canada Customs*]
TPA	TASS [*Towed Array SONAR System*] Probability Area (NVT)
TPA	Technical Practice Aid (ADA)
TPA	Technical Publications Agent (MCD)
TPA	Technical Publications Announcement
TPA	Telemetry Power Amplifier
TPA	Telepanel, Inc. [*Vancouver Stock Exchange symbol*]
TPA	Telephone Pioneers of America (EA)
TPA	Temperature-Programmed Analysis
TPA	Tennis Professionals Association [*Canada*]
TPa	Terapascal [*Pressure unit*]
TPA	Terephthalic Acid [*Also, TA*] [*Organic chemistry*]
TPA	Test Plans and Analysis
TPA	Test Preparation Area [*NASA*] (KSC)
TPA	Test Project Agreement (NG)
TPA	Tetradecanoylphorbolacetate [*Also, PMA, PTA*] [*Organic chemistry*]
TPA	Tetrapropylammonium [*Chemical radical*]
TPA	Texture Profile Analysis [*Food technology*]
TPA	Theta Phi Alpha [*Sorority*]
TPA	Timber Producers Association of Michigan and Wisconsin (EA)
TPA	Tissue Plasminogen Activator [*Anticlotting agent*]
TPA	Tissue Polypeptide Antigen [*Immunochemistry*]
TPA	Toll Pulse Accepter [*Telecommunications*] (TEL)
TPA	Tons per Annum (ADA)
TPA	Top Pumparound [*Chemical engineering*]
TPA	T'oung Pao. Archives [*A publication*]
TPA	Tournament Players Association (EA)
TPA	Track Production Area [*Air Force*]
TPA	Trade Practices Act [*Australia*] (ADA)
TPA	Traffic Pattern Altitude [*Aviation*]
TPA	Training Problem Analysis (MCD)
TPA	Trans-Pacific Airlines Ltd.
TPA	Transfer of Pay Account [*Military*]
TPA	Transient Program Area
TPA	Transmission Products Association (EA)
TPA	Travel by Personal Auto Authorized [*Military*]
TPA	Travel Professionals Association (EA)
TPA	Travelers Protective Association of America [*St. Louis, MO*] (EA)
TPA	Trim Power Assembly
TPA	Triphenylamine [*Organic chemistry*]
TPA	Truck Performance Analysis
TPA	Tunable Parametric Amplifier
TPA	Turboprop Aircraft
TPA	Turbopump Assembly (KSC)
TPA	Tutmonda Parolspuro-Asocio [*Universal Association for Speech Tracing - UAST*] (EAIO)
TPA	Type of Professional Activity
TPAA........	Travelers Protective Association of America (EA)
TPAC........	Technology Policy and Assessment Center [*Georgia Institute of Technology*] [*Research center*] (RCD)

TPAC......... Telescope Precision Angle Counter
TP-AD .... Technical Publications - Administration [*Naval Facilities Engineering Command Publications*]
TPAD .... Trunnion Pin Attachment Device [*NASA*]
TPAEDP ... Topics in Paediatrics [*A publication*]
TPAM........ Teleprocessing Access Method
TPAM........ Three-Phase Aquatic Microcosms [*Technique for study of waters*]
TPAMF ..... Transpacific Asbestos Capital Shares [*NASDAQ symbol*] (NQ)
TPAOH ..... Tetrapropylammonium Hydroxide [*Organic chemistry*]
TPAP........ Time-Phased-Action Plan [*DoD*]
TPAPA ...... Transactions and Proceedings. American Philological Association [*A publication*]
TP A Ph A ... Transactions and Proceedings. American Philological Association [*A publication*]
TPAPOABITCOS ... [*The*] Precentor and Prebendary of Alton Borealis in the Church of Sarum [*Pseudonym used by Arthur Ashley Sykes*]
TPAR......... Tactical Penetration Aids Rocket
TPARR...... TRADOC Program Analysis and Resource Review [*Military*] (MCD)
TPAT........ Test Point Algorithm Technique (MCD)
TPAWA..... Tennis Professionals Association of Western Australia
TPAX........ Tampax, Inc. [*NASDAQ symbol*] (NQ)
TPB........... Nebraska Library Commission, Lincoln, NE [*OCLC symbol*] (OCLC)
TPB............ Tape Playback BIT [*Binary Digit*] [*Data processing*]
TPB............ Tarnished Plant Bug [*Entomology*]
TPB............ Tennessee Philological Bulletin [*A publication*]
TPB............ Tetraphenylbutadiene [*Organic chemistry*]
TPB............ Tetraphenylbutane [*Organic chemistry*]
TpB............ Trypan Blue [*Biological stain*]
TPB............ Tryptone Phosphate Broth
T(PBEIST) ... Transport - Planning Board European Inland Surface Transport (NATG)
TPBF .... Total Pulmonary Blood Flow [*Physiology*]
TPBI .... Third Party Bodily Injury [*Insurance*] (AIA)
TPBK........ Tape Block
T(PBOS).... Transport - Planning Board Ocean Shipping (NATG)
TPBR........ Top Brass Enterprises, Inc. [*Merrick, NY*] [*NASDAQ symbol*] (NQ)
TPBS .... Tetrapropylenbenzenesulfonate [*Organic chemistry*]
TPBT .... Technical Papers for the Bible Translator [*A publication*] (BJA)
TPBVP ...... Two-Point Boundary Value Problem
TPC............ Nebraska Library Commission, Lincoln, NE [*OCLC symbol*] (OCLC)
TPC............ Tactical Pilotage Chart
TPC............ Tangential Period Correction
TPC............ Technical Prime Contractor
TPC............ Technical Progress Committee [*British*] (DCTA)
TPC............ Technical Protein Colloid
TPC............ Telecommunications Planning Committee [*Civil Defense*]
TPC............ Telemetry Preprocessing Computer (MCD)
TPC............ Telephone Pickup Coil
TPC............ Territorial Production Complex [*Russian*]
TPC............ Test Point Controller
TPC............ Texas Petroleum Corp. [*Vancouver Stock Exchange symbol*]
TPC............ Thermafor Pyrolytic Cracking [*A chemical process developed by Surface Combustion*]
TP & C ...... Thermal Protection and Control (NASA)
TPC............ Thermally Protected Composite
TPC............ Thromboplastic Plasma Component [*Factor VIII*] [*Also, AHF, AHG, PTF*] [*Hematology*]
TPC............ Thymolphthalein complexone [*Analytical reagent*]
TPC............ Time Polarity Control
TPC............ Time Projection Chamber [*High-energy physics*]
TPC............ Tire Performance Criteria [*General Motors Corp.*]
TPC............ Tons per Centimeter (DCTA)
TPC............ Topical Pulmonary Chemotherapy [*Medicine*]
TPC............ Topographic Center [*Defense Mapping Agency*]
TPC............ Total Package Contract
TPC............ Total Plasma Cholesterol [*Clinical chemistry*]
TPC............ Total Program Costs (KSC)
TPC............ Total Protein Concentration
TPC............ Tournament Players Championship
TPC............ Trade Policy Committee [*Advisory to President*] [*Abolished, 1963*]
TPC............ Trade Practices Cases [*A publication*] (APTA)
TPC............ Training Plans Conference
TPC............ Trans-Pacific Freight Conference of Japan/Korea Agent, San Francisco CA [*STAC*]
TPC............ Transistor Photo Control
TPC............ Transport Plane Commander
TPC............ Transvascular Protein Clearance [*Medicine*]
TPC............ Travaux Publics Canada [*Public Works Canada - PWC*]
TPC............ Travel by Privately-Owned Conveyance Permitted for Convenience [*Military*] (AFM)
TPC............ Treated Paper Copier [*Reprography*]
TPC............ Tricalcium Phosphate Ceramic [*Inorganic chemistry*]
TPC............ Triple Paper-Covered [*Wire insulation*] (DEN)

TPC........... Triple-Product Convolver [*Acousto-optic technology*] (RDA)
TPC........... Turbopump Control
TPC........... Turns per Centimeter [*Yarn*]
TPC........... Twentynine Palms [*California*] [*Seismograph station code, US Geological Survey*] (SEIS)
TPC........... Twisted Pair Cable
TPCA........ Test Procedure Change Authorization (NATG)
TPCB .... [*The*] Personal Computer Book
TPCC......... TPC Communications, Inc. [*NASDAQ symbol*] (NQ)
TPCCA...... Topics in Current Chemistry [*A publication*]
TPCCOA .. Telephone Provincial Clerical and Contract Officers' Association [*A union*] [*British*]
TPCD........ Trade Practices Commission. Decisions and Determinations [*A publication*] (APTA)
TPCDD...... Trade Practices Commission. Decisions and Determinations [*A publication*] (APTA)
TPCF .... Treponema Pallidum Complement Fixation [*Clinical chemistry*]
TPCK........ Tosylamidophenylethyl Chloromethyl Ketone [*Organic chemistry*]
TPCN........ Task Plan Change Notice (MCD)
TPCO .... Teleprinter Coordinator
TPCP .... Trainer Power Control Panel
TPCR........ Task Plan Change Request (MCD)
TPCS .... Torquay Pottery Collectors' Society (EA)
TPCU........ Thermal Preconditioning Unit
TPCV .... Turbine Power Control Valve
TPCWDL .. Colorado. Division of Wildlife. Technical Publication [*A publication*]
TPD .... Five Associated University Libraries, Rochester, NY [*OCLC symbol*] (OCLC)
TPD .... South African Law Reports, Transvaal Provincial Division [*South Africa*] [*A publication*] (DLA)
T/PD......... Table of Personnel Distribution (NATG)
TPD .... Tape Playback Discriminator
TPD .... Tapped (MSA)
TPD .... Temperature-Programmed Desorption [*Catalysis*]
TPD .... Temporary Partial Disablement [*Insurance*] (AIA)
TPD .... Terminal Protective Device (MSA)
TPD .... Terracamp Development [*Vancouver Stock Exchange symbol*]
TPD .... Test Plasma Produced by Discharge (MCD)
TPD .... Test Point Data
TPD .... Test Procedure Deviation [*Nuclear energy*] (NRCH)
TPD .... Test Procedure Drawing [*NASA*] (KSC)
TPD .... Theophylline, Proxyphylline, and Dyphylline [*Antineoplastic drug regimen*]
TPD .... Thermoplastic Photoconductor Device
TPD .... Time Pulse Distributor (MCD)
TPD .... Toilet Paper Dispenser [*Technical drawings*]
TPD .... Tons per Day
TPD .... Torque Proportioning Differential [*Automotive engineering*]
TPD .... Total Permanent Disablement [*Insurance*] (AIA)
TPD .... Total Purity by Difference [*Gas analysis*]
TPD .... Tournament Players Division of the Professional Golfers Association of America [*Later, TPA*]
TPD .... Training Programs Directorate [*Army*]
TPD .... Transient Photodichroism [*Physics*]
TPD .... Tumor-Producing Dose [*Virology*]
TPDB........ Tape Deblock
TPDC........ Training and Performance Data Center [*Military*]
TPDLRI..... Textile Printers and Dyers Labor Relations Institute (EA)
TPDS........ Tape Playback Discriminator System
TPDS .... Test Procedures Development System (NASA)
TPDS-T ... Target Practice Discarding Sabot-Tracer [*Projectile*] (MCD)
TPDT........ Triple-Pole, Double-Throw [*Switch*]
TPE........... Five Associated University Libraries, Rochester, NY [*OCLC symbol*] (OCLC)
TPE........... T-Pulse Effectiveness [*Neurology*]
TPE........... Tactical Performance Evaluation
TPE........... Taipei [*Taiwan*] [*Airport symbol*] (OAG)
TPE............ Technology, People, Environment [*National Science Foundation project*]
TPE........... Test Planning and Evaluation
TP & E .... Test Planning and Evaluation (MCD)
TPE........... Test Project Engineer (NASA)
TPE........... Thermoplastic Elastomer [*Plastics technology*]
TPE........... Threshold Photoelectron [*Spectroscopy*]
TPE........... Total Potential Energy
TPE........... Transaction Processing Executive (MCD)
TPE........... Transport Planning and Economics [*British*]
TPE........... Triple Crown Electronics, Inc. [*Toronto Stock Exchange symbol*]
TPE........... Turbopropeller Engine
TPE........... Two-Photon Excitation [*Fluorescence spectrometry*]
TPEA........ Television Program Export Association (EA)
TPED........ Trade and Professional Exhibits Directory [*Later, TSW*] [*A publication*]
T-PEES .... Triplane Elevated Evaluation System [*Army*] (RDA)
TPEMA..... Telephone Engineer and Management [*A publication*]
TPEMDZ .. Topics in Perinatal Medicine [*A publication*]
TPEN......... Tetrakis(pyridylmethyl)ethylenediamine [*Organic chemistry*

TPer............	Tetradi Perevodcika [*A publication*]
TPESP........	Technical Panel on the Earth Satellite Program
TPET..........	Terrapet Energy Corp. [*NASDAQ symbol*] (NQ)
TPETA........	Techniques du Petrole [*A publication*]
TPEX..........	TPEX Exploration, Inc. [*NASDAQ symbol*] (NQ)
TPEY..........	Tellurite-Polymyxin-Egg Yolk [*Agar*] [*Microbiology*]
TPF.............	[*The*] Pygmy Fund (EA)
TPF.............	Tactical Patrol Force [*Police*]
TPF.............	Tailored Probability Forecast
TPF.............	Tampa, FL [*Location identifier*] [*FAA*] (FAAL)
TPF.............	Telemetry Processing Facility (MCD)
TPF.............	Temporary Program File [*Data processing*]
TPF.............	Terminal Phase Finalization [*or Finish*] [*NASA*] (KSC)
TPF.............	Tetraphenylfuran [*Organic chemistry*]
TPF.............	Thai Patriotic Front [*Communist-directed activity outside Thailand*] [*Merged with TIM*]
TPF.............	Theoretical Point of Fog (MSA)
TPF.............	Thymus Permeability Factor
TPF.............	Time Prism Filter [*Telecommunications*] (TEL)
TPF.............	Total Package Fielding [*Army*]
TPF.............	Total Peaking Factor [*Nuclear energy*] (NRCH)
TPF.............	Trainer Parts Fabrication (AAG)
TPF.............	Transfer Phase Final (MCD)
TPF.............	Tri-Pacific Resources Ltd. [*Vancouver Stock Exchange symbol*]
TPF.............	Tube and Pipe Fabricators Association, International (EA)
TPF.............	Tug Processing Facility [*NASA*] (NASA)
TPF.............	Two-Phase Flow
TPFC..........	[*The*] Platters Fan Club (EA)
TPF & C.......	Towers, Perrin, Forster & Crosby [*Compensation and actuarial consulting company*]
TPFDD........	Time-Phased Force Deployment Data [*Military*] (AABC)
TPFDL........	Time-Phased Force Deployment List [*Military*] (AFM)
TPFDL........	Troop Program Field Deployment List [*Military*]
TPFI...........	Terminal Pin Fault Insertion
TPFP..........	Transkei People's Freedom Party [*South Africa*] [*Political party*] (PPW)
TPFW.........	Thermoplastic Fan Wheel
TPFW.........	Three-Phase Full Wave
TPG...........	Tapping
TPG...........	Technology Planning Guide [*Military*] (AFIT)
TPG...........	Telecom Publishing Group (EISS)
TPG...........	Telecommunication Program Generator
TPG...........	Teletype Preamble Generator
TPG...........	Thermionic Power Generator
TPG...........	Timing Pulse Generator
TPG...........	Topping (FAAC)
TPG...........	Total Pressure Gauge
TPG...........	Town Planning and Local Government Guide [*A publication*] (APTA)
TPG...........	Trinity Peninsula Group [*Geology*]
TPG...........	Triphenylguanidine [*Organic chemistry*]
TPG...........	Trypticase, Peptone, Glucose
TPGC.........	Temperature-Programmed Gas Chromatography
TPGS.........	[*The*] Pennsylvania German Society (EA)
TPGS.........	Tocopherol Polyethylene Glycol Succinate [*Organic chemistry*]
TPH...........	Telephony [*A publication*]
TPH...........	Theosophical Publishing House
TPH...........	Thromboembolic Pulmonary Hypertension [*Medicine*]
TPh...........	Tijdschrift voor Philosophie [*A publication*]
TPH...........	Tonopah [*Nevada*] [*Seismograph station code, US Geological Survey*] (SEIS)
TPH...........	Tonopah, NV [*Location identifier*] [*FAA*] (FAAL)
TPH...........	Tons per Hour
TPH...........	Total Possessed Hours (MCD)
TPH...........	Triumph Resources Corp. [*Vancouver Stock Exchange symbol*]
TPH...........	University of Texas, Health Science Center at Houston, School Public Health, Houston, TX [*OCLC symbol*] (OCLC)
TPHA.........	Treponema Pallidum Hemagglutination
TPHA.........	Truman Philatelic and Historical Association (EA)
TPHASAP ...	Telephone as Soon as Possible (NOAA)
TPHAT.......	Telephone at [*Followed by time*] (NOAA)
TPHAYC....	Telephone at Your Convenience (NOAA)
TPHC........	Time-to-Pulse Height Converter
TPhl..........	Turfan Pahlavi (BJA)
TPHO........	Telephotograph
TPhS.........	Transactions. Philological Society [*A publication*]
TPhS.........	Transactions. Philosophical Society [*London and Strassburg*] [*A publication*]
TPHSDY....	Trends in Pharmacological Sciences [*A publication*]
TPHSG......	Troop Housing [*Army*] (AABC)
TPHW.......	Three-Phase Half Wave
TPI............	[*The*] Progress Interview
TPI............	Tape Phase Inverter
TPI............	Tape-Position Indicator (DEN)
TPI............	Tapini [*Papua New Guinea*] [*Airport symbol*] (OAG)
TPI............	Target Position Indicator
TPI............	Task Parameter Interpretation
TPI............	Tax Planning Ideas [*A publication*] (DLA)
TPI............	Tax and Price Index
TPI............	Taxpayer Inquiry [*IRS*]
TPI............	Teatro Popolare Italiano [*Italian theatrical troupe*]

TPI............	Technical Proficiency Inspection [*Military*]
TPI............	Teeth per Inch [*of cog wheels*]
TPI............	Tennessee Polytechnic Institute
TPI............	Terminal Phase Ignition [*NASA*]
TPI............	Terminal Phase Initiate [*NASA*] (KSC)
TPI............	Terminal Phase Insertion [*NASA*]
TPI............	Test Program Instruction (MCD)
TPI............	Thermal Protection Investigation
TPI............	Thermo Process Systems, Inc. [*AMEX symbol*] (SPSG)
TPI............	Threads per Inch
TPI............	Time Perception Inventory [*Test*]
TPI............	Timing Pulse Idler
TPI............	Tire Pressure Indicating System (MCD)
TPI............	Tons per Inch
TPI............	Total Positive Income [*IRS*]
TPI............	Totally and Permanently Incapacitated [*Insurance*] (ADA)
T & PI.......	Totally and Permanently Incapacitated [*Insurance*] (ADA)
TPI............	Town Planning Institute [*Later, Royal Town Planning Institute*] [*British*] (ILCA)
TPI............	Tracks per Inch [*Magnetic storage devices*] [*Data processing*]
TPI............	TRADOC Procurement Instruction (MCD)
TPI............	Training Plan Information (MCD)
TPI............	Transmission Performance Index [*Telecommunications*] (TEL)
TPI............	Treponema pallidum Immobilization [*or Immobilizing*] [*Clinical chemistry*]
TPI............	Trim Position Indicator
TPI............	Triosephosphate Isomerase [*An enzyme*]
TPI............	Triphosphoinositide [*Biochemistry*]
TPI............	Tropical Products Institute [*Overseas Development Administration*] [*British*] (DS)
TPI............	Truss Plate Institute (EA)
TPI............	Tuned Port Fuel Injection
TPI............	Turns per Inch
TPIA.........	Treponema pallidum Immune Adherence [*Clinical chemistry*]
TPIC.........	Town Planning Institute of Canada
TPIE.........	TPI Enterprises, Inc. [*NASDAQ symbol*] (NQ)
TPIF.........	Thornton Pacific Investment Fund
TPIM........	Tool Process Instruction Manual (MCD)
TPIN.........	True Personal Identification Number [*Banking*]
TPIPAR....	Trudy Tsentral'nogo Nauchno-Issledovatel'skogo i Proektno-Konstruktorskogo Instituta Profilaktiki Pnevmokoniozov i Tekhniki Bezopasnosti [*A publication*]
TPIRA.......	Trudy Gosudarstvennyi Institut po Proektirovaniyu i Issledovatel'skim Rabotam v Neftedobyvayushchei Promyshlennosti [*A publication*]
TPI Rep Trop Prod Inst ...	TPI Report. Tropical Products Institute [*A publication*]
TPIS.........	Tire Pressure Indicating System (MCD)
TPIX.........	Telepictures Corp. [*NASDAQ symbol*] (NQ)
TPJ...........	Tangkuban-Prahu [*Java*] [*Seismograph station code, US Geological Survey*] [*Closed*] (SEIS)
TPJ...........	Tennessee Poetry Journal [*A publication*]
TPJSL.......	Transactions and Proceedings. Japan Society (London) [*A publication*]
TPK..........	Test of Practical Knowledge
TPK..........	Tulare Free Public Library, Tulare, CA [*OCLC symbol*] (OCLC)
TPK..........	Turnpike
TPK..........	Turns per Knot [*Navy*] (CAAL)
TPKE........	Turnpike (MCD)
TPKrR.......	Theologicka Priloha (Krestanske Revue) [*A publication*] (BJA)
TPL..........	Table Producing Language [*1971*] [*Data processing*] (IID)
TPL..........	Tabular Parts List
TPL..........	Target Position Location (MCD)
TPL..........	Technical Publications Library (MCD)
TPL..........	Temple [*Texas*] [*Airport symbol*] (OAG)
TPL..........	Temple, TX [*Location identifier*] [*FAA*] (FAAL)
TPL..........	Terminal per Line [*Telecommunications*]
TPL..........	Terminal Processing Language
TPL..........	Test Parts List
TPL..........	Test Plan (CAAL)
TPL..........	Test Plan Log (MCD)
TPL..........	Test Point Logic
TPL..........	Texas Pacific Land Trust [*NYSE symbol*] (SPSG)
TPL..........	Text Processing Language [*Data processing*]
TPL..........	THERE Programming Language [*Data processing*]
TPL..........	Tocopilla [*Chile*] [*Seismograph station code, US Geological Survey*] (SEIS)
TPL..........	Toll Pole Line [*Telecommunications*] (TEL)
TPL..........	Tons Poids Lourd [*Deadweight Tons*] [*French*]
TPL..........	Topsail [*Ship's rigging*] (ROG)
TPL..........	Toronto Public Library [*UTLAS symbol*]
TPL..........	Training Parts List (AAG)
TPL..........	Transistorized Portable Laboratory
TPL..........	Trap Processing Line
TPL..........	Triple (MSA)
TPL..........	Triumph Petroleums Limited [*Vancouver Stock Exchange symbol*]
TPL..........	Troop Program List [*Army*]
TPL..........	Tropicalized (MSA)

TPL............	Trust for Public Land (EA)
TPL............	Tunable Pulsed LASER
TPL............	Turns per Layer
TPL............	Twyford Plant Laboratories Ltd. [British] (IRUK)
TPLA.........	[The] Product Liability Alliance (EA)
TPLA.........	Triphenyllead Acetate [Organic chemistry]
TPLA.........	Turkish People's Liberation Army (PD)
TPLAAV ...	Tidsskrift foer Planteavl [A publication]
TPLAB	Tape Label [Data processing]
TPLAF........	Thai People's Liberation Armed Forces [Thailand]
TPLD.........	Test Planning Liaison Drawing (AAG)
TPLF	Tigre People's Liberation Front [Ethiopia] [Political party] (PD)
TPLG.........	Topologix, Inc. [NASDAQ symbol] (NQ)
TPLGG......	Town Planning and Local Government Guide [A publication] (APTA)
TP & LGG ...	Town Planning and Local Government Guide [A publication] (APTA)
T-PLL........	T-Cell Prolymphocytic Leukemia [Oncology]
TPLOA......	Teploenergetika [Moscow] [A publication]
TPLP	Teeco Properties LP [NASDAQ symbol] (NQ)
TPLP	Tobacco Products Liability Project (EA)
TPLP	Turkish People's Liberation Party [Political party] (PD)
TPLP/F......	Turkish People's Liberation Party/Front
TPLQ-A.....	Town Planning Quarterly [New Zealand] [A publication]
TPLR-A.....	Town Planning Review [United Kingdom] [A publication]
TPLS	Technology in Public Libraries Section [Public Library Association]
TPLS	Terminal Position Location System
TPLS	Texas Panhandle Library System [Library network]
TPLS	Tunable Pulsed LASER System
T/PLT........	Tapping Plate [Automotive engineering]
TPLW........	Triple Wall
TPM	Tape Preventive Maintenance
TPM	Tape Processing Machine
TPM	Technical Performance Measurement System [NASA]
TPM	Technical Performance Module (MCD)
TPM	Telemetry Processor Module
TPM	Tepoztlan [Mexico] [Seismograph station code, US Geological Survey] (SEIS)
TPM	Terminal Phase Maneuver [Aerospace] (MCD)
TPM	Terminal Phase Midcourse [Aerospace] (MCD)
TPM	Test Performance Management [Army]
TPM	Test Planning Manager [NASA] (KSC)
TPM	Theoretical Platers per Meter [Chromatography]
TPM	Thermal Power Monitor [Nuclear energy] (NRCH)
TPM	Timber Products Manufacturers (EA)
TPM	Title Page Mutilated
TPM	Tons per Minute
TPM	Tons per Month
TPM	Torpedo Prize Money [British military] (DMA)
TPM	Total Downtime for Preventive Scheduled Maintenance [Quality control] (MCD)
TPM	Total Particulate Matter [The "tar" of cigar and cigarette smoke]
TPM	Total Passive Motion
TPM	Total Polar Material [Analytical chemistry]
TPM	Total Population Management [Department of Agriculture]
TPM	Tours par Minute [Revolutions per Minute] [French]
TPM	Transfer Phase Midcourse [Aerospace] (MCD)
TPM	Transfiguration Prison Ministries (EA)
TPM	Transmission and Processing Model
TPM	Trigger Pricing Mechanism
TPM	Triplate Module
TPM	Tubular Products Manual [A publication] (EAAP)
TPMA.......	Thermodynamic Properties of Metals and Alloys (KSC)
TPMA.......	Timber Products Manufacturers Association [Later, TPM]
TPMAD5....	Tropical Pest Management [A publication]
TPMF	Tax Practitioner Master File [IRS]
TPMG	[The] Provost Marshal General [Army]
TPMGA.....	Teoriya i Praktika Metallurgii [A publication]
TPMM	Teleprocessing Multiplexer Module
TPMM	Triphenylmethyl Methacrylate [Organic chemistry]
TP-MO......	Technical Publications - Maintenance Operation [Naval Facilities Engineering Command Publications]
TPMP.......	Tender Production Management Program
TPMP.......	Texas Pacific-Missouri Pacific Terminal [Railroad of New Orleans] [AAR code]
TPMV.......	Tomato (Peru) Mosaic Virus
TPMXA....	Tecnica Pecuaria en Mexico [A publication]
TPN	Pan American University, Library, Edinburg, TX [OCLC symbol] (OCLC)
TPN	Sandoz Pharmaceuticals [Research code symbol]
TPN	Tapini [Papua New Guinea] [Seismograph station code, US Geological Survey] [Closed] (SEIS)
TPN	Tetrachlorophthalodinitrile [Organic chemistry]
TPN	Thalamic Projection Neurons [Neurology]
TPN	Total Parenteral Nutrition
TPN	Total Petroleum (North America) Ltd. [AMEX symbol] [Toronto Stock Exchange symbol] (SPSG)
TPN	Triphosphopyridine Nucleotide [See NADP] [Biochemistry]

TP & N.....	Triple Pole and Neutral [Switch]
TP & ND...	Theft, Pilferage, and Nondelivery [Insurance] (ADA)
TPND	Theft, Pilferage, and Nondelivery [Insurance]
TPNEG......	Travel Will Be Performed at No Expense to the Government [Military]
TPNF........	Tijdschrift voor Privaatrecht, Notariaat, en Fiscaalrecht [A publication]
TPNG	Territory of Papua and New Guinea
TPNG	Topping (AAG)
TPNH.......	Triphosphopyridine Nucleotide (Reduced) [See NADPH] [Biochemistry]
TPNL........	Townsend Plan National Lobby (EA)
T/PNL.......	Trim Panel [Automotive engineering]
TPNO	Tree Planters' Notes [A publication]
TPNPAI	Trudy Polyarnogo Nauchno-Issledovatel'skogo i Proektnogo Instituta Morskogo Rybnogo Khozyaistva i Okeanografii [A publication]
TPNS........	Teleprocessing Network Simulator
TPO	Nederlands Transport [A publication]
TPO	Sandoz Pharmaceuticals [Research code symbol]
TPO	Tanalian Point, AK [Location identifier] [FAA] (FAAL)
TPO	Tank Pressurizing Orifice (KSC)
TPO	Technical Planning Office
TPO	Technical Project Officer
TPO	Technology Planning Objectives (MCD)
TPO	Telecommunications Program Objective [Army] (AABC)
TPO	Temperature-Programmed Oxidation [For surface analysis]
Tpo............	Tempo [Record label] [Germany]
TPO	TEMPO Enterprises, Inc. [AMEX symbol] (SPSG)
TPO	Tentative Program Objectives [Navy]
TPO	Test of Perceptual Organization [Neuropsychology test]
TPO	Test Program Outline [Military]
TPO	Thermoplastic Olefinic [Elastomer]
TPO	Thyroid Peroxidase [An enzyme]
TPO	Track Production Officer [NATO Air Defense Ground Environment] (NATG)
TPO	Transportation Packaging Order (AFM)
TPO	Traveling Post Office
TPO	Tree Preservation Order [Town planning] [British]
TPO	Tryptophan Oxygenase [Also, TO, TP] [An enzyme]
TPO	Tuned Plate Oscillator
TPOD	Test Plan of the Day
TPOH.......	[The] Pursuit of Happiness [Rock music group]
TPOM	Tentative Program Objectives Memorandum [Military] (CAAL)
TPOM	Tube Propagation d'Ondes Magnetron
TPorH.......	Highland Hospital, Portland, TN [Library symbol] [Library of Congress] (LCLS)
TPORT.....	Transport
TPOS.........	Track Position
TPow........	Tygodnik Powszechny [A publication]
TPP...........	Tarapoto [Peru] [Airport symbol] (OAG)
TPP...........	Technical Performance Parameter (MCD)
TPP...........	Technology Program Plan [Military] (AFIT)
TPP...........	Telephony Preprocessor [Telecommunications] (TEL)
TPP...........	Teletype Page Printer
TPP...........	Teppco Partners LP [NYSE symbol] (SPSG)
TPP...........	Test Point Pace (KSC)
TPP...........	Test Program Plan (MCD)
TPP...........	Tetraphenylporphine [Organic chemistry]
TPP...........	Tetraphenylporphyrin [Biochemistry]
TPP...........	Textured Peanut Protein [Food industry]
TPP...........	Thermal Power Plant (CINC)
TPP...........	Thermal Protection Panel
TPP...........	Thermally Protected Plastic
TPP...........	Thiamine Pyrophosphate [Also, DPT, TDP] [Biochemistry]
TPP...........	Thomson Professional Publishing [The Thomson Corp.]
TP & P......	Time, Place, and Person
TPP...........	Toledo Progressive Party [Belize] [Political party] (PPW)
TPP...........	Total Package Procurement [Government contracting]
TPP...........	Total Program Planning/Procurement
TPP...........	Trained Profile Panel [Sensory testing]
TPP...........	Trans-Pluto Probe
TPP...........	Transducer Power Programmer
TP & P......	Transients, Patients, and Prisoners [Military]
TPP...........	Transients, Patients, and Prisoners [Military]
TPP...........	Transport Policies and Programme [British] (DCTA)
TPP...........	Transuranium Processing Plant
TPP...........	Tri-Power Petroleum Corp. [Toronto Stock Exchange symbol]
TPP...........	Trinidad [Pointe-A-Pierre] [Trinidad-Tobago] [Seismograph station code, US Geological Survey] (SEIS)
TPP...........	Triphenyl Phosphite [Organic chemistry]
TPP...........	Tripolyphosphate [Food industry]
TPP...........	True Path Party [Turkey] [Political party]
TPP...........	Two-Phase Principle
TPPADK ...	Trends and Perspectives in Parasitology [A publication]
TPPC........	Total Package Procurement Concept [Government contracting]
TPPC........	Trans-Pacific Passenger Conference [Later, PCC] (EA)
TPPD........	Technical Program Planning Division [Air Force] (MCD)
TPPE	Two-Photon Photoemission Spectroscopy

TPPEP....... Turkey Point Performance Enforcement Program [*Nuclear energy*]   (NRCH)
TPPGM..... Tentative Planning and Programming Guidance Memorandum [*Navy*]   (NVT)
TPPha........ Transactions. College of Physicians of Philadelphia [*A publication*]
TPPIS........ Treasury Payroll/Personnel Information System
TP-PL........ Technical Publications - Planning [*Naval Facilities Engineering Command Publications*]
TPPN........ Total Peripheral Parenteral Nutrition
TPPS .... Tape Post-Processing System
TPPS .... Tetraphenylporphinesulfonate [*Reagent*]
TPPS .... Tops Markets, Inc. [*Buffalo, NY*] [*NASDAQ symbol*]   (NQ)
TP-PU .... Technical Publications - Public Utilities [*Naval Facilities Engineering Command Publications*]
TPPYA ...... Topical Problems of Psychotherapy [*A publication*]
TPPYAL..... Aktuelle Fragen der Psychotherapie [*A publication*]
TPQ .... AMIGOS [*Access Method for Indexed Data Generalized for Operating System*] Bibliographic Council, Dallas, TX [*OCLC symbol*]   (OCLC)
TPQ .... Government of Quebec [*Canada*] [*FAA designator*]   (FAAC)
TPQ .... Tepic [*Mexico*] [*Airport symbol*]
T P Q .... Theologisch-Praktische Quartalschrift [*A publication*]
TPQ .... Threshold Planning Quantity [*Hazardous substances*]
TPQI........ Teacher-Pupil Question Inventory
TPQS .... Theologisch-Praktische Quartalschrift [*A publication*]
TPR........... AMIGOS [*Access Method for Indexed Data Generalized for Operating System*] Bibliographic Council, Dallas, TX [*OCLC symbol*]   (OCLC)
TPR........... Tamper-Protected Recording [*3M Co.*]
TPR........... Tape Programmed Row [*Data scanner*]
TPR........... Taper   (MSA)
TPR........... Team Power Rating [*Hockey*]
TPR........... Technical Program Review
TPR........... Technical Progress Report
TPR........... Technical Proposal Requirement   (MCD)
TPR........... Telecommunications Product Review [*A publication*]
TPR........... Teleprinter   (AAG)
TPR........... Telescopic Photographic Recorder
TPR........... Temperature Profile Recorder   (AAG)
TPR........... Temperature-Programmed Reaction [*Chemistry*]
TPR........... Temperature-Programmed Reduction [*For analysis of surfaces*]
TPR........... Temperature, Pulse, Respiration [*Medicine*]
TPr............ Tempo Presente [*A publication*]
TPR........... Temporary Price Reduction
TPR........... Terrain Profile Recorder
TPR........... Test Performance Recorder
TPR........... Test Phase Report
TPR........... Test Problem Report [*NASA*]   (NASA)
TPR........... Test Procedure Record   (NATG)
TPR........... Thermoplastic Rubber
TPR........... Three Penny Review [*A publication*]
TPR........... Tijdschrift voor Privaatrecht [*A publication*]
TPR........... Tom Price [*Australia*] [*Airport symbol*]
TPR........... Total Peripheral Resistance
TPR........... Total Pulmonary Resistance [*Cardiology*]
TPR........... Trade Practices Reports [*Australia*] [*A publication*]
TPR........... Trained Personnel Requirements [*Air Force*]
TPR........... Transmitter Power Rating
TPR........... Trapped Pressure Ratio [*Gas analysis*]
TPR........... Trooper
TPRC........ Thermophysical Properties Research Center [*DoD*]
TPRC........ Trade Policy Research Centre [*British*]   (ECON)
TPRD........ Technology Planning and Research Division [*Central Electricity Generating Board*] [*British*]   (IRUK)
TPRG........ Technology Performance Requirements Guideline
TPRI........ Teacher-Pupil Relationship Inventory
TPRI........ Time Problems Inventory [*Test*]
TPRI........ Total Peripheral Resistance Index
TPRL........ Thermophysical Properties Research Laboratory [*Purdue University*] [*Research center*]   (RCD)
TPRRD..... Technik-Index ueber Plasmaphysikalische Forschung und Fusionsreaktoren [*A publication*]
TPRS .... Temperature-Programmed Reaction Spectroscopy
TPRS .... Temperature-Programmed Reaction System
TPRS .... Trade Practices Reporting Service [*A publication*]   (APTA)
TPRSL....... Transactions and Proceedings. Royal Society of Literature [*A publication*]
TPRU........ Technical Processing and Reporting Unit   (CAAL)
TPRU........ Tropical Pesticides Research Unit [*Later, Centre for Overseas Pest Research*] [*British*]
TPRV........ Transient Peak Reverse Voltage
TPrzPI....... Trudy Przeval'skogo Pedagogiceskogo Instituta [*A publication*]
TPS........... Bibliographic Center for Research, Denver, CO [*OCLC symbol*]   (OCLC)
TPS........... [*The*] Planetary Society
TPS........... [*The*] Pope Speaks [*A publication*]
TPS........... Tandem Propeller Submarine
TPS........... Tangent Plane System   (MUGU)
TPS........... Tank Pressure Sensing   (AAG)
TPS.......... Tape Plotting System

TPS........... Tape Processing System   (CMD)
TPS............ Tape Punch Subassembly
TPS............ Task Parameter Synthesizer
TPS............ Technical Publishing Society [*Later, STC*]
TPS............ Technical Publishing Software [*Interleaf, Inc.*]
TPS............ Technology Policy Statement [*1982*] [*India*]
TPS............ Technopolymer Structure [*Engineering plastics*]
TPS............ Telecommunications Programming System
TPS............ Telemation Program Services
TPS............ Telemetry Processing System [*Space Flight Operations Facility, NASA*]
TPS............ Terminal Performance Specification
TPS............ Terminal Polling System
TPS............ Terminals per Station [*Telecommunications*]
TPS............ Test Pilot School [*Navy*]
TPS............ Test Plotting System
TPS............ Test Point Selector
TPS............ Test Preparation Sheet [*NASA*]   (AAG)
TPS............ Test Procedure Specification [*NASA*]   (KSC)
TPS............ Test Program Set   (MCD)
TPS............ Theologie Pastorale et Spiritualite [*A publication*]
TPS............ Thermal Protection System [*or Subsystem*]
TPS............ Thermoplastic Storage
TPS............ Thomas Paine Society [*Nottingham, England*]   (EAIO)
TPS............ Threat Platform Simulator [*Military*]   (CAAL)
TPS............ Throttle Position Sensor [*Automotive engineering*]
TPS............ Total Parameter Space [*Statistics*]
TPS............ Total Product Support
TPS............ Tough Plastic-Sheathed
TPS............ TPA of America [*AMEX symbol*]   (SPSG)
TPS............ Trade Promotion Services Group [*British*]
TPS............ Trail Pilot Sensor
TPS............ Tramp Power Supply
TPS............ Trans Rampart Industry [*Vancouver Stock Exchange symbol*]
TPS............ Transaction Processing System [*Trademark of Software Consulting Service, Inc.*]
TPS............ Transactions. Philological Society [*London*] [*A publication*]
TPS............ Transactions per Second
TPS............ Transduodenal Pancreatic Sphincteroplasty
TPS............ Translunar Propulsion Stage [*Aerospace*]   (AAG)
TPS............ Trapani [*Italy*] [*Airport symbol*]   (OAG)
TPS............ Tree Pruning System
TPS............ Trigger-Price System [*Department of the Treasury*]
TPS............ Troops [*Military*] [*British*]
TPS............ Tube Pin Straightener
TPS............ Tumor Polysaccharidal Substance [*Oncology*]
TPS............ Turkey Point Station [*Nuclear energy*]   (NRCH)
TPS............ Turner Program Services [*Broadcasting*]
TPS............ Tuvalu Philatelic Society   (EA)
TPSB .... Telemetry Processing System Buffer [*Space Flight Operations Facility, NASA*]
TPSB .... Thomas Paine Society. Bulletin [*A publication*]
TPSC .... Test Planning and Status Checker [*Data processing*]
TPSC .... Trade Policy Staff Committee [*Federal interagency group*]
TPSE .... Thermal Protection Subsystem Experiments   (NASA)
TPSE .... (Tritylphenyl)sulfonylethanol [*Organic chemistry*]
TPSF .... Telephonie sans Fil [*Wireless Telephony*]
TPSF .... Terminal Profile Security File [*IRS*]
TPSFA....... Tohoku Psychologica Folia [*A publication*]
TPSI .... Torque Pressure in Pounds per Square Inch
TPSL .... Tyoevaeen ja Pienviljelijaein Sosialidemokraattinen Liitto [*Social Democratic League of Workers and Smallholders*] [*Finland*] [*Political party*]   (PPE)
TPSM .... Tepatshimuwin. Journal d'Information des Attikamekes et des Montagnais [*A publication*]
TPSN........ Transposition   (AAG)
TPSN........ Troop Program Sequence Number [*Military*]
TPSO........ Triphenylstibine Oxide [*Organic chemistry*]
TPSP .... Tape Punch Subassembly Panel
TPSRS....... Theologie Pastorale et Spiritualite. Recherches et Syntheses [*A publication*]
TPSS........ Thermal Protection System Selection
TPST .... Training and Personnel Systems Technology   (MCD)
TPST .... Triple-Pole, Single-Throw [*Switch*]
TPSTe....... Triisopropylbenzenesulfonyl Tetrazolide [*Organic chemistry*]
TPT........... Air Transport Corp. [*Detroit, MI*] [*FAA designator*]   (FAAC)
TPT........... Bibliographic Center for Research, Denver, CO [*OCLC symbol*]   (OCLC)
TPT........... Tail Pipe Temperature   (NG)
TPT........... Tappet [*Mechanical engineering*]
TPT........... Tappit Resources [*Vancouver Stock Exchange symbol*]
TPT........... Target Practice [*Ammunition*] with Tracer
TPT........... Telecommunication Products Plus Technology [*Pennwell Publishing Co.*] [*Littleton, MA*]   (TSSD)
TPT........... Teleprinter Planning Table
TPT........... Temporary Part Time [*Personnel*]   (MCD)
TPT........... Test Pilot Training
TPT........... Tetraisopropyl Titanate [*Organic chemistry*]
TPT........... Third-Party Transaction [*Business term*]
TPT........... Time to Peak Tension

TPT............ Time Period Tape [*Database*] [*Arbitron Ratings Co.*] [*Information service or system*]   (CRD)

TPT............ Time Priority Table

TPT............ Tiputa [*Tuamotu Archipelago*] [*Seismograph station code, US Geological Survey*]   (SEIS)

TPT............ Total Pressure Transducer

TPT............ Totul pentru Tara [*"All for the Fatherland"*] [*Romania*] [*Political party*]   (PPE)

TPT............ Trade Practices Tribunal [*Australia*]

TPT............ Training Proficiency Test [*Army*]   (INF)

TPT............ Transonic Pressure Tunnel [*NASA*]

TPT............ Transport

TPT............ Trenton-Princeton Traction Co. [*Absorbed into Consolidated Rail Corp.*] [*AAR code*]

TPT............ Troop Proficiency Trainer

TPT............ Trumpet

TPT............ Typhoid-Paratyphoid [*Medicine*]

TPTA......... Thiophosphoryl Triamide [*Fertilizer technology*]

TPTA......... Tin Triphenyl [*or* Triphenyltin] Acetate [*Organic chemistry*]

TPTC......... Triphenyltin Chloride [*Organic chemistry*]

TPTD......... Test Pilot Training Division

TPTD......... Transported

TPTE......... (Tritylphenyl)thioethanol [*Organic chemistry*]

TPTF......... Tributyl Phosphate Task Force   (EA)

TPTG......... Tuned Plate Tuned Grid [*Electronic tube*]

TPTH......... Triphenyltin Hydroxide [*Organic chemistry*]

TPTN......... Toilet Partition [*Technical drawings*]

TPTOL...... True Position Tolerance   (MSA)

TPTR......... Topps and Trousers [*NASDAQ symbol*]   (NQ)

TPTR......... Transporter

TPTR......... Trumpeter

TPTRL...... Time-Phased Transportation Requirements List [*Military*]   (AABC)

TPTS........ Two-Phase Thermosyphon [*Heat exchanger*]

TPTX........ Thyroparathyroidectomized [*Medicine*]

TPTZ........ Triphenyltetrazolium Chloride [*Also, RT, TTC*] [*Chemical indicator*]

TPTZ......... Tris(pyridyl)-s-triazine [*Analytical chemistry*]

TPU .... Capitol Consortium Network, Washington, DC [*OCLC symbol*]   (OCLC)

TPU .... Tape Preparation Unit

TPU .... Tarn Pure Technology Corp. [*Vancouver Stock Exchange symbol*]

TPU .... Task Processing Unit

TPU .... Telecommunications Processing Unit

TPU .... Text Processing Utility [*Data processing*]

TPU .... Thermoplastic Urethane [*Plastics technology*]

TPU .... Troop Program Unit [*Army*]   (AABC)

TPU .... Trunk Processing Unit [*Bell System*]

TPU .... Turbopower Unit

TPUC........ Telephone Pickup Coil

TPUG .... Toronto PET Users Group [*Canada*]

TP/UMF ... Total Package/Unit Materiel Fielding [*Army*]   (RDA)

TPUN .... Test Procedure Update Notice   (NASA)

TPUS......... Transportation and Public Utilities Service [*Later, part of Transportation and Communication Service, GSA*]

TPV........... Capitol Consortium Network, Washington, DC [*OCLC symbol*]   (OCLC)

TPV........... Thermophotovoltaic

TPV........... Thermoplastic Vulcanizate [*Plastics technology*]

TPV........... Tonopah [*Nevada*] [*Seismograph station code, US Geological Survey*] [*Closed*]   (SEIS)

TPV........... Total Pore Volume [*Geology*]

TPV........... Transverse Pallial Vein

TPV........... Triple Polio Vaccine [*Medicine*]

TPW .... Tenth-Power Width

TPW .... Title Page Wanting

TP & W...... Toledo, Peoria & Western Railroad Co.

TPW .... Toledo, Peoria & Western Railroad Co. [*AAR code*]

TPW .... Tons per Week

TPW .... True Polar Wandering [*Geophysics*]

TPWBH .... Tax Paid Wine Bottling House

TPWG .... Test Planning Working Group [*Military*]

TPWIC....... Theater Prisoner of War Information Center

TPWU .... Tanganyika Plantation Workers Union

TPWU .... Tea Plantation Workers' Union [*Kenya*]

TPX........... Total Pancreatectomy [*Medicine*]

TPX........... Transponder   (KSC)

TPY........... FEDLINK [*Federal Library and Information Network*], Washington, DC [*OCLC symbol*]   (OCLC)

TPY........... Tapestry   (ADA)

TPY........... Tons per Year

TPY........... Trans-Provincial Airlines Ltd. [*Prince Rupert, BC*] [*FAA designator*]   (FAAC)

TPZ........... FEDLINK [*Federal Library and Information Network*], Washington, DC [*OCLC symbol*]   (OCLC)

TPZ........... Thioperazine [*or* Thioproperazine] [*Tranquilizer*]

TQ.............. [*The*] Questers   (EA)

TQ.............. Tale Quale [*Of Conditions on Arrival*] [*Latin*]

TQ.............. Texas Quarterly [*A publication*]

TQ.............. Theatre Quarterly [*A publication*]

TQ.............. Theologische Quartalschrift [*Tuebingen*] [*A publication*]

TQ.............. Thought Quality [*Psychology*]

TQ.............. Three-Quarter Midget [*Horse racing*]

TQ.............. Three-Quarter Size [*Car racing*]

TQ.............. Timbre de Quittance [*Receipt Stamp*] [*French*]

TQ.............. Tocopherolquinone [*Vitamin E*] [*Biochemistry*]

TQ.............. Toronto Quarterly [*A publication*]

TQ.............. Trans Oceanic Airways Ltd. [*Great Britain*] [*ICAO designator*]   (FAAC)

TQ.............. Transition Quarter [*Between fiscal years 1976 and 1977*]

TQ.............. Tri-Quarterly [*A publication*]

TQ.............. Tyrolean Airways [*Austria*] [*ICAO designator*]   (ICDA)

TQ-3.......... Tocotrienolquinone [*Biochemistry*]

TQA........... Abilene, TX [*Location identifier*] [*FAA*]   (FAAL)

TQA........... ILLINET [*Illinois Library Information Network*], Springfield, IL [*OCLC symbol*]   (OCLC)

TQAGA ..... Technique Agricole [*A publication*]

TQB........... ILLINET [*Illinois Library Information Network*], Springfield, IL [*OCLC symbol*]   (OCLC)

TQC........... Indiana Cooperative Library Services Authority, Indianapolis, IN [*OCLC symbol*]   (OCLC)

TQC........... Technical Quality Control [*Telecommunications*]   (TEL)

TQC........... Time, Quality, Cost

TQC........... Total Quality Control

TQCA......... Textile Quality Control Association   (EA)

TQCM....... Thermoelectric Quartz Crystal Microbalance

TQD........... Indiana Cooperative Library Services Authority, Indianapolis, IN [*OCLC symbol*]   (OCLC)

TQD........... Ter Quaterve in Die [*Three or Four Times a Day*] [*Pharmacy*]

TQE........... Michigan Library Consortium, Detroit, MI [*OCLC symbol*]   (OCLC)

TQE........... Technical Quality Evaluation [*Polaris*]

TQE........... Technique de l'Eau et de l'Assainissement [*A publication*]

TQE........... Tekamah, NE [*Location identifier*] [*FAA*]   (FAAL)

TQE........... Timer Queue Element

TQF........... Michigan Library Consortium, Detroit, MI [*OCLC symbol*]   (OCLC)

TQF........... Threshold Quality Factor

TQG........... MIDLNET [*Midwest Regional Library Network*], St. Louis, MO [*OCLC symbol*]   (OCLC)

TQH........... MIDLNET [*Midwest Regional Library Network*], St. Louis, MO [*OCLC symbol*]   (OCLC)

TQH........... Tahlequah, OK [*Location identifier*] [*FAA*]   (FAAL)

TQI .... MINITEX [*Minnesota Interlibrary Teletype Exchange*], Minneapolis, MN [*OCLC symbol*]   (OCLC)

TQI .... Training Quality Index [*Military*]   (CAAL)

TQJ........... MINITEX [*Minnesota Interlibrary Teletype Exchange*], Minneapolis, MN [*OCLC symbol*]   (OCLC)

TQK........... NELINET [*New England Library Information Network*], Newton, MA [*OCLC symbol*]   (OCLC)

TQL........... NELINET [*New England Library Information Network*], Newton, MA [*OCLC symbol*]   (OCLC)

TQM........... OCLC [*Online Computer Library Center*] Western Services Center, Claremont, CA [*OCLC symbol*]   (OCLC)

TQM........... Total Quality Management

TQM.......... Transport Quartermaster

TQMG....... [*The*] Quartermaster General [*Army*]

TQMS .... Technical Quartermaster Sergeant

TQMS .... Triple Quadrupole Mass Spectrometer

TQMS .... Troop Quartermaster-Sergeant [*British military*]   (DMA)

TQN........... OCLC [*Online Computer Library Center*] Western Services Center, Claremont, CA [*OCLC symbol*]   (OCLC)

TQO........... OHIONET, Columbus, OH [*OCLC symbol*]   (OCLC)

TQP........... OHIONET, Columbus, OH [*OCLC symbol*]   (OCLC)

TQP........... Transistor Qualification Program

TQPF......... [*The*] Valley/Wall Blake [*Anguilla Island*] [*ICAO location identifier*]   (ICLI)

TQQ.......... Pennsylvania Area Library Network, Philadelphia, PA [*OCLC symbol*]   (OCLC)

TQQPRI.... Tentative Qualitative Quantitative Personnel Requirements Information [*Army*]

TQR........... Pennsylvania Area Library Network, Philadelphia, PA [*OCLC symbol*]   (OCLC)

TQR........... Saginaw, MI [*Location identifier*] [*FAA*]   (FAAL)

TQR........... Tenquille Resources Ltd. [*Vancouver Stock Exchange symbol*]

TQS........... Pittsburgh Regional Library Center, Pittsburgh, PA [*OCLC symbol*]   (OCLC)

TQS........... Theologische Quartalschrift [*A publication*]

TQS........... Tres Esquinas [*Colombia*] [*Airport symbol*]   (OAG)

TQT........... Pittsburgh Regional Library Center, Pittsburgh, PA [*OCLC symbol*]   (OCLC)

TQT........... Transistor Qualification Test

TQTP........ Transistor Qualification Test Program

TQU........... Southeastern Library Network, Atlanta, GA [*OCLC symbol*]   (OCLC)

TQV .... Southeastern Library Network, Atlanta, GA [*OCLC symbol*]   (OCLC)

TQW.......... Pittsburgh, PA [*Location identifier*] [*FAA*]   (FAAL)

TQW......... State University of New York, OCLC [*Online Computer Library Center*], Albany, NY [*OCLC symbol*]   (OCLC)

TQX	State University of New York, OCLC [*Online Computer Library Center*], Albany, NY [*OCLC symbol*] (OCLC)
TQY	Tanquery Resources Ltd. [*Vancouver Stock Exchange symbol*]
TQY	Wisconsin Library Consortium, Madison, WI [*OCLC symbol*] (OCLC)
TQZ	Wisconsin Library Consortium, Madison, WI [*OCLC symbol*] (OCLC)
TR	Caines' Term Reports [*New York*] [*A publication*] (DLA)
TR	Compania de Aviacion Trans-Europa [*Spain*] [*ICAO designator*] (ICDA)
TR	Gabon [*Aircraft nationality and registration mark*] (FAAC)
TR	Stewardsman Recruit [*Navy*]
TR	Table Ronde [*A publication*]
TR	Tactical Reconnaissance (NATG)
TR	Talyllyn Railway [*Wales*]
TR	Tank Regiment (MCD)
TR	Tape Reader
TR	Tape Recorder
TR	Tape Register
TR	Tape Resident
TR	Tare (ROG)
TR	Target Recognition (AFM)
TR	Tariff Reform
TR	Task Register [*Data processing*] (BYTE)
TR	Tax Rate
TR	Taxation Reports [*England*] [*A publication*] (DLA)
TR	Teaching and Research [*Medicine*]
TR	Team Recorder [*Sports*]
TR	Tear [*Deltiology*]
TR	Technical Readiness
TR	Technical Regulation
TR	Technical Report
TR	Technical Reporter [*World Council of Credit Unions*] [*A publication*]
TR	Technical Representative
TR	Technical Requirement (MCD)
TR	Technical Review [*Nuclear energy*] (NRCH)
TR	Technology Review [*A publication*]
TR	Telegraphe Restant [*Telegram to Be Called for at a Telegraph Office*] [*French*] (ROG)
TR	Telephone Rentals [*Commercial firm*]
TR	Tell-Rimah (BJA)
TR	Temperature Range
TR	Temperature Recorder
TR	Temperature, Rectal [*Medicine*]
TR	Temporary Resident
TR	Tempore Regis [*In the Time of the King*] [*Latin*]
TR	Terbium [*Chemical element*] [*Symbol is Tb*] (ROG)
TR	Term Reports [*Legal*] [*British*]
TR	Term Reports, English King's Bench [*Durnford and East's Reports*] [*England*] [*A publication*] (DLA)
TR	Terminal Ready [*Data processing*]
TR	Terminal Rendezvous
TR	Terminal Repeat [*Genetics*]
TR	Terminalischer Reiz [*Terminal Stimulus*] [*German*] [*Psychology*]
TRX	Terms of Reference
TR	Territorial Reserve [*British military*] (DMA)
TR	Test Regulation (MCD)
TR	Test Report
TR	Test Request
TR	Test-Retest
TR	Test Routine (AAG)
TR	Test Run
T & R	Testing and Regulating Department [*Especially, in a wire communications maintenance division*]
TR	Textus Receptus (BJA)
TR	Thalamic Radiation [*Neurology*]
TR	Theatre Research [*A publication*]
TR	Theatre Royal (ROG)
TR	Thematic Resource Nomination [*National Register of Historic Places*]
TR	Theodore [*Teddy*] Roosevelt [*US president, 1858-1919*]
TR	Theologische Revue [*Muenster*] [*A publication*]
TR	Theologische Rundschau [*A publication*]
TR	Therapeutic Radiology
TR	Thioredoxin [*Also, TD, Trx*] [*Biochemistry*]
TR	Thioredoxin Reductase [*An enzyme*]
TR	Threaded Rod
TR	Threat Reaction [*Military*] (CAAL)
TR	Throws Right-Handed [*Baseball*]
TR	Thrust Reverser (MCD)
TR	Thyroid Hormone Receptor [*Endocrinology*]
TR	Tijdschrift voor Rechtsgeschiedenis [*A publication*]
TR	Time Rate [*Payment system*]
TR	Time Record (MCD)
TR	Time to Repetition [*Medicine*]
TR	Time Resolved [*Fluoroscopy*]
TR	Time to Retrofire
TR	Time-to-Retrograde [*NASA*] (KSC)
T/R	Time of Rise (MSA)

TR	Timed-Release [*Pharmacy*]
TR	Tinctura [*Tincture*] [*Pharmacy*]
TR	Tirailleur Regiments [*Military*]
TR	Tobacco Reporter [*A publication*]
TR	Tone Relevant
TR	Tons Registered [*Shipping*]
TR	Tool Resistant [*Rating for safes*]
TR	Toothed Ring [*Technical drawings*]
TR	Tootsie Roll Industries, Inc. [*NYSE symbol*] (SPSG)
TR	Topical Report [*Nuclear energy*] (NRCH)
TR	Torpedo Reconnaissance Aircraft [*Navy*]
TR	Torque Synchro Receiver (MUGU)
TR	Total Regulation
TR	Total Revenue
TR	Touchdowns Running [*Football*]
TR	Touche Remnant [*Investment firm*] [*British*]
TR	Towel Rack (MSA)
TR	Tower
TR	Trace
TR	Tracer
TR	Track
TR	Tracking RADAR
TR	Tract
TR	Trade
TR	Traffic Route [*Telecommunications*] (TEL)
TR	Tragedy
TR	Trailer (AAG)
TR	Train (ADA)
TR	Trainer (AAG)
TR	Training (ROG)
TR	Training Regulations [*Military*]
TR	Training Requirements
TR	Tramway (ROG)
TR	Transaction
TR	Transaction Record
TR	Transatlantic Review [*A publication*]
TR	Transbrasil SA Linhas Aereas [*Brazil*] [*ICAO designator*] (FAAC)
T/R	Transceiver
TR	Transcontinental Resources [*Vancouver Stock Exchange symbol*]
Tr	Transcript (DLA)
TR	Transducers [*JETDS nomenclature*] [*Military*] (CET)
TR	Transfer (DEN)
TR	Transfer Register
TR	Transfer Reset
TR	Transformation Ratio
TR	Transformer (DEN)
T-R	Transformer-Rectifier
TR	Transfusion Reaction [*Medicine*]
TR	Transfusion Receptors [*Oncology*]
TR	Transient Response (IEEE)
TR	Transilluminator [*Chromatography*]
TR	Transitive
TR	Translate [*or Translation, or Translator*]
TR	Translation Register
tr	Translator
TR	Transmission Report [*Telecommunications*] (TEL)
T-R	Transmit-Receive
TR	Transmitter
TR	Transom (MSA)
TR	Transport
TR	Transportability Report [*Army*]
TR	Transportation [*or Travel*] Request [*Military*]
TR	Transportation Science [*A publication*] (EAAP)
TR	Transpose
TR	Transverse (DEN)
Tr	Tratta [*Bill of Exchange*] [*Italian*] [*Business term*]
Tr	Tratte [*Draft*] [*German*] [*Business term*]
TR	Travel and Relocation
T/R	Travel Request
TR	Travel Required [*Civil Service*]
TR	Trawler
TR	Treasurer
TR	Treasury Receipt
TR	Treatise (ROG)
TR	Treaty (ROG)
TR	Treble [*Music*]
TR	Treble [*Knitting*]
TR	Trees [*Ecology*]
TR	Triad [*A publication*]
TR	Trial (ROG)
TR	Trial Report
TR	Tributary (ROG)
TR	Tricuspid Regurgitation [*Cardiology*]
TR	Trident Aircraft Ltd. [*Canada*] [*ICAO aircraft manufacturer identifier*] (ICAO)
TR	Trigonal [*Molecular geometry*]
TR	Trillo [*Trill*] [*Music*]
tr	Trinidad and Tobago [*MARC country of publication code*] [*Library of Congress*] (LCCP)

TR .... Trip Report
TR .... Triple Reduction (DS)
TR .... Triple Screw [*Shipping*] (DS)
Tr .... Tristia [*of Ovid*] [*Classical studies*] (OCD)
Tr .... Tristram's Consistory Judgments [*England*] [*A publication*] (DLA)
TR .... Tritium Ratio [*Measure of tritium activity*] [*AEC*]
TR .... Tritium Recovery [*Nuclear energy*] (NRCH)
Tr .... Trityl [*Organic chemistry*]
tr .... Trityl [*As substituent on nucleoside*] [*Biochemistry*]
Tr .... Trivium [*A publication*]
TR .... Troop
TR .... Trouble Report
TR .... Trough (ADA)
TR .... Troupe (ROG)
TR .... Truck
TR .... True (FAAC)
TR .... Trumpet
TR .... Trunnion [*Pivot*]
TR .... Truro [*British depot code*]
TR .... Truss (MSA)
TR .... Trust
T/R .... Trust Receipt [*Banking*]
TR .... Trustee
TR .... Tubercular Rueckstand [*Medicine*]
TR .... Tuberculin Residue [*Medicine*]
TR .... Tunnel Rectifier
TR .... Turbine Rate (NVT)
TR .... Turkey [*ANSI two-letter standard code*] (CNC)
TR .... Turkish Reactor
TR .... Turnaround Requirements (MCD)
T & R .... Turner and Russell's English Chancery Reports [*1822-25*] [*A publication*] (DLA)
Tr .... Y Traethodydd [*A publication*]
1TR .... One Turn Right [*Dance terminology*]
Tra .... Epistulae ad Traianum [*of Pliny the Younger*] [*Classical studies*] (OCD)
TRA .... La Tuyere a Reverse Aval [*Concorde*]
TRA .... RADAR Transfer of Control Message [*Communications*] (FAAC)
TRA .... Tackle Representatives Association (EA)
TRA .... Taiwan Railway Administration (DCTA)
TRA .... Tandem Rotary Activator
TRA .... Tape Recorder Amplifier
TRA .... Taramajima [*Japan*] [*Airport symbol*] (OAG)
TRA .... Tax Reform Act [*1969, 1976, 1984, 1986*]
TRA .... Technical Review and Analysis
TRA .... Technical Risk Assessment (MCD)
TRA .... Television/Radio Age [*A publication*]
TRA .... Temporary Restricted Area [*USSR*] (NATG)
TRA .... Terrain-Related Accident [*Aviation*]
TRA .... Test Requirement Analysis (CAAL)
TRA .... Textile Refinishers Association (EA)
TRA .... Theodore Roosevelt Association (EA)
TRA .... Thoroughbred Racing Associations (EA)
TRA .... Thrace Requirements Analysis [*Military*]
TRA .... Tinctura [*Tincture*] [*Pharmacy*] (ROG)
TRA .... Tire and Rim Association (EA)
TRA .... Tournament of Roses Association [*Later, TOR*] (EA)
TRA .... Toward Revolutionary Art [*A publication*]
TRA .... Tracan Oil & Gas [*Vancouver Stock Exchange symbol*]
TRA .... Trade Readjustment Allowance [*or Assistance*]
TRA .... Trade Recovery Act
TRA .... Trade Relations Association (EA)
TrA .... Traduction Automatique [*The Hague*] [*A publication*]
TRA .... Training [*A publication*]
TRA .... Training
TRA .... Training Readjustment Allowance (OICC)
TRA .... Training Requirements Analysis [*NASA*] (NASA)
TRA .... Transfer
TRA .... Transportation Reform Alliance
TRA .... Transracial Adoption
TRA .... Travnik [*Yugoslavia*] [*Seismograph station code, US Geological Survey*] [*Closed*] (SEIS)
TrA .... Triangulum Australe [*Constellation*]
TRA .... Triaxial Recording Accelerometer
TRA .... Tripoli Rocketry Association (EA)
TRA .... Triumph Register of America (EA)
TRA .... Tubular Reactor Assembly [*Nuclear energy*] (NRCH)
TRA .... Turnaround Requirements Analysis [*NASA*] (NASA)
TRA .... United States Army TRADOC, Institute for Military Assistance, Library, Fort Bragg, NC [*OCLC symbol*] (OCLC)
TRAA .... Towing and Recovery Association of America (EA)
TRAAC ...... Transit Research and Attitude Control [*Navy satellite*]
TRAACS ... Transit Research and Attitude Control Satellite [*Navy*] (IEEE)
Tr A Am Physicians ... Transactions. Association of American Physicians [*A publication*]
TRAB .... Triaminobenzene [*Organic chemistry*]
Trabajos Estadist ... Trabajos de Estadistica [*A publication*]

Trabajos Estadist Investigacion Oper ... Trabajos de Estadistica y de Investigacion Operativa [*A publication*]
Trab Antrop Etnol ... Trabalhos. Sociedade Portuguesa de Antropologia e Etnologia [*A publication*]
Trab Antropol Etnol ... Trabalhos de Antropologia e Etnologia [*A publication*]
Trab Cent Bot Junta Invest Ultramar ... Trabalhos. Centro de Botanica. Junta de Investigacoes do Ultramar [*A publication*]
Trab Cient Univ Cordoba ... Trabajos Cientificos de la Universidad de Cordoba [*A publication*]
Trab Compostelanos Biol ... Trabajos Compostelanos de Biologia [*A publication*]
Trab 5 Cong Med Latino-Am ... Trabajos Presentados al Quinto Congreso Medico Latino-Americano [*A publication*]
Trab Dep Bot Fisiol Veg Univ Madrid ... Trabajos. Departamento de Botanica y Fisiologia Vegetal. Universidad de Madrid [*A publication*]
TrabEsta.... Trabajos de Estadistica [*A publication*]
Trab Estac Agric Exp Leon ... Trabajos. Estacion Agricola Experimental de Leon [*A publication*]
Trab Estadistica ... Trabajos de Estadistica y de Investigacion [*A publication*]
Trab Geol... Trabajos de Geologia [*A publication*]
Trab Geol Oviedo Univ Fac Cienc ... Trabajos de Geologia. Oviedo Universidad. Facultad de Ciencias [*A publication*]
Trab Inst Cajal Invest Biol ... Trabajos. Instituto Cajal de Investigaciones Biologicas [*A publication*]
Trab Inst Econ Prod Ganad Ebro ... Trabajos. Instituto de Economia y Producciones Ganaderas del Ebro [*A publication*]
Trab Inst Esp Entomol ... Trabajos. Instituto Espanol de Entomologia [*A publication*]
Trab Inst Esp Oceanogr ... Trabajos. Instituto Espanol de Oceanografia [*A publication*]
Trab Inst Fisiol Fac Med Univ Lisboa ... Trabajos. Instituto de Fisiologia. Faculdade de Medicina. Universidade do Lisboa [*A publication*]
Trab Inst Nac Cienc Med (Madrid) ... Trabajos. Instituto Nacional de Ciencias Medicas (Madrid) [*A publication*]
Trab Inst Oceanogr Univ Recife ... Trabalhos. Instituto Oceanografico. Universidade do Recife [*A publication*]
Trab Investigacao 79 ... Trabalhos de Investigacao 79 [*A publication*]
Trab Investigacao 80 ... Trabalhos de Investigacao 80 [*A publication*]
Trab Lab Bioquim Quim Apl Inst Alonso Barba ... Trabajo. Laboratorio de Bioquimica y Quimica Aplicada. Instituto "Alonso Barba" [*A publication*]
Trab Oceanogr Univ Fed Pernambuco ... Trabalhos Oceanograficos. Universidade Federal de Pernambuco [*A publication*]
TRABOT... Terrier RADAR and Beacon Orientation Test (MUGU)
Trab Pesqui Inst Nutr Univ Bras ... Trabalhos e Pesquisas. Instituto de Nutricao. Universidade do Brasil [*A publication*]
Trab Pr Hist ... Trabajos de Prehistoria [*A publication*]
TRAC......... DTIC [*Defense Technical Information Center*] Technical Awareness Circular [*Information service or system*] (CRD)
TRAC......... Tandem Razor and Cartridge [*Gillette Co.*]
TRAC......... Target Research Analysis Center (CINC)
TRAC......... Tax Reform Action Coalition (EA)
TRAC......... Technical Reports Announcement Checklist
TRAC......... Telecommunications Research and Action Center [*Washington, DC*] [*Information service or system*] [*Telecommunications*] (TSSD)
TRAC......... Telescoping Rotor Aircraft Concept (MCD)
TRAC......... Test of Reading Affective Cues [*Psychology*]
TRAC......... Texas Reconfigurable Array Computer
TRAC......... Text Reckoning and Compiling [*Data processing*]
TRAC......... Textiles Research Advisory Committee [*Australia*]
TRAC......... Thermally Regenerative Alloy Cell
TRAC......... Tracer (AABC)
TRAC......... Tractor (AAG)
TRAC......... Trade Reform Action Coalition [*Washington, DC*] (EA)
TRAC......... TRADOC Analysis Command
TRAC......... Transaction Reporting and Control System (MCD)
TRAC......... Transient Radiation Analysis by Computer (KSC)
TRAC......... Transient Reactor Analysis Code (NRCH)
TRAC......... Transportation Account Code (AFM)
TrAC......... Trends in Analytical Chemistry [*A publication*]
TRACAB... Terminal RADAR Approach Control Cab [*Aviation*] (FAAC)
TRACAD... Training for [*US Military Academy*] Cadets (NVT)
TRACALS ... Traffic Control Approach and Landing System [*Aviation electronics*]
TRACAP... Transient Circuit Analysis Program [*Data processing*]
TRACC...... Target Review and Adjustment for Continuous Control (MCD)
TRACDR... Tractor-Drawn
TRACE...... Tactical Readiness and Checkout Equipment
TRACE...... Tactical Resources and Combat Effectiveness Model (MCD)
TRACE...... Tape-Controlled Recording Automatic Checkout Equipment [*Component of automatic pilot*] [*Aviation*]
TRACE...... Task Reporting and Current Evaluation
TRACE...... Taxiing and Routing of Aircraft Coordinating Equipment (MCD)
TRACE...... Taxiway Routing and Coordination Equipment [*Aviation*]
TRACE...... Technical Report Analysis, Condensation, Evaluation
TRACE...... Teleprocessing Recording for Analysis by the Customer (IEEE)

TRACE...... Test Equipment for Rapid Automatic Checkout and Evaluation [*Pan American Airways*]
TRACE...... Time-Shared Routines for Analysis, Classification, and Evaluation (DIT)
TRACE...... Tolls Recording and Computing Equipment (IEEE)
TRACE...... Toronto Region Aggregation of Computer Enthusiasts [*Canada*]
TRACE...... Total Resource Allocation Cost Estimating (RDA)
TRACE...... Total Risk Assessing Cost Estimate [*Army*] (RDA)
TRACE...... Trace Remote Atmospheric Chemical Evaluation [*National Center for Atmospheric Research*]
TRACE...... Track Retrieve and Account for Configuration of Equipment (MCD)
TRACE...... Tracking and Communications, Extraterrestrial
TRACE...... Traffic Routing and Control Equipment (MCD)
TRACE...... Trane Air Conditioning Economics [*The Trane Co.*]
TRACE...... Transistor Radio Automatic Circuit Evaluator
TRACE...... Transport and Atmospheric Chemistry Near the Equator
TRACE...... Transportable Automated Control Environment
Trace Anal ... Trace Analysis [*A publication*]
Trace & M ... Tracewell and Mitchell's United States Comptroller's Decisions [*A publication*] (DLA)
TRACEN... Training Center
TRACE-P.. Total Risk Assessing Cost Estimate - Production [*Army*] (RDA)
TRACERS ... Teleprocessed Record and Card Entry Reporting System (MCD)
Tracers Exogram Oil Gas Rev ... Tracer's Exogram and Oil and Gas Review [*A publication*]
TRACES.... Technology in Retrospect and Critical Events in Science [*IITRI*]
Trace Subst Environ Health ... Trace Substances in Environmental Health [*A publication*]
Trace Subst Environ Health Proc Univ Mo Annu Conf ... Trace Substances in Environmental Health. Proceedings. University of Missouri. Annual Conference [*A publication*]
TRACEX ... Amphibious Tractor Exercise [*Navy*] (NVT)
Tracey Evidence ... Tracey's Cases on Evidence [*A publication*] (DLA)
TRACH ..... Trachea [*or Tracheotomy*] [*Medicine*]
Trach.......... Trachiniae [*of Sophocles*] [*Classical studies*] (OCD)
TRACHY.. Tracheotomy (DSUE)
TRACINFO ... Tracer, Number as Indicated. Furnish Information Immediately or Advise
TRACIRS ... [*The*] Recording and Controlling of In-Transit Requisition System [*Army*]
TRACIS..... Traffic Records Criminal Justice Information System (OICC)
TRACKEX ... Tracking Exercise [*Navy*] (NVT)
Track Field Q Rev ... Track and Field Quarterly Review [*A publication*]
Track Tech ... Track Technique [*A publication*]
TRAC-MTRY ... TRADOC [*Training and Doctrine Command*] Analysis Command-Monterey [*California*] [*Army*] (GRD)
TRACOMDLANT ... Training Command, Atlantic Fleet [*Navy*]
TRACOMDPAC ... Training Command, Pacific Fleet [*Navy*]
TRACOMDSUBPAC ... Training Command, Submarines, Pacific Fleet [*Navy*]
TRACOMDWESTCOAST ... Training Command, West Coast [*Navy*]
TRACOMP ... Tracking Comparison
TRACON .. Terminal RADAR Control [*FAA*]
TRACS...... Tool Record Accountability System [*NASA*] (NASA)
TRACS...... Travel Accounting Control System [*Citicorp Diners Club*]
TRACS...... Triangulation Ranging and Crossfix System [*Military*] (CAAL)
tract........... Traction
Tract Sel Khozmashiny ... Tractory i Sel Khozmashiny [*A publication*]
Tracts Math Nat Sci ... Tracts in Mathematics and Natural Science [*A publication*]
TRACY...... Technical Reports Automated Cataloging - Yes [*National Oceanic and Atmospheric Administration*]
TRAD .... Terminal RADAR [*Aviation*] (FAAC)
Trad .... Traditio [*A publication*]
TRAD .... Tradition
TRAD .... Traditional Industries, Inc. [*NASDAQ symbol*] (NQ)
TRADA ..... Timber Research and Development Association [*United Kingdom*] [*Research center*] (IRC)
TRADAC... Trajectory Determination and Acquisition Computation
TRADAD .. Trace to Destination and Advise [*Military*]
TrADAT.... (Triazolyl-Azo) diaminotoluene [*Organic chemistry*]
TRADCOM ... Transportation Corps Research and Development Command [*Army*]
Trad Dep Exploit Util Bois Univ Laval ... Traduction. Departement d'Exploitation et Utilisation des Bois. Universite Laval [*A publication*]
TRADE...... Tracking RADAR Angle Deception Equipment (NG)
TRADE...... Training Devices (RDA)
Trade Cas .. Trade Cases [*Commerce Clearing House*] [*A publication*] (DLA)
Trade Cas CCH ... Trade Cases. Commerce Clearing House [*A publication*]
Trade and Commer ... Trade and Commerce [*A publication*]
Trade Commod Mark Summaries C Exports ... Trade by Commodities. Market Summaries. Series C. Exports [*A publication*]
Trade Commod Mark Summaries C Imports ... Trade by Commodities. Market Summaries. Series C. Imports [*A publication*]
Trade D...... Trade Digest [*A publication*] (APTA)

Trade Dig... Trade Digest [*A publication*] (APTA)
Trade Ind ... Trade and Industry [*A publication*]
Trade and Ind ... Trade and Industry [*A publication*]
Trade Ind Bul ... Trade and Industry Bulletin [*A publication*]
Trademark Bull ... Bulletin. United States Trademark Association Series [*A publication*] (DLA)
Trademark Bull (NS) ... Trademark Bulletin. United States Trademark Association (New Series) [*New York*] [*A publication*] (DLA)
Trade-Mark Rep ... Trade-Mark Reporter [*A publication*]
Trademark Rptr ... Trademark Reporter [*A publication*]
Trade Mks J ... Trade Marks Journal [*A publication*]
Trade News N ... Trade News North [*A publication*]
Trade R ...... Trade Review. Swedish Chamber of Commerce for Australia [*A publication*] (APTA)
TRADER... Training Devices Requirements Office [*TRADOC*] (MCD)
TRADER... Transient Radiation Effects Recorder (MCD)
Trade Reg Rep ... Trade Regulation Reporter [*Commerce Clearing House*] [*A publication*] (DLA)
Trade Reg Rep CCH ... Trade Regulation Reporter. Commerce Clearing House [*A publication*]
Trade Reg Rev ... Trade Regulation Review [*A publication*] (DLA)
TRADES ... TRADOC Data Evaluation Study (MCD)
Trades Union D ... Trades Union Digest [*A publication*] (APTA)
TRADET... Training Detachment [*Navy*]
TRADEVCO ... Trading & Development Bank Ltd. [*Liberia*]
Tra Devel Aust ... Training and Development in Australia [*A publication*]
TRADEVMAN ... Training Devices Man [*Navy rating*]
TRADEX... Target Resolution and Discrimination Experiment [*ARPA*]
TRADEX... Trade Data Element Exchange
Trad Greec ... Trade with Greece [*A publication*]
TRADIC... Transistorized Airborne Digital Computer [*Air Force*]
TRADIS ... Tape Repeating Automatic Data Integration System
TRADIS .... Tropical Resources for Agricultural Development Information System [*Overseas Development Natural Resources Institute*] [*Great Britain*] [*Information service or system*] (IID)
Traditional Kent Bldgs ... Traditional Kent Buildings [*A publication*]
Trad Mus... Traditional Music [*A publication*]
TRADOC .. Training and Doctrine Command [*Army*]
TRADOC-R .. Training and Doctrine Command Regulation [*Army*]
TRADSTAT ... World Trade Statistics Database [*Data-Star*] [*Great Britain*] [*Information service or system*] (IID)
Trad Un Dig ... Trades Union Digest [*A publication*]
TRAE......... Transport Airlift Estimator [*Air Force*]
TRAEA...... Technical Report Series. IAEA [*International Atomic Energy Agency*] [*A publication*]
TRAEX...... Training and Experience [*Military*] (AFM)
TRAF......... Traffic
TRAFCO... Television, Radio and Film Communications [*of the Methodist Church*]
TRAFF ...... Traffic (ROG)
Traff Cas.... Railway, Canal, and Road Traffic Cases [*A publication*] (DLA)
Traff Educ ... Traffic Education [*A publication*]
Traff Engng ... Traffic Engineering [*A publication*]
Traff Engng Control ... Traffic Engineering and Control [*A publication*]
TRAFFIC .. Trade Records Analysis of Flora and Fauna in Commerce [*An association*]
Traffic Dig Rev ... Traffic Digest and Review [*A publication*]
Traffic Eng ... Traffic Engineering [*A publication*]
Traffic Eng Contr ... Traffic Engineering and Control [*A publication*]
Traffic Eng & Control ... Traffic Engineering and Control [*A publication*]
Traffic Manage ... Traffic Management [*A publication*]
Traffic Q .... Traffic Quarterly [*A publication*]
Traffic Qly ... Traffic Quarterly [*A publication*]
Traffic Saf ... Traffic Safety [*A publication*]
Traffic Saf Res Rev ... Traffic Safety Research Review [*A publication*]
Traff Q .... Traffic Quarterly [*A publication*]
TRAFOLPERS ... Transfer Following Enlisted Personnel
TRAG .... Traffic Responsive Advance Green [*Control strategy*]
TRAG .... Tragedy
Trag .... Tragoedopodagra [*of Lucian*] [*Classical studies*] (OCD)
TRAGB...... Trudy po Radiatsionnoi Gigiene Leningradskii Nauchno-Issledovatel'skii Institut Radiatsionnoi Gigieny [*A publication*]
TRAI......... Tackle Representatives Association International [*Later, TSSAA*] (EA)
TRAIB .... Trudy Astrofizicheskogo Instituta Akademiya Nauk Kazakhskoi SSR [*A publication*]
TRAIF ...... Torso Restraint Assembly with Integrated Flotation
TRAIN...... Telerail Automated Information Network [*Association of American Railroads*]
TRAIN...... To Restore American Independence Now [*An association*]
TRAIN...... Tourist Railway Association, Inc. (EA)
Train .... Training [*A publication*]
train........... Training
Train Agric Rural Dev ... Training for Agriculture and Rural Development [*A publication*]
TRAINBASEFOR ... Training Base Force, Pacific Fleet [*Navy*]
TRAINCON ... Training Conference (MCD)

Train Dev Aust ... Training and Development in Australia [*A publication*] (APTA)
Train & Devel J ... Training and Development Journal [*A publication*]
Train Dev J ... Training and Development Journal [*A publication*]
TRAINDIV ... Training Division [*Canadian Navy*]
Training & Dev J ... Training and Development Journal [*A publication*]
TRAINLANT ... Training Atlantic Fleet [*Navy*]
Train Off.... Training Officer [*A publication*]
TRAINPACHQ ... Training Group Pacific Headquarters [*Canadian Navy*]
TRAINRON ... Training Squadron [*Later, SERRON*] [*Navy*]
Train Sch B ... Training School Bulletin [*A publication*]
TRA INT'L ... Tackle Representatives Association International [*Later, TSSAA*] (EA)
TRAIS .... Transportation Research Activities Information Service [*Department of Transportation*]
Traite du Mar ... Pothier's Traite du Contrat de Mariage [*A publication*] (DLA)
Trait Surf... Traitements de Surface [*A publication*]
Trait Therm ... Traitement Thermique [*A publication*]
TRAJ .... Trajectory (AAG)
Tr Akad Med Nauk SSSR ... Trudy Akademii Meditsinskikh Nauk SSSR [*A publication*]
Tr Akad Nauk Gruz SSR Inst Sist Upr ... Trudy Akademii Nauk Gruzinskoi SSR Institut Sistem Upravleniya [*A publication*]
Tr Akad Nauk Kaz SSR Inst Mikrobiol Virusol ... Trudy Akademiia Nauk Kazakhskoi SSR Institut Mikrobiologii i Virusologii [*A publication*]
Tr Akad Nauk Latv SSR Inst Mikrobiol ... Trudy Akademii Nauk Latviiskoi SSR Institut Mikrobiologii [*A publication*]
Tr Akad Nauk Litov SSR Inst Biol ... Trudy Akademii Nauk Litovskoi SSR Institut Biologii [*A publication*]
Tr Akad Nauk Lit SSR Ser V ... Trudy Akademii Nauk Litovskoi SSR. Seriya V [*A publication*]
Tr Akad Nauk Lit SSR Ser V Biol Nauki ... Trudy Akademii Nauk Litovskoi SSR. Seriya V. Biologicheskie Nauki [*A publication*]
Tr Akad Nauk SSSR Inst Biol Vnutr Vod ... Trudy Akademiia Nauk SSSR Institut Biologii Vnutrennikh Vod [*A publication*]
Tr Akad Nauk SSSR Karel Fil ... Trudy Akademii Nauk SSSR Karel'skii Filial [*A publication*]
Tr Akad Nauk SSSR Sibirsk Otd Biol Inst ... Trudy Akademiia Nauk SSSR Sibirskoe Otdelenie. Biologicheskii Institut [*A publication*]
Tr Akad Nauk Tadzh SSR ... Trudy Akademii Nauk Tadzhikskoi SSR [*A publication*]
Tr Akad Nauk Turkm SSR ... Trudy Akademii Nauk Turkmenskoi SSR [*A publication*]
Tr Akad Neft Promsti ... Trudy Akademiya Neftyanoi Promyslennosti [*A publication*]
Tr Akad Stroit Arkhit SSSR Zapadno Sib Fil ... Trudy Akademiya Stroitel'stva i Arkhitektury SSSR Zapadno-Sibirskii Filial [*A publication*]
Trak Sel'khozmashiny ... Traktory i Sel'khozmashiny [*USSR*] [*A publication*]
Trakt Landmasch ... Traktor und die Landmaschine [*A publication*]
TRAK TROL ... Trackless Trolley [*Freight*]
Trakt Sel'khozmash ... Traktory i Sel'khozmashiny [*A publication*]
TRALA...... Truck Renting and Leasing Association (EA)
TRALANT ... Fleet Training Command, Atlantic [*Navy*]
TRALINET ... TRADOC Library Information Network (MCD)
Tr Alma At Gos Med Inst ... Trudy Alma Atinskii Gosudarstvennyi Meditsinskii Institut [*A publication*]
Tr Alma-At Med Inst ... Trudy Alma-Atinskogo Meditsinskogo Instituta [*A publication*]
Tr Alma At Nauchno Issled Proektn Inst Stroit Mater ... Trudy Alma-Atinskogo Nauchno-Issledovatel'skogo i Proektnogo Instituta Stroitel'nykh Materialov [*A publication*]
Tr Alma-At Zoovet Inst ... Trudy Alma-Atinskogo Zooveterinarnogo Instituta [*A publication*]
Tr Altai Gorno Metall Nauchno Issled Inst Akad Nauk Kaz SSR ... Trudy Altaiskogo Gorno-Metallurgicheskogo Nauchno-Issledovatel'skogo Instituta Akademiya Nauk Kazakhskoi SSR [*A publication*]
Tr Altai Politekh Inst ... Trudy Altaiskogo Politekhnicheskogo Instituta [*A publication*]
Tr Altai Skh Inst ... Trudy Altaiskogo Sel'skokhozyaistvennogo Instituta [*A publication*]
TRAM .... Target Recognition Attack Multisensor [*DoD*]
TRAM .... Tensioned Replacement Alongside Method (MCD)
TRAM .... Test Reliability and Maintenance Program [*Navy*] (NVT)
TRAM .... Tracking RADAR Automatic Monitoring (AFM)
TRAM .... Training Readiness Analysis Monitor (MCD)
Tr Am Acad Ophth ... Transactions. American Academy of Ophthalmology and Otolaryngology [*A publication*]
Tr Am Ass Genito-Urin Surg ... Transactions. American Association of Genito-Urinary Surgeons [*A publication*]
Tr Am Fish Soc ... Transactions. American Fisheries Society [*A publication*]
TRAMID... Training for [*US Naval Academy/Naval Reserve Officers Training Corps*] Midshipmen (NVT)
TRAMIS ... TRADOC [*Training and Doctrine Command*] Management Information System [*Army*]
TRAMIT ... Especialidades Farmaceuticas en Tramite de Registro [*Ministerio de Sanidad y Consumo*] [*Spain*] [*Information service or system*] (CRD)

Tr Am Micr Soc ... Transactions. American Microscopical Society [*A publication*]
Tr Am Neurol A ... Transactions. American Neurological Association [*A publication*]
TRAMOD ... Training Requirements Analysis Model (MCD)
Tr Am Ophth Soc ... Transactions. American Ophthalmological Society [*A publication*]
TRAMP..... Temperature Regulation and Monitor Panel
TRAMP..... Test Retrieval and Memory Print [*Data processing*]
TRAMP..... Time-Shared Relational Associative Memory Program [*Data processing*] (IEEE)
TRAMPCO ... Thioguanine, Rubidomycin [*Daunorubicin*], ara-C, Methotrexate, Prednisolone, Cyclophosphamide, Oncovin [*Vincristine*] [*Antineoplastic drug regimen*]
TRAMPCOL ... Thioguanine, Rubidomycin [*Daunorubicin*], ara-C, Methotrexate, Prednisolone, Cyclophosphamide, Oncovin [*Vincristine*], L-Asparaginase [*Antineoplastic drug regimen*]
TRAMPL .. TRADOC Master Priority List (MCD)
TRAMPS .. Temperature Regulator and Missile Power Supply
TRAMPS .. Traffic Measure and Path Search [*Telecommunications*] (TEL)
Tr Am Soc Artific Int Organs ... Transactions. American Society for Artificial Internal Organs [*A publication*]
Tr Am Soc Trop Med ... Transactions. American Society of Tropical Medicine [*A publication*]
Tr Amur Skh Opytn Stn ... Trudy Amurskoi Sel'skokhozyaistvennoi Opytnoi Stantsii [*A publication*]
TRAN .... Transaction
TRAN .... Transformer
TRAN .... Transient (AABC)
TRAN .... Transit
TRAN .... Transmit
TRAN .... Transport
TRANA ..... Transfusion [*Philadelphia*] [*A publication*]
TRANC ..... Transient Center [*Marine Corps*]
TRAND ..... Tone Reproduction and Neutral Determination [*Chart*] [*Printing technology*]
TRANDIR ... Translation Director (IEEE)
TRANET..... Tracking [*or Transit*] Network [*Navy*]
TRANET..... Transnational Network for Appropriate/Alternative Technologies
Tr Angarsk Fil Irkutsk Politekh Inst ... Trudy Angarskogo Filiala Irkutskogo Politekhnicheskogo Instituta [*A publication*]
TRAN-PRO ... Transaction Processing [*Data processing*]
Tranq .... De Tranquillitate Animi [*of Seneca the Younger*] [*Classical studies*] (OCD)
TRANQ..... Tranquillo [*Quietly*] [*Music*] (ROG)
TRANS...... Telemetry Redundancy Analyzer System
TRANS...... Transaction
Trans.......... Transactions. Institute of Professional Engineers [*New Zealand*] [*A publication*]
TRANS...... Transcript (ADA)
TRANS...... Transfer (AAG)
TRANS...... Transformer (AFM)
TRANS...... Transient (AFIT)
TRANS...... Transistor (ADA)
TRANS...... Transition (ROG)
TRANS...... Transitive
TRANS...... Transitory
TRANS...... Translation
Trans.......... Translator (DLA)
TRANS...... Transmission
TRANS...... Transmittance (AAG)
TRANS...... Transparent (MSA)
TRANS...... Transport [*or Transportation*] (AAG)
TRANS...... Transpose [*Proofreading*]
TRANS...... Transverse
TRANSA..... Transaction (MSA)
Trans AACE ... Transactions. American Association of Cost Engineers [*A publication*]
TRANSAC ... Transistorized Automatic Computer
Trans Acad Sci St Louis ... Transactions. Academy of Science of St. Louis [*A publication*]
Transact Am Phil Ass ... Transactions and Proceedings. American Philological Association [*A publication*]
Transact Cumb Ant ... Transactions. Cumberland and Westmorland Antiquarian and Archaeological Society [*A publication*]
Transact Dumfries ... Transactions. Dumfriesshire and Galloway Natural History and Antiquarian Society [*A publication*]
Transact Essex ... Essex Archaeology and History. The Transactions of the Essex Archaeological Society [*A publication*]
Transact Lond ... Transactions. London and Middlesex Archaeological Society [*A publication*]
Transact Roy Soc Canada ... Transactions. Royal Society of Canada [*A publication*]
Trans Act Soc Aust & NZ ... Transactions. Actuarial Society of Australia and New Zealand [*A publication*] (APTA)
Transact South Stafford ... Transactions. South Staffordshire Archaeological and Historical Society [*A publication*]
Trans Actuar Soc S Afr ... Transactions. Actuarial Society of South Africa [*A publication*]

Transact Worc ... Transactions. Worcestershire Archaeological Society [*A publication*]

Trans Agric Engng Soc (Tokyo) ... Transactions. Agricultural Engineering Society (Tokyo) [*A publication*]

Trans AIChE ... Transactions. AIChE [*American Institute of Chemical Engineers*] [*A publication*]

Trans AIME Metall Soc ... Transactions. AIME [*American Institute of Mining, Metallurgical, and Petroleum Engineers*] Metallurgical Society [*A publication*]

Trans All-India Inst Ment Health ... Transactions. All-India Institute of Mental Health [*A publication*]

Trans All Union Sci Res Inst Confect Ind ... Transactions. All-Union Scientific Research Institute of the Confectionery Industry [*A publication*]

Trans All Union Sci Res Inst Veg Oils Margarine ... Transactions. All-Union Scientific Research Institute for Vegetable Oils and Margarine [*A publication*]

Trans Am Acad Ophthalmol Oto-Laryngol ... Transactions. American Academy of Ophthalmology and Oto-Laryngology [*A publication*]

Trans Am Assoc Cost Eng ... Transactions. American Association of Cost Engineers [*A publication*]

Trans Am Assoc Genito-Urin Surg ... Transactions. American Association of Genito-Urinary Surgeons [*A publication*]

Trans Am Assoc Obstet Gynecol ... Transactions. American Association of Obstetricians and Gynecologists [*A publication*]

Trans Am Assoc Obstet Gynecol Abdom Surg ... Transactions. American Association of Obstetricians, Gynecologists, and Abdominal Surgeons [*A publication*]

Trans Am Brew Inst ... Transactions. American Brewing Institute [*A publication*]

Trans Am Broncho-Esophagol Assoc ... Transactions. American Broncho-Esophagological Association [*A publication*]

Trans Am Ceram Soc ... Transactions. American Ceramic Society [*A publication*]

Trans Am Clin Climatol Assoc ... Transactions. American Clinical and Climatological Association [*A publication*]

Trans Am Coll Cardiol ... Transactions. American College of Cardiology [*A publication*]

Trans Am Crystallogr Assoc ... Transactions. American Crystallographic Association [*A publication*]

Trans Am Electroch Soc ... Transactions. American Electrochemical Society [*A publication*]

Trans Am Entomol Soc (Phila) ... Transactions. American Entomological Society (Philadelphia) [*A publication*]

Trans Am Ent Soc ... Transactions. American Entomological Society [*A publication*]

Trans Amer Acad Ophthalmol Otolaryngol ... Transactions. American Academy of Ophthalmology and Otolaryngology [*A publication*]

Trans Amer Ass Cereal Chem ... Transactions. American Association of Cereal Chemists [*A publication*]

Trans Amer Electro-Chem Soc ... Transactions. American Electrochemical Society [*A publication*]

Trans Amer Foundrymen's Soc ... Transactions. American Foundrymen's Society [*A publication*]

Trans Amer Geophys Union ... Transactions. American Geophysical Union [*A publication*]

Trans Amer Math Soc ... Transactions. American Mathematical Society [*A publication*]

Trans Amer Microscop Soc ... Transactions. American Microscopical Society [*A publication*]

Trans Amer Nucl Soc ... Transactions. American Nuclear Society [*A publication*]

Trans Am Fisheries Soc ... Transactions. American Fisheries Society [*A publication*]

Trans Am Fish Soc ... Transactions. American Fisheries Society [*A publication*]

Trans Am Foundrymen's Assoc Q ... Transactions. American Foundrymen's Association [*Later, American Foundrymen's Society*]. Quarterly [*A publication*]

Trans Am Geophys Union ... Transactions. American Geophysical Union [*A publication*]

Trans Am Goiter Assoc ... Transactions. American Goiter Association [*A publication*]

Trans Am Gynecol Soc ... Transactions. American Gynecological Society [*A publication*]

Trans Am Inst Chem Eng ... Transactions. American Institute of Chemical Engineers [*A publication*]

Trans Am Inst Electr Eng ... Transactions. American Institute of Electrical Engineers [*A publication*]

Trans Am Inst Electr Eng Part 1 ... Transactions. American Institute of Electrical Engineers. Part 1. Communication and Electronics [*A publication*]

Trans Am Inst Electr Eng Part 2 ... Transactions. American Institute of Electrical Engineers. Part 2. Applications and Industry [*A publication*]

Trans Am Inst Electr Eng Part 3 ... Transactions. American Institute of Electrical Engineers. Part 3. Power Apparatus and Systems [*A publication*]

Trans Am Inst Ind Eng ... Transactions. American Institute of Industrial Engineers [*A publication*]

Trans Am Inst Min Eng ... Transactions. American Institute of Mining Engineers [*A publication*]

Trans Am Inst Min Metall Eng ... Transactions. American Institute of Mining and Metallurgical Engineers [*A publication*]

Trans Am Inst Min Metall Pet Eng ... Transactions. American Institute of Mining, Metallurgical, and Petroleum Engineers [*A publication*]

Trans Am Math Soc ... Transactions. American Mathematical Society [*A publication*]

Trans Am Microsc Soc ... Transactions. American Microscopical Society [*A publication*]

Trans Am Neurol Assoc ... Transactions. American Neurological Association [*A publication*]

Trans Am Nucl Soc ... Transactions. American Nuclear Society [*A publication*]

Trans Am Nucl Soc Suppl ... Transactions. American Nuclear Society. Supplement [*A publication*]

Trans Am Ophthalmol Soc ... Transactions. American Ophthalmological Society [*A publication*]

Trans Am Otol Soc ... Transactions. American Otological Society [*A publication*]

Trans Am Philos Soc ... Transactions. American Philosophical Society [*A publication*]

Trans Am Soc Agric Eng Gen Ed ... Transactions. American Society of Agricultural Engineers. General Edition [*A publication*]

Trans Am Soc Agric Engrs ... Transactions. American Society of Agricultural Engineers [*A publication*]

Trans Am Soc Agric Engrs Gen Edn ... Transactions. American Society of Agricultural Engineers. General Edition [*A publication*]

Trans Am Soc Artif Intern Organs ... Transactions. American Society for Artificial Internal Organs [*A publication*]

Trans Am Soc Art Int Org ... Transactions. American Society for Artificial Internal Organs [*A publication*]

Trans Am Soc Heat Air-Cond Eng ... Transactions. American Society of Heating and Air-Conditioning Engineers [*A publication*]

Trans Am Soc Met ... Transactions. American Society for Metals [*A publication*]

Trans Am Soc Ophthalmol Otolaryngol Allergy ... Transactions. American Society of Ophthalmologic and Otolaryngologic Allergy [*A publication*]

Trans Am Soc Steel Treat ... Transactions. American Society for Steel Treating [*A publication*]

Trans Am Ther Soc ... Transactions. American Therapeutic Society [*A publication*]

Trans Am Urol Assoc ... Transactions. American Urological Association [*A publication*]

Trans Ancient Monuments Soc ... Transactions. Ancient Monuments Society [*A publication*]

Trans Anglesey Antiq Soc Fld Club ... Transactions. Anglesey Antiquarian Society and Field Club [*A publication*]

Trans Ann Anthracite Conf Lehigh Univ ... Transactions. Annual Anthracite Conference of Lehigh University [*A publication*]

Trans Ann Meet Am Laryngol Assoc ... Transactions. Annual Meeting. American Laryngological Association [*A publication*]

Trans Annu Conf Can Nucl Soc ... Transactions. Annual Conference. Canadian Nuclear Society [*A publication*]

Trans Annu Meet Allen O Whipple Surg Soc ... Transactions. Annual Meeting. Allen O. Whipple Surgical Society [*A publication*]

Trans Annu Tech Conf Am Soc Qual Control ... Transactions. Annual Technical Conference. American Society for Quality Control [*A publication*]

Trans Annu Tech Conf ASQC ... Transactions. Annual Technical Conference. American Society for Quality Control [*A publication*]

Trans Annu Tech Conf Soc Vac Coaters ... Transactions. Annual Technical Conference. Society of Vacuum Coaters [*A publication*]

Trans Ap .... Transcript Appeals [*New York*] [*1867-68*] [*A publication*]   (DLA)

Trans App ... Transcript Appeals [*New York*] [*A publication*]   (DLA)

Trans Appeal R ... New York Transcript Appeals Reports [*A publication*]   (DLA)

Trans Architect Archaeol Soc Durham Northumberland ... Transactions. Architectural and Archaeological Society of Durham and Northumberland [*A publication*]

Trans Architect Inst Jpn ... Transactions. Architectural Institute of Japan [*A publication*]

Trans ASAE ... Transactions. ASAE [*American Society of Agricultural Engineers*] [*A publication*]

Trans ASME ... Transactions. American Society of Mechanical Engineers [*A publication*]

Trans ASME J Appl Mech ... Transactions. American Society of Mechanical Engineers. Journal of Applied Mechanics [*A publication*]

Trans ASME J Biomech Eng ... Transactions. ASME [*American Society of Mechanical Engineers*] Series K. Journal of Biomechanical Engineering [*A publication*]

Trans ASME J Biomech Engng ... Transactions. American Society of Mechanical Engineers. Journal of Biomechanical Engineering [*A publication*]

Trans ASME J Dyn Syst Meas & Control ... Transactions. American Society of Mechanical Engineers. Journal of Dynamic Systems Measurement and Control [*A publication*]

Trans ASME J Energy Resour Technol ... Transactions. American Society of Mechanical Engineers. Journal of Energy Resources Technology [*A publication*]

Trans ASME J Eng Gas Turbines Power ... Transactions. ASME [*American Society of Mechanical Engineers*] Journal of Engineering for Gas Turbines and Power [*A publication*]

Trans ASME J Eng Ind ... Transactions. ASME [*American Society of Mechanical Engineers*] Series B. Journal of Engineering for Industry [*A publication*]

Trans ASME J Eng Mater and Technol ... Transactions. ASME [*American Society of Mechanical Engineers*] Series H. Journal of Engineering Materials and Technology [*A publication*]

Trans ASME J Engng Ind ... Transactions. American Society of Mechanical Engineers. Journal of Engineering for Industry [*A publication*]

Trans ASME J Engng Mater & Technol ... Transactions. American Society of Mechanical Engineers. Journal of Engineering Materials and Technology [*A publication*]

Trans ASME J Engng Power ... Transactions. American Society of Mechanical Engineers. Journal of Engineering for Power [*A publication*]

Trans ASME J Eng Power ... Transactions. ASME [*American Society of Mechanical Engineers*] Series A. Journal of Engineering for Power [*A publication*]

Trans ASME J Fluids Eng ... Transactions. ASME [*American Society of Mechanical Engineers*] Series I. Journal of Fluids Engineering [*A publication*]

Trans ASME J Fluids Engng ... Transactions. American Society of Mechanical Engineers. Journal of Fluids Engineering [*A publication*]

Trans ASME J Heat Transfer ... Transactions. American Society of Mechanical Engineers. Journal of Heat Transfer [*A publication*]

Trans ASME J Lubr Technol ... Transactions. American Society of Mechanical Engineers. Journal of Lubrication Technology [*A publication*]

Trans ASME J Mech Des ... Transactions. American Society of Mechanical Engineers. Journal of Mechanical Design [*A publication*]

Trans ASME J Pressure Vessel Technol ... Transactions. American Society of Mechanical Engineers. Journal of Pressure Vessel Technology [*A publication*]

Trans ASME J Sol Energy Eng ... Transactions. ASME [*American Society of Mechanical Engineers*] Journal of Solar Energy Engineering [*A publication*]

Trans ASME J Sol Energy Engng ... Transactions. American Society of Mechanical Engineers. Journal of Solar Energy Engineering [*A publication*]

Trans ASME J Tribol ... Transactions. ASME [*American Society of Mechanical Engineers*] Journal of Tribology [*A publication*]

Trans ASME Ser A ... Transactions. ASME [*American Society of Mechanical Engineers*] Series A. Journal of Engineering for Power [*A publication*]

Trans ASME Ser A J Eng Power ... Transactions. ASME [*American Society of Mechanical Engineers*] Series A. Journal of Engineering for Power [*A publication*]

Trans ASME Ser B ... Transactions. ASME [*American Society of Mechanical Engineers*] Series B. Journal of Engineering for Industry [*A publication*]

Trans ASME Ser B J Eng Ind ... Transactions. ASME [*American Society of Mechanical Engineers*] Series B. Journal of Engineering for Industry [*A publication*]

Trans ASME Ser C ... Transactions. ASME [*American Society of Mechanical Engineers*] Series C. Journal of Heat Transfer [*A publication*]

Trans ASME Ser C J Heat Transfer ... Transactions. ASME [*American Society of Mechanical Engineers*] Series C. Journal of Heat Transfer [*A publication*]

Trans ASME Ser D ... Transactions. ASME [*American Society of Mechanical Engineers*] Series D [*A publication*]

Trans ASME Ser E ... Transactions. ASME [*American Society of Mechanical Engineers*] Series E. Journal of Applied Mechanics [*A publication*]

Trans ASME Ser E J Appl Mech ... Transactions. ASME [*American Society of Mechanical Engineers*] Series E. Journal of Applied Mechanics [*A publication*]

Trans ASME Ser F ... Transactions. ASME [*American Society of Mechanical Engineers*] Series F. Journal of Lubrication Technology [*A publication*]

Trans ASME Ser F J Lubr Technol ... Transactions. ASME [*American Society of Mechanical Engineers*] Series F. Journal of Lubrication Technology [*A publication*]

Trans ASME Ser G ... Transactions. ASME [*American Society of Mechanical Engineers*] Series G. Journal of Dynamic Systems. Measurement and Control [*A publication*]

Trans ASME Ser GJ Dynamic Systems ... Transactions. ASME [*American Society of Mechanical Engineers*] Series G. Journal of Dynamic Systems. Measurement and Control [*A publication*]

Trans ASME Ser G J Dynamic Systems Measurement and Control ... Transactions. ASME [*American Society of Mechanical Engineers*] Series G. Journal of Dynamic Systems. Measurement and Control [*A publication*]

Trans ASME Ser G J Dyn Syst Meas and Control ... Transactions. ASME [*American Society of Mechanical Engineers*] Series G. Journal of Dynamic Systems. Measurement and Control [*A publication*]

Trans ASME Ser H ... Transactions. ASME [*American Society of Mechanical Engineers*] Series H. Journal of Engineering Materials and Technology [*A publication*]

Trans ASME Ser H J Eng Mater and Technol ... Transactions. ASME [*American Society of Mechanical Engineers*] Series H. Journal of Engineering Materials and Technology [*A publication*]

Trans ASME Ser I ... Transactions. ASME [*American Society of Mechanical Engineers*] Series I. Journal of Fluids Engineering [*A publication*]

Trans ASME Ser I J Fluids Eng ... Transactions. ASME [*American Society of Mechanical Engineers*] Series I. Journal of Fluids Engineering [*A publication*]

Trans ASME Ser J J Pressure Vessel Technol ... Transactions. ASME [*American Society of Mechanical Engineers*] Series J. Journal of Pressure Vessel Technology [*A publication*]

Trans ASME Ser K ... Transactions. ASME [*American Society of Mechanical Engineers*] Series K [*A publication*]

Trans ASME Ser K J Biomech Eng ... Transactions. ASME [*American Society of Mechanical Engineers*] Series K. Journal of Biomechanical Engineering [*A publication*]

Trans Assoc Am Physicians ... Transactions. Association of American Physicians [*A publication*]

Trans Assoc Ind Med Off ... Transactions. Association of Industrial Medical Officers [*A publication*]

Trans Assoc Life Ins Med Dir Am ... Transactions. Association of Life Insurance Medical Directors of America [*A publication*]

Transatl R ... Transatlantic Review [*A publication*]

Trans Aust Coll Ophthalmol ... Transactions. Australian College of Ophthalmologists [*A publication*]

Trans B'ham Warwks Arch Soc ... Transactions. Birmingham and Warwickshire Archaeological Society [*A publication*]

Trans Biochem Soc ... Transactions. Biochemical Society [*A publication*]

Trans Birmingham Warwickshire Archaeol Soc ... Transactions. Birmingham and Warwickshire Archaeological Society [*A publication*]

Trans Bose Res Inst ... Transactions. Bose Research Institute [*A publication*]

Trans Bose Res Inst (Calcutta) ... Transactions. Bose Research Institute (Calcutta) [*A publication*]

Trans Bot Soc Edinb ... Transactions and Proceedings. Botanical Society of Edinburgh [*A publication*]

Trans Br Bryol Soc ... Transactions. British Bryological Society [*A publication*]

Trans Br Ceram Soc ... Transactions. British Ceramic Society [*A publication*]

Trans Bristol Gloucestershire Archaeol Soc ... Transactions. Bristol and Gloucestershire Archaeological Society [*A publication*]

Trans Bristol Gloucestershire Arch Soc ... Transactions. Bristol and Gloucestershire Archaeological Society [*A publication*]

Trans Brit Mycol Soc ... Transactions. British Mycological Society [*A publication*]

Trans Br Mycol Soc ... Transactions. British Mycological Society [*A publication*]

Trans Br Soc Hist Pharm ... Transactions. British Society for the History of Pharmacy [*A publication*]

Trans Br Soc Study Orthod ... Transactions. British Society for the Study of Orthodontics [*A publication*]

Transc A .... Transcript Appeals [*New York*] [*A publication*]   (DLA)

Trans Caernarvonshire Hist Soc ... Transactions. Caernarvonshire Historical Society [*A publication*]

Trans Cambridge Philos Soc ... Transactions. Cambridge Philosophical Society [*A publication*]

Trans Can Inst Mining Soc NS ... Transactions. Canadian Institute of Mining and Metallurgy and Mining Society of Nova Scotia [*A publication*]

Trans Can Inst Min Metall ... Transactions. Canadian Institute of Mining and Metallurgy and Mining Society of Nova Scotia [*A publication*]

Trans Can Inst Min Metall Min Soc NS ... Transactions. Canadian Institute of Mining and Metallurgy and Mining Society of Nova Scotia [*A publication*]

Trans Can Min Inst ... Transactions. Canadian Mining Institute [*A publication*]

Trans Can Nucl Soc ... Transactions. Canadian Nuclear Society [*A publication*]

Trans Can Soc Mech Eng ... Transactions. Canadian Society of Mechanical Engineers [*A publication*]

Trans Can Soc Mech Engrs ... Transactions. Canadian Society of Mechanical Engineers [*A publication*]

Trans Cardiff Nat Soc ... Transactions. Cardiff Naturalists Society [*A publication*]

Trans Cardiff Natur Soc ... Transactions. Cardiff Naturalists Society [*A publication*]

Trans Cave Res Group GB ... Transactions. Cave Research Group of Great Britain [*A publication*]

TRANSCEIVER ... Transmitter-Receiver　(NATG)

Trans Cent Sci Res Inst Confect Ind ... Transactions. Central Scientific Research Institute of the Confectionery Industry [*A publication*]

Trans Ceylon Coll ... Transactions. Ceylon College of Physicians [*A publication*]

Trans Chalmers Univ Technol (Gothenburg) ... Transactions. Chalmers University of Technology (Gothenburg) [*Sweden*] [*A publication*]

Trans Chem Div Am Soc Qual Control ... Transactions. Chemical Division. American Society for Quality Control [*A publication*]

Trans Chin Assoc Adv Sci ... Transactions. Chinese Association for the Advancement of Science [*A publication*]

Trans Citrus Eng Conf ... Transactions. Citrus Engineering Conference [*A publication*]

Trans Coll Med S Afr ... Transactions. College of Medicine of South Africa [*A publication*]

Trans Coll Physicians Philadelphia ... Transactions. College of Physicians of Philadelphia [*A publication*]

TRANSCOM ... Transportable Communications

TRANSCON ... Transcontinental　(MCD)

Trans Conf Cold Inj ... Transactions. Conference on Cold Injury [*A publication*]

Trans Conf Glaucoma ... Transactions. Conference on Glaucoma [*A publication*]

Trans Conf Group Processes ... Transactions. Conference on Group Processes [*A publication*]

Trans Conf Group Soc Adm Hist ... Transactions. Conference Group for Social and Administrative History [*A publication*]

Trans Conf Neuropharmacol ... Transactions. Conference on Neuropharmacology [*A publication*]

Trans Conf Physiol Prematurity ... Transactions. Conference on Physiology of Prematurity [*A publication*]

Trans Conf Polysaccharides Biol ... Transactions. Conference on Polysaccharides in Biology [*A publication*]

Trans Conn Acad Arts Sci ... Transactions. Connecticut Academy of Arts and Sciences [*A publication*]

Trans Corn Inst Eng ... Transactions. Cornish Institute of Engineers [*A publication*]

TRANSCR ... Transcribed

Transcr A ... Transcript Appeals [*New York*] [*A publication*]　(DLA)

TRANSCRON ... Transcription　(ROG)

Trans C S Peirce Soc ... Transactions. C. S. Peirce Society [*A publication*]

Transcult Psychiat Res ... Transcultural Psychiatric Research Review [*A publication*]

Trans Cumberland Westmorland Antiq Archaeol Soc N Ser ... Transactions. Cumberland and Westmorland Antiquarian and Archaeological Society. New Series [*A publication*]

TRANSDEC ... SONAR Transducer Test and Evaluation Center, Naval Electronics Laboratory [*San Diego, CA*] [*Navy*]

TRANSDEF ... Transducer Evaluation Facility

Trans Denbighshire Hist Soc ... Transactions. Denbighshire Historical Society [*A publication*]

Trans Desert Bighorn Counc ... Transactions. Desert Bighorn Council [*A publication*]

TRANSDIV ... Transport Division [*Navy*]

Transducer Technol ... Transducer Technology [*A publication*]

Trans Dumfries Galloway Nat Hist Antiq Soc ... Transactions. Dumfriesshire and Galloway Natural History and Antiquarian Society [*A publication*]

Trans Dumfriesshire Galloway Natur Hist Antiq Soc ... Transactions. Dumfriesshire and Galloway Natural History and Antiquarian Society [*A publication*]

Trans Dumfriesshire Galloway Natur Hist Ant Soc ... Transactions. Dumfriesshire and Galloway Natural History and Antiquarian Society [*A publication*]

Trans Dynam Dev ... Transactions. Dynamics of Development [*A publication*]

Trans East Lothian Antiq Field Nat Soc ... Transactions. East Lothian Antiquarian and Field Naturalists' Society [*A publication*]

TRANSEC ... Transmission Security [*Communications*]

Trans Econ & Oper Anal ... Transport Economics and Operational Analysis [*A publication*]　(APTA)

TRANSED ... Transition Education

Trans Edinb Geol Soc ... Transactions. Edinburgh Geological Society [*A publication*]

Trans Edinburgh Geol Soc ... Transactions. Edinburgh Geological Society [*A publication*]

Trans Electrochem Soc ... Transactions. Electrochemical Society [*A publication*]

Trans Electr Supply Auth Eng Inst NZ ... Transactions. Electric Supply Authority Engineers' Institute of New Zealand, Inc. [*A publication*]

Trans Electr Supply Eng Inst ... Transactions. Annual Conference. Electric Supply Authority Engineers' Institute of New Zealand, Inc.

Trans E Lothian Antiq Fld Natur Soc ... Transactions. East Lothian Antiquarian and Field Naturalists' Society [*A publication*]

Trans Eng Inst Can ... Transactions. Engineering Institute of Canada [*A publication*]

Trans Engl Ceram Circle ... Transactions. English Ceramic Circle [*A publication*]

Trans Engl Ceram Soc ... Transactions. English Ceramic Society [*A publication*]

Trans Essex Arch Soc ... Transactions. Essex Archaeological Society [*A publication*]

Trans Est Agric Acad ... Transactions. Estonian Agricultural Academy [*A publication*]

Trans Eur Orthod Soc ... Transactions. European Orthodontic Society [*A publication*]

TRANSF ... Transferred

TRANSF ... Transformer　(AAG)

Trans Fac Hortic Chiba Univ ... Transactions. Faculty of Horticulture. Chiba University [*A publication*]

Trans Farady Soc ... Transactions. Faraday Society [*A publication*]

TRANSFAX ... Facsimile Transmission [*Telecommunications*]

TRANSFD ... Transferred　(ROG)

Trans Fed-Prov Wildl Conf ... Transactions. Federal-Provincial Wildlife Conference [*A publication*]

TRANSFIG ... Transfiguration

TRANSFLTNG ... Transitional Flight Training　(NVT)

TRANSFORM ... Trade-Off Analysis - Systems/Force Mix Analysis [*Military*]

Transform (Papeterie) ... Transformation (Supplement to La Papeterie) [*A publication*]

Trans Geol Soc Glasg ... Transactions. Geological Society of Glasgow [*A publication*]

Trans Geol Soc S Afr ... Transactions. Geological Society of South Africa [*A publication*]

Trans Geotherm Resour Counc ... Transactions. Geothermal Resources Council [*United States*] [*A publication*]

Trans Glasgow Univ Orient Soc ... Transactions. Glasgow University Oriental Society [*A publication*]

Trans Greenwich Lewisham Antiq Soc ... Transactions. Greenwich and Lewisham Antiquarian Society [*A publication*]

TRANSGRPPHIBFOR ... Transportation Group Amphibious Forces [*Navy*]

TRANSGRPSOPAC ... Transport Group, South Pacific Force [*Navy*]

Trans Gulf Coast Ass Geol Soc ... Transactions. Gulf Coast Association of Geological Societies [*A publication*]

Trans Gulf Coast Assoc Geol Soc ... Transactions. Gulf Coast Association of Geological Societies [*A publication*]

Trans Gulf Coast Mol Biol Conf ... Transactions. Gulf Coast Molecular Biology Conference [*A publication*]

Trans Halifax Antiq Society ... Transactions. Halifax Antiquarian Society [*A publication*]

Trans Hawick Archaeol Soc ... Transactions. Hawick Archaeological Society [*A publication*]

Trans Hertfordshire Nat Hist Field Club ... Transactions. Hertfordshire Natural History Society and Field Club [*A publication*]

Trans Hertfordshire Nat Hist Soc Field Club ... Transactions. Hertfordshire Natural History Society and Field Club [*A publication*]

Trans Highl Agric Soc Scotl ... Transactions. Highland and Agricultural Society of Scotland [*A publication*]

Trans Hist Soc Ghana ... Transactions. Historical Society of Ghana [*A publication*]

Trans Hist Soc Lancashire Cheshire ... Transactions. Historic Society of Lancashire and Cheshire [*A publication*]

Trans Hunter Archaeol Soc ... Transactions. Hunter Archaeological Society [*A publication*]

Trans Hunter Soc ... Transactions. Hunterian Society [*A publication*]

Trans ILA ... Transactions. International Law Association [*1873-1924*] [*A publication*]　(DLA)

Trans Illinois State Acad Sci ... Illinois State Academy of Science. Transactions [*A publication*]

Trans Ill St Acad Sci ... Transactions. Illinois State Academy of Science [*A publication*]

Trans Ill State Acad Sci ... Transactions. Illinois State Academy of Science [*A publication*]

Trans Ill State Hortic Soc ... Transactions. Illinois State Horticultural Society [*A publication*]

Trans Ill State Hortic Soc Ill Fruit Counc ... Transactions. Illinois State Horticultural Society and the Illinois Fruit Council [*A publication*]

Trans Ill St Hort Soc ... Transactions. Illinois State Horticultural Society [*A publication*]

Trans Illum Eng Soc ... Transactions. Illuminating Engineering Society [*A publication*]

TRANSIM ... Transit Simplified Receiver [*Satellite navigation system*]

Trans I Mar E ... Transactions. Institute of Marine Engineers [*A publication*]

Trans Indiana Acad Ophthalmol Otolaryngol ... Transactions. Indiana Academy of Ophthalmology and Otolaryngology [*A publication*]

Trans Indian Ceram Soc ... Transactions. Indian Ceramic Society [*A publication*]

Trans Indian Inst Chem Eng ... Transactions. Indian Institute of Chemical Engineers [*A publication*]

Trans Indian Inst Met ... Transactions. Indian Institute of Metals [*A publication*]

Trans Indian Inst Metals ... Transactions. Indian Institute of Metals [*A publication*]

Trans Indian Soc Desert Technol Univ Cent Desert Stud ... Transactions. Indian Society of Desert Technology and University Centre of Desert Studies [*A publication*]

Trans Ind Inst Chem Eng ... Transactions. Indian Institute of Chemical Engineers [*A publication*]

Trans Inf Process Soc Jpn ... Transactions. Information Processing Society of Japan [*A publication*]

Trans Inst Act Aust & NZ ... Transactions. Institute of Actuaries of Australia and New Zealand [*A publication*] (APTA)

Trans Inst Br Geogr New Ser ... Transactions. Institute of British Geographers. New Series [*A publication*]

Trans Inst Brit Geogr ... Transactions. Institute of British Geographers [*A publication*]

Trans Inst Chem Eng ... Transactions. Institution of Chemical Engineers [*A publication*]

Trans Inst Chem Eng (London) ... Transactions. Institution of Chemical Engineers (London) [*A publication*]

Trans Inst Chem Engrs ... Transactions. Institution of Chemical Engineers [*A publication*]

Trans Inst Civ Eng Ir ... Transactions. Institution of Civil Engineers of Ireland [*A publication*]

Trans Inst Electr Eng Jap ... Transactions. Institute of Electrical Engineers of Japan [*A publication*]

Trans Inst Electr Eng Jap Overseas Ed ... Transactions. Institute of Electrical Engineers of Japan. Overseas Edition [*A publication*]

Trans Inst Electr Eng Jpn ... Transactions. Institute of Electrical Engineers of Japan [*A publication*]

Trans Inst Electr Eng Jpn B ... Transactions. Institute of Electrical Engineers of Japan. Part B [*A publication*]

Trans Inst Electr Eng Jpn C ... Transactions. Institute of Electrical Engineers of Japan. Part C [*A publication*]

Trans Inst Electr Eng Jpn Part A ... Transactions. Institute of Electrical Engineers of Japan. Part A [*A publication*]

Trans Inst Electr Eng Jpn Part B ... Transactions. Institute of Electrical Engineers of Japan. Part B [*A publication*]

Trans Inst Electr Eng Jpn Part C ... Transactions. Institute of Electrical Engineers of Japan. Part C [*A publication*]

Trans Inst Electr Eng Jpn Sect E ... Transactions. Institute of Electrical Engineers of Japan. Section E [*A publication*]

Trans Inst Electron & Commun Eng Jap A ... Transactions. Institute of Electronics and Communication Engineers of Japan. Part A [*A publication*]

Trans Inst Electron & Commun Eng Jap B ... Transactions. Institute of Electronics and Communication Engineers of Japan. Part B [*A publication*]

Trans Inst Electron & Commun Eng Jap C ... Transactions. Institute of Electronics and Communication Engineers of Japan. Part C [*A publication*]

Trans Inst Electron & Commun Eng Jap D ... Transactions. Institute of Electronics and Communication Engineers of Japan. Part D [*A publication*]

Trans Inst Electron Commun Eng Jap Sect J Part A ... Transactions. Institute of Electronics and Communication Engineers of Japan. Section J. Part A [*A publication*]

Trans Inst Electron Commun Eng Jap Sect J Part C ... Transactions. Institute of Electronics and Communication Engineers of Japan. Section J. Part C [*A publication*]

Trans Inst Electron Commun Eng Jap Sect J Part D ... Transactions. Institute of Electronics and Communication Engineers of Japan. Section J [*Japanese*] Part D [*A publication*]

Trans Inst Electron and Commun Eng Jpn Part A ... Transactions. Institute of Electronics and Communication Engineers of Japan. Part A [*A publication*]

Trans Inst Electron and Commun Eng Jpn Part B ... Transactions. Institute of Electronics and Communication Engineers of Japan. Part B [*A publication*]

Trans Inst Electron Commun Eng Jpn Part B ... Transactions. Institute of Electronics and Communication Engineers of Japan. Part B [*A publication*]

Trans Inst Electron and Commun Eng Jpn Part C ... Transactions. Institute of Electronics and Communication Engineers of Japan. Part C [*A publication*]

Trans Inst Electron and Commun Eng Jpn Part D ... Transactions. Institute of Electronics and Communication Engineers of Japan. Part D [*A publication*]

Trans Inst Electron and Commun Eng Jpn Sect E ... Transactions. Institute of Electronics and Communication Engineers of Japan. Section E [*A publication*]

Trans Inst Electron Commun Eng Jpn Sect E (Engl) ... Transactions. Institute of Electronics and Communication Engineers of Japan. Section E (English) [*A publication*]

Trans Inst Eng Aust ... Transactions. Institution of Engineers of Australia [*A publication*]

Trans Inst Eng Aust Civ Eng ... Transactions. Institution of Engineers of Australia. Civil Engineering [*A publication*]

Trans Inst Eng Aust Electr Eng ... Transactions. Institution of Engineers of Australia. Electrical Engineering [*A publication*]

Trans Inst Eng Aust Mech Eng ... Transactions. Institution of Engineers of Australia. Mechanical Engineering [*A publication*]

Trans Inst Engrs Aust Civ Engng ... Transactions. Institution of Engineers of Australia. Civil Engineering [*A publication*]

Trans Inst Engrs Aust Mech Engng ... Transactions. Institution of Engineers of Australia. Mechanical Engineering [*A publication*]

Trans Inst Eng Shipbuilders Scot ... Transactions. Institution of Engineers and Shipbuilders in Scotland [*A publication*]

Trans Inst Gas Eng ... Transactions. Institution of Gas Engineers [*England*] [*A publication*]

Trans Inst Mar Eng ... Transactions. Institute of Marine Engineers [*A publication*]

Trans Inst Mar Eng Conf Pap ... Transactions. Institute of Marine Engineers. Conference Papers [*A publication*]

Trans Inst Mar Engrs ... Transactions. Institute of Marine Engineers [*A publication*]

Trans Inst Mar Eng Ser C ... Transactions. Institute of Marine Engineers. Series C [*A publication*]

Trans Inst Mar Eng Tech Meet Pap ... Transactions. Institute of Marine Engineers. Technical Meeting Papers [*A publication*]

Trans Inst Marine Eng ... Transactions. Institute of Marine Engineers [*A publication*]

Trans Inst Meas & Control ... Transactions. Institute of Measurement and Control [*A publication*]

Trans Inst Meas Control ... Transactions. Institute of Measurement and Control [*A publication*]

Trans Inst Measmt Control ... Transactions. Institute of Measurement and Control [*A publication*]

Trans Inst Met Finish ... Transactions. Institute of Metal Finishing [*A publication*]

Trans Inst Min Eng ... Transactions. Institution of Mining Engineers [*A publication*]

Trans Inst Mining Met Sect A ... Transactions. Institution of Mining and Metallurgy. Section A. Mining Industry [*A publication*]

Trans Inst Mining Met Sect B ... Transactions. Institution of Mining and Metallurgy. Section B. Applied Earth Science [*A publication*]

Trans Inst Mining Met Sect C ... Transactions. Institution of Mining and Metallurgy. Section C [*A publication*]

Trans Inst Min Metall ... Transactions. Institution of Mining and Metallurgy [*A publication*]

Trans Inst Min Metall (Ostrava) Min Geol Ser ... Transactions. Institute of Mining and Metallurgy (Ostrava). Mining and Geological Series [*A publication*]

Trans Inst Min Metall Sec A ... Transactions. Institution of Mining and Metallurgy. Section A. Mining Industry [*A publication*]

Trans Inst Min Metall Sec B ... Transactions. Institution of Mining and Metallurgy. Section B. Applied Earth Science [*A publication*]

Trans Inst Min Metall Sec C ... Transactions. Institution of Mining and Metallurgy. Section C [*United Kingdom*] [*A publication*]

Trans Inst Min Metall Sect A Min Ind ... Transactions. Institution of Mining and Metallurgy. Section A. Mining Industry [*A publication*]

Trans Inst Min Metall Sect B Appl Earth Sci ... Transactions. Institution of Mining and Metallurgy. Section B. Applied Earth Science [*United Kingdom*] [*A publication*]

Trans Instn Chem Engrs ... Transactions. Institution of Chemical Engineers [*A publication*]

Trans Instn E Shipb Scot ... Transactions. Institution of Engineers and Shipbuilders in Scotland [*A publication*]

Trans Instn Min Metall ... Transactions. Institution of Mining and Metallurgy [*A publication*]

Trans Inst Plast Ind ... Transactions. Institute of the Plastics Industry [*A publication*]

Trans Inst Prof Eng ... Transactions. Institution of Professional Engineers of New Zealand [*A publication*]

Trans Inst Prof Eng NZ ... Transactions. Institution of Professional Engineers. New Zealand Civil Engineering Section [*A publication*]

Trans Inst Prof Eng NZ Civ Eng Sect ... Transactions. Institution of Professional Engineers of New Zealand. Civil Engineering Section [*A publication*]

Trans Inst Prof Eng NZ Electr Mech Chem Eng Sect ... Transactions. Institution of Professional Engineers of New Zealand. Electrical/Mechanical/Chemical Engineering Section [*A publication*]

Trans Inst Prof Eng NZ EMCh ... Transactions. Institution of Professional Engineers of New Zealand. Electrical/Mechanical/Chemical Engineering Section [*A publication*]

Trans Inst Pure Chem Reagents (Moscow) ... Transactions. Institute of Pure Chemical Reagents (Moscow) [*A publication*]

Trans Inst Rubber Ind ... Transactions. Institution of the Rubber Industry [*A publication*]

Trans Inst Water Eng ... Transactions. Institution of Water Engineers [*A publication*]

Trans Inst Weld (London) ... Transactions. Institute of Welding (London) [*A publication*]

Trans Int Assoc Math and Comput Simulation ... Transactions. International Association for Mathematics and Computers in Simulation [*A publication*]

Trans Int Astron Union ... Transactions. International Astronomical Union [*A publication*]

Trans Int Ceram Congr ... Transactions. International Ceramic Congress [*A publication*]

Trans Int Conf Endod ... Transactions. International Conference on Endodontics [*A publication*]

Trans Int Conf Oral Surg ... Transactions. International Conference on Oral Surgery [*A publication*]

Trans Int Conf Or Ja ... Transactions. International Conference of Orientalists in Japan [*A publication*]

Trans Int Conf Soil Sci ... Transactions. International Conference of Soil Science [*A publication*]

Trans Int Congr Agr Eng ... Transactions. International Congress of Agricultural Engineering [*A publication*]

Trans Int Congr Agric Engng ... Transactions. International Congress for Agricultural Engineering [*A publication*]

Trans Int Congr Entomol ... Transactions. International Congress of Entomology [*A publication*]

Trans Int Congr Soil Sci ... Transactions. International Congress of Soil Science [*A publication*]

Trans Intl... Journal pour le Transport International [*A publication*]

Trans Int Soc Geotherm Eng ... Transactions. International Society for Geothermal Engineering [*A publication*]

Trans Iowa State Hortic Soc ... Transactions. Iowa State Horticultural Society [*A publication*]

Trans Iowa St Hort Soc ... Transactions. Iowa State Horticultural Society [*A publication*]

Trans Iron Steel Inst Jap ... Transactions. Iron and Steel Institute of Japan [*A publication*]

Trans Iron Steel Inst Jpn ... Transactions. Iron and Steel Institute of Japan [*A publication*]

TRANSIS ... Transportation Safety Information System [*Department of Transportation*]   (IID)

TRANSISTOR ... Transfer Resistor

TRANSITEX ... Transit Exercise   (NVT)

Transition Met Chem ... Transition Metal Chemistry [*A publication*]

Transit J .... Transit Journal [*A publication*]

Transit L Rev ... Transit Law Review [*A publication*]

Transit Met Chem (Weinheim Ger) ... Transition Metal Chemistry (Weinheim, Germany) [*A publication*]

Transit Packag ... Transit Packaging [*A publication*]

Trans Japan Soc Civ Engrs ... Transactions. Japan Society of Civil Engineers [*A publication*]

Trans Japan Soc Compos Mater ... Transactions. Japan Society for Composite Materials [*A publication*]

Trans Japan Soc Mech Engrs Ser B ... Transactions. Japan Society of Mechanical Engineers. Series B [*A publication*]

Trans Japan Soc Mech Engrs Ser C ... Transactions. Japan Society of Mechanical Engineers. Series C [*A publication*]

Trans Jap Inst Met ... Transactions. Japan Institute of Metals [*A publication*]

Trans Jap Inst Metals ... Transactions. Japan Institute of Metals [*A publication*]

Trans Jap Soc Aeronaut Space Sci ... Transactions. Japan Society for Aeronautical and Space Sciences [*A publication*]

Trans Jap Soc Mech Eng ... Transactions. Japan Society of Mechanical Engineers [*A publication*]

Trans Jap Weld Soc ... Transactions. Japan Welding Society [*A publication*]

Trans J Br Ceram Soc ... Transactions and Journal. British Ceramic Society [*A publication*]

Trans and J Br Ceram Soc ... Transactions and Journal. British Ceramic Society [*A publication*]

Trans J Brit Ceram Soc ... Transactions and Journal. British Ceramic Society [*A publication*]

Trans J Plast Inst ... Transactions and Journal. Plastics Institute [*England*] [*A publication*]

Trans Jpn Inst Met ... Transactions. Japan Institute of Metals [*A publication*]

Trans Jpn Inst Met Suppl ... Transactions. Japan Institute of Metals. Supplement [*A publication*]

Trans Jpn Pathol Soc ... Transactions. Japanese Pathological Society [*A publication*]

Trans Jpn Soc Aeronaut and Space Sci ... Transactions. Japan Society for Aeronautical and Space Sciences [*A publication*]

Trans Jpn Soc Aeronaut Space Sci ... Transactions. Japan Society for Aeronautical and Space Sciences [*A publication*]

Trans Jpn Soc Civ Eng ... Transactions. Japan Society of Civil Engineers [*A publication*]

Trans Jpn Soc Irrig Drain Reclam Eng ... Transactions. Japanese Society of Irrigation Drainage and Reclamation Engineering [*A publication*]

Trans Jpn Soc Mech Eng Ser B ... Transactions. Japan Society of Mechanical Engineers. Series B [*A publication*]

Trans Jpn Weld Soc ... Transactions. Japan Welding Society [*A publication*]

Trans Jt Mtg Comm Int Soc Soil Sci ... Transactions. Joint Meeting of Commissions. International Society of Soil Science [*A publication*]

Trans JWRI ... Transactions. JWRI [*Japanese Welding Research Institute*] [*A publication*]

Trans K Acad Sci ... Transactions. Kentucky Academy of Science [*A publication*]

Trans Kans Acad Sci ... Transactions. Kansas Academy of Science [*A publication*]

Trans Kansai Ent Soc ... Transactions. Kansai Entomological Society [*A publication*]

Transkei Dev Rev ... Transkei Development Review [*A publication*]

Trans Koll Geneeskd S-Afr ... Transaksies. Kollege van Geneeskunde van Suid-Afrika [*A publication*]

Trans Korean Inst Electr Eng ... Transactions. Korean Institute of Electrical Engineers [*A publication*]

Trans Korean Soc Mech Eng ... Transactions. Korean Society of Mechanical Engineers [*Republic of Korea*] [*A publication*]

Trans KY Acad Sci ... Transactions. Kentucky Academy of Science [*A publication*]

TRANSL ... Translation   (AAG)

Trans Lancashire Cheshire Antiq Soc ... Transactions. Lancashire and Cheshire Antiquarian Society [*A publication*]

TRANSLANG ... Translator Language [*Data processing*]

TRANSLANT ... Transports, Atlantic Fleet [*Navy*]

TRANSLANTEX ... Transatlantic Training Exercise   (MCD)

Translat ..... Translation   (BJA)

Trans Latv Branch All Union Soc Soil Sci ... Transactions. Latvian Branch. All-Union Society of Soil Science [*A publication*]

Transl Beltone Inst Hear Res ... Translations. Beltone Institute for Hearing Research [*A publication*]

Transl Commonw Sci Industr Res Organ (Aust) ... Translation. Commonwealth Scientific and Industrial Research Organisation (CSIRO) (Australia) [*A publication*]

Transld Contents Lists Russ Period ... Translated Contents Lists of Russian Periodicals [*A publication*]

Transl Dep Fish For (Can) ... Translation. Department of Fisheries and Forestry (Ottawa, Canada) [*A publication*]

Trans Leeds Geol Assoc ... Transactions. Leeds Geological Association [*A publication*]

Trans Leicestershire Archaeol Hist Soc ... Transactions. Leicestershire Archaeological and Historical Society [*A publication*]

Transl Fac For Univ BC ... Translation. Faculty of Forestry. University of British Columbia [*A publication*]

Transl For Comm (Lond) ... Translation. Forestry Commission (London) [*A publication*]

Trans Lich S Staffs Arch Hist Soc ... Transactions. Lichfield and South Staffordshire Archaeological and Historical Society [*A publication*]

Trans Linn Soc Lond ... Transactions. Linnean Society of London [*A publication*]

Trans Linn Soc NY ... Transactions. Linnaean Society of New York [*A publication*]

TRANSLIT ... Transliteration

Trans Liverpool Eng Soc ... Transactions. Liverpool Engineering Society [*A publication*]

Trans LJ .... Transportation Law Journal [*A publication*]

TRANSLOC ... Trade-Off Analysis Systems/Force Mix   (MCD)

TRANSLOC ... Transportable LORAN-C   (MCD)

Trans Lond Middx Archaeol Soc ... Transactions. London and Middlesex Archaeological Society [*A publication*]

Trans London Middlesex Archaeol Soc ... Transactions. London and Middlesex Archaeological Society [*A publication*]

Trans London M'sex Arch ... Transactions. London and Middlesex Archaeological Society [*A publication*]

Trans London Msex Arch Soc ... Transactions. London and Middlesex Archaeological Society [*A publication*]

Transl Reg-Index ... Translations Register-Index [*A publication*]

Transl Rev ... Translation Review [*A publication*]

Transl Russ Game Rep ... Translations of Russian Game Reports [*A publication*]

Transl Soviet Agr US Joint Publ Res Serv ... Translations on Soviet Agriculture. United States Joint Publications Research Service [*A publication*]

Transl US For Prod Lab (Madison) ... Translation. United States Forest Products Laboratory (Madison) [*A publication*]

TRANSM ... Transmission   (AFM)

TRANSMAN ... Enlisted Transfer Manual [*Military*]

Trans Manchester Assoc Eng ... Transactions. Manchester Association of Engineers [*A publication*]

Trans Mass Hort Soc ... Transactions. Massachusetts Horticultural Society [*A publication*]

Trans Math Monographs ... Translations of Mathematical Monographs. American Mathematical Society [*A publication*]

Transm & Distrib ... Transmission and Distribution [*A publication*]

Transm Distrib ... Transmission and Distribution [*A publication*]

Trans Med Soc Lond ... Transactions. Medical Society of London [*A publication*]

Trans Med Soc London ... Transactions. Medical Society of London [*A publication*]

Trans Meet Commns II & IV Int Soc Soil Sci ... Transactions. Meeting of Commissions II and IV. International Society of Soil Science [*A publication*]

Trans Metall Soc AIME ... Transactions. Metallurgical Society of AIME [*American Institute of Mining, Metallurgical, and Petroleum Engineers*] [*A publication*]

Trans Metall Soc AIME (Am Inst Min Metall Pet Eng) ... Transactions. Metallurgical Society of AIME (American Institute of Mining, Metallurgical, and Petroleum Engineers) [*A publication*]

Trans Met Heat Treat ... Transactions of Metal Heat Treatment [*China*] [*A publication*]

Trans Min Geol Metall Inst India ... Transactions. Mining, Geological, and Metallurgical Institute of India [*A publication*]

Trans Mining Geol Met Inst India ... Transactions. Mining, Geological, and Metallurgical Institute of India [*A publication*]

Trans Min Metall Alumni Assoc ... Transactions. Mining and Metallurgical Alumni Association [*Japan*] [*A publication*]

Trans Min Metall Assoc (Kyoto) ... Transactions. Mining and Metallurgical Association (Kyoto) [*A publication*]

TRANSMO ... Transportation Model [*Military*]

Trans MO Acad Sci ... Transactions. Missouri Academy of Science [*A publication*]

Trans MO Acad Scie ... Transactions. Missouri Academy of Science [*A publication*]

TRANSMON ... Transmission (ROG)

Trans Monumental Brass Soc ... Transactions. Monumental Brass Society [*A publication*]

Trans Morris C Res Counc ... Transactions. Morris County Research Council [*A publication*]

Trans Mosc Math Soc ... Transactions. Moscow Mathematical Society [*A publication*]

Trans Moscow Math Soc ... Transactions. Moscow Mathematical Society [*A publication*]

TRANSMTG ... Transmitting

Trans Mycol Soc Jap ... Transactions. Mycological Society of Japan [*A publication*]

Trans Mycol Soc Japan ... Transactions. Mycological Society of Japan [*A publication*]

Trans Mycol Soc Jpn ... Transactions. Mycological Society of Japan [*A publication*]

Transn........ Transition [*A publication*]

Trans N Amer Wildlife Conf ... Transactions. North American Wildlife and Natural Resources Conference [*A publication*]

Trans N Am Wildl Nat Resour Conf ... Transactions. North American Wildlife and Natural Resources Conference [*A publication*]

Trans Nat Hist Northumberl Durham Newcastle Upon Tyne ... Transactions. Natural History Society of Northumberland, Durham, and Newcastle-Upon-Tyne [*A publication*]

Trans Nat Hist Soc Formosa ... Transactions. Natural History Society of Formosa [*A publication*]

Trans Nat Hist Soc Northumberl Durham Newcastle-Upon-Tyne ... Transactions. Natural History Society of Northumberland, Durham, and Newcastle-Upon-Tyne [*Later, Natural History Society of Northumbria. Transactions*] [*A publication*]

Trans Nat Hist Soc Northumbria ... Transactions. Natural History Society of Northumbria [*A publication*]

Transnational Data Rep ... Transnational Data Report [*A publication*]

Transnatl ... Transnational (DLA)

Transnatl Data Rep ... Transnational Data Report [*A publication*]

Trans Natl Inst Sci India ... Transactions. National Institute of Sciences. India [*A publication*]

Transnat'l Rep ... Transnational Reporter [*A publication*] (DLA)

Trans Natl Res Inst Met ... Transactions. National Research Institute for Metals [*Japan*] [*A publication*]

Trans Natl Res Inst Met (Tokyo) ... Transactions. National Research Institute for Metals (Tokyo) [*A publication*]

Trans Natl Saf Congr ... Transactions. National Safety Congress [*United States*] [*A publication*]

Trans Nat Res Inst Metals (Tokyo) ... Transactions. National Research Institute for Metals (Tokyo) [*A publication*]

Trans Nat Vac Symp ... Transactions. National Vacuum Symposium [*A publication*]

Trans Nebr Acad Sci ... Transactions. Nebraska Academy of Sciences [*A publication*]

Trans NEC Instn E Ship ... Transactions. North East Coast Institution of Engineers and Shipbuilders [*United Kingdom*] [*A publication*]

Trans NE Cst Instn Engrs Shipbldrs ... Transactions. North East Coast Institution of Engineers and Shipbuilders [*United Kingdom*] [*A publication*]

Trans Newbury Dist Fld Club ... Transactions. Newbury District Field Club [*A publication*]

Trans Newcomen Soc Study His Eng Technol ... Transactions. Newcomen Society for the Study of the History of Engineering and Technology [*A publication*]

Trans New Engl Obstet Gynecol Soc ... Transactions. New England Obstetrical and Gynecological Society [*United States*] [*A publication*]

Trans New Orleans Acad Ophthalmol ... Transactions. New Orleans Academy of Ophthalmology [*A publication*]

Trans News ... Transport News [*New Zealand*] [*A publication*]

Trans New York Acad Sci Ser II ... Transactions. New York Academy of Sciences. Series II [*A publication*]

Trans NJ Obstet Gynecol Soc ... Transactions. New Jersey Obstetrical and Gynecological Society [*A publication*]

Trans North Am Wildl Conf ... Transactions. North American Wildlife Conference [*A publication*]

Trans North Am Wildl Nat Res Conf ... Transactions. North American Wildlife and Natural Resources Conference [*A publication*]

Trans North Am Wildl Nat Resour Conf ... Transactions. North American Wildlife and Natural Resources Conference [*A publication*]

Trans North East Coast Inst Eng Shipbuild ... Transactions. North East Coast Institution of Engineers and Shipbuilders [*United Kingdom*] [*A publication*]

Trans Northeast Sect Wildl Soc ... Transactions of the Northeast Section. Wildlife Society [*A publication*]

Trans NY Acad Sci ... Transactions. New York Academy of Sciences [*A publication*]

Trans NZ Inst Eng ... Transactions. New Zealand Institution of Engineers, Incorporated [*A publication*]

Trans NZ Inst Eng CE ... Transactions. New Zealand Institution of Engineers, Incorporated. Civil Engineering Section [*A publication*]

Trans NZ Inst Eng EMCh ... Transactions. New Zealand Institution of Engineers, Incorporated. Electrical/Mechanical/Chemical Engineering Section [*A publication*]

Trans NZ Inst Eng Inc Civ Eng Sect ... Transactions. New Zealand Institution of Engineers, Incorporated. Civil Engineering Section [*A publication*]

Trans NZ Inst Eng Inc Electr Mech Chem Eng Sect ... Transactions. New Zealand Institution of Engineers, Incorporated. Electrical/Mechanical/Chemical Engineering Section [*A publication*]

Trans Ophthalmol Soc Aust ... Transactions. Ophthalmological Society of Australia [*A publication*]

Trans Ophthalmol Soc NZ ... Transactions. Ophthalmological Society of New Zealand [*A publication*]

Trans Ophthalmol Soc UK ... Transactions. Ophthalmological Societies of the United Kingdom [*A publication*]

Trans Ophthal Soc Aust ... Transactions. Ophthalmological Society of Australia [*A publication*] (APTA)

Trans Opt Soc ... Transactions. Optical Society [*A publication*]

TRANSP ... Transparency (AAG)

TRANSP ... Transportation

Transp........ Transporter [*A publication*] (APTA)

Trans PA Acad Ophthalmol Otolaryngol ... Transactions. Pennsylvania Academy of Ophthalmology and Otolaryngology [*A publication*]

TRANSPAC ... Thermal Structure Monitoring Program in the Pacific [*Marine science*] (MSC)

Trans-Pac.. Trans-Pacific [*A publication*]

TRANSPAC ... Transpacific

Trans Pac Coast Obstet Gynecol Soc ... Transactions. Pacific Coast Obstetrical and Gynecological Society [*United States*] [*A publication*]

Trans Pac Coast Oto-Ophthalmol Soc ... Transactions. Pacific Coast Oto-Ophthalmological Society [*A publication*]

Trans Pac Coast Oto-Ophthalmol Soc Annu Meet ... Transactions. Pacific Coast Oto-Ophthalmological Society. Annual Meeting [*United States*] [*A publication*]

TRANSPACMAG ... Trans-Pacific Magnetic Anomaly Study [*National Oceanic and Atmospheric Administration*] (NOAA)

Trans Papers (L) Brit G ... Institute of British Geographers (Liverpool). Transactions and Papers [*A publication*]

Transp Aust ... Transport Australia [*A publication*] (APTA)

Transp Commun Rev ... Transport and Communication Review [*A publication*]

Trans Peirce Soc ... Transactions. Charles S. Peirce Society [*A publication*]

Transp Eng ... Transportation Engineering [*A publication*]

Transp Eng J ASCE ... Transportation Engineering Journal. ASCE [*American Society of Civil Engineers*] [*A publication*]

Transp Engng ... Transportation Engineering [*Formerly, Traffic Engineering*] [*A publication*]

Transp Engng J Proc ASCE ... Transportation Engineering Journal. Proceedings of the American Society of Civil Engineers [*A publication*]

Transp Engr ... Transport Engineer [*A publication*]

Trans Peninsula Hortic Soc ... Transactions. Peninsula Horticultural Society [*A publication*]

Transp En J ... Transportation Engineering Journal. ASCE [*American Society of Civil Engineers*] [*A publication*]

TRANSPHIBLANT ... Transports, Amphibious Force, Atlantic Fleet [*Navy*]

TRANSPHIBPAC ... Transports, Amphibious Force, Pacific Fleet [*Navy*]

Trans Philol Soc ... Transactions. Philological Society [*A publication*]

Trans Phil Soc ... Transactions. Philological Society [*A publication*]

Transp His ... Transportation History [*A publication*]

Transp Hist ... Transport History [*A publication*]

TRANSPIRE ... Transpiration-Cooled Stacked Platelet Injection (MCD)

Transp J..... Transport Journal [*A publication*]

Transp J..... Transportation Journal [*A publication*]

Transp J of Aust ... Transport Journal of Australia [*A publication*] (APTA)

Transp Khranenie Nefti Nefteprod ... Transport i Khranenie Nefti i Nefteproduktov [*USSR*] [*A publication*]

transpl........ Transplant

TRANSPLAN ... Transaction Network Service Planning Model [*Telecommunications*] (TEL)

Transplan P ... Transplantation Proceedings [*A publication*]

Transplan R ... Transplantation Reviews [*A publication*]

Transplant ... Transplantation [*A publication*]

Transplant Bull ... Transplantation Bulletin [*A publication*]

Transplant Clin Immunol ... Transplantation and Clinical Immunology [*A publication*]

Transplant Immunol Clin ... Transplantation et Immunologie Clinique [*A publication*]

Transplantn Proc ... Transplantation Proceedings [*A publication*]

Transplant Proc ... Transplantation Proceedings [*A publication*]
Transplant Proc Suppl ... Transplantation Proceedings. Supplement [*A publication*]
Transplant Rev ... Transplantation Reviews [*A publication*]
Transplant Soc Int Cong Proc ... Transplantation Society. International Congress. Proceedings [*A publication*]
Transp L J ... Transportation Law Journal [*A publication*]
Transp Manage ... Transport Management [*A publication*]
Transp-Med Vesti ... Transportno-Meditsinski Vesti [*A publication*]
Transp News ... Transport News of New Zealand [*A publication*]
Transp News Dig ... Transport News Digest [*A publication*]
Transportat ... Transportation [*A publication*]
Transportation J ... Transportation Journal [*A publication*]
Transportation Plann Tech ... Transportation Planning and Technology [*London*] [*A publication*]
Transportation Q ... Transportation Quarterly [*A publication*]
Transportation Res ... Transportation Research [*A publication*]
Transportation Res Part A ... Transportation Research. Part A. General [*A publication*]
Transportation Res Part B ... Transportation Research. Part B. Methodological [*A publication*]
Transportation Sci ... Operations Research Society of America. Transportation Science Section. Transportation Science [*A publication*]
Transport and Communications Bul Asia and Pacific ... Transport and Communications Bulletin for Asia and the Pacific [*A publication*]
Transport D ... Transport Digest [*A publication*]   (APTA)
Transport Theory Statist Phys ... Transport Theory and Statistical Physics [*A publication*]
Trans Powder Metall Assoc India ... Transactions. Powder Metallurgy Association of India [*A publication*]
Transp Plann Tech ... Transportation Planning and Technology [*A publication*]
Transp Plann Technol ... Transportation Planning and Technology [*A publication*]
Transp Plan and Technol ... Transport Planning and Technology [*A publication*]
Transp Policy Decision Making ... Transport Policy and Decision Making [*A publication*]
Transp Porous Media ... Transport in Porous Media [*A publication*]
Transp Q .... Transportation Quarterly [*A publication*]
Transp Res ... Transportation Research [*A publication*]
Transp Res Board Spec Rep ... Transportation Research Board. Special Report [*A publication*]
Transp Res Board Transp Res Rec ... Transportation Research Board. Transportation Research Record [*A publication*]
Transp Res News ... Transportation Research News [*A publication*]
Transp Res Part A ... Transportation Research. Part A. General [*A publication*]
Transp Res Part A Gen ... Transportation Research. Part A. General [*England*] [*A publication*]
Transp Res Part B ... Transportation Research. Part B. Methodological [*A publication*]
Transp Res Rec ... Transportation Research Record [*United States*] [*A publication*]
Transp Revs ... Transport Reviews [*A publication*]
Trans Princeton Conf Cerebrovasc Dis ... Transactions. Princeton Conference on Cerebrovascular Diseases [*A publication*]
Transp Road Res Lab (GB) TRRL Rep ... Transport and Road Research Laboratory (Great Britain). TRRL Report [*A publication*]
Trans Proc Birmingham Arch Soc ... Transactions and Proceedings. Birmingham Archaeological Society [*A publication*]
Trans Proc Bot Soc Edinb ... Transactions and Proceedings. Botanical Society of Edinburgh [*A publication*]
Trans Proc Geol Soc S Afr ... Transactions and Proceedings. Geological Society of South Africa [*A publication*]
Trans Proc Palaeontol Soc Jap ... Transactions and Proceedings. Palaeontological Society of Japan [*A publication*]
Trans Proc Palaeontol Soc Japan New Ser ... Transactions and Proceedings. Palaeontological Society of Japan. New Series [*A publication*]
Trans Proc Palaeontol Soc Jpn New Ser ... Transactions and Proceedings. Palaeontological Society of Japan. New Series [*A publication*]
Trans Proc Perthshire Soc Natur Sci ... Transactions and Proceedings. Perthshire Society of Natural Science [*A publication*]
Trans Proc R Soc South Aust ... Transactions and Proceedings. Royal Society of South Australia [*A publication*]
Trans Proc Torquay Natur Hist Soc ... Transactions and Proceedings. Torquay Natural History Society [*A publication*]
Transp Sci ... Transportation Science [*A publication*]
Transp Stroit ... Transportnoe Stroitel'stvo [*USSR*] [*A publication*]
Transp Theo ... Transport Theory and Statistical Physics [*A publication*]
Transp Theory Stat Phys ... Transport Theory and Statistical Physics [*A publication*]
Transp Th St P ... Transport Theory and Statistical Physics [*A publication*]
Transp Traffic ... Transport and Traffic [*A publication*]
Trans Q Am Soc Met ... Transactions Quarterly. American Society for Metals [*A publication*]
Trans R ...... Transatlantic Review [*A publication*]

Trans Radnorshire Soc ... Transactions. Radnorshire Society [*A publication*]
Trans R Can Inst ... Transactions. Royal Canadian Institute [*A publication*]
Trans R Entomol Soc Lond ... Transactions. Royal Entomological Society of London [*A publication*]
Trans R Ent Soc Lond ... Transactions. Royal Entomological Society of London [*A publication*]
Trans Res A ... Transportation Research. Part A. General [*A publication*]
Trans Res Abstr ... Transportation Research Abstracts [*A publication*]
Trans Res B ... Transportation Research. Part B. Methodological [*A publication*]
Trans R Geol Soc (Corn) ... Transactions. Royal Geological Society (Cornwall) [*A publication*]
Trans R Highl Agric Soc Scotl ... Transactions. Royal Highland and Agricultural Society of Scotland [*A publication*]
Trans Rhod Sci Assoc ... Transactions. Rhodesia Scientific Association [*A publication*]
Trans RINA ... Transactions. Royal Institutions of Naval Architects [*London*] [*A publication*]
Trans R Instn Naval Archit ... Quarterly Transactions. Royal Institution of Naval Architects [*London*] [*A publication*]
TRANSRON ... Transport Squadron [*Navy*]
Trans Royal Soc Can Sect 1 Sect 2 and Sect 3 ... Transactions. Royal Society of Canada. Section 1, Section 2, and Section 3 [*A publication*]
Trans Roy Inst Technol (Stockholm) ... Transactions. Royal Institute of Technology (Stockholm) [*A publication*]
Trans Roy Inst Tech (Stockholm) ... Transactions. Royal Institute of Technology (Stockholm) [*A publication*]
Trans Roy Soc Canada ... Transactions. Royal Society of Canada [*A publication*]
Trans Roy Soc Canada 4 ... Transactions. Royal Society of Canada. Chemical, Mathematical, and Physical Sciences. Fourth Series [*A publication*]
Trans Roy Soc NZ Bot ... Transactions. Royal Society of New Zealand. Botany [*A publication*]
Trans Roy Soc S Aust ... Royal Society of South Australia. Transactions [*A publication*]   (APTA)
Trans Roy Soc South Africa ... Transactions. Royal Society of South Africa [*A publication*]
Trans R Sch Dent (Stockh Umea) ... Transactions. Royal Schools of Dentistry (Stockholm and Umea) [*A publication*]
Trans R Soc Arts ... Transactions. Royal Society of Arts [*A publication*]
Trans R Soc Can ... Transactions. Royal Society of Canada [*A publication*]
Trans R Soc Can Sect 3 ... Transactions. Royal Society of Canada. Section 3. Chemical, Mathematical, and Physical Sciences [*A publication*]
Trans R Soc Can Sect 4 ... Transaction. Royal Society of Canada. Section 4. Geological Sciences Including Mineralogy [*A publication*]
Trans R Soc Can Sect 5 ... Transactions. Royal Society of Canada. Section 5. Biological Sciences [*A publication*]
Trans R Soc Can Sect 1 2 3 ... Transactions. Royal Society of Canada. Section 1, Section 2, and Section 3 [*A publication*]
Trans R Soc Edinb ... Transactions. Royal Society of Edinburgh [*A publication*]
Trans R Soc Edinb Earth Sci ... Transactions. Royal Society of Edinburgh. Earth Sciences [*A publication*]
Trans R Soc Edinburgh ... Transactions. Royal Society of Edinburgh [*A publication*]
Trans R Soc Edinburgh Earth Sci ... Transactions. Royal Society of Edinburgh. Earth Sciences [*A publication*]
Trans R Soc NZ ... Transactions. Royal Society of New Zealand [*A publication*]
Trans R Soc NZ Biol Sci ... Transactions. Royal Society of New Zealand. Biological Science [*A publication*]
Trans R Soc NZ Bot ... Transactions. Royal Society of New Zealand. Botany [*A publication*]
Trans R Soc NZ Earth Sci ... Transactions. Royal Society of New Zealand. Earth Science [*A publication*]
Trans R Soc NZ Gen ... Transactions. Royal Society of New Zealand. General [*A publication*]
Trans R Soc NZ Geol ... Transactions. Royal Society of New Zealand. Geology [*A publication*]
Trans R Soc NZ Zool ... Transactions. Royal Society of New Zealand. Zoology [*A publication*]
Trans R Soc S Afr ... Transactions. Royal Society of South Africa [*A publication*]
Trans R Soc S Aust ... Transactions. Royal Society of South Australia [*A publication*]   (APTA)
Trans R Soc South Aust ... Transactions. Royal Society of South Australia [*A publication*]   (APTA)
Trans R Soc Trop Med Hyg ... Transactions. Royal Society of Tropical Medicine and Hygiene [*A publication*]
Trans Russ Inst Appl Chem ... Transactions. Russian Institute of Applied Chemistry [*A publication*]
Trans SAEST ... Transactions. SAEST [*Society for Advancement of Electrochemical Science and Technology*] [*A publication*]
Trans S Afr Inst Civ Eng ... Transactions. South African Institution of Civil Engineers [*A publication*]
Trans S Afr Inst Elec Eng ... Transactions. South African Institute of Electrical Engineers [*A publication*]

Trans S Afr Inst Electr Eng ... Transactions. South African Institute of Electrical Engineers [*A publication*]
Trans San Diego Soc Nat Hist ... Transactions. San Diego Society of Natural History [*A publication*]
TransSBA ... Transactions. Society of Biblical Archaeology [*London*] [*A publication*]　(BJA)
Trans Sci .... Transportation Science [*A publication*]
Trans Sci Soc China ... Transactions. Science Society of China [*A publication*]
Trans SHASE ... Transactions. Society of Heating, Air Conditioning, and Sanitary Engineers [*Japan*] [*A publication*]
Trans SHASE Japan ... Transactions. SHASE [*Society of Heating, Air Conditioning, and Sanitary Engineers*] (Japan) [*A publication*]
Trans Shikoku Entomol Soc ... Transactions. Shikoku Entomological Society [*A publication*]
Trans Shikoku Ent Soc ... Transactions. Shikoku Entomological Society [*A publication*]
Trans Shropshire Archaeol Soc ... Transactions. Shropshire Archaeological Society [*A publication*]
Trans SMPE ... Transactions. Society of Motion Picture Engineers [*A publication*]
Trans Soc Adv Electrochem Sci Technol ... Transactions. Society for Advancement of Electrochemical Science and Technology [*A publication*]
Trans Soc Br Ent ... Transactions. Society for British Entomology [*A publication*]
Trans Soc Br Entomol ... Transactions. Society for British Entomology [*A publication*]
Trans Soc Heat Air Cond Sanit Eng Jpn ... Transactions. Society of Heating, Air Conditioning, and Sanitary Engineers of Japan [*A publication*]
Trans Soc Ill Eng ... Transactions. Illuminating Engineering Society [*A publication*]
Trans Soc Instr Control Eng ... Transactions. Society of Instrument and Control Engineers [*Japan*] [*A publication*]
Trans Soc Instrum and Control Eng ... Transactions. Society of Instrument and Control Engineers [*A publication*]
Trans Soc Instrum Control Eng ... Transactions. Society of Instrument and Control Engineers [*A publication*]
Trans Soc Instrum & Control Engrs (Japan) ... Transactions. Society of Instrument and Control Engineers (Japan) [*A publication*]
Trans Soc Instrum Technol ... Transactions. Society of Instrument Technology [*England*] [*A publication*]
Trans Soc Min Eng AIME ... Transactions. Society of Mining Engineers. AIME [*American Institute of Mining, Metallurgical, and Petroleum Engineers*] [*A publication*]
Trans Soc Min Engrs AIME ... Transactions. Society of Mining Engineers. AIME [*American Institute of Mining, Metallurgical, and Petroleum Engineers*] [*A publication*]
Trans Soc Motion Pict Eng ... Transactions. Society of Motion Picture Engineers [*A publication*]
Trans Soc Mot Pict Eng ... Transactions. Society of Motion Picture Engineers [*A publication*]
Trans Soc NAME ... Transactions. Society of Naval Architects and Marine Engineers [*A publication*]
Trans Soc Naval Architects Mar Eng ... Transactions. Society of Naval Architects and Marine Engineers [*A publication*]
Trans Soc Occup Med ... Transactions. Society of Occupational Medicine [*A publication*]
Trans Soc Pathol Jpn ... Transactiones Societatis Pathologicae Japonicae [*Japan*] [*A publication*]
Trans Soc Pet Eng AIME ... Transactions. Society of Petroleum Engineers of AIME [*American Institute of Mining, Metallurgical, and Petroleum Engineers*] [*A publication*]
Trans Soc Rheol ... Transactions. Society of Rheology [*A publication*]
Trans Southwest Fed Geol Soc ... Transactions. Southwestern Federation of Geological Societies [*A publication*]
Trans SPWLA Annu Log Symp ... Transactions. SPWLA [*Society of Professional Well Log Analysts*] Annual Logging Symposium [*A publication*]
Trans S Staffordshire Archaeol Hist Soc ... Transactions. South Staffordshire Archaeological and Historical Society [*A publication*]
Trans S Staffs Archaeol Hist Soc ... Transactions. South Staffordshire Archaeological and Historical Society [*A publication*]
Trans S Staffs Arch Hist Soc ... Transactions. South Staffordshire Archaeological and Historical Society [*A publication*]
Trans State Inst Appl Chem ... Transactions. State Institute of Applied Chemistry [*A publication*]
Trans St John's Hosp Dermatol Soc ... Transactions. St. John's Hospital Dermatological Society [*A publication*]
Trans Stud Coll Physicians Phila ... Transactions and Studies. College of Physicians of Philadelphia [*A publication*]
Trans Suffolk Natur Soc ... Transactions. Suffolk Naturalists' Society [*A publication*]
Trans Symp Carl Neuberg Soc ... Carl Neuberg Society for International Scientific Relations. Transactions of the Symposium [*A publication*]
Trans Tech Sect Can Pulp and Pap Assoc ... Transactions. Technical Section. Canadian Pulp and Paper Association [*A publication*]
Trans Tech Sect Can Pulp Pap Assoc ... Transactions. Technical Section. Canadian Pulp and Paper Association [*A publication*]

Trans 8th Int Congr Soil Sci ... Transactions. 8th International Congress of Soil Science [*A publication*]
Trans Thoroton Soc Nottinghamshire ... Transaction. Thoroton Society of Nottinghamshire [*A publication*]
Trans Thoroton Soc Notts ... Transactions. Thoroton Society of Nottinghamshire [*A publication*]
Transtl .... Transitional　(DLA)
Trans Tokyo Univ Fish ... Transactions. Tokyo University of Fisheries [*A publication*]
Trans Tottori Soc Agric Sci ... Transactions. Tottori Society of Agricultural Sciences [*A publication*]
Trans Tottori Soc Agr Sci ... Transactions. Tottori Society of Agricultural Science [*A publication*]
Trans Tuberc Soc Scotl ... Transactions. Tuberculosis Society of Scotland [*A publication*]
Trans Udgivet Dan Ing ... Transactions. Udgivet af Dansk Ingenioeren [*Denmark*] [*A publication*]
Trans Univ Cent Desert Stud (Jodhpur India) ... Transactions. University Centre of Desert Studies (Jodhpur, India) [*A publication*]
Trans Utah Acad Sci ... Transactions. Utah Academy of Sciences [*A publication*]
TRANSV ... Transvaal [*South Africa*]　(ROG)
TRANSV ... Transverse　(AAG)
Transvaal Agric J ... Transvaal Agricultural Journal [*A publication*]
Transvaal Mus Bull ... Transvaal Museum. Bulletin [*A publication*]
Transvaal Mus Mem ... Transvaal Museum. Memoirs [*A publication*]
Transvaal Mus Monogr ... Transvaal Museum. Monograph [*A publication*]
Transvaal Mus Rep ... Transvaal Museum. Report [*A publication*]
Transvaal Nat Conserv Div Annu Rep ... Transvaal Nature Conservation Division. Annual Report [*A publication*]
Trans Vac Symp ... Transactions. Vacuum Symposium [*A publication*]
Trans Wagner Free Inst Sci Philadelphia ... Transactions. Wagner Free Institute of Science of Philadelphia [*A publication*]
Trans West Sect Am Urol Assoc ... Transactions. Western Section of the American Urological Association [*A publication*]
Trans West Surg Ass ... Transactions. Western Surgical Association [*A publication*]
Trans Wis Acad Sci ... Transactions. Wisconsin Academy of Sciences, Arts, and Letters [*A publication*]
Trans Wis Acad Sci Arts Lett ... Transactions. Wisconsin Academy of Sciences, Arts, and Letters [*A publication*]
Trans Wisc Acad Sci ... Transactions. Wisconsin Academy of Sciences, Arts, and Letters [*A publication*]
Trans & Wit ... Transvaal and Witswatersrand Reports [*A publication*]　(DLA)
Trans Woolhope Naturalists ... Transactions. Woolhope Naturalists' Field Club [*A publication*]
Trans Woolhope Natur Fld Club ... Transactions. Woolhope Naturalists' Field Club [*Herefordshire*] [*A publication*]
Trans Worc Arch Soc ... Transactions. Worcestershire Archaeological Society [*A publication*]
Trans Worcestershire Archaeol Soc 3 Ser ... Transactions. Worcestershire Archaeological Society. Series 3 [*A publication*]
Trans Worcs Arch Soc ... Transaction. Worcestershire Archaeological Society [*A publication*]
Trans Worcs Arc Soc ... Transactions. Worcestershire Archaeological Society [*A publication*]
Trans World Energy Conf ... Transactions. World Energy Conference [*A publication*]
Transylvania J Med ... Transylvania Journal of Medicine [*A publication*]
Trans Zimbabwe Sci Assoc ... Transactions. Zimbabwe Scientific Association [*A publication*]
Trans Zimb Sci Assoc ... Transactions. Zimbabwe Scientific Association [*A publication*]
Trans Zool Soc Lond ... Transactions. Zoological Society of London [*A publication*]
Tran USA .. Transportation USA [*A publication*]
TRAP .... Tank, Racks, Adapters, Pylons [*Military*]
TRAP .... Tape Recorder Action Plan [*Committee*] [*NASA/Air Force*]
TRAP .... Tartrate Resistant Acid Phosphatase [*An enzyme*]
TRAP .... Terminal Radiation Airborne Program [*Air Force*]
TRAP .... Thioguanine, Rubidomycin [*Daunorubicin*], Cytosine arabinoside [*ara-C*], Prednisone [*Antineoplastic drug regimen*]
TRAP .... Time Response Approximation
TRAP .... Tracker Analysis Program　(MCD)
TRAP .... Trapezoid　(MSA)
TRAP .... Treasury Relief Aid Project
TRAP .... Tyrosine-Rich Amelogenin Polypeptide [*Biochemistry of dental enamel*]
TRAPAC ... Fleet Training Command, Pacific [*Navy*]
TRAPATT ... Trapped Plasma Avalanche Triggered Transit [*Bell Laboratories*]
TRAPCON ... Transportable RADAR Approach Control [*Army*]
Tr A Ph A .. Transactions and Proceedings. American Philological Association [*A publication*]
TRAPP .... Training and Retention as Permanent Party [*Army*]　(AABC)
Tr App .... Transcript Appeals [*New York*] [*1867-68*] [*A publication*]　(DLA)
TRAPS ...... Tactical Rapid Access Processing System　(KSC)
TRAPS ...... Transportable Reliable Acoustic Path SONAR　(MCD)

TRAPS ...... Troop Reaction and Posture Sequence   (MCD)
TRAPV ...... Trap on Overflow BIT [*Binary Digit*] Set [*Data processing*]
TRAQA ...... Traffic Quarterly [*A publication*]
TRAR .... Total Radiation Absolute Radiometer [*NASA*]
Tr Arkhang Lesotekh Inst ... Trudy Arkhangel'skogo Lesotekhnicheskogo Instituta [*A publication*]
Tr Arkt Antarkt Nauchno-Issled Inst ... Trudy Arkticheskogo i Antarkticheskogo Nauchno-Issledovatel'skogo Instituta [*A publication*]
Tr Arm Geol Upr ... Trudy Armyanskogo Geologicheskogo Upravleniya [*A publication*]
Tr Arm Inst Stroim Sooruzh ... Trudy Armyanskogo Instituta Stroimaterialov i Sooruzhenii [*A publication*]
Tr Arm Nauchno Issled Inst Gidrotekh Melior ... Trudy Armyanskogo Nauchno-Issledovatel'skogo Instituta Gidrotekhniki i Melioratsii [*A publication*]
Tr Arm Nauchno Issled Inst Vinograd Vinodel Plodovod ... Trudy Armyanskogo Nauchno-Isseldovatel'skogo Instituta Vinogradarstva Vinodeliya i Plodovodstva
Tr Arm Nauchno-Issled Inst Zhivotnovod Vet ... Trudy Armyanskogo Nauchno-Issledovatel'skogo Instituta Zhivotnovodstva i Veterinarii [*A publication*]
Tr Arm Nauchno-Issled Vet Inst ... Trudy Armyanskogo Nauchno-Issledovatel'skogo Veterinarnogo Instituta [*A publication*]
Tr Arm Protivochumn Stn ... Trudy Armyanskoi Protivochumnoi Stantsii [*A publication*]
TRARON .. Training Squadron
TRAS .... Training Requirements Analysis System [*Army*]
TRASA ...... Traktory i Sel'khozmashiny [*A publication*]
TRASANA ... TRADOC [*Training and Doctrine Command*] Systems Analysis Activity [*White Sands Missile Range, NM*] [*Army*]
Trasfus Sangue ... Trasfusione del Sangue [*A publication*]
TRASH ...... Trash Remover and Satellite Hauler [*Proposed device to remove orbiting space debris*]
TRASH ...... Tsunami Research Advisory System of Hawaii
Tr Ashkhab Nauchno Issled Inst Epidemiol Gig ... Trudy Ashkhabadskogo Nauchno-Issledovatel'skogo Instituta Epidemiologii i Gigieny [*A publication*]
TRASOP ... Tax Reduction Act Stock Ownership Plan
Trasp .... Trasporti. Rivista di Politica, Economia, e Tecnica [*A publication*]
Trasp Pubbl ... Trasporti Pubblici [*A publication*]
TRASSO ... TRADOC Systems Staff Officer [*or Office*] [*Army*]
TRASTA ... Training Station [*Navy*]
Tr Astrakh Gos Med Inst ... Trudy Astrakhanskogo Gosudarstvennogo Meditinskogo Instituta [*A publication*]
Tr Astrakh Gos Zapov ... Trudy Astrakhanskogo Gosudarstvennogo Zapovednika [*A publication*]
Tr Astrakh Tekh Inst Rybn Promsti Khoz ... Trudy Astrakhanskogo Tekhnicheskogo Instituta Rybnoi Promyshlennosti i Khozyaistva [*A publication*]
Tr Astrofiz Inst Akad Nauk Kaz SSR ... Trudy Astrofizicheskogo Instituta Akademiya Nauk Kazakhskoi SSR [*Kazakh SSR*] [*A publication*]
TRAT .... Torpedo Readiness Assistance Team
TRAT .... Trade Aptitude Test [*Vocational guidance test*]
TRAT .... Travelers REIT [*Boston, MA*] [*NASDAQ symbol*]   (NQ)
TRAT .... Triacetylhexahydrotriazine [*Organic chemistry*]
TRATE ...... Trace Test and Evaluation
TRATEL ... Tracking through Telemetry [*Air Force*]
Tr Atl Nauchno-Issled Inst Ryb Khoz Okeanogr ... Trudy Atlanticheskii Nauchno-Issledovatel'skii Institut Rybnogo Khozyaistva i Okeanografii [*USSR*] [*A publication*]
Tratt .... Trattenuto [*Music*]
Tratt Met ... Trattamenti dei Metalli [*A publication*]
Tr At Zoovet Inst ... Trudy Alma-Atinskogo Instituta [*A publication*]
TRAU .... Tanganyika Railway African Union
TrAu .... Triangulum Australe [*Constellation*]
TRAV .... Training Availability [*Navy*]   (NVT)
TRAV .... Travancore [*India*]   (ROG)
Trav .... Travel [*A publication*]
Trav .... Travel/Holiday [*A publication*]
Trav .... Travelling [*A publication*]
TRAV .... Travels [*or Traveler*]
TRAV .... Traverse   (AABC)
TRAVA ...... Travaux [*A publication*]
Trav Act Pop ... Travaux de l'Action Populaire [*A publication*]
Travailleur Can ... Travailleur Canadien [*A publication*]
Trav Alphabet ... Travail de l'Alphabetisation [*A publication*]
Trav Assoc H Capitant ... Travaux. Association Henri Capitant [*A publication*]
Travaux du Com Franc de Droit Internat Prive ... Travaux. Comite Francais de Droit International Prive [*Paris, France*] [*A publication*]   (DLA)
Travaux et Conf Univ Libre de Brux ... Travaux et Conferences. Universite Libre de Bruxelles. Faculte de Droit [*Brussels, Belgium*] [*A publication*]   (DLA)
Travaux Sem Anal Convexe ... Travaux. Seminaire d'Analyse Convexe [*A publication*]
Trav Bur Geol ... Travaux du Bureau Geologique [*A publication*]

TRAVC ...... Travail Canada [*Labour Canada - LC*]
Trav CCI .... Travaux de la CCI [*Chambre de Commerce Internationale*] [*A publication*]
Trav Cent Rech Etudes Oceanogr ... Travaux. Centre de Recherches et d'Etudes Oceanographiques [*A publication*]
TRAVCHAR ... Cost Travel Chargeable
Trav Chim Aliment Hyg ... Travaux de Chimie Alimentaire et d'Hygiene [*A publication*]
Trav-Cochin ... Indian Law Reports, Kerala Series [*A publication*]   (DLA)
Trav Com Int Etude Bauxites Alumine Alum ... Travaux. Comite International pour l'Etude des Bauxites, de l'Alumine, et de l'Aluminium [*A publication*]
Trav Com Int Etude Bauxites Oxydes Hydroxydes Alum ... Travaux. Comite International pour l'Etude des Bauxites, des Oxydes, et des Hydroxydes d'Aluminium [*A publication*]
Trav Communaux ... Travaux Communaux [*France*] [*A publication*]
Trav C Ph R ... Travaux de Linguistique et de Litterature. Centre de Philologie et de Litteratures Romanes. Universite de Strasbourg [*A publication*]
Trav Doc Geogr Trop ... Travaux et Documents de Geographie Tropicale [*A publication*]
Trav Doc ORSTOM ... Travaux et Documents. ORSTOM [*Office de la Recherche Scientifique et Technique d'Outre-Mer*] [*A publication*]
TRAVEL ... Transportable Vertical Erectable Launcher
Trav Geophys (Prague) ... Travaux Geophysiques (Prague) [*A publication*]
Trav/Holiday ... Travel/Holiday [*A publication*]
Trav Hum .. Travail Humain [*A publication*]
Trav Humain ... Travail Humain [*A publication*]
Trav Hum Ren ... Travaux d'Humanisme et Renaissance [*A publication*]
Trav Inst Franc Et And ... Travaux. Institut Francais d'Etudes Andines [*A publication*]
Trav Inst Franc Et Andines ... Travaux. Institut Francais d'Etudes Andines [*A publication*]
Trav Inst Geol Anthropol Prehist Fac Sci Poitiers ... Travaux. Institut de Geologie et d'Anthropologie Prehistorique. Faculte des Sciences de Poitiers [*A publication*]
Trav Inst L ... Travaux. Institut de Linguistique de Lund [*A publication*]
Trav Inst Med Super ... Travaux. Institut Medical Superieur [*A publication*]
Trav Inst Rech Sahar ... Travaux. Institut de Recherches Sahariennes [*A publication*]
Trav Inst Sci Cherifien Fac Sci Rabat Ser Gen ... Travaux. Institut Scientifique Cherifien et Faculte des Sciences de Rabat. Serie Generale [*A publication*]
Trav Inst Sci Cherifien Fac Sci Ser Sci Phys ... Travaux. Institut Scientifique Cherifien et Faculte des Sciences. Serie: Sciences Physiques [*A publication*]
Trav Inst Sci Cherifien Fac Sci Ser Zool ... Travaux. Institut Scientifique Cherifien et Faculte des Sciences. Serie Zoologie [*A publication*]
Trav Inst Sci Cherifien Ser Bot ... Travaux. Institut Scientifique Cherifien. Serie Botanique [*A publication*]
Trav Inst Sci Cherifien Ser Bot Biol Veg ... Travaux. Institut Scientifique Cherifien. Serie Botanique et Biologique Vegetale [*A publication*]
Trav Inst Sci Cherifien Ser Geol Geogr Phys ... Travaux. Institut Scientifique Cherifien. Serie Geologie et Geographie Physique [*A publication*]
Trav Inst Sci Cherifien Ser Sci Phys ... Travaux. Institut Scientifique Cherifien. Serie Sciences Physiques [*A publication*]
Trav Inst Sci Cherifien Ser Zool ... Travaux. Institut Scientifique Cherifien. Serie Zoologique [*A publication*]
Trav Inst Speleo "Emile Racovitza" ... Travaux. Institut de Speleologie "Emile Racovitza" [*A publication*]
Trav IRS .... Travaux. Institut de Recherches Sahariennes [*A publication*]
TRAVIS ..... Traffic Retrieval Analysis Validation and Information System [*Telecommunications*]   (TEL)
Trav Jeunes Sci ... Travaux des Jeunes Scientifiques [*A publication*]
Trav et Jours ... Travaux et Jours [*A publication*]
Trav Lab Anthropol Prehist Ethnol Pays Mediterr Occid ... Travaux. Laboratoire d'Anthropologie de Prehistoire et d'Ethnologie des Pays de la Mediterranee Occidentale [*A publication*]
Trav Lab For Toulouse ... Travaux. Laboratoire Forestier de Toulouse [*A publication*]
Trav Lab For Toulouse Tome I Artic Divers ... Travaux. Laboratoire Forestier de Toulouse. Tome I. Articles Divers [*A publication*]
Trav Lab For Toulouse Tome II Etud Dendrol ... Travaux. Laboratoire Forestier de Toulouse. Tome II. Etudes Dendrologiques [*A publication*]
Trav Lab For Toulouse Tome V Geogr For Monde ... Travaux. Laboratoire Forestier de Toulouse. Tome V. Geographie Forestier du Monde [*A publication*]
Trav Lab For Univ Toulouse ... Travaux. Laboratoire Forestier. Universite de Toulouse [*A publication*]
Trav Lab Geol Ec Norm Super (Paris) ... Travaux. Laboratoire de Geologie. Ecole Normale Superieure (Paris) [*A publication*]
Trav Lab Geol Fac Sci Grenoble ... Travaux. Laboratoire de Geologie. Faculte des Sciences de Grenoble [*A publication*]
Trav Lab Geol Fac Sci Grenoble Mem ... Travaux. Laboratoire de Geologie. Faculte des Sciences de Grenoble. Memoires [*A publication*]

Trav Lab Geol Fac Sci Lyon ... Travaux. Laboratoire de Geologie. Faculte des Sciences de Lyon [*A publication*]
Trav Lab Geol Fac Sci Univ Bordeaux ... Travaux. Laboratoire de Geologie. Faculte des Sciences. Universite de Bordeaux [*A publication*]
Trav Lab Geol Hist Paleontol Cent St Charles Univ Provence ... Travaux. Laboratoire de Geologie Historique et de Paleontologie. Centre Saint Charles. Universite de Provence [*A publication*]
Trav Lab Hydrobiol Piscic Univ Grenoble ... Travaux. Laboratoire d'Hydrobiologie et de Pisciculture. Universite de Grenoble [*A publication*]
Trav Lab Hydrogeol Geochim Fac Sci Univ Bordeaux ... Travaux. Laboratoire d'Hydrogeologie Geochimie. Faculte des Sciences Universite de Bordeaux [*A publication*]
Trav Lab Matiere Med Pharm Galenique Fac Pharm (Paris) ... Travaux. Laboratoires de Matiere Medicale et de Pharmacie Galenique. Faculte de Pharmacie (Paris) [*A publication*]
Trav Lab Microbiol Fac Pharm Nancy ... Travaux. Laboratoire de Microbiologie. Faculte de Pharmacie de Nancy [*A publication*]
Trav LJ ...... Travancore Law Journal [*India*] [*A publication*] (DLA)
Trav Lorient ... Travaux. Societe Lorientaise d'Archeologie [*A publication*]
Trav LR ...... Travancore Law Reports [*India*] [*A publication*] (DLA)
Trav LT ...... Travancore Law Times [*India*] [*A publication*] (DLA)
Travl Wkly ... Travel Weekly [*A publication*]
Trav Mem ... Travaux et Memoires. Centre de Recherche d'Histoire et Civilisation Byzantine [*Paris*] [*A publication*]
Trav Mem Bur Int Poids Mes ... Travaux et Memoires. Bureau International des Poids et Mesures [*A publication*]
Trav Met Deform ... Travail des Metaux par Deformation [*A publication*]
Trav et Meth ... Travail et Methodes [*A publication*]
Trav Mus Hist Nat "Gr Antipa" ... Travaux. Museum d'Histoire Naturelle "Grigore Antipa" [*A publication*]
Trav Mus Hist Nat "Grigore Antipa" ... Travaux. Museum d'Histoire Naturelle "Grigore Antipa" [*A publication*]
TRAVNEC ... Subject Travel Was Necessary at This Time and Time Consumed in Administrative Channels Prevented Written Orders Being Issue
Trav Pech Que ... Travaux sur les Pecheries du Quebec [*A publication*]
Trav Peint .. Travaux de Peinture [*A publication*]
Trav Quebec ... Travail Quebec [*A publication*]
Trav et Rech ... Travaux et Recherches [*A publication*]
Trav Rech Haut Comite Et Inform Alcool ... Travaux et Recherches. Haut Comite d'Etude et d'Information sur l'Alcoolisme [*A publication*]
Trav Sci Cent Rech Sci Proj Ind Vini (Sofia) ... Travaux Scientifiques. Centre de Recherches Scientifiques et de Projections de l'Industrie Vinicole (Sofia) [*A publication*]
Trav Sci Parc Natl Vanoise ... Travaux Scientifiques. Parc National de la Vanoise [*A publication*]
Trav Sect Scient Tech Inst Fr Pondichery ... Travaux. Section Scientifique et Technique. Institut Francais de Pondichery [*A publication*]
Trav Sect Sci Tech Inst Franc Pondichery ... Travaux. Section Scientifique et Technique. Institut Francais de Pondichery [*A publication*]
Trav Sect Sci Tech Inst Fr Pondichery ... Travaux. Section Scientifique et Technique. Institut Francais de Pondichery [*A publication*]
Trav Secur ... Travail et Securite [*A publication*]
Trav et Soc ... Travail et Societe [*A publication*]
Trav Soc Bot Geneve ... Travaux. Societe Botanique de Geneve [*A publication*]
Trav Soc Pharm Montp ... Travaux. Societe de Pharmacie de Montpellier [*A publication*]
Trav Soc Pharm Montpellier ... Travaux. Societe de Pharmacie de Montpellier [*France*] [*A publication*]
Trav Soc Sci Lettres Wroclaw ... Travaux. Societe des Sciences et des Lettres de Wroclaw [*A publication*]
Trav Sta Rech Groenendaal ... Travaux. Station de Recherches des Eaux et Forets. Groenendaal-Hoeilaart [*A publication*]
Trav-Syndicalisme Bibl ... Travail-Syndicalisme. Bibliographie [*A publication*]
Tr Avtom Svarke Flyusom ... Trudy po Avtomaticheskoi Svarke pod Flyusom [*A publication*]
Trav & Tw L of N ... Travers and Twiss on Law of Nations [*A publication*] (DLA)
TRAWL ..... Tape Read and Write Library
T Ray .... [*Sir Thomas*] Raymond's English King's Bench Reports [*83 English Reprint*] [*1660-84*] [*A publication*] (DLA)
Tray Lat Max ... Trayner's Latin Maxims and Phrases, Etc. [*A publication*] (DLA)
Tray Leg Max ... Trayner's Latin Maxims and Phrases [*A publication*] (ILCA)
T Raym ...... [*Sir Thomas*] Raymond's English King's Bench Reports [*83 English Reprint*] [*A publication*] (DLA)
T Raym (Eng) ... [*Sir Thomas*] Raymond's English King's Bench Reports [*83 English Reprint*] [*A publication*] (DLA)
Tr Azerb Gos Nauchno Issled Proektn Inst Neft Promsti ... Trudy Azerbaidzhanskii Gosudarstvennyi Nauchno-Issledovatel'skii i Proektnyi Institut Neftyanoi Promyshlennosti [*A publication*]

Tr Azerb Gos Pedagog Inst ... Trudy Azerbaidzhanskogo Gosudarstvennogo Pedagogicheskogo Instituta [*A publication*]
Tr Azerb Gos Univ Ser Khim ... Trudy Azerbaidzhanskogo Gosudarstvennogo Universiteta. Seriya Khimicheskaya [*A publication*]
Tr Azerb Ind Inst ... Trudy Azerbaidzhanskogo Industrial'nogo Instituta [*A publication*]
Tr Azerb Inst Nefti Khim ... Trudy Azerbaidzhanskogo Instituta Nefti i Khimii [*A publication*]
Tr Azerb Nauchno Issled Inst Buren Neft Gazov Skvazhin ... Trudy Azerbaidzhanskogo Nauchno-Issledovatel'skogo Instituta po Bureniyu Neftyanykh i Gazovykh Skvazhin [*A publication*]
Tr Azerb Nauchno Issled Inst Energ ... Trudy Azerbaidzhanskogo Nauchno-Issledovatel'skogo Instituta Energetiki [*A publication*]
Tr Azerb Nauchno-Issled Inst Gig Tr Prof Zabol ... Trudy Azerbaidzhanskogo Nauchno-Issledovatel'skogo Instituta Gigieny Truda i Professional'nykh Zabolevaniya [*A publication*]
Tr Azerb Nauchno Issled Inst Lesn Khoz Agrolesomelior ... Trudy Azerbaidzhanskogo Nauchno-Issledovatel'skogo Instituta Lesnogo Khozyaistva i Agrolesomelioratsii [*A publication*]
Tr Azerb Nauchno-Issled Inst Med Parazitol Trop Med ... Trudy Azerbaidzhanskogo Nauchno-Issledovatel'skogo Instituta Meditsinskoi Parazitologii i Trophicheskoi Meditsiny [*A publication*]
Tr Azerb Nauchno Issled Inst Ovoshchevod ... Trudy Azerbaidzhanskogo Nauchno-Issledovatel'skogo Instituta Ovoshchevodstva [*A publication*]
Tr Azerb Nauchno Issled Inst Virusol Mikrobiol Gig ... Trudy Azerbaidzhanskogo Nauchno-Issledovatel'skogo Instituta Virusologii Mikrobiologii i Gigieny [*A publication*]
Tr Azerb Nauchno Issled Inst Zemled ... Trudy Azerbaidzhanskogo Nauchno-Issledovatel'skogo Instituta Zemledeliya [*A publication*]
Tr Azerb Nauchno Issled Vet Inst ... Trudy Azerbaidzhanskogo Nauchno-Issledovatel'skogo Veterinarnogo Instituta [*A publication*]
Tr Azerb Nauchno Issled Vet Opytn Stn ... Trudy Azerbaidzhanskoi Nauchno-Issledovatel'skoi Veterinarnoi Opytnoi Stantsii [*A publication*]
Tr Azerb Neft Nauchno Issled Inst ... Trudy Azerbaidzhanskogo Neftyanogo Nauchno-Issledovatel'skogo Instituta [*A publication*]
Tr Azerb Otd Tsentr Nauchno Issled Inst Osetr Khoz ... Trudy Azerbaidzhanskogo Otdeleniya Tsentral'nogo Nauchno-Issledovatel'skogo Instituta Osetrovgo Khozyaistva [*A publication*]
Tr Azerb Politekh Inst ... Trudy Azerbaidzhanskogo Politekhnicheskogo Instituta [*A publication*]
Tr Azerb Skh Inst ... Trudy Azerbaidzhanskogo Sel'skokhozyaistvennogo Instituta [*A publication*]
Tr Azerb Vet Nauchno Issled Inst ... Trudy Azerbaidzhanskogo Veterinarnogo Nauchno-Issledovatel'skogo Instituta [*A publication*]
Tr Azovsko Chernomorsk Nauchn Rybokhoz Stn ... Trudy Azovsko-Chernomorskoi Nauchnoi Rybokhozyaistvennoi Stantsii [*A publication*]
Tr Azovskogo Nauchno Issled Inst Rybn Khoz ... Trudy Azovskogo Nauchno-Issledovatel'skogo Instituta Rybnogo Khozyaistva [*A publication*]
TRB .... Signature for Washington correspondent's column in "New Republic" magazine [*Said to have been derived by reversing the initialism for Brooklyn Rapid Transit: BRT*]
TRB .... Tactical Review Board [*Military*] (CAAL)
TRB .... Tapered Roller Bearing
TRB .... Tax Review Board [*Canada*]
TRB .... Technical Reference Branch [*Department of Transportation*] (IID)
TRB .... Technical Review Board [*NASA*] (KSC)
TRB .... Tennyson Research Bulletin [*A publication*]
TRB .... Test Requirement Bulletins [*NASA*] (KSC)
TRB .... Test Review Board [*NASA*] (NASA)
TRB .... Tom Robinson Band
TRB .... Torpedo Recovery Boat
TRB .... Trabaccolo [*Small coasting vessel of the Adriatic*] (DS)
TRB .... Transportation Research Board (EA)
TRB .... Trapped Radiation Belt
TRB .... Treble
TRB .... [*The*] Tribune Co. [*NYSE symbol*] (SPSG)
TRB .... Trombone [*Music*]
TRB .... Troop Basis (MUGU)
TRB .... Turbo [*Colombia*] [*Airport symbol*] (OAG)
TRB .... United States Army TRADOC, Engineering School Library and Learning Resource Center, Fort Belvoir, VA [*OCLC symbol*] (OCLC)
Tr Baik Limnol Stn Akad Nauk SSSR Vost Sib Fil ... Trudy Baikal'skoi Limnologicheskoi Stantsii Akademiya Nauk SSSR Vostochno-Sibirskii Filial [*A publication*]
Tr Bakinsk Nauchno-Issled Inst Travmatol Ortop ... Trudy Bakinskogo Nauchno-Issledovatel'skogo Instituta Travmatologii Ortopedii [*A publication*]
Tr Bakinskogo Nauchno Issled Inst Travmatol Ortop ... Trudy Bakinskogo Nauchno-Issledovatel'skogo Instituta Travmatologii Ortopedii [*A publication*]

Tr Balt Nauchno Issled Inst Rybn Khoz ... Trudy Baltiiskogo Nauchno-Issledovatel'skogo Instituta Rybnogo Khozyaistva [*A publication*]
Tr Bashk Gos Nauchno Issled Proektn Inst Neft Promsti ... Trudy Bashkirskii Gosudarstvennyi Nauchno-Issledovatel'skii i Proektnyi Institut Neftyanoi Promyshlennosti [*A publication*]
Tr Bashk Gos Zapov ... Trudy Bashkirskogo Gosudarstvennogo Zapovednika [*A publication*]
Tr Bashk Nauchno-Issled Inst Pererab Nefti ... Trudy Bashkirskii Nauchno-Issledovatel'skii Institut po Pererabotke Nefti [*USSR*] [*A publication*]
Tr Bashk Nauchno Issled Inst Sel'sk Khoz ... Trudy Bashkirskogo Nauchno-Issledovatel'skogo Instituta Sel'skogo Khozyaistva [*A publication*]
Tr Bashk Nauchno Issled Inst Stroit ... Trudy Bashkirskii Nauchno-Issledovatel'skii Institut po Stroitel'stvu [*A publication*]
Tr Bashk S-Kh Inst ... Trudy Bashkirskogo Sel'skokhozyaistvennogo Instituta [*A publication*]
Tr Batum Bot Sada Akad Nauk Gruz SSR ... Trudy Batumskogo Botanicheskogo Sada Akademii Nauk Gruzinskoi SSR [*A publication*]
Tr Belgorod Gos Skh Opytn Stn ... Trudy Belgorodskoi Gosudarstvennoi Sel'skokhozyaistvennoi Opytnoi Stantsii [*A publication*]
Tr Belgorod Tekhnol Inst Stroit ... Trudy Belgorodskogo Tekhnologicheskogo Instituta Stroitel'nyhmaterialov [*A publication*]
Tr Belomorsk Biol Stn Mosk Gos Univ ... Trudy Belomorskoi Biologicheskoi Stantsii Moskovskogo Gosudarstvennogo Universiteta [*A publication*]
Tr Beloruss Nauchno-Issled Inst Melior Vodn Khoz ... Trudy Belorusskogo Nauchno-Issledovatel'skogo Instituta Melioratsii i Vodnogo Khozyaistva [*A publication*]
Tr Beloruss Nauchno-Issled Inst Pishch Promsti ... Trudy Belorusskogo Nauchno-Issledovatel'skogo Instituta Pishchevoi Promyshlennosti [*A publication*]
Tr Beloruss Nauchno Issled Inst Pochvoved ... Trudy Belorusskii Nauchno-Issledovatel'skii Institut Pochvovedenii [*A publication*]
Tr Beloruss Nauchno Issled Inst Promsti Prodovol Tovarov ... Trudy Belorusskii Nauchno-Issledovatel'skii Institut Promyshlennosti Prodovol'stvennykh Tovarov [*A publication*]
Tr Beloruss Nauchno Issled Inst Rybn Khoz ... Trudy Belorusskogo Nauchno-Issledovatel'skogo Instituta Rybnogo Khozyaistva [*A publication*]
Tr Beloruss Nauchno Issled Inst Zhivotnovod ... Trudy Belorusskii Nauchno-Issledovatel'skii Institut Zhivotnovodstva [*A publication*]
Tr Beloruss Naucno-Issled Inst Pishch Prom-Sti ... Trudy Belorusskogo Nauchno-Issledovatel'skogo Instituta Pishchevoi Promyshlennosti [*A publication*]
Tr Beloruss Sel'skokhoz Akad ... Trudy Belorusskoi Sel'skokhozyaistvennoi Akademii [*A publication*]
Tr Beloruss Skh Akad ... Trudy Belorusskoi Sel'skokhozyaistvennoi Akademii [*A publication*]
Tr Berdyanskii Opytn Neftemaslozavod ... Trudy Berdyanskii Opytnyi Neftemaslozavod [*A publication*]
TRBF .... Total Renal Blood Flow [*Medicine*]
TRBIDM ... Trends in Biotechnology [*A publication*]
Tr Biogeokhim Lab Akad Nauk SSSR ... Trudy Biogeokhimicheskoi Laboratorii Akademii Nauk SSSR [*A publication*]
Tr Biol Inst Akad Nauk SSSR Sib Otd ... Trudy Biologicheskogo Instituta Akademiya Nauk SSSR Sibirskoe Otdelenie [*A publication*]
Tr Biol Inst Zapadno-Sib Fil Akad Nauk SSSR ... Trudy Biologicheskogo Instituta Zapadno-Sibirskogo Filiala Akademii Nauk SSSR [*A publication*]
Tr Biol Nauchno Issled Inst Biol Stn Permsk Gos Univ ... Trudy Biologicheskogo Nauchno-Issledovatel'skogo Instituta i Biologicheskoi Stantsii pri Permskom Gosudarstvennom Universitete [*A publication*]
Tr Biol Nauchno Issled Inst Molotov Gos Univ ... Trudy Biologicheskogo Nauchno-Issledovatel'skogo Instituta pri Molotovskom Gosudarstvennom Universitete [*A publication*]
Tr Biol Pochv Inst Dalnevost Nauchn Tsentr Akad Nauk SSSR ... Trudy Biologo-Pochvennogo Instituta Dal'nevostochnyi Nauchnyi Tsentr Akademiya Nauk SSSR [*A publication*]
Tr Biol Stn Borok Akad Nauk SSSR ... Trudy Biologicheskoi Stantsii "Borok" Akademii Nauk SSSR [*A publication*]
TRBK .... Trustbank Savings FSB [*NASDAQ symbol*] (NQ)
Trbl .... Tractatenblad [*A publication*]
TRBL .... Trouble (FAAC)
TRBL .... Troubleshooting (NASA)
Tr Blagoveshch Gos Med Inst ... Trudy Blagoveshchenskogo Gosudarstvennogo Meditsinskogo Instituta [*A publication*]
Tr Blagoveshch Skh Inst ... Trudy Blagoveshchenskogo Sel'skokhozyaistvennogo Instituta [*A publication*]
TRBMA ..... Texas Reports on Biology and Medicine [*A publication*]
TRBN .... Trombone [*Music*]
Tr Bot Inst Akad Nauk SSSR ... Trudy Botanicheskogo Instituta Akademii Nauk SSSR [*A publication*]
Tr Bot Inst Akad Nauk SSSR Ser 4 ... Trudy Botanicheskogo Instituta Akademii Nauk SSSR. Seriya 4 [*A publication*]

Tr Bot Inst Akad Nauk SSSR Ser 5 ... Trudy Botanicheskogo Instituta Akademiya Nauk SSSR. Seriya 5. Rastitel'noe Syr'ye [*A publication*]
Tr Bot Inst Akad Nauk SSSR Ser 6 ... Trudy Botanicheskogo Instituta Akademiya Nauk SSSR. Seriya 6. Introduktsiya Rastenii i Zelenoe [*A publication*]
Tr Bot Inst Akad Nauk Tadzhikskoi SSR ... Trudy Botanicheskogo Instituta Akademiya Nauk Tadzhikskoi SSR [*A publication*]
Tr Bot Inst Akad Nauk Tadzh SSR ... Trudy Botanicheskogo Instituta Akademiya Nauk Tadzhikskoi SSR [*A publication*]
Tr Bot Inst Azerb Fil Akad Nauk SSSR ... Trudy Botanicheskogo Instituta Azerbaidzhanskii Filial Akademii Nauk SSSR [*A publication*]
Tr Bot Inst V L Komarova Akad Nauk SSSR Ser VII ... Trudy Botanicheskogo Instituta Imeni V. L. Komarova Akademiya Nauk SSSR. Seriya VII [*A publication*]
Tr Bot Sada Akad Nauk Ukr SSR ... Trudy Botanicheskogo Sada Akademii Nauk Ukrainskoi SSR [*A publication*]
Tr Bot Sada Tashk Akad Nauk Uzb SSR ... Trudy Botanicheskogo Sada v Tashkente Akademii Nauk Uzbekskoi SSR [*A publication*]
Tr Bot Sada Tashkente Akad Nauk Uzb SSR ... Trudy Botanicheskogo Sada v Tashkente Akademii Nauk Uzbekskoi SSR [*A publication*]
Tr Bot Sada Zapadn-Sib Fil Akad Nauk SSSR ... Trudy Botanicheskogo Sada Zapadno-Sibirskogo Filiala Akademii Nauk SSSR [*A publication*]
Tr Bot Sadov Akad Nauk Kaz SSR ... Trudy Botanicheskikh Sadov Akademii Nauk Kazakhskoi SSR [*A publication*]
TRBP .... Trainable Retractable Bow Propeller
Tr Bryansko Lesokhoz Inst ... Trudy Bryanskogo Lesokhozyaistvennogo Instituta [*A publication*]
TRBU .... Treasury Bulletin
Tr Bukhar Obl Opytn Skh Stn ... Trudy Bukharskoi Oblastnoi Opytnoi Sel'skokhozyaistvennoi Stantsii [*A publication*]
Tr Burat Inst Estest Nauk Buryat Fil Sib Otd Akad Nauk SSSR ... Trudy Buryatskogo Instituta Estestvennykh Nauk. Buryatskii Filial. Sibirskoe Otdelenie. Akademiya Nauk SSSR [*A publication*]
Tr Buryat-Mong Nauchno-Issled Vet Opytn Stn ... Trudy Buryat-Mongol'skoi Nauchno-Issledovatel'skoi Veterinarnoi Opytnoi Stantsii [*A publication*]
Tr Buryat Mong Zoovet Inst ... Trudy Buryat-Mongol'skogo Zooveterinarnogo Instituta [*A publication*]
Tr Buryat S-Kh Inst ... Trudy Buryatskogo Sel'skokhozyaistvennogo Instituta [*A publication*]
Tr Buryat Zoovet Inst ... Trudy Buryatskogo Zooveterinarnogo Instituta [*A publication*]
TRC .... [*The*] Radiochemical Centre [*British*]
TRC .... [*The*] Ranchero Club (EA)
TRC .... [*The*] Revitalization Corps (EA)
TRC .... Tanned Red Cell [*Clinical chemistry*]
TRC .... Tape Reader Calibrator
TRC .... Tape Reader Control
TRC .... Tape Record Coordinator [*Data processing*]
TRC .... Tape Relay Center (NATG)
TRC .... Taylor Ranch [*California*] [*Seismograph station code, US Geological Survey*] (SEIS)
TrC .... Tayloreed Corporation, Rochester, NY [*Library symbol*] [*Library of Congress*] (LCLS)
TRC .... Technical Repair Center [*Air Force*] (AFIT)
TRC .... Technical Research Center (MCD)
TRC .... Technical Resources Center [*Syracuse University*] [*Research center*]
TRC .... Technical Review Committee [*International Atomic Energy Agency*] (NRCH)
TRC .... Technology Reports Centre [*British*]
TRC .... Technology Resource Center [*Information service or system*] (IID)
TRC .... Tejon Ranch Co. [*AMEX symbol*] (SPSG)
TRC .... Telemetry and Remote Control (IEEE)
TRC .... Temperature Recording Controller
TRC .... Teryl Resources Corp. [*Vancouver Stock Exchange symbol*]
TRC .... Test Readiness Certificate (AAG)
TRC .... Textile Research Council [*British*]
TRC .... Thermal Regenerative Cracking [*Hydrocarbon pyrolysis process*]
TRC .... Thermodynamics Research Center [*College Station, TX*] [*Department of Commerce*] (GRD)
TRC .... Thoroughbred Racing Communications [*An association*] (EA)
TRC .... Thrombosis Research Center [*Temple University*] [*Research center*] (RCD)
TRC .... Tierce [*Unit of measurement*]
TRC .... Tithe Rent-Charge
TRC .... Token Ring Controller
TRC .... Topic [*Record label*] [*Great Britain*]
TRC .... Toroidal Propellant Container
TRC .... Torreon [*Mexico*] [*Airport symbol*] (OAG)
TRC .... Total Relevant Cost
TRC .... Total Residual Chlorine [*Environmental chemistry*]
TRC .... Total-Response Chromatogram
TRC .... Total Ridge Count [*Anthropology*]
TRC .... Tough Rubber-Sheathed Cable

TRC	Tracking, RADAR-Input, and Correlation
TRC	Trade Relations Council of the United States (EA)
TRC	Traffic Records Committee (EA)
TRC	Transcaribbean (MCD)
TRC	Transmit/Receive Control Unit
TRC	Transportation Research Center [*Ohio*]
TRC	Transverse Redundancy Check [*Data processing*] (IBMDP)
TRC	Travelers Research Center [*Oceanography*]
trc	Treble Crochet
TRC	Tricon International Airlines [*Dallas, TX*] [*FAA designator*] (FAAC)
TRC	Triumph Roadster Club (EA)
TRC	Trona Railway Company [*AAR code*]
TRC	Type Requisition Code [*Military*]
TRC	United States Army TRADOC, Fort Leavenworth Post Library, Commander, General Staff, Fort Leavenworth, KS [*OCLC symbol*] (OCLC)
TRCA........	Tricycle Racing Club of America
TRC-AS.....	Transmit/Receive Control Unit-Asynchronous Start/Stop
TRCC........	T-Carrier Restoration Control Center [*Bell System*]
TRCC........	Theodore Roosevelt Centennial Commission [*Government agency*] [*Terminated, 1959*]
TR8CCA....	TR8 Car Club of America (EA)
TRCCC.......	Tracking RADAR Central Control Console [*BMEWS*]
TRCE........	Tactical Radio Communications Equipment
TRCE........	Terrace [*Classified advertising*] (ADA)
TRCE........	Thermionic Reactor Critical Experiment [*NASA*]
TRCE........	Trace
TRCE........	Trace Products [*NASDAQ symbol*] (NQ)
Tr Ch..........	Transactions of the High Court of Chancery (Tothill's Reports) [*A publication*] (DLA)
Tr Chelyab Gos Pedagog Inst ...	Trudy Chelyabinskii Gosudarstvennyi Pedagogicheskii Institut [*A publication*]
Tr Chelyab Inst Mekh Elektrif Selsk Khoz ...	Trudy Chelyabinskogo Instituta Mekhanizatsii i Elektrifikatsii Sel'skogo Khozyaistva [*A publication*]
Tr Chelyab Politekh Inst ...	Trudy Chelyabinskii Politekhnicheskii Institut [*USSR*] [*A publication*]
Tr Chernomorsk Biol Stan Varna ...	Trudove na Chernomorskata Biologichna Stantsiya v Varna [*A publication*]
TRCHI.......	Tanned Red Cell Hemagglutination Inhibition Test [*Immunology*]
Tr Chimkent Obl Skh Opytn Stn Kaz SSR ...	Trudy Chimkentskoi Oblastnoi Sel'skokhozyaistvennoi Opytnoi Stantsii. Kazakhskaya SSR [*A publication*]
Tr Chuv Skh Inst ...	Trudy Chuvashskogo Sel'skokhozyaistvennogo Instituta [*A publication*]
Tr Chuv Skh Opytn Stn ...	Trudy Chuvashskoi Sel'skokhozyaistvennoi Opytnoi Stantsii [*A publication*]
TRCI..........	Technology Research Corporation [*Clearwater, FL*] [*NASDAQ symbol*] (NQ)
TRCO	Technical Representative of the Contracting Officer (MCD)
TRCO	Trade and Commerce [*A publication*]
TRCO	Transportation Research Command [*Army*] (KSC)
TRCO	Trico Products Corp. [*NASDAQ symbol*] (NQ)
Tr Coll Physicians Phila ...	Transactions and Studies. College of Physicians of Philadelphia [*A publication*]
Tr Conf ULB ...	Travaux et Conferences. Universite Libre de Bruxelles [*A publication*]
TRCONS...	Theater Rate Consolidation Data File [*Military*]
Tr Consist J ...	Tristram's Consistory Judgments [*1872-90*] [*England*] [*A publication*] (DLA)
TRCP........	Tape Recorder Control Panel (MCD)
TRCR........	Tracer (MSA)
TRCR........	Tractor
TRCR........	Trail Riders of the Canadian Rockies (EA)
TRCRA......	Tobacco Research Council. Research Paper [*A publication*]
TRCS	Tactical Radio Communications System
TRCS	Techniques for Determining RADAR Cross Section [*Air Force*]
TRC-SC	Transmit/Receive Control Unit-Synchronous Character
TRC-SF	Transmit/Receive Control Unit-Synchronous Framing
TRCVR......	Transceiver (CET)
TRD	Registry of Tissue Reactions to Drugs [*Later, DETP*] (EA)
TRD	Test Requirements Document [*NASA*] (AAG)
TRD	Thread (AAG)
TRD	Toyota Racing Development [*Toyota Motor Corp.*]
TRD	Transferred (ROG)
TRD	Trapped Radiation Detector
TRD	Tread
TRD	Trivandrum [*India*] [*Seismograph station code, US Geological Survey*] (SEIS)
TRD	Trivandrum [*India*] [*Geomagnetic observatory code*]
TRD	Trondheim [*Norway*] [*Airport symbol*] (OAG)
TRD	Trouble Reporting Desk [*NASA*] (KSC)
TRD	Troudor Resources, Inc. [*Vancouver Stock Exchange symbol*]
TRD	Try Repeating Dose [*Medicine*]
TRD	Turbine Reduction Drive
TRD	United States Army TRADOC, Fort Dix Post Library, Fort Dix, NJ [*OCLC symbol*] (OCLC)
Tr Dagest Gos Pedagog Inst ...	Trudy Dagestanskogo Gosudarstvennogo Pedagogicheskogo Instituta [*A publication*]

Tr Dagest Gos Pedagog Inst Estestv-Geogr Fak ...	Trudy Dagestanskogo Gosudarstvennogo Pedagogicheskogo Instituta Estestvenno-Geograficheskii Fakul'tet [*A publication*]
Tr Dagest S-Kh Inst ...	Trudy Dagestanskogo Sel'skokhozyaistvennogo Instituta [*A publication*]
Tr Dalnevost Fil Akad Nauk SSSR Ser Geol ...	Trudy Dal'nevostochnogo Filiala Akademii Nauk SSSR. Seriya Geologicheskaya [*A publication*]
Tr Dalnevost Fil Akad Nauk SSSR Ser Khim ...	Trudy Dal'nevostochnogo Filiala Akademii Nauk SSSR. Seriya Khimicheskaya [*A publication*]
Tr Dalnevost Geol Razved Tresta ...	Trudy Dal'nevostochnogo Geologo-Razvedochnogo Tresta [*A publication*]
Tr Dal'nevost Gos Med Inst ...	Trudy Dal'nevostochnogo Gosudarstvennogo Meditsinskogo Instituta [*A publication*]
Tr Dalnevost Gos Univ ...	Trudy Dal'nevostochnogo Gosudarstvennogo Universiteta [*A publication*]
Tr Dalnevost Gos Univ Ser 4 ...	Trudy Dal'nevostochnogo Gosudarstvennogo Universiteta. Seriya 4. Lesnye Nauki [*A publication*]
Tr Dalnevost Gos Univ Ser 5 ...	Trudy Dal'nevostochnogo Gosudarstvennogo Universiteta. Seriya 5. Sel'skoe Khozyaistvo [*A publication*]
Tr Dalnevost Gos Univ Ser 7 ...	Trudy Dal'nevostochnogo Gosudarstvennogo Universiteta. Seriya 7. Fizika i Khimiya [*A publication*]
Tr Dalnevost Gos Univ Ser 8 ...	Trudy Dal'nevostochnogo Gosudarstvennogo Universiteta. Seriya 8. Biologiya [*A publication*]
Tr Dalnevost Gos Univ Ser 11 ...	Trudy Dal'nevostochnogo Gosudarstvennogo Universiteta. Seriya 11. Geologiya [*A publication*]
Tr Dalnevost Gos Univ Ser 12 ...	Trudy Dal'nevostochnogo Gosudarstvennogo Universiteta. Seriya 12. Gornoe Delo [*A publication*]
Tr Dalnevost Gos Univ Ser 13 ...	Trudy Dal'nevostochnogo Gosudarstvennogo Universiteta. Seriya 13. Tekhnika [*A publication*]
Tr Dalnevost Gos Univ Ser 15 ...	Trudy Dal'nevostochnogo Gosudarstvennogo Universiteta. Seriya 15. Matematika [*A publication*]
Tr Dalnevost Kraev Nauchno Issled Inst ...	Trudy Dal'nevostochnogo Kraevogo Nauchno-Issledovatel'skogo Instituta [*A publication*]
Tr Dalnevost Nauchno Issled Gidrometeorol Inst ...	Trudy Dal'nevostochnogo Nauchno-Issledovatel'skogo Gidrometeorologicheskogo Instituta [*A publication*]
Tr Dalnevost Nauchno Issled Vet Inst ...	Trudy Dal'nevostochnogo Nauchno-Issledovatel'skogo Veterinarnogo Instituta [*A publication*]
Tr Dalnevost Politekh Inst ...	Trudy Dal'nevostochnogo Politekhnicheskogo Instituta [*A publication*]
Tr Dalnevost Tekh Inst Rybn Promsti Khoz ...	Trudy Dal'nevostochnogo Tekhnicheskogo Instituta Rybnoi Promyshlennosti i Khozyaistva [*A publication*]
Tr Darvinsk Gos Zapov ...	Trudy Darvinskogo Gosudarstvennogo Zapovednika [*A publication*]
TRDC	Transport Research and Development Command [*Army*] (MCD)
TRDCBC ...	Datum Collection. Tokai Regional Fisheries Research Laboratory [*A publication*]
TRDE	Transparent Rotating Disk Electrode [*Electrochemistry*]
TRDG	Trading (DCTA)
TRDI.........	Trim Die (AAG)
TRDIA.......	Transmission and Distribution [*A publication*]
Tr Din Raz ...	Trudy po Dinamike Razvitiya [*A publication*]
TRDJSDOPII ...	[*The*] Reverend Doctor Jonathan Swift, Dean of Patrick's in Ireland [*Pseudonym used by Jonathan Swift*]
TRDL.........	Tactical Reconnaissance Data Link (MCD)
TR & DL....	Tung Research and Development League [*Defunct*] (EA)
TRDM	Tactical Reconnaissance Data Marking
TRDMRK ...	Trademark
Tr Dnepropetr Inst Inzh Zheleznodorozhn Transp ...	Trudy Dnepropetrovskogo Instituta Inzhenerov Zheleznodorozhnogo Transporta [*A publication*]
Tr Dnepropetr Khim Tekhnol Inst ...	Trudy Dnepropetrovskogo Khimiko-Tekhnologicheskogo Instituta [*A publication*]
Tr Dnepropetr S-Kh Inst ...	Trudy Dnepropetrovskogo Sel'skokhozyaistvennogo Instituta [*A publication*]
Tr Donbasskaya Nauchno Issled Lab ...	Trudy Donbasskaya Nauchno-Issledovatel'skaya Laboratoriya [*A publication*]
Tr Donetsk Gos Med Inst ...	Trudy Donetskogo Gosudarstvennogo Meditsinskogo Instituta [*A publication*]
Tr Donetsk Ind Inst ...	Trudy Donetskogo Industrial'nogo Instituta [*Ukrainian SSR*] [*A publication*]
Tr Donetsk Politekh Inst Ser Fiz Mat ...	Trudy Donetskogo Politekhnicheskogo Instituta. Seriya Fiziko-Matematicheskaya [*A publication*]
Tr Donetsk Politekh Inst Ser Khim Tekhnol ...	Trudy Donetskogo Politekhnicheskogo Instituta. Seriya Khimiko-Tekhnologicheskaya [*A publication*]
Tr Donetsk Politekh Inst Ser Metall ...	Trudy Donetskogo Politekhnicheskogo Instituta. Seriya Metallurgicheskaya [*A publication*]
Tr Donetsk Politekh Inst Ser Stroit ...	Trudy Donetskogo Politekhnicheskogo Instituta. Seriya Stroitel'naya [*A publication*]

TRDR .... Test Readiness Design Review
TRDS........ Towards (ROG)
TRDT .... Trim and Drill Template (MCD)
TRDT .... Triple Rotating Directional Transmission [*Military*] (CAAL)
TRDTO ..... Tracking RADAR Data Takeoff
TRDx........ Texas Red-Labeled Dextran
TRDY .... Trudy Corp. [*NASDAQ symbol*] (NQ)
TRE .... Telecommunications Research Establishment [*British military*] (DMA)
TRE .... Tempore Regis Edwardi [*In the Time of King Edward*] [*Latin*] (DLA)
TRE .... Terratech Resources, Inc. [*Toronto Stock Exchange symbol*]
TRE .... Theologische Realenzyklopaedie [*A publication*]
TRE .... Thyroid Hormone Response Element [*Endocrinology*]
TRE .... Thyroid-Responsive Element [*Genetics*]
TRE .... Tidal Regenerator Engine
TRE .... Timing Read Error
TRE .... Tiree Island [*Scotland*] [*Airport symbol*] (OAG)
TRE .... Total Rare Earths (NRCH)
TRE .... Total Resource Effectiveness Index [*Environmental Protection Agency*]
TRE .... Toxicity Reduction Evaluation
TRE .... Training Equipment (KSC)
TRE .... Training Readiness Evaluation (MCD)
TRE .... Training-Related Expenses [*Work Incentive Program*]
TRE .... Transient Radiation Effects
TRE .... Treasury
TRE .... Tremont Corp. [*NYSE symbol*] (SPSG)
TRE .... Trent University [*UTLAS symbol*]
TRE .... Trente [*Italy*] [*Seismograph station code, US Geological Survey*] [*Closed*] (SEIS)
TRE .... True Radiation Emittance
TRE .... Trusts and Estates [*A publication*]
TRE .... United States Army TRADOC, Fort Eustis Post Library and Translation School Library, Fort Eustis, VA [*OCLC symbol*] (OCLC)
TREA........ [*The*] Retired Enlisted Association (EA)
TREA & A ... [*The*] Real Estate Appraiser and Analyst [*Society of Real Estate Appraisers*] [*A publication*]
Tread.......... Treadway's South Carolina Constitutional Reports [*A publication*] (DLA)
Tread.......... Treadway's South Carolina Law Reports [*1812-16*] [*A publication*] (DLA)
TREAD...... Troop Recognition and Detection (MCD)
Tread Const ... Treadway's South Carolina Constitutional Reports [*A publication*] (DLA)
Treadway Const (SC) ... Treadway's South Carolina Constitutional Reports [*A publication*] (DLA)
TREAS ...... Treasurer (EY)
TREAS ...... Treasury (ROG)
Treas Dec... Treasury Decisions under Customs and Other Laws [*United States*] [*A publication*] (DLA)
Treas Dec Int Rev ... Treasury Decisions under Internal Revenue Laws [*A publication*] (DLA)
Treas Dept Cir ... Treasury Department Circular [*A publication*] (DLA)
Treas Regs ... United States Treasury Regulations [*A publication*] (DLA)
TREAT...... Transient Radiation Effects Automated Tabulation
TREAT...... Transient Reactor Test Facility
TREAT...... Treatment (AAG)
TREAT...... Trouble Report Evaluation and Analysis Tool (MCD)
Treatise Anal Chem ... Treatise on Analytical Chemistry [*A publication*]
Treatise Mater Sci Technol ... Treatise on Materials Science and Technology [*A publication*]
Treatises Sect Med Sci Pol Acad Sci ... Treatises of the Section of Medical Sciences. Polish Academy of Sciences [*A publication*]
Treat Tro.... Treatise on Trover and Conversion [*A publication*] (DLA)
TREB........ Treble (ROG)
Treballs Inst Bot Barc ... Treballs. Institut Botanic de Barcelona [*A publication*]
TREC........ Tracking RADAR Electronic Component (AFM)
TREC........ Transistor Radiation Effects Compilation [*Program*] (MCD)
TREC........ Treco [*NASDAQ symbol*] (NQ)
TRECOM ... Transportation Research and Engineering Command (MUGU)
TRED .... TDA [*Taxpayer Delinquent Account*] Report Edit Data [*IRS*]
TRED .... Transmitting and Receiving Equipment Development (MCD)
Tred.......... Tredgold's Cape Colony Reports [*A publication*] (DLA)
TREDS ...... TRADOC Educational Data System
TREDS-NRI ... TRADOC [*Training and Doctrine Command*] Educational Data System - Nonresident Instruction [*Army*]
TREE........ Aspen Leaf, Inc. [*NASDAQ symbol*] (NQ)
TREE........ Transient Radiation Effects on Electronics [*Military*]
TREE........ Trustee
Tree Crops J ... Tree Crops Journal [*A publication*]
Tree Farm Proc ... Trees on Farms. Proceedings of a Seminar on Economic and Technical Aspects of Commercial Plantations. Agro-Forestry and Shelter Belts on Farms [*A publication*]
TREELS.... Time-Resolved Electron Energy-Loss Spectroscopy
Tree Plant Notes ... Tree Planters' Notes [*A publication*]
Tree Plant Notes US For Serv ... Tree Planter's Notes. United States Forest Service [*A publication*]
Tree-Ring Bull ... Tree-Ring Bulletin [*A publication*]

TREES ...... Time-Resolved Europium Excitation Spectroscopy
TREES ...... Transient Radiation Effects on Electronic Systems [*Air Force*] (MCD)
Trees Mag ... Trees Magazine [*A publication*]
Trees Nat Resour ... Trees and Natural Resources [*A publication*]
TREESS..... Tactical Reflected and Emitted Energy Suppression System
Trees S Afr ... Trees in South Africa [*A publication*]
Trees Victoria's Resour ... Trees and Victoria's Resources [*A publication*]
TREET ...... [*A*] programming language (CSR)
T Regswet .. Tydskrif vir Regswetenskap [*A publication*]
Trehern...... British and Colonial Prize Cases [*A publication*] (DLA)
TREKA...... Technical Reports. Engineering Research Institute. Kyoto University [*A publication*]
Tr Eksp Nauchno Issled Inst Metallorezhushchikh Stankov ... Trudy Eksperimental'nyi Nauchno-Issledovatel'skii Institut Metallorezhushchikh Stankov [*A publication*]
TREKZINE ... Trek Magazine [*Generic term for a publication of interest to fans of the television program "Star Trek"*]
TREL........ Transitron Electronic Corp. [*NASDAQ symbol*] (NQ)
Tr Elem Med ... Trace Elements in Medicine [*A publication*]
TREM........ Tape Reader Emulator Module
TREM........ TRADOC Research Center [*Monterey, CA*] [*Army*] (GRD)
Trem.......... Tremaine's Pleas of the Crown [*England*] [*A publication*] (DLA)
Trem PC .... Tremaine's Pleas of the Crown [*England*] [*A publication*] (DLA)
TREN .... Trenwick Group, Inc. [*NASDAQ symbol*] (NQ)
tren............ Tris(aminoethyl)amine [*Organic chemistry*]
TRENA...... Tokyo Toritsu Eisei Kenkyusho Kenkyu Nempo [*A publication*]
TREND ..... Trade-Offs for Lifting Reentry Vehicle Evaluation and Nominal Design
TREND ..... Transportation Research News [*A publication*]
TREND ..... Tropical Environmental Data
Trend Eng ... Trends in Engineering [*A publication*]
Trend Eng Univ Wash ... Trends in Engineering. University of Washington [*A publication*]
Trend Prognosticke Inf ... Trend Prognosticke Informace [*A publication*]
Trends Anal Chem ... Trends in Analytical Chemistry [*A publication*]
Trends Analyt Chem ... Trends in Analytical Chemistry [*A publication*]
Trends Auton Pharmacol ... Trends in Autonomic Pharmacology [*A publication*]
Trends Biochem Sci ... Trends in Biochemical Sciences [*A publication*]
Trends Biochem Sci (Pers Ed) ... Trends in Biochemical Sciences (Personal Edition) [*Netherlands*] [*A publication*]
Trends Biochem Sci (Ref Ed) ... Trends in Biochemical Sciences (Reference Edition) [*Netherlands*] [*A publication*]
Trends Biot ... Trends in Biotechnology [*A publication*]
Trends Biotechnol ... Trends in Biotechnology [*A publication*]
Trends Ed .. Trends in Education [*A publication*]
Trends in Ed ... Trends in Education [*A publication*]
Trends Educ ... Trends in Education [*A publication*]
Trends Fluoresc ... Trends in Fluorescence [*A publication*]
Trends Gen ... Trends in Genetics [*A publication*]
Trends Genet ... Trends in Genetics [*A publication*]
Trends Haematol ... Trends in Haematology [*A publication*]
Trends Neurosci ... Trends in Neurosciences [*Netherlands*] [*A publication*]
Trends Perspect Parasitol ... Trends and Perspectives in Parasitology [*A publication*]
Trends and Perspect Signal Process ... Trends and Perspectives in Signal Processing [*A publication*]
Trends Pharmacol Sci ... Trends in Pharmacological Sciences [*A publication*]
Trends Tech Contemp Dent Lab ... Trends and Techniques in the Contemporary Dental Laboratory [*A publication*]
Tr Energ Inst Akad Nauk Az SSR ... Trudy Energeticheskogo Instituta Akademiya Nauk Azerbaidzhanskoi SSR [*A publication*]
Tr Energ Inst Az SSR ... Trudy Energeticheskogo Instituta Azerbaidzhanskoi SSR [*A publication*]
Tr Energ Inst Im I G Es'mana Akad Nauk Azerb SSR ... Trudy Energeticheskogo Instituta Imeni I. G. Es'mana Akademiya Nauk Azerbaidzhanskoi SSR [*Azerbaidzhan SSR*] [*A publication*]
TR (Eng).... Term Reports [*99-101 English Reprint*] [*A publication*] (DLA)
TRENS...... Transcutaneous Random Electrical Nerve Stimulator [*Medicine*]
Trent LJ..... Trent Law Journal [*A publication*]
Tr Entom Soc London ... Transactions. Entomological Society of London [*A publication*]
Trep............ Treponema [*Microbiology*]
Tr Eq.......... Fonblanque's Treatise of Equity [*A publication*] (DLA)
Tr Erevan Gos Inst Usoversh Vrachei ... Trudy Erevanskogo Gosudarstvennogo Instituta Usovershenstvovaniya Vrachei [*A publication*]
Tr Erevan Med Inst ... Trudy Erevanskogo Meditsinskogo Instituta [*A publication*]
Tr Erevan Zootekh Vet Inst ... Trudy Erevanskogo Zootekhnichesko-Veterinarnogo Instituta [*A publication*]
Tr Erevan Zoovet Inst ... Trudy Erevanskogo Zooveterinarnogo Instituta [*A publication*]
TRES .... Tayside Rehabilitation Engineering Services [*United Kingdom*] (IRUK)

TRES .... Terminal Retrieval and Enquiry Services [*Department of Employment*] [*British*]
TRES .... Thermally Regenerative Electrochemical System [*Power source*]
TRES .... Time-Resolved Emission Spectra
TRESI .... Target Resolution Extraction of Statistical Invariances
TRESNET ... Trent Interlibrary Loan and Communication Network [*Canada*] [*Information service or system*] (IID)
TRESNET ... Trent Resource Sharing Network [*Ontario Library Service Trent*] [*Richmond Hill, ON*] [*Telecommunications*] (TSSD)
Tr and Est ... Trusts and Estates [*A publication*]
Tr Estestvennonauchn Inst Molotov Gos Univ ... Trudy Estestvennonauchnogo Instituta pri Molotovskom Gosudarstvennom Universitete [*A publication*]
Tr Estestvennonauchn Inst Permsk Gos Univ ... Trudy Estestvennonauchnogo Instituta pri Permskom Gosudarstvennom Universitete [*A publication*]
Tr Estestv Inst Permsk Gos Univ Radiospektrosk ... Trudy Estestvennonauchnogo Instituta pri Permskom Gosudarstvennom Universitete Imeni A. M. Gor'kogo Radiospektroskopiy [*A publication*]
TRev .... Theologische Revue [*A publication*]
T Rev .... Translation Review [*A publication*]
Trev Tax Suc ... Trevor's Taxes on Succession [*4th ed.*] [*1881*] [*A publication*] (DLA)
TREX .... Intrex Financial Services, Inc. [*NASDAQ symbol*] (NQ)
Trex .... Tyrannosaurus Rex [*A dinosaur*]
TRF .... T-Cell Replacing Factor [*Biochemistry*]
TRF .... Tank Range-Finder
TRF .... Tariff
TRF .... Technical Reference File
TRF .... Technical Replacement Factor
TRF .... Tele-Radio Systems Ltd. [*Toronto Stock Exchange symbol*]
TRF .... Terminal Renal Failure [*Medicine*]
TRF .... Test Tube and Ring-Shaped Forms [*AIDS cytology*]
TRF .... Thermal Radiation at Microwave Frequencies
TRF .... Thymus-Cell Replacing Factor [*Immunology*]
TRF .... Thyrotrophin-Releasing Factor [*Later, TRH*] [*Endocrinology*]
TRF .... Tragicorum Romanorum Fragmenta [*A publication*] (OCD)
TRF .... Transducer Repair Facility
TRF .... Transfer (AABC)
TRF .... Transferrin [*Also, T, TF*] [*Biochemistry*]
TRF .... Transportation Research Forum (EA)
TRF .... Transportation Research Foundation
TRF .... Tuna Research Foundation (EA)
TRF .... Tuned Radio Frequency
TRF .... Turf Research Foundation [*Defunct*] (EA)
TRF .... United States Army TRADOC, Fort McClellan, Fort McClellan, AL [*OCLC symbol*] (OCLC)
TRFA .... Triple Revolving Fund Account (AABC)
TRFA .... Trustees for Alaska. Newsletter [*A publication*]
TRFAD ..... Thomas Roderick Fraser and Andrew Dewar [*Pseudonym*]
TRFB .... Tariff Board [*Canada*]
TRFC .... Tanya Roberts Fan Club (EA)
TRFC .... Tex Ritter Fan Club (EA)
TRFC .... Traffic (MSA)
TRFC .... Tristan Rogers Fan Club (EA)
TRFCA ...... Tea Research Foundation (Central Africa) (EAIO)
TRFCS .... Temperature Rate Flight Control System
Tr Ferg Politekh Inst ... Trudy Ferganskogo Politekhnicheskogo Instituta [*A publication*]
TRFI .... Trans Financial Bancorp, Inc. [*Bowling Green, KY*] [*NASDAQ symbol*] (NQ)
Tr (Fifteenth) Internat Cong Hyg and Demog ... Transactions. Fifteenth International Congress on Hygiene and Demography [*A publication*]
Tr Fiz Inst Akad Nauk SSSR ... Trudy Fizicheskogo Instituta Imeni P. N. Lebedeva Akademiya Nauk SSSR [*A publication*]
Tr Fiz Inst Im Lebedeva ... Trudy Ordena Lenina Fizicheskogo Instituta Imeni P. N. Lebedeva [*A publication*]
Tr Fiz Inst Im P N Lebedeva Akad Nauk SSSR ... Trudy Fizicheskogo Instituta Imeni P. N. Lebedeva Akademiya Nauk SSSR [*USSR*] [*A publication*]
Tr Fiziol Biokhim Rast ... Trudy po Fiziologii i Biokhimii Rastenii [*Estonian SSR*] [*A publication*]
Tr Fiziol Lab Akad Nauk SSSR ... Trudy Fiziologicheskoi Laboratorii Akademii Nauk SSSR [*A publication*]
Tr Fiziol Patol Zhen ... Trudy Fiziologicheskoi Patologii Zhenshchiny [*A publication*]
Tr Fiz Mosk Gorn Inst ... Trudy po Fizike Moskovskii Gornyi Institut [*A publication*]
Tr Fiz Poluprovodn ... Trudy po Fizike Poluprovodnikov [*A publication*]
Tr Fiz Tekh Inst Akad Nauk Turkm SSR ... Trudy Fiziko-Tekhnicheskogo Instituta Akademiya Nauk Turkmenskoi SSR [*A publication*]
Tr Frunz Politekh Inst ... Trudy Frunzenskogo Politekhnicheskogo Instituta [*A publication*]
TRFS .... Trace Fuselage Station (MCD)
TRG .... [*The*] Record Group [*Funded by N. V. Philips*]
TRG .... T-Cell Rearranging Gene [*Genetics*]

TRG .... Tactical Reconnaissance Group
TRG .... Tauranga [*New Zealand*] [*Airport symbol*] (OAG)
TRG .... Technical Research Group, Inc. (MCD)
TRG .... Telecommunications Research Group [*Culver City, CA*] [*Telecommunications*] (TSSD)
TRG .... Tertiary Research Group [*British*]
TRG .... Tijdschrift voor Rechtsgeschiedenis [*A publication*]
TRG .... Track-Rich Grains[*s*] [*Cosmic-ray path in meteorites*]
TRG .... Trailing (AAG)
TRG .... Training
T/R & G..... Transmit, Receive, and Guard (MSA)
TRG .... Travail et Methodes. Revue des Nouvelles au Service de l'Entreprise [*A publication*]
TRG .... [*The*] Triangle Corp. [*AMEX symbol*] (SPSG)
TRG .... Trilogy Resource Corp. [*Toronto Stock Exchange symbol*]
TRG .... Triton Research Group (EA)
TRG .... Trudeau, R. G., Bloomfield Hills MI [*STAC*]
TRG .... Tuned Rotor Gyro (MCD)
TRG .... United States Army TRADOC, Fort Benning Post and Infantry School Library, Fort Benning, GA [*OCLC symbol*] (OCLC)
TRGA .... Trust Co. of Georgia [*NASDAQ symbol*] (NQ)
TRGEE2.... Trends in Genetics [*A publication*]
Tr Gelmintol Lab ... Trudy Gel'mintologicheskoi Laboratorii [*A publication*]
Tr Gel'mintol Lab Akad Nauk SSSR ... Trudy Gel'mintologicheskaya Laboratoriya Akademiya Nauk SSSR [*A publication*]
Tr Geofiz Inst Akad Nauk SSSR ... Trudy Geofizicheskogo Instituta Akademiya Nauk SSSR [*A publication*]
Tr Geol Bulg Ser Geokhm Mineral Petrogr ... Trudove Vurkhu Geologiyata na Bulgariya. Seriya Geokhimaya Mineralogiya i Petrografiya [*A publication*]
Tr Geol Bulg Ser Inzh Geol Khidrogeol ... Trudove Vurkhu Geologiyata na Bulgariya. Seriya Inzhenerna Geologiya i Khidrogeologiya [*A publication*]
Tr Geol Bulg Ser Paleonto ... Trudove Vurkhu Geologiyata na Bulgariya. Seriya Paleontologiya [*A publication*]
Tr Geol Inst Akad Nauk Gruz SSR ... Trudy Geologicheskogo Instituta Akademiya Nauk Gruzinskoi SSR [*A publication*]
Tr Geol Inst Akad Nauk Gruz SSR Geol Ser ... Trudy Geologicheskogo Instituta Akademiya Nauk Gruzinskoi SSR. Geologicheskaya Seriya [*A publication*]
Tr Geol Inst Akad Nauk Gruz SSR Mineral Petrogr Ser ... Trudy Geologicheskogo Instituta Akademiya Nauk Gruzinskoi SSR. Mineralogo-Petrograficheskaya Seriya [*A publication*]
Tr Geol Inst Akad Nauk SSSR ... Trudy Geologicheskogo Instituta Akademiya Nauk SSSR [*A publication*]
Tr Geol Inst (Kazan) ... Trudy Geologicheskogo Instituta (Kazan) [*A publication*]
Tr Geol Zavod Soc Repub Makedonija ... Trudovei na Geoloskiot Zavod na Socijalisticka Republika Makedonija [*A publication*]
Tr Geom Semin ... Trudy Geometriceskogo Seminara [*A publication*]
TrgGpRM ... Training Group, Royal Marines [*British*]
TRGH .... Trough [*Freight*]
Tr GIAP..... Trudy GIAP [*A publication*]
Tr Gidrometeorol Nauchno-Issled Tsentr SSSR ... Trudy Gidrometeorologicheskii Nauchno-Issledovatel'skii Tsentral'nogo SSSR [*A publication*]
Tr "Giprotsement" ... Trudy "Giprotsement" [*A publication*]
TRGL......... Toreador Royalty Corp. [*NASDAQ symbol*] (NQ)
TRGLA...... Triangle [*English Edition*] [*A publication*]
TrGlasgUOrS ... Transactions. Glasgow University Oriental Society [*Hertford, England*] [*A publication*]
Tr Glav Bot Sada ... Trudy Glavnogo Botanicheskogo Sada [*A publication*]
Tr Glavgeologii (Gl Upr Geol Okhr Nedr) Uzb SSR ... Trudy Glavgeologii (Glavnoe Upravlenie Geologii i Okhrany Nedr) Uzbekskoi SSR [*A publication*]
TRGLB...... Triangle [*A publication*]
Tr Gl Bot Sada ... Trudy Glavnogo Botanicheskogo Sada [*A publication*]
Tr Gl Bot Sada Akad Nauk SSSR ... Trudy Glavnogo Botanicheskogo Sada Akademiya Nauk SSSR [*A publication*]
Tr Gl Geofiz Obs ... Trudy Glavnoi Geofizicheskoi Observatorii [*USSR*] [*A publication*]
Tr Gl Geo Obs ... Trudy Glavnoi Geofizicheskoi Observatorii [*A publication*]
Tr Golovn Nauchno-Issled Inst Tsem Mashinostr ... Trudy Golovnoi Nauchno-Issledovatel'skii Institut Tsementnogo Mashinostroeniya [*A publication*]
Tr Goriiskogo Gos Pedagog Inst ... Trudy Goriiskogo Gosudarstvennogo Pedagogicheskogo Instituta [*A publication*]
Tr Gor'k Golovn Skh Inst ... Trudy Gor'kovskii Golovnoi Sel'skokhozyaistvennyi Institut [*A publication*]
Tr Gor'k Gos Med Inst ... Trudy Gor'kovskogo Gosudarstvennogo Meditsinskogo Instituta [*A publication*]
Tr Gor'k Gos Nauchno Issled Inst Gig Tr Profbolezn ... Trudy Gor'kovskii Gosudarstvennyi Nauchno-Issledovatel'skii Institut Gigieny Truda i Profbolezni [*A publication*]
Tr Gork Gos Pedagog Inst ... Trudy Gor'kovskogo Gosudarstvennogo Pedagogicheskogo Instituta [*A publication*]
Tr Gork Inst Inzh Vodn Transp ... Trudy Gor'kovskogo Instituta Inzhenerov Vodnogo Transporta [*A publication*]
Tr Gork Inzh Stroit Inst ... Trudy Gor'kovskogo Inzhenero-Stroitel'nogo Instituta [*A publication*]

Tr Gork Nauchno Issled Pediatr Inst ... Trudy Gor'kovskogo Nauchno-Issledovatel'skogo Pediatricheskogo Instituta [*A publication*]

Tr Gor'k Nauchno-Issled Vet Opytn Stn ... Trudy Gor'kovskoi Nauchno-Issledovatel'skoi Veterinarnoi Opytnoi Stantsii [*A publication*]

Tr Gork Politekh Inst ... Trudy Gor'kovskogo Politekhnicheskogo Instituta [*A publication*]

Tr Gor'k S-Kh Inst ... Trudy Gor'kovskogo Sel'skokhozyaistvennogo Instituta [*A publication*]

Tr Gorno Geol Inst Akad Nauk SSSR Ural Fil ... Trudy Gorno-Geologicheskogo Instituta Akademiya Nauk SSSR Ural'skii Filial [*A publication*]

Tr Gorno Geol Inst Akad Nauk SSSR Zapadno Sib Fil ... Trudy Gorno-Geologicheskogo Instituta Akademiya Nauk SSSR Zapadno-Sibirskii Filial [*A publication*]

Tr Gos Astron Inst Im Shternberga ... Trudy Gosudarstvennogo Astronomicheskogo Instituta Imeni P. K. Shternberga [*A publication*]

Tr Gos Astron Inst Mosk Gos Univ ... Trudy Gosudarstvennogo Astronomicheskogo Instituta Moskovskii Gosudarstvennyi Universitet [*A publication*]

Tr Gos Dorozhn Proektno Izyskatel'skii Nauchno Issled Inst ... Trudy Gosudarstvennyi Dorozhnyi Proektno-Izyskatel'skii i Nauchno-Issledovatel'skii Institut [*A publication*]

Tr Gos Gidrol Inst ... Trudy Gosudarstvennogo Gidrologicheskogo Instituta [*A publication*]

Tr Gos Inst Prikl Khim ... Trudy Gosudarstvennyi Institut Prikladnoi Khimii [*A publication*]

Tr Gos Inst Proekt Issled Rab Neftedobyvayushchei Prom-Sti ... Trudy Gosudarstvennyi Institut po Proektirovaniyu i Issledovatel'skim Rabotam v Neftedobyvayushchei Promyshlennosti [*USSR*] [*A publication*]

Tr Gos Inst Usoversh Vrachei I M Lenina ... Trudy Gosudarstvennogo Instituta Usovershenstvovaniya Vrachei I. M. Lenina [*A publication*]

Tr Gos Issled Elektrokeram Inst ... Trudy Gosudarstvennogo Issledovatel'skogo Elektrokeramicheskogo Instituta [*USSR*] [*A publication*]

Tr Gos Issled Keram Inst ... Trudy Gosudarstvennogo Issledovatel'skogo Keramicheskogo Instituta [*A publication*]

Tr Gos Makeev Nauchno-Issled Inst Bezop Rab Gorn Prom-Sti ... Trudy Gosudarstvennyi Makeevskii Nauchno-Issledovatel'skii Institut po Bezopasnosti Rabot v Gornoi Promyshlennosti [*Ukrainian SSR*] [*A publication*]

Tr Gos Nauchno Eksp Inst Grazhdanskikh Prom Inzh Sooruzh ... Trudy Gosudarstvennyi Nauchno-Eksperimental'nogo Instituta Grazhdanskikh Promyshlennykh i Inzhenernykh Sooruzhenii [*A publication*]

Tr Gos Nauchno Issled Elektrokeram Inst ... Trudy Gosudarstvennogo Nauchno-Issledovatel'skogo Elektrokeramicheskogo Instituta [*A publication*]

Tr Gos Nauchno Issled Inst Gornokhim Syr ... Trudy Gosudarstvennogo Nauchno-Issledovatel'skogo Instituta Gornokhimicheskogo Syr'ya [*A publication*]

Tr Gos Nauchno-Issled Inst Gornokhim Syr'ya ... Trudy Gosudarstvennogo Nauchno-Issledovatel'skogo Instituta Gornokhimicheskogo Syr'ya [*USSR*] [*A publication*]

Tr Gos Nauchno Issled Inst Keram Promsti ... Trudy Gosudarstvennogo Nauchno-Issledovatel'skogo Instituta Keramicheskoi Promyshlennosti [*A publication*]

Tr Gos Nauchno Issled Inst Khim Promsti ... Trudy Gosudarstvennogo Nauchno-Issledovatel'skogo Instituta Khimicheskoi Promyshlennosti [*A publication*]

Tr Gos Nauchno-Issled Inst Prom Sanit Ochistke Gazov ... Trudy Gosudarstvennogo Nauchno-Issledovatel'skogo Instituta po Promyshlennoi i Sanitarnoi Ochistke Gazov [*USSR*] [*A publication*]

Tr Gos Nauchno Issled Inst Psikhiatrii ... Trudy Gosudarstvennogo Nauchno-Issledovatel'skogo Instituta Psikhiatrii [*A publication*]

Tr Gos Nauchno-Issled Inst Stroit Keram ... Trudy Gosudarstvennyi Nauchno-Issledovatel'skii Institut Stroitel'noi Keramiki [*USSR*] [*A publication*]

Tr Gos Nauchno-Issled Inst Ukha Gorla Nosa ... Trudy Gosudarstvennogo Nauchno-Issledovatel'skogo Instituta Ukha Gorla i Nosa [*A publication*]

Tr Gos Nauchno Issled Keram Inst ... Trudy Gosudarstvennogo Nauchno-Issledovatel'skogo Keramicheskogo Instituta [*A publication*]

Tr Gos Nauchno-Issled Proekt Inst Splavov Obrab Tsvet Met ... Trudy Gosudarstvennyi Nauchno-Issledovatel'skii i Proektnyi Institut Splavov i Obrabotki Tsvetnykh Metallov [*USSR*] [*A publication*]

Tr Gos Nauchno Issled Proektn Inst "Gipromorneft" ... Trudy Gosudarstvennogo Nauchno-Issledovatel'skogo i Proektnogo Instituta "Gipromorneft" [*A publication*]

Tr Gos Nauchno-Issled Proektn Inst Splavov Obrab Tsvetn Met ... Trudy Gosudarstvennyj Nauchno-Issledovatel'skij i Proektnyj Institut Splavov i Obrabotki Tsvetnykh Metallov [*A publication*]

Tr Gos Nauchno Issled Rentgeno Radiol Inst ... Trudy Gosudarstvennyi Nauchno-Issledovatel'skii Rentgeno-Radiologicheskii Institut [*A publication*]

Tr Gos Nauchno-Kontrol'n Inst Vet Prep ... Trudy Gosudarstvennogo Nauchno-Kontrol'nogo Instituta Veterinarnykh Preparatov [*A publication*]

Tr Gos Nikitskii Bot Sad ... Trudy Gosudarstvennyi Nikitskii Botanicheskii Sad [*A publication*]

Tr Gos Okeanogr Inst ... Trudy Gosudarstvennogo Okeanograficheskogo Instituta [*A publication*]

Tr Gos Opt Inst ... Trudy Gosudarstvennogo Opticheskogo Instituta [*USSR*] [*A publication*]

Tr Gos Proektno Issled Inst Vostokgiprogaz ... Trudy Gosudarstvennyi Proektno-Issledovatel'skii Institut "Vostokgiprogaz" [*A publication*]

Tr Gos Proektno Konstr Nauchno Issled Inst Morsk Transp ... Trudy Gosudarstvennyi Proektno-Konstruktorskii i Nauchno-Issledovatel'skii Institut Morskogo Transporta [*A publication*]

Tr Gos Soyuzn Nauchno Issled Trakt Inst ... Trudy Gosudarstvennyi Soyuznyi-Nauchno-Issledovatel'skii Traktornyi Institut [*A publication*]

Tr Gos Tsentr Nauchno Issled Inst Tekhnol Organ Proizvod ... Trudy Gosudarstvennyi Tsentral'nyi Nauchno-Issledovatel'skii Institut Tekhnologii i Organizatsii Proizvodstva [*A publication*]

Tr Gos Vses Dorozhn Nauchno Issled Inst ... Trudy Gosudarstvennyi Vsesoyuznyi Dorozhnyi Nauchno-Issledovatel'skii Institut [*A publication*]

Tr Gos Vses Inst Proekt Nauchno-Issled Rab Giprotsement ... Trudy Gosudarstvennogo Vsesoyuznogo Instituta po Proektirovaniyu i Nauchno-Issledovatel'skim Rabotam "Giprotsement" [*A publication*]

Tr Gos Vses Inst Proekt Nauchno-Issled Rab Tsem Promsti ... Trudy Gosudarstvennogo Vsesoyuznyi Instituta po Proektirovaniyu i Nauchno-Issledovatel'skim Rabotam v Tsementnoi Promyshlennosti [*A publication*]

Tr Gos Vses Proektn Nauchno-Issled Inst Tsem Prom-Sti ... Trudy Gosudarstvennyi Vsesoyuznyi Proektnyi i Nauchno-Issledovatel'skii Institut Tsementnoi Promyshlennosti [*USSR*] [*A publication*]

TRGP........ Tactical Reconnaissance Group [*Air Force*]

Tr Grozn Neft Inst ... Trudy Groznenskii Neftyanoi Institut [*A publication*]

Tr Gruz Nauchno-Issled Inst Energ ... Trudy Gruzinskogo Nauchno-Issledovatel'skogo Instituta Energetiki [*Georgian SSR*] [*A publication*]

Tr Gruz Nauchno-Issled Inst Gidrotekh Melior ... Trudy Gruzinskogo Nauchno-Issledovatel'skogo Instituta Gidrotekhniki i Melioratsii [*A publication*]

Tr Gruz Politekh Inst ... Trudy Gruzinskogo Politekhnicheskogo Instituta [*Georgian SSR*] [*A publication*]

Tr Gruz S-kh Inst ... Trudy Gruzinskogo Sel'skokhozyaistvennogo Instituta [*A publication*]

TRGT........ Target (AAG)

TRH.......... Technical Reference Handbook

TRH.......... Test Requirements Handbook (MUGU)

TRH.......... Their Royal Highnesses

TRH.......... Thyrotrophin-Releasing Hormone [*Formerly, TRF*] [*Endocrinology*]

TRH.......... Transatlantic Holdings [*NYSE symbol*] (SPSG)

TRH.......... Truss Head [*Engineering*]

TRH.......... United States Army TRADOC, Fort Benjamin Harrison Library System, Fort Benjamin Harrison, IN [*OCLC symbol*] (OCLC)

TRHADS... Topical Reviews in Haematology [*A publication*]

TRHAZCON ... Training Hazardous Condition (MCD)

Tr & H Pr... Troubat and Haly's Pennsylvania Practice [*A publication*] (DLA)

Tr & H Prec Ind ... Train and Heard's Precedents of Indictment [*A publication*] (DLA)

TRH-R....... Thyrotrophin-Releasing Hormone Receptor [*Endocrinology*]

TRHS .... Transactions. Royal Historical Society [*A publication*]

TRHUA..... Travail Humain [*A publication*]

TRI............ Bristol, TN [*Location identifier*] [*FAA*] (FAAL)

TRI............ [*The*] Refractories Institute (EA)

TRI............ Tactical Reconnaissance/Intelligence [*Air Force*] (AFM)

TRI............ Technical Report Instruction (AAG)

TRI............ Technical Research Institute [*Japan*]

TRI............ Telecomputer Research, Incorporated [*Bala Cynwyd, PA*] [*Information service or system*] [*Telecommunications*] (TSSD)

TRI............ Telemanagement Resources International, Inc. (TSSD)

TRI............ Textile Research Institute (EA)

TRI............ Time-Reversal Invariance [*Physics*]

TRI............ Tin Research Institute (EA)

TRI............ Tire Retreading Institute (EA)

TRI............ Torsion Reaction Integrating

TRI............ Total Response Index [*Psychology*]

TRI............ Toxic Chemical Release Inventory [*National Library of Medicine*] [*Information service or system*] (CRD)

TRI............ Toxics Release Inventory [*Environmental Protection Agency*]

TRI............ Transaction Routing Index
TRI............ Translation Research Institute　(EA)
TR-I......... Translations Register - Index　(MCD)
TRI............ Transpacific Resources, Inc. [Toronto Stock Exchange symbol]
TRI............ Transponder Receiver Isolation
TRI............ Transportation Research Institute [Carnegie-Mellon University]
TRI............ Transportation Research Institute [Oregon State University] [Research center]　(RCD)
TRI............ Tri-City Airport [Tennessee] [Airport symbol]　(OAG)
TRI............ Tri-College Library, Moorhead, MN [OCLC symbol]　(OCLC)
TRI............ Tri-State Airlines, Inc. [White Lake, NY] [FAA designator]　(FAAC)
TRI............ Triangle Industries, Inc. [NYSE symbol]　(SPSG)
Tri............. Triangulation
Tri............ Triangulum [Constellation]
TRI........... Triassic [Period, era, or system] [Geology]
Tri............ Tribuna [A publication]
TRI.......... Trichloroethylene [Anesthesiology]
TRI.......... Tricycle　(AAG)
TRI.......... Trieste [Grotta Gigante] [Italy] [Seismograph station code, US Geological Survey]　(SEIS)
TRI.......... Triode　(AAG)
TRI.......... Tropical Research Institute [Smithsonian Institution]
TRI.......... Trucking Research Institute [Research center]　(RCD)
TRI.......... Tuboreticular Inclusions [Hematology]
TRIA........ Telemetry Range Instrumentation Aircraft
TRIA........ Temperature Removable Instrument Assembly [Nuclear energy]　(NRCH)
TRIA........ Triacontanol [Plant growth regulator]
TRIA........ Triangle Industries, Inc. [NASDAQ symbol]　(NQ)
Tria.......... Triangulum [Constellation]
TRIAC...... Test Resources Improvement Advisory Council [Military]
TRIAC...... Triiodothyroacetic Acid [Endocrinology]
TRIAC...... Triode Alternating Current Semiconductor Switch
TRIAD...... Target Resolving Information Augmentation Device　(MCD)
TRIAL....... Technique to Retrieve Information from Abstracts of Literature [Data processing]
Trial Advoc Q ... Trial Advocate Quarterly [A publication]　(DLA)
Trial Diplomacy J ... Trial Diplomacy Journal [A publication]
Trial Dpl J ... Trial Diplomacy Journal [A publication]
Trial Law Forum ... Trial Lawyers Forum [A publication]　(DLA)
Trial Law G ... Trial Lawyer's Guide [A publication]
Trial Law Guide ... Trial Lawyer's Guide [A publication]
Trial Law Q ... Trial Lawyers Quarterly [A publication]
TRIB........ Tire Retread Information Bureau
TRIB........ Transfer Rate of Information BITs [Binary Digits] [Dial telephone network] [American National Standards Institute]
TRIB........ Tri-Basin Resources Ltd. [NASDAQ symbol]　(NQ)
TRIB........ Tribal
TRIB........ Tribulation　(DSUE)
Trib.......... Tribunal
Trib.......... Tribunale [Ordinary Court of First Instance] [Italian]　(DLA)
TRIB........ Tribunus [Tribune] [Latin]　(OCD)
TRIB........ Tributary
TRIB........ Tribute　(ADA)
Trib Admin ... Tribunaux Administratifs [French]　(DLA)
Trib Arb Mixtes ... Tribunaux Arbitraux Mixtes [French]　(DLA)
Trib CEBEDEAU ... Tribune. CEBEDEAU [Centre Belge d'Etude et de Documentation des Eaux et de l'Air] [A publication]
Trib Con ... Tribunal des Conflits [Tribunal of Conflicts] [French]　(DLA)
TRIBE....... Teaching and Research in Bicultural Education [Indian organization in Maine]
TriBeCa ..... Triangle Below Canal Street [Artists' colony in New York City] [See also NoHo, SoHo, SoSo]
Trib Farm (Curitiba) ... Tribuna Farmaceutica (Curitiba) [A publication]
Tri Bish...... Trial of the Seven Bishops [A publication]　(DLA)
Trib Mus.... Tribune Musical [A publication]
Trib Odontol ... Tribuna Odontologica [A publication]
Tribol Int ... Tribology International [A publication]
Tribol Lubrificazione ... Tribologia e Lubrificazione [A publication]
Tribologia & Lubr ... Tribologia e Lubrificazione [A publication]
Tribology ... Tribology International [A publication]
Tribology Int ... Tribology International [A publication]
TRIB POT ... Tribunicia Potestas [Latin]　(OCD)
Tribuna Postale ... Tribuna Postale e delle Telecomunicazioni [A publication]
TRIC.......... Trachoma-Inclusion Conjunctivitis [Ophthalmology]
TRIC.......... Tracking RADAR Input and Correlation　(MSA)
TRIC.......... Transaction Identification Code [Military]　(AFIT)
TRIC.......... Transit Research Information Center [Department of Transportation] [Washington, DC]　(GRD)
TRIC........ Tri-Chem, Inc. [NASDAQ symbol]　(NQ)
TRIC........ Tricks for Research in Cancer
TRIC........ Triclinic [Crystallography]
TRICAP .... Triple Capability [Army]
TRICC....... Tariff Rules of the Interstate Commerce Commission
TRICE ...... Transistorized Realtime Incremental Computer
Trich .... Trichomonas [A protozoan] [Medicine]
Trich .... Trichoptera [Entomology]
TRICI .... Trichinopoli Cigar　(DSUE)

TRICINE... Tris(hydroxymethyl)methylglycine [Biochemical analysis]
TRICL....... Triclinic
TRICS ...... Threat Reactive Integrated Combat System
TRICS ...... Trajectory Incremental Correction System　(MCD)
TRID......... Track Identity
TRID......... Triduum [Three Days] [Latin]　(ADA)
TRIDAC.... Three-Dimensional Analog Computer [British]　(MCD)
TRIDENT ... South Atlantic Cooperative Investigation Phase [Marine science]　(MSC)
TRIDO ...... Table Ronde Internationale pour le Developpement de l'Orientation [International Round Table for the Advancement of Counselling - IRTAC]　(EAIO)
TRIDOP.... Tridoppler
Tri E of Cov ... Trial of the Earl of Coventry [A publication]　(DLA)
Trier Archiv ... Trierisches Archiv [A publication]
TriererThZ ... Trierer Theologische Zeitschrift [Trier] [A publication]
TriererZ..... Trierer Zeitschrift fuer Geschichte und Kunst des Trierer Landes und Seiner Nachbargebiete [A publication]
Trierer Z Gesch Kunst ... Trierer Zeitschrift fuer Geschichte und Kunst des Trierer Landes und Seiner Nachbargebiete [A publication]
TRI-FED ... Triathlon Federation/USA　(EA)
TRIFED/USA ... Triathlon Federation/USA [Later, TRI-FED]　(EA)
TRIFLATE ... Trifluoromethanesulfonate [Organic chemistry]
TRIFLIC ... Trifluoromethanesulfonic [Organic chemistry]
triFMA ...... Time-Resolved Immunofluorometric Assay [Clinical chemistry]
TRIG......... Triangulation　(AABC)
TRIG......... Trigger　(AAG)
trig............ Triglycerides [Clinical chemistry]
TRIG......... Trigonal [Crystallography]
TRIG......... Trigonometry
TRIGA....... Training Reactor, Isotopes General Atomic [Nuclear energy]
TRIGA....... Traitement Industrial des Gadoues [French company]
TRIGAT ... Third Generation Antitank [Army]
TRIGLYME ... Triethylene Glycol Dimethyl Ether [Organic chemistry]
TRIGON ... Trigonometry　(ROG)
TRII.......... Travelers Realty Income Investors [Boston, MA] [NASDAQ symbol]　(NQ)
TRIL......... Trilogy Ltd. [NASDAQ symbol]　(NQ)
TRIM........ Inertia Dynamics Corp. [Chandler, AZ] [NASDAQ symbol]　(NQ)
TRIM........ Tailored Reliable Integrated Modular
TRIM........ Tailored Retrieval and Information Management
TRIM........ Targets, Receivers, Impacts, and Methods
TRIM........ Tax Reform Immediately　(EA)
TRIM........ Tax Reform Information Materials
TRIM........ Technical Requirements Identification Matrix　(MCD)
TRIM........ Technique for Report and Index Management [Information service or system] [No longer available]　(IID)
TRIM........ Test Rules for Inventory Management
TRIM........ Thin Region Integral Method
TRIM........ Throw Away/Repair Implications on Maintenance
TRIM........ Timely Responsive Integrated Multiuse System　(MCD)
TRIM........ Trails, Roads, and Interdiction Missions [or Multisensor] [Navy]
TRIM........ Training Relation and Instruction Mission [Military] [Vietnam, France, United States]
TRIM........ Training Requirements and Information Management System [Navy]
TRIM........ Transformation of Imagery [Data processing] [NASA]
TRI-M .... Tri-M Music Honor Society [Acronym is based on former name, Modern Music Masters Society]　(EA)
TRIM........ Trimmer [Mining engineering]
Trim Econ .. Trimestre Economico [A publication]
Trimes Econ ... Trimestre Economico [A publication]
TRIMET ... Trimethylolethane [Organic chemistry]
TRIMIS..... Tri-Service Medical Information Systems [Military]
TRIMM..... Triple Missile Mount　(MCD)
TRIMMS .. Telecom Canada Remote Interface Monitoring and Management System
TRIMMS .. Total Refinement and Integration of Maintenance Management Systems [Army]
Trim Pol..... Trimestre Politico [A publication]
TRIMS ...... Trade-Related Investment Measures [International finance]　(ECON)
TRIMS ...... Training Requirements and Information Management System　(MCD)
TRIMS ...... Transportation Integrated Management System [Air Force]
TRIN .... Trans-Industries, Inc. [NASDAQ symbol]　(NQ)
TRIN .... Trans International Airlines
TRIN .... Trinity
Trin .... Trinity Term [British] [Legal term]　(DLA)
TRINCO.... Trincomalee [Sri Lanka port city]　(DSUE)
Tr Indiana Med Soc ... Transactions. Indiana State Medical Society [A publication]
TRI Newsl ... Textile Research Institute. Newletter [A publication]
Trinidad LR ... Trinidad Law Reports [A publication]　(DLA)
Trinidad Tobago Min Petrol Mines Mon Bull ... Trinidad and Tobago. Ministry of Petroleum and Mines. Monthly Bulletin [A publication]

Trinity J..... Trinity Journal [*A publication*]
Trinity Sem R ... Trinity Seminary Review [*A publication*]
Trinkwasser-Verord ... Trinkwasser-Verordnung [*A publication*]
Tr Inst Biol Akad Nauk Latv SSR ... Trudy Institut Biologii Akademiya Nauk Latviiskoi SSR [*A publication*]
Tr Inst Biol Akad Nauk SSSR Ural Fil ... Trudy Instituta Biologii Akademiya Nauk SSSR Ural'skii Filial [*USSR*] [*A publication*]
Tr Inst Biol Bashk Univ ... Trudy Instituta Biologii Bashkirskogo Universiteta [*A publication*]
Tr Inst Biol Ural Fil Akad Nauk SSSR ... Trudy Instituta Biologii Ural'skogo Filiala Akademii Nauk SSSR [*A publication*]
Tr Inst Biol Vnutr Vod Akad Nauk SSSR ... Trudy Instituta Biologii Vnutrennikh Vod Akademii Nauk SSSR [*A publication*]
Tr Inst Biol Yakutsk Fil Sib Otd Akad Nauk SSSR ... Trudy Instituta Biologii Yakutskii Filial Sibirskogo Otdeleniya Akademii Nauk SSSR [*A publication*]
Tr Inst Bot Akad Nauk Azerb SSR ... Trudy Instituta Botaniki Akademiya Nauk Azerbaidzhanskoi SSR [*A publication*]
Tr Inst Bot Akad Nauk Kazakh SSR ... Trudy Instituta Botaniki Akademiya Nauk Kazakhskoi SSR [*A publication*]
Tr Inst Bot Akad Nauk Kaz SSR ... Trudy Instituta Botaniki Akademii Nauk Kazakhskoi SSR [*A publication*]
Tr Inst Chist Khim Reakt ... Trudy Instituta Chistykh Khimicheskikh Reaktivov [*A publication*]
Tr Inst Ehkol Rast Zhivotn ... Trudy Instituta Ehkologii Rastenij i Zhivotnykh [*A publication*]
Tr Inst Ehlektrokhim Akad Nauk SSSR Ural Fil ... Trudy Instituta Ehlektrokhimii Akademiya Nauk SSSR Ural'skij Filial [*A publication*]
Tr Inst Ehlektrokhim Ural Nauch Tsentr Akad Nauk SSSR ... Trudy Instituta Ehlektrokhimii Ural'skij Nauchnyj Tsentr Akademiya Nauk SSSR [*A publication*]
Tr Inst Ekol Rast Zhivotn ... Trudy Instituta Ekologii Rastenii i Zhivotnykh [*USSR*] [*A publication*]
Tr Inst Ekol Rast Zhivotn Ural Fil Akad Nauk SSSR ... Trudy Instituta Ekologii Rastenii i Zhivotnykh Ural'skogo Filiala Akademii Nauk SSSR [*A publication*]
Tr Inst Ekol Rast Zhivotn Ural Nauchn Tsentr Akad Nauk SSSR ... Trudy Instituta Ekologii Rastenii i Zhivotnykh Ural'skii Nauchnyi Tsentr Akademiya Nauk SSSR [*USSR*] [*A publication*]
Tr Inst Eksp Biol Akad Nauk Kaz SSR ... Trudy Instituta Eksperimental'noi Biologii Akademiya Nauk Kazakhskoi SSR [*A publication*]
Tr Inst Eksper Biol Akad Nauk Eston SSR ... Trudy Instituta Eksperimental'noi Biologii Akademiya Nauk Estonskoi SSR [*A publication*]
Tr Inst Eksp Klin Khir Gematol ... Trudy Instituta Eksperimental'noi i Klinicheskoi Khirurgii i Gematologii [*A publication*]
Tr Inst Eksp Klin Med Akad Nauk Latv SSR ... Trudy Instituta Eksperimental'noi i Klinicheskoi Meditsiny Akademii Nauk Latviiskoi SSR [*A publication*]
Tr Inst Eksp Klin Onkol Akad Med Nauk SSSR ... Trudy Instituta Eksperimental'noi Klinicheskoi Onkologii Akademiya Meditsinskikh Nauk SSSR [*USSR*] [*A publication*]
Tr Inst Eksp Med Akad Med Nauk SSR ... Trudy Instituta Eksperimental'noi Meditsiny Akademii Meditsinskikh Nauk SSR [*A publication*]
Tr Inst Eksp Med Akad Nauk Latv SSR ... Trudy Instituta Eksperimental'noi Meditsiny Akademii Nauk Latviiskoi SSR [*A publication*]
Tr Inst Eksp Med Akad Nauk Lit SSR ... Trudy Instituta Eksperimental'noi Meditsiny Akademii Nauk Litovskoi SSR [*A publication*]
Tr Inst Eksp Meteorol ... Trudy Institut Eksperimental'noi Meteorologii [*USSR*] [*A publication*]
Tr Inst Elektrokhim Ural Nauchn Tsentr Akad Nauk SSSR ... Trudy Instituta Elektrokhimii Ural'skii Nauchnyi Tsentr Akademiya Nauk SSSR [*USSR*] [*A publication*]
Tr Inst Energ Akad Nauk BSSR ... Trudy Instituta Energetiki Akademiya Nauk Belorusskoi SSR [*Belorussian SSR*] [*A publication*]
Tr Inst Epidemiol Mikrobiol (Frunze) ... Trudy Instituta Epidemiologii i Mikrobiologii (Frunze) [*A publication*]
Tr Inst Fiz Akad Nauk Azerb SSR ... Trudy Instituta Fiziki Akademiya Nauk Azerbaidzhanskoi SSR [*Azerbaidzhan SSR*] [*A publication*]
Tr Inst Fiz Akad Nauk Est SSR ... Trudy Instituta Fiziki Akademii Nauk Estonskoi SSR [*A publication*]
Tr Inst Fiz Akad Nauk Gruz SSR ... Trudy Instituta Fiziki Akademiya Nauk Gruzinskoi SSR [*Georgian SSR*] [*A publication*]
Tr Inst Fiz Astron Akad Nauk Ehst SSR ... Trudy Instituta Fiziki i Astronomii Akademiya Nauk Ehstonskoj SSR [*A publication*]
Tr Inst Fiziol Akad Nauk Gruz SSR ... Trudy Instituta Fiziologii Akademiya Nauk Gruzinskoi SSR [*Georgian SSR*] [*A publication*]
Tr Inst Fiziol Akad Nauk Kaz SSR ... Trudy Instituta Fiziologii Akademiya Nauk Kazakhskoi SSR [*A publication*]
Tr Inst Fiziol Akad Nauk SSSR ... Trudy Instituta Fiziologii Akademiya Nauk SSSR [*A publication*]
Tr Inst Fiziol Im I P Pavlova Akad Nauk SSSR ... Trudy Instituta Fiziologii Imeni I. P. Pavlova Akademii Nauk SSSR [*A publication*]
Tr Inst Fiziol Im I P Pavlova Akad Nauk SSSR ... Trudy Instituta Fiziologii Imeni I. P. Pavlova Akademii Nauk SSSR [*A publication*]
Tr Inst Fiziol Rast Im K A Timiryazeva ... Trudy Instituta Fiziologii Rastenii Imeni K. A. Timiryazeva [*A publication*]

Tr Inst Fiz Met Ural Nauchn Tsent Akad SSSR ... Trudy Instituta Fiziki Metallov Ural'skogo Nauchnogo Tsentra Akademiya Nauk SSSR [*USSR*] [*A publication*]
Tr Inst Fiz Vys Ehnerg ... Trudy Instituta Fiziki Vysokikh Ehnergij [*A publication*]
Tr Inst Fiz Vys Energ Akad Nauk Kaz SSR ... Trudy Instituta Fiziki Vysokikh Energii Akademiya Nauk Kazakhskoi SSR [*Kazakh SSR*] [*A publication*]
Tr Inst Fiz Zemli Akad Nauk SSSR ... Trudy Instituta Fiziki Zemli Akademiya Nauk SSSR [*USSR*] [*A publication*]
Tr Inst Genet Akad Nauk SSSR ... Trudy Instituta Genetiki Akademii Nauk SSSR [*A publication*]
Tr Inst Genet Sel Akad Nauk Az SSR ... Trudy Instituta Genetiki i Selektsii Akademii Nauk Azerbaidzhanskoi SSR [*A publication*]
Tr Inst Geofiz Akad Nauk Gruz SSR ... Trudy Instituta Geofiziki Akademiya Nauk Gruzinskoi SSR [*Georgian SSR*] [*A publication*]
Tr Inst Geogr Akad Nauk SSSR ... Trudy Instituta Geografii Akademii Nauk SSSR [*A publication*]
Tr Inst Geol Akad Nauk Est SSR ... Trudy Instituta Geologii Akademiya Nauk Estonskoi SSR [*Estonian SSR*] [*A publication*]
Tr Inst Geol Akad Nauk Tadzh SSR ... Trudy Instituta Geologii Akademiya Nauk Tadzhikskoi SSR [*A publication*]
Tr Inst Geol Geofiz Akad Nauk SSSR Sib Otd ... Trudy Instituta Geologii i Geofiziki Akademiya Nauk SSSR Sibirskoe Otdelenie [*USSR*] [*A publication*]
Tr Inst Geol Korisnikh Koplain Akad Nauk Ukr RSR ... Trudy Institut Geologii Kori Korisnikh Koplain Akademiya Nauk Ukrains'koi RSR [*Ukrainian SSR*] [*A publication*]
Tr Inst Geol Nauk Akad Nauk Kaz SSR ... Trudy Instituta Geologicheskikh Nauk Akademiya Nauk Kazakhskoi SSR [*Kazakh SSR*] [*A publication*]
Tr Inst "Giproninemetallorud" ... Trudy Instituta "Giproninemetallorud" [*A publication*]
Tr Inst Goryuch Iskop (Moscow) ... Trudy Instituta Goryuchikh Iskopaemykh (Moscow) [*A publication*]
Tr Inst Istor Estestvozn Tekh Akad Nauk SSSR ... Trudy Instituta Istorii Estestvoznaniya i Tekhniki Akademiya Nauk SSSR [*USSR*] [*A publication*]
Tr Inst Khig Okhr Tr Prof Zabol ... Trudove na Instituta po Khigiena. Okhrana na Truda i Profesionalni Zabolyavaniya [*A publication*]
Tr Inst Khim Akad Nauk Kirg SSR ... Trudy Instituta Khimii Akademiya Nauk Kirgizskoi SSR [*A publication*]
Tr Inst Khim Akad Nauk SSSR Ural Fil ... Trudy Instituta Khimii Akademiya Nauk SSSR Ural'skii Filial [*USSR*] [*A publication*]
Tr Inst Khim Akad Nauk Tadzh SSR ... Trudy Instituta Khimii Akademiya Nauk Tadzhikskoi SSR [*A publication*]
Tr Inst Khim Akad Nauk Turkm SSR ... Trudy Instituta Khimii Akademiya Nauk Turkmenskoi SSR [*A publication*]
Tr Inst Khim Akad Nauk Uzb SSR ... Trudy Instituta Khimii Akademiya Nauk Uzbekskoi SSR [*A publication*]
Tr Inst Khim Metall Akad Nauk SSSR Ural Fil ... Trudy Instituta Khimii i Metallurgii Akademiya Nauk SSSR Ural'skii Filial [*A publication*]
Tr Inst Khim Nauk Akad Nauk Kaz SSR ... Trudy Instituta Khimicheskikh Nauk Akademiya Nauk Kazakhskoi SSR [*A publication*]
Tr Inst Khim Nefti Prir Solei Akad Nauk Kaz SSR ... Trudy Instituta Khimii Nefti i Prirodnykh Solei Akademiya Nauk Kazakhskoi SSSR [*A publication*]
Tr Inst Khim Ural Nauchn Tsentr Akad Nauk SSSR ... Trudy Instituta Khimii Ural'skii Nauchnyi Tsentr Akademiya Nauk SSSR [*A publication*]
Tr Inst Klin Eksp Kardiol ... Trudy Instituta Klinicheskoi i Eksperimental'noi Kardiologii [*A publication*]
Tr Inst Klin Eksp Kardiol Akad Nauk Gruz SSR ... Trudy Instituta Klinicheskoi i Eksperimental'noi Kardiologii Akademiya Nauk Gruzinskoi SSR [*A publication*]
Tr Inst Klin Eksp Khir Akad Nauk Kaz SSR ... Trudy Instituta Klinicheskoi i Eksperimental'noi Khirurgii Akademiya Nauk Kazakhskoi SSR [*A publication*]
Tr Inst Klin Eksp Nevrol Gruz SSR ... Trudy Instituta Klinicheskoi i Eksperimental'noi Nevrologii Gruzinskoi SSR [*A publication*]
Tr Inst Kom Stand Mer Izmer Prib Sov Minist SSSR ... Trudy Institutov Komiteta Standartov Mer i Izmeritel'nykh Priborov pri Sovete Ministrov SSSR [*A publication*]
Tr Inst Kraev Eksp Med Akad Nauk Uzb SSR ... Trudy Instituta Kraevoi Eksperimental'noi Meditsiny Akademiya Nauk Uzbekskoi SSR [*A publication*]
Tr Inst Kraev Med Akad Nauk Kirg SSR ... Trudy Instituta Kraevoi Meditsiny Akademii Nauk Kirgizskoi SSR [*A publication*]
Tr Inst Kraev Patol Akad Nauk Kaz SSR ... Trudy Instituta Kraevoi Patologii Akademii Nauk Kazakhskoi SSR [*A publication*]
Tr Inst Kristallogr Akad Nauk SSSR ... Trudy Instituta Kristallografii Akademiya Nauk SSSR [*A publication*]
Tr Inst Lesa Akad Nauk Gruzin SSR ... Trudy Instituta Lesa Akademiya Nauk Gruzinskoi SSR [*A publication*]
Tr Inst Lesa Akad Nauk Gruz SSR ... Trudy Instituta Lesa Akademii Nauk Gruzinskoi SSR [*A publication*]

Tr Inst Lesa Akad Nauk SSSR ... Trudy Instituta Lesa Akademii Nauk SSSR [*A publication*]
Tr Inst Lesa Drev Akad Nauk SSSR Sib Otd ... Trudy Instituta Lesa i Drevesiny Akademiya Nauk SSSR Sibirskoe Otdelenie [*A publication*]
Tr Inst Lesokhoz Probl Khim Drev Akad Nauk Latv SSR ... Trudy Instituta Lesokhozyaistvennykh Problem i Khimii Drevesiny Akademiya Nauk Latviiskoi SSR [*Latvian SSR*] [*A publication*]
Tr Inst Malyarii Med Parazitol ... Trudy Instituta Malyarii i Meditsinskoi Parazitologii [*A publication*]
Tr Inst Mat Mekh Akad Nauk Az SSR ... Trudy Instituta Matematiki i Mekhaniki Akademii Nauk Azerbajdzhanskoj SSR [*A publication*]
Tr Inst Mekh Obrab Polezn Iskop ... Trudy Instituta Mekhanicheskoi Obrabotki Poleznykh Iskopaemykh [*A publication*]
Tr Inst Melior Vodn Bolotnogo Khoz Akad Nauk B SSR ... Trudy Instituta Melioratsii Vodnogo i Bolotnogo Khozyaistva Akademiya Nauk Belorusskoi SSR [*A publication*]
Tr Inst Merzlotoved Akad Nauk SSSR ... Trudy Instituta Merzlotovedeniya Akademiya Nauk SSSR [*A publication*]
Tr Inst Metall Akad Nauk SSSR ... Trudy Instituta Metallurgii Akademiya Nauk SSSR [*A publication*]
Tr Inst Metall Akad Nauk SSSR Ural Nauchn Tsentr ... Trudy Instituta Metallurgii Akademiya Nauk SSSR Ural'skii Nauchnyi Tsentr [*A publication*]
Tr Inst Metall Im A A Baikova Akad Nauk SSSR ... Trudy Instituta Metallurgii Imeni A. A. Baikova Akademiya Nauk SSSR [*USSR*] [*A publication*]
Tr Inst Metall Obogashch Akad Nauk Kaz SSR ... Trudy Instituta Metallurgii i Obogashcheniya Akademiya Nauk Kazakhskoi SSR [*A publication*]
Tr Inst Metallofiz Metall Akad Nauk SSSR Ural Fil ... Trudy Instituta Metallofiziki Metallurgii Akademiya Nauk SSSR Ural'skii Filial [*A publication*]
Tr Inst Metall (Sverdlovsk) ... Trudy Instituta Metallurgii (Sverdlovsk) [*A publication*]
Tr Inst Met (Leningrad) ... Trudy Instituta Metallov (Leningrad) [*A publication*]
Tr Inst Mikrobiol Akad Nauk Latv SSR ... Trudy Instituta Mikrobiologii Akademii Nauk Latviiskoi SSR [*A publication*]
Tr Inst Mikrobiol Akad Nauk SSSR ... Trudy Instituta Mikrobiologii Akademii Nauk SSSR [*A publication*]
Tr Inst Mikrobiol Virusol Akad Nauk Kaz SSR ... Trudy Instituta Mikrobiologii i Virusologii Akademii Nauk Kazakhskoi SSR [*A publication*]
Tr Inst Morfol Zhivotn Akad Nauk SSSR ... Trudy Instituta Morfologii Zhivotnykh Akademii Nauk SSSR [*A publication*]
Tr Inst Mosk Inst Tonkoi Khim Tekhnol ... Trudy Instituta Moskovskii Institut Tonkoi Khimicheskoi Tekhnologii [*A publication*]
Tr Inst Nefti Akad Nauk Az SSR ... Trudy Instituta Nefti Akademiya Nauk Azerbaidzhanskoi SSR [*A publication*]
Tr Inst Nefti Akad Nauk Kaz SSR ... Trudy Instituta Nefti Akademiya Nauk Kazakhoskoi SSR [*A publication*]
Tr Inst Nefti Akad Nauk SSSR ... Trudy Instituta Nefti Akademiya Nauk SSSR [*A publication*]
Tr Inst Norm Patol Fiziol Akad Med Nauk SSSR ... Trudy Instituta Normal'noi i Patologicheskoi Fiziologii Akademii Meditsinskikh Nauk SSSR [*A publication*]
Tr Inst Nov Lub Syrya ... Trudy Instituta Novogo Lubyanogo Syr'ya [*A publication*]
Tr Inst Obogashch Tverd Goryuch Iskop ... Trudy Instituta Obogashcheniya Tverdykh Goryuchikh Iskopaemykh [*USSR*] [*A publication*]
Tr Inst Okeanol Akad Nauk SSSR ... Trudy Instituta Okeanologii Akademiya Nauk SSSR [*A publication*]
Tr Inst Onkol Akad Med Nauk SSSR ... Trudy Instituta Onkologii Akademiya Meditsinskikh Nauk SSSR [*A publication*]
Tr Inst Org Katal Elektrokhim Akad Nauk Kaz SSR ... Trudy Instituta Organicheskogo Kataliza i Elektrokhimii Akademiya Nauk Kazakhskoi SSR [*Kazakh SSR*] [*A publication*]
Tr Inst Pastera ... Trudy Instituta Imeni Pastera [*A publication*]
Tr Inst Pochvoved Agrokhim Akad Nauk Az SSR ... Trudy Instituta Pochvovedeniya i Agrokhimii Akademii Nauk Azerbaidzhanskoi SSR [*A publication*]
Tr Inst Pochvoved Agrokhim AN UzSSR ... Trudy Instituta Pochvovedeniya i Agrokhimii Akademii Nauk UzSSR [*A publication*]
Tr Inst Pochvoved Akad Nauk Gruz SSR ... Trudy Instituta Pochvovedeniya Akademii Nauk Gruzinskoi SSR [*A publication*]
Tr Inst Pochvoved Akad Nauk Kaz SSR ... Trudy Instituta Pochvovedeniya Akademii Nauk Kazakhskoi SSR [*A publication*]
Tr Inst Pochvoved (Tashkent) ... Trudy Instituta Pochvovedeniya (Tashkent) [*A publication*]
Tr Inst Polevod Akad Nauk Gruz SSR ... Trudy Instituta Polevodstva Akademii Nauk Gruzinskoi SSR [*A publication*]
Tr Inst Polio Virusn Entsefalitov Akad Med Nauk SSSR ... Trudy Instituta Poliomielita i Virusnykh Entsefalitov Akademii Meditsinskikh Nauk SSSR [*A publication*]
Tr Inst Prikl Geofiz ... Trudy Instituta Prikladnoi Geofiziki [*USSR*] [*A publication*]

Tr Inst Prikl Khim Elektrokhim Akad Nauk Gruz SSR ... Trudy Instituta Prikladnoi Khimii i Elektrokhimii Akademiya Nauk Gruzinskoi SSR [*A publication*]
Tr Inst Proektn Nauchno-Issled Inst Ural Promstroiniiproekt ... Trudy Instituta Proektnyi i Nauchno-Issledovatel'skii Institut Ural'skii Promstroiniiproekt [*A publication*]
Tr Inst Razrab Neft Gazov Mestorozhd Akad Nauk Az SSR ... Trudy Instituta Razrabotki Neftyanykh i Gazovykh Mestorozhdenii Akademiya Nauk Azerbaidzhanskoi SSR [*A publication*]
Tr Inst Sadovod Vinograd Vinodel Akad Nauk Gruz SSR ... Trudy Instituta Sadovodstva Vinogradarstva i Vinodeliya Gruzinskoi SSR [*A publication*]
Tr Inst Sadovod Vinograd Vinodel (Tiflis) ... Trudy Instituta Sadovodstva Vinogradarstva i Vinodeliya (Tiflis) [*A publication*]
Tr Inst Sel Semenovod Khlop (Tashkent) ... Trudy Instituta Selektsii i Semenovodstva Khlopchatnika (Tashkent) [*A publication*]
Tr Inst Sist Upr Akad Nauk Gruz SSR ... Trudy Institut Sistem Upravleniya Akademiya Nauk Gruzinskoj SSR [*A publication*]
Tr Inst Stroit Dela Akad Nauk Gruz SSR ... Trudy Instituta Stroitel'nogo Dela Akademiya Nauk Gruzinskoi SSR [*A publication*]
Tr Inst Stroit Mater Miner Proiskhozhd Stekla ... Trudy Instituta Stroitel'nykh Materialov Mineral'nogo Proiskhozhdeniya i Stekla [*A publication*]
Tr Inst Stroit Mekh Seismostoikosti Akad Nauk Gruz SSR ... Trudy Instituta Stroitel'noi Mekhaniki i Seismostoikosti Akademiya Nauk Gruzinskoi SSR [*A publication*]
Tr Inst Stroit Stroimat Akad Nauk Kazakhskoi SSR ... Trudy Instituta Stroitel'stva i Stroimaterialov Akademiya Nauk Kazakhskoi SSR [*A publication*]
Tr Inst Teor Astron ... Trudy Instituta Teoreticeskoi Astronomii [*USSR*] [*A publication*]
Tr Inst Teor Geofiz Akad Nauk SSSR ... Trudy Instituta Teoreticheskoi Geofiziki Akademiya Nauk SSSR [*A publication*]
Tr Inst Torfa Akad Nauk B SSR ... Trudy Instituta Torfa Akademiya Nauk Belorusskoi SSR [*A publication*]
Tr Inst Vinograd Vinodel Akad Nauk Arm SSR ... Trudy Instituta Vinogradarstva i Vinodeliya Akademii Nauk Armyanskoi SSR [*A publication*]
Tr Inst Vinograd Vinodel Akad Nauk Gruz SSR ... Trudy Instituta Vinogradarstva i Vinodeliya Akademii Nauk Gruzinskoi SSR [*A publication*]
Tr Inst Vses Nauchno-Issled Inst Tsellyul Bum Prom-Sti ... Trudy Instituta. Vsesoyuznyi Nauchno-Issledovatel'skii Institut Tsellyulozno-Bumazhnoi Promyshlennosti [*USSR*] [*A publication*]
Tr Inst Vulkanol Akad Nauk SSSR Sib Otd ... Trudy Instituta Vulkanologii Akademiya Nauk SSSR Sibirskoe Otdelenie [*A publication*]
Tr Inst Vyssh Nervn Deya Akad Nauk SSSR Fiziol ... Trudy Instituta Vysshei Nervnoi Deyatel'nosti Akademii Nauk SSSR. Seriya Fiziologicheskaya [*A publication*]
Tr Inst Vyssh Nervn Deyat Akad Nauk SSSR Ser Fiziol ... Trudy Instituta Vysshei Nervnoi Deyatel'nosti Akademii Nauk SSSR. Seriya Fiziologicheskaya [*A publication*]
Tr Inst Vyssh Nervn Deyat Ser Fiziol ... Trudy Instituta Vysshei Nervnoi Deyatel'nosti. Seriya Fiziologicheskaya [*A publication*]
Tr Inst Vyssh Nervn Deyat Ser Patofiziol ... Trudy Instituta Vysshei Nervnoi Deyatel'nosti. Seriya Patofiziologicheskaya [*A publication*]
Tr Inst Yad Fiz Akad Nauk Kaz SSR ... Trudy Instituta Yadernoi Fiziki Akademiya Nauk Kazakhskoi SSR [*A publication*]
Tr Inst Zasch Rast (Tiflis) ... Trudy Instituta Zashchity Rastenii (Tiflis) [*Georgian SSR*] [*A publication*]
Tr Inst Zashch Rast Akad Nauk Gruz SSR ... Trudy Instituta Zashchity Rastenii Akademii Nauk Gruzinskoi SSR [*A publication*]
Tr Inst Zashch Rast (Tiflis) ... Trudy Instituta Zashchity Rastenii (Tiflis) [*A publication*]
Tr Inst Zemled Akad Nauk Azerb SSR ... Trudy Instituta Zemledeliya Akademiya Nauk Azerbaidzhanskoi SSR [*A publication*]
Tr Inst Zemled Kaz Fil Akad Nauk SSSR ... Trudy Instituta Zemledeliya Kazakhskogo Filiala Akademii Nauk SSSR [*A publication*]
Tr Inst Zemled (Leningrad) Razdel 3 ... Trudy Instituta Zemledeliya (Leningrad). Razdel 3. Pochvovedenie [*A publication*]
Tr Inst Zhivotnovod Akad Nauk Turkm SSR ... Trudy Instituta Zhivotnovodstva Akademii Nauk Turkmenskoi SSR [*A publication*]
Tr Inst Zhivotnovod Dagest Fili Akad Nauk SSSR ... Trudy Instituta Zhivotnovodstva Dagestanskogo Filiala Akademii Nauk SSSR [*A publication*]
Tr Inst Zhivotnovod Minist Skh Uzb SSR ... Trudy Instituta Zhivotnovodstva Ministerstvo Sel'skokhozyaistva Uzbekistanskoi SSR [*A publication*]
Tr Inst Zhivotnovod (Tashkent) ... Trudy Instituta Zhivotnovodstva (Tashkent) [*A publication*]
Tr Inst Zool Akad Nauk Az SSR ... Trudy Instituta Zoologii Akademii Nauk Azerbaidzhanskoi SSR [*A publication*]
Tr Inst Zool Akad Nauk Gruz SSR ... Trudy Instituta Zoologii Akademii Nauk Gruzinskoi SSR [*A publication*]
Tr Inst Zool Akad Nauk Kazakh SSR ... Trudy Instituta Zoologii Akademii Nauk Kazakhskoi SSR [*A publication*]
Tr Inst Zool Akad Nauk Kaz SSR ... Trudy Instituta Zoologii Akademii Nauk Kazakhskoi SSR [*A publication*]

Tr Inst Zool Akad Nauk Ukr SSR ... Trudy Instituta Zoologii Akademii Nauk Ukrainskoi SSR [*A publication*]
Tr Inst Zool Biol (Kiev) ... Trudy Instytutu Zoolohiyi ta Biolohiyi (Kiev) [*A publication*]
Tr Inst Zool Parazitol Akad Nauk Tadzh SSR ... Trudy Instituta Zoologii i Parazitologii Akademiya Nauk Tadzhikskoi SSR [*A publication*]
Tr Inst Zool Parazitol Akad Nauk Uzb SSR ... Trudy Instituta Zoologii i Parazitologii Akademii Nauk Uzbekskoi SSR [*A publication*]
Tr Inst Zool Parazitol Akad Tadzh SSR ... Trudy Instituta Zoologii i Parazitologii Akademiya Nauk Tadzhikskoi SSR [*A publication*]
Tr Inst Zool Parazitol Kirg Fil Akad Nauk SSR ... Trudy Instituta Zoologii i Parazitologii Kirgizskogo Filiala Akademii Nauk SSR [*A publication*]
Trin Tob For ... Trinidad and Tobago Forester [*A publication*]
Trint T .... Trinity Term [*British*] [*Legal term*]   (DLA)
TRIOS .... Thermionic Reactor for Installed Oceanic Service   (KSC)
Trip .... All India Reporter, Tripura [*A publication*]   (DLA)
TRIP .... [*The*] Road Information Program   (EA)
TRIP .... Tartar Reliability Improvement Plan [*Military*]
TRIP .... Technical Reports Indexing Project   (KSC)
TRIP .... Test Requirement Implementation Plan   (CAAL)
TRIP .... Thunderstorm Research International Project [*Meteorology*]
TRIP .... Transformation-Induced Plasticity [*Steel*]
Tri per P ..... Trials per Pais [*A publication*]   (DLA)
TRIP .... Triplicate   (AABC)
Trip .... Tripoli
Trip .... Tripolitania [*Libya*]   (BJA)
TRipLH ..... Lauderdale County Hospital, Ripley, TN [*Library symbol*] [*Library of Congress*]   (LCLS)
TRIPLTEE ... True Temperature Tunnel [*Acronym pronounced, "Triple T"*]
TRIPOD .... Transit Injector Polaris Derived   (AAG)
TRIPOLD ... Transit Injector Polaris Derived
Tripp .... Tripp's Reports [*5, 6 Dakota*] [*A publication*]   (DLA)
TRIPREC ... Triplet Recall [*Neuropsychology test*]
TRIPS .... Transformation-Induced Plasticity (Steel)
TRIPS .... Triplets [*Slang*]   (DSUE)
TriQ .... Tri-Quarterly [*A publication*]
Tri-Quar .... Tri-Quarterly [*A publication*]
TriQuart .... Tri-Quarterly [*A publication*]
Tr IREA ...... Trudy IREA [*A publication*]
Tr Irkutsk Gorometall Inst ... Trudy Irkutskogo Gornometallurgicheskogo Instituta [*A publication*]
Tr Irkutsk Gos Univ ... Trudy Irkutskogo Gosudarstvennogo Universiteta [*A publication*]
Tr Irkutsk Inst Nar Khoz ... Trudy Irkutskogo Instituta Narodnogo Khozyaistva [*A publication*]
Tr Irkutsk Nauchno Issled Inst Epidemiol Mikrobiol ... Trudy Irkutsk Nauchno-Issledovatel'skogo Instituta Epidemiologii i Mikrobiologii [*A publication*]
Tr Irkutsk Politekh Inst ... Trudy Irkutskogo Politekhnicheskogo Instituta [*USSR*] [*A publication*]
TRIS .... Transportation Research Information Services [*National Academy of Sciences*] [*Washington, DC*] [*Bibliographic database*]
Tris .... Tris(2,3-dibromopropyl)phosphate [*Also, TDBP, TDBPP, Tris-BP*] [*Flame retardant, mutagen*]
TRIS .... Tris(hydroxymethyl)aminomethane [*Also, THAM*] [*Biochemical analysis*]
TrIs .... Trito-Isaiah   (BJA)
TRISAFE .. Triple Redundancy Incorporating Self-Adaptive Failure Exclusion   (MCD)
TRISAT ..... Target Recognition through Integral Spectrum Analysis Techniques   (MCD)
Tris-BP ...... Tris(2,3-dibromopropyl)phosphate [*Also, TDBP, TDBPP, Tris*] [*Flame retardant, mutagen*]
TRISECT .. Total Reconnaissance Intelligence System Evaluation and Comparison Technique   (MCD)
TRISNET ... Transportation Research Information Services Network [*Department of Transportation*] [*Library network*]
Tris Pr Pr ... Tristram's Probate Practice [*25th ed.*] [*1978*] [*A publication*]   (DLA)
Trist .... Supplement to 4 Swabey and Tristram's Probate and Divorce Reports [*England*] [*A publication*]   (DLA)
TRIST .... Traveling Image Storage Tube   (MCD)
Trist .... Tristram's Consistory Judgments [*England*] [*A publication*]   (DLA)
Tri State Med J (Greensburo NC) ... Tri-State Medical Journal (Greensburo, North Carolina) [*A publication*]
Tri State Med J (Shreveport LA) ... Tri-State Medical Journal (Shreveport, Louisiana) [*A publication*]
Tristram ...... Tristram's Consistory Judgments [*1872-90*] [*A publication*]   (DLA)
Tristram ..... Tristram's Probate Practice [*25th ed.*] [*1978*] [*A publication*]   (DLA)
Tristram ..... Tristram's Supplement to 4 Swabey and Tristram [*A publication*]   (DLA)
TRISYLL .. Trisyllable   (ROG)
TRIT .... Tritura [*Triturate*] [*Pharmacy*]

TRITAC .... DIFAR Triangular Tactic   (NVT)
TRITAC .... Tri-Service Tactical Communications System [*DoD*]
TRITC ...... Tetramethyl Rhodamine Isothiocyanate [*Organic chemistry*]
TRIUMF ... Tri-University-Meson Facility [*Nuclear research facility at the University of British Columbia*]
TRIUN ...... Department of Trusteeship and Information from Non-Self-Governing Territories of the United Nations
Tr Ivanov Khim Tekhnol Inst ... Trudy Ivanovskogo Khimiko-Tekhnologicheskogo Instituta [*A publication*]
Tr Ivanov Med Inst ... Trudy Ivanovskogo Meditsinskogo Instituta [*A publication*]
Tr Ivanov Skh Inst ... Trudy Ivanovskogo Sel'skokhozyaistvennogo Instituta [*A publication*]
TRIX .... Total Rate Imaging with X-Rays
TRIYA .... Trade and Industry [*A publication*]
Tr Izhevsk Med Inst ... Trudy Izhevskogo Meditsinskogo Instituta [*A publication*]
Tr Izhevsk Otd Vses Fiziol Ova ... Trudy Izhevskogo Otdeleniya Vsesoyuznogo Fiziologicheskogo Obshchestva [*A publication*]
Tr Izhevsk Skh Inst ... Trudy Izhevskogo Sel'skokhoziastvennogo Instituta [*A publication*]
Tr Izuch Radiya Radioakt Rud ... Trudy po Izucheniyu Radiya i Radioaktivnykh Rud [*A publication*]
TRJ .... Tarija [*Bolivia*] [*Seismograph station code, US Geological Survey*]   (SEIS)
TRJ .... Thermocouple Reference Junction
TRJ .... Towards Racial Justice [*British*]
TRJ .... United States Army TRADOC, Fort Jackson, Fort Jackson, SC [*OCLC symbol*]   (OCLC)
Tr Japan Path Soc ... Transactions. Japanese Pathological Society [*A publication*]
TRJaVUZ ... Trudy Kafedry Russkogo Jazyka Vuzov Vostocnoj Sibiri i Dal'nego Vostoka [*A publication*]
Tr Judge J ... Trial Judges' Journal [*A publication*]   (DLA)
TRJWD ..... Transactions. JWRI [*Japanese Welding Research Institute*] [*A publication*]
TRK .... Roche Products Ltd. [*Great Britain*] [*Research code symbol*]
TRK .... Tank Range-Finder Kit
TRK .... Tarakan [*Indonesia*] [*Airport symbol*]   (OAG)
TRK .... Track   (AAG)
TRK .... Truck   (AAG)
TRK .... Truckee, CA [*Location identifier*] [*FAA*]   (FAAL)
TRK .... Trunk   (AAG)
TRK .... United States Army TRADOC, Fort Knox, Library Service Center, RSL Section, Fort Knox, KY [*OCLC symbol*]   (OCLC)
TRKA .... Trak Auto Corp. [*NASDAQ symbol*]   (NQ)
Tr Kafedry Avtomob Trakt Vses Zaochn Mashinostroit Inst ... Trudy Kafedry Avtomobili i Traktory Vsesoyuznyi Zaochnyi Mashinostroitel'nyi Institut [*A publication*]
Tr Kafedry Gosp Khir Lech Fak Sarat Med Inst ... Trudy Kafedry Gospital'noi Khirurgii i Lechebnogo Fakul'teta Saratovskogo Meditsinskogo Instituta [*A publication*]
Tr Kafedry Kozhnykh Vener Bolezn Tashk ... Trudy Kafedry Kozhnykh i Venericheskikh Boleznei Tashkentskii Meditsinskii Institut [*A publication*]
Tr Kafedry Kozhnykh Vener Bolezn Tashk Med Inst ... Trudy Kafedry Kozhnykh i Venericheskikh Boleznei Tashkentskii Meditsinskii Institut [*A publication*]
Tr Kafedry Norm Anat Sarat Gos Med Inst ... Trudy Kafedry Normal'noi Anatomii Saratovskogo Gosudarstvennogo Meditsinskogo Instituta [*A publication*]
Tr Kafedry Oper Khir Topogr Anat Tbilis Gos Med Inst ... Trudy Kafedry Operativnoi Khirurgii i Topograficheskoi Anatomii Tbilisskogo Gosudarstvennogo Meditsinskogo Instituta [*A publication*]
Tr Kafedry Pochvoved Biol Poch Fak Kaz Gos Univ ... Trudy Kafedry Pochvovedeniya Biologo-Pochvennogo Fakul'teta Kazakhskii Gosudarstvennyi Universitet [*A publication*]
Tr Kafedry Pochvoved Biol Pochv Fak Kaz Gos Univ ... Trudy Kafedry Pochvovedeniya Biologo-Pochvennogo Fakul'teta Kazakhskii Gosudarstvennyi Universitet [*A publication*]
Tr Kafedry Teor Eksp Fiz Kaliningr Gos Univ ... Trudy Kafedry Teoreticheskoi i Eksperimental'noi Fiziki Kaliningradskii Gosudarstvennyi Universitet [*A publication*]
Tr Kalinin Gos Med Inst ... Trudy Kalininskogo Gosudarstvennogo Meditsinskogo Instituta [*A publication*]
Tr Kaliningr Nauchno Issled Vet Stn ... Trudy Kaliningradskoi Nauchno-Issledovatel'skoi Veterinarnoi Stantsii [*A publication*]
Tr Kaliningr Tekh Inst Rybn Promsti Khoz ... Trudy Kaliningradskogo Tekhnicheskogo Instituta Rybnoi Promyshlennosti i Khozyaistva [*A publication*]
Tr Kalinin Politekh Inst ... Trudy Kalininskii Politekhnicheskii Institut [*USSR*] [*A publication*]
Tr Kalinin Torf Inst ... Trudy Kalininskogo Torfyanogo Instituta [*A publication*]
Tr Kaluzhskoi Gos Obl Skh Opytn Stn ... Trudy Kaluzhskoi Gosudarstvennoi Oblastnoi Sel'skokhozyaistvennoi Opytnoi Stantsii [*A publication*]

Tr Kamenetsk Podolsk Skh Inst ... Trudy Kamenetsk-Podolskogo Sel'skokhozyaistvennogo Instituta [*A publication*]

Tr Kamenets Podol'sk Skh Inst ... Trudy Kamenets-Podol'skogo Sel'skokhozyaistvennogo Instituta [*A publication*]

Tr Kandalakshskogo Gos Zapov ... Trudy Kandalakshskogo Gosudarstvennogo Zapovednika [*A publication*]

Tr Kansas Acad Sc ... Transactions. Kansas Academy of Science [*A publication*]

Tr Karagandin Bot Sada ... Trudy Karagandinskogo Botanicheskogo Sada [*A publication*]

Tr Karel Fil Akad Nauk SSSR ... Trudy Karel'skogo Filiala Akademii Nauk SSSR [*A publication*]

Tr Karelo-Fin Uchit Inst ... Trudy Karelo-Finskogo Uchitel'skogo Instituta [*A publication*]

Tr Karel Otd Gos Nauchno Issled Inst Ozern Rechn Rybn Khoz ... Trudy Karel'skogo Otdeleniya Gosudarstvennogo Nauchno-Issledovatel'skogo Instituta Ozernogo i Rechnogo Rybnogo Khozyaistva [*A publication*]

Tr Kasp Nauchno Issled Inst Rybn Khoz ... Trudy Kaspiiskii Nauchno-Issledovatel'skii Institut Rybnogo Khozyaistva [*A publication*]

Tr Kaunas Gos Med Inst ... Trudy Kaunasskogo Gosudarstvennogo Meditsinskogo Instituta [*A publication*]

Tr Kavk Inst Miner Syrya ... Trudy Kavkazskogo Instituta Mineral'nogo Syr'ya [*A publication*]

Tr Kazan Aviats Inst ... Trudy KAI. Kazanskij Ordena Trudovogo Krasnogo Znameni Aviatsionnyj Institut Imeni A. N. Tupoleva [*A publication*]

Tr Kazan Aviats Inst Ser Khim ... Trudy Kazanskogo Aviatsionogo Instituta. Seriya Khimicheskaya [*A publication*]

Tr Kazan Fil Akad Nauk SSSR Ser Geol Nauk ... Trudy Kazanskogo Filiala Akademii Nauk SSSR. Seriya Geologicheskikh Nauk [*A publication*]

Tr Kazan Fil Akad Nauk SSSR Ser Khim Nauk ... Trudy Kazanskogo Filiala Akademii Nauk SSSR. Seriya Khimicheskikh Nauk [*A publication*]

Tr Kazan Gor Astron Obs ... Trudy Kazanskoi Gorodskoi Astronomicheskoi Observatorii [*A publication*]

Tr Kazan Gos Inst Usoversh Vrachei ... Trudy Kazanskogo Gosudarstvennogo Instituta Usovershenstvovaniya Vrachei [*A publication*]

Tr Kazan Inst Usoversh Vrachei Im V I Lenina ... Trudy Kazanskogo Instituta Usovershenstvovaniya Vrachei Imeni V. I. Lenina [*A publication*]

Tr Kazan Inzh Stroit Inst ... Trudy Kazanskogo Inzhenerno-Stroitel'nogo Instituta [*A publication*]

Tr Kazan Khim Tekhnol Inst ... Trudy Kazanskogo Khimiko-Tekhnologicheskogo Instituta [*A publication*]

Tr Kazan Med Inst ... Trudy Kazanskogo Meditsinskogo Instituta [*A publication*]

Tr Kazan Nauchno-Inst Onkol Radiol ... Trudy Kazanskogo Nauchno-Issledovatel'skogo Instituta Onkologii i Radiologii [*A publication*]

Tr Kazan Nauchno-Issled Inst Onkol Radiol ... Trudy Kazanskogo Nauchno-Issledovatel'skogo Instituta Onkologii i Radiologii [*A publication*]

Tr Kazan Nauchno-Issled Inst Travmatol Ortop ... Trudy Kazanskogo Nauchno-Issledovatel'skogo Instituta Travmatologii i Ortopedii [*A publication*]

Tr Kazan Nauchno Issled Vet Inst ... Trudy Kazanskogo Nauchno-Issledovatel'skogo Veterinarnogo Instituta [*A publication*]

Tr Kazan S-Kh Inst ... Trudy Kazanskogo Sel'skokhozyaistvennogo Instituta [*A publication*]

Tr Kaz Fil Akad Stroit Arkhit SSSR ... Trudy Kazakhskogo Filiala Akademiya Stroitel'stva i Arkhitektury SSSR [*A publication*]

Tr Kaz Gos Pedagog Inst ... Trudy Kazanskii Gosudarstvennyi Pedagogicheskii Institut [*A publication*]

Tr Kaz Gos Skh Inst ... Trudy Kazakhskogo Gosudarstvennogo Sel'skokhozyaistvennogo Instituta [*A publication*]

Tr Kaz Inst Epidemiol Mikrobiol Gig ... Trudy Kazakhskii Institut Epidemiologii Mikrobiologii Gigieny [*A publication*]

Tr Kaz Inst Klin Eksp Khir Akad Med Nauk SSSR ... Trudy Kazakhskogo Instituta Klinicheskoi i Eksperimental'noi Khirurgii Akademiya Meditsinskikh Nauk SSSR [*A publication*]

Tr Kaz Inst Klin Ekst Khir ... Trudy Kazakhskogo Instituta Klinicheskoi i Eksperimental'noi Khirurgii [*A publication*]

Tr Kaz Inst Usoversh Vrachei Im V I Lenina ... Trudy Kazakhskogo Instituta Usovershenstvovaniya Vrachei Imeni V. I. Lenina [*A publication*]

Tr Kaz Nauchno-Issled Gidrometeorol Inst ... Trudy Kazakhskogo Nauchno-Issledovatel'skogo Gidrometeorologicheskogo Instituta [*A publication*]

Tr Kaz Nauchno Issled Inst Glaznykh Bolezn ... Trudy Kazakhskogo Nauchno-Issledovatel'skogo Instituta Glaznykh Boleznei [*A publication*]

Tr Kaz Nauchno-Issled Inst Lesn Khoz ... Trudy Kazakhskogo Nauchno-Issledovatel'skogo Instituta Lesnogo Khozyaistva [*A publication*]

Tr Kaz Nauchno-Issled Inst Lesn Khoz Agrolesomelior ... Trudy Kazakhskogo Nauchno-Issledovatel'skogo Instituta Lesnogo Khozyaistva i Agrolesomelioratsii [*A publication*]

Tr Kaz Nauchno Issled Inst Miner Syrya ... Trudy Kazakhskogo Nauchno-Issledovatel'skogo Instituta Mineral'nogo Syr'ya [*A publication*]

Tr Kaz Nauchno-Issled Inst Onkol Radiol ... Trudy Kazakhskogo Nauchno-Issledovatel'skogo Instituta Onkologii i Radiologii [*A publication*]

Tr Kaz Nauchno Issled Inst Tuberk ... Trudy Kazakhskogo Nauchno-Issledovatel'skogo Instituta Tuberkuleza [*A publication*]

Tr Kaz Nauchno Issled Inst Vodn Khoz ... Trudy Kazakhskogo Nauchno-Issledovatel'skogo Instituta Vodnogo Khozyaistva [*A publication*]

Tr Kaz Nauchno Issled Inst Zashch Rast ... Trudy Kazakhskogo Nauchno-Issledovatel'skogo Instituta Zashchity Rastenii [*A publication*]

Tr Kaz Nauchno Issled Inst Zemled ... Trudy Kazakhskogo Nauchno-Issledovatel'skogo Instituta Zemledeliya [*A publication*]

Tr Kaz Nauchno Issled Kozhno Venerol Inst ... Trudy Kazakhskogo Nauchno-Issledovatel'skogo Kozhno-Venerologicheskogo Instituta [*A publication*]

Tr Kaz Nauchno-Issled Vet Inst ... Trudy Kazakhskogo Nauchno-Issledovatel'skogo Veterinarnogo Instituta [*A publication*]

Tr Kaz Opytn Stn Pchelovod ... Trudy Kazakhskoi Opytnoi Stantsii Pchelovodstva [*A publication*]

Tr Kaz Politekh Inst ... Trudy Kazakhskogo Politekhnicheskogo Instituta [*Kazakh SSR*] [*A publication*]

Tr Kaz S-Kh Inst ... Trudy Kazakhskogo Sel'skokhozyaistvennogo Instituta [*A publication*]

Tr Kaz S-Kh Inst Ser Agron ... Trudy Kazakhskogo Sel'skokhozyaistvennogo Instituta. Seriya Agronomii [*A publication*]

TRKD .... Tracked

TRKDR ...... Truck-Drawn

Tr Kemer Gos Skh Opytn Stn ... Trudy Kemerovskoi Gosudarstvennoi Sel'skokhozyaistvennoi Opytnoi Stantsii [*A publication*]

Tr Kemer Obl Gos S-Kh Opytn Stn ... Trudy Kemerovskoi Oblastnoi Gosudarstvennoi Sel'skokhozyaistvennoi Opytnoi Stantsii [*A publication*]

Tr Kerch Ikhtiol Lab ... Trudy Kerchenskoi Ikhtiologicheskoi Laboratorii [*A publication*]

Tr Kerch Nauchn Rybokhoz Stn ... Trudy Kerchenskoi Nauchnoi Rybokhozyaistvennoi Stantsii [*A publication*]

TRKG .... Tracking (AAG)

TrKH .... Die Transkriptionen des Hieronymus in Seinem Kommentarwerken [*A publication*] (BJA)

Tr Khabar Inst Inzh Zheleznodorozhn Transp ... Trudy Khabarovskogo Instituta Inzhenerov Zheleznodorozhnogo Transporta [*A publication*]

Tr Khabar Med Inst ... Trudy Khabarovskogo Meditsinskogo Instituta [*A publication*]

Tr Khabar Politekh Inst ... Trudy Khabarobskogo Politekhnicheskogo Instituta [*A publication*]

Tr Khark Aviats Inst ... Trudy Khar'kovskogo Aviatsionnogo Instituta [*A publication*]

Tr Khar'k Avtodorozhn Inst ... Trudy Khar'kovskogo Avtodorozhnogo Instituta [*A publication*]

Tr Khar'k Avtomob Dorozhn Inst ... Trudy Khar'kovskogo Avtomobil'no-Dorozhnogo Instituta [*A publication*]

Tr Khark Avtomob Dorozhnogo Instituta ... Trudy Khar'kovskogo Avtomobil'no-Dorozhnogo Instituta [*A publication*]

Tr Khar'k Farm Inst ... Trudy Khar'kovskogo Farmatsevticheskogo Instituta [*A publication*]

Tr Khark Gos Farm Inst ... Trudy Khar'kovskogo Gosudarstvennogo Farmatsevticheskogo Instituta [*A publication*]

Tr Khar'k Gos Med Inst ... Trudy Khar'kovskii Gosudarstvennyi Meditsinskii Institut [*A publication*]

Tr Khark Inst Gorn Mashinostr Avtom Vychisl Tekh ... Trudy Khar'kovskogo Instituta Gornogo Mashinostroeniya. Avtomatiki i Vychislitel'noi Tekhniki [*A publication*]

Tr Khark Inst Inzh Zheleznodorozhn Transp ... Trudy Khar'kovskogo Instituta Inzhenerov Zheleznodorozhnogo Transporta [*A publication*]

Tr Khark Inzh Ekon Inst ... Trudy Khar'kovskogo Inzhenerno-Ekonomicheskogo Instituta [*A publication*]

Tr Khark Khim Tekhnol Inst ... Trudy Khar'kovskogo Khimiko-Tekhnologicheskogo Instituta [*A publication*]

Tr Khar'k Med Inst ... Trudy Khar'kovskogo Meditsinskogo Instituta [*A publication*]

Tr Khark Nauchno Issled Khim Farm Inst ... Trudy Khar'kovskogo Nauchno-Issledovatel'skogo Khimiko-Farmatsevticheskogo Instituta [*A publication*]

Tr Khar'kov Med Inst ... Trudy Khar'kovskogo Meditsinskogo Instituta [*A publication*]

Tr Khark Politekh Inst ... Trudy Khar'kovskogo Politekhnicheskogo Instituta [*A publication*]

Tr Khar'k S-Kh Inst ... Trudy Khar'kovskogo Sel'skokhozyaistvennogo Instituta [*A publication*]

Tr Khar'k Skh Inst Im V V Dokuchaeva ... Trudy Khar'kovskii Sel'skokhozyaistvennyi Institut Imeni V. V. Dokuchaeva [*A publication*]

TRKHD ..... Truck Head

Tr Khim Inst Im L Ya Karpova ... Trudy Khimicheskogo Instituta Imeni L. Ya. Karpova [*A publication*]

Tr Khim Khim Tekhnol ... Trudy po Khimii i Khimicheskoi Tekhnologii [*A publication*]

Tr Khim-Metall Inst Akad Nauk Kaz SSR ... Trudy Khimiko-Metallurgicheskogo Instituta Akademiya Nauk Kazakhskoj SSR [*A publication*]

Tr Khim Metall Inst Akad Nauk SSSR Sib Otd ... Trudy Khimiko-Metallurgicheskogo Instituta Akademiya Nauk SSSR Sibirskoe Otdelenie [*A publication*]

Tr Khim Prir Soedin ... Trudy po Khimii Prirodnykh Soedinenii [*A publication*]

Tr Kiev Gor Obl Nauchn Ova Dermatol ... Trudy Kievskogo Gorodskogo Oblastnogo Nauchnogo Obshchestva Dermatologii [*A publication*]

Tr Kiev Politekh Inst ... Trudy Kievskogo Politekhnicheskogo Instituta [*A publication*]

Tr Kiev Tekhnol Inst Pishch Promsti ... Trudy Kievskogo Tekhnologicheskogo Instituta Pishchevoi Promyshlennosti [*A publication*]

Tr Kiev Vet Inst ... Trudy Kievskogo Veterinarnogo Instituta [*A publication*]

Tr Kirg Gos Med Inst ... Trudy Kirgizskogo Gosudarstvennogo Meditsinskogo Instituta [*A publication*]

Tr Kirg Gos Univ Ser Fiz Nauk ... Trudy Kirgizskogo Gosudarstvennogo Universiteta. Seriya Fizicheskikh Nauk [*A publication*]

Tr Kirg Inst Epidemiol Mikrobiol Gig ... Trudy Kirgizskogo Instituta Epidemiologii, Mikrobiologii, i Gigieny [*A publication*]

Tr Kirgiz Nauch Issled Inst Zemled ... Trudy Kirgizskogo Nauchno-Issledovatel'skogo Instituta Zemledeliya [*A publication*]

Tr Kirg Lesn Opytn Stn ... Trudy Kirgizskoi Lesnoi Opytnoi Stantsii [*A publication*]

Tr Kirg Nauchno-Issled Inst Onkol Radiol ... Trudy Kirgizskogo Nauchno-Issledovatel'skoi Instituta Onkologii i Radiologii [*A publication*]

Tr Kirg Nauchno-Issled Inst Pochvoved ... Trudy Kirgizskogo Nauchno-Issledovatel'skogo Instituta Pochvovedeniya [*A publication*]

Tr Kirg Nauchno Issled Inst Zemled ... Trudy Kirgizskogo Nauchno-Issledovatel'skogo Instituta Zemledeliya [*A publication*]

Tr Kirg Nauchno-Issled Inst Zhivotnovod ... Trudy Kirgizskogo Nauchno-Issledovatel'skogo Instituta Zhivotnovodstva [*A publication*]

Tr Kirg Nauchno-Issled Inst Zhivotnovod Vet ... Trudy Kirgizskogo Nauchno-Issledovatel'skogo Instituta Zhivotnovodstva i Veterinarii [*A publication*]

Tr Kirg Opytno-Sel Stn Sakh Svekle ... Trudy Kirgizskoi Opytno-Selektsionnoi Stantsii po Sakharnoi Svekle [*A publication*]

Tr Kirg Opytn Stn Khlopkovod ... Trudy Kirgizskoi Opytnoi Stantsii Khlopkovodstva [*A publication*]

Tr Kirg S-Kh Inst ... Trudy Kirgizskogo Sel'skokhozyaistvennogo Instituta [*A publication*]

Tr Kirg Skh Inst Ser Agron ... Trudy Kirgizskogo Sel'skokhozyaistvennogo Seriya Agronomii [*A publication*]

Tr Kirg Univ Ser Biol Nauk ... Trudy Kirgizskogo Universiteta Seriya Biologicheskikh Nauk [*A publication*]

Tr Kirov Obl Nauchno Issled Inst Kraeved ... Trudy Kirovskogo Oblastnogo Nauchno-Issledovatel'skogo Instituta Kraevedeniya [*A publication*]

Tr Kirov Otd Vses Fiziol Ova ... Trudy Kirovskogo Otdeleniya Vsesoyuznogo Fiziologicheskogo Obshchestva [*A publication*]

Tr Kirov S-Kh Inst ... Trudy Kirovskogo Sel'skokhozyaistvennogo Instituta [*A publication*]

Tr Kishinev Gos Med Inst ... Trudy Kishinevskogo Gosudarstvennogo Meditsinskogo Instituta [*A publication*]

Tr Kishinev Politekh Inst ... Trudy Kishinevskii Politekhnicheskii Institut [*A publication*]

Tr Kishinev S-Kh Inst ... Trudy Kishinevskogo Sel'skokhozyaistvennogo Instituta [*A publication*]

Tr Kishinev S-Kh Inst Im M V Frunze ... Trudy Kishinevskii Sel'skokhozyaistvennyi Institut Imeni M. V. Frunze [*USSR*] [*A publication*]

Tr Klin Nervn Bolezn Mosk Obl Nauchno-Issled Klin Inst ... Trudy Kliniki Nervnykh Boleznei Moskovskogo Oblastnogo Nauchno-Issledovatel'skogo Klinicheskogo Instituta [*A publication*]

Tr Klin Otd Nauchno Issled Inst Gig Tr Profzabol ... Trudy Klinicheskogo Otdeleniya Nauchno-Issledovatel'skogo Instituta Gigieny Truda i Profzabolevanii [*A publication*]

TRKMTD ... Truck-Mounted (AABC)

Tr Kolomenskogo Fil Vses Zaochn Politekh Inst ... Trudy Kolomenskogo Filiala Vsesoyuznogo Zaochnogo Politekhnicheskogo Instituta [*A publication*]

Tr Kom Anal Khim Akad Nauk SSSR ... Trudy Komissii po Analiticheskoi Khimii Akademiya Nauk SSSR [*USSR*] [*A publication*]

Tr Kom Borbe s Korroz Met Akad Nauk SSSR ... Trudy Komissii po Bor'be s Korroziei Metallov Akademiya Nauk SSSR [*A publication*]

Tr Komi Fil Akad Nauk SSSR ... Trudy Komi Filiala Akademii Nauk SSSR [*A publication*]

Tr Kom Irrig Akad Nauk SSSR ... Trudy Komissii po Irrigatsii Akademiya Nauk SSSR [*A publication*]

Tr Kom Okhr Prir Ural Fil Akad Nauk SSSR ... Trudy Komissii po Okhrane Prirody Ural'skogo Filiala Akademii Nauk SSSR [*A publication*]

Tr Kom Pirom Vses Nauchno Issled Inst Metrol ... Trudy Komissii po Pirometrii Vsesoyuznyi Nauchno-Issledovatel'skii Institut Metrologii [*A publication*]

Tr Kompleksn Eksped Dnepropetr Univ ... Trudy Kompleksnoi Ekspeditsii Dnepropetrovskogo Universiteta [*A publication*]

Tr Kompleksn Eksped Sarat Univ Izuch Volgogr Sarat Vodokhran ... Trudy Kompleksnoi Ekspeditsii Saratovskogo Universiteta po Izucheniyu Volgogradskogo i Saratovskogo Vodokhranilishch [*A publication*]

Tr Kompleksn Yuzhn Geol Eksped Akad Nauk SSSR ... Trudy Kompleksnoi Yuzhnoi Geologicheskoi Ekspeditsii. Akademiya Nauk SSSR [*A publication*]

Tr Kom Spektros Akad Nauk SSSR ... Trudy Komissii po Spektroskopii Akademiya Nauk SSSR [*USSR*] [*A publication*]

Tr Koord Soveshch Gidrotekh ... Trudy Koordinatsionnykh Soveshchanyi po Gidrotekhnike [*A publication*]

Tr Kostrom Skh Inst ... Trudy Kostromskogo Sel'skokhozyaistvennogo Instituta "Karavaevo" [*A publication*]

TRKR .... Tracker

Tr Kranoyarsk Nauchno Issled Inst Selsk Khoz ... Trudy Krasnoyarskogo Nauchno-Issledovatel'skogo Instituta Sel'skogo Khozyaistva [*A publication*]

Tr Krasnodar Fil Vses Neftegazov Nauchno Issled Inst ... Trudy Krasnodarskii Filial Vsesoyuznogo Neftegazovogo Nauchno-Issledovatel'skogo Instituta [*A publication*]

Tr Krasnodar Gos Pedagog Inst ... Trudy Krasnodarskogo Gosudarstvennogo Pedagogicheskogo Instituta [*A publication*]

Tr Krasnodar Inst Pishch Promsti ... Trudy Krasnodarskogo Instituta Pishchevoi Promyshlennosti [*A publication*]

Tr Krasnodar Nauchno-Issled Inst Pishch Promsti ... Trudy Krasnodarskogo Nauchno-Issledovatel'skogo Instituta Pischevoi Promyshlennosti [*A publication*]

Tr Krasnodar Nauchno-Issled Inst Selsk Khoz ... Trudy Krasnodarskogo Nauchno-Issledovatel'skogo Instituta Sel'skogog Khozyaistva [*A publication*]

Tr Krasnodar Politekh Inst ... Trudy Krasnodarskogo Politekhnicheskogo Instituta [*A publication*]

Tr Krasnoyarsk Gos Med Inst ... Trudy Krasnoyarskogo Gosudarstvennogo Meditsinskogo Instituta [*A publication*]

Tr Krasnoyarsk Med Inst ... Trudy Krasnoyarskogo Meditsinskogo Instituta [*A publication*]

Tr Krasnoyarsk Nauchno Issled Inst Sel'sk Khoz ... Trudy Krasnoyarskogo Nauchno-Issledovatel'skogo Instituta Sel'skogo Khozyaistva [*A publication*]

Tr Krasnoyarsk S-Kh Inst ... Trudy Krasnoyarskogo Sel'skokhozyaistvennogo Instituta [*A publication*]

Tr Krym Fil Akad Nauk Ukr SSR ... Trudy Krymskogo Filiala Akademiya Nauk Ukrainskoi SSR [*A publication*]

Tr Krym Gos Med Inst ... Trudy Krymskogo Gosudarstvennogo Meditsinskogo Instituta [*A publication*]

Tr Krym Gos Med Inst Im I V Stalina ... Trudy Krymskogo Gosudarstvennogo Meditsinskogo Instituta Imeni I. V. Stalina [*A publication*]

Tr Krym Gos Skh Opytn Stn ... Trudy Krymskoi Gosudarstvennoi Sel'skokhozyaistvennoi Opytnoi Stantsii [*A publication*]

Tr Krym Gosud Sel'skokhoz Opyt Sta ... Trudy Krymskoi Gosudarstvennoi Sel'skokhozyaistvennoi Opytnoi Stantsii [*A publication*]

Tr Krym Med Inst ... Trudy Krymskogo Meditsinskogo Instituta [*A publication*]

Tr Krym Obl Gos Skh Opytn Stn ... Trudy Krymskoi Oblastnoi Gosudarstvennoi Sel'skokhozyaistvennoi Opytnoi Stantsii [*A publication*]

Tr Krym Opytno Sel Stn VIR ... Trudy Krymskoi Opytno Selektsionnoi Stantsii VIR [*A publication*]

Tr Krym Skh Inst ... Trudy Krymskogo Sel'skokhozyaistvennogo Instituta [*A publication*]

Tr Krym S-Kh Inst Im M I Kalinina ... Trudy Krymskogo Sel'skokhozyaistvennogo Instituta Imeni M. I. Kalinina [*A publication*]

TRKUA ..... Technology Reports. Kansai University [*A publication*]

Tr Kuban Otd Vses Ova Genet Sel ... Trudy Kubanskoe Otdelenie Vsesoyuznogo Obshchestva Genetikovi Selektsionerov [*A publication*]

Tr Kuban S-Kh Inst ... Trudy Kubanskogo Sel'skokhozyaistvennogo Instituta [*A publication*]

Tr Kuibyshev Aviats Inst ... Trudy Kuibyshevskii Aviatsionnyi Institut [*USSR*] [*A publication*]

Tr Kuibyshev Gos Nauchno-Issled Inst Neft Prom-Sti ... Trudy Kuibyshevskii Gosudarstvennyi Nauchno-Issledovatel'skii Institut Neftyanoi Promyshlennosti [*USSR*] [*A publication*]

Tr Kuibyshev Inzh-Stroit Inst ... Trudy Kuibyshevskii Inzhenerno-Stroitel'nyi Institut [*A publication*]

Tr Kuibyshev Med Inst ... Trudy Kuibyshevskii Meditsinskii Instituta [*A publication*]

Tr Kuibyshev Nauchno-Issled Inst Neft Promsti ... Trudy Kuibyshevskii Nauchno-Issledovatel'skii Institut Neftyanoi Promyshlennosti [*A publication*]

Tr Kuibyshev S-Kh Inst ... Trudy Kuibyshevskogo Sel'skokhozyaistvennogo Instituta [*A publication*]

Tr Kurgan Mashinostroit Inst ... Trudy Kurganskogo Mashinostroitel'nogo Instituta [*A publication*]

Tr Kurortol ... Trudy po Kurortologii [*A publication*]
Tr Kursk Med Inst ... Trudy Kurskogo Meditsinskogo Instituta [*A publication*]
Tr Kutais Skh Inst ... Trudy Kutaisskogo Sel'skokhozyaistvennogo Instituta [*A publication*]
TRKWHL ... Trick Wheel
TRL............ Tariff Reform League [*British*]   (ROG)
TRL............ Telecom Australia Research Laboratories
TRL............ Terrell, TX [*Location identifier*] [*FAA*]   (FAAL)
TRL............ Test Readiness List [*NASA*]   (NASA)
TRL............ Thermodynamics Research Laboratory [*National Institute of Standards and Technology*]   (MCD)
TRL............ Tool Room Lathe
TRL............ Trading Law [*British*]
TRL............ Trail   (MCD)
TRL............ Training Research Laboratory [*Army Research Institute for the Behavioral and Social Sciences*]   (RDA)
TRL............ Transistor Resistor Logic
trl............ Translator [*MARC relator code*] [*Library of Congress*]   (LCCP)
TrL............ Transmitted Light [*Microscopy*]
TRL............ Transuranium Research Laboratory [*AEC*]
TRL............ Trax Petroleums [*Vancouver Stock Exchange symbol*]
TRL............ Trial   (ROG)
TRL............ Trillo [*Trill*] [*Music*]   (ROG)
TRL............ Trunk Register Link [*Telecommunications*]   (TEL)
TRL............ United States Department of Transportation, Library, Washington, DC [*OCLC symbol*]   (OCLC)
TRLA........ Trans Louisiana Gas [*NASDAQ symbol*]   (NQ)
Trla............ Triola [*Record label*] [*Finland*]
TRLA........ Truck Renting and Leasing Association   (EA)
Tr Lab Biokhim Fiziol Zhivotn Inst Biol Akad Nauk Latv SSR ... Trudy Laboratorii Biokhimii i Fiziologii Zhivotnykh Instituta Biologii Akademiya Nauk Latviiskoi SSR [*A publication*]
Tr Lab Eksp Biol Mosk Zooparka ... Trudy Laboratorii Eksperimental'noi Biologii Moskovskogo Zooparka [*A publication*]
Tr Lab Evol Ekol Fiziol Akad Nauk SSSR Inst Fiziol Rast ... Trudy Laboratorii Evolyutsionnoi i Ekologicheskoi Fiziologii Akademiya Nauk SSSR Institut Fiziologii Rastenii [*A publication*]
Tr Lab Fiziol Zhivotn Inst Biol Akad Nauk Lit SSR ... Trudy Laboratorii Fiziologii Zhivotnykh Instituta Biologii Akademii Nauk Litovskoi SSR [*A publication*]
Tr Lab Geol Dokembr Akad Nauk SSSR ... Trudy Laboratorii Geologii Dokembriya Akademiya Nauk SSSR [*A publication*]
Tr Lab Geol Uglya Akad Nauk SSSR ... Trudy Laboratorii Geologii Uglya Akademiya Nauk SSSR [*A publication*]
Tr Lab Gidrogeol Probl Akad Nauk SSSR ... Trudy Laboratorii Gidrogeologicheskikh Problem Akademiya Nauk SSSR [*USSR*] [*A publication*]
Tr Lab Izuch Belka Akad Nauk SSSR ... Trudy Laboratorii po Izucheniyu Belka Akademiya Nauk SSSR [*A publication*]
Tr Lab Lesoved Akad Nauk SSSR ... Trudy Laboratorii Lesovedeniya Akademiya Nauk SSSR [*A publication*]
Tr Lab Ozeroved Leningr Gos Univ ... Trudy Laboratorii Ozerovedeniya Leningradskii Gosudarstvennyi Universitet [*A publication*]
Tr Lab Sapropelevykh Otlozh Akad Nauk SSSR ... Trudy Laboratorii Sapropelevykh Otlozhenii Akademiya Nauk SSSR [*A publication*]
Tr Lab Vulkanol Akad Nauk SSSR ... Trudy Laboratorii Vulkanologii Akademiya Nauk SSSR [*A publication*]
Tr Latviiskogo Nauchno-Issled Inst Zhivotnovod Vet ... Trudy Latviiskogo Nauchno-Issledovatel'skogo Instituta Zhivotnovodstva i Veterinarii [*A publication*]
Tr Latv Inst Eksp Klin Med Akad Med Nauk SSSR ... Trudy Latviiskogo Instituta Eksperimental'noi i Klinicheskoi Meditsiny Akademii Meditsinskikh Nauk SSSR [*A publication*]
Tr Latv Nauchno Issled Inst Gidrotekh Melior ... Trudy Latviiskogo Nauchno-Issledovatel'skogo Instituta Gidrotekhniki i Melioratsii [*A publication*]
Tr Latv Nauchno-Issled Inst Zhivotnovod Vet ... Trudy Latviiskogo Nauchno-Issledovatel'skogo Instituta Zhivotnovodstva i Veterinarii [*A publication*]
Tr Latv Sel'kh Akad ... Trudy Latviiskaia Sel'skokhoziaistvennaia Akademiia [*A publication*]
Tr Latv S-Kh Akad ... Trudy Latviiskoi Sel'skokhoziaistvennoi Akademii [*A publication*]
Tr Law Guide ... Trial Lawyer's Guide [*A publication*]
Tr Law Q ... Trial Lawyers Quarterly [*A publication*]
TRLB........ Temporarily Replaced by Lighted Buoy Showing Same Characteristic [*Maps and charts*]
Tr Legochn Patol Inst Eksp Klin Med Est SSR ... Trudy po Legochnoi Patologii Institut Eksperimental'noi i Klinicheskoi Meditsiny Estonskoi SSR [*A publication*]
Tr Leningrad Tekhnol Inst Tsellyul-Bumazh Prom ... Trudy Leningradskogo Tekhnologicheskogo Instituta Tsellyulozno-Bumazhnoi Promyshlennosti [*A publication*]
Tr Leningr Elektrotekh Inst Svyazi ... Trudy Leningradskii Elektrotekhnicheskii Institut Svyazi [*A publication*]
Tr Leningr Geol Upr ... Trudy Leningradskogo Geologicheskogo Upravleniya [*A publication*]

Tr Leningr Gidrometeorol Inst ... Trudy Leningradskii Gidrometeorologicheskii Institut [*A publication*]
Tr Leningr Gos Nauchno Issled Inst Travmatol Ortop ... Trudy Leningradskogo Gosudarstvennogo Nauchno-Issledovatel'skogo Instituta Travmatologii i Ortopedii [*A publication*]
Tr Leningr Ind Inst ... Trudy Leningradskii Industrial'nogo Instituta [*A publication*]
Tr Leningr Inst Epidemiol Mikrobiol ... Trudy Leningradskogo Instituta Epidemiologii i Mikrobiologii [*A publication*]
Tr Leningr Inst Inzh Kommunal'n Stroit ... Trudy Leningradskii Institut Inzhenerov Kommunal'nogo Stroitel'stva [*A publication*]
Tr Leningr Inst Inzh Zheleznodorozhn Transp ... Trudy Leningradskii Institut Inzhenerov Zheleznodorozhnogo Transporta [*A publication*]
Tr Leningr Inst Kinoinzh ... Trudy Leningradskogo Instituta Kinoinzhenerov [*A publication*]
Tr Leningr Inst Sov Torg ... Trudy Leningradskii Institut Sovetskoi Torgovli [*A publication*]
Tr Leningr Inst Tochn Mekh Opt ... Trudy Leningradskii Institut Tochnoi Mekhaniki i Optiki [*A publication*]
Tr Leningr Inst Usoversh Vrachei ... Trudy Leningradskogo Instituta Usovershenstvovaniya Vrachei [*A publication*]
Tr Leningr Inst Vaktsin Syvorotok ... Trudy Leningradskogo Instituta Vaktsin i Syvorotok [*A publication*]
Tr Leningr Inst Vodn Transp ... Trudy Leningradskogo Instituta Vodnogo Transporta [*A publication*]
Tr Leningr Inzh Ekon Inst ... Trudy Leningradskogo Inzhenerno-Ekonomicheskogo Instituta [*A publication*]
Tr Leningr Inzh Ekon Inst Im Pal'miro Tol'yatti ... Trudy Leningradskii Inzhenerno-Ekonomicheskii Institut Imeni Pal'miro Tol'yatti [*A publication*]
Tr Leningr Khim-Farm Inst ... Trudy Leningradskogo Khimiko-Farmatsevticheskogo Instituta [*A publication*]
Tr Leningr Khim Tekhnol Inst ... Trudy Leningradskogo Khimiko-Tekhnologicheskogo Instituta [*A publication*]
Tr Leningr Korablestroit Inst ... Trudy Leningradskogo Korablestroitel'nogo Instituta [*A publication*]
Tr Leningr Korablestroit'nogo Inst ... Trudy Leningradskogo Korablestroitel'nogo Instituta [*USSR*] [*A publication*]
Tr Leningr Lesotekh Akad ... Trudy Leningradskoi Lesotekhnicheskoi Akademii [*A publication*]
Tr Leningr Med Inst ... Trudy Leningradskogo Meditsinskogo Instituta [*A publication*]
Tr Leningr Mekh Tekhnol Inst Kholod Promsti ... Trudy Leningradskogo Mekhaniko-Tekhnologicheskogo Instituta Kholodil'noi Promyshlennosti [*A publication*]
Tr Leningr Met Zavod ... Trudy Leningradskii Metallicheskii Zavod [*A publication*]
Tr Leningr Nauchno-Issled Inst Antibiot ... Trudy Leningradskogo Nauchno-Issledovatel'skogo Instituta Antibiotiki [*A publication*]
Tr Leningr Nauchno-Issled Inst Epidemiol Mikrobiol ... Trudy Leningradskogo Nauchno-Issledovatel'skogo Instituta Epidemiologii i Mikrobiologii [*A publication*]
Tr Leningr Nauchno Issled Inst Neirokhir ... Trudy Leningradskogo Nauchno-Issledovatel'skogo Instituta Neirokhirurgii [*A publication*]
Tr Leningr Nauchno Issled Inst Radiats Gig ... Trudy Leningradskogo Nauchno-Issledovatel'skogo Instituta Radiatsii i Gigieny [*A publication*]
Tr Leningr Nauchno Issled Inst Tuberk ... Trudy Leningradskogo Nauchno-Issledovatel'skogo Instituta Tuberkuleza [*A publication*]
Tr Leningr Nauchno Issled Inst Vaktsin Syvorotok ... Trudy Leningradskii Nauchno-Issledovatel'skii Institut Vaktsin i Syvorotok [*A publication*]
Tr Leningr Nauchno-Issled Konstr Inst Khim Mashinostr ... Trudy Leningradskii Nauchno-Issledovatel'skii i Konstruktorskii Institut Khimicheskogo Mashinostroeniya [*USSR*] [*A publication*]
Tr Leningr Nauchno Issled Psikhonevrol Inst ... Trudy Leningradskogo Nauchno-Issledovatel'skogo Psikhonevrologisheskogo Instituta [*A publication*]
Tr Leningr Nauchno Ova Patologoanat ... Trudy Leningradskogo Nauchnogo Obshchestva Patologoanatomov [*A publication*]
Tr Leningr Ova Anat Gistol Embriol ... Trudy Leningradskogo Obshchestva Anatomov, Gistologov, i Embriologov [*A publication*]
Tr Leningr O-Va Estestvoispyt ... Trudy Leningradskogo Obshchestva Estestvoispytatelei [*A publication*]
Tr Leningr Pediatr Med Inst ... Trudy Leningradskogo Pediatricheskogo Meditsinskogo Instituta [*A publication*]
Tr Leningr Politekh Inst ... Trudy Leningradskogo Politekhnicheskogo Instituta Imeni M. I. Kalinina [*A publication*]
Tr Leningr Politekh Inst Im M I Kalinina ... Trudy Leningradskogo Politekhnicheskogo Instituta Imeni M. I. Kalinina [*USSR*] [*A publication*]
Tr Leningr Sanit-Gig Med Inst ... Trudy Leningradskogo Sanitarno-Gigienicheskogo Meditsinskogo Instituta [*A publication*]
Tr Leningr Tekhnol Inst Im Lensoveta ... Trudy Leningradskogo Tekhnologicheskogo Instituta Imeni Lensoveta [*A publication*]

Tr Leningr Tekhnol Inst Kholod Prom-St' ... Trudy Leningradskogo Tekhnologicheskogo Instituta Kholodil'noi Promyshlennosti [*A publication*]

Tr Leningr Tekhnol Inst Pishch Prom-Sti ... Trudy Leningradskogo Tekhnologicheskogo Instituta Pishchevoi Promyshlennosti [*A publication*]

Tr Leningr Tekhnol Inst Tsellyul Bum Promsti ... Trudy Leningradskogo Tekhnologicheskogo Instituta Tsellyulozno-Bumazhnoi Promyshlennosti [*A publication*]

Tr Leningr Teknol Inst ... Trudy Leningradskogo Tekhnologicheskogo Instituta [*USSR*] [*A publication*]

Tr Leningr Tekst Inst ... Trudy Leningradskogo Tekstil'nogo Instituta [*A publication*]

Tr Leningr Tsentr Gos Travmatol Inst ... Trudy Leningradskogo Tsentral'nogo Gosudarstvennogo Travmatologicheskogo Instituta [*A publication*]

Tr Leningr Voen Mekh Inst ... Trudy Leningradskii Voenno-Mekhanicheskii Institut [*A publication*]

Tr Lesotekh Akad ... Trudy Lesotekhnicheskoi Akademii [*A publication*]

TRLFSW ... Tactical Range Landing Force Support Weapon

TRLGA ...... Translog [*A publication*]

Tr Limnol Inst Sib Otd Akad Nauk SSSR ... Trudy Limnologicheskogo Instituta Siberskogo Otdeleniya. Akademii Nauk SSSR [*A publication*]

Tr Litov Inst Eksp Klin Med Akad Med Nauk SSSR ... Trudy Litovskogo Instituta Eksperimental'noi i Klinicheskoi Meditsiny Akademii Meditsinskikh Nauk SSSR [*A publication*]

Tr Litov Inst Eksp Med Akad Med Nauk SSSR ... Trudy Litovskogo Instituta Eksperimental'noi Meditsiny Akademii Meditsinskikh Nauk SSSR [*A publication*]

Tr Litov Nauchno Issled Geologorazves Inst ... Trudy Litovskogo Nauchno-Issledovatel'skogo Geologorazvedochnogo Instituta [*A publication*]

Tr Litov Nauchno Issled Inst Lesn Khoz ... Trudy Litovskogo Nauchno-Issledovatel'skogo Instituta Lesnogo Khozyaistva [*A publication*]

Tr Litov Nauchno Issled Inst Vet ... Trudy Litovskogo Nauchno-Issledovatel'skogo Instituta Veterinarii [*A publication*]

Tr LNIIA ... Trudy LNIIA [*Leningrad Nauchno-Issledovatel'skii Institut Antibiotikov*] [*A publication*]

TRLP .... Transport Landplane [*Navy*]

TRLR .... Trailer

Tr LR .... Trinidad Law Reports [*A publication*]   (DLA)

TRLS .... Thousand Trails, Inc. [*NASDAQ symbol*]   (NQ)

TRLSC .... Time-Resolved Liquid Scintillation Counting [*Analytical procedure*]

TRLU .... TISEO RADAR Logic Unit [*Air Force*]   (MCD)

Tr Lugansk S-Kh Inst ... Trudy Luganskogo Sel'skokhozyaistvennoi Instituta [*A publication*]

TRLY .... Trolley

TRM .... Task Response Module [*Office furniture*]

TRM .... Tay River Petroleum [*Vancouver Stock Exchange symbol*]

TRM .... Telecommunications Regulatory Monitor [*A publication*]

TRM .... Terminal Response Monitor

TRM .... Test Request Message [*Data processing*]

TRM .... Test Requirements Manual

TRM .... Test Responsibility Matrix   (MCD)

TRM .... Theater Rates Model [*Military*]

TRM .... Thermal, CA [*Location identifier*] [*FAA*]   (FAAL)

TRM .... Thermal Remanent Magnetization [*Geophysics*]   (IEEE)

TRM .... Thermal Resistance Measurement

TRM .... Thermoremanence

TRM .... Thermoremanent Magnetism [*or Magnetization*]

TRM .... Thickness Readout Module

TRM .... Time Ratio Modulation

TRM .... Time Release Mechanism [*Martin-Baker seat system*] [*Aviation*]   (NG)

TRM .... Topics in Health Record Management [*A publication*]

TRM .... Totally Reflective Mirror

Tr M .... Traditional Music [*A publication*]

TRM .... TRADOC Resources Management   (MCD)

TRM .... TRADOC [*Training and Doctrine Command*] Review of Manpower

TRM .... Turner [*Maine*] [*Seismograph station code, US Geological Survey*]   (SEIS)

TRM .... United States Army TRADOC, Fort Monroe Post Library and Headquarters Technical Library, Fort Monroe, VA [*OCLC symbol*]   (OCLC)

Tr Magadan Zon Nauchno Issled Inst Selsk Khoz Sev Vostoka ... Trudy Magadanskogo Zonal'nogo Nauchno-Issledovatel'skogo Instituta Sel'skogo Khozyaistva Severo-Vostoka [*A publication*]

TRMAP ..... Theater Rate Mapping Data File [*Military*]

Tr Marii Gos Pedagog Inst ... Trudy Mariiskii Gosudarstvennyi Pedagogicheskii Institut [*A publication*]

Tr Mater Donetsk Med Inst ... Trudy i Materialy Donetskii Meditsinskii Institut [*A publication*]

Tr Mater Donetsk Nauchno Issled Inst Fiziol Tr ... Trudy i Materialy Donetskii Nauchno-Issledovatel'skii Institut Fiziologii Truda [*A publication*]

Tr Mater Leningr Inst Organ Okhr Tr ... Trudy i Materialy Leningradskii Institut Organizatsii i Okhrany Truda [*A publication*]

Tr Mater Nauchno Issled Inst Fiziol Tr (Stalino) ... Trudy i Materialy Nauchno-Issledovatel'skii Institut Fiziologii Truda (Stalino) [*A publication*]

Tr Mater Pervogo Ukr Inst Rab Med ... Trudy i Materialy Pervogo Ukrainskogo Instituta Rabochei Meditsiny [*A publication*]

Tr Mater Ukr Gos Inst Patol Gig Tr ... Trudy i Materialy Ukrainskogo Gosudarstvennogo Instituta Patologii i Gigieny Truda [*A publication*]

Tr Mater Ukr Gos Inst Rab Med ... Trudy i Materialy Ukrainskogo Gosudarstvennogo Instituta Rabochei Meditsiny [*A publication*]

Tr Mater Ukr Tsentr Inst Gig Tr Profzabol ... Trudy i Materialy Ukrainskii Tsentral'nyi Institut Gigieny Truda i Profzabolevanii [*A publication*]

Tr Mat Inst Akad Nauk SSSR ... Trudy Matematicheskogo Instituta Akademiya Nauk SSSR [*A publication*]

TRMC .... Time-Resolved Microwave Conductivity [*Physical chemistry*]

TRMCA ..... Transition Metal Chemistry [*New York*] [*A publication*]

TRMD .... Trimmed

TRME .... Theater Readiness Monitoring Equipment   (MCD)

TRMEA ..... Trattamenti dei Metalli [*A publication*]

Tr Med and Phys Soc Bombay ... Transactions. Medical and Physical Society of Bombay [*A publication*]

Tr Metrol Inst SSSR ... Trudy Metrologiceskih Institutov SSSR [*A publication*]

Tr Mezhdunar Konf Fiz Vys Energ ... Trudy Mezhdunarodnaya Konferentsiya po Fizike·Vysokikh Energii [*A publication*]

Tr Mezhdunar Simp Geterog Katal ... Trudy Mezhdunarodnogo Simpoziuma po Geterogennomu Katalizu [*A publication*]

Tr Mezhdunar Simp Tsitoekol ... Trudy Mezhdunarodnogo Simpoziuma po Tsitoekologii [*A publication*]

TRMF .... Test Report Management Forms   (MCD)

TRMF .... Theater Readiness Monitoring Facility [*Missile testing*]

TRMF .... Theodore Roethke Memorial Foundation   (EA)

Tr MFTI Ser "Obshch Mol Fiz" ... Trudy Moskovskogo Fiziko-Tekhnicheskogo Instituta. Seriya "Obshchaya i Molekulyarnaya Fizika" [*A publication*]

TRMG .... Tread Rubber Manufacturers Group   (EA)

TRMG .... Trimming

TRMI .... Tubular Rivet and Machine Institute   (EA)

Tr Mineral Inst Akad Nauk SSSR ... Trudy Mineralogicheskogo Instituta Akademiya Nauk SSSR [*A publication*]

Tr Mineral Muz Akad Nauk SSSR ... Trudy Mineralogicheskogo Muzeya Akademiya Nauk SSSR [*USSR*] [*A publication*]

Tr Minniya Nauchnoizsled Proekto Konstr Inst ... Trudove na Minniya Nauchnoizsledovatelski i Proektno Konstruktorski Institut [*A publication*]

Tr Minsk Gos Med Inst ... Trudy Minskogo Gosudarstvennogo Meditsinskogo Instituta [*A publication*]

TRMK .... Trustmark Corp. [*NASDAQ symbol*]   (SPSG)

TRML .... Terminal   (AFM)

TRML .... Tropical Research Medical Laboratory [*Army*]

TRMM ...... Tropical Rainfall Measuring Mission [*Proposed satellite*]

Tr Moldav Nauch Issled Inst Orosh Zemled Ovoshchev ... Trudy Moldavskogo Nauchno-Issledovatel'skogo Instituta Oroshaemogo Zemledeliya i Ovoshchevodstva [*A publication*]

Tr Mold Nauchno Issled Inst Epidemiol Mikrobiol Gig ... Trudy Moldavskii Nauchno-Issledovatel'skii Institut Epidemiologii, Mikrobiologii, i Gigieny [*A publication*]

Tr Mold Nauchno Issled Inst Gig Epidemiol ... Trudy Moldavskii Nauchno-Issledovatel'skii Institut Gigieny i Epidemiologii [*A publication*]

Tr Mold Nauchno Issled Inst Oroshaemogo Zemled Ovoshchevod ... Trudy Moldavskogo Nauchno-Issledovatel'skogo Instituta Oroshaemogo Zemledeliya i Ovoshchevodstva [*A publication*]

Tr Mold Nauchno-Issled Inst Orosh Zemled Ovoshchevod ... Trudy Moldavskogo Nauchno-Issledovatel'skogo Instituta Oroshaemogo Zemledeliya i Ovoshchevodstva [*A publication*]

Tr Mold Nauchno Issled Inst Pishch Promsti ... Trudy Moldavskogo Nauchno-Issledovatel'skogo Instituta Pishchevoi Promyshlennosti [*A publication*]

Tr Mold Nauchno Issled Inst Tuberk ... Trudy Moldavskogo Nauchno-Issledovatel'nogo Instituta Tuberkuleza [*A publication*]

Tr Mold Nauchno Issled Inst Zhivotnovod Vet ... Trudy Moldavskii Nauchno-Issledovatel'skii Institut Zhivotnovodstva i Veterinarii [*A publication*]

Tr Molodykh Uch Dagest Nauchno Issled Inst Selsk Khoz ... Trudy Molodykh Uchenykh Dagestanskii Nauchno-Issledovatel'skii Institut Sel'skogo Khozyaistva [*A publication*]

Tr Molodykh Uch Spets Chuv Skh Inst ... Trudy Molodykh Uchenykh Spetsial'nogo Chuvashskogo Sel'skokhozyaistvennogo Instituta [*A publication*]

Tr Molodykh Uch Ukr Skh Akad ... Trudy Molodykh Uchenykh Ukrainskoi Sel'skokhozyaistvennoi Akademii [*A publication*]

Tr Molodykh Uch Yakutsk Univ ... Trudy Molodykh Uchenykh Yakutskogo Universiteta [*A publication*]

Tr Molotov Gos Med Inst ... Trudy Molotovskogo Gosudarstvennogo Meditsinskogo Instituta [*A publication*]

Tr Mord Gos Zapovednika Im P G Smirovicha ... Trudy Mordovskogo Gosudarstvennogo Zapovednika Imeni P. G. Smirovicha [*A publication*]

Tr Morsk Biol Stn Stalin ... Trudove na Morskata Biologichna Stantsiya v Stalin [*A publication*]

Tr Morsk Gidrofiz Inst Akad Nauk Ukr SSR ... Trudy Morskogo Gidrofizicheskogo Instituta Akademiya Nauk Ukrainskoj SSR [*A publication*]

Tr Morsk Rybn Inst Ser A (Gdynia Pol) ... Trudy Morskogo Rybnogo Instituta. Seriya A. Okeanografiya i Promyslovaya Ikhtiologiya (Gdynia, Poland) [*A publication*]

Tr Morsk Rybn Inst Ser B (Gdynia Pol) ... Trudy Morskogo Rybnogo Instituta. Seriya B (Gdynia, Poland) [*A publication*]

Tr Mosk Aviats Inst Im S Ordzhonikidze Sb Statei ... Trudy Moskovskij Aviatsionnyj Institut Imeni S. Ordzhonikidze Sbornik Statei [*USSR*] [*A publication*]

Tr Mosk Aviats Tekhnol Inst ... Trudy Moskovskij Aviatsionnyj Tekhnologicheskij Institut [*A publication*]

Tr Mosk Avtomob Dorozhn Inst ... Trudy Moskovskogo Avtomobil'no Dorozhnogo Instituta [*A publication*]

Tr Mosk Ehnerg Inst ... Trudy Moskovskogo Ordena Lenina Ehnergiticheskogo Instituta [*A publication*]

Tr Mosk Energ Inst ... Trudy Moskovskogo Energeticheskogo Instituta [*USSR*] [*A publication*]

Tr Mosk Energ Inst Fiz ... Trudy Moskovskogo Energeticheskogo Instituta Fizika [*USSR*] [*A publication*]

Tr Mosk Fiz Tekh Inst ... Trudy Moskovskii Fiziko-Tekhnicheskii Institut [*A publication*]

Tr Mosk Fiz Tekh Inst Ser "Obshch Mol Fiz" ... Trudy Moskovskogo Fiziko-Tekhnicheskogo Instituta. Seriya "Obshchaya i Molekulyarnaya Fizika" [*A publication*]

Tr Mosk Geol Razved Inst ... Trudy Moskovskogo Geologo-Razvedochnogo Instituta [*A publication*]

Tr Mosk Geol Upr ... Trudy Moskovskogo Geologicheskogo Upravlenie [*A publication*]

Tr Mosk Gor Bakteriol Inst ... Trudy Moskovskii Gorodskoi Bakteriologicheskii Institut [*A publication*]

Tr Mosk Gor Inst Epidemiol Bakteriol ... Trudy Moskovskii Gorodskoi Institut Epidemiologii i Bakteriologii [*A publication*]

Tr Mosk Gor Nauchno Issled Inst Epidemiol Bakteriol ... Trudy Moskovskii Gorodskoi Nauchno-Issledovatel'skii Institut Epidemiologii i Bakteriologii [*A publication*]

Tr Mosk Gor Nauchno Issled Inst Skoroi Pomoshchi ... Trudy Moskovskogo Gorodskogo Nauchno-Issledovatel'skogo Instituta Skoroi Promoshchi [*A publication*]

Tr Mosk Gorn Inst ... Trudy Moskovskogo Gornogo Instituta [*A publication*]

Tr Mosk Inst Elektron Mashinostr ... Trudy Moskovskii Institut Elektronnogo Mashinostroeniya [*USSR*] [*A publication*]

Tr Mosk Inst Epidemiol Mikrobiol Gig ... Trudy Moskovskii Institut Epidemiologii, Mikrobiologii, i Gigieny [*A publication*]

Tr Mosk Inst Inzh Gor Stroit ... Trudy Moskovskogo Instituta Inzhenerov Gorodskogo Stroitel'stva [*A publication*]

Tr Mosk Inst Inzh Zheleznodorozhn Transp ... Trudy Moskovskogo Instituta Inzhenerov Zheleznodorozhnogo Transporta [*A publication*]

Tr Mosk Inst Khim Mashinostr ... Trudy Moskovskogo Instituta Khimicheskogo Mashinostroeniya [*A publication*]

Tr Mosk Inst Nar Khoz ... Trudy Moskovskogo Instituta Narodnogo Khozyaistva [*A publication*]

Tr Mosk Inst Neftekhim Gazov Prom-Sti Im I M Gubkina ... Trudy Moskovskii Institut Neftekhimicheskoi i Gazovoi Promyshlennosti Imeni I. M. Gubkina [*USSR*] [*A publication*]

Tr Mosk Inst Neftekhim Gaz Promsti ... Trudy Moskovskii Institut Neftekhimicheskoi i Gazovoi Promyshlennosti [*A publication*]

Tr Mosk Inst Radiotekh Elektron Avtom ... Trudy Moskovskogo Instituta Radiotekhniki, Elektroniki, i Avtomatiki [*A publication*]

Tr Mosk Inst Tonkoi Khim Tekhnol ... Trudy Moskovskogo Instituta Tonkoi Khimicheskoi Tekhnologii [*A publication*]

Tr Mosk Inzh Ekon Inst ... Trudy Moskovskogo Inzhenerno-Ekonomicheskogo Instituta [*A publication*]

Tr Mosk Khim-Tekhnol Inst ... Trudy Moskovskogo Khimiko-Tekhnologicheskogo Instituta Imeni D. I. Mendeleeva [*A publication*]

Tr Mosk Mat O-Va ... Trudy Moskovskogo Matematicheskogo Obshchestva [*A publication*]

Tr Mosk Med Stomatol Inst ... Trudy Moskovskogo Meditsinskogo Stomatologichesko Instituta [*A publication*]

Tr Mosk Nauchno-Issled Inst Epidemiol Mikrobiol ... Trudy Moskovskogo Nauchno-Issledovatel'skogo Instituta Epidemiologii i Mikrobiologii [*A publication*]

Tr Mosk Nauchno Issled Inst Epidemiol Mikrobiol Gig ... Trudy Moskovskii Nauchno-Issledovatel'skii Institut Epidemiologii, Mikrobiologii, i Gigieny [*A publication*]

Tr Mosk Nauchno-Issled Inst Psikhiatr ... Trudy Moskovskogo Nauchno-Issledovatel'skogo Instituta Psikhiatrii [*A publication*]

Tr Mosk Nauchno-Issled Inst Ukha Gorla Nosa ... Trudy Moskovskogo Nauchno-Issledovatel'skogo Instituta Ukha Gorla i Nosa [*A publication*]

Tr Mosk Nauchno Issled Inst Virusn Prep ... Trudy Moskovskii Nauchno-Issledovatel'skii Institut Virusnykh Preparatov [*A publication*]

Tr Mosk Neft Inst ... Trudy Moskovskii Neftyanoi Institut [*A publication*]

Tr Mosk Obl Nauchno Issled Klin Inst Prakt Nevropatol ... Trudy Moskovskogo Oblastnogo Nauchno-Issledovatel'skogo Klinicheskogo Instituta Prakticheskoi Nevropatologii [*A publication*]

Tr Mosk Obshch Ispyt Otedel Biol ... Trudy Moskovskoe Obshchestvo Ispytatelei Prirody Otedel Biologicheskii [*A publication*]

Tr Mosk O-Va Ispyt Prir ... Trudy Moskovskogo Obshchestva Ispytatelei Prirody [*USSR*] [*A publication*]

Tr Mosk O-Va Ispyt Prir Otd Biol ... Trudy Moskovskogo Obshchestva Ispytatelei Prirody Otdel Biologicheskii [*USSR*] [*A publication*]

Tr Mosk Radiotekh Elektron Avtomat ... Trudy Moskovskogo Instituta Radiotekhniki, Elektroniki, i Avtomatiki [*USSR*] [*A publication*]

Tr Mosk Tekh Inst Rybn Prom-Sti Khoz ... Trudy Moskovskogo Tekhnologicheskogo Instituta Rybnoi Promyshlennosti i Khozyaistva [*USSR*] [*A publication*]

Tr Mosk Tekhnol Inst Myasn Molochn Prom-Sti ... Trudy Moskovskogo Tekhnologicheskogo Instituta Myasnoi Molochnoi Promyshlennosti [*A publication*]

Tr Mosk Tekhnol Inst Pishch Promsti ... Trudy. Moskovskii Tekhnologicheskii Institut Pishchevoi Promyshlennosti [*A publication*]

Tr Mosk Torf Inst ... Trudy Moskovskogo Torfyanogo Instituta [*A publication*]

Tr Mosk Vet Akad ... Trudy Moskovskoi Veterinarnoi Akademii [*A publication*]

Tr Mosk Vyssh Tekh Uchil ... Trudy Moskovskogo Vysshego Tekhnicheskogo Uchilishcha [*USSR*] [*A publication*]

TRMPDU ... University of Maryland. Sea Grant Program. Technical Report [*A publication*]

TRMR .... Trimmer [*Mining engineering*]

TRMS .... Technical Requirements Management System

TRMS .... Test Resource Management System [*TECOM*] (RDA)

TRMT .... Terminate (FAAC)

TRMT .... Treatment (AFM)

Tr Murm Biol Stn ... Trudy Murmanskoi Biologicheskoi Stantsii [*A publication*]

Tr Murm Morsk Biol Inst ... Trudy Murmanskogo Morskogo Biologicheskogo Instituta [*A publication*]

TRMW ...... Triangle Microwave, Inc. [*NASDAQ symbol*] (NQ)

TRN .... OCLC [*Online Computer Library Center*] Training Symbol, Columbus, OH [*OCLC symbol*] (OCLC)

TRN .... Technical Research Note (IEEE)

TRN .... Temporary Record Number

TRN .... Teriton Resources Ltd. [*Vancouver Stock Exchange symbol*]

TRN .... Thomson Regional Newspapers [*The Thomson Corp.*] [*Publishing*]

TRN .... Trade Name (MSA)

TRN .... Train (FAAC)

TRN .... Transfer (DEN)

TRN .... Transformation Research Network [*Canada*] [*Research center*] (RCD)

TRN .... Transmit (BUR)

TRN .... Trinidad [*Trinidad-Tobago*] [*Seismograph station code, US Geological Survey*] (SEIS)

TRN .... Trinity Industries, Inc. [*NYSE symbol*] (SPSG)

TRN .... Trunnion (NASA)

TRN .... Turin [*Italy*] [*Airport symbol*] (OAG)

tRNA .... Ribonucleic Acid, Transfer [*Replaces sRNA*] [*Biochemistry, genetics*]

TRNA .... Topolino Register of North America (EA)

Tr Nakhich Kompleksn Zon Opytn Stn ... Trudy Nakhichevanskoi Kompleksnoi Zonal'noi Opytnoi Stantsii [*A publication*]

Tr Nakhich Kompleksn Zon Stn ... Trudy Nakhichevanskaya Kompleksnaya Zonal'naya Stantsiya [*A publication*]

Tr Nauch Issled Inst Klopkovod (Tashkent) ... Trudy Nauchno-Issledovatel'skii Institut po Khlopkovodstvu (Tashkent) [*A publication*]

Tr Nauchn Konf Stalinskogo Gos Pedagog Inst ... Trudy Nauchnoi Konferentsii Stalinskogo Gosudarstvennogo Pedagogicheskogo Instituta [*A publication*]

Tr Nauchn Korresp Inst Stroit Dela Akad Nauk Gruz SSR ... Trudy Nauchnykh Korrespondentov Instituta Stroitel'nogo Dela Akademiya Nauk Gruzinskoi SSR [*A publication*]

Tr Nauchno Issled Dizeln Inst ... Trudy Nauchno-Issledovatel'skogo Dizel'nogo Instituta [*A publication*]

Tr Nauchno-Issled Gidrometerol Inst (Alma-Ata) ... Trudy Nauchno-Issledovatel'skogo Gidrometeorologicheskogo Instituta (Alma-Ata) [*Kazakh SSR*] [*A publication*]

Tr Nauchno-Issled Inst Betona Zhelezobetona ... Trudy Nauchno-Issledovatel'skogo Instituta Betona i Zhelezobetona [*USSR*] [*A publication*]

Tr Nauchno Issled Inst Biol Biofiz Tomsk Gos Univ ... Trudy Nauchno-Issledovatel'skogo Instituta Biologii i Biofiziki pri Tomskom Gosudarstvennom Universitete [*A publication*]

Tr Nauchno-Issled Inst Biol Khar'k Gos Univ ... Trudy Nauchno-Issledovatel'skogo Instituta Biologii Khar'kovskogo Gosudarstvennogo Universiteta [*A publication*]

Tr Nauchno-Issled Inst Dobyche Pererab Slantsev ... Trudy Nauchno-Issledovatel'skogo Instituta po Dobyche i Pererabotke Slantsev [*USSR*] [*A publication*]

Tr Nauchno-Issled Inst Eksp Klin Ter Gruz SSR ... Trudy Nauchno-Issledovatel'skogo Instituta Eksperimental'noi i Klinicheskoi Terapii Gruzinskoi SSR [*A publication*]

Tr Nauchno-Issled Inst Epidemiol Mikrobiol ... Trudy Nauchno-Issledovatel'skogo Instituta Epidemiologii i Mikrobiologii [*A publication*]

Tr Nauchno Issled Inst Fiziol ... Trudy Nauchno-Issledovatel'skogo Instituta Fiziologii [*A publication*]

Tr Nauchno-Issled Inst Fiziol Patol Zhen ... Trudy Nauchno-Issledovatel'skogo Instituta Fiziologii i Patologii Zhenshchiny [*A publication*]

Tr Nauchno-Issled Inst Geol Arktiki ... Trudy Nauchno-Issledovatel'skogo Instituta Geologii Arktiki [*USSR*] [*A publication*]

Tr Nauchno Issled Inst Geol Mineral ... Trudy Nauchno-Issledovatel'skogo Instituta Geologii i Mineralogii [*A publication*]

Tr Nauchno Issled Inst Gidrometeorol Priborostr ... Trudy Nauchno-Issledovatel'skii Institut Gidrometeorologicheskogo Priborostroeniya [*A publication*]

Tr Nauchno Issled Inst Gig Vodn Transp ... Trudy Nauchno-Issledovatel'skogo Instituta Gigieny Vodnoi Transportatsii [*A publication*]

Tr Nauchno Issled Inst Kabeln Prom ... Trudy Nauchno-Issledovatel'skogo Instituta Kabel'noi Promyshlennosti [*A publication*]

Tr Nauchno Issled Inst Kamnya Silik ... Trudy Nauchno-Issledovatel'skogo Instituta Kamnya i Silikatov [*A publication*]

Tr Nauchno-Issled Inst Kartofel'nogo Khoz ... Trudy Nauchno-Issledovatel'skogo Instituta Kartofel'nogo Khozyaistva [*A publication*]

Tr Nauchno Issled Inst Klin Eksp Khir ... Trudy Nauchno-Issledovatel'skogo Instituta Klinicheskoi i Eksperimental'noi Khirurgii [*A publication*]

Tr Nauchno-Issled Inst Kraev Patol (Alma-Ata) ... Trudy Nauchno-Issledovatel'skogo Instituta Kraevoi Patologii (Alma-Ata) [*A publication*]

Tr Nauchno-Issled Inst Legk Met ... Trudy Nauchno-Issledovatel'skogo Instituta Legkikh Metallov [*A publication*]

Tr Nauchno-Issled Inst Med Parazitol Trop Med Gruz SSR ... Trudy Nauchno-Issledovatel'skogo Instituta Meditsinskoi Parazitologii i Tropicheskoi Meditsiny Gruzinskoi SSR [*A publication*]

Tr Nauchno Issled Inst Mekh Rybn Promsti ... Trudy Nauchno-Issledovatel'skogo Instituta Mekhanizatsii Rybnoi Promyshlennosti [*A publication*]

Tr Nauchno Issled Inst Mestnoi Topl Promsti ... Trudy Nauchno-Issledovatel'skogo Instituta Mestnoi i Toplivnoi Promyshlennosti [*A publication*]

Tr Nauchno Issled Inst Minist Radiotekh Promsti SSSR ... Trudy Nauchno-Issledovatel'skogo Instituta Ministerstvo Radiotekhnicheskoi Promyshlennosti SSSR [*A publication*]

Tr Nauchno Issled Inst Neftekhim Proizvod ... Trudy Nauchno-Issledovatel'skii Institut Neftekhimicheskikh Proizvodstv [*A publication*]

Tr Nauchno Issled Inst Okhr Tr Prof Zabol ... Trudy Nauchno-Issledovatel'skogo Instituta Okhrany Truda i Professional'nykh Zabolevanii [*A publication*]

Tr Nauchno Issled Inst Onkol Gruz SSR ... Trudy Nauchno-Issledovatel'skogo Instituta Onkologii Gruzinskoi SSR [*A publication*]

Tr Nauchno Issled Inst Onkol (Tiflis) ... Trudy Nauchno-Issledovatel'skii Institut Onkologii (Tiflis) [*A publication*]

Tr Nauchno Issled Inst Osnovnoi Khim ... Trudy Nauchno-Issledovatel'skogo Instituta Osnovnoi Khimii [*A publication*]

Tr Nauchno Issled Inst Pishch Promsti ... Trudy Nauchno-Issledovatel'skogo Instituta Pishchevoi Promyshlennosti [*A publication*]

Tr Nauchno Issled Inst Pochvoved Agrokhim Melior (Tiflis) ... Trudy Nauchno-Issledovatel'skogo Instituta Pochvovedeniya Agrokhimii i Melioratsii (Tiflis) [*A publication*]

Tr Nauchno Issled Inst Pochvoved Agrokhim Yerevan ... Trudy Nauchno-Issledovatel'skogo Instituta Pochvovedeniya i Agrokhimii Yerevan [*A publication*]

Tr Nauchno Issled Inst Pochvoved Tadzh SSR ... Trudy Nauchno-Issledovatel'skogo Instituta Pochvovedeniya Tadzhikskoi SSR [*A publication*]

Tr Nauchno-Issled Inst Profil Pnevmokoniozov ... Trudy Nauchno-Issledovatel'skogo Instituta Profilaktiki i Pnevmokoniozov [*A publication*]

Tr Nauchno-Issled Inst Rentgenol Radiol Onkol Az SSR ... Trudy Nauchno-Issledovatel'skogo Instituta Rentgenologii Radiologii i Onkologii Azerbaidzhanskoi SSR [*A publication*]

Tr Nauchno Issled Inst Rezin Promsti ... Trudy Nauchno-Issledovatel'skogo Instituta Rezinovoi Promyshlennosti [*A publication*]

Tr Nauchno Issled Inst Rybn Khoz (Riga) ... Trudy Nauchno-Issledovatel'skogo Instituta Rybnogo Khozyaistva (Riga) [*A publication*]

Tr Nauchno-Issled Inst Sadovod Vinograd Vinodel (Tashkent) ... Trudy Nauchno-Issledovatel'skogo Instituta Sadovodstva. Vinogradarstva i Vinodeliya (Tashkent) [*A publication*]

Tr Nauchno-Issled Inst Sel'sk Khoz Krainego Sev ... Trudy Nauchno Issledovatel'skogo Instituta Sel'skogo Khozyaistva Krainego Severa [*A publication*]

Tr Nauchno Issled Inst Shinnoi Promsti ... Trudy Nauchno-Issledovatel'skogo Instituta Shinnoi Promyshlennosti [*A publication*]

Tr Nauchno Issled Inst Sin Spirtov Org Prod ... Trudy Nauchno-Issledovatel'skii Institut Sinteticheskikh Spirtov i Organicheskikh Produktov [*A publication*]

Tr Nauchno-Issled Inst Slantsev ... Trudy Nauchno-Issledovatel'skogo Instituta Slantsev [*USSR*] [*A publication*]

Tr Nauchno Issled Inst Teploenerg Priborostr ... Trudy Nauchno-Issledovatel'skii Institut Teploenergeticheskogo Priborostroeniya [*A publication*]

Tr Nauchno Issled Inst Transp Khraneniyu Nefti Nefteprod ... Trudy Nauchno-Issledovatel'skii Institut po Transportu i Khraneniyu Nefti i Nefteproduktov [*A publication*]

Tr Nauchno Issled Inst Tuberk ... Trudy Nauchno-Issledovatel'skogo Instituta Tuberkuleza [*A publication*]

Tr Nauchno-Issled Inst Udobr Insektofungits ... Trudy Nauchno-Issledovatel'skii Institut po Udobreniyam i Insektofungitsidam [*USSR*] [*A publication*]

Tr Nauchno Issled Inst Virusol Mikrobiol Gig ... Trudy Nauchno-Issledovatel'skogo Instituta Virusologii Mikrobiologii Gigieny [*A publication*]

Tr Nauchno Issled Inst Zashch Rast Uzb SSR ... Trudy Nauchno-Issledovatel'skogo Instituta Zashchity Rastenii Uzbekskoi SSR [*A publication*]

Tr Nauchno Issled Inst Zhivotnovod (Tashkent) ... Trudy Nauchno-Issledovatel'skogo Instituta Zhivotnovodstva (Tashkent) [*A publication*]

Tr Nauchno Issled Inst Zhivotnovod Uzb Akad Skh Nauk ... Trudy Nauchno-Issledovatel'skogo Instituta Zhivotnovodstva. Uzbekskaya Akademiya Sel'skokhozyaistvennykh Nauk [*A publication*]

Tr Nauchno Issled Khim Inst Mosk Univ ... Trudy Nauchno-Issledovatel'skogo Khimicheskogo Instituta Moskovskii Universitet [*A publication*]

Tr Nauchno Issled Konstr Inst Mekh Rybn Prom-Sti ... Trudy Nauchno-Issledovatel'skogo i Konstruktorskogo Instituta Mekhanizatsii Rybnoi Promyshlennosti [*A publication*]

Tr Nauchno Issled Lab Geol Zarub Stran ... Trudy Nauchno-Issledovatel'skaya Laboratoriya Geologii Zarubezhnykh Stran [*A publication*]

Tr Nauchno Issled Proektn Inst Mekh Obrab Polezn Iskop ... Trudy Nauchno-Issledovatel'skii i Proektnyi Institut Mekhanicheskoi Obrabotki Poleznykh Iskopaemykh [*A publication*]

Tr Nauchno Issled Protivochumn Inst Kavk Zakavk ... Trudy Nauchno-Issledovatel'skogo Protivochumnogo Instituta Kavkaza i Zakavkaz'ya [*A publication*]

Tr Nauchno Issled Sekt Mosk Fil Inst "Orgenergostroi" ... Trudy Nauchno-Issledovatel'skogo Sektora Moskovskogo Filiala Instituta "Orgenergostroi" [*A publication*]

Tr Nauchno Issled Sel'sk Khoz Krainego Sev ... Trudy Nauchno-Issledovatel'skogo Instituta Sel'skogo Khozyaistva Krainego Severa [*A publication*]

Tr Nauchno Issled Tekhnokhim Inst Bytovogo Obsluzhivaniya ... Trudy Nauchno-Issledovatel'skogo Tekhnokhimicheskogo Instituta Bytovogo Obsluzhivaniya [*A publication*]

Tr Nauchno Issled Vet Inst Tadzh SSR ... Trudy Nauchno-Issledovatel'skogo Veterinarnogo Instituta Tadzhikskoi SSR [*A publication*]

Tr Nauchnoizsled Inst Cherna Metal ... Trudove na Nauchnoizsledovatelskiya Institut po Cherna Metallurgiya [*A publication*]

Tr Nauchnoizsled Inst Epidemio Mikrobiol ... Trudove na Nauchnoizsledovatelskiya Instituta po Epidemiologiya i Mikrobiologiya [*A publication*]

Tr Nauchnoizsled Inst Farm ... Trudove na Nauchnoizsledovatelskiya Instituta po Farmatsiya [*A publication*]

Tr Nauchnoizsled Inst Okhr Tr Prof Zabol ... Trudove na Nauchnoizsledovatelskiya Instituta po Okhrana na Truda i Profesionalnite Zabolyavaniya [*A publication*]

Tr Nauchnoizsled Inst Stroit Mater (Sofia) ... Trudove na Nauchnoizsledovatelskiya Instituta po Stroitelni Materiali (Sofia) [*A publication*]

Tr Nauchnoizsled Inst Tekst Promst (Sofia) ... Trudove na Nauchnoizsledovatelskiya Instituta po Tekstilna Promishlenost (Sofia) [*A publication*]

Tr Nauchnoizsled Inst Vodosnabdyavane Kanaliz Sanit Tekh ... Trudove na Nauchnoizsledovatelskiya Institut po Vodosnabdyavane. Kanalizatsiya i Sanitarna Tekhnika [*Bulgaria*] [*A publication*]

Tr Nauchnoizsled Khim Farm Inst ... Trudove na Nauchnoizsledovatelskiya Khimiko-Farmatsevtichen Institut [*A publication*]

Tr Nauchnoizsled Proektokonstr Tekhnol Inst Tekst Promst ... Trudove na Nauchnoizsledovatelskiya. Proektokonstruktorski i Tekhnologicheski Institut po Tekstilna Promishlenost [*A publication*]
Tr Nauchno Khim Farm Inst ... Trudy Nauchnogo Khimiko Farmatsevtecheskogo Instituta [*A publication*]
Tr Nauchno Proizvod Konf Agron Buryat Zoovet Inst ... Trudy Nauchno-Proizvodstvennoi Konferentsii po Agronomii Buryatskii Zooveterinarnyi Institut [*A publication*]
Tr Nauchno-Tekh Konf Leningr Elek-Tekh Inst Svyazi ... Trudy Nauchno-Tekhnicheskoi Konferentsii Leningradskogo Elektro-Tekhnicheskogo Instituta Svyazi [*USSR*] [*A publication*]
Tr Nauchno Tekh Konf Leningr Elektrotekh Inst Svyazi ... Trudy Nauchno-Tekhnicheskoi Konferentsii Leningradskogo Elektrotekhnicheskogo Instituta Svyazi [*A publication*]
Tr Nauchno Tekh Ova Chern Metall ... Trudy Nauchno-Tekhnicheskogo Obshchestva Chernoi Metallurgii [*A publication*]
Tr Nauchn Ova Stud Erevan Gos Univ ... Trudy Nauchnogo Obshchestva Studentov Erevanskii Gosudarstvennyi Universitet [*A publication*]
Tr Nauchn Stud Ova Gork Politekh Inst ... Trudy Nauchnogo Studencheskogo Obshchestva Gor'kovskii Politekhnicheskii Institut [*A publication*]
TRNBKL ... Turnbuckle [*Aerospace*]   (AAG)
TRNCAP ... Training Capability [*Military*]
TRN CRD ... Turn Coordination   (MSA)
TRND .... Turned   (MSA)
TRNE .... Trainee   (AABC)
Tr New York Acad Sc ... Transactions. New York Academy of Sciences [*A publication*]
TRNF .... Theologische Rundschau. Neue Folge [*A publication*]
TRNFR .... Transfer   (KSC)
TRNG .... Training
TRNGA ..... Traffic Engineering [*United States*] [*A publication*]
TRNGL ...... Triangle   (MSA)
TRNGR .... Turning Gear
TRNI .... Trans-Industries, Inc. [*NASDAQ symbol*]   (NQ)
Tr NII Metrol Vyssh Uchebn Zaved ... Trudy NII [*Nauchno-Issledovatel'skogo Instituta*] Metrologii Vysshikh Uchebnykh Zavedeniy [*USSR*] [*A publication*]
Tr Nikitsk Bot Sada ... Trudy Nikitskogo Botanicheskogo Sada [*A publication*]
Tr Nikolaev Korablestroit Inst ... Trudy Nikolaevskogo Korablestroitel'nogo Instituta [*A publication*]
Tr NIRMMI ... Trudy NIRMMI [*A publication*]
Tr Nizhnednepr Nauchno-Issled Stn Obleseniyu Peskov ... Trudy Nizhnedneprovskoi Nauchno-Issledovatel'skoi Stantsii po Obleseniyu Peskov [*A publication*]
Tr Nizhnevolzh Nauchno Issled Inst Geol Geofiz ... Trudy Nizhnevolzhskogo Nauchno-Issledovatel'skogo Instituta Geologii i Geofiziki [*A publication*]
TRNJA ...... Transportation Journal [*A publication*]
TRNO .... Terrano Corp. [*NASDAQ symbol*]   (NQ)
Tr Norilsk Vech Ind Inst ... Trudy Noril'skogo Vechernego Industrial'nogo Instituta [*A publication*]
Tr Nov Appar Metod ... Trudy po Novoi Apparature i Metodikam [*A publication*]
Tr Novocherkassk Politekh Inst ... Trudy Novocherkasskogo Politekhnicheskogo Instituta [*USSR*] [*A publication*]
Tr Novocherk Inzh Melior Inst ... Trudy Novocherkasskogo Inzhenerno-Meliorativnogo Instituta [*A publication*]
Tr Novocherk Politekh Inst ... Trudy Novocherkasskogo Politekhnicheskogo Instituta [*A publication*]
Tr Novocherk Vet Inst ... Trudy Novocherkasskogo Veterinarnogo Instituta [*A publication*]
Tr Novocherk Zootekh Vet Inst ... Trudy Novocherkasskogo Zootekhnichesko-Veterinarnogo Instituta [*A publication*]
Tr Novokuz Gos Inst Usoversh Vrach ... Trudy Novokuznetskogo Gosudarstvennogo Instituta Usovershenstvovaniya Vrachei [*A publication*]
Tr Novokuz Gos Inst Usoversh Vrachei ... Trudy Novokuznetskogo Gosudarstvennogo Instituta Usovershenstvovaniya Vrachei [*A publication*]
Tr Novokuz Gos Pedagog Inst ... Trudy Novokuznetskogo Gosudarstvennogo Pedagogicheskogo Instituta [*A publication*]
Tr Novosib Gos Med Inst ... Trudy Novosibirskogo Gosudarstvennogo Meditsinskogo Instituta [*A publication*]
Tr Novosib Inst Inzh Zheleznodorozhn Transp ... Trudy Novosibirskogo Instituta Inzhenerov Zheleznodorozhnogo Transporta [*A publication*]
Tr Novosib Inzh Stroit Inst ... Trudy Novosibirskogo Inzhenerno-Stroitel'nogo Instituta [*A publication*]
Tr Novosib Skh Inst ... Trudy Novosibirskogo Sel'skokhozyaistvennogo Instituta [*A publication*]
T & RNP .... Transportation and Recruiting Naval Personnel [*Budget appropriation title*]
TRNPS ...... Transpose   (MSA)
TRNR .... Touche Remnant Natural Resources [*Investment fund*] [*British*]
TRNR .... Trainer   (AAG)
TRNS .... Transition   (AABC)

TRNS .... Transmation, Inc. [*NASDAQ symbol*]   (NQ)
TRNSMT .. Transmitter
TRNSN ..... Transition   (MSA)
TRNSP ...... Transport [*or Transportation*]   (AFM)
TRNSPN ... Transportation   (KSC)
TRNSPR ... Transporter   (KSC)
TRNT .... TransNet Corp. [*NASDAQ symbol*]   (NQ)
TRNTBL ... Turntable   (MSA)
TR (NY) .... Caines' Term Reports [*New York*] [*A publication*]   (DLA)
TRO .... Taree [*Australia*] [*Airport symbol*]   (OAG)
TRO .... Tarron Industry [*Vancouver Stock Exchange symbol*]
TRO .... Tax Reduction Option
TRO .... Technical Records Office [*or Officer*] [*British*]
TRO .... Technical Reviewing Office   (AFM)
TRO .... Temporary Restraining Order
TRO .... Terminal Release Order [*Military*]   (AFIT)
TRO .... Test Requirements Outline
TRO .... Transportation Officer
TRO .... Trico Industries, Inc. [*NYSE symbol*]   (SPSG)
Tro .... Troades [*of Euripides*] [*Classical studies*]   (OCD)
Tro .... Troilus and Cressida [*Shakespearean work*]
TRO .... Tromsoe [*Norway*] [*Geomagnetic observatory code*]
TRO .... Tromsoe [*Norway*] [*Seismograph station code, US Geological Survey*]   (SEIS)
TRO .... Tropical [*Broadcasting antenna*]
TRO .... Truck Route Order [*Army*]   (AABC)
TRO .... United States Army TRADOC, Fort Sill Post Library, Fort Sill, OK [*OCLC symbol*]   (OCLC)
TROA .... [*The*] Retired Officers Association   (EA)
TROANO ... [*Don Juan*] De Tro y Ortolano [*Acronym identifies manuscript discovered in library of Don Juan De Tro y Ortolano in 1866*]
TROB .... Twenty-First Century Robotics [*NASDAQ symbol*]   (NQ)
Tr Obedin Semin Gidrotekh Vodokhoz Stroit ... Trudy Ob'edinennogo Seminara po Gidrotekhnicheskomu i Vodokhozyaistvennomu Stroitel'stvu [*A publication*]
TROC .... Tritium Removal with Organic Compound [*Nuclear energy*]
TROC .... Trocadero [*London*]   (DSUE)
TROC .... Trochiscus [*Lozenge*] [*Pharmacy*]   (ROG)
TROCA ..... Tangible Reinforcement Operant Conditioning Audiometry
TROCH ..... Trochiscus [*Lozenge*] [*Pharmacy*]
Tr Odess Gidrometeorol Inst ... Trudy Odesskogo Gidrometeorologicheskogo Instituta [*A publication*]
Tr Odess Nauchno-Issled Inst Epidemiol Mikrobiol ... Trudy Odesskogo Nauchno-Issledovatel'skogo Instituta Epidemiologii i Mikrobiologii [*A publication*]
Tr Odess S-Kh Inst ... Trudy Odesskogo Sel'skokhozyaistvennogo Instituta [*A publication*]
Tr Odess Tekhnol Inst ... Trudy Odesskogo Tekhnologicheskogo Instituta [*A publication*]
Tr Odess Tekhnol Inst Konservn Promsti ... Trudy Odesskogo Tekhnologicheskogo Instituta Konservnoi Promyshlennosti [*A publication*]
Tr Odess Tekhnol Inst Pishch Kholod Promsti ... Trudy Odesskogo Tekhnologicheskogo Instituta Pishchevoi i Kholodil'noi Promyshlennosti [*A publication*]
TRODI .... Touchdown Rate of Descent Indicator [*Aviation*]
TROEA ..... Tekko Rodo Eisei [*Japan*] [*A publication*]
TROF .... Trough [*Meteorology*]   (FAAC)
Tr Okeanog Kom Akad Nauk SSSR ... Trudy Okeanograficheskoi Komissii. Akademiya Nauk SSSR [*A publication*]
TROL .... Tapeless Rotorless On-Line Cryptographic Equipment   (NATG)
Trol .... Troland [*Unit of light intensity at the retina*]
TROLAMINE ... Triethanolamine [*Organic chemistry*] [*USAN*]
TROLL .... [*A*] programming language [*1966*]   (CSR)
TRom .... Tribuna Romaniei [*A publication*]
TROM .... Trombone
TROMB .... Tromba [*Trumpet*] [*Music*]   (ROG)
TROMB .... Trombone
TROMEX ... Tropical Oceanographic and Meteorological Experiment [*National Science Foundation*]
TROMP ...... Trompette [*Trumpets*] [*Music*]
Tr Omsk Gos Nauchno-Issled Inst Epidemiol Mikrobiol Gig ... Trudy Omskogo Gosudarstvennogo Nauchno-Issledovatel'skogo Instituta Epidemiologii Mikrobiologii i Gigieny [*A publication*]
Tr Omsk Inst Molochn Khoz Omsk Zon Stn Molochn Khoz ... Trudy Omskogo Instituta Molochnogo Khozyaistva i Omskoi Zonal'noi Stantsii po Molochnomu Khozyaistvu [*A publication*]
Tr Omsk Med Inst Im M I Kalinina ... Trudy Omskogo Meditsinskogo Instituta Imeni M. I. Kalinina [*A publication*]
Tromso Mus Skr ... Tromsoe Museum. Skrifter [*A publication*]
TRON .... [*The*] Real-Time Operating System Nucleus [*Data processing*]   (PCM)
TRON .... Trion, Inc. [*NASDAQ symbol*]   (NQ)
TROO .... Transponder On-Off
TROP .... Tropical
Trop .... Tropical Agriculture [*A publication*]
TROP .... Tropopause [*Meteorology*]   (FAAC)
Trop Abstr ... Tropical Abstracts [*A publication*]

TROPAG... Tropical Agriculture [*Royal Tropical Institute*] [*Bibliographic database*] [*Netherlands*]
Trop Agr .... Tropical Agriculture [*A publication*]
Trop Agr (Ceylon) ... Tropical Agriculturist (Ceylon) [*A publication*]
Trop Agric ... Tropical Agriculture [*A publication*]
Trop Agric (Colombo) ... Tropical Agriculturist (Colombo) [*A publication*]
Trop Agri (Ceylon) ... Tropical Agriculturist (Ceylon) [*A publication*]
Trop Agric Res Ser ... Tropical Agriculture Research Series [*A publication*]
Trop Agric Res Ser (Japan) ... Tropical Agriculture Research Series (Japan) [*A publication*]
Trop Agricst Mag Ceylon Agric Soc ... Tropical Agriculturist and Magazine. Ceylon Agricultural Society [*A publication*]
Trop Agri (Trinidad) ... Tropical Agriculture (Trinidad) [*A publication*]
Trop Agron Tech Memo Aust CSIRO Div Trop Crops Pastures ... Australia. Commonwealth Scientific and Industrial Research Organisation. Division of Tropical Crops and Pastures. Tropical Agronomy. Technical Memorandum [*A publication*] (APTA)
Trop Anim Health Prod ... Tropical Animal Health and Production [*A publication*]
Trop Anim Prod ... Tropical Animal Production [*Dominican Republic*] [*A publication*]
TROPARC ... Center for Tropical and Subtropical Architecture Planning and Construction [*University of Florida*] [*Research center*] (RCD)
TROPB...... Tropenlandwirt [*A publication*]
Trop Build Res Notes Div Build Res CSIRO ... Tropical Building Research Notes. Division of Building Research. Commonwealth Scientific and Industrial Research Organisation [*A publication*] (APTA)
Trop Dent J ... Tropical Dental Journal [*A publication*]
Trop Dis Bull ... Tropical Diseases Bulletin [*A publication*]
Trop Doct... Tropical Doctor [*A publication*]
Trop Ecol ... Tropical Ecology [*A publication*]
Tropenlandwirt (Germany FR) ... Tropenlandwirtschaft (Germany, Federal Republic) [*A publication*]
Tropenmed P ... Tropenmedizin und Parasitologie [*A publication*]
Tropenmed Parasitol ... Tropenmedizin und Parasitologie [*A publication*]
TROPEX... Tropical Experiment [*Proposed by BOMEX*]
Trop For Notes ... Tropical Forest Notes [*A publication*]
Trop Gastroenterol ... Tropical Gastroenterology [*A publication*]
Trop Geogr Med ... Tropical and Geographical Medicine [*A publication*]
Trop Geo Me ... Tropical and Geographical Medicine [*A publication*]
Trop Grain Legume Bull ... Tropical Grain Legume Bulletin [*A publication*]
Trop Grassl ... Tropical Grasslands [*A publication*]
Trop Grasslands ... Tropical Grasslands [*A publication*]
Trop Grasslds ... Tropical Grasslands [*A publication*] (APTA)
Trophoblast Res ... Trophoblast Research [*A publication*]
Tropical Ag ... Tropical Agriculturist [*A publication*]
TROPICS ... Tour Operators Integrated Computer System [*Airline ticket system*]
TROPM .... Tropical Man [*Leiden*] [*A publication*]
Trop Man... Tropical Man [*Leiden*] [*A publication*]
TROPMED ... Regional Project for Tropical Medicine and Public Health [*SEAMEO*] [*Research center*] [*Thailand*] (IRC)
Trop Med... Tropical Medicine [*A publication*]
Trop Med Hyg News ... Tropical Medicine and Hygiene News [*A publication*]
Trop Med Parasitol ... Tropical Medicine and Parasitology [*A publication*]
Trop Med Res Stud Ser ... Tropical Medicine Research Studies Series [*A publication*]
TROPO ..... Tropospheric
Trop Pest Bull ... Tropical Pest Bulletin [*A publication*]
Trop Pestic Res Inst Annu Rep ... Tropical Pesticides Research Institute. Annual Report [*A publication*]
Trop Pestic Res Inst Misc Rep ... Tropical Pesticides Research Institute. Miscellaneous Report [*A publication*]
Trop Pest Manage ... Tropical Pest Management [*A publication*]
Trop Prod Inst Crop Prod Dig ... Tropical Products Institute. Crop and Product Digest [*A publication*]
Trop Prod Inst Rep ... Tropical Products Institute. Report [*A publication*]
TROPRAN ... Tropical Regional Analysis [*National Weather Service*]
Trop Sci ..... Tropical Science [*A publication*]
Trop Sci Cent Occas Pap (San Jose Costa Rica) ... Tropical Science Center. Occasional Paper (San Jose, Costa Rica) [*A publication*]
Trop Stored Prod Inf ... Tropical Stored Products Information [*A publication*]
Trop Stored Prod Inform ... Tropical Stored Products Information [*A publication*]
Trop Subtrop Pflwelt ... Tropische und Subtropische Pflanzenwelt [*A publication*]
Trop Vet..... Tropical Veterinarian [*A publication*]
Trop Vet Bull ... Tropical Veterinary Bulletin [*A publication*]
Trop Woods ... Tropical Woods [*A publication*]
Trop Woods Yale Univ Sch For ... Tropical Woods. Yale University School of Forestry [*A publication*]
Tr Opytn Stn Plodovod Akad Nauk Gruz SSR ... Trudy Opytnoi Stantsii Plodovodstva Akademii Nauk Gruzinskoi SSR [*A publication*]
Trop Zool ... Tropical Zoology [*A publication*]
Tr Orenb Gos Med Inst ... Trudy Orenburgskogo Gosudarstvennogo Meditsinskogo Instituta [*A publication*]

Tr Orenb Nauchno Issled Inst Molochno Myasn Skotovod ... Trudy Orenburgskii Nauchno-Issledovatel'skii Instituta Molochno-Myasnogo Skotovodstva [*A publication*]
Tr Orenb Obl Otd Vseross-Nauchn O-Va Ter ... Trudy Orenburgskogo Oblastnogo Otdeleniya Vserossiiskogonauchnogo Obshchestva Terapevtov [*A publication*]
Tr Orenb Otd Vses Fiziol Ova ... Trudy Orenburgskogo Otdeleniya Vsesoyuznogo Fiziologicheskogo Obshchestva [*A publication*]
Tr Orenb Otd Vses Ova Fiziol ... Trudy Orenburgskogo Otdeleniya Vsesoyuznogo Obshchestva Fiziologov [*A publication*]
Tr Orenb Otd Vses Ova Fiziol Biokhim Farmakol ... Trudy Orenburgskogo Otdeleniya Vsesoyuznogo Obshchestva Fiziologov, Biokhimikov, i Farmakologov [*A publication*]
Tr Orenb Skh Inst ... Trudy Orenburgskogo Sel'skokhozyaistvennogo Instituta [*A publication*]
TROS......... Tape Resident Operating System [*Data processing*] (IEEE)
TROS......... Transformer Read Only Storage
TROSA...... Tropical Science [*A publication*]
TROSCOM ... Troop Support Command [*Formerly, MECOM*] [*Army*] [*St. Louis, MO*]
Tr Otd Fiziol Biofiz Rast Akad Nauk Tadzh SSR ... Trudy Otdel Fiziologii i Biofiziki Rastenii Akademiya Nauk Tadzhikskoi SSR [*A publication*]
Tr Otd Geol Buryat Fil Sib Otd Akad Nauk SSSR ... Trudy Otdela Geologii Buryatskii Filial Sibirskoe Otdelenie Akademiya Nauk SSSR [*A publication*]
Tr Otd Gorn Dela Metall Akad Nauk Kirg SSR ... Trudy Otdela Gornogo Dela i Metallurgii Akademiya Nauk Kirgizskoi SSR [*A publication*]
Tr Otd Pochvoved Akad Nauk Kirg SSR ... Trudy Otdela Pochvovedeniya Akademiya Nauk Kirgizskoi SSR [*A publication*]
Tr Otd Pochvoved Dagest Fil Akad Nauk SSSR ... Trudy Otdela Pochvovedeniya Dagestanskogo Filiala. Akademii Nauk SSSR [*A publication*]
TROTTS ..... Theater Realignment of Traffic Transportation Support (MCD)
TROU .... Tround International, Inc. [*NASDAQ symbol*] (NQ)
Troub & H Prac ... Troubat and Haly's Pennsylvania Practice [*A publication*] (DLA)
Troub Lim Partn ... Troubat on Limited Partnership [*A publication*] (DLA)
Trouser....... Trouser Press [*A publication*]
TROV .... Tethered Remotely Operational Vehicle [*Marine science*] (MSC)
Tr O-Va Fiziol Azerb ... Trudy Obshchestva Fiziologov Azerbaidzhana [*A publication*]
TROW .... T. Rowe Price Associates, Inc. [*Baltimore, MD*] [*NASDAQ symbol*] (NQ)
Trow D & Cr ... Trower's Debtor and Creditor [*1860*] [*A publication*] (DLA)
Trow Eq ..... Trower's Manual of the Prevalance of Equity [*1876*] [*A publication*] (DLA)
T Roy Ent S ... Transactions. Royal Entomological Society of London [*A publication*]
T Roy Soc C ... Transactions. Royal Society of Canada [*A publication*]
TRP............ Maryland State Police [*Pikesville, MD*] [*FAA designator*] (FAAC)
TRP............ Table of Replaceable Parts
TRP............ Tamper Resistant Packaging [*Food and Drug Administration*]
TRP............ Tangible Research Property [*Business*]
TRP............ Target Reference Point (AABC)
TRP............ Target Reporting Parameters (MCD)
TRP............ Technical Requirements Package (MCD)
TRP............ Television Remote Pickup
TRP............ Terminal Rendezvous Phase
TRP............ Threat Recognition Processor [*Navy*] (MCD)
TRP............ Thunderstorm Research Project [*Environmental Science Services Administration*]
TRP............ Timber Rights Purchase
TRP............ Time to Repair Part
TRP............ Timing Release Pin
TRP............ Trade Pattern (MSA)
TRP............ Traffic Regulation Point [*Military*]
TRP............ Trainable Retractable Propeller
TRP............ Training Review Panel (CAAL)
TRP............ TransCanada Pipelines Ltd. [*NYSE symbol*] [*Toronto Stock Exchange symbol*] [*Vancouver Stock Exchange symbol*] (SPSG)
TrP............ Transpatent [*German*] (DLA)
TRP............ Transportation Proceedings [*A publication*]
TRP............ Tree Point, AK [*Location identifier*] [*FAA*] (FAAL)
TRP............ Trefpunt [*A publication*]
TRP............ Tricommand Review Panel [*Military*] (AFIT)
TRP............ Tripped
TRP............ Troop (AFM)
TRP............ Trujillo [*Peru*] [*Seismograph station code, US Geological Survey*] (SEIS)
Trp............ Tryptophan [*Also, W*] [*An amino acid*]
TRP............ Tubular Reabsorption [*or Resorption*] of Phosphate
TRPA......... Tryptophan-Rich Prealbumin [*Biochemistry*]
Tr Pacific Coast Oto-Ophth Soc ... Transactions. Pacific Coast Oto-Ophthalmological Society [*A publication*]

Tr Paleontol Inst Akad Nauk SSSR ... Trudy Paleontologicheskogo Instituta Akademiya Nauk SSSR [*A publication*]

Tr Path Soc London ... Transactions. Pathological Society of London [*A publication*]

TRPB......... Thoroughbred Racing Protective Bureau (EA)

TRPC......... Tasmanian Rural Promotions Committee [*Australia*]

TRPC......... Tradicion. Revista Peruana de Cultura [*A publication*]

TRPCAR ... Troop Carrier [*Military*] (CINC)

TRPCAR(M) ... Troop Carrier (Medium) (CINC)

TRPCL...... Tropical (FAAC)

TRPCO...... Tropical Continental [*American air mass*] (FAAC)

TRPCSq.... Troop Carrier Squadron [*Air Force*]

Tr Pechoro Ilychskogo Gos Zapov ... Trudy Pechoro-Ilychskogo Gosudarstvennogo Zapovednika [*A publication*]

Tr Permsk Biol Nauchno Issled Inst ... Trudy Permskogo Biologicheskogo Nauchno-Issledovatel'skogo Instituta [*A publication*]

Tr Permsk Farm Inst ... Trudy Permskogo Farmatseuticheskogo Instituta [*A publication*]

Tr Permsk Gos Med Inst ... Trudy Permskii Gosudarstvennyi Meditsinskii Institut [*A publication*]

Tr Permsk Gos Nauchno-Issled Proektn Inst Neft Prom-Sti ... Trudy Permskij Gosudarstvennyj Nauchno-Issledovatel'skij i Proektnyj Institut Neftyanoj Promyshlennosti [*A publication*]

Tr Permsk Gos Skh Inst ... Trudy Permskogo Gosudarstvennogo Sel'skokhozyaistvennogo Instituta [*A publication*]

Tr Permsk Nauchno Issled Inst Vaktsin Syvorotok ... Trudy Permskogo Nauchno-Issledovatel'skogo Instituta Vaktsin i Syvorotok [*A publication*]

Tr Permsk S-Kh Inst ... Trudy Permskogo Sel'skokhozyaistvennogo Instituta [*A publication*]

Tr Perv Mosk Med Inst Im I M Sechenova ... Trudy Pervogo Moskovskogo Meditsinskogo Instituta Imeni I. M. Sechenova [*A publication*]

Tr 1 Pervogo Mosk Med Inst ... Trudy 1 Pervogo Moskovskogo Meditsinskogo Instituta [*USSR*] [*A publication*]

Tr Pervogo Mosk Pedagog Inst ... Trudy Pervogo Moskovskogo Pedagogicheskogo Instituta [*A publication*]

Tr Petergof Biol Inst Leningr Gos Univ ... Trudy Petergofskogo Biologicheskogo Instituta. Leningradskii Gosudarstvennyi Universitet [*A publication*]

Tr Petergof Estest Nauchn Inst ... Trudy Petergofskogo Estestvenno-Nauchnogo Instituta [*A publication*]

Tr Petrogr Inst Akad Nauk SSSR ... Trudy Petrograficheskogo Instituta. Akademiya Nauk SSSR [*A publication*]

TRPF .... Tax Resisters' Penalty Fund (EA)

TRPGDA... Tripropylene Glycol Diacrylate [*Organic chemistry*]

TRPH .... Triumph Capital, Inc. [*NASDAQ symbol*] (NQ)

TRPI .... Training Requirement Priority Index

TRPL .... Terneplate [*Materials*]

TRPLA ...... Transplantation [*A publication*]

Tr Plodoovoshchn Inst ... Trudy Plodoovoshchnogo Instituta [*A publication*]

Tr Plodovoshchn Inst Im I V Michurina ... Trudy Plodovoshchnogo Instituta Imeni I. V. Michurina [*A publication*]

Tr Plodovo-Yagodnogo Inst Im Akad R R Shredera ... Trudy Plodovo-Yagodnogo Instituta Imeni Akademika R. R. Shredera [*A publication*]

TRPLYR.... Trapping Layer (FAAC)

TRPM........ Plymouth/Blackburne [*Montserrat Island*] [*ICAO location identifier*] (ICLI)

Trp-mRNA ... Ribonucleic Acid, Messenger - Tryptophan Constitutive [*Biochemistry, genetics*]

TRPN .... Transportation

TRPNA2.... Trudy Rostovskogo Gosudarstvennogo Nauchno-Issledovatel'skogo Protivochumnogo Instituta Narkomzdrava SSSR [*A publication*]

TRPO .... Track Reference Printout

Tr Poch Inst V V Dokuchaeva Akad Nauk SSSR ... Trudy Pochvennogo Instituta Imeni V. V. Dokuchaeva Akademiya Nauk SSSR [*A publication*]

Tr Pochv Inst Im V V Dokuchaeva Akad Nauk SSSR ... Trudy Pochvennogo Instituta Imeni V. V. Dokuchaeva Akademii Nauk SSSR [*A publication*]

Tr Polyar Nauchno-Issled Proekt Inst Morsk Ryb Khoz Okeanogr ... Trudy Polyarnyi Nauchno-Issledovatel'skii i Proektnyi Institut Morskogo Rybnogo Khozyaistva i Okeanografii [*USSR*] [*A publication*]

TRPPA ...... Transplantation Proceedings [*A publication*]

TRPRB ...... Transplantation Reviews [*A publication*]

Tr Prik Bot Genet Sel Ser 10 ... Trudy po Prikladnoi Botanike. Genetike i Selektsii. Seriya 10. Dendrologiya i Dekorativnoe Sadovodstvo [*A publication*]

Tr Prikl Bot Genet Sel ... Trudy po Prikladnoi Botanike Genetike i Selektsii [*USSR*] [*A publication*]

Tr Prikl Bot Genet Selek ... Trudy po Prikladnoi Botanike Genetike i Selektsii [*A publication*]

Tr Prikl Bot Genet Sel Ser 1 ... Trudy po Prikladnoi Botanike. Genetike i Selektsii. Seriya 1. Sistematika, Geografia, i Ekologia Rastenii [*A publication*]

Tr Prikl Bot Genet Sel Ser 2 ... Trudy po Prikladnoi Botanike. Genetike i Selektsii. Seriya 2. Genetika, Selektsiya, i Tsitologiya Rastenii [*A publication*]

Tr Prikl Bot Genet Sel Ser 3 ... Trudy po Prikladnoi Botanike. Genetike i Selektsii. Seriya 3. Fiziologiya, Biokhimiya, i Anatomiya Rastenii [*A publication*]

Tr Prikl Bot Genet Sel Ser 4 ... Trudy po Prikladnoi Botanike. Genetike i Selektsii. Seriya 4. Semenovedenie i Semennoi Kontrol [*A publication*]

Tr Prikl Bot Genet Sel Ser 5 ... Trudy po Prikladnoi Botanike. Genetike i Selektsii. Seriya 5. Zernovye Kul'tury [*A publication*]

Tr Prikl Bot Genet Sel Ser 6 ... Trudy po Prikladnoi Botanike. Genetike i Selektsii. Seriya 6. Ovoshchnye Kul'tury [*A publication*]

Tr Prikl Bot Genet Sel Ser 9 ... Trudy po Prikladnoi Botanike. Genetike i Selektsii. Seriya 9. Tekhnicheskie Kul'tury [*A publication*]

Tr Prikl Bot Genet Sel Ser 11 ... Trudy po Prikladnoi Botanike. Genetike i Selektsii. Seriya 11. Novye Kul'tury i Voprosy Introduktsii [*A publication*]

Tr Prikl Bot Genet Sel Ser 13 ... Trudy po Prikladnoi Botanike. Genetike i Selektsii. Seriya 13. Regeraty i Bibliografia [*A publication*]

Tr Prikl Bot Genet Sel Ser 14 ... Trudy po Prikladnoi Botanike. Genetike i Selektsii. Seriya 14. Osvoenie Pustyn [*A publication*]

Tr Prikl Bot Genet Sel Ser 15 ... Trudy po Prikladnoi Botanike. Genetike i Selektsii. Seriya 15. Severnoe (Pripolyarnoe) Zemledelie [*A publication*]

Tr Prikl Bot Genet Sel Ser A ... Trudy po Prikladnoi Botanike. Genetike i Selektsii. Seriya A. Sotsialisticheskoe [*A publication*]

Tr Primorsk S-Kh Inst ... Trudy Primorskogo Sel'skokhozyaistvennogo Instituta [*A publication*]

Tr Priokso Terrasnogo Gos Zapov ... Trudy Priokso-Terrasnogo Gosudarstvennogo Zapovednika [*A publication*]

Tr Probl Lab Khim Vysokomol Soedin Voronezh Gos Univ ... Trudy Problemnoi Laboratorii Khimii Vysokomolekulyarnykh Soedinenii. Voronezhskii Gosudarstvennyi Universitet [*A publication*]

Tr Probl Lab Osad Form Osad Rud Tashk Gos Univ ... Trudy Problemnoi Laboratorii Osadochnykh Formatsii i Osadochnykh Rud Tashkentskii Gosudarstvennyi Universitet [*A publication*]

Tr Probl Lab Silik Mater Konstr Voronezh Inzh Stroit Inst ... Trudy Problemnoi Laboratorii Silikatnykh Materialov i Konstruktsii Voronezhskii Inzhenerno-Stroitel'nyi Institut [*A publication*]

Tr Probl Temat Soveshch Akad Nauk SSSR Zool Inst ... Trudy Problemnykh i Tematicheskikh Soveshchanii Akademiya Nauk SSSR Zoologicheskii Institut [*A publication*]

Tr Proizvod Nauchno-Issled Inst Inzh Izyskaniyam Stroit ... Trudy Proizvodstvennyi i Nauchno-Issledovatel'skii Institut po Inzhenernym Izyskaniyam v Stroitel'stve [*A publication*]

TRPS .... Temperature Regulating Power Supply

TRPS .... Troops

TRPSC....... Triple Screw

Tr Pskov Obl Gos Skh Opytn Stn ... Trudy Pskovskoi Oblastnoi Gosudarstvennoi Sel'skokhozyaistvennoi Opytnoi Stantsii [*A publication*]

TRPT......... Time to Reach Peak Tension

Tr Pushkin Nauchno-Issled Lab Razvedeniya S-Kh Zhivotn ... Trudy Pushkinskoi Nauchno-Issledovatel'skoi Laboratorii Razvedeniya Sel'skokhozyaistvennykh Zhivotnykh [*A publication*]

TRPX......... TRP Energy Sensors [*NASDAQ symbol*] (NQ)

TRQ........... Task Ready Queue

TRQ........... Torque (AAG)

TRQ........... Total Requirements (AAG)

TRQ........... United States Army TRADOC, Fort Ord, CDEC Library, Fort Ord, CA [*OCLC symbol*] (OCLC)

TRQUD..... Transportation Quarterly [*A publication*]

TRR........... [*The*] Research Ranch [*An association*] (EA)

TRR........... [*The*] Rohmer Review [*A publication*]

TRR........... Tactical Range Recorder [*Navy*]

TRR........... Tactical Reaction Reconnaissance

TRR........... Tape Read Register

TRR........... Target Ranging RADAR

TRR........... Tarraleah [*Tasmania*] [*Seismograph station code, US Geological Survey*] (SEIS)

TRR........... Teaching and Research Reactor

TRR........... Test Readiness Review [*NASA*] (NASA)

TRR........... Test and Research Reactor [*Nuclear energy*] (NRCH)

TRR........... Tethered RADAR Reflector

TRR........... Thailand Research Reactor

TRR........... Theoretical Research Report

TRR........... Topical Report Request [*or Review*] [*Nuclear energy*] (NRCH)

TRR........... Trade Regulation Reporter [*A publication*] (DLA)

TRR........... Trader Resource Corp. [*Toronto Stock Exchange symbol*]

TRR........... Transfer Relay Rack (CAAL)

TRR........... TRC Companies, Inc. [*AMEX symbol*] (SPSG)

TRR........... True Rate of Return [*Finance*] (ADA)

TRR........... United States Army TRADOC, Fort Rucker Post Library and Aviation School Library, Fort Rucker, AL [*OCLC symbol*] (OCLC)

TRRA........ Tera Corp. [*NASDAQ symbol*] (NQ)

TRRA........ Terminal Railroad Association of St. Louis [*AAR code*]

TRRA........ Tilt Rotor Research Aircraft

Tr Radiat Gig Leningr Nauchno-Issled Inst Radiats Gig ... Trudy po
    Radiatsionnoi Gigiene Leningradskii Nauchno-
    Issledovatel'skii Institut Radiatsionnoi Gigieny [*USSR*] [*A
    publication*]
Tr Radiats Gig ... Trudy po Radiatsionnoi Gigiene [*A publication*]
Tr Radiats Gig Leningr Nauchno-Issled Inst Radiats Gig ... Trudy po
    Radiatsionnoi Gigiene Leningradskij Nauchno-
    Issledovatel'skij Institut Radiatsionnoj Gigieny [*A
    publication*]
Tr Radievogo Inst Akad Nauk SSSR ... Trudy Radievogo Instituta
    Akademiya Nauk SSSR [*A publication*]
Tr Radiotekh Inst ... Trudy Radiotekhnicheskogo Instituta [*USSR*] [*A
    publication*]
Tr Radiotekh Inst Akad Nauk SSSR ... Trudy Radiotekhnicheskogo Instituta
    Akademiya Nauk SSSR [*A publication*]
TRRAPS.... Transportable Reliable Acoustic Path Sonobuoy   (NVT)
TRRB........ Test Readiness Review Board [*NASA*]
TRRB........ Transportation Research Board. Special Report [*United States*]
    [*A publication*]
TRRC........ Test Resources Review Committee [*DoD*]
TRRC........ Textile Resource and Research Center   (EA)
TRRE........ H & S Treat & Release, Inc. [*Brooklyn, NY*] [*NASDAQ
    symbol*]   (NQ)
TRRE........ Transportation Research Record [*A publication*]
TRREB...... Transportation Research [*A publication*]
TRRED...... Transportation Research Record [*A publication*]
Tr Resp Inst Epidemiol Mikrobiol ... Trudove na Respublikanskiya Instituta
    po Epidemiologiya i Mikrobiologiya [*A publication*]
Tr Resp Opytn Stn Kartofeln Ovoshchn Khoz Kaz SSR ... Trudy
    Respublikanskoi Opytnoi Stantsii Kartofel'nogo i
    Ovoshchnogo Khozyaistva Kazakhskaya SSR [*A
    publication*]
Tr Resp Ova Ftiziatrov Nauchno Issled Inst Tuberk Kaz SSR ... Trudy
    Respublikanskogo Obshchestva Ftiziatrov Nauchno-
    Issledovatel'skogo Instituta Tuberkuleza Kazakhskoi SSR
    [*A publication*]
Tr Resp Stn Zashch Rast ... Trudy Respublikanskoi Stantsii Zashchity
    Rastenii [*A publication*]
TRRF........ [*The*] Refrigeration Research Foundation   (EA)
TRRF........ Training Review File [*IRS*]
TRRFDP ... Israel. Agricultural Research Organization. Division of Forestry.
    Triennial Report of Research [*A publication*]
TRRG .... Tax Reform Research Group   (EA)
TRRIA ...... Translations Register-Index [*A publication*]
Tr Rizh Inst Inzh Grazhdanskoi Aviats ... Trudy Rizhskogo Instituta
    Inzhenerov Grazhdanskoi Aviatsii [*A publication*]
Tr Rizh Nauchno Issled Inst Travmatol Ortop ... Trudy Rizhskii Nauchno-
    Issledovatel'skii Institut Travmatologii i Ortopedii [*A
    publication*]
TRRL........ Tooling Rejection and Rework Laboratory
TRRL........ Transport and Road Research Laboratory [*Departments of the
    Environment and Transport*] [*Information service or
    system*]   (IID)
TRRL Lab Rep ... TRRL [*Transport and Road Research Laboratory*]
    Laboratory Report [*A publication*]
TRRL Rep ... TRRL [*Transport and Road Research Laboratory*] Report [*A
    publication*]
TRRL Suppl Rep ... TRRL [*Transport and Road Research Laboratory*]
    Supplementary Report [*A publication*]
TRRN .... Terrain   (FAAC)
Tr Ross Inst Prikl Khim ... Trudy Rossiiskogo Instituta Prikladnoi Khimii [*A
    publication*]
Tr Rostov na Donu Inst Inzh Zheleznodorozhn Transp ... Trudy Rostovskogo-
    na-Donu Instituta Inzhenerov Zheleznodorozhnogo
    Transporta [*A publication*]
Tr Rostov-Na-Donu Inzh Stroit Inst ... Trudy Rostovskii-Na-Donu
    Inzhenerno Stroitel'nyi Institut [*A publication*]
Tr Roy Soc Edinb ... Transactions. Royal Society of Edinburgh [*A publication*]
Tr Roy Soc Trop Med Hyg ... Transactions. Royal Society of Tropical
    Medicine and Hygiene [*A publication*]
TRRR........ Trilateral Range and Range Rate System
TRRS........ Transport and Road Research Laboratory. Supplementary
    Report [*A publication*]
TRR of ST L ... Terminal Railroad Association of St. Louis
TRRT........ Test Results Review Team [*Nuclear energy*]   (NRCH)
TRRT........ Tooling Rejection and Rework Tag
Tr Ryazan Med Inst ... Trudy Ryazanskogo Meditsinskogo Instituta [*A
    publication*]
Tr Ryazan Radiotekh Inst ... Trudy Ryazanskogo Radiotekhnicheskogo
    Instituta [*USSR*] [*A publication*]
TRS............ Tactical RADAR System
TRS............ Tactical Radio Set
TRS............ Tactical Reconnaissance Squadron [*Air Force*]
TRS............ Tactical Reconnaissance System
TRS............ Tape Recorder Subsystem
TRS............ Target Range Servo
TRS............ Technical Repair Standards
TRS............ Technical Requirements Specification   (MCD)
TRS............ Technical Research Ship
TRS............ Teleoperator Retrieval System [*NASA*]
TRS............ Terrestrial Radio System

TRS.......... Test Requirement Specification   (MCD)
TRS.......... Test Requirements Summary   (MUGU)
TRS.......... Test Research Service [*Defunct*]   (EA)
TRS.......... Test Research Station
TRS.......... Test Response Spectrum   (IEEE)
TRS.......... Tetrahedral Research Satellite
TRS.......... Textes Religieux Sumeriens du Louvre [*A publication*]   (BJA)
TRS.......... Theatre Recording Society   (EA)
TRS.......... Theologische Rundschau [*A publication*]
TRS.......... Thermal Radiation Simulator
TRS.......... Thermal Reactor Safety [*Nuclear energy*]   (NRCH)
TRS.......... Third Readiness State   (AAG)
TRS.......... Thorson Aviation, Inc. [*Aberdeen, SD*] [*FAA
    designator*]   (FAAC)
TRS.......... Threat Reaction System
TRS.......... Ticket Reservation Systems, Inc.
TRS.......... Time Reference System   (MCD)
TRS.......... Time-Resolved Spectrometry
TRS.......... Toll Room Switch [*Telecommunications*]   (TEL)
TRS.......... Top Right Side   (MCD)
TRS.......... Torry Research Station [*British*]
TRS.......... Total Reduced Sulfur [*Environmental chemistry*]
TRS.......... Total Reducing Sugars [*Food science*]
TRS.......... Tough Rubber-Sheathed [*Cable*]   (DEN)
TRS.......... Traceability and Reporting System
TRS.......... Training Reservation System   (MCD)
trs .... Traites [*Drafts*] [*French*] [*Business term*]
TRS.......... Transfer   (ADA)
TRS.......... Transportable Relay Station
TRS.......... Transportation Research [*A publication*]
TRS.......... Transpose   (ROG)
TRS.......... Transverse Rupture Strength [*Metallurgy*]
TRS.......... Traumatic Surgery [*Medical specialty*]   (DHSM)
TRS.......... Travel Related Services Co., Inc.
TRS.......... Treasure Island Resources [*Vancouver Stock Exchange symbol*]
TRS.......... Tree-Ring Society   (EA)
TRS.......... Trieste [*Campo Marzio*] [*Italy*] [*Seismograph station code, US
    Geological Survey*] [*Closed*]   (SEIS)
TRS.......... Trieste [*Italy*] [*Airport symbol*]   (OAG)
TRS.......... Tropical Revolving Storm [*Meteorology*]
TRS.......... Troubleshooting Record Sheet [*NASA*]   (NASA)
TRS.......... Truss [*Shipping*]
TRS.......... Trust America Services [*AMEX symbol*]   (SPSG)
TRS.......... Trustees
TRS.......... Tuboreticular Structure [*Cytology*]
TRS.......... Tug Rotational System [*NASA*]   (NASA)
TRS.......... United States Department of Transportation, Transportation
    System Center, Cambridge, MA [*OCLC symbol*]   (OCLC)
TRSA........ Tax Reduction and Simplification Act of 1977
TRSA........ Terminal RADAR Service Area   (FAAC)
TRSA........ Textile Rental Services Association of America   (EA)
TRSAA...... Transaction. Royal Society of South Africa [*A publication*]
Tr Sakhalin Obl Stn Zashch Rast ... Trudy Sakhalinskaya Oblastnaya
    Stantsiya Zashchity Rastenii [*A publication*]
Tr Samark Gos Univ ... Trudy Samarkandskogo Gosudarstvennogo
    Universiteta [*A publication*]
Tr Samar Skh Inst ... Trudy Samarskogo Sel'skokhozyaistvennogo Instituta
    [*A publication*]
Tr Sarat Avtomob Dorozhn Inst ... Trudy Saratovskogo Avtomobil'no-
    Dorozhnogo Instituta [*A publication*]
Tr Sarat Inst Mekh Selsk Khoz ... Trudy Saratovskogo Instituta
    Mekhanizatsii Sel'skogo Khozyaistva [*A publication*]
Tr Sarat Med Inst ... Trudy Saratovskogo Meditsinskogo Instituta [*A
    publication*]
Tr Sarat Nauchno Issled Vet Stn ... Trudy Saratovskoi Nauchno-
    Issledovatel'skogo Veterinarnoi Stantsii [*A publication*]
Tr Sarat Otd Vses Nauchno Issled Inst Ozern Rechn Rybn Khoz ... Trudy
    Saratovskogo Otdeleniya Vsesoyuznogo Nauchno-
    Issledovatel'skogo Instituta Ozernogo i Rechnogo Rybn
    Khoz [*A publication*]
Tr Sarat Ova Estestvoispyt Lyubit Estestvozn ... Trudy Saratovskogo
    Obshchestva Estestvoispytatelei i Lyubitelei
    Estestvoznaniya [*A publication*]
Tr Sarat S-Kh Inst ... Trudy Saratovskogo Sel'skokhozyaistvennogo Instituta
    [*A publication*]
Tr Sarat Zootekh Vet Inst ... Trudy Saratovskogo Zootekhnicheskogo
    Veterinarnogo Instituta [*A publication*]
Tr Sary Chelekskogo Gos Zap ... Trudy Sary Chelekskogo Gosudarstvennogo
    Zapovednikia [*A publication*]
TRSB........ Time Reference Scanning Beam [*Aviation*]
TRSBG...... Transcribing   (MSA)
TRSBR...... Transcriber   (MSA)
TR/SBS.... Teleoperator Retrieval/Skylab Boost System
    [*Aerospace*]   (MCD)
TRSC........ Transactions. Royal Society of Canada [*A publication*]
TRSC........ Triad Systems Corporation [*NASDAQ symbol*]   (NQ)
TRSCA...... Transactions. Royal Society of Canada [*A publication*]
TRSCB...... Transcribe   (MSA)
TRSCB...... Transportation Science [*A publication*]
TRSD........ Test Requirements/Specification Document [*NASA*]   (MCD)
TRSD........ Total Radiance Spectral Distribution

TRSD......... Total Rated Service Date [*Air Force*]   (AFM)
TRSD......... Transferred
TRSD......... Transposed
Tr Sekt Astrobot Akad Nauk Kazakh SSR ... Trudy Sektora Astrobotaniki Akademiya Nauk Kazakhskoi SSR [*A publication*]
Tr Sekt Astrobot Akad Nauk Kaz SSR ... Trudy Sektora Astrobotaniki Akademiya Nauk Kazakhskoi SSR [*A publication*]
Tr Sekt Energ Azerb Fil Akad Nauk SSSR ... Trudy Sektora Energetiki Azerbaidzhanskogo Filiala Akademii Nauk SSSR [*A publication*]
Tr Sekt Fiziol Akad Nauk Az SSR ... Trudy Sektora Fiziologii Akademiya Nauk Azerbaidzhanskoi SSR [*A publication*]
Tr Sekt Fiziol Zhivotn Inst Biol Akad Nauk Latv SSR ... Trudy Sektora Fiziologii Zhivotnykh Instituta Biologii Akademiya Nauk Latviiskoi SSR [*A publication*]
Tr Sel Agrotekh Zashch Rast ... Trudy po Selektsii Agrotekhnike i Zashchite Rastenii [*A publication*]
Tr Semin "Bionika Mat Model Biol" ... Trudy Seminara "Bionika i Matematicheskoe Modelirovanie v Biologii" [*A publication*]
Tr Semin Zharostoikim Mater ... Trudy Seminara po Zharostoikim Materialam [*A publication*]
Tr Semipalat Med Inst ... Trudy Semipalatinskogo Meditsinskogo Instituta [*A publication*]
Tr Semipalat Zoovet Inst ... Trudy Semipalatinskogo Zooveterinarnogo Instituta [*A publication*]
Tr Ser......... Treaty Series [*A publication*]   (DLA)
Tr Sess Kom Opred Absol Vozrasta Geol Form Akad Nauk SSSR ... Trudy Sessii Komissii po Opredeleniyu Absolyutnogo Vozrasta Geologicheskikh Formatsii Akademiya Nauk SSSR [*A publication*]
Tr Sevansk Gidrobiol Stn ... Trudy Sevanskoi Gidrobiologicheskoi Stantsii [*A publication*]
Tr Sevastop Biol Stn Akad Nauk Ukr SSR ... Trudy Sevastopol'skoi Biologicheskoi Stantsii Akademii Nauk Ukrainskoi SSR [*A publication*]
Tr Sevastop Biol Stn Im A D Kovalenskogo Akad Nauk Ukr SSR ... Trudy Sevastopol'skoi Biologicheskoi Stantsii Imeni A. D. Kovalenskogo Akademii Nauk Ukrainskoi SSR [*A publication*]
Tr Severokavkazskogo Gornometall Inst ... Trudy Severokavkazskogo Gornometallurgicheskogo Instituta [*USSR*] [*A publication*]
Tr Sev Kavk Gornometall Inst ... Trudy Severo-Kavkazskogo Gornometallurgicheskogo Instituta [*A publication*]
Tr Sev Nauchno Issled Inst Gidrotekh Melior ... Trudy Severnyi Nauchno-Issledovatel'skii Institut Gidrotekhniki i Melioratsii [*A publication*]
Tr Sev-Oset Med Inst ... Trudy Severo-Osetinskogo Meditsinskogo Instituta [*A publication*]
Tr Sev-Oset S-kh Inst ... Trudy Severo-Osetinskogo Sel'skokhozyaistvennogo Instituta [*A publication*]
Tr Sev Vost Kompleksn Inst Dalnevost Tsentr Akad Nauk SSSR ... Trudy Severo-Vostochnogo Kompleksnogo Instituta Dal'nevostochnyi Tsentr Akademiya Nauk SSSR [*A publication*]
Tr Sev Zapadn Nauchno Issled Inst Sel'sk Khoz ... Trudy Severo. Zapadnogo Nauchno-Issledovatel'skogo Instituta Sel'skogo Khozyaistva [*A publication*]
Tr Sev Zapadn Zaochn Politekh Inst ... Trudy. Severo-Zapadnyi Zaochnyi Politekhnicheskii Institut [*A publication*]
TRSF......... Torque-Regulated Speed Follower
TRSG......... Third Reich Study Group   (EA)
TRSG......... Track RADAR Simulation Group [*Military*]   (CAAL)
TRSH......... Trim Shell
TRSI......... Test of Retail Sales Insight
Tr Sib Fiz Tekh Inst Tomsk Gos Univ ... Trudy Sibirskogo Fiziko-Tekhnicheskogo Instituta pri Tomskom Gosudarstvennom Universitete [*USSR*] [*A publication*]
Tr Sib Gos Nauchno Issled Inst Metrol ... Trudy Sibirskii Gosudarstvennyi Nauchno-Issledovatel'skii Institut Metrologii [*A publication*]
Tr Sib Lesotekh Inst ... Trudy Sibirskogo Lesotekhnicheskogo Instituta [*A publication*]
Tr Sib Metall Inst ... Trudy Sibirskogo Metallurgicheskogo Instituta [*A publication*]
Tr Sib Nauch-Issled Inst Zhivotn ... Trudy Sibirskogo Nauchno-Issledovatel'skogo Instituta Zhivotnovodstva [*A publication*]
Tr Sib Nauchno-Issled Inst Energ ... Trudy Sibirskogo Nauchno-Issledovatel'skogo Instituta Energetiki [*USSR*] [*A publication*]
Tr Sib Nauchno-Issled Inst Geol Geofiz Miner Syr'ya ... Trudy Sibirskogo Nauchno-Issledovatel'skogo Instituta Geologii, Geofiziki, i Mineral'nogo Syr'ya [*A publication*]
Tr Sib Nauchno Issled Inst Lesn Promsti ... Trudy Sibirskii Nauchno-Issledovatel'skii Institut Lesnoi Promyshlennosti [*A publication*]
Tr Sib Otd Gos Nauchno-Issled Inst Ozern Rechn Rybn Khoz ... Trudy Sibirskogo Otdela Gosudarstvennogo Nauchno-Issledovatel'skogo Instituta Ozernogo i Rechnogo Rybnogo Khozyaistva [*A publication*]

Tr Sib Tekhnol Inst ... Trudy Sibirskogo Tekhnologicheskogo Instituta [*A publication*]
Tr Sikhote-Alinsk Gos Zapov ... Trudy Sikhote-Alinskogo Gosudarstvennogo Zapovednika [*A publication*]
Tr Skh Samarkanskogo Inst ... Trudy Sel'skokhozyaistvennogo Samarkanskogo Instituta [*A publication*]
TRSL......... Toms River Signal Laboratory [*Army*]   (MCD)
TRSL......... Transactions. Royal Society of Literature [*A publication*]
TRSL......... Transnational Industries, Inc. [*NASDAQ symbol*]   (NQ)
TRSLA......... TRW Space Log [*A publication*]
Tr Smolensk Gos Med Inst ... Trudy Smolenskogo Gosudarstvennogo Meditsinskogo Instituta [*A publication*]
Tr Smolensk Nauchno Issled Vet Stn ... Trudy Smolenskoi Nauchno-Issledovatel'skoi Veterinarnoi Stantsii [*A publication*]
TRSN......... Torsion   (MSA)
TRSN......... Transition   (FAAC)
TRSN......... Transition [*Indian and Northern Affairs, Canada*] [*A publication*]
TRSOC...... Trademark Society, Inc.
Tr Soc Trop Med and Hyg (London) ... Transactions. Society of Tropical Medicine and Hygiene (London) [*A publication*]
Tr Solyanoi Lab Vses Inst Galurgii Akad Nauk SSSR ... Trudy Solyanoi Laboratorii Vsesoyuznyi Institut Galurgii Akademiya Nauk SSSR [*A publication*]
Tr Sov Antarkt Eksped ... Trudy Sovetskoi Antarkticheskoi Ekspeditsii [*USSR*] [*A publication*]
Tr Soveshch Ikhtiol Kom Akad Nauk SSSR ... Trudy Soveshchanii Ikhtiologicheskoi Komissii Akademii Nauk SSSR [*A publication*]
Tr Soveshch Morfogen Rast ... Trudy Soveshchanii po Morfogenezu Rastenii [*A publication*]
Tr Soveshch Poliploidiya Selek Akad Nauk SSSR ... Trudy Soveshchaniya Poliploidiya i Selektsiya Akademiya Nauk SSSR [*A publication*]
Tr Sovmestnaya Sov Mong Nauchno Issled Geol Eksped ... Trudy Sovmestnaya Sovetsko-Mongol'skaya Nauchno-Issledovatel'skaya Geologicheskaya Ekspeditsiya [*A publication*]
Tr Sov Sekts Mezhdunar Assots Pochvovedov ... Trudy Sovetskoi Sektsii Mezhdunarodnoi Assotsiatsii Pochvovedov [*A publication*]
Tr Soyuzn Geologopoisk Kontora ... Trudy Soyuznaya Geologopoiskovaya Kontora [*A publication*]
Tr Soyuznogo Nauchno-Issled Inst Priborostr ... Trudy Soyuznogo Nauchno-Issledovatel'skogo Instituta Priborostroeniya [*USSR*] [*A publication*]
Tr Soyuzn Trest Razved Burovykh Rab ... Trudy Soyuznyi Trest Razvedochno-Burovykh Rabot [*A publication*]
TRSP......... Total Radiance Spectral Polarization
TRSP......... Transport Seaplane [*Navy*]
Trsp............. Transportieren [*Transport*] [*German*] [*Business term*]
TRSP......... Tri-Star Pictures, Inc. [*New York, NY*] [*NASDAQ symbol*]   (NQ)
TRSq......... Tactical Reconnaissance Squadron [*Air Force*]   (AFM)
TRSR......... Taxi and Runway Surveillance RADAR
Tr Sredneaziat Gos Univ ... Trudy Sredneaziatskogo Gosudarstvennogo Universiteta [*A publication*]
Tr Sredneaziat Gos Univ Ser 6 ... Trudy Sredneaziatskogo Gosudarstvennogo Universiteta. Seriya 6. Khimiya [*A publication*]
Tr Sredneaziat Gos Univ Ser 9 ... Trudy Sredneaziatskogo Gosudarstvennogo Universiteta. Seriya 9. Meditsina [*A publication*]
Tr Sredneaziat Gos Univ Ser 10 ... Trudy Sredneaziatskogo Gosudarstvennogo Universiteta. Seriya 10. Sel'skoe Khozyaistvo [*A publication*]
Tr Sredneaziat Gos Univ Ser 11 ... Trudy Sredneaziatskogo Gosudarstvennogo Universiteta. Seriya 11. Tekhnika [*A publication*]
Tr Sredneaziat Gos Univ Ser 13 ... Trudy Sredneaziatskogo Gosudarstvennogo Universiteta. Seriya 13. Varia [*A publication*]
Tr Sredneaziat Gos Univ Ser 7a ... Trudy Sredneaziatskogo Gosudarstvennogo Universiteta. Seriya 7a. Geologiya [*A publication*]
Tr Sredneaziat Gos Univ Ser 8a ... Trudy Sredneaziatskogo Gosudarstvennogo Universiteta. Seriya 8a. Zoologiya [*A publication*]
Tr Sredneaziat Gos Univ Ser 8b ... Trudy Sredneaziatskogo Gosudarstvennogo Universiteta. Seriya 8b. Botanika [*A publication*]
Tr Sredneaziat Gos Univ Ser 7d ... Trudy Sredneaziatskogo Gosudarstvennogo Universiteta. Seriya 7d. Pochvovedenie [*A publication*]
Tr Sredneaziat Nauchno Issled Gidrometeorol Institut ... Trudy Sredneaziat Nauchno-Issledovatel'skii Gidrometeorologicheskii Institut [*A publication*]
Tr Sredneaziat Nauchno Issled Inst Geol Miner Syrya ... Trudy Sredneaziatskii Nauchno-Issledovatel'skii Institut Geologii i Mineral'nogo Syr'ya [*A publication*]
Tr Sredneaziat Nauchno Issled Inst Irrig ... Trudy Sredneaziatskogo Nauchno-Issledovatel'skogo Instituta Irrigatsii [*A publication*]

Tr Sredneaziat Nauchno Issled Inst Lesn Khoz ... Trudy Sredneaziatskogo Nauchno-Issledovatel'skogo Instituta Lesnogo Khozyaistva [*A publication*]

Tr Sredne-Aziat Nauchno-Issled Protivochumn Inst ... Trudy Sredne-Aziatskogo Nauchno-Issledovatel'skogo Protivochumnogo Instituta [*A publication*]

Tr Sredne Volzh Skh Inst ... Trudy Sredne-Volzhskogo Sel'skokhozyaistvennogo Instituta [*A publication*]

TRSS .... Triple Screw Ship

T Rs S Afr ... Transactions. Royal Society of South Africa [*A publication*]

TRSSCOMM ... Technical Research Ship Special Communications [*System*] [*Pronounced "triss-com"*] [*Navy*]

TRSSGM .. Tactical Range Surface-to-Surface Guided Missile

TRSSM ..... Tactical Range Surface-to-Surface Missile

TRST .... Throttle Reset

TRST .... TrustCo Bank Corp. NY [*NASDAQ symbol*] (NQ)

TRSTA ...... Transactions. Royal Society of Tropical Medicine and Hygiene [*A publication*]

Tr Stalinab Astron Obs ... Trudy Stalinabadskoi Astronomicheskoi Observatorii [*A publication*]

Tr Stalinab Gos Med Inst ... Trudy Stalinabadskogo Gosudarstvennogo Meditsinskogo Instituta [*A publication*]

Tr Stalingr S-Kh Inst ... Trudy Stalingradskogo Sel'skokhozyaistvennogo Instituta [*A publication*]

Tr Stalinskogo Gos Med Inst ... Trudy Stalinskogo Gosudarstvennogo Meditsinskogo Instituta [*A publication*]

Tr Stalinskogo Gos Pedagog Inst ... Trudy Stalinskogo Gosudarstvennogo Pedagogicheskogo Instituta [*A publication*]

Tr Stavrop Kraev Nauchno-Issled Vet Stn ... Trudy Stavropol'skoi Kraevoi Nauchno-Issledovatel'skoi Veterinarnoi Stantsii [*A publication*]

Tr Stavrop Nauchno Issled Inst Selsk Khoz ... Trudy Stavropol'skogo Nauchno-Issledovatel'skogo Instituta Sel'skogo Khozyaistva [*A publication*]

Tr Stavropol Sel'skokhoz Inst ... Trudy Stavropol'skogo Sel'skokhozyaistvennogo Instituta [*A publication*]

Tr Stavrop S-Kh Inst ... Trudy Stavropol'skogo Sel'skokhozyaistvennogo Instituta [*A publication*]

Tr Stomatol Lit SSR ... Trudy Stomatologov Litovskoi SSR [*A publication*]

T Rs Trop M ... Transactions. Royal Society of Tropical Medicine and Hygiene [*A publication*]

Tr Stud Nauchno Tekh Ova Mosk Vyssh Tekh Uchil ... Trudy Studencheskogo Nauchno-Tekhnicheskogo Obshchestva Moskovskoe Vysshe Tekhnicheskoe Uchilishche [*A publication*]

Tr Stud Nauchn Ova Azerb Gos Med Inst ... Trudy Studencheskogo Nauchnogo Obshchestva Azerbaidzhanskii Gosudarstvennyi Meditsinskii Institut [*A publication*]

Tr Stud Nauchn Ova Khark Politekh Inst ... Trudy Studencheskogo Nauchnogo Obshchestva Khar'kovskii Politekhnicheskii Institut [*A publication*]

Tr Sukhum Bot Sada ... Trudy Sukhumskogo Botanicheskogo Sada [*A publication*]

Tr Sukhum Opytn Stn Efiromaslichn Kult ... Trudy Sukhumskoi Opytnoi Stantsii Efiromaslichnykh Kultur [*A publication*]

TRSV .... Tobacco Ring Spot Virus

Tr Sverdl Gorn Inst ... Trudy Sverdlovskogo Gornogo Instituta [*A publication*]

Tr Sverdl Med Inst ... Trudy Sverdlovskogo Meditsinskogo Instituta [*A publication*]

Tr Sverdl Nauchno Issled Inst Lesn Promsti ... Trudy Sverdlovskii Nauchno-Issledovatel'skii Institut Lesnoi Promyshlennosti [*A publication*]

Tr Sverdl Nauchno Issled Vet Stn ... Trudy Sverdlovskoi Nauchno-Issledovatel'skoi Veterinarnoi Stantsii [*A publication*]

Tr Sverdl Skh Inst ... Trudy Sverdlovskogo Sel'skokhozyaistvennogo Instituta [*A publication*]

TRSY .... Treasury (AABC)

Tr SZPI ..... Trudy SZPI [*Severo-Zapadnyi Zaochnyi Politekhnicheskii Institut*] [*A publication*]

TRT .... San Antonio, TX [*Location identifier*] [*FAA*] (FAAL)

TRT .... TACFIRE Remote Terminal (MCD)

TRT .... Technical Review Team [*Nuclear energy*] (NRCH)

TRT .... Television Resource Teachers [*Canada*]

TRT .... Tempo di Restituzione Termica [*Thermal Restitution Test*] [*Italian*] [*Medicine*]

TRT .... Torpedo Rocket Thrown

TRT .... Trademark Registration Treaty

TRT .... Traffic Route Testing [*Telecommunications*] (TEL)

trt .... Treatment [*Medicine*]

TRT .... Treherbert [*Cardiff*] [*Welsh depot code*]

TRT .... Trent Regional Library System [*UTLAS symbol*]

TRT .... Tretes [*Java*] [*Seismograph station code, US Geological Survey*] (SEIS)

TRT .... Trim Template (MCD)

TRT .... Trinity Resources Ltd. [*Toronto Stock Exchange symbol*]

Trt .... Trityl [*Biochemistry*]

TRT .... Tuned Receiver Tuner

TRT .... Turkish Radio & Television Corp.

TRT .... Turret (AABC)

TRT .... United States Army TRADOC, Fort Bliss, Fort Bliss, TX [*OCLC symbol*] (OCLC)

TrT₃ .... Total Reverse Triiodothyronine

Tr Tadzh Astron Obs ... Trudy Tadzhikskoi Astronomicheskoi Observatorii [*A publication*]

Tr Tadzh Gos Med Inst ... Trudy Tadzhikskogo Gosudarstvennogo Meditsinskogo Instituta [*A publication*]

Tr Tadzh Med Inst ... Trudy Tadzhikskogo Meditsinskogo Instituta [*A publication*]

Tr Tadzh Nauchno Issled Inst Pochvoved ... Trudy Tadzhikskogo Nauchno-Issledovatel'skogo Instituta Pochvovedeniya [*A publication*]

Tr Tadzh Nauchno Issled Inst Selsk Khoz ... Trudy Tadzhikskogo Nauchno-Issledovatel'skogo Instituta Sel'skogo Khozyaistva [*A publication*]

Tr Tadzh Nauchno-Issled Inst Zemled ... Trudy Tadzhikskogo Nauchno-Issledovatel'skogo Instituta Zemledeliya [*A publication*]

Tr Tadzh Politekh Inst ... Trudy Tadzhikskogo Politekhnicheskogo Instituta [*A publication*]

Tr Taganrog Radiotekh Inst ... Trudy Taganrogskogo Radiotekhnicheskogo Instituta [*A publication*]

Tr Tallin Pedagog Inst ... Trudy Tallinskogo Pedagogicheskogo Instituta [*Estonian SSR*] [*A publication*]

Tr Tallin Politekh Inst ... Trudy Tallinskogo Politekhnicheskogo Instituta [*Estonian SSR*] [*A publication*]

Tr Tallin Politekh Inst Ser A ... Trudy Tallinskogo Politekhnicheskogo Instituta. Seriya A [*Estonian SSR*] [*A publication*]

Tr Tambov Inst Khim Mashinostr ... Trudy Tambovskogo Instituta Khimicheskogo Mashinostroeniya [*USSR*] [*A publication*]

Tr Tashk Farm Inst ... Trudy Tashkentskogo Farmatsevticheskogo Instituta [*A publication*]

Tr Tashk Gos Univ ... Trudy Tashkentskogo Gosudarstvennogo Universiteta Imeni V. I. Lenina [*A publication*]

Tr Tashk Gos Univ Im V I Lenina ... Trudy Tashkentskogo Gosudarstvennogo Universiteta Imeni V. I. Lenina [*USSR*] [*A publication*]

Tr Tashk Inst Inzh Irrig Mekh Selsk Khoz ... Trudy Tashkentskogo Instituta Inzhenerov Irrigatsii i Mekhanizatsii Sel'skogo Khozyaistva [*A publication*]

Tr Tashk Inst Inzh Zh Zheleznodorozhn Transp ... Trudy Tashkentskogo Instituta Inzhenerov Zheleznodorozhnogo Transporta [*A publication*]

Tr Tashk Nauchno Issled Inst Vaktsin Syvorotok ... Trudy Tashkentskogo Nauchno-Issledovatel'skogo Instituta Vaktsin i Syvorotok [*A publication*]

Tr Tashk Politekh Inst ... Trudy Tashkentskogo Politekhnicheskogo Instituta [*A publication*]

Tr Tashk S-Kh Inst ... Trudy Tashkentskogo Sel'skokhozyaistvennogo Instituta [*A publication*]

Tr Tatar Gos Nauchno Issled Proektn Inst Neft Promsti ... Trudy Tatarskii Gosudarstvennyi Nauchno-Issledovatel'skii i Proektnyi Institut Neftyanoi Promyshlennosti [*A publication*]

Tr Tatar Nauchno Issled Inst Selsk Khoz ... Trudy Tatarskii Nauchno-Issledovatel'skii Institut Sel'skogo Khozyaistva [*A publication*]

Tr Tatar Neft Nauchno Issled Inst ... Trudy Tatarskii Neftyanoi Nauchno-Issledovatel'skii Institut [*A publication*]

Tr Tatar Otd Gos Nauchno Issled Inst Ozern Rechn Rybn Khoz ... Trudy Tatarskogo Otdeleniya Gosudarstvennogo Nauchno-Issledovatel'skogo Instituta Ozernogo i Rechnogo Rybnogo Khozyaistva [*A publication*]

Tr Tatar Resp Mezhved Sb ... Trudy Tatarskii Respublikanskii Mezhvedomstvennyi Sbornik [*A publication*]

Tr Tatar Resp Skh Opytn Stn ... Trudy Tatarskoi Respublikanskoi Sel'skokhozyaistvennoi Opytnoi Stantsii [*A publication*]

Tr Tatar Respub Gosud Sel'skokhoz Opyt Sta ... Trudy Tatarskoi Respublikanskoi Gosudarstvennoi Sel'skokhozyaistvennoi Opytnoi Stantsii [*A publication*]

Tr Tbilis Bot Inst Akad Nauk Gruz SSR ... Trudy Tbilisskogo Botanicheskogo Instituta Akademiya Nauk Gruzinskoi SSR [*A publication*]

Tr Tbilis Gos Med Inst ... Trudy Tbilisskogo Gosudarstvennogo Meditsinskogo Instituta [*A publication*]

Tr Tbilis Gos Pedagog Inst ... Trudy Tbilisskogo Gosudarstvennogo Pedagogiceskogo Instituta Imeni A. S. Pushkina [*A publication*]

Tr Tbilis Gos Univ ... Trudy Tbilisskogo Gosudarstvennogo Universiteta [*A publication*]

Tr Tbilis Gos Univ Im Stalina ... Trudy Tbilisskogo Gosudarstvennogo Universiteta Imeni Stalina [*A publication*]

Tr Tbilis Gos Univ Inst Prikl Mat ... Trudy Tbilisskii Gosudarstvennyi Universitet Institut Prikladnoi Matematiki [*A publication*]

Tr Tbilis Inst Lesa ... Trudy Tbilisskogo Instituta Lesa [*A publication*]

Tr Tbilis Inst Poliklin Funkts Nervn Zabol ... Trudy Tbilisskogo Instituta i Polikliniki Funktsional'nykh Nervnykh Zabolevanii [*A publication*]

Tr Tbilis Inst Usoversh Vrachei ... Trudy Tbilisskogo Instituta Usovershenstvovaniya Vrachei [*A publication*]

Tr Tbilis Mat Inst ... Trudy Tbilisskogo Ordena Trudovogo Krasnogo Znameni Matematicheskogo Instituta [*A publication*]

Tr Tbilis Nauchno-Issled Gidrometeorol Inst ... Trudy Tbilisskogo Nauchno-Issledovatel'skogo Gidrometeorologicheskogo Instituta [*A publication*]

Tr Tbilis Nauchno Issled Inst Priborostr Sredstv Avtom ... Trudy Tbilisskogo Nauchno-Issledovatel'skogo Instituta Priborostroeniya i Sredstv Avtomatizatsii [*A publication*]

Tr Tbilissk Bot Inst ... Trudy Tbilisskogo Botanicheskogo Instituta [*A publication*]

TRTC........ Tactical Record Traffic Center (MCD)

TRTC........ Trio-Tech International [*NASDAQ symbol*] (NQ)

TRTD .... Treated (MSA)

Tr Tekhnol Inst Pishch Promsti (Kiev) ... Trudy Tekhnologicheskogo Instituta Pishchevoi Promyshlennosti (Kiev) [*A publication*]

Tr Teor Polya ... Trudy po Teorii Polya [*USSR*] [*A publication*]

Tr Ternop Gos Med Inst ... Trudy Ternopol'skii Gosudarstvennyi Meditsinskii Institut [*A publication*]

TRTF .... Tactical Reconnaissance Task Force (CINC)

TRTF .... Tactical Record Traffic Facsimile (MCD)

TRTF .... Tasking Requirements and Tasking File (MCD)

TRTG........ Tactical RADAR Threat Generator (MCD)

TRTG........ Treating

TRTHB...... Traitement Thermique [*A publication*]

TRTI .... Transtech Industries, Inc. [*NASDAQ symbol*] (NQ)

TRTL .... Transistor-Resistor-Transistor Logic (IEEE)

TRTMT...... Treatment (MSA)

Tr Tom Nauchno Issled Inst Kabeln Promsti ... Trudy Tomskogo Nauchno-Issledovatel'skogo Instituta Kabel'noi Promyshlennosti [*A publication*]

Tr Tomsk Gos Univ ... Trudy Tomskogo Gosudarstvennogo Universiteta [*USSR*] [*A publication*]

Tr Tomsk Gos Univ Im V V Kuibysheva ... Trudy Tomskogo Gosudarstvennogo Universiteta Imeni V. V. Kuibysheva [*A publication*]

Tr Tomsk Gos Univ Ser Khim ... Trudy Tomskogo Gosudarstvennogo Universiteta Imeni V. V. Kuibysheva. Seriya Khimicheskaya [*USSR*] [*A publication*]

Tr Tomsk Inst Radioehlektron Ehlektron Tekh ... Trudy Tomskogo Instituta Radioehlektroniki i Ehlektronnoj Tekhniki [*A publication*]

Tr Tomsk Med Inst ... Trudy Tomskogo Meditsinskogo Instituta [*A publication*]

Tr Tomsk Nauchno-Issled Inst Kabel'n Promsti ... Trudy Tomskogo Nauchno-Issledovatel'skogo Instituta Kabel'noi Promyshlennosti [*A publication*]

Tr Tomsk Nauchno-Issled Inst Vaksiny Syvorotok ... Trudy Tomskogo Nauchno-Issledovatel'skogo Instituta Vaktsiny i Syvorotok [*A publication*]

TRTP .... Toxicology Research and Testing Program [*National Institutes of Health*]

TRTR .... [*National Organization of*] Test, Research, and Training Reactors (EA)

Tr Transp Energ Inst Akad Nauk SSSR Sib Otd ... Trudy Transportno-Energeticheskogo Instituta Akademiya Nauk SSSR Sibirskoe Otdelenie [*A publication*]

Tr Troitsk Vet Inst ... Trudy Troitskogo Veterinarnogo Instituta [*A publication*]

TRTS .... Tactical Record Traffic System (MCD)

TRTS .... Track RADAR Test Set (MCD)

TRTS .... Triple Redundant Timing Systems (MCD)

Tr Tselinograd Sel'skokhoz Inst ... Trudy Tselinogradskogo Sel'skokhozyaistvennogo Instituta [*A publication*]

Tr Tselinogr Gos Med Inst ... Trudy Tselinogradskii Gosudarstvennyi Meditsinskii Institut [*A publication*]

Tr Tselinogr Med Inst ... Trudy Tselinogradskogo Meditsinskogo Instituta [*A publication*]

Tr Tselinogr S-Kh Inst ... Trudy Tselinogradskogo Sel'skokhozyaistvennogo Instituta [*A publication*]

Tr Tsent Aerol Obs ... Trudy Tsentral'noi Aerologicheskoi Observatorii [*USSR*] [*A publication*]

Tr Tsent Nauchno-Issled Gornorazved Inst ... Trudy Tsentral'nyi Nauchno-Issledovatel'skii Gornorazvedochnyi Institut [*USSR*] [*A publication*]

Tr Tsent Nauchno-Issled Inst Tekhnol Mashinostr ... Trudy Tsentral'nyi Nauchno-Issledovatel'skii Institut Tekhnologii i Mashinostroeniya [*USSR*] [*A publication*]

Tr Tsent Nauchno-Issled Proekt-Konst Kotloturbinnogo Inst ... Trudy Tsentral'nogo Nauchno-Issledovatel'skogo i Proektno-Konstruktorskogo Kotloturbinnogo Instituta [*USSR*] [*A publication*]

Tr Tsentr Aerol Obs ... Trudy Tsentral'noi Aerologicheskoi Observatorii [*A publication*]

Tr Tsentr Aptechn Nauchno-Issled Inst ... Trudy Tsentral'nogo Aptechnogo Nauchno-Issledovatel'skogo Instituta [*A publication*]

Tr Tsentr Chernozemn Gos Zapov ... Trudy Tsentral'nogo Chernozemnogo Gosudarstvennogo Zapovednika [*A publication*]

Tr Tsentr Genet Lab I V Michurina ... Trudy Tsentral'noi Genetiki Laboratorii I. V. Michurina [*A publication*]

Tr Tsentr Genet Lab Vses Akad Skh Nauk ... Trudy Tsentral'noi Geneticheskoi Laboratorii Vsesoyuznaya Akademiya Sel'skokhozyaistvennykh Nauk [*A publication*]

Tr Tsentr Inst Prognozov ... Trudy Tsentral'nogo Instituta Prognozov [*A publication*]

Tr Tsentr Inst Travmatol Ortop ... Trudy Tsentral'nogo Instituta Travmatologii i Ortopedii [*A publication*]

Tr Tsentr Inst Usoversh Vrachei ... Trudy Tsentral'nogo Instituta Usovershenstvovaniya Vrachei [*A publication*]

Tr Tsentr Kaz Geol Upr ... Trudy Tsentral'no-Kazakhstanskogo Geologicheskogo Upravleniya [*A publication*]

Tr Tsentr Kom Vodookhr ... Trudy Tsentral'nogo Komiteta Vodookhraneniya [*A publication*]

Tr Tsentr Nauchno Issled Avtomob Avtomot Inst ... Trudy Tsentral'nyi Nauchno-Issledovatel'skii Avtomobil'nyi i Avtomotornyi Institut [*A publication*]

Tr Tsentr Nauchno-Issled Dezinfekts Inst ... Trudy Tsentral'nogo Nauchno-Issledovatel'skogo Dezinfektsionnogo Instituta [*A publication*]

Tr Tsentr Nauchno Issled Dizeln Inst ... Trudy Tsentral'nogo Nauchno-Issledovatel'skogo Dizel'nogo Instituta [*A publication*]

Tr Tsentr Nauchno-Issled Gornorazved Inst ... Trudy Tsentral'nyj Nauchno-Issledovatel'skij Gornorazvedochnyj Institut [*A publication*]

Tr Tsentr Nauchno Issled Inst Faner Mebeli ... Trudy Tsentral'nogo Nauchno-Issledovatel'skogo Instituta Fanery i Mebeli [*A publication*]

Tr Tsentr Nauchno Issled Inst Khim Pishch Sredstv ... Trudy Tsentral'nogo Nauchno-Issledovatel'skogo Instituta Khimii Pishchevykh Sredstv [*A publication*]

Tr Tsentr Nauchno Issled Inst Konditer Promsti ... Trudy Tsentral'nogo Nauchno-Issledovatel'skogo Instituta Konditerskoi Promyshlennosti [*A publication*]

Tr Tsentr Nauchno Issled Inst Krakhmalo Patochn Promsti ... Trudy Tsentral'nyi Nauchno-Issledovatel'skii Institut Krakhmalo-Patochnoi Promyshlennosti [*A publication*]

Tr Tsentr Nauchno Issled Inst Kurortol Fizioter ... Trudy Tsentral'nogo Nauchno-Issledovatel'skogo Instituta Kurortologii i Fizioterapii [*A publication*]

Tr Tsentr Nauchno Issled Inst Osetr Khoz Nauk SSR ... Trudy Tsentral'nogo Nauchno-Issledovatel'skogo Instituta Osetrovogo Khozyaistva Nauk SSR [*A publication*]

Tr Tsentr Nauchno Issled Inst Rentgenol Radiol ... Trudy Tsentral'nogo Nauchno-Issledovatel'skogo Instituta Rentgenologii i Radiologii [*A publication*]

Tr Tsentr Nauchno Issled Inst Sakh Promsti Moscow ... Trudy Tsentral'nogo Nauchno-Issledovatel'skogo Instituta Sakharnoi Promyshlennosti Moscow [*A publication*]

Tr Tsentr Nauchno-Issled Inst Spirt Likero-Vodochn Prom-Sti ... Trudy Tsentral'nogo Nauchno-Issledovatel'skogo Instituta Spirtovoi i Likero-Vodochnoi Promyshlennosti [*USSR*] [*A publication*]

Tr Tsentr Nauchno Issled Inst Stroit Konstr ... Trudy Tsentral'nyi Nauchno-Issledovatel'skii Institut Stroitel'nykh Konstruktsii [*A publication*]

Tr Tsentr Nauchno Issled Inst Tekhnol Sudostr ... Trudy Tsentral'nyi Nauchno-Issledovatel'skii Institut Tekhnologii Sudostroeniya [*A publication*]

Tr Tsentr Nauchno Issled Inst Tuberk ... Trudy Tsentral'nogo Nauchno-Issledovatel'skogo Instituta Tuberkuleza [*A publication*]

Tr Tsentr Nauchno Issled Lab Novosib Med Inst ... Trudy Tsentral'noi Nauchno-Issledovatel'skoi Laboratorii Novosibirskogo Meditsinskogo Instituta [*A publication*]

Tr Tsentr Nauchno Issled Morsk Flota ... Trudy Tsentral'nyi Nauchno-Issledovatel'skii Institut Morskogo Flota [*A publication*]

Tr Tsentr Nauchno Issled Proektno Konstr Kotloturbinnyi Inst ... Trudy Tsentral'nyi Nauchno-Issledovatel'skii i Proektno-Konstruktorskii Kotloturbinnyi Institut [*A publication*]

Tr Tsentr Nauchno-Issled Rentgeno-Radiol Inst ... Trudy Tsentral'nogo Nauchno-Issledovatel'skogo Rentgeno-Radiologicheskogo Instituta [*A publication*]

Tr Tsentr Nauchno Issled Stn Skh Ispol'z Stochnykh Vod ... Trudy Tsentral'noi Nauchno-Issledovatel'skoi Stantsii po Sel'skokhozyaistvennomu Ispol'zovaniyu Stochnykh Vod [*A publication*]

Tr Tsentr Nauchnoizsled Inst Ribovud Varna Bulg Akad Nauk ... Trudove na Tsentralniya Nauchnoizsledovatelski Institut po Ribovudstvo i Ribolov. Varna. Bulgarska Akademiya na Naukite [*A publication*]

Tr Tsentr Sib Bot Sada ... Trudy Tsentral'nogo Sibirskogo Botanicheskogo Sada [*A publication*]

TRTT .... Tactical Record Traffic Terminal [*Army*] (MCD)

Tr & TT ..... Trial and Tort Trends [*A publication*] (DLA)

TRTTF ...... Trinity Resources Ltd. [*NASDAQ symbol*] (NQ)

Tr Tul Gos Skh Opytn Stn ... Trudy Tul'skoi Gosudarstvennoi Sel'skokhozyaistvennoi Opytnoi Stantsii [*A publication*]

Tr Tul Mekh Inst ... Trudy Tul'skogo Mekhanicheskogo Instituta [*A publication*]

Tr Turkm Bot Sada Akad Nauk Turkm SSR ... Trudy Turkmenskogo Botanicheskogo Sada Akademii Nauk Turkmenskoi SSR [*A publication*]

Tr Turkm Fil Vses Neft Nauchno Issled Inst ... Trudy Turkmenskogo Filiala Vsesoyuznogo Neftyanogo Nauchno-Issledovatel'skogo Instituta [*A publication*]

Tr Turkm Gos Med Inst ... Trudy Turkmenskogo Gosudarstvennogo Meditsinskogo Instituta [*A publication*]

Tr Turkm Nauchno-Issled Inst Kozhynykh Bolezn ... Trudy Turkmenskogo Nauchno-Issledovatel'skogo Instituta Kozhynykh Boleznei [*A publication*]
Tr Turkm Nauchno Issled Trakhomatoznogo Inst ... Trudy Turkmenskogo Nauchno-Issledovatel'skogo Trakhomatoznogo Instituta [*A publication*]
Tr Turkm Politekh Inst ... Trudy Turkmenskogo Politekhnicheskogo Instituta [*A publication*]
Tr Turkm Skh Inst ... Trudy Turkmenskogo Sel'skokhozyaistvennogo Instituta [*A publication*]
Tr Turkm S-Kh Inst Im M Kalinina ... Trudy Turkmenskogo Sel'skokhozyaistvennogo Instituta Imeni M. I. Kalinina [*A publication*]
Tr Turk Nauchno Issled Inst Kozhynykh Bolezn ... Trudy Turkmenskogo Nauchno-Issledovatel'skogo Instituta Kozhynykh Boleznei [*A publication*]
Tr Tuvinskoi Gos Skh Opytn Stn ... Trudy Tuvinskoi Gosudarstvennoi Sel'skokhozyaistvennoi Opytnoi Stantsii [*A publication*]
Tr Tyazan Radiotekh Inst ... Trudy Tyazanskogo Radiotekhnicheskogo Instituta [*A publication*]
Tr Tyumen Ind Inst ... Trudy Tyumenskogo Industrial'nogo Instituta [*A publication*]
Tr Tyumen Otd Vses Nauchn Ova Anat Gistol Embriol ... Trudy Tyumenskogo Otdeleniya Vsesoyuznogo Nauchnogo Obshchestva Anatomov, Gistologov, i Embriologov [*A publication*]
Tr Tyumenskogo Ind Inst ... Trudy Tyumenskogo Industrial'nogo Instituta [*USSR*] [*A publication*]
TRU .... Taurus Resources [*Vancouver Stock Exchange symbol*]
TRU .... Test Replaceable Unit
TRu .... Theologische Rundschau [*Tuebingen*] [*A publication*]
TRU .... Time Release Unit　(MCD)
TRU .... Transformer-Rectifier Unit　(MCD)
TRU .... Transmit-Receive Unit
TRU .... Transportable Radio Unit [*Military*]
TRU .... Transuranic [*or Transuranium*] [*Chemistry*]
TRU .... Transuranium Processing Plant　(NRCH)
TRU .... Trouw [*A publication*]
TRU .... Truancy [*FBI standardized term*]
Tru .... Trueman's New Brunswick Equity Cases [*1876-93*] [*A publication*]　(DLA)
TRU .... Trujillo [*Peru*] [*Airport symbol*]　(OAG)
TRU .... Truk [*Caroline Islands*] [*Seismograph station code, US Geological Survey*] [*Closed*]　(SEIS)
TRU .... Truncated Variant [*Genetics*]
TRU .... United States Army TRADOC, Fort Hood, Fort Hood, TX [*OCLC symbol*]　(OCLC)
TRUB .... Temporarily Replaced by Unlighted Buoy [*Maps and charts*]
Trubn Proizvod Urala ... Trubnoe Proizvodstvo Urala [*A publication*]
Truck & Bus Trans ... Truck and Bus Transportation [*A publication*]　(APTA)
Truck & Bus Transp ... Truck and Bus Transportation [*A publication*]　(APTA)
Truck Bus Transpn ... Truck and Bus Transportation [*A publication*]　(APTA)
Truck Off-Highw Ind ... Truck and Off-Highway Industries [*United States*] [*A publication*]
TRUD .... Time Remaining until Dive [*Air Force*]
Trud po Mezhdunar Pravo ... Trudovo po Mezhdunarodno Pravo [*Studies on International Law*] [*Sofia, Bulgaria*] [*A publication*]　(DLA)
Trud Viss Ikonom Inst Karl Marks-Sofia ... Trudove. Vissija Ikonomiceski Institut Karl Marks-Sofija [*A publication*]
Trudy Akad Nauk Litov SSR ... Trudy Akademii Nauk Litovskoi SSR [*A publication*]
Trudy Akad Nauk Litov SSR Ser A Obsc Nauki ... Trudy Akademii Nauk Litovskoj SSR. Serija A. Obscestvennye Nauki [*A publication*]
Trudy Akad Nauk Litov SSR Ser B ... Trudy Akademii Nauk Litovskoi SSR. Serija B [*A publication*]
Trudy Altai Politehn Inst ... Trudy Altaiskii Politehniceskii Institut Imeni I. I. Polizunova [*A publication*]
Trudy Altaisk Politehn Inst ... Trudy Altaiskii Politehniceskii Institut Imeni I. I. Polizunova [*A publication*]
Trudy Altaisk Sel'khoz Inst ... Trudy Altaiskogo Sel'skokhozyaistvennogo Instituta [*A publication*]
Trudy Altajsk Politehn Inst ... Trudy Altajskogo Politehniceskogo Instituta [*A publication*]
Trudy Andizhan Ped Inst ... Trudy Andizhanskii Gosudarstvennyi Pedagogicheskii Institut [*A publication*]
Trudy A N Tadzh ... Trudy Akademiia Nauk Tadzhikskoi SSR [*Stalinabad, USSR*] [*A publication*]
Trudy Arhangel Lesotehn Inst ... Trudy Arhangel'skogo Lesotehniceskogo Instituta Imeni V. V. Kuibysheva [*A publication*]
Trudy Arkhangel Lesotekh Inst Im V V Kuibysheva ... Trudy Arkhangel'skogo Ordena Trudovogo Kraskogo Znameni Lesotekhnicheskogo Instituta Imeni V. V. Kuibysheva [*A publication*]
Trudy Armyansk Nauchno-Issled Inst Vinograd Vinodel Plodov ... Trudy Armyanskogo Nauchno-Issledovatel'skogo Instituta Vinogradarstva Vinodeliya i Plodovodstva [*A publication*]

Trudy Armyansk Nauchno-Issled Inst Zhivot Vet ... Trudy Armyanskogo Nauchno-Issledovatel'skogo Instituta Zhivotnovodstva i Veterinarii [*A publication*]
Trudy Aspirantov Gruzin Sel'-Khoz Inst ... Trudy Aspirantov Gruzinskogo Sel'skokhozyaistvennogo Instituta [*A publication*]
Trudy Azerbajdzansk Opytn Sta ... Trudy Azerbajdzanskogo Opytnoj Stancii [*A publication*]
Trudy Azerb Nauchno-Issled Inst Gidrotekh Melior ... Trudy Azerbaidzhanskogo Nauchno-Issledovatel'skogo Instituta Gidrotekhniki i Melioratsii [*A publication*]
Trudy Azerb Nauchno-Issled Inst Zhivot ... Trudy Azerbaidzhanskogo Nauchno-Issledovatel'skogo Instituta Zhivotnovodstva [*A publication*]
Trudy Azerb Vet Inst ... Trudy Azerbaidzhanskogo Nauchno-Issledovatel'skogo Veterinarnogo Instituta [*A publication*]
Trudy Bashkir Nauch Isst Sel Khoz ... Trudy Bashkirskogo Nauchnogo Instituta Sel'skogo Khozyaistva [*A publication*]
Trudy Baskir S-H Inst ... Trudy Bashkirskogo Sel'skokhozyaistvennogo Instituta [*A publication*]
Trudy Belorussk Nauchno-Issled Inst Pochv ... Trudy Belorusskogo Nauchno-Issledovatel'skogo Instituta Pochvovedeniya [*A publication*]
Trudy Belorussk Sel'-Khoz Akad ... Trudy Belorusskoi Sel'skokhozyaistvennoi Akademii [*A publication*]
Trudy Biol Inst Sib Otd Akad Nauk SSSR ... Trudy Biologicheskogo Instituta Sibirskoe Otdelenie Akademiya Nauk SSSR [*A publication*]
Trudy Bot Inst Akad Nauk SSSR Ser VI ... Trudy Botaniceskij Institut Akademiya Nauk SSSR. Serija VI [*A publication*]
Trudy Burjat Inst Obsc Nauk ... Trudy Burjatskogo Instituta Obscestvennyh Nauk [*A publication*]
Trudy Buryat Mongol Nauchno-Issled Vet Opyt Sta ... Trudy Buryat-Mongol'skoi Nauchno-Issledovatel'skoi Veterinarnoi Opytnoi Stantsii [*A publication*]
Trudy Buryatsk Sel'khoz Inst ... Trudy Buryatskogo Sel'skokhozyaistvennogo Instituta [*A publication*]
Trudy CNIIKA ... Trudy Gosudarstvennyi Vsesojuznyi Central'nyi Naucno-Issledovatel'skii Institut Kompleksnoi Avtomatizacii [*A publication*]
Trudy Dagest Nauchno-Issled Inst Sel Khoz ... Trudy Dagestanskogo Nauchno-Issledovatel'skogo Instituta Sel'skogo Khozyaistva [*A publication*]
Trudy Doneck Politehn Inst ... Trudy Doneckogo Politehniceskogo Instituta [*A publication*]
Trudy Don Zonal'Inst Sel'Khoz ... Trudy Donskogo Zonal'nogo Instituta Sel'skogo Khozyaistva [*A publication*]
Trudy Ermit ... Trudy Gosudarstvennogo Ermitazha [*A publication*]
Trudy Fiz Inst Lebedev ... Trudy Fizicheskogo Instituta Imeni P. N. Lebedeva [*A publication*]
Trudy Frunze Politehn Inst ... Trudy Frunzenskogo Politehniceskogo Instituta [*A publication*]
Trudy Geogr Fak Kirgiz Univ ... Trudy Geograficheskogo Fakul'teta Kirgizskogo Universiteta [*A publication*]
Trudy Geometr Sem ... Trudy Geometriceskogo Seminara [*A publication*]
Trudy Geom Sem Kazan Univ ... Trudy Geometriceskogo Seminara Kazanskii Universitet [*A publication*]
Trudy G Ermitazh ... Trudy Gosudarstvennogo Ermitazha [*A publication*]
Trudy Glav Geofiz Obs ... Trudy Glavnoi Geofizicheskoi Observatorii Imeni A. I. Voeikova [*A publication*]
Trudy Gor'kov Politehn Inst ... Trudy Gor'kovskogo Politehniceskii Institut [*A publication*]
Trudy Gor'kov Sel'-Khoz Inst ... Trudy Gor'kovskogo Sel'skokhozyaistvennogo Instituta [*A publication*]
Trudy Gorsk Sel'-Khoz Inst ... Trudy Gorskogo Sel'skokhozyaistvennogo Instituta [*A publication*]
Trudy Gos Gidrol Inst ... Trudy Gosudarstvennogo Gidrologicheskogo Instituta [*A publication*]
Trudy Gruz Nauchno-Issled Pishch Prom ... Trudy Gruzinskii Nauchno-Issledovatel'skii Institut Pishchevoi Promyshlennosti [*A publication*]
Trudy Gruz Sel'-Khoz Inst ... Trudy Gruzinskogo Sel'skokhozyaistvennogo Instituta Imeni L. P. Beriya [*A publication*]
Trudy Inst Biol Ural Fil (Sverdlovsk) ... Trudy Instituta Biologii Ural'skii Filial Akademiya Nauk SSSR (Sverdlovsk) [*A publication*]
Trudy Inst Bot (Alma-Ata) ... Trudy Instituta Botaniki Akademiya Nauk Kazakhskoi SSR (Alma-Ata) [*A publication*]
Trudy Inst Etnogr ... Trudy Instituta Etnografii [*A publication*]
Trudy Inst Fiziol (Baku) ... Trudy Instituta Fiziologii Akademiya Nauk Azerbaidzhanskoi SSR (Baku) [*A publication*]
Trudy Inst Fiziol I P Pavlova ... Trudy Instituta Fiziologii Imeni I. P. Pavlova Akademii Nauk SSSR [*A publication*]
Trudy Inst Genet ... Trudy Instituta Genetiki Akademiya Nauk SSR [*A publication*]
Trudy Inst Istor Estestvoznan Tehn ... Trudy Instituta Istorii Estestvoznanija i Tehniki [*A publication*]
Trudy Inst Jaz Lit Ist Komi Fil Akad Nauk SSSR ... Trudy Instituta Jazyka, Literatury, i Istorii Komi Filiala Akademii Nauk SSSR [*A publication*]
Trudy Inst Mat i Meh Ural Naucn Centr Akad Nauk SSSR ... Trudy Instituta Matematiki i Mehaniki Ural'skii Naucnyi Centr Akademija Nauk SSSR [*A publication*]

Trudy Inst Mat i Mekh Ural Nauchn Tsentr Akad Nauk SSSR ... Trudy Instituta Matematiki i Mekhaniki Ural'skii Nauchnyi Tsentr Akademiya Nauk SSSR [*A publication*]
Trudy Inst Pochv Agrokhim (Baku) ... Trudy Instituta Pochvovedeniya i Agrokhimii Akademiya Nauk Azerbaidzhanskoi SSR (Baku) [*A publication*]
Trudy Inst Sistem Upravleniya Akad Nauk Gruzin SSR ... Trudy Instituta Sistem Upravleniya Akademiya Nauk Gruzinskoi SSR [*A publication*]
Trudy Inst Teoret Astronom ... Trudy Instituta Teoreticeskoi Astronomii [*A publication*]
Trudy Inst Zool Parazit (Tashkent) ... Trudy Instituta Zoologii i Parazitologii Akademiya Nauk Uzbekskoi SSR (Tashkent) [*A publication*]
Trudy Irkutsk Gos Univ ... Trudy Irkutskogo Gosudarstvennogo Universiteta [*A publication*]
Trudy Ist-Kraev Muz Mold ... Trudy Istoriko-Kraevedcheskogo Muzeia Moldavskoi SSR [*A publication*]
Trudy Izevsk Sel'skohozjaistv Inst ... Trudy Izevskii Sel'skohozjaistvennyi Institut [*A publication*]
Trudy Kabardino-Balkarsk Gos Sel'khoz Opyt Sta ... Trudy Kabardino-Balkarskoi Gosudarstvennoi Sel'skokhozyaistvennoi Opytnoi Stantsii [*A publication*]
Trudy Kaf Teorii Funkcii i Funkcional Anal Moskov Gos Univ ... Moskovskii Gosudarstvennyi Universitet. Mehaniko-Matematiceskii Fakul'tet. Kafedra Teorii Funkcii i Funkcional'nogo Analiza. Trudy [*A publication*]
Trudy Karagand Gos Med Inst ... Trudy Karagandinskii Gosudarstvennyi Meditsinskii Institut [*A publication*]
Trudy Karel' Fil Akad Nauk SSSR ... Trudy Karel'skogo Filiala Akademii Nauk SSSR [*A publication*]
Trudy Kavkaz Gos Zapov ... Trudy Kavkazskogo Gosudarstvennogo Zapovednika [*A publication*]
Trudy Kazakh Opyt Sta Pchelov ... Trudy Kazakhskoi Opytnoi Stantsii Pchelovodstva [*A publication*]
Trudy Kazakh Sel'-Khoz Inst ... Trudy Kazakhskogo Sel'skokhozyaistvennogo Instituta [*A publication*]
Trudy Kazan Aviacion Inst ... Trudy Kazanskogo Aviacionnogo Instituta. Matematika i Mehanika [*A publication*]
Trudy Kazan Gorod Astronom Observator ... Trudy Kazanskoi Gorodskoi Astronomiceskoi Observatorii [*A publication*]
Trudy Kazan Gos Pedagog Inst ... Trudy Kazanskogo Gosudarstvennogo Pedagogicheskogo Instituta [*A publication*]
Trudy Kazan Sel'-Khoz Inst ... Trudy Kazanskogo Sel'skokhozyaistvennogo Instituta [*A publication*]
Trudy Kazan S-H Inst ... Trudy Kazanskogo Sel'skokhozyaistvennogo Instituta [*A publication*]
Trudy Kemerov Gos Sel Khoz Opyt Sta ... Trudy Kemerovskoi Gosudarstvennoi Sel'skokhozyaistvennoi Opytnoi Stantsii [*A publication*]
Trudy Kharkov Opyt Sta Pchelov ... Trudy Khar'kovskaya Opytnaya Stantsiya Pchelovodstva [*A publication*]
Trudy Kharkov Sel'-Khoz Inst ... Trudy Khar'kovskogo Sel'skokhozyaistvennogo Instituta [*A publication*]
Trudy Kirgiz Gos Univ Ser Biol Nauk ... Trudy Kirgizskogo Gosudarstvennogo Universiteta. Seriya Biologicheskikh Nauk Zoologiya-Fiziologiya [*A publication*]
Trudy Kirgiz Gos Univ Ser Mat Nauk ... Trudy Kirgizskogo Gosudarstvennogo Universiteta. Serija Matematiceskih Nauk [*A publication*]
Trudy Kirgiz Nauchno-Issled Inst Zeml ... Trudy Kirgizskogo Nauchno-Issledovatel'skogo Instituta Zemledeliya [*A publication*]
Trudy Kirgiz Sel'-Khoz Inst ... Trudy Kirgizskogo Sel'skokhozyaistvennogo Instituta [*A publication*]
Trudy Kishinev Sel'-Khoz Inst ... Trudy Kishinevskogo Sel'skokhozyaistvennogo Instituta [*A publication*]
Trudy Kolomen Filiala Vsesojuz Zaocn Politehn Inst ... Trudy Kolomenskogo Filiala Vsesojuznyi Zaocnyi Politehniceskii Institut [*A publication*]
Trudy Kom Analit Khim ... Trudy Komissii po Analiticheskoi Khimii Akademiya Nauk SSSR [*A publication*]
Trudy Komi Fil Akad Nauk SSSR ... Trudy Komi Filiala Akademii Nauk SSSR [*A publication*]
Trudy Komi Filiala Akad Nauk SSSR ... Trudy Komi Filiala Akademii Nauk SSSR [*A publication*]
Trudy Konf Pochv Sib Dal'n Vostoka Akad Nauk SSSR ... Trudy Konferentsiya Pochvovedov Sibiri i Dal'nego Vostoka Akademiya Nauk SSSR [*A publication*]
Trudy Kuban Sel'-Khoz Inst ... Trudy Kubanskogo Sel'skokhozyaistvennogo Instituta [*A publication*]
Trudy (Kujbys Aviac) Inst ... Trudy (Kujbysevskij Aviacionnyj) Institut [*A publication*]
Trudy Latv Sel'-Khoz Inst ... Trudy Latviiskogo Sel'skokhozyaistvennogo Instituta [*A publication*]
Trudy Leningrad Tehnolog Inst Holod Promysl ... Trudy Leningradskogo Tehnologicheskogo Instituta Holodil'noi Promyslennosti [*A publication*]
Trudy Leningr Gidromet Inst ... Trudy Leningradskogo Gidrometeorologicheskogo Instituta [*A publication*]
Trudy Leningr Inst Kul't ... Trudy Leningradskii Institut Kul'tury [*A publication*]

Trudy Leningr Obshch Estest ... Trudy Leningradskogo Obshchestva Estestvoispytatelei [*A publication*]
Trudy Litov Nauchno-Issled Inst Zeml ... Trudy Litovskogo Nauchno-Issledovatel'skogo Instituta Zemledeliya [*A publication*]
Trudy Mat Inst Steklov ... Trudy Matematiceskogo Instituta Imeni V. A. Steklova [*A publication*]
Trudy Metrolog Inst SSSR ... Trudy Metrologiceskih Institutov SSSR [*A publication*]
Trudy Mold Akad Nauk ... Trudy Ob'edinennoi Nauchnoi Sessii Moldavskii Filial Akademii Nauk SSR [*A publication*]
Trudy Mol Ucen Kirigiz Univ ... Trudy Molodyh Ucenyh Kirigizskogo Universiteta [*A publication*]
Trudy Mosk Ordena Lenina Sel'Khoz Akad ... Trudy Moskovskoi Ordena Lenina Sel'sko-Khozyaistvennoi Akademii Imeni K. A. Timiryazeva [*A publication*]
Trudy Moskov Elektrotehn Inst Svjazi ... Trudy Moskovskogo Elektrotehniceskogo Instituta Svjazi [*A publication*]
Trudy Moskov Inst Inzen Zelezno-Doroz Transporta ... Trudy Moskovskogo Instituta Inzenernov Zeleznodoroznogo Transporta [*A publication*]
Trudy Moskov Inst Istoriji ... Trudy Moskovskogo Instituta Istoriji, Filosofiji, i Literatury [*A publication*]
Trudy Moskov Inst Radiotehn Elektron i Avtomat ... Trudy Moskovskogo Instituta Radiotekhniki, Elektroniki, i Avtomatiki [*A publication*]
Trudy Moskov Mat Obsc ... Trudy Moskovskogo Matematiceskogo Obscestva [*A publication*]
Trudy Moskov Mat Obshch ... Trudy Moskovskogo Matematicheskogo Obshchestva [*A publication*]
Trudy Moskov Orden Lenin Energet Inst ... Trudy Moskovskogo Ordena Lenina Energeticeskogo Instituta [*A publication*]
Trudy Nakhich Kompleks Zonal Opyt Sta ... Trudy Nakhichevanskoi Kompleksnoi Zonal'noi Opytnoi Stantsii [*A publication*]
Trudy Nauch Inst Udobr Insektofung ... Trudy Nauchnogo Instituta po Udobreniyam i Insektofungitsidam Imeni Ya. V. Satoilova [*A publication*]
Trudy Nauchno-Issled Inst Pchelov ... Trudy Nauchno-Issledovatel'skogo Instituta Pchelovodstva [*A publication*]
Trudy Nauchno-Issled Inst Prud Rybn Khoz ... Trudy Nauchno-Issledovatel'skogo Instituta Prudovogo Rybnogo Khozyaistva [*A publication*]
Trudy Nauchno-Issled Inst Sel'Khoz Severn Zaural'ya ... Trudy Nauchno-Issledovatel'skogo Instituta Sel'skogo Khozyaistva Severnogo Zaural'ya [*A publication*]
Trudy Nauc-Issled Inst Sociol Kul't ... Trudy Nauchno-Issledovatel'skogo Instituta Sociologiceskoj Kul'tury [*A publication*]
Trudy Novocherk Inzh-Melior Inst ... Trudy Novocherkasskogo Inzhenerno-Meliorativnogo Instituta [*A publication*]
Trudy Obshch Estest Imp Kazan Univ ... Trudy Obshchestva Estestvoispytatelei pri Imperatordkom Kazanskom Universitete Kazan [*A publication*]
Trudy Obsh Dietsk Vrach Moskve ... Trudy Obshchestva Dietskikh Vrachei v Moskve [*A publication*]
Trudy Omsk Vet Inst ... Trudy Omskogo Veterinarnogo Instituta [*A publication*]
Trudy Omsk Vyss Skoly Milicii ... Trudy Omskogo Vyssej Skoly Milicii [*A publication*]
Trudy Ped Inst Gruzin SSR Ser Fiz i Mat ... Trudy Pedagogiceskih Institutov Gruzinskoi SSR. Serija Fiziki i Matematiki [*A publication*]
Trudy Plodov Inst ... Trudy Plodovoshchnogo Instituta Imeni I. V. Michurina [*A publication*]
Trudy Prikl Bot Genet Selek ... Trudy po Prikladnoi Botanike Genetike i Selektsii [*A publication*]
Trudy Przeval'sk Gos Ped Inst ... Trudy Przeval'skogo Gosudarstvennogo Pedagogiceskogo Instituta [*A publication*]
Trudy Radiats Gig Leningr Nauchno-Issled Inst Radiats Gig ... Trudy Radiatsii i Gigieny Leningradskogo Nauchno-Issledovatel'skogo Instituta Radiatsii Gigieny [*A publication*]
Trudy Rjazan Radiotehn Inst ... Trudy Rjazanskogo Radiotehniceskogo Instituta [*A publication*]
Trudy Russk Ent Obshch ... Trudy Russkogo Entomologicheskogo Obshchestva [*A publication*]
Trudy Samarkand Gos Univ ... Trudy Samarkandskogo Gosudarstvennogo Universiteta Imeni Alisera Navoi [*A publication*]
Trudy Samarkand Gos Univ NS ... Ministerstvo Vyssego i Srednego Obrazovanija UzSSR Trudy Samarkandskogo Gosuda rstvennogo Universiteta Imeni A. Navoi Novaja Serija [*A publication*]
Trudy Samarkand Univ ... Trudy Samarkandskogo Universiteta [*A publication*]
Trudy Saratov Inst Meh S-H ... Trudy Saratovskogo Instituta Mehanizacii Sel'skogo-Hozjaistva [*A publication*]
Trudy Saratov Nauchno-Issled Vet Sta ... Trudy Saratovskoi Nauchno-Issledovatel'skoi Veterinarnoi Stantsii [*A publication*]
Trudy Saratov Sel'-Khoz Inst ... Trudy Saratovskogo Sel'skokhozyaistvennogo Instituta [*A publication*]
Trudy Saratov Zootekh Vet Inst ... Trudy Saratovskogo Zootekhnicheskogo Veterinarnogo Instituta [*A publication*]

Trudy Sem Kraev Zadacham ... Trudy Seminara po Kraevym Zadacham [*A publication*]

Trudy Sem Mat Fiz Nelinien Koleban ... Trudy Seminara po Matematiceskoi Fizike i Nelinienym Kolebanijam [*A publication*]

Trudy Sem Petrovsk ... Trudy Seminara Imeni I. G. Petrovskogo [*A publication*]

Trudy Sem Vektor Tenzor Anal ... Trudy Seminara po Vektornomu i Tenzornomu Analizu s ih Prilozenijami k Geometrii. Mehanike i Fizike [*A publication*]

Trudy Sibirsk Fiz-Tehn Inst ... Trudy Sibirskogo Fiziko-Tehniceskogo Instituta Imeni Akademika V. D. Kuznecova [*A publication*]

Trudy SibNIIE ... Trudy Sibirskii Nauchno-Issledovatel'skii Institut Energetiki [*A publication*]

Trudy Solikam Sel'-Khoz Opyt Sta ... Trudy Solikamskoi Sel'skokhozyaistvennoi Opytnoi Stantsii [*A publication*]

Trudy Stavropol' Sel'-Khoz Inst ... Trudy Stavropol'skogo Sel'skokhozyaistvennogo Instituta [*A publication*]

Trudy Sverdlovsk Sel'-Khoz Inst ... Trudy Sverdlovskogo Sel'skokhozyaistvennogo Instituta [*A publication*]

Trudy Tadzhik Nauchno-Issled Inst Sel Khoz ... Trudy Tadzhikskogo Nauchno-Issledovatel'skogo Instituta Sel'skogo Khozyaistva [*A publication*]

Trudy Tadzik Politehn Inst ... Trudy Tadzikskogo Politehniceskogo Instituta [*A publication*]

Trudy Tallinsk Politehn Inst ... Trudy Tallinskogo Politekhnicheskogo Instituta [*A publication*]

Trudy Taskent Gos Univ ... Trudy Taskentskogo Gosudarstvennogo Universiteta Imeni V. I. Lenina. Matematika [*A publication*]

Trudy Tatar Nauchno-Issled Inst Sel'Khoz ... Trudy Tatarskii Nauchno-Issledovatel'skii Institut Sel'skogo Khozyaistva [*A publication*]

Trudy Tatar Respub Gos Sel-Khoz Opyt Sta ... Trudy Tatarskoi Respublikanskoi Gosudarstvennoi Sel'skokhozyaistvennoi Opytnoi Stantsii [*A publication*]

Trudy Tbilisk Univ Fiz-Mat Estestv Nauki ... Trudy Tbilisskogo Universiteta Fiziko-Matematiceskie i Estestvennyi Nauki [*A publication*]

Trudy Tbiliss Mat Inst Razmadze Akad Nauk Gruzin SSR ... Trudy Tbilisskogo Matematiceskogo Instituta Imeni A. M. Razmadze Akademija Nauk Gruzinskoi SSR [*A publication*]

Trudy Tbiliss Univ ... Trudy Tbilisskogo Universiteta Fiziko-Matematiceskie i Estestvennyi Nauki [*A publication*]

Trudy Tomsk Gos Univ ... Trudy Tomskogo Gosudarstvennogo Universiteta [*A publication*]

Trudy Tomsk Univ ... Trudy Tomskogo Universiteta [*A publication*]

Trudy Tsent Chernoz Gos Zapov ... Trudy Tsentral'nogo Chernozemnogo Gosudarstvennogo Zapovednika [*A publication*]

Trudy Tsent Sib Bot Sada ... Trudy Tsentral'nogo Sibirskogo Botanicheskogo Sada [*A publication*]

Trudy Turkmen Sel'Khoz Inst ... Trudy Turkmenskogo Sel'sko-Khozyaistvennogo Instituta [*A publication*]

Trudy Ufmsk Aviac Inst ... Trudy Ufimskogo Aviacionnogo Instituta [*A publication*]

Trudy Ukr Gidromet Inst ... Trudy Ukrainskogo Gidrometeorologicheskogo Instituta [*A publication*]

Trudy Ul'yanov Sel'khoz Inst ... Trudy Ul'yanovskogo Sel'skokhozyaistvennogo Instituta [*A publication*]

Trudy Univ Druzby Narod ... Trudy Universiteta Druzhby Narodov Imeni Patrisa Lumumby [*A publication*]

Trudy Ural Politehn Inst ... Trudy Ural'skogo Politehniceskogo Instituta [*A publication*]

Trudy Volgogr Opytno-Melior Sta ... Trudy Volgogradskoi Opytno-Meliorativnoi Stantsii [*A publication*]

Trudy Vologod Sel'khoz Inst ... Trudy Vologodskogo Sel'skokhozyaistvennogo Instituta [*A publication*]

Trudy Voronezh Zoovetinst ... Trudy Voronezhskogo Zooveterinarnogo Instituta [*A publication*]

Trudy Vost Kazakh Gos Opyt Sta ... Trudy Vostochno-Kazakhstanskaya Gosudarstvennaya Sel'skokhozyaistvennaya Opytnaya Stantsiya [*A publication*]

Trudy Vost-Sibir Tehnol Inst ... Trudy Vostochno-Sibirskogo Tekhnologicheskogo Instituta [*A publication*]

Trudy Vses Aerogeol Tresta ... Trudy Vsesoyuznogo Aerogeologicheskogo Tresta [*A publication*]

Trudy Vses Ent Obshch ... Trudy Vsesoyuznogo Entomologicheskogo Obshchestva [*A publication*]

Trudy Vses Nauchno-Issled Geol Inst ... Trudy Vsesoyuznogo Nauchno-Issledovatel'skogo Geologicheskogo Instituta [*A publication*]

Trudy Vses Nauchno-Issled Inst Sakharn Svekly Sakhara ... Trudy Vsesoyuznogo Nauchno-Issledovatel'skogo Instituta Sakharnoi Svekly i Sakhara [*A publication*]

Trudy Vses Nauchno-Issled Inst Torf Prom ... Trudy Vsesoyuznogo Nauchno-Issledovatel'skogo Instituta Torfyanoi Promyshlennosti [*A publication*]

Trudy Vses Nauchno-Issled Inst Udobr Agrotekh Agropochv ... Trudy Vsesoyuznogo Nauchno-Issledovatel'skogo Instituta Udobrenii Agrotekhniki i Agropochvovedeniya [*A publication*]

Trudy Vses Nauchno-Issled Inst Vet Sanit Ektoparazit ... Trudy Vsesoyuznogo Nauchno-Issledovatel'skogo Instituta Veterinarnoi Sanitarii i Ektoparazitologii [*A publication*]

Trudy Vses Nauchno-Issled Inst Zashch Rast ... Trudy Vsesoyuznogo Nauchno-Issledovatel'skogo Instituta Zashchity Rasteni [*A publication*]

Trudy Vsesojuz Nauc-Issled Inst Sov Zakon ... Trudy Vsesoyuznogo Nauchno-Issledovatel'skogo Instituta Sovetskogo Zakonodatel'stva [*A publication*]

Trudy Vsesojuz Nauc-Issled Inst Zascity Rast ... Trudy Vsesojuznogo Naucno-Issledovatel'skogo Instituta Zascity Rastenij [*A publication*]

Trudy Vsesojuz Naucno-Issled Inst Elektromeh ... Trudy Vsesojuznogo Naucno-Issledovatel'skogo Instituta Elektromehaniki [*A publication*]

Trudy Vsesojuz Zaocn Energet Inst ... Trudy Vsesojuznogo Zaocnogo Energeticeskogo Instituta [*A publication*]

Trudy Vses Ordena Lenina Inst Eksp Vet ... Trudy Vsesoyuznogo Ordena Lenina Instituta Eksperimental'noi Veterinarii [*A publication*]

Trudy VTI ... Trudy Vsesojuznogo Teplotehniceskogo Instituta [*A publication*]

Trudy Vychisl Tsentra Tartu Gos Univ ... Trudy Vychislitel'nogo Tsentra Tartuskii Gosudarstvennyi Universitet [*A publication*]

Trudy Vycisl Centra Akad Nauk Gruzin SSR ... Trudy Vycislitel'nogo Centra Akademija Nauk Gruzinskoi SSR [*A publication*]

Trudy Vycisl Centra Tartu Gos Univ ... Trudy Vycislitel'nogo Centra Tartuskii Gosudarstvennyi Universitet [*A publication*]

Trudy Zool Inst (Leningr) ... Trudy Zoologicheskogo Instituta Akademiya Nauk SSSR (Leningrad) [*A publication*]

True............ Trueman's New Brunswick Reports [*A publication*]   (DLA)

Trueman Eq Cas ... Trueman's New Brunswick Equity Cases [*A publication*]   (DLA)

Truem Eq Cas ... Trueman's New Brunswick Equity Cases [*A publication*]   (DLA)

Tru Est....... Trusts and Estates [*A publication*]

TRUF........ Transferable Revolving Underwriting Facility [*Finance*]   (ADA)

Tr Ufim Aviats Inst ... Trudy Ufimskogo Aviatsionnogo Instituta [*A publication*]

Tr Ufim Nauchno-Issled Inst Gig Profzabol ... Trudy Ufimskogo Nauchno-Issledovatel'skogo Instituta Gigieny i Profzabolevanii [*A publication*]

Tr Ufim Neft Naucho-Issled Inst ... Trudy Ufimskii Neftyanoi Nauchno-Issledovatel'skii Institut [*A publication*]

TRUFOS ... True Unidentified Flying Objects

TRUGA ..... Trudy Ukrainskii Nauchno-Issledovatel'skii Geologo-Razvedochnyi Institut [*A publication*]

TRUK .... Builders Transport, Inc. [*NASDAQ symbol*]   (NQ)

Tr Ukr Gos Nauchno-Issled Inst Prikl Khim ... Trudy Ukrainskogo Gosudarstvennogo Nauchno-Issledovatel'skogo Instituta Prikladnoi Khimii [*A publication*]

Tr Ukr Inst Eksp Endokrinol ... Trudy Ukrainskogo Instituta Eksperimental'noi Endokrinologii [*A publication*]

Tr Ukr Nauch-Issled Gidrometeorol Inst ... Trudy Ukrainskogo Nauchno-Issledovatel'skogo Gidrometeorologicheskogo Instituta [*A publication*]

Tr Ukr Nauchno Issled Geol Razved Inst ... Trudy Ukrainskii Nauchno-Issledovatel'skii Geologo-Razvedochnyi Institut [*A publication*]

Tr Ukr Nauchno-Issled Gidrometeorol Inst ... Trudy Ukrainskogo Nauchno-Issledovatel'skogo Gidrometeorologicheskogo Instituta [*Ukrainian SSR*] [*A publication*]

Tr Ukr Nauchno Issled Inst Klin Med ... Trudy Ukrainskogo Nauchno-Issledovatel'skogo Instituta Klinicheskoi Meditsiny [*A publication*]

Tr Ukr Nauchno Issled Inst Konservn Promsti ... Trudy Ukrainskogo Nauchno-Issledovatel'skogo Instituta Konservnoi Promyshlennosti [*A publication*]

Tr Ukr Nauchno-Issled Inst Lesn Khoz Agrolesomelior ... Trudy Ukrainskogo Nauchno-Issledovatel'skogo Instituta Lesnogo Khozyaistva i Agrolesomelioratsii [*A publication*]

Tr Ukr Nauchno Issled Inst Pishch Promsti ... Trudy Ukrainskii Nauchno-Issledovatel'skii Institut Pishchevoi Promyshlennosti [*A publication*]

Tr Ukr Nauchno-Issled Inst Prir Gazov ... Trudy Ukrainskii Nauchno-Issledovatel'skii Institut Prirodnykh Gazov [*A publication*]

Tr Ukr Nauchno-Issled Inst Rastenievod Sel Genet ... Trudy Ukrainskogo Nauchno-Issledovatel'skogo Instituta Rastenievodstva Selektsii i Genetiki [*A publication*]

Tr Ukr Naucho-Issled Inst Spirt Likero Vodochn Promsti ... Trudy Ukrainskii Nauchno-Issledovatel'skii Institut Spirtovoi i Likero-Vodochnoi Promyshlennosti [*A publication*]

Tr Ukr Nauchno-Issled Inst Zernovogo Khoz ... Trudy Ukrainskogo Nauchno-Issledovatel'skogo Instituta Zernovogo Khozyaistva [*A publication*]

Tr Ul'vanovsk Gos Opytn Stn Zhivotnovod ... Trudy Ul'vanovskaya Gosudarstvennaya Opytnaya Stantsiya Zhivotnovodstva [*A publication*]

Tr Ulyanovsk Politekh Inst ... Trudy Ul'yanovskii Politekhnicheskii Institut [*A publication*]

Tr Ul'yanovsk S-Kh Inst ... Trudy Ul'yanovskogo Sel'skokhozyaistvennogo Instituta [*A publication*]

Tr Ul'yanovsk Skh Opytn Stn ... Trudy Ul'yanovskoi Sel'skokhozyaistvennoi Opytnoi Stantsii [*A publication*]

TRUMP..... Target Radiation Ultraviolet Measurement Program (AAG)

TRUMP..... Technical Review Updated Manuals and Publications (MCD)

TRUMP..... Teller Register Unit Monitoring Program (IEEE)

TRUMP..... Threat Reaction Upgrade Modernization (MCD)

TRUMP..... Total Revision and Upgrading of Maintenance Procedures [*Marine Corps*]

TRUMP..... Transportable Understanding Mechanism Package [*Software system*] (IT)

TRUMP..... Tribal Class Update and Modernization Project [*Canadian Navy*]

TRUN........ Trunnion [*Pivot*] (KSC)

TRUNANG ... Trunnion Angle (MCD)

Tr Univ Druzhby Nar ... Trudy Universiteta Druzhby Narodov [*USSR*] [*A publication*]

Tr Univ Druzhby Nar Fiz ... Trudy Universiteta Druzhby Narodov. Fizika [*USSR*] [*A publication*]

Tr Univ Druzhby Nar Im Patrisa Lumumby ... Trudy Universiteta Druzhby Narodov Imeni Patrisa Lumumby [*A publication*]

Tr Univ Druzhby Nar Ser Fiz ... Trudy Universiteta Druzhby Narodov Imeni Patrisa Lumumby. Seriya Fizika [*A publication*]

Truppie ...... Trucker with Upscale Living Quarters in His or Her Vehicle [*Lifestyle classification*]

Tr Upr Geol Okhr Nedr Sov Minist Kirg SSR ... Trudy Upravleniya Geologii i Okhrany Nedr pri Sovete Ministrov Kirgizskoi SSR [*A publication*]

Tru Railw Rep ... Truman's American Railway Reports [*A publication*] (DLA)

Tr Ural Elektromekh Inst Inzh Zheleznodorozhn ... Trudy Ural'skogo Elektromekhanicheskogo Instituta Inzhenerov Zheleznodorozhnogo Transporta [*A publication*]

Tr Ural Ind Inst ... Trudy Ural'skogo Industrial'nogo Instituta [*A publication*]

Tr Ural Lesotekh Inst ... Trudy Ural'skogo Lesotekhnicheskogo Instituta [*A publication*]

Tr Ural Nauchno-Issled Inst Chern Met ... Trudy Ural'skogo Nauchno-Issledovatel'skogo Instituta Chernykh Metallov [*A publication*]

Tr Ural Nauchno-Issled Inst Sel'sk Khoz ... Trudy Ural'skogo Nauchno-Issledovatel'skogo Instituta Sel'skogo Khozyaistva [*A publication*]

Tr Ural Nauchno-Issled Khim Inst ... Trudy Ural'skogo Nauchno-Issledovatel'skogo Khimicheskogo Instituta [*A publication*]

Tr Ural Nauchno-Issled Proekt Inst Mednoi Promsti ... Trudy Ural'skii Nauchno-Issledovatel'skii i Proektnyi Institut Mednoi Promyshlennosti [*USSR*] [*A publication*]

Tr Ural Nauchno-Issled Proektn Inst Mednoi Promsti ... Trudy Ural'skii Nauchno-Issledovatel'skii i Proektnyi Institut Mednoi Promyshlennosti [*A publication*]

Tr Ural Otd Gos Nauchno-Issled Inst Ozern Rechn Rybn Khoz ... Trudy Ural'skogo Otdeleniya Gosudarstvennyi Nauchno-Issledovatel'skii Institut Ozernogo i Rechnogo Rybnogo Khozyaistva [*A publication*]

Tr Ural Otd Mosk Ova Ispyt Prir ... Trudy Ural'skogo Otdeleniya Moskovskogo Obshchestva Ispytatelei Prirody [*A publication*]

Tr Ural Otd Sib Nauchno-Issled Inst Rybn Khoz ... Trudy Ural'skogo Otdeleniya Sibirskogo Nauchno-Issledovatel'skogo Instituta Rybnogo Khozyaistva [*A publication*]

Tr Ural Politekh Inst ... Trudy Ural'skogo Politekhnicheskogo Instituta Imeni S. M. Kirova [*A publication*]

Tr Ural Politekh Inst Im S M Kirova ... Trudy Ural'skogo Politekhnicheskogo Instituta Imeni S. M. Kirova [*USSR*] [*A publication*]

TRURON.. Truronensis [*Signature of the Bishop of Truro*] [*Latin*] (ROG)

TRUST...... Toluidine Red Unheated Serum Test

TRUST...... Transportable Units and Self-Sufficient Teams (MCD)

TRUST...... Trieste United States Troops

Trust Bull... Trust Bulletin [*A publication*]

Trust Co Mag ... Trust Companies Magazine [*1904-38*] [*A publication*] (DLA)

Trust Lett... Trust Letter. American Bankers Association [*A publication*] (ILCA)

Trust Newsl ... Trust Newsletter [*National Trust of Australia*] [*A publication*] (APTA)

Trust Nletter ... Trust Newsletter [*National Trust of Australia*] [*A publication*] (APTA)

Trusts & Es ... Trusts and Estates [*A publication*]

Trusts & Est ... Trusts and Estates [*A publication*]

Trust Terr.. Trust Territory Reports [*A publication*] (DLA)

TRUT .... Time Remaining until Transition [*Air Force*]

Tr Uzb Geol Upr ... Trudy Uzbekskogo Geologicheskogo Upravlenie [*A publication*]

Tr Uzb Gos Nauchno-Issled Inst Kurortol Fizioter ... Trudy Uzbekskogo Gosudarstvennogo Nauchno-Issledovatel'skogo i Instituta Kurortologii i Fizioterapii [*A publication*]

Tr Uzb Inst Malyarii Med Parazitol ... Trudy Uzbekistanskogo Instituta Malyarii i Meditsinskoi Parazitologii [*A publication*]

Tr Uzb Nauchno-Issled Inst Fizioter Kurortol ... Trudy Uzbekistanskogo Nauchno-Issledovatel'skogo Instituta Fizioterapii i Kurortologii [*A publication*]

Tr Uzb Nauchno-Issled Inst Ortop Travmatol Prot ... Trudy Uzbekistanskogo Nauchno-Issledovatel'skogo Instituta Ortopedii Travmatologii i Protezirovaniya [*A publication*]

Tr Uzb Nauchno-Issled Inst Ortop Travmatol Protez ... Trudy Uzbekistanskogo Nauchno-Issledovatel'skogo Instituta Ortopedii Travmatologii i Protezirovaniya [*A publication*]

Tr Uzb Nauchno-Issled Inst Vet ... Trudy Uzbekskogo Nauchno-Issledovatel'skogo Instituta Veterinarii [*A publication*]

TRV .... Tank Recovery Vehicle [*Army*] (AABC)

TRV .... Thrust Reduction Valve

TRV .... Timing Relay Valve

TRV .... Tobacco Rattle Virus

TRV .... Torpedo-Recovery Vessel [*Navy*] [*British*]

TRV .... Transient Recovery Voltage (IEEE)

TRV .... Traverse

TRV .... Treviso [*Italy*] [*Seismograph station code, US Geological Survey*] [*Closed*] (SEIS)

TRV .... Trivandrum [*India*] [*Airport symbol*] (OAG)

TRV .... Trove Resources [*Vancouver Stock Exchange symbol*]

TRV .... United States Army TRADOC, Fort Lee Post, Logistic Center, Logistic, Quartermaster, Fort Lee, VA [*OCLC symbol*] (OCLC)

TRVA .... Thermally Released Volatile Aromatics [*i.e., odors*] [*Slang*]

Tr VAMI ... Trudy VAMI [*A publication*]

TRVB........ Tables of Redemption Values for US Savings Bonds

TRVED8.... Theory of Science Development [*A publication*]

TRVEH ..... Tracked Vehicle (AABC)

Tr Velikoluk S-Kh Inst ... Trudy Velikolukskogo Sel'skokhozyaistvennogo Instituta [*A publication*]

Tr Vinnitsk Gos Med Inst ... Trudy Vinnitskogo Gosudarstvennogo Meditsinskogo Instituta [*A publication*]

Tr Vissh Inst Nar Stop (Varna Bulg) ... Trudove na Visshiya Institut za Narodno Stopanstvo "D. Blagoev" (Varna Bulgaria) [*A publication*]

Tr Vissh Pedagog Inst (Plovdiv) Mat Fiz Khim Biol ... Trudove na Visshiya Pedagogicheski Institut (Plovdiv). Matematika, Fizika, Khimiya, Biologiya [*A publication*]

TRVL........ Truvel Corp. [*NASDAQ symbol*] (NQ)

Tr Vladivost Nauchno Issled Inst Epidemiol Mikrobiol Gig ... Trudy Vladivostokskogo Nauchno-Issledovatel'skogo Instituta Epidemiologii, Mikrobiologii, i Gigieny [*A publication*]

TRVLG...... Traveling (MSA)

TRVLMT.. Travel Limit

TRVLR...... Traveler (MSA)

TRVM .... Transistorized Voltmeter

TRVM .... TRV Minerals Corp. [*NASDAQ symbol*] (NQ)

Tr VNIGRI ... Trudy VNIGRI [*Vsesoyuznogo Neftyanogo Nauchno-Issledovatel'skogo Geologorazvedochnogo Instituta*] [*A publication*]

Tr VNIIEI ... Trudy VNIIEI [*Vsesoyuznogo Nauchno-Issledovatel'skogo i Proektno-Tekhnologicheskogo Instituta Elektrougol'nykh Izdelii*] [*A publication*]

Tr VNII Fiz-Tekh Radiotekh Izmer ... Trudy Vsesoyuznyj Nauchno-Issledovatel'skij Institut Fiziko-Tekhnicheskikh i Radiotekhnicheskikh Izmerenij [*A publication*]

Tr Volgogr Gos Nauchno-Issled Proektn Inst Neft Promsti ... Trudy Volgogradskii Gosudarstvennyi Nauchno-Issledovatel'skii i Proektnyi Institut Neftyanoi Promyshlennosti [*A publication*]

Tr Volgogr Med Inst ... Trudy Volgogradskogo Meditsinskogo Instituta [*A publication*]

Tr Volgogr Nauchno-Issled Inst Neft Gazov Promsti ... Trudy Volgogradskii Nauchno-Issledovatel'skii Institut Neftyanoi i Gazovoi Promyshlennosti [*A publication*]

Tr Volgogr Opytno Melior Stn ... Trudy Volgogradskaya Opytno-Meliorativnaya Stantsiya [*A publication*]

Tr Volgogr Otd Gos Nauchno-Issled Inst Ozern Rechn Rybn Khoz ... Trudy Volgogradskogo Otdeleniya Gosudarstvennogo Nauchno-Issledovatel'skogo Instituta Ozernogo i Rechnogo Rybnogo Khozyaistva [*A publication*]

Tr Volgogr S-Kh Inst ... Trudy Volgogradskogo Sel'skokhozyaistvennogo Instituta [*A publication*]

Tr Vologod Molochn Inst ... Trudy Vologodskogo Molochnogo Instituta [*A publication*]

Tr Vologod Molochno Khoz Inst ... Trudy Vologodskogo Molochno-Khozyaistvennogo Instituta [*A publication*]

Tr Volzh Kamskogo Gos Zapov ... Trudy Volzhsko-Kamskogo Gosudarstvennogo Zapovednika [*A publication*]

Tr Voronezh Gos Med Inst ... Trudy Voronezhskii Gosudarstvennyi Meditsinskii Institut [*A publication*]

Tr Voronezh Gos Univ ... Trudy Voronezhskogo Gosudarstvennogo Universiteta [*A publication*]

Tr Voronezh Gos Zapov ... Trudy Voronezhskogo Gosudarstvennogo Zapovednika [*A publication*]

Tr Voronezh Inzh Stroit Inst ... Trudy Voronezhskogo Inzhenerno-Stroitel'nogo Instituta [*A publication*]

Tr Voronezh Khim Tekhnol Inst ... Trudy Voronezhskogo Khimiko-Tekhnologicheskogo Instituta [*A publication*]

Tr Voronezh Med Inst ... Trudy Voronezhskogo Meditsinskogo Instituta [*A publication*]

Tr Voronezh Nauchno Issled Vet Stn ... Trudy Voronezhskoi Nauchno-Issledovatel'skoi Veterinarnoi Stantsii [*A publication*]

Tr Voronezh Stn Zashch Rast ... Trudy Voronezhskogo Stantsii Zashchity Rastenii [*A publication*]

Tr Voronezh Tekhnol Inst ... Trudy Voronezhskogo Tekhnologicheskogo Instituta [*A publication*]

Tr Voronezh Zoovet Inst ... Trudy Voronezhskogo Zooveterinarnogo Instituta [*A publication*]

Tr Voroshil Gorno Metall Inst ... Trudy Voroshilovskogo Gorno-Metallurgicheskogo Instituta [*A publication*]

Tr Voroshilovgr S-Kh Inst ... Trudy Voroshilovgradskogo Sel'skokhozyaistvennogo Instituta [*A publication*]

Tr Vost Inst Ogneuporov ... Trudy Vostochnogo Instituta Ogneuporov [*USSR*] [*A publication*]

Tr Vost Kaz Gos Skh Opytn Stn ... Trudy Vostochno-Kazakhskoi Gosudarstvennoi Sel'skokhozyaistvennoi Opytnoi Stantsii [*A publication*]

Tr Vost Nauchno Issled Gornorudn Inst ... Trudy Vostochnogo Nauchno-Issledovatel'skogo Gornorudnogo Instituta [*A publication*]

Tr Vost-Sib Fil Akad Nauk SSSR ... Trudy Vostochno-Sibirskogo Filiala Akademii Nauk SSSR [*A publication*]

Tr Vost Sib Geol Inst Akad Nauk SSSR Sib Otd ... Trudy Vostochno-Sibirskogo Geologicheskogo Instituta Akademiya Nauk SSSR Sibirskoe Otdelenie [*A publication*]

Tr Vost Sib Geol Upr ... Trudy Vostochno-Sibirskogo Geologicheskogo Upravleniya [*A publication*]

Tr Vost Sib Tekhnol Inst ... Trudy Vostochno-Sibirskogo Tekhnologicheskogo Instituta [*A publication*]

TRVSA ...... Travail et Securite [*A publication*]

Tr Vseross Konf Khir Flebol ... Trudy Vserossiiskoi Konferentsii Khirurgov po Flebologii [*A publication*]

Tr Vseross Nauchno Issled Inst Sakh Svekly Sakhara ... Trudy Vserossiiskogo Nauchno-Issledovatel'skogo Instituta Sakharnoi Svekly i Sakhara [*A publication*]

Tr Vses Aerogeol Tresta ... Trudy Vsesoyuznogo Aerogeologicheskogo Tresta [*A publication*]

Tr Vses Alyum Magnievyi Inst ... Trudy Vsesoyuznyi Alyuminievo-Magnievyi Institut [*A publication*]

Tr Vses Elektrotekh Inst ... Trudy Vsesoyuznogo Elektrotekhnicheskogo i Instituta [*A publication*]

Tr Vses Entomol Obshch ... Trudy Vsesoyuznogo Entomologicheskogo Obshchestva [*A publication*]

Tr Vses Entomol O-Va ... Trudy Vsesoyuznogo Entomologicheskogo Obshchestva [*A publication*]

Tr Vses Geol Razved Obedin ... Trudy Vsesoyuznogo Geologo-Razvedochnogo Ob'edineniya [*A publication*]

Tr Vses Gidrobiol O-Va ... Trudy Vsesoyuznogo Gidrobiologicheskogo Obshchestva [*A publication*]

Tr Vses Gos Nauchno Issled Proektn Inst Khim Fotogr Promsti ... Trudy Vsesoyuznogo Gosudarstvennogo Nauchno-Issledovatel'skogo Proektnogo Instituta Khimiko-Fotograficheskoi Promyshlennosti [*A publication*]

Tr Vses Inst Eksp Med ... Trudy Vsesoyuznogo Instituta Eksperimental'noi Meditsiny [*A publication*]

Tr Vses Inst Eksp Vet ... Trudy Vsesoyuznogo Instituta Eksperimental'noi Veterinarii [*USSR*] [*A publication*]

Tr Vses Inst Gel'mintol ... Trudy Vsesyuznogo Instituta Gel'mintologii [*A publication*]

Tr Vses Inst Rastenievod ... Trudy Vsesoyuznogo Instituta Rastenievodstva [*A publication*]

Tr Vses Inst Rast Prob Pop Vyssh Rast ... Trudy Vsesoyuznyi Institut Rastenievodstva Problema Populatsii u Vysshikh Rastenii [*A publication*]

Tr Vses Inst Sodovoi Promsti ... Trudy Vsesoyuznogo Instituta Sodovoi Promyshlennosti [*A publication*]

Tr Vses Inst Zashch Rast ... Trudy Vsesoyuznogo Instituta Zashchity Rastenii [*A publication*]

Tr Vses Mekh Tekhnol Inst Konservn Promsti ... Trudy Vsesoyuznogo Mekhaniko-Tekhnologicheskogo Instituta Konservnoi Promyshlennosti [*A publication*]

Tr Vses Nauch-Isled Inst Zashch Rast ... Trudy Vsesoyuznogo Nauchno-Issledovatel'skogo Instituta Zashchity Rastenii [*A publication*]

Tr Vses Nauch-Issled Inst Lub Kul't ... Trudy Vsesoyuznyi Nauchno-Issledovatel'skii Institut Lubyanykh Kul'ture [*A publication*]

Tr Vses Nauch-Issled Inst Ptitsevod ... Trudy Vsesoyuznogo Nauchno-Issledovatel'skogo Instituta Ptitsevodstva [*A publication*]

Tr Vses Nauch-Issled Inst Zerna Prod Ego Pererab ... Trudy Vsesoyuznyi Nauchno-Issledovatel'skii Institut Zerna i Produktov Ego Pererabotki [*A publication*]

Tr Vses Nauch-Issled Inst Zhivotnovod ... Trudy Vsesoyuznyi Nauchno-Issledovatel'skii Institut Zhivotnovodstva [*A publication*]

Tr Vses Nauchn Inzh Tekh Ova Metall ... Trudy Vsesoyuznogo Nauchnogo Inzhenerno-Tekhnicheskogo Obshchestva Metallurgov [*A publication*]

Tr Vses Nauchn-Issled Inst Spirt Likero-Vodoch Prom ... Trudy Vsesoyuznogo Nauchno-Issledovatel'skogo Instituta Spirtovoi i Likero-Vodochnoi Promyshlennosti [*USSR*] [*A publication*]

Tr Vses Nauchno Issled Alyum Magnievyi Inst ... Trudy Vsesoyuznyi Nauchno-Issledovatel'skii Alyuminievo-Magnievyi Institut [*A publication*]

Tr Vses Nauchno Issled Eksp Konstr Inst Prodovol Mashinostr ... Trudy Vsesoyuznyi Nauchno-Issledovatel'skii i Eksperimental'no-Konstruktorskii Institut Prodovol'stvennogo Mashinostroeniya [*A publication*]

Tr Vses Nauchno-Issled Galurgii ... Trudy Vsesoyuznogo Nauchno-Issledovatel'skogo Instituta Galurgii [*A publication*]

Tr Vses Nauchno-Issled Geol Inst ... Trudy Vsesoyuznogo Nauchno-Issledovatel'skogo Geologicheskogo Instituta [*A publication*]

Tr Vses Nauchno Issled Geologorazved Inst ... Trudy Vsesoyuznogo Nauchno-Issledovatel'skogo Geologorazvedochnogo Instituta [*A publication*]

Tr Vses Nauchno-Issled Geologorazved Neft Inst ... Trudy Vsesoyuznyi Nauchno-Issledovatel'skii Geologorazvedochnyi Neftyanoi Instituta [*A publication*]

Tr Vses Nauchno-Issled Inst Abrazivov Shlifovaniya ... Trudy Vsesoyuznyi Nauchno-Issledovatel'skii Institut Abrazivov i Shlifovaniya [*A publication*]

Tr Vses Nauchno-Issled Inst Antibiot ... Trudy Vsesoyuznogo Nauchno-Issledovatel'skogo Instituta Antibiotikov [*A publication*]

Tr Vses Nauchno-Issled Inst Aviats Mater ... Trudy Vsesoyuznogo Nauchno-Issledovatel'skogo Instituta Aviatsionnykh Materialov [*A publication*]

Tr Vses Nauchno-Issled Inst Burovoi Tekh ... Trudy Vsesoyuznyi Nauchno-Issledovatel'skii Institut Burovoi Tekhniki [*A publication*]

Tr Vses Nauchno-Issled Inst Efirnomaslichn Kult ... Trudy Vsesoyuznogo Nauchno-Issledovatel'skogo Instituta Efirnomaslichnykh Kul'tur [*A publication*]

Tr Vses Nauchno-Issled Inst Elektromekh ... Trudy Vsesoyuznogo Nauchno-Issledovatel'skogo Instituta Elektromekhaniki [*A publication*]

Tr Vses Nauchno-Issled Inst Elektroterm Oborudovaniya ... Trudy Vsesoyuznogo Nauchno-Issledovatel'skogo Instituta Elektrotermicheskogo Oborudovaniya [*A publication*]

Tr Vses Nauchno-Issled Inst Fermentn Spirt Promsti ... Trudy Vsesoyuznyi Nauchno-Issledovatel'skii Institut Fermentnoi i Spirtovoi Promyshlennosti [*A publication*]

Tr Vses Nauchno-Issled Inst Fiziol Biokhim Pitan Skh Zhivotn ... Trudy Vsesoyuznogo Nauchno-Issledovatel'skogo Instituta Fiziologii, Biokhimii, i Pitaniya Sel'skokhozyaistvennykh Zhivotnykh [*A publication*]

Tr Vses Nauchno-Issled Inst Fiziol Biokhim Skh Zhivotn ... Trudy Vsesoyuznogo Nauchno-Issledovatel'skogo Instituta Fiziologii i Biokhimii Sel'skokhozyaistvennykh Zhivotnykh [*A publication*]

Tr Vses Nauchno-Issled Inst Galurgii ... Trudy Vsesoyuznogo Nauchno-Issledovatel'skogo Instituta Galurgii [*A publication*]

Tr Vses Nauchno Issled Inst Geofiz Metodov Razved ... Trudy Vsesoyuznyi Nauchno-Issledovatel'skii Institut Geofizicheskikh Metodov Razvedki [*A publication*]

Tr Vses Nauchno Issled Inst G Gidrotekh Melior ... Trudy Vsesoyuznogo Nauchno-Issledovatel'skogo Instituta Gidrotekhniki i Melioratsii [*A publication*]

Tr Vses Nauchno Issled Inst Gidrogeol Inzh Geol ... Trudy Vsesoyuznogo Nauchno-Issledovatel'skogo Instituta Gidrogeologii i Inzhenernoi Geologii [*A publication*]

Tr Vses Nauchno-Issled Inst Gidrotekh Melior ... Trudy Vsesoyuznogo Nauchno-Issledovatel'skogo Instituta Gidrotekhniki i Melioratsii [*A publication*]

Tr Vses Nauchno-Issled Inst Ikusstv Zhidk Topl Gaza ... Trudy Vsesoiuznogo Nauchno-Issledovatel'skogo Instituta Iskusstvennogo Zhidkogo Topliva i Gaza [*USSR*] [*A publication*]

Tr Vses Nauchno Issled Inst Iskusstv Zhidk Topl Gaza ... Trudy Vsesoyuznogo Nauchno-Issledovatel'skogo Instituta Iskusstvennogo Zhidkogo Topliva i Gaza [*A publication*]

Tr Vses Nauchno Issled Inst Karakulevod ... Trudy Vsesoyuznogo Nauchno-Issledovatel'skogo Instituta Karakulevodstva [*A publication*]

Tr Vses Nauchno-Issled Inst Khim Pererab Gazov ... Trudy Vsesoyuznogo Nauchno-Issledovatel'skogo Instituta Khimicheskoi Pererabotki Gazov [*A publication*]

Tr Vses Nauchno-Issled Inst Khim Reakt ... Trudy Vsesoyuznogo Nauchno-Issledovatel'skogo Instituta Khimicheskikh Reaktivov [*A publication*]

Tr Vses Nauchno-Issled Inst Khlebopek Promsti ... Trudy Vsesoyuznyi Nauchno-Issledovatel'skii Institut Khlebopekarnoi Promyshlennosti [*A publication*]

Tr Vses Nauchno-Issled Inst Khlopkovod ... Trudy Vsesoyuznogo Nauchno-Issledovatel'skogo Instituta Khlopkovodstva [*A publication*]

Tr Vses Nauchno-Issled Inst Khlopkovod Nov Raionov ... Trudy Vsesoyuznogo Nauchno-Issledovatel'skii Institut Khlopkovodstva Novykh Raionov [*A publication*]
Tr Vses Nauchno Issled Inst Konditer Promsti ... Trudy Vsesoyuznogo Nauchno-Issledovatel'skogo Instituta Konditerskoi Promyshlennosti [*A publication*]
Tr Vses Nauchno-Issled Inst Konservn Ovoshchesush Prom-sti ... Trudy Vsesoyuznogo Nauchno-Issledovatel'skogo Instituta Konservnoi i Ovoshchesushyl'noi Promyshlennosti [*A publication*]
Tr Vses Nauchno Issled Inst Korml S-Kh Zhivotn ... Trudy Vsesoyuznogo Nauchno-Issledovatel'skogo Instituta Kormleniya Sel'skokhozyaistvennykh Zhivotnykh [*A publication*]
Tr Vses Nauchno Issled Inst Krakhmaloprod ... Trudy Vsesoyuznyi Nauchno-Issledovatel'skii Institut Krakhmaloproduktov [*A publication*]
Tr Vses Nauchno-Issled Inst L'na ... Trudy Vsesoyuznogo Nauchno-Issledovatel'skogo Instituta L'na [*A publication*]
Tr Vses Nauchno-Issled Inst Med Instrum Oborudovaniya ... Trudy Vsesoyuznogo Nauchno-Issledovatel'skogo Instituta Meditsinskikh Instrumentov Oborudovaniya [*A publication*]
Tr Vses Nauchno-Issled Inst Med Priborostr ... Trudy Vsesoyuznogo Nauchno-Issledovatel'skogo Instituta Meditsinskikh Priborostroenii [*A publication*]
Tr Vses Nauchno Issled Inst Metod Tekh Razved ... Trudy Vsesoyuznogo Nauchno-Issledovatel'skogo Instituta Metodiki i Tekhniki Razvedki [*A publication*]
Tr Vses Nauchno-Issled Inst Molochn Prom-St ... Trudy Vsesoyuznogo Nauchno-Issledovatel'skogo Instituta Molochnoi Promyshlennost [*A publication*]
Tr Vses Nauchno-Issled Inst Morsk Ryb Khoz Okeanogr ... Trudy Vsesoyuznogo Nauchno-Issledovatel'skogo Instituta Morskogo Rybnogo Khozyaistva i Okeanografii [*USSR*] [*A publication*]
Tr Vses Nauchno-Issled Inst Morsk Rybn Khoz Okeanogr ... Trudy Vsesoyuznogo Nauchno-Issledovatel'skogo Instituta Morskogo Rybnogo Khozyaistva i Okeanografii [*A publication*]
Tr Vses Nauchno-Issled Inst Myasn Prom-St ... Trudy Vsesoyuznogo Nauchno-Issledovatel'skogo Instituta Myasnoi Promyshlennost [*A publication*]
Tr Vses Nauchno-Issled Inst Pererab Ispol'z Topl ... Trudy Vsesoyuznogo Nauchno-Issledovatel'skogo Instituta Pererabotki i Ispol'zovaniya Topliva [*USSR*] [*A publication*]
Tr Vses Nauchno-Issled Inst Pererab Nefti ... Trudy Vsesoyuznyj Nauchno-Issledovatel'skij Institut po Pererabotke Nefti [*A publication*]
Tr Vses Nauchno-Issled Inst Pererab Slantsev ... Trudy Vsesoyuznogo Nauchno-Issledovatel'skogo Instituta po Pererabotke Slantsev [*USSR*] [*A publication*]
Tr Vses Nauchno Issled Inst Pivo Bezalkogol'n Promsti ... Trudy Vsesoyuznogo Nauchno-Issledovatel'skogo Instituta Pivo-Bezalkogol'noi Promyshlennosti [*A publication*]
Tr Vses Nauchno Issled Inst Pivovar Promsti ... Trudy Vsesoyuznyi Nauchno-Issledovatel'skii Institut Pivovarennoi Promyshlennosti [*A publication*]
Tr Vses Nauchno-Issled Inst Podzemn Gazif Uglei ... Trudy Vsesoyuznyi Nauchno-Issledovatel'skii Institut Podzemnoi Gazifikatsii Uglei [*USSR*] [*A publication*]
Tr Vses Nauchno-Issled Inst Prir Gazov ... Trudy Vsesoyuznyi Nauchno-Issledovatel'skii Institut Prirodnykh Gazov [*USSR*] [*A publication*]
Tr Vses Nauchno-Issled Inst Prod Brozheniya ... Trudy Vsesoyuznyi Nauchno-Issledovatel'skii Institut Produktov Brozheniya [*USSR*] [*A publication*]
Tr Vses Nauchno Issled Inst Proizvod Pishch Prod Kartofelya ... Trudy Vsesoyuznyi Nauchno-Issledovatel'skii Institut po Proizvodstvu Pishchevykh Produktov iz Kartofelya [*A publication*]
Tr Vses Nauchno-Issled Inst Prud Rybn Khoz ... Trudy Vsesoyuznogo Nauchno-Issledovatel'skogo Instituta Prudovogo Rybnogo Khozaistva [*A publication*]
Tr Vses Nauchno-Issled Inst Radiat Tekh ... Trudy Vsesoyuznyj Nauchno-Issledovatel'skij Institut Radiatsionnoj Tekhniki [*A publication*]
Tr Vses Nauchno-Issled Inst Rastit Masel Margarina ... Trudy Vsesoyuznogo Nauchno-Issledovatel'skogo Instituta Rastitel'nykh Masel i Margarina [*A publication*]
Tr Vses Nauchno-Issled Inst Sint Nat Dushistykh Veshchestv ... Trudy Vsesoyuznogo Nauchno-Issledovatel'skogo Instituta Sinteticheskikh i Natural'nykh Dushistykh Veshchestv [*A publication*]
Tr Vses Nauchno Issled Inst Solvanoi Promsti ... Trudy Vsesoyuznyi Nauchno-Issledovatel'skii Institut Solvanoi Promyshlennosti [*A publication*]
Tr Vses Nauchno-Issled Inst Spirt Prom-Sti ... Trudy Vsesoyuznogo Nauchno-Issledovatel'skogo Instituta Spirtovoi Promyshlennosti [*USSR*] [*A publication*]

Tr Vses Nauchno-Issled Inst Stand Obraztsov Spektr Etalonov ... Trudy Vsesoyuznogo Nauchno-Issledovatel'skogo Instituta Standartnykh Obraztsov i Spektral'nykh Etalonov [*USSR*] [*A publication*]
Tr Vses Nauchno Issled Inst Steklyannogo Volokna ... Trudy Vsesoyuznogo Nauchno-Issledovatel'skogo Instituta Steklyannogo Volokna [*A publication*]
Tr Vses Nauchno-Issled Inst Torf Prom-Sti ... Trudy Vsesoyuznogo Nauchno-Issledovatel'skogo Instituta Torfyanoi Promyshlennosti [*USSR*] [*A publication*]
Tr Vses Nauchno-Issled Inst Udobr Agropochvoved ... Trudy Vsesoyuznogo Nauchno-Issledovatel'skogo Instituta Udobreniya i Agropochvovedeniya [*A publication*]
Tr Vses Nauchno-Issled Inst Vet Sanit ... Trudy Vsesoyuznogo Nauchno-Issledovatel'skogo Instituta Veterinarnoi Sanitarii [*A publication*]
Tr Vses Nauchno-Issled Inst Vet Sanit Ektoparazitol ... Trudy Vsesoyuznogo Nauchno-Issledovatel'skogo Instituta Veterinarnoi Sanitarii i Ektoparazitologii [*A publication*]
Tr Vses Nauchno-Issled Inst Yad Geofiz Geokhim ... Trudy Vsesoyuznyi Nauchno-Issledovatel'skii Institut Yadernoi Geofiziki i Geokhimii [*USSR*] [*A publication*]
Tr Vses Nauchno-Issled Inst Zashch Rast ... Trudy Vsesoyuznogo Nauchno-Issledovatel'skogo Instituta Zashchity Rastenii [*A publication*]
Tr Vses Nauchno-Issled Inst Zerna Prod Pererab ... Trudy Vsesoyuznogo Nauchno-Issledovatel'skogo Instituta Zerna i Produktov Ego Pererabotki [*A publication*]
Tr Vses Nauchno-Issled Inst Zheleznodorozhn Transp ... Trudy Vsesoyuznogo Nauchno-Issledovatel'skogo Instituta Zheleznodorozhnogo Transporta [*A publication*]
Tr Vses Nauchno-Issled Inst Zheleznodorzhn ... Trudy Vsesoyuznogo Nauchno-Issledovatel'skogo Instituta Zheleznodorozhnogo Transporta [*A publication*]
Tr Vses Nauchno Issled Inst Zhirov ... Trudy Vsesoyuznyi Nauchno-Issledovatel'skii Institut Zhirov [*A publication*]
Tr Vses Nauchno-Issled Inst Zhivotn Syr'ya Pushn ... Trudy Vsesoyuznogo Nauchno-Issledovatel'skogo Instituta Zhivotnogo Syr'ya Pushniny [*A publication*]
Tr Vses Nauchno-Issled Inst Zolota Redk Met ... Trudy Vsesoyuznogo Nauchno-Issledovatel'skogo Instituta Zolota i Redkikh Metallov [*USSR*] [*A publication*]
Tr Vses Nauchno-Issled Konstr Inst Avtog Mashinostr ... Trudy Vsesoyuznogo Nauchno-Issledovatel'skogo i Konstruktorskogo Instituta Avtogennogo Mashinostroeniya [*USSR*] [*A publication*]
Tr Vses Nauchno Issled Konstr Inst Nauchn Priborostr ... Trudy Vsesoyuznyi Nauchno-Issledovatel'skii i Konstruktorskii Institut Nauchnogo Priborostroeniya [*A publication*]
Tr Vses Nauchno Issled Proektn Inst Galurgii ... Trudy Vsesoyuznogo Nauchno-Issledovatel'skogo i Proektnogo Instituta Galurgii [*A publication*]
Tr Vses Nauchno-Issled Proektn Inst Mekh Obrab Polezn Iskop ... Trudy Vsesoyuznyi Nauchno-Issledovatel'skii i Proektnyi Institut Mekhanicheskoi Obrabotki Poleznykh Iskopaemykh [*A publication*]
Tr Vses Neftegazov Nauchno-Issled Inst ... Trudy Vsesoyuznyi Neftegazovyi Nauchno-Issledovatel'skii Institut [*A publication*]
Tr Vses Neft Nauchno-Issled Geologorazved Inst ... Trudy Vsesoyuznogo Neftyanogo Nauchno-Issledovatel'skogo Geologorazvedochnogo Instituta [*USSR*] [*A publication*]
Tr Vses Neft Nauchno-Issled Inst Tekh Bezop ... Trudy Vsesoyuznyi Neftyanoi Nauchno-Issledovatel'skii Institut po Tekhnike Bezopasnosti [*A publication*]
Tr Vses O Genet Sel Kuban Otd ... Trudy Vsesoyuznoe Obshchestvo Genetikov i Selektsionerov Kubanskoe Otdelenie [*A publication*]
Tr Vses O-Va Fiziol Biokhim Farmakol ... Trudy Vsesoyuznogo Obshchestva Fiziologov Biokhimikov i Farmakologov [*A publication*]
Tr Vses S-Kh Inst Zaochn Obraz ... Trudy Vsesoyuznogo Sel'skokhozyaistvennogo Instituta Zaochnogo Obrazovaniva [*A publication*]
Tr Vses Teplotekh Nauchno-Issled Inst ... Trudy Vsesoyuznyi Teplotekhnikii Nauchno-Issledovatel'skii Institut [*USSR*] [*A publication*]
Tr Vses Tsentr Nauchno Issled Inst Zhirov ... Trudy Vsesoyuznogo Tsentral'nogo Nauchno-Issledovatel'skogo Instituta Zhirov [*A publication*]
Tr Vses Zaochn Energ Inst ... Trudy Vsesoyuznogo Zaochnogo Energeticheskogo Instituta [*A publication*]
Tr Vses Zaochn Inst Inzh Zheleznodorozhn Transp ... Trudy Vsesoyuznyi Zaochnyi Institut Inzhenerov Zheleznodorozhnogo Transporta [*A publication*]
Tr Vses Zaochn Inst Pishch Promsti ... Trudy Vsesoyuznyi Zaochnyi Institut Pishchevoi Promyshlennosti [*A publication*]
TRVTDJ.... Tropical Veterinarian [*A publication*]
Tr VTI........ Trudy VTI [*USSR*] [*A publication*]
Tr Vtorogo Leningr Med Inst ... Trudy Vtorogo Leningradskogo Meditsinskogo Instituta [*A publication*]
Tr Vtorogo Mosk Med Inst ... Trudy Vtorogo Moskovskogo Meditsinskogo Instituta [*A publication*]
TRVV........ Time Radius and Velocity Vector

Tr Vysokogorn Geofiz Inst ... Trudy Vysokogornyj Geofizicheskij Institut [*A publication*]	
TRW .... Tactical Reconnaissance Wing [*Air Force*]　(MCD)	
TRW .... Tarawa [*Kiribati*] [*Airport symbol*]　(OAG)	
TRW .... Trade Winds Resources [*Vancouver Stock Exchange symbol*]	
TRW .... Trail Riders of the Wilderness [*Later, AFA*]　(EA)	
TRW .... Trans Western Airlines of Utah [*Logan, UT*] [*FAA designator*]　(FAAC)	
TRW .... TRW, Inc. [*Formerly, Thompson Ramo Wooldridge, Inc.*] [*NYSE symbol*]　(SPSG)	
TRW .... United States Army TRADOC, Fort Leonard Wood Post Library, Fort Leonard Wood, MO [*OCLC symbol*]　(OCLC)	
TRWA .... Trackway	
TRWC .... Threat Responsive Weapon Control [*Military*]　(CAAL)	
TRWG .... Tactical Reconnaissance Wing [*Air Force*]	
TRW IND ... TRW Information Networks Division [*TRW, Inc.*] [*Torrance, CA*]　(TSSD)	
TRWOA .... Traffic World [*A publication*]	
TRWOV .... Transit Without Visa	
Trx .... Thioredoxin [*Also, TD, TR*] [*Biochemistry*]	
TRX .... Transaction	
TRX .... Trenton, MO [*Location identifier*] [*FAA*]　(FAAL)	
TRX .... Tri-State Resources Ltd. [*Vancouver Stock Exchange symbol*]	
TRX .... Triplex	
TRX .... Two-Region Physics Critical Experiment　(NRCH)	
TRX .... United States Army TRADOC, Ordnance and Chemical School Library, Aberdeen Proving Ground, MD [*OCLC symbol*]　(OCLC)	
TRY .... Teens for Retarded Youth [*Program in Fairfax County, Virginia*]	
TRY .... Toronto Railway	
TRY .... Tororo [*Uganda*] [*Airport symbol*]　(OAG)	
TRY .... Tri-Arc Energy Ltd. [*Vancouver Stock Exchange symbol*]	
TRY .... Troy [*New York*] [*Seismograph station code, US Geological Survey*]　(SEIS)	
TRY .... Truly　(ROG)	
TRY .... United States Army TRADOC, TRADOC System Analysis [*TRASANA*], White Sands Range, NM [*OCLC symbol*]　(OCLC)	
Tr Yakutsk Fil Akad Nauk SSSR Ser Fiz ... Trudy Yakutskogo Filiala Akademiya Nauk SSSR Seriya Fizicheskaya [*A publication*]	
Tr Yakutsk Fil Akad Nauk SSSR Ser Geol ... Trudy Yakutskogo Filiala Akademii Nauk SSSR Seriya Geologicheskaya [*A publication*]	
Tr Yakutsk Nauchno-Issled Inst Selsk Khoz ... Trudy Yakutskogo Nauchno-Issledovatel'skogo Instituta Sel'skogo Khozyaistva [*A publication*]	
Tr Yakutsk Nauchno-Issled Inst Tuberk ... Trudy Yakutskogo Nauchno-Issledovatel'skii Instituta Tuberkuleza [*A publication*]	
Tr Yakutsk Otd Sib Nauchno-Issled Inst Rybn Khoz ... Trudy Yakutskogo Otdeleniya Sibirskogo Nauchno-Issledovatel'skogo Instituta Rybnogo Khozyaistva [*A publication*]	
Tr Yalt Nauchno-Issled Inst Fiz Metodov Lech Med Klimatol ... Trudy Yaltinskogo Nauchno-Issledovatel'nogo Instituta Fizicheskikh Metodov Lecheniya i Meditsinskoi Klimatologii [*A publication*]	
Tr Yarosl Med Inst ... Trudy Yaroslavskogo Meditsinskogo Instituta [*A publication*]	
Tr Yarosl Skh Inst ... Trudy Yaroslavskogo Sel'skokhozyaistvennogo Instituta [*A publication*]	
Tryb Spold ... Trybuna Spoldzielcza [*A publication*]	
Trye Jus Filiz ... Trye's Jus Filizarii [*A publication*]　(ILCA)	
TRZ .... Taradale [*New Zealand*] [*Seismograph station code, US Geological Survey*]　(SEIS)	
TRZ .... Thioridazine [*Tranquilizer*]	
TRZ .... Tiruchirappalli [*India*] [*Airport symbol*]　(OAG)	
TrZ .... Trierer Zeitschrift [*A publication*]	
Tr Z .... Trierer Zeitschrift fuer Geschichte und Kunst des Trierer Landes und Seiner Nachbargebiete [*A publication*]	
TRZ .... United States Army Intelligence Center and School Library, Fort Huachuca, AZ [*OCLC symbol*]　(OCLC)	
Tr Zakavk Nauchno-Issled Gidrometeorol Inst ... Trudy Zakavkazskogo Nauchno-Issledovatel'skogo Gidrometeorologicheskogo Instituta [*A publication*]	
Tr Zapadno Sib Fil Akad Stroit Arkhit SSSR ... Trudy Zapadno-Sibirskii Filial Akademiya Stroitel'stva i Arkhitektury SSSR [*A publication*]	
TRZO .... Terrazzo [*Classified advertising*]　(ADA)	
Tr Zool Inst Akad Nauk SSSR ... Trudy Zoologicheskogo Instituta Akademiya Nauk SSSR [*A publication*]	
TS .... Air Benin [*Benin*] [*ICAO designator*]　(FAAC)	
TS .... Iraq [*Later, BZ*] [*License plate code assigned to foreign diplomats in the US*]	
Ts .... Skin Temperature [*Medicine*]	
TS .... [*The*] Steamboaters　(EA)	
Ts .... T Suppressor [*Cell*] [*Immunology*]	
TS .... Tailshaft Survey	
TS .... Tall Salicornia Zone [*Ecology*]	
TS .... Tangent to Spiral	

TS .... Tank Steamer	
TS .... Taoist Sanctuary [*Later, DS*]　(EA)	
TS .... Taper Shank [*Screw*]	
TS .... Taper Sided	
T/S .... Target Seeker	
TS .... Target Strength	
TS .... Task Statement　(MCD)	
TS .... Task-Switched [*Data processing*]　(BYTE)	
TS .... Tasto Solo [*Bass without Accompaniment*] [*Music*]	
TS .... Tax Shelter	
TS .... Taxis Services Proprietary Ltd. [*Australia*]	
TS .... Taxpayers' Society [*British*]	
TS .... Taylor-Schechter Collection. University Library [*Cambridge, England*]　(BJA)	
TS .... Teacher Survey	
TS .... Teachers Section [*Library Education Division*] [*American Library Association*]	
TS .... Team Supervisor　(FAAC)	
TS .... Technical School　(ADA)	
T and S ...... Technical and Scientific Information [*United Nations Development Program*]	
TS .... Technical Secretariat　(NATG)	
TS .... Technical Specification　(MCD)	
TS .... Technical Support　(NASA)	
TS .... Ted Smith Aircraft [*ICAO aircraft manufacturer identifier*]　(ICAO)	
TS .... Telecommunications System	
TS .... Telegraph System　(MSA)	
TS .... Television, Sound Channel	
TS .... Telophase Society [*Commercial firm*]　(EA)	
T-S .... Temperature-Salinity [*Oceanography*]	
TS .... Temperature Sensitive	
TS .... Temperature Switch	
TS .... Template Set-Up　(MCD)	
TS .... Temporal Stem [*Brain anatomy*]	
TS .... Ten Silhouettes [*Psychological testing*]	
TS .... Tennyson Society　(EA)	
TS .... Tensile Strength	
TS .... Tensile Stress	
TS .... Tentative Specification	
TS .... Teratology Society　(EA)	
TS .... Terminal [*or Greater*] Sensation	
TS .... Terminal Service	
TS .... Terminal Strip　(DEN)	
TS .... Terminal Student　(OICC)	
TS .... Terra Santa [*Jerusalem*] [*A publication*]　(BJA)	
TS .... Test Items [*JETDS nomenclature*] [*Military*]　(CET)	
TS .... Test Set　(KSC)	
TS .... Test Site [*NASA*]　(NASA)	
TS .... Test Solution [*of a chemical*] [*Medicine*]	
TS .... Test Specification　(MSA)	
T/S .... Test Stand　(AAG)	
TS .... Test Station [*NASA*]　(MCD)	
TS .... Test Stimulus	
TS .... Test Summary	
TS .... Textes Sogdiens. Edites. Traduits et Commentes [*A publication*]　(BJA)	
TS .... Texts and Studies [*Cambridge*] [*A publication*]　(BJA)	
TS .... Theatre Studies [*A publication*]	
TS .... Theatre Survey [*A publication*]	
TS .... Theological Studies [*A publication*]	
TS .... Theologische Studien [*Utrecht*] [*A publication*]　(BJA)	
TS .... Theosophical Society	
TS .... Thermal Microscope Stage	
TS .... Thermal Spray [*Also, THSP*] [*Coating technology*]	
TS .... Thermal Stethoscope [*Medical instrumentation*]	
TS .... Thermal Synchrotron [*High-energy physics*]	
TS .... Thermosetting [*Plastics technology*]	
TS .... Thermospray [*Also, TSP*] [*Ionization*] [*Physics*]	
T/S .... Third Stage [*Aerospace*]　(AAG)	
T & S .... Thomson and Steger's Tennessee Statutes [*A publication*]　(ILCA)	
TS .... Thoracic Surgery [*Medicine*]	
TS .... Thoreau Society　(EA)	
TS .... Threaded Stud	
TS .... Three Stooges Club　(EA)	
TS .... Thunderstorm [*Meteorology*]　(FAAC)	
TS .... Thymidylate Synthase [*Also, ThS*] [*An enzyme*]	
TS .... Thymostimulin [*Endocrinology*]	
T/S .... Thyroid:Serum [*Radioiodide ratio*]	
TS .... Tibet Society　(EA)	
TS .... Tide Surveyor [*British*]　(ROG)	
TS .... Tidewater Southern Railway Co. [*AAR code*]	
TS .... Tijdschrift voor Skandinanistiek [*A publication*]	
T v S .... Tijdschrift voor Strafrecht [*A publication*]	
TS .... Till Sale	
TS .... Time Scheduled　(NASA)	
TS .... Time Shack [*NAS operations desk*]	
TS .... Time Sharing [*Data processing*]	
TS .... Time Slot [*Telecommunications*]　(TEL)	
TS .... Time Switch　(MSA)	

TS	Timing Selector
TS	Timing System (MCD)
TS	Tip Speed
TS	Tippers [*Shipping*] (DCTA)
TS	Titan Society (EA)
T2S	Titration System Software [*Metter Instruments*]
TS	Today Show [*Television program*]
TS	Today's Speech [*A publication*]
TS	Tolkien Society [*Hove, East Sussex, England*] (EAIO)
TS	Toll Switching [*Trunk*] [*Telecommunications*] (TEL)
TS	Too Short [*Symbol stamped in shoes which are not actually of the size marked*]
TS	Tool Sharpness
TS	Tool Steel
TS	Tool Storage
TS	Tool Strength (ADA)
TS	Top Secret
TS	Top Spare
TS	Torch Soldering
TS	Torpedo Station (MCD)
TS	Torstar Corp. [*Toronto Stock Exchange symbol*]
Ts	Tosyl [*Also, Tos*] [*Organic chemistry*]
TS	Total Solids [*Medicine*]
TS	Totally Smutted [*Plant pathology*]
T and S	Touch and Stay
TS	Tough Situation [*Bowdlerized version*]
TS	Tough Stuff
TS	Tourette Syndrome [*Neurology*]
TS	Touring Sedan [*As in Olds 98 TS*]
TS	Tower Station
ts	Tracheosyringeal [*Neuroanatomy of birds*]
TS	Tracking Scope
TS	Tracking System (AAG)
TS	Trade Study (MCD)
TS	Trademark Society (EA)
TS	Traffic Superintendent [*British*] (DCTA)
TS	Trained Soldier [*British military*] (DMA)
TS	Training Ship
TS	Training Squadron [*British military*] (DMA)
TS	Transaction Services (MCD)
TS	Transfer Set
TS	Transient Source
TS	Transient State (AAG)
TS	Transient Synovitis [*Medicine*]
TS	Transit Storage
TS	Transmission Service [*Telecommunications*]
TS	Transmission Set
TS	Transmittal Sheet [*Military*]
TS	Transmitted Shock
TS	Transmitter Station
TS	Transplantation Society (EA)
TS	Transport Service (ROG)
TS	Transport Ship (ROG)
TS	Transport and Supply
TS	Transsexual [*Medicine*]
T/S	Transtage [*Upper stage for Titan III C rocket*]
TS	Transvaal Supreme Court Reports [*South Africa*] [*A publication*] (DLA)
TS	Transverse Section [*Medicine*]
TS	Transverse System [*Cytology*]
TS	Travel Supplement [*Publishing*]
TS	Travelling Showmen [*Public-performance tariff class*] [*British*]
TS	Treasury Solicitor [*British*]
TS	Treasury Stock
TS	Treatment System [*Nuclear energy*] (NRCH)
TS	Treaty Series [*A publication*] (ILCA)
TS	Tree Sparrow [*Ornithology*]
TS	Tres Sage [*Wisest*] [*Presiding officer in the French rite*] [*Freemasonry*]
TS	Tribology Series [*Elsevier Book Series*] [*A publication*]
TS	Tricuspid Stenosis [*Cardiology*]
TS	Trinidad Sector [*World War II*]
TS	Triple Strength
TS	Troubleshoot (MCD)
ts	Trucial States [*United Arab Emirates*] [*MARC country of publication code*] [*Library of Congress*] (LCCP)
TS	Trust Secretary
TS	Tub-Sized [*Paper*]
TS	Tube Sheet (MSA)
TS	Tuberous Sclerosis [*Medicine*]
TS	Tubular [*Tracheal*] Sound
TS	Tumor Specific [*Medicine*]
TS	Tuning Stability
TS	Tunisia [*Aircraft nationality and registration mark*] (FAAC)
ts	Turboshaft Engine (IEEE)
T/S	Turn-In Slip [*Military*]
TS	Turner Society [*London, England*] (EAIO)
T-S	Turonian-Santonian [*Paleontology*]
TS	Tutto Solo [*All by Itself*] [*Music*]
TS	Twin Screw (ADA)
TS	Two-Stage Least Squares [*Statistics*]
TS	Tyneside Scottish [*British military*] (DMA)
T & S	Type and Screen
TS	Type Specification
TS	Typescript
TS	United States Treaty Series [*A publication*] (DLA)
T2S	Technology Transfer Society (EA)
TSA	Aloha Airlines, Inc. [*Air carrier designation symbol*]
TSA	[*The*] Securities Association [*British*]
TSA	Tablettes Sumeriennes Archaiques [*A publication*] (BJA)
TSA	Taipei-Sung Shan [*Taiwan*] [*Airport symbol*] (OAG)
TSA	Tamworth Swine Association (EA)
TSA	Target Signature Analysis
TSA	Target System Alternatives (MCD)
TSA	Targhee Sheep Association (EA)
TSA	Tariff Schedules of the United States, Annotated
T & SA	Task and Skill Analysis (AAG)
TSA	Tasmanian School of Arts [*Australia*]
TSA	Tax-Sheltered Annuity
TSA	Teater SA. Quarterly for South African Theater [*A publication*]
TSA	Technical Supplemental Allowance [*Military*]
TSA	Technical Support Activity [*Army*] (RDA)
TSA	Technical Support Agent (MCD)
TSA	Technology Student Association (EA)
TSA	Tele-Systems Associates, Inc. [*Bloomington, MN*] [*Telecommunications service*] (TSSD)
TSA	Telegraph System Analyzer
TSA	Test Site Activation [*NASA*] (KSC)
TSA	Test Start Approval [*NASA*] (NASA)
TSA	Test Support Agent (MCD)
TSA	Texas Shrimp Association (EA)
TSA	Textile Salesmen's Association [*Defunct*] (EA)
TSA	Theater Service Area (MCD)
TS in A	Theosophical Society in America (EA)
TSA	Thermal Swing Adsorption [*Chemical engineering*]
TSA	Time Series Analysis
TSA	Time-Shared Amplifier
TSA	Time Slot Access
TSA	Time Study Analysis
TSA	Tolkien Society of America
TSA	Toluenesulfonic Acid [*Organic chemistry*]
TSA	Tom Skinner Associates (EA)
TSA	Tourette Syndrome Association (EA)
TSA	Track Subsystem Analyst (MUGU)
TSA	Track Supply Association
TSA	Training Services Agency [*Department of Employment*] [*British*]
TSA	Training Situation Analysis [*Navy*]
TSA	Training Support Agency [*Army*]
TSA	Trans America Industries [*Vancouver Stock Exchange symbol*]
TSA	Trans Sierra Airline [*Cupertino, CA*] [*FAA designator*] (FAAC)
TSA	Transition State Analog
TSA	Transportation Service, Army
TSA	Transportation Standardization Agency [*DoD*]
TSA	Transportation Stores Assignment [*British*]
TSA	Tripoli Science Association (EA)
TSA	Troop Support Agency [*Army*] (AABC)
TSA	Troubleshooting Aid (MCD)
TSA	Trypticase Soy Agar [*Cell growth medium*]
TSA	Tube Support Assembly [*Nuclear energy*] (NRCH)
TSA	Tuberous Sclerosis Association of Great Britain
TSA	Tumor-Specific Antigens [*Immunology*]
T2SA	Turkish Studies Association (EA)
TSA	Two-Step Antenna
TSA	Type-Specific Antibody [*Immunology*]
TSA	University of Texas, Health Science Center at San Antonio, San Antonio, TX [*OCLC symbol*] (OCLC)
TSAA	Tobacco Salesmen's Association of America (EA)
TSAA	Tuberous Sclerosis Association of America [*Also known as American Tuberous Sclerosis Association and Asociacion de Esclerosis Tuberosa de America*] (EA)
TSaab	Thyroid-Stimulating Autoantibody [*Endocrinology*]
TSAB	Theatre-Screen Advertising Bureau [*Defunct*]
TSAb	Thyroid-Stimulating Antibodies [*Endocrinology*]
TSABF	Troop Support Agency Bagger Fund (MCD)
TSAC	Target Signature Analysis Center (MCD)
TSAC	Testing Accessories (AAG)
TSAC	Time Slot Assignment Circuit [*Telecommunications*] (TEL)
TSAC	Title, Subtitle, and Caption
TSAC	Topographic Scientific Advisory Committee [*Terminated, 1973*] [*Army*] (EGAO)
TSAC	Tracking System Analytical Calibration
TSACA	Transactions. South African Institution of Civil Engineers [*A publication*]
TSAD	Test System Analysis Directorate [*Army*] (MCD)
TSAE	Training Support Activity - Europe (MCD)
TSAEA	Transactions. South African Institute of Electrical Engineers [*A publication*]
TSAF	Transportation Service for the Army in the Field (MCD)
TSAF	Typical System Acquisition Flow
TSAFA	Traffic Safety [*A publication*]
TSAG	Tracking System Analysis Group [*NASA*]

TSAG......... Trivalent Sodium Antimony Gluconate [*Pharmacology*]
TsAGI....... Tsentralyni Aero-Gidrodinamichescky Institute [*Institute of Aeronautical Research*] [*USSR*]
TSAK........ Test Stand Adapter Kit
TSAK........ Training Support Activity - Korea (MCD)
TSAM....... [*The*] Skill Alignment Module [*Army*] (INF)
TSAM....... Time Series Analysis and Modeling [*Software*]
TSAM....... Training Surface-to-Air Missile
TSamU ...... Trudy Samarkandskogo Gosudarstvennogo Universiteta Imeni Alisera Navoi [*A publication*]
TSAP........ Time Series Analysis Package
TSAR........ Telemetry System Application Requirements
TSAR........ Throttleable Solid Augmented Rocket (MCD)
TSAR........ Time Sows and Reaps [*Acronym used in name of Tsar Publishing Co.*]
TSAR........ Timed Scanned Array RADAR
TSAR........ TransAmerica Solar Auto Run [*In name of solar-powered car TSAR Phoenix*]
TSAR........ Transmission Security Analysis Report (AFM)
TSARC...... Test Schedule and Review Committee [*Army*] (AABC)
TSARCOM ... Troop Support and Aviation Materiel Readiness Command [*Army*]
TSAT........ Tube-Slide Agglutination Test [*Clinical chemistry*]
TSAU........ Time Slot Access Unit [*Telecommunications*] (TEL)
TSAZ........ Target Seeker-Azimuth
TSB........... [*The*] School Brigade [*Army*] (INF)
TSB........... Technical Service Bulletin
TSB........... Temporary Stowage Bag [*NASA*] (KSC)
TSB........... Terminal Status Block [*Data processing*] (IBMDP)
TSB........... Textiles Surveillance Body [*Textile trade agreement*]
TSB........... Theological Studies (Baltimore) [*A publication*]
TSB........... Thermally Stabilized Burner [*Engineering*]
TSB........... Thoreau Society. Bulletin [*A publication*]
TSb........... Thrust Section Blower (AAG)
TSb........... Tjurkologiceskij Sbornik [*A publication*]
TSB........... Towed SONAR Body
TSB........... Toxic Substances Bulletin [*A publication*]
TSB........... Trade Show Bureau (EA)
TSB........... Transportation Services Branch [*Air Force*]
TSB........... Trustee Savings Bank [*British*]
TSB........... Trypticase Soy Broth [*Cell growth medium*]
TSB........... Tsumeb [*Namibia*] [*Airport symbol*] (OAG)
TSB........... Twin Sideband
TSB........... Two Complete Science Adventure Books [*A publication*]
TSBA........ Transactions of the Society of Biblical Archaeology [*London*] [*A publication*] (BJA)
TSB(CI)..... Trustee Savings Bank (Channel Islands) [*British*]
TSBD........ Tracking Servobridge Detector (MCD)
TSBFA....... Traditional Siamese Breeders and Fanciers Association (EA)
TS-3 Bibliograf Informacija ... TS-3 Bibliografija Informacija [*A publication*]
TSBK........ Taunton Savings Bank [*Taunton, MA*] [*NASDAQ symbol*] (NQ)
TSBMD..... Tellus. Series B. Chemical and Physical Meteorology [*A publication*]
T S Booklet ... Thoreau Society. Booklet [*A publication*]
TSBUD...... Tennessee Survey of Business [*A publication*]
Ts BW P R ... Tijdschrift voor Bestuurswetenschappen en Publiek Recht [*A publication*]
TSBY......... Tuscola & Saginaw Bay Railway Co., Inc. [*AAR code*]
TSC........... Passed a Territorial Army Course in Staff Duties [*British*]
TSC........... Tactical Support Center
TSC........... Tanker Service Committee
TSC........... Tape Station Conversion (CET)
TSC........... Target Selection Console (MCD)
TSC........... Tarleton State College [*Later, TSU*] [*Texas*]
TSC........... Technical Services Corp. [*Burma*] (DS)
TSC........... Technical Standing Committee [*Australia*]
TSC........... Technical Subcommittee
TSC........... Technical Support Center [*Nuclear energy*] (NRCH)
TSC........... Techniscope Development [*Vancouver Stock Exchange symbol*]
TSC........... Teleconferencing Systems Canada Ltd. [*Etobicoke, ON*] [*Telecommunications service*] (TSSD)
TSC........... Teledyne Systems Corporation
TSC........... Telephone Software Connection, Inc.
TSC........... Television Scan Converter
TSC........... Terminal Sterilization Chamber
TSC........... Terrestrial Science Center (MCD)
tsc............. Territorial Staff Course [*British military*] (DMA)
TSC........... Test Acquisition Module Self Check (CAAL)
TSC........... Test Set Computer
TSC........... Test Set Connection
TSC........... Test Setup Complete [*NASA*] (NASA)
TSC........... Test Shipping Cask [*Nuclear energy*] (NRCH)
TSC........... Test Steering Committee [*Military*]
TSC........... Test Support Controller [*or Coordinator*] [*NASA*] (KSC)
TSC........... Texas Southmost College
TSC........... Thermal Stress Crack [*Plastics*]
TSC........... Thermal Surface Coating
TSC........... Thermally Stimulated Conductivity [*or Currents*]
TSC........... Thiosemicarbazide [*Organic chemistry*]

TSC........... Three-State Control [*Data processing*]
TSC........... Time Sharing Control Task [*Data processing*] (BUR)
TSC........... Tonic Sol-Fa College [*London*]
TSC........... Top Secret Control (MCD)
TSC........... Total System Control [*Architecture*]
TSC........... Total System Cost [*Aviation*]
TSC........... Totally Self-Checking
TSC........... Towson State University, Towson, MD [*OCLC symbol*] (OCLC)
TSC........... Training Support Center [*Army*] (MCD)
TSC........... Transit Switching Center [*Telecommunications*] (TEL)
TSC........... Transmitter Start Code [*Bell System*]
TSC........... Transportation Systems Center [*Department of Transportation*] [*Cambridge, MA*]
TSC........... Troop Support Command [*Formerly, MECOM*] [*Army*]
TSC........... Trouble-Shooting Checklist [*Test for academic institutions*]
TSC........... Tuscaloosa Oil & Gas [*Vancouver Stock Exchange symbol*]
TSCA........ Target Satellite Controlled Approach (MUGU)
TSCA........ Textile Supplies and Credit Association (EA)
TSCA........ TIGA Sailboard Class Association [*Defunct*] (EA)
TSCA........ Timing Single-Channel Analyzer
TSCA........ Tool Subcontract Authorization (AAG)
TSCA........ Top Secret Control Agency (MCD)
TSCA........ Toxic Substances Control Act [*1976*]
TSCA........ Traditional Small Craft Association (EA)
TSCAP ...... Thermally Stimulated Capacitance [*Photovoltaic energy systems*]
TSCAPP.... Toxic Substances Control Act Plant and Production Data [*Chemical Information Systems, Inc.*] [*Information service or system*]
TSCATS.... Toxic Substances Control Act Test Submissions [*Environmental Protection Agency*] [*Database*]
TSCC........ Telemetry Standards Coordination Committee
TSCC........ Test Support Control Center [*NASA*] (KSC)
TSCC........ Top Secret Control Channels [*Military*]
TSCC........ TSC Corporation [*NASDAQ symbol*] (NQ)
TSCD........ Test Specification and Criteria Document (MCD)
TSCD........ Tool Specification Control Drawing (MCD)
TSCDP...... Technical Service Career Development Program [*Military*]
TSCF .... Task Schedule Change Form [*Nuclear energy*] (NRCH)
TSCF .... Template Set-Up Check Fixture (MCD)
TSCF .... Top Secret Cover Folder (AAG)
TSCGD...... GRS [*Gesellschaft fuer Reaktorsicherheit*] Translations. Safety Codes and Guides [*A publication*]
Tschermaks Mineralog u Petrog Mitt ... Tschermaks Mineralogische und Petrographische Mitteilungen [*A publication*]
Tschermaks Mineral Petrogr Mitt ... Tschermaks Mineralogische und Petrographische Mitteilungen [*A publication*]
TSCHLT ... Test Support Center High-Level Terminal (CAAL)
Tsch Min Pe ... Tschermaks Mineralogische und Petrographische Mitteilungen [*A publication*]
TSCI .... Techscience Industries [*NASDAQ symbol*] (NQ)
TSCIXS ..... Tactical Support Center Information Exchange Subsystem
TSCLT....... Transportable Satellite Communications Link Terminal
TSCM........ Taylor Series Correction Method
TSCM........ Technical Surveillance Countermeasures [*Program*] [*Air Force*]
TSCM........ Test Station Configuration Model (MCD)
TSCN........ Trainer Specification Change Notice (MCD)
TSCO........ Test Support Coordination Office [*NASA*] (MCD)
TSCO........ Test Support Coordinator (NASA)
TSCO........ Top Secret Control Officer [*Military*]
TSCOM..... TS Communications [*Springfield, IL*] [*Telecommunications*] (TSSD)
TSCP .... Top Secret Control Proceeding [*Navy*]
TSCP .... Training Simulator Control Panel [*NASA*] (MCD)
TSCPA ...... Transactions and Studies. College of Physicians of Philadelphia [*A publication*]
TSCPAM .. Tentative Summary CPAM [*Military*] (CAAL)
TSCR .... Telecom Securitor Cellular Radio Ltd. [*British*]
TSCRA...... Texas and Southwestern Cattle Raisers Association (EA)
TSCRS...... Teacher's Self-Control Rating Scale
TSCS .... Tactical Satellite Communications System [*Air Force*] (CET)
TSCS .... Tactical Software Control Site [*Missile system evaluation*] (RDA)
TSCS .... Tennessee Self-Concept Scale [*Psychology*]
TSCS .... Top Secret Control Section [*Navy*]
TSCT .... Transportable Satellite Communications Terminal
TSCVT ..... TACSATCOM Single Channel Vehicular Terminal System (MCD)
TSCVT ..... Thomas Self-Concept Values Test [*Psychology*]
TSCW....... Top Secret Codeword (MCD)
TSD .... Tactical Situation Display
TSD .... Tactical and Staff Duties [*British military*] (DMA)
TSD .... TARAN [*Tactical Attack RADAR and Navigation*] System Data
TSD .... Target Skin Distance
TSD .... Tay-Sachs Disease [*Medicine*]
TSD .... Technical Support Document
TSD .... Temperature-Dependent Sex Determination
TSD .... Temperature-Salinity-Density-Depth [*Oceanography*]

TSD .... Tertiary of the Order of St. Dominic [*Roman Catholic religious order*]
TSD .... Test Start Date [*NASA*]   (NASA)
TSD .... Theater Shipping Document [*Military*]
TSD .... Theory of Signal Detection
TSD .... Thermally Stimulated Depolarization [*Chemistry*]
TSD .... Thermionic Specific Detector [*Analytical instrumentation*]
TSD .... Third-Degree Stochastic Dominance [*Agricultural statistics*]
TSD .... Time-Speed-Distance [*Driving skills*]
TSD .... Time Synchronization Device
TSD .... Torque Screwdriver
TSD .... Total Spectral Density
TSD .... Track Situation Display
TSD .... Traffic Situation [*Status*] Display
TSD .... Transient Signal Detector
TSD .... Transportation Stores Depot [*British military*]   (DMA)
TSD .... Treatment, Storage, or Disposal [*Hazardous waste management*]
TSD .... Triple-Sequence Diffusion
TSD .... Tubeless Steel Disc [*Wheel*] [*Automotive engineering*]
TSD .... United States Army TRADOC, Fort Devens, USAISD, Fort Devens, MA [*OCLC symbol*]   (OCLC)
TSDA........ Theory of Signal Detection Analysis
TSDB........ SCB [*Statistika Centralbyran*] Time Series Data Base [*Sweden*] [*Information service or system*]   (CRD)
TSDC........ Tennessee State Data Center [*Tennessee State Planning Office*] [*Nashville*] [*Information service or system*]   (IID)
TSDC........ Thermally Stimulated Discharge Current [*Voltage-induced polarization*]
TSDD .... Temperature-Salinity-Density-Depth   (IEEE)
TSDF........ Tactical Software Development Facility
TSDF........ Target System Data File
TSDF........ Treatment, Storage, and Disposal Facility [*Hazardous waste*]
TS-DHFR ... Thymidylate Synthetase Dihydrofolate Reductase [*Biochemistry*]
TSDI .... Tactical Situation Display Indicator
TSDK........ Torque Screwdriver Kit
TSDL........ Tuebingen Studien zur Deutschen Literatur [*A publication*]
TSDM....... Time-Shared Data Management [*System*] [*Data processing*]   (IEEE)
TS/DMS ... Time-Shared/Data Management System
TSDOS..... Time-Shared Disk Operating System [*Data processing*]   (IEEE)
T/SDPS..... Tube/Sea Differential Pressure Subsystem
TSDR........ Treatment, Storage, Disposal, or Recycling [*Hazardous waste management*]
TSDS .... Technological Services Delivery System [*UNIDO*]
TSDS .... Two-Speed Destroyer Sweeper [*Military*]
TSDTA ...... Tenside-Detergents [*A publication*]
TSDU .... Target System Data Update
TS D/W ..... Tons Deadweight   (DS)
TSE............ Memphis, TN [*Location identifier*] [*FAA*]   (FAAL)
TSE............ Tactical Support Element   (AFM)
TSE............ Tactical Support Equipment [*Military*]   (MCD)
TSE............ Target State Estimator   (MCD)
TSE............ Target Support Element   (MCD)
TSE............ Technical Support Effort
TSE............ Technical Support Equipment
TSE............ Tender Support Equipment
TSE............ Terminal Source Editor
TSE............ Test Scoring Equipment
TSE............ Test Set Electrical
TSE............ Test of Spoken English
TSE............ Test Support Equipment [*NASA*]
TSE............ Testicular Self-Examination
TSE............ Texas South-Eastern Railroad Co. [*AAR code*]
TSE............ Texas Studies in English [*A publication*]
TSE............ Tokyo Stock Exchange [*Japan*]
TSE............ Toronto Stock Exchange [*Toronto, ON*]
TSE............ Total Subsystem Evaluation
TSE............ Transmission Secondary Emission [*Physics*]
TSE............ Transportation Support Equipment   (NASA)
TSE............ Tulane Studies in English [*A publication*]
TSE............ Turboshaft Engine
TSEA........ Training Subsystem Effectiveness Analysis
TSEC........ Taft Sanitary Engineering Center
TSEC........ Telecommunications Security [*Army*]   (AABC)
TSEC........ Terminal Secondary RADAR Beacon [*Aviation*]   (FAAC)
TSEC........ Top Secret   (MCD)
TSEC........ Transierra Explorations Corporation [*NASDAQ symbol*]   (NQ)
TSED........ Training Simulators Engineering Department
TSEE .... Test Support Equipment Evaluation   (MCD)
TSEE .... Thermally Stimulated Exoelectron Emission [*Dosimetry*]
TSEG .... Tactical Satellite Communications Executive Steering Group
TSEG .... Toronto Stock Exchange - Gold
TS-EI .... Thermospray-Electron Ionization [*Chemistry*]
TSEI .... Toronto Stock Exchange - Industrials
TSEI .... Transportation Safety Equipment Institute   (EA)
Tselliul Bum Karton ... Tselliuloza, Bumaga, i Karton [*USSR*] [*A publication*]
TSEM........ Toronto Stock Exchange - Mines
TSEM........ Transmission Secondary Emission Multiplier [*Physics*]

Tsem Rastvory Krepleniya Glubokikh Skvazhin ... Tsementnye Rastvory dlya Krepleniya Glubokikh Skvazhin [*A publication*]
Tsentr Nauchno Issled Dizel'n Inst Tr ... Tsentral'nyi Nauchno-Issledovatel'skii Dizel'nyi Institut Trudy [*A publication*]
Tsentr Nauchno-Issled Inst Bum Sbor Tr ... Tsentral'nyi Nauchno-Issledovatel'skii Institut Bumagi Sbornik Trudov [*A publication*]
Tsentr Nauchno-Issled Inst Olovyannoi Promsti Nauchny Tr ... Tsentral'nyi Nauchno-Issledovatel'skii Institut Olovyannoi Promyshlennosti Nauchnye Trudy [*A publication*]
Tsentr Nauchno-Issled Inst Tekhnol Mashinostr Sb ... Tsentral'nyi Nauchno-Issledovatel'skii Institut Tekhnologii i Mashinostroeniya Sbornik [*A publication*]
Tsentr Ref Med Zh Ser A ... Tsentral'nyi Referativnyi Meditsinskii Zhurnal. Seriya A. Biologiya, Teoreticheskie Problemy Meditsiny [*A publication*]
Tsentr Ref Med Zh Ser B ... Tsentral'nyi Referativnyi Meditsinskii Zhurnal. Seriya B. Vnutrennye Bolezni [*A publication*]
Tsentr Ref Med Zh Ser G ... Tsentral'nyi Referativnyi Meditsinskii Zhurnal. Seriya G. Mikrobiologiya, Gigiena, i Sanitariya [*A publication*]
Tsentr Ref Med Zh Ser V ... Tsentral'nyi Referativnyi Meditsinskii Zhurnal. Seriya V. Khirurgiya [*A publication*]
TSEO........ Toronto Stock Exchange - Oils
TSEQ........ Time Sequenced [*NASA*]   (KSC)
T & SER.... Tilbury & Southend Railway [*British*]   (ROG)
TSERR ...... Type of Leaf Serration [*Botany*]
TSES .... Technical Simulation and Evaluation System
TSES .... Transportable Satellite Earth Station
TSESG....... Tactical Satellite Executive Steering Group
TSewU....... University of the South, Sewanee, TN [*Library symbol*] [*Library of Congress*]   (LCLS)
TSewU-T ... University of the South, School of Theology, Sewanee, TN [*Library symbol*] [*Library of Congress*]   (LCLS)
TSF............ Tab Sequence Format
TSF............ Tactical Strike Fighter   (MCD)
TSF............ Telephone Service Fitting
TSF............ Ten-Statement FORTRAN [*Data processing*]   (IEEE)
TSF............ Ten Story Fantasy [*A publication*]
TSF............ Terminal Sterilization Facility
TSF............ Test Aankoop [*A publication*]
TSF............ Tetraselenofulvalene [*Organic chemistry*]
TSF............ Textured Soy Flour
TSF............ Thai Support Foundation   (EA)
TSF............ Theological Students Fellowship   (EA)
TSF............ Theological Students Fellowship. Bulletin [*A publication*]
TSF............ Thermally Stable Fuel   (MCD)
TSF............ Thin Solid Films   (IEEE)
TSF............ Thrombopoietic Stimulating Factor [*Medicine*]
TSF............ Tower Shielding Facility [*Nuclear energy*]
TSF............ Track Synthesis Frequency
TSF............ Transverse Shear Force
TSF............ Treasury Security Force [*Department of the Treasury*]
TSF............ Tri-State Flite Services, Inc. [*Dubuque, IA*] [*FAA designator*]   (FAAC)
TSF............ Triceps Skinfold [*Medicine*]
TSF............ Truncation Safety Factor [*In biological systems*]
TSF............ Two-Seater Fighter [*Air Force*] [*British*]
TSFA .... Two-Step Formal Advertising   (MCD)
TSF Bul .... TSF [*Theological Students Fellowship*] Bulletin [*A publication*]
TSFC .... Tactical Support Functional Components   (NVT)
TSFC .... Thrust Specific Fuel Consumption
TSFC .... Tom Sneva Fan Club   (EA)
TSFC .... Tribune/Swab-Fox Companies, Inc. [*Tulsa, OK*] [*NASDAQ symbol*]   (NQ)
TSFC .... Twisted Sister Fan Club   (EA)
TSFET...... Theater Service Forces, European Theater [*World War II*]
TSFMES ... Thomas Say Foundation. Monographs [*A publication*]
TSFO........ Training Set, Fire Observation   (MCD)
TSFO........ Transportation Support Field Office [*Federal disaster planning*]
TSFR .... Transfer   (AFM)
TSFS......... Trunk Servicing Forecasting System [*Telecommunications*]   (TEL)
TSFSOILITU ... [*The*] Search for Signs of Intelligent Life in the Universe [*Lily Tomlin one-woman show written by Jane Wagner*]
TSFSR....... Transcaucasian Soviet Federation Socialist Republic
TSFTA....... Trudy Sibirskogo Fiziko-Tekhnicheskogo Instituta pri Tomskom Gosudarstvennom Universitete [*A publication*]
TSG........... [*The*] Stelle Group   (EA)
TSG........... [*The*] Surgeon General [*Army*]
TSG........... Tanacross, AK [*Location identifier*] [*FAA*]   (FAAL)
TSG........... Technical Specialty Group [*AIAA*]
TSG........... Technical Steering Group   (OICC)
TSG........... Technical Subgroup   (NATG)
TSG........... Technology Support Group
TSG........... Territorial Support Group [*Scotland Yard*] [*British*]
TSG........... Test Signal Generator
TSG........... Test and Switching Gear [*NASA*]   (KSC)
TSG........... Time Signal Generator
TSG........... Timeslot Generator [*Telecommunications*]   (TEL)
TSG........... Timing Systems Group [*NASA*]

TSG............	Tracking Signal Generator
TSG............	Transglobe Resources [*Vancouver Stock Exchange symbol*]
TSG............	Transport Supplement Grant [*British*]
TSG............	Transversely Adjusted Gap (IEEE)
TSG............	Travel Security Guide [*Control Risks Information Services - CRIS*] [*London, England*] [*Information service or system*] (IID)
TSG............	Tri-Service Group [*NATO*]
TSG............	Troubleshooting Guide (MCD)
TSG............	Truebner's Simplified Grammars [*A publication*]
TSG............	United States Army TRADOC, Fort Gordon, United States Army Signal School and Fort Gordon, Fort Gordon, GA [*OCLC symbol*] (OCLC)
TSGA.........	Three-Conductor, Shipboard, General Use, Armor Cable
TSGAD.....	Tri-Service Group on Air Defense [*NATO*] (NATG)
TSGB........	Tensor Society of Great Britain
TSGCEE....	Tri-Service Group on Communications and Electronic Equipment [*NATO*] (NATG)
TSGF........	T-Suppressor-Cell Growth Factor [*Immunology*]
TSGMS.....	Test Set Guided Missile Set [*or System*]
TSGP........	Test Sequence Generator Program [*European Space Research and Technology Center*] (NASA)
TSGR........	Thunderstorm with Hail [*Meteorology*]
TSGS........	Time Series Generation System
TSGT........	Technical Sergeant [*Military*]
TSGT........	Throgmorton Secured Growth Trust [*Commercial firm*] [*British*]
TSGT(C)....	Technical Sergeant (Commissary) [*Marine Corps*]
TsGw.........	Tydskrif vir Geesteswetenskappe [*A publication*]
TSH...........	Temperature Switch, High [*Nuclear energy*] (NRCH)
TSH	Their Serene Highnesses
TSH	Thermodynamic Suppression Head
TSH	Thyroid-Stimulating Hormone [*Thyrotrophin*] [*Also, TTH*] [*Endocrinology*]
TSH	Tijdschrift voor Sociale Hygiene [*A publication*]
TSH	Toluenesulfonyl Hydrazide [*Organic chemistry*]
TSh	Torah Shelemah [*A publication*] (BJA)
TSH	TSC Shannock Corp. [*Toronto Stock Exchange symbol*] [*Vancouver Stock Exchange symbol*]
TSH	Tshikapa [*Zaire*] [*Airport symbol*] (OAG)
TSHC	Two-Stage Hydrocracker [*Chemical engineering*]
TSHIDP	Tsurumi University Dental Journal [*A publication*]
TSHIRTS ...	TSHIRTS: the Society Handling the Interchange of Remarkable T-Shirts (EA)
TSHR	Thyrotropin-Stimmulating Hormone Receptor [*Endocrinology*]
TSHWR.....	Thundershower [*Meteorology*] (FAAC)
TSI...........	Target Signature Investigation
TSI...........	Tax Shelter Insider [*Newsletter Management Corp.*] [*Defunct*] [*Information service or system*] (CRD)
TSI...........	Tayson Systems, Inc. [*Telecommunications service*] (TSSD)
TSI...........	Technical Standardization Inspection [*Military*]
TSI...........	Technology and Science of Informatics [*A publication*]
TSI...........	Telebase Systems, Incorporated [*Information service or system*] (IID)
TSI...........	Teleconferencing Systems International, Inc. [*Elk Grove Village, IL*] (TSSD)
TSI...........	Teleguard System International [*Vancouver Stock Exchange symbol*]
TSI...........	Television Services International [*British*]
TSI...........	[*Degangi-Berk*] Test of Sensory Integration
TSI...........	Test of Social Insight [*Psychology*]
TSI...........	Test Support Instructions [*NASA*] (KSC)
TSI...........	Tests of Social Intelligence [*Psychology*]
TSI...........	Theological School Inventory [*Psychology*]
TSI...........	Threshold Signal-to-Interference Ratio (IEEE)
TSI...........	Threshold Soot Index
TSI...........	Thyroid-Stimulating Immunoglobulin [*Endocrinology*]
TSI...........	Time-Significant Item (MCD)
TSI...........	Time Slot Interchange [*Telecommunications*] (TEL)
TSI...........	Time Sterile Indicator
TSI...........	Tons per Square Inch (MCD)
TSI...........	Total Sum Insured (AIA)
TSI...........	Trans-Service Inc., Bala-Cynwyd PA [*STAC*]
TSI...........	Transmitting Subscriber Information [*Data processing*]
TSI...........	Transport Studies and Inquiries [*British*]
TSI...........	Transportation Safety Institute [*Department of Transportation*]
TSI...........	Triad Systems Integration Corp.
TSI...........	Triple Sugar-Iron [*Agar*] [*Microbiology*]
tsi	Tsimshian [*MARC language code*] [*Library of Congress*] (LCCP)
TSI...........	Turbo Sport Intercooler [*Automotive engineering*]
TSI...........	Turkish Standards Institution
TSIA	Trading Stamp Institute of America (EA)
TSIA	Triple Sugar-Iron Agar [*Microbiology*]
TSIAJ........	This Scherzo Is a Joke [*Used by American composer Charles Edward Ives*]
TSIC	Transducer Systems, Incorporated [*NASDAQ symbol*] (NQ)
TSID.........	Track Sector Identification
TSIE	Transformed Special Index of the External Standard [*Scintillation analysis*]
TSIFL........	Trade Society of Iron Foundry Labourers [*A union*] [*British*]

T/SIG	Turn Signal [*Automotive engineering*]
TSIGA	Trudy Sibirskogo Nauchno-Issledovatel'skogo Instituta Geologii, Geofiziki, i Mineral'nogo Syr'ya [*A publication*]
TSII	TSI, Incorporated [*NASDAQ symbol*] (NQ)
TSIL	Time-Significant Item List (AAG)
TSIM	(Trimethylsilyl)imidazole [*Also, TMSIM*] [*Organic chemistry*]
TSIMS.......	Telemetry Simulation Submodule
TSIN.........	Total Soluble Inorganic Nitrogen [*Analytical chemistry*]
TSIN..........	Transgenic Sciences, Inc. [*NASDAQ symbol*] (NQ)
TSIO..........	Time-Shared Input/Output [*Data processing*]
TSI-OH	Tube Sheet Inlet and Outlet Head (MSA)
TSIR	Total System Integration Responsibility
Tsirk Shemakh Astrofiz Obs ...	Tsirkulyar Shemakhinskoi Astrofizicheskoi Observatorii [*Azerbaidzhan SSR*] [*A publication*]
TSIS..........	Total Specifications Information System
TSIT	Technical Service Intelligence Team [*Military*]
TsIT	Tijdschrift voor Indische Taal-, Land-, en Volkenkunde [*A publication*]
TSITA	Tsitologiya [*A publication*]
Tsititiksiny Sovrem Med ...	Tsititiksiny e Sovremennoi Meditsine [*A publication*]
Tsitol..........	Tsitologiya [*A publication*]
Tsitol Genet ...	Tsitologiya i Genetika [*A publication*]
Tsitol Genet Akad Nauk Ukr SSR ...	Tsitologiya i Genetika. Akademiya Nauk Ukrainsoi SSR [*A publication*]
Tsitologiya Genet ...	Tsitologiya i Genetika [*A publication*]
TSIU	Telephone System Interface Unit
TSJ	Toxic Substances Journal [*A publication*]
TSJ	Tsushima [*Japan*] [*Airport symbol*] (OAG)
TSJC..........	Trinidad State Junior College [*Colorado*]
TSJSN.......	Transactions. Samuel Johnson Society of the Northwest [*A publication*]
TSJSNW ...	Transactions. Samuel Johnson Society of the Northwest [*A publication*]
Ts Jur Foer Finland ...	Tidskrift Utgiven av Juridiska Foereningen i Finland [*A publication*]
TSK...........	Computer Task Group, Inc. [*NYSE symbol*] (SPSG)
TSK...........	Fort Hamilton Post Library, Morale Support Activities, Brooklyn, NY [*OCLC symbol*] (OCLC)
TSK...........	Task
TSK...........	Theologische Studien und Kritiken [*A publication*]
TSK...........	Time Shift Keying
TSK...........	Torque Screwdriver Kit
TSK...........	Tsukuba - Telemeter [*Japan*] [*Seismograph station code, US Geological Survey*] (SEIS)
Ts Kad Lmk ...	Tijdschrift voor Kadaster en Landmeetkunde [*A publication*]
TSKHAY...	Bulletin. Freshwater Fisheries Research Laboratory [*Tokyo*] [*A publication*]
TSKT	Test Kit (AAG)
TSKTA	Toyo Shokuhin Kogyo Tanki Daigaku. Toyo Shokuhin Kenkyusho Kenkyu Hokokusho [*A publication*]
TSKZA	Tekhnika v Sel'skom Khozyaistve [*A publication*]
TSL...........	Chicago, IL [*Location identifier*] [*FAA*] (FAAL)
TSL...........	[*The*] Software Link, Inc. [*Software manufacturer*]
TSL...........	Temporary Storage Location
TSL...........	Tennessee Studies in Literature [*A publication*]
TSL...........	Test Set Logic
TSL...........	Test Source Library
TSL...........	Test Stand Level (AAG)
TSL...........	Test Support List (CAAL)
TSL...........	Texas Short Line Railway [*AAR code*]
TSL...........	Thin Shock Layer
TSL...........	Top of Slab [*Technical drawings*]
TSL...........	Torsatron/Stellarator Laboratory [*University of Wisconsin - Madison*] [*Research center*] (RCD)
TSL...........	Total Service Life [*Telecommunications*] (TEL)
TSL...........	Trans Siberian Landbridge (DS)
TSL...........	Travaux. Classe I de Linguistique, de Litterature, et de Philosophie. Societe des Sciences et des Lettres de Lodz [*A publication*]
TSL...........	Triservice LASER
TSL...........	Tristate Logic [*Electronics*]
TSL...........	Troop Safety Line
TSL...........	Troubleshooting Loop
TSL...........	Tsaile [*Navajo Community College*] [*Arizona*] [*Seismograph station code, US Geological Survey*] (SEIS)
TSL...........	Two-Stage Liquefaction [*Chemical engineering*]
TSL...........	Typesetting Lead (MSA)
TSL...........	United States Army TRADOC, Defense Language Institute, Presidio of Monterey, CA [*OCLC symbol*] (OCLC)
TSLAET	Technician of the Society of Licensed Aircraft Engineers and Technologists [*British*] (DBQ)
TS Lang	Typological Studies in Language [*A publication*]
TSLCC-E...	Total System Life Cycle Cost-Effectiveness
TSLCN	Texas State Library Communication Network [*Library network*]
TSLD.........	Troubleshooting Logic Diagram (NASA)
TSLI	Time Since Last Inspection (MCD)
TSLI	TSL, Inc. [*NASDAQ symbol*] (NQ)
TS Lit........	Trierer Studien zur Literatur [*A publication*]
Ts LJ.........	Tulsa Law Journal [*A publication*]

TSLL	Texas Studies in Literature and Language [*A publication*]
TSLS	Triservice LASER Seeker [*DoD*]
TSLS	Two-Stage Least Squares [*Statistics*]
TSM	Methodist Theological School in Ohio, Delaware, OH [*OCLC symbol*] (OCLC)
TSM	Tactical Survey Meter
TSM	Tail Service Mast [*NASA*] (KSC)
TSM	Tandem Scanning Microscope
TSM	Target Signature Model
TSM	Target-to-Surface-to-Missile Path
TSM	Tentative Standard Method [*of analysis*]
TSM	Terminal Support Module
TSM	Tesoro Sacro-Musical [*A publication*]
TSM	Test Site Manager [*Army*]
TSM	Test Standards Module
TSM	Test Support Manager [*NASA*] (KSC)
TSM	Texte des Spaeten Mittelalters [*A publication*]
TSM	Time Scheduled Maintenance
TSM	Time-Shared Monitor System [*Data processing*] (IEEE)
TSM	Ton Statute Mile (AAG)
TSM	Total Scheduled Maintenance [*Army*]
TSM	Total Suspended Matter [*Environmental science*]
TSM	Total System Management Concept (MCD)
TSM	Trade Study Management (NASA)
TSM	TRADOC System Manager [*Army*]
TSM	Training and Doctrine Command System Manager [*Army*] (MCD)
TSM	Training Site Manager (MCD)
TSM	Training System Manager (MCD)
TSM	Transportation Systems Management
TSM	Trends. Financieel Economisch Magazine [*A publication*]
TSM	Tri-State Motor Transit Co. of Delaware [*AMEX symbol*] (SPSG)
TSM	Troop Sergeant-Major [*British military*] (DMA)
TSM	Type, Series, and Model (MCD)
TSM	Type-Specific M (Protein) [*Immunology*]
TSMC	Technical Supply Management Code
TSMC	Transportation Supply and Maintenance Command
TSMDA	Test-Section Melt-Down Accident [*Nuclear energy*] (NRCH)
TSMDAL ..	Trudy Sverdlovskogo Gosudarstvennogo Meditsinskogo Instituta [*A publication*]
TSMG	Thompson Submachine Gun
TSMNO	Transmitting Capability Out of Service (FAAC)
TSMO	TACSATCOM Management Office
TSMO	TRADOC Systems Management Office [*Military*] (RDA)
TSMOK	Transmitting Capability Returned to Service (FAAC)
TSMRD9 ..	Canada. Fisheries and Marine Service. Resource Development Branch. Maritimes Region Technical Report. Series Mar-T [*A publication*]
TSMS	Tobacco Strippers Mutual Society [*A union*] [*British*]
TSMT	Transmit
TSMTS	Tri-State Motor Tariff Service
TSMYDU ...	Thailheimer's Synthetic Methods of Organic Chemistry. Yearbook [*A publication*]
TSN	[*The*] Sports Network [*Cable-television system*] [*Information service or system*] (IID)
TSN	Tailshaft Renewed
TSN	Tan Son Nhut [*Air base*] [*Vietnam*]
TSN	Tape Serial Number [*Data processing*]
TSN	Tecsyn International, Inc. [*Toronto Stock Exchange symbol*]
TSN	Temporary Sort Number [*Data processing*]
TSN	Test Sequence Network (CAAL)
TSN	Thymosin [*A thymus hormone*]
TSN	Tianjin [*China*] [*Airport symbol*] (OAG)
TSN	Time since New [*Navy*] (NG)
TSN	Traffic Safety Now (EA)
TSN	Trimethoprim, Sulfamethoxazole, Nystatin [*Medicine*]
TSN	Tsingtau [*Republic of China*] [*Seismograph station code, US Geological Survey*] (SEIS)
TSN	United States Army TRADOC, Fort Wadsworth, Chaplains Center Library, Fort Wadsworth, NY [*OCLC symbol*] (OCLC)
TSNA	Tobacco-Specific Nitrosamine [*Biochemistry*]
TsNAG	Tijdschrift. Koninklijk Nederlandsch Aardrijkskundig Genootschap [*A publication*]
TSNG	Tseng Labs, Inc. [*Newtown, PA*] [*NASDAQ symbol*] (NQ)
TSNGA	Trudy. Sredneaziatskii Nauchno-Issledovatel'skii Institut Geologii i Mineral'nogo Syr'ya [*A publication*]
TSNI	(Toluenesulfonyl)nitroimidazole [*Organic chemistry*]
TSNL Index Series ...	Texas System of Natural Laboratories. Index Series [*A publication*]
TSNSDH...	US National Oceanic and Atmospheric Administration. Northeast Fisheries Center Sandy Hook Laboratory. Technical Series Report [*A publication*]
TSNT	(Toluenesulfonyl)nitrotriazole [*Organic chemistry*]
TSNT	Transient (FAAC)
TsNTL	Tijdschrift voor Nederlandsche Taal- en Letterkunde [*A publication*]
TSO	Carrollton, OH [*Location identifier*] [*FAA*] (FAAL)
TSo	Fayette County Free Library, Somerville, TN [*Library symbol*] [*Library of Congress*] (LCLS)

TSO	Information Society [*A publication*]
TSO	Isles Of Scilly-Tresco [*Airport symbol*] (OAG)
TSO	Table Structure Overview [*NASA*]
TSO	Tactical Surveillance Officer (MCD)
TSO	Technical Service Organization [*A generic term*]
TSO	Technical Specification Order
TSO	Technical Staff Officer
TSO	Technical Standard Order [*FAA*]
TSO	Technical Standing Order (KSC)
TSO	Technical Support Organization [*AEC*]
TSO	Telecommunications Service Order [*Telecommunications*] (TEL)
TSO	Telephone Service Observation [*Telecommunications*] (TEL)
TSO	Terminator Sensor Output
TSO	Tesoro Petroleum Corp. [*NYSE symbol*] (SPSG)
TSO	Test Site Office [*NASA*]
TSO	Test Support Operations [*NASA*] (KSC)
TSO	Thrust Section Observer (AAG)
TSO	Time-Sharing Option [*Data processing*]
TSO	Time Since Overhaul [*of engine, or other equipment*]
TSO	Town Suboffice
TSO	Trans Southern Airways [*Florence, SC*] [*FAA designator*] (FAAC)
TSO	Transportation Supply Officer [*Military*]
TSO	Tulsa [*Oklahoma*] [*Seismograph station code, US Geological Survey*] [*Closed*] (SEIS)
TSOA	Technical Standard Order Authorization (MCD)
TSOA	Triumph Sports Owners Association (EA)
T Soc R	Tijdschrift voor Sociaal Recht en van de Arbeidsgerechten [*A publication*]
T Soc Rheol ...	Transactions. Society of Rheology [*A publication*]
TSODB	Time Series Oriented Database
TSOET	Tests of Elementary Training [*Military*] [*British*]
TSOF	TSO Financial Corp. [*Wilmington, DE*] [*NASDAQ symbol*] (NQ)
TSOL	[*The*] Sound of London [*Record label*]
TSOL	True Sounds of Liberty [*Musical group*]
TSOP	[*The*] Sound of Philadelphia [*Song*]
TSOP	Tactical Standing Operating Procedure [*Army*]
TSOP	Technical Standard Operating Procedure [*NASA*] (KSC)
TSOP	Thin Small-Outline Package [*Data processing*]
TSOR	Tentative Specific Operational Requirement [*Military*]
TSORT	Transmission System Optimum Relief Tool [*Telecommunications*] (TEL)
TSOS	Time-Sharing Operating System [*Data processing*] (IEEE)
TSOSC	Test Set Operational Signal Converter (AAG)
TSP	[*The*] Sentencing Project (EA)
TSP	Teaspoonful (GPO)
TSP	Technical Specification
TSP	Technical Support Package [*NASA*]
TSP	Tehachapi, CA [*Location identifier*] [*FAA*] (FAAL)
TSP	Telemetry Simulation Program
TSP	Telephone Switching Planning (ADA)
TSP	Teleprocessing Services Program [*General Service Administration*]
TSP	Telesphere Communications, Inc. [*AMEX symbol*] (SPSG)
TSP	Temperature-Sensitive Period
TSP	Temporary Standard Practice [*or Procedure*] (AAG)
TSP	Test Site Position [*NASA*] (KSC)
TSP	Test Software Program [*NASA*] (NASA)
TSP	Test Status Panel (MCD)
TSP	Test Support Package
TSP	Test Support Plan [*Army*]
TSP	Test Support Position
TSP	Test Support Program
TSP	Tesuque Peak [*New Mexico*] [*Seismograph station code, US Geological Survey*] (SEIS)
TSP	Textured Soy Protein [*Food industry*]
TSP	Thermospray [*Also, TS*] [*Ionization*] [*Physics*]
TSP	Theta Sigma Phi [*Later, Women in Communications*]
TSP	Threat Support Plan (MCD)
TSP	Thrombospondin [*or Thrombin-Sensitive Protein*] [*Hematology*]
TSP	Thyroid-Stimulating Hormone of the Prepituitary Gland [*Endocrinology*]
TSP	Time Sorting Program
TSP	Time and Space Processing (MCD)
TSP	Toronto Sun Publishing Corp. [*Toronto Stock Exchange symbol*]
TSP	Torpedo Seaplane [*Navy*]
TSP	Torpedo Setting Panel [*Military*] (CAAL)
TSP	Total Serum Protein [*Medicine*]
TSP	Total Suspended Particulates
TSP	Total Systems Performance [*MODCOMP*]
TSP	Traffic Service Position [*Telephone*]
TSP	Trans Penn Airlines [*Reedsville, PA*] [*FAA designator*] (FAAC)
TSP	Transponder
TSP	Transshipment Point (AFM)
TSP	Traveling Salesman Problem [*Mathematics*]
TSP	Traveling Scholar Program (EA)

TSP............	Trial Shot Point
TSP............	Tribal Sovereignty Program [*Later, SGFID*] (EA)
TSP............	Trimethylsilyl Propionate [*Organic chemistry*]
TSP............	Triple-Super Phosphates
TSP............	Triservice Program [*Military*]
TSP............	Trisodium Phosphate [*Inorganic chemistry*]
TSP............	Tropical Spastic Paraparesis [*Neurology*]
TSP............	Tube Support Plate [*Nuclear energy*] (NRCH)
TSP............	Tulane Studies in Philosophy [*A publication*]
TSP............	Twisted Shielded Pairs [*Cables*] (NASA)
TSP............	United States Army TRADOC, Carlisle Barracks, Carlisle Barracks, PA [*OCLC symbol*] (OCLC)
TSPA........	Triethylenethiophosphoramide [*Also, THioTEPA*] [*Antineoplastic drug*]
TSPAC......	Transpacific (FAAC)
TSPAK......	Time Series Package [*Bell System*]
TSPC........	Thermal Sciences and Propulsion Center [*Purdue University*] [*Research center*] (RCD)
TSPC........	Toxic Substances Priority Committee [*Terminated, 1984*] [*Environmental Protection Agency*] (EGAO)
TSPC........	Tropical Stored Products Centre [*Tropical Products Institute*] [*Overseas Development Administration*] [*British*] (DS)
TSPEC......	Test Specification (MSA)
TSPED......	Trade Shows and Professional Exhibits Directory [*Formerly, TPED*] [*Later, TSW*] [*A publication*]
TsPhil........	Tijdschrift voor Philosophie [*A publication*]
TSPI..........	Time-Space-Position-Information (MCD)
TSPIRS.....	Timber Sales Program Information Reporting System [*Department of the Interior*]
TSPM........	Total Suspended Particulate Matter
TSPMA.....	Travaux. Societe de Pharmacie de Montpellier [*A publication*]
TSpMH.....	South Pittsburg Municipal Hospital, South Pittsburg, TN [*Library symbol*] [*Library of Congress*] (LCLS)
TSPP.........	Technetium Stannous Pyrophosphate [*Radiochemistry*]
TSPP.........	Tetrasodium Pyrophosphate [*Inorganic chemistry*]
TSPP.........	Training System Procurement Package
T & S Pr.....	Tillinghast and Shearman's New York Practice [*A publication*] (DLA)
TSPR........	Total Systems Performance Reliability [*or Responsibility*] (MCD)
TSPR........	Training System Program Requirements (MCD)
TSPS.........	Time-Sharing Programming System [*Data processing*] (IEEE)
TSPS.........	Traffic Service Position System [*Telecommunications*]
TSPSCAP ...	Traffic Service Position System Real-Time Capacity Program [*Telecommunications*] (TEL)
TSpTC.......	Trained Special Teacher's Certificate [*Australia*]
TSP-Z........	Trisodium Phosphate - Zephiran [*Clinical chemistry*]
TSQ	T2 Medical, Inc. [*AMEX symbol*] (SPSG)
TSQ	Technical Services Quarterly [*A publication*]
TSQ	Time and Super Quick
TSQ	Trade Specialty Qualification (MCD)
TSQ	Triple Stage Quadrupole [*Instrumentation*]
TSQLS.......	Thundersqualls [*Meteorology*] (FAAC)
TSR...........	[*The*] Shopper Report [*A publication*]
TSR...........	Tactical SONAR Range (NVT)
TSR...........	Tactical Strike and Reconnaissance
TSR...........	Tactical Studies Rules [*In corporation name TSR, Inc.*]
TSR...........	Technical Sales Representative
TSR...........	Technical Services Report [*A publication*] (EAAP)
TSR...........	Technical Services Representative (MCD)
TSR...........	Technical Status Review [*NASA*] (NASA)
TSR...........	Technical Study Report
TSR...........	Technical Summary Report
TSR...........	Technically Specified Natural Rubber
TSR...........	Telecommunications Service Request (CET)
TSR...........	Telemarketing Sales Representative
TSR...........	Temporary Storage Register
TSR...........	Tensile Strength Retention [*Textile technology*]
TSR...........	Terminate and Stay Resident [*Data processing*]
TSR...........	Test Schedule Request
TSR...........	Test Status Report [*NASA*] (NASA)
TSR...........	Test Support Requirements (KSC)
TSR...........	Testosterone Sterilized Rat
TSR...........	Texas Star Airlines [*Ft. Worth, TX*] [*FAA designator*] (FAAC)
TSR...........	Thermal Shock Rig [*Nuclear energy*] (NRCH)
TSR...........	Thermally Stable Resin
TSR...........	Thermochemical Sulfate Reduction [*Chemistry*]
TSR...........	Tijdschrift voor Sociaal Recht [*A publication*]
TSR...........	Tile-Shingle Roof [*Technical drawings*]
TSR...........	Time Sharing Resources, Inc. [*Information service or system*] (IID)
TSR...........	Time Status Register
TSR...........	Time to Sustained Respirations [*Obstetrics*]
TSR...........	Timisoara [*Romania*] [*Airport symbol*] (OAG)
TSR...........	Tokyo Shoko Research Ltd. [*Database producer*] [*Japan*]
TSR...........	Torpedo-Spotter Reconnaissance [*Obsolete*] [*Military*] [*British*]
TSR...........	Total Shoulder Replacement [*Medicine*]
TSR...........	Total Solar Radiation [*Botany*]
TSR...........	Total Stress Range [*Nuclear energy*] (NRCH)
TSR...........	Total System Responsibility
TSR...........	Towed SONAR Response
TSR...........	Tower Shielding Reactor [*Nuclear energy*]
TSR...........	Trade Study Report
TSR...........	Trans-Siberian Railway
TSR...........	Transistor Saturable Reactor
TSR...........	Transportable Surveillance RADAR (MCD)
TSR...........	Traveling Stock Reserve
TSR...........	Tri-Star Resources [*Vancouver Stock Exchange symbol*]
TSR...........	Tsuruga [*Japan*] [*Seismograph station code, US Geological Survey*] (SEIS)
TSR...........	Turbine Shaft Rate [*Military*] (CAAL)
TSR...........	Turnover Summary Report [*Military*]
TSR...........	United States Army TRADOC, Redstone Arsenal, USAMMCS [*United States Army Missile and Munitions Center School*] Technical Library, Redstone Arsenal, AL [*OCLC symbol*] (OCLC)
TSRA........	Total System Requirements Analysis (NASA)
TSRA........	Training Support Requirements Analysis (MCD)
TSRB........	Top Salaries Review Board [*British*]
TSRC........	Theta-Sensitive Regulatory Cell [*Hypothetical*] [*Hematology*]
TSRC........	Tubular and Split Rivet Council [*Later, TRMI*] (EA)
TSRE........	Tropospheric Scatter Radio Equipment (AAG)
TS-3 Referativnyi Sb ...	TS-3 Referativnyi Sbornik [*A publication*]
TSRI..........	Technical Skill Reenlistment Incentive
TSRI..........	TSR, Incorporated [*Hauppauge, NY*] [*NASDAQ symbol*] (NQ)
TSRL.........	[*The*] Special Relief League (EA)
TSRL.........	Total Support Requirements List (AAG)
TSRLD......	TRRL [*Transport and Road Research Laboratory*] Supplementary Report [*A publication*]
TSRLL.......	Tulane Studies in Romance Languages and Literature [*A publication*]
TSRLM.....	Tandem Scanning Reflected Light Microscopy
TSRMP.....	Training System Resource Management Plan [*Army*]
TSRO........	Two-Stage Reverse Osmosis [*Chemical engineering*]
TSRP........	Technical Support Real Property
TSRP........	Toll Service Results Plan [*Bell System*]
TSRS........	Training Site Requirements Study [*DoD*]
TSRT........	Teacher Situation Reaction Test
TSRTAMAA ...	Tactical Surveillance, Reconnaissance, and Target Acquisition Mission Area Analysis (MCD)
TSRU........	Tuberculosis Surveillance Research Unit (EAIO)
TSRV........	Torpedo Ship Ranging Vessel [*Canadian Navy*]
TSRVA.......	Times Science Review [*A publication*]
TSS............	New York [*New York*] E. 34th Street [*Airport symbol*] (OAG)
TSS............	[*The*] Safety Society (EA)
TSS............	St. Andrews School, St. Andrews, TN [*Library symbol*] [*Library of Congress*] (LCLS)
TSS............	[*The*] Super Show (ITD)
TSS............	TACFIRE Software Specialist (MCD)
TSS............	Tactical Strike System
TSS............	Tangential Signal Sensitivity
TSS............	Tape Search System
TSS............	Target Selector Switch
TSS............	Target Sensing Switch
TSS............	Task-State Segment [*Operating system data structure*] [*Data processing*]
TSS............	Technical Sales Seminars [*Department of Commerce*]
TSS............	Technical Specification Sheet
TSS............	Technical Support Services
TSS............	Telecommunication Switching System
TSS............	Teletype Switching System [*or Subsystem*]
TSS............	Temporary Storage Site [*DoD*]
TSS............	Tensile Shear Specimen [*Plastics technology*]
TSS............	Terminal Security System [*Data processing*]
TSS............	Terminal Send Side
TSS............	Terminal Support System
TSS............	Test Set Simulator
TSS............	Thrust Stand System
TSS............	Time-Sharing System [*Data processing*]
TSS............	Toll Switching System [*Telecommunications*] (TEL)
TSS............	Topographic Support System [*Army*] (RDA)
TSS............	Toroidal Space Station
TSS............	Toroidal Support Submarine
TSS............	Total Soluble Sulfur [*Analytical chemistry*]
TSS............	Total Subscriber Satisfaction [*HBO (Home Box Office) rating system*]
TSS............	Total Suspended Solids [*Environmental chemistry*]
TSS............	Total System Services, Inc. [*NYSE symbol*] (SPSG)
TSS............	TOW [*Tube-Launched, Optically Tracked, Wire-Guided (Weapon)*] Subsystem [*Army*]
TSS............	Toxic Shock Syndrome [*Medicine*]
TSS............	Trainer System Software
TSS............	Training Services [*Job Training and Partnership Act*] (OICC)
TSS............	Training Subsystem (MCD)
TSS............	Transistor Servo Simulator
TSS............	Transition State Spectroscopy [*Physics*]
TSS............	Transmission Surveillance System [*Bell System*]
TSS............	Transparent Semiconductor Shutter
TSS............	Trend-Set Industry [*Vancouver Stock Exchange symbol*]
TSS............	Tropospheric Scatter System
TSS............	Trunk Servicing System [*Bell System*]

TSS .... Tsurugisan [*Anabuki*] [*Japan*] [*Seismograph station code, US Geological Survey*] (SEIS)
TSS .... Tug Structural Support [*NASA*] (NASA)
TSS .... Turbine Steam Ship
TSS .... Turner's Syndrome Society of the US (EA)
TSS .... Twin-Screw Steamer [*Nautical*]
TSS .... Typographic Support System (MCD)
TSS .... United States Army TRADOC, Fort Story, Fort Story, VA [*OCLC symbol*] (OCLC)
TSSA .... Tackle and Shooting Sports Agents Association (EA)
TSSA .... Telecommunications Sales Superintendents' Association [*A union*] [*British*]
TSSA .... Telemetry Subcarrier Spectrum Analyzer
TSSA .... Test Scorer and Statistical Analyzer [*Data processing*]
TSSA .... Test Site Support Activity [*NASA*]
TSSA .... Thunderstorm with Sandstorm [*Meteorology*]
TSSA .... Trade Show Services Association [*Defunct*] (EA)
TSSA .... Transport Salaried Staff's Association [*A union*] [*British*] (DCTA)
TSSAA ...... Tackle and Shooting Sports Agents Association (EA)
TSSC .... Target Selection and Seeking Console
TSSC .... Target System Service Charge (NG)
TSSC .... Toxic Substances Strategy Committee [*Nuclear energy*] (NRCH)
TSS-C .... Transmission Surveillance System - Cable [*Telecommunications*] (TEL)
TS & SCP .. Task, Schedule, and Status Control Plan (AAG)
TSSCS ...... Tactical Synchronous Satellite Communication System
TSSD .... Telecommunications Systems and Services Directory [*A publication*]
TSSDT ...... Thrust Subsystem Design Team [*NASA*]
TSSE .... Tactical Security Support Equipment [*Military*]
TSSE .... Toxic Shock Syndrome Exotoxin
TSSI .... Telephone Support Systems, Incorporated [*NASDAQ symbol*] (NQ)
TSSIC .... Tool and Stainless Steel Industry Committee (EA)
TSSL .... TSS Ltd. [*NASDAQ symbol*] (NQ)
TSSM .... Thruster Subsystem Module [*NASA*]
TSSM .... Total Ship Simulation Model
TSSNM ...... Technologist Section of the Society of Nuclear Medicine (EA)
TSSP .... Tactical Satellite Signal Processor (RDA)
TSSP .... Thickness-Sensitive Solar Paint [*Coating technology*]
TSSP .... Two Stripper in Series Permeater [*Chemical engineering*]
TSSPS ...... Tsentralniya Suvet na Profesionalnite Suyuzi [*Central Council of Trade Unions*] [*Bulgaria*]
TSSR .... Theater Stock Status Report [*Military*]
TSSSP ...... Tennessee Study of State Science Policy [*National Science Foundation*] (EA)
TSSST ...... Time-Space-Space-Space-Time [*Telecommunications*] (TEL)
TSST .... Toxic Shock Syndrome Toxin [*Medicine*]
TSSU .... Test Signal Switching Unit (MCD)
TsSV .... Tijdschrift voor de Studie van de Verlichting [*A publication*]
TST .... [*The*] Science Teacher [*A publication*]
TST .... Tail Stop and Turning [*Automotive engineering*]
TST .... Technical and Scholastic Test [*Vocational guidance test*]
TST .... Telemetry Simulation Terminal
TST .... Television Signal Tracer (DEN)
TST .... Temperature Sensing Transducer
TST .... Test (AAG)
TST .... Test Support Table
TST .... Textile Science and Technology [*Elsevier Book Series*] [*A publication*]
TSt .... Texts and Studies [*A publication*] (BJA)
TST .... Thermistor Sterilization Test
TST .... Threshold Setting Tracer
TST .... Time-Sharing Terminals, Inc.
TST .... Time-Space-Time [*Digital switching*] [*Telecommunications*] (TEL)
TST .... Total Surface Tested
TST .... Toxic Shock Toxin [*Biochemistry*]
TST .... Trang [*Thailand*] [*Airport symbol*] (OAG)
TST .... Transaction Step Task
TST .... Transition State Theory [*Physical chemistry*]
TST .... Transmission Scheme Translator (MCD)
TST .... Transmission System Test (MCD)
TST .... Treadmill Stress Testing [*Physiology*]
TST .... Triceps Skinfold Thickness [*Medicine*]
TST .... Trilogy Screening Technique
TST .... Trust
TST .... Twenty Statements Test
TST .... Two-Station Training
TST .... United States Army TRALINET, Systems Center, ATPL-AOT, Fort Monroe, VA [*OCLC symbol*] (OCLC)
TSTA .... Technology Security Technical Assessment [*DoD*]
TSTA .... Transmission, Signaling, and Test Access
TSTA .... Tritium Systems Test Assembly (MCD)
TSTA .... Tumor-Specific Transplantation Antigen [*Immunology*]
TSTC .... Target Selection and Tracking Console
TSTC .... Testamatic Corp. [*Albany, NY*] [*NASDAQ symbol*] (NQ)
TSTC(MTC) ... Trained Secondary Teacher's Certificate (Melbourne Teachers College) [*Australia*]

TSTD .... Total Ship Test Director [*Navy*] (CAAL)
TSTE .... Training System Test and Evaluation (MCD)
TSTEE....... Trustee
TSTEQ ...... Test Equipment
TSTFLT .... Test Set Fault (AAG)
TSTG......... Testing (MSA)
TSTIA .... Trudy Sibirskogo Tekhnologicheskogo Instituta [*A publication*]
TsTK.......... Tidsskrift for Teologi og Kirke [*Oslo*] [*A publication*]
TSTKA ...... Tsuchi To Kiso [*A publication*]
TStL & KC ... Toledo, St. Louis & Kansas City Railroad
TSTM........ Media Logic, Inc. [*NASDAQ symbol*] (NQ)
TSTM........ Thunderstorm [*Meteorology*] (FAAC)
TSTN........ Triple-Supertwist-Nematic [*Focus*]
TSTNG...... Testing
TSTO......... Test Site Tool Order [*NASA*] (AAG)
TSTO......... Testing Tool (AAG)
TSTP .... Test of Selected Topics in Physics
TSTP .... Thermistor Sterilization Test Program
TSTP .... Total Ship Test Program [*Navy*] (CAAL)
TSTP .... Traffic Safety Training Program
TSTPAC.... Transmission and Signaling Test Plan and Analysis Concept [*Telecommunications*] (TEL)
TSTP/AFS ... Total Ship Test Program/Active Fleet Surface Ships [*Navy*] (CAAL)
TSTPI........ Tapered Steel Transmission Pole Institute [*Inactive*] (EA)
TSTP/SP... Total Ship Test Program/Ship Production [*Navy*] (CAAL)
TSTR .... Telstar Corp. [*NASDAQ symbol*] (NQ)
TSTR .... Tester (MSA)
TSTR .... Transistor (AAG)
TSTRZ ...... Transistorized (MSA)
TSTS .... Tail Section Test Stand (AAG)
TSTS .... Thermal Sight Test Set [*Army*]
TSTS .... Third Stage Test Set [*Aerospace*] (MCD)
TSTS .... Thrust Structure Test Stand (AAG)
TSTS .... Tomahawk System Test Set
TSTS .... Tracking System Test Set (AAG)
TSU .... Tabiteuea South [*Kiribati*] [*Airport symbol*] (OAG)
TSU .... Tandem Signal Unit [*Telecommunications*] (TEL)
TSU .... Tape Search Unit (CET)
TSU .... Tarleton State University [*Formerly, TSC*] [*Texas*]
TSU .... Task-Specific Utility
TSU .... Technical Service Unit
TSU .... Telecommunications Study Unit [*American Topical Association*] (EA)
TSU .... Telephone Signal Unit [*Telecommunications*] (TEL)
TSU .... Telescope Sight Unit (MCD)
TSU .... Tennessee State University, Nashville, TN [*Library symbol*] [*Library of Congress*] [*OCLC symbol*] (LCLS)
TSU .... Test Signal Unit [*Telecommunications*] (TEL)
TSU .... Texas Southern University
TSU .... Thermal Systems Unit (KSC)
TSU .... This Side Up
TSU .... Time Standard Unit
TSU .... Trans-Species Unlimited [*Later, ARM*] (EA)
TSU .... Transfer Switch Unit (AAG)
TSU .... Transportation System Utilization Program [*Department of Energy*]
TSU .... Triple Sugar-Urea Base [*Agar*] [*Microbiology*]
TSU .... Tsu [*Japan*] [*Seismograph station code, US Geological Survey*] (SEIS)
TSU .... Tsumeb [*South-West Africa*] [*Geomagnetic observatory code*]
TSU .... Tulsa-Sapulpa Union Railway Co. [*AAR code*]
Tsukuba-Daigaku Shakaigaku J ... Tsukuba-Daigaku Shakaigaku Journal [*A publication*]
Tsukuba J Math ... Tsukuba Journal of Mathematics [*A publication*]
Tsukuba Univ Inst Geosci Annu Rep ... Tsukuba University. Institute of Geoscience. Annual Report [*A publication*]
Tsukumo Earth Sci ... Tsukumo Earth Science [*A publication*]
Tsurumi Univ Dent J ... Tsurumi University. Dental Journal [*A publication*]
TSUS......... Tariff Schedules of the United States
TSUSA ...... Tariff Schedules of the United States, Annotated
TSV........... Terminal Stage Vehicle
TSV........... Thru-Sight Video [*Army training device*] (INF)
TSV........... Tobacco Streak Virus
TSV........... Townsville [*Australia*] [*Airport symbol*] (OAG)
TSV........... Turbine Stop Valve [*Nuclear energy*] (NRCH)
TSV........... Twin Springs [*Nevada*] [*Seismograph station code, US Geological Survey*] [*Closed*] (SEIS)
Tsvet Metal ... Tsvetnye Metally [*A publication*]
Tsvetn Met ... Tsvetnye Metally [*A publication*]
Tsvetn Metall ... Tsvetnaya Metallurgiya [*A publication*]
Tsvetn Metall Nauchno Tekh Sb ... Tsvetnaya Metallurgiya-Nauchno-Tekhnicheskii Sbornik [*A publication*]
Tsvetn Metall (Ordzhonikidze, USSR) ... Tsvetnaya Metallurgiya (Ordzhonikidze, USSR) [*A publication*]
TSVP .... Tournez s'il Vous Plait [*Please Turn Over*] [*See also PTO*] [*French*]
TSVR........ Total Systemic Vascular Resistance
TSVS .... Time Sharing - Virtual System [*Data processing*] (MCD)
Tsvtn Metall Nauchno Tekh Byull ... Tsvetnaya Metallurgiya-Nauchno-Tekhnicheskii Byulleten [*A publication*]

TsVUB.......	Tijdschrift van de Vrije Universiteit van Brussel [*A publication*]
TsVV.........	Tydskrif vir Volkskunde en Volkstaal [*A publication*]
TSW..........	Prace Wroclawskiego Towarzystwa Naukowego [*A publication*]
TSW..........	Southwestern Baptist Theological Seminary, Fort Worth, TX [*OCLC symbol*] (OCLC)
TSW..........	T Switch Cell [*Immunology*]
TSW..........	Technical Scope of Work
T & SW......	Temperance and Social Welfare [*Free Church*] [*British*]
TSW..........	Temperature Switch (MSA)
TSW..........	Test Software (MCD)
TSW..........	Test Switch
TSW..........	Three Banks Review [*A publication*]
TSW..........	Time Switch [*Telecommunications*] (TEL)
TSW..........	Trade Shows Worldwide [*Formerly, TSPED*] [*A publication*]
TSW..........	Transfer Switch
TSW..........	Transmitting Slide Wire
TSW..........	Trau, Schau, Wem [*Trust, but Be Careful Whom*] [*German*] [*Motto of Christian I, Elector of Saxony (1560-91)*]
TSW..........	Tropical Summer Winter [*Vessel load line mark*]
tsw............	Tswana [*MARC language code*] [*Library of Congress*] (LCCP)
TSW..........	Turbine-Building Service Water [*Nuclear energy*] (NRCH)
TSWE........	Test of Standard Written English
TsWK	Tydskrif vir Wetenskap en Kuns [*A publication*]
TSWL........	Tulsa Studies in Women's Literature [*A publication*]
TSWP........	Training Scheme for Widow Pensioners [*Australia*]
TSWTT	Test Switch Thrust Termination
TSWV........	Tomato Spotted Wilt Virus
TSX...........	Telephone Satellite, Experimental
TSX...........	Texscan Corp. [*AMEX symbol*] (SPSG)
TSX...........	Time-Sharing Executive [*Modular Computer Systems*] [*Data processing*]
TSX...........	True Seed Exchange [*Later, SSE*] (EA)
TSX-4	Touring Sport Extra-4WD [*In automotive name Ghia Vignale TSX-4*]
TSY..........	Tech-Sym Corp. [*NYSE symbol*] (SPSG)
TSYKDE ...	Annual Report. Tobacco Research Institute. Taiwan Tobacco and Wine Monopoly Bureau [*A publication*]
TSZGK......	Thueringisch-Saechsische Zeitschrift fuer Geschichte und Kunst [*A publication*]
TT	Chad [*Aircraft nationality and registration mark*] (FAAC)
TT	Taal en Tongval [*Antwerpen*] [*A publication*]
TT	TABA [*Transportes Aereos da Bacia Amazonica SA*] [*Brazil*] [*ICAO designator*] (FAAC)
TT	Tablet Triturate [*Pharmacy*]
TT	Tactical Training [*Followed by location*] [*Military*]
TT	Tactile Tension [*Ophthalmology*]
TT	Taiga Times '71 [*A publication*]
TT	Tail-to-Tail [*Polymer structure*]
TT	Talar Tilt [*Angle of ankle joint*]
TT	Talith and Tefillin (BJA)
TT	Talmud Torah (BJA)
TT	Tanganyika Territory
TT	Tank Top (DS)
TT	Tank Truck [*Freight*]
T & T........	Tanqueray [*Gin*] and Tonic
TT	Tantato Resources, Inc. [*Vancouver Stock Exchange symbol*]
TT	Target Towing Aircraft [*Navy*]
T & T........	Tax and Tip
TT	Teacher Training
TT	Technical Team
TT	Technical Test
TT	Technical Training (OICC)
TT	Technical Translation [*A publication*] [*Obsolete*]
T & T........	Technicals and Turnovers [*Basketball*]
TT	Technology Transfer (DS)
TT	Teetotaler [*Slang*]
TT	Telecommunications Technician [*British military*] (DMA)
TT	Telegraphic Transfer [*of funds*] [*Banking*]
TT	Teletype
TT	Teletypewriter [*Telecommunications*]
TT	Teletypewriter and Facsimile Apparatus [*JETDS nomenclature*] [*Military*] (CET)
TT	Tell Taanach (BJA)
TT	Tempelurkunden aus Tello [*A publication*] (BJA)
TT	Temperature Transmitter [*Nuclear energy*] (NRCH)
TT	Temporarily Transferred [*Telecommunications*] (TEL)
TT	Tendon Transfer [*Surgery*]
TT	Teologisk Tidsskrift [*A publication*]
T/T...........	Terminal Timing (KSC)
tt...............	Terminus Technicus (BJA)
TT	Test Temperature [*Nuclear energy*] (NRCH)
TT	Testamentary Trust [*Legal term*]
TT	Tetanus Toxoid [*Medicine*]
TT	Tetrathionate [*Nutrient broth*] [*Microbiology*]
TT	Theologisch Tijdschrift [*A publication*]
TT	Theology Today [*A publication*]
TT	Theorie en Techniek [*A publication*]
TT	Thermal-Tow
TT	Thermometric Titrimetry
TT	Think Time [*Computer order entry*]
TT	Thomas Thorpe [*Publisher of a 1609 edition of Shakespeare's sonnets*]
TT	Thrombin Time [*Hematology*]
TT	Thrust Termination
TT	Thymol Turbidity [*Clinical chemistry*]
TT	Tibial Tubercle [*Anatomy*]
TT	Ticarcillin and Tobramycin [*Antibacterial mixture*]
TT	Tidningarnas Telegrambyra [*Press agency*] [*Sweden*]
TT	Tight Torso [*Women's fashions*]
TT	Tile Threshold (MSA)
TT	Tilt Trailers (DCTA)
T & T........	Time and Temperature
T & T........	Time and Tide [*A publication*]
TT	Time and Tide [*A publication*]
TT	Times [*London*] [*A publication*]
T/T...........	Timetable (DS)
T/T...........	Timing and Telemetry
Tt...............	Titus [*New Testament book*] (BJA)
TT	Tobacco Tax Ruling Term (DLA)
TT	Tobramycin-Ticarcillin [*Antibiotic combination*]
TT	[*The*] Toledo Terminal Railroad Co. [*AAR code*]
TT	Tolytriazole [*Organic chemistry*]
TT	Tooling Template (MCD)
T & T........	Tools and Tillage [*A publication*]
TT	Torpedo Tube
TT	Total Run Time [*Robotic assay*]
TT	Total Task Chaining [*Psychology*]
TT	Total Temperature (MCD)
TT	Total Thyroxine [*Endocrinology*]
TT	Total Time (MSA)
TT	Totus Tuus [*All Yours*] [*Latin*]
TT	Tourist Trophy [*Motorcycle racing*] [*British*]
TT	Townsend Thoreson [*Company running English Channel ferries*]
TT	Tracking Telescope
TT	Traffic Tester [*Telecommunications*] (TEL)
TT	Training Text
TT	Trans-Texas Airways
TT	Transaction Terminal (BUR)
TT	Transit Time [*of blood through heart and lungs*]
TT	Transmitting Tract [*Botany*]
TT	Transonic Tunnel [*NASA*]
TT	Transport [*A publication*]
T & T........	Transportation and Transportability
TT	TransTechnology Corp. [*NYSE symbol*] (SPSG)
TT	Transthoracic [*Medicine*]
T/T...........	Travel/Tourism
TT	Travel and Tourism Program [*Association of Independent Colleges and Schools specialization code*]
TT	Tree Test [*Psychology*]
TT	Tree Tops
TT	Trees for Tomorrow (EA)
TT	Tributary Team [*Military*]
TT	Tricycle and Tail Skid [*Aerospace*] (AAG)
T/T...........	Trienoic/Tetraenoic [*Ratio of unsaturated chemicals*]
TT	Trigesimo-Secundo [*Book from 10 to 12-1/2 centimeters in height*] [*Bibliography*]
TT	Trinidad and Tobago [*ANSI two-letter standard code*] (CNC)
TT	Trinity Term
TT	Troop Test
TT	Trust Termination
tt...............	Trust Territory of the Pacific Islands [*MARC country of publication code*] [*Library of Congress*] (LCCP)
TT	Trust Territory of the Pacific Islands [*Postal code*]
TT	Tuberculin Tested [*Milk*]
TT	Tufted Titmouse [*Ornithology*]
TT	Turbine Tanker
TT	Turbine Trip (IEEE)
TT	Turntable (ADA)
TT	Turret Trainer [*British military*] (DMA)
TT	Tyne and Tees [*50th Northumbrian Division*] [*British military*] (DMA)
TT₃............	Total Triiodothyronine [*Endocrinology*]
TT4............	Total Thyroxine [*Endocrinology*]
TT's...........	Tripoli Trots [*Term used by entertainers in World War II*]
TTA...........	Tan Tan [*Morocco*] [*Airport symbol*] (OAG)
TTA...........	Tatalina [*Alaska*] [*Seismograph station code, US Geological Survey*] (SEIS)
TTA	Telecommunications and Telephone Association [*Arlington, VA*] [*Telecommunications service*] (TSSD)
TTA...........	Test Target Array (AFM)
TTA...........	Theatre Television Authority (EA)
TTA...........	Thenoyltrifluoroacetone [*Also, TTB*] [*Organic chemistry*]
TTA...........	Thermomechanical Test Area [*NASA*] (NASA)
TTA...........	Thrust Termination Assembly
TTA...........	Time to Apogee [*Aerospace*] (MCD)
TTA...........	Tolyltriazole [*Organic chemistry*]
TTA...........	Total Tangible Assets [*Business term*] (ADA)
TTA...........	Total Titratable Acidity [*Analytical chemistry*]
TTA...........	Trade and Tourism Alliance [*Defunct*] (EA)
TTA...........	Traffic Trunk Administration [*Telecommunications*] (TEL)

TTA .... Train Travellers Association [*Australia*]
T & TA ...... Training and Technical Assistance   (OICC)
TTA .... Trans-Texas Airways
TTA .... Transit Time Accelerometer
TTA .... Transtracheal Aspiration [*Medicine*]
TTA .... Travel Time Authorized
TTA .... Travel and Tourism Association   (EA)
TTA .... Triplet-Triplet Annihilation [*Spectroscopy*]
TTA .... Tritolylamine [*Organic chemistry*]
TTA .... Turbine-Alternator Assembly   (MCD)
TTAB .... Tetradecyltrimethylammonium Bromide [*Organic chemistry*]
TTAB .... Trademark Trial and Appeal Board [*of Patent Office*]
TTAD .... Temporary Tour of Active Duty [*Military*]
TTADB ..... Tactical Terrain Analysis Database [*Army*]
TTAE .... Turk Tarih. Arkeologya ve Etnografya Dergisi [*A publication*]
TTAF .... Technical Training Air Force
TTagPI ...... Trudy Taganrogskogo Gosudarstvennogo Pedagogiceskogo Instituta [*A publication*]
TTAP .... Telemetry Technical Analysis Position   (MCD)
TTAPS ...... [*R. P.*] Turco, [*O. B.*] Toon, [*T. P.*] Ackerman, [*J. B.*] Pollack, and [*Carl*] Sagan [*Authors of a paper on the biological and climatological effects of nuclear war*]
TTAT .... TACFIRE Training Assistance Team   (MCD)
TTAT .... Torpedo Tube Acceptance Trials [*Navy*]   (NG)
TTAV .... TTAV [*Technical Teachers Association of Victoria*] News [*A publication*]   (APTA)
TTAWA ..... Typewriter Trade and Allied Workers' Association [*A union*] [*British*]
TTB .... Tanker, Transport, Bomber [*Requirements*] [*Air Force*]
TTB .... Target Triggered Burst
TTB .... Tatuoca [*Brazil*] [*Geomagnetic observatory code*]
TTB .... Technical Test Battery [*Aptitude test*]
TTB .... Teletypewriter Buffer   (CET)
TTB .... Tetragonal Tungsten Bronze
TTB .... Time to Blackout
TTB .... Toll Testboard [*Telecommunications*]   (TEL)
TTB .... Trifluoro(thienyl)butanedione [*Also, TTA*] [*Organic chemistry*]
TTb .... Trudy Tbilisskogo Pedagogiceskogo Instituta [*A publication*]
TTB .... Typing Test for Business
TTBB .... First Tenor, Second Tenor, First Bass, and Second Bass [*in all-male choral groups*]
TTBOY ...... To the Best of You [*An association*]   (EA)
TTBT .... Threshold Test Ban Treaty [*1974*]
TTBWR ..... Twisted Tape Boiling Water Reactor   (IEEE)
TTC .... Tape to Card
TTC .... Target Track Central
TTC .... Target Tracking Console   (MCD)
TTC .... Tatung [*Republic of China*] [*Seismograph station code, US Geological Survey*]   (SEIS)
TTC .... Teacher Training College
TTC .... Technical Training Center [*Air Force*]
TTC .... Technical Training Command [*Army Air Forces*] [*World War II*]
TTC .... Technology Transfer Centre [*University of New England*] [*Australia*]
TTC .... Telecommunication Training Centre [*Fiji*] [*Telecommunications*]   (TSSD)
TTC .... Telemetry, Tracking, and Command   (NASA)
TTC .... Telephone Terminal Cables   (KSC)
TTC .... Teletypewriter Center [*Military*]
TTC .... Television Training Centre Ltd. [*British*]   (CB)
TTC .... Temperature Test Chamber
TTC .... Tender to Contract Policy [*Export Credits Guarantee Department*] [*British*]
TTC .... Terminating Toll Center   (DEN)
TTC .... Test Transfer Cask [*Nuclear energy*]   (NRCH)
TTC .... [*The*] Thomson Corp.
TTC .... Tight Tape Contact
TTC .... Time to Circularize Orbit   (MCD)
TTC .... Time to Control
TTC .... Tin Telluride Crystal
TTC .... Tobacco Tax Council   (EA)
TTC .... Tobramycin, Ticarcillin, and Cephalothin
TTC .... Toro Company [*NYSE symbol*]   (SPSG)
TTC .... Tow Target Cable
TT & C ...... Tracking, Telemetry, and Command
TTC .... Tracking, Telemetry, and Command
TTC .... Tracking, Telemetry, and Control [*NASA*]   (NASA)
TT & C ...... Tracking, Telemetry, and Control [*NASA*]   (MCD)
TTC .... Training Technology Centers [*Army*]
TTC .... Transient Temperature Control
TTC .... Translation Thrust Control
TTC .... Transportation Test Center [*Department of Transportation*] [*Pueblo, CO*]   (GRD)
TTC .... Travel for Tomorrow Council   (EA)
TTC .... Travelmaster Travel Club   (EA)
TTC .... Treasure Trove Club   (EA)
TTC .... Triphenyltetrazolium Chloride [*Also, RT, TPTZ*] [*Chemical indicator*]
TTC .... Tropic Test Center [*Army*]   (MCD)
TTC .... Tube Temperature Control

TTC .... Tubulinyl Tyrosine Carboxypeptidase
TTC .... Tunnel Thermal Control   (NASA)
TTCA .... T-Ten Class Association   (EA)
TTCA .... Thiothiazolidinecarboxylic Acid [*Organic chemistry*]
T/TCA .... Thrust/Translation Control Assembly [*NASA*]   (KSC)
TTCA .... Tibetan Terrier Club of America   (EA)
TTCC .... [*The*] Technical Cooperation Committee [*Army*]   (AABC)
TTCE .... Tooth-to-Tooth Composite Error
TTC/FES .. Tender to Contract and Forward Exchange Supplement [*Export Credits Guarantee Department*] [*British*]   (DS)
TTCI .... Transient Temperature Control Instrument
TTC & M ... Telemetry, Tracking, Command, and Monitoring
TTCMA .... Turk Tip Cemiyeti Mecmuasi [*A publication*]
TTCMSC ... Tonga and Tin Can Mail Study Circle   (EA)
TTCO .... Trustcorp, Inc. [*Formerly, Toledo Trustcorp*] [*NASDAQ symbol*]   (NQ)
TTCP .... Scarborough/Crown Point, Tobago [*Trinidad and Tobago*] [*ICAO location identifier*]   (ICLI)
TTCP .... [*The*] Technical Cooperation Program [*US, UK, Canada, Australia*] [*Research*]
TTCP .... Tripartite Technical Cooperation Program [*Military*]   (NG)
TTCS .... Target Tracking and Control System   (MCD)
TTCS .... Toy Train Collectors Society   (EA)
TTCS .... Truck Transportable Communications Station
TTCT .... Torrance Tests of Creative Thinking [*Educational test*]
TTCU .... Teletypewriter Control Unit   (AABC)
TTCV .... Tracking, Telemetry, Command, and Voice [*Aerospace*]
TTD .... Tactical Terrain Data [*Army*]
TTD .... Tank Training Devices   (MCD)
TTD .... Teachers Training Diploma
TTD .... Technical Test Director
TTD .... Technical Training Detachment
TTD .... Temporary Text Delay
TTD .... Temporary Total Disablement [*Insurance*]   (AIA)
TTD .... Temporary Travel Document   (NATG)
TTD .... Tetraethylthiuram Disulfide [*Also, TETD*] [*Organic chemistry*]
TTD .... Textile Technology Digest [*A publication*]
TTD .... Things to Do
TTD .... [*The*] Third Degree [*A publication*]   (EAAP)
TTD .... Total Time to Doctorate
TTD .... Totals to Date   (MCD)
TTD .... Transponder Transmitter Detector
TTD .... Transportation Technical Data [*Army*]
TTD .... Troutdale, OR [*Location identifier*] [*FAA*]   (FAAL)
TTDI .... Teacher Training in Developing Institutions
TTDR .... Tracking Telemetry Data Receiver   (AAG)
TTDT .... Tactical Test Data Translator   (MUGU)
TTE .... Talks to Teachers of English [*A publication*]
TTE .... Task Training Exercise
TT & E ...... Technical Test and Evaluation
TTE .... Technical Training Engineer
TTE .... Technical Training Equipment   (MCD)
TTE .... Telephone Terminal Equipment
TTE .... Temporary Test Equipment   (AAG)
TTE .... Tentative Tables of Equipment
TTE .... Ternate [*Indonesia*] [*Airport symbol*]   (OAG)
TTE .... Texpress. Economisch en Technisch Weekblad voor de Textiel en Kledingindustrie en Handel in de Benelux [*A publication*]
TTE .... Thermal Transient Equipment [*Nuclear energy*]   (NRCH)
TTE .... Time to End
TTE .... Time to Event [*NASA*]   (KSC)
T & TE ...... Tool and Test Equipment [*DoD*]   (AFIT)
TTE .... Tool and Test Equipment [*DoD*]
TTE .... Total Tax Expenditures [*Economics*]
TTE .... Total Transportation Expenditure [*Department of Transportation*]
TTE .... Trailer Test Equipment   (AAG)
TTE .... Trigon Tech, Inc. [*Vancouver Stock Exchange symbol*]
TTEB ..... Transfert de la Technologie de l'Energie dans les Batiments [*Buildings Energy Technology Transfer Program*] [*Canada*]
TTEC .... Teletypewriter Technician
TTEC .... Transpirator Technologies, Inc. [*NASDAQ symbol*]   (NQ)
T & TEC .... Trinidad & Tobago Electricity Commission
T Tech .... Track Technique Annual [*A publication*]
TTEE .... Trustee
TTeF .... Tetratellurafulvalene [*Organic chemistry*]
TTEGDA .... Tetraethylene Glycol Diacrylate [*Organic chemistry*]
TTEK .... Taunton Technologies, Inc. [*NASDAQ symbol*]   (CTT)
TTEKA ...... Tokyo Toritsu Eisei Kenkyusho Kenkyu Hokoku [*A publication*]
TTEL .... Tool and Test Equipment List [*NASA*]   (NASA)
TTele .... Tatar Tele Hem Adebijaty [*A publication*]
TTEM .... Tooling Test Equipment Team   (AAG)
TTEP .... Training and Training Equipment   (MCD)
TTET .... Turbine Transport Evaluation Team [*FAA*]   (MUGU)
TTF .... Tactical Task Force   (AFM)
TTF .... Tanker Task Force   (AFM)
TTF .... Target Towing Flight [*British military*]   (DMA)
TTF .... Test to Failure   (NATG)

TTF............ Tetrathiofulvalene [*Organic chemistry*]
TTF............ Thai Fund [*NYSE symbol*]   (SPSG)
TTF............ Timber Trades Federation   (DAS)
TTF............ Time to Failure
TTF............ Time to Fire [*Military*]   (CAAL)
TTF............ Tone Telegraph Filter
TTF............ Training Task Force
TTF............ Transient Time Flowmeter [*Nuclear energy*]   (NRCH)
TTF............ Transistor Test Fixture
TTF............ Trend Type Forecast   (ADA)
TTF............ Two/Ten Foundation   (EA)
TTFA........ Thallium Trifluoroacetate [*Organic chemistry*]
TTFA........ Training Technology Field Activity [*Army*]
TTFB........ Tetrachlorotrifluoromethylbenzimidazole [*Organic chemistry*]
TTFC........ Tactical and Technical Fire Control   (MCD)
TTFC........ Tanya Tucker Fan Club   (EA)
TTFD........ Thiamine Tetrahydrofurfuryl Disulfide [*Pharmacology*]
TTFF........ Time to First Fix [*Quality control*]
TTFN........ Ta Ta for Now
TTF & T.... Technology Transfer, Fabrication, and Test   (RDA)
TTFT........ Tetra(trifluoromethyl)thiophene [*Organic chemistry*]
TTF-TCNQ ... Tetrathiafulvene-Tetracyanoquinodimethane [*Organic chemistry*]
TTFTT....... Terminal Tax Filing Time Trauma
TTFW....... Too Tacky for Words [*Slang*]
TTG .... General Trustco of Canada [*Toronto Stock Exchange symbol*]
TTG .... Gibson General Hospital, Trenton, TN [*Library symbol*] [*Library of Congress*]   (LCLS)
TTG .... Technical Translation Group   (IEEE)
TTG .... Test Target Generator
TTG .... Time to Go [*Air Force*]
TTG .... Titograd [*Yugoslavia*] [*Seismograph station code, US Geological Survey*]   (SEIS)
TTG .... Tobacco Tax Guide [*Internal Revenue Service*]
TTG .... Travel Trade Gazette UK [*A publication*]
TTG .... Travel with Troops Going
TTGA....... Tellurite-Taurocholate-Gelatin Agar [*Microbiology*]
TTGAC...... Travel and Tourism Government Affairs Council   (EA)
TTGD........ Time-to-Go Dial
TTH .... Thyrotrophic Hormone [*Also, TSH*] [*Endocrinology*]
TTh.......... Tijdschrift voor Theologie [*Wageningen*] [*A publication*]
TTH.......... Title Tech, Inc. [*Vancouver Stock Exchange symbol*]
TTHA........ Triethylenetetraminehexaacetic Acid [*Organic chemistry*]
TTHE .... Thermal Transient Histogram Equivalent [*Nuclear energy*]   (NRCH)
TTHFC...... Tom T. Hall Fan Club   (EA)
TTHM....... Total Trihalomethane [*Analytical chemistry*]
T Th Z....... Trierer Theologische Zeitschrift [*A publication*]
TTI............ Tactical Target Illustration   (AFM)
TTI............ [*Robert A.*] Taft Institute of Government   (EA)
TTI............ [*The*] Teachers, Incorporated   (EA)
TTI............ Technical Tape, Incorporated [*AMEX symbol*]   (SPSG)
TTI............ Technology Transfer Institute [*Santa Monica, CA*] [*Telecommunications*]   (TSSD)
TTI............ Teletype Test Instruction   (KSC)
TTI............ Texas Transportation Institute [*Texas A & M University*] [*Research center*]
TTI............ TIE/Telecommunications Canada Ltd. [*Toronto Stock Exchange symbol*]
TTI............ Time to Intercept [*Missiles*]   (NG)
TTI............ Time-Temperature Index
TTI............ Time Temperature Indicator   (IEEE)
TTI............ Time Template Indicator
TTI............ Training-Testing Intervals
TTI............ Transthoracic Impedance [*Medicine*]
TTI............ Travel Trends International [*Commercial firm*] [*British*]
TTI............ Traveling Ticket Inspector   (DCTA)
TTI............ True Total Ion
TTI............ Tuck Tummy In [*Slang*]
TTI............ Tulane Tax Institute [*A publication*]
TTI............ Turner Teleport, Incorporated [*Atlanta, GA*] [*Telecommunications service*]   (TSSD)
TTIA........ Tube Temperature Indication and Alarm
TTIC........ Test Technology Information Center   (MCD)
TTIC........ Tropical Timber Information Center [*College of Environmental Science and Forestry at Syracuse*] [*Research center*]   (RCD)
TTIDA...... Teknisk Tidskrift [*Sweden*] [*A publication*]
TTIF .... Training Taxpayer Information File [*IRS*]
TTIG........ Training Task Indentification Guide
TTII.......... Therapeutic Technologies, Inc. [*AMEX symbol*]   (NQ)
TTIIA .... Trudy Tashkentskogo Instituta Inzhenerov Irrigatsii i Mekhanizatsii Sel'skogo Khozyaistva [*A publication*]
T Times..... These Times [*A publication*]
TTIPS....... Ticker Tape Information Processing System [*Online stock information service*]
TTIS .... Traveling Trickle Irrigation System
TTIS Publ .. TTIS [*Translation and Technical Information Service*] Publication [*A publication*]
TTITS........ Thrust Termination Initiator Test Set

TTJ .... Thermo Technology International [*Vancouver Stock Exchange symbol*]
TTJ .... Timber Trades Journal and Wood Processing [*A publication*]
TTJ .... Tottori [*Japan*] [*Airport symbol*]   (OAG)
TTK .... Terminate Task Key
TTK .... Tie Trunk [*Telecommunications*]
TTK .... Tokyo Tsushin Kogyo [*Tokyo Telecommunications Engineering Co.*]
TTK .... Turk Tarih Kurumu [*A publication*]
TTK .... Two-Tone Keying
TTK "Belleten" ... Turk Tarih Kurumu "Belleten" [*A publication*]
TTKi .... Tidsskrift for Teologi og Kirke [*Oslo*] [*A publication*]
TTKLAJ .... Trudy Turkmenskogo Nauchno-Issledovatel'skogo Instituta Klimatologii Kurortologii i Fizicheskikh Metodov Lecheniya [*A publication*]
TTKMA..... Trudy Tambovskogo Instituta Khimicheskogo Mashinostroeniya [*A publication*]
TTKSA ..... Tokyo-Toritsu Kogyo Shoreikan Hokoku [*A publication*]
TTL........... Tatalina [*Alaska*] [*Seismograph station code, US Geological Survey*] [*Closed*]   (SEIS)
TTL........... Teletype Telling
TTL........... Texas Tech University, School of Law Library, Lubbock, TX [*OCLC symbol*]   (OCLC)
TTL........... Theological Translation Library [*A publication*]
TTL........... Thomson T-Line [*Commercial firm*] [*British*]
TTL........... Through the Lens [*Trademark of Spiratone, Inc.*]
TTL........... Title [*Online database field identifier*] [*Data processing*]
TTL........... To Take Leave
TTL........... Torotel, Inc. [*AMEX symbol*]   (SPSG)
TTL........... Torrent Resources Limited [*Vancouver Stock Exchange symbol*]
TTL........... Total Time to Launch [*NASA*]   (KSC)
TTL........... TRADOC Troop List   (MCD)
TTL........... Transistor-Transistor Logic [*Also, T²L*]
TT & L...... Treasury Tax and Loan Account [*Banking*]
TTL........... Tribal Trust Land [*Zimbabwe*]
TTL........... Tribothermoluminescence
TTL........... Tubulinyl Tyrosine Ligase
TTL........... Turtle Island [*Fiji*] [*Airport symbol*]   (OAG)
TTL........... Twin Trapezoidal Links [*Mazda*] [*Automotive engineering*]
TTLC........ Themes and Topics of Literature Criticism [*A publication*]
TTLC........ Total Threshold Limit Concentration [*Environmental chemistry*]
TTLM........ Through-the-Lens Light Metering   (MCD)
TTLPA ...... Tekstil'naya Promyshlennost [*A publication*]
TTLR......... Tanganyika Territory Law Reports [*1921-47*] [*A publication*]   (DLA)
TTLS .... Team Training Launch Station   (AAG)
TTL-S .... Transistor-Transistor Logic - Schottky
TTM .... Tactical Target Materials
TTM .... Tactical Telemetry
TTM .... Taiwan Trade Monthly [*A publication*]
TTM .... Temperature Test Model
T/TM........ Test and Training Monitor   (AAG)
T/TM........ Thailand Tobacco Monopoly   (DS)
TTM .... Thermal Test Model
TTM .... Transit Time Modulation   (DEN)
TTM .... Turtle Mountains [*California*] [*Seismograph station code, US Geological Survey*]   (SEIS)
TTM .... Two-Tone Modulation
TTMA .... Truck Trailer Manufacturers Association   (EA)
TTMA .... Tufted Textile Manufacturers Association [*Later, CRI*]   (EA)
TTMAD ..... Testing-Teaching Module of Auditory Discrimination [*Child development test*]
TTMC....... Tactical Target Materials Catalogue   (MCD)
T/TMC...... Traffic/Traffic Management and Control [*British*]
TTMCFC .. Theater-Type Mobilization Corps Force Capabilities [*Military*]
TTMCFO .. Theater-Type Mobilization Corps Force Objective [*Military*]
TTME....... Tech:Time, Inc. [*Nokomis, FL*] [*NASDAQ symbol*]   (NQ)
TTMF .... Touch-Tone Multifrequency   (CET)
TTMM ...... Tergotrochanteral Muscle Motoneuron [*Zoology*]
TTMM ...... True Tape Motion Monitor
TTMP........ Tactical Targets Materials Program   (AFM)
TTMP........ Transit Time Magnetic Pumping
TTMS........ Telephoto Transmission Measuring Set
TTMTA..... Tungsram Technische Mitteilungen [*A publication*]
TTN .... Taitung [*Taito*] [*Republic of China*] [*Seismograph station code, US Geological Survey*]   (SEIS)
TTN .... Technology Transfer Network [*Michigan State Department of Commerce*] [*Lansing, MI*] [*Information service or system*]   (IID)
TT/N .... Test Tone to Noise Ratio [*Telecommunications*]   (TEL)
TTN .... [*The*] Titan Corp. [*NYSE symbol*]   (SPSG)
TTN .... Transient Tachypnea of Newborn [*Gynecology*]
TTN .... Trenton [*New Jersey*] [*Airport symbol*]   (OAG)
TTN .... Trenton, NJ [*Location identifier*] [*FAA*]   (FAAL)
TTN .... Trevecca Nazarene College, Nashville, TN [*OCLC symbol*]   (OCLC)
TTN .... Triton Canada Resources Ltd. [*Toronto Stock Exchange symbol*]
TTN .... Tumor Site, T-Stage, N-Stage [*Oncology*]

TTNA	Trinidad and Tobago National Alliance [*Political party*] (PPW)
TTNF	Two/Ten National Foundation [*Later, TTF*] (EA)
TTNG	Tightening (MSA)
TTNN	(Tetrahydrotetramethylnaphthyl) Naphthoic Acid [*Antineoplastic drug*]
TTNP	Tactical Telephone Numbering Plan (MCD)
TTNPB	((Tetrahydrotetramethylnaphthalenyl)propenyl)benzoic Acid [*Antineoplastic drug*]
TTNS	TOW [*Tube-Launched, Optically Tracked, Wire-Guided (Weapon)*] Thermal Night Sight [*Night vision device*] [*Army*] (RDA)
TTO	Tactical Technology Office [*Arlington, VA*] [*DoD*] (GRD)
TTO	Telecommunications Technical Officer [*British*]
TTO	Terminal Training Objective [*Army*] (INF)
TTO	To Take Out [*Medicine*]
TTO	Total Toxic Organics [*Environmental chemistry*]
TTO	Traffic Trunk Order [*Telecommunications*] (TEL)
TTO	Transit Tracers in the Ocean [*Oceanography*]
TTO	Transmitter Turn-Off
TTO	Travel and Transportation Order
TTO	Trinidad and Tobago [*ANSI three-letter standard code*] (CNC)
T Today	Theology Today [*A publication*]
TTOI	TEMPEST Technologies, Inc. [*NASDAQ symbol*] (NQ)
T Tokyo U F	Transactions. Tokyo University of Fisheries [*A publication*]
TTOMT	Tank Turret Organizational Maintenance Trainer [*Army*]
TTomU	Trudy Tomskogo Gosudarstvennogo Universiteta [*A publication*]
TTOR	Transtector Systems, Inc. [*Hayden Lake, ID*] [*NASDAQ symbol*] (NQ)
TTOS	Toy Train Operating Society (EA)
TTOY	Tyco Toys, Inc. [*NASDAQ symbol*] (NQ)
TTP	Tactical Targeting Program (AFM)
TTP	Tactics, Techniques, and Procedures
TTP	Tamarind Technical Papers [*A publication*]
TTP	Tape-to-Print
T & TP	Terry and the Pirates [*Pop music group*]
TTP	Tetilla Peak [*New Mexico*] [*Seismograph station code, US Geological Survey*] (SEIS)
TTP	Thermistor Test Program
TTP	Thrombotic Thrombocytopenic Purpura [*Medicine*]
TTP	Thymidine Triphosphate [*Biochemistry*]
TTP	Time to Perigee (MCD)
TTP	Total Taxable Pay
TTP	Total Temperature Probe (MCD)
TTP	Trainer Test Procedure [*Army*]
TT & P	Training, Transient and Patient
TTP	Transverse Thrust Propeller
TTP	Trick-Taking Potential [*Statistics*]
TTP	Trudy Tallinskogo Politekhnicheskogo Instituta. Seriya B, XX [*A publication*]
TTP	Tu-Tahl Petroleum, Inc. [*Vancouver Stock Exchange symbol*]
TTP	Turn toward Peace [*Later, WWWC*] [*An association*] (EA)
TTPC	Titanium Toroidal Propellant Container
TTPE	Total Taxable Pay Earned
TTPES	Torpedo Tube Pump Ejection System [*Navy*] (CAAL)
TTPFC	Terry and the Pirates Fan Club (EA)
TTPG	(Thenoylthio)propionylglycine [*Biochemistry*]
TTPH	Team Trainer, Pearl Harbor
TTPI	Trudy Tbilisskogo Gosudarstvennogo Pedagogiceskogo Instituta [*A publication*]
TTPI	Trust Territory of the Pacific Islands
TTPP	Port-Of-Spain/Piarco, Trinidad [*Trinidad and Tobago*] [*ICAO location identifier*] (ICLI)
TTPR	Trainer Test Procedures and Results [*Army*]
TTPS	Port-Of-Spain/Port-Of-Spain, Trinidad [*Trinidad and Tobago*] [*ICAO location identifier*] (ICLI)
TTP & S	Trainees, Transients, Patients, and Students Program [*Military*]
TTQ	Murphy, NC [*Location identifier*] [*FAA*] (FAAL)
TTQ	Tuebinger Theologische Quartalschrift [*A publication*]
TTQAP	Teletherapy Treatment Quality Assurance Program [*Nuclear energy*] (NRCH)
TTQS	Tuebinger Theologische Quartalschrift (Stuttgart) [*A publication*]
TTR	Tab-Tronic Recorder (DIT)
TTR	Tactical Technical Requirements (RDA)
TTR	Tana Toraja [*Indonesia*] [*Airport symbol*] (OAG)
TTR	Tape-Reading Tripping Relay
TTR	Target Track [*or Tracking*] RADAR [*Air Force*]
TTR	Target Tracking Receiver [*Military*] (CAAL)
TTR	Tarl Town Reports [*New South Wales*] [*A publication*] (DLA)
TTR	Teletypewriter Translator (CET)
TTR	Thermal Test Reactor [*Nuclear energy*] (AAG)
TTR	Thermal Timing Relay
TTR	Thermal Transpiration Ratio
TTR	Thermotolerance Ratio [*Roentgenology*]
TTR	Tijuana & Tecate Railway Co. [*AAR code*]
TTR	Time to Repair [*Military*] (CAAL)
TTR	Time-Temperature Recorder
TTR	Tonopah Test Range
TTR	Toshiba Training Reactor [*Japan*] (NRCH)
TTR	Total Tank Requirement
TTR	Transient Thermal Radiation
TTR	Transthyretin [*Biochemistry*]
TTR	Travel with Troops Returning
TTR	Triplet-Triplet Resonance [*Physics*]
TTR	Trust Territory Reports of Pacific Island [*A publication*] (DLA)
TTR	Type-Token Ratio [*Education of the hearing-impaired*]
TTRA	Tetra Systems, Inc. [*NASDAQ symbol*] (NQ)
TTrA	Textes et Traitement Automatique [*A publication*]
TTRA	Travel and Tourism Research Association (EA)
TTRB	Timken Tapered Roller Bearing
TTRC	Transistorized Thyratron Ring Counter
TTRE	Task Training Remedial Exercise [*Army*]
TTrIC	Trained Technical Instructor's Certificate [*Australia*]
TTRIF	Trident Resources [*NASDAQ symbol*] (NQ)
TTRS	Torture and Trauma Rehabilitation Service [*Australia*]
TTRSA	Twisted Telephone Radio, Shielded, Armored
TTRT	Target Token Rotation Time [*Data processing*]
TTS	TACFIRE Training System (MCD)
TTS	Tactical Test Set (MCD)
TTS	Tank Thermal Site
TTS	Target Trajectory Sensor
TTS	Tarleton State University, Dick Smith Library, Stephenville, TX [*OCLC symbol*] (OCLC)
TTS	Technical Training Squadron (MCD)
TTS	Tele-Tech Services [*McAfee, NJ*] [*Information service or system*] [*Telecommunications*] (TSSD)
TTS	Telecom Technology Showcase [*British*]
TTS	Telecommunications Terminal Systems
TTS	Telemetry Transmission System
TTS	Teletype Switching Facilities (FAAC)
TTS	Teletypesetter
TTS	Teletypewriter System
TTS	Temperature Test Set
TTS	Temporary Threshold Shift
TTS	Terminal Testing Section [*Social Security Administration*]
TTS	Terrain Trend System (MCD)
TTS	Test and Training Satellite [*Also, TATS, TETR*] [*NASA*]
TTS	Thanks to Scandinavia (EA)
TTS	[*The*] Theban Tombs Series [*London*] [*A publication*] (BJA)
TTS	Thermal Transfer Standard
TTS	Thomas Tallis Society [*British*]
TTS	Thule Tracking Station (MCD)
TTS	Thurstone Temperament Schedule [*Psychology*]
TTS	Tintina Mines Ltd. [*Toronto Stock Exchange symbol*]
TTS	Tissue Type Specific [*Antigen*]
TTS	Tracker Test Set [*Dragon*] (MCD)
TTS	Trade Testing Section [*Australia*]
TTS	[*The*] Training School at Vineland [*An association*] (EA)
TTS	Transactions. Thoroton Society [*A publication*]
TTS	Transdermal Therapeutic System [*Medicine*]
TTS	Transducer Tubing System
TTS	Transistor-Transistor Logic Schottky Barrier (IEEE)
TTS	Transmission Test Set (IEEE)
TTS	Transponder Test Set
TTS	Transportable Telemetry Set
TTS	True to Scale
TTS	Tsaratanana [*Madagascar*] [*Airport symbol*] (OAG)
TTSA	Tactical Traffic and System Analysis (MCD)
TTSA	Transition Training Squadron, Atlantic [*Navy*]
TTSC	TSC, Inc. of California [*NASDAQ symbol*] (NQ)
TTSD	Telephone Tracking System Directory (MCD)
TTSF	Test and Timesharing Facility [*Social Security Administration*]
TTSF	Time to Subsequent Fix [*Quality control*]
TTSF	Tongass [*National Forest*] Timber Supply Fund [*Department of the Interior*]
TTSI	TTS, Inc. [*NASDAQ symbol*] (NQ)
TTSP	Training Test Support Package [*Army*]
TTSP	Transition Training Squadron, Pacific [*Navy*]
TTSPB	Transport Theory and Statistical Physics [*A publication*]
TTSPN	Two Terminal Series Parallel Networks
TTSS	[*The*] Trumpeter Swan Society (EA)
TTSt	Trierer Theologische Studien [*Trier*] [*A publication*] (BJA)
TTSU	Tracker Test Set Supplemental Unit (MCD)
T & T Sup	Trinidad and Tobago Supreme Court Judgments [*A publication*] (ILCA)
TTT	Tactical Training Team [*Military*] (CAAL)
TTT	Taitung [*Taiwan*] [*Airport symbol*] (OAG)
TTT	Tallulah, LA [*Location identifier*] [*FAA*] (FAAL)
TTT	Tatiko-Tekhnicheskye-Trebovaniya [*Tactical Technical Requirement*] [*for military materiel*] [*USSR*] (RDA)
TTT	Telecom USA, Inc. [*NYSE symbol*] (CTT)
TTT	Tetrathiotetracene [*Organic chemistry*]
TTT	Texas College, Tyler, TX [*OCLC symbol*] (OCLC)
TTT	Teylers Theologisch Tijdschrift [*A publication*]
TTT	Thymol Turbidity Test [*Clinical chemistry*]
TTT	Time to Target (AAG)
TTT	Time Temperature Transformation
TTT	Time, Temperature, Turbulence [*Fuel technology*]
TTT	Time to Turn [*Ship or aircraft*]
TTT	Tolbutamide Tolerance Test [*Clinical chemistry*]

TTT............ Trade Token Topics [*A publication*]
TTT............ Training of Teacher Trainers
TTT............ Transamerican Trailer Transport
TTT............ Trilateral Tracking Technique
TTT............ Trinidad & Tobago Television Co.
TTT............ True Temperature Tunnel
TTTA......... Teletypewriter Terminal Assembly
TTTE......... Tri-National Tornado Training Establishment [*British military*]   (DMA)
TTU .... Tantalus Resources Ltd. [*Vancouver Stock Exchange symbol*]
TTU .... Target Transfer Unit   (MCD)
TTU .... Tartu [*Dorpat, Jurjeio*] [*USSR*] [*Seismograph station code, US Geological Survey*] [*Closed*]   (SEIS)
TTU .... Tennessee Technical University, Cookville, TN [*OCLC symbol*]   (OCLC)
TTU .... Terminal Timing Unit [*NASA*]   (KSC)
TTU .... Tetuan [*Morocco*] [*Airport symbol*]   (OAG)
TTU .... Thrust Termination Unit   (MSA)
TTU .... Timing Terminal Unit   (NASA)
TTuGS....... Church of Jesus Christ of Latter-Day Saints, Genealogical Society Library, Tennessee South District Branch, Tullahoma, TN [*Library symbol*] [*Library of Congress*]   (LCLS)
TTUV News ... TTUV (Technical Teachers Union of Victoria) News [*A publication*]
TTV .... Teletape Video
TTV .... Tenth Thickness Value [*Nuclear energy*]   (NRCH)
TTV .... Termination, Test, and Verification   (NASA)
TTV .... Territorial Petroleum [*Vancouver Stock Exchange symbol*]
TTV .... Thermal Test Vehicle
TTV .... Tow Test Vehicle [*Aerospace*]
TTVM .... Thermal Transfer Voltmeter
TTVP........ Trentiner Tiroler Volkspartei [*Trentino Tirol People's Party*] [*Italy*] [*Political party*]   (PPE)
TTW .... Tactical Training Wing [*Air Force*]
TTW .... Teletypewriter [*Telecommunications*]
TTW .... Test [*A publication*]
TTW......... Total Temperature and Weight
TTWB........ Turbine Trip with Bypass [*Nuclear energy*]   (NRCH)
TTWL........ Twin Tandem Wheel Loading [*Aviation*]
TTWS....... Terminal Threat Warning System
TTX .... Teletex [*Telecommunications*]
TTX .... Tetrodotoxin [*A poison*] [*Biochemistry*]
TTX .... Thiothixene [*Tranquilizer*]
TTX .... Tultex Corp. [*NYSE symbol*]   (SPSG)
TTX .... Tut Enterprises, Inc. [*Toronto Stock Exchange symbol*]
TTY .... Teletype   (CAAL)
TTY .... Teletypewriter [*Telecommunications*]
TTY .... Telex-Type [*Terminal*]
TTY .... Torque-to-Yield [*Automotive engineering*]
TTYA......... Teletypewriter Assembly
TTYD .... Tele-Typewriters for the Deaf [*An association*]
TTYQ/RSS ... Teletypewriter Query-Reply Subsystem   (CET)
TTZ............ Tactical-Technical Assignment [*Army*]   (RDA)
TTZ............ Titizima [*Bonin Islands*] [*Seismograph station code, US Geological Survey*] [*Closed*]   (SEIS)
TTZ............ Transformation Toughened Zirconia [*Metallurgy*]
TTZ............ Treats, Inc. [*Toronto Stock Exchange symbol*]
TTZ............ Trierer Theologische Zeitschrift [*A publication*]
TTZED...... TIZ. Tonindustrie-Zeitung [*A publication*]
TTZGAB ... Trudy Respublikanskogo Nauchno-Issledovatel'skogo Instituta Tuberkuleza Ministerstva Zdravookhraneniya Gruzinskoi SSR [*A publication*]
TTZP.......... Piarco, Trinidad [*Trinidad and Tobago*] [*ICAO location identifier*]
TU............. Ivory Coast [*Aircraft nationality and registration mark*]   (FAAC)
TU............. Societe Tunisienne de l'Air [*Tunisia*] [*ICAO designator*]
TU............. Tanking Unit   (AAG)
TU............. Tanners' Union [*British*]
TU............. Tape Unit
TU............. Task Unit [*Military*]
TU............. Taxicrinic Unit [*Data processing*]
TU............. Technical Service Unit [*Military*]
TU............. Technische Ueberwachung [*Technological Supervising*] [*A publication*]
TU............. Technische Universitat [*Technical University*] [*German*]
TU............. Technology Utilization
TU............. Tenebrio Unit [*Endocrinology*]
TU............. Terminal Unit
TU............. Testo Unico [*Consolidated Statutes*] [*Italian*]   (ILCA)
TU............. Texte und Untersuchungen zur Geschichte der Altchristlichen Literatur [*Berlin*] [*A publication*]
TU............. Thank You [*Communications operator's procedural remark*]
TU............. Thermal Unit
TU............. Thulium [*Chemical element*] [*Symbol is Tm*]   (ROG)
TU............. Timing Unit
TU............. Torah Umesorah - National Society for Hebrew Day Schools   (EA)
TU............. Toxic Unit [*Medicine*]
TU............. Trade Union

TU............. Traffic Unit
TU............. Training Unit [*Army*]
TU............. Transfer Unconditionally
TU............. Transfer Unit   (AAG)
TU............. Transmission Unit [*Telecommunications*]
TU............. Transport Unit   (MCD)
TU............. Transuranium [*Chemistry*]
TU............. Tritium Unit [*Nuclear energy*]
TU............. Trophic Unit [*Analytical biochemistry*]
TU............. Trout Unlimited   (EA)
TU............. Tuba
TU............. Tube
Tu............. Tubercle [*Anatomy*] [*Medicine*]
TU............. Tuberculin Unit
TU............. Tudor   (ROG)
TU............. Tuesday
TU............. Tugboatmen's Union [*British*]
TU............. Tuition
TU............. Tulane University [*New Orleans, LA*]
TU............. Tundra Times [*A publication*]
TU............. Tunis Airline   (DS)
TU............. Tupolev [*USSR*] [*ICAO aircraft manufacturer identifier*]   (ICAO)
TU............. Turbidity Unit
TU............. Turkey [*NATO*]   (AFM)
tu.............. Turkey [*MARC country of publication code*] [*Library of Congress*]   (LCCP)
TU............. Type Unique [*French standard troop train, World War I*]
TU............. University of Tennessee, Knoxville, TN [*Library symbol*] [*Library of Congress*]   (LCLS)
T$_3$U .... Triiodothyronine Uptake [*Endocrinology*]
TUA .... AT & T, Americus [*NYSE symbol*]   (SPSG)
TUA .... Syndicat International des Travailleurs Unis de l'Automobile, de l'Aerospatiale, et de l'Outillage Agricole d'Amerique [*International Union, United Automobile, Aerospace, and Agricultural Implement Workers of America - UAW*] [*Canada*]
TUA .... Telecommunications Users' Association   (TSSD)
TUA .... Telephone Users Association   (EA)
TuA .... Texte und Arbeiten [*Beuron*] [*A publication*]   (BJA)
TUA .... Time Use Analysis [*Test*]
TUA .... Tuai [*New Zealand*] [*Seismograph station code, US Geological Survey*]   (SEIS)
TUA .... Tulcan [*Ecuador*] [*Airport symbol*]   (OAG)
TUAC .... Trade Union Advisory Committee [*British*]   (DAS)
TUAC .... Union Internationale des Travailleurs Unis de l'Alimentation et du Commerce [*United Food and Commercial Workers Union*] [*Canada*]
TUAC OECD ... Trade Union Advisory Committee to the Organization for Economic Cooperation and Development [*Paris, France*]   (EAIO)
TuAF......... Turkish Air Force
T/U/Ag...... Trustee under Agreement [*Legal term*]   (DLA)
TUAGAT ... Tunisie Agricole. Revue Mensuelle Illustree [*A publication*]
TUAL .... Tentative Unit Allowance List [*Air Force*]   (AFM)
TUAR .... Turning Arbor
TUB .... Temporary Unlighted Buoy [*Maps and charts*]
TUB .... Troop Unit Basis [*Military*]
TUB .... Tubing   (AAG)
TUB .... Tubingen [*Federal Republic of Germany*] [*Seismograph station code, US Geological Survey*]   (SEIS)
TUB .... Tubuai Island [*Austral Islands*] [*Airport symbol*]   (OAG)
TUB .... Tubular [*Automotive engineering*]
TUB .... Tulane University. Bulletin [*A publication*]
TUB .... [*The*] Unborn Book [*A publication*]
TUBA ...... John Phillip Tuba Corp. [*NASDAQ symbol*]   (NQ)
TUBA .... Tubists Universal Brotherhood Association   (EA)
TUBE........ Terminating Unfair Broadcasting Excesses [*Student legal action organization*]   (EA)
TUBE........ Trans-Urban Bicentennial Exposition
TUBEA...... Tubercle [*A publication*]
tuberc .... Tuberculosis [*Medicine*]
Tuberc Res ... Tuberculosis Research [*A publication*]
Tuberc Respir Dis ... Tuberculosis and Respiratory Diseases [*A publication*]
Tuberculol Thorac Dis ... Tuberculology and Thoracic Diseases [*A publication*]
Tuberk Forschungsinst Borstel Jahresber ... Tuberkulose Forschungsinstitut Borstel. Jahresbericht [*A publication*]
Tuberk Grenzgeb Einzeldarst ... Tuberkulose und Ihre Grenzgebiete in Einzeldarstellungen [*A publication*]
Tuberk Ihre Grenzgeb Einzeldarst ... Tuberkulose und Ihre Grenzgebiete in Einzeldarstellungen [*A publication*]
TUBITAK ... Scientific and Technical Research Council of Turkey [*Ankara*] [*Information service or system*]   (IID)
TUBLR...... Tubular [*Freight*]
TUBS......... Tubular Tires [*Cyclist term*] [*British*]   (DSUE)
Tubular Struct ... Tubular Structures [*A publication*]
TUBWPL ... Technische Universitaet Berlin. Arbeitspapiere zur Linguistik/Working Papers in Linguistics [*A publication*]
TUC .... Teaching Usefulness Classification [*of a hospital patient*]
TUC .... Technology Utilization Center

TUC .... Telecommunications Users Coalition (EA)
TUC .... Teleordering Users' Council [British]
TUC .... Temporary Unemployment Compensation [Labor]
TUC .... Time of Useful Consciousness [Medicine]
TUC .... Tracer Resources [Vancouver Stock Exchange symbol]
TUC .... Trade [or Trades] Union Council
TUC .... Trades Union Congress [British]
TUC .... Transportation, Utilities, Communications
Tuc .... Tucana [Constellation]
TUC .... Tucson [Arizona] [Geomagnetic observatory code]
TUC .... Tucson [Arizona] [Seismograph station code, US Geological Survey] (SEIS)
TUC .... Tucuman [Argentina] [Airport symbol] (OAG)
TUC .... Type Unit Code (CINC)
TUC .... University of Tennessee at Chattanooga, Chattanooga, TN [OCLC symbol] (OCLC)
TUCA .... Tilt-Up Concrete Association (EA)
TUCA .... Transient Undercooling Accident [Nuclear energy]
TUCA .... Turning Cam [Tool] (AAG)
TUCC ...... Transport Users' Consultative Council [British] (ILCA)
TUCC ...... Triangle Universities Computation Center [Durham, NC]
TUCE .... Test of Understanding of College Economics
TUCHA ..... Type Unit Characteristics
Tu Civ LF.. Tulane Civil Law Forum [A publication] (DLA)
Tuck .... Tucker and Clephane's Reports [21 District of Columbia] [1892-93] [A publication] (DLA)
TUCK .... Tucker Drilling Co., Inc. [NASDAQ symbol] (NQ)
Tuck .... Tucker's New York Surrogate's Court Reports [A publication] (DLA)
Tuck .... Tucker's Reports [District of Columbia] [A publication] (DLA)
Tuck .... Tucker's Reports [156-175 Massachusetts] [A publication] (DLA)
Tuck .... Tucker's Select Cases [Newfoundland] [A publication] (DLA)
Tuck Bl Com ... Tucker's Blackstone's Commentaries [A publication] (DLA)
Tuck & C.... Tucker and Clephane's Reports [21 District of Columbia] [A publication] (DLA)
Tuck & Cl... Tucker and Clephane's Reports [21 District of Columbia] [1892-93] [A publication] (DLA)
Tuck Dist of Col ... Tucker's District of Columbia Appeals [A publication] (DLA)
Tucker........ Tucker's New York Surrogate's Court Reports [A publication] (DLA)
Tucker's Blackstone ... Tucker's Blackstone's Commentaries [A publication] (DLA)
Tuck Lect... Tucker's Lectures [A publication] (DLA)
Tuck Pl ...... Tucker's Pleadings [A publication] (DLA)
Tuck Sel Cas ... Tucker's Select Cases [1817-28] [Newfoundland] [A publication] (DLA)
Tuck Sur .... Tucker's Surrogate Reports, City of New York [A publication] (DLA)
Tuck Surr... Tucker's Surrogate Reports, City of New York [A publication] (DLA)
TUCN .... Trades Union Congress of Nigeria
Tucn .... Tucana [Constellation]
TUCOPS ...... [The] Universal Coterie of Pipe Smokers (EA)
TUCOSP .. Tehran Union Catalogue of Scientific Periodicals [A publication]
TUCR .... Troop Unit Change Request
TUCRC..... Trade Union Community Research Centre [Hobart, Australia]
TUCSA...... Trade Union Council of South Africa
TUCT .... Taxation Unpaid Companies Tax Act [Australia] (ADA)
TUD.......... Tambacounda [Senegal] [Airport symbol] (OAG)
TUD.......... Technology Utilization Division [NASA] (IEEE)
TUD.......... Total Urethral Discharge [Medicine]
TUD.......... Trudy Universiteta Druzhby Narodov Imeni Patrisa Lumumby [A publication]
TUD.......... Tugold Resources, Inc. [Vancouver Stock Exchange symbol]
TUDC....... Tauroursodeoxycholate [Biochemistry]
TUDCA....... Tauroursodeoxycholic Acid [Biochemistry]
Tud Cas Merc Law ... Tudor's Leading Cases on Mercantile Law [3 eds.] [1860-84] [A publication] (DLA)
Tud Cas RP ... Tudor's Leading Cases on Real Property [4 eds.] [1856-98] [A publication] (DLA)
Tud Char Tr ... Tudor's Charitable Trusts [2nd ed.] [1871] [A publication] (DLA)
Tud Char Trusts ... Tudor's Charitable Trusts [2nd ed.] [1871] [A publication] (DLA)
Tud Ert Agrartud Egy Godollo ... Tudomanyos Ertesito-Agrartudomanyi Egyetem Godollo [A publication]
Tud Ert Agrartud Egy Godollo (Hung) ... Tudomanyos Ertesito-Agrartudomanyi Egyetem Godollo (Hungary) [A publication]
Tud Mezogazd ... Tudomany es Mezogazdasag [A publication]
Tud & Musz Tajek ... Tudomanyos es Muszaki Tajekoztatas [A publication]
TUDNL ..... Trudy Universiteta Druzhby Narodov Imeni Patrisa Lumumby [Moscow] [A publication]
Tudom Musz Tajek ... Tudomanyos es Muszaki Tajekoztatas [A publication]
Tudor Lead Cas Real Prop ... Tudor's Leading Cases on Real Property [A publication] (DLA)
Tudor's LCML ... Tudor's Leading Cases on Mercantile Law [A publication] (DLA)

Tudor's LCRP ... Tudor's Leading Cases on Real Property [A publication] (DLA)
TUDS .... Tunnel Detection System (MCD)
Tud-Szerv Tajekoz ... Tudomanyszervezesi Tajekoztato [A publication]
TUE .... Tolerance of Unrealistic Experience [Psychometrics]
TUE .... Trainer Unique Equipment [Navy]
TUE .... Tuesday (AFM)
TUE .... Tupile [Panama] [Airport symbol] (OAG)
TUE .... University of Tokyo (EDUCATSS) [UTLAS symbol]
TUEL .... Trade Union Educational League
Tuerk Z Hyg Exp Biol ... Tuerkische Zeitschrift fuer Hygiene und Experimentelle Biologie [A publication]
TUES........ Tuesday (EY)
TUES........ Tuesday Morning, Inc. [Dallas, TX] [NASDAQ symbol] (NQ)
TUeV Mitt Mitglieder Tech Ueberwach-Ver Bayern ... TUeV [Technischer Ueberwachungs-Verein] Mitteilungen fuer die Mitglieder. Technischer Ueberwachungs-Verein Bayern [German Federal Republic] [A publication]
TUF .... Tactical Undercover Function [Chicago police operation]
TUF .... Thermal Utilization Factor (MCD)
TUF .... Tours [France] [Airport symbol] (OAG)
TUF .... Trade Union Federation [British] (EY)
TUF .... Transmitter Underflow
TUF .... Umweltmagazin. Fachzeitschrift fuer Umwelttechnik in Industrie und Kommune [A publication]
TUFA........ Total Unsaturated Fatty Acid [of foodstuffs]
TUFA........ Trans Unsaturated Fatty Acids
TUFCDF ... Thorium-Uranium Fuel Cycle Development Facility [Nuclear energy]
TUFEC...... Thailand-UNESCO Fundamental Education Centre
TUFF-TUG ... Tape Update of Formatted Files-Format Table Tape Updater and Generator [Data processing]
TUFI........ This Umbrella Folds Itself [Trademark for type of umbrella]
TUFL......... Trade Unionists for Labour [British]
TU-FM ...... University of Tennessee Center for the Health Sciences/ Memphis Department of Family Medicine, Memphis, TN [Library symbol] [Library of Congress] (LCLS)
TUFMIS ... Tactical Unit Financial Management Information System
TUFPB ...... Proceedings. Faculty of Science. Tokai University [A publication]
Tufs Folia Med ... Tufs Folia Medica [A publication]
Tufts Coll Studies ... Tufts College Studies [A publication]
Tufts Dent Outlook ... Tufts Dental Outlook [A publication]
Tufts Health Sci Rev ... Tufts Health Science Review [A publication]
TUFX........ Turning Fixture
TUG .... Maritrans Partners LP [NYSE symbol] (SPSG)
TUG .... Tape Unit Group [Telecommunications] (TEL)
TUG .... Telecommunications Users Group [Montclair, NJ] [Telecommunications service] (TSSD)
TUG .... Teleram Users Group (EA)
TUG .... Total Urinary Gonadotropin [Clinical chemistry]
TUG .... Towed Universal Glider
TUG .... TRANSAC [Transistorized Automatic Computer] Users Group
TUG .... Transtex Universal Gateway [Data processing]
TUG .... Tuguegarao [Philippines] [Airport symbol] (OAG)
TUGAL ..... Texte und Untersuchungen zur Geschichte der Altchristlichen Literatur [A publication]
TU Gazette ... University of Tasmania. Gazette [A publication] (APTA)
TUGEA...... Teknisk Ukeblad [A publication]
TUGPS...... Taxe Unique Globale sur les Presentations de Service [Service tax] [French] (IMH)
TUGRA ..... Report of Investigations. University of Texas at Austin. Bureau of Economic Geology [A publication]
TUH .... Review of Economic Conditions [Ankara] [A publication]
TUH .... Tullahoma, TN [Location identifier] [FAA] (FAAL)
TU-H .... University of Tennessee Center for the Health Sciences/ Knoxville, Preston Medical Library, Knoxville, TN [Library symbol] [Library of Congress] (LCLS)
TUHC........ Tucker Holding Company, Inc. [NASDAQ symbol] (NQ)
TUHTKP... Time Urgent Hard Target Kill Potential (MCD)
TUI .... Green Bay, WI [Location identifier] [FAA] (FAAL)
TUI .... Tool Usage Instructions (MCD)
TUI .... Trade Union Immunities [British]
TUI .... Trade Union International
TUI .... Trade Unions International of Transport Workers (EAIO)
TUI .... Trypsin Units Inhibited [Food technology]
TUI .... Tuinderij. Vakblad voor de Intensieve Groenteteelt [A publication]
TUI .... Tuition (DSUE)
TUI .... Turaif [Saudi Arabia] [Airport symbol] (OAG)
TUIAFPW ... Trade Unions International of Agriculture, Forestry, and Plantation Workers [See also UISTAFP] [Prague, Czechoslovakia] (EAIO)
TUIFU....... [The] Ultimate in Foul Ups [Military slang] [Bowdlerized version]
TUII.......... TU International, Incorporated [NASDAQ symbol] (NQ)
TUIMWE ... Trade Unions International of Miners and Workers in Energy [See also UISMTE] (EAIO)
TUIPAE ..... Trade Unions International of Public and Allied Employees [Berlin, Federal Republic of Germany] (EAIO)
TUIR .... Time until in Range

TUIRC....... Trade Union Information and Research Centre [*Sydney, Australia*]

TUITW...... Trade Unions International of Transport Workers (EAIO)

TUIWC...... Trade Unions International of Workers in Commerce [*Prague, Czechoslovakia*] (EAIO)

TUJ........... Tubouterine Junction [*Anatomy*]

TUJ........... Tum [*Ethiopia*] [*Airport symbol*] (OAG)

TUK.......... Nantucket, MA [*Location identifier*] [*FAA*] (FAAL)

TuK........... Text und Kritik [*A publication*]

TUK.......... Tuckahoe Financial Corp. [*Toronto Stock Exchange symbol*]

TUK.......... Turbat [*Pakistan*] [*Airport symbol*] (OAG)

tuk............. Turkmen [*MARC language code*] [*Library of Congress*] (LCCP)

TUKMAT ... Trudy Ukrainskogo Nauchno-Issledovatel'skogo Instituta Klinicheskoi Meditsiny [*A publication*]

TuL........... Tod und Leben nach der Vorstellungen der Babylonier [*A publication*] (BJA)

TUL.......... Tula Peak, New Mexico [*Spaceflight Tracking and Data Network*] [*NASA*]

Tu L .... Tulane Law Review [*A publication*]

TUL .... Tulsa [*University of Oklahoma*] [*Oklahoma*] [*Seismograph station code, US Geological Survey*] (SEIS)

TUL .... Tulsa [*Oklahoma*] [*Airport symbol*] (OAG)

TUL .... Tulsa [*Oklahoma*] [*Geomagnetic observatory code*]

TUL .... Tulsa City-County Library System, Tulsa, OK [*OCLC symbol*] (OCLC)

TU-L.......... University of Tennessee, Law Library, Knoxville, TN [*Library symbol*] [*Library of Congress*] (LCLS)

TULACS ... Tactical Unit Location and Communication System (MCD)

Tulane Law R ... Tulane Law Review [*A publication*]

Tulane L Rev ... Tulane Law Review [*A publication*]

Tulane St ... Tulane Studies in English [*A publication*]

Tulane Stud Eng ... Tulane Studies in English [*A publication*]

Tulane Stud Geol ... Tulane Studies in Geology [*A publication*]

Tulane Stud Geol Paleontol ... Tulane Studies in Geology and Paleontology [*A publication*]

Tulane Stud Phil ... Tulane Studies in Philosophy [*A publication*]

Tulane Stud Zool ... Tulane Studies in Zoology [*A publication*]

Tulane Stud Zool Bot ... Tulane Studies in Zoology and Botany [*A publication*]

Tulane U Stud Eng ... Tulane University. Studies in English [*A publication*]

TU Law R .. University of Tasmania. Law Review [*A publication*] (APTA)

TULC........ Trade Union Leadership Council (EA)

TULCC...... Triangle University Library Cooperative Committee [*Library network*]

Tul Civ LF ... Tulane Civil Law Forum [*A publication*] (DLA)

TULE......... Transistorized Universal Logic Elements

TULF........ Tamil United Liberation Front [*Sri Lanka*] (PD)

Tul Gorn Inst Nauchn Tr ... Tul'skii Gornyi Institut Nauchnye Trudy [*A publication*]

Tul Gos Pedagog Inst Uch Zap Fiz Tekh Nauk ... Tul'skii Gosudarstvennyi Pedagogicheskii Institut Uchenye Zapiski Fiziko-Tekhnicheskie Nauki [*A publication*]

Tul Gos Ped Inst Ucen Zap Mat Kaf ... Tul'skii Gosudarstvennyi Pedagogiceskii Institut Imeni L. N. Tolstogo Ucenye Zapiski Matematiceskih Kafedr [*A publication*]

Tul LR....... Tulane Law Review [*A publication*]

Tul L Rev ... Tulane Law Review [*A publication*]

Tu LR........ Tulane Law Review [*A publication*]

TULRA...... Trade Union and Labour Relations Act [*1974 and 1976*] [*British*] (DCTA)

TULS........ TRON [*The Real-Time Operating System Nucleus*] Universal Language System [*Data processing*]

TULS........ Tulsa World [*A publication*]

TULSA....... Petroleum Abstracts [*Online*]

Tulsa Bs C ... Tulsa Business Chronicle [*A publication*]

Tulsa Geol Soc Dig ... Tulsa Geological Society. Digest [*A publication*]

Tulsa Geol Soc Digest ... Tulsa Geological Society. Digest [*A publication*]

Tulsa L J... Tulsa Law Journal [*A publication*]

Tulsa Med ... Tulsa Medicine [*A publication*]

Tul Tax Inst ... Tulane Tax Institute [*A publication*]

Tul Tidelands Inst ... Tulane Mineral and Tidelands Law Institute [*A publication*]

TUM.......... Technical University in Munich [*Federal Republic of Germany*]

TuM.......... Texte und Materialien der Frau Professor Hilprecht Collection of Babylonian Antiquities im Eigentum der Univerisitaet Jena [*A publication*] (BJA)

TuM.......... Torah Umesorah - National Society for Hebrew Day Schools

TUM........ Total Unscheduled Maintenance Time

TUM........ Trades Union Movement

TUM........ Tumut [*Australia*] [*Airport symbol*] (OAG)

TUM........ Tumwater [*Washington*] [*Seismograph station code, US Geological Survey*] (SEIS)

TUM........ Tuning Unit Member (IEEE)

TUM.......... University of Tennessee, Center for the Health Sciences, Memphis, TN [*OCLC symbol*] (OCLC)

TU-M......... University of Tennessee Medical Units, Memphis, TN [*Library symbol*] [*Library of Congress*] (LCLS)

TUM.......... [*The*] Unsatisfied Man [*A publication*]

TUMA....... Tumacacori National Monument

TU-MDC... University of Tennessee, Downtown Memphis Center, Memphis, TN [*Library symbol*] [*Library of Congress*] (LCLS)

TUME .... [*The*] Ultimate Musical Experience [*Rock music group*]

TUMEA .... Tunisie Medicale [*A publication*]

Tumor Diagn ... Tumor Diagnostik [*A publication*]

Tumor Diagn Ther ... Tumor Diagnostik und Therapie [*A publication*]

Tumor Res ... Tumor Research [*A publication*]

Tumour Biol ... Tumour Biology [*A publication*]

TU-MS...... University of Tennessee Center for the Health Sciences Library, Stollerman Library, Memphis, TN [*Library symbol*] [*Library of Congress*] (LCLS)

TuMV .... Turnip Mosaic Virus

TUN........... Flint, MI [*Location identifier*] [*FAA*] (FAAL)

TUN........... Technical University of Nova Scotia [*UTLAS symbol*]

TUN........... Tennessee State University, Downtown Campus, Nashville, TN [*OCLC symbol*] (OCLC)

TUN........... Transfer Unconditionally

TUN........... Tuning (AAG)

TUN........... Tunis [*Tunisia*] [*Seismograph station code, US Geological Survey*] [*Closed*] (SEIS)

TUN........... Tunis [*Tunisia*] [*Airport symbol*] (OAG)

TUN........... Tunisia [*ANSI three-letter standard code*] (CNC)

TUN........... Turner Energy & Resources [*Vancouver Stock Exchange symbol*]

TUNA....... Tunable Attribute Display Subsystem (CAAL)

Tuners JL .. Tuners' Journal [*A publication*]

TUNG........ Tungsten (AAG)

Tungsram Tech Mitt ... Tungsram Technische Mitteilungen [*A publication*]

TUNICAT ... Tunicatae [*Coated*] [*Pharmacy*]

Tunis Agric ... Tunisie Agricole [*A publication*]

TUNISAIR ... Societe Tunisienne de l'Air [*Airline*] [*Tunisia*]

Tunisie Agr ... Tunisie Agricole [*A publication*]

Tunisie Agric Rev Mens Illus ... Tunisie Agricole. Revue Mensuelle Illustree [*A publication*]

Tunisie Econ ... Tunisie Economique [*A publication*]

Tunis Med ... Tunisie Medicale [*A publication*]

TUNL........ Triangle Universities Nuclear Laboratory [*Research center*] (RCD)

TUNL........ Tunnel

Tunnels Ouvrages Souterr ... Tunnels et Ouvrages Souterrains [*A publication*]

Tunnels Tunnell ... Tunnels and Tunnelling [*A publication*]

Tunnlg Technol Newsl ... Tunneling Technology Newsletter [*A publication*]

Tunn Technol Newsl ... Tunneling Technology Newsletter [*United States*] [*A publication*]

Tunn Tunn ... Tunnels and Tunnelling [*A publication*]

Tunn Tunnlg ... Tunnels and Tunnelling [*A publication*]

TUNX........ Tunex International, Inc. [*NASDAQ symbol*] (NQ)

TUO........... Taupo [*New Zealand*] [*Airport symbol*] (OAG)

TUO........... Technology Utilization Office [*NASA*]

TUO........... Teuton Resources Corp. [*Vancouver Stock Exchange symbol*]

TUO........... Tucson Observatory [*Arizona*] [*Seismograph station code, US Geological Survey*] (SEIS)

TUOC........ Tactical Unit Operations Center (AFM)

TUP .... Technology Utilization Program [*Defunct*]

TUP .... Telephony User Part [*Telecommunications*] (TEL)

TUP .... Temple University Press

TUP .... Torres United Party [*Australia*] [*Political party*]

TUP .... Tovarystvo Ukrainskykh Progresystiv [*Ukrainian Progressive Association*] [*Russian*] [*Political party*] (PPE)

TUP .... Trickle Up Program (EA)

TUP .... Tupelo [*Mississippi*] [*Airport symbol*] (OAG)

TUP .... Tupik [*USSR*] [*Seismograph station code, US Geological Survey*] (SEIS)

TUP .... Twin Unit Pack [*for vehicles*]

Tup App...... Tupper's Appeal Reports [*Ontario*] [*A publication*] (DLA)

TUPC........ T. U. P. Charlton's Georgia Reports [*A publication*] (DLA)

T U P Charlt ... T. U. P. Charlton's Georgia Reports [*A publication*] (DLA)

TUPE........ Tanganyika Union of Public Employees

TUPE........ Tupelo National Battlefield

TUPJ .... Roadtown/Beef Island [*Virgin Islands*] [*ICAO location identifier*] (ICLI)

TUPMA .... Trudy Ural'skii Nauchno-Issledovatel'skii i Proektnyi Institut Mednoi Promyshlennosti [*A publication*]

TUPONA .. [*The*] United Provinces of North America [*See also EFISGA*] [*Suggested early name for Canada*]

Tupp.......... Tupper's Appeal Reports [*Ontario*] [*A publication*] (DLA)

Tupp.......... Tupper's Upper Canada Practice Reports [*A publication*] (DLA)

Tupp App... Tupper's Appeal Reports [*Ontario*] [*A publication*] (DLA)

Tupper ...... Tupper's Appeal Reports [*Ontario*] [*A publication*] (DLA)

Tupper ...... Tupper's Upper Canada Practice Reports [*A publication*] (DLA)

TUPS........ Technical User Performance Specifications [*US Independent Telephone Association*] [*Telecommunications*] (TEL)

TUPW .... Virgin Gorda [*Virgin Islands*] [*ICAO location identifier*] (ICLI)

TUR .... American Turners [*An association*]

TUR .... Temporary Unattached Register [*Employment*] [*British*]

TUR .... Traffic Usage Recorder [*Telecommunications*]

TUR .... Transurethral Resection [*of prostate gland*]

TUR.......... Tucurui [Brazil] [Airport symbol] (OAG)
TUR.......... Turbat [USSR] [Seismograph station code, US Geological Survey] [Closed] (SEIS)
TUR.......... Turbine
TUR.......... Turkey [ANSI three-letter standard code] (CNC)
tur............. Turkish [MARC language code] [Library of Congress] (LCCP)
TUR.......... Turkish Economy [A publication]
TUR.......... Turner Corp. [AMEX symbol] (SPSG)
Tur .... Turner's Reports [35-48 Arkansas] [A publication] (DLA)
Tur .... Turner's Reports [99-101 Kentucky] [A publication] (DLA)
Tur .... Turner's Select Pleas of the Forest [Selden Society Publication, Vol. 13] [A publication] (DLA)
TUR.......... Turret (MSA)
TURB .... Turbine (AAG)
TURB .... Turbulence
TURBC...... Turbulence (FAAC)
TURBO ...... Turbocharger [Automotive engineering]
TURBOALT ... Turboalternator (AAG)
TURBOCAT .. Turbine-Powered Catapult
TURBOGEN ... Turbogenerator (AAG)
Turbomachinery Int ... Turbomachinery International [A publication]
Turbomach Int ... Turbomachinery International [A publication]
TURBT...... Turbulent (FAAC)
Turbul Meas Liq Proc Symp ... Turbulence Measurements in Liquids. Proceedings of Symposium [A publication]
Turc............ Turcica. Revue d'Etudes Turques [A publication]
TURCO ..... Turnaround Control [Navy]
TURDOK .. Turkish Scientific and Technical Documentation Centre [Scientific and Technical Research Council of Turkey] [Ankara]
TUREA...... Tumor Research [A publication]
TURF......... Thorium-Uranium Recycle Facility [Oak Ridge National Laboratory]
TURF......... Turf Paradise, Inc. [NASDAQ symbol] (NQ)
Turf Bull .... Turf Bulletin [A publication]
Turf Cult .... Turf Culture [A publication]
TURK .... Turkey
Turk AD .... Turk Arkeoloji Dergisi [A publication]
Turk AEC Ankara Nucl Res Cent Tech J ... Turkish Atomic Energy Commission. Ankara Nuclear Research Center. Technical Journal [A publication]
Turk Ark Derg ... Turk Arkeoloji Dergisi [A publication]
Turk Biol Derg ... Turk Biologi Dergisi [A publication]
Turk Bitki Koruma Derg ... Turkiye Bitki Koruma Dergisi [A publication]
Turk Bull Hyg Exp Biol ... Turkish Bulletin of Hygiene and Experimental Biology [A publication]
Turk Cerrahi Cemiy Mecm ... Turk Cerrahi Cemiyeti Mecmuasi [A publication]
Turkest ...... Turkestan
Turkey Prod ... Turkey Producer [A publication]
Turk Fiz Dernegi Bul ... Turk Fizik Dernegi Bulteni [A publication]
Turk For Pol Rep ... Turkish Foreign Policy Report [A publication]
Turk Gen Kim Kurumu Derg B ... Turkiye Genel Kimyagerler Kurumu Dergisi-B [A publication]
Turk Hemsire Derg ... Turk Hemsireler Dergisi [A publication]
Turk Hifzissihha Tecr Biol Mecm ... Turk Hifzissihha ve Tecrubi Biologi Mecmuasi [A publication]
Turk Hij Deney Biyol Derg ... Turk Hijiyen ve Deneysel Biyoloji Dergisi [A publication]
Turk Hij Deneysel Biyol Derg ... Turk Hijiyen ve Deneysel Biyoloji Dergisi [A publication]
Turk Hij Tecr Biyol Derg ... Turk Hijiyen ve Tecruby Biyoloji Dergisi [A publication]
Turk J Biol ... Turkish Journal of Biology [A publication]
Turk Jeol Kurumu Bul ... Turkiye Jeoloji Kurumu Bulteni [A publication]
Turk Jeomorfologlar Dernegi Yayini ... Turkiye Jeomorfologlar Dernegi. Yayini [A publication]
Turk J Nucl Sci ... Turkish Journal of Nuclear Sciences [A publication]
Turk J Pediatr ... Turkish Journal of Pediatrics [A publication]
Turk Ljiyen Tecruebi Biyol Dergisi ... Turk Ljiyen ve Tecruebi Biyoloji Dergisi [A publication]
Turkmen Gos Univ Ucen Zap ... Turkmenskii Gosudarstvennyi Universitet Imeni A. M. Gor'kogo Ucenye Zapiski [A publication]
Turk Mikrobiyol Cemiy Derg ... Turk Mikrobiyoloji Cemiyeti Dergisi [A publication]
Turk Miner Res Explor Bull ... Turkey. Mineral Research and Exploration Institute. Bulletin [A publication]
Turkm Iskra ... Turkmenskaya Iskra [USSR] [A publication]
TurkmSSR ... Turkmen Soviet Socialist Republic
Turk Publ Adm Annu ... Turkish Public Administration Annual [A publication]
Turk Ship... Turkish Shipping [A publication]
Turk Tar Derg ... Turk Tarih. Arkeologya ve Etnografya Dergisi [A publication]
Turk Tip Akad Mecm ... Turkiye Tip Akademisi Mecmuasi [A publication]
Turk Tip Cemiy Mecm ... Turkiye Tip Cemiyeti Mecmuasi [A publication]
Turk Tip Cem Mecm ... Turkiye Tip Cemiyeti Mecmuasi [Turkey] [A publication]
Turk Tip Dern Derg ... Turk Tip Dernegi Dergisi [A publication]
Turk Tip Encumeni Ars ... Turkiye Tip Encumeni Arsivi [A publication]
Turn .... Turner's Reports [35-48 Arkansas] [A publication] (DLA)

Turn .... Turner's Reports [99-101 Kentucky] [A publication] (DLA)
Turn .... Turner's Select Pleas of the Forest [Selden Society Publication, Vol. 13] [A publication] (DLA)
Turn Anglo Sax ... Turner's History of the Anglo Saxon [A publication] (DLA)
TURNBKLE ... Turnbuckle[s] [Freight]
Turnbull Libr Rec ... Turnbull Library Record [A publication]
Turn Ch Pr ... Turner's Practice of the Court of Chancery [4th ed.] [1821] [A publication] (DLA)
Turn Cop.... Turner on Copyright in Designs [1849] [A publication] (DLA)
Turn & P .... Turner and Phillips' English Chancery Reports [A publication] (DLA)
Turn Pat.... Turner on Patents [1851] [A publication] (DLA)
Turn & Ph ... Turner and Phillips' English Chancery Reports [A publication] (DLA)
Turn Pr ...... Turnbull's Practice [New York] [A publication] (DLA)
Turn Qui Tit ... Turner on Quieting Titles [A publication] (DLA)
Turn & R.... Turner and Russell's English Chancery Reports [37 English Reprint] [A publication] (DLA)
Turn Rec .... Turnbull Library Record [New Zealand] [A publication]
Turn & R (Eng) ... Turner and Russell's English Chancery Reports [37 English Reprint] [A publication] (DLA)
Turn & Rus ... Turner and Russell's English Chancery Reports [37 English Reprint] [A publication] (DLA)
Turn & Russ ... Turner and Russell's English Chancery Reports [37 English Reprint] [A publication] (DLA)
Turon Yliopiston Julk Sar A-II ... Turon Yliopiston Julkaisuja. Sarja A-II [A publication]
TURP........ Transurethral Resection of the Prostate [Medicine]
TURPS...... Terrestrial Unattended Reactor Power System
TURQ........ Turquoise (ROG)
Tur & R...... Turner and Russell's English Chancery Reports [37 English Reprint] [1822-24] [A publication] (DLA)
TURRA ..... Turrialba [Costa Rica] [A publication]
Turrialba.... Turrialba. Revista Interamericana de Ciencias Agricolas [A publication]
Tur & Ru.... Turner and Russell's English Chancery Reports [37 English Reprint] [1822-24] [A publication] (DLA)
Tur & Rus .. Turner and Russell's English Chancery Reports [37 English Reprint] [1822-24] [A publication] (DLA)
TURS........ Terminal Usage Reporting System [Data processing]
Tu & Rus.... Turner and Russell's English Chancery Reports [1822-24] [A publication] (DLA)
TUS .... Tailored Upper Stage (MCD)
TUS .... Treasurer of the United States (AFM)
TUS .... Tucson [Arizona] [Airport symbol] (OAG)
TUS .... Tugboat Underwriting Syndicate [Defunct] (EA)
TUS .... Tuscarora [New York] [Seismograph station code, US Geological Survey] [Closed] (SEIS)
TUS .... Tushaun Resources, Inc. [Vancouver Stock Exchange symbol]
TUS .... Tuskegee Institute, Tuskegee, AL [OCLC symbol] (OCLC)
TUS .... Tussis [Cough] [Pharmacy]
TUSA........ Third United States Army [Terminated, 1973]
TUSA........ Trekville USA (EA)
TUSAB...... [The] United States Army Band (AABC)
TUSAC...... [The] United States Army Chorus (AABC)
TUSAFG ... [The] United States Air Force Group, American Mission for Aid to Turkey
TUSAS ..... Twayne's United States Authors Series [A publication]
TUSC........ Technology Use Studies Center [Southeastern State College]
TUSC........ Tuscarora Plastics, Inc. [NASDAQ symbol] (NQ)
Tusc.......... Tusculanae Disputationes [of Cicero] [Classical studies] (OCD)
TU-SI........ University of Tennessee, Space Institute Library, Tullahoma, TN [Library symbol] [Library of Congress] (LCLS)
Tuskegee Exp ... Tuskegee Normal and Industrial Institute. Experiment Station. Publications [A publication]
TUSLA...... Trudy Ukrainskii Nauchno-Issledovatel'skii Institut Spirtovoi i Likero-Vodochnoi Promyshlennosti [A publication]
TUSLOG... Turkish-United States Logistic Group
TUSLOG... [The] United States Logistics Group [Military] (AABC)
TUSQA ..... Quarterly Bulletin. Faculty of Science. Tehran University [A publication]
TUSSI .... Temple University Short Syntax Inventory [Educational test]
TUSSIL..... Tussilago [Coltsfoot] [Pharmacology] (ROG)
TUSS MOL ... Tussi Molesta [When the Cough Is Troublesome] [Pharmacy]
Tussock Grassl Mt Lands Inst Annu Rep ... Tussock Grasslands and Mountain Lands Institute. Annual Report [A publication]
TUSS URG ... Tussi Urgente [When the Cough Is Troublesome] [Pharmacy]
TUST......... Texarkana Union Station Trust [AAR code]
TUT .... Tafuna, AS [Location identifier] [FAA] (FAAL)
TUT .... Transistor under Test (IEEE)
TUT .... Travailleurs Unis du Telegraphe [United Telegraph Workers - UTW] [Canada]
TUT .... Travailleurs Unis des Transports [United Transportation Union - UTU] [Canada]
TUT .... Tube Template (MCD)
TUT .... Tube under Test (MSA)
TUT .... Tucson - Telemeter [Arizona] [Seismograph station code, US Geological Survey] [Closed] (SEIS)

tut .... Turko-Tataric [*MARC language code*] [*Library of Congress*] (LCCP)

TUT .... University of Saint Thomas, Houston, TX [*OCLC symbol*] (OCLC)

TUT's .... Totally Unified Theories [*Cosmology*]

Tutkimuksia Res Rep ... Tutkimuksia Research Reports [*A publication*]

Tutkimus Tek ... Tutkimus ja Tekniikka [*A publication*]

TUTNB ..... Tunneling Technology Newsletter [*A publication*]

TUTOR ..... [*A*] programming language (CSR)

TUTT........ Tropical Upper Tropospheric Trough [*Meteorology*]

Tutt & C..... Tuttle and Carpenter's Reports [*52 California*] [*A publication*] (DLA)

Tutt & Carp ... Tuttle and Carpenter's Reports [*52 California*] [*A publication*] (DLA)

Tuttle .... Tuttle and Carpenter's Reports [*52 California*] [*A publication*] (DLA)

Tuttle & Carpenter ... Tuttle and Carpenter's Reports [*52 California*] [*A publication*] (DLA)

TUTUB ..... Tunnels and Tunnelling [*A publication*]

TUU........... Huntington, WV [*Location identifier*] [*FAA*] (FAAL)

TUU........... Tabuk [*Saudi Arabia*] [*Airport symbol*] (OAG)

TUUL .... Trade Union Unity League

TUUL .... Transurethral Ultrasonic Uterolithotripsy [*Urology*]

TUV .... Tenants Union of Victoria [*Australia*]

TUV .... Tucupita [*Venezuela*] [*Airport symbol*] (OAG)

TUV .... Tuvalu [*ANSI three-letter standard code*] (CNC)

TUVMAG ... Trudy Ufimskogo Nauchno-Issledovatel'skogo Instituta Vaktsin i Syvorotok Imeni I. I. Mechnikova [*A publication*]

TUW........... Trustee under Will [*Legal term*] (DLA)

TUW........... Tubala [*Panama*] [*Airport symbol*] (OAG)

TUWAH.... Trade Union Women of African Heritage (EA)

TUWC........ Tactical Utilization Working Committee [*Navy*] (MCD)

TUWR .... Turning Wrench [*Tool*] (AAG)

TUX........... Tuxedo (DSUE)

TUX........... Tuxpeno [*Race of maize*]

TUXX .... Al's Formal Wear, Inc. [*NASDAQ symbol*] (NQ)

TUY .... Tulum [*Mexico*] [*Airport symbol*] [*Obsolete*] (OAG)

TuZ............ Texte und Zeichen [*A publication*]

TUZI.......... Tuzigoot National Monument

TV .... Taff Vale Railway [*Wales*]

TV .... Target Valve (MCD)

T/V .... Target Vehicle [*Air Force*] (AAG)

TV .... Target Vulnerability (MCD)

TV .... Telefunken Variable Microgroove [*Record label*] [*Germany*]

TV .... Television [*A publication*]

TV .... Television

TV .... Television, Vision Channel

TV .... Terminal Velocity [*Navy*]

TV .... Test Vehicle

T & V .... Test and Verify Programs [*Data processing*] (MDG)

TV .... Tetrazolium Violet [*Also, TZV*]

TV .... Thames Valley [*England*]

TV .... Theater of War [*Soviet*] (MCD)

TV .... Thermal Vacuum

TV .... Throttle Valve

TV .... Thrust Vector [*Aerospace*] (NASA)

TV .... Tidal Volume [*Amount of air that moves in and out of lungs under given conditions*] [*Physiology*]

TV .... Time Variation of Gain

TV .... Total Value

TVCL .... Total Volume

TV .... Trans America Airlines, Inc. [*ICAO designator*] (FAAC)

TV .... Transfer Vector

TV .... Transfer and Void (MCD)

TV .... Transfer Voucher (AFM)

TV .... Transport Vehicle [*Military*]

TV .... Transversion [*Molecular biology*]

TV .... Transvestite [*Medicine*]

TV .... Traverse (IEEE)

TV .... Treji Varti [*A publication*]

TV .... Trichomonas vaginalis [*A protozoan*] [*Medicine*]

TV .... Trinidad Volunteers [*British military*] (DMA)

TV .... Trip Valve [*Railroad term*]

TV .... Tube Tester [*JETDS nomenclature*] [*Military*] (CET)

TV .... Tunica Vaginalis [*Anatomy*]

tv .... Tuvalu [*gn (Gilbert and Ellice Islands) used in records cataloged before October 1978*] [*MARC country of publication code*] [*Library of Congress*] (LCCP)

TV .... Tuvalu [*ANSI two-letter standard code*] (CNC)

TV .... Tzertovnyia Viedomosti [*A publication*]

Tv .... Ventral Touch Neurons [*of a leech*]

TV .... [*The*] Voluntaryists (EA)

TV5 .... Television Francophone par Satellite (EAIO)

TVA .... 369th Veterans' Association (EA)

TVA .... Morafenobe [*Madagascar*] [*Airport symbol*] (OAG)

TVA .... Tax on Value Added [*European manufacturing tax*]

TVA .... Taxe a la Valeur Ajoutee [*Value-Added Tax*] [*French*] [*Business term*]

TVA .... Television Age [*A publication*]

TvA .... Television Associates Network [*Canada*]

TVA .... Temporary Variance Authority [*or Authorization*] [*NASA*] (AAG)

TVA .... Temporary Volume Allowance

TVA .... Temporary Voluntary Allowance

TVA .... Tennessee Valley Authority [*Also, an information service or system*]

TVA .... Tennessee Valley Authority, Technical Library, Knoxville, TN [*OCLC symbol*] (OCLC)

TVA .... Textile Veterans Association (EA)

TVA .... Thrust Vector Actuator

TVA .... Thrust Vector Alignment [*Aerospace*] (MCD)

TVA .... Torah Va'Avodah (BJA)

TVA .... Tuned Vertical Array (CAAL)

TVA Bibliogr Tenn Val Auth Tech Libr ... TVA Bibliography. Tennessee Valley Authority. Technical Library [*A publication*]

TVAC........ Thrust Vector Activation Control [*Aerospace*]

TVAC........ Time-Varying Adaptive Correlation

TVA Chem Eng Rept ... Tennessee Valley Authority. Chemical Engineering Report [*A publication*]

Tvaett Ind ... Tvaett Industrin [*A publication*]

TVAHVF... Textile Veterans Association Hospitalized Veterans Fund [*Defunct*] (EA)

TVAR .... Test Variance (NASA)

TV-ARBS .. Television Angle Rate Bombing System (MCD)

Tvarinnictvo Ukr ... Tvarinnictvo Ukraini [*A publication*]

Tvarynnytstvo Ukr ... Tvarynnytstvo Ukrainy [*A publication*]

TVAT........ Television Air Trainer

TVA Tech Rept ... Tennessee Valley Authority. Technical Report [*A publication*]

TVB .... Cabool, MO [*Location identifier*] [*FAA*] (FAAL)

TvB .... Television Bureau of Advertising [*New York, NY*] (EA)

TVB .... Total Volatile Bases [*Chemistry*]

TVB .... Treu und Bestaendig [*Faithful and Steadfast*] [*German*] [*Motto of Johann Georg, Margrave of Brandenburg (1577-1624)*]

TVBN .... Total Volatile Basic Nitrogen [*Food analysis*]

TVBS .... Television Broadcast Satellite [*NASA*]

TVBTA ...... Trudy Vsesoyuznyi Nauchno-Issledovatel'skii Institut Burovoi Tekhniki [*A publication*]

TVC .... Televideo Consultants, Inc. [*Evanston, IL*] [*Telecommunications*] (TSSD)

TVC .... Temperature Valve Control

TVC .... Thermal Vacuum Chamber (NASA)

TVC .... Thermal Voltage Converter

TVC .... Thoracic Vena Cava [*Medicine*]

TVC .... Throttle Valve Control

TVC .... Thrust Vector Control [*Aerospace*]

TVC .... Tientsin Volunteer Corps [*British military*] (DMA)

TVC .... Time-Varying Coefficient

TVC .... Timed Vital Capacity

TVC .... Torsional Vibration Characteristics

TVC .... Total Annual Variable Cost

TVC .... Total Variable Cost Curve [*Economics*]

TVC .... Total Viable Cells [*Microbiology*]

TVC .... Total Volume Capacity [*Physiology*]

TVC .... Traverse City [*Michigan*] [*Airport symbol*] (OAG)

TVC .... Triple Voiding Cystogram [*Medicine*]

TVCA........ Thrust Vector Control Actuator [*Aerospace*] (NASA)

TVCA........ Thrust Vector Control Assembly [*Aerospace*]

TVCAM..... Television Camera and Control Equipment

TVCD .... Thrust Vector Control Driver [*Aerospace*] (NASA)

TVCL .... Toxic Victims Compensation Legislation

TV Commun ... TV Communications [*A publication*]

TVCS......... Television Communications Subsystem

TVCS......... Thrust Vector Control System [*Aerospace*] (KSC)

TVCS......... Tyler Vocational Card Sort [*Guidance*]

TVD .... Teatr Voennykh Deistvii [*Theater of Military Operations*] [*USSR*]

TVD .... Television Digest [*A publication*]

TVD .... Television Display (MCD)

TVD .... Thermal Voltaic Detection [*Analytical chemistry*]

TVD .... Toxic Vapor Detector

TVD .... Toxic Vapor Disposal [*NASA*] (KSC)

TVD .... Transmissable Virus Dementia [*Psychiatry*]

TVD .... Travaux sur Voltaire et le Dix-Huitieme Siecle [*A publication*]

TVD .... True Vertical Depth [*Diamonds*]

TVD .... Tuned Viscoelastic Damper

TVDALV... Triple Vessel Disease with Abnormal Left Ventricle [*Cardiology*]

TVDC .... Test Volts, Direct Current

TVDC .... Tidewater Virginia Development Council

TVDP........ Terminal Vector Display Unit

TVDR .... Tag Vector Display Register

TVDY .... Television Deflection Yoke

TVE .... Technology Validation Experiment (SDI)

TVE .... Television Espanola [*Television network*] [*Spain*]

TVE .... Test Vehicle Engine (AAG)

TVE .... Thermal Vacuum Environment

TVE .... Tijdschrift voor Economie [*A publication*]

TVE .... Tricuspid Valve Echophonocardiogram [*Cardiology*]

TVED .... Tuned Viscoelastic Damper

TVEI......... Technical and Vocational Education Initiative [*Manpower Services Commission*] [*British*]
TVEL........ Track Velocity
TVER........ Tumor Virus Epidemiology Repository [*National Institutes of Health*]
T Ver Nederlandse Mg ... Tijdschrift van de Vereeniging voor Nederlandse Muziekgeschiedenis [*A publication*]
TVERS...... Television Evaluation and Renewal Standards [*Student legal action organization*]
TVEXPIS .. Television Experiment Interconnecting Station [*NASA*]   (NASA)
TVF........... Tactile Vocal Fremitus [*Medicine*]
TVF........... Tape Velocity Fluctuation
TVF........... Templeton Value Fund [*NYSE symbol*]   (SPSG)
TVF........... Thief River Falls [*Minnesota*] [*Airport symbol*]   (OAG)
TVF........... Tidskrift foer Teknisk-Vettenskaplig Forskning [*A publication*]
TVF........... Total Variable Factor Curve [*Economics*]
TVFA........ Total Volatile Fatty Acid [*of foodstuffs*]
TVFS........ Tactical Vehicle Fleet Simulation   (MCD)
TVFT........ Television Flyback Transformer
TVF Tek Vetensk Forsk ... TVF. Teknisk Vetenskaplig Forskning [*A publication*]
TVG .... Tavares & Gulf R. R. [*AAR code*]
TVG .... Threshold Voltage Generator
TVG .... Tijdschrift voor Geschiedenis [*A publication*]
TVG .... Time Variation of Gain
TVG .... Triggered Vacuum Gap
TVG .... TV Guide [*A publication*]
TvG .... Tydskrif vir Geesteswetenskappe [*A publication*]
TVGDHS .. Television Ground Data Handling System [*NASA*]
TVH........ Total Vaginal Hysterectomy [*Gynecology*]
TVI........... Television Interference [*Communications*]
TVI........... Temperament and Values Inventory [*Interpersonal skills and attitudes test*]
TVI........... Thomasville, GA [*Location identifier*] [*FAA*]   (FAAL)
TVI........... Total Vision, Incorporated [*Houston, TX*]   (TSSD)
TVI........... Transient Voltage Indicator
TVI........... Turbo Vapor Injector
TVI........... Tutored Videotape Instruction
TVIC........ Television Input Converter
TVIC........ Television Interference Committee
TVID........ Television Frame Identification Data [*NASA*]
TVIE........ TVI Corp. [*NASDAQ symbol*]   (NQ)
TVIG........ Television and Inertial Guidance
TVIIJ........ Trudy Vojennogo Instituta Inostrannykh Jazykov [*A publication*]
TVIIJa...... Trudy Vojennogo Instituta Inostrannykh Jazykov [*A publication*]
TV Int .... Television International [*A publication*]
TVIS .... Time Video Information Services, Inc.   (IID)
T-VIS........ Toyota's Variable Induction System [*Automotive engineering*]
TVIS .... Tropical Vegetable Information Service [*Asian Vegetable Research and Development Center*] [*Information service or system*]   (IID)
TVIS .... Turbine Vibration Indication System   (NG)
TVIST....... Television Information Storage Tube
TVIV........ Taco Viva, Inc. [*NASDAQ symbol*]   (NQ)
TVJ .... Thomas Jefferson University, Philadelphia, PA [*OCLC symbol*]   (OCLC)
TVK .... Target Value Kills   (MCD)
TVK .... Toimihenkilo - ja Virkamiesjarjestojen Keskusliitto [*Confederation of Intellectual and Government Workers*] [*Finland*]
TVKMF..... Theodore Von Karman Memorial Foundation   (EA)
TVL.......... Lake Tahoe [*California*] [*Airport symbol*]   (OAG)
TVL.......... Tenth Value Layer
TVL.......... Tijdschrift voor Liturgei [*A publication*]
TVL.......... Townsville [*Australia*] [*Seismograph station code, US Geological Survey*] [*Closed*]   (SEIS)
TVL.......... Transverse Vertical Longitudinal
TVL.......... Travel   (AABC)
TvL.......... Tydskrif vir Letterkunde [*A publication*]
TVLA........ Taco Villa, Inc. [*NASDAQ symbol*]   (NQ)
TVLADVP ... Travel Advance Payment [*TDY*]
TVLALWADV ... Travel Allowance Advance [*in PCS*]
TVLALWS ... Travel Allowance on Separation [*Army*]
Tvl Educ News ... Transvaal Educational News [*A publication*]
TVLF........ Transportable Very-Low-Frequency [*Transmitter*]
TVLRO...... Television Licensing and Records Office [*Post Office*] [*British*]
TVM .... Tachometer Voltmeter
TVM .... Target Via Missile [*Aviation*]
TVM .... Television Monitor [*Video only*]
TVM .... Thrust Vectoring Motor [*Aerospace*]   (MUGU)
TVM .... TOW [*Tube-Launched, Optically Tracked, Wire-Guided (Weapon)*] Visual Module [*Army*]
TVM .... Track-Via-Missile
TVM .... Trailer Van Mount
TVM .... Transistorized Voltmeter
TVM .... TRV Minerals Corp. [*Vancouver Stock Exchange symbol*]
TVMS....... Test of Visual-Motor Skills [*Sensorimotor skills test*]
TVMV .... Tobacco Vein Mottling Virus

TVN .... Television News, Inc.
TVN .... Televisora Nacional [*Television network*] [*Venezuela*]
TVN .... Test Verification Network [*NASA*]   (NASA)
TVN .... Total Volatile Nitrogen [*Analytical chemistry*]
TVNZ .... Television, New Zealand
TVO .... Taravao [*Society Islands*] [*Seismograph station code, US Geological Survey*]   (SEIS)
TVO .... Tractor Vaporizing Oil [*Automotive engineering*]
TVOC .... Television Operations Center [*NASA*]   (KSC)
T Volkskd Volkstaal ... Tydskrif vir Volkskunde en Volkstaal [*A publication*]
TVOP .... Television Observation Post   (CET)
TVOP .... [*The*] Vista Organization Partnership LP [*NASDAQ symbol*]   (NQ)
TVOR .... Terminal VHF [*Very-High Frequency*] Omnidirectional Range
TVOR .... Terminal Visual Omnirange
TVOR .... Translational Vestibulo-Ocular Reflex [*Ophthalmology*]
TVP........... Tamil Vimukhti Peramena [*Sri Lanka*] [*Political party*]   (PPW)
TVP........... Television and Video Production [*A publication*]
TVP........... Test Verification Program [*NASA*]   (NASA)
TVP........... Textured Vegetable Protein [*Trademark of Archer Daniels Midland Co. for soybean product*]
TVP........... Thermo-Photo-Voltaic
TVP........... Tricuspid Valve Prolapse [*Cardiology*]
TVP........... True Vapor Pressure
TVP........... Victoria Public Library, Victoria, TX [*OCLC symbol*]   (OCLC)
TVPC........ TOW [*Tube-Launched, Optically Tracked, Wire-Guided (Weapon)*] Vehicle Power Conditioner   (MCD)
TVPED...... Tennessee Valley Perspective [*A publication*]
TVPPA...... Tennessee Valley Public Power Association   (EA)
TVPRA...... Teoriya Veroyatnostei i Ee Primeneniya [*A publication*]
TVPS .... Test of Visual-Perceptual Skills
TV Q .... Television Quarterly [*A publication*]
TVQ .... Top Visual Quality
TVR .... Tadcaster Volunteer Rifles [*British military*]   (DMA)
TVR .... Temperature Variation of Resistance [*Electricity*]
TVR .... Tennessee Valley Region
TVR .... Thermal Vapor Recompressors [*For evaporators*]
TVR .... Time Variable Reflectivity   (MCD)
TVR .... Tonic Vibration Reflex [*or Response*] [*Medicine*]
TVR .... Trajectory Velocity RADAR   (MCD)
TVR .... Tricuspid Valve Replacement [*Cardiology*]
TV Radio A ... Television/Radio Age [*A publication*]
TV/Radio Age ... Television/Radio Age [*A publication*]
TV/Radio Age Int ... Television/Radio Age International [*A publication*]
TVRB........ Tactical Vehicle Review Board [*Army*]   (AABC)
TVRCC....... TVR Car Club [*Later, TVRCCNA*]   (EA)
T Vred .... Tijdschrift voor Vrederechters [*A publication*]
TVRG .... Tijdschrift voor Rechtsgeschiedenis [*A publication*]
TVRI........ Televisi Republik Indonesia [*Television network*]
TVRM....... Television Receiver/Monitor
TVRN .... Tavern
TVRO .... Television Receive Only [*Telecommunications*]
TVRP....... Television Reading Program
TVRS........ Television Video Recording System   (MCD)
TVS........... Stedebouw en Volkshuisvesting [*A publication*]
TVS........... Tactical Vocoder System
TVS........... Telemetry Video Spectrum
TVS........... Telephone Video System [*NEC America, Inc.*] [*Wood Dale, IL*] [*Telecommunications*]   (TSSD)
TVS........... Television Subsystem [*Spacecraft*]
TVS........... Thermal [*or Thermostatic*] Vacuum Switch [*Automotive engineering*]
TVS........... Thrust Vector System [*Aerospace*]
TVS........... Total Volatile Solids [*Analytical chemistry*]
TVS........... Toxic Vapor Suit [*NASA*]   (NASA)
TVS........... Transient Voltage Suppressor
TVS........... Tube-Vehicle System   (MCD)
TVS........... Volunteer State Community College, Gallatin, TN [*OCLC symbol*]   (OCLC)
TVSA........ Thrust Vector Position Servo Amplifier [*Aerospace*]
TVSC........ Television Videotape Satellite Communications [*Group W Productions*] [*Pittsburgh, PA*]   (TSSD)
TVSD........ Time-Varying Spectral Display
TVSG........ Television Signal Generator
TVSM........ Television System Monitor
TVSM........ Time-Varying Sequential Measuring [*Device*]
TVSO........ Television Space Observatory
TV SPOTTS ... Tuneful Viewer's Society for the Preservation of Television Theme Songs
TVSS .... Television Systems Section
TVSSIS .... Television Subsystem Interconnecting Station [*NASA*]   (NASA)
TVSU........ Television Sight Unit
TVSV........ Kingstown/Arnos Vale [*St. Vincent*] [*ICAO location identifier*]   (ICLI)
TVSV........ Thermostatic Vacuum Switching Valve [*Automotive engineering*]
TVT .... Target Verification Test [*Military*]   (CAAL)
TVT .... Television Terminal   (CMD)
TVT .... Television Trainer/Tapes   (MCD)
TVT .... Television Typewriter
TVT .... Thermal Vacuum Test

TVT	Tijdschrift voor Theologie [*A publication*]
TVT	Tiverton, OH [*Location identifier*] [*FAA*] (FAAL)
TVT	Tunica Vaginalis Testis [*Anatomy*]
TVTA........	Thermal Vacuum Test Article (NASA)
TVTK........	Television Technology Corp. [*NASDAQ symbol*] (NQ)
TV TR........	Television Tower [*Mast*]
TVTV........	Thermostatic Vacuum Transmitting Valve [*Automotive engineering*]
TVTV........	Top Value Television [*Group of 26 young people who photographed the 1972 Democratic convention and presented it on TV*]
TVU	Taveuni [*Fiji*] [*Airport symbol*] (OAG)
TVU	Television Unlimited [*Australia*]
TVU	Total Volume Urine [*in 24 hours*]
TVUAAG ..	Trudy Vsesoyuznogo Nauchno-Issledovatel'skogo Instituta Udobrenii Agrotekhniki i Agropochvovedeniya Imeni Gedroitsa [*A publication*]
TVUB	Tijdschrift van de Vrige Universiteit van Brussel [*A publication*]
TVV	Thermal Vacuum Valve [*Automotive engineering*]
TVVS........	Tijdschrift voor Vennootschappen, Verenigingen, en Stichtingen [*A publication*]
TVW	Total Ventricular Weight [*Cardiology*]
TVX	Target Vehicle Experimental [*Air Force*]
TVX	Tulip Virus X
TVX	TVX Mining Corp. [*Formerly, Treasure Valley Explorations Ltd.*] [*Toronto Stock Exchange symbol*]
TVXCA......	Travaux Communaux [*A publication*]
TVXG	TVX Broadcast Group, Inc. [*Virginia Beach, VA*] [*NASDAQ symbol*] (NQ)
TVY	Tavoy [*Burma*] [*Airport symbol*] (OAG)
TVYTA......	Teplofizika Vysokikh Temperatur [*A publication*]
TW	Journal of Technical Writing and Communication [*A publication*]
TW	Tactical Warning (MCD)
TW	Tail Warning [*RADAR*] (NATG)
TW	Tail Wind
TW	Tailwater
TW	Taiwan [*ANSI two-letter standard code*] (CNC)
TW	Tankwagon
TW	Tap Water [*Medicine*]
TW	Tapes and Recording Wires [*JETDS nomenclature*] [*Military*] (CET)
TW	Tapwe [*A publication*]
TW	Taxiway [*Aviation*]
TW	Teamwork (MSA)
TW	Technical Works [*Air Force*] (MCD)
TW	Temperature Well (MSA)
TW	Tempered Water
TW	Temporary Warrant
TW	Terawatt
TW	Terre Wallonne [*A publication*]
TW	Test Weight
TW	Textil-Wirtschaft [*Textile Industry*] [*Deutscher Fachverlag GmbH*] [*Information service or system*] (IID)
TW	Thermal Wire (KSC)
TW	Thermit Welding
TW	Thermoplastic Wire
TW	Third World [*A publication*]
T-W..........	Three-Wheeler [*Type of motorcycle*]
TW	Thrilling Wonder Stories [*A publication*]
T/W	Thrust-to-Weight
TW	Thumbwheel (MCD)
TW	Tight Wrapped (MSA)
TW	Tile Wainscot [*Technical drawings*]
TW	Time Word
TW	Top of Wall [*Technical drawings*]
TW	Torpedo Water
TW	Total Body Water
TW	Total Weight
TW	Total Woman [*Title of a 1973 book by Marabel Morgan and of TV seminars based on this book*]
TW	Total Work
TW	Trail Watcher (CINC)
TW	Trans World Airlines, Inc. [*ICAO designator*]
TW	Transit Working [*Telecommunications*] (TEL)
TW	Travel Warrant
TW	Travel Writer [*A publication*] (EAAP)
TW	Traveling Wave
TW	Trow [*Ship's rigging*] (ROG)
TW	Tru-Wall Group Ltd. [*Toronto Stock Exchange symbol*]
TW	True Watt (MSA)
TW	Trustee under Will [*Legal term*] (DLA)
TW	TW Services [*NYSE symbol*] (SPSG)
TW	Twaddell [*Specific gravity scale*] [*Physics*]
TW	Twin Screw (DS)
TW	Twister (AAG)
Tw	Tworczosc [*A publication*]
TW	Typewriter (AAG)
TW3..........	That Was The Week That Was [*Also, TWTWTW*] [*Television program of English origin*]
TWA..........	Tap Water Agar [*Microbiology*]
TWA..........	Textile Waste Association [*Later, Textile Fibers and By-Products Association*] (EA)
TWA..........	Thames Water Authority [*British*]
TWA..........	Tijdschrift voor Sociale Wetenschappen [*A publication*]
TWA..........	Time Weighted Average [*Data sampling*]
TWA..........	Tooling Work Authorization
TWA..........	Toy Wholesalers Association of America (EA)
TWA..........	Trailing Wire Antenna [*on aircraft*]
TWA..........	Trans World Airlines, Inc. [*NYSE symbol*] [*Air carrier designation symbol*] [*Humorously interpreted as "Try Walking Across" and "Teeny Weeny Airlines"*] (SPSG)
TWA..........	Transaction Work Area
TWA..........	Transactions. Wisconsin Academy of Sciences, Arts, and Letters [*A publication*]
TWA..........	Transcontinental & Western Airlines [*Later, Trans World Airlines, Inc.*]
TWA..........	Traveling-Wave Amplifier
TWA..........	Trelew [*Argentina*] [*Geomagnetic observatory code*]
TWA..........	[*The*] Waferboard Association [*Later, SBA*] (EA)
TWA..........	[*The*] Woman Activist (EA)
TW/AA.....	Tactical Warning/Attack Assessment
TWAC	Tactical Weather Analysis Center (MCD)
Twad	Twaddell [*Physics*]
TWADL.....	Two-Way Air Data Link [*Tactical Air Command*]
TWAES.....	Tactical Warfare Analysis and Evaluation System (MCD)
TWALNDG ...	Turnaway Landing [*Navy*] (NVT)
TWAP........	Thin Wire Analysis Program [*Air Force*]
TWAR	Taiwan Acute Respiratory Disease [*Pneumonia-causing chlamydia strain named after the ailment that results from it*]
TWAS........	Third World Academy of Sciences [*Trieste, Italy*] (EAIO)
TWAS........	Twayne's World Authors Series [*A publication*]
TWASPIT ...	Therapeutic Work Aid Station for Physically Inactive Thinkers (MCD)
TWAT	Traveling-Wave Amplifier Tube
TWB	Toowoomba [*Australia*] [*Airport symbol*] (OAG)
TWB	Total Water Burden [*Environmental science*]
TWB	Transsonischer Windkanal Braunschweig [*Federal Republic of Germany*]
TWB	Traveling-Wave Beam [*LASER*]
TWB	Typewriter Buffer
TWB	Wayland Baptist College, Plainview, TX [*OCLC symbol*] (OCLC)
TWBC........	Total White Blood Cells [*Medicine*]
TWBC........	Transworld Bancorp [*NASDAQ symbol*] (NQ)
TWBFA.....	Treeing Walker Breeders and Fanciers Association (EA)
TWBNT.....	Theologisches Woerterbuch zum Neuen Testament [*A publication*] (BJA)
TWBS........	Traditional Wooden Boat Society [*Defunct*] (EA)
TWC	Suao [*Republic of China*] [*Seismograph station code, US Geological Survey*] (SEIS)
TWC	Tennessee Wesleyan College
TWC	Texas Wesleyan College
TWC	Texas Wesleyan College, Fort Worth, TX [*OCLC symbol*] (OCLC)
TWC	Texas Western College [*Later, UTEP*]
TWC	Theater Weather Central [*Military*]
TWC	Three-Way Catalyst [*Vehicle exhaust control*]
TWC	Truncated Whitworth Coarse [*Thread*] (MSA)
TwC..........	Twentieth Century [*A publication*]
TWC	[*The*] Weather Channel [*Cable TV programming service*]
TWC	[*The*] Wordsworth Circle [*A publication*]
TWCA	T. W. Cape and Associates [*Atlanta, GA*] [*Telecommunications service*] (TSSD)
TWCRT.....	Traveling-Wave Cathode-Ray Tube (IEEE)
TWCS........	Test of Work Competency and Stability [*Psychology*]
TWCS........	Through-Water Communications System [*Navy*] (CAAL)
TWD	Hualien [*Republic of China*] [*Seismograph station code, US Geological Survey*] (SEIS)
TWD	Tactical Weapons Delivery
TWD	Tail Wags Dog [*Airspace effects*]
TWD	Thermal Warning Device (MCD)
TWD	Torpedo Wire Dispenser
TWD	Toward
TWD	Tween Deck [*on a ship*] (DS)
TWD	Twisted Double Shielded (MCD)
TWDC	Tyne and Wear Development Corp. [*British*] (ECON)
TWDD	Two-Way/Delay Dial [*Telecommunications*] (TEL)
TWDRA	Report. Texas Water Development Board [*A publication*]
TWDS......	Tactical Water Distribution System (MCD)
TWE	Tap Water Enema [*Medicine*]
TWE	Test of Written English [*Educational test*]
TWE	Textile Waste Exchange [*Later, Textile Fibers and By-Products Association*]
TWE	Thumb Wheel Encoder
TWE	Trans-Western Exploration, Inc. [*Toronto Stock Exchange symbol*]
TWE	[*The*] Washington Establishment
TWEA	Trading with the Enemy Act
TWEB........	Transcribed Weather Broadcast

TWEC........ [*Isaac N.*] Thut World Education Center [*University of Connecticut*] [*Research center*] (RCD)
TWEC........ Twenty-First Century Envelope Company, Inc. [*NASDAQ symbol*] (NQ)
Tweener ..... Between Two Outfielders [*Baseball*] [*Also, a lifestyle classification*]
TWEN .... 20th Century Industries [*NASDAQ symbol*] (NQ)
Twen Cen ... Twentieth Century [*A publication*] (APTA)
Twen Ct Lit ... Twentieth Century Literature [*A publication*]
Twent Cent ... Twentieth Century [*A publication*] (APTA)
Twent Cen V ... Twentieth Century Views [*A publication*]
TWEP........ Terminate with Extreme Prejudice [*To kill*] [*Counterintelligence*]
TWERL..... Tropical Wind, Energy Conversion, and Reference Level [*National Science Foundation*]
TWERLE .. Tropical Wind, Energy Conversion, and Reference Level Experiment [*National Science Foundation*]
TWEX....... Trans-Western Exploration, Inc. [*NASDAQ symbol*] (NQ)
TWF......... Third World Forum [*Cairo, Egypt*] (EAIO)
TWF......... Third World Foundation [*London, England*] (EAIO)
TWFA....... Transylvanian World Federation (EAIO)
TWF......... Trasco Wind-Force [*Vancouver Stock Exchange symbol*]
TWF......... Truncated Whitworth Fine [*Thread*] (MSA)
TWF......... Twin Falls [*Idaho*] [*Airport symbol*] (OAG)
TWF......... Yuli [*Republic of China*] [*Seismograph station code, US Geological Survey*] [*Closed*] (SEIS)
TWF1........ Yuli [*Republic of China*] [*Seismograph station code, US Geological Survey*] (SEIS)
TWFC....... 21st Century Communications, Inc. [*NASDAQ symbol*]
TWFC....... Tom Wopat Fan Club (EA)
TWFS....... TW Holdings, Inc. [*NASDAQ symbol*] (NQ)
TWG......... Taitung [*Republic of China*] [*Seismograph station code, US Geological Survey*] (SEIS)
TWG......... Technical Working Group [*of the Conference on the Discontinuance of Nuclear Weapon Tests*]
TWG......... Telemetry Working Group
TWG......... Test Working Group [*in various federal government agencies*] (KSC)
TWG......... Transfer Working Group (MCD)
TWG......... Transsonischer Windkanal Goettingen [*Federal Republic of Germany*]
TWGC....... Treatment of War Gas Casualties (MCD)
TWGI .... [*The*] Westwood Group, Incorporated [*Boston, MA*] [*NASDAQ symbol*] (NQ)
TWGSS ..... Tank Weapons Gunnery Simulation System (MCD)
TWH......... Catalina Island [*California*] [*Airport symbol*] [*Obsolete*] (OAG)
TWH......... Houston Baptist University, Houston, TX [*OCLC symbol*] (OCLC)
TWh......... Terawatt Hour (ADA)
TWH......... Toronto Western Hospital [*UTLAS symbol*]
TWHBEA ... Tennessee Walking Horse Breeders' and Exhibitors' Association (EA)
TWHBEAA ... Tennessee Walking Horse Breeders' and Exhibitors' Association of America [*Later, TWHBEA*] (EA)
TWHD...... Tons per Workable Hatch per Day [*Shipping*]
TWHF....... Technoserve's World Harvest Fund (EA)
TWHL....... Tail Wheel [*Aviation*]
TWHO ...... [*The*] White House Office
TWHTA .... Tennessee Walking Horse Trainers' Association [*Later, Walking Horse Trainers Association*]
TW(I)........ Tail Warning (Indicator) [*RADAR*] (DEN)
TWI .... Threat Warning Information [*Air Force*]
TWI .... Trade-Weighted Index (ADA)
TWI .... Training with Industry Program [*Army*] (RDA)
twi........... Twi [*MARC language code*] [*Library of Congress*] (LCCP)
TWI .... Twilight (FAAC)
TWI .... [*The*] Way International [*An association*] (EA)
TWI .... [*The*] Welding Institute [*Information service or system*] (IID)
TWI .... Wichita, KS [*Location identifier*] [*FAA*] (FAAL)
TWI .... [*The*] Women's Institute (EA)
TWIB........ This Week in Baseball [*Television program*]
TWIC....... Theater Watch Intelligence Condition (NATG)
TWICE...... This Week in Consumer Electronics [*A publication*]
TWID .... Two-Way/Immediate Dial [*Telecommunications*] (TEL)
TWIDS...... Threat Warning Information Display System (MCD)
TWIF........ Tug-of-War International Federation [*Zevenhuizen, Netherlands*] (EAIO)
TWIG .... Tandem Wing in Sound Effect (MCD)
TWIMC..... To Whom It May Concern
TWIN .... Together Women in Neighborhoods
TWI-N....... Twi-Night [*or Twilight-Night*] [*Doubleheader in baseball*]
TWIRP ...... [*The*] Woman Is Requested to Pay [*Some claim that this acronym, originally a designation for certain school dances, evolved into a slang term denoting any male unable to afford a date*]
TWIS........ Technical Writing Improvement Society
TWIS........ Technically Workable Ideal System [*Industrial engineering*]
T Wisc Ac .. Transactions. Wisconsin Academy of Sciences, Arts, and Letters [*A publication*]
TWITAS.... Third World Institute of Theatre Arts Studies

TWITW..... [*The*] Wind in the Willows [*Book by Kenneth Grahame*]
TWIU .... Tobacco Workers International Union [*Later, BCTWIU*] (EA)
TWIX........ Teletypewriter Message
TWJ......... Tack Welded Joint
TWK......... Hsinying [*Republic of China*] [*Seismograph station code, US Geological Survey*] (SEIS)
TWK......... Too Well Known
TWK......... Tool Welders Kit
TWK......... Traveling-Wave Klystron
TWK......... Typewriter Keyboard
TWL......... Leased Teletypewriter Service
TWL .... Telex World Letter [*MCI International, Inc.*] [*Rye Brook, NY*] (TSSD)
TWL .... Top Water Level
TWL .... Total Weight Loss (MCD)
TWL .... Traveling-Wave LASER
TWL .... Tuberculosis Welfare League [*Defunct*] (EA)
TWL .... Twin Lakes [*California*] [*Seismograph station code, US Geological Survey*] (SEIS)
TWL .... Twin Wheel Loading [*Aviation*]
TWLA....... Turkish Women's League of America (EA)
TWLOA ... Technik Wlokienniczy [*A publication*]
TWLS....... Twayne's World Leaders Series [*A publication*]
TWLT....... Twilight
TWM......... Kaohsiung [*Republic of China*] [*Seismograph station code, US Geological Survey*] [*Closed*] (SEIS)
TWM .... Tape Wrapping Machine
TWM .... Traveling-Wave MASER
TWM .... Two-Way Mirror
TWM1 .... Kaohsiung [*Republic of China*] [*Seismograph station code, US Geological Survey*] (SEIS)
TW-MAE-W ... Third World Movement Against the Exploitation of Women [*Quezon City, Philippines*] (EAIO)
TWMAS.... Tobacco Workers' Mutual Assistance Society [*A union*] [*British*]
TWMBK.... Traveling-Wave Multiple-Beam Klystron (MSA)
TWMC ...... Trans World Music Corporation [*Albany, NY*] [*NASDAQ symbol*] (NQ)
TWMC ...... Transport, Wages, Maintenance, and Care
TWMIP..... Third World Moving Images Project (EA)
TWMP ..... Track Width Mine Plow (MCD)
TWMR ..... Tungsten Water Moderated Reactor (KSC)
TWN........ Taiwan [*ANSI three-letter standard code*] (CNC)
TWN........ Taiwan Fund, Inc. [*NYSE symbol*] (SPSG)
TWN........ Thomas Wolfe Newsletter [*A publication*]
TWN........ Town (MCD)
TWN......... Twin Eagles Resources, Inc. [*Vancouver Stock Exchange symbol*]
TWN......... Twin Peaks [*California*] [*Seismograph station code, US Geological Survey*] (SEIS)
Tw Nat P.... Twiss. Law of Nations in Time of Peace [*2nd ed.*] [*1884*] [*A publication*] (DLA)
Tw Nat W .. Twiss. Law of Nations in Time of War [*2nd ed.*] [*1875*] [*A publication*] (DLA)
TWNG...... Towing
TWNT ...... Theologisches Woerterbuch zum Neuen Testament [*A publication*] (BJA)
TWO......... Meishan [*Republic of China*] [*Seismograph station code, US Geological Survey*] (SEIS)
TWO......... Neoucom Processing Center, Rootstown, OH [*OCLC symbol*] (OCLC)
TWO......... Ontario, CA [*Location identifier*] [*FAA*] (FAAL)
TWO......... This Week Only (ADA)
TWO......... Tooling Work Order (MCD)
TWOATAF ... Second Allied Tactical Air Force Central Europe
TWOC...... Taken Without Owner's Consent
TWODS .... [*The*] World of Dark Shadows (EA)
T Wolfe New ... Thomas Wolfe Newsletter [*A publication*]
T Wolfe Rev ... Thomas Wolfe Review [*A publication*]
TWOM...... Traveling-Wave Optical MASER
Tworzywa Sztuczne Med ... Tworzywa Sztuczne'w Medycynie [*A publication*]
TWOS ...... Total Warrant Officer System [*Army*]
TWOS ...... Tropical Wind Observing Ships [*Marine science*] (MSC)
TW/OT ..... Travel without Troops
Two-Year College Math J ... Two-Year College Mathematics Journal [*A publication*]
Two-Yr Coll Math J ... Two-Year College Mathematics Journal [*A publication*]
TWP .... Task Work Package (KSC)
TWP .... Technological War Plan
TWP .... Torwood [*Australia*] [*Airport symbol*] [*Obsolete*] (OAG)
TWP .... Total Wave Pressure
TWP .... Township
TWP .... Traveling-Wave Phototube
TWP .... Trawler Petroleum Explorations Ltd. [*Vancouver Stock Exchange symbol*]
TWP .... Trial Work Period [*Social Security Administration*] (OICC)
TWP .... Trondheim Workingpapers [*A publication*]
TWP .... True Whig Party [*Liberia*]
TWP .... Twisted Wire Pair
TWP .... Two Pesos, Inc. [*AMEX symbol*] (SPSG)

TWP	[*The*] Washington Post [*A publication*]
TWPA.......	Traveling-Wave Parametric Amplifier
TWPB.......	Total Work Package Budget (MCD)
TWPL.......	Teletypewriter, Private Line
TWPLA.....	Turkish Workers' and Peasants' Liberation Army
TWPP.......	Truncated Whitworth, British Standard Pipe (Parallel) [*Thread*]
TWPS.......	Traveling-Wave Phase Sifter
TWQ.........	Third World Quarterly [*A publication*]
TWQ.........	Tungshih [*Republic of China*] [*Seismograph station code, US Geological Survey*] (SEIS)
TWR	Tactical Weather RADAR
TWR	Tape Write Register
TWR	Theater War Reserves [*Army*]
TWR	Thomas Wolfe Review [*A publication*]
TWR	Threat Warning RADAR
TWR	Threat Warning Receiver
TWR	Tool Wear Rate
TWR	Torpedo Weapons Receiver
TWR	Total Wrist Replacement [*Medicine*]
TWR	Tower (AAG)
TWR	TransWorld Radio (EA)
TWR	Traveling-Wave Resonator
TWR	Twin Richfield Oils Ltd. [*Toronto Stock Exchange symbol*]
TWRA	Transpacific Westbound Rate Agreement (DS)
TWRG	Towering (FAAC)
TWRI........	Texas Water Resources Institute [*Department of the Interior*] [*Texas A & M University*] [*Research center*] (RCD)
TWRL.......	Taylor Woodrow Research Laboratories [*British*] (IRUK)
TWRS.......	Towers
TWRX	[*The*] Software Toolworks, Inc. [*NASDAQ symbol*] (NQ)
TWS..........	Southwestern at Memphis, Memphis, TN [*OCLC symbol*] (OCLC)
TWS..........	Tactical Warning System (AAG)
TWS..........	Tactical Weapon System (NG)
TWS..........	Tactical Weather Station [*Military*]
TWS..........	Tail Warning Set [*or System*] [*Aerospace*] (MCD)
TWS..........	Tartar Weapons System
TWS..........	Teletypewriter Exchange Service
TWS..........	Terrier Weapons System
TWS..........	Test of Written Spelling [*Education*]
TWS..........	Thermal Weapon Sight [*Army*] (INF)
TWS..........	Thermal Wire Stripper
TWS..........	Thomas Wolfe Society (EA)
TWS..........	Thrilling Wonder Stories [*A publication*]
TWS..........	Track-while-Scan [*Communications*]
TWS..........	Truncated Whitworth Special [*Thread*] (MSA)
TWS..........	Tsunami Warning System [*National Oceanic and Atmospheric Administration*]
TWS..........	Twin-Wheel Stripper
TWS..........	[*The*] Wilderness Society [*Australia*]
TWS..........	[*The*] Wildlife Society (EA)
TWSB.......	Twin Sideband
TWSC.......	Twin Screw
TWSEAS...	Tactical Warfare Simulation, Evaluation, and Analysis System [*Marine Corps*] (MCD)
TWSO	Tactical Weapon Systems Operation
TWSP	Tactical Warfare Simulation Program
TWSR.......	Track-while-Scan RADAR
TWSRO.....	Track-while-Scan on Receive Only (NG)
TWSRS	Track-while-Scan RADAR Simulator
TWST.......	Torus Water Storage Tank (IEEE)
TWST.......	Twistee Treat Corp. [*NASDAQ symbol*] (NQ)
TWSUA.....	Taiwan Sugar [*A publication*]
TWT	Ingenieursblad [*A publication*]
TWT	Sturgis, KY [*Location identifier*] [*FAA*] (FAAL)
TWT	Tawi-Tawi [*Philippines*] [*Airport symbol*] (OAG)
TWT	Torpedo Water Tube
TWT	Toy World Test [*Psychology*]
TWT	Transonic Wind Tunnel [*NASA*] (AAG)
TWT	Transworld Corp. [*NYSE symbol*] (SPSG)
TWT	Travel with Troops
TWT	Traveling-Wave Tube [*Radio*]
TWT	Tri-West Resources Ltd. [*Vancouver Stock Exchange symbol*]
TWT	Tritiated Waste Treatment [*Subsystem*] (MCD)
TWT	Two-Way-Traffic-in-Ideas Conference [*of Labor Party*] [*British*]
TWT	West Texas State University, Canyon, TX [*OCLC symbol*] (OCLC)
TWT	[*The*] Write Thing [*An association*] (EA)
TWTA	Traveling-Wave Tube Amplifier [*Radio*]
TWTHF.....	Twentieth Century Energy [*NASDAQ symbol*] (NQ)
TWTWTW ...	That Was The Week That Was [*Also, TW3*] [*Television program of English origin*]
TWU..........	Tactical Weapons Unit [*British military*] (DMA)
TWU..........	Tata Workers' Union [*India*]
TWU..........	Tawau [*Malaysia*] [*Airport symbol*] (OAG)
TWU..........	Technical Writing Unit [*NASA*]
TWU..........	Telecommunications Workers Union [*Canada*]
TWU..........	Texas Woman's University
TWU..........	Tobacco Workers' Union [*British*] (DCTA)
TWU..........	Transport Workers' Union [*British*]
TWU..........	Transport Workers Union of America (EA)

TWU..........	University of the South, Sewanee, TN [*OCLC symbol*] (OCLC)
TWUA.......	Textile Workers Union of America [*Later, ACTWU*]
TWV	Two-Wire Vertical [*Grape culture*]
TWW	Independent Television for Wales and the West of England
TWWP	Third World Women's Project (EA)
TWWS.......	Two-Way/Wink Start [*Telecommunications*] (TEL)
TWX	Telegraphic Message (MSA)
TWX	Teletypewriter Exchange Service [*Western Union*] [*Term also used generically for teletypewriter message*]
TWX	Time Warner, Inc. [*NYSE symbol*] (SPSG)
TWX	Time Wire Transmission
TWX	Transport en Opslag. Maandblad voor Managers en Medewerkers op het Gebied van Intern Transport, Opslag, Magazijntechniek, en Distributietechniek [*A publication*]
TWXIL......	TWX Interlibrary Loan Network [*Library network*]
TWY	Taxiway [*Aviation*] (AAG)
TWY	Twenty (ADA)
TWYL.......	Taxiway-Link [*Aviation*]
TWZ	Neifu [*Republic of China*] [*Seismograph station code, US Geological Survey*] (SEIS)
TWZO	Trade Wind Zone Oceanography
TX	Nondramatic Literary Works [*US Copyright Office class*]
TX	Tax
TX	TELEX
TX	Terminating Toll Operator [*Telecommunications*] (TEL)
TX	Tested Extra (MCD)
TX	Texaco, Inc. [*NYSE symbol*] (SPSG)
TX	Texas [*Postal code*]
TX	Texas Reports [*A publication*] (DLA)
Tx.............	Texas State Library and Historical Commission, Austin, TX [*Library symbol*] [*Library of Congress*] (LCLS)
TX	Thromboxane [*Also, T, TA, Tx*] [*Biochemistry*]
Tx.............	Thyroidectomy [*Medicine*]
TX	Time to Equipment Reset [*Data processing*] (MDG)
TX	Torque Transmitter
TX	Traction [*Medicine*]
TX	Transformer
TX	Translation Hand Controller X-Axis Direction (MCD)
TX	Transmitter
Tx.............	Transplant [*or Transplantation*] [*Medicine*]
TX	Transportes Aereos Nacionales, SA [*Honduras*] [*ICAO designator*] (FAAC)
TX	Treatment
TX	Treble Cash Ruling [*Business term*]
T & X.........	Type and Crossmatch [*Clinical chemistry*]
TXA	Texas A & M University, College Station, TX [*OCLC symbol*] (OCLC)
TXA	Texas American Bancshares, Inc. [*NYSE symbol*] (SPSG)
TXA	Thromboxane A [*Also, TA, TxA*] [*Biochemistry*]
TxAb.........	Abilene Public Library, Abilene, TX [*Library symbol*] [*Library of Congress*] (LCLS)
TxAbC	Abilene Christian University, Abilene, TX [*Library symbol*] [*Library of Congress*] (LCLS)
TxAbH......	Hardin-Simmons University, Abilene, TX [*Library symbol*] [*Library of Congress*] (LCLS)
TxAbM	McMurry College, Abilene, TX [*Library symbol*] [*Library of Congress*] (LCLS)
TxAl..........	Stella Hill Memorial Library, Alto, TX [*Library symbol*] [*Library of Congress*] (LCLS)
TxAlpS	Sul Ross State University, Alpine, TX [*Library symbol*] [*Library of Congress*] (LCLS)
TxAlvC	Alvin Junior College, Alvin, TX [*Library symbol*] [*Library of Congress*] (LCLS)
TxAm.........	Amarillo Public Library, Amarillo, TX [*Library symbol*] [*Library of Congress*] (LCLS)
TxAmC	Amarillo College, Amarillo, TX [*Library symbol*] [*Library of Congress*] (LCLS)
TxAmM	Mason & Hanger-Silas Mason Co., Inc., Pantex Plant Library, Amarillo, TX [*Library symbol*] [*Library of Congress*] (LCLS)
TxAmSP....	Southwestern Public Service Co., Amarillo, TX [*Library symbol*] [*Library of Congress*] (LCLS)
TxAmV	United States Veterans Administration Hospital, Amarillo, TX [*Library symbol*] [*Library of Congress*] (LCLS)
TxAng........	Brazoria County Library, Angleton, TX [*Library symbol*] [*Library of Congress*] (LCLS)
TXAPA.....	Toxicology and Applied Pharmacology [*A publication*]
TxArB........	Arlington Baptist Junior College, Arlington, TX [*Library symbol*] [*Library of Congress*] (LCLS)
TxAr-G	Arlington Public Library, Genealogy Department, Arlington, TX [*Library symbol*] [*Library of Congress*] (LCLS)
TxArJ	Jet Research Center, Inc., Arlington, TX [*Library symbol*] [*Library of Congress*] (LCLS)
TxArU	University of Texas at Arlington, Arlington, TX [*Library symbol*] [*Library of Congress*] (LCLS)
TxAtH	Henderson County Junior College, Athens, TX [*Library symbol*] [*Library of Congress*] (LCLS)
TxAu..........	Austin Public Library, Austin, TX [*Library symbol*] [*Library of Congress*] (LCLS)

TxAuA .... Charles E. Stevens American Atheist Library and Archives, Inc., Austin, TX [*Library symbol*] [*Library of Congress*] (LCLS)

TxAu-AT ... Austin Public Library, Austin-Travis County Collection, Austin, TX [*Library symbol*] [*Library of Congress*] (LCLS)

TxAuC .... Concordia Lutheran College, Austin, TX [*Library symbol*] [*Library of Congress*] (LCLS)

TxAuCC..... Austin Community College, Austin, TX [*Library symbol*] [*Library of Congress*] (LCLS)

TxAuCH .... Church Historical Society, Austin, TX [*Library symbol*] [*Library of Congress*] (LCLS)

TxAuDR .... Daughters of the Republic of Texas Museum, Austin, TX [*Library symbol*] [*Library of Congress*] (LCLS)

TxAuE .... Episcopal Theological Seminary of the Southwest, Austin, TX [*Library symbol*] [*Library of Congress*] (LCLS)

TxAuEd ..... Texas Education Agency, Austin, TX [*Library symbol*] [*Library of Congress*] (LCLS)

TxAuGS..... Church of Jesus Christ of Latter-Day Saints, Genealogical Society Library, Austin Branch, Austin, TX [*Library symbol*] [*Library of Congress*] (LCLS)

TxAuHi...... Texas State Department of Highways and Public Transportation, Materials and Tests Research Library, Austin, TX [*Library symbol*] [*Library of Congress*] (LCLS)

TxAuHT .... Huston-Tillotson College, Austin, TX [*Library symbol*] [*Library of Congress*] (LCLS)

TxAuL .... Legislative Library Board, Legislative Reference Library, Austin, TX [*Library symbol*] [*Library of Congress*] (LCLS)

TxAuLBJ... Lyndon B. Johnson School of Public Affairs, Lyndon Baines Johnson Library, Austin, TX [*Library symbol*] [*Library of Congress*] (LCLS)

TxAuM ...... Texas Medical Association, Austin, TX [*Library symbol*] [*Library of Congress*] (LCLS)

TxAuMH.... Texas Department of Mental Health and Mental Retardation, Austin, TX [*Library symbol*] [*Library of Congress*] (LCLS)

TxAuP .... Austin Presbyterian Theological Seminary, Austin, TX [*Library symbol*] [*Library of Congress*] (LCLS)

TxAuPW .... Texas Department of Parks and Wildlife, Austin, TX [*Library symbol*] [*Library of Congress*] (LCLS)

TxAuR .... Radian Corp., Austin, TX [*Library symbol*] [*Library of Congress*] (LCLS)

TxAuSE..... Saint Edward's University, Austin, TX [*Library symbol*] [*Library of Congress*] (LCLS)

TxAuSHos ... Austin State Hospital, Austin, TX [*Library symbol*] [*Library of Congress*] (LCLS)

TxAuT .... Tracor, Inc., Technical Library, Austin, TX [*Library symbol*] [*Library of Congress*] (LCLS)

TxAuW ...... Texas Water Development Board, Austin, TX [*Library symbol*] [*Library of Congress*] (LCLS)

TXB .... Abilene Public Library, Abilene, TX [*OCLC symbol*] (OCLC)

TXB .... TextielVisie. Vakblad voor de Textielbranche [*A publication*]

TXB .... Thromboxane B [*Also, TB, TxB*] [*Biochemistry*]

TxBea .... Tyrrell Public Library, Beaumont, TX [*Library symbol*] [*Library of Congress*] (LCLS)

TxBeaAM ... Beaumont Art Museum, Beaumont, TX [*Library symbol*] [*Library of Congress*] (LCLS)

TxBeaE...... Beaumont Enterprise & Journal, Beaumont, TX [*Library symbol*] [*Library of Congress*] (LCLS)

TxBeaG...... Gulf States Utilities Co., Beaumont, TX [*Library symbol*] [*Library of Congress*] (LCLS)

TxBeaL...... Lamar University, Beaumont, TX [*Library symbol*] [*Library of Congress*] (LCLS)

TxBeaMC ... Mobil Chemical Co., Research and Development Laboratory, Beaumont, TX [*Library symbol*] [*Library of Congress*] (LCLS)

TxBeaSE ... Saint Elizabeth Hospital, Health Science Library, Beaumont, TX [*Library symbol*] [*Library of Congress*] (LCLS)

TxBee........ Bee County Public Library, Beeville, TX [*Library symbol*] [*Library of Congress*] (LCLS)

TxBeeC...... Bee County College, Beeville, TX [*Library symbol*] [*Library of Congress*] (LCLS)

TxBelM ..... Mary Hardin-Baylor College, Belton, TX [*Library symbol*] [*Library of Congress*] (LCLS)

TxBHi........ Brownsville Historical Association, Brownsville, TX [*Library symbol*] [*Library of Congress*] (LCLS)

TxBl........... Bellaire City Library, Bellaire, TX [*Library symbol*] [*Library of Congress*] (LCLS)

TXBL......... Taxable

TxBlT .... Texaco, Inc., Bellaire, TX [*Library symbol*] [*Library of Congress*] (LCLS)

TxBor......... Hutchinson County Library, Borger, TX [*Library symbol*] [*Library of Congress*] (LCLS)

TxBorF ..... Frank Phillips College, Borger, TX [*Library symbol*] [*Library of Congress*] (LCLS)

Tx-BPH ..... Texas Regional Library, Division for the Blind and Physically Handicapped, Austin, TX [*Library symbol*] [*Library of Congress*] (LCLS)

TXBRA ...... Texas Business Review [*A publication*]

TxBrd......... Brownwood Public Library, Brownwood, TX [*Library symbol*] [*Library of Congress*] (LCLS)

TxBrdH ..... Howard Payne College, Brownwood, TX [*Library symbol*] [*Library of Congress*] (LCLS)

TxBreB ..... Blinn College, Brenham, TX [*Library symbol*] [*Library of Congress*] (LCLS)

TxBry......... Bryan Public Library, Bryan, TX [*Library symbol*] [*Library of Congress*] (LCLS)

TxBryA ..... Allen Academy, Bryan, TX [*Library symbol*] [*Library of Congress*] (LCLS)

TxBs .... Howard County Library, Big Spring, TX [*Library symbol*] [*Library of Congress*] (LCLS)

TxBS......... Texas Southmost College, Brownsville, TX [*Library symbol*] [*Library of Congress*] (LCLS)

TxBsaA...... Ambassador College, Big Sandy, TX [*Library symbol*] [*Library of Congress*] (LCLS)

TxBsH .... Howard County Junior College, Big Spring, TX [*Library symbol*] [*Library of Congress*] (LCLS)

TxBsV........ United States Veterans Administration Hospital, Big Spring, TX [*Library symbol*] [*Library of Congress*] (LCLS)

TxBUC ...... Union Carbide Corp., Chemicals and Plastics Library, Brownsville, TX [*Library symbol*] [*Library of Congress*] (LCLS)

TX Bus Rev ... Texas Business Review [*A publication*]

TxBy .... Sterling Municipal Library, Baytown, TX [*Library symbol*] [*Library of Congress*] (LCLS)

TxByH....... Humble Oil & Refining Co., Technical Library, Baytown, TX [*Library symbol*] [*Library of Congress*] (LCLS)

TxByH-E... Humble Oil & Refining Co., Engineering Division Library, Baytown, TX [*Library symbol*] [*Library of Congress*] (LCLS)

TxByL........ Lee College, Baytown, TX [*Library symbol*] [*Library of Congress*] (LCLS)

TXC .... Abilene Christian University, Abilene, TX [*OCLC symbol*] (OCLC)

TXC .... Texaco Canada, Inc. [*AMEX symbol*] [*Toronto Stock Exchange symbol*] [*Vancouver Stock Exchange symbol*] (SPSG)

TXC .... Thurman, CO [*Location identifier*] [*FAA*] (FAAL)

TxCarP ...... Panola College, Carthage, TX [*Library symbol*] [*Library of Congress*] (LCLS)

TxCaW ...... West Texas State University, Canyon, TX [*Library symbol*] [*Library of Congress*] (LCLS)

TxCc .... La Retama Public Library, Corpus Cristi, TX [*Library symbol*] [*Library of Congress*] (LCLS)

TxCcD .... Del Mar College, Corpus Christi, TX [*Library symbol*] [*Library of Congress*] (LCLS)

TxCcGS ..... Church of Jesus Christ of Latter-Day Saints, Genealogical Society Library, Corpus Christi Branch, Corpus Christi, TX [*Library symbol*] [*Library of Congress*] (LCLS)

TxCcMST ... Art Museum of South Texas, Corpus Christi, TX [*Library symbol*] [*Library of Congress*] (LCLS)

TxCcNHi... Nueces County Historical Society, La Retama Public Library, Corpus Christi, TX [*Library symbol*] [*Library of Congress*] (LCLS)

TxCcT....... Texas A & I University at Corpus Christi, Corpus Christi, TX [*Library symbol*] [*Library of Congress*] (LCLS)

TxCcU .... University of Corpus Christi, Corpus Christi, TX [*Library symbol*] [*Library of Congress*] [*Obsolete*] (LCLS)

TxCeN .... Northwood Institute of Texas, Cedar Hill, TX [*Library symbol*] [*Library of Congress*] (LCLS)

TX Ci .... Texas Civil Appeals Reports [*A publication*] (DLA)

TxCiC .... Cisco Junior College, Cisco, TX [*Library symbol*] [*Library of Congress*] (LCLS)

TxClaC ...... Clarendon College, Clarendon, TX [*Library symbol*] [*Library of Congress*] (LCLS)

TxClcU ...... University of Houston at Clear Lake City, Houston, TX [*Library symbol*] [*Library of Congress*] (LCLS)

TxCle .... Cleburne Public Library, Cleburne, TX [*Library symbol*] [*Library of Congress*] (LCLS)

TxCli.......... Nellie Pederson Civic Library, Clifton, TX [*Library symbol*] [*Library of Congress*] (LCLS)

TxClv .... Cleveland Public [*Charles O. Austin Memorial*] Library, Cleveland, TX [*Library symbol*] [*Library of Congress*] (LCLS)

TxClwC...... Celanese Corp., Clarkwood, TX [*Library symbol*] [*Library of Congress*] (LCLS)

TxCM .... Texas A & M University, College Station, TX [*Library symbol*] [*Library of Congress*] (LCLS)

TxCM-M.... Texas A & M University, Medical Sciences Library, College Station, TX [*Library symbol*] [*Library of Congress*] (LCLS)

TXCO .... [*The*] Exploration Company [*NASDAQ symbol*] (NQ)

TxComf..... Comfort Public Library, Comfort, TX [*Library symbol*] [*Library of Congress*] (LCLS)

TxComS..... East Texas State University, Commerce, TX [*Library symbol*] [*Library of Congress*] (LCLS)

TxComS-M ... East Texas State University, Museum, Commerce, TX [*Library symbol*] [*Library of Congress*] (LCLS)

TxCoN....... Navarro Junior College, Corsicana, TX [*Library symbol*] [*Library of Congress*] (LCLS)

TxConM .... Montgomery County Memorial Library, Conroe, TX [*Library symbol*] [*Library of Congress*] (LCLS)
TxCr.......... Crockett Public Library, Crockett, TX [*Library symbol*] [*Library of Congress*] (LCLS)
TX Cr .... Texas Criminal Appeals Reports [*A publication*] (DLA)
TxCrMA.... Mary Allen Junior College, Crockett, TX [*Library symbol*] [*Library of Congress*] (LCLS)
TxCvS........ ARCO Chemical Co., Channelview, TX [*Library symbol*] [*Library of Congress*] (LCLS)
TxCvT .... Texas Butadine & Chemical Corp., Channelview, TX [*Library symbol*] [*Library of Congress*] (LCLS)
TXCYA...... Toxicology [*A publication*]
TXD .... McMurry College, Abilene, TX [*OCLC symbol*] (OCLC)
TXD .... Telephone Exchange (Digital) [*Telecommunications*] (TEL)
TXD .... Transmit Data [*Data processing*]
TxDa.......... Dallas Public Library, Dallas, TX [*Library symbol*] [*Library of Congress*] (LCLS)
TxDaABC ... AMIGOS [*Access Method for Indexed Data Generalized for Operating System*] Bibliographic Council, Dallas, TX [*Library symbol*] [*Library of Congress*] (LCLS)
TxDaAC .... Anderson, Clayton & Co., Foods Division Technical Library, Dallas, TX [*Library symbol*] [*Library of Congress*] (LCLS)
TxDaAR-G ... Atlantic Richfield Co., Geoscience Library, Dallas, TX [*Library symbol*] [*Library of Congress*] (LCLS)
TxDaAR-R ... Atlantic Richfield Co., R and D Library, Dallas, TX [*Library symbol*] [*Library of Congress*] (LCLS)
TxDaAR-T ... Atlantic Richfield Co., Technical Library, Dallas, TX [*Library symbol*] [*Library of Congress*] (LCLS)
TxDaB .... Dallas Baptist College, Dallas, TX [*Library symbol*] [*Library of Congress*] (LCLS)
TxDaBC..... Bishop College, Dallas, TX [*Library symbol*] [*Library of Congress*] (LCLS)
TxDaBM ... Burgess-Manning Co., Dallas, TX [*Library symbol*] [*Library of Congress*] (LCLS)
TxDaBU .... Baylor University in Dallas, Dallas, TX [*Library symbol*] [*Library of Congress*] (LCLS)
TxDaCC .... Christian College of the Southwest, Dallas, TX [*Library symbol*] [*Library of Congress*] (LCLS)
TxDaCCD ... Callier Center for Communication Disorders, Dallas, TX [*Library symbol*] [*Library of Congress*] (LCLS)
TxDaCiA ... Court of Civil Appeals, Dallas, TX [*Library symbol*] [*Library of Congress*] (LCLS)
TxDaCL..... Core Laboratories, Inc., Dallas, TX [*Library symbol*] [*Library of Congress*] (LCLS)
TxDaCR .... Collins Radio Co., Dallas, TX [*Library symbol*] [*Library of Congress*] (LCLS)
TxDaCS..... Dallas County Community College System, Dallas, TX [*Library symbol*] [*Library of Congress*] (LCLS)
TxDaDC .... Dallas Christian College, Dallas, TX [*Library symbol*] [*Library of Congress*] (LCLS)
TxDaDF .... DeGoyler Foundation, Dallas, TX [*Library symbol*] [*Library of Congress*] (LCLS)
TxDaDL .... Dallas County Law Library, Dallas, TX [*Library symbol*] [*Library of Congress*] (LCLS)
TxDaDM... DeGoyler and MacNaughton Library, Dallas, TX [*Library symbol*] [*Library of Congress*] (LCLS)
TxDaE .... El Centro College, Dallas, TX [*Library symbol*] [*Library of Congress*] (LCLS)
TxDaET..... East Texas State University, Metroplex Center, Dallas, TX [*Library symbol*] [*Library of Congress*] (LCLS)
TxDaFR..... Federal Reserve Bank of Dallas, Dallas, TX [*Library symbol*] [*Library of Congress*] (LCLS)
TxDaGS..... Church of Jesus Christ of Latter-Day Saints, Genealogical Society Library, Dallas Branch, Dallas, TX [*Library symbol*] [*Library of Congress*] (LCLS)
TxDaHi ..... Dallas Historical Society, Dallas, TX [*Library symbol*] [*Library of Congress*] (LCLS)
TxDaJS ..... Johnson and Swanson, Law Library, Dallas, TX [*Library symbol*] [*Library of Congress*] (LCLS)
TxDaL .... Lone Star Gas Co., Dallas, TX [*Library symbol*] [*Library of Congress*] (LCLS)
TxDaM...... Southern Methodist University, Dallas, TX [*Library symbol*] [*Library of Congress*] (LCLS)
TxDaME ... Mobil Exploration & Producing Services, Inc., Dallas, TX [*Library symbol*] [*Library of Congress*] (LCLS)
TxDaMF ... Dallas Museum of Fine Arts, Dallas, TX [*Library symbol*] [*Library of Congress*] (LCLS)
TxDaM-L.. Southern Methodist University, Law Library, Dallas, TX [*Library symbol*] [*Library of Congress*] (LCLS)
TxDaM-P.. Southern Methodist University, Perkins School of Theology, Dallas, TX [*Library symbol*] [*Library of Congress*] (LCLS)
TxDaM-SE ... Southern Methodist University, Science/Engineering Library, Dallas, TX [*Library symbol*] [*Library of Congress*] (LCLS)
TxDaMV ... Mountain View College, Dallas, TX [*Library symbol*] [*Library of Congress*] (LCLS)
TxDaP .... Dallas Power & Light Co., Dallas, TX [*Library symbol*] [*Library of Congress*] (LCLS)
TxDaPO .... Placid Oil Co. Exploration Library, Dallas, TX [*Library symbol*] [*Library of Congress*] (LCLS)

TxDaPP..... Planned Parenthood of Northeast Texas, Dallas, TX [*Library symbol*] [*Library of Congress*] (LCLS)
TxDaR ...... Richland College, Dallas, TX [*Library symbol*] [*Library of Congress*] (LCLS)
TxDaRI..... Rockwell International, Collins Radio Group, Technical Information Center, Dallas, TX [*Library symbol*] [*Library of Congress*] (LCLS)
TxDaS ...... University of Texas, Health Science Center at Dallas, Dallas, TX [*Library symbol*] [*Library of Congress*] (LCLS)
TxDaSM.... Mobil Research & Development Corp., Dallas, TX [*Library symbol*] [*Library of Congress*] (LCLS)
TxDaTI-A ... Texas Instruments, Inc., Apparatus Division Library, Dallas, TX [*Library symbol*] [*Library of Congress*] (LCLS)
TxDaTI-C ... Texas Instruments, Inc., Central Research and Engineering Library, Dallas, TX [*Library symbol*] [*Library of Congress*] (LCLS)
TxDaTI-IS ... Texas Instruments, Inc., IS & S Library, Dallas, TX [*Library symbol*] [*Library of Congress*] (LCLS)
TxDaTI-S.. Texas Instruments, Inc., Semiconductor Division, Dallas, TX [*Library symbol*] [*Library of Congress*] (LCLS)
TxDaTI-SS ... Texas Instruments, Inc., Science Services Division, Dallas, TX [*Library symbol*] [*Library of Congress*] (LCLS)
TxDaTS..... Dallas Theological Seminary and Graduate School, Dallas, TX [*Library symbol*] [*Library of Congress*] (LCLS)
TxDaU....... University of Dallas, Irving, TX [*Library symbol*] [*Library of Congress*] (LCLS)
TxDaUSAF ... United States Army and Air Force Exchange Service, Dallas, TX [*Library symbol*] [*Library of Congress*] (LCLS)
TxDaUSFD ... United States Food and Drug Administration, Dallas, TX [*Library symbol*] [*Library of Congress*] (LCLS)
TxDaVA .... United States Veterans Administration Hospital, Dallas, TX [*Library symbol*] [*Library of Congress*] (LCLS)
TXDE .... Toluene-Xylene-Dioxane-Ethanol [*Scintillation solvent*]
TxDeni...... Denison Public Library, Denison, TX [*Library symbol*] [*Library of Congress*] (LCLS)
TxDeniG.... Grayson County College, Denison, TX [*Library symbol*] [*Library of Congress*] (LCLS)
TxDib........ T. L. L. Temple Memorial Library, Diboll, TX [*Library symbol*] [*Library of Congress*] (LCLS)
TxDN........ North Texas State University, Denton, TX [*Library symbol*] [*Library of Congress*] (LCLS)
TxDN-Hi... North Texas State University, State Historical Collection, Denton, TX [*Library symbol*] [*Library of Congress*] (LCLS)
TxDpS .... Shell Oil Co., Deer Park, TX [*Library symbol*] [*Library of Congress*] (LCLS)
TxDpSC..... Shell Chemical Co., Deer Park, TX [*Library symbol*] [*Library of Congress*] (LCLS)
TxDunv..... Duncanville Public Library, Duncanville, TX [*Library symbol*] [*Library of Congress*] (LCLS)
TxDW........ Texas Woman's University, Denton, TX [*Library symbol*] [*Library of Congress*] (LCLS)
TXE .... El Paso Community College, El Paso, TX [*OCLC symbol*] (OCLC)
TxE .... El Paso Public Library, El Paso, TX [*Library symbol*] [*Library of Congress*] (LCLS)
TXE .... Tax Executive [*A publication*]
TXE .... Telephone Exchange (Electronics) [*Telecommunications*] (IEEE)
TXE .... Telephone Exchange (Equipment) [*Telecommunications*]
TxEC .... El Paso Community College, El Paso, TX [*Library symbol*] [*Library of Congress*] (LCLS)
TXECB ...... Toxicological and Environmental Chemistry Reviews [*A publication*]
TxEdP........ Pan American University, Edinburg, TX [*Library symbol*] [*Library of Congress*] (LCLS)
TxEGS....... Church of Jesus Christ of Latter-Day Saints, Genealogical Society Library, El Paso Branch, El Paso, TX [*Library symbol*] [*Library of Congress*] (LCLS)
TxEHD...... Hotel-Dieu Medical-Nursing Educational Media Center, El Paso, TX [*Library symbol*] [*Library of Congress*] (LCLS)
TXEL........ Texcel International, Inc. [*NASDAQ symbol*] (NQ)
TXEN .... Texas Energies, Inc. [*NASDAQ symbol*] (NQ)
TxENG ...... El Paso Natural Gas Co., Technical Information Center, El Paso, TX [*Library symbol*] [*Library of Congress*] (LCLS)
TxEU .... University of Texas at El Paso, El Paso, TX [*Library symbol*] [*Library of Congress*] (LCLS)
TxEWB....... United States Army, William Beaumont General Hospital, Medical and Technical Library, El Paso, TX [*Library symbol*] [*Library of Congress*] (LCLS)
TXF............ Corpus Christi State University, Corpus Christi, TX [*OCLC symbol*] (OCLC)
TxF .... Fort Worth Public Library, Fort Worth, TX [*Library symbol*] [*Library of Congress*] (LCLS)
TXF............ Texfi Industries, Inc. [*NYSE symbol*] (SPSG)
TxFACM... Amon Carter Museum of Western Art, Fort Worth, TX [*Library symbol*] [*Library of Congress*] (LCLS)
TxFAl .... Alcon Laboratories, Inc., Fort Worth, TX [*Library symbol*] [*Library of Congress*] (LCLS)
TxFbAD .... United States Army, Air Defense School, Fort Bliss, TX [*Library symbol*] [*Library of Congress*] (LCLS)

TxFBH ...... Bell Helicopter Co., Fort Worth, TX [*Library symbol*] [*Library of Congress*] (LCLS)

TxFCB .... Carter & Burgess, Inc., Fort Worth, TX [*Library symbol*] [*Library of Congress*] (LCLS)

TxFCC .... Fort Worth Christian College, Fort Worth, TX [*Library symbol*] [*Library of Congress*] (LCLS)

TxFCO .... Texas College of Osteopathic Medicine, Fort Worth, TX [*Library symbol*] [*Library of Congress*] (LCLS)

TxFF .... Fort Worth Art Museum, Fort Worth, TX [*Library symbol*] [*Library of Congress*] (LCLS)

TxFFAA .... United States Federal Aviation Administration, Fort Worth, TX [*Library symbol*] [*Library of Congress*] (LCLS)

TxFG .... General Dynamics/Convair Aerospace Division, Fort Worth, TX [*Library symbol*] [*Library of Congress*] (LCLS)

TxFGS .... Church of Jesus Christ of Latter-Day Saints, Genealogical Society Library, Fort Worth Branch, North Richland Hills, Fort Worth, TX [*Library symbol*] [*Library of Congress*] (LCLS)

TxFhH .... Darnell Army Hospital, Medical Library, Fort Hood, TX [*Library symbol*] [*Library of Congress*] (LCLS)

TxFJPS ..... John Peter Smith Hospital, Fort Worth, TX [*Library symbol*] [*Library of Congress*] (LCLS)

TxFK .... Kimbell Art Museum, Fort Worth, TX [*Library symbol*] [*Library of Congress*] (LCLS)

TxFM .... Fort Worth Museum of Science and History, Fort Worth, TX [*Library symbol*] [*Library of Congress*] (LCLS)

TxFNA ...... United States National Archives and Record Center, Fort Worth, TX [*Library symbol*] [*Library of Congress*] (LCLS)

TxFNIMH ... National Institute of Mental Health, Clinical Research Center Medical Library, Fort Worth, TX [*Library symbol*] [*Library of Congress*] (LCLS)

TxFrB .... Brazosport Junior College, Freeport, TX [*Library symbol*] [*Library of Congress*] (LCLS)

TxFrD .... Dow Chemical Co., Texas Division, Freeport, TX [*Library symbol*] [*Library of Congress*] (LCLS)

TxFS .... Southwestern Baptist Theological Seminary, Fort Worth, TX [*Library symbol*] [*Library of Congress*] (LCLS)

TxFshBH... Brooke General Hospital, Medical Library, Fort Sam Houston, TX [*Library symbol*] [*Library of Congress*] (LCLS)

TxFshM..... Medical Field Service School, Fort Sam Houston, TX [*Library symbol*] [*Library of Congress*] (LCLS)

TxFSJ .... Saint Joseph Hospital, Medical and Nursing Library, Fort Worth, TX [*Library symbol*] [*Library of Congress*] (LCLS)

TxFT .... Tarrant County Junior College, Fort Worth, TX [*Library symbol*] [*Library of Congress*] (LCLS)

TxFTC .... Texas Christian University, Fort Worth, TX [*Library symbol*] [*Library of Congress*] (LCLS)

TxFTE .... Texas Electric Service Co., Fort Worth, TX [*Library symbol*] [*Library of Congress*] (LCLS)

TxFTM ...... Terrell's Laboratories Medical Library, Fort Worth, TX [*Library symbol*] [*Library of Congress*] (LCLS)

TxFT-NE... Tarrant County Junior College, Northeast Campus, Hurst, TX [*Library symbol*] [*Library of Congress*] (LCLS)

TxFT-S ...... Tarrant County Junior College, South Campus, Fort Worth, TX [*Library symbol*] [*Library of Congress*] (LCLS)

TxFTW ...... Texas Wesleyan College, Fort Worth, TX [*Library symbol*] [*Library of Congress*] (LCLS)

TXG .... Austin Public Library, Austin, TX [*OCLC symbol*] (OCLC)

TXG .... Taxiing [*Aviation*] (FAAC)

TxGA .... United States Army, Army Engineering District, Office of Administrative Services, Galveston, TX [*Library symbol*] [*Library of Congress*] (LCLS)

TxGaiC ...... Cooke County Junior College, Gainsville, TX [*Library symbol*] [*Library of Congress*] (LCLS)

TxGar .... Nicholson Memorial Library, Garland, TX [*Library symbol*] [*Library of Congress*] (LCLS)

TxGarD ..... Dresser Industries, Inc., Garland, TX [*Library symbol*] [*Library of Congress*] (LCLS)

TxGarV...... Varo, Inc., Texas Division, Garland, TX [*Library symbol*] [*Library of Congress*] (LCLS)

TxGat......... Gatesville Public Library, Gatesville, TX [*Library symbol*] [*Library of Congress*] (LCLS)

TxGC .... Galveston Community College, Galveston, TX [*Library symbol*] [*Library of Congress*] (LCLS)

TxGeoS...... Southwestern University, Georgetown, TX [*Library symbol*] [*Library of Congress*] (LCLS)

TxGilGS... Church of Jesus Christ of Latter-Day Saints, Genealogical Society Library, Longview Branch, Gilmer, TX [*Library symbol*] [*Library of Congress*] (LCLS)

TxGML ..... Texas A & M University, Moody College of Marine Sciences and Maritime Resources, Galveston, TX [*Library symbol*] [*Library of Congress*] (LCLS)

TxGoS........ Spanish Texas Microfilm Center, Goliad, TX [*Library symbol*] [*Library of Congress*] (LCLS)

TxGR .... Rosenberg Library, Galveston, TX [*Library symbol*] [*Library of Congress*] (LCLS)

TxGrp .... Grand Prairie Memorial Library, Grand Prairie, TX [*Library symbol*] [*Library of Congress*] (LCLS)

TxGUSFW ... United States National Marine Fisheries Service, Biological Laboratory, Galveston, TX [*Library symbol*] [*Library of Congress*] (LCLS)

TxH .... Houston Public Library, Houston, TX [*Library symbol*] [*Library of Congress*] (LCLS)

TXH.......... Transfer on Index High

TXH.......... University of Houston, Houston, TX [*OCLC symbol*] (OCLC)

TxHaJ .... Jarvis Christian College, Hawkins, TX [*Library symbol*] [*Library of Congress*] (LCLS)

TxHAM..... Houston Academy of Medicine for Texas Medical Center, Houston, TX [*Library symbol*] [*Library of Congress*] (LCLS)

TxHAWD ... Arnold, White & Durkee, Houston, TX [*Library symbol*] [*Library of Congress*] (LCLS)

TxHBa .... National Lead Industries, Inc., Baroid Division, Houston, TX [*Library symbol*] [*Library of Congress*] (LCLS)

TxHBB ...... Baker, Botts, Shepherd & Coates, Houston, TX [*Library symbol*] [*Library of Congress*] (LCLS)

TxHBC ...... Houston Baptist University, Houston, TX [*Library symbol*] [*Library of Congress*] (LCLS)

TxHBec ..... Bechtel Group, Inc., Technical Library, Houston, TX [*Library symbol*] [*Library of Congress*] (LCLS)

TxHBR ...... Brown & Root, Inc., Technical Library, Houston, TX [*Library symbol*] [*Library of Congress*] (LCLS)

TxHC......... Houston Community College System, Houston, TX [*Library symbol*] [*Library of Congress*] (LCLS)

TxHCC ...... Continental Carbon Co., Houston, TX [*Library symbol*] [*Library of Congress*] (LCLS)

TxHCG...... Columbia Gulf Transmission Co., Houston, TX [*Library symbol*] [*Library of Congress*] (LCLS)

TxHCI .... Cameron Iron Works, Inc., Houston, TX [*Library symbol*] [*Library of Congress*] (LCLS)

TxHCS ...... Community Welfare Planning Association, Social Research Library, Houston, TX [*Library symbol*] [*Library of Congress*] (LCLS)

TxHDC...... Dow Chemical Co., E and CS Information Center, Houston, TX [*Library symbol*] {*Library of Congress*] (LCLS)

TxHDE...... Dresser Industries, Inc., Lane-Wells Co., Houston, TX [*Library symbol*] [*Library of Congress*] (LCLS)

TxHDom.... Dominican College, Houston, TX [*Library symbol*] [*Library of Congress*] (LCLS)

TxHe.......... Edwards Public Library, Henrietta, TX [*Library symbol*] [*Library of Congress*] (LCLS)

TxHE......... United States Air Force, Base Library, Ellington AFB, Houston, TX [*Library symbol*] [*Library of Congress*] (LCLS)

TxHebO..... Our Lady of Guadalupe Parish Library, Hebbronville, TX [*Library symbol*] [*Library of Congress*] (LCLS)

TxHE-NA ... United States Air Force, National Aerospace Education Library, Ellington AFB, Houston, TX [*Library symbol*] [*Library of Congress*] (LCLS)

TxHF.......... Captain Theodore C. Freeman Memorial Library, Houston, TX [*Library symbol*] [*Library of Congress*] (LCLS)

TxHFE ...... Fluor Engineers & Constructors, Fluor Houston Library, Houston, TX [*Library symbol*] [*Library of Congress*] (LCLS)

TxHFO...... Fluor Ocean Services, Engineering Library, Houston, TX [*Library symbol*] [*Library of Congress*] (LCLS)

TxHFR ..... Freelance Research Service, Houston, TX [*Library symbol*] [*Library of Congress*] (LCLS)

TxHG......... Gulf Coast Bible College, Houston, TX [*Library symbol*] [*Library of Congress*] (LCLS)

TxHGO ..... Gulf Oil Co.-US, Central Reference Library, Houston, TX [*Library symbol*] [*Library of Congress*] (LCLS)

TxHGP...... Gulf Publishing Co., Houston, TX [*Library symbol*] [*Library of Congress*] (LCLS)

TxHGS ...... Church of Jesus Christ of Latter-Day Saints, Genealogical Society Library, Houston Branch, Houston, TX [*Library symbol*] [*Library of Congress*] (LCLS)

TxHGS-E.. Church of Jesus Christ of Latter-Day Saints, Genealogical Society Library, Houston East Branch, Houston, TX [*Library symbol*] [*Library of Congress*] (LCLS)

TxHH .... Black, Syvalls & Bryson, Inc., HOMCO Division, Houston, TX [*Library symbol*] [*Library of Congress*] (LCLS)

TxHHC ..... Houston Chronicle, Houston, TX [*Library symbol*] [*Library of Congress*] (LCLS)

TxHHG ..... Houston-Galveston Area Council Library, Houston, TX [*Library symbol*] [*Library of Congress*] (LCLS)

TxHHH ..... Herman Hospital, Houston, TX [*Library symbol*] [*Library of Congress*] (LCLS)

TxHHL...... Houston Lighting & Power Co., Houston, TX [*Library symbol*] [*Library of Congress*] (LCLS)

TxHHO ..... Humble Oil & Refining Co., General Services Library, Houston, TX [*Library symbol*] [*Library of Congress*] (LCLS)

TxHHO-E ... Humble Oil & Refining Co., Marketing Research Library, Houston, TX [*Library symbol*] [*Library of Congress*] (LCLS)

TxHHOM ... Houston Oil and Mineral Corp., Corporate Library, Houston, TX [*Library symbol*] [*Library of Congress*] (LCLS)

TxHHP...... Houston Post, Houston, TX [*Library symbol*] [*Library of Congress*] (LCLS)

TxHHT...... Hughes Tool Co., Houston, TX [*Library symbol*] [*Library of Congress*] (LCLS)

TxHI.......... International Business Machines Corp., Corporation Library, Houston, TX [*Library symbol*] [*Library of Congress*] (LCLS)

TXHI........ THT, Inc. [*Formerly, Texas Hitech, Inc.*] [*NASDAQ symbol*] (NQ)

TxHiC....... Hill Junior College, Hillsboro, TX [*Library symbol*] [*Library of Congress*] (LCLS)

TxHIR...... Institute of Religion, Texas Medical Center, Houston, TX [*Library symbol*] [*Library of Congress*] (LCLS)

TXHL........ Texas Health Letter [*A publication*]

TxHLD...... City of Houston Legal Department, Houston, TX [*Library symbol*] [*Library of Congress*] (LCLS)

TxHLJ....... Memorial Baptist Hospital, Lillie Jolly School of Nursing, Houston, TX [*Library symbol*] [*Library of Congress*] (LCLS)

TxHLS...... Lunar Science Institute, Houston, TX [*Library symbol*] [*Library of Congress*] (LCLS)

TxHLT...... Layne Texas Co., Houston, TX [*Library symbol*] [*Library of Congress*] (LCLS)

TxHM........ Museum of Fine Arts, Houston, TX [*Library symbol*] [*Library of Congress*] (LCLS)

TxHMa...... Magcobar Corp., Houston, TX [*Library symbol*] [*Library of Congress*] (LCLS)

TxHMC..... Houston Academy of Medicine, Houston, TX [*Library symbol*] [*Library of Congress*] (LCLS)

TxHMc..... McClelland Engineers, Inc., Houston, TX [*Library symbol*] [*Library of Congress*] (LCLS)

TxHMM.... Milwhite Co., Houston, TX [*Library symbol*] [*Library of Congress*] (LCLS)

TxHMon.... Monsanto Co., Houston, TX [*Library symbol*] [*Library of Congress*] (LCLS)

TxHN....... National Association of Corrosion Engineers, Houston, TX [*Library symbol*] [*Library of Congress*] (LCLS)

TxHNASA ... National Aeronautics and Space Administration, Manned Spacecraft Center, Technical Library, Houston, TX [*Library symbol*] [*Library of Congress*] (LCLS)

TxHNH..... North Harris County College, Houston, TX [*Library symbol*] [*Library of Congress*] (LCLS)

TxHP........ Texas Research Institute of Mental Sciences, Houston, TX [*Library symbol*] [*Library of Congress*] (LCLS)

TxHPC...... Pace Company, Houston, TX [*Library symbol*] [*Library of Congress*] (LCLS)

TxHPen..... Pennzoil Exploration Library, Houston, TX [*Library symbol*] [*Library of Congress*] (LCLS)

TxHPH...... Port of Houston World Trade Center, Houston, TX [*Library symbol*] [*Library of Congress*] (LCLS)

TxHPI....... Prudential Insurance Co. of America, Houston, TX [*Library symbol*] [*Library of Congress*] (LCLS)

TxHPT...... Petro-Tex Chemical Corp., Research Library, Houston, TX [*Library symbol*] [*Library of Congress*] (LCLS)

TxHR........ Rice University, Houston, TX [*Library symbol*] [*Library of Congress*] (LCLS)

TxHRa...... Raymond International, Inc., Houston, TX [*Library symbol*] [*Library of Congress*] (LCLS)

TxHRH..... Roy M. Huffington, Inc., Library, Houston, TX [*Library symbol*] [*Library of Congress*] (LCLS)

TxHRI....... Houston Research Institute, Houston, TX [*Library symbol*] [*Library of Congress*] (LCLS)

TxHSB...... Southern Bible College, Houston, TX [*Library symbol*] [*Library of Congress*] (LCLS)

TxHSD...... Shell Development Co., Bellaire Research Center, Houston, TX [*Library symbol*] [*Library of Congress*] (LCLS)

TxHSDW .. Shell Oil Development Co., Westhollow Research Center Library, Houston, TX [*Library symbol*] [*Library of Congress*] (LCLS)

TxHSJM... San Jacinto Museum of History Association, Deer Park, TX [*Library symbol*] [*Library of Congress*] (LCLS)

TxHSOC ... Standard Oil Company of Texas, Houston, TX [*Library symbol*] [*Library of Congress*] (LCLS)

TxHSOF.... Shell Oil Co., Information and Library Services Library, Houston, TX [*Library symbol*] [*Library of Congress*] (LCLS)

TxHSOIC ... Shell Oil Co., Information and Computing Services Center Library, Houston, TX [*Library symbol*] [*Library of Congress*] (LCLS)

TxHSP....... Shell Pipe Line Corp., R and D Library, Houston, TX [*Library symbol*] [*Library of Congress*] [*Obsolete*] (LCLS)

TxHSR...... Southwestern Research Institute, Houston, TX [*Library symbol*] [*Library of Congress*] (LCLS)

TxHST...... University of Saint Thomas, Houston, TX [*Library symbol*] [*Library of Congress*] (LCLS)

TxHSTC.... South Texas Junior College, Houston, TX [*Library symbol*] [*Library of Congress*] (LCLS)

TxHSTL.... South Texas College of Law, Houston, TX [*Library symbol*] [*Library of Congress*] (LCLS)

TxHSU...... Superior Oil Exploration Library, Houston, TX [*Library symbol*] [*Library of Congress*] (LCLS)

TxHSW..... Schlumberger Well Services, Houston, TX [*Library symbol*] [*Library of Congress*] (LCLS)

TxHTC...... Transcontinental Gas Pipe Line Corp., Houston, TX [*Library symbol*] [*Library of Congress*] (LCLS)

TxHTE...... Texas Eastern Transmission Corp., Houston, TX [*Library symbol*] [*Library of Congress*] (LCLS)

TxHTen..... Tennessee Gas Transmission Co., Houston, TX [*Library symbol*] [*Library of Congress*] (LCLS)

TxHTexG.. Texas Gas Exploration Co., Houston, TX [*Library symbol*] [*Library of Congress*] (LCLS)

TxHTexO ... Texasgulf Oil & Gas Co., Houston, TX [*Library symbol*] [*Library of Congress*] (LCLS)

TxHTG...... Trunkline Gas Co., Houston, TX [*Library symbol*] [*Library of Congress*] (LCLS)

TxHTGP ... Tennessee Gas Pipeline Co., Houston, TX [*Library symbol*] [*Library of Congress*] (LCLS)

TxHTGS.... Texas Gulf Sulphur Co., Inc., Houston, TX [*Library symbol*] [*Library of Congress*] (LCLS)

TxHTI ...... Texas Instruments, Inc., Houston, TX [*Library symbol*] [*Library of Congress*] (LCLS)

TxHTide.... Getty Oil Co., Houston, TX [*Library symbol*] [*Library of Congress*] (LCLS)

TxHTide(Res) ... Getty Oil Co., Exploration and Production Research Library, Houston, TX [*Library symbol*] [*Library of Congress*] (LCLS)

TxHTI-I .... Texas Instruments, Inc., Industrial Products Division, Houston, TX [*Library symbol*] [*Library of Congress*] (LCLS)

TxHTM..... Texas Manufacturers Association, Houston, TX [*Library symbol*] [*Library of Congress*] (LCLS)

TxHTO...... Tenneco Oil Co., Exploration Research Library, Houston, TX [*Library symbol*] [*Library of Congress*] (LCLS)

TxHTRW .. TRW Systems Group, Houston, TX [*Library symbol*] [*Library of Congress*] (LCLS)

TxHTSU ... Texas Southern University, Houston, TX [*Library symbol*] [*Library of Congress*] (LCLS)

TxHTu....... Turner, Collie & Braden, Inc., Houston, TX [*Library symbol*] [*Library of Congress*] (LCLS)

TxHU .... University of Houston, Houston, TX [*Library symbol*] [*Library of Congress*] (LCLS)

TxHUC...... Union Carbide Corp., Houston, TX [*Library symbol*] [*Library of Congress*] (LCLS)

TxHU-D.... University of Houston, Downtown College, Houston, TX [*Library symbol*] [*Library of Congress*] (LCLS)

TxHU-L.... University of Houston, Law School, Houston, TX [*Library symbol*] [*Library of Congress*] (LCLS)

TxHurT..... Tarrant County Junior College District, Hurst, TX [*Library symbol*] [*Library of Congress*] (LCLS)

TxHUSC ... United States Department of Commerce, Houston Field Office Library, Houston, TX [*Library symbol*] [*Library of Congress*] (LCLS)

TxHuT....... Sam Houston State University, Huntsville, TX [*Library symbol*] [*Library of Congress*] (LCLS)

TxHUTP ... Union Texas Petroleum Co., Houston, TX [*Library symbol*] [*Library of Congress*] (LCLS)

TxHVA...... United States Veterans Administration Hospital, Houston, TX [*Library symbol*] [*Library of Congress*] (LCLS)

TxHVE...... Vinson, Elkins, Searls, Connally & Smith, Law Library, Houston, TX [*Library symbol*] [*Library of Congress*] (LCLS)

TxHW........ Welex Division, Halliburton Co., Houston, TX [*Library symbol*] [*Library of Congress*] (LCLS)

TxHWB..... World Book Encyclopaedia Science Service, Inc., Houston, TX [*Library symbol*] [*Library of Congress*] (LCLS)

TxHWG..... Western Geophysical Co., Houston, TX [*Library symbol*] [*Library of Congress*] (LCLS)

TxHWH .... Westbury Senior High School, Houston, TX [*Library symbol*] [*Library of Congress*] (LCLS)

TxHWN .... Western Natural Gas Co., Houston, TX [*Library symbol*] [*Library of Congress*] (LCLS)

TXI............ Southwest Texas State University, San Marcos, TX [*OCLC symbol*] (OCLC)

TXI............ Texas Industries, Inc. [*NYSE symbol*] (SPSG)

TXI............ Texas International Airlines, Inc. [*Air carrier designation symbol*]

TXI............ Torex Minerals Ltd. [*Vancouver Stock Exchange symbol*]

TXI............ Transfer with Index Incremented

TxIr........... Irving Municipal Library, Irving, TX [*Library symbol*] [*Library of Congress*] (LCLS)

TxIrS .... Irving Independent School District, Irving, TX [*Library symbol*] [*Library of Congress*] (LCLS)

TXJ........... University of Texas at San Antonio, San Antonio, TX [*OCLC symbol*] (OCLC)

TxJaB........ Baptist Missionary Association Theological Seminary, Jacksonville, TX [*Library symbol*] [*Library of Congress*] (LCLS)

TxJaC........ Jacksonville College, Jacksonville, TX [*Library symbol*] [*Library of Congress*] (LCLS)

TxJaL........ Lon Morris College, Jacksonville, TX [*Library symbol*] [*Library of Congress*] (LCLS)

TXK .... Stephen F. Austin University, Nacogdoches, TX [*OCLC symbol*] (OCLC)

TXK .... Telephone Exchange (Crossbar) [*Telecommunications*] (TEL)

TXK .... Texarkana [*Arkansas*] [*Airport symbol*] (OAG)

TxKeeS ...... Southwestern Union College, Keene, TX [*Library symbol*] [*Library of Congress*] (LCLS)

TxKerS ...... Schreiner Institute, Kerrville, TX [*Library symbol*] [*Library of Congress*] (LCLS)

TXKF .... Bermuda Naval Air Station [*Bermuda*] [*ICAO location identifier*] (ICLI)

TxKiC .... Central Texas College, Killeen, TX [*Library symbol*] [*Library of Congress*] (LCLS)

TxKilC ...... Kilgore College, Kilgore, TX [*Library symbol*] [*Library of Congress*] (LCLS)

TxKT .... Texas A & I University, Kingsville, TX [*Library symbol*] [*Library of Congress*] (LCLS)

TXL .... Berlin [*West Germany*] [*Airport symbol*] (OAG)

TXL .... Lubbock City-County Libraries, Lubbock, TX [*OCLC symbol*] (OCLC)

TxL .... Lubbock City-County Libraries, Lubbock, TX [*Library symbol*] [*Library of Congress*] (LCLS)

TX L .... Texas Law Review [*A publication*]

TXL .... Transfer on Index Low

TxLaH .... United States Air Force, Base Library, Lackland Air Force Base, TX [*Library symbol*] [*Library of Congress*] (LCLS)

TxLaM .... United States Air Force, Wilford Hall Medical Center, Lackland AFB, TX [*Library symbol*] [*Library of Congress*] (LCLS)

TxLapU ...... Upjohn Co., Polymer Chemicals Division Library, La Porte, TX [*Library symbol*] [*Library of Congress*] (LCLS)

TxLar .... Laredo Public Library, Laredo, TX [*Library symbol*] [*Library of Congress*] (LCLS)

TxLarC ...... Laredo Junior College, Laredo, TX [*Library symbol*] [*Library of Congress*] (LCLS)

TxLarU ...... Laredo State University, Laredo, TX [*Library symbol*] [*Library of Congress*] (LCLS)

TxLC .... Lubbock Christian College, Lubbock, TX [*Library symbol*] [*Library of Congress*] (LCLS)

TxLcD .... Soil and Water Conservation Districts Foundation, Davis Conservation Library, League City, TX [*Library symbol*] [*Library of Congress*] (LCLS)

TxLeS .... South Plains College, Levelland, TX [*Library symbol*] [*Library of Congress*] (LCLS)

TxLib .... Liberty City Library, Liberty, TX [*Library symbol*] [*Library of Congress*] (LCLS)

TxLivP .... Polk County Enterprise, Livingston, TX [*Library symbol*] [*Library of Congress*] (LCLS)

TX LJ .... Texas Law Journal [*A publication*] (DLA)

TxLjB .... Brazosport College, Lake Jackson, TX [*Library symbol*] [*Library of Congress*] (LCLS)

TxLMH ...... Methodist Hospital, Lubbock, TX [*Library symbol*] [*Library of Congress*] (LCLS)

TxLoL .... LeTourneau College, Longview, TX [*Library symbol*] [*Library of Congress*] (LCLS)

TX LR .... Texas Law Review [*A publication*]

TXLRA .... Texas Law Review [*A publication*]

TxLT .... Texas Tech University, Lubbock, TX [*Library symbol*] [*Library of Congress*] (LCLS)

TxLTM ...... Texas Tech University, School of Medicine at Lubbock, Lubbock, TX [*Library symbol*] [*Library of Congress*] (LCLS)

TxLufA ...... Angelina College, Lufkin, TX [*Library symbol*] [*Library of Congress*] (LCLS)

TxLufFS ...... Texas Forest Service, Forest Products Laboratory Library, Lufkin, TX [*Library symbol*] [*Library of Congress*] (LCLS)

TxLufK ...... Kurth Memorial Library, Lufkin, TX [*Library symbol*] [*Library of Congress*] (LCLS)

TXM .... Middle Tennessee State University, Murfreesboro, TN [*OCLC symbol*] (OCLC)

TXM .... Tank Exchange Model

Tx-M .... Texas State Medical Library, Austin, TX [*Library symbol*] [*Library of Congress*] (LCLS)

TXM .... Trimel Corp. [*Toronto Stock Exchange symbol*]

TxMaIC ...... ICI America, Inc., Darco Experimental Laboratory Library, Marshall, TX [*Library symbol*] [*Library of Congress*] (LCLS)

TxMaW ..... Wiley College, Marshall, TX [*Library symbol*] [*Library of Congress*] (LCLS)

TxMCa ...... McAllen Memorial Library, McAllen, TX [*Library symbol*] [*Library of Congress*] (LCLS)

TxMcaH .... Hidelgo County Library System, McAllen, TX [*Library symbol*] [*Library of Congress*] (LCLS)

TxMcgR .... North American Rockwell Corp., Solid Rocket Division, McGregor, TX [*Library symbol*] [*Library of Congress*] (LCLS)

TxMck .... McKinney Memorial Public Library, McKinney, TX [*Library symbol*] [*Library of Congress*] (LCLS)

TXMDA .... Texas Medicine [*A publication*]

TxMe .... Mesquite Public Library, Mesquite, TX [*Library symbol*] [*Library of Congress*] (LCLS)

TxMeE ...... Eastfield College, Mesquite, TX [*Library symbol*] [*Library of Congress*] (LCLS)

TxMM .... Midland County Public Library, Midland, TX [*Library symbol*] [*Library of Congress*] (LCLS)

TXMX .... Southwest Cafes, Inc. [*NASDAQ symbol*] (SPSG)

TXN .... Houston Public Library, Houston, TX [*OCLC symbol*] (OCLC)

TXN .... Taxation

TXN .... Texas Instruments, Inc. [*NYSE symbol*] (SPSG)

TXN .... Texas Northern Oil & Gas [*Vancouver Stock Exchange symbol*]

TXN .... Texas Satellite Network [*Telecommunications service*] (TSSD)

TXN .... Tunxi [*China*] [*Airport symbol*] (OAG)

TxNacS ...... Stephen F. Austin State University, Nacogdoches, TX [*Library symbol*] [*Library of Congress*] (LCLS)

TXNO .... Technogenetics, Inc. [*New York, NY*] [*NASDAQ symbol*] (NQ)

TXO .... Texico, NM [*Location identifier*] [*FAA*] (FAAL)

TXO .... University of Texas of the Permian Basin, Odessa, TX [*OCLC symbol*] (OCLC)

TxOC .... Odessa College, Odessa, TX [*Library symbol*] [*Library of Congress*] (LCLS)

TxOE .... Ector County Public Library, Odessa, TX [*Library symbol*] [*Library of Congress*] (LCLS)

TxOEP .... El Paso Products Co., Odessa, TX [*Library symbol*] [*Library of Congress*] (LCLS)

TxOGS ...... Church of Jesus Christ of Latter-Day Saints, Genealogical Society Library, Odessa Stake Branch, Odessa, TX [*Library symbol*] [*Library of Congress*] (LCLS)

TXOL .... Texoil, Inc. [*NASDAQ symbol*] (NQ)

TXON .... Texon Energy Corp. [*NASDAQ symbol*] (NQ)

TxOr .... Orange Public Library, Orange, TX [*Library symbol*] [*Library of Congress*] (LCLS)

TXOrD ...... E. I. Du Pont de Nemours & Co., Sabine River Works, Orange, TX [*Library symbol*] [*Library of Congress*] (LCLS)

TXP .... El Paso Public Library, El Paso, TX [*OCLC symbol*] (OCLC)

TxP .... Pasadena Public Library, Pasadena, TX [*Library symbol*] [*Library of Congress*] (LCLS)

TxPaIMS .. Institute of Marine Science, University of Texas, Port Aransas, TX [*Library symbol*] [*Library of Congress*] (LCLS)

TxParC ...... Paris Junior College, Paris, TX [*Library symbol*] [*Library of Congress*] (LCLS)

TxPC .... Champion Papers, Inc., Pasadena, TX [*Library symbol*] [*Library of Congress*] (LCLS)

TxPE .... Ethyl Corp., Pasadena, TX [*Library symbol*] [*Library of Congress*] (LCLS)

TxPlao .... Plano Public Library, Plano, TX [*Library symbol*] [*Library of Congress*] (LCLS)

TxPlW .... Wayland Baptist College, Plainview, TX [*Library symbol*] [*Library of Congress*] (LCLS)

TxPnT .... Texas-United States Chemical Co., Process Engineering Section, R and D Library, Port Neches, TX [*Library symbol*] [*Library of Congress*] (LCLS)

TxPo .... Gates Memorial Library, Port Arthur, TX [*Library symbol*] [*Library of Congress*] (LCLS)

TXPRD ...... Tax Period

TxPS .... San Jacinto College, Pasadena, TX [*Library symbol*] [*Library of Congress*] (LCLS)

TxPT .... Tenneco Chemicals, Inc., Pasadena, TX [*Library symbol*] [*Library of Congress*] (LCLS)

TxPvC .... Prairie View Agricultural and Mechanical College, Prairie View, TX [*Library symbol*] [*Library of Congress*] (LCLS)

TXPYR ...... Taxpayer

TXQ .... University of Texas, Austin, Law Library, Austin, TX [*OCLC symbol*] (OCLC)

TXR .... Lamar University, Beaumont, TX [*OCLC symbol*] (OCLC)

TXR .... Susitna Valley, AK [*Location identifier*] [*FAA*] (FAAL)

TXR .... Tank Exchange Ratio (MCD)

TXR .... Triex Resources Ltd. [*Vancouver Stock Exchange symbol*]

TxRaC .... Ranger Junior College, Ranger, TX [*Library symbol*] [*Library of Congress*] (LCLS)

TXRC .... Texas Export [*AAR code*]

TxReTR ..... Texas Research Foundation, Renner, TX [*Library symbol*] [*Library of Congress*] (LCLS)

TXRF .... Total-Reflection X-Ray Fluorescence [*Analytical chemistry*]

TxRi .... Richardson Public Library, Richardson, TX [*Library symbol*] [*Library of Congress*] (LCLS)

TxRiA .... Anderson Clayton Foods [*of Anderson, Clayton & Co.*], Richardson, TX [*Library symbol*] [*Library of Congress*] (LCLS)

TxRiS .... Sun Oil Co., Richardson, TX [*Library symbol*] [*Library of Congress*] (LCLS)

TXRX .... Transmitter-Receiver

TXS .... Hardin-Simmons University, Abilene, TX [*OCLC symbol*] (OCLC)

TXS .... Taxpayer Service [*IRS*]

TXS .... Telephone Exchange (Strowger) [*Telecommunications*] (TEL)

TXS .... Texas Star Resources Corp. [*Vancouver Stock Exchange symbol*]

TxSa .... San Antonio Public Library, San Antonio, TX [*Library symbol*] [*Library of Congress*] (LCLS)

TxSaBAM ... United States Air Force, School of Aerospace Medicine, Brooks Air Force Base, San Antonio, TX [*Library symbol*] [*Library of Congress*] (LCLS)

TxSaBHR ... United States Air Force, Human Resources Laboratory Library, Brooks Air Force Base, San Antonio, TX [*Library symbol*] [*Library of Congress*] (LCLS)

TxSaBM.... Bexar County Medical Library Association, San Antonio, TX [*Library symbol*] [*Library of Congress*] (LCLS)

TxSaC....... San Antonio College, San Antonio, TX [*Library symbol*] [*Library of Congress*] (LCLS)

TxSaGH .... Robert B. Green Memorial Hospital, San Antonio, TX [*Library symbol*] [*Library of Congress*] (LCLS)

TxSaGS..... Church of Jesus Christ of Latter-Day Saints, Genealogical Society Library, San Antonio Branch, San Antonio, TX [*Library symbol*] [*Library of Congress*] (LCLS)

TxSaI........ Incarnate Word College, San Antonio, TX [*Library symbol*] [*Library of Congress*] (LCLS)

TxSal .... Tom Green County Library, San Angelo, TX [*Library symbol*] [*Library of Congress*] (LCLS)

TxSalA ...... Angelo State University, San Angelo, TX [*Library symbol*] [*Library of Congress*] (LCLS)

TxSaO .... Our Lady of the Lake College, San Antonio, TX [*Library symbol*] [*Library of Congress*] (LCLS)

TxSaOC..... Oblate College of the Southwest, San Antonio, TX [*Library symbol*] [*Library of Congress*] (LCLS)

TxSaSFRE ... Southwest Foundation for Research and Education, San Antonio, TX [*Library symbol*] [*Library of Congress*] (LCLS)

TxSaSM .... Saint Mary's University, San Antonio, TX [*Library symbol*] [*Library of Congress*] (LCLS)

TxSaSM-L ... Saint Mary's University, Law Library, San Antonio, TX [*Library symbol*] [*Library of Congress*] (LCLS)

TxSaSP...... St. Philip's College, San Antonio, TX [*Library symbol*] [*Library of Congress*] (LCLS)

TxSaSR ..... Southwest Research Institute, San Antonio, TX [*Library symbol*] [*Library of Congress*] (LCLS)

TxSaStJ..... Saint John's Seminary, San Antonio, TX [*Library symbol*] [*Library of Congress*] (LCLS)

TxSaT....... Trinity University, San Antonio, TX [*Library symbol*] [*Library of Congress*] (LCLS)

TxSaT-W... Trinity University, Whitsett Library Museum, San Antonio, TX [*Library symbol*] [*Library of Congress*] (LCLS)

TxSaU .... University of Texas at San Antonio, San Antonio, TX [*Library symbol*] [*Library of Congress*] (LCLS)

TxSaUS..... United Services Automobile Association, San Antonio, TX [*Library symbol*] [*Library of Congress*] (LCLS)

TxSaV........ United States Veterans Administration Hospital, San Antonio, TX [*Library symbol*] [*Library of Congress*] (LCLS)

Tx-SC .... Texas State Law Library, Austin, TX [*Library symbol*] [*Library of Congress*] (LCLS)

TxSE......... Texas Studies in English [*A publication*]

TxSeTL...... Texas Lutheran College, Seguin, TX [*Library symbol*] [*Library of Congress*] (LCLS)

TxShA ...... Austin College, Sherman, TX [*Library symbol*] [*Library of Congress*] (LCLS)

TxShpM .... United States Air Force, Regional Hospital, Medical Library, Sheppard AFB, TX [*Library symbol*] [*Library of Congress*] (LCLS)

TxSiW ...... Rob and Bessie Welder Wildlife Foundation, Sinton, TX [*Library symbol*] [*Library of Congress*] (LCLS)

TxSjM .... San Jacinto Museum of History Association, San Jacinto Monument, TX [*Library symbol*] [*Library of Congress*] (LCLS)

TxSmS...... Southwest Texas State University, San Marcos, TX [*Library symbol*] [*Library of Congress*] (LCLS)

TxSn .... Scurry County Library, Snyder, TX [*Library symbol*] [*Library of Congress*] (LCLS)

TxSvT .... Tarleton State University, Stephenville, TX [*Library symbol*] [*Library of Congress*] (LCLS)

TxSw......... Sweetwater City-County Library, Sweetwater, TX [*Library symbol*] [*Library of Congress*] (LCLS)

TXT .... Texas Southern University, Houston, TX [*OCLC symbol*] (OCLC)

TXT .... Text

TXT .... Textron, Inc. [*NYSE symbol*] (SPSG)

TxTA .... American Oil Co. [*Later, Amoco Oil Co.*], Texas City, TX [*Library symbol*] [*Library of Congress*] (LCLS)

TxTCM ..... College of the Mainland, Texas City, TX [*Library symbol*] [*Library of Congress*] (LCLS)

TxTe .... Texarkana Public Library, Texarkana, TX [*Library symbol*] [*Library of Congress*] (LCLS)

TxTeC....... Texarkana College, Texarkana, TX [*Library symbol*] [*Library of Congress*] (LCLS)

TxTeET ..... East Texas State University, Texarkana, TX [*Library symbol*] [*Library of Congress*] (LCLS)

TxTehW .... Westminster College, Tehuacana, TX [*Library symbol*] [*Library of Congress*] (LCLS)

TxTemC..... Temple Junior College, Temple, TX [*Library symbol*] [*Library of Congress*] (LCLS)

TxTemH .... Scott and White Memorial Hospital, Temple, TX [*Library symbol*] [*Library of Congress*] (LCLS)

TxTerS....... Southwestern Christian College, Terrell, TX [*Library symbol*] [*Library of Congress*] (LCLS)

TxTeS........ East Texas State University at Texarkana, Texarkana, TX [*Library symbol*] [*Library of Congress*] (LCLS)

TXTL......... Textile (MSA)

TXTLE ...... Textile

TxTMC ..... Monsanto Co., Texas City, TX [*Library symbol*] [*Library of Congress*] (LCLS)

TXTN .... Textone, Inc. [*NASDAQ symbol*] (NQ)

TxTUC ...... Union Carbide Corp., Chemicals and Plastics Division, Texas City, TX [*Library symbol*] [*Library of Congress*] (LCLS)

TxTy .... Tyler Carnegie Public Library, Tyler, TX [*Library symbol*] [*Library of Congress*] (LCLS)

TxTyB....... Butler College, Tyler, TX [*Library symbol*] [*Library of Congress*] (LCLS)

TxTyC....... Texas Eastern University, Tyler, TX [*Library symbol*] [*Library of Congress*] (LCLS)

TxTyT....... Texas College, Tyler, TX [*Library symbol*] [*Library of Congress*] (LCLS)

TXU .... Tabou [*Ivory Coast*] [*Airport symbol*] (OAG)

txu .... Texas [*MARC country of publication code*] [*Library of Congress*] (LCCP)

TXU .... Texas Utilities Co. [*NYSE symbol*] (SPSG)

TXU .... Texoro Resources Ltd. [*Vancouver Stock Exchange symbol*]

TxU........... University of Texas, Austin, TX [*Library symbol*] [*Library of Congress*] (LCLS)

TXU .... University of Texas at El Paso, El Paso, TX [*OCLC symbol*] (OCLC)

TxU-A....... University of Texas, M. D. Anderson Hospital and Tumor Institute, Houston, TX [*Library symbol*] [*Library of Congress*] (LCLS)

TxU-B....... University of Texas, Business Administration and Economics Library, Austin, TX [*Library symbol*] [*Library of Congress*] (LCLS)

TxU-D ...... University of Texas, School of Dentistry, Houston, TX [*Library symbol*] [*Library of Congress*] (LCLS)

TxU-Da ..... University of Texas at Dallas, Richardson, TX [*Library symbol*] [*Library of Congress*] (LCLS)

TxU-Hu ..... Humanities Research Center, University of Texas, Austin, TX [*Library symbol*] [*Library of Congress*] (LCLS)

TxU-J .... University of Texas, Lyndon Baines Johnson Presidential Library, Austin, TX [*Library symbol*] [*Library of Congress*] (LCLS)

TxU-L........ University of Texas, Law Library, Austin, TX [*Library symbol*] [*Library of Congress*] (LCLS)

TxU-M ...... University of Texas, Medical School, Galveston, TX [*Library symbol*] [*Library of Congress*] (LCLS)

TxU-O .... University of Texas of the Permian Basin, Odessa, TX [*Library symbol*] [*Library of Congress*] (LCLS)

TxU-PH..... University of Texas, School of Public Health, Houston, TX [*Library symbol*] [*Library of Congress*] (LCLS)

TxU-STM ... University of Texas Medical School at San Antonio, San Antonio, TX [*Library symbol*] [*Library of Congress*] (LCLS)

TxUvS........ Southwest Texas Junior College, Uvalde, TX [*Library symbol*] [*Library of Congress*] (LCLS)

TXV .... Fairfield, CA [*Location identifier*] [*FAA*] (FAAL)

TXV .... Texas Business Review [*A publication*]

TXV .... Textil Revue. Fachblatt fuer Textilhandel, Konfektionsindustrie, und Textilindustrie [*A publication*]

TXV .... University of Houston, Victoria Center, Victoria, TX [*OCLC symbol*] (OCLC)

TxVeC........ Vernon Regional Junior College, Vernon, TX [*Library symbol*] [*Library of Congress*] (LCLS)

TxVi.......... Victoria Public Library, Victoria, TX [*Library symbol*] [*Library of Congress*] (LCLS)

TxViC .... Victoria College, Victoria, TX [*Library symbol*] [*Library of Congress*] (LCLS)

TxVidGS.... Church of Jesus Christ of Latter-Day Saints, Genealogical Society Library, Beaumont Branch, Vidor, TX [*Library symbol*] [*Library of Congress*] (LCLS)

TxViHU..... University of Houston, Victoria Center, Victoria, TX [*Library symbol*] [*Library of Congress*] (LCLS)

TxW.......... Waco-McLennan County Library, Waco, TX [*Library symbol*] [*Library of Congress*] (LCLS)

TXW .... Waco-McLennan County Library, Waco, TX [*OCLC symbol*] (OCLC)

TxWaS....... Southwestern Assemblies of God College, Waxahachie, TX [*Library symbol*] [*Library of Congress*] (LCLS)

TxWB .... Baylor University, Waco, TX [*Library symbol*] [*Library of Congress*] (LCLS)

TxWB-B ..... Baylor University, Armstrong Browning Library, Waco, TX [*Library symbol*] [*Library of Congress*] (LCLS)

TxWB-L ..... Baylor University, Law School Library, Waco, TX [*Library symbol*] [*Library of Congress*] (LCLS)

TxWB-Mus ... Baylor University, Museum Collection, Waco, TX [*Library symbol*] [*Library of Congress*] (LCLS)

TxWeaC .... Weatherford College, Weatherford, TX [*Library symbol*] [*Library of Congress*] (LCLS)

TxWeiM .... Weimar Mercury, Weimar, TX [*Library symbol*] [*Library of Congress*] (LCLS)

TxWFM ..... Masonic Grand Lodge of Texas, Waco, TX [*Library symbol*] [*Library of Congress*] (LCLS)

TxWhaC .... Wharton County Junior College, Wharton, TX [*Library symbol*] [*Library of Congress*] (LCLS)

TxWhaW ... Wharton County Library, Wharton, TX [*Library symbol*] [*Library of Congress*] (LCLS)

TxWic	Kemp Public Library, Wichita Falls, TX [*Library symbol*] [*Library of Congress*] (LCLS)
TxWicM	Midwestern State University, Wichita Falls, TX [*Library symbol*] [*Library of Congress*] (LCLS)
TxWM	McClennan Community College, Waco, TX [*Library symbol*] [*Library of Congress*] (LCLS)
TxWPQ	Paul Quinn College, Waco, TX [*Library symbol*] [*Library of Congress*] (LCLS)
TxWV	United States Veterans Administration Hospital, Waco, TX [*Library symbol*] [*Library of Congress*] (LCLS)
TXX	Southwestern University, Georgetown, TX [*OCLC symbol*] (OCLC)
TY	Air Caledonie [*France*] [*ICAO designator*] (FAAC)
TY	Dahomey [*Aircraft nationality and registration mark*] (FAAC)
TY	Talmud Yerushalmi (BJA)
TY	Tax Year
TY	Tebul [*or Tevul*] Yom (BJA)
Ty	Temporary
TY	Territorial Yeomanry [*British military*] (DMA)
TY	Territory
TY	Thank You
Ty	Thyroxine [*Also, T4, Thx*] [*An amino acid*] [*Endocrinology*]
TY	Total Yield (AABC)
TY	Translation Hand Controller Y-Axis Direction (MCD)
TY	Transposon Yeast [*Genetics*]
TY	Tri-Continental Corp. [*NYSE symbol*] (SPSG)
TY	Truly
TY	Tyler's Quarterly Historical and Genealogical Magazine [*A publication*]
Ty	Tyndale New Testament Commentaries [*A publication*] (BJA)
TY	Type
TY	Typhoid Fever (DSUE)
TYA	Steele Aviation [*Fresno, CA*] [*FAA designator*] (FAAC)
TYA	Tygas Resources Corp. [*Vancouver Stock Exchange symbol*]
TYAA	Textured Yarn Association of America (EA)
Tyazh Mashinostr ...	Tyazhelie Mashinostroenie [*A publication*]
TYC	Toby Creek Resources Ltd. [*Vancouver Stock Exchange symbol*]
TYC	Trinity College, Hartford, CT [*OCLC symbol*] (OCLC)
TYC	Two-Year[-Old] Course [*Horse racing*]
TYC	Tyco Laboratories, Inc. [*NYSE symbol*] (SPSG)
TYC	Tylerdale Connecting [*AAR code*]
T-YCDT	Ten-Year Chinese Dong Tang [*Turmoil*] Cycle [*Reference to the Kuomintang's defeat in 1946-48, Mao's Great Leap Forward in 1956, the Cultural Revolution in 1966, and the Gang of Four's fall in 1976*] [*Term coined by William Safire*]
TYCO	Tylenol and Codeine [*Pharmacy*]
TYCOM	Type Commander
TYD	Temporary Duty (MCD)
TyD	Trabajos y Dias [*A publication*]
tyd	Type Designer [*MARC relator code*] [*Library of Congress*] (LCCP)
TYDAC	Typical Digital Automatic Computer
TYDE	Type Designators (MSA)
TYDNAP ...	Annual Report. Tokyo College of Pharmacy [*A publication*]
TYDS	Transactions. Yorkshire Dialect Society [*A publication*]
Tydskr Dieetkd Huishoudkd ...	Tydskrif vir Dieetkunde en Huishoudkunde [*South Africa*] [*A publication*]
Tydskr Natuurwet ...	Tydskrif vir Natuurwetenskappe [*A publication*]
Tydskr Natuurwetenskap ...	Tydskrif vir Natuurwetenskappe. Suid-Afrikaanse Akademie vir Wetenskap en Kuns [*A publication*]
Tydskr S-Afr Ver Spraak Gehoorheelkd ...	Tydskrif van die Suid-Afrikaanse Vereniging vir Spraaken Gehoorheelkunde [*A publication*]
Tydskr S-Afr Vet Ver ...	Tydskrif. Suid-Afrikaanse Veterinere Vereniging [*A publication*]
Tydskr Skoon Lug ...	Tydskrif vir Skoon Lug [*A publication*]
Tydskr Tandheelkd Ver S-Afr ...	Tydskrif. Tandheelkundige Vereniging van Suid-Afrika [*A publication*]
Tydskr Wet Kuns ...	Tydskrif vir Wetenskap en Kuns [*A publication*]
TYE	Tye Explorations, Inc. [*Vancouver Stock Exchange symbol*]
TYE	Tyonek, AK [*Location identifier*] [*FAA*] (FAAL)
TYF	Panama City, FL [*Location identifier*] [*FAA*] (FAAL)
TYF	Tung Yeun Feng [*Republic of China*] [*Seismograph station code, US Geological Survey*] (SEIS)
TYFSOK ...	Thank You for Shopping Our K-Mart [*or Kresge's*] [*Slogan of K-Mart Corp.*]
TYG	Temple Youth Group [*Local groups of National Federation of Temple Youth, sometimes called TYG-ers, pronounced "tigers"*]
TYG	Trypticase, Yeast-Extract, Glucose [*Cell growth medium*]
tyg	Typographer [*MARC relator code*] [*Library of Congress*] (LCCP)
TygP	Tygodnik Powszechny [*A publication*]
TYGR	Tigera Group, Inc. [*NASDAQ symbol*] (NQ)
TYH	Tihany [*Hungary*] [*Geomagnetic observatory code*]
TYI	Rocky Mount, NC [*Location identifier*] [*FAA*] (FAAL)
TYK	Toyooka [*Japan*] [*Seismograph station code, US Geological Survey*] (SEIS)
TYKNAQ ..	Annual Report. Tohoku College of Pharmacy [*A publication*]
TYL	Talara [*Peru*] [*Airport symbol*] (OAG)
TYL	TANU [*Tanganyika African National Union*] Youth League [*Tanganyika*]
TYL	Tyler Corp. [*NYSE symbol*] (SPSG)
Tyl	Tyler's Vermont Supreme Court Reports [*1800-03*] [*A publication*] (DLA)
Tyl Boun	Tyler on Boundaries, Fences, Etc. [*A publication*] (DLA)
TYLC	Tomato Yellow Leaf Curl [*Plant pathology*]
TYLCV	Tomato Yellow Leaf Curl Virus
Tyl Eccl L ..	Tyler's American Ecclesiastical Law [*A publication*] (DLA)
Tyl Eject.	Tyler on Ejectment and Adverse Enjoyment [*A publication*] (DLA)
Tyler.	Tyler's Vermont Reports [*1800-03*] [*A publication*] (DLA)
Tyler Ej	Tyler on Ejectment and Adverse Enjoyment [*A publication*] (DLA)
Tyler's	Tyler's Quarterly Historical and Genealogical Magazine [*A publication*]
Tyler's Quar ...	Tyler's Quarterly Historical and Genealogical Magazine [*A publication*]
Tyler Steph Pl ...	Tyler's Edition of Stephen on Principles of Pleading [*A publication*] (DLA)
Tyl Fix	Tyler on Fixtures [*A publication*] (DLA)
Tyl Inf	Tyler on Infancy and Coverture [*A publication*] (DLA)
TYLN	Tylan Corp. [*NASDAQ symbol*] (NQ)
Tyl Part.	Tyler on Partnership [*A publication*] (DLA)
Tyl St Pl.	Tyler's Edition of Stephen on the Principles of Pleading [*A publication*] (DLA)
Tyl Us	Tyler on Usury, Pawns, and Loans [*A publication*] (DLA)
TYLX	Tylox Resources Corp. [*NASDAQ symbol*] (NQ)
TYMNET ...	Timeshare, Inc. Network [*Telecommunications*] (TEL)
tymp	Tympany
TYMV	Turnip Yellow Mosaic Virus
TYN	Taiyuan [*China*] [*Airport symbol*] (OAG)
TYN	Taiyuan [*China*] [*Seismograph station code, US Geological Survey*] (SEIS)
TYN	Taywin Resources Ltd. [*Vancouver Stock Exchange symbol*]
TYNAA	Tydskrif vir Natuurwetenskappe [*A publication*]
Tyndale Bul ...	Tyndale Bulletin [*A publication*]
TyndHB	Tyndale House Bulletin [*Cambridge*] [*A publication*] (BJA)
Tyng	Tyng's Reports [*2-17 Massachusetts*] [*A publication*] (DLA)
TYO	Tokyo [*Japan*] [*Airport symbol*] (OAG)
TYO	Tokyo Newsletter [*A publication*]
TYO	Two-Year-Old [*Horse racing*] (ROG)
Tyoevaeen Taloudell Tutkimus Katsaus ...	Tyoevaeen Taloudellinen Tutkimuslaitos Katsaus [*A publication*]
TYOG	Take Your Own Gadgets
TYP	Transitional Year Program [*Brandeis University*] (EA)
TY-P	Trial Y-Plane
Typ.	Typed (BJA)
TYP.	Typical (AAG)
TYP.	Typography [*or Typographer*] (AAG)
TYP.	[*The*] Youth Project (EA)
TYPER	Typographical Error (AAG)
TYPH	Typhoon
TYPL	Type-Plate
Typ News ...	Typewriting News [*A publication*]
TYPNO	Teletypewriter Communications Interrupted (FAAC)
Typo.	Typographed [*Philately*]
TYPO	Typographical
TYPOE	Ten Year Plan for Ocean Exploration [*National Council on Marine Resources and Engineering Development*] (MSC)
TYPOG	Typographer [*or Typography*]
Typographical J ...	Typographical Journal [*A publication*]
Typogr Monatsbl ...	Typographische Monatsblaetter [*A publication*]
TYPOK	Teletypewriter Communications Resumed (FAAC)
TYPOUT. ...	Typewriter Output
TYPSTG. ...	Typesetting (MSA)
TYPW	Typewriter (ADA)
TYPWRT ..	Typewriter
TYPWRTR ...	Typewriter
TYQ	Indianapolis, IN [*Location identifier*] [*FAA*] (FAAL)
TYR	Tyler [*Texas*] [*Airport symbol*] (OAG)
TYR	Tyrone [*County in Ireland*] (ROG)
Tyr	Tyrosine [*Also, Y*] [*An amino acid*]
Tyr	Tyrwhitt and Granger's English Exchequer Reports [*1830-35*] [*A publication*] (DLA)
TYRE.	Export Tyre Holding Co. [*NASDAQ symbol*] (NQ)
Tyre Jus Filiz ...	Tyre's Jus Filizarii [*A publication*] (DLA)
Tyres & Access ...	Tyres and Accessories [*A publication*]
Tyr & Gr	Tyrwhitt and Granger's English Exchequer Reports [*1830-35*] [*A publication*] (DLA)
Tyr Trig	Tyranni Triginta [*of Scriptores Historiae Augustae*] [*Classical studies*] (OCD)
Tyrw	Tyrwhitt and Granger's English Exchequer Reports [*1830-35*] [*A publication*] (DLA)
Tyrw & G ...	Tyrwhitt and Granger's English Exchequer Reports [*1835-36*] [*A publication*] (DLA)
Tyrw & G (Eng) ...	Tyrwhitt and Granger's English Exchequer Reports [*1835-36*] [*A publication*] (DLA)
TYRX	Tyrex Oil Co. [*NASDAQ symbol*] (NQ)
TYS	Knoxville [*Tennessee*] [*Airport symbol*] (OAG)

TYS............ Overzicht van de Economische Ontwikkeling [*A publication*]
TYS............ Tensile Yield Strength
TYS............ Tyler Resources, Inc. [*Toronto Stock Exchange symbol*]
TYS............ Tyseley [*British depot code*]
TYS............ Tyson Valley [*Missouri*] [*Seismograph station code, US
              Geological Survey*] (SEIS)
TYSD........ Total Years Service Date
TYSN........ Tyson Foods, Inc. [*NASDAQ symbol*] (NQ)
TYSP........ Tibetan Youth Sponsorship Programs (EA)
TYT .... Nantucket, MA [*Location identifier*] [*FAA*] (FAAL)
TYT .... Type Training [*Navy*] (NVT)
TYTIPT..... Type Training in Port [*Navy*] (NVT)
Tytler Mil Law ... Tytler on Military Law and Courts-Martial [*A
              publication*] (DLA)
Tyt Mil L ... Tytler on Military Law and Courts-Martial [*3rd ed.*] [*1812*] [*A
              publication*] (DLA)
TYTV........ Tomato Yellow Top Virus
TYU.......... Tyuratam [*Satellite launch complex*] [*USSR*]
TYV .... Little Rock, AR [*Location identifier*] [*FAA*] (FAAL)
TYVM .... Thank You Very Much
TYX .... Tylox Resources Corp. [*Vancouver Stock Exchange symbol*]
TYY .... Abilene, TX [*Location identifier*] [*FAA*] (FAAL)
TYZ .... Taylor [*Arizona*] [*Airport symbol*] [*Obsolete*] (OAG)
TZ.............. American Trans Air, Inc. [*ICAO designator*] (FAAC)
TZ.............. Der Treue Zionswaechter [*Altona*] [*A publication*] (BJA)
TZ.............. Mali [*Aircraft nationality and registration mark*] (FAAC)
TZ.............. Tactical Zone [*Military*] (AABC)
tz................. Tanzania [*MARC country of publication code*] [*Library of
              Congress*] (LCCP)
TZ.............. Terrazo [*Technical drawings*]
TZ.............. Theologische Zeitschrift [*A publication*]
TZ.............. Tidal Zone
TZ.............. Time Zero
TZ.............. Times of Zambia [*A publication*]
TZ.............. Transition Zone [*in plant growth*] [*Botany*]
TZ.............. Translation Hand Controller Z-Axis Direction (NASA)
TZ.............. Transmitter Zone [*Telecommunications*] (TEL)
TZ.............. Transportation Zone [*Department of Transportation*]
TZ.............. Trennzahl Values [*For carrier gas flow rates*] [*Chromatography*]
TZ.............. Trierer Zeitschrift [*A publication*]
TZ.............. Tropical Zodiac
TZ.............. [*The*] Twilight Zone [*Television program created by Rod
              Serling*]
TZ.............. Twilight-Zoner [*Undecided voter*] [*Political slang*]
TZ.............. United Republic of Tanzania [*ANSI two-letter standard
              code*] (CNC)
TZA .... Finanzierung, Leasing, Factoring [*A publication*]
TZA .... United Republic of Tanzania [*ANSI three-letter standard
              code*] (CNC)
TZBas....... Theologische Zeitschrift (Basel) [*A publication*]
TZC .... Tetrazolium Chloride Agar [*Biological stain*]
TZC .... Trizec Corp. Ltd. [*Toronto Stock Exchange symbol*]
TZD .... True Zenith Distance [*Navigation*]
TZE........... Topaz Exploration Ltd. [*Vancouver Stock Exchange symbol*]
TZE........... Transfer on Zero
TZG .... Thermofit Zap Gun
TZI............ Traditiones. Zbornik Instituta za Slovensko Narodopisje [*A
              publication*]
TZJ .... Tubular Zippered Jacket
TZKRA...... Tonindustrie-Zeitung und Keramische Rundschau [*A
              publication*]
TZM .... Titanium-Zirconium-Molybdenum [*Alloy*]
TZN .... South Andros [*Bahamas*] [*Airport symbol*] (OAG)
TZN .... Tchaikazan Enterprises, Inc. [*Vancouver Stock Exchange
              symbol*]
TZNSDW ... Topographie und Zytologie Neurosekretorischer Systeme [*A
              publication*]
TZP........... Temperate Zone Phase
TZP........... Time Zero Pulse
TZP........... Triazolopyridazine [*Potential antianxiety drug*]
TZ Prakt Metallbearb ... TZ fuer Praktische Metallbearbeitung [*A
              publication*]
TZR .... Torrez Resources Ltd. [*Vancouver Stock Exchange symbol*]
TZS........... Terzake Subsidies [*A publication*]
TZTh .... Tuebinger Zeitschrift fuer Theologie [*A publication*] (BJA)
TZV .... Tetrazolium Violet [*Also, TV*]
TZX .... Trabzon [*Turkey*] [*Airport symbol*] (OAG)
TZY .... Warsaw, IN [*Location identifier*] [*FAA*] (FAAL)
TZZ........... Tabubil [*Papua New Guinea*] [*Seismograph station code, US
              Geological Survey*] (SEIS)

U

U	Audio and Power Connectors [*JETDS nomenclature*] [*Military*] (CET)
u------	Australasia [*MARC geographic area code*] [*Library of Congress*] (LCCP)
U	Benzon [*Denmark*] [*Research code symbol*]
U	Eased Up [*Horse racing*]
U	Eaton Laboratories, Inc. [*Research code symbol*]
U	Electric Tension [*Symbol*] [*IUPAC*]
u	Group Velocity [*Symbol*] (DEN)
U	Intensity Unknown [*Meteorology*] (FAAC)
U	Internal Energy [*Symbol*] [*Thermodynamics*]
U	Intrinsic Energy [*Symbol*] [*Physics*]
U	Quartermon Versor [*Symbol of a function*] [*Mathematics*] (ROG)
U	Shape Descriptor [*U-turn, for example. The shape resembles the letter for which it is named*]
U	Thermal Transmittance per Unit of Area [*Heat transmission symbol*]
U	Uafhaengige Parti [*Independent Party*] [*Denmark*] [*Political party*] (PPE)
U	Ubiquinone [*Coenzyme Q*] [*Also, CoQ, Q, UQ*] [*Biochemistry*]
u	Uebersetzen [*Translate*] [*German*]
U	Ugly Sky [*Navigation*]
U	Ugly Threatening Weather [*Meteorology*]
U	Ugutio [*Huguccio*] [*Deceased, 1210*] [*Authority cited in pre-1607 legal work*] (DSA)
U	Uhr [*Clock*] [*German*]
U	Uitgelezen [*A publication*]
U	Ullage (AAG)
U	Ultraphon & Supraphon [*Record label*] [*Czechoslovakia*]
U	Umpire [*Baseball*]
U	Unbalanced
U	Unburned [*Ecology*]
U	Uncirculated
U	Unclassified
U	Uncle [*Phonetic alphabet*] [*Royal Navy*] [*World War I*] [*Pre-World War II*] [*World War II*] (DSUE)
U	Uncle
U	Uncommon Species
U	Und [*And*] [*German*]
U	Under
U	Underfloor (NASA)
U	Underwater [*Missile launch environment symbol*]
U	Unemployed Parent [*Aid to Families with Dependent Children*] (OICC)
U	Unemployment
U	Unified
U	Uniform
U	Uniform [*Phonetic alphabet*] [*International*] (DSUE)
U	Uniformly Labeled [*Also, UL*] [*Compound, with radioisotope*]
U	Union [*or Unionist*]
U	Union Association [*Major league in baseball, 1884*]
U	Unionist Party [*Northern Ireland*] [*Political party*]
U	Unit
U	United
U	Universal
U	Universal/Unrestricted [*Film certificate*] [*British*]
U	Universitas [*A publication*]
U	University
U	Unknown
U	Unlimited [*Aviation*] (FAAC)
U	Unlimited Time [*Broadcasting term*]
U	Unoccupied
U	Unpleasant
U	Unrestricted [*Aviation*] (FAAC)
U	Unseated Rider [*Horse racing*]
u .҂.	Unser [*Our*] [*German*]
U	Unsymmetrical
U	Unter [*Among*] [*German*]
U	Untreated [*Medicine*]
U	Unwatched [*With reference to a light*] [*Maps and charts*]
U	Up [*or Upper*]
u	Up (quark) [*Atomic physics*]
U	Update [*Data processing*]
U	Upjohn Co. [*Research code symbol*]
U	Upper (ROG)
U	Upper Bow [*Music*] (ROG)
U	Upper-Class Speech [*"Non-U" designates the opposite*]
U	Upper School [*British*]
U	Uranium [*Chemical element*]
U	Urban [*District Council*] [*British*]
U	Urban Association [*Baseball*]
U	Urgent
U	Uridine [*One-letter symbol; see Urd*]
U	Urinal (ROG)
U	Urinate [*or Urine*] [*Medicine*]
U	Urological Surgery [*Medical specialty*] (DHSM)
U	Urology [*Medical Officer designation*] [*British*]
U	Urschrift [*Original, as of a document*] [*German military*]
U	Uruguay [*IYRU nationality code*]
U	USAIR Group [*NYSE symbol*] (SPSG)
U	Use
U	Utah
U	Utah Reports [*A publication*] (DLA)
U	Utah State Library, Salt Lake City, UT [*Library symbol*] [*Library of Congress*] (LCLS)
U	Utendus [*To Be Used*] [*Pharmacy*]
U	Utility [*Economics*]
U	Utility [*Designation for all US military aircraft*]
U	UTVA Aircraft Factory [*Yugoslavia*] [*ICAO aircraft manufacturer identifier*] (ICAO)
U	You [*Communications*] (FAAC)
U2	Popular music group
U²	Unclassified, Unlimited [*DoD*]
5U	Niger [*Aircraft nationality and registration mark*] (FAAC)
9U	Burundi [*Aircraft nationality and registration mark*] (FAAC)
U (Bomb)	[*A*] theoretical uranium-encased atomic or hydrogen bomb, the shell of which would be transformed into deadly radioactive dust upon detonation (MUGU)
UA	Ukrainian Soviet Socialist Republic [*ISO two-letter standard code*] (CNC)
UA	Ultra-Audible
UA	Umbilical Artery [*Anatomy*]
UA	Unable to Approve Arrival for the Time Specified [*Aviation*] (FAAC)
UA	Unanesthetized [*Physiology*]
UA	Unauthorized Absence (MUGU)
UA	Unavailable
UA	Unburned plus Ash [*Ecology*]
UA	Und Andere [*And Others*] [*German*]
UA	Under Age [*i.e., entitled neither to a daily rum ration nor money instead*] [*See also G, T*] [*Obsolete*] [*Navy*] [*British*]
U/A	Under Agreement [*Legal term*] (DLA)
UA	Understanding Aging (EA)
UA	Underwater Actuator
UA	Underwater Association for Scientific Research [*Margate, Kent, England*] (EAIO)
U/A	Underwriting Account [*Insurance*]
UA	Uniform Allowance [*Military*]
UA	Union des Artistes [*Union of Artists*] [*Canada*]
UA	Union Association [*Major league in baseball, 1884*]
U/A	Unit of Account [*European Monetary Agreement*] (EY)
UA	Unit Assets [*Army*]
UA	United Air Lines, Inc. [*ICAO designator*]
ua	United Arab Republic [*Egypt*] [*MARC country of publication code*] [*Library of Congress*] (LCCP)
UA	United Artists Communications, Inc.
UA	United Asia [*A publication*]
UA	United Association of Journeymen and Apprentices of the Plumbing and Pipe Fitting Industry of the United States and Canada (OICC)
UA	Universidad de Antioquia [*Colombia*] [*A publication*]

U of A.........	University of Alaska [*Anchorage, AK*]
UA..............	University of Alaska [*Anchorage, AK*]
UA..............	University of Arizona [*Tucson, AZ*]
U of A.........	University of Arkansas [*Fayetteville, AR*]
UA..............	Unnumbered Acknowledge [*or Acknowledgment*] [*Telecommunications*] (IEEE)
UA..............	Unstable Angina [*Medicine*]
UA..............	Upper Arm
UA..............	Ural-Altaische Jahrbuecher [*A publication*]
UA..............	Urban Anthropology [*A publication*]
UA..............	Urbanized Area (OICC)
UA..............	Uric Acid
UA..............	Urinalysis [*Medicine*] (KSC)
UA..............	User Area [*Information storage*]
UA..............	Usque Ad [*As Far As*] [*Latin*] (ADA)
UA..............	Uterine Aspiration [*Medicine*]
U3A...........	University of the Third Age [*Australia*]
UAA...........	Undergarment Accessories Association (EA)
UAA...........	Union des Avocats Arabes [*Arab Lawyers Union - ALU*] (EAIO)
UAA...........	United Action for Animals (EA)
UAA...........	United African Appeal (EA)
UAA...........	United American and Australasian Film Productions (ADA)
UAA...........	United Arab Airlines
UAA...........	Universitet i Bergen. Arbok. Historisk-Antikvarisk Rekke [*A publication*]
UAA...........	University of Alaska, Anchorage
UAA...........	University Athletic Association (EA)
UAA...........	University Aviation Association (EA)
UAA...........	Uracil Adenine Adenine [*Genetics*]
UAA...........	Urban Affairs Association (EA)
UAA...........	User Action Analyzer
UAA...........	Utility Arborist Association (EA)
UAAA........	Alma-Ata [*USSR*] [*ICAO location identifier*] (ICLI)
UAAF........	United Action Armed Forces [*A publication*]
UAAN........	Uzunagach [*USSR*] [*ICAO location identifier*] (ICLI)
UAAR........	United Activists for Animal Rights (EA)
UAAS	Ukrainian Academy of Arts and Sciences in the US (EA)
UAAS	Union Africaine des Artistes de Spectacle [*Union of African Performing Artists - UAPA*] (EAIO)
UAAUSA ..	Ukrainian Artists Association in USA (EA)
UAB..........	Unemployment Assistance Board
UAB..........	University of Alabama in Birmingham
UAB..........	University of Alberta Biotron [*University of Alberta*] [*Research center*] (RCD)
UAB..........	University Appointments Board [*British*] (DAS)
UAB..........	Until Advised By [*Aviation*] (FAAC)
u-ac---........	Ashmore and Cartier Islands [*MARC geographic area code*] [*Library of Congress*] (LCCP)
UAC..........	Unicorp American Corporation [*AMEX symbol*] (SPSG)
UAC..........	Unified Arab Command (BJA)
UAC..........	Uniform Annual Cost
UAC..........	Uninterrupted Automatic Control
UAC..........	Union Army of Commemoration
UAC..........	United African Company
UAC..........	United Aircraft Corporation [*Later, United Technologies Corp.*]
UAC..........	United American Croats
UAC..........	United Association of Coremakers [*A union*] [*British*]
UAC..........	Universal Area Code [*Bureau of Census*]
UAC..........	Universidad de Antioquia (Colombia) [*A publication*]
UAC..........	Universities Advisory Council
UAC..........	University of Alberta, Faculty of Library Science, Edmonton, AL, Canada [*OCLC symbol*] (OCLC)
UAC..........	University Analytical Center [*University of Arizona*] [*Research center*] (RCD)
UAC..........	Unusual Appearing Child [*Medicine*]
UAC..........	Upper Area Control Center [*Aviation*]
UAC..........	Utility Airplane Council [*Defunct*] (EA)
UAC..........	Utility Assemble Compool
UACA........	Union of Australian College Academics
UACA........	United American Contractors Association (EA)
UACC........	Universal Autograph Collectors Club (EA)
UACC........	Upper Area Control Center [*Aviation*]
UACCDD..	University Affiliated Cincinnati Center for Developmental Disorders [*University of Cincinnati*] [*Research center*] (RCD)
UACCI......	United Association of Christian Counselors International (EA)
UACES......	University Association for Contemporary European Studies [*British*]
UACL	United Aircraft of Canada Limited
UACMC	Union Arabe de Ciment et des Materiaux de Construction [*Arab Union for Cement and Building Materials - AUCBM*] (EAIO)
UACN........	Unified Automated Communication Network
UACN........	University of Alaska Computer Network [*Research center*] (RCD)
UACNPM ...	United American and Captive Nations Patriotic Movement (EA)
UACRL......	United Aircraft Corporation Research Laboratory (KSC)
UACSC......	United Aircraft Corporate Systems Center (KSC)

UACTE......	Universal Automatic Control and Test Equipment
UAD..........	Salinas, CA [*Location identifier*] [*FAA*] (FAAL)
UAD..........	Underwater Acoustic Decoupler
UAD..........	Undetermined Aerodynamic Disturbance (MCD)
UAD..........	Unit Assembly Drawing
UADBU......	Unattended Automatic Dial Back Up [*Telecommunications*]
UADC........	Universal Air Data Computer
UADP........	Uniform Automated [*or Automatic*] Data Processing
UADPS......	Uniform Automated [*or Automatic*] Data Processing System
UADPS-ICP ...	Uniform Automated [*or Automatic*] Data Processing System for Inventory Control Points [*Navy*]
UADPS/INAS ...	Uniform Automated [*or Automatic*] Data Processing System/Industrial Naval Air Station
UADPS-SP ...	Uniform Automated [*or Automatic*] Data Processing System for Stock Points [*Navy*]
UADS	User Attribute Data Set [*Data processing*] (MDG)
UADV........	University of Alberta Devonian Botanic Garden [*Canada*]
UADW.......	Universal Alliance of Diamond Workers [*See also AUOD*] [*Antwerp, Belgium*] (EAIO)
UAE..........	Unilateral Absence of Excretion [*Medicine*]
UAE..........	United Arab Emirates
UAEAC	Union Aduanera y Economica del Africa Central [*Central African Customs and Economic Union - CACEU*] [*Spanish*]
UAEC	United Artists Entertainment Co. [*NASDAQ symbol*] (NQ)
UAEE	Union des Associations Europeennes d'Etudiants [*Union of European Student Associations*]
UAegAl.....	Urkunden die Aegyptischen Altertums [*A publication*]
UAEI	United American Energy, Incorporated [*NASDAQ symbol*] (NQ)
UAEM.......	Union of Associations of European Meat Meal Producers [*See also UAPEFV*] [*Later, Eurpoean Renderers Association - EURA*] (EAIO)
UA/EM	University Association for Emergency Medicine (EA)
UAERA	United States. Air Force. School of Aerospace Medicine. Technical Report [*A publication*]
UAES	Utah Agricultural Experiment Station [*Utah State University*] [*Research center*] (RCD)
UAF	Ultimate Asbestos Fibril
UAF	Unit Authorization File
UAF	University-Affiliated Facility
UAF	University of Alaska, Fairbanks
UAF	Upper Atmospheric Facilities Program [*Washington, DC*] [*National Science Foundation*] (GRD)
UAFA	Union of Arab Football Associations (EAIO)
UAFC	Universal Air Freight Corporation
UAFF	Frunze [*USSR*] [*ICAO location identifier*] (ICLI)
UAFMMEEC ...	Union of Associations of Fish Meal Manufacturers in the EEC (EAIO)
UAF-MR ...	University-Affiliated Facility for the Mentally Retarded
UAFRA.......	Uniform Aircraft Financial Responsibility Act [*National Conference of Commissioners on Uniform State Laws*]
UAFSC......	Utilization Air Force Specialty Code
UAFS/T	Universal Aircraft Flight Simulator/Trainer
UAFUR......	Urgent Amplified Failure of Unsatisfactory Report
UAFZAG...	Contributions. Faculty of Science. University College of Addis Ababa (Ethiopia). Series C. Zoology [*A publication*]
UAG..........	Underwater Acoustic Group [*British*]
UAG..........	Union of Anarchist Groups [*British*]
UAG..........	Untersuchungen zur Altorientalischen Geschichte [*H. Winckler*] [*A publication*] (BJA)
UAG..........	Upper Atmosphere Geophysics (KSC)
UAG..........	Uracil Adenine Guanine [*Genetics*]
UAG..........	USSR. Academy of Science. Proceedings. Geographical Series [*A publication*]
UAGA	Uniform Anatomical Gift Act [*For organ donation*]
UAH	Ua Huka [*Marquesas Islands*] [*Airport symbol*] (OAG)
UAH	Union of Arab Historians (EA)
UAH	University of Alabama in Huntsville
UAHC.......	Union of American Hebrew Congregations (EA)
UAHS.......	Ulster Architectural Heritage Society
UAI	Union Academique Internationale [*International Academic Union - IAU*] (EAIO)
UAI	Union des Associations Internationales [*Union of International Associations - UIA*] (EAIO)
UAI	Union Astronomique Internationale [*International Astronomical Union - IAU*]
UAI	Universal Azimuth Indicator
UAI	Urban Affairs Institute (EA)
UAI	Uterine Activity Interval [*Obstetrics*]
UAICC.......	Underwater Acoustic Interference Coordinating Committee [*Military*]
UAIDE	Users of Automatic Information Display Equipment (EA)
UAII	Chimkent [*USSR*] [*ICAO location identifier*] (ICLI)
UAIM	United Andean Indian Mission [*Superseded by Ecuador Concerns Committee*]
UAIMS......	United Aircraft Information Management System
UAIRA	US Aircraft Cl A [*NASDAQ symbol*] (NQ)
UAJ	Union of Arab Jurists [*Baghdad, Iraq*] (EAIO)
UAJ	Ural-Altaische Jahrbuecher [*A publication*]
UAJb	Ural-Altaische Jahrbuecher [*A publication*]

UAJG	Union d'Action des Jeunes de Guinee [*Guinean Union of Youth Action*]
UAK..........	Narssarssuaq [*Greenland*] [*Airport symbol*] (OAG)
UAL...........	UAL Corp. [*NYSE symbol*] (SPSG)
UAL...........	Ukrainian American League (EA)
UAL...........	Unit Area Loading (AAG)
UAL...........	Unit Authorization List
UAL...........	Unite Arithmetique et Logique [*Arithmetic and Logic Unit - ALU*] [*French*]
UAL...........	United Air Lines, Inc. [*Air carrier designation symbol*]
UAL...........	Universal Airline Codes (MCD)
UAL...........	Upper Acceptance Limit
UAL...........	Urea-Ammonia Liquor
UAL...........	User Adaptive Language
UALE	Universala Artista Ligo de Esperantistoj [*Universal Artist League of Esperantists*] (EAIO)
UALI	Unit Authorization List Item
UALR LJ...	University of Arkansas at Little Rock. Law Journal [*A publication*]
UAM..........	Ultrasonically Assisted Machining [*Manufacturing term*]
UAM..........	Und Anderes Mehr [*And So Forth*] [*German*]
UAM..........	Underwater-to-Air Missile [*Air Force*]
UAM..........	Union Africaine et Malagache [*African and Malagasy Union*] [*Later, Common Afro-Malagasy Organization*]
UAM..........	United American Mechanics (EA)
UAM..........	United Asset Management Corp. [*NYSE symbol*] (SPSG)
UAM..........	United States Medical Intelligence and Information Agency, Frederick, MD [*OCLC symbol*] (OCLC)
UAMBD....	Union Africaine et Mauricienne de Banques pour le Developpement [*African and Mauritian Union of Development Banks*] (EAIO)
UAMC.......	Utility Assemble Master Compool
UAMCT.....	Union of Automobile, Motorcycle, and Cycle Technology
UAMH	University of Alberta Microfungus Collection and Herbarium [*Canada*]
UAMR.......	United Association of Manufacturers' Representatives (EA)
UAMS	Ukrainian Academy of Medical Sciences (EA)
UAMS	Upper Atmosphere Mass Spectrometer
UAN	United Animal Nations (EAIO)
UAN	Urea-Ammonium Nitrate [*Fertilizer*]
UAN	Uric Acid Nitrogen
UANAS	Urea-Ammonium Nitrate Ammonium Sulfate [*Fertilizer*]
UANC........	United African National Congress
UANC........	United African National Council [*Zimbabwe*] [*Political party*] (PPW)
UANM	United African Nationalist Movement (EA)
UANM	Universal African Nationalist Movement (EA)
UAO	Unconventional Aerial Object
UAO	Und Andere Orte [*And Elsewhere*] [*German*]
UAO	Unexplained Aerial Object
UAOD	United Ancient Order of Druids [*Freemasonry*] (ROG)
UAOO	Kzyl-Orda [*USSR*] [*ICAO location identifier*] (ICLI)
UAP...........	Ua Pou [*Marquesas Islands*] [*Airport symbol*] (OAG)
UAP...........	UAP, Inc. [*Toronto Stock Exchange symbol*]
UAP...........	Unabhaengige Arbeiterpartei [*Independent Labor Party*] [*Federal Republic of Germany*] [*Political party*] (PPE)
UAP...........	Unidentified Atmospheric Phenomena
UAP...........	Union Africaine de Physique [*African Union of Physics - AUP*] (EAIO)
UAP...........	Union of American Physicians [*Later, UAPD*] (EA)
UAP...........	United Amateur Press (EA)
UAP...........	United Australia Party [*Political party*]
UAP...........	Universal Availability of Publications [*International Federation of Library Associations*]
UAP...........	University-Affiliated Program
UAP...........	Unmanned Airborne Position (MCD)
UAP...........	Upper Air Project
UAP...........	Upper Arlington Public Library, Upper Arlington, OH [*OCLC symbol*] (OCLC)
UAP...........	Urea-Ammonium Phosphate [*Organic chemistry*]
UAP...........	User Area Profile
UAP...........	Utility Amphibian Plane [*Navy*]
UAPA	Union of African Performing Artists [*See also UAAS*] (EAIO)
UAPA	United Amateur Press Association [*Later, UAP*] (EA)
UAPA	United American Progress Association (EA)
UAPD	Union of American Physicians and Dentists (EA)
UAPEFV ...	Union des Associations des Producteurs Europeens de Farine de Viande [*Union of Associations of European Meat Meal Producers - UAEM*] [*Later, European Renderers Association - EURA*] (EAIO)
UAPT	United Association for the Protection of Trade [*British*]
UAQ	San Juan [*Argentina*] [*Airport symbol*] (OAG)
UAQUA.....	Urban Affairs Quarterly [*A publication*]
UAR...........	Underwater Acoustic Resistance
UAR...........	Underwater Angle Receptacle
UAR...........	Uniform Airman Record
UAR...........	Unit Address Register
UAR...........	United Arab Republic [*Egypt and Syria*] [*Obsolete*]
UAR...........	Upper Air Route
UAR...........	Upper Atmosphere Research
UAR...........	Use as Required (MSA)

UARCO	UARCO, Inc. [*Formerly, United Autographic Register Company*]
UAREP......	Universities Associated for Research and Education in Pathology (EA)
UAR Geol Surv Miner Res Dep Pap ...	United Arab Republic. Geological Survey and Mineral Research Department. Papers [*A publication*]
UARI	University of Alabama Research Institute (KSC)
UAR Inst Oceanogr Fish Bull ...	United Arab Republic. Institute of Oceanography and Fisheries. Bulletin [*A publication*]
UARJ Anim Prod ...	United Arab Republic. Journal of Animal Production [*A publication*]
UARJ Bot ...	United Arab Republic. Journal of Botany [*A publication*]
UARJ Chem ...	United Arab Republic. Journal of Chemistry [*A publication*]
UARJ Geol ...	United Arab Republic. Journal of Geology [*A publication*]
UAR J Microbiol ...	United Arab Republic. Journal of Microbiology [*A publication*]
UARJ Pharm Sci ...	United Arab Republic. Journal of Pharmaceutical Sciences [*A publication*]
UAR J Phys ...	United Arab Republic. Journal of Physics [*A publication*]
UARJ Soil Sci ...	United Arab Republic. Journal of Soil Science [*A publication*]
UARJ Vet Sci ...	United Arab Republic. Journal of Veterinary Science [*A publication*]
U Ark Little Rock LJ ...	University of Arkansas at Little Rock. Law Journal [*A publication*]
UARL	United Aircraft Research Laboratories
UAR Minist Agric Agrar Reform Tech Bull ...	United Arab Republic. Ministry of Agriculture and Agrarian Reform. Technical Bulletin [*A publication*]
UAR Minist Agric Tech Bull ...	United Arab Republic. Ministry of Agriculture. Technical Bulletin [*A publication*]
UARR	Uralsk [*USSR*] [*ICAO location identifier*] (ICLI)
UARRSI	Universal Aerial Refueling Receptacle Slipaway Installation (MCD)
UARS	Underwater Acoustic Receiving System [*Navy*] (MCD)
UARS	Unmanned Arctic Research Submersible
UARS	Upper Atmosphere Research Satellite (MCD)
UAR (South Reg) Minist Agric Hydrobiol Dep Notes Mem ...	United Arab Republic (Southern Region). Ministry of Agriculture. Hydrobiological Department. Notes and Memoirs [*A publication*]
UART	Universal Asynchronous Receiver/Transmitter
UAS	Ulster Archaeological Society
UAS	Uniform Accounting System (OICC)
UAS	Union of African States
UAS	Unit Approval System [*for approval of aircraft materials, parts, and appliances*] [*FAA*]
UAS	Unit Assets by State [*Army*]
UAS	United Arab States
UAS	University Air Squadrons
UAS	University of Alabama. Studies [*A publication*]
UAS	Unmanned Aerial [*or Aerospace*] Surveillance
UAS	Unusual Aerial Sighting (ADA)
UAS	Upper Atmospheric Sounder
UAS	Upstream Activating Sequence [*Genetics*]
UAS	Upstream Activation Site [*Genetics*]
UAS	Uralic and Altaic Series. Indiana University. Publications [*A publication*]
UAS	Urea-Ammonium Sulfate [*Fertilizer*]
UAS	Urgent Action Service International [*British Library*]
UAS (Hebbal) Monogr Ser ...	UAS (Hebbal) Monograph Series [*A publication*]
UASI..........	UAS Automation Systems, Incorporated [*Bristol, CT*] [*NASDAQ symbol*] (NQ)
UASS........	Unmanned Aerial Surveillance System (MCD)
UASSS	Underwater Acoustic Sound Source System
UAST........	Universal Association for Speech Tracing [*See also TPA*] (EAIO)
u-at---	Australia [*MARC geographic area code*] [*Library of Congress*] (LCCP)
UAT..........	Ultraviolet Acquisition Technique
UAT..........	Under Armor Tow (MCD)
UAT..........	Underway Acceptance Trials (MCD)
UAT..........	Union Aeromaritime de Transport [*Privately-owned French airline*]
UAT..........	Until Advised by the Tower [*Aviation*] (FAAC)
UAT..........	Urban Arts Theatre (EA)
UAT..........	User Acceptance Test (MCD)
UATA........	Aralsk [*USSR*] [*ICAO location identifier*] (ICLI)
UATC........	United Artists Theatre Circuit, Inc.
UATE	Universal Automatic Test Equipment
UATI	Union de Asociaciones Tecnicas Internacionales [*Union of International Engineering Organizations - UIEO*] [*Spanish*] (ASF)
UATI	Union des Associations Techniques Internationales [*Union of International Technical Associations - UITA*] (EAIO)
u-at-ne	New South Wales [*MARC geographic area code*] [*Library of Congress*] (LCCP)
u-at-no........	Northern Territory [*Australia*] [*MARC geographic area code*] [*Library of Congress*] (LCCP)

UATP	Universal Air Travel Plan [*Commercial airlines credit system*]
u-at-qn........	Queensland [*MARC geographic area code*] [*Library of Congress*] (LCCP)
UATR	Chelkar [*USSR*] [*ICAO location identifier*] (ICLI)
u-at-sa	South Australia [*MARC geographic area code*] [*Library of Congress*] (LCCP)
UATT	Aktyubinsk [*USSR*] [*ICAO location identifier*] (ICLI)
u-at-tm	Tasmania [*MARC geographic area code*] [*Library of Congress*] (LCCP)
u-at-vi.........	Victoria [*MARC geographic area code*] [*Library of Congress*] (LCCP)
u-at-we	Western Australia [*MARC geographic area code*] [*Library of Congress*] (LCCP)
UAU	Universities Athletics Union [*British*]
UAUM.......	Underwater-to-Air-to-Underwater Missile [*Air Force*]
UAUOC.....	United American Ukrainian Organizations Committee (EA)
UA/USA.....	UNESCO Association/USA (EA)
UAV...........	Ukrainian American Veterans (EA)
UAV...........	University of the Andes [*Merida*] [*Venezuela*] [*Seismograph station code, US Geological Survey*] (SEIS)
UAV...........	Unmanned Aerial [*or Air*] Vehicle (RDA)
UAVA	Untersuchungen zur Assyriologie und Vorderasiatischen Archaeologie [*A publication*]
UAW..........	International Union, United Automobile, Aerospace, and Agricultural Implement Workers of America [*Also known as United Auto Workers*] (EA)
UAWB.......	Universal Air Waybill [*Shipping*] (DS)
UAW-CAP ...	United Auto Workers Community Action Program (EA)
UAWFA	United Auto Workers, Family Auxiliary (EA)
UAWG.......	Um Antwort Wird Gebeten [*Please Reply*] [*German*]
UAWIU	United Allied Workers International Union (EA)
UAX...........	Unit Automatic Exchange
UAZ..........	East Hartford, CT [*Location identifier*] [*FAA*] (FAAL)
UB.............	Burma Airways Corp. [*Burma*] [*ICAO designator*] (ICDA)
Ub	Ubertus de Bobio [*Flourished, 1214-37*] [*Authority cited in pre-1607 legal work*] (DSA)
UB.............	Ultimobranchial [*Bodies*] [*Medicine*]
UB.............	Umno Baru [*New Umno*] [*Malaysia*] [*Political party*]
UB.............	Unaccompanied Baggage (MCD)
UB.............	Underwater Battery [*Navy*]
UB.............	Undistributed Budget (MCD)
UB.............	Unemployment Benefits [*Unemployment insurance*] (OICC)
UB.............	Unicbank [*Unique Bank*] [*Hungary*]
UB.............	Union Bank [*British*] (ROG)
UB.............	Union of Burma Airways [*ICAO designator*] (FAAC)
UB.............	United Benefice
UB.............	United Biscuits [*Commercial firm*] [*British*]
UB.............	United Brethren in Christ
UB.............	United Brotherhood [*Also written VC for secrecy*] [*Fenianism*] (ROG)
UB.............	University Bookman [*A publication*]
UB.............	Upper Bench [*Legal*] [*British*] (ROG)
UB.............	Upper Bound
UB.............	Upper Brace (MCD)
UB.............	Urban Buecher [*A publication*]
UB.............	Urea Briquettes [*Agronomy*]
UB.............	Usage Block (MSA)
UB.............	Utility Bridge (NASA)
UB.............	Uttara Bharati [*A publication*]
UB1...........	University of Connecticut, Stamford Branch, Stamford, CT [*OCLC symbol*] (OCLC)
UB2...........	University of Connecticut, Hartford Branch, West Hartford, CT [*OCLC symbol*] (OCLC)
UB3...........	University of Connecticut, Southeastern Branch, Groton, CT [*OCLC symbol*] (OCLC)
UB4...........	University of Connecticut, MBA Library, Hartford, CT [*OCLC symbol*] (OCLC)
UB40..........	Name of British band, derived from code number on a British unemployment form
UBA	Uberaba [*Brazil*] [*Airport symbol*] (OAG)
UBA	Ulan Bator [*Mongolia*] [*Geomagnetic observatory code*]
UBA	Ulusal Basin Ajansi [*News agency*] [*Turkey*] (MENA)
UBA	Unblocking Acknowledge [*Telecommunications*] (TEL)
UBA	Undenatured Bacterial Antigen
UBA	Underwater Breathing Apparatus [*Navy*] (CAAL)
UBA	Union of Burma Airways
UBA	United Baltic Appeal (EA)
UBA	United Bank for Africa Ltd.
UBA	United Breweries of America (EA)
UBA	Universal Beer Agar [*Brewery bacteria culture medium*]
UBA	Universitet i Bergen. Arbok. Historisk-Antikvarisk Rekke [*A publication*]
UBAEC......	Union of Burma Atomic Energy Centre
UBAF........	Union des Banques Arabes et Francaises [*Union of Arab and French Banks*] [*France*]
UBAK	United Bancorp of Alaska, Inc. [*NASDAQ symbol*] (NQ)
Ubal..........	Ubaldus [*Authority cited in pre-1607 legal work*] (DSA)
U Baltimore L Rev ...	University of Baltimore. Law Review [*A publication*]
U Balt LR ..	University of Baltimore. Law Review [*A publication*]
U Balt L Rev ...	University of Baltimore. Law Review [*A publication*]
UBAN........	Union Bancorp, Inc. [*NASDAQ symbol*] (NQ)

UBARI......	Union of Burma Applied Research Institute
UBAT	Ultrasonic Bioassay Tank [*Aerospace*]
UBATS.....	Ultrasonic Bioassay Tank System [*Aerospace*]
UBAZ	United Bancorp of Arizona [*NASDAQ symbol*] (NQ)
UBB	Union Bank of Bavaria
UBB	Union of Burma Bank (DS)
UBB	Universal Building Block
UBBA	United Boys' Brigades of America [*Later, BGBA*] (EA)
UBBC	Unsaturated (Vitamin) B$_{12}$ Binding Capacity
Ub Bo	Ubertus de Bobio [*Flourished, 1214-37*] (DSA)
Ub de Bo ...	Ubertus de Bobio [*Flourished, 1214-37*] [*Authority cited in pre-1607 legal work*] (DSA)
UBBR	University Bureaus of Business Research
UBC	Uniform Broadband Channel [*Telecommunications*]
UBC	Uniform Building Code (NRCH)
UBC..........	United Black Christians (EA)
UBC	United Brotherhood of Carpenters and Joiners of America (EA)
UBC	United Business Communications, Inc. [*Atlanta, GA*] [*Telecommunications*] (TSSD)
UBC	Universal Bibliographic Control
UBC	Universal Block Channel
UBC	Universal Buffer Controller
UBC	University of British Columbia [*Vancouver, BC*]
UBC	University of British Columbia Library [*UTLAS symbol*]
UBC	Used Beverage Can
UBCA	United Black Church Appeal (EA)
UBC Alumni Chronicle ...	Alumni Association. University of British Columbia. Chronicle [*A publication*]
UBcGS......	Church of Jesus Christ of Latter-Day Saints, Genealogical Society Library, Brigham City South Branch, Brigham City, UT [*Library symbol*] [*Library of Congress*] (LCLS)
UBCHEA ..	United Board for Christian Higher Education in Asia (EA)
UBcI..........	National Indian Training Center, Brigham City, UT [*Library symbol*] [*Library of Congress*] (LCLS)
UBCIO	University of British Columbia Institute of Oceanography [*Canada*] (MSC)
UBCJ........	United Brotherhood of Carpenters and Joiners of America
UBCL........	Union of Black Clergy and Laity of the Episcopal Church [*Later, UBE*] (EA)
UBC Legal N ...	University of British Columbia. Legal Notes [*A publication*]
UBC Legal Notes ...	University of British Columbia. Legal Notes [*A publication*]
UBCLN	University of British Columbia. Legal News [*A publication*] (DLA)
UBC LR.....	University of British Columbia. Law Review [*A publication*]
UBC L Rev ...	University of British Columbia. Law Review [*A publication*]
UBC Notes ...	University of British Columbia. Legal Notes [*A publication*] (DLA)
UBCNREP ...	University of British Columbia. Programme in Natural Resource Economics. Resources Paper [*A publication*]
UBCP........	Unibancorp, Inc. [*Chicago, IL*] [*NASDAQ symbol*] (NQ)
UBcT	Thiokol Chemical Corp., Utah Division, Brigham City, UT [*Library symbol*] [*Library of Congress*] (LCLS)
UBCW	United Brick and Clay Workers of America [*Later, ABCWIU*] (EA)
UBD..........	Bureau of Land Management, Billings, MT [*OCLC symbol*] (OCLC)
UBD..........	Universal Business Directory for the Pacific Islands [*A publication*]
UBD..........	Utility Binary Dump [*Data processing*]
UBDA........	Uniform Brain Death Act [*National Conference of Commissioners on Uniform State Laws*]
UBDC.......	Urban Bikeway Design Collaborative (EA)
UBDd.......	You Be Darned [*Bowdlerized version*] (DSUE)
UBDI	Underwater Battery Director Indicator
UBDMA	United Better Dress Manufacturers Association (EA)
UBE	Union of Black Episcopalians (EA)
UBE	Union Bouddhique d'Europe [*Buddhist Union of Europe - BUE*] (EAIO)
UBE	Universal Bus Exercisor (NASA)
UBEA	United Business Education Association [*Later, NBEA*]
UBEA Forum ...	United Business Education Association. Forum [*A publication*]
UBeGS.......	Church of Jesus Christ of Latter-Day Saints, Genealogical Society Library, Beaver Branch, Beaver, UT [*Library symbol*] [*Library of Congress*] (LCLS)
UBF	Universal Boss Fitting
UBF	Universal Buddhist Fellowship (EA)
UBFA	United Black Fund of America (EA)
UBFC	Underwater Battery Fire Control [*Navy*]
UBFCS	Underwater Battery Fire Control System [*Navy*]
UBG	Newberg, OR [*Location identifier*] [*FAA*] (FAAL)
UBG	Ultimobranchial Glands [*Endocrinology*]
UBG	Underground Building [*National Security Agency*]
UBHC.......	Unburned Hydrocarbon [*Also, UHC*] [*Fuel technology*]
UBHJ	University of Birmingham. Historical Journal [*A publication*]
UBHR	User Block Handling Routine [*Data processing*] (IBMDP)
UBI	Buin [*Papua New Guinea*] [*Airport symbol*] (OAG)
UBI	Ultraviolet Blood Irradiation
UBI	Universal Battlefield Identification

UBIC.........	Universal Bus Interface Controller (NASA)
UBIP..........	Ubiquitous Immunopoietic Polypeptide [*Immunochemistry*]
U Birmingham Hist J ...	University of Birmingham. Historical Journal [*A publication*]
UBIT.........	Unrelated Business Income Tax
UBITRON ...	Undulating Beam Interaction Electron Tube
UBJ..........	Ube [*Japan*] [*Airport symbol*] (OAG)
UBJSA	Union of Burma. Journal of Science and Technology [*A publication*]
UBK..........	Unbleached Kraft [*Pulp and paper processing*]
UBK..........	US Banknote Corp. [*AMEX symbol*] (SPSG)
UBKA	Universitaetsbibliothek Karlsruhe [*Karlsruhe University Library*] [*Information retrieval*]
UBKHA.....	Uspekhi Biologicheskoi Khimii [*A publication*]
UBKR	United Bankers, Inc. [*NASDAQ symbol*] (NQ)
UBKS........	United Banks of Colorado, Inc. [*NASDAQ symbol*] (NQ)
ubl	Ublich [*Usual*] [*German*]
UBL...........	Unbleached (MSA)
UBL..........	Unblocking [*Telecommunications*] (TEL)
UBL..........	Undifferentiated B-Cell Lymphoma [*Medicine*]
UBL..........	United Beverages [*Vancouver Stock Exchange symbol*]
UBLDP......	Union Belge et Luxembourgeoise de Droit Penal [*Belgian and Luxembourg Association of Penal Law*] (EAIO)
UBLR........	University of Baltimore. Law Review [*A publication*]
UBLSLJ	University of Botswana, Lesotho, and Swaziland Law Journal [*A publication*] (DLA)
UBLU	United Building Labourers' Union [*British*]
UBM.........	Ultrasonic Bonding Machine
UBM..........	University of Bridgeport, Bridgeport, CT [*OCLC symbol*] (OCLC)
UBMT	United Savings Bank FA [*Great Falls, MT*] [*NASDAQ symbol*] (NQ)
UBN..........	United Business Network [*United Business Communications, Inc.*] [*Atlanta, GA*] [*Telecommunications*] [*Defunct*] (TSSD)
UBN..........	University Bank NA [*AMEX symbol*] (SPSG)
UBNK.......	Union Bank [*NASDAQ symbol*] (SPSG)
UBO..........	Uinta Basin Array [*Utah*] [*Seismograph station code, US Geological Survey*] [*Closed*] (SEIS)
UBO..........	Uinta Basin Observatory
UBO..........	Unemployment Benefit Office [*British*]
UBO..........	Unidentified Bright Object
UBOA.......	United Bus Owners of America (EA)
U-BOOT....	Unterseeboot [*Submarine*] [*German*]
UBP	Ubon Ratchathani [*Thailand*] [*Airport symbol*] (OAG)
UBP	Underwater Battery Plot [*Antisubmarine warfare*]
UBP	Unit Beat Policing
UBP	United Bahamian Party [*Political party*] (PPW)
UBP	United Bermuda Party [*Political party*] (PPW)
UBP	Upward Bound Programs [*Department of Labor*]
U-BPH.......	Utah State Library Commission, Division of the Blind and Physically Handicapped, Salt Lake City, UT [*Library symbol*] [*Library of Congress*] (LCLS)
UBPLOT ...	Underwater Battery Plotting Room [*Navy*] (NVT)
UBPR........	Uniform Bank Performance Report [*Federal Financial Institutions Examination Council*]
UB Pr	Upper Bench Precedents Tempore Car. I [*A publication*] (DLA)
UBPVLS....	Uniform Boiler and Pressure Vessel Laws Society (EA)
UBR..........	Uniform Business Rate [*Taxation*] [*British*]
UBR..........	United Bison Resources [*Vancouver Stock Exchange symbol*]
UBR..........	University of British Columbia Retrospective Conversion [*UTLAS symbol*]
UBR..........	Upper Burma Rulings [*India*] [*A publication*] (DLA)
U Brdgpt LR ...	University of Bridgeport. Law Review [*A publication*]
UBRF........	Upper Branchial Filament
U Bridgeport L Rev ...	University of Bridgeport. Law Review [*A publication*]
U Brit Col L Rev ...	University of British Columbia. Law Review [*A publication*]
U Brit Colum L Rev ...	University of British Columbia. Law Review [*A publication*]
UBS	Columbus, MS [*Location identifier*] [*FAA*] (FAAL)
UBS	Uniform Bearing Stress
UBS	Union Bank of Switzerland
UBS	Union Broadcasting System [*Fictitious broadcasting organization in film "Network"*]
UBS	Unit Backspace Character [*Data processing*]
UBS	United Bible Societies [*Stuttgart, Federal Republic of Germany*] (EA)
UBS	United Broadcasting System [*Network in TV series "America 2-Night"*]
UBS	Universal Builders Supply Co.
UBS	University of British Columbia, School of Librarianship, Vancouver, BC, Canada [*OCLC symbol*] (OCLC)
UBS	University of Buffalo. Studies [*A publication*]
UBS	US Bioscience, Inc. [*AMEX symbol*] (SPSG)
UBSA........	United Business Schools Association [*Later, AICS*] (EA)
UBSB.......	United Bible Societies. Bulletin [*London*] [*A publication*]
UBSC	United Building Services Corporation of Delaware [*NASDAQ symbol*] (NQ)
UBSF.........	United Bank FSB [*NASDAQ symbol*] (NQ)

UBSI.........	United Bankshares, Inc. [*NASDAQ symbol*] (NQ)
UBSO	Uinta Basin Seismological Observatory
UBT..........	Ubatuba [*Brazil*] [*Airport symbol*] [*Obsolete*] (OAG)
UBT..........	Universal Boattail Thor [*NASA*]
UBT..........	Universal Book Tester [*Measures performance of binding*]
UBTA	Union Bank & Trust [*NASDAQ symbol*] (NQ)
UBTC	University Bank & Trust Company [*Newton, MA*] [*NASDAQ symbol*] (NQ)
UB/TIB	Universitatsbibliothek Hannover und Technische Informationsbibliothek [*University Library of Hannover and Technical Information Library*] [*Information service or system*] (IID)
UBTM	United Bellows Tankage Module
UBU..........	UNESCO [*United Nations Educational, Scientific, and Cultural Organization*] Journal of Information Science, Librarianship, and Archives Administration [*A publication*]
UBV	Ultraviolet-Blue-Visual [*Photometric system*]
UBW	Kuparuk, AK [*Location identifier*] [*FAA*] (FAAL)
UBW	Unbewusste [*Unconscious Mind*] [*Psychology*]
UBW	University of Connecticut, Waterbury Branch, Waterbury, CT [*OCLC symbol*] (OCLC)
UBWPS.....	United Bargemen and Watermen's Protective Society [*A union*] [*British*]
UBX	Cuba, MO [*Location identifier*] [*FAA*] (FAAL)
UBZ	Upper Border Zone [*Geology*]
UBZC	UBZ Corporation [*NASDAQ symbol*] (NQ)
UBZHA.....	Ukrayinski Biokhimichnyi Zhurnal [*A publication*]
UC...........	Linea Aerea del Cobre Ltda. [*Chile*] [*ICAO designator*] (FAAC)
UC.............	National Union Catalogue [*A publication*]
UC.............	Ulcerative Colitis [*Medicine*]
UC.............	Ultimate Collider [*Particle accelerator*]
UC.............	Umbilical Cable [*or Connector*]
UC.............	Umbilical Cable Unit Cooler [*Aerospace*] (AAG)
UC.............	Una Corda [*With one string or with the soft pedal*] [*Music*]
UC.............	Unaccompanied Child [*Airline notation*]
Uc.............	Uncanny Stories [*A publication*]
UC.............	Uncirculated Coins [*Numismatics*]
U/C.............	Unclassified
UC.............	Unclipping [*Medicine*]
UC.............	Uncut Edges [*Bookbinding*]
UC.............	Undeducted Contributions
U/C.............	Under Carriage (MCD)
UC.............	Under Charge
UC.............	Under Construction
U/C.............	Under Conversion (NATG)
U/C.............	Under Cover (ADA)
U/C.............	Under Current (NASA)
UC.............	Undercut [*Technical drawings*]
UC.............	Underfashion Club (EA)
UC.............	Underwater Communications (MCD)
UC.............	Undifferentiated Carcinoma [*Oncology*]
UC.............	Unemployment Compensation
UC.............	UNESCO [*United Nations Educational, Scientific, and Cultural Organization*] Chronicle [*A publication*]
UC.............	Unichannel
Uc.............	Uniform, Coarse-Grained [*Soil*]
UC.............	Union Caledonienne [*Caledonian Union*] [*Political party*] (PPW)
UC.............	Union Camerounaise [*Cameroonese Union*] [*Political party*]
UC.............	Union Constitutionelle [*Constitutional Union*] [*Morocco*] [*Political party*] (PPW)
UC.............	Unit Call [*Also known as CCS*] [*Telecommunications*]
UC.............	Unit Chairman
UC.............	Unit Clerk
UC.............	Unit Cooler
UC.............	Unit Cost
UC.............	Unit Count (AFIT)
UC.............	United Canada Insurance Co.
UC.............	United Christian [*Australia*] [*Political party*]
uc.............	United States Miscellaneous Caribbean Islands [*MARC country of publication code*] [*Library of Congress*] (LCCP)
UC.............	Unity College [*London, England*]
UC.............	University of California
UC.............	University of Cincinnati [*Ohio*]
UC.............	University College
UC.............	University Colleges [*Public-performance tariff class*] [*British*]
UC.............	Unoperated Control
UC.............	Unsatisfactory Condition (NASA)
UC.............	Untreated Controls [*Medicine*]
UC.............	Up Converter
UC.............	Uplink Command
UC.............	Upper Canada
UC.............	Upper Cylinder
UC.............	Uppercase [*Typography*] (ADA)
UC.............	Uranium Canada Ltd.
UC.............	Urbis Conditae [*From the Foundation of the City; that is, of Rome*] [*Latin*]
UC.............	Urea Clearance [*Clinical chemistry*]
U & C	Urethral and Cervical [*Medicine*]
UC.............	Urinary Catheter [*Medicine*]

UC............ Usable Control
UC............ Using Command
U & C .... Usual and Customary
UC............ Usual Health-Care [*Medicine*]
UC............ Utility Car [*British*]
UC............ Utility Cargo
UC............ Utility Corridor
UC1........... Utilization Control
UC1........... Underwater Control Rating 1st Class [*British military*]   (DMA)
UC2........... Underwater Control Rating 2nd Class [*British military*]   (DMA)
UCA.......... Under Color Addition [*Printing technology*]
UCA.......... Uniform Chart of Accounts [*DoD*]
UCA.......... Uniform Companies Act [*A publication*]   (APTA)
UCA.......... United Carters' Association [*A union*] [*British*]
UCA........ United Collision [*Vancouver Stock Exchange symbol*]
UCA........ United Congressional Appeal   (EA)
UCA........ United States Court of Appeals for the District of Columbia, Judges Library, Washington, DC [*OCLC symbol*]   (OCLC)
UCA.......... Unitized Component Assembly [*Aerospace*]
UCA.......... Units Consistency Analyzer [*Data processing*]
UCA.......... Universal Calibration Adapter
UCA.......... Upper Control Area   (NATG)
UCA.......... Utah Code, Annotated [*A publication*]   (DLA)
UCA.......... Utica [*New York*] [*Airport symbol*]   (OAG)
UCACEP... United Council of Associations of Civil Employees of Pakistan
UCAE....... United Carters' Association of England [*A union*]
UCAE........ Universities Council for Adult Education [*British*]
UCAM....... Camera Enterprises, Inc. [*NASDAQ symbol*]   (NQ)
UCAM....... United Campuses to Prevent Nuclear War   (EA)
UCAN....... Union of Catholic Asian News [*Kwun Tong, Hong Kong*]   (EAIO)
UCAN....... Utilities Conservation Action Now [*Federal Energy Administration*]
UCANF ..... United Canso Oil & Gas Ltd. [*NASDAQ symbol*]   (NQ)
UCAP .... United Coconut Association of the Philippines   (DS)
UC App ..... Upper Canada Appeal Reports [*A publication*]   (DLA)
UC App (Can) ... Upper Canada Appeal Reports [*A publication*]   (DLA)
UC App Rep ... Upper Canada Appeal Reports [*A publication*]   (DLA)
UCAR....... United Carolina Bancshares Corp. [*NASDAQ symbol*]   (NQ)
UCAR....... University Corporation for Atmospheric Research   (EA)
UCARCIDE ... Union Carbide Biocide [*Trademark*] [*Union Carbide Corp.*]
UCARS...... Uniform Cost Accounting and Reporting System
UCAS........ Uniform Cost Accounting Standards   (MCD)
UCAS .... Union of Central African States   (EY)
UCASBJ.... Agro Sur [*A publication*]
UCATA ..... Uniform Contribution Among Tortfeasors Act [*National Conference of Commissioners on Uniform State Laws*]
UCATT...... Union of Construction, Allied Trades, and Technicians [*British*]
UCAVJ...... Union Continentale Africaine des Villes Jumelees [*Continental African Union of Twin Cities*]
UCB.......... Canadian Union Catalogue of Books [*National Library of Canada*] [*Information service or system*]   (IID)
UCB.......... UCB [*Belgium*] [*Research code symbol*]
UCB.......... UCB Chemie [*Germany*] [*Research code symbol*]
UCB.......... Unconjugated Bilirubin
UCB.......... Union Chimique Belge [*Belgium*]
UCB.......... Union de Credit pour le Batiment [*French*]
UCB.......... Unit Control Block   (MCD)
UCB.......... United Cambridge Mines [*Vancouver Stock Exchange symbol*]
UCB.......... United Commercial Bank Ltd. [*Bangladesh*]
UCB.......... Universal Character Buffer
UCB.......... University of California, Berkeley
UCB.......... University of California, Berkeley School of Library and Information Science, Berkeley, CA [*OCLC symbol*]   (OCLC)
UCBC .... Parti de l'Unite et de la Communaute Belgo-Congolaise [*Political party*]
UCBI......... United Central Bancshares [*NASDAQ symbol*]   (NQ)
UCBLL...... Language Laboratory [*Research center*]   (RCD)
UCBSRP ... University of California, Berkeley, Sulfur Recovery Process
UCBT .... Universal Circuit Board Tester
UCBWM ... United Church Board for World Ministries   (EA)
UCC .... Computing Center [*University of Rochester*] [*Research center*]   (RCD)
UCC .... Uccle [*Belgium*] [*Seismograph station code, US Geological Survey*]   (SEIS)
UCC .... Uccle [*Belgium*] [*Later, DOU*] [*Geomagnetic observatory code*]
UCC .... Umbilical Checkout Cable
UCC .... Unadjusted Contractual Changes
UCC .... Uniform Classification Committee [*Later, NRFC*]   (EA)
UCC .... Uniform Code Council   (EA)
UCC .... Uniform Commercial Code [*National Conference of Commissioners on Uniform State Laws*]
UCC .... Uniform Commercial Code Law Journal [*A publication*]
UCC .... Uniform Credit Code
UCC .... Union Camp Corporation [*NYSE symbol*]   (SPSG)
UCC .... Union Carbide Canada Ltd. [*Toronto Stock Exchange symbol*]
UCC .... Union Carbide Corporation   (KSC)
UCC .... United Cancer Council   (EA)
UCC .... United Church of Christ
UCC .... Universal Checkout Console   (NASA)

UCC.......... Universal Copyright Convention
UCC......... University of California. Chronicle [*A publication*]
UCC......... University College, Cardiff [*Wales*]
UCC......... University College Computer [*London, England*]   (DEN)
UCC......... University College, Cork [*Ireland*]
UCC.......... University Computer Center [*New Mexico State University*] [*Research center*]   (RCD)
UCC.......... University Computer Center [*San Diego State University*] [*Research center*]   (RCD)
UCC......... University Computer Center [*North Dakota State University*] [*Research center*]   (RCD)
UCC.......... University Computer Center [*Oklahoma State University*] [*Research center*]   (RCD)
UCC.......... University Computer Center [*University of Minnesota*] [*Research center*]   (RCD)
UCC.......... University Computing Company [*International computer bureau*]
UCC.......... University of Corpus Christi [*Texas*] [*Closed, 1973*]
UCC........... Upper Canada College
UCC........... Upper Control Center   (NATG)
UCC........... Urgent Care Center [*Medicine*]
UCC........... Uruguay Collectors Club   (EA)
UCC........... Utility Control Console
UCC........... Yucca Flat, NV [*Location identifier*] [*FAA*]   (FAAL)
UC/CA ...... Current Anthropology. University of Chicago [*A publication*]
UCCA .... Ukrainian Congress Committee of America   (EA)
UCCA .... Universities Central Council on Admission [*British*]
UCCC .... Computing Center [*University of Cincinnati*] [*Research center*]   (RCD)
UCCC .... Uniform Consumer Credit Code [*National Conference of Commissioners on Uniform State Laws*]
UCCC .... Unmarried-Catholics Correspondence Club   (EA)
UCCCCWCS ... United Church of Christ Coordinating Center for Women in Church and Society   (EA)
UCCCRJ ... United Church of Christ Commission for Racial Justice   (EA)
UCCE .... Union des Capitales de la Communaute Europeenne [*Union of Capitals of the European Community*]
UCCE .... Universal Craftsmen Council of Engineers   (EA)
UCC/EMC ... Union Carbide and Carbon/Electric Metallurgical Company   (AAG)
UCCEW .... University of Cape Coast. English Department. Workpapers [*A publication*]
UCCF........ United Campus Christian Fellowship [*Defunct*]
UC Ch........ Upper Canada Chancery Reports [*1849-82*] [*A publication*]   (DLA)
UC Cham ... Upper Canada Chambers Reports [*A publication*]   (DLA)
UC Chamb ... Upper Canada Chambers Reports [*1846-52*] [*A publication*]   (DLA)
UC Cham (Can) ... Upper Canada Chambers Reports [*1846-52*] [*A publication*]   (DLA)
UC Chan.... Upper Canada Chancery Reports [*A publication*]   (DLA)
UC Ch (Can) ... Upper Canada Chancery Reports [*A publication*]   (DLA)
UC Ch Rep ... Upper Canada Chancery Reports [*1849-82*] [*A publication*]   (DLA)
UCC Law Letter ... Uniform Commercial Code Law Letter [*A publication*]   (DLA)
UCCL/GC ... United Church Coalition for Lesbian/Gay Concerns   (EA)
UCCLJ .... Uniform Commercial Code Law Journal [*A publication*]
UCC-ND.... Union Carbide Corporation - Nuclear Division   (MCD)
UCCP .... Upper Canada Common Pleas Reports [*A publication*]   (DLA)
UCCP (Can) ... Upper Canada Common Pleas Reports [*A publication*]   (DLA)
UCCPD ..... Upper Canada Common Pleas Division Reports [*Ontario*] [*A publication*]   (DLA)
UCCPL...... United Citizens Coastal Protection League   (EA)
UCCR .... Upper Canada Court Records [*Report of Ontario Bureau of Archives*] [*A publication*]   (DLA)
UCCRC...... University of Chicago Cancer Research Center [*Research center*]   (RCD)
UCC Rep Serv ... Uniform Commercial Code Reporting Service [*A publication*]   (DLA)
UCCRL...... Union Carbide and Carbon Research Laboratories   (AAG)
UCCRP...... Union College Character Research Project   (EA)
UCCRS...... Underwater Coded Command Release System
UCCS........ Ultrasonic Chemical Cleaning System
UCCS........ United Cabinet and Chairmakers' Society [*A union*] [*British*]
UCCS........ Universal Camera Control System
UCCS........ University Classification and Compensation System
UCD.......... Unchanged Charge Distribution [*Fission*]
UCD.......... Uniform Call Distribution [*Telephone system*]
UCD.......... Union de Centro Democratico [*Union of the Democratic Center*] [*Spain*] [*Political party*]   (PPE)
UCD.......... United Canadian Shares Ltd. [*Toronto Stock Exchange symbol*]
UCD.......... University of California, Davis
UCD.......... University of California (Davis). Law Review [*A publication*]
UCd.......... University College, Dublin [*Ireland*]
UCd.......... Urine Cadmium Level
UCD.......... Urine Collection Device [*NASA*]   (MCD)
UCD.......... Usual Childhood Diseases [*Medicine*]
UCDA........ University and College Designers Association   (EA)

UC Davis L Rev ... University of California (Davis). Law Review [*A publication*] (DLA)
UCDC .... Ulster Constitution Defence Committee [*Northern Ireland*]
UCDC .... Uniado do Centro Democrata Cristao [*Union of the Christian Democratic Center*] [*Portugal*] [*Political party*] (PPE)
UCDCC ..... Union Centro y Democratica Cristiana de Catalunya [*Union of the Center and Christian Democrats of Catalonia*] [*Spain*] [*Political party*] (PPE)
UCdE .... Emery County Library, Castle Dale, UT [*Library symbol*] [*Library of Congress*] (LCLS)
UCDEC ..... Union Chretienne Democrate d'Europe Centrale [*Christian Democratic Union of Central Europe - CDUCE*] (EAIO)
UCdH .... Emery County High School, Castle Dale, UT [*Library symbol*] [*Library of Congress*] (LCLS)
UCDL .... Union Chretienne Democrate Libanaise [*Lebanese Christian Democratic Union*] [*Political party*] (PPW)
UCD LR ..... University of California (Davis). Law Review [*A publication*]
UCD L Rev ... UCD [*University of California, Davis*] Law Review [*A publication*]
UCDP .... Uncorrected Data Processor
UCDPE ...... University of California (Davis). Publications in English [*A publication*]
UCDS .... Unit Chemical Defense Study (MCD)
UCDWN .... Until Cleared Down [*Aviation*] (FAAC)
UCDWR .... University of California Division of War Research
UCE .... UCCEL Corp. [*NYSE symbol*] (SPSG)
UCE .... Union Canadienne des Etudiants
UCE .... Unit Checkout Equipment
UCE .... Unit Correction Entry
UCEA .... Uniform Conservation Easement Act [*National Conference of Commissioners on Uniform State Laws*]
UCEA .... Uniform Criminal Extradition Act [*National Conference of Commissioners on Uniform State Laws*]
UCEA .... Union Chimique Elf-Aquitaine [*France*]
UCEA .... University Council for Educational Administration (EA)
UCE & A .... Upper Canada Error and Appeal Reports [*1846-66*] [*A publication*] (DLA)
UCEA .... Used Clothing Exporters Association of America (EA)
UCEC .... Utility Commission Engineers Conference
UC/EDCC ... Economic Development and Cultural Change. University of Chicago [*A publication*]
UCE LINALUX-HAINAUT ... Union des Centrales Electriques de Liege-Namur-Luxembourg-Hainaut [*Belgium*]
UCEMT .... University Consortium in Educational Media and Technology [*Later, UCIDT*]
Ucenyje Zapiski Belorusskogo Gosud Univ ... Ucenyje Zapiski Belorusskogo Gosudarstvennogo Universiteta [*A publication*]
Ucenyje Zapiski Jaroslav ... Ucenyje Zapiski Jaroslavskogo Universiteta [*A publication*]
Ucenyje Zapiski Leningrad ... Ucenyje Zapiski Leningradskogo Gosudarstvennogo Universiteta [*A publication*]
Ucenyje Zapiski Leningrad Pedag Inst ... Ucenyje Zapiski Leningradskogo Gosudarstvennogo Pedagogiceskogo Instituta [*A publication*]
Ucenyje Zapiski Moskov Gosud Pedag Inst ... Ucenyje Zapiski Moskovskogo Gosudarstvennogo Pedagogiceskogo Instituta Inostraunych Jazykov [*A publication*]
Ucenyje Zapiski Moskva ... Ucenyje Zapiski Moskovskogo Gosudarstvennogo Universiteta Imeni Lononosova [*A publication*]
Ucenyje Zapiski (Tomsk) ... Ucenyje Zapiski Tomskogo Gosudarstvennogo Universiteta Imeni Kujbyseva (Tomsk) [*A publication*]
Ucen Zap Azerb Gosud Univ Ser Ist Filos Nauk ... Ucenye Zapiski. Azerbajdzanskij Gosudarstvennyj Universitet. Serija Istoriceskih i Filosofskih Nauk [*A publication*]
Ucen Zap Azerb Univ Ser Ist Filos Nauk ... Ucenye Zapiski. Azerbajdzanskij Universitet. Serija Istoriceskih i Filosofskih Nauk [*A publication*]
Ucen Zap CAGI ... Ucenyi Zapiski Central'nogo Aero-Gidrodinamiceskogo Instituta [*A publication*]
Ucen Zap Dal'nevost Univ ... Ucenye Zapiski Dal'nevostocnogo Universiteta [*A publication*]
Ucen Zap Dusan Gos Pedag Inst ... Ucenye Zapiski Dusanbinskogo Gosudarstvennogo Pedagogiceskogo Instituta [*A publication*]
Ucen Zap Erevan Gos Univ Estestv Nauki ... Ucenye Zapiski Erevanskogo Gosudarstvennogo Universiteta Estestvennye Nauki [*A publication*]
Ucen Zap Hakas Nauc-Issled Inst Jaz Lit Ist ... Ucenye Zapiski Hakasskogo Naucno-Issledovatel'skogo Instituta Jazyka, Literatury, i Istorii [*A publication*]
Ucen Zap Ivanov Univ ... Ucenye Zapiski Ivanovskogo Universitet [*A publication*]
Ucen Zap Kaf Obsc Nauk Leningr Filos ... Ucenye Zapiski Kafedr Obscestvennykh Nauk Vuzov Leningrada Filosofija [*A publication*]
Ucen Zap Kaf Obsc Nauk Vuzov G Leningr Filos ... Ucenye Zapiski Kafedr Obscestvennykh Nauk Vuzov Goroda Leningrada Filosofskih [*A publication*]

Ucen Zap Kaf Obsc Nauk Vuzov G Leningr Probl Nauc Kommunizma ... Ucenye Zapiski Kafedr Obscestvennykh Nauk Vuzov Goroda Leningrada Problemy Naucnogo Kommunizma [*A publication*]
Ucen Zap Kalmyk Nauc-Issled Inst Jaz Lit Ist ... Ucenye Zapiski Kalmykskogo Naucno-Issledovatel'skogo Instituta Jazyka, Literatury, i Istorii [*A publication*]
Ucen Zap Karel Ped Inst Ser Fiz-Mat Nauk ... Ucenye Zapiski Karel'skii Pedagogiceskii Institut. Serija Fiziko-Matematiceskih Nauk [*A publication*]
Ucen Zap Kazan Pedag Inst ... Ucenye Zapiski. Kazanskij Pedagogiceskij Institut [*A publication*]
Ucen Zap Latv Univ ... Ucenye Zapiski. Latvijskogo Universiteta [*A publication*]
Ucen Zap Lening Pedag Inst ... Ucenye Zapiski. Leningradskij Pedagogiceskij Institut [*A publication*]
Ucen Zap Moskov Pedag Inst ... Ucenye Zapiski. Moskovskogo Pedagogiceskogo Instituta [*A publication*]
Ucen Zap Perm Univ ... Ucenye Zapiski Permskogo Universiteta [*A publication*]
Ucen Zap Statist ... Ucenyi Zapiski po Statistike Akademija Nauk SSSR Central'nyi Ekonomiko-Matematiceskii Institut [*A publication*]
Ucen Zap Vyss Part Skola CK KPSS ... Ucenye Zapiski. Vyssaja Partijnaja Skola pri CK KPSS [*A publication*]
UCEP .... Upper Critical End Points [*Supercritical extraction*]
UCEPCEE ... Union du Commerce des Engrais des Pays de la Communaute Economique Europeenne [*Union of the Fertilizer Trade of Countries of the EEC*] [*Hasselt, Belgium*] (EAIO)
UCER .... University Center for Energy Research [*Oklahoma State University*] [*Research center*] (RCD)
UC Err & App ... Upper Canada Error and Appeal Reports [*1846-66*] [*A publication*] (DLA)
UC Err & App (Can) ... Upper Canada Error and Appeal Reports [*1846-66*] [*A publication*] (DLA)
UCES .... University Center for Environmental Studies [*Virginia Polytechnic Institute and State University*] [*Research center*] (RCD)
U Ceylon LR ... University of Ceylon. Law Review [*A publication*] (DLA)
UCF .... Union Culturelle Francais [*French Cultural Union*]
UCF .... Unit Control File [*Air Force*]
UCF .... United Cat Federation (EA)
UCF .... United Companies Financial Corp. [*AMEX symbol*] (SPSG)
UCF .... United Cooperative Farmers, Inc.
UCF .... University of Central Florida [*Orlando, FL*]
UCF .... Utility Control Facility
UCFA .... Uniform Comparative Fault Act [*National Conference of Commissioners on Uniform State Laws*]
UCFA .... Union pour la Communaute Franco-Africaine [*Union for the Franco-African Community*] [*Niger*]
UCFAC .... United Council of Filipino Associations in Canada
UCFC .... UniCARE Financial Corporation [*Irvine, CA*] [*NASDAQ symbol*] (NQ)
UCFC .... United Community Funds and Councils of America [*Later, UWA*] (EA)
UCFE .... Unemployment Compensation, Federal Employees
UCFML ..... Union des Communistes de France Marxiste-Leniniste [*Marxist-Leninist Union of Communists of France*] [*Political party*] (PPW)
UCFRU ..... Utah Cooperative Fishery Research Unit [*Utah State University*] [*Research center*] (RCD)
UCG .... Underground Coal Gasification
UCG .... Unidirectional Categorical Grammar
UCG .... University College Galway [*Ireland*]
UCG .... Urinary Chorionic Gonadotrophin [*Endocrinology*]
UCGA .... University Center in Georgia, Inc. [*Library network*]
UCGF .... Undergraduate Computer Graphics Facility [*Stevens Institute of Technology*] [*Research center*] (RCD)
UCH .... China Business Review [*A publication*]
UCH .... University of Connecticut, Health Center Library, Farmington, CT [*OCLC symbol*] (OCLC)
UCHD .... Usual Childhood Diseases [*Medicine*]
Uchen Zap Azerb Gos Univ Ser Biol Nauk ... Uchenye Zapiski Azerbaidzhanskogo Gosudarstvennogo Universiteta. Seriya Biologicheskikh Nauk [*A publication*]
Uchen Zap Azerb Gos Univ Ser Fiz Mat Nauk ... Uchenye Zapiski Azerbaidzhanskogo Gosudarstvennogo Universiteta. Seriya Fiziko-Matematicheskikh Nauk [*A publication*]
Uchen Zap Dal'nevost Univ ... Uchenye Zapiski Dal'nevostochnogo Universiteta [*A publication*]
Uchen Zap Gor'kov Gos Pedag Inst ... Uchenye Zapiski Gor'kovskogo Gosudarstvennogo Pedagogicheskogo Instituta [*A publication*]
Uchen Zap Gor'kov Gos Univ Ser Biol ... Uchenye Zapiski Gor'kovskogo Gosudarstvennogo Universiteta Imeni N. I. Lobachevskogo. Seriya Biologichevskaya [*A publication*]
Uchen Zap Gor'k Univ Ser Biol ... Uchenye Zapiski Gor'kovskogo Universiteta. Seriya Biologiya [*A publication*]
Uchen Zap Kabardino-Balkar Gos Univ ... Uchenye Zapiski Kabardino-Balkarskogo Gosudarstvennogo Universiteta [*A publication*]

Uchen Zap Kabardino-Balkars Univ ... Uchenye Zapiski Kabardino-Balkarskogo Gosudarstvennogo Universiteta [*A publication*]

Uchen Zap Kazan Gos Univ ... Uchenye Zapiski Kazanskogo Gosudarstvennogo Universiteta [*A publication*]

Uchen Zap Kazan Vet Inst ... Uchenye Zapiski Kazanskogo Veterinarnogo Instituta [*A publication*]

Uchen Zap Kirovabad Ped Inst ... Uchenye Zapiski Kirovabadskii Pedagogicheskii Institut [*A publication*]

Uchen Zap Kishinev Univ ... Uchenye Zapiski Kishinevskii Gosudarstvennyi Universitet [*A publication*]

Uchen Zap Kursk Pedagog Inst ... Uchenye Zapiski Kurskii Gosudarstvennyi Pedagogicheskii Institut [*A publication*]

Uchen Zap Leningr Gos Pedagog Inst Gertsena ... Uchenye Zapiski Leningradskogo Gosudarstvennogo Pedagogicheskogo Instituta Gertsena [*A publication*]

Uchen Zap Mosk Gos Univ ... Uchenye Zapiski Moskovskogo Gosudarstvennogo Universiteta [*A publication*]

Uchen Zap Novgorod Golovn Pedagog Inst ... Uchenye Zapiski Novgorodskogo Golovnogo Pedagogicheskogo Instituta [*A publication*]

Uchen Zap Petrozavodsk Gos Univ ... Uchenye Zapiski Petrozavodskogo Gosudarstvennogo Universiteta [*A publication*]

Uchen Zap Ryazan Gos Pedagog Inst ... Uchenye Zapiski Ryazanskogo Gosudarstvennogo Pedagogicheskii Instituta [*A publication*]

Uchen Zap Sel Khoz Dal'n Vost (Vladivostok) ... Uchenye Zapiski Sel'skogo Khozyaistva Dal'nogo Vostoka (Vladivostok) [*A publication*]

Uchen Zap Tartu Gos Univ ... Uchenye Zapiski Tartuskogo Gosudarstvennogo Universiteta [*A publication*]

Uchen Zap TsAGI ... Uchenye Zapiski Tsentral'nogo Aero-Gidrodinamicheskogo Instituta (TsAGI) [*A publication*]

Uchen Zap Ural Univ ... Uchenye Zapiski Ural'skogo Gosudarstvennogo Universiteta Imeni A. M. Gor'kogo [*A publication*]

Uchen Zap Yaroslav Gos Pedagog Inst ... Uchenye Zapiski Yaroslavskii Gosudarstvennyi Pedagogicheskii Institut [*A publication*]

Uchet Finan Kolkhoz Sovkhoz ... Uchet i Finansy v Kolkhozakh i Sovkhozakh [*A publication*]

UCHF .... Uncoupled Hartree-Fock [*Physical chemistry*]

U Chicago L Rev ... University of Chicago. Law Review [*A publication*]

U Chi L Rec ... University of Chicago. Law School. Record [*A publication*]

U Chi L Rev ... University of Chicago. Law Review [*A publication*]

UCHILS .... University of Chicago Law School (DLA)

U Chi L Sch Rec ... University of Chicago. Law School. Record [*A publication*]

U Chi LS Conf Series ... University of Chicago. Law School. Conference Series [*A publication*]

U Chi L S Rec ... University of Chicago. Law School. Record [*A publication*]

UCHSC ..... University of Colorado Health Sciences Center [*Denver*]

Uch Tr Gork Gos Med Inst ... Uchenye Trudy Gorkovskogo Gosudarstvennogo Meditsinskogo Instituta [*A publication*]

Uch Tr Gor'k Med Inst ... Uchenye Trudy Gor'kovskii Meditsinskii Institut [*A publication*]

Uch Zap Anat Gistol Embriol Resp Sredn Azii Kaz ... Uchenye Zapiski Anatomov Gistologov i Embriologov Respublik Srednei Azii i Kazakhstana [*A publication*]

Uch Zap Azerb Gos Inst Usoversh Vrachei ... Uchenye Zapiski Azerbaidzhanskii Gosudarstvennyi Institut Usovershenstvovaniya Vrachei [*A publication*]

Uch Zap Azerb Gos Uiv Im S M Kirova ... Uchenye Zapiski Azerbaidzhan-Gosudarstvennogo Universiteta Imeni S. M. Kirova [*A publication*]

Uch Zap Azerb Gos Univ ... Uchenye Zapiski Azerbaidzhanskogo Gosudarstvennogo Universiteta [*A publication*]

Uch Zap Azerb Gos Univ Im S M Kirova ... Uchenye Zapiski Azerbaidzhanskogo Gosudarstvennogo Universiteta Imeni S. M. Kirova [*A publication*]

Uch Zap Azerb Gos Univ Ser Biol Nauk ... Uchenye Zapiski Azerbaidzhanskogo Gosudarstvennogo Universiteta. Seriya Biologicheskikh Nauk [*A publication*]

Uch Zap Azerb Gos Univ Ser Fiz Mat Nauk ... Uchenye Zapiski Azerbaidzhanskogo Gosudarstvennogo Universiteta. Seriya Fiziko-Matematicheskikh Nauk [*A publication*]

Uch Zap Azerb Gos Univ Ser Geol Geogr Nauk ... Uchenye Zapiski Azerbaidzhanskogo Gosudarstvennogo Universiteta. Seriya Geologo-Geograficheskikh Nauk [*A publication*]

Uch Zap Azerb Gos Univ Ser Khim Nauk ... Uchenye Zapiski Azerbaidzhanskogo Gosudarstvennogo Universiteta Imeni S. M. Kirova. Seriya Khimicheskikh Nauk [*Azerbaidzhan SSR*] [*A publication*]

Uch Zap Azerb Inst Nefti Khim Ser 9 ... Uchenye Zapiski Azerbajdzhanskij Institut Nefti i Khimii. Seriya 9 [*A publication*]

Uch Zap Azerb Inst Usoversh Vrachei ... Uchenye Zapiski Azerbaidzhanskii Institut Usovershenstvovaniya Vrachei [*A publication*]

Uch Zap Azerb Med Inst ... Uchenye Zapiski Azerbaidzhanskogo Meditsinskogo Instituta [*A publication*]

Uch Zap Azerb Med Inst Klin Med ... Uchenye Zapiski Azerbaidzhanskogo Meditsinskogo Instituta Klinicheskoi Meditsiny [*A publication*]

Uch Zap Azerb Politekh Inst ... Uchenye Zapiski Azerbaidzhanskii Politekhnicheskii Institut [*A publication*]

Uch Zap Azerb Skh Inst ... Uchenye Zapiski Azerbaidzhanskogo Sel'skokhozyaistvennogo Instituta [*A publication*]

Uch Zap Azerb Skh Inst Ser Agron ... Uchenye Zapiski Azerbaidzhanskogo Sel'skokhozyaistvennogo Instituta. Seriya Agronomii [*A publication*]

Uch Zap Azerb S-Kh Inst Ser Vet ... Uchenye Zapiski Azerbaidzhanskogo Sel'skokhozyaistvennogo Instituta. Seriya Veterinarii [*A publication*]

Uch Zap Azerb Univ Ser Biol Nauk ... Uchenye Zapiski Azerbaidzhanskogo Universiteta. Seriya Biologicheskoi Nauki [*A publication*]

Uch Zap Bashk Univ ... Uchenye Zapiski Bashkirskogo Universiteta [*A publication*]

Uch Zap Beloruss Gos Univ ... Uchenye Zapiski Belorusskogo Gosudarstvennogo Universiteta [*A publication*]

Uch Zap Beloruss Inst Inzh Zheleznodorozhn Transp ... Uchenye Zapiski Belorusskii Institut Inzhenerov Zheleznodorozhnogo Transporta [*A publication*]

Uch Zap Bel'tskii Pedagog Inst ... Uchenye Zapiski Bel'tskii Pedagogicheskii Institut [*A publication*]

Uch Zap Biol Fak Kirg Univ ... Uchenye Zapiski Biologicheskogo Fakul'teta Kirgizskogo Universiteta [*A publication*]

Uch Zap Biol Fak Osnovn Gos Pedagog Inst ... Uchenye Zapiski Biologicheskogo Fakul'teta Osnovnogo Gosudarstvennogo Pedagogicheskogo Instituta [*A publication*]

Uch Zap Birskogo Gos Pedagog Inst ... Uchenye Zapiski Birskogo Gosudarstvennogo Pedagogicheskogo Instituta [*A publication*]

Uch Zap Brest Gos Pedagog Inst ... Uchenye Zapiski Brestskii Gosudarstvennyi Pedagogicheskii Institut [*A publication*]

Uch Zap Brst Gos Pedagog Inst ... Uchenye Zapiski Brestskii Gosudarstvennyi Pedagogicheskii Institut [*A publication*]

Uch Zap Bukhar Gos Pedagog Inst ... Uchenye Zapiski Bukharskii Gosudarstvennyi Pedagogicheskii Institut [*A publication*]

Uch Zap Buryat Gos Pedagog Inst ... Uchenye Zapiski Buryatskii Gosudarstvennyi Pedagogicheskii Institut [*A publication*]

Uch Zap Buryat Mong Pedagog Inst ... Uchenye Zapiski Buryat-Mongol'skii Pedagogicheskii Institut [*A publication*]

Uch Zap Checheno Ingush Gos Pedagog Inst ... Uchenye Zapiski Checheno-Ingushskii Gosudarstvennyi Pedagogicheskii Institut [*A publication*]

Uch Zap Chelyab Gos Pedagog Inst ... Uchenye Zapiski Chelyabinskogo Gosudarstvennogo Pedagogicheskogo Instituta [*A publication*]

Uch Zap Chit Gos Pedagog Inst ... Uchenye Zapiski Chitinskii Gosudarstvennyi Pedagogicheskii Institut [*A publication*]

Uch Zap Chuv Gos Pedagog Inst ... Uchenye Zapiski Chuvashskii Gosudarstvennyi Pedagogicheskii Institut [*A publication*]

Uch Zap Dagest Gos Pedagog Inst ... Uchenye Zapiski Dagestanskii Gosudarstvennyi Pedagogicheskii Institut [*A publication*]

Uch Zap Dagest Gos Univ ... Uchenye Zapiski Dagestanskogo Gosudarstvennogo Universiteta [*A publication*]

Uch Zap Dal'nevost Gos Univ ... Uchenye Zapiski Dal'nevostochnyi Gosudarstvennyi Universitet [*A publication*]

Uch Zap Dushanb Gos Pedagog Inst ... Uchenye Zapiski Dushanbinskii Gosudarstvennyi Pedagogicheskii Institut [*A publication*]

Uch Zap Erevan Gos Univ ... Uchenye Zapiski Erevanskii Gosudarstvennyi Universitet [*A publication*]

Uch Zap Erevan Univ ... Uchenye Zapiski Erevanskii Universitet [*A publication*]

Uch Zap Erevan Univ Estestv Nauk ... Uchenye Zapiski Erevanskogo Universiteta Estestvennykh Nauk [*A publication*]

Uch Zap Gomel Gos Pedagog Inst ... Uchenye Zapiski Gomel'skii Gosudarstvennyi Pedagogicheskii Institut [*A publication*]

Uch Zap Gomel Gos Pedagog Inst Im V P Chkalova ... Uchenye Zapiski Gomel'skogo Gosudarstvennogo Pedagogicheskogo Instituta Imeni V. P. Chkalova [*A publication*]

Uch Zap Gor'k Gos Med Inst Im S M Kirova ... Uchenye Zapiski Gor'kovskogo Gosudarstvennogo Meditsinskogo Instituta Imeni S. M. Kirova [*A publication*]

Uch Zap Gor'k Gos Pedagog Inst ... Uchenye Zapiski Gor'kovskogo Gosudarstvennogo Pedagogicheskogo Instituta [*A publication*]

Uch Zap Gor'k Gos Pedagog Inst Im A M Gor'kogo ... Uchenye Zapiski Gor'kovskogo Gosudarstvennogo Pedagogicheskogo Instituta Imeni A. M. Gor'kogo [*A publication*]

Uch Zap Gor'k Gos Univ ... Uchenye Zapiski Gor'kovskogo Gosudarstvennogo Universiteta [*A publication*]

Uch Zap Gor'k Univ ... Uchenye Zapiski Gor'kovskogo Universiteta [*A publication*]

Uch Zap Gor'k Univ Ser Biol ... Uchenye Zapiski Gor'kovskogo Universiteta. Seriya Biologiya [*A publication*]

Uch Zap Gorno-Altai Gos Pedagog Inst ... Uchenye Zapiski Gorno-Altaiskogo Gosudarstvennogo Pedagogicheskogo Instituta [*A publication*]

Uch Zap Gos Inst Fiz Kul't Im P F Lesgafta ... Uchenye Zapiski Gosudarstvennogo Instituta Fizicheskoi Kul'tury Imeni P. F. Lesgafta [*A publication*]

Uch Zap Gos Nauchno-Issled Inst Glazn Bolezn Im Gel'Mgol'Tsa ... Uchenye Zapiski Gosudarstvennogo Nauchno-Issledovatel'skogo Instituta Glaznykh Boleznei Imeni Gel'Mgol'Tsa [*A publication*]

Uch Zap Gos Nauchno-Issled Inst Glaznykh Bolezn ... Uchenye Zapiski Gosudarstvennogo Nauchno-Issledovatel'skogo Instituta Glaznykh Boleznei [*A publication*]

Uch Zap Gos Pedagog Inst ... Uchenye Zapiski Gosudarstvennogo Pedagogicheskogo Instituta Imeni T. G. Shevchenko [*A publication*]

Uch Zap Gos Pedagog Inst Im T G Shevchenko ... Uchenye Zapiski Gosudarstvennogo Pedagogicheskogo Instituta Imeni T. G. Shevchenko [*A publication*]

Uch Zap Grozn Gos Pedagog Inst ... Uchenye Zapiski Groznenskogo Gosudarstvennogo Pedagogicheskogo Instituta [*A publication*]

Uch Zap Imp Yur'ev Univ ... Uchenyya Zapiskik Imperatorskogo Yur'evskago Universiteta [*A publication*]

Uch Zap Irkutsk Gos Pedagog Inst ... Uchenye Zapiski Irkutskii Gosudarstvennyi Pedagogicheskii Institut [*A publication*]

Uch Zap Irkutsk Inst Nar Khoz ... Uchenye Zapiski Irkutskii Institut Narodnogo Khozyaistva [*A publication*]

Uch Zap Ivanov Gos Pedagog Inst ... Uchenye Zapiski Ivanovskogo Gosudarstvennogo Pedagogicheskogo Instituta [*A publication*]

Uch Zap Kabard Balkar Gos Univ ... Uchenye Zapiski Kabardino-Balkarskii Gosudarstvennyi Universitet [*A publication*]

Uch Zap Kabard-Balkar Nauchno-Issled Inst ... Uchenye Zapiski Kabardino-Balkarskogo Nauchno-Issledovatel'skogo Instituta [*A publication*]

Uch Zap Kabard Gos Pedagog Inst ... Uchenye Zapiski Kabardinskogo Gosudarstvennogo Pedagogicheskogo Instituta [*A publication*]

Uch Zap Kalinin Gos Pedagog Inst ... Uchenye Zapiski Kalininskii Gosudarstvennyi Pedagogicheskii Institut [*A publication*]

Uch Zap Kaliningr Gos Pedagog Inst ... Uchenye Zapiski Kaliningradskogo Gosudarstvennogo Pedagogicheskogo Instituta [*A publication*]

Uch Zap Kaliningr Gos Univ ... Uchenye Zapiski Kaliningradskii Gosudarstvennyi Universitet [*A publication*]

Uch Zap Karagand Gos Med Inst ... Uchenye Zapiski Karagandinskii Gosudarstvennyi Meditsinskii Institut [*A publication*]

Uch Zap Karagand Med Inst ... Uchenye Zapiski Karagandinskogo Meditsinskogo Instituta [*A publication*]

Uch Zap Karelo Fin Gos Univ Biol Nauki ... Uchenye Zapiski Karelo-Finskogo Gosudarstvennogo Universiteta Biologicheskie Nauki [*A publication*]

Uch Zap Karelo Fin Gos Univ Fiz Mat Nauki ... Uchenye Zapiski Karelo-Finskogo Gosudarstvennogo Universiteta Fiziko Matematicheskie Nauki [*A publication*]

Uch Zap Karelo-Fin Pedagog Inst ... Uchenye Zapiski Karelo-Finskogo Pedagogicheskogo Instituta [*A publication*]

Uch Zap Karel Pedagog Inst ... Uchenye Zapiski Karel'skogo Pedagogicheskogo Instituta [*A publication*]

Uch Zap Karsh Gos Pedagog Inst ... Uchenye Zapiski Karshinskii Gosudarstvennyi Pedagogicheskii Institut [*A publication*]

Uch Zap Kazan Gos Pedagog Inst ... Uchenye Zapiski Kazanskii Gosudarstvennyi Pedagogicheskii Institut [*A publication*]

Uch Zap Kazan Gos Univ ... Uchenye Zapiski Kazanskii Gosudarstvennyi Universitet [*USSR*] [*A publication*]

Uch Zap Kazan Univ ... Uchenye Zapiski Kazanskogo Universiteta [*A publication*]

Uch Zap Kazan Vet Inst ... Uchenye Zapiski Kazanskogo Veterinarnogo Instituta [*A publication*]

Uch Zap Kazan Yuridicheskogo Inst ... Uchenye Zapiski Kazanskogo Yuridicheskogo Instituta [*A publication*]

Uch Zap Kaz Gos Uiv Im S M Kirova ... Uchenye Zapiski Kazakhskogo Gosudarstvennogo Universiteta Imeni S. M. Kirova [*A publication*]

Uch Zap Kaz Gos Univ ... Uchenye Zapiski Kazakhskii Gosudarstvennyi Universitet [*A publication*]

Uch Zap Kemer Gos Pedagog Inst ... Uchenye Zapiski Kemerovskogo Gosudarstvennogo Pedagogicheskogo Instituta [*A publication*]

Uch Zap Khabar Gos Pedagog Inst ... Uchenye Zapiski Khabarovskogo Gosudarstvennogo Pedagogicheskogo Instituta [*A publication*]

Uch Zap Khabar Gos Pedagog Inst Biol Khim Nauk ... Uchenye Zapiski Khabarovskii Gosudarstvennyi Pedagogicheskii Institut Biologii i Khimicheskikh Nauk [*A publication*]

Uch Zap Khabar Gos Pedagog Inst Ser Biol ... Uchenye Zapiski Khabarovskii Gosudarstvennyi Pedagogicheskii Institut. Seriya Biologiya [*A publication*]

Uch Zap Khabar Gos Pedagog Inst Ser Estestv Nauk ... Uchenye Zapiski Khabarovskii Gosudarstvennyi Pedagogicheskii Institut. Seriya Estestvennykh Nauk [*A publication*]

Uch Zap Khabar Nauchno-Issled Inst Epidemiol Mikrobiol ... Uchenye Zapiski Khabarovskogo Nauchno-Issledovatel'skogo Instituta Epidemiologii i Mikrobiologii [*A publication*]

Uch Zap Khar'k Univ Tr Biol Fak Genet Zool ... Uchenye Zapiski Khar'kovskogo Universiteta Trudy Biologicheskogo Fakul'teta po Genetlike i Zoologii [*A publication*]

Uch Zap Khark Univ Tr Nauchno Issled Inst Biol Biol Fak ... Uchenye Zapiski Khar'kovskogo Universiteta Trudy Nauchno-Issledovatel'skogo Instituta Biologii i Biologicheskogo Fakul'teta [*A publication*]

Uch Zap Kiev Nauchno-Isled Rentgeno Radiol Onkol Inst ... Uchenye Zapiski Kievskogo Nauchno-Issledovatel'skogo Rentgeno Radiologicheskogo i Onkologicheskogo Instituta [*A publication*]

Uch Zap Kirg Zhen Pedagog Inst ... Uchenye Zapiski Kirgizskii Zhenskii Pedagogicheskii Institut [*A publication*]

Uch Zap Kirovab Pedagog Inst ... Uchenye Zapiski Kirovabadskii Pedagogicheskii Institut [*A publication*]

Uch Zap Kirov Gos Pedagog Inst ... Uchenye Zapiski Kirovskogo Gosudarstvennogo Pedagogicheskogo Instituta [*A publication*]

Uch Zap Kishinev Gos Univ ... Uchenye Zapiski Kishinevskogo Gosudarstvennogo Universiteta [*A publication*]

Uch Zap Komsomol'skogo-Na-Amure Gos Pedagog Inst ... Uchenye Zapiski Komsomol'skogo-Na-Amure Gosudarstvennogo Pedagogicheskogo Instituta [*A publication*]

Uch Zap Kostrom Gos Pedagog Inst ... Uchenye Zapiski Kostromskoi Gosudarstvennyi Pedagogicheskii Institut [*A publication*]

Uch Zap Kuibyshev Gos Pedagog Inst ... Uchenye Zapiski Kuibyshevskogo Gosudarstvennogo Pedagogicheskogo Instituta [*A publication*]

Uch Zap Kursk Gos Pedagog Inst ... Uchenye Zapiski Kurskogo Gosudarstvennogo Pedagogicheskogo Instituta [*A publication*]

Uch Zap Latv Gos Univ ... Uchenye Zapiski Latvijskogo Gosudarstvennogo Universiteta Imeni Petra Stuchki [*A publication*]

Uch Zap Latv Gos Univ Astron ... Uchenye Zapiski Latvijskogo Gosudarstvennogo Universiteta Imeni Petra Stuchki. Astronomiya [*A publication*]

Uch Zap Latv Univ ... Uchenye Zapiski Latvijskogo Universiteta [*A publication*]

Uch Zap Lenigr Gos Univ Ser Fiz Nauk ... Uchenye Zapiski Leningradskogo Gosudarstvennogo Universiteta. Seriya Fizicheskikh Nauk [*A publication*]

Uch Zap Leninab Gos Pedagog Inst ... Uchenye Zapiski Leninabadskogo Gosudarstvennogo Pedagogicheskogo Instituta [*A publication*]

Uch Zap Lening Gos Im A A Zhadanova Ser Fiz Geol Nauk ... Uchenye Zapiski Leningradskogo Gosudarstvennogo Universiteta Imeni A. A. Zhdanova. Seriya Fizicheskikh i Geologicheskikh Nauk [*USSR*] [*A publication*]

Uch Zap Leningr Gos Inst ... Uchenye Zapiski Leningradskogo Gosudarstvennogo Instituta [*A publication*]

Uch Zap Leningr Gos Pedagog Inst Im A I Gertsena ... Uchenye Zapiski Leningradskogo Gosudarstvennogo Pedagogicheskogo Instituta Imeni A. I. Gertsena [*A publication*]

Uch Zap Leningr Gos Univ Im A A Zhdanova Ser Biol Nauk ... Uchenye Zapiski Leningradskogo Gosudarstvennogo Universiteta Imeni A. A. Zhdanova. Seriya Biologicheskikh Nauk [*USSR*] [*A publication*]

Uch Zap Leningr Gos Univ Im A A Zhdanova Ser Fiz Nauk ... Uchenye Zapiski Leningradskogo Gosudarstvennogo Universiteta Imeni A. A. Zhdanova. Seriya Fizicheskikh Nauk [*USSR*] [*A publication*]

Uch Zap Leningr Gos Univ Im A A Zhdanova Ser Geogr Nauk ... Uchenye Zapiski Leningradskogo Gosudarstvennogo Universiteta Imeni A. A. Zhdanova. Seriya Geograficheskikh Nauk [*A publication*]

Uch Zap Leningr Gos Univ Im A A Zhdanova Ser Geol Nauk ... Uchenye Zapiski Leningradskogo Gosudarstvennogo Universiteta Imeni A. A. Zhdanova. Seriya Geologicheskikh Nauk [*A publication*]

Uch Zap Leningr Gos Univ Ser Biol Nauk ... Uchenye Zapiski Leningradskogo Gosudarstvennogo Universiteta. Seriya Biologicheskikh Nauk [*A publication*]

Uch Zap Leningr Gos Univ Ser Fiz Geol Nauk ... Uchenye Zapiski Leningradskogo Gosudarstvennogo Universiteta. Seriya Fizicheskikh i Geologicheskikh Nauk [*A publication*]

Uch Zap Leningr Gos Univ Ser Geogr Nauk ... Uchenye Zapiski Leningradskogo Gosudarstvennogo Universiteta. Seriya Geograficheskikh Nauk [*A publication*]

Uch Zap Leningr Gos Univ Ser Geol Nauk ... Uchenye Zapiski Leningradskogo Gosudarstvennogo Universiteta. Seriya Geologicheskikh Nauk [*A publication*]

Uch Zap Leningr Gos Univ Ser Khim Nauk ... Uchenye Zapiski Leningradskogo Gosudarstvennogo Universiteta. Seriya Khimicheskikh Nauk [*A publication*]

Uch Zap Leningr Gos Univ Ser Mat Nauk ... Uchenye Zapiski Leningradskogo Gosudarstvennogo Ordena Lenina Universita Imeni A. A. Zhdanova. Seriya Matematicheskikh Nauk [*A publication*]

Uch Zap Marii Gos Pedagog Inst ... Uchenye Zapiski Mariiskii Gosudarstvennyi Pedagogicheskii Institut [*A publication*]

Uch Zap Michurinsk Gos Pedagog Inst ... Uchenye Zapiski Michurinskii Gosudarstvennyi Pedagogicheskii Institut [*A publication*]

Uch Zap Mo Gos Univ ... Uchenye Zapiski Moskovskii Gosudarstvennyi Universitet [*A publication*]

Uch Zap Molotov Gos Univ Im A M Gor'kogo ... Uchenye Zapiski Molotovskogo Gosudarstvennogo Universiteta Imeni A. M. Gor'kogo [*A publication*]

Uch Zap Mord Gos Univ ... Uchenye Zapiski Mordovskii Gosudarstvennyi Universitet [*A publication*]

Uch Zap Mord Univ ... Uchenye Zapiski Mordovskogo Universiteta [*A publication*]

Uch Zap Mosk Gor Pedagog Inst ... Uchenye Zapiski Moskovskogo Gorodskogo Pedagogicheskogo Instituta [*A publication*]

Uch Zap Mosk Gos Pedagog Inst ... Uchenye Zapiski Moskovskii Gosudarstvennyi Pedagogicheskii Institut [*A publication*]

Uch Zap Mosk Gos Pedagog Inst Im Lenina ... Uchenye Zapiski Moskovskogo Gosudarstvennogo Pedagogicheskogo Instituta Imeni Lenina [*A publication*]

Uch Zap Mosk Gos Univ ... Uchenye Zapiski Moskovskii Gosudarstvennyi Universitet [*USSR*] [*A publication*]

Uch Zap Mosk Gos Zaochn Pedagog Inst ... Uchenye Zapiski Moskovskii Gosudarstvennyi Zaochnyi Pedagogicheskii Institut [*A publication*]

Uch Zap Mosk Inst Tonkoi Khim Tekhnol ... Uchenye Zapiski Moskovskogo Instituta Tonkoi Khimicheskoi Tekhnologii [*A publication*]

Uch Zap Mosk Nauchno-Issled Inst Gig ... Uchenye Zapiski Moskovskii Nauchno-Issledovatel'skii Institut Gigieny [*A publication*]

Uch Zap Mosk Nauchno-Issled Inst Glaznym Bolezn ... Uchenye Zapiski Moskovskogo Nauchno-Issledovatel'skogo Instituta po Glaznym Boleznam [*A publication*]

Uch Zap Mosk Obl Pedagog Inst ... Uchenye Zapiski Moskovskogo Oblastnogo Pedagogicheskogo Instituta [*A publication*]

Uch Zap Murom Gos Pedagog Inst ... Uchenye Zapiski Muromskii Gosudarstvennyi Pedagogichskii Institut [*A publication*]

Uch Zap Namanganskii Gos Pedagog Inst ... Uchenye Zapiski Namanganskii Gosudarstvennyi Pedagogicheskii Institut [*A publication*]

Uch Zap Nauchno Issled Inst Geol Arktiki Reg Geol ... Uchenye Zapiski Nauchno-Issledovatel'skogo Instituta Geologii Arktiki Regional'naya Geologiya [*A publication*]

Uch Zap Nauchno-Issled Inst Geol Arkt Reg Geol ... Uchenye Zapiski Nauchno-Issledovatel'skogo Instituta Geologii Arktiki Regional'naya Geologiya [*A publication*]

Uch Zap Nauchno-Issled Inst Izuch Lepry ... Uchenye Zapiski Nauchno-Issledovatel'skogo Instituta po Izucheniyu Lepry [*A publication*]

Uch Zap Novgorod Golovn Gos Pedagog Inst ... Uchenye Zapiski Novgorodskii Golovnoi Gosudarstvennyi Pedagogicheskii Institut [*A publication*]

Uch Zap Novgorod Gos Pedagog ... Uchenye Zapiski Novgorodskogo Gosudarstvennogo Pedagogicheskogo Instituta [*A publication*]

Uch Zap Novgorod Gos Pedagog Inst ... Uchenye Zapiski Novgorodskogo Gosudarstvennogo Pedagogicheskogo Instituta [*A publication*]

Uch Zap Novosib Inst Sov Koop Torg ... Uchenye Zapiski Novosibirskii Institut Sovetskoi Kooperativnoi Torgovli [*A publication*]

Uch Zap Novozybkovskii Gos Pedagog Inst ... Uchenye Zapiski Novozybkovskii Gosudarstvennyi Pedagogicheskii Institut [*A publication*]

Uch Zap Omsk Gos Pedagog Inst ... Uchenye Zapiski Omskogo Gosudarstvennogo Pedagogicheskogo Instituta [*A publication*]

Uch Zap Orenb Gos Pedagog Inst ... Uchenye Zapiski Orenburgskii Gosudarstvennyi Pedagogicheskii Institut [*A publication*]

Uch Zap Orenb Otd Vses Nauchn Ova Anat Gistol Embriol ... Uchenye Zapiski Orenburgskogo Otdela Vsesoyuznogo Nauchnogo Obshchestva Anatomov, Gistologov, i Embriologov [*A publication*]

Uch Zap Orlov Gos Pedagog Inst ... Uchenye Zapiski Orlovskogo Gosudarstvennogo Pedagogicheskogo Instituta [*A publication*]

Uch Zap Osh Gos Pedagog Inst ... Uchenye Zapiski Oshskii Gosudarstvennyi Pedagogicheskii Institut [*A publication*]

Uch Zap Penz Gos Pedagog Inst ... Uchenye Zapiski Penzenskogo Gosudarstvennogo Pedagogicheskogo Instituta [*A publication*]

Uch Zap Penz S-Kh Inst ... Uchenye Zapiski Penzenskogo Sel'skokhozyaistvennogo Instituta [*A publication*]

Uch Zap Perm Gos Pedagog Inst ... Uchenye Zapiski Permskii Gosudarstvennyi Pedagogicheskii Institut [*A publication*]

Uch Zap Perm Gos Univ ... Uchenye Zapiski Permskij Gosudarstvennyj Universitet Imeni A. M. Gor'kogo [*A publication*]

Uch Zap Permsk Univ Im A M Gor'korgo ... Uchenye Zapiski Permskogo Universiteta Imeni A. M. Gor'kogo [*A publication*]

Uch Zap Perm Univ Im A M Gor'kogo ... Uchenye Zapiski Permskogo Universiteta Imeni A. M. Gor'kogo [*A publication*]

Uch Zap Petropavlovsk Gos Inst ... Uchenye Zapiski Petropavlovskogo Gosudarstvennogo Instituta [*A publication*]

Uch Zap Petrozavodsk Gos Univ Fiz Mat Nauki ... Uchenye Zapiski Petrozavodskogo Gosudarstvennogo Universiteta Fiziko-Matematicheskie Nauki [*A publication*]

Uch Zap Petrozavodsk Inst ... Uchenye Zapiski Petrozavodskogo Instituta [*A publication*]

Uch Zap Petrozavodsk Univ ... Uchenye Zapiski Petrozavodskogo Universiteta [*A publication*]

Uch Zap Pskov Gos Pedagog Inst ... Uchenye Zapiski Pskovskogo Gosudarstvennogo Pedagogicheskogo Instituta [*A publication*]

Uch Zap Pskov Pedagog Inst Estestv Nauk ... Uchenye Zapiski Pskovskogo Pedagogicheskogo Instituta Estestvennykh Nauk [*A publication*]

Uch Zap Pyatigorsk Farm Inst ... Uchenye Zapiski Pyatigorskii Farmatsevticheskii Institut [*A publication*]

Uch Zap Pyatigorsk Gos Nauchno Issled Balneol Inst ... Uchenye Zapiski Pyatigorskii Gosudarstvennyi Nauchno-Issledovatel'skii Bal'neologicheskii Institut [*A publication*]

Uch Zap Rizh Politekh Inst ... Uchenye Zapiski Rizhskii Politekhnicheskii Institut [*A publication*]

Uch Zap Rostov Na Donu Gos Pedagog Inst Fiz Mat Fak ... Uchenye Zapiski Rostovskii-Na-Donu Gosudarstvennyi Pedagogicheskii Institut Fiziko-Matematicheskii Fakul'tet [*A publication*]

Uch Zap Rostov Na Donu Gos Univ ... Uchenye Zapiski Rostovskogo-Na-Donu Gosudarstvennogo Universiteta [*A publication*]

Uch Zap Rostov-Na-Donu Univ Im V M Molotova ... Uchenye Zapiski Rostovskogo-Na-Donu Universiteta Imeni V. M. Molotova [*A publication*]

Uch Zap Rostov Na Donu Univ V M Molotva ... Uchenye Zapiski Rostovskogo-Na-Donu Universiteta Imeni V. M. Molotova [*A publication*]

Uch Zap Ryazan Gos Pedagog Inst ... Uchenye Zapiski Ryazanskogo Gosudarstvennogo Pedagogicheskogo Instituta [*A publication*]

Uch Zap Rybinsk Gos Pedagog Inst ... Uchenye Zapiski Rybinskii Gosudarstvennyi Pedagogicheskii Institut [*A publication*]

Uch Zap Sarat Gos Pedagog Inst ... Uchenye Zapiski Saratovskogo Gosudarstvennogo Pedagogicheskogo Instituta [*A publication*]

Uch Zap Sarat Gos Univ ... Uchenye Zapiski Saratovskogo Gosudarstvennogo Universiteta [*A publication*]

Uch Zap Sev Oset Gos Pedagog Inst ... Uchenye Zapiski Severo-Osetinskii Gosudarstvennyi Pedagogicheskii Institut [*A publication*]

Uch Zap Sev-Oset Gos Pedagog Inst Im K L Khetagurova ... Uchenye Zapiski Severo-Osetinskogo Gosudarstvennogo Pedagogicheskogo Instituta Imeni K. L. Khetagurova [*A publication*]

Uch Zap Smolensk Gos Pedagog Inst ... Uchenye Zapiski Smolenskogo Gosudarstvennogo Pedagogicheskogo Instituta [*A publication*]

Uch Zap Sredneaziat Nauchno-Issled Inst Geol Miner Syr'ya ... Uchenye Zapiski Sredneaziatskii Nauchno-Issledovatel'skii Institut Geologii i Mineral'nogo Syr'ya [*A publication*]

Uch Zap Stavrop Gos Med Inst ... Uchenye Zapiski Stavropol'skogo Gosudarstvennogo Meditsinskogo Instituta [*A publication*]

Uch Zap Sverdl Gos Pedagog Inst ... Uchenye Zapiski Sverdlovskii Gosudarstvennyi Pedagogicheskii Institut [*A publication*]

Uch Zap Tadzh Gos Univ ... Uchenye Zapiski Tadzhikskogo Gosudarstvennogo Universiteta [*A publication*]

Uch Zap Tartu Gos Univ ... Uchenye Zapiski Tartuskogo Gosudarstvennogo Universiteta [*Estonian SSR*] [*A publication*]

Uch Zap Tashk Gos Pedagog Inst ... Uchenye Zapiski Tashkentskogo Gosudarstvennogo Pedagogicheskogo Instituta [*A publication*]

Uch Zap Tashk Vech Pedagog Inst ... Uchenye Zapiski Tashkentskii Vechernii Pedagogicheskii Institut [*A publication*]

Uch Zap Tirasp Gos Pedagog Inst ... Uchenye Zapiski Tiraspol'skii Gosudarstvennyi Pedagogicheskii Institut [*A publication*]

Uch Zap Tomsk Gos Pedagog Inst ... Uchenye Zapiski Tomskogo Gosudarstvennogo Pedagogicheskogo Instituta [*A publication*]

Uch Zap Tomsk Gos Univ ... Uchenye Zapiski Tomskogo Gosudarstvennogo Universiteta [*A publication*]

Uch Zap TsAGI ... Uchenye Zapiski TsAGI [*Tsentral'nogo Aero-Gidrodinamicheskogo Instituta*] [*USSR*] [*A publication*]

Uch Zap Tsentr Nauchno-Issled Inst Olovyannoi Promsti ... Uchenye Zapiski Tsentral'nyi Nauchno-Issledovatel'skii Institut Olovyannoi Promyshlennosti [*A publication*]

Uch Zap Tul Gos Pedagog Inst Fiz Tekh Nauki ... Uchenye Zapiski Tul'skii Gosudarstvennyi Pedagogicheskii Institut Fiziko-Tekhnicheskie Nauki [*USSR*] [*A publication*]

Uch Zap Turkm Gos Pedagog Inst Ser Estest Nauk ... Uchenye Zapiski Turkmenskii Gosudarstvennyi Pedagogicheskii Institut Seriya Estestvennykh Nauk [*A publication*]

Uch Zap Turkm Gos Univ ... Uchenye Zapiski Turkmenskogo Gosudarstvennogo Universiteta [*A publication*]

Uch Zap Tyumen Gos Pedagog Inst ... Uchenye Zapiski Tyumenskogo Gosudarstvennogo Pedagogicheskogo Instituta [*A publication*]

Uch Zap Udmurt Gos Pedagog Inst ... Uchenye Zapiski Udmurtskogo Gosudarstvennogo Pedagogicheskogo Instituta [*A publication*]

Uch Zap Udmurt Pedagog Inst ... Uchenye Zapiski Udmurtskogo Pedagogicheskogo Instituta [*A publication*]

Uch Zap Ukr Inst Eksp Endokrinol ... Uchenye Zapiski Ukrainskii Institut Eksperimental'noi Endokrinologii [*A publication*]

Uch Zap Ukr Nauchno Issled Inst Gig Tr Profzabol ... Uchenye Zapiski Ukrainskii Nauchno-Issledovatel'skii Institut Gigieny Truda i Profzabolevanii [*A publication*]

Uch Zap Ukr Tsentr Inst Gig Tr Profzabol ... Uchenye Zapiski Ukrainskii Tsentral'nyi Institut Gigieny Truda i Profzabolevanii [*A publication*]

Uch Zap Ul'yanovsk Pedagog Inst ... Uchenye Zapiski Ul'yanovskii Pedagogicheskii Institut [*A publication*]

Uch Zap Ural Gos Univ ... Uchenye Zapiski Ural'skogo Gosudarstvennogo Universiteta [*USSR*] [*A publication*]

Uch Zap Ural Gos Univ Im A M Gor'kogo ... Uchenye Zapiski Ural'skogo Gosudarstvennogo Universiteta Imeni A. M. Gor'kogo [*A publication*]

Uch Zap Ussur Gos Pedagog Inst ... Uchenye Zapiski Ussuriiskii Gosudarstvennyi Pedagogicheskii Institut [*A publication*]

Uch Zap Velikoluk Gos Pedagog Inst ... Uchenye Zapiski Velikolukskii Gosudarstvennyi Pedagogicheskii Institut [*A publication*]

Uch Zap Vitebsk Gos Pedagog Inst Im S M Kirova ... Uchenye Zapiski Vitebskogo Gosudarstvennogo Pedagogicheskogo Instituta Imeni S. M. Kirova [*A publication*]

Uch Zap Vitebsk Vet Inst ... Uchenye Zapiski Vitebskogo Veterinarnogo Instituta [*A publication*]

Uch Zap Vladimir Gos Pedagog Inst Ser Bot ... Uchenye Zapiski Vladimirskogo Gosudarstvennogo Pedagogicheskogo Institut. Seriya Botanika [*A publication*]

Uch Zap Vladimir Gos Pedagog Inst Ser Fiz ... Uchenye Zapiski Vladimirskii Gosudarstvennyi Pedagogicheskii Institut. Seriya Fizika [*A publication*]

Uch Zap Vladimir Gos Pedagog Inst Ser Fiziol Rast ... Uchenye Zapiski Vladimirskii Gosudarstvennyi Pedagogicheskii Institut. Seriya Fiziologiya Rastenii [*A publication*]

Uch Zap Vladimir Gos Pedagog Inst Ser Khim ... Uchenye Zapiski Vladimirskii Gosudarstvennyi Pedagogicheskii Institut. Seriya Khimiya [*A publication*]

Uch Zap Volgogr Gos Pedagog Inst ... Uchenye Zapiski Volgogradskogo Gosudarstvennogo Pedagogicheskogo Instituta [*A publication*]

Uch Zap Vologod Gos Pedagog Inst ... Uchenye Zapiski Vologodskii Gosudarstvennyi Pedagogicheskii Institut [*A publication*]

Uch Zap Vybors Gos Pedagog Inst ... Uchenye Zapiski Vyborskii Gosudarstvennyi Pedagogicheskii Institut [*A publication*]

Uch Zap Yakutsk Gos Univ ... Uchenye Zapiski Yakutskogo Gosudarstvennogo Universiteta [*A publication*]

Uch Zap Yakutsk Inst ... Uchenye Zapiski Yakutskogo Instituta [*A publication*]

Uch Zap Yarosl Gos Pedagog Inst ... Uchenye Zapiski Yaroslavskii Gosudarstvennyi Pedagogicheskii Institut [*A publication*]

Uch Zap Yarosl Tekhnol Inst ... Uchenye Zapiski Yaroslavskogo Tekhnologicheskogo Instituta [*A publication*]

UCI .... Imperial Chemical Industries [*Great Britain*]

UCI .... Union Cycliste Internationale [*International Cycling Union*] [*Geneva, Switzerland*]   (EA)

UCI .... Unione Coltivatori Italiana [*Farmers Union*] [*Italy*]   (EY)

UCI .... Unit Construction Index

UCI .... United Charity Institutions of Jerusalem   (EA)

UCI .... Universite Cooperative Internationale [*International Cooperative University*]

UCI .... University of California at Irvine

UCI .... Urinary Catheter In [*or Input*] [*Medicine*]

UCI .... User-Communication Interface [*Telecommunications*]

UCI .... Utility Card Input

UCI .... Utility Communicators International   (EA)

UCIB .... USAFE Command Intelligence Brief   (MCD)

UCID .... Independent Democratic Union of Cape Verde [*Political party*]   (PD)

UCIDT .... University Consortium for Instructional Development and Technology   (EA)

UC/IG .... Informaciones Geograficas. Universidad de Chile [*A publication*]

UCIIM .... Unione Cattolica Italiana Insegnanti Medi

UCIM .... UCI Medical Affiliates, Inc. [*Fort Lauderdale, FL*] [*NASDAQ symbol*]   (NQ)

UCIMT ...... University Center for Instructional Media and Technology [*University of Connecticut*] [*Research center*]   (RCD)

UCIMU ..... Unione Costruttori Italiani Macchine Utensili [*Machine Tool Manufacturers Union*] [*Italy*]   (EY)

UCINA ...... Unione Nazionale Cantieri e Industrie Nautiche ed Affini [*Shipyard and Nautical Industries Union*] [*Italy*]   (EY)

U Cin LR .... University of Cincinnati. Law Review [*A publication*]

U Cin L Rev ... University of Cincinnati. Law Review [*A publication*]

UCIP .... Union Catholique Internationale de la Presse [*International Catholic Union of the Press*]   (EAIO)

UCIR .... University Center for International Rehabilitation [*Michigan State University*] [*Research center*]   (RCD)

UCIS .... Unemployment Compensation Interpretation Service   (DLA)

UCIS .... University Center for International Studies [*University of Pittsburgh*] [*Research center*]   (IID)

UCIS .... University Computing and Information Services [*Villanova University*] [*Research center*]   (RCD)

UCIS .... Uprange Computer Input System

UCISS .... Union Catholique Internationale de Service Social [*Catholic International Union for Social Service*] [*Brussels, Belgium*]   (EAIO)

UCIT .... United Cities Gas Co. [*NASDAQ symbol*]   (NQ)

UCITS .... Undertakings for Collective Investment in Transferable Securities [*European Community*]

UCJ .... Unsatisfied Claim and Judgment [*State driver insurance*]

UCJG .... Alliance Universelle des Unions Chretiennes de Jeunes Gens [*World Alliance of Young Men's Christian Associations*]

UC Jur ...... Upper Canada Jurist [*A publication*]   (DLA)

UC Jur (Can) ... Upper Canada Jurist [*A publication*]   (DLA)

UCK .... Union Culturelle Katangaise [*Katangan Cultural Union*]

UCKB .... Upper Canada King's Bench Reports, Old Series [*1831-44*] [*A publication*]   (DLA)

UCKB (Can) ... Upper Canada King's Bench Reports, Old Series [*1831-44*] [*A publication*]   (DLA)

UCL .... Ulnar Collateral Ligament [*Anatomy*]

UCL .... Uncomfortable Loudness [*Audiometry*]

UCL .... Universal Consolidated Limited [*British*]

UCL .... University of Calgary Library [*UTLAS symbol*]

UCL .... University Catholique de Louvain [*Belgium*]   (MCD)

UCL .... University of Chicago. Law Review [*A publication*]

UCL .... University College of London   (KSC)

UCL .... University of Connecticut, Law Library, West Hartford, CT [*OCLC symbol*]   (OCLC)

UCL .... Unocal Corp. [*NYSE symbol*]   (SPSG)

UCL .... Update Control List

UCL .... Upper Confidence Level [*Industrial engineering*]   (IEEE)

UCL .... Upper Confidence Limit [*Statistics*]

UCL .... Upper Control Limit [*Nuclear energy*]

UCL .... Urea Clearance [*Test*] [*Medicine*]

UCLA .... University of California, Los Angeles [*Databank originator*]

UCLA .... University at the Corner of Lenox Avenue [*Nickname for "The Tree of Life," a Harlem bookstore*]

UCLA-Alaska L Rev ... UCLA [*University of California, Los Angeles*]-Alaska Law Review [*A publication*]   (DLA)

UCLA Forum Med Sci ... UCLA [*University of California, Los Angeles*] Forum in Medical Sciences [*A publication*]

UCLA Intra L Rev ... UCLA [*University of California, Los Angeles*] Intramural Law Review [*A publication*]   (DLA)

UCLA J Envt'l L & Pol'y ... UCLA [*University of California, Los Angeles*] Journal of Environmental Law and Policy [*A publication*]   (DLA)

UCLA/JLAL ... Journal of Latin American Lore. University of California. Latin American Center [*A publication*]

UCLA Law R ... UCLA [*University of California, Los Angeles*] Law Review

UCLA Law Rev ... University of California at Los Angeles. Law Review [*A publication*]   (DLA)

UCLA L Rev ... University of California at Los Angeles. Law Review [*A publication*]   (DLA)

UCLA Pac Basin J ... UCLA [*University of California at Los Angeles*] Pacific Basin Law Journal [*A publication*]   (DLA)

UCLA Slav S ... UCLA [*University of California at Los Angeles*] Slavic Studies [*A publication*]

UCLA Symp Mol Cell Biol ... UCLA [*University of California, Los Angeles*] Symposia on Molecular and Cellular Biology [*A publication*]

UCLA (Univ Calif Los Ang) Symp Mol Cell Biol New Ser ... UCLA (University of California at Los Angeles) Symposia on Molecular and Cellular Biology. New Series [*A publication*]

UCLA (Univ Cal Los Angeles)-Alaska Law R ... UCLA (University of California, Los Angeles)-Alaska Law Review [*A publication*]

UCLA (Univ Cal Los Angeles) J Environmental Law and Policy ... UCLA (University of California, Los Angeles) Journal of Environmental Law and Policy [*A publication*]

UCLA (Univ Cal Los Angeles) Pacific Basin Law J ... UCLA (University of California, Los Angeles) Pacific Basin Law Journal [*A publication*]

UCLC .... Utah College Library Council [*Library network*]

UCLEA ...... University and College Labor Education Association   (EA)

UCLG .... United Cement, Lime, Gypsum, and Allied Workers International Union [*Formerly, CLGW*]   (EA)

UCLJ .... University of California, La Jolla

UCLJ .... Upper Canada Law Journal [*1855-1922*] [*A publication*]   (DLA)

UCLJ (Can) ... Upper Canada Law Journal [*A publication*]   (DLA)

UCLJ NS ... Upper Canada Law Journal, New Series [*A publication*]   (DLA)

UCLJ NS (Can) ... Upper Canada Law Journal, New Series [*A publication*]   (DLA)

UCLJ OS ... Canada Law Journal, Old Series [*A publication*]   (DLA)

UCLM .... Unity of Czech Ladies and Men [*Later, CSA*]   (EA)

UCLR .... University of Ceylon. Law Review [*A publication*]   (DLA)

UCLR .... University of Chicago. Law Review [*A publication*]

UCLR .... University of Cincinnati. Law Review [*A publication*]

UCLR .... University of Colorado. Law Review [*A publication*]

UCLRL ...... University of California Lawrence Radiation Laboratory

UCLT .... Until Cleared to Land by the Tower [*Aviation*]   (FAAC)

UCM......... Can You Come and See Me?
UCM......... Union des Croyants Malagaches [*Malagasy Christian Union*]
UCM......... Universal Christian Movement (EA)
UCM......... Universal Communications Monitor
UCM......... University Christian Movement [*Formerly, NSCF*] [*Defunct*]
UCM......... Unresolved Complex Mixture
UCMAE .... United Carters' and Motormen's Association of England [*A union*]
UCMJ....... Uniform Code of Military Justice
UCML....... Unit Committed Munitions List
UCMP ...... UniComp, Inc. [*NASDAQ symbol*] (NQ)
UCMP ...... Union Catalog of Medical Periodicals [*A publication*]
UCMS ...... Unit Capability Measurement System (AFM)
UCMS ...... United Christian Missionary Society (EA)
UCMSA..... UCLA [*University of California, Los Angeles*] Forum in Medical Sciences [*A publication*]
UCMSU .... United Chain Makers' and Strikers' Union [*British*]
UCMT ...... Unglazed Ceramic Mosaic Tile [*Technical drawings*]
UCN.......... Ultracold Neutron
UCN.......... Unemployment Compensation News [*James E. Frick, Inc.*] [*Information service or system*] (CRD)
UCN.......... Uniform Control Number (NASA)
UCN.......... Union Civica Nacional [*National Civic Union*] [*Dominican Republic*] [*Political party*] (PPW)
UCNC........ Union Carbide Nuclear Corporation
UCNI......... Unclassified Controlled Nuclear Information [*Department of Energy*]
UCNI......... Unified Communications Navigation Identification
UCNS........ Universities Committee for Non-Teaching Staff [*British*]
UCNSA/SA ... Suplemento Antropologico. Universidad Catolica de Nuestra Senora de la Asuncion [*A publication*]
UCNT........ Undifferentiated Carcinoma of Nasopharyngeal Type [*Oncology*]
UCNT .... University College of the Northern Territory [*Australia*]
UCNW........ University College of North Wales
UCNY........ Underfashion Club of New York [*Formerly, CBWC*] (EA)
UCO.......... Union Corporation [*NYSE symbol*] (SPSG)
UCO.......... Universal Code [*Used for giving transport aircraft meteorological information in wartime*] (NATG)
UCO.......... Universal Weather Landing Code
UCO.......... Urinary Catheter Out [*or Output*] [*Medicine*]
UCO.......... Utility Compiler
UCOA........ United Coasts Corp. [*NASDAQ symbol*] (NQ)
UCOD........ University Clearing Office for Developing Countries
UCOFT...... Unit Combat Fire Trainer [*Army*]
U-COFT ... Unit Conduct of Fire Trainer [*Army*]
UCOIP ...... University of Chicago. Oriental Institute. Publications [*A publication*]
UCOL........ Union des Colons du Katanga [*Settlers' Union of Katanga*]
U Colo LR ... University of Colorado. Law Review [*A publication*]
U Colo L Rev ... University of Colorado. Law Review [*A publication*]
U Color L Rev ... University of Colorado. Law Review [*A publication*]
U Colo Stud ... University of Colorado. Studies [*A publication*]
UCOM....... Unified Command [*DoD*]
UCOM....... Union Catalog of Medical Monographs and Multimedia [*Medical Library Center of New York*] [*No longer available online*] [*Information service or system*] (CRD)
UCON ...... Utility Control
UCONN ... University of Connecticut
UCOP....... University of Cambridge. Oriental Publications [*A publication*]
UCOPOM ... Union Europeenne du Commerce de Gros des Pommes de Terre [*European Union of the Wholesale Potato Trade*] [*Common Market*]
UCOS .... Upper Canada King's Bench Reports, Old Series [*1831-44*] [*A publication*] (DLA)
UCOS .... Uprange Computer Output System
UCOSDDEEC ... Union of Cafe Owners and Soft Drink Dealers of the European Economic Community [*Paris, France*] (EAIO)
UCOSL...... University of Colorado School of Law (DLA)
UCOWR.... Universities Council on Water Resources (EA)
UCP .... New Castle, PA [*Location identifier*] [*FAA*] (FAAL)
UCP .... Ubiquitous Crystallization Process [*Photovoltaic energy systems*]
UCP .... Unified Command Plan [*Military*] (AFM)
UCP .... Uniform Customs and Practice for Documentary Credits [*International Chamber of Commerce*] [*A publication*]
UC & P....... Uniform Customs and Practice for Documentary Credits [*International Chamber of Commerce*] [*A publication*] (DS)
UCP .... Uninterruptable Computer Power
UCP .... Union Comorienne pour le Progres [*Comorian Union for Progress*] (PD)
UCP .... United Christian Party [*Australia*] [*Political party*] (ADA)
UCP .... United Country Party [*Australia*] [*Political party*]
UCP .... Universal Commercial Paper [*Investment term*]
UCP .... University of California. Publications in Classical Philology [*A publication*]
UCP .... University of Connecticut, Health Center Library, Processing Center, Farmington, CT [*OCLC symbol*] (OCLC)
UCP .... Update Control Process [*Telecommunications*] (TEL)
UCP .... Urinary C-Peptide [*Urology*]

UCP .... Urinary Coproporphyrin [*Urology*]
UCP .... Utilities Conservation Program [*Navy*] (NG)
UCP .... Utility Control Program
UCPA .... United Cerebral Palsy Associations (EA)
UCPA .... University of California. Publications in Classical Archaeology [*A publication*]
UCPC .... University of Connecticut Paleobotanical Collection
UCPE......... Unit of Comparative Plant Ecology [*Natural Environment Research Council*] [*British*] (IRUK)
UCPES ...... University of California. Publications in English Studies [*A publication*]
UCPF........ United Church Peace Fellowship [*Defunct*] (EA)
UCPFS ..... University of California. Publications in Folklore Studies [*A publication*]
UCPh .... Universitas Carolina: Philologica [*A publication*]
UCPL........ University of California. Publications in Linguistics [*A publication*]
UCPM ...... University of California. Publications in Music [*A publication*]
UCPMP..... University of California. Publications in Modern Philology [*A publication*]
UCPMPh... University of California. Publications in Modern Philology [*A publication*]
UCPN .... Union des Chefs et des Populations du Nord [*Union of Chiefs and Peoples of the North*] [*Togo*]
UCPP........ Urban Crime Prevention Program [*Federal government*]
UCPPh ..... University of California. Publications in Classical Philology [*A publication*]
UCPR .... Upper Canada Practice Reports [*A publication*] (DLA)
UC Pract .... Upper Canada Practice Reports [*1850-1900*] [*A publication*] (DLA)
UC Pr (Can) ... Upper Canada Practice Reports [*A publication*] (DLA)
UCPREF ... United Cerebral Palsy Research and Educational Foundation (EA)
UC Pr R ... Upper Canada Practice Reports [*A publication*] (DLA)
UCPSP ...... University of California. Publications in Semitic Philology [*A publication*]
UCPSPh... University of California. Publications in Semitic Philology [*A publication*]
UCPT........ Urinary Coproporphyrin Test [*Urology*]
UCPTE...... Union for the Coordination of the Production and Transport of Electric Power (EAIO)
UCPTE...... Union pour la Coordination de la Production et du Transport de l'Electricite [*Union for the Coordination of the Production and Transport of Electric Power - UCPTE*] (EAIO)
UCPU .... Universal Central Processor Unit [*Computer hardware*]
UCPU .... Urine Collection and Pretreatment Unit (NASA)
UCQ......... University College Quarterly [*A publication*]
UCQB .... Upper Canada Queen's Bench Reports [*A publication*] (DLA)
UC QB OS ... Upper Canada Queen's Bench Reports, Old Series [*A publication*] (DLA)
UC QB OS (Can) ... Upper Canada Queen's Bench Reports, Old Series [*A publication*] (DLA)
UCR.......... Committee on Uniform Crime Records (EA)
UCR.......... Unconditioned Reflex [*or Response*] [*Psychometrics*]
UCR.......... Under-Color Removal [*Printing technology*]
UCR.......... Uniform Crime Reports [*FBI*]
UCR.......... Union Centriste et Radicale [*France*] [*Political party*] (EY)
UCR.......... Union Civica Radical [*Radical Civic Union*] [*Argentina*] (PD)
UCR.......... Union Confederale des Retraites [*France*] (EY)
UCR.......... Unit Card Reader
UCR.......... Unit Cost Report [*Military*] (RDA)
UCR.......... University of California, Riverside (IID)
UCR.......... University of Ceylon. Review [*A publication*]
UCR.......... University of Cincinnati. Law Review [*A publication*]
UCR.......... Unsatisfactory Condition Report [*NASA*]
UCR.......... Upper Canada Reports [*A publication*] (DLA)
UCR.......... User Control Routine (MCD)
UCR.......... Usual, Customary, and Reasonable Charges [*Medicine*]
UCR.......... Utah Coal Route [*AAR code*]
UCRC .... Underground Construction Research Council
UCRC .... Union Canadienne des Religieuses Contemplatives
UCRC .... United Civil Rights Committee
UC Rep ...... Upper Canada Reports [*A publication*] (DLA)
UC Rep FM Univ Calif Berkeley Dep Mech Eng ... UC. Report FM. University of California, Berkeley. Department of Mechanical Engineering [*A publication*]
UCRG .... Union des Clubs pour le Renouveau de la Gauche [*Union of Clubs for the Renovation of the Left*] [*France*] [*Political party*] (PPE)
UCRI .... Union Carbide Research Institute (KSC)
UCRI .... Union Civica Radical Intransigente [*Left-wing radical political party*] [*Argentina*]
UCRIFER ... Unione Costruttori e Riparatori Ferrotramviari [*Rolling Stock Manufacturers Union*] [*Italy*] (EY)
U-CRIS...... Utah Computer Retrieval Information Service [*Utah State Office of Education*] (OLDSS)
UCRL .... University of California Radiation Laboratory (MCD)
UCRL .... University of California Research Laboratory (KSC)
UCrow........ Upstart Crow [*A publication*]

UCRP .... Union Civica Radical del Pueblo [*Moderate radical political party*] [*Argentina*]

UCR/RCS ... Revista de Ciencias Sociales. Universidad de Costa Rica [*A publication*]

UCS .... Canadian Union Catalogue of Serials [*National Library of Canada*] [*Information service or system*]   (IID)

UC/S .... Signs. University of Chicago Press [*A publication*]

UCS .... Southern Utah State College, Cedar City, UT [*Library symbol*] [*Library of Congress*]   (LCLS)

UCS .... Unbalanced Current Sensing   (MCD)

UCS .... Unclosed Contract Status [*Military*]   (AFIT)

UCS .... Unconditioned Stimulus [*Psychometrics*]

UCS .... Unconscious [*Medicine*]

UCS .... Underwater Cable System

UCS .... Underwater Communications System

UCS .... Unican Security Systems Ltd. [*Toronto Stock Exchange symbol*]

UCS .... Uniform Chromaticity Scale [*Illuminant*]

UCS .... Uniform Communications System

UCS .... Union of Concerned Scientists   (EA)

UCS .... Unit of Coastal Sedimentation [*NERC*] [*British*]

UCS .... Unit Cost of Sales

UCS .... Unit-Count System

UCS .... United Cable Service [*Australia*]

UCS .... United Community Services

UCS .... United Computing Systems, Inc.

UCS .... United Concerned Students   (EA)

UCS .... United States Army Corps of Engineers, Sacramento, Sacramento, CA [*OCLC symbol*]   (OCLC)

UCS .... Universal Call Sequence

UCS .... Universal Camera Site   (KSC)

UCS .... Universal Card Scanner [*Data processing*]   (DIT)

UCS .... Universal Cargo Sling

UCS .... Universal Character Set [*Data processing*]

UCS .... Universal Classification System

UCS .... Universal Command System   (KSC)

UCS .... Universal Connector Strip

UCS .... Universal Control System   (NASA)

UCS .... University Computer Services [*Ball State University*] [*Research center*]   (RCD)

UCS .... University Computing Services [*State University of New York at Buffalo*] [*Research center*]   (RCD)

UCS .... University Computing Services [*University of Southern California*] [*Research center*]   (RCD)

UCS .... Urine Collection System [*NASA*]   (KSC)

UCS .... User Control Store

UCS .... Utilities Control System [*NASA*]   (KSC)

UCS .... Utility Consulting Services [*Petroleum Information Corp.*] [*Information service or system*]   (IID)

UCSA .... Ukrainian Canadian Servicemen's Association

UCSA .... Uniform Controlled Substances Act [*National Conference of Commissioners on Uniform State Laws*]

UCSA .... Union des Confederations Sportives Africaines [*Association of African Sports Confederations - AASC*] [*Yaounde, Cameroon*]   (EAIO)

UCSA .... United Chian Societies of America [*Later, CSA*]   (EA)

UCSB .... University of California, Santa Barbara

UCSBS ...... Ukrainian Catholic Soyuz of Brotherhoods and Sisterhoods   (EA)

UCSC .... University of California, Santa Cruz

UCSC .... University City Science Center [*Research center*]   (RCD)

UCSD .... Universal Communications Switching Device

UCSD .... University of California, San Diego

UC-SDRL ... University of Cincinnati Structural Dynamics Research Laboratory

UCSEL ...... University of California Structural Engineering Laboratory   (KSC)

UCSF .... University of California, San Francisco

UCSGS ...... University of Colorado. Studies. General Series [*A publication*]

UCSJ .... Union of Councils for Soviet Jews   (EA)

UCSL .... Union Congolaise des Syndicats Libres [*Congolese Union of Free Syndicates*] [*Leopoldville*]

UCSL .... University of California. Studies in Linguistics [*A publication*]

UCSLL ...... University of Colorado. Studies. Series in Language and Literature [*A publication*]

UCSM .... Utility Control Strategy Model [*Developed at Carnegie Mellon University for acid rain analysis*]

UCSMB ..... Union des Carrieres et Scieries de Marbres de Belgique [*Belgium*]   (EY)

UCSMP ..... University of California. Studies in Modern Philology [*A publication*]

UCSR .... Ukrainian Center for Social Research   (EA)

UCSR .... Union Catalogue of Sound Recordings [*Australia*]

UCSR .... Unionist Committee for Social Reform [*British*]

UCSS .... Universal Communications Switching System   (MCD)

UC/SSL ..... University of California/Space Sciences Laboratory   (KSC)

UCSSLL .... University of Colorado. Studies. Series in Language and Literature [*A publication*]

UCST .... Upper Critical-Solution-Temperature

UCSTR ...... Universal Code Synchronous Transmitter Receiver

UCSU .... United Carters' and Storemen's Union [*British*]

UCSUR ...... University Center for Social and Urban Research [*University of Pittsburgh*] [*Research center*]   (RCD)

UCSUS ...... Ukrainian Catholic Students of the United States [*Defunct*]   (EA)

UCT .... Order of United Commercial Travelers of America [*Columbus, OH*]   (EA)

UCT .... Ultrasonic Computed Tomography [*For examining interiors of solids*]

UCT .... Unchanged Conventional Treatment [*Medicine*]

UCT .... Underwater Construction Team [*Navy*]   (NVT)

UCT .... Union Carbide Canada Equipment Trust Units [*Toronto Stock Exchange symbol*]

UCT .... Unite Centrale de Traitement [*Central Processing Unit - CPU*] [*French*]

UCT .... United Cable Television Corp. [*NYSE symbol*]   (SPSG)

UCT .... Units Compatibility Test

UCT .... Universal Coordinated Time

UCT .... University of Cape Town [*South Africa*]

UCT .... University of Connecticut [*Storrs*] [*Connecticut*] [*Seismograph station code, US Geological Survey*]   (SEIS)

UCT .... Urine Culture Tube [*Clinical chemistry*]

UCTA .... University and College Theatre Association   (EA)

UCTA .... Urine Collection/Transfer Assembly [*Apollo*] [*NASA*]

UCTC .... Union Camerounaise des Travailleurs Croyants [*Cameroonese Union of Believing Workers*]

UCTC .... United Counties Bancorporation [*NASDAQ symbol*]   (NQ)

UCTF .... Union Culturelle et Technique de Langue Francaise [*French-Language Cultural and Technical Union*] [*Paris, France*]   (EA)

UCTL .... Up Control [*Aerospace*]   (AAG)

UCTPA ...... United Coppersmiths Trade Protection Association [*A union*] [*British*]

UCTS .... United Chairmakers' Trade Society [*A union*] [*British*]

UCTS .... United Church Training School

UCTSE ...... University of Cape Town. Studies in English [*A publication*]

UCU .... University of California Union List, Berkeley, CA [*OCLC symbol*]   (OCLC)

UCU .... Utilicorp United, Inc. [*NYSE symbol*] [*Toronto Stock Exchange symbol*]   (SPSG)

UCV .... Uncontrolled Variable

UCV .... Unimproved Capital Value [*Business term*]   (ADA)

UCV .... United Confederate Veterans

UCW .... Union of Communications Workers [*British*]   (ECON)

UCW .... Unit Control Word [*Data processing*]   (BUR)

UCW .... United Church Women of the National Council of Churches   (EA)

UCW .... University College of Wales

UCW .... University of Connecticut, Storrs, CT [*OCLC symbol*]   (OCLC)

UCWA ...... United Construction Workers Association   (OICC)

UCWE ...... Underwater Countermeasures and Weapons Establishment [*British*]

UCWR ...... Upon Completion Thereof Will Return To [*Air Force*]

UCWRE .... Underwater Countermeasures and Weapons Research Establishment [*British military*]   (DMA)

UCX .... UC Corp. [*Formerly, Universal Communication Systems, Inc.*] [*AMEX symbol*]   (SPSG)

UCX .... Unemployment Compensation, Ex-Serviceman

UCY .... Union City, TN [*Location identifier*] [*FAA*]   (FAAL)

UCY .... United Caribbean Youth

UCYM ...... United Christian Youth Movement [*Defunct*]   (EA)

Uc Zap Adyg Nauc-Issled Inst Jaz Lit Ist ... Ucenye Zapiski Adygejoskogo Naucno-Issledovatel'skogo Instituta Jazyka, Literatury, i Istorii [*A publication*]

Uc Zap Bask Univ Filol N ... Ucenye Zapiski. Baskirskij Gosudarstvennyj Universitet. Filolog. Nauki [*A publication*]

Uc Zap Dal'nevost Univ ... Ucenye Zapiski. Dal'nevostocnyj Universitet [*A publication*]

Uc Zap Daug Ped Inst ... Ucenye Zapiski. Daugavpilskij Pedagogiceskij Institut [*A publication*]

Uc Zap IMO ... Ucenye Zapiski Institut Mezdunarodnych Otnosenij [*A publication*]

Uc Zap Inst Sl Ved ... Ucenye Zapiski Instituta Slavjanovedenija [*A publication*]

Uc Zap Kar Ped Inst ... Ucenye Zapiski Karel'skogo Pedagogiceskogo Instituta [*A publication*]

Uc Zap Kaz Univ ... Ucenye Zapiski. Kazachskij Universitet [*A publication*]

Uc Zap Kis Gos Univ ... Ucenye Zapiski. Kisinevskij Gosudarstvennyj Universitet [*A publication*]

Uc Zap Leningr Ped Inst Im ... Ucenye Zapiski. Leningradskij Pedagogiceskij Institut Imeni Gercena [*A publication*]

Uc Zap LGPI ... Ucenye Zapiski. Leningradskij Gosudarstvennyj Pedagogiceskij Institut Imeni A. I. Gercena [*A publication*]

Uc Zap MGPI ... Ucenye Zapiski Moskovskogo Gosudarstvennogo Pedagogiceskogo Instituta Imeni Lenina [*A publication*]

Uc Zap Mosk Bibl Inst ... Ucenye Zapiski. Moskovskij Bibliotecnyj Institut [*A publication*]

Uc Zap Omsk Ped Inst ... Ucenye Zapiski. Omsskij Pedagogiceskij Institut [*A publication*]

Uc Zap Perm Gos Univ ... Ucenye Zapiski Permskij Gosudarstvennyj Universitet [*A publication*]

Uc Zap Stavr Med Inst ... Ucenye Zapiski. Stavropol'skij Medicinskij Institut [*A publication*]
Uc Zap Stavropol Gos Pedag Inst ... Ucenye Zapiski. Stavropol'skij Gosudarstvennyj Pedagogiceskij Institut [*A publication*]
Uc Zap Tomsk Ped Inst ... Ucenye Zapiskij. Tomskij Pedagogiceskij Institut [*A publication*]
Uc Zap Tuv Nauc Issle Inst Jaz Lit Ist ... Ucenye Zapiski. Tuvinskij Naucno-Issledovatel'skij Institut Jazyka, Literatury, Istorii [*A publication*]
UD .... Fast Air Ltda. [*Chile*] [*ICAO designator*] (FAAC)
UD .... Ulnar Deviation [*Medicine*]
UD .... Ultimate Dependability [*Automotive designation*]
UD .... Unable to Approve Departure for the Time Specified [*Aviation*] (FAAC)
UD .... Unavoidable Delay
UD .... Undated
U/D .... Under Deck (ADA)
UD .... Underground Distribution (MSA)
UD .... Underwater Demolition [*Navy*] (NVT)
UD .... Undesirable Discharge [*Military*]
UD .... Undetected Defect
UD .... Undifferentiated (BJA)
UD .... Undiluted
UD .... Unidentifiable (BJA)
UD .... Uniflow Diesel [*Nissan-designed engine*]
UD .... Unit Designation
UD .... Unit Diary
UD .... Unit Director
UD .... Unit Dose [*Medicine*]
UD .... Unity-and-Diversity World Council (EA)
UD .... Universal Dipole (DEN)
UD .... University of Denver [*Colorado*]
U of D .... University of Detroit [*Michigan*]
U of D .... University of Dublin [*Ireland*]
UD .... Unlawful Detainer [*Legal term for an eviction proceeding*]
UD .... Unlisted Drugs [*A publication*]
UD .... Unplanned Derating [*Electronics*] (IEEE)
U/D .... Up/Down (KSC)
UD .... Update [*Data processing*] (NASA)
UD .... Upper Deck [*Naval*]
UD .... Urban District
UD .... Urethral Discharge [*Medicine*]
UD .... Uroporphyrinogen Decarboxylase [*Also, UDase*] [*An enzyme*]
UD .... Usable Depth (MCD)
UD .... Usage Data
UD .... Ut Dictum [*As Directed*] [*Latin*]
UD .... Utility Dog [*Dog show term*]
UDA .... Ulster Defence Association
UDA .... Ultrasonic Detergent Action
UDA .... Union for Democratic Action
UDA .... United States Department of the Interior, Alaska Resources, Anchorage, AK [*OCLC symbol*] (OCLC)
UDA .... Universal Detective Association [*Defunct*] (EA)
UDA .... Urban Development Agency [*British*]
UDA .... Urtica Dioica Agglutinin [*Biochemistry*]
UDAA .... Unlawfully Driving Away Auto
UDAC .... Urban Design Advisory Council [*Australia*]
UDAC .... User Digital Analog Controller
UDAG .... Urban Development Action Grant [*HUD*]
Udal .... Udal's Fiji Law Reports [*A publication*] (DLA)
UDAM .... Universal Digital Avionics Module (MCD)
UDAP .... Universal Digital Autopilot
UDAR .... Universal Digital Adaptive Recognizer (IEEE)
UDAS .... Unified Direct Access System (BUR)
UDAS .... Universal Data Acquisition System
UDAS .... Universal Database Access Service [*Telecommunications*] (TSSD)
UDase .... Uroporphyrinogen Decarboxylase [*Also, UD*] [*An enzyme*]
UDAT .... Unidata Systems, Inc. [*NASDAQ symbol*] (NQ)
U Day LR ... University of Dayton. Law Review [*A publication*]
U Dayton L Rev ... University of Dayton. Law Review [*A publication*]
UDB .... Unified Data Base
UDB .... Union Democratique Bretonne - Unvaniezh Demokratel Breizh [*Breton Democratic Union*] [*France*] [*Political party*] (PPW)
UDB .... Up-Data Buffer [*Data processing*]
UDC .... National Park Service, National Capital Region, Washington, DC [*OCLC symbol*] (OCLC)
UDC .... UDC - Universal Development [*NYSE symbol*] (SPSG)
UDC .... Ultrasonic Doppler Cardioscope [*Heartbeat monitor*]
UDC .... Underdeveloped Countries
UDC .... Underwater Decompression Computer [*Navy*] (CAAL)
UDC .... Uniao Democratica de Cabo Verde [*Democratic Union of Cape Verde*]
UDC .... Union of the Democratic Centre [*Sahara*] [*Political party*] (PPW)
UDC .... Union for Democratic Communications (EA)
UDC .... Union of Democratic Control [*British*]
UDC .... Union Democratica Cristiana [*Christian Democratic Union*] [*Bolivia*] [*Political party*] (PPW)

UDC .... Union Democratique Centrafricaine [*Central African Democratic Union*] [*Political party*] (PPW)
UDC .... Union Democratique du Centre [*Democratic Union of the Center*] [*Switzerland*] [*Political party*] (PPE)
UDC .... Unit Deployment of Containers (MCD)
UDC .... United Daughters of the Confederacy (EA)
UDC .... Unity-and-Diversity Council [*Later, UD*] (EA)
UDC .... Universal Decimal Classification [*Online database field identifier*]
UDC .... Universal Digital Control
UDC .... Universal Disk Controller [*Central Point Software*]
UDC .... University of the District of Columbia
UDC .... Up-Down Counter
UDC .... Upper Dead Center
UDC .... Urban Development Corporation [*New York State agency*]
UDC .... Urban District Council [*British*]
UDC .... Ursodeoxycholate [*Biochemistry*]
UDC .... Ursodeoxycholic Acid
UDC .... User Designation Codes [*Navy*] (NG)
UDC .... User Dissemination Circuit [*Air Force Weather Center*]
UDC .... Usual Diseases of Childhood [*Medicine*]
UDCA .... Undesirable Discharge, Trial by Civil Authorities [*Navy*]
UDCA .... Union pour la Defense des Commercants et des Artisans [*Union for the Defense of Traders and Artisans*] [*France*] [*Political party*] (PPE)
UDCA .... Ursodeoxycholic Acid [*Pharmacology*]
UDCCS ...... Uniform Data Classification Code Structure [*Navy*] (NG)
UDCS .... United Data Collection System (MCD)
UDCV .... Uniao Democratica de Cabo Verde [*Democratic Union of Cape Verde*]
UDD .... Bermuda Dunes, CA [*Location identifier*] [*FAA*] (FAAL)
UDD .... Bureau of Land Management, Denver, Denver, CO [*OCLC symbol*] (OCLC)
UDD .... Uddeholm [*Sweden*] [*Seismograph station code, US Geological Survey*] (SEIS)
UDD .... Ulster Diploma in Dairying
UDD .... Union Democratique Dahomeenne [*Benin*] [*Political party*]
UDDA .... Uniform Determination of Death Act [*National Conference of Commissioners on Uniform State Laws*]
UDDE .... Undesirable Discharge, Desertion without Trial [*Navy*]
UDDEHOLM ... Uddeholms Aktiebolag [*Business term*] [*Sweden*]
UDDF .... Up and Down Drafts [*Meteorology*] (FAAC)
UDDIA ...... Union Democratique pour la Defense des Interets Africains [*Democratic Union to Defend African Interests*]
UDDL .... Ultrasonic Dispersive Delay Line
UDDS .... Urban Dynamometer Driving Schedule [*EPA engine test*]
UDE .... Underwater Detection Establishment [*British*] (MCD)
UDE .... Undetermined Etiology
UDE .... Union Douaniere Equatoriale [*Equatorial Customs Union*]
UDE .... United States Fish and Wildlife Service, Region 2, Albuquerque, NM [*OCLC symbol*] (OCLC)
UDE .... Universal Data Entry
UDEAC ..... Union Douaniere et Economique de l'Afrique Centrale [*Central African Customs and Economic Union*] (EAIO)
UDEAO ..... Union Douaniere des Etats de l'Afrique et l'Ouest [*Customs Union of West African States*] [*Later, CEAO*]
UDEC .... Unitized Digital Electronic Calculator (MCD)
UDECMA-KMPT ... Parti Democratique Chretien Malgache [*Malagasy Christian Democratic Party*] [*Political party*] (PPW)
UDEFEC ... Union Democratique des Femmes Camerounaises [*Cameroonese Democratic Women's Union*]
UDENAMO ... Uniao Democratica Nacional de Mocambique [*Mozambican National Democratic Union*] [*Later, FRELIMO*] [*Political party*]
Udenrigspolit Skr Ser 15 ... Udenrigspolitiske Skrifter. Serie 15 [*A publication*]
UDET .... Universal Digital Element Tester (MCD)
U Det J Urb L ... University of Detroit. Journal of Urban Law [*A publication*]
U Det L J ... University of Detroit. Law Journal [*A publication*]
U Det L Rev ... University of Detroit. Law Review [*A publication*] (DLA)
UDETO ..... Union Democratique Togolaise [*Togolese Democratic Union*]
U Detroit LJ ... University of Detroit. Law Journal [*A publication*]
U of Detroit LJ ... University of Detroit. Law Journal [*A publication*]
UDF .... Boise Interagency Fire Center, Boise, ID [*OCLC symbol*] (OCLC)
UDF .... Federation Guadeloupeenne de l'Union pour la Democratie Francaise [*Guadeloupe Federation of the Union for French Democracy*] [*Political party*] (PPW)
UDF .... UHF [*Ultrahigh Frequency*] Direction Finder (FAAC)
UDF .... Ulster Defence Force
UDF .... Unducted Fan [*Type of prop engine developed by General Electric Co.*]
UDF .... Union Defence Force [*British*]
UDF .... Union of Democratic Forces [*Bulgaria*] [*Political party*]
UDF .... Union pour la Democratie Francaise [*Union for French Democracy*] [*French Guiana*] [*Political party*] (PPW)
UDF .... Union pour la Democratie Francaise [*Union for French Democracy*] [*Reunion*] [*Political party*] (PPW)
UDF .... Union pour la Democratie Francaise [*Union for French Democracy*] [*France*] [*Political party*] (PPW)

UDF .... Union pour la Democratie Francaise [*Union for French Democracy*] [*New Caledonia*] [*Political party*]   (PPW)

UDF .... Uniroyal, Dunlop, and Firestone [*Alternative translation of South Africa's UDF, United Democratic Front. Translation refers to method of execution consisting of forcing a tire around the victim's body and setting it on fire*]

UDF .... Unit Derating Factor [*Electronics*]   (IEEE)

UDF .... Unit Development Folder   (MCD)

UDF .... United Democratic Front [*South Africa*] [*Political party*]   (PPW)

UDF .... United Democratic Front [*India*] [*Political party*]   (PPW)

UDF .... Upside-Down Flipper

UDF .... User-Defined Function [*Data processing*]   (PCM)

UDF .... Utility and Data Flow   (NASA)

UDFAA ..... Upholstery and Decorative Fabrics Association of America [*Defunct*]   (EA)

UDFAM .... User-Defined File Access Method [*Data processing*]   (IT)

UDFE .... Undesirable Discharge, Fraudulent Enlistment [*Navy*]

UDFMA .... Upholstery and Drapery Fabric Manufacturers Association [*Later, UFMA*]

UDFT .... Union Democratique des Femmes Tunisiennes [*Democratic Union of Tunisian Women*]

UDG .... National Fisheries Center, Kearneysville, WV [*OCLC symbol*]   (OCLC)

UDG .... Unit Derated Generation [*Electronics*]   (IEEE)

UD(G) .... United Distillers (Guiness) [*Commercial firm*]

UDH .... National Park Service, Harpers Ferry Center, Harpers Ferry, WV [*OCLC symbol*]   (OCLC)

UDH .... Universal Die Holder

UDH .... Unplanned Derated Hours [*Electronics*]   (IEEE)

UDHS .... Unit Demand History Summary [*Military*]   (AABC)

UDI .... Uberlandia [*Brazil*] [*Airport symbol*]   (OAG)

UDI .... Udine [*Italy*] [*Seismograph station code, US Geological Survey*]   (SEIS)

UDI .... Unilateral Declaration of Independence [*of Southern Rhodesia*]

UDI .... Union Democratica Independiente [*Independent Democratic Union*] [*Chile*] [*Political party*]   (PPW)

UDI .... Union Democratique des Independants [*Democratic Union of Independents*] [*France*] [*Political party*]   (PPE)

UDI .... Unique Data Item   (MCD)

UDI .... United Dominion Industries Ltd. [*NYSE symbol*]   (SPSG)

UDI .... United States Department of the Interior, Natural Resources Library, Washington, DC [*OCLC symbol*]   (OCLC)

UDI .... Utility Data Institute [*Information service or system*]   (IID)

UDIA .... United Dairy Industry Association   (EA)

UDID .... Unique Data Item Description   (MCD)

U-Dink ...... Upper Class - Double [*or Dual*] Income, No Kids [*Lifestyle classification*]

UDIR .... USAREUR Daily Intelligence Report   (MCD)

UDIRL .... University of Durham Industrial Research Laboratories [*British*]

UDIT .... Union pour la Defense des Interets du Tchad [*Union for the Defense of Chadian Interests*]

UDITPA .... Uniform Division of Income for Tax Purposes Act

UDITS .... Universal Digital Test Set

UDJ .... Northern Prairie Wildlife Research Center, Jamestown, ND [*OCLC symbol*]   (OCLC)

UDJM .... Union Democratique de la Jeunesse Marocaine [*Democratic Union of Moroccan Youth*]

UDJV .... Union Democratique de la Jeunesse Voltaique [*Voltaic Democratic Youth Union*]

UDK .... United States Fish and Wildlife Service, Alaska Area Office, Anchorage, AK [*OCLC symbol*]   (OCLC)

UDK .... Upper Deck

UDKKB ..... Utsunomiya Daigaku Kyoikugakubu Kiyo, Dai-2-Bu [*A publication*]

UDL .... Bureau of Land Management, Boise District Office, Boise, ID [*OCLC symbol*]   (OCLC)

UDL .... Ultrasonic Delay Line

UDL .... Underwater Data Link   (MCD)

UDL .... Uniform Data Language

UDL .... Uniform Data Link

UDL .... Unit Detail Listings [*Air Force*]

UDL .... Unit Document Listing   (MCD)

UDL .... Universal Development Laboratory [*Computer debugger*] [*Orion Instruments*]

UDL .... Untersuchungen zur Deutschen Literaturgeschichte [*A publication*]

UDL .... Up-Data Link [*Data processing*]

UdLH .... Universidad de la Habana [*A publication*]

UDLP .... United Democratic Labour Party [*Trinidad and Tobago*] [*Political party*]   (PPW)

UDLP .... United Dominica Labour Party [*Political party*]   (PPW)

UDM .... National Mine Health and Safety Academy, Beckley, WV [*OCLC symbol*]   (OCLC)

UDM .... Union of Democratic Mineworkers [*British*]

UDM .... Union Democratique Mauritanienne [*Mauritanian Democratic Union*] [*Political party*]   (PD)

UDM .... Universal Drafting Machine Corp.

UDM .... Upright Drilling Machine

UDMA ...... United Dance Merchants of America   (EA)

UDMH ...... Unsymmetrical Dimethylhydrazine [*Rocket fuel base, convulsant poison*]

UDMH/H ... Unsymmetrical Dimethylhydrazine Hydrazine Blend   (NASA)

UDN .... National Park Service, National Register Division, Washington, DC [*OCLC symbol*]   (OCLC)

UDN .... Ulcerative Dermal Necrosis [*Medicine*]

UDN .... Underwater Doppler Navigation

UDN .... Uniao Democratica Nacional [*National Democratic Union*] [*Brazil*]

UDN .... Union Democrata Nacional [*National Democratic Union*] [*El Salvador*] [*Political party*]   (PPW)

UDN .... Union Democratica Nicaraguense [*Nicaraguan Democratic Union*] [*Political party*]   (PD)

UDNGA .... Utsonomiya Daigaku Nogakubu Gakujutsu Hokoku [*A publication*]

UDO .... United States Fish and Wildlife Service, Billings, MT [*OCLC symbol*]   (OCLC)

Udobr Urozhai ... Udobrenie i Urozhai [*A publication*]

Udobr Urozhai Kom Khim Nar Khaz SSSR ... Udobrenie i Urozhai. Komitet po Khimaisatsii Narodnogo Khozyaistva SSSR [*A publication*]

Udobr Urozhai Minist Sel'sk Khoz SSSR ... Udobrenie i Urozhai. Ministerstvo Sel'skogo Khozyaistva SSSR [*A publication*]

UDOFT ..... Universal Digital Operational Flight Trainer [*Navy*]

UDOP........ UHF [*Ultrahigh Frequency*] Doppler System

UDOP........ Ultrahigh Doppler   (NASA)

UDP .... National Park Service, Denver, Denver, CO [*OCLC symbol*]   (OCLC)

UDP .... Ulster Diploma in Poultry Husbandry

UDP .... Uniao Democratica Popular [*Portugal*]

UDP .... Unidad Democratica Popular [*Democratic Popular Unity*] [*Bolivia*] [*Political party*]   (PPW)

UDP .... Unidad Democratica Popular [*Popular Democratic Unity*] [*Peru*] [*Political party*]   (PPW)

UDP .... Unification du Droit Prive

UDP .... Union pour la Democratie Populaire [*Union for People's Democracy*] [*Senegal*] [*Political party*]   (PPW)

UDP .... United Data Processing   (BUR)

UDP .... United Democratic Party [*Belize*] [*Political party*]   (PD)

UDP .... United Democratic Party [*Basotho*] [*Political party*]   (PPW)

UDP .... Uridine Diphosphate [*Biochemistry*]

UDP .... User Datagram Protocol   (BYTE)

UDPAG ..... Uridine(diphospho)acetylglucosamine [*Biochemistry*]

UDPG........ Uridine Diphosphate Glucose [*Biochemistry*]

UDPGA ..... Uridine Diphosphate Glucuronic Acid [*Biochemistry*]

UDPGDH ... Uridinediphosphoglucose Dehydrogenase [*An enzyme*]

UDPGT ..... Uridine Diphosphate Glucuronosyltransferase [*An enzyme*] [*Biochemistry*]

UDPIA ...... Uniform Disclaimer of Property Interests Act [*National Conference of Commissioners on Uniform State Laws*]

UDPK .... United Democratic Party of Kurdistan [*Political party*]   (BJA)

UDPL .... United Dated Parts List [*Configuration listing*]   (MCD)

UDPM .... Union Democratique du Peuple Malien [*Mali People's Democratic Union*] [*Political party*]   (PPW)

UDPS........ Union pour la Democratie et le Progres Social [*Democratic Union of Social Progress*] [*Political party*] [*Zaire*]

UDPT .... Union Democratique des Populations Togolaises [*Democratic Union of Togolese People*]

UDQ .... Bureau of Land Management, Library, New Orleans, New Orleans, LA [*OCLC symbol*]   (OCLC)

UDQ .... University of Denver. Quarterly [*A publication*]

UDR .... Udaipur [*India*] [*Airport symbol*]   (OAG)

UDR .... Ulster Defence Regiment [*Military unit*] [*British*]

UDR .... Undersampling Ratio

UDR .... Union pour la Defense de la Republique [*Union for the Defense of the Republic*] [*France*] [*Political party*]   (PPE)

UDR .... Union pour la Democratie Francaise [*Union for French Democracy*] [*Martinique*] [*Political party*]   (PPW)

UDR .... United Dominion Realty Trust, Inc. [*NYSE symbol*]   (SPSG)

UDR .... United States Department of the Interior, Bureau of Reclamation, Denver, CO [*OCLC symbol*]   (OCLC)

UDR .... Universal Digital Readout

UDR .... Universal Document Reader   (BUR)

UDR .... University of Dayton. Review [*A publication*]

UDR .... Urgent Data Request [*GIDEP*]

UDR .... Usage Data Report

UDR .... Utility Data Reduction

UDRA........ Uniform Divorce Recognition Act [*National Conference of Commissioners on Uniform State Laws*]

UDRA........ United Drag Racers Association   (EA)

UDRC........ Utility Data Retrieval Control

UDRI .... University of Dayton Research Institute [*Ohio*]

UDRO .... Utility Data Retrieval Output

UDRP .... Uridine Diribose Phosphate [*Biochemistry*]

UDRPS...... Ultrasonic Data Recording and Processing System   (NRCH)

UDRS .... Universal Driver Rating System [*Harness racing*]

UDRT/RAD ... Union Democratique pour le Respect du Travail - Respect voor Arbeid en Democratie [*Democratic Union for the Respect of Labor*] [*Belgium*] [*Political party*]   (PPW)

U/DRV ...... Underdrive [*Automotive engineering*]

UDS .... Office of Surface Mining Reclamation and Enforcement, Region V, Denver, CO [*OCLC symbol*]   (OCLC)
UDS .... Ultraviolet Detector System
UDS .... Unified Data System [*Data processing*]
UDS .... Union Democratique Senegalaise [*Senegalese Democratic Union*]
UDS .... Unit Data System [*Military*]
UDS .... Universal Data Set   (CMD)
UDS .... Universal Data System [*Army*]
UDS .... Universal Data Systems [*Hardware manufacturer*]
UDS .... Universal Digital Switch   (MCD)
UDS .... Universal Distributed System [*UNIVAC*]
UDS .... Universal Documentation System [*NASA*]
UDS .... Unscheduled DNA Synthesis [*Genetics*]
UDS .... Urban Data Service [*International City Management Association*]   (IID)
UDS .... Urban Decision Systems, Inc. [*Information service or system*]   (IID)
UDS .... Utility Data Systems [*Information service or system*]   (IID)
UDS .... Utilization and Disposal Service [*Functions transferred to Property Management and Disposal Service*] [*General Services Administration*]
UDSG .... Union Democratique et Sociale Gabonaise [*Gabonese Democratic and Social Union*]
UDSKD .... Udenrigspolitiske Skrifter. Serie 15 [*A publication*]
UDSM .... Union des Democrates Sociaux de Madagascar [*Union of Social Democrats of Madagascar*]
UDSM .... Union Departementale de Syndicats du Mungo [*Departmental Union of the Trade Unions of Mungo*] [*Cameroon*]
UDSR .... Union Democratique et Socialiste de la Resistance [*Democratic and Socialist Union of the Resistance*] [*France*] [*Political party*]   (PPE)
UDSR .... United Duroc Swine Registry   (EA)
UDT .... Underdeck Tonnage
UDT .... Underwater Demolition Team [*Navy*]
UDT .... Union of Democratic Thais in the US   (EA)
UDT .... United States Fish and Wildlife Service, Science Reference Library, Twin Cities, MN [*OCLC symbol*]   (OCLC)
UDT .... United Tire & Rubber Co. Ltd. [*Toronto Stock Exchange symbol*]
UDT .... Universal Data Transcriber [*Navy*]
UDT .... Upgraded Data Terminal   (MCD)
UDT .... User Display Terminal
UDT .... Utility Dog Tracker [*Degree of obedience training*]
UDTC .... User-Dependent-Type Code
UDTD .... Updated   (MSA)
UDTDET... Underwater Demolition Team Detachment [*Navy*]   (NVT)
UDT/EOD ... Underwater Demolition Team/Explosive Ordnance Proposal [*Navy*]   (MCD)
UDTI .... Universal Digital Transducer Indicator
UDTPHIBSPAC ... Underwater Demolition Teams, Amphibious Forces, Pacific Fleet [*Navy*]
UDTS .... Universal Data Transfer Service [*ITT World Communications, Inc.*] [*Secaucus, NJ*] [*Telecommunications*]   (TSSD)
UDTS .... Universal Data Transmission System [*For international access*]
UDTUNIA ... Uniform Disclaimer of Transfers under Nontestamentary Instruments Act [*National Conference of Commissioners on Uniform State Laws*]
UDTX .... Utility Dog and Tracking Excellent [*Degree of obedience training*]
UDU .... National Maritime Museum, San Francisco, CA [*OCLC symbol*]   (OCLC)
UDU .... Unabhaengige Demokratische Union [*Independent Democratic Union*] [*Austria*] [*Political party*]   (PPE)
UDU .... Underwater Demolition Unit
UDUAL ..... Union de Universidades de America Latina [*Union of Latin American Universities*] [*Mexico*]
UDucGS .... Church of Jesus Christ of Latter-Day Saints, Genealogical Society Library, Duchesne Branch, Stake Center, Duchesne, UT [*Library symbol*] [*Library of Congress*]   (LCLS)
UDUF .... Undesirable Discharge, Unfitness [*Navy*]
UDUPA ..... Uniform Distribution of Unclaimed Property Act [*National Conference of Commissioners on Uniform State Laws*]
UDURA ..... Udobrenie i Urozhai [*Ministerstvo Sel'skogo Khozyaistva SSSR*] [*A publication*]
UDV .... Union Democratique Voltaique [*Voltaic Democratic Union*] [*Banned, 1974*]
UD-Ve .... Union Democratique pour la Cinquieme Republique [*Democratic Union for the Fifth Republic*] [*France*] [*Political party*]   (PPE)
UDW .... Ultradeep Water
UDW .... Western Energy and Land Use Team, Fort Collins, CO [*OCLC symbol*]   (OCLC)
UDX .... Office of Surface Mining Reclamation and Enforcement, Washington, DC [*OCLC symbol*]   (OCLC)
UDX .... Utility Dog Excellent [*Dog show term*] [*Canada*]
UDY .... USGS [*United States Geological Survey*] Water Resources Division, New York District, Albany, NY [*OCLC symbol*]   (OCLC)

UDZ .... United States Department of the Interior, Western Archeological Center, Tucson, AZ [*OCLC symbol*]   (OCLC)
UE .... Ultrasonic Engineering   (MCD)
UE .... Unexpired   (ADA)
UE .... Unit Entry
UE .... Unit Equipment [*as authorized to an Air Force unit*]
UE .... Unit Establishment
UE .... Unit Exception   (CMD)
UE .... United Air Services [*South Africa*] [*ICAO designator*]   (FAAC)
UE .... United Electrical, Radio, and Machine Workers of America   (EA)
UE .... United Electrical, Radio, and Machine Workers of Canada [*See also OUE*]
UE .... United Electrodynamics   (AAG)
UE .... United Empire [*Canada*]
UE .... Unity of Empire [*Award*] [*British*]
UE .... Universale Economica [*A publication*]
UE .... University Extension
UE .... Until Exhausted
UE .... Update and Ephemeria   (MUGU)
UE .... Upper Entrance [*Theater*]
UE .... Upper Epidermis [*Botany*]
UE .... Upper Extremity [*Medicine*]
UE .... Urinary Energy [*Nutrition*]
UE .... Use of English [*A publication*]
UE .... User Equipment
UE .... Uterine Epithelium [*Medicine*]
UEA .... Graphic Arts Union Employers of America   (EA)
UEA .... Ulex europeus Agglutinin [*Immunology*]
UEA .... Unattended Equipment Area
UEA .... Union Europeenne de l'Ameublement [*European Furniture Manufacturers Federation*]   (EAIO)
UEA .... Union Europeenne des Aveugles [*European Blind Union - EBU*]   (EAIO)
UEA .... United Egg Association   (EA)
UEA .... United Epilepsy Association [*Later, EFA*]   (EA)
UEA .... United Evangelical Action [*A publication*]
UEA .... Universala Esperanto Asocio [*Universal Esperanto Association*]   (EAIO)
UEA .... University of East Anglia [*England*]
UEA .... Uranium Enrichment Associates [*Bechtel Corp., Union Carbide Corp., Westinghouse Electric Corp.*]
UEAC .... Unit Equipment Aircraft
UEAC .... United European American Club
UEAI .... Ulex Europaeus Agglutinin I
UEAI .... Union Europeenne des Arabisants et des Islamisants [*European Union of Arab and Islamic Studies - EUAIS*]   (EAIO)
U East LJ .. University of the East. Law Journal [*Manila, Philippines*] [*A publication*]   (DLA)
UEAtc .... Union Europeenne pour l'Agrement Technique dans la Construction [*European Union of Agrement*]   (EAIO)
Ueb .... Uebereinkommen [*Agreement*] [*German*]   (ILCA)
UEB .... Ultrasonic Epoxy Bonder
UEB .... Unexploded Bomb
UEB .... Union Economique BENELUX
UEB .... Upper Equipment Bay [*NASA*]   (KSC)
UEBC .... Union Espanola Benefica de California   (EA)
Ueberr Tb .. Uebereuter Taschenbuecher [*A publication*]
Uebersee Rdsch ... Uebersee Rundschau [*A publication*]
UEC .... Union Electric Company
UEC .... Union des Etudiants Communistes [*France*]
UEC .... Union Europeenne de la Carrosserie [*European Union of Coachbuilders - EUC*] [*Belgium*]
UEC .... Union Europeenne des Experts Comptables Economiques et Financiers [*European Union of Public Accountants*]
UEC .... Unit Endurance Chamber   (MCD)
UEC .... United Engineering Center
UEC .... United Ethnic Communities of South Australia
UEC .... Unmanned Equipment Cabinet
UEC .... Urban Elderly Coalition   (EA)
UEC .... Urban Environment Conference   (EA)
UEC .... USS Engineers & Consultants, Inc. [*Information service or system*]   (IID)
UECA .... Underground Engineering Contractors Association [*Later, ECA*]   (EA)
UECB .... Union Europeenne des Commerces du Betail
UECBV ...... Union Europeenne du Commerce du Betail et de la Viande [*European Livestock and Meat Trading Union*]   (EAIO)
UECL .... Union Europeenne des Constructeurs de Logements [*European Union of Independent Building Contractors*]
UECS .... Unified Electronic Computer System [*Air Force*]
UECU .... Union for Experimenting Colleges and Universities [*Later, UI*]   (EA)
UED .... Uranian Electrostatic Discharge [*Planetary science*]
UEDC .... Union Europeenne Democrate Chretienne [*European Christian Democratic Union*]
UEDS .... Uniao de Esquerda para a Democracia Socialista [*Left Union for Social Democracy*] [*Portugal*] [*Political party*]   (PPE)
UEE .... Queenstown [*Australia*] [*Airport symbol*]   (OAG)
UEE .... Unit Essential Equipment [*Military*]   (NATG)

UEE.........	US Commercial Newsletter [*The Hague*] [*A publication*]
UEEB........	Union des Exploitations Electriques en Belgique
UEEBA.....	Bulletin. Utah Engineering Experiment Station [*A publication*]
UEEJ........	Union Europeenne des Etudiants Juifs [*European Union of Jewish Students - EUJS*] (EA)
UEES Report ...	Utah. Engineering Experiment Station. Report [*A publication*]
UEF	Uniform Electric Field
UEF	Union Europaeischer Forstberufsverbaende [*Union of European Foresters*] [*Teningen-Heimbach, Federal Republic of Germany*] (EAIO)
UEF	Union Europeenne des Federalistes
UEF	Union Europeenne Feminine [*European Union of Women*]
UEF	Upper End Fitting [*Nuclear energy*] (NRCH)
UEFA........	Union of European Football Associations [*Switzerland*] (EAIO)
UEFJA	Uniform Enforcement of Foreign Judgments Act [*National Conference of Commissioners on Uniform State Laws*]
UEFS........	United Enginemen's Friendly Society [*A union*] [*British*]
UEI	Union of Educational Institutions [*British*]
UEI	Union Energy [*Toronto Stock Exchange symbol*] (SPSG)
UEIC.........	United East India Company
UEIES	Uppsala English Institute. Essays and Studies [*A publication*]
UEIS	United Engineering Information System
UEITP	Union Europeenne des Industries de Transformation de Pomme de Terre [*European Union of the Potato Processing Industries*]
UEJ...........	Unattended Expendable Jammer (MCD)
UEJ...........	University of Edinburgh. Journal [*A publication*]
UEJDC......	Union Europeenne des Jeunes Democrates-Chretiens [*European Union of Young Christian Democrats*]
UEK	Elmira, NY [*Location identifier*] [*FAA*] (FAAL)
UEL	Quelimane [*Mozambique*] [*Airport symbol*] (OAG)
UEL	Underwater Environmental Laboratory [*General Electric Co.*]
UEL	United Empire Loyalist
UEL	Uomini e Libri [*A publication*]
UEL	Upper Electrical Limit [*Nuclear energy*] (NRCH)
UEL	Upper Explosive Limit
UEL	Usage Exception List (MCD)
UE Law J...	University of the East. Law Journal [*Manila, Philippines*] [*A publication*] (DLA)
UELF........	Union des Editeurs de Langue Francaise (EAIO)
UELJ	UE [*University of the East*] Law Journal [*Manila*] [*A publication*]
UELL........	Chulman [*USSR*] [*ICAO location identifier*] (ICLI)
UEM.........	Union Electrica Madrilena [*Spain*]
UEM.........	Union Europeenne de Malacologie [*European Malacological Union*]
UEM.........	Union Evangelique Mondiale [*World Evangelical Fellowship*]
UEM.........	Unite Electromagnetique [*Electromagnetic Unit*]
UEM.........	Universal Electron Microscope
UEM.........	University Extension Manuals [*A publication*]
UEMC......	Unidentified Endosteal Marrow Cell [*Hematology*]
UEMN.......	Union des Ecrivains du Monde Noir [*World Union of Black Writers - WUBW*] (EAIO)
UEMO.......	Union Europeenne des Medecins Omnipraticiens [*European Union of General Practitioners*] (EA)
UEMS	Unione Europea di Medicina Sociale [*European Union of Social Medicine - EUSM*] (EAIO)
UEMTA	European Union for the Prevention of Cruelty to Animals (EAIO)
UEN..........	Unisave Energy Ltd. [*Vancouver Stock Exchange symbol*]
UENDC.....	Union Europeenne des Negociants Detaillants en Combustibles [*European Union of Merchant Dealers in Combustibles*] [*Switzerland*]
UEO..........	Kume Jima [*Japan*] [*Airport symbol*] (OAG)
UEO..........	Union of Electrical Operatives [*British*]
UEO..........	Union de l'Europe Occidentale [*Western European Union - WEU*] (EAIO)
UEO..........	Unit Emplaning Officer [*Military*] [*British*]
UEOA........	Union des Etudiants Ouest Africains [*Union of West African Students*]
UEP..........	Underwater Electric Potential
UEP..........	Unequal Error Protection (IEEE)
UEP..........	Uniform External Pressure
UEP..........	Union Electric Co. [*NYSE symbol*] (SPSG)
UEP..........	Union Europeenne de Paiements
UEP..........	Union Europeenne de Pedopsychiatres [*European Union for Child Psychiatry*]
UEP..........	Unit Evolutionary Period
UEP..........	United Egg Producers (EA)
UEP..........	Unplanned Event Pickup [*NASA*] (KSC)
UEP..........	Unusual End of Program [*Data processing*]
UEPEDY...	US Environmental Protection Agency. Office of Air and Waste Management. EPA-450 [*A publication*]
UEPMD	Union Europeenne des Praciciens en Medecine Dentaire [*European Union of Dental Medicine Practitioners*] (EAIO)
UEPR........	Unsatisfactory Equipment Performance Report [*Military*] (AABC)

UEPS.........	Union Europeenne de la Presse Sportive [*European Sports Press Union*] (EAIO)
UEPS........	United Elvis Presley Society (EAIO)
UER	Union Europeenne de Radiodiffusion [*European Broadcasting Union - EBU*] (EAIO)
UER	Unique Equipment Register (NASA)
UER	Unite d'Enseignement et de Recherche [*Units of Teaching and Research*] [*University of Paris*]
UER	Uniunea Evreilor Romani (BJA)
UER	Unplanned Event Record [*NASA*] (KSC)
UER	Unsatisfactory Equipment Report
UER	Ust-Elegest [*USSR*] [*Seismograph station code, US Geological Survey*] (SEIS)
UERA	Umbilical Ejection Relay Assembly (AAG)
UERA	Uniform Extradition and Rendition Act [*National Conference of Commissioners on Uniform State Laws*]
UERD	Underwater Explosives Research Division [*Navy*]
UERDC	Underwater Explosion Research and Development Center [*Navy*] (CAAL)
UERE	Ultrasonic Echo Ranging Equipment
UERE	User Equivalent Range Error
UERG	Universitywide Energy Research Group [*University of California*] [*Research center*] (RCD)
UERL........	Underwater Explosives Research Laboratory
UERL........	Unplanned Event Record Log [*NASA*] (KSC)
UERMWA ...	United Electrical, Radio, and Machine Workers of America
UERP........	Unione Europea di Relazioni Pubbliche [*European Union of Public Relations - International Service Organization - EURPISO*] (EAIO)
UERPS	Uniform Excess Reporting Procedures [*DoD*]
UERS........	Unusual Event Recording System [*Jet transport*]
UERT	Union Explosivos-Rio Tinto [*Spain*]
UERT	Universal Engineer Tractor, Rubber-Tired [*Army*]
UES	Snow College, Ephraim, UT [*Library symbol*] [*Library of Congress*] (LCLS)
UES	Uniform Emission Standard (DCTA)
UES	UNISA [*University of South Africa*] English Studies [*A publication*]
UES	United Engineering Steels [*Commercial firm*] [*British*]
UES	Universal Environmental Shelter (KSC)
UES	University Extension Series [*A publication*]
UES	Upper Esophageal Sphincter [*Anatomy*]
UES	Upstream Expression Sequence [*Genetics*]
UES	Waukesha, WI [*Location identifier*] [*FAA*] (FAAL)
UESA........	Ukrainian Engineers' Society of America (EA)
UESC........	Union Electric Steel Corporation [*NASDAQ symbol*] (NQ)
UESD	Uniao da Esquerda Socialista Democratica [*Union of the Socialist and Democratic Left*] [*Portugal*] [*Political party*] (PPW)
UESEG......	United Earth Sciences Exploration Group [*British*]
UESK........	Unit Emergency Supply Kit
UESK........	Unit Essential Spares Kit [*Military*] (AFM)
UESPDE ...	University of Tasmania. Environmental Studies Working Paper [*A publication*]
UESS........	United Education & Software, Inc. [*NASDAQ symbol*] (NQ)
UEST........	Institute of Urban and Environmental Studies [*Brock University*] [*Canada*] [*Research center*] (RCD)
UET	Quetta [*Pakistan*] [*Airport symbol*] (OAG)
UET	Unattended Earth Terminal
UET	Unit Equipment Table [*Military*]
UET	United Engineering Trustees (EA)
UET	Universal Emulating Terminal
UET	Universal Engineer Tractor [*Later, BEST*] [*Army*]
UET	Ur Excavations: Texts [*London*] [*A publication*] (BJA)
UETA........	Universal Engineer Tractor, Armored [*Army*]
UETRT......	Universal Engineer Tractor, Rubber-Tired [*Army*]
UEVP	Union Europeenne des Veterinaires Practiciens [*European Union of Practising Veterinary Surgeons*] (EAIO)
UEW.........	United Electrical Workers
UEWS	Ultimate Elastic Wall Stress [*Mechanical engineering*]
UEX..........	Underexposed [*Photography*]
UEX..........	Ur Excavations [*A publication*] (BJA)
UF	All Cargo Airlines Ltd. [*Great Britain*] [*ICAO designator*] (FAAC)
UF	Ugarit-Forschungen [*A publication*]
UF	Ulster Folklife [*Belfast*] [*A publication*]
UF	Ultrafilter [*or Ultrafiltration*]
UF	Ultrafine
UF	Ultrasonic Frequency (MSA)
UF	Unavailability Factor [*Electronics*] (IEEE)
UF	Underground Feeder
UF	Unemployed Father (OICC)
UF	Uni Air International [*France*] [*ICAO designator*] (ICDA)
UF	Unified Forces [*Military*]
UF	Union Fidelity Corp. [*NYSE symbol*] (SPSG)
UF	Union de Fribourg: Institut International des Sciences Sociales et Politiques [*Union de Fribourg: International Institute of Social and Political Sciences*] [*Fribourg/Pensier, Switzerland*] (EAIO)
UF	Unit of Fire [*Military*] (MUGU)
UF	United Focus [*Later, Omni Learning Institute*] (EA)

UF............	United Force [*Guyana*] (PD)
UF............	United Foundation
UF............	United Front [*Political party*] [*Sri Lanka*] (FEA)
UF............	Uniterra Foundation (EA)
UF............	Universities Funding Council [*British*]
UF............	University of Florida [*Gainesville*]
UF............	Unknown Factor
UF............	Unofficial Funds [*British*]
U & F	Unterricht und Forschung [*A publication*]
UF............	Upper Air Fallout [*Civil Defense*]
UF............	Urea Formaldehyde
UF............	Used For
UF............	Utility File
UF............	Utilization Factor
UFA..........	Ukrainian Fraternal Association (EA)
UFA..........	Unesterified Fatty Acid [*Biochemistry*]
UFA..........	Uniform Firearms Act
UFA..........	Uniformed Firefighters Association
UFA..........	Union des Femmes d'Algerie [*Union of Algerian Women*]
UFA..........	Union of Flight Attendants (EA)
UFA..........	United Families of America (EA)
UFA..........	United Fathers of America (EA)
UFA..........	United Federation of Australia
UFA..........	University Film Association [*Later, UFVA*] (EA)
UFA..........	Universum-Film Aktien-Gesellschaft [*German motion picture company*]
UFA..........	Unsaturated Fatty Acid [*Organic chemistry*]
UFA..........	Until Further Advised
UFA..........	Usable Floor Area [*Classified advertising*] (ADA)
UFA..........	Use Frequency Analysis
UFAA........	United Food Animal Association (EA)
UFAC........	Unlawful Flight to Avoid Custody
UFAC........	Upholstered Furniture Action Council (EA)
UFAED......	Unit Forecast Authorization Equipment Data (AFM)
UFAJ........	University Film Association. Journal [*A publication*]
UFAM........	Universal File Access Method
UFAP........	Union Francaise des Annuaires Professionels [*French Union for Professional Yearbooks*] [*Trappes*] [*Information service or system*] (IID)
UFAP........	Universal-Fine Ammonium Perchlorate [*Organic chemistry*] (MCD)
UFAP........	Unlawful Flight to Avoid Prosecution
UFA Rev Union Fed Coop Agric Suisse ...	UFA Revue. Union des Federations Cooperatives Agricoles de la Suisse [*A publication*]
UFAS........	Unified Flight Analysis System [*NASA*]
UFAT........	Unlawful Flight to Avoid Testimony
UFAW........	Universities Federation for Animal Welfare [*British*]
UFAW Courr ...	UFAW [*Universities Federation for Animal Welfare*] Courrier [*A publication*]
UFAWU....	United Fishermen and Allied Workers' Union [*Canada*]
UFBC........	United Financial Banking Companies, Inc. [*NASDAQ symbol*] (NQ)
UFBK........	United Federal Bancorp, Inc. [*NASDAQ symbol*] (NQ)
UFBS........	Union des Francais de Bon Sens [*Union of Frenchmen of Good Sense*] [*Political party*] (PPW)
UFBS........	United Friendly Boilermakers' Society [*A union*] [*British*]
UFBTAD...	Universidad de la Republica del Uruguay. Facultad de Agronomia. Estacion Experimental de Paysandu Dr. Mario A. Cassinoni. Boletin Tecnico [*A publication*]
UFC	Unidirectional Filamentary Composite
UFC	Unified Fire Control (MCD)
UFC	Uniform Freight Classification
UFC	Union des Facteurs du Canada [*Letter Carriers' Union of Canada - LCUC*]
UFC	Unit Funded Costs (MCD)
UFC	United Flight Classification
UFC	United Flowers-by-Wire Canada
UFC	United Free Church [*Scotland*]
UFC	Universal Flight Computer
UFC	Universal Foods Corporation [*NYSE symbol*] (SPSG)
UFC	Universal Frequency Counter
UFC	Universities Funding Council [*British*] (ECON)
UFC	Urinary Free Cortisol
UFCA	Uniform Fraudulent Conveyance Act [*National Conference of Commissioners on Uniform State Laws*]
UFCA	United Film Carriers Association [*Defunct*] (EA)
UFCA	Urethane Foam Contractors Association (EA)
UFCC........	Underwater Fire Control Computer [*Navy*] (CAAL)
UFCC........	Uniform Freight Classification Committee
UFCE........	Union Federaliste des Communautes Ethniques Europeennes [*Federal Union of European Nationalities*]
UFCG	Underwater Fire Control Group
UFCP........	Up-Front Control Panel (MCD)
UFCS........	UF-6 Chemical Feed Station [*Nuclear energy*] (NRCH)
UFCS........	Underwater Fire Control System
UFCS........	United Fellowship for Christian Service [*Later, BMMFI*] (EA)
UFCS........	United Fire & Casualty Co. [*NASDAQ symbol*] (NQ)
UFCS........	Universal Fire Control System
UFCS........	Up-Front Control Set (MCD)
UFCT........	United Federation of College Teachers [*AFL-CIO*]
UFCW	United Food and Commercial Workers International Union (EA)
UFCWIU...	United Food and Commercial Workers International Union (EA)
UFD	Davis County Library, Farmington, UT [*Library symbol*] [*Library of Congress*] (LCLS)
UFD	Ultrafast Detection
UFD	Union des Forces Democratiques [*Union of Democratic Forces*] [*France*] [*Political party*] (PPE)
UFD	United Foods, Inc. [*AMEX symbol*] (SPSG)
UFD	Universal Firing Device [*Military*] (AABC)
UFD	User File Directory (NASA)
UFDC........	Union des Femmes Democratiques du Canada
UFDC........	United Federation of Doll Clubs (EA)
UFDC........	Universal Flight Director Computer
UFE	Union des Francais a l'Etranger [*Union of French Citizens Abroad*] [*Political party*] (PPW)
UFE	Union des Groupements Professionnels de l'Industrie de le Feculerie de Pommes de Terre [*Union of Professional Groups of the Potato Starch Industry*]
UFE	Universal Field Element (MCD)
UFEA........	Union Financiere pour l'Europe et l'Afrique [*Financial Union for Europe and Africa*] [*French*]
UFEBB	Bulletin. Faculty of Education. Utsunomiya University [*A publication*]
UFEMAT ...	Federation Europeenne des Associations Nationales des Negociants en Materiaux de Construction [*European Association of National Builders Merchants Associations*] (EAIO)
UFEMTO ...	Union des Femmes du Togo [*Togolese Women's Union*]
UFER........	Mouvement International pour l'Union Fraternelle entre les Races et les Peuples [*International Movement for Fraternal Union among Races and Peoples*]
UFESA	United Fire Equipment Service Association (EA)
UFF	U-Landshjaelp fra Folk til Folk [*Development Aid from People to People*] (EAIO)
UFF...........	Ufficiale [*Official, Officer*] (EY)
UFF...........	Ulster Freedom Fighters
UFF...........	Union et Fraternite Francaise [*French Union and Fraternity*] [*Political party*] (PPE)
UFF...........	UnionFed Financial [*NYSE symbol*] (SPSG)
UFF...........	United Freedom Front (EA)
UF-F	Universal Flip-Flop [*Data processing*]
UFF...........	University Film Foundation (EA)
UFFCS.......	IEEE Ultrasonics, Ferroelectrics, and Frequency Control Society (EA)
UFFI	Urea-Formaldehyde Foam Insulation
UFFT.........	Upplands Fornminnesfoerenings Tidskrift [*A publication*]
UFFVA	United Fresh Fruit and Vegetable Association (EA)
UFGCC......	Ultrafine Ground Calcium Carbonate [*Inorganic chemistry*]
UFGI	United Financial Group, Incorporated [*NASDAQ symbol*] (NQ)
UFH	Upper Facial Height [*Medicine*]
UFi............	Fillmore City Library, Fillmore, UT [*Library symbol*] [*Library of Congress*] (LCLS)
UFI	Unifi, Inc. [*NYSE symbol*] (SPSG)
UFI	Union des Foires Internationales [*Union of International Fairs*] (EAIO)
UFI	Unit Fault Isolation (MCD)
UFI	Universal Fermi Interaction
UFI	Usage Frequency Indicator
UFI	User Friendly Interface
UFIB..........	Union Federazioni Italiane Bocce [*Italian lawn bowling, or boccie, organization*]
UFIDA.......	Union Financiere Internationale pour le Developpement de l'Afrique [*International Financial Union for the Development of Africa*]
Ufim Aviacion Inst Trudy ...	Ufimskii Aviacionnyi Institut Imeni Ordzonikidze Trudy [*A publication*]
UFIPTE.....	Union Franco-Iberique pour la Coordination de la Production et du Transport de l'Electricite [*Franco-Iberian Union for Coordinating the Production and Transmission of Electricity*] (EAIO)
UFIRS	Uniform Fire Incident Reporting System [*National Fire Protection Association*]
UFIRS	Universal Far Infrared Sensor (MCD)
UFIZA.......	Ukrainskii Fizicheskii Zhurnal [*A publication*]
UFJC.........	United Fund for Jewish Culture [*Defunct*] (EA)
UFKT........	Universitetsforlagets Kronikktjeneste [*A publication*]
UFL	Underfull Employment [*Economics*]
UFL	Upper Flammable Limit
U Fla LR ...	University of Florida. Law Review [*A publication*]
U Fla L Rev ...	University of Florida. Law Review [*A publication*]
UFLC........	Union Internationale des Femmes Liberales Chretiennes [*International Union of Liberal Christian Women*]
U Florida L Rev ...	University of Florida. Law Review [*A publication*]
UFLT........	Uniflite, Inc. [*NASDAQ symbol*] (NQ)
UFM	Uganda Freedom Movement (PD)
UFM	Union Fleuve de Mano [*Mano River Union - MRU*] (EAIO)
UFM	United Financial Management Ltd. [*Toronto Stock Exchange symbol*]

UFM.........	University for Man [*Manhattan, KS*]
UFM.........	Upper Figure of Merit
UFM.........	User to File Manager
UFMA......	United Fur Manufacturers Association (EA)
UFMA......	Upholstered Furniture Manufacturers Association (EA)
UFMA......	Upholstery Fabric Manufacturers Association [*Defunct*] (EA)
UFMCC.....	Universal Fellowship of Metropolitan Community Churches (EA)
UFMH.......	University of Florida. Monographs. Humanities Series [*A publication*]
UFMOP	Unintentional Frequency Modulation on Pulse (MCD)
UFMT	Urban Federation for Music Therapists [*Later, AAMT*] (EA)
UFN.........	UniCare Financial Corp. [*AMEX symbol*] (SPSG)
UFN.........	Union Franco-Nigerienne [*French-Nigerian Union*]
UFN.........	Until Further Notice
UFN.........	Uspechi Fiziceskich Nauk [*A publication*]
UFNAA	Uspekhi Fizicheskikh Nauk [*A publication*]
UFNSHD ..	Unfinished
UFO.........	Ultralight Flight Organization (EA)
UFO.........	Unidentified Flying Object [*"Flying saucers"*] [*Facetious translation: "Undue Fuss Over"*]
UFO.........	Uniform Field Organization [*DoD*]
UFO.........	Unit Families Officer [*Military*] [*British*]
UFO.........	United 510 Owners (EA)
UFO.........	Universal Fiber Optic (MCD)
UFO.........	Unlimited Freak-Out [*Slang*] (DSUE)
UFO.........	Unwanted Falling Objects (MCD)
UFO.........	User Friendly Operating System [*UFO Systems, Inc.*]
UFOA.......	Union des Femmes de l'Ouest Africain [*West African Women's Union*]
UFOAAL...	Anales. Facultad de Odontologia. Universidad de la Republica [*Uruguay*] [*A publication*]
UFOCAT...	UFO [*Unidentified Flying Object*] Catalog [*Center for Unidentified Flying Object Studies*]
UFOIC......	UFO [*Unidentified Flying Object*] Investigation Center [*Australia*] [*Defunct*]
UFOIN	UFO Investigators Network [*British*]
UFOIRC....	Unidentified Flying Object Information Retrieval Center, Inc. (EA)
UFOP	Ultrafast-Opening Parachute (NG)
UFOPIA....	Unidentified Flying Objects Phenomena Investigations, Australia
UFOR.......	UFO [*Unidentified Flying Object*] Research [*Australia*]
UFORDAT ...	Umweltforschungsdatenbank [*Data Bank for Environmental Research Projects*] [*Deutsches Umweltbundesamt*] [*Federal Republic of Germany*] [*Information service or system*] (CRD)
UFOS	Unacceptable Face of Socialism (DSUE)
UFOs	United Flying Octogenarians (EA)
UFP.........	Ultrafine Powder [*Materials processing*]
UFP.........	Under Frequency Protector (MCD)
UFP.........	Unemployed Full Pay [*Military*] [*British*]
UFP.........	United Federal Party [*Northern Rhodesia*]
UFP.........	United Federation of Planets
UFP.........	Universal Folded Plate [*Structural system*] (RDA)
UFP.........	Utility Facilities Program [*Data processing*] (IBMDP)
UFPA........	University Film Producers Association [*Later, UFVA*] (EA)
UFPC........	United Federation of Postal Clerks [*Formerly, NFPOC*] [*Later, APWU*] (EA)
UFP-ICP ...	Ultrafine Particle Inductively Coupled Plasma [*Spectrometry*]
UFPO	Underground Facilities Protective Organization (EA)
UFR.........	UF-6 Recovery Room [*Nuclear energy*] (NRCH)
UFR.........	Under Frequency Relay
UFR.........	Unfinanced Requirement [*Army*]
UFR.........	Urine Flow Rate
UFRCC......	Uniform Federal Regional Council City
UFRM	United Federal Savings & Loan of Rocky Mount [*NASDAQ symbol*] (NQ)
UFRWO	United Federation of Russian Workers' Organizations of USA and Canada (EA)
UFS..........	Ulster Folklife Society (EA)
UFS..........	Ultimate Factor of Safety
UFS..........	Under Frequency Sensing (MCD)
UFS..........	United Features Syndicate [*Commercial firm*]
UFS..........	Universal Freight Services [*Commercial firm*] (DS)
UFS..........	Unnormalized Floating Subtract
UFSA........	Ukrainian Free Society of America (EA)
UFSB........	University Savings Bank [*NASDAQ symbol*] (NQ)
UFSI-IWA ...	Universities Field Staff International - Institute of World Affairs
UFSJ	Unitarian Fellowship for Social Justice
UFSL.........	Union Federal Savings & Loan Association [*Los Angeles, CA*] [*NASDAQ symbol*] (NQ)
UFSS	Unified Flexible Spacecraft Simulation
UFST	Unifast Industries, Inc. [*NASDAQ symbol*] (NQ)
UFST	United Federation of Canadian Star Trekkers
UFT	Finance and Trade Review [*A publication*]
UFT	Ultrasonic Frequency Transformer [*or Translator*]
UFT	United Federation of Teachers [*New York*]
UFT	United Fly Tyers (EA)

UFTA........	Uniform Fraudulent Transfer Act [*National Conference of Commissioners on Uniform State Laws*]
UFTAA......	Universal Federation of Travel Agents' Associations [*Formed by a merger of International Federation of Travel Agencies and Universal Organization of Travel Agents' Associations*] (EAIO)
UFTR........	University of Florida Teaching Reactor
UFTS	United Furnishing Trades Society [*A union*] [*British*]
UFU..........	United Fishermen Union [*British*]
UFU..........	Utility Flight Unit [*Navy*]
UFUR	Universal Furniture Ltd. [*NASDAQ symbol*] (NQ)
UFV..........	Unsymmetrical Free Vibration
UFVA	University Film and Video Association (EA)
UFVF	University Film and Video Foundation (EA)
UFW	United Farm Workers of America (EA)
UFW	United Furniture Workers of America (EA)
UFWA	United Farm Workers of America
UFWA	United Furniture Workers of America
UFWDA	United Four-Wheel Drive Associations (EA)
UFWOC	United Farm Workers Organizing Committee [*Later, UFW*]
UFWU	United Farm Workers Union
UG	Norfolk Island Airlines [*Australia*] [*ICAO designator*] (ICDA)
UG	Radio Frequency Connectors [*JETDS nomenclature*] [*Military*] (CET)
ug..............	Uganda [*MARC country of publication code*] [*Library of Congress*] (LCCP)
UG	Uganda [*ANSI two-letter standard code*] (CNC)
UG	Uganda Airlines Corp. [*ICAO designator*] (FAAC)
Ug	Ugaritica [*Paris*] [*A publication*]
Ug	Ugutio [*Huguccio*] [*Deceased, 1210*] [*Authority cited in pre-1607 legal work*] (DSA)
UG	Uncertain Glory: Folklore and the American Revolution [*A publication*]
UG	Undergarment
UG	Undergraduate
UG	Underground [*Technical drawings*]
Ug	Uniform, Fine-Grained [*Soil*]
UG	Unite Guyanaise [*Guyanese Unity*] [*Political party*] (PPW)
UG	Universal Generalization [*Rule of quantification*] [*Logic*]
UG	Universal Government
UG	Upgrading Training [*Job Training and Partnership Act*] (OICC)
UG	Urban Gorillas (EA)
UG	Urogenital [*Medicine*]
UG	US-North Africa (Gibraltar) Convoy [*World War II*]
UG	User Group [*Data processing*]
UG	Uteroglobin [*Physiology*]
UGA..........	Uganda [*ANSI three-letter standard code*] (CNC)
uga............	Ugaritic [*MARC language code*] [*Library of Congress*] (LCCP)
UGA..........	Ugashik [*Alaska*] [*Airport symbol*] (OAG)
UGA..........	Ugashik, AK [*Location identifier*] [*FAA*] (FAAL)
UGA..........	Underwriters Grain Association (EA)
UGA..........	United Golfers' Association (EA)
UGA..........	Unity Gain Amplifier
UGA..........	Unscreened Granulated Aluminate [*Inorganic chemistry*]
UGA..........	Untersuchungen zur Geschichte und Altertumskunde Agyptens [*A publication*]
UGA..........	Uracil Guanine Adenine [*Genetics*]
UGA..........	Urgeschichtlicher Anzeiger [*A publication*]
UGAA.......	Untersuchungen zur Geschichte und Altertumskunde Aegyptens [*K. Sethe*] [*A publication*] (BJA)
UGAL........	Union des Groupements d'Achat Cooperatifs de Detaillants de l'Europe [*Association of Cooperative Retailer-Owned Wholesalers of Europe - ACROWE*] (EAIO)
UGAM......	United Gaming, Inc. [*NASDAQ symbol*] (SPSG)
UGAN	Uganda
Uganda Dep Agric Annu Rep ...	Uganda. Department of Agriculture. Annual Report [*A publication*]
Uganda Dep Agric Mem Res Div Ser II Veg ...	Uganda. Department of Agriculture. Memoirs of the Research Division. Series II. Vegetation [*A publication*]
Uganda For Dep Tech Note ...	Uganda. Forest Department. Technical Note [*A publication*]
UgandaJ	Uganda Journal [*A publication*]
Uganda Leg Focus ...	Uganda Legal Focus [*A publication*] (DLA)
Uganda LF ...	Uganda Law Focus [*A publication*] (DLA)
Uganda LR ...	Uganda Protectorate Law Reports [*1904-51*] [*A publication*] (DLA)
Uganda Natl Parks Dir Rep ...	Uganda National Parks Director's Report [*A publication*]
UGAPB	Publication. Utah Geological Association [*A publication*]
Ugarit F	Ugarit-Forschungen. Internationales Jahrbuch fuer die Altertumskunde Syrien-Palaestinas [*A publication*]
UGAS	Union Gas Systems [*NASDAQ symbol*] (NQ)
UGB..........	Pilot Point, AK [*Location identifier*] [*FAA*] (FAAL)
UGB..........	Union Giovantu Benadir [*Benadir Youth Union*] [*Somalia*]
UGB..........	Union de Guerreros Blancos [*White Warriors' Union*] [*El Salvador*] [*Political party*] (PD)
UGB..........	United Gulf Bank [*Middle East*]
UGB..........	Unity Gain Bandwidth
UGBW.......	Unity Gain Bandwidth

UGC.......... Ukrainian Gold Cross (EA)
UGC.......... Ultrasonic Grating Constant
UGC.......... United Gold Corp. [*Vancouver Stock Exchange symbol*]
UGC.......... United Nations Food and Agriculture Organization Intergovernmental Committee [*World Food Program*]
UGC.......... Unity Gain Crossover
UGC.......... Universal Guided Column
UGC.......... University Grants Commission [*India*]
UGC.......... University Grants Committee [*British*]
UGC.......... Urgench [*USSR*] [*Airport symbol*] (OAG)
UGCAA..... Union Generale des Cooperatives Agricoles d'Approvisionnement
UGCW...... United Glass and Ceramic Workers of North America
UGD......... United Greenwood [*Vancouver Stock Exchange symbol*]
UGDP........ University Group Diabetes Program [*Study group involving 12 medical schools*] [*Defunct*]
UGE......... Undergraduate Engineering Program [*Air Force*]
UGEAO..... Union Generale des Etudiants d'Afrique Occidentale [*General Union of West African Students*]
UGEC........ Union Generale des Etudiants Congolais [*General Union of Congolese Students*]
UGEE........ Yerevan/Zvartnots [*USSR*] [*ICAO location identifier*] (ICLI)
UGEED..... Union Generale des Etudiants et Eleves Dahomeens
U Gefl AWG ... Um Gefaellige Antwort Wird Gebeten [*The Favor of an Answer Is Requested*] [*German*] [*Correspondence*]
UGEG........ Union Generale des Etudiants Guineens [*General Union of Guinean Students*]
UGEM....... Union Generale des Etudiants du Maroc [*General Union of Moroccan Students*]
UGEMA.... Union Generale des Etudiants Musulmans d'Algerie [*General Union of Moslem Students of Algeria*]
UGEN........ University Genetics Co. [*NASDAQ symbol*] (NQ)
Ugeskr Agron Hortonomer ... Ugeskrift foer Agronomer og Hortonomer [*A publication*]
Ugeskr Jordbrug ... Ugeskrift foer Jordbrug [*A publication*]
Ugeskr Laeg ... Ugeskrift foer Laeger [*A publication*]
Ugeskr Landm ... Ugeskrift foer Landmaend [*A publication*]
Ugeskr Landmaend ... Ugeskrift foer Landmaend [*A publication*]
UGET .... Union Generale des Etudiants Tunisiens [*General Union of Tunisian Students*]
Ug F .... Ugarit-Forschungen [*A publication*]
UGF.......... Unidentified Growth Factor
UGF.......... United Givers Fund
UGF.......... Unserviceable Generation Factor [*Military*]
UGF.......... US-North Africa (Gibraltar) Convoy-Fast [*World War II*]
UGGG........ Tbilisi/Novoalexeyevka [*USSR*] [*ICAO location identifier*] (ICLI)
UGGI........ Union Geodesique et Geophysique Internationale [*International Union of Geodesy and Geophysics*]
UGGI Chron ... UGGI [*Union Geodesique et Geophysique Internationale*] Chronicle [*A publication*]
UGGSC ..... Uggscombe [*England*]
UGH.......... Uveitis-Glaucoma-Hyphemia [*Ophthalmology*]
UGHA........ United in Group Harmony Association (EA)
UGHP........ Undergraduate Helicopter Pilot Training [*Army*]
UGI.......... Uganik [*Alaska*] [*Airport symbol*] (OAG)
UGI.......... UGI Corp. [*Formerly, United Gas Improvement Co.*] [*NYSE symbol*] (SPSG)
UGI.......... Union Geographique Internationale [*International Geographical Union*]
UGI.......... Upper Gastrointestinal [*Medicine*]
UGIB......... Upper Gastrointestinal Bleeding [*Medicine*]
UGI Bull .... UGI [*Union Geographique Internationale*] Bulletin [*A publication*]
UGIH........ Upper Gastrointestinal Tract Hemorrhage [*Medicine*]
UGIMA ..... Unione Generale degli Industriali Apuani del Marmo ed Affini [*Marble Industry Union*] [*Italy*] (EY)
UgJ........... Uganda Journal [*A publication*]
UGJA .... United Galician Jews of America [*Defunct*] (EA)
UGL.......... Uglegorsk [*USSR*] [*Seismograph station code, US Geological Survey*] (SEIS)
UGL.......... Uitgelezen. Documentatieoverzicht Bibliotheek en Documentatiedienst Ministerie van Sociale Zaken [*A publication*]
UGL.......... Utility General
UGLAA ..... Ugeskrift foer Laeger [*A publication*]
UGLAS...... Uniform General Ledger Accounting Structure (NVT)
UGLE .... United Grand Lodge of England [*Masonry*]
UGLE .... Universal Graphics Language Executive (MCD)
Ugleobogat Oborudovanie ... Ugleobogatitel'noe Oborudovanie [*A publication*]
Ug LF........ Uganda Law Focus [*A publication*] (DLA)
UGLI .... Universal Gate for Logic Implementation [*Data processing*] (MCD)
UGLIAC.... United Gas Laboratories Internally Programmed Automatic Computer
UGLJ........ University of Ghana. Law Journal [*A publication*]
Ug LR .... Uganda Law Reports [*Africa*] [*A publication*] (DLA)
UGLRC ..... Upper Great Lakes Regional Commission [*Department of Commerce*]
UgM........... Ugaritic Manual [*A publication*] (BJA)

UG/M........ Umdrehungen je Minute [*Revolutions per Minute*] [*German*]
UGM........ Underwater Guided Missile [*DoD*] (MCD)
UGM .... University of Georgia. Monographs [*A publication*]
UGM .... Urogenital Mesenchyme [*Medicine*]
UGMA....... Uniform Gifts to Minors Act [*National Conference of Commissioners on Uniform State Laws*]
UGML....... Universal Guided Missile Launcher [*Navy*] (MCD)
UGMM..... Mukhrani [*USSR*] [*ICAO location identifier*] (ICLI)
UGN .... Waukegan, IL [*Location identifier*] [*FAA*] (FAAL)
UGNCO ... Unit Gas Noncommissioned Officer [*Army*] [*World War II*]
UGND ...... Underground (AABC)
UGNE....... Unigene Laboratories, Inc. [*NASDAQ symbol*] (NQ)
UGO .... Uige [*Angola*] [*Airport symbol*] [*Obsolete*] (OAG)
UGO .... Unigesco, Inc. [*Toronto Stock Exchange symbol*]
UGO .... Unit Gas Offices [*Army*] [*World War II*]
UGO .... Unmanned Geophysical Observatory [*National Science Foundation*]
UGOC....... United Greek Orthodox Charities [*Defunct*] (EA)
Ugol' Ukr .. Ugol' Ukrainy [*A publication*]
UGOT....... Urine Glutamic-Oxaloacetic Transaminase [*An enzyme*]
UGOUA .... Ugol' Ukrainy [*A publication*]
UGP......... Union des Gaullistes de Progres [*Union of Progressive Gaullists*] [*France*] [*Political party*] (PPE)
UGP......... United Global Petroleum, Inc. [*Vancouver Stock Exchange symbol*]
UGPA .... Undergraduate Grade-Point Average [*Higher education*]
UGPCC...... Uniform Grocery Product Code Council [*Later, UPCC*] (EA)
UGPP....... Uridine Diphosphoglucose Pyrophosphorylase [*An enzyme*]
Ug Pr LR ... Uganda Protectorate Law Reports [*Africa*] [*A publication*] (DLA)
UGR.......... Ultrasonic Grain Refinement
UGR.......... United Gunn Resources [*Vancouver Stock Exchange symbol*]
UGR.......... Universal Graphic Recorder [*Raytheon Co.*]
UGRE .... Undergraduate Record Examination [*Education*]
UGRR........ Underground Railroad [*A smuggling system*] [*Criminal slang*]
UGS .... Unattended Ground Sensors
UGS .... Uniaxial Gyrostabilizer
UGS .... Union de la Gauche Socialiste
UGS .... Union Graduate School [*Yellow Springs, Ohio*]
UGS .... Union des Guineens au Senegal [*Union of Guineans in Senegal*] [*Political party*] (PD)
UGS .... United Grounders' Society [*A union*] [*British*]
UGS .... Upper Group Stop [*Nuclear energy*] (NRCH)
UGS .... Upper Guide Structure [*Nuclear energy*] (NRCH)
UGS .... Urogenital Sinus [*Anatomy*]
UGS .... Urogenital System [*Medicine*]
UGS .... US-North Africa (Gibraltar) Convoy-Slow [*World War II*]
UGSA .... Union Generale des Syndicats Algeriens [*General Federation of Algerian Trade Unions*]
UGSP....... United Galaxy Sanitation Patrol [*In TV series "Quark"*]
UGSS........ Sukhumi [*USSR*] [*ICAO location identifier*] (ICLI)
UgT.......... Ugaritic Textbook [*A publication*] (BJA)
UGT......... Underground Test (MCD)
UGT......... Union General de Trabajadores de Espana [*General Union of Spanish Workers*] [*In exile*]
UGT.......... United Bible Societies' Greek New Testament [*A publication*] (BJA)
UGT.......... Upgrade Training [*Military*] (AFM)
UGT.......... Upgraded Third-Generation Enroute Software Program [*Data processing*] (MCD)
UGT......... Urgent
UGT......... Urogenital Tract [*Medicine*]
UGTA .... Union Generale des Travailleurs Algeriens [*General Union of Algerian Workers*]
UGTAN..... Union Generale des Travailleurs d'Afrique Noire [*General Union of Workers of Black Africa*]
UGTC .... Union Generale des Travailleurs du Cameroun [*General Union of Workers of Cameroon*]
UGTC .... Union Generale des Travailleurs Centrafricains [*General Union of Central African Workers*]
UGTCI...... Union Generale des Travailleurs de la Cote D'Ivoire [*General Union of Workers of the Ivory Coast*]
UGTD....... Uniform Geometrical Theory of Diffraction (MCD)
UGTD........ Union Generale des Travailleurs du Dahomey [*General Union of Workers of Dahomey*]
UGTG .... Union Generale des Travailleurs de la Guadeloupe (PD)
UGTK .... Union Generale des Travailleurs du Kamerun [*General Union of Workers of the Cameroon*]
UGTM ...... Union Generale des Travailleurs du Maroc [*General Union of Workers of Morocco*]
UGTM .... Union Generale des Travailleurs de Mauritanie [*General Union of Workers of Mauritania*]
UGTP .... Uniao Geral dos Trabalhadores de Portugal [*General Workers Union*] [*Portugal*] (EY)
UGTS .... Union Generale des Travailleurs du Senegal [*General Union of Workers of Senegal*]
UGTT .... Union Generale de Travailleurs Tunisiens [*General Federation of Tunisian Workers*]
UGW......... United Garment Workers of America (EA)
UH .... Air-Cushion Vehicle built by Universal Hovercraft [*US*] [*Usually used in combination with numerals*]

UH	Bristow Helicopters Group Ltd. [*Great Britain*] [*ICAO designator*] (FAAC)
UH	Ugaritic Handbook [*C. H. Gordon*] [*A publication*] (BJA)
UH	Ukrainian Herald [*A publication*]
UH	Unavailable Hours [*Electronics*] (IEEE)
UH	Underhatch
UH	Unit Head
UH	Unit Heater [*Technical drawings*]
UH	United Humanitarians (EA)
UH	Universidad de la Habana [*A publication*]
UH	University of Hawaii [*Honolulu, HI*]
UH	Upper Half
UH	Upper Hemispherical (MCD)
UH	US Home Corp. [*NYSE symbol*] (SPSG)
UH	Utah [*Obsolete*] (ROG)
UH	Utility Helicopter [*Military*] (AABC)
UHA	Ukrains'ka Halyts'ka Armiia
UHA	Ultrahigh Altitude
UHA	Unexpected Home Attack [*Medicine*]
UHA	Union House of Assembly [*South Africa*] (DAS)
UHA	Universitets- och Hogskoleambetet [*National Board of Universities and Colleges*] [*Ministry of Education and Cultural Affairs*] [*Information service or system*] (IID)
UHA	Upper Half Assembly
UHAA	United Horological Association of America [*Later, AWI*]
UHAB	Urban Homesteading Assistance Board (EA)
UHAC	United Hellenic American Congress (EA)
U Hart St L	University of Hartford. Studies in Literature [*A publication*]
U Hawaii L Rev	University of Hawaii. Law Review [*A publication*]
U Haw LR	University of Hawaii. Law Review [*A publication*]
UHBP	Ekimcham [*USSR*] [*ICAO location identifier*] (ICLI)
UHC	Ultimate Holding Company
UHC	Unburned Hydrocarbon [*Also, UBHC*] [*Fuel technology*]
UHC	Under Honorable Conditions [*Military*]
UHC	Unit Hardware Cost (MCD)
UHC	Universal Health Care Ltd. [*Australia*]
UHC	University of Houston at Clear Lake City, Houston, TX [*OCLC symbol*] (OCLC)
UHCC	University of Houston Coastal Center [*Research center*] (RCD)
UHCMWIU	United Hatters, Cap, and Millinery Workers International Union
UHCO	Universal Holding Corporation [*NASDAQ symbol*] (NQ)
UHCP	United Heritage Corp. [*NASDAQ symbol*] (NQ)
UHCS	Ultrahigh Capacity Storage
UHDDS	Uniform Hospital Discharge Data Set [*National Center for Health Statistics*]
UHE	Uherske Hradiste [*Czechoslovakia*] [*Airport symbol*] [*Obsolete*] (OAG)
UHE	Ultimate Hour Estimate (MCD)
UHE	Ultrahigh Efficiency [*Arc lamp*]
UHE	Ultrahigh Energy
UH/ED	Economia y Desarrollo. Universidad de La Habana [*A publication*]
UHELP	[*A*] programming language (CSR)
UHF	Ulster Historical Foundation (EA)
UHF	Ultrahigh-Frequency [*Electricity of radio waves*]
UHF	Uniform Heat Flux [*Engineering*]
UHF	United Health Foundations [*Defunct*]
UHF	Unrestricted Hartree-Fock [*Wave-Function*]
UHFDF	Ultrahigh-Frequency Direction Finder
UHFF	Ultrahigh-Frequency Filter
UHFG	Ultrahigh-Frequency Generator
UHF/HF	Ultrahigh-Frequency/High-Frequency (MCD)
UHFJ	Ultrahigh-Frequency Jammer
UHFO	Ultrahigh-Frequency Oscillator
UHFR	Ultrahigh-Frequency Receiver
UHFS	Unsteady Heat Flux Sensor
UHG	Urban History Group [*Defunct*] (EA)
UHHH	Khabarovsk/Novy [*USSR*] [*ICAO location identifier*] (ICLI)
UHHO	Troitskoye [*USSR*] [*ICAO location identifier*] (ICLI)
UHI	Upper Head Injection [*Nuclear energy*] (NRCH)
UHi	Utah State Historical Society, Salt Lake City, UT [*Library symbol*] [*Library of Congress*] (LCLS)
UHJA	United Hungarian Jews of America (EA)
UHK	University of Hard Knocks [*West Virginia*] [*"University" founded by Jim Comstock and based on the expression "school of hard knocks"*]
UHL	Unge Hoyres Landsforbund [*Norway*] [*Political party*] (EAIO)
UHL	User Header Label (CMD)
UHLCADS	Ultra-High-Level Container Airdrop System [*Military*] (MCD)
UHLI	United Home Life Insurance Co. [*Greenwood, IN*] [*NASDAQ symbol*] (NQ)
UHMC	Upper Harbour Mooring Committee [*Australia*]
UHML	Lavrentiya [*USSR*] [*ICAO location identifier*] (ICLI)
UHMR	Beringovsky [*USSR*] [*ICAO location identifier*] (ICLI)
UHMS	Ultrasonic Helmet Mounted Sight [*Army*] (MCD)
UHMS	Undersea and Hyperbaric Medical Society (EA)
UHMW	Ultrahigh Molecular Weight
UHMW-PE	Ultrahigh Molecular Weight Polyethylene [*Organic chemistry*]
UHP	Ugaritic-Hebrew Philology [*Rome*] [*M. Dahood*] [*A publication*] (BJA)
UHP	Ultra-High Performance [*in UHP Imposer, a product of Opti-Copy, Inc.*]
UHP	Ultrahigh Power
UHP	Ultrahigh Purity
UHP	Undergraduate Helicopter Pilot Training [*Army*]
UHPFB	University of Hawaii Press
UHPFB	Untreated Hard Pressed Fiberboard
UHPS	Underground Hydro-Pumped Storage [*Room*]
UHPT	Undergraduate Helicopter Pilot Training (MCD)
UHQ	Utah Historical Quarterly [*A publication*]
UHR	Ultrahigh Resistance
UHR	Ultrahigh Resolution
UHR	United Hearne Resources Ltd. [*Vancouver Stock Exchange symbol*]
UHR	Upper Hybrid Resonance [*Spectroscopy*]
UHRA	United Hunts Racing Association [*Later, NSHA*]
UHR-ESCA	Ultrahigh-Resolution Electron Spectrometer for Chemical Analysis
UHRN	United Hearne Resources Ltd. [*NASDAQ symbol*] (NQ)
UHS	Ultimate Heat Sink [*Nuclear energy*] (NRCH)
UHS	Ultrahigh Speed
UHS	Unit Handling System
UHS	Unitarian Historical Society [*Later, UUHS*] (EA)
UHS	United HIAS Service (EA)
UHS	Universalist Historical Society [*Later, UUHS*] (EA)
UHS	University of Health Sciences - Chicago Medical School
UHSA	United Halsingian Society of America [*Defunct*] (EA)
UHS-CMS	University of Health Sciences - Chicago Medical School
UHSI	Universal Health Services, Inc. [*NASDAQ symbol*] (NQ)
UHT	Ultrahigh Temperature
UHT	Ultrasonic Hardness Tester
UHT	Underheat
UHT	Unit Horizontal Tail
UHT	United Hebrew Trades of the State of New York (EA)
UHT	Universal Hand Tool
UHT	Universal Health Realty [*NYSE symbol*] (SPSG)
UHT	Universal Horizontal Tail [*Aviation*] (NG)
UHTPB	Unsaturated Hydroxyl-Terminated Polybutadiene [*Organic chemistry*]
UHTREX	Ultrahigh-Temperature Reactor Experiment [*Nuclear energy*]
UHTV	Unmanned Hypersonic Test Vehicle (MCD)
UHV	Ultrahigh Vacuum
UHV	Ultrahigh Voltage
UHV	Under Hatch Valve
UHVA	United Hellenic Voters of America (EA)
UHVC	Ultrahigh Vacuum Chamber
UHVS	Ultrahigh Vacuum System
UI	Societe de Transport Aerien du Rwanda [*ICAO designator*] (FAAC)
UI	Uj Iras [*A publication*]
U/I	Under Instructions (ADA)
UI	Underground Injection [*of wastes*]
UI	Underwear Institute [*Later, NKMA*] (EA)
UI	Undifferentiated Infiltrating [*Tumor*] [*Oncology*]
UI	Unemployment Insurance
UI	Unexplained Infertility
U/I	Unidentified
UI	Union Institute (EA)
UI	Union Interparlementaire [*Inter-Parliamentary Union*] (EAIO)
UI	Union-Intersection [*Statistics*]
UI	Unit of Issue (KSC)
UI	United Inches
UI	United Inns, Inc. [*NYSE symbol*] (SPSG)
ui	United Kingdom Miscellaneous Islands [*MARC country of publication code*] [*Library of Congress*] (LCCP)
UI	Universal Instantiation [*Rule of quantification*] [*Logic*]
U of I	University of Illinois [*Urbana, IL*]
U of I	University of Iowa [*Iowa City, IA*] (OICC)
UI	Unreported Income [*IRS*]
UI	Uranium Institute [*London, England*] (EAIO)
UI	Urban Initiatives (EA)
UI	Urban Institute (EA)
UI	Urinary Infection [*Medicine*]
UI	USE, Incorporated [*Acronym is now organization's official name*] (EA)
UI	User Interface
UI	Ut Infra [*As Below*] [*Latin*]
UIA	Ukrainian Institute of America (EA)
UIA	Ultrasonic Industry Association (EA)
UIA	Unemployment Insurance Act [*Canada*]
UIA	Union of International Associations [*See also UAI*] [*Brussels, Belgium*] (EAIO)
UIA	Union of International Associations. Documents [*A publication*]
UIA	Union Internationale des Architectes [*International Union of Architects*] (EAIO)
UIA	Union Internationale des Avocats [*International Union of Lawyers*]
UIA	Union Internationale Contre l'Alcoolisme

UIA .... Union Internationale des Syndicats des Industries Alimentaires
UIA .... Unit Identifier Applications   (MCD)
UIA .... United Israel Appeal   (EA)
UIA .... Universidad Iberoamericana, Mexico, DF, Mexico [*OCLC symbol*]   (OCLC)
UIA .... Uranium Institute of America   (EA)
UIA .... Usable Inside Area   (MCD)
UIAA .... Chita/Kadala [*USSR*] [*ICAO location identifier*]   (ICLI)
UIAA .... Union Internationale des Associations d'Alpinisme [*International Union of Alpine Associations*] [*Switzerland*]
UIAA .... Union Internationale des Associations d'Annonceurs [*International Union of Advertisers Associations*]
UIAA .... Union Internationale des Assureurs Aeronautiques
UIACM ..... Union Internationale des Automobile-Clubs Medicaux [*International Union of Associations of Doctor-Motorists*]
UIAL .... United Italian American League   (EA)
UIALC ...... United Italian American Labor Council   (EA)
UIAMS ...... Union Internationale d'Action Morale et Sociale [*International Union for Moral and Social Action*]
UIAPME ... Union Internationale de l'Artisanat et des Petites et Moyennes Entreprises [*International Association of Crafts and Small and Medium-Sized Enterprises*]
UIAPPA .... Union Internationale des Associations de Prevention de la Pollution Atmospherique [*International Union of Air Pollution Prevention Associations*]   (EAIO)
UIARVEP ... Unione Italiana Agenti Rappresentati Viaggiatori e Piazzisti [*Italian Union of Agents and Travelers*]
UIASPPA ... Uniform Individual Accident and Sickness Policy Provisions Act [*National Association of Insurance Commissioners*]
UIAT .... Union Internationale des Syndicats des Industries de l'Alimentation et des Tabacs
UIATF .... United Indians of All Tribes Foundation   (EA)
UIB .... Quibdo [*Colombia*] [*Airport symbol*]   (OAG)
UIB .... Union Internationale des Maitres Boulangers [*International Union of Master Bakers*]
UIB .... Unione Italiana Bancari [*Italian Union of Bank Employees*]
UIBB .... Bratsk [*USSR*] [*ICAO location identifier*]   (ICLI)
UIBC .... Unsaturated Iron-Binding Capacity [*Clinical chemistry*]
UIBPIP ...... United International Bureau for the Protection of Intellectual Property [*Superseded by WIPO*]
UIBWM .... Trade Unions International of Workers of Building, Wood, and Building Materials Industries
UIC .... Ufficio Italiano dei Cambi [*Italian Exchange Office*]   (IMH)
UIC .... Ultraviolet Image Converter
UIC .... Underground Injection Control [*Environmental Protection Agency*]
UIC .... Unemployment Insurance Code   (OICC)
UIC .... Unemployment Insurance Commission [*Canada*]
UIC .... Unidad de Izquierda Comunista [*Unity of the Communist Left*] [*Mexico*] [*Political party*]   (PPW)
UIC .... Union of International Conventions
UIC .... Union Internationale des Chemins de Fer [*International Union of Railways*]   (EAIO)
UIC .... Union Internationale de Cristallographie [*International Union of Crystallography*]   (EAIO)
UIC .... Unit Identification Code [*Army*]   (AABC)
UIC .... United Industrial Corporation [*NYSE symbol*]   (SPSG)
UIC .... Upper Information Center [*Aviation*]
UIC .... Urban Information Center [*Milwaukee Urban Observatory*] [*Information service or system*] [*Ceased operations*]   (IID)
UIC .... Urinary Immune Complex
UIC .... User Identification Code
UICA .... Union of Independent Colleges of Art   (EA)
UICA .... Union Internationale des Constructeurs d'Ascenseurs [*International Union of Elevator Constructors - IUEC*]
UICANY ... United Irish Counties Association of New York   (EA)
UICB .... Union Internationale des Centres du Batiment [*International Union of Building Centers*] [*British*]
UICC .... Union Internationale Contre le Cancer [*International Union Against Cancer*] [*Switzerland*]
UICC .... University of Illinois at Chicago Circle
UICC Monogr Ser ... UICC [*Union Internationale Contre le Cancer*] Monograph Series [*A publication*]
UICC Tech Rep Ser ... UICC [*Union Internationale Contre le Cancer*] Technical Report Series [*A publication*]
UICGF .... Union Internationale du Commerce en Gros de la Fleur [*International Union for the Wholesale Flower Trade*]
UICI .... United Insurance Companies, Inc. [*NASDAQ symbol*]   (NQ)
UICIO .... Unit Identification Code Information Officer [*Military*]   (AABC)
UICM .... Union Internationale Catholique des Classes Moyennes [*International Catholic Union of the Middle Classes*]
UICN .... Union Internationale pour la Conservation de la Nature et de Ses Ressources [*International Union for Conservation of Nature and Natural Resources*]
UICO .... UNICO, Inc. [*NASDAQ symbol*]   (NQ)
UICP .... Uniform Inventory Control Points System [*Military*]
UICP .... Union Internationale de la Couverture et Plomberie   (EA)
UICPA .... Union Internationale de Chimie Pure et Appliquee [*International Union of Pure and Applied Chemistry*]

UICR .... Union Internationale des Chauffeurs Routiers [*International Union of Lorry Drivers - IULD*]   (EAIO)
UICSM ...... University of Illinois Committee on School Mathematics
UICT .... Union Internationale Contre la Tuberculose [*International Union Against Tuberculosis - IUAT*]   (EAIO)
UICTMR .. Union Internationale Contre la Tuberculose et les Maladies Respiratoires [*International Union Against Tuberculosis and Lung Disease - IUATLD*]   (EAIO)
UICWA ..... United Infants' and Children's Wear Association   (EA)
UID .... Selected Decisions by Umpire for Northern Ireland, Respecting Claims to Benefit [*A publication*]   (DLA)
UID .... Unemployment Insurance Department
UID .... Usable Inside Depth   (MCD)
UIDA .... Union Internationale des Organisations de Detaillants de la Branche Alimentaire [*International Federation of Grocers' Associations*]
UIDA .... United Indian Development Association   (EA)
UIDAC ...... Unione Italiana Dipendenti Aziende Commerciali ed Affini [*Italian Union of Commerical and Allied Workers*]
UIE .... UNESCO Institute for Education
UIE .... Union Internationale d'Editeurs [*International Publishers Association - IPA*]   (EAIO)
UIE .... Union Internationale d'Electrothermie [*International Union for Electroheat*]   (EAIO)
UIE .... Union Internationale des Etudiants [*International Union of Students - IUS*]   (EAIO)
UIEA .... Union Internationale des Etudiants en Architecture [*International Union of Students in Architecture*]
UIEC .... Union Internationale de l'Exploitation Cinematographique [*International Union of Cinematographic Exhibitors*]   (EAIO)
UIEIS .... Union Internationale pour l'Etude des Insectes Sociaux [*International Union for the Study of Social Insects - IUSSI*] [*Netherlands*]
UIEO .... Union of International Engineering Organizations
UIEP .... Union Internationale des Entrepreneurs de Peinture
UIEPB .... Union Internationale des Employes Professionnels et de Bureau
UIES .... Union Internationale d'Education pour la Sante [*International Union of Health Education - IUHE*] [*Paris, France*]   (EAIO)
UIES .... Union Internationale des Employes de Service
UIES .... Union Internationale d'Etudes Sociales [*International Union for Social Studies*]
UIEUA ...... Upravlenie Yadernymi Energeticheskimi Ustanovkami [*A publication*]
UIF .... Ultraviolet Interference Filter
UIF .... Unfavorable Information File [*Military*]
UIF .... Union Immobiliere de France
UIF .... Universal Intermolecular Force
UIF .... Unserviceable Items File
UIF .... USLIFE Income Fund, Inc. [*NYSE symbol*]   (SPSG)
UIFA .... Union Internationale des Femmes Architectes [*International Union of Women Architects - IUWA*]   (EAIO)
UIFI .... Union Internationale des Fabricants d'Impermeables
UIFL .... Union Internationale des Federations de Detaillants en Produits Laitiers
uig .... Uigur [*MARC language code*] [*Library of Congress*]   (LCCP)
UIG .... Uniglobe International Energy Corp. [*Vancouver Stock Exchange symbol*]
UIG .... User Instruction Group
UIGDC ...... Unione Internazionale des Giovani Democratici Cristiana [*International Union of Young Christian Democrats*]
UIGSE .... Union Internationale des Guides et Scouts d'Europe [*International Union of European Guides and Scouts - IUEGS*] [*Chateau Landon, France*]   (EAIO)
UIH .... Urban and Industrial Health   (KSC)
UIHE .... Union Internationale de l'Humanisme et de l'Ethique
UIHMSU .. Union Internationale d'Hygiene et de Medecine Scolaires et Universitaires [*International Union of School and University Health and Medicine - IUSUHM*] [*Brussels, Belgium*]   (EAIO)
UIHPS .... Union Internationale d'Histoire et de Philosophie des Sciences
UII .... Universal Identification Interface [*Allen-Bradley Co.*]
UII .... Utila Island [*Honduras*] [*Airport symbol*] [*Obsolete*]   (OAG)
UIIG .... Union Internationale de l'Industrie du Gaz [*International Gas Union - IGU*] [*Paris, France*]   (EAIO)
UIII .... Irkutsk [*USSR*] [*ICAO location identifier*]   (ICLI)
UIII .... Urban Information Interpreters, Incorporated   (IID)
UIIO .... Ust-Ordynsky [*USSR*] [*ICAO location identifier*]   (ICLI)
UIIPI .... Unione Italiana Lavoratori Pubblico Impiego [*Public Office Workers Union*] [*Italy*]   (EY)
UIJA .... Union Internationale des Journalistes Agricoles [*International Union of Agricultural Journalists*]
UIJDC .... Union Internationale de Jeunesse Democrate Chretienne [*International Union of Young Christian Democrats*]
UIJPLF ..... Union Internationale des Journalistes et de la Presse de Langue Francaise [*International Union of French-Language Journalists and Press - IUFLJP*]   (EAIO)
UIJS .... Union Internationale de la Jeunesse Socialiste [*International Union of Socialist Youth*]
UIKB .... Bodaybo [*USSR*] [*ICAO location identifier*]   (ICLI)

UIKK	Kirensk [*USSR*] [*ICAO location identifier*] (ICLI)
UIKW	Vitim [*USSR*] [*ICAO location identifier*] (ICLI)
UIL	Quillayute, WA [*Location identifier*] [*FAA*] (FAAL)
UIL	Unione Italiana del Lavoro [*Italian Union of Labor*]
UIL	United Illuminating Co. [*NYSE symbol*] (SPSG)
UIL	UNIVAC Interactive Language [*Data processing*] (IEEE)
UIL	University of Iowa, School of Library Science, Iowa City, IA [*OCLC symbol*] (OCLC)
UILA	Unione Italiana Lavoratori Assicurazioni [*Italian Union of Insurance Workers*]
UILAM	Unione Italiana Lavoratori Albergo e Mensa [*Italian Union of Hotel and Restaurant Workers*]
UILAS	Unione Italiana Lavoratori Assicurazioni [*Assurance Company Workers Union*] [*Italy*] (EY)
UILC	Unione Italiana Lavoratori Chimici [*Italian Union of Chemical Workers*]
UILE	Union Internationale pour la Liberte d'Enseignement [*International Union for the Liberty of Education*]
UIL-GAS	Unione Italiana Lavoratori Aziende Gas [*Italian Union of Gas Workers*]
UILI	Union Internationale des Laboratoires Independents [*International Union of Independent Laboratories*] [*Elstree, Hertfordshire, England*] (EAIO)
UILIA	Unione Italiana Lavoratori Industrie Alimentari [*Italian Union of Food-Processing Workers*]
UILIAS	Unione Italiana Lavoratori Industrie Alimentari Saccariferi [*Food Workers Union*] [*Italy*] (EY)
UILIC	Unione Italiana Lavoratori Imposte Consumo [*Italian Union of Food Tax Levy Workers*]
UILL	University of Illinois. Studies in Language and Literature [*A publication*]
U Ill LB	University of Illinois. Law Bulletin [*A publication*] (DLA)
U Ill L Bull	University of Illinois. Law Bulletin [*A publication*] (DLA)
U Ill L F	University of Illinois. Law Forum [*A publication*]
U Ill L Forum	University of Illinois. Law Forum [*A publication*]
U Ill LR	University of Illinois. Law Review [*A publication*]
U Ill L Rev	University of Illinois. Law Review [*A publication*]
UILM	Unione Italiana Lavoratori Metallurgici [*Italian Metalworkers' Union*]
UILPEM	Unione Italiana Lavoratori Petrolieri e Metanieri [*Italian Union of Oil and Methane Gas Workers*]
UILS	Unione Italiana Lavoratori Saccariferi [*Italian Union of Sugar Industry Workers*]
UILT	Unione Italiana Lavoratori delle Terra [*Italian Union of Landworkers*]
UILT	Unione Italiana Lavoratori Tessili [*Italian Union of Textile Workers*]
UILTATEP	Unione Italiana Lavoratori Trasporti Ausiliari Traffico e Portuali [*Transport and Associated Workers Union*] [*Italy*] (EY)
UILTRAS	Unione Italiana Trasporti ed Ausiliari del Traffico [*Italian Union of Transport Workers and Auxiliary Services*]
UILTuCS	Unione Italiana Lavoratori Turismo Commercio e Servizi [*Tourism industry*] [*Italy*] (EY)
UILU	University of Illinois, Urbana
UILVECA	Unione Italiana Lavoratori Vetro, Ceramica, ed Abrasivi [*Italian Union of Glass, Ceramics, and Abrasive Workers*]
UIM	Quitman, TX [*Location identifier*] [*FAA*] (FAAL)
UIM	Ufficio Informazioni Militare [*Office of Military Information*] [*Italian*]
UIM	Ultra-Intelligent Machine
UIM	Ultrasonic Interferometer Manometer [*Instrumentation*]
UIM	Union of International Motorboating (EA)
UIM	Union Internationale des Magistrats [*International Association of Judges - IAJ*] (EAIO)
UIM	Union Internationale des Metis [*International Union of Individuals of Mixed Parentage*]
UIM	Union Internationale Monarchiste [*Weinsberg, Federal Republic of Germany*] (EAIO)
UIM	Union Internationale Motonautique [*Union of International Motorboating*] (EAIO)
UIM	Unione Italiana Marittimi [*Italian Union of Seamen*]
UIMC	Union Internationale des Services Medicaux des Chemins de Fer [*International Union of Railway Medical Services*]
UIMEC	Unione Italiana Mezzadri e Coltivatori Diretti [*Land Workers Union*] [*Italy*] (EY)
UIMI	United Indian Missions, International (EA)
UIMJ	Union Internationale des Maisons de Jeunesse [*Service de la FIJC*]
UIMP	Union Internationale pour la Protection de la Moralite Publique
UIMVT	Union Internationale Contre les Maladies Veneriennes et les Treponematoses [*International Union Against the Venereal Diseases and the Treponematoses - IUVDT*]
UIN	Quincy [*Illinois*] [*Airport symbol*] (OAG)
UIN	USR Industries, Inc. [*AMEX symbol*] (SPSG)
UINA	Uintah Energy Corp. [*NASDAQ symbol*] (NQ)
UIND	USR Industries, Inc. [*NASDAQ symbol*] (NQ)
UINF	Union Internationale de la Navigation Fluviale [*International Union for Inland Navigation - IUIN*] (EAIO)
UINL	Union Internationale du Notariat Latin [*International Union of Latin Notaries*]
UINN	Nizhneudinsk [*USSR*] [*ICAO location identifier*] (ICLI)
UINP	Unit of Insect Neurophysiology and Pharmacology [*University of Cambridge*] [*British*] (IRUK)
UIO	Quito [*Ecuador*] [*Airport symbol*] (OAG)
UIO	Union Internationale des Orientalistes [*International Union of Orientalists*]
UIO	United Infertility Organization (EA)
UIO	Units in Operation [*Business term*]
UIO	Utility Iterative Operation
UIOD	User Input/Output Devices [*Data processing*] (RDA)
UIOF	Union Internationale des Organismes Familiaux [*International Union of Family Organizations - IUFO*] [*France*]
UIOOT	Union Internationale des Organismes Officiels de Tourisme [*International Union of Official Travel Organizations*]
UIOVD	Union Internationale des Ouvriers du Vetement pour Dames [*International Ladies' Garment Workers' Union - ILGW*]
U Iowa L Rev	University of Iowa. Law Review [*A publication*] (DLA)
UIP	Quimper [*France*] [*Airport symbol*] (OAG)
UIP	Unallowable Items Program [*IRS*]
UIP	Unfair Industrial Practice
UIP	Union Internationale d'Associations de Proprietaires de Wagons Particuliers [*International Union of Private Railway Truck Owners' Associations*] (EAIO)
UIP	Union Internationale de Patinage [*International Skating Union - ISU*] [*Davos-Platz, Switzerland*] (EAIO)
UIP	Union Internationale de Physique Pure et Appliquee [*International Union of Pure and Applied Physics*]
UIP	Union Internationale des Publicitaires
UIP	Union Interparlementaire
UIP	Unione Italiana Pescatori [*Italian Union of Fishermen*]
UIP	United Ireland Party
UIP	University of Illinois Press
UIP	Usable in Place (MCD)
UIP	Usual Interstitial Pneumonia [*Medicine*]
UIPA	United Indian Planners Association [*Defunct*] (EA)
UIPC	Underground Injection Practices Council (EA)
UIPC	Union Internationale de la Presse Catholique [*International Catholic Press Union*]
UIPCG	Union Internationale de la Patisserie, Confiserie, Glacerie [*International Union of Bakers and Confectioners*]
UIPD	Ulrich's International Periodicals Directory [*A publication*]
UIPE	Union Internationale de Protection de l'Enfance [*International Union for Child Welfare - IUCW*] [*Geneva, Switzerland*] (EA)
UIPFB	Union Internationale de la Propriete Fonciere Batie [*International Union of Landed Property Owners*]
UIPI	Union Internacional de Proteccion a la Infancia [*International Union for Child Welfare*]
UIPI	Union Internationale de la Propriete Immobiliere [*International Union of Property Owners*] [*Paris, France*] (EAIO)
UIPM	Union Internationale de la Presse Medicale [*International Union of the Medical Press*]
UIPMB	Union Internationale de Pentathlon Moderne et Biathlon [*International Union for Modern Pentathlon and Biathlon*] (EAIO)
UIPN	Union Internationale pour la Protection de la Nature [*International Union for the Protection of Nature - IUPN*] [*Later, IUCN*]
UIPPA	Union Internationale de Physique Pure et Appliquee [*International Union of Pure and Applied Physics*]
UIPPI	Union Internationale pour la Protection de la Propriete Industrielle [*International Union for the Protection of Industrial Property*]
UIPRE	Union Internationale de la Presse Radiotechnique et Electronique [*Freiburg, Federal Republic of Germany*] (EAIO)
UIPVT	Union Internationale Contre le Peril Venerien et la Treponematose [*International Union Against the Venereal Diseases and the Treponematoses*]
UIQ	Upper Inner Quadrant [*Anatomy*]
UIR	Quirindi [*Australia*] [*Airport symbol*] [*Obsolete*] (OAG)
UIR	Union Internationale des Radioecologistes [*International Union of Radioecologists - IUR*] (EAIO)
UIR	Union Internationale des Rembourreurs de l'Amerique du Nord [*Upholsterers' International Union of North America - UIU*] [*Canada*]
UIR	Unitary Irreducible Representation
UIR	United International Research, Inc.
UIR	University-Industry Research Program [*University of Wisconsin-Madison*] [*Information service or system*] (IID)
UIR	Upper Flight Information Region [*Aviation*] (FAAC)
UIR	Upper Information Region (NATG)
UIR	Urban Intelligence Reports (CINC)
UIR	User Instruction Register
UIRC	Universal Interline Reservations Code
UIRD	Union Internationale de la Resistance et de la Deportation [*International Union of Resistance and Deportee Movements*]
UIRR	University-Industry Research Relationship

UIR/Res Newsl ... UIR [*University-Industry Research Program*]/Research Newsletter [*A publication*]
UIS .... Ulster-Irish Society　(EA)
UIS .... Unemployment Insurance Service [*Department of Labor*]
UIS .... Union Immobiliere de Supermarches et Centres Commerciaux [*French*]
UIS .... Union Internationale de Secours [*International Relief Union*]
UIS .... Union Internationale de Speleologie [*International Union of Speleology - IUS*]　(EAIO)
UIS .... Union Internationale des Syndicats des Travailleurs des Transports [*Trade Unions International of Transport Workers*]　(EAIO)
UIS .... Unisys Corp. [*NYSE symbol*]　(SPSG)
UIS .... Unit Identification System
UIS .... United Information Services, Inc.　(IID)
UIS .... Universal Isolation Switch
UIS .... Unlimited Intermediate Storage [*Industrial engineering*]
UIS .... Upper Internals Structure [*Nuclear energy*]　(NRCH)
UISA .... United Inventors and Scientists of America　(EA)
UISAE .... Union Internationale des Sciences Anthropologiques et Ethnologiques [*International Union of Anthropological and Ethnological Sciences - IUAES*]　(EAIO)
UISB .... Union Internationale des Sciences Biologiques [*International Union of Biological Sciences*]
UISC .... Unreported Interstate Shipment of Cigarettes
UISDC .... Unemployment Insurance Service Design Center [*Department of Labor*]
UISE .... Union Internationale de Secours aux Enfants
UISG .... Union Internationale des Superieures Majeures [*International Union of Superiors General*] [*Rome, Italy*]　(EAIO)
UISIF .... Union Internationale des Societies d'Ingenieurs Forestiers [*International Union of Societies of Foresters - IUSF*] [*Ottawa, ON*]　(EAIO)
UISJM ...... Upper Internals Structure Jacking Mechanism [*Nuclear energy*]　(NRCH)
UISM .... Union Internationale des Syndicats des Mineurs [*Miners' Trade Unions International*]
UISMM ..... Union Internationale des Syndicats des Industries Metallurgiques et Mecaniques
UISMTE ... Union Internationale des Syndicats des Mineurs et des Travailleurs de l'Energie [*Trade Unions International of Miners and Workers in Energy - TUIMWE*]　(EAIO)
UISN .... Union Internationale des Sciences de la Nutrition [*International Union of Nutritional Sciences - IUNS*] [*Wageningen, Netherlands*]　(EA)
UISP .... Union Internationale des Societes de la Paix [*International Union of Peace Societies*]
UISP .... Union Internationale des Syndicats de Police [*International Union of Police Syndicates*]　(EAIO)
UISPI .... Urethane Institute, Society of the Plastics Industry　(EA)
UISPP .... Union Internationale des Sciences Prehistoriques et Protohistoriques [*International Union of Prehistoric and Protohistoric Sciences*]
UISPTT ..... Union Internationale Sportive des Postes, des Telephones, et des Telecommunications [*International Sports Union of Post, Telephone, and Telecommunications Services - ISUPTTS*] [*Switzerland*]
UISTABP ... Union Internacional de Sindicatos de Trabajadores de la Agricultura, de los Bosques, y de las Plantaciones [*Trade Unions International of Agricultural, Forestry, and Plantation Workers*]
UISTAF ..... Union Internationale des Syndicats des Travailleurs Agricoles et Forestiers et des Organisations des Paysans Travailleurs
UISTAFP .. Union Internationale des Syndicats des Travailleurs de l'Agriculture, des Forets, et des Plantations [*Trade Unions International of Agriculture, Forestry, and Plantation Workers - TUIAFPW*] [*Prague, Czechoslovakia*]　(EAIO)
UISTAV .... Union Internationale pour la Science, la Technique, et les Applications du Vide [*International Union for Vacuum Science, Technique, and Applications - IUVSTA*]　(EAIO)
UISTC .... Union Internationale des Syndicats des Travailleurs du Commerce [*Trade Unions International of Workers in Commerce*]
UISTICPS ... Union Internationale des Syndicats des Travailleurs des Industries Chimiques du Petrole et Similaires
UIT .... Jaluit [*Marshall Islands*] [*Airport symbol*]　(OAG)
UIT .... Ultraviolet Imaging Telescope
UIT .... Union des Independants de Tananarive [*Union of Independents of Tananarive*]
UIT .... Union Internationale de Tir [*International Shooting Union*] [*Federal Republic of Germany*] [*See also IS*]　(EAIO)
UIT .... Union Internationale des Typographes [*International Typographical Union - ITU*]
UIT .... Unit Impulse Train
UIT .... Unit Investment Trusts [*Standard and Poor's Corp.*] [*Information service or system*]
UITA .... Union of International Technical Associations [*See also UATI*] [*ICSU*] [*Paris, France*]　(EAIO)
UITA .... Union Internationale des Travailleurs de l'Alimentation et des Branches Connexes [*International Union of Food and Allied Workers Associations*]

UITAM ..... Union Internationale de Mecanique Theorique et Appliquee [*International Union of Theoretical and Applied Mechanics*]
UITBB .... Union Internationale des Syndicats des Travailleurs du Batiment, du Bois, et des Materiaux de Construction [*Trade Unions International of Workers of the Building, Wood, and Building Materials Industries*]
UITCA ...... International Union of Co-operative and Associated Tourism　(EAIO)
Uitg .... Uitgave [*Edition*] [*Netherlands*]　(ILCA)
Uitgaben Natuurwet Stud Suriname Ned Antillen ... Uitgaben Natuurwetenschappelijke Studichring voor Suriname en de Nederlandse Antillen [*A publication*]
Uitg Natuurwet Studiekring Suriname Ned Antillen ... Uitgaven Natuurwetenschappelijke Studiekring voor Suriname en de Nederlandse Antillen [*A publication*]
Uitg Natuurwet Werkgroep Ned Antillen (Curacao) ... Uitgaven. Natuurwetenschappelijke Werkgroep Nederlandse Antillen (Curacao) [*A publication*]
UITP .... Union Internationale des Transports Publics [*International Union of Public Transport*]　(EAIO)
UIT Rep ..... UIT [*Ulsan Institute of Technology*] Report [*A publication*]
Uitvoerige Versl Sticht Bosbouwproefstn De Dorschkamp ... Uitvoerige Verslagen van de Stichting Bosbouwproefstation "De Dorschkamp" [*A publication*]
Uitvoer Versl Bosbouwproefsta ... Uitvoerige Verslagen van de Stichting Bosbouwproefstation "De Dorschkamp" [*A publication*]
UIU .... Universal Interactive Unit [*Telecommunications*]
UIU .... University of Illinois, Urbana, IL [*OCLC symbol*]　(OCLC)
UIU .... Upholsterers' International Union of North America [*Absorbed by USWA*]
UIU .... Upper Iowa University [*Fayette*]
UIUC .... University of Illinois, Urbana-Champaign
UIUH .... Khorinsk [*USSR*] [*ICAO location identifier*]　(ICLI)
UIUSD ...... Union Internationale Universitaire Socialiste et Democratique [*International Union of Social Democratic Teachers*]
UIUU .... Ulan-Ude/Mukhino [*USSR*] [*ICAO location identifier*]　(ICLI)
UIV .... Union Internationale des Villes et Pouvoirs Locaux [*International Union of Local Authorities*]
UIW .... United Iron Workers
UIW .... Usable Inside Width　(MCD)
UIWU .... United Israel World Union　(EA)
UIWV .... United Indian War Veterans, USA　(EA)
UIZ .... Utica, MI [*Location identifier*] [*FAA*]　(FAAL)
UJ .... Air Lanka [*Sri Lanka*] [*ICAO designator*]　(FAAC)
UJ .... Uganda Journal [*A publication*]
UJ .... Ungarische Jahrbuecher [*A publication*]
UJ .... Union Jack
UJ .... Union Joint　(MSA)
UJ .... Unique Jargon
UJ .... Uniwersytet Jagiellonski [*A publication*]
U de J .... Ursulines of Jesus [*Roman Catholic women's religious order*]
UJ .... Uyoku Jiten [*A publication*]
UJA .... United Jewish Appeal　(EA)
UJAFJP .... United Jewish Appeal - Federation of Jewish Philanthropies of New York　(EA)
UJB .... UJB Financial Corp. [*Formerly, United Jersey Banks*] [*NYSE symbol*]　(SPSG)
UJB .... Umbilical Junction Box
U Jb .... Ungarische Jahrbuecher [*A publication*]
U Jb .... Ural-Altaische Jahrbuecher [*A publication*]
UJC .... Union Jack Club [*British military*]　(DMA)
UJC .... Union de la Jeunesse Congolaise [*Congolese Youth Union*]
UJC .... Union Junior College [*New Jersey*]
UJC .... Universal Japanese Coupe [*Automotive engineering*]
UJC .... Urbana Junior College [*Ohio*]
UJC .... Urgency Justification Code [*Military*]　(AFIT)
UJCC(M-L) ... Union de la Jeunesse Communiste du Canada (Marxiste-Leniniste)
UJCD .... Union de la Jeunesse de la Cote d'Ivoire [*Ivory Coast Youth Union*]
UJCD Union Jeunes Chir Dent ... UJCD. Union des Jeunes Chirurgiens-Dentistes [*A publication*]
UJCL .... Universal Job Control Language
UJCML ..... Union des Jeunesses Communistes Marxistes-Leninistes [*Union of Young Marxist-Leninist Communists*] [*France*] [*Political party*]　(PPE)
UJCT Rep ... UJCT [*Ulsan Junior College of Technology*] Report [*Republic of Korea*] [*A publication*]
UJD .... Ultriusque Juris Doctor [*Doctor of Either Law; i.e., Canon Law or Civil Law*]
UJDG .... Union de la Jeunesse Democratique Gabonaise [*Union of Democratic Youth of Gabon*]
UJDK .... Union de la Jeunesse Democratique du Kongo [*Union of Democratic Youth of the Congo*]
UJDS .... Universitetsjubilaeets Danske Samfund [*A publication*]
UJE .... Universal Jewish Encyclopedia [*New York*] [*1939-1943*] [*A publication*]　(BJA)
UJEKO ...... Union de la Jeunesse Congolaise [*Congolese Youth Union*]
UJF .... Unsatisfied Judgment Fund [*Insurance*]

UJH.......... International Union of Journeymen Horseshoers of the United States and Canada
UJISLAA.. UNESCO [*United Nations Educational, Scientific, and Cultural Organization*] Journal of Information Science, Librarianship, and Archives Administration [*A publication*]
UJJ........... Ujjain [*India*] [*Geomagnetic observatory code*]
UJL........... Uninet Japan Limited [*Telecommunications*]
UJNR....... United States-Japan Cooperative Program on Natural Resources
U/JNT...... Universal Joint [*Automotive engineering*]
UJS........... Universal Jamming System
UJ (SC)..... Unreported Judgments (Supreme Court) [*India*] [*A publication*]
UJSC/EA.. ECA [*Estudios Centroamericanos*]. Universidade Centroamericana Jose Simeon Canas [*San Salvador*] [*A publication*]
UJSP........ United States-Japan Science Program   (MSC)
UJT........... Ultrasonic Journal Tester
UJT........... Unijunction Transistor
UJTS........ United Jewish Teachers Seminary [*Montreal*] [*A publication*] (BJA)
UK............ Air UK Ltd. [*Great Britain*] [*ICAO designator*]   (FAAC)
Uk............. British Library, London, United Kingdom [*Library symbol*] [*Library of Congress*]   (LCLS)
UK............ Pfizer Ltd. [*Great Britain*] [*Research code symbol*]
'Uk............. 'Ukzin   (BJA)
UK............ Unabkoemmlich [*Indispensable, irreplaceable*] [*German military - World War II*]
UK............ Union Carbide Corp. [*NYSE symbol*] [*Wall Street slang name: "Ukelele"*]   (SPSG)
UK............ Union Katangaise [*Katanga Union*]
UK............ Unit Check
UK............ United Kingdom
uk .... United Kingdom [*MARC country of publication code*] [*Library of Congress*]   (LCCP)
UK............ University of Kansas [*Lawrence, KS*]
U d K........ Universum der Kunst [*A publication*]
UK............ Unknown [*A publication*]
UK............ Unknown
UK............ Unknown Worlds [*A publication*]
UK............ Urokinase [*An enzyme*]
UKA.......... Ulster King-at-Arms
UKA.......... United Kingdom Alliance
UkAc......... Accrington Public Library, Accrington, United Kingdom [*Library symbol*] [*Library of Congress*]   (LCLS)
UKAC....... United Kingdom Automation Council [*London, England*]
UKADGE.. United Kingdom Air Defense Ground Environment
UKADR.... United Kingdom NATO Air Defense Region   (NATG)
UKAEA..... United Kingdom Atomic Energy Authority [*London, England*] [*Databank originator and operator*]
UKAEL...... United Kingdom Association for European Law [*British*]
UKaGS...... Church of Jesus Christ of Latter-Day Saints, Genealogical Society Library, Kanab Branch, Stake Center, Kanab, UT [*Library symbol*] [*Library of Congress*]   (LCLS)
UKAIRCCIS ... United Kingdom Air Forces Command, Control, and Information System
U Kan City L Rev ... University of Kansas City. Law Review [*A publication*]
U Kan LR... University of Kansas. Law Review [*A publication*]
U Kan L Rev ... University of Kansas. Law Review [*A publication*]
U of Kansas City L Rev ... University of Kansas City. Law Review [*A publication*]
U of Kansas L Rev ... University of Kansas. Law Review [*A publication*]   (DLA)
U Kans Publ ... University of Kansas. Publications. Library Series [*A publication*]
UKAPC...... United Kingdom Agricultural Production Committee
UKAPE...... United Kingdom Association of Professional Engineers [*A union*]
UKARC..... United Kingdom Agricultural Research Council
UKASE..... University of Kansas Automated Serials
UKASS...... United Kingdom Amalgamated Society of Shipwrights [*A union*]
UKASTA... United Kingdom Agricultural Supply Trade Association   (DS)
UK At Energy Auth At Weapons Res Establ Lib Bibliogr ... United Kingdom. Atomic Energy Authority. Atomic Weapons Research Establishment. Library Bibliography [*A publication*]
UK At Energy Auth At Weapons Res Establ Rep Ser NR ... United Kingdom. Atomic Energy Authority. Atomic Weapons Research Establishment. Report. Series NR [*A publication*]
UK At Energy Auth At Weapons Res Establ Rep Ser O ... United Kingdom. Atomic Energy Authority. Atomic Weapons Research Establishment. Report. Series O [*A publication*]
UK At Energy Auth At Weapons Res Establ Rep Ser R ... United Kingdom. Atomic Energy Authority. Atomic Weapons Research Establishment. Report. Series R [*A publication*]
UK At Energy Auth Auth Health Saf Branch Mem ... United Kingdom. Atomic Energy Authority. Authority Health and Safety Branch. Memorandum [*A publication*]
UK At Energy Auth Auth Health Saf Branch Rep ... Initialism. Atomic Energy Authority. Authority Health and Safety Branch. Report [*A publication*]

UK At Energy Auth Dev Eng Group DEG Rep ... United Kingdom. Atomic Energy Authority. Development and Engineering Group. DEG Report [*A publication*]
UK At Energy Auth Harwell Lab Mem ... United Kingdom Atomic Energy Authority. Harwell Laboratory. Memorandum [*A publication*]
UK At Energy Auth Harwell Lab Rep ... United Kingdom Atomic Energy Authority. Harwell Laboratory. Report [*A publication*]
UK At Energy Auth Health Saf Code Auth Code ... United Kingdom. Atomic Energy Authority. Health and Safety Code. Authority Code [*A publication*]
UK At Energy Auth Ind Group IG Rep ... United Kingdom. Atomic Energy Authority. Industrial Group. IG Report [*A publication*]
UK At Energy Auth Prod Group PG Rep ... United Kingdom. Atomic Energy Authority. Production Group. PG Report [*A publication*]
UK At Energy Auth Radiochem Cent Mem ... United Kingdom. Atomic Energy Authority. Radiochemical Centre. Memorandum [*A publication*]
UK At Energy Auth Radiochem Cent Rep ... United Kingdom Atomic Energy Authority. Radiochemical Centre. Report [*A publication*]
UK At Energy Auth React Group Rep ... United Kingdom. Atomic Energy Authority. Reactor Group. Report [*A publication*]
UK At Energy Auth React Group TRG Rep ... United Kingdom. Atomic Energy Authority. Reactor Group. TRG Report [*A publication*]
UK At Energy Auth Res Group Culham Lab Rep ... United Kingdom. Atomic Energy Authority. Research Group. Culham Laboratory. Report [*A publication*]
UK At Energy Auth Res Group Culham Lab Transl ... United Kingdom. Atomic Energy Authority. Research Group. Culham Laboratory. Translation [*A publication*]
UK At Energy Auth Saf Reliab Dir SRD Rep ... United Kingdom. Atomic Energy Authority. Safety and Reliability Directorate. SRD Report [*A publication*]
UK At Energy Res Establ Anal Method ... United Kingdom. Atomic Energy Research Establishment. Analytical Method [*A publication*]
UK At Energy Res Establ Bibliogr ... United Kingdom. Atomic Energy Research Establishment. Bibliography [*A publication*]
UK At Energy Res Establ Health Phys Med Div Res Prog Rep ... United Kingdom. Atomic Energy Research Establishment. Health Physics and Medical Division. Research Progress Report [*A publication*]
UK At Energy Res Establ Lect ... United Kingdom. Atomic Energy Research Establishment. Lectures [*A publication*]
UK At Energy Res Establ Memo ... United Kingdom. Atomic Energy Research Establishment. Memorandum [*A publication*]
UK At Energy Res Establ Rep ... United Kingdom. Atomic Energy Research Establishment. Report [*A publication*]
UK At Energy Res Establ Transl ... United Kingdom. Atomic Energy Research Establishment. Translation [*A publication*]
UkAul .... Ashton-Under-Lyne Public Library, Ashton-Under-Lyne, United Kingdom [*Library symbol*] [*Library of Congress*]   (LCLS)
UKAWG.... United Kingdom Asian Women's Conference [*London, England*]
UKAWPCM ... United Kingdom Association of Wood Packing Case Makers [*A union*]
UkB........... Birmingham Public Libraries, Birmingham, United Kingdom [*Library symbol*] [*Library of Congress*]   (LCLS)
UKB .... United Kingdom Base [*World War II*]
UKB .... Universal Keyboard [*Data processing*]   (AABC)
UKB .... Unvaniezh Kevredel Breizh [*Federalist Union of Brittany - FUB*] [*Bannalec, France*]   (EAIO)
UKBB .... Kiev/Borispol [*USSR*] [*ICAO location identifier*]   (ICLI)
UKBC .... United Kingdom Bomber Command   (NATG)
UKBelQU ... Queen's University of Belfast, Belfast, United Kingdom [*Library symbol*] [*Library of Congress*]   (LCLS)
UKBHU...... United Kingdom Band of Hope Union   (EAIO)
UkBl .... Blackpool Central Library, Blackpool, United Kingdom [*Library symbol*] [*Library of Congress*]   (LCLS)
UkBlG .... Blackpool Gazette & Herald Ltd., Blackpool, United Kingdom [*Library symbol*] [*Library of Congress*]   (LCLS)
UkBoN....... Bolton Evening News, Bolton, United Kingdom [*Library symbol*] [*Library of Congress*]   (LCLS)
UkBot .... Burton-On-Trent Public Library, Burton-On-Trent, United Kingdom [*Library symbol*] [*Library of Congress*]   (LCLS)
UkBP .... Birmingham Post & Mail Ltd., Birmingham, United Kingdom [*Library symbol*] [*Library of Congress*]   (LCLS)
UkBrP........ Bristol Evening Post, Bristol, United Kingdom [*Library symbol*] [*Library of Congress*]   (LCLS)
UKBS......... United Kingdom Base Section [*World War II*]
UkBU......... Birmingham University, Birmingham, United Kingdom [*Library symbol*] [*Library of Congress*]   (LCLS)
UKC.......... Ukrainian Gold Cross   (EA)
UKC.......... Unit Kind Code [*Military*]   (AFIT)
UKC.......... United Kennel Club   (EA)
UKC.......... University of Kansas City [*Later, University of Missouri at Kansas City*]
UKC.......... University of Kansas City. Review [*A publication*]

UKCC	United Kingdom Central Council [*for Nursing, Midwifery, and Health Visiting*]
UKCC	United Kingdom Commercial Corporation
UkCh	Chelmsford Library, Chelmsford, United Kingdom [*Library symbol*] [*Library of Congress*] (LCLS)
UKCHH	United Kingdom or Continent (Havre to Hamburg) (ROG)
UKCICC....	United Kingdom Commanders-in-Chiefs' Committee
UKCIS	United Kingdom Chemical Information Service [*University of Nottingham*] [*Nottingham, England*] [*Information broker, databank originator, and host*]
UKCMET ...	United Kingdom Council for Music Education and Training (EAIO)
UkCoE	Essex County Newspapers Ltd., Colchester, United Kingdom [*Library symbol*] [*Library of Congress*] (LCLS)
UK Cont	United Kingdom or Continent [*Shipping*] (DS)
UK/Cont (BH) ...	United Kingdom or Continent (Bordeaux-Hamburg) [*Shipping*] (DS)
UK/Cont (GH) ...	United Kingdom or Continent (Gibraltar-Hamburg) [*Shipping*] (DS)
UK/Cont (HH) ...	United Kingdom or Continent (Havre-Hamburg) [*Shipping*] (DS)
UKCOSA...	United Kingdom Council for Overseas Student Affairs (DS)
UkCov	Coventry Corp., Coventry, United Kingdom [*Library symbol*] [*Library of Congress*] (LCLS)
UkCr	Croydon Library, Croydon, United Kingdom [*Library symbol*] [*Library of Congress*] (LCLS)
UKCR	United Kingdom Communication Region [*Air Force*] (MCD)
UKCR	University of Kansas City. Review [*A publication*]
UkCrA	Croydon Advertiser, Croydon, United Kingdom [*Library symbol*] [*Library of Congress*] (LCLS)
UkCraT	Cranfield Institute of Technology, Cranfield, Bedfordshire, United Kingdom [*Library symbol*] [*Library of Congress*] (LCLS)
UkCrC	Coulsdon Library, Croydon, United Kingdom [*Library symbol*] [*Library of Congress*] (LCLS)
UkCrP	Purley Library, Croydon, United Kingdom [*Library symbol*] [*Library of Congress*] (LCLS)
UKCRv	University of Kansas City. Review [*A publication*]
UKCS........	United Kingdom Continental Shelf
UkCU	Cambridge University, Cambridge, United Kingdom [*Library symbol*] [*Library of Congress*] (LCLS)
UkCwN	North Wales Weekly News, Conway, United Kingdom [*Library symbol*] [*Library of Congress*] (LCLS)
UKD...........	Unusual Killing Device [*Counterintelligence*]
UkDo	Doncaster Public Library, Doncaster, United Kingdom [*Library symbol*] [*Library of Congress*] (LCLS)
UkDw.........	Dewsbury Central Library, Dewsbury, United Kingdom [*Library symbol*] [*Library of Congress*] (LCLS)
UkE...........	Edinburgh Public Library, Edinburgh, United Kingdom [*Library symbol*] [*Library of Congress*] (LCLS)
UKE	Uke Resources [*Vancouver Stock Exchange symbol*]
UKE	Ukelele (DSUE)
UkEc..........	Eccles Public Library, Central Library, Eccles, United Kingdom [*Library symbol*] [*Library of Congress*] (LCLS)
UKEMS.....	United Kingdom Environmental Mutagen Society (EAIO)
UkENL......	National Library of Scotland, Edinburgh, United Kingdom [*Library symbol*] [*Library of Congress*] (LCLS)
UkEPh.......	Pharmaceutical Society of Great Britain, Scottish Department, Edinburgh, United Kingdom [*Library symbol*] [*Library of Congress*] (LCLS)
UkERCP....	Royal College of Physicians, Edinburgh, United Kingdom [*Library symbol*] [*Library of Congress*] (LCLS)
UkERCS....	Royal College of Surgeons, Edinburgh, United Kingdom [*Library symbol*] [*Library of Congress*] (LCLS)
UkES	Scottish Central Library, Edinburgh, United Kingdom [*Library symbol*] [*Library of Congress*] (LCLS)
UkEU........	University of Edinburgh, Edinburgh, United Kingdom [*Library symbol*] [*Library of Congress*] (LCLS)
UKF	United Karate Federation (EA)
UKFF.........	Simferopol [*USSR*] [*ICAO location identifier*] (ICLI)
UKFO	United Kingdom for Orders [*Shipping*]
UkGM	Mitchell Library, Glasgow, United Kingdom [*Library symbol*] [*Library of Congress*] (LCLS)
UkGO	George Outram & Co. Ltd., Glasgow, United Kingdom [*Library symbol*] [*Library of Congress*] (LCLS)
UkGP........	Royal Faculty of Procurators in Glasgow, Glasgow, United Kingdom [*Library symbol*] [*Library of Congress*] (LCLS)
UkGU	University of Glasgow, Glasgow, United Kingdom [*Library symbol*] [*Library of Congress*] (LCLS)
UKH	United Keno Hill Mines Ltd. [*Toronto Stock Exchange symbol*]
UkHA	Atomic Energy Research Establishment, Didcot, Oxfordshire, United Kingdom [*Library symbol*] [*Library of Congress*] (LCLS)
UKHAD	United Kingdom and Havre, Antwerp, and Dunkirk [*Shipping*] (DS)
UkHe	Heywood Public Library, Heywood, Lancashire, United Kingdom [*Library symbol*] [*Library of Congress*] (LCLS)
UKHE........	Petrovskoye [*USSR*] [*ICAO location identifier*] (ICLI)
UKHEF	United Kingdom Home Economics Federation [*British*]
UKHH	United Kingdom and Havre-Hamburg [*Shipping*] (DS)
UKHT........	United Kingdom Housing Trust
UkHu.........	Huddersfield Public Libraries, Huddersfield, United Kingdom [*Library symbol*] [*Library of Congress*] (LCLS)
UKI	Ukiah [*California*] [*Seismograph station code, US Geological Survey*] (SEIS)
UKI	Ukiah, CA [*Location identifier*] [*FAA*] (FAAL)
UKIAS.......	United Kingdom Immigrants Advisory Service
UKIBEK	United Kingdom Insurance Brokers European Committee
UKII..........	Kishinev [*USSR*] [*ICAO location identifier*] (ICLI)
UKIP.........	United Kingdom Import Plan
UKIRT.......	United Kingdom Infrared Telescope
UKITO	United Kingdom Information Technology Organization
UKJATFOR ...	United Kingdom Joint Airborne Task Force [*British military*] (DMA)
UK Jt Fire Res Organ Fire Res Tech Pap ...	United Kingdom. Joint Fire Research Organization. Fire Research Technical Paper [*A publication*]
UkK	Keighley Central Library, Keighley, United Kingdom [*Library symbol*] [*Library of Congress*] (LCLS)
UKK..........	Urho Kekkonen [*President of Finland*]
UkKi	Kilmarnock Public Library, Central Library, Dick Institute, Kilmarnock, United Kingdom [*Library symbol*] [*Library of Congress*] (LCLS)
UKKK	Kiev/Zhulyany [*USSR*] [*ICAO location identifier*] (ICLI)
UKKS	Semyenovka [*USSR*] [*ICAO location identifier*] (ICLI)
UkKuK......	Knapp, Drewett & Sons Ltd., Kingston-Upon-Thames, United Kingdom [*Library symbol*] [*Library of Congress*] (LCLS)
UKL	Utashik Lake [*Alaska*] [*Seismograph station code, US Geological Survey*] (SEIS)
UkLA	Associated Newspapers Ltd., London, United Kingdom [*Library symbol*] [*Library of Congress*] (LCLS)
UKLA	Ukalaha [*Quzinkie High School, Alaska*] [*A publication*]
UkLB	Beaverbrook Newspapers Ltd., London, United Kingdom [*Library symbol*] [*Library of Congress*] (LCLS)
UkLBOA ...	British Optical Association, London, United Kingdom [*Library symbol*] [*Library of Congress*] (LCLS)
UkLC	Chemical Society, London, United Kingdom [*Library symbol*] [*Library of Congress*] (LCLS)
UkLCS......	Institute of Commonwealth Studies, London, United Kingdom [*Library symbol*] [*Library of Congress*] (LCLS)
UkLe	Leeds City Library, Leeds, United Kingdom [*Library symbol*] [*Library of Congress*] (LCLS)
UKLF	United Kingdom Land Forces [*Military*]
UkLG........	Guildhall Library, Aldermanbury, London, United Kingdom [*Library symbol*] [*Library of Congress*] (LCLS)
UkLH	Hampstead Public Libraries, Central Library, London, United Kingdom [*Library symbol*] [*Library of Congress*] (LCLS)
UkLHu	A. J. Hurley Ltd., London, United Kingdom [*Library symbol*] [*Library of Congress*] (LCLS)
UkLi..........	Liverpool Public Libraries, Liverpool, United Kingdom [*Library symbol*] [*Library of Congress*] (LCLS)
UkLin.........	City of Lincoln Public Library, Lincoln, United Kingdom [*Library symbol*] [*Library of Congress*] (LCLS)
UkLIO	India Office Library and Records, Foreign and Commonwealth Office, London, United Kingdom [*Library symbol*] [*Library of Congress*] (LCLS)
UkLIP.......	IPC Newspapers Ltd., London, United Kingdom [*Library symbol*] [*Library of Congress*] (LCLS)
UkLiP	Liverpool Daily Post & Echo Ltd., Liverpool, United Kingdom [*Library symbol*] [*Library of Congress*] (LCLS)
UkLiU.......	University of Liverpool, Liverpool, United Kingdom [*Library symbol*] [*Library of Congress*] (LCLS)
UkLJ.........	Jews' College, London, United Kingdom [*Library symbol*] [*Library of Congress*] (LCLS)
UKLL.........	Lvov [*USSR*] [*ICAO location identifier*] (ICLI)
UkLLA	Library Association, London, United Kingdom [*Library symbol*] [*Library of Congress*] (LCLS)
UkLLT......	Lambeth Public Libraries, Tate Central Library, London, United Kingdom [*Library symbol*] [*Library of Congress*] (LCLS)
UkLMS.....	Morning Star Co-Operative Society, London, United Kingdom [*Library symbol*] [*Library of Congress*] (LCLS)
UkLNw......	North West London Press Ltd., London, United Kingdom [*Library symbol*] [*Library of Congress*] (LCLS)
UkLPh	Pharmaceutical Society of Great Britain, London, United Kingdom [*Library symbol*] [*Library of Congress*] (LCLS)
UkLPo	H. Pordes, Publisher and Bookseller, London, United Kingdom [*Library symbol*] [*Library of Congress*] (LCLS)
UkLPR	Public Record Office, London, United Kingdom [*Library symbol*] [*Library of Congress*] (LCLS)
UkLQ........	Friends Reference Library, London, United Kingdom [*Library symbol*] [*Library of Congress*] (LCLS)
UKLR	University of Kansas. Law Review [*A publication*] (DLA)
UkLRCP....	Royal College of Physicians, London, United Kingdom [*Library symbol*] [*Library of Congress*] (LCLS)
UkLRCS....	Royal College of Surgeons of England, London, United Kingdom [*Library symbol*] [*Library of Congress*] (LCLS)
UkLRSM...	Royal Society of Medicine, London, United Kingdom [*Library symbol*] [*Library of Congress*] (LCLS)
UkLS	Science Museum, London, United Kingdom [*Library symbol*] [*Library of Congress*] (LCLS)

UkLTh....... Thomasons Ltd., London, United Kingdom [*Library symbol*] [*Library of Congress*] (LCLS)
UkLU........ University of London, London, United Kingdom [*Library symbol*] [*Library of Congress*] (LCLS)
UkLuH ...... Home Counties Newspapers Ltd., Luton, United Kingdom [*Library symbol*] [*Library of Congress*] (LCLS)
UkLU-K.... University of London, Kings College, London, United Kingdom [*Library symbol*] [*Library of Congress*] (LCLS)
UkLW....... Wellcome Historical Medical Library, London, United Kingdom [*Library symbol*] [*Library of Congress*] (LCLS)
UkLWa...... Wandsworth Borough News Co. Ltd., London, United Kingdom [*Library symbol*] [*Library of Congress*] (LCLS)
UKM......... UK MARC [*United Kingdom Machine-Readable Cataloging*] [*Source file*] [*UTLAS symbol*]
UKM......... United Kingdom Fund [*NYSE symbol*] (SPSG)
UkMa .... Manchester Public Libraries, Central Library, Manchester, United Kingdom [*Library symbol*] [*Library of Congress*] (LCLS)
UkMaG ..... Guardian Newspapers Ltd., Manchester, United Kingdom [*Library symbol*] [*Library of Congress*] (LCLS)
UK MARC ... UK [*British Library*] Machine Readable Catalogue [*Bibliographic database*]
UKMC....... University of Kentucky Medical Center [*Lexington, KY*]
UkMe......... Public Libraries, Central Library, Merthyr-Tydfil, United Kingdom [*Library symbol*] [*Library of Congress*] (LCLS)
UKMF .... United Kingdom Mobile Force
UKMF(A) ... United Kingdom Mobile Force (Air) [*British military*] (DMA)
UKMF(L).. United Kingdom Mobile Force (Land) [*British military*] (DMA)
UkMg .... Margate Public Library, Margate, United Kingdom [*Library symbol*] [*Library of Congress*] (LCLS)
UK Miner Stat ... United Kingdom Mineral Statistics [*A publication*]
UKMJB..... Ukrainian Mathematical Journal [*English Translation*] [*A publication*]
UKML....... United Knitwear Manufacturers League (EA)
UKMO....... United Kingdom Meteorological Office
UKMRC .... United Kingdom Medical Research Council
UKN......... Unknown (KSC)
UKN......... Waukon, IA [*Location identifier*] [*FAA*] (FAAL)
UKNCIAWPRC ... United Kingdom National Committee of the International Association on Water Pollution Research and Control (EAIO)
UK/NL ...... United Kingdom/Netherlands (MCD)
UKNND .... United Kingdom National Nutrient Databank [*Ministry of Agriculture and Royal Society of Chemistry*]
UkNr......... Norwich Public Libraries, Norwich, United Kingdom [*Library symbol*] [*Library of Congress*] (LCLS)
UKNR....... University of Kansas Nuclear Reactor
UkNrE....... Eastern Counties Newspapers Ltd., Norwich, United Kingdom [*Library symbol*] [*Library of Congress*] (LCLS)
UKNSDC .. United Kingdom National Serials Data Centre [*Information service or system*] (EISS)
UKO .... Unverhofft Kommt Oft [*The Unexpected Often Happens*] [*Motto of Franz, Duke of Pomerania (1577-1620)*]
UKOA....... United Kingdom Offshore Operators' Association
UKOLUG ... United Kingdom On-Line User Group [*Information service or system*] (IID)
UKOO .... Odessa/Tsentralny [*USSR*] [*ICAO location identifier*] (ICLI)
UKOOA ..... United Kingdom Offshore Operators' Association (DS)
UKOP .... United Kingdom Official Publications [*Information service or system*] (IID)
UKORN..... Ukrains'kij Katolic'kij Oseredok Religijnogo Navcannja
UkOxU...... Oxford University, Bodleian Library, Oxford, United Kingdom [*Library symbol*] [*Library of Congress*] (LCLS)
UkOxU-AS ... Oxford University, All Souls College, Oxford, United Kingdom [*Library symbol*] [*Library of Congress*] (LCLS)
UkOxU-N ... Oxford University, Nuffield College, Oxford, United Kingdom [*Library symbol*] [*Library of Congress*] (LCLS)
UkOxU-Rh ... Oxford University, Bodleian Library, Rhodes House, Oxford, United Kingdom [*Library symbol*] [*Library of Congress*] (LCLS)
UKPA .... United Kingdom Patternmakers' Association [*A union*]
UKPA .... United Kingdom Pilots Association (DS)
UKPCA...... United Kingdom Postal Clerks' Association [*A union*]
UkPe......... Sandeman Public Library, Perth, United Kingdom [*Library symbol*] [*Library of Congress*] (LCLS)
UKPG .... United Kingdom Press Gazette [*A publication*]
UKPHS ..... University of Kansas. Publications. Humanistic Studies [*A publication*]
UKPI........ United Kingdom Provident Institute [*Commercial firm*]
UKPJA ...... Ukrainian Physics Journal [*A publication*]
UKPO .... United Kingdom Post Office [*Telecommunications*] (TEL)
UKPPD...... United Kingdom Paper and Packaging Directory [*A publication*]
UkPS .... Portsmouth & Sunderland Newspapers Ltd., Portsmouth, Hants, United Kingdom [*Library symbol*] [*Library of Congress*] (LCLS)
UKR .... Ukraine
ukr............. Ukrainian [*MARC language code*] [*Library of Congress*] (LCCP)

UKR.......... Ukrainian Soviet Socialist Republic [*ISO three-letter standard code*] (CNC)
UKR.......... Uranian Kilometric Radiation [*Planetary science*]
UKRA .... United Kingdom Reading Association [*British*]
Ukrain Fiz Z ... Ukrainskii Fizicheskii Zhurnal [*A publication*]
Ukrain Fiz Zh ... Akademiya Nauk Ukrainskoi SSR. Otdelenie Fiziki. Ukrainskii Fizicheskii Zhurnal [*A publication*]
Ukrain Geometr Sb ... Ukrainskii Geometriceskii Sbornik [*A publication*]
Ukrain Geom Sb ... Ukrainskii Geometriceskii Sbornik [*A publication*]
Ukrainian Math J ... Ukrainian Mathematical Journal [*A publication*]
Ukrainian Q ... Ukrainian Quarterly [*A publication*]
Ukrain Mat Z ... Ukrainskii Matematicheskii Zhurnal [*A publication*]
Ukrain Mat Zh ... Akademiya Nauk Ukrainskoi SSR. Institut Matematiki. Ukrainskii Matematicheskii Zhurnal [*A publication*]
Ukrain Phys J ... Ukrainian Physics Journal [*A publication*]
Ukr Biochim Z ... Ukrains'kyj Biochimicnyj Zurnal [*A publication*]
Ukr Biokhim ... Ukrainskii Biokhimicheski Zhurnal [*A publication*]
Ukr Biokhim Zh ... Ukrainskij Biokhimicheskij Zhurnal [*A publication*]
Ukr Biokhim Zh (1946-1977) ... Ukrains'kii Biokhimichnii Zhurnal (1946-1977) [*Ukrainian SSR*] [*A publication*]
Ukr Bot Z... Ukrains'kyj Botanicnyj Zurnal [*A publication*]
Ukr Bot Zh ... Ukrayins'kyi Botanichnyi Zhurnal [*A publication*]
Ukr Chim Z ... Ukrainskij Chimiceskij Zurnal [*A publication*]
UKREP...... United Kingdom Permanent Representative [*EEC*] (DS)
UK Report ... Economic Progress Report (United Kingdom) [*A publication*]
Ukr Fiz Z ... Ukrains'kyj Fizycnyj Zurnal [*A publication*]
Ukr Fiz Zh ... Ukrainskii Fizichnii Zhurnal [*A publication*]
Ukr Fiz Zh ... Ukrainskij Fizicheskij Zhurnal [*A publication*]
Ukr Fiz Zh (Kiev) ... Ukrayinskoyi Fizichnij Zhurnal (Ukrainian Edition) (Kiev) [*A publication*]
Ukr Geom Sb ... Ukrainskij Geometricheskij Sbornik [*A publication*]
UkrI .... Ukrajins'kyj Istoryk [*A publication*]
UkRiH .... Richmond Herald Ltd., Richmond, Surrey, United Kingdom [*Library symbol*] [*Library of Congress*] (LCLS)
Ukr Ist Zhurnal ... Ukrainskyi Istorichnyi Zhurnal [*A publication*]
Ukr J Biochem ... Ukrainian Journal of Biochemistry [*A publication*]
Ukr J Chem ... Ukrainian Journal of Chemistry [*A publication*]
UKRK .... Ukrains'ka Kooperativna Rada Kanadi
UkrK......... Ukrajins'ka Knyha [*A publication*]
Ukr Khem Zh ... Ukrains'ka Khemichnii Zhurnal [*A publication*]
Ukr Khim Zh ... Ukrainskii Khimicheskii Zhurnal [*A publication*]
UkrM......... Ukrajins'ka Mova i Literatura v Skoli [*A publication*]
Ukr Math J ... Ukrainian Mathematical Journal [*A publication*]
Ukr Mat Zh ... Ukrainskij Matematicheskij Zhurnal [*A publication*]
Ukr Mov .... Ukrajins'ke Movnoznavstvo [*A publication*]
Ukr Nauchno Issled Inst Eksp Vet Nauchn Tr ... Ukrainskii Nauchno-Issledovatel'skii Institut Eksperimental'noi Veterinarii Nauchnye Trudy [*A publication*]
Ukr Nauchno Issled Inst Fiziol Rast Nauchn Tr ... Ukrainskii Nauchno-Issledovatel'skii Institut Fiziologii Rastenii Nauchnye Trudy [*A publication*]
Ukr Nauchno Issled Inst Pishch Promsti Sb Tr ... Ukrainskii Nauchno-Issledovatel'skii Institut Pishchevoi Promyshlennosti Sbornik Trudov [*A publication*]
UkRoS .... G. & A. N. Scott Ltd., Rochdale, United Kingdom [*Library symbol*] [*Library of Congress*] (LCLS)
Ukr Phys J ... Ukrainian Physics Journal [*A publication*]
Ukr Poligr Inst Nauchn Zap ... Ukrainskii Poligraficheskii Institut Nauchnye Zapiski [*A publication*]
Ukr Q........ Ukrainian Quarterly [*A publication*]
Ukr Quart .. Ukrainian Quarterly [*A publication*]
UkrR......... Ukrainian Review [*A publication*]
UkrS .... Ukrajins'kyj Samostijnyk [*A publication*]
UkrSSR .... Ukranian Soviet Socialist Republic
UKS .... United Kingdom Subsatellite
UKSA .... United Kingdom Shipmakers' Association [*A union*]
UKSASS.... United Kingdom Society of Amalgamated Smiths and Strikers [*A union*]
UKSATA... United Kingdom-South Africa Trade Association
UKSC........ United Kingdom Society of Coachmakers [*A union*]
UKSG .... United Kingdom Serials Group
UkSh......... Sheffield City Libraries, Central Library, Sheffield, United Kingdom [*Library symbol*] [*Library of Congress*] (LCLS)
UkShU....... University of Sheffield, Sheffield, United Kingdom [*Library symbol*] [*Library of Congress*] (LCLS)
UkSlO........ Slough Observer Ltd., Slough, United Kingdom [*Library symbol*] [*Library of Congress*] (LCLS)
UkSsB........ John H. Burrows & Sons Ltd., Southend-On-Sea, United Kingdom [*Library symbol*] [*Library of Congress*] (LCLS)
UKST........ United Kingdom Schmidt Telescope
UkSta........ Stamford Public Library and Museum, Stamford, United Kingdom [*Library symbol*] [*Library of Congress*] (LCLS)
UKSTC...... United Kingdom Strike Command (NATG)
UKSTU...... United Kingdom Schmidt Telescope Unit
UkSw........ Swansea Public Library, Swansea, United Kingdom [*Library symbol*] [*Library of Congress*] (LCLS)
UKT .... Quakertown, PA [*Location identifier*] [*FAA*] (FAAL)
UKT .... United Kingdom Tariff (DS)
UKTA .... United Kingdom Trade Agency
UKTD .... United Kingdom Treasury Delegation

UKTM .... UK [*United Kingdom*] Trade Marks [*The Patent Office*] [*London, England*] [*Information service or system*] (IID)
UKTOTC... United Kingdom Tariff and Overseas Trade Classification (DS)
UK Trends ... Economic Trends (United Kingdom) [*A publication*]
UKTS........ United Kingdom Treaty Series [*A publication*]
UKTTSMA ... United Kingdom Timber Trade Shipowners Mutual Association Ltd. (DS)
UKU........... Nuku [*Papua New Guinea*] [*Airport symbol*] (OAG)
UKU........... Ukrains'kii Katolic'kij Universitet
UKUSA ..... United Kingdom-United States Agreement [*Intelligence*] [*1947*]
UKV........... Underground Keybox Vault (NATG)
UKVA .... Uitgaven der Koninklijke Vlaamse Academie voor Taal- en Letterkunde [*A publication*]
UKW.......... Ultrakurzwelle [*Ultrashort wave*] [*German*]
UKWAL..... United Kingdom West Africa Line [*Shipping*]
UkWE........ Eton College, Windsor, Berks, United Kingdom [*Library symbol*] [*Library of Congress*] (LCLS)
UKWE....... Ultrakurzwellenempfaenger [*Very-High-Frequency Receiver*] [*German*]
UkWg .... County Borough of Wigan Public Libraries, Central Library, Wigan, United Kingdom [*Library symbol*] [*Library of Congress*] (LCLS)
UkWoE...... Express & Star Ltd., Wolverhampton, United Kingdom [*Library symbol*] [*Library of Congress*] (LCLS)
UkWr......... Wrexham Public Library, Wrexham, United Kingdom [*Library symbol*] [*Library of Congress*] (LCLS)
UKY........... United Kingdom Energy [*Vancouver Stock Exchange symbol*]
'Ukz......... 'Ukzin (BJA)
UKZHA..... Ukrainskii Khimicheskii Zhurnal [*A publication*]
UL............. Lansa, SRL [*Honduras*] [*ICAO designator*] (ICDA)
UL............. Ugaritic Literature [*C. H. Gordon*] [*A publication*] (BJA)
Ul .... Uldericus de Bamberg [*Flourished, 12th century*] [*Authority cited in pre-1607 legal work*] (DSA)
Ul .... Ulisse [*A publication*]
UL............. Ulitsa [*Street*] (EY)
UL............. Ultralinear
UL............. Ultralow
UL............. Unauthorized Launch
UL............. Underload (NASA)
UL............. Underwriters Laboratories (EA)
UL............. Uniformly Labeled [*Compound, with radioisotope*] [*Also, U*]
UL............. Unilever ADR [*NYSE symbol*] (SPSG)
UL............. Union Liberal [*Liberal Union*] [*Spain*] [*Political party*] (PPW)
UL............. Union List
UL............. Unionist Liberal [*British*] (ROG)
UL............. United Left [*Political party*] [*Peru*]
UL............. Universal League (EAIO)
UL............. Universal Life [*Insurance*]
UL............. Universala Ligo [*Defunct*] (EA)
u/l............. Unlimited [*Water depth*]
UL............. Unterlafette [*Bottom carriage*] [*German military - World War II*]
U e L .... Uomini e Libri [*A publication*]
UL............. Up Left [*The rear left portion of a stage*] [*A stage direction*]
UL............. Up Link [*Data processing*]
UL............. Upper Laterals [*Botany*]
UL............. Upper Left [*S-band antenna*] (NASA)
UL............. Upper Leg
UL............. Upper Level [*Nuclear energy*] (NRCH)
UL............. Upper Limb [*Upper edge of sun, moon, etc.*] [*Navigation*]
UL............. Upper Limit
UL............. Upper Lobe [*Anatomy*]
U & L .... Upper and Lower (MSA)
UL............. Urban League (MCD)
UL............. Usage List (MSA)
UL............. User Language [*Data processing*] (DIT)
UL............. Utility Lead [*Telecommunications*] (TEL)
ULA .... San Julian [*Argentina*] [*Airport symbol*] (OAG)
ULA .... UCLA [*University of California, Los Angeles*] Law Review [*A publication*]
ULA .... Ulamona Field Station [*New Britain*] [*Seismograph station code, US Geological Survey*] (SEIS)
ULA .... Uncommitted Logic Array [*Semiconductor technology*]
ULA .... Uniform Laws, Annotated [*A publication*] (DLA)
ULA .... Utah State University, Logan, UT [*Library symbol*] [*Library of Congress*] (LCLS)
ULAA........ Ukrainian Library Association of America (EA)
ULAA .... United Latin Americans of America (EA)
ULAAA ..... Ultra Light Aircraft Association of Australia
ULAB .... Unilab Corp. [*NASDAQ symbol*] (NQ)
ULAC .... Union Latinoamericana de Ciegos [*Latin American Blind Union - LABU*] [*Montevideo, Uruguay*] (EAIO)
ULAE .... Universal Limited Art Editions
ULAEY ...... Union of Latin American Ecumenical Youth (EA)
ULAIDS ..... Universal Locator Airborne Integrated Data System (MCD)
ULAJE .... Union Latino-Americaine des Jeunesses Evangeliques [*Union of Latin American Evangelical Youth*]
ULAJE .... Union Latinoamericana de Juventudes Ecumenicas [*Union of Latin American Ecumenical Youth - ULAEY*] (EAIO)
ULAK .... Kotlas [*USSR*] [*ICAO location identifier*] (ICLI)

ULANG..... User Language [*Data processing*]
ULAPC...... Union Latino-Americaine de la Presse Catholique
ULAS........ University of Louisville Archaeological Survey [*Research center*] (RCD)
ULASM..... Undersea Multichannel Large-Scale Scattering Meter [*NASA*] (MCD)
ULAST...... Union Latino Americana de Sociedades de Tisiologia [*Latin American Union of Societies of Phthisiology*]
ULB .... Underwater Locator Beacon (MCD)
ULB .... Universal Logic Block (IEEE)
ULBA .... Universal Love and Brotherhood Association [*Kyoto, Japan*] (EAIO)
UlbR .... Ulbandus Review [*A publication*]
ULB-VUB Inter-Univ High Energ Rep ... ULB-VUB [*Universite Libre de Bruxelles - Vrije Universiteit Brussel*] Inter-University Institute for High Energies. Report [*A publication*]
ULC .... Cache County Public Library, Logan, UT [*Library symbol*] [*Library of Congress*] (LCLS)
ULC .... Philippines Civil Liberties Union (PD)
ULC .... Underwriters' Laboratories of Canada
ULC .... Uniform Loop Clock
ULC .... Union Library Catalogue
ULC .... Union de la Lutte Communiste [*Burkina Faso*] [*Political party*] (EY)
ULC .... Unit Ledger Card [*Data processing*]
ULC .... Unit Level Code (AFM)
ULC .... Unit Level Computers [*Army*]
ULC .... Unitary Launch Concept [*or Control*] (AAG)
ULC .... United Labor Congress [*Nigeria*]
ULC .... Universal Life Church
ULC .... Universal Load Cell
ULC .... Universal Logic Circuit
ULC .... Upper Left Center [*The rear left center portion of a stage*] [*A stage direction*]
U & LC...... Uppercase and Lowercase [*i.e., capital and small letters*] [*Typography*]
ULC .... Urban Libraries Council (EA)
ULC .... Utah State Library, Salt Lake City, UT [*OCLC symbol*] (OCLC)
ULCA .... Ukrainian Life Cooperative Association (EA)
ULCBAJ.... Uchenye Zapiski Leningradskogo Ordena Lenina Gosudarstvennogo Universiteta Imeni A. A. Zhdanova. Seriya Biologicheskikh Nauk [*A publication*]
ULCC .... Ulster Loyalist Central Coordinating Committee [*Ireland*]
ULCC .... Ultralarge Crude Carrier [*Oil tanker*]
ULCER...... Underwater Launch Control Energy Requirements
ULCER...... Underwater Launch Current and Energy Recorder
ULCHi....... Cache Valley Historical Society, Logan, UT [*Library symbol*] [*Library of Congress*] (LCLS)
ULCJ .... University Law College. Journal. Rajputana University [*India*] [*A publication*] (DLA)
ULCM .... United Lutheran Church Men [*Defunct*] (EA)
ULCP........ University Laboratory Cooperative Program
ULCS........ Unit Level Circuit Switch (CAAL)
ULD.......... Ultrasonic Leak Detector
ULD.......... Ultrasonic Light Diffraction
ULD.......... Unit Load Demand [*Nuclear energy*] (NRCH)
ULD.......... Unit Load Device [*Shipping containers*]
ULD.......... Unit Logic Device
ULD.......... Upper Level Deck [*Cargo containers*]
ULD.......... Upper-Limb Disorder [*Medicine*] (ECON)
ULDEST..... Ultimate Destination [*Army*] (AABC)
ULDF .... United Left Democratic Front [*India*] [*Political party*] (PPW)
ULDMI ..... Ultraprecise LASER Distance Measuring Instrument
ULDP .... Ulster Loyalist Democratic Party [*Northern Ireland*] [*Political party*] (PPW)
ULDS........ Union Liberale-Democratique Suisse [*Liberal Democratic Union of Switzerland*] [*Political party*] (PPE)
ULE .... Sule [*Papua New Guinea*] [*Airport symbol*] (OAG)
ULE .... Ultralow Expansion [*Trademark, Corning Glass Works*]
ULE .... Unit Location Equipment (MCD)
ULEA .... University Labor Education Association [*Later, UCLEA*]
ULECA ...... Ultralow Energy Charge Analyzer [*Instrumentation*]
ULES........ University of Lancaster Engineering Services [*British*] (IRUK)
ULew........ Lewiston Public Library, Lewiston, UT [*Library symbol*] [*Library of Congress*] (LCLS)
ULEWAT ... Ultralow-Energy Wide-Angle Telescope
ULF .... Ultralow Frequency
ULF .... United Labour Front [*Trinidad and Tobago*] (PD)
ULF .... University Labour Federation [*British*]
ULF .... Upper Limiting Frequency (ADA)
ULFIS .... University Libraries Free Information Service [*Australia*]
ULFJ .... Ultralow-Frequency Jammer
ULFO........ Ultralow-Frequency Oscillator
ULG.......... Upholstery Leather Group [*Later, AG*] (EA)
ULGCS...... United Lesbian and Gay Christian Scientists (EA)
ULGLAM ... Eugenics Laboratory. Memoirs [*A publication*]
ULGS........ Church of Jesus Christ of Latter-Day Saints, Genealogical Society Library, Cache Branch, Logan, UT [*Library symbol*] [*Library of Congress*] (LCLS)
ULH.......... Ukrains'ka Literaturna Hazeta [*A publication*]

ULH..........	Universidad de la Habana [*A publication*]
ULI	ULI - the Urban Land Institute (EA)
ULI	Underwriters Laboratories, Incorporated [*Also, UL*]
ULI	Union pour la Langue Internationale Ido [*Union for the International Language Ido*]
ULI	Uniono por la Linguo Internaciona Ido [*International Language Union*] (EA)
ULI	Universal Logic Implementer
ULI	[*The*] Urban Land Institute [*An association*] (EAAP)
ULI	Urban Law Institute of Antioch School of Law (EA)
ULIA	Unattached List, Indian Army
ULIB.........	Utility Library [*National Center for Atmospheric Research*]
ULIDAT....	Umweltliteraturedatenbank [*Data Bank for Environmental Literature*] [*Deutsches Umweltbundesamt*] [*Federal Republic of Germany*] [*Information service or system*] (CRD)
ULI Lm Rep ...	Urban Land Institute. Landmark Report [*A publication*]
ULI Res Rep ...	Urban Land Institute. Research Report [*A publication*]
ULIS.........	Uniform Law on the International Sale of Goods
ULI Spe Rep ...	Urban Land Institute. Special Report [*A publication*]
ULJ	Bedford, MA [*Location identifier*] [*FAA*] (FAAL)
Ul'janovsk Gos Ped Inst Ucen Zap ...	Ul'janovskii Gosudarstvennyi Pedagogiceskii Institut Imeni I. N. Ul'janova. Ucennyi Zapiski [*A publication*]
ULL	Savoonga, AK [*Location identifier*] [*FAA*] (FAAL)
ULL	Ullage [*NASA*] (KSC)
ULL	Unit Local Loading (AAG)
ULL	Unitarian Laymen's League
ULL	United States Department of Labor, Washington, DC [*OCLC symbol*] (OCLC)
ULL	Upper Lip Length [*Medicine*]
ULLA	Ultra-Low-Level Air-Drop [*British military*] (DMA)
ULLC.......	Unit Level Learning Center
ULLDPE ..	Ultra Linear Low-Density Polyethylene [*Plastics technology*]
ULLL........	Leningrad/Pulkovo [*USSR*] [*ICAO location identifier*] (ICLI)
ULLOS......	University of London. London Oriental Series [*A publication*]
ULLS	Ultrasonic Liquid Level Sensor
ULLS........	Unit Level Logistics System [*Army*]
Ullst DG	Ullstein Deutsche Geschichte [*A publication*]
Ullst Kr	Ullstein-Buecher. Kriminalromane [*A publication*]
Ullst Kunst ...	Ullstein-Kunstgeschichte [*A publication*]
ULLV........	Unmanned Lunar Logistics Vehicle [*OMSF*]
ULM.........	Meiji University, Maruzen Co. Ltd. [*UTLAS symbol*]
ULM.........	Mine Safety and Health Administration, Denver, Denver, CO [*OCLC symbol*] (OCLC)
ULM.........	New Ulm [*Minnesota*] [*Airport symbol*] [*Obsolete*] (OAG)
ULM.........	New Ulm Flight Service, Inc. [*New Ulm, MN*] [*FAA designator*] (FAAC)
ULM.........	Ultramar Capital Corp. [*Toronto Stock Exchange symbol*]
ULM.........	Ultrasonic Light Modulator
ULM.........	Undersea [*or Underwater*] Long-Range Missile [*Navy*]
ULM.........	Union List of Manuscripts [*Canada*] [*A publication*]
ULM.........	Universal Line Multiplexer
ULM.........	Universal Logic Module
ULMA	University Laboratory Managers Association [*Later, ALMA*] (EA)
Ulm L Rec ...	Ulman's Law Record [*New York*] [*A publication*] (DLA)
ULMS.......	Undersea [*or Underwater*] Long-Range Missile System [*Redesignated "Trident"*] [*Navy*]
ULMS.......	Union List of Montana Serials [*Library network*]
ULMS.......	Unit Level Message Switch
ULN.........	Ulan Bator [*Mongolia*] [*Airport symbol*] (OAG)
ULN.........	United Lincoln Resources, Inc. [*Vancouver Stock Exchange symbol*]
ULN..........	University of Lowell, North Campus, Lowell, MA [*OCLC symbol*] (OCLC)
ULN..........	Upper Limits of Normal [*Medicine*]
ULNN.......	United Lincoln Resources, Inc. [*NASDAQ symbol*] (NQ)
ULO..........	Occupational Safety and Health Administration, Technical Data Center, Washington, DC [*OCLC symbol*] (OCLC)
ULO..........	Unilateral Ovariectomy [*Gynecology*]
ULO..........	United Labour Organization [*Burma*]
ULO..........	Unmanned Launch Operations [*NASA*] (KSC)
ULO..........	Unmanned Lunar Orbiter [*NASA*] (MCD)
ULOL........	Velikiye Luki [*USSR*] [*ICAO location identifier*] (ICLI)
U Lond I Cl ...	University of London. Institute of Classical Studies. Bulletin [*A publication*]
ULOS	Unliquidated Obligations (MCD)
ULOSSOM ...	Union List of Selected Serials of Michigan [*Wayne State University Libraries*] [*Information service or system*] [*Ceased*] (IID)
ULOTC	University of London Officer Training Corps [*British military*] (DMA)
ULOW.......	Unmanned Launch Operations - Western Test Range [*NASA*] (KSC)
ULP	Quilpie [*Australia*] [*Airport symbol*] (OAG)
Ulp	[*Domitius*] Ulpianus [*Deceased, 228*] [*Authority cited in pre-1607 legal work*] (DSA)
ULP	Ulster Petroleums Ltd. [*Toronto Stock Exchange symbol*]
ULP	Unfair Labor Practice [*Department of Labor*]
ULP	Uniform Latex Particles

ULP	Unleaded Petrol [*British*] (ADA)
ULP	Utilitaire Logique Processor [*Programming language*] [*Data processing*] [*French*] (CSR)
ULP	Utility Landplane [*Navy*]
ULPA........	Uniform Limited Partnership Act [*National Conference of Commissioners on Uniform State Laws*]
ULPA.......	United Lightning Protection Association (EA)
Ulpia	[*Domitius*] Ulpianus [*Deceased, 228*] [*Authority cited in pre-1607 legal work*] (DSA)
ULPOD	Urban Law and Policy [*A publication*]
ULPR.......	Ultralow-Pressure Rocket
ULQ..........	Tulua [*Colombia*] [*Airport symbol*] (OAG)
ULQ..........	Utah Foreign Language Quarterly [*A publication*]
ULR	Uganda Law Reports [*A publication*] (DLA)
ULR	Uganda Protectorate Law Reports [*1904-51*] [*A publication*] (DLA)
ULR	Ultralinear Rectifier
ULR	Uniform Law Review [*A publication*] (DLA)
ULR	Union Labor Report [*Bureau of National Affairs*] [*Information service or system*] (CRD)
ULR	Union Law Review [*South Africa*] [*A publication*] (DLA)
ULR	United Liberty Resources Ltd. [*Vancouver Stock Exchange symbol*]
ULR	University Law Review [*United States*] [*A publication*] (DLA)
ULR	University of Leeds. Review [*A publication*]
ULR	Utah Law Review [*A publication*]
ULR	Utilities Law Reporter [*A publication*] (DLA)
ULRA	United Lithuanian Relief Fund of America (EA)
ULRED......	UCLA [*University of California, Los Angeles*] Law Review [*A publication*]
ULRF........	Urban Land Research Foundation (EA)
Ulrich's Q ..	Ulrich's Quarterly [*A publication*]
Ulrich's Qtly ...	Ulrich's Quarterly [*A publication*]
ULRSA	Union and League of Romanian Societies of America (EA)
ULS	ULS Capital Corp. [*Toronto Stock Exchange symbol*]
ULS..........	Ultimatist Life Society (EA)
ULS..........	Ultrasystems, Inc. [*AMEX symbol*] (SPSG)
ULS..........	Ultraviolet Light Stabilizer
ULS..........	Ulysses, KS [*Location identifier*] [*FAA*] (FAAL)
ULS..........	Union List of Serials [*A publication*]
ULS..........	Unit Level Switchboard (MCD)
ULS..........	United Lutheran Society (EA)
ULS..........	University Libraries Section [*Association of College and Research Libraries*]
ULS...........	University of Lowell, South Campus, Lowell, MA [*OCLC symbol*] (OCLC)
ULS..........	Unsecured Loan Stock (DCTA)
ULS..........	Upward-Looking SONAR
ULSA........	Ultralow Sidelobe Antenna [*Air Force*] (MCD)
UL Sci Mag ...	UL [*University of Liberia*] Science Magazine [*A publication*]
ULSI........	Ultralarge-Scale Integration [*of circuits*] [*Semiconductor technology*]
ULSIA	Uniform Land Security Interest Act [*National Conference of Commissioners on Uniform State Laws*]
ULSP........	Unified Legal Services Program
ULSPD......	Ultrasonics Symposium. Proceedings [*A publication*]
ULSS	Underwater LASER Surveying System (MCD)
ULSSCL....	Union List of Scientific Serials in Canadian Libraries [*A publication*]
ULSSSHCL ...	Union List of Serials in the Social Sciences and Humanities Held by Canadian Libraries [*National Library of Canada*] [*Information service or system*] (CRD)
ULSTD......	Union Label and Service Trades Department (of AFL-CIO) [*American Federation of Labor and Congress of Industrial Organizations*] (EA)
Ulster Folk ...	Ulster Folklife [*A publication*]
Ulster J Arch ...	Ulster Journal of Archaeology [*A publication*]
Ulster J Archaeol 3 Ser ...	Ulster Journal of Archaeology. Series 3 [*A publication*]
Ulster Med J ...	Ulster Medical Journal [*A publication*]
ULSV........	Unmanned Launch Space Vehicles [*NASA*] (KSC)
ULT	Ultimate (AAG)
ULT	Ultimate Corp. [*NYSE symbol*] (SPSG)
ULT	Ultime [*Lastly*] [*Pharmacy*]
ULT	Ultralow Tar [*Cigarettes*] [*Tobacco industry*]
ULT	Ultralow Temperature
ULT	Ultramar PLC [*Toronto Stock Exchange symbol*]
ULT	Ultramarine [*Philately*] (ROG)
ULT	Uniform Low-Frequency Technique
ULT	Unione per la Lotta alla Tubercolosi [*Union of Anti-Tuberculosis Association Workers*] [*Italy*]
ULT	United Lodge of Theosophists (EA)
ULT	Upper Layer Thickness [*Of ocean waters*] [*Oceanography*]
ULTA	Uniform Land Transactions Act [*National Conference of Commissioners on Uniform State Laws*]
ULTB........	Ultra Bancorporation [*NASDAQ symbol*] (NQ)
ULTC.......	Urban Library Trustees Council [*Later, ULC*] (EA)
ULTI........	Ultralow-Temperature Isotropic [*Carbon*]
Ultim Real Mean ...	Ultimate Reality and Meaning [*A publication*]
ULTK	Ultrak, Inc. [*NASDAQ symbol*] (NQ)
ULTO........	Ultimo [*In the Month Preceding the Present*] [*Latin*]

ULT PRAESCR ... Ultimo Praescriptus [*The Last Ordered*] [*Pharmacy*] (ROG)
ULTRA ... Ultramarine [*Philately*] (ROG)
ULTRA..... Ultrasonics [*A publication*]
ULTRACOM ... Ultraviolet Communications
ULTRAJ ... Ultrajectum [*Utrecht*] [*Imprint*] [*Latin*] (ROG)
Ultramicrosc ... Ultramicroscopy [*A publication*]
Ultraschall Med ... Ultraschall in der Medizin [*A publication*]
Ultrason..... Ultrasonics [*A publication*]
Ultrason Imaging ... Ultrasonic Imaging [*A publication*]
Ultrason Symp Proc ... Ultrasonics Symposium. Proceedings [*A publication*]
Ultrasound Annu ... Ultrasound Annual [*A publication*]
Ultrasound Med Biol ... Ultrasound in Medicine and Biology [*A publication*]
Ultrasound Med & Biol ... Ultrasound in Medicine and Biology [*A publication*]
Ultrasound Teach Cases ... Ultrasound Teaching Cases [*A publication*]
Ultrastruct Pathol ... Ultrastructural Pathology [*A publication*]
ULTRA-X ... Universal Language for Typographic Reproduction Applications
ULTRD..... Ultramicroscopy [*A publication*]
Ult Real...... Ultimate Reality and Meaning [*A publication*]
ULTSIGN ... Ultimate Assignment
ULTT.......... Tallin [*USSR*] [*ICAO location identifier*] (ICLI)
ULU.......... Gulu [*Uganda*] [*Airport symbol*] (OAG)
ULV .... Ultralow Volume
ULVA .... USS [*United States Ship*] Liberty Veterans Association (EA)
ULW .... Unsafe Landing Warning
ULWA ...... Union of Latin Writers and Artists [*Paris, France*] (EAIO)
ULWB ...... Belozyorsk [*USSR*] [*ICAO location identifier*] (ICLI)
ULWC ...... Ultra-Lightweight Coated [*Paper*]
ULWT ...... Totma [*USSR*] [*ICAO location identifier*] (ICLI)
ULWW ...... Vologda [*USSR*] [*ICAO location identifier*] (ICLI)
ULY .... Ulyanovsk [*USSR*] [*Airport symbol*] (OAG)
Ul'yanovsk Skh Opytn Stn Tr ... Ul'yanovskaya Sel'skokhozyaistvennaya Opytnaya Stantsiya Trudy [*A publication*]
ULYSSES ... University Library System for the Satisfaction of Enquiries [*Australia*]
ULz .... Ukrajins'ke Literaturoznavstvo [*A publication*]
ULZP........ United Labor Zionist Party [*Later, LZA*] (EA)
UM .... Air Manila, Inc. [*Philippines*] [*ICAO designator*] (FAAC)
UM .... Salt Lake County Library System, Midvale, UT [*Library symbol*] [*Library of Congress*] (LCLS)
UM .... Ugaritic Manual [*C. H. Gordon*] [*A publication*] (BJA)
UM .... Umbilical Mast [*NASA*] (KSC)
UM .... Umot Me'uhadot [*United Nations*] [*Hebrew*]
Um .... Umschau [*A publication*]
UM .... Unable to Maintain [*Aviation*] (FAAC)
UM .... Unaccompanied Minor [*Airline passenger*]
UM .... Under-Mentioned [*i.e., mentioned later in a document*]
UM .... Underwater Mechanic
Um .... Uniform, Medium-Grained [*Soil*]
UM .... Uninflated Movement [*Australia*]
UM .... Uninsured Motorists [*Insurance*]
UM .... Unio Mallorquina [*Majorcan Union*] [*Political party*] (PPW)
UM .... Union Movement Party [*British*]
UM .... Unione Maniferro [*Somalia*]
UM .... Unit of Measure (MCD)
UM .... Unitas Malacologica [*An association*] (EAIO)
UM .... United Medical Corp. [*AMEX symbol*] (SPSG)
UM .... United States Minor Outlying Islands [*ANSI two-letter standard code*] (CNC)
UM .... Universal Machine Gun (MCD)
UM .... Universal Measuring Microscope
UM .... Universal Monitor (MCD)
UM .... Universidad de Mexico [*A publication*]
UM .... University of Manitoba [*Canada*]
UM .... University of Massachusetts [*Amherst, MA*]
UM .... University of Miami [*Florida*]
U of M....... University of Michigan [*Ann Arbor, MI*]
UM .... University Microfilms [*A publication*]
UM .... University of Missouri Press
U/M........... Unmanned (NASA)
UM .... Unmarried
UM .... Unpopular Magnetic Fields
UM .... Unpriced Material
UM .... Unscheduled Maintenance
UM .... Upper Magazine [*Typography*]
UM .... Upper Motor [*Neurons*] [*Medicine*]
UM .... Uromodulin
UM .... Useful Method
UM .... User Manual (MCD)
U & M....... Utilization/Reutilization and Marketing [*DoD*]
UMA .... Ultrasonic Manufacturers Association [*Later, UIA*] (EA)
UMA......... Uniform - Memory - Access [*Data processing*]
UMA......... Union Mathematique Africaine [*African Mathematical Union - AMU*] (EA)
UMA......... Union Medicale Arabe [*Arab Medical Union*] (EAIO)
UMA......... Union Membership Agreement (DCTA)
UMA......... Union Mondiale des Aveugles [*World Blind Union - WBU*] (EA)
UMA......... Union de Mujeres Americanas [*United Women of the Americas*]

UMA......... United Maritime Administration
UMA......... United Maritime Authority
UMA......... United Methodist Association of Health and Welfare Ministries (EA)
UMA......... Universal Measurement Assembly (MCD)
UMA......... Universal Measuring Amplifier (KSC)
UMA......... University of Mid-America [*Consortium of six midwestern universities*]
UMA......... Unmanned Aircraft [*Aviation*]
UMA......... Unscheduled Maintenance Action [*Military*] (AABC)
UMa......... Ursa Major [*Constellation*]
UMAA....... United Martial Arts Association (EA)
UMAB...... University of Maryland at Baltimore
UMAC...... UMI [*University Microfilms International*] Article Clearinghouse [*Information service or system*] (IID)
UMAD...... Umatilla Army Depot [*Oregon*] (AABC)
UMAH ...... Union Mondiale d'Avancee Humaine [*World Union for Human Progress*]
U Maine L Rev ... University of Maine. Law Review [*A publication*] (DLA)
UMaj .... Ursa Major [*Constellation*]
U of Malaya L Rev ... University of Malaya. Law Review [*A publication*] (DLA)
UMan .... Manti City Library, Manti, UT [*Library symbol*] [*Library of Congress*] (LCLS)
UMANA.... Ukrainian Medical Association of North America (EA)
UMANA.... Uspekhi Matematicheskikh Nauk [*A publication*]
UMAP...... ULTIMAP International Corp. [*NASDAQ symbol*] (NQ)
UMAP...... University of Michigan Assembly Program
U Mary L Forum ... University of Maryland Law Forum [*A publication*] (DLA)
UMASS..... University of Massachusetts [*Amherst, MA*]
UMASS..... Unlimited Machine Access from Scattered Sites [*Data processing*]
UMB......... Ultramicrobacteria
Umb .... Umbelliferyl [*Biochemistry*]
UMB......... Umberatana [*Australia*] [*Seismograph station code, US Geological Survey*] (SEIS)
UMB......... Umberto's Pasta Enterprises, Inc. [*Vancouver Stock Exchange symbol*]
UMB......... Umbilical (MCD)
umb .... Umbundu [*MARC language code*] [*Library of Congress*] (LCCP)
UMB......... Umnak, AK [*Location identifier*] [*FAA*] (FAAL)
UMB......... Union Medicale Balkanique [*Balkan Medical Union*] (EAIO)
UMB......... Union Mondiale de Billard [*World Billiards Union - WBU*] [*Switzerland*]
UMB......... United Merchant Bar [*Commercial firm*] [*British*]
UMB......... Universal Masonic Brotherhood (EA)
UMB......... Universal Medical Buildings, Inc. [*NYSE symbol*] (SPSG)
UMB......... Universal Missile Building (MCD)
UMB......... University of Pennsylvania. Museum Bulletin [*A publication*]
UMBA...... United Mortgage Bankers of America [*Philadelphia, PA*] (EA)
UMBC...... Umbilical Cord [*Aerospace engineering*]
UMBC...... United Malayan Banking Corporation
UMBC...... University of Maryland, Baltimore County
UMBC Econ R ... UMBC Economic Review [*Kuala Lumpur*] [*A publication*]
UMBE...... UMB Equities, Inc. [*Milwaukee, WI*] [*NASDAQ symbol*] (NQ)
UMBL...... Umbilical (AAG)
UMBP...... University Museum. Bulletin (Philadelphia) [*A publication*]
UMBR...... Unclad-Metal Breeder Reactor
UMBR ...... Universal Multiple Bomb Rack (NG)
UMBS...... University of Michigan Biological Station [*Research center*] (RCD)
UMBS ...... University of Pennsylvania. University Museum. Publications of the Babylonian Section [*A publication*]
UMB V ...... Umbilical Vein [*Anatomy*]
UMC......... Ukrainian Museum of Canada [*UTLAS symbol*]
UMC......... Underwater Manifold Centre [*Shell Oil Co.*] [*British*]
UMC......... Unibus Microchannel
UMC......... Unified Management Corp. Database [*Information service or system*] (CRD)
UMC......... Uniform Motion Coupling
UMC......... Uniform Moving Charge
UMC......... Uninsured Motorists Coverage [*Insurance*]
UMC......... Union du Moyen-Congo [*Union of the Middle Congo*]
UMC......... Unit Mail Clerk
UMC......... Unit Mobility Center [*Military*] (AFIT)
UMC......... United Maritime Council
UMC......... United Methodist Church
UMC......... United Mining Corporation [*Vancouver Stock Exchange symbol*]
UMC......... United Motor Courts
UMC......... Universal Match Corporation
UmC......... Universal Microfilming Corporation, Salt Lake City, UT [*Library symbol*] [*Library of Congress*] [*Obsolete*] (LCLS)
UMC......... University of Maryland, College Park, MD [*OCLC symbol*] (OCLC)
UMCA ...... Ultra Marathon Cycling Association (EA)
UMCA ...... Union Monetaria Centroamericana [*Central American Monetary Union*] [*El Salvador*]
UMCA....... United Mining Councils of America (EA)

UMCA....... Universities Mission to Central Africa [*Later, USPG*] [*British*]
UMCA....... Uraba, Medellin & Central Airways, Inc.
UMCAA.... Union Medicale du Canada [*A publication*]
UMCC...... United Maritime Consultative Committee
UMCE....... UMC Electronics [*NASDAQ symbol*]   (NQ)
UMCEES.. University of Maryland Center for Environmental and Estuarine Studies
UMCI........ Universal Money Centers, Inc. [*NASDAQ symbol*]   (NQ)
UMCJA..... University of Michigan. Medical Center. Journal [*A publication*]
UMCMP ... University of Michigan. Contributions in Modern Philology [*A publication*]
UMCO...... United Michigan Corporation [*NASDAQ symbol*]   (NQ)
UMCOM... United Methodist Communications [*Information service or system*]   (IID)
UMCOR.... United Methodist Committee on Relief   (EA)
UMCP ...... Unit Maintenance Collection Point [*Army*]   (INF)
UMCP ...... University of Maryland, College Park
UM/CR ..... Unsatisfactory Material/Condition Report   (MCD)
UMCS .... Uniwersytet Marii Curie-Sklodowskiej [*A publication*]
UMD .... Ultrasonic Material Dispersion
UMD .... Unit Manning Document [*DoD*]
UMD .... Unit Movement Data [*Military*]
UMD .... Unitized Microwave Devices
UMD .... University of Maryland [*College Park, MD*]
UMD .... University of Medicine and Dentistry of New Jersey
UMDA....... Uniform Marriage and Divorce Act [*National Conference of Commissioners on Uniform State Laws*]
UMDA...... United Micronesia Development Association
UMDC...... Union Mondiale Democrate Chretienne [*Christian Democratic World Union*]
UMDK...... United Movement for Democracy in Korea [*Later, UMDUK*]   (EA)
U Md LF .. University of Maryland Law Forum [*A publication*]   (DLA)
UMDNJ .... University of Medicine and Dentistry of New Jersey [*Newark*]
UMDUK.... United Movement for Democracy and Unification in Korea   (EA)
UME.......... Umea [*Sweden*] [*Seismograph station code, US Geological Survey*]   (SEIS)
UME.......... Umea [*Sweden*] [*Airport symbol*]   (OAG)
UME.......... Uniform Manufacturers Exchange   (EA)
UME.......... Unit Mission Equipment   (AAG)
UME.......... Unit Mobility Equipment
UME.......... Unit Monthly Equipment   (MSA)
UME.......... United Ministries in Education [*Later, HEMT/UMHE*]   (EA)
UME.......... University of Maryland, Eastern Shore, Princess Anne, MD [*OCLC symbol*]   (OCLC)
UmE.......... University Music Editions, New York, NY [*Library symbol*] [*Library of Congress*]   (LCLS)
UME.......... Unpredictable Main Event
UME.......... Urethane Mixing Equipment
UMEA....... Universala Medicina Esperanto Asocio [*Universal Medical Esperanto Association*]   (EAIO)
UMEA Psychol Rep ... UMEA Psychological Reports [*A publication*]
UMEA Psychol Reports ... UMEA Psychological Reports [*A publication*]
UMEB .... United Maritime Executive Board
UMEC....... Union Mondiale des Enseignants Catholiques [*World Union of Catholic Teachers*] [*Rome, Italy*]
UMED...... Unimed, Inc. [*NASDAQ symbol*]   (NQ)
UMEJ........ Union Mondiale des Etudiants Juifs [*World Union of Jewish Students - WUJS*]   (EAIO)
UMEMPS ... Union of Middle Eastern and Mediterranean Pediatric Societies [*See also USPMOM*] [*Athens, Greece*]   (EAIO)
UMES .... United Mechanical Engineers' Society [*A union*] [*British*]
UMES .... University of Maryland, Eastern Shore
UmF.......... National Cash Register Co., New York, NY [*Library symbol*] [*Library of Congress*]   (LCLS)
UMF......... Ultramicrofiche
UMF......... Uniform Magnetic Field
UMF......... University of Maine at Farmington, Farmington, ME [*OCLC symbol*]   (OCLC)
UMFC ...... United Methodist Free Churches
UMFCBMA ... United Male and Female Cardboard Box Makers' Association [*A union*] [*British*]
UMFDC .... Union Mundial de Mujeres Democrata Cristianas [*World Union of Christian Democratic Women*] [*Venezuela*] [*Political party*]   (EAIO)
Umform Tech ... Umform Technik [*A publication*]
UMFP........ Unit Materiel Fielding Point [*Army*]   (RDA)
Umfrev Off Cor ... Umfreville's Office of Coroner [*A publication*]   (DLA)
UMFS........ United Mutual Fund Selector [*United Business Service Co.*]
UMG........ Universal Machine Gun   (MCD)
UMG .... Universal Matchbox Group Ltd. [*NYSE symbol*]   (SPSG)
UMG .... Universal Mercator Grid   (NVT)
UMHE....... United Ministries in Higher Education [*Later, HEMT/UMHE*]   (EA)
UMHI........ United Mobile Homes, Incorporated [*Eatontown, NJ*] [*NASDAQ symbol*]   (NQ)
UMHK ...... Union Miniere du Haut Katanga [*Mining Company of Upper Katanga*]

UMHP....... Union Mondiale des Societes d'Histoire Pharmaceutique [*World Organization of Societies of Pharmaceutical History*]
UMHS....... University of Miami. Hispanic Studies [*A publication*]
UMI.......... Udruzena Metalna Industrija [*Belgrade, Yugoslavia*]
UMI.......... Ukrainian Music Institute in America
UMI.......... Underway Material Inspection [*Navy*]   (NVT)
UMI.......... Union Mathematique Internationale [*International Mathematical Union - IMU*]   (EAIO)
UMI.......... Union de Melillenses Independientes [*Political party*] [*Spanish North Africa*]   (MENA)
UMI.......... Union Mundial pro Interlingua   (EA)
UMI.......... Unit Movement Identifier [*Army*]   (AABC)
UMI.......... United Methodist Information [*Database*] [*United Methodist Communications*] [*Information service or system*]   (CRD)
UMI.......... United States Minor Outlying Islands [*ANSI three-letter standard code*]   (CNC)
UMI.......... University Microfilms International [*Database producer*]   (IID)
UMi .... Ursa Minor [*Constellation*]
U Miami LR ... University of Miami. Law Review [*A publication*]
U Miami L Rev ... University of Miami. Law Review [*A publication*]
UMICH..... University of Michigan [*Ann Arbor, MI*]
U Mich Bus R ... University of Michigan. Business Review [*A publication*]
U Mich J Law Reform ... University of Michigan. Journal of Law Reform [*A publication*]
U Mich J L Ref ... University of Michigan. Journal of Law Reform [*A publication*]
UMIFA...... Uniform Management of Institutional Funds Act [*National Conference of Commissioners on Uniform State Laws*]
UMII .... Vitebsk [*USSR*] [*ICAO location identifier*]   (ICLI)
UMIN........ United Mining Corp. [*Reno, NV*] [*NASDAQ symbol*]   (NQ)
UMin........ Ursa Minor [*Constellation*]
UMINF ..... United Movement of Iranian National Forces   (EA)
UMIP .... Uniform Material Issue Priority [*Navy*]
UMIPS..... Uniform Material Issue Priority System [*Navy*]   (NG)
UMIS........ Urban Management Information System
U Missouri at KCL Rev ... University of Missouri at Kansas City. Law Review [*A publication*]
UMIST...... University of Manchester Institute of Science and Technology [*British*] [*Databank originator and research institute*]
UMIX .... User-Manufacturer Information Exchange
UMJ .... Ukrainian Mathematical Journal [*A publication*]
Umjet Rij ... Umjetnost Rijeci [*A publication*]
UMJL....... Union Mondiale pour un Judaisme Liberal
UMJOA .... Ulster Medical Journal [*A publication*]
UMK......... University of Missouri at Kansas City, Kansas City, MO [*OCLC symbol*]   (OCLC)
UMKC...... University of Missouri at Kansas City
UMKCLR ... University of Missouri at Kansas City. Law Review [*A publication*]
UMKC L Rev ... University of Missouri at Kansas City. Law Review [*A publication*]
UML.......... Universal Mission Load [*Military*]   (AABC)
UML.......... University of Missouri, Columbia School of Library and Information Science, Columbia, MO [*OCLC symbol*]   (OCLC)
U of MLB .. University of Missouri. Law Bulletin [*A publication*]   (DLA)
UMLC .... Institute of Estate Planning, University of Miami Law Center   (DLA)
UMLC .... Universal Multiline Controller
UMLC .... University of Miami Law Center   (DLA)
UMLER..... Universal Machine Language Equipment Register [*Association of American Railroads*] [*Information service or system*]   (CRD)
UMLR .... University of Malaya. Law Review [*A publication*]
UMLR .... University of Miami. Law Review [*A publication*]
UMLRB..... University of Miami. Law Review [*A publication*]
UMLS........ Ukrajins'ka Mova i Literatura v Skoli [*A publication*]
UMM .... Summit, AK [*Location identifier*] [*FAA*]   (FAAL)
UMM .... Union Mondiale du Mapam [*World Union of Mapam - WUM*]   (EAIO)
UMM .... United Merchants & Manufacturers, Inc. [*NYSE symbol*]   (SPSG)
UMM .... Universal Measuring Machine
UMM .... University of Manitoba Medical Library [*UTLAS symbol*]
UMMAN.. Ukrains'ka Mogiljans'ko-Mazepins'ka Akademija Nauk
UM-MaP... University of Maryland Mathematics Project
UMMC...... Union Metal Manufacturing [*NASDAQ symbol*]   (NQ)
UMMH ..... Unscheduled Maintenance Manhours   (MCD)
UMMIPS.. Uniform Materiel Movement and Issue Priority System [*Military*]   (AFM)
UMMJ ...... University of Manitoba. Medical Journal [*A publication*]
UMML...... Unione Medicale Mediterranea Latina [*Latin Mediterranean Medical Union - LMMU*] [*Mantua, Italy*]   (EAIO)
UMML...... University of Miami Marine Laboratory [*Florida*]
UMMM..... Minsk/Loshitsa [*USSR*] [*ICAO location identifier*]   (ICLI)
UMMPA3 ... Contributions. Museum of Paleontology. University of Michigan [*A publication*]
UMMZ...... University of Michigan Museum of Zoology
UMN .... Monett, MO [*Location identifier*] [*FAA*]   (FAAL)

UMN .... Union pour la Majorite Nouvelle [*Union for the New Majority*] [*France*] [*Political party*]   (PPE)

UMN .... Union des Musiciens Nordiques [*Nordic Musicians' Union - NMU*]   (EAIO)

UMN .... Unsatisfactory Material Notice   (MSA)

UMN .... Upper Motor Neuron [*Medicine*]

UMN .... Uspechi Matematiceskich Nauk [*A publication*]

UMNCF .... United Merchant Navy Christian Fellowship [*British*]

UMNL....... Upper Motor Neuron Lesion [*Neurology*]

UMNO ...... United Malays National Organization [*Malaysia*] [*Political party*]

UMO .... Umbertino's Restaurant [*Vancouver Stock Exchange symbol*]

UMO .... Unconventional Military Operations   (MCD)

UMO .... University of Maine, Orono

UMO .... Unmanned Orbital [*NASA*]   (NASA)

UMOA ...... Union Monetaire Ouest-Africaine [*West African Monetary Union*]

U MO B Law Ser ... University of Missouri. Bulletin. Law Series [*A publication*]   (DLA)

U MO Bull L Ser ... University of Missouri. Bulletin. Law Series [*A publication*]   (DLA)

UMOC....... Ugly Man on Campus [*Contest*]

UMOES .... Universal Masonic Order of the Eastern Star   (EA)

UMOFC .... Union Mondiale des Organisations Feminines Catholiques [*World Union of Catholic Women's Organizations - WUCWO*] [*Canada*]

U MO-Kansas City L Rev ... University of Missouri at Kansas City. Law Review [*A publication*]

U MO KCL Rev ... University of Missouri at Kansas City. Law Review [*A publication*]

UMOL....... Unmanned Orbital Laboratory

U MO L Bull ... University of Missouri. Law Bulletin [*A publication*]   (DLA)

UMOS....... U-Grooved Metal Oxide Semiconductors   (MCD)

UMoS .... University of Missouri. Studies [*A publication*]

UMOSBESL ... Union Mondiale des Organisations Syndicales sur Base Economique et Sociale Liberale [*World Union of Liberal Trade Union Organizations*]

UMOSEA ... Union Mondiale pour la Sauvegarde de l'Enfance et de l'Adolescence [*World Union for the Safeguard of Youth*]

UMP......... Umpire   (DSUE)

UMP......... Uniformly Most Powerful Test [*Statistics*]

UMP......... Uninflated Movement Party [*Australia*] [*Political party*]   (ADA)

UMP......... Union of Moderate Parties [*Vanuatu*] [*Political party*]   (PPW)

UMP......... Upper Mantle Project

UMP......... Upper Merion & Plymouth Railroad Co. [*AAR code*]

UMP......... Upward Mobility Program

UMP......... Uridine Monophosphate [*Biochemistry*]

UMPAL..... University of Minnesota. Pamphlets on American Literature [*A publication*]

UMPAW ... University of Minnesota. Pamphlets on American Writers [*A publication*]

UMPEAL ... University of Miami. Publications in English and American Literature [*A publication*]

UMPG....... University of Maine at Portland/Gorham

UMpGS..... Church of Jesus Christ of Latter-Day Saints, Genealogical Society Library, Mount Pleasant Branch, Stake Center, Mount Pleasant, UT [*Library symbol*] [*Library of Congress*]   (LCLS)

UMPLIS ... Informations- und Dokumentationssystem Umwelt [*Environmental Information and Documentation System*] [*Berlin*] [*Information retrieval*]

UMPLL.... University of Michigan. Publications in Language and Literature [*A publication*]

UMPR....... Uniform Military Personnel Record   (AFM)

UMPS........ Union Mondiale des Pioniers de Stockholm [*World Union of Stockholm Pioneers*]   (EAIO)

UMPT .... Ultrahigh-Frequency Multi-Platform Transceiver [*Navy*]   (MCD)

UMpW ...... Wasatch Academy, Mount Pleasant, UT [*Library symbol*] [*Library of Congress*]   (LCLS)

UMR......... Ultraviolet Mitogenic Radiation

UMR......... Unimar Indonesian Participating Units [*AMEX symbol*]   (SPSG)

UMR......... Unipolar Magnetic Regions

UMR......... Unit Mail Room [*Air Force*]   (AFM)

UMR......... University of Missouri at Rolla

UMR......... University of Missouri at Rolla, Library, Rolla, MO [*OCLC symbol*]   (OCLC)

UMR......... Unsatisfactory Material Report [*Military*]   (AABC)

UMR......... Upper Maximum Range

UMR......... Usual Marketing Requirement [*Business term*]

UMR......... Woomera [*Australia*] [*Airport symbol*]   (OAG)

UMRB....... Upper Mississippi River Basin

UMRCC ... Upper Mississippi River Conservation Committee   (EA)

UMREL..... Upper Midwest Regional Educational Laboratory, Inc.

UMREMP ... Upper Mississippi River Environmental Management Program [*Federal government*]

UMRG....... Ergli [*USSR*] [*ICAO location identifier*]   (ICLI)

UMRI Ne .. UMRI [*University of Michigan Research Institute*] News [*A publication*]

UMRL....... Union Mondiale des Romains Libres [*World Union of Free Romanians - WUFR*] [*Creteil, France*]   (EAIO)

UMR-MEC Conf Energy Resour Proc ... UMR-MEC [*University of Missouri, Rolla - Missouri Energy Council*] Conference on Energy Resources. Proceedings [*A publication*]

UMRR....... Riga/Spilve [*USSR*] [*ICAO location identifier*]   (ICLI)

UMRR....... University of Missouri Research Reactor

UMRW...... Ventspils [*USSR*] [*ICAO location identifier*]   (ICLI)

UMS......... Ukrajins'ka Mova v Skoli [*A publication*]

UMS......... Ultrasonic Motion Sensor   (MCD)

UMS......... Unattended Machinery Spaces   (DS)

UMS......... Unfederated Malay States

UMS......... United Missionary Society

UMS......... Universal Maintenance Standards

UMS......... Universal Memory System [*Intel Corp.*]

UMS......... Universal Military Service

UMS......... University of Maine. Studies [*A publication*]

UMS......... University of Michigan. Studies [*A publication*]

UMS......... University of Missouri at St. Louis, St. Louis, MO [*OCLC symbol*]   (OCLC)

UMS......... University of Missouri. Studies [*A publication*]

UMS......... Unmanned Multifunction Satellite

UMS......... Upstream Modulation Sequence [*Genetics*]

UMSA ...... United States Marine Safety Association   (EA)

UMSA ...... Utah-Manhattan-Sundt & Associates   (AAG)

UMSB ...... United Missouri Bancshares, Inc. [*NASDAQ symbol*]   (NQ)

Umsch........ Umschau [*A publication*]

Umschau.... Umschau in Wissenschaft und Technik [*A publication*]

Umsch Fortschr Wiss Tech ... Umschau ueber die Fortschritte in Wissenschaft und Technik [*A publication*]

Umsch Wiss und Tech ... Umschau in Wissenschaft und Technik [*A publication*]

Umsch Wiss Tech ... Umschau in Wissenschaft und Technik [*A publication*]

UMSDC .... Unscheduled Maintenance Sample Data Collection   (MCD)

UMSE .... Unconditional Mean Square Error [*Statistics*]

UMSE .... University of Mississippi. Studies in English [*A publication*]

UMSE .... Unmanned Surveillance Equipment

UMSHS .... University of Michigan. Studies. Humanistic Series [*A publication*]

UMSN .... Union Mondiale de Ski Nautique [*World Water Ski Union - WWSU*] [*Montreaux, Switzerland*]   (EAIO)

UMSOA .... Umi To Sora [*A publication*]

UMSP........ Universal Microscope Spectro-Photometer

UMSP........ User Maintenance Support Plan   (MCD)

UMSPA..... Uniform Metric System Procedure Act [*National Conference of Commissioners on Uniform State Laws*]

UMSR .... Universal Movement for Scientific Responsibility [*See also MURS*]   (EAIO)

UMSSS ..... UDAM [*Universal Digital Avionics Module*] Microprocessor Software Support System   (MCD)

Ums St G ... Umsatzsteuergesetz [*A publication*]

Umst G....... Umstellungsgesetz [*A publication*]

UMT......... Ultrasonic Material Testing

UMT......... Umiat, AK [*Location identifier*] [*FAA*]   (FAAL)

UMT......... Union Marocaine du Travail [*Moroccan Labor Union*]

UMT......... Unit of Medical Time [*Each 4-hour period after 40-hour work week*] [*British*]

UMT......... United Methodist Today [*A publication*]

UMT......... United Milk Tasmania Ltd. [*Australia*]

UMT......... Universal Microwave Trainer

UMT......... Universal Military Training [*Participants known as Umtees*] [*Army*] [*Post World War II*]

UMTA .... Urban Mass Transportation Act [*1964*]

UMTA .... Urban Mass Transportation Administration [*Department of Transportation*]

UMTD....... Using Mails to Defraud

UMTR .... Universal Movement Theater Repertory [*Defunct*]

UMTR .... University of Maryland Teaching Reactor   (NRCH)

UMTRAP ... Uranium Mill Trailings Remedial Action Program [*Department of Energy*]

UMTRI..... University of Michigan Transportation Research Institute [*Research center*]   (RCD)

UMTRIS ... Urban Mass Transportation Research Information Service [*National Academy of Sciences*] [*Database*]   (IID)

UMTRI (Univ Mich Transportation Research Inst) ... UMTRI (University Michigan Transportation Research Institute) Research Review [*A publication*]

UMTS .... Universal Military Training Service [*or System*]   (GPO)

UMTSA..... Universal Military Training and Service Act

UMu .... Murray Public Library, Murray, UT [*Library symbol*] [*Library of Congress*]   (LCLS)

UMU .... Uplink Multiplexer Unit   (MCD)

UMUKY.... Universal Money Centers PLC ADR [*NASDAQ symbol*]   (NQ)

UMUS....... Unbleached Muslin

UMVBA6 .. Contributions. Laboratory of Vertebrate Biology. University of Michigan [*A publication*]

UMVF .... Union Mondiale des Voix Francaises [*World Union of French-Speakers - WUFS*]   (EAIO)

UMVF .... Unmanned Vertical Flight [*NASA*]   (NASA)

UMW......... Ultramicrowaves

UMW......... Umwelt [*A publication*]

UMW......... Upper Midwest
UMWA...... International Union, United Mine Workers of America [*Also known as UMW*] (EA)
UMWA...... United Machine Workers' Association [*A union*] [*British*]
Umwelt Inf Bundesminist Innern ... Umwelt. Informationen des Bundesministers des Innern zur Umweltplanung und zum Umweltschutz [*A publication*]
Umweltpolit Umweltplanung ... Umweltpolitik und Umweltplanung [*A publication*]
Umwelt-Rep ... Umwelt-Report [*A publication*]
Umweltschutz Gesundheitstech ... Umweltschutz. Gesundheitstechnik [*A publication*]
Umweltschutz - Staedtereinig ... Umweltschutz - Staedtereinigung [*A publication*]
Umwelt Z Biol Stn Wilhelminenberg ... Umwelt Zeitschrift der Biologischen Station Wilhelminenberg [*A publication*]
UMW J ..... United Mine Workers. Journal [*A publication*]
UMWLA ... Umwelt Zeitschrift der Biologischen Station Wilhelminenberg [*A publication*]
Umw Planungsrecht ... Umwelt- und Planungsrecht [*A publication*]
UMWSF.... United Methodist Women in Switzerland and in France (EAIO)
Umw St G .. Umwandlungssteuergesetz [*A publication*]
UMWTA ... Umwelt [*A publication*]
UMWW..... Vilnius [*USSR*] [*ICAO location identifier*] (ICLI)
UMx .... University of Mexico [*A publication*]
UMZHA.... Ukrainskii Matematicheskii Zhurnal [*A publication*]
UN .... Nephi Public Library, Nephi, UT [*Library symbol*] [*Library of Congress*] (LCLS)
UN .... Unable (FAAC)
UN .... Unassigned [*Telecommunications*] (TEL)
UN .... Underworld Nobility [*Used by Walter Winchell to refer to mobsters in television series "The Untouchables"*]
UN .... Unico National (EA)
UN .... Unified (AAG)
UN .... Unilever NV [*NYSE symbol*] (SPSG)
UN .... Union (MSA)
UN .... Union Flag [*Navy*] [*British*]
UN .... Union Nacional [*National Union*] [*Spain*] [*Political party*] (PPE)
UN .... Union Nationale [*National Union*] [*Canada*] [*Political party*]
UN .... Unit (AAG)
UN .... United
UN .... United Nations (EA)
UN .... University
UN .... Unknown [*Telecommunications*] (TEL)
UN .... Untreated [*Medicine*]
UN .... Urea-Nitrogen [*Medicine*]
UNA .... Ukrainian National Association (EA)
UNA .... Unalaska [*Alaska*] [*Seismograph station code, US Geological Survey*] [*Closed*] (SEIS)
UNA .... Underwear-Negligee Associates (EA)
UNA .... Unione Nazionale dell'Avicoltura [*Aviculture Union*] [*Italy*] (EY)
UNA .... United Nations Association
UNA .... United Native Americans (EA)
UNA .... United States Naval Academy, Annapolis, MD [*OCLC symbol*] (OCLC)
UNA .... Universal Network Achitecture [*Telecommunications*]
UNA .... Universal Night Answering [*Telecommunications*] (TEL)
UNAAA..... Ukrainian National Aid Association of America (EA)
UNAAF..... Unified Action Armed Forces [*Military*]
UNAB....... Unabridged (ADA)
Unabashed Libn ... Unabashed Librarian [*A publication*]
UNABR..... Unabridged
UNAC....... United Nations Appeal for Children
UNAC....... United Nations Association in Canada (EAIO)
UNACC..... Unaccompanied
UNACOM ... Universal Army Communication System
UNACOMA ... Unione Nazionale Costruttori Macchine Agricole [*Farm Machinery Manufacturers Union*] [*Italy*] (EY)
UNA Commun ... UNA [*Utah Nurses Association*] Communique [*A publication*]
UNADE..... Union Nacional Democratica [*National Democratic Union*] [*Ecuador*] [*Political party*] (PPW)
UNADS..... UNIVAC Automated Documentation System [*Data processing*]
UNAEC..... United Nations Atomic Energy Commission [*Superseded by Disarmament Commission, 1952*]
UNAECC .. United Nations Atomic Energy Control Commission
UNAF....... Universities National Antiwar Fund
UNAFEI.... United Nations Asia and Far East Institute for the Prevention of Crime and Treatment of Offenders
UNAFPA... Union des Associations des Fabricants de Pates Alimentaires de la Communaute Economique Europeenne [*Union of Organizations of Manufacturers of Pasta Products in the European Economic Community*]
UNAGA..... Union Agriculture [*A publication*]
UNAH....... Universidad Nacional Autonoma, Tegucigalpa [*Honduras*]
UNAIS....... United Nations Association International Service [*British*]
UNAKI...... Union des Colons Agricoles du Kivu [*Union of Agricultural Settlers of Kivu*] [*Congo - Leopoldville*]

UNALC ..... User Network Access Link Control
UNALOT .. Unallotted (AABC)
UNALTD .. Unaltered (ROG)
UNAM ...... Unico American Corp. [*NASDAQ symbol*] (NQ)
UNAMACE ... Universal Automatic Map Compilation Equipment
UNAMAP ... Users Network for Applied Modeling of Air Pollution [*Set of computer simulation models being developed by Battelle for EPA*]
UNAMI..... Uniao Nacional Africana de Mocambique Independente [*Mozambique*] [*Political party*]
UNAM/RMS ... Revista Mexicana de Sociologia. Universidad Nacional Autonoma de Mexico. Instituto de Investigaciones Sociales [*A publication*]
UNAN ...... Unanimous
UNANSD ... Unanswered (ROG)
UNA Nursing J ... UNA Nursing Journal [*Royal Victorian College of Nursing*] [*A publication*] (APTA)
UNA Nurs J ... UNA [*Utah Nurses Association*] Nursing Journal [*A publication*]
UNAP........ Union Nationale Progressite [*National Progressive Union*] [*Burundi*]
UNAPEC... United Nations Action Program for Economic Cooperation
Un Apic...... Union Apicole [*A publication*]
UNAPOC.. United National Association of Post Office Craftsmen [*Later, APWU*]
UNAPPD... Unappointed (ROG)
UNAPV..... Unable to Approve (FAAC)
UNAR....... Unable to Approve Altitude Requested [*Aviation*] (FAAC)
UNAR....... Union Nationale Ruandaise [*Ruanda National Union*]
UNARU..... Union Nationale Africaine du Ruanda-Urundi [*African National Union of Ruanda-Urundi*]
UNASA ..... Unasylva [*A publication*]
UNASABEC ... Union Nationale des Syndicats Agricoles Forestiers, des Bois, de l'Elevage, et de la Peche du Cameroun [*National Union of Farmers, Fishermen, Forest Guards, and Timber Workers of Cameroun*]
UNASGD .. Unassigned (AABC)
UNASGN .. Unassigned [*Navy*] (NVT)
UNASSD... Unassembled
UNAT........ Union Nationale des Agriculteurs Tunisiens [*National Union of Tunisian Farmers*]
UNATAC .. Union d'Assistance Technique pour l'Automobile et la Circulation Routiere [*Union of Technical Assistance for Motor Vehicle and Road Traffic*] [*Geneva, Switzerland*] (EAIO)
UNATRACAM ... Union des Associations Traditionelles du Cameroun [*Union of Traditional Associations of Cameroon*]
UNATRACO ... Union Nationale des Travailleurs du Congo [*National Union of Workers of the Congo*]
UNATT ..... Unattached (ROG)
UNATT ..... Unattended (ADA)
UNATTRIB ... Unattributed
UNA-UK ... United Nations Association of Great Britain and Northern Ireland (EAIO)
UNA-USA ... United Nations Association of the United States of America (EA)
Unauth .... Unauthorized (DLA)
UNAUTHD ... Unauthorized (AABC)
Unauth Prac News ... Unauthorized Practice News [*A publication*]
UNAVBL... Unavailable (FAAC)
UNAVEM ... United Nations Angola Verification Mission
UNAVIC ... United Nations Audiovisual Information Center
UNB.......... Fredericton [*New Brunswick*] [*Seismograph station code, US Geological Survey*] (SEIS)
UNB.......... Kanab, UT [*Location identifier*] [*FAA*] (FAAL)
UNB.......... Unbound (ROG)
UNB.......... Unexploded Booklet [*Philately*]
UNB.......... United Nations Beacon
UNB.......... Universal Navigation Beacon
UNB.......... University of New Brunswick [*Canada*]
UNB.......... University of New Brunswick Library [*UTLAS symbol*]
UNBAL ..... Unbalanced [*Telecommunications*] (TEL)
UNBB........ Barnaul [*USSR*] [*ICAO location identifier*] (ICLI)
UNBC........ Union National Corporation [*NASDAQ symbol*] (NQ)
UnBCh....... United Board Chaplain [*British military*]
UNBCL ..... University of Nebraska College of Law [*Lincoln, NE*] (DLA)
Un Bd Ch ... United Board Chaplain [*British military*] (DMA)
UNBIS....... United Nations Bibliographic Information System [*United Nations Headquarters*] (IID)
Un Bi Soc Bull ... United Bible Societies. Bulletin [*A publication*]
UNBJ........ United National Bancorp [*NASDAQ symbol*] (NQ)
UNB Law Journal ... University of New Brunswick. Law Journal [*A publication*]
UNB L J ... University of New Brunswick. Law Journal [*A publication*]
UNBLK ..... Unblanking (MSA)
UNBLSJ.... University of New Brunswick. Law School. Journal [*A publication*] (DLA)
UNBS .... United Buying Service International, Inc. [*NASDAQ symbol*] (NQ)
UNBSA ..... United Nations Bureau of Social Affairs
UNBT........ United Nations "Blue Top" [*A publication*]

UNBTAO..   United Nations Bureau of Technical Assistance Operations
UN Bul.......   United Nations Bulletin [*A publication*]
UN Bull.....   United Nations Bulletin [*A publication*]
UN/C.........   Chungara. Universidad del Norte. Departamento de Antropologia [*A publication*]
UNC..........   UNC, Inc. [*Formerly, United Nuclear Corporation*] [*NYSE symbol*]   (SPSG)
Unc............   Uncanny Stories [*A publication*]
UNC..........   Uncertain   (ADA)
UNC..........   Uncirculated [*Numismatics*]
UNC..........   Unclassified   (KSC)
UNC..........   Uncle   (DSUE)
UNC..........   Unified Coarse [*Thread*]
UNC..........   Union Nationale Camerounaise [*Cameroon National Union*]
UNC..........   Union Nouvelle Caledonienne [*Political party*] [*New Caledonia*]   (FEA)
UNC..........   United Corporations Ltd. [*Toronto Stock Exchange symbol*]
UNC..........   United National Convention [*Ghana*] [*Political party*]   (PPW)
UNC..........   United Nations Command
UNC..........   United Network Company [*TV broadcasting network*]
UNC..........   United New Conservationists   (EA)
UNC..........   Universal Navigation Computer
UNC..........   University of North Carolina [*Chapel Hill, NC*]
UNC..........   University of Northern Colorado [*Formerly, Colorado State College*] [*Greeley*]
UNC..........   Uranyl Nitrate Concentrate [*Nuclear energy*]
UNCA.......   United Nations Correspondents Association   (EA)
UNCA.......   United Neighborhood Centers of America   (EA)
UNCAA .....   United Nations Centre Against Apartheid   (EA)
UNCACK ..   United Nations Civil Assistance Command, Korea
UNCAFE...   United Nations Commission for Asia and the Far East
UNCAH ...   Union Nacional de Campesinas Autenticos de Honduras [*National Union of Authentic Peasants of Honduras*]   (PD)
UNCAST...   United Nations Conference on Applications of Science and Technology [*1963*]
UNCASTD ...   United Nations Advisory Committee on the Application of Science and Technology to Development   (ASF)
UNCAT .....   Uncatalogued   (ADA)
UNCC........   Unable to Contact Company Radio   (FAAC)
UNCC........   Union Nationale des Cheminots du Cameroun [*National Union of Railway Workers of Cameroon*]
UNCC.......   University of North Carolina at Charlotte
UNC-CH ...   University of North Carolina at Chapel Hill
UN CCOP Newslett ...   United Nations Committee for Coordination of Joint Prospecting. Newsletter [*A publication*]
UNCCP ......   United Nations Conciliation Commission for Palestine
UNCDF......   United Nations Capital Development Fund
UNCE.......   Novokuznetsk [*USSR*] [*ICAO location identifier*]   (ICLI)
UNCE.......   United Nations Commission for Europe
UNCERT...   Uncertainty [*Standard deviation*] [*Data processing*]
UNCF.......   United Companies Financial Corp. [*NASDAQ symbol*]   (NQ)
UNCF.......   United Negro College Fund   (EA)
UNCG.......   Uncage
UNCG.......   University of North Carolina, Greensboro
UNCHBP ..   Center for Housing, Building, and Planning [*United Nations*]
UNCHE.....   United Nations Conference on the Human Environment   (MSC)
UNCHR.....   United Nations Centre for Human Rights   (EAIO)
UNCHR.....   United Nations High Commissioner for Refugees   (DLA)
UN Chron..   United Nations Chronicle [*A publication*]
UNCHS.....   United Nations Center for Human Settlement [*Research center*] [*Kenya*]   (IRC)
UNCI........   United Nations Committee on Information   (EA)
UNCID......   Uniform Rules of Conduct for Interchange of Trade Data by Teletransmission [*ICC Publishing Co.*] [*A publication*]
UNCIO......   Documents. United Nations Conference on International Organization [*A publication*]
UNCIO......   United Nations Conference on International Organization [*San Francisco, 1945*]
UNCIP......   United Nations Commission for India and Pakistan
UNCITRAL ...   United Nations Commission on International Trade Law
UNCIVPOL ...   United Nations Civilian Police [*Peace-keeping force in Cyprus*]
UNCIWC ..   United Nations Commission for Investigation of War Criminals
UNCL........   Kolpashevo [*USSR*] [*ICAO location identifier*]   (ICLI)
UNCLAS...   Unclassified   (AABC)
UNCLE .....   United Network Command for Law and Enforcement [*Fictitious intelligence organization in various television series*]
UNCLOS...   United Nations Conference on the Law of the Sea
UNCLP......   Unclamp
UNCM......   User Network Control Machine
UNCMAC ...   United Nations Command Military Armistice Commission
UNCMD....   United Nations Command
UNCN ......   United Nations Censorship Network
UNCOA.....   UNESCO [*United Nations Educational, Scientific, and Cultural Organization*] Courier [*A publication*]
UNCOD ....   United Nations Conference on Desertification
UNCOK.....   United Nations Committee on Korea

UNCOL.....   Universal Computer Oriented Language [*Programming language*] [*Data processing*]
UN Comm Int'l Trade LYB ...   United Nations Commission on International Trade Law. Yearbook [*A publication*]   (DLA)
uncomp.......   Uncomplicated
uncon........   Unconscious
UNCON ....   Uncontainerable Goods [*Shipping*]   (DS)
uncond........   Unconditioned
UNCONDL ...   Unconditional   (ROG)
UNCONFD ...   Unconfirmed   (ROG)
Unconsol Laws ...   Unconsolidated Laws [*A publication*]   (DLA)
UNCOPUOS ...   United Nations Committee on the Peaceful Uses of Outer Space
uncorr........   Uncorrected
Uncov ....   Uncover
UNCP........   United Nations Conference of Plenipotentiaries
UNCR ......   United Nations Command (Rear)
UNCR ....   University of North Carolina. Record. Research in Progress [*A publication*]
UNCRD.....   United Nations Center for Regional Development
UNCSCL...   University of North Carolina. Studies in Comparative Literature [*A publication*]
UNCSF......   United Nations Command Security Force [*Military*]   (INF)
UNCSGL...   University of North Carolina. Studies in Germanic Languages and Literatures [*A publication*]
UNCSGLL ...   University of North Carolina. Studies in Germanic Languages and Literatures [*A publication*]
UNCSRL...   University of North Carolina. Studies in the Romance Languages and Literatures [*A publication*]
UNCSRLL ...   University of North Carolina. Studies in the Romance Languages and Literatures [*A publication*]
UNCSTD...   United Nations Center for Science and Technology for Development [*Later, CSTD*]   (EAIO)
UNCSTD...   United Nations Centre for Science and Technology for Development   (EA)
UNCT.......   Unctus [*Smeared*] [*Pharmacy*]
UNCT.......   Uncut   (ROG)
UNCTAD..   United Nations Conference on Trade and Development
UNCTD.....   Uncoated
UNCURK..   United Nations Commission for the Unification and Rehabilitation of Korea
UNCW......   Novy Vasyugan [*USSR*] [*ICAO location identifier*]   (ICLI)
UND ....   Kunduz [*Afghanistan*] [*Airport symbol*] [*Obsolete*]   (OAG)
UND ....   Undecaprenol [*Organic chemistry*]
UND ....   Under   (AAG)
und ....   Undetermined [*MARC language code*] [*Library of Congress*]   (LCCP)
Und ....   Undivided   (DLA)
UND ....   Union Nationale et Democratique [*National Democratic Union*] [*Monaco*] [*Political party*]   (PPW)
UND ....   Unit Derating [*Electronics*]   (IEEE)
UND ....   University of National Defense [*Formerly, Industrial College of the Armed Forces and National War College*]
UND ....   University of North Dakota, Grand Forks, ND [*OCLC symbol*]   (OCLC)
UND ....   University of Notre Dame [*Indiana*]   (KSC)
UND ....   Urgency of Need Designator [*Military*]   (AFM)
UND ....   User Need Date   (KSC)
UNDA ....   Uniform Narcotic Drug Act [*National Conference of Commissioners on Uniform State Laws*]
Und Art Cop ...   Underwood on Art Copyright [*A publication*]   (DLA)
UNDAT....   United Nations Development Advisory Team
UNDBK.....   Undivided Back [*Deltiology*]
UNDC.......   Undercurrent
UNDC.......   United Nations Disarmament Commission [*Also, DC, DC(UN)*]
UNDCC.....   United Nations Development Cooperation Cycle
Und Child ..   Understanding the Child [*A publication*]
Und Ch Pr ...   Underhill's Chancery Procedure [*1881*] [*A publication*]   (DLA)
Und Conv ...   Underhill on New Conveyancing [*1925*] [*A publication*]   (DLA)
UNDED.....   Undercurrents [*A publication*]
UNDED.....   Undereducated
UNDEF .....   Undefined
UNDEL.....   Unione Nazionale Dipendenti Enti Locali [*National Union of Local Government Employees*] [*Italy*]
UNDELORDCAN ...   Undelivered Orders Cancelled [*Military*]
UNDERC..   University of North Dakota Energy Research Center [*Grand Forks, ND*] [*Department of Energy*]   (GRD)
Undercur....   Undercurrents [*A publication*]
Underground Eng ...   Underground Engineering [*A publication*]
Underground Min Symp ...   Underground Mining Symposia [*A publication*]
Underground Water Conf Aust Newsl ...   Underground Water Conference of Australia. Newsletter [*A publication*]   (APTA)
Undergr Wat Supply Pap (Tasm) ...   Underground Water Supply Papers (Tasmania) [*A publication*]   (APTA)
Underhill Ev ...   Underhill on Evidence [*A publication*]   (DLA)
Under Lttr ...   Underwater Letter [*A publication*]
UNDERSD ...   Undersea   (ROG)
Undersea Biomed Res ...   Undersea Biomedical Research [*A publication*]
Undersea Technol ...   Undersea Technology [*A publication*]
UNDERSECNAV ...   Under Secretary of the Navy

Under Sign ... Under the Sign of Pisces/Anais Nin and Her Circle [*A publication*]
UNDERSTG ... Understanding (ROG)
UNDERTG ... Undertaking (ROG)
Underwater Inf Bull ... Underwater Information Bulletin [*A publication*]
Underwater J ... Underwater Journal [*A publication*]
Underwater J & Inf Bull ... Underwater Journal and Information Bulletin [*A publication*]
Underwater J Inf Bull ... Underwater Journal and Information Bulletin [*A publication*]
Underwater Nat ... Underwater Naturalist [*A publication*]
Underwater Sci Technol J ... Underwater Science and Technology Journal [*A publication*]
Underw J Inf Bull ... Underwater Journal and Information Bulletin [*A publication*]
Underwriters Lab Stand ... Underwriters Laboratories. Standards [*A publication*]
Underwrit Lab Bull Res ... Underwriters Laboratories. Bulletin of Research [*A publication*]
UNDET ..... Undetermined
UNDETM ... Undetermined (AABC)
UNDEX ..... Underwater Explosion [*Navy*]
UNDEX ..... United Nations Index [*A publication*]
UNDF .... Underfrequency
UNDG .... Undergoing (AABC)
UNDH .... Unit Derated Hours [*Electronics*] (IEEE)
UNDHR .... United Nations Declaration of Human Rights (BJA)
UNDI .... United Nations Document Index
Un Dk .... Under Deck Tank [*on a ship*] (DS)
UNDK .... Undock [*NASA*] (KSC)
UNDLD ..... Undelivered (FAAC)
UNDLD ..... Underload
UNDO .... Ukrainian National Democratic Organization
UNDO .... Union for National Draft Opposition
UN Doc ...... United Nations Documents [*A publication*]
UN Doc E .. United Nations Documents. Economic and Social Council [*A publication*]
Und-Oder-Nor Steuerungstech ... Und-Oder-Nor und Steuerungstechnik [*A publication*]
Und-Oder-Nor & Steuerungstech ... Und-Oder-Nor und Steuerungstechnik [*A publication*]
UNDOF ..... United Nations Disengagement Observer Force [*Damascus, Syria*]
UNDP .... United Nations Development Programme (EA)
UNDP .... University of Notre Dame Press
Und Part .... Underhill on Parternship [*10th ed.*] [*1975*] [*A publication*] (DLA)
UNDP/FAO Pakistan Nat For Res Train Proj Rep ... UNDP [*United Nations Development Programme*]/FAO [*Food and Agriculture Organization of the United Nations*] Pakistan National Forestry Research and Training Project Report [*A publication*]
UNDRO .... United Nations Disaster Relief Office (EAIO)
UND SHER ... Under Sheriff (DLA)
Und Torts .. Underhill on Torts [*A publication*] (DLA)
Und Tr .... Underhill on Trusts and Trustees [*A publication*] (DLA)
UNDV .... Undervoltage
UNDW ..... Underwater (KSC)
UNDWC .... Ultrasonically Nebulized Distilled Water Challenge
UNE .... Qacha's Nek [*Lesotho*] [*Airport symbol*] (OAG)
UNE .... Umweltschutzdienst. Informationsdienst fuer Umweltfragen [*A publication*]
UNE .... Underground Nuclear Explosion
UNE .... United Nations European Headquarters [*Geneva, Switzerland*]
UNE .... Universal Nonlinear Element
UNE .... University of North Dakota, Law Library, Grand Forks, ND [*OCLC symbol*] (OCLC)
UNEA .... Unearth [*A publication*]
UNEASICO ... Union des Etudiants et Anciens des Instituts Sociaux de Congo [*Congolese Union of Students and Former Students of Social Institutes*]
UNEC .... Union Nationale des Etudiants Camerounais [*National Union of Cameroonese Students*]
UNEC .... United Nations Education Conference
UNEC .... Unnecessary (FAAC)
UNECA ..... United Nations Economic Commission for Africa (EA)
UNECO ..... Union Economique du Congo [*Economic Union of the Congo*] [*Usumbura*]
UNECOLAIT ... Union Europeenne du Commerce Laitier [*European Milk Trade Union*] [*Common Market*]
UN Econ Comm Asia Far East Water Resour Ser ... United Nations Economic Commission for Asia and the Far East. Water Resources Series [*A publication*]
UN Econ Comm Eur Comm Agr Prob Work Party Mech Agr AGRI/WP ... United Nations Economic Commission for Europe. Committee on Agricultural Problems. Working Party on Mechanization of Agriculture AGRI/WP [*A publication*]
UN Econo Comm Asia Far East Miner Resour Develop Ser ... United Nations Economic Commission for Asia and the Far East. Mineral Resources Development Series [*A publication*]

UNECOSOC ... United Nations Economic and Social Council. Official Record [*A publication*] (DLA)
UNEDA ..... United Nations Economic Development Administration
UN (Educ Sci Cult Organ) Cour ... UNESCO (United Nations Educational, Scientific, and Cultural Organization) Courier [*A publication*]
UNEEG ..... Union Nationale des Eleves et Etudiants de la Guadeloupe [*National Union of Pupils and Students of Guadeloupe*] (PD)
UNEEM .... Union Nationale des Eleves et Etudiants du Mali [*National Union of Pupils and Students of Mali*] (PD)
UNEF .... Unified Extra Fine [*Thread*]
UNEF .... United Nations Emergency Force [*to separate hostile forces of Israel and Egypt*]
UNEF .... United Nations Environment Fund
UNEGA ..... Union Europeenne des Fondeurs et Fabricants de Corps Gras Animaux [*European Union of Animal Fat Producers*] (EA)
UNEM .... Union Nationale des Etudiants du Maroc [*National Union of Moroccan Students*] (PD)
Unempl Ins Rep ... Unemployment Insurance Reports [*Commerce Clearing House*] [*A publication*] (DLA)
Unempl Ins Rep (CCH) ... Unemployment Insurance Reports (Commerce Clearing House) [*A publication*] (DLA)
Unemployment Ins Statis ... Unemployment Insurance Statistics [*A publication*]
Unempl Unit Bull Briefing ... Unemployment Unit Bulletin and Briefing [*A publication*]
UNEP .... United Nations Environment Programme [*Kenya*] [*Database originator*] (EAIO)
UNEP .... University of New England Press [*Australia*] (ADA)
UNEP/IRS ... United Nations Environment Programme/International Referral System
UNEPPA .... United Nations Environment Programme Participation Act of 1973
UNERG ..... United Nations Conference on New and Renewable Sources of Energy [*1981*]
UNESCAP ... United Nations Economic and Social Commission for Asia and the Pacific
UNESCO .. United Nations Educational, Scientific, and Cultural Organization [*France*] [*Database originator and operator*] [*Research center*]
UNESCO B Li ... UNESCO [*United Nations Educational, Scientific, and Cultural Organization*] Bulletin for Libraries [*A publication*]
UNESCO Bul Lib ... UNESCO [*United Nations Educational, Scientific, and Cultural Organization*] Bulletin for Libraries [*A publication*]
UNESCO Bull Lib ... UNESCO [*United Nations Educational, Scientific, and Cultural Organization*] Bulletin for Libraries [*A publication*]
UNESCO Bull Libr ... UNESCO [*United Nations Educational, Scientific, and Cultural Organization*] Bulletin for Libraries [*A publication*]
UNESCO Cour ... UNESCO [*United Nations Educational, Scientific, and Cultural Organization*] Courier [*A publication*]
UNESCO Inf Circ ... Australian National Advisory Committee for UNESCO [*United Nations Scientific, Educational, and Cultural Organization*]. Information Circular [*A publication*] (APTA)
UNESCO/IRE ... International Review of Education. United Nations Educational, Scientific, and Cultural Organization. Institute for Education [*A publication*]
UNESCO J Inf Sci Librarianship and Arch Adm ... UNESCO [*United Nations Educational, Scientific, and Cultural Organization*] Journal of Information Science, Librarianship, and Archives Administration [*A publication*]
UNESCO Nat Resour Res ... United Nations Educational, Scientific, and Cultural Organization. Natural Resources Research [*A publication*]
UNESCOR ... United Nations Economic and Social Council Official Record [*A publication*] (DLA)
UNESCO-ROSTA ... UNESCO Regional Office for Science and Technology in Africa [*See also BRUSTA*] [*Nairobi, Kenya*] (EAIO)
UNESCOSFY ... UNESCO Special Fund for Youth (EAIO)
UNESCO Tech Pap Mar Sci ... UNESCO [*United Nations Educational, Scientific, and Cultural Organization*] Technical Papers in Marine Science [*A publication*]
UNESDA .. Union of EEC Soft Drinks Associations (EAIO)
UNESEM ... Union Europeenne des Sources d'Eaux Minerales du Marche Commun [*European Union of Natural Mineral Water Sources of the Common Market*] (EAIO)
UNESOB ... United Nations Economic and Social Office in Beirut
UNET .... United Energy Technology [*NASDAQ symbol*] (NQ)
UNETAS ... United Nations Emergency Technical Aid Service
UNETPSA ... United Nations Educational and Training Program for Southern Africa
UNEV .... Unevaluated (MCD)
unev .... Uneven [*Quality of the bottom*] [*Nautical charts*]
UNEW .... United Newspapers PLC [*NASDAQ symbol*] (NQ)

U Newark L Rev ... University of Newark. Law Review [*A publication*] (DLA)
U New Brunswick LJ ... University of New Brunswick. Law Journal [*A publication*]
U New South Wales LJ ... University of New South Wales. Law Journal [*A publication*]
U New S Wales LJ ... University of New South Wales. Law Journal [*A publication*]
UNEX........ Unexecuted
UNEXPL... Unexplained
UNEXPL... Unexploded
UNEXPL... Unexplored
UNEXSO .. Underwater Explorers Society (EA)
UNF.......... Unfinished [*Technical drawings*]
UNF.......... Unfused (KSC)
UNF.......... Unified Fine [*Thread*]
UNF.......... Unifirst Corp. [*NYSE symbol*] (SPSG)
UNF.......... Union Flights [*Sacramento, CA*] [*FAA designator*] (FAAC)
UNF.......... Union Freight R. R. [*AAR code*]
UNF.......... United National Front [*Lebanese*] (BJA)
UNF.......... Universal National Fine (MCD)
UNF.......... University of North Dakota, Medical Library, Grand Forks, ND [*OCLC symbol*] (OCLC)
UNFAO..... United Nations Food and Agriculture Organization
UNFAO (Organ) World Soil Resour Rep ... United Nations. FAO (Food and Agriculture Organization) World Soil Resources Reports [*A publication*]
UNFAV ..... Unfavorable
UNFB .... United Nations Film Board
UNFC .... Universal Fuels Company [*NASDAQ symbol*] (NQ)
UNFDAC ... United Nations Fund for Drug Abuse Control
UNFF .... United First Federal Savings & Loan [*NASDAQ symbol*] (NQ)
UNFGA ..... Unternehmensforschung [*A publication*]
UNFI .... Unfinished
UNFICYP ... United Nations Forces in Cyprus (DMA)
UNFIN .... Unfinished
UNFKA ..... Uspekhi Nauchnoi Fotografii [*A publication*]
UNFO .... Unidentified Nonflying Objects
UNFP .... Union Nationale des Forces Populaires [*National Union of Popular Forces*] [*Political party*] [*Morocco*]
UNFP .... United National Federal Party [*Zimbabwe*] [*Political party*] (PPW)
UNFPA....... United Nations Fund for Population Activities
UNFR .... Uniforce Temporary Personnel, Inc. [*New Hyde Park, NY*] [*NASDAQ symbol*] (NQ)
UNFSSTD ... United Nations Financing System for Science and Technology for Development (EY)
UNFT .... Union Nationale des Femmes de Tunisie [*National Union of Tunisian Women*]
UNFTP....... Unified Navy Field Test Program (MCD)
UNFURNOTE ... Until Further Notice [*Military*]
UNG .... Kiunga [*Papua New Guinea*] [*Airport symbol*] (OAG)
UNG .... Ungava [*Canada*]
UNG .... Unguentum [*Ointment*] [*Pharmacy*]
UNG .... Union Gas Ltd. [*AMEX symbol*] [*Delisted*] [*Toronto Stock Exchange symbol*] (SPSG)
UNGA .... United Nations General Assembly (MCD)
UNGAOR ... United Nations General Assembly Official Record [*A publication*] (DLA)
Ungar Fil L ... Ungar Film Library [*A publication*]
Ungarische Rundschau ... Ungarische Rundschau fuer Historische und Sociale Wissenschaften [*A publication*]
UNGEGN ... United Nations Group of Experts on Geographical Names
Ungerer's Bull ... Ungerer's Bulletin [*A publication*]
Ung Forstwiss Rundsch ... Ungarische Forstwissenschaftliche Rundschau [*A publication*]
Un of Gh LJ ... University of Ghana. Law Journal [*A publication*] (DLA)
Ung Jhb ..... Ungarische Jahrbuecher [*A publication*]
UNGOMAP ... United Nations Good Offices Mission in Afghanistan and Pakistan
UNGR........ Ungermann-Bass, Inc. [*NASDAQ symbol*] (NQ)
UNGT........ Unguentum [*Ointment*] [*Pharmacy*]
UN-GTDI ... United Nations Guidelines for Trade Data Interchange
Ung Z Berg Huettenwes Bergbau ... Ungarische Zeitschrift fuer Berg und Huettenwesen. Bergbau [*A publication*]
UNH .... United Homes, Inc. [*Vancouver Stock Exchange symbol*]
UNH .... Uranyl Nitrate Hexahydrate [*Inorganic chemistry*]
UNHC .... United Nations High Commission (BJA)
UNHCC..... University of New Haven Computer Center [*Research center*] (RCD)
UNHCR..... United Nations High Commission [*or Commissioner*] for Refugees
UNHJ .... University of Newcastle. Historical Journal [*A publication*] (APTA)
UNHNOCY ... United Nations Headquarters Nongovernmental Organizations Committee on Youth (EA)
UNHQ........ United Nations Headquarters (EA)
UNHRC..... United Nations Human Rights Commission (BJA)
UNHRD .... Unheard (FAAC)
UNI............ Athens/Albany, OH [*Location identifier*] [*FAA*] (FAAL)
UNI............ Undistributed Net Income [*Banking*]

Uni .... Unicorn [*Record label*]
UNI............ Unicorp Canada Corp. [*Toronto Stock Exchange symbol*]
UNI............ Uniform (DSUE)
UNI............ Union Island [*Windward Islands*] [*Airport symbol*] (OAG)
UNI............ Union Nationale pour l'Independence [*National Union for Independence*] [*Djibouti*] (PPW)
UNI............ Union Nationale des Independents [*National Union of Independents*] [*Monaco*] (PPE)
UNI............ United News of India Ltd. [*News agency*] (FEA)
UNI............ United States International Airways
UNI............ Unity Railways Co. [*AAR code*]
Uni .... Universe Science Fiction [*A publication*]
UNI............ University (ADA)
UNI............ University of Northern Iowa [*Cedar Falls, IA*] (OICC)
UNI............ User Network Interface [*Data processing*]
UNIA .... Universal Negro Improvement Association [*Organization led by Marcus Aurelius Garvey*]
UNIA & ACLW ... Universal Negro Improvement Association and African Communities League of the World (EA)
UNIADUSEC ... Union Internationale des Associations de Diplomes Universitaires en Sciences Economiques et Commerciales
UNIATEC ... Union Internationale des Associations Techniques Cinematographiques [*International Union of Technical Cinematograph Associations - IUTCA*] (EAIO)
UNIBID..... UNISIST International Centre for Bibliographic Descriptions [*UNESCO*] [*Information service or system*] (IID)
UNIBUS.... Universal Bus [*Digital Equipment Corp.*]
UNIC .... Union Internationale des Cinemas [*International Union of Cinemas*] (EAIO)
UNIC .... United International Club, Inc.
UNIC .... United Nations Information Centre
UNICA ...... Asociacion de Universidades del Caribe [*Association of Caribbean Universities and Research Institutes*] (EA)
UNICA ...... Association of Caribbean Universities and Research Institutes (EAIO)
UNICA ...... Union Internationale du Cinema Non Professionnel [*International Union of Amateur Cinema*] (EAIO)
UNICAP.... Universidade Catolica de Pernambuco [*Brazil*]
UNICCAP ... Universal Cable Circuit Analysis Program [*Bell System*]
UNICE ...... Union of Industrial and Employers' Confederations of Europe (EAIO)
UNICE ...... Union des Industries de la Communaute Europeenne [*Union of Industries of the European Community*] [*Belgium*]
UNICEF..... United Nations Children's Fund [*Acronym is based on former name, United Nations International Children's Emergency Fund*] (EA)
UNICHAL ... Union Internationale des Distributeurs de Chaleur [*International Union of Heat Distributors*] (EAIO)
UNICIS ..... Unit Concept Indexing System
UNICIV Rep ... UNICIV [*School of Civil Engineering, University of New South Wales*] Report [*A publication*] (APTA)
UNICO ...... Union pour les Interets du Peuple Congolais [*Union for the Interests of the Congolese People*]
UNICO ...... Universal Cooperatives (EA)
UNICOCYM ... Union Internationale du Commerce et de la Reparation du Cycle et du Motocycle [*International Union of Cycle and Motorcycle Trade and Repair*] [*Federal Republic of Germany*]
UNICOL ... Union des Colons de la Province Orientale [*Union of Settlers in Orientale Province*]
UNICOM ... Underwater Integration Communication
UNICOM ... Unidad Informativa Computable [*Computerized Information Unit*] [*Mexico*] [*Information service or system*] (IID)
UNICOM ... Unified Communications [*Radio station*]
UNICOM ... Universal Components [*Construction*]
UNICOM ... Universal Integrated Communication System [*Military*]
UNICOMP ... Universal Compiler (IEEE)
UNICON ... Unidensity Coherent Light Recording (IEEE)
Unicorn J ... Unicorn Journal [*A publication*]
UNICYP.... United Nations International Force, Cyprus
UNID........ Unidentified (FAAC)
UNIDA ...... Unidia [*A publication*]
UNIDAHO ... Union des Independants du Dahomey [*Independents Union of Dahomey*]
UNIDENT ... Unidentified
UNIDF ...... United Nations Industrial Development Fund
UNIDIR ..... United Nations Institute for Disarmament Research [*Research center*] [*Switzerland*] (IRC)
UNIDO...... United Nations Industrial Development Organization [*Austria*] [*Also, an information service or system*] (IID)
UNIDROIT ... Institut International pour l'Unification du Droit Prive [*International Institute for the Unification of Private Law*] (EAIO)
Unidroit Yb ... International Institute for the Unification of Private Law. Yearbook [*Rome, Italy*] [*A publication*] (DLA)
UNIEF....... USEUCOM [*United States European Command*] Nuclear Interface Element Fastbreak (MCD)
UNIEP....... Union Internationale des Entrepreneurs de Peinture [*International Union of Master Painters - IUMP*] (EAIO)
Unif........... Unified (DLA)
UNIF .... Uniflex, Inc. [*NASDAQ symbol*] (NQ)

UNIF .... Uniform (AFM)
UNIF .... Uniformity
UNIFAC.... Universal Functional Activity Coefficient [*Chemical engineering*]
Unif C Code ... Uniform Commercial Code Law Journal [*A publication*]
UNIFE....... Union des Industries Ferroviaires Europeennes [*Union of European Railway Industries*] (EA)
UNIFEM... United Nations Development Fund for Women (EA)
UNIFET .... Unipolar Field-Effect Transistor
Unific LYB ... Unification of Law Yearbook [*A publication*] (DLA)
UNIFIL .... United Nations Interim Force in Lebanon
Unif L Conf ... Proceedings, Uniform Law Conference of Canada [*A publication*] (DLA)
Unif L Conf ... Uniform Law Conference [*A publication*]
Unif L Conf Can ... Uniform Law Conference of Canada [*A publication*] (DLA)
UNIFOR ... Unified Forces [*Military*]
UNIFORCE ... United Defense Force [*Established by the Brussels Treaty*] (NATG)
Uniform City Ct Act ... New York Uniform City Court Act [*A publication*]
Uniform City Ct Act ... Uniform City Court Act [*A publication*] (DLA)
Uniform Dist Ct Act ... New York Uniform District Court Act [*A publication*]
Uniform Dist Ct Act ... Uniform District Court Act [*A publication*] (DLA)
Uniform Just Ct Act ... New York Uniform Justice Court Act [*A publication*]
Uniform L Rev ... Uniform Law Review [*A publication*] (DLA)
UNI-FREDI ... Universal Flight Range and Endurance Data Indicator
Unif Sys Citation ... Uniform System of Citation [*Legal term*] (DLA)
UNIG........ University Graphics, Inc. [*Atlantic Highlands, NJ*] [*NASDAQ symbol*] (NQ)
UNIGABON ... Union Interprofessionnelle du Gabon [*Inter-Trade Union of Gabon*]
UNIH .... United Healthcare Corp. [*Minnetonka, MN*] [*NASDAQ symbol*] (NQ)
UNIHI....... University of Hawaii [*Honolulu, HI*] (NOAA)
UNII .... Yeniseysk [*USSR*] [*ICAO location identifier*] (ICLI)
UNIIMOG ... United Nations Iran-Iraq Military Observer Group
UNILAC ... Universal Linear Accelerator
unilat.......... Unilateral
Uni Ljubljai Teh Fak Acta Tech Ser Chim ... Univerza v Ljubljani. Tehniska Fakulteta. Acta Technica. Series Chimica [*A publication*]
UNIMA..... Union Internationale de Grands Magasins [*International Union of Department Stores*]
UNIMA..... Union Internationale de la Marionnette [*International Puppeteers Union*] [*France*]
UNIMA..... Unione Nazionale Imprese di Meccanizzazione Agricola [*Agricultural Mechanization Enterprises Union*] [*Italy*] (EY)
UNIMARC ... Universal Machine Readable Cataloging (ADA)
UNIMA-USA ... American Center of the Union Internationale de la Marionette (EA)
UNIMERC ... Universal Numeric Coding System [*Distilling industry*]
UNIMOD ... Unified Modular Plant [*Nuclear energy*]
UNIN........ Unilife Corp. [*NASDAQ symbol*] (NQ)
Un Ins Co ... Unemployment Insurance Code [*A publication*] (DLA)
UN Int Mtg Oilfield Dev Techniques ... United Nations International Meeting on Oilfield Development Techniques [*A publication*]
UNIO........ United Nations Information Organization
Union Agric ... Union Agriculture [*A publication*]
Union Burma J Life Sci ... Union of Burma. Journal of Life Sciences [*A publication*]
Union Burma J Sci and Technol ... Union of Burma. Journal of Science and Technology [*A publication*]
Union Burma J Sci Technol ... Union of Burma. Journal of Science and Technology [*A publication*]
Union Carbide Met Rev ... Union Carbide Metals Review [*A publication*]
UNION FLEURS ... Union Internationale du Commerce de Gros en Fleurs [*International Union of the Wholesale Flower Trade*]
Union Int Sci Biol Ser A Gen ... Union Internationale des Sciences Biologiques. Serie A. Generale [*A publication*]
Union Int Sci Biol Ser B Colloq ... Union Internationale des Sciences Biologiques. Serie B. Colloques [*A publication*]
Union Lab Rep BNA ... Union Labor Report. Bureau of National Affairs [*A publication*]
Union Med Can ... Union Medicale du Canada [*A publication*]
Union Med Mexico ... Union Medica de Mexico [*A publication*]
Union Med (Paris) ... Union Medicale (Paris) [*A publication*]
Union Oceanogr Fr ... Union des Oceanographes de France [*France*] [*A publication*]
Union Pac LDB ... Union Pacific Law Department. Bulletin [*A publication*] (DLA)
Union Pharm ... Union Pharmaceutique [*A publication*]
Union Rec .. Union Recorder [*A publication*] (APTA)
Union S Afr Dep Commer Ind Div Fish Invest Rep ... Union of South Africa. Department of Commerce and Industries. Division of Fisheries. Investigational Report [*A publication*]
Union Soc Fr Hist Nat Bull Trimest ... Union des Societes Francaises d'Histoire Naturelle. Bulletin Trimestriel [*A publication*]
Union S Q R ... Union Seminary. Quarterly Review [*A publication*]
Union Tank Car Co Graver Water Cond Div Tech Repr ... Union Tank Car Company. Graver Water Conditioning Division. Technical Reprint [*A publication*]

Union Univ Q ... Union University. Quarterly [*A publication*]
UNIP .... United National Independence Party [*Nigeria*] [*Political party*]
UNIP .... United National Independence Party [*Trinidad and Tobago*] [*Political party*] (PPW)
UNIP .... United National Independence Party [*Zambia*] [*Political party*] (PD)
UNIPAC... Unified Prediction and Analysis Code (MCD)
UNIPAC.... Unit Packaging
UNIPAC.... Universal Payload Accommodation Capsule
UNIPEDE ... Union Internationale de Producteurs et Distributeurs d'Energie Electrique [*International Union of Producers and Distributors of Electrical Energy*] [*France*]
UNIPI........ Unione Industriali Pastai Italiani [*Pasta Manufacturers Union*] [*Italy*] (EY)
UNIPOCONGO ... Union des Populations Rurales du Congo [*Union of Rural People of the Congo*]
UNIPOL.... Universal Problem-Oriented Language [*Data processing*] (MCD)
UNIPOL.... Universal Procedure-Oriented Language
UNIPRO ... Unite et Progres du Burundi [*Unity and Progress of Burundi*]
UNIPRO ... Universal Processor [*Data processing*]
UNIPZ...... United National Independence Party of Zambia
Uni of Q LR ... University of Queensland. Law Review [*A publication*] (APTA)
UNIQUAC ... Universal Quasichemical [*Chemical engineering*]
UNIQUE... Uniform Inquiry Update Element
UNIR .... Unemployment Insurance Review [*A publication*]
UNIR .... Union de Izquierda Revolucionaria [*Union of the Revolutionary Left*] [*Peru*] [*Political party*] (PPW)
UNIR .... Union Nationale pour l'Initiative et la Responsabilite [*National Union for Initiative and Responsibility*] [*France*] [*Political party*] (PPW)
UNIR .... United-Guardian, Inc. [*NASDAQ symbol*] (NQ)
UNIRAC ... Union Involved Racketeering [*FBI undercover investigation*]
UNIRAR ... Universal Radio Relay
UNIS .... Ukrainian National Information Service (EA)
UNIS .... Underwater Television and Inspection System
UNIS .... Unison
UNIS .... United Nations Information Service
UNIS .... United Nations International School
UNISA....... University of South Africa
UNISA Engl Stud ... UNISA [*University of South Africa*] English Studies [*A publication*]
UNISAP ... UNIVAC Share Assembly Program [*Sperry UNIVAC*] [*Data processing*] (IEEE)
UNISA Psychol ... UNISA [*University of South Africa*] Psychologia [*A publication*]
UNISCAMTA ... Union Territoriale des Syndicats de Cadres, Agents de Maitrise, Techniciens, et Assimiles du Senegal [*Territorial Union of Leaders, Supervising Personnel, and Related Workers of Senegal*]
UNISCAN ... United Kingdom and Scandinavia (NATG)
UNISCO.... Union des Interets Sociaux Congolais [*Congolese Union of Social Interests*]
UNISIST... Universal System for Information in Science and Technology [*UNESCO*] [*Zagreb, Yugoslavia*]
UNISOR ... University Isotope Separator at Oak Ridge
UNISPACE ... United Nations Conference on the Exploration and Peaceful Uses of Outer Space
UNISPEC ... Universal Spectroscopy [*Trademark*] [*Kevex Corp.*]
UNISTAR ... UNIVAC Storage and Retrieval System [*Sperry UNIVAC*] [*Data processing*]
UNISTAR ... User Network for Information Storage, Transfer Acquisition, and Retrieval (MCD)
UNISTAT ... University Science Statistics Project [*Information service or system*] (IID)
UNISTOCK ... Union Professionnelle des Stockeurs de Cereales dans la CEE [*Organization of Cereal Storage Firms in the European Economic Community*]
UNISURV G Rep ... UNISURV G Report. School of Surveying. University of New South Wales [*A publication*] (APTA)
UNISURV Rep ... UNISURV Report. School of Surveying. University of New South Wales [*A publication*] (APTA)
UNISWEP ... Unified Switching Equipment Practice (MCD)
UNISYS .... United Information Systems [*Formed by a merger of Burroughs Corp. and Sperry UNIVAC*]
UNIT .... Unitarian
UNIT .... Universal Numerical Interchange Terminal
UNITA ...... Uniao Nacional para a Independencia Total de Angola [*National Union for the Complete Independence of Angola*]
Unit Aborig Messenger ... United Aborigines' Messenger [*A publication*] (APTA)
Unita R ...... Unitarian Review [*A publication*]
UNITAR.... United Nations Institute for Training and Research [*Research center*] [*New York*] [*ICSU*]
UNITAR Prepr or Proc ... UNITAR [*United Nations Institute for Training and Research*] Preprints or Proceedings [*A publication*]
UNITAS.... United International Antisubmarine Warfare
Uni-Taschenb ... Uni-Taschenbuecher [*A publication*]
Unitas Int ... Unitas. Revue Internationale [*A publication*]

Uni of Tas LR ... University of Tasmania. Law Review [*A publication*] (APTA)
Uni-TB....... Uni-Taschenbuecher [*A publication*]
United Dent Hosp Syd Inst Dent Res Annu Rep ... United Dental Hospital of Sydney. Institute of Dental Research. Annual Report [*A publication*]
United Dent Hosp Sydney Inst Dent Res Annu Rep ... United Dental Hospital of Sydney. Institute of Dental Research. Annual Report [*A publication*]
United Fresh Fruit Veg Assoc Yearb ... United Fresh Fruit and Vegetable Association. Yearbook [*A publication*]
United Plant Assoc South India Sci Dep Bull ... United Planters' Association of Southern India. Scientific Department. Bulletin [*A publication*]
United Service Q ... United Service Quarterly [*A publication*] (APTA)
United Serv Rev ... United Services Review [*A publication*]
UNITEL.... Universal Teleservice [*Satellite information service*]
UNITEL.... University Information Technology Corporation [*MIT-Harvard*]
UNITNG... Unit Training (NVT)
UNITOPOS ... Unit to Which Ordered Will Operate in an Overseas Area a Contemplated Continuous Period of One Year or More [*Military*]
UNITOR ... United Nations International TOKAMAK Reactor [*Proposed experimental fusion power plant*]
UNITRAC ... Universal Trajector Compiler (IEEE)
UNITREP ... Unit Status and Identity Report [*DoD*]
Unit Univ Chr ... Unitarian Universalist Christian [*A publication*]
UNIUM..... Union Nationale des Intellectuels et Universitaires Malgaches [*National Union of Intellectuals and University People of Madagascar*]
UNIV........ Univation, Inc. [*Milpitas, CA*] [*NASDAQ symbol*] (NQ)
UNIV........ Universal (AFM)
UNIV........ Universalist
Univ .... Universitas [*A publication*]
UNIV........ University (AFM)
Univ .... Universo [*A publication*]
UNIVA...... Universitas [*A publication*]
Univ Abidjan Dep Geol Ser Doc ... Universite d'Abidjan. Departement de Geologie. Serie Documentation [*A publication*]
UNIVAC ... Universal Automatic Computer [*Remington Rand Corp.*] [*Early computer*]
Univ Adelaide Cent Precambrian Res Spec Pap ... University of Adelaide. Centre for Precambrian Research. Special Paper [*A publication*]
Univ Aff/Aff Univ ... University Affairs/Affaires Universitaires [*A publication*]
Univ Agric Sci (Bangalore) Curr Res ... University of Agricultural Sciences (Bangalore). Current Research [*A publication*]
Univ Agric Sci (Bangalore) Misc Ser ... University of Agricultural Sciences (Bangalore). Miscellaneous Series [*A publication*]
Univ Agric Sci (Bangalore) Res Ser ... University of Agricultural Sciences (Bangalore). Research Series [*A publication*]
Univ Agric Sci (Hebbal Bangalore) Annu Rep ... University of Agricultural Sciences (Hebbal, Bangalore). Annual Report [*A publication*]
Univ Agric Sci (Hebbal Bangalore) Ext Ser ... University of Agricultural Sciences (Hebbal, Bangalore). Extension Series [*A publication*]
Univ Agric Sci (Hebbal Bangalore) Stn Ser ... University of Agricultural Sciences (Hebbal, Bangalore). Station Series [*A publication*]
Univ Agric Sci (Hebbal Bangalore) Tech Ser ... University of Agricultural Sciences (Hebbal, Bangalore). Technical Series [*A publication*]
Univ Alaska Agric Exp Stn Bull ... University of Alaska. Agricultural Experiment Station. Bulletin [*A publication*]
Univ Alaska Inst Mar Sci Rep ... University of Alaska. Institute of Marine Science. Report [*A publication*]
Univ Alaska IWR (Inst Water Resour) Ser ... University of Alaska. IWR (Institute of Water Resources) Series [*A publication*]
Univ Alberta Agric Bull ... University of Alberta. Agriculture Bulletin [*A publication*]
Univ Alberta Agric For Bull ... University of Alberta. Agriculture and Forestry Bulletin [*A publication*]
Univ Alberta Dep Civ Eng Struct Eng Rep ... University of Alberta. Department of Civil Engineering. Structural Engineering Report [*A publication*]
Univ Alberta Fac Agric Bull ... University of Alberta. Faculty of Agriculture. Bulletins [*A publication*]
Univ Alexandria Fac Eng Bull Chem Eng ... University of Alexandria. Faculty of Engineering. Bulletin. Chemical Engineering [*A publication*]
Univ Alger Trav Inst Rech Sahariennes ... Universite d'Alger. Travaux. Institut de Recherches Sahariennes [*A publication*]
Univ Allahabad Stud ... University of Allahabad. Studies [*A publication*]
Univ Allahabad Stud Biol Sect ... University of Allahabad. Studies. Biology Section [*A publication*]
Univ Allahabad Stud Bot Sect ... University of Allahabad. Studies. Botany Section [*A publication*]
Univ Allahabad Stud Chem Sect ... University of Allahabad. Studies. Chemistry Section [*A publication*]

Univ Allahabad Stud Math Sect ... University of Allahabad. Studies. Mathematics Section [*A publication*]
Univ Allahabad Stud New Ser ... University of Allahabad. Studies. New Series [*A publication*]
Univ Allahabad Stud Phys Sect ... University of Allahabad. Studies. Physics Section [*A publication*]
Univ Allahabad Stud Zool Sect ... University of Allahabad. Studies. Zoology Section [*A publication*]
Univ Ankara Fac Agri Publ ... Universite d'Ankara. Faculte de l'Agriculture. Publications [*A publication*]
Univ Ankara Fac Sci Commun Ser A ... Universite d'Ankara. Faculte des Sciences. Communications. Serie A. Mathematiques, Physique, et Astronomie [*A publication*]
Univ Ankara Fac Sci Commun Ser A2 ... Universite d'Ankara. Faculte des Sciences. Communications. Serie A2. Physique [*A publication*]
Univ Ankara Fac Sci Commun Ser C ... Universite d'Ankara. Faculte des Sciences. Communications. Serie C. Sciences Naturelles [*A publication*]
Univ Ankara Yearb Fac Agric ... University of Ankara. Yearbook. Faculty of Agriculture [*A publication*]
Univ Antioquia ... Universidad de Antioquia [*Colombia*] [*A publication*]
UNIVAR ... Universal Valve Action Recorder
Univ Ariz Coop Ext Serv Bull ... University of Arizona. Cooperative Extension Service. Bulletin [*A publication*]
Univ Ariz Coop Ext Serv Circ ... University of Arizona. Cooperative Extension Service. Circular [*A publication*]
Univ Ariz Coop Ext Serv Ser P ... University of Arizona. Cooperative Extension Service. Series P [*A publication*]
Univ Arkansas Eng Exp Stn Res Rep Ser ... University of Arkansas. Engineering Experiment Station. Research Report Series [*A publication*]
Univ Arkansas Lecture Notes in Math ... University of Arkansas. Lecture Notes in Mathematics [*A publication*]
Univ Austral Chile Fac Cienc Agrar Agro Sur ... Universidad Austral de Chile. Facultad de Ciencias Agrarias. Agro Sur [*A publication*]
Univ Auton Barcelona Col Univ Gerona Secc Cienc An ... Universidad Autonoma de Barcelona. Colegio Universitario de Gerona. Seccion de Ciencias. Anales [*A publication*]
Univ Auton Potosina Inst Geol Metal Foll Tec ... Universidad Autonoma Potosina. Instituto de Geologia y Metalurgia. Folleto Tecnico [*A publication*]
Univ Baghdad Nat Hist Res Cent Annu Rep ... University of Baghdad. Natural History Research Center. Annual Report [*A publication*]
Univ Baghdad Nat Hist Res Cent Publ ... University of Baghdad. Natural History Research Center. Publication [*A publication*]
Univ Bahia Esc Geol Publ Avulsa ... Universidade de Bahia. Escola de Geologia. Publicacao Avulsa [*A publication*]
Univ B Aires Fac Agron Vet Bol Tec Inf ... Universidad de Buenos Aires. Facultad de Agronomia y Veterinaria. Boletin Tecnico Informativo [*A publication*]
Univ BC Bot Gard Tech Bull ... University of British Columbia. Botanical Garden. Technical Bulletin [*A publication*]
Univ BC Res For Annu Rep ... University of British Columbia. Research Forest. Annual Report [*A publication*]
Univ Beograd Publ Elektrotehn Fak Ser Mat Fiz ... Univerzitet u Beogradu. Publikacije Elektrotehnickog Fakulteta. Serija Matematika i Fizika [*A publication*]
Univ Beograd Tehn Fiz ... Univerzitet u Beogradu. Tehnicka Fizika [*A publication*]
Univ Beograd Zb Radova Gradevin Fak ... Univerzitet u Beogradu. Zbornik Radova Gradevinskog Fakulteta u Beogradu [*A publication*]
Univ Bergen Arb Naturv R ... Universitetet i Bergen Arbok. Naturvitenskapelig Rekke [*A publication*]
Univ Bergen Arbok Med Rekke ... Universitetet i Bergen Arbok Medisinsk Rekke [*A publication*]
Univ Bergen Arbok Naturvitensk Rekke ... Universitetet i Bergen Arbok. Naturvitenskapelig Rekke [*A publication*]
Univ Bergen Arsmeld ... Universitetet i Bergen Arsmelding [*A publication*]
Univ Bergen Med Avh ... Universitetet i Bergen Medisinske Avhandlinger [*A publication*]
Univ Bergen Skr ... Universitetet i Bergen Skrifter [*A publication*]
Univ Botswana Swazil Agric Res Div Annu Rep ... University of Botswana and Swaziland. Agricultural Research Division. Annual Report [*A publication*]
Univ Botswana Swaziland Agric Res Div Annu Rep ... University of Botswana, Swaziland. Agricultural Research Division. Annual Report [*A publication*]
Univ Bras Cent Estud Zool Avulso ... Universidade do Brasil. Centro de Estudos Zoologicos Avulso [*A publication*]
Univ Brasov Lucrari Stiint ... Universitatea din Brasov. Lucrari Stiintifice [*A publication*]
Univ of Brit Columbia L Rev ... University of British Columbia. Law Review [*A publication*]
Univ British Columbia Law R ... University of British Columbia. Law Review [*A publication*]
Univ Bruxelles Inst Phys Bull ... Universite de Bruxelles. Institut de Physique. Bulletin [*A publication*]

Univ Buenos Aires Fac Agrom Vet Bol ... Universidad de Buenos Aires. Facultad de Agronomia y Veterinaria. Boletin [*A publication*]
Univ Buenos Aires Inst Anat Publ ... Universidad de Buenos Aires. Instituto de Anatomia. Publicacion [*A publication*]
Univ Burundi Rev ... Universite du Burundi. Revue [*A publication*]
UNIVC ...... Universal Energy Corporation [*NASDAQ symbol*] (NQ)
Univ Calicut Zool Monogr ... University of Calicut. Zoological Monograph [*A publication*]
Univ Calif Agric Ext Serv ... University of California. Agricultural Extension Service [*A publication*]
Univ Calif (Berkeley) Publ Agric Sci ... University of California (Berkeley). Publications in Agricultural Sciences [*A publication*]
Univ Calif (Berkeley) Publ Bot ... University of California (Berkeley). Publications in Botany [*A publication*]
Univ Calif (Berkeley) Publ Eng ... University of California (Berkeley). Publications in Engineering [*A publication*]
Univ Calif (Berkeley) Publ Entomol ... University of California (Berkeley). Publications in Entomology [*A publication*]
Univ Calif (Berkeley) Publ Health ... University of California (Berkeley). Publications in Public Health [*A publication*]
Univ Calif (Berkeley) Publ Pharmacol ... University of California (Berkeley). Publications in Pharmacology [*A publication*]
Univ Calif (Berkeley) Publ Zool ... University of California (Berkeley). Publications in Zoology [*A publication*]
Univ Calif (Berkeley) Sanit Eng Res Lab Rep ... University of California (Berkeley). Sanitary Engineering Research Laboratory. Report [*A publication*]
Univ Calif (Berkly) Publ Pathol ... University of California (Berkeley). Publications in Pathology [*A publication*]
Univ Calif Bull ... University of California. Bulletin [*A publication*]
Univ of Calif Davis L Rev ... University of California at Davis. Law Review [*Davis, California*] [*A publication*] (DLA)
Univ Calif Div Agric Sci Bull ... University of California. Division of Agricultural Sciences. Bulletin [*A publication*]
Univ Calif Div Agric Sci Leafl ... University of California. Division of Agricultural Sciences. Leaflet [*A publication*]
Univ Calif Lawrence Livermore Lab Rep ... University of California. Lawrence Livermore Laboratory. Report [*A publication*]
Univ Calif (Los Angeles) Symp Mol Cell Biol ... University of California (Los Angeles). Symposia on Molecular and Cellular Biology [*A publication*]
Univ California Los Angeles L Rev ... University of California at Los Angeles. Law Review [*Los Angeles, California*] [*A publication*] (DLA)
Univ Calif Publ Am Archaeol Ethnol ... University of California. Publications in American Archaeology and Ethnology [*A publication*]
Univ Calif Publ Bot ... University of California. Publications in Botany [*A publication*]
Univ of Calif Publ in English Ling M Ph ... University of California. Publications in English, Linguistics, Modern Philology [*A publication*]
Univ Calif Publ Ent ... University of California. Publications in Entomology [*A publication*]
Univ Calif Publ Entomol ... University of California. Publications in Entomology [*A publication*]
Univ Calif Publ Geol Sci ... University of California. Publications in Geological Sciences [*A publication*]
Univ Calif Publications Zool ... University of California. Publications in Zoology [*A publication*]
Univ Calif Publ Physiol ... University of California. Publications in Physiology [*A publication*]
Univ Calif Publ Psychol ... University of California. Publications in Psychology [*A publication*]
Univ Calif Publs Ent ... University of California. Publications in Entomology [*A publication*]
Univ Calif Publ Zool ... University of California. Publications in Zoology [*A publication*]
Univ Calif Sea Water Convers Lab Rep ... University of California. Sea Water Conversion Laboratory. Report [*A publication*]
Univ Calif Univ Los Angeles Publ Biol Sci ... University of California. University at Los Angeles. Publications in Biological Sciences [*A publication*]
Univ Calif Univ Los Angeles Publ Math Phys Sci ... University of California. University at Los Angeles. Publications in Mathematical and Physical Sciences [*A publication*]
Univ Calif Water Resour Cent Contrib ... University of California. Water Resources Center. Contribution [*A publication*]
Univ Camb Dep Appl Biol Mem Rev Ser ... University of Cambridge. Department of Applied Biology. Memoirs. Review Series [*A publication*]
Univ Cambridge Dep Eng Rep CUDE/A-Aerodyn ... University of Cambridge. Department of Engineering. Report. CUDE [*Cambridge University Department of Engineering*]/A-Aerodynamics [*A publication*]
Univ Cambridge Dep Eng Rep CUDE/A-Thermo ... University of Cambridge. Department of Engineering. Report. CUDE [*Cambridge University Department of Engineering*]/A-Thermo [*A publication*]

Univ Cambridge Dep Eng Rep CUDE/A-Turbo ... University of Cambridge. Department of Engineering. Report. CUDE [*Cambridge University Department of Engineering*]/A-Turbo [*A publication*]
Univ Cambridge Inst Anim Pathol Rep Dir ... University of Cambridge. Institute of Animal Pathology. Report of the Director [*A publication*]
Univ Canterbury Publ ... University of Canterbury. Publications [*A publication*]
Univ Cathol Louvain Fac Sci Agron Lab Biochim Nutr Publ ... Universite Catholique de Louvain. Faculte des Sciences Agronomiques. Laboratoire de Biochimie de la Nutrition. Publication [*A publication*]
Univ Cathol Louv Inst Agron Mem ... Universite Catholique de Louvain. Institut Agronomique. Memoires [*A publication*]
Univ Catol Bolivar ... Universidad Catolica Bolivariana [*A publication*]
Univ Cent Desert Stud Trans (Jodhpur India) ... University Centre of Desert Studies. Transactions (Jodhpur, India) [*A publication*]
Univ Cent Venez Inst Mater Modelos Estruct Bol Tec ... Universidad Central de Venezuela. Instituto de Materiales y Modelos Estructurales. Boletin Tecnico [*A publication*]
Univ Chic ... Library of the University of Chicago [*A publication*]
Univ of Chicago L Rev ... University of Chicago. Law Review [*A publication*]
Univ Chicago Publ ... University of Chicago. Publications [*A publication*]
Univ Chicago Rep ... University of Chicago. Reports [*A publication*]
Univ Chic L ... University of Chicago. Law Review [*A publication*]
Univ Chic M ... University of Chicago. Magazine [*A publication*]
Univ Chic Rec ... University of Chicago. Record [*A publication*]
Univ of Chi Law Rev ... University of Chicago. Law Review [*A publication*]
Univ Chile Dep Prod Agric Publ Misc Agric ... Universidad de Chile. Departamento de Produccion Agricola. Publicaciones Miscelaneas Agricolas [*A publication*]
Univ Chile Fac Agron Dep Sanid Veg Bol Tec ... Universidad de Chile. Facultad de Agronomia. Departamento Sanidad Vegetal. Boletin Tecnico [*A publication*]
Univ Chile Fac Agron Publ Misc Agric ... Universidad de Chile. Facultad de Agronomia. Publicaciones Miscelaneas Agricolas [*A publication*]
Univ Chile Fac Cienc Fis Mat An ... Universidad de Chile. Facultad de Ciencias Fisicas y Matematicas. Anales [*A publication*]
Univ Chile Fac Cienc Fis Mat Inst Geol Publ ... Universidad de Chile. Facultad de Ciencias Fisicas y Matematicas. Instituto de Geologia. Publicacion [*A publication*]
Univ Chile Fac Cienc For Bol Tec ... Universidad de Chile. Facultad de Ciencias Forestales. Boletin Tecnico [*A publication*]
Univ Chile Fac Cienc For Manual ... Universidad de Chile. Facultad de Ciencias Forestales. Manual [*A publication*]
Univ Chile Fac Quim Farm Tesis Quim Farm ... Universidad de Chile. Facultad de Quimica y Farmacia. Tesis de Quimicos Farmaceuticos [*A publication*]
Univ Chile Inst Invest Ensayes Mater Inf Tec ... Universidad de Chile. Instituto de Chile. Instituto de Investigaciones y Ensayes de Materiales. Informe Tecnico [*A publication*]
Univ of Cincinnati L Rev ... University of Cincinnati. Law Review [*A publication*]
Univ Cincin Stud ... University of Cincinnati. Studies [*A publication*]
Univ of Cinc Law Rev ... University of Cincinnati. Law Review [*A publication*]
Univ Cluj-Napoca Gradina Bot Contrib Bot ... Universitatea din Cluj-Napoca Gradina Botanica Contributii Botanice [*A publication*]
Univ Col Eng Exp Stn Bull ... University of Colorado. Engineering Experiment Station. Bulletin [*A publication*]
Univ Coll Dublin Agric Fac Rep ... University College of Dublin. Agricultural Faculty. Report [*A publication*]
Univ Coll Dublin Fac Gen Agric Res Rep ... University College of Dublin. Faculty of General Agriculture. Research Report [*A publication*]
Univ Coll Wales (Aberystwyth) Memorandum ... University College of Wales (Aberystwyth). Memorandum [*A publication*]
Univ of Colorado L Rev ... University of Colorado. Law Review [*A publication*]
Univ Color Stud Ser A ... University of Colorado. Studies. Series A. General Series [*A publication*]
Univ Color Stud Ser B ... University of Colorado. Studies. Series B. Studies in the Humanities [*A publication*]
Univ of Colo Studies ... University of Colorado. Studies [*A publication*]
Univ Colo Stud Ser Anthropol ... University of Colorado. Studies. Series in Anthropology [*A publication*]
Univ Colo Stud Ser Biol ... University of Colorado. Studies. Series in Biology [*A publication*]
Univ Colo Stud Ser Chem Pharm ... University of Colorado. Studies. Series in Chemistry and Pharmacy [*A publication*]
Univ Colo Stud Ser D ... University of Colorado. Studies. Series D. Physical and Biological Sciences [*A publication*]
Univ Colo Stud Ser Earth Sci ... University of Colorado. Studies. Series in Earth Sciences [*A publication*]
Univ Col Stud ... University of Colorado. Studies [*A publication*]
Univ Col Stud Ser C ... University of Colorado. Studies. Series C. Studies in the Social Sciences [*A publication*]
Univ Conn Occas Pap Biol Sci Ser ... University of Connecticut. Occasional Papers. Biological Science Series [*A publication*]

Univ Craiova An Ser 3 ... Universitatea din Craiova. Analele. Seria a/3. Stiinte Agricole [*A publication*]
Univ Craiova An Ser Biol Med Stiinte Agric ... Universitatea din Craiova. Analele. Seria. Biologie, Medicina, Stiinte Agricole [*A publication*]
Univ Craiova An Ser Mat Fiz Chim Electroteh ... Universitatea din Craiova. Analele. Seria. Matematica, Fizica, Chimie, Electrotehnica [*A publication*]
Univ D .... Doctor of the University
Univ Debaters Annual ... University Debaters' Annual [*A publication*]
Univ Del Mar Lab Inf Ser Publ ... University of Delaware. Marine Laboratories. Information Series Publication [*A publication*]
Univ Durban-Westville J ... University of Durban-Westville. Journal [*A publication*]
Univ Durban-Westville Tydskr ... Universiteit van Durban-Westville. Tydskrif [*A publication*]
Univ Durham King's Coll Dep Civ Eng Bull ... University of Durham. King's College. Department of Civil Engineering. Bulletin [*A publication*]
Univ Edinb Pfizer Med Monogr ... University of Edinburgh. Pfizer Medical Monographs [*A publication*]
Univ Edinburgh J ... University of Edinburgh. Journal [*A publication*]
UNIVER .... Universal Inverter and Register (MCD)
Universe Nat Hist Ser ... Universe Natural History Series [*A publication*]
Univers Farm ... Universal Farmacia [*A publication*]
Universitas (Bogota) ... Universitas Pontificia Universidad Catolica Javeriana (Bogota) [*A publication*]
Universities Q ... Universities Quarterly [*A publication*]
University of Singapore School of Archre Jnl ... University of Singapore. School of Architecture. Journal [*A publication*]
University of Southern Calif School of Archre Yearbook ... University of Southern California. School of Architecture. Yearbook [*A publication*]
Univ Fed Pernambuco Esc Quim Dep Technol Publ Avulsa ... Universidade Federal de Pernambuco. Escola de Quimica. Departamento de Technologia. Publicacao Avulsa [*A publication*]
Univ Fed Pernambuco Inst Biocienc Publ Avulsa ... Universidade Federal de Pernambuco. Instituto de Biociencias. Publicacao Avulsa [*A publication*]
Univ Fed Pernambuco Inst Micol Publ ... Universidade Federal de Pernambuco. Instituto de Micologia. Publicacao [*A publication*]
Univ Fed Pernambuco Mem Inst Biocienc ... Universidade Federal de Pernambuco. Memorias do Instituto de Biociencias [*A publication*]
Univ Fed Rio De Janeiro Inst Geocienc Geol Bol ... Universidade Federal do Rio De Janeiro. Instituto de Geociencias. Geologia. Boletim [*A publication*]
Univ Fed Rio De J Inst Geocienc Bol Geol ... Universidade Federal do Rio De Janeiro. Instituto de Geociencias. Boletim Geologia [*A publication*]
Univ Fed Rio De J Inst Geocienc Dep Geol Contrib Dida ... Universidade Federal do Rio De Janeiro. Instituto de Geociencias. Departamento de Geologia. Contribuicao Didatica [*A publication*]
Univ Fed Rural Rio Grande Do Sul Dep Zootec Bol Tec ... Universidade Federal Rural do Rio Grande Do Sul. Departamento do Zootecnia. Boletin Tecnico [*A publication*]
Univ Fed Vicosa Bibl Centr Ser Bibliogr Espec ... Universidade Federal de Vicosa. Biblioteca Central. Serie Bibliografias Especializadas [*A publication*]
Univ Fed Vicosa Ser Tec Bol ... Universidade Federal de Vicosa. Serie Tecnica. Boletin [*A publication*]
Univ Ferrara Ann Sez 6 ... Universita di Ferrara. Annali. Sezione 6. Fisiologia e Chimica Biologica [*A publication*]
Univ Ferrara Mem Geopaleontol ... Universita di Ferrara. Memorie Geopaleontologiche [*A publication*]
Univ Fla Agric Ext Serv Circ ... University of Florida. Agricultural Extension Service. Circular [*A publication*]
Univ Fla Coastal Oceanogr Eng Lab Rep UFL COEL TR ... University of Florida. Coastal and Oceanographic Engineering Laboratory. Report. UFL/COEL/TR [*A publication*]
Univ Fla Coop Ext Serv Bull ... University of Florida. Cooperative Extension Service. Bulletin [*A publication*]
Univ Fla Inst Food Agric Sci Annu Res Rep ... University of Florida. Institute of Food and Agricultural Sciences. Annual Research Report [*A publication*]
Univ Fla Inst Food Agri Sci Publ ... University of Florida. Institute of Food and Agricultural Sciences. Publication [*A publication*]
Univ Fla Inst Gerontol Ser ... University of Florida. Institute of Gerontology Series [*A publication*]
Univ Fla Publ Biol Sci Ser ... University of Florida. Publications. Biological Science Series [*A publication*]
Univ Fla Water Resour Res Cent Publ ... University of Florida. Water Resources Research Center. Publication [*A publication*]
Univ of Florida L Rev ... University of Florida. Law Review [*A publication*]
Univ Fl SSM ... University of Florida. Social Sciences Monograph [*A publication*]
Univ For Bois (Sopron) Publ Sci ... Universite Forestiere et du Bois (Sopron). Publications Scientifiques [*A publication*]

Univ Forst Holzwirtsch (Sopron) Wiss Mitt ... Universitaet fuer Forst- und Holzwirtschaft (Sopron). Wissenschaftliche Mitteilungen [*A publication*]
Univ For Timber Ind (Sopron) Sci Publ ... University of Forestry and Timber Industry (Sopron). Scientific Publications [*A publication*]
Univ F Study ... University Film Study Center. Newsletter [*A publication*]
Univ GA Mar Sci Cent Tech Rep Ser ... University of Georgia. Marine Science Center. Technical Report Series [*A publication*]
Univ Gaz .... University Gazette [*University of Melbourne*] [*A publication*] (APTA)
Univ Genova Pubbl Ist Mat ... Universita di Genova. Pubblicazioni dell'Istituto di Matematica [*A publication*]
Univ Geograd Radovi Zavoda za Fiz ... Univerzitet u Geogradu Radovi. Zavoda za Fiziku [*A publication*]
Univ Ghana Agric Irrig Res Stn (Kpong) Annu Rep ... University of Ghana. Agricultural Irrigation Research Station (Kpong). Annual Report [*A publication*]
Univ Ghana Agric Res Stn (Kpong) Annu Rep ... University of Ghana. Agricultural Research Station (Kpong). Annual Report [*A publication*]
Univ of Ghana LJ ... University of Ghana. Law Journal [*London, England*] [*A publication*] (DLA)
Univ de Grenoble Annales n s Sci ... Universite de Grenoble. Sciences-Medecine. Annales [*A publication*]
Univ Hawaii Coll Trop Agric Dep Pap ... University of Hawaii. College of Tropical Agriculture. Departmental Paper [*A publication*]
Univ Hawaii Coop Ext Ser Misc Publ ... University of Hawaii. Cooperative Extension Service. Miscellaneous Publication [*A publication*]
Univ Hawaii Hawaii Inst Geophys Bienn Rep ... University of Hawaii. Hawaii Institute of Geophysics. Biennial Report [*A publication*]
Univ Hawaii Hawaii Inst Geophys Rep HIG ... University of Hawaii. Hawaii Institute of Geophysics. Report HIG [*A publication*]
Univ Hawaii Occas Pap ... University of Hawaii. Occasional Papers [*A publication*]
Univ Hawaii Res Publ ... University of Hawaii. Research Publications [*A publication*]
Univ Hisp An Ser Med ... Universidad Hispalense. Anales. Serie Medicina [*A publication*]
Univ H Sch J ... University High School. Journal [*A publication*]
Univ Human Rights ... Universal Human Rights [*A publication*]
Univ Hum Rts ... Universal Human Rights [*A publication*]
Univ IL Law ... University of Illinois. Law Forum [*A publication*]
Univ Ill Grad Sc Libr Sci Occas Pap ... University of Illinois. Graduate School of Library Science. Occasional Papers [*A publication*]
Univ of Illinois L Forum ... University of Illinois. Law Forum [*A publication*]
Univ Ill L Forum ... University of Illinois. Law Forum [*A publication*]
Univ Ill Urbana-Champaign Water Resour Cent Res Rep ... University of Illinois at Urbana-Champaign. Water Resources Center. Research Report [*A publication*]
Univ Ill Urbana-Champaign Water Resour Cent Spec Rep ... University of Illinois at Urbana-Champaign. Water Resources Center. Special Report [*A publication*]
Univ Indore Res J Sci ... University of Indore. Research Journal. Science [*A publication*]
Univ Ind Santander Bol Geol ... Universidad Industrial de Santander. Boletin de Geologia [*A publication*]
Univ Iowa Monogr Studies in Med ... University of Iowa. Monographs. Studies in Medicine [*A publication*]
Univ Iowa Stud Nat Hist ... University of Iowa. Studies in Natural History [*A publication*]
Univ J Busan Natl Univ ... University Journal. Busan National University [*South Korea*] [*A publication*]
Univ J Busan Sanup Univ ... University Journal. Busan Sanup University [*A publication*]
Univ J of Business ... University Journal of Business [*A publication*]
Univ J Nat Sci Ser ... University Journal. Natural Sciences Series. Busan National University [*Republic of Korea*] [*A publication*]
Univ Joensuu Publ Sci ... University of Joensuu. Publications in Sciences [*A publication*]
Univ Jyvaskyla Stud Sport Phys Educ Health ... University of Jyvaskyla. Studies in Sport, Physical Education, and Health [*A publication*]
Univ Kansas Sci Bull ... University of Kansas. Science Bulletin [*A publication*]
Univ Kans Mus Nat Hist Misc Publ ... University of Kansas. Museum of Natural History. Miscellaneous Publication [*A publication*]
Univ Kans Mus Nat Hist Monogr ... University of Kansas. Museum of Natural History. Monograph [*A publication*]
Univ Kans Paleontol Contrib Artic ... University of Kansas. Paleontological Contributions. Article [*A publication*]
Univ Kans Paleontol Contrib Monogr ... University of Kansas. Paleontological Contributions. Monograph [*A publication*]
Univ Kans Paleontol Contrib Pap ... University of Kansas. Paleontological Contributions. Paper [*A publication*]
Univ Kans Primary Rec Psychol Publ ... University of Kansas. Primary Records in Psychology. Publication [*A publication*]
Univ Kans Publ Mus Nat Hist ... University of Kansas. Publications. Museum of Natural History [*A publication*]
Univ Kans Sci Bull ... University of Kansas. Science Bulletin [*A publication*]

Univ Kans Sci Bull Suppl ... University of Kansas. Science Bulletin. Supplement [*A publication*]
Univ KC R ... University of Kansas City. Review [*A publication*]
Univ K Inst Min Miner Res Tech Rep ... University of Kentucky. Institute for Mining and Minerals Research. Technical Report [*A publication*]
Univ Kiril Metodij-Skopje Fac Math ... Universite Kiril et Metodij-Skopje. Faculte des Mathematiques [*A publication*]
Univ KY Coll Agric Coop Ext Ser Rep ... University of Kentucky. College of Agriculture. Cooperative Extension Service. Report [*A publication*]
Univ KY Coop Ext Serv Circ ... University of Kentucky. Cooperative Extension Service. Circular [*A publication*]
Univ KY Coop Ext Serv 4-H ... University of Kentucky. Cooperative Extension Service. 4-H [*A publication*]
Univ KY Coop Ext Serv Leafl ... University of Kentucky. Cooperative Extension Service. Leaflet [*A publication*]
Univ KY Coop Ext Serv Misc ... University of Kentucky. Cooperative Extension Service. Miscellaneous [*A publication*]
Univ KY Eng Exp Stn Bull ... University of Kentucky. Engineering Experiment Station. Bulletin [*A publication*]
Univ KY Inst Min Miner Res Rep IMMR ... University of Kentucky. Institute for Mining and Minerals Research. Report IMMR [*A publication*]
Univ KY Inst Min Miner Res Tech Rep IMMR ... University of Kentucky. Institute for Mining and Minerals Research. Technical Report. IMMR [*A publication*]
Univ KY Off Res Eng Ser Bull ... University of Kentucky. Office of Research and Engineering Services. Bulletin [*A publication*]
Univ KY Publ Anthropol Archaeol ... University of Kentucky. Publications in Anthropology and Archaeology [*A publication*]
Univ Laval Dep Exploit Util Bois Note Rech ... Universite Laval. Departement d'Exploitation et Utilisation des Bois. Note de Recherches [*A publication*]
Univ Laval Dep Exploit Util Bois Note Tech ... Universite Laval. Departement d'Exploitation et Utilisation des Bois. Note Technique [*A publication*]
Univ L Coll J ... University Law College. Journal. Rajputana University [*India*] [*A publication*]   (DLA)
Univ Leeds Med J ... University of Leeds. Medical Journal [*A publication*]
Univ Lesn Khoz Derevoobrab Prom-Sti (Sopron) Nauchn Publ ... Universitet Lesnogo Khozyaistva i Derevoobrabatyvaoushchei Promyshlennosti (Sopron) Nauchnye Publikatsii [*A publication*]
Univ Libre Bruxelles Inter-Univ Inst High Energ Rep ... Universite Libre de Bruxelles. Inter-University Institute for High Energies. Report [*A publication*]
Univ Liege Fac Sci Appl Coll Publ ... Universite de Liege. Faculte des Sciences Appliques. Collection des Publications [*Belgium*] [*A publication*]
Univ Lisboa Fac Farm Bol ... Universidade de Lisboa. Faculdade de Farmacia. Boletim [*A publication*]
Univ Lisboa Rev Fac Cienc A 2 ... Universidade de Lisboa. Revista da Faculdade de Ciencias. 2. Serie A. Ciencias Matematicas [*A publication*]
Univ Lisboa Revista Fac Ci A ... Universidade de Lisboa. Revista da Faculdade de Ciencas. 2. Serie A. Ciencias Matematicas [*A publication*]
Univ Liverp Rec ... University of Liverpool. Recorder [*A publication*]
Univ London Galton Lab Univ Coll Eugen Lab Mem ... University of London. Galton Laboratory. University College Eugenics Laboratory. Memoirs [*A publication*]
Univ Lond Univ Coll Galton Lab Eugen Lab Mem ... University of London. University College. Galton Laboratory. Eugenics Laboratory. Memoirs [*A publication*]
Univ LR ..... University Law Review [*A publication*]   (DLA)
Univ L Rev ... University Law Review [*A publication*]   (DLA)
Univ Lund Dep Anat Commun ... University of Lund. Department of Anatomy. Communications [*A publication*]
Univ M .... University Magazine [*Montreal*] [*A publication*]
Univ Madr Fac Vet Publ ... Universidad de Madrid. Facultad de Veterinaria. Publicacion [*A publication*]
Univ Maine Orono Life Sci Agric Exp Stn Annu Rep ... University of Maine at Orono. Life Sciences and Agriculture Experiment Station. Annual Report [*A publication*]
Univ Maine Orono Life Sci Agric Exp Stn Tech Bull ... University of Maine at Orono. Life Sciences and Agriculture Experiment Station. Technical Bulletin [*A publication*]
Univ Maine Orono Maine Agric Exp Stn Ann Rep ... University of Maine at Orono. Maine Agricultural Experiment Station. Annual Report [*A publication*]
Univ of Maine Studies ... University of Maine. Studies [*A publication*]
Univ of Manila L Gaz ... University of Manila. Law Gazette [*Manila, Philippines*] [*A publication*]   (DLA)
Univ Maria Curie-Sklodowsk Ann Sect B ... Universitas Maria Curie-Sklodowsk. Annales. Sectio B [*A publication*]
Univ Mass Dep Geol Contrib ... University of Massachusetts. Department of Geology. Contribution [*A publication*]
Univ MD Nat Resour Inst Contrib ... University of Maryland. Natural Resources Institute. Contribution [*A publication*]

Univ MD Sea Grant Program Tech Rep ... University of Maryland. Sea Grant Program. Technical Report [*A publication*]
Univ MD Water Resour Res Cent Tech Rep ... University of Maryland. Water Resources Research Center. Technical Report [*A publication*]
Univ MD Water Resour Res Cent WRRC Spec Rep ... University of Maryland. Water Resources Research Center. WRRC Special Report [*A publication*]
Univ Med Rec (London) ... Universal Medical Record (London) [*A publication*]
Univ Melb Gaz ... University of Melbourne. Gazette [*A publication*]   (APTA)
Univ Melb Sch For Bull ... University of Melbourne. School of Forestry. Bulletin [*A publication*]   (APTA)
Univ Miami Law R ... University of Miami. Law Review [*A publication*]
Univ Miami Law Rev ... University of Miami. Law Review [*A publication*]
Univ of Miami L Rev ... University of Miami. Law Review [*A publication*]
Univ Miami Rosenstiel Sch Mar Atmos Sci Annu Rep ... University of Miami. Rosenstiel School of Marine and Atmospheric Science. Annual Report [*A publication*]
Univ Miami Rosenstiel Sch Mar Atmos Sci Res Rev ... University of Miami. Rosenstiel School of Marine and Atmospheric Science. Research Review [*A publication*]
Univ Miami Sea Grant Program Sea Grant Field Guide Ser ... University of Miami. Sea Grant Program. Sea Grant Field Guide Series [*A publication*]
Univ Miami Sea Grant Program Sea Grant Tech Bull ... University of Miami. Sea Grant Program. Sea Grant Technical Bulletin [*A publication*]
Univ Mich (Ann Arbor) Off Res Adm Res News ... University of Michigan (Ann Arbor). Office of Research Administration. Research News [*A publication*]
Univ Mich Bus R ... University of Michigan. Business Review [*A publication*]
Univ Mich Bus Rev ... University of Michigan. Business Review [*A publication*]
Univ Mich Dep Nav Archit Mar Eng Rep ... University of Michigan. Department of Naval Architecture and Marine Engineering. Report [*A publication*]
Univ of Michigan J of Law Reform ... University of Michigan. Journal of Law Reform [*A publication*]
Univ Mich Inst Sci Tech Rep ... University of Michigan. Institute of Science and Technology. Report [*A publication*]
Univ Mich J Law Reform ... University of Michigan. Journal of Law Reform [*A publication*]
Univ Mich Med Bull ... University of Michigan. Medical Bulletin [*A publication*]
Univ Mich Med Cent J ... University of Michigan. Medical Center. Journal [*A publication*]
Univ Mich Mus Anthropol Tech Rep ... University of Michigan. Museum of Anthropology. Technical Reports [*A publication*]
Univ Mich Mus Zool Circ ... University of Michigan. Museum of Zoology. Circular [*A publication*]
Univ Minn Agric Ext Serv Ext Bull ... University of Minnesota. Agricultural Extension Service. Extension Bulletin [*A publication*]
Univ Minn Agric Ext Serv Ext Folder ... University of Minnesota. Agricultural Extension Service. Extension Folder [*A publication*]
Univ Minn Agric Ext Serv Ext Pam ... University of Minnesota. Agricultural Extension Service. Extension Pamphlet [*A publication*]
Univ Minn Agric Ext Serv Misc ... University of Minnesota. Agricultural Extension Service. Miscellaneous Publications [*A publication*]
Univ Minn Agric Ext Serv Misc Publ ... University of Minnesota. Agricultural Extension Service. Miscellaneous Publications [*A publication*]
Univ Minn Agric Ext Serv Spec Rep ... University of Minnesota. Agricultural Extension Service. Special Report [*A publication*]
Univ Minn Contin Med Educ ... University of Minnesota. Continuing Medical Education [*A publication*]
Univ Minn Med Bull ... University of Minnesota. Medical Bulletin [*A publication*]
Univ Mississippi Stud Engl ... University of Mississippi. Studies in English [*A publication*]
Univ of Missouri at Kansas City L Rev ... University of Missouri at Kansas City. Law Review [*A publication*]
Univ Missouri Stud ... University of Missouri. Studies [*A publication*]
Univ MO Bull Eng Exp Stn Ser ... University of Missouri. Bulletin. Engineering Experiment Station Series [*A publication*]
Univ MO Eng Exp Sta Eng Ser Bull ... University of Missouri. Engineering Experiment Station. Engineering Series. Bulletin [*A publication*]
Univ Montreal Chercheurs ... Universite de Montreal. Chercheurs [*A publication*]
Univ MO Sch Mines Metall Bull Tech Ser ... University of Missouri. School of Mines and Metallurgy. Bulletin. Technical Series [*A publication*]
Univ MO Stud ... University of Missouri. Studies [*A publication*]
Univ of MO Studies ... University of Missouri. Studies [*A publication*]
Univ Mus Bull Univ PA ... University Museum. Bulletin. University of Pennsylvania [*A publication*]
Univ Nac Auton Mex Inst Geol An ... Universidad Nacional Autonoma de Mexico. Instituto de Geologia. Anales [*A publication*]

Univ Nac Auton Mex Inst Geol Bol ... Universidad Nacional Autonoma de Mexico. Instituto de Geologia. Boletin [*A publication*]

Univ Nac Auton Mex Inst Geol Paleontol Mex ... Universidad Nacional Autonoma de Mexico. Instituto de Geologia. Paleontologica Mexicana [*A publication*]

Univ Nac Auton Mex Inst Geol Rev ... Universidad Nacional Autonoma de Mexico. Instituto de Geologia. Revista [*A publication*]

Univ Nac Cordoba Fac Cienc Med Rev ... Universidad Nacional de Cordoba. Facultad de Ciencias Medicas. Revista [*A publication*]

Univ Nac Cuyo Fac Cien Agrar Bol Tec ... Universidad Nacional de Cuyo. Facultad de Ciencias Agrarias. Boletin Tecnico [*A publication*]

Univ Nac de Cuyo Fac Cienc Agrar Bol de Ext ... Universidad Nacional de Cuyo. Facultad de Ciencias Agrarias. Boletin de Extension [*A publication*]

Univ Nac Cuyo Fac Cienc Fis-Quim Mat Ses Quim Argent ... Universidad Nacional de Cuyo. Facultad de Ciencias Fisico-Quimico Matematicas. Sesiones Quimicas Argentinas [*A publication*]

Univ Nac Cuyo Inst Pet Publ ... Universidad Nacional de Cuyo. Instituto del Petroleo. Publicacion [*A publication*]

Univ Nac Eva Peron Fac Cienc Fisicomat Publ Ser 2 ... Universidad Nacional de Eva Peron. Facultad de Ciencias Fisicomatematicas. Publicaciones. Serie 2. Revista [*A publication*]

Univ Nac La Plata Fac Agron Lab Zool Agric Bol ... Universidad Nacional de La Plata. Facultad de Agronomia. Laboratorio de Zoologia Agricola. Boletin [*A publication*]

Univ Nac La Plata Fac Cienc Nat Mus Ser Tec Didact ... Universidad Nacional de La Plata. Facultad de Ciencias Naturales y Museo. Serie Tecnica y Didactica [*A publication*]

Univ Nac La Plata Notas Mus Bot ... Universidad Nacional de La Plata. Notas del Museo. Botanica [*A publication*]

Univ Nac La Plata Notas Mus Geol ... Universidad Nacional de La Plata. Notas del Museo. Geologia [*A publication*]

Univ Nac La Plata Notas Mus Zool ... Universidad Nacional de La Plata. Notas del Museo. Zoologia [*A publication*]

Univ Nac La Plata Publ Fac Cienc Fisicomat ... Universidad Nacional de La Plata. Publicaciones. Facultad de Ciencias Fisicomatematicas [*A publication*]

Univ Nac La Plata Publ Fac Cienc Fisicomat Ser 2 ... Universidad Nacional de La Plata. Publicaciones. Facultad de Ciencias Fisicomatematicas. Serie 2. Revista [*A publication*]

Univ Nac Tucuman Fac Agron Misc ... Universidad Nacional de Tucuman. Facultad de Agronomia. Miscelanea [*A publication*]

Univ Nac Tucuman Fac Agron Zootec Misc ... Universidad Nacional de Tucuman. Facultad de Agronomia y Zootecnia. Miscelanea [*A publication*]

Univ Nac Tucuman Fac Agron Zootec Publ Espec ... Universidad Nacional de Tucuman. Facultad de Agronomia y Zootecnia. Publicacion Especial [*A publication*]

Univ Nac Tucuman Fac Agron Zootec Ser Didact ... Universidad Nacional de Tucuman. Facultad de Agronomia y Zootecnia. Serie Didactica [*A publication*]

Univ Nac Tucuman Fund Inst Miguel Lillo Misc ... Universidad Nacional de Tucuman. Fundacion e Instituto Miguel Lillo. Miscelanea [*A publication*]

Univ Nac Tucuman Inst Fis Publ ... Universidad Nacional de Tucuman. Instituto de Fisica. Publicacion [*A publication*]

Univ Nac Tucuman Inst Geol Min Rev ... Universidad Nacional de Tucuman. Instituto de Geologia y Mineria. Revista [*A publication*]

Univ Nac Tucuman Inst Ing Quim Pub ... Universidad Nacional de Tucuman. Instituto de Ingenieria Quimica. Publicacion [*A publication*]

Univ Nac Tucuman Rev Ser A ... Universidad Nacional de Tucuman. Facultad de Ciencias Exactas y Tecnologia. Revista. Serie A. Matematicas y Fisica Teorica [*A publication*]

Univ de Nancy Fac d Lettres Annales de l'Est ... Universite de Nancy. Faculte des Lettres. Annales de l'Est [*A publication*]

Univ Natal Wattle Res Inst Rep ... University of Natal. Wattle Research Institute. Report [*A publication*]

Univ Nebr Coll Agric Home Econ Q ... University of Nebraska. College of Agriculture and Home Economics. Quarterly [*A publication*]

Univ NE Bul ... University of New England. Bulletin [*A publication*] (APTA)

Univ N Engl Annu Rep ... University of New England. Annual Report [*A publication*]

Univ N Engl Explor Soc Aust Rep ... University of New England. Exploration Society of Australia. Report [*A publication*]

Univ Nev Mackay Sch Mines Geol Min Ser Bull ... University of Nevada. Mackay School of Mines. Geological and Mining Series. Bulletin [*A publication*]

Univ Nev Max C Fleischmann Coll Agric R ... University of Nevada. Max C. Fleischmann College of Agriculture. R Series [*A publication*]

Univ Nev Max C Fleischmann Coll Agric Rep ... University of Nevada. Max C. Fleischmann College of Agriculture. Report [*A publication*]

Univ Nev Max C Fleischmann Coll Agric Ser B ... University of Nevada. Max C. Fleischmann College of Agriculture. B Series [*A publication*]

Univ Nev Max C Fleischmann Coll Agric T Ser ... University of Nevada. Max C. Fleischmann College of Agriculture. T Series [*A publication*]

Univ of New Brunswick LJ ... University of New Brunswick. Law Journal [*A publication*]

Univ Newcastle Tyne Med Gaz ... University of Newcastle Upon Tyne. Medical Gazette [*A publication*]

Univ Newcastle Upon Tyne Rep Dove Mar Lab Third Ser ... University of Newcastle Upon Tyne. Report of the Dove Marine Laboratory. Third Series [*A publication*]

Univ New Eng Bull ... University of New England. Bulletin [*A publication*] (APTA)

Univ New South Wales Occas Pap ... University of New South Wales. Occasional Papers [*Australia*] [*A publication*]

Univ NM Bull Biol Ser ... University of New Mexico. Bulletin. Biological Series [*A publication*]

Univ NM Bull Geol Ser ... University of New Mexico. Bulletin. Geological Series [*A publication*]

Univ NM Inst Meteorit Spec Publ ... University of New Mexico. Institute of Meteoritics. Special Publication [*A publication*]

Univ NM Publ Anthropol ... University of New Mexico. Publications in Anthropology [*A publication*]

Univ NM Publ Biol ... University of New Mexico. Publications in Biology [*A publication*]

Univ NM Publ Geol ... University of New Mexico. Publications in Geology [*A publication*]

Univ NM Publ Meteorit ... University of New Mexico. Publications in Meteoritics [*A publication*]

Univ Nottingham Dep Agric Hortic Misc Publ ... University of Nottingham. Department of Agriculture and Horticulture. Miscellaneous Publication [*A publication*]

Univ u Novom Sadu Zb Rad Prirod-Mat Fak ... Univerzitet u Novom Sadu. Zbornik Radova Prirodno-Matematickog Fakulteta [*A publication*]

Univ NSW Law J ... University of New South Wales. Law Journal [*A publication*]

Univ NSW LJ ... University of New South Wales. Law Journal [*A publication*] (APTA)

Univ of NSW LJ ... University of New South Wales. Law Journal [*A publication*] (APTA)

Univ NSW Occas Pap ... University of New South Wales. Occasional Papers [*A publication*] (APTA)

Univ NSW Q ... University of New South Wales. Quarterly [*A publication*] (APTA)

Univ Orange Free State Publ Ser C ... University of the Orange Free State. Publication. Series C [*A publication*]

Univ Oriente Inst Oceanogr Bol ... Universidad de Oriente. Instituto Oceanografico. Boletin [*A publication*]

Univ Oriente Inst Oceanogr Bol Bibliogr ... Universidad de Oriente. Instituto Oceanografico. Boletin Bibliografico [*A publication*]

Univ Oxford Dept Eng Sci Rep ... University of Oxford. Department of Engineering. Science Reports [*A publication*]

Univ PA Bull Vet Ext Q ... University of Pennsylvania. Bulletin. Veterinary Extension Quarterly [*A publication*]

Univ Palermo Ann Fac Econom e Commercio ... Universita di Palermo. Annali della Facolta di Economia e Commercio [*A publication*]

Univ Palermo Ann Fac Econom Commercio ... Universita di Palermo. Annali della Facolta di Economia e Commercio [*A publication*]

Univ PA Libr Chron ... University of Pennsylvania. Library Chronicle [*A publication*]

Univ PA Med Bull ... University of Pennsylvania. Medical Bulletin [*A publication*]

Univ of PA Pub Pol Econ ... University of Pennsylvania. Publications in Political Economy [*A publication*]

Univ Paris Conf Palais Decouverte Ser A ... Universite de Paris. Conferences du Palais de la Decouverte. Serie A [*A publication*]

Univ Penn Law Rev ... University of Pennsylvania. Law Review [*A publication*]

Univ of Pennsylvania L Rev ... University of Pennsylvania. Law Review [*A publication*]

Univ Perspect ... University Perspectives [*A publication*]

Univ Peshawar J ... University of Peshawar. Journal [*A publication*]

Univ of Pittsburgh L Rev ... University of Pittsburgh. Law Review [*A publication*]

Univ Pontif Bolivariana Publ Trimest ... Universidad Pontificia Bolivariana. Publicacion Trimestral [*A publication*]

Univ Pontif Bolivar Publ Trimest ... Universidad Pontificia Bolivariana. Publicacion Trimestral [*A publication*]

Univ Pretoria Publ Ser 2 ... University of Pretoria. Publications. Series 2. Natural Sciences [*A publication*]

Univ Q........ Universalist Quarterly Review [*Boston*] [*A publication*]

Univ Q........ Universities Quarterly [*London*] [*A publication*]

Univ Qd Agric Dep Pap ... University of Queensland. Agriculture Department. Papers [*A publication*] (APTA)

Univ Qd Bot Dep Pap ... University of Queensland. Botany Department. Papers [*A publication*] (APTA)

Univ Qd Ent Dep Pap ... University of Queensland. Entomology Department. Papers [*A publication*] (APTA)

Univ Q Gaz ... University of Queensland. Gazette [*A publication*] (APTA)

Univ Q Law J ... University of Queensland. Law Journal [*A publication*] (APTA)

Univ Qld Gaz ... University of Queensland. Gazette [*A publication*]   (APTA)
Univ Qld Law J ... University of Queensland. Law Journal [*A publication*]   (APTA)
Univ Q LJ ... University of Queensland. Law Journal [*A publication*]   (APTA)
Univ Quart ... Universities Quarterly [*A publication*]
Univ of Queensland LJ ... University of Queensland. Law Journal [*A publication*]
Univ Queensl Comput Cent Pap ... University of Queensland. Computer Centre. Papers [*A publication*]
Univ Queensl Great Barrier Reef Comm Heron Isl Res Stn ... University of Queensland. Great Barrier Reef Committee. Heron Island Research Station [*A publication*]
Univ Queensl Pap Dep Bot ... University of Queensland. Papers. Department of Botany [*A publication*]
Univ Queensl Pap Dep Chem ... University of Queensland. Papers. Department of Chemistry [*A publication*]
Univ Queensl Pap Dep Entomol ... University of Queensland. Papers. Department of Entomology [*A publication*]
Univ Queensl Pap Dep Geol ... University of Queensland. Papers. Department of Geology [*A publication*]
Univ Queensl Pap Dep Zool ... University of Queensland. Papers. Department of Zoology [*A publication*]
Univ Queensl Pap Fac Vet Sci ... University of Queensland. Papers. Faculty of Veterinary Science [*A publication*]
Univ R .... Universal Review [*A publication*]
Univ R .... University Review [*A publication*]
Univ Reading Natl Inst Res Dairy Bienn Rev ... University of Reading. National Institute for Research in Dairying. Biennial Reviews [*A publication*]
Univ Reading Natl Inst Res Dairy Rep ... University of Reading. National Institute for Research in Dairying. Report [*A publication*]
Univ Rec .... University Record [*A publication*]
Univ Repub Fac Agron Bol (Montev) ... Universidad de la Republica. Facultad de Agronomia. Boletin (Montevideo) [*A publication*]
Univ Repub (Montevideo) Fac Agron Bol ... Universidad de la Republica (Montevideo). Facultad de Agronomia. Boletin [*A publication*]
Univ Rhod Fac Med Res Lect Ser ... University of Rhodesia. Faculty of Medicine. Research Lecture Series [*A publication*]
Univ of Richmond L Not ... University of Richmond. Law Notes [*Richmond, Virginia*] [*A publication*]   (DLA)
Univ of Richmond L Rev ... University of Richmond. Law Review [*A publication*]
Univ RI Mar Publ Ser ... University of Rhode Island. Marine Publication Series [*A publication*]
Univ Rio Grande Do Sul Esc Geol Avulso ... Universidade do Rio Grande Do Sul. Escola de Geologia. Avulso [*A publication*]
Univ Rio Grande Do Sul Esc Geol Bol ... Universidade do Rio Grande Do Sul. Escola de Geologia. Boletim [*A publication*]
Univ Rio Grande Do Sul Esc Geol Notas Estud ... Universidad do Rio Grande Do Sul. Escola de Geologia. Notas e Estudos [*A publication*]
Univ Rochester Lib Bull ... University of Rochester. Library Bulletin [*A publication*]
Univ Rochester Libr Bull ... University of Rochester. Library Bulletin [*A publication*]
Univ Roma Ist Autom Not ... Universita di Roma. Istituto di Automatica. Notiziario [*A publication*]
Univ Roorkee Res J ... University of Roorkee. Research Journal [*A publication*]
Univ Rural Pernambuco Comun Tec ... Universidade Rural de Pernambuco. Comunicado Tecnico [*A publication*]
Univ of San Fernando Valley L Rev ... University of San Fernando Valley. Law Review [*Sepulveda, California*] [*A publication*]   (DLA)
Univ of San Francisco L Rev ... University of San Francisco. Law Review [*A publication*]
Univ Sao Paulo Esc Politec Geol Metal Bol ... Universidade de Sao Paulo. Escola Politecnica, Geologia, e Metalurgia. Boletim [*A publication*]
Univ Sao Paulo Esc Super Agric Luiz De Queiroz Bol Tec Cient ... Universidade de Sao Paulo. Escola Superior de Agricultura Luiz De Queiroz. Boletim Tecnico Cientifico [*A publication*]
Univ Sao Paulo Fac Filos Cienc Let Bol Bot ... Universidade de Sao Paulo. Faculdade de Filosofia, Ciencias, e Letras. Boletim. Botanica [*A publication*]
Univ Sao Paulo Fac Filos Cienc Let Bol Geol ... Universidade de Sao Paulo. Faculdade de Filosofia, Ciencias, e Letras. Boletim. Geologia [*A publication*]
Univ Sao Paulo Fac Filos Cienc Let Bol Mineral ... Universidade de Sao Paulo. Faculdade de Filosofia, Ciencias, e Letras. Boletim. Mineralogia [*A publication*]
Univ Sao Paulo Fac Filos Cienc Let Bol Quim ... Universidade de Sao Paulo. Faculdade de Filosofia, Ciencias, e Letras. Boletim. Quimica [*A publication*]
Univ Sao Paulo Inst Geocienc Astron Bol ... Universidade de Sao Paulo. Instituto de Geociencias e Astronomia. Boletim [*A publication*]

Univ Sao Paulo Inst Geocienc Bol IG ... Universidade de Sao Paulo. Instituto de Geociencias. Boletim IG [*Instituto de Geociencias*] [*A publication*]
Univ SC Governmental R ... University of South Carolina. Governmental Review [*A publication*]
Univ Sevilla Publ Ser Med ... Universidad de Sevilla. Publicaciones. Serie Medicina [*A publication*]
Univ S Inst of Crim Proceeding ... University of Sydney. Institute of Criminology. Proceedings [*Australia*] [*A publication*]
Univ Skopje Sumar Fak God Zb ... Univerzitet vo Skopje. Sumarski Fakultet. Godisen Zbornik [*A publication*]
Univ South Calif Allan Hancock Found ... University of Southern California. Allan Hancock Foundation [*A publication*]
Univs Q ...... Universities Quarterly [*A publication*]
Univ Strathclyde Annu Rep ... University of Strathclyde. Annual Report [*A publication*]
Univ Strathclyde Res Rep ... University of Strathclyde. Research Report [*A publication*]
Univ Stud ... University Studies in History and Economics [*A publication*]   (APTA)
Univ Stud Hist ... University Studies in History [*A publication*]   (APTA)
Univ Stud Hist Ec ... University Studies in History and Economics [*A publication*]   (APTA)
Univ Stud Hist Econ ... University Studies in History and Economics [*A publication*]
Univ Studies ... University Studies in History and Economics [*A publication*]   (APTA)
Univ Studies ... University Studies in Western Australian History [*A publication*]   (APTA)
Univ Studies Math ... University Studies in Mathematics [*A publication*]
Univ Studi Trieste Fac Econ Commer Ist Merceol Pubbl ... Universita degli Studi di Trieste. Facolta di Economia e Commercio. Istituto di Merceologia. Pubblicazione [*A publication*]
Univ Studi Trieste Fac Ing Ist Chim App Pubbl ... Universita degli Studi di Trieste. Facolta di Ingegneria. Istituto di Chimica Applicata. Pubblicazioni [*A publication*]
Univ Studi Trieste Fac Sci Ist Chim Pubbl ... Universita degli Studi di Trieste. Facolta di Scienze. Istituto di Chimica. Pubblicazioni [*A publication*]
Univ Studi Trieste Fac Sci Ist Geol Pubbl ... Universita degli Studi di Trieste. Facolta di Scienze. Istituto di Geologia. Pubblicazioni [*A publication*]
Univ Studi Trieste Fac Sci Ist de Mineral Pubbl ... Universita degli Studi di Trieste. Facolta di Scienze. Istituto di Mineralogia. Pubblicazione [*A publication*]
Univ Studi Trieste Ist Chim Farm Tossicol Pubbl ... Universita degli Studi di Trieste. Istituto di Chimica Farmaceutica e Tossicologica. Pubblicazioni [*A publication*]
Univ Studi Triest Fac di Sci Ist Geol Pubbl ... Universita degli Studi di Trieste. Facolta di Scienze. Istituto di Geologia. Pubblicazioni [*A publication*]
Univ Stud Math (Jaipur) ... University Studies in Mathematics (Jaipur) [*A publication*]
Univ Stud Trieste Fac Farm Ist Chim Farm Tossicol Pubbl ... Universita degli Studi di Trieste. Facolta di Farmacia. Istituto di Chimica, Farmaceutica, e Tossicologica. Pubblicazioni [*A publication*]
Univ Stud Trieste Fac Farm Ist Tec Farm Pubbl ... Universita degli Studi di Trieste. Facolta di Farmacia. Istituto di Tecnica Farmaceutica. Pubblicazioni [*A publication*]
Univ Stud Trieste Ist Tec Farm Pubbl ... Universita degli Studi di Trieste. Istituto di Tecnica Farmaceutica. Pubblicazioni [*A publication*]
Univ Stud Univ Neb ... University Studies. University of Nebraska [*A publication*]
Univ Stud W Aust Hist ... University Studies in Western Australian History [*A publication*]
Univ Sydney Med J ... University of Sydney. Medical Journal [*A publication*]
Univ Syd Post Grad Ctee Med Bull ... University of Sydney. Postgraduate Committee in Medicine. Bulletin [*A publication*]   (APTA)
Univ Tas Gaz ... University of Tasmania. Gazette [*A publication*]   (APTA)
Univ of Tas LR ... University of Tasmania. Law Review [*A publication*]
Univ Tas LR ... University of Tasmania. Law Review [*A publication*]   (APTA)
Univ Tasmania Environ Stud Occas Pap ... University of Tasmania. Environmental Studies. Occasional Paper [*A publication*]
Univ Tasmania Environ Stud Work Pap ... University of Tasmania. Environmental Studies. Working Paper [*A publication*]
Univ of Tasmania L Rev ... University of Tasmania. Law Review [*A publication*]
Univ Tas News ... University of Tasmania. News [*A publication*]
Univ Teheran Fac Agron Bull ... Universite de Teheran. Faculte d'Agronomie. Bulletin [*A publication*]
Univ Tenn Rec ... University of Tennessee. Record [*A publication*]
Univ Tenn Surv Bus ... University of Tennessee. Survey of Business [*A publication*]
Univ Tex Austin Bur Econ Geol Handb ... University of Texas at Austin. Bureau of Economic Geology. Handbook [*A publication*]
Univ Tex Austin Bur Econ Geol Miner Resour Circ ... University of Texas at Austin. Bureau of Economic Geology. Mineral Resource Circular [*A publication*]

Univ Tex Austin Bur Econ Geol Res Note ... University of Texas at Austin. Bureau of Economic Geology. Research Note [*A publication*]

Univ Tex Austin Cent Highw Res Res Rep ... University of Texas at Austin. Center for Highway Research. Research Report [*A publication*]

Univ Tex Austin Cent Res Water Resour Tech Rep ... University of Texas at Austin. Center for Research in Water Resources. Technical Report [*A publication*]

Univ Tex Bull ... University of Texas. Bulletin [*A publication*]

Univ Tex Bur Econ Geol Publ ... University of Texas. Bureau of Economic Geology. Publication [*A publication*]

Univ Tex Bur Econ Geol Rep Invest ... University of Texas. Bureau of Economic Geology. Report of Investigations [*A publication*]

Univ Tex MD Anderson Symp Fundam Cancer Res ... University of Texas. M. D. Anderson Symposium on Fundamental Cancer Research [*A publication*]

Univ Timisoara An Stiinte Fiz Chim ... Universitatea din Timisoara. Analele. Stiinte Fizice-Chimice [*A publication*]

Univ TLR ... University of Tasmania. Law Review [*A publication*]

Univ Toledo Law R ... University of Toledo. Law Review [*A publication*]

Univ of Toledo L Rev ... University of Toledo. Law Review [*A publication*]

Univ Toronto Biol Ser ... University of Toronto. Biological Series [*A publication*]

Univ Toronto Fac For Tech Rep ... University of Toronto. Faculty of Forestry. Technical Report [*A publication*]

Univ Toronto Inst Environ Sci Eng Publ EH ... University of Toronto. Institute of Environmental Sciences and Engineering. Publication EH [*A publication*]

Univ Toronto Inst Environ Stud Publ EH ... University of Toronto. Institute for Environmental Studies. Publication EH [*A publication*]

Univ Toronto Law J ... University of Toronto. Law Journal [*A publication*]

Univ of Toronto LJ ... University of Toronto. Law Journal [*A publication*]

Univ Toronto Med J ... University of Toronto. Medical Journal [*A publication*]

Univ Toronto Q ... University of Toronto. Quarterly [*A publication*]

Univ Toronto Stud Biol Ser ... University of Toronto. Studies. Biological Series [*A publication*]

Univ Toronto Stud Geol Ser ... University of Toronto. Studies. Geological Series [*A publication*]

Univ Toronto Stud Pap Chem Lab ... University of Toronto. Studies. Papers from the Chemical Laboratories [*A publication*]

Univ Toronto Stud Pathol Ser ... University of Toronto. Studies. Pathological Series [*A publication*]

Univ Toronto Stud Physiol Ser ... University of Toronto. Studies. Physiological Series [*A publication*]

Univ Toronto Stud Phys Ser ... University of Toronto. Studies. Physics Series [*A publication*]

Univ Toronto Undergrad Dent J ... University of Toronto Undergraduate Dental Journal [*A publication*]

Univ Tor Q ... University of Toronto. Quarterly [*A publication*]

Univ Tripoli Bull Fac Eng ... University of Tripoli. Bulletin. Faculty of Engineering [*A publication*]

Univ of Tulsa LJ ... University of Tulsa. Law Journal [*Tulsa, Oklahoma*] [*A publication*] (DLA)

Univ Udaipur Res J ... University of Udaipur. Research Journal [*A publication*]

Univ Udaipur Res Stud ... University of Udaipur. Research Studies [*A publication*]

Univ Umea Commun Res Unit Proj Rep ... University of Umea. Communication Research Unit. Project Report [*A publication*]

Univ Utah Anthropol Pap ... University of Utah. Anthropological Papers [*A publication*]

Univ Utah Biol Ser ... University of Utah. Biological Series [*A publication*]

Univ V ... University Vision [*A publication*]

Univ VA News Letter ... University of Virginia. News Letter [*A publication*]

Univ WA Ann L Rev ... University of Western Australia. Annual Law Review [*A publication*]

Univ WA Law Rev ... University of Western Australia. Law Review [*A publication*] (APTA)

Univ WA L Rev ... University of Western Australia. Law Review [*A publication*] (APTA)

Univ Warsaw Dep Radiochem Publ ... University of Warsaw. Department of Radiochemistry. Publication [*A publication*]

Univ Wash Coll Fish Tech Rep ... University of Washington. College of Fisheries. Technical Report [*A publication*]

Univ Wash Eng Exp Stn Bull ... University of Washington. Engineering Experiment Station. Bulletin [*A publication*]

Univ Wash Eng Exp Stn Rep ... University of Washington. Engineering Experiment Station. Report [*A publication*]

Univ Wash Eng Exp Stn Tech Note ... University of Washington. Engineering Experiment Station. Technical Note [*A publication*]

Univ Wash Inst For Prod Contrib ... University of Washington. Institute of Forest Products. Contributions [*A publication*]

Univ Wash Publ Biol ... University of Washington. Publications in Biology [*A publication*]

Univ Wash Publ Fish ... University of Washington. Publications in Fisheries [*A publication*]

Univ Wash Publ Fish New Ser ... University of Washington. Publications in Fisheries. New Series [*A publication*]

Univ Wash Publ Geol ... University of Washington. Publications in Geology [*A publication*]

Univ Wash Publ Oceanogr ... University of Washington. Publications in Oceanography [*A publication*]

Univ Waterloo Biol Ser ... University of Waterloo. Biology Series [*A publication*]

Univ Waterloo Fac Environ Stud Occas Pap ... University of Waterloo. Faculty of Environmental Studies. Occasional Paper [*A publication*]

Univ of West Australia L Rev ... University of Western Australia. Law Review [*A publication*]

Univ Western Australia Law R ... University of Western Australia. Law Review [*A publication*]

Univ Western Ontario Series in Philos Sci ... University of Western Ontario. Series in Philosophy of Science [*A publication*]

Univ West Indies Reg Res Cent Soil Land Use Surv ... University of the West Indies. Regional Research Centre. Soil and Land Use Surveys [*A publication*]

Univ West Ont Med J ... University of Western Ontario. Medical Journal [*A publication*]

Univ West Ont Ser Philos Sci ... University of Western Ontario. Series in Philosophy in Science [*A publication*]

Univ Windsor R ... University of Windsor. Review [*A publication*]

Univ Wis Coll Agric Life Sci Res Div Bull ... University of Wisconsin. College of Agricultural and Life Sciences. Research Division. Bulletin [*A publication*]

Univ Wis Coll Agric Life Sci Res Div Res Rep ... University of Wisconsin. College of Agricultural and Life Sciences. Research Division. Research Report [*A publication*]

Univ Wis Eng Exp Stn Rep ... University of Wisconsin. Engineering Experiment Station. Report [*A publication*]

Univ Wis-Madison Coll Agric Life Sci Res Div Res Bull ... University of Wisconsin-Madison. College of Agricultural and Life Sciences. Research Division. Research Bulletin [*A publication*]

Univ Wis Milw Field Stn Bull ... University of Wisconsin-Milwaukee. Field Stations Bulletin [*A publication*]

Univ Wis Sea Grant Coll Tech Rep ... University of Wisconsin. Sea Grant College. Technical Report [*A publication*]

Univ Wis Sea Grant Program Tech Rep ... University of Wisconsin. Sea Grant Program. Technical Report [*A publication*]

Univ Wis Water Resour Cent Eutrophication Inf Prog Lit Rev ... University of Wisconsin. Water Resources Center. Eutrophication Information Program. Literature Review [*A publication*]

Univ Witwatersrand Dep Geogr Environ Stud Occas Pap ... University of the Witwatersrand. Department of Geography and Environmental Studies. Occasional Paper [*A publication*]

Univ of Wyoming Publ ... University of Wyoming. Publications [*A publication*]

Univ Wyo Publ ... University of Wyoming. Publications [*A publication*]

Univ Yaounde Fac Sci Ann Ser 3 ... Universite de Yaounde. Faculte des Sciences. Annales. Serie 3. Biologie-Biochimie [*A publication*]

Uniw Adama Mickiewicza Poznaniu Inst Chem Ser Chem ... Uniwersytet Imienia Adama Mickiewicza w Poznaniu. Instytut Chemii. Seria Chemia [*A publication*]

Uniw Adama Mickiewicza Poznaniu Ser Astron ... Uniwersytet Imienia Adama Mickiewicza w Poznaniu. Seria Astronomia [*A publication*]

Uniw Adama Mickiewicza Poznaniu Ser Biol ... Uniwersytet Imienia Adama Mickiewicza w Poznaniu. Seria Biologia [*A publication*]

Uniw Adama Mickiewicza Poznaniu Ser Chem ... Uniwersytet Imienia Adama Mickiewicza w Poznaniu. Seria Chemia [*A publication*]

Uniw Adama Mickiewicza w Poznaniu Ser Fiz ... Uniwersytet Imienia Adama Mickiewicza w Poznaniu. Seria Fizyka [*A publication*]

Uniw Gdanski Wydz Mat Fiz Chem Zesz Nauk Ser Chem ... Uniwersytet Gdanski Wydzial Matematyki, Fizyki, Chemii, Zeszyty Naukowe. Seria Chemia [*A publication*]

Uniw Lodz Acta Univ Lodz Ser 2 ... Uniwersytet Lodzki. Acta Universitatis Lodziensis. Seria 2 [*A publication*]

Uniw Marii Curie-Sklodowskiej Ann Sect AA ... Uniwersytet Marii Curie-Sklodowskiej. Annales. Sectio AA. Physica et Chemia [*A publication*]

Uniw Slaski w Katowicach Prace Nauk ... Uniwersytet Slaski w Katowicach. Prace Naukowe [*A publication*]

Uniw Slaski w Katowicach Prace Naukowe ... Uniwersytet Slaski w Katowicach. Prace Naukowe [*A publication*]

Uniw Slaski w Katowicach Prace Naukowe Prace Mat ... Uniwersytet Slaski w Katowicach. Prace Naukowe. Prace Matematyczne [*A publication*]

Uniw Slaski w Katowicach Prace Nauk-Prace Mat ... Uniwersytet Slaski w Katowicach. Prace Naukowe. Prace Matematyczne [*A publication*]

Unix ... [*An*] operating system developed by Bell Laboratories [*Software*]

UNJBS ... United Nations Joint Board of Strategy

UNJC ... Unified National J Series Coarse [*Thread*]

UNJEF ... Unified National J Series Extra Fine [*Thread*]

UNJF ... Unified National J Series Fine [*Thread*]

UNJS......... Unified National J Series Special [*Thread*]
UN Juridical YB ... United Nations Juridical Year Book [*A publication*] (DLA)
UN Jur YB ... United Nations Juridical Year Book [*A publication*] (DLA)
UNK.......... Unalakleet [*Alaska*] [*Airport symbol*] (OAG)
UNK.......... Unknown (AFM)
Unk .... Unknown Worlds [*A publication*]
UNK.......... Zeitschrift fuer Operations Research [*A publication*]
UNKA........ Abakan [*USSR*] [*ICAO location identifier*] (ICLI)
UNKI........ Vanavara [*USSR*] [*ICAO location identifier*] (ICLI)
UNKK........ Krasnoyarsk [*USSR*] [*ICAO location identifier*] (ICLI)
UNKN ...... Unknown
UNKO .... Sovetsky Rudnik [*USSR*] [*ICAO location identifier*] (ICLI)
UNKRA..... United Nations Korean Reconstruction Agency
UNKT........ Podkamennaya Tunguska [*USSR*] [*ICAO location identifier*] (ICLI)
UNK UNK ... Unknown Unknowns [*Design engineering*]
UNKW....... Baykit [*USSR*] [*ICAO location identifier*] (ICLI)
UNKWN ... Unknown
UNL.......... Umwelt. Forschung, Gestaltung, Schutz [*A publication*]
UNL.......... United Leader Resources, Inc. [*Vancouver Stock Exchange symbol*]
UNL.......... University of Nebraska - Lincoln
UNL.......... University of New Brunswick Law Library [*UTLAS symbol*]
UNL.......... Unlimited
UNL.......... Unloading
UNLA........ Uganda National Liberation Army [*Political party*]
UNLA........ Unione Nazionale per la Lotta Contra l'Analfabatismo [*Union for the Struggle Against Illiteracy*] [*Italy*]
UNLCH..... Unlatch (MCD)
UNLF .... Ugandan National Liberation Front [*Political party*] (PD)
UNLGTD.. Unlighted (FAAC)
UNL/H...... Humanitas. Universidad de Nuevo Leon. Centro de Estudios Humanisticos [*A publication*]
UNLIM ..... Unlimited
UNLIQ...... Unliquidated
UNLIS ...... United National Life Insurance Society (EA)
UNLK....... Unlock
UNLKG..... Unlocking
UNLL........ United Nations League of Lawyers
UNLOS ..... United Nations Law of the Sea [*Conference*]
UNLPM/R ... Revista. Museo de La Plata. Universidad Nacional de La Plata. Facultad de Ciencias Naturales y Museo [*A publication*]
UNLR .... United Nations Law Reports [*A publication*] (DLA)
UNLV .... University of Nevada, Las Vegas
UNM .... National University of Mexico [*Mexico*] [*Seismograph station code, US Geological Survey*] [*Closed*] (SEIS)
UNM .... Unified Miniature
UNM .... United Nations Medal [*Military decoration*]
UnM .... University Microfilms International, Ann Arbor, MI [*Library symbol*] [*Library of Congress*] (LCLS)
UNM .... University of Nebraska, Medical Center, Omaha, NE [*OCLC symbol*] (OCLC)
UNM .... Unmarried
UNM .... UNUM Corp. [*NYSE symbol*] (SPSG)
UNMA ...... Uni-Marts, Inc. [*State College, PA*] [*NASDAQ symbol*] (NQ)
UNMA ...... Unified Network Management Architecture [*Data processing*]
UNMAC.... United Nations Mixed Armistice Commission
Unman Syst ... Unmanned Systems [*A publication*]
UNMC....... United Nations Mediterranean Command (BJA)
UNMC....... United Nations Mediterranean Commission
UNMC....... University of Nebraska Medical Center [*Omaha, NB*]
UNMCB.... Unscheduled Not Mission Capable Both [*Maintenance and supply*] (MCD)
UNMCM... Unscheduled Not Mission Capable Maintenance (MCD)
UNMD ...... Unmanned (KSC)
Un Med Can ... Union Medicale du Canada [*A publication*]
UNMEM... United Nations Middle East Mission (EY)
UNM/JAR ... Journal of Anthropological Research. University of New Mexico. Department of Anthropology [*A publication*]
UNMKD.... Unmarked
UnM-L....... University Microfilms Ltd., Penn, Buckinghamshire, United Kingdom [*Library symbol*] [*Library of Congress*] (LCLS)
UNMO's.... United Nations Military Observers (BJA)
UN Mo Bul ... Monthly Bulletin of Statistics. United Nations [*A publication*]
UN Mo Chron ... UN Monthly Chronicle [*A publication*]
UNMOGIP ... United Nations Military Observer Group for India and Pakistan (AABC)
UNMON... Unable to Monitor (FAAC)
Unm Ox ..... Unmuzzled Ox [*A publication*]
UNMSC.... United Nations Military Staff Committee (AABC)
UNMT....... United Nations Multilateral Treaties [*A publication*] (DLA)
UNMTD.... Unmounted
UNN .... Unternehmung. Schweizerische Zeitschrift fuer Betriebswirtschaft [*A publication*]
UNNB........ University National Bank & Trust Co. [*NASDAQ symbol*] (NQ)
UNNE........ Universidad Nacional del Nordeste [*Argentina*]
UNNECY .. Unnecessary (ROG)
UNNEFO .. United Nations of the New Emerging Forces [*Indonesia*]

UNNN .... Novosibirsk/Tolmachevo [*USSR*] [*ICAO location identifier*] (ICLI)
Unnumbered Rep US Dep Agric Econ Stat Coop Serv Stat Res Div ... Unnumbered Report. United States Department of Agriculture. Economics, Statistics, and Cooperatives Service. Statistical Research Division [*A publication*]
UNNUS..... Uralic News and Notes from the United States [*A publication*]
UNO......... Unicorn Resources [*Vancouver Stock Exchange symbol*]
UNO .... Unified Nimbus Observatory (MCD)
UNO .... Union Nacional Odriista [*Peruvian political party*]
UNO .... United Nations Observer Corps (BJA)
UNO .... United Nations Organization [*ICSU*]
UNO .... United Nicaraguan Opposition
UNO .... University of Nebraska at Omaha
UNO .... University of New Orleans [*Louisiana*]
UNO .... Uno Restaurant Corp. [*AMEX symbol*] (SPSG)
UNO .... Utility Night Observer
UNOBSD.. Unobserved (ROG)
UNOC .... Union Nationale des Ouvriers Congolais [*National Union of Congolese Workers*]
UNOC .... United Nations Operation in the Congo
UNO-CARA-PEN ... Union Internationale pour la Cooperation Culturelle [*International Union for Cultural Co-operation*]
UNODIR... Unless Otherwise Directed
UNOEOA ... United Nations Office for Emergency Operations in Africa (EA)
Unof .... Unofficial Reports [*A publication*] (DLA)
UNOFFL... Unofficial (FAAC)
UNOG .... United Nations Organization - Geneva
UNOGIL... United Nations Observer Group in Lebanon
UNOINDC ... Unless Otherwise Indicated
UNOLS ..... University National Oceanographic Laboratory System [*National Science Foundation*]
UNOO .... United Nations Oceanographic Organization (NOAA)
UNOP....... Unopened (ADA)
UNOP....... Unopposed
UNOPAR.. Universal Operator Performance Analyzer and Recorder
UNORDCAN ... Unexecuted Portion of Orders Cancelled
UNOREQ ... Unless Otherwise Requested (NVT)
UNOS........ United Network for Organ Sharing [*Database*] (EA)
U Notr D St ... University of Notre Dame. Studies in the Philosophy of Religion [*A publication*]
UNP.......... Union Nacional Paraguaya [*Paraguayan political party*]
UNP.......... Union Pacific Corp. [*NYSE symbol*] (SPSG)
UNP.......... United National Party [*Sri Lanka*] [*Political party*] (PPW)
UNP.......... United Nations Philatelists (EA)
UNP.......... United Northern Petroleum Corp. [*Vancouver Stock Exchange symbol*]
UNP.......... Unpaged
UNP.......... Unpostable [*Data processing*]
UNPA .... Unione Nazionale Protezione Antiaere [*Italy*]
UNPA .... United Nations Participation Act of 1945
UNPA........ United Nations Postal Administration
UN-PAAERD ... United Nations Programme of Action for African Economic Recovery and Development [*1986-1990*]
UNPAC ..... Union Pacific Railroad Co.
UNPAD..... Universitas Negeri Padjadjaran [*Indonesia*]
Unpartizan R ... Unpartizan Review [*A publication*]
UNPC .... United Nations Palestine Commission
UNPCC ..... United Nations Palestine Conciliation Commission (BJA)
UNPD........ Unpaid (AABC)
UNPERF.. Unperformed [*Music*]
UNPERFD ... Unperformed (ROG)
UNPIK ...... United Nations Partisan Infantry Korea
UNPOC ..... United Nations Peace Observation Commission
Unpop R...... Unpopular Review [*A publication*]
Un Prac News ... Unauthorized Practice News [*A publication*]
UNPS .... Unified Network Planning Study
UNPS .... United Nations Philatelic Society (EA)
UNPS .... Universal Power Supply
UNPUB ..... Unpublished
UNPUBD.. Unpublished
UNQ .... Providence, RI [*Location identifier*] [*FAA*] (FAAL)
UNQ .... Unique Resources Ltd. [*Vancouver Stock Exchange symbol*]
UNQTE..... Unquote
UNQUAL ... Unqualified (AABC)
unr............. Ukrainian Soviet Socialist Republic [*MARC country of publication code*] [*Library of Congress*] (LCCP)
UNR.......... Ukrains'ka Natsional'na Rada
UNR.......... Uniao Nacional Republicana [*National Republican Union*] [*Portugal*] [*Political party*] (PPE)
UNR.......... Unicorp Resources Ltd. [*Toronto Stock Exchange symbol*]
UN R......... United Nations Review [*A publication*]
UNRCCFE ... United Nations Regional Cartographic Conferences on Asia and the Far East (NOAA)
UNRDBL .. Unreadable (FAAC)
UNREF..... United Nations Refugee Fund
UNREF..... Unreformed (ROG)
UNREL..... Unreliable
UNREP ..... Underway Replenishment [*Military*]

Unrep Cr C ... Bombay Unreported Criminal Cases [*1862-98*] [*India*] [*A publication*]   (DLA)
Unrep NY Est TC ... Unreported New York Estate Tax Cases [*Prentice-Hall, Inc.*] [*A publication*]   (DLA)
Unrep Wills Cas ... Unreported Wills Cases [*Prentice-Hall, Inc.*] [*A publication*]   (DLA)
UN Res ...... United Nations Resolutions [*A publication*]   (DLA)
UN Rev ...... United Nations Review [*A publication*]
UNRF .... Uganda National Rescue Front   (PD)
UNRGLTD ... Unregulated
UNRI .... UNR Industries, Inc. [*NASDAQ symbol*]   (NQ)
UNRIAA ... United Nations Reports of International Arbitral Awards [*A publication*]   (DLA)
UNRIPS .... United Nations Regional Institute for Population Studies [*Legon, Ghana*]   (EAIO)
UNRISD.... United Nations Research Institute for Social Development   (EA)
UNROD .... United Nations Relief Operation in Dacca
UNRP .... University of Nottingham. Research Publications [*A publication*]
UNRPR ..... United Nations Relief for Palestine Refugees
UNRR .... Unable to Approve Route Requested [*Aviation*]   (FAAC)
UNRRA ..... United Nations Relief and Rehabilitation Administration [*"United Nations" in this body's name derives from the wartime alliance of this name, not from any affiliation with the postwar international organization*]
UNRRC ..... United Nations Relief and Rehabilitation Conference
UNRS .... Union pour la Nouvelle Republique Senegalaise [*Union for the New Senegalese Republic*] [*Political party*]
UNRSTD... Unrestricted   (FAAC)
UNRTD..... United Nations Resources and Transport Division
UNRWA.... United Nations Relief and Works Agency for Palestine Refugees in the Near East [*Austria*]   (PD)
UNRWAPR ... United Nations Relief and Works Agency for Palestine Refugees in the Near East [*Austria*]   (DLA)
UNRWAPRNE ... United Nations Relief and Works Agency for Palestine Refugees in the Near East [*Pronounced: "Unwrap me"*] [*Austria*]
UNS .... Umnak, AK [*Location identifier*] [*FAA*]   (FAAL)
UNS .... Unified Numbering Systems [*for metals*]   (MCD)
UNS .... Unified Special [*Thread*]
UNS .... United News Shops [*British*]
UNS .... Universal News Service [*Great Britain*]
UNS .... Universal Night Sight
UNS .... University of Nebraska. Studies [*A publication*]
UNS .... Unsymmetrical
UNSA .... United Financial Corporation of South Carolina, Inc. [*NASDAQ symbol*]   (NQ)
UNSAC ..... United Nations Scientific Advisory Committee [*ICSU*]
UNSAT ...... Unsatisfactory   (AABC)
unsat........... Unsaturated [*Chemistry*]
UNSATFY ... Unsatisfactory
UNSB .... United Bank, A Savings Bank [*NASDAQ symbol*]   (NQ)
UNSBL...... Unseasonable   (FAAC)
UNSC .... United Nations Security Council
UNSC .... United Nations Social Commission
UNSCC...... United Nations Standards Co-Ordinating Committee
UNSCC...... University of Nevada System Computing Center [*Research center*]   (RCD)
UNSCCUR ... United Nations Scientific Conference on the Conservation and Utilization of Resources
UNSCEAR ... United Nations Scientific Committee on the Effects of Atomic Radiation
UNSCOB .. United Nations Special Committee on the Balkans [*Greece*]
UNSCOP... United Nations Special Committee on Palestine
UNSCOR .. United Nations Security Council Official Records [*A publication*]   (DLA)
UNSD .... Unsweetened   (ROG)
UNSDD...... United Nations Social Development Division
UNSDRI... United Nations Social Defense Research Institute [*UN/Italy*]
UNSE .... United Security Financial Corp. of Illinois [*NASDAQ symbol*]   (NQ)
UN Sec Bur Soc Aff Ser K ... United Nations Secretariat. Bureau of Social Affairs. Series K [*A publication*]
UNSECNAV ... Under Secretary of the Navy
UnSemQR ... Union Seminary. Quarterly Review [*New York*] [*A publication*]
Unsere Heim ... Unsere Heimat. Zeitschrift des Vereines fuer Landeskunde von Niederoesterreich und Wien [*A publication*]
Unser Sozial Dorf ... Unser Sozialistisches Dorf [*A publication*]
Un Serv M ... United Service Magazine [*A publication*]
Un Serv (Phila) ... United Service (Philadelphia) [*A publication*]
UNSF........ United Nations Special Fund
UNSFH ..... United Nations Security Forces, Hollandia   (AABC)
UNSG .... United Nations Secretary General
UNSI .... United Service Source, Inc. [*NASDAQ symbol*]   (NQ)
UNSKED... Unscheduled   (FAAC)
UNSL .... UNSL Financial Corp. [*Formerly, United Saving & Loan Association*] [*NASDAQ symbol*]   (NQ)
UNSM .... United Nations Service Medal [*Military decoration*]
UNSO........ United Nations Sudano-Sahelian Office
UNSPD ..... Underground Space [*A publication*]

UNSPDPM ... United Nations Subcommission on the Prevention of Discrimination and the Protection of Minorities [*Geneva, Switzerland*]   (EAIO)
UNSS........ United Nations Sales Section [*for UN documents*]
UNST .... Union Nordique pour la Sante et le Travail [*Nordic Union for Health and Work*]   (EAIO)
UNSTBL.... Unstable
UNSTD ..... Union Nationale des Syndicats des Travailleurs du Dahomey [*National Federation of Workers' Unions of Dahomey*]
UNSTDY... Unsteady
UNSTHV .. Union Nationale des Syndicats des Travailleurs de la Haute Volta [*National Federation of Workers' Unions of the Upper Volta*]
UNSTL...... Unsettle   (FAAC)
UNSU........ United Nations Staff Union   (EA)
UNSU........ United Nations Study Unit [*Philatelic organization*]   (EA)
UNSUB ..... Unknown Subject [*FBI*] [*Acronym also used as title of television series*]
UNSUPPR ... Unsuppressed   (MSA)
UNSV .... United Savings Association [*Miami Lakes, FL*] [*NASDAQ symbol*]   (NQ)
UNSVC ...... Unserviceable   (AABC)
UNSVM .... United Nations Service Medal
UNSW .... University of New South Wales [*Australia*]
UNSWLJ .. University of New South Wales. Law Journal [*A publication*]   (APTA)
UNSWR .... University of New South Wales Regiment [*Australia*]
UNSYM .... Unsymmetrical
UN Symp Dev Use Geotherm Resour Abstr ... United Nations Symposium on the Development and Use of Geothermal Resources. Abstracts [*A publication*]
UN Symp Dev Use Geotherm Resour Proc ... United Nations Symposium on the Development and Use of Geothermal Resources. Proceedings [*A publication*]
UnT........... Uncanny Tales [*A publication*]
UNT.......... Undergraduate Navigator Training [*Air Force*]   (AFM)
UNT.......... Underground Nuclear Test
UNT.......... Unit Corp. [*NYSE symbol*]   (SPSG)
UNT.......... Unitas [*Finland*] [*A publication*]
UNT.......... United Tariff Bureau, Inc., New York NY [*STAC*]
UNT.......... Unst [*Scotland*] [*Airport symbol*]   (OAG)
UNT.......... Untersuchungen zum Neuen Testament [*A publication*]
UNT.......... Uppsala Nya Tidning [*A publication*]
UNTA .... Union Nationale des Travailleurs Angolais [*National Union of Angolan Workers*]
UNTA....... United Nations Technical Assistance
UNTAA ..... United Nations Technical Assistance Administration
UNTAC ..... United Nations Transitional Authority for Cambodia
UNTAF ..... United Nations Technical Assistance Fellowship
UNTAG..... United Nations Transition Assistance Group
UNTC .... Unable to Establish Contact   (FAAC)
UNTC .... Union Nationale des Travailleurs Congolais [*National Union of Congolese Workers*]
UNTC .... United Nations Trusteeship Council   (DLA)
UNTCI ...... Union Nationale des Travailleurs de Cote d'Ivoire [*National Union of Ivory Coast Workers*]
UNTCOK.. United Nations Temporary Committee on Korea
UNTCOR.. United Nations Trusteeship Council Official Record [*A publication*]   (DLA)
UNTD........ First United Bancshares, Inc. [*El Dorado, AR*] [*NASDAQ symbol*]   (NQ)
UNTD........ University Naval Training Division [*Canada*]
UNTDED.. United Nations Data Elements Directory [*A publication*]
UNTE .... Unit Corp. [*NASDAQ symbol*]   (NQ)
UNTEA ..... Undersea Technology [*A publication*]
UNTEA ..... United Nations Temporary Executive Authority [*Supervised transfer of Netherlands New Guinea to Indonesia*]
Unternehm ... Unternehmung. Schweizerische Zeitschrift fuer Betriebswirtschaft [*A publication*]
Unternehmungsfuehrung im Gewerbe ... Unternehmungsfuehrung im Gewerbe und Gewerbliche [*A publication*]
Unters Angebot Nachfrage Miner Rohst ... Untersuchungen ueber Angebot und Nachfrage Mineralischer Rohstoffe [*A publication*]
UNTFDPP ... United Nations Trust Fund for Development Planning and Projections
UNTFSD... United Nations Trust Fund for Social Development
UNTG........ United Nations Theatre Group   (EA)
UNTHD .... Unthreaded
UNTM....... Union Nationale des Travailleurs du Mali [*National Union of Malian Workers*]
UNTN........ Union Nationale des Travailleurs Nigeriens [*National Union of Nigerian Workers*]
UNTP .... Universidad de Tucuman. Publications [*A publication*]
Un Trav Dec ... Unreported Travancore Decisions [*A publication*]   (DLA)
UNTS .... Undergraduate Navigator Training System [*Air Force*]
UNTS .... Union Nationale des Travailleurs du Senegal [*National Union of Workers of Senegal*]
UNTS .... United Nations Treaty Series [*Project*] [*University of Washington*]
UNTSO ..... United Nations Truce Supervision Organization

UNTT........ Union Nationale des Travailleurs du Togo [*National Union of Togolese Workers*]
UNTT........ United Nations Trust Territory
UNTW....... Untwist
UNTY........ Unity Healthcare Holding Co., Inc. [*NASDAQ symbol*]   (NQ)
UNU .... Juneau, WI [*Location identifier*] [*FAA*]   (FAAL)
UNU .... United Nations University [*Tokyo*]
UNUMO ... Universal Underwater Mobile [*Robot*]
UNUSBL... Unusable
UNUSL ...... Unusual   (ROG)
UNV.......... State College, PA [*Location identifier*] [*FAA*]   (FAAL)
UNV.......... United Nations Volunteers   (EAIO)
UNV.......... Unitel Video, Inc. [*AMEX symbol*]   (SPSG)
Unverd ...... Unverified
UNVS-A .... Universo [*Italy*] [*A publication*]
UNVX........ Universal Trading Exchange, Inc. [*NASDAQ symbol*]   (NQ)
UNWAL Rev ... University of Western Australia. Law Review [*A publication*]   (APTA)
UN W Bul ... United Nations Weekly Bulletin [*A publication*]
UNWCC.... Unions' Nation-Wide Coordinating Council for Oil and Allied Industries   (EA)
UNWCC.... United Nations War Crimes Commission [*"United Nations" in this body's name derives from the wartime alliance of this name, not from any affiliation with the postwar international organization*]
UNWG ...... United Nations Women's Guild   (EA)
UNWLA .... Ukrainian National Women's League of America   (EA)
UNWMG .. Utility Nuclear Waste Management Group   (EA)
UnwmK...... Unwatermarked [*Philately*]
UN World ... United Nations World [*A publication*]
UNWR....... Unwritten   (ROG)
UNWRAP ... United We Resist Additional Packaging [*Student legal action organization*]
UNWRF .... United Westland Resources [*NASDAQ symbol*]   (NQ)
UNWS....... Uniwest Financial Corp. [*NASDAQ symbol*]   (NQ)
UNWSA .... Unterrichtswissenschaft [*A publication*]
UNX......... Underground Nuclear Explosion
UNX......... Univex Mining Corp. [*Vancouver Stock Exchange symbol*]
UNY......... San Antonio, TX [*Location identifier*] [*FAA*]   (FAAL)
UNY......... United Nations of Yoga [*Stockholm, Sweden*]   (EAIO)
UNY......... University of New York   (ROG)
UNYB........ United Nations Year Book [*A publication*]   (DLA)
UNYFA ..... Ukrainian National Youth Federation of America [*Later, Ukrainian Youth Association of America*]   (EA)
UNYOM ... United Nations Yemen Observation Mission
u-nz---........ New Zealand [*MARC geographic area code*] [*Library of Congress*]   (LCCP)
UNZ......... Unzendake [*Japan*] [*Seismograph station code, US Geological Survey*]   (SEIS)
UO .... Empresa Aero Uruguay SA [*ICAO designator*]   (FAAC)
UO .... Trans-Union [*France*] [*ICAO designator*] [*Obsolete*]   (FAAC)
UO .... Ukrainica Occidentalia [*Winnipeg*] [*A publication*]
UO .... Ulm-Oberschwaben [*A publication*]
UO .... Und Oefters [*And Often*] [*German*]
UO .... Undelivered Orders [*Army*]   (AABC)
UO .... Union Office   (ROG)
UO .... Union Railroad of Oregon [*AAR code*]
UO .... Unit Operator   (NRCH)
UO .... University of Oxford   (ROG)
UO .... Urinary Output [*Medicine*]
U & O........ Use and Occupancy [*Real estate*]
U/O............ Used On   (MSA)
UO .... Weber County Library, Ogden, UT [*Library symbol*] [*Library of Congress*]   (LCLS)
UOA .... Unattached Officers' Association [*A union*] [*British*]
UOA .... United Ostomy Association   (EA)
UOA .... University of Arizona [*Arizona*] [*Seismograph station code, US Geological Survey*] [*Closed*]   (SEIS)
UOA .... Use of Other Automobiles [*Insurance*]
UOA .... Used on Assembly
UOBI........ United Oklahoma Bankshares, Incorporated [*NASDAQ symbol*]   (NQ)
UOBTPS ... United Operative Bricklayers' Trade Protection Society [*A union*] [*British*]
UOC.......... Ultimate Operating Capability
UOC.......... Ultimate Operational Configuration   (AAG)
UOC.......... Unequilibrated Ordinary Chondrites
UOC.......... Unilens Optical [*Vancouver Stock Exchange symbol*]
UOC.......... Union de l'Ouest Cameroun [*Union of West Cameroon*]
UOC.......... Unit of Choice
UOC.......... United Orpington Club   (EA)
UOC.......... Universal Output Computer
UOC.......... Unusual Occurrence Control
UOC.......... Uranium Ore Concentrate
UOC.......... Useable on Code   (MCD)
UOCA....... United Orpington Club of America [*Later, UOC*]   (EA)
UOCB....... Uncrossed Olivocochlear Bundle [*Otology*]
UOCC....... Unilens Optical Corp. [*NASDAQ symbol*]   (NQ)
UOCMWD ... Union of Operative Card Makers and Wire Drawers [*British*]
UOCO ...... Union Oil Company
UODDL..... User-Oriented Data Display Language [*Data processing*]

UODG .... Underwater Ordnance Development Group
UOE.......... Unit of Error   (MCD)
UOEF .... Union de Obreros Estivadores de Filipinos [*Union of Longshoremen of the Philippines*]
UOF.......... Unplanned Outage Factor [*Electronics*]   (IEEE)
UOFS .... United States Forest Service, Intermountain Range and Experiment Station Library, Ogden, UT [*Library symbol*] [*Library of Congress*]   (LCLS)
UOGC....... United Order of the Golden Cross [*Defunct*]   (EA)
UOGF....... Uranium Off-Gas Filter [*Nuclear energy*]   (NRCH)
UOGS .... Church of Jesus Christ of Latter-Day Saints, Genealogical Society Library, Ogden Branch, Ogden, UT [*Library symbol*] [*Library of Congress*]   (LCLS)
UOH......... Unplanned Outage Hours [*Electronics*]   (IEEE)
UOHC ...... Under Other than Honorable Conditions [*Discharge*] [*Military*]
UOI.......... University of Illinois [*Record label*]
UOI.......... User On-Line Interaction [*Data processing*]
UOIL........ Unioil [*NASDAQ symbol*]   (NQ)
UOIW....... United Optical and Instrument Workers of America
UOJC .... Union of Orthodox Jewish Congregations of America   (EA)
UOJCA...... Union of Orthodox Jewish Congregations of America   (EA)
UOK......... University of Oklahoma [*Record label*]
UOL.......... Underwater Object Locator
UOL.......... Utility Octal Load
UOL.......... Utility-Oriented Language   (MCD)
UOLS .... Underwater Object Location and Search Operations [*Navy*]   (NVT)
U of Omaha Bull ... Night Law School Bulletin. University of Omaha [*A publication*]   (DLA)
UOMCA..... United Orthodox Ministers and Cantors Association of America and Canada   (EA)
UOMGCU ... United Operative Masons' and Granite Cutters' Union [*British*]
UOMS....... Union des Originaires de Mauritanie du Sud [*Union of Natives of South Mauritania*]
UOMS....... Unmanned Orbital Multifunction Satellite
UOO .... Undelivered Orders Outstanding [*Military*]   (AFM)
UOP.......... Understanding of the Problem   (MCD)
UOP.......... Unit Operating Procedure   (NRCH)
UOP.......... University of the Pacific [*Stockton, CA*]
UOP.......... Urine Output [*Physiology*]
UOPA....... Uranium Ore Processing Association
UOPDP ..... Union Ouvriere et Paysanne pour la Democratie Proletarienne [*Peasant and Worker Union for Proletarian Democracy*] [*France*] [*Political party*]   (PPE)
UOPG....... United Osteopathic Physicians Guild [*Australia*]
UOPH .... Unaccompanied Officer Personnel Housing [*Navy*]
UOQ .... Upper Outer Quadrant [*Anatomy*]
UOr........... Orem City Library, Orem, UT [*Library symbol*] [*Library of Congress*]   (LCLS)
UOR......... Uniform Officer Record
UOR......... Unplanned Outage Rate [*Electronics*]   (IEEE)
UOR......... Urgent Operation Requirement
UORUSC .. Union of Orthodox Rabbis of the US and Canada   (EA)
UOS.......... Sewanee, TN [*Location identifier*] [*FAA*]   (FAAL)
UOS.......... Ultraviolet Ozone Spectrometer   (MCD)
UOS.......... Undelivered Orders Schedule [*Army*]
UOS.......... Underwater Ordnance Station [*Navy*]
UOS.......... United Order of Smiths [*A union*] [*British*]
UOS.......... University of the South [*Record label*]
UOS.......... Unless Otherwise Specified   (MSA)
UOS.......... Unmanned Orbital Satellite
UOSAT ..... University of Surrey Satellite
UOSM....... Urinary Osmolarity [*Medicine*]
UOT.......... Uncontrollable Overtime
UOT.......... Union, SC [*Location identifier*] [*FAA*]   (FAAL)
UOT.......... Unit of Trading
UOT.......... Upper Outer Tube
UOTASP.... United Order of the Total Abstaining Sons of the Phoenix   (ROG)
UOTC........ University Officers Training Corps [*British military*]   (DMA)
UOTHC.... Under Other than Honorable Conditions [*Discharge*] [*Military*]
UOTS .... United Order True Sisters   (EA)
UOV .... Union Ouvriere du Viet-Nam [*Vietnam Labor Union*] [*South Vietnam*]
UOV .... Units of Variance
UOW .... Weber State College, Ogden, UT [*Library symbol*] [*Library of Congress*]   (LCLS)
UOX.......... Oxford, MS [*Location identifier*] [*FAA*]   (FAAL)
UOX.......... University [*Mississippi*] [*Airport symbol*]   (OAG)
UP............. Air Foyle Ltd. [*Great Britain*] [*ICAO designator*]   (FAAC)
UP............. Journal of Urban Planning and Development [*A publication*]
UP............. Lab. UPSA [*France*] [*Research code symbol*]
UP............. Oregon Short Line R. R. [*of Union Pacific Railroad Co.*] [*AAR code*]
UP............. Oregon-Washington R. R. & Navigation [*of Union Pacific Railroad Co.*] [*AAR code*]
UP............. Provo Public Library, Provo, UT [*Library symbol*] [*Library of Congress*]   (LCLS)
UP............. Ulster Parliament   (DAS)
UP............. Ultra Presse [*Press agency*] [*Colombia*]

UP............. Umbilical Pin
UP............. Uncertainty Principle [*Quantum mechanics*]
UP............. Uncertified Patient [*British*]
UP............. Under-Proof [*Of spirituous liquors*] [*Distilling*]
UP............. Under Provisions Of [*Military*]
UP............. Undergraduate Program [*Subject area tests*]
UP............. Unearned Premium [*Insurance*]
UP............. Unemployed Parent [*Department of Health and Human Services*]
UP............. Union Pacific Corp.
UP............. Union Patriotica [*Patriotic Union*] [*Spain*] [*Political party*] (PPE)
UP............. Union Patriotica [*Patriotic Union*] [*Colombia*] [*Political party*]
UP............. Union Popular [*Popular Union*] [*Uruguay*] (PD)
UP............. Union del Pueblo [*Union of the People*] [*Mexico*] (PD)
UP............. Uniprocessor
UP............. Unit Pack
UP............. Unit Price
UP............. United Party [*Papua New Guinea*] [*Political party*] (PPW)
UP............. United Party [*Gambia*] [*Political party*] (PPW)
UP............. United Presbyterian
UP............. United Press [*Merged with International News Service to form UPI*]
UP............. United Provinces [*India*]
up .... United States Miscellaneous Pacific Islands [*MARC country of publication code*] [*Library of Congress*] (LCCP)
UP............. Universal Processor [*TRW, Inc.-Motorola, Inc.*] [*Data processing*]
UP............. University Presses [*General term applied to presses of various universities*]
UP............. Uniwersytet Imienia Adama Mickiewicza w Poznaniu [*A publication*]
UP............. Unpostable [*Data processing*]
UP............. Unrealized Profit
UP............. Unrotated Projectile [*Rocket*]
UP............. Unsolicited Proposal (MCD)
UP............. Unstained Pollen [*Botany*]
UP............. Unterrichtspraxis [*A publication*]
UP............. Update [*Online database field identifier*] [*Data processing*]
UP............. Upper (ADA)
UP............. Upper Peninsula [*Michigan*]
UP............. Upper Proof (ROG)
UP............. Ureteropelvic [*Anatomy*]
UP............. Uridine Phosphorylase [*An enzyme*]
U/P............ Urine-Plasma Ratio [*Clinical chemistry*]
UP............. Uroporphyrin [*Biochemistry*]
UP............. Urticaria Pigmentosa [*Dermatology*]
UP............. User Program (MCD)
UP............. Utility Path (IEEE)
UP............. Utility Program (MCD)
U & P......... Uttering and Publishing [*Legal term*]
UPA........... Ukrains'ka Povstans'ka Armiia
UPA........... Ultimate Players Association (EA)
UPA........... Uncooled Parametric Amplifier
UPA........... Uniao das Populacoes de Angola [*Angolan People's Union*] [*Later, NFLA*]
UPA........... Uniform Partnership Act
UPA........... Union Panamericana [*Pan-American Union*] [*Washington, DC*]
UPA........... Union of Poles in America (EA)
UPA........... Union Postale Arabe [*Arab Postal Union*]
UPA........... Unique Product Advantage [*Advertising*]
UPA........... Unitary Pole Approximation
UPA........... United Patternmakers Association
UPA........... United Producers of America [*Motion picture company*]
UPA........... University Photographers Association of America
UPA........... University Press of America
UPA........... Urokinase Plasminogen Activator [*An enzyme*]
UPAA......... University Photographers Association of America (EA)
UPAC........ Unemployed and Poverty Action Council (EA)
UPAC........ Unidad de Poder Adquisitivo Constante [*Savings Certificates with Constant Purchasing Power*] [*Spanish*]
UPAC........ Unificacion y Progreso [*Unification and Progress*] [*Mexico*] [*Political party*] (PPW)
UPAC........ United Parents of Absconded Children [*Defunct*] (EA)
UPACS...... Universal Performance Assessment and Control System
UPADI...... Union Pan-Americana de Asociaciones de Igenieros [*Pan American Federation of Engineering Societies*] [*Uruguay*] (EAIO)
UPAE........ Union Postal de las Americas y Espana [*Postal Union of the Americas and Spain - PUAS*] (EAIO)
UPAJ......... Union Panafricaine des Journalistes
UPAL......... Utrechtse Publikaties voor Algemene Literatuurwetenschap [*A publication*]
U PA Law Rev ... University of Pennsylvania. Law Review and American Law Register [*A publication*]
U PA LR.... University of Pennsylvania. Law Review [*A publication*]
U PA L Rev ... University of Pennsylvania. Law Review [*A publication*]
UPAM....... United People's Association of Matabeleland [*Zimbabwe*] [*Political party*] (PPW)
UPAO........ University Professors for Academic Order (EA)

UPAP......... Union Pan Africaine des Postes [*Pan African Postal Union - PAPU*] (EAIO)
UPAP......... Urban Planning Assistance Program
U-PARC .... University of Pittsburgh Applied Research Center [*Research center*] (RCD)
UPARR....... Urban Park and Recreation Recovery
UPAS........ Uniform Performance Assessment System [*Education*]
UPAT .... Union Panafricaine des Telecommunications [*Pan African Telecommunications Union - PATU*] (EAIO)
UPB .... Brigham Young University, Provo, UT [*Library symbol*] [*Library of Congress*] (LCLS)
UPB .... Union Patriotica Bonairiana [*Bonaire Patriotic Union*] [*Netherlands Antilles*] [*Political party*] (PPW)
UPB .... United Press of Bangladesh
UPB .... Universal Patents Bureau [*British*] (ROG)
UPB .... Universidad Pontificia Bolivariana [*A publication*]
UPB .... Upper Bound
UP/BA....... Unitary Payroll Benefit Accounting (MCD)
Up Ben Pr .. Upper Bench Precedents Tempore Car. I [*England*] [*A publication*] (DLA)
Up Ben Pre ... Upper Bench Precedents Tempore Car. I [*A publication*] (DLA)
UPB-L .... Brigham Young University, J. Reuben Clark Law Library, Provo, UT [*Library symbol*] [*Library of Congress*] (LCLS)
UPC .... Pennsylvania State University, Commonwealth Campuses, University Park, PA [*OCLC symbol*] (OCLC)
UPC .... Uganda People's Congress [*Suspended*]
UPC .... Underwater Pipe Cutter
UPC .... Uniform Practice Code
UPC .... Uniform Probate Code
UPC .... Union of the Corsican People [*France*]
UPC .... Union Planters Corp. [*NYSE symbol*] (CTT)
UPC .... Union des Populations Camerounaises [*Union of Cameroonian Peoples*] (PD)
UPC .... Union pour le Progres Comorien [*Union for Comorian Progress*] [*Political party*] (PPW)
UPC .... Union Progressiste Congolaise [*Congolese Progressive Union*]
UPC .... Union del Pueblo Canario [*Union of the Canarian People*] [*Spain*] [*Political party*] (PPE)
UPC .... Unione di u Populu Corsu [*Union of the Corsican People*] [*France*] [*Political party*] (PPE)
UPC .... Unit of Packed Cells [*Hemology*]
UPC .... Unit of Processing Capacity
UPC .... Unit Processing Code (AFM)
UPC .... Unit Production Cost
UPC .... United Power Company [*British*]
UPC .... United Presbyterian Church
UPC .... Universal Peripheral Controller
UPC .... Universal Product Code [*Inventory control*]
UPC .... Unpostable Code [*Data processing*]
UPC .... USPCI, Inc. [*NYSE symbol*] (SPSG)
UPCA .... Uniform Planned Community Act [*National Conference of Commissioners on Uniform State Laws*]
UPCC .... Uniform Product Code Council [*Formerly, UGPCC*] (EA)
UPCHUK.. University Program for the Comprehensive Handling and Utilization of Knowledge [*Humorous*]
UPCO........ Union Progressiste Congolaise [*Congolese Progressive Union*]
UPCO........ United Presidential Corporation [*NASDAQ symbol*] (NQ)
UPCON..... Upgraded Constellation (MCD)
UPCS........ Universal Philatelic Cover Society
UP/CSEC ... Cuban Studies/Estudios Cubanos. University of Pittsburg. University Center for International Studies. Center for Latin American Studies [*A publication*]
UPD.......... Underpotential Deposition [*Electrochemistry*]
UPD.......... Unit Power Density [*Lighting*]
UPD.......... Unpaid (ADA)
UPD.......... Update
UPD.......... Urban Planning Directorate [*British*]
UPD.......... Uredba o Porezu na Dobit iz Deviznog Poslovanja [*Decree on the Tax on Profit in Foreign Exchange Operations*] [*Yugoslavian*]
UPDA .... United Plastics Distributors Association [*Later, NAPD*] (EA)
UPDATE... Unlimited Potential Data through Automation Technology in Education (IEEE)
Update .... Update on Law-Related Education [*A publication*]
UPDEA ..... Union des Producteurs, Transporteurs, et Distributeurs d'Energie Electrique d'Afrique [*Union of Producers, Conveyors, and Distributors of Electric Power in Africa - UPDEA*] (EAIO)
UPDFT...... Updraft (MSA)
UPDFTS... Updrafts (FAAC)
UPDMA.... United Popular Dress Manufacturers Association [*Later, LACA*] (EA)
UPDRS...... Unified Parkinson's Disease Rating Scale
UP/E.......... Ethnology. University of Pittsburgh [*A publication*]
UPE .... Union Panafricaine des Etudiants [*All Africa Students Union - AASU*] (EAIO)
UPE .... Unit Proficiency Exercise
UPE .... Unitary Pole Expansion
UPE .... Upstream Promoter Element [*Genetics*]

UPEB......... Union de Paises Exportadores de Banano [*Union of Banana-Exporting Countries - UBEC*]   (EAIO)
UPECO ..... Union Progressiste Congolaise [*Congolese Progressive Union*]
UPEI......... Union Petroliere Europeenne Independante [*Independent European Petroleum Union*]   (EAIO)
UPEI......... University of Prince Edward Island [*Canada*]
UPEN .... Upper Peninsula Energy Corp. [*NASDAQ symbol*]   (NQ)
UPEP......... Undergraduate Preparation of Educational Personnel [*Office of Education*]
UPEQUA .. Union Progressiste de l'Equateur [*Progressive Union of Equateur Province*] [*Congo - Leopoldville*]
UPES........ Ultraviolet Photoelectron Spectroscopy
UPET........ Urokinase Pulmonary Embolism Trial
UPEU .... Uganda Public Employees' Union
UPF .... Uganda Popular Front [*Political party*]   (PD)
UPF .... Union pour la France [*France*] [*Political party*]
UPF .... United Parkinson Foundation   (EA)
UPF .... United Patriotic Front
UPF .... United People's Front [*Singapore*] [*Political party*]   (PPW)
UPF .... Unofficial Personnel Folder
UPFAW..... United Packinghouse Food and Allied Workers [*Later, UFCWIU*]   (EA)
UPFD .... United Pesticide Formulators and Distributors Association   (EA)
UPFDA...... United Pesticide Formulators and Distributors Association
UPFF .... Universal Proutist Farmers Federation   (EA)
UPFM........ Union Progressive des Femmes Marocaines [*Progressive Union of Moroccan Women*]
UPFT........ Uluslararasi Para Fonu Teskilati [*International Monetary Fund Organization*] [*Turkish*]
UPG........... Ujung Pandang [*Indonesia*] [*Airport symbol*]   (OAG)
UPG........... Union des Populations de Guinee [*Guinea People's Union*]   (PD)
UPG........... Union Progressiste Guineenne [*Guinean Progressive Union*]
UPG........... United Pacific Gold [*Vancouver Stock Exchange symbol*]
UPG........... United Parents under God   (EA)
UPG........... Unpaying Guest [*In a rooming or boarding house*]
UPG........... Upgrade [*Data processing*]
UPGGAZ .. Uchenye Zapiski Permskogo Universiteta Imeni A. M. Gor'kogo [*A publication*]
UPGMA .... Unweighted Pair-Group Method with Arithmetic Means [*Phylogenetic analysis*]
UPGRADE ... University of Pittsburgh Generalized Recording and Dissemination Experiment
UPGRADE ... User-Prompted Graphic Data Evaluation [*US Council on Environmental Quality*]
UPGS........ Church of Jesus Christ of Latter-Day Saints, Genealogical Society Library, Utah Valley Branch, Provo, UT [*Library symbol*] [*Library of Congress*]   (LCLS)
UPGS......... Unione Progressista della Gioventu Somala [*Progressive Union of Somali Youth*]
UPGWA .... International Union, United Plant Guard Workers of America   (EA)
UPH........... Unaccompanied Personnel Housing [*Military*]
UPH........... Underground Pumped Hydro [*Energy storage*]
UPH........... Union Patriotique Haitienne [*Haitian Patriotic Union*]   (EA)
UPH........... Union of Platers Helpers [*British*]
UPHA........ United Professional Horsemen's Association   (EA)
UPHC........ United Party of Haitian Communists
UPHCI...... Undistributed Personal Holding Company Income
UPHD........ Uphold [*Law*]   (ROG)
UPHD........ Upholstered
UPHEWA ... United Presbyterian Health, Education, and Welfare Association [*Later, PHEWA*]   (EA)
UPHG........ Upholstering
UPHPISEC ... Union for the Protection of the Human Person by International, Social, and Economic Cooperation [*Defunct*]   (EA)
UPHR........ Up Here [*A publication*]
UPHSTR... Upholster
UPHTDE .. Annual Research Reviews. Ultrastructural Pathology of Human Tumors [*A publication*]
UPI .... Fayetteville/Fort Bragg, NC [*Location identifier*] [*FAA*]   (FAAL)
UPI .... United Press International   (EA)
UPI .... Upper Plenum Injection [*Nuclear energy*]   (NRCH)
UPI .... Uteroplacental Insufficiency [*Medicine*]
UPIA .... Underwater Photography Instruction Association [*Defunct*]   (EA)
UPIA .... Uniform Principal and Income Act [*National Conference of Commissioners on Uniform State Laws*]
UPICV....... Uniao dos Povos das Ilhas do Cabo Verde [*Union of the Peoples of the Cape Verde Islands*]
UPIF .... Universal Proutist Intellectual Federation   (EA)
UPIGO ...... Union Professionnelle Internationale des Gynecologues et Obstetriciens [*International Union of Professional Gynecologists and Obstetricians*]
UPIN .... United Press International Newspictures
UPIR......... Uniform Photographic Interpretation Report [*Military*]   (AFM)
U Pit Law... University of Pittsburgh. Law Review [*A publication*]
UPITN........ United Press International Television News

U Pitt L R .. University of Pittsburgh. Law Review [*A publication*]
U Pitt L Rev ... University of Pittsburgh. Law Review [*A publication*]
U of Pitt L Rev ... University of Pittsburgh. Law Review [*A publication*]
UPIU .... United Paperworkers International Union   (EA)
UPJ .... Underwater Pump Jet
UPJ .... Upjohn Co. [*NYSE symbol*]   (SPSG)
UPJ .... Ureteropelvic Junction [*Anatomy*]
UPK .... United Park City Mines Co. [*NYSE symbol*]   (SPSG)
UPK .... Unpopped Kernel [*Popcorn*]
UPK .... Upkeep Period [*Navy*]   (NVT)
UPL .... Unidentified Process Loss
UPL .... Union Populaire Locale [*Political party*] [*Wallis and Futuna Islands*]   (FEA)
UPL .... Unit Personnel List [*Army*]
UPL .... Universal Programming Language [*Data processing*]   (BUR)
UPL .... Universal Publications, London [*British*]
UPL .... Upala [*Costa Rica*] [*Airport symbol*] [*Obsolete*]   (OAG)
UPL .... Uplink
UPL .... Uranium Product Loadout [*Nuclear energy*]   (NRCH)
UPL .... User Programming Language [*Burroughs Corp.*] [*Data processing*]   (IEEE)
UPLAC...... Union des Producteurs de Levure-Aliment de la CEE [*Union of Dried Yeast Producers of the Common Market*]
UP/LAIL... Latin American Indian Literatures. University of Pittsburgh. Department of Hispanic Languages and Literatures [*A publication*]
UPLD .... Upland [*Plateau, highland*] [*Board on Geographic Names*]
UPLF........ Universal Payload Fairing [*NASA*]   (KSC)
UPLF........ Universal Proutist Labour Federation   (EA)
UPLG .... Union Populaire pour la Liberation de la Guadeloupe [*Popular Union for the Liberation of Guadeloupe*]   (PD)
UPLI......... United Poets Laureate International   (EA)
UPLK........ Uplink (NASA)
UPLR........ Uganda Protectorate Law Reports [*1904-51*] [*A publication*]   (DLA)
UPLR........ United Provinces Law Reports [*India*] [*A publication*]   (DLA)
U of PLR.... University of Pennsylvania. Law Review [*A publication*]
U of PL Rev ... University of Pennsylvania. Law Review [*A publication*]
UPLT........ United Provinces Law Times [*India*] [*A publication*]   (DLA)
UPLV........ Upper Leg Vein [*Anatomy*]
UPM .... Pennsylvania State University, University Park, PA [*OCLC symbol*]   (OCLC)
UPM .... Uganda Patriotic Movement   (PD)
UPM .... Ultrapure Metal
UPM .... Union du Peuple Malgache [*Malagasy People's Union*]
UPM .... Union Pontificale Missionnaire [*Pontifical Missionary Union - PMU*] [*Later, PMUPR*]
UPM .... Union Progressiste Mauritanienne [*Mauritanian Progressive Union*]
UPM .... Union Progressiste Melanesienne [*Political party*] [*New Caledonia*]   (FEA)
UPM .... Union del Pueblo de Melilla [*Political party*] [*Spanish North Africa*]   (MENA)
UPM .... Unione Politica Maltese [*Maltese Political Union*] [*Political party*]   (PPE)
UPM .... Unit Production Manager [*Filmmaking*]
UPM .... United People's Movement [*Antigua*] [*Political party*]   (PPW)
UPM .... United People's Movement [*St. Vincent*] [*Political party*]   (PPW)
UPM .... Universal Permissive Module [*Nuclear energy*]   (IEEE)
UPM .... Unreached Peoples Mission   (EA)
UPMB........ University of Pennsylvania. Museum Bulletin [*A publication*]
UPMFF ..... University of Pennsylvania. Monographs in Folklore and Folklife [*A publication*]
UPMI .... Union Progressiste Melanesienne [*Progressive Melanesian Union*] [*New Caledonia*] [*Political party*]   (PPW)
UPMR .... Unit Personnel Management Roster
UPN........... Union del Pueblo Navarrese [*Union of the Navarrese People*] [*Spain*] [*Political party*]   (PPW)
UPN........... United Party of Nigeria
UPN........... Uruapan [*Mexico*] [*Airport symbol*]   (OAG)
UPNCA ..... United Pants and Novelties Contractors Association [*Defunct*]   (EA)
UPNE .... University Press of New England
U P News... Unauthorized Practice News [*A publication*]
UPNI .... Unionist Party of Northern Ireland [*Political party*]   (PPW)
UP (Noth) ... Ueberlieferungsgeschichte des Pentateuch (M. Noth) [*A publication*]   (BJA)
UPNS .... Ukrainian Philatelic and Numismatic Society   (EA)
UPO........... Undistorted Power Output
UPO........... Unidentified Paleontological Object
UPO........... Unit Personnel Office [*or Officer*] [*Military*]
UPortR...... University of Portland. Review [*A publication*]
UPOS .... Utility Program Operating System   (IEEE)
UPOV .... Union Internationale pour la Protection des Obtentions Vegetales [*International Union for the Protection of New Varieties of Plants*]   (EAIO)
UPP .... Hawi, HI [*Location identifier*] [*FAA*]   (FAAL)
UPP .... Ultraprecision Parachute   (NG)
UPP .... UNESCO Publications and Periodicals
UPP .... Unionist Progressive Party [*Political party*] [*Egypt*]

UPP .... United Papermakers and Paperworkers [*Later, UPIU*]   (EA)
UPP .... United Peasants' Party [*Poland*] [*Political party*]   (PD)
UPP .... United People's Party [*Sierra Leone*] [*Political party*]
UPP .... United People's Party [*Grenada*] [*Political party*]   (PPW)
UPP .... United Press of Pakistan
UPP .... United Progressive Party [*Zambia*] [*Political party*]
UPP .... United Progressive Party [*Trinidad and Tobago*] [*Political party*]   (PPW)
UPP .... Universal PROM Programmer
UPP .... Upolu Point [*Hawaii*] [*Airport symbol*]   (OAG)
UPP .... Uppsala [*Sweden*] [*Seismograph station code, US Geological Survey*]   (SEIS)
UPP .... Urea (Prilled) in Paper Packets [*Agronomy*]
UPP .... User Parameter Processing   (NASA)
UPP .... Utility Print Punch
UPPA .... United People's Party of Arunachal [*India*] [*Political party*]   (PPW)
UPPC .... Universal Pin Pack Connector
UPPE .... Ultraviolet Photometric and Polarimetric Explorer
UPPF .... United Presbyterian Peace Fellowship   (EA)
UPPG .... Union des Paysans Pauvres de la Guadeloupe   (PD)
UPPIAI ..... Uchenye Zapiski Permskogo Gosudarstvennogo Pedagogicheskogo Instituta [*A publication*]
UPPN .... Union Postale des Pays du Nord [*Nordic Postal Union - NPU*]   (EAIO)
UPPN .... United People's Party of Nigeria
UPPOE ...... University of Pittsburgh Production Organization Exercise [*Simulation game*]
UPPP .... Uvulo-Palato-Pharyngoplasty [*Surgical procedure*] [*Initials are derived from the name of the problem the procedure cures*]
UPPS .... Ultimate Plant Protection System [*Nuclear energy*]   (NRCH)
UPPS .... Unified Pilot Publication System [*American Chemical Society*]
Uppsala Univ G Inst B ... Uppsala University. Geological Institution. Bulletin [*A publication*]
Upps Arsskr ... Uppsala Universitets Arsskrift [*A publication*]
Upps Univ Geol Inst Bull ... Uppsala University. Geological Institution. Bulletin [*A publication*]
UPr .... Ucilisten Pregled [*A publication*]
UPR .... Ultraportable RADAR   (MCD)
UPR .... Ultrasonic Parametric Resonance   (IEEE)
UPR .... Ultraviolet Proton Radiation
UPR .... Uniform Parole Reports [*Law Enforcement Assistance Administration*]
UPR .... Union des Populations Rurales [*Union of Rural People*] [*Lomela-Kasai*]
UPR .... University of Puerto Rico [*Mayaguez, PR*]
UPR .... Upper   (AAG)
UPR .... Uranium Production Reactor [*Nuclear energy*]
UPR .... Urethral Profile at Rest [*Medicine*]
Upravlenie Slozn Sistemami ... Upravlenie Sloznymi Sistemami. Rizskii Politehniceskii Institut [*A publication*]
Upravlyaemye Sistemy ... Upravlyaemye Sistemy Institut Matematiki Institut Kataliza Sibirskogo Otdeleniya Akademii Nauk SSSR [*A publication*]
Uprawa Rosl Nawozenie ... Uprawa Roslin i Nawozenie [*A publication*]
UPR Co ...... Union Pacific Railroad Company [*A publication*]
UPR/CS ..... Caribbean Studies. University of Puerto Rico. Institute of Caribbean Studies [*A publication*]
UPrE .... College of Eastern Utah, Price, UT [*Library symbol*] [*Library of Congress*]   (LCLS)
UPREAL ... Unit Property Record and Equipment Authorization List
UPREC ...... Upon Receipt
UPREL ...... Unit Property Record and Equipment List
UP Res Dig ... UP [*University of the Philippines*] Research Digest [*A publication*]
UPRG .... Unit Personnel Records Group [*Air Force*]   (AFM)
UPRGp ...... Unit Personnel Records Group [*Air Force*]   (AFM)
UPrGS .... Church of Jesus Christ of Latter-Day Saints, Genealogical Society Library, Price Branch, Price, UT [*Library symbol*] [*Library of Congress*]   (LCLS)
UPRI .... Up-Right, Inc. [*NASDAQ symbol*]   (NQ)
UPRI .... Uteroplacental Respiratory Insufficiency [*Gynecology*]
UPRICO .... University of Puerto Rico [*Mayaguez, PR*]
Uprochnyayushchaya Term Termomekh Obrab Prokata ... Uprochnyayushchaya Termicheskaya i Termomekhanicheskaya Obrabotka Prokata [*A publication*]
UPROCO .. Union Progressiste du Congo [*Progressive Union of the Congo*] [*Niangara*]
UPRONA .. Union pour le Progres National [*Union for National Progress*] [*Burundi*] [*Political party*]   (PPW)
UPRP .... Union des Paysans Ruraux et Progressistes [*Union of Rural and Progressive Farmers*] [*Congo-Kasai*]
UPRR .... Union Pacific Railroad Co.
Upr Sist Mash ... Upravlyayushchie Sistemy i Mashiny [*Ukrainian SSR*] [*A publication*]
Upr Yad Energ Ustanovkami ... Upravlenie Yadernymi Energeticheskimi Ustanovkami [*A publication*]
UPS .... Ultraviolet Photoemission Spectroscopy
UPS .... Uncontested Physical Searches [*CIA term for break-ins*]
UPS .... Under Provisions of Section [*Military*]

UPS .... Underground Press Syndicate [*Later, APS*]   (EA)
UPS .... Underwater Photographic Society   (EA)
UP & S .... Uniform Printing and Supply
UPS .... Uniform Procurement System
UPS .... Uninterruptible Power Supply [*or System*]
UPS .... Union Progressiste Senegalaise [*Senegalese Progressive Union*] [*Political party*]
UPS .... Unit Personnel Section [*Military*]
UPS .... Unit Price Standards   (MCD)
UPS .... Unit Proficiency System   (AAG)
UPS .... United Parcel Service
UPS .... United Peregrine Society   (EA)
UPS .... Universal Polar Stereographic Grid
UPS .... Universal Press Syndicate Co.
UPS .... Universal Processing System
UPS .... Universities and Public Schools Battalions [*Military units*] [*British*] [*World War I*]
UPS .... Upright Perigee Stage [*Aerospace*]   (MCD)
UPS .... Urethral Profile under Stress [*Medicine*]
UPS .... Uterine Progesterone System [*Contraceptive device*]
UPSA .... Ukrainian Political Science Association in the United States   (EA)
UPSA .... Ukrainian Professional Society of America   (EA)
UPSA .... Uniform Program Salary Administration   (MCD)
Upsala J Med Sci ... Upsala Journal of Medical Sciences [*A publication*]
Upsala J Med Sci Suppl ... Upsala Journal of Medical Sciences. Supplement [*A publication*]
UPSEELL ... University of Pennsylvania. Studies in East European Languages and Literatures [*A publication*]
UPSF .... Universal Proutist Student Federation   (EA)
UPSI .... User Program Sense Indicator
UPSI .... User Program Switch Indicator [*Data processing*]
UPSIS .... United States Political Science Information Service [*University of Pittsburgh*]   (IID)
Ups J Med Sci ... Upsala Journal of Medical Sciences [*A publication*]
Ups J Med Sci Suppl ... Upsala Journal of Medical Sciences. Supplement [*A publication*]
UPSLP ...... Upslope   (FAAC)
UPSN .... University Peace Studies Network   (EA)
UPSR .... Unit Proficiency System Requirements   (AAG)
UPSS .... Ukrainska Partiia Samostiinykiv-Sotsiialistiv [*Ukrainian Party of Socialist-Independentists*] [*Russian*] [*Political party*]   (PPE)
UPSS .... United Postal Stationery Society   (EA)
UPSSL ...... University of Puget Sound School of Law   (DLA)
Ups Sto ...... Upshur's Review of Story on the Constitution [*A publication*]   (DLA)
UPSTAGE ... Upper-Stage Guidance Experiment
UPSTARS ... Universal Propulsion Stabilization, Retardation, and Separation [*Air Force*]
UPSTART ... Universal Parachute Support Tactical and Research Target [*NG*]
UPSTEP ..... Undergraduated Pre-Service Teacher Education Program [*National Science Foundation*]   (EA)
UPSUB ...... Submit Draft to a Superior for Approval [*From George Orwell's novel, "1984"*]
UPT .... Undergraduate Pilot Training [*Air Force*]
UPT .... Undistributed Profits Tax   (IMH)
UP & T .... Unit Personnel and Tonnage Table [*Military*]
UPT .... University Patents, Inc. [*AMEX symbol*]   (SPSG)
UPT .... Upgrade Pilot Training
UPT .... Urgent Postal Telegram
UPT .... US Platinum [*Vancouver Stock Exchange symbol*]
UPT .... User Process Table
UPTA .... Uniform Perpetuation of Testimony Act [*National Conference of Commissioners on Uniform State Laws*]
UPTA .... United Parent-Teachers Association of Jewish Schools   (EA)
UPTAS ...... Utility Practical Transport Aircraft System [*Army*]
UPTC .... Union Panafricaine des Travailleurs Croyants [*Pan-African Union of Believing Workers*]
UPTD .... Unit Pulmonary Toxicity Dose [*Deep-sea diving*]
UPTF .... Upper Plenum Test Facility [*Nuclear energy*]   (NRCH)
UPT-H .... Undergraduate Pilot Training - Helicopter [*Air Force*]
UPTLM ...... Up-Link Telemetry [*NASA*]   (NASA)
UP/TM ...... Tiers Monde. Universite de Paris. Institut d'Etude du Developpement Economique et Social [*Paris*] [*A publication*]
Upt Mar W ... Upton on Maritime Warfare and Prize [*A publication*]   (DLA)
UPTP .... Universal Package Test Panel
UPTT .... Unit Personnel and Tonnage Table [*Military*]   (AABC)
Upt Tr Mar ... Upton on Trade-Marks [*A publication*]   (DLA)
UPU .... Union Postale Universelle [*Universal Postal Union*] [*Switzerland*] [*Also, an information service or system*]   (IID)
UPUC .... Unauthorized Publication or Use of Communications
UPUC .... Universal Postal Union Collectors   (EA)
UPUC .... Universal Postal Union Convention
U Puget Sound L Rev ... University of Puget Sound. Law Review [*A publication*]
UPUP .... Ulster Popular Unionist Party [*Northern Ireland*] [*Political party*]   (PPW)

UPUP	Ulster Progressive Unionist Party [*Northern Ireland*] [*Political party*] (PPW)
UPUS	United Public Utility Systems
UPUSA......	UPU [*Universal Postal Union*] Staff Association (EAIO)
UPV	Unfired Pressure Vessel
UPV	Universal Pre-Vent, Inc. [*Vancouver Stock Exchange symbol*]
UPVC	Unfired Pressure Vessel Code (AAG)
UPVC	Unplasticized Polyvinyl Chloride
UP Vet	UP [*University of the Philippines*] Veterinarian [*A publication*]
UPW	Union of Post Office Workers [*British*] (DCTA)
UPW	United Port Workers' Union [*Ceylon*]
UPW	United Presbyterian Women (EA)
UPW	United Public Workers of America
UPWA	Union of Polish Women in America (EA)
UPWA	United Packinghouse Workers of America [*Later, UFCWIU*]
UPWA	United Polish Women of America (EA)
UPWARD ...	Understanding Personal and Racial Dignity [*Navy program*]
UPWBA	Uniwersytet Imienia Adama Mickiewicza w Poznaniu. Wydzial Biologii i Nauk o Ziemi. Prace. Seria Geologia [*A publication*]
UPWD......	Upward (MSA)
UPWF.......	Ukrainian Patriarchal World Federation (EA)
UPWT	Unitary Plan Wind Tunnel (KSC)
UPY	Union of People's Youth [*Bulgaria*]
UPYF........	Universal Proutist Youth Federation (EA)
UPz	Urkunden der Ptolemaerzeit [*U. Wilcken*] [*A publication*] (BJA)
UQ	Fronte dell'Uomo Qualunque; Uomo Qualunque [*Common Man Front*] [*Italy*] [*Political party*] (PPE)
UQ	Ubiquinone [*Also, CoQ, Q, U*] [*Biochemistry*]
UQ	Ukrainian Quarterly [*A publication*]
UQ	Ultraquick [*Flashing*] Light [*Navigation signal*]
UQ	United African Airline [*Libya*] [*ICAO designator*] (ICDA)
UQ	Universities Quarterly [*A publication*]
UQ	University of Queensland [*Australia*]
UQ	Upper Quadrant [*Anatomy*]
UQ	Upper Quadrile
UQAC.......	Universite du Quebec a Chicoutimi [*Canada*]
UQAH	Universite du Quebec a Hull [*Canada*]
UQAM......	Universite du Quebec a Montreal [*Canada*]
UQAR	Universite du Quebec a Rimouski [*Canada*]
UQB..........	Universite de Quebec [*UTLAS symbol*]
UQC..........	Underwater Telephone [*Navy*] (CAAL)
UQCP........	Uniform Quality Control Program
UQE..........	Queen [*Alaska*] [*Airport symbol*] [*Obsolete*] (OAG)
UQGS.......	Uniform Quality Grading System [*Tires*]
UQL..........	Unacceptable Quality Level
UQL..........	University of Queensland Library [*Australia*]
UQLJ........	University of Queensland. Law Journal [*A publication*] (APTA)
UQOT.......	Unquote (FAAC)
UQP..........	Universities and the Quest for Peace [*An association*]
UQP..........	University of Queensland. Papers [*A publication*]
UQP..........	University of Queensland Press [*Australia*]
UQS..........	Nuiqsut Village, AK [*Location identifier*] [*FAA*] (FAAL)
Uqs...........	'Uqsin (BJA)
U Qsld P SS ...	University of Queensland. Papers. Social Sciences [*A publication*]
UQT	User Queue Table
U Queens L J ...	University of Queensland. Law Journal [*A publication*]
U of Queensl LJ ...	University of Queensland. Law Journal [*A publication*]
U Queensl LJ ...	University of Queensland. Law Journal [*A publication*]
U Queens LR ...	University of Queensland. Law Review [*A publication*]
UQY..........	Kansas City, MO [*Location identifier*] [*FAA*] (FAAL)
UR.............	AeroSun International, Inc. [*ICAO designator*] (FAAC)
UR.............	[*The*] Item Requested Is Under Revision By the Proponent. Copies of Edition Presently in Use Are Not Available [*Advice of supply action code*] [*Army*]
UR.............	Lab. J. Uriach & Cia. SA [*Spain*] [*Research code symbol*]
UR.............	Lloyd's Universal Register of Shipping [*British*] (ROG)
UR.............	Red Carpet Airlines, Inc. [*ICAO designator*] (ICDA)
UR.............	Uganda Rifles [*British military*] (DMA)
UR.............	Ukrainian Review [*London*] [*A publication*]
UR.............	Ullage Rocket (KSC)
UR.............	Umjetnost Rijeci [*A publication*]
UR.............	Unconditioned Response [*Psychometrics*]
UR.............	Under the Rule [*Business term*]
U/R...........	Underrange (IEEE)
UR.............	Underreporter [*IRS*]
UR.............	Undulator Radiation [*High-energy physics*]
UR.............	Unfinanced Requirement [*Army*] (AABC)
URz...........	Unfractionated Reservoir [*Geology*]
UR.............	Unfunded Requirement [*Military*] (AFIT)
UR.............	Uniao Republicana [*Republican Union*] [*Portugal*] [*Political party*] (PPE)
UR.............	Unidentified Remittance [*IRS*]
UR.............	Uniform Regulations
UR.............	Unit Record [*Data processing*]
UR.............	Unit Register
UR.............	Unitatis Redintegratio [*Decree on Ecumenism*] [*Vatican II document*]
UR............	University Relations
UR............	University Review [*A publication*]
UR............	University of Rochester [*New York*] (KSC)
UR............	Unprogrammed Requirements (MCD)
UR............	Unreleasable (MCD)
UR............	Unreliable (MCD)
UR............	Unsatisfactory Report
U/R...........	Up Range [*NASA*] (KSC)
UR............	Up Right [*The rear right portion of a stage*] [*A stage direction*]
UR............	Upper Rail
UR............	Upper Respiratory [*Medicine*]
UR............	Upper Right (MCD)
UR............	Uranium (ROG)
UR............	Urban Rat [*Virus*]
UR............	Urinal (MSA)
UR............	Urine
UR............	Urology
UR............	User Requirements [*Nuclear energy*] (NRCH)
ur..............	USSR [*Union of Soviet Socialist Republics*] [*MARC country of publication code*] [*Library of Congress*] (LCCP)
UR............	Uti Rogas [*Be It as You Desire*] [*Used by Romans to express assent to a proposition*] [*Latin*]
UR............	Utility Room (MSA)
UR............	Utilization Review [*Preferred provider organization*] [*Medicine*]
UR............	Your
URA..........	United Red Army [*Japan*] (PD)
URA..........	United Republicans of America
URA..........	Universities Research Association (EA)
URA..........	Upper Respiratory Allergy [*Medicine*]
Ura..........	Uracil [*Biochemistry*]
URA..........	Urakawa [*Japan*] [*Seismograph station code, US Geological Survey*] (SEIS)
Ura..........	Urania [*Record label*] [*USA, Europe, etc.*]
URA..........	Uranium Recycle Acid [*Nuclear energy*] (NRCH)
URA..........	Urban Redevelopment Authority
URA..........	Urban Renewal Administration [*of HHFA*] [*Terminated*]
URA..........	Urine Receptacle Assembly [*NASA*] (MCD)
URA..........	User Requirements Analysis
URA..........	Utilization Review Agency [*Insurance*]
URAAA	Urania [*Poland*] [*A publication*]
URAC.......	Union des Republiques de l'Afrique Centrale [*Union of Central African Republics*]
URACTY...	Your Activity
URAD.......	Unit for Research on Addictive Drugs [*University of Aberdeen*] [*United Kingdom*] (IRUK)
URAD.......	[*Reference*] Your Radio [*Message*] [*Military*]
URAEP.....	University of Rochester Atomic Energy Project
URAF	Unidentified Remittance Amount File [*IRS*]
URAI	Universities Research Association, Incorporated
Ural Gos Univ Mat Zap ...	Ural'skii Gosudarstvennyi Universitet Imeni A. M. Gor'kogo Ural'skoe Matematiceskoe Obscestvo Matematiceskie Zapiski [*A publication*]
Ural Metall ...	Ural'skaya Metallurgiya [*A publication*]
Ural Politehn Inst Sb ...	Ural'skii Politehniceskii Institut Imeni S. M. Kirova Sbornik [*A publication*]
URAM.......	Unrelated Adult Man
Uranium Abstr ...	Uranium Abstracts [*A publication*]
Uranium Min Metall ...	Uranium Mining and Metallurgy [*A publication*]
Uran Supply ...	Uranium Supply and Demand. Perspectives to 1995 [*A publication*]
URAPA	Uniform Rendition of Accused Persons Act [*National Conference of Commissioners on Uniform State Laws*]
URARPAA ...	Uniform Relocation Assistance and Real Property Acquisition Act [*1970*] (OICC)
URARPAPA ...	Uniform Relocation Assistance and Real Property Acquisition Policies Act of 1970
URARRED ...	US Army Readiness Command (MCD)
URAS	Union des Republicains d'Action Sociale [*Union of Republicans of Social Action*] [*France*] [*Political party*] (PPE)
URAUZ.....	You Are Authorized (FAAC)
URAW.......	Unrelated Adult Woman
URB	Union Regionale de Bamileke [*Regional Union of Bamileke*] [*Cameroon*]
URB	University Resources Board [*Australia*]
URB	University of Riyad. Bulletin. Faculty of Arts [*Saudi Arabia*] [*A publication*]
URB	Unridable Bicycle
URB	Urban
URB	Urbana College, Urbana, OH [*OCLC symbol*] (OCLC)
URB	Urubupunga [*Brazil*] [*Airport symbol*] (OAG)
Urb Aff Abstr ...	Urban Affairs Abstracts [*A publication*]
Urb Aff Ann R ...	Urban Affairs Annual Review [*A publication*]
Urb Aff Q ...	Urban Affairs Quarterly [*A publication*]
Urb Aff Quart ...	Urban Affairs Quarterly [*A publication*]
Urb Aff Rep ...	Urban Affairs Reporter [*Commerce Clearing House*] [*A publication*] (DLA)
URBAMET ...	Urbanisme, Amenagement, Equipments, et Transports [*Reseau URBAMET*] [*France*] [*Information service or system*] (CRD)

Urban Abs ... Urban Abstracts [*A publication*]
Urban Aff Abs ... Urban Affairs Abstracts [*A publication*]
Urban Affairs Q ... Urban Affairs Quarterly [*A publication*]
Urban Anthr ... Urban Anthropology [*A publication*]
Urban Data Service Rept ... Urban Data Service Report [*A publication*]
Urban Des ... Urban Design [*A publication*]
Urban Design Intl ... Urban Design International [*A publication*]
Urban Des Int ... Urban Design International [*A publication*]
Urban Des Q ... Urban Design Quarterly [*A publication*]
Urban Ecol ... Urban Ecology [*A publication*]
Urban Ed ... Urban Education [*A publication*]
Urban Educ ... Urban Education [*A publication*]
Urban For .. Urban Forum [*A publication*]
Urban Hist ... Urban History Review [*Revue d'Histoire Urbaine*] [*A publication*]
Urban Hist R ... Urban History Review [*A publication*]
Urban Hist Yearb ... Urban History Yearbook [*A publication*]
URBANICOM ... Association Internationale Urbanisme et Commerce [*International Association for Town Planning and Distribution*] (EAIO)
Urban Innov Abroad ... Urban Innovation Abroad [*A publication*]
Urban Inst Policy Res Rep ... Urban Institute. Policy and Research Report [*A publication*]
URBANK .. Urban Development Bank
Urban L Ann ... Urban Law Annual [*A publication*]
Urban Law ... Urban Lawyer [*A publication*]
Urban Law An ... Urban Law Annual [*A publication*]
Urban Law Ann ... Urban Law Annual [*A publication*] (ILCA)
Urban Lif C ... Urban Life and Culture [*Later, Urban Life*] [*A publication*]
Urban LJ ... University of Detroit. Journal of Urban Law [*A publication*] (DLA)
Urban L Rev ... Urban Law Review [*A publication*] (DLA)
Urban R ..... Urban Review [*A publication*]
Urban Rev ... Urban Review [*A publication*]
Urban Soc C ... Urban and Social Change Review [*A publication*]
Urban Stud ... Urban Studies [*A publication*]
Urban Syst ... Urban Systems [*A publication*]
Urb Anthrop ... Urban Anthropology [*A publication*]
Urban Transp Abroad ... Urban Transportation Abroad [*A publication*]
URBC .... Uninfected Red Blood Cells [*Hematology*]
URBCOM ... [*The*] Urban Communications Game
URBE .... Urban Ecology [*Netherlands*] [*A publication*]
URBH .... Urban Health [*A publication*]
URBK .... Union Rheinische Braunkohlen Kraftstoff [*West Germany*]
Urb L Ann ... Urban Law Annual [*A publication*]
Urblaw .... Urban Law and Policy [*A publication*] (ILCA)
Urb Law ..... Urban Lawyer [*A publication*]
Urb Law Pol ... Urban Law and Policy [*A publication*]
Urb Life ..... Urban Life [*A publication*]
Urb Life & Cult ... Urban Life and Culture [*Later, Urban Life*] [*A publication*]
Urb L and P ... Urban Law and Policy [*A publication*]
Urb L and Poly ... Urban Law and Policy [*A publication*]
Urb L Rev .. Urban Law Review [*A publication*]
URBM ...... Ultimate Range Ballistic Missile [*Air Force*]
URBN-A .... Urbanisme [*France*] [*A publication*]
URBOE ..... Ultimatist Religious Bodies on Earth (EA)
URBPOP ... Urban Population File (MCD)
URBS-A ..... Urban Studies [*United Kingdom*] [*A publication*]
Urb Soc Change R ... Urban and Social Change Review [*A publication*]
Urb Stud .... Urban Studies [*A publication*]
URC .... Uganda Railways Corporation (DCTA)
URC .... Ultrasonic Resin Cleaner [*Nuclear energy*] (NRCH)
URC .... Uniform Rules for Collections
URC .... Union de Rassemblement et du Centre [*France*] [*Political party*] (ECON)
URC .... Unit Record Card
URC .... Unit Record Control
URC .... United Reform Church in England and Wales
URC .... University Research Centre [*British*]
URC .... Upper Rib Cage [*Anatomy*]
URC .... Ursuline College Library, Pepper Pike, OH [*OCLC symbol*] (OCLC)
URC .... Urumqi [*China*] [*Airport symbol*] (OAG)
URC .... Utility Radio Communication
URCC .... University of Rochester Cancer Center [*Research center*] (RCD)
URCF .... Unidentified Remittance Control File [*IRS*]
URCG .... Uniform Rules for Contract Guarantees
URCLK ...... Universal Receiver Clock
URCO .... Union des Ressortissants du Congo pour la Defense et la Promotion du Congo [*Union of Congolese for the Defense and Promotion of the Congo*]
URCS .... Uniform Ration Cost System (MCD)
URD .... New York, NY [*Location identifier*] [*FAA*] (FAAL)
URD .... Underground Residential Distribution [*Cable*]
URD .... Union Republicana Democratica [*Democratic Republican Union*] [*Puerto Rico, Venezuela*]
URD .... Upper Respiratory Disease [*Medicine*]
urd .... Urdu [*MARC language code*] [*Library of Congress*] (LCCP)
Urd .... Uridine [*Also, U*] [*A nucleoside*]
URD .... User Requirements Document (MCD)

URDA .... Uniform Retirement Date Act [*National Conference of Commissioners on Uniform State Laws*]
URDA .... Urban Resources Development Agency (OICC)
URDIS .... Your Dispatch [*Military*]
Urdmurt i Glazov Ped Inst Ucen Zap ... Urdmurtskogo i Glazovskogo Pedagogiceskogo Instituta Ucenye Zapiski [*A publication*]
Urdmurt Ped Inst Ucen Zap ... Urdmurtskogo Pedagogiceskogo Instituta Ucenye Zapiski [*A publication*]
URDP .... Ukrains'ka Revoliutsiino-Demokratychna Partiia
URDS .... Unregistered Dealing System [*Australia*]
URE .... Undergraduate Record Examination [*Education*]
URE .... Unintentional Radiation Exploitation (AFM)
URE .... User Range Error
URECD ...... Urban Ecology [*A publication*]
UREHE ..... Union for Research and Experimentation in Higher Education [*Later, UECU*]
UREKA ..... Unlimited Resources Ensure Keen Answers
Uremia Invest ... Uremia Investigation [*A publication*]
UREP .... Unit Representative [*Military*] (INF)
UREP .... University Research Expeditions Programs
URES .... University Residence Environment Scale [*Student attitudes test*]
URESA ...... Uniform Reciprocal Enforcement of Support Act
U-REST ..... Universal Range, Endurance, Speed, and Time (NG)
ureth .... Urethra [*Anatomy*]
Urethane .... Urethane Plastics and Products [*A publication*]
Urethane Plast Prod ... Urethane Plastics and Products [*A publication*]
URETS ...... University Real Estate Trust [*NASDAQ symbol*] (NQ)
URev .... University Review [*Dublin*] [*A publication*]
URF .... Ukrainian Research Foundation [*Defunct*] (EA)
URF .... Unassigned Reading Frame [*Genetics*]
URF .... Unidentified Reading Frame [*Genetics*]
URF .... Unidentified Remittance File [*IRS*]
URF .... Union des Services Routiers des Chemins de Fer Europeens [*Union of European Railways Road Services*]
URF .... United Religious Front [*Israel*] (BJA)
URF .... United Republican Fund
URF .... Uterine-Relaxing Factor [*Endocrinology*]
URFDA-NYC ... United Retail Fish Dealers Association of New York City (EA)
URG .... Underway Replenishment Group [*Military*]
URG .... Unit Review Group [*Nuclear energy*] (NRCH)
URG .... United Rayore Gas [*Vancouver Stock Exchange symbol*]
URG .... Universal Radio Group
URG .... Urban Regeneration Grant [*British*]
URG .... Urgent (AFM)
URG .... Urheberrechtsgesetz [*German Copyright Act*] (DLA)
URG .... Uruguaiana [*Brazil*] [*Airport symbol*] (OAG)
URGAB .... Urologe. Ausgabe A [*A publication*]
URGE .... Urgent Care Centers of America [*NASDAQ symbol*] (NQ)
URGENT .. Universal Relevance Group Enterprise in a National Theater [*Theater workshop*]
URGR .... Underway Replenishment Group [*Military*]
URGYA ..... Urology [*Ridgewood, NJ*] [*A publication*]
URHB .... Urban Renewal Handbook
URi .... Richmond City Library, Richmond, UT [*Library symbol*] [*Library of Congress*] (LCLS)
URI .... Union Research Institute, Kowloon, Hong Kong [*Library symbol*] [*Library of Congress*] (LCLS)
URI .... United Research, Incorporated
URI .... University Research Initiative [*DoD*] (RDA)
URI .... University of Rhode Island
URI .... Unpublished Research Information [*Conducted by National Science Foundation*]
URI .... Upper Respiratory Infection [*Medicine*]
URI .... Uranium Resources, Inc. [*Vancouver Stock Exchange symbol*]
URI .... Uribe [*Colombia*] [*Airport symbol*] [*Obsolete*] (OAG)
URICA ...... Universal Real-Time Information Control and Administration (MCD)
URICA ...... Universal Real-Time Machine Readable Information Cataloguing and Administration [*Australia*]
URICA ...... University of Rhode Island Computer Access [*University of Rhode Island Library*] (OLDSS)
URICA ...... Using Reading in Creative Activities
U Rich LN ... University of Richmond. Law Notes [*A publication*] (DLA)
U Rich LR ... University of Richmond. Law Review [*A publication*]
U Rich L Rev ... University of Richmond. Law Review [*A publication*]
U Richmond L Rev ... University of Richmond. Law Review [*A publication*]
URifGS ...... Church of Jesus Christ of Latter-Day Saints, Genealogical Society Library, Richfield Branch, Richfield, UT [*Library symbol*] [*Library of Congress*] (LCLS)
URII .... Ukrainian Research and Information Institute [*Defunct*] (EA)
URIMA ..... University Risk and Insurance Managers Association [*Later, URMIA*] (EA)
URINA ...... Urologia Internationalis [*A publication*]
URINT ...... Unintentional Radiation Intelligence (MCD)
URIPS .... Undersea Radioisotope Power Supply
URIR .... Unified Radioactive Isodromic Regulator
URISA .... Urban and Regional Information Systems Association (EA)
URIX .... Uranium Resources, Inc. [*NASDAQ symbol*] (NQ)
URIZR .... Your Recommendation Is Requested (FAAC)

URJA.........	United Roumanian Jews of America (EA)
Urk.............	Urkunde [*Document, Deed, Instrument*] [*German*] (ILCA)
Urk.............	Urkunden des Aegyptischen Altertums [*G. Steindorff*] [*Leipzig*] [*A publication*] (BJA)
URKK.......	Krasnodar [*USSR*] [*ICAO location identifier*] (ICLI)
URL..........	University of Regina Library [*UTLAS symbol*]
URL..........	Unrequited Love [*Slang*]
URL..........	Unrestricted Line Officer [*Navy*]
URL..........	Upper Reference Limit [*Analytical chemistry*]
URL..........	User Requirements Language [*Data processing*]
URLA.......	Uniform Reciprocal Licensing Act [*State law*] [*Insurance*]
URLAA	Urban Land [*A publication*]
URLB........	University of Rochester. Library Bulletin [*A publication*]
URLBB	Urologe. Ausgabe B [*A publication*]
Url Cl........	Urling's Legal Guide for the Clergy [*A publication*] (DLA)
Url For Pat ...	Urling on Foreign Patents [*A publication*] (DLA)
URLGA	Urologe [*A publication*]
URLH........	Urban Renewal and Low Income Housing [*A publication*]
URLTR......	[*Reference*] Your Letter [*Military*]
Url Trust....	Urling on the Office of a Trustee [*A publication*] (DLA)
URM.........	Uncle Remus Museum (EA)
URM..........	University Reform Movement [*in Latin America*]
URM..........	Unlimited Register Machine
URM..........	Urban Renewal Manual
URM..........	Uriman [*Venezuela*] [*Airport symbol*] (OAG)
URMGM...	[*Reference*] Your Mailgram [*Military*]
URMIA	University Risk Management and Insurance Association [*Madison, WI*] (EA)
URMIS......	Uniform Retail Meat Identity Standard [*Pronounced "er-miss"*]
URMK.......	Kislovodsk [*USSR*] [*ICAO location identifier*] (ICLI)
UR M-L.....	Uniao Revolucionaria, Marxista-Leninista [*Marxist-Leninist Revolutionary Union*] [*Portugal*] [*Political party*] (PPE)
URMM......	Mineralnye Vody [*USSR*] [*ICAO location identifier*] (ICLI)
URMSG	[*Reference*] Your Message [*Military*]
URN..........	Covington/Cincinnati, OH [*Location identifier*] [*FAA*] (FAAL)
URN..........	Ultrahigh Radio Navigation (NATG)
URN..........	Uniform Random Numerator [*Data processing*]
URN..........	Unique Record Number [*Data processing*] (ADA)
URN..........	Unique Reference Number [*Customs*] (DS)
URN..........	Urine (NASA)
URNEA	Urologiya i Nefrologiya [*A publication*]
Urner Miner Freund ...	Urner Mineralien Freund [*A publication*]
URNF........	Unidentified Remittance Name File [*IRS*]
URNG........	Unidad Revolucionaria Nacional Guatemalteca [*Guatemalan National Revolutionary Unity*] [*Political party*] (PD)
URO..........	United Restitution Organization
URO..........	United Rink Operators [*Defunct*] (EA)
URO..........	Urology
URO..........	Uroporphyrin [*Biochemistry*]
URO..........	Uroporphyrinogen [*Biochemistry*]
URO..........	User Readout (MCD)
URO..........	Ustredni Rada Odboru [*Central Council of Trade Unions*] [*Czechoslovakia*]
UROBA	United Russian Orthodox Brotherhood of America (EA)
UROC........	United Railroad Operating Crafts [*Defunct*]
UROEA	UNESCO [*United Nations Educational, Scientific, and Cultural Organization*] Regional Office for Education in Asia and Oceania (DLA)
UROGEN ...	Uroporphyrinogen [*Biochemistry*]
UROL........	Urology
UROLA	UNEP [*United Nations Environmental Programme*] Regional Office for Latin America (EAIO)
Urol Ausg A ...	Urologe. Ausgabe A [*A publication*]
Urol Clin North Am ...	Urologic Clinics of North America [*A publication*]
Urol Cutaneous Rev ...	Urologic and Cutaneous Review [*A publication*]
Urol Int	Urologia Internationalis [*A publication*]
Urol Intern ...	Urologia Internationalis [*A publication*]
Urol Internat ...	Urologia Internationalis [*A publication*]
Urol i Nefrol ...	Urologiya i Nefrologiya [*A publication*]
Urol Nefrol (Mosk) ...	Urologiia i Nefrologiia (Moskva) [*A publication*]
Urol Nephrol Sz ...	Urologiai es Nephrologiai Szemle [*Hungary*] [*A publication*]
Urologe	Urologe. Ausgabe A [*A publication*]
Urologe A...	Urologe. Ausgabe A. Zeitschrift fuer Klinische und Praktische Urologie [*A publication*]
Urologe B...	Urologe. Ausgabe B. Organ des Berufsverbandes der Deutschen Urologen [*A publication*]
Urol Panam ...	Urologia Panamericana [*A publication*]
Urol Pol ...	Urologia Polska [*A publication*]
Urol Radiol ...	Urologic Radiology [*A publication*]
Urol Res.....	Urological Research [*A publication*]
Urol Suppl (Treviso) ...	Urologia. Supplemento (Treviso) [*A publication*]
Urol Surv ...	Urological Survey [*A publication*]
UROP........	Undergraduate Research Opportunities Program [*Pronounced "your-op"*] [*Massachusetts Institute of Technology*]
UROS........	Uroporphyrinogen I Synthase [*An enzyme*]
URP..........	Undergraduate Research Participation [*National Science Foundation project*] [*Defunct*] (EA)
URP..........	Underreporter Program [*IRS*]
URP..........	Unique Radiolytic Product [*Food technology*]
URP..........	Unit Record Processor
URP..........	United Reef Petroleums Ltd. [*Toronto Stock Exchange symbol*]
URP..........	Unmanned Recovery Platform [*Navy*] (NVT)
URP..........	Untersuchungen zur Romanischen Philologie [*A publication*]
URP..........	Upper-Stage Reusable Payload
URP..........	Urban Renewal Project [*HUD*] (OICC)
URPE........	Union for Radical Political Economics (EA)
URPE........	Union des Resistants pour une Europe Unie [*Union of Resistance Veterans for a United Europe*]
URPE........	Union Revolucionaria Popular Ecuatoriana [*Ecuadorean Popular Revolutionary Union*] [*Political party*] (PPW)
URPG	President's Urban and Regional Policy Group [*Terminated, 1978*] (EGAO)
URPP........	Undergraduate Research Participation Program [*Formerly, URP*] (EA)
URPT-A	Urban and Rural Planning Thought [*India*] [*A publication*]
URQ..........	Unsatisfactory Report Questionnaire
URQ..........	Upper Right Quadrant [*Medicine*]
URR..........	Ultra-Rapid Reader [*Data processing*]
URR..........	Union Railroad Co. [*Pittsburgh, PA*] [*AAR code*]
URR..........	Unit Readiness Report [*Army*] (AABC)
URR..........	United Redford Resources, Inc. [*Vancouver Stock Exchange symbol*]
URR..........	Universities Research Reactor [*British*]
URR..........	Upstream Regulatory Region [*Genetics*]
URR..........	Urrao [*Colombia*] [*Airport symbol*] (OAG)
URR..........	Utilization Research Report
URRC	Urological Rehabilitation and Research Center [*University of Alabama in Birmingham*] [*Research center*] (RCD)
URRM	Morozovsk [*USSR*] [*ICAO location identifier*] (ICLI)
URRR	Rostov-Na-Donu [*USSR*] [*ICAO location identifier*] (ICLI)
URS..........	Ugurusu [*Japan*] [*Seismograph station code, US Geological Survey*] (SEIS)
URS..........	Unate Ringe Sum [*Logic expression*] (IEEE)
Urs	Underwriters [*Insurance*]
URS..........	UNESCO Relations Staff
URS..........	Uniform Reporting System
URS..........	Union of Railway Signalmen [*British*]
URS..........	Unit Reference Sheet [*Military*] (AABC)
URS..........	United Research Service (MCD)
URS..........	Universal Reference System
URS..........	Universal Regulating System
URS..........	University Research Support [*Department of Energy*]
URS..........	Update Report System (TEL)
URS..........	Urban Resource Systems (EA)
URS..........	URS Corp. [*NYSE symbol*] (SPSG)
URS..........	Ursinus College, Collegeville, PA [*OCLC symbol*] (OCLC)
URS..........	Utilization Reporting System (MCD)
URSA	Unit Replacement System Analysis [*Military*]
URSA	United Russia Societies Association [*London*]
URSA	Urban and Rural Systems Associates
URSER......	[*Reference*] Your Serial [*Military*]
URSI..........	Union Radio Scientifique Internationale [*International Union of Radio Science*] [*Also, ISRU*] [*Belgium*]
URSNSC ...	Union Regionale des Syndicats du Nyong-et-Sanaga
URSP........	Universal RADAR Signal Processor
URSR........	Ukrains'ka Radjans'ka Socialistyczna Respublika [*A publication*]
URSS........	Sochi [*USSR*] [*ICAO location identifier*] (ICLI)
URSS.........	Union des Republiques Socialistes Sovietiques [*Union of Socialist Soviet Republics; USSR*]
URSTM.....	Unite de Recherche et de Service en Technologie Minerale de l'Abitibi-Temiscamingue [*University of Quebec at Abitibi- Temiscamingue*] [*Canada*] [*Research center*] (RCD)
URSUA	Urological Survey [*A publication*]
URSW	Union Regionale des Syndicats du Wouri [*Regional Union of Wouri Unions*]
URT..........	Surat Thani [*Thailand*] [*Airport symbol*] (OAG)
URT..........	Unit Recruit Training [*Army*] (AABC)
URT..........	Universal RADAR Tracker
URT..........	University Research and Training [*Programs*]
URT..........	Upper Respiratory Tract [*Medicine*]
URT..........	Upright (MSA)
Urt.............	Urteil [*Judgment, Decision*] [*German*] (ILCA)
URT..........	USP Real Estate Investment Trust [*AMEX symbol*] (SPSG)
URT..........	Utility Radio Transmitter
URTA	University Resident Theatre Association (EA)
URTEL......	[*Reference*] Your Telegram [*Military*]
URTI	Universite Radiophonique et Televisuelle Internationale [*International Radio-Television University*]
URTI	Upper Respiratory Tract Infection [*Medicine*]
URTIA......	Uniform Rights of the Terminally Ill Act [*National Conference of Commissioners on Uniform State Laws*]
URTNA	Union des Radio-Televisions Nationales Africaines [*African National Radio-Television Union*]
URTU	United Road Transport Union [*British*] (DCTA)
URTWAE ...	United Road Transport Workers' Association of England [*A union*]
URTX	URI Therm-X, Inc. [*NASDAQ symbol*] (NQ)
URU..........	Uruguay
URV..........	Undersea Research Vehicle [*or Vessel*]

URW.........	Ultrasonic Ring Welder
URW.........	United Racquetsports for Women (EA)
URW.........	United Rubber, Cork, Linoleum, and Plastic Workers of America (EA)
URWA......	United Railroad Workers of America
URWC......	Urinal Water Closet (MSA)
URX.........	Ubersee Rundschau [*A publication*]
URY.........	Gurayat [*Saudi Arabia*] [*Airport symbol*] (OAG)
URY.........	Union Railway of Memphis [*AAR code*]
URY.........	Uruguay [*ANSI three-letter standard code*] (CNC)
URZ.........	Uroozgan [*Afghanistan*] [*Airport symbol*] [*Obsolete*] (OAG)
US............	Military Airlift Command [*Air Force*] [*ICAO designator*] (FAAC)
US............	Ubi Supra [*In the Place Mentioned Above*] [*Latin*]
US............	Ultrasonic Spectroscopy
US............	Ultrasound
U/S..........	Unassorted (ROG)
US............	Uncle Sam
US............	Unconditional Selection
US............	Unconditional Surrender
US............	Unconditioned Stimulus [*Psychometrics*]
US............	Under Secretary
US............	Underlying Stock [*Finance*]
U/S..........	Underside
US............	Undersize (AAG)
US............	Underspeed (MSA)
US............	Underwriters' Special Request
U/S..........	Unhelpful, Helpless, Useless Persons [*From abbreviation for "unserviceable"*]
U & S	Unified and Specified [*or Strategic*] Command (MCD)
US............	Uniform System
US............	Union Settlement Association (EA)
US............	Unit Separator [*Control character*] [*Data processing*]
US............	United Serpents (EA)
US............	United Service (EA)
US............	United Sisters (EA)
US............	United States [*ANSI two-letter standard code*]
us..............	United States [*MARC country of publication code*] [*Library of Congress*] (LCCP)
US............	United States Supreme Court Reports [*A publication*] (DLA)
US............	Unites States of America [*IYRU nationality code*] (IYR)
US............	Universal Service [*News agency*]
US............	Universale Studium [*A publication*]
US............	Unknown Significance
US............	Unlike-Sexed
US............	Unregistered Stock [*Finance*]
US............	Unserviceable
U/S..........	Unsorted
US............	Up Stage [*Away from audience*] [*A stage direction*]
US............	Update State [*Online database field identifier*]
US............	Upper Stage (MCD)
US............	Uprighting Subsystem [*NASA*] (KSC)
US............	US Ammunition Co. [*Vancouver Stock Exchange symbol*]
US............	US Supreme Court Reports (GPO)
US............	Useless
US............	Uterine Stroma
US............	Uusi Suomi [*A publication*]
US1...........	United States 1 Worksheets [*A publication*]
USA..........	INFO-DOC [*ACCORD*] [*UTLAS symbol*]
USA..........	Liberty All-Star Equity [*NYSE symbol*] (SPSG)
USA..........	Ukiyo-E Society of America (EA)
USA...........	Ullage Simulation Assembly (MCD)
USA...........	Ultrasonic Agitation
USA...........	Ultrastable Arc Lamp
USA...........	Ultraviolet Spectral Analysis
US of A	Under Secretary of the Army
USA...........	Underwater Society of America (EA)
USA...........	Unicycling Society of America [*Later, USA, Inc.*] (EA)
USA...........	Union of South Africa
USA...........	Union Syndicale de l'Agriculture [*Union of Agricultural Workers*] [*Morocco*]
USA	United Scenic Artists (EA)
USA..........	United Secularists of America (EA)
USA...........	United Shareholders Association (EA)
USA...........	United Shareowners of America (EA)
USA...........	United Shoppers Association
USA...........	United Sidecar Association [*Later, USCA*] (EA)
USA...........	United Soccer Association [*Later, NASL*]
USA	United Socialist Alliance [*Sri Lanka*] [*Political party*]
USA...........	United Spoilers of America [*Later, MERCPAC*] (EA)
USA...........	United Sprint Association (EA)
USA	United States [*ANSI three-letter standard code*]
USA..........	United States of ACORN [*Publication of the Association of Community Organizations for Reform Now*]
USA..........	United States of America
USA..........	United States Army
USA..........	United States Automobile Association, San Antonio, TX [*OCLC symbol*] (OCLC)
USA..........	United Steelworkers of America
USA..........	United Student Aid Funds (EA)
USA..........	United Students for America [*Defunct*] (EA)

USA	United Support of Artists [*In USA for Africa, the chorus of American pop stars who recorded "We Are the World" to benefit famine victims in Africa*]
USA	United Synagogue of America (EA)
USA	Unity for Safe Airtravel [*Program of Air Line Pilots Association*]
USA	Universal Subject Access [*Librarianship*]
USA	Unix Systems Association (EA)
USA	Unsegmented Storage Analyzer [*Instrumentation*]
USA	Urban Sanitary Authority [*British*]
USA	Utility Shareholders Association (EA)
USAA	United Specialty Agents Alliance [*Also known as USA Alliance*] (EA)
USAA	United States Academy of Arms (EA)
USAA	United States Arbitration Act [*A publication*] (DLA)
USAA	United States Armor Association (EA)
USAA	United States Athletes Association (EA)
USAA	US Albacore Association (EA)
USAA	US Armbrust Association (EA)
USAA	US Armor Association (EA)
USAA	United States Army Audit Agency
USAA	US Amputee Athletic Association (EA)
USAAAVS ...	United States Army Agency for Aviation Safety [*Formerly, USABAAR*] (AABC)
USAAAWR ...	United States Army Audit Agency, Washington Region
USAAB......	United States Army Aviation Board
USAABELCTBD ...	United States Army Airborne and Electronics Board [*Later, USAAESWBD*]
USA/ABF ...	USA Amateur Boxing Federation (EA)
USAABMDA ...	United States Army Advanced Ballistic Missile Defense Agency (AABC)
USAABMU ...	United States Army Aircraft Base Maintenance Unit (AABC)
USAAC......	United States Army Administration Center [*Obsolete*] (AABC)
USAAC......	United States Army Air Corps
USAACDA ...	United States Army Aviation Combat Developments Agency [*CDC*]
USAACEBD ...	United States Army Airborne Communications and Electronics Board
USAADAT ...	United States Army Alcohol and Drug Abuse Team Training (MCD)
USAADB...	United States Army Air Defense Board
USAADCEN ...	United States Army Air Defense Center
USAADCENFB ...	United States Army Air Defense Center and Fort Bliss (AABC)
USAADCS ...	United States Army Air Defense Center and School
USAADEA ...	United States Army Air Defense Engineering Agency [*Formerly, USASADEA*] [*AEC*]
USAADMAC ...	United States Army Aeronautical Depot Maintenance Center
USAADS ...	United States Army Air Defense School (AABC)
USAADTA ...	United States Army Aircraft Development Test Activity
USAADTC ...	United States Army Armor and Desert Training Center
USAADVCOM ...	United States Army Advance Command
USAAEFA ...	United States Army Aviation Engineering Flight Activity [*Edwards Air Force Base, CA*]
USAAESWBD ...	United States Army Airborne, Electronics, and Special Warfare Board (AABC)
USAAF......	United States Army Air Forces
USAAFIME ...	United States Army Air Forces in the Middle East
USAAFINO ...	United States Army Aviation Flight Information and Nav-Aids Office (AABC)
USAAFIO ...	United States Army Aviation Flight Information Office
USAAFO...	United States Army Avionics Field Office [*Formerly, USASAFO*]
USAAFUK ...	United States Army Air Forces in the United Kingdom
USAAGAR ...	United States Army Advisor Group O - Army Reserve (AABC)
USAAGDPSC ...	United States Army Adjutant General Data Processing Service Center (AABC)
USAAGNG ...	United States Army Advisory Group (National Guard) (AABC)
USAAGPC ...	United States Army Adjutant General Publications Center
USAAGS...	United States Army Adjutant General's School (AABC)
USAALS ...	United States Army Aviation Logistics School (INF)
USAAMA ...	United States Army Advent Management Agency (MUGU)
USAAMC ...	United States Army Aeromedical Center
USAAMC ...	United States Army Artillery and Missile Center
USAAML ...	United States Army Aviation Materiel Laboratories
USAAMR & DL ...	United States Army Air Mobility Research and Development Laboratory [*Also, AMR & DL, USAAMRDL*]
USAAMRDL ...	United States Army Air Mobility Research and Development Laboratory [*Also, AMR & DL, USAAMR & DL*]
USAAMS..	United States Army Artillery and Missile School [*Later, Field Artillery School*]
USAAPDT ...	United States Army Aviation Precision Demonstration Team (AABC)
USAAPSA ...	United States Army Ammunition Procurement and Supply Agency
USAARC...	United States Antiaircraft Replacement Center

USAARCOM ... United States Army Armament Command
USAARDC ... United States Army Aberdeen Research and Development Center
USAARENBD ... United States Army Armor and Engineer Board   (AABC)
USAARL ... United States Army Aeromedical Research Laboratory [*Ft. Rucker, AL*]   (AABC)
USAARMA ... United States Assistant Army Attache
USAARMBD ... United States Army Armor Board
USAARMC ... United States Army Armor Center [*Fort Knox, KY*]
USAARMHRU ... United States Army Armor Human Research Unit [*Fort Knox, KY*]   (AABC)
USAARMS ... United States Army Armor School
USAARTYBD ... United States Army Artillery Board
USAARU ... United States Army Aeromedical Research Unit
USAAS ... United States Army Air Services [*World War II*]
USAASC ... United States Army Air Service Command
USAASCFBH ... United States Army Administrative School Center and Fort Benjamin Harrison   (AABC)
USAASD ... United States Army Aeronautical Services Detachment
USAASD-E ... United States Army Aeronautical Services Detachment, Europe   (AABC)
USAASD-LA ... United States Army Aeronautical Services Detachment, Latin America   (AABC)
USAASD-PAC ... United States Army Aeronautical Services Detachment, Pacific   (AABC)
USAASL ... United States Army Atmospheric Sciences Laboratory   (RDA)
USAASO ... United States Army Aeronautical Services Office   (AABC)
USAASTA ... United States Army Aviation Systems Test Activity [*Also, AASTA*]
USAATBD ... United States Army Arctic Test Board
USAATC ... United States Army Arctic Test Center
USAATCO ... United States Army Air Traffic Coordinating Officer
USAATMS ... United States Army Air Traffic Management System
USAAVA ... United States Army Audio-Visual Agency   (AABC)
USAAVCOM ... United States Army Aviation Materiel Command   (AABC)
USAAVLABS ... United States Army Aviation Materiel Laboratories   (AABC)
USAAVNBD ... United States Army Aviation Board
USAAVNC ... United States Army Aviation Center [*CONARC*]
USAAVNDTA ... US Army Aviation Development Test Activity [*Fort Rucker, AL*]   (GRD)
USAAVNHRU ... United States Army Aviation Human Research Unit [*Ft. Rucker, AL*]   (AABC)
USAAVNS ... United States Army Aviation School [*CONARC*]
USAAVNTA ... United States Army Aviation Test Activity   (AABC)
USAAVNTBD ... United States Army Aviation Test Board
USAAVRADCOM ... United States Army Aviation Research and Development Command
USAAVS ... United States Agency for Aviation Safety   (MCD)
USAAVSCOM ... United States Army Aviation Systems Command [*Obsolete*]   (AABC)
USAB .... United States Air Base   (AAG)
USAB .... United States Army, Berlin   (AABC)
USAB .... US Animal Bank   (EA)
USAB .... USA Bancorp, Inc. [*NASDAQ symbol*]   (NQ)
USABA ...... US Association for Blind Athletes   (EA)
USABAAR ... United States Army Board for Aviation Accident Research [*Later, USAAAVS*]
USABDA ... United States Amateur Ballroom Dancers Association   (EA)
USABESRL ... United States Behavioral Science Research Laboratory [*Obsolete*]   (IEEE)
USABF ...... United States Amateur Baseball Federation
USA-BIAC ... USA - Business and Industry Advisory Committee to the OECD [*Organization for Economic Cooperation and Development*]   (EA)
USABIOLABS ... United States Army Biological Laboratories   (AABC)
USABRL ... United States Army Ballistic Research Laboratories   (AABC)
USABVAPAC ... United States Army Broadcasting and Visual Activities, Pacific
USAC .... Union des Syndicats Autonomes Camerounais [*Federation of Cameroonese Autonomous Unions*]
USAC .... United States Air Corps
USAC .... United States Alpine Club [*Defunct*]
USAC .... United States of America Confederation [*Later, USAC/RS*]   (EA)
USAC .... United States Apparel Council [*Defunct*]   (EA)
USAC .... United States Archery Congress   (EA)
USAC .... United States Army Corps   (AABC)
USAC .... United States Auto Club   (EA)
USAC .... Urban Information Systems Inter-Agency Committee [*HUD*] [*Terminated*]   (EGAO)
USAC .... US Antimony Corporation [*NASDAQ symbol*]   (NQ)
USAC .... US Aquaculture Council [*Defunct*]   (EA)
USAC .... User Services Advisory Committee [*NERComP*]
USAC .... Utah State Agricultural College
USACA ...... United States Advanced Ceramics Association
USACA ...... United States Allied Commission Austria
USACA ...... United States Army Civil Affairs [*World War II*]
USACA ...... United States Army Communications Agency
USACA ...... US A-Division Catamaran Association   (EA)
USACAA ... United States Army Concepts Analysis Agency   (AABC)

USACAC ... United States Army Combined Arms Center   (AABC)
USACAC ... United States Army Continental Army Command [*CONARC*] [*Superseded by FORSCOM*]
USACAF ... United States Army Construction Agency, France
USACAK ... United States Army Construction Agency, Korea
US-ACAN ... United States Advisory Committee on Antarctic Names [*1947-*]
USACARMSCDA ... United States Army Combined Arms Combat Developments Agency
USACAS ... United States Army Civil Affairs School
USACATB ... United States Army Combat Arms Training Board   (AABC)
USACBRWOC ... United States Army Chemical, Biological, and Radiological Weapons Orientation Course   (AABC)
USACBRWOCAAB ... United States Army Chemical, Biological, and Radiological Weapons Orientation Course Academic Advisory Board   (AABC)
USACC ...... United States Army Communications Command   (AABC)
USACC ...... US-Arab Chamber of Commerce   (EA)
USACC ...... USA Convertible Club   (EA)
USACC-A ... United States Army Communications Command - Alaska   (AABC)
USACCA ... United States Army Congressional Correspondence Agency   (AABC)
USACC-AMC ... United States Army Communications Command - Army Materiel Command   (AABC)
USACC COMMAGCY-HSC ... United States Army Communications Command Communications Agency - Health Services Command   (AABC)
USACC COMMAGCY-MTMC ... United States Army Communications Command Communications Agency - Military Traffic Management Command   (AABC)
USACC COMMAGCY-USACIDC ... United States Army Communications Command Communications Agency - United States Army Criminal Investigation Command   (AABC)
USACC COMMAGCY-USAINTC ... United States Army Communications Command Communications Agency - United States Army Intelligence Center
USACC-CONUS ... United States Army Communications Command - Continental United States   (AABC)
USACC-EUR ... United States Army Communications Command - Europe   (AABC)
USACC-FORCES ... United States Army Communications Command - Forces   (AABC)
USACCIA ... United States Army Chemical Corps Intelligence Agency
USACCL ... United States Army Coating and Chemical Laboratory   (AABC)
USACCO ... United States Army Commercial Communications Office
USACC-PAC ... United States Army Communications Command - Pacific   (AABC)
USACC-R/FMD ... United States Army Communications Command Radio and Frequency Management Division
USACCSA ... United States Army Command and Control Support Agency
USACC-SAFCA ... United States Army Communications Command Safeguard Communications Agency
USACCSD ... United States Army Command and Control Support Detachment   (AABC)
USACC SIG GP (AD) ... United States Army Communications Command Signal Group (AD)
USACC-SO ... United States Army Communications Command - South   (AABC)
USACC-T ... United States Army Communications Command - Thailand   (AABC)
USACCTC ... United States Army Chemical Corps Technical Committee
USACC-TRADOC ... United States Army Communications Command - Training and Doctrine Command   (AABC)
USACDA ... United States Arms Control and Disarmament Agency
USACDA ... United States Army Catalog Data Agency   (AABC)
USACDC ... United States Army Combat Developments Command
USACDCADA ... United States Army Combat Developments Command Air Defense Agency [*Fort Bliss, TX*]   (AABC)
USACDCAGA ... United States Army Combat Developments Command Adjutant General Agency
USACDCARMA ... United States Army Combat Developments Command Armor Agency [*Fort Knox, KY*]   (AABC)
USACDCARTYA ... United States Army Combat Developments Command Artillery Agency   (AABC)
USACDCAVNA ... United States Army Combat Developments Command Aviation Agency [*Fort Rucker, AL*]   (AABC)
USACDCCA ... United States Army Combat Developments Command Combined Arms Agency [*Fort Leavenworth, KS*]
USACDCCAA ... United States Army Combat Developments Command Civil Affairs Agency [*Fort Gordon, GA*]   (AABC)
USACDCCAG ... United States Army Combat Developments Command Combat Army Group [*Obsolete*] [*Fort Leavenworth, KS*]   (AABC)
USACDCCARMSA ... United States Army Combat Developments Command Combat Arms Agency
USACDCCBRA ... United States Army Combat Developments Command Chemical-Biological-Radiological Agency [*Fort McClellan, AL*]   (AABC)
USACDCCEA ... United States Army Combat Developments Command Communications-Electronics Agency [*Fort Monmouth, NJ*]   (AABC)

USACDCCHA ... United States Army Combat Developments Command Chaplain Agency [*Fort Lee, VA*] (AABC)
USACDCCOMSG ... United States Army Combat Developments Command Combat Systems Group (AABC)
USACDCCONFG ... United States Army Combat Developments Command Concept and Force Design Group (AABC)
USACDCCSG ... United States Army Combat Developments Command Combat Support Group [*Obsolete*] [*Fort Belvoir, VA*] (AABC)
USACDCCSSG ... United States Army Combat Developments Command Combat Service Support Group [*Obsolete*] [*Fort Lee, VA*] (AABC)
USACDCDPFO ... United States Army Combat Developments Command Data Processing Field Office (AABC)
USACDCEA ... United States Army Combat Developments Command Engineer Agency [*Later, USACDCENA*] [*Fort Belvoir, VA*] (AABC)
USACDCEC ... United States Army Combat Developments Command Experimentation Center [*or Command*] [*Fort Ord, CA*] (AABC)
USACDCENA ... United States Army Combat Developments Command Engineer Agency [*Formerly, USACDCEA*] (AABC)
USACDCFAA ... United States Army Combat Developments Command Field Artillery Agency [*Fort Sill, OK*] (AABC)
USACDCFINA ... United States Army Combat Developments Command Finance Agency (AABC)
USACDCIA ... United States Army Combat Developments Command Infantry Agency [*Later, USACDCINA*] [*Fort Benning, GA*] (AABC)
USACDCIAS ... United States Army Combat Developments Command Institute of Advanced Studies [*Obsolete*] [*Carlisle Barracks, PA*] (AABC)
USACDCICAS ... United States Army Combat Developments Command Institute of Combined Arms and Support [*Obsolete*] [*Fort Leavenworth, KS*] (AABC)
USACDCIDDFO ... United States Army Combat Developments Command Internal Defense and Development Field Office (AABC)
USACDCILC ... United States Army Combat Developments Command Institute of Land Combat [*Obsolete*] [*Alexandria, VA*] (AABC)
USACDCINA ... United States Army Combat Developments Command Infantry Agency [*Formerly, USACDCIA*] (AABC)
USACDCINCSG ... United States Army Combat Developments Command Intelligence and Control Systems Group (AABC)
USACDCINS ... United States Army Combat Developments Command Institute of Nuclear Studies [*Obsolete*] [*Fort Bliss, TX*] (AABC)
USACDCINTA ... United States Army Combat Developments Command Intelligence Agency [*Fort Holabird, MD*] (MCD)
USACDCISA ... United States Army Combat Developments Command Institute of Systems Analysis [*Obsolete*] [*Fort Belvoir, VA*] (AABC)
USACDCISS ... United States Army Combat Developments Command Institute of Special Studies [*Obsolete*] [*Fort Belvoir, VA*] (AABC)
USACDCISSO ... United States Army Combat Developments Command Institute of Strategic and Stability Operations [*Obsolete*] (AABC)
USACDCJAA ... United States Army Combat Developments Command Judge Advocate Agency [*Charlottesville, VA*] (AABC)
USACDCMA ... United States Army Combat Developments Command Maintenance Agency [*Aberdeen Proving Ground, MD*] (AABC)
USACDCMPA ... United States Combat Developments Command Military Police Agency [*Fort Gordon, GA*] (AABC)
USACDCMSA ... United States Army Combat Developments Command Medical Service Agency [*Fort Sam Houston, TX*] (AABC)
USACDCNG ... United States Army Combat Developments Command Nuclear Group [*Fort Bliss, TX*]
USACDCNUA ... United States Army Combat Developments Command Nuclear Agency (AABC)
USACDCOA ... United States Army Combat Developments Command Ordnance Agency [*Aberdeen Proving Ground, MD*]
USACDCPALSG ... United States Army Combat Developments Command Personnel and Logistics Systems Group (AABC)
USACDCPASA ... United States Army Combat Developments Command Personnel and Administrative Services Agency [*Fort Benjamin Harrison, IN*] (AABC)
USACDCQA ... United States Army Combat Developments Command Quartermaster Agency [*Fort Lee, VA*]
USACDCSA ... United States Army Combat Developments Command Supply Agency [*Later, USACDCSUA*] [*Fort Lee, VA*] (AABC)
USACDCSAG ... United States Army Combat Developments Command Systems Analysis Group [*Fort Belvoir, VA*] (AABC)
USACDCSOA ... United States Army Combat Developments Command Special Operations Agency (AABC)
USACDCSSI ... United States Army Combat Developments Command Strategic Studies Institute (AABC)
USACDCSUA ... United States Army Combat Developments Command Supply Agency [*Formerly, USACDCSA*] (AABC)

USACDCSWA ... United States Army Combat Developments Command Special Warfare Agency [*Fort Bragg, NC*] (AABC)
USACDCSWCAG ... United States Army Combat Developments Command Special Warfare and Civil Affairs Group [*Fort Belvoir, VA*]
USACDCSWG ... United States Army Combat Developments Command Special Warfare Group
USACDCTA ... United States Army Combat Developments Command Transportation Agency [*Fort Eustis, VA*] (AABC)
USACE ...... United States Army Corps of Engineers [*Merged with General Equipment Command*]
USACEBD ... United States Army Airborne Communications and Electronics Board (AABC)
USACECDA ... United States Army Communications-Electronics Combat Developments Agency [*Fort Huachuca, AZ*]
USACEEIA ... United States Army Communications-Electronics Engineering Installation Agency [*Fort Huachuca, AZ*] (AABC)
USACEEIA-PAC ... United States Army Communications-Electronics Engineering Installation Agency-Pacific (RDA)
USACEEIA-WH ... United States Army Communications-Electronics Engineering Installation Agency - Western Hemisphere (AABC)
USACEIBN ... United States Army Communications-Electronics Installation Battalion (AABC)
USACENCDCSA ... United States Army Corps of Engineers National Civil Defense Computer Support Agency (AABC)
USACESSEC ... United States Army Computer Systems Support and Evaluation Command
USACGSC ... United States Army Command and General Staff College
USACHB ... United States Army Chaplain Board
USACHS ... United States Army Chaplain School
USACI ...... United States Advisory Commission on Information
USACICD ... United States Army Criminal Investigation Command [*Formerly, USACIDA*] (AABC)
USACIDA ... United States Army Criminal Investigation Division Agency [*Later, USACICD*] (AABC)
USACIECA ... United States Advisory Commission on International Educational and Cultural Affairs
USACII ..... United States of America Standard Code for Information Interchange (NOAA)
USACIL .... United States Army Criminal Investigation Laboratory (AABC)
USACIR .... United States Army Criminal Investigation Repository
USACISO ... United States Army Counterinsurgency Support Office, Okinawa [*Obsolete*] (AABC)
USACIU .... United States Army Command Information Unit (AABC)
USACJE .... United Synagogue of America Commission on Jewish Education (EA)
USACM ..... US Association for Computational Mechanics (EA)
USACMA ... United States Army Club Management Agency (AABC)
USACMLC ... United States Army Chemical Center [*Later, United States Army Ordnance and Chemical Center and School*]
USACMLCB ... United States Army Chemical Corps Board
USACMLCS ... United States Army Chemical Center and School [*Later, United States Army Ordnance and Chemical Center and School*] (AABC)
USACMLCSCH ... United States Army Chemical Corps School
USACMLRDL ... United States Army Chemical Research and Development Laboratories
USACMLS ... United States Army Chemical School (AABC)
USACMR ... United States Army Court of Military Review (AABC)
USACMS .. United States Army Command Management School
USACOJE ... United Synagogue of America Commission on Jewish Education (EA)
USACOMISA ... United States Army Communications Management Information Systems Activity
USACOMZEUR ... United States Army Communications Zone, Europe
USACOR ... US Association for the Club of Rome (EA)
USACPEB ... United States Army Central Physical Evaluation Board (AABC)
USACRAPAC ... United States Army Command Reconnaissance Activities, Pacific Command
USACRC ... United States Army Crime Records Center (AABC)
USACRF ... United States Army Counterintelligence Records Facility (MCD)
USACRREL ... United States Army Cold Regions Research and Engineering Laboratory (AABC)
USAC/RS ... United States Amateur Confederation of Roller Skating (EA)
USACRTC ... United States Army Cold Regions Test Center (INF)
USACS ...... United States Army Combat Surveillance Agency (AAG)
USACS ...... United States Army Courier Service (AABC)
USACSA ... United States Army Combat Surveillance Agency
USACSA ... United States Army Communications Systems Agency (AABC)
USACSC ... United States Army Computer Systems Command [*Fort Belvoir, VA*]
USACSG ... United States Army CINPAC Support Group
USACSLA ... United States Army Communications Security Logistics Agency (AABC)
USACSR ... United States Air Corps Specialist Reserve
USACSS ... United States Army Chief of Support Services
USACSS .... United States Army Combat Surveillance School (AABC)
USACSSAA ... United States Army Computer Systems Selection and Acquisition Agency (AABC)

USACSSC ... United States Army Computer Systems Support and Evaluation Command (IEEE)
USACSSEA ... United States Army Computer Systems Support and Evaluation Agency (AABC)
USACSSEC ... United States Army Computer Systems Support and Evaluation Command
USACSTA ... United States Army Courier Station (AABC)
USACSTATC ... United States Army Combat Surveillance and Target Acquisition Training Command
USACT ...... United States Accident Containment Team [*Government agency in 1985 movie "Warning Sign"*]
USACTA ... US Army Central TMDE [*Test, Measurement, and Diagnostic Equipment*] Activity (RDA)
USACTC ... . United States Army Clothing and Textile Center
USACTMC ... United States Army Clothing and Textile Materiel Center
USACWL .. United States Army Chemical Warfare Laboratory
USAD .... United States Army Dispensary (AABC)
USADA ..... United States Army Amateur Dancers Association (EA)
USADACS ... United States Army Defense Ammunition Center and School (AABC)
USADATCOM ... United States Army Data Support Command
USADC ..... United States Army Data Support Command
USADC ..... United States Army Dental Clinic
USADCJ ... United States Army Depot Command, Japan (AABC)
USADEG .. United States Army Dependents' Education Group (AABC)
USADIP .... United States Army Deserter Information Point (AABC)
USADJ ...... United States Army Depot, Japan (AABC)
USADOFL ... United States Army Diamond Ordnance Fuze Laboratory [*Later, HDL*]
USADP ...... Uniform Shipboard Automatic Data Processing
USADPC ... United States Army Data Processing Center
USADPS ... Uniform Automatic Data Processing System [*Navy*]
USADRB ... United States Army Discharge Review Board (AABC)
USADSC ... United States Army Data Services and Administrative Systems Command
USADTC ... United States Army Armor and Desert Training Center (AABC)
USAE .... United States Army Engineer (AABC)
USAEAGSC ... United States Army, Europe, Adjutant General Support Center (AABC)
USAEARA ... United States Army Equipment Authorization Review Activity (AABC)
USAEARC ... United States Army Equipment Authorizations Review Center (AABC)
USAEB ...... United States Army Engineer Board
USAEC ...... United States Army Electronics Command [*Obsolete*]
USAEC ...... United States Atomic Energy Commission
USAECA ... United States Army Electronics Command Computation Agency [*Obsolete*] (AABC)
USAECAV ... United States Army Engineer Construction Agency, Vietnam
USAECBDE ... United States Army Engineer Center Brigade (AABC)
USAECFB ... United States Army Engineer Center and Fort Belvoir (AABC)
USAECOM ... United States Army Electronics Command [*Obsolete*]
USAECR ... United States Army Engineer Center Regiment (AABC)
USAEC Rep CONF ... US Atomic Energy Commission. Report. CONF [*A publication*]
USAEC Rep GJO ... United States. Atomic Energy Commission. Report GJO [*A publication*]
USAEC Res Dev Rep AEC-TR ... US Atomic Energy Commission. Research and Development Report. AEC-TR [*A publication*]
USAEC Res Dev Rep ANL ... US Atomic Energy Commission. Research and Development Report. ANL [*A publication*]
USAEC Res Dev Rep BNL ... US Atomic Energy Commission. Research and Development Report. BNL [*A publication*]
USAEC Res Dev Rep COO ... US Atomic Energy Commission. Research and Development Report. COO [*A publication*]
USAEC Res Dev Rep HASL ... US Atomic Energy Commission. Research and Development Report. HASL [*A publication*]
USAEC Res Dev Rep HW ... US Atomic Energy Commission. Research and Development Report. HW [*A publication*]
USAEC Res Dev Rep LAMS (LA) ... US Atomic Energy Commission. Research and Development Report. LAMS (LA) [*A publication*]
USAEC Res Dev Rep LF ... US Atomic Energy Commission. Research and Development Report. LF [*A publication*]
USAEC Res Dev Rep NYO ... US Atomic Energy Commission. Research and Development Report. NYO [*A publication*]
USAEC Res Dev Rep ORINS ... US Atomic Energy Commission. Research and Development Report. ORINS [*A publication*]
USAEC Res Dev Rep ORNL ... US Atomic Energy Commission. Research and Development Report. ORNL [*A publication*]
USAEC Res Dev Rep ORO ... US Atomic Energy Commission. Research and Development Report. ORO [*A publication*]
USAEC Res Dev Rep RLO ... US Atomic Energy Commission. Research and Development Report. RLO [*A publication*]
USAEC Res Dev Rep SCR ... US Atomic Energy Commission. Research and Development Report. SCR [*A publication*]
USAEC Res Dev Rep TID ... US Atomic Energy Commission. Research and Development Report. TID [*A publication*]
USAEC Res Dev Rep UCD ... US Atomic Energy Commission. Research and Development Report. UCD [*A publication*]

USAEC Res Dev Rep UCLA ... US Atomic Energy Commission. Research and Development Report. UCLA [*A publication*]
USAEC Res Dev Rep UCRL ... US Atomic Energy Commission. Research and Development Report. UCRL [*A publication*]
USAEC Res Dev Rep UCSF ... US Atomic Energy Commission. Research and Development Report. UCSF [*A publication*]
USAEC Res Dev Rep UH ... US Atomic Energy Commission. Research and Development Report. UH [*A publication*]
USAEC Res Dev Rep UR ... US Atomic Energy Commission. Research and Development Report. UR [*A publication*]
USAEC Res Dev Rep WT ... US Atomic Energy Commission. Research and Development Report. WT [*A publication*]
USAEC Symp Ser ... US Atomic Energy Commission. Symposium Series [*A publication*]
USAECV(P) ... United States Army Engineer Command, Vietnam (Provisional)
USAED ...... United States Army Engineer District
USAEDE ... United States Army Engineer Division, Europe (AABC)
USAEDH .. United States Army Engineer Division, Huntsville (AABC)
USAEDLMV ... United States Army Engineer Division, Lower Mississippi Valley (AABC)
USAEDM ... United States Army Engineer Division, Mediterranean (AABC)
USAEDMR ... United States Army Engineer Division, Missouri River (AABC)
USAEDNA ... United States Army Engineer Division, North Atlantic (AABC)
USAEDNC ... United States Army Engineer Division, North Central (AABC)
USAEDNE ... United States Army Engineer Division, New England (AABC)
USAEDNP ... United States Army Engineer Division, North Pacific (AABC)
USAEDOR ... United States Army Engineer Division, Ohio River (AABC)
USAEDPO ... United States Army Engineer Division, Pacific Ocean (AABC)
USAEDSA ... United States Army Engineer Division, South Atlantic (AABC)
USAEDSP ... United States Army Engineer Division, South Pacific (AABC)
USAEDSW ... United States Army Engineer Division, Southwestern (AABC)
USAEEA ... United States Army Enlistment Eligibility Activity (AABC)
USAEFMA ... United States Army Electronics Command Financial Management Agency [*Obsolete*] (AABC)
USAEGD ... United States Army Engineer, Gulf District
USAEGIMRADA ... US Army Engineer, Geodesy, Intelligence, and Mapping Research and Development Agency (NOAA)
USAEHA .. United States Army Environmental Hygiene Agency [*Aberdeen Proving Ground, MD*] (AABC)
USAEHL .. United States Army Environmental Health Laboratory
USAEIGHT ... Eighth United States Army (CINC)
USAEIS ... United States Army Electronic Intelligence and Security (AABC)
USAELRO ... United States Army Electronics Logistics Research Office
USAELRU ... United States Army Electronics Research Unit
USAEMA ... United States Army Electronics Materiel Agency [*Formerly, USASSA*]
USAEMAFHPO ... United States Army Electronics Materiel Agency, Fort Huachuca Procurement Office
USAEMAFMPO ... United States Army Electronics Materiel Agency, Fort Monmouth Procurement Office
USAEMAPICO ... United States Army Electronics Materiel Agency, Plant Inventory Control Office
USAEMAWPO .. United States Army Electronics Materiel Agency, Washington Procurement Office
USAEMCA ... United States Army Engineer Mathematical Computation Agency (AABC)
USAEMSA ... United States Army Electronics Materiel Support Agency [*Formerly, USASMSA*]
USAENGCOMEUR ... United States Army Engineer Command, Europe (AABC)
USAENPG ... United States Army Engineer Power Group (RDA)
USAENPG-ED ... United States Army Engineer Power Group Engineering Division [*Fort Belvoir, VA*]
USAEPA ... United States Army Electronics Command Patent Agency [*Obsolete*] (AABC)
USAEPG ... United States Army Electronic Proving Ground [*Fort Huachuca, AZ*]
USAEPMARA ... United States Army, Europe, Personnel Management and Replacement Activity (AABC)
USAEPOC ... United States Army Engineer Procurement Office, Chicago
USAERA ... United States Army Electronics Command Logistics Research Agency [*Obsolete*] (AABC)
USAERADCOM ... United States Army Electronics Research and Development Command (RDA)
USAERDA ... United States Army Electronic Research and Development Agency
USAERDAW ... United States Army Electronics Research and Development Activity, White Sands [*New Mexico*] (AABC)
USAERDL ... United States Army Electronics Research and Development Laboratory [*Formerly, USASRDL*] (MCD)
USAEREC ... United States Army Enlisted Records and Evaluation Center (MCD)
USAERG ... United States Army Engineer Reactor Group (AABC)
USAERLO ... United States Army Electronics Regional Labor Office
US Aeros P ... United States Aerospace Industry Profile [*A publication*]

US Aerosp Med Res Lab Tech Rep AMRL-TR ... United States. Aerospace Medical Research Laboratory. Technical Report. AMRL-TR [*A publication*]
US Aerosp Res Lab Rep ... United States. Aerospace Research Laboratories. Reports [*A publication*]
USAES ...... United States Army Engineer School
USAES ...... United States Association of Evening Students   (EA)
USAESC ... United States Army Electronics Support Command   (AABC)
USAET & DL (ECOM) ... United States Army Electronics Technology and Devices Laboratory (Electronics Command)   (AABC)
USAETL ... United States Army Engineer Topographic Laboratories [*Fort Belvoir, VA*]
USAEU ..... United States Army Exhibit Unit   (AABC)
USAEUR... United States Army, Europe   (MCD)
USAEWES ... United States Army Engineer Waterways Experiment Station
US of AF.... Under Secretary of the Air Force
USAF........ United States Aikido Federation   (EA)
USAF........ United States Air Force [*Washington, DC*]
USAF........ United States Army Forces
USAF........ United Student Aid Fund
USAF........ United Students of America Foundation   (EA)
USAF........ US Aquaculture Federation   (EA)
USAF........ USA Foundation   (EA)
USAFA...... United States Air Force Academy [*Colorado*]
USAFA...... US-Albania Friendship Association   (EA)
USAFA...... USA Finn Association   (EA)
USAFABD ... United States Army Field Artillery Board [*Fort Sill, OK*]   (AABC)
USAFAC... United States Army Finance and Accounting Center   (AABC)
USAFACFS ... United States Army Field Artillery Center and Fort Sill   (AABC)
USAFACS ... United States Air Force Air Crew School
USAFADWC ... United States Air Force Air Defense Weapons Center   (MCD)
USAF AFHRL ... United States. Air Force. Human Resources Laboratory [*A publication*]
USAFAG... United States Air Force Auditor General
USAFAGOS ... United States Air Force's Air-Ground Operations School
USAFALCENT ... United States Air Force Airlift Center
USAFAPC ... United States Air Force Airframe Production Contract
USAFAPS ... United States Air Force Air Police School
USAFAS.... United States Army Field Artillery School [*Fort Sill, OK*]   (AABC)
USAFAVLO ... United States Air Force Audiovisual Liaison Office
USAFB ...... United States Army Field Band   (AABC)
USAFBI..... United States Army Forces in the British Isles
USAFBMD ... United States Air Force Ballistic Missile Division
USAFBMS ... United States Air Force Basic Military School
USAFBS.... United States Air Force Bandsman School   (AFM)
USAFBS.... United States Air Force Bombardment School
USAFCBI ... United States Forces, China, Burma, India [*World War II*]
USAFCBIT ... United States Forces, China, Burma, India Theater [*World War II*]
USAFCC ... United States Army Forces in Central Canada [*World War II*]
USAF CMR ... United States Air Force Court of Military Review   (AFM)
USAFCO... United States Air Force, Southern Command   (MCD)
USAFCRL ... United States Air Force Cambridge Research Laboratories
USAFD...... United States Air Force Dictionary [*A publication*]
USAFE...... United States Air Force in Europe
USAFEC ... United States Army Forces in Eastern Canada [*World War II*]
USAFECI ... United States Air Force Extension Course Institute
USAF/EDA ... Society of United States Air Force Flight Surgeons   (EA)
USAFEHL .... United States Air Force Environmental Health Laboratory
USAFEL... United States Air Force Epidemiological Laboratory   (AFM)
USAFESA ... United States Army Facilities Engineering Support Agency   (AABC)
USAFESA-ED ... United States Army Facilities Engineering Support Agency Engineering Division
USAFESA-RT ... United States Army Facilities Engineering Support Agency Research and Technology Division
USAFESA-RTD ... United States Army Facilities Engineering Support Agency Research and Technology Division
USAFESA-TS ... United States Army Facilities Engineering Support Agency - Technology Support Division
USAFESA-TSD ... United States Army Facilities Engineering Support Agency - Technology Support Division
USAFETAC ... United States Air Force Environmental Technical Applications Center [*Scott Air Force Base, IL*]   (AFM)
USAFETO ... United States Army Forces, European Theater of Operations [*World War II*]
USAFETPS ... United States Air Force Experimental Test Pilot School
USAFEURPCR ... United States Air Force European Postal and Courier Region   (AFM)
USAFF ...... USA Film Festival   (EA)
USAFFE... United States Army Forces, Far East [*World War II*]
USAFFGS ... United States Air Force Flexible Gunnery School
USAFFSR ... United States Air Force Flight Safety Research
USAFH ..... United States Air Force Hospital
USAFHA... USA Field Hockey Association   (EA)
USAFHD .. United States Air Force Historical Division
USAFHG... United States Air Force Honor Guard

USAFHRC ... United States Air Force Historical Research Center
USAFI .... United States Armed Forces Institute
USAFIA ... United States Army Forces in Australia
USAFIB..... United States Army Aviation Flight Information Bulletin   (FAAC)
USAFIC..... United States Association of Firearm Instructors and Coaches   (EA)
USAFICA ... United States Army Forces in Central Africa [*World War II*]
USAFICPA ... United States Army Forces in Central Pacific Area
USAFIFC.. United States Air Force Instrument Flight Center   (AFM)
USAFIK... United States Army Forces in Korea
USAFIL..... United States Army Forces in Liberia [*World War II*]
USAFIME ... United States Armed Forces in Middle East
USAFINCISCOM ... United States Army Finance and Comptroller Information Systems Command   (AABC)
USAFINTEL ... United States Air Force Intelligence Publication
USAFINZ ... United States Army Forces in New Zealand
USAFIP(NL) ... United States Army Forces in the Philippines (Northern Luzon) [*World War II*]
USAFISPA ... United States Army Forces in the South Pacific Area
USAFIT..... United States Air Force Institute of Technology
USAFIWS ... United States Air Force Interceptor Weapons School
USAFLANT ... United States Air Forces, Atlantic   (AABC)
USAFMC.. United States Association of Former Members of Congress   (EA)
USAFMD ... United States Army Frequency Management Directorate   (MCD)
USAFMEPCR ... United States Air Force Mideast Postal and Courier Region   (AFM)
USAFMEPCS ... United States Air Force Mideast Postal and Courier Service   (AFM)
USAFMIDPAC ... United States Army Forces, Middle Pacific [*World War II*] [*See AFMIDPAC*]
USAFMPC ... United States Air Force Military Personnel Center
USAFMTC ... United States Air Force Marksmanship Training Center
USAFMTO ... United States Army Forces, Mediterranean Theater of Operations [*World War II*]
USAF NR .. United States. Air Force. News Release [*A publication*]
USAF/NRD ... United States Air Force, National Range Division
USAFNS ... United States Air Force Navigation School
USAF Nucl Saf ... USAF [*United States Air Force*] Nuclear Safety [*A publication*]
USAFO...... United States Army Field Office   (RDA)
USAFOB... USA Federation of Bocce   (EA)
USAFOCA ... United States Army Field Operating Cost Agency   (AABC)
USAFOCS ... United States Air Force Officer Candidate School
USAFOEHL ... United States Air Force Occupational and Environmental Health Laboratory [*Brooks Air Force Base, TX*]
USAFOF ... United States Army Flight Operations Facility   (AABC)
USAFOMC ... US Air Force Occupational Measurement Center [*Randolph Air Force Base, TX*]   (GRD)
USAFOSR ... United States Air Force Office of Scientific Research
USAFP ...... Uniformed Services Academy of Family Physicians   (EA)
USAFPAC ... United States Air Forces, Pacific
USAFPACPCR ... United States Air Force Pacific Postal and Courier Region
USAFPCS ... United States Air Force Postal and Courier Service
USAFPCS Eur-Me Rgn ... United States Air Force Postal and Courier Service, Europe-Mideast Region   (AFM)
USAFPCS LA Rgn ... United States Air Force Postal and Courier Service, Latin American Region   (AFM)
USAFPCS Pac Rgn ... United States Air Force Postal and Courier Service, Pacific Region   (AFM)
USAFPCS US Rgn ... United States Air Force Postal and Courier Service, United States Region   (AFM)
USAFPDC ... United States Air Force Personnel Development Center
USAFPEB ... United States Air Force Physical Evaluation Board   (AFM)
USAFPLREP ... United States Air Force Plant Representative Office
USAFPOA ... United States Army Forces, Pacific Ocean Areas [*World War II*]
USAFPRO ... United States Air Force Plant Representative Office
USAFPS.... United States Air Force Pilot School
USAFR ...... Union of South Africa
USAFR ...... United States Air Force Representative   (AFM)
USAFR ...... United States Air Force Reserve
USAFRD... United States Air Force Recruiting Detachment
USAFRED ... United States Air Force Forces, Readiness Command
USAFRG ... United States Air Force Recruiting Group
USAFRHL ... United States Air Force Radiological Health Laboratory
USAFRO... United States Air Force Recruiting Office
USAFROTC ... United States Air Force Reserve Officer Training Corps
USAFRR ... United States Air Force Resident Representative   (MCD)
USAFRS.... United States Air Force Recruiting Service
USAFS..... United States Army Finance School   (AABC)
USAFSA.... United States Army Forces in South America
USAFSA.... United States Army Forces, South Atlantic [*World War II*]
USAFSAAS ... United States Air Force School of Applied Aerospace Sciences   (AFM)
USAFSACS ... United States Air Force School of Applied Cryptologic Sciences   (AFM)
USAFSAM ... United States Air Force School of Aerospace Medicine
USAFSAM/ED ... Society of United States Air Force Flight Surgeons   (EA)

USAFSAWC ... United States Air Force Special Air Warfare Center (AFM)
USAFSBSS ... United States Air Force Standard Base Supply System
USAFSC.... United States Army Food Service Center (AABC)
USAFSE .... United States Air Force Supervisory Examination (AFM)
USAFSG ... United States Army Field Support Group (AABC)
USAFSO ... United States Air Forces Southern Command (AABC)
USAFSOC ... United States Air Force Special Operations Center (AFM)
USAFSOF ... United States Air Force Special Operations Force (AFM)
USAFSOS ... United States Air Force Special Operations School (AFM)
USAFSPA ... United States Air Force Security Policy Academy
USAFSRA ... United States Air Force Special Reporting Agency
USAFSS .... United States Air Force Security Service [*Later, AFESC*]
USAFSTC ... United States Air Force Special Treatment Center (AFM)
USAFSTC ... United States Army Foreign Science and Technology
   Center (AABC)
USAFSTRIKE ... United States Air Forces Strike Command (AABC)
USAFTAC ... United States Air Force Technical Applications Center (MCD)
USAFTALC ... United States Air Force Tactical Airlift Center (AFM)
USAFTARC ... United States Air Force Tactical Air Reconnaissance
   Center (AFM)
USAFTAWC ... United States Air Force Tactical Air Warfare Center (AFM)
USAF TESTPLTSCH ... United States Air Force Test Pilot School
USAFTFWC ... United States Air Force Tactical Fighter Weapons
   Center (AFM)
USAFTPS ... United States Air Force Test Pilot School (MCD)
USAFTS.... United States Air Force Technical School
USAFTTS ... United States Air Force Technical Training School
USAF-USPCR ... United States Air Force - United States Postal Courier
   Region (AFM)
USAFWPLO ... United States Air Force Water Port Logistics Office
USAFWPO ... United States Air Force Water Port Liaison Office [*or
   Officer*] (AFM)
USAG .... United States Army Garrison (AABC)
USAG .... United States Army in Greece
USAGEM ... US Atlantic and Gulf Ports/Eastern Mediterranean and North
   African Freight Conference [*New York, NY*] (EA)
USAGETA ... United States Army General Equipment Test Activity (AABC)
USAGF ...... United States Army Ground Forces (MUGU)
USAGG ..... United States Army Group, American Mission for Aid to
   Greece
USAGIMRADA ... United States Army Geodesy Intelligence and Mapping
   Research and Development Agency (AABC)
USAGMPA ... United States Army General Materiel and Petroleum Activity
USAGMPC ... United States Army General Materiel and Parts
   Center (AABC)
USAGPC... United States Adjutant General Publications Center
US Agric .... United States. Department of Agriculture. Publications [*A
   publication*]
US Agric Mark Serv AMS Series ... United States. Agriculture Marketing
   Service. AMS Series [*A publication*]
US Agric Res Serv ARS-NC ... US Agricultural Research Service. ARS-NC [*A
   publication*]
US Agric Res Serv ARS-NE ... US Agricultural Research Service. ARS-NE [*A
   publication*]
US Agric Res Serv ARS-S ... US Agricultural Research Service. ARS-S [*A
   publication*]
US Agric Res Serv ARS-W ... US Agricultural Research Service. ARS-W [*A
   publication*]
US Agric Res Serv CA ... US Agricultural Research Service. CA [*A
   publication*]
US Agric Res Serv East Reg Res Lab Publ ... United States. Agricultural
   Research Service. Eastern Regional Research Laboratory.
   Publication [*A publication*]
US Agric Res Serv Mark Res Rep ... US Agricultural Research Service.
   Marketing Research Report [*A publication*]
US Agric Res Serv North Cent Reg Rep ... United States. Agricultural
   Research Service. North Central Region. Report [*A
   publication*]
US Agric Res Serv Northeast Reg Rep ARS NE ... US Agricultural Research
   Service. Northeastern Region Report. ARS-NE [*A
   publication*]
US Agric Res Serv South Reg Rep ... US Agricultural Research Service.
   Southern Region Report [*A publication*]
USAGSC ... United States Army General Supplies Commodity Center
USAH .... United States Army Hospital
USAHA ..... United States Army Animal Health Association (EA)
USAHAC ... United States Army Headquarters Area Command
USAHC ..... United States Army Health Clinic (AABC)
USAHEL... United States Army Human Engineering Laboratories (AABC)
USAHOME ... United States Army Homes [*Prefabricated houses, shipped
   overseas*]
USAHS ...... United States Army Hospital Ship
USAHSC... United States Army Health Service Command
USAHSDSA ... United States Army Health Services Data Systems
   Agency (AABC)
USAHTN .. United States Army Hometown News Center (AABC)
USAI......... US-Asia Institute (EA)
USAIA ...... United States Army Institute of Administration (AABC)
USAIB .... United States Army Infantry Board
USAIC....... United States Army Infantry Center [*Fort Benning, GA*]
USAIC....... United States Army Intelligence Command

USAICA .... United States Army Interagency Communications
   Agency (AABC)
USAICS..... United States Army Intelligence Center and School [*Fort
   Huachuca, AZ*] (AABC)
USAID....... United States Agency for International Development [*Also,
   AID*]
USAIDR .... United States Army Institute of Dental Research (AABC)
USAIDSC ... United States Army Information and Data Systems Command
USAIDSCOM ... United States Army Information and Data Systems
   Command (AABC)
USAIG....... United States Aircraft Insurance Group
USAIGC.... United States Association of Independent Gymnastic
   Clubs (EA)
USAIIA ..... United States Army Imagery Interpretation Agency (AABC)
USAIIC ..... United States Army Imagery Interpretation Center (AABC)
USAILC .... United States Army International Logistics Center
USAILCOM ... United States Army International Logistics
   Command (AABC)
USAILG.... United States Army International Logistics Group (AABC)
USAIMA... United States Army Institute for Military Assistance [*Fort
   Bragg, NC*] (AABC)
USAIMC... United States Army Inventory Management Center (AABC)
USAIMS ... United States Army Institute for Military Systems (AABC)
USAIN....... United States Agricultural Information Network
USA Inc..... Unicycling Society of America, Incorporated (EA)
USAINFHRU ... United States Army Infantry Human Research Unit [*Ft.
   Benning, GA*] (AABC)
USAINSB ... United States Army Intelligence Security Board
USAINSBD ... United States Army Intelligence and Security Board (MCD)
USAINSCOM ... United States Army Intelligence and Security Command
USAINTA ... United States Army Intelligence Agency (AABC)
USAINTB ... United States Army Intelligence Board
USAINTC ... United States Army Intelligence Center
USAINTCA ... United States Army Intelligence Corps Agency
USAINTELMDA ... United States Army Intelligence Materiel Developments
   Agency (AABC)
USAINTS ... United States Army Intelligence School
USAIPSG ... United States Army Industrial and Personnel Security Group
USAIRA ... United States Army Air Attache
USAIRC .... United States Army Ionizing Radiation Center
US Air Force Acad Tech Rep ... US Air Force Academy. Technical Report [*A
   publication*]
US Air Force Aeronaut Syst Div Tech Note ... United States. Air Force.
   Aeronautical Systems. Division Technical Note [*A
   publication*]
US Air Force Aeronaut Syst Div Tech Rep ... US Air Force. Aeronautical
   Systems. Division Technical Report [*A publication*]
US Air Force Cambridge Res Lab Instrum Pap ... United States. Air Force.
   Cambridge Research Laboratories. Instrumentation Papers
   [*A publication*]
US Air Force Cambridge Res Lab Phy Sci Res Pap ... United States. Air
   Force. Cambridge Research Laboratories. Physical Sciences
   Research Papers [*A publication*]
US Air Force Hum Resour Lab Tech Rep AFHRL-TR ... US Air Force.
   Human Resources Laboratory. Technical Report AFHRL-
   TR
US Air Force Syst Command Air Force Flight Dyn Lab Tech Rep ... United
   States. Air Force. Systems Command Air Force Flight
   Dynamics Laboratory. Technical Report [*A publication*]
US Air Force Syst Command Air Force Mater Lab Tech Rep AFML ... United
   States. Air Force. Systems Command Air Force Materials
   Laboratory. Technical Report AFML [*A publication*]
US Air Force Syst Command Res Technol Div Tech Doc Rep ASD ... United
   States. Air Force. Systems Command Research and
   Technology Division. Technical Documentary Report.
   ASD [*A publication*]
US Air Force Tech Doc Rep ... United States. Air Force. Technical
   Documentary Report [*A publication*]
US Air Force Tech Doc Rep AFSWC-TDR ... US Air Force. Technical
   Documentary Report. AFSWC-TDR [*A publication*]
US Air Force Tech Doc Rep AMRL-TDR ... US Air Force. Technical
   Documentary Report. AMRL-TDR [*A publication*]
US Air Force Tech Doc Rep ARL-TDR ... US Air Force. Technical
   Documentary Report. ARL-TDR [*A publication*]
US Air Force Tech Doc Rep ASD-TDR ... US Air Force. Technical
   Documentary Report. ASD-TDR [*A publication*]
US Air Force Tech Doc Rep RTD-TDR ... US Air Force. Technical
   Documentary Report. RTD-TDR [*A publication*]
US Air Force Tech Doc Rep SAM-TDR ... US Air Force. Technical
   Documentary Report. SAM-TDR [*A publication*]
US Air Force Tech Doc Rep SEG-TDR ... US Air Force. Technical
   Documentary Report. SEG-TDR [*A publication*]
US Air Force WADC Tech Rep ... United States. Air Force. Wright Air
   Development Center. Technical Report [*A publication*]
US Air Force Weapons Lab Tech Rep AFWL-TR ... United States. Air Force.
   Weapons Laboratory Technical Report AFWL-TR [*A
   publication*]
US Air Force Wright Air Dev Cent Tech Notes ... US Air Force. Wright Air
   Development Center. Technical Notes [*A publication*]
US Air Force Wright Air Dev Cent Tech Rep ... US Air Force. Wright Air
   Development Center. Technical Report [*A publication*]

USAIRLO ... United States Air Liaison Officer (CINC)
USAIRMILCOMUN ... United States Air Force Representative, UN Military Staff Committee
USAIRR .... United States Army Investigative Records Repository (AABC)
USAIS .... United States Army Infantry School
USAISC ..... United States Army Information Systems Command [*Fort Huachuca, AZ*]
USAISR ..... United States Army Institute of Surgical Research [*Ft. Sam Houston, TX*] (AABC)
USA-ITA ... United States Association of Importers of Textiles and Apparel (EA)
USAITAC ... United States Army Intelligence and Threat Analysis Center (AABC)
USAITAD ... United States Army Intelligence Threat Analysis Detachment
USAITC .... United States Army Intelligence Training Center
USAITFG ... United States Army Intelligence Threats and Forecasts Group (AABC)
USAJAPA ... United States Amateur Jai Alai Players Association (EA)
USAJFKCENMA ... United States Army John Fitzgerald Kennedy Center for Military Assistance (AABC)
USAJFKCENSPWAR ... United States Army John Fitzgerald Kennedy Center for Special Warfare [*Airborne*] (AABC)
USAJHGSOWA ... United States Army Joint Household Goods Shipping Office of the Armed Forces
USAJSC .... United States Army Joint Support Command (AABC)
USAKF ...... USA Karate Federation (EA)
USA-KKA ... USA-Korean Karate Association (EA)
USAKORSCOM ... United States Army Korea Support Command (AABC)
US des AL ... Union Syndicale des Artistes Lyriques [*French*] (ROG)
USALA ...... United States Amateur Lacrosse Association
USALAPA ... United States Army Los Angeles Procurement Agency (AABC)
USALC ..... United States Army Logistics Center
USALCA ... United States Army Logistic Control Activity (AABC)
USALCJ .... United States Army Logistics Center, Japan (AABC)
USALDC ... United States Army Logistics Data Center
USALDJ .... United States Army Logistics Depot, Japan
USALDRHRU ... United States Army Leadership Human Research Unit [*Presidio of Monterey, CA*] (AABC)
USALDSRA ... United States Army Logistics Doctrine, Systems and Readiness Agency [*New Cumberland Army Depot, Harrisburg, PA*] (AABC)
USALEA ... United States Army Logistics Evaluation Agency (AABC)
USALGPM ... United States Army Liaison Group, Project Michigan
USALMC .. United States Army Logistics Management Center [*Fort Lee, VA*]
USALOGC ... United States Army Logistics Center (AABC)
USALS ...... United States Army Language School
USALSA ... United States Army Legal Services Agency (AABC)
USALWL .. United States Army Limited War Laboratory (AABC)
USAM .... Unified Space Applications Mission (MCD)
USAM .... Union des Syndicats Autonomes de Madagascar [*Federation of Malagasy Autonomous Unions*]
USAM .... Unique Sequential Access Method
USAM .... United States Army Mothers Organization, National (EA)
USAM .... United States Automated Mail Service [*Telecommunications*] (TSSD)
USAM .... US Attorney's Manual [*A publication*] (DLA)
USAMAA ... United States Army Memorial Affairs Agency (AABC)
USAMANRRDC ... United States Army Manpower Resources Research and Development Center (AABC)
USAMAPLA ... United States Army Military Assistance Program Logistics Agency
USAMARDA ... US Army Manpower Requirements and Documentation Agency
USAMB ..... United States Army Maintenance Board (AABC)
USAMBRDL ... United States Army Medical Bioengineering Research and Development Laboratory [*Fort Detrick, MD*] [*Later, USABRDL*] (AABC)
USAMBRL ... United States Army Medical Biomechanical Research Laboratory [*Walter Reed Army Medical Center*] (AABC)
USAMC ..... United States Army Materiel Command [*Alexandria, VA*]
USAMC ..... United States Army Medical Corps
USAMC ..... United States Army Missile Command [*Obsolete*]
USAMC ..... United States Army Mobility Command [*Later, Troop Support Command*]
USAMC ..... United States Army Munitions Command [*Later, Armaments Command*]
USAMCALMSA ... United States Army Materiel Command Automated Logistics Management Systems Agency (AABC)
USAMCC ... United States Army Metrology and Calibration Center (AABC)
USAMCFG ... United States Army Medical Center, Fort Gordon (AABC)
USAMCFO ... United States Army Materiel Command Field Office (RDA)
USAMCFSA ... United States Army Materiel Command Field Safety Agency (AABC)
USAMC-IRO ... United States Army Materiel Command Inventory Research Office
USAMCI & SA ... United States Army Materiel Command Installations and Service Agency (AABC)
USAMC-ITC ... United States Army Materiel Command Intern Training Center

USAMCLDC ... United States Army Materiel Command Logistics Data Center
USAMCLSSA ... United States Army Materiel Command Logistic Systems Support Agency (AABC)
USAMCSFO ... United States Army Materiel Command Surety Field Office
USAMD .... United States Army Missile Detachment (AABC)
USAMDAR ... United States Army Medical Depot Activity, Ryukyu Islands (AABC)
USAMDPC ... United States Army Maintenance Data Processing Center
USAMEAF ... United States Army Middle East Air Forces [*World War II*]
USAMEC ... United States Army Mobility Equipment Command [*Obsolete*]
USAMECOM ... United States Army Mobility Equipment Command [*Obsolete*] (AABC)
USAMEDCOMEUR ... United States Army Medical Command, Europe (AABC)
USAMEDDBD ... United States Army Medical Department Board (RDA)
USAMEDLAB ... United States Army Medical Laboratory
USAMEDS ... United States Army Medical Service
USAMEDSVS ... United States Army Medical Service Veterinary School (AABC)
USAMEDTC ... United States Army Medical Training Center [*Ft. Sam Houston, TX*] (AABC)
USAMEERU ... United States Army Medical Environmental Engineering Research Unit
USAMEOS ... United States Army Medical Equipment and Optical School (AABC)
USAMERCC ... United States Army Middle East Regional Communications Command
USAMERDC ... United States Army Mobility Equipment Research and Development Center (AABC)
USAMERDL ... United States Army Medical Equipment Research and Development Laboratory (AABC)
USAMETA ... United States Army Management Engineering Training Activity [*Rock Island, IL*] (AABC)
USAMFSS ... United States Army Medical Field Service School (AABC)
USAMGIK ... United States Army Military Government in Korea
USAMHRC ... United States Army Military History Research Collection (AABC)
USAMICOM ... United States Army Missile Command [*Obsolete*] (AABC)
USAMIDA ... United States Army Major Item Data Agency (AABC)
USAMIIA ... United States Army Medical Intelligence and Information Agency (AABC)
USAML ..... United States Army Medical Laboratory (AABC)
USAMMA ... United States Army Medical Materiel Agency (AABC)
USAMMAE ... United States Army Materiel Management Agency, Europe
USAMMAPAC ... United States Army Medical Materiel Agency, Pacific (AABC)
USAMMC ... United States Army Maintenance Management Center (AABC)
USAMMCS ... United States Army Missile and Munitions Center School (AABC)
USA-MMDA ... US Army Medical Materiel Development Activity (RDA)
USAMMT ... United States Army Military Mail Terminal
USAMN .... United States Army Mothers, National (EA)
USAMOAMA ... United States Army Medical Optical and Maintenance Activity
USAMOCOM ... United States Army Mobility Command [*Later, Troop Support Command*]
USAMOMA ... United States Army Medical Optical and Maintenance Agency (AABC)
USAMP ..... United States Army Maintenance Plant
USAMP ..... United States Army Mine Planter
USAMP & CS/TCTFM ... United States Army Military Police and Chemical Schools/Training Center and Fort McClellan
USAMPHIBFOR ... United States Amphibious Forces (AABC)
USAMPS .. United States Army Military Police School (AABC)
USAMPTAO ... United States Army Military Personnel and Transportation Assistance Office (AABC)
USAMRAA ... United States Army Medical Research Acquisition Agency
USAMRICD ... United States Army Medical Research Institute for Chemical Defense [*Aberdeen Proving Ground, MD*] (RDA)
USAMRIID ... United States Army Medical Research Institute of Infectious Diseases [*Fort Detrick, MD*] (AABC)
USAMRL ... United States Army Medical Research Laboratory [*Fort Knox, KY*] (AABC)
USAMRN ... United States Army Medical Research and Nutrition (MCD)
USAMRNL ... United States Army Medical Research and Nutrition Laboratory [*Denver, CO*] (AABC)
USAMRU ... United States Army Medical Research Unit [*Malaysia, Panama*] (AABC)
USAMRU-E ... United States Army Medical Research Unit - Europe (INF)
USAMS ... United States Army Management School
USAMSAA ... United States Army Materiel Systems Analysis Agency
USAMSMADHS ... United States Army Medical Service Meat and Dairy Hygiene School
USAMSSA ... United States Army Management Systems Support Agency
USAM & TTC ... United States Army Mechanical and Technical Training Center [*Also called MECHTECH*]
USAMTU ... United States Army Marksmanship Training Unit
USAMU .... United States Army Marksmanship Unit [*Fort Benning, GA*]
USAMUCOM ... United States Army Munitions Command [*Later, Armaments Command*]

USAMUFD ... United States Army Medical Unit, Fort Detrick [*Maryland*] (AABC)
USAMV .... United States Association of Museum Volunteers [*Later, AAMV*] (EA)
USAN .... United States Adopted Name [*Drugs*]
USANA ..... United States Army Nuclear Agency (AABC)
USANAFBA ... United States Army, Navy, and Air Force Bandsmen's Association [*Defunct*]
USANAVEUR ... United States Navy, Europe
USANC ..... United States Army Nurse Corps
USANCA ... US Army Nuclear and Chemical Agency (RDA)
USANCG .. United States Army Nuclear Cratering Group (AABC)
USANCSG ... United States Army Nuclear and Chemical Surety Group [*Formerly, USANWSG*] (AABC)
USANDL ... United States Army Nuclear Defense Laboratory (AABC)
USANF ...... United States Auxiliary Naval Force
U San Fernando Valley L Rev ... University of San Fernando Valley. Law Review [*A publication*] (DLA)
U San Fernando VL Rev ... University of San Fernando Valley. Law Review [*A publication*] (DLA)
U San Francisco L Rev ... University of San Francisco. Law Review [*A publication*]
U San Fran LR ... University of San Francisco. Law Review [*A publication*]
U San Fran L Rev ... University of San Francisco. Law Review [*A publication*]
USANG ..... United States Army National Guard
USanGS ..... Church of Jesus Christ of Latter-Day Saints, Genealogical Society Library, Santaquin Stake Branch, Santaquin, UT [*Library symbol*] [*Library of Congress*] (LCLS)
USANIBC ... United States Army Northern Ireland Base Command [*World War II*]
USANIF .... United States Army Northern Ireland Force [*World War II*]
USA-NLABS ... United States Army Natick Laboratories
USANP ...... United South African National Party
USANWCG ... United States Army Nuclear Weapon Coordination Group
USANWSG ... United States Army Nuclear Weapon Surety Group [*Later, USANCSG*]
USANWTC ... United States Army Northern Warfare Training Center (AABC)
USAOAC .. United States Army Ordnance Ammunition Command [*Merged with Munitions Command, which later became Armaments Command*]
USAOCBRL ... United States Army Ordnance Corps Ballistic Research Laboratory
USAOCCCL ... United States Army Ordnance Corps Coating and Chemical Laboratory
USAOCCS ... United States Army Ordnance-Chemical Center and School
USAOCDPS ... United States Army Ordnance Corps Development and Proof Services
USAOC & S ... United States Army Ordnance Center and School [*Later, United States Army Ordnance and Chemical Center and School*] (AABC)
USAOD ..... United States Army Ordnance District
USAOEC ... United States Army Officer Evaluation Center
USAOGMS ... United States Army Ordnance Guided Missile School
USAOMC ... United States Army Ordnance Missile Command [*Later, Missile Command*]
USAOMSA ... United States Army Ordnance Missile Support Agency (AAG)
USAORDCORPS ... United States Army Ordnance Corps
USAORP ... United States Army Oversea Research Program
USAORRF ... United States Army Ordnance Rocket Research Facility
USAOSA ... United States Army Overseas Supply Agency (CINC)
USAOSANO ... United States Army Overseas Supply Agency, New Orleans
USAOSANY ... United States Army Overseas Supply Agency, New York
USAOSASF ... United States Army Overseas Supply Agency, San Francisco
USAOSREPLSTA ... United States Army Oversea Replacement Station
USAOSWAC ... United States Army Ordnance Special Weapons-Ammunition Command
USAOWC ... United States Army Ordnance Weapons Command [*Merged with Missile Command*]
USAP .... United States Antarctic Program [*National Science Foundation*]
US Ap .... United States Appeals Reports [*A publication*] (DLA)
USAPA ... United States Army Photographic Agency [*Obsolete*]
USAPACDA ... United States Army Personnel and Administration Combat Developments Activity (AABC)
USAPAE ... United States Army Procurement Agency, Europe (AABC)
USAPATACE ... United States Army Publications and Training Aids Center, Europe
USAPAV ... United States Army Procurement Agency, Vietnam
USAPC ... United States Army Petroleum Center
USAPC ...... United States Army Pictorial Center
USAPCC ... United States Army Personnel Coordination Center
USAPDA ... United States Army Physical Disability Agency
USAPDC ... United States Army Property Disposal Center [*Merged with Defense Logistics Services Center*]
USAPDCE ... United States Army Petroleum Distribution Command, Europe (AABC)
USAPDSC ... United States Army Personnel Data Support Center (AABC)
USAPDSK ... United States Army Petroleum Distribution System, Korea (AABC)
USAPEB ... United States Army Physical Evaluation Board (AABC)

USAPEQUA ... United States Army Productions Equipment Agency
USAPERSCEN ... United States Army Personnel Center
USAPG ...... United States Army Participation Group (AABC)
USAPHC ... United States Army Primary Helicopter Center (AABC)
USAPHS ... United States Army Primary Helicopter School
USAPIA .... United States Army Personnel Information Activity (AABC)
USAPIC .... United States Army Photointerpretation Center
USAPO ..... United States Antarctic Projects Office
USAPO ..... USA Plowing Organization (EA)
USAPOP ... United States Army Port Operations, Pusan (AABC)
US App ...... United States Appeals Reports [*A publication*] (DLA)
US App (DC) ... United States Court of Appeals Reports (District of Columbia) [*A publication*]
USAPRC ... United States Army Physical Review Council (AABC)
USAPRDC ... United States Army Polar Research and Development Center
USAPRO ... United States Army Personnel Research Office
USAPSG ... United States Army Personnel Security Group (AABC)
USAPT ...... United States Army Parachute Team
USAPWA ... United Stone and Allied Products Workers of America [*Later, USWA*] (EA)
USAQMC ... United States Army Quartermaster Corps [*Merged with Supply and Maintenance Command*]
USAQMCENFL ... United States Army Quartermaster Center and Fort Lee (AABC)
USAQMS ... United States Army Quartermaster School
USAQMTC ... United States Army Quartermaster Training Command
USAR .... Uniform Systems of Accounts and Reports for Certified Air Carriers [*Civil Aeronautics Board*]
USAR .... United States Army Aeronautical Reserve
USAR .... United States Air Army Reserve
USARA ..... United States Air Racing Association [*Formerly, PRPA*] (EA)
USARA ...... US Army Ranger Association (EA)
US-Arab Commer ... US-Arab Commerce [*A publication*]
USARACS ... United States Army Alaska Communications Center
USARADBD ... United States Army Air Defense Board
USARADCOM ... United States Army Air Defense Command
USARADSCH ... United States Army Air Defense School
USARADSCH ... United States Army Research and Development School (AAG)
USARAE ... United States Army Reserve Affairs, Europe (AABC)
USARAL ... United States Army, Alaska
USARB .... United States Army Retraining Brigade (AABC)
USARBCO ... United States Army Base Command, Okinawa (AABC)
USARC ...... United States Army Reserve Center (AABC)
USARCARIB ... United States Army, Caribbean
USARCC ... US Association of Roller Canary Culturists (EA)
USA-RCEC ... USA-Republic of China Economic Council (EA)
USARCEN ... United States Army Records Center
USARCENT ... United States Army Forces, Central Command
USARCPC ... United States Army Reserve Components Personnel Center (AABC)
USARCS ... United States Army Claims Service (AABC)
USARctBad ... United States Army Recruiter Badge [*Military decoration*] (AABC)
USARDA ... United States Army Regional Dental Activity (AABC)
USARDAISA ... United States Army Research, Development, and Acquisition Information Systems Agency (AABC)
USARDL ... United States Army Research and Development Laboratories
USARDORAG ... United States Army Research and Development Operational Research Advisory Group (AABC)
USARDSG-GE ... United States Army Research, Development, and Standardization Group - Germany (RDA)
USAREC ... United States Army Recruiting Command (AABC)
USARECSTA ... United States Army Reception Station
USARENBD ... United States Army Armor and Engineer Board (RDA)
USAREPG ... United States Army Electronic Proving Ground
USARET-RSGSTA ... United States Army Returnee - Reassignment Station
USAREUR ... United States Army, Europe
USAREURAGLO ... United States Army, Europe, Adjutant General Liaison Office (AABC)
USAREURCSTC ... United States Army, Europe, Combat Support Training Center (AABC)
USAREURORDCOM ... United States Army European Ordnance Command
USARF ...... United States Army Reserve Forces
USARFA ... United States of America Rugby Fives Association (EA)
USARFANT ... United States Army Forces, Antilles
USARFEO ... United States Army Frequency Engineering Office (MCD)
USARFT ... United States Army Forces, Taiwan
USARFU ... United States of America Rugby Football Union (EA)
US Argonne Nat Lab Biol Med Res Div Semiannu Rep ... United States. Argonne National Laboratory. Biological and Medical Research Division. Semiannual Report [*A publication*]
US Argonne Natl Lab Rep ... US Argonne National Laboratory. Report [*A publication*]
USARHAW ... United States Army, Hawaii
USARIA .... United States Army Rock Island Arsenal
USARIBSS ... United States Army Research Institute for the Behavioral and Social Sciences (AABC)
USARIEM ... United States Army Research Institute of Environmental Medicine [*Natick, MA*] (AABC)

USARIS..... United States Army Information School [*Fort Slocum, New Rochelle, NY*]

USARJ ...... United States Army, Japan

USARK...... United States Army, Korea (MCD)

USARLANT ... United States Army Forces, Atlantic (AABC)

USARLT ... United States Army Reserve Losses Tally

USARMA ... United States Army Attache

USARMCOM ... United States Army Armament Command

US Armed Forces Food Container Inst Libr Bull ... United States. Armed Forces Food and Container Institute. Library Bulletin [*A publication*]

US Armed Forces Med J ... US Armed Forces. Medical Journal [*A publication*]

US Armed Forc Med J ... United States. Armed Forces Medical Journal [*A publication*]

USARMIS ... United States Army Mission

USARMLO ... United States Army Liaison Officer

USARMY ... Uncle Sam Ain't Released Me Yet

US Army Armament Res Dev Command Tech Rep ... US Army. Armament Research and Development Command. Technical Report [*A publication*]

US Army Behav Sci Res Lab Tech Res Note ... US Army. Behavioral Science Research Laboratory. Technical Research Note [*A publication*]

US Army Behav Syst Res Lab Tech Res Note ... United States. Army. Behavior and Systems Research Laboratory. Technical Research Note [*A publication*]

US Army Behav Syst Res Lab Tech Res Rep ... United States. Army. Behavior and Systems Research Laboratory. Technical Research Report [*A publication*]

US Army Coastal Eng Res Cent Misc Pap ... United States. Army. Coastal Engineering Research Center. Miscellaneous Paper [*A publication*]

US Army Coastal Eng Res Cent Tech Memo ... US Army. Coastal Engineering Research Center. Technical Memorandum [*A publication*]

US Army Corps Eng Cold Reg Res Eng Lab Res Rep ... United States. Army Corps of Engineers. Cold Regions Research and Engineering Laboratory [*Hanover, New Hampshire*]. Research Report [*A publication*]

US Army Corps Eng Cold Reg Res Eng Lab Tech Rep ... United States. Army Corps of Engineers. Cold Regions Research and Engineering Laboratory [*Hanover, New Hampshire*]. Technical Report [*A publication*]

US Army Corps of Engineers Comm Tidal Hydraulics Rept ... United States. Army Corps of Engineers. Committee on Tidal Hydraulics. Report [*A publication*]

US Army Corps Engineers Waterways Expt Sta Misc Paper ... United States. Army Corps of Engineers. Waterways Experiment Station. Miscellaneous Paper [*A publication*]

US Army Corps Engineers Waterways Expt Sta Tech Rept ... United States. Army Corps of Engineers. Waterways Experiment Station. Technical Report [*A publication*]

US Army Diamond Ord Fuze Lab Tech Rep ... US Army. Diamond Ordnance Fuze Laboratories. Technical Report [*A publication*]

US Army Diamond Ordnance Fuze Lab Tech Rep ... United States. Army. Diamond Ordnance Fuze Laboratories. Technical Report [*A publication*]

US Army Eng Waterw Exp Stn Tech Rep ... US Army Engineers. Waterways Experiment Station. Technical Report [*A publication*]

US Army Med Res Lab Rep ... United States. Army. Medical Research Laboratory. Report [*A publication*]

US Army Natick Lab Tech Rep Microbiol Ser ... US Army. Natick Laboratories. Technical Report. Microbiology Series [*A publication*]

USARO ..... United States Army Research Office

USA-ROCEC ... USA-Republic of China Economic Council [*Crystal Lake, IL*] (EA)

USAROD .. United States Army Research Office (Durham)

USAROTC ... United States Army Reserve Officer Training Corps

USAROTCR ... United States Army Reserve Officers' Training Corps Region (AABC)

USARP ...... US Antarctic Research Program (EA)

USARPA ... United States Army Radio Propagation Agency (AABC)

USARPAC ... United States Army, Pacific

USARPACINTS ... United States Army Pacific Intelligence School (AABC)

USARPERCEN ... United States Army Reserve Personnel Center

USARR ...... United States Army Readiness Regions (AABC)

USARRACL ... United States Army Reserve Report Activity Control List

USARRADCOM ... United States Army Armament Research and Development Command (RDA)

USARRED ... United States Army Forces, Readiness Command

USARS ...... US Army Regimental System (INF)

USARSA ... United States Amateur Roller Skating Association [*Later, USAC/RS*] (EA)

USARSA ... United States Army School of the Americas [*Fort Benning, AR*] (INF)

USARSCV ... United States Army Support Command, Vietnam [*Obsolete*]

USARSG ... United States Army Standardization Group

USARSO... United States Army Forces, Southern Command

USARSO-PR ... United States Army Forces, Southern Command - Puerto Rico (AABC)

USARSOUTHCOM ... United States Army Forces, Southern Command

USARSSO ... United States Army Safeguard Systems Office

USARSTRIKE ... United States Army Forces Strike Command (AABC)

USARSUPTHAI ... United States Army Support, Thailand (AABC)

USART ...... Universal Synchronous/Asynchronous Receiver and Transmitter [*Data processing*]

USARTL ... United States Army Research and Technical Labs (MCD)

USARTLS ... United States Army Reserve Troop List by State

USARUCU ... United States Army Reserve Unit Commander Unit

USARV...... United States Army Vietnam [*Obsolete*]

USARYIS ... United States Army, Ryukyu Islands

USAS......... United States Air Service

USAS......... United States Airspace System (NOAA)

USAS......... United States of America Standard (IEEE)

USAS......... United States Antarctic Service [*1939-41*] [*Navy*]

USAS......... US Aquatic Sports (EA)

USAS......... USA Waste Services, Inc. [*NASDAQ symbol*] (NQ)

USASA ... United States Army Security Agency

USASAALA ... United States Army Security Assistance Agency, Latin America (AABC)

USASAC ... United States Army Security Assistance Center

USASAC ... US Army Security Affairs Command (RDA)

USASACDA ... United States Army Security Agency Combat Development Activity (AABC)

USASACDSA ... United States Army Security Agency Command Data Systems Activity (AABC)

USASADEA ... United States Army Signal Air Defense Engineering Agency [*Later, USAADEA*]

USASAE ... United States Army Security Agency, Europe (AABC)

USASAFLOG ... United States Army Safeguard Logistics Command

USASAFO ... United States Army Signal Avionics Field Office [*Later, USAAFO*]

USASAFS ... United States Army Security Agency Field Station

USASAFSCOM ... United States Army Safeguard System Command (AABC)

USASAPAC ... United States Army Security Agency, Pacific (AABC)

USASASA ... United States Army Security Agency Systems Activity (AABC)

USASASA ... United States Army Small Arms Systems Agency

USASASSA ... United States Army Security Agency Signal Security Activity (AABC)

USASATCOMA ... United States Army Satellite Communications Agency (AABC)

USASATC & S ... United States Army Security Agency Training Center and School (AABC)

USASATEC ... United States Army Security Agency Test and Evaluation Center (AABC)

USASATSA ... United States Army Signal Aviation Test Support Activity

USASC ...... United States Army Safety Center

USASC ...... United States Army Signal Corps [*Merged with Communications and Electronics Command*]

USASC ...... United States Army Subsistence Center

USASC ...... United States Army Support Center

USASCA ... United States Army Safeguard Communications Agency (RDA)

USASCAF ... United States Army Service Center for the Armed Forces (AABC)

USASCC ... United States Army Strategic Communications Command

USASC & FG ... United States Army Signal Center and Fort Gordon (AABC)

USASCH... United States Army Support Command, Hawaii (AABC)

USASCHEUR ... United States Army School, Europe [*Obsolete*] (AABC)

USASCII... United States of America Standard Code for Information Interchange

USASCOCR ... United States of America Standard Character Set for Optical Character Recognition [*Data processing*]

USASCR ... United States Army Support Center, Richmond (AABC)

USASCS.... United States Army Signal Center and School

USASCSA ... United States Army Signal Communications Security Agency

USASCSOCR ... United States of America Standard Character Set for Optical Character Recognition [*Data processing*]

USASCV ... United States Army Support Command, Vietnam [*Obsolete*]

USASD...... United States Army Student Detachment (AABC)

USASDC ... United States Army Strategic Defense Command

USASEA ... United States Army Signal Engineering Agency

USASESA ... United States Army Signal Equipment Support Agency (MCD)

USASESS ... United States Army Southeastern Signal School (AABC)

USASETAF ... United States Army Southern European Task Force

USASEUR ... United States Army School, Europe [*Obsolete*]

USASEW .. US Department of Agriculture. Soil Conservation Service. SCS-TP [*A publication*]

USASEXC ... United States Armed Services Exploitation Center (AABC)

USASF ..... United States Army Special Forces (CINC)

USASFG ... United States Army Special Forces Group

USASFGV ... United States Army Special Forces Group, Vietnam

USASFV... United States Army Special Forces, Vietnam [*Obsolete*]

USASG(Aus) ... United States Army Standardization Group (Australia) (AABC)

USASG(Ca) ... United States Army Standardization Group (Canada) (AABC)

USASG(UK) ... United States Army Standardization Group (United Kingdom) (AABC)

USASGV ... United States Army Support Group, Vietnam [*Obsolete*]

USASI .... United States of America Standards Institute [*Formerly, ASA*] [*Later, ANSI*]

USASIGC ... United States Army Signal Corps [*Merged with Communications and Electronics Command*]

USASIGS ... United States Army Signal School   (AABC)

USASIMSA ... United States Army Signal Materiel Support Agency [*Later, USAEMSA*]

USASIS..... United States Army Strategic Intelligence School

USASLE.... Uniform Securities Agent State Law Examination [*Investment term*]

USASMA .. United States Army Sergeant Major Academy   (AABC)

USASMC.. United States Army Supply and Maintenance Command

USASMCOM ... United States Army Supply and Maintenance Command   (MUGU)

USASMSA ... United States Army Signal Materiel Support Agency [*Later, USAEMSA*]

USASOPAC ... United States Army Support Office, Pacific   (AABC)

USASOS ... United States Army Services of Supply

USASPSAE .. United States Army Special Services Agency, Europe   (AABC)

USASPTAP ... United States Army Support Activity, Philadelphia   (AABC)

USASPTC ... United States Army Support Center   (AABC)

USASPTCC ... United States Army Support Command, Chicago

USASPTCM ... United States Army Support Center, Memphis   (AABC)

USASPTCP ... United States Army Support Center, Philadelphia   (AABC)

USASPTCR ... United States Army Support Center, Richmond   (AABC)

USASRDL ... United States Army Signal Research and Development Laboratory [*Later, USAERDL*]

USASRU... United States Army Surgical Research Unit   (AABC)

USASSA.... United States Army Signal Supply Agency [*Later, USAEC*]

USASSAFMPO ... United States Army Signal Supply Agency, Fort Monmouth Procurement Office

USASSAMRO ... United States Army Signal Supply Agency, Midwestern Regional Office

USASSAUSAEPGPO ... United States Army Signal Supply Agency, United States Army Electronic Proving Ground Procurement Office

USASSAWPO ... United States Army Signal Supply Agency, Washington Procurement Office

USASSAWRO ... United States Army Signal Supply Agency, Western Regional Office

USASSC & FBH ... United States Army Soldier Support Center and Fort Benjamin Harrison   (AABC)

USASSD ... United States Army Special Security Detachment

USASSG ... United States Army Special Security Group   (AABC)

USASTAF ... United States Army Southern European Task Force

USASTAF ... United States Army Strategic Air Forces in the Pacific

USASTC ... United States Army Signal Training Center [*Fort Gordon, GA*]

USASTCFM ... United States Army Signal Training Command and Fort Monmouth

USASTRATCOM ... United States Army Strategic Communications Command [*Later, USACC*]   (AABC)

USASTRATCOM-A ... United States Army Strategic Communications Command - Alaska   (AABC)

USASTRATCOM-CONUS ... United States Army Strategic Communications Command - Continental United States   (AABC)

USASTRATCOM-EUR ... United States Army Strategic Communications Command - Europe   (AABC)

USASTRATCOM-PAC ... United States Army Strategic Communications Command - Pacific   (AABC)

USASTRATCOM-SIGGP-T ... United States Army Strategic Communications Command Signal Group - Thailand   (AABC)

USASTRATCOM-SO ... United States Army Strategic Communications Command - South   (AABC)

USASTRATCOM-V ... United States Army Strategic Communications Command - Vietnam [*Obsolete*]   (AABC)

USASUPCOM-CRB ... United States Army Support Command - Cam Ranh Bay [*Obsolete*]   (AABC)

USASUPCOM-QN ... United States Army Support Command - Qui Nhon [*Obsolete*]   (AABC)

USASUPCOM-SGN ... United States Army Support Command - Saigon [*Obsolete*]   (AABC)

USASWL .. United States Army Signals Warfare Laboratory

USASWS... United States Army Special Warfare School

USAT........ United States Army Transport

USATAC.. United States Army Terrain Analysis Center   (MCD)

USATAC... United States Army Training Center, Engineer [*Fort Leonard Wood, MO*]

USATACOM ... United States Army Tank-Automotive Command [*Obsolete*]

USATAFO ... United States Army Transportation Aviation Field Office

USATATSA ... United States Army Transportation Aircraft Test and Support Activity

USATA(WH) ... United States Army Transportation Agency (White House)   (AABC)

USATB...... United States Army Training Board

USATC...... United States Army Topographic Command

USATC...... United States Army Training Center

USATC...... United States Army Transportation Center and School

USATC .... United States Assault Training Center [*World War II*]

USATCA ... United States Army Terminal Command, Atlantic

USATCAD ... United States Army Training Center, Air Defense

USATCARMOR ... United States Army Training Center, Armor [*Fort Knox, KY*]

USATCBASIC ... United States Army Training Center, Basic

USATCD... United States Army Training Center, Air Defense

USATCEFLW ... United States Army Training Center, Engineer, Fort Leonard Wood [*Missouri*]   (AABC)

USATCENGR ... United States Army Training Center, Engineer

USATCEUR ... United States Army Terminal Command, Europe   (AABC)

USATC FA ... United States Army Training Center, Field Artillery [*Fort Sill, OK*]   (AABC)

USATCFE ... United States Army Transportation Center and Fort Eustis   (AABC)

USATCFLW ... United States Army Training Center and Fort Leonard Wood   (AABC)

USATCG... United States Army Terminal Command, Gulf   (AABC)

USATCINF ... United States Army Training Center, Infantry

USATCO... Universal Satellite Corporation [*New York, NY*] [*Telecommunications*]   (TSSD)

USATCO... US Air Traffic Controllers Organization [*Defunct*]   (EA)

USATCP... United States Army Terminal Command, Pacific

USATCRTSA ... United States Army Transportation Corps Road Test Support Activity

USATDA... United States Army Training Device Agency

USATDGL ... United States Army Terminal Detachment, Great Lakes   (AABC)

USATEA... United States Army Transportation Engineering Agency   (AABC)

USATEC... United States Army Test and Evaluation Command [*Obsolete*]

USATECOM ... United States Army Test and Evaluation Command [*Obsolete*]

USATHAMA ... United States Army Toxic and Hazardous Materials Agency   (RDA)

USATIA.... United States Army Transportation Intelligence Agency

USATL.... United States Army Technical Library   (DIT)

USATLA ... USA Toy Library Association   (EA)

USATMACE ... United States Army Traffic Management Agency, Central Europe   (AABC)

USATMC ... United States Army Transportation Materiel Command

USATMC ... United States Army Troop Medical Clinic   (AABC)

US Atom Energy Commn Pub ... US Atomic Energy Commission. Publication [*A publication*]

US Atomic Energy Comm Map Prelim Map ... United States. Atomic Energy Commission. Map. Preliminary Map [*A publication*]

US Atomic Energy Comm Rept ... US Atomic Energy Commission. Report [*A publication*]

USATOPOCOM ... United States Army Topographic Command   (AABC)

USATOWA ... United States Amateur Tug of War Association   (EA)

USATRADOC ... United States Army Training and Doctrine Command

USATRASANA ... United States Army TRADOC Systems Analysis Activity   (AABC)

USATRC... United States Army Transportation Research Command

USATRECOM ... United States Army Transportation Research and Engineering Command

USATREOG ... United States Army Transportation Environmental Operations Group   (AABC)

USATRFSTA ... United States Army Transfer Station

USATRML ... United States Army Tropical Research Medical Laboratory

USATROSCOM ... United States Army Troop Support Command

USATSA ... United States Army Technical Support Activity   (AABC)

USATSC ... United States Army Terrestrial Sciences Center   (AABC)

USATSC ... United States Army Training Support Center

USATSCH ... United States Army Transportation School

USATSG ... United States Army TMDE [*Test, Measurement, and Diagnostic Equipment*] Support Group

USATT ...... Union des Syndicats Autonomes des Travailleurs Tchadiens [*Federation of Autonomous Workers Unions of Chad*]

USATTAY ... United States Army Transportation Test Activity, Yuma [*Arizona*]   (AABC)

USATTB ... United States Army Transportation Terminal, Brooklyn

USATTC ... United States Army Transportation Training Command

USATTC ... United States Army Tropic Test Center   (AABC)

USATTCA ... United States Army Transportation Terminal Command, Atlantic

USATTCARC ... United States Army Transportation Terminal Command, Arctic

USATTCG ... United States Army Transportation Terminal Command, Gulf

USATTCP ... United States Army Transportation Terminal Command, Pacific

USATTU... United States Army Transportation Terminal Unit   (AABC)

USATUC... United States Army Terminal Unit, Canaveral   (AABC)

USAUD3 ... US Air Force Academy. Technical Report [*A publication*]

US Auto Ind ... Structural Change in the United States Automobile Industry [*A publication*]

USAV .... United Savings Life Insurance [*NASDAQ symbol*]   (NQ)

US Av... United States Aviation Reports [*A publication*]   (DLA)

USAVA... USA Victory Alliance   (EA)

USAVETS ... United States Army Veterinary School

US Aviation Rep ... United States Aviation Reports [*A publication*]   (DLA)

US Avi Rep ... United States Aviation Reports [*A publication*]   (DLA)

US Av R..... United States Aviation Reports [*A publication*]   (DLA)
USAW .... Underwater Security Advance Warnings [*Navy*]
USAWC..... United States Army War College
USAWC..... United States Army Weapons Command [*Later, Armaments Command*]
USAWECOM ... United States Army Weapons Command [*Later, Armaments Command*]   (AABC)
USAWES .. United States Army Waterways Experiment Station   (AABC)
USAWF..... United States Amateur Wrestling Foundation   (EA)
USAWOA ... United States Army Warrant Officers Association   (EA)
USB .... Unified S-Band   (MCD)
USB .... United Society of Brushmakers [*A union*] [*British*]
USB .... United States Banker [*A publication*]
USB .... United States Bases [*British*] [*World War II*]
USB .... Universal Serials and Book Exchange, Inc. [*ACCORD*] [*UTLAS symbol*]
USB .... Upflow Sludge Blanket [*Reactor, wastewater treatment*]
USB .... Upper Sideband
USB .... Upper Surface Blown [*Jet flap*] [*Aviation*]
USB .... US Bass   (EA)
USB .... Uspechi Sovremennoj Biologii [*A publication*]
USBA........ Union Syndicale des Bases Americaines [*Union of American Base Workers*] [*Morocco*]
USBA........ United Savings Bank [*Salem, OR*] [*NASDAQ symbol*]   (NQ)
USBA........ United States Badminton Association   (EA)
USBA........ United States Bartenders Association   (EA)
USBA........ United States Boardsailing Association   (EA)
USBA........ United States Brewers Association [*Defunct*]   (EA)
USBA........ US Base Association   (EA)
USBA........ US Biathlon Association   (EA)
USBA........ US Boomerang Association   (EA)
US Banker ... United States Banker [*A publication*]
USBATU ... United States - Brazil Aviation Training Unit
USBBC...... United States Beef Breeds Council   (EA)
USBBS ...... United States Bureau of Biological Survey [*Terminated, 1940; later, Fish and Wildlife Service*]
USBBY...... US Board on Books for Young People   (EA)
USBC........ United States Bureau of the Census   (OICC)
USBC........ US Bancorp [*NASDAQ symbol*]   (NQ)
USBCA...... United States Braille Chess Association   (EA)
USBCC...... United States Border Collie Club   (EA)
USBCJ....... US Business Committee on Jamaica [*New York, NY*]   (EA)
USBE........ Unified S-Band Equipment
USBE........ Universal Serials and Book Exchange, Inc. [*Acronym now used as official name of association*]   (EA)
US Beach Erosion Board Bull Tech Memo Tech Rept ... United States. Beach Erosion Board. Bulletin. Technical Memorandum. Technical Report [*A publication*]
USBEP ...... United States Bureau of Engraving and Printing
USBER...... United States Mission, Berlin
USBF........ United States Baseball Federation   (EA)
USBF........ United States Bocce Federation   (EA)
USBF........ United States Brewers Foundation [*Later, USBA*]
USBF........ United States Bureau of Fisheries [*Terminated*]
USBF........ US Bobsled and Skeleton Federation   (EA)
USBFA ...... US Bass Fishing Association [*Later, USB*]   (EA)
USBFDC ... United States Bureau of Foreign and Domestic Commerce
USBG .... United States Bartenders Guild [*Later, USBA*]   (EA)
USBG .... United States Botanic Garden
USBGA...... United States Blind Golfer's Association   (EA)
USBGN ..... United States Bureau on Geographical Names [*Terminated, 1947; later, Board on Geographical Names*]
USBIA .... United States Bowling Instructors Association   (EA)
USBIA .... United States Bureau of Insular Affairs
USBIA .... Uspekhi Sovremennoi Biologii [*A publication*]
USBIC....... United States Business and Industrial Council [*Washington, DC*]   (EA)
USBISS ..... United Society of Boilermakers and Iron and Steel Shipbuilders [*A union*] [*British*]
USBJA ...... United States Barrel Jumping Association   (EA)
USBK........ United Savings Bank [*Vienna, VA*] [*NASDAQ symbol*]   (NQ)
USBL........ United States Bureau of Lighthouses
USBL........ Usable   (FAAC)
USBLM...... United States Bureau of Land Management [*Department of the Interior*]
USBLS....... United States Bureau of Labor Statistics
USBM .... United States Bureau of Mines [*Department of the Interior*]
USBMG .... United States Berlin Mission in Germany
USBN .... United States Bureau of Navigation
USBNP...... United States Bureau of Navy Personnel [*Terminated*]
USBP........ United States Border Patrol [*Department of the Treasury*]
USBP........ USBANCORP, Inc. [*NASDAQ symbol*]   (NQ)
USBPA ...... United States Bicycle Polo Association   (EA)
USBPR ...... United States Bureau of Public Roads
USBR........ United States Bureau of Reclamation [*Department of the Interior*] [*See also BOR*]
USBRO...... United States Base Requirements Overseas [*Military*]   (AABC)
USBS........ Unified S-Band System [*Radio*]
USBS........ United States Bureau of Standards
USBSA ...... United States Beet Sugar Association   (EA)
USBSA ...... United States Boardsailing Association   (EA)

USBSF....... US Bobsled and Skeleton Federation   (EA)
USBSSW... United Society of Boilermakers, Shipbuilders, and Structural Workers [*A union*] [*British*]
USBTA...... United States Board of Tax Appeals [*Later, the Tax Court of the United States*]
USBTC...... University-Small Business Technology Consortium   (EA)
USBTC...... US Battery Trade Council
US Bur Am Ethnology Bull ... US Bureau of American Ethnology. Bulletin [*A publication*]
US Bur Commer Fish Rep Cal Year ... US Bureau of Commercial Fisheries. Report for the Calendar Year [*A publication*]
US Bureau Sport Fish Wildl Invest Fish Control ... US Bureau of Sport Fisheries and Wildlife. Investigations in Fish Control [*A publication*]
USBurEducBul ... United States. Bureau of Education. Bulletins [*A publication*]
USBurEducCirc ... United States. Bureau of Education. Circulars [*A publication*]
US Bur Mines Bull ... United States. Bureau of Mines. Bulletin [*A publication*]
US Bur Mines Inf Circ ... US Bureau of Mines. Information Circular [*A publication*]
US Bur Mines Inform Circ ... United States. Bureau of Mines. Information Circular [*A publication*]
US Bur Mines Miner Yearb ... United States. Bureau of Mines. Minerals Yearbook [*A publication*]
US Bur Mines New Publ ... United States. Bureau of Mines. New Publications Monthly List [*A publication*]
US Bur Mines Rep Invest ... United States. Bureau of Mines. Report of Investigations [*A publication*]
US Bur Mines Rept Inv ... US Bureau of Mines. Report of Investigations [*A publication*]
US Bur Mines Tech Pa ... United States. Bureau of Mines. Technical Paper [*A publication*]
US Bur Mines Tech Prog Rep ... United States. Bureau of Mines. Technical Progress Report [*A publication*]
US Bur Reclam Div Des Dams Br Rep ... United States. Department of the Interior. Bureau of Reclamation. Division of Design [*Denver, Colorado*]. Dams Branch Report [*A publication*]
US Bur Reclam Eng Monogr ... United States. Department of the Interior. Bureau of Reclamation. Engineering Monographs [*A publication*]
US Bur Reclam Res Rep ... United States. Department of the Interior. Bureau of Reclamation. Research Report [*A publication*]
US Bur Reclam Tech Rec Des Constr ... United States. Department of the Interior. Bureau of Reclamation. Technical Record of Design and Construction. Dams and Powerplants [*A publication*]
US Bur Soils B ... US Bureau of Soils. Bulletin [*A publication*]
US Bur Sport Fish Wildl Invest Fish Control ... United States. Bureau of Sport Fisheries and Wildlife. Investigations in Fish Control [*A publication*]
US Bur Sport Fish Wildl Resour Publ ... United States. Bureau of Sport Fisheries and Wildlife. Resource Publication [*A publication*]
US Bur Sport Fish Wildl Res Rep ... US Bureau of Sport Fisheries and Wildlife. Research Report [*A publication*]
US Bur Sport Fish Wildl Tech Pap ... US Bureau of Sport Fisheries and Wildlife. Technical Papers [*A publication*]
USBWA..... United States Basketball Writers Association   (EA)
USC .... Ultrasonic Storage Cell
USC .... Under Separate Cover
USC .... Union of Sephardic Congregations   (EA)
USC .... Union Sociale Camerounaise [*Cameroonese Social Union*]
USC .... Unitarian Service Committee [*Later, UUSC*] [*Post-World War II*]
USC .... United Satellite Communications [*Cable TV programming service*]
USC .... United Service Club [*Charter jet service to Europe for servicemen and dependents*]
USC .... United Sisters of Charity   (EA)
USC .... United States Catalog [*A bibliographic publication*]
USC .... United States Citizen
USC .... United States Code [*Legal term*]
USC .... United States of Colombia
USC .... United States Congress
USC .... United States Custom Service, Washington, DC [*OCLC symbol*]   (OCLC)
USC .... United States Customs
USC .... United States Strasser Club
USC .... United Survival Clubs   (EA)
USC .... Universal Specimen Chamber
USC .... University of Santa Clara [*California*]
USC .... University Scholarships of Canada
USC .... University of South Carolina [*Columbia, SC*]
USC .... University of Southern California [*Los Angeles*] [*Seismograph station code, US Geological Survey*]   (SEIS)
USC .... University of Southern California [*Los Angeles, CA*]
USC .... University Statistics Center [*New Mexico State University*] [*Research center*]   (RCD)
USC .... Up Stage Center [*Away from audience*] [*A stage direction*]

USC	User Service Center (MCD)
USC	User Support Center (MCD)
USC	USLICO Corporation [*NYSE symbol*] (SPSG)
USCA	Under Secretary for Civil Aviation
USCA	Uniformed Services Contingency Act
USCA	United Sidecar Association (EA)
USCA	United States Canoe Association (EA)
USCA	United States Code Annotated [*Law*] [*Based on official USC*]
USCA	United States Copper Association [*Later, American Bureau of Metal Statistics*] (EA)
USCA	United States Courts of Appeals
USCA	United States Croquet Association (EA)
USCA	United States Curling Association (EA)
USCA	US Canola Association (EA)
USCAA	United States Corporate Athletics Association (EA)
USCA App ...	United States Code, Annotated, Appendix [*A publication*] (DLA)
USCAB	United States Congressional Advisory Board (EA)
USCAC	United States Continental Army Command [*Superseded by FORSCOM*]
USCAD	University of Southern California. Abstracts of Dissertations [*A publication*]
USCAL	University of Southern California, Aeronautical Laboratory (MCD)
US Cal Sch L Tax Inst ...	University of Southern California School of Law Tax Institute (DLA)
USCAM	United States Civil Aviation Mission (AFM)
US & Can Av ...	United States and Canadian Aviation Reports [*A publication*]
USCANS ...	Unified S-Band Communication and Navigation System [*NASA*]
USCANW ...	US Committee Against Nuclear War (EA)
USCAPP ...	Advanced Professional Programs, University of Southern California Law Center (DLA)
USC App ...	United States Code Appendix [*A publication*] (DLA)
USCAR	United States Civil Administration, Ryukyu Islands
US Cath	United States Catholic [*A publication*]
US Cath Hist Rec ...	US Catholic Historical Society. Historical Records and Studies [*A publication*]
US Cath M ...	United States Catholic Magazine [*A publication*]
US Cath S ...	United States Catholic Historical Society. Historical Records and Studies [*A publication*]
US & C Avi Rep ...	United States and Canadian Aviation Reports [*A publication*]
US & C Av R ...	United States and Canadian Aviation Reports [*A publication*]
USCB	United States Customs Bonded
USCBC	US-China Business Council (EA)
USCBRA ...	United States CB Radio Association (EA)
USCC	Union des Syndicats Croyants du Cameroun [*Federation of Cameroonese Believers' Unions*]
USCC	United Society of Cork Cutters [*A union*] [*British*]
USCC	United States Calorimetry Conference
USCC	United States Camaro Club (EA)
USCC	United States Catholic Conference (EA)
USCC	United States Cellular Corporation [*Park Ridge, IL*] [*Telecommunications*] (TSSD)
USCC	United States Chamber of Commerce
USCC	United States Circuit Court
USCC	United States Citizens' Congress [*Defunct*]
USCC	United States Commerical Company [*World War II*]
USCC	United States Cotton Commission
USCC	United States Court of Claims [*Abolished, 1982*]
USCC	United States Criminal Code
USCC	United States Criminal Court
USCC	United States Customs Court [*Later, United States Court of International Trade*]
USCC	United Student Christian Council in United States
USCC	US Cancellation Club (EA)
USCC	US Capital Corporation [*NASDAQ symbol*] (NQ)
USCCA	United States Circuit Court of Appeals
USCCA	United States Circuit Court of Appeals Reports [*A publication*] (DLA)
USCCCA ...	United States Cross Country Coaches Association (EA)
USCCEC ...	United States Committee for Care of European Children [*Post-World War II*]
USCCHO ..	United States Conference of City Health Officers (EA)
USCCHSO ...	United States Conference of City Human Service Officials (EA)
USCCPA ...	United States Court of Customs and Patent Appeals [*Abolished, 1982*]
USCCSA ...	US Corporate Council on South Africa (EA)
USCDC	United States Civil Defense Council (EA)
USCEA	US Council for Energy Awareness (EA)
USCEC	University of Southern California, Engineering Center (MCD)
USCEF	US-China Education Foundation (EA)
USCEFI	United Social, Cultural, and Educational Foundation of India
USCEI	United States - China Educational Institute (EA)
US Cem Frct ...	United States Cement Consumption Forecast 1981-86. Market and Economic Research [*A publication*]
USCE/NPD ...	United States Army, Corps of Engineers, North Pacific Division (NOAA)

USCENTAF ...	United States Central Command - Air Forces
USCENTCOM ...	United States Central Command
US Cert Den ...	Certiorari Denied by United States Supreme Court [*Legal term*] (DLA)
US Cert Dis ...	Certiorari Dismissed by United States Supreme Court [*Legal term*] (DLA)
USCESS	US Cultural Exchange and Sports Society (EA)
USCF	United States Chess Federation (EA)
USCF	United States Churchill Foundation [*Later, WCF*]
USCF	United States Cycling Federation (EA)
USCFSTI AD Rep ...	United States. Clearinghouse for Federal Scientific and Technical Information. AD Reports [*A publication*]
USCFSTI PB Rep ...	United States. Clearinghouse for Federal Scientific and Technical Information. PB Report [*A publication*]
USC & G....	United States Coast and Geodetic Survey [*Later, National Ocean Survey*] (MUGU)
USCG	United States Coast Guard
USCG	United States Consul General
USCGA	United States Coast Guard Academy [*New London, CT*]
USCGA	United States Coast Guard Auxiliary
USCGAD...	United States Coast Guard Air Detachment
USC-GARP ...	United States Committee for the Global Atmospheric Research Program [*Defunct*] (EA)
USCGAS ...	United States Coast Guard Air Station
USCGASB ...	United States Coast Guard Aircraft and Supply Base
USCGAUX ...	United States Coast Guard Auxiliary (EA)
USCGB......	United States Coast Guard Base
USCG-B	United States Coast Guard Office of Boating Safety
USCGC......	United States Coast Guard Cutter
USCG-C	United States Coast Guard Office of Chief of Staff
USCGD	United States Coast Guard Depot
USC Gov'l Rev ...	University of South Carolina. Governmental Review [*A publication*] (DLA)
USCGR......	United States Coast Guard Reserve
USCGRC....	United States Coast Guard Receiving Center
USCGR(T) ...	United States Coast Guard, Reserve (Temporary)
USCGR(W) ...	United States Coast Guard, Reserve (Women)
USC & GS ...	United States Coast and Geodetic Survey [*Later, National Ocean Survey*]
USCGS......	United States Coast and Geodetic Survey [*Later, National Ocean Survey*]
USCGSCF ...	United States Coast Guard Shore Communication Facilities
USCGTS ...	United States Coast Guard Training Station
USCH	University of South Carolina Herbarium
US Chil Bur Pub ...	United States. Children's Bureau. Publications [*A publication*]
US China Bus R ...	US-China Business Review [*Washington, DC*] [*A publication*]
USCHRB...	US Council for Human Rights in the Balkans (EA)
USCHS......	United States Capitol Historical Society (EA)
USCHS......	US Catholic Historical Society (EA)
USCI.........	United Satellite Communications Incorporated
USCIA	United States Customs Inspectors' Association Port of New York (EA)
USCIAA	United States Committee of the International Association of Art (EA)
USCIB	United States Communications Intelligence Board [*Later, National Security Agency*]
USCIB	United States Council for International Business (EA)
USCIB/IC ...	United States Communications Intelligence Board Intelligence Committee [*Obsolete*]
USCICC ...	United States Council of the International Chamber of Commerce [*Later, USCIB*] (EA)
USCICSW ...	United States Committee of the International Council on Social Welfare (EA)
USCID	US Committee on Irrigation and Drainage (EA)
USCIDFC ...	US Committee on Irrigation, Drainage, and Flood Control [*Later, USCID*] (EA)
USCIIC......	United States Civilian Internee Information Center [*Army*] (AABC)
USCIIC(Br) ...	United States Civilian Internee Information Center (Branch) [*Army*] (AABC)
USCINCAFRED ...	United States Commander-in-Chief, Air Force Forces, Readiness Command
USCINCARRED ...	United States Commander-in-Chief, Army Forces, Readiness Command
USCINCCENT ...	Commander-in-Chief, United States Central Command
USCINCEUR ...	United States Commander-in-Chief, Europe
USCINCLANT ...	Commander-in-Chief, United States Atlantic Command
USCINCPAC ...	Commander-in-Chief, United States Pacific Command
USCINCRED ...	United States Commander-in-Chief, Readiness Command
USCINCREDCOM ...	Commander-in-Chief, US Readiness Command (MCD)
USCINCSO ...	United States Commander-in-Chief, Southern Command (AFM)
US Cir Ct Rep DC ...	Hayward and Hazelton's United States Circuit Court Reports [*District of Columbia*] [*A publication*] (DLA)
USCISCO ...	United States Counterinsurgency Support Office
USCJ	United Society of Carpenters and Joiners [*A union*] [*British*]
USCJE.......	United Synagogue Commission on Jewish Education [*Later, USACJE*] (EA)

USCL......... United Society for Christian Literature [*British*]
USCL........ United States Coalition for Life (EA)
USCLA...... United States Club Lacrosse Association (EA)
USCLHO .. United States Conference of Local Health Officers (EA)
USCM .... Unit Simulated Combat Mission (AAG)
USCM .... United States Conference of Mayors (EA)
USCM .... Usibelli Coal Miner [*Usibelli, AK*] [*A publication*]
USCMA..... United States Catholic Mission Association (EA)
USCMA..... United States Cheese Makers Association (EA)
USCMA..... United States Court of Military Appeals
USCMA..... United States Crutch Manufacturers Association (EA)
USCMA Adv Op ... United States Court of Military Appeals, Advance
          Opinions [*A publication*] (DLA)
USCMC..... United States Catholic Mission Council (EA)
USCMH .... United States Commission of Maritime History (MSC)
USCMI...... United States Commission on Mathematical Instruction
USCO .... United States Committee for the Oceans (EA)
USCO .... US Commercial Office [*Department of Commerce, Department
          of State*] (IMH)
USCOA ..... Uniformed Services Contingency Option Act
US Coast and Geod Survey Pub ... US Coast and Geodetic Survey. Publication
          [*A publication*]
US Coast Geod Surv Magnetograms Hourly Values MHV ... US Department
          of Commerce. Coast and Geodetic Survey. Magnetograms
          and Hourly Values MHV [*A publication*]
USCOB...... United States Commander, Berlin
US Code Cong & Ad News ... United States Code Congressional and
          Administrative News [*A publication*] (DLA)
USCOLD... United States Committee on Large Dams of the International
          Commission on Large Dams (EA)
USCOMEAST ... United States Commander, Eastern Atlantic (MCD)
USCOMEASTLANT ... United States Commander, Naval Forces, Eastern
          Atlantic (NATG)
US Comp St ... United States Compiled Statutes [*A publication*] (DLA)
USCOMSUBGRUEASTLANT ... United States Commander, Submarines
          Group, Eastern Atlantic (NATG)
USCONARC ... United States Continental Army Command [*Superseded by
          FORSCOM*]
US Cond Rep ... Peters' Condensed United States Reports [*A
          publication*] (DLA)
US Const.... United States Constitution [*A publication*] (DLA)
US Consum Marketing Serv C & MS ... US Consumer and Marketing Service.
          C & MS [*A publication*]
USCP........ United States Capitol Police
USCPAA ... United States Cerebral Palsy Athletic Association (EA)
USCPFA.... US-China Peoples Friendship Association (EA)
USCPSHHM ... United States Committee to Promote Studies of the History
          of the Habsburg Monarchy [*Later, SAHH*] (EA)
USCR........ United States Committee for Refugees (EA)
USCR........ US Census Report [*Database*] [*Business Publishers, Inc.*]
          [*Information service or system*] (CRD)
USCRA...... United States Citizens' Rights Association (EA)
USCS........ United States Coast Survey
USCS........ United States Code Service [*A publication*] (DLA)
USCS........ United States Commercial Standard
USCS........ United States Conciliation Service [*Functions transferred to
          Federal Mediation and Conciliation Service, 1947*]
USCS........ United States Customary System [*System of units used in the
          US*]
USCS........ United States Customs Service (MCD)
USCS........ Universal Ship Cancellation Society (EA)
USCS........ Urine Sampling and Collection System [*NASA*]
USCS........ US Commercial Service [*International Trade Administration*]
USCSB...... United States Communications Security Board
USCSC...... United States Chefs Ski Club (EA)
USCSC...... United States Civil Service Commission [*Later, MSPB*]
USCSC...... United States Collegiate Sports Council (EA)
USCSC...... United States Cuban Sugar Council [*Defunct*] (EA)
USC/SCC ... Studies in Comparative Communism. University of Southern
          California [*A publication*]
USCSCV ... US Committee for Scientific Cooperation with Vietnam (EA)
USCSE ...... United States Civil Service Examination
USC-SFI.... United States Committee-Sports for Israel (EA)
USCSRA .... United States Cane Sugar Refiners' Association (EA)
USCSSB.... United States Cap Screw Service Bureau [*Later, Cap Screw and
          Special Threaded Products Bureau*] (EA)
USCT......... Union des Syndicats Confederes du Togo [*Federation of
          Confederated Unions of Togo*]
USCT........ United States Colored Troops [*Civil War*]
USCTA...... United States Combined Training Association (EA)
US Ct Cl ... United States Court of Claims (DLA)
US-CUES ... US Campaign for the University of El Salvador (EA)
USCUN ..... United States Committee for the United Nations [*Later, UNA-
          USA*]
USCV........ Union Scientifique Continentale de Verre [*European Union for
          the Scientific Study of Glass - EUSSG*] (EAIO)
USCWC..... United States Chemical Warfare Committee
USCWCC.. United States Conference for the World Council of
          Churches (EA)
USCWF ..... US Council for World Freedom (EA)

USC-WHO ... United States Committee for the World Health
          Organization (EA)
USD .... Ultimate Strength Design (IEEE)
USD .... Ultrasonic Separation Detector
USD .... Under Seas Defense Exposition (ITD)
USD .... Uniao Social Democratico [*Social Democratic Union*]
          [*Portugal*] [*Political party*] (PPE)
USD .... Unified School District
USD .... United Society of Drillers [*A union*] [*British*]
USD .... United States Dispensatory [*Pharmacology*]
USD .... United States Diving, Inc. (EA)
USD .... United States Dollars
USD .... Universal Standard Data
USD .... University Science Development [*National Science
          Foundation*]
USD .... University of South Dakota [*Vermillion, SD*]
USD .... University of South Dakota, Vermillion, SD [*OCLC
          symbol*] (OCLC)
USD .... Uranium Series Dating
USD .... Urban Sanitary District [*British*]
USD .... User-Supplied Data
USDA .... Uniform Simultaneous Death Act [*National Conference of
          Commissioners on Uniform State Laws*]
USDA .... United Square Dancers of America (EA)
USDA .... United States Department of Agriculture [*Washington, DC*]
          [*Database originator*]
USDA .... United States Disarmament Administration [*Transferred to US
          Arms Control and Disarmament Agency, 1961*]
USDA .... United States Duffers' Association (EA)
USDA .... US Darting Association (EA)
USDA .... US Disc Sports Association (EA)
USDA Agr Econ Rep ... US Department of Agriculture. Agricultural
          Economic Report [*A publication*]
USDA Agr Handb ... United States. Department of Agriculture. Agricultural
          Handbook [*A publication*]
USDA Bur Biol Surv Bull ... US Department of Agriculture. Bureau of
          Biological Survey. Bulletin [*A publication*]
USDA Fert ... US Department of Agriculture. Fertilizer Supply [*A
          publication*]
USDA For Ser Res Bull PNW US Pac Northwest For Range Exp Stn ...
          USDA [*United States Department of Agriculture*]. Forest
          Service. Resource Bulletin PNW-United States. Pacific
          Northwest Forest and Range Experiment Station [*A
          publication*]
USDA For Ser Res Pap PSW US Pac Southwest For Range Exp Stn ... USDA
          [*United States Department of Agriculture*]. Forest Service.
          Research Paper PSW-United States. Pacific Southwest
          Forest and Range Experiment Station [*A publication*]
USDA For Serv Gen Tech Rep INT Intermt For Range Exp Stn ... USDA
          [*United States Department of Agriculture*]. Forest Service.
          General Technical Report INT-United States.
          Intermountain Forest and Range Experiment Station [*A
          publication*]
USDA For Serv Gen Tech Rep NC US North Cent For Exp Stn ... USDA
          [*United States Department of Agriculture*]. Forest Service.
          General Technical Report NC-United States. North Central
          Forest Experiment Station [*A publication*]
USDA For Serv Gen Tech Rep NE NE For Exp Stn ... USDA [*United States
          Department of Agriculture*]. Forest Service. General
          Technical Report NE-United States. Northeastern Forest
          Experiment Station [*A publication*]
USDA For Serv Gen Tech Rep PSW US Pac Southwest For Exp Stn ... USDA
          [*United States Department of Agriculture*]. Forest Service.
          General Technical Report PSW-United States. Pacific
          Southwest Forest and Range Experiment Station [*A
          publication*]
USDA For Serv Gen Tech Rep SE US Southeast For Exp Stn ... USDA
          [*United States Department of Agriculture*]. Forest Service.
          General Technical Report SE-United States. Southeastern
          Forest Experiment Station [*A publication*]
USDA For Serv Res Note FPL US For Prod Lab ... USDA [*United States
          Department of Agriculture*]. Forest Service. Research Note
          FPL-United States. Forest Products Laboratory [*A
          publication*]
USDA For Serv Res Note ITF Inst Trop For ... USDA [*United States
          Department of Agriculture*]. Forest Service. Research Note
          ITF-United States. Institute of Tropical Forestry [*A
          publication*]
USDA For Serv Res Note (PNW) ... USDA [*United States Department of
          Agriculture*]. Forest Service. Research Note (Pacific
          Northwest) [*A publication*]
USDA For Serv Res Note PSW US Pac Southwest For Range Exp St ...
          USDA [*United States Department of Agriculture*]. Forest
          Service. Research Note PSW-United States. Pacific
          Southwest Forest and Range Experiment Station [*A
          publication*]
USDA For Serv Res Note RM US Rocky Mt For Range Exp Stn ... USDA
          [*United States Department of Agriculture*]. Forest Service.
          Research Note RM-United States. Rocky Mountain Forest
          and Range Experiment Station [*A publication*]

USDA For Serv Res Note SE US Southeast For Exp Stn ... USDA [*United States Department of Agriculture*]. Forest Service. Research Note SE-United States. Southeastern Forest Experiment Station [*A publication*]

USDA For Serv Resour Bull NC US North Cent For Exp Stn ... USDA [*United States Department of Agriculture*]. Forest Service. Resource Bulletin NC-United States. North Central Forest Experiment Station [*A publication*]

USDA For Serv Res Pap INT US Intermt For Range Exp Stn ... USDA [*United States Department of Agriculture*]. Forest Service. Research Paper INT-United States. Intermountain Forest and Range Experiment Station [*A publication*]

USDA For Serv Res Pap NC US North Cent For Exp Stn ... USDA [*United States Department of Agriculture*]. Forest Service. Research Paper NC-United States. North Central Forest Experiment Station [*A publication*]

USDA For Serv Res Pap NE US Northeast For Exp Stn ... USDA [*United States Department of Agriculture*]. Forest Service. Research Paper NE-United States. Northeastern Forest Experiment Station [*A publication*]

USDA For Serv Res Pap (PNW) ... USDA [*United States Department of Agriculture*]. Forest Service. Research Paper (Pacific Northwest) [*A publication*]

USDA For Serv Res Pap RM US Rocky Mt For Range Exp Stn ... USDA [*United States Department of Agriculture*]. Forest Service. Research Paper RM-United States. Rocky Mountain Forest and Range Experiment Station [*A publication*]

USDA For Serv Res Pap SO ... USDA [*United States Department of Agriculture*]. Forest Service. Research Paper SO [*A publication*]

USDA-FSVP ... USDA-Forest Service Volunteers Program   (EA)

USDAO..... United States Defense Attache Office [*or Officer*]   (AABC)

USDA PA ... United States. Department of Agriculture. PA [*Program Aid*] [*A publication*]

USDA Prod Res Rep ... United States. Department of Agriculture. Production Research Report [*A publication*]

USDA RDD ... USDA [*United States Department of Agriculture*] Regional Document Delivery [*Library network*]

USDASL... USDA [*United States Department of Agriculture*] Sedimentation Laboratory [*Research center*]   (RCD)

USDAW .... Union of Ship Distributive and Allied Workers [*British*]   (DCTA)

USDB .... United States Disciplinary Barracks [*Military*]

USDC .... Underwater Search, Detection, Classification   (AAG)

USDC .... United States Defense Committee   (EA)

USDC .... United States Department of Commerce

USDC .... United States District of Columbia   (DLA)

USDC .... United States District Court

USDC .... US Design Corporation [*NASDAQ symbol*]   (NQ)

USDCFO... United States Defense Communication Field Office   (NATG)

USDC Haw ... United States District Court, District of Hawaii   (DLA)

USDC Haw ... United States District Court, District of Hawaii, Reports [*A publication*]   (DLA)

USDC Hawaii ... United States District Court, District of Hawaii   (DLA)

USDC Hawaii ... United States District Court, District of Hawaii, Reports [*A publication*]   (DLA)

USDD .... United States Department of Defense

USDE .... United States Department of Education

USDE .... United States Department of Energy   (MCD)

USDEL...... United States Delegate   (NOAA)

USDELIADB ... United States Delegation, Inter-American Defense Board   (AABC)

US Dep Agric Agric Handb ... US Department of Agriculture. Agriculture Handbook [*A publication*]

US Dep Agric Agric Inf Bull ... US Department of Agriculture. Agriculture Information Bulletin [*A publication*]

US Dep Agric Agric Monogr ... United States. Department of Agriculture. Agriculture Monograph [*A publication*]

US Dep Agric Agric Res Serv ARS Ser ... United States. Department of Agriculture. Agricultural Research Service. ARS Series [*A publication*]

US Dep Agric Agric Res Serv Rep ... United States. Department of Agriculture. Agricultural Research Service. Report [*A publication*]

US Dep Agric Agric Res Serv Stat Bull ... United States. Department of Agriculture. Agricultural Research Service. Statistical Bulletin [*A publication*]

US Dep Agric Bull ... United States. Department of Agriculture. Bulletin [*A publication*]

US Dep Agric Circ ... US Department of Agriculture. Circular [*A publication*]

US Dep Agric Conserv Res Rep ... US Department of Agriculture. Conservation Research Report [*A publication*]

US Dep Agric Farmers' Bull ... US Department of Agriculture. Farmers' Bulletin [*A publication*]

US Dep Agric For Serv For Prod Lab Rep ... United States. Department of Agriculture. Forest Service. Forest Products Laboratory. Report [*A publication*]

US Dep Agric For Serv Res Note (PNW) ... United States. Department of Agriculture. Forest Service. Research Note (Pacific Northwest) [*A publication*]

US Dep Agric For Serv Res Pap NC ... United States. Department of Agriculture. Forest Service. Research Paper NC [*A publication*]

US Dep Agric For Serv Res Pap (PNW) ... US Department of Agriculture. Forest Service. Research Paper (Pacific Northwest) [*A publication*]

US Dep Agric Home Econ Res Rep ... United States. Department of Agriculture. Home Economics Research Report [*A publication*]

US Dep Agric Home Gard Bull ... US Department of Agriculture. Home and Garden Bulletin [*A publication*]

US Dep Agric Index-Cat Med Vet Zool Spec Publ ... United States. Department of Agriculture. Index-Catalogue of Medical and Veterinary Zoology. Special Publication [*A publication*]

US Dep Agric Index-Cat Med Vet Zool Suppl ... United States. Department of Agriculture. Index-Catalogue of Medical and Veterinary Zoology. Supplement [*A publication*]

US Dep Agric Leafl ... US Department of Agriculture. Leaflet [*A publication*]

US Dep Agric Mark Res Rep ... United States. Department of Agriculture. Marketing Research Report [*A publication*]

US Dep Agric Misc Publ ... US Department of Agriculture. Miscellaneous Publications [*A publication*]

US Dep Agric Northeast For Exp Stn Stn Pap ... United States. Department of Agriculture. Northeastern Forest Experiment Station. Station Paper [*A publication*]

US Dep Agric Plant Inventory ... US Department of Agriculture. Plant Inventory [*A publication*]

US Dep Agric Prod Res Rep ... US Department of Agriculture. Production Research Report [*A publication*]

US Dep Agric Res Serv Mark Res Rep ... United States. Department of Agriculture. Agricultural Research Service. Marketing Research Report [*A publication*]

US Dep Agric Sci Educ Adm Agric Res Man ... US Department of Agriculture. Science and Education Administration. Agricultural Research Manual [*A publication*]

US Dep Agric Sci Educ Adm Agric Res Results ARR-S ... US Department of Agriculture. Science and Education Administration. Agricultural Research Results. ARR-S [*A publication*]

US Dep Agric Sci Educ Adm Agric Res Results ARR-W ... US Department of Agriculture. Science and Education Administration. Agricultural Research Results. ARR-W [*A publication*]

US Dep Agric Sci Educ Adm Bibliogr Lit Agric ... US Department of Agriculture. Science and Education Administration. Bibliographies and Literature of Agriculture [*A publication*]

US Dep Agric Soil Conserv Ser Soil Surv ... United States. Department of Agriculture. Soil Conservation Service. Soil Survey [*A publication*]

US Dep Agric Soil Conserv Serv SCS-TP ... US Department of Agriculture. Soil Conservation Service. SCS-TP [*A publication*]

US Dep Agric Soil Conserv Serv Soil Surv Invest Rep ... US Department of Agriculture. Soil Conservation Service. Soil Survey Investigation Report [*A publication*]

US Dep Agric Soil Surv ... United States. Department of Agriculture. Soil Survey [*A publication*]

US Dep Agric Stat Bull ... US Department of Agriculture. Statistical Bulletin [*A publication*]

US Dep Agric Tech Bull ... US Department of Agriculture. Technical Bulletin [*A publication*]

US Dep Agric Util Res Rep ... United States. Department of Agriculture. Utilization Research Report [*A publication*]

US Dep Agric Yearb Agric ... US Department of Agriculture. Yearbook of Agriculture [*A publication*]

US Dep Commer Natl Bur Stand Tech Note ... US Department of Commerce. National Bureau of Standards. Technical Note [*A publication*]

US Dep Commer Natl Mar Fish Serv Circ ... US Department of Commerce. National Marine Fisheries Service. Circular [*A publication*]

US Dep Commer Natl Mar Fish Serv Spec Sci Rep Fish ... US Department of Commerce. National Marine Fisheries Service. Special Scientific Report. Fisheries [*A publication*]

US Dep Commer Off Tech Serv PB Rep ... United States. Department of Commerce. Office of Technical Services. PB Report [*A publication*]

US Dep Energy Bartlesville Energy Technol Cent Pet Prod Surv ... US Department of Energy. Bartlesville Energy Technology Center. Petroleum Product Surveys [*A publication*]

US Dep Energy Bartlesville Energy Technol Cent Publ ... US Department of Energy. Bartlesville Energy Technology Center. Publications [*A publication*]

US Dep Energy Environ Meas Lab Environ Rep ... US Department of Energy. Environmental Measurements Laboratory. Environmental Report [*A publication*]

US Dep Health Educ Welfare Annu Rep ... US Department of Health, Education, and Welfare [*Later, US Department of Health and Human Services*] Annual Report [*A publication*]

US Dep Health Educ Welfare DHEW Publ (FDA) ... United States. Department of Health, Education, and Welfare. DHEW [*Department of Health, Education, and Welfare*] Publication. (FDA) [*Food and Drug Administration*] [*A publication*]

US Dep Health Educ Welfare DHEW Publ (NIH) ... US Department of Health, Education, and Welfare [*Later, US Department of Health and Human Services*] DHEW Publication (NIH) [*A publication*]

US Dep Health Educ Welfare Health Serv Adm Publ HSA ... United States. Department of Health, Education, and Welfare. Health Services Administration. Publication HSA [*Health Services Administration*] [*A publication*]

US Dep Health Educ Welfare Natl Inst Ment Health Sci Monogr ... US Department of Health, Education, and Welfare. National Institute of Mental Health. Science Monographs [*A publication*]

US Dep Health Hum Serv Natl Inst Ment Health Sci Monogr ... US Department of Health and Human Services. National Institute of Mental Health. Science Monographs [*A publication*]

US Dep Inter Bur Mines New Publ ... United States. Department of the Interior. Bureau of Mines. New Publications [*A publication*]

US Dep Inter Conserv Yearb ... US Department of the Interior. Conservation Yearbook [*A publication*]

US Dep Inter Fish Wildl Res Rep ... United States. Department of the Interior. Fish and Wildlife Service. Research Report [*A publication*]

US Dep Inter MESA Inf Rep ... US Department of the Interior. Mining Enforcement and Safety Administration. Informational Report [*A publication*]

US Dep Inter Off Libr Serv Bibliogr Ser ... United States. Department of the Interior. Office of Library Services. Bibliography Series [*A publication*]

US Dep State Bur Public Aff Backgr Notes ... United States. Department of State. Bureau of Public Affairs. Background Notes [*A publication*]

US Dept Agriculture Tech Bull Yearbook ... United States. Department of Agriculture. Technical Bulletin. Yearbook [*A publication*]

US Dept HEW Publ ... US Department of Health, Education, and Welfare [*Later, US Department of Health and Human Services*] Publications [*A publication*]

US Dept HHS Publ ... US Department of Health and Human Services. Publications [*A publication*]

US Dept Int ... United States Department of the Interior   (DLA)

US Dep Transp (Rep) DOT/TST ... US Department of Transportation (Report). DOT/TST [*A publication*]

USDESEA ... United States Dependent Schools, European Area [*Army*]

USDF .... United States Dressage Federation   (EA)

USDFRC ... US Dairy Forage Research Center [*Research center*]   (RCD)

USDGA ..... United States Durum Growers Association   (EA)

USDH .... United States Direct Hire [*Military*]

USDHE & W ... United States Department of Health, Education, and Welfare

USDHUD ... United States Department of Housing and Urban Development

USDI .... United States Department of the Interior

US Dig .... United States Digest [*A publication*]   (DLA)

USDISBad ... United States Distinguished International Shooter Badge [*Military decoration*]   (AABC)

US Dist Ct Haw ... United States District Court District of Hawaii   (DLA)

USDJ .... United States Department of Justice

USDJ .... United States District Judge

USDL .... United States Department of Labor

USDLGI .... United States Defense Liaison Group, Indonesia [*Army*]   (AABC)

USDO .... United States Disbursing Officer

USDOC ...... United States Department of Commerce

USDOCO .. United States Documents Officer   (AFM)

USDOCOLANDSOUTHEAST ... United States Document Office, Allied Land Forces, Southeastern Europe   (AABC)

USDOD .... United States Department of Defense

USDOE ..... United States Department of Energy [*Also, an information service or system*]

USDOI ...... United States Department of the Interior   (MCD)

USDOT ..... United States Department of Transportation   (MCD)

USD(P) ...... Undersecretary of Defense for Policy   (MCD)

US Dp Agr B ... US Department of Agriculture. Bulletin [*A publication*]

US Dp Int .. US Department of the Interior. Publication [*A publication*]

USDR .... United States Divorce Reform   (EA)

USDRE ...... Office of the Under Secretary of Defense for Research and Engineering

USDS .... United States Department of State

USDS .... US Disc Sports Association   (EA)

USDSA ...... United States Deaf Skiers Association   (EA)

USDSEA ... United States Dependent Schools, European Area [*Army*]   (AABC)

USDT .... United States Department of Transportation

USDT .... United States Department of the Treasury

USDTA ...... United States Dental Tennis Association   (EA)

USDTP ...... Ukrainska Sotsial Demokraticheskaia Truda Partiia [*Ukrainian Social Democratic Labor Party*] [*Russian*] [*Political party*]   (PPE)

USDW .... Underground Sources of Drinking Water

USE .... Encyclopedia of United States Reports [*A publication*]   (DLA)

USE .... Underground Service Entrance

USE .... Undersea Scientific Expedition

USE .... Unified S-Band Equipment

USE .... Unit Support Equipment

USE .... United States Economic Problems [*British*] [*World War II*]

USE .... United States Embassy

USE .... United States Envelope Co.

USE .... UNIVAC Scientific Exchange [*Later, UI, USE, Inc.*]

USE .... University of South Dakota, Law Library, Vermillion, SD [*OCLC symbol*]   (OCLC)

USE .... University Space Experiments

USE .... Unmanned Surveillance Equipment

USE .... US English [*An association*]   (EA)

USE .... Wauseon, OH [*Location identifier*] [*FAA*]   (FAAL)

USEA .... Undersea   (AABC)

USEASA ... United States Eastern Amateur Ski Association [*Later, ESA*]

USEC .... United States Endurance Cup [*Car racing*]

USEC .... United States Mission to European Communities [*Department of State*]

USEC .... United System of Electronic Computers   (IEEE)

USEC .... Universal Security Instruments, Inc. [*NASDAQ symbol*]   (NQ)

USECC ...... United States Employees' Compensation Commission [*Functions transferred to Federal Security Agency, 1946*]

USECOM ... United States Army Electronics Command [*Obsolete*]

US Econ P ... United States Economic Policies Affecting Industrial Trade [*A publication*]

US Econ Res Serv Foreign Agric Econ Rep ... US Economic Research Service. Foreign Agricultural Economic Report [*A publication*]

US Ec Outlk ... US Economic Outlook [*A publication*]

USEE .... United States Exploring Expedition [*1838-42*] [*Navy*]

USEEM ..... United States Establishment and Enterprise Microdata Base [*Brookings Institution*]

USEES ...... United States Naval Engineering Experiment Station [*Annapolis, MD*]

USEFP ...... United States Educational Foundation in Pakistan

USEG .... US Energy Corp. [*NASDAQ symbol*]   (NQ)

US Egg .... United States Egg and Poultry Magazine [*A publication*]

USEI .... United States Society of Esperanto Instructors [*Later, AATE*]

USELMCENTO ... United States Element Central Treaty Organization   (AFM)

USEM .... United States Egg Marketers   (EA)

USEMA ..... [*The*] United States Electronic Mail Association

USEMB ..... United States Embassy   (MCD)

USEMS ..... United Steam Engine Makers' Society [*A union*] [*British*]

USEN .... USENCO, Inc. [*NASDAQ symbol*]   (NQ)

US Energy Res Dev Adm Rep CONF ... United States. Energy Research and Development Administration. Report CONF [*A publication*]

US Energy Res Dev Adm (Rep) GJO ... US Energy Research and Development Administration (Report) GJO [*Grand Junction Office*] [*A publication*]

US Environ Prot Agency Munic Constr Div Rep ... United States. Environmental Protection Agency. Municipal Construction Division. Report [*A publication*]

US Environ Prot Agency Natl Environ Res Cent Ecol Res Ser ... US Environmental Protection Agency. National Environmental Research Center. Ecological Research Series [*A publication*]

US Environ Prot Agency Off Air Qual Plann Stand Tech Rep ... US Environmental Protection Agency. Office of Air Quality Planning and Standards. Technical Report [*A publication*]

US Environ Prot Agency Off Air Waste Manage EPA-450 ... US Environmental Protection Agency. Office of Air and Waste Management. EPA-450 [*A publication*]

US Environ Prot Agency Off Pestic Programs Rep ... United States. Environmental Protection Agency. Office of Pesticide Programs. Report [*A publication*]

US Environ Prot Agency Off Radiat Programs EPA ... US Environmental Protection Agency. Office of Radiation Programs. EPA [*A publication*]

US Environ Prot Agency Off Radiat Programs EPA-ORP ... US Environmental Protection Agency. Office of Radiation Programs. EPA-ORP [*A publication*]

US Environ Prot Agency Off Radiat Programs Tech Rep ... United States. Environmental Protection Agency. Office of Radiation Programs. Technical Report [*A publication*]

US Environ Prot Agency Off Radiat Programs Tech Rep ORP-SID ... US Environmental Protection Agency. Office of Radiation Programs. Technical Reports ORP-SID [*A publication*]

US Environ Prot Agency Off Res Dev Rep EPA ... United States. Environmental Protection Agency. Office of Research and Development. Report EPA [*A publication*]

US Environ Prot Agency Off Res Dev Res Rep Ecol Res Ser ... US Environmental Protection Agency. Office of Research and Development. Research Reports. Ecological Research Series [*A publication*]

US Environ Prot Agency Publ AP Ser ... US Environmental Protection Agency. Publication. AP Series [*A publication*]

USEO .... United States Employment Opportunities

USEO .... United States Engineer Office

USEORD ... Use Order [*Navy*]   (NVT)

USEP .... United States Escapee Program

USEPA .... United States Environmental Protection Agency

US EPA Ecol Res ... US Environmental Protection Agency. Ecological Research [*A publication*]
US EPA Envir Health Res ... US Environmental Protection Agency. Environmental Health Effects Research [*A publication*]
US EPA Envir Monit ... United States. Environmental Protection Agency. Environmental Monitoring [*A publication*]
US EPA Envir Prot Technol ... US Environmental Protection Agency. Environmental Protection Technology [*A publication*]
US EPA Socioecon Studies ... United States. Environmental Protection Agency. Socioeconomic Environmental Studies [*A publication*]
US Eq Dig ... United States Equity Digest [*A publication*]   (DLA)
USER .... Ultra-Small Electronics Research [*DoD*]
USERC ...... US Environment and Resources Council   (EA)
USERDA ... United States Energy Research and Development Administration [*Superseded by Department of Energy, 1977*]
USERIA .... Ultrasensitive Enzymatic Radioimmunoassay [*Clinical chemistry*]
USERID .... User Identification [*Data processing*]
USER INC ... Urban Scientific and Educational Research, Incorporated   (EA)
USERS ...... Uniform Socio-Economic Reporting System [*Financial reporting system for voluntary health and welfare organizations*]
U Serv M ... United Service Magazine [*A publication*]
USES .... United States Employment Service [*Department of Labor*]
USES .... US Energy Search [*NASDAQ symbol*]   (NQ)
USESF ...... United States Exchange Stabilization Fund
US-ESRIC ... US-El Salvador Research and Information Center   (EA)
USESSA .... United States Environmental Science Services Administration   (AABC)
USET .... United South and Eastern Tribes   (EA)
USET .... United States Equestrian Team   (EA)
USEUCOM ... United States European Command
USEX .... US Exploration Corp. [*NASDAQ symbol*]   (NQ)
USF .... Lommen Health Science Library, University of South Dakota, Vermillion, SD [*OCLC symbol*]   (OCLC)
USF .... Und So Fort [*And So Forth*] [*German*]
USF .... Uniaxial Stress Field
USF .... United Scleroderma Foundation   (EA)
USF .... United Socialist Front [*Thailand*] [*Political party*]   (PD)
USF .... United States Fleet
USF .... United States Forces   (CINC)
USF .... University of San Francisco [*California*]
USF .... University of Santa Fe [*A publication*]
USFA .... United Sports Fans of America   (EA)
USFA .... United States Fencing Association   (EA)
USFA .... United States Forces in Austria
USFA .... United States Fuel Administration [*Terminated*]
USFA .... US Farmers Association   (EA)
US Fachbuch ... U & S [*Urban & Schwarzenberg*] Fachbuch [*A publication*]
USFADTC ... United States Fleet Air Defense Training Center
USFAIRWINGMED ... United States Fleet Air Wing, Mediterranean   (NATG)
US Farm .... US Farm News [*A publication*]
USFARS .... United States Federation of Amateur Roller Skaters [*Later, USAC-RS*]   (EA)
USFBI .... United States Forces, British Isles [*World War II*]
USFC .... United States Foil Company
USFCA ...... United States Fencing Coaches Association   (EA)
USFCC ...... United States Fire Companies Conference [*Defunct*]   (EA)
USFCC ...... US Federation for Culture Collections   (EA)
USFCF ...... USF Constellation Foundation   (EA)
USFCT ...... United States Forces, China Theater
US Fed Railroad Adm Rep ... US Federal Railroad Administration. Report [*A publication*]
USFET ...... United States Forces, European Theater [*American headquarters for occupation of Germany after SHAEF was dissolved*] [*World War II*]
USFF .... United States Filter Corp. [*NASDAQ symbol*]   (SPSG)
USFF .... United States Flag Foundation   (EA)
USFFL ...... United States Flag Football League   (EA)
USF & G ... United States Fidelity & Guaranty Co.
USFGC ...... US Feed Grains Council   (EA)
USFHA ..... USA Field Hockey Association   (EA)
USFI .... Unione Sindacale Ferrovieri Italiani [*National Union of Italian Railway Workers*]
USFIA .... United States Forces in Australia
USFIP .... United States Forces in the Philippines
USFIS .... United States Foundation for International Scouting   (EA)
USFISC ...... United States Foreign Intelligence Surveillance Court
US Fish and Wildlife Service Fishery Bull ... US Fish and Wildlife Service. Fishery Bulletin [*A publication*]
US Fish Wildl Serv Biol Rep ... US Fish and Wildlife Service. Biological Report [*A publication*]
US Fish Wildl Serv Biol Serv Program FWS-OBS ... US Fish and Wildlife Service. Biological Services Program. FWS-OBS [*A publication*]
US Fish Wildl Serv Bur Commer Fish Fish Leafl ... US Fish and Wildlife Service. Bureau of Commercial Fisheries. Fishery Leaflet [*A publication*]

US Fish Wildl Serv Bur Commer Fish Stat Dig ... US Fish and Wildlife Service. Bureau of Commercial Fisheries. Statistical Digest [*A publication*]
US Fish Wildl Serv Bur Sport Fish Wildl EGL ... US Fish and Wildlife Service. Bureau of Sport Fisheries and Wildlife. EGL [*A publication*]
US Fish Wildl Serv Circ ... US Fish and Wildlife Service. Circular [*A publication*]
US Fish Wildl Serv Fish Bull ... US Fish and Wildlife Service. Fishery Bulletin [*A publication*]
US Fish Wildl Serv Fish Distrib Rep ... US Fish and Wildlife Service. Fish Distribution Report [*A publication*]
US Fish Wildl Serv Fish Wildl Leafl ... US Fish and Wildlife Service. Fish and Wildlife Leaflet [*A publication*]
US Fish Wildl Serv FWS-OBS ... US Fish and Wildlife Service. Biological Services Program. FWS-OBS [*A publication*]
US Fish Wildl Serv Invest Fish Control ... US Fish and Wildlife Service. Investigations in Fish Control [*A publication*]
US Fish Wildl Serv N Am Fauna ... US Fish and Wildlife Service. North American Fauna [*A publication*]
US Fish Wildl Serv Resour Publ ... US Fish and Wildlife Service. Resource Publication [*A publication*]
US Fish Wildl Serv Res Rep ... US Fish and Wildlife Service. Research Report [*A publication*]
US Fish Wildl Serv Spec Sci Rep Fish ... US Fish and Wildlife Service. Special Scientific Report. Fisheries [*A publication*]
US Fish Wildl Serv Spec Sci Rep Wildl ... US Fish and Wildlife Service. Special Scientific Report. Wildlife [*A publication*]
US Fish Wildl Serv Tech Pap ... US Fish and Wildlife Service. Technical Papers [*A publication*]
US Fish Wildl Serv Wildl Leafl ... US Fish and Wildlife Service. Wildlife Leaflet [*A publication*]
US Fish Wildl Serv Wildl Res Rep ... US Fish and Wildlife Service. Wildlife Research Report [*A publication*]
US Fish Wild Serv Fish Bull ... US Fish and Wildlife Service. Fishery Bulletin [*A publication*]
USFJ .... United States Forces, Japan   (CINC)
USFK .... United States Forces, Korea
USFL .... US Football League   (EA)
USFLQ ...... USF Language Quarterly [*A publication*]
USFLR ...... University of San Francisco. Law Review [*A publication*]
USF L Rev ... University of San Francisco. Law Review [*A publication*]
USFMG ..... United States Fastener Manufacturing Group   (EA)
USFMG ..... United States Foreign Medical Graduate   (DHSM)
USFMIA ... United States Fishmeal Importers Association [*Defunct*]   (EA)
USFOA ...... United States Forces, Occupation Austria [*World War II*]
USFOA ...... Uspekhi Fotoniki [*A publication*]
USFODA ... US Fish and Wildlife Service. Biological Services Program. FWS-OBS [*A publication*]
USFODA ... US Fish and Wildlife Service. FWS-OBS [*A publication*]
US Food Drug Adm DHEW Publ ... United States. Food and Drug Administration. DHEW [*Department of Health, Education, and Welfare*] Publication [*A publication*]
USFOR ...... United States Forces
USFORAZ ... United States Forces in Azores
US Forest Serv Agr Hdb ... United States. Forest Service. Agriculture Handbooks [*A publication*]
US Forest Serv Res Note ... US Forest Service. Research Notes [*A publication*]
US Forest Serv Res Paper ... US Forest Service. Research Papers [*A publication*]
US For Prod Lab Rep ... United States. Forest Products Laboratory. Reports [*A publication*]
US For Prod Lab Res Note FPL ... United States. Forest Products Laboratory. Research Note FPL [*A publication*]
US For Prod Lab Tech Notes ... United States. Forest Products Laboratory. Technical Notes [*A publication*]
US For Serv AIB ... US Forest Service. AIB [*A publication*]
US For Serv Cent States For Exp Stn Misc Release ... United States. Forest Service. Central States Forest Experiment Station. Miscellaneous Release [*A publication*]
US For Serv Div State Priv For North Reg Rep ... US Forest Service. Division of State and Private Forestry. Northern Region Report [*A publication*]
US For Serv For Insect & Dis Leafl ... US Forest Service. Forest Insect and Disease Leaflet [*A publication*]
US For Serv For Insect & Dis Manage North Reg Rep ... US Forest Service. Forest Insect and Disease Management. Northern Region Report [*A publication*]
US For Serv For Pest Leafl ... US Forest Service. Forest Pest Leaflet [*A publication*]
US For Serv For Pest Manage North Reg Rep ... US Forest Service. Forest Pest Management. Northern Region Report [*A publication*]
US For Serv For Prod Lab Annu Rep ... US Forest Service. Forest Products Laboratory. Annual Report [*A publication*]
US For Serv For Prod Lab Gen Tech Rep FPL ... United States. Forest Service. Forest Products Laboratory. General Technical Report FPL [*A publication*]
US For Serv For Resour Rep ... United States. Forest Service. Forest Resource Report [*A publication*]

US For Serv For Res What's New West ... US Forest Service. Forestry Research. What's New in the West [*A publication*]
US For Serv Gen Tech Rep INT ... US Forest Service. General Technical Report. INT [*A publication*]
US For Serv Gen Tech Rep NC ... US Forest Service. General Technical Report. NC [*A publication*]
US For Serv Gen Tech Rep NE ... US Forest Service. General Technical Report. NE [*A publication*]
US For Serv Gen Tech Rep PNW ... US Forest Service. General Technical Report. PNW [*A publication*]
US For Serv Gen Tech Rep PSW ... US Forest Service. General Technical Report. PSW [*A publication*]
US For Serv Gen Tech Rep RM ... US Forest Service. General Technical Report. RM [*A publication*]
US For Serv Gen Tech Rep SE ... US Forest Service. General Technical Report. SE [*A publication*]
US For Serv Gen Tech Rep SO ... US Forest Service. General Technical Report. SO [*A publication*]
US For Serv Gen Tech Rep WO ... US Forest Service. General Technical Report. WO [*A publication*]
US For Serv Northeast For Exp Stn Ann Rep ... United States. Forest Service. Northeastern Forest Experiment Station. Annual Report [*A publication*]
US For Serv Northeast For Exp Stn Annu Rep ... US Forest Service. Northeastern Forest Experiment Station. Annual Report [*A publication*]
US For Serv Northeast For Exp Stn Stn Pap ... United States. Forest Service. Northeastern Forest Experiment Station. Station Paper [*A publication*]
US For Serv North Reg Coop For Pest Manage Rep ... US Forest Service. Northern Region. Cooperative Forestry and Pest Management Report [*A publication*]
US For Serv North Reg For Environ Prot ... US Forest Service. Northern Region. Forest Environmental Protection [*A publication*]
US For Serv Pac Northwest For Range Experiment Stn Res Notes ... United States. Forest Service. Pacific Northwest Forest and Range Experiment Station. Research Notes [*A publication*]
US For Serv Pac Northwest For Range Exp Stn Ann Rep ... United States. Forest Service. Pacific Northwest Forest and Range Experiment Station. Annual Report [*A publication*]
US For Serv Pac Northwest For Range Exp Stn Annu Rep ... US Forest Service. Pacific Northwest Forest and Range Experiment Station. Annual Report [*A publication*]
US For Serv Pac Northwest For Range Exp Stn Res Pap ... United States. Forest Service. Pacific Northwest Forest and Range Experiment Station. Research Paper [*A publication*]
US For Serv Pac Northwest For Range Exp Stn Res Pap PNW ... US Forest Service. Pacific Northwest Forest and Range Experiment Station. Research Paper PNW [*A publication*]
US For Serv Pac Northwest For Range Exp Stn Res Prog ... US Forest Service. Pacific Northwest Forest and Range Experiment Station. Research Progress [*A publication*]
US For Serv Pac Southwest For Range Exp Stn Misc Pap ... United States. Forest Service. Pacific Southwest Forest and Range Experiment Station. Miscellaneous Paper [*A publication*]
US For Serv Res Note FPL ... US Forest Service. Research Note. FPL [*A publication*]
US For Serv Res Note Inst Trop For ... United States. Forest Service. Research Note. Institute of Tropical Forestry [*A publication*]
US For Serv Res Note INT ... US Forest Service. Research Note. INT [*A publication*]
US For Serv Res Note Intermt For Range Exp Sta ... United States. Forest Service. Research Note. Intermountain Forest and Range Experiment Station [*A publication*]
US For Serv Res Note ITF ... US Forest Service. Research Note. ITF [*A publication*]
US For Serv Res Note NC ... US Forest Service. Research Note. NC [*A publication*]
US For Serv Res Note NE ... US Forest Service. Research Note. NE [*A publication*]
US For Serv Res Note Nth Cent For Exp Sta ... United States. Forest Service. Research Note. North Central Forest Experiment Station [*A publication*]
US For Serv Res Note Ntheast For Exp Sta ... United States. Forest Service. Research Note. Northeastern Forest Experiment Station [*A publication*]
US For Serv Res Note Nth For Exp Sta ... United States. Forest Service. Research Note. Northern Forest Experiment Station [*A publication*]
US For Serv Res Note Pacif Nthwest For Range Exp Sta ... United States. Forest Service. Research Note. Pacific Northwest Forest and Range Experiment Station [*A publication*]
US For Serv Res Note Pacif Sthwest For Range Exp Sta ... US Forest Service. Research Note. Pacific Southwest Forest and Range Experiment Station [*A publication*]
US For Serv Res Note PNW ... US Forest Service. Research Note. PNW [*A publication*]
US For Serv Res Note PSW ... US Forest Service. Research Note. PSW [*A publication*]
US For Serv Res Note RM ... US Forest Service. Research Note. RM [*A publication*]

US For Serv Res Note Rocky Mt For Range Exp Sta ... US Forest Service. Research Note. Rocky Mountain Forest and Range Experiment Station [*A publication*]
US For Serv Res Note SE ... US Forest Service. Research Note. SE [*A publication*]
US For Serv Res Note SO ... US Forest Service. Research Note. SO [*A publication*]
US For Serv Res Note Stheast For Exp Sta ... US Forest Service. Research Note. Southeastern Forest Experiment Station [*A publication*]
US For Serv Res Note Sth For Exp Sta ... United States. Forest Service. Research Note. Southern Forest Experiment Station [*A publication*]
US For Serv Res Note US For Prod Lab (Madison) ... US Forest Service. Research Note. US Forest Products Laboratory (Madison, Wisconsin) [*A publication*]
US For Serv Resour Bull INT ... US Forest Service. Resource Bulletin. INT [*A publication*]
US For Serv Resour Bull NC ... US Forest Service. Resource Bulletin. NC [*A publication*]
US For Serv Resour Bull NE ... US Forest Service. Resource Bulletin. NE [*A publication*]
US For Serv Resour Bull PNW ... US Forest Service. Resource Bulletin. PNW [*A publication*]
US For Serv Resour Bull PSW ... US Forest Service. Resource Bulletin. PSW [*A publication*]
US For Serv Resour Bull SE ... US Forest Service. Resource Bulletin. SE [*A publication*]
US For Serv Resour Bull SO ... US Forest Service. Resource Bulletin. SO [*A publication*]
US For Serv Resource Bull Intermt For Range Exp Sta ... United States. Forest Service. Resource Bulletin. Intermountain Forest and Range Experiment Station [*A publication*]
US For Serv Resource Bull Nth Cent For Exp Sta ... US Forest Service. Resource Bulletin. North Central Forest Experiment Station [*A publication*]
US For Serv Resource Bull Ntheast For Exp Sta ... US Forest Service. Resource Bulletin. Northeastern Forest Experiment Station [*A publication*]
US For Serv Resource Bull Nth For Exp Sta ... US Forest Service. Resource Bulletin. Northern Forest Experiment Station [*A publication*]
US For Serv Resource Bull Pacif Nthwest For Range Exp Sta ... United States. Forest Service. Pacific Northwest Forest and Range Experiment Station. Resource Bulletin [*A publication*]
US For Serv Resource Bull Pacif Sthwest For Range Exp Sta ... US Forest Service. Resource Bulletin. Pacific Southwest Forest and Range Experiment Station [*A publication*]
US For Serv Resource Bull Stheast For Exp Sta ... US Forest Service. Resource Bulletin. Southeastern Forest Experiment Station [*A publication*]
US For Serv Resource Bull Sth For Exp Sta ... US Forest Service. Resource Bulletin. Southern Forest Experiment Station [*A publication*]
US For Serv Res Pap FPL ... US Forest Service. Research Paper. FPL [*A publication*]
US For Serv Res Pap Inst Trop For ... US Forest Service. Research Paper. Institute of Tropical Forestry [*A publication*]
US For Serv Res Pap INT ... US Forest Service. Research Paper. INT [*A publication*]
US For Serv Res Pap Intermt For Range Exp Sta ... US Forest Service. Research Paper. Intermountain Forest and Range Experiment Station [*A publication*]
US For Serv Res Pap ITF ... US Forest Service. Research Paper. ITF [*A publication*]
US For Serv Res Pap NC ... US Forest Service. Research Paper. NC [*A publication*]
US For Serv Res Pap NE ... US Forest Service. Research Paper. NE [*A publication*]
US For Serv Res Pap Nth Cent For Exp Sta ... US Forest Service. Research Paper. North Central Forest Experiment Station [*A publication*]
US For Serv Res Pap Ntheast For Exp Sta ... US Forest Service. Research Paper. Northeastern Forest Experiment Station [*A publication*]
US For Serv Res Pap Nth For Exp Sta ... United States. Forest Service. Research Paper. Northern Forest Experiment Station [*A publication*]
US For Serv Res Pap Pacif Nthwest For Range Exp Sta ... US Forest Service. Research Paper. Pacific Northwest Forest and Range Experiment Station [*A publication*]
US For Serv Res Pap Pacif Sthwest For Range Exp Sta ... US Forest Service. Research Paper. Pacific Southwest Forest and Range Experiment Station [*A publication*]
US For Serv Res Pap PNW ... US Forest Service. Research Paper. PNW [*A publication*]
US For Serv Res Pap PSW ... US Forest Service. Research Paper. PSW [*A publication*]
US For Serv Res Pap RM ... US Forest Service. Research Paper. RM [*A publication*]

US For Serv Res Pap Rocky Mt For Range Exp Sta ... United States. Forest Service. Research Paper. Rocky Mountain Forest and Range Experiment Station [*A publication*]

US For Serv Res Pap SE ... US Forest Service. Research Paper. SE [*A publication*]

US For Serv Res Pap SO ... US Forest Service. Research Paper. SO [*A publication*]

US For Serv Res Pap Stheast For Exp Sta ... US Forest Service. Research Paper. Southeastern Forest Experiment Station [*A publication*]

US For Serv Res Pap Sth For Exp Sta ... US Forest Service. Research Paper. Southern Forest Experiment Station [*A publication*]

US For Serv Res Pap US For Prod Lab (Madison) ... United States. Forest Service. Research Paper. United States Forest Products Laboratory (Madison, Wisconsin) [*A publication*]

US For Serv Res Pap WO ... US Forest Service. Research Paper. WO [*A publication*]

US For Serv Rocky Mount For Range Exp Stn For Sur Release ... United States. Forest Service. Rocky Mountain Forest and Range Experiment Station. Forest Survey Release [*A publication*]

US For Serv Rocky Mount For Range Exp Stn Res Notes ... United States. Forest Service. Rocky Mountain Forest and Range Experiment Station. Research Notes [*A publication*]

US For Serv Rocky Mount For Range Exp Stn Stn Pap ... United States. Forest Service. Rocky Mountain Forest and Range Experiment Station. Station Paper [*A publication*]

US For Serv Southeast For Exp Stn For Surv Release ... United States. Forest Service. Southeastern Forest Experiment Station. Forest Survey Release [*A publication*]

US For Serv Southeast For Exp Stn Res Notes ... United States. Forest Service. Southeastern Forest Experiment Station. Research Notes [*A publication*]

US For Serv Southeast For Exp Stn Stn Pap ... United States. Forest Service. Southeastern Forest Experiment Station. Station Paper [*A publication*]

US For Serv South For Exp Stn Annu Rep ... US Forest Service. Southern Forest Experiment Station. Annual Report [*A publication*]

US For Serv South For Exp Stn For Surv Release ... United States. Forest Service. Southern Forest Experiment Station. Forest Survey Release [*A publication*]

US For Serv Tech Bull ... US Forest Service. Technical Bulletin [*A publication*]

US For Serv Tree Plant Notes ... US Forest Service. Tree Planters' Notes [*A publication*]

USFP .... Union Socialiste des Forces Populaires [*Socialist Union of Popular Forces*] [*Morocco*] [*Political party*] (PPW)

USFP .... United States Federation of Pelota (EA)

USFP .... United States Forces, Police

USFR .... United States Fleet Reserve

USFS .... United Society of Fitters and Smiths [*A union*] [*British*]

USFS .... United States Foreign Service [*Department of State*]

USFS .... United States Forest Service

USFS .... United States Frequency Standard

USFSA ...... United States Figure Skating Association (EA)

USFSS .... United States Fleet SONAR School

USFSS .... US Federation of Scholars and Scientists (EA)

USFTA ...... United States Floor Tennis Association [*Defunct*] (EA)

USFU .... Unglazed Structural Facing Units [*Technical drawings*]

USFV .... United States Forces, Vietnam

USFVL Rev ... University of San Fernando Valley. Law Review [*A publication*] (DLA)

USFWS ..... United States Fish and Wildlife Service [*Department of the Interior*]

USFWSWRR ... United States. Fish and Wildlife Service. Wildlife Research Report [*A publication*]

USG .... U. S. Grant Mining [*Vancouver Stock Exchange symbol*]

USG .... Ultrasonic Space Grating

USG .... Ultrasonography

USG .... Ulysses Simpson Grant [*US general and president, 1822-1885*]

USG .... Union of Superiors General (EA)

USG .... United States Gauge

USG .... United States Government

USG .... USG Corp. [*NYSE symbol*] (SPSG)

USGA .... Ulysses S. Grant Association (EA)

USGA .... United States Golf Association (EA)

USGA .... US Green Alliance (EA)

USGA Green Sect Rec US Golf Assoc ... USGA Green Section Record. US Golf Association [*A publication*]

USGC .... US Geodynamics Committee (EA)

USGCC/A ... United States Group Control Council/Austria [*World War II*]

USGCC/G ... United States Group Control Council/Germany [*World War II*]

USGCLR ... United States-German Committee on Learning and Remembrance (EA)

USGCM .... United States Government Correspondence Manual

US Geog G S Rocky Mtn Reg (Powell) ... United States Geographical and Geological Survey of the Rocky Mountain Region (Powell) [*A publication*]

US Geol S Bul ... United States. Geological Survey. Bulletin [*A publication*]

US Geol S Professional Pa ... United States. Geological Survey. Professional Paper [*A publication*]

US Geol Surv Annu Rep ... United States. Geological Survey. Annual Report [*A publication*]

US Geol Surv Bull ... United States. Geological Survey. Bulletin [*A publication*]

US Geol Surv Circ ... United States. Geological Survey. Circular [*A publication*]

US Geol Surv Coal Invest Map ... US Geological Survey. Coal Investigations Map [*A publication*]

US Geol Survey Bull ... United States. Geological Survey. Bulletin [*A publication*]

US Geol Survey Circ ... US Geological Survey. Circular [*A publication*]

US Geol Survey Coal Inv Map ... US Geological Survey. Coal Investigations Map [*A publication*]

US Geol Survey Geol Quad Map ... United States. Geological Survey. Geological Quadrangle Map [*A publication*]

US Geol Survey Geol Quadrangle Map ... US Geological Survey. Geologic Quadrangle Map [*A publication*]

US Geol Survey Geophys Inv Map ... US Geological Survey. Geophysical Investigations Map [*A publication*]

US Geol Survey Hydrol Inv Atlas ... US Geological Survey. Hydrologic Investigations Atlas [*A publication*]

US Geol Survey Index Geol Mapping US ... US Geological Survey. Index to Geologic Mapping in the United States [*A publication*]

US Geol Survey Mineral Inv Field Studies Map ... US Geological Survey. Mineral Investigations Field Studies Map [*A publication*]

US Geol Survey Mineral Inv Res Map ... US Geological Survey. Mineral Investigations Resource Map [*A publication*]

US Geol Survey Misc Geol Inv Map ... United States. Geological Survey. Miscellaneous Geologic Investigations Map [*A publication*]

US Geol Survey Oil and Gas Inv Chart ... US Geological Survey. Oil and Gas Investigations Chart [*A publication*]

US Geol Survey Oil and Gas Inv Map ... United States. Geological Survey. Oil and Gas Investigations Map [*A publication*]

US Geol Survey Prof Paper ... US Geological Survey. Professional Paper [*A publication*]

US Geol Survey Water-Supply Paper ... United States. Geological Survey. Water-Supply Paper [*A publication*]

US Geol Surv Geol Quadrangle Map ... US Geological Survey. Geologic Quadrangle Map [*A publication*]

US Geol Surv Geophys Invest Map ... United States. Geological Survey. Geophysical Investigations Map [*A publication*]

US Geol Surv Hydrol Invest Atlas ... US Geological Survey. Hydrologic Investigations Atlas [*A publication*]

US Geol Surv Miner Invest Field Stud Map ... United States. Department of the Interior. Geological Survey. Mineral Investigations Field Studies Map [*A publication*]

US Geol Surv Misc Field Stud Map ... US Geological Survey. Miscellaneous Field Studies Map [*A publication*]

US Geol Surv Misc Geol Invest Map ... United States. Geological Survey. Miscellaneous Geologic Investigations Map [*A publication*]

US Geol Surv Oil Gas Invest Chart ... US Geological Survey. Oil and Gas Investigations Chart [*A publication*]

US Geol Surv Oil Gas Invest Map ... US Geological Survey. Oil and Gas Investigations Map [*A publication*]

US Geol Surv Open-File Rep ... US Geological Survey. Open-File Report [*A publication*]

US Geol Surv Prof Pap ... United States. Geological Survey. Professional Paper [*A publication*]

US Geol Surv Trace Elem Memo Rep ... United States. Geological Survey. Trace Elements Memorandum Report [*A publication*]

US Geol Surv Water-Resour Invest ... US Geological Survey. Water-Resources Investigations [*A publication*]

US Geol Surv Water-Supply Pap ... US Geological Survey. Water-Supply Paper [*A publication*]

USGF .... United States Gymnastics Federation (EA)

US G Geog S Terr (Hayden) ... United States Geological and Geographies Survey of the Territories (Hayden) [*A publication*]

USGIPU .... United States Group of the Inter-Parliamentary Union (EA)

USGL .... US Gold Corp. [*NASDAQ symbol*] (SPSG)

USGLI .... United States Government Life Insurance

USGLW ...... Union of Saddlers and General Leather Workers [*British*]

USGM ...... United States Government Manual [*A publication*] (OICC)

US Gov Res Dev Rep ... US Government Research and Development Reports [*A publication*]

US Gov Res Rep ... US Government Research Reports [*A publication*]

US Govt Paper Spec Std ... US Government Paper. Specification Standards [*A publication*]

US Govt Res Develop Rept ... United States Government Research and Development Reports [*A publication*]

US Govt Res Rept ... United States Government Research Report [*A publication*]

USGPM ..... United States Government Purchasing Mission [*World War II*]

USGPO ..... United States Government Printing Office

USGR .... United States Government Report (IEEE)

USGRA ...... United States Government Report Announcements (IID)

USGRDR ... United States Government Research and Development Reports [*Later, GRA*]

USGRDR-I ... United States Government Research and Development Reports Index [*Later, GRI*]

USGRR ...... United States Government Research Reports [*National Bureau of Standards publication*]

USGS......... United States Geological Survey [*Reston, VA*] [*Databank originator*]
USGSA...... United States Grass Ski Association (EA)
USGSA...... United States Gymnastic Safety Association
USGS An Rp PPB W-S P Mon Min Res G Atlas Top Atlas ... United States. Geological Survey. Annual Report. Professional Paper. Bulletin. Water-Supply Paper Monograph. Mineral Resources Geology Atlas [*A publication*]
USGSB...... United States. Geological Survey. Bulletin [*A publication*]
USGSC...... United States. Geological Survey. Circular [*A publication*]
USGSPP.... United States. Geological Survey. Professional Paper [*A publication*]
USGS Terr ... United States Geological Survey of the Territories [*A publication*]
USGW....... Underwater-to-Surface Guided Weapon (MCD)
US Gym Fed Gym News ... United States Gymnastic Federation. Gymnastic News [*A publication*]
U SH.......... Shilling [*Monetary unit in Uganda*]
USH.......... United Scientific Holdings [*Defense equipment manufacturer*] [*British*]
USH.......... Ushuaia [*Argentina*] [*Airport symbol*] (OAG)
USH.......... USLIFE Corp. [*NYSE symbol*] (SPSG)
USHA....... United States Handball Association (EA)
USHA........ United States Housing Authority [*Functions transferred to Public Housing Commissioner, 1947*]
USHB....... Uniformed Services Health Benefits
USHBP..... Uniformed Services Health Benefits Program
USHC........ United States Housing Corporation [*Terminated, 1952*]
USHC........ US Healthcare, Inc. [*NASDAQ symbol*] (NQ)
USHCA...... US Horse Cavalry Association (EA)
USHCC ..... US Hispanic Chamber of Commerce (EA)
USHDA.... United States Highland Dancing Association (EA)
USHDI ..... United States Historical Documents Institute
USHE........ Upstream Heat Exchanger (AAG)
USHG........ United States Home Guard
USHGA..... United States Hop Growers Association
USHGA..... US Hang Gliding Association (EA)
USHH .... Khanty-Mansiysk [*USSR*] [*ICAO location identifier*] (ICLI)
USHI .... US Health, Incorporated [*NASDAQ symbol*] (NQ)
USHIGEO ... United States National Committee for the History of Geology (EA)
USHL .... United States Hockey League
USHL .... United States Hydrograph Laboratory
USHL .... United States Hygienic Laboratory
USHMAC ... United States Health Manpower Advisory Council
USHMC .... US Holocaust Memorial Council (EA)
USHO........ United States Hydrographic Office [*Later, Naval Oceanographic Office*]
USHP .... United States Helium Plant [*Amarillo, TX*]
USHSLA ... US Hide, Skin, and Leather Association (EA)
USHTA ..... United States Handicap Tennis Association (EA)
USHWA ... United States Harness Writers' Association (EA)
USHWC.... US Helsinki Watch Committee (EA)
US Hydrog Office Pub ... US Hydrographic Office. Publication [*A publication*]
USI .... Mabaruma [*Guyana*] [*Airport symbol*] (OAG)
USI .... Ultrasonic System [*Vancouver Stock Exchange symbol*]
USI .... Ultraviolet Spectroheliographic Instrument
USI .... United Schools International [*New Delhi, India*] (EAIO)
USI .... United Sons of Israel (EA)
USI .... United States Information Agency, Washington, DC [*OCLC symbol*] (OCLC)
USI .... United States Investor [*A publication*]
USI .... Universal Software Interface [*MRI Systems Corp.*]
USI .... Unlawful Sexual Intercourse
USI .... Unresolved Safety Issue [*Nuclear energy*] (NRCH)
USI .... Update Software Identity (MCD)
USI .... US, Incorporated (EA)
USI .... US Intec, Inc. [*AMEX symbol*] (SPSG)
USI .... User Software Integration Subsystem [*Space Flight Operations Facility, NASA*]
USI .... User/System Interface
USI .... Usine Nouvelle [*A publication*]
USIA.......... United States Information Agency [*Formerly called BECA, it later became known as ICA or USICA, then again as USIA*]
USIAC....... United States Inter-American Council [*Later, COA*] (EA)
USIAEA .... United States Mission to the International Atomic Energy Agency
USIA/PC... Problems of Communism. United States Information Agency [*A publication*]
USIB.......... United States Intelligence Board [*Later, NFIB*] [*National Security Council*]
US-IBP Anal Ecosyst Program Interbiome Abstr ... US-IBP [*International Biological Program*] Analyses of Ecosystems Program. Interbiome Abstracts [*A publication*]
US-IBP Ecosyst Anal Stud Abstr ... US-IBP [*International Biological Program*] Ecosystem Analysis Studies Abstracts [*A publication*]
US-IBP Synth Ser ... US-IBP [*International Biological Program*] Synthesis Series [*A publication*]

USIC.......... Undersea Instrument Chamber [*Marine science*] (MSC)
USIC.......... Union Sportive Interuniversitaire Canadienne
USIC.......... United States Industrial Council (EA)
USIC.......... United States Information Center [*Department of State*] (MCD)
USICA....... United States International Communication Agency [*Also, ICA*] [*Formerly called BECA and USIA, it later became known again as USIA*]
USICC....... United States Industrial Chemical Company (KSC)
USICC Rep ... United States Interstate Commerce Commission Reports [*A publication*] (DLA)
USICCVR ... United States Interstate Commerce Commission Valuation Reports [*A publication*] (DLA)
US ICDBL ... US Branch of the International Committee for the Defense of the Breton Language (EA)
USICF .... Union Sportive Interuniversitaire Canadienne Feminine
USICID ..... United States National Committee, International Commission on Irrigation and Drainage
US/ICID.... US Committee on Irrigation and Drainage [*Formerly, USCIDFC*] (EA)
US/ICOMOS ... United States Committee of the International Council on Monuments and Sites (EA)
USIDF ...... United States Icelandic Defense Forces (MCD)
USIFA .... US International Fireball Association (EA)
USIHR ...... US Institute of Human Rights (EA)
USIITA ..... United States Indian International Travel Agency, Inc.
USILA .... United States Intercollegiate Lacrosse Association (EA)
USIMC...... United States International Marketing Center [*American Embassy, London*] (CB)
USIMCA ... United States International Moth Class Association (EA)
USINCC.... United States International Narcotics Control Commission
US Ind Outlk ... United States Industrial Outlook [*A publication*]
Usine Nouv ... Usine Nouvelle [*A publication*]
Usine Nouv Ed Suppl ... Usine Nouvelle. Edition Supplementaire [*France*] [*A publication*]
Usine Nouv M ... Usine Nouvelle. Monthly Edition [*A publication*]
Usine Nouv Suppl ... Usine Nouvelle. Edition Supplementaire [*A publication*]
Using Govt P ... Using Government Publications. Volume 2. Finding Statistics and Using Special Techniques [*A publication*]
USINOA .... US Immigration and Naturalization Officers' Association (EA)
US Inst Text Res Bull ... United States Institute for Textile Research. Bulletin [*A publication*]
USINT....... United States Interests Section [*Foreign Service*]
US Interdep Comm Atmos Sci Rep ... US Interdepartmental Committee for Atmospheric Sciences. Report [*A publication*]
USIO .... United States Industrial Outlook [*A publication*]
USIO .... Unlimited Sequential Input/Output
USIP .... United Solomon Islands Party (PPW)
USIP .... University of Stockholm Institute of Physics
USIPC .... US Institute of Peace (EA)
USIPC .... Uniformed Services Identification and Privilege Card (AFM)
USIPU ...... United States Inter-Parliamentary Union (EA)
USIRB ...... United States Internal Revenue Bonded
USIS .... Ultraviolet Stratospheric Imaging Spectrometer (MCD)
USIS .... United States Information Service [*Name used abroad for USIA offices*]
USISA .... United States International Sailing Association (EA)
USISA .... United States International Skating Association
USISCA ..... US Islands 17 Class Association [*Defunct*] (EA)
USISL....... United States Information Service Library (DIT)
USISSA ..... United States International Speed Skating Association (EA)
US-ISY ...... US International Space Year Association (EA)
USIT .... Unit Share Investment Trust
USITA .... United States Independent Telephone Association (EA)
USITA .... United States International Tempest Association (EA)
USITC .... United States International Trade Commission
USITC Pub ... United States International Trade Commission. Publication [*A publication*] (DLA)
USITT .... United States Institute for Theatre Technology (EA)
USIU .... United States International University [*San Diego, CA*]
USJ.......... United States Jaycees (EA)
USJ........... United States Judo (EA)
USJA .... United States Judo Association (EA)
USJAC ..... US-Japan Culture Center (EA)
US JAYCEE ... United States Junior Chamber of Commerce [*Later, United States Jaycees*] (EA)
USJB .... Union Saint-Jean-Baptiste (EA)
USJBC ...... US-Japan Business Council (EA)
USJCA ...... United States Joint Communication Agency (NATG)
USJCC ...... United States Junior Chamber of Commerce [*Later, United States Jaycees*] (EA)
USJCC ...... US-Japan Culture Center (EA)
USJCIRPTE ... United States-Japan Committee on Industry Related Policies and Their Trade Effects [*Acronym pronounced "use-jay-krip-tee"*]
USJCS....... United States Joint Chiefs of Staff (NATG)
US-JCSC... United States-Japan Committee on Scientific Cooperation [*Department of State*] (NOAA)
USJF .... United States Judo Federation (EA)
USJF .... United States Justice Foundation (EA)
USJNRP ... United States/Japan Natural Resources Panel

US Joint Publ Res Serv Transl E Eur Agr Forest Food Ind ... United States. Joint Publication Research Service. Translations on East European Agriculture, Forestry, and Food Industries [*A publication*]
USJPRS .... United States Joint Publications Research Service
US-JTC ..... United States-Japan Trade Council   (EA)
USJTF....... United States Joint Task Force   (AABC)
US Jur .... United States Jurist [*A publication*]   (DLA)
USJUWTF ... United States Joint Unconventional Warfare Task Force   (AABC)
USK .... Ultrasonic Kit
USK .... United States Forces, Korea
USKA .... United States Kart Association [*Defunct*]   (EA)
USKBA...... United Strictly Kosher Butchers Association
USKBTC ... United States Kerry Blue Terrier Club   (EA)
USKEC...... US-Korea Economic Council [*Later, KS*]   (EA)
USKF .... United States Korfball Federation   (EA)
USKHA ..... Uspekhi Khimii [*A publication*]
USKOREA ... United States Forces Korea
Uskor Mosk Inzh-Fiz Inst Sb Statei ... Uskoriteli. Moskovskii Inzherno-Fizicheskii Institut. Sbornik Statei [*USSR*] [*A publication*]
USKOS...... US-Korea Society [*Later, KS*]   (EA)
USI............ Salt Lake City Public Library, Salt Lake City, UT [*Library symbol*] [*Library of Congress*]   (LCLS)
USL............ Underwater Sound Laboratory [*New London, CT*] [*Navy*]
USL............ Unemployed Supernumerary List [*Military*] [*British*]
USL............ Unique Suppliers List
USL .... Unit Spares List
USL............ United Satellites Limited [*London, England*] [*Telecommunications*]   (TSSD)
USL .... United Soccer League   (EA)
USL ...... United States Laws   (DLA)
USL .... United States Legation
USL............ Up Stage Left [*Away from audience*] [*A stage direction*]
USL............ US Leasing International, Inc. [*NYSE symbol*]   (SPSG)
USL............ US Long Distance [*Vancouver Stock Exchange symbol*]
USL............ Useless Loop [*Australia*] [*Airport symbol*]   (OAG)
USL............ Usual   (ROG)
USLA........ United States Committee for Justice to Latin American Political Prisoners [*Defunct*]   (EA)
USLA........ United States Lifesaving Association   (EA)
USLA........ United States Luge Association   (EA)
USLANT... United States Atlantic Subarea [*NATO*]
US Law Ed ... United States Supreme Court Reports, Lawyers' Edition [*A publication*]   (DLA)
US Law Int ... United States Law Intelligencer and Review [*Providence and Philadelphia*] [*A publication*]   (DLA)
US Law Jour ... United States Law Journal [*A publication*]   (DLA)
US Law Mag ... United States Law Magazine [*A publication*]   (DLA)
US Law R... United States Law Review [*A publication*]
USIC .... Church of Jesus Christ of Latter-Day Saints, Historian's Office, Salt Lake City, UT [*Library symbol*] [*Library of Congress*]   (LCLS)
USLC........ United States Locals Collectors   (EA)
USLCA ...... United States Lacrosse Coaches' Association   (EA)
USLCMBA ... US Letter Carriers Mutual Benefit Association [*Washington, DC*]   (EA)
USID .... Daughters of Utah Pioneers Museum Library, Salt Lake City, UT [*Library symbol*] [*Library of Congress*]   (LCLS)
USLD........ Ultrasonic Link Detector
USLD........ Union des Syndicats Libres du Dahomey [*Federation of Free Unions of Dahomey*]
USLDMA ... United States Lanolin and Derivative Manufacturers Association   (EA)
USLE......... Universal Soil Loss Equation [*Agricultural engineering*]
USL Ed...... Lawyers' Edition, United States Supreme Court Reports [*A publication*]   (DLA)
USL Ed 2d ... Lawyers' Edition, United States Supreme Court Reports, Second Series [*A publication*]   (DLA)
USIGS........ Church of Jesus Christ of Latter-Day Saints, Genealogical Society Library, Salt Lake City, UT [*Library symbol*] [*Library of Congress*]   (LCLS)
USL & H.... United States Longshoremen and Harborworkers Act
USLH .... University of Southwestern Louisiana Herbarium
USLHS..... United States Lighthouse Society   (EA)
US Lit Gaz ... United States Literary Gazette [*A publication*]
USLJ .... United States Law Journal [*New Haven and New York*] [*A publication*]   (DLA)
USIL .... Latter-Day Saints Museum, Salt Lake City, UT [*Library symbol*] [*Library of Congress*]   (LCLS)
USLL......... Utah Studies in Literature and Linguistics [*A publication*]
USL Mag... United States Law Magazine [*A publication*]   (DLA)
USLO .... United States Liaison Office [*or Officer*]
USLO .... University Students for Law and Order
US Long Term ... United States Long-Term Review [*A publication*]
USlOr........ Oregon Short Line Law Department, Salt Lake City, UT [*Library symbol*] [*Library of Congress*] [*Obsolete*]   (LCLS)
USLO SACA ... United States Liaison Officer to Supreme Allied Commander, Atlantic   (MUGU)
USIP .... Pioneer Memorial Museum, Salt Lake City, UT [*Library symbol*] [*Library of Congress*]   (LCLS)

USLP........ United States Labor Party
USLR........ United States Law Review [*A publication*]
USL Rev .... United States Law Review [*A publication*]
USLS .... United States Lake Survey [*Marine science*]   (MSC)
USLS .... United States Lighthouse Society   (EA)
USLSA ...... United States League of Savings Associations [*Later, USLSI*]
USLSA ...... United States Livestock Sanitary Association [*Later, United States Animal Health Association*]   (EA)
USLSI....... United States League of Savings Institutions [*Chicago, IL*]   (EA)
USLSO ...... United States Logistics Support Office   (AFM)
USlStM ..... College of Saint Mary-of-the-Wasatch, Salt Lake City, UT [*Library symbol*] [*Library of Congress*] [*Obsolete*]   (LCLS)
USIT .... Utah Technical College at Salt Lake, Salt Lake City, UT [*Library symbol*] [*Library of Congress*]   (LCLS)
USLTA...... United States Lawn Tennis Association [*Later, USTA*]   (EA)
USLTC ...... United States Lakeland Terrier Club   (EA)
USLW .... United States Law Week [*Bureau of National Affairs*] [*A publication*]   (DLA)
USIW .... Westminster College, Salt Lake City, UT [*Library symbol*] [*Library of Congress*]   (LCLS)
USLW BNA ... United States Law Week. Bureau of National Affairs [*A publication*]
USM .... Underwater-to-Surface Missile [*Air Force*]
USM .... Uniform Staffing Methodologies [*DoD*]
USM .... Union des Syndicats de Monaco [*Union of Monaco Trade Unions*]   (EY)
USM .... United Service Magazine [*A publication*]
USM .... United States Mail
USM .... United States Marine
USM .... United States Mint
USM .... United States Minutemen [*Defunct*]   (EA)
USM .... United States Representative to the Military Committee Memorandum [*NATO*]   (NATG)
USM .... University of Southern Mississippi
USM .... Unlisted Securities Market [*London Stock Exchange*]
USM .... Unsaponifiable Matter [*Organic analytical chemistry*]
USM .... Unscheduled Maintenance
USM .... US Cellular [*AMEX symbol*]   (SPSG)
UsM........... US Microfilm Corp., Jacksonville, FL [*Library symbol*] [*Library of Congress*]   (LCLS)
USM .... Usine Nouvelle [*A publication*]
USMA ...... Union Special Corp. [*NASDAQ symbol*]   (NQ)
USMA ...... United States Maritime Administration
USMA ...... United States Military Academy [*West Point, NY*]
USMA ...... United States Military Attache
USMA ...... United States Monopoly Association   (EA)
USMA ...... US Metric Association   (EA)
USMAC..... United States Marine Air Corps
USMAC..... United States Military Assistance Command
USMACSV ... United States Military Assistance Command, South Vietnam [*Obsolete*]
USMACTHAI ... United States Military Assistance Command, Thailand [*Obsolete*]   (AFM)
USMACV ... United States Military Assistance Command, Vietnam [*Obsolete*]
USMAG .... United States Military Advisory Group
USMAPS .. United States Military Academy Preparatory School
USMAPU ... United States Military Academy Preparatory Unit
USMARC ... Advisory Committee for the US Meat Animal Research Center [*Terminated, 1977*]   (EGAO)
USMATS .. United States Military Air Transport Service [*Later, Military Airlift Command*]
USMB .... United States Marine Barracks
USMB .... United States Metric Board [*Terminated*]
USMBHA ... US-Mexico Border Health Association   (EA)
USMBP..... US-Mexico Border Program   (EA)
USMC .... United States Marine Corps
USMC .... United States Maritime Commission [*Functions transferred to Department of Commerce, 1950*]
USMCA..... United States Men's Curling Association [*Later, USCA*]   (EA)
USMCA..... US Mariner Class Association   (EA)
USMCA..... US Mirror Class Association   (EA)
USMCAM ... United States Military Community Activity, Mannheim
USMCAS .. United States Marine Corps Air Station
USMCB..... United States Marine Corps Base   (MCD)
USMCC..... United States Mint - Carson City   (ROG)
USMCCCA ... US Marine Corps Combat Correspondents Association   (EA)
USMCDIA ... United States Marine Corps Drill Instructors Association   (EA)
USMCEB.. United States Military Communications Electronics Board   (NVT)
USMCOC ... United States-Mexico Chamber of Commerce [*See also CCMEU*]   (EA)
USMCP..... United States Military Construction Program   (CINC)
USMCR..... United States Marine Corps Reserve
USMCR(AF) ... United States Marine Corps Reserve (Aviation Fleet)
USMCR(AO) ... United States Marine Corps Reserve (Aviation, Organized)
USMCR(AV) ... United States Marine Corps Reserve (Aviation, Volunteer)
USMCR(F) ... United States Marine Corps Reserve (Fleet)
USMCR(LS) ... United States Marine Corps Reserve (Limited Service)
USMCR(NAV) ... United States Marine Corps Reserve (Naval Aviators)

USMCR(NAVO) ... United States Marine Corps Reserve (Graduate Aviation Cadets, Volunteer)

USMCR(NAVT) ... United States Marine Corps Reserve (Aviation Specialist Transport Pilot, Volunteer)

USMCR(O) ... United States Marine Corps Reserve (Organized)

USMCRTC ... United States Marine Corps Reserve Training Center

USMCR(V) ... United States Marine Corps Reserve (Volunteer)

USMCR(VS) ... United States Marine Corps Reserve (Volunteer Specialists)

USMCR(W) ... United States Marine Corps Reserve (Women)

USMCSS... United States Marine Corps Selective Service Selectee

USMCSSV ... United States Marine Corps Selective Service Volunteer

USMC(W) ... United States Marine Corps (Women)

USMCWR ... United States Marine Corps Women's Reserve

USMD .... US Medical Enterprises, Inc. [*Santa Monica, CA*] [*NASDAQ symbol*] (NQ)

USMECBL ... United States Mission to the European Communities in Belgium and Luxembourg

US Med ..... US Medicine [*A publication*]

USMEF ..... United States Meat Export Federation (EA)

USMEMILCOMUN ... United States Members, United Nations Military Staff Committee

USMEOUN ... United States Mission to the European Office of the United Nations

USMEPC .. United States Military Enlistment Processing Command

USMEPCOM ... United States Military Entrance Processing Command

USMES ..... Unified Science and Mathematics for Elementary Schools [*National Science Foundation*]

USMF .... United States Sports Massage Federation (EA)

USMG .... United States Medical Graduate

USMH .... United States Marine Hospital

USMHS .... United States Marine Hospital Service

USMI .... Universal Software Market Identifier [*Technique Learning*] [*Information service or system*] (IID)

USMI .... US Mineral & Royalty Corp. [*NASDAQ symbol*] (NQ)

USMIAEAA ... United States Mission to the International Atomic Energy Agency in Austria

USMICC ... United States Military Information Control Committee (AFM)

USMID...... Ultrasensitive Microwave Infrared Detector

USMILADREP ... United States Military Advisor's Representative (CINC)

USMILADREPSMPO ... United States Military Advisor's Representative, Southeast Asia Treaty Organization, Military Planning Office (CINC)

USMILATTACHE ... United States Military Attache

USMILCOMUN ... United States Delegation, United Nations Military Staff Committee

USMILLIAS ... United States Military Liaison Office

USMILTAG ... United States Military Technical Advisory Group (AFM)

USMITT ... United States Masters International Track Team [*Defunct*] (EA)

USMKA .... Uspekhi Mikrobiologii [*A publication*]

USML Mag ... United States Monthly Law Magazine [*A publication*] (DLA)

USMLMCINCGSFG ... United States Military Liaison Mission to Commander-in-Chief, Group Soviet Forces, Germany (AABC)

USMLO .... United States Military Liaison Office

USMLS ..... United States Museum Librarian Society (EA)

USMM ...... Union Socialiste des Musulmans Mauritaniens [*Socialist Union of Mauritanian Moslems*]

USMM ...... United States Merchant Marine

USMMA .. United States Merchant Marine Academy [*Kings Point, NY*]

USMMCC ... United States Merchant Marine Cadet Corps

USMMVETS WW2 ... US Merchant Marine Veterans of World War II (EA)

USMNAM ... United States Military North African Mission [*World War II*]

US Month Law Mag ... United States Monthly Law Magazine [*A publication*] (DLA)

USMP........ United States Mallard Project [*Army*]

USMPA..... United States Modern Pentathlon Association (EA)

USMPBA .. United States Modern Pentathlon and Biathlon Association [*Later, USMPA*] (EA)

USMPTC .. United States Modern Pentathlon Training Center [*Military*] (AABC)

USMR .... US Mutual Financial Corp. [*NASDAQ symbol*] (NQ)

USMS........ Unattended Sensor Monitoring System

USMS........ United States Maritime Service

USMS........ United States Marshall Service [*Department of Justice*]

USMS....... United States Mint - San Francisco (ROG)

USMSA .... United States Marine Safety Association (EA)

USMSGS .. United States Maritime Service Graduate Station

USMSMI .. United States Military Supply Mission to India (AFM)

USMSOS .. United States Maritime Service Officers School

USMSR .... United States Military Specification Requirements (MCD)

USMSSB... United States Machine Screw Service Bureau [*Defunct*] (EA)

USMSTS... United States Maritime Service Training School

USMSTS... United States Maritime Service Training Ship

USMSTS... United States Maritime Service Training Station

USMT .... United States Military Transport

USMTM ... United States Military Training Mission (MCD)

USMTMSA ... United States Military Training Mission to Saudi Arabia

USMWR ... United States Mission Weekly Report [*Military*]

USMWW .. United Society of Mechanical Wood Workers [*A union*] [*British*]

USMX .... USMX, Inc. [*Formerly, US Minerals & Explorations Co.*] [*NASDAQ symbol*] (NQ)

USN........... Ultrasonic Nebulizer

USN........... Under Secretary of the Navy

USN........... Union des Scolaires Nigeriens [*Union of Nigerian Scholars*]

USN........... United States Navy

USNA .... United States National Army

USNA .... United States Naval Academy [*Annapolis, MD*]

USNA .... United States Naval Aircraft

USNAAA .. United States Naval Academy Alumni Association

USNAAA .. United States Naval Academy Athletic Association

USNA ANNA ... United States Naval Academy, Annapolis [*Maryland*]

USNAAS... United States Naval Auxiliary Air Station

USNAB ..... United States Naval Advanced Base [*World War II*]

USNAB ..... United States Naval Amphibious Base

USNAC ..... United States of America National Committee of the International Dairy Federation (EA)

USNAC ..... United States Naval Administrative Command

USNAC ..... United States Naval Air Corps

USNACC... United States Naval Member of the Allied Control Commission [*Germany*]

USNADC .. United States Naval Air Development Center

USNA-EPRD ... United States Naval Academy Energy-Environment Study Group and Development Team

USNA-EW ... United States Naval Academy Division of Engineering and Weapons

USNAF...... United States Naval Avionics Facility

USNAHALO ... United States NATO Hawk Liaison Office [*Missiles*] (NATG)

USNAMTC ... United States Naval Air Missile Test Center

USNARS... United States National Archives and Records Service (DIT)

USNAS..... United States Naval Air Service

USNAS..... United States Naval Air Station

USNASA Conf Publ ... United States. National Aeronautics and Space Administration. Conference Publication [*A publication*]

USNATC... United States Naval Air Training Center

US Natl Aeronaut Space Admin Spec Publ ... US National Aeronautics and Space Administration. Special Publication [*A publication*]

US Natl Bur Stand Handb ... US National Bureau of Standards. Handbook [*A publication*]

US Natl Bur Stand J Res ... United States. National Bureau of Standards. Journal of Research [*A publication*]

US Natl Bur Stand J Res Sec A ... US National Bureau of Standards. Journal of Research. Section A [*A publication*]

US Natl Cancer Inst Carcinog Tech Rep Ser ... US National Cancer Institute. Carcinogenesis Technical Report Series [*A publication*]

US Natl Clgh Drug Abuse Inf Rep Ser ... US National Clearinghouse for Drug Abuse. Information Report Series [*A publication*]

US Natl Fert Dev Cent Bull Y ... United States National Fertilizer Development Center. Bulletin Y [*A publication*]

US Natl Ind Pollut Control Counc Publ ... US National Industrial Pollution Control Council. Publications [*A publication*]

US Natl Inst Drug Abuse Res Issues ... US National Institute on Drug Abuse. Research Issues [*A publication*]

US Natl Inst Health Natl Toxicol Program Tech Rep Ser ... US National Institutes of Health. National Toxicology Program Technical Report Series [*A publication*]

US Natl Inst Health Publ ... US National Institutes of Health. Publication [*A publication*]

US Natl Lab (Oak Ridge Tenn) Rev ... United States National Laboratory (Oak Ridge, Tennessee). Review [*A publication*]

US Natl Mar Fish Serv Curr Fish Stat ... US National Marine Fisheries Service. Current Fisheries Statistics [*A publication*]

US Natl Mar Fish Serv Fish Bull ... US National Marine Fisheries Service. Fishery Bulletin [*A publication*]

US Natl Mar Fish Serv Fish Facts ... US National Marine Fisheries Service. Fishery Facts [*A publication*]

US Natl Mar Fish Serv Mar Fish Rev ... US National Marine Fisheries Service. Marine Fisheries Review [*A publication*]

US Natl Mar Fish Serv Rep Natl Mar Fish Serv ... US National Marine Fisheries Service. Report of the National Marine Fisheries Service [*A publication*]

US Natl Mar Fish Serv Stat Dig ... US National Marine Fisheries Service. Statistical Digest [*A publication*]

US Natl Mus Bull ... US National Museum. Bulletin [*A publication*]

US Natl Mus Bull Proc ... United States National Museum. Bulletin. Proceedings [*A publication*]

US Natl Oceanic Atmos Adm Environ Data Serv Tech Memo ... United States. National Oceanic and Atmospheric Administration. Environmental Data Service. Technical Memorandum [*A publication*]

US Natl Oceanic Atmos Adm Key Oceanogr Rec Doc ... US National Oceanic and Atmospheric Administration. Key to Oceanographic Records Documentation [*A publication*]

US Natl Oceanog Data Center Pub ... US National Oceanographic Data Center. Publication [*A publication*]

US Natl Park Serv Ecol Serv Bull ... US National Park Service. Ecological Services Bulletin [*A publication*]

US Natl Park Serv Fauna Natl Parks US Fauna Ser ... US National Park Service. Fauna of the National Parks of the United States. Fauna Series [*A publication*]

US Natl Park Service Nat History Handb Ser ... US National Park Service. Natural History Handbook Series [*A publication*]

US Natl Park Serv Natl Cap Reg Sci Rep ... US National Park Service. National Capitol Region Scientific Report [*A publication*]

US Natl Park Serv Nat Resour Rep ... US National Park Service. Natural Resources Report [*A publication*]

US Natl Park Serv Occas Pap ... US National Park Service. Occasional Paper [*A publication*]

US Natl Park Serv Sci Monogr Ser ... US National Park Service. Scientific Monograph Series [*A publication*]

US Natl Sci Found Res Appl Natl Needs Rep ... United States. National Science Foundation. Research Applied to National Needs Report [*A publication*]

US Nat Mus Bull ... United States National Museum. Bulletin [*A publication*]

US Nat Mus Rept ... United States National Museum. Reports [*A publication*]

USNATO .. United States Mission to the North Atlantic Treaty Organization [*Department of State*]   (NATG)

USNATRA ... United States Naval Training

US Nav Aerosp Med Inst (Pensacola) Monogr ... US Naval Aerospace Medical Institute (Pensacola). Monograph [*A publication*]

US Nav Aerosp Med Inst (Pensacola) NAMI ... US Naval Aerospace Medical Institute (Pensacola). NAMI [*A publication*]

US Nav Aerosp Med Res Lab (Pensacola) NAMRL ... US Naval Aerospace Medical Research Laboratory (Pensacola). NAMRL [*A publication*]

US Nav Aerosp Med Res Lab (Pensacola) Spec Rep ... US Naval Aerospace Medical Research Laboratory (Pensacola). Special Report [*A publication*]

US Nav Air Dev Cent NADC ... US Naval Air Development Center. NADC [*A publication*]

US Naval Aerospace Med Inst ... US Naval Aerospace Medical Institute [*A publication*]

US Naval Med Bull ... United States Naval Medical Bulletin [*A publication*]

US Naval Ordnance Test Sta NAVORD Report ... United States. Naval Ordnance Test Station. NAVORD Report [*A publication*]

US Naval Res Lab Shock Vib Bull ... United States. Naval Research Laboratories. Shock and Vibration Bulletin [*A publication*]

US Naval Submar Med Cent Rep ... US Naval Submarine Medical Center. Report [*A publication*]

US Nav Civ Eng Lab Tech Rep ... United States. Department of the Navy. Naval Civil Engineering Laboratory [*Port Hueneme, California*]. Technical Report [*A publication*]

USNAVEUR ... United States Naval Forces Europe   (MCD)

US Nav Inst Proc ... US Naval Institute. Proceedings [*A publication*]

US Nav Med Bull ... United States Naval Medical Bulletin [*A publication*]

US Nav Med Res Lab Rep ... US Naval Medical Research Laboratory. Report [*A publication*]

US Nav Oceanogr Off Spec Publ ... US Naval Oceanographic Office. Special Publication [*A publication*]

US Nav Postgrad Sch Tech Rep/Res Paper ... United States. Naval Postgraduate School. Technical Report/Research Paper [*A publication*]

USNAVPRO ... United States Navy Plan Representative Office

US Nav Sch Aviat Med Monogr ... US Naval School of Aviation Medicine. Monograph [*A publication*]

US Nav Sch Aviat Med Res Rep ... US Naval School of Aviation Medicine. Research Report [*A publication*]

US Nav Ship Eng Cent Ship Struct Com Rep ... United States. Department of the Navy. Naval Ship Engineering Center. Ship Structure Committee. Report [*A publication*]

US Nav Ship Res Dev Cent Rep ... United States. Naval Ship Research and Development Center. Report [*A publication*]

USNAVSO ... United States Navy Forces Southern Command   (AFM)

USNAVSOUTHC ... United States Navy Southern Command

USNAVSOUTHCOM ... United States Navy Southern Command

US Nav Submar Med Cent Memo Rep ... US Naval Submarine Medical Center. Memorandum Report [*A publication*]

US Nav Submar Med Cent Rep ... United States. Naval Submarine Medical Center. Report [*A publication*]

US Nav Submar Med Res Lab Memo Rep ... United States. Naval Submarine Medical Research Laboratory. Memorandum Report [*A publication*]

US Nav Submar Med Res Lab Rep ... US Naval Submarine Medical Research Laboratory. Report [*A publication*]

USNAVSUPACT ... United States Naval Supply Activity   (CINC)

USNAVWEASERV ... United States Naval Weather Service

US Navy Electronics Lab Rept ... United States. Navy Electronics Laboratory. Report [*A publication*]

US Navy Med ... US Navy Medicine [*A publication*]

USNAVYMILCOMUN ... United States Naval Representative, United Nations Military Staff Committee

USNB .... United States Naval Base   (MUGU)

USNC .... United States National Commission for UNESCO [*of the Department of State*]

USNC .... United States National Committee [*IEC*]

USNCB ...... United States National Central Bureau

USNCB ...... United States Naval Construction Battalion [*SEABEES*] [*BUDOCKS; later, FEC, NFEC*]

USNCBS ... US National Committee for Byzantine Studies   (EA)

USNC/CIE ... US National Committee of the Commission Internationale de l'Eclairage [*International Commission on Illumination*]   (EA)

USNCEREL ... United States Naval Civil Engineering Research and Evaluation Laboratory

USNCFID ... United States National Committee for Federation Internationale de Documentation

USNC/IBP ... United States National Committee for the International Biological Program [*Defunct*]   (EA)

USNCIEC ... United States National Committee of the International Electrotechnical Commission

USNC-IGY ... United States National Committee for the International Geophysical Year

USNCIPS ... United States National Committee of the International Peat Society   (EA)

USNCPNM ... United States National Committee for the Preservation of Nubian Monuments [*Defunct*]   (EA)

USNCSCOR ... US National Committee for the Scientific Committee on Oceanic Research   (EA)

USNCSM & FE ... United States National Council on Soil Mechanics and Foundation Engineering

USNC-STR ... United States National Committee for Solar-Terrestrial Research   (MCD)

USNC/TAM ... US National Committee on Theoretical and Applied Mechanics   (EA)

USNC/UPSI ... United States National Committee/International Union of Radio Science   (MCD)

USNC-URSI ... United States National Committee for the Union Radio Scientifique Internationale [*International Union of Radio Science*]   (EA)

USNCWEC ... United States National Committee of the World Energy Conference   (EA)

USNCWFD ... US National Committee for World Food Day   (EA)

USNDC ..... United States Nuclear Data Committee [*Nuclear Regulatory Commission*]

USNDD ..... United States Naval Drydocks

USNEDS ... United States Navy Experimental Diving Station

USNEL ...... United States Naval Electronics Laboratory

USNELM ... United States Naval Forces, Eastern Atlantic and Mediterranean   (MCD)

US News .... US News and World Report [*A publication*]

US News World Rep ... US News and World Report [*A publication*]

USNFCLC ... US National Federation of Christian Life Communities   (EA)

USNFEC ... US National Fruit Export Council [*Defunct*]   (EA)

USNFP ...... US Nicaragua Friendship Project   (EA)

USNFPN ... US Nuclear Free Pacific Network   (EA)

USNFR ...... United States Naval Fleet Reserve

USNG .... United States National Guard

USNH .... United States Naval Hospital

USNH .... United States, North of Cape Hatteras [*Shipping*]

USNHO .... United States Navy Hydrographic Office [*Later, NOO*]   (NATG)

USNI .... United States Naval Institute   (EA)

USN-I .... United States Regular Navy - Inductee

USN-I-CB ... United States Regular Navy - Inductee - Construction Battalion

USNID ...... United States National Institute of Dance   (EA)

US N Inst Proc ... United States. Naval Institute. Proceedings [*A publication*]

USNIP .... United States. Naval Institute. Proceedings [*A publication*]

USN(I)(SA) ... United States Navy (Inductee) (Special Assignment)

USNL .... United States Navy League

USNLO ..... United States Naval Liaison Officer

USNM .... United States National Museum [*Smithsonian Institution*]

USNMATOEROF ... United States Mission to the North Atlantic Treaty Organization and European Regional Organizations in France

USNMDL ... United States Navy Mine Defense Laboratory   (MUGU)

USNMF ..... United States Naval Missile Facility

USNMF ..... United States Navy Memorial Foundation   (EA)

USNMR ... United States National Military Representative

USNMSC ... United States Navy Medical Service Corps

USNMTC ... United States Naval Missile Test Center [*Point Mugu, CA*]   (AAG)

USNO .... United Sabah National Organization [*Malaysia*] [*Political party*]   (PPW)

USNO .... United States Naval Observatory

USNOA ..... United States Norton Owners' Association   (EA)

USNOADS ... United States Naval Observatory Automated Data Service [*Database*] [*Information service or system*]   (CRD)

USNOBSY ... United States Naval Operating Bases System

USNOF ..... United States NOTAM Office   (FAAC)

USNOO ..... United States Naval Oceanographic Office [*Marine science*]   (MSC)

US North Cent For Exp Stn Res Pap NC ... US North Central Forest Experiment Station. Research Paper NC [*A publication*]

US (Noth) .. Ueberlieferungsgeschichtliche Studien (M. Noth) [*A publication*]   (BJA)

USNOTS ... United States Naval Ordnance Test Station

USNOWSP ... United States National Ocean-Wide Survey Program   (NOAA)

USNP .... United States Naval Prison

USNP .... United States Newspaper Program [*National Foundation on the Arts and the Humanities*] [*Information service or system*] (IID)
USNPACMISTESCEN ... US Navy Pacific Missile Test Center
USNPG ..... United States Naval Proving Ground
USNPGS... United States Naval Postgraduate School (MUGU)
USNPS...... United States Naval Postgraduate School
USNR .... United States Naval Reserve
USNR .... United States Navy Regulations
USNRB....... United States Naval Repair Base
USNRC ..... United States Nuclear Regulatory Commission (NRCH)
USNRDL... United States Naval Radiological Defense Laboratory
USNRDL... United States Navy Research and Development Laboratory
USN(Ret).. United States Navy (Retired)
USNRF...... United States Naval Reserve Force
USNRL....... United States Naval Research Laboratory
USNRM ..... United States Merchant Marine Reserve
USNRM1 .. United States Merchant Marine Reserve Seagoing
USNRM2 .. United States Merchant Marine Reserve Coastal Defense
USNRO ..... United States Organized Naval Reserve
USNRO1 ... United States Organized Naval Reserve Seagoing
USNRO2... United States Organized Naval Reserve Aviation
USNRP...... United States National Reference Preparation [*Centers for Disease Control*]
USNRS...... United States Navy Recruiting Station
USNR & SL ... United States Navy Radio and Sound Laboratory [*San Diego, CA*]
USNRSV ... United States Naval Reserve, Selective Volunteer
USNRTC... United States Naval Reserve Training Center
USNRV ..... United States Naval Reserve, Volunteer
USNR(W) ... United States Naval Reserve (Women's Reserve)
USNS........ United States Naval Ship [*Civilian manned*]
USNS......... United States Naval Station
USNS........ Universal Stabilized Night Sight
USNSA...... United States National Student Association [*Later, USSA*]
USNSC ...... United States Naval Safety Code
USNSISSMFE ... US National Society for the International Society of Soil Mechanics and Foundation Engineering (EA)
USNSMC ... United States Naval Submarine Medical Center
USNSMSES ... United States Navy Ship Missile System Engineering Station
USNSO ..... United States Navy Southern Command
USNSPS.... United States National Stockpile Purchase Specification [*for metals*]
USN-SV .... United States Regular Navy Selective Volunteer
USNTC...... United States Naval Training Center
USNTDC... United States Naval Training Device Center
USNTI....... United States Navy Travel Instructions
US NTIS AD Rep ... United States. National Technical Information Service. AD Report [*A publication*]
USNTIS PB Rep ... United States. National Technical Information Service. PB Report [*A publication*]
USNTPS ... United States Naval Test Pilot School
USNTS...... United States Naval Training School
USNUSL... United States Navy Underwater Sound Laboratory [*BUSHIPS; later, ESC, NESC*]
USNWC .... United States Naval War College
USNWR .... US News and World Report [*A publication*]
USNZC...... United States-New Zealand Council (EA)
USO.......... Under Secretary of the Navy's Office
USO.......... Unidentified Submarine Object
USO.......... Unit Security Officer (AAG)
USO.......... United Service Organizations, Inc. (EA)
USO.......... United Siscoe Mines, Inc. [*Toronto Stock Exchange symbol*]
USO.......... Universal Service Order [*Bell System*] (TEL)
USO.......... Unmanned Seismological Observatory
USO.......... US Office - UTLAS Corp. [*UTLAS symbol*]
USOA .... Uniform System of Accounts [*Telecommunications*] (TEL)
USOA .... United Shoppers of America, Inc. [*NASDAQ symbol*] (NQ)
USOA .... United States Olympic Association [*Later, USOC*]
USOA .... United States Othello Association (EA)
USOA .... United States Overseas Airlines
US Oak Ridge Natl Lab Radiat Shield Inf Cent Rep ... United States. Oak Ridge National Laboratory. Radiation Shielding Information Center. Report [*A publication*]
USOAS...... United States Mission to the Organization of American States [*Department of State*]
USO-ASPCC ... USO [*United Service Organizations*]-All Service Postal Chess Club [*Later, ASPCC*] (EA)
USOC .... Uniform Service Order Code [*Bell System*] (TEL)
USOC .... United States Olympic Committee (EA)
USOCA ..... United States Office of Consumer Affairs
USOCA ..... US 1 Class Association (EA)
USOCA ..... US Out of Central America (EA)
U So Cal Tax Inst ... University of Southern California Tax Institute (DLA)
U So Carol ... University of South Carolina. Business and Economic Review [*A publication*]
USOCDC .. US Overseas Cooperative Development Committee (EA)
USO-CLAT ... US Relations Office of CLAT [*Central Latinoamericana de Trabajadores*] (EA)
USOE .... United States Office of Education [*Later, USDE*]

USOECD... United States Mission to the Organization for Economic Cooperation and Development [*Department of State*]
USOF .... United States Orienteering Federation (EA)
USOFA...... Under Secretary of the Army
USOFAF ... Under Secretary of the Air Force
US Office Ed Bul ... United States. Office of Education. Bulletin [*A publication*]
US Office Ed Circ ... United States. Office of Education. Circulars [*A publication*]
US Office Ed Pub ... United States. Office of Education. Publications [*A publication*]
US Office Ed Voc Div Bul ... United States. Office of Education. Vocational Division. Bulletin [*A publication*]
US Office Saline Water Research and Devel Progress Rept ... United States. Office of Saline Water Research and Development. Progress Report [*A publication*]
US Off Libr Serv Bibliogr Ser ... US Office of Library Service. Bibliography Series [*A publication*]
US Off Nav Res Rep ACR ... United States. Office of Naval Research. Report ACR [*A publication*]
US Off Pub Roads B ... US Office of Public Roads. Bulletin [*A publication*]
US Off Saline Water Res Dev Prog Rep ... United States. Office of Saline Water Research and Development. Progress Report [*A publication*]
USOID ...... United States Oversea Internal Defense [*Army*] (AABC)
USOL .... US Oil Co. [*NASDAQ symbol*] (NQ)
USOLTA... Uniform Simplification of Land Transfers Act [*National Conference of Commissioners on Uniform State Laws*]
USOM....... United States Operations Mission [*Military*]
USOMC .... United States Ordnance Missile Command
USONIA ... United States of North America [*Name of a cooperative community in Pleasantville, NY designed by Frank Lloyd Wright*]
USONR..... United States Office of Naval Research
USOPA...... United States Ordnance Producers Association [*Inactive*] (EA)
USOSP...... United States Ocean Survey Plan (NOAA)
US Outlook ... United States Industrial Outlook [*A publication*]
USOVA ..... United States Outdoor Volleyball Association (EA)
USp............ Springville City Library, Springville, UT [*Library symbol*] [*Library of Congress*] (LCLS)
USP........... Ultrasensitive Position (AFM)
USP........... Under the Sign of Pisces [*A publication*]
USP........... Underwater Sound Projection
USP........... Uniform Specification Program (AAG)
USP........... Unique Selling Point
USP........... Unique Selling Proposition [*Advertising*]
USP........... Unit Stream Power [*Hydrology*]
USP........... Unit Support Plan (MCD)
USP........... United Socialist Party [*Tongsa Dang*] [*Republic of Korea*] [*Political party*] (PPW)
USP........... United States Patent
USP........... United States Penitentiary
USP........... United States Pharmacopeia [*Following name of a substance, signifies substance meets standards set by USP*]
USP........... United States Pharmacopeial Convention [*Database producer*] (EA)
USP........... United States Postal Service Library, Washington, DC [*OCLC symbol*] (OCLC)
USP........... United States Property
USP........... Universal Signal Processor
USP........... Upper Sequential Permissive [*Nuclear energy*] (NRCH)
USP........... Upper Solution Point
USP........... Urban Studies Project
USP........... US Precious Metals, Inc. [*Toronto Stock Exchange symbol*] [*Vancouver Stock Exchange symbol*]
USP........... Usage Sensitive Pricing [*Telecommunications*]
USP........... Utility Seaplane [*Navy, Coast Guard*]
USP........... Utility Summary Program
USPA........ Uniform Single Publication Act [*National Conference of Commissioners on Uniform State Laws*]
USPA........ Uniformed Services Pay Act
USPA........ United States Parachute Association (EA)
USPA........ United States Passport Agency [*Department of State*]
USPA........ United States Pilots Association (EA)
USPA........ United States Polo Association (EA)
USPA........ United States Potters' Association (EA)
USPA........ US Patents Alert [*Derwent, Inc.*] [*Database*]
USPA........ US Psychotronics Association (EA)
US Pacific RR Expl ... US War Department. Pacific Railroad Explorations [*A publication*]
US Pac Northwest For Range Exp Stn Res Note PNW ... US Pacific Northwest Forest and Range Experiment Station. Research Note PNW [*A publication*]
USPACOM ... United States Pacific Command [*Military*]
USPAK...... US-Pakistan Economic Council (EA)
US Pap Maker ... United States Paper Maker [*A publication*]
US Pat Off Off Gaz US Pat Off Pat ... US Patent Office. Official Gazette of the United States Patent Office. Patents [*A publication*]
US Pat Q.... United States Patent Quarterly [*A publication*] (DLA)
US Pat Quar ... United States Patent Quarterly [*A publication*] (DLA)
US Pat Quart ... United States Patent Quarterly [*A publication*] (DLA)

US Pat Trademark Off Off Gaz US Pat Trademark Off Pat ... US Patent and Trademark Office. Official Gazette of the United States Patent and Trademark Office. Patents [*A publication*]
Usp Biol Chim ... Uspechi Biologiceskoj Chimii [*A publication*]
Usp Biol Khim ... Uspekhi Biologicheskoi Khimii [*USSR*] [*A publication*]
USPC........ Union des Syndicats Professionels du Cameroun [*Federation of Professional Trade Unions of Cameroon*]
USPC........ United States Parole Commission [*Formerly, United States Parole Board*]
USPC........ United States Peace Corps   (EA)
USPC........ United States Pony Clubs   (EA)
USPC........ United States Procurement Committee
USPC........ United States Purchasing Commission
USPC........ US Peace Council   (EA)
USPC........ US Playing Card Corp. [*NASDAQ symbol*]   (NQ)
USPCA...... United States Police Canine Association   (EA)
USPCF...... US Professional Cycling Federation [*Later, USPRO*]   (EA)
Usp Chim... Uspechi Chimii [*A publication*]
USPCS...... US Philatelic Classics Society   (EA)
USPCU...... US Postal Chess Union   (EA)
USPD........ Unabhaengige Sozialdemokratische Partei Deutschlands [*Independent Social Democratic Party of Germany*] [*Political party*]   (PPE)
USPD........ US Publicity Director [*A publication*]
USPDCA... United States Professional Diving Coaches Association   (EA)
USPDI....... United States Professional Development Institute [*Silver Spring, MD*]
USPDLTR ... [*Reference*] Your Speedletter [*Military*]
USP & DO ... United States Property and Disbursing Officer
USPDO..... United States Property and Disbursing Officer
USPE........ United States Purchasing Exchange
USPEC...... United States Paper Exporters Council   (EA)
Uspehi Fiz Nauk ... Akademija Nauk SSSR. Uspehi Fiziceskih Nauk [*A publication*]
Uspehi Mat Nauk ... Akademija Nauk SSSR i Moskovskoe Matematiceskoe Obscestvo. Uspehi Matematiceskih Nauk [*A publication*]
Uspekhi Fiz Nauk ... Uspekhi Fiziceskih Nauk [*A publication*]
Uspekhi Mat Nauk ... Uspekhi Matematicheskikh Nauk [*A publication*]
USPEPA.... United States Poultry and Egg Producers Association   (EA)
USPF........ US Powerlifting Federation   (EA)
Usp Fizic N ... Uspechi Fiziceskich Nauk [*A publication*]
Usp Fiziol Nauk ... Uspekhi Fiziologicheskikh Nauk [*A publication*]
Usp Fiz Nau ... Uspekhi Fizicheskikh Nauk [*A publication*]
Usp Fiz Nauk ... Uspekhi Fizicheskii Nauk [*A publication*]
USPFO...... United States Property and Fiscal Officer [*Military*]
Usp Foton ... Uspekhi Fotoniki [*A publication*]
Usp Fotoniki ... Uspekhi Fotoniki [*A publication*]
US/PFUN ... United States People for the United Nations [*Defunct*]   (EA)
USPG........ Uniform System of Accounts Prescribed for Natural Gas Companies
USPG........ United Society for the Propagation of the Gospel [*Formed by a merger of Society for the Propagation of the Gospel in Foreign Parts and UMCA*]   (EAIO)
USpGS....... Church of Jesus Christ of Latter-Day Saints, Genealogical Society Library, Springville Branch, Springville, UT [*Library symbol*] [*Library of Congress*]   (LCLS)
USPh .... United States Pharmacopoeia
US Pharm ... US Pharmacist [*A publication*]
USPHD5 ... US Pharmacist [*A publication*]
USPHS...... United States Postal History Society [*Defunct*]   (EA)
USPHS...... United States Public Health Service
USPHSR.... United States Public Health Service Reserve
USPHT..... United States Precision Helicopter Team
USPI........ University Science Partners, Inc. [*NASDAQ symbol*]   (NQ)
USPIN....... United States Pacific Issues Network   (EA)
USPIRG .... US Public Interest Research Group   (EA)
Usp Kh...... Uspekhi Khimii [*A publication*]
Usp Khim... Uspekhi Khimii [*A publication*]
Usp Khim Fosfororg Seraorg Soedin ... Uspekhi Khimii Fosfororganicheskikh i Seraorganicheskikh Soedinenii [*A publication*]
Usp Khim Tekhnol Polim ... Uspekhi Khimii i Tekhnologii Polimerov [*A publication*]
USPL........ Uniform System of Accounts, Public Utilities, and Licensees [*Federal Power Commission*]
USPL........ Unpriced Spare Parts List
USPLS....... United States Public-Land Surveys
USPLTA.... United States Professional Lawn Tennis Association [*Later, USPTA*]   (EA)
USPM....... United Society of Pattern Makers [*A union*] [*British*]
USPM........ US Precious Metals, Inc. [*Vancouver, BC*] [*NASDAQ symbol*]   (NQ)
Usp Mat Nauk ... Uspekhi Matematicheskikh Nauk [*A publication*]
USPMF..... US Patent Model Foundation   (EA)
Usp Mikrobiol ... Uspekhi Mikrobiologii [*A publication*]
Usp Mol Biol ... Uspekhi na Molekulyarnata Biologiya [*A publication*]
USPMOM ... Union des Societes de Pediatrie du Moyen-Orient et de la Mediterranee [*Union of Middle Eastern and Mediterranean Pediatric Societies - UMEMPS*] [*Athens, Greece*]   (EAIO)
USPN .... US Pawn, Inc. [*NASDAQ symbol*]   (NQ)
Usp Nauchn Fotogr ... Uspekhi Nauchnoi Fotografii [*A publication*]

USPO .... United Sabah People's Organization [*Pertubuhan Rakyat Sabah Bersatu*] [*Malaysia*] [*Political party*]   (PPW)
USPO .... United States Patent Office [*Department of Commerce*]
USPO .... United States Post Office [*Later, United States Postal Service*]
US Posture ... United States Military Posture [*A publication*]
USPP .... United States Pacifist Party [*Political party*]   (EA)
USPP .... United States Park Police [*Department of the Interior*]
USPP .... University Science Policy Planning [*Program*] [*National Science Foundation*]
USPPA ...... United States Pulp Producers Association [*Later, API*]   (EA)
USPPI ...... United States Producer Price Index [*Database*] [*Department of Labor*] [*Information service or system*]   (CRD)
USPPS...... US Possessions Philatelic Society   (EA)
USPQ .... United States Patents Quarterly
USPQ BNA ... United States Patents Quarterly. Bureau of National Affairs [*A publication*]
USPRO...... US Professional Cycling Federation   (EA)
USPS .... United States Postal Service
USPS .... United States Power Squadrons   (EA)
USPSA ...... US Practical Shooting Association   (EA)
USPSD ..... United States Political Science Documents [*Information service or system*] [*A publication*]
USPSDA ... United States Private Security and Detective Association   (EA)
USPSF...... United States Pigeon Shooting Federation [*Defunct*]   (EA)
Usp Sovrem Biol ... Uspekhi Sovremennoi Biologii [*A publication*]
Usp Sovrem Genet ... Uspekhi Sovremennoi Genetiki [*A publication*]
USPT........ United Societies of Physiotherapists   (EA)
USPTA ...... United States Physical Therapy Association   (EA)
USPTA ...... United States Pony Trotting Association   (EA)
USPTA ...... United States Professional Tennis Association   (EA)
USPTA ...... US Paddle Tennis Association   (EA)
USPTO ...... United States Patent and Trademark Office
USPTR ...... United States Professional Tennis Registry   (EA)
US Publ H Rep ... US Public Health Report [*A publication*]
US Public Health Serv Public Health Monogr ... United States. Public Health Service. Public Health Monograph [*A publication*]
US Public Health Serv Radiol Health Data Rep ... US Public Health Service. Radiological Health Data and Reports [*A publication*]
USPWIC ... United States Prisoner of War Information Center [*Army*]   (AABC)
USPWIC(Br) ... United States Prisoner of War Information Center (Branch) [*Army*]   (AABC)
USQ.......... United States Quarterly Book Review [*A publication*]
US Q Bk R ... United States Quarterly Book Review [*A publication*]
USQBL...... United States Quarterly Book List [*A publication*]
USQBR...... United States Quarterly Book Review [*A publication*]
USQR .... Union Seminary. Quarterly Review [*A publication*]
US Quartermaster Food Container Inst Armed Forces Libr Bull ... US Quartermaster Food and Container Institute for the Armed Forces. Library Bulletin [*A publication*]
USR .... Ukrainska Partiia Sotsialistov Revolyutsionerov [*Ukrainian Socialist Revolutionary Party*] [*Russian*] [*Political party*]   (PPE)
USR .... Ultrasonic Radiation
USR .... Under Speed Relay   (MCD)
USR .... Union Seminary. Review [*A publication*]
USR .... Unit Status Report [*Army*]
USR .... United States [*Supreme Court*] Reports
USR .... United States Reserves
USR .... Up Stage Right [*Away from audience*] [*A stage direction*]
USR .... US Shoe Corp. [*NYSE symbol*]   (SPSG)
USR .... User Service Request
USR .... User Service Routine [*Digital Equipment Corp.*]
USR .... User Status Reporting   (MCD)
USR .... Usher of the Scarlet Rod   (ROG)
USRA .... United Sportsman Racers Association   (EA)
USRA .... United States Racquetball Association   (EA)
USRA .... United States Railway Association [*In 1974, superseded United States Railroad Administration, which had been absorbed by the Department of Transportation in 1939*] [*Terminated in 1987*]
USRA .... United States Revolver Association   (EA)
USRA .... United States Rowing Association   (EA)
USRA .... United Street Rod Association   (EA)
USRA .... Universities Space Research Association   (EA)
USRAC ..... US Repeating Arms Company
USRAD ..... United States Fleet Shore Radio Station
USR-Borotbists ... Ukrainska Partiia Sotsialistov Revolyutsionerov-Borotbists [*Ukrainian Socialist Revolutionary Party-Fighters*] [*Russian*] [*Political party*]   (PPE)
USRCMM ... US Region of Congregation of Mariannhill Missionaries [*Later, CMM*]   (EA)
USRCPAC ... United States Reserve Components and Personnel Administration Center
USRCS ...... United States Revenue Cutter Service
USRCSI..... United States Red Cedar Shingle Industry
USRD .... Underwater Sound Reference Detachment [*Navy*] [*Orlando, FL*]
USRDA ..... US Recommended Daily Allowance [*Nutrition*]
USRE........ US Facilities Corp. [*Costa Mesa, CA*] [*NASDAQ symbol*]   (NQ)

USREC...... United States Environment and Resources Council [*Marine science*] (MSC)
USREDA... United States Rice Export Development Association [*Later, RCMD*]
USREDCOM ... United States Readiness Command
US Reg....... United States Register [*Philadelphia*] [*A publication*] (DLA)
US Reh Den ... Rehearing Denied by United States Supreme Court [*Legal term*] (DLA)
US Reh Dis ... Rehearing Dismissed by United States Supreme Court [*Legal term*] (DLA)
US Rep....... United States Reports [*A publication*] (DLA)
US Rep (L Ed) ... United States Supreme Court Reports, Lawyers' Edition [*A publication*] (DLA)
USREPMC ... United States Representative to the Military Committee [*NATO*] (NATG)
USREPMILCOMLO ... United States Representative to the Military Committee Liaison Office [*NATO*] (NATG)
USREPMILCOMUN ... United States Representative, Military Staff Committee, United Nations
USREPOF ... United States Navy Reporting Office [*or Officer*]
US Res Developm Rep ... United States Government Research and Development Reports [*A publication*]
US Rev St .. United States Revised Statutes [*A publication*] (DLA)
USRFP ...... US Requests for Proposals [*Washington Representative Service*] [*Information service or system*] [*Defunct*] (CRD)
USRI......... US Resources, Incorporated [*Columbus, OH*] [*NASDAQ symbol*] (NQ)
USRL......... Laryak [*USSR*] [*ICAO location identifier*] (ICLI)
USRL......... Underwater Sound Reference Laboratory [*Navy*]
USRL......... US Realty Partners Limited Partnership [*Greenville, SC*] [*NASDAQ symbol*] (NQ)
USRM .... United States Revenue Marine
USRN .... Nizhnevartovsk [*USSR*] [*ICAO location identifier*] (ICLI)
USRNMC ... United States Representative to NATO Military Committee (AABC)
USRO .... Ultrasmall Structures Research Office [*University of Michigan*] [*Research center*] (RCD)
USRO .... United States Mission to NATO and European Regional Organizations
USRO .... United States Navy Routing Office
USRP......... United States Refugee Program
USRPA...... United States Racing Pigeon Association [*Defunct*] (EA)
USRR......... Surgut [*USSR*] [*ICAO location identifier*] (ICLI)
USRRC...... United States Road Racing Championship
USRR Lab Bd Dec ... Decisions of the United States Railroad Labor Board [*A publication*] (DLA)
USRS......... United States Reclamation Service
USRS......... United States Revised Statutes
USRS......... United States Robotics Society (CSR)
USRS......... United States Rocket Society (EA)
USRS......... United States Rowing Society (EA)
USRSA ...... United States Racquet Stringers Association (EA)
USRSG...... United States Representative, Standing Group [*Military*] (AABC)
USRT........ Universal Synchronous Receiver/Transmitter
USRTA...... United States Recreational Tennis Association (EA)
USS........... Ultrasound Scanning
USS........... Ultraviolet Scanning Spectrometer
US of S....... Under Secretary of State
USS........... Underwater Sound Source
USS........... Unified S-Band System [*Radio*]
USS........... Union Syndicale Suisse [*Swiss Federation of Trade Unions*]
USS........... United Scholarship Service [*Later, NCAIAE, NCAIE*]
USS........... United Seamen's Service (EA)
USS........... United States Naval Vessel
USS........... United States Sellers [*Standard threads*] (DEN)
USS........... United States Senate
USS........... United States Ship
USS........... United States Standard
USS........... United States Steamer
USS........... United States Surgical Corp. [*NYSE symbol*] (SPSG)
USS........... United States Swimming, Inc. (EA)
USS........... United Superannuation Services Proprietary Ltd. [*Australia*]
USS........... United Swedish Societies (EA)
USS........... Universities Superannuation Scheme
USS........... US Steel Canada, Inc. [*Toronto Stock Exchange symbol*]
USS........... US Steel Corp. [*Also, USSC*] [*Later, USX Corp.*]
USS........... USAF [*United States Air Force*] Security Service
USS........... Usage Sensitive Service [*Telecommunications*]
USS........... User Support System (MCD)
USS........... Utility Support Structure (MCD)
USSA........ Underground Security Storage Association [*Defunct*]
USSA........ Uniaxial Split-Sphere Apparatus [*Mineralogy*]
USSA........ Union Suisse des Syndicats Autonomes [*Swiss Association of Autonomous Unions*]
USSA........ United Saw Service Association (EA)
USSA........ United States Salvage Association (EA)
USSA........ United States Security Authority [*for NATO affairs*]
USSA........ United States Ski Association (EA)
USSA........ United States Snowshoe Association (EA)

USSA........ United States Sports Academy (EA)
USSA........ United States Standard Atmosphere (KSC)
USSA........ United States Student Association (EA)
USSA........ United States Swimming Association (EA)
USSA........ United Sugar Samplers' Association [*Defunct*]
USSA........ US Sidewinder Association (EA)
USSA........ US Soling Association (EA)
USSAC...... United States Army Ambulance Service Association [*Defunct*] (EA)
USSAC...... United States Security Authority for CENTO Affairs (AABC)
USSAF ...... United States Strategic Air Force [*Later, Strategic Air Command*]
USSAF ...... US Sports Acrobatic Federation (EA)
USSAFE.... United States Strategic Air Forces in Europe
USSAG...... United States Support Activities Group [*Military*]
USSAH...... United States Soldiers' and Airmen's Home (AABC)
USSALEP ... US-South Africa Leader Exchange Program (EA)
USSAS ...... United States Security Authority for SEATO Affairs (AABC)
USSB........ United States Satellite Broadcasting Co., Inc. [*Minneapolis, MN*] [*Telecommunications*] (TSSD)
USSB........ United States Shipping Board [*Terminated, 1933*]
USSB........ United States Shipping Board Decisions [*A publication*] (DLA)
USSBA ..... United States Seniors Bowling Association [*Later, Seniors Division of the American Bowling Congress*] (EA)
USSBB ...... United States Shipping Board Bureau Decisions [*A publication*] (DLA)
USSBD ...... United States Savings Bonds Division [*Department of the Treasury*]
USSBF....... United States Skibob Federation (EA)
USSBIA..... United States Stone and Bead Importers Association (EA)
USSBL...... United States Stickball League (EA)
USSBS...... United States Strategic Bombing Survey [*Disbanded, 1946*]
USSC........ United States Servas Committee (EA)
USSC....... United States Strike Command [*Military combined Tactical Air Command and Strategic Army Command Force*]
USSC........ United States Supreme Court
USSC........ US Steel Corporation [*Also, USS*] [*Later, USX Corp.*] (MCD)
USSC........ US Systems Corporation (EA)
USSCA ..... US Ski Coaches Association (EA)
US-SCAN ... United States Special Committee on Antarctic Names [*1943-47*]
US Sci Educ Adm Agric Res Man ... US Science and Education Administration. Agricultural Research Manual [*A publication*]
USSC Rep ... United States Supreme Court Reports [*A publication*] (DLA)
USSCT ...... United States Supreme Court
USSDP....... Uniformed Services Savings Deposits Program (AABC)
USSE........ Severouralsk [*USSR*] [*ICAO location identifier*] (ICLI)
USSE......... Ultrasonic Soldering Equipment
USSE......... University of Saga. Studies in English [*A publication*]
USSEA ...... United States Scientific Export Association
USSEA ...... United States Society for Education through Art (EA)
USSEA ...... United States Space Education Association (EA)
USSECMILCOMUN ... [*The*] Secretary, United States Delegation United Nations Military Staff Committee
US Seed Rep ... United States Seed Reporter [*A publication*]
USSEF....... United States Ski Educational Foundation (EA)
US Serv M ... United States Service Magazine [*A publication*]
USSES....... US Sheep Experiment Station [*University of Idaho*] [*Research center*] (RCD)
USSF .... Ulster Special Service Force [*British military*] (DMA)
USSF .... United States Soccer Federation (EA)
USSF .... United States Softball Federation
USSF .... United States Space Foundation (EA)
USSF .... United States Special Forces
USSF .... United States Steel Foundation
USSF .... United States Surfing Federation (EA)
USSF .... United States Swimming Foundation (EA)
USSFA ...... United States Soccer Football Association [*Later, USSF*] (EA)
USSFFA .... United Soft Serve and Fast Food Association [*Later, NSSFFA*] (EA)
USSF(P)..... United States Special Forces (Provisional) (CINC)
USSFR....... US Scottish Fiddling Revival (EA)
USSG........ United States Standard Gauge
USSGA...... United States Seniors Golf Association [*Defunct*] (EA)
USSGA...... Uspekhi Sovremennoi Genetiki [*A publication*]
USSGREP ... United States Standing Group Representative [*NATO*] (AABC)
USSH .... United States Soldiers' Home
US Ship Struct Com Rep ... United States. Ship Structure Committee. Report [*A publication*]
USSI.......... Ivdel [*USSR*] [*ICAO location identifier*] (ICLI)
USSI.......... Ultrasonic Soldering Iron
USSI.......... United Software Security, Incorporated [*Vienna, VA*] [*NASDAQ symbol*] (NQ)
USSI.......... United States Strategic Institute (EA)
USSI.......... USS Interphase (EA)
USSIA .... United States Shellac Importers Association (EA)
USSIAFCM ... USS Intrepid Association of Former Crew Members (EA)
USSID....... United States Signal Intelligence Directive (AABC)
US-SIOP ... United States Single Integrated Operational Plan (NATG)
USSIS........ United States Signals Intellignce System (MCD)

USSLL....... United States Savings and Loan League [*Later, USLSI*] (EA)
USSMA..... US Spanish Merchants Association (EA)
USSNBA .... USS [*United States Ship*] Natoma Bay Association (EA)
USSOA...... USS [*United States Ship*] Oklahoma Association (EA)
USSOCOM ... United States Special Operations Command [*DoD*]
US Soil Conserv Service Sedimentation Bull (TP) ... United States. Soil Conservation Service. Sedimentation Bulletin (Technical Publication) [*A publication*]
US Soil Conserv Serv Soil Surv ... US Soil Conservation Service. Soil Survey [*A publication*]
USSOUTHCOM ... United States Southern Command [*Air Force*]
USSP .... User Systems Support Plan
USSPA ...... United States Student Press Association [*Superseded by CPS*]
USSPACECOM ... United States Space Command
USSPC ...... US Student Pugwash Committee (EA)
USSPEI..... Union des Syndicats des Services Publics Europeens et Internationaux [*European and International Public Services Union*] [*Later, EUROFEDOP*] (EAIO)
USSPG ...... United States Senate Press Photographers Gallery (EA)
USSPG ...... US Sweetener Producers Group [*Later, ASA*] (EA)
USSPL....... United Ship Scrapers' Protection League [*A union*] [*British*]
USSPPG.... United States Senate Press Photographers Gallery (EA)
USSR .... State Music Trust [*Record label*] [*USSR*]
USSR......... Uninterrupted Sustained Silent Reading
USSR......... Union of Soviet Socialist Republics [*See also SSSR, CCCP*]
U d SSR ..... Union der Sozialistischen Sowjetrepubliken [*A publication*]
USSRA ...... United States Squash Racquets Association (EA)
USSR Comp Info B ... USSR. Union of Composers. Information Bulletin [*A publication*]
USSR Computational Math and Math Phys ... USSR Computational Mathematics and Mathematical Physics [*A publication*]
USSR Comput Math Math Phys ... USSR Computational Mathematics and Mathematical Physics [*A publication*]
USSR Comput Math and Math Phys ... USSR Computational Mathematics and Mathematical Physics [*A publication*]
USSRM ..... State Music Trust [*78 RPM*] [*Record label*] [*USSR*]
USSRN...... Under Secretary of State for the Royal Navy [*British*]
USSR Rep Earth Sci ... USSR Report. Earth Sciences [*Arlington*] [*A publication*]
USSR Rep Eng Equip ... USSR Report. Engineering Equipment [*A publication*]
USSS .... Sverdlovsk [*USSR*] [*ICAO location identifier*] (ICLI)
USSS .... Undersea Surveillance System (MCD)
USSS .... United States Secret Service [*Department of the Treasury*]
USSS .... United States Steamship
USSS .... Unmanned Sensing Satellite System
USSS .... US Shelter Corp. [*NASDAQ symbol*] (NQ)
USSSA ...... United States Slo-Pitch Softball Association (EA)
USSSA ...... United States Snowshoe Association (EA)
USSSI........ United Stamp Society for Shut-Ins (EA)
USSSI........ United States Satellite Systems, Incorporated [*Defunct*] (TSSD)
USSSI....... United States Synchronized Swimming, Incorporated (EA)
USSSMA .. US Shake and Shingle Manufacturers Association (EA)
USSSO...... United States Sending State Office [*Navy*]
USSS/UD ... United States Secret Service Uniformed Division
USSTAF.... United States Strategic Air Force [*Later, Strategic Air Command*]
USSTAFE ... United States Strategic Tactical Air Force, Europe
US Stat ...... United States Statutes at Large [*A publication*] (DLA)
US Steel News ... United States Steel News [*A publication*]
US St at L.. United States Statutes at Large [*A publication*] (DLA)
USSTRICOM ... United States Strike Command [*Military combined Tactical Air Command and Strategic Army Command Force*]
USSTS....... US Student Travel Service (EA)
US St Tr..... United States State Trials [*Wharton*] [*A publication*] (DLA)
US Sup Ct ... United States Supreme Court Reporter [*A publication*] (DLA)
US Sup Ct (L Ed) ... United States Supreme Court Reports, Lawyers' Edition [*A publication*] (DLA)
US Sup Ct R ... United States Supreme Court Reporter [*West*] [*A publication*] (DLA)
US Sup Ct Rep ... United States Supreme Court Reporter [*A publication*] (DLA)
US Sup Ct Reps ... Supreme Court Reporter [*A publication*] (DLA)
USSWA..... United States Ski Writers Association [*Later, NASJA*] (EA)
UST .... Ultrasonic Test
UST .... Ultrasonic Transducer [*Crystal*] [*Used in measuring human cardiac output*]
UST .... Unblocked Serial Telemetry (MCD)
UST .... Underground Storage Tank [*Environmental Protection Agency*]
UST .... Undersea Technology
UST .... Uniform Specification Tree
UST .... Union Senegalaise du Travail [*Senegalese Labor Union*]
UST .... Union Socialiste Tchadienne [*Chadian Socialist Union*]
UST .... Unit Security Technician
UST .... United States Testing Co., Inc. (NASA)
UST .... United States Time
UST .... United States Treaties and Other International Agreements [*A publication*] (DLA)
UST .... Universal Servicing Tool (NASA)
UST .... University of Saint Thomas [*Texas*]

UST .... UST, Inc. [*Formerly, US Tobacco*] [*NYSE symbol*] (SPSG)
UST .... Ustilago [*A fungus*]
UST .... Ustus [*Burnt*] [*Pharmacy*]
USTA........ Union des Syndicats des Travailleurs Algeriens [*Federation of Unions of Algerian Workers*]
USTA........ United States Telephone Association (EA)
USTA........ United States Tennis Association, Inc. (EA)
USTA........ United States Trademark Association (EA)
USTA........ United States Trotting Association (EA)
USTA........ United States Twirling Association (EA)
USTA........ Unlisted Securities Trading Act [*1936*]
USTA........ US Tornado Association (EA)
USTA........ US Triathlon Association [*Later, TRI-FED*] (EA)
USTA........ US Trivia Association (EA)
U-Stadtbibliothek ... Universitaets- und Stadtbibliothek [*A publication*]
USTAF....... United States/Thai Forces
USTA/NJTL ... USTA [*United States Tennis Association*] National Junior Tennis League (EA)
US Tariff Comm Rep ... United States. Tariff Commission. Reports [*A publication*]
US Tariff Comm TC Publ ... United States. Tariff Commission. TC Publication [*A publication*]
Ustav Jad Fyz Cesk Akad Ved Rep ... Ustav Jaderne Fyziky Ceskoslovenska Akademia Ved. Report [*A publication*]
Ustav Vedeckotech Inf Sb UVTI Genet Slechteni ... Ustav Vedeckotechnickych Informaci. Sbornik UVTI. Genetika a Slechteni [*A publication*]
Ustav Vedeckotech Inf Sb UVTI Melior ... Ustav Vedeckotechnickych Informaci. Sbornik UVTI. Rada. Meliorace [*A publication*]
Ustav Vedeckotech Inf Zemed ... Ustav Vedeckotechnickych Informaci pro Zemedelstvi [*A publication*]
Ustav Vedeckotech Inf Zemed Sb UVTIZ Melior ... Ustav Vedeckotechnickych Informaci pro Zemedelstvi. Sbornik UVTIZ. Rada. Meliorace [*A publication*]
Ustav Vedeckotech Inf Zemed Stud Inf Ochr Rostl ... Ustav Vedeckotechnickych Informaci pro Zemedelstvi Studijni Informace Ochrana Rostlin [*A publication*]
Ustav Vyzk Vyuziti Paliv Monogr ... Ustav pro Vyzkum a Vyuziti Paliv Monografie [*A publication*]
US Tax Cas ... United States Tax Cases [*Commerce Clearing House*] [*A publication*] (DLA)
US Tax Cas CCH ... US Tax Cases. Commerce Clearing House [*A publication*]
US Tax Rpt ... United States Tax Report [*A publication*]
US Tb........ U & S [*Urban & Schwarzenberg*] Taschenbuecher [*A publication*]
USTB........ United States Travel Bureau
USTB........ UST Corp. [*NASDAQ symbol*] (NQ)
USTC........ United States Tariff Commission [*Later, ITC*]
USTC........ United States Tax Cases [*Commerce Clearing House*] [*A publication*] (DLA)
USTC........ United States Testing Company, Inc.
USTC........ United States Tourist Council (EA)
USTC........ United States Transportation Commission [*Proposed commission to consolidate CAB, ICC, and FMC*]
USTC........ US-Tibet Committee (EA)
USTC........ US Trade Center [*Mexico*] (IMH)
USTC........ US Trust Corporation [*NASDAQ symbol*] (NQ)
USTCA...... United States Track Coaches Association [*Later, TFA/USA*]
USTC Jl BG ... United States Tobacco and Candy Journal Buyer's Guide [*A publication*]
USTC Jrl... United States Tobacco and Candy Journal [*A publication*]
USTC & TBA ... US Tennis Court and Track Builders Association (EA)
USTD .... Union des Syndicats des Travailleurs du Dahomey [*Federation of Workers' Unions of Dahomey*]
USTD .... United States Treasury Department
USTD .... United States Treaty Development [*A publication*] (DLA)
USTDA...... United States Truck Drivers Association
USTDC...... United States Forces, Taiwan Defense Command (CINC)
USTDC...... US Travel Data Center (EA)
US TEL ...... US Telephone, Inc. [*Dallas, TX*] [*Telecommunications*] (TSSD)
USTES ...... United States Training and Employment Service [*Abolished, 1971*] [*Department of Labor*]
USTF .... United States Tuna Foundation (EA)
USTFA...... United States Trout Farmers Association (EA)
USTFF...... United States Track and Field Federation [*Later, TFA/USA*]
USTFFA.... United States Touch and Flag Football Association (EA)
U St G .... Umsatzsteuergesetz [*A publication*]
UStG .... Umsatzsteuergesetz [*German Turnover Tax Act*] (DLA)
USTG .... Union Syndicale des Travailleurs de Guinee [*Guinean Federation of Workers*]
UStgD........ Dixie College, St. George, UT [*Library symbol*] [*Library of Congress*] (LCLS)
UStgGS...... Church of Jesus Christ of Latter-Day Saints, Genealogical Society Library, St. George Branch, St. George, UT [*Library symbol*] [*Library of Congress*] (LCLS)
UStgW .... Washington County Library, St. George, UT [*Library symbol*] [*Library of Congress*] (LCLS)
USTHF...... US Team Handball Federation (EA)
USTI.......... United Systems Technology, Inc. [*NASDAQ symbol*] (NQ)

USTIIC...... United States Technical Industrial Intelligence Committee (MCD)
USTJ......... United States Tobacco Journal [*A publication*]
USTL......... US Telephone, Inc. [*NASDAQ symbol*] (NQ)
USTOA..... United States Tour Operators Association (EA)
USTOL...... Ultrashort Takeoff and Landing [*Aviation*] (MCD)
USTOPS... United States Travelers' Overseas Personalized Service [*Also known as TOPS*]
USTR........ United States Trade Representative [*Formerly, SRTN*] [*Executive Office of the President*]
USTR........ United Stationers, Inc. [*NASDAQ symbol*] (NQ)
USTRA...... United States Touring Riders Association (EA)
USTRANSCOM ... United States Transportation Command
USTRC...... United States Transportation Research Command [*Army*]
U St Rd...... Umsatzsteuer-Rundschau [*A publication*]
US Treas Dept ... United States Treasury Department (DLA)
US Treas Reg ... United States Treasury Regulations [*A publication*] (DLA)
US Treaty Ser ... United States Treaty Series [*A publication*] (DLA)
USTS......... Union Syndicale des Travailleurs du Soudan [*Federation of Sudanese Workers*] [*Mali*]
USTS......... United States Time Standard [*National Institute of Standards and Technology*]
USTS......... United States Transmission Systems, Inc. [*Secaucus, NJ*] (TSSD)
USTS......... United States Travel Service [*Replaced by United States Travel and Tourism Administration*] [*Department of Commerce*]
USTSA...... US Targhee Sheep Association (EA)
USTSA...... US Telecommunications Suppliers Association [*Later, TIA*] (EA)
USTTA...... United States Table Tennis Association (EA)
USTTA...... United States Travel and Tourism Administration [*Formerly, US Travel Service*] [*Department of Commerce*]
USTTI....... US Telecommunications Training Institute [*Washington, DC*] [*Telecommunications*] (TSSD)
USTU........ Ultrasonic Test Unit
USTU........ US Taekwondo Union (EA)
USTU........ US Taxpayers Union (EA)
USTV........ Universal Subscription Television
USTV........ Unmanned Supersonic Test Vehicle (MCD)
USTVA...... United States Tennessee Valley Authority
Ust Ved Inf MZLVH Rostl Vyroba ... Ustav Vedeckotechnickych Informaci. Ministerstva Zemedelstvi. Lesniho a Vodnlho Hospodarstvi. Rostlinna Vyroba [*A publication*]
Ust Ved Inf MZLVH Stud Inf Pudoz ... Ustav Vedeckotechnickych Informaci. MZLVH [*Ministerstva Zemedelstvi. Lesniho a Vodnlho Hospodarstvi*] Studijni Informace Pudoznalstvi a Meliorace [*A publication*]
Ust Ved Inf MZ Rostl Vyroba ... Ustav Vedeckotechnickych Informaci. Ministerstva Zemedelstvi. Rostlinna Vyroba [*A publication*]
Ust Ved Inf MZVZ Rostl Vyroba ... Ustav Vedeckotechnickych Informaci. Ministerstva Zemedelstvi a Vyzivy. Rostlinna Vyroba [*A publication*]
USTW....... Sovetsky [*USSR*] [*ICAO location identifier*] (ICLI)
USTWA..... US Tennis Writers Association (EA)
USTZD...... Unsensitized
USU.......... Unbundled Stock Unit [*Investment term*] [*Obsolete*]
USU.......... Uniformed Services University of the Health Sciences Library, Bethesda, MD [*OCLC symbol*] (OCLC)
USU.......... United Stevedores' Union [*British*]
USU.......... Usually
USUA........ United States Ultralight Association (EA)
USUARIOI ... Association of Maritime Transport Users in the Central American Isthmus [*Guatemala, Guatemala*] (EAIO)
USUB........ Unglazed Structural Unit Base [*Technical drawings*]
USUCA..... United Steel Workers' Union of Central Africa [*Rhodesia and Nyasaland*]
USUG........ US Sugar Corp. [*NASDAQ symbol*] (NQ)
USUHS..... Uniformed Services University of the Health Sciences [*DoD*] [*Bethesda, MD*] (EGAO)
US/UK....... United States/United Kingdom
USUMS..... Utah State University. Monograph Series [*A publication*]
USUN........ United States United Nations Delegation (CINC)
USURP...... Usurpandus [*To Be Used*] [*Pharmacy*]
USUSA...... United Societies of the United States of America [*McKeesport, PA*] (EA)
USV .... U-Save Foods Ltd. [*Vancouver Stock Exchange symbol*]
USV .... United States Volunteers [*Civil War*]
USV .... Unmanned Strike Vehicle
USVAAD... United States Veteran's Administration Administrator's Decisions [*A publication*] (DLA)
USVAC...... United States Veterans' Assistance Center (OICC)
USVB........ United States Veterans Bureau
USVBA...... United States Volleyball Association (EA)
USVBA...... US Venetian Blind Association (EA)
USVBDD... United States Veterans Bureau Director's Decisions [*A publication*] (DLA)
USVC........ US LICO Corporation [*Formerly, United Services Life Insurance*] [*NASDAQ symbol*] (NQ)

US Veterans Adm (W) Dep Med Surg Bull Prosthet Res ... United States. Veterans Administration (Washington, DC). Department of Medicine and Surgery. Bulletin of Prosthetics Research [*A publication*]
US Veterans Bureau Med Bull ... United States. Veterans Bureau. Medical Bulletin [*A publication*]
USVH........ United States Veterans Hospital
USVIP....... Uniformed Services Voluntary Insurance Program
USVMD.... Urine Specimen Volume Measuring Device
USVMS..... Urine Sample Volume Measurement System (MCD)
USVR........ US Vacation Resorts [*NASDAQ symbol*] (NQ)
USVS........ United Services Advisors, Inc. [*San Antonio, TX*] [*NASDAQ symbol*] (NQ)
USVT........ Universal Stray Voltage Tester
USW .... Ultrashort Wave
USW .... Ultrasonic Welding
USW .... Und So Weiter [*And So Forth*] [*German*]
USW .... Under Secretary of War [*Obsolete*]
USW .... Undersea Warfare
USW .... United Steelworkers [*Trade union*] [*British*]
USW .... Universitaets-Seminar fuer Wirtschaft [*Wiesbaden*] [*A publication*]
USW .... US West, Inc. [*NYSE symbol*] (SPSG)
USW .... US Wheat Associates (EA)
USWA .... American Association for Study of the United States in World Affairs (EA)
USWA .... United Shoe Workers of America [*Later, ACTWU*] (EA)
USWA .... United States Wayfarer Association (EA)
USWA .... United Steelworkers of America [*Also known as USW*] (EA)
USWAB.... United States Warehouse Act Bonded
USWACC ... United States Women's Army Corps Center
USWACS .. United States Women's Army Corps School
USWAP..... United South West Africa Party [*Namibia*] [*Political party*]
USWAP..... United Steel Workers' Association of the Philippines
US War Dp Chief Eng An Rp ... United States. War Department. Chief of Engineers. Annual Report [*A publication*]
US Waterw Exp Stn Contract Rep ... United States. Waterways Experiment Station. Contract Report [*A publication*]
US Waterw Exp Stn Misc Pap ... United States. Waterways Experiment Station. Miscellaneous Paper [*A publication*]
US Waterw Exp Stn Res Rep ... United States. Waterways Experiment Station. Research Report [*A publication*]
US Waterw Exp Stn Tech Rep ... United States. Waterways Experiment Station. Technical Report [*A publication*]
US Waterw Exp Stn (Vicksburg Miss) Misc Pap ... United States. Waterways Experiment Station (Vicksburg, Mississippi). Miscellaneous Paper [*A publication*]
US Waterw Exp Stn (Vicksburg Miss) Res Rep ... United States. Waterways Experiment Station (Vicksburg, Mississippi). Research Report [*A publication*]
US Waterw Exp Stn (Vicksburg Miss) Tech Rep ... United States. Waterways Experiment Station (Vicksburg, Mississippi). Technical Report [*A publication*]
USWB .... United States Weather Bureau [*Later, National Weather Service*]
USWBC..... United States War Ballot Commission [*World War II*]
USWCA..... United States Women's Curling Association (EA)
USWF........ United States Weightlifting Federation (EA)
USWF........ United States Wrestling Federation (EA)
USWGA .... United States Wholesale Grocers' Association [*Later, NAWGA*] (EA)
USWI........ United States West Indies
USWISOMWAGMOHOTM ... United Single Women in Search of Men Who Aren't Gay, Married, or Hung-Up on Their Mothers [*Fictitious association*]
USWLA..... United States Women's Lacrosse Association (EA)
USWN....... US WEST NewVector Group, Inc. [*NASDAQ symbol*] (NQ)
US Women's Bur Bul ... United States. Women's Bureau. Bulletin [*A publication*]
USWP........ United States Water Polo (EA)
USWSRA .. United States Women's Squash Racquets Association (EA)
USWSSB... United States Wood Screw Service Bureau [*Defunct*] (EA)
USWTCA ... United States Women's Track Coaches Association (EA)
USWV .... United Spanish War Veterans (EA)
USX .... Ultrasoft X-Ray
USX .... US Steel Corp. [*Formerly, USS, USSC*]
USXFS..... Ultrasoft X-Ray Fluorescence [*Spectroscopy*]
USXRS ..... Ultrasoft X-Ray Spectroscopy
USXX......... US Technologies, Inc. [*NASDAQ symbol*] (NQ)
USY .... United Synagogue Youth (EA)
USY .... US Pay-Tel, Inc. [*Vancouver Stock Exchange symbol*]
USYC........ United States Youth Council (EA)
USYEC...... US Yugoslav Economic Council (EA)
USYRU ..... US Yacht Racing Union (EA)
USYSA...... United States Youth Soccer Association (EA)
USZI......... United States Zone of the Interior
UT............. Conference Internationale pour l'Unite Technique des Chemins de Fer
UT............. Tooele Public Library, Tooele, UT [*Library symbol*] [*Library of Congress*] (LCLS)
UT............. Ugaritic Text [*A publication*]

UT............. Ultrasonic Test
UT............. Ultrathin
UT............. Umbilical Tower [Aerospace]
UT............. Uncontrolled Term [Online database field identifier]
UT............. Under the Tongue [Pharmacy]
U/T........... Under Training [British military]   (DMA)
U/T........... Under Trust [Legal term]   (DLA)
UT............. Underway Trials [Shipbuilding]
UT............. Unemployed Time [Military] [British]
UT............. Unexpired Term [Real estate] [British]   (ROG)
UT............. Union Terminal Railway Co. [AAR code]
UT............. Union de Transports Aeriens [France] [ICAO
              designator]   (FAAC)
UT............. Unit   (MCD)
UT............. Unit Tester   (NASA)
UT............. Unit Trust   (ILCA)
UT............. United Technologies Corp.
UT............. United Telecommunications, Inc. [NYSE symbol]   (SPSG)
UT............. United Territory
UT............. United Together   (EA)
UT............. Universal Time [Astronomy]
UT............. Universal Torpedo   (MCD)
UT............. Universal Trainer
UT............. Universal Turret   (MCD)
U of T........ University of Toronto [Ontario]
UT............. University of Toronto [Ontario]
UT............. University of Tulsa [Oklahoma]
UT............. Unser Tsait/Unzer Tsayt [A publication]
UT............. Unspecified Temperature
UT............. Untested
U/T........... Untrained
UT............. Up Through [Parapsychology]
UT............. Up Time
UT............. Upper Torso
UT............. Urinary Tract [Medicine]
UT............. User Test
UT............. User's Terminal   (MCD)
UT............. Utah [Postal code]
UT............. Utah Music Educator [A publication]
UT............. Utah Reports [A publication]   (DLA)
UT............. Utah Territory [Prior to statehood]
UT............. Utendum [To Be Used] [Pharmacy]   (ROG)
UT............. Utilitiesman [Navy rating]
UT............. Utility   (BUR)
UT............. Utility Boat
UT............. Utility Player
UT1........... Utilitiesman, First Class [Navy rating]
UT2........... Utilitiesman, Second Class [Navy rating]
UT3........... Utilitiesman, Third Class [Navy rating]
UTA.......... Ultrasonic Thermal Action
UTA.......... Union de Transports Aeriens [Air Transport Union] [Private
              airline] [France]   (EY)
UTA.......... Unit Training Assembly [Military]   (AABC)
UTA.......... Unit Trust Association [British]
UTA.......... United Technologies Automotive
UTA.......... United Typothetae of America [Later, Printing Industries of
              America]
UTA.......... University of Texas at Arlington
UTA.......... Upper Terminal Area   (NATG)
UTA.......... Urban Transportation Administration [HUD]
UTA.......... User Transfer Address
UTAA........ Unit Trust Association of Australia
UTAC........ Union Tunisienne de l'Artisanat et du Commerce [Tunisian
              Union of Artisans and Merchants]
UTACV ..... Urban Tracked Air-Cushion Vehicle [Transit] [Department of
              Transportation]
UTAD........ Utah Army Depot   (AABC)
UTAH........ Utah Railway Co. [AAR code]
UTAH........ Utah Shale Land & Minerals Corp. [NASDAQ symbol]   (NQ)
Utah .... Utah Supreme Court Reports [A publication]   (DLA)
Utah Acad Sci Proc ... Utah Academy of Sciences, Arts, and Letters.
              Proceedings [A publication]
Utah Ac Sc Tr ... Utah Academy of Sciences. Transactions [A publication]
Utah Admin Bull ... State of Utah Bulletin [A publication]   (DLA)
Utah Admin R ... Administrative Rules of Utah [A publication]   (DLA)
Utah Ag Exp ... Utah. Agricultural Experiment Station. Publications [A
              publication]
Utah Agric Exp Stn Bull ... Utah. Agricultural Experiment Station. Bulletin [A
              publication]
Utah Agric Exp Stn Circ ... Utah. Agricultural Experiment Station. Circular
              [A publication]
Utah Agric Exp Stn Res Rep ... Utah. Agricultural Experiment Station.
              Research Report [A publication]
Utah Agric Exp Stn Spec Rep ... Utah. Agricultural Experiment Station.
              Special Report [A publication]
Utah Agric Exp Stn Utah Resour Ser ... Utah. Agricultural Experiment
              Station. Utah Resources Series [A publication]
Utah Bar Bull ... Utah Bar Bulletin [A publication]
Utah B Bull ... Utah Bar Bulletin [A publication]
Utah BJ ..... Utah Bar Journal [A publication]
Utah Code Ann ... Utah Code, Annotated [A publication]   (DLA)

Utah 2d ...... Utah Reports, Second Series [A publication]   (DLA)
Utah Dep Nat Resour Tech Publ ... Utah. Department of Natural Resources.
              Technical Publication [A publication]
Utah Dep Nat Resour Water Cir ... Utah. Department of Natural Resources.
              Water Circular [A publication]
Utah Dept Nat Resources Tech Pub ... Utah. Department of Natural
              Resources. Division of Water Rights. Technical Publication
              [A publication]
Utah Div Water Resources Coop Inv Rept ... Utah. Division of Water
              Resources. Cooperative Investigations Report [A
              publication]
Utah Econ and Bus R ... Utah Economic and Business Review [A publication]
Utah Eng Exp Stn Bull ... Utah. Engineering Experiment Station. Bulletin [A
              publication]
Utah Farm Home Sci ... Utah Farm and Home Science [A publication]
Utah Geol .. Utah Geology [A publication]
Utah Geol Assoc Publ ... Utah Geological Association. Publication [A
              publication]
Utah Geol and Mineralog Survey Bull ... Utah. Geological and Mineralogical
              Survey. Bulletin [A publication]
Utah Geol and Mineralog Survey Circ ... Utah. Geological and Mineralogical
              Survey. Circular [A publication]
Utah Geol and Mineralog Survey Quart Rev ... Utah. Geological and
              Mineralogical Survey. Quarterly Review [A publication]
Utah Geol and Mineralog Survey Spec Studies ... Utah. Geological and
              Mineralogical Survey. Special Studies [A publication]
Utah Geol and Mineralog Survey Water Resources Bull ... Utah. Geological
              and Mineralogical Survey. Water Resources Bulletin [A
              publication]
Utah Geol Mineral Surv Bull ... Utah. Geological and Mineralogical Survey.
              Bulletin [A publication]
Utah Geol Mineral Surv Circ ... Utah. Geological and Mineralogical Survey.
              Circular [A publication]
Utah Geol Mineral Surv Spec Stud ... Utah. Geological and Mineralogical
              Survey. Special Studies [A publication]
Utah Geol Mineral Surv Water Resour Bull ... Utah. Geological and
              Mineralogical Survey. Water Resources Bulletin [A
              publication]
Utah Geol Miner Surv Circ ... Utah. Geological and Mineralogical Survey.
              Circular [A publication]
Utah Geol Miner Surv Q Rev ... Utah. Geological and Mineralogical Survey.
              Quarterly Review [A publication]
Utah Geol Miner Surv Notes ... Utah. Geological and Mineralogical
              Survey. Survey Notes [A publication]
Utah Geol Soc Guidebook to Geology of Utah ... Utah Geological Society.
              Guidebook to the Geology of Utah [A publication]
Utah Hist Q ... Utah Historical Quarterly [A publication]
Utah Hist Quar ... Utah Historical Quarterly [A publication]
Utah Hist Quart ... Utah Historical Quarterly [A publication]
Utah IC Bull ... Utah Industrial Commission. Bulletin [A publication]   (DLA)
Utah Lib..... Utah Libraries [A publication]
Utah Lib Assn Newsl ... Utah Library Association. Newsletter [A publication]
Utah Libr... Utah Libraries [A publication]
Utah LR... Utah Law Review [A publication]
Utah L Rev ... Utah Law Review [A publication]
Utah M ...... Utah Genealogical and Historical Magazine [A publication]
Utah Med Bull ... Utah Medical Bulletin [A publication]
Utah PUC ... Utah Public Utilities Commission Report [A
              publication]   (DLA)
Utah R .... Utah Reports [A publication]   (DLA)
Utah Resour Ser Utah Agr Exp Sta ... Utah Resources Series. Utah
              Agricultural Experiment Station [A publication]
Utah Sci..... Utah Science [A publication]
Utah Sci Utah Agric Exp Stn ... Utah Science. Utah Agricultural Experiment
              Station [A publication]
Utah State Engineer Bienn Rept Tech Pub ... Utah State Engineer. Biennial
              Report. Technical Publications [A publication]
Utah State Engineer Inf Bull ... Utah State Engineer. Information Bulletin [A
              publication]
Utah State Eng Off Basic Data Rep ... Utah. State Engineer's Office. Basic
              Data Report [A publication]
Utah State Eng Tech Publ ... Utah State Engineer. Technical Publication [A
              publication]
Utah State Med J ... Utah State Medical Journal [A publication]
Utah State Univ Agric Exp Stn Bull ... Utah State University. Agricultural
              Experiment Station. Bulletin [A publication]
Utah Univ Anthropol Papers Bull ... Utah University. Anthropological Papers.
              Bulletin [A publication]
Utah Univ Eng Exp Stn Tech Pap ... Utah University. Engineering
              Experiment Station. Technical Paper [A publication]
Utah Univ Eng Expt Sta Bull ... Utah University. Engineering Experiment
              Station. Bulletin [A publication]
UTAP .... Unified Transportation Assistance Program [Proposed]
UTAP .... Urban Transportation Assistance Program [Canada]
UTAS........ Underwater Target-Activated Sensor   (MCD)
U Tas LR ... University of Tasmania. Law Review [A publication]
U Tasmania L Rev ... University of Tasmania. Law Review [A publication]
U Tasm L Rev ... University of Tasmania. Law Review [A publication]
UTASN ..... University of Texas at Austin School of Nursing
UT/AT....... Underway Trial/Acceptance Trial [Navy]   (NVT)

UTATA ..... Uniform Testamentary Additions to Trusts Act [*National Conference of Commissioners on Uniform State Laws*]
UTB .... Muttaburra [*Australia*] [*Airport symbol*]   (OAG)
UTB .... Uni Taschenbuecher GmbH [*German publishers cooperative*]
UTB .... United Tariff Bureau
UTB .... Universitaets-Taschenbuecher [*A publication*]
UTB .... University of Toronto Library, Brieflisted Records [*UTLAS symbol*]
UTB .... Utilitiesman, Boilerman [*Navy rating*]
UTBC .... Union Trust Bancorp [*NASDAQ symbol*]   (NQ)
UT BJ .... Utah Bar Journal [*A publication*]
UTBK .... United Bancorp, Inc. [*Salt Lake City, UT*] [*NASDAQ symbol*]   (NQ)
UTBN .... Utah Bancorp [*NASDAQ symbol*]   (NQ)
UTC .... Uncle Tom's Cabin [*Title of book by Harriet Beecher Stowe*]
UTC .... Underwater Training Centre [*British*]
UTC .... Union de Trabajadores Campesinos [*Agricultural Workers' Union*] [*El Salvador*]   (PD)
UTC .... Union des Travailleurs Congolais [*Union of Congolese Workers*]
UTC .... Unit Test Cases   (NASA)
UTC .... Unit Time Coding
UTC .... Unit Total Cost
UTC .... Unit Training Center [*Military*]
UTC .... Unit Type Code   (AFM)
UTC .... United Canso Oil & Gas Ltd. [*Toronto Stock Exchange symbol*]
UTC .... United States Tax Court, Library, Washington, DC [*OCLC symbol*]   (OCLC)
UTC .... United Technologies Corporation [*Information service or system*]   (IID)
UTC .... United Trust & Credit [*Finance group*] [*British*]
UTC .... Universal Test Console   (KSC)
UTC .... Universal Time Code
UTC .... Universal Time Coordinated [*The universal time emitted by coordinated radio stations*]
UTC .... University Teachers Certificate
UTC .... University of Tennessee at Chattanooga
UTC .... University Training Corps [*British*]
UTC .... Urban Technology Conference
UTC .... Urban Training Center
UTC .... Utilities Telecommunications Council   (EA)
UTC .... Utilities, Transportation, Communication
UTC .... Utilitiesman, Chief [*Navy rating*]
UTCA .... Constructionman Apprentice, Utilitiesman, Striker [*Navy rating*]
UTCA .... Utica Bankshares Corp. [*NASDAQ symbol*]   (NQ)
UTCAA ..... Uncle Tom Cobley and All [*Refers to everyone*] [*Slang*] [*British*]   (DSUE)
UTCC .... University of Tennessee at Knoxville Computer Center [*Research center*]   (RCD)
UTCEU ..... Universidad de Tucuman. Cuadernos de Extension Universitaria [*A publication*]
UTCL .... Union des Travailleurs Communistes Libertaires [*Union of Libertarian Communist Workers*] [*France*] [*Political party*]   (PPW)
UTCLK ...... Universal Transmitter Clock
UTCM .... Utilitiesman, Master Chief [*Navy rating*]
UTCN .... Constructionman, Utilitiesman, Striker [*Navy rating*]
UTCPTT ... Union Internationale des Organismes Touristiques et Culturels des Postes et des Telecommunications [*International Union of Tourist and Cultural Associations in the Postal and Telecommunications Services*]
UTCS .... Urasenke Tea Ceremony Society   (EA)
UTCS .... Urban Traffic Control System
UTCS .... Utilitiesman, Senior Chief [*Navy rating*]
UTCT .... Undermanned Tank Crew Test [*Military*]   (MCD)
UTD .... Kermisgids [*A publication*]
UTD .... Undetermined
UTD .... United
UTD .... United Investors Management Co. Non-Voting [*NYSE symbol*]   (SPSG)
UTD .... Universal Transfer Device
UTD .... University of Texas at Dallas   (MCD)
UTD .... Uranium-Thorium Dating
UTD .... User Terminal and Display Subsystem [*Space Flight Operations Facility, NASA*]
UTDC .... Urban Transportation Development Corporation [*Canada*]
UTDD .... Dushanbe [*USSR*] [*ICAO location identifier*]   (ICLI)
UTDEMS ... University of Tulsa. Department of English. Monograph Series [*A publication*]
UT DICT ... Ut Dictum [*As Directed*] [*Latin*]
UTDO .... Oktyabrsky [*USSR*] [*ICAO location identifier*]   (ICLI)
UTE .... Chandler, AZ [*Location identifier*] [*FAA*]   (FAAL)
UTE .... Underwater Tracking Equipment   (MCD)
UTE .... Union Technique de l'Electricite [*France*]
UTE .... Universal Test Equipment
UTE .... Utilization of Theoretical Energy
UTEC .... Universal Test Equipment Compiler   (KSC)
U Tech Umweltmag ... U das Technische Umweltmagazin [*West Germany*] [*A publication*]
UTED .... Dzhizak [*USSR*] [*ICAO location identifier*]   (ICLI)

UTEELRAD ... Utilization of Enemy Electromagnetic Radiation   (MSA)
UTEL .... United Telecontrol Electronics, Inc. [*NASDAQ symbol*]   (NQ)
UTEND ...... Utendus [*To Be Used*] [*Pharmacy*]
UTEP .... University of Texas at El Paso
UTEPDF ... University of Tasmania. Environmental Studies Occasional Paper [*A publication*]
UTES .... Unit Training Equipment Site [*Military*]   (AABC)
UTET .... Unione Tipografico-Editrice Torinese [*Publisher*] [*Italy*]
UTET Boll Ed ... UTET [*Unione Tipigrafico-Editrice Torinese*] Bollettino Editoriale [*A publication*]
UTF .... Underwater Tank Facility
UTF .... Underwater Test Facility [*GE*]
UTF .... Valparaiso [*Chile*] [*Seismograph station code, US Geological Survey*]   (SEIS)
U T Fac L Rev ... University of Toronto. Faculty of Law. Review [*A publication*]
UT Faculty LR ... Faculty of Law Review. University of Toronto [*A publication*]
UTFO .... Untouchable Force Organization [*Rap recording group*]
UTFS .... University of Toronto. French Series [*A publication*]
UTG .... University of Toronto Library, Government Documents [*UTLAS symbol*]
UTGA .... United Tobacco Growers Association   (EA)
UT & GS ... Uplink Text and Graphics System   (NASA)
UTGT .... Under Thirty Group for Transit [*Defunct*]   (EA)
UTH .... Udon Thani [*Thailand*] [*Airport symbol*]   (OAG)
UTH .... Union Texas Petroleum Holdings, Inc. [*NYSE symbol*]   (SPSG)
UTH .... Upper Turret Half
UTHS .... University of Texas. Hispanic Studies [*A publication*]
UTHSCSA ... University of Texas Health Science Center at San Antonio
UTI .... International Universal Time [*Telecommunications*]   (TEL)
UTI .... Union Telegraphique Internationale   (MSC)
UTI .... United Transport International [*Bennett's, Transport*] [*British*]
UTI .... Universal Trident Industries Ltd. [*Vancouver Stock Exchange symbol*]
UTI .... Urinary Tract Infection [*Medicine*]
UTIA .... University of Toronto, Institute of Aerophysics   (MCD)
UTIAS ...... University of Toronto, Institute for Aerospace Studies [*Research center*]   (MCD)
UTIC .... USAREUR Tactical Intelligence Center   (MCD)
UTICI .... Union Technique des Ingenieurs Conseils [*French*]
UT-IG .... University of Texas at Austin Institute for Geophysics [*Research center*]   (RCD)
UTIL .... Utility [*or Utilization*]   (AFM)
Utilitas Math ... Utilitas Mathematica [*A publication*]
Util L Rep .. Utilities Law Reporter [*Commerce Clearing House*] [*A publication*]   (DLA)
Util L Rep CCH ... Utilities Law Reports. Commerce Clearing House [*A publication*]
UTILN .... Utilitarian   (AAG)
Util Sect Newl ... Utility Section Newsletter [*A publication*]   (DLA)
UT INF ..... Ut Infra [*As Below*] [*Latin*]   (ADA)
UTIPS .... Upgraded Tactical Information Processing System [*Data processing*]
UTIRS .... United Tiberias Institutions Relief Society   (EA)
UTJ .... Uterotubal Junction [*Medicine*]
UTK .... University of Tennessee, Knoxville
UTK .... Utirik [*Marshall Islands*] [*Airport symbol*]   (OAG)
UTL .... Unit Transmission Loss
UTL .... Unit Transmittal Letter [*Army*]
UTL .... UNITIL Corp. [*AMEX symbol*]   (SPSG)
UTL .... UnivEd Technologies Ltd. [*United Kingdom*]   (IRUK)
UTL .... Universal Transporter Loader   (MCD)
UTL .... University of Toledo, College of Law, Toledo, OH [*OCLC symbol*]   (OCLC)
UTL .... University of Toronto Library [*UTLAS symbol*]
UTL .... Up Telecommunications Switch
UTL .... User Trailer Label   (CMD)
UTLAS ...... UTLAS International Canada [*Formerly, University of Toronto Library Automation System*] [*Library network*]
UTLC .... University of Tennessee College of Law   (DLA)
UTLC .... UTL Corporation [*NASDAQ symbol*]   (NQ)
UTLD .... Utah Test of Language Development [*Education*]
UTLJ .... University of Toronto. Law Journal [*A publication*]
UTLL .... Utilitech, Inc. [*NASDAQ symbol*]   (NQ)
UTLM .... Up Telemetry   (MCD)
UTLR .... University of Tasmania. Law Review [*A publication*]
UT LR .... Utah Law Review [*A publication*]
UTLY .... Utility   (BUR)
UTM .... Union des Travailleurs de Mauritanie [*Union of Workers of Mauritania*]
UTM .... Union des Travailleurs de Mayotte [*Comoros*]   (PD)
UTM .... Universal Test Message
UTM .... Universal Testing Machine
UTM .... Universal Transverse Mercator [*Cartography*]
UTM .... Universal Turing Machine [*Mathematical model*] [*Data processing*]   (BYTE)
UTMA .... Uniform Transfers to Minors Act [*National Conference of Commissioners on Uniform State Laws*]
UTMA .... United Tank Makers' Association [*A union*] [*British*]

UTMAWTU ... United Turners', Machinists', and Athletic Woodworkers' Trade Union [*British*]
UTMB ...... University of Texas Medical Branch [*Galveston*]
UTMCI ...... Union des Travailleurs de la Moyenne Cote d'Ivoire [*Union of Middle Ivory Coast Workers*]
UTMC/K ... University of Tennessee Medical Center/Knoxville
UTMD .... Utah Medical Products, Inc. [*NASDAQ symbol*]   (NQ)
UTMDAH ... University of Texas, M. D. Anderson Hospital
UTML .... Utility Motor Launch
UTN .... Upington [*South Africa*] [*Airport symbol*]   (OAG)
UTN .... Utensil   (MSA)
UTNOTREQ ... Utilization of Government Facilities Not Required as It Is Considered Such Utilization Would Adversely Affect Performance of Assigned Temporary Duty
UTNRS ...... Underwater Terrain Navigation and Reconnaissance Simulator   (MCD)
UTO .... Indian Mountain, AK [*Location identifier*] [*FAA*]   (FAAL)
UTO .... United Telephone Organizations
UTO .... United Towns Organisation [*See also FMVJ*] [*Paris, France*]   (EAIO)
UTO .... Utopia Creek [*Alaska*] [*Airport symbol*]   (OAG)
UTOA .... United Truck Owners of America   (EA)
UTOA .... United TVRO [*Television Receive Only*] Owners Association   (EA)
UTOC .... United Technologies Online Catalog [*United Technologies Corp.*] [*Information service or system*]   (IID)
UTOCO ..... Utah Oil Company
UTOG .... Unitog Co. [*NASDAQ symbol*]   (NQ)
UTOL .... Universal Translator Oriented Language
UTOLCL ... University of Toledo College of Law   (DLA)
U Toledo Intra LR ... University of Toledo. Intramural Law Review [*A publication*]   (DLA)
U Toledo L Rev ... University of Toledo. Law Review [*A publication*]
U Tol Law ... University of Toledo. Law Review [*A publication*]
U Tol LR .... University of Toledo. Law Review [*A publication*]
U Tol L Rev ... University of Toledo. Law Review [*A publication*]
UTOPIA .... Universal Terminalized Online Printing and Investigative Aid [*Bancroft-Parkman, Inc.*] [*Information service or system*]
Utopian E ... Utopian Eyes [*A publication*]
U Tor Fac LR ... University of Toronto. Faculty of Law. Review [*A publication*]
U Tor Law J ... University of Toronto. Law Journal [*A publication*]
U Tor LJ ... University of Toronto. Law Journal [*A publication*]
U Tor L Rev ... University of Toronto. School of Law. Review [*A publication*]   (DLA)
U Toronto Fac L Rev ... University of Toronto. Faculty of Law. Review [*A publication*]
U Toronto Faculty L Rev ... University of Toronto. Faculty of Law. Review [*A publication*]
U Toronto L J ... University of Toronto. Law Journal [*A publication*]
U Toronto Q ... University of Toronto. Quarterly [*A publication*]
U Toronto Sch L Rev ... University of Toronto. School of Law. Review [*A publication*]   (DLA)
UTP .... Unified Test Plan
UTP .... Unit Territory Plan
UTP .... Unit Test Plan
UTP .... United Teaching Profession   (MCD)
UTP .... United Trade Press (Holdings) Ltd. [*Commercial firm*] [*British*]
UTP .... Universal Tape Processor
UTPC .... Universal Test Point   (CAAL)
UTP .... Unlisted Trading Privileges
UTP .... Upper Thames Patrol [*British military*]   (DMA)
UTP .... Upper Trip Point
UTP .... Upper Turning Point
UTP .... Uridine Triphosphatase [*An enzyme*]
UTP .... Uridine Triphosphate [*Biochemistry*]
UTP .... User Test Program [*Army*]
UTP .... Utah Power & Light Co. [*NYSE symbol*]   (SPSG)
UTP .... Utapao [*Thailand*] [*Airport symbol*] [*Obsolete*]   (OAG)
UTP .... Utility Tape Processor
UTPA .... Uniform Trustees' Powers Act [*National Conference of Commissioners on Uniform State Laws*]
UTPase ...... Uridine Triphosphatase [*An enzyme*]
UTPL .... Urban Transportation Planning Laboratory [*University of Pennsylvania*] [*Research center*]   (RCD)
UTPLF ...... Universita di Torino. Pubblicazioni della Facolta di Lettere e Filosofia [*A publication*]
UTPMS ..... Unit Trust Portfolio Management Service [*Investment term*] [*British*]
UTPS .... UMTA [*Urban Mass Transit Administration*] Transportation Planning System
UTQ .... Hinesville, GA [*Location identifier*] [*FAA*]   (FAAL)
UTQ .... University of Toronto. Quarterly [*A publication*]
UTQA .... Uutuqtwa. Bristol Bay High School [*A publication*]
UTQG .... Uniform Tire Quality Grade
UTR .... Underwater Tracking Range
UTR .... Union Transportation [*AAR code*]
UTR .... Unitrode Corp. [*NYSE symbol*]   (SPSG)
UTR .... Universal Torah Registry   (EA)
UT R .... University of Tampa. Review [*A publication*]

UTR .... University of Toronto, Thomas Fisher Rare Book Library [*UTLAS symbol*]
UTR .... University Training Reactor
UTR .... Unprogrammed Transfer Register
UTR .... Untranslated Region [*Genetics*]
UTR .... Up Time Ratio
UTR .... Urticarial Transfusion Reaction [*Medicine*]
UTRA .... Upper Torso Restraint Assembly
UTRAO ..... Radio Astronomy Observatory [*University of Texas at Austin*] [*Research center*]   (RCD)
UTRC .... Union Theatre Repertory Co. [*Australia*]
UTRC .... United Technologies Research Centre
Utredn Norsk Tretekn Inst ... Utredning. Norsk Treteknisk Institutt [*A publication*]
UTREP ...... University of Tennessee Rehabilitation Engineering Program
UTRF .... Update Training File [*IRS*]
UTRK .... US Truck Lines, Inc. of Delaware [*NASDAQ symbol*]   (NQ)
Utr Micropaleontol Bull ... Utrecht Micropaleontological Bulletins [*A publication*]
Utr Micropaleontol Bull Spec Publ ... Utrecht Micropaleontological Bulletins. Special Publication [*A publication*]
UTROAA .. Units to Round Out the Active Army
UTRON ..... Utility Squadron [*Navy*]
UTRONFWDAREA ... Utility Squadron, Forward Area [*Navy*]
UTRP .... Underwater Tactical Range, Pacific
UTRR .... University of Teheran Research Reactor
UTRTD ...... Untreated
UTRX .... Unitronix Corp. [*NASDAQ symbol*]   (CTT)
UTS .... Huntsville, TX [*Location identifier*] [*FAA*]   (FAAL)
UTS .... Ullrich-Turner Syndrome [*Genetics*]
UTS .... Ultimate Tensile Strength [*or Stress*]
UTS .... Umbilical Test Set
UTS .... Underwater Telephone System
UTS .... Unified Transfer System [*Computer to translate Russian to English*]
UTS .... Union Theological Seminary
UTS .... Union des Travailleurs du Senegal [*Senegalese Workers Union*]
UTS .... Unit Training Standard
UTS .... Unit Trouble Shooting
UTS .... United Tanners' Society [*A union*] [*British*]
UTS .... United Theological Seminary, Dayton, OH [*OCLC symbol*]   (OCLC)
UTS .... United Tri-Star Resources Ltd. [*Toronto Stock Exchange symbol*]
UTS .... Universal Terminal System [*Sperry UNIVAC*] [*Data processing*]
UTS .... Universal Test Station
UTS .... Universal Thrust Stand
UTS .... Universal Time Sharing [*Data processing*]   (IEEE)
UTS .... Universal Time Standards   (NG)
UTS .... University of Technology, Sydney [*Australia*]
UTS .... University Tutorial Series [*A publication*]
UTS .... Unmanned Teleoperator Spacecraft   (MCD)
UTS .... Update Transaction System   (TEL)
UTS .... Urine-Transfer System [*Apollo*] [*NASA*]
UTS .... Utsunomiya [*Japan*] [*Seismograph station code, US Geological Survey*]   (SEIS)
UTSCB ...... Utah Science [*A publication*]
UTSCC ...... University of Texas System Cancer Center [*Houston, TX*] [*Research center*]
U of T School of LR ... School of Law. Review. Toronto University [*Canada*] [*A publication*]   (DLA)
UTSE .... United Transport Service Employees [*Later, BRAC*]   (EA)
UTSE .... University of Texas. Studies in English [*A publication*]
UTS-FO ..... Union Territoriale des Syndicats - Force Ouvrieres [*Territorial Federation of Trade Unions - Workers' Force*] [*French Somaliland*]
UTSH .... University of Tennessee. Studies in the Humanities [*A publication*]
UTSI .... University of Tennessee Space Institute
UTSL .... University of Texas School of Law   (DLA)
UTSM .... Tamdy-Bulak [*USSR*] [*ICAO location identifier*]   (ICLI)
UTSMS ...... University of Texas Southwestern Medical School
UTSN .... Used Truck Sales Network   (EA)
UTSS .... Samarkand [*USSR*] [*ICAO location identifier*]   (ICLI)
UTST .... Termez [*USSR*] [*ICAO location identifier*]   (ICLI)
UT SUP ...... Ut Supra [*As Above*] [*Latin*]
UT SUPR .. Ut Supra [*As Above*] [*Latin*]
UTSV .... Union Theological Seminary in Virginia
UTT .... Umtata [*South Africa*] [*Airport symbol*]   (OAG)
UTT .... UT Technologies [*Vancouver Stock Exchange symbol*]
UTT .... Utility Tactical Transport   (MCD)
UTT .... Uttering [*FBI standardized term*]
UTTA .... United Thoroughbred Trainers of America   (EA)
Uttar Pradesh Dir Geol Min Monogr ... Uttar Pradesh. Directorate of Geology and Mining. Monograph [*A publication*]
Uttar Pradesh J Zool ... Uttar Pradesh Journal of Zoology [*A publication*]
Uttar Pradesh State Dent J ... Uttar Pradesh State Dental Journal [*A publication*]
UTTAS ...... Utility Tactical Transport Aircraft System [*Helicopter*] [*Military*]

UTTBA...... Bulletin. International Union Against Tuberculosis [*A publication*]
UTTC .... Universal Tape-to-Tape Converter
UTTL......... Uttlesford [*England*]
UTTR .... Utah Test and Training Range [*Air Force*]
UTTS......... Union Territoriale du Senegal des Travailleurs [*Senegalese Workers Union*]
UTTS........ Universal Target Tracking Station   (MCD)
UTTT......... Tashkent/Yuzhny [*USSR*] [*ICAO location identifier*]   (ICLI)
UTU........... Ultrasonic Test Unit
UTU........... Underway Training Unit
UTU........... United Transportation Union   (EA)
UTU........... Ustupo [*Panama*] [*Airport symbol*]   (OAG)
utu .... Utah [*MARC country of publication code*] [*Library of Congress*]   (LCCP)
UTUC........ Uganda Trades' Union Congress
UTUC........ United Trades Union Congress [*India*]
UTV .... Uncompensated Temperature Variation   (TEL)
UTV .... Underwater Television
UTV .... Universal Test Vehicle [*Military*]
UTVI .... United Television, Incorporated [*NASDAQ symbol*]   (NQ)
UTVS........ Ucebni Texty Vysokych Skol [*A publication*]
UTW .... Ultrathin Window [*Spectroscopy*]
UTW .... Under the Wing [*Aircraft*]
UTW .... United Telegraph Workers [*Later, C/UBC*]   (EA)
UTW .... Utilitiesman, Water and Sanitation [*Navy rating*]
UTWA .... United Textile Workers of America   (EA)
UTWG .... Utility Wing [*Navy*]   (MUGU)
UTWING .. Utility Wing [*Navy*]
UTWINGSERVLANT ... Utility Wing, Service Force, Atlantic [*Navy*]
UTWINGSERVPAC ... Utility Wing, Service Force, Pacific [*Navy*]
UTX .... Jupiter, FL [*Location identifier*] [*FAA*]   (FAAL)
UTX .... United Technologies Corp. [*NYSE symbol*]   (SPSG)
UTY .... Utility Air, Inc. [*Moberly, MO*] [*FAA designator*]   (FAAC)
UU .... Reunion Air Service [*France*] [*ICAO designator*]   (FAAC)
UU .... Uglies Unlimited   (EA)
UU .... Ulster Unionist Party
UU .... Ultimate User [*Nuclear energy*]
UU .... Unemployment Unit [*An association*] [*British*]
UU .... Unicorns Unanimous [*An association*]   (EA)
UU .... Union University [*Tennessee*]
UU .... University of Utah, Salt Lake City, UT [*Library symbol*] [*Library of Congress*]   (LCLS)
UU .... Urine Urobilinogen [*Clinical chemistry*]
UU .... User Unit   (MCD)
UUA .... Southern Utah State College, Cedar City, UT [*OCLC symbol*]   (OCLC)
UUA .... Unitarian Universalist Society for Alcohol and Drug Education
UUA .... UNIVAC Users Association [*Later, AUUA*]
UUA .... Uppsala Universitets Arsskrift [*A publication*]
UUABCWG ... Unitarian Universalist Association Black Concerns Working Group   (EA)
UUAC....... United Unionist Action Council [*Northern Ireland*]
UUARC..... United Ukrainian American Relief Committee   (EA)
UUA/WO ... Unitarian Universalist Association of Congregations-Washington Office   (EA)
UUA/WOSC ... Unitarian Universalist Association-Washington Office for Social Concern [*Later, UUA/WOSJ*]   (EA)
UUA/WOSJ ... Unitarian Universalist Association of Congregations-Washington Office for Social Justice   (EA)
UUB.......... Brigham Young University, School of Library and Information Science, Provo, UT [*OCLC symbol*]   (OCLC)
UUBCWG ... Unitarian Universalist Black Concerns Working Group   (EA)
UUBP .... Bryansk [*USSR*] [*ICAO location identifier*]   (ICLI)
UUC........... Salt Lake County Library System, Salt Lake City, UT [*OCLC symbol*]   (OCLC)
UUC........... United University Club [*British*]
UUCA....... United Underwear Contractors Association [*Defunct*]   (EA)
UUCD....... USA-USSR Citizens' Dialogue [*Inactive*]   (EA)
UUCF....... Unitarian Universalist Christian Fellowship   (EA)
UUCP....... Unix-to-Unix Copy Program [*Data processing*]
UUD .... Logan Public Library, Logan, UT [*OCLC symbol*]   (OCLC)
UUE .... University of Utah, Eccles Health Science Library, Salt Lake City, UT [*OCLC symbol*]   (OCLC)
UUE .... Use until Exhausted
UUEE .... Moskva/Sheremetyevo [*USSR*] [*ICAO location identifier*]   (ICLI)
UUEM....... Kalini/Migalovo [*USSR*] [*ICAO location identifier*]   (ICLI)
UUEW....... United Unions for Employees and Workers [*Lebanon*]
UUFSJ ...... Unitarian Universalist Fellowship for Social Justice   (EA)
UUGS........ Unitarian and Universalist Genealogical Society [*Defunct*]   (EA)
UUHS....... Unitarian Universalist Historical Society   (EA)
UUIP .... Uppsala University Institute of Physics [*Sweden*]
UUK......... Kuparuk, AK [*Location identifier*] [*FAA*]   (FAAL)
UU-L......... University of Utah, Law Library, Salt Lake City, UT [*Library symbol*] [*Library of Congress*]   (LCLS)
UULGC..... Unitarian Universalist Lesbian Gay Caucus   (EA)
UUM .... Underwater-to-Underwater Missile [*Air Force*]
UU-M........ University of Utah, Library of Medical Sciences, Salt Lake City, UT [*Library symbol*] [*Library of Congress*]   (LCLS)

UUM .... University of Utah, Salt Lake City, UT [*OCLC symbol*]   (OCLC)
UUMA....... Unitarian Universalist Ministers Association   (EA)
UUMN ...... Unitarian Universalist Musicians' Network   (EA)
UUMPS .... Unitarian Universalist Ministers' Partners Society   (EA)
UUN .... Urinary Urea Nitrogen [*Clinical medicine*]
UUO .... Weber State College, Ogden, UT [*OCLC symbol*]   (OCLC)
UUOO ...... Voronezh [*USSR*] [*ICAO location identifier*]   (ICLI)
UUP.......... Salt Lake City Public Library, Salt Lake City, UT [*OCLC symbol*]   (OCLC)
UUPP .... Unused Undeducted Purchase Price
UU/PS....... Peasant Studies. University of Utah. Department of History [*A publication*]
UUR.......... Under Usual Reserves
UURWAW ... United Union of Roofers, Waterproofers, and Allied Workers   (EA)
UUS........... Utah State University, Logan, UT [*OCLC symbol*]   (OCLC)
UUSAE .... Unitarian Universalist Society for Alcohol Education [*Later, UUA*]   (EA)
UUSC .... Unitarian Universalist Service Committee   (EA)
UUSS........ University of Utah Seismograph Stations [*Research center*]   (RCD)
UUT........... Unit under Test
UUU.......... Manumu [*Papua New Guinea*] [*Airport symbol*]   (OAG)
UUUC........ United Ulster Unionist Coalition [*Northern Ireland*]
UUUM ...... Moskva [*USSR*] [*ICAO location identifier*]   (ICLI)
UUUM ...... United Ulster Unionist Movement [*Northern Ireland*]
UUUP........ United Ulster Unionist Party [*Northern Ireland*] [*Political party*]   (PPW)
UUUU .... Moskva [*USSR*] [*ICAO location identifier*]   (ICLI)
UUV.......... Unter Ueblicher Vorbehalt [*Errors and Omissions Excepted*] [*German*]
UUW .... Westminster College, Salt Lake City, UT [*OCLC symbol*]   (OCLC)
UUWF........ Unitarian Universalist Women's Federation   (EA)
UU/WPQ .. Western Political Quarterly. University of Utah [*A publication*]
UUWW ...... Moskva/Vnukovo [*USSR*] [*ICAO location identifier*]   (ICLI)
UUYEP ...... US-USSR Youth Exchange Program   (EA)
UUYT........ Ust-Kulom [*USSR*] [*ICAO location identifier*]   (ICLI)
UUYY........ Syktyvkar [*USSR*] [*ICAO location identifier*]   (ICLI)
UUZ.......... Utah State Library, Processing Center, Salt Lake City, UT [*OCLC symbol*]   (OCLC)
UV............. Ultra Vans   (EA)
UV............. Ultraviolet [*Electromagnetic spectrum range*]
UV............. Ultravisible
UV............. Umbilical Vein [*Medicine*]
UV............. Under Voltage
UV............. Underwater Vehicle
UV............. Union Valdotaine [*Valdotaine Union*] [*Italy*] [*Political party*]   (EAIO)
UV............. Universal Aviation, Inc. [*ICAO designator*]   (FAAC)
uv............... Upper Volta [*MARC country of publication code*] [*Library of Congress*]   (LCCP)
UV............. Urinary Volume [*Physiology*]
UV............. Uterine Vein [*Anatomy*]
UV............. Uterine Volume
UV............. Utility Value [*Psychology*]
UVA.......... Ultraviolet Light, Long Wave
UVA.......... Uvalde Aero Service [*Uvalde, TX*] [*FAA designator*]   (FAAC)
UVA.......... Uvalde, TX [*Location identifier*] [*FAA*]   (FAAL)
UVAL........ Ultraviolet Argon LASER
UVAN........ Ukrainian Academy of Arts and Sciences of Canada
UVAN........ Ukrains'ka Vil'na Akademjia Nauk
UVAR .... University of Virginia Reactor
UVAS........ Unmanned Vehicle for Aerial Surveillance   (MCD)
UVASER ... Ultraviolet Amplification by Stimulated Emission of Radiation
UVASERS ... Ultraviolet Amplification by Stimulated Emission of Radiation System
UV-B......... Ultraviolet Band
UVBF........ Umbilical Vein Blood Flow
UVC.......... Pennsylvania State University, Capitol Campus, Middletown, PA [*OCLC symbol*]   (OCLC)
UVC.......... Ultrahigh Vacuum Chamber
UVC.......... Ultraviolet Communications System
UVC.......... Uniform Vehicle Code
UVC.......... Union Valley Corporation [*AMEX symbol*]   (SPSG)
UVCA .... Uniform Vehicle Code Annotated
UVCB .... Unknown or Variable Composition, Complex Reaction Products, and Biological Materials [*Chemical Abstracts Services*]
UVCE .... Unconfined Vapor Cloud Explosion
UVD.......... Ultrasonic Vapor Degresser
UVD.......... Ultraviolet Detector
UVD.......... Undervoltage Device
UVD.......... Unintegrated Viral DNA [*Deoxyribonucleic Acid*] [*Pathology*]
UVD.......... Upper Vas Deferens [*Anatomy*]
UVDC........ Urban Vehicle Design Competition
UVD-SV ... Upper Vas Deferens-Seminal Vesicle Complex [*Anatomy*]
UVE.......... Ouvea [*Loyalty Islands*] [*Airport symbol*]   (OAG)
UV-EPROMS ... Ultraviolet-Erasable Programmable Read-Only Memories [*Data processing*]

UVES.........	Ukrains'ka Ekonomicna Visoka Skola v Mjunhenj
UVF...........	St. Lucia [*West Indies*] Hewanorra Airport [*Airport symbol*] (OAG)
UVF...........	Ulster Volunteer Force
UVF...........	Ultraviolet Filter
UVF...........	Ultraviolet Floodlight (AAG)
UVF...........	Unmanned Vertical Flight [*NASA*] (NASA)
UVFLT......	Ultraviolet Floodlight
UVG...........	UV [*Ultraviolet*] Spectrometry Group [*British*]
UVGS........	Church of Jesus Christ of Latter-Day Saints, Genealogical Society Library, Uintah Basin Branch, Vernal, UT [*Library symbol*] [*Library of Congress*] (LCLS)
UVH	Univentricular Heart [*Cardiology*]
UVI...........	Ultraviolet Irradiation
UVI...........	Uvira [*Zaire*] [*Seismograph station code, US Geological Survey*] [*Closed*] (SEIS)
UVIC	University of Victoria [*British Columbia*]
UVIL.........	Ultraviolet Inspection Light
UVIL.........	Ultraviolet Ion LASER
UVIRSG	Ultraviolet Infrared Scene Generator
UVL...........	New Valley [*Egypt*] [*Airport symbol*] (OAG)
UVL...........	Ultraviolet Lamp
UVL...........	Ultraviolet LASER
UVL...........	Ultraviolet Light
UVL...........	Universal Voltronics Corp. [*AMEX symbol*] (SPSG)
UVL...........	Untersuchungen zur Vergleichenden Literatur [*Hamburg*] [*A publication*]
UVLI........	Ustav Vedeckych Lekarskych Informaci [*Institute for Medical Information*] [*Czechoslovakia*] [*Database operator*] [*Information service or system*] (IID)
UVLS........	Ultraviolet Light Stabilizer
UVM.........	Ultraviolet Meter
UVM.........	Universitas Viridis Montis [*University of the Green Mountains; i.e., University of Vermont*]
UVM.........	University of Virginia. Magazine [*A publication*]
UVMag......	University of Virginia. Magazine [*A publication*]
UVMC.......	United Voluntary Motor Corps (EA)
UVN.........	Unionville [*Nevada*] [*Seismograph station code, US Geological Survey*] [*Closed*] (SEIS)
UVNO	Ultraviolet Nitric-Oxide Experiment
UVO	Uvol [*Papua New Guinea*] [*Airport symbol*] (OAG)
UVP...........	Ultrahigh Vacuum Pump
UVP...........	Ultraviolet Photometry
UVP...........	Unified Vocational Preparation [*Manpower Services Commission*] [*British*]
UVPJU......	Uganda Vernacular, Primary and Junior Secondary Teachers' Union
UVPROM ...	Ultraviolet Programmable Read Only Memory
UVPS........	Ultrahigh Vacuum Pumping Station
UVR...........	Uitenhage Volunteer Rifles [*British military*] (DMA)
UVR...........	Ultraviolet Radiation
UVR...........	Ultraviolet Radiometer (MCD)
UVR...........	Ultraviolet Receiver
UVR...........	Ultraviolet Rocket
UVR...........	Under Voltage Relay
UVR...........	University of Virginia Reactor
UVR...........	User Visible Resources
UVS...........	Ultraviolet Spectrometer
UVS	Under Voltage Sensing (MCD)
UVS	United Voluntary Services (EA)
UVS	Unmanned Vehicle System
UVSC.......	Ultraviolet Solar Constant
UVSC.......	Uranium Ventilation Scrubber Cell [*Nuclear energy*] (NRCH)
UVSP.......	Ultraviolet Spectral Photometer
UV Spectrom Group Bull ...	UV Spectrometry Group. Bulletin [*A publication*]
UVT........	Ultraviolet Transmission
UVT........	Ultraviolet Tube
UVT........	Universal Voltage Tester
UVT........	Usable Vector Table
UVTB	United Vermont Bancorporation [*Rutland, VT*] [*NASDAQ symbol*] (NQ)
UVTEI.......	Ustredi Vedeckych, Technickych, a Ekonomickych Informaci [*Czechoslovakia*] [*Information service or system*] (IID)
UVV...........	Universal Corp. [*NYSE symbol*] (SPSG)
UVV...........	Upward Vertical Velocity [*Meteorology*] (FAAC)
UV-VIS.......	Ultraviolet/Visible [*Spectroscopy*]
UVVO.......	United Vietnam Veterans Organization (EA)
UVX...........	Univar Corp. [*Formerly, VWR United Corp.*] [*NYSE symbol*] (SPSG)
UW	Air Rwanda [*Rwanda*] [*ICAO designator*] (ICDA)
UW	Service des Transports Publics Aeriens [*Portugal*] [*ICAO designator*] (FAAC)
UW	Ultimate Weapon (AAG)
UW	Ultrasonic Wave
UW	Unburned, Warmed [*Ecology*]
UW	Unconventional Warfare [*Army*]
U/W	Under Will [*Legal term*] (DLA)
UW	Underwater
UW	Underwater Weapons [*British*]
U/W	Underway (NVT)
U/W	Underwriter [*Insurance*]

UW	United Way (OICC)
UW	United Weldors International Union
UW	University of Washington [*Seattle, WA*]
U of W.......	University of Washington [*Seattle, WA*]
U of W.......	University of Windsor [*Ontario*]
UW	University of Wisconsin [*Madison, WI*] (MCD)
UW	Untere Winkelgruppe [*Angles up to 45*] [*German military - World War II*]
UW	Uppity Women [*An association*] (EA)
UW	Upset Welding
UW	Us Wurk [*A publication*]
UW	Usable Width (MCD)
U/W	Used With
UW	Utility Water (AAG)
UWA.........	Ukrainian Workingmen's Association [*Later, UFA*] (EA)
UWA.........	United Way of America (EA)
UWA.........	United Weighers Association (EA)
UWA.........	United Women of the Americas (EA)
UWA.........	United World Atheists (EA)
UWA.........	User Working Area
UWA.........	Uwajima [*Japan*] [*Seismograph station code, US Geological Survey*] (SEIS)
UWA.........	Ware, MA [*Location identifier*] [*FAA*] (FAAL)
UWAC.......	Ukrainian Women's Association of Canada
UWAGE....	Union Women's Alliance to Gain Equality [*Defunct*] (EA)
UWAL.......	Underwater Wide-Angle Lens
UWAL.......	University of Washington Aeronautical Laboratory (MCD)
UWALR	University of Western Australia. Law Review [*A publication*] (APTA)
UWAL Rev ...	University of Western Australia. Law Review [*A publication*]
UWARC	United Whiteruthenian [*Byelorussian*] American Relief Committee (EA)
U Wash L Rev ...	University of Washington. Law Review [*A publication*] (DLA)
UWASIS ...	United Way of America Services Identification System
UWAT.......	User Written Application Test [*Data processing*]
UWATU....	Underway Training Unit
UW Austl L Rev ...	University of Western Australia. Law Review [*A publication*]
UWAVM...	Underwater Antivehicle Mine (MCD)
UWB.........	Universal White Brotherhood [*An association*] (EAIO)
UWBBR	University of Wisconsin - Madison Bureau of Business Research [*Research center*] (RCD)
UWBS	Uniform Work Breakdown Structure
UWC.........	Ulster Workers' Council
UWC.........	Underwater Communications [*Navy*] (CAAL)
UWC.........	Universal Water Charts [*Air Force*]
UWC.........	Universal Winding Company (MCD)
UWC.........	Widener College, Chester, PA [*OCLC symbol*] (OCLC)
UWCCARG ...	University of Washington. Contributions. Cloud and Aerosol Research Group [*A publication*]
UWCCCM ...	Union of Watch, Clock, and Clock Case Makers [*British*]
UWCCPGR ...	University of Washington. Contributions. Cloud Physics Group. Collections from Reprints [*A publication*]
UWCETG ...	University of Washington. Contributions. Energy Transfer Group. Collections from Reprints [*A publication*]
UWCS	Underwater Weapons Control System
UWCSS....	Universal Weapon Control Stabilization System
UWD	Underwater Weapons Department [*British military*] (DMA)
UWD	UWD [*Umweltschutz-Dienst*] Informationsdienst fuer Umweltfragen [*A publication*]
UWDD	Undersea Warfare Development Division [*Navy*] (MCD)
UWE.........	University Women of Europe (EA)
UWE.........	Uwekahuna [*Hawaii*] [*Seismograph station code, US Geological Survey*] (SEIS)
UWEN.......	United Western Energy [*NASDAQ symbol*] (NQ)
UWERT	United World Education and Research Trust (EAIO)
U West Aust Ann L Rev ...	University of Western Australia. Annual Law Review [*A publication*]
U of West Aust L Rev ...	University of Western Australia. Law Review [*A publication*]
U Western Aust Ann L Rev ...	University of Western Australia. Annual Law Review [*A publication*]
U Western Aust L Rev ...	University of Western Australia. Law Review [*A publication*]
U Western Ont L Rev ...	University of Western Ontario. Law Review [*A publication*]
U West LA L Rev ...	University of West Los Angeles. Law Review [*A publication*]
U West Los Angeles L Rev ...	University of West Los Angeles. Law Review [*A publication*]
UWF.........	United World Federalists [*Later, World Federalists Association*] (EA)
UWF.........	University of West Florida [*Pensacola*]
UWFC	Underwater Fire Control [*Navy*] (CAAL)
UWFCS	Underwater Fire Control System
UWFPC.....	Union Wallisienne et Futunienne pour la Caledonie [*Wallisian and Futunian Union for Caledonia*] [*Political party*] (PPW)
UWG.........	Gesetz Gegen den Unlauteren Wettbewerb [*Law Against Unfair Competition*] [*German*] (DLA)

UWGB....... University of Wisconsin at Green Bay
UWH........ Underwater Habitat
UWH........ Underwater Welding Habitat [*Deep-sea diving*]
UW-HF ..... Upset Welding-High Frequency
UWI.......... Dalton, GA [*Location identifier*] [*FAA*]   (FAAL)
UWI.......... United Way International   (EA)
UWI.......... United Westburne Industries Ltd. [*Toronto Stock Exchange symbol*]
UWI.......... University of the West Indies [*Jamaica*]
UW-I......... Upset Welding-Induction
UWI/CQ ... Caribbean Quarterly. University of the West Indies [*A publication*]
UWI/JCH ... Journal of Caribbean History. University of the West Indies. Department of History and Caribbean Universities Press [*A publication*]
UWINDS .. Upper Winds   (FAAC)
U Windsor L Rev ... University of Windsor. Law Review [*A publication*]   (DLA)
UWI/SES ... Social and Economic Studies. University of the West Indies. Institute of Social and Economic Research [*A publication*]
UWIST...... University of Wales Institute of Science and Technology [*British*]
UWKD...... Kazan [*USSR*] [*ICAO location identifier*]   (ICLI)
UWL........ New Castle, IN [*Location identifier*] [*FAA*]   (FAAL)
UWL........ Underwater Launch
UWL........ University of Winnipeg Library [*UTLAS symbol*]
UWL........ Utowana Lake [*New York*] [*Seismograph station code, US Geological Survey*]   (SEIS)
UWLA LR ... University of West Los Angeles. Law Review [*A publication*]
UWLA L Rev ... University of West Los Angeles. Law Review [*A publication*]
UWLA Rev ... University of West Los Angeles. School of Law. Law Review [*A publication*]   (DLA)
UWM........ Uniform Wave Motion
UWM........ United World Mission   (EA)
UWM........ University of Wisconsin at Milwaukee
UWM........ University of Wisconsin at Milwaukee [*Wisconsin*] [*Seismograph station code, US Geological Survey*]   (SEIS)
UWMAK... University of Wisconsin TOKAMAK
UWNE...... Brotherhood of Utility Workers of New England   (EA)
UWNR...... University of Wisconsin - Madison Nuclear Reactor Laboratory [*Research center*]   (RCD)
UWO .... University of Western Ontario   (MCD)
UWO .... University of Western Ontario Library [*UTLAS symbol*]
UWO .... University of Western Ontario, School of Library and Information Science, London, ON, Canada [*OCLC symbol*]   (OCLC)
UWOA ...... Unclassified without Attachment
UWOA ...... Unconventional Warfare Operations Area [*Army*]   (AABC)
UWOL Rev ... University of Western Ontario. Law Review [*A publication*]
UWOMA6 ... University of Western Ontario. Medical Journal [*A publication*]
UWO Med J ... UWO [*University of Western Ontario*] Medical Journal [*A publication*]
UW Ont L Rev ... University of Western Ontario. Law Review [*A publication*]
UWOPGS ... University of Warwick. Occasional Papers in German Studies [*A publication*]
UWO (Univ West Ont) Med J ... UWO (University of Western Ontario) Medical Journal [*A publication*]
UWP......... United Workers' Party [*St. Lucia*] [*Political party*]   (PPW)
UWP......... United Workers' Party [*Hungary*] [*Political party*]   (PPW)
UWP......... Up with People   (EA)
UWPC....... United World Press Cooperative [*Later, The Peoples Media Cooperative*]   (EA)
UWPFAO ... University of Washington Publications in Fisheries. New Series [*A publication*]
UWPLL..... University of Washington. Publications in Language and Literature [*A publication*]
UWPP .... Penza [*USSR*] [*ICAO location identifier*]   (ICLI)
UWR........ Underwater Range   (MUGU)
U/Wr .... Underwriter [*Insurance*]   (DLA)
UWR........ Unexpected Wildlife Refuge   (EA)
UWR........ United Water Resources, Inc. [*NYSE symbol*]   (SPSG)
UWR........ University of Windsor. Review [*A publication*]
UWRC...... Urban Wildlife Research Center   (EA)
UW-RF ...... University of Wisconsin-River Falls
UWRFAY ... Research in Fisheries. Annual Report. School of Fisheries. University of Washington [*A publication*]
UWRR....... University of Wyoming Research Reactor
UWS........ Undersea Weapon System
UWS........ University of Western Sydney [*Australia*]
UWS........ Unmanned Weather Station
UWS........ User Work Station   (NASA)
UWSAMBS ... United Women's Societies of the Adoration of the Most Blessed Sacrament [*Later, NUWSAMBS*]   (EA)
UWSB .... Union Warren Savings Bank [*Boston, MA*] [*NASDAQ symbol*]   (NQ)
UWSDDMS ... Underwater Weapons System Design Disclosure Management Systems   (KSC)
UWSRD ..... Underwater Weapons Systems Reliability Data   (KSC)
UWST .... United Western Corp. [*NASDAQ symbol*]   (NQ)
UWT......... Underwater Telephone

UWT......... Uniform Wave Train
UWT......... Unit Weight   (MSA)
UWTCA..... Umschau in Wissenschaft und Technik [*A publication*]
UWTM..... Underwater Team   (MSA)
UWTR...... Underwater   (AABC)
UWTR...... University of Washington Training Reactor
UWU .... Los Angeles, CA [*Location identifier*] [*FAA*]   (FAAL)
UWU .... Utility Workers Union of America
UWUA...... Utility Workers Union of America   (EA)
UWW........ University without Walls [*Twenty-one-university consortium*]
UWWR...... Unpublished Scholarly Writings on World Religions   (BJA)
UWWW..... Kuybyshev/Kurumoch [*USSR*] [*ICAO location identifier*]   (ICLI)
UX............. Lotus Airways [*Egypt*] [*ICAO designator*]   (FAAC)
UXAA....... Unexploded Antiaircraft [*Shell*]
UXAPB...... Unexploded Antipersonnel Bomb
UXB........ Unexploded Bomb
UXC......... Unocal Exploration Corp. [*NYSE symbol*]   (SPSG)
UXGB .... Unexploded Gas Bomb
UXIB .... Unexploded Incendiary Bomb
UXM......... Universal Extension Mechanism   (KSC)
UXO......... Unexploded Ordnance
UXOI........ Unexploded Ordnance Incident
UXPM...... Unexploded Parachuted Mine
UXS .... Unexploded Shell [*British military*]   (DMA)
UXTGM..... Unexploded Type G Mine
UXW......... South Bend, IN [*Location identifier*] [*FAA*]   (FAAL)
UY............. Cameroon Airlines [*ICAO designator*]   (FAAC)
UY............. Unit Years [*Electronics*]   (IEEE)
UY............. Universal Youth
UY............. Uruguay [*ANSI two-letter standard code*]   (CNC)
uy............... Uruguay [*MARC country of publication code*] [*Library of Congress*]   (LCCP)
UYA........... University Year for ACTION [*Refers to federal program, ACTION, which is not an acronym*]
UYAP .... Unconstrained Youth Allowances Package [*Australia*]
UYC......... Uxbridge Yeomanry Cavalry [*British military*]   (DMA)
UYF .... London, OH [*Location identifier*] [*FAA*]   (FAAL)
UYL .... Nyala [*Sudan*] [*Airport symbol*]   (OAG)
UYLNA ..... Ukrainian Youth League of North America [*Defunct*]   (EA)
UYN.......... Yulin [*China*] [*Airport symbol*]   (OAG)
UZ............. Uhrzuender [*Clockwork fuze*] [*German military - World War II*]
UZ............. United Aviation Services SA [*Great Britain*] [*ICAO designator*]   (FAAC)
UZ............. Upper Zone [*Geology*]
UZ............. Ustredna Zidov [*Slovakia*] [*A publication*]
U Zambia LB ... University of Zambia. Law Bulletin [*A publication*]   (DLA)
UZAstPI .... Ucenye Zapiski Astrachanskogo Gosudarstvennogo Pedagogiceskogo Instituta [*A publication*]
UZAzPI..... Ucenye Zapiski Pedagogiceskogo Instituta Jazykov Imeni M. F. Achundova. Serija Filologiceskaja [*A publication*]
UZAzU ...... Ucenye Zapiski Azerbajdzanskogo Gosudarstvennogo Universiteta Imeni S. M. Kirova. Jazyk i Literatura [*A publication*]
uzb............. Uzbek [*MARC language code*] [*Library of Congress*]   (LCCP)
UZBasU .... Ucenye Zapiski Baskirskogo Gosudarstvennogo Universiteta. Serija Filologiceskich Nauk [*A publication*]
Uzb Biol Zh ... Uzbekskii Biologicheskii Zhurnal [*A publication*]
Uzbek Biol Zh ... Uzbekskii Biologiceskii Zhurnal [*A publication*]
Uzbek Geol Zh ... Uzbekskii Geologiceskii Zhurnal [*A publication*]
Uzbek Iztim Fanlar ... Uzbekiztonda Iztimoii Fanlar [*A publication*]
Uzbek Khim Zh ... Uzbekskii Khimiceskii Zhurnal [*A publication*]
Uzb Khim Zh ... Uzbekskii Khimiceskii Zhurnal [*A publication*]
UZBurPI.... Ucenye Zapiski Burjatskogo Gosudarstvennogo Pedagogiceskogo Instituta Imeni Dorzi Banzarova. Istoriko-Filologiceskaja Serija. Ulan-Ude [*A publication*]
UZBZA...... Uzbekskii Biologiceskii Zhurnal [*A publication*]
UZCerepPI ... Ucenye Zapiski Cerepoveckogo Gosudarstvennogo Pedagogiceskogo Instituta [*A publication*]
UZChabPI ... Ucenye Zapiski Chabarovskogo Gosudarstvennogo Pedagogiceskogo Instituta [*A publication*]
UZChakNII ... Ucenye Zapiski Chakasskogo Naucno-Issledovatel'skogo Instituta Jazyka, Literatury, i Istorii [*A publication*]
UZCharU .. Ucenye Zapiski Charkovskogo Universiteta Imeni A. M. Gorkogo Trudy Filologiceskogo Fakul'teta [*A publication*]
UZCIngPI ... Ucenye Zapiski Ceceno-Ingusskogo Pedagogiceskogo Instituta. Serija Filolo Giceskaja [*A publication*]
UZCuvNII ... Ucenye Zapiski Naucno-Issledovatel'skogo Instituta Jazyka, Literatury, Istorii, i Ekonomiki Pri Sovete Ministrov Cuvasskoj ASSR [*A publication*]
UZDag...... Ucenye Zapiski Dagestanskogo Filiala Akademii Nauk SSSR. Serija Filologiceskaja [*A publication*]
UZDagU.... Ucenye Zapiski Dagestanskogo Gosudarstvennogo Universiteta. Serija Filologiceskaja [*A publication*]
UZDalU.... Ucenye Zapiski Dal'nevostocnogo Universiteta. Serija Filologiceskaja [*A publication*]
UZDusPI... Ucenye Zapiski Dusanbinskogo Gosudarstvennogo Pedagogiceskogo Instituta Imeni T. G. Seveenko Filologiceskaja Serija [*A publication*]

UZElPI...... Ucenye Zapiski Elabuzskogo Gosudarstvennogo Pedagogiceskogo Instituta. Serija Istorii i Filologii [*A publication*]

UZEnPI..... Ucenye Zapiski Enisejskogo Gosudarstvennogo Pedagogiceskogo Instituta Kafedra Russkogo Jazyka [*A publication*]

UZErevU .. Ucenye Zapiski Erevanskogo Gosudarstvennogo Universiteta. Serija Filologiceskich Nauk [*A publication*]

UZGIYa..... Ucenye Zapiski Gor'kovskii Pedagogicheskii Institut Inostrannykh Yazykov [*Gor'kii*] [*A publication*]

UZGorPI ... Ucenye Zapiski Gor'kovskogo Gosudarstvennogo Pedagogiceskogo Instituta Imeni M. Gor'kogo. Serija Filologiceskaja [*A publication*]

UZGorPIIJa ... Ucenye Zapiski Gor'kovskogo Pedagogiceskogo Instituta Inostrannych Jazykov [*A publication*]

UZGorU .... Ucenye Zapiski Gor'kovskogo Universiteta Imeni N. I. Lobacevskogo. Serija Istoriko-Filologiceskaja [*A publication*]

UZGPI....... Ucenye Zapiski Gor'kovskii Gosudarstvennyi Pedagogicheskii Institut [*Gor'kii*] [*A publication*]

UZGurPI ... Ucenye Zapiski Gur'evskogo Gosudarstvennogo Pedagogiceskogo Instituta. Serija Istoriko-Filologiceskaja [*A publication*]

UZGZA ..... Uzbekskii Geologicheskii Zhurnal [*A publication*]

UZH .... Uzhgorod [*Unuar*] [*USSR*] [*Seismograph station code, US Geological Survey*]   (SEIS)

UZII.......... Ucenye Zapiski Instituta Istorii [*A publication*]

UZIMach .. Ucenye Zapiski Instituta Istorii, Jazyka, i Literatury Imeni G. Cadasy. Serija Filologiceskaja. Machackala [*A publication*]

UZIMO ..... Ucenye Zapiski Institut Mezdunarodnych Otnosenij [*A publication*]

UZIPI .... Ucenye Zapiski Irkutskii Pedagogicheskii Institut [*Irkutsk*] [*A publication*]

UZIrkutPI ... Ucenye Zapiski Irkutskogo Gosudarstvennogo Pedagogiceskogo Instituta Inostrannych Jazykov [*A publication*]

UZISL .... Ucenye Zapiski Instituta Slavjanovedenija [*A publication*]

UZIV .... Ucenye Zapiski Instituta Vostokovedenija Akademija Nauk SSSR [*A publication*]

UZIVAz..... Ucenye Zapiski Instituta Vostokovedenija Akademii Nauk Azerbajdzanskoj SSSR [*A publication*]

UZK .... Indianapolis, IN [*Location identifier*] [*FAA*]   (FAAL)

UZKa .... Ucenye Zapiski Kalininskii Gosudarstvennyi Pedagogicheskii Institut [*Kalinin*] [*A publication*]

UZKalinPI ... Ucenye Zapiski Kalininskogo Pedagogiceskogo Instituta Imeni M. I. Kalinina. Serija Filologiceskaja [*A publication*]

UZKalPI... Ucenye Zapiski Kaluzskogo Gosudarstvennogo Pedagogiceskogo Instituta [*A publication*]

UZKaragPI ... Ucenye Zapiski Karagandinskogo Pedagogiceskogo Instituta Filologiceskie Nauki [*A publication*]

UZKarelPI ... Ucenye Zapiski Karel'skogo Pedagogiceskogo Instituta [*A publication*]

UZKarPI ... Ucenye Zapiski Karsinskogo Gosudarstvennogo Pedagogiceskogo Instituta. Filologiceskaja Serija [*A publication*]

UZKazanU ... Ucenye Zapiski Kazanskogo Universiteta Imeni V. I. Ul'janova'lenina [*A publication*]

UZKBI....... Ucenye Zapiski Kabardino-Balkarskij Naucno-Issledovatel'skij Institut pri Sovete Ministrov Kbassr [*A publication*]

UZKemPI .. Ucenye Zapiski Kemerovskogo Gosudarstvennogo Pedagogiceskogo Instituta [*A publication*]

UZKGPI.... Ucenye Zapiski Kujbysevskogo Gosudarstvennogo Pedagogiceskogo Instituta Imeni V. V. Kujbyseva [*A publication*]

UZKi .... Ucenye Zapiski Kishinevskii Universitet [*Kishinev*] [*A publication*]

UZKirovPI ... Ucenye Zapiski Kirovabadskogo Pedagogiceskogo Instituta [*A publication*]

UZKisU ..... Ucenye Zapiski Kisinevskogo Gosudarstvennogo Universiteta [*A publication*]

UZKokPI... Ucenye Zapiski Kokandskogo Pedagogiceskogo Instituta Imeni Mukimi. Serija Filologiceskaja [*A publication*]

UZKolPI.... Ucenye Zapiski Kolomenskogo Gosudarstvennogo Pedagogiceskogo Instituta Istoriko-Filologiceskij Fakul'tet Kafedry Russkogo Jazyka [*A publication*]

UZKomPI ... Ucenye Zapiski Komi Gosudarstvennogo Pedagogiceskogo Instituta Kafedra Russkogo Jazyka [*A publication*]

UZKr .... Ucenye Zapiski Krasnodarskii Pedagogicheskii Institut [*Krasnodar*] [*A publication*]

UZKujPI.... Ucenye Zapiski Kujbysevskogo Gosudarstvennogo Pedagogiceskogo Instituta Imeni V. V. Kujbyseva [*A publication*]

UZKVA ..... Uchenye Zapiski Kazanskogo Veterinarnogo Instituta [*A publication*]

UZKZA ..... Uzbekskii Khimicheskii Zhurnal [*A publication*]

UZLa .... Ucenye Zapiski Latviiskii Gosudarstvennyi Universitet [*Riga*] [*A publication*]

UZLenPI ... Ucenye Zapiski Leningradskogo Pedagogiceskogo Instituta Imeni S. M. Kirova [*A publication*]

UZLPedI ... Ucenye Zapiski Leningradskogo Pedagogiceskogo Instituta Imeni A. I. Gercena [*A publication*]

UZLPI .... Ucenye Zapiski Leningradskogo Pedagogiceskogo Instituta Imeni A. I. Gercena [*A publication*]

UZLU .... Ucenye Zapiski Leningradskogo Gosudarstvennogo Ordena Lenina Universiteta Imeni A. A. Zdanova [*A publication*]

UZLU-FN ... Ucenye Zapiski Leningradskogo Universiteta. Serija Filologiceskikh Nauk [*A publication*]

UZl'VovU .. Ucenye Zapiski l'Vovskogo Gosudarstvennogo Universiteta [*A publication*]

UZMagPI ... Ucenye Zapiski Magnitorskogo Gosudarstvennogo Pedagogiceskogo Instituta [*A publication*]

UZMIK ..... Ucenye Zapiski Moskovskii Gosudarstvennyi Institut Kul'tury [*Moscow*] [*A publication*]

UZMKrup ... Ucenye Zapiski Moskovskogo Oblastnogo Pedagogiceskogo Instituta Imeni N. K. Krupskoj [*A publication*]

UZMOPI... Ucenye Zapiski Moskovskii Oblastnoi Pedagogicheskii Institut Imeni N. K. Krupskoi [*Moscow*] [*A publication*]

UZMorU ... Ucenye Zapiski Mordovskogo Universiteta. Serija Filologiceskich Nauk [*A publication*]

UZMPedI ... Ucenye Zapiski Moskovskogo Gosudarstvennogo Pedagogiceskogo Instituta [*A publication*]

UZMPI...... Ucenye Zapiski Moskovskii Gosudarstvennyi Pedagogicheskii Institut Imeni Lenina [*Moscow*] [*A publication*]

UZMPI...... Ucenye Zapiski Moskovskogo Gosudarstvennogo Pedagogiceskogo Instituta Imeni Potemkina [*A publication*]

UZMPIIJa ... Ucenye Zapiski Moskovskogo Gosudarstvennogo Pedagogiceskogo Instituta Inostrannych Jazykov [*A publication*]

UZMU...... Ucenye Zapiski Moskovskogo Universiteta [*A publication*]

UZNovPI... Ucenye Zapiski Novgorodskogo Gosudarstvennogo Pedagogicesko Instituta Kafedra Russkogo Jazyka [*A publication*]

UZOrenPI ... Ucenye Zapiski Orenburgskogo Gosudarstvennogo Pedagogiceskogo Instituta Imeni V. P. Ckalova [*A publication*]

UZPe .... Ucenye Zapiski Penzenskii Pedagogicheskii Institut [*Penza*] [*A publication*]

UZPer....... Ucenye Zapiski Permskii Universitet [*Perm'*] [*A publication*]

UZPerm..... Ucenye Zapiski Permskogo Gosudarstvennogo Universiteta Imeni A. M. Gor'kogo [*A publication*]

UZPs .... Ucenye Zapiski Pskovskii Pedagogicheskii Institut [*Pskov*] [*A publication*]

UZPU .... Ucenye Zapiski Petrozavodskogo Universiteta Filologiceskie Nauk [*A publication*]

uzr .... Uzbek Soviet Socialist Republic [*MARC country of publication code*] [*Library of Congress*]   (LCCP)

UZRA .... United Zionist Revisionists of America [*Later, Herut - USA*]   (EA)

UZRjazPI .. Ucenye Zapiski Rjazanskogo Gosudarstvennogo Pedagogiceskogo Instituta [*A publication*]

UZRovPI ... Ucenye Zapiski Rovenskogo Gosudarstvennogo Pedagogiceskogo Instituta Filologiceskij Fakul'tet [*A publication*]

UZSachPI ... Ucenye Zapiski Sachtinskogo Gosudarstvennogo Pedagogiceskogo Instituta [*A publication*]

UZSarPedI ... Ucenye Zapiski Saratovskogo Gosudarstvennogo Pedagogiceskogo Instituta [*A publication*]

UZSGU ..... Ucenye Zapiski Saratovskogo Gosudarstvennogo Universiteta [*A publication*]

UZSmolPI ... Ucenye Zapiski Smolenskogo Gosudarstvennogo Pedagogiceskogo Instituta [*A publication*]

UZSterPI... Ucenye Zapiski Sterlitamakskogo Gosudarstvennogo Pedagogiceskogo Instituta. Serija Filologiceskaja [*A publication*]

UZTar....... Ucenye Zapiski Tartusskii Universitet [*Tartu*] [*A publication*]

UZTarU..... Ucenye Zapiski Tartuskogo Gosudarstvennogo Universiteta [*A publication*]

UZTasPIIn ... Ucenye Zapiski Taskentskogo Pedagogiceskogo Instituta Inostrannych Jazykov [*A publication*]

UZTasPINiz ... Ucenye Zapiski Taskentskogo Pedagogiceskogo Instituta Imeni Nizami [*A publication*]

UZTFA...... Uchenye Zapiski Tul'skii Gosudarstvennyi Pedagogicheskii Institut Fiziko-Tekhnicheskie Nauki [*A publication*]

UZTI......... Ucenye Zapiski Tikhookeanskogo Instituta [*A publication*]

UZTjPI...... Ucenye Zapiski Tjumenskogo Pedagogiceskogo Instituta Kafedra Russkogo Jazyka [*A publication*]

UZTomU ... Ucenye Zapiski Tomskogo Universiteta Imeni V. V. Kujbyseva [*A publication*]

UZToU ...... Ucenye Zapiski Tomskii Universitet [*Tomsk*] [*A publication*]

UZTPI....... Ucenye Zapiski Tomskii Gosudarstvennyj Pedagogiceskij Institut [*A publication*]

UZTuvNII ... Ucenye Zapiski Tuvinskogo Naucno-Issledovatel'skogo Instituta Jazyka, Literatury, i Istorii [*A publication*]

UZU.......... Curuzu Cuatia [*Argentina*] [*Airport symbol*]   (OAG)

UZUlPI ..... Ucenye Zapiski Ul'janovskogo Gosudarstvennogo Pedagogiceskogo Instituta Imeni I. N. Ul'janova [*A publication*]

UZUPI....... Ucenye Zapiski Ural'skogo Pedagogiceskogo i Ucitel'skogo Instituta Imeni Puskina [*A publication*]

UZUzPI..... Ucenye Zapiski Uzbekskogo Respublikanskogo
       Pedagogiceskogo Instituta Kafedra Russkogo Jazyka i
       Literatury [*A publication*]
UZVinPI.... Ucenye Zapiski Vinnickogo Gosudarstvennogo
       Pedagogiceskogo Instituta Kafedra Russkogo Jazyka i
       Literatury [*A publication*]
UZVolPI.... Ucenye Zapiski Vologodskogo Gosudarstvennogo
       Pedagogiceskogo Instituta [*A publication*]
UZW.......... Und Zwar [*That Is*] [*German*]

V

V................ Abstracted Valuation Decisions [*A publication*]   (DLA)
V................ Deflection of the Vertical
V................ Digestum Vetus [*A publication*]   (DSA)
V................ Electric Potential [*Symbol*] [*IUPAC*]
V................ Electromotive Force [*Symbol*] [*See also E, EMF*] [*Electrochemistry*]   (DEN)
V................ Five [*Roman numeral*]
V................ Five Dollars [*Slang*]
V................ Five-Year Sentence [*Criminal slang*]
V................ Fixed-Wing Aircraft [*Navy symbol*]
V................ Frequency [*Spectroscopy*]
V................ Potential Difference [*Symbol*]
V................ Potential Energy [*Symbol*] [*IUPAC*]
V................ Promotional Fare [*Also, K, L, Q*] [*Airline fare code*]
V................ Ranger-Parachutist [*Army skill qualification identifier*]   (INF)
V................ [*A*] Safe [*Criminal slang*]
V................ Sanol Arzneimittel Dr. Schwarz [*Germany*] [*Research code symbol*]
V................ Shape Descriptor [*V-sign, for example. The shape resembles the letter for which it is named.*]
v................ Specific Volume [*Symbol*] [*IUPAC*]
V................ Staff Transport [*When V is the first of two letters in a military aircraft designation*]
V................ Unusual Visibility
V................ V3 London Gun [*British military*]   (DMA)
V................ Vacated [*Same case vacated*] [*Used in Shepard's Citations*] [*Legal term*]   (DLA)
V................ Vaccella [*Flourished, 12th century*] [*Authority cited in pre-1607 legal work*]   (DSA)
V................ Vaccinated [*Medicine*]
V................ Vacuole
V................ Vacuum   (AAG)
V................ Vagabond
V................ Vale   (ROG)
V................ Valencia [*A publication*]
V................ Valine [*One-letter symbol; see Val*]
V................ Valley   (ROG)
V................ Value
V................ Valve
V................ Van
V................ Van Container [*Shipping*]   (DS)
V................ Vanadium [*Chemical element*]
V................ Vancouver Stock Exchange [*Canada*]
V................ Vapor
V................ Variable
V................ Variable Region [*Immunochemistry*]
V................ Variant [*Genetics*]
V................ Variation
V................ Variety [*A publication*]
V................ Variety Theatres and Shows [*Public-performance tariff class*] [*British*]
V................ Varnish   (AAG)
V................ Varnish-Treated [*Insulation*]   (MSA)
V................ Varsity
V................ Vascular Tissue [*Botany*]
V................ Vatican City
V................ Vector [*Mathematics*]
V................ Vedi [*See*] [*Italian*]   (ILCA)
V................ Veen, Publishers [*Holland*]
V................ Vehicles   (MCD)
V................ Vein
V................ Vel [*Or*] [*Pharmacy*]
V................ Velocity
V................ Vendor   (AAG)
V................ Venerable
V................ Venereology [*Medical Officer designation*] [*British*]
V................ Venezuela [*IYRU nationality code*]   (IYR)
V................ Venous [*Medicine*]
V................ Venstre [*Liberal Party*] [*Norway*] [*Political party*]   (PPE)
V................ Venstre (Liberale Parti) [*Liberal Party*] [*Denmark*] [*Political party*]   (PPE)

V................ Vent
V................ Ventilator
V................ Ventral
V................ Ventur [*Quality of carburetor barrel*] [*Automotive engineering*]
V................ Venturi [*Automotive engineering*]
V................ Venue
V................ Verapamil [*A coronary vasodilator*]
V................ Verb
V................ Verbal
V................ Verbo [*A publication*]
V................ Verfassung [*Constitution*] [*German*]   (ILCA)
V................ Verfuegung [*Order, Decree*] [*German*]   (ILCA)
V................ Vergeltung [*Retaliation*] [*German*]
V................ Vermessung [*Survey*] [*German military*]
V................ Vermiculite
V................ Vermont Reports [*A publication*]   (DLA)
V................ Verordnung [*Decree, Regulation, Ordinance*] [*German*]   (ILCA)
V................ Verse
V................ Versicle
V................ Versiculo [*In Such a Way*] [*Latin*]   (ROG)
V................ Version
V................ Verso
V................ Versus [*Against*]
V................ Vert [*Heraldry*]
V................ Verte [*Turn Over*]
V................ Vertex
V................ Vertical [*RADAR*]
V................ Vertical in Line [*Aircraft engine*]
V................ Verticillium Wilt [*Plant pathology*]
V................ Very
V................ Vespers
V................ Veto   (OICC)
V................ Via [*By Way Of*] [*Latin*]   (ADA)
V................ Vibrio [*Microbiology*]
V................ Vic [*Phonetic alphabet*] [*Pre-World War II*]   (DSUE)
V................ Vicar [*or Vicarage*]
V................ Vice [*In a position or title*]
v................ Vicinal [*Also, vic*] [*Chemistry*]
V................ Victor [*Phonetic alphabet*] [*World War II*] [*International*]   (DSUE)
V................ Victoria
V................ Victory [*As in "the V campaign" in Europe, during World War II*]
V................ Victualling [*British military*]   (DMA)
V................ Village
V................ Vinblastine [*See VBL*]
V................ Vincentius Hispanus [*Deceased, 1248*] [*Authority cited in pre-1607 legal work*]   (DSA)
V................ Vincristine [*Also, LCR, O, V, VC, VCR*] [*Antineoplastic drug*]
V................ Vinegar [*Phonetic alphabet*] [*Royal Navy*] [*World War I*]   (DSUE)
V................ Violet
V................ Violin [*Music*]
V................ Virgin
V................ Virginia Reports [*A publication*]   (DLA)
V................ Virulent
V................ Virus
V................ Viscosity
V................ Viscount [*or Viscountess*]
V................ Vise Break Distance [*Stress test for steel*]
V................ Visibility
V................ Vision [*A publication*]
V................ Vision
V................ Visit
V................ Visiting Practice Only [*Chiropody*] [*British*]
V................ Visual
V................ Visual Acuity [*Also, VA*] [*Ophthalmology*]
V................ Visual Magnitude [*When followed by a two-digit number*]
V................ Vivra, Inc. [*NYSE symbol*]   (SPSG)
V................ Vixisti [*You Lived*] [*Latin*]

V................	Vixit [*He Lived*] [*Latin*]
V................	Vocative
V................	Voce [*Voice*] [*Latin*]
V................	Voice
V................	Voice Data [*NASA*]
V................	Void [*Decision or finding held invalid for reasons given*] [*Used in Shepard's Citations*] [*Legal term*] (DLA)
V................	Voir [*See*] [*French*] (ILCA)
V................	Volcano (ROG)
V................	Volt [*Symbol*] [*SI unit of electric potential difference*]
V................	Voltage
V................	Voltare [*Turn Over*] [*Latin*] (ROG)
V................	Volti [*Turn Over*] [*Music*]
V................	Voltmeter
V................	Volts
V................	Volume [*Bibliography*]
V................	Volume [*Symbol*] [*IUPAC*]
V................	Voluntary Aided School [*British*]
V................	Volunteer [*US Naval Reserve*]
V................	Von [*Of, From*] [*German*]
V................	VOR [*Very-High-Frequency Omnidirectional Range*] Federal Airway [*Followed by identification*]
V................	Vous [*You*] [*French*] (ROG)
V................	Vowel
V................	VTOL [*Vertical Takeoff and Landing*] [*or STOL - Short Takeoff and Landing*] [*when V is the second or only letter in a military aircraft designation*]
V................	Vulgate [*Latin translation of the Bible*] [*A publication*] (BJA)
V................	Wrong Verb Form [*Used in correcting manuscripts, etc.*]
V-1............	Vergeltungswaffe 1 [*Pilotless flying bomb employed by the Germans*] [*World War II*]
V₂............	Takeoff Safety Speed [*Aviation*]
V-2............	Vergeltungswaffe 2 [*Rocket bomb employed by the Germans*] [*World War II*]
V3.............	Takeoff Speed Over Screen [*Aviation code*] (AIA)
V4.............	Steady Initial Climb Speed [*Aviation code*] (AIA)
5V.............	Togo [*Aircraft nationality and registration mark*] (FAAC)
6V.............	Senegal [*Aircraft nationality and registration mark*] (FAAC)
9V.............	Singapore [*Aircraft nationality and registration mark*] (FAAC)
V (Bomb)....	Vergeltungswaffe Bomb [*German "vengeance weapon"*]
VA.............	Alveolar Ventilation
VA.............	Attack Squadron [*Symbol*] (MCD)
VA.............	Avian Aircraft Ltd. [*Canada*] [*ICAO aircraft manufacturer identifier*] (ICAO)
VA.............	End of Work [*Morse telephony*] (FAAC)
VA.............	Gilmer's Virginia Reports [*A publication*] (DLA)
VA.............	University of Virginia, Charlottesville, VA [*OCLC symbol*] (OCLC)
Va.............	Vacarius [*Flourished, 1144-70*] [*Authority cited in pre-1607 legal work*] (DSA)
Va.............	Vaccella [*Flourished, 12th century*] [*Authority cited in pre-1607 legal work*] (DSA)
VA.............	Vacuum Aspiration [*Medicine*]
Va.............	Valid [*Decision or finding held valid for reasons given*] [*Used in Shepard's Citations*] [*Legal term*] (DLA)
VA.............	Valium Anonymous (EA)
V and A......	Valuable and Attractive [*A marking used by RAF on such supplies as watches and cameras*] [*British*]
VA.............	Value Added (ADA)
VA.............	Value Analysis
Va.............	Valuta [*Exchange Equivalent*] [*German*] [*Banking*]
VA.............	Variable Annuity
Va.............	Vasari [*A publication*]
VA.............	Vatican City [*ANSI two-letter standard code*] (CNC)
VA.............	Vehicle Analyst (MCD)
VA.............	Vehicular Accident [*British police*]
VA.............	Velocity at Apogee (MCD)
VA.............	Venezolana Internacional de Aviacion Sociedad Anonima (VIASA) [*Venezuela*] [*ICAO designator*] (ICDA)
VA.............	Ventral Area [*Anatomy*]
VA.............	Ventricular Aneurysm [*Cardiology*]
VA.............	Ventricular Arrhythmia [*Cardiology*]
VA.............	Verb Active
VA.............	Verbal Adjective
VA.............	VERLORT [*Very-Long-Range Tracking*] Azimuth [*NASA*]
VA.............	Vermiculite Association (EA)
VA.............	Verpflegungsausgabestelle [*Rations distributing point*] [*German military - World War II*]
VA.............	Vertebral Artery [*Anatomy*]
VA.............	Vesicular-Arbuscular [*Mycorrhiza*] [*Botany*]
VA.............	[*Department of*] Veterans Affairs [*Formerly, Veterans Administration*]
V-A............	Vibroacoustic (NASA)
VA.............	Vibroacoustic Test (NASA)
VA.............	Vicar Apostolic
VA.............	Vice Admiral [*Also, VADM, VADML*]
VA.............	Vickers-Armstrong Gun
V-A............	Vickers-Armstrong Ltd.
VA.............	Victims Anonymous (EA)
V & A	Victoria and Albert Museum [*London, England*]

VA.............	Victoria and Albert Order [*British*]
VA.............	Victualling Allowance [*British military*] (DMA)
VA.............	Video Amplifier
V/A...........	Video/Analog (NASA)
V/A...........	Video/Audio [*Telecommunications*]
VA.............	Vincent's Angina [*Medicine*]
VA.............	Viola [*Music*]
VA.............	Virginia [*Postal code*]
VA.............	Virginia Reports [*A publication*] (DLA)
VA.............	Virginia Supreme Court Reports [*A publication*] (DLA)
VA.............	Virtual Address
VA.............	Virus-Antibody [*Immunology*]
VA.............	Visual Acuity [*Also, V*] [*Ophthalmology*]
VA.............	Visual Aid
VA.............	Visual Approach [*Aviation*] (FAAC)
VA.............	Visual Arts [*US Copyright Office class*]
VA.............	Visual Training Aid Specialist [*Navy*]
VA.............	Vita Apollonii [*of Philostratus*] [*Classical studies*] (OCD)
VA.............	Vital Area (NRCH)
VA.............	Voice of America
V-A............	Volt-Ampere (AAG)
VA.............	Voltaire Alternative
VA.............	Voluntary Aid (ADA)
VA.............	Volunteer Artillery [*Military*] [*British*] (ROG)
V of A	Volunteers of America (EA)
VA.............	Vorausabteilung [*Advance detachment*] [*German military - World War II*]
VA.............	Vorderasiatische Abteilung der Staatlichen Museen zu Berlin [*A publication*]
VA.............	Vorderasien (BJA)
VA.............	Vote America (EA)
VA.............	Votre Altesse [*Your Highness*] [*French*]
V/A...........	Voucher Attached [*Banking*]
VA.............	Voyage Alliance [*Later, IVA*] (EA)
VA.............	Vulnerable Area (NATG)
VAA...........	Vaasa [*Finland*] [*Airport symbol*] (OAG)
VAA...........	Vegetarian Association of America (EA)
VAA...........	Vehicle Assembly Area [*NASA*] (MCD)
VAA...........	Venezuelan American Association of the United States (EA)
VAA...........	Verhandelingen. Koninklijke Akademie van Wetenschappen te Amsterdam [*A publication*]
VAA...........	Verticillium albo-atrium [*A fungus*]
VAA...........	Vietnamese American Association
VAA...........	Viewpoint Adapter Assembly (NASA)
VAA...........	Voice Access Arrangement
VAAC........	Vanadyl Acetylacetonate [*Organic chemistry*]
VAAC........	Victorian AIDS [*Acquired Immune Deficiency Syndrome*] Action Committee [*Australia*]
VA Acts......	Acts of the General Assembly, Commonwealth of Virginia [*A publication*] (DLA)
VAADA.....	Victorian Association of Alcohol and Drug Agencies [*Australia*]
VA Ag Dept ...	Virginia. Department of Agriculture and Immigration. Publications [*A publication*]
VA Ag Exp ...	Virginia Polytechnic Institute. Agricultural Experiment Station. Publications [*A publication*]
VA Agric Exp Stn Bull ...	Virginia. Agricultural Experiment Station. Bulletin [*A publication*]
VA Agric Exp Stn Tech Bull ...	Virginia. Agricultural Experiment Station. Technical Bulletin [*A publication*]
VAAH........	Ahmadabad [*India*] [*ICAO location identifier*] (ICLI)
VAAHDJ...	Virchows Archiv. A. Pathological Anatomy and Histopathology [*A publication*]
VAAK........	Akola [*India*] [*ICAO location identifier*] (ICLI)
VAAL	Vaal Reefs Exploration and Mining Co. Ltd. [*NASDAQ symbol*] (NQ)
VAAL	Victorian Aborigines Advancement League [*Australia*]
VAAP	USSR Copyright Agency [*Acronym is based on Russian name*]
VAAP	Volunteer Army Ammunition Plant (AABC)
VA App......	Virginia Appeals [*A publication*] (DLA)
VAAR........	Vinyl Alcohol Acetate Resin [*NASA*] (KSC)
VAAS........	Vermont Academy of Arts and Sciences
VAAU.......	Aurangabad [*India*] [*ICAO location identifier*] (ICLI)
VAAUS......	Venezuelan American Association of the United States (EA)
VAB..........	Van Allen Belts
VAB..........	Variable Action Button (NVT)
VAB..........	Vehicle Assembly Building [*NASA*] (AFM)
VAB..........	Vehicule de l'Avant Blinde [*Armored Personnel Carrier*] [*French*]
VAB	Vertical Axis Bearing
VAB	Vinblastine, Actinomycin D, Bleomycin [*Antineoplastic drug regimen*]
VAB	Voice Answer Back
VAB	Vorderasiatische Bibliothek [*H. Winckler and A. Jeremias*] [*Leipzig*] [*A publication*] (BJA)
vab............	Vry aan Boord [*Free on Board*] [*Afrikaans*] [*Shipping*]
VABA........	Value Added by Advertising
VABA........	Victorian Amateur Boxing Association [*Australia*]
VA BAJ	Virginia Bar Association. Journal [*A publication*]
VA Bar News ...	Virginia Bar News [*A publication*] (DLA)
VABB.........	Bombay [*India*] [*ICAO location identifier*] (ICLI)

VABBA...... Vestsi Akademii Navuk BSSR. Seryya Biyalagichnykh Navuk [*A publication*]
VABCD...... Vinblastine, Adriamycin, Bleomycin, CCNU [*Lomustine*], Dacarbazine [*Antineoplastic drug regimen*]
VABD........ Van Allen Belt Dosimeter
VABF........ Bombay [*India*] [*ICAO location identifier*] (ICLI)
VABF........ Variety Artistes' Benevolent Fund [*British*] (ROG)
VABF........ Virginia Beach Federal Savings Bank [*NASDAQ symbol*] (NQ)
VABFA...... Vestsi Akademii Navuk BSSR. Seryya Fizika-Tekhnichnykh Navuk [*A publication*]
VABI........ Bilaspur [*India*] [*ICAO location identifier*] (ICLI)
VAB-I........ Vinblastine, Actinomycin D [*Dactinomycin*], Bleomycin [*Antineoplastic drug regimen*]
VAB-II...... Vinblastine, Actinomycin D [*Dactinomycin*], Bleomycin, Cisplatin [*Antineoplastic drug regimen*]
VAB-III..... Vinblastine, Actinomycin D [*Dactinomycin*], Bleomycin, Cisplatin, Chlorambucil, Cyclophosphamide [*Antineoplastic drug regimen*]
VABJ........ Bhuj [*India*] [*ICAO location identifier*] (ICLI)
VABL........ Victorian Amateur Boxing League [*Australia*]
VABM....... Belgaum [*India*] [*ICAO location identifier*] (ICLI)
VABM....... Vertical Angle Bench Mark
VABO....... Baroda/Vadodara [*India*] [*ICAO location identifier*] (ICLI)
VABP....... Bhopal [*India*] [*ICAO location identifier*] (ICLI)
VABPDE ... Virchows Archiv. B. Cell Pathology Including Molecular Pathology [*A publication*]
VABPF...... Vice Admiral British Pacific Fleet
VABR .... Vehicle Assembly Building Repeater [*NASA*] (KSC)
VABV .... Bhaunagar [*India*] [*ICAO location identifier*] (ICLI)
VAC......... Alternating Current Volts
VAC......... Fifth Amphibious Corps
VAC......... Vacancy [*Real estate*] (ADA)
VAC......... Vacant (AFM)
VAC......... Vacate
VAC......... Vacation
Vac......... Vaccella [*Flourished, 12th century*] [*Authority cited in pre-1607 legal work*] (DSA)
VAC......... Vaccination [*or Vaccine*] [*Medicine*]
VAC......... Vacuolar Apical Compartment [*Cytology*]
VAC......... Vacuum (AABC)
VAC......... Value-Added Carrier [*Telecommunications*]
VAC......... Variable Air Capacitor
VAC......... Variance at Completion (MCD)
VAC......... Vector Analog Computer
VAC......... Vehicle Assembly and Checkout [*NASA*] (NASA)
VAC......... Verified Audit Circulation [*Newspaper auditing firm*] [*Advertising*]
VAC......... Vermont American Corporation [*AMEX symbol*] (SPSG)
VAC......... Vertical Air Current
VAC......... Veterans Administration Center
VAC......... Veterans Affairs Canada [*See also AACC*]
VAC......... Vice-Admiralty Court [*British*]
VAC......... Victor Analog Computer [*Data processing*]
VAC......... Victorian AIDS [*Acquired Immune Deficiency Syndrome*] Council [*Australia*]
VAC......... Video Amplifier Chain
VAC......... Vidicon Alignment Coil
VAC......... Vincristine, Actinomycin D, Cyclophosphamide [*Antineoplastic drug regimen*]
VAC......... Vincristine, Adriamycin, Cyclophosphamide [*Also, VACY*] [*Antineoplastic drug regimen*]
VAC......... Visual Aid Console
VAC......... Vital Area Center (CAAL)
VAC......... Volt-Ampere Characteristics [*Microwave emission*]
VAC......... Volts Alternating Current
VAC......... Voluntary Action Center
VAC......... Volunteer Adviser Corps (EA)
VACAB...... Veterans Administration Contract Appeals Board
VACAPES ... Virginia Capes [*Navy*] (CAAL)
VA Cas....... Virginia Cases (Brockenbrough and Holmes) [*A publication*] (DLA)
VA Cas....... Virginia Criminal Cases [*3-4 Virginia*] [*1789-1826*] [*A publication*] (DLA)
VA Cavalcade ... Virginia Cavalcade [*A publication*]
Vacc .... Vaccella [*Flourished, 12th century*] [*Authority cited in pre-1607 legal work*] (DSA)
vacc .... Vaccinate
VACC .... Value-Added Common Carrier [*Telecommunications*]
VAcC .... Visual Acuity with Spectacle Correction
VACCI...... Vaccine [*Medicine*]
VACCJ ...... VACC [*Victorian Automobile Chamber of Commerce*] Journal [*A publication*] (APTA)
VAcCL...... Visual Acuity with Contact Lens Correction
VACE....... Verification and Checkout Equipment
VACF....... Vietnamese-American Children's Fund [*Defunct*] (EA)
VACHA ..... Virginias Automated Clearing House Association
VA Ch Dec ... Wythe's Virginia Chancery Reports [*1788-99*] [*A publication*] (DLA)
VA Cir....... Virginia Circuit Court Opinions [*A publication*] (DLA)
VACM ...... Vector Averaging Current Meter [*Marine science*] (MSC)

VACM .... Vincristine, Adriamycin, Cyclophosphamide, Methotrexate [*Antineoplastic drug regimen*]
Vac Microbalance Tech ... Vacuum Microbalance Techniques [*A publication*]
VA Col Dec ... Virginia Colonial Decisions (Randolph and Barrandall) [*A publication*] (DLA)
VACP........ Vacation Publications, Inc. [*NASDAQ symbol*] (NQ)
VACR........ Visual Aircraft Recognition (MCD)
VACRS ..... Vocational Assistance Commission for Retired Servicemen (CINC)
VACSAT ... Vaccine Satellite Program (MCD)
VACT........ Alternating Current Test Volts (MSA)
VACTERL ... Vertebral, Anal, Cardiac, Tracheosophageal, Renal, and Limb [*Defects*]
VACTL...... Vertical Assembly Component Test Laboratory
VACU .... Virtual Access Control Unit
VACUA ..... Vacuum [*A publication*]
VACURG .. Veterans Administration Cooperative Urological Research Group
Vacuum Chem ... Vacuum Chemistry [*Japan*] [*A publication*]
Vacuum R .. Vacuum Review [*A publication*] (APTA)
VACW .... Alternating Current Working Volts (MSA)
VACY .... Vincristine, Adriamycin, Cyclophosphamide [*Also, VAC*] [*Antineoplastic drug regimen*]
VAD......... Vacuum Arc Degassing [*Metal technology*]
VAD......... Val d'Or Explorations [*Vancouver Stock Exchange symbol*]
VAD......... Valdosta, GA [*Location identifier*] [*FAA*] (FAAL)
VAD......... Value Added and Data [*Communications network*]
VAD......... Value-Added Dealer [*Business term*]
VAD......... Value-Added Distributor
VAD......... Value-Added Driver [*Data processing*] (PCM)
VAD......... Vandenberg Addendum Document [*Air Force*] (NASA)
VAD......... Vapor Axial Deposition [*Optical fiber technology*]
VAD......... Velocity-Azimuth Display
VAD......... Ventricle-Assist Device [*Cardiology*]
VAD......... Vereinigte Arbeitnehmerpartei Deutschland [*United Employees' Party of Germany*] [*Federal Republic of Germany*] [*Political party*] (PPW)
VAD......... Veterans' Affairs Decisions, Appealed Pension and Civil Service Retirement Cases [*United States*] [*A publication*] (DLA)
VAD......... Voltmeter Analog-to-Digital Converter
VAD......... Voluntary Aid Detachment [*British World War I nursing unit*]
VAD......... Vulcan Air Defense (MCD)
VADA .... VFR [*Visual Flight Rules*] Arrival Delay Advisory [*Aviation*] (FAAC)
VADAC ..... Voice Analyzer Data Converter
VADC .... Video Analog to Digital Converter
VADC .... Voice Analyzer and Data Converter (MCD)
VADE .... Vandenberg Automatic Data Equipment [*Air Force*]
VADE .... Vandenberg Automatic Data Evaluation [*Air Force*]
VADE .... Versatile Automatic Data Exchange (MCD)
VADE .... Voice Analog to Digital Encoder
VA Dec...... Virginia Decisions [*A publication*] (DLA)
VA Dent J ... Virginia Dental Journal [*A publication*]
VA Dept Highways Div Tests Geol Yearbook ... Virginia. Department of Highways. Division of Tests. Geological Yearbook [*A publication*]
VA Dept Labor and Industry Ann Rept ... Virginia. Department of Labor and Industry. Annual Report [*A publication*]
VADER ...... Vacuum Arc Double-Electrode Remelting [*Metallurgy*]
VADES...... Victorian Association for Dance Education in Schools [*Australia*]
VADF .... Vietnamese Air Defense Force (MCD)
VADIC....... Vincristine, Adriamycin, DIC [*Dacarbazine*] [*Antineoplastic drug regimen*]
VADIS....... Voice and Data Integrated System [*Telecommunications*] (TEL)
VA Div Geol Bull ... Virginia. Division of Geology. Bulletin [*A publication*]
VA Div Geology Bull Reprint Ser ... Virginia. Division of Geology. Bulletin. Reprint Series [*A publication*]
VA Div Mineral Res Bull Inf Circ Mineral Res Circ ... Virginia. Division of Mineral Resources. Bulletin. Information Circular. Mineral Resources Circular [*A publication*]
VA Div Miner Resour Bull ... Virginia. Division of Mineral Resources. Bulletin [*A publication*]
VA Div Miner Resour Inf Cir ... Virginia. Division of Mineral Resources. Information Circular [*A publication*]
VA Div Miner Resour Miner Resour Rep ... Virginia. Division of Mineral Resources. Mineral Resources Report [*A publication*]
VA Div Miner Resour Rep Invest ... Virginia. Division of Mineral Resources. Report of Investigations [*A publication*]
VADM....... Vice Admiral [*Also, VA, VADML*]
VADM....... Virtual Axial Dipole Moment [*Geophysics*]
VADML .... Vice Admiral [*Also, VA, VADM*] (FAAC)
VADMS..... Voice-Analog-Digital Manual Switch (MCD)
VADS .... Value Added and Data Services
VADS .... Velocity-Aligned Doppler Spectroscopy
VADS .... Vendor Automated Data System (MCD)
VADS .... Veterans Assistance Discharge System (MCD)
VADS .... Visual-Aural Digit Span Test [*Educational test*]
VADS .... Vulcan Air Defense Systems (MCD)
VAE .... Vinta Exploration Ltd. [*Vancouver Stock Exchange symbol*]

VAE .... Vinyl Acetate - Ethylene [*Organic chemistry*]
VAE .... Votre Altesse Electorale [*Your Electoral Highness*] [*French*]
VAEBAI .... Agricultural Experiment Station. University of Vermont. Bulletin [*A publication*]
VAEDAI.... Victorian Aboriginal Employment Development Association, Inc. [*Australia*]
VAEP........ Variable, Attributes, Error Propagation (IEEE)
Vaerml Bergsmannafoeren Ann ... Vaermlaendska Bergsmannafoereningens Annaler [*A publication*]
VAES......... Voice-Activated Encoding System
VAE VA Agric Econ VA Polytech Inst State Univ Coop Ext Serv ... VAE. Virginia Agricultural Economics. Virginia Polytechnic Institute and State University. Cooperative Extension Service [*A publication*]
VAEVC...... Vinyl Acetate - Ethylene - Vinyl Chloride [*Organic chemistry*]
Vaextskyddsanst-Notiser ... Vaextskyddsanstalt-Notiser [*A publication*]
VAF .... Valence [*France*] [*Airport symbol*] (OAG)
VAF .... Vane Airflow [*Automotive engineering*]
VAF .... Vendor Approval Form
VAF .... Vernacular Architecture Forum (EA)
VAF .... Vietnamese Air Force (MCD)
VAFAC...... Vincristine, Amethopterin [*Methotrexate*], Fluorouracil, Adriamycin, Cyclophosphamide [*Antineoplastic drug regimen*]
VA Farm Econ VA Polytech Inst Agr Ext Serv ... Virginia Farm Economics. Virginia Polytechnic Institute. Agricultural Extension Service [*A publication*]
VAFB........ Valley Federal Savings Bank [*NASDAQ symbol*] (NQ)
VAFB........ Vandenberg Air Force Base [*California*]
VAFD........ Valley Federal Savings Bank [*NASDAQ symbol*] (NQ)
VA Fish Lab Educ Ser ... Virginia Fisheries Laboratory. Educational Series [*A publication*]
VA Fruit..... Virginia Fruit [*A publication*]
VAG.......... Vagabond (DSUE)
VAG.......... Vaginal [*Medicine*]
VAG.......... Vaginitis [*Medicine*]
VAG.......... Vagrancy [*FBI standardized term*]
VAG.......... Vananda Gold [*Vancouver Stock Exchange symbol*]
VAG.......... Vancouver Art Gallery [*Canada*]
VAG.......... Varginha [*Brazil*] [*Airport symbol*] (OAG)
VAG.......... Vastgoed [*A publication*]
VAG.......... Vernacular Architecture Group [*British*]
Vaga.......... Vagabond [*A publication*]
VAGA........ Vagabond Hotels [*NASDAQ symbol*] (NQ)
VAGA........ Visual Artists and Galleries Association (EA)
VA Geol Surv Circ ... Virginia. Geological Survey. Circular [*A publication*]
VA Geol Survey Bull ... Virginia. Geological Survey. Bulletin [*A publication*]
VA Geol Surv Repr Ser ... Virginia. Geological Survey. Reprint Series [*A publication*]
VAGO........ Goa [*India*] [*ICAO location identifier*] (ICLI)
VAGO........ Vanderbilt Gold Corp. [*NASDAQ symbol*] (NQ)
VA GSB ... Virginia. Geological Survey. Bulletin [*A publication*]
VAH.......... Heavy Attack Squadron [*Symbol*] (MCD)
VAH.......... Vaihoa [*Tuamotu Archipelago*] [*Seismograph station code, US Geological Survey*] (SEIS)
VAH.......... Vertical Array Hydrophone
VAH.......... Veterans Administration Hospital [*Later, VAMC*]
VAH.......... Virilizing Adrenal Hyperplasia [*Medicine*]
VAH.......... Vitiated Air Heater
VAHD....... Veterinary and Animal Husbandry Department [*Burma*] (DS)
VA Hist Soc Coll ... Virginia Historical Society. Collections [*A publication*]
VA Horse Ind Yearb ... Virginia Horse Industry Yearbook [*A publication*]
VAHR........ Veterans Administration Hospital Representative [*Red Cross*]
VAHS........ Virus-Associated Hemophagocytic Syndrome [*Medicine*]
VAI .... Vanimo [*Papua New Guinea*] [*Airport symbol*] (OAG)
VAI .... Vassar Attitude Inventory [*Education*]
VAI .... Ventilation Air Intake [*Hovercraft*]
VA & I....... Verb Active and Intransitive (ROG)
VAI .... Video Arts International, Inc.
VAI .... Video-Assisted Instruction
VAI .... Visual Alignment Indicators [*Tire maintenance*]
VAI .... Vorticity Area Index [*Meteorology*]
VA IC Ops ... Virginia Industrial Commission Opinions [*A publication*] (DLA)
VAID .... Indore [*India*] [*ICAO location identifier*] (ICLI)
VAIL......... Vail Associates [*NASDAQ symbol*] (NQ)
VA Inst Mar Sci Spec Sci Rep ... Virginia Institute of Marine Science. Special Scientific Report [*A publication*]
Vaizey .... Vaizey's Law of Settlements [*1887*] [*A publication*] (DLA)
VAJ........... Vajont [*Belluno*] [*Italy*] [*Seismograph station code, US Geological Survey*] (SEIS)
VAJB .... Jabalpur [*India*] [*ICAO location identifier*] (ICLI)
VA J Ed ..... Virginia Journal of Education [*A publication*]
VA J Educ ... Virginia Journal of Education [*A publication*]
VA J Int L ... Virginia Journal of International Law [*A publication*]
VA J Intl L ... Virginia Journal of International Law [*A publication*]
VAJJ .... Bombay/Juhu [*India*] [*ICAO location identifier*] (ICLI)
VAJM........ Jamnagar [*India*] [*ICAO location identifier*] (ICLI)
VA J Nat Resources L ... Virginia Journal of Natural Resources Law [*A publication*]

VA J Nat Resour Law ... Virginia Journal of Natural Resources Law [*A publication*]
VAJODH .. Lantbrukshogskolan Vaxtskyddsrapporter Jordbruk [*A publication*]
VA Jour Sci ... Virginia Journal of Science [*A publication*]
VA J Sci..... Virginia Journal of Science [*A publication*]
VAK .... Chevak [*Alaska*] [*Airport symbol*] (OAG)
VAK .... Vertical Access Kit (NASA)
VAK .... Vertical Assembly Kit (NASA)
Vakbl Biol ... Vakblad voor Biologen [*A publication*]
VAKD .... Khandwa [*India*] [*ICAO location identifier*] (ICLI)
VAKE .... Kandla [*India*] [*ICAO location identifier*] (ICLI)
Vak Inf...... Vakuum Information [*A publication*]
VAKP........ Kolhapur [*India*] [*ICAO location identifier*] (ICLI)
VAKS........ Keshod [*India*] [*ICAO location identifier*] (ICLI)
Vakstudie... Fiscale Encyclopedie de Vakstudie [*A publication*]
VAKT .... Visual, Association, Kinesthetic, Tactile [*With reference to reading*]
VAKT .... Visual-Auditory-Kinesthetic-Tactual
VAKTA...... Vakuum-Technik [*A publication*]
Vak-Tech ... Vakuum-Technik [*A publication*]
Vak-Technik ... Vakuum-Technik [*A publication*]
VAL .... Light Attack Aircraft [*Symbol*] (MCD)
VAL .... Plattsburgh, NY [*Location identifier*] [*FAA*] (FAAL)
VAL .... University of Virginia, Law Library, Charlottesville, VA [*OCLC symbol*] (OCLC)
Val............. Valcausus [*Gualcosius*] [*Flourished, 11th-12th century*] [*Authority cited in pre-1607 legal work*] (DSA)
VAL .... Valentia [*Ireland*] [*Seismograph station code, US Geological Survey*] (SEIS)
VAL .... Valentia [*Ireland*] [*Geomagnetic observatory code*]
VAL .... Valid [*or Validation*] (KSC)
Val............. Valine [*Also, V*] [*An amino acid*]
VAL .... Valley (MSA)
Val............. Valley Girl [*Lifestyle classification*]
VAL .... Valspar Corp. [*AMEX symbol*] (SPSG)
VAL .... Valuation
VAL .... Valuation [*A publication*]
VAL .... Value
VAL .... Value Investment Corp. [*Toronto Stock Exchange symbol*]
Val............. Valuta [*Exchange Equivalent*] [*German*] [*Banking*]
VAL .... Valuta [*Currency*] [*Afrikaans*] [*Business term*]
VAL .... Valve
VAL .... Variable Angle Launcher
VAL .... Vehicle Authorization List [*Military*] (AFM)
VAL .... Vertical Assault Lift
VAL .... Vicarm Arm Language
VAL .... Vieques Air Link [*Caribbean airline*]
VA L .... Virginia Law Review [*A publication*]
VAL .... Visual Approach and Landing Chart [*Aviation*]
VAL .... Vortex Arc LASER
VAL .... Vulnerability Assessment Laboratory [*White Sands Missile Range, NM*] [*Military*] (RDA)
VALA .... Victorian Amateur Lacrosse Association [*Australia*]
Valachica ... Acta Valachica. Studii si Materiale de Istorie a Culturii [*A publication*]
VA Law J ... Virginia Law Journal [*Richmond*] [*A publication*] (DLA)
VA Law R ... Virginia Law Review [*A publication*]
VA Law Rev ... Virginia Law Review [*A publication*]
VALB........ Veterans of the Abraham Lincoln Brigade (EA)
VALCO ..... Volta Aluminum Company Ltd.
Val Com ... Valen's Commentaries [*A publication*] (DLA)
VALD .... Valued (ROG)
val dec .... Valeur Declaree [*Declared Value*] [*French*] [*Business term*]
VA L Dig.... Virginia Law Digest [*A publication*] (DLA)
VALDN ..... Validation
VALE........ [*The*] Valley Railroad Co. [*AAR code*]
Vale Evesham Hist Soc Res Pap ... Vale of Evesham Historical Society. Research Papers [*A publication*]
VALEUROP ... Fonds Commun de Placement Principalement Investi en Valeurs Europeennes [*French*] [*Business term*]
VALI......... Validate (AABC)
VA Lib Bul ... Virginia Library Bulletin [*A publication*]
VA Libn ..... Virginia Librarian [*A publication*]
VALID....... Validation (NASA)
VA LJ .... Virginia Law Journal [*A publication*] (DLA)
VALL......... Vortex Arc LASER Light
Vallalatvez -Szerv ... Vallalatvezetes-Vallalatszervezes [*A publication*]
VALM .... Valmont Industries, Inc. [*NASDAQ symbol*] (NQ)
VALN .... Vallen Corp. [*NASDAQ symbol*] (NQ)
VALN .... Valuation
VALN .... Victorian Adult Literacy News [*A publication*] (APTA)
VALNET... Veterans Administration Library Network [*Veterans Administration*] [*Washington, DC*]
VALOR ..... Veterans Administration Libraries Online Resources
VALP........ Valex Petroleum, Inc. [*NASDAQ symbol*] (NQ)
VALP........ Vortex Arc LASER Pump
Valparaiso Univ Law R ... Valparaiso University. Law Review [*A publication*]
Valparaiso Univ L Rev ... Valparaiso University. Law Review [*A publication*]
VALPO...... Valparaiso (DSUE)
VA LR........ Virginia Law Review [*A publication*]

VALRA...... Variable-Area Light-Reflecting Assembly [*Invented by T. C. Howard of Synergetics, Inc.*]
VA L Reg ... Virginia Law Register [*A publication*]   (DLA)
VA L Reg NS ... Virginia Law Register, New Series [*A publication*]   (DLA)
Val Rep...... Valuation Reports, Interstate Commerce Commission [*A publication*]   (DLA)
Val Rep ICC ... Valuation Reports, Interstate Commerce Commission [*A publication*]   (DLA)
VA L Rev ... Virginia Law Review [*A publication*]
VALS........ Value and Lifestyle [*Classifications*] [*Marketing*]
Valsa.......... Valsalva [*A publication*]
VALSAS.... Variable Length Word Symbolic Assembly System   (IEEE)
VALT........ Valtek, Inc. [*NASDAQ symbol*]   (NQ)
VALT........ VTOL [*Vertical Takeoff and Landing*] Approach and Landing Technology [*Program*]
Valt Maatalouskoetoiminnan Julk ... Valtion Maatalouskoetoiminnan Julkaisuja [*A publication*]
VALT(S).... Vulnerability and Lethality Test (System)   (MCD)
Valt Tek Tutkimuskeskus Reaktorilab Tied ... Valtion Teknillinen Tutkimuskeskus. Reaktorilaboratorio. Tiedonanto [*A publication*]
Valt Tek Tutkimuslaitos Julk ... Valtion Teknillinen Tutkimuslaitos. Julkaisu [*A publication*]
Valt Tek Tutkimuslaitos Tiedotus Sar 2 ... Valtion Teknillinen Tutkimuslaitos. Tiedotus. Sarja 2. Metalli [*A publication*]
Valt Tek Tutkimuslaitos Tiedotus Sar 4 ... Valtion Teknillinen Tutkimuslaitos. Tiedotus. Sarja 4. Kemia [*A publication*]
Valt Tek Tutkimuslaitos Tiedotus Sar 1 Puu ... Valtion Teknillinen Tutkimuslaitos. Tiedotus. Sarja 1. Puu [*A publication*]
Valt Tek Tutkimuslaitos Tied Sar 2 ... Valtion Teknillinen Tutkimuslaitos. Tiedotus. Sarja 2. Metalli [*A publication*]
Valt Tek Tutkimuslaitos Tied Sar 3 ... Valtion Teknillinen Tutkimuslaitos. Tiedotus. Sarja 3. Rakennus [*A publication*]
Valt Tek Tutkimuslaitos Tied Sar I PUU ... Valtion Teknillinen Tutkimuslaitos Tiedotus. Sarja I. PUU [*A publication*]
VALU .... Value Line, Inc. [*NASDAQ symbol*]   (NQ)
VALUE...... Validated Aircraft Logistics Utilization Evaluation [*Navy*]
VALUE...... Visible Achievement Liberates Unemployment [*DoD project for disadvantaged youth*]
Value Eng .. Value Engineering [*A publication*]
Value Line ... Value Line Investment Survey [*A publication*]
Val U LR.... Valparaiso University. Law Review [*A publication*]
Val U L Rev ... Valparaiso University. Law Review [*A publication*]
VALUON.. Valuation
Valvo Tech Inf Ind ... Valvo Technische Informationen fuer die Industrie [*A publication*]
VA L Wk Dicta Comp ... Virginia Law Weekly Dicta Compilation [*A publication*]   (DLA)
VALY........ Vallicorp Holdings, Inc. [*NASDAQ symbol*]   (NQ)
VAM.......... Medium Attack Aircraft [*Navy symbol*]   (NVT)
VAM.......... University of Virginia, C. Moore Health Sciences Library, Charlottesville, VA [*OCLC symbol*]   (OCLC)
VAM.......... Vacuum-Assisted Molding [*Automotive technology*]
VAM.......... Value Aluminizing Machine
VAM.......... Vamos [*Greece*] [*Seismograph station code, US Geological Survey*]   (SEIS)
VAM.......... Vector Airborne Magnetometer   (IEEE)
VAM.......... Vehiculos Automotores Mexicanos [*Commercial firm*]
VAM.......... Vending and Affixing Machine
VAM.......... Vesicular Arbuscular Mycorrhizae [*Botany*]
VAM.......... Veterans Administration Matters [*FBI standardized term*]
VAM.......... Vinyl Acetate Monomer [*Organic chemistry*]
VA M........ Virginia Magazine of History and Biography [*A publication*]
VAM.......... Virtual Access Method
VAM.......... Vista Mines, Inc. [*Toronto Stock Exchange symbol*]
VAM.......... Visual Approach Monitor [*Aviation*]
VAM.......... Vogel's Approximation Method
VAM.......... Voltammeter
VAM.......... VP-16-213 [*Etoposide*], Adriamycin, Methotrexate [*Antineoplastic drug regimen*]
VA Mag Hist ... Virginia Magazine of History and Biography [*A publication*]
VA Mag Hist Biog ... Virginia Magazine of History and Biography [*A publication*]
VA Mag Hist Biogr ... Virginia Magazine of History and Biography [*A publication*]
VAMC....... Veterans Administration Medical Center [*Formerly, VAH*]
VAMCO...... Village & Marketing Corporation [*Jamaica*]
VAMD...... Virginia & Maryland Railroad [*AAR code*]
VA Med..... Virginia Medical [*A publication*]
VA Med Mon ... Virginia Medical Monthly [*Later, Virginia Medical*] [*A publication*]
VAMFO.... Variable Angle Monochromatic Fringe Observation [*Film thickness determination*]
VA Miner.... Virginia Minerals [*A publication*]
VAMIS...... Virginia Medical Information System [*Library network*]
VAMOS.... Verified Additional Military Occupational Specialty
VAMOSC.. Visibility and Management of Operating and Support Costs [*Army*]
VAMP....... Value Analysis of Management Practices   (MCD)
VAMP....... Vandenberg Atlas Modification Program [*Air Force*]   (MCD)

VAMP....... Variable [*or Visual*] Anamorphic Motion Picture [*Training device to provide realistic environment during simulated flight training*]   (MCD)
VAMP....... Vector Arithmetic Multiprocessor [*Data processing*]   (IEEE)
VAMP....... Vietnam Ammunition Program   (AFM)
VAMP....... Vincristine, Actinomycin, Methotrexate, Prednisone [*Antineoplastic drug regimen*]
VAMP....... Vincristine Amethopterin [*Antitumor agent*]
VAMP....... Vincristine, Amethopterin [*Methotrexate*], Mercaptopurine, Prednisone [*Antineoplastic drug regimen*]
VAMP....... Visual-Acoustic-Magnetic Pressure   (IEEE)
VAMP....... Visual-Acoustic-Magnetic Program [*NOO*]
VAMP...... Visual Anamorphic Motion Picture   (AIA)
VAMP....... Vulnerability Assessment Modeling Program [*Air Force*]
VAMR....... Vernon's Annotated Missouri Rule [*A publication*]   (DLA)
VAMROC ... Veterans Administration Medical and Regional Office Center
VAMS....... Vernon's Annotated Missouri Statutes [*A publication*]   (DLA)
VAMS....... Victor Airspeed Measuring System   (MCD)
VAMS....... Visual Analog Mood Scale
VAMSI...... Visual Approach Multiple Slope Indicator [*Aviation*]
VAMT....... Vertical Assault Medium Transport   (MCD)
VAN.......... Northern Virginia Community College, Springfield, VA [*OCLC symbol*]   (OCLC)
VAN.......... Value-Added Network [*Data processing*] [*Telecommunications*]
VAN.......... Van [*Turkey*] [*Airport symbol*]   (OAG)
VAN.......... Vance, SC [*Location identifier*] [*FAA*]   (FAAL)
VAN.......... Vandeno [*Race of maize*]
VAN.......... Vanderbilt Law Review [*A publication*]
Van............ Vanguard [*Record label*]
Van............ Vanguard Science Fiction [*A publication*]
VAN.......... Vanguard Tracking Station [*NASA*]   (NASA)
VAN.......... Vanier College [*UTLAS symbol*]
VAN.......... Vannovskaya [*USSR*] [*Seismograph station code, US Geological Survey*]   (SEIS)
VAN.......... Vanwin Resources Corp. [*Vancouver Stock Exchange symbol*]
VAN.......... Variable Area Nozzle
VAN.......... Vestnik Akademii Nauk SSSR [*A publication*]
VAN.......... Voluntary Action News [*A publication*]
VAN.......... Vorlaeufige Arbeitsnormen
VANA........ Victorian Authorised Newsagents' Association [*Australia*]
VANB........ Vesci Akademii Navuk BSSR [*A publication*]
Vancoram Rev ... Vancoram Review [*A publication*]
Vand........... De Bello Vandalico [*of Procopius*] [*Classical studies*]   (OCD)
VAND....... Nanded [*India*] [*ICAO location identifier*]   (ICLI)
VAND....... Vacuum-Air-Nitrogen Distribution
VAND....... Van Den Bergh [*Liver function test*]
VAND....... Van Dusen Air, Inc. [*NASDAQ symbol*]   (NQ)
Vanderbilt J Transnat'l L ... Vanderbilt Journal of Transnational Law [*A publication*]
Vanderbilt LR ... Vanderbilt Law Review [*A publication*]   (DLA)
Vanderbilt Univ Abs Theses Bull ... Vanderbilt University. Abstracts of Theses. Bulletin [*A publication*]
Vander L ... Vanderlinden's Laws of Holland [*A publication*]   (DLA)
Vander Law ... Vanderbilt Law Review [*A publication*]
Vanderstr ... Vanderstraaten's Reports [*1869-71*] [*Ceylon*] [*A publication*]   (DLA)
Vanderstraaten ... Vanderstraaten's Decisions in Appeal, Supreme Court [*1869-71*] [*Sri L.*] [*A publication*]   (DLA)
Vand Int..... Vanderbilt International [*A publication*]
Vand J Trans L ... Vanderbilt Journal of Transnational Law [*A publication*]
Vand J Transnatl L ... Vanderbilt Journal of Transnational Law [*A publication*]
Vand LR..... Vanderbilt Law Review [*A publication*]
Vand L Rev ... Vanderbilt Law Review [*A publication*]
VAND UNIV Q ... Vanderbilt University Quarterly [*Tennessee*] [*A publication*]   (ROG)
VANF........ VanFed Bancorp [*NASDAQ symbol*]   (CTT)
VANFIS..... Visible and Near-Visible Frequency Intercept System [*Navy*]
Van Fleet Coll Attack ... Van Fleet on Collateral Attack [*A publication*]   (DLA)
Van Hey Eq ... Van Heythuysen's Equity Draftsman [*2nd ed.*] [*1828*] [*A publication*]   (DLA)
Van Hey Mar Ev ... Van Heythuysen on Maritime Evidence [*A publication*]   (DLA)
Van Hey Rud ... Van Heythuysen's Rudiments of English Law [*A publication*]   (DLA)
VANHP...... Virginia Natural Heritage Program [*Virginia State Department of Conservation and Historic Resources*] [*Information service or system*]   (IID)
VANIS....... Volume Analysis Information System Software
Van K........ Van Koughnet's Reports [*15-21 Upper Canada Common Pleas*] [*1864-71*] [*A publication*]   (DLA)
Van K & H ... Upper Canada Common Pleas Reports [*1864-71*] [*A publication*]   (DLA)
Van L .... Vander Linden's Practice [*Cape Colony*] [*A publication*]   (DLA)
Van N......... Van Ness' Prize Cases, United States District Court, District of New York [*A publication*]   (DLA)
VAN N....... Van Norden Magazine [*New York*] [*A publication*]   (ROG)

Van Ness Prize Cas ... Van Ness' Prize Cases, United States District Court, District of New York [*A publication*] (DLA)
VANP........ Nagpur [*India*] [*ICAO location identifier*] (ICLI)
VANR........ Nasik Road [*India*] [*ICAO location identifier*] (ICLI)
VANS .... Value Added Network Service [*Data processing*] [*Telecommunications*]
VANS .... Van Schaack & Co. [*NASDAQ symbol*] (NQ)
VANS .... Vehicle Austere Night Sight [*Army*] (MCD)
Van Sant Ch J ... Van Santvoord's Lives of the Chief Justices of the United States [*A publication*] (DLA)
Van Sant Eq Pr ... Van Santvoord's Equity Practice [*A publication*] (DLA)
Van Sant Pl ... Van Santvoord's Pleadings [*A publication*] (DLA)
Van Sant Prec ... Van Santvoord's Precedents [*A publication*] (DLA)
VAN SSSR ... Vestnik Akademii Nauk SSSR [*A publication*]
Vant .... [*Sebastianus*] Vantius [*Flourished, 16th century*] [*Authority cited in pre-1607 legal work*] (DSA)
VA Num..... Virginia Numismatist [*A publication*]
VA Nurse... Virginia Nurse [*A publication*]
VA Nurse Q ... Virginia Nurse Quarterly [*Later, Virginia Nurse*] [*A publication*]
VANUSL... Vanderbilt University School of Law (DLA)
VANWACE ... Vulnerability Analysis of Nuclear Weapons in Allied Command, Europe [*Army*] (AABC)
VANZ........ Vanzetti Systems, Inc. [*NASDAQ symbol*] (NQ)
Van Zee Ld ... Van Zee tot Land [*A publication*]
VAO........... Veterans Administration Office
VAO........... Voting Assistance Officer
VAOKN...... Visual Acuity by Optokinetic Nystagmus
VAOR........ VHF [*Very-High-Frequency*] Aural Omnirange
VAP .... Photographic Squadron (Heavy) [*Navy symbol*] (NVT)
VAP .... Vaginal Acid Phosphatase [*An enzyme*]
VAP .... Valence-Alternation Pair [*Solid-state physics*]
VAP .... Value-Added Process [*Data processing*] (PCM)
VAP .... Vaporization [*or Vaporizer*] (KSC)
VAP .... Vehicle Antenna Position [*NASA*]
VAP .... Velocity Analysis Program
VAP .... Vertical Axis Pivots
VAP .... Veteran Air Pilots
VAP .... Vibrationally Adiabatic Potential [*Chemical physics*]
VAP .... Videotex Access Point [*Data processing*] (IT)
VAP .... Vinblastine, Actinomycin D [*Dactinomycin*], Platinol [*Cisplatin*] [*Antineoplastic drug regimen*]
VAP .... Vincristine, Adriamycin, Prednisone [*Antineoplastic drug regimen*]
VAP .... Vincristine, Adriamycin, Procarbazine [*Antineoplastic drug regimen*]
VAP .... Voluntary Assistance Program
VAPA .... Video Alliance for the Performing Arts (EA)
VAPC........ Vector Adaptive Predictive Coding [*Telecommunications*]
VAPC........ Veterans Administration Prosthetics Center [*Later, VAREC*]
VAP-Cyclo ... Vincristine, Adriamycin, Prednisolone, Cyclophosphamide [*Antineoplastic drug regimen*]
VAPH........ Visual Acuity with Pin Hole
VAPHD..... Virchows Archiv. A. Pathological Anatomy and Histology [*A publication*]
VAPI......... Visual Approach Path Indicator [*Aviation*]
VAPO .... Pune [*India*] [*ICAO location identifier*] (ICLI)
VAPO .... Vaporizing Oil
VA Polytech Inst Bull Eng Expt Sta Ser ... Virginia Polytechnic Institute. Bulletin. Engineering Experiment Station Series [*A publication*]
VA Polytech Inst Eng Ext Ser Cir ... Virginia Polytechnic Institute. Engineering Extension Series. Circular [*A publication*]
VA Polytech Inst Res Div Bull ... Virginia Polytechnic Institute. Research Division. Bulletin [*A publication*]
VA Polytech Inst Res Div Wood Res Wood Constr Lab Bull ... Virginia Polytechnic Institute. Research Division. Wood Research and Wood Construction Laboratory [*Blacksburg*]. Bulletin [*A publication*]
VA Polytech Inst State Univ Res Div Bull ... Virginia Polytechnic Institute and State University. Research Division. Bulletin [*A publication*]
VA Polytech Inst State Univ Res Div Monogr ... Virginia Polytechnic Institute and State University. Research Division. Monograph [*A publication*]
VA Polytech Inst State Univ Res Div Rep ... Virginia Polytechnic Institute and State University. Research Division. Report [*A publication*]
VA Polytech Inst State Univ Sch For Wildl Resour Publ FWS ... Virginia Polytechnic Institute and State University. School of Forestry and Wildlife Resources. Publication FWS [*A publication*]
VA Polytech Inst State Univ VA Water Resour Res Cent Bull ... Virginia Polytechnic Institute and State University. Virginia Water Resources Research Center. Bulletin [*A publication*]
VA Polytech Inst State Univ Water Resour Res Cent Bull ... Virginia Polytechnic Institute and State University. Water Resources Research Center. Bulletin [*A publication*]
VAPR........ Porbandar [*India*] [*ICAO location identifier*] (ICLI)
VAPR........ Veterans Administration Procurement [*or Purchase*] Regulations

VAPS........ V/STOL Approach System (MCD)
VAPS........ Victorian Association for Peace Studies [*Australia*]
VAPS........ Volume, Article [*or Chapter*], Paragraph, Sentence [*Numbers*] [*Indexing*]
VAQ.......... Visiting Airmen's Quarters [*Air Force*]
VAQ.......... Visual Air Quality
VA Q R ..... Virginia Quarterly Review [*A publication*]
VA Q Rev.. Virginia Quarterly Review [*A publication*]
VAR.......... Corps of Volunteers Artillery Regiment [*British military*] (DMA)
VA R .... Gilmer's Virginia Reports [*A publication*] (DLA)
VAR.......... Reactive Volt-Ampere
VAR.......... Vacuum Arc Remelting [*Steel alloy*]
VAR.......... Validation Analysis Report [*Social Security Administration*]
VAR.......... Value-Added Remarketer [*or Reseller or Retailer*] [*Business term*]
VAR.......... VANAIR, Inc. [*Gasport, NY*] [*FAA designator*] (FAAC)
VAR.......... Varanasi [*India*] [*Seismograph station code, US Geological Survey*] (SEIS)
VAR.......... Variable (AFM)
Var.......... Variae [*of Cassiodorus*] [*Classical studies*] (OCD)
VAR.......... Varian Associates [*NYSE symbol*] (SPSG)
VAR.......... Variance Analysis Report (MCD)
VAR.......... Variant [*Numismatics*]
VAR.......... Variation
VAR.......... Variegated
var .... Varietas [*Variety*] [*Biology*]
VAR.......... Variety
VAR.......... Variety [*A publication*]
VAR.......... Various
VAR.......... Varitech Resources [*Vancouver Stock Exchange symbol*]
VAR.......... Varna [*Bulgaria*] [*Airport symbol*] (OAG)
VAR.......... Varnish [*Technical drawings*]
Var.......... Varsity [*Record label*]
VAR.......... Vector Autoregressive Model [*Mathematics*]
VAR.......... Vendor Approval Request (AAG)
VAR.......... Verification Analysis Report (NASA)
VAR.......... Vertical Acceleration Ramp
VAR.......... Vertical Air Rocket (NATG)
VAR.......... Veterans Administration Regulations
VAR.......... Victorian Administrative Reports [*Australia*] [*A publication*]
VAR.......... Video-Audio Range [*Radio*]
VAR.......... Vintage Austin Register [*Ashover, Derbyshire, England*] (EAIO)
VAR.......... Visual-Aural Range [*Radio*]
VAR.......... Volt-Ampere Reactive
VAR.......... Voltage in Acceptable Range (MCD)
VAR.......... Voltage Adjusting Rheostat
VAR.......... Voluntary Auto Restraints [*Import quotas on automobiles*]
VAR.......... Volunteer Air Reserve [*Air Force*]
VAR.......... Votre Altesse Royale [*Your Royal Highness*] [*French*]
VAR.......... Vrij Anti-Revolutionaire Partij [*Free Anti-Revolutionary Party*] [*Netherlands*] [*Political party*] (PPE)
VARA .... Vereiniging van Arbeiders Radio Amateurs
VARAD ..... Varying Radiation (IEEE)
VA R Ann .. Virginia Reports, Annotated [*A publication*] (DLA)
Vara Palsd ... Vara Palsdjur [*A publication*]
VARBLK.... Variable Block [*Data processing*]
VARC .... Variable Axis Rotor Control System [*Telecommunications*] (TEL)
VARC .... Victorian Accident Rehabilitation Council [*Australia*]
VARC .... Virginia Associated Research Campus [*Later, Continuous Electron Beam Accelerator Facility*] [*Research center*] (RCD)
vard .... Varied [*Quality of the bottom*] [*Nautical charts*]
VAREC...... Veterans Administration Rehabilitation Engineering Center [*Formerly, VAPC*]
VA Rep Anno ... Virginia Reports, Annotated [*A publication*] (DLA)
VARES...... Vega Aircraft RADAR Enhancing System [*FAA*]
VARG........ Ratnagiri [*India*] [*ICAO location identifier*] (ICLI)
VARGUS... Variable Generator of Unfamiliar Stimuli [*Computer program*]
VARHM.... Var-Hour Meter [*Electricity*]
Vari........... Variegation [*A publication*]
VARI......... Varityper
VARIA....... Variamento [*In a Varied Style*] [*Music*] (ROG)
Varian Instrum Appl ... Varian Instrument Applications [*A publication*]
VARICAP ... Variable Capacitor
VARIG...... Viacao Aerea Rio-Grandense [*Airline*] [*Brazil*] (FAAC)
Varilna Teh ... Varilna Tehnika [*A publication*]
VARION ... Variation (ROG)
Various Publ Ser ... Various Publications Series [*Aarhus*] [*A publication*]
VARISTOR ... Variable Resistor
VARITRAN ... Variable-Voltage Transformer (IEEE)
VARK........ Rajkot [*India*] [*ICAO location identifier*] (ICLI)
VAR LECT ... Varia Lectio [*Variant Reading*] [*Latin*] (ROG)
VARM....... Varmeter [*Engineering*]
Varme- o Sanit-Tek ... Vearme- och Saniteteknikern [*A publication*]
VARN........ Variation (FAAC)
VARN........ Varnish
var nov........ Varietas Nova [*New Variety*] [*Biology*]
VARO........ Veterans Administration Regional Office (AFM)

VARP......... Raipur [*India*] [*ICAO location identifier*]   (ICLI)
VARP......... Vietnam Asset Reconciliation Procedure [*Military*]   (AABC)
VARPC...... Veterans Administration Records Processing Center
VARR .... Variable Range Reflector   (IEEE)
VARR .... Visual-Aural Radio Range   (MSA)
VARS......... Various   (ROG)
VARS......... Vertical Azimuth Reference System   (NATG)
VARS......... Vocational Adaptation Rating Scales [*Test*]
Var Sci Inst Rebois Tunis ... Varietes Scientifiques. Institut de Reboisement de Tunis [*A publication*]
VARSITY ... University [*British*]   (ROG)
Var Spom ... Varstvo Spomenikov [*A publication*]
VART .... Volunteer Air Reserve Training [*Air Force*]
VARTA Spez Rep ... VARTA Spezial Report [*West Germany*] [*A publication*]
VARTU ..... Volunteer Air Reserve Training Unit [*Air Force*]
VARVS...... Variable Acuity Remote Viewing System   (MCD)
VAS .... Sivas [*Turkey*] [*Airport symbol*]   (OAG)
VAS .... Value-Added Service [*Telecommunications*]   (TEL)
VAS .... Value-Added Statement   (ADA)
VAS .... Vassijaure [*Sweden*] [*Seismograph station code, US Geological Survey*] [*Closed*]   (SEIS)
VAS .... Vector Addition System
VAS .... Venomological Artifact Society   (EA)
VAS .... Vesicle Attachment Sites [*Neurology*]
VAS .... Veterinary Assistant Surgeon [*British military*]   (DMA)
VAS .... Vibration Analysis System
VAS .... VISSR [*Visible-Infrared Spin Scan Radiometer*] Atmospheric Sounder [*NASA*]
VAS .... Visual Analog [*Pain*] Scale
VAS .... Visual Analysis System [*Military*]
VAS .... Visual Attack System
VAS .... Visual Augmentation System
VAS .... Vorderasiatische Schriftdenkmaeler der Koeniglichen [*or Staatlichen*] Museen zu Berlin [*A publication*]
VAS .... Vortex Advisory System [*FAA*]
VASA........ Sihora [*India*] [*ICAO location identifier*]   (ICLI)
VASA........ Victorian Amateur Swimming Association [*Australia*]
VASA........ Viola d'Amore Society of America   (EA)
Vasa Suppl ... Vasa Supplementum [*A publication*]
VA SBA ..... Virginia State Bar Association, Reports [*A publication*]   (DLA)
VASC........ Vascular
VASC........ Verbal Auditory Screen for Children
VASC........ Vision and Autonomous Systems Laboratory, Carnegie Mellon University [*Research center*]   (RCD)
VAsC .... Visual Acuity without Spectacle Correction [*Unaided*]
VASCA...... Vacation and Senior Citizens Association   (EA)
VASCAR .... Visual Average Speed Computer and Recorder [*Speed trap*]
Vasc Dis .... Vascular Diseases [*A publication*]
Vasc Surg... Vascular Surgery [*A publication*]
VASD .... Veroeffentlichungen. Deutsche Akademie fuer Sprache und Dichtung [*A publication*]
VaSd .... Vorderasiatische Schriftdenkmaeler der Koeniglichen [*or Staatlichen*] Museen zu Berlin [*A publication*]
VASE......... Variable Angle Spectroscopic Ellipsometer
Vasenlisten ... Vasenlisten zur Griechischen Heldensage [*A publication*]   (OCD)
VASG........ Songadh [*India*] [*ICAO location identifier*]   (ICLI)
VAS of GB ... Vasectomy Advancement Society of Great Britain
VASI......... Visual Approach Slope Indicator [*Aviation*]
VASI......... Volunteer Ambulance School of Instruction [*Military*] [*British*]   (ROG)
VASIM...... Voltage and Synchro Interface Module
VASIS....... Visual Approach Slope Indicator System [*Aviation*]
VASL........ Sholapur [*India*] [*ICAO location identifier*]   (ICLI)
VA Social Science J ... Virginia Social Science Journal [*A publication*]
VASOG...... Veterans Administration Surgical Oncology Group
VASP........ Value-Added Service Provider [*Agreement*]   (IT)
VASP........ Variable Automatic Synthesis Program [*NASA*]
VASP........ Viacao Aerea Sao Paulo SA [*Airline*] [*Brazil*]
Vasq .... [*Ferdinand*] Vasquez Menchaca [*Deceased, 1566*] [*Authority cited in pre-1607 legal work*]   (DSA)
VASRD...... Veterans Administration Schedule for Rating Disabilities   (AABC)
VASS........ Variable Angle Sample Spinning [*Physics*]
VASS........ Visual Analysis Subsystem [*Military*]
VASS........ Visually Activated Switch System   (MCD)
Vassar Bros Inst Tr ... Vassar Brothers Institute. Transactions [*A publication*]
VASSEL.... Validation of ASW [*Antisubmarine Warfare*] Subsystem Effectiveness Levels [*Navy*]   (CAAL)
VASSS....... Van Alen Simplified Scoring System [*Tennis*]
VAST........ Versatile Automatic Specification Tester
VAST........ Virtual Archival Storage Technology [*Data processing*]
VA State Lib Bull ... Virginia State Library. Bulletin [*A publication*]
Vasterbotten ... Vasterbottens Lans Hambygdsforenings Arsbok [*A publication*]
Vastergotlands Fornminnesforen Tidskr ... Vastergotlands Fornminnesforenings Tidskrift [*A publication*]
Vastmanlands Fornminnesforen Arsskr ... Vastmanlands Fornminnesforenings Arsskrift [*A publication*]

VASTT ...... Versatile Aerial Simulation TOW [*Tube-Launched, Optically Tracked, Wire-Guided (Weapon)*] Target   (MCD)
VASU .... Surat [*India*] [*ICAO location identifier*]   (ICLI)
Vasuti Tud Kut Intez Evk ... Vasuti Tudomanyos Kutato Intezet Evkoenyve [*Hungary*] [*A publication*]
VAS VITR ... Vas Vitreum [*A Glass Vessel*] [*Pharmacy*]
VAT .... Vacuum Arc Thrustor Program   (MCD)
VAT .... Value-Added Tax
VAT .... Vane Air Temperature [*Automotive engineering*]
VAT .... Variable Area Turbine
VAT .... Variant Antigenic Type [*Genetics, immunology*]
VAT .... Varity Corp. [*NYSE symbol*] [*Toronto Stock Exchange symbol*] [*Vancouver Stock Exchange symbol*]   (SPSG)
VAT .... Vatican
VAT .... Vatican City [*ANSI three-letter standard code*]   (CNC)
VAT .... Vatomandry [*Madagascar*] [*Airport symbol*]   (OAG)
VAT .... Ventricular Activation Time [*Cardiology*]
VAT .... Veterinary Aptitude Test
VAT .... Vibration Acceptance Test
VAT .... Vibroacoustic Test   (NASA)
VAT .... Vinyl Asbestos Tile [*Technical drawings*]
VAT .... Virtual Address Translation
VAT .... Visual Acquisition Technique
VAT .... Visual Action Time
VAT .... Visual Apperception Test [*Psychology*]
VAT .... Vitro Assistance Team
VAT .... Vocational Apperception Test [*Psychology*]
VAT .... Voice-Activated Typewriter
VAT .... Volt-Ampere Tester
VAT .... Voltage Amplifier Tube
VAT .... Vulnerability Analysis Team   (MCD)
VATA .... Vibroacoustic Test Article   (NASA)
VA Tax R... Virginia Tax Review [*A publication*]
Va Tax Rev ... Virginia Tax Review [*A publication*]   (DLA)
VatBA........ Biblioteca Apostolica Vaticana, Vatican City, Vatican City [*Library symbol*] [*Library of Congress*]   (LCLS)
VATD .... Vincristine, ara-C [*Cytarabine*], Thioguanine, Daunorubicin [*Antineoplastic drug regimen*]
VATE........ Versatile Automatic Test Equipment [*Computers*]
V-ATE .... Vertical Anisotropic Etch [*Raytheon Co.*]
VA Teach... Virginia Teacher [*A publication*]
VATEJ .... Victorian Association for the Teaching of English. Journal [*A publication*]   (APTA)
VATER...... Vascular Tracheoesophageal-Limb-Reduction [*Endocrinology*]
VATER...... Vertebral, Anal, Tracheal, Esophageal, Renal
VATF........ Vibration and Acoustic Test Facility   (NASA)
VAtf .... Visual Acuity with Trial Frame
VATH........ Vinblastine, Adriamycin, Thiotepa [*Antineoplastic drug regimen*]
VATH........ Vinblastine, Adriamycin, Thiotepa, Halotestin [*Fluoxymesterone*] [*Antineoplastic drug regimen*]
VATISJ ..... VATIS [*Victorian Association of Teachers in Independent Schools*] Journal [*A publication*]   (APTA)
VATLIT..... Very Advanced Technology Light Twin   (MCD)
VATLS .... Visual Airborne Target Locator System [*Military*]
VATR .... Variable Aperture Target Recognition   (MCD)
VATRD8 ... Lantbrukshogskolan Vaxtskyddsrapporter Tradgard [*A publication*]
VATRD8 ... Sveriges Landbruksuniversitet Vaxtskyddsrapporter Tradgard [*A publication*]
VA Truck Exp ... Virginia Truck Experiment Station. Publications [*A publication*]
VATS........ Vehicle Anti-Theft System [*General Motors Corp.*]
VATS........ Vehicle Automatic Test System
VATS........ Vernon's Annotated Texas Statutes [*A publication*]   (DLA)
VATS........ Vertical-Lift Airfield for Tactical Support   (NVT)
VATS........ Video-Augmented Tracking System   (MCD)
VATS/SNAP ... Video-Augmented Tracking System/Single Seat Night Attack Program   (MCD)
Vatt .... Vattel's Law of Nations [*A publication*]   (DLA)
Vattel .... Vattel's Law of Nations [*A publication*]   (DLA)
Vattel Law Nat ... Vattel's Law of Nations [*A publication*]   (DLA)
VATTR...... Value Added Tax Tribunal Reports [*A publication*]
VA/TVTA ... Vibroacoustic/Thermal/Vacuum Test Article   (NASA)
VATW........ Varity Corp. [*NASDAQ symbol*]   (NQ)
VAU.......... Vertical Accelerometer Unit
VAU.......... Vertical Arithmetic Unit
vau............. Virginia [*MARC country of publication code*] [*Library of Congress*]   (LCCP)
VAU.......... Volume Accumulator Unit
VAU.......... Volunteer Air Units
VAUB........ Vehicle Authorization Utilization Board [*Military*]
VAUD........ Vaudeville
Vaug......... Vaughan's English Common Pleas Reports [*124 English Reprint*] [*A publication*]   (DLA)
Vaugh........ Vaughan's English Common Pleas Reports [*124 English Reprint*] [*A publication*]   (DLA)
Vaughan..... Vaughan's English Common Pleas Reports [*124 English Reprint*] [*A publication*]   (DLA)
Vaughan (Eng) ... Vaughan's English Common Pleas Reports [*124 English Reprint*] [*A publication*]   (DLA)

VA Univ Ph Soc B Sc S ... Virginia University. Philosophical Society. Bulletin. Scientific Series [*A publication*]
VAUSSI .... Veteran's Association of the USS [*United States Ship*] Iowa (EA)
VAUX .... Vauxhall [*Automobile*]   (DSUE)
Vaux .... Vaux's Recorder's Decisions [*1841-45*] [*Philadelphia, PA*] [*A publication*]   (DLA)
Vaux (PA) ... Vaux's Recorder's Decisions [*1841-45*] [*Philadelphia, PA*] [*A publication*]   (DLA)
Vaux Rec Dec ... Vaux's Recorder's Decisions [*1841-45*] [*Philadelphia, PA*] [*A publication*]   (DLA)
VAV .... Variable Air Volume
VAV .... Vava'u [*Tonga Island*] [*Airport symbol*]   (OAG)
VAV .... Veroeffentlichungen zum Archiv fuer Voelkerkunde [*A publication*]
VAV .... VP-16-213 [*Etoposide*], Adriamycin, Vincristine [*Antineoplastic drug regimen*]
VAVP .... Variable Angle, Variable Pitch
VAVS .... Veterans Administration Voluntary Service
VAW .... Carrier Airborne Early Warning Squadron [*Navy symbol*]   (NVT)
VAW .... Valley Airways, Inc. [*McAllen, TX*] [*FAA designator*]   (FAAC)
VAW .... Vertical Arc Welder
VA Water Resour Res Cent Bull ... Virginia Water Resources Research Center. Bulletin [*A publication*]
VA Wildl .... Virginia Wildlife [*A publication*]
VAWM .... Washim [*India*] [*ICAO location identifier*]   (ICLI)
VAWT .... Vertical Axis Wind Turbine [*Power generator*] [*See also VAWTG*]
VAWTG .... Vertical Axis Wind Turbine Generator [*Also, VAWT*]
VAX .... Alexandria Public Library, Alexandria, VA [*OCLC symbol*]   (OCLC)
VAX .... Heavy Attack Aircraft, Experimental
VAX .... Trademark of Digital Equipment Corp.
VAX .... Virtual Address Extension [*Data processing*]
Vaxtekol Stud ... Vaxtekologiska Studier [*A publication*]
Vaxt-Nar-Nytt ... Vaxt-Narings-Nytt [*A publication*]
Vaxtodling Inst Vaxtodlingslara Lantbrukshogsk ... Vaextodling. Institutionen foer Vaextodlingslara. Lantbrukshoegskolan [*A publication*]
Vaxtskyddsnotiser Sver Lantbruksuniver ... Vaxtskyddsnotiser. Sveriges Lantbruksuniversitet [*A publication*]
VAY .... Valandovo [*Yugoslavia*] [*Seismograph station code, US Geological Survey*]   (SEIS)
Vayr .... Vayikra Rabba   (BJA)
Vazduhoplovni Glas ... Vazduhoplovni Glasnik [*Yugoslavia*] [*A publication*]
VB .... Bombing Plane [*Navy symbol*]
VB .... Bretagne Air Services [*France*] [*ICAO designator*]   (FAAC)
VB .... Dive Bomber Squadron [*Navy symbol*]
VB .... Valence Bond   (DEN)
VB .... Valve Box
VB .... Vanity Bar [*Classified advertising*]   (ADA)
VB .... Vapor Barrier [*Boots*] [*Army*]   (INF)
VB .... Vascular Bundle [*Botany*]
VB .... Ventrobasal Complex [*Brain anatomy*]
VB .... Verb
Vb .... Verordeningenblad [*A publication*]
VB .... Vertical Beam [*of light*]
VB .... Vertical Bomb [*Air Force*]
VB .... Vertical Main Boiler [*on a ship*]   (DS)
V & B .... Vesey and Beames' English Chancery Reports [*35 English Reprint*] [*A publication*]   (DLA)
VB .... Veterinary Bulletin [*Database*] [*Commonwealth Bureau of Animal Health*] [*Information service or system*]   (CRD)
VB .... Viable Birth [*Medicine*]
VB .... Vibration   (AAG)
VB .... Victoria Bitter [*Australia*]   (ADA)
VB .... Vinblastine, Bleomycin [*Antineoplastic drug regimen*]
VB .... Vir Bonus [*A Good Man*] [*Latin*]
vb .... Virgin Islands, British [*MARC country of publication code*] [*Library of Congress*]   (LCCP)
VB .... Viven and Bassiere [*Rifle grenade*]
VB .... Voelkischer Beobachter [*A publication*]
VB .... Voice Band [*Telecommunications*]
VB .... Voice Bank [*Telecommunications*]   (TEL)
VB .... Voks Bulletin [*A publication*]
VB .... Volunteer Battalion [*Military*]
VB .... Vorgeschobener Beobachter [*Forward Observer*] [*German military*]
V/b .... Vragbrief [*Consignment-Note; Bill of Lading*] [*Afrikaans*] [*Business term*]
VB .... Vulgate Bible
VBA .... NIMO [*Nederlands Instituut voor Maatschappelijke Opbouw*] Kroniek. Nieuwsbulletin [*A publication*]
VBA .... Vegetarian Brotherhood of America [*Defunct*]   (EA)
VBA .... Veterans Benefits Administration [*Department of Veterans Affairs*]
VBA .... Vibrating Beam Accelerometer [*Inertial sensor*]   (IEEE)
VBA .... Vincristine, BCNU [*Carmustine*], Adriamycin [*Antineoplastic drug regimen*]
VBAA .... Vanilla Bean Association of America   (EA)

VBAC .... Vaginal Birth After Caesarean [*Obstetrics*]
VBAN .... Ann [*Burma*] [*ICAO location identifier*]   (ICLI)
VBAN .... V Band Corp. [*NASDAQ symbol*]   (NQ)
VBAP .... Vincristine, BCNU [*Carmustine*], Adriamycin, Prednisone [*Antineoplastic drug regimen*]
VBAS .... Anisakan [*Burma*] [*ICAO location identifier*]   (ICLI)
VBAS .... Von Braun Astronomical Society   (EA)
VB (B) .... Voelkischer Beobachter (Berlin) [*A publication*]
vbb .... Volgens Bygaande Brief [*According to Accompanying Letter*] [*Afrikaans*] [*Correspondence*]
VBBM .... Bhamo [*Burma*] [*ICAO location identifier*]   (ICLI)
Vb Bo .... Verordeningenblad Bedrijfsorganisatie [*A publication*]
VBBP .... Bokepyin [*Burma*] [*ICAO location identifier*]   (ICLI)
VBBS .... Bassein [*Burma*] [*ICAO location identifier*]   (ICLI)
VBBVE6 .... Verhandlungen des Berliner Botanischen Vereins [*A publication*]
VBC .... Bridgewater College, Bridgewater, VA [*OCLC symbol*]   (OCLC)
VBC .... Variable Boost Control [*System*] [*Automotive engineering*]
VBC .... Venetian Blind Council [*Formerly, VBI*]
VBC .... Vinylbenzyl Chloride [*Organic chemistry*]
VBC .... Vogel-Bonner Citrate [*Growth medium*]
VBCI .... Coco Island [*Burma*] [*ICAO location identifier*]   (ICLI)
VBCS .... Victorian Bing Crosby Society   (EAIO)
VBD .... Vector-Borne Disease
VBD .... Veronal-Buffered Diluent
VBD .... Vertebrobasilar Dolichoectasia [*Medicine*]
VBD .... Vinblastine, Bleomycin, Diamminedichloroplatinum [*Cisplatin*] [*Antineoplastic drug regimen*]
VBD .... Voice Band Data   (KSC)
VBDMA ...... Vinylbenzyldimethylamine [*Organic chemistry*]
VBE .... Vibrating Plate Extractor [*Chemical engineering*]
VBelGrN .... Vesci Akademii Navuk Belaruskaj SSR. Seryja Gramadskich Navuk [*A publication*]
VBF .... Bomber-Fighter Squadron [*Navy symbol*]
VBF .... Bombing-Fighting Aircraft [*Navy symbol*]
VBF .... Vibrated Fluid Bed [*Chemical engineering*]
VBF .... Vibratory Bowl Feeder
VBG .... Lompoc, CA [*Location identifier*] [*FAA*]   (FAAL)
VBGG .... Gangaw [*Burma*] [*ICAO location identifier*]   (ICLI)
VBGH .... Volunteer Battalion Gordon Highlanders [*British military*]   (DMA)
VBGQ .... Vacuum Brazed - Gas Quenched
VBGW .... Gwa [*Burma*] [*ICAO location identifier*]   (ICLI)
VBHB .... Hmawbi [*Burma*] [*ICAO location identifier*]   (ICLI)
VBHH .... Hebo [*Burma*] [*ICAO location identifier*]   (ICLI)
VBHL .... Homalin [*Burma*] [*ICAO location identifier*]   (ICLI)
VBHN .... Htilin [*Burma*] [*ICAO location identifier*]   (ICLI)
VBI .... Venetian Blind Institute [*Later, VBC*]   (EA)
VBI .... Vertical Blanking Interval [*Telecommunications*]
VBI .... Video Bible Institute [*Defunct*]   (EA)
VBI .... Vital Bus Inverter [*Data processing*]   (IEEE)
V-BIG .... Ventricular Bigeminy [*Medicine*]
VBJ .... Vacuum Bell Jar
VBKG .... Kengtung [*Burma*] [*ICAO location identifier*]   (ICLI)
VBKK .... Kutkai [*Burma*] [*ICAO location identifier*]   (ICLI)
VBKM .... Kalemyo [*Burma*] [*ICAO location identifier*]   (ICLI)
VBKP .... Kyaukpyu [*Burma*] [*ICAO location identifier*]   (ICLI)
VBKTPS .... Vierteljahrschrift fuer Bibelkunde, Talmudische, und Patristische Studien [*A publication*]
VBKU .... Kyauktu [*Burma*] [*ICAO location identifier*]   (ICLI)
VBL .... BOCES [*Boards of Cooperative Educational Services*], Monroe 1, Penfield, NY [*OCLC symbol*]   (OCLC)
Vbl .... Vakblad [*A publication*]
VBL .... Vakblad voor de Bloemisterij [*A publication*]
VBL .... Vector Biology Laboratory [*University of Notre Dame*] [*Research center*]   (RCD)
VBL .... Verbal
VBl .... Verordnungsblatt [*Official Gazette*] [*German*]   (ILCA)
VBL .... Vertical-Blank [*Data processing*]   (BYTE)
VBL .... Vinblastine, Vincaleukoblastine [*Velban, Vincaleukoblastine*] [*Also, V, Ve, VLB*] [*Antineoplastic drug*]
VBL .... Voyager Biological Laboratory [*NASA*]
VBLK .... Loikaw [*Burma*] [*ICAO location identifier*]   (ICLI)
VBLN .... Lonekin [*Burma*] [*ICAO location identifier*]   (ICLI)
VBLO .... Langkho [*Burma*] [*ICAO location identifier*]   (ICLI)
VBLS .... Lashio [*Burma*] [*ICAO location identifier*]   (ICLI)
V BLT .... Vee Built [*Ship classification term*]   (DS)
VBLY .... Lanywa [*Burma*] [*ICAO location identifier*]   (ICLI)
VBM .... BOCES [*Boards of Cooperative Educational Services*], Monroe 2, Orleans, Spencerport, NY [*OCLC symbol*]   (OCLC)
VBM .... Vincristine, Bleomycin, Methotrexate [*Antineoplastic drug regimen*]
VBMA .... Vacuum Bag Manufacturers Association   (EA)
VBMH .... Mong-Hpayak [*Burma*] [*ICAO location identifier*]   (ICLI)
VBMI .... Mongyai [*Burma*] [*ICAO location identifier*]   (ICLI)
VBMK .... Myitkyina [*Burma*] [*ICAO location identifier*]   (ICLI)
VBML .... Meiktila [*Burma*] [*ICAO location identifier*]   (ICLI)
VBMM .... Moulmein [*Burma*] [*ICAO location identifier*]   (ICLI)
VBMN .... Manaung [*Burma*] [*ICAO location identifier*]   (ICLI)
VBMO .... Momeik [*Burma*] [*ICAO location identifier*]   (ICLI)
VBMP .... Mong Pyin [*Burma*] [*ICAO location identifier*]   (ICLI)

VBMR .... Ventilation Barrier Machine Room [*Nuclear energy*]　(NRCH)
VBMS....... Mong-Hsat [*Burma*] [*ICAO location identifier*]　(ICLI)
VBMT .... Mong Tong [*Burma*] [*ICAO location identifier*]　(ICLI)
VBMU .... Myauk U [*Burma*] [*ICAO location identifier*]　(ICLI)
VB (Mu)..... Voelkischer Beobachter (Muenich) [*A publication*]
VBMW .... Magwe [*Burma*] [*ICAO location identifier*]　(ICLI)
VBMWMO ... Vintage BMW Motorcycle Owners　(EA)
VBN .... Verbal Noun
VBN .... Veterans Bedside Network　(EA)
VBN .... Victorian Bar News [*A publication*]　(APTA)
VBND .... VeloBind, Inc. [*NASDAQ symbol*]　(NQ)
VBNIDQ ... Vogelkundliche Berichte aus Niedersachsen [*A publication*]
VBNM ...... Naungmon [*Burma*] [*ICAO location identifier*]　(ICLI)
VBNP .... Nampong [*Burma*] [*ICAO location identifier*]　(ICLI)
VBNS........ Namsang [*Burma*] [*ICAO location identifier*]　(ICLI)
VBNT .... Namtu [*Burma*] [*ICAO location identifier*]　(ICLI)
VBNU........ Nyaung U [*Burma*] [*ICAO location identifier*]　(ICLI)
VBO .... Bouwwereld. Universeel Veertiendaags Vaktijdschrift voor de
　　　　Bouwnijverheid [*A publication*]
VBO .... Oswego County BOCES [*Boards of Cooperative Educational
　　　　Services*], Mexico, NY [*OCLC symbol*]　(OCLC)
VBo .... Verordeningenblad Bedrijfsorganisatie [*A publication*]
VBO .... Veterans Benefits Office
VBOB .... Veterans of the Battle of the Bulge　(EA)
VBOMP ..... Virtual Base Organization and Maintenance Processor
VBOS .... Veronal-Buffered Oxalated Saline
VBot .... Verstreute Boghazkoei-Texte [*A. Goetze*] [*A
　　　　publication*]　(BJA)
VBP........... Vacuum Backing Pump
VBP........... Virtual Block Processor
VBP........... Vortex Breakdown Position
VBPA......... Pa-An [*Burma*] [*ICAO location identifier*]　(ICLI)
VBPB .... Phaungbyin [*Burma*] [*ICAO location identifier*]　(ICLI)
VBPE .... Paletwa [*Burma*] [*ICAO location identifier*]　(ICLI)
VBPF .... Variable Bandpass Filter
VBPG......... Pegu [*Burma*] [*ICAO location identifier*]　(ICLI)
VBPI .... Pearl Island [*Burma*] [*ICAO location identifier*]　(ICLI)
VBPK........ Pauk [*Burma*] [*ICAO location identifier*]　(ICLI)
VBPL........ Pinlebu [*Burma*] [*ICAO location identifier*]　(ICLI)
VBPP .... Papun [*Burma*] [*ICAO location identifier*]　(ICLI)
VBPR......... Prome [*Burma*] [*ICAO location identifier*]　(ICLI)
VBPT .... Putao [*Burma*] [*ICAO location identifier*]　(ICLI)
VBPU .... Pakokku [*Burma*] [*ICAO location identifier*]　(ICLI)
VBPW........ Palaw [*Burma*] [*ICAO location identifier*]　(ICLI)
VBQ .... Visvabharati Quarterly [*A publication*]
VBR .... Vacuum Bottoms Recycle [*Petroleum refining*]
VBR .... Variable BIT [*Binary Digit*] Rate [*Telecommunications*]
VBR .... Ventricle Brain Ratio [*Medicine*]
VBR .... Vinyl Bromide [*Organic chemistry*]
VBR .... Virginia Blue Ridge Railway [*AAR code*]
VBRA......... Sittwe [*Burma*] [*ICAO location identifier*]　(ICLI)
VBRM ...... Mandalay [*Burma*] [*ICAO location identifier*]　(ICLI)
VBRN .... Mergui [*Burma*] [*ICAO location identifier*]　(ICLI)
VBRR........ Rangoon/Mingaladon [*Burma*] [*ICAO location
　　　　identifier*]　(ICLI)
VBS........... Vacation Bible Schools　(EA)
VBS........... Variable Ballast System
VBS........... Veronal-Buffered Saline
VBS........... Virtual Bragg Scattering [*Physics*]
VBSA......... Saw [*Burma*] [*ICAO location identifier*]　(ICLI)
VBSFA ...... Vestsi Akademii Navuk BSSR. Seryya Fizika-Matematychnykh
　　　　Navuk [*A publication*]
VBSK........ Sinkaling Khamti [*Burma*] [*ICAO location identifier*]　(ICLI)
VBSKA ...... Vestsi Akademii Navuk BSSR. Seryya Khimichnykh Navuk [*A
　　　　publication*]
VBSL......... Salingyi [*Burma*] [*ICAO location identifier*]　(ICLI)
VBSO........ Sidoktaya [*Burma*] [*ICAO location identifier*]　(ICLI)
VBST .... Shante [*Burma*] [*ICAO location identifier*]　(ICLI)
VBSW........ Shinbweyang [*Burma*] [*ICAO location identifier*]　(ICLI)
VBSY........ Sandoway [*Burma*] [*ICAO location identifier*]　(ICLI)
VBT .... Bombing, Torpedo Plane [*Navy symbol*]
VBT .... Tabak Plus [*A publication*]
VBT .... Valence-Bond Theory [*Physical chemistry*]
VBT .... Videos for Business and Training [*A publication*]
VBTL........ Tachilek [*Burma*] [*ICAO location identifier*]　(ICLI)
VBTN .... Tanai [*Burma*] [*ICAO location identifier*]　(ICLI)
VBTPS....... Vierteljahrschrift fuer Bibelkunde, Talmudische, und
　　　　Patristische Studien [*A publication*]
VBTV........ Tavoy [*Burma*] [*ICAO location identifier*]　(ICLI)
VBTY........ Tanyang [*Burma*] [*ICAO location identifier*]　(ICLI)
VBU .... Vibrating Bag Unloader
VBULE...... Vestibule [*Classified advertising*]　(ADA)
VBV .... Documentatieblad voor Onderwijs en Wetenschappen [*A
　　　　publication*]
VBV .... Vanuabalavu [*Fiji*] [*Airport symbol*]　(OAG)
VBVP........ Kawthaung [*Burma*] [*ICAO location identifier*]　(ICLI)
VBVT........ Valley Bank [*NASDAQ symbol*]　(NQ)
VBW .... Bridgewater, VA [*Location identifier*] [*FAA*]　(FAAL)
VBW .... Vakbondskrant van Nederland [*A publication*]
VBW .... Video Bandwidth
VBW .... Vortraege der Bibliothek Warburg [*A publication*]

VBWR .... Vallecitos Boiling Water Reactor
VBY .... Visby [*Sweden*] [*Airport symbol*]　(OAG)
VBYE........ Ye [*Burma*] [*ICAO location identifier*]　(ICLI)
VC.............. British Aircraft Corp. Ltd. [*ICAO aircraft manufacturer
　　　　identifier*]　(ICAO)
VC.............. Circular Velocity
VC.............. Color Vision [*Ophthalmology*]
VC.............. Composite Aircraft Squadron [*Navy symbol*]
VC.............. Creditreform Databank [*Verband der Vereine Creditreform eV*]
　　　　[*Information service or system*]　(IID)
VC.............. Cruise Speed [*Aviation*]
VC.............. St. Vincent and the Grenadines [*ANSI two-letter standard
　　　　code*]　(CNC)
VC.............. Vacuolated Cell
VC.............. Valuable Cargo
VC.............. Valuation Clause
VC.............. Vaporizer Concentrate [*Nuclear energy*]　(NRCH)
VC.............. Variable Capacitor　(DEN)
VC.............. Variable Charge　(DCTA)
VC.............. [*Total*] Variable Costs
VC.............. Varnished Cambric [*Insulation*]
VC.............. Vasoconstrictor [*Medicine*]
VC.............. Vatel Club　(EA)
vc .... Vatican City [*MARC country of publication code*] [*Library of
　　　　Congress*]　(LCCP)
VC.............. Vector Character　(NASA)
V/C .... Vector Control　(KSC)
Vc.............. Vecuronium [*A muscle relaxant*]
VC.............. Vegetative Capability [*Biology*]
VC.............. Vehicular Communications　(MCD)
VC.............. Velocity Character　(MCD)
VC.............. Velocity Compounded
VC.............. Velocity Counter　(KSC)
VC.............. Vena Cava [*Anatomy*]
VC.............. Vendor Call　(MCD)
VC.............. Vendor Code　(MCD)
VC.............. Vendor Contact
VC.............. Venereal Case [*Medical slang*]
VC.............. Venice Committee　(EA)
VC.............. Ventilated Containers [*Shipping*]　(DCTA)
VC.............. Ventilatory Capacity [*Physiology*]
VC.............. Ventricular Complex [*Cardiology*]
VC.............. Ventricular Coupling [*Cardiology*]
VC.............. Venture Capital [*Finance*]
VC.............. Verb-Consonant [*Education of the hearing-impaired*]
VC.............. Verbi Causa [*For Example*] [*Latin*]
VC.............. Verification Condition
VC.............. Vernair Flying Services [*United Kingdom*] [*ICAO
　　　　designator*]　(ICDA)
VC.............. Vernal Conjunctivitis [*Ophthalmology*]
VC.............. Versatility Code
VC.............. Vertical Curve
VC.............. Veterinary Corps [*Military*]
VC.............. Vicar Choral
VC.............. Vice Chairman [*or Chairperson or Chairwoman*]
VC.............. Vice Chancellor
VC.............. Vice-Chancellor's Courts [*England*]　(DLA)
VC.............. Vice Commodore [*Navy*]　(NVT)
VC.............. Vice Consul
VC.............. Victoria Cross [*British*]
VC.............. Video Channel [*Auckland, NZ*]
VC.............. Video Correlator
VC.............. Videodisc Controller
VC.............. Vietcong [*Vietnamese Communists*]
VC.............. Vigilance Committee
VC.............. Vigiliae Christianae [*A publication*]
VC.............. Village of Childhelp　(EA)
VC.............. Vinyl Chloride [*Organic chemistry*]
VC.............. Violoncello [*Music*]
VC.............. Vir Clarissimus [*A Most Illustrious Man*] [*Latin*]
VC.............. Virginia Cavalcade [*A publication*]
VC.............. Virginia Central Railway [*AAR code*]
VC.............. Virtual Circuit
VC.............. Viscous Criterion
VC.............. Visiting Committee [*British*]
VC.............. Vista Chemical [*NYSE symbol*]　(SPSG)
VC.............. Visual Capacity [*Acuity*]
VC.............. Visual Cortex
VC.............. Visum Cultum [*Seen Cultivated*] [*Botany*]　(ROG)
VC.............. Vital Capacity
VC.............. Vitreous Carbon
VC.............. Vitrified Clay [*Technical drawings*]
VC.............. Vocal Cord
VC.............. Voice Ciphony　(CET)
VC.............. Voice Coil
VC.............. Volt-Coulomb　(DEN)
VC.............. Voltage Comparator [*or Compensator*]　(DEN)
VC.............. Volume of Compartment [*Technical drawings*]
VC.............. Volume Control　(DEN)
VC.............. Voluntary Closing [*Prosthesis*] [*Medicine*]
VC.............. Volunteer Consultant [*Red Cross*]

VC .... Volunteer Corps
v/c .... Vossa Conta [*Your Account*] [*Portuguese*] [*Business term*]
VC .... Voters for Choice [*Later, VFC*] (EA)
v/c .... Votre Compte [*Your Account*] [*French*] [*Business term*]
VC .... Voyage Charter
VC .... Vuelta de Correo [*Return Mail*] [*Spanish*]
VC's .... Vocal Chords [*Musical slang*]
VCA .... Valve Control Amplifier (MDG)
VCA .... Vancomycin-Colistin-Anisomycin [*Growth-inhibiting mixture*] [*Microbiology*]
VCA .... Vanished Children's Alliance (EA)
VCA .... Vehicle Checkout Area
VCA .... Venture Clubs of the Americas (EA)
VCA .... Vestnik Ceske Akademie Ved a Umeni [*A publication*]
VCA .... Vestnik Ceskoslovenske Akademie Ved [*A publication*]
VCA .... Veteran Corps of Artillery, State of New York, Constituting the Military Society of the War of 1812 (EA)
VCA .... Victims of Crime Assistance Act
VCA .... Victorian College of the Arts [*Australia*]
VCA .... Viewdata Corporation of America, Inc. [*Miami Beach, FL*] [*Telecommunications*] (TSSD)
VCA .... Vinchina [*Argentina*] [*Seismograph station code, US Geological Survey*] (SEIS)
VCA .... Viral Capsid Antibody [*Hematology*]
VCA .... Viral Capsular Antigen [*Immunology*]
VCA .... Virtual City Associates Ltd. [*London, England*] [*Telecommunications*] (TSSD)
VCA .... Visual Course Adapter (MUGU)
VCA .... Vitrified China Association [*Defunct*]
VC of A ...... Vizsla Club of America (EA)
VCA .... Voice Connecting Arrangement [*Telecommunications*] (TEL)
VCA .... Voltage Control of Amplification
VCA .... Voluntary Care Association [*Australia*]
VCAB .... Victorian Curriculum and Assessment Board [*Australia*]
VCAD .... Vertical Contact Analog Display
VC Adm ..... Victoria Reports, Admiralty [*A publication*] (DLA)
VCAM .... Volunteer Committees of Art Museums (EA)
VCAMCUS ... Volunteer Committees of Art Museums of Canada and the United States (EA)
VCAP .... Vehicle Charging and Potential Experiment (NASA)
VCAP .... Vincristine, Cyclophosphamide, Adriamycin, Prednisone [*Antineoplastic drug regimen*]
V-CAP III ... VP-16-213 [*Etoposide*], Cyclophosphamide, Adriamycin, Platinol [*Cisplatin*] [*Antineoplastic drug regimen*]
VCAR .... Vector Aeromotive Corp. [*NASDAQ symbol*] (NQ)
VCARE...... Veterans Council for American Rights and Equality (EA)
VCAS........ Vice-Chief of the Air Staff [*British*]
VCASS........ Visually Coupled Airborne Systems Simulator (IEEE)
VCAW .... Movement Against War and Fascism, Victorian Council [*Australia*]
VCB .... CBNU Learning Resources Center, Virginia Beach, VA [*OCLC symbol*] (OCLC)
VCB .... Construction Battalion [*USNR classification*]
VCB .... Vertical Location of the Center of Buoyancy
VCB .... Visual Control Board
VCBA........ Variable Control Block Area [*Data processing*]
VCBFE ...... Vauxhall College of Building and Further Education [*London, England*]
VCBI......... Colombo/Katunayake [*Sri Lanka*] [*ICAO location identifier*] (ICLI)
VCC .... Vancouver Community College Library [*UTLAS symbol*]
VCC .... Variable Ceramic Capacitor
VCC .... Variable Characteristic Car (ADA)
VCC .... Variable Command Count (MCD)
VCC .... Vasoconstrictor Center [*Physiology*]
VCC .... Vehicle Crew Chief [*NASA*] (KSC)
VCC .... Verification Code Counter (MCD)
VCC .... Vermilion Community College, Ely, MN [*OCLC symbol*] (OCLC)
VCC .... Versatile Corporation [*Toronto Stock Exchange symbol*]
VCC .... Vertical Centering Control
VCC .... Vice-Chancellor's Courts (DLA)
VCC .... Video Coaxial Connector
VCC .... Video Compact Cassette [*Video recorder*] [*Philips*]
VCC .... Vietcong Captured
VCC .... Village Community Centre [*Australia*]
VCC .... Virginia Community College System
VCC .... Viscous-Damped Converter Clutch [*Automotive engineering*]
VCC .... Visual Communications Congress
VCC .... Vogelback Computing Center [*Northwestern University*] [*Research center*] (RCD)
VCC .... Voice Control Center [*NASA*] (KSC)
VCC .... Voltage Coefficient of Capacitance
VCC .... Voltage-Controlled Capacitor
VCC .... Voluntary Census Committee (EA)
VCC .... Volunteer Cadet Corps [*British*]
VCC .... Volunteer Capital Corp. [*NYSE symbol*] (SPSG)
VCC .... Vuilleumier Cycle Cooler
VCCA .... Anuradhapura [*Sri Lanka*] [*ICAO location identifier*] (ICLI)
VCCA .... Vintage Chevrolet Club of America (EA)
VCCB........ Batticaloa [*Sri Lanka*] [*ICAO location identifier*] (ICLI)

VCCC......... Colombo/Ratmalana [*Sri Lanka*] [*ICAO location identifier*] (ICLI)
VCCC....... Vuilleumier Cycle Cryogenic Cooler
VCCG .... Galoya/Amparai [*Sri Lanka*] [*ICAO location identifier*] (ICLI)
VCCJ .... Jaffna/Kankesanturai [*Sri Lanka*] [*ICAO location identifier*] (ICLI)
VCCN .... Valley Capital Corp. [*NASDAQ symbol*] (NQ)
VCCS........ Visually Coupled Control System (MCD)
VCCS........ Voltage-Controlled Current Source [*Electronics*]
VCCT........ Trincomalee/China Bay [*Sri Lanka*] [*ICAO location identifier*] (ICLI)
VCCUS...... Venezuelan Chamber of Commerce of the United States
VCCW ...... Wirawila [*Sri Lanka*] [*ICAO location identifier*] (ICLI)
VCD.......... Vapor Compression Distillation
VCD.......... Variable-Capacitance Diode
VCD.......... Verification Control Document (NASA)
VCD.......... Vernier Engine Cutoff [*Aerospace*]
VCD.......... Vibrational Circular Dichroism [*Spectrometry*]
VCD.......... Victoria Diego Resource Corp. [*Vancouver Stock Exchange symbol*]
VCD.......... Visiting Card (BJA)
VCD.......... Voltage Crossing Detector
VCDS........ Vapor Compression Distillation Subsystem (NASA)
VCDS........ Vice-Chief of Defence Staff [*British*]
VCDS(P & L) ... Vice Chief of Defence Staff Personnel and Logistics [*British*] (RDA)
VCE .... Vapor Compression Evaporation
VCE .... Variable Cycle Engine (MCD)
VCE .... Vehicle Condition Evaluation (MCD)
VCE .... Venice [*Italy*] [*Airport symbol*] (OAG)
VCE .... Vertical Centrifugal
VCE .... Vice
VCE .... Voice (NASA)
VCEL........ Vanguard Cellular Systems, Inc. [*NASDAQ symbol*] (NQ)
Vcela Morav ... Vcela Moravska [*A publication*]
VC Eq........ Victoria Reports, Equity [*A publication*] (DLA)
VCF.......... Vapor Chamber Fin
VCF.......... Variable Crystal Filter (DEN)
Vcf............ Velocity of Circumferential Fiber Shortening [*Cardiology*]
VCF.......... Venture Capital Fund [*Finance*]
VCF.......... Verified Circulation Figure [*Advertising*]
VCF.......... Vietnam-Canada Foundation
VCF.......... Vincristine, Cyclophosphamide, Fluorouracil [*Antineoplastic drug regimen*]
VCF.......... Visual Comfort Factor
VCF.......... Voltage-Controlled Filter
VCF.......... Voltage-Controlled Frequency (IEEE)
VCFC........ Vik Chandler Fan Club (EA)
VCFUSA ... Vietnamese Catholic Federation in the USA (EA)
VCG .... Calcutta Volunteer Guards [*British military*] (DMA)
VCG .... Vapor Crystal Growth [*Materials processing*]
VCG .... Vectorcardiogram [*Medicine*]
VCG .... Vehicle Control Group
VCG .... Verification Condition Generator
VCG .... Vertical Location of the Center of Gravity
VCG .... Vice-Consul General [*British*] (ROG)
VCG .... Video Command Generator (MCD)
VCG .... Voltage-Controlled Generator
VCGS........ Vapor Crystal Growth System [*Materials processing*]
VCGS........ Vice Chief of the General Staff [*in the field*] [*Military*] [*British*] (RDA)
VCH.......... Veterinary Convalescent Hospital
VCH.......... Vichadero [*Uruguay*] [*Airport symbol*] [*Obsolete*] (OAG)
VCH.......... Victoria County History [*Classical studies*] (OCD)
VCH.......... Video Concert Hall
VCH.......... Vinylcyclohexene [*Organic chemistry*]
VCHO....... Vicar Choral
VCHP........ Variable Conductance Heat Pipe
VCHP........ Vegas Chips, Inc. [*NASDAQ symbol*] (NQ)
VChr .... Vigiliae Christianae [*A publication*]
V Christ ..... Vetera Christianorum [*A publication*]
VCI .... Variety Clubs International (EA)
VCI .... Velocity Change Indicator (NASA)
VCI .... Vibration Control Index
VCI .... Videtics International Corp. [*Vancouver Stock Exchange symbol*]
VCI .... Vietcong Infrastructure
VCI .... Virtual Circuit Identifier [*Data processing*]
VCI .... Visual Comfort Index
VCI .... Volatile Corrosion Inhibitor [*See also VPI*] [*Metallurgy*]
VCID .... Very Close in Defense
VCIGS....... Vice-Chief of the Imperial General Staff [*British*]
VCIM .... Varnished Cambric Insulation Material
VCINS....... Vietcong Infrastructure Neutralization System
VCIP........ Veterans Cost-of-Instruction Program [*Higher Education Act*]
VCIS .... Voluntary Cooperative Information System [*American Public Welfare Association*] (EGAO)
V-CITE...... Vertical-Cargo Integration Test Equipment [*NASA*] (MCD)
VC-K........ Eli Lilly & Co. [*Canada*] [*Research code symbol*]
VCK .... Veckans Affarer [*A publication*]
VCK .... Video Camera Kit

VCK	Vietcong Killed
VC KIA(BC) ...	Vietcong Killed in Action (Body Count)
VC KIA(POSS) ...	Vietcong Killed in Action (Possible)
VCL	Vehicle Checkout Laboratory
VCL	Vertical Center Line
VCL	Violincello [Music]
VCL	Voice Communications Laboratory
VCL	Voluntary College Letter [British]
VCLE	Versicle
VCLF	Vertical Cask-Lifting Fixture [Nuclear energy] (NRCH)
VCLK	Video Clock [Data processing]
VCLLO	Violoncello [Music]
VCLO	Voltage-Controlled Local Oscillator
VCM	Vacuum (AAG)
VCM	Ventilation Control Module [NASA]
VCM	Veracruz [Mexico] [Seismograph station code, US Geological Survey] (SEIS)
VCM	Vertical Current Meter
VCM	Vertical Cutter Motion
VCM	Vibrating Coil Magnetometer
VCM	Victoria College of Music [London] (ROG)
VCM	Viking Continuation Mission [NASA]
VCM	Vinyl Chloride Monomer [Organic chemistry]
VCM	Visual Countermeasure
VCM	Volatile Combustible Material
VCM	Volatile Condensable Material
VCM	Voltage-Controlled Multivibrator
VCM	Voorhees College, Denmark, SC [OCLC symbol] (OCLC)
VCMA	Vacuum Cleaner Manufacturers Association (EA)
VCmax	Maximum Viscous Response [Medicine]
VCMP	Vincristine, Cyclophosphamide, Melphalan, Prednisone [Antineoplastic drug regimen]
VCN	Christopher Newport College, Newport News, VA [OCLC symbol] (OCLC)
VCN	Millville, NJ [Location identifier] [FAA] (FAAL)
VCN	Vancomycin-Colistin-Nystatin [Growth-inhibiting mixture] [Microbiology]
VCN	Vendor Contract Notice
VCN	Verification Completion Notice (NASA)
VCN	Vibrio cholerae Neuraminidase [An enzyme]
VCN	Vinyl Cyanide [Organic chemistry]
VCN	Visual Communications Network, Inc. [Cambridge, MA]
VCN	Vulcan Resources [Vancouver Stock Exchange symbol]
VCNM	Vice Chief of Naval Material Command
VCNO	Vice Chief of Naval Operations
VCNS	Vice-Chief of the Naval Staff [British]
VCNTY	Vicinity (AFM)
VC/NVA	Vietcong/North Vietnamese Army
VCO	Glendale, AZ [Location identifier] [FAA] (FAAL)
VCO	Variable Cycle Operation
VCO	Vehicle Control Officer [Air Force] (AFM)
VCO	Verbal Concrete Object
VCO	Verbit & Company, Consultants to Management [Bala Cynwyd, PA] [Telecommunications] (TSSD)
VCO	Vertical Control Operator [Military]
VCO	Viceroy's Commissioned Officer [British military] (DMA)
VCO	Voice-Controlled Oscillator [Telecommunications] (TEL)
VCO	Voltage-Controlled Oscillator
VCOA	Volkswagen Convertible Owners of America (EA)
VCoA	Volvo Club of America (EA)
VCOD	Vertical Carrier Onboard Delivery
VCOFGWBS ...	Vietnamese Cross of Gallantry with Bronze Star [Military decoration] (AABC)
VCOFGWGS ...	Vietnamese Cross of Gallantry with Gold Star [Military decoration] (AABC)
VCOFGWP ...	Vietnamese Cross of Gallantry with Palm [Military decoration] (AABC)
VCOFGWSS ...	Vietnamese Cross of Gallantry with Silver Star [Military decoration] (AABC)
VCOI	Veterans Cost-of-Instruction
V Conv R	Victorian Conveyancing Cases [Australia] [A publication]
VCOP	Variable Control Oil Pressure (MSA)
VCOR	Vencor, Inc. [NASDAQ symbol] (NQ)
VCOS	Vice-Chiefs of Staff [British]
VCOT	VFR [Visual Flight Rules] Conditions on Top [Aviation] (FAAC)
VCOV	Volunteer Consultant for Office of Volunteers [Red Cross]
VCP	Sao Paulo [Brazil] Viracopos Airport [Airport symbol] (OAG)
VCP	Valosin-Containing Protein [Biochemistry]
VCP	Vehicle Check Point [Military]
VCP	Vehicle Collecting Point
VCP	Velocity Control Programmer
VCP	VERDAN [Versatile Differential Analyzer] Checkout Panel
VCP	Veterinary Collecting Post [British military] (DMA)
VCP	Veterinary Creolin-Pearson
VCP	Video Cassette Player
VCP	Vincristine, Cyclophosphamide, Prednisone [Antineoplastic drug regimen]
VCP	Virtual Counterpoise Procedure [Physical chemistry]
VCP	Virus Cancer Program [National Cancer Institute]

VCP	Voluntary Cooperation Program [World Meteorological Organization] [United Nations]
VCPA	Virginia-Carolina Peanut Association (EA)
VCPA	Virginia Crab Packers Association [Defunct] (EA)
VCPI	Virtual Control Program Interface [Data processing] (PCM)
VCPM	Video-Enhanced Contrast Polarization Microscopy
VCPOR	Vanguardia Comunista del Partido Obrero Revolucionario [Bolivia] [Political party] (PPW)
VCPS	Velocity Control Propulsion Subsystem [NASA]
VCPS	Video Copyright Protection Society [British]
VC PW	Vietcong Prisoner of War
VCR	Go-Video, Inc. [AMEX symbol] (SPSG)
VCR	Vacuum Contact Relay
VCR	Valclair Resources Ltd. [Vancouver Stock Exchange symbol]
VCR	Valuation by Components Rule (ADA)
VCR	Variable Compression Ratio
VCR	Vasoconstrictive [Physiology]
VCR	Vertical Crater Retreat [Mining technology]
VCR	Video Cassette Recorder
VCR	Vincristine [Also, LCR, O, V, VC] [Antineoplastic drug]
VCR	Visual Control Room
VCR	Viva Cristo Rey [Long Live Christ the King] [Spanish]
VCR	Vocal Character Recognition
VCR	Voltage Coefficient of Resistance
VCRAS	Office of Vice Chancellor for Research and Advanced Study [University of Alaska] [Research center] (RCD)
VCRC	Vector Control Research Centre [India]
VCRE	Vari-Care, Inc. [NASDAQ symbol] (NQ)
VC Rep	Vice-Chancellor's Reports [English, Canadian] [A publication] (DLA)
VCRI	Video Communications & Radio, Inc. [NASDAQ symbol] (NQ)
VCRT	Variable Contrast Resolution Test [Optics]
VCS	Cruiser-Scouting Aircraft Squadron [Navy symbol]
VCS	Vacuum Control Switch
VCS	Validation Control System
VCS	Vane Control System (MCD)
VCS	Vapor Coating System
VCS	Vapor Cooling System
VCS	Variable Correlation Synchronization
VCS	Vasoconstrictor Substance [Physiology]
VCS	Vehicular Communications System
VCS	Velocity Cutoff System (KSC)
VCS	Ventilation Control System [NASA] (KSC)
VCS	Verbal Communication Scales [Educational testing]
VCS	Verification Control Sheet (NASA)
VCS	Vernier Control System
VCS	Veterans Canteen Service [Veterans Administration]
VCS	Veterinary Cancer Society (EA)
VC of S	Vice Chief of Staff
VCS	Vice Chief of Staff
VCS	Video Cassette System
VCS	Video Clutter Suppression (CAAL)
VCS	Video Communications System
VCS	Video Computer System [Atari, Inc.]
VCS	Video Contrast Seeker
VCS	Vietcong Suspect
VCS	Viking Change Status [NASA]
VCS	Virginia & Carolina Southern R. R. [AAR code]
VCS	Visual Call Sign [Communications]
VCS	Visually Coupled System (IEEE)
VCS	Vocabulary Comprehension Scale [Educational test]
VCS	Voice Command System [Ground Communications Facility, NASA]
VCS	Voice Control Switch [NASA]
VCS	Voltage Calibration Set
VCS	Voltage-Current-Sequence (MCD)
VCSA	Vice Chief of Staff, Army [Formerly, VC of SA]
VC of SA	Vice Chief of Staff, Army [Later, VCSA] (AABC)
VC/SAF	Vice Chief of Staff, Air Force
VCSAV	Vestnik Ceskoslovenske Akademie Ved [A publication]
VCS Bul	VCS [Victorian Computer Society] Bulletin [A publication] (APTA)
VCSEL	Vertical-Cavity Surface Emitting LASER
VCSFO	Veterans Canteen Service Field Office [Veterans Administration]
VCSI	VCS, Inc. [NASDAQ symbol] (NQ)
VCSL	Voice Call Signs List
VCSP	Voice Call Signs Plan
VCSR	Voltage-Controlled Shift Register
VCSS	Value Creation Study Society (CINC)
VCSS	Voice Communications Security System
VCT	St. Vincent and the Grenadines [ANSI three-letter standard code] (CNC)
VCT	Variable Cycle Technology
VCT	Vector [A publication]
VCT	Venous Clotting Time [Clinical chemistry]
VCT	Victoria [Texas] [Airport symbol] (OAG)
VCT	Vidicon Camera Tube
VCT	Vinyl Composition Tile
VCT	Vitrified Clay Tile [Technical drawings]

VCT .... Voice Code Translation (BUR)
VCT .... Voltage Control Transfer
VCT .... Voltage Curve Tracer
VCT .... Volume Control Tank [*Nuclear energy*] (NRCH)
VCTA General J ... Victorian Commercial Teachers' Association. General Journal [*A publication*] (APTA)
VCTCA ...... Virtual Channel to Channel Adapter
VCTD .... Vendor Contract Technical Data
v/cte .... Votre Compte [*Your Account*] [*French*] [*Business term*]
VCTR .... Vector (NASA)
VCTR .... Vector Graphic, Inc. [*NASDAQ symbol*] (NQ)
VCTS .... Variable Cockpit Training System (MCD)
VCTY .... Vicinity (NVT)
VCU .... Video Control Unit (MCD)
VCU .... Videocystourethrography [*Medicine*]
VCU .... Virginia Commonwealth University
VCU .... Viscous Coupling Unit [*Automotive engineering*]
VCU .... Voiding Cystourethrogram [*Medicine*]
VCU .... Voltage Control Unit
VCUG .... Vesicoureterogram [*Urology*]
VCUG .... Voiding Cystourethrogram [*Medicine*]
VCV .... Clinch Valley College of the University of Virginia, Wise, VA [*OCLC symbol*] (OCLC)
VCV .... Vacuum Check Valve
VCV .... Vacuum Control Valve [*Automotive engineering*]
VCV .... Victorville, CA [*Location identifier*] [*FAA*] (FAAL)
VCV .... Vietnam Combat Veterans (EA)
VCVS .... Vehicle Component Verification System [*Automotive engineering*]
VCVS .... Voltage-Controlled Voltage Source
VCXO .... Voltage-Controlled Crystal Oscillator
VCY .... Valley City, ND [*Location identifier*] [*FAA*] (FAAL)
VCY .... Ventura County Railway Co. [*Army*]
VCYAN ..... Victorian Country Youth Affairs Network [*Australia*]
VCZ .... Vinylcarbazole [*Organic chemistry*]
VD .... Double Vibrations [*Cycles*]
VD .... Leo Pharm. Products [*Denmark*] [*Research code symbol*]
VD .... Photographic Squadron [*Navy symbol*]
VD .... RTZ Services Ltd. [*United Kingdom*] [*ICAO designator*] (ICDA)
VD .... Valuation Decisions [*A publication*] (DLA)
VD .... Vandyke [*Graphics*]
VD .... Vapor Density
VD .... Various Dates [*Bibliography*]
VD .... Vault Door (AAG)
Vd .... Vend [*Sell*] [*French*] [*Business term*]
VD .... Venereal Disease
VD .... Ventilating Deadlight [*Technical drawings*]
VD .... Ventricular Dilator [*Neuron*] [*Medicine*]
VD .... Verbal Discrimination [*Psychology*]
VD .... Verbum Domini [*Rome*] [*A publication*] (BJA)
VD .... Vertical Drive
VD .... Viceroy-Designate [*British*]
VD .... Victoria Docks [*British*] (ROG)
VD .... Victorian Decoration [*British*]
VD .... Video Decoder
VD .... Video Disk (BUR)
VD .... Violent Defectives [*British*]
VD .... Virtual Data
VD .... Visiting Dignitary
V/D .... Voice/Data (BUR)
VD .... Void (AAG)
VD .... Voltage Detector
VD .... Voltage Drop (MSA)
VD .... Volume Deleted [*Finance*]
VD .... Volume Discount [*Investment term*]
VD .... Volume of Distribution
VD .... Volunteer Decoration [*British*]
VDA .... Valve Drive Amplifier
VDA .... Valve Driver Assembly (NASA)
VDA .... Variable Data Area (NASA)
VDA .... Variable Depth ASDIC (NATG)
VDA .... Vendor Data Article
VDA .... Versatile Drone Autopilot (MCD)
VDA .... Vertical Danger Angle [*Navigation*]
V & DA ..... Video and Data Acquisition (MCD)
V & DA ..... Video and Data Processing Assembly (NASA)
VDA .... Video Dimension Analysis [*Sports medicine*]
VDA .... Video Distribution Amplifier
VDA .... Viola d'Amore [*Music*]
VDA .... Visual Discriminatory Acuity
VDA .... Volksbund fuer das Deutschtum im Ausland [*NAZI Germany*]
VDAC .... Vaginal Delivery after Caesarean [*Obstetrics*]
VDAC .... Vendor Data Article Control
VDAC .... Voltage-Dependent, Anion-Selective Channels [*In the membrane of a mitochondrion*]
VDA/D ..... Video Display Adapter with Digital Enhancement [*AT & T*]
VDAM ...... Virtual Data Access Method (IEEE)
VDAS .... Vibration Data Acquisition System (KSC)
VDAS .... Voltage-Dependent, Anion-Selective [*Proteins*] [*Biochemistry*]

VDASD ..... Veroeffentlichungen. Deutsche Akademie fuer Sprache und Dichtung [*A publication*]
VDB .... Brooklyn College, Brooklyn, NY [*OCLC symbol*] (OCLC)
VdB .... Van Den Bergh [*Liver function test*]
VDB .... Vector Data Buffer
VDB .... Very Dear Brother [*Freemasonry*]
VDB .... Victor D. Brenner [*Designer's mark, when appearing on US coins*]
VDB .... Video Display Board
VDB .... Vrijzinnige-Democratische Bond [*Radical Democratic League*] [*Netherlands*] [*Political party*] (PPE)
VDBA .... Victorian Deer Breeders Association [*Australia*]
VDBG .... Battambang [*Kampuchea*] [*ICAO location identifier*] (ICLI)
VDC .... Van Dorn Company [*NYSE symbol*] (SPSG)
VDC .... Vanadocene Dichloride [*Antineoplastic drug*]
VDC .... Variable Diode Circuit
VDC .... Vasodilator Center [*Physiology*]
VDC .... Vendor Data Control (MCD)
VDC .... Ventilation Duct Chase [*Nuclear energy*] (NRCH)
VDC .... Venture Development Corporation [*Natick, MA*] [*Telecommunications*] (TSSD)
VDC .... Video-Documentary Clearinghouse (EA)
VDC .... Voltage to Digital Converter
VDC .... Voltage Doubler Circuit
VDC .... Volts Direct Current
VDC .... Volunteer Defense Corps
VDC .... Volunteer Development Corps (EA)
VDCC .... Voltage-Dependent Calcium Channel [*Neurobiology*]
VDCP .... Video Data Collection Program
VDCT .... Direct-Current Test Volts
VDCU .... Videograph Display Control Unit
VDCW ...... Direct-Current Working Volts
VDD .... Verification Description Document (NASA)
VDD .... Version Description Document (KSC)
VDD .... Video Detector Diode
VDD .... Visual Display Data
VDD .... Voice Digital Display
VDDI .... Voyager Data Detailed Index [*NASA*] (KSC)
VDDL .... Voyager Data Distribution List [*NASA*] (KSC)
VDDP .... Video Digital Data Processing
VDDR .... Vitamin D-Dependent Rickets [*Medicine*]
VDDS .... Voice/Document Delivery System [*Data processing*]
VDDS .... Voyager Data Description Standards [*NASA*] (KSC)
VDE .... Vacuum Deposition Equipment
VDE .... Valverde [*Canary Islands*] [*Airport symbol*] (OAG)
VDE .... Variable Displacement Engine
VDE .... Variable Display Equipment
VDE .... Verband Deutscher Elektrotechniker [*Association of German Electrical Engineers*]
VDEF .... Vie de France Corp. [*McLean, VA*] [*NASDAQ symbol*] (NQ)
VDEFA ..... VDE [*Verband Deutscher Elektrotechniker*] Fachberichte [*A publication*]
VDE Fachber ... VDE [*Verband Deutscher Elektrotechniker*] Fachberichte [*A publication*]
VDEh .... Verein Deutscher Eisenhuttenleute [*German Iron and Steel Engineers Association*] [*Information service or system*] (IID)
VDEL .... Variable Delivery
VDEL .... Venereal Disease Experimental Laboratory
VDEO .... Video Station, Inc. [*NASDAQ symbol*] (NQ)
VDET .... Voltage Detector (IEEE)
VDETS ..... Voice Data Entry Terminal System
VDEV .... "V" Device [*Military decoration*] (AABC)
VDEW (Ver Dtsch Elektrizitaetswerke) Informationsdienst ... VDEW (Vereinigung Deutscher Elektrizitaetswerke) Informationsdienst (German Federal Republic) [*A publication*]
VDF .... Very-High-Frequency Direction-Finding
VDF .... Vibration Damping Fastener
VDF .... Video Frequency
VDF .... Vinylidene Fluoride [*Organic chemistry*]
VDF .... Vorkaempfer Deutscher Freiheit. Series [*Munich*] [*A publication*]
VDFAN ..... Vestnik Dal'nevostochnogo Filiala Akademii Nauk SSSR [*A publication*]
VDFG .... Variable Diode Function Generator
VDG .... Royal Inniskilling Dragoon Guards [*Military unit*] [*British*]
VDG .... Vehicle Data Guide
VDG .... Venereal Disease Gonorrhea
VDG .... Vertical and Direction Gyro
VDG .... Vertical Display Generator (NG)
VDG .... Video Display Generator
VdgB .... Vereinigung der Gegenseitigen Bauernhilfe [*Mutual Farmers' Aid Society*] [*Germany*]
VDGIA ...... Verhandlungen. Deutsche Gesellschaft fuer Innere Medizin [*A publication*]
VDGKA ..... Verhandlungen. Deutsche Gesellschaft fuer Kreislaufforschung [*A publication*]
VDGPA ..... Verhandlungen. Deutsche Gesellschaft fuer Pathologie [*A publication*]

VDGRA ..... Verhandlungen. Deutsche Gesellschaft fuer Rheumatologie [*A publication*]
VdGSA ...... Viola da Gamba Society of America (EA)
VdGSA ...... Viola da Gamba Society of America. Journal [*A publication*]
VDH .... Valvular Disease of the Heart [*Medicine*]
VDH .... Van Der Hout Associates Ltd. [*Toronto Stock Exchange symbol*]
VDI .... Vat Dye Institute [*Later, American Dye Manufacturers Institute*] (EA)
VDI .... Vendor Documentation Inventory (NASA)
VDI .... Verein Deutscher Ingenieure [*Society of German Engineers*]
VDI .... Vertical Direction Indicator (CAAL)
VDI .... Vertical Display Indicator (NG)
VDI .... Vestnik Drevnei Istorii [*A publication*]
VDI .... Vidalia, GA [*Location identifier*] [*FAA*] (FAAL)
VDI .... Video Display Input
VDI .... Video Display Interface
VDI .... Virtual Device Interface [*Computer technology*]
VDI .... Visual Display Input
VDI .... Voluntary Data Inquiry
VDI Ber ..... VDI [*Verein Deutscher Ingenieure*] Berichte [*A publication*]
VDICAPP ... VDI [*Verein Deutscher Ingenieure*]-Commission on Air Pollution Prevention (EAIO)
VDIEO ...... Vendor Data Information Engineering Order (MCD)
VDIFA .... VDI [*Verein Deutscher Ingenieure*] Forschungsheft [*A publication*]
VDI Forschungsh ... VDI [*Verein Deutscher Ingenieure*] Forschungsheft [*A publication*]
VDIG .... Vertical Display Indicator Group
VDIKRL .... VDI [*Verein Deutscher Ingenieure*]-Kommission Reinhaltung der Luft [*VDI - Commission on Air Pollution Prevention*] (EAIO)
VDI-N .... VDI-Nachrichten [*VDI-Verlag GmbH*] [*Database*]
VDI Nachr ... Verein Deutscher Ingenieure. Nachrichten [*A publication*]
VDISK .... Virtual Disk [*Data processing*]
VDI Z .... VDI [*Verein Deutscher Ingenieure*] Zeitschrift [*A publication*]
VDI Z Fortschr Ber Reihe 5 ... VDI [*Verein Deutscher Ingenieure*] Zeitschriften. Fortschritt-Berichte. Reihe 5. Grund- und Werkstoffe [*A publication*]
VDJ .... Variable-Diversity-Joining [*Genetics*]
VDK .... Vicinal Diketone [*Organic chemistry*]
VDKC .... Kompong Cham [*Kampuchea*] [*ICAO location identifier*] (ICLI)
VDKH .... Kompong Chnang [*Kampuchea*] [*ICAO location identifier*] (ICLI)
VDKT .... Kratie [*Kampuchea*] [*ICAO location identifier*] (ICLI)
VDL .... Van Diemen's Land [*Former name of Tasmania*]
VDL .... Variable Delay Line
VDL .... Vasodepressor Lipid [*Physiology*]
VDL .... Ventilating Deadlight
VDL .... Video Data Link (NVT)
VDL .... Vienna Definition Language [*1960*] [*Data processing*] (CSR)
VDL .... Voice Direct Line
VDLF .... Variable Depth Launch Facility (AAG)
VDM .... Variable Direction Microphone
VDM .... Varian Data Machines
VDM .... Vasodepressor Material [*Physiology*]
VDM .... Vector Dominance Model [*Physics*]
VDM .... Vector Drawn Map
VDM .... Vehicle Deadlined for Maintenance (AFM)
VDM .... Verbi Dei Minister [*Minister, or Preacher, of the Word of God*] [*Latin*]
VDM .... Vereinigte Deutsche Metallwerke AG [*United German Metal Workers*]
VDM .... Vibration Damping Mount
VDM .... Video Delta Modulation
VDM .... Viedma [*Argentina*] [*Airport symbol*] (OAG)
VDM .... Vienna Development Method [*Data processing*]
VDM .... Virtual Dipole Moment [*Geodesy*]
VDMA .... Verband Deutscher Maschinen- und Anlagenbau eV [*German Machine Construction Union*] [*Federal Republic of Germany*] (EY)
VDME .... Vibrating Dropping Mercury Electrode [*Electrochemistry*]
VDMIE ...... Verbum Domini Manet in Eternum [*The Word of the Lord Endureth Forever*] [*Latin*]
VDMOS .... Vertical Double Diffused Metal Oxide Semiconductor (MCD)
VDMS .... Video Delta Modulation System
VDMS .... Vocal Data Management System
VDMSC ..... Volunteer Durham Medical Staff Corps [*British military*] (DMA)
VDN .... Varudeklarationsnamnden [*Labeling system*] [*Sweden*]
VDN .... Vedron Ltd. [*Toronto Stock Exchange symbol*]
VDN .... Vereinigte Deutsche Nickel-Werke Aktiengesellschaft [*United German Nickel Works Joint Stock Company*] [*Business term*]
VdN .... Voix des Notres [*Record label*] [*France*]
VDNAA ..... VDI [*Verein Deutscher Ingenieure*] Nachrichten [*A publication*]
VDNCOA ... Veterans Division of the Non-Commissioned Officers Association of the USA (EA)

VDNH .... VD [*Venereal Disease*] National Hotline [*Later, NSTDH*] (EA)
VDO .... Videotron Groupe Ltee. SV [*Toronto Stock Exchange symbol*]
VDOP .... Vertical Dilution of Precision
VD/OS .... Vacuum Distillation/Overflow Sampler [*Nuclear energy*] (NRCH)
VDP .... Vacuum Diffusion Pump
VDP .... Vehicle Deadlined for Parts
VDP .... Verenigde Democratische Partijen [*United Democratic Parties*] [*Surinam*] [*Political party*] (PPW)
VDP .... Vertical Data Processing
VDP .... Vertical Dipole (MCD)
VDP .... Vibration Diagnostic Program
VDP .... Vibration-Dissociation Process
VDP .... Video Data Processor
VDP .... Videodisc Player [*RCA Corp.*]
VDP .... Vincristine, Daunorubicin, Prednisone [*Antineoplastic drug regimen*]
VDP .... Visual Descent Point [*Aviation*] (FAAC)
VDP .... Volunteer Reservists in Drill Pay Status [*Navy*]
VDP .... Von Deutscher Poeterey [*A publication*]
VDPh .... Verhandlung. Versammlung Deutscher Philologen [*A publication*]
VDPI .... Vehicle Direction and Position Indicator
VDPI .... Voyager Data Processing Instructions [*NASA*] (KSC)
VDPP .... Phnom-Penh [*Kampuchea*] [*ICAO location identifier*] (ICLI)
VDPS .... Voice Data Processor System
VDPT .... Pongtuk [*Kampuchea*] [*ICAO location identifier*] (ICLI)
VDQ .... Visual Display of Quality
VDQS .... Vins Delimites de Qualite Superieure [*Designation on French wine labels*]
VDR .... Vader Group, Inc. [*AMEX symbol*] (SPSG)
VDR .... Validated Data Record
VDR .... Variable Deposit Requirement [*Business term*] (ADA)
VDR .... Variable Diameter Rotor
VDR .... Vehicle Deselect Request [*NASA*] (KSC)
VDR .... Vendor Data Request
VDR .... Venous Diameter Ratio [*Cancer detection*]
VDR .... Video Disc Recorder
VDR .... Vitamin D Receptor [*Genetics*]
VDR .... Voice & Data Resources, Inc. [*Ashbury Park, NJ*] [*Information service or system*] [*Telecommunications*] (TSSD)
VDR .... Voice Digitization Rate
VDR .... Voltage-Dependent Resistor (DEN)
VDR .... Voyage Data Recorder
VDRA .... Voice and Data Recording Auxiliary [*NASA*] (KSC)
VDRE .... Vitamin D-Responsive Element [*Biochemistry*]
VDRG .... Vendor Data Release Group (MCD)
VDRL .... Venereal Disease Research Laboratory
VDRT .... Venereal Disease Reference Test [*of Harris*]
VDRY .... Vacu-Dry Co. [*NASDAQ symbol*] (NQ)
VDS .... Vadso [*Norway*] [*Airport symbol*] (OAG)
VDS .... Vapor Deposited Silica [*Optical fiber technology*]
VDS .... Vapor Detection System
VDS .... Variable Depth SONAR
VDS .... Vasodilator Substance [*Physiology*]
VDS .... Vehicle Description Summary [*General Motors Corp.*]
VDS .... Vehicle Dynamics Simulator [*NASA*] (NASA)
VDS .... Velocita di Sedimentazione [*Sedimentation Rate*] [*Medicine*]
VDS .... Vendor Data Service
VDS .... Vendor Direct Shipment
VDS .... Venereal Disease Syphilis
VDS .... Veroeffentlichungen. Deutsche Schillergesellschaft [*A publication*]
VDS .... Vertical Display System [*Navy*]
VDS .... Video Digitizer System (MCD)
VDS .... Vindesine [*Also, E*] [*Antineoplastic drug*]
VDS .... Viola d'Amore Society (EA)
VDS .... Visual Display System
VDS .... Visual Docking Simulator
VDS .... Voice Data Switch
VDSA .... Veut Dieu Saint Amour [*Knights Templar*] [*Freemasonry*]
VDSA .... Video Superstores of America, Inc. [*NASDAQ symbol*] (NQ)
VDSM .... Internationaler Verband der Stadt-, Sport-, und Mehrzweckhallen [*International Federation of City, Sport, and Multi-Purpose Halls*] (EAIO)
VDSP .... Videospection, Inc. [*NASDAQ symbol*] (NQ)
VDSR .... Siem-Reap [*Kampuchea*] [*ICAO location identifier*] (ICLI)
VDSS .... Variable Depth SONAR System
VDSS .... Volume of Distribution at Steady State
VDST .... Stung Treng [*Kampuchea*] [*ICAO location identifier*] (ICLI)
VDSV .... Sihanouk [*Kampuchea*] [*ICAO location identifier*] (ICLI)
VDT .... Van Doorne's Transmissie BV [*Netherlands*] [*Automotive engineering*]
VDT .... Varactor Diode Test
VDT .... Variable Deflection Thruster [*Helicopter*]
VDT .... Variable Density Tunnel
VDT .... Variable Depth Transducer [*Navy*] (NVT)
VDT .... Variable Differential Transformer
VDT .... Vehicle Data Table [*NASA*] (MCD)
VDT .... Video Data Terminal [*Data processing*]

VDT .... Video [*or Visual*] Display Terminal [*Data processing*]
VDT .... Videotex World [*A publication*]
VDTA .... Vacuum Dealers Trade Association   (EA)
VDTIAX.... Flemish Veterinary Journal [*A publication*]
VDTJ .... Voprosy Dialektologii Tjurkskich Jazykov [*A publication*]
VDTT .... Very Difficult to Test [*Audiology*]
VDU........... Refugio, TX [*Location identifier*] [*FAA*]   (FAAL)
VdU............ Verband der Unabhaengigen [*League of Independents*] [*Dissolved, 1956*] [*Austria*]   (PPE)
VDU........... Video [*or Visual*] Display Unit [*Data processing*]
VDV .... Vacuum Differential Valve [*Automotive engineering*]
VDV .... Vojski Drzavne Varnosti [*Yugoslavia*]
VDV .... Vozdushno-Desantnye Voiska [*Airborne Troops*] [*An autonomous command*] [*USSR*]
VD-VF .... Vacuum Distillation - Vapor Filtration
VDVS........ Voeune Sai [*Kampuchea*] [*ICAO location identifier*]   (ICLI)
VDW .... Venus Departure Window [*NASA*]
VDW .... Very Deep Water
VDX .... Vandorex Energy [*Vancouver Stock Exchange symbol*]
VDYK .... Van Dyk Research Corp. [*NASDAQ symbol*]   (NQ)
VDZ........... Valdez [*Alaska*] [*Airport symbol*]   (OAG)
VE .... AVENSA Aerovias Venezolanas SA [*Venezuela*] [*ICAO designator*]   (FAAC)
Ve .... Biblioteca Nacional, Caracas, Venezuela [*Library symbol*] [*Library of Congress*]   (LCLS)
VE .... Vaginal Epithelium [*Endocrinology*]
VE .... Vaginal Examination [*Medicine*]
VE .... Value Effectiveness
VE .... Value Engineering [*Military*]
VE .... Varicose Eczema [*Medicine*]
VE .... Vehicle Experimental   (MCD)
Ve .... Velban [*See VBL*]
VE .... Velocity Equipment   (MCD)
VE .... Velocity Error
ve .... Venezuela [*MARC country of publication code*] [*Library of Congress*]   (LCCP)
VE .... Venezuela [*ANSI two-letter standard code*]   (CNC)
VE .... Ventilating Equipment   (MSA)
VE .... Verbal Emotional (Stimuli) [*Psychology*]
V-E............ VERLORT [*Very-Long-Range Tracking*] Elevation [*NASA*]
VE .... Vermont Music Educators News [*A publication*]
VE .... Vernal Equinox
VE .... Vernier Engine [*as a modifier*]   (AAG)
VE .... Vertical Exaggeration [*Geology*]
Ve .... Vesey, Senior's, English Chancery Reports [*27, 28 English Reprint*] [*A publication*]   (ILCA)
VE .... Vesicular Exanthema [*Virus*]
VE .... Vestnik Evropy [*A publication*]
VE .... Veuve [*Widow*] [*French*]   (ROG)
VE .... Victory in Europe [*as in VE-Day*]
VE .... Vidatron Enterprise Ltd. [*Vancouver Stock Exchange symbol*]
V & E .... Vinethene and Ether
VE .... Visalia Electric Railroad Co. [*AAR code*]
VE .... Visual Efficiency
VE .... Vocational Education   (OICC)
VE .... Voltage Efficiency [*Electrochemistry*]
VE .... Volume Ejection [*Medicine*]
VE .... Voluntary Effort [*A cost containment program established by AHA, AMA, and FAH*]
VE .... Votre Eminence [*Your Eminence*] [*French*]
VE .... Vox Evangelica [*A publication*]
V-E (Day) .. Victory in Europe Day [*World War II*]
VEA .... Value Engineering Audit
VEA .... Vehicle Engineering Analysis
VEA .... Veliger Escape Aperture
VEA .... Veterans Educational Assistance [*Act*]
VEA .... Viral Envelope Antigens [*Immunology*]
VEA .... Vocational Education Act [*1963*]
VEA .... Voluntary Employment Agreement [*Australia*]
VEAB Ert.. VEAB Ertesitoe [*Hungary*] [*A publication*]
VEAMCOP ... Viking Error Analysis Monte Carlo Program [*Data processing*]
VEAN .... Along [*India*] [*ICAO location identifier*]   (ICLI)
VEAP........ Veterans Educational Assistance Program [*DoD*]
VEAT........ Agartala [*India*] [*ICAO location identifier*]   (ICLI)
VEAZ........ Aizwal [*India*] [*ICAO location identifier*]   (ICLI)
Veazey....... Veazey's Reports [*36-44 Vermont*] [*A publication*]   (DLA)
VEB .... Financieel Ekonomische Tijd [*A publication*]
VEB .... Variable Elevation Beam [*RADAR*]
VE & B...... Vehicle Energy and Biotechnology   (MCD)
VEB .... Ventricular Ectopic Beats [*Cardiology*]
VEB .... Venus Entry Body [*NASA*]
Ve & B....... Vesey and Beames' English Chancery Reports [*35 English Reprint*] [*A publication*]   (DLA)
VEB .... Vneshekonombank [*State Bank for Foreign Economic Affairs*] [*USSR*]
VEB .... Vocational Education Board   (OICC)
VEBA........ Calcutta (Behala) [*India*] [*ICAO location identifier*]   (ICLI)
VEBA........ Vereinigte Elektrizitaets und Bergwerks, AG [*Holding company*] [*Germany*]

VEBA........ Voluntary Employee Benefit Association [*Type of trust established by a company, a union, or both to provide members with various insurance benefits*]
VEBC........ Berachampa [*India*] [*ICAO location identifier*]   (ICLI)
VEBD .... Baghdogra [*India*] [*ICAO location identifier*]   (ICLI)
VEBG .... Balurghat [*India*] [*ICAO location identifier*]   (ICLI)
VEBK .... Bokaro [*India*] [*ICAO location identifier*]   (ICLI)
VEBL .... Barbil [*India*] [*ICAO location identifier*]   (ICLI)
VEBR........ Visual Evoked Brain Response
VEBS........ Bhubaneswar [*India*] [*ICAO location identifier*]   (ICLI)
VEB Verlag Tech Mon Tech Rev ... VEB [*Volkseigener Betrieb*] Verlag Technik. Monthly Technical Review [*A publication*]
VEBW........ Vacuum Electron Beam Welder
VEC .... Vacation Exchange Club   (EA)
VEC .... Value Engineering Change
VEC .... Variable Energy Cyclotron   (IEEE)
VEC .... Vector   (KSC)
VEC .... Vector Control   (MUGU)
VEC .... Vertical Electrical Chase [*Nuclear energy*]   (NRCH)
VeC .... Vertice (Coimbra) [*A publication*]
VEC .... Vibration Exciter Control
VEC .... Video-Enhanced Contrast Technique [*Microscopy*]
VEC .... Voice Equivalent Channel   (MCD)
VeCAL....... Archivo del Libertador, Caracas, Venezuela [*Library symbol*] [*Library of Congress*]   (LCLS)
VECAS ...... Vertical Escape Collision Avoidance System [*Aviation*]
VECC......... Calcutta [*India*] [*ICAO location identifier*]   (ICLI)
VECC......... Value Engineering Control Committee [*Military*]
VECC......... Variable Energy Content Curves   (NOAA)
VECF......... Calcutta [*India*] [*ICAO location identifier*]   (ICLI)
VECHCC... Voluntary Effort to Contain Health Care Costs   (EA)
VECI......... Vehicular Equipment Complement Index   (IEEE)
VECIB .... Vehicle Engineering Change Implementation Board   (NASA)
VECK........ Chakulia [*India*] [*ICAO location identifier*]   (ICLI)
VECM .... Vocational Education Curriculum Materials Database [*University of California, Berkeley*] [*Information service or system*]   (CRD)
VECO .... Cooch-Behar [*India*] [*ICAO location identifier*]   (ICLI)
VECO .... Vernier Engine Cutoff [*Aerospace*]
VECOS ...... Vehicle Checkout Set
VECP .... Value Engineering Change Proposal [*Military*]
VECP......... Visually Evoked Cortical Potential [*Neurophysiology*]
VECR........ Vendor Engineering Change Request [*DoD*]
VECS........ Vocational Education Curriculum Specialists   (OICC)
Vect .... De Vectigalibus [*of Xenophon*] [*Classical studies*]   (OCD)
V-ECT .... Ventricular Ectopy
VECTAC .... Vectored Attack [*Navy*]   (NVT)
VECTAR ... Value, Expertise, Client, Time, Attorney, Result [*Lawyer evaluation method*]
VECTRAN ... [*A*] programming language   (CSR)
VECX......... Car Nicobar [*India*] [*ICAO location identifier*]   (ICLI)
VED .... Vacuum Energy Diverter
VED........... Vacuum Erection Device [*Medicine*]
VED........... Ventricular Ectopic Depolarization
VED........... Victoria Education Department [*Australia*]
VED........... Viscoelastic Damper
VED........... Volumetric Energy Density [*of fuels*]
VEDAR ... Visible Energy Detection and Ranging
Veda Tech Mladezi ... Veda a Technika Mladezi [*Czechoslovakia*] [*A publication*]
Veda Tech SSSR ... Veda a Technika v SSSR [*A publication*]
Veda Vyzk Potravin Prum ... Veda a Vyzkum v Potravinarskem Prumyslu [*A publication*]
Veda Vyzk Prum Sklarskem ... Veda a Vyzkum v Prumyslu Sklarskem [*A publication*]
Veda Vyzk Prum Text ... Veda a Vyzkum v Prumyslu Textilnim [*A publication*]
VEDB .... Dhanbad [*India*] [*ICAO location identifier*]   (ICLI)
Vedeckovyzk Uhelny Ustav Sb Vyzk Pr ... Vedeckovyzkumny Uhelny Ustav Sbornik Vyzkumnych Praci [*Czechoslovakia*] [*A publication*]
Ved Inf CSAV ... Vedecke Informace CSAV [*Ceskoslovenska Akademie Ved*] [*A publication*]
Ved Kes ... Vedanta Kesari [*Madras*] [*A publication*]
VeDo .... Verbum Domino [*A publication*]
Ved Prace Ustr Vyzk Ustavu Rost Vyr (Praha) ... Vedecke Prace Ustredniho Vyzkumneho Ustavu Rostlinne Vyroby (Praha) [*A publication*]
Ved Prace Vyskum Ust Lesn Hosp Zvolen ... Vedecke Prace Vyskumny Ustav Lesneho Hospodarstva v Zvolene [*A publication*]
Ved Prace Vysk Ustavu Kukurice Trnave ... Vedecke Prace Vyskumneho Ustavu Kukurice v Trnave [*A publication*]
Ved Prace Vysk Ustavu Rastlinnej Vyr ... Vedecke Prace Vyskumneho Ustavu Rastlinnej Vyroby [*A publication*]
Ved Prace Vysk Ustavu Zavlahov Hospod Bratislave ... Vedecke Prace Vyskumneho Ustavu Zavlahoveho Hospodarstva v Bratislave [*A publication*]
Ved Prace Vysk Ustavu Zivoc Nitre ... Vedecke Prace Vyskumneho Ustavu Zivocisnej Vyroby v Nitre [*A publication*]

Ved Prace Vyzkum Ust Melior ... Vedecke Prace Vyzkumneho Ustavu Zemedelsko-Lesnickych Melioraci CSAZV [*Ceskoslovenska Akademie Zemedelskych Ved*] v Praze [*A publication*]

Ved Pr Cesk Zemed Muz ... Vedecke Prace Ceskoslovenskeho Zemedelskeho Muzea [*A publication*]

Ved Pr Lab Podoznalectva Bratisl ... Vedecke Prace Laboratoria Podoznalectva v Bratislave [*A publication*]

Ved Pr Ustavu Zelinarskeho Olomouci ... Vedecke Prace Ustavu Zelinarskeho v Olomouci [*A publication*]

Ved Pr Ustr Vyzk Ust Rostl Vyroby Praze-Ruzyni ... Vedecke Prace Ustredniho Vyzkumneho Ustavu Rostlinne Vyroby v Praze-Ruzyni [*A publication*]

Ved Pr VSCHK (Slatinany) ... Vedecke Prace VSCHK [*Vyzkumna Stanice pro Chov Koni*] (Slatinany) [*A publication*]

Ved Pr Vysk Ustav Rastl Vyroby Piestanoch ... Vedecke Prace Vyskumneho Ustavu Rastlinnej Vyroby v Piestanoch [*A publication*]

Ved Pr Vysk Ustavu Chov Hydiny Ivanka Dunaji ... Vedecke Prace Vyskumneho Ustavu pro Chov Hydiny v Ivanka pri Dunaji [*A publication*]

Ved Pr Vysk Ustavu pro Chov Hydiny Ivanka pri Dunaji ... Vedecke Prace Vyskumneho Ustavu pro Chov Hydiny v Ivanka pri Dunaji [*A publication*]

Ved Pr Vysk Ustavu Chov Skotu Caz Rapotine ... Vedecke Prace Vyskumneho Ustavu pro Chov Skotu Caz v Rapotine [*A publication*]

Ved Pr Vysk Ustavu Kukurice Trnave ... Vedecke Prace Vyskumneho Ustavu Kukurice v Trnave [*A publication*]

Ved Pr Vysk Ustavu Lesn Hospod Zvolene ... Vedecke Prace Vyskumneho Ustavu Lesneho Hospodarstva v Zvolene [*A publication*]

Ved Pr Vysk Ustavu Lesn Hospod v Zvolene ... Vedecke Prace Vyskumneho Ustavu Lesneho Hospodarstva v Zvolene [*A publication*]

Ved Pr Vysk Ustavu Luk Pasienkov Banskej Bystrici ... Vedecke Prace Vyskumneho Ustavu Luk a Pasienkov v Banskej Bystrici [*A publication*]

Ved Pr Vysk Ustavu Ovciar Trencine ... Vedecke Prace Vyskumneho Ustavu Ovciarskeho v Trencine [*A publication*]

Ved Pr Vysk Ustavu Podoznalectva Vyz Rastl Bratislave ... Vedecke Prace Vyskumneho Ustavu Podoznalectva a Vyzivy Rastlin v Bratislave [*A publication*]

Ved Pr Vysk Ustavu Podoznalectva Vyz Rastlin Bratisl ... Vedecke Prace Vyskumneho Ustavu Podoznalectva a Vyzivy Rastlin v Bratislave [*A publication*]

Ved Pr Vysk Ustavu Rastlinnej Vyroby Piestanoch ... Vedecke Prace Vyskumneho Ustavu Rastlinnej Vyroby v Piestanoch [*A publication*]

Ved Pr Vysk Ustavu Rastl Vyroby Piestanoch ... Vedecke Prace Vyskumneho Ustavu Rastlinnej Vyroby v Piestanoch [*A publication*]

Ved Pr Vysk Ustavu Zavlahoveho Hospod Bratisl ... Vedecke Prace Vyskumneho Ustavu Zavlahoveho Hospodarstva v Bratislave [*A publication*]

Ved Pr Vysk Ustavu Zivocisnej Vyroby Nitre ... Vedecke Prace Vyskumneho Ustavu Zivocisnej Vyroby v Nitre [*A publication*]

Ved Pr Vysk Ustav Zavlahov Hospod ... Vedecke Prace Vyskumny Ustavu Zavlahoveho Hospodarstva [*A publication*]

Ved Pr Vysk Ustav Zivoc Vyroby Nitre ... Vedecke Prace Vyskumneho Ustavu Zivocisnej Vyroby v Nitre [*A publication*]

Ved Pr Vysk Ust Rastl Vyroby Piestanoch ... Vedecke Prace Ustredniho Vyskumneho Ustavu Rastlinnej Vyroby Piestanoch [*A publication*]

Ved Pr Vysk Ust Rastl Vyroby Praze-Ruzyni ... Vedecke Prace Ustredniho Vyskumneho Ustavu Rastlinnej Vyroby CSAZV [*Ceskoslovenska Akademie Zemedelskych Ved*] v Praze-Ruzyni [*A publication*]

Ved Pr Vyzk Stanice Chov Koni Slatinany ... Vedecke Prace Vyzkumna Stanice pro Chov Koni Slatinany [*A publication*]

Ved Pr Vyzk Ustav Melior ... Vedecke Prace. Vyzkumny Ustav Melioraci [*A publication*]

Ved Pr Vyzk Ustavu Bramborarskeho Havlickove Brode ... Vedecke Prace Vyzkumneho Ustavu Bramborarskeho v Havlickove Brode [*A publication*]

Ved Pr Vyzk Ustavu Chov Prasat Kostelci Nad Orlice ... Vedecke Prace Vyzkumneho Ustavu pro Chov Prasat v Kostelci Nad Orlice [*A publication*]

Ved Pr Vyzk Ustavu Chov Skotu Caz Rapotine ... Vedecke Prace Vyzkumneho Ustavu pro Chov Skotu Caz v Rapotine [*A publication*]

Ved Pr Vyzk Ustavu Krmivarskeho CSAZV Brne ... Vedecke Prace Vyzkumneho Ustavu Krmivarskeho CSAZV [*Ceskoslovenska Akademie Zemedelskych Ved*] v Brne [*A publication*]

Ved Pr Vyzk Ustavu Melior Praze ... Vedecke Prace Vyzkumneho Ustavu Melioraci v Praze [*A publication*]

Ved Pr Vyzk Ustavu Melior Praze Zbraslavi ... Vedecke Prace Vyzkumneho Ustavu Melioraci v Praze or Zbraslavi [*A publication*]

Ved Pr Vyzk Ustavu Obilnarskeho Kromerizi ... Vedecke Prace Vyzkumneho Ustavu Obilnarskeho v Kromerizi [*A publication*]

Ved Pr Vyzk Ustavu Okrasneho Zahradnictvi Pruhonicich ... Vedecke Prace Vyzkumneho Ustavu Okrasneho Zahradnictvi v Pruhonicich [*A publication*]

Ved Pr Vyzk Ustavu Ovilnarskeho Kromerizi ... Vedecke Prace Vyzkumneho Ustavu Ovilnarskeho v Kromerizi [*A publication*]

Ved Pr Vyzk Ustavu Rostl Vyroby Praze Ruzyni ... Vedecke Prace Vyzkumnych Ustavu Rostlinne Vyroby v Praze-Ruzyni [*A publication*]

Ved Pr Vyzk Ustavu Vcelarskeho Dole Libcic ... Vedecke Prace Vyzkumneho Ustavu Vcelarskeho v Dole u Libcic [*A publication*]

Ved Pr Vyzk Ustavu Vet CSAZV Brne ... Vedecke Prace Vyzkumneho Ustavu Veterinarni CSAZV [*Ceskoslovenska Akademie Zemedelskych Ved*] v Brne [*A publication*]

Ved Pr Vyzk Ustavu Vet Lek Brne ... Vedecke Prace Vyzkumneho Ustavu Veterinarniho Lekarstvi v Brne [*Czechoslovakia*] [*A publication*]

Ved Pr Vyzk Ustavu Zavlahoveho Hospod Bratislave ... Vedecke Prace Vyzkumneho Ustavu Zavlahoveho Hospodarstva v Bratislave [*A publication*]

Ved Pr Vyzk Ust Vcelar v Dole u Libcic ... Vedecke Prace Vyzkumneho Ustavu Vcelarskeho v Dole u Libcic [*A publication*]

VEDR .... Value Engineering Design Review

VEDS .... Vehicle Emergency Detection System [*NASA*] (KSC)

VEDS .... Vocational Education Data System

Ved Svet ..... Vedecky Svet [*A publication*]

VEDZ .... Deparizo [*India*] [*ICAO location identifier*] (ICLI)

VEE .... Vagina, Ectocervix, and Endocervix [*Cytopathology*]

VEE .... Veeco Instruments, Inc. [*NYSE symbol*] (SPSG)

VEE .... Venetie [*Alaska*] [*Airport symbol*] (OAG)

VEE .... Venezuelan Equine Encephalomyelitis [*Virus*]

Veeartsenijk Blad Nederl-Indie ... Veeartsenijkundige Bladen voor Nederlandsch-Indie [*A publication*]

VEECO .... Vacuum Electronics Engineering Company (MCD)

VEED .... Veeco Instruments, Inc. [*NASDAQ symbol*] (NQ)

VEEG .... Vector Electroencephalograph

VEEGA ...... Venus-Earth-Earth-Gravity-Assist [*Spacecraft trajectory*]

VEEI .... Vehicle Electrical Engine Interface [*NASA*] (NASA)

VEEP .... Vice President

VEER .... Variable Emergence Electronically Rotated (MCD)

VEESS .... Vehicle Engine Exhaust Smoke System [*Army*] (RDA)

Veeteelt Zuivelber ... Veeteelt- en Zuivelberichten [*A publication*]

VEF .... Variable Electronic Filter

VEF .... Viscoelastic Fiber

VEF .... Viscoelastic Flow

VEF .... Vision Educational Foundation (EA)

VEF .... Visually Evoked Field [*Neurophysiology*]

VEFCA ...... Value Engineering Functional Cost Analysis

VEFCO .... Vertical Function Checkout

VEF Inf Bul ... VEF [*Victorian Employers' Federation*] Information Bulletin [*A publication*] (APTA)

VEG .... Maikwak [*Guyana*] [*Airport symbol*] (OAG)

VEG .... Value Engineering Guideline

Veg .... Vega [*Record label*] [*France*]

VEG .... Vegetable [*or Vegetation*] (KSC)

VEGA .... Vega Biotechnologies, Inc. [*NASDAQ symbol*] (NQ)

VEGA .... Venera [*Venus*] and Gallei [*Halley*] [*Russian spacecraft*]

VEGANET ... Vegetarian Awareness Network (EA)

Veg Crops Ser Calif Univ Dept Veg Crops ... Vegetable Crops Series. California University. Department of Vegetable Crops [*A publication*]

Vegetarian Mo ... Vegetarian Monthly [*A publication*] (APTA)

Veg Ex .... Vegetable Exchange [*Dietetics*]

VEGG .... Ventura Entertainment Group, Ltd. [*NASDAQ symbol*] (NQ)

Veg Grower ... Vegetable Grower [*A publication*] (APTA)

Veg Grow News ... Vegetable Growers News [*A publication*]

VEGIL .... Vehicle Equipment and Government-Furnished Infrared Locator

VEGK .... Gorakhpur [*India*] [*ICAO location identifier*] (ICLI)

VEGL .... Value Engineering Guideline

Veg Situat TVS US Dep Agric Econ Res Serv ... Vegetable Situation. United States Department of Agriculture. Economic Research [*A publication*]

VEGT .... Gauhati [*India*] [*ICAO location identifier*] (ICLI)

Veg Times ... Vegetarian Times [*A publication*]

VEGY .... Gaya [*India*] [*ICAO location identifier*] (ICLI)

Vegyip Kut Intez Kozl ... Vegyipari Kutato Intezetek Kozlemenyei [*A publication*]

VEH .... Emory and Henry College, Emory, VA [*OCLC symbol*] (OCLC)

VEH .... Valence Effective Hamiltonian [*Physical chemistry*]

VEH .... Vehicle (AFM)

VEH .... Veterinary Evacuation Hospital

VEHID .... Vehicle Identification [*NASA*] (MCD)

VEHK .... Hirakud [*India*] [*ICAO location identifier*] (ICLI)

Veh News Ltr ... Experimental Vehicle Newsletter [*A publication*]

Veh Syst Dyn ... Vehicle System Dynamics [*A publication*]

VEI .... Value Engineered Indicator (NG)

VEI .... Value Engineering Incentive [*Office of Federal Procurement Policy*]

VEI .... Vehicle End Item (NASA)

VEI .... Volcanic Explosivity Index [*Measure of amounts of gas and ash that reach the atmosphere*]

VEIM .... Imphal [*India*] [*ICAO location identifier*] (ICLI)

VEIS .... Vocational Education Information System

VEITA .... Vietnam Era Veterans Inter-Tribal Association (EA)

VEJ............ DHZ Markt. Vakblad voor de Doe het Zelf Ondernemer [*A publication*]
VEJH........ Jharsuguda [*India*] [*ICAO location identifier*]   (ICLI)
VEJP .... Jeypore [*India*] [*ICAO location identifier*]   (ICLI)
VEJS......... Jamshedpur [*India*] [*ICAO location identifier*]   (ICLI)
VEJT .... Jorhat [*India*] [*ICAO location identifier*]   (ICLI)
VEK .... Veterana Esperantista Klubo [*Esperantist Club of Veterans - ECV*]   (EAIO)
VEKH .... Katihar [*India*] [*ICAO location identifier*]   (ICLI)
VEKJ .... Keonjhar [*India*] [*ICAO location identifier*]   (ICLI)
VEKM .... Kamalpur [*India*] [*ICAO location identifier*]   (ICLI)
VEKN .... Konark [*India*] [*ICAO location identifier*]   (ICLI)
VEKR........ Kailashahar [*India*] [*ICAO location identifier*]   (ICLI)
VEKU .... Silchar/Kumbhirgram [*India*] [*ICAO location identifier*]   (ICLI)
VEKW .... Khowai [*India*] [*ICAO location identifier*]   (ICLI)
VEL........... Vehicle Emissions and Fuel Economy Laboratory [*Texas A & M University*] [*Research center*]   (RCD)
Vel.............. Vela [*Constellation*]
VEL........... Vellum
VEL........... Velocity   (AFM)
Vel............. Veltro' [*A publication*]
VEL........... Vernal [*Utah*] [*Airport symbol*]   (OAG)
VEL........... Virginia Electric & Power Co. [*NYSE symbol*]   (SPSG)
VELARC... Vertical Ejection Launch Aero-Reaction Control   (MCD)
VELC........ Velcro Industries NV [*NASDAQ symbol*]   (NQ)
VELCOR... Velocity Correction
VELCRO... Velour and Crochet [*Interlocking nylon tapes - one with tiny loops, the other with tiny hooks - invented as a reusable fastener by George de Mestral*]
VELF........ Velocity Filter   (IEEE)
VELG........ Velocity Gain   (AAG)
VELKDDR ... Vereinigte Evangelisch-Lutherische Kirche in der Deutschen Demokratischen Republik [*United Evangelical-Lutheran Church of the German Democratic Republic*] [*German Democratic Republic*]   (EY)
Vell Pat...... Velleius Paterculus [*First century AD*] [*Classical studies*]   (OCD)
Vel Lt Trap ... Velvet Light Trap [*A publication*]
VELOC....... Velocity
VELR........ Lilabari/North Lakhimpur [*India*] [*ICAO location identifier*]   (ICLI)
VELXF ...... Velvet Exploration Co. Ltd. [*NASDAQ symbol*]   (NQ)
VEM .... Eastern Mennonite College, Harrisonburg, VA [*OCLC symbol*]   (OCLC)
VEM .... Value Engineering Model   (NG)
VEM .... Vasoexcitor Material [*Physiology*]
VEM .... Vendor Engineering Memorandum   (MCD)
VEM .... Versatile Exercise Mine [*Navy*] [*British*]
VEM .... Vertical Extent of Mortality [*Intertidal organisms*]
Vema Res Ser ... Vema Research Series [*A publication*]
VEMASID ... Vehicle Magnetic Signature Duplicator   (MCD)
VEMH....... Malda [*India*] [*ICAO location identifier*]   (ICLI)
VEMN....... Mohanbari [*India*] [*ICAO location identifier*]   (ICLI)
VEMS........ Vehicle and Equipment Maintenance System [*Software*]
VEMZ .... Mazuffarpur [*India*] [*ICAO location identifier*]   (ICLI)
VEN .... Hawaiian Sky Tours [*Honolulu, HI*] [*FAA designator*]   (FAAC)
VEN .... Variable Exhaust Nozzle
Ven.......... Vendome [*Record label*] [*France*]
VEN .... Venerable
VEN .... Venetian
VEN .... Venezuela [*ANSI three-letter standard code*]   (CNC)
VEN .... Venice [*Italy*] [*Seismograph station code, US Geological Survey*] [*Closed*]   (SEIS)
VEN .... Venite [*95th Psalm*]
VEN .... Venture [*A publication*]
VEN .... Venture Gold Corp. [*Vancouver Stock Exchange symbol*]
VEN .... Venture Science Fiction [*A publication*]
VEN .... Venture Stores, Inc. [*NYSE symbol*]   (SPSG)
Ven............ Venus and Adonis [*Shakespearean work*]
VenAmCham ... Venezuelan-American Chamber of Commerce and Industry   (EA)
Vend.......... Vending Times [*A publication*]
Vend.......... Vending Times International Buyers Guide and Directory [*A publication*]
VEND........ Vendor   (KSC)
VEND........ Venerated
VENDAC .. Vendor Data Control
Vend Intnl ... Vending International [*A publication*]
VENET...... Venetian   (ROG)
VEN EX..... Venditione Exponas [*Writ of Execution for Sheriff to Sell Goods*] [*Latin*]   (ROG)
VENEZ...... Venezuela
Venez Dir Geol Bol Geol ... Venezuela. Direccion de Geologia. Boletin de Geologia [*A publication*]
Venez Dir Geol Bol Geol Publ Esp ... Venezuela. Direccion de Geologia. Boletin de Geologia. Publicacion Especial [*A publication*]
Venez Inst Nac Nutr Publ ... Venezuela. Instituto Nacional de Nutricion. Publicacion [*A publication*]

Venez Min Minas Hidrocarburos Dir Geol Bol Geol ... Venezuela. Ministerio de Minas e Hidrocarburos. Direccion de Geologia. Boletin de Geologia [*A publication*]
Venez Odontol ... Venezuela Odontologica [*A publication*]
Venez Univ Cent Esc Geol Minas Lab Petrogr Geoquimica Inf ... Venezuela. Universidad Central. Escuela de Geologia y Minas. Laboratorio de Petrografia y Geoquimica. Informe [*A publication*]
Venez UTD ... Venezuela Up-to-Date [*A publication*]
VEN FA..... Venire Facias [*Writ to Sheriff to Summon Jury*] [*Latin*]   (ROG)
Vengarskaya Farmakoter ... Vengarskaya Farmakoterapiya [*A publication*]
Veng Zh Gorn Dela Metall Gorn Delo ... Vengerskii Zhurnal Gornogo Dela i Metallurgii. Gornoe Delo [*A publication*]
VENP....... Nawapara [*India*] [*ICAO location identifier*]   (ICLI)
VENP .... Vincristine, Endoxan [*Cyclophosphamide*], Natulan [*Procarbazine*], Prednisone [*Antineoplastic drug regimen*]
VenPK........ Venizelikon Phileleftheron Komma [*Venizelist Liberal Party*] [*Greek*] [*Political party*]   (PPE)
VENR .... Veneer
VENT .... Ventilation   (AFM)
VENT .... Ventilator
VENT .... Ventricular [*Cardiology*]
VENT .... Ventriloquist
Vent........... Ventris' English Common Pleas Reports [*86 English Reprint*] [*A publication*]   (DLA)
Vent........... Ventris' English King's Bench Reports [*A publication*]   (DLA)
VENT .... Venturian Corp. [*NASDAQ symbol*]   (NQ)
Vent (Eng) ... Ventris' English Common Pleas Reports [*86 English Reprint*] [*A publication*]   (DLA)
Vent (Eng) ... Ventris' English King's Bench Reports [*A publication*]   (DLA)
Vent Forth ... Venture Forth [*A publication*]
Vent Kond Vozdukha Zdanii ... Ventilyatsiya i Konditsionirovanie Vozdukha Zdanii [*A publication*]
Vent Kond Vozdukha Zdanii Sooruzh ... Ventilyatsiya i Konditsionirovanie Vozdukha Zdanii Sooruzhenii [*A publication*]
Vent Ochistka Vozdukha ... Ventilyatsiya i Ochistka Vozdukha [*A publication*]
ventr .... Ventral
Ventr .... Ventris' English Common Pleas Reports [*86 English Reprint*] [*A publication*]   (DLA)
Ventr Dev... News from Venture Development Corporation [*A publication*]
ventric .... Ventricular
Vent Shakht Rudn ... Ventilyatsiya Shakht i Rudnikov [*A publication*]
Venul........... Venuleius Saturninus [*Flourished, 2nd century*] [*Authority cited in pre-1607 legal work*]   (DSA)
VENUS...... Valuable and Effective Network Utility Services   (BUR)
VENUS...... Video-Enhanced User System [*Video conferencing*]
VENUS...... Vulcain Experimental Nuclear Study [*Nuclear reactor*] [*Belgium*]
Venus Jpn J Malacol ... Venus: The Japanese Journal of Malacology [*A publication*]
VEO .... Value Engineering Organization
VEO .... Veronex Resources Ltd. [*Vancouver Stock Exchange symbol*]
VEOA .... Victorian Education Officers Association [*Australia*]
VEOFA....... Vestnik Oftal'mologii [*A publication*]
VEOS........ Versatile Electro-Optical System   (MCD)
VEP........... Value Engineering Program
VEP........... Value Engineering Proposal [*Army*]   (RDA)
VEP........... Vector Equilibrium Principle [*Crystallography*]
VEP........... Verbrauchsendpreis [*Retail Sales Price*] [*German*] [*Business term*]
VEP........... Verpakken. Het Vakblad voor de Verpakkende Industrie en Verpakkingsindustrie [*A publication*]
VEP........... Vertical Extrusion Press
VEP........... Veterans Education Project   (EA)
VEP........... Visually Evoked Potential [*Neurophysiology*]
VEP........... Vocational Exploration Program [*Office of Youth Programs*]
VEP........... Vojno-Ekonomski Pregled [*A publication*]
VEP........... Voter Education Project
VEPA........ Vincristine, Endoxan [*Cyclophosphamide*], Prednisone, Adriamycin [*Antineoplastic drug regimen*]
VEPA........ Vocational Education Planning Areas   (OICC)
VEPB........ Port Blair [*India*] [*ICAO location identifier*]   (ICLI)
VEPCO...... Virginia Electric & Power Company
VEPG...... Pasighat [*India*] [*ICAO location identifier*]   (ICLI)
VEPG........ Value Engineering Program Guideline
VEPH........ Panagarh [*India*] [*ICAO location identifier*]   (ICLI)
VEPIS....... Vocational Education Program Information System
VEPL........ Vendor Engineering Procurement Liaison   (MCD)
VEPM........ Value Engineering Program Manager [*Military*]   (AABC)
VEPN........ Phulbani [*India*] [*ICAO location identifier*]   (ICLI)
VEPP........ Padampur [*India*] [*ICAO location identifier*]   (ICLI)
VEPR........ Value Engineering Program Requirement [*Office of Federal Procurement Policy*]   (NG)
VEPT........ Patna [*India*] [*ICAO location identifier*]   (ICLI)
VEQ .... Visiting Enlisted Quarters [*Army*]   (AABC)
VEQUD...... Veterinary Quarterly [*A publication*]
VER .... Boonville, MO [*Location identifier*] [*FAA*]   (FAAL)
VER .... Veracruz [*Mexico*] [*Airport symbol*]   (OAG)
VER .... Verandah [*Classified advertising*]   (ADA)
VER .... Verapamil [*A coronary vasodilator*]

VeR .... Verbum (Rio De Janeiro) [*A publication*]
VER .... Verein [*Association*] [*German*]
Ver .... Vereniging [*Association*] [*Dutch*]   (ILCA)
VER .... Verfkroniek [*A publication*]
VER .... Verge   (ROG)
VER .... Verify   (AFM)
VER .... Verit Industries [*AMEX symbol*]   (SPSG)
Ver .... Veritas [*A publication*]
VER .... Vermifuge [*Destroying Worms*] [*Pharmacy*]   (ROG)
VER .... Vermilion   (ROG)
VER .... Vermillion Resources [*Vancouver Stock Exchange symbol*]
VER .... Vermont   (ROG)
Ver .... Vermont Reports [*A publication*]   (DLA)
VER .... Vernier [*Engine*]   (AAG)
Ver .... Verri [*A publication*]
Ver .... Versamento [*Payment*] [*Italian*] [*Business term*]
VER .... Verse
VER .... Version   (ROG)
Ver .... Versty [*A publication*]
VER .... Vert [*Heraldry*]
VER .... Vertical   (KSC)
VER .... Vertical Earth Rate
VER .... Verwaltungsfuehrung Organisation Personalwesen [*A publication*]
VER .... Veterans Employment Representative [*Department of Labor*]
VER .... Visual Evoked Response
VER .... Voluntary Export Restraints
VERA .... Ranuna [*India*] [*ICAO location identifier*]   (ICLI)
VERA .... Variable Eddington Radiation Approximation   (MCD)
VERA .... Versatile Experimental Reactor Assembly   (DEN)
VERA .... Veterans' Employment and Readjustment Act of 1972
VERA .... Vision Electric Recording Apparatus [*BBC*]
VERAD9 .. Veterinary Radiology [*A publication*]
VERAS ...... Vehicule Experimental de Recherches Aerothermodynamique et Structurale [*Glider*] [*France*]
VERB........ Verbatim   (MSA)
VERB........ Verbessert [*Improved*] [*German*]
VERB........ Victor Electrowriter Remote Blackboard [*Educational device of Victor Comptometer Corp.*]
Verb C........ Verbum Caro [*A publication*]
VERB ET LIT ... Verbatim et Literatim [*Word for Word, An Exact Copy*] [*Latin*]   (ROG)
Ver Bibl Landes NRW Mitt ... Verband der Bibliotheken des Landes Nordrhein-Westfalen. Mitteilungsblatt [*A publication*]
Ver Bl........ Verordeningblad voor het Bezette Nederlandse Gebied [*A publication*]
Verb Sap .... Verbum Sapienti Sat Est [*A Word to the Wise Is Sufficient*] [*Latin*]
VERC........ Ranchi [*India*] [*ICAO location identifier*]   (ICLI)
VERC........ Vacation Eligibility and Request Card [*Military*]
VERC........ Vehicle Effectiveness Remaining Converter
VERDAN .. Versatile Differential Analyzer
Ver Destill Ztg ... Vereinigte Destillateur-Zeitungen [*A publication*]
VERDIN.... Antijam MODEM [*Modulate, Demodulate*], Very-Low Frequency   (CAAL)
Verdi Newsl ... Verdi Newsletter [*A publication*]
VERDT...... Verdict   (ROG)
Ver Dtsch Ing Z ... Verein Deutscher Ingenieure. Zeitschrift [*A publication*]
Ver Dtsch Ing Z Fortschr Ber Reihe 5 ... Verein Deutscher Ingenieure. Zeitschriften. Fortschritt-Berichte. Reihe 5. Grund- und Werkstoffe [*A publication*]
Vereinigung Schweizer Petroleum-Geologen u Ingenieure Bull ... Vereinigung Schweizerischer Petroleum-Geologen und Ingenieure. Bulletin [*A publication*]
Vereinte Nationen ... Zeitschrift fuer die Vereinten Nationen und Ihre Sonderorganisationen [*A publication*]
Ver Erdk Dresden Mitt ... Verein fuer Erdkunde zu Dresden. Mitteilungen [*A publication*]
Ver Erdk Leipzig Mitt ... Verein fuer Erdkunde zu Leipzig. Mitteilungen [*A publication*]
Ver Exploit Proefzuivelboerderij Hoorn Versl ... Vereniging tot Exploitatie eener Proefzuivelboerderij te Hoorn. Verslag [*A publication*]
Verfahrenstech ... Verfahrenstechnik International [*A publication*]
Verfass Recht Uebersee ... Verfassung und Recht in Uebersee [*A publication*]
Verfassung u -Wirklichkeit ... Verfassung und Verfassungswirklichkeit [*A publication*]
VerfGH...... Verfassungsgerichtshof [*Provincial Constitutional Court*] [*German*]   (DLA)
Verfinst TNO Circ ... Verfinstituut TNO [*Nederlands Centrale Organisatie voor Toegepast - Natuurwetenschappelijk Onderzoek*] Circulaire [*A publication*]
Ver Freunde Naturg Mecklenberg Arch ... Verein der Freunde der Naturgeschichte in Mecklenburg. Archiv [*A publication*]
Ver Freunden Erdk Leipzig Jber ... Verein von Freunden der Erdkunde zu Leipzig. Jahresbericht [*A publication*]
VERG .... Rayaguda [*India*] [*ICAO location identifier*]   (ICLI)
Verg........... Vergil [*First century BC*] [*Classical studies*]   (OCD)
Ver f d Gesch Berlins Schr ... Verein fuer die Geschichte Berlins. Schriften [*A publication*]

Ver f Gesch Dresdens Mitt ... Verein fuer Geschichte Dresdens. Mitteilungen [*A publication*]
VERGL...... Vergleische [*Compare*] [*German*]   (ROG)
Verh Anat Ges ... Verhandlungen. Anatomische Gesellschaft [*A publication*]
Verhandl Deutsch Path Gesellsch ... Verhandlungen. Deutsche Pathologische Gesellschaft [*A publication*]
Verhandl Deutsch Zool Gesellsch ... Verhandlungen. Deutsche Zoologische Gesellschaft [*A publication*]
Verhandl DPG ... Verhandlungen. Deutsche Physikalische Gesellschaft [*Stuttgart*] [*A publication*]
Verhandl Geol Bundesanstalt ... Verhandlungen. Geologische Bundesanstalt [*A publication*]
Verhandl Gesellsch Deutsch Naturf u Aerzte ... Verhandlungen. Gesellschaft Deutscher Naturforscher und Aerzte [*A publication*]
Verhandl Naturw Ver Hamburg ... Verhandlungen. Naturwissenschaftlicher Verein in Hamburg [*A publication*]
Verhandl Naturw Ver Karlsruhe ... Verhandlungen. Naturwissenschaftlicher Verein in Karlsruhe [*A publication*]
Verhandl Schweiz Naturf Gesellsch ... Verhandlungen. Schweizerische Naturforschende Gesellschaft [*A publication*]
Verhandlungsber Kolloid-Ges ... Verhandlungsberichte. Kolloid-Gesellschaft [*A publication*]
VerhBer Dt Zool Ges ... Verhandlungsbericht. Deutsche Zoologische Gesellschaft [*A publication*]
Verh Bot Ver Prov Brandenb ... Verhandlungen. Botanischer Verein der Provinz Brandenburg [*A publication*]
Verh Dt Ges Angew Ent ... Verhandlungen. Deutsche Gesellschaft fuer Angewandte Entomologie [*A publication*]
Verh Dtsch Ges Angew Entomol ... Verhandlungen. Deutsche Gesellschaft fuer Angewandte Entomologie [*A publication*]
Verh Dtsch Ges Exp Med ... Verhandlungen. Deutsche Gesellschaft fuer Experimentelle Medizin [*A publication*]
Verh Dtsch Ges Inn Med ... Verhandlungen. Deutsche Gesellschaft fuer Innere Medizin [*A publication*]
Verh Dtsch Ges Kreislaufforsch ... Verhandlungen. Deutsche Gesellschaft fuer Kreislaufforschung [*A publication*]
Verh Dtsch Ges Pathol ... Verhandlungen. Deutsche Gesellschaft fuer Pathologie [*A publication*]
Verh Dtsch Ges Rheumatol ... Verhandlungen. Deutsche Gesellschaft fuer Rheumatologie [*A publication*]
Verh Dtsch Ges Verdau Stoffwechselkr ... Verhandlungen der Deutschen Gesellschaft fuer Verdauungs- und Stoffwechselkrankheiten [*A publication*]
Verh Dtsch Phys Ges ... Verhandlungen. Deutsche Physikalische Gesellschaft [*A publication*]
Verh Dtsch Zool Ges ... Verhandlungen. Deutsche Zoologische Gesellschaft [*A publication*]
Verh Dt Zool Ges Bonn ... Verhandlungen. Deutsche Zoologische Gesellschaft in Bonn [*Rhein*] [*A publication*]
Verh Dt Zool Ges Erlangen ... Verhandlungen. Deutsche Zoologische Gesellschaft in Erlangen [*A publication*]
Verh Dt Zool Ges Frankfurt ... Verhandlungen. Deutsche Zoologische Gesellschaft in Frankfurt [*A publication*]
Verh Dt Zool Ges Goett ... Verhandlungen. Deutsche Zoologische Gesellschaft in Goettingen [*A publication*]
Verh Dt Zool Ges Graz ... Verhandlungen. Deutsche Zoologische Gesellschaft in Graz [*A publication*]
Verh Dt Zool Ges Hamburg ... Verhandlungen. Deutsche Zoologische Gesellschaft in Hamburg [*A publication*]
Verh Dt Zool Ges Jena ... Verhandlungen. Deutsche Zoologische Gesellschaft in Jena [*A publication*]
Verh Dt Zool Ges (Kiel) ... Verhandlungen. Deutsche Zoologische Gesellschaft (Kiel) [*A publication*]
Verh Dt Zool Ges (Tuebingen) ... Verhandlungen. Deutsche Zoologische Gesellschaft (Tuebingen) [*A publication*]
Verh Dt Zool Ges (Wien) ... Verhandlungen. Deutsche Zoologische Gesellschaft (Wien) [*A publication*]
Verh Dt Zool Ges (Wilhelmshaven) ... Verhandlungen. Deutsche Zoologische Gesellschaft (Wilhelmshaven) [*A publication*]
Verh Geol Bundesanst ... Verhandlungen. Geologische Bundesanstalt [*A publication*]
Verh Geol Bundesanst Bundeslaenderser ... Verhandlungen. Geologische Bundesanstalt. Bundeslaenderserie [*A publication*]
Verh Ges Dsch Naturfrsch Aerzte ... Verhandlungen. Gesellschaft Deutscher Naturforscher und Aerzte [*A publication*]
Verh Hist Nied Bay ... Verhandlungen. Historischer Vereine von Niederbayern [*A publication*]
Verh Hist Oberpfalz ... Verhandlungen. Historischer Vereine von Oberpfalz und Regensburg [*A publication*]
Verh Inst Praev Geneeskd ... Verhandelingen. Instituut voor Praeventieve Geneeskunde [*A publication*]
Verh Int Psychother Kongr ... Verhandlungen. Internationaler Psychotherapie Kongress [*A publication*]
Verh Int Ver Theor Angew Limnol ... Verhandlungen der Internationalen Vereinigung fuer Theoretische und Angewandte Limnologie [*A publication*]
Ver Hist ..... Verae Historiae [*of Lucian*] [*Classical studies*]   (OCD)
Verh K Acad Geneeskd Belg ... Verhandelingen. Koninklijke Academie voor Geneeskunde van Belgie [*A publication*]

Verh K Acad Wet Lett & Schone Kunsten Belg ... Verhandelingen. Koninklijke Academie voor Wetenschappen. Letteren en Schone Kunsten van Belgie [*A publication*]

Verh K Acad Wet Lett Schone Kunsten Belg Kl Wet ... Verhandelingen. Koninklijke Academie voor Wetenschappen. Letteren en Schone Kunsten van Belgie. Klasse der Wetenschappen [*A publication*]

Verh K Acad Wet Lett en Schone Kunsten Belg Kl Wet ... Verhandelingen. Koninklijke Academie voor Wetenschappen. Letteren en Schone Kunsten van Belgie. Klasse der Wetenschappen [*A publication*]

Verh K Akad Wet Amsterdam Afd Natuurkd ... Verhandelingen. Koninklijke Akademie van Wetenschappen te Amsterdam. Afdeeling Natuurkunde [*A publication*]

Verh K Ned Akad Wet Afd Natuurkd Reeks 1 ... Verhandelingen. Koninklijke Nederlandse Akademie van Wetenschappen. Afdeling Natuurkunde. Reeks 1 [*A publication*]

Verh K Ned Akad Wet Afd Natuurkd Reeks 2 ... Verhandelingen. Koninklijke Nederlandse Akademie van Wetenschappen. Afdeling Natuurkunde. Reeks 2 [*A publication*]

Verh K Ned Akad Wet Afd Natuurkd Tweede Reeks ... Verhandelingen. Koninklijke Nederlandse Akademie van Wetenschappen. Afdeling Natuurkunde. Tweede Reeks [*A publication*]

Verh K Ned Akad Wetensch Afd Natuurk Reeks 1 ... Verhandelingen. Koninklijke Nederlandse Akademie van Wetenschappen. Afdeling Natuurkunde. Reeks 1 [*Netherlands*] [*A publication*]

Verh K Ned Akad Wetensch Afd Natuurk Reeks 2 ... Verhandelingen. Koninklijke Nederlandse Akademie van Wetenschappen. Afdeling Natuurkunde. Reeks 2 [*Netherlands*] [*A publication*]

Verh K Ned Geol Mijnbouwkd Genoot ... Verhandelingen. Koninklijke Nederlands Geologisch Mijnbouwkundig Genootschap [*A publication*]

Verh K Ned Geol Mijnbouwkd Genoot Geol Ser ... Verhandelingen. Koninklijke Nederlandse Geologisch Mijnbouwkundig Genootschap. Geologische Serie [*A publication*]

Verh K Ned Geol Mijnbouwkd Genoot Mijnbouwkd Ser ... Verhandelingen. Koninklijke Nederlandse Geologisch Mijnbouwkundig Genootschap. Mijnbouwkundige Serie [*A publication*]

Verh Konink Acad Wetensch Belgie ... Verhandelingen. Koninklijke Academie voor Wetenschappen. Letteren en Schone Kunsten van Belgie [*A publication*]

Verh Kon Nederl Ak Wetensch Afd Lett ... Verhandelingen. Koninklijke Nederlandse Akademie van Wetenschappen. Afdeling Letterkunde [*A publication*]

Verh K Vlaam Acad Geneesk Belg ... Verhandelingen. Koninklijke Vlaamse Academie voor Geneeskunde van Belgie [*Belgium*] [*A publication*]

Verh K Vlaam Acad Geneeskd Belg ... Verhandelingen. Koninklijke Vlaamse Academie voor Geneeskunde van Belgie [*A publication*]

Verh K Vlaam Acad Wetensch Belg Kl Wetensch ... Verhandelingen. Koninklijke Vlaamse Academie voor Wetenschappen, Letteren, en Schone Kunsten van Belgie. Klasse der Wetenschappen [*Belgium*] [*A publication*]

Verh K Vlaam Acad Wet Lett Schone Kunsten Belg Kl Wet ... Verhandelingen. Koninklijke Vlaamse Academie voor Wetenschappen, Letteren, en Schone Kunsten van Belgie. Klasse der Wetenschappen [*A publication*]

Verh Naturforsch Ges Basel ... Verhandlungen. Naturforschende Gesellschaft in Basel [*A publication*]

Verh Naturforsch Ver Bruenn ... Verhandlungen. Naturforschender Verein in Bruenn [*A publication*]

Verh Natur-Med Ver Heidelb ... Verhandlungen. Naturhistorisch-Medizinischer Verein zu Heidelberg [*A publication*]

Verh Naturwiss Ver Hamb ... Verhandlungen des Naturwissenschaftlichen Vereins in Hamburg [*A publication*]

Verh Ornithol Ges Bayern ... Verhandlungen. Ornithologische Gesellschaft in Bayern [*A publication*]

Verh Phys-Med Ges Wuerzb ... Verhandlungen. Physikalisch-Medizinische Gesellschaft in Wuerzburg [*A publication*]

Verh Phys-Med Ges Wuerzburg ... Verhandlungen. Physikalisch-Medizinische Gesellschaft in Wuerzburg [*A publication*]

Verh Rijksinst Natuurbeheer ... Verhandelingen. Rijksinstituut voor Natuurbeheer [*A publication*]

Verh Schweiz Naturf Ges ... Verhandlungen. Schweizerische Naturforschende Gesellschaft [*A publication*]

Verh Schweiz Naturforsch Ges ... Verhandlungen. Schweizerische Naturforschende Gesellschaft [*A publication*]

Verh Schweiz Naturforsch Ges Wiss Teil ... Verhandlungen. Schweizerische Naturforschende Gesellschaft. Wissenschaftlicher Teil [*A publication*]

Verh Ver Schweiz Physiol ... Verhandlungen. Verein der Schweizer Physiologen [*A publication*]

Verh Zool-Bot Ges Wien ... Verhandlungen. Zoologisch-Botanische Gesellschaft in Wien [*A publication*]

VERI .... Veritec, Inc. [*Calabasas Park, CA*] [*NASDAQ symbol*] (NQ)

VERI .... Vineyard Environmental Research Institute [*Research center*] (RCD)

VERIC .... Vocational Education Resources Information Center

VERIF .... Verification (MSA)

VeritCarit ... Veritatem in Caritate. Orgaan van de Protestanse Theologische Faculteit te Brussel [*A publication*] (BJA)

VERK .... Rourkela [*India*] [*ICAO location identifier*] (ICLI)

Verkehrsmed Grenzgeb ... Verkehrsmedizin und Ihre Grenzgebiete [*A publication*]

Verkehrsmed Ihre Grenzgeb ... Verkehrsmedizin und Ihre Grenzgebiete [*German Democratic Republic*] [*A publication*]

VerkF .... Verkuendigung und Forschung [*Munich*] [*A publication*]

Verksamheten Stift Rasforadl Skogstrad ... Verksamheten. Stiftelsen foer Rasforadling av Skogstrad [*A publication*]

VERL .... Raxaul [*India*] [*ICAO location identifier*] (ICLI)

VERLORT ... Very-Long-Range Tracking [*NASA*]

Ver LR ...... Vermont Law Review [*A publication*]

VERM .... Vermilion (ROG)

VERM .... Vermont

Verm .... Vermont Reports [*A publication*] (DLA)

Vermess-Inf ... Vermessungs-Informationen [*A publication*]

Verm Nox Weeds Destr Board Leafl ... Leaflet. Vermin and Noxious Weeds Destruction Board [*Victoria*] [*A publication*] (APTA)

Verm Nox Weeds Destrn Bd (Melb) Surv ... Vermin and Noxious Weeds Destruction Board (Melbourne). Survey [*A publication*] (APTA)

Vermont Bs ... Vermont Business [*A publication*]

Vermont Geol Survey Bull ... Vermont. Geological Survey. Bulletin [*A publication*]

Vermont Lib ... Vermont Libraries [*A publication*]

Vermont L Rev ... Vermont Law Review [*A publication*]

Vermont R ... Vermont Reports [*A publication*] (DLA)

Vermont Regist Nurse ... Vermont Registered Nurse [*A publication*]

Vermont Rep ... Vermont Reports [*A publication*] (DLA)

Vermt .... Vermont Reports [*A publication*] (DLA)

VERN .... Rangeilunda [*India*] [*ICAO location identifier*] (ICLI)

VERN .... Vernacular (ADA)

VERN .... Vernier [*Engineering*]

Vern .... Vernon's English Chancery Reports [*23 English Reprint*] [*A publication*] (DLA)

Vernacular Architect ... Vernacular Architecture [*A publication*]

Vernacular Archre ... Vernacular Architecture [*A publication*]

Vernacular Bldg ... Vernacular Building [*A publication*]

VERNAV ... Vertical Navigation System

Vern (Eng) ... Vernon's English Chancery Reports [*23 English Reprint*] [*A publication*] (DLA)

Verniciature Decor ... Verniciature e Decorazioni [*A publication*]

VERNITRAC ... Vernier Tracking by Automatic Correlation [*Aerospace*]

Vernon's Ann CCP ... Vernon's Annotated Texas Code of Criminal Procedure [*A publication*] (DLA)

Vernon's Ann Civ St ... Vernon's Annotated Texas Civil Statutes [*A publication*] (DLA)

Vernon's Ann PC ... Vernon's Annotated Texas Penal Code [*A publication*] (DLA)

Vern & S .... Vernon and Scriven's Irish King's Bench Reports [*1786-88*] [*A publication*] (DLA)

Vern & Sc ... Vernon and Scriven's Irish King's Bench Reports [*1786-88*] [*A publication*] (DLA)

Vern & Scr ... Vernon and Scriven's Irish King's Bench Reports [*1786-88*] [*A publication*] (DLA)

Vern & Scriv ... Vernon and Scriven's Irish King's Bench Reports [*1786-88*] [*A publication*] (DLA)

Vern & S (Ir) ... Vernon and Scriven's Irish King's Bench Reports [*1786-88*] [*A publication*] (DLA)

Veroeff Bundesanst Alp Landwirtsch Admont ... Veroeffentlichungen. Bundesanstalt fuer Alpine Landwirtschaft in Admont [*A publication*]

Veroeff Dtsch Geod Komm Reihe A ... Veroeffentlichungen. Deutsche Geodaetische Kommission. Bayerische Akademie der Wissenschaften. Reihe A [*West Germany*] [*A publication*]

Veroeffentlich Schweizer Gesellsch Medizin Naturwissensch ... Veroeffentlichungen. Schweizerische Gesellschaft fuer Geschichte der Medizin und der Naturwissenschaft [*A publication*]

Veroeffentlichungen Volkskunde Kulturgesch ... Veroeffentlichungen zur Volkskunde und Kulturgeschichte [*A publication*]

Veroeffentl J-Vet-Ber Beamt Tieraerzte Preuss ... Veroeffentlichungen aus den Jahres-Veterinaer-Berichten. Beamtete Tieraerzte Preussen [*A publication*]

Veroeffentl Leibniz-Archivs ... Veroeffentlichungen. Leibniz-Archiv [*A publication*]

Veroeffentl Wiss Photolab ... Veroeffentlichungen. Wissenschaftliche Photo-Laboratorien [*A publication*]

Veroeff Geobot Inst Eidg Tech Hochsch Stift Ruebel Zuer ... Veroeffentlichungen. Geobotanisches Institut. Eidgenoessische Technische Hochschule Stiftung Ruebel in Zuerich [*A publication*]

Veroeff Geobot Inst Eidg Tech Hochsch Stift Ruebel Zuerich ... Veroeffentlichungen. Geobotanisches Institut. Eidgenoessische Technische Hochschule Stiftung Ruebel in Zuerich [*A publication*]

Veroeff Geobot Inst Ruebel ... Veroeffentlichungen. Geobotanisches Institut Ruebel [*A publication*]

Veroeff Inst Meeresforsch Bremerhaven ... Veroeffentlichungen. Institut fuer Meeresforschung in Bremerhaven [*A publication*]

Veroeff Inst Meeresforsch Bremerhaven Suppl ... Veroeffentlichungen. Institut fuer Meeresforschung in Bremerhaven. Supplement [*A publication*]

Veroeff Kaiser Wilhelm Inst Silikatforsch Berlin Dahlem ... Veroeffentlichungen. Kaiser-Wilhelm-Institut fuer Silikatforschung in Berlin-Dahlem [*A publication*]

Veroeff Landwirtsch Chem Bundesversuchsanst (Linz) ... Veroeffentlichungen. Landwirtschaftlich-Chemische Bundesversuchsanstalt (Linz) [*A publication*]

Veroeff Meteorol Dienstes DDR ... Veroeffentlichungen. Meteorologischer Dienst. Deutsche Demokratische Republik [*A publication*]

Veroeff Meterol Hydrol Dienstes DDR ... Veroeffentlichungen. Meteorologischer und Hydrologischer Dienst. Deutsche Demokratische Republik [*A publication*]

Veroeff Morphol Pathol ... Veroeffentlichungen aus der Morphologischen Pathologie [*A publication*]

Veroeff Mus (Potsdam) ... Veroeffentlichungen des Museums fuer Ur- und Fruehgeschichte (Potsdam) [*A publication*]

Veroeff Naturhist Mus (Basel) ... Veroeffentlichungen. Naturhistorischer Museum (Basel) [*A publication*]

Veroeff Naturh Mus (Wien) ... Veroeffentlichungen. Naturhistorischer Museum (Wien) [*A publication*]

Veroeff Naturschutz Landschaftspflege Baden Wuerttemb ... Veroeffentlichungen fuer Naturschutz und Landschaftspflege in Baden-Wuerttemberg [*A publication*]

Veroeff Naturschutz Landschaftspflege Baden-Wuerttemb Beih ... Veroeffentlichungen fuer Naturschutz und Landschaftspflege in Baden-Wuerttemberg. Beihefte [*A publication*]

Veroeff Oe Ur Frueh Gesch ... Veroeffentlichungen der Oesterreichischen Arbeitsgemeinschaft fuer Ur- und Fruehgeschichte [*A publication*]

Veroeff Pathol ... Veroeffentlichungen aus der Pathologie [*A publication*]

Veroeff Reichsgesundheitsamts ... Veroeffentlichungen. Reichsgesundheitsamt [*A publication*]

Veroeff Ueberseemus (Bremen) Reihe A ... Veroeffentlichungen. Ueberseemuseum (Bremen). Reihe A [*A publication*]

Veroeff Wiss Photo Lab (Wolfen) ... Veroeffentlichungen. Wissenschaftliche Photo-Laboratorien (Wolfen) [*A publication*]

Veroeff Wiss Zent Lab Photogr Abt AGFA ... Veroeffentlichungen. Wissenschaftliches Zentral Laboratorium. Photographische Abteilung AGFA [*A publication*]

Veroeff Zentralinst Phys Erde ... Veroeffentlichungen. Zentralinstitut Physik der Erde [*Czechoslovakia*] [*A publication*]

Veroeff Zool Staatssamml (Muench) ... Veroeffentlichungen. Zoologische Staatssammlung (Muenchen) [*A publication*]

Veroeff Zool StSamml (Muench) ... Veroeffentlichungen. Zoologische Staatssammlung (Muenchen) [*A publication*]

Veroff Inst Agrarmet Univ (Leipzig) ... Veroeffentlichungen. Institut fuer Agrarmeteorologie und des Agrarmeteorologischen Observatoriums. Karl Marx-Universitaet (Leipzig) [*A publication*]

Veroff Land-Hauswirtsch Auswertungs-Informationsdienst ... Veroeffentlichungen. Land- und Hauswirtschaftlicher Auswertungs- und Informationsdienst [*A publication*]

VERP .... Vertical Effective Radiated Power (MCD)

Verpack Chemiebetr ... Verpackung im Chemiebetrich [*A publication*]

Verpack Mag ... Verpackungs-Magazin [*A publication*]

Verpack-Rundsch ... Verpackungs-Rundschau [*A publication*]

Verpl Cont ... Verplanck on Contracts [*A publication*] (DLA)

Verpl Ev ..... Verplanck on Evidence [*A publication*] (DLA)

Verr .... In Verrem [*of Cicero*] [*Classical studies*] (OCD)

Ver Rep ...... Vermont Reports [*A publication*] (DLA)

Verre Silic Ind ... Verre et Silicates Industriels [*A publication*]

Verres Refract ... Verres et Refractaires [*A publication*]

Verres Refract Part 1 ... Verres et Refractaires. Part 1. Articles Originaux [*A publication*]

Verres Refract Part 2 ... Verres et Refractaires. Part 2. Documentation [*A publication*]

Verre Text Plast Renf ... Verre Textile, Plastiques Renforces [*France*] [*A publication*]

Verrigtinge Kongr S-Afr Genet Ver ... Verrigtinge van die Kongres van die Suid-Afrikaanse Genetiese Vereniging [*A publication*]

VERS .... Versed Sine [*Engineering*] (KSC)

VERS .... Versicherung [*Insurance*] [*German*] [*Business term*]

VERS .... Version (ROG)

Ver Schweizer Petroleum-Geologen u Ingenieure Bull ... Vereinigung Schweizerischer Petroleum-Geologen und Ingenieure. Bulletin [*A publication*]

Ver Schweiz Pet-Geol Ing Bull ... Vereinigung Schweizerischer Petroleum-Geologen und Ingenieure. Bulletin [*A publication*]

versk .... Verskuldig [*Due*] [*Afrikaans*] [*Business term*]

Vers Landbouwkd Onderz ... Verslagen van Landbouwkundige Onderzoekingen [*A publication*]

Versl Interprov Proeven Proefstn Akkerbouw Lelystad (Neth) ... Verslagen van Interprovinciale Proeven. Proefstation voor de Akkerbouw Lelystad (Netherlands) [*A publication*]

Versl Interprov Proeven Proefstn Akkerbouw (Wageningen) ... Verslagen van Interprovinciale Proeven. Proefstation voor de Akkerbouw (Wageningen) [*A publication*]

Versl Landbouwkd Onderz A ... Verslagen van Landbouwkundige Onderzoekingen A. Rijkslandbouwproefstation en Bodemkundig Instituut te Groningen [*A publication*]

Versl Landbouwkd Onderz (Agric Res Rep) ... Verslagen van Landbouwkundige Onderzoekingen (Agricultural Research Reports) [*A publication*]

Versl Landbouwkd Onderz B ... Verslagen van Landbouwkundige Onderzoekingen B. Bodemikundig Instituut te Groningen [*A publication*]

Versl Landbouwkd Onderz C ... Verslagen van Landbouwkundige Onderzoekingen C. Rijkslandbouwproefstation te Hoorn [*A publication*]

Versl Landbouwkd Onderz E ... Verslagen van Landbouwkundige Onderzoekingen E. Rijkslandbouwproefstation voor Veevoederonderzoek te Wageningen [*A publication*]

Versl Landbouwkd Onderz G ... Verslagen van Landbouwkundige Onderzoekingen G. Onderzoekingen Uitgevoerd in Opdracht van den Algemeenen Nederlandschen Zuivelbond [*A publication*]

Versl Landbouwkd Onderz Rijkslandbouwproefstn ... Verslagen van Landbouwkundige Onderzoekingen der Rijkslandbouwproefstations [*A publication*]

Versl Landbouwk Onderz ... Verslagen van Landbouwkundige Onderzoekingen [*A publication*]

Versl Landbouwk Onderz Cent Lanbouwpubl Landbouwdoc ... Verslagen van Landbouwkundige Onderzoekingen. Centrum voor Landbouwpublikatien en Landbouwdocumentatie [*A publication*]

Versl Landbouwk Onderz Ned ... Verslagen van het Landbouwkundig Onderzoek in Nederland [*A publication*]

Versl Meded Kon Vl Ak Taal & Letterk ... Verslagen en Mededeelingen. Koninklijke Vlaamse Akademie voor Taal- en Letterkunde [*A publication*]

Versl Meded K Vlaam Acad Taal Lett ... Verslagen en Mededeelingen. Koninklijke Vlaamse Academie voor Taal- en Letterkunde [*A publication*]

Versl Meded Rijkslandbouwconsul Westelijk Drenthe ... Verslagen en Mededelingen van het Rijkslandbouwconsulentschap Westelijk Drenthe [*A publication*]

Versl Tien-Jarenplan Graanonderzoek Sticht Nederl Graan-Cent ... Verslagen. Tien-Jarenplan voor Graanonderzoek. Stichting Nederlands Graan-Centrum [*A publication*]

Versl Ver Chem Tech Landbouwkd Advis ... Verslagen der Vereniging van Chemisch-Technischen. Landbouwkundig Adviseurs [*A publication*]

VERSO ...... Reverso [*Left-Hand Page of Open Book*] (ROG)

VERST ...... Versatile

Verstaendliche Wiss ... Verstaendliche Wissenschaft [*A publication*]

Versuchsergeb Bundesanst Pflanzenbau Samenpruefung Wien ... Versuchsergebnisse der Bundesanstalt fuer Pflanzenbau und Samenpruefung in Wien [*A publication*]

Versuchsgrubenges Quartalsh ... Versuchsgrubengesellschaft Quartalshefte [*West Germany*] [*A publication*]

VERT .... Venture Evaluation and Review Technique

Vert .... Vermont Reports [*A publication*] (DLA)

VERT .... Vertebrate

VERT .... Vertical (MCD)

Vert .... Vertical Lights [*Navigation signal*]

VERT .... Vertical Polarization (AFM)

VERT .... Verticom, Inc. [*Sunnyvale, CA*] [*NASDAQ symbol*] (NQ)

VERTAR ... Versatile Test Analysis RADAR (MCD)

VERTEB ... Vertebrate

Vertebr Hung ... Vertebrata Hungarica [*A publication*]

Vertebr Palasiat ... Vertebrata Palasiatica [*A publication*]

Vertebr Palasiatica ... Vertebrata Palasiatica [*A publication*]

VERTEX ... Vertical Transport and Exchange [*Oceanographic research program*]

Vert File Ind ... Vertical File Index [*A publication*]

Ver f Thuer Gesch u Alt Ztsch ... Verein fuer Thueringische Geschichte und Altertumskunde. Zeitschrift [*A publication*]

VERTIC .... Verification Technology Information Centre [*British*] (CB)

VERTIJET ... Vertical Takeoff and Landing Jet [*Aircraft*]

VERTOL ... Vertical Takeoff and Landing [*Also, VTOL*]

VERTREP ... Vertical Replenishment [*Navy*] (NVT)

VERU .... Rupsi [*India*] [*ICAO location identifier*] (ICLI)

Ver Vaterl Naturk Wuerttemberg Jahresh ... Verein fuer Vaterlaendische Naturkunde in Wuerttemberg. Jahreshefte [*A publication*]

Ver Verbr Naturwiss Kenntnisse Wien Schr ... Verein zur Verbreitung Naturwissenschaftlicher Kenntnisse in Wien. Schriften [*A publication*]

Verwaltung ... Zeitschrift fuer Verwaltungswissenschaft [*A publication*]

Verwarm Vent ... Verwarming en Ventilatie [*A publication*]

VerwG .... Verwaltungsgericht [*Administrative Court or Tribunal*] [*German*]

VerwGH ..... Verwaltungsgerichtshof [*District Administrative Court of Appeal*] [*German*] (DLA)

Verw Pr ...... Die Verwaltungspraxis [*A publication*] (ILCA)

VERY .... Vanderbilt Energy Corp. [*NASDAQ symbol*] (NQ)

Verzam Overdruk Plantenziektenk Dienst (Wageningen) ... Verzamelde Overdrukken. Plantenziektenkundige Dienst (Wageningen) [*A publication*]

Verzekerings-Arch ... Verzekerings-Archief [*A publication*]
VES........... Vacuum Evaporator System
VES........... Vapor Extraction System [*Engineering*]
VES........... Variable Elasticity of Substitution [*Industrial production*]
VES........... Variable Explanation Sheet [*Army*]
VES........... Vehicle Ecological System   (AAG)
VES........... Vehicle Engagement Simulator   (MCD)
VES........... Versailles, OH [*Location identifier*] [*FAA*]   (FAAL)
Ves .... Vesey, Senior's, English Chancery Reports [*27, 28 English Reprint*] [*A publication*]   (DLA)
VES........... Vesica [*Bladder*] [*Latin*]   (ADA)
VES........... Vesicula [*Blister*] [*Latin*]   (ADA)
VES........... Vespere [*In the Evening*] [*Latin*]   (ADA)
VES........... Vessel   (AABC)
VES........... Vestaur Securities, Inc. [*NYSE symbol*]   (SPSG)
VES........... Veterans Employment Service [*Later, VETS*] [*of USES*]
VES........... Veterinary Evacuating Station [*British military*]   (DMA)
VES........... Victorian Era Series [*A publication*]
VES........... Vieques Air Link, Inc. [*Vieques, PR*] [*FAA designator*]   (FAAC)
VES........... Visual Effects Simulator   (MCD)
VES........... Visual Efficiency Scale
VES........... Vulcan Engagement Simulator   (MCD)
VESADE ... Elektronmikroskopievereniging van Suidelike Afrika. Verrigtings [*Electron Microscopy Society of Southern Africa. Proceedings*] [*A publication*]
Ves Akad Nauk Kirg SSR ... Vestnik Akademii Nauk Kirgizskoi SSR [*A publication*]
Ves & B ...... Vesey and Beames' English Chancery Reports [*35 English Reprint*] [*A publication*]   (DLA)
Ves & Bea .. Vesey and Beames' English Chancery Reports [*35 English Reprint*] [*A publication*]   (DLA)
Ves & Beam ... Vesey and Beames' English Chancery Reports [*35 English Reprint*] [*A publication*]   (DLA)
Ves & B (Eng) ... Vesey and Beames' English Chancery Reports [*35 English Reprint*] [*A publication*]   (DLA)
VESC .... Vehicle Equipment Safety Commission
VESCAC ... Victorian Education Service Conciliation and Arbitration Commission [*Australia*]
VESCA(S) ... Vessels and Cargo
VESCF...... Variable Eletronegativity Self-Consistent Field [*Physics*]
Vesci Akad Navuk BSSR Ser Fiz-Mat Navuk ... Vesci Akademii Navuk BSSR. Seryja Fizika-Matematycnyh Navuk [*A publication*]
Vesci Ak BSSR ... Vesci Akademii Navuk BSSR [*A publication*]
Ves Drev Istor ... Vestnik Drevnei Istorii [*A publication*]
VESE .... Value Engineering Staff Engineer
VESG......... Vocational Education Services Grant   (OICC)
VESI .... Victor Educational Services Institute [*Educational division of Victor Comptometer Corp.*]
Vesic........... Vesicula [*Blister*] [*Latin*]
vesic........... Vesicular
Vesientutkimuslaitoksen Julk ... Vesientutkimuslaitoksen Julkaisuja [*A publication*]
Ves Jr......... Vesey, Junior's, English Chancery Reports [*30-34 English Reprint*] [*A publication*]   (DLA)
Ves Jr (Eng) ... Vesey, Junior's, English Chancery Reports [*30-34 English Reprint*] [*A publication*]   (DLA)
Ves Jr Suppl ... Supplement to Vesey, Junior's, English Chancery Reports, by Hovenden [*34 English Reprint*] [*A publication*]   (DLA)
Ves Jun ...... Vesey, Junior's, English Chancery Reports [*30-34 English Reprint*] [*A publication*]   (DLA)
Ves Jun Supp ... Supplement to Vesey, Junior's, English Chancery Reports, by Hovenden [*34 English Reprint*] [*A publication*]   (DLA)
Ves Jun Supp (Eng) ... Supplement to Vesey, Junior's, English Chancery Reports, by Hovenden [*34 English Reprint*] [*A publication*]   (DLA)
Vesn Zavod Geol Geofiz Istraz NR Srb ... Vesnik Zavod za Geoloska i Geofizicka Istrazivanja NR Srbije [*A publication*]
Vesn Zavod Geol Geofiz Istraz Ser A ... Vesnik Zavod za Geoloska i Geofizicka Istrazivanja. Serija A. Geologija [*A publication*]
Vesn Zavod Geol Geofiz Istraz Ser C ... Vesnik Zavod za Geoloska i Geofizicka Istrazivanja. Serija C. Priminjena Geofizika [*A publication*]
VESO......... Vocalization of the Egyptian Syllabic Orthography [*W. F. Albright*] [*A publication*]   (BJA)
VESP .... Value Engineering Supplier Program
Vesp........... Vespae [*Wasps*] [*of Aristophanes*] [*Classical studies*]   (OCD)
VESP .... Vesper [*Evening*] [*Pharmacy*]
VESP .... Vesper Corp. [*NASDAQ symbol*]   (NQ)
VESPER.... Vehicle Sizing and Performance   (MCD)
VESR......... Vallecitos Experimental Superheat Reactor
VESR......... Value Engineering Study Request   (MCD)
VESS .... Vehicle Exhaust Smoke System   (MCD)
VESS .... Visual Environment Simulation System   (MCD)
Ves Sen ...... Vesey, Senior's, English Chancery Reports [*27, 28 English Reprint*] [*A publication*]   (DLA)
Ves Sen Supp ... Supplement to Vesey, Senior's, English Chancery Reports [*28 English Reprint*] [*A publication*]   (DLA)
Ves Sr......... Vesey, Senior's, English Chancery Reports [*27, 28 English Reprint*] [*A publication*]   (DLA)
Ves Sr (Eng) ... Vesey, Senior's, English Chancery Reports [*27, 28 English Reprint*] [*A publication*]   (DLA)

Ves Sr Supp ... Supplement to Vesey, Senior's, English Chancery Reports [*28 English Reprint*] [*1747-56*] [*A publication*]   (DLA)
Ves Sr Supp (Eng) ... Supplement to Vesey, Senior's, English Chancery Reports [*28 English Reprint*] [*A publication*]   (DLA)
Ves Supp.... Supplement to Vesey, Junior's, English Chancery Reports, by Hovenden [*34 English Reprint*] [*1789-1817*] [*A publication*]   (DLA)
VEST .... Vestibule   (MSA)
VEST .... Vestro Foods, Inc. [*NASDAQ symbol*]   (NQ)
VEST .... Vestry [*Ecclesiastical*]   (ROG)
VEST .... Volunteer Engineers, Scientists, and Technicians [*An association*]
Vest Akad Nauk SSSR ... Vestnik Akademii Nauk SSSR [*A publication*]
Vest Ces Akad Zemed ... Vestnik Ceskoslovenske Akademie Zemedelske [*A publication*]
Vest Csl Spol Zool ... Vestnik Ceskoslovenske Spolecnosti Zoologicke [*A publication*]
Vest Dal'nevost Fil Akad Nauk SSSR ... Vestnik Dal'nevostochnogo Filiala Akademii Nauk SSSR [*A publication*]
Vest Gos Muz Gruz ... Vestnik Gosudarstvennogo Muzeja Gruzii Imeni Akademika S. N. Dzhanashia [*A publication*]
Vest Inst Pchelovodstva ... Vestnik Institut Pchelovodstva [*A publication*]
Vest Ist Mirov Kul't ... Vestnik Istorii Mirovoi Kul'tury [*A publication*]
Vest Khar'k Univ Radiofiz Elektron ... Vestnik Khar'kovskogo Universiteta. Radiofizika, Elektronika [*USSR*] [*A publication*]
Vest Latv PSR Akad ... Vestis Latvijas Pasomju Socialistikas Republikas Zinatu Akademija [*Riga, USSR*] [*A publication*]
Vest Leningr Gos Univ Ser Biol ... Vestnik Leningradskogo Gosudarstvennogo Universiteta. Seriya Biologii [*A publication*]
Vest Leningr Inst ... Vestnik Leningradskogo Instituta [*A publication*]
Vest Mikrobiol Epidemiol Parazitol ... Vestnik Mikrobiologii, Epidemiologii, i Parazitologii [*A publication*]
Vest Mosk Gos Univ Ser VI ... Vestnik Moskovskogo Gosudarstvennogo Universiteta. Seriya VI [*A publication*]
Vest Mosk Inst Biol Pochv ... Vestnik Moskovskogo Instituta. Seriya Biologiya, Pochvovedenie [*A publication*]
Vest Mosk Inst Geogr ... Vestnik Moskovskogo Instituta Geografii [*A publication*]
Vest Mosk Univ Ser Biol Pochv Geol Geogr ... Vestnik Moskovskogo Universiteta. Seriya Biologii, Pochvovedeniya, Geologii, Geografii [*A publication*]
Vest Mosk Univ Ser 15 Vychisl Mat Kibern ... Vestnik Moskovskogo Universiteta. Seriya 15. Vychislitel'naya Matematika i Kibernetika [*USSR*] [*A publication*]
Vestn Akad Med Nauk SSSR ... Vestnik Akademii Meditsinskikh Nauk SSSR [*A publication*]
Vestn Akad Nauk Belorussk SSR Ser Obsc Nauk ... Vestnik Akademii Nauk Belorusskoj SSR. Serija Obscestvennyh Nauk [*A publication*]
Vestn Akad Nauk Kazah SSR ... Vestnik Akademii Nauk Kazahskoj SSR [*A publication*]
Vestn Akad Nauk Kazakh SSR ... Vestnik Akademiya Nauk Kazakhskoi SSR [*A publication*]
Vestn Akad Nauk Kaz SSR ... Vestnik Akademii Nauk Kazakhskoi SSR [*A publication*]
Vestn Akad Nauk SSSR ... Vestnik Akademii Nauk SSSR [*A publication*]
Vest Nauchno-Issled Inst Pchel ... Vestnik Nauchno-Issledovatel'skii Institut Pchelovodstva [*A publication*]
Vestn Beloruss Gos Univ Ser 1 ... Vestnik Belorusskogo Gosudarstvennogo Universiteta. Seriya 1. Matematika, Fizika, Mekhanika [*A publication*]
Vestn Beloruss Gos Univ Ser 2 Biol Khim Geol Geogr ... Vestnik Belorusskogo Gosudarstvennogo Universiteta. Seriya 2. Biologiya, Khimiya, Geologiya, Geografiya [*A publication*]
Vestn Beloruss Univ ... Vestnik Belorusskogo Universiteta [*A publication*]
Vestn Cesk Akad Zemed ... Vestnik Ceskoslovenske Akademie Zemedelske [*A publication*]
Vestn Cesk Akad Zemed Ved ... Vestnik Ceskoslovenske Akademie Zemedelskych Ved [*A publication*]
Vestn Ceskoslov Akad Zemed Ved ... Vestnik Ceskoslovenske Akademie Zemedelskych Ved [*A publication*]
Vestn Cesk Spol Zool ... Vestnik Ceskoslovenske Spolecnosti Zoologicke [*A publication*]
Vestn Chkal Otd Vses Khim O-Va Im D I Mendeleeva ... Vestnik Chkalovckogo Otdeleniya Vsesoyuznogo Khimicheskogo Obshchestva Imeni D. I. Mendeleeva [*A publication*]
Vestn Dermatol Venerol ... Vestnik Dermatologii i Venerologii [*A publication*]
Vestn Drevnej Istor ... Vestnik Drevnej Istorii. Revue d'Histoire Ancienne [*A publication*]
Vestn Drevn Ist ... Vestnik Drevnei Istorii [*A publication*]
Vestn Elektroprom-Sti ... Vestnik Elektropromyshlennosti [*USSR*] [*A publication*]
Vestn Elektrotekh ... Vestnik Elektrotekhniki [*A publication*]
Vestn Gos Muz Gruz ... Vestnik Gosudarstvennogo Muzeja Gruzii [*A publication*]
Vestn Gosud Muz Gruzii ... Vestnik Gosudarstvennogo Muzeja Gruzii Imeni Akademika S. N. Dzhanashia [*A publication*]
Vestn Gruz Bot Ova ... Vestnik Gruzinskogo Botanicheskogo Obshchestva [*A publication*]
Vestnik Akad Nauk Kazah SSR ... Vestnik Akademii Nauk Kazahskoj SSR [*A publication*]

Vestnik Akad Nauk Kazakh SSR ... Vestnik Akademii Nauk Kazakhskoi SSR [*A publication*]

Vestnik Akad Nauk SSSR ... Vestnik Akademii Nauk SSSR [*A publication*]

Vestnik Beloruss Gos Univ Ser 1 ... Vestnik Belorusskogo Gosudarstvennogo Universiteta Imeni V. I. Lenina. Naucnyi Zurnal. Seriya 1. Matematika, Fizika, Mekhanika [*A publication*]

Vestnik Har'kov Gos Univ ... Vestnik Har'kovskogo Gosudarstvennogo Universiteta [*A publication*]

Vestnik Har'kov Politehn Inst ... Vestnik Har'kovskogo Politehniceskogo Instituta [*A publication*]

Vestnik Jaroslav Univ ... Vestnik Jaroslavskogo Universiteta [*A publication*]

Vestnik Karakalpak Fil Akad Nauk UzSSR ... Akademija Nauk UzSSR. Karakalpakskii Filial. Vestnik [*A publication*]

Vestnik K Ceske Spolec Nauk v Praze Trida Mat Prirod ... Vestnik Kralovske Ceske Spolecnosti Nauk v Praze Trida Matematicko Prirodovedecka [*A publication*]

Vestnik Khar'kov Gos Univ ... Vestnik Khar'kovskogo Gosudarstvennogo Universiteta. Seriya Mekhaniko-Matematicheskaya. Zapiski Mekhaniko-Matematicheskogo Fakul'teta i Khar'kovskogo Matematicheskogo Obshchestva [*A publication*]

Vestnik Kiev Politehn Inst Ser Tehn Kibernet ... Vestnik Kievskogo Politehniceskogo Instituta. Serija Tehniceskoi Kibernetiki [*A publication*]

Vestnik Leningrad Univ Fiz Him ... Vestnik Leningradskogo Universiteta. Fizika i Himija [*A publication*]

Vestnik Leningrad Univ Fiz Khim ... Vestnik Leningradskogo Universiteta. Fizika i Khimiya [*A publication*]

Vestnik Leningrad Univ Math ... Vestnik Leningrad University. Mathematics [*A publication*]

Vestnik Leningrad Univ Mat Mekh Astronom ... Vestnik Leningradskogo Universiteta. Matematika, Mekhanika, Astronomiya [*A publication*]

Vestnik Leningrad Univ Ser Fiz Khim ... Vestnik Leningradskogo Universiteta. Seriya Fiziki i Khimii [*A publication*]

Vestnik Leningr Gosud Univ ... Vestnik Leningradskogo Gosudarstvennogo Universiteta [*A publication*]

Vestnik L'vov Politehn Inst ... Vestnik L'vovskogo Politehniceskogo Instituta [*A publication*]

Vestnik Mikrobiol i Epidemiol ... Vestnik Mikrobiologii i Epidemiologii [*A publication*]

Vestnik Mikrobiol Epidemiol i Parazitol ... Vestnik Mikrobiologii, Epidemiologii, i Parazitologii [*A publication*]

Vestnik Moskov Univ Ser III Fiz Astronom ... Vestnik Moskovskogo Universiteta. Serija III. Fizika, Astronomija [*A publication*]

Vestnik Moskov Univ Ser I Mat Meh ... Vestnik Moskovskogo Universiteta. Serija I. Matematika, Mehanika [*A publication*]

Vestnik Moskov Univ Ser XV Vycisl Mat Kibernet ... Vestnik Moskovskogo Universiteta. Serija XV. Vycislitel'naja Matematika i Kibernetika [*A publication*]

Vestnik Mosk Univ Ser Khim ... Vestnik Moskovskogo Universiteta. Seriya 2. Khimiya [*A publication*]

Vestnik Obsh Vet (S Peterburg) ... Vestnik Obshchestvennoi Veterinarii (S. Peterburg) [*A publication*]

Vestnik Rentg i Radiol ... Vestnik Rentgenologii i Radiologii [*A publication*]

Vestnik Sovrem Vet ... Vestnik Sovremennoi Veterinarii [*A publication*]

Vestnik Statist ... Vestnik Statistiki [*A publication*]

Vestnik Ustredniho Ustavu Geol ... Vestnik Ustredniho Ustavu Geologickeho [*A publication*]

Vestn Inzh Tekh ... Vestnik Inzhenerov i Tekhnikov [*USSR*] [*A publication*]

Vestn Jaroslav Univ ... Vestnik Jaroslavskogo Universiteta [*A publication*]

Vestn Kabard Balkar Nauc-Issled Inst ... Vestnik Kabardino-Balkarskogo Naucno-Issledovatel'skogo Instituta [*A publication*]

Vestn Karakalp Fil Akad ... Vestnik Karakalpakskogo Filiala Akademii Nauk Uzbekskoi SSR [*A publication*]

Vestn Karakalp Fil Akad Nauk Uzb SSR ... Vestnik Karakalpakskogo Filiala Akademii Nauk Uzbekskoi SSR [*A publication*]

Vestn Kaz Fil Akad Nauk SSSR ... Vestnik Kazakhskogo Filiala Akademii Nauk SSSR [*A publication*]

Vestn Khar'k Politekh Inst ... Vestnik Khar'kovskogo Politekhnicheskogo Instituta [*Ukrainian SSR*] [*A publication*]

Vestn Khark Univ ... Vestnik Khar'kovskogo Universiteta [*A publication*]

Vestn Khar'k Univ Astron ... Vestnik Khar'kovskogo Universiteta. Astronomiya [*Ukrainian SSR*] [*A publication*]

Vestn Khar'k Univ Geol Geogr ... Vestnik Khar'kovskogo Universiteta. Geologiya i Geografiya [*Ukrainian SSR*] [*A publication*]

Vestn Khar'k Univ Ser Biol ... Vestnik Khar'kovskogo Universiteta. Seriya Biologicheskaya [*A publication*]

Vestn Khar'k Univ Ser Geol ... Vestnik Khar'kovskogo Universiteta. Seriya Geologicheskaya [*Ukrainian SSR*] [*A publication*]

Vestn Khar'k Univ Ser Khim ... Vestnik Khar'kovskogo Universiteta. Seriya Khimicheskaya [*A publication*]

Vestn Khar'k Univ Vopr Ehlektrokhim ... Vestnik Khar'kovskogo Universiteta. Voprosy Ehlektrokhimii [*A publication*]

Vestn Khir ... Vestnik Khirurgii Imeni I. I. Grekova [*A publication*]

Vestn Khir Im I I Grekova ... Vestnik Khirurgii Imeni I. I. Grekova [*A publication*]

Vestn Kiev Politekh Inst Ser Mashinostr ... Vestnik Kievskogo Politekhnicheskogo Instituta. Seriya Mashinostroeniya [*A publication*]

Vestn Kiev Politekh Inst Ser Priborostr ... Vestnik Kievskogo Politekhnicheskogo Instituta. Seriya Priborostroeniya [*A publication*]

Vestn Kiev Politekh Inst Ser Teploenerg ... Vestnik Kievskogo Politekhnicheskogo Instituta. Seriya Teploenergetiki [*A publication*]

Vestn Kral Ceske Spol Nauk Trida Mat Prirodoved ... Vestnik Kralovske Ceske Spolecnosti Nauk Trida Matematicko Prirodovedecka [*A publication*]

Vestn La Upr Metallopromsti ... Vestnik Lavnogo Upravleniya Metallopromyshlennosti [*A publication*]

Vestn Leningrad Univ Ser Biol ... Vestnik Leningradskogo Universiteta. Seriya Biologii [*A publication*]

Vestn Leningr Univ ... Vestnik Leningradskogo Universiteta [*A publication*]

Vestn Leningr Univ Biol ... Vestnik Leningradskogo Universiteta. Biologiya [*A publication*]

Vestn Leningr Univ Fiz & Khim ... Vestnik Leningradskogo Universiteta. Fizika i Khimiya [*A publication*]

Vestn Leningr Univ Geol Geogr ... Vestnik Leningradskogo Universiteta. Geologiya, Geografiya [*A publication*]

Vestn Leningr Univ Ist Jaz Lit ... Vestnik Leningradskogo Universiteta. Istorija, Jazyka, i Literatury [*A publication*]

Vestn Leningr Univ Mat Mekh Astron ... Vestnik Leningradskogo Universiteta. Matematika, Mekhanika, Astronomiya [*A publication*]

Vestn Leningr Univ Ser Ekon Filos Pravo ... Vestnik Leningradskogo Universiteta. Serija Ekonomiki, Filosofii, i Pravo [*A publication*]

Vestn Leningr Univ Ser Fiz Khim ... Vestnik Leningradskogo Universiteta. Seriya Fiziki i Khimii [*USSR*] [*A publication*]

Vestn Leningr Univ Ser Geol Geogr ... Vestnik Leningradskogo Universiteta. Seriya Geologii i Geografii [*USSR*] [*A publication*]

Vestn Leningr Univ Ser Mat Fiz Khim ... Vestnik Leningradskogo Universiteta. Seriya Matematiki, Fiziki, i Khimii [*A publication*]

Vestn Leningr Univ Ser Mat Mekh & Astron ... Vestnik Leningradskogo Universiteta. Seriya Matematika, Mekhanika, i Astronomiya [*A publication*]

Vestn Lening Univ Ser Biol Geogr Geol ... Vestnik Leningradskogo Universiteta. Seriya Biologii, Geografii, i Geologii [*A publication*]

Vestn L'viv Derzh Univ Ser Fiz ... Vestnik L'vivs'kogo Derzhavnogo Universitetu. Seriya Fizichna [*Ukrainian SSR*] [*A publication*]

Vestn Mashinostr ... Vestnik Mashinostroeniya [*A publication*]

Vestn Metallopromsti ... Vestnik Metallopromyshlennosti [*A publication*]

Vestn Minist Zdrav ... Vestnik Ministerstva Zdravotnictvi [*Czechoslovakia*] [*A publication*]

Vestn Moskovskogo Univ Fiz-Astron ... Vestnik Moskovskogo Universiteta. Seriya Fizika-Astronomiya [*A publication*]

Vestn Moskovskogo Univ Khim ... Vestnik Moskovskogo Universiteta. Seriya Khimiya [*A publication*]

Vestn Moskov Univ Ser 6 ... Vestnik Moskovskogo Universiteta. Seriya 6 [*A publication*]

Vestn Moskov Univ Ser Ekon ... Vestnik Moskovskogo Universiteta. Serija Ekonomika [*A publication*]

Vestn Moskov Univ Ser Filos ... Vestnik Moskovskogo Universiteta. Serija Filosofija [*A publication*]

Vestn Moskov Univ Ser Geogr ... Vestnik Moskovskogo Universiteta. Serija Geografija [*A publication*]

Vestn Moskov Univ Ser Ist ... Vestnik Moskovskogo Universiteta. Serija Istorija [*A publication*]

Vestn Moskov Univ Ser Pravo ... Vestnik Moskovskogo Universiteta. Serija Pravo [*A publication*]

Vestn Moskov Univ Teorija Nauc Kommunizma ... Vestnik Moskovskogo Universiteta Teorija Naucnogo Kommunizma [*A publication*]

Vestn Mosk Univ ... Vestnik Moskovskogo Universiteta [*A publication*]

Vestn Mosk Univ Biol Pochvoved ... Vestnik Moskovskogo Universiteta. Biologiya, Pochvovedenie [*A publication*]

Vestn Mosk Univ Fiz Astron ... Vestnik Moskovskogo Universiteta. Fizika, Astronomiya [*A publication*]

Vestn Mosk Univ Geogr ... Vestnik Moskovskogo Universiteta. Geografiya [*A publication*]

Vestn Mosk Univ Geol ... Vestnik Moskovskogo Universiteta. Geologiya [*A publication*]

Vestn Mosk Univ Khim ... Vestnik Moskovskogo Universiteta. Khimiya [*A publication*]

Vestn Mosk Univ Mat Mekh ... Vestnik Moskovskogo Universiteta. Matematika, Mekhanika [*A publication*]

Vestn Mosk Univ Ser 1 ... Vestnik Moskovskogo Universiteta. Seriya 1. Matematika, Mekhanika [*A publication*]

Vestn Mosk Univ Ser 3 ... Vestnik Moskovskogo Universiteta. Seriya 3. Fizika, Astronomiya [*A publication*]

Vestn Mosk Univ Ser 15 ... Vestnik Moskovskogo Universiteta. Seriya 15. Vychislitel'naya Matematika i Kibernetika [*A publication*]

Vestn Mosk Univ Ser 16 Biol ... Vestnik Moskovskogo Universiteta. Seriya 16. Biologiya [*A publication*]

Vestn Mosk Univ Ser 6 Biol Pochvoved ... Vestnik Moskovskogo Universiteta. Seriya 6. Biologiya, Pochvovedenie [*A publication*]

Vestn Mosk Univ Ser Biol Pochvoved Geol Geogr ... Vestnik Moskovskogo Universiteta. Seriya Biologii, Pochvovedeniya, Geologii, Geografii [*A publication*]

Vestn Mosk Univ Ser 3 Fiz Astron ... Vestnik Moskovskogo Universiteta. Seriya 3. Fizika, Astronomiya [*A publication*]

Vestn Mosk Univ Ser Fiz-Mat Estestv Nauk ... Vestnik Moskovskogo Universiteta. Seriya Fiziko-Matematicheskikh i Estestvennykh Nauk [*USSR*] [*A publication*]

Vestn Mosk Univ Ser 5 Geogr ... Vestnik Moskovskogo Universiteta. Seriya 5. Geografiya [*A publication*]

Vestn Mosk Univ Ser 4 Geol ... Vestnik Moskovskogo Universiteta. Seriya 4. Geologiya [*A publication*]

Vestn Mosk Univ Ser II ... Vestnik Moskovskogo Universiteta. Nauchnyj Zhurnal. Seriya II. Khimiya [*A publication*]

Vestn Mosk Univ Ser 2 Khim ... Vestnik Moskovskogo Universiteta. Seriya 2. Khimiya [*A publication*]

Vestn Mosk Univ Ser 1 Mat Mekh ... Vestnik Moskovskogo Universiteta. Seriya 1. Matematika, Mekhanika [*A publication*]

Vestn Mosk Univ Ser Mat Mekh Astron Fiz Khim ... Vestnik Moskovskogo Universiteta. Seriya Matematiki, Mekhaniki, Astronomii, Fiziki, Khimii [*A publication*]

Vestn Mosk Univ Ser 17 Pochvoved ... Vestnik Moskovskogo Universiteta. Seriya 17. Pochvovedenie [*A publication*]

Vestn Mosk Univ Ser 16 Ser Biol ... Vestnik Moskovskogo Universiteta. Seriya 16. Seriya Biologiia [*A publication*]

Vestn Mosk Univ Ser 15 Vychisl Mat Kibern ... Vestnik Moskovskogo Universiteta. Seriya 15. Vychislitel'naya Matematika i Kibernetika [*A publication*]

Vestn Nauchn Inf Zabaik Fil Geogr Ova SSSR ... Vestnik Nauchnoi Informatsii Zabaikal'skogo Filiala Geograficheskogo Obshchestva SSSR [*A publication*]

Vestn Nauchno-Issled Inst Gidrobiol (Dnepropetr) ... Vestnik Nauchno-Issledovatel'skogo Instituta Gidrobiologii (Dnepropetrovski) [*A publication*]

Vestn Obsc Nauk Akad Nauk Arm SSR ... Vestnik Obscestvennyh Nauk. Akademija Nauk Armjanskoj SSR [*A publication*]

Vestn Oftal'mol ... Vestnik Oftal'mologii [*A publication*]

Vestn ORL ... Vestnik Oto-Rino-Laringologii [*A publication*]

Vestn Otorinolaringol ... Vestnik Otorinolaringologii [*A publication*]

Vestn Protivovozdushnoi Oborony ... Vestnik Protivovozdushnoi Oborony [*A publication*]

Vestn Rentgenol Radiol ... Vestnik Rentgenologii i Radiologii [*A publication*]

Vestn Respub Inst Okhr Prir Estestvennonauchn Muz Titograde ... Vestnik Respublikanskogo Instituta za Okhranu Prirodyi Estestvennonauchnogo Muzeya v Titograde [*A publication*]

Vestn Sel'skokhoz Nauki (Alma-Ata) ... Vestnik Sel'skokhozyaistvennoi Nauki (Alma-Ata) [*A publication*]

Vestn Sel'skokhoz Nauki (Moscow) ... Vestnik Sel'skokhozyaistvennoi Nauki (Moscow) [*A publication*]

Vestn S-Kh Nauki (Alma-Ata) ... Vestnik Sel'skokhozyaistvennoi Nauki (Alma-Ata) [*Kazakh SSR*] [*A publication*]

Vestn S-Kh Nauki Kaz ... Vestnik Sel'skokhozyaistvennoi Nauki Kazakhstana. Ezhemesiachnyi Nauchnyi Zhurnal [*A publication*]

Vestn S-Kh Nauki (Mosc) ... Vestnik Sel'skokhozyaistvennoi Nauki (Moscow) [*A publication*]

Vestn Slov Kem Drus ... Vestnik Slovenskega Kemijskega Drustva [*A publication*]

Vestn Sots Rastenievod ... Vestnik Sotsialisticheskogo Rastenievodstva [*A publication*]

Vestn Stand ... Vestnik Standartizatsii [*A publication*]

Vestn Statis ... Vestnik Statistiki [*A publication*]

Vestn Statist ... Vestnik Statistiki [*A publication*]

Vestn Statniho Geol Ustavu Cesk Repub ... Vestnik Statniho Geologickiho Ustavu Ceskoslovenske Republiky [*A publication*]

Vestn Stud Nauchn Ova Kazan Gos Univ Estestv Nauki ... Vestnik Studencheskogo Nauchnogo Obshchestva Kazanskii Gosudarstvennyi Universitet Estestvennye Nauki [*A publication*]

Vestn Tbilis Bot Sada Akad Nauk Gruz SSR ... Vestnik Tbilisskogo Botanicheskogo Sada Akademii Nauk Gruzinskoi SSR [*A publication*]

Vestn Uradu Vynalezy Objevy ... Vestnik Uradu pro Vynalezy a Objevy [*A publication*]

Vestn Uradu Vynalezy Objevy Cast A Vynalezy ... Vestnik Uradu pro Vynalezy a Objevy. Cast A. Vynalezy [*A publication*]

Vestn Uradu Vynalezy Objevy Cast B Ochr Znamky Prum Vzory ... Vestnik Uradu pro Vynalezy a Objevy. Cast B. Ochranne Znamky. Prumyslovy Vzory [*A publication*]

Vestn Uradu Vynalezy Objevy Ochr Znamky Prum Vzory ... Vestnik Uradu pro Vynalezy a Objevy. Ochranne Znamky. Prumyslovy Vzory [*A publication*]

Vestn Uradu Vynalezy Objevy Vynalezy ... Vestnik Uradu pro Vynalezy a Objevy. Vynalezy [*A publication*]

Vestn USSR Acad Med Sci ... Vestnik. USSR Academy of Medical Science [*A publication*]

Vestn Ustred Ustavu Geol ... Vestnik Ustredniho Ustavu Geologickeho [*A publication*]

Vestn Vyssh Shk ... Vestnik Vysshej Shkoly [*A publication*]

Vestn Vyzk Ustavu Zemed ... Vestnik Vyzkumnych Ustavu Zemedelskych [*A publication*]

Vestn Zapadno Sib Geol Upr ... Vestnik Zapadno-Sibirskogo Geologicheskogo Upravleniya [*A publication*]

Vestn Zapadno Sib i Novosib Geol Upr ... Vestnik Zapadno-Sibirskogo i Novosibirskogo Geologicheskikh Upravlenii [*A publication*]

Vestn Zashch Rast ... Vestnik Zashchity Rastenii [*A publication*]

Vestn Zool ... Vestnik Zoologii [*A publication*]

Vestn Zool Zool Rec ... Vestnik Zoologii/Zoological Record [*A publication*]

Vest Oftal (Kiev) ... Vestnik Oftal'mologii (Kiev) [*A publication*]

Vest Oftal (Mosk) ... Vestnik Oftal'mologii (Moskva) [*A publication*]

Vest Oto-Rino-Lar ... Vestnik Otorinolaringologii [*A publication*]

Vest Sel'-Khoz Nauki (Alma-Ata) Minist Sel Khoz Kazakh SSR ... Vestnik Sel'skokhozyaistvennoi Nauki (Alma-Ata). Ministerstvo Sel'skogo Khozyaistva Kazakhskoi SSR [*A publication*]

Vest Sel-Khoz Nauki (Mosk) ... Vestnik Sel'skokhozyaistvennoi Nauki (Moskva) [*USSR*] [*A publication*]

Vestsi Akad Navuk BSSR Khim Navuk ... Vestsi Akademii Navuk Belaruskai SSR. Khimichnykh Navuk [*A publication*]

Vestsi Akad Navuk BSSR Ser ... Vestsi Akademii Navuk Belaruskai SSR. Seriya [*A publication*]

Vestsi Akad Navuk BSSR Ser Biyal Navuk ... Vestsi Akademii Navuk Belaruskai SSR. Seryya Biyalagichnykh Navuk [*A publication*]

Vestsi Akad Navuk BSSR Ser Fiz-Ehnerg Navuk ... Vestsi Akademii Navuk BSSR. Seryya Fizika-Ehnergetychnykh Navuk [*A publication*]

Vestsi Akad Navuk BSSR Ser Fiz-Mat ... Vestsi Akademii Navuk BSSR. Seriya Fizika-Matematicheskikh [*A publication*]

Vestsi Akad Navuk BSSR Ser Fiz-Mat Navuk ... Vestsi Akademii Navuk BSSR. Seryya Fizika-Matematychnykh Navuk [*A publication*]

Vestsi Akad Navuk BSSR Ser Fiz-Tekh Navuk ... Vestsi Akademii Navuk BSSR. Seryya Fizika-Tekhnichnykh Navuk [*A publication*]

Vestsi Akad Navuk BSSR Ser Gramadskikh Navuk ... Vestsi Akademii Navuk BSSR. Seryya Gramadskikh Navuk [*Belorussian SSR*] [*A publication*]

Vestsi Akad Navuk BSSR Ser Khim ... Vestsi Akademii Navuk BSSR. Seriya Khimicheskikh [*USSR*] [*A publication*]

Vestsi Akad Navuk BSSR Ser Khim Navuk ... Vestsi Akademii Navuk Belaruskai SSR. Seryya Khimichnykh Navuk [*A publication*]

Vestsi Akad Navuk BSSR Ser Sel'skagas Navuk ... Vestsi Akademii Navuk Belaruskai SSR. Seryya Sel'skagaspadar Navuk [*A publication*]

Vestsi Belarus Akad Navuk Ser Biyal Navuk ... Vestsi Belaruskaya Akademiya Navuk. Seryya Biyalagichnykh Navuk [*A publication*]

Vestsyi Akad Navuk BSSR Ser Fyiz-Ehnerg Navuk ... Vestsyi Akademhyiyi Navuk BSSR. Seryya Fyizyika-Ehnergetychnykh Navuk [*A publication*]

Vestsyi Akad Navuk BSSR Ser Fyiz-Mat Navuk ... Vestsyi Akademhyiyi Navuk BSSR. Seryya Fyizyika-Matehmatychnykh Navuk [*A publication*]

Vestsyi Akad Navuk BSSR Ser Fyiz-Tehkh Navuk ... Vestsyi Akademhyiyi Navuk BSSR. Seryya Fyizyika-Tehkhnyichnykh Navuk [*A publication*]

Vestsyi Akad Navuk BSSR Ser Khyim Navuk ... Vestsyi Akademhyiyi Navuk BSSR. Seryya Khyimyichnykh Navuk [*A publication*]

Vest Ustred Ust Geol ... Vestnik Ustredniho Ustavu Geologickeho [*A publication*]

Vest Zool.... Vestnik Zoologii [*A publication*]

VES UR ..... Vesica Urinaria [*Urinary Bladder*]

VESV.......... Vesicular Exanthema Swine Virus

Veszpremi Vegyip Egy Tud Ulesszakanak Eloadasai ... Veszpremi Vegyipari Egyetem Tudomanyos Ulesszakanak Eloadasai [*Hungary*] [*A publication*]

Veszprem Koezl ... Veszprem Megyei Muzeumok Koezlemenyei [*A publication*]

Veszprem Megyei Muz ... Veszprem Megyei Muzeumok Koezlemenyei [*A publication*]

Veszprem Megyei Muz Koezlem ... Veszprem Megyei Muzeumok Koezlemenyei [*A publication*]

Veszprmi Vegyip Egy Kozl ... Veszpremi Vegyipari Egyetem Kozlemenyei [*A publication*]

VET .... Care Vet Pharmacy [*Vancouver Stock Exchange symbol*]

VET .... Value Engineering Training

VET .... Vehicle Elapsed Time (MCD)

VET .... Verbal Test

V & ET...... Verification and Evaluation Tests (MCD)

VET .... Versatile Engine Tester

VET .... Vestigial Testes [*Anatomy*]

VET .... Veteran (AFM)

VET .... Veterans Administration, Somerville, NJ [*OCLC symbol*] (OCLC)

Vet............. Veterinaria [*A publication*]

VET .... Veterinary (AFM)

VET .... Vibrational Energy Transfer [*LASER*] (MCD)

VET .... Victorian Equity Trust [*Australia*]

VET .... Video Editing Terminal [*Data processing*]

VET .... Vidicon Electron Tube
Vet Anesth ... Veterinary Anesthesia [*A publication*]
Vet Annu.... Veterinary Annual [*A publication*]
Vet Arh ...... Veterinarski Arhiv [*A publication*]
Vet Bull...... Veterinary Bulletin [*A publication*]
Vet Bull (London) ... Veterinary Bulletin (London) [*A publication*]
Vet Bull (Weybridge Eng) ... Veterinary Bulletin (Weybridge, England) [*A publication*]
Vet Cas...... Veterinarsky Casopis [*A publication*]
Vet Cas (Kosice) ... Veterinarsky Casopis (Kosice) [*A publication*]
VetChr .... Vetera Christianorum [*A publication*]
Vet Clin North Am ... Veterinary Clinics of North America [*A publication*]
Vet Clin North Am Equine Pract ... Veterinary Clinics of North America. Equine Practice [*A publication*]
Vet Clin North Am Food Anim Pract ... Veterinary Clinics of North America. Food Animal Practice [*A publication*]
Vet Clin North Am (Large Anim Pract) ... Veterinary Clinics of North America (Large Animal Practice) [*A publication*]
Vet Clin North Am (Small Anim Pract) ... Veterinary Clinics of North America (Small Animal Practice) [*A publication*]
Vet Clin Pathol ... Veterinary Clinical Pathology [*A publication*]
VETDOC... Veterinary Literature Documentation [*Derwent Publications Ltd.*] [*Bibliographic database*] [*London, England*]
Vet Econ..... Veterinary Economics [*A publication*]
Vetensk Publ Tek Hoegsk Helsingfors ... Vetenskapliga Publikationer. Tekniska Hoegskolan i Helsingfors [*A publication*]
Vetensk Soc i Lund Arsbok ... Vetenskaps-Societeten i Lund. Aarsbok [*A publication*]
Vetera Chr ... Vetera Christianorum [*A publication*]
Ve Tes .... Vetus Testamentum [*A publication*]
Vet Espan .. Veterinaria Espanola [*A publication*]
VETF........ Value Engineering Task Force
Vet Glas ..... Veterinarski Glasnik [*A publication*]
Vet Glasn ... Veterinarski Glasnik [*A publication*]
Vet Hist...... Veterinary History Bulletin. Veterinary History Society [*A publication*]
Vet Hum Toxicol ... Veterinary and Human Toxicology [*A publication*]
Vet Immunol Immunopathol ... Veterinary Immunology and Immunopathology [*A publication*]
Vet Insp Annu Inst Vet Insp NSW ... Veterinary Inspector Annual. Institute of Veterinary Inspectors of New South Wales [*A publication*]
Vet Int........ Veteres Intrationes [*A publication*]   (DLA)
Vet Ital....... Veterinaria Italiana [*A publication*]
VETJ .... Tezu [*India*] [*ICAO location identifier*]   (ICLI)
Vet J.......... Veterinary Journal [*A publication*]
Vet J and Ann Comp Path ... Veterinary Journal and Annals of Comparative Pathology [*A publication*]
Vet J (Bratislava) ... Veterinary Journal (Bratislava) [*A publication*]
VETK........ Tarakeshwar [*India*] [*ICAO location identifier*]   (ICLI)
Vet Mag...... Veterinary Magazine [*A publication*]
Vet MB ...... Bachelor of Veterinary Medicine
Vet Med..... Veterinarni Medicina [*A publication*]
Vet Med ..... Veterinary Medicine [*A publication*]
Vet Med ..... Veterinary Medicine and Small Animal Clinician [*A publication*]
Vet Med Nauki ... Veterinarno Meditsinski Nauki [*A publication*]
Vet Med Nauki (Sofia) ... Veterinarno Meditsinski Nauki (Sofia) [*A publication*]
Vet Med (Prague) ... Veterinarni Medicina (Prague) [*A publication*]
Vet Med (Praha) ... Veterinarni Medicina (Praha) [*A publication*]
Vet Med Rev ... Veterinary Medical Review [*A publication*]
Vet Med/SAC ... Veterinary Medicine and Small Animal Clinician [*A publication*]
Vet Med Sci ... Veterinary Medical Science [*A publication*]
Vet Med & Small Anim Clin ... Veterinary Medicine and Small Animal Clinician [*A publication*]
Vet Med Small Anim Clin ... Veterinary Medicine and Small Animal Clinician [*A publication*]
Vet Microbiol ... Veterinary Microbiology [*Netherlands*] [*A publication*]
VETMIS.... Vertical Technical Management Information System   (MCD)
Vet Na B .... Old Natura Brevium [*A publication*]   (DLA)
VETNAL... Veterinariya [*Moscow*] [*A publication*]
Vet N B ...... Vetus Natura Brevium [*A publication*]   (DSA)
Vet N Br..... Old Natura Brevium [*A publication*]   (ILCA)
Vet News.... Veterinary News [*A publication*]
Vet Obozr... Veterinarnoe Obozrienie [*A publication*]
Vet Parasitol ... Veterinary Parasitology [*A publication*]
Vet Path..... Veterinary Pathology [*A publication*]
Vet Pathol ... Veterinary Pathology [*A publication*]
Vet Pathol (Suppl) ... Veterinary Pathology. Supplement [*A publication*]
Vet Q......... Veterinary Quarterly [*A publication*]
Vet QQJ Vet Sci ... Veterinary Quarterly. Quarterly Journal of Veterinary Science [*A publication*]
Vet Radiol ... Veterinary Radiology [*A publication*]
Vet Rec....... Veterinary Record [*A publication*]
Vet Res Commun ... Veterinary Research Communications [*A publication*]
Vet Resp Mezhved Temat Nauchn Sb ... Veterinariya Respublikanskii Mezhvedomstvennyi Tematicheskii Nauchnyi Sbornik [*A publication*]

Vet Resp Mizhvid Temat Nauk Zb ... Veterinariya Respublikanskyu Mizhvidomchyi Tematychnyi Naukovyi Zbirnyk [*A publication*]
Vet Rev...... Veterinary Review [*A publication*]
VETRONICS ... Vehicle Electronics [*Program*] [*Army*]
Vetro Silic.. Vetro e Silicati [*A publication*]
VETS........ Animed, Inc. [*Roslyn, NY*] [*NASDAQ symbol*]   (NQ)
VETS........ Tusra [*India*] [*ICAO location identifier*]   (ICLI)
VETS........ Vehicle Electrical Test System   (ADA)
VETS........ Vertical Engine Test Stand
VETS........ Veterans' Employment and Training Service [*Department of Labor*]
VetSb........ Veterinarna Sbirka [*A publication*]
Vet Sb (Bratislava) ... Veterinarsky Sbornik (Bratislava) [*A publication*]
Vet Sbirka ... Veterinarna Sbirka [*A publication*]
Vet Sbir (Sof) ... Veterinarna Sbirka (Sofia) [*A publication*]
Vet Sb (Sofia) ... Veterinarna Sbirka (Sofia) [*A publication*]
VetSci........ Veterinary Science
Vet Sci Commun ... Veterinary Science Communications [*A publication*]
Vet Stars ... Vets Stars and Stripes for Peace [*A publication*]
Vet Surg .... Veterinary Surgery [*A publication*]
Vet Surgery ... Veterinary Surgery [*A publication*]
Vett Cens ... De Veterum Censura [*of Dionysius Halicarnassensis*] [*Classical studies*]   (OCD)
Vet Test..... Vetus Testamentum [*A publication*]
Vet Toxicol ... Veterinary Toxicology [*A publication*]
Vet Urug .... Veterinaria Uruguay [*A publication*]
Vetus Test ... Vetus Testamentum [*A publication*]
Vet World .. Veterinary World [*A publication*]
VETX........ Vertex Industries, Inc. [*Clifton, NJ*] [*NASDAQ symbol*]   (NQ)
Vet Zh (Bratislava) ... Veterinarnyi Zhurnal (Bratislava) [*A publication*]
Vet Zootec Rev Peru ... Veterinaria y Zootecnia Revista Peruana [*A publication*]
VEUK .... Utkela [*India*] [*ICAO location identifier*]   (ICLI)
VEV .... Barakoma [*Solomon Islands*] [*Airport symbol*]   (OAG)
VEV .... Vernier Engine Vibration [*Aerospace*]
VEV .... Verre Oosten. Orgaan van de Landenkamers Verre Oosten [*A publication*]
VEV .... Vietnam Era Veterans   (OICC)
VEV .... Vlaams Economisch Verbond
VEV .... Voice-Excited VOCODER
VEVA .... Vereingung der Europaischen Verbande des Automatenwirtschaft [*Federation of European Coin-Machine Associations*]   (EAIO)
VEV Ber..... VEV [*Vlaams Economisch Verband*] Berichten [*A publication*]
VEVERP ... Vietnam Era Veteran Recruitment Program
VEVITA ... Vietnam Era Veterans Inter-Tribal Association   (EA)
VEVZ........ Vishakhapatnam [*India*] [*ICAO location identifier*]   (ICLI)
VEWAA ... Vocational Evaluation and Work Adjustment Association   (EA)
VEWS....... Very Early Warning System
VEWU .... Vietnam Educational Workers' Union [*North Vietnam*]
VEX .... Tioga, ND [*Location identifier*] [*FAA*]   (FAAL)
VEXP....... Virtual Machine Experience
VEY .... Vestmannaeyjar [*Iceland*] [*Airport symbol*]   (OAG)
Vez .... Vezey's [*or Vesey's*] English Chancery Reports [*A publication*]   (DLA)
Vezelinst TNO Delft VI Pam ... Vezelinstituut TNO [*Nederlands Centrale Organisatie voor Toegepast-Natuurwetenschappelijk Onderzoek*] Delft VI Pamflet [*A publication*]
Vezetestud ... Vezetestudomany [*A publication*]
VEZO .... Zero [*India*] [*ICAO location identifier*]   (ICLI)
VF .... British Air Ferries Ltd.   (FAAC)
VF .... De Vrije Fries [*A publication*]
VF .... Fighter Plane [*Navy symbol*]
VF .... Fighter Squadron [*Navy symbol*]
VF .... Flaps-Down Speed [*Aviation*]
VF .... Valley Forge Corp. [*AMEX symbol*]   (SPSG)
VF .... Value Foundation   (EA)
VF .... Vaporizer Feed [*Nuclear energy*]   (NRCH)
VF .... Variable Factor [*Economics*]
VF .... Variable Frequency [*Electricity*]   (MSA)
VF .... Variant Frequency [*Biology*]
VF .... Vector Field
VF .... Velocity Failure
VF .... Ventral Funiculus [*Anatomy*]
VF .... Ventricular Fibrillation [*Also, vent fib, VFIB*] [*Cardiology*]
VF .... Verification of Function
VF .... Verkuendigung und Forschung [*Munich*] [*A publication*]
VF .... Vertical File
VF .... Vertical Flight   (NASA)
VF .... Very Fair
VF .... Very Fine [*Condition*] [*Antiquarian book trade, numismatics, etc.*]
VF .... Very Fine Soil [*Agronomy*]
VF .... VFW [*Vereinigte Flugtechnische Werke*]-Fokker [*Federal Republic of Germany*] [*ICAO aircraft manufacturer identifier*]   (ICAO)
VF .... Vicarius Foraneus [*Vicar-Forane*] [*Latin*]
VF .... Video Frequency
VF .... View Factor
VF .... Viewfinder [*Photography*]

VF .... Vilagirodalmi Figyelo [*A publication*]
VF .... Villers Foundation [*Later, Families USA Foundation*]   (EA)
VF .... Vinyl Fabric [*Technical drawings*]
VF .... Vinylferrocene [*Organic chemistry*]
VF .... Virile Female Project [*RJ Reynolds Tobacco Co. marketing strategy for proposed Dakota brand*]
VF .... Vision Foundation   (EA)
VF .... Vision Frequency
VF .... Visiting Friends [*An association*]   (EA)
VF .... Visual Field
VF .... Visual Flight [*Aviation*]   (FAAC)
VF .... Vocal Fremitus
VF .... Voice Foundation   (EA)
VF .... Voice Frequency [*Communications*]
V/F .... Voltage to Frequency [*Converter*] [*Data processing*]
VF .... Volunteer Fireman
VF .... Voprosy Filologii [*A publication*]
VF .... Voprosy Filosofii [*A publication*]
VF .... Vulcanized Fiber
VFA .... Variation Flow Analysis
VFA .... Victoria Falls [*Zimbabwe*] [*Airport symbol*]   (OAG)
VFA .... Video Free America   (EA)
VFA .... Video Frequency Amplifier
VFA .... Videotape Facilities Association   (EA)
VFA .... Visual Flight Attachment [*Aviation*]   (RDA)
VFA .... Volatile Fatty Acid [*Organic chemistry*]
VFA .... Volunteer Fire Alarm   (TEL)
VFAS......... Vertical Force Accounting System
VFAS/TL .. Vertical Force Accounting System/Troop List   (MCD)
VFAT........ Visual Functioning Assessment Tool [*Educational test*]
VF AW....... Fighter Squadron - All Weather [*Navy symbol*]   (MCD)
VFAX........ Heavier-than-Air Fighter/Attack/Experimental [*Aircraft*]
VFB.......... Fighter Bombing Plane [*Navy symbol*]
VFB.......... Vertical Format Buffer
VFB.......... Vierteljahrschrift fuer Bibelkunde, Talmudische, und Patristische Studien [*A publication*]
VFBK........ Eastern Bancorp, Inc. [*Formerly, Vermont Federal Bank FSB*] [*NASDAQ symbol*]   (NQ)
VFC........... Ferrum College, Ferrum, VA [*OCLC symbol*]   (OCLC)
VFC........... Variable File Channel
VFC........... Variable Frequency Control
VFC........... Vertical Format Control
VFC........... Very Fine Cognac
VFC........... VF Corporation [*NYSE symbol*]   (SPSG)
VFC........... Video Frequency Carrier [*or Channel*]   (CET)
VFC........... Visual Field Control [*Aviation*]
VFC........... Voice Frequency Carrier [*or Channel*]
VFC........... Volatile Flavor Compound
VFC........... Voltage to Frequency Converter
VFC........... Volunteer Field Consultant [*Red Cross*]
VFC........... Voters for Choice/Friends of Family Planning   (EA)
VFCBA9 .... Forests Commission Victoria. Bulletin [*A publication*]
VFC/FFP... Voters for Choice/Friends of Family Planning [*Later, VFC*]   (EA)
VFCS .... Vehicle Flight Control System
VFCT........ Voice Frequency Carrier [*or Channel*] Telegraph [*or Teletype*]
VFCTT ...... Voice Frequency Carrier Teletype   (MSA)
VFD .... Vacuum Fluorescent Display [*Data processing*]
VFD .... Value for Duty [*Business term*]
VFD .... Variable Frequency Drive [*Instrumentation*]
VFD .... Verified Free Distribution [*British*]
VFD .... Vocal Feedback Device [*Aid for stutterers developed at the University of Pittsburgh by Dr. George Shames*]
VFD .... Volunteer Fire Department
VFDBA...... VFDB [*Vereinigung zur Foerderung des Deutschen Brandschutzes eV*] Zeitschrift [*A publication*]
VFDB (Ver Foerd Dtch Brandschutzes) Z ... VFDB (Vereinigung zur Foerderung des Deutschen Brandschutzes eV) Zeitschrift [*A publication*]
VFDB Z ..... Vereinigung zur Foerderung des Deutschen Brandschutzes. Zeitschrift [*A publication*]
VFDF........ Very Fast Death Factor
VFDM .... Vsemirnaia Federatsiia Demokraticheskoi Molodezhi [*World Federation of Democratic Youth*]
VFDMIS ... Vertical Force Development Management Information Systems
VFDR........ Variable-Flow Directed Rocket
VFE.......... Vendor-Furnished Equipment   (NASA)
VFED......... Valley Federal Savings & Loan Association [*NASDAQ symbol*]   (NQ)
VFER........ Veterans Federal Employment Representative [*Civil Service Commission*]
VFF........... Valence Force Field
VFF........... Victorian Farmers' Federation [*Australia*]
VFF........... Voice Frequency Filter
VFFM........ Vestlandets Forstilige Forsoksstasjon. Meddelelse [*A publication*]
VFFT .... Voice Frequency Facility Terminal [*Telecommunications*]   (TEL)
VFG .... Valley Fig Growers   (EA)
VFG .... Visual Flight Guide [*A publication*]   (APTA)

VfGH .... Verfassungsgerichtshof [*Provincial Constitutional Court*] [*German*]   (ILCA)
VFH .... Vacuum Film Handling
VFH .... Vertical Flow Horizontal
VFHG .... Versammlungen der Freunde des Humanistischen Gymnasiums [*A publication*]
VFHS........ Valley Forge Historical Society   (EA)
VFHT .... Vacuum Film Handling Technique
VFI........... Verification Flight Instrumentation   (NASA)
VFI........... Vinyl Fabrics Institute [*Later, Chemical Fabrics and Film Association*]   (EA)
VFI........... Visual Field Information [*Aviation*]
VFI........... Vocational Foundation, Incorporated   (EA)
VFI........... Volunteers for Israel   (EA)
VFIB .... Ventricular Fibrillation [*Also, vent fib, VF*] [*Cardiology*]
VFil........... Voprosy Filologii [*A publication*]
VFL........... LeMoyne College, Syracuse, NY [*OCLC symbol*]   (OCLC)
VFL........... Variable Field Length   (MCD)
VFL........... Variable Focal Length
VFL........... Victorian Football League [*Australia*] [*Receives television coverage in the US through the Entertainment and Sports Programming Network*]
VFL........... Voice Frequency Line [*Telecommunications*]   (TEL)
VFLA........ Volume Folding and Limiting Amplifier
VFLC .... Video Fluorometric Detection Liquid Chromatograph
VFLT .... Visual Flight [*Aviation*]   (FAAC)
VF(M)....... Fighter Plane (Two-Engine) [*Navy symbol*]
VFM .... Jahresberichte ueber die Veraenderungen und Fortschritte im Militaerwesen [*A publication*]
VFM .... Vacuum Forming Machine
VFM .... Value for Money [*Accounting*]
VFM .... Vendor-Furnished Material   (MCD)
VFM .... Vertical Flight Maneuver
VFMED...... Variable Format Message Entry Device [*Data processing*]   (MCD)
VF(N)........ Night Fighter Squadrons [*Navy symbol*]
VFN .... Verticillium Wilt, Fusarium Wilt, Nematode Resistance [*Tomato culture*]
VFO .... Vandenberg Field Office [*Air Force*]   (MCD)
VFO .... Vaporized Fuel Oil [*Process*]
VFO .... Variable Frequency Oscillator
VFO .... Viking Flight Operations [*NASA*]
VFON......... Volunteer Flight Officers Network
VFOX .... Vicon Fiber Optics Corp. [*NASDAQ symbol*]   (NQ)
VFP........... Fighter Squadron, Photo [*Navy symbol*]   (MCD)
VFP........... Vacuum Flash Pyrolysis
VFP........... Vacuum Fore Pump
VFP........... Variable-Factor Programming
VFP........... Variance Frequency Processor   (MCD)
VFP........... Veterans for Peace   (EA)
VFP........... Volunteers for Peace   (EA)
VFP........... Vsemirnaja Federacija Profsojuzov [*World Federation of Trade Unions*]
VFPR .... Via Flight Planned Route [*Aviation*]   (FAAC)
VFR........... Vehicle Flight Readiness   (KSC)
VFR........... Vehicle Force Ratio   (MCD)
VFR........... Verein fuer Raumschiffahrt [*Society for Space Travel*] [*Germany*]
VFR........... Victorian Fiction Research Guides [*A publication*]
VFR........... Visiting Friends and Relatives [*Airlines*]
VFR........... Visual Flight Rules [*Aviation*]
VFR........... Volunteer Field Representative [*Red Cross*]
VFRA........ Volume Footwear Retailers of America [*Later, FDRA*]
VFRC........ Valley Forge Research Center [*University of Pennsylvania*] [*Research center*]   (RCD)
VFRCTS .... Visual Flight Rules Control Tower Simulator [*Aviation*]   (MCD)
VFRSA ...... VFR [*Visual Flight Rules*] Restrictions Still Apply [*Aviation*]   (FAAC)
VFS .... Vapor Feed System
VFS .... Variable Frequency Synthesizer [*Ariel Corp.*] [*Data processing*]
VFS .... Ventilated Flight Suit
VFS .... Veterinary Field Services [*Australia*]
VFS .... Victorian Flying School [*Australia*]
VFS .... Visual Flight Simulator
VFS .... Voice from the Silence [*An association*]   (EA)
VFS .... Volume Fraction of Solids in a Slurry
VFSB .... Verein der Freunde Schloss Blutenburg [*Association of Friends of Schloss Blutenburg - AFSB*] [*Munich, Federal Republic of Germany*]   (EAIO)
VFSB .... Virginia First Savings Bank FSB [*NASDAQ symbol*]   (NQ)
VFSC .... Vermont Financial Services Corporation [*NASDAQ symbol*]   (NQ)
Vf Sch G.... Verfassungsschutzgesetz [*A publication*]
VFSL .... Valdosta Federal Savings & Loan Association [*NASDAQ symbol*]   (NQ)
VFSS.......... Voice Frequency Signaling System
VFSSMCQ ... Victorian Federation of State Schools Mothers Clubs. Quarterly Review [*A publication*]   (APTA)
VFSW .... Variable Frequency Sine Wave

VFSW........ Vierteljahrsschrift fuer Sozial- und Wirtschaftsgeschichte [*A publication*]
VFT........... Vacuum Form Tool   (MCD)
VFT........... Vacuum Friction Test
VFT........... Velocity False Target [*Military*]   (CAAL)
VFT........... Ventricular Fibrillation Threshold [*Cardiology*]
VFT........... Verification Flight Test   (MCD)
VFT........... Vertical Flight Test   (MCD)
VFT........... Very Fast Train [*Proposed*] [*Australia*]   (ADA)
VFT........... Viking Flight Team [*NASA*]
VFT........... Voice Frequency Telegraphy   (NATG)
VFT........... Voice Frequency Terminal
VFTG........ Voice Frequency Telegraphy
VFTTA ...... Visa for Travel to Australia   (ADA)
VFU .... Van Wert, OH [*Location identifier*] [*FAA*]   (FAAL)
VFU .... Vertical Format Unit   (BUR)
VFU .... Vocabulary File Utility
VFUNDW ... Voluntary Fund for the United Nations Decade for Women   (EA)
VFV........... Variable Fuel Vehicle [*General Motors Corp.*] [*Automotive engineering*]
VFV........... Venus Flyby Vehicle [*NASA*]
VFVC........ Vacuum Freezing, Vapor Compression [*Desalination*]
VFW .... Variable/Fixed Wavelength [*Electronics*]
VFW .... Verwaltungsamt fuer Wirtschaft [*Executive Committee for Economics*] [*Germany*]
VFW .... Veterans of Foreign Wars of the USA   (EA)
VFW .... Veterans of Future Wars [*Facetious organization formed by Princeton students in 1930's*]
VFY........... Verify   (AFM)
VG............. British Virgin Islands [*ANSI two-letter standard code*]   (CNC)
VG............. Central Caraibes SA [*Haiti*] [*ICAO designator*]   (FAAC)
VG............. Grundriss der Vergleichenden Grammatik der Semitischen Sprachen [*A publication*]   (BJA)
VG............. Light Transport Plane [*Single-engine*] [*Navy symbol*]
VG............. Validity Generalization Testing   (OICC)
VG............. Varga Aircraft Corp. [*ICAO aircraft manufacturer identifier*]   (ICAO)
VG............. Variable Geometry [*Refers to an aircraft that is capable of altering the sweep of the wings while in flight*]   (NATG)
VG............. Vector Generator [*Computer graphics*]
VG............. Velocity Gravity
VG............. Ventricular Gallop [*Cardiology*]
VG............. Verbi Gratia [*For Example*] [*Latin*]
V & G .... Vergangenheit und Gegenwart [*A publication*]
VG............. Vertical Grain
V-G .... Vertical Gust   (MCD)
VG............. Vertical Gyro   (MCD)
VG............. Verwaltungsgesellschaft fuer Industrielle Unternehmungen Friedrich Flick GmbH [*Frederick Flick Management Association for Industrial Enterprises*] [*Federal Republic of Germany*]
VG............. Very Good [*Condition*] [*Antiquarian book trade, numismatics, etc.*]
VG............. Vibration Greatness
VG............. Vicarius Generalis [*Vicar-General*] [*Latin*]
VG............. Vice Grand [*Freemasonry*]   (ROG)
VG............. Vinylguaiacol [*Biochemistry*]
VG............. Vocational Guidance   (ADA)
VG............. Voice Grade [*Telecommunications*]   (TEL)
VG............. Volksgrenadier [*Title given to infantry divisions with distinguished combat records*] [*Germany*] [*World War II*]
VG............. Voltage Gain
VG............. Volunteer Guards [*British military*]   (DMA)
VG............. Votre Grace [*Your Grace*] [*French*]
VG............. Votre Grandeur [*Your Highness*] [*French*]
Vg............. Vulgate [*Latin translation of the Bible*]   (BJA)
VGA........... Vapor Generation Accessory [*Instrumentation*]
VGA........... Variable Gain Amplifier
VGA........... Vertical Gyro Alignment
VGA........... Very General Algorithm   (KSC)
VGA........... Video Graphics Array [*Computer technology*]
VGA........... Vijayawada [*India*] [*Airport symbol*]   (OAG)
VGA........... Virginia Air Cargo, Inc. [*Charlottesville, VA*] [*FAA designator*]   (FAAC)
VGAA........ Vegetable Growers Association of America [*Defunct*]   (EA)
VGAM........ Vector Graphics Access Method
VGAT........ Visual General Aviation Trainer
VGB........... British Virgin Islands [*ANSI three-letter standard code*]   (CNC)
VGBAW .... Verhandlungen der Geologischen Bundesanstalt in Wien [*A publication*]
VGBD........ Virtual Grain Boundary Dislocation
Vgbl........... Bayerische Vorgeschichtsblaetter [*A publication*]
VGC........... Variable Gas Capacitor
VGC........... Velocity Gate Capture [*Military*]   (CAAL)
VGC........... Verdstone Gold Corp. [*Vancouver Stock Exchange symbol*]
VGC........... Very Good Condition [*Doll collecting*]
VGC........... Vesterheim Genealogical Center
VGC........... Video Graphics Controller [*Apple Computer, Inc.*]
VGC........... Viscosity Gravity Constant
VGCA .... Voice Gate Circuit Adaptors [*Data processing*]   (MCD)

VGCB .... Cox's Bazar [*Bangladesh*] [*ICAO location identifier*]   (ICLI)
VGCF........ Vapor-Phase-Grown Carbon Fiber
VGCH........ Vent Gas Collection Header [*Nuclear energy*]   (NRCH)
VGCI......... Veta Grande Companies [*NASDAQ symbol*]   (NQ)
VGCL........ Vietnam General Confederation of Labor
VGCM .... Comilla [*Bangladesh*] [*ICAO location identifier*]   (ICLI)
VGD........... Valentine Gold [*Vancouver Stock Exchange symbol*]
VGDIP .... Very God-Damned Important Person
VGE .... Video-Game Epilepsy [*Neurology*]
VGE .... Visual Gross Error
VGEBA...... Verhandlungen. Geologische Bundesanstalt (Austria) [*A publication*]
VGEG .... Chittagong [*Bangladesh*] [*ICAO location identifier*]   (ICLI)
VGF .... Escort Fighter Squadron [*Navy symbol*]
VGF .... Vaccinia Growth Factor [*Biochemistry*]
VGF .... Virus Growth Factor [*Biochemistry*]
VGFR......... Dhaka [*Bangladesh*] [*ICAO location identifier*]   (ICLI)
VGFTU....... Vietnam General Federation of Trade Unions [*North Vietnam*]
VGG .... Valhalla Gold Group [*Vancouver Stock Exchange symbol*]
VGH .... Vancouver General Hospital
VGH .... Velocity, Normal Gravity, and Height
VGH .... Verwaltungsgerichtshof [*A publication*]
VGH .... Very Good Health [*Medicine*]
VGH .... Veterinary General Hospital
VGHN......... Vaughn Communications, Inc. [*NASDAQ symbol*]   (NQ)
VGHQ .... Dhaka [*Bangladesh*] [*ICAO location identifier*]   (ICLI)
VGI .... Variable Geometry Inlet
VGI .... Vertical Gyro Indicator
VGIEMTP ... Veroeffentlichungen. Grabmann Institut zur Erforschung der Mittelalterlichen Theologie und Philosophie [*A publication*]
VGIN.......... Virgin Group PLC [*NASDAQ symbol*]   (NQ)
VGIS......... Ishurdi [*Bangladesh*] [*ICAO location identifier*]   (ICLI)
VGJ........... Vorgeschichtliches Jahrbuch [*A publication*]
VGJR.......... Jessore [*Bangladesh*] [*ICAO location identifier*]   (ICLI)
VGLI.......... Veterans Group Life Insurance
VGLIS .... Video Guidance, Landing, and Imaging System [*NASA*]
VGLKV...... Vierteljahrsschrift fuer Geschichte und Landeskunde Vorarlbergs [*A publication*]
VGLL......... Valstybine Grozines Literaturos Leidykla [*A publication*]
V/GLLD .... Vehicular/Ground LASER Locator Designator   (MCD)
VGLM .... Lalmonirhat [*Bangladesh*] [*ICAO location identifier*]   (ICLI)
VGM.......... George Mason University, Fairfax, VA [*OCLC symbol*]   (OCLC)
VGM......... Ventriculogram [*A roentgenogram*]
VGM......... VGM Capital Corp. [*Formerly, Vestgron Mines Ltd.*] [*Toronto Stock Exchange symbol*]
VGM.......... Vice Grand Master   (BJA)
VGM.......... Villa Grajales [*Mexico*] [*Seismograph station code, US Geological Survey*] [*Closed*]   (SEIS)
VGML .... Vegetarian Meal [*Airline notation*]
VGMU .... Vulcan Gunner Monitor Unit   (MCD)
VGN.......... Variable Geometry Nozzle
VGN.......... Virginian Railway Co. [*AAR code*]
VGO.......... Vacuum Gas Oil [*Petroleum technology*]
VGO.......... Vereinigte Gruenen Oesterreich [*United Green Party of Austria*] [*Political party*]   (EY)
VGO.......... Vicar General's Office [*British*]   (ROG)
VGO.......... Vickers Gas Operated [*British military*]   (DMA)
VGO.......... Vigo [*Spain*] [*Airport symbol*]   (OAG)
VGOR....... Vandenberg Ground Operations Requirement [*Air Force*]   (NASA)
VGOR....... Vehicle Ground Operation Requirements [*NASA*]   (NASA)
VGP .... Vehicle Ground Point [*NASA*]   (NASA)
VGP .... Victorian Government Publications [*A publication*]   (APTA)
VGP .... Virtual Geomagnetic Pole [*Geophysics*]
VGPI......... Visual Glide Path Indicator
VGPI......... Visual Ground Position Indicator   (NATG)
VGPO....... Velocity Gate Pulloff [*Military*]   (CAAL)
VGQ .... Vocational Guidance Quarterly [*A publication*]
VGR.......... Variable Geometry Rotor
VGRJ......... Rajshahi [*Bangladesh*] [*ICAO location identifier*]   (ICLI)
VGS .... Escort-Scouting Squadron [*Navy symbol*]
VGS .... Variable Geometry Structure
VGS .... Variable-Grade Gravity Sewer
VGS .... Vehicle Generating System
VGS .... Velocity Gate Stealer [*Military*]   (CAAL)
VGS .... Visual Guidance System [*Aviation*]   (FAAC)
VGS .... Volunteer Gliding Schools [*British*]
VGSD .... Saidpur [*Bangladesh*] [*ICAO location identifier*]   (ICLI)
VGSG .... Thakuragaon [*Bangladesh*] [*ICAO location identifier*]   (ICLI)
VGSH .... Shamshernagar [*Bangladesh*] [*ICAO location identifier*]   (ICLI)
VGSI......... Visual Glide Slope Indicator
VGSY........ Sylhet Osmani [*Bangladesh*] [*ICAO location identifier*]   (ICLI)
VGT.......... Las Vegas [*Nevada*] North Terminal [*Airport symbol*]   (OAG)
VGT.......... Las Vegas, NV [*Location identifier*] [*FAA*]   (FAAL)
VGT .... National Victoria & Grey Trustco Ltd. [*Toronto Stock Exchange symbol*]
VGT.......... Variable Geometry Turbocharger [*Automotive engineering*]
VGT .... Vehicle Ground Test [*NASA*]   (NASA)
VGTE .... Vulcan Gunner Tracking Evaluation   (MCD)

VGTJ......... Dhaka/Tejgaon [*Bangladesh*] [*ICAO location identifier*]   (ICLI)
VGTSA...... Voprosy Gigieny Truda v Slantsevoi Promyshlennosti
                Estonskoi SSR [*A publication*]
VGU.......... Des Moines, IA [*Location identifier*] [*FAA*]   (FAAL)
VGV.......... Vacuum Gate Valve
VG & VF..... Vicar General and Vicar Foreign [*British*]   (ROG)
VGVT........ Vertical Ground Vibration Test   (MCD)
VGW......... Variable Geometry Wing [*Aircraft*]
VGWA...... Variable Geometry Wing Aircraft   (AAG)
VGWO...... Velocity Gate Walkoff [*Military*]   (CAAL)
VGX.......... Velocity to Be Gained [*Body X-Axis*] [*NASA*]   (NASA)
VGY.......... Velocity to Be Gained [*Body Y-Axis*] [*NASA*]   (NASA)
VGZ.......... Velocity to Be Gained [*Body Z-Axis*] [*NASA*]   (NASA)
VGZR .... Dhaka/Zia International [*Bangladesh*] [*ICAO location
                identifier*]   (ICLI)
VH .... Air Volta [*Upper Volta*] [*ICAO designator*]   (FAAC)
VH .... Ambulance Plane [*Navy symbol*]
VH .... Australia [*Aircraft nationality and registration mark*]   (FAAC)
VH .... Rescue Squadrons [*Navy symbol*]
VH .... Vacuum Housing
VH .... Vaginal Hysterectomy [*Gynecology*]
VH .... Varia Historia [*of Aelianus*] [*Classical studies*]   (OCD)
VH .... Variable Heavy
V/H........... Velocity/Height
VH .... Venice Hospital [*Venice, FL*]
VH .... Vent Hole [*Technical drawings*]
VH .... Vermont History [*A publication*]
V & H........ Vertical and Horizontal [*Telecommunications*]   (TSSD)
VH .... Very Heavy [*Cosmic ray nuclei*]
VH .... Very High
VH .... Veterans Hospital
VH .... Vickers Hardness Number [*Also, HV, VHN*]   (AAG)
VH .... Vir Honestus [*A Worthy Man*] [*Latin*]
VH .... Viral Hepatitis [*Medicine*]
V/H........... Vulnerability/Hardness [*Refers to a weapon system's weakness
                and capabilities in withstanding adverse operating
                environments*]
VH-1 .... Video Hits One [*Cable-television system*] [*Companion to
                MTV*]
VHA......... Van Houten Associates [*Information service or system*]   (IID)
VHA....... Variable Housing Allowance   (MCD)
VHA.......... Very High Altitude
VHA.......... Very High Aluminum [*Rock composition*]
VHA.......... Voluntary Hospitals of America   (EA)
VHAA........ Very High Altitude Abort [*NASA*]   (KSC)
VHAAH .... Vitterhets, Historie- och Antikvitets-Akademiens Handlingar [*A
                publication*]
VHB........... Buffalo and Erie County Public Library, Buffalo, NY [*OCLC
                symbol*]   (OCLC)
VHB........... Very Heavy Bombardment [*Air Force*]
VHB........... Very High Bond Tape [*3M Co.*]
Vh BAG ..... Verhandlungen. Berliner Gesellschaft fuer Anthropologie,
                Ethnologie, und Urgeschichte [*A publication*]
VHBW....... Very-High-Speed Black and White [*Photography*]
VHC........... Hollins College, Hollins College, VA [*OCLC symbol*]   (OCLC)
VHC........... Saurimo [*Angola*] [*Airport symbol*]   (OAG)
VHC........... Ventech Healthcare Corp., Inc. [*Toronto Stock Exchange
                symbol*]
VHC........... Vertical Hold Control
VHC........... Very High Contrast [*Liquid crystal display*]
VHC........... Very Highly Commended
VHCH .... Cheung Chau [*Hong Kong*] [*ICAO location identifier*]   (ICLI)
VHCL .... VHC Limited [*New York, NY*] [*NASDAQ symbol*]   (NQ)
VHD .... Valvular Heart Disease
VHD .... Video High Density [*Television*]
VHDL........ Very-High Density Lipoprotein [*Biochemistry*]
VHDL........ VHSIC [*Very-High-Speed Integrated Circuit*] Hardware
                Description Language [*Data processing*]
VHDV....... Very High Dollar Value
VHE.......... Very-High Energy
VHE.......... Volatile Human Effluents
VHEDD8... Vogelkundliche Hefte Edertal [*A publication*]
VH Eq Dr... Van Heythuysen's Equity Draftsman [*2nd ed.*] [*1828*] [*A
                publication*]   (DLA)
VHF.......... Vacuum Hydrogen Furnace
VHF.......... Very-High-Frequency [*Electronics*]
VHF.......... Visual Half-Field
VHF/AM.... Very-High-Frequency, Amplitude Modulated   (NASA)
VHF/DF.... Very-High-Frequency Direction-Finding
VHFF......... Very-High-Frequency Filter
VHF-FM ... Very-High-Frequency, Frequency Modulated   (NOAA)
VHFG........ Very-High-Frequency Generator
VHFI .... Very-High-Frequency Indeed [*Ultrahigh frequency*] [*British*]
VHFJ......... Very-High-Frequency Jammer
VHFO........ Very-High-Frequency Oscillator
VHFOR..... Very-High-Frequency Omnirange   (AFM)
VHFR........ Very-High-Frequency Receiver
VHFS......... Videnskabernes Selskabs Historisk-Filologiske Skrifter [*A
                publication*]
VHFT .... Very-High-Frequency Termination
VHG .... Vertragshilfegesetz [*A publication*]

VHHH....... Hong Kong/International [*Hong Kong*] [*ICAO location
                identifier*]   (ICLI)
VHHK .... Hong Kong [*Hong Kong*] [*ICAO location identifier*]   (ICLI)
VHI........... Valhi, Incorporated [*NYSE symbol*]   (SPSG)
VHIP .... Vehicle Hit Indicator, Pyrotechnic
VHis.......... Vida Hispanica [*A publication*]
VHIS .... Vietnam Head Injury Study
VHJ .... Victorian Historical Journal [*A publication*]   (APTA)
VHKT .... Kai Tak [*Hong Kong*] [*ICAO location identifier*]   (ICLI)
VHL.......... Viceroy Homes Ltd. [*Toronto Stock Exchange symbol*]
VHL.......... Von Hippel-Lindau Disease
VHLH....... Very Heavy Lift Helicopter
VHLL .... Very-High-Level Language
VHM .... Victorian Historical Magazine [*Australia*] [*A publication*]
VHM .... Virtual Hardware Monitor [*Data processing*]   (IEEE)
VHM .... Visitation Nuns [*Roman Catholic religious order*]
VHM .... Vista Hermosa [*Mexico*] [*Seismograph station code, US
                Geological Survey*] [*Closed*]   (SEIS)
VHMCP .... Voluntary Home Mortgage Credit Program [*of HHFA*]
                [*Terminated*]
VHN .... Van Horn, TX [*Location identifier*] [*FAA*]   (FAAL)
VHN .... Verhandlungen. Historischer Vereine von Niederbayern [*A
                publication*]
VHN .... Vickers Hardness Number [*Also, HV, VH*]
VHO .... Very High Output
VHO .... Vila Coutinho [*Mozambique*] [*Airport symbol*]
                [*Obsolete*]   (OAG)
VHO .... Vista Hermosa [*Mexico*] [*Seismograph station code, US
                Geological Survey*]   (SEIS)
VHO .... Volatile Halogenated Organic [*Analytical chemistry*]
VHOC....... Volatile Halogenated Organic Compound [*Environmental
                chemistry*]
VHOL....... Very-High-Order Language
VHP.......... County of Henrico Public Library, Richmond, VA [*OCLC
                symbol*]   (OCLC)
VHP.......... Variable Horsepower
VHP.......... Very High Performance
VHP.......... Very High Polarization [*Raw sugar grade*]
VHP.......... Very High Pressure
VHP.......... Vooruitstrewende Hervormings Partij [*Progressive Reform
                Party*] [*Surinam*] [*Political party*]   (PPW)
VHPA .... Vietnam Helicopter Pilots Association   (EA)
VHPF .... Victorian Health Promotion Foundation [*Australia*]
VHR.......... Very-Highly Repeated [*Genetics*]
VHR.......... Video-to-Hardcopy Recorder
VHRR .... Very High Resolution Radiometer [*NASA*]
VHRTG ..... Veterans' Hospital Radio and Television Guild   (EA)
VHS .... Hampden-Sydney College, Hampden-Sydney, VA [*OCLC
                symbol*]   (OCLC)
VHS .... Honorary Surgeon to the Viceroy of India
VHS .... Versatile High Speed [*Copier*]
VHS .... Very High Speed [*Copier*]
VHS .... Victorian House of Studies
VHS .... Video Home System
VHS .... Viral Hemorrhagic Septicemia [*Medicine*]
VHS-C ...... Video Home System - Compact
VHSI .... Very-High-Speed Integrated [*Electronics*]
VHSIC....... Very-High-Speed Integrated Circuit [*Electronics*]
VHSK .... Sek Kong [*Hong Kong*] [*ICAO location identifier*]   (ICLI)
VHSKA ..... Vital and Health Statistics. Series 11 [*United States*] [*A
                publication*]
VHSOC ..... Very-High-Speed Optic Cable
VHS & RA ... Veterans Health Services and Research Administration
                [*Department of Veterans Affairs*]
VHST .... Very-High-Speed Transit
VHSTA...... Victorian High School Teachers' Association [*Australia*]
VHT.......... VMS Hotel Investments Fund [*AMEX symbol*]   (SPSG)
VHTR....... Very-High-Temperature Reactor [*Nuclear energy*]
V/HUD...... Vertical/Heads-Up Display [*Aviation*]   (MCD)
VHUP....... Veterinary Hospital of the University of Pennsylvania
VHVNB..... Verhandlungen. Historischer Verein von Niederbayern [*A
                publication*]
VHVOR..... Verhandlungen. Historischer Verein von Oberpfalz und
                Regensburg [*A publication*]
VHW .... Verband Hannoverscher Warmblutzuchter [*Verden, Federal
                Republic of Germany*]   (EAIO)
VHY.......... Vess, Henry, Kansas City MO [*STAC*]
VI .... Congregation of the Incarnate Word and the Blessed Sacrament
                [*Roman Catholic women's religious order*]
VI .... Inertial Velocity
VI .... Societe de Travail Aerien [*Algeria*] [*ICAO designator*]   (FAAC)
VI .... Vaginal Irrigation [*Medicine*]
VI .... Valley Industries, Inc. [*NYSE symbol*]   (SPSG)
VI .... Value Included Entry [*Business term*]
VI .... Values Inventory [*Management test*]
VI .... Vancouver Island
VI .... Variable Interval [*Reinforcement schedule*]
VI .... Vasoinhibitory [*Medicine*]
VI .... Vector International   (EA)
VI .... Vegetation Index
VI .... Vendor Item [*Sales*]   (AAG)

VI	Vent Isolation [*Nuclear energy*] (NRCH)
VI	Verb Intransitive
VI	Vermiculite Institute [*Defunct*]
VI	Vertical Interval [*Mapmaking*]
VI	Veterinary Inspector (ADA)
VI	Vial
Vi.	Viator [*A publication*]
VI	Vibration Institute (EA)
VI	Victoria Institute [*British*] (DAS)
VI	Video Integrator
Vi.	Vincentius Hispanus [*Deceased, 1248*] [*Authority cited in pre-1607 legal work*] (DSA)
VI	Vinegar Institute (EA)
VI	Viol [*A publication*]
VI	Violet
VI	Virgin Islands Reports [*A publication*] (DLA)
VI	Virgin Islands of the US [*ANSI two-letter standard code*] (CNC)
VI	Virgin Islands of the US [*Postal code*]
vi.	Virgin Islands of the US [*MARC country of publication code*] [*Library of Congress*] [*IYRU nationality code*] (LCCP)
Vi.	Virginia State Library, Richmond, VA [*Library symbol*] [*Library of Congress*] (LCLS)
VI	Virgo Intacta [*Medicine*]
Vi.	Virulence [*Antigen*] [*Immunology*]
VI	Viscosity Improver [*Element in multigrade engine oil*]
VI	Viscosity Index
VI	Visual Identification
VI	Visual Impairment
VI	Visual Inspection
Vi.	Vivianus Tuscus [*Flourished, 13th century*] [*Authority cited in pre-1607 legal work*] (DSA)
V & I	Voix et Images. Etudes Quebecoises [*A publication*]
VI	Volume Index [*Medicine*] (DHSM)
VI	Volume Indicator [*Radio equipment*]
VI	Volume Investigation [*Three-dimensional imaging technology developed at The Toronto Hospital in Canada*]
VI	Voluntary Indefinite [*Status*] [*Army*] (INF)
VI	Voluntary Interceptor [*World War II*] [*British*]
VI	Volunteers for Israel (EA)
VI	Voprosy Istorii [*A publication*]
VIA	Arlington County Department of Libraries, Arlington, VA [*OCLC symbol*] (OCLC)
VIA	Valorisation de l'Innovation dans l'Ameublement [*Committee to Promote Innovation in Furniture Design*] [*France*]
VIA	Variable Income Annuity
VIA	Venezolana Internacional de Aviacion SA [*Venezuelan airline*]
VIA	Viacom, Inc. [*AMEX symbol*] (SPSG)
VIA	Viaduct
V & IA	Victorian and Interstate Airways [*Australia*]
VIA	Video Image Analysis
VIA	Videotex Industry Association (EA)
VIA	Viral Interval Antigen [*Virology*]
VIA	Virus Inactivating Agency [*Medicine*]
VIA	Virus Infection Associated Antigen [*Immunology*]
VIA	Vision Institute of America [*Later, VSP*] (EA)
VIA	Vocational Interests and Vocational Aptitudes [*Psychology*]
VIA	Voice Interactive Avionics [*Army*]
VIA	Volunteers in Asia (EA)
ViAb	Washington County Public Library, Abingdon, VA [*Library symbol*] [*Library of Congress*] (LCLS)
VIABLE	Vertical Installation Automated Baseline [*Army*]
ViAc	Eastern Shore Public Library, Accomac, VA [*Library symbol*] [*Library of Congress*] (LCLS)
VIAC	Victorian Industrial Appeals Court [*Australia*]
VIAC	Vienna Allied Command [*British military*] (DMA)
VIAFF	Vancouver International Amateur Film Festival [*Canada*]
VIAG	Agra [*India*] [*ICAO location identifier*] (ICLI)
VIAG	Vereinigte Industrie-Unternehmungen AG [*Industrial Enterprise Association*] [*Business term*] [*Federal Republic of Germany*]
VIAH	Aligarh [*India*] [*ICAO location identifier*] (ICLI)
ViAl	Alexandria Library, Alexandria, VA [*Library symbol*] [*Library of Congress*] (LCLS)
VIAL	Allahabad [*India*] [*ICAO location identifier*] (ICLI)
ViAlA	United States Army Material Command Headquarters, Technical Library, Alexandria, VA [*Library symbol*] [*Library of Congress*] (LCLS)
ViAlbS	Southside Virginia Community College, Christanna Campus, Alberta, VA [*Library symbol*] [*Library of Congress*] (LCLS)
ViAlD	Defense Technical Information Center, Cameron Station, Alexandria, VA [*Library symbol*] [*Library of Congress*] (LCLS)
ViAlDL	Defense Logistics Agency, Cameron Station, Alexandria, VA [*Library symbol*] [*Library of Congress*] (LCLS)
ViAlP	Jacob Simpson Payton Library, Alexandria, VA [*Library symbol*] [*Library of Congress*] (LCLS)
ViAlTh	Protestant Episcopal Theological Seminary in Virginia, Alexandria, VA [*Library symbol*] [*Library of Congress*] (LCLS)

ViAnGS	Church of Jesus Christ of Latter-Day Saints, Genealogical Society Library, Annandale Branch, Annandale, VA [*Library symbol*] [*Library of Congress*] (LCLS)
ViAnN	Northern Virginia Community College, Annandale, VA [*Library symbol*] [*Library of Congress*] (LCLS)
Viansa	Vicky and Sam [*Sebastiani*] [*Brand name of wines made by the Sebastianis*]
VIAP	Vanuatu Independent Alliance Party [*Political party*] (PPW)
VIAR	Amritsar [*India*] [*ICAO location identifier*] (ICLI)
ViAr	Arlington County Department of Libraries, Arlington, VA [*Library symbol*] [*Library of Congress*] (LCLS)
ViAr-A	Arlington County Department of Libraries, Aurora Hills Branch, Arlington, VA [*Library symbol*] [*Library of Congress*] (LCLS)
ViArAL	Center for Applied Linguistics, Arlington, VA [*Library symbol*] [*Library of Congress*] (LCLS)
ViAr-Ch	Arlington County Department of Libraries, Cherrydale Branch, Arlington, VA [*Library symbol*] [*Library of Congress*] (LCLS)
ViAr-Cl	Arlington County Department of Libraries, Clarendon Branch, Arlington, VA [*Library symbol*] [*Library of Congress*] (LCLS)
ViAr-F	Arlington County Department of Libraries, Fairlington Branch, Arlington, VA [*Library symbol*] [*Library of Congress*] (LCLS)
ViAr-G	Arlington County Department of Libraries, Glencarlyn Branch, Arlington, VA [*Library symbol*] [*Library of Congress*] (LCLS)
ViArHD	United States Historical Documents Institute, Inc., Arlington, VA [*Library symbol*] [*Library of Congress*] (LCLS)
ViArM	Marymount College, Arlington, VA [*Library symbol*] [*Library of Congress*] (LCLS)
ViArNG	National Graduate University, Arlington, VA [*Library symbol*] [*Library of Congress*] (LCLS)
ViAr-W	Arlington County Department of Libraries, Westover Branch, Arlington, VA [*Library symbol*] [*Library of Congress*] (LCLS)
VIAS	Voice Interference Analysis Set
VIASA	Venezolana Internacional de Aviacion Sociedad Anonima [*Airline*] [*Venezuela*]
ViAsM	Mobil Chemical Co., Industrial Chemicals Division, Ashland, VA [*Library symbol*] [*Library of Congress*] (LCLS)
ViAsR	Randolph-Macon College, Ashland, VA [*Library symbol*] [*Library of Congress*] (LCLS)
Viata Med	Viata Medicala. Revista a Unuinii Societatelor de Stiinte Medicale din Republica Socialista [*Romania*] [*A publication*]
Viata Med (Buchar)	Viata Medicala (Bucharest) [*A publication*]
Viata Med (Medii Sanit)	Viata Medicala. Revista de Informare Profesionala se Stiintifica a Cadrelor (Medii Sanitare) [*A publication*]
Viator Med	Viator. Medieval and Renaissance Studies [*A publication*]
VIB	Vanilla Information Bureau (EA)
VIB	Veal Infusion Broth [*Immunology*]
VIB	Vertical Integration Building [*NASA*]
VIB	Vibraphone [*Music*]
VIB	Vibrate (AAG)
VIB	Vitamin Information Bureau [*Commercial firm*] (EA)
VIB	Volunteer Infantry Brigade [*British military*] (DMA)
VIBG	Vibrating (AAG)
VIBGYOR	Violet, Indigo, Blue, Green, Yellow, Orange, Red [*Mnemonic for the colors of the spectrum*]
VIBH	Banihal [*India*] [*ICAO location identifier*] (ICLI)
VIBI	Virgini Immaculatae Bavaria Immaculata [*To the Immaculate Virgin Immaculate Bavaria*] [*Latin*] [*Motto of the Order of St. George of Bavaria*]
VIBJ	Virgin Islands Bar Journal [*A publication*]
VIBK	Bikaner [*India*] [*ICAO location identifier*] (ICLI)
VIBL	Bakshi Ka Talab [*India*] [*ICAO location identifier*] (ICLI)
ViBlbV	Virginia Polytechnic Institute and State University, Blacksburg, VA [*Library symbol*] [*Library of Congress*] (LCLS)
ViBluC	Bluefield College, Bluefield, VA [*Library symbol*] [*Library of Congress*] (LCLS)
VIBN	Varanasi [*India*] [*ICAO location identifier*] (ICLI)
VIBN	Vibration (AAG)
Vi-BPH	Virginia State Library for the Visually and Physically Handicapped, Richmond, VA [*Library symbol*] [*Library of Congress*] (LCLS)
VIBR	Kulu/Bhuntar [*India*] [*ICAO location identifier*] (ICLI)
VIBR	Vibration
VIBRA	Vehicle Inelastic Bending Response Analysis [*Computer program*]
VIBRAM	Vitale Bramani [*Inventor of rubber soles for boots used in mountain climbing*]
ViBrC	Bridgewater College, Bridgewater, VA [*Library symbol*] [*Library of Congress*] (LCLS)
VIBROT	Vibrational-Rotational [*Spectra*] [*Data processing*]
ViBS	Sullins College, Bristol, VA [*Library symbol*] [*Library of Congress*] (LCLS)
VIBS	Vocabulatory, Information, Block Design, Similarities [*Psychology*]

Vib Spectra Struct ... Vibrational Spectra and Structure [*A publication*]
VIBT......... Bhatinda [*India*] [*ICAO location identifier*] (ICLI)
ViBV .... Virginia Intermont College, Bristol, VA [*Library symbol*] [*Library of Congress*] (LCLS)
VIBW........ Bhiwani [*India*] [*ICAO location identifier*] (ICLI)
VIBY.......... Bareilly [*India*] [*ICAO location identifier*] (ICLI)
ViC............. McIntire Public Library, Charlottesville, VA [*Library symbol*] [*Library of Congress*] (LCLS)
VIC .... University of Victoria Library [*UTLAS symbol*]
VIC .... Value Incentive Clause [*General Services Administration*]
VIC .... Values Inventory for Children [*Attitude test*]
VIC .... Vapor Injection Curing [*Plastics technology*]
VIC .... Variable Instruction Computer
VIC .... Varnish Insulating Compound
VIC .... Vasoinhibitory Center [*Physiology*]
VIC .... Vehicle Intercommunications System   (MCD)
VIC .... Very Important Cargo [*Shipping*]
VIC .... Very Important Contributors [*Political*]
VIC .... Very Important Customer
VIC .... Veterinary Investigation Centre [*Ministry of Agriculture, Fisheries, and Food*] [*British*]
VIC .... Vicar [*or Vicarage*]
VIC .... Vices [*Times*] [*Pharmacy*]
vic.............. Vicinal [*Also, v*] [*Chemistry*]
VIC .... Vicinity (AABC)
Vic............. Victor [*Record label*]
VIC .... Victoria [*British Columbia*] [*Seismograph station code, US Geological Survey*] (SEIS)
VIC .... Victoria [*State in Australia*]
VIC .... Victoria [*British Columbia*] [*Geomagnetic observatory code*]
VIC .... Vienna International Centre [*United Nations*]
VIC .... Viking Integrated Change [*NASA*]
VIC .... Virgin Islands Code [*A publication*] (DLA)
VIC .... Virgin Islands Corporation [*Intended to promote VI economic development, dissolved 1966*] [*Department of the Interior*]
VIC .... Virginia Intermont College
VIC .... Virginia State Library, Richmond, VA [*OCLC symbol*] (OCLC)
VIC .... Virtual Interaction Controller
VIC .... Visibility of Intransit Cargo [*Shipping*]
VIC .... Visitor Information Center [*Kennedy Space Center*]
VIC .... Visual Information Center [*Oldsmobile*] [*Automotive engineering*]
VIC .... Vortex in Cell
VIC .... VSC Tech, Inc. [*Vancouver Stock Exchange symbol*]
VICA.......... Video Corporation of America [*NASDAQ symbol*] (NQ)
VICA.......... Vision Industry Council of America (EA)
VICA.......... Vocational Industrial Clubs of America (EA)
Vic ACR..... Victorian Accident Compensation Reports [*Australia*] [*A publication*]
ViCAF........ United States Army, Foreign Science and Technical Center, Charlottesville, VA [*Library symbol*] [*Library of Congress*] (LCLS)
ViCAHi...... Abermarle County Historical Society, Charlottesville, VA [*Library symbol*] [*Library of Congress*] (LCLS)
VIC and ALB ... Victoria and Albert Museum [*London*] (DSUE)
VICAM...... Virtual Integrated Communications Access Method [*Sperry UNIVAC*]
VICANA.... Vietnamese Cultural Association of North America (EA)
VICAP....... Violent Criminal Apprehension Program [*Quantico, VA*] [*National Center for the Analysis of Violent Crime*] [*Department of Justice*]
VICAR....... Video Image Communication and Retrieval
Vic Assn Teach Eng J ... Victorian Association for the Teaching of English. Journal [*A publication*] (APTA)
Vicat.......... Vicat's Vocabularium Juris Utriusque ex Variis Ante Editis [*A publication*] (DLA)
Vicat Voc Jur ... Vicat's Vocabularium Juris Utriusque ex Variis Ante Editis [*A publication*] (DLA)
Vic Bar News ... Victorian Bar News [*A publication*] (APTA)
VICBETI ... Victorian Inventory of Community Based Employment and Training Initiatives [*Australia*]
VIC C........ Victoria Cross (DSUE)
Vic CC........ County Court Reports (Victoria) [*A publication*] (APTA)
Vic Chamber of Manufactures Econ Serv ... Victorian Chamber of Manufactures. Economic Service [*A publication*] (APTA)
Vic Chap News ... Victorian Chapter Newsletter [*Australian College of Education*] [*A publication*] (APTA)
Vic Comm Teach Assn General J ... Victorian Commercial Teachers' Association. General Journal [*A publication*] (APTA)
Vic Comput ... Vic Computing [*A publication*]
Vic Conf Soc Welfare Proc ... Victorian Conference of Social Welfare. Proceedings [*A publication*] (APTA)
Vic Creditman ... Victorian Creditman [*A publication*] (APTA)
Vic Dairyfarmer ... Victorian Dairyfarmer [*A publication*] (APTA)
Vic Dep Agric Tech Bull ... Victoria. Department of Agriculture. Technical Bulletin [*A publication*] (APTA)
VICE.......... Vast Integrated Communications Environment [*Carnegie Mellon University*] [*Pittsburgh, PA*]

Vic Ed Gaz ... Education Gazette and Teachers Aid (Victoria) [*A publication*] (APTA)
Vic Elec Contractor ... Victorian Electrical Contractor [*A publication*] (APTA)
Vic Employers' Federation AR ... Victorian Employers' Federation. Annual Report [*A publication*] (APTA)
Vicenza Econ ... Vicenza Economica [*A publication*]
VICF......... Victoria Financial Corp. [*NASDAQ symbol*] (NQ)
Vic Fam Alm ... Victorian Family Almanac [*A publication*]
VICFIT...... Victoria Council on Fitness and General Health [*Australia*]
Vic For Comm Bull ... Victoria. Forests Commission. Bulletin [*A publication*] (APTA)
VICG .... Chandigarh [*India*] [*ICAO location identifier*] (ICLI)
VICGEN.... Vicar General's Office [*British*]
Vic Geogr J ... Victorian Geographical Journal [*A publication*] (APTA)
Vic Govt Gaz ... Victorian Government Gazette [*A publication*] (APTA)
Vic His J ... Victorian Historical Journal [*A publication*]
Vic Hist J... Victorian Historical Journal [*A publication*]
Vic Hist Mag ... Victorian Historical Magazine [*A publication*] (APTA)
Vic Hortic Dig ... Victorian Horticultural Digest [*A publication*] (APTA)
ViChT........ John Tyler Community College, Chester, VA [*Library symbol*] [*Library of Congress*] (LCLS)
VICI.......... Vantage Information Consultants, Incorporated [*Information service or system*] (IID)
VICI.......... Velocity Indicating Coherent Integrator
VICI.......... Video Console Indexing
VICI.......... Voice Input Child Identicant [*Pronounced "Vicki"*] [*Young robot in television show "Small Wonder"*]
VICI.......... Voice Input Code Identifier (MCD)
Vic Inst Coll News ... Victoria Institute of Colleges. Newsletter [*A publication*] (APTA)
Vic Inst Ed Res Bull ... Victoria Institute of Educational Research. Bulletin [*A publication*]
VICK......... Vicksburg National Military Park
VICL......... Vienna International Centre Library [*Information service or system*] (IID)
Vic Legal Exec ... Victorian Legal Executive [*A publication*] (APTA)
ViClR........ Robbins Mills, Inc., Clarksville, VA [*Library symbol*] [*Library of Congress*] (LCLS)
Vic LSAJ ... Victorian LSA [*Limbless Soldiers' Association*] Journal [*A publication*] (APTA)
VICM .... VICOM, Inc. [*Eden Prairie, MN*] [*NASDAQ symbol*] (NQ)
VicN.......... Victorian Naturalist [*A publication*]
Vic Nat...... Victorian Naturalist [*A publication*] (APTA)
Vic Naturalist ... Victorian Naturalist [*A publication*] (APTA)
VIC News .. Victoria Institute of Colleges. Newsletter [*A publication*] (APTA)
VICO .... Virginia International Company
VICO .... Volkswagen Insurance Company
ViCoC .... Castle Hill Museum, Cobham, VA [*Library symbol*] [*Library of Congress*] (LCLS)
VICOED.... Visual Communications Education
VICOM ..... Visual Communications Management
VICOMP... Victorian Government Computing Service [*Australia*]
VICON ...... Visual Confirmation [*of voice takeoff clearing system*] [*Aviation*]
VICORE.... Visual Conceptual Reading
ViCou .... Walter Cecil Rawls Library and Museum, Courtland, VA [*Library symbol*] [*Library of Congress*] (LCLS)
ViCovI........ Industrial Rayon Corp., Covington, VA [*Library symbol*] [*Library of Congress*] (LCLS)
ViCovW ..... West Virginia Pulp & Paper Co., Covington, VA [*Library symbol*] [*Library of Congress*] (LCLS)
ViCP .... Piedmont Virginia Community College, Learning Resources Center, Charlottesville, VA [*Library symbol*] [*Library of Congress*] (LCLS)
Vic Parl Deb ... Victorian Parliamentary Debates [*A publication*] (APTA)
Vic Parl Parl Deb ... Victoria. Parliament. Parliamentary Debates [*A publication*] (APTA)
Vic Poultry J ... Victorian Poultry Journal [*A publication*] (APTA)
VICR......... Victor Technologies [*NASDAQ symbol*] (NQ)
ViCRA .... National Radio Astronomy Observatory, Charlottesville, VA [*Library symbol*] [*Library of Congress*] (LCLS)
Vic Railways Newsletter ... Victorian Railways Newsletter [*A publication*] (APTA)
Vic Resour ... Victoria's Resources [*A publication*] (APTA)
Vic Resources ... Victoria's Resources [*A publication*] (APTA)
Vic Rev...... Victorian Review [*A publication*] (APTA)
VICS.......... Variable Inertia Charging System [*Mazda Motor Co.*] [*Automotive engineering*]
VICS.......... Verbal Interaction Category System [*Student teacher test*]
VICS.......... Vocational Information through Computer Systems [*Philadelphia School District*] [*Pennsylvania*] [*Information service or system*] (IID)
Vic's Res .... Victoria's Resources [*A publication*]
Vic Stat Pub ... Victorian Statistics Publications [*A publication*] (APTA)
Vic Sup Ct FC ... Victorian Supreme Court Full Court [*Australia*]
ViCT .... Institute of Textile Technology, Charlottesville, VA [*Library symbol*] [*Library of Congress*] (LCLS)
VICT.......... Victoria Bankshares, Inc. [*NASDAQ symbol*] (NQ)
Vict............. Victorian Reports [*A publication*]

VICTA....... Valett Inventory of Critical Thinking Abilities [*Child development test*]
Vict Acts .... Victoria Acts of Parliament [*A publication*] (DLA)
Vict Cancer News ... Victorian Cancer News [*A publication*] (APTA)
Vict CS....... Victorian Consolidated Statutes [*A publication*] (ILCA)
Vict Dairyfmr ... Victorian Dairyfarmer [*A publication*] (APTA)
Vic Teachers J ... Victorian Teachers Journal [*A publication*] (APTA)
Vic Teach J ... Victorian Teachers Journal [*A publication*] (APTA)
Vict For Comm Bull ... Victoria. Forests Commission. Bulletin [*A publication*] (APTA)
Vict For Comm For Tech Pap ... Victoria. Forests Commission. Forestry Technical Paper [*A publication*] (APTA)
Vict For Comm Misc Publ ... Victoria. Forests Commission. Miscellaneous Publication [*A publication*] (APTA)
Vict Geogr J ... Victorian Geographical Journal [*A publication*] (APTA)
Vict Geol Surv Bull ... Victoria. Geological Survey. Bulletin [*A publication*] (APTA)
Vict Geol Surv Mem ... Victoria. Geological Survey. Memoirs [*A publication*] (APTA)
Vict Hist Mag ... Victorian Historical Magazine [*A publication*] (APTA)
Vict Hort Dig ... Victorian Horticultural Digest [*A publication*] (APTA)
Vict L .... Victorian Law Journal [*A publication*] (DLA)
Vict L (Austr) ... Victorian Reports (Law)(Australia) [*A publication*] (ILCA)
Vict LJ .... Victorian Law Journal [*A publication*] (APTA)
Vict LR....... Victorian Law Reports [*A publication*]
Vict LR Min ... Victorian Mining Law Reports [*Australia*] [*A publication*] (DLA)
Vict LT....... Victorian Law Times [*A publication*] (APTA)
Vict Nat...... Victorian Naturalist [*A publication*]
Vict Naturalist ... Victorian Naturalist [*A publication*] (APTA)
Vict Newsl ... Victorian Newsletter [*A publication*]
Victoria Country Roads Board Eng Note ... Victoria. Country Roads Board. Engineering Note [*A publication*] (APTA)
Victoria Country Roads Board Tech Bull ... Victoria. Country Roads Board. Technical Bulletin [*A publication*] (APTA)
Victoria Dep Agric Res Proj Ser ... Victoria. Department of Agriculture. Research Project Series [*A publication*] (APTA)
Victoria Dep Agric Tech Bull ... Victoria. Department of Agriculture. Technical Bulletin [*A publication*] (APTA)
Victoria Dep Agric Tech Rep Ser ... Victoria. Department of Agriculture. Technical Report Series [*A publication*] (APTA)
Victoria Fish Wildl Dep Fish Contrib ... Victoria. Fisheries and Wildlife Department. Fisheries Contribution [*Australia*] [*A publication*]
Victoria Fish Wildl Dep Wildl Contrib ... Victoria. Fisheries and Wildlife Department. Wildlife Contribution [*A publication*]
Victoria Geol Bull ... Victoria. Geological Survey. Bulletin [*A publication*] (APTA)
Victoria Geol Surv Mem ... Victoria. Geological Survey. Memoirs [*A publication*]
Victoria Inst Tr ... Victoria Institute or Philosophical Society of Great Britain. Journal of the Transactions [*A publication*]
Victoria Inst (Trinidad) Pr ... Victoria Institute (Trinidad). Proceedings [*A publication*]
Victoria Mines Dep Annu Rep ... Victoria. Mines Department. Annual Report [*A publication*]
Victoria Mines Dep Groundwater Invest Program Rep ... Victoria. Mines Department. Groundwater Investigation Program. Report [*Australia*] [*A publication*]
Victoria Minist Conserv Environ Stud Program Proj Rep ... Victoria. Ministry for Conservation. Environmental Studies Program. Project Report [*A publication*] (APTA)
Victorian Entomol ... Victorian Entomologist [*A publication*]
Victorian Hist J ... Victorian Historical Journal [*A publication*]
Victorian Hist Mag ... Victorian Historical Magazine [*A publication*]
Victorian Nat ... Victorian Naturalist [*A publication*]
Victorian Natl Parks Assoc J ... Victorian National Parks Association. Journal [*A publication*] (APTA)
Victorian Railw ... Victorian Railways [*A publication*] (APTA)
Victorian Stud ... Victorian Studies [*A publication*]
Victorian Vet Proc ... Victorian Veterinary Proceedings [*A publication*]
Victoria's Resour ... Victoria's Resources [*A publication*]
Victoria State Rivers Water Supply Comm Annu Rep ... Victoria. State Rivers and Water Supply Commission. Annual Report [*A publication*]
Victoria Univ Antarct Data Ser ... Victoria University of Wellington. Antarctic Data Series [*New Zealand*] [*A publication*]
Vict Poet .... Victorian Poetry [*A publication*]
Vict Poetry ... Victorian Poetry [*A publication*]
Vict R .... Victorian Reports (Australian) [*A publication*] (DLA)
Vict Rep ..... Victorian Reports [*A publication*]
Vict Rep (Adm) ... Victorian Reports (Admiralty) [*A publication*] (DLA)
Vict Rep (Austr) ... Victorian Reports (Australian) [*A publication*]
Vict Rep (Eq) ... Victorian Reports (Equity) [*A publication*]
Vict Rep (Law) ... Victorian Reports (Law) [*A publication*]
Vict Res...... Victoria's Resources [*A publication*] (APTA)
Vict Resour ... Victoria's Resources [*A publication*] (APTA)
Vict Rev...... Victorian Review [*A publication*]
Vict Soil Conserv Auth TC ... Victoria. Soil Conservation Authority. TC Report [*A publication*] (APTA)

Vict Soil Conserv Auth TC Rep ... Victoria. Soil Conservation Authority. TC Report [*A publication*] (APTA)
Vict Stat..... Victorian Statutes [*General Public Acts*] [*Australia*] [*A publication*] (DLA)
Vict Stat R Regs & B ... Victorian Statutory Rules, Regulations, and By-Laws [*Australia*] [*A publication*] (DLA)
Vict St Tr ... Victorian State Trials [*Australia*] [*A publication*] (DLA)
Vict Stud .... Victorian Studies [*A publication*]
Vict U C L Rev ... Victoria University. College Law Review [*A publication*]
Vict UL Rev ... Victoria University. Law Review [*A publication*] (DLA)
Vict U of Wellington L Rev ... Victoria University of Wellington. Law Review [*A publication*]
Vict U Well L Rev ... Victoria University of Wellington. Law Review [*A publication*]
Vict Vet Proc ... Australian Veterinary Association. Victorian Division. Annual General Meeting. Proceedings [*A publication*] (APTA)
Vict Vet Proc ... Australian Veterinary Association. Victorian Division. Victorian Veterinary Proceedings [*A publication*] (APTA)
Vic Veg Grower ... Victorian Vegetable Grower [*A publication*] (APTA)
Vic Vet Proc ... Victorian Veterinary Proceedings [*A publication*] (APTA)
ViCVH....... Virginia Highway Research Council, Charlottesville, VA [*Library symbol*] [*Library of Congress*] (LCLS)
VICX......... Kanpur/Chakeri [*India*] [*ICAO location identifier*] (ICLI)
Vic Yrbk..... Victoria Yearbook [*A publication*] (APTA)
ViD........... Danville Public Library, Danville, VA [*Library symbol*] [*Library of Congress*] (LCLS)
VID .... Vide [*or Videte*] [*See*] [*Latin*]
VID .... Video (AAG)
VID .... Video-Data [*Computer graphics*] (BYTE)
VID .... Video Image Display Assembly [*Space Flight Operations Facility, NASA*]
Vid............. Vidian's Exact Pleader [*1684*] [*A publication*] (DLA)
VID .... Vidin [*Bulgaria*] [*Airport symbol*] (OAG)
VID .... Vidipress Nieuwsbrief [*A publication*]
VID .... Vienna Institute for Development (EAIO)
VID .... Virtual Image Display (MCD)
VID .... Visual Identification (CAAL)
VID .... Volunteers for International Development [*Later, Peaceworkers*] (EA)
VID .... Vspomogatel'nye Istoricheskie Distsipliny [*A publication*]
ViDA......... Averette College, Danville, VA [*Library symbol*] [*Library of Congress*] (LCLS)
VIDA .... Ventricular Impulse Detector and Alarm [*Cardiology*]
Vida Agr .... Vida Agricola [*A publication*]
Vida Agric ... Vida Agricola [*A publication*]
VIDAC....... Visual Information Display and Control
VidaL........ Vida Literaria [*A publication*]
Vida Med... Vida Medica [*A publication*]
VIDAMP... Video Amplifier
Vida Odontol ... Vida Odontologica [*A publication*]
VIDAP...... Vibration Data Accuracy Program
VIDAR...... Velocity Integration, Detection, and Ranging (NG)
VIDAS....... Video Image Digitiser and Storage System [*Sirton Computer*] [*London, England*]
VIDAS...... Vitek ImmunoDiagnostic Assay System
VIDAT...... Visual Data Acquisition
ViDC......... Danville Community College, Danville, VA [*Library symbol*] [*Library of Congress*] (LCLS)
VIDC .... Video Connection of America [*NASDAQ symbol*] (NQ)
VIDC .... Virgin Islands Department of Commerce (EA)
VIDD .... Delhi/Safdarjung [*India*] [*ICAO location identifier*] (ICLI)
VIDD........ Vehicle Intrusion Detection Device
VIDD .... Vertical Interval Data Detector (NASA)
VIDE......... Video Display Corp. [*NASDAQ symbol*] (NQ)
VIDEM...... Vietnam Demonstration [*FBI security file*]
Videnskabs-Selsk Christiana Forh ... Videnskabs-Selskabet i Christiania. Forhandlingar [*A publication*]
Vidensk Medd Dan Naturhist Foren ... Videnskabelige Meddelelser fra Dansk Naturhistorisk Forening [*A publication*]
Vidensk Medd Dan Naturhist Foren Khobenhavn ... Videnskabelige Meddelelser fra Dansk Naturhistorisk Forening i Khobenhavn [*A publication*]
Video......... Video-Tronics [*A publication*] (APTA)
VIDEO...... Visual Data Entry On-Line [*Data processing*]
Videodical.. [*Special-Interest*] Video Cassette Issued Periodically
Video Mktg ... Video Marketing Newsletter [*A publication*]
Video Syst ... Video Systems [*A publication*]
Vide Tech-Appl ... Vide. Technique-Applications [*France*] [*A publication*]
VIDF......... Delhi [*India*] [*ICAO location identifier*] (ICLI)
VIDF......... Vertical Side of Intermediate Distribution Frame [*Telecommunications*] (TEL)
VIDF......... Video Frequency (IEEE)
Vid Game T ... Video Games Today [*A publication*]
VIDI.......... Visual Input Detection Instrumentation (MCD)
VIDN........ Dehra Dun [*India*] [*ICAO location identifier*] (ICLI)
VIDO......... Paralax Video Enterprises, Inc. [*New York, NY*] [*NASDAQ symbol*] (NQ)
VIDO........ Veterinary Infectious Disease Organization [*University of Saskatchewan*] [*Canada*] [*Research center*] (RCD)

VIDP.......... Delhi/Indira Gandhi International [*India*] [*ICAO location identifier*] (ICLI)
VIDPI........ Visually Impaired Data Processors International (EA)
VIDR .... Dadri [*India*] [*ICAO location identifier*] (ICLI)
ViDR .... Dan River Mills Co., Danville, VA [*Library symbol*] [*Library of Congress*] (LCLS)
ViDS .... Stratford College, Danville, VA [*Library symbol*] [*Library of Congress*] (LCLS)
VIDS.......... Vertical Instruments Display System (MCD)
VIDS.......... Video Science Technology, Inc. [*Dallas, TX*] [*NASDAQ symbol*] (NQ)
VIDS.......... Virtual Image Display System
VIDSL .... Veroeffentlichungen. Institut fuer Deutsche Sprache und Literatur. Deutsche Akademie der Wissenschaften zu Berlin [*A publication*]
VIDS/MAF ... Visual Information Display System/Maintenance Action Form (NVT)
VIDV .... Veroeffentlichungen. Institut fuer Deutsche Volkskunde. Deutsche Akademie der Wissenschaften zu Berlin [*A publication*]
Vidya B ...... Vidya. Section B. Sciences [*A publication*]
Vidya Bhar ... Vidya Bharati [*Bangalore*] [*A publication*]
VIE............. Vampire Information Exchange (EA)
VIE............. Vibration Isolation Equipment (RDA)
VIE............. Victorian Institute of Engineers [*Australia*]
VIE............. Vienna [*Austria*] [*Airport symbol*] (OAG)
VIE............. Vienna [*Wien-Hohewarte*] [*Austria*] [*Seismograph station code, US Geological Survey*] (SEIS)
vie............... Vietnamese [*MARC language code*] [*Library of Congress*] (LCCP)
VIE............. Viewpoint [*A publication*]
VIE............. Vigilance, Initiative, Excellence [*Aerospace Defense Command's acronym for the Zero Defects Program*]
VIE............. Villeneuve Resources [*Vancouver Stock Exchange symbol*]
VIE............. Voluntary Import Expansion [*International trade*] (ECON)
VIE............. Volunteers in Education
Vie Acad Acad Sci (Paris) ... Vie Academique. Academie des Sciences (Paris) [*A publication*]
Vie Agric Meuse ... Vie Agricole de la Meuse [*A publication*]
Vie Agric et Rurale ... Vie Agricole et Rurale [*A publication*]
Vie Camp ... Vie a la Campagne [*A publication*]
Vie Econ (Berne) ... Vie Economique (Berne) [*A publication*]
ViEIM........ Merck & Co., Inc., Stonewall Process Development Library, Elkton, VA [*Library symbol*] [*Library of Congress*] (LCLS)
Vie Med ..... Vie Medicale [*A publication*]
Vie Med Can Fr ... Vie Medicale au Canada Francais [*A publication*]
Vie Milie A ... Vie et Milieu. Serie A. Biologie Marine [*A publication*]
Vie Milie B ... Vie et Milieu. Serie B. Oceanographie [*A publication*]
Vie Milie C ... Vie et Milieu. Serie C. Biologie Terrestre [*A publication*]
Vie Milieu Ser A ... Vie et Milieu. Serie A. Biologie Marine [*France*] [*A publication*]
Vie Milieu Ser A Biol Mar ... Vie et Milieu. Serie A. Biologie Marine [*A publication*]
Vie Milieu Ser B Oceanogr ... Vie et Milieu. Serie B. Oceanographie [*A publication*]
Vie Milieu Ser C Biol Terr ... Vie et Milieu. Serie C. Biologie Terrestre [*A publication*]
ViEmoE ..... Emory and Henry College, Emory, VA [*Library symbol*] [*Library of Congress*] (LCLS)
ViEmP .... Greenville County Library, Emporia, VA [*Library symbol*] [*Library of Congress*] (LCLS)
Vie Mus ..... Vie Musicale [*A publication*]
Vie Mus Belge ... Vie Musicale Belge [*A publication*]
Vien........... Viennola [*Record label*] [*Austria*]
Vienna Circle Coll ... Vienna Circle Collection [*A publication*]
VIEO .... Vendor's Item Engineering Order
Vie Ped ...... Vie Pedagogique [*A publication*]
VIER Bul ... Victorian Institute of Educational Research. Bulletin [*A publication*] (APTA)
VIER Bull ... Victorian Institute of Educational Research. Bulletin [*A publication*] (APTA)
VIERS .... Virgin Islands Ecological Research Station
Vierteljahreschr Gerichtl Med Oeff Sanitaetswes ... Vierteljahrschrift fuer Gerichtliche Medizin und Oeffentliches Sanitaetswesen [*A publication*]
Vierteljahressch Wirtschaftsforsch ... Vierteljahresschrift Wirtschaftsforschung [*West Germany*] [*A publication*]
Vierteljahrschr Prakt Pharm ... Vierteljahrschrift fuer Praktische Pharmazie [*A publication*]
Vierteljahrsh Zeitgesch ... Vierteljahrshefte fuer Zeitgeschichte [*A publication*]
Vierteljahrsschr Naturforsch Ges (Zuer) ... Vierteljahrsschrift. Naturforschende Gesellschaft (Zuerich) [*A publication*]
Vierteljahrsschr Naturforsch Ges (Zuerich) ... Vierteljahrsschrift. Naturforschende Gesellschaft (Zuerich) [*A publication*]
Vierteljahrsschr Soz Wirtschgesch ... Vierteljahrsschrift fuer Sozial- und Wirtschaftsgeschichte [*A publication*]
Vierteljahrsschr f Wiss Philos ... Vierteljahrsschrift fuer Wissenschaftliche Philosophie und Soziologie [*A publication*]

Viert Naturf Ges Zuerich ... Vierteljahrschrift der Naturforschenden Gesellschaft in Zuerich [*A publication*]
Vier Zeitg... Vierteljahrshefte fuer Zeitgeschichte [*A publication*]
VIESA .... Vocational Interest, Experience, and Skill Assessment [*Vocational guidance test*]
Vie Sci Econ ... Vie et Sciences Economiques [*A publication*]
Vie et Sciences Econs ... Vie et Sciences Economiques [*A publication*]
Vie Soc .... Vie Sociale [*A publication*]
Vietnam Chim Acta ... Vietnamica Chimica Acta [*A publication*]
Viet Stud ... Vietnamese Studies [*Hanoi*] [*A publication*]
VIEW......... Virtual Interface Environment Workstation
VIEW......... Visible, Informative, Emotionally Appealing, Workable [*Package evaluation in marketing*]
VIEW......... Vital Information for Education and Work (OICC)
Vie Wallonne ... La Vie Wallonne. Revue Mensuelle Illustree [*A publication*]
View Bot..... View from the Bottom [*A publication*]
Viewdata ... Viewdata and Television User [*A publication*]
Vieweg Stud Aufbaukurs Math ... Vieweg Studium. Aufbaukurs Mathematik [*A publication*]
Vieweg Tracts Pure Appl Phys ... Vieweg Tracts in Pure and Applied Physics [*A publication*]
Viewpoints Biol ... Viewpoints in Biology [*A publication*]
Viewpoint Ser Aust Conserv Fdn ... Viewpoint Series. Australian Conservation Foundation [*A publication*] (APTA)
Viewpoints Teach & Learn ... Viewpoints in Teaching and Learning [*A publication*]
VIEWS ...... Vibration Indicator Early Warning System (MCD)
VIEWS ...... Virtual Interactive Environment Workstation [*NASA*] (BYTE)
VIEWS ...... Vocational Information and Evaluation Work Samples [*Vocational guidance test*]
Views & R .. Views and Reviews [*A publication*]
ViF .... Fairfax County Public Library, Fairfax, VA [*Library symbol*] [*Library of Congress*] (LCLS)
VIF............ Vale International Airlines, Inc. [*Nashville, TN*] [*FAA designator*] (FAAC)
VIF............ Vanier Institute of the Family [*Canada*]
VIF............ Variance Inflation Factor [*Statistics*]
VIF............ Vertical Infrared Fuze (CAAL)
VIF............ Video Information [*Winslow Associates*] [*Information service or system*] [*No longer available*] (IID)
VIF............ Virion Infectivity Factor [*Genetics*]
VIF............ Virus-Induced Interferon [*Cell biology*]
VIF............ Visual Image Formula [*of psychotherapist Joseph Bird's self-help theory*]
ViFarL .... Longwood College, Farmville, VA [*Library symbol*] [*Library of Congress*] (LCLS)
VIFB .... Farrukhabad [*India*] [*ICAO location identifier*] (ICLI)
ViFbE........ United States Army Engineer School, Fort Belvoir, VA [*Library symbol*] [*Library of Congress*] (LCLS)
ViFbEM..... United States Army, Engineer Museum, Fort Belvoir, VA [*Library symbol*] [*Library of Congress*] (LCLS)
ViF-BPH ... Fairfax County Public Library, Services for the Blind and Physically Handicapped, Alexandria, VA [*Library symbol*] [*Library of Congress*]
VIFC......... VTOL [*Vertical Takeoff and Landing*] Integrated Flight Control
VIFD......... Faridkot [*India*] [*ICAO location identifier*] (ICLI)
ViFeAM..... United States Army, Air Mobility Research and Development Laboratory, Fort Eustis, VA [*Library symbol*] [*Library of Congress*] (LCLS)
ViFeAT ...... United States Army Transportation School, Fort Eustis, VA [*Library symbol*] [*Library of Congress*] (LCLS)
ViFerF........ Ferrum College, Ferrum, VA [*Library symbol*] [*Library of Congress*] (LCLS)
VIFF .... Vectoring in Forward Flight (MCD)
ViFGM ...... George Mason College [*Later, George Mason University*], Fairfax, VA [*Library symbol*] [*Library of Congress*] (LCLS)
VIFI......... Voyager Information Flow Instructions [*NASA*] (KSC)
ViFlL........ United States Army Logistics Management Center, Fort Lee, VA [*Library symbol*] [*Library of Congress*] (LCLS)
ViFlQ........ Quartermaster Technical Library, Fort Lee, VA [*Library symbol*] [*Library of Congress*] (LCLS)
ViFmTD .... United States Army, Training and Doctrine Command Library, Fort Monroe, VA [*Library symbol*] [*Library of Congress*] (LCLS)
ViFmTS ..... United States Army Tralinet Systems Center, Fort Monroe, VA [*Library symbol*] [*Library of Congress*] (LCLS)
ViFmUS.... United States Army Field Forces Library, Fort Monroe, VA [*Library symbol*] [*Library of Congress*] (LCLS)
ViFmyA .... United States Army, Fort Meyer Post Library, Fort Meyer, VA [*Library symbol*] [*Library of Congress*] (LCLS)
ViFraC .... Camp Manufacturing Co., Franklin, VA [*Library symbol*] [*Library of Congress*] (LCLS)
ViFraPC..... Paul D. Camp Community College, Franklin, VA [*Library symbol*] [*Library of Congress*] (LCLS)
ViFre.......... Central Rappahannock Regional Library, Fredericksburg, VA [*Library symbol*] [*Library of Congress*] (LCLS)
ViFreJM.... James Monroe Memorial Foundation, Fredericksburg, VA [*Library symbol*] [*Library of Congress*] (LCLS)

ViFreM...... Mary Washington College of the University of Virginia, Fredericksburg, VA [*Library symbol*] [*Library of Congress*]   (LCLS)

ViFroA....... American Viscose Co., Front Royal, VA [*Library symbol*] [*Library of Congress*]   (LCLS)

VIFS......... Village Financial Services Ltd. [*NASDAQ symbol*]   (NQ)

VIFSC....... VTOL [*Vertical Takeoff and Landing*] Integrated Flight System Control

VIFZ......... Ferojpur [*India*] [*ICAO location identifier*]   (ICLI)

VIG........... Vaccinia Immune Globulin [*Medicine*]

VIG........... Van Kampen Merritt Investment Grade [*NYSE symbol*]   (SPSG)

VIG........... Video Image Generator

VIG........... Video Integrating Group

Vig............ Vigente [*In Force*] [*Italian*]   (ILCA)

VIG........... Vigil   (ROG)

VIG........... Vigilant Identification   (MCD)

VIG........... Vignette   (ADA)

VIG........... Vigoroso [*With Vigor*] [*Music*]   (ROG)

VIG........... Visible Gold, Inc. [*Vancouver Stock Exchange symbol*]

VIG........... Vojnoistoriski Glasnik [*A publication*]

VIGB......... Variable Inlet Guide Blades   (MCD)

Vig C......... Vigiliae Christianae [*A publication*]

Vig Chr ..... Vigiliae Christianae [*A publication*]

ViGcS........ Scott County Library, Gate City, VA [*Library symbol*] [*Library of Congress*]   (LCLS)

VIGIL....... Vertical Indicating Gyro Internally Lighted   (MCD)

Vigil Chris ... Vigiliae Christianae [*A publication*]

Vigl............ Viglius ab Ayta Zuichemus [*Deceased, 1577*] [*Authority cited in pre-1607 legal work*]   (DSA)

VIGN........ Guna [*India*] [*ICAO location identifier*]   (ICLI)

VIGORN ... Vigorniensis [*Signature of the Bishops of Worcester*] [*Latin*]   (ROG)

ViGpD....... Deepsea Ventures, Inc., Gloucester Point, VA [*Library symbol*] [*Library of Congress*]   (LCLS)

ViGpM...... Virginia Institute of Marine Science, Gloucester Point, VA [*Library symbol*] [*Library of Congress*]   (LCLS)

VIGR .... Gwalior [*India*] [*ICAO location identifier*]   (ICLI)

VIGS......... Vertical Impact Guidance System [*Army*]   (MCD)

VIGS......... Video Disc Gunnery Simulator [*Army*]   (INF)

VIGS......... Visual Glide Slope

VIH........... Rolla/Vichy, MO [*Location identifier*] [*FAA*]   (FAAL)

VIH........... Velocity Impact Hardening

ViHa .... Charles H. Taylor Memorial Library, Hampton, VA [*Library symbol*] [*Library of Congress*]   (LCLS)

ViHaI........ Hampton Institute, Hampton, VA [*Library symbol*] [*Library of Congress*]   (LCLS)

ViHal........ Halifax County-South Boston Regional Library, Halifax, VA [*Library symbol*] [*Library of Congress*]   (LCLS)

ViHaNASA ... National Aeronautics and Space Administration, Langley Research Center, Hampton, VA [*Library symbol*] [*Library of Congress*]   (LCLS)

ViHar........ Rockingham Public Library, Harrisonburg, VA [*Library symbol*] [*Library of Congress*]   (LCLS)

ViHarEM .. Eastern Mennonite College, Harrisonburg, VA [*Library symbol*] [*Library of Congress*]   (LCLS)

ViHarT ...... James Madison University, Harrisonburg, VA [*Library symbol*] [*Library of Congress*]   (LCLS)

ViHaT....... Thomas Nelson Community College, Hampton, VA [*Library symbol*] [*Library of Congress*]   (LCLS)

ViHaV....... United States Veterans Administration Center, Medical Library, Hampton, VA [*Library symbol*] [*Library of Congress*]   (LCLS)

ViHdsC...... Hampden-Sydney College, Hampden-Sydney, VA [*Library symbol*] [*Library of Congress*]   (LCLS)

ViHi .... Virginia Historical Society, Richmond, VA [*Library symbol*] [*Library of Congress*]   (LCLS)

ViHo .... Hollins College, Hollins College, VA [*Library symbol*] [*Library of Congress*]   (LCLS)

ViHop .... Appomattox Regional Library, Hopewell, VA [*Library symbol*] [*Library of Congress*]   (LCLS)

ViHopA ..... Allied Corp., Hopewell, VA [*Library symbol*] [*Library of Congress*]   (LCLS)

ViHopAT ... American Tobacco Co., Department of Research and Development, Hopewell, VA [*Library symbol*] [*Library of Congress*]   (LCLS)

ViHopHC .. Hercules Powder Co. [*Later, Hercules, Inc.*], Cellulose Products Division, Hopewell, VA [*Library symbol*] [*Library of Congress*]   (LCLS)

ViHopHV .. Hercules Powder Co. [*Later, Hercules, Inc.*], Virginia Cellulose Division, Hopewell, VA [*Library symbol*] [*Library of Congress*]   (LCLS)

VIHR .... Hissar [*India*] [*ICAO location identifier*]   (ICLI)

VII............ Vacuum-Impregnated Inductor

VII............ Vicon Industries, Incorporated [*AMEX symbol*]   (SPSG)

VII............ Viscosity Index Improver [*for motor oil*]

VII............ Vocational Interest Inventory [*Vocational guidance test*]

VIIS .... Virgin Islands National Park

Viitor Soc ... Viitorul Social [*A publication*]

VIJ............ Vera Institute of Justice   (EA)

VIJ............ Virgin Gorda [*British Virgin Islands*] [*Airport symbol*]   (OAG)

VIJ............ Vishveshvaranand Indological Journal [*A publication*]

Vijes (Zagreb) ... Vijesti Muzealaca i Konservatora (Zagreb) [*A publication*]

VIJN.......... Jhansi [*India*] [*ICAO location identifier*]   (ICLI)

VIJO......... Jodhpur [*India*] [*ICAO location identifier*]   (ICLI)

VIJP .... Jaipur [*India*] [*ICAO location identifier*]   (ICLI)

VIJR .... Jaiselmer [*India*] [*ICAO location identifier*]   (ICLI)

VIJU .... Jammu [*India*] [*ICAO location identifier*]   (ICLI)

VIK .... Kavik River, AK [*Location identifier*] [*FAA*]   (FAAL)

VIK .... Vik [*Iceland*] [*Seismograph station code, US Geological Survey*] [*Closed*]   (SEIS)

VIK .... Viking International Air Freight, Inc. [*Minneapolis, MN*] [*FAA designator*]   (FAAC)

Vik .... Viking. Norsk Arkeologisk Selskap [*A publication*]

VIKA......... Kanpur [*India*] [*ICAO location identifier*]   (ICLI)

VIKA......... Viking Air Lines

VIKD .... Kud [*India*] [*ICAO location identifier*]   (ICLI)

ViKeS........ Southside Virginia Community College, John H. Daniel Campus, Keysville, VA [*Library symbol*] [*Library of Congress*]   (LCLS)

VIKG .... Viking Freight, Inc. [*NASDAQ symbol*]   (NQ)

Viking Fund Publ Anthropol ... Viking Fund Publication in Anthropology [*A publication*]

VIKJ .... Khajuraho [*India*] [*ICAO location identifier*]   (ICLI)

VIK Mitt... VIK [*Vereinigung Industrielle Kraftwirtschaft*] Mitteilungen [*A publication*]

VIKO .... Kota [*India*] [*ICAO location identifier*]   (ICLI)

Vikram Quart Res J Vikram University ... Vikram. Quarterly Research Journal of Vikram University [*A publication*]

VIL........... Dakhla [*Mauritania*] [*Airport symbol*]   (OAG)

ViL........... Jones Memorial Library, Lynchburg, VA [*Library symbol*] [*Library of Congress*]   (LCLS)

VIL........... University of Victoria Law Library [*UTLAS symbol*]

VIL........... Vendor Item List [*Sales*]   (AAG)

VIL........... Vertical Injection Logic [*Data processing*]

VIL........... Very Important Ladies

VIL........... Very Important Launch   (MUGU)

VIL........... Villa Mercy [*Maryland*] [*Seismograph station code, US Geological Survey*] [*Closed*]   (SEIS)

VIL........... Village

Vi-L........... Virginia State Law Library, Richmond, VA [*Library symbol*] [*Library of Congress*]   (LCLS)

VIL........... Vivisection Investigation League   (EA)

VIL........... VTI Industries, Inc. [*Vancouver Stock Exchange symbol*]

ViLanAF.... United States Air Force, Langley Air Force Base Library, Langley AFB, VA [*Library symbol*] [*Library of Congress*]   (LCLS)

Vilas.......... Vilas' Criminal Reports [*1-5 New York*] [*A publication*]   (DLA)

ViLaw....... Brunswick-Greensville Regional Library, Lawrenceville, VA [*Library symbol*] [*Library of Congress*]   (LCLS)

ViLawS ...... Saint Paul's College, Lawrenceville, VA [*Library symbol*] [*Library of Congress*]   (LCLS)

Vil & Br...... Vilas and Bryant's Edition of the Wisconsin Reports [*A publication*]   (DLA)

ViLBW....... Babcock & Wilcox Co., Lynchburg, VA [*Library symbol*] [*Library of Congress*]   (LCLS)

ViLC .... Lynchburg College, Lynchburg, VA [*Library symbol*] [*Library of Congress*]   (LCLS)

ViLCV........ Central Virginia Community College, Lynchburg, VA [*Library symbol*] [*Library of Congress*]   (LCLS)

VILD......... Ludhaiha [*India*] [*ICAO location identifier*]   (ICLI)

V I Lenin Sakharth Politekh Inst Samecn Srom ... V. I. Leninis Sahelobis Sromis Citheli Drosis Ordenosani Sakharthvelos Politekhnikuri Instituti. Samecniero Sromebi [*A publication*]

VILIOR ..... Vladimir Ilyich Lenin, Initiator of the October Revolution [*Given name popular in Russia after the Bolshevik Revolution*]

VILK......... Lucknow [*India*] [*ICAO location identifier*]   (ICLI)

VILL......... Village

Vill........... Villandry Festival [*Record label*] [*France*]

Villanova L Rev ... Villanova Law Review [*A publication*]

Vill L Rev... Villanova Law Review [*A publication*]

Vilniaus Valstybinis Univ Mokslo Darb ... Vilniaus Valstybinis Universitetas Mokslo Darbai [*A publication*]

ViLoGH..... Gunston Hall Plantation Library, Lorton, VA [*Library symbol*] [*Library of Congress*]   (LCLS)

VILP .... Lalitpur [*India*] [*ICAO location identifier*]   (ICLI)

VILP .... Vector Impedance Locus Plotter

ViLRM ...... Randolph-Macon Woman's College, Lynchburg, VA [*Library symbol*] [*Library of Congress*]   (LCLS)

VILTAR .... Viltrevy [*Stockholm*] [*A publication*]

VILTCH .... Verapamil, Imipramine, Lidocaine, Tamoxifen, Chlorpromazine, Haloperidol [*Antineoplastic drug regimen*]

ViLuV........ Virginia Oak Tannery, Luray, VA [*Library symbol*] [*Library of Congress*]   (LCLS)

Vil V .... Village Voice [*A publication*]

ViLx.......... Botetourt-Rockbridge Regional Library, Lexington, VA [*Library symbol*] [*Library of Congress*]   (LCLS)

ViLxV .... Virginia Military Institute, Lexington, VA [*Library symbol*] [*Library of Congress*]   (LCLS)

ViLxW .... Washington and Lee University, Lexington, VA [Library symbol] [Library of Congress] (LCLS)
ViLxW-L ... Washington and Lee University, Law Library, Lexington, VA [Library symbol] [Library of Congress] (LCLS)
VIM .... Vacuum Induction Melting [Metallurgy]
VIM .... Vendor Initial Measurement [Sales]
VIM .... Ventral Intersegmental Muscles [Anatomy]
VIM .... Vertical Improved Mail [Mail-delivery system for large buildings in which all tenants pick up their mail from lockboxes in a central mailroom]
VIM .... Vibration Isolation Module
VIM .... Video Intensified Microscopy
VIM .... Vinyl Insulation Material
VIM .... Vision Intensified Microscopy
VIM .... Vocational Instructional Materials Section (EA)
ViMan........ Ruffner-Carnegie Public Library, Manassas, VA [Library symbol] [Library of Congress] [Obsolete] (LCLS)
ViManCo .. Prince William County Public Library, Manassas, VA [Library symbol] [Library of Congress] (LCLS)
ViMarC ..... Marion Junior College, Marion, VA [Library symbol] [Library of Congress] (LCLS)
ViMat .... Mathews Memorial Library, Mathews, VA [Library symbol] [Library of Congress] (LCLS)
VIMBA...... Veroeffentlichungen. Institut fuer Meeresforschung in Bremerhaven [A publication]
ViMcC .... Central Intelligence Agency, McLean, VA [Library symbol] [Library of Congress] (LCLS)
ViMelE ...... Eastern Shore Community College, Learning Resources Center, Melfa, VA [Library symbol] [Library of Congress] (LCLS)
VIMEX...... Visit Mexico [Airline fares]
VIMG .... Moga [India] [ICAO location identifier] (ICLI)
VIMHEX.... Venezuela International Meteorological and Hydrological Experiment [Colorado State University project]
ViMidL...... Lord Fairfax Community College, Learning Resources Center, Middletown, VA [Library symbol] [Library of Congress] (LCLS)
ViMiN .... Notre Dame Institute, Middleburg, VA [Library symbol] [Library of Congress] (LCLS)
ViMiNS ..... National Sporting Library, Inc., Middleburg, VA [Library symbol] [Library of Congress] (LCLS)
VIMP........ Vertical Impulse
VIMS........ Mandasor [India] [ICAO location identifier] (ICLI)
VIMS........ Vehicle Integrated Management System
VIMS........ Virginia Institute of Marine Science [College of William and Mary] [Research center]
VIMTPG ... Virtual Interactive Machine Test Program Generator
ViMtvL...... Mount Vernon Ladies' Association of the Union, Mount Vernon, VA [Library symbol] [Library of Congress] (LCLS)
VIMVAR... Vacuum Induction Melt, Vacuum Arc Remelt
ViMvD....... E. I. Du Pont de Nemours & Co., Martinsville, VA [Library symbol] [Library of Congress] (LCLS)
VIN .... Miami, FL [Location identifier] [FAA] (FAAL)
ViN .... Norfolk Public Library, Norfolk, VA [Library symbol] [Library of Congress] (LCLS)
VIN .... Vehicle Identification Number
VIN .... Vendor Identification Number [Sales] (MCD)
VIN .... Victorian Industrial Notes [A publication]
Vin........... Vincentius Hispanus [Deceased, 1248] [Authority cited in pre-1607 legal work] (DSA)
Vin........... Vinduet [A publication]
VIN .... Vineyard [California] [Seismograph station code, US Geological Survey] [Closed] (SEIS)
VIN .... Vintage Enterprises, Inc. [AMEX symbol] (SPSG)
VIN .... Vinum [Wine] [Pharmacy] (ROG)
VIN .... Vinyl [Technical drawings]
VIN .... Voltage Input (TEL)
Vin Abr ...... Supplement to Viner's Abridgment of Law and Equity [England] [A publication] (DLA)
Vin Abr (Eng) ... Viner's Abridgment of Law and Equity [1741-53] [A publication] (DLA)
Vina Q....... Vina Quarterly [A publication]
ViNarC ...... Celanese Corp., Narrows, VA [Library symbol] [Library of Congress] (LCLS)
Vinar Obz .. Vinarsky Obzor [A publication]
ViNC......... Chrysler Art Museum, Jean Outland Chrysler Library, Norfolk, VA [Library symbol] [Library of Congress] (LCLS)
Vinc.......... Vincentius Hispanus [Deceased, 1248] [Authority cited in pre-1607 legal work] (DSA)
Vinc Cr L ... Vincent's Manual of Criminal Law [A publication] (DLA)
Vinc Cr & Lib ... Vincent on Criticism and Libel [A publication] (DLA)
Vincent de Franch ... Vincentius de Franchis [Deceased, 1601] [Authority cited in pre-1607 legal work] (DSA)
Vin Comm ... Viner's Abridgment [or Commentaries] [A publication] (DLA)
VIND........ Vicarious Interpolations Not Desired
VIND........ Vindication (ROG)
VIndJ........ Vishveshvaranand Indological Journal [A publication]
ViNE.......... Eastern Virginia Medical School, Norfolk, VA [Library symbol] [Library of Congress] (LCLS)
ViNe.......... Newport News Public Library, Newport News, VA [Library symbol] [Library of Congress] (LCLS)

ViNeC........ Christopher Newport College, Newport News, VA [Library symbol] [Library of Congress] (LCLS)
ViNeM....... Mariners' Museum, Newport News, VA [Library symbol] [Library of Congress] (LCLS)
ViNeN........ Newport News Shipbuilding & Dry Dock Co., Newport News, VA [Library symbol] [Library of Congress] (LCLS)
Viner Abr ... Viner's Abridgment of Law and Equity [1741-53] [A publication] (DLA)
VINES....... Virtual Networking Software [Banyan Systems]
ViNeV........ Virginia Associated Research Center, Newport News, VA [Library symbol] [Library of Congress] (LCLS)
VINFA....... Volunteers in the National Forests Act of 1972
Vingt Siecle Feder ... Vingtieme Siecle Federaliste [A publication]
VINH........ Nuh [India] [ICAO location identifier] (ICLI)
Vinifera Wine Grow J ... Vinifera Wine Growers Journal [A publication]
Vini Ital...... Vini d'Italia [A publication]
VINITI ...... Vsesoyuznyy Institut Nauchnoy i Tekhnicheskoy Informatsii [All-Union Institute of Scientific and Technical Information] [USSR]
VINL......... Naranaup [India] [ICAO location identifier] (ICLI)
ViNM........ Norfolk County Medical Society, Inc., Norfolk, VA [Library symbol] [Library of Congress] (LCLS)
ViNMoN.... Monsanto Chemical Co., Norfolk, VA [Library symbol] [Library of Congress] (LCLS)
Vinn ad Inst ... Vinnius' Commentary on the Institutes of Justinian [A publication] (DLA)
ViNO .... Old Dominion University, Norfolk, VA [Library symbol] [Library of Congress] (LCLS)
VINO........ WINE, Inc. [NASDAQ symbol] (NQ)
Vinodel Vinograd SSSR ... Vinodelie i Vinogradarstvo SSSR [A publication]
Vinograd Plodovod (Budapest) ... Vinogradarstvo i Plodovodstvo (Budapest) [A publication]
Vinograd Vinar (Budapest) ... Vinogradarstvo i Vinarstvo (Budapest) [A publication]
Vinograd Vinorobstvo ... Vinogradarstvo i Vinorobstvo [A publication]
ViNott........ Nottoway County Library, Nottoway, VA [Library symbol] [Library of Congress] (LCLS)
Vin Palaeot ... Vincentius Palaeotus [Deceased, 1498] [Authority cited in pre-1607 legal work] (DSA)
ViNR......... F. S. Royster Guano Co., Norfolk, VA [Library symbol] [Library of Congress] (LCLS)
ViNS .... Norfolk State College, Norfolk, VA [Library symbol] [Library of Congress] (LCLS)
VINS........ Velocity Inertia Navigation System
ViNSC .... United States Armed Forces Staff College, Norfolk, VA [Library symbol] [Library of Congress] (LCLS)
Vin Supp .... Supplement to Viner's Abridgment of Law and Equity [A publication] (DLA)
ViNT.......... Norfolk Testing Laboratories, Norfolk, VA [Library symbol] [Library of Congress] (LCLS)
VINT .... Video Integrate (NVT)
VInt........... Vie Intellectuelle [A publication] (BJA)
VINT .... Vintage Group, Inc. [NASDAQ symbol] (NQ)
VINT² .... Vehicle Integrated Intelligence [Army]
Vint Can Law ... Vinton's American Canon Law [A publication] (DLA)
ViNWe....... Virginia Wesleyan College, Norfolk, VA [Library symbol] [Library of Congress] (LCLS)
Vinyls Polym ... Vinyls and Polymers [Japan] [A publication]
VIO .... Heavy [Used to qualify interference or static reports] [Telecommunications] (FAAC)
VIO .... Veroeffentlichungen. Institut fuer Orientforschung. Deutsche Akademie der Wissenschaften zu Berlin [A publication]
VIO .... Very Important Object (DCTA)
VIO .... Veterinary Investigation Officer [Ministry of Agriculture, Fisheries, and Food] [British]
VIO .... Video Input/Output
VIO .... Violet (AAG)
VIO .... Violino [Violin] [Music] (ROG)
VIO .... Vior Miniere d'Exploration Societe, Inc. [Toronto Stock Exchange symbol]
VIO .... Virtual Input/Output [Data processing] (IBMDP)
VIO .... Visual Intercept Officer [Navy]
VIOC......... Variable Input-Output Code
VIODAWB ... Deutsche Akademie der Wissenschaften zu Berlin. Institut fuer Orientforschung. Veroeffentlichungen [A publication]
VIOL......... Viola [Music] (ROG)
VIOLE...... Violone [Double Bass] [Music] (ROG)
VIOLENT ... Viewers Intent on Listing Violent Episodes on Nationwide Television [Student legal action organization]
VIOLO .... Violino [Violin] [Music] (ROG)
ViOr.......... Orange County Public Library, Orange, VA [Library symbol] [Library of Congress] (LCLS)
VIP........... Value Improving Products
VIP........... Value in Performance
VIP........... Variable Incentive Pay [Military] (NVT)
VIP........... Variable Individual Protection [Insurance]
VIP........... Variable Inductance Pickup
VIP........... Variable Information Processing [Naval Ordnance Laboratory] [Information retrieval]
VIP............ Variable Input Phototypesetter
VIP............ Variable Interest Plus [Banking]

VIP............ Vasoactive Inhibitory Principle [*Biochemistry*]
VIP............ Vasoactive Intestinal Peptide [*or Polypeptide*] [*Biochemistry*]
VIP............ Vector Instruction Processor
VIP............ Vermont Information Processes, Inc. [*Information service or system*] (IID)
VIP............ Versatile Information Processor [*Data processing*]
VIP............ Very Important Passenger
VIP............ Very Important Person
VIP............ Very Important Poor
VIP............ Very Important Pregnancy [*In book title, "VIP Program"*]
VIP............ Vice President (AAG)
VIP............ Video Inertial Pointing [*System*] [*NASA*]
VIP............ Video Integrator and Processor
VIP............ Viewers in Profile [*A. C. Nielsen Co. reports for television industry*]
VIP............ Virgil Partch [*Cartoonist*]
VIP............ Viscosity-Index Improver [*for motor oil*]
VIP............ Visible Ink Press [*Publisher*]
VIP............ Vision Information Program (IID)
VIP............ Visit-Investigate-Purchase [*Department of Commerce program*]
VIP............ Visitor Information Publications (EA)
VIP............ Visual Identification Point (AFM)
VIP............ Visual Image Projection
VIP............ Visual Information Processing
VIP............ Visual Information Projection
VIP............ Visual Input [*System*] [*AT & T*]
VIP............ Visual Integrated Presentation [*Aviation*] (FAAC)
VIP............ Voice Integrated Presentations [*Telecommunications*] (RDA)
VIP............ Voix et Images du Pays [*University of Quebec*] [*A publication*]
VIP............ Volume Inverse Pricing [*Business term*]
VIP............ Vulcan Packaging, Inc. [*Toronto Stock Exchange symbol*]
VIP............ Vulcanized Interlinked Polyethylene [*Union Carbide Corp.*]
VIPA......... Victorian Interior Plantscapers Association [*Australia*]
VIPA......... Volunteers in the Parks Act of 1969
ViPe.......... Vita e Pensiero [*Milan*] [*A publication*]
VIPER....... Verifiable Integrated Processor for Enhanced Reliability [*Data processing*] (BYTE)
VIPER....... Video Processing and Electronic Reduction (IEEE)
ViPet......... Petersburg Public Library, Petersburg, VA [*Library symbol*] [*Library of Congress*] (LCLS)
ViPetA....... Allied Chemical Corp., Fibers Division, Technical Center Library, Petersburg, VA [*Library symbol*] [*Library of Congress*] (LCLS)
ViPetS........ Virginia State College, Petersburg, VA [*Library symbol*] [*Library of Congress*] (LCLS)
VIPI......... Very Important Person Indeed
VIPI.......... Volunteers in Probation, Incorporated [*Later, VIP Division of National Council on Crime and Delinquency*] (EA)
VIPID....... Visual Information Processing Interface Device (MCD)
VIPK......... Pathankot [*India*] [*ICAO location identifier*] (ICLI)
VIPL......... Patiala [*India*] [*ICAO location identifier*] (ICLI)
VIPL......... Vulcan Packaging Limited [*Formerly, Vulcan Industrial Packaging Limited*] [*NASDAQ symbol*] (NQ)
ViPo.......... Portsmouth Public Library, Portsmouth, VA [*Library symbol*] [*Library of Congress*] (LCLS)
ViPoN........ Norfolk Naval Hospital, Portsmouth, VA [*Library symbol*] [*Library of Congress*] (LCLS)
ViPoVC...... Virginia Chemicals, Inc., Portsmouth, VA [*Library symbol*] [*Library of Congress*] (LCLS)
ViPoVS...... Virginia Smelting Co., Portsmouth, VA [*Library symbol*] [*Library of Congress*] (LCLS)
VIPP......... Variable Information Processing Package
VIPP......... Venda Independent People's Party [*Political party*] (PPW)
ViPrA......... American Cyanamid Co., Pigments Division, Piney River, VA [*Library symbol*] [*Library of Congress*] (LCLS)
VIPRA....... Vest Individual Protective Reflective Adjustable [*System*] [*Military*] (INF)
VIPS......... Variable Item Processing System
VIPS......... Verbal Instruction Programmed System
VIPS......... Versatile Isotope Power System (MCD)
VIPS......... Veterans in Public Service Act
VIPS......... Video Image Processing System
VIPS......... Video Interactive Processing System
VIPS......... Voice Information Processing System [*UNISYS Corp.*] [*Blue Bell, PA*] [*Telecommunications service*] (TSSD)
VIPS......... Voice Interruption Priority System
VIPT.......... Nainital (Pantnagar) [*India*] [*ICAO location identifier*] (ICLI)
VIPT......... Vinland Property Trust [*NASDAQ symbol*] (NQ)
VIPTI........ Visually Impaired Piano Tuners International (EA)
ViPur......... Purcellville Library, Purcellville, VA [*Library symbol*] [*Library of Congress*] (LCLS)
VIQ............ Neillsville, WI [*Location identifier*] [*FAA*] (FAAL)
VIQG......... Qazigund [*India*] [*ICAO location identifier*] (ICLI)
ViQM........ United States Marine Corps Schools, Quantico, VA [*Library symbol*] [*Library of Congress*] (LCLS)
ViQM-E..... United States Marine Corps Schools, Educational Center, Quantico, VA [*Library symbol*] [*Library of Congress*] (LCLS)
VIR .... A. H. Robins Co., Richmond, VA [*OCLC symbol*] (OCLC)
VIR .... Point Barrow, AK [*Location identifier*] [*FAA*] (FAAL)

ViR............. Richmond Public Library, Richmond, VA [*Library symbol*] [*Library of Congress*] (LCLS)
VIR .... Si Vires Permittant [*If the Strength Will Bear It*] [*Pharmacy*] (ROG)
VIR .... Variable Interest Rate
VIR .... Vendor Information Request [*Sales*]
VIR .... Vendor Item Release [*Sales*]
VIR .... Vertical Interval Reference [*Automatic color adjustment*] [*Television*]
ViR............. Viata Romaneasca [*Bucharest*] [*A publication*]
VIR .... Victoria Imperatrix Regina [*Victoria Empress and Queen*] (ILCA)
VIR .... Victorian Industrial Reports [*A publication*]
VIR .... Virco Manufacturing Corp. [*AMEX symbol*] (SPSG)
VIR .... Virgin Islands of the US [*ANSI three-letter standard code*] (CNC)
Vir .... Virginia Cases (Brockenbrough and Holmes) [*A publication*] (DLA)
Vir .... Virgin's Reports [*52-60 Maine*] [*A publication*] (DLA)
Vir .... Virgo [*Constellation*]
VIR .... Viridis [*Green*] [*Pharmacy*]
Vir .... Virittaja [*A publication*]
VIR .... Virology
VIR .... Virtuoso [*A publication*]
VIR .... Virulent
VIR .... Visible [*or Visual*] and Infrared Radiometer [*NASA*]
VIR .... Vulcanized India Rubber
ViRa.......... Radford College, Radford, VA [*Library symbol*] [*Library of Congress*] (LCLS)
ViRA......... Richmond Academy of Medicine, Richmond, VA [*Library symbol*] [*Library of Congress*] (LCLS)
VIRA......... Vehicular Infrared Alarm (MCD)
VIRA......... Venus International Reference Atmosphere [*Meteorology*]
VIRA......... Video Review Award
VIRA......... Viratek, Inc. [*NASDAQ symbol*] (NQ)
VIRA......... Voprosy Istorii Religii i Ateizma. Sbornik Statei [*Moscow*] [*A publication*]
Vira-A........ Vidarabine [*Also, ara-A*] [*Biochemistry*]
VIRAD...... Virtual RADAR Defense [*Army*] (MCD)
ViRaP .... Radford Public Library, Radford, VA [*Library symbol*] [*Library of Congress*] (LCLS)
ViRAV ...... Atlantic Varnish & Paint Co., Richmond, VA [*Library symbol*] [*Library of Congress*] (LCLS)
VIRB......... Raibarelli/Fursatganj [*India*] [*ICAO location identifier*] (ICLI)
ViRC......... Museum of the Confederacy, Richmond, VA [*Library symbol*] [*Library of Congress*] (LCLS)
Virc Arch A ... Virchows Archiv. A. Pathological Anatomy and Histology [*A publication*]
Virc Arch B ... Virchows Archiv. B. Cell Pathology [*A publication*]
ViRCC .... [*The*] Computer Co., Richmond, VA [*Library symbol*] [*Library of Congress*] (LCLS)
Virchows Arch Abt A ... Virchows Archiv. Abteilung A. Pathologische Anatomie [*A publication*]
Virchows Arch Abt A Pathol Anat ... Virchows Archiv. Abteilung A. Pathologische Anatomie [*A publication*]
Virchows Arch Abt B ... Virchows Archiv. Abteilung B. Zellpathologie [*A publication*]
Virchows Arch Abt B Zellpathol ... Virchows Archiv. Abteilung B. Zellpathologie [*A publication*]
Virchows Arch A Pathol Anat Histol ... Virchows Archiv. A. Pathological Anatomy and Histology [*A publication*]
Virchows Arch A Pathol Anat Histopathol ... Virchows Archiv. A. Pathological Anatomy and Histopathology [*A publication*]
Virchows Arch B Cell Pathol ... Virchows Archiv. B. Cell Pathology [*A publication*]
Virchows Arch B Cell Pathol Incl Mol Pathol ... Virchows Archiv. B. Cell Pathology Including Molecular Pathology [*A publication*]
Virchows Arch Path Anat ... Virchows Archiv fuer Pathologische Anatomie [*A publication*]
Virchows Arch Pathol Anat Physiol Klin Med ... Virchows Archiv fuer Pathologische Anatomie und Physiologie und fuer Klinische Medizin [*A publication*]
Virch PM... Virchow on Post Mortem Examinations [*A publication*] (DLA)
ViRCU .... Virginia Commonwealth University, Richmond, VA [*Library symbol*] [*Library of Congress*] (LCLS)
ViRCU-A... Virginia Commonwealth University, Academic Division, Richmond, VA [*Library symbol*] [*Library of Congress*] (LCLS)
ViRCU-H .. Virginia Commonwealth University, Health Sciences Division, Richmond, VA [*Library symbol*] [*Library of Congress*] (LCLS)
VIREDF .... Virus Research [*A publication*]
ViREP........ Virginia Electric & Power Co., Richmond, VA [*Library symbol*] [*Library of Congress*] (LCLS)
ViREx........ Experiment, Inc., Richmond, VA [*Library symbol*] [*Library of Congress*] (LCLS)
ViRFR........ Federal Reserve Bank of Richmond, Richmond, VA [*Library symbol*] [*Library of Congress*] (LCLS)
VIRG .... Reengus [*India*] [*ICAO location identifier*] (ICLI)
ViRG.......... Richmond Guano Co., Richmond, VA [*Library symbol*] [*Library of Congress*] (LCLS)

VIRG .... Virgin
Virg .... Virgin's Reports [*52-60 Maine*] [*A publication*] (DLA)
Virg .... Virgo [*Constellation*]
Virg Cas ..... Virginia Cases (Brockenbrough and Holmes) [*A publication*] (DLA)
Virgin .... Virgin's Reports [*52-60 Maine*] [*A publication*] (DLA)
Virginia Div Mineral Rsources Rept Inv ... Virginia. Division of Mineral Resources. Report of Investigations [*A publication*]
Virginia Jour Sci ... Virginia Journal of Science [*A publication*]
Virginia J Sci ... Virginia Journal of Science [*A publication*]
Virginia Med Month ... Virginia Medical Monthly [*Later, Virginia Medical*] [*A publication*]
Virginia Miner ... Virginia Minerals [*Charlottesville*] [*A publication*]
Virginia M Month ... Virginia Medical Monthly [*A publication*]
Virginia Polytech Inst Research Div Bull ... Virginia Polytechnic Institute. Research Division. Bulletin [*A publication*]
Virginia Polytech Inst Research Div Mon ... Virginia Polytechnic Institute. Research Division. Monograph [*A publication*]
Virginia Q R ... Virginia Quarterly Review [*A publication*]
Virgin Pilo ... Virginian-Pilot [*A publication*]
Virg J Int'l L ... Virginia Journal of International Law [*A publication*]
Virg LJ ... Virginia Law Journal [*Richmond*] [*A publication*] (DLA)
ViRGS........ Church of Jesus Christ of Latter-Day Saints, Genealogical Society Library, Richmond Stake Branch, Richmond, VA [*Library symbol*] [*Library of Congress*] (LCLS)
Virg & Star L ... Virginian-Pilot and Ledger-Star [*A publication*]
ViRHC....... Henrico County Public Library, Richmond, VA [*Library symbol*] [*Library of Congress*] (LCLS)
VIRIS .... Visible/Infrared Intelligent Spectrometer
VIRL......... Visual Impairment Reference Libraries [*Australia*]
Vir LJ........ Virginia Law Journal [*A publication*] (DLA)
VIRM .... Variable-Interest-Rate Mortgage [*Real estate*]
ViRMu....... Virginia Museum of Fine Arts, Richmond, VA [*Library symbol*] [*Library of Congress*] (LCLS)
VIRNS....... Velocity Inertia RADAR Navigation System
ViRo .... Roanoke Public Library, Roanoke, VA [*Library symbol*] [*Library of Congress*] (LCLS)
ViRoA .... American Viscose Co., Roanoke, VA [*Library symbol*] [*Library of Congress*] (LCLS)
Virol .... Virology [*A publication*]
Virol Abstr ... Virology Abstracts [*A publication*]
Virol Monogr ... Virology Monographs [*A publication*]
ViRoNW.... Norfolk & Western Railway Co., Roanoke, VA [*Library symbol*] [*Library of Congress*] (LCLS)
ViRoV .... Virginia Western Community College, Brown Library, Roanoke, VA [*Library symbol*] [*Library of Congress*] (LCLS)
ViRPM ...... Philip Morris Research Center, Richmond, VA [*Library symbol*] [*Library of Congress*] (LCLS)
VIRPO....... Victorian Irrigation Research and Promotion Organisation [*Australia*]
ViRPol .... W. P. Poythress Co., Richmond, VA [*Library symbol*] [*Library of Congress*] (LCLS)
Vir Q R...... Virginia Quarterly Review [*A publication*]
ViRR .... Reynolds Metals Co., Richmond, VA [*Library symbol*] [*Library of Congress*] (LCLS)
VIRR......... Visible [*or Visual*] and Infrared Radiometer [*NASA*]
ViRRC .... J. Sargeant Reynolds Community College, Downtown Campus, Richmond, VA [*Library symbol*] [*Library of Congress*] (LCLS)
ViRR-E....... Reynolds Metals Co., Executive Office Library, Richmond, VA [*Library symbol*] [*Library of Congress*] (LCLS)
VIR & Regs ... Virgin Islands Rules and Regulations [*A publication*] (DLA)
ViRRob ...... A. H. Robins Co., Richmond, VA [*Library symbol*] [*Library of Congress*] (LCLS)
ViRR-P ...... Reynolds Metals Co., Packaging Research Division, Richmond, VA [*Library symbol*] [*Library of Congress*] (LCLS)
ViRR-T ...... Reynolds Metals Co., Technical Information Services Library, Richmond, VA [*Library symbol*] [*Library of Congress*] (LCLS)
VIRS .... Veroeffentlichungen. Institut fuer Romanische Sprachwissenschaft. Deutsche Akademie der Wissenschaften zu Berlin [*A publication*]
Virt............ De Virtutibus [*of Philo*] (BJA)
Virt............ Virtually (ILCA)
ViRU......... University of Richmond, Richmond, VA [*Library symbol*] [*Library of Congress*] (LCLS)
ViRUCA .... United States Circuit Court of Appeals, Fourth Circuit, Richmond, VA [*Library symbol*] [*Library of Congress*] (LCLS)
Viruly's Tech Maandbl Wasind ... Viruly's Technisch Maandblad voor de Wasindustrie [*A publication*]
Virus Res ... Virus Research [*A publication*]
Virus Res Suppl ... Virus Research. Supplement [*A publication*]
ViRUT .... Union Theological Seminary, Richmond, VA [*Library symbol*] [*Library of Congress*] (LCLS)
ViRUV .... United Virginia Bankshares, Inc., Richmond, VA [*Library symbol*] [*Library of Congress*] (LCLS)
ViRV .... United States Veterans Administration Hospital, Richmond, VA [*Library symbol*] [*Library of Congress*] (LCLS)

ViRVal...... Valentine Museum, Richmond, VA [*Library symbol*] [*Library of Congress*] (LCLS)
ViRVB .... Virginia Baptist Historical Society, University of Richmond, Richmond, VA [*Library symbol*] [*Library of Congress*] (LCLS)
ViRVI........ Virginia Institute for Scientific Research, Richmond, VA [*Library symbol*] [*Library of Congress*] (LCLS)
ViRVM ...... Valentine Meat Juice Co., Richmond, VA [*Library symbol*] [*Library of Congress*] (LCLS)
ViRVU ...... Virginia Union University, Richmond, VA [*Library symbol*] [*Library of Congress*] (LCLS)
VIS............ Minority Vendor Information Service [*National Minority Supplier Development Council, Inc.*] (IID)
VIS............ Variance Index Score [*Statistics*]
VIS............ Vector Instruction Set [*Data processing*]
VIS............ Vegetarian Information Service (EA)
VIS............ Vehicle Information System [*Automotive engineering*]
VIS............ Verification Information System (NASA)
VIS............ Veroeffentlichungen. Institut fuer Slawistik. Deutsche Akademie zu Berlin [*A publication*]
VIS............ Veterinary Investigation Service [*Ministry of Agriculture, Fisheries, and Food*] [*British*]
VIS............ Vibration Isolation System
VIS............ Videotex Information System [*Radio Shack*] [*Information service or system*] (IID)
VIS............ Vietnamese Information Service
VIS............ Virtual Information Storage (BUR)
VIS............ Visalia [*California*] [*Airport symbol*] (OAG)
VIS............ Viscosity
VIS............ Viscount [*or Viscountess*]
VIS............ Viscount Resources Ltd. [*Vancouver Stock Exchange symbol*]
VIS............ Vishakhapatnam [*Andhra, Waltair*] [*India*] [*Seismograph station code, US Geological Survey*] (SEIS)
VIS............ Visible [*or Visibility*] (AFM)
VIS............ Visit [*or Visitor*]
VIS............ Vista
VIS............ Visual
VIS............ Visual Imagery System [*NASA*]
VIS............ Visual Information Storage
VIS............ Visual Information System
VIS............ Visual Instrumentation Subsystem
VIS............ Visual Spectrophotometry
VIS............ VNR [*Van Nostrand Reinhold*] Information Services (IID)
VIS............ Voice Information Service [*Telecommunications*]
VIS............ Voice Intercom Subsystem (MCD)
VIs .... Voprosy Istorii [*Moscow*] [*A publication*]
ViSa .... Salem Public Library, Salem, VA [*Library symbol*] [*Library of Congress*] (LCLS)
VISA .... Ventricular Inhibiting Synchronous with Atrium [*Cardiac pacemaker*] [*Trademark*]
VISA .... [*The*] Vista Organization Ltd. [*New York, NY*] [*NASDAQ symbol*] (NQ)
VISA .... Vocational Interest and Sophistication Assessment [*Vocational guidance test*]
Vis Aids News ... Visual Aids News [*A publication*] (APTA)
Vis Aids Rev ... Visual Aids Review [*A publication*] (APTA)
VISAR .... Velocity Interferometer System for Any Reflector (MCD)
ViSaRC .... Roanoke College, Salem, VA [*Library symbol*] [*Library of Congress*] (LCLS)
Vis Arts..... Visual Arts [*A publication*]
ViSaV........ United States Veterans Administration Hospital, Salem, VA [*Library symbol*] [*Library of Congress*] (LCLS)
VISB .... Sikandrabad [*India*] [*ICAO location identifier*] (ICLI)
Visbl Lang ... Visible Language [*A publication*]
VISC .... Video Disc
visc .... Visceral
VISC .... Viscosity (AAG)
VISC .... Viscount [*or Viscountess*]
VISC .... Visual Industries, Inc. [*NASDAQ symbol*] (NQ)
VISC .... Vitreous Infusion Suction Cutter [*Ophthalmology*]
VISCA Rev Visayas State Coll Agric ... VISCA Review. Visayas State College of Agriculture [*A publication*]
VISCO .... Visual Systems Corporation
VISCOM... Visual Communications
VIS-COM-UK ... Visual Communications Exhibition and Conference, United Kingdom (ITD)
VISCT .... Viscount [*or Viscountess*]
Vis Educ..... Visual Education [*A publication*]
Vish Indo J ... Vishveshvaranand Indological Journal [*Hoshiarpur*] [*A publication*]
VISI .... VisionTech, Inc. [*Roswell, GA*] [*NASDAQ symbol*] (NQ)
VISI .... Volar Intercalated Segment Instability [*Orthopedics*]
Visible Lang ... Visible Language [*A publication*]
VISID .... Visual Identification (MSA)
Vis Ind ...... Vision Index [*A publication*]
Visindafelag Isl Greinar ... Visindafelag Islendinga. Greinar [*A publication*]
Visindafelag Isl Rit ... Visindafelag Islendinga. Rit [*A publication*]
VISION.... Volunteers in Service to India's Oppressed and Neglected (EA)
Vision Res ... Vision Research [*A publication*]
Vision Res Suppl ... Vision Research. Supplement [*A publication*]

VISIT......... Project VISIT - Vehicle Internal Systems Investigative Team (EA)
VISITS ...... Very Important Small Institution Travel Support
VISl........... Veroeffentlichungen. Institut fuer Slawistik. Deutsche Akademie der Wissenschaften zu Berlin [A publication]
VisL .... Visible Language [A publication]
VIS LAB .... Visibility Laboratory [Research center] (RCD)
VISM........ Simla [India] [ICAO location identifier] (ICLI)
VISMEM .. Visual Memory Task [Neuropsychology test]
VISMOD... Visual Modifications [Program] [Army] (RDA)
VISMR....... Viscometer [Engineering]
VISN........ Vision Interfaith Satellite Network
Visn Akad Nauk Ukr RSR ... Visnyk Akademiyi Nauk Ukrayins'koyi RSR [A publication]
Visnik Kiiv Univ Ser Mat Meh ... Visnik Kiivs'kogo Universitetu. Serija Matematiki ta Mehaniki [A publication]
Visnik Kiiv Ser Mat Mekh ... Visnik Kiivs'kogo Universitetu. Serija Matematiki ta Mekhaniki [A publication]
Visnik L'viv Derz Univ Ser Meh-Mat ... Visnik L'vivs'kogo Ordena Lenina Derzavogo Universitetu Imeni Ivana Franka. Serija Mehaniko-Matematicna [A publication]
Visnik L'viv Politehn Inst ... Visnik L'vivs'kogo Politehnicnogo Institutu [A publication]
Visn Kharkiv Univ Astron ... Visnik Kharkivs'kogo Universitetu. Astronomiya [Ukrainian SSR] [A publication]
Visn Kharkiv Univ Radiofiz ... Visnik Kharkivs'kogo Universitetu. Radiofizika [Ukrainian SSR] [A publication]
Visn Kharkiv Univ Radiofiz Elektron ... Visnik Kharkivs'kogo Universitetu. Radiofizika i Elektronika [Ukrainian SSR] [A publication]
Visn Kiiv Politekh Inst Ser Khim Mashinobuduv Tekhnol ... Visnik Kiivs'kogo Politekhnichnogo Institutu. Seriya Khimichnogo Mashinobuduvannya ta Tekhnologii [Ukrainian SSR] [A publication]
Visn Kiiv Univ Ser Astron ... Visnik Kiivs'kogo Universitetu. Seriya Astronomii [Ukrainian SSR] [A publication]
Visn Kiiv Univ Ser Astron Fiz Khim ... Visnik Kiivs'kogo Universitetu. Seriya Astronomii, Fiziki, ta Khimii [A publication]
Visn Kiiv Univ Ser Biol ... Visnik Kiivs'kogo Universitetu. Seriya Biologii [Ukrainian SSR] [A publication]
Visn Kiiv Univ Ser Fiz ... Visnik Kiivs'kogo Universitetu. Seriya Fiziki [A publication]
Visn Kiiv Univ Ser Fiz Khim ... Visnik Kiivs'kogo Universitetu. Seriya Fiziki ta Khimii [Ukrainian SSR] [A publication]
Visn Kiiv Univ Ser Geol Geogr ... Visnik Kiivs'kogo Universitetu. Seriya Geologii ta Geografii [A publication]
Visn Kiiv Univ Ser Khim ... Visnik Kiivs'kogo Universitetu. Seriya Khimii [Ukrainian SSR] [A publication]
Visn Kiyiv Univ Ser Fiz ... Visnik Kiyivs'kogo Universitetu. Seriya Fizika [Ukrainian SSR] [A publication]
Visn Kyyiv Univ Ser Biol ... Visnyk Kyyivs'koho Universytetu. Seriya Biolohiyi [A publication]
Visn L'viv Derzh Univ Ser Biol ... Visnik L'vivs'kogo Derzhavnogo Universitetu. Seriya Biologichna [A publication]
Visn L'viv Derzh Univ Ser Fiz ... Visnik L'vivs'kii Derzhavnii Universitet Imeni Ivana Franka. Seriya Fizichna [Ukrainian SSR] [A publication]
Visn L'viv Derzh Univ Ser Geol ... Visnik L'vivs'kogo Derzhavnogo Universitetu. Seriya Geologichna [A publication]
Visn L'viv Derzh Univ Ser Khim ... Visnik L'vivs'kogo Derzhavnogo Universitetu Imeni Ivana Franka. Seriya Khimichna [Ukrainian SSR] [A publication]
Visn L'viv Univ Ser Biol Heohr ... Visnyk L'vivs'koho Universytetu. Seriya Biolohiyi, Heohrafiyi, ta Heolohiyi [A publication]
Visn L'viv Univ Ser Biol Heohr Heol ... Visnyk L'vivs'koho Universytetu. Seriya Biolohiyi, Heohrafiyi, ta Heolohiyi [A publication]
Visn Sil-Hospod Nauky ... Visnyk Sil'kohospodars'koyi Nauky [A publication]
Visn Sil's'kohospod Nauki ... Visnyk Sil's'kohospodars'koy Nauki [A publication]
Visn Tsentr Resp Bot Sad Akad Nauk Ukr RSR ... Visnik Tsentral'nii Respublikans'kii Botanichnii Sad Akademiya Nauk Ukrains'koi RSR [A publication]
Visnyk Akad Nauk Ukr RSR ... Visnyk Akademiyi Nauk Ukrayins'koyi RSR [A publication]
VISP .... Saharanpur/Sarsawa [India] [ICAO location identifier] (ICLI)
VISPAC..... Videotex Information Service Providers Association of Canada [Defunct] (IID)
ViSpN........ National Technical Information Service, Springfield, VA [Library symbol] [Library of Congress] (LCLS)
VISR.......... Srinagar [India] [ICAO location identifier] (ICLI)
VISR.......... Virginia Institute for Scientific Research [University of Richmond] [Research center] (MCD)
VISR .... Viscount Resources Ltd. [NASDAQ symbol] (NQ)
Vissh Inst Arkhit Stroit Sofiya God ... Vissh Institut po Arkhitektura i Stroitelstvo-Sofiya. Godishnik [A publication]
VISSI......... Visindafelag Islendinga. Societas Scientiarum Islandica [A publication]
VISSR....... Visible-Infrared Spin Scan Radiometer [NASA]
VIST .... Satna [India] [ICAO location identifier] (ICLI)
ViSt........... Staunton Public Library, Staunton, VA [Library symbol] [Library of Congress] (LCLS)

VISTA .... Variable Interlace System for Television Applications
VISTA .... Verbal Information Storage and Text Analysis [in FORTRAN computer language]
VISTA .... Very Intelligent Surveillance and Target Acquisition [Army] (RDA)
VISTA .... Videodisc Interpersonal Skills Training and Assessment (INF)
VISTA .... Viewing Instantly Security Transactions Automatically [Wall Street]
VISTA .... Visual Information for Satellite Telemetry Analysis
VISTA .... Visually Impaired Secretarial/Transcribers Association [Indianapolis, IN] (EA)
VISTA .... Volunteers in Service to America (EA)
Vistas Astron ... Vistas in Astronomy [A publication]
Vistas Astronaut ... Vistas in Astronautics [A publication]
Vistas Bot .. Vistas in Botany [A publication]
Vistas Volunt ... Vistas for Volunteers [A publication]
ViSte .... Sterling Public Library, Sterling, VA [Library symbol] [Library of Congress] (LCLS)
Visti Akad Nauk Ukr RSR ... Visti Akademii Nauk Ukrains'koi RSR [A publication]
Visti Inst Fiz Khim Akad Nauk Ukr RSR ... Visti Institutu Fizichnoi Khimii Akademiya Nauk Ukrains'koi RSR [A publication]
Visti Ukr Nauk Dosl Inst Fiz Khim ... Visti Ukrains'kogo Naukovo Doslidchogo Institutu Fizichnoi Khimii [A publication]
ViStM .... Mary Baldwin College, Staunton, VA [Library symbol] [Library of Congress] (LCLS)
VISTRAC ... Visual Target Reconnaissance and Acquisition (MCD)
ViStrR....... Robert E. Lee Memorial Association, Stratford Hall, Stratford, VA [Library symbol] [Library of Congress] (LCLS)
Visual Aids R ... Visual Aids Review [A publication] (APTA)
Visual Com ... Studies in Visual Communication [A publication]
Visual Ed ... Visual Education [A publication]
Visual Med ... Visual Medicine [A publication]
Visual Sonic Med ... Visual Sonic Medicine [A publication]
ViSwC....... Sweet Briar College, Sweet Briar, VA [Library symbol] [Library of Congress] (LCLS)
VISX .... VISX, Inc. [NASDAQ symbol] (NQ)
VIT............ Roanoke, VA [Location identifier] [FAA] (FAAL)
VIT............ Van Kampen Merritt Intermediate Term High Income Trust [NYSE symbol] (SPSG)
VIT............ Variable Impedance Tube
VIT............ Vertically Integrated Team [Engineering]
VIT............ Very Important Traveler
VIT............ Vibration Isolation Table
VIT............ Victoria Resources [Vancouver Stock Exchange symbol]
VIT............ Vineyard [Telemeter] [California] [Seismograph station code, US Geological Survey] [Closed] (SEIS)
Vit .... Vita [of Josephus] [Classical studies] (OCD)
Vit .... Vitae Parallelae [of Plutarch] [Classical studies] (OCD)
VIT............ Vital
VIT............ Vital Speeches of the Day [A publication]
VIT............ Vitamin
Vit .... Vitellius [of Suetonius] [Classical studies] (OCD)
VIT............ Vitoria [Spain] [Airport symbol] (OAG)
VIT............ Vitreous (AAG)
Vita .... Vita. Revue Bimensuelle. Confederation de l'Alimentation Belge [A publication]
VITA......... Vitalink Communications Corp. [NASDAQ symbol] (NQ)
VITA......... VMEbus International Trade Association (EA)
VITA......... Volunteer Income Tax Assistance Program [Internal Revenue Service]
VITA......... Volunteers in Technical Assistance (EA)
Vita Hum ... Vita Humana [A publication]
Vita Int...... Vita International [A publication]
Vita Ital...... Vita Italiana [A publication]
VITAL .... Variably Initialized Translator for Algorithmic Languages [Data processing]
VITAL .... VAST [Versatile Avionics Shop Test] Interface Test Application Language
VITAL .... Virtual Image Takeoff and Landing [Simulator] (MCD)
Vital C........ Vital Christianity [A publication]
Vital Health Stat 1 ... Vital and Health Statistics. Series 1. Programs and Collection Procedures [United States] [A publication]
Vital Health Stat 2 ... Vital and Health Statistics. Series 2. Data Evaluation and Methods Research [United States] [A publication]
Vital Health Stat 3 ... Vital and Health Statistics. Series 3. Analytical Studies [United States] [A publication]
Vital Health Stat 4 ... Vital and Health Statistics. Series 4. Documents and Committee Reports [United States] [A publication]
Vital Health Stat 10 ... Vital and Health Statistics. Series 10. Data from the National Health Survey [United States] [A publication]
Vital Health Stat 11 ... Vital and Health Statistics. Series 11. Data from the National Health Survey [United States] [A publication]
Vital Health Stat 13 ... Vital and Health Statistics. Series 13. Data from the National Health Survey [United States] [A publication]
Vital Health Stat 14 ... Vital and Health Statistics. Series 14. Data on National Health Resources [United States] [A publication]
Vital Health Stat 20 ... Vital and Health Statistics. Series 20. Data from the National Vital Statistics System [United States] [A publication]

Vital Health Stat 21 ... Vital and Health Statistics. Series 21. Data from the National Vital Statistics System [*United States*] [*A publication*]
Vital Health Stat 23 ... Vital and Health Statistics. Series 23. Data from the National Survey of Family Growth [*United States*] [*A publication*]
Vital Health Statist Ser 2 Data Evaluation Methods Res ... Vital and Health Statistics. Series 2. Data Evaluation and Methods Research [*A publication*]
Vital S HD ... Monthly Vital Statistics Report. Hospital Discharge Survey Data [*US*] [*A publication*]
Vital S HI .. Monthly Vital Statistics Report. Health Interview Survey [*US*] [*A publication*]
Vital S HS ... Monthly Vital Statistics Report. Health Statistics [*US*] [*A publication*]
Vital S MS ... Monthly Vital Statistics Report. Advance Report of Final Mortality Statistics. 1981 [*US*] [*A publication*]
Vital Speeches ... Vital Speeches of the Day [*A publication*]
Vital Speeches Day ... Vital Speeches of the Day [*A publication*]
Vital St A ... Monthly Vital Statistics Report. Annual Summary of Births, Deaths, Marriages, and Divorces. 1983 [*US*] [*A publication*]
Vital Stat .... Monthly Vital Statistics Report. Births, Marriages, Divorces, and Deaths [*US*] [*A publication*]
Vital St N ... Monthly Vital Statistics Report. Advance Report of Final Natality Statistics. 1981 [*US*] [*A publication*]
Vitalstoffe .. Vitalstoffe Zivilisationskrankheiten [*A publication*]
Vitalst Zivilisationskr ... Vitalstoffe Zivilisationskrankheiten [*A publication*]
Vita Luc ..... Vita Lucani [*of Suetonius*] [*Classical studies*]   (OCD)
Vitam D Dig ... Vitamin D Digest [*A publication*]
Vitam Eksp Klin ... Vitaminy v Eksperimente i Klinike [*A publication*]
Vitam Horm ... Vitamins and Hormones [*A publication*]
Vita Mon .... Vita Monastica [*A publication*]
Vitam Resur Ikh Ispol'z ... Vitaminnye Resursy i Ikh Ispol'zovanie [*A publication*]
Vitams Horm ... Vitamins and Hormones [*A publication*]
VITAP ...... Viking Targeting Analysis Program [*NASA*]
VITAS ...... Visual Target Acquisition System [*Navy*]   (MCD)
VITAS ...... Vocational Interest, Temperament, and Aptitude System [*Aptitude test*]
Vit Auct ...... Vitarum Auctio [*of Lucian*] [*Classical studies*]   (OCD)
VITB .... Vocational and Industrial Training Board [*Singapore*]   (DS)
VITC .... Vertical Internal Time Code [*Electronic musical instruments*]
VITC .... Victoria Creations, Inc. [*Warwick, RI*] [*NASDAQ symbol*]   (NQ)
VITEK ...... Life Technology   (MCD)
Vitel .... Vitellus [*Yolk*] [*Pharmacy*]
VITIC .... Viticulture
Vitic Arboric ... Viticulture, Arboriculture [*A publication*]
Vitic Enol (Budapest) ... Viticulture and Enology (Budapest) [*A publication*]
VITIS-VEA ... VITIS-Viticulture and Enology Abstracts [*International Food Information Service*] [*Information service or system*]   (IID)
Viti-Vinic (Budapest) ... Viti-Viniculture (Budapest) [*A publication*]
VITL .... Vitality Unlimited [*NASDAQ symbol*]   (NQ)
Vit Ov Sol .. Vitello Ovi Solutus [*Dissolved in the Yolk of an Egg*] [*Pharmacy*]
VITR .... Vitramon, Inc. [*NASDAQ symbol*]   (NQ)
VITR .... Vitreum [*Glass*] [*Latin*]   (ADA)
Vitr .... Vitruvius [*First century BC*] [*Classical studies*]   (OCD)
VITRAN ... Vibration Transient Analysis   (MCD)
VITS .... Vertical Interval Test Signal   (IEEE)
VITT .... Vehicle Integration Test Team [*NASA*]   (MCD)
ViU .... University of Virginia, Charlottesville, VA [*Library symbol*] [*Library of Congress*]   (LCLS)
VIU .... Vehicle in Use
VIU .... Video Interface Unit   (MCD)
VIU .... Voice Intercommunications Unit
VIU .... Voice Interface Unit [*Telecommunications*]   (TEL)
VIUD .... Udaipur [*India*] [*ICAO location identifier*]   (ICLI)
ViU-ES ...... University of Virginia, School of General Studies, Eastern Shore Branch, Wallops Island, VA [*Library symbol*] [*Library of Congress*]   (LCLS)
ViU-H .... University of Virginia Medical Center, Health Sciences Library, Charlottesville, VA [*Library symbol*] [*Library of Congress*]   (LCLS)
ViU-L .... University of Virginia, Law Library, Charlottesville, VA [*Library symbol*] [*Library of Congress*]   (LCLS)
ViU-Mu ..... University of Virginia, Music Library, Charlottesville, VA [*Library symbol*] [*Library of Congress*]   (LCLS)
VIURAM ... Video Interface Unit Random Access Memory
ViU-ST ...... University of Virginia, Science/Technology Information Center, Charlottesville, VA [*Library symbol*] [*Library of Congress*]   (LCLS)
VIV .... Variable Inlet Vane [*Nuclear energy*]   (NRCH)
VIV .... Vivace [*Lively*] [*Music*]
Viv .... Vivarium [*A publication*]
VIV .... Vivian, LA [*Location identifier*] [*FAA*]   (FAAL)
VIV .... Vivid-Inventive-Vital [*Spring fashions*]
VIV .... Vivigani [*Papua New Guinea*] [*Airport symbol*]   (OAG)
VIV .... Vlaamse Ingenieurs-Vereniging

VIVA .... Victory in Vietnam Association
VIVA .... Virgin Islands Visitors Association
VIVA .... Visually Impaired Veterans of America   (EA)
VIVA .... Voices in Vital America
Vivar .... Vivarium. A Journal for Mediaeval Philosophy and the Intellectual Life of the Middle Ages [*A publication*]
ViVb .... Department of Public Libraries and Information, City of Virginia Beach, Reference Department, Virginia Beach, VA [*Library symbol*] [*Library of Congress*]   (LCLS)
ViVbGS ..... Church of Jesus Christ of Latter-Day Saints, Genealogical Society Library, Norfolk Virginia Stake Branch, Virginia Beach, VA [*Library symbol*] [*Library of Congress*]   (LCLS)
ViVbRE ..... Association for Research and Enlightenment, Virginia Beach, VA [*Library symbol*] [*Library of Congress*]   (LCLS)
VIVED ...... Virtual Visual Environment Display [*Helmet equipped with liquid crystal display screens viewed through wide-angle lenses*] [*NASA*]
Vivi .... Vivianus Tuscus [*Flourished, 13th century*] [*Authority cited in pre-1607 legal work*]   (DSA)
VIVI .... Vivienda [*Mexico*] [*A publication*]
VIVI .... Vivigen, Inc. [*NASDAQ symbol*]   (NQ)
Vivia .... Vivianus Tuscus [*Flourished, 13th century*] [*Authority cited in pre-1607 legal work*]   (DSA)
VIVL .... Verhandlungen der Internationalen Vereinigung fuer Theoretische und Angewandte Limnologie [*A publication*]
ViW .... College of William and Mary, Williamsburg, VA [*Library symbol*] [*Library of Congress*]   (LCLS)
ViWaR ...... Rappahannock Community College, North Campus, Warsaw, VA [*Library symbol*] [*Library of Congress*]   (LCLS)
ViWarUS ... United States Army, Post Library, Vint Hill Farms Station, Warrenton, VA [*Library symbol*] [*Library of Congress*]   (LCLS)
ViWb .... Waynesboro Public Library, Waynesboro, VA [*Library symbol*] [*Library of Congress*]   (LCLS)
ViWbD ...... E. I. Du Pont de Nemours & Co., Benger Laboratory, Waynesboro, VA [*Library symbol*] [*Library of Congress*]   (LCLS)
ViWbF .... Fairfax Hall Junior College, Waynesboro, VA [*Library symbol*] [*Library of Congress*]   (LCLS)
ViWC .... Colonial Williamsburg, Inc., Williamsburg, VA [*Library symbol*] [*Library of Congress*]   (LCLS)
ViWI .... Institute of Early American History and Culture, Williamsburg, VA [*Library symbol*] [*Library of Congress*]   (LCLS)
ViWiN .... United States National Aeronautics and Space Administration, Technical Library, Wallops Island, VA [*Library symbol*] [*Library of Congress*]   (LCLS)
ViWisC ...... Clinch Valley College of the University of Virginia, Wise, VA [*Library symbol*] [*Library of Congress*]   (LCLS)
ViW-L .... College of William and Mary, Law School, Williamsburg, VA [*Library symbol*] [*Library of Congress*]   (LCLS)
ViWn .... Handley Library, Winchester, VA [*Library symbol*] [*Library of Congress*]   (LCLS)
ViWnS .... Shenandoah College and Conservatory of Music, Winchester, VA [*Library symbol*] [*Library of Congress*]   (LCLS)
ViWyC .... Wytheville Community College, Wytheville, VA [*Library symbol*] [*Library of Congress*]   (LCLS)
VIX .... Vitoria [*Brazil*] [*Airport symbol*]   (OAG)
VIX .... Vixit [*He Lived*] [*Latin*]
VIY .... Nashville, TN [*Location identifier*] [*FAA*]   (FAAL)
VIY .... Visserij. Voorlichtingsblad voor de Nederlandse Visserij [*A publication*]
ViYNW ...... United States Naval Weapons Station, Yorktown, VA [*Library symbol*] [*Library of Congress*]   (LCLS)
VIZ .... Videlicet [*Namely*] [*Latin*]
Viz .... Vizardinus [*Guizzardinus*] [*Deceased, 1222*] [*Authority cited in pre-1607 legal work*]   (DSA)
VIZ .... Vizianagram [*India*] [*Seismograph station code, US Geological Survey*]   (SEIS)
Vizar .... Vizardinus [*Guizzardinus*] [*Deceased, 1222*] [*Authority cited in pre-1607 legal work*]   (DSA)
Vizgazdalkodasi Tud Kut Intez Tanulmanyok Kut Eredmenyek ... Vizgazdalkodasi Tudomanyos Kutato Intezet Tanulmanyok es Kutatasi Eredmenyek [*A publication*]
Viz Koezl .... Vizuegyi Koezlemenyek [*A publication*]
Viz Pr .... Vizard's Practice of the Court in Banc [*A publication*]   (DLA)
Vizugyi Kozl ... Vizugyi Kozlemenyek [*A publication*]
Vizugyi Kozlem ... Vizugyi Kozlemenyek [*A publication*]
VizV .... Vizantiiskii Vremenik [*A publication*]
Viz Vrem ... Vizantijskij Vremennik [*A publication*]
VJ .... Sempati Air Transport P.T. [*Indonesia*] [*ICAO designator*]   (FAAC)
VJ .... Utility Plane [*Navy symbol*]
VJ .... V-Joint [*Technical drawings*]
VJ .... Vacuum-Jacketed   (KSC)
VJ .... Variable Joining [*Genetics*]
VJ .... Vassar Journal of Undergraduate Studies [*A publication*]
VJ .... Ventriculojugular [*Medicine*]
VJ .... Video Jockey [*Television version of disc jockey; originated on all-rock-music cable station MTV*]
VJ .... Visiting Judges [*British*]
VJ .... Voprosy Jazykoznanija [*Lvov*] [*A publication*]

V-J (Day)... Victory over Japan [*Japanese surrender, World War II, 14 August 1945*]
VJA............ Adelphi University, Garden City, NY [*OCLC symbol*]   (OCLC)
VJA............ V-8 Juice Agar [*Microbiology*]
VJa............. Voprosy Jazykoznanija [*Moscow*] [*A publication*]
VJaL......... Voprosy Jazyka i Literatury [*A publication*]
VJB............ Verdan Junction Box
VJB............ Victorian Judgements Bulletin [*Australia*] [*A publication*]
Vjber .... Vierteljahresberichte [*A publication*]
VJC............ Vallejo Junior College [*California*]
VJC............ Vermont Junior College
VJC............ Virginia Junior College [*Minnesota*] [*Later, Mesabi Community College*]
Vjes A Muz Zagreb ... Vjesnik Arheoloskog Muzeja u Zagrebu [*A publication*]
Vjes Dal ..... Vjesnik za Arheologiju i Historiju Dalmatinsku [*Bulletin d'Archeologie et d'Histoire Dalmates*] [*A publication*]
Vjesn Bibliot Hrv ... Vjesnik Bibliotekara Hrvatske [*A publication*]
VJH .... Victorian Journal of History [*A publication*]
Vjhber Probl Entwickllaend ... Vierteljahresberichte Probleme der Entwicklungslaender [*A publication*]
Vjhefte Zeitgesch ... Vierteljahrshefte fuer Zeitgeschichte [*A publication*]
Vjh WF ...... Vierteljahreshefte fuer Wirtschaftsforschung [*A publication*]
Vjh Wirtsch-Forsch ... Vierteljahreshefte fuer Wirtschaftsforschung [*A publication*]
V Jh f Z...... Vierteljahrshefte fuer Zeitgeschichte [*A publication*]
Vjh Zeitg.... Vierteljahrshefte fuer Zeitgeschichte [*A publication*]
Vjh Zeitgesch ... Vierteljahreshefte fuer Zeitgeschichte [*A publication*]
V Jh ZG ..... Vierteljahrshefte fuer Zeitgeschichte [*A publication*]
VJJ .... Johnson & Johnson Dental Products Co., Science Information Center, East Windsor, NJ [*OCLC symbol*]   (OCLC)
VJLB .... Veterans Jewish Legion. Bulletin [*A publication*]
VJ Lit........ Deutsche Vierteljahrsschrift fuer Literaturwissenschaft und Geistesgeschichte [*A publication*]
VJMC........ Vintage Japanese Motorcycle Club   (EA)
Vj Nat Ges (Zuer) ... Vierteljahresschrift der Naturforschenden Gesellschaft (Zuerich) [*A publication*]
Vj NGZ...... Vierteljahrsschrift. Naturforschende Gesellschaft [*Zuerich*] [*A publication*]
VJNRL...... Virginia Journal of Natural Resources Law [*A publication*]   (DLA)
Vjschr Naturf Ges (Zuerich) ... Vierteljahrsschrift. Naturforschende Gesellschaft (Zuerich) [*A publication*]
Vjschr Soz- und Wirtschaftsgesch ... Vierteljahrschrift fuer Sozial- und Wirtschaftsgeschichte [*A publication*]
Vj SR......... Vierteljahresschrift fuer Sozialrecht [*A publication*]
VJTA........ Veterans' Job Training Act
VJWPh...... Vierteljahrsschrift fuer Wissenschaftliche Philosophie [*A publication*]
VK............ Airbus Industrie [*France*] [*ICAO designator*]   (FAAC)
VK............ Vedanta Kesari [*Mylapore*] [*A publication*]
VK............ Ventral Wall, Kidney [*Anatomy*]
VK............ Verbundkatalog Maschinenlesbarer Katalogdaten Deutscher Bibliotheken [*Deutsches Bibliotheksinstitut*] [*Federal Republic of Germany*] [*Information service or system*]   (CRD)
VK............ Vertical Keel
VK............ Voelkische Kultur [*A publication*]
VK............ Volkskrant [*A publication*]
VKA.......... Vienna-Kobenzl [*Austria*] [*Seismograph station code, US Geological Survey*]   (SEIS)
VKA.......... Volatile Keying Assembly   (AFM)
VKAW....... Verhandelingen. Koninklijke Akademie van Wetenschappen [*A publication*]
VKC.......... Canisius College, Buffalo, NY [*OCLC symbol*]   (OCLC)
VKC.......... Tijdschrift voor Vervoerswetenschap [*A publication*]
VKC.......... Van Kampen Merritt California Municipal Trust [*AMEX symbol*]   (CTT)
VKCSN...... Vestnik Kralovske Ceske Spolecnosti Nauk [*A publication*]
VKE .... Von Karman Equation
VKF.......... Von Karman Gas Dynamics Facility [*Air Force*] [*Arnold Air Force Base, TN*]
VKF.......... Voprosy Klassicekoj Filologii [*A publication*]
VKFLA ...... Voprosy Kurortologii, Fizioterapii, i Lechebnoi Fizicheskoi Kul'tury [*A publication*]
VKH.......... Vogt-Koyanagi-Harada [*Syndrome*] [*Ophthalmology*]
VKI .... Von Karman Institute   (NATG)
VKIFD....... Von Karman Institute for Fluid Dynamics [*Belgium*]
VKL.......... Verhandelingen. Koninklijke Akademie van Wetenschappen. Letterkunde [*Elsevier Book Series*] [*A publication*]
VKN.......... Barre-Montpelier, VT [*Location identifier*] [*FAA*]   (FAAL)
VKN.......... Verhandelingen. Koninklijke Akademie van Wetenschappen. Natuurkunde [*Elsevier Book Series*] [*A publication*]
VKNA........ Verhandelingen. Koninklijke Nederlandse Akademie van Wetenschappen. Afdeling Letterkunde [*A publication*]
VKNAL...... Verhandelingen. Koninklijke Nederlandse Akademie van Wetenschappen. Afdeling Letterkunde [*A publication*]
VKNAW .... Verhandelingen. Koninklijke Nederlandse Akademie van Wetenschappen [*A publication*]
VKO.......... Moscow [*USSR*] Vnukovo Airport [*Airport symbol*]   (OAG)
VKP .... Verkaufspreis [*Selling Price*] [*German*]
VKR .... Volkstum und Kultur der Romanen [*A publication*]

VKR .... Voprosy Kul'tury Reci [*A publication*]
VKS........... Vicksburg, MS [*Location identifier*] [*FAA*]   (FAAL)
VKS........... Vlees en Vleeswaren [*A publication*]
VKSI......... Vikonics, Inc. [*NASDAQ symbol*]   (NQ)
VKSt .... Verkaufsstelle [*Sales Outlet*] [*German*]
VKT .... Vane Kindergarten Test [*Child development test*]
VKT .... Vehicle Kit Test
VKyjU....... Visnyk Kyjivs'koho Universytetu [*A publication*]
VL .... Deutsche Vierteljahrsschrift fuer Literaturwissenschaft und Geistesgeschichte [*A publication*]
VL .... Eagleair Ltd. [*Arnarflug hf*] [*Iceland*] [*ICAO designator*]   (FAAC)
VL .... Valmet OY [*Finland*] [*ICAO aircraft manufacturer identifier*]   (ICAO)
VL .... Value Line Investment Survey [*Finance*]
V-L............ Van Langenhoven [*Rifle*]
VL .... Vandalia Line [*Railroad*]
V/L............ Vapor-to-Liquid
VL .... Vapor Return Line
VL .... Varia Lectio [*Variant Reading*] [*Latin*]
VL .... Variable Light [*Immunology*]
VL .... Vario-Losser [*Electronics*]
VL .... Velar Lobe
VL .... Ventralis Lateralis [*Brain anatomy*]
VL .... Ventrolateral [*Anatomy*]
VL .... Vereinigte Linke [*United Left*] [*Federal Republic of Germany*] [*Political party*]   (PPW)
VL .... Vereniging Lucht [*Clean Air Society in the Netherlands - CLAN*] [*Delft, Netherlands*]   (EAIO)
VL .... Vertical Ladder [*Technical drawings*]
VL .... Vertical Landing   (MCD)
VL .... Vestre Landsret [*Western Court of Appeal*] [*Denmark*]   (ILCA)
VL .... Vetenskaps-Societeten i Lund [*A publication*]
VL .... Vice Lieutenant [*British*]
VL .... Vide Locum [*See the Place Indicated*] [*Latin*]
VL .... Videlicet [*Namely*] [*Latin*]
VL .... Video Logic   (IEEE)
V & L........ Vie et Langage [*A publication*]
VL .... View Loss
VL .... Viking Lander [*NASA*]
VL .... Ville
VL .... Violation of Lawful [*Order*] [*Military*]
VL .... Violin [*Music*]   (ROG)
VL .... Vision, Left Eye
VL .... Visual Laydown
VL .... Voprosy Literatury [*A publication*]
VL .... Vraie Lumiere [*True Light*] [*French*] [*Freemasonry*]   (ROG)
VL .... Vulgar Latin
VLA .... Vachel Lindsay Association   (EA)
VLA .... Valhalla Energy Corp. [*Vancouver Stock Exchange symbol*]
VLA .... Vandalia, IL [*Location identifier*] [*FAA*]   (FAAL)
VLA .... Vertical Landing Aid [*Military*]   (CAAL)
VLA .... Vertical Launch ASROC [*Antisubmarine Rocket*]
VLA .... Vertical Line Array
VLA .... Very Large Array [*Radioscope*]
VLA .... Very Late Activation Antigen [*Immunology*]
VLA .... Very Low Altitude
VLA .... Veterans' Land Act [*Canada*]
VLA .... Video Logarithmic Amplifier
VLa .... Vie et Langage [*A publication*]
VLA .... Viola [*Music*]
VLA .... Visual Landing Aid
VLA .... Vladivostok [*USSR*] [*Seismograph station code, US Geological Survey*]   (SEIS)
VLA .... Vladivostok [*USSR*] [*Geomagnetic observatory code*]
VLA .... Voice of Liberty Association   (EA)
VLA .... Volume Limiting Amplifier
VLA .... Volunteer Lawyers for the Arts   (EA)
Vlaams Diergeneeskd Tijdschr ... Vlaams Diergeneeskundig Tijdschrift [*A publication*]
Vlaams Diergeneesk Tijdschr ... Vlaams Diergeneeskundig Tijdschrift [*A publication*]
VLAB........ Vipont Pharmaceutical, Inc. [*Formerly, Vipont Laboratories*] [*NASDAQ symbol*]   (SPSG)
VLAC........ Vertical Lift Aircraft Council   (EA)
VLAD .... Vertical Line Array DIFAR   (MCD)
VLADD ..... Visual Low-Angle Drogue Delivery   (AFM)
Vladimir Gos Ped Inst Ucen Zap ... Vladimirskii Gosudarstvennyi Pedagogiceskii Institut Imeni P. I. Lebedeva-Poljanskogo. Ucenyi Zapiski [*A publication*]
Vladimir Vecer Politehn Inst Sb Naucn Trudov ... Vladimirskii Vecernyi Politehniceskii Institut. Sbornik Naucnyh Trudov [*A publication*]
Vladivost Med Inst Sb Nauchn Tr ... Vladivostokskii Meditsinskii Institut. Sbornik Nauchnykh Trudov [*A publication*]
VLAM .... Variable Level Access Method [*Data processing*]
VLAM .... Vlamertinghe [*City in Flanders*] [*Army*] [*World War I*]   (DSUE)
VLAN .... VMS Strategic Land Trust [*NASDAQ symbol*]   (NQ)
V Lang ...... Visible Language [*A publication*]
VLAO .... Vientiane [*Laos*] [*ICAO location identifier*]   (ICLI)

VLAP......... Attopeu [*Laos*] [*ICAO location identifier*]   (ICLI)
VLAP......... Vietnam Laboratory Assistance Program [*Naval Oceanographic Office*]
VLAPA..... Vietnam Laboratory Assistance Program, Army   (RDA)
VLAR......... VFR [*Visual Flight Rules*] Low-Altitude High-Speed Routes [*Aviation*]   (FAAC)
VLAT........ Very Large Array Telescope [*NASA*]
VLATME.. Very-Lighweight Air Traffic Management Equipment   (MCD)
VLB.......... Glider [*Special*] [*Navy symbol*]
VLB.......... Vacuum Lens Blank
VLB.......... Very Long Baseline
VLB.......... Verzeichnis Lieferbarer Buecher [*List of Deliverable Books, i.e., books in print*] [*Germany*]
VLB.......... Vincaleukoblastine [*Also, V, VBL, Ve*] [*Antineoplastic drug*]
VLB.......... Visual LASER Beam
VLBA........ Very Long Baseline Array
VLBI......... Very Long Baseline Interferometer [*or Interferometry*]
VLBI......... Viking Lander Biological Instrument [*NASA*]
VLBR........ Very Low Birth Rate
VLBW....... Very Low Birth Weight [*Medicine*]
VLC .... Longwood College, Farmville, VA [*OCLC symbol*]   (OCLC)
VLC .... Nortankers, Inc. [*AMEX symbol*]   (SPSG)
VLC .... Valencia [*Spain*] [*Airport symbol*]   (OAG)
VLC .... Viking Lander Capsule [*NASA*]
VLC .... Violoncello [*Music*]
VLC .... Vital Load Center   (MSA)
VLCC........ Very Large Cargo [*or Crude*] Carrier [*Oil tanker*]
VLCD .... Very-Low-Calorie Diet
VLCE .... Visible LASER Communication Experiment
VLCF .... Vectored Lift Cannon Fighter [*Air Force*]   (MCD)
VLCF .... Victoria League for Commonwealth Fellowship [*British*]
VLCFA ..... Very-Long-Chain Saturated Fatty Acid [*Organic chemistry*]
VLCHV ..... Very-Low-Cost Harassment Vehicle   (MCD)
VLCM....... ValCom, Inc. [*NASDAQ symbol*]   (NQ)
VLCR........ Variable Length Cavity Resonance
VLCS .. Voltage-Logic-Current-Switching [*Electronics*]
VLCTY ..... Velocity   (FAAC)
VLD .... Vacuum Leak Detector
VLD .... Valdez [*Alaska*] [*Seismograph station code, US Geological Survey*] [*Closed*]   (SEIS)
VLD .... Valdosta [*Georgia*] [*Airport symbol*]   (OAG)
VLD .... Vendor List of Drawings
VLD .... Victorian Licensing Decisions [*A publication*]   (APTA)
VLD .... Village and Local Development
VLD .... Visual Laydown Delivery   (AFM)
VLD .... Vulnerability/Lethality Division [*Ballistic Research Laboratory*]   (RDA)
VLDB........ Very-Large Data Base   (ADA)
VLDBS ..... Very-Large Data Base System
VLDF........ Very-Low Delay Fuze [*Military*]   (CAAL)
VLDL........ Very-Low-Density Lipoprotein [*Biochemistry*]
VLDTA8.... Veldtrust [*Johannesburg*] [*A publication*]
VLDTN ..... Validation   (AAG)
VLE........... Landing-Gear-Extended Speed [*Aviation*]
VLE........... V & L Enterprises [*ACCORD*] [*UTLAS symbol*]
VLE........... Valle, AZ [*Location identifier*] [*FAA*]   (FAAL)
VLE........... Vapor-Liquid Equilibrium
VLE........... Victorian Legal Executive [*A publication*]   (APTA)
VLE........... Violone [*Violins*] [*Music*]
VLE........... Visible Light Emission
VLEASS.... Very Long Endurance Acoustic Submarine Simulator
VLED........ Visible Light-Emitting Diodes
V Lenin Fiz ... Vestnik Leningradskogo Universiteta. Seriya Fiziki i Khimii [*A publication*]
V Lenin Mek ... Vestnik Leningradskogo Universiteta. Seriya Matematiki i Mekhaniki [*A publication*]
VLenU ...... Vestnik Leningradskogo Gosudarstvennogo Universiteta [*A publication*]
VLF........... Installatie [*A publication*]
VLF........... Variable Length Field
VLF........... Vectored Lift Fighter   (MCD)
VLF........... Vertical Launch Facility
VLF........... Very-Low Fluence [*Physics*]
VLF .... Very-Low-Frequency [*Electronics*]
VLFG........ Valley Forge Scientific Corp. [*NASDAQ symbol*]   (NQ)
VLFJ........ Very-Low-Frequency Jammer [*Electronics*]
VLFR........ Very-Low-Frequency Receiver [*Electronics*]
VLFS .... Variable Low-Frequency Standard
VLG .... Maximum Landing Gear Operating Speed [*Aviation code*]   (AIA)
VLG .... Valerie Gold Resources [*Vancouver Stock Exchange symbol*]
VLG .... Vertical Load Gun
VLG .... Villa Gesell [*Argentina*] [*Airport symbol*]   (OAG)
VLG .... Village   (MCD)
VLG .... Visible Light Generator
VLG .... Vlaamse Gids [*A publication*]
VLGE........ Village Super Market, Inc. [*NASDAQ symbol*]   (NQ)
VLH......... Very Large Herbivores
VLH.......... Very Lightly Hinged [*Philately*]
VLH.......... Volatile Liquid Hydrocarbon

VLHS........ Bane Houei Say [*Laos*] [*ICAO location identifier*]   (ICLI)
VLI............ Port Vila [*Vanuata*] [*Airport symbol*]   (OAG)
VLI............ Variable Life Insurance
VLI............ Very-Low Inertia
VLI............ Video Load Impedance
VLIA......... Virus-Like Infectious Agent [*Medicine*]
VLIB......... Valodas un Literaturas Instituta Biletens [*A publication*]
VLID......... Valid Logic Systems, Inc. [*NASDAQ symbol*]   (NQ)
VLIR......... Valodas un Literaturas Instituta Raksti [*A publication*]
VLIS .... Viking Lander Imaging System [*NASA*]
VLIS .... Viking Library System [*Library network*]
VLIS .... VLI Corp. [*NASDAQ symbol*]   (NQ)
VLit........... Voprosy Literatury [*A publication*]
VLIW........ Very Long Instruction Word [*Computer architecture*] [*Multiflow Computer, Inc.*]
Vliyanie Rab Sred Svoistva Mater ... Vliyanie Rabochikh Sred na Svoistva Materialov [*A publication*]
VLJ .... Val Joyeux [*France*] [*Later, CLF*] [*Geomagnetic observatory code*]
VLJaTas.... Voprosy Literaturovedenija i Jazykoznanija (Taskent) [*A publication*]
VLKG .... Khong Island [*Laos*] [*ICAO location identifier*]   (ICLI)
VLKT........ Kene Thao [*Laos*] [*ICAO location identifier*]   (ICLI)
VLL........... Amigo Airways [*Harlingen, TX*] [*FAA designator*]   (FAAC)
VLL........... Valladolid [*Spain*] [*Airport symbol*]   (OAG)
VLLB........ Luang Prabang [*Laos*] [*ICAO location identifier*]   (ICLI)
VLLC........ Very Long Linear Collider [*USSR*] [*Proposed*]
VLLD........ Vehicular LASER Locator Designator
VLLN........ Luong Nam Tha [*Laos*] [*ICAO location identifier*]   (ICLI)
VLLO........ Violoncello [*Music*]
VLM .... Variable Length Multiply
VLM .... Visceral Larval Migrans [*Medicine*]
VLM .... Vortex Lattice Method
VLMR........ Value Merchants, Inc. [*NASDAQ symbol*]   (SPSG)
VLMS....... Villa-Lobos Music Society   (EA)
VLMS....... Vintage Light Music Society [*British*]
VLMTRC.. Volumetric
VLN .... Training Glider [*Navy symbol*]
VLN .... Valencia [*Venezuela*] [*Airport symbol*]   (OAG)
VLN .... Vanua-Lava [*Sola*] [*New Hebrides*] [*Seismograph station code, US Geological Survey*]   (SEIS)
VLN .... Very Low Nitrogen [*Fuel technology*]
VLN .... Villebon Resources Ltd. [*Vancouver Stock Exchange symbol*]
VLN .... Violin [*Music*]
VLNT .... Violent   (FAAC)
VLO .... Maximum Speed to Extend or Retract Landing Gear [*Aviation code*]   (AIA)
VLO .... Valero Energy Corp. [*NYSE symbol*]   (SPSG)
VLO .... Vereniging van Luguaart Onderhoudbedrywe [*Association of Aviation Maintenance Organizations*]   (EAIO)
VLO .... Vertical Lockout
VLON....... Verwaltungslexikon [*Administration Dictionary*] [*NOMOS Datapool*] [*Information service or system*]
VLONAB ... Agricultural Research Reports [*Wageningen*] [*A publication*]
VLOS........ Oudomsay [*Laos*] [*ICAO location identifier*]   (ICLI)
VLP........... Valero Natural Gas Partners LP [*NYSE symbol*]   (SPSG)
VLP........... Valpar Resources [*Vancouver Stock Exchange symbol*]
VLP........... Valparaiso [*Chile*] [*Seismograph station code, US Geological Survey*]   (SEIS)
VLP........... Vaporizing Liquid Plenum
VLP........... Vasopressin-Like Peptide [*Biochemistry*]
VLP........... Vertical Landing Point   (AFM)
VLP........... Vertical Long Period
VLP........... Video Long Player [*Video disk system*] [*Philips/MCA*]
VLP........... Vincristine, L-Asparaginase, Prednisone [*Antineoplastic drug regimen*]
VLP........... Virus-Like Particle
VLPE........ Very Long Period Experiment [*Geophysics*]
VLPK........ Paksane [*Laos*] [*ICAO location identifier*]   (ICLI)
VLPP........ Very Low Pressure Pyrolysis
VLPS........ Pakse [*Laos*] [*ICAO location identifier*]   (ICLI)
VLPS .... Vandenberg Launch Processing System [*Aerospace*]   (MCD)
VLPV........ Phong Savanh [*Laos*] [*ICAO location identifier*]   (ICLI)
VLR........... Randolph-Macon Woman's College, Lynchburg, VA [*OCLC symbol*]   (OCLC)
VLR........... Transport Glider [*Navy symbol*]
VLR........... Valar Resources Ltd. [*Vancouver Stock Exchange symbol*]
VLR........... Vanderbilt Law Review [*A publication*]
VLR........... Variable Loan Rate [*Business term*]
VLR........... Vertical-Looking RADAR
VLR........... Very Long Range
VLR........... Very Low Range
VLR........... Victorian Law Reports [*A publication*]   (APTA)
VLR........... Violation of Law of Road [*Traffic offense charge*]
VLR........... Virginia Law Review [*A publication*]
VLR .... Voluntary Loss Rate [*of Air Force officers resigning before retirement*]
VLR (Adm) ... Victorian Law Reports (Admiralty) [*A publication*]   (APTA)
VLR (E) ..... Victorian Law Reports (Equity) [*A publication*]   (APTA)
VLR (Eq) ... Victorian Law Reports (Equity) [*A publication*]

VLR (IP & M) ... Victorian Law Reports (Insolvency, Probate, and Matrimonial) [*A publication*] (APTA)
VLR (L) ..... Victorian Law Reports (Law) [*A publication*] (APTA)
VLR (M) .... Victorian Law Reports (Mining) [*A publication*] (APTA)
VLR (P & M) ... Victorian Law Reports (Probate and Matrimonial) [*A publication*] (APTA)
VLRSN ...... Violation of Lawful Regulation Issued by the Secretary of the Navy
VLS .... Vacuum Loading System
VLS .... Valesdir [*Vanuata*] [*Airport symbol*] (OAG)
VLS .... Valsamata [*Kephallenia*] [*Greece*] [*Seismograph station code, US Geological Survey*] (SEIS)
VLS .... Valstieciu Liaudininku Sajunga [*Peasant Populist Union*] [*Lithuania*] [*Political party*] (PPE)
VLS .... Vandenberg Launch Site [*Aerospace*] (MCD)
VLS .... Vapor-Liquid-Solid
VLS .... Vertical Launch System [*Military*]
VLS .... Vertical Liquid Spring
VLS .... Very Long Shot [*A photograph or motion picture sequence taken from a considerable distance*]
VLS .... Very Low Speed
VLS .... Viking Lander System [*NASA*] (KSC)
VLS .... Village Voice. Literary Supplement [*A publication*]
VLS .... Virtual Linkage System [*or Subsystem*]
VLS .... Visible Light Sensors (MCD)
VLS .... Visual Lunacy Society (EA)
VLS .... Volume Loadability Speed (IEEE)
VLS .... Vry Langs Skip [*Free Alongside Ship*] [*Afrikaans*]
VLSB .... Sayaboury [*Laos*] [*ICAO location identifier*] (ICLI)
VLSI .... Very-Large-Scale Integration [*of circuits*] [*Electronics*]
VLSI .... VLSI Technology, Inc. [*NASDAQ symbol*] (NQ)
VLSIC .... Very-Large-Scale Integrated Circuit [*Electronics*]
VLSIIC ...... VLSI Implementation Centre [*Research center*] [*Queen's University, Kingston*] [*Canada*]
VLSK .... Savannakhet [*Laos*] [*ICAO location identifier*] (ICLI)
VLSM .... Vertical Launched Standard Missile (MCD)
VLSN .... Sam Neua [*Laos*] [*ICAO location identifier*] (ICLI)
VLSV .... Saravane [*Laos*] [*ICAO location identifier*] (ICLI)
VLSW .... Virtual Line Switch
VLT .... Van Kampen Merritt Ltd. [*NYSE symbol*] (SPSG)
VLT .... Vault Explorations, Inc. [*Vancouver Stock Exchange symbol*]
VLT .... Vehicle Licensing and Traffic [*British*]
VLT .... Very Large Telescope [*Proposed*] [*European Southern Observatory*]
VLT .... Very Low Titanium [*Geology*]
VLT .... Victorian Law Times [*A publication*] (APTA)
VLT .... Video Layout Terminal [*Data processing*]
VLT .... Volute
VLTG .... Voltage (AAG)
VLTK .... Thakhek [*Laos*] [*ICAO location identifier*] (ICLI)
VLTSV ..... Virusoid Lucerne Transient Streak Virus
VLTT .... Vehicular Leger Toot Terrain [*Light All-Terrain Vehicle*] [*French*] (MCD)
VLU .... Vacuum Lifting Unit
VLU .... Vestnik Leningradskogo Gosudarstvennogo Universiteta [*A publication*]
VLU .... Vestnik Leningradskogo Universiteta. Seriya Istorii, Jazyka, i Literatura [*A publication*]
VLU .... Video Logic Unit (MCD)
VLU .... Worldwide Value Fund [*NYSE symbol*] (SPSG)
VLUist .... Vestnik Leningradskogo Gosudarstvennogo Universiteta [*A publication*]
VLV .... Valdivia [*Chile*] [*Seismograph station code, US Geological Survey*] (SEIS)
VLV .... Valera [*Venezuela*] [*Airport symbol*] (OAG)
VLV .... Valve (AAG)
VLV .... Velvet Exploration Co. Ltd. [*Vancouver Stock Exchange symbol*]
VLV .... Very-Low Volume
VLV .... Visna Lentivirus
VLvivU .... Visnyk L'vivs'koho Derzavnoho Universytetu [*A publication*]
VLVL .... Video Library, Inc. [*San Diego, CA*] [*NASDAQ symbol*] (NQ)
VLVM ...... Vlastivedny Vestnik Moravsky [*A publication*]
v-LVN .... Ventral Lateral Ventricular Nerve [*Anatomy*]
VLVS .... Voltage-Logic-Voltage-Switching [*Electronics*]
VLVT .... Vientiane/Wattay [*Laos*] [*ICAO location identifier*] (ICLI)
VLW .... Village Level Workers [*India*]
VLW .... Washington and Lee University, Lexington, VA [*OCLC symbol*] (OCLC)
VLXG .... Xieng Khouang [*Laos*] [*ICAO location identifier*] (ICLI)
VLXK .... Xieng Khouang (Plaine Des Jarres) [*Laos*] [*ICAO location identifier*] (ICLI)
VLY .... Valley (MCD)
VLY .... Valley Oil & Gas [*Vancouver Stock Exchange symbol*]
VLZ .... Valdez [*Alaska*] [*Seismograph station code, US Geological Survey*] (SEIS)
VM .... Abacus Air [*West Germany*] [*ICAO designator*] (FAAC)
VM .... V-Mail Specialists [*Navy*]
VM .... Validation Material [*Social Security Administration*]
VM .... Valles Marineris [*A filamentary mark on Mars*]
VM .... Vasomotor [*Physiology*]

VM .... Vastus Medialis [*A muscle*]
VM .... Vector Message
VM .... Velocity Meter
VM .... Velocity Modulation
VM .... Ventilation Management
VM .... Verslagen en Mededeelingen [*A publication*]
VM .... Vertical Magnet
VM .... Vertical Meridian [*Optics, Eye anatomy*]
VM .... Vestibular Membrane [*Medicine*]
VM .... Victory Medal [*British*]
VM .... Vietminh (CINC)
vm .... Vietnam [*MARC country of publication code*] [*Library of Congress*] (LCCP)
VM .... Vir Magnificus [*A Great Man*] [*Latin*]
VM .... Viral Myocarditis [*Medicine*]
V & M .... Virgin and Martyr [*Church calendars*]
VM .... Virgin and Martyr [*Church calendars*]
VM .... Virtual Machine [*Data processing*]
VM .... Virtual Memory [*Data processing*] (MCD)
VM .... VM Software, Inc. [*NYSE symbol*] [*Later, SMX*] (CTT)
VM .... Voennoe Ministerstvo [*Ministry of War*] [*1950-53; merged into the Ministry of Defense*] [*Russian*]
VM .... Voice Modulation
VM .... Volatile Matter
VM .... Volksmarine
VM .... Voltmeter
V/m .... Volts per Meter [*Also, VPM*]
V/M .... Volts per Mil (DEN)
VM .... Vorigen Monats [*Of Last Month*] [*German*]
VM .... Votre Majeste [*Your Majesty*] [*French*]
VM .... Voyager Mars [*NASA*]
VMA .... Marine Attack Squadron [*Navy symbol*] (NVT)
VMA .... Valid Memory Address [*Data processing*]
VMA .... Valve Manufacturers Association of America (EA)
VMA .... Vanillylmandelic Acid [*Also, HMMA*] [*Biochemistry*]
VMA .... Vehicle Maintenance Area
VMA .... Vero Monmouth Airlines [*Vero Beach, FL*] [*FAA designator*] (FAAC)
VMA .... Virtual Machine Assist [*IBM Corp.*]
VMA .... Virtual Memory Allocation
VMA .... Visual Maneuverability Aids (MCD)
VMAAI ..... Violin Makers Association of Arizona International (EA)
VMA(AW) ... Marine Attack Squadron (All-Weather) [*Navy symbol*] (NVT)
VMAD .... Vincristine, Methotrexate, Adriamycin, Actinomycin D [*Antineoplastic drug regimen*]
VMAP .... Video Map Equipment
VMAPS ..... Virtual Memory Array Processing System
VMarJa ..... Voprosy Marijskogo Jazykoznanija [*A publication*]
VMAVA ..... Verdun-Meuse-Argonne Veterans Association (EA)
VMAW ...... Verslagen en Mededeelingen. Koninklijke Akademie van Wetenschappen [*A publication*]
VMAX .... Maximum Velocity
VMB .... Marine Medium and Heavy Patrol Bomber Squadron [*Land-based and seaplane*] [*Navy symbol*]
VMB .... Mary Baldwin College, Staunton, VA [*OCLC symbol*] (OCLC)
VMB .... Vandringar Med Boeker [*A publication*]
VMB .... Vermont Motor Rate Bureau Inc., Barre VT [*STAC*]
VMBC .... Vintage Motor Bike Club (EA)
VMBF .... Marine Fighter Bomber Squadron [*Navy symbol*]
VMBLOK ... Virtual Machine Control Block [*Data processing*] (IBMDP)
VMBR .... Visual Motor Behavior Rehearsal [*Psychology*]
VMC .... James Madison University, Harrisonburg, VA [*OCLC symbol*] (OCLC)
VMC .... Variable Message Cycle
VMC .... Variable Mica Capacitor
VMC .... Vasomotor Center [*Physiology*]
VMC .... Velocity Minimum Control (AAG)
VMC .... Veritable Master of Crewelwork
VMC .... Vertical Motion Compensation (CAAL)
VMC .... Victorian Marathon Club [*Australia*]
VMC .... Viet Montagnard Cong
VMC .... Villa Madonna College [*Kentucky*]
VMC .... Villa Maria College [*Erie, PA*]
VMC .... Ville Marie [*Quebec*] [*Seismograph station code, US Geological Survey*] [*Closed*] (SEIS)
VMC .... Virginia Medical College
VMC .... Visual Meteorological Conditions [*Aviation*]
VMC .... Void Metallic Composite
VMC .... Vulcan Materials Company [*NYSE symbol*] (SPSG)
Vmca .... Minimum Control Speed in Air [*Aviation code*] (AIA)
VMCB .... Virtual Machine Control Block
VMCCA ..... Veteran Motor Car Club of America (EA)
VMCF .... Virtual Machine Communication Facility
Vmcg .... Minimum Control Speed on the Ground [*Aviation code*] (AIA)
VMCJ .... Marine Composite Reconnaissance [*Photo*] Squadron [*Navy symbol*]
Vmcl .... Minimum Control Speed for the Landing Approach [*Aviation code*] (AIA)
VMCM .... Vector-Measuring Current Meter [*Instrumentation*]
VM/CMS .. Virtual Machine/Conversational Monitor System [*Data processing*]

VMCP....... Vincristine, Melphalan, Cyclophosphamide, Prednisone [*Antineoplastic drug regimen*]
VMCR....... Volunteer Marine Corps Reserve
VMD.......... Doctor of Veterinary Medicine
VMD.......... Marine Photographic Squadron [*Navy symbol*]
VMD.......... Vertical Magnetic Dipole (IEEE)
VMD.......... Volume Median Diameter [*Particle size*]
VMDF....... Vertical Side of Main Distribution Frame [*Telecommunications*] (TEL)
VMDI....... Vector Miss Distance Indicator
VMDKA..... Voprosy Meditsinskoi Khimii [*A publication*]
VMDP....... Veterinary Medical Data Program [*Association of Veterinary Medical Data Program Participants*] [*Information service or system*] (IID)
VME.......... British Columbia Ministry of Education [*UTLAS symbol*]
VME.......... Villa Mercedes [*Argentina*] [*Airport symbol*] (OAG)
VME.......... Vinyl Methyl Ether [*Organic chemistry*]
VME.......... Virtual Machine Environment [*International Computers Ltd.*]
VME.......... Volvo, Michigan, Euclid [*In company name VME Americas, Inc.*]
VMEC....... Vehicle Mounted Explosive Container (MCD)
VMF.......... Marine Fighter Squadron [*Navy symbol*]
VMF.......... Vacuum Melting Furnace
VMF.......... Verenigde Machinefabrieken NV [*Association of Machine Factories*] [*Business term*] [*Netherlands*]
VMF.......... Vertical Maintenance Facility (NASA)
VMFA...... Marine Fighter Attack Squadron [*Navy symbol*] (NVT)
VMFAT..... Marine Fighter Attack Training Squadron [*Navy symbol*]
VMF(AW) ... Marine Fighter Squadron (All-Weather) [*Navy symbol*] (NVT)
VMFI......... Voltage Monitor and Fault Indicating
VMF(N)..... Marine Night Fighter Squadron [*Navy symbol*]
VMG.......... Vickers Machine Gun [*British military*] (DMA)
VMG.......... Video Mapping Group
VMG.......... Video Mixer Group
VMG.......... VMS Mortgage Investment Fund [*NYSE symbol*] (SPSG)
VMG.......... Voluntary Movement Group (EAIO)
VMGR....... Marine Aerial Refueler/Transport Squadron [*Navy symbol*] (NVT)
VMGSE..... Vehicle Measuring Ground Support Equipment (KSC)
VMH.......... Misericordia Hospital, Medical Library, Bronx, NY [*OCLC symbol*] (OCLC)
VMH.......... Ventral Medial Hypothalamus [*Anatomy*]
VMH.......... Victoria Medal of Honour
VMHB....... Virginia Magazine of History and Biography [*A publication*]
VMHI........ Victorian Military History Institute [*Defunct*] (EA)
VMI.......... Developmental Test of Visual-Motor Integration [*Beery & Buktenica*]
VMI.......... Meubel. Weekblad voor de Meubelindustrie, Meubelhandel, Woninginrichting, en Toeleveringsbedrijven [*A publication*]
VMI.......... Variable Moment of Inertia [*Nuclear physics*]
VMI.......... Vertical Markets Information Database [*Amidon/Litman Associates*] [*Information service or system*] (CRD)
VMI.......... Vertical Motion Index (PCM)
VMI.......... Vibration Measurement Integrator
VMI.......... Videodisc-Mouse Interface
VMI.......... Virginia Military Institute [*Lexington, VA*]
VMI.......... Virginia Military Institute, Lexington, VA [*OCLC symbol*] (OCLC)
VMI.......... Visual Maneuvering Indicator (MCD)
VMI.......... Voicemail International, Incorporated [*Cupertina, CA*] [*Telecommunications*] (TSSD)
VMIA........ Vinyl Metal Industry Association [*Defunct*] (EA)
VMIC........ Vermont Maple Industry Council (EA)
VMID........ Virtual Machine Identifier
VMIG........ View-Master Ideal Group, Inc. [*NASDAQ symbol*] (NQ)
VMII 1986 ... Vertical Markets Information Index 1986 [*Amidon/Litman Associates*] [*A publication*]
V/mil.......... Volts per Mil
VMIRL...... VMI [*Virginia Military Institute*] Research Laboratories [*Research center*] (RCD)
VMJ.......... Marine Utility Squadron [*Navy symbol*]
VMJ.......... Vertical Multijunction [*Solar cell*]
VMJ/BIV ... Boletin Indigenista Venezolano. Organo de la Comision Indigenista. Ministerio de Justicia [*A publication*]
VMK.......... Vita-Metall-Keramik [*German dental material for crowns and bridgework*]
VMKA....... Verslagen en Mededeelingen. Koninklijke Akademie voor Nederlandse Taal- en Letterkunde [*A publication*]
VMKey..... Voice Master Key
VMKT....... Victory Markets [*NASDAQ symbol*] (NQ)
VMKVA .... Verslagen en Mededeelingen. Koninklijke Vlaamse Akademie voor Taal- en Letterkunde [*A publication*]
VML.......... Marine Glider Squadron [*Navy symbol*]
VML.......... Mohawk Valley Library Association, Schenectady County Public Library, Schenectady, NY [*OCLC symbol*] (OCLC)
VML.......... Valley Migrant League (EA)
VML.......... Virtual Memory Linking [*Data processing*]
VMLH....... Ventromedial and Lateral Hypothalami [*Neuroanatomy*]
VMLI......... Veterans Mortgage Life Insurance

VMLP......... VMS Mortgage Investors LP [*Chicago, IL*] [*NASDAQ symbol*] (NQ)
VMLS/MLA ... Veterinary Medical Libraries Section/Medical Library Association (EA)
VMM........ Vacuum Melting Module
V & MM .... Vandalism and Malicious Mischief [*Insurance*]
VMM........ Vehicle Model Movement
VMM........ Vertical Milling Machine
VMM........ Video Map Module
VMM........ Virtual Machine Monitor [*Data processing*] (IEEE)
VMM........ Virtual Memory Manager [*Data processing*] (BYTE)
VMM........ Volunteer Missionary Movement [*London Colney, Hertfordshire, England*] (EAIO)
VMMC..... Macau [*Macau*] [*ICAO location identifier*] (ICLI)
VMMC..... Veterans Memorial Medical Center
VMMMA ... Vestnik Moskovskogo Universiteta. Seriya 1. Matematika, Mekhanika [*A publication*]
VMMOA... Virginia Medical Monthly [*Later, Virginia Medical*] [*A publication*]
VMMPS.... Vehicle Management and Mission Planning System [*NASA*]
VMN........ Ventromedial Nucleus [*Brain anatomy*]
VMO........ Marine Observation Squadron [*Navy symbol*]
VMO........ Maximum Operating Speed (MCD)
VMO........ Vastus Medialis Obliquus [*Muscle*]
VMO........ Velocity-Modulated Oscillator
VMO........ Very Massive Object [*Astronomy*]
VMO........ Visiting Medical Officer (ADA)
VMO(AS) ... Marine Observation Squadron (Artillery Spotting) [*Navy symbol*]
VMOGA.... Vestnik Moskovskogo Universiteta. Seriya 5. Geografiya [*A publication*]
VMOR...... VMS Mortgage Investors LP III [*NASDAQ symbol*] (NQ)
VMOS...... V-Groove Metal-Oxide Semiconductor (MCD)
VMOS...... Virtual Memory Operating System [*Sperry UNIVAC*] [*Data processing*] (IEEE)
V Mosk Fiz ... Vestnik Moskovskogo Universiteta. Seriya Fiziki i Astronomii [*A publication*]
V Mosk Mekh ... Vestnik Moskovskogo Universiteta. Seriya Matematiki i Mekhaniki [*A publication*]
V Mosk U Kh ... Vestnik Moskovskogo Universiteta. Seriya Khimiya [*A publication*]
VMOW...... Vice Minister of War (MCD)
VMP.......... Value as Marine Policy [*Insurance*] (DS)
VMP.......... Variable Major Protein [*Genetics*]
VM & P...... Varnish Makers' and Painters' Naphtha
vMP.......... Ventral Midline Precursor [*Neuroanatomy*]
VMP.......... Vertically Moored Platform [*Offshore drilling*]
VMP.......... Visiting Medical Practitioner
VMPA....... Vancouver Museums and Planetarium Association [*Canada*]
VMPP........ Vincristine, Melphalan, Prednisone, Procarbazine [*Antineoplastic drug regimen*]
VM-26PP .. VM-26 [*Teniposide*], Procarbazine, Prednisone [*Antineoplastic drug regimen*]
VMR.......... Marine Transport Squadron [*Navy symbol*]
VMR.......... Variance to Mean Rate
VMR.......... Vasomotor Rhinitis [*Medicine*]
VMR.......... Victoria Mounted Rifles [*British military*] (DMA)
VMR.......... Violation Monitor and Remover [*Bell System*]
VMR.......... Volumetric Mixing Ratio
VMRB....... Vereinigte Metallwerke Ranshofen-Berndorf [*AG*]
VMRC....... Virginia Mason Research Center [*Virginia Mason Hospital and Mason Clinic*] [*Research center*] (RCD)
VMRI........ Veterinary Medical Research Institute [*Iowa State University*] [*Research center*] (RCD)
VMRMDS ... Vehicle-Mounted Road Mine Detector System
VMRO....... Vnatreshna Makedonska Revolucionerna Organizacija [*Internal Macedonian Revolutionary Organization (Known popularly among English-speaking nations as the IMRO)*] [*Yugoslavia*] [*Political party*] (PPE)
VMRO....... Vutreshna Makidoniski Revoliutsionna Organizatsiia [*Internal Macedonian Revolutionary Organization*] [*Bulgaria*] [*Political party*] (PPE)
VMRO(U) ... Vnatresna Makedonska Revolucionerna Organizacija (Udruzena) [*Internal Macedonian Revolutionary Organization (United)*] [*Yugoslavia*] [*Political party*] (PPE)
VMRR....... Vendor Material Review Report [*NASA*] (KSC)
VMRS....... Vehicle Maintenance Reporting Standard [*American Trucking Association*]
VMRS....... Vessel Movement Reporting System
VMS.......... Valve Mounting System
VMS.......... Variable Mass System
VMS.......... Vehicle Management System
VMS.......... Vehicle Monitoring System (RDA)
VMS.......... Velocity Measurement System
VMS.......... Vertical Motion Simulator [*NASA*]
VMS.......... Vibration Measuring System
VMS.......... Victorian Military Society (EAIO)
VMS.......... Video Modulation System
VMS.......... Video Movie System [*For video recording tapes*]
VMS.......... Videofile Microwave System

VMS	Viewfinder-Metering System (KSC)
VMS	Virtual Memory Operating System [*Data processing*]
VMS	Visual Memory Scale [*Educational test*]
VMS	Visual Motion Simulator (MCD)
VMS	Voice Messaging System [*Telecommunications*]
VMSA	Victorian Motor Schools Association [*Australia*]
VMSB	Marine Scout Bombing Squadron [*Navy symbol*]
VMSDA	Vysokomolekulyarnye Soedineniya [*A publication*]
VMSEA	Vehicle Monitoring System Electronics Assembly (RDA)
Vmsl	Minimum Speed in a Stall [*Aviation code*] (AIA)
Vmso	Minimum Speed in a Stall, Flaps Down [*Aviation code*] (AIA)
VMSODA	Vie et Milieu. Serie AB. Biologie Marine et Oceanographie [*A publication*]
VMSP	Volunteer Management Support Program [*ACTION*]
VMT	Validate Master Tape
VMT	Van Kampen Merritt Municipal Income Trust [*NYSE symbol*] (CTT)
VMT	Variable Microcycle Timing
VMT	Variable Mu Tube [*Electronics*]
VMT	Vehicle-Miles Traveled
VMT	Velocity-Modulated Transistor [*Solid-state physics*]
VMT	Velocity-Modulated Tube
VMT	Very Many Thanks
VMT	Video Matrix Terminal
VMT	Virtual Memory Technique [*Data processing*] (MDG)
VMT	Voltage-Modulated Transmission [*Electronics*]
VMT	Von Mises Theory
VMTA	Victorian Music Teachers Association [*Australia*]
VMTB	Marine Torpedo Bomber Squadron [*Navy symbol*]
VMTC	Vehicle and Machinery Stores Trade Corp. [*Burma*] (DS)
VMTG	VMS Mortgage Investors LP II [*Chicago, IL*] [*NASDAQ symbol*] (NQ)
VMTSS	Virtual Machine Time-Sharing System [*Data processing*] (IEEE)
VMU	Baimuru [*Papua New Guinea*] [*Airport symbol*] (OAG)
Vmu	Minimum Unstick Speed [*Aviation code*] (AIA)
VMU	Vestnik Moskovskogo Gosudarstvennogo Universiteta [*A publication*]
VMUBA	Vestnik Moskovskogo Universiteta. Seriya 6. Biologiya, Pochvovedenie [*A publication*]
VMUFA	Vestnik Moskovskogo Universiteta. Seriya 3. Fizika, Astronomiya [*A publication*]
VMUGA	Vestnik Moskovskogo Universiteta. Seriya 4. Geologiya [*A publication*]
VMUist	Vestnik Moskovskogo Gosudarstvennogo Universiteta [*A publication*]
VMUKA	Vestnik Moskovskogo Universiteta. Seriya 2. Khimiya [*A publication*]
VMUZh	Vestnik Moskovskogo Universiteta Zhurnalistika [*A publication*]
VMV	Viola Mottle Virus
VMVBORG	Verslagen en Mededeelingen van de Vereeniging tot Beoefening van Overijsselsch Recht en Geschiedenis [*A publication*]
VMVOVR	Verslagen en Mededeelingen van de Vereeniging tot Uitgaaf van der Bronnen van het Oud-Vaderlandsche Recht [*A publication*]
VMW	Mary Washington College, Fredericksburg, VA [*OCLC symbol*] (OCLC)
VMW	Vierteljahrschrift fuer Musikwissenschaft [*A publication*]
V Mw	Vierteljahrsschrift fuer Musikwissenschaft [*A publication*]
VMWWI	Victory Medal World War I [*British*]
VMWWII	Victory Medal World War II [*British*]
VMXI	VMX, Incorporated [*NASDAQ symbol*] (NQ)
VMY	York College of the City University of New York, Jamaica, NY [*OCLC symbol*] (OCLC)
VN	Hang Khong Vietnam [*Vietnam*] [*ICAO designator*] (FAAC)
VN	Training Plane [*Navy symbol*]
VN	Vakstudie-Nieuws [*A publication*]
VN	Van Ness' Prize Cases [*United States*] [*A publication*] (DLA)
VN	Vangold Resources, Inc. [*Vancouver Stock Exchange symbol*]
VN	(Vanillyl)nonanamide [*Biochemistry*]
VN	Vegetative Nucleus [*Botany*]
VN	Ventral Nerve [*Neuroanatomy*]
VN	Ventral Nozzle
VN	Verb Neuter
VN	Verbal Noun
VN	Verify Number If No Answer [*Telecommunications*] (TEL)
VN	Victorian Navy [*Australia*]
VN	Victorian Newsletter [*A publication*]
VN	Vietnam [*ANSI two-letter standard code*] (CNC)
vn	Vietnam, North [*vm (Vietnam) used in records cataloged after January 1978*] [*MARC country of publication code*] [*Library of Congress*] (LCCP)
VN	VietNow (EA)
VN	Violin [*Music*]
VN	Virus Neutralization
VN	Visiting Nurse
VN	Vladimir Nabokov [*In book title, "VN: The Life and Art of Vladimir Nabokov"*]
VN	Vocational Nurse
VN	Vomeronasal [*Anatomy*]
VN	Von Neumann [*Procedure*] [*Statistics*]
VN	Vulnerability Number
VNA	Air Viet-Nam
VNA	Jetstream International Airlines [*Latrobe, PA*] [*FAA designator*] (FAAC)
VNA	Mercy Hospital, Library, Watertown, NY [*OCLC symbol*] (OCLC)
VNA	Vienna, GA [*Location identifier*] [*FAA*] (FAAL)
VNA	Vietnam News Agency
VNA	Vietnamese National Army
VNA	Visiting Nurse Association
VNAA	Visiting Nurse Associations of America (EA)
VNAF	Vietnam Air Force
VNAF	Vietnam Armed Forces
VNAF I & M	Vietnam Air Force Improvement and Modernization Program
VNAGA2	Archives Geologiques du Vietnam [*A publication*]
VNAS	Vehicle Navigation Aid System
VNAV	Vertical Navigation Mode (IEEE)
VNAWAG	Koninklijke Nederlandse Akademie van Wetenschappen. Verhandelingen. Afdeling Natuurkunde. Tweede Reeks [*A publication*]
V N B	Vetus Natura Brevium [*A publication*] (DSA)
VNB	Wadhams Hall Seminary College, Library, Ogdensburg, NY [*OCLC symbol*] (OCLC)
VNBG	Bajhang [*Nepal*] [*ICAO location identifier*] (ICLI)
VNBJ	Bhojpur [*Nepal*] [*ICAO location identifier*] (ICLI)
VNBL	Baglung [*Nepal*] [*ICAO location identifier*] (ICLI)
VNBP	Bharatpur [*Nepal*] [*ICAO location identifier*] (ICLI)
VNBP	Valley National Bancorp [*Formerly, Valley National Bancorp of Passaic*] [*NASDAQ symbol*] (NQ)
VNBR	Bajura [*Nepal*] [*ICAO location identifier*] (ICLI)
VNBT	Baitadi [*Nepal*] [*ICAO location identifier*] (ICLI)
VNBW	Bhairawa [*Nepal*] [*ICAO location identifier*] (ICLI)
VNC	North Country Reference and Research Resources Council, Union List of Serials, Canton, NY [*OCLC symbol*] (OCLC)
VNC	Variable Neutralizing Capacitor
VNC	Venice, FL [*Location identifier*] [*FAA*] (FAAL)
VNC	Ventral Nerve Cord [*Neuroanatomy*]
VNC	VNC Video Network [*Vancouver Stock Exchange symbol*]
VNC	Voice Numerical Control
VNC	Votes National Committee (EA)
VNCCI	Volunteer - The National Center [*Later, NVC*] (EA)
VNCF	Vietnam-Canada Foundation
VNCG	Chandragarhi [*Nepal*] [*ICAO location identifier*] (ICLI)
VNCP	Valley National Corporation [*NASDAQ symbol*] (NQ)
VNCS	Vietnam Christian Service [*Defunct*] (EA)
VND	Jefferson Community College, Library, Watertown, NY [*OCLC symbol*] (OCLC)
VND	Vanda [*Antarctica*] [*Seismograph station code, US Geological Survey*] (SEIS)
VND	Vprasanja Nasih Dni [*A publication*]
VNDG	Dang [*Nepal*] [*ICAO location identifier*] (ICLI)
VNDH	Dhangarhi [*Nepal*] [*ICAO location identifier*] (ICLI)
VNDP	Dolpa [*Nepal*] [*ICAO location identifier*] (ICLI)
VNDR	Dhorpatan [*Nepal*] [*ICAO location identifier*] (ICLI)
VNDT	Doti [*Nepal*] [*ICAO location identifier*] (ICLI)
VNE	Ogdensburg Public Library, Ogdensburg, NY [*OCLC symbol*] (OCLC)
VNE	Velocity Never to Exceed
VNE	Verbal Nonemotional (Stimuli) [*Psychology*]
VNESE	Vietnamese
Vnesn Torg	Vnesnjaja Torgovlja [*A publication*]
VNETF	Vietnam Expediting Task Force [*Military*]
VNF	Paul Smiths College, Library, Paul Smiths, NY [*OCLC symbol*] (OCLC)
VNF	Vietnam Foundation (EA)
VNFH	Vjesnik Narodnog Fronta Hrvatske [*A publication*]
VNG	Ventral Surface, Nephridial Gland [*Anatomy*]
VNG	W. Alton Jones Cell Science Center Library, Lake Placid, NY [*OCLC symbol*] (OCLC)
VNGGA	Verhandelingen. Koninklijke Nederlands Geologisch Mijnbouwkundig Genootschap. Geologische Serie [*A publication*]
VNGK	Gorkha [*Nepal*] [*ICAO location identifier*] (ICLI)
VNHP	Vermont Natural Heritage Program [*Information service or system*] (IID)
VNI	Violini [*Violins*] [*Music*]
VNIC	Voltage Negative Immittance Converter
VNIIMP	Vsesoiuznyi Nauchno-Issledovatel'skii Institut Miasnoi Promyshlennosti [*All-Union Scientific Research Institute of the Meat Industry*]
Vnitr Lek	Vnitrni Lekarstvi [*A publication*]
VNJI	Jiri [*Nepal*] [*ICAO location identifier*] (ICLI)
VNJL	Jumla [*Nepal*] [*ICAO location identifier*] (ICLI)
VNJP	Janakpur [*Nepal*] [*ICAO location identifier*] (ICLI)
VNJS	Jomsom [*Nepal*] [*ICAO location identifier*] (ICLI)
VNKT	Kathmandu/International [*Nepal*] [*ICAO location identifier*] (ICLI)

VNL........... Bogalusa, LA [*Location identifier*] [*FAA*]   (FAAL)
VNL........... Variable Neodymium LASER
VNL........... Via Net Loss [*Telecommunications*]
VNL........... Victorian Newsletter [*A publication*]
VNL........... Vrij Nederland [*A publication*]
VNLD........ Lamidada [*Nepal*] [*ICAO location identifier*]   (ICLI)
VNLF........ Via Net Loss Factor   (TEL)
VNLK........ Lukla [*Nepal*] [*ICAO location identifier*]   (ICLI)
VNLT........ Langtang [*Nepal*] [*ICAO location identifier*]   (ICLI)
VNM......... Tijdschrift van de Vereeniging voor Nederlandse
                 Muziekgeschiedenis [*A publication*]
VNM......... Vietnam [*ANSI three-letter standard code*]   (CNC)
VNMA...... Manang [*Nepal*] [*ICAO location identifier*]   (ICLI)
VNMC....... Vietnam Marine Corps
VNMG....... Meghauli [*Nepal*] [*ICAO location identifier*]   (ICLI)
VNMN...... Mahendranagar [*Nepal*] [*ICAO location identifier*]   (ICLI)
VNN .... Eastern Virginia Medical Authority, Norfolk, VA [*OCLC
                 symbol*]   (OCLC)
VNN .... Mount Vernon, IL [*Location identifier*] [*FAA*]   (FAAL)
VNN .... Vacant National Number [*Telecommunications*]   (TEL)
VNN .... Vietnam Navy
VNNG....... Nepalgung [*Nepal*] [*ICAO location identifier*]   (ICLI)
VNO .... Cruising Speed [*Aviation code*]   (AIA)
VNO .... Value Not Obtained
VNO .... Vilnius [*USSR*] [*Airport symbol*]   (OAG)
VNO .... Vital National Objective   (AAG)
VNO .... Vomeronasal Organ [*Anatomy*]
VNO .... Vornado, Inc. [*NYSE symbol*]   (SPSG)
VNP .... Venda National Party [*Political party*]   (PPW)
VNPK....... Pokhara [*Nepal*] [*ICAO location identifier*]   (ICLI)
VNPL........ Phaplu [*Nepal*] [*ICAO location identifier*]   (ICLI)
VNR .... Van Nostrand Reinhold Co., Inc. [*Publisher*]
VNR .... Variable Navigation Ratio
VNR .... Veneer [*Technical drawings*]
VNR .... VFR [*Visual Flight Rules*] Not Recommended [*Pilot brief*]
                 [*Aviation*]   (FAAC)
VNR .... Video News Release [*A news release in the form of video tape*]
VNR .... Vietnam Reactor
VNRB....... Rajbiraj [*Nepal*] [*ICAO location identifier*]   (ICLI)
VNRK........ Rukumkot (Chaurjhari) [*Nepal*] [*ICAO location
                 identifier*]   (ICLI)
VNRN....... Vladimir Nabokov Research Newletter [*A publication*]
VNRP........ Rolpa [*Nepal*] [*ICAO location identifier*]   (ICLI)
VNRS........ Vietnamese National Railway System   (CINC)
VNRT........ Rumjatar [*Nepal*] [*ICAO location identifier*]   (ICLI)
VNS .... Bondsspaarbanken [*A publication*]
VNS .... Norfolk State College, Norfolk, VA [*OCLC symbol*]   (OCLC)
VNS .... Vagus Nerve Stimulation [*Physiology*]
VNS .... Varanasi [*India*] [*Airport symbol*]   (OAG)
VNS .... Vasomotor Nervous System [*Physiology*]
VNS .... Ventral Nervous System [*Neuroanatomy*]
VNS .... Very North Shore [*Women's Wear Daily*]
VNS .... Visiting Nurse Service
VNS .... Vladimir Nabokov Society   (EA)
VNSB....... Syanboche [*Nepal*] [*ICAO location identifier*]   (ICLI)
VnSc......... Florence Williams Public Library, Christiansted, St. Croix, VI
                 [*Library symbol*] [*Library of Congress*]   (LCLS)
VNSF........ Vietnamese Special Forces   (CINC)
VNSI........ Simara [*Nepal*] [*ICAO location identifier*]   (ICLI)
VNSK .... Surkhet [*Nepal*] [*ICAO location identifier*]   (ICLI)
VNSL....... Variable Nozzle Slow Landing   (MCD)
VNSM....... Kathmandu [*Nepal*] [*ICAO location identifier*]   (ICLI)
VNSP........ Vacant Nozzle Shield Plug [*Nuclear energy*]   (NRCH)
VNSR .... Safebagar [*Nepal*] [*ICAO location identifier*]   (ICLI)
VnSt.......... Saint Thomas Public Library, Charlotte Amalie, VI [*Library
                 symbol*] [*Library of Congress*]   (LCLS)
VNST........ Simikot [*Nepal*] [*ICAO location identifier*]   (ICLI)
VnStC....... College of the Virgin Islands, St. Thomas, VI [*Library symbol*]
                 [*Library of Congress*]   (LCLS)
VNT .... Variable-Nozzle Turbocharger [*Automotive engineering*]
VNT .... Ventora Resources Ltd. [*Vancouver Stock Exchange symbol*]
VNTJ........ Taplejung [*Nepal*] [*ICAO location identifier*]   (ICLI)
VNTP........ Tikapur [*Nepal*] [*ICAO location identifier*]   (ICLI)
VNTR .... Tumlingtar [*Nepal*] [*ICAO location identifier*]   (ICLI)
VNTR .... Variable Number of Tandem Repeats [*Genetics*]
VNTRF....... Ventora Resources Ltd. [*NASDAQ symbol*]   (NQ)
VNTS........ Vertical Nutrient-Solution Transport System [*i.e., plant stem*]
                 [*Slang*]
VNU.......... Verenigde Nederlandse Uitgeversbedrijven [*Publishing group*]
                 [*Netherlands*]
VNV.......... Vlaamsch Nationaal Verbond [*Flemish National League*]
                 [*Dissolved*] [*Belgium*] [*Political party*]   (PPE)
VNVO....... Verbal-Nonverbal Operation [*Psychometrics*]
VNVT....... Biratnagar [*Nepal*] [*ICAO location identifier*]   (ICLI)
VNW........ Van Wert, OH [*Location identifier*] [*FAA*]   (FAAL)
VNXL....... Vane Axial
VNY .... Van Nuys, CA [*Location identifier*] [*FAA*]   (FAAL)
VNZ........... Schweizerische Handelskammer in den Niederlanden.
                 Mitteilungen an die Mitglieder [*A publication*]
VO............. Battleship Observation Squadron [*Navy symbol*]
VO............. De Verborum Obligationibus [*A publication*]   (DLA)

Vo............. Initial Velocity
VO............. Observation Plane [*Navy symbol*]
VO............. [*The*] Seagram Co. Ltd. [*NYSE symbol*] [*Toronto Stock
                 Exchange symbol*] [*Vancouver Stock Exchange symbol*]
VO............. Valve Oscillator   (DEN)
VO............. Varying Order [*British*]
VO............. Vehicle Operations [*NASA*]   (NASA)
VO............. Verb-Object [*Education of the hearing-impaired*]
VO............. Verbal Orders
VO............. Verbindungsoffizier [*Liaison Officer*] [*German military - World
                 War II*]
VO............. Vernehmungsoffizier [*Interrogation Officer*] [*German military -
                 World War II*]
VO............. Verordnung [*Decree, Regulation, Ordinance*]
                 [*German*]   (ILCA)
VO............. Verpflegungsoffizier [*Mess Officer*] [*German military - World
                 War II*]
VO............. Verso
VO............. Vertical Oculus
VO............. Very Old [*Wines and spirits*]
VO............. Vesnjani Orbriji [*Kyjiv*] [*A publication*]
VO............. Veterinary Officer [*British*]
VO............. Victorian Order [*British*]   (ROG)
VO............. Viking Orbiter [*NASA*]
VO............. Violation of [*Local*] Ordinance
VO............. Violino [*Violin*] [*Music*]   (ROG)
VO............. Visa Office [*Department of State*]
VO............. Vocal   (AAG)
VO............. Voice [*A publication*]
VO............. Voice   (AAG)
VO............. Voice Over [*Commentary read over a program*] [*Television*]
Vo............. Voices [*A publication*]
VO............. Volatile Oil
VO............. Volcanic Origin   (AAG)
VO............. Volt   (ROG)
VO............. Volume
VO............. Voluntary Opening [*Prosthesis*] [*Medicine*]
VO............. Von Oben [*From the Top*] [*German*]
v/o............ Vossa Ordem [*Your Order*] [*Business term*] [*Portuguese*]
VO............. VOTEC, Servicos Aereos Regionais SA [*Brazil*] [*ICAO
                 designator*]   (ICDA)
VO............. Voucher   (MCD)
VOA......... Vehicule d'Observation d'Artillerie [*French*]
VOA......... Vibrational Optical Activity [*Spectroscopy*]
VOA......... Voice of America [*United States Information Agency*]
VOA......... Volkswagen of America
VOA......... Volunteers of America   (EA)
VOA......... Voorlichter [*A publication*]
VO-AG ...... Vocational Agriculture [*Education*]
VOAPA ..... Vultee Owners and Pilots Association   (EA)
VOAR....... St. John's, NF [*AM radio station call letters*]
VOARS....... Velocity over Altitude Ratio Sensor   (MCD)
VOB.......... Vacuum Optical Bench
VOB.......... Volume over Bark [*Forestry*]
VOBANC .. Voice Band Compression   (CET)
VOBG....... Bangalore [*India*] [*ICAO location identifier*]   (ICLI)
VOBI .... Bellary [*India*] [*ICAO location identifier*]   (ICLI)
VOBL BZ .. Verordnungsblatt fuer die Britische Zone [*Official Gazette of
                 the Former British Zone of Occupation*]
                 [*German*]   (ILCA)
VOBR....... Bidar [*India*] [*ICAO location identifier*]   (ICLI)
VOBZ....... Vijayawada [*India*] [*ICAO location identifier*]   (ICLI)
VOC.......... Observation Spotter Squadron [*Navy symbol*]
VOC.......... Onondaga Community College, Syracuse, NY [*OCLC
                 symbol*]   (OCLC)
VOC.......... Variable Oil Capacitor
VOC.......... Variable Output Circuit   (DEN)
VOC.......... Vehicle Observer Corps [*Road Haulage Association*]
                 [*British*]   (DCTA)
VOC.......... Vehicle Out of Commission [*Army*]   (AFIT)
VOC.......... Verbal Orders of the Commander
VOC.......... Vincent Owners Club   (EA)
VOC.......... Virago Owners Club   (EA)
VOC.......... VM. Voorlichtingsblad van het Ministerie van Volksgezondheid
                 en Milieuhygiene [*A publication*]
VOC.......... Vocabulary [*Linguistics*]
VOC.......... Vocal   (ADA)
VOC.......... Vocational
VOC.......... Vocative
VOC.......... Voice of Calvary [*An association*]
VOC.......... Voice-Operated Coder
VOC.......... Voice Order Circuit   (CET)
VOC.......... Volatile Organic Compound [*Environmental chemistry*]
VOC.......... Volunteer Officer Candidate [*Army*]
VOCA....... Victims of Crime Act of 1984
VOCA....... Voice of China and Asia Missionary Society   (EA)
VOCA....... Voice Communications Assembly [*Ground Communications
                 Facility, NASA*]
VOCA .... Voice Output Communications Aid
VOCA .... Voltmeter Calibrator
VOCA .... Volunteers in Overseas Cooperative Assistance   (EA)

VOCAB ..... Vocabulary
VOCAL ..... Vessel Ordnance Allowance List
VOCAL ..... Victims of Child Abuse Laws   (EA)
VOCAL ..... Victims of Crime Assistance League [*Australia*]
VOCAL ..... Victims of Crime and Leniency   (EA)
VOCAP ..... VP-16-213 [*Etoposide*], Oncovin [*Vincristine*],
        Cyclophosphamide, Adriamycin, Platinol [*Cisplatin*]
        [*Antineoplastic drug regimen*]
Voc Aspect Ed ... Vocational Aspect of Education [*A publication*]
VOCAT ..... Vocational
VOCAT ..... Vocative [*Grammar*]   (ROG)
Vocat Asp Educ ... Vocational Aspect of Education [*A publication*]
Vocat Guid ... Vocational Guidance Quarterly [*A publication*]
Vocational Aspect ... Vocational Aspect of Education [*A publication*]
Vocat Train Bull ... Vocational Training. Bulletin [*A publication*]
Vocat Training ... Vocational Training [*A publication*]
VOCB .... Coimbatore [*India*] [*ICAO location identifier*]   (ICLI)
VOCC .... Cochin [*India*] [*ICAO location identifier*]   (ICLI)
VOC-ED.... Vocational Education   (OICC)
VocEd Insider ... VocEd Business and Office Insider. Journal of the American
        Vocational Association [*A publication*]
Voc Educ.... Vocational Education [*A publication*]
Voc Educ M ... Vocational Education Magazine [*A publication*]
VOCG........ Verbal Orders of Commanding General
Voc Guid Q ... Vocational Guidance Quarterly [*A publication*]
VOCL .... Calicut [*India*] [*ICAO location identifier*]   (ICLI)
VOCM....... St. John's, NF [*AM radio station call letters*]
VOCM....... Vehicle Out of Commission for Maintenance [*Military*]
VOCM-FM ... St. John's, NF [*FM radio station call letters*]
VOCNA..... Velocette Owners Club of North America   (EA)
VOCO........ Verbal Orders of Commanding Officer
VOCODER ... Voice Coder
VOCOM.... Voice Communications
VOCP .... Cuddapah [*India*] [*ICAO location identifier*]   (ICLI)
VOCP .... Vehicle Out of Commission for Parts [*Military*]
VocRehab... Vocational Rehabilitation   (OICC)
VOCS .... Verbal Orders of the Chief of Staff
VOCX .... Carnicobar [*India*] [*ICAO location identifier*]   (ICLI)
VOD.......... Old Dominion University, Norfolk, VA [*OCLC
        symbol*]   (OCLC)
VOD.......... Vacuum Oxygen Decarburization [*Stainless-steel processing*]
VOD.......... Vehicle On-Board Delivery
VOD.......... Velocity of Detonation   (IEEE)
VOD.......... Veno-Occlusive Disease [*of the liver*]
VOD.......... Vertical On-Board Delivery [*Navy*]   (NVT)
VOD.......... Via Omnidirect   (FAAC)
VOD.......... Vision, Right Eye
VODACOM ... Voice Data Communications
VODARO ... Vertical Ozone Distribution from the Absorption and Radiation
        of Ozone   (AAG)
VODAS ..... Voice-Operated Device Antising   (CET)
VODAT ..... Voice-Operated Device for Automatic Transmission
VODC........ Viking Orbiter Design Change [*NASA*]
VODER ..... Voice Coder
VODER ..... Voice-Operated Demonstrator
VODG....... Dundigul [*India*] [*ICAO location identifier*]   (ICLI)
VODK....... Donakonda [*India*] [*ICAO location identifier*]   (ICLI)
VODK........ [*The*] Voice of Democratic Kampuchea [*Radio station of the
        Red Khmers*]   (PD)
Vodn Hospod ... Vodni Hospodarstvi [*A publication*]
Vodn Hospod Rada B ... Vodni Hospodarstvi. Rada B [*A publication*]
Vodni Hospod ... Vodni Hospodarstvi [*A publication*]
Vodni Hospod A ... Vodni Hospodarstvi. Rada A [*Czechoslovakia*] [*A
        publication*]
Vodni Hospod Rada B ... Vodni Hospodarstvi. Rada B [*A publication*]
Vodn Resur ... Vodnye Resursy [*USSR*] [*A publication*]
Vodohospod Cas ... Vodohospodarsky Casopis [*A publication*]
Vodopodgot Ochistka Prom Stokov ... Vodopodgotovka i Ochistka
        Promyshlennykh Stokov [*A publication*]
Vodorosli Griby Sib Dal'nego Vostoka ... Vodorosli i Griby Sibiri i Dal'nego
        Vostoka [*A publication*]
Vodosnabzh Kanaliz Gidrotekh Sooruzh ... Vodosnabzhenie Kanalizatsiya
        Gidrotekhnicheskie Soooruzheniya [*A publication*]
Vodosnabzh Sanit Tekh ... Vodosnabzhenie i Sanitarnaya Tekhnika [*A
        publication*]
Vodos Sanit Tekhn ... Vodosnabzhenie i Sanitarnaya Tekhnika [*A
        publication*]
VODP........ Verbal Orders by Direction of the President
VOE.......... Venus Orbit Ejection [*NASA*]   (MCD)
VOE.......... Visual Order Error
VOE.......... Vocational Office Education [*NASA employment program*]
VOEC .... Vegetable Oil Export Corporation   (EA)
VOECRN .. Vietnamese Organization to Exterminate Communists and
        Restore the Nation   (EA)
Voedingsmiddelen Technol ... Voedingsmiddelen Technologie [*A publication*]
Voegel Rheinl ... Voegel des Rheinlandes [*A publication*]
VOEI .... Veroeffentlichungen. Osteuropa-Institut [*A publication*]
Voen Khim ... Voennaya Khimiya [*A publication*]
Voen Med Delo ... Voenno Meditsinsko Delo [*A publication*]

Voen Med Fak Sarat Medinst Sb Nauchn Tr ... Voenno-Meditsinskii
        Fakul'tet pri Saratovskom Medinstitute. Sbornik
        Nauchnykh Trudov [*A publication*]
Voen-Med Zh ... Voenno-Meditsinskii Zhurnal [*A publication*]
Voenna Tekh ... Voenna Tekhnika [*Bulgaria*] [*A publication*]
Voenno-Ist Zhurnal ... Voenno-Istoricheskii Zhurnal [*A publication*]
Voenno-Med Zh ... Voenno-Meditsinskii Zhurnal [*A publication*]
Voenno Med Zhurnal (Leningrad) ... Voenno-Meditsinskii Zhurnal
        (Leningrad) [*A publication*]
Voenno-Med Zhurnal (S Peterburg) ... Voenno-Meditsinskii Zhurnal (S.
        Peterburg) [*A publication*]
Voen Sanit Delo ... Voenno-Sanitarnoe Delo [*A publication*]
Voen Vest... Voennyi Vestnik [*USSR*] [*A publication*]
Voen Znaniya ... Voennye Znaniya [*USSR*] [*A publication*]
Voet Com ad Pand ... Voet's Commentarius ad Pandectas [*A
        publication*]   (DLA)
VOF.......... Covington, GA [*Location identifier*] [*FAA*]   (FAAL)
VOF.......... Observation Fighter Squadron [*Navy symbol*]
VOF.......... Variable Operating Frequency   (NATG)
VOF.......... Vennootschap Onder Firma [*Limited Partnership*]
        [*Dutch*]   (ILCA)
VOF.......... Vsesoiuznoe Obshchestvo Filatelistov [*or Fizioterapistov*]
vlof........... Lift-Off Speed [*Aviation code*]   (AIA)
VOG......... Observation Plane Squadron [*Navy symbol*]
VOG......... Vanguard Operations Group
VOG......... Vectoroculogram
VOG......... Vessel Off-Gas [*Nuclear energy*]   (NRCH)
Vog........... Vogue [*Record label*] [*France*]
VOG......... Volgograd [*USSR*] [*Airport symbol*]   (OAG)
VOGAA..... Voice-Operated Gain-Adjusting Amplifier [*NASA*]
VOGAD..... Voice-Operated Gain-Adjusting Device [*NASA*]
VOGB....... Gulbarga [*India*] [*ICAO location identifier*]   (ICLI)
Vogelkd Hefte Edertal ... Vogelkundliche Hefte Edertal [*A publication*]
VOGIN...... Nederlandse Vereniging van Gebruikers van Online Informatie-
        Systemen [*Netherlands Association of Users of Online
        Information Systems*] [*Amsterdam*]   (IID)
Vog Liv....... Vogue Living [*A publication*]   (APTA)
VOGOV.... Verbal Orders of the Governor
VOGT........ Vogart Crafts Corp. [*NASDAQ symbol*]   (NQ)
VOH .... Grootkeuken. Voedingsblad voor Instellingen en Bedrijven [*A
        publication*]
VOH .... Vohemar [*Madagascar*] [*Airport symbol*]   (OAG)
VOHCA...... Veterans Omnibus Health Care Act of 1976
VOHY....... Hyderabad [*India*] [*ICAO location identifier*]   (ICLI)
VOI........... Vehicle Ordnance Installation
VOI........... Video Output Impedance
VOI........... Vocational Opinion Index   (OICC)
VOI........... Voinjama [*Liberia*] [*Airport symbol*]   (OAG)
VOIB .... Veroeffentlichungen. Abteilung fuer Slavische Sprachen und
        Literaturen. Osteuropa-Institut [*Slavisches Seminar*]. Freie
        Universitaet Berlin [*A publication*]
VOIC .... Voicemail International, Inc. [*NASDAQ symbol*]   (NQ)
VOICE...... Victims of Incest Can Emerge   (EA)
Voice .... Village Voice [*A publication*]
VOICE...... Vocabulary of Intelligence Concept Expressions
VOICE...... Voice of Informed Community Expression
VOICE...... Volunteer Oil Industry Communications Effort [*Program*]
        [*Phillips Petroleum Co.*]
VOIR .... Venus Orbiting and Imaging RADAR [*NASA*]
VOIS......... Visual Observation Instrumentation Subsystem [*Lunar space
        program*]
VOIS......... Visual Observation Integration Subsystem   (AAG)
VOIS......... Voice-Operated Inspection System [*Software*]
VOIT .... Voit Corp. [*NASDAQ symbol*]   (NQ)
Voith Forsch Konstr ... Voith Forschung und Konstruktion [*A publication*]
Voith Res & Constr ... Voith Research and Construction [*A publication*]
VOIZD ...... Voice of Z-39 [*Later, Information Standards Quarterly*] [*A
        publication*]
Vojenskozdrav Knih ... Vojenskozdravotnicka Knihovna [*A publication*]
Vojen Zdrav Listy ... Vojenske Zdravotnicke Listy [*A publication*]
Vojnoekon Pregl ... Vojnoekonomski Pregled [*Yugoslavia*] [*A publication*]
Vojnosanit Pregl ... Vojnosanitetski Pregled [*A publication*]
VOK.......... Camp Douglas, WI [*Location identifier*] [*FAA*]   (FAAL)
VOK.......... Volkskrant [*A publication*]
VOK.......... Vry op Kaai [*Free on Quay*] [*Afrikaans*]
VOKM....... Khamampet [*India*] [*ICAO location identifier*]   (ICLI)
VOKS .... Soviet Union Society for Cultural Relations with Foreign
        Countries. Weekly News Bulletin [*A publication*]
VOKS .... Vsesoiuznoe Obshchestvo Kul'turnoi Sviazi s Zagranitsei [*All-
        Union Society for Cultural Relations with Foreign
        Countries*] [*USSR*]
VOL.......... Variable Orientation Launcher   (AAG)
Vol........... Volans [*Constellation*]
VOL.......... Volante [*Lightly and Rapidly*] [*Music*]   (ROG)
VOL.......... Volatilis [*Volatile*] [*Pharmacy*]
Vol........... Volcanic [*Quality of the bottom*] [*Nautical charts*]
VOL.......... Volcano [*Maps and charts*]
VOL.......... Volume   (EY)
VOL.......... Voluntary [*or Volunteer*]   (AFM)
VOLA .... Volume, American Stock Exchange [*Selection symbol*]
VOLAD ..... Voice of the Lakes [*A publication*]

VOLAG ..... Voluntary Agency [*Generic term for a charitable organization*]
VOLAR ..... Volunteer Army [*Project, absorbed by MVA, 1972*]
Vol Ash ..... Volcanic Ash [*Quality of the bottom*] [*Nautical charts*]
VOLB .... Volunteer Bancshares, Inc. [*Jackson, TN*] [*NASDAQ symbol*]　(NQ)
VOLC .... Volcanics [*Lithology*]
VOLC .... Volcano
Volcani Inst Agric Res Div For Ilanot Leafl ... Volcani Institute of Agricultural Research. Division of Forestry. Ilanot Leaflet [*A publication*]
Volcani Inst Agric Res Div Sci Publ Pam ... Volcani Institute of Agricultural Research. Division of Scientific Publications. Pamphlet [*A publication*]
Volcanol Bull Jpn Meterol Agency ... Volcanological Meteorological Bulletin. Japan Meteorological Agency [*A publication*]
Volcanol Soc Jap Bull ... Volcanological Society of Japan. Bulletin [*A publication*]
VOLCAS ... Voice-Operated Loss Control and Suppressor
VOLCOM ... Value of Life Committee　(EA)
Vol Effort Q ... Voluntary Effort Quarterly [*A publication*]
VOLERE ... Voluntary/Legal/Regulatory　(IEEE)
Vol Feeding Mgt ... Volume Feeding Management [*A publication*]
Volgograd Gos Ped Inst Ucen Zap ... Volgogradskogo Gosudarstvennogo Pedagogiceskogo Instituta Imeni A. S. Serafimovica Ucenye Zapiski [*A publication*]
VOLIR .... Volumetric Indicating RADAR
VOLKS ...... Volkswagen [*Automobile*]　(DSUE)
Volksm ...... Volksmusik [*A publication*]
Volksmus ... Volksmusik. Zeitschrift fuer das Musikalische Laienschaffen [*A publication*]
Volkstum Landschaft ... Volkstum und Landschaft. Heimatblaetter der Muensterlaendische Tageszeitung [*A publication*]
Volleyball Mag ... Volleyball Magazine [*A publication*]
Volleyball Tech J ... Volleyball Technical Journal [*A publication*]
VOLMET ... Meteorological Information for Aircraft in Flight [*Aviation code*]　(FAAC)
Voln .... Volans [*Constellation*]
VOLN .... Volume, New York Stock Exchange [*Selection symbol*]
Vologod Gos Ped Inst Ucen Zap ... Vologodskii Gosudarstvennyi Pedagogiceskii Institut. Ucenye Zapiski [*A publication*]
Vologod I Cerepovec Gos Ped Inst Ucen Zap ... Vologodskii Gosudarstvennyi Pedagogiceskii Institut. Cerepoveckii Gosudarstvennyi Pedagogiceskii Institut. Ucenye Zapiski [*A publication*]
Vo LR .... Villanova Law Review [*A publication*]
Volr .... Volunteer [*British military*]　(DMA)
VOLRA ..... Volta Review [*A publication*]
VOLRY ...... Voluntary
VOLS .... Voluntary Overseas Libraries Service
VOLSCAN ... Volumetric Scanning RADAR
VOLSER ... Volume/Serial
VOLT .... Volt Information Sciences, Inc. [*NASDAQ symbol*]　(NQ)
VOLT .... Volume, Toronto Stock Exchange [*Selection symbol*]
VOLTAN .. Voltage Amperage Normalizer
Volta R ...... Volta Review [*A publication*]
Volt Electr Trade Mon ... Volt. Electrical Trade Monthly [*Japan*] [*A publication*]
VOLUG ...... Victorian Online Users Group [*Australia*]
Volunt Action ... Voluntary Action [*A publication*]
Volunt Action Leadersh ... Voluntary Action Leadership [*A publication*]
Volunt Adm ... Volunteer Administration [*A publication*]
Volunt Forum Abs ... Voluntary Forum Abstracts [*A publication*]
Volunt Housing ... Voluntary Housing [*A publication*]
Volunt Leader ... Volunteer Leader [*A publication*]
VOLV .... Volvendus [*To Be Rolled*] [*Pharmacy*]　(ADA)
VOLV .... Volvo AB [*Sweden*] [*NASDAQ symbol*]　(NQ)
VOLVEND ... Volvendus [*To Be Rolled*] [*Pharmacy*]
VOLY .... Voluntary　(ROG)
Volz Mat Sb ... Volzskii Matematiceskii Sbornik [*A publication*]
VOM .... Nux Vomica Strychnia [*Strychnine-producing plant*] [*Pharmacy*]　(ROG)
VOM .... Volcano Resources Corp. [*Vancouver Stock Exchange symbol*]
VOM .... Volt-Ohm Meter
VOM .... Volt-Ohm-Milliammeter
VOMD .... Madurai [*India*] [*ICAO location identifier*]　(ICLI)
VOMD .... VAFB [*Vandenberg Air Force Base*] Operations and Maintenance Documentation [*NASA*]
VOMF .... Madras [*India*] [*ICAO location identifier*]　(ICLI)
VOMG .... Magadi [*India*] [*ICAO location identifier*]　(ICLI)
VOMH .... Mahad [*India*] [*ICAO location identifier*]　(ICLI)
VOMI .... Volksdeutsche Mittelstelle [*NAZI Germany*]
VOML .... Mangalore [*India*] [*ICAO location identifier*]　(ICLI)
VOMM ...... Madras [*India*] [*ICAO location identifier*]　(ICLI)
VOM URG ... Vomitione Urgente [*The Vomiting Being Troublesome*] [*Pharmacy*]　(ROG)
VOMY .... Mysore [*India*] [*ICAO location identifier*]　(ICLI)
VON .... Avon, CO [*Location identifier*] [*FAA*]　(FAAL)
VON .... Vestnik Otdelenija Obscestvennych Nauk. Akademija Nauk Gruzinskoj SSR [*A publication*]
VON .... Victorian Order of Nurses
VON .... Vons Companies [*NYSE symbol*]　(SPSG)
VONEA ..... Voprosy Neirokhirurgii [*A publication*]

Von H Const Hist ... Von Holst's Constitutional History of the United States [*A publication*]　(DLA)
Von Ihr Str for L ... Von Ihring's Struggle for Law [*A publication*]　(DLA)
VONJY ...... Elan Populaire pour l'Unite Nationale [*Popular Impulse for National Unity*] [*Malagascar*] [*Political party*]　(PPW)
Von Roll Mitt ... Von Roll Mitteilungen [*A publication*]
VONS .... Committee for the Defense of Persons Unjustly Persecuted [*Czechoslovakia*] [*Political party*]　(PD)
VONS .... Nagarjunsagar [*India*] [*ICAO location identifier*]　(ICLI)
VOofA .... Vasa Order of America [*Cranston, RI*]　(EA)
Voorh Code ... Voorhies' Code [*New York*] [*A publication*]　(DLA)
Voorh Cr Jur ... Voorhies' Criminal Jurisprudence of Louisiana [*A publication*]　(DLA)
Voorh St ..... Voorhies' Louisiana Revised Statutes [*A publication*]　(DLA)
Voorlichting Onderz ... Voorlichting en Onderzoek [*A publication*]
VOP .... Valued as in Original Policy [*Insurance*]
VOP .... Vertical Ozone Profile
VOP .... Very Old Pale [*Designation on brandy labels*]
VOP .... Viral Oncology Program [*National Cancer Institute*]
VOPA .... Verbal Order Purchase Agreement [*Sales*]
VOPAN ..... Voice Pitch Analysis [*Consumer Response Corp.*]
VOPB .... Port Blair [*India*] [*ICAO location identifier*]　(ICLI)
VOPB .... Voice of the People of Burma [*Radio station of the Burma Communist Party*]　(PD)
Vop Bot Akad Nauk Litov SSR Inst Bot ... Voprosy Botaniki. Akademiya Nauk Litovskoi SSR. Institut Botaniki [*A publication*]
Vop Ekol .... Voprosy Ekologii [*A publication*]
Vop Erozii Povysh Prod Sklon Zemel' Moldavii ... Voprosy Erozii i Povysheniya Produktivnosti Sklonovykh Zemel' Moldavii [*A publication*]
Vop Fil .... Voprosy Filosofii [*A publication*]
Vop Filos .... Voprosy Filosofii [*A publication*]
Vop Genez Krypnomashtabn Kartir Pochv Kazan Univ ... Voprosy Genezisa i Krypnomashtabnoi Kartirovanii Pochv Kazanskii Universitet [*A publication*]
Vop Geogr Mordovsk ASSR ... Voprosy Geografii Mordovskoi ASSR [*A publication*]
VopIst .... Voprosy Istorii [*A publication*]
Vop Istor .... Voprosy Istorii [*A publication*]
Vop Med Kh ... Voprosy Meditsinskoi Khimii [*A publication*]
Vop Mikrobiol Akad Nauk Armyan SSR ... Voprosy Mikrobiologii. Akademiya Nauk Armyanskoi SSR [*A publication*]
VOPNAV .. Vice Chief of Naval Operations
VOPO .... Volkspolizei [*Also, VP*]
VOPP .... Veterinary Medicine, Optometry, Podiatry, and Pharmacy [*HEW program*]
Vop Pitan ... Voprosy Pitaniya [*A publication*]
Vop Psikhol ... Voprosy Psikhologii [*A publication*]
VOPR .... Voice-Operated Relay
Vopr Antropol ... Voprosy Antropologii [*A publication*]
Vopr At Nauki Tekh Ser Fiz Plazmy Probl Upr Termodad Reakts ... Voprosy Atomnoi Nauki i Tekhniki. Seriya Fizika Plazmy i Problemy Upravlyaemykh Termodadernykh Reaktsii [*Ukrainian SSR*] [*A publication*]
Vopr At Nauki Tekh Ser Fiz Vys Energ At Yadra ... Voprosy Atomnoi Nauki i Tekhniki. Seriya Fizika Vysokikh Energii i Atomnogo Yadra [*Ukrainian SSR*] [*A publication*]
Vopr At Nauki Tekh Ser Obshch Yad Fiz ... Voprosy Atomnoi Nauki i Tekhniki. Seriya Obshchaya i Yadernaya Fizika [*Ukrainian SSR*] [*A publication*]
Vopr At Nauki Tekh Ser Radiats Tekh ... Voprosy Atomnoi Nauki i Tekhniki. Seriya Radiatsionnaya Tekhnika [*A publication*]
Vopr At Nauki Tekh Ser Yad Konstanty ... Voprosy Atomnoi Nauki i Tekhniki. Seriya Yadernye Konstanty [*A publication*]
Vopr Bezopasn Ugol'n Shakhtakh ... Voprosy Bezopasnosti v Ugol'nykh Shakhtakh [*A publication*]
Vopr Biokhim ... Voprosy Biokhimii [*A publication*]
Vopr Biokhim Mozga ... Voprosy Biokhimii Mozga [*A publication*]
Vopr Biokhim Nervn Myshechnoi Sist ... Voprosy Biokhimii Nervnoi i Myshechnoi Sistem [*Georgian SSR*] [*A publication*]
Vopr Biokhim Nervn Sist ... Voprosy Biokhimii Nervnoi Sistemy [*A publication*]
Vopr Biol.... Voprosy Biologii [*A publication*]
Vopr Biol Kraev Med ... Voprosy Biologii i Kraevoi Meditsiny [*A publication*]
Vopr Biol Semennogo Rezmnozheniya ... Voprosy Biologii Semennogo Reszmnozheniya [*A publication*]
Vopr Bor'by Silikozom Sib ... Voprosy Bor'by s Silikozom v Sibiri [*A publication*]
Vopr Cenoobraz ... Voprosy Cenoobrazovanija [*A publication*]
Vopr Chetvertechn Geol ... Voprosy Chetvertechnoi Geologii [*A publication*]
Vopr Din Prochn ... Voprosy Dinamiki i Prochnosti [*A publication*]
Vopr Din Teor Rasprostr Seism Voln ... Voprosy Dinamicheskoi Teorii Rasprostraneniya Seismicjeskikh Voln [*USSR*] [*A publication*]
Vopr Dozim Zasch Izluch Mosk Inzh Fiz Inst Sb Statei ... Voprosy Dozimetrii i Zaschity ot Izluchenii. Moskovskii Inzhenerno Fizicheskii Institut Sbornik Statei [*USSR*] [*A publication*]
Vopr Dozim Zashch Izluch ... Voprosy Dozimetrii i Zashchity ot Izluchenii [*A publication*]
Vopr Ekol Biotsenol ... Voprosy Ekologii i Biotsenologii [*A publication*]
Vopr Ekon ... Voprosy Ekonomiki [*A publication*]

Vopr Eksp Klin Radiol ... Voprosy Eksperimental'noi i Klinicheskoi Radiologii [*Ukrainian SSR*] [*A publication*]
Vopr Eksp Onkol ... Voprosy Eksperimental'noi Onkologii [*A publication*]
Vopr Endokrinol Obmena Veshchestv ... Voprosy Endokrinologii i Obmena Veshchestv [*A publication*]
Vopr Endokrinol Obmena Veshchestv Resp Mezhved Sb ... Voprosy Endokrinologii Obmena Veshchestvennyi Respublikanskoi Mezhvedomstvennyi Sbornik [*A publication*]
Vopr Energ ... Voprosy Energetiki [*A publication*]
Vopr Erozii Povysh Prod Sklonovykh Zemel Mold ... Voprosy Erozii i Povysheniya Produktivnosti Sklonovykh Zemel' Moldavii [*A publication*]
Vopr Etiol Patog Opukholei ... Voprosy Etiologii i Patogeneza Opukholei [*A publication*]
Vopr Filos .. Voprosy Filosofii [*A publication*]
Vopr Fiz Gorn Porod ... Voprosy Fiziki Gornykh Porod [*A publication*]
Vopr Fiziol Akad Nauk Azerb SSR Sekt Fiziol ... Voprosy Fiziologii Akademiya Nauk Azerbaidzhanskoi SSR. Sektor Fiziologii [*Azerbaidzhan SSR*] [*A publication*]
Vopr Fiziol Biokhim Kul't Rast ... Voprosy Fiziologii i Biokhimii Kul'turnykh Rastenii [*A publication*]
Vopr Fiziol Biokhim Zool Parazitol ... Voprosy Fiziologii, Biokhimii, Zoologii, i Parazitologii [*A publication*]
Vopr Fiziol Chel Zhivotn ... Voprosy Fiziologii Cheloveka i Zhivotnykh [*A publication*]
Vopr Fiziol Rast Mikrobiol ... Voprosy Fiziologii Rastenii i Mikrobiologii [*A publication*]
Vopr Fiz Tverd Tela ... Voprosy Fiziki Tverdogo Tela [*A publication*]
Vopr Fiz Zasch Reaktorov ... Voprosy Fiziki Zashchity Reaktorov [*USSR*] [*A publication*]
Vopr Fiz Zashch Reakt ... Voprosy Fiziki Zashchity Reaktorov [*A publication*]
Vopr Fotosint ... Voprosy Fotosinteza [*A publication*]
Vopr Gazotermodin Energoustanovok ... Voprosy Gazotermodinamiki Energoustanovok [*Ukrainian SSR*] [*A publication*]
Vopr Gematol Pereliv Krovi Krovozamenitelei ... Voprosy Gematologii Perelivaniya Krovi i Krovozamenitelei [*A publication*]
Vopr Geogr ... Voprosy Geografii [*A publication*]
Vopr Geogr Dal'nego Vostoka ... Voprosy Geografii Dal'nego Vostoka [*A publication*]
Vopr Geogr Kaz ... Voprosy Geografii Kazakhstana [*A publication*]
Vopr Geogr Mordov ASSR ... Voprosy Geografii Mordovskoi ASSR [*A publication*]
Vopr Geokhim Tipomorfizm Miner ... Voprosy Geokhimii i Tipomorfizm Mineralov [*A publication*]
Vopr Geol Buren Neft Gazov Skvazhin ... Voprosy Geologii i Bureniya Neftyanykh i Gazovykh Skvazhin [*A publication*]
Vopr Geol Metallog Kol'sk Poluostrova ... Voprosy Geologii i Metallogenii Kol'skogo Poluostrova [*A publication*]
Vopr Geol Metod Razved Zolota ... Voprosy Geologii i Metodiki Razvedki Zolota [*A publication*]
Vopr Geol Mineral Kolsk Poluostrova ... Voprosy Geologii i Mineralogii Kol'skogo Poluostrova [*A publication*]
Vopr Geol Mineral Rudn Mestorozhd Ukr ... Voprosy Geologii i Mineralogii Rudnykh Mestorozhdenii Ukrainy [*A publication*]
Vopr Geol Neftegazonsn Uzb ... Voprosy Geologii i Neftegazonosnosti Uzbekistana [*A publication*]
Vopr Geol Neftenosn Sredn Povolzh'ya ... Voprosy Geologii i Neftenosnosti Srednego Povolzh'ya [*A publication*]
Vopr Geol Tadzh ... Voprosy Geologii Tadzhikistana [*A publication*]
Vopr Geol Uzb ... Voprosy Geologii Uzbekistana [*A publication*]
Vopr Geol Vost Okrainy Russ Platformy Yuzhn Urala ... Voprosy Geologii Vostochnoi Okrainy Russkoi Platformy i Yuzhnogo Urala [*A publication*]
Vopr Geol Yuzhn Urala Povolzh'ya ... Voprosy Geologii Yuzhnogo Urala i Povolzh'ya [*A publication*]
Vopr Geomorfol Geol Bashk ... Voprosy Geomorfologii i Geologii Bashkirii [*A publication*]
Vopr Gerontol Geriatr ... Voprosy Gerontologii i Geriatrii [*A publication*]
Vopr Gidrodin Teploobmena Kriog Sist ... Voprosy Gidrodinamiki i Teploobmena v Kriogennykh Sistemakh [*A publication*]
Vopr Gidrogeol Inzh Geol Ukr ... Voprosy Gidrogeologii i Inzhenernoi Geologii Ukrainy [*A publication*]
Vopr Gidrol ... Voprosy Gidrologii [*A publication*]
Vopr Gidrotekh ... Voprosy Gidrotekhniki [*A publication*]
Vopr Gig Pitan ... Voprosy Gigieny Pitaniya [*A publication*]
Vopr Gig Tr Profpatol Prom Toksikol ... Voprosy Gigieny Truda Profpatologii i Promyshlennoi Toksikologii [*A publication*]
Vopr Gig Tr Slants Promsti Est SSR ... Voprosy Gigieny Truda v Slantsevoi Promyshlennosti Estonskoi SSR [*A publication*]
Vopr Ikhtiol ... Voprosy Ikhtiologii [*A publication*]
Vopr Immunol ... Voprosy Immunologii [*A publication*]
Vopr Infekts Patol Immunol ... Voprosy Infektsionnoi Patologii i Immunologii [*A publication*]
Vopr Inf Teor Prakt ... Voprosy Informatsionnoi Teorii i Praktiki [*A publication*]
Vopr Introd Rast Zelenogo Stroit ... Voprosy Introduktsii Rastenii i Zelenogo Stroitel'stva [*A publication*]
Vopr Inzh Geol Gruntoved ... Voprosy Inzhenernoi Geologii i Gruntovedeniya [*A publication*]

Vopr Inzh Seismol ... Voprosy Inzhenernoi Seismologii [*USSR*] [*A publication*]
Vopr Issled Ispol'z Pochv Mold ... Voprosy Issledovaniya i Ispol'zovaniya Pochvovedeniya Moldavii [*A publication*]
Vopr Issled Lessovykh Gruntov Osn Fundam ... Voprosy Issledovaniya Lessovykh Gruntov Osnovanii i Fundamentov [*A publication*]
Vopr Ist ...... Voprosy Istorii [*A publication*]
Vopr Ist KPSS ... Voprosy Istorii KPSS [*Kommunisticheskaya Partiya Sovietskogo Soyuza*] [*A publication*]
Vopr Istor .. Voprosy Istorii [*A publication*]
Vopr Istor Estestvozn Tekh ... Voprosy Istorii Estestvoznaniya i Tekhniki [*A publication*]
Vopr Ist Udm ... Voprosy Istorii Udmurtii [*A publication*]
Vopr Karstoved ... Voprosy Karstovedeniya [*A publication*]
Vopr Khim Biokhim Sist Soderzh Marganets Polifenoly ... Voprosy Khimii i Biokhimii Sistem. Soderzhashchikh Marganets i Polifenoly [*A publication*]
Vopr Khim Khim Tekhnol ... Voprosy Khimii i Khimicheskoj Tekhnologii [*USSR*] [*A publication*]
Vopr Kinet Katal ... Voprosy Kinetiki i Kataliza [*A publication*]
Vopr Klin Eksp Onkol ... Voprosy Klinicheskoi i Eksperimental'noi Onkologii [*A publication*]
Vopr Klin Eskp Khir ... Voprosy Klinicheskoi i Eksperimental'noi Khirurgii [*A publication*]
Vopr Klin Lech Zlokach Novoobraz ... Voprosy Kliniki i Lecheniya Zlokachestvennykh Novoobrazovanii [*A publication*]
Vopr Klin Med ... Voprosy Klinicheskoi Meditsiny [*A publication*]
Vopr Kommunal'n Gig ... Voprosy Kommunal'noi Gigieny [*A publication*]
Vopr Kosmog ... Voprosy Kosmogonii [*A publication*]
Vopr Kraev Patol Akad Nauk Uzb SSR ... Voprosy Kraevoi Patologii Akademii Nauk Uzbekskoi SSR [*A publication*]
Vopr Kriog Tekh ... Voprosy Kriogennoi Tekhniki [*A publication*]
Vopr Kurortol Fizioter (Frunze) ... Voprosy Kurortologii i Fizioterapii (Frunze) [*A publication*]
Vopr Kurortol Fizioter Lech Fiz Kul't ... Voprosy Kurortologii, Fizioterapii, i Lechebnoi Fizicheskoi Kul'tury [*A publication*]
Vopr Kurortol Revatol ... Voprosy Kurortologii i Revmatologii [*A publication*]
Vopr Leikozol ... Voprosy Leikozologii [*A publication*]
Vopr Leprol Dermatol ... Voprosy Leprologii i Dermatologii [*A publication*]
Vopr Lesoved ... Voprosy Lesovedeniya [*A publication*]
Vopr Litol Petrogr ... Voprosy Litologii i Petrografii [*A publication*]
Vopr Magmat Metamorf ... Voprosy Magmatizma i Metamorfizma [*A publication*]
Vopr Magmat Metamorfiz ... Voprosy Magmatizma i Metamorfizma [*USSR*] [*A publication*]
Vopr Magn Gidrodin Akad Nauk Latv SSR Inst Fiz ... Voprosy Magnitnoi Gidrodinamiki. Akademiya Nauk Latviiskoi SSR. Institut Fiziki [*Latvian SSR*] [*A publication*]
Vopr Med Khim ... Voprosy Meditsinskoi Khimii [*A publication*]
Vopr Med Khim Akad Med Nauk SSR ... Voprosy Meditsinskoi Khimii Akademiya Meditsinskikh Nauk SSSR [*A publication*]
Vopr Med Teor Klin Prakt Kurortnogo Lech ... Voprosy Meditsinskoi Teorii Klinicheskoi Praktiki i Kurortnogo Lecheniya [*A publication*]
Vopr Med Virusol ... Voprosy Meditsinskoi Virusologii [*A publication*]
Vopr Mekh ... Voprosy Mekhanika [*USSR*] [*A publication*]
Vopr Mekh Real'nogo Tverd Tela ... Voprosy Mekhaniki Real'nogo Tverdogo Tela [*A publication*]
Vopr Metalloved Korroz Met ... Voprosy Metallovedeniya i Korrozii Metallov [*A publication*]
Vopr Metod Nauki ... Voprosy Metodologii Nauki [*A publication*]
Vopr Mikrobiol ... Voprosy Mikrobiologii [*A publication*]
Vopr Mikrodozim ... Voprosy Mikrodozimetrii Ministerstvo Vysshego i Srednego Spetsial'nogo Obrazovaniya SSSR [*A publication*]
Vopr Mineral Osad Obraz ... Voprosy Mineralogii Osadochnykh Obrazonanii [*A publication*]
Vopr Neftekhim ... Voprosy Neftekhimii [*A publication*]
Vopr Neirokhir ... Voprosy Neirokhirurgii [*A publication*]
Vopr Obsc Nauk ... Voprosy Obscestvennyh Nauk [*A publication*]
Vopr Obshch Khim Biokhim ... Voprosy Obshchei Khimii i Biokhimii [*A publication*]
Vopr Okhr Materin Det ... Voprosy Okhrany Materinstva i Detstva [*A publication*]
Vopr Onkol ... Voprosy Onkologii [*A publication*]
Vopr Onkol (Leningr) ... Voprosy Onkologii (Leningrad) [*A publication*]
Vopr Org Geokhim Gidrogeol Neftegazonsn Basseinov Uzb ... Voprosy Organicheskoi Geokhimii i Gidrogeologii Neftegazonosnykh Basseinov Uzbekistana [*A publication*]
Voprosy Dinamiki i Procnosti ... Rizskii Politehniceskii Institut. Voprosy Dinamiki i Procnosti [*A publication*]
Voprosy Filos ... Voprosy Filosofii [*A publication*]
Voprosy Gidrotekh ... Voprosy Gidrotekhniki [*A publication*]
Voprosy Informatsion Teorii i Praktiki ... Akademiya Nauk SSSR. Vsesoyuznyi Institut Nauchnoi i Tekhnicheskoi Informatsii. Voprosy Informatsionnoi Teorii i Praktiki [*A publication*]
Voprosy Istor Estestvoznan i Tehn ... Voprosy Istorii Estestvoznanija i Tehniki [*A publication*]
Voprosy Kibernet (Moscow) ... Voprosy Kibernetiki (Moscow) [*A publication*]

Voprosy Kibernet (Tashkent) ... Voprosy Kibernetiki (Tashkent) [*A publication*]
Voprosy Teor Sistem Avtomat Upravleniya ... Leningradskii Universitet Voprosy Teorii Sistem Avtomaticheskogo Upravleniya [*A publication*]
Voprosy Vychisl i Prikl Mat ... Akademiya Nauk Uzbekskoi SSR. Trudy Ordena Trudovogo Krasnogo Znameni Instituta Kibernetiki s Vychislitel'nym Tsentrom. Voprosy Vychislitel'noi i Prikladnoi Matematiki [*A publication*]
Vopr Patol Krovi Krovoobrashch ... Voprosy Patologii Krovi i Krovoobrashcheniya [*A publication*]
Vopr Pediatr Ohkr Materin Det ... Voprosy Pediatrii i Ohkrany Materinstva i Detstva [*A publication*]
Vopr Peredachi Inf ... Voprosy Peredachi Informatsii [*Ukrainian SSR*] [*A publication*]
Vopr Pitan ... Voprosy Pitaniya [*A publication*]
Vopr Prikl Geokhim ... Voprosy Prikladnoi Geokhimii [*A publication*]
Vopr Prikl Radiogeol ... Voprosy Prikladnoi Radiogeologii [*A publication*]
Vopr Prochn Plast Met ... Voprosy Prochnosti i Plastichnosti Metallov [*A publication*]
Vopr Proekt Sodovykh Zavodov ... Voprosy Proekhitovaniya Sodovykh Zavodov [*A publication*]
Vopr Proizvod Stali ... Voprosy Proizvodstva Stali [*A publication*]
Vopr Proizvod Vaktsin Syvorotok ... Voprosy Proizvodstva Vaktsin i Syvorotok [*A publication*]
Vopr Psikhiat Nevropatol ... Voprosy Psikhiatrii i Nevropatologii [*USSR*] [*A publication*]
Vopr Psikhiatr Nevropatol ... Voprosy Psikhiatrii i Nevropatologii [*A publication*]
Vopr Psikhol ... Voprosy Psikhologii [*A publication*]
Vopr Radiobiol ... Voprosy Radiobiologii [*A publication*]
Vopr Radiobiol Akad Nauk Arm SSR ... Voprosy Radiobiologii. Akademiya Nauk Armyanskoi SSR [*A publication*]
Vopr Radiobiol Biol Deistviya Tsitostatich Prep ... Voprosy Radiobiologii i Biologicheskogo Deistviya Tsitostaticheskikh Preparatov [*A publication*]
Vopr Radiobiol Biol Dejstv Tsitostatich Prep ... Voprosy Radiobiologii i Biologicheskogo Dejstviya Tsitostaticheskikh Preparatov [*USSR*] [*A publication*]
Vopr Radiobiol Klin Radiol ... Voprosy Radiobiologii i Klinicheskoi Radiologii [*A publication*]
Vopr Radiobiol Sb Tr ... Voprosy Radiobiologii. Sbornik Trudov [*Armenian SSR*] [*A publication*]
Vopr Radiobiol (Yerevan) ... Voprosy Radiobiologii (Yerevan) [*A publication*]
Vopr Radioelektron ... Voprosy Radioelektroniki [*A publication*]
Vopr Ratsion Pitan ... Voprosy Ratsional'nogo Pitaniya [*A publication*]
Vopr Razved Geofiz ... Voprosy Razvedochnoi Geofiziki [*A publication*]
Vopr Razvit Gazov Promsti Ukr SSR ... Voprosy Razvitiya Gazovoi Promyshlennosti Ukrainskoi SSR [*A publication*]
Vopr Razvit Licnosti ... Voprosy Razvitija Licnosti [*A publication*]
Vopr Reg Geol Metallog Zabaikal'ya ... Voprosy Regional'noi Geologii i Metallogenii Zabaikal'ya [*A publication*]
Vopr Rentgenol Onkol ... Voprosy Rentgenologii i Onkologii [*A publication*]
Vopr Revm ... Voprosy Revmatizma [*A publication*]
Vopr Rud Geofiz ... Voprosy Rudnoi Geofiziki [*USSR*] [*A publication*]
Vopr Rud Geofiz Minist Geol Okhr Nedr SSSR ... Voprosy Rudnoi Geofiziki. Ministerstvo Geologii i Okhrany Nedr SSSR [*USSR*] [*A publication*]
Vopr Rudn Geofiz ... Voprosy Rudnoi Geofiziki [*A publication*]
Vopr Rudn Radiom ... Voprosy Rudnoi Radiometrii [*A publication*]
Vopr Rudn Transp ... Voprosy Rudichnogo Transporta [*A publication*]
Vopr Sel'sk Lesn Khoz Dal'nego Vostoka ... Voprosy Sel'skogo i Lesnogo Khozyaistva Dal'nego Vostoka [*A publication*]
Vopr Sel'sk Lesn Khoz Dal'n Vost ... Voprosy Sel'skogo i Lesnogo Khozyaistva Dal'nego Vostoka [*A publication*]
Vopr Sov Finno-Ugroved ... Voprosy Sovetskogo Finno-Ugrovedenija [*A publication*]
Vopr Stereokhim ... Voprosy Stereokhimii [*A publication*]
Vopr Strat Takt Marks-Lenin Partij ... Voprosy Strategii i Taktiki Marksistsko-Leninskih Partij [*A publication*]
Vopr Sudebno-Med Ekspert ... Voprosy Sudebno-Meditsinskoi Ekspertizy [*A publication*]
Vopr Sud Med Ekspertnoi Prakt ... Voprosy Sudebnoi Meditsiny i Ekspertnoi Praktiki [*A publication*]
Vopr Tekhnol Obrab Vody Prom Pit'evogo Vodoshnabzh ... Voprosy Tekhnologii Obrabotki Vody Promyshlennogo i Pit'evogo Vodosnabzheniya [*A publication*]
Vopr Tekhnol Tovaroved Izdelii Legk Promsti ... Voprosy Tekhnologii i Tovarovedeniya Izdelii Legkoi Promyshlennosti [*A publication*]
Vopr Tekhnol Ulavlivaniya Pererab Prod Koksovaniya ... Voprosy Tekhnologii Ulavlivaniya i Pererabotki Produktov Koksovaniya [*A publication*]
Vopr Tekh Teplofiz ... Voprosy Tekhnicheskoi Teplofiziki [*Ukrainian SSR*] [*A publication*]
Vopr Teor At Stolknovenii ... Voprosy Teorii Atomnykh Stolknovenii [*USSR*] [*A publication*]
Vopr Teorii Metod Ideol Raboty ... Voprosy Teorii i Metodov Ideologiceskoj Raboty [*A publication*]
Vopr Teor Plazmy ... Voprosy Teorii Plazmy [*A publication*]

Vopr Teplofiz Yad Reakt ... Voprosy Teplofiziki Yadernykh Reaktorov [*USSR*] [*A publication*]
Vopr Teploobmena Termodin ... Voprosy Teploobmena i Termodinamiki [*A publication*]
Vopr Termodin Geterogennykh Sist Teor Poverkhn Yavlenii ... Voprosy Termodinamiki Geterogennykh Sistemi Teorii Poverkhnostnykh Yavlenii [*A publication*]
Vopr Tuberk (Riga) ... Voprosy Tuberkuleza (Riga) [*A publication*]
Vopr Urol ... Voprosy Urologii [*A publication*]
Vopr Vet Virusol ... Voprosy Veterinarnoi Virusologii [*A publication*]
Vopr Virusol ... Voprosy Virusologii [*A publication*]
Vopr Vodn Khoz ... Voprosy Vodnogo Khozyaistva [*A publication*]
Vopr Vychisl Mat Tekh (Tashkent) ... Voprosy Vychislitel'noi Matematiki i Tekhniki (Tashkent) [*A publication*]
VOPSA ...... Voprosy Psikhologii [*A publication*]
VOPT .... Voice of the People of Thailand [*Radio station of the Communist Party of Thailand*] (PD)
Vop Virus ... Voprosy Virusologii [*A publication*]
Vop Virusol ... Voprosy Virusologii [*A publication*]
VOQ .... Visiting Officers' Quarters [*Military*]
VOR .... Vehicle off the Road [*British*]
VOR .... Vertical Omnidirectional Radio
VOR .... Very-High-Frequency Omnidirectional Range
VOR .... Vestibulo-Ocular Reflex [*Neurology*]
VOR .... Visual Omnirange [*Directional Beacon*] [*Aviation*] (NG)
VOR .... Voice-Operated Relay
VOR .... Vortex Science Fiction [*A publication*]
VORDAC ... VHF [*Very-High-Frequency*] Omnidirectional Range/Distance-Measuring for Air Coverage
VORDME ... VHF [*Very-High-Frequency*] Omnidirectional Range/Distance-Measuring Equipment (CET)
VOR/DMET ... VHF [*Very-High-Frequency*] Omnidirectional Range/Distance-Measuring Equipment Compatible with TACAN
VOR-FIX ... Vestibuloocular Reflex with Fixation Light [*Ophthalmology*]
VORG .... Ramagundam [*India*] [*ICAO location identifier*] (ICLI)
vorh .... Vorhanden [*In Stock*] [*German*]
VORHDW ... Voegel des Rheinlandes [*A publication*]
VORLA ..... Vestnik Oto-Rino-Laringologii [*A publication*]
Vorlesungen Fachbereich Math Univ Essen ... Vorlesungen aus dem Fachbereich Mathematik. Universitaet Essen [*A publication*]
Vorlesungen Math Inst Giessen ... Vorlesungen. Mathematisches Institut Giessen [*A publication*]
VORLOC .. VHF [*Very-High-Frequency*] Omnirange Localizer (CET)
VORM ...... Ramnad [*India*] [*ICAO location identifier*] (ICLI)
VORM .... Vormittags [*In the Morning*] [*German*]
Voronez Gos Univ Trudy Mat Fak ... Voronezskii Gosudarstvennyi Universitet Imeni Leninskogo Komsomola. Trudy Matematiceskogo Fakul'teta [*A publication*]
Voronez Gos Univ Trudy Naucn Issled Inst Mat VGU ... Voronezskii Ordena Lenina Gosudarstvennyi Universitet Imeni Leninskogo Komsomola. Trudy Naucno-Issledovatel'skogo Instituta Matematiki [*A publication*]
Voronez Gos Univ Trudy Sem Funkcional Anal ... Ministerstvo Vyssego Obrazovanija SSSR Voronezskii Gosudarstvennyi Universitet Trudy Seminara po Funkcional'nomu Analizu [*A publication*]
Voronez Tehn Inst Trudy ... Voronezskii Tehnologiceskii Institut. Trudy [*A publication*]
VORR .... Raichur [*India*] [*ICAO location identifier*] (ICLI)
VORS .... Vestibulo-Ocular Reflex Suppression [*Ophthalmology*]
Vorsokr ...... Fragmente der Vorsokratiker [*A publication*] (OCD)
VORT .... Vorticity (FAAC)
VORTAC ... Variable Omnirange Tactical (NASA)
VORTAC ... VHF [*Very-High-Frequency*] Omnirange TACAN
VORTEX ... Venus Orbiter Radiometric Temperature Experiment [*NASA*]
Vortr Gesamtgeb Bot ... Vortraege aus dem Gesamtgebiet der Botanik [*A publication*]
Vortr Pflanzenz Deut Landwirt Ges Pflanzenzuchtabt ... Vortraege fuer Pflanzenzuchter. Deutsche Landwirtschaftliche Gesellschaft Pflanzenzuchtabteilung [*A publication*]
VORY .... Rajahmundry [*India*] [*ICAO location identifier*] (ICLI)
VOS .... Observation Scout Plane [*Navy symbol*]
VOS .... Vehicle Origin Survey [*R. L. Polk & Co.*] [*Information service or system*] (IID)
VOS .... Vehicle on Stand (MCD)
VOS .... Veterans of Safety (EA)
VOS .... Veterinary Orthopaedic Society (EA)
VOS .... Viking Orbiter System [*NASA*]
VOS .... Virtual Operating System
VOS .... Visicoder Oscillograph System
VOS .... Vision, Left Eye
VOS .... Vitello Ovi Solutus [*Dissolved in the Yolk of an Egg*] [*Pharmacy*] (ROG)
VOS .... Voice-Operated Switch [*or System*]
VOS .... Voluntary Observing Ships [*Marine science*] (MSC)
Vos .... Voskhod (BJA)
VOS .... Vostok [*USSR*] [*Geomagnetic observatory code*]
vos .... Vry op Skip [*Free on Ship*] [*Afrikaans*]
vos .... Vry op Spoor [*Free on Rail*] [*Afrikaans*]
VOSA .... Verbal Orders of the Secretary of the Army

VOSAA ..... Vox Sanguinis [*A publication*]
VOSAF ..... Verbal Orders of the Secretary of the Air Force
VoSanD ...... Voenno-Sanitarnoe Delo [*A publication*]
VOSC .... VAST [*Versatile Avionics Shop Test*] Operating System Code
VOSH .... Volunteer Optometric Services to Humanity/
                   International (EA)
VOSL .... Variable Operating and Safety Level
VOST .... Volatile Organic Sampling Train [*For air analysis*]
V Ost Geschichtsv ... Veroeffentlichungen. Verband Oesterreichischer
                   Geschichts- Vereine [*A publication*]
VOSTGOSTORG ... All-Union Association for Trade with the Countries of
                   the East
Vost Neft .... Vostochnaya Neft [*A publication*]
VOSW .... Very Old Scotch Whisky
VOT .... Valve Opening Time [*Nuclear energy*] (NRCH)
VOT .... Very Old Tawny [*Wines and spirits*]
VOT .... VHF [*Very-High-Frequency*] Omnitest
VOT .... Vision of Tomorrow [*A publication*]
VOT .... Vocational Office Trainee
VOT .... Voice Onset Time
VOT .... Voplex Corp. [*AMEX symbol*] (SPSG)
VOT .... VOR [*Very-High-Frequency Omnidirectional Range*] Test
                   Signal (CET)
VOT .... Vorticity (FAAC)
vot .... Votic [*MARC language code*] [*Library of Congress*] (LCCP)
VOTA .... Vibration Open Test Assembly [*Nuclear energy*] (NRCH)
VOTACT ... Validation of Theoretical Automatic Checkout
                   Techniques (MCD)
VOTAG ..... Verbal Orders of the Adjutant General
VOTC .... Volume Table of Contents [*Data processing*]
VOTCA ..... Victims of Terrorism Compensation Act
VO-TECH ... Vocational-Technical
VOTJ .... Tanjore [*India*] [*ICAO location identifier*] (ICLI)
VOTM .... Vacuum-Operated Throttle Modulator [*Automotive
                   engineering*]
VOTP .... Tirupeti [*India*] [*ICAO location identifier*] (ICLI)
VOTR .... Tiruchchirappalli [*India*] [*ICAO location identifier*] (ICLI)
VOTV .... Trivandrum [*India*] [*ICAO location identifier*] (ICLI)
VOTX .... Tambaram [*India*] [*ICAO location identifier*] (ICLI)
VOTX .... Votrax International, Inc. [*NASDAQ symbol*] (NQ)
VOU .... Voucher (AFM)
VOU .... Vouglans [*France*] [*Seismograph station code, US Geological
                   Survey*] (SEIS)
VOV .... Verband Oeffentlicher Verkehrsbetriebe eV [*Association of
                   Public Transport*] [*Federal Republic of Germany*] (EY)
VOV .... Very Old Version
VOV .... Video Output Voltage
VOVB .... Vikarabad [*India*] [*ICAO location identifier*] (ICLI)
VOVR .... Vellore [*India*] [*ICAO location identifier*] (ICLI)
VOW .... Voice of Women
VOWA .... Warangal [*India*] [*ICAO location identifier*] (ICLI)
VOWR .... St. John's, NF [*AM radio station call letters*]
VOX .... Audiovox Corp. Class A [*AMEX symbol*] (SPSG)
VOX .... Voice-Operated Keying [*Data processing*]
VOX .... Voice-Operated Transmission
VOX .... Voice Output Exchange
VOX POP ... Vox Populi [*Voice of the People*] [*Latin*]
Vox Sang .... Vox Sanguinis [*A publication*]
Vox Sanguin ... Vox Sanguinis [*A publication*]
VoxTh .... Vox Theologica [*Assen*] [*A publication*]
VoxTheol .... Vox Theologica [*Assen*] [*A publication*]
VOY .... Viceroy Resources Corp. [*Toronto Stock Exchange symbol*]
                   [*Vancouver Stock Exchange symbol*]
voy .... Voyage (DS)
VOYA .... Voice of Youth Advocates [*A publication*]
Vozes .... Vozes Revista Catolica de Cultura [*A publication*]
Voz Farm (Lima) ... Voz Farmaceutica (Lima) [*A publication*]
VOZNA ..... Voennye Znaniya [*A publication*]
Vozr .... Vozrozdenie [*A publication*]
VP .... All India Reporter, Vindhya Pradesh [*1951-57*] [*A
                   publication*] (DLA)
VP .... Patrol Plane [*Navy symbol*]
VP .... Patrol Squadron [*Navy symbol*]
VP .... United Kingdom Colonies and Protectorates [*Aircraft
                   nationality and registration mark*] (FAAC)
VP .... Vacant Property (ADA)
VP .... Vacuum Packaged
VP .... Vacuum Pickup
VP .... Vacuum Pump
V & P .... Vagotomy and Pyloroplasty [*Medicine*]
VP .... Validation Plan [*Social Security Administration*]
VP .... Valve Pit (AAG)
VP .... Valve Positioner
VP .... Vanishing Point [*Term in art/drawing*]
VP .... Vanuaaku Pati [*New Hebrides*] [*Political party*] (PD)
VP .... Vanuatu Pati (PD)
VP .... Vapor Pressure
VP .... Variable Pitch [*as, an aircraft propeller*]
VP .... Variable Procedure (AAG)
VP .... Variable Property
VP .... Variant Pinocytic [*Cell*] [*Medicine*]

VP .... Variegate Porphyria [*Medicine*]
VP .... Various Paging [*Bibliography*]
vp .... Various Places [*MARC country of publication code*] [*Library of
                   Congress*] (LCCP)
VP .... Various Publishers [*Bibliography*]
VP .... Vasopressin [*Endocrinology*]
VP .... Vector Processor
VP .... Velocity Pressure
V & P .... Vendor and Purchaser [*Sales*] (ROG)
VP .... Venereal Pamphlet [*Navy*]
VP .... Venous Pressure [*Medicine*]
VP .... Vent-Clearing Pressure [*Nuclear energy*] (NRCH)
VP .... Vent Pipe [*Technical drawings*]
V-P .... Ventilation-Perfusion Scintigraphy
VP .... Ventral Pioneer [*Neuron*]
VP .... Ventral Posterior [*Anatomy*]
VP .... Ventriculoperitoneal [*Medicine*]
VP .... Verb Passive
VP .... Verb Phrase
VP .... Verification Polarization (NASA)
VP .... Verifying Punch (CMD)
VP .... Verstell Propeller (MCD)
VP .... Vertical Planning (NG)
VP .... Vertical Polarization
VP .... Vest Pocket
VP .... Viacao Aerea Sao Paulo, SA [*Brazil*] [*ICAO
                   designator*] (FAAC)
VP .... Vice President
VP .... Vice-Principal [*British*]
VP .... Victorian Poetry [*A publication*]
VP .... Video Processor (NVT)
VP .... Videoplayer
VP .... Vietnam Press
VP .... Viewpoint (NASA)
VP .... Vincristine and Prednisone [*Antineoplastic drug regimen*]
VP .... Vinylphenol [*Biochemistry*]
VP .... Vinylpyrrolidinone [*Organic chemistry*]
VP .... Viral Particle [*Medicine*]
VP .... Viral Protein [*Biochemistry, genetics*]
VP .... Virtual Pitch [*Neurophysiology*]
VP .... Virtual Processor
VP .... Visa Petition
VP .... Visitor's Passport [*British*]
VP .... Vita e Pensiero [*A publication*]
V e P .... Vita e Pensiero [*A publication*]
VP .... Vivre et Penser [*A publication*] (BJA)
VP .... Voce del Passato [*A publication*]
VP .... Voges-Proskauer [*Bacteriology*]
VP .... Void in Part [*Decision or finding held invalid in part for reasons
                   given*] [*Used in Shepard's Citations*] [*Legal term*] (DLA)
VP .... Volkspartie [*People's Party*] [*Liechtenstein*] [*Political
                   party*] (PPE)
VP .... Volkspolizei [*Also, VOPO*]
VP .... Voluntary Patient [*British*]
VP .... Vorposten [*Outpost*] [*German military*]
VP .... Vossa Paternidade [*Yours Paternally*] [*Portuguese*]
V & P .... Votes and Proceedings [*A publication*] (APTA)
VP .... Voting Pool [*Said of disposition of stocks*]
VP .... Vulnerable Period [*Physiology*]
VP .... Vulnerable Point
VP-16-213 ... Vepeside [*Etoposide*] [*Antineoplastic drug*]
VPA .... Valproic Acid [*Anticonvulsant compound*]
VPA .... Vascular Permeability Assay [*Clinical chemistry*]
VPA .... Vehicle Power Adapter
VPA .... Verpackung. Schweizerische Fachzeitschrift fuer Verpackung,
                   Technologie, Package Design, Marketing [*A publication*]
VPA .... Vibration Pickup Amplifier
VPA .... Victorian Planning Appeal Decisions [*A publication*] (APTA)
VPA .... Videotape Production Association (EA)
VPA .... Virtual Population Analysis
VPA .... Visual Packaging Association (EA)
VPA .... Volatile Profile Analysis [*Food chemistry*]
VPA .... Volume Purchase Agreement [*Sales*]
VPA .... Vote Profile Analysis
VPAM .... Virtual Partitioned Access Method
VPAP .... Voluntary Petroleum Allocation Program [*Presidential*]
VPARD ...... Veterinary Parasitology [*A publication*]
VPB .... Medium and Heavy Patrol Bomber Squadron [*Land based and
                   seaplane*] [*Navy symbol*]
VPB .... Patrol-Bombing Plane [*Navy symbol*]
VPB .... Vendors per Block [*Sales*]
VPB .... Ventricular Premature Beat [*Cardiology*]
VPB .... Vertical Plot Board [*Navy*]
VPB .... Vinblastine, Platinol [*Cisplatin*], Bleomycin [*Antineoplastic
                   drug regimen*]
VPBA .... Varipolarization Beacon Antenna
VPBA .... Virginia Poultry Breeders Association (EA)
VPBC .... Virginia Poultry Breeders Club [*Later, VPBA*] (EA)
VPB(HL) ... Patrol Bomber, Four-Engine, Landplane [*Navy symbol*]
VPB(HS) ... Patrol Bomber, Four-Engine, Seaplane [*Navy symbol*]
VPB(ML) .. Patrol Bomber, Two-Engine, Landplane [*Navy symbol*]

VPB(MS)... Patrol Bomber, Two-Engine, Seaplane [*Navy symbol*]
VPC .... La Vente par Correspondance [*Mail Order*] [*Business term*]
          [*French*]
VPC .... Vacuum Pump Chamber
VPC .... Vapor Permeation Curing [*Plastics technology*]
VPC .... Vapor-Phase Chromatography
VPC .... Variable Padder Capacitor
VPC .... Ventricular Premature Contraction [*Cardiology*]
VPC .... Verpackungsberater [*A publication*]
VPC .... Veterinary Products Committee [*British*]
VPC .... Video Processor Control   (MCD)
VPC .... Visual Punch Card
VPC .... Voltage Phasing Control   (DEN)
VPC .... Voltage to Pulse Converter
VPC .... Volume Packed Cells
VPC .... Volume-Pulse-Charge
VPC .... Volunteer Program Consultant [*Red Cross*]
VPC .... Volunteers for Peaceful Change   (EA)
VPC .... Vulval Precursor Cell [*Genetics*]
VPCA........ Video Prelaunch Command Amplifier
VPCDS...... Video Prelaunch Command Data System [*Air Force*]
VPCE........ Vapor Phase Catalytic Exchange   (MCD)
VPCMF ..... Vincristine, Prednisone, Cyclophosphamide, Methotrexate,
          Fluorouracil [*Antineoplastic drug regimen*]
VPCPr ...... Vincristine, Prednisone, Vinblastine, Chlorambucil,
          Procarbazine [*Antineoplastic drug regimen*]
VPD .... Vapor-Phase Deacidification [*of books and documents*]
VPD .... Vapor Pressure Deficit [*Meteorology*]
VPD .... Variation per Day [*Navigation*]
VPD .... Vehicle Performance Data
VPD .... Vehicles per Day [*Military*]   (AFM)
VPD .... Ventricular Premature Depolarization [*Cardiology*]
VPD .... Vertically Polarized Dipole   (MCD)
VPD .... Victorian Parliamentary Debates [*A publication*]
VPD .... Vierte Partei Deutschlands [*Fourth Party of Germany*] [*Federal
          Republic of Germany*] [*Political party*]   (PPW)
VPD .... Villa Park Dam [*California*] [*Seismograph station code, US
          Geological Survey*]   (SEIS)
VPD .... Vremennik Puskinskogo Doma [*A publication*]
VPDF........ Vacuum Pump Discharge Filter
VPE.......... Vapor-Phase Epitaxy
VPE.......... Vehicle Positioning Equipment   (MCD)
VPE........ Video Processing Equipment
VPen .... Vita e Pensiero [*A publication*]
VPF.......... Vacuum Pump Filter
VPF.......... Variable Parts Feeder
VPF.......... Variable Phase Filter
VPF.......... Vascular-Permeability Factor [*Medicine*]
VPF.......... Vertical Processing Facility [*NASA*]   (MCD)
VPF.......... Vibratory Pan Feeder
VPF.......... Viscoplastic Flow
VPFAS...... Vice President of the Faculty of Architects and Surveyors
          [*British*]   (DBQ)
VPFG........ Variable Phase Function Generator
VPG .... Variable-Rate Pulse Generator
VPGS........ Venous Pressure Gradient Support Stocking
VPGS........ Vice-President of the Geological Society [*British*]
VPH.......... Variation per Hour [*Navigation*]
VPH.......... Vehicles per Hour [*Traffic*]   (AFM)
VPH.......... Veterans of Pearl Harbor   (EA)
VPH.......... Volkspolizeihelfer
VPHD........ Vertical Payload Handling Device [*NASA*]   (MCD)
VPI.......... Vacuum Pressure Impregnation   (IEEE)
VPI.......... Valve Position Indicator   (KSC)
VPI.......... Vapor-Phase Inhibitor [*See also VCI*] [*Chemical technology*]
VPI.......... Vendor Parts Index [*Sales*]
VPI.......... Vertical Point of Intersection [*Transportation*]
VPI.......... Vessel Patentcy Index [*Medicine*]
VPI.......... Vintage Petroleum [*NYSE symbol*]   (SPSG)
VPI.......... VIP Dynasty International Marketing Corp. [*Vancouver Stock
          Exchange symbol*]
VPI.......... Virginia Polytechnic Institute and State University [*Blacksburg*]
VPI.......... Virginia Polytechnic Institute and State University, Blacksburg,
          VA [*OCLC symbol*]   (OCLC)
VPI.......... Vocational Preference Inventory [*Psychology*]
VPII.......... Vita Plus Industries, Incorporated [*NASDAQ symbol*]   (NQ)
VPIMD...... Vilniaus Pedagoginio Instituto Mokslo Darbai [*A publication*]
VPITA ...... Voprosy Pitaniya [*A publication*]
VPJT .... Vertical Power Jump Test
VPK .... Valley Airpark, Inc. [*Fort Collins, CO*] [*FAA
          designator*]   (FAAC)
VPK .... Vehicle per Kilometer   (AABC)
VPK .... Verdi Peak [*California*] [*Seismograph station code, US
          Geological Survey*]   (SEIS)
VPK .... Vest Pocket Kodak [*Camera*]
VPK .... Volts Peak   (NASA)
VPKA........ Volkspolizeikreisamt
VP(L)........ US Navy Patrol Squadron (Land)   (CINC)
VPL.......... Variable Pulse LASER
VPL........... Vendor Parts List   (AAG)
VPL........... Ventral Posterolateral [*Anatomy*]

VPL............ Virginia Beach Public Library System, Virginia Beach, VA
          [*OCLC symbol*]   (OCLC)
VPL............ Visible Panty Line [*In reference to clothing*]
VPL............ Volunteer Prison League [*Defunct*]   (EA)
VPL............ Vulcano Piano [*Lipari Islands*] [*Seismograph station code, US
          Geological Survey*]   (SEIS)
VPLCC...... Vehicle Propellant Loading Control Center
VPLEA...... Victorian Public Librarians Expo Association [*Australia*]
VPLS .... Vice-President of the Linnaean Society [*British*]
VPLX........ Videoplex, Inc. [*Somerset, NJ*] [*NASDAQ symbol*]   (NQ)
VPM .... Vacuum Pumping Module
VPM .... Variation per Minute [*Navigation*]
VPM .... Vascular Permeability Mediator [*Hematology*]
VPM .... Vehicle Project Manager [*NASA*]   (NASA)
VPM .... Vehicles per Mile
VPM .... Velocity Preset Module   (MCD)
VPM .... Vendor Part Modification   (AAG)
VPM .... Versatile Packaging Machine
VPM .... Vertical Panel Mount
VPM .... Vertical Polarization Mode
VPM .... Vibrations per Minute
VPM .... Voix du Peuple Murundi [*Voice of the Murundi People*]
VPM .... Volts per Meter [*Also, V/m*]
VPM .... Volts per Mil
VPM .... Volumes per Million [*Measure of gas contamination*]
VPMA ...... Vegetable Parchment Manufacturers Association [*Later,
          API*]   (EA)
VPMLL ..... Valstybine Politines ir Mokslines Literatu [*A publication*]
VPMOS..... Verified Primary Military Occupational Specialty
VPMR ...... Vanguard Party of the Malagasy Revolution
VPMS....... Virchow-Pirquet Medical Society   (EA)
VPN .... Vendor Parts Number
VPN .... Vickers Pyramid Number [*Hardness test*]
VPN .... Victorian Periodicals Newsletter [*A publication*]
VPN .... Virtual Page Number
VPN .... Virtual Private Network [*US Sprint Communications Co.*]
          [*Atlanta, GA*]   (TSSD)
VPN .... Vopnafjordur [*Iceland*] [*Airport symbol*]   (OAG)
VPNL........ Variable Pulse Neodymium LASER
VPO .... Vapor Phase Oxidation [*Chemical processing*]
VPO .... Vapor Pressure Osmometer [*or Osmometry*] [*Analytical
          chemistry*]
VPO .... Vienna Philharmonic Orchestra
VPO .... Viking Project Office [*NASA*]   (KSC)
VPOF........ Vacuum-Processed Oxide Free
VPP .... Vacuum Pickup Pencil
VPP........... Value Payable by Post
VPP........... Variable Pitch Propeller
VPP........... Vegetable Protein Products [*Food technology*]
VPP........... Velocity per Performance
VPP........... Vertical Pinpoint   (AFM)
VPP........... Vertical Pouch Packager
VPP........... Very Public Person
VPP........... Viral Porcine Pneumonia [*Veterinary medicine*]
VPP........... Viscous Plastic Processing [*Materials science and technology*]
V P-P....... Volt Peak-to-Peak   (NASA)
VPP........... Voluntary Projects Programme [*British*]
VPP........... Voluntary Protection Program [*OSHA*]
VPP........... Volunteer Political Party [*Northern Ireland*]
VPPB........ Vendor Provisioning Parts Breakdown   (AAG)
VPPD....... Vice Presidential Protective Division [*US Secret Service*]
VPPS .... Vehicle Parking Protection Services [*British*]
VPR .... Valveless Pulse Rocket
VPR .... Vaporize   (MSA)
VPR .... Variable Parameter Regression [*Statistics*]
VPR .... Ventricle Pressure Response [*Cardiology*]
VPR .... Verpackungs-Rundschau [*A publication*]
VPR .... Virtual PPI [*Plan-Position Indicator*] Reflectoscope [*RADAR*]
VPR .... Vital Pacific Resources Ltd. [*Vancouver Stock Exchange
          symbol*]
VPR .... Voluntary Price Reduction   (AABC)
VPRC....... Volume of Packed Red Cells [*Hematology*]
VPRES...... Vice-President
VPRF....... Variable Pulse Repetition Frequency   (IEEE)
VPRGS...... Vice-President of the Royal Geographical Society [*British*]
VPRI......... Vice-President of the Royal Institute [*British*]
VPR-NMP ... Virtual PPI [*Plan-Position Indicator*] Reflectoscope with
          Navigational Microfilm Projector [*RADAR*]
VPRON..... US Navy Patrol Squadron   (CINC)
VPRS........ Vice-President of the Royal Society [*British*]
VPRT........ Vector Pressure Ratio Transducer
VPS........... Fort Walton Beach [*Florida*] [*Airport symbol*]   (OAG)
VP(S)....... US Navy Patrol Squadron (Sea-Based)   (CINC)
VPS........... Vacuum Pickup System
VPS........... Vacuum Pipe Still [*Chemical engineering*]
VPS........... Vacuum Pump System
VPS........... Valparaiso, FL [*Location identifier*] [*FAA*]   (FAAL)
VPS........... Vanguard Planning Summary [*Air Force*]
VPS........... Variable Parameter System
VPS........... Variable Power Supply   (MCD)
VPS........... Vatican Philatelic Society   (EA)

VPS........... Vernier Propulsion System [*Aerospace*]
VPS........... Versatile Pacific Shipyards [*Shipbuilder*] [*Vancouver, Canada*]
VPS........... Vibrations per Second
VPS........... Vibrator Power Supply
VPS........... Video-Pac Systems Ltd. [*Hollywood, CA*] [*Telecommunications service*]   (TSSD)
VPS........... Vinylpolysilane [*Organic chemistry*]
VPS........... Visitor Program Service of Meridian House International   (EA)
VPS........... Visual Programs Systems
VPS........... Voice Processing System [*Data processing*]   (IT)
VPS........... Volcan Poas [*Costa Rica*] [*Seismograph station code, US Geological Survey*]   (SEIS)
VPS........... Voluntary Product Standard [*National Bureau of Standards*]
VPSA........ Vice-President of the Society of Antiquaries [*British*]
VPSB........ Veterans Placement Service Board [*Post-World War II*]
VPSS........ Vector Processing Subsystem
VPSW........ Virtual Program Status Word
VPT........... Patrol Torpedo Plane [*Navy symbol*]
VPT........... Ventral Posterior Thalamic [*Electrode for stimulation*]
VPT........... Vibratron Pressure Transducer
VPT........... Video Pulse Termination
VPT........... Voice plus Telegraph [*Telecommunications*]   (TEL)
VPT........... Volume-Price Trend [*Finance*]
VPTAR....... Variable Parameter Terrain-Avoidance RADAR
VPTRM..... Viscous Partial Thermoremanent Magnetization [*Geophysics*]
VPU........... Pace University Library, Union List of Serials, New York, NY [*OCLC symbol*]   (OCLC)
VPU........... Vacuum Penetration Unit
VPU........... Vibrator Power Unit   (MSA)
VPUA........ Vibration Pickup Amplifier
VPUG........ Ventura Publisher User's Group   (EA)
VPVCPr..... Vincristine, Prednisone, Vinblastine, Chlorambucil, Procarbazine [*Antineoplastic drug regimen*]
VPVLBZ.... Scientific Works. Forest Research Institute in Zvolen [*A publication*]
VPVMA3... Vedecke Prace Vyzkumneho Ustavu Melioraci v Praze [*A publication*]
VPVMA3... Vedecke Prace Vyzkumneho Ustavu Melioraci v Zbraslavi [*A publication*]
VPVZB9.... Scientific Works. Research Institute of Animal Production at Nitra [*A publication*]
VPW......... Ventral Prostate Weight [*Medicine*]
VPW......... Vertically Polarized Wave
VPW......... Vorarbeiten zum Pommerschen Woerterbuch [*A publication*]
VPX.......... Pineville, WV [*Location identifier*] [*FAA*]   (FAAL)
VPY.......... Vinylpyridine [*Organic chemistry*]
VPZ........... Valparaiso [*Indiana*] [*Airport symbol*]   (OAG)
VPZ........... Valparaiso, IN [*Location identifier*] [*FAA*]   (FAAL)
VPZ........... Virtual Processing Zero
VPZS........ Vice-President of the Zoological Society [*British*]
VQ............. Aermediterranea Linee Aeree Mediterranee SpA [*Italy*] [*ICAO designator*]   (FAAC)
VQ............. Fleet Air Reconnaissance Squadron [*Navy symbol*]   (CINC)
VQ............. United Kingdom Colonies and Protectorates [*Aircraft nationality and registration mark*]   (FAAC)
V/Q........... Ventilation/Perfusion [*Quotient*] [*Medicine*]
VQ............. Vermont Quarterly [*A publication*]
VQ............. Very Quick [*Flashing*] Light [*Navigation signal*]
VQ............. Virtual Quantum
VQ............. Visvabharati Quarterly [*A publication*]
VQ............. Voluntary Quit [*Unemployment insurance*] [*Bureau of Labor Statistics*]   (OICC)
VQA.......... Al Sigl Center Library, Rochester, NY [*OCLC symbol*]   (OCLC)
VQA.......... Vendor Quality Assurance
VQAR....... Vendor Quality Assurance Representative [*Nuclear energy*]   (NRCH)
VQB.......... Bausch & Lomb, Inc., Library, Rochester, NY [*OCLC symbol*]   (OCLC)
VQC.......... Canandaigua Veterans Administration Medical Center Library, Canandaigua, NY [*OCLC symbol*]   (OCLC)
VQC.......... Variable Quartz Capacitor
VQC.......... Vendor Quality Certification
VQD.......... Center for Governmental Research Library, Rochester, NY [*OCLC symbol*]   (OCLC)
VQD.......... Vendor Quality Defect
VQE.......... Colgate-Rochester Divinity School, Library, Rochester, NY [*OCLC symbol*]   (OCLC)
VQE.......... San Antonio, TX [*Location identifier*] [*FAA*]   (FAAL)
VQF.......... Convalescent Hospital for Children, Library, Rochester, NY [*OCLC symbol*]   (OCLC)
VQG.......... Eastman Dental Center, Basil G. Bibby Library, Rochester, NY [*OCLC symbol*]   (OCLC)
VQH......... Eastman Kodak Co., KAD Library, Rochester, NY [*OCLC symbol*]   (OCLC)
VQI........... Eastman Kodak Co., Business Library, Rochester, NY [*OCLC symbol*]   (OCLC)
VQJ.......... Eastman Kodak Co., Engineering Division, Library, Rochester, NY [*OCLC symbol*]   (OCLC)
VQK.......... Eastman Kodak Co., Health and Safety Laboratory, Library, Rochester, NY [*OCLC symbol*]   (OCLC)
V Qk Fl...... Very-Quick Flashing Light

VQL........... Eastman Kodak Co., Photographic Technology Library, Rochester, NY [*OCLC symbol*]   (OCLC)
VQL........... Variable Quantization Level [*Algorithm developed by Aydin Monitor Corp.*] [*Telecommunications*]
VQM......... Detroit, MI [*Location identifier*] [*FAA*]   (FAAL)
VQM......... Eastman Kodak Co., Research Laboratories, Library, Rochester, NY [*OCLC symbol*]   (OCLC) .
VQMG....... Vice-Quartermaster-General
VQN.......... General Railway Signal Co., Library, Rochester, NY [*OCLC symbol*]   (OCLC)
VQO .... Genesee Hospital, Stabins Health Science Library, Rochester, NY [*OCLC symbol*]   (OCLC)
VQO .... Provincetown, MA [*Location identifier*] [*FAA*]   (FAAL)
VQOL........ Victorian Quality of Life [*Survey*] [*Australia*]
VQP.......... Highland Hospital, Williams Health Science Library, Rochester, NY [*OCLC symbol*]   (OCLC)
VQQ......... Mixing Equipment Co., Library, Rochester, NY [*OCLC symbol*]   (OCLC)
VQR.......... Virginia Quarterly Review [*A publication*]
VQS .... Isla De Vieques, PR [*Location identifier*] [*FAA*]   (FAAL)
VQS .... Mobil Chemical Co., Plastics Division, Research Library, Macedon, NY [*OCLC symbol*]   (OCLC)
VQS .... Valve Qualification Study
VQS .... Vieques [*Puerto Rico*] [*Airport symbol*]   (OAG)
VQS .... Vieques [*Puerto Rico*] [*Later, SJG*] [*Geomagnetic observatory code*]
VQS .... Vieques [*Puerto Rico*] [*Seismograph station code, US Geological Survey*] [*Closed*]   (SEIS)
VQT.......... Monroe Community College, L. V. Good Library, Rochester, NY [*OCLC symbol*]   (OCLC)
VQT.......... Viewers for Quality Television   (EA)
VQU.......... Monroe Community Hospital, Medical-Nursing Library, Rochester, NY [*OCLC symbol*]   (OCLC)
VQV.......... Monroe County Department of Health, Library, Rochester, NY [*OCLC symbol*]   (OCLC)
VQV.......... Vacaville, CA [*Location identifier*] [*FAA*]   (FAAL)
VQW......... Monroe Development Center, Library, Rochester, NY [*OCLC symbol*]   (OCLC)
VQX.......... Park Ridge Hospital, Medical Library, Rochester, NY [*OCLC symbol*]   (OCLC)
VQY.......... Pennwalt Corp., Pharmaceutical Division, Library, Rochester, NY [*OCLC symbol*]   (OCLC)
VQZ.......... R. T. French Co., Library, Rochester, NY [*OCLC symbol*]   (OCLC)
VQZD....... Vendor Quality Zero Defects
VR............. Fleet Tactical Support [*Navy symbol*]   (NVT)
VR............. Transport Plane [*Multiengine*] [*Navy symbol*]
VR............. Transport Squadron [*Navy symbol*]
VR............. Transportes Aereos de Cabo Verde [*Portugal*] [*ICAO designator*]   (FAAC)
VR............. United Kingdom Colonies and Protectorates [*Aircraft nationality and registration mark*]   (FAAC)
VR............. Vagabonds Removed [*Prison van nickname used during reign of VR, Victoria Regina*] [*British*]   (DSUE)
V of R .... Vale of Rheidol Light Railway [*Wales*]
VR............. Vale of Rheidol Light Railway [*Wales*]
VR............. Validation and Recovery
VR............. Validation Report [*Army*]
VR............. Valley Resources, Inc. [*AMEX symbol*]   (SPSG)
VR............. Valtionrautatiet [*Finnish State Railways*]
VR............. Valuation Reports, Interstate Commerce Commission [*A publication*]   (DLA)
VR............. Valve Replacement [*Cardiology*]
VR............. Vanguardia Revolucionaria [*Revolutionary Vanguard*] [*Peru*] [*Political party*]   (PPW)
VR............. Variable Ratio [*Reinforcement*]
VR............. Variable Reluctance
VR............. Variant Reading
VR............. Veer [*Aviation*]   (FAAC)
VR............. Vehicle Recovery
VR............. Velocity, Relative   (MCD)
VR............. Vendor Rating [*Sales*]
VR............. Venous Return [*Medicine*]
VR............. Ventilation Rate
VR............. Ventral Root [*of a spinal nerve*] [*Anatomy*]
VR............. Ventricular Rate [*Cardiology*]
VR............. Verb Reflexive
VR............. Verification Receiver
V/R........... Verkoopsrekening [*Account Sales*] [*Business term*] [*Afrikaans*]
V-R............ VERLORT [*Very-Long-Range Tracking*] Range [*NASA*]
VR............. Vermont Reports [*A publication*]   (DLA)
VR............. Vertical Resistance
VR............. Vertical Retort
VR............. Very Respectfully [*Letter closing*]
VR............. Vested Right
VR............. Veterinary and Remount Service [*British military*]
VR............. VFR [*Visual Flight Rules*] Military Training Routes [*Aviation*]   (FAAC)
VR............. Viata Romaneasca [*Bucharest*] [*A publication*]
V-R............ Vibrational-Rotational [*Chemical kinetics*]
VR............. Vicar Rural

VR............ Victoria Regina [*Queen Victoria*]
VR............ Victorian Reports [*A publication*]   (APTA)
VR............ Video Recorder   (NASA)
VR............ Viera i Razum [*A publication*]
VR............ Villanova Law Review [*A publication*]
VR............ Virtual Route [*Data processing*]
VR............ Viscous Response [*Medicine*]
VR............ Vision, Right Eye
VR............ Visit Request   (AAG)
VR............ Visor
VR............ Visual Reconnaissance
VR............ Visual Resources [*A publication*]
VR............ Vital Records [*Genealogy*]
VR............ Vocal Resonance
VR............ Vocational Rehabilitation
VR............ Voice of Reason [*Later, Americans for Religious Liberty*]   (EA)
VR............ Volja Rossii [*A publication*]
VR............ Voltage Reference   (DEN)
VR............ Voltage Regulator
VR............ Voltage Relay
VR............ Voltage Repair
VR............ Volume Reduction [*Nuclear energy*]   (NRCH)
VR............ Voluntary Returnees [*Immigration Service*]
VR............ Volunteer Regiment [*British military*]   (DMA)
VR............ Volunteer Reserve   (BJA)
VR............ Vox Reformata: Australasian Journal for Christian Scholarship [*A publication*]   (APTA)
VR............ Vox Romanica [*A publication*]
VR............ Voyage Repairs [*Navy*]   (NVT)
Vr .... Vroom's Law Reports [*30-85 New Jersey*] [*A publication*]   (DLA)
VR............ Vulcanized Rubber
VR............ Vulnerability Reduction [*Military*]   (RDA)
VR............ Webb, A'Beckett, and Williams' Victorian Reports [*1870-72*] [*Australia*] [*A publication*]   (DLA)
VRA .... Radford College, Radford, VA [*OCLC symbol*]   (OCLC)
VRA .... Rough-Air [*or Turbulence*] Speed [*Aviation*]
VRA .... Varadero [*Cuba*] [*Airport symbol*]   (OAG)
VRA .... Vertical Reference Attitude
VRA .... Vertical Rising Aircraft
VRA .... Veterans Readjustment Appointment
VRA .... [*The*] Victorian Railways of Australia   (DCTA)
VRA .... Viking RADAR Altimeter [*NASA*]
VRA .... Vocational Rehabilitation Act [*1973*]
VRA .... Vocational Rehabilitation Administration [*Later, Social and Rehabilitation Service*] [*HEW*]
VRA .... Vocational Rehabilitation Association
VRA .... Voltage Reference Amplifier
VRA .... Voltage Regulator Alarm
VRA .... Voluntary Restraint Arrangement [*Import quotas*]
VRA .... Voluntary Restriction Agreement [*Pact between the US and Japan on automotive imports*]
VRA .... Voting Rights Act [*1965, 1970, 1975*]
VRA .... Vraag en Aanbod voor Techniek, Nijverheid, Bouwvak, en Handel [*A publication*]
Vrach Delo ... Vrachebnoe Delo [*A publication*]
Vrach Gaz ... Vrachebnaia Gazeta [*A publication*]
VRAD........ Vertically Referenced Attitude Display
VR (Adm)... Victorian Reports (Admiralty) [*A publication*]   (DLA)
VRAH....... Vertical Receiving Array Hydrophone
VRAM ...... Variable Random Access Memory [*Data processing*]
VRAM ...... Variable Rate Adaptive Multiplexing [*Telecommunications*]   (TEL)
VRAM ...... Video Random Access Memory
VRAM ...... Virtual Random Access Memory [*Data processing*]
VRARA...... Voprosy Radiobiologii. Sbornik Trudov [*A publication*]
Vrashchenie i Prilivnye Deform Zemli ... Vrashchenie i Prilivnye Deformatsii Zemli [*A publication*]
VRASS ...... Voice Recognition and Synthesis System [*Aviation*] [*Navy*]
VRB .... Variable
VRB .... Variable Reenlistment Bonus [*Military*]   (AABC)
VRB .... Vehicle Retaining Board
VRB .... Vero Beach [*Florida*] [*Airport symbol*]   (OAG)
VRB .... Vero Beach, FL [*Location identifier*] [*FAA*]   (FAAL)
VRB .... Verordeningenblad Bedrijfsorganisatie [*A publication*]
VRB .... Veterans' Review Board [*Australia*]
VRB .... VHF [*Very-High-Frequency*] Recovery Beacon [*NASA*]   (KSC)
VRB .... Violet Red Bile [*Microorganism growth medium*]
VRB .... Voice Rotating Beacon
VRB .... Volunteer Reenlistment Bonus
VRBA ...... Violet Red Bile Agar [*Microorganism growth medium*]
VRBB........ VR Business Brokers, Inc. [*Boston, MA*] [*NASDAQ symbol*]   (NQ)
VRBG ...... Viceroy's Bodyguard [*British military*]   (DMA)
VRBL........ Variable   (FAAC)
VRBM ...... Variable Range Ballistic Missile [*DoD*]   (MCD)
VRC .... Fleet Tactical Support Squadron Carrier [*Navy symbol*]   (CINC)
VRC .... Vampire Research Center   (EA)
VRC .... Varco International, Inc. [*NYSE symbol*]   (SPSG)
VRC .... Variable Reluctance Cartridge

VRC .... Vehicle Research Corporation
VRC .... Vertical Redundancy Check [*Telecommunications*]   (BUR)
VRC .... Vibrating Reed Capacitor
VRC .... Victoria Rifles of Canada   (DMA)
VRC .... Virac [*Philippines*] [*Airport symbol*]   (OAG)
VRC .... Virginia Commonwealth University, Richmond, VA [*OCLC symbol*]   (OCLC)
VRC .... Virtual Redundancy Check [*Data processing*]
VRC .... Viscometer Recorder-Controller
VRC .... Visual Record Computer
VR & C....... Vocational Rehabilitation and Counseling Service [*Veterans Administration*]
VRC .... Volunteer Rifle Corps [*Military*] [*British*]   (ROG)
VRCA .... Voice Recording Assembly [*Ground Communications Facility, NASA*]
VRCAMS .. Vehicle-Road Compatibility Analysis and Modification System   (RDA)
VRCCC...... Vandenberg Range Communications Control Center [*Air Force*]   (MCD)
VRCI......... Variable Resistive Components Institute   (EA)
VRCODX .. Veterinary Research Communications [*A publication*]
VRCS........ Vernier [*Engine*] Reaction Control System [*Aerospace*]   (NASA)
VRCS........ Veterinary and Remount Conducting Section [*British military*]   (DMA)
VRCTR .... Varactor   (MSA)
VRD.......... Vacuum-Tube Relay Driver
VRD.......... Vehicle Reception Depot [*British military*]   (DMA)
VRD.......... Victoria River Downs [*Australia*]
VRD.......... Voltage Regulating Diode
VRD.......... Volunteer Reserve Decoration [*British*]
VRDDO...... Variable Retention of Diatomic Differential [*Physics*]
VRDEA ...... Vrachebnoe Delo [*A publication*]
VRDS........ Vacuum Residuum Desulfurization [*Petroleum refining*]
VRDV .... Vacuum Retard Delay Valve [*Automotive engineering*]
VRDX .... Verdix Corp. [*NASDAQ symbol*]   (NQ)
VRE .... Venezuelan Economic Review [*A publication*]
VRE .... Vermont Research Corp. [*AMEX symbol*]   (SPSG)
VRE .... Vibrating Reed Electrometer
VR (F) .... Victorian Reports (Equity) [*A publication*]   (APTA)
VRE .... Voltage Regulator-Exciter
VR (E)........ Webb, A'Beckett, and Williams' Victorian Equity Reports [*1870-72*] [*Australia*] [*A publication*]   (DLA)
Vrednaya Polezn Fauna Bespozvon Mold ... Vrednaya i Poleznaya Fauna Bespozvonochnykh Moldavii [*A publication*]
V/REG....... Voltage Regulator [*Automotive engineering*]
Vremennik Gl Palaty Mer Vesov ... Vremennik Glavnoi Palaty Mer i Vesov [*A publication*]
VREO .... Vanguard Real Estate Fund I [*NASDAQ symbol*]   (NQ)
VR (Eq)...... Victorian Reports (Equity) [*A publication*]
VRES......... VICORP Restaurants, Inc. [*NASDAQ symbol*]   (NQ)
VREST ...... Vacuum Restrictor [*Automotive engineering*]
V Rev.......... Very Reverend
VRF.......... Ferry Squadron [*Navy symbol*]   (NVT)
VRF.......... Vascular Research Foundation
VRF.......... Versatile Repair Facility
VRF.......... Vertical Removal Fixture   (NASA)
VRF.......... Vietnam Refugee Fund   (EA)
VRF.......... Visual Recording Facility   (MCD)
VRFI......... Voice Reporting Fault Indicator
VRFWS .... Vehicle Rapid Fire Weapon System [*Army*]
VRFWSS.... Vehicle Rapid-Fire Weapons System Successor   (IEEE)
VRFY .... Verify   (MSA)
VRG .... Vegetarian Resource Group   (EA)
VRG .... Visual Reference Gate [*Aviation*]   (FAAC)
VRG .... Vocationally Related Annual Goal
VRGC........ Voucher Register and General Control [*Military*]   (AABC)
VRGN........ Gan [*Maldives*] [*ICAO location identifier*]   (ICLI)
VRGN........ Viragen, Inc. [*NASDAQ symbol*]   (NQ)
VRH.......... Var-Hour Meter [*Electricity*]
VRH.......... Vertical Receiving Hydrophone
VR(HL)..... Transport, Four-Engine, Landplane [*Navy symbol*]
VRHMU.... Visor Rectical Helmet Mounted Unit [*Navy*]   (MCD)
VR(HS)..... Transport, Four-Engine, Seaplane [*Navy symbol*]
VRHU........ Hanimaadhoo [*Maldives*] [*ICAO location identifier*]   (ICLI)
VRI .... Varistor [*Telecommunications*]   (TEL)
VRI .... Varitech Investors Corp. [*Toronto Stock Exchange symbol*]
VRI .... Vehicle Research Institute [*Society of Automotive Engineers*]
VRI .... Verbal Response Inventory
VRI .... Veterans Reopened Insurance
VRI .... Victoria Regina et Imperatrix [*Victoria, Queen and Empress*]
VR et I...... Victoria Regina et Imperatrix [*Victoria, Queen and Empress*]
VRI .... Viral Respiratory Infection [*Medicine*]
VRI .... Visual Rule Instrument Landing   (AAG)
VRI .... Vrincioaia [*Romania*] [*Seismograph station code, US Geological Survey*]   (SEIS)
VRI .... Vulcanized Rubber Installation
VR (IE & M) ... Victorian Reports (Insolvency, Ecclesiastical, and Matrimonial) [*A publication*]   (APTA)
VRIFS........ Vector Recurrent Iterated Function System [*Iterated Systems, Inc.*] [*Digital imaging*]

Vrije Univ Brussel Inter-Univ Inst High Energ Rep ... Vrije Universiteit Brussel. Inter-University Institute for High Energies. Report [*A publication*]
VRIL......... Vendor Repairable Items List
VRIS......... Varistor [*Electronics*]
VRIS......... Vietnam Refugee and Information Services
VRISL...... Vancouver Island, BC, Canada   (FAAC)
VRJa......... Voprosy Russkogo Jazykoznanija [*A publication*]
VRK .... Varkaus [*Finland*] [*Airport symbol*]   (OAG)
VRK .... Video Recorder Kit
VRK .... Viral Respiratory Kit [*Medicine*]
VRKD .... Kadhdhoo [*Maldives*] [*ICAO location identifier*]   (ICLI)
VRL .... Validation Reject Listing   (MCD)
VRL .... Vanterra Resources Limited [*Vancouver Stock Exchange symbol*]
VRL .... Vertical Recovery Line [*NASA*]   (NASA)
VRL .... Vertical Reference Line [*Technical drawings*]
VRL .... Veterinary Research Laboratory [*Montana State University*] [*Research center*]
VRL .... Vibration Research Laboratory [*Stanford University*]   (MCD)
VR (L)....... Victorian Reports (Law) [*A publication*]   (APTA)
VRL .... Vila Real [*Portugal*] [*Airport symbol*]   (OAG)
VRL .... Virus Reference Laboratory
VRL .... Voprosy Russkoi Literatury. Respublikanskii Mezhvedomstvennyi Nauchnyi Sbornik [*A publication*]
VR (Law) ... Victorian Law Reports (Law) [*A publication*]
VRLN .... Varlen Corp. [*NASDAQ symbol*]   (NQ)
VRLTRY ... Vale of Rheidol Light Railway [*Wales*]
VRLY......... Voltage Relay
VRM .... Randolph-Macon College, Ashland, VA [*OCLC symbol*]   (OCLC)
VRM .... Van Riebeeck Medal [*British military*]   (DMA)
VRM .... Variable Range Marker [*RADAR technology*]
VRM .... Variable-Rate Mortgage [*Real estate*]
VRM .... Variable Reluctance Microphone
VRM .... Vendor Receiving Memorandum [*Sales*]
VRM .... Venus RADAR Mapper [*Planetary exploration*]
VRM .... Vermiculite [*Technical drawings*]
VRM .... Viscous Remanant Magnetization
VRM .... Voice Recognition Module [*Data processing*]
VRM .... Voltage Regulator Module
VRM .... Volumetric Redox Measurement [*Analytical chemistry*]
VR(ML)...... Transport, Two-Engine, Landplane [*Navy symbol*]
VRMM ...... Male/International [*Maldives*] [*ICAO location identifier*]   (ICLI)
VR(MS)..... Transport, Two-Engine, Seaplane [*Navy symbol*]
VRMS....... Voltage Root Mean Square
VRN .... Vernier [*Engine*]   (AAG)
VRN .... Vernitron Corp. [*AMEX symbol*]   (SPSG)
VRN .... Verona [*Italy*] [*Airport symbol*]   (OAG)
VRN .... Vessel Radiated Noise
VR Newsletter ... Victorian Railways Newsletter [*A publication*]   (APTA)
VRNF .... Von Recklinghausen Neurofibromatosis [*Medicine*]
VRNR .... Vernier [*Engine*]   (NASA)
VRO .... Roanoke College, Salem, VA [*OCLC symbol*]   (OCLC)
VRO .... Variable Ratio Oiling
VRO .... Varo, Inc. [*NYSE symbol*]   (SPSG)
VRO .... Verified Record Output [*Data processing*]
VRO .... Veterinary Research Officer [*British*]
VRo .... Viata Romaneasca [*A publication*]
VROA .... Verslagen Omtrent's Rijks Oude Archieven [*A publication*]
VROC .... Vertical Rate of Climb [*Aviation*]
VROM ...... Vocabulary Read-Only Memory [*Data processing*]
VROOM.... Vintage Racers of Old Motorcycles   (EA)
Vroom .... Vroom's Law Reports [*30-85 New Jersey*] [*A publication*]   (DLA)
Vroom (G D W) ... [*G. D. W.*] Vroom's Law Reports [*36-63 New Jersey*] [*A publication*]   (DLA)
VROOMM ... Virtual Real-Time Object-Oriented Memory Manager [*Data processing*]
Vroom (NJ) ... Vroom's Law Reports [*30-85 New Jersey*] [*A publication*]   (DLA)
Vroom (P D) ... [*P. D.*] Vroom's Law Reports [*30-35 New Jersey*] [*A publication*]   (DLA)
VRP .... Richmond Public Library, Richmond, VA [*OCLC symbol*]   (OCLC)
VRP .... Vapor Reheat Process
VRP .... Variable Reluctance Pickup
VRP .... Vector-to-Raster Processor [*Computer graphics terminology*]
VRP .... Ventral Root Potential [*Neurophysiology*]
VRP .... Vestra Reverendissima Paternitas [*Your Very Reverend Paternity*] [*Latin*]
VRP .... Visual Record Printer
VRP .... Voyageur Representant Placier [*Traveling Salesman*] [*French*]
VR-PC .... Vanguardia Revolucionaria - Proletario Comunista [*Revolutionary Vanguard - Proletarian Communist*] [*Peru*] [*Political party*]   (PPW)
VRPF .... Voltage-Regulated Plate Filament
VRPS .... Vintage Radio and Phonograph Society   (EA)
VRPS .... Voltage-Regulated Power Supply

VRR .... Rochester Regional Research Library Council, Rochester, NY [*OCLC symbol*]   (OCLC)
VRR .... Validity, Repeatability, and Reliability [*Examination*]
VRR .... Valley Railroad
VRR .... Verification Readiness Review   (NASA)
VRR .... Vero Aero [*Vero Beach, FL*] [*FAA designator*]   (FAAC)
VRR .... Veterans Reemployment Rights
VRR .... Vibrating Reed Relay
VRR .... Visual Radio Range
VRR .... Visual Rapid Reorder   (MCD)
VRRC .... Vehicle Radio Remote Control
VRRI......... Vocational and Rehabilitation Research Institute [*University of Calgary*] [*Research center*]   (RCD)
VRS............ Rochester 3R's Union List of Serials, Rochester, NY [*OCLC symbol*]   (OCLC)
VRS............ Vacuum Relief System [*Nuclear energy*]   (NRCH)
VRS............ Vehicle Registration System [*Army*]
VRS............ Vehicular RADIAC [*Radioactivity Detection, Indication, and Computation*] System
VRS............ Velocity Response Shape   (CET)
VRS............ Veterinary and Remount Service [*British military*]   (DMA)
VRS............ Video Reception System
VRS............ Video Relay System
VRS............ Visual Reference System
VRS............ Visual Response System
VRS............ Vocational Rehabilitation Services
VRS............ Voice Recording Subsystem
VRS............ Volume Reduction and Solidification [*Hazardous waste disposal*]
VRS............ Volunteer Reserve Section
VRS............ Vortex Rate Sensor
VRS............ Voter Research & Surveys [*Commercial firm*]
VRSA........ Versa Technologies, Inc. [*NASDAQ symbol*]   (NQ)
VRSA........ Voice Reporting Signal Assembly
VRSI .... Viral Response Systems, Incorporated [*Greenwich, CT*] [*NASDAQ symbol*]   (NQ)
VRSP .... Voltage Regulator Supervisory Panel   (MCD)
VRSS .... Voice Reporting Signal System
VRSY .... Varitronic Systems, Inc. [*NASDAQ symbol*]   (NQ)
VRT .... Vacuum Rectifying Tube
VRT .... Variable Reluctance Transducer
VRT .... Vernon, TX [*Location identifier*] [*FAA*]   (FAAL)
VRT .... Visual Recognition Threshold
VRT .... Vocational Rehabilitation Therapist
VRT .... Voltage Reference Tube
VRT .... Voltage Regulator Tube
VRT .... Volume-Rendering Technique [*Computer graphics*]   (BYTE)
VRT .... Voluntary Reserve Training [*British military*]   (DMA)
VRTC........ Vehicle Research and Test Center [*National Highway Traffic Safety Administration*]   (GRD)
V-RTIF ...... Vandenberg Real Time Interface   (MCD)
VRTMOTN ... Vertical Motion   (FAAC)
VRTX .... Virtual Real-Time Executive
VRTX .... Vortec Corp. [*NASDAQ symbol*]   (NQ)
VRTY .... Variety   (MSA)
VRU .... University of Richmond, Richmond, VA [*OCLC symbol*]   (OCLC)
VRU .... Velocity Reference Unit
VRU .... Verfassung und Recht in Uebersee [*A publication*]
VRU .... Vertical Reference Unit   (MCD)
VRU .... Virtual Resource Unit   (MCD)
VRU .... Voice Response Unit
VRU .... Voltage Readout Unit
VRU.......... Vryburg [*South Africa*] [*Airport symbol*]   (OAG)
VRV .... Vacuum Regulator Valve [*Automotive engineering*]
VRV .... Viper Retrovirus
VRX .... Vestor Exploration [*Vancouver Stock Exchange symbol*]
VRX .... Virtual Resource Executive [*Software*] [*NCR Corp.*]
VRY .... Fayetteville/Fort Bragg, NC [*Location identifier*] [*FAA*]   (FAAL)
VRY .... Vaeroy [*Norway*] [*Airport symbol*]   (OAG)
VRYG .... Varying
VS .... Air Antisubmarine Squadron [*Navy*]
VS .... Intercontinental Airlines Ltd. [*Nigeria*] [*ICAO designator*]   (FAAC)
VS .... La Vie Spirituelle [*Paris*] [*A publication*]
VS .... Search Plane [*Navy symbol*]
VS .... Shore-Based Search Squadron [*Navy symbol*]
VS .... Single Vibrations [*Half cycles*]
VS .... Staging Velocity [*NASA*]   (NASA)
VS .... Vaccination Scar [*Medicine*]
VS .... Vacuum Switch
VS .... Vaginal Stroma
VS .... Valley & Siletz Railroad Co. [*AAR code*]
VS .... Vapor Seal [*Technical drawings*]
VS .... Vapor Suppression [*Nuclear energy*]   (NRCH)
VS .... Variable Speed   (IEEE)
VS .... Variable Sweep   (IEEE)
VS .... Variance Score [*Statistics*]
VS .... Vascular Strand [*Botany*]
VS .... Vectoring Service

VS .... Vegan Society [*Oxford, England*] (EAIO)
VS .... Vehicle Station [*NASA*] (KSC)
VS .... Velocity Search (MCD)
V/S............ Vendor Supplier [*Sales*] (MCD)
VS .... Venerable Sage [*Freemasonry*] (ROG)
VS .... Venesection [*Medicine*]
VS .... Venstresocialisterne [*Left Socialists Party*] [*Denmark*] [*Political party*] (PPE)
VS .... Vent Stack [*Technical drawings*]
VS .... Ventilation System [*NASA*]
VS .... Ventral Subiculum [*Brain anatomy*]
VS .... Venture Capital/Special Situations [*Business term*]
VS .... Verbal Scale
VS .... Verbum Salutis [*Paris*] [*A publication*]
VS .... Vergilian Society (EA)
VS .... Vermont Statutes [*A publication*] (DLA)
VS .... Vernacular Society (EA)
V & S........ Vernon and Scriven's Irish King's Bench Reports [*1786-88*] [*A publication*] (DLA)
VS .... Verse
VS .... Versus [*Against*] [*Latin*]
VS .... Vertical [*Activity*] Sensor [*Physiology*]
VS .... Vertical Software [*AI Software*] [*Data processing*]
VS .... Vertical Speed [*Aviation*]
VS .... Vertical Stereoscopic [*Photograph*]
VS .... Vertical Stripes [*Navigation markers*]
VS .... Vertical System [*Government arrangement*] (OICC)
VS .... Very Small Inclusions [*Diamond clarity grade*]
VS .... Very Soluble
VS .... Very Strong [*Spectral*]
VS .... Very Superior
VS .... Very Susceptible [*Plant pathology*]
VS .... Vesicular Sound [*in auscultation of chest*] [*Medicine*]
VS .... Vesicular Stomatitis [*Also, VSV*] [*Virus*]
V of S .... Veterans of Safety (EA)
VS .... Veterinary Surgeon
VS .... Vibration Seconds
VS .... Victorian Society (EA)
VS .... Victorian Studies [*A publication*]
VS .... Vida Sobrenatural [*A publication*]
VS .... Vide Supra [*See Above*] [*Latin*]
VS .... Videnskabs Selskapet Skrifter [*A publication*]
VS .... Video Selection
vs .... Vietnam, South [*vm (Vietnam) used in records cataloged after January 1978*] [*MARC country of publication code*] [*Library of Congress*] (LCCP)
VS .... Vieux Style [*Old Style*] [*French*]
VS .... Villas
VS .... Violoncello Society (EA)
VS .... Virgil Society (EA)
VS .... Virtual Storage [*Data processing*]
VS .... Virtual System
VS .... Visceral Sinus
VS .... Visible Supply
VS .... Vista Resources, Inc. [*NYSE symbol*] (SPSG)
VS .... Visual Signaling [*Military*]
VS .... Visual Storage [*Data processing*]
VS .... Visum Siccum [*Seen in a Dried State*] [*Botany*] (ROG)
VS .... Vitae Sophistarum [*of Philostratus*] [*Classical studies*] (OCD)
VS .... Vital Signs [*Medicine*]
VS .... Vivisection
VS .... Vocal Students Practice Aid Records [*Record label*]
VS .... Vocal Synthesis
VS .... Voicespondence Club (EA)
VS .... Volatile Solids [*Environmental science*]
VS .... Voltaire Society (EA)
VS .... Volti Subito [*Turn Over Quickly*] [*Music*]
VS .... Voltmeter Switch (MSA)
VS .... Volumetric Solution
VS .... Voluntary Sterilization
VS .... Voorschrift [*Rule, Order*] [*Dutch*] (ILCA)
VS .... Votre Seigneurie [*Your Lordship*] [*French*]
VS .... Vulcan Society (EA)
V2S .... V-Groove on Two Sides [*Lumber*]
VSA .... By Visual Reference to the Ground [*Aviation*] (FAAC)
VSA .... Mitteilungsblatt. Vereinigung Schweizerischer Angestelltenverbaende [*A publication*]
VSA .... Vancouver School of Art
VSA .... Variable Stability Aircraft (NASA)
VSA .... Variant-Specific Surface Antigen [*Genetics, immunology*]
VSA .... Vehicle Security Association (EA)
VSA .... Velocity Sensor Antenna
VSA .... Vereinigung Schweizerischer Angestelltenverbande [*Federation of Swiss Employees' Societies*]
VSA .... Verification Site Approval [*NASA*] (MCD)
VSA .... Vermont Statutes, Annotated [*A publication*] (DLA)
VSA .... Vernier Solo Accumulator [*Aerospace*] (AAG)
VS & A...... Veronis, Suhler & Associates, Inc. [*Telecommunications service*] (TSSD)
VSA .... Vertical Sensor Assembly
VSA .... Very Special Arts (EA)

VSA .... Vibrating String Accelerometer
VSA .... Victorian Society in America (EA)
VSA .... Victualling Store Allowance [*British military*] (DMA)
VSA .... Videocom Satellite Associates [*Dedham, MA*] [*Telecommunications*] (TSSD)
VSA .... Videographic Systems of America, Inc. [*Information service or system*] [*Ceased operation*] (IID)
VSA .... Villahermosa [*Mexico*] [*Airport symbol*] (OAG)
VSA .... Vintage Sailplane Association (EA)
VSA .... Violin Society of America (EA)
VSA .... Violin Society of America. Journal [*A publication*]
VSA .... Viscoelastic Stress Analysis
VSA .... Visual Skills Appraisal [*Child development test*]
VSA .... Voltage-Sensitive Amplifier
VSA/1800 ... Volvo Sports America 1800 (EA)
vSAA.......... Very Severe Aplastic Anemia [*Hematology*]
V-SAC ...... Vehicle Speed Activated Converter [*Automotive engineering*]
VSAD .... Vacuum Spark Advance Disconnect [*Auto air pollution control device*]
V/SAF .... Vulnerability and Survivability of the Armed Forces (MCD)
VSAL......... Berichte. Verhandlungen der Saechsischen Akademie der Wissenschaften zu Leipzig [*A publication*]
VSAL......... Visual Technology [*NASDAQ symbol*] (NQ)
VSAM....... Virtual Sequential Access Method
VSAM....... Virtual Storage Access Method [*Data processing*]
VSAM....... Virtual System Access Method
VSAT........ Very Small Aperture Terminal [*Telecommunications*] (TSSD)
VSAV........ Vydavtel'stvo Slovenskej Akademie Vied [*A publication*]
VSB........... Scout-Bombing Plane [*Navy symbol*]
VSB........... Sweet Briar College Library, Sweet Briar, VA [*OCLC symbol*] (OCLC)
VSB........... Venae Sectio Brachii [*Bleeding in the Arm*] [*Pharmacy*] (ROG)
VSB........... Vent and Supply Bay
VSB........... Vestigial Sideband [*Radio*]
VSB........... Victorian Studies Bulletin [*A publication*]
VSB........... Video Source Book [*A publication*]
VSB........... Visible (FAAC)
VSB........... Vision. The European Business Magazine [*A publication*]
VSB........... Volunteer Services for the Blind [*Later, ASB*] (EA)
VSB-AM... Vestigial Sideband - Amplitude Modulation
VSBC........ VSB Bancorp, Inc. [*NASDAQ symbol*] (CTT)
VSBD-PdA ... Volkssozialistische Bewegung Deutschlands - Partei der Arbeit [*People's Socialist Movement of Germany - Party of Labor*] [*Federal Republic of Germany*] (PD)
VSBF .... Vestigial Sideband Filter
VSBL........ Visible (MSA)
VSBS .... Very Small Business System
VSBY........ Visibility [*Aviation*] (FAAC)
VSBYDR ... Visibility Decreasing Rapidly [*Aviation*] (FAAC)
VSBYIR... Visibility Increasing Rapidly [*Aviation*] (FAAC)
VSC........... Valdosta State College [*Georgia*]
VSC........... Variable Speech Control [*Device that permits distortion-free rapid playback of speech recorded on tape*]
VSC........... Variable Speed Chopper
VSC........... Varnville [*South Carolina*] [*Seismograph station code, US Geological Survey*] (SEIS)
VSC........... Vehicle Sectoring Code
VSC........... Vehicle System Control
VSC........... Vendor Shipping Configuration (AAG)
VSC........... Ventral Spinal Cord [*Anatomy*]
VSC........... Vermont State College
VSC........... Vibration Safety Cutoff [*NASA*] (KSC)
VSC........... Vidicon Camera System (MCD)
V-S/C........ Viking Spacecraft [*NASA*]
VSC........... Vincentian Sisters of Charity [*Roman Catholic religious order*]
VSC........... Virginia State College [*Petersburg*]
VSC........... Virginia State College, Petersburg, VA [*OCLC symbol*] (OCLC)
VSC........... Virtual Subscriber Computer
VSC........... Vocations for Social Change [*Employment clearinghouse*] [*Defunct*] (EA)
VSC........... Volatile Sulfur Compound [*Chemistry*]
VSC........... Voltage-Saturated Capacitor
VSC........... Volunteer Staff Corps [*British*] (ROG)
VSCA........ Vacation and Senior Citizens Association (EA)
VSCA........ Vietnamese Senior Citizens Association (EA)
VSCC........ Victorian Spoon Collectors Club [*Australia*]
VSCC........ Voltage-Sensitive Calcium Channel [*Physiology*]
VSCCA...... Vintage Sports Car Club of America (EA)
VSCDF ...... Vatican's Sacred Congregation for the Doctrine of the Faith
VSCE........ Variable Stream Control Engine [*NASA*] (MCD)
VSCF........ Variable Speed Constant Frequency
V Sch G .... Verfassungsschutzgesetz [*A publication*]
VSCNY...... Vedanta Society of the City of New York (EA)
VSCOA...... Victorian Standing Committee on Adoption [*Australia*]
VSD .... Valve Solenoid Driver
VSD .... Variable Slope Delta
VSD .... Variable Speed Drive
VSD .... Vendor's Shipping Document
VSD .... Vendredi, Samedi, Dimanche [*A publication*]
VSD .... Ventricular Septal Defect [*Cardiology*]
VSD .... Versatile Signal Device

VSD	Vertical Situation Display
VSD	Video Subcarrier Detector
VSD	Village Self-Development
VSD	Virtually Safe Dose [*Toxicology*]
VSDA	Video Software Dealers Association (EA)
VSD/ADI ..	Vertical Situation Display/Attitude Director Indicator (MCD)
VSDC........	Victorian School for Deaf Children [*Australia*]
VSDM	Variable Slope Delta Modulation
VSDR........	Vieteljahrsheft zur Statistik des Deutschen Reichs [*Germany*]
VSE...........	Steam Explosion in Vessel [*Nuclear energy*] (NRCH)
VSE...........	Vancouver Stock Exchange [*Canada*]
VSE...........	Vessel (Reactor) Steam Explosion [*Nuclear energy*] (IEEE)
VSE...........	Virtual Storage Extension [*IBM Corp.*] [*Data processing*]
Vse	Vsesvit [*Kiev*] [*A publication*]
VSEC........	VSE Corporation [*NASDAQ symbol*] (NQ)
VSEGEI.....	Vsesojuznyj Naucno-Issledovatel'skij Geologiceskij Institut [*Moskau*] [*A publication*]
VSEL........	Vickers Shipbuilding and Engineering Ltd. [*British*]
VSEPR	Valence-Shell Electron Pair Repulsion [*Theory of molecular structure*]
VSERC	Victorian Solar Energy Research Council [*Australia*]
Vses Geogr O-Vo Izv ...	Vsesoyuznoye Geograficheskoye Obshchestvo. Izvestiya [*A publication*]
Vses Nauchno Issled Geol Inst Inf Sb ...	Vsesoyuznyi Nauchno-Issledovatel'skii Geologicheskii Institut. Informatsionnyi Sbornik [*A publication*]
Vses Nauchno-Issled Geol Inst Tr ...	Vsesoyuznyy Nauchno-Issledovatel'skiy Geologicheskiy Institut. Trudy [*A publication*]
Vses Nauchno-Issled Geologorazved Neft Inst Tr ...	Vsesoyuznyy Nauchno-Issledovatel'skiy Geologorazvedochnyi Neftyanoy Institut. Trudy [*A publication*]
Vses Nauchno Issled Inst Eksp Vet Im Ya R Kovalenko Byull ...	Vsesoyuznyi Nauchno-Issledovatel'skii Institut Eksperimental'noi Veterinarii Imeni Ya. R. Kovalenko. Byulleten [*A publication*]
Vses Nauchno Issled Inst Geofiz Metodov Razved Tr ...	Vsesoyuznyi Nauchno-Issledovatel'skii Institut Geofizicheskikh Metodov Razvedki. Trudy [*A publication*]
Vses Nauchno Issled Inst Gidrogeol Inzh Geol Tr ...	Vsesoyuznyi Nauchno-Issledovatel'skii Institut Gidrogeologii i Inzhenernoi Geologii. Trudy [*A publication*]
Vses Nauchno Issled Inst Khlopkovod Sb Nauchn Rab Aspir ...	Vsesoyuznyi Nauchno-Issledovatel'skii Institut Khlopkovodstva. Sbornik Nauchnykh Rabot Aspirantov [*A publication*]
Vses Nauchno Issled Inst Konditer Promsti Tr ...	Vsesoyuznyi Nauchno-Issledovatel'skii Institut Konditerskoi Promyshlennosti. Trudy [*A publication*]
Vses Nauchno Issled Inst Solyanoi Promsti Tr ...	Vsesoyuznyi Nauchno-Issledovatel'skii Institut Solyanoi Promyshlennosti. Trudy [*A publication*]
Vses Nauchno Issled Inst Tsellyul Bum Promsti Sb Tr ...	Vsesoyuznyi Nauchno-Issledovatel'skii Institut Tsellyulozno-Bumazhnoi Promyshlennosti. Sbornik Trudov [*A publication*]
Vses Nauchno Issled Inst Zhirov Tr ...	Vsesoyuznyi Nauchno-Issledovatel'skii Institut Zhirov. Trudy [*A publication*]
Vses Nauchno Issled Khim Farm Inst Khim Med ...	Vsesoyuznyi Nauchno-Issledovatel'skii Khimiko-Farmatsevticheskii Institut. Khimiya i Meditsina [*A publication*]
Vses Nauchno Issled Proektn Inst Galurgii Tr ...	Vsesoyuznyi Nauchno-Issledovatel'skii i Proektnyi Institut Galurgii. Trudy [*A publication*]
Vses Nauchno Issled Proektn Inst Mekh Obrab Polezn Iskop Tr ...	Vsesoyuznyi Nauchno-Issledovatel'skii i Proektnyi Institut Mekhanicheskoi Obrabotki Poleznykh Iskopaemykh. Trudy [*A publication*]
Vses Nauchn O-Vo Neirokhir ...	Vsesoyuznoe Nauchnoe Obshchestvo Neirokhirurgii [*A publication*]
Vses Neft Nauchno Issled Geologorazved Inst Tr ...	Vsesoyuznyi Neftyanoi Nauchno-Issledovatel'skii Geologorazvedochnyi Institut. Trudy [*A publication*]
Vsesojuz Zaocn Politehn Inst Sb Trudov ...	Vsesojuznyi Zaocnyi Politehniceskii Institut. Sbornik Trudov [*A publication*]
Vsesoyunaya Nauchno Metod Konf Vet Patologoanat ...	Vsesoyuznaya Nauchno-Metod Konferentsiya Veterinarnykh Patologoanatomov [*A publication*]
Vsesoyuznoe Paleont Obshch Ezhegodnik ...	Vsesoyuznoe Paleontologicheskoe Obshchestvo Ezhegodnik [*A publication*]
VSF...........	Antisubmarine Fighter Squadron [*Navy*]
VSF...........	Springfield [*Vermont*] [*Airport symbol*] (OAG)
VSF...........	Springfield, VT [*Location identifier*] [*FAA*] (FAAL)
VSF...........	Vestigial Sideband Filter
VSF...........	Vitreous Silica Fabric
VSF...........	Voice Store and Forward [*Voice messaging*]
VSFC	Vince Smith Fan Club (EA)
VSFP	Venous Stop-Flow Pressure [*Medicine*]
VSFR	Vertical Seismic Floor Response (IEEE)
VSG	Variable Speed Gear (DEN)
VSG	Variable [*or Variant*] Surface Glycoprotein [*Biochemistry*]
VSG	Vernier Step Gauge [*Aerospace*]
VSG	Versatile Signal [*or Symbol*] Generator
VSG	Vierteljahrsschrift fuer Sozial- und Wirtschaftsgeschichte [*A publication*]
VSG	Vulture Study Group (EAIO)
VSH..........	Vie Economique. Rapports Economiques et de Statistique Sociale [*A publication*]
VSH..........	Village Self-Help
VSH..........	Vishay Intertechnology, Inc. [*NYSE symbol*] (SPSG)
VSH..........	Vishnu Resources [*Vancouver Stock Exchange symbol*]
VSHPS	Vernier Solo Hydraulic Power System [*Aerospace*] (AAG)
VSI	College of Staten Island, St. George Campus Library, Staten Island, NY [*OCLC symbol*] (OCLC)
VSI	Vendor Shipping Instruction
VSI	Vertical Signal [*or Situation*] Indicator [*Helicopters*]
VSI	Vertical Speed Indicator [*Aviation*]
VSI	Very Seriously Ill [*Army*] (AABC)
VSI	Video Simulation Interface (NASA)
VSI	Video Sweep Integrator
VSI	Videoconferencing Systems, Incorporated [*Norcross, GA*] [*Telecommunications service*] (TSSD)
VSI...........	Vinyl Siding Industry (EA)
VSI...........	Vsemirnaja Istorija [*A publication*]
VSI...........	Vuesenoria Ilustrisima [*Your Illustrious Ladyship (or Lordship)*] [*Spanish*]
VS Ilma......	Vossa Senhoria Ilustrissima [*Your Illustrious Lordship*] [*Portuguese*]
VSIP	Valence State Ionization Potentials [*of atoms*]
VS Ja (M) ...	Voprosy Slavjanskogo Jazykoznanija (Moskva) [*A publication*]
VSJW	Vise Jaw [*Tool*] (AAG)
VSL..........	Metaal en Kunststof [*A publication*]
VSL..........	Special Libraries Cataloguing, Inc. [*UTLAS symbol*]
VSL..........	State Library of Victoria [*Australia*]
VSL..........	Valve Signal Light
VSL..........	Variable Safety Level
VSL..........	Variable Specification List
VSL..........	Ventilation Sampling Line (IEEE)
VSL..........	Vermont State Department of Libraries, Montpelier, VT [*OCLC symbol*] (OCLC)
VSL..........	Vessel (FAAC)
VSL..........	Vetenskaps-Societeten i Lund [*A publication*]
VSL..........	Viscous Shock Layer
VSL..........	Volume of the Sacred Law [*Freemasonry*]
VSL..........	VS Services Limited [*Toronto Stock Exchange symbol*]
VSLA	Vetenskaps-Societeten i Lund. Aarsbok [*A publication*]
VSL Bibs....	Research Service Bibliographies. State Library of Victoria [*A publication*] (APTA)
VSLE	Very Small Local Exchange [*Telecommunications*] (TEL)
VSLF	VMS Strategic Land Fund II [*NASDAQ symbol*] (CTT)
VSLI	Veterans Special Life Insurance [*Veterans Administration*]
VSlJa.........	Voprosy Slavjanskogo Jazykoznanija [*A publication*]
VSlJa (Lvov) ...	Voprosy Slavjanskogo Jazykoznanija (Lvov) [*A publication*]
VSlJa (Moskva) ...	Voprosy Slavjanskogo Jazykoznanija (Moskva) [*A publication*]
V Sl Jaz......	Voprosy Slavjanskogo Jazykoznanija [*A publication*]
VSLS	Very Slightly Soluble
VSM	Vascular Smooth Muscle [*Anatomy*]
VSM	Vehicle State Monitor
VSM	Vestigial Sideband Modulation
VSM	Vibrating Sample Magnetometer
VSM	Video Switching Matrix (KSC)
VSM	Vietnam Service Medal [*Military decoration*] (AFM)
VSM	Virtual Storage Manager (BUR)
VSM	Virtual Storage Memory [*Data processing*] (MCD)
VSM	Voice Switch Monitor (MCD)
VSMA	Vibrating Screen Manufacturers Association (EA)
VSMC	Vascular Smooth Muscle Cell [*Cytology*]
VSMF	Visual Search Microfilm File [*Trademark*] [*Data processing*]
VSMOS	Verified Secondary Military Occupational Specialty
VSMPA	Victorian Secondary Masters' Professional Association [*Australia*]
VSMS	Video Switching Matrix System
VSMS	Vineland Social Maturity Scale [*Psychology*]
VSN	Scout-Training Plane [*Navy symbol*]
VSN	Video Switching Network (MCD)
VSN	Vision
VSN	Volume-Sequence-Number [*Data processing*]
VSNL........	Videsh Sanchar Nigam Ltd. [*India*] [*Telecommunications service*] (TSSD)
VSN(M).....	Training Plane, 2-Engine [*Navy symbol*]
VSNP........	Viking Society for Northern Research [*British*]
VSNS	Virgil C. Summer Nuclear Station (NRCH)
VSNY	Vegetarian Society of New York (EA)
VSO	Handel. Zeitschrift fuer Theorie und Praxis des Innenhandels in der Deutschen Demokratischen Republik [*A publication*]
VSO	Scout Observation Plane [*Navy symbol*]
VSO	Valdosta Southern Railroad [*AAR code*]
VSO	Verso (BJA)
VSO	Very Special Old
VSO	Very Stable Oscillator
VSO	Very Superior Old [*Designation on brandy labels*]
VSO	Victualling Stores Officer [*British military*] (DMA)

VSO .... Voluntary Service Overseas [*Military*]
VSOE......... Venice Simplon Orient-Express [*London-to-Venice train*]
VSOP........ Very Superior Old Pale [*Designation on brandy labels. Facetious French translation is "Versez sans Oublier Personne," or "Pour without Forgetting Anyone"*]
V Soz WG .. Vierteljahrsschrift fuer Sozial- und Wirtschaftsgeschichte [*A publication*]
VSP........... Variable Size Parameter [*Thermodynamics*]
VSP........... Vectored Slipstream Principle
VSP........... Vehicle Scheduling Program [*Data processing*]
VSP........... Vehicle Synthesis Program [*Aerospace*]
VSP........... Vertical Seismic Profile [*Geology*]
VSP........... Vertical Speed [*Aviation*] (FAAC)
VSP........... Victorian Socialist Party [*Australia*] [*Political party*]
VSP........... Video Signal Processor
VSP........... Video System Processor [*Telecommunications*] (TSSD)
VSP........... Vikki's Special People (EA)
VSP........... Virtual Switching Point [*Telecommunications*] (TEL)
VSP........... Vision Service Plan National (EA)
V SP......... Visum Sponanteum [*Seen Wild*] [*Botany*] (ROG)
V SP......... Visum Sporadicum [*Seen Wild*] [*Botany*] (ROG)
VSPA........ Vacation Spa Resorts, Inc. [*NASDAQ symbol*] (NQ)
VSPC........ Virtual Storage Personal Computing [*IBM Corp.*] [*Data processing*]
V/SPD ...... Variable Speed
VSPEP....... Vehicle Sizing and Performance Evaluation Program (MCD)
VSPP .... Vangiya Sahitya Parisat Patrika [*A publication*]
VSPRITES ... Virtual Sprites [*Amiga computer hardware*]
VSPS .... Vernier Solo Power Supply [*Aerospace*] (AAG)
VSPX........ Vehicle Scheduling Program Extended [*Data processing*]
VSQ .... St. Vladimir's Seminary. Quarterly [*A publication*]
VSQ .... Very Special Quality
VSR .... Vacuum Short Resid [*Petroleum technology*]
VSR .... Validation Summary Report
VSR .... Vallecitos Experimental Superheat Reactor (NRCH)
VSR .... Versar, Inc. [*AMEX symbol*] (SPSG)
VSR .... Vertical Storage and Retrieval Systems
VSR .... Very Short Range
VSR .... Very Short Run [*Printing technology*]
VSR .... Very Special Reserve (ADA)
VSR .... Vibration Sensitive Relay
VSR .... Vietnam Supply Rate [*Military*] (MCD)
VSR........... Vincit Sapientia Robur [*Wisdom Overcomes Strength*] [*Latin*] [*Motto of Johann Ernst, Duke of Saxony-Eisenach (1566-1638)*]
VSR........... Visual Security Range (NATG)
VSR........... Voltage-Sensing Relay
VSRADWS ... Very-Short-Range Air Defense Weapon System (NATG)
VSRBM ..... Very-Short-Range Ballistic Missile
VSRGSR.... Very-Short-Range Ground Surveillance RADAR (MCD)
VSS .... V/STOL Support Ship
VSS........... Vampire Studies Society [*Defunct*] (EA)
VSS........... Vapor Saver System [*Automobile*]
VSS........... Variable Slit Set
VSS........... Variable SONAR System
VSS........... Variable Stability System [*Aviation*]
VSS........... Vascular Surgical Society [*British*]
VSS........... Vassouras [*Brazil*] [*Geomagnetic observatory code*]
VSS........... Vector Scoring System [*Navy*] (MCD)
VSS........... Vehicle Speed Sensor [*Automotive engineering*]
VSS........... Vehicle Stability System [*Truck engineering*]
VSS........... Vehicle Surveillance System
VSS........... Vehicle System Simulator
VSS........... Velocity Sensor System
VSS........... Versions (ROG)
VSS........... Vertical Sounding System
VSS........... Vertical Spike Soderberg [*Pot*] [*Aluminum processing*]
VSS........... Vertical Support Structure
VSS........... Vessel Support System (MCD)
VSS........... Victor Scoring System
VSS........... Videnskabs Selskapet Skrifter [*A publication*]
VSS........... Video Select Switch (MCD)
VSS........... Video Signal Simulator (NATG)
VSS........... Video Storage System [*or Subsystem*]
VSS........... Video Supervisory Signal
VSS........... Virtual Storage System [*SEMIS*]
VSS........... Visual Sensor Set
VSS........... Visual Systems Simulator [*FAA*]
VSS........... Vital Signs Stable [*Medicine*]
VSS........... Vocabulary Switching System [*Data processing*]
VSS........... Voice Signaling System
VSS........... Voice Storage System [*AT & T*]
VSS........... VoiceStation System [*Sydis, Inc.*] [*San Jose, CA*] (TSSD)
VSS........... Volatile Suspended Solids [*Environmental science*]
VSS........... Voltage-Sensing Switch
VSS........... Voltage to Substrate and Sources [*Microelectronics*]
VSS........... Voyager Spacecraft Subsystem [*NASA*]
VSSC .... Vedanta Society of Southern California (EA)
VSSF......... Videnskabs Selskapet Skrifter. Forhandlingar [*A publication*]
VSSM .... Video Scanner Switch Matrix
VSSP .... Vendor Standard Settlement Program (AAG)

VSSR .... Vierteljahrsschrift fuer Sozialrecht [*A publication*]
VSSRBP .... Vysoka Skola Zemedelska v Praze Fakulta Provozne Ekonomicka v Ceskych Budejovicich Sbornik Referatu [*A publication*]
VSSSN ...... Verification Status Social Security Number (AABC)
VSSTU ...... Victorian State School Teachers' Union [*Australia*]
VS Suppl... Vie Spirituelle. Supplement [*A publication*]
VST........... St. Thomas [*Virgin Islands*] [*Seismograph station code, US Geological Survey*] (SEIS)
VST........... Valve Seat (MSA)
VST........... Valve Setpoint Tolerance [*Nuclear energy*] (NRCH)
VST........... Vancouver School of Theology [*University of British Columbia*]
VST........... Vanstates Resources Ltd. [*Vancouver Stock Exchange symbol*]
VST........... Variable Stability Trainer [*Aviation*]
VST........... Vasteras [*Sweden*] [*Airport symbol*] (OAG)
VST........... Venom Skin Test [*Immunology*]
VST........... Video Scroller Terminal [*Data processing*]
VST........... Video System Test
VST........... Visit (NVT)
VST........... VMS Short Term Income Trust [*AMEX symbol*] (SPSG)
VST........... Vocational Skills Training [*Funds*] [*Job Corps*]
VST........... Volume Sensitive Tariff [*Telecommunications*] (TEL)
VSTA........ Victoria Station [*NASDAQ symbol*] (NQ)
VSTA........ Virus-Serum-Toxin Act
VSTAG...... Vandenberg Shuttle Turnaround Analysis Group [*NASA*] (NASA)
VSTAR ...... Variable Search and Track Air Defense RADAR
VSTC .... Vermont State Teachers College
VSTCB ...... Vuoto, Scienza, e Tecnologia [*A publication*]
V St DV ...... Vermoegensteuer- Durchfuehrungsverordnung [*A publication*]
V St G .... Vermoegensteuergesetz [*A publication*]
VSTI .... Versus Tech, Inc. [*NASDAQ symbol*] (NQ)
VStil.......... Voprosy Stilistiki [*A publication*]
VSTKJ....... Vesientutkimuslaitoksen Julkaisuja [*Publications. Finnish Water Research Institute*] [*A publication*]
VSTM........ Valve Stem (MSA)
VSTO........ Vertical/Short Takeoff [*and Landing*] (MCD)
V/STOL .... Vertical/Short Takeoff and Landing [*Aircraft*]
VSTP .... Visual Satellite Tracking Program
VSTR .... Ventral Striatum [*Neurology*]
VSTR .... Vestar, Inc. [*NASDAQ symbol*] (NQ)
VSTR .... Volt Second Transfer Ratio
VSTSP ...... Visit Ship in Port [*Navy*] (NVT)
VSTT .... Variable Speed Tactical Trainer [*Air Force*] (MCD)
VSTT .... Variable Speed Training Target
VSTU .... Victorian School Teachers' Union [*Australia*]
VSUH .... Virginia State University Herbarium
VSV........... Vacuum Switching Valve [*Automotive engineering*]
VSV........... Vesicular Stomatitis Virus [*Also, VS*]
VSv........... Vokrug Sveta [*Moscow*] [*A publication*]
VSVG........ Vesicular Stomatitis Virus Glycoprotein [*Biochemistry*]
VSVVS ...... Vereinigung Schweizerischer Versuchs und Vermittlungstellen fuer Saatkartoffeln [*Solothurn*] [*A publication*]
VSW .... Variable Sweep Wing
VSW .... Vertrau Schau Wem [*Trust, but Be Careful Whom*] [*German*] [*Motto of Johann Georg, Duke of Wohlau (1552-92)*]
VSW .... Very Short Wave
VSW .... Vierteljahrsschrift fuer Sozial- und Wirtschaftsgeschichte [*A publication*]
VSW .... Visual Studies Workshop (EA)
VSW .... Vitrified Stoneware
VSW .... Voltage Standing Wave
V f SWG .... Vierteljahrsschrift fuer Sozial- und Wirtschaftsgeschichte [*A publication*]
VSWG .... Vierteljahrsschrift fuer Sozial- und Wirtschaftsgeschichte [*A publication*]
VSWR........ Visual Standing Wave Ratio (NASA)
VSWR........ Voltage Standing-Wave Ratio
VSX........... Navy Submarine Attack Airplane - Experimental (MCD)
VSYNC...... Vertical Synchronous [*Data processing*]
VSystems ... Video Systems [*A publication*]
VT .... Air-Cushion Vehicle built by Vosper Thorneycroft [*England*] [*Usually used in combination with numerals*]
VT .... Air Polynesie [*France*] [*ICAO designator*] (FAAC)
VT .... India [*Aircraft nationality and registration mark*] (FAAC)
Vt .... State of Vermont, Department of Libraries, Montpelier, VT [*Library symbol*] [*Library of Congress*] (LCLS)
VT .... Target-on-Threshold Speed [*Aviation*]
VT .... Torpedo Plane [*Navy symbol*]
VT .... Training Squadron [*Navy symbol*] (NVT)
VT .... Vacuum Tube [*Electronics*]
VT .... Validation Testing (MCD)
VT .... Valitocin [*Endocrinology*]
VT .... Vaportight (MSA)
VT .... Variable Thrust
VT .... Variable Time [*Fuse*] [*Also known as a "proximity fuse"*]
VT .... Variable Transformer
VT .... Variable Transmission (ADA)
VT .... Vascular Time
VT .... Vasotocin

VT	Vat Petroleum [*Vancouver Stock Exchange symbol*]
VT	Vehicle Theft
VT	Vehicular Technology (MCD)
V-T	Velocity Time (MUGU)
VT	Vent (NASA)
VT	Ventricular Tachycardia [*Cardiology*]
VT	Verb Transitive
VT	Verfuegungstruppen (BJA)
VT	Vermont [*Postal code*]
VT	Vermont Reports [*A publication*] (DLA)
VT	Verotoxin [*Biochemistry*]
VT	Vertical Tabulation [*Data processing*]
VT	Vertical Tail
VT	Vetus Testamentum [*Old Testament*] [*of the Bible*] [*Latin*]
VT	Vetus Testamentum [*A publication*]
VT	Vibration Testing
V-T	Vibrational-to-Translational [*Energy transfer*]
VT	Victa Ltd. [*Aviation Division*] [*Australia*] [*ICAO aircraft manufacturer identifier*] (ICAO)
VT	Video Terminal
VT	Video Times [*A publication*]
VT	Videotape
VT	Viere i Tzerkov [*A publication*]
VT	Vinyl Tile [*Technical drawings*]
VT	Virtual Terminal (BYTE)
VT	Vision Test [*Ophthalmology*]
VT	Visual Telegraphy
VT	Visual Toss
VT	Vocational-Technical
V & T	Vodka and Tonic
VT	Voice Tube [*Technical drawings*]
V & T	Volume and Tension [*of pulse*]
VT	Voting Trust [*Investment term*]
VTA	Vacuum-Tube Amplifier
VTA	Variable Transfer Address
VTA	Varnished Tube Association
VTA	Ventral Tegmental Area [*Anatomy*]
VTA	Verkeerskunde [*A publication*]
VTA	Vertical Tracking Angle [*of a phonograph cartridge*]
VTA	Vision Test Apparatus [*Ophthalmology*]
VTAADS...	Vertical the Army Authorization Document System
VTAB........	Vertical Tabulation Character [*Data processing*]
VTAC........	Video Timing and Control
VTAC........	VOR [*Very-High-Frequency Omnidirectional Range*] Collocated with TACAN (FAAC)
V-TACH....	Ventricular Tachycardia [*Cardiology*]
VT Admin Comp ...	Vermont Administrative Procedure Compilation [*A publication*] (DLA)
VT Ag Exp ...	Vermont. Agricultural Experiment Station. Publications [*A publication*]
VT Agric Exp Stn Bull ...	Vermont. Agricultural Experiment Station. Bulletin [*A publication*]
VTAJX	Navy Trainer Advanced Jet - Experimental (MCD)
VTAM	Virtual Telecommunications [*or Teleprocessing*] Access Method [*IBM Corp.*] [*Data processing*]
VTAM	Virtual Terminal Access Method
VTAM	VORTEX [*Varian Omnitask Real-Time Executive*] Telecommunications Access Method
VTAME.....	Virtual Telecommunications Access Method Entry
VTAS........	Visual Target Acquisition System [*Navy*]
VtB............	Fletcher Free Library, Burlington, VT [*Library symbol*] [*Library of Congress*] (LCLS)
VTB	Torpedo-Bombing Plane [*Navy symbol*]
VTB	Velocity Test Barrel
VtB............	Verfahrenstechnische Berichte [*Chemical and Process Engineering Abstracts*] [*Information service or system*] [*A publication*]
VtB............	Verkehrswasserbaubibliothek [*Bundesanstalt fuer Wasserbau*] [*Database*]
VTB	Vinyl T-Butylstyrene [*Organic chemistry*]
VTB	Vlaamsche Toeristenbond
VTB	Voltage Time to Breakdown (DEN)
VTB	Volunteer Talent Bank [*American Association of Retired Persons*]
VTBA........	Bangkok [*Thailand*] [*ICAO location identifier*] (ICLI)
VT BA........	Vermont Bar Association Reports [*A publication*] (DLA)
VTBB........	Bangkok [*Thailand*] [*ICAO location identifier*] (ICLI)
VtBC	Champlain College, Burlington, VT [*Library symbol*] [*Library of Congress*] (LCLS)
VTBC........	Chanthaburi [*Thailand*] [*ICAO location identifier*] (ICLI)
VTBD	Bangkok/International [*Thailand*] [*ICAO location identifier*] (ICLI)
VTBE........	Saraburi [*Thailand*] [*ICAO location identifier*] (ICLI)
VtBef..........	Rockingham Free Public Library, Bellows Falls, VT [*Library symbol*] [*Library of Congress*] (LCLS)
VtBenn.......	Bennington Free Library, Bennington, VT [*Library symbol*] [*Library of Congress*] (LCLS)
VtBennC	Bennington College, Bennington, VT [*Library symbol*] [*Library of Congress*] (LCLS)
VtBennM ...	Bennington Museum, Inc., Bennington, VT [*Library symbol*] [*Library of Congress*] (LCLS)

VtBennP	Putnam Memorial Hospital, Medical Library, Bennington, VT [*Library symbol*] [*Library of Congress*]
VTBF.........	Chachoengsao/Phanom Sarakhan [*Thailand*] [*ICAO location identifier*] (ICLI)
VtBFB.......	Grand Lodge of Vermont, F & AM Library, Burlington, VT [*Library symbol*] [*Library of Congress*] (LCLS)
VTBG	Kanchanaburi [*Thailand*] [*ICAO location identifier*] (ICLI)
VTBH........	Lop Buri/Sa Pran Nak [*Thailand*] [*ICAO location identifier*] (ICLI)
VTBHA	Vuoriteollisuus/Bergshanteringen [*A publication*]
VTBI.........	Prachin Buri [*Thailand*] [*ICAO location identifier*] (ICLI)
VTBJ	Phetchaburi/Tha Yang [*Thailand*] [*ICAO location identifier*] (ICLI)
VTBK........	Nakhon Pathom/Kamphaeng Saen [*Thailand*] [*ICAO location identifier*] (ICLI)
VTBL........	Lop Buri [*Thailand*] [*ICAO location identifier*] (ICLI)
VTBM	Phetchaburi/Maruk [*Thailand*] [*ICAO location identifier*] (ICLI)
VTBN	Prachuap Khiri Khan/Pran Buri [*Thailand*] [*ICAO location identifier*] (ICLI)
VTBP........	Prachuap Khiri Khan [*Thailand*] [*ICAO location identifier*] (ICLI)
VTBR........	Ratchaburi [*Thailand*] [*ICAO location identifier*] (ICLI)
VtBran	Brandon Free Public Library, Brandon, VT [*Library symbol*] [*Library of Congress*] (LCLS)
VTBR Case ...	Victorian Taxation Board of Review Case [*Australia*] [*A publication*]
VtBrt	Brooks Memorial Library, Brattleboro, VT [*Library symbol*] [*Library of Congress*] (LCLS)
VtBrtS........	School for International Training, Brattleboro, VT [*Library symbol*] [*Library of Congress*] (LCLS)
VTBS........	Chon Buri/Sattahip [*Thailand*] [*ICAO location identifier*] (ICLI)
VTBT........	Chon Buri/Bang Phra [*Thailand*] [*ICAO location identifier*] (ICLI)
VtBT..........	Trinity College, Burlington, VT [*Library symbol*] [*Library of Congress*] (LCLS)
VTBU	Rayong/Utapao [*Thailand*] [*ICAO location identifier*] (ICLI)
VT Bul	Vermont. Free Public Library Commission and State Library. Bulletin [*A publication*]
VTBW........	Prachin Buri/Watthana Nakhon [*Thailand*] [*ICAO location identifier*] (ICLI)
VTC	Vandenberg Test Center [*Air Force*]
VTC	Variable Trimmer Capacitor
VTC	Vehicular Traffic Control
VTC	Veractor Tuned Microwave Cavity
VTC	Viable Titanium Composite
VTC	Video Tape Center [*Commercial firm*] [*British*]
VTC	Vidicon Television Camera
VTC	Vitronics Corp. [*AMEX symbol*] (SPSG)
VTC	Volunteer Training Corps [*An organization for home defense*] [*British*] [*World War I*]
VTC	Voting Trust Certificate [*or Company*] [*Investment term*]
VTCA........	Chiang Rai/Chiang Khong [*Thailand*] [*ICAO location identifier*] (ICLI)
VTCA........	Vernon's Texas Codes, Annotated [*A publication*] (DLA)
VTCA........	Vintage Thunderbird Club of America [*Later, VTCI*] (EA)
VtCasT......	Castleton State College, Castleton, VT [*Library symbol*] [*Library of Congress*] (LCLS)
VTCB........	Chiang Rai/Ban Chiang Kham [*Thailand*] [*ICAO location identifier*] (ICLI)
VTCC........	Chiang Mai [*Thailand*] [*ICAO location identifier*] (ICLI)
VTCC........	Variable Temperature Compensation Capacitor
VTCCHE...	Tidewater Consortium, Librarians' Networking Committee [*Library network*]
VTCD	Nan/Chiang Klang [*Thailand*] [*ICAO location identifier*] (ICLI)
VTCE........	Nan/Ban Pua [*Thailand*] [*ICAO location identifier*] (ICLI)
VTCE........	Vehicle Team Combat Exercise [*Army*] (INF)
VTCF........	Uttaradit (West) [*Thailand*] [*ICAO location identifier*] (ICLI)
VTCH	Mae Hong Son [*Thailand*] [*ICAO location identifier*] (ICLI)
VTCI.........	Mae Hong Son/Pai [*Thailand*] [*ICAO location identifier*] (ICLI)
VTCI.........	Vintage Thunderbird Club International (EA)
VTCK........	Mae Hong Son/Khun Yuam [*Thailand*] [*ICAO location identifier*] (ICLI)
VTCL........	Lampang [*Thailand*] [*ICAO location identifier*] (ICLI)
VTCN	Nan [*Thailand*] [*ICAO location identifier*] (ICLI)
VTC News ...	Vocational Training Council. Newsletter [*New Zealand*] [*A publication*]
VTCP........	Phrae [*Thailand*] [*ICAO location identifier*] (ICLI)
VTCR........	Chiang Rai [*Thailand*] [*ICAO location identifier*] (ICLI)
VTCS.........	Mae Hong Son/Mae Sariang [*Thailand*] [*ICAO location identifier*] (ICLI)
VTCS........	Variable Thermal Control Surface
VTCS.........	Vega Target Control System [*Computer flight control of test vehicles*]
VTCS.........	Vehicular Traffic Control System (IEEE)
VTCS.........	Video Telemetering Camera Systems (AAG)
VTD	Aircraft (Training) [*Navy symbol*]
VTD	Variable Time Delay

VTD .... Vertical Tape Display (KSC)
VTD .... Vision Testing Device [*Ophthalmology*]
VTDC .... Vacuum Tube Development Committee [*Columbia University*] (MCD)
VTDI .... Variable Threshold Digital Input
VTE .... Variable Thrust Engine
vte .... Vente [*Sale*] [*Business term*] [*French*]
VTE .... Vertical Tube Effects [*Desalination*]
VTE .... Vertical Tube Evaporation [*Desalination*]
VTE .... Vibration Test Equipment
VTE .... Vicarious Trial and Error [*Psychology*]
VTE .... Vientiane [*Laos*] [*Airport symbol*] (OAG)
VTE .... Viscous Transonic Equation
VTEC........ Verotoxin-Producing Escherichia Coli
V-TECS ..... Vocational Technical Education Consortium of States (OICC)
VTEK........ Vodavi Technology Corp. [*NASDAQ symbol*] (NQ)
VTEL .... Vitel Fiber Optics Corp. [*NASDAQ symbol*] (NQ)
VTERL ...... Veterinary Toxicology and Entomology Research Laboratory [*Department of Agriculture*] [*College Station, TX*] (GRD)
VTERM..... Variable Temperature Electrical Resistivity Measurement [*Physics*]
VTES .... Variable Thrust Engine System
VTES .... Vinyltriethoxysilane [*Organic chemistry*]
VTEX........ Vertex Communications Corp. [*Kilgore, TX*] [*NASDAQ symbol*] (NQ)
VTF........... Vacuum Test Furnace
VTF........... Variable Time, Fragmentation [*Military*] (CAAL)
VTF........... Venezuelan Trust Fund [*Inter-American Development Bank*]
VTF........... Vertical Test Facility [*NASA*]
VTF........... Vertical Test Fixture
VTF........... Vertical Test Flight (MCD)
VTF........... Vertical Tracking Force [*of a phonograph cartridge*]
VTF........... Voltage Transfer Function
VT Farm & Home Sci ... Vermont Farm and Home Science [*A publication*]
VT Farm Home Sci ... Vermont Farm and Home Science [*A publication*]
VTFDA...... Ankara Universitesi. Veteriner Fakultesi. Dergisi [*A publication*]
VTFE........ Vertical Tube Foam Evaporation [*Chemical engineering*]
VTFS .... Visual Technology Flight Simulator (MCD)
VTFT .... Value Task Force Team
VTG .... Vantage [*Washington*] [*Seismograph station code, US Geological Survey*] (SEIS)
VTG .... Vitellogenin [*Biochemistry*]
VTG .... Vojno-Tehnicki Glasnik [*A publication*]
VTG .... Volume Thoracic Gas [*Medicine*]
VTG .... Voting [*Business term*]
VT Geol Sur Econ Geol ... Vermont. Geological Survey. Economic Geology [*A publication*]
VT Geol Surv Bull ... Vermont. Geological Survey. Bulletin [*A publication*]
VT Geol Surv Water Resour Dep Environ Geol ... Vermont. Geological Survey. Water Resources Department. Environmental Geology [*A publication*]
VTGO........ Vacations to Go, Inc. [*Houston, TX*] [*NASDAQ symbol*] (NQ)
VThB .... Vocabulaire de Theologie Biblique [*A publication*] (BJA)
VtHi.......... Vermont Historical Society, Montpelier, VT [*Library symbol*] [*Library of Congress*] (LCLS)
VT His S.... Vermont Historical Society. Proceedings [*A publication*]
VT Hist ..... Vermont History [*A publication*]
VtHS......... Vermont Historical Society. Proceedings [*A publication*]
VTI............ Statens Vag- och Trafikinstitut [*Swedish Road and Traffic Research Institute*] [*Linkoping*] [*Information service or system*] (IID)
VTI............ Valparaiso Technical Institute [*Indiana*]
VTI............ Vanguard Technologies International, Inc. [*AMEX symbol*] (SPSG)
VTI............ Vermont Telecommunications, Incorporated [*Winooski, VT*] [*Telecommunications*] (TSSD)
VTI............ Video Terminal Interface
VTI............ Vinton, IA [*Location identifier*] [*FAA*] (FAAL)
VTI............ Volume Thickness Index
VTI............ Voluntary Termination Incentive [*Business term*]
VTIP .... Visual Target Identification Point (AFM)
VTJ........... Johnson State College, Johnson, VT [*OCLC symbol*] (OCLC)
VtJoT........ Johnson State College, Johnson, VT [*Library symbol*] [*Library of Congress*] (LCLS)
VTK .... Viatech, Inc. [*AMEX symbol*] (SPSG)
VTL........... Vacuum-Tube Launcher
VTL........... Variable Threshold Logic
VTL........... Vertical Turret Lathe
VTL........... Video Tape Lecture
VTL........... Vientitakuulaitos [*Export credit agency*] [*Finland*]
VT Lib....... Vermont Libraries [*A publication*]
VTLM........ Vitalmetrics, Inc. [*NASDAQ symbol*] (NQ)
Vt-LR........ Vermont Legislative Council, Montpelier, VT [*Library symbol*] [*Library of Congress*] (LCLS)
VT L Rev.... Vermont Law Review [*A publication*]
VTLS .... Virginia Technical Library System [*Virginia Polytechnic Institute and State University Center for Library Automation*] [*Information service or system*]
VtLyL .... Lyndon State College, Lyndonville, VT [*Library symbol*] [*Library of Congress*] (LCLS)

VTM .... Vacuum-Tube Module
VTM .... Vehicle Test Meter [*TACOM*] [*Army*] (RDA)
VTM .... Vehicles to the Mile [*Military*]
VTM .... Versatile Tracking Mount (MCD)
VTM .... Vibration Test Module (MCD)
VTM .... Voltage Tunable Magnetron
VtMan ...... Mark Skinner Public Library, Manchester, VT [*Library symbol*] [*Library of Congress*] (LCLS)
VtMarC ..... Marlboro College, Marlboro, VT [*Library symbol*] [*Library of Congress*] (LCLS)
VTMC .... Viable Titanium Matrix Composite
VTMDA..... Veterinarni Medicina [*A publication*]
VTMIDB... Annual Research Reviews. Vitamin-Trace Mineral-Protein Interactions [*A publication*]
VtMiM ...... Middlebury College, Middlebury, VT [*Library symbol*] [*Library of Congress*] (LCLS)
VtMiS........ Sheldon Art Museum, Middlebury, VT [*Library symbol*] [*Library of Congress*] (LCLS)
VTMO....... Voltage Tunable Microwave Oscillator
VtMor .... Morristown Centennial Library, Morrisville, VT [*Library symbol*] [*Library of Congress*] (LCLS)
VTMoV ..... Velvet Tobacco Mottle Virus
VTMRJa ... Voprosy Teorii i Metodiki Izucenijy Russkogo Jazyka [*A publication*]
VtMS .... Office of the Secretary of State, State Papers Division, Montpelier, VT [*Library symbol*] [*Library of Congress*] (LCLS)
VTMS....... Vessel Traffic Management System (DS)
VTMS....... Vinyltrimethysilane [*Organic chemistry*]
VtN .... Brown Public Library, Northfield, VT [*Library symbol*] [*Library of Congress*] (LCLS)
VT(N) .... Night Torpedo Bomber Squadron [*Navy symbol*]
VTN .... Valentine, NE [*Location identifier*] [*FAA*] (FAAL)
VTN .... Ventral Tegmental Nuclei [*Neuroanatomy*]
VTN .... Verification Test Network [*NASA*] (MCD)
VTN .... Video Tape Network (EA)
VTN .... Vitran Corp., Inc. [*Toronto Stock Exchange symbol*]
VTNA .... VTAM Telecommunications Network Architecture
VTNC .... VTN Corporation [*NASDAQ symbol*] (NQ)
VTNF....... Variable Time Non-Fragmenting [*Military*] (CAAL)
VtNN .... Norwich University, Northfield, VT [*Library symbol*] [*Library of Congress*] (LCLS)
VTNS........ Voltage Tunable Noise Source
VTO.......... Vertical Takeoff
VTO.......... Viable Terrestrial Organism
VTO.......... Visual Training Officer [*Navy*]
VTO.......... Vocational Training Officer [*Navy*]
VTO.......... Voltage Tunable Oscillator
VTOC....... Volume Table of Contents [*Data processing*]
VTOGW..... Vertical Takeoff Gross Weight
VTOHL ..... Vertical Takeoff and Horizontal Landing
VTOL .... Vertical Takeoff and Landing [*Also, VERTOL*] [*Acronym used for a type of aircraft*]
VTop .... Voprosy Toponomastiki [*A publication*]
VTOVL...... Vertical Takeoff Vertical Landing
VTP.......... Valid Target Presentation [*Military*] (CAAL)
VTP.......... Vandenberg Test Program [*Air Force*]
VTP.......... Vehicle Test Plan [*NASA*] (NASA)
VTP.......... Vendor Test Procedure
VTP.......... Verification Test Plan [*or Program*] (NASA)
VTP.......... VIEWDATA Terminal Program
VTP.......... Virtual Terminal Protocol
VTP.......... Visual Transmitter Power
VTPA .... Vertical Turbine Pump Association [*Defunct*]
VTPA .... (Vinylthiazolidinylidene)phenylamine [*Organic chemistry*]
VTPAI .... Victorian Town Planning Appeals Tribunal. Index of Appeals Decisions [*A publication*] (APTA)
VTPH .... Prachuap Khiri Khan/Hua Hin [*Thailand*] [*ICAO location identifier*] (ICLI)
VTPI .... Nakhon Sawan/Takhli [*Thailand*] [*ICAO location identifier*] (ICLI)
VtPifi .... Free Library, Pittsfield, VT [*Library symbol*] [*Library of Congress*] (LCLS)
VTPL........ Pretchabun/Lom Sak [*Thailand*] [*ICAO location identifier*] (ICLI)
VtPlaG....... Goddard College, Plainfield, VT [*Library symbol*] [*Library of Congress*] (LCLS)
VTPM....... Tak/Mae Sot [*Thailand*] [*ICAO location identifier*] (ICLI)
VTPN....... Nakhon Sawan [*Thailand*] [*ICAO location identifier*] (ICLI)
VtPom .... Abbott Memorial Library, Pomfret, VT [*Library symbol*] [*Library of Congress*] (LCLS)
VtPouG ..... Green Mountain College, Poultney, VT [*Library symbol*] [*Library of Congress*] (LCLS)
VTPP........ Phitsanulok [*Thailand*] [*ICAO location identifier*] (ICLI)
Vt-PR........ Vermont Public Records Library, Montpelier, VT [*Library symbol*] [*Library of Congress*] (LCLS)
VTPR........ Vertical Temperature Profile [*or Profiling*] Radiometer
VTPS .... Phitsanulok/Sarit Sena [*Thailand*] [*ICAO location identifier*] (ICLI)
VTPS .... Vibration Test Plotting System
VTPT......... Tak [*Thailand*] [*ICAO location identifier*] (ICLI)

VTPU .... Uttaradit [*Thailand*] [*ICAO location identifier*]   (ICLI)
VtPuW .... Windham College, Putney, VT [*Library symbol*] [*Library of Congress*]   (LCLS)
VTPY......... Tak/Sam Ngao [*Thailand*] [*ICAO location identifier*]   (ICLI)
VtQ .... Vermont Quarterly [*A publication*]
VTR .... McGrath, AK [*Location identifier*] [*FAA*]   (FAAL)
VTR .... Value of Time Research [*British*]
VTR .... Variable Tandem Repetition [*Genetics*]
VTR .... Vector   (FAAC)
VTR .... Vehicle Track Recovery [*Military*]
VTR .... Vehicle Tracking Receiver
VTR .... Vendor Trouble Report
VTR .... Verification Test Report   (NASA)
VTR .... Vermont Railway, Inc. [*AAR code*]
VT R .... Vermont Reports [*A publication*]   (DLA)
VTR .... Vertical Radial   (MSA)
VTR .... Vertical Test Range
VTR .... Veto Resources Ltd. [*Vancouver Stock Exchange symbol*]
VTR .... Videotape Recorder [*or Recording*]
VTR .... Vintage Triumph Register   (EA)
VTR .... Virginia Tax Review [*A publication*]
VTR .... Voltage Transformation Ratio [*Physics*]
VTRA .... Victorian Trotting and Racing Association [*Australia*]
VTRAN ..... Vast Translator   (KSC)
VtRaStM ... Saint Mary's Seminary, Randolph, VT [*Library symbol*] [*Library of Congress*]   (LCLS)
VTRB......... Variable Trim Reentry Body   (MCD)
VT Regist Nurse ... Vermont Registered Nurse [*A publication*]
VT Rep....... Vermont Reports [*A publication*]   (DLA)
VTRO .... Vitro Diagnostics [*NASDAQ symbol*]   (CTT)
VtRoc........ Rochester Public Library, Rochester, VT [*Library symbol*] [*Library of Congress*]   (LCLS)
VTRR......... Visual Target RADAR Ranging
VTRS......... Videotape Recording System
VTRS......... Videotape Response System
VTRS......... Visual Technology Research Simulator   (CAAL)
VTRX........ Ventrex Laboratories, Inc. [*NASDAQ symbol*]   (NQ)
VTS........... IEEE Vehicular Technology Society   (EA)
VTS........... Vandenberg Tracking Station [*Air Force*]
VTS........... Variable Time Step
VTS........... Variable Tracking Strategy   (MCD)
VTS........... Venture Touring Society   (EA)
VTS........... Versatile Training Systems   (MCD)
VTS........... Vertical Test Site [*NASA*]   (MCD)
VTS........... Vertical Test Stand [*NASA*]   (KSC)
VTS........... Vertical Test System   (NASA)
VTS........... Vertical Thrust Stand
VTS........... Vessel Traffic Service [*Harbor RADAR system*] [*Coast Guard*]
VTS........... Vetus Testamentum. Supplementum [*Leiden*] [*A publication*]
VTS........... Vibration Test Specification
VTS........... Vibration Test System
VTS........... Viewfinder Tracking System
VTS........... Virginia Theological Seminary, Alexandria, VA [*OCLC symbol*]   (OCLC)
VTS........... Visual Typing System   (MCD)
VTS........... Vitosha [*Bulgaria*] [*Seismograph station code, US Geological Survey*]   (SEIS)
VTS........... Vocational Training Scheme [*British*]
VTS........... Vocational Training Service
VTS........... Vote Tally System
VTS........... Vulcan Training System   (MCD)
VTSA......... Satun [*Thailand*] [*ICAO location identifier*]   (ICLI)
VTSB......... Surat Thani [*Thailand*] [*ICAO location identifier*]   (ICLI)
VTSC......... Narathiwat [*Thailand*] [*ICAO location identifier*]   (ICLI)
VTSD......... Chumpon [*Thailand*] [*ICAO location identifier*]   (ICLI)
VTSD......... Variable-Temperature Stepwise Desorption [*Chemical engineering*]
VTSE......... Vehicle Team Subcaliber Exercise [*Army*]   (INF)
VTSH........ Songkhla [*Thailand*] [*ICAO location identifier*]   (ICLI)
VtShelM .... Shelburne Museum, Inc., Research Library, Shelburne, VT [*Library symbol*] [*Library of Congress*]   (LCLS)
VTSI .... Vac-Tec Systems, Incorporated [*NASDAQ symbol*]   (NQ)
VTSK........ Pattani [*Thailand*] [*ICAO location identifier*]   (ICLI)
VTSN........ Nakhon Si Thammarat [*Thailand*] [*ICAO location identifier*]   (ICLI)
VTSO........ Surat Thani/Don Nok [*Thailand*] [*ICAO location identifier*]   (ICLI)
VTSP......... Phuket [*Thailand*] [*ICAO location identifier*]   (ICLI)
VTSPS....... Vsesoyuznyy Tsentral'nyy Sovet Professional'nykh Soyuzov [*All-Union Central Council of Trade Unions*] [*USSR*]
VTSR........ Ranong [*Thailand*] [*ICAO location identifier*]   (ICLI)
VTSS .... Songkhla/Hat Yai [*Thailand*] [*ICAO location identifier*]   (ICLI)
VTST .... Trang [*Thailand*] [*ICAO location identifier*]   (ICLI)
VTST .... Variant Transition State Theory [*Chemical physics*]
VT Stat Ann ... Vermont Statutes, Annotated [*A publication*]   (DLA)
VT St G Rp ... Vermont State Geologist. Report [*A publication*]
VtStjA........ St. Johnsbury Atheneum, St. Johnsbury, VT [*Library symbol*] [*Library of Congress*]   (LCLS)
VtStjF .... Fairbanks Museum of Natural Science, St. Johnsbury, VT [*Library symbol*] [*Library of Congress*]   (LCLS)
VTSuppl .... Vetus Testamentum. Supplementum [*Leiden*] [*A publication*]

Vt-SWRL... Vermont Department of Libraries, Southwest Regional Library, Rutland, VT [*Library symbol*] [*Library of Congress*]   (LCLS)
VTSY........ Ya La [*Thailand*] [*ICAO location identifier*]   (ICLI)
VTT .... Vacuum Thermal Testing
VTT .... Vacuum-Tube Transmitter
VTT .... Valtion Teknillinen Tutkimuskeskus [*Technical Research Center of Finland*] [*Espoo*] [*Information service or system*]   (IID)
VTT .... Variable Threshold Transistor
VTTC......... Vocational Technical and Training Corp. [*Australia*]
VTTJA ...... Valtion Teknillinen Tutkimuslaitos. Julkaisu [*A publication*]
VTU .... Las Tunas [*Cuba*] [*Airport symbol*]   (OAG)
VTU .... Oxnard, CA [*Location identifier*] [*FAA*]   (FAAL)
VTU .... University of Vermont, Bailey Library, Burlington, VT [*OCLC symbol*]   (OCLC)
VtU .... University of Vermont, Burlington, VT [*Library symbol*] [*Library of Congress*]   (LCLS)
vtu .... Vermont [*MARC country of publication code*] [*Library of Congress*]   (LCCP)
V + TU..... Voice plus Teleprinter Unit
VTU .... Volunteer Reserve Training Unit [*Coast Guard*]
VTU .... Volunteer Training Unit
VTUA .... Kalasin/Ban Na Khu [*Thailand*] [*ICAO location identifier*]   (ICLI)
VTUB .... Bakhon Phanom/Mukdahan [*Thailand*] [*ICAO location identifier*]   (ICLI)
VTUC .... Chaiyaphum [*Thailand*] [*ICAO location identifier*]   (ICLI)
VTUD .... Udon Thani [*Thailand*] [*ICAO location identifier*]   (ICLI)
VTUE .... Sakon Nakhon/Nam Phung Dam (North) [*Thailand*] [*ICAO location identifier*]   (ICLI)
VTUF......... Sakon Nakhon/Nam Phung Dam (South) [*Thailand*] [*ICAO location identifier*]   (ICLI)
VTUG .... Chaiyaphum/Phu Khieo [*Thailand*] [*ICAO location identifier*]   (ICLI)
VTUH .... Nakhon Ratchasima/Pak Chong [*Thailand*] [*ICAO location identifier*]   (ICLI)
VTUI .... Sakon Nakhon/Bankhai [*Thailand*] [*ICAO location identifier*]   (ICLI)
VTUK .... Khon Kaen [*Thailand*] [*ICAO location identifier*]   (ICLI)
VTUL .... Loei [*Thailand*] [*ICAO location identifier*]   (ICLI)
VTUM ...... Nongkhai [*Thailand*] [*ICAO location identifier*]   (ICLI)
VtU-Med ... University of Vermont, College of Medicine, Burlington, VT [*Library symbol*] [*Library of Congress*]   (LCLS)
VTU(MMS) ... Volunteer Training Unit (Merchant Marine Safety)
VTUN........ Nakhon Ratchasima [*Thailand*] [*ICAO location identifier*]   (ICLI)
VTUP .... Nakhon Phanom [*Thailand*] [*ICAO location identifier*]   (ICLI)
VTUR .... Roi Et [*Thailand*] [*ICAO location identifier*]   (ICLI)
VTUS........ Sakon Nakhon [*Thailand*] [*ICAO location identifier*]   (ICLI)
VTUT .... Ubon Ratchathani/Loeng Nok Tha [*Thailand*] [*ICAO location identifier*]   (ICLI)
VTUU .... Ubon Ratchathani [*Thailand*] [*ICAO location identifier*]   (ICLI)
VTUW ...... Nakhon Phanom (West) [*Thailand*] [*ICAO location identifier*]   (ICLI)
VtU-W ...... University of Vermont and State Agricultural College, Wilbur Collection, Burlington, VT [*Library symbol*] [*Library of Congress*]   (LCLS)
VTUZ .... Khon Kaen/Nam Phung Dam [*Thailand*] [*ICAO location identifier*]   (ICLI)
VTV .... Vacuum Transmitting Valve [*Automotive engineering*]
VT(V)........ Vacuum-Tube (Voltmeter)   (DEN)
VTV .... Value Television [*Television program*]
VTV .... Verification Test Vehicle [*Military*]   (CAAL)
VtVe......... Bixby Memorial Free Library, Vergennes, VT [*Library symbol*] [*Library of Congress*]   (LCLS)
VT Verfahrenstech ... VT. Verfahrenstechnik [*A publication*]
VTVM........ Vacuum-Tube Voltmeter
VTW .... Variable Transmission Window
VtWeo........ Wilder Memorial Library, Weston, VT [*Library symbol*] [*Library of Congress*]   (LCLS)
VtWinoS .... Saint Michael's College, Winooski, VT [*Library symbol*] [*Library of Congress*]   (LCLS)
VTX .... Vacuum-Tube Transmitter
VTX .... Ventex Energy [*Vancouver Stock Exchange symbol*]
VTX .... Vertex
VTX .... Vertex [*A publication*]
VTX .... Videotex [*Telecommunications*]
VTX .... Vortex   (AAG)
VTX .... VTX Electronics [*AMEX symbol*]   (SPSG)
VTXTS ...... Navy Jet Trainer   (MCD)
VTXX........ Vertz Corp. [*NASDAQ symbol*]   (NQ)
VTY .... Vatovaky [*Madagascar*] [*Seismograph station code, US Geological Survey*]   (SEIS)
VTY .... Virkamiesten ja Tyoentekijaein Yhteisjaerjestoe [*Joint Organization of Civil Servants and Workers*] [*Finland*]   (EY)
VTZ .... Vishakhapatnam [*India*] [*Airport symbol*]   (OAG)
VU............. Societe Air Ivoire [*Ivory Coast*] [*ICAO designator*]   (FAAC)
VU............. Utility Squadron [*Navy symbol*]   (MCD)

VU............ Validation Unit (AAG)
VU............ Vanity Unit [Classified advertising] (ADA)
VU............ Vanuatu [ANSI two-letter standard code] (CNC)
VU............ Varicose Ulcer [Medicine]
VU............ Vaterlaendische Union [Patriotic Union] [Liechtenstein]
         [Political party] (PPE)
VU............ Vehicle Unit (KSC)
VU............ Vehicle Utility (MCD)
VU............ Very Urgent
VU............ Voice of Uganda [A publication]
VU............ Voice Unit [Signal amplitude measurement]
VU............ Volksunite [United People's Party] [Belgium] [Political party]
VU............ Volume Unit [Signal amplitude measurement]
VU............ Von Unten [From the Bottom] [German]
VUA.......... Valorous Unit Award [Military decoration]
VUA.......... Verbal Underachievers [Education]
VUA.......... Virtual Unit Address (BUR)
VUB.......... Variational Upper Bound
VUB.......... Vrije Universiteit Brussel [Free University of Brussels]
         [Belgium] [Information service or system] (IID)
VUBN........ Valley Utah Bancorporation [Salt Lake City, UT] [NASDAQ
         symbol] (NQ)
VUBT .... Vuebotics Corp. [NASDAQ symbol] (NQ)
VUCC .... Computer Center [Vanderbilt University] [Research
         center] (RCD)
VUCDT ..... Ventilation Unit Condensate Drain Tank (IEEE)
VUCLR...... Victoria University. College Law Review [A publication]
VUCS........ Ventilation Umbilical Connector System
VUE.......... Upper Hudson Library Federation, Albany, NY [OCLC
         symbol] (OCLC)
Vues Econ Aquitaine ... Vues sur l'Economie d'Aquitaine [A publication]
VuF .... Verkuendigung und Forschung [A publication]
VUF .... Vertical Upward Force
VuG.......... Vergangenheit und Gegenwart [A publication]
VUHZ....... Vyzkumny Ustav Hutnictvi Zeleza, Dobra [Dobra Iron and
         Steel Research Institute] [Information service or
         system] (IID)
VUL.......... Vulcan [Taviliu] [New Britain] [Seismograph station code, US
         Geological Survey] (SEIS)
VUL.......... Vulcan International Corp. [AMEX symbol] (SPSG)
VUL.......... Vulcanize (AAG)
VUL.......... Vulnerary [Medicine to heal wounds] (ROG)
Vul........... Vulpecula [Constellation]
VULBS ..... Virginia Union List of Biomedical Serials [Library network]
VULC .... Vanguard Unionist Loyalist Coalition [Northern Ireland]
         [Political party]
VULC .... Vulcanize
VULCAN .. [A] programming language (CSR)
VULG .... Vulgar
VULG .... Vulgate [Version of the Bible]
Vulkanol Seismol ... Vulkanologiya i Seismologiya [A publication]
Vulp .... Vulpecula [Constellation]
VULR .... Valparaiso University. Law Review [A publication]
VULREP ... Vulnerability Report [Navy] (NVT)
VULT .... Voprosy Uzbekskogo Jazyka i Literatury [A publication]
Vultei .... [Hermannus] Vulteius [Deceased, 1634] [Authority cited in pre-
         1607 legal work] (DSA)
VUMD....... Vilniaus Valstybinio V. Kapsuko Vardo Universiteto Mokslo
         Darbai [A publication]
VUMS .... Vyzkumny Ustav pro Matematickych Stroju [Research Institute
         for Mathematical Machines] [Czechoslovakia]
VUN.......... Vunikawai [Fiji] [Seismograph station code, US Geological
         Survey] (SEIS)
VUNC....... Voice of United Nations Command
Vuorit Bergshant ... Vuoriteollisuus/Bergshanteringen [A publication]
Vuoto....... Vuoto, Scienza, e Tecnologia [A publication]
Vuoto Sci Tecnol ... Vuoto, Scienza, e Tecnologia [A publication]
VUP.......... Valledupar [Colombia] [Airport symbol] (OAG)
VUP.......... Vela Uniform Platform
VUPP........ Vanguard Unionist Progressive Party [Northern Ireland]
         [Political party]
VUQ.......... Dayton, OH [Location identifier] [FAA] (FAAL)
VUR.......... Vesicoureteral Reflex [Nephrology]
VURB-A .... Vie Urbaine [France] [A publication]
VUS .... Versatile Upper Stage [NASA]
VUSA .... Visit USA [Airline fare]
VUSH........ Vanderbilt University. Studies in the Humanities [A
         publication]
VUT .... Union Theological Seminary Library, Richmond, VA [OCLC
         symbol] (OCLC)
VUT .... Vanuatu [ANSI three-letter standard code] (CNC)
Vutr Boles ... Vutreshni Bolesti [A publication]
VUTS........ Verification Unit Test Set (AFM)
VUU .... Virginia Union University [Richmond]
VUU .... Virginia Union University, Richmond, VA [OCLC
         symbol] (OCLC)
VUV .... Vacuum Ultraviolet
VUW.......... Eugene Isle, LA [Location identifier] [FAA] (FAAL)
VUWLR .... Victoria University of Wellington. Law Review [A publication]
VUWL Rev ... Victoria University of Wellington. Law Review [A publication]
VUZ........... Birmingham, AL [Location identifier] [FAA] (FAAL)

VV............ First and Second Violins [Music] (ROG)
VV............ Nile Valley Aviation Co. [Egypt] [ICAO designator] (FAAC)
VV............ Vaccinia Virus
VV............ Vacuum Valve
V/V .... Validation/Verification (CAAL)
VV............ Vanguard Ventures [Vancouver Stock Exchange symbol]
VV............ Veins [Medicine]
VV............ Velocity Vector (AAG)
VV............ Velocity-Volume
VV............ Vent Valve
VV............ Verbs (ADA)
V & V .... Verification and Validation [Data processing]
VV............ Verses
VV............ Vertebral Vein [Anatomy]
V/V .... Vertical Velocity
VV............ Vestron, Inc. [NYSE symbol] (SPSG)
V-V .... Vibrational-to-Vibrational [Energy transfer]
VV............ Vibrio Vulnificus [A microorganism]
VV............ Vice Versa
VV............ Victims for Victims (EA)
VV............ Vietnam Veterans (OICC)
VV............ Village Voice [A publication]
VV............ Violini [Violins] [Music]
VV............ Visna Virus
VV............ Vista Ventures [Commercial firm] [British]
VV............ Visum Vivum [Seen Alive] [Botany] (ROG)
VV............ Viva Voce [Spoken Aloud] [Latin] (ADA)
VV............ Vizantiiskii Vremenik [A publication]
VV............ Voices [Music]
VV............ Volk und Volkstum [A publication]
V/V .... Volume/Volume
V for V .... Volunteers for Vision [Defunct] (EA)
v/v .... Votre Ville [Your City] [French]
vv.............. Vragvry [Carriage Free] [Afrikaans]
VV............ Vulva and Vagina [Physiology]
VVA .... Southern Adirondack Library System, Saratoga Springs, NY
         [OCLC symbol] (OCLC)
VVa .... Vida Vasca [A publication]
VVA .... Vietnam Veterans of America (EA)
Vva .... Viuva [Widow] [Portuguese]
VVAA .... Vietnam Veterans Association of Australia
VVAG .... Vietnam Veterans Arts Group [Later, CTVWA] (EA)
VVAOVI..... Vietnam Veterans Agent Orange Victims (EA)
VVAP........ Mouvement Socialiste Occitan - Volem Viure al Pais
         [Occitanian Socialist Movement] [France] [Political
         party] (PPW)
VVAW ...... Vietnam Veterans Against the War (EA)
VVB .... Baruch College, New York, NY [OCLC symbol] (OCLC)
VVB .... Mahanoro [Madagascar] [Airport symbol] (OAG)
VVBAA..... Venetian and Vertical Blind Association of America [Defunct]
VVBM .... Buonmethuot/Chung Duc [Viet Nam] [ICAO location
         identifier] (ICLI)
VVC .... Colgate University, Hamilton, NY [OCLC symbol] (OCLC)
VVC .... Variable Vacuum Capacitor
VVC .... Vertical Velocity Console
VVC .... Villavicencio [Colombia] [Airport symbol] (OAG)
VVC .... Voltage Variable Capacitor
VVCB........ Caobang [Viet Nam] [ICAO location identifier] (ICLI)
VVCC........ Viri Clarissimi [Most Illustrious Men] [Latin]
VVCD .... Voltage Variable Capacitance Diode
VVCEC....... Voice and Video Control and Editing Components (MCD)
VVCO .... US Video Vending Corporation [Iselin, NJ] [NASDAQ
         symbol] (NQ)
VVCS........ Conson [Viet Nam] [ICAO location identifier] (ICLI)
VVCS........ Vernier Velocity Correction System [Aerospace] (KSC)
VVCT........ Cantho [Viet Nam] [ICAO location identifier] (ICLI)
VVCUS..... Veteran Vespa Club, US (EA)
VVD.......... Downstate Medical Center, SUNY [State University of New
         York], Brooklyn, NY [OCLC symbol] (OCLC)
VVD.......... Valid Verifiable Defense [Stamped on dismissed traffic tickets]
VVD.......... Valverde [Canary Islands] [Seismograph station code, US
         Geological Survey] (SEIS)
VVD.......... Volkspartij voor Vrijheid en Democratie [People's Party for
         Freedom and Democracy] [Netherlands] [Political
         party] (EAIO)
VVD.......... Voltage Variable Diode
VVDB .... Dienbienphu [Viet Nam] [ICAO location identifier] (ICLI)
VVDL .... Dalat/Lienkhuong [Viet Nam] [ICAO location
         identifier] (ICLI)
VVDN........ Danang [Viet Nam] [ICAO location identifier] (ICLI)
VVDS........ Video Verter Decision Storage
VVDStRL.. Veroeffentlichungen der Vereinigung der Deutschen
         Staatsrechtslehrer [Proceedings of the Society of German
         Teachers of Public Law] [A publication] (ILCA)
VVE .... Erie Community College-North, Buffalo, NY [OCLC
         symbol] (OCLC)
VVF........... New York Medical College, New York, NY [OCLC
         symbol] (OCLC)
VVF........... Veseco Vaginal Fistula [Medicine]
VVG .... New York State Institute for Research in Mental Retardation,
         Staten Island, NY [OCLC symbol] (OCLC)

VVGF.........	Vincent Van Gogh Foundation (EA)
VVGL	Hanoi/Gialam [*Viet Nam*] [*ICAO location identifier*] (ICLI)
VVH..........	Daemen College, Buffalo, NY [*OCLC symbol*] (OCLC)
VVH..........	Very Very Heavy [*Cosmic ray nuclei*]
VVH.........	Veterans Vigil of Honor (EA)
VVHR.......	Vibration Velocity per Hour
VVI	Beth Israel Medical Center, New York, NY [*OCLC symbol*] (OCLC)
VVI	Vertical Velocity Indicator (MCD)
VVI	Vice Viewers International (EA)
VVI	Vietnam Veterans, Incorporated (EA)
VVI	Vietnam Veterans Institute [*Research center*] (RCD)
VVI	Vocational Values Inventory [*Guidance in education*]
VVI	Voltage Variation Indicator
VVIC.........	Vietnam Era Veterans in Congress (EA)
VVIP........	Very, Very Important Person
VVIR........	Voice and Vision of the Iranian Revolution [*Iranian television*]
VVIRA......	Vietnam Veterans Institute for Research and Advocacy (EA)
VVIS.........	Vision Communication Corp. [*Formerly, Videovision, Inc.*] [*NASDAQ symbol*] (NQ)
VVITA.......	Vietnam Veterans Inter-Tribal Association (EA)
VVJ...........	John Jay College of Criminal Justice, New York, NY [*OCLC symbol*] (OCLC)
VVK	New York Academy of Medicine, New York, NY [*OCLC symbol*] (OCLC)
VVK	Van Vleck [*Quantum mechanics*]
VVK	Vastervik [*Sweden*] [*Airport symbol*] (OAG)
VVKP........	Kep [*Viet Nam*] [*ICAO location identifier*] (ICLI)
VVL	Mount Sinai School of Medicine of the City University of New York, New York, NY [*OCLC symbol*] (OCLC)
VVL	Vee en Vlees. Het Vakblad voor Handelaar en Producent [*A publication*]
VVLK........	Laokay [*Viet Nam*] [*ICAO location identifier*] (ICLI)
VV LL........	Variae Lectiones [*Variant Readings*] [*Latin*]
VVLP........	Vietnam Veterans Leadership Program [*ACTION*]
VVM	Memorial Sloan-Kettering Cancer Center, New York, NY [*OCLC symbol*] (OCLC)
VVM.........	Vector Voltmeter
VVM.........	Velocity Vector Measurement
VVM.........	Vlastivedny Vestnik Moravsky [*A publication*]
VVMC.......	Voice and Video Monitoring Component (MCD)
VVMF.......	Vietnam Veterans Memorial Fund (EA)
VVMS.......	Velocity Vector Measurement System
VVN	Niagara University, Niagara University, NY [*OCLC symbol*] (OCLC)
VVNB	Hanoi/Noibai [*Viet Nam*] [*ICAO location identifier*] (ICLI)
VVNS	Nasan [*Viet Nam*] [*ICAO location identifier*] (ICLI)
VVNT	Nhatrang [*Viet Nam*] [*ICAO location identifier*] (ICLI)
VVnW.......	Veterans of the Vietnam War (EA)
VVO	New York Medical College, Westchester Medical Center, Valhalla, NY [*OCLC symbol*] (OCLC)
VVO	Very Very Old [*Designation on brandy labels*]
VVOH	Vacuum Valve Operating Handle
VVP	Bard College, Annandale-On-Hudson, NY [*OCLC symbol*] (OCLC)
VVPB........	Hue/Phubai [*Viet Nam*] [*ICAO location identifier*] (ICLI)
VVPK........	Pleiku/Cu-Hanh [*Viet Nam*] [*ICAO location identifier*] (ICLI)
VVPP........	Variable Volume Piston Pump
VVPQ........	Phuquoc [*Viet Nam*] [*ICAO location identifier*] (ICLI)
VVQ	Roosevelt Hospital, Medical Library, New York, NY [*OCLC symbol*] (OCLC)
VVQN........	Quinhon [*Viet Nam*] [*ICAO location identifier*] (ICLI)
VVR	Rockland Community College, Suffern, NY [*OCLC symbol*] (OCLC)
VVR	Vancouver Ventures [*Vancouver Stock Exchange symbol*]
VVR	Variable Voltage Rectifier
VVR	Vehicle Vapor Recovery [*Automobile*]
VVR	Viewdata/Videotex Report [*Link Resources Corp.*] [*Information service or system*] (CRD)
VVRG	Rachgia [*Viet Nam*] [*ICAO location identifier*] (ICLI)
VVRI.........	Veterinary Virus Research Institute [*New York State Veterinary College*]
VVRM	Vortex Valve Rocket Motor (MCD)
VVRS.......	Viscous Vortex Rate Sensor
VVS...........	Connellsville, PA [*Location identifier*] [*FAA*] (FAAL)
VVS...........	Sarah Lawrence College, Bronxville, NY [*OCLC symbol*] (OCLC)
VVS...........	Vein Ventures Ltd. [*Vancouver Stock Exchange symbol*]
VVS...........	Very Very Slightly Flawed [*Gems*]
VVS...........	Very, Very Small Inclusions [*Diamond clarity grade*]
VVS...........	Very Very Superior
VVS...........	Voenno-Vozdushnye Sily [*Army Air Forces*] [*Part of the MO*] [*USSR*]
VVS...........	Voice Verification System
VVSA........	Velocity Vector Sensor Assembly
VVSO	Very, Very Superior Old [*Designation on brandy labels*]
VVSOP......	Very, Very Superior Old Pale [*Designation on brandy labels*]
VVSS........	Vertical Volute Spring Suspension [*Technical drawings*]
VVS Tidsk Energ VVS-Tek ...	VVS. Tidskrift foer Energi- och VVS [*Vaerme, Ventilation, Sanitet*]-Teknik [*A publication*]
VVS Tidskr Vaerme Vent Sanit Kyltetek ...	VVS. Tidskrift foer Vaerme, Ventilation, Sanitet, och Kylteteknik [*A publication*]
VVS Tidskr Varme Vent Sanit ...	VVS. Tidskrift foer Vaerme, Ventilation, Sanitet [*Sweden*] [*A publication*]
VVS-VMF ...	Voenno-Vozdushnye Sily - Voenno-Morskogo Flota [*Naval Air Force*] [*USSR*]
VVT	Teachers College, Columbia University, New York, NY [*OCLC symbol*] (OCLC)
VVT	Velocity Variation Tube
VVT	Venturi Vacuum Transducer [*Engineering*]
VVT	Visual-Verbal Test [*Psychology*]
VVTBA......	Vaeg- och Vattenbyggaren [*A publication*]
VVTC........	Vendor-Vendee Technical Committee
VVTS.........	Hochiminh/Tansonnhat [*Viet Nam*] [*ICAO location identifier*] (ICLI)
VVU	New York University, Medical Center, New York, NY [*OCLC symbol*] (OCLC)
VVUU Zpr ...	VVUU [*Vedeckovyzkumny Uhelny Ustav*] Ostrava-Radvanice Zprava [*A publication*]
VVV	Ortonville, MN [*Location identifier*] [*FAA*] (FAAL)
VVV	Utica College of Syracuse University, Utica, NY [*OCLC symbol*] (OCLC)
VVVH........	Vinh [*Viet Nam*] [*ICAO location identifier*] (ICLI)
VVVT........	Vungtau [*Viet Nam*] [*ICAO location identifier*] (ICLI)
VVVV	Hanoi [*Viet Nam*] [*ICAO location identifier*] (ICLI)
VVW	Westchester Library System, Yonkers, NY [*OCLC symbol*] (OCLC)
VVWCA	Vintage Volkswagen Club of America (EA)
VV:WT	Vaccinia Virus: Wild Type [*Virology*]
VVX	Nassau Community College, Garden City, NY [*OCLC symbol*] (OCLC)
VVY	St. Luke's Hospital, Bolling Medical Library, New York, NY [*OCLC symbol*] (OCLC)
VVZ	Medical Library Center of New York, New York, NY [*OCLC symbol*] (OCLC)
VW	Air Concept [*Federal Republic of Germany*] [*ICAO aircraft manufacturer identifier*] (ICAO)
VW	Early Warning Squadron [*Symbol*] (MCD)
Vw	Maximum Winch Launching Speed [*Gliders*] (AIA)
VW	Transportes Aereos Trafe SA [*ICAO designator*] (FAAC)
VW	Very Weak [*Spectral*]
VW	Very Worshipful
VW	Vessel Wall
VW	Vie Wallonne [*A publication*]
VW	View (MCD)
VW	Volkswagen [*German automobile*]
VW	Volkswagenwerk Aktiengesellschaft [*Volkswagen Joint Stock Company*] [*Business term*] [*Federal Republic of Germany*]
VWA	Vacuum Window Assembly
VWA	Vendor Working Authority
VWA	Verband der Weiblichen Angestellten [*Association of Female Employees*] [*West Germany*]
VWA	Vintage Wireless Association [*British*]
VWA	Volume-Weighted Average [*Statistics*]
VWAC	Victorian Women's Advisory Council to the Premier [*Australia*]
VWB	Bronx Community College Library, Bronx, NY [*OCLC symbol*] (OCLC)
VWBN	Valley West Bancorp [*Springfield, OR*] [*NASDAQ symbol*] (NQ)
VWC	Villa Walsh College [*New Jersey*]
VWC	Vulcan Wheeled Carrier
VWCA	Volkswagen Club of America (EA)
VWCC	Victorian Women's Consultative Council [*Australia*]
VWCL........	Volkswagen Caminhoes Limitada [*Brazil*]
VWD........	Vereinigte Wirtschaftsdienste [*Press agency*] [*West Germany*]
VWD........	Video-West Distributors Ltd. [*Vancouver Stock Exchange symbol*]
VWD........	Vinyl Window and Door Institute (EA)
vWD..........	Von Willebrand's Disease [*Medicine*]
VWDU......	Viewing Window Deicing Unit
VWE	Vanadium Wire Equilibration [*Nuclear energy*] (NRCH)
VWED	Vanadium Wire Equilibration Device [*Nuclear energy*] (NRCH)
VWF	Vehicle Work Flow
VWF	Vibration-Induced White Finger [*Medicine*]
vWf............	Von Willebrand factor [*Also, vWF, VWF*] [*Hematology*]
VWFC........	Very-Wide-Field Camera
VWG.........	Vital Wheat Gluten [*Vegetable protein*]
VWGA	Vinifera Wine Growers Association (EA)
VWH	Vale of White Horse [*Hounds*]
VWH	Vertical Weld Head
VWHA.......	Vertical Weld Head Assembly
VWL	College of William and Mary, Law School, Williamsburg, VA [*OCLC symbol*] (OCLC)
VWL	Variable Word Length
VWM........	College of William and Mary, Williamsburg, VA [*OCLC symbol*] (OCLC)
VWM........	Virginia Woolf Miscellany [*A publication*]
VWM........	Volume-Weighted Mean [*Statistical technique*]
VWMP	Vietnam Women's Memorial Project (EA)

VWN......... Virginia Woolf Newsletter [*A publication*]
VWO......... Valves Wide Open [*Nuclear energy*] (NRCH)
VWO......... Woolsey, GA [*Location identifier*] [*FAA*] (FAAL)
VWOA...... Veteran Wireless Operators Association (EA)
VWOA...... Volkswagen of America
VWP......... Variable Width Pulse
VWP......... Vietnam Workers' Party [*Political party*] (PPW)
VWPI........ Vacuum Wood Preservers Institute (EA)
VWQ........ Virginia Woolf Quarterly [*A publication*]
VWR......... North Country Reference and Research Resources Council, Canton, NY [*OCLC symbol*] (OCLC)
VWR......... Volkswirtschaftsrat [*Political Economy Bureau*] [*German*]
VWRRC..... Virginia Water Resources Research Center [*Virginia Polytechnic Institute and State University*] [*Research center*] (RCD)
VWRS........ Vibrating Wire Rate Sensor
VWRX .... VWR Corp. [*Seattle, WA*] [*NASDAQ symbol*] (NQ)
VWS .... Valdez, AK [*Location identifier*] [*FAA*] (FAAL)
VWS .... Variable Word Size
VWS .... Virginia Woolf Society (EA)
VWS .... Voice Warning System
VWSG ...... Victorian Wader Study Group [*Australia*]
VWSS....... Vertical Wire Sky Screen (KSC)
VWSWCA ... Volkswagen Split Window Club of America (EA)
VWTA ...... Vintage White Truck Association (EA)
VW-TCA ... Volkswagen Toy Collectors of America (EA)
VWU......... Chincoteague Island, VA [*Location identifier*] [*FAA*] (FAAL)
VWV......... Waterville, OH [*Location identifier*] [*FAA*] (FAAL)
VWW........ Velocity of Wireless Waves
VWWI .... Veterans of World War I of USA (EA)
VWY .... Visway Transport, Inc. [*Toronto Stock Exchange symbol*]
VX............. Air Development Squadron [*Navy*]
VX............. Experimental Squadron [*Symbol*] (MCD)
VX............. Nerve Gas [*US Chemical Corps symbol*]
VX............. Transvalair [*Switzerland*] [*ICAO designator*] (FAAC)
VX............. Vanex Resources Ltd. [*Vancouver Stock Exchange symbol*]
VX............. Vauxhall [*Automobile*] [*British*]
VX............. Velocity along the X-Axis (NASA)
VX............. Veronex Resources Ltd. [*AMEX symbol*] (SPSG)
VX............. Vertex [*Medicine*]
VX............. Vivas, Care [*May You Live, Dear One*] [*Latin*]
VX............. Voice
VX............. Volume Unknown [*Medicine*]
VX-1........... OPTEVFOR [*Operational Test and Evaluation Force*] Air Test and Evaluation Squadron One, Naval Air Station, Patuxent River, MD (CAAL)
VX-4........... OPTEVFOR [*Operational Test and Evaluation Force*] Air Test and Evaluation Squadron Four, Naval Air Station, Pt. Mugu, CA (CAAL)
VX-5........... OPTEVFOR [*Operational Test and Evaluation Force*] Air Test and Evaluation Squadron Five, Naval Weapons Center, China Lake, CA (CAAL)
VXA .... Harlem Hospital Center, Health Sciences Library, New York, NY [*OCLC symbol*] (OCLC)
VXC .... Lichinga [*Mozambique*] [*Airport symbol*] (OAG)
VXD.......... New York University, College of Dentistry Library, New York, NY [*OCLC symbol*] (OCLC)
VXE .... Elmira College, Elmira, NY [*OCLC symbol*] (OCLC)
VXE .... Sao Vicente [*Cape Verde Islands*] [*Airport symbol*] (OAG)
VXF.......... State University of New York, College of Environmental Science and Forestry, Syracuse, NY [*OCLC symbol*] (OCLC)
VXG .... New York Botanical Garden Library, Bronx, NY [*OCLC symbol*] (OCLC)
VXH.......... Herkimer County Community College, Herkimer, NY [*OCLC symbol*] (OCLC)
VXI .... Iona College, New Rochelle, NY [*OCLC symbol*] (OCLC)
VXJ .... Jewish Theological Seminary of America, New York, NY [*OCLC symbol*] (OCLC)
VXL .... Albany Medical College, Schaffer Library of Health Sciences, Albany, NY [*OCLC symbol*] (OCLC)
VXLB........ Verex Laboratories, Inc. [*NASDAQ symbol*] (NQ)
VXM .... General Theological Seminary, St. Mark's Library, New York, NY [*OCLC symbol*] (OCLC)
VXN.......... New York State Department of Health, Albany, NY [*OCLC symbol*] (OCLC)
VXO.......... Houghton College, Houghton, NY [*OCLC symbol*] (OCLC)
VXO.......... Variable Crystal Oscillator
VXO.......... Vaxjo [*Sweden*] [*Airport symbol*] (OAG)
VXP .... State University of New York, College of Optometry, New York, NY [*OCLC symbol*] (OCLC)
VXR .... Rochester Museum and Science Center, Rochester, NY [*OCLC symbol*] (OCLC)
VXR .... Vertex Resources Ltd. [*Vancouver Stock Exchange symbol*]
VXT .... Tompkins-Cortland Community College, Dryden, NY [*OCLC symbol*] (OCLC)
VXU .... Chautauqua-Cattaraugus Library System, Jamestown, NY [*OCLC symbol*] (OCLC)
VXV .... Hudson Valley Community College, Troy, NY [*OCLC symbol*] (OCLC)
VXW .... Vassar College, Poughkeepsie, NY [*OCLC symbol*] (OCLC)

VXX .... Long Island University, C. W. Post Center, Greenvale, NY [*OCLC symbol*] (OCLC)
VXX .... Venturex Resources [*Vancouver Stock Exchange symbol*]
VXY .... Centro de Estudios Puertorriquenos, New York, NY [*OCLC symbol*] (OCLC)
VXZ .... Dowling College, Oakdale, NY [*OCLC symbol*] (OCLC)
VY .... Abelag Airways [*Belgium*] [*ICAO designator*] (ICDA)
VY .... Air Belgium [*Belgium*] [*ICAO designator*] (FAAC)
VY .... Valley (ADA)
VY .... Various Years [*Bibliography*]
VY .... Velocity along the Y-Axis (NASA)
VY .... Very (ROG)
VY .... Victualling Yard [*Obsolete*] [*Navy*] [*British*] (ROG)
VY .... Vyquest, Inc. [*AMEX symbol*] (SPSG)
VYA .... Molloy College, Rockville Centre, NY [*OCLC symbol*] (OCLC)
Vya............ Voprosy Yazykoznaniya [*Moscow*] [*A publication*]
VYB .... St. Barnabas Medical Staff Library, Livingston, NJ [*OCLC symbol*] (OCLC)
VYB .... Vivian, Younger & Bond Ltd.
VYB .... Vyborg [*USSR*] [*Seismograph station code, US Geological Survey*] [*Closed*] (SEIS)
Vyber Inf Organ Vypocetni Tech ... Vyber Informaci z Organizacni a Vypocetni Techniky [*A publication*]
VYBN .... Valley Bancorporation [*NASDAQ symbol*] (NQ)
VYC .... Cornell University, Medical College, New York, NY [*OCLC symbol*] (OCLC)
Vychisl Metody Progam ... Vychislitel'nye Metody i Programmirovanie [*A publication*]
Vychisl Metody & Program ... Vychislitel'nye Metody i Programmirovanie [*A publication*]
Vychisl Metody i Programmirovanie ... Moskovskii Universitet. Sbornik Rabot Vychislitelnogo Tsentra Moskovskogo Universiteta. Vychislitel'nye Metody i Programmirovanie [*A publication*]
Vychisl Prikl Mat ... Kievskii Gosudarstvennyi Universitet Mezhvedomstvennyi Nauchnyi Sbornik Vychislitel'naya i Prikladnaya Matematika [*A publication*]
Vychisl Seismol ... Vychislitel'naya Seismologiya [*USSR*] [*A publication*]
Vychisl Sist ... Vychislitel'nye Sistemy [*A publication*]
Vychisl Tekhn i Voprosy Kibernet ... Leningradskii Gosudarstvennyi Universitet Vychislitel'nyi Tsentr Moskovskii Gosudarstvennyi Universitet Vychislitel'nyi Tsentr Vychislitel'naya Tekhnika i Voprosy Kibernetiki [*A publication*]
Vychisl Tekh i Vopr Kibern ... Vychislitel'naya Tekhnika i Voprosy Kibernetiki [*A publication*]
Vycisl Mat i Vycisl Tehn (Kharkov) ... Vycislitel'naja Matematika i Vycislitel'naja Tehnika (Kharkov) [*A publication*]
Vycisl Metody i Programmirovanie ... Vycislitel'nye Metody i Programmirovanie. Moskovskii Universitet. Sbornik Rabot Vycislitel'nogo Centra Moskovskogo Universiteta [*A publication*]
Vycisl Prikl Mat (Kiev) ... Vycislitel'naja i Prikladnaja Matematika (Kiev) [*A publication*]
Vycisl Sistemy ... Akademija Nauk SSSR. Sibirskoe Otdelenie. Institut Matematiki. Vycislitel'nye Sistemy. Sbornik Trudov [*A publication*]
Vycisl Tehn v Masinostroen ... Vycislitel'naja Tehnika v Masinostroenii [*A publication*]
Vycisl Tehn i Voprosy Kibernet ... Vycislitel'naja Tehnika i Voprosy Kibernetiki [*A publication*]
VYD .... Capital District Library Council, Troy, NY [*OCLC symbol*] (OCLC)
VYD .... Vryheid [*South Africa*] [*Airport symbol*] (OAG)
VYE .... Manhattanville College, Purchase, NY [*OCLC symbol*] (OCLC)
Vyestsi Akad Navuk BSSR Syer Biyal Navuk ... Vyestsi Akademii Navuk BSSR. Syeryya Biyalagichnykh Navuk [*A publication*]
Vyestsi Akad Navuk BSSR Syer Syel' Skahaspad Navuk ... Vyestsi Akademii Navuk BSSR. Syeryya Syel' Skahaspadarchukh Navuk [*A publication*]
VYF........... Fordham University, Bronx, NY [*OCLC symbol*] (OCLC)
VYG .... Finger Lakes Library System, Ithaca, NY [*OCLC symbol*] (OCLC)
VYGS........ Vermont Yankee Generating Station [*Nuclear energy*] (NRCH)
VYI .... Kahului, HI [*Location identifier*] [*FAA*] (FAAL)
Vyisn Akad Nauk Ukr RSR ... Vyisnik Akademyiyi Nauk Ukrayins'koyi RSR [*A publication*]
Vyisn Kiyiv Unyiv Ser Astron ... Vyisnik Kiyivs'kogo Unyiversitetu. Seryiya Astronomii [*A publication*]
Vyisn Kiyiv Unyiv Ser Fyiz ... Vyisnik Kiyivs'kogo Unyiversitetu. Seryiya Fyizika [*USSR*] [*A publication*]
Vyisn L'vyiv Derzh Unyiv Ser Fyiz ... Vyisnik L'vyivs'kij Derzhavnij Unyiversitet Imeni I. Franka. Seryiya Fyizichna [*A publication*]
Vyisn Syil'skogospod Nauki ... Vyisnik Syil'skogospodars'koyi Nauki [*A publication*]
VYJ........... Martinsburg, WV [*Location identifier*] [*FAA*] (FAAL)
VYK .... Christ the King Seminary, East Aurora, NY [*OCLC symbol*] (OCLC)
VYK .... Colombia, SC [*Location identifier*] [*FAA*] (FAAL)

VYL .... Lehman College, Bronx, NY [*OCLC symbol*]　(OCLC)
VYM .... United States Merchant Marine Academy, Kings Point, NY
　　　　　　 [*OCLC symbol*]　(OCLC)
VYN .... Dallas-Fort Worth, TX [*Location identifier*] [*FAA*]　(FAAL)
VYN .... Union Theological Seminary, New York, NY [*OCLC
　　　　　　 symbol*]　(OCLC)
VYNAA ..... Vynalezy [*A publication*]
Vynohrad Vynorobstvo ... Vynohradarstvo i Vynorobstvo [*A publication*]
VYNP .... Vermont Yankee Nuclear Plant　(NRCH)
VYNPS ...... Vermont Yankee Nuclear Power Station　(NRCH)
VYQ .... Upstate Medical Center, Syracuse, NY [*OCLC
　　　　　　 symbol*]　(OCLC)
VYR .... Rome Air Development Center, Griffiss AFB, NY [*OCLC
　　　　　　 symbol*]　(OCLC)
VYS .... St. Bonaventure University, St. Bonaventure, NY [*OCLC
　　　　　　 symbol*]　(OCLC)
VYS .... Visceral Yolk Sac [*Embryology*]
Vysk Pra Odboru Pap Celul ... Vyskumne Prace z Odboru Papiera a Celulozy
　　　　　　 [*A publication*]
Vyskum Pr Odboru Papiera Celulozy ... Vyskumne Prace z Odboru Papiera a
　　　　　　 Celulozy [*A publication*]
Vysk Ustav Lesn Hospod Zvolene Lesn Stud ... Vyskumny Ustav Lesneho
　　　　　　 Hospodarstvavo Zvolene Lesnicke Studie [*A publication*]
Vysk Ustav Ovciar Trencine Ved Pr ... Vyskumny Ustav Ovciarsky v
　　　　　　 Trencine. Vedecke Prace [*A publication*]
Vysokomol Soed ... Vysokomolekulyarnye Soedineniya [*A publication*]
Vysokomol Soedin ... Vysokomolekulyarnye Soedineniya [*A publication*]
Vysokomol Soedin Geterotsepnye Vysokomol Soedin ... Vysokomolekulyarnye
　　　　　　 Soedineniya Geterotsepnye Vysokomolekulyarnye
　　　　　　 Soedineniya [*USSR*] [*A publication*]
Vysokomol Soedin Ser A ... Vysokomolekulyarnye Soedineniya. Seriya A [*A
　　　　　　 publication*]
Vysokomol Soedin Ser B ... Vysokomolekulyarnye Soedineniya. Seriya B [*A
　　　　　　 publication*]
Vysokomol Soedin Vses Khim Ovo ... Vysokomolekulyarnye Soedineniya
　　　　　　 Vsesoyuznoe Khimicheskoe Obshchestvo [*A publication*]
Vyso Soed A ... Vysokomolekulyarnye Soedineniya. Seriya A [*A publication*]
Vyso Soed B ... Vysokomolekulyarnye Soedineniya. Seriya B [*A publication*]
Vyssh Nervn Deyat Norme Patol ... Vysshaya Nervnaya Deyatel'nost v
　　　　　　 Norme i Patologii [*A publication*]
Vyssh Uchebn Zaved Izv Geol Razved ... Vysshoye Uchebnoye Zavedeniye.
　　　　　　 Izvestiya Geologiya i Razvedka [*A publication*]
Vys Sk Chem-Technol Praze Sb Oddil Chem Inz ... Vysoka Skola Chemicko-
　　　　　　 Technologicka v Praze. Sbornik. Oddil. Chemicke
　　　　　　 Inzenyrstvi [*A publication*]
Vys Soed B ... Vysokomolekulyarnye Soedineniya. Seriya B [*A publication*]
VYT .... Clarkson College of Technology, Potsdam, NY [*OCLC
　　　　　　 symbol*]　(OCLC)
Vytr Boles .. Vytreshni Bolesti [*A publication*]
VyV .... Verdad y Vida [*Milan*] [*A publication*]
VYV .... Wegvervoer [*A publication*]
Vyzk Ustav Vodohospodar Pr Stud ... Vyzkumny Ustav Vodohospodarsky.
　　　　　　 Prace a Studie [*A publication*]
Vyzk Ustav Vodohospod Pr Stud ... Vyzkumny Ustav Vodohospodarsky.
　　　　　　 Prace a Studie [*A publication*]
Vyz Lidu ..... Vyziva Lidu [*A publication*]
Vyznach Prisnovod Vodor Ukr RSR ... Vyznachnyk Prisnovodnykh
　　　　　　 Vodorostei Ukrains'koi RSR
Vyz Rodine ... Vyziva v Rodine [*A publication*]
VyzS .... Vyzvol'nyj Sljax [*A publication*]
Vyz Zdravie ... Vyzica a Zdravie [*A publication*]
VZ .... Nefertiti Aviation [*Egypt*] [*ICAO designator*]　(FAAC)
VZ .... Varicella-Zoster [*Also, VZV*] [*A virus*]
VZ .... Velocity along the Z-Axis　(NASA)
V f Z .... Vierteljahrshefte fuer Zeitgeschichte [*A publication*]
VZ .... Virtual Zero
Vz .... Vizardinus [*Guizzardinus*] [*Deceased, 1222*] [*Authority cited in
　　　　　　 pre-1607 legal work*]　(DSA)
VZ .... Vostocnye Zapiski [*A publication*]
Vzar .... Vizardinus [*Guizzardinus*] [*Deceased, 1222*] [*Authority cited in
　　　　　　 pre-1607 legal work*]　(DSA)
V Zashch Mira ... V Zashchitu Mira [*A publication*]
VZB .... State University of New York at Stony Brook, Health Sciences
　　　　　　 Library, Stony Brook, NY [*OCLC symbol*]　(OCLC)
VZC .... Clinton-Essex-Franklin Library, Plattsburgh, NY [*OCLC
　　　　　　 symbol*]　(OCLC)
VZD .... Vendor Zero Defect
VZE .... Mercy College, Dobbs Ferry, NY [*OCLC symbol*]　(OCLC)
VZF .... St. Francis College, Brooklyn, NY [*OCLC symbol*]　(OCLC)
VZG .... St. Joseph's College Library, Suffolk Campus, Patchogue, NY
　　　　　　 [*OCLC symbol*]　(OCLC)
V f ZG .... Vierteljahreshefte fuer Zeitgeschichte [*A publication*]
VZH .... Hartwick College, Oneonta, NY [*OCLC symbol*]　(OCLC)
VZI .... Stony Brook Institute for Advanced Studies of World Religions,
　　　　　　 Stony Brook, NY [*OCLC symbol*]　(OCLC)
VZIG .... Varicella-Zoster Immune Globulin
VZJ .... St. John Fisher College, Rochester, NY [*OCLC
　　　　　　 symbol*]　(OCLC)
VZK .... King's College, Briarcliff Manor, NY [*OCLC symbol*]　(OCLC)
VZL .... Pace University, Law Library, White Plains, NY [*OCLC
　　　　　　 symbol*]　(OCLC)

VZL .... Vinzolidine [*Antineoplastic drug*]
VZM .... Margaret Woodbury Strong Museum, Rochester, NY [*OCLC
　　　　　　 symbol*]　(OCLC)
VZM .... Von Zeipel Method
VZN .... College of New Rochelle, New Rochelle, NY [*OCLC
　　　　　　 symbol*]　(OCLC)
Vznik Pocatky Slov ... Vznik a Pocatky Slovanu [*Origine et Debuts des Slaves*]
　　　　　　 [*A publication*]
VZO .... Coatesville, PA [*Location identifier*] [*FAA*]　(FAAL)
VZP .... Pace University, New York, NY [*OCLC symbol*]　(OCLC)
VZP .... Verenigde Verzekeringspers. Wekelijks Verschijnend Vakblad
　　　　　　 voor het Verzekeringswezen in Binnenland en Buitenland
　　　　　　 [*A publication*]
VZQ .... Pratt Institute, Brooklyn, NY [*OCLC symbol*]　(OCLC)
VZR .... Roswell Park Memorial Institute, Buffalo, NY [*OCLC
　　　　　　 symbol*]　(OCLC)
VZRPAS .... Veterinaria y Zootecnia Revista Peruana [*A publication*]
Vzryvnoe Delo Nauchno-Tekh Gorn O-Vo Sb ... Vzryvnoe Delo. Nauchno-
　　　　　　 Tekhnicheskoe Gornoe Obshchestvo Sbornik [*USSR*] [*A
　　　　　　 publication*]
VZS .... Skidmore College, Saratoga Springs, NY [*OCLC
　　　　　　 symbol*]　(OCLC)
VZS .... Valdez South [*Alaska*] [*Seismograph station code, US
　　　　　　 Geological Survey*]　(SEIS)
VZT .... St. Joseph's College, Brooklyn, NY [*OCLC symbol*]　(OCLC)
VZU .... Pace University, Pleasantville, Pleasantville, NY [*OCLC
　　　　　　 symbol*]　(OCLC)
VZV .... College of Mount Saint Vincent, New York, NY [*OCLC
　　　　　　 symbol*]　(OCLC)
VZV .... Varicella-Zoster Virus [*Also, VZ*]
VZW .... College of White Plains, White Plains, NY [*OCLC
　　　　　　 symbol*]　(OCLC)
VZW .... Valdez West [*Alaska*] [*Seismograph station code, US Geological
　　　　　　 Survey*]　(SEIS)
VZX .... Western New York Library Resources Council, Buffalo, NY
　　　　　　 [*OCLC symbol*]　(OCLC)
VZY .... Montefiore Hospital, Bronx, NY [*OCLC symbol*]　(OCLC)
VZZ .... International Museum of Photography, Eastman House,
　　　　　　 Rochester, NY [*OCLC symbol*]　(OCLC)

W

W............... Climatic Data for the World [*A publication*]
W............... Coast Guard Ship [*When precedes vessel classification*] [*Navy symbol*]
W............... Diameter of Driving-Wheel in Inches [*Railroad term*]
W............... Electrical Energy [*Symbol*]   (DEN)
w............... Flow Rate [*Heat transmission symbol*]
W............... Indefinite Ceiling [*Meteorology*]   (FAAC)
w............... Load per Unit of Length
W............... Requires an Engineer [*Search and rescue symbol that can be stamped in sand or snow*]
W............... Total Load
w----- .... Tropics [*MARC geographic area code*] [*Library of Congress*]   (LCCP)
W............... Tryptophan [*One-letter symbol; see Trp*]
W............... Waehrung [*Currency*] [*German*]
W............... Waffle [*Used in correcting manuscripts, etc.*]
W............... Wages [*Economics*]
W............... Waist   (ADA)
W............... Wait Time [*Data processing*]
W............... Wales
W............... Walk [*Baseball*]
W............... Wall
W............... Wallace Laboratories [*Research code symbol*]
W............... Waltz [*Music*]
W............... Wander AG [*Switzerland*] [*Research code symbol*]
W............... Wanderer Books [*Publisher's imprint*]
W............... Wanting
W............... War
W............... Warden
W............... Wardroom [*Aerospace*]
W............... Warehouse
W............... Warhead [*Nuclear*]   (NG)
W............... Warm
W............... Warner-Lambert Pharmaceutical Co. [*Research code symbol*]
W............... Warning [*Railroad signal arm*] [*British*]
W............... Warning Area [*Followed by identification*]
W............... Warrant [*A document entitling holder to purchase a given issue of stock*] [*Investment term*]
W............... Washington Reports [*1890-1939*] [*A publication*]   (DLA)
W............... Waste
W............... Watch Time
W............... Water
W............... Water Point [*British Waterways Board sign*]
W............... Water Vapor Content
W............... Waterloo [*Army*] [*British*]   (ROG)
W............... Watermeyer's Cape Of Good Hope Supreme Court Reports [*A publication*]   (DLA)
W............... Watt [*Symbol*] [*SI unit of power*]   (GPO)
W............... Wattle [*Ornithology*]
W............... Watt's Pennsylvania Reports [*A publication*]   (DLA)
W............... Wave Height Correction
W............... Weak [*Spectral*]
W............... Weather
W............... Weather Aircraft Equipped with Meteorological Gear [*Designation for all US military aircraft*]
W............... Weather Review [*A publication*]
W............... Web
W............... Weber Fraction [*Psychology*]
W............... Wednesday
W............... Week
W............... Weekblad van het Recht [*A publication*]
W............... Weekend Travel [*Also, Z*] [*Airline fare code*]
w............... Weekly
W............... Weekly Dose [*Medicine*]
W............... Weeping [*Shrub*]
W............... Weight
W............... Weld   (DAS)
W............... Welding Program [*Association of Independent Colleges and Schools specialization code*]
W............... Welsh [*or Welch*]

W............... Wendell's Reports [*1826-41*] [*New York*] [*A publication*]   (DLA)
W............... Wesleyan
W............... West [*or Western*]
W............... West Point, NY [*Mint mark when appearing on US coins*]
W............... Westcoast Energy, Inc. [*Toronto Stock Exchange symbol*]
W............... Westcoast Energy, Inc. [*Vancouver Stock Exchange symbol*]
W............... Westerhout [*Astronomy*]
W............... Westinghouse [*as in "Group W"*]
W............... Westvaco Corp. [*NYSE symbol*]   (SPSG)
W............... Wet
W............... Wet Dew
W............... Wheaton's Reports [*14-25 United States*] [*A publication*]   (DLA)
W............... Wheeled [*Vehicles*]   (NATG)
W............... Whip
W............... Whiskey [*Phonetic alphabet*] [*International*]   (DSUE)
W............... White [*Light, buoy, beacon*]
W............... White Return [*Round trip fare for specified period*] [*British*]
W............... Whitehorse Star [*A publication*]
W............... Whole [*Response*] [*Medicine*]
W............... Whole Word Designator [*Data processing*]
W............... Whorls and Compounds [*Fingerprint description*]
W............... Wicked   (DAS)
W............... Wicket
W............... Wide
W............... Widow [*or Widower*]
W............... Width
W............... Wife
W............... Will Advise [*Business term*]
w............... Will Factor [*Psychology*]
W............... Wille [*Will Factor*] [*Psychology*]
W............... William [*Phonetic alphabet*] [*Royal Navy*] [*World War I*] [*Pre-World War II*] [*World War II*]   (DSUE)
W............... William (King of England)   (DLA)
W............... Wilson's [*or Willson's*] Reports [*Texas Civil Cases, Court of Appeals*] [*A publication*]   (DLA)
W............... Winch   (DS)
W............... Wind [*In reference to wind velocity*]
W............... Window   (NASA)
W............... Windward [*Botany*]
W............... Wins [*Sports*]
W............... Winter [*A publication*]
W............... Winter [*Vessel load line mark*]
W............... Wire
W............... Wisconsin Reports [*A publication*]   (DLA)
W............... With
W............... Withdrawal
W............... Without Voice Facilities on Range or Radiobeacon Frequency
W............... Witwatersrand Local Division Reports [*South Africa*] [*A publication*]   (DLA)
W............... Wolfram [*Tungsten*] [*Chemical element*]
W............... Woman   (ADA)
W............... Women's Reserve, Unlimited Service [*USNR officer designation*]
W............... Won [*Monetary unit in the Republic of Korea*]
W............... Won [*Sports statistics*]
W............... Wood
W............... Wooden [*Shipping*]   (ROG)
W............... Woody Plant [*Botany*]
W............... Word
W............... Work [*or w*] [*Symbol*] [*IUPAC*]
W............... Workmen's Compensation [*Insurance*]
W............... World
w............... WORLDSCALE [*Worldwide Tanker Nominal Freight Scale*]   (DS)
W............... Worshipful [*Freemasonry*]
W............... Wortkunst [*A publication*]
W............... [*Alfred*] Wotquenne [*When used in identifying C. P. E. Bach's compositions, refers to cataloging of his works by musicologist Wotquenne*]

W.............. Wright's Ohio Reports [*1831-34*] [*A publication*]   (DLA)
W.............. Write
W.............. Writer Officer [*British military*]
W.............. Wrong
W.............. Wyoming Reports [*A publication*]   (DLA)
1/W.......... One-Way
1-W .... Selective Service Class [*for Conscientious Objector Performing Alternate Service Contributing to Maintenance of National Health, Safety, or Interest*]
W2............ Second Statute of Westminster [*A publication*]   (DSA)
W-2.......... Wage and Tax Statement [*IRS*]
W2............ William II [*German emperor and king of Prussia, 1888-1918*]   (DSUE)
3W............ Three-Wire   (MSA)
W-4 .... Employee's Withholding Allowance Certificate [*IRS*]
4W............ Four-Wire
4-W .... Selective Service Class [*for Conscientious Objector Who Has Completed Alternate Service Contributing to National Health, Safety, or Interest*]
4W............ Yemen Arab Republic [*Aircraft nationality and registration mark*]   (FAAC)
5W............ Western Samoa [*Aircraft nationality and registration mark*]   (FAAC)
6W............ Senegal [*Aircraft nationality and registration mark*]   (FAAC)
3W's.......... [*The*] Who, What, or Where Game [*Also, WWW*] [*Television show*]
3W's.......... Worry, Want, and Wickedness [*Causes of insanity, according to Victorian medical theory*]
5W's.......... Who, What, When, Where, Why [*Journalism*]
W (Colds)... Whole Colds [*Medicine*]
WA............ Appleton Public Library, Appleton, WI [*Library symbol*] [*Library of Congress*]   (LCLS)
WA............ Independent Watchmen's Association
WA............ Voice of Washington Music [*A publication*]
WA............ Wabash Railroad Co. [*NYSE symbol*]   (SPSG)
WA............ Wadsworth Athneneum [*Hartford, CT*]
WA............ Wage Record [*Social Security Administration*]   (OICC)
WA............ Wainscot
WA............ Waiver
WA............ Walking Association   (EA)
WA............ War Aims [*British*]
WA............ Warbirds of America [*Later, WB*] [*An association*]   (EA)
WA............ Warm Air
W/A .... Warrant of Arrest
Wa............ Warsaw [*A publication*]
WA............ Washer
WA............ Washington [*State*] [*Postal code*]
Wa............ Washington Reports [*A publication*]   (DLA)
Wa............ Washington State Library, Olympia, WA [*Library symbol*] [*Library of Congress*]   (LCLS)
WA............ Wassmer Aviation [*France*] [*ICAO aircraft manufacturer identifier*]   (ICAO)
WA............ Water Agar [*Microbiology*]
WA............ Water Authority [*British*]   (DCTA)
WA............ Watertown Arsenal [*Massachusetts*] [*Army*]
Wa............ Watts' Reports [*1890-1939*] [*A publication*]   (DLA)
WA............ Waveform Analyzer
WA............ Weapon Armourer [*British military*]   (DMA)
WA............ Weapons Analyst [*British military*]   (DMA)
WA............ Weapons Assignment   (NVT)
WA............ Weather Almanac [*A publication*]
WA............ Weather Atlas of the United States [*A publication*]
WA............ Wedge Action [*British military*]   (DMA)
WA............ Weighted Average [*Accounting*]
WA............ Weizmann Israel Archives [*Rehovoth*]   (BJA)
WA............ Welfare Administration [*Became Social and Rehabilitation Service*] [*HEW*]
WA............ Wellness Associates   (EA)
Wa............ Wellsiania [*An association*]   (EA)
WA............ Weltwirtschaftliches Archiv [*A publication*]
WA............ West Africa
WA............ West Africa [*A publication*]
WA............ Western Airlines, Inc. [*ICAO designator*]
WA............ Western Approaches [*to Great Britain and Ireland*] [*Obsolete*]
WA............ Western Area
WA............ Western Australia
W of A........ [*The*] Western Railway of Alabama
WA............ [*The*] Western Railway of Alabama [*AAR code*]
WA............ Westminster Abbey [*London*]
WAE........... When Awake
WA............ Wide Angle [*Photography*]
WA............ Will Adjust   (AABC)
WA............ Williams Act [*1968*]
WA............ Wire Armored [*Cables*]
WA............ Wire Assembly   (MSA)
WA............ Wire Association [*Later, WAI*]
WA............ Wissenschaftliche Annalen [*A publication*]
WA............ With Answers
WA............ With Average [*Insurance*]
WA............ Withholding Agent   (DLA)

WA............ Wohl Associates [*Bala Cynwyd, PA*] [*Telecommunications*]   (TSSD)
WA............ Women's Reserve, Aviation Nonflying Duties [*USNR officer designation*]
WA............ Womenwealth Ambika [*London, England*]   (EAIO)
WA............ Woolknit Associates   (EA)
WA............ Woolwich Armstrong Gun
WA............ Word Add
WA............ Word After [*Message handling*]
WA............ Work Assignment   (MCD)
WA............ Work Authorization   (MCD)
WA............ Workers Anonymous [*Mythical organization devoted to helping human beings overcome their desire to lead productive lives; created by columnist Arthur Hoppe in satirizing short work week and early retirement schemes*]
WA............ Workmanship Assurance
WA............ Workshop Assembly [*Torpedo*]
WA............ World Archaeology [*A publication*]
WA............ Wright Aeronautical Corp.   (KSC)
WA............ Writing Ability
WA............ Writing Academy   (EA)
WA1.......... Wongan Hills [*Australia*] [*Seismograph station code, US Geological Survey*]   (SEIS)
WA2.......... Wagin [*Australia*] [*Seismograph station code, US Geological Survey*]   (SEIS)
WA3.......... Talbot Brook [*Australia*] [*Seismograph station code, US Geological Survey*]   (SEIS)
W-4A .... Wage Withholding Form [*Revised version*] [*IRS*]
WaA.......... Aberdeen Public Library, Aberdeen, WA [*Library symbol*] [*Library of Congress*]   (LCLS)
WAA.......... Wabash Motor Freight Tariff Association, Springfield IL [*STAC*]
WAA.......... Wales [*Alaska*] [*Airport symbol*]   (OAG)
WAA.......... Wales, AK [*Location identifier*] [*FAA*]   (FAAL)
WAA.......... War Assets Administration [*For disposal of US surplus war property*] [*Post-World War II*]
WAA.......... Warden's Association of America [*Later, NAAWS*]   (EA)
WAA.......... Waris [*Papua New Guinea*] [*Seismograph station code, US Geological Survey*]   (SEIS)
WAA.......... Wartime Aircraft Activity   (AFM)
Wa A.......... Washington Appellate Reports [*A publication*]   (DLA)
WAA.......... Water-Augmented Air Jet
WAA.......... Water Authorities Association [*British*]   (ECON)
WAA.......... Watermark Association of Artisans   (EA)
WAA.......... Welded Aluminum Alloy
WAA.......... West Australian Airways   (ADA)
WAA.......... Western Amateur Astronomers   (EA)
WAA.......... Western Awning Association [*Later, NPEA*]   (EA)
WAA.......... Wide-Aperture Array   (MCD)
WAA.......... Wien Air Alaska [*Air carrier designation symbol*]
WAA.......... Women's Action Alliance   (EA)
WAA.......... Worker Adjustment Assistance
WAA.......... World Aluminum Abstracts [*Aluminum Association*] [*Information service or system*] [*A publication*]   (IID)
WAA.......... World American Airlift   (FAAC)
WAA.......... World Atlatl Association   (EA)
WAA.......... Writing Assistants' Association [*A union*] [*British*]
WAAA .... Ujung Pandang/Hasanuddin [*Indonesia*] [*ICAO location identifier*]   (ICLI)
WAAA ...... Walleye Anglers Association of America [*Defunct*]   (EA)
WAAA ...... Western Armenian Athletic Association   (EA)
WAAA ...... Winston-Salem, NC [*AM radio station call letters*]
WAAAF..... Women's Auxiliary Australian Air Force
WAAB .... Bau Bau/Betoambari [*Indonesia*] [*ICAO location identifier*]   (ICLI)
WAABI...... National Women's Association of Allied Beverage Industries   (EA)
WAAC ...... Valdosta, GA [*FM radio station call letters*]
WAAC ...... War Artists' Advisory Committee [*British military*]   (DMA)
WAAC ...... West African Airways Corporation
WAAC ...... Western Australian AIDS [*Acquired Immune Deficiency Syndrome*] Council
WAAC ...... Women's Army Auxiliary Corps [*Name later changed to WAC*] [*World War II*]
WAAC ...... World Academy of Arts and Culture   (EA)
WAACC's Motor Ind ... WAACC's [*Western Australian Automobile Chamber of Commerce*] Motor Industry [*A publication*]
WAAD...... Westinghouse Air Arm Division
WAADS .... Washington Air Defense Sector [*ADC*]
WAAE ...... World Association for Adult Education
WAAF ...... Women's Auxiliary Air Force [*Functioned under direct command of RAF*] [*World War II*] [*British*]
WAAF ...... Worcester, MA [*FM radio station call letters*]
WAAFB.... Walker Air Force Base   (AAG)
WAAG...... Galesburg, IL [*FM radio station call letters*]
WaAG........ Grays Harbor College, Aberdeen, WA [*Library symbol*] [*Library of Congress*]   (LCLS)
WAAG...... Malimpung [*Indonesia*] [*ICAO location identifier*]   (ICLI)
WAAH...... Houghton, MI [*FM radio station call letters*]
WAAI .... Hurlock, MD [*FM radio station call letters*]
WAAI .... Malili [*Indonesia*] [*ICAO location identifier*]   (ICLI)

WAAIC...... Women's Association of the African Independent Churches
WAAJ....... Huntsville, AL [*AM radio station call letters*]
WAAJ....... Mamuju/Tampa Padang [*Indonesia*] [*ICAO location identifier*] (ICLI)
WAAJ....... Water-Augmented Air Jet
WAAK...... Dallas, NC [*AM radio station call letters*]
WAAL...... Binghamton, NY [*FM radio station call letters*]
WAAL...... Ponggaluku [*Indonesia*] [*ICAO location identifier*] (ICLI)
WaAlVA.... United States Veterans Administration Hospital, American Lake, WA [*Library symbol*] [*Library of Congress*] (LCLS)
WAAM...... Ann Arbor, MI [*AM radio station call letters*]
WAAM...... Masamba/Andi Jemma [*Indonesia*] [*ICAO location identifier*] (ICLI)
WAAM...... Wide-Area Antiarmor Munitions [*Military*] (MCD)
WAAMA... Woman's Auxiliary to the American Medical Association [*Later, AMAA*] (EA)
WAAMAC ... Weight, Alignment, and Mass Center Determination Equipment (AAG)
WAAMMS ... Women's Auxiliary of the American Merchant Marine [*World War II*]
WaAn........ Anacortes Public Library, Anacortes, WA [*Library symbol*] [*Library of Congress*] (LCLS)
WAAN....... West African Archaeological Newsletter [*A publication*]
WA Ann LR ... University of Western Australia. Annual Law Review [*A publication*] (APTA)
WAAO-FM ... Andalusia, AL [*FM radio station call letters*]
WAAP....... East Lansing, MI [*AM radio station call letters*]
WAAP....... Kolaka/Pomalaa [*Indonesia*] [*ICAO location identifier*] (ICLI)
WAAP....... World Association for Animal Production [*Rome, Italy*] (EAIO)
WAAPM ... Wide-Area Antipersonnel Mine [*Military*]
WAAQ....... Big Rapids, MI [*FM radio station call letters*]
WAAR....... Raha/Sugi Manuru [*Indonesia*] [*ICAO location identifier*] (ICLI)
WAAR...... Wartime Aircraft Activity Reporting [*System*]
WAAR...... Western Australian Arbitration Reports [*A publication*] (APTA)
WA Arb R ... Western Australian Arbitration Reports [*A publication*] (APTA)
WaArI........ Indian Ridge Treatment Center, Staff Library, Arlington, WA [*Library symbol*] [*Library of Congress*] (LCLS)
WaArI-R.... Indian Ridge Treatment Center, Resident Library, Arlington, WA [*Library symbol*] [*Library of Congress*] (LCLS)
WA Art Gall Bull ... Western Australian Art Gallery. Bulletin [*A publication*] (APTA)
WAAS .... Soroako [*Indonesia*] [*ICAO location identifier*] (ICLI)
WAAS .... Warning and Attack Assessment (MCD)
WAAS .... Wide-Area Active Surveillance [*Military*] (MCD)
WAAS .... Women's Auxiliary Army Service [*British*]
WAAS .... World Academy of Art and Science [*Solna, Sweden*] (EA)
WAASC .... Women's Auxiliary Army Service Corps [*British*]
WAASDT ... Western Australian Association of School Dental Therapists
WAAT .... Makale/Pongtiku [*Indonesia*] [*ICAO location identifier*] (ICLI)
WAATS..... Weights Analysis for Advanced Transportation Systems [*NASA*]
WaAu........ Auburn Public Library, Auburn, WA [*Library symbol*] [*Library of Congress*] (LCLS)
WAAU....... Kendari/Wolter Monginsidi [*Indonesia*] [*ICAO location identifier*] (ICLI)
WaAuG...... Green River Community College, Auburn, WA [*Library symbol*] [*Library of Congress*] (LCLS)
WAAV .... Wilmington-Leland, NC [*AM radio station call letters*]
WAAVP..... World Association for the Advancement of Veterinary Parasitology [*Thessaloniki, Greece*] (EAIO)
WAAW....... Williston, SC [*FM radio station call letters*]
WAAX....... Gadsden, AL [*AM radio station call letters*]
WAAY-TV ... Huntsville, AL [*Television station call letters*]
WAAZ .... Ujung Pandang [*Indonesia*] [*ICAO location identifier*] (ICLI)
WAAZ-FM ... Crestview, FL [*FM radio station call letters*]
WAB......... Aero Industries, Inc. [*Richmond, VA*] [*FAA designator*] (FAAC)
WAB......... Wabag [*Papua New Guinea*] [*Seismograph station code, US Geological Survey*] (SEIS)
WAB......... Wabash Railroad System [*AAR code*] [*Obsolete*]
WAB......... Waffenabwurfbehaelter [*Parachute Weapons Container*] [*German military - World War II*]
WAB......... Wage Adjustment Board [*World War II*]
WAB......... Wage Appeals Board [*Department of Labor*]
WAB......... Water-Activated Battery
WAB......... Westamerica Bancorporation [*AMEX symbol*] (SPSG)
WAB......... Western Actuarial Bureau [*Later, ISO*] (EA)
WAB......... Western Aphasia Battery [*Neuropsychology test*]
WAB......... When Authorized By
WAB......... Wine Advisory Board [*Later, WAG*] (EA)
WAB......... World Association for Buiatrics [*Hanover, Federal Republic of Germany*] (EAIO)
WABA....... Aguadilla, PR [*AM radio station call letters*]
WABA .... Women's American Basketball Association (EA)

WABASH VLY ALSA ... Wabash Valley Area Library Services Authority [*Library network*]
WaBB .... Bellevue Community College, Bellevue, WA [*Library symbol*] [*Library of Congress*] (LCLS)
WABB .... Biak/Frans Kaisiepo [*Indonesia*] [*ICAO location identifier*] (ICLI)
WABB ...... Mobile, AL [*AM radio station call letters*]
WABB-FM ... Mobile, AL [*FM radio station call letters*]
WABC .... New York, NY [*AM radio station call letters*]
WABCO .... Westinghouse Air Brake Company
WABC-TV ... New York, NY [*Television station call letters*]
WABD ...... Fort Campbell, KY [*AM radio station call letters*]
WABD ...... Moanamani [*Indonesia*] [*ICAO location identifier*] (ICLI)
WABE ...... Atlanta, GA [*FM radio station call letters*]
WaBe .... Bellingham Public Library, Bellingham, WA [*Library symbol*] [*Library of Congress*] (LCLS)
WABE ...... Western Allenbee Oil & Gas Co. Ltd. [*NASDAQ symbol*] (NQ)
WABE ...... Western Association of Broadcast Engineers [*Canada*]
WaBeCo..... Whatcom County Public Library, Bellingham, WA [*Library symbol*] [*Library of Congress*] (LCLS)
WaBeSJ ..... Saint Joseph Hospital, Bellingham, WA [*Library symbol*] [*Library of Congress*] (LCLS)
WaBeSL .... Saint Luke's Hospital, Bellingham, WA [*Library symbol*] [*Library of Congress*] (LCLS)
WaBeW ..... Western Washington State College [*Later, WWU*], Bellingham, WA [*Library symbol*] [*Library of Congress*] (LCLS)
WABF........ Fairhope, AL [*AM radio station call letters*]
WABF........ Numfor/Jemburwo [*Indonesia*] [*ICAO location identifier*] (ICLI)
WaBfM ...... Mission Creek Youth Camp, Staff Library, Belfair, WA [*Library symbol*] [*Library of Congress*] (LCLS)
WaBfM-R ... Mission Creek Youth Camp, Resident Library, Belfair, WA [*Library symbol*] [*Library of Congress*] (LCLS)
WABG ...... Greenwood, MS [*AM radio station call letters*]
WABG ...... Waghete [*Indonesia*] [*ICAO location identifier*] (ICLI)
WaBGS...... Church of Jesus Christ of Latter-Day Saints, Genealogical Society Library, Bellevue Branch, Bellevue, WA [*Library symbol*] [*Library of Congress*] (LCLS)
WABG-TV ... Greenwood, MS [*Television station call letters*]
WABI........ Bangor, ME [*AM radio station call letters*]
WABI........ Nabire [*Indonesia*] [*ICAO location identifier*] (ICLI)
WABI........ Western Australian Biographical Index [*A publication*] (APTA)
WABI-TV ... Bangor, ME [*Television station call letters*]
WABJ........ Adrian, MI [*AM radio station call letters*]
WABK....... Gardiner, ME [*AM radio station call letters*]
WABK-FM ... Gardiner, ME [*FM radio station call letters*]
WABL....... Amite, LA [*AM radio station call letters*]
WABL....... Ilaga [*Indonesia*] [*ICAO location identifier*] (ICLI)
WABLC..... Wilmington Area Biomedical Libraries [*Library network*]
WABN...... Kokonau [*Indonesia*] [*ICAO location identifier*] (ICLI)
WABN-FM ... Abingdon, VA [*FM radio station call letters*]
WABO....... Serui/Sujarwo Condronegoro [*Indonesia*] [*ICAO location identifier*] (ICLI)
WABO....... Waynesboro, MS [*AM radio station call letters*]
WABO-FM ... Waynesboro, MS [*FM radio station call letters*]
WaBOH..... Overlake Hospital, Medical Library, Bellevue, WA [*Library symbol*] [*Library of Congress*] (LCLS)
WaBP .... Puget Sound Power and Light Co., Bellevue, WA [*Library symbol*] [*Library of Congress*] (LCLS)
WABP....... Timika/Tembagapura [*Indonesia*] [*ICAO location identifier*] (ICLI)
Wa-BPH.... Washington Regional Library for the Blind and Physically Handicapped, Seattle, WA [*Library symbol*] [*Library of Congress*] (LCLS)
WABQ....... Cleveland, OH [*AM radio station call letters*]
WaBr .... Kitsap Regional Library, Bremerton, WA [*Library symbol*] [*Library of Congress*] (LCLS)
WABR ...... West Asia Blocking Ridge [*Meteorology*]
WABR-FM ... Tifton, GA [*FM radio station call letters*]
WaBrH ...... Harrison Memorial Hospital, Bremerton, WA [*Library symbol*] [*Library of Congress*] (LCLS)
WaBrNP.... United States Navy, Puget Sound Naval Shipyard, Engineering Library, Bremerton, WA [*Library symbol*] [*Library of Congress*] (LCLS)
WaBrNR.... United States Navy, Naval Regional Medical Center, Bremerton, WA [*Library symbol*] [*Library of Congress*] (LCLS)
WaBrNS.... United States Navy, Naval Submarine Base, Bangor Library, Bremerton, WA [*Library symbol*] [*Library of Congress*] (LCLS)
WaBrO ...... Olympic College, Bremerton, WA [*Library symbol*] [*Library of Congress*] (LCLS)
WaBrOC.... Olympic Center, Bremerton, WA [*Library symbol*] [*Library of Congress*] (LCLS)
WABS....... Arlington, VA [*AM radio station call letters*]
WaBS........ Bellevue School District, Instructional Materials Center, Bellevue, WA [*Library symbol*] [*Library of Congress*] (LCLS)
WABSIH... Society for Italic Handwriting, Western American Branch [*Later, WASIH*] (EA)
WABT .... Dundee, IL [*FM radio station call letters*]

WABT .... Enarotali [*Indonesia*] [*ICAO location identifier*] (ICLI)
WABTOC ... When Authorized by the Oversea Commander [*Military*]
WABU .... Biak/Manuhua [*Indonesia*] [*ICAO location identifier*] (ICLI)
WaBucR ..... Rainier School, Staff Library, Buckley, WA [*Library symbol*] [*Library of Congress*] (LCLS)
WaBucR-R ... Rainier School, Resident Library, Buckley, WA [*Library symbol*] [*Library of Congress*] (LCLS)
WABV .... Abbeville, SC [*AM radio station call letters*]
WABW ...... Waren [*Indonesia*] [*ICAO location identifier*] (ICLI)
W A'B & W ... Webb, A'Beckett, and Williams' Reports [*A publication*] (APTA)
W A'B & W Eq ... Webb, A'Beckett, and Williams' Equity Reports [*A publication*] (APTA)
W A'B & W IE & M ... Webb, A'Beckett, and Williams' Insolvency, Ecclesiastical, and Matrimonial Reports [*A publication*] (APTA)
W A'B & W Min ... Webb, A'Beckett, and Williams' Mining Cases [*A publication*] (APTA)
WABW-TV ... Pelham, GA [*Television station call letters*]
WABX .... Clare, MI [*AM radio station call letters*]
WABY .... Albany, NY [*AM radio station call letters*]
WABZ .... Biak [*Indonesia*] [*ICAO location identifier*] (ICLI)
WABZ-FM ... Albemarle, NC [*FM radio station call letters*]
WAC .... Waca [*Ethiopia*] [*Airport symbol*] (OAG)
WAC .... Wake Analysis and Control (MCD)
WAC .... War Assets Corporation [*Post-World War II*] [*Succeeded by War Assets Administration*]
WAC .... Weapon Arming Computer (MCD)
WAC .... Weapons Assignment Console
WAC .... Weber Aircraft Company
WAC .... Weighted Average Coupon [*Finance*]
WAC .... Wells American Corporation [*AMEX symbol*] (SPSG)
WAC .... Welsh Arts Council (EAIO)
WAC .... West Africa Command [*World War II*]
WAC .... West Africa Committee (EA)
WAC .... Western Archeological Center [*Department of the Interior*] (GRD)
WAC .... Western Athletic Conference
WAC .... Wolfe Angel Committee [*Defunct*] (EA)
WAC .... Women's Advisory Committee [*Trades Union Congress*] [*British*] (DCTA)
WAC .... Women's Advisory Council [*Australia*]
WAC .... Women's Aerobic Circuit [*Exercise regimen at some health spas*]
WAC .... Women's Army Corps [*Formerly, WAAC*] [*Abolished, 1978*] (GPO)
WAC .... Women's Auxiliary Corps [*British*] (DAS)
WAC .... Work Accomplishment Code [*Military*] (AFIT)
WAC .... Work Activities Center
WAC .... Work Assignment Card (MCD)
WAC .... Work and Occupations [*A publication*]
WAC .... Worked All Continents [*Contacted at least one station on all continents*] [*Amateur radio*]
WAC .... Working Alternating Current (DEN)
WAC .... Workshop Arts Centre [*Australia*]
WAC .... World Aeronautical Chart [*Air Force*] [*A publication*] (APTA)
WAC .... World Affairs Center for the United States [*Later, FPA*]
WAC .... World Area Code (MCD)
WAC .... World Assistance Corps [*Paris, France*] (EAIO)
WAC .... Wright Aeronautical Corporation (MCD)
WAC .... Write Address Counter
WACA ..... Ithaca, NY [*Television station call letters*]
WACA ..... Walnut Canyon National Monument
WACA .... West African Court of Appeal, Selected Judgments [*A publication*] (DLA)
WACA .... Western Agricultural Chemicals Association (EA)
WACA ...... Winchester Arms Collectors Association (EA)
WACA ...... Women's Apparel Chains Associations (EA)
WACA ...... World Airlines Clubs Association [*Montreal, PQ*] (EAIO)
WACA ...... World Association of Center Associates (EA)
WACAAI ... Women's Africa Committee of the African-American Institute (EA)
WACAP ..... Western Australian Chip & Pulp Co.
WACAS ..... Wave and Current Advisory Service [*British*]
WACASC .. West African Consolidated Administrative Service Center [*Foreign Service*]
WACB .... Kittanning, PA [*AM radio station call letters*]
WACB .... Women's Army Classification Battery (AABC)
WACC .... Washing Corrosion Control (MCD)
WACC .... Weighted Average Cost of Capital [*Accounting*] (ADA)
WACC .... World Africa Chamber of Commerce (EA)
WACC .... World Association for Christian Communication
WACCC ..... Worldwide Air Cargo Commodity Classification (DS)
WACCM .... World Association for Chinese Church Music (EAIO)
WACD .... Alexander City, AL [*AM radio station call letters*]
WACE ...... Chicopee, MA [*AM radio station call letters*]
WaCeC ..... Centralia College, Centralia, WA [*Library symbol*] [*Library of Congress*] (LCLS)
WaCeM ..... Maple Lane School, Staff Library, Centralia, WA [*Library symbol*] [*Library of Congress*] (LCLS)

WaCeW ..... Weyerhaeuser Co., Forestry Research Center, Centralia, WA [*Library symbol*] [*Library of Congress*] (LCLS)
WACF .... Paris, IL [*FM radio station call letters*]
WACG-FM ... Augusta, GA [*FM radio station call letters*]
WACH ...... Columbia, SC [*Television station call letters*]
WACH ...... Wedge Adjustable Cushioned Heel [*Orthopedics*]
WACH ...... West African Clearing House (EAIO)
WACH ...... Worship Arts Clearing House (EA)
WACHA .... Wisconsin Automated Clearing House Association
WaChehG ... Green Hill School, Staff Library, Chehalis, WA [*Library symbol*] [*Library of Congress*] (LCLS)
WaChehYS ... Washington State Twin City Center for Youth Services, Chehalis, WA [*Library symbol*] [*Library of Congress*] (LCLS)
WaChenE .. Eastern Washington State College, Cheney, WA [*Library symbol*] [*Library of Congress*] (LCLS)
WACI .... Atlantic City, NJ [*Television station call letters*]
WACI .... Western Approaches Convoy Instructions [*British military*] (DMA)
WACI .... Women's Army Corps of India [*British military*] (DMA)
WACIID .... Winter Advanced Course for Immunology and Infectious Diseases [*Japan International Friendship and Welfare Foundation*]
WACK .... Newark, NY [*AM radio station call letters*]
WACK .... Wait before Transmitting Positive Acknowledgment
WaCl .... Asotin County Library, Clarkston, WA [*Library symbol*] [*Library of Congress*] (LCLS)
WACL ...... Wacoal Corp. [*Japan*] [*NASDAQ symbol*] (NQ)
WACL ...... Waycross, GA [*AM radio station call letters*]
WACL ...... Worcester Area Cooperating Libraries [*Worcester, MA*] [*Library network*]
WACL .... World Anti-Communist League [*Seoul, Republic of Korea*] (EAIO)
WaClvSC ... Spruce Canyon Correctional Center, Staff Library, Colville, WA [*Library symbol*] [*Library of Congress*] (LCLS)
WaClvSC-R .. Spruce Canyon Correctional Center, Resident Library, Colville, WA [*Library symbol*] [*Library of Congress*] (LCLS)
WACM ...... West Springfield, MA [*AM radio station call letters*]
WACM ...... Western Association of Circuit Manufacturers
WACO ...... Waco, TX [*AM radio station call letters*]
WACO ...... Waterman Marine [*NASDAQ symbol*] (NQ)
WACO ...... Written Advice of Contracting Officer [*Military*]
WaCol .... Whitman County Library, Colfax, WA [*Library symbol*] [*Library of Congress*] (LCLS)
WACP .... Western Acceptance Corp. [*NASDAQ symbol*] (NQ)
WACPAC ... Whimsical Alternative Coalition Political Action Committee (EA)
WACQ ...... Tallassee, AL [*AM radio station call letters*]
WACQ-FM ... Tallassee, AL [*FM radio station call letters*]
WACR ...... Columbus, MS [*AM radio station call letters*]
WA Craftsman ... Western Australian Craftsman [*A publication*] (APTA)
WACRAL ... World Association of Christian Radio Amateurs and Listeners [*Hull, England*] (EAIO)
WACRAX ... Cocoa Research Institute. Council for Scientific and Industrial Research. Annual Report [*A publication*]
WACRES .. Women's Army Corps Reserve
WACR-FM ... Columbus, MS [*FM radio station call letters*]
WACRI ...... West African Cocoa Research Institution
WACS .... Weather Analysis Computer System [*Accu-Weather, Inc.*]
WACS .... West African College of Surgeons [*See also COAC*] (EAIO)
WACS .... Wire Automated Check System (MCD)
WACS .... Workshop Attitude Control System (MCD)
WACS .... World Association of Cooks Societies (EA)
WACSM .... Women's Army Corps Service Medal [*Military decoration*]
WACS-TV ... Dawson, GA [*Television station call letters*]
WACT .... Tuscaloosa, AL [*AM radio station call letters*]
WACT-FM ... Tuscaloosa, AL [*FM radio station call letters*]
WACU ...... West African Customs Union
WACV ...... Montgomery, AL [*AM radio station call letters*]
WACVA ..... Women's Army Corps Veterans Association (EA)
WACX ...... Leesburg, FL [*Television station call letters*]
WACY ...... Fenton, MI [*AM radio station call letters*]
WACY 2000 ... World Association for Celebrating the Year 2000 [*London, England*]
WACZ .... Dansville, NY [*FM radio station call letters*]
WAD .... Andriamena [*Madagascar*] [*Airport symbol*] (OAG)
WAD .... Waddy Lake Resources, Inc. [*Toronto Stock Exchange symbol*] [*Vancouver Stock Exchange symbol*]
WAD .... Warta Ekonomi Maritim. Facts and Analysis in Communications, Commerce, and Finance [*A publication*]
WAD .... Washington Aqueduct Division [*Army*]
WAD .... Weapon Assignment Display [*Air Force*]
WAD .... Wide-Angle Optics Weapon Assignment Display [*DoD*]
WAD .... William Addison Dwiggins [*American type designer and illustrator, 1880-1956*]
WAD .... Work Authorization and Delegation
WAD .... Work Authorization Document [*NASA*]
WAD .... World Association of Detectives (EA)
WAD .... World Aviation Directory [*A publication*]

WAD.......... World Wide Military Command Control System Automated Data Processing
Wa 2d........ Washington State Reports, Second Series [*A publication*] (DLA)
WADA....... Shelby, NC [*AM radio station call letters*]
WADA....... Wissenschaftliche Annalen. Deutsche Akademie [*A publication*]
WADAAA ... Washington District Army Audit Agency (MUGU)
WADB....... Point Pleasant, NJ [*FM radio station call letters*]
WADC....... Parkersburg, WV [*AM radio station call letters*]
WADC....... Western Air Defense Command
WADC....... Wright Air Development Center [*Air Force*]
WADC Tech Rept ... Wright Air Development Center. Technical Report [*A publication*]
W ADD...... With Added [*Freight*]
WADD....... Wright Air Development Division [*Air Force*]
Wad Dig..... Waddilove's Digest of Ecclesiastical Cases [*1849*] [*A publication*] (DLA)
WADE....... Wadesboro, NC [*AM radio station call letters*]
WADE....... World Association of Document Examiners (EA)
Wade Am Mining Law ... Wade on American Mining Law [*A publication*] (DLA)
Wade Attachm ... Wade on Attachment and Garnishment [*A publication*] (DLA)
WADEBR ... Wadebridge [*England*]
Wade Min ... Wade on American Mining Law [*A publication*] (DLA)
WA Democrat ... West Australian Democrat [*A publication*] (APTA)
Wade Not... Wade on the Law of Notice [*A publication*] (DLA)
Wade Retro L ... Wade on Retroactive Laws [*A publication*] (DLA)
WADEX .... Words and Authors Index [*Computer-produced index*]
WADF....... Western Air Defense Force
WADFFU ... Women's Association for the Defense of Four Freedoms for Ukraine (EA)
WADH ...... Wadham College [*Oxford University*] (ROG)
WADI........ Corinth, MS [*FM radio station call letters*]
WADJ....... Somerset, PA [*AM radio station call letters*]
WADK....... Newport, RI [*AM radio station call letters*]
WADL....... Mount Clemens, MI [*Television station call letters*]
WADL....... Wiener Arbeiten zur Deutschen Literatur [*A publication*]
Wadley Med Bull ... Wadley Medical Bulletin [*A publication*]
WADM...... Decatur, IN [*AM radio station call letters*]
Wad Mar & Div ... Waddilove on Marriage and Divorce [*1864*] [*A publication*] (DLA)
WADN....... Concord, MA [*AM radio station call letters*]
WADNA.... Women and Development Network of Australia
WADO....... New York, NY [*AM radio station call letters*]
WADR....... Remsen, NY [*AM radio station call letters*]
WADR....... Weight Analysis Data Report
WADS....... Ansonia, CT [*AM radio station call letters*]
WADS ...... Wide-Angle Display System
WADS ...... Wide-Area Data Service [*Data transmission service*]
WAD/SO... Work Authorization Document/Shop Order (NASA)
Wadsworth Ath Bul ... Wadsworth Atheneum. Bulletin [*A publication*]
WADT....... Western Australian Diamond Trust
WADU....... Norco, LA [*AM radio station call letters*]
W Adv....... Wesleyan Advocate [*A publication*]
WADVBS ... World Association of Daily Vacation Bible Schools [*Later, VBS*] (EA)
WADX....... Trenton, GA [*AM radio station call letters*]
WaE.......... Everett Public Library, Everett, WA [*Library symbol*] [*Library of Congress*] (LCLS)
WAE.......... Waterkampioen [*A publication*]
WAE.......... Weapon Aiming Error
WAE......... When [*or While*] Actually Employed [*Government short jobs*]
WAE.......... Wilfred American Educational Corp. [*NYSE symbol*] (SPSG)
WAE.......... Wills and Administration of Estates [*Law*]
WaEawC.... Canyon View Group Home, East Wenatchee, WA [*Library symbol*] [*Library of Congress*] (LCLS)
WAEB ...... Allentown, PA [*AM radio station call letters*]
WAEB-FM ... Allentown, PA [*FM radio station call letters*]
WAEC .... Atlanta, GA [*AM radio station call letters*]
WAEC .... War Agricultural Executive Committee [*British*] (DAS)
Wa-Ec....... Washington State Library, Ecology Department, Olympia, WA [*Library symbol*] [*Library of Congress*] (LCLS)
WAEC .... West African Economic Community [*Ivory Coast, Mali, Mauritania, Niger, Senegal, Upper Volta*] (ASF)
WAED....... Western Australia Education Department
WAED....... Westinghouse Aerospace Electrical Division
WA Ed Circ ... Education Circular. Education Department of Western Australia [*A publication*] (APTA)
WaEdE ...... Edmonds Community College, Edmonds, WA [*Library symbol*] [*Library of Congress*] (LCLS)
WAEDM ... World Association for Emergency and Disaster Medicine [*Bristol, England*] (EAIO)
WA Educ News ... WA Education News. Education Department of Western Australia [*A publication*] (APTA)
WaEE .... Everett Community College, Everett, WA [*Library symbol*] [*Library of Congress*] (LCLS)
WaEG........ Everett General Hospital, Medical Library, Everett, WA [*Library symbol*] [*Library of Congress*] (LCLS)
WA Egg Marketing Board Nletter ... Western Australia. Egg Marketing Board. Newsletter [*A publication*] (APTA)

WaEGS...... Church of Jesus Christ of Latter-Day Saints, Genealogical Society Library, Everett, Washington Stake Branch, Everett, WA [*Library symbol*] [*Library of Congress*] (LCLS)
WAEJ........ World Association of Esperanto Journalists [*See also TEJA*] [*Cittadella, Italy*] (EAIO)
WaEJP ...... Washington State Office of Juvenile Parole Services, Everett, WA [*Library symbol*] [*Library of Congress*] (LCLS)
WaEl.......... Ellensburg Public Library, Ellensburg, WA [*Library symbol*] [*Library of Congress*] (LCLS)
WAEL....... Mayaguez, PR [*AM radio station call letters*]
WaElC....... Central Washington State College, Ellensburg, WA [*Library symbol*] [*Library of Congress*] (LCLS)
WAELD..... Wave Electronics [*A publication*]
WA Electr Contract ... WA [*Western Australian*] Electrical Contractor [*A publication*] (APTA)
WAEL-FM ... Maricao, PR [*FM radio station call letters*]
WAEMA ... Western and English Manufacturers Association [*Denver, CO*] (EA)
WAEM-FM ... Marseilles, IL [*FM radio station call letters*]
WAEO....... La Grange, IN [*FM radio station call letters*]
WaEp........ Ephrata Public Library, Ephrata, WA [*Library symbol*] [*Library of Congress*] (LCLS)
WAEP....... World Association for Element Building and Prefabrication [*Hamburg, Federal Republic of Germany*] (EAIO)
WAEPA..... War Agencies Employees Protective Association
WAEPA..... Worldwide Assurance for Employees of Public Agencies [*Falls Church, VA*] (EA)
WaEPH ...... Providence Hospital, Everett, WA [*Library symbol*] [*Library of Congress*] (LCLS)
WaEpS....... Sunrise Group Home, Ephrata, WA [*Library symbol*] [*Library of Congress*] (LCLS)
WAER ...... Syracuse, NY [*FM radio station call letters*]
WAER ...... World Association for Educational Research [*See also AMSE*] [*Ghent, Belgium*] (EAIO)
Waerme Kaeltetch ... Waerme- und Kaeltetechnik [*A publication*]
Waerme und Stoffuebertrag ... Waerme- und Stoffuebertragung [*A publication*]
Waerme- Stoffuebertrag ... Waerme- und Stoffuebertragung [*A publication*]
Waerme Stoffuebertrag/Thermo Fluid Dyn ... Waerme- und Stoffuebertragung/Thermo and Fluid Dynamics [*A publication*]
Waermetech ... Waermetechnik [*A publication*]
WAERSA .. World Agricultural Economics and Rural Sociology Abstracts [*A publication*]
WAES....... Charlotte, NC [*AM radio station call letters*]
WAES....... Workshop on Alternative Energy Strategies
WAEV....... Savannah, GA [*FM radio station call letters*]
WAEW...... Crossville, TN [*AM radio station call letters*]
WAEY ...... Princeton, WV [*AM radio station call letters*]
WAEY-FM ... Princeton, WV [*FM radio station call letters*]
WaEYS...... Washington State Center for Youth Services, Everett, WA [*Library symbol*] [*Library of Congress*] (LCLS)
WAEZ-FM ... Milton, WV [*FM radio station call letters*]
WAF......... Wafer (AAG)
Wa-F.......... Washington State Film Library, Olympia, WA [*Library symbol*] [*Library of Congress*] (LCLS)
WAF......... West Africa [*A publication*]
WAF......... West African Forces [*British military*] (DMA)
WAF .... Width across Flats (MSA)
WAF .... Wiring around Frame (MSA)
WAF......... With All Faults [*i.e., to be sold as is*]
WAF .... Woman Activist Fund (EA)
WAF .... Women in the Air Force
WAF .... Women's Aglow Fellowship (EA)
WAF .... Women's Auxiliary Force [*British*] [*World War I*] [*Later, Victory Corps*]
WAF .... Word Address Format
WAF .... World Apostolate of Fatima [*The Blue Army*] (EAIO)
WAF .... Wound Angiogensis Factor [*Biochemistry*]
WAF .... WTC, Inc. [*AMEX symbol*] (SPSG)
WAFAH .... West African Federation of Associations for the Advancement of Handicapped Persons [*See also FOAPH*] [*Bamako, Mali*] (EAIO)
WAFB....... Baton Rouge, LA [*Television station call letters*]
WAFB....... Warren Air Force Base [*Wyoming*] (AAG)
WAFC....... Clewiston, FL [*AM radio station call letters*]
WAFC....... Wendel Adkins Fan Club (EA)
WAFC....... West African Fisheries Commission
WAFC....... Western Area Frequency Coordinator
WAFC-FM ... Clewiston, FL [*FM radio station call letters*]
WAF/CP ... Women and Foundations/Corporate Philanthropy (EA)
WAFE....... Wives of the Armed Forces, Emeritus [*Defunct*] (EA)
WAFF....... Huntsville, AL [*Television station call letters*]
WAFF....... Wartime Fuel Factors
WAFF....... West African Frontier Force
WAFF....... Western Australian Farmers' Federation
WAFFLE... Wide-Angle Fixed-Field Locating Equipment
WAFG....... Fort Lauderdale, FL [*FM radio station call letters*]
WAFK....... Saraland, AL [*AM radio station call letters*]
WAFL........ Milford, DE [*FM radio station call letters*]

W Af LR .... West African Law Reports [*A publication*] (DLA)
WAFLT Forum ... Washington Association of Foreign Language Teachers. Forum [*A publication*]
WAFM ...... Amory, MS [*FM radio station call letters*]
WaForC ..... Clearwater Correctional Center, Staff Library, Forks, WA [*Library symbol*] [*Library of Congress*] (LCLS)
WaForC-R ... Clearwater Correctional Center, Resident Library, Forks, WA [*Library symbol*] [*Library of Congress*] (LCLS)
Wa For LR ... Wake Forest Law Review [*A publication*]
WAFP........ Woody Allen's Fall Picture [*Designation reflecting the filmmaker's reluctance to provide information about his movies in advance of their commercial release*] [*See also WASP*]
W AFR...... West Africa
W Afr........ West Africa [*A publication*]
W Afr App ... West African Court of Appeal Reports [*A publication*] (DLA)
W Africa .... West Africa [*A publication*]
W African Rel ... West African Religion [*A publication*]
W Afr J Arc ... West African Journal of Archaeology [*A publication*]
WA Fruitgrower ... Western Australian Fruitgrower [*A publication*] (APTA)
WAFS........ Atlanta, GA [*AM radio station call letters*]
WAFS........ Women's Air Force Services [*British military*] (DMA)
WAFS........ Women's Auxiliary Ferrying Squadron [*Part of Air Transport Command*] [*World War II*]
WAFS........ Women's Auxiliary Fire Service [*British*] [*World War II*]
WAFS........ World Area Forecast System [*Meteorology*]
WaFsWS ... Western State Hospital, Staff Library, Fort Steilacoom, WA [*Library symbol*] [*Library of Congress*] (LCLS)
WAFT........ Valdosta, GA [*FM radio station call letters*]
WAFT........ Wichita Auditory Fusion Test
WaFtl......... United States Army, Fort Lewis Library System, Grandstaff Library, Fort Lewis, WA [*Library symbol*] [*Library of Congress*] (LCLS)
WaFW .... Whatcom Community College, Ferndale, WA [*Library symbol*] [*Library of Congress*] (LCLS)
WAFWA.... Western Association of Fish and Wildlife Agencies (EA)
WaFwS ...... Federal Way School District Central Library, Federal Way, WA [*Library symbol*] [*Library of Congress*] (LCLS)
WAFX........ Suffolk, VA [*FM radio station call letters*]
WAFY........ Middletown, MD [*FM radio station call letters*]
WAG......... Wagon (MSA)
WAG......... Walgreen Co. [*NYSE symbol*] (SPSG)
WAG......... Wanganui [*New Zealand*] [*Airport symbol*] (OAG)
WAG......... Warfare Analysis Group [*Navy*]
WAG......... Water-Alternating Gas [*Petroleum engineering*]
WAG......... Wellsville, Addison & Galeton Railroad Corp. [*AAR code*]
WAG......... Wiederaufbaugesellschaft fuer die Juedische Bevoelkerung der Bucovina [*A publication*] (BJA)
WAG......... Wild Aim Guess [*Bowdlerized version*]
WAG......... Wine Appreciation Guild (EA)
WAG......... Wireless Air Gunner [*British military*] (DMA)
WAG......... World Agricultural Economics and Rural Sociology Abstracts [*A publication*]
WAG......... World Area Grid (MCD)
WAG......... Writers' Action Group [*British*]
WaGal...... Intermediate School District 113, Instructional Materials Center, Galvin, WA [*Library symbol*] [*Library of Congress*] (LCLS)
WAGA-TV ... Atlanta, GA [*Television station call letters*]
WAGB ...... Wildfowlers' Association of Great Britain
WAGC...... Centre, AL [*AM radio station call letters*]
WaGc......... Grand Coulee Public Library, Grand Coulee, WA [*Library symbol*] [*Library of Congress*] (LCLS)
WAGC...... World Amateur Golf Council (EA)
WAGCOM ... War Game Comparison (MCD)
WAGE...... Leesburg, VA [*AM radio station call letters*]
WAGE...... Union Women's Alliance to Gain Equality [*Defunct*] (EA)
WAGEA .... Waste Age [*A publication*]
Wage & Hour Cas BNA ... Wage and Hour Cases. Bureau of National Affairs [*A publication*]
Wage & Hour Rep ... Wage and Hour Reporter [*Bureau of National Affairs*] [*A publication*] (DLA)
Wage-Price Law and Econ R ... Wage-Price Law and Economics Review [*A publication*]
Wage-Price L & Econ Rev ... Wage-Price Law and Economics Review [*A publication*]
Wage-Pr L ... Wage-Price Law and Economics Review [*A publication*]
WAGE$..... Women Achieving Greater Economic Status [*Commercial firm*] (EA)
WAGF ...... Dothan, AL [*AM radio station call letters*]
WAGFEI ... Women's Action Group on Excision and Infibulation [*London, England*] (EAIO)
WAGG...... Birmingham, AL [*AM radio station call letters*]
WAGG...... Western Australia Government Gazette [*A publication*] (APTA)
Wagga Hist Soc News ... Wagga Wagga and District Historical Society. Newsletter [*A publication*] (APTA)
WAGGGS ... World Association of Girl Guides and Girl Scouts [*See also AMGE*] [*London, England*] (EAIO)
WAGH ...... Fort Mitchell, AL [*FM radio station call letters*]

WaGhP...... Purdy Treatment Center for Women, Gig Harbor, WA [*Library symbol*] [*Library of Congress*] (LCLS)
WAGI-FM ... Gaffney, SC [*FM radio station call letters*]
WAGL....... Lancaster, SC [*AM radio station call letters*]
WAGM-TV ... Presque Isle, ME [*Television station call letters*]
WAGN....... Menominee, MI [*AM radio station call letters*]
Wagner Free Inst Sci Bull Cards ... Wagner Free Institute of Science. Bulletin. Cards [*A publication*]
Wagner Free I Sc Tr ... Wagner Free Institute of Science [*Philadelphia*]. Transactions [*A publication*]
WAGO...... Reading, PA [*AM radio station call letters*]
WA Govt Gaz ... Western Australia Government Gazette [*A publication*] (APTA)
WAGP....... Beaufort, SC [*FM radio station call letters*]
WAGR....... Lumberton, NC [*AM radio station call letters*]
WAGR ...... Wald, Arnold, Goldberg, Rushton [*Test*] [*Statistics*]
WAGR ...... Wilms Tumor, Aniridia, Genitourinary Abnormalities, and Mental Retardation [*Syndrome*] [*Medicine*]
WAGR ...... Windscale Advanced Gas-Cooled Reactor
WAGRO .... Warsaw Ghetto Resistance Organization (EA)
WAGS ...... Bishopville, SC [*AM radio station call letters*]
WAGS ...... Weighted Agreement Scores
WAGS ...... Western Australian Genealogical Society
WAGS ...... Wireless Air Gunners School [*British military*] (DMA)
WAGS ...... Worldwide Atmospheric Gravity Wave Study [*Ionospheric physics*]
WAGSO .... Wiener Archiv fuer Geschichte des Slawentums und Osteuropas [*A publication*]
Wag St ...... Wagner's Missouri Statutes [*A publication*] (DLA)
Wag Stat .... Wagner's Missouri Statutes [*A publication*] (DLA)
WAGT ...... Augusta, GA [*Television station call letters*]
WAGY ...... Forest City, NC [*AM radio station call letters*]
WAH .... Wahluke [*Washington*] [*Seismograph station code, US Geological Survey*] (SEIS)
WAH .... Westair Holding, Inc. [*AMEX symbol*] (CTT)
WAH .... Womack Army Hospital Medical Library, Fort Bragg, NC [*OCLC symbol*] (OCLC)
WAH .... Writings on American History [*A publication*]
WAHA...... Wide-Angle High Aperture (MCD)
WAHC...... West African Health Community (EA)
WAHC...... World Airlines Hobby Club (EA)
WAHD ...... Wilson, NC [*FM radio station call letters*]
WaHi .... Washington State Historical Society, Tacoma, WA [*Library symbol*] [*Library of Congress*] (LCLS)
WA Hist Soc J ... Western Australian Historical Society. Journal and Proceedings [*A publication*] (APTA)
WAHLC .... World Association for Hebrew Language and Culture (EAIO)
WAHO ...... World Arabian Horse Organization [*Windermere, England*] (EAIO)
WAHR...... Huntsville, AL [*FM radio station call letters*]
WAHS...... Auburn Heights, MI [*FM radio station call letters*]
WAHS ...... World Airline Historical Society (EA)
WAHSJ..... Western Australian Historical Society. Journal [*A publication*] (ADA)
WAHT...... Annville-Cleona, PA [*AM radio station call letters*]
WAHVM... World Association for the History of Veterinary Medicine [*Hanover, Federal Republic of Germany*] (EAIO)
WAI .... Antsohihy [*Madagascar*] [*Airport symbol*] (OAG)
WAI .... Wairiri [*Glentunnel*] [*New Zealand*] [*Seismograph station code, US Geological Survey*] [*Closed*] (SEIS)
WAI .... Walk Around Inspection
WAI .... Wall Street Journal. European Edition [*A publication*]
WAI .... Water Absorption Index [*Analytical chemistry*]
WAI .... Water Alcohol Injection (MCD)
WAI .... Wire Association International (EA)
WAI .... Work in America Institute (EA)
WAIA .... St. Augustine Beach, FL [*AM radio station call letters*]
WAIA Ct ... Western Australian Industrial Appeal Court
WAIC .... Springfield, MA [*FM radio station call letters*]
WAICA..... Women's Auxiliary of the ICA [*International Chiropractors Association*] (EA)
WAID .... Clarksdale, MS [*FM radio station call letters*]
WAID........ Wage and Information Documents [*IRS*]
WAIF....... Cincinnati, OH [*FM radio station call letters*]
WAIF........ World Adoption International Fund
WAIG .... Western Australian Industrial Gazette [*A publication*] (APTA)
WAIHA ..... Warm Autoimmune Hemolytic Anemia [*Medicine*]
WAIJ .... Grantsville, MD [*FM radio station call letters*]
WAIK .... Galesburg, IL [*AM radio station call letters*]
Waikato Univ Antarct Res Unit Rep ... Waikato University. Antarctic Research Unit. Reports [*A publication*]
WAIL........ Key West, FL [*FM radio station call letters*]
WAIM ...... Anderson, SC [*AM radio station call letters*]
WAIN .... Columbia, KY [*AM radio station call letters*]
WAIN .... Wainwright Bank & Trust Co. [*NASDAQ symbol*] (CTT)
WA Ind Gaz ... Western Australian Industrial Gazette [*A publication*] (APTA)
WA Indus Gaz ... Western Australian Industrial Gazette [*A publication*] (APTA)
WAIN-FM ... Columbia, KY [*FM radio station call letters*]
WAIOP ...... Will Accept, If Offered, the Position of _____ (FAAC)

WAIP......... World Association for Infant Psychiatry [*Later, WAIPAD*] (EA)
WAIPAD... World Association for Infant Psychiatry and Allied Disciplines (EA)
WAIQ........ Montgomery, AL [*Television station call letters*]
WAIR........ Atlanta, MI [*FM radio station call letters*]
WAIRC..... Western Australian Industrial Relations Commission
W Air Trans ... World Air Transport Statistics [*A publication*]
WAIS......... Buchtel, OH [*AM radio station call letters*]
WAIS......... Wechsler Adult Intelligence Scale [*Education*]
WAIS......... Western Australian Institute of Sport
WAIS-R... Wechsler Adult Intelligence Scale-Revised [*Test*]
WAIT........ Crystal Lake, IL [*AM radio station call letters*]
WAIT........ Weighted Average Inlet Temperature [*Chemical engineering*]
WAIT........ Western Australia Institute of Technology [*Database originator and operator*]
Wait Act & Def ... Wait's Actions and Defences [*A publication*] (DLA)
Wait Co...... Wait's New York Annotated Code [*A publication*] (DLA)
Wait Dig .... Wait's New York Digest [*A publication*] (DLA)
WAIT-FM ... Woodstock, IL [*FM radio station call letters*]
Wait L & P ... Wait's Law and Practice in New York Justices' Courts [*A publication*] (DLA)
Wait Pr ...... Wait's New York Practice [*A publication*] (DLA)
WAITRO.. World Association of Industrial and Technological Research Organizations [*Arhus, Denmark*]
Waits Prac ... Wait's New York Practice [*A publication*] (DLA)
Wait St Pap ... Wait's State Papers of the United States [*A publication*] (DLA)
Wait Tab Ca ... Wait's New York Table of Cases [*A publication*] (DLA)
WAIV-FM ... Jacksonville, FL [*FM radio station call letters*]
WAJ.......... Wajima [*Japan*] [*Seismograph station code, US Geological Survey*] (SEIS)
WAJ.......... Water-Augmented Jet
WAJ.......... World Association of Judges (EA)
WAJA....... Arso [*Indonesia*] [*ICAO location identifier*] (ICLI)
WAJA....... Franklin, NC [*AM radio station call letters*]
WAJA....... West African Journal of Archaeology [*A publication*]
WAJB....... Bokondini [*Indonesia*] [*ICAO location identifier*] (ICLI)
WAJC....... Indianapolis, IN [*FM radio station call letters*]
WAJCSC... W. Alton Jones Cell Science Center, Inc. [*Research center*] (RCD)
WAJD....... Gainesville, FL [*AM radio station call letters*]
WAJD....... Wakde [*Indonesia*] [*ICAO location identifier*] (ICLI)
WAJE....... West African Journal of Education [*A publication*]
WAJF....... Decatur, AL [*AM radio station call letters*]
WAJI........ Fort Wayne, IN [*FM radio station call letters*]
WAJI........ Sarmi/Orai [*Indonesia*] [*ICAO location identifier*] (ICLI)
WAJJ .... Jayapura/Sentani [*Indonesia*] [*ICAO location identifier*] (ICLI)
WAJK....... Kiwirok [*Indonesia*] [*ICAO location identifier*] (ICLI)
WAJK....... La Salle, IL [*FM radio station call letters*]
WAJL....... Lereh [*Indonesia*] [*ICAO location identifier*] (ICLI)
WAJL....... Pine Castle-Sky Lake, FL [*AM radio station call letters*]
WAJM.... Mulia [*Indonesia*] [*ICAO location identifier*] (ICLI)
WAJML.... West Africa Journal of Modern Language [*A publication*]
WAJM-TV ... Palatka, FL [*Television station call letters*]
WAJN .... Ashland City, TN [*AM radio station call letters*]
WAJO .... Marion, AL [*AM radio station call letters*]
WAJO .... Oksibil [*Indonesia*] [*ICAO location identifier*] (ICLI)
WAJR....... Morgantown, WV [*AM radio station call letters*]
WAJR....... Waris [*Indonesia*] [*ICAO location identifier*] (ICLI)
WAJS....... Senggeh [*Indonesia*] [*ICAO location identifier*] (ICLI)
WAJU .... Ubrub [*Indonesia*] [*ICAO location identifier*] (ICLI)
WAJW....... Wamena [*Indonesia*] [*ICAO location identifier*] (ICLI)
WAJY....... New Ellenton, SC [*FM radio station call letters*]
WAJZ........ Jayapura Sector [*Indonesia*] [*ICAO location identifier*] (ICLI)
WAK......... Ankazoabo [*Madagascar*] [*Airport symbol*] (OAG)
WAK......... Wackenhut Corp. [*NYSE symbol*] (SPSG)
WAK......... Wait Acknowledge
wak............ Wakashan [*MARC language code*] [*Library of Congress*] (LCCP)
WAK......... Wakkanai [*Japan*] [*Seismograph station code, US Geological Survey*] (SEIS)
WAK......... Water Analyzer Kit
WAK......... Wearable Artificial Kidney
WAK....... Write Access Key
WAKA....... Akimuga [*Indonesia*] [*ICAO location identifier*] (ICLI)
WAKA .... Selma, AL [*Television station call letters*]
Wakayama Med Rep ... Wakayama Medical Reports [*A publication*]
WAKC-TV ... Akron, OH [*Television station call letters*]
WAKD....... Mindiptanah [*Indonesia*] [*ICAO location identifier*] (ICLI)
WAKE .... Bade [*Indonesia*] [*ICAO location identifier*] (ICLI)
WAKE .... Valparaiso, IN [*AM radio station call letters*]
Wake Forest Intra L Rev ... Wake Forest Intramural Law Review [*A publication*] (DLA)
Wake Forest L Rev ... Wake Forest Law Review [*A publication*]
Wake For L Rev ... Wake Forest Law Review [*A publication*]
Wake For Univ Dev Nations Monogr Ser Ser II Med Behav Sci ... Wake Forest University. Developing Nations Monograph Series. Series II. Medical Behavioral Science [*A publication*]

Wake For Unive Dev Nations Monogr Ser Ser II Med Behav Sci ... Wake Forest University. Developing Nations Monograph Series. Series II. Medical Behavioral Science [*A publication*]
WaKel........ Kelso Public Library, Kelso, WA [*Library symbol*] [*Library of Congress*] (LCLS)
WaKeM .... Mid-Columbia Regional Library, Kennewick, WA [*Library symbol*] [*Library of Congress*] (LCLS)
WaKenS..... Saint Thomas Seminary, Kenmore, WA [*Library symbol*] [*Library of Congress*] (LCLS)
WAKG .... Agats [*Indonesia*] [*ICAO location identifier*] (ICLI)
WAKG .... Danville, VA [*FM radio station call letters*]
WAKH...... Abohoy [*Indonesia*] [*ICAO location identifier*] (ICLI)
WAKH...... McComb, MS [*FM radio station call letters*]
WAKI .... McMinnville, TN [*AM radio station call letters*]
WaKiN....... Northwest College, Kirkland, WA [*Library symbol*] [*Library of Congress*] (LCLS)
WAKK .... McComb, MS [*AM radio station call letters*]
WAKK .... Merauke/Mopah [*Indonesia*] [*ICAO location identifier*] (ICLI)
WAKM .... Franklin, TN [*AM radio station call letters*]
WAKN ...... Primapun [*Indonesia*] [*ICAO location identifier*] (ICLI)
WAKO....... Lawrenceville, IL [*AM radio station call letters*]
WAKO....... Okaba [*Indonesia*] [*ICAO location identifier*] (ICLI)
WAKO-FM ... Lawrenceville, IL [*FM radio station call letters*]
WAKP .... Kepi [*Indonesia*] [*ICAO location identifier*] (ICLI)
WAKQ .... Paris, TN [*FM radio station call letters*]
WAKR .... Akron, OH [*AM radio station call letters*]
Waksman Inst Microbiol Rutgers Univ Annu Rep ... Waksman Institute of Microbiology. Rutgers University. Annual Report [*A publication*]
WAKT .... Tanah Merah [*Indonesia*] [*ICAO location identifier*] (ICLI)
WAKW .... Cincinnati, OH [*FM radio station call letters*]
WAKX .... Duluth, MN [*FM radio station call letters*]
WAKY .... Greensburg, KY [*AM radio station call letters*]
WAL .... Chincoteague, VA [*Location identifier*] [*FAA*] (FAAL)
WAL .... Lawrence University, Appleton, WI [*Library symbol*] [*Library of Congress*] (LCLS)
WAL .... Wahlco Environment Systems [*NYSE symbol*] (SPSG)
wal............ Walamo [*MARC language code*] [*Library of Congress*] (LCCP)
Wal .... Waldorf [*Record label*]
WAL .... Wallace [*Idaho*] [*Seismograph station code, US Geological Survey*] (SEIS)
WAL .... Walloon (ROG)
WAL .... Walsh College, Canton, OH [*OCLC symbol*] (OCLC)
Wa-L......... Washington State Law Library, Olympia, WA [*Library symbol*] [*Library of Congress*] (LCLS)
WAL .... Waterloo Resources, Inc. [*Vancouver Stock Exchange symbol*]
WAL .... Watertown Arsenal Laboratory [*Massachusetts*] [*Army*]
WAL .... We Are Lost [*Army*]
WAL .... Weather Almanac [*A publication*]
WAL .... Western Airlines, Inc. [*Facetious translation: What an Airline*]
WAL .... Western Allegheny Railroad Co. [*AAR code*]
WAL .... Western American Literature [*A publication*]
W-AL........ Westinghouse-Astronuclear Laboratories
WAL .... Wide-Angle Lens
WAL .... World Association of Lawyers (EA)
WAL .... Wright Aeronautical Laboratories (MCD)
WALA News ... West African Library Association. News [*A publication*]
WALA-TV ... Mobile, AL [*Television station call letters*]
WALB....... Walbro Corp. [*NASDAQ symbol*] (NQ)
WALB-TV ... Albany, GA [*Television station call letters*]
WALC .... West African Lands Committee. Report [*A publication*] (ILCA)
WALC .... Worldwide Aviation Logistics Conference (RDA)
Wal Ch....... Walker's Michigan Chancery Reports [*A publication*] (DLA)
WALD .... Waldbaum, Inc. [*NASDAQ symbol*] (NQ)
Wald .... Walden [*Record label*]
WALD .... Walterboro, SC [*AM radio station call letters*]
WALD-FM ... Walterboro, SC [*FM radio station call letters*]
WALDO ...... Wichita Automatic Linear Data Output
WALDO ...... Winona Tri College University Library Network [*Library network*]
WALE....... Providence, RI [*AM radio station call letters*]
WALF....... Alfred, NY [*FM radio station call letters*]
Walf Cust... Walford's Laws of the Customs [*1846*] [*A publication*] (DLA)
Walford's Antiq ... Walford's Antiquarian and Bibliographer [*A publication*]
Walf Part... Walford's Parties to Actions [*1842*] [*A publication*] (DLA)
Walf Railw ... Walford on Railways [*2nd ed.*] [*1846*] [*A publication*] (DLA)
WALG .... Albany, GA [*AM radio station call letters*]
WALH...... Mountain City, GA [*AM radio station call letters*]
WALI .... Cumberland, MD [*AM radio station call letters*]
Wal Jr .... [*J. W.*] Wallace's United States Circuit Court Reports [*A publication*] (DLA)
WALK ...... Patchogue, NY [*AM radio station call letters*]
Walk .... Walker's Michigan Chancery Reports [*A publication*] (DLA)
Walk .... Walker's Pennsylvania Reports [*1855-85*] [*A publication*] (DLA)
Walk .... Walker's Reports [*96, 109 Alabama*] [*A publication*] (DLA)
Walk .... Walker's Reports [*22-25, 38-51, 72-88 Texas*] [*1-10 Civil Appeals Texas*] [*A publication*] (DLA)
Walk .... Walker's Reports [*1 Mississippi*] [*A publication*] (DLA)
Walk Am Law ... Walker's American Law [*A publication*] (DLA)

Walk Bank L ... Walker's Banking Law [2nd ed.] [1885] [A publication]   (DLA)
Walk Ch..... Walker's Michigan Chancery Reports [A publication]   (DLA)
Walk Chanc Rep ... Walker's Michigan Chancery Reports [A publication]   (DLA)
Walk Ch Cas ... Walker's Michigan Chancery Reports [A publication]   (DLA)
Walk Ch Mich ... Walker's Michigan Chancery Reports [A publication]   (DLA)
Walk Com L ... Walker's Theory of the Common Law [A publication]   (DLA)
Walk Eq Pl ... Walker's Equity Pleader's Assistant [A publication]   (DLA)
Walker....... Walker's Michigan Chancery Reports [A publication]   (DLA)
Walker....... Walker's Pennsylvania Reports [1855-85] [A publication]   (DLA)
Walker....... Walker's Reports [96, 109 Alabama] [A publication]   (DLA)
Walker....... Walker's Reports [22-25, 38-51, 72-88 Texas] [1-10 Civil Appeals Texas] [A publication]   (DLA)
Walker....... Walker's Reports [1 Mississippi] [A publication]   (DLA)
Walker's Ch R ... Walker's Michigan Chancery Reports [A publication]   (DLA)
Walk Exec ... Walker and Elgood's Executors and Administrators [6th ed.] [1926] [A publication]   (DLA)
WALK-FM ... Patchogue, NY [FM radio station call letters]
Walk Int..... Walker's Introduction to American Law [A publication]   (DLA)
Walk LA Dig ... Walker's Louisiana Digest [A publication]   (DLA)
Walk (Mic) Ch ... Walker's Michigan Chancery Reports [A publication]   (DLA)
Walk Mich ... Walker's Michigan Chancery Reports [A publication]   (DLA)
Walk Michig Rep ... Walker's Michigan Chancery Reports [A publication]   (DLA)
Walk Miss ... Walker's Reports [1 Mississippi] [A publication]   (DLA)
Walk PA .... Walker's Pennsylvania Reports [1855-85] [A publication]   (DLA)
Walk Pat.... Walker on Patents [A publication]   (DLA)
Walk Tex... Walker's Reports [22-25, 38-51, 72-88 Texas] [1-10 Civil Appeals Texas] [A publication]   (DLA)
Walk Wills ... Walker on Wills [A publication]   (DLA)
WALL....... Middletown, NY [AM radio station call letters]
Wall .... Wallace's Nova Scotia Reports [A publication]   (DLA)
Wall .... Wallace's Supreme Court Reports [68-90 United States] [1863-74] [A publication]   (DLA)
Wall .... Wallace's United States Circuit Court Reports [A publication]   (DLA)
WALL....... Wallachian   (ROG)
WALL........ Wallingford [Municipal borough in England]
Wall .... Wallis' Irish Chancery Reports [A publication]   (DLA)
Wal by L .... Wallis' Irish Chancery Reports, by Lyne [A publication]   (DLA)
Wall .... Wallis' Philadelphia Reports [1855-85] [Pennsylvania] [A publication]   (DLA)
WALL....... Walloon   (ROG)
Wallace Jr Rept ... [J. W.] Wallace, Junior's, United States Circuit Court Reports [A publication]   (DLA)
Wallaces F ... Wallaces Farmer [A publication]
Walla Walla Coll Publ ... Walla Walla College. Publications [A publication]
Wall CC..... Wallace's United States Circuit Court Reports [A publication]   (DLA)
Wallerstein Lab Commun ... Wallerstein Laboratories. Communications [A publication]
Wallerstein Lab Commun Sci Pract Brew ... Wallerstein Laboratories. Communications on the Science and Practice of Brewing [A publication]
Wallis........ Wallis' Irish Chancery Reports [A publication]   (DLA)
Wallis (Ir).. Wallis' Irish Chancery Reports [A publication]   (DLA)
Wallis by L ... Wallis' Irish Chancery Reports, by Lyne [1776-91] [A publication]   (DLA)
Wallis by Lyne ... Wallis' Irish Chancery Reports, by Lyne [1766-91] [A publication]   (DLA)
Wall Jr....... [J. W.] Wallace's United States Circuit Court Reports [A publication]   (DLA)
Wall Jr CC ... [J. W.] Wallace's United States Circuit Court Reports [A publication]   (DLA)
Wall Lyn.... Wallis' Irish Chancery Reports, by Lyne [1776-91] [A publication]   (DLA)
Wall Pr ...... Wallace's Principles of the Laws of Scotland [A publication]   (DLA)
Wallraf-Richartz Jahr ... Wallraf-Richartz Jahrbuch [A publication]
Wall Rep.... Wallace's "The Reporters" [A publication]   (DLA)
Wall Rep.... Wallace's Supreme Court Reports [68-90 United States] [A publication]   (DLA)
Wall SC ..... Wallace's Supreme Court Reports [68-90 United States] [A publication]   (DLA)
Wall Sen .... [J. B.] Wallace's United States Circuit Court Reports [A publication]   (DLA)
Wall St J.... Wall Street Journal [A publication]
Wall St J East Ed ... Wall Street Journal. Eastern Edition [A publication]
Wall St J Midwest Ed ... Wall Street Journal. Midwest Edition [A publication]
Wall St Jnl ... Wall Street Journal [A publication]
Wall St J Three Star East Ed ... Wall Street Journal. Three Star Eastern Edition [A publication]
Wall St R Bk ... Wall Street Review of Books [A publication]
Wall Str J .. Wall Street Journal [A publication]
Wall St T ... Wall Street Transcript [A publication]

WALM ...... Albion, MI [AM radio station call letters]
WALMS ...... West African Language Monograph Series [A publication]
WALO .... Humacao, PR [AM radio station call letters]
WaLo .... Longview Public Library, Longview, WA [Library symbol] [Library of Congress]   (LCLS)
WaLoGS.... Church of Jesus Christ of Latter-Day Saints, Genealogical Society Library, Longview Stake Branch, Longview, WA [Library symbol] [Library of Congress]   (LCLS)
WaLoL....... Lower Columbia College, Longview, WA [Library symbol] [Library of Congress]   (LCLS)
WALOPT ... Weapons Allocation and Desired Ground-Zero Optimizer [Military]
WALP....... Weapons Assignment Linear Program
WALP....... World Association of Law Professors   (EA)
Wal Prin .... Wallace's Principles of the Laws of Scotland [A publication]   (DLA)
Walp Rub .... Walpole's Rubric of Common Law [A publication]   (DLA)
WALR ...... Athens, GA [FM radio station call letters]
WALR ...... University of Western Australia. Law Review [A publication]
Wa LR....... Washington Law Review [A publication]
WALR ...... West African Law Reports [Gambia, Ghana, and Sierra Leone] [A publication]   (DLA)
WALR ...... Western Australian Law Reports [A publication]   (APTA)
WaLrC....... Cedar Creek Youth Camp, Littlerock, WA [Library symbol] [Library of Congress]   (LCLS)
WALRC Bull ... Western Australia Law Reform Commission. Bulletin [A publication]
WALRPA... Western Australian Light Railway Preservation Association
WALRUS.. Water and Land Resources Use Simulation
WALS....... Walshire Assurance Co. [NASDAQ symbol]   (NQ)
WALS....... Western Aboriginal Legal Service [Australia]
WALS....... World Association of Law Students   (EA)
Walsh........ Walsh's Irish Registry Cases [A publication]   (DLA)
Walsh's R .. Walsh's American Review [A publication]
Wal Sr........ [J. B.] Wallace's United States Circuit Court Reports [A publication]   (DLA)
Wal Steve J ... Wallace Stevens Journal [A publication]
WALT....... Meridian, MS [AM radio station call letters]
WALT....... West's Automatic Law Terminal
Walter....... Walter's Reports [14-16 New Mexico] [A publication]   (DLA)
Walter Andree Nottbeck Found Sci Rep ... Walter and Andree de Nottbeck Foundation. Scientific Reports [A publication]
Walter C .... Walter's Code [A publication]   (DLA)
Walter Reed Army Med Cent Prog Notes ... Walter Reed Army Medical Center. Progress Notes [A publication]
Walter Reed Gen Hosp Dep Med Prog Notes ... Walter Reed General Hospital. Department of Medicine. Progress Notes [A publication]
Walters J ... Walters Art Gallery [Baltimore]. Journal [A publication]
Walt H & W ... Walton on Husband and Wife [Scotland] [A publication]
Walt Lim.... Walter's Statute of Limitations [4th ed.] [A publication]   (DLA)
WALTSTOW ... Walthamstow [England]
Walt Whit R ... Walt Whitman Review [A publication]
Wal US Rep ... Wallace's United States Reports [A publication]   (DLA)
WALV ...... Cleveland, TN [FM radio station call letters]
WALX ...... Selma, AL [FM radio station call letters]
WALY ...... Bellwood, PA [FM radio station call letters]
WALZ....... Machias, ME [FM radio station call letters]
WAM........ Ambatondrazaka [Madagascar] [Airport symbol]   (OAG)
WAM........ Appleton Memorial Hospital, Appleton, WI [Library symbol] [Library of Congress]   (LCLS)
WAM........ Emirates News Agency [United Arab Emirates]   (MENA)
WAM........ Walleye Measurements Program
WAM........ Wambrook [Australia] [Seismograph station code, US Geological Survey]   (SEIS)
WAM........ Warburton Minerals [Vancouver Stock Exchange symbol]
WAM........ Weight after Melt [Metallurgy]
WAM........ Weighted Average Maturity [Finance]
WAM........ Western Apparel Manufacturers Show   (ITD)
WAM........ Western Associated Modelers   (EA)
WAM........ Western Australian Museum
WAM........ White Australia Movement
WAM........ Wide-Area Mine [Military]   (MCD)
WAM........ Wiltshire Archaeological Magazine [A publication]
WAM........ Women in Advertising and Marketing   (EA)
WAM........ Women's Action Movement
WAM........ Words a Minute
WAM........ Worth Analysis Model   (IEEE)
wam........... Writer of Accompanying Material [MARC relator code] [Library of Congress]   (LCCP)
WAMA ...... Galela/Gamarmalamo [Indonesia] [ICAO location identifier]   (ICLI)
WAMA ...... Tampa, FL [AM radio station call letters]
WAMA ...... Weight after Mars Arrival [NASA]
WA Manuf ... West Australian Manufacturer [A publication]   (APTA)
WA Manufacturer ... West Australian Manufacturer [A publication]   (APTA)
WaMaS ..... Sno-Isle Regional Library, Marysville, WA [Library symbol] [Library of Congress]   (LCLS)
WAMB ...... Donelson, TN [AM radio station call letters]

WAMB...... Kotamubagu/Mopait [*Indonesia*] [*ICAO location identifier*] (ICLI)
WAMC...... Albany, NY [*FM radio station call letters*]
WAMC...... Tentena [*Indonesia*] [*ICAO location identifier*] (ICLI)
WAMD...... Aberdeen, MD [*AM radio station call letters*]
WAMD...... Jailolo/Kuripasai [*Indonesia*] [*ICAO location identifier*] (ICLI)
WAME...... Charlotte, NC [*AM radio station call letters*]
WaMeH.... Eastern State Hospital, Medical Lake, WA [*Library symbol*] [*Library of Congress*] (LCLS)
WaMeI ...... Interlake School, Staff Library, Medical Lake, WA [*Library symbol*] [*Library of Congress*] (LCLS)
WaMeL ..... Lakeland Village School, Medical Lake, WA [*Library symbol*] [*Library of Congress*] (LCLS)
WaMeP ..... Pine Lodge Correctional Center, Staff Library, Medical Lake, WA [*Library symbol*] [*Library of Congress*] (LCLS)
WaMeP-R ... Pine Lodge Correctional Center, Resident Library, Medical Lake, WA [*Library symbol*] [*Library of Congress*] (LCLS)
WAMF ...... Tallahassee, FL [*FM radio station call letters*]
WAMFLEX ... Wave Momentum Flux Experiment [*National Science Foundation*]
WAMG...... Gallatin, TN [*AM radio station call letters*]
WAMG...... Gorontalo/Jalaluddin [*Indonesia*] [*ICAO location identifier*] (ICLI)
WAMH...... Amherst, MA [*FM radio station call letters*]
WAMH .... Tahuna/Naha [*Indonesia*] [*ICAO location identifier*] (ICLI)
WAMI....... Opp, AL [*AM radio station call letters*]
WAMI .... Toli Toli/Lalos [*Indonesia*] [*ICAO location identifier*] (ICLI)
WAMI .... Washington, Alaska, Montana, and Idaho [*Program for states without medical schools*]
WAMI-FM ... Opp, AL [*FM radio station call letters*]
WaMiH ..... Highline Community College, Midway, WA [*Library symbol*] [*Library of Congress*] (LCLS)
WA Mining & Commercial R ... West Australian Mining and Commercial Review [*A publication*] (APTA)
WAMIS..... Watershed Management Information System
WAMJ....... South Bend, IN [*AM radio station call letters*]
WAMK...... Kao/Kuabang [*Indonesia*] [*ICAO location identifier*] (ICLI)
WAMK...... Kingston, NY [*FM radio station call letters*]
WAML ...... Laurel, MS [*AM radio station call letters*]
WaMl......... Moses Lake Public Library, Moses Lake, WA [*Library symbol*] [*Library of Congress*] (LCLS)
WAML ...... Palu/Mutiara [*Indonesia*] [*ICAO location identifier*] (ICLI)
WAML ...... Watertown Arsenal Medical Laboratory [*Massachusetts*] [*Army*]
WAML ...... Western Association of Map Libraries (EA)
WAML ...... Wright Aero Medical Laboratory [*Air Force*]
WaMlB...... Big Bend Community College, Moses Lake, WA [*Library symbol*] [*Library of Congress*] (LCLS)
WaMlGS ... Church of Jesus Christ of Latter-Day Saints, Genealogical Society Library, Moses Lake Branch, Moses Lake, WA [*Library symbol*] [*Library of Congress*] (LCLS)
WAMM..... Manado/Sam Ratulangi [*Indonesia*] [*ICAO location identifier*] (ICLI)
WAMM..... Women Against Military Madness (EA)
WAMM..... Woodstock, VA [*AM radio station call letters*]
WAMN...... Green Valley, WV [*AM radio station call letters*]
WAMN...... Melangguane [*Indonesia*] [*ICAO location identifier*] (ICLI)
WAMO...... Pittsburgh, PA [*AM radio station call letters*]
WAMOC... Women's Auxiliary to the Military Order of the Cootie (EA)
WAMOD... Wave Motion [*A publication*]
WAMO-FM ... Pittsburgh, PA [*FM radio station call letters*]
WaMonR... Washington State Reformatory, Monroe, WA [*Library symbol*] [*Library of Congress*] (LCLS)
WaMonT ... Twin Rivers Correctional Center, Monroe, WA [*Library symbol*] [*Library of Congress*] (LCLS)
WAMOSCOPE ... Wave-Modulated Oscilloscope
WAMP ...... Poso/Kasigunou [*Indonesia*] [*ICAO location identifier*] (ICLI)
WAMPRI ... Western Australian Mining and Petroleum Research Institute
WAMPUM ... Wage and Manpower Process Utilizing Machine [*Bureau of Indian Affairs*]
WAMPUM ... Wartime Availability of Medical Personnel upon Mobilization
WAMQ...... Bada [*Indonesia*] [*ICAO location identifier*] (ICLI)
WAMQ...... Loretto, PA [*AM radio station call letters*]
WAMR...... Morotai/Pitu [*Indonesia*] [*ICAO location identifier*] (ICLI)
WAMR...... Venice, FL [*AM radio station call letters*]
WAMRAC ... World Association of Methodist Radio Amateurs and Clubs
WAMS...... Weapon Aiming and Mode Selector (MCD)
WAMS ...... Wilmington, DE [*AM radio station call letters*]
WAMS ...... Women's Automotive Maintenance Staff
WAMSTAS ... Wide-Area Mine Seismic Target Acquisition Sensor [*Military*] (MCD)
WAMT ...... Ternate/Babullah [*Indonesia*] [*ICAO location identifier*] (ICLI)
WAMT ...... Titusville, FL [*AM radio station call letters*]
WaMtJF.... John Fluke Manufacturing Co., Mountlake Terrace, WA [*Library symbol*] [*Library of Congress*] (LCLS)
WAMTMTS ... Western Area, Military Traffic Management and Terminal Service (AABC)
WaMtv....... Mount Vernon Public Library, Mount Vernon, WA [*Library symbol*] [*Library of Congress*]

WaMtvGS ... Church of Jesus Christ of Latter-Day Saints, Genealogical Society Library, Mount Vernon Branch, Mount Vernon, WA [*Library symbol*] [*Library of Congress*] (LCLS)
WaMtvS .... Skagit Valley College, Mount Vernon, WA [*Library symbol*] [*Library of Congress*] (LCLS)
WAMU...... Washington, DC [*FM radio station call letters*]
WAMU...... Washington Mutual Savings Bank [*NASDAQ symbol*] (NQ)
WAMU...... West African Monetary Union
WAMU...... Wuasa [*Indonesia*] [*ICAO location identifier*] (ICLI)
WAMV...... Amherst, VA [*AM radio station call letters*]
WAMW..... Luwuk/Bubung [*Indonesia*] [*ICAO location identifier*] (ICLI)
WAMW..... Washington, IN [*AM radio station call letters*]
WAMW-FM ... Washington, IN [*FM radio station call letters*]
WAMX...... Ann Arbor, MI [*FM radio station call letters*]
WAMY...... Amory, MS [*AM radio station call letters*]
WAMY...... World Assembly of Muslim Youth [*Riyadh, Saudi Arabia*] (EAIO)
WAMZ...... Louisville, KY [*FM radio station call letters*]
WAMZ...... Menado Sector [*Indonesia*] [*ICAO location identifier*] (ICLI)
WAn.......... Antigo Public Library, Antigo, WI [*Library symbol*] [*Library of Congress*] (LCLS)
WAN......... Wang Laboratories, Inc. [*AMEX symbol*] (SPSG)
WAN......... Wanigan
WAN......... Wanliss Street [*New Britain*] [*Seismograph station code, US Geological Survey*] (SEIS)
WAN......... Western Air Navigation Ltd. [*Australia*]
WAN......... Wide Area Network [*Telecommunications*]
WAN......... Women's Aquatic Network (EA)
WAN......... Women's Royal Australian Naval Service [*World War II*] (DSUE)
WAN......... Work Authorization Number (NASA)
WANA...... Anniston, AL [*AM radio station call letters*]
WANA...... Woodworking Association of North America (EA)
WANADA ... Western Australian Network of Alcohol and Other Drug Agencies
WANAP .... Washington [*DC*] National Airport
WaNasY ... Naselle Youth Camp, Staff Library, Naselle, WA [*Library symbol*] [*Library of Congress*] (LCLS)
WaNasY-R ... Naselle Youth Camp, Resident Library, Naselle, WA [*Library symbol*] [*Library of Congress*] (LCLS)
WA Nat...... Western Australian Naturalist [*A publication*] (APTA)
WANATCA ... Western Australian Nut and Tree Crop Association
WANATCA (West Aust Nut & Tree Crop Assoc) Yearb ... WANATCA (West Australian Nut and Tree Crop Association) Yearbook [*A publication*]
WA Naturalist ... Western Australian Naturalist [*A publication*] (APTA)
WANB....... Waynesburg, PA [*AM radio station call letters*]
WANB-FM ... Waynesburg, PA [*FM radio station call letters*]
WAND....... Decatur, IL [*Television station call letters*]
WAND...... Women and Development Unit (EA)
WAND...... Women's Action for Nuclear Disarmament (EA)
WAND EF ... WAND [*Women's Action for Nuclear Disarmament*] Education Fund (EA)
Wandell ... Wandell's New York Reports [*A publication*] (DLA)
WANE-TV ... Fort Wayne, IN [*Television station call letters*]
WA News... West Australian News [*A publication*] (APTA)
WANG....... Western Australian Natural Gas Proprietary Ltd.
WANL....... Albany, GA [*AM radio station call letters*]
WANL....... Westinghouse-Astronuclear Laboratories
WANM....... Tallahassee, FL [*AM radio station call letters*]
WANN ...... Annapolis, MD [*AM radio station call letters*]
WANO ...... Pineville, KY [*AM radio station call letters*]
WANQ....... Delmar, NY [*AM radio station call letters*]
WANRDN ... Walter and Andree de Nottbeck Foundation. Scientific Reports [*A publication*]
WANS .... Anderson, SC [*AM radio station call letters*]
WANS .... Women's Australian National Service
WANS-FM ... Anderson, SC [*FM radio station call letters*]
WANST..... Wanstead [*England*]
WANT....... Richmond, VA [*AM radio station call letters*]
WANT....... Wantage [*Urban district in England*]
WANT....... Warrant Apprehension Narcotics Team [*In US Marshal Service's "Operation WANT"*]
WANV....... Waynesboro, VA [*AM radio station call letters*]
WANV-FM ... Staunton, VA [*FM radio station call letters*]
WANY....... Albany, KY [*AM radio station call letters*]
WANY-FM ... Albany, KY [*FM radio station call letters*]
WAO.......... Outagamie County Hospital, Appleton, WI [*Library symbol*] [*Library of Congress*] (LCLS)
WaO .... Timberland Regional Library, Olympia, WA [*Library symbol*] [*Library of Congress*] (LCLS)
WAO......... Weapons Assignment Officer [*Air Force*] (AFM)
WAO......... Women's American ORT (EA)
WAOA...... Melbourne, FL [*FM radio station call letters*]
WaOAP..... Washington State Office of Adult Probation and Parole, Olympia, WA [*Library symbol*] [*Library of Congress*] (LCLS)
WaOAr...... State of Washington Department of General Administration, Division of Archives and Records Management, Olympia, WA [*Library symbol*] [*Library of Congress*] (LCLS)

WaOB........ Washington State Department of Public Assistance, Ben Tidball Memorial Library, Olympia, WA [*Library symbol*] [*Library of Congress*] (LCLS)
WAOB...... Winamac, IN [*AM radio station call letters*]
WAOC....... St. Augustine, FL [*AM radio station call letters*]
WaOE........ Evergreen State College, Olympia, WA [*Library symbol*] [*Library of Congress*] (LCLS)
WaOEd...... Washington State Department of Education, Olympia, WA [*Library symbol*] [*Library of Congress*] (LCLS)
WaOEng.... Washington State Energy Office, Olympia, WA [*Library symbol*] [*Library of Congress*] (LCLS)
WaOGS ..... Church of Jesus Christ of Latter-Day Saints, Genealogical Society Library, Olympia Branch, Olympia, WA [*Library symbol*] [*Library of Congress*] (LCLS)
WAOK....... Atlanta, GA [*AM radio station call letters*]
WaOLI ...... State of Washington Department of Labor and Industries Libraries, Olympia, WA [*Library symbol*] [*Library of Congress*] (LCLS)
WaOLN ..... Washington Library Network, Olympia, WA [*Library symbol*] [*Library of Congress*] (LCLS)
WaONR..... Washington State Department of Natural Resources, Division of Geology and Earth Resources, Olympia, WA [*Library symbol*] [*Library of Congress*] (LCLS)
WAOPA .... Western Australian Overseas Projects Authority
WAOR....... Niles, MI [*FM radio station call letters*]
WaOrtS ..... Washington Soldiers' Home, Staff Library, Orting, WA [*Library symbol*] [*Library of Congress*] (LCLS)
WaOrtS-R ... Washington Soldiers' Home, Resident Library, Orting, WA [*Library symbol*] [*Library of Congress*] (LCLS)
WAOS .... Austell, GA [*AM radio station call letters*]
WAOS .... Wide-Angle Optical System
WaOSM .... Saint Martin's College, Olympia, WA [*Library symbol*] [*Library of Congress*] (LCLS)
WaOSP...... Saint Peter's Hospital, Olympia, WA [*Library symbol*] [*Library of Congress*] (LCLS)
WaOT .... Washington State Department of Transportation, Olympia, WA [*Library symbol*] [*Library of Congress*] (LCLS)
WaOTC ..... Olympia Technical Community College, Olympia, WA [*Library symbol*] [*Library of Congress*] (LCLS)
WAOV....... Vincennes, IN [*AM radio station call letters*]
WAOW-TV ... Wausau, WI [*Television station call letters*]
WAP .... Institute of Paper Chemistry, Appleton, WI [*Library symbol*] [*Library of Congress*] (LCLS)
WAP .... Wandering Atrial Pacemaker [*Cardiology*]
WAP .... Wapentake [*Subdivision of some English shires*]
WAP .... Warner Audio Publishing
W Ap .... Washington Appellate Reports [*A publication*] (DLA)
WAP .... Wax Appearance Point [*Temperature at which waxy substances in fuel start to precipitate*]
WAP .... Weak Anthropic Principle [*Term coined by authors John Barrow and Frank Tipler in their book, "The Anthropic Cosmological Principle"*]
WAP .... Weight after Processing [*Metallurgy*]
WAP .... Werkabgabepreis [*Plant Delivered Price*] [*German*]
WAP .... Whey Acidic Protein
WAP .... Wide-Angle Panorama [*Photography*] [*NASA*]
WAP .... Wideband Acoustical Processor (CAAL)
WAP .... Women Against Pornography (EA)
WAP .... Women's Action Program [*HEW*]
WAP .... Work Activity Program
WAP .... Work Analysis Program [*Data processing*] (BUR)
WAP .... Work Assignment Procedure
WAPA .... Amahai [*Indonesia*] [*ICAO location identifier*] (ICLI)
WaPa .... Pasco Public Library, Pasco, WA [*Library symbol*] [*Library of Congress*] (LCLS)
WAPA .... San Juan, PR [*AM radio station call letters*]
WAPA .... Western Area Power Administration [*Department of Energy*]
WAPA .... White American Political Association (EA)
WAP (A)..... Work and People (Australia) [*A publication*]
WaPaAp .... Washington State Office of Adult Probation and Parole, Pasco, WA [*Library symbol*] [*Library of Congress*] (LCLS)
WaPaC ...... Columbia Basin College, Pasco, WA [*Library symbol*] [*Library of Congress*] (LCLS)
WaPaGS .... Church of Jesus Christ of Latter-Day Saints, Genealogical Society Library, Pasco Branch, Pasco, WA [*Library symbol*] [*Library of Congress*] (LCLS)
WA Parent & Cit ... Western Australian Parent and Citizen [*A publication*] (APTA)
WA Parent & Citizen ... Western Australian Parent and Citizen [*A publication*] (APTA)
WA Parl Deb ... Western Australia. Parliamentary Debates [*A publication*] (APTA)
WAPA-TV ... San Juan, PR [*Television station call letters*]
WAPB....... Bula [*Indonesia*] [*ICAO location identifier*] (ICLI)
WAPC....... Banda [*Indonesia*] [*ICAO location identifier*] (ICLI)
WAPC .... Women's Auxiliary Police Corps [*British*] [*World War II*]
WAPCB..... West African Produce Control Board [*World War II*]
WAPCOS ... Water and Power Development Consultancy Services
WAPD....... Dobo [*Indonesia*] [*ICAO location identifier*] (ICLI)
WAPD....... Western Air Procurement District
WAPE........ Mangole [*Indonesia*] [*ICAO location identifier*] (ICLI)

WAPE-FM ... Jacksonville, FL [*FM radio station call letters*]
WAPET..... West Australian Petroleum Proprietary Ltd.
WAPF....... McComb, MS [*AM radio station call letters*]
WAPF........ West African Pharmaceutical Federation [*Lagos, Nigeria*] (EAIO)
WAPG ...... Arcadia, FL [*AM radio station call letters*]
WAPG ...... High-Endurance Coast Guard Cutter [*Later, WHEC*] (CINC)
WAPH....... Labuhu/Usman Sadik [*Indonesia*] [*ICAO location identifier*] (ICLI)
WAPI........ Birmingham, AL [*AM radio station call letters*]
WAPI........ Saumlaki [*Indonesia*] [*ICAO location identifier*] (ICLI)
WAPI........ World Aerial Photographic Index [*Meteorology*]
WAPI-FM ... Birmingham, AL [*FM radio station call letters*]
WAPL........ Langgur/Dumatubun [*Indonesia*] [*ICAO location identifier*] (ICLI)
WAPL........ Western Aerial Photography Laboratory [*Department of Agriculture*]
WAPLA..... Water, Air, and Soil Pollution [*A publication*]
WAPL-FM ... Appleton, WI [*FM radio station call letters*]
WaPlP .... Pacific Lutheran University, Parkland, WA [*Library symbol*] [*Library of Congress*] (LCLS)
WAPME..... Writers and Artists for Peace in the Middle East (EA)
WAPN....... Holly Hill, FL [*FM radio station call letters*]
WAPN....... Sanana [*Indonesia*] [*ICAO location identifier*] (ICLI)
WAPO....... Jasper, TN [*AM radio station call letters*]
WAPOA ..... Water Power [*England*] [*A publication*]
WaPoN ..... North Olympic Library System, Port Angeles, WA [*Library symbol*] [*Library of Congress*] (LCLS)
WaPoP....... Peninsula College, Port Angeles, WA [*Library symbol*] [*Library of Congress*] (LCLS)
WAPOR .... World Association for Public Opinion Research (EA)
WAPP........ Ambon/Pattimura [*Indonesia*] [*ICAO location identifier*] (ICLI)
WAPP........ Berryville, VA [*FM radio station call letters*]
Wap Pr R ... Waples on Proceedings in Rem [*A publication*] (DLA)
WAPPS ..... Work Aptitude Profile and Practice Set [*Test*]
WAPR .... Avon Park, FL [*AM radio station call letters*]
WAPR .... Namlea [*Indonesia*] [*ICAO location identifier*] (ICLI)
WAPR .... World Association for Psychosocial Rehabilitation (EAIO)
WAPR .... World Association for Psychosocial Rehabilitation - US Branch (EA)
WAPRA.... Wissenschaftliche Abhandlungen der Physikalische-Technischen Reichsanstalt [*A publication*]
WA Primary Princ ... WA Primary Principal. West Australian Primary Principals Association [*A publication*] (APTA)
WA Primary Principal ... West Australian Primary Principals Association [*A publication*]
WAPS........ Akron, OH [*FM radio station call letters*]
WAPS........ Selaru [*Indonesia*] [*ICAO location identifier*] (ICLI)
WaPS........ Washington State University, Pullman, WA [*Library symbol*] [*Library of Congress*] (LCLS)
WAPS........ Weighted Airman Promotion System [*Air Force*]
WAPS........ Women of the American Press Service [*Accredited American women war correspondents*] [*World War II*]
WAPS........ World Association of Pathology Societies
WaPS-V..... Washington State University, Veterinary Medical Library, Pullman, WA [*Library symbol*] [*Library of Congress*] (LCLS)
WAPT........ Jackson, MS [*Television station call letters*]
WAPT........ Taliabu [*Indonesia*] [*ICAO location identifier*] (ICLI)
WAPT........ Wichita Auditory Processing Test [*Child development test*]
WAPT....... Wild Animal Propagation Trust [*Defunct*]
WAPT........ Work Area Pointer Table [*Data processing*]
WaPuS....... Washington State University, Western Washington Research and Extension Center, Puyallup, WA [*Library symbol*] [*Library of Congress*] (LCLS)
WAPW ...... Atlanta, GA [*FM radio station call letters*]
WAPX-FM ... Clarksville, TN [*FM radio station call letters*]
WAPY .... Apalachicola, FL [*FM radio station call letters*]
WAPZ........ Ambon Sector [*Indonesia*] [*ICAO location identifier*] (ICLI)
WAPZ....... Wetumpka, AL [*AM radio station call letters*]
WAQ......... Antsalova [*Madagascar*] [*Airport symbol*] (OAG)
WAQE-FM ... Rice Lake, WI [*FM radio station call letters*]
WaQGS ..... Church of Jesus Christ of Latter-Day Saints, Genealogical Society Library, Quincy Branch, Quincy, WA [*Library symbol*] [*Library of Congress*] (LCLS)
WAQI....... Miami, FL [*AM radio station call letters*]
WAQI-FM ... Goulds, FL [*FM radio station call letters*]
WAQP....... Saginaw, MI [*Television station call letters*]
WAQT....... Carrollton, AL [*FM radio station call letters*]
WAQX....... Syracuse, NY [*AM radio station call letters*]
WAQX-FM ... Manlius, NY [*FM radio station call letters*]
WAQY....... Springfield, MA [*FM radio station call letters*]
WAR......... Warrant
WAR......... Warrenton Railroad Co. [*AAR code*]
WAR......... Warrior Industry Ltd. [*Vancouver Stock Exchange symbol*]
WAR......... Warsaw [*Poland*] [*Seismograph station code, US Geological Survey*] (SEIS)
WAR......... Warwickshire (ROG)
WAR......... Wassermann Antigen Reaction [*Test for syphilis*] [*Medicine*]
WAR......... We Are Ridiculous [*Antiwar slogan*]

WAR......... Weapon Accuracy and Results [*Model*] (MCD)
WAR......... West African Regiment [*Military unit*] [*British*]
WAR......... Western Australian Reports [*A publication*] (APTA)
WAR......... White Aryan Resistance (EA)
WAR......... Whiteruthenian American Relief (EA)
WAR......... Wisconsin Academy. Review [*A publication*]
WAR......... With All Risks [*Insurance*]
WAR......... Work Acquisition Routine
WAR......... Work Authorization Report [*or Request*] [*NASA*] (MCD)
WAR......... World Administrative Radio Conference for Space
         Communication
WAR......... World Affairs Report [*Database*] [*California Institute of
         International Studies*] [*Information service or
         system*] (CRD)
WARA....... Attleboro, MA [*AM radio station call letters*]
War Adv Att ... Warren's Adventures of an Attorney in Search of Practice [*A
         publication*] (DLA)
WARAMS ... Wartime Alignment of Reserve and Active Medical Systems
WARB....... Covington, LA [*AM radio station call letters*]
WARBA .... Water Resources Bulletin [*A publication*]
War Bell..... Ward on Belligerent and Neutral Powers [*A
         publication*] (DLA)
Warburg & Courtauld Inst Jnl ... Warburg and Courtauld Institute. Journal [*A
         publication*]
WARC....... Meadville, PA [*FM radio station call letters*]
War C......... War Cry [*A publication*]
WARC....... Washington Archaeological Research Center [*Washington State
         University*] [*Research center*] (RCD)
WARC....... Wharton Applied Research Center [*University of Pennsylvania*]
         [*Research center*] (RCD)
WARC....... World Administrative Radio Conference [*Also known as
         IAARC*] [*Takes place every 20 years*] [*Held in 1979 in
         Geneva, Switzerland*] [*International Telecommunications
         Union*]
WARC....... World Alliance of Reformed Churches [*Formed by a merger of
         Alliance of the Reformed Churches throughout the World
         Holding the Presbyterian System and International
         Congregational Council*] (EAIO)
WARCAD ... War Department - Civil Affairs Division [*Obsolete*]
WARCAT ... Workload and Resources Correlation Analysis Technique
         [*Army*]
W Arch ...... Western Architect [*A publication*]
WARC-MAR ... World Administrative Radio Conference for Maritime
         Mobile Telecommunications
WARCO.... War Correspondent (DSUE)
War Cr L..... Warren's Ohio Criminal Law [*A publication*] (DLA)
WARC-ST ... World Administrative Radio Conference for Space
         Telecommunications
WARD....... Pittston, PA [*AM radio station call letters*]
Ward......... Warden's State Reports [*2, 4 Ohio*] [*A publication*] (DLA)
WARD....... Wardship
WARDA.... West Africa Rice Development Association
Ward AW .. Ward's Auto World [*A publication*]
Warden...... Warden's State Reports [*2, 4 Ohio*] [*A publication*] (DLA)
Warden's Law & Bk Bull ... Warden's Weekly Law and Bank Bulletin [*Ohio*]
         [*A publication*] (DLA)
Warden & Smith ... Warden and Smith's State Reports [*3 Ohio*] [*A
         publication*] (DLA)
War Dept BCA ... United States War Department, Decisions of Board of
         Contract Adjustment [*A publication*] (DLA)
Ward Just.. Ward's Justice of the Peace [*A publication*] (DLA)
Ward Leg ... Ward on Legacies [*A publication*] (DLA)
Ward Nat ... Ward's Law of Nations [*A publication*] (DLA)
WARDS..... Welfare of Animals Used for Research in Drugs and Therapy
Wards Auto ... Ward's Automotive Reports [*A publication*]
Ward's Bull ... Ward's Bulletin [*A publication*]
Ward & Sm ... Warden and Smith's State Reports [*3 Ohio*] [*A
         publication*] (DLA)
Wards Yrbk ... Ward's Automotive Yearbook [*A publication*]
WaRe......... Renton Public Library, Renton, WA [*Library symbol*] [*Library
         of Congress*] (LCLS)
WARE .... Ware, MA [*AM radio station call letters*]
Ware .... Ware's United States District Court Reports [*A
         publication*] (DLA)
WAREH .... Water Research [*A publication*]
WAREH .... Wareham [*Municipal borough in England*]
Warehousing Superv Bull ... Warehousing Supervisor's Bulletin [*United
         States*] [*A publication*]
War Emerg Proc Inst Mech Eng ... War Emergency Proceedings. Institution of
         Mechanical Engineers [*A publication*]
WARES..... Workload and Resources Evaluation System [*Navy*]
Ware's CC Rep ... Ware's United States District Court Reports [*A
         publication*] (DLA)
Ware's Rep ... Ware's United States District Court Reports [*A
         publication*] (DLA)
WaRetV ..... Washington Veterans' Home, Medical Library, Retsil, WA
         [*Library symbol*] [*Library of Congress*] (LCLS)
WaRetV-R ... Washington Veterans' Home, Resident Library, Retsil, WA
         [*Library symbol*] [*Library of Congress*] (LCLS)
WaReVG ... Valley General Hospital, Renton, WA [*Library symbol*]
         [*Library of Congress*] (LCLS)

WAREX..... Warrant Issued for Extradite
WARF....... Jasper, AL [*AM radio station call letters*]
WARF....... Warfare (AFM)
WARF....... Wartime Active Replacement Factors (AABC)
WARF....... Weekly Audit Report File [*IRS*]
WARF....... Wide-Aperture Research Facility [*For hurricane detection*]
WARG....... Summit, IL [*FM radio station call letters*]
WARH....... Dayton, VA [*AM radio station call letters*]
WARHD.... Warhead (AAG)
War Hung ... War on Hunger [*A publication*]
WARI .... Abbeville, AL [*AM radio station call letters*]
WaRi......... Richland Public Library, Richland, WA [*Library symbol*]
         [*Library of Congress*] (LCLS)
WARI .... Wheezing Associated with Respiratory Injections
WaRiAR .... Atlantic Richfield Hanford Co., Richland, WA [*Library symbol*]
         [*Library of Congress*] (LCLS)
WaRiB .... Battelle Memorial Institute, Pacific Northwest Laboratory,
         Richland, WA [*Library symbol*] [*Library of
         Congress*] (LCLS)
WaRiBN .... Battelle-Northwest Hospital, Life Science Library, Richland,
         WA [*Library symbol*] [*Library of Congress*] (LCLS)
WaRiGS .... Church of Jesus Christ of Latter-Day Saints, Genealogical
         Society Library, Richland Branch, Richland, WA [*Library
         symbol*] [*Library of Congress*] (LCLS)
WaRiMC... Mid-Columbia Mental Health Center, Richland, WA [*Library
         symbol*] [*Library of Congress*] (LCLS)
WArI-R..... Indian Ridge Treatment Center, Resident Library, Arlington,
         WA [*Library symbol*] [*Library of Congress*] (LCLS)
WaRit........ Ritzville Public Library, Ritzville, WA [*Library symbol*]
         [*Library of Congress*] (LCLS)
WARK ...... Hagerstown, MD [*AM radio station call letters*]
WARKS..... Warwickshire [*County in England*]
WARL ...... Cloverdale, VA [*AM radio station call letters*]
WARLA..... Wide-Aperture Radio Location Array
WARLOCE ... Wartime Lines of Communication, Europe (AABC)
WARLOG ... Wartime Logistics (AABC)
War L St ... Warren's Law Studies [*A publication*] (DLA)
WARM...... Scranton, PA [*AM radio station call letters*]
WARM..... Weapons Assignment Research Model [*Military*]
WARM...... Wood and Solid Fuel Association of Retailers and
         Manufacturers (EA)
WARMA ... Waerme [*A publication*]
WARMAPS ... Wartime Manpower Planning System
War Med.... War Medicine [*A publication*]
WARMEDY ... Warm, Family Comedy [*Type of television show*]
WARM-FM ... York, PA [*FM radio station call letters*]
WARN...... Falmouth, VA [*AM radio station call letters*]
WARN...... Warner Electric Brake & Clutch Co. [*NASDAQ symbol*] (NQ)
WARN...... Warning (NASA)
WARN...... Weather Amateur Radio Network (NOAA)
WARN...... Women of All Red Nations (EA)
WARN...... Worker Adjustment and Retraining Notification Act [*1988*]
WARNA.... Worker Adjustment and Retraining Notification Act [*1988*]
WARNORD ... Warning Order [*Military*] (INF)
WARO....... Claremont, VA [*AM radio station call letters*]
War Op...... Warwick's Opinions [*City Solicitor of Philadelphia, PA*] [*A
         publication*] (DLA)
WARP .... Bangor, ME [*AM radio station call letters*]
WARP .... Worldwide Ammunition Reporting Program (NG)
WARP .... Worldwide AUTODIN [*Automatic Digital Information
         Network*] Restoral Plan (CET)
WARPAC ... Wartime Repair Parts Consumption (MCD)
WARPATH ... World Association to Remove Prejudice Against the
         Handicapped
War Prof Dut ... Warren. Moral, Social, and Professional Duties of Attorneys
         and Solicitors [*2nd ed.*] [*1851*] [*A publication*] (DLA)
Warr.......... Warrant [*A document entitling holder to purchase a given issue
         of stock*] [*Investment term*]
WARR ...... Warranty (MSA)
WARR ...... Warrenton, NC [*AM radio station call letters*]
WARR ...... Water Resources Research [*A publication*]
WARRAMP ... Wartime Requirements for Ammunition, Materiel, and
         Personnel
WARRC..... Western Aerospace Rescue and Recovery Center [*Air Force*]
WARRF.... Warrior Research Ltd. [*NASDAQ symbol*] (NQ)
WARRT..... Warrant (ROG)
Wars .... [*The*] Jewish Wars [*of Josephus*] [*A publication*] (BJA)
WARS....... Warfare Analysis and Research System [*Navy*]
WARS....... Wide-Area Remote Sensors
WARS....... Worldwide Ammunition Reporting System [*Military*]
Warsaw Agric Univ SGGW-AR Ann Anim Sci ... Warsaw Agricultural
         University. SGGW-AR [*Szkola Glowna Gospodarstwa
         Wiejskiego - Akademia Rolnicza*] Annals. Animal Science
         [*A publication*]
WARSCAP ... Wartime Support Capability
WARSIC ... Water Resources Scientific Information Center [*US Geological
         Survey*] [*Reston, VA*] [*Database originator*] (IT)
WARSL..... War Reserve Stockage List (MCD)
WART ...... Port Orange, FL [*AM radio station call letters*]
WART ...... Weighted Average Remaining Term [*Finance*]

WART .... Wenceslaus Anxiety Representation Taxonomy [*Satirical psychology term*]
Warta Geol ... Warta Geologi [*A publication*]
Warta Geol (Kuala Lumpur) ... Warta Geologi (Kuala Lumpur) [*A publication*]
Warth Code ... West Virginia Code [*1899*] [*A publication*] (DLA)
WARU .... Peru, IN [*AM radio station call letters*]
WARU-FM ... Peru, IN [*FM radio station call letters*]
WARV .... Warwick-East Greenwich, RI [*AM radio station call letters*]
Warv Abst ... Warvelle on Abstracts of Title [*A publication*] (DLA)
Warv El RP ... Warvelle's Elements of Real Property [*A publication*] (DLA)
Warv V & P ... Warvelle's Vendors and Purchasers of Real Property [*A publication*] (DLA)
WARW ..... Warwickshire [*County in England*]
WARWICKS ... Warwickshire [*County in England*]
Warwick's Op ... Warwick's Opinions [*City Solicitor of Philadelphia, PA*] [*A publication*] (DLA)
WARWS .... Warwickshire [*County in England*]
WARX ...... Hagerstown, MD [*FM radio station call letters*]
WARY .... Valhalla, NY [*FM radio station call letters*]
WaS .... Seattle Public Library, Seattle, WA [*Library symbol*] [*Library of Congress*] (LCLS)
WAs .... Vaughn Public Library, Ashland, WI [*Library symbol*] [*Library of Congress*] (LCLS)
WAS .... Wadley Southern Railway Co. [*AAR code*] [*Obsolete*]
WAS .... Wallops Station [*Later, WFC*] [*NASA*]
WAS .... War at Sea (NVT)
WAS .... Ward Atmosphere Scale [*Psychology*]
WAS .... Ware Resources Ltd. [*Vancouver Stock Exchange symbol*]
WAS .... Warner & Swasey Co., Solon, OH [*OCLC symbol*] (OCLC)
WAS .... Washington [*District of Columbia*] [*Airport symbol*] (OAG)
WAS .... Washington [*District of Columbia*] [*Seismograph station code, US Geological Survey*] [*Closed*] (SEIS)
was .... Washo [*MARC language code*] [*Library of Congress*] (LCCP)
WAS .... Waste-Activated Sludge
WAS .... Waste International [*A publication*]
WAS .... Waynesburg Southern [*AAR code*]
WAS .... Weapons Alert System [*NORAD*] (MCD)
WAS .... Weekly Arrival Schedule [*Military*] (AFIT)
WAS .... Wide Analysis Sheet
WAS .... Wide-Angle Sensor
WAS .... Wideband Antenna System
WAS .... Wildlife Art Society [*Australia*]
WAS .... Wiskott-Aldrich Syndrome [*Immunology*]
WAS .... Witchcraft and Sorcery [*A publication*]
WAS .... Women's Addiction Service [*National Institute of Mental Health*]
WAS .... Worcester Archaeological Society. Transactions [*A publication*]
WAS .... Worked All States [*Contacted at least one station in all states*] [*Amateur radio*]
WAS .... World Animal Science [*Elsevier Book Series*] [*A publication*]
WAS .... World Aquaculture Society (EA)
WAS .... World Archaeological Society (EA)
WAS .... World Around Songs (EA)
WAS .... World Artifex Society (EAIO)
WAS .... World Association for Sexology (EA)
WASA .... Havre De Grace, MD [*AM radio station call letters*]
WaSA .... Seattle Art Museum, Seattle, WA [*Library symbol*] [*Library of Congress*] (LCLS)
WASA ...... West African Shipper's Association (DS)
WASA ...... Women's All-Star Association (EA)
WaSAA ...... Catholic Archdiocese of Seattle, Archives, Seattle, WA [*Library symbol*] [*Library of Congress*] (LCLS)
WaSAB ...... Atomic Bomb Casualty Commission, Seattle, WA [*Library symbol*] [*Library of Congress*] (LCLS)
WASAC ..... Working Group of the Army Study Advisory Committee (AABC)
WASAG ..... Washington Special Action Group [*National Security Council*]
WASAL ..... Wisconsin Academy of Sciences, Arts, and Letters
WASAR .... Wide Application System Adapter
WASB .... Brockport, NY [*AM radio station call letters*]
WaSB .... Pacific Northwest Bibliographic Center, Seattle, WA [*Library symbol*] [*Library of Congress*] (LCLS)
WASB .... Steenkol/Bintuni [*Indonesia*] [*ICAO location identifier*] (ICLI)
WaSBa ...... Battelle Human Affairs Research Center, Seattle, WA [*Library symbol*] [*Library of Congress*] (LCLS)
WASBB ..... Waerme- und Stoffuebertragung [*A publication*]
WaSBo .... [*The*] Boeing Co., Commercial Airplane Group, Technical Libraries, Seattle, WA [*Library symbol*] [*Library of Congress*] (LCLS)
WaSBo-A ... [*The*] Boeing Co., Aerospace Division, Technical Library, Kent, WA [*Library symbol*] [*Library of Congress*] (LCLS)
WASC .... Ransiki/Abresso [*Indonesia*] [*ICAO location identifier*] (ICLI)
WaSC .... Seattle Central Community College, Seattle, WA [*Library symbol*] [*Library of Congress*] (LCLS)
WASC .... Spartanburg, SC [*AM radio station call letters*]
WASC .... West Africa Supply Centre [*World War II*]
WASC .... Western Association of Schools and Colleges (EA)
WASC .... White Anglo-Saxon Catholic
WASC .... Williams Awareness Sentence Completion [*Personality development test*] [*Psychology*]

WASCAL .. Wide-Angle Scanning Array Lens Antenna
WascanaR ... Wascana Review [*A publication*]
WaSC-N .... North Seattle Community College, Seattle, WA [*Library symbol*] [*Library of Congress*] (LCLS)
WaSCO ..... Children's Orthopedic Hospital and Medical Center, Seattle, WA [*Library symbol*] [*Library of Congress*] (LCLS)
WASCO ..... War Safety Council
WaSC-S ..... South Seattle Community College, Seattle, WA [*Library symbol*] [*Library of Congress*] (LCLS)
WaSC-Sh ... Shoreline Community College, Seattle, WA [*Library symbol*] [*Library of Congress*] [*Obsolete*] (LCLS)
WASD .... Wide-Angle Self-Destruct (MCD)
WASE .... Fort Knox, KY [*FM radio station call letters*]
WASE .... Kebar [*Indonesia*] [*ICAO location identifier*] (ICLI)
WASE .... Saint Elizabeth Hospital, Appleton, WI [*Library symbol*] [*Library of Congress*] (LCLS)
WASEC ..... Warner Amex Satellite Entertainment Company [*Cable television*]
Waseda Polit Stud ... Waseda Political Studies [*A publication*]
Waseda Pol Studies ... Waseda Political Studies [*A publication*]
WaSelY ...... Yakima Valley School, Selah, WA [*Library symbol*] [*Library of Congress*] (LCLS)
WASF .... Fak Fak/Torea [*Indonesia*] [*ICAO location identifier*] (ICLI)
WaSF .... Fircrest School, Staff Library, Seattle, WA [*Library symbol*] [*Library of Congress*] (LCLS)
WASF .... Water Authorities Superannuation Fund [*British*]
WaSFC ...... Firland Correctional Center, Staff Library, Seattle, WA [*Library symbol*] [*Library of Congress*] (LCLS)
WaSFC-R .. Firland Correctional Center, Resident Library, Seattle, WA [*Library symbol*] [*Library of Congress*] (LCLS)
WaSF-R ..... Fircrest School, Resident Library, Seattle, WA [*Library symbol*] [*Library of Congress*] (LCLS)
WaSFRC ... Federal Records Center, Seattle, WA [*Library symbol*] [*Library of Congress*] (LCLS)
WASG ...... Atmore, AL [*AM radio station call letters*]
WaSG .... Seattle Genealogical Society, Seattle, WA [*Library symbol*] [*Library of Congress*] (LCLS)
WASGFC .. Western Association of State Game and Fish Commissioners [*Later, Western Association of Fish and Wildlife Agencies*] (EA)
WaSGH ..... Group Health Cooperative of Puget Sound, Medical Library, Seattle, WA [*Library symbol*] [*Library of Congress*] (LCLS)
WASGIC ... Western Australian State Government Insurance Commission (ECON)
WaSGS ...... Church of Jesus Christ of Latter-Day Saints, Genealogical Society Library, Seattle North Branch, Seattle, WA [*Library symbol*] [*Library of Congress*] (LCLS)
WaSGS ...... Good Samaritan Hospital, Seattle, WA [*Library symbol*] [*Library of Congress*] (LCLS)
WaSh .... Shelton Public Library, Shelton, WA [*Library symbol*] [*Library of Congress*] (LCLS)
WaSH .... Virginia Mason Hospital, Medical Library, Seattle, WA [*Library symbol*] [*Library of Congress*] (LCLS)
WASH ...... Washer (AAG)
WASH ...... Washington (AAG)
Wash .... Washington Reports [*A publication*] (DLA)
Wash .... Washington State Reports [*A publication*] (DLA)
Wash .... Washington Territory Reports [*1854-88*] [*A publication*] (DLA)
WASH ...... Washington Trust Bancorp, Inc. [*NASDAQ symbol*] (NQ)
Wash .... Washington's Reports [*1, 2 Virginia*] [*A publication*] (DLA)
Wash .... Washington's Reports [*16-23 Vermont*] [*A publication*] (DLA)
Wash .... Washington's United States Circuit Court Reports [*A publication*] (DLA)
Wash Actions Health ... Washington Actions on Health [*A publication*]
Wash Admin Code ... Washington Administrative Code [*A publication*] (DLA)
Wash Admin Reg ... Washington State Register [*A publication*] (DLA)
Wash Ag Exp ... Washington. Agricultural Experiment Station. Publications [*A publication*]
Wash Agric Exp Stn Bull ... Washington. Agricultural Experiment Station. Bulletin [*A publication*]
Wash Agric Exp Stn Cir ... Washington. Agricultural Experiment Station. Circular [*A publication*]
Wash Agric Exp Stn Stn Circ ... Washington. Agricultural Experiment Station. Station Circular [*A publication*]
Wash Agric Exp Stn Tech Bull ... Washington. Agricultural Experiment Station. Technical Bulletin [*A publication*]
Wash App ... Washington Appellate Reports [*A publication*] (DLA)
Washb Easem ... Washburn on Easements and Servitudes [*A publication*] (DLA)
Wash B News ... Washington Bar News [*A publication*] (DLA)
Washb Real Prop ... Washburn on Real Property [*A publication*] (DLA)
Wash Bsn J ... Washington Business Journal [*A publication*]
Washburn .. Washburn's Reports [*18-23 Vermont*] [*A publication*] (DLA)
Washburn Coll Lab N H B ... Washburn College. Laboratory of Natural History. Bulletin [*A publication*]
Washburn L J ... Washburn Law Journal [*A publication*]
Wash Bus L Rpr ... Washington Business Law Reporter [*A publication*]

WaShC ...... Washington Correction Center, Staff Library, Shelton, WA [*Library symbol*] [*Library of Congress*] (LCLS)

WASHCAP ... Washington Operations Capabilities System

Wash CC.... Washington's United States Circuit Court Reports [*A publication*] (DLA)

Wash CCR ... Washington's United States Circuit Court Reports [*A publication*] (DLA)

Wash Co .... Washington County Reports [*Pennsylvania*] [*A publication*] (DLA)

Wash Co (PA) ... Washington County Reports [*Pennsylvania*] [*A publication*] (DLA)

Wash Co R ... Washington County Reports [*Pennsylvania*] [*A publication*] (DLA)

Wash Co Repr ... Washington County Reports [*Pennsylvania*] [*A publication*] (DLA)

WaSHCR... Fred Hutchinson Cancer Research Center, Seattle, WA [*Library symbol*] [*Library of Congress*] (LCLS)

WaShC-R .. Washington Correction Center, Resident Library, Shelton, WA [*Library symbol*] [*Library of Congress*] (LCLS)

Wash Cr L ... Washburn on Criminal Law [*A publication*] (DLA)

Wash 2d..... Washington Reports, Second Series [*A publication*] (DLA)

Wash Dec... Washington Decisions [*A publication*] (DLA)

Wash Dep Ecol State Water Program Bienn Rep ... Washington. Department of Ecology. State Water Program. Biennial Report [*A publication*]

Wash Dep Ecol Tech Rep ... Washington. Department of Ecology. Technical Report [*A publication*]

Wash Dep Ecol Water Supply Bull ... Washington. Department of Ecology. Water Supply Bulletin [*A publication*]

Wash Dep Fish Annu Rep ... Washington. Department of Fisheries. Annual Report [*A publication*]

Wash Dep Fish Fish Res Pap ... Washington. Department of Fisheries. Fisheries Research Papers [*A publication*]

Wash Dep Fish Res Bull ... Washington. Department of Fisheries. Research Bulletin [*A publication*]

Wash Dep Fish Tech Rep ... Washington. Department of Fisheries. Technical Report [*A publication*]

Wash Dep Water Resour Water Supply Bull ... Washington. Department of Water Resources. Water Supply Bulletin [*A publication*]

Wash Dig... Washburn's Vermont Digest [*A publication*] (DLA)

Wash Div Geol Earth Resour Geol Map ... Washington. Division of Geology and Earth Resources. Geologic Map [*A publication*]

Wash Div Geol Earth Resour Inf Circ ... Washington. Division of Geology and Earth Resources. Information Circular [*A publication*]

Wash Div Mines Geol Bull ... Washington. Department of Natural Resources. Division of Mines and Geology. Bulletin [*A publication*]

Wash Div Mines Geol Inform Circ ... Washington. Department of Conservation. Division of Mines and Geology. Information Circular [*A publication*]

Wash Div Mines Geol Rep Invest ... Washington. Department of Conservation. Division of Mines and Geology. Report of Investigations [*A publication*]

Wash Div Mines Min Rep Invest ... Washington. Division of Mines and Mining. Report of Investigations [*A publication*]

Wash Ease ... Washburn on Easements and Servitudes [*A publication*] (DLA)

Wash Fin Rep (BNA) ... Washington Financial Reports (Bureau of National Affairs) [*A publication*] (DLA)

WASH-FM ... Washington, DC [*FM radio station call letters*]

Wash Geol Earth Resour Div Bull ... Washington. Department of Natural Resources. Geology and Earth Resources Division. Bulletin [*A publication*]

Wash GSB ... Washington. Geological Survey. Bulletin [*A publication*]

Wash & Haz PEI ... Washburton and Hazard's Reports [*Prince Edward Island, Canada*] [*A publication*] (DLA)

Wash Health Costs Let ... Washington Health Costs Letter [*A publication*]

Wash His Q ... Washington Historical Quarterly [*A publication*]

Wash His S ... Washington State Historical Society. Publications [*A publication*]

Wash Hist Q ... Washington Historical Quarterly [*A publication*]

WaSHi....... Seattle Historical Society, Seattle, WA [*Library symbol*] [*Library of Congress*] (LCLS)

Washington Acad Sci Jour ... Washington Academy of Sciences. Journal [*A publication*]

Washington Dept Water Resources Water Supply Bull ... Washington. Department of Water Resources. Water Supply Bulletin [*A publication*]

Washington Div Mines and Geology Bull ... Washington. Division of Mines and Geology. Bulletin [*A publication*]

Washington Div Mines and Geology Geol Map ... Washington. Division of Mines and Geology. Geologic Map [*A publication*]

Washington Div Mines and Geology Inf Circ ... Washington. Division of Mines and Geology. Information Circular [*A publication*]

Washington and Lee L Rev ... Washington and Lee Law Review [*A publication*]

Washington L Rev ... Washington Law Review [*A publication*]

Washington M ... Washington Monthly [*A publication*]

Washington Univ L Quart ... Washington University. Law Quarterly [*A publication*]

WaSHIR..... ITT Rayonier, Inc., Olympic Research Center, Shelton, WA [*Library symbol*] [*Library of Congress*] (LCLS)

Wash Journ Rev ... Washington Journalism Review [*A publication*]

Wash Jur ... Washington Jurist [*A publication*] (DLA)

Wash Law Re ... Washington Law Review [*A publication*]

Wash Law Rep ... Washington Law Reporter [*District of Columbia*] [*A publication*] (DLA)

Wash and Lee LR ... Washington and Lee Law Review [*A publication*]

Wash & Lee L Rev ... Washington and Lee Law Review [*A publication*]

Wash Legis Serv ... Washington Legislative Service (West) [*A publication*] (DLA)

Wash LR.... Washington Law Review [*A publication*]

Wash LR (Dist Col) ... Washington Law Reporter (District of Columbia) [*A publication*] (DLA)

Wash L Rep ... Washington Law Reporter [*District of Columbia*] [*A publication*] (DLA)

Wash L Rev ... Washington Law Review [*A publication*]

Wash M ..... Washington Monthly [*A publication*]

Wash Med Ann ... Washington Medical Annals [*A publication*]

WASHMIC ... Washington Military Industrial Complex

Wash Mon ... Washington Monthly [*A publication*]

Wash News Beat ... Washington News Beat [*A publication*]

Wash Nurse ... Washington Nurse [*A publication*]

WASHO.... Western Association of State Highway Officials

Wash Post ... Washington Post [*A publication*]

Wash Prop L Rpr ... Washington Property Law Reporter [*A publication*]

Wash Public Policy Notes ... Washington Public Policy Notes [*A publication*]

Wash PUR ... Washington Public Utility Commission Reports [*A publication*] (DLA)

Wash Q...... Washington Quarterly [*A publication*]

Wash Rep .. Washington Report [*A publication*]

Wash Rep Med Health ... Washington Report on Medicine and Health [*A publication*]

Wash Rev Code ... Revised Code of Washington [*A publication*] (DLA)

Wash Rev Code Ann ... Washington Revised Code, Annotated [*A publication*] (DLA)

Wash RP.... Washburn on Real Property [*A publication*] (DLA)

Wash SBA ... Washington State Bar Association. Proceedings [*A publication*] (DLA)

Wash St ..... Washington State Reports [*A publication*] (DLA)

Wash State Coll Agric Exp Stn Tech Bull ... Washington State College. Washington Agricultural Experiment Station. Institute of Agricultural Sciences. Technical Bulletin [*A publication*]

Wash State Coll Research Studies ... Washington State College. Research Studies [*A publication*]

Wash State Council Highway Research Eng Soils Manual ... Washington State. Council for Highway Research Engineering. Soils Manual [*A publication*]

Wash State Dent J ... Washington State Dental Journal [*A publication*]

Wash State For Prod Inst Bull New Wood Use Ser ... Washington State Forest Products Institute. Bulletins. New Wood-Use Series [*A publication*]

Wash State Hortic Assoc Proc ... Proceedings. Washington State Horticultural Association [*A publication*]

Wash State Inst Technol Circ ... Washington State Institute of Technology. Circular [*A publication*]

Wash State Inst Technology Bull ... Washington State Institute of Technology. Bulletin [*A publication*]

Wash State Inst Technol Tech Rep ... Washington State Institute of Technology. Technical Report [*A publication*]

Wash State J Nurs ... Washington State Journal of Nursing [*A publication*]

Wash State Univ Agric Exp Stn Tech Bull ... Washington State University. Agricultural Experiment Station. Institute of Agricultural Sciences. Technical Bulletin [*A publication*]

Wash State Univ Agric Res Cent Res Bull ... Washington State University. Agricultural Research Center. Research Bulletin [*A publication*]

Wash State Univ Coll Agric Res Cent Bull ... Washington State University. College of Agriculture. Research Center. Bulletin [*A publication*]

Wash State Univ Coll Agric Res Cent Tech Bull ... Washington State University. College of Agriculture. Research Center. Technical Bulletin [*A publication*]

Wash State Univ Coll Eng Bull ... Washington State University. College of Engineering. Bulletin [*A publication*]

Wash State Univ Coll Eng Circ ... Washington State University. College of Engineering. Circular [*A publication*]

Wash State Univ Coop Ext Serv Ext Bull ... Washington State University. Cooperative Extension Service. Extension Bulletin [*A publication*]

Wash State Univ Ext Ser Ext Bull ... Washington State University. Extension Service. Extension Bulletin [*A publication*]

Wash State Univ Ext Serv EM ... Washington State University. Extension Service. EM [*A publication*]

Wash State Univ Int Symp Particleboard Proc ... Washington State University. International Symposium on Particleboard. Proceedings [*A publication*]

Wash State Univ Publ Geol Sci ... Washington State University. Publications in Geological Sciences [*A publication*]

Wash State Univ Symp Particleboard Proc ... Washington State University. Symposium on Particleboard. Proceedings [*A publication*]

Wash St G An Rp ... Washington State Geologist. Annual Report [*A publication*]

WASH T.... Washington Territory (ROG)
Wash T ...... Washington Territory Opinions [*1854-64*] [*A publication*] (DLA)
Wash T ...... Washington Territory Reports [*1854-88*] [*A publication*] (DLA)
Wash Ter ... Washington Territory Opinions [*1854-64*] [*A publication*] (DLA)
Wash Ter ... Washington Territory Reports [*1854-88*] [*A publication*] (DLA)
Wash Ter NS ... Allen's Washington Territory Reports, New Series [*A publication*] (DLA)
Wash Terr ... Washington Territory Opinions [*1854-64*] [*A publication*] (DLA)
Wash Terr ... Washington Territory Reports [*1854-88*] [*A publication*] (DLA)
Wash Ty .... Washington Territory Opinions [*1854-64*] [*A publication*] (DLA)
Wash Ty .... Washington Territory Reports [*1854-88*] [*A publication*] (DLA)
Wash UJ Urb & Contemp L ... Washington University. Journal of Urban and Contemporary Law [*A publication*] (DLA)
Wash U L Q ... Washington University. Law Quarterly [*A publication*]
Wash UL Rev ... Washington University. Law Review [*A publication*] (DLA)
Wash Univ Bull ... Washington University. Bulletin [*A publication*]
Wash Univ Dent J ... Washington University. Dental Journal [*A publication*]
Wash Univ Dep Geol Sci Abstr Res ... Washington University. Department of Geological Sciences. Abstracts of Research [*A publication*]
Wash Univ Pub G ... Washington University. Publications in Geology [*A publication*]
Wash Univ St Hum Ser ... Washington University. Studies. Humanistic Series [*A publication*]
Wash Univ St Sci Ser ... Washington University. Studies. Scientific Series [*A publication*]
Wash Univ Stud Lang & Lit ... Washington University. Studies. Language and Literature [*A publication*]
Wash Univ Stud Sci & Tech ... Washington University. Studies. Science and Technology [*A publication*]
Wash Univ Stud Sci & Tech NS ... Washington University. Studies. Science and Technology. New Series [*A publication*]
Wash Univ Stud Social & Philos Sci ... Washington University. Studies. Social and Philosophical Sciences [*A publication*]
Wash Univ Stud Social & Philos Sci NS ... Washington University. Studies. Social and Philosophical Sciences. New Series [*A publication*]
Wash VA ... Washington's Reports [*1, 2 Virginia*] [*A publication*] (DLA)
WASI........ Inanwatan [*Indonesia*] [*ICAO location identifier*] (ICLI)
WASI........ Whimbey Analytical Skills Inventory [*Educational test*]
WASIA...... Women's Armed Services Integration Act of 1948
WaSIF ...... International Fisheries Commission, Seattle, WA [*Library symbol*] [*Library of Congress*] (LCLS)
WASIH ..... Western American Society for Italic Handwriting [*Formerly, WABSIH*] (EA)
WASK....... Kaimana (Utarom) [*Indonesia*] [*ICAO location identifier*] (ICLI)
WaSK .... King County Medical Society, Seattle, WA [*Library symbol*] [*Library of Congress*] (LCLS)
WASK....... Lafayette, IN [*AM radio station call letters*]
WaSKC...... King County Library System, Seattle, WA [*Library symbol*] [*Library of Congress*] (LCLS)
WASK-FM ... Lafayette, IN [*FM radio station call letters*]
WASL....... Dyersburg, TN [*FM radio station call letters*]
WAsM .... Memorial Medical Center, Health Sciences Library, Ashland, WI [*Library symbol*] [*Library of Congress*] (LCLS)
WASM ...... Merdei [*Indonesia*] [*ICAO location identifier*] (ICLI)
WaSM .... Mountaineers, Inc., Seattle, WA [*Library symbol*] [*Library of Congress*] (LCLS)
WASM ...... White Anglo-Saxon Male
Wasmann J Biol ... Wasmann Journal of Biology [*A publication*]
WASME...... World Assembly of Small and Medium Enterprises [*See also AMPME*] [*New Delhi, India*] (EAIO)
WAsN........ Northland College, Ashland, WI [*Library symbol*] [*Library of Congress*] (LCLS)
WASNA .... Western Apicultural Society of North America (EA)
WaSNH..... Northwest Hospital, Effie M. Storey Learning Center, Seattle, WA [*Library symbol*] [*Library of Congress*] (LCLS)
WaSnqE..... Echo Glen Children's Center, Staff Library, Snoqualmie, WA [*Library symbol*] [*Library of Congress*] (LCLS)
WaSnqE-R ... Echo Glen Children's Center, Resident Library, Snoqualmie, WA [*Library symbol*] [*Library of Congress*] (LCLS)
WASO ...... Babo [*Indonesia*] [*ICAO location identifier*] (ICLI)
WASO ...... Women's Association for Symphony Orchestras [*Later, AMSO*] (EA)
WASOG .... World Association on Sarcoidosis and Other Granulomatous Disorders (EAIO)
WASP....... Brownsville, PA [*AM radio station call letters*]
WASP........ MARINALG International, World Association of Seaweed Processors (EA)
WaSp .... Spokane Public Library, Spokane, WA [*Library symbol*] [*Library of Congress*] (LCLS)
WASP....... Wait-and-See Parsing [*Data processing*] (BYTE)
WASP....... War Air Service Program [*Department of Commerce*]

WASP....... Water, Air, and Soil Pollution [*A publication*]
WASP....... Water Spectrum [*A publication*]
WASP....... Water and Steam Program [*NASA*]
WASP....... Weather-Atmospheric Sounding Projectile [*Research rocket*]
WASP....... Weber Advanced Spatial Perception Test [*Vocational guidance test*]
WASP....... Weightless Analysis Sounding Probe [*NASA*]
WASP....... Westinghouse Advanced Systems Planning Group
WASP....... White Anglo-Saxon Protestant
WASP....... White Appalachian Southern Protestant [*Chicago slang*]
WASP....... White Ashkenazi Sabra with Pull [*Israeli variation on White Anglo-Saxon Protestant*]
WASP....... Wide Antiarmor Minimissile (MCD)
WASP....... Williams Aerial Systems Platform [*One-man flying platform*]
WASP....... Wind-Assisted Ship Propulsion (DS)
WASP....... Window Atmosphere Sounding Projectile [*NASA*]
WASP....... Women's Airforce Service Pilots [*World War II*]
WASP....... Woody Allen's Spring Picture [*Designation reflecting the filmmaker's reluctance to provide information about his movies in advance of their commercial release*] [*See also WAFP*]
WASP....... Work Activity Sampling Plan
WASP....... Workshop Analysis and Scheduling Programming
WASP....... World Association of Societies of Pathology - Anatomic and Clinical (EA)
WASP....... World Associations for Social Psychiatry (EA)
WASP....... Wrap-Around Simulation Program [*Military*] (CAAL)
WASPA ..... White Anglo-Saxon Protestant Ambulatory [*Extension of WASP; indicates the necessity of being able-bodied as an additional requirement for success*]
WASPB .... Water Spectrum [*A publication*]
WaSpBM... United States Bureau of Mines, Mining Research Center, Spokane, WA [*Library symbol*] [*Library of Congress*] (LCLS)
WaSpBMW ... United States Bureau of Mines, Western Field Operations Center, Spokane, WA [*Library symbol*] [*Library of Congress*] (LCLS)
WaSPC ...... Seattle Pacific College, Seattle, WA [*Library symbol*] [*Library of Congress*] (LCLS)
WaSpCN ... Center for Nursing Education, Spokane, WA [*Library symbol*] [*Library of Congress*] (LCLS)
WaSpCo..... Spokane County Library, Spokane, WA [*Library symbol*] [*Library of Congress*] (LCLS)
WaSpD ...... Deaconess Hospital, School of Nursing, Spokane, WA [*Library symbol*] [*Library of Congress*] (LCLS)
WaSPe ...... Perkins, Coie, Stone, Olsen & Williams, Seattle, WA [*Library symbol*] [*Library of Congress*] (LCLS)
WaSpG ...... Gonzaga University, Spokane, WA [*Library symbol*] [*Library of Congress*] (LCLS)
WaSpGL.... Church of Jesus Christ of Latter-Day Saints, Genealogical Society Library, Spokane Branch, Spokane, WA [*Library symbol*] [*Library of Congress*] (LCLS)
WaSpG-L .. Gonzaga University, Law Library, Spokane, WA [*Library symbol*] [*Library of Congress*] (LCLS)
WaSpGS.... United States Geological Survey, Spokane, WA [*Library symbol*] [*Library of Congress*] (LCLS)
WaSpH ..... Holy Family Hospital, Spokane, WA [*Library symbol*] [*Library of Congress*] (LCLS)
WaSPH ..... United States Public Health Service Hospital, Medical Service Library, Seattle, WA [*Library symbol*] [*Library of Congress*] (LCLS)
WaSpHiE .. Eastern Washington State Historical Society, Museum Library, Spokane, WA [*Library symbol*] [*Library of Congress*] (LCLS)
WaSpIn...... Intermediate School District 101, Professional Materials Library, Spokane, WA [*Library symbol*] [*Library of Congress*] (LCLS)
WaSpJ .... Jesuit Archives of the Province of Oregon, Spokane, WA [*Library symbol*] [*Library of Congress*] (LCLS)
WaSpJP .... Washington State Office of Juvenile Parole Services, Spokane, WA [*Library symbol*] [*Library of Congress*] (LCLS)
WaSpJS..... Jesuit Scholastic Library, Spokane, WA [*Library symbol*] [*Library of Congress*] (LCLS)
WaSPM..... Providence Hospital, Medical Library and Learning Resource Center, Seattle, WA [*Library symbol*] [*Library of Congress*] (LCLS)
WaSpM ..... Spokane County Medical Library, Spokane, WA [*Library symbol*] [*Library of Congress*] (LCLS)
WaSpMF... Murphey Favre, Inc., Spokane, WA [*Library symbol*] [*Library of Congress*] (LCLS)
WaSpN ...... Fort Wright College, Spokane, WA [*Library symbol*] [*Library of Congress*] (LCLS)
WASP-NN ... White Anglo-Saxon Protestant Native Born of Native Parents
WaSPoD.... Population Dynamics, Seattle, WA [*Library symbol*] [*Library of Congress*] (LCLS)
Was Polit ... Waseda Political Studies [*A publication*]
WaSpPS .... Spokane Public Schools, Curriculum Library, Spokane, WA [*Library symbol*] [*Library of Congress*] (LCLS)
WASPRU .. West African Stored Products Research Unit
WaSPS ...... Seattle Public Schools, Library Technical Service, Seattle, WA [*Library symbol*] [*Library of Congress*] (LCLS)

WaSpS....... Spokane Community College, Spokane, WA [*Library symbol*] [*Library of Congress*] (LCLS)
WASPS ..... Women's Agricultural Security Production Service [*British military*] (DMA)
WASPS ..... Women's Auxiliary Service Platoon
WaSpSF .... Spokane Falls Community College, Spokane, WA [*Library symbol*] [*Library of Congress*] (LCLS)
WaSpSH.... Sacred Heart Medical Center, Spokane, WA [*Library symbol*] [*Library of Congress*] (LCLS)
WaSpSL .... Saint Luke's Hospital, Spokane, WA [*Library symbol*] [*Library of Congress*] (LCLS)
WaSpSL .... Spokane County Law Library, Spokane, WA [*Library symbol*] [*Library of Congress*] (LCLS)
WaSpStM ... Saint Michael's Institute, Spokane, WA [*Library symbol*] [*Library of Congress*] (LCLS)
WaSpVA.... United States Veterans Administration Hospital, Spokane, WA [*Library symbol*] [*Library of Congress*] (LCLS)
WaSpW ..... Whitworth College, Spokane, WA [*Library symbol*] [*Library of Congress*] (LCLS)
WASPWWII ... Women Airforce Service Pilots WWII (EA)
WaSpYS.... Washington State Center for Youth Services, Spokane, WA [*Library symbol*] [*Library of Congress*] (LCLS)
WASR....... Manokwari/Rendani [*Indonesia*] [*ICAO location identifier*] (ICLI)
WASR....... Wolfeboro, NH [*AM radio station call letters*]
WASRA..... Western Australian Smallbore Rifle Association
WASRAID ... Western Australian Sports and Recreation Association for the Intellectually Disabled
WaSS........ Schick's Schadel Hospital, Medical Library, Seattle, WA [*Library symbol*] [*Library of Congress*] (LCLS)
WASS........ Sorong/Jefman [*Indonesia*] [*ICAO location identifier*] (ICLI)
Wass .... Wassermann [*Test for syphilis*]
WASS........ Wavefront Analysis of Spatial Sampling [*Aircraft landing approach*]
WASS....... Wide-Area Active Surveillance System [*Military*] (MCD)
WaSSB ...... Washington State Office for the Services for the Blind, Seattle, WA [*Library symbol*] [*Library of Congress*] (LCLS)
Wasser- Energiewirt ... Wasser- und Energiewirtschaft [*A publication*]
Wasser Luft Betr ... Wasser, Luft, und Betrieb [*A publication*]
Wasserwirtsch-Wassertech ... Wasserwirtschaft-Wassertechnik [*A publication*]
Wasserwirt-Wassertech ... Wasserwirtschaft-Wassertechnik [*A publication*]
WaSSh....... Shoreline Community College, Seattle, WA [*Library symbol*] [*Library of Congress*] (LCLS)
WaSSH...... Swedish Hospital Medical Center, Seattle, WA [*Library symbol*] [*Library of Congress*] (LCLS)
W Assn Map Lib Inf Bull ... Western Association of Map Libraries. Information Bulletin [*A publication*]
WASSP ..... Wire Arc Seismic Section Profiler
WaSSW..... Shannon & Wilson, Inc., Seattle, WA [*Library symbol*] [*Library of Congress*] (LCLS)
Wasswirt Wasstech ... Wasserwirtschaft-Wassertechnik [*A publication*]
WAST....... Ashtabula, OH [*AM radio station call letters*]
WAST........ Teminabuan [*Indonesia*] [*ICAO location identifier*] (ICLI)
WASTE..... Wisdom, Acclaim, and Status through Expenditures [*Fictional government agency in book "Alice in Blunderland"*]
Waste Disposal & Water Manage in Aust ... Waste Disposal and Water Management in Australia [*A publication*] (APTA)
Waste Disposal Water Manage Aust ... Waste Disposal and Water Management in Australia [*A publication*] (APTA)
Waste Dispos Water Manage Aust ... Waste Disposal and Water Management in Australia [*A publication*]
Waste Disp Recyc Bull ... Waste Disposal and Recycling Bulletin [*A publication*]
WaSteM .... McNeil Island Correction Center, Steilacoom, WA [*Library symbol*] [*Library of Congress*] (LCLS)
Waste Manage ... Waste Management [*A publication*]
Waste Manage Pap ... Waste Management Paper [*London*] [*A publication*]
Waste Mgmt Inf Bull ... Waste Management Information Bulletin [*A publication*]
Waste Mgmt Res ... Waste Management Research [*A publication*]
Wastes Eng ... Wastes Engineering [*A publication*]
Wastes Mgmt ... Wastes Management [*A publication*]
WaSU .... Seattle University, Seattle, WA [*Library symbol*] [*Library of Congress*] (LCLS)
WASU-FM ... Boone, NC [*FM radio station call letters*]
WaSUN ..... United Nursing Homes, Seattle, WA [*Library symbol*] [*Library of Congress*] (LCLS)
WaSVA...... United States Veterans Administration Hospital, Seattle, WA [*Library symbol*] [*Library of Congress*] (LCLS)
WASV-TV ... Asheville, NC [*Television station call letters*]
WASW ...... Wasior [*Indonesia*] [*ICAO location identifier*] (ICLI)
WASWC.... World Association of Soil and Water Conservation (EA)
WaSWG .... West Seattle General Hospital, Seattle, WA [*Library symbol*] [*Library of Congress*] (LCLS)
WASZ........ Ashland-Lineville, AL [*FM radio station call letters*]
WaT .... Tacoma Public Library, Tacoma, WA [*Library symbol*] [*Library of Congress*] (LCLS)
WAT .... University of Waterloo Library [*UTLAS symbol*]
WAT .... Water [*Automotive engineering*]

Wat .... Watermeyer's Cape Of Good Hope Supreme Court Reports [*1857*] [*South Africa*] [*A publication*] (DLA)
WAT .... Watertown Free Public Library, Watertown, MA [*OCLC symbol*] (OCLC)
WAT .... Watheroo [*Australia*] [*Seismograph station code, US Geological Survey*] [*Closed*] (SEIS)
WAT .... Watheroo [*Australia*] [*Later, GNA*] [*Geomagnetic observatory code*]
WAT .... Weapons Assignment Technician (AFM)
WAT......... Web Action Time (MCD)
WAT......... Weight, Altitude, and Temperature (IEEE)
WAT .... Weight Average Temperature [*Chemical engineering*]
WAT .... Wet Anode Tantalum
WAT .... What Acronym's That? [*A publication*] (APTA)
WAT .... White Adipose Tissue [*Physiology*]
WAT .... Wideband Adapter Transformer
WAT .... Word Association Test [*Psychology*]
WAT's ...... Wide-Angle [*Galilean*] Telescopes
WATA .... Boone, NC [*AM radio station call letters*]
WATA .... Wisconsin Automatic Test Apparatus
WATA .... World Association of Travel Agencies (EAIO)
WaTAC ..... Allenmore Community Hospital, Tacoma, WA [*Library symbol*] [*Library of Congress*] (LCLS)
WaTAH..... United States Army [*Madigan*] General Hospital, Tacoma, WA [*Library symbol*] [*Library of Congress*] (LCLS)
Wat Aust ... Water in Australia [*A publication*] (APTA)
Wat Bull..... Water Bulletin [*A publication*]
WATC .... Atlanta, GA [*Television station call letters*]
WATC .... [*The*] Washington Terminal Company [*AAR code*]
WATC .... Western Australian Tourism Commission
WATC .... Women's Ambulance and Transportation Corps
WaTCC..... Tacoma Community College, Tacoma, WA [*Library symbol*] [*Library of Congress*] (LCLS)
Wat CGH... Watermeyer's Cape Of Good Hope Reports [*South Africa*] [*A publication*] (DLA)
WaTCH ..... Mary Bridge Children's Health Center, Tacoma, WA [*Library symbol*] [*Library of Congress*] (LCLS)
WATCH .... Watchers Against Television Commercial Harrassment [*Student legal action organization*]
WATCH .... Working Group on the Assessment of Toxic Chemicals [*British*]
WATCH .... World Against Toys Causing Harm
WATCIM ... Waterloo Centre for Integrated Manufacturing [*University of Waterloo*] [*Canada*] [*Research center*] (RCD)
WaTCJ ...... Cascadia Juvenile Diagnostic Center, Tacoma, WA [*Library symbol*] [*Library of Congress*] (LCLS)
Wat Con..... Watkins on Conveyancing [*9th ed.*] [*1845*] [*A publication*] (DLA)
Wat Cop..... Watkins on Copyholds [*6th ed.*] [*1829*] [*A publication*] (DLA)
Wat Cr Dig ... Waterman's Criminal Digest [*United States*] [*A publication*] (DLA)
Wat Cr Proc ... Waterman's Criminal Procedure [*A publication*] (DLA)
WATD ...... Brockton, MA [*AM radio station call letters*]
WaTD .... Doctors Hospital, Tacoma, WA [*Library symbol*] [*Library of Congress*] (LCLS)
WATD-FM ... Marshfield, MA [*FM radio station call letters*]
WATDOC ... Water Resources Document Reference Centre [*Canadian Department of Fisheries and the Environment*] [*Database*] (IID)
WA Teachers J ... Western Australian Teachers' Journal [*A publication*] (APTA)
WA Teach J ... Western Australian Teachers' Journal [*A publication*] (APTA)
WATER..... Women's Alliance for Theology, Ethics, and Ritual (EA)
Water Air and Soil Pollut ... Water, Air, and Soil Pollution [*A publication*]
Water Air Soil Pollut ... Water, Air, and Soil Pollution [*A publication*]
Water Am Inst Chem Eng ... Water. American Institute of Chemical Engineers [*A publication*]
Water A S P ... Water, Air, and Soil Pollution [*A publication*]
Water Biol Syst ... Water in Biological Systems [*A publication*]
Water Electrolyte Metab Proc Symp ... Water and Electrolyte Metabolism. Proceedings of the Symposium [*A publication*]
Water E & M ... Water Engineering and Management [*A publication*]
Water Eng ... Water and Wastes Engineering [*A publication*]
WATERF .. Waterford [*County in Ireland*] (ROG)
WATERFD ... Waterford [*County in Ireland*]
Water Invest Mich Geol Surv Div ... Water Investigation. Michigan Geological Survey Division [*A publication*]
Water Law Newsl ... Water Law Newsletter [*United States*] [*A publication*]
Water Manage News ... Water Management News [*A publication*]
Water Manage Techn Rep Colorado State Univ ... Colorado State University. Water Management Technical Report [*A publication*]
Watermeyer ... Watermeyer's Cape Of Good Hope Reports [*South Africa*] [*A publication*] (DLA)
Water Poll Abstr ... Water Pollution Abstracts [*A publication*]
Water Poll Cont Fed J ... Water Pollution Control Federation. Journal [*A publication*]
Water Poll Control Fed J ... Water Pollution Control Federation. Journal [*A publication*]
Water Pollut Contr Fed J ... Water Pollution Control Federation. Journal [*A publication*]
Water Pollut Control ... Water Pollution Control [*A publication*]

Water Pollut Control (Don Mills Can) ... Water and Pollution Control (Don Mills, Canada) [*A publication*]

Water Pollut Control (London) ... Water Pollution Control (London) [*A publication*]

Water Pollut Control Res Ser ... Water Pollution Control Research Series [*A publication*]

Water Pollut Res Can ... Water Pollution Research in Canada [*A publication*]

Water Pollut Res (Stevenage) ... Water Pollution Research (Stevenage) [*A publication*]

Water Purif Liquid Wastes Treat ... Water Purification and Liquid Wastes Treatment [*Japan*] [*A publication*]

Water Qual Instrum ... Water Quality Instrumentation [*A publication*]

Water Res .. Water Research [*A publication*]

Water Res Cent Notes Water Res ... Water Research Centre. Notes on Water Research [*A publication*]

Water Res Found Aust Annu Rep Balance Sheet ... Water Research Foundation of Australia Limited. Annual Report and Balance Sheet [*A publication*]

Water Res Found Aust Bull ... Water Research Foundation of Australia Limited. Bulletin [*A publication*]

Water Res Found Aust Lted Ann Rep Balance Sheet ... Water Research Foundation of Australia Limited. Annual Report and Balance Sheet [*A publication*]

Water Res Found of Aust Newsl ... Water Research Foundation of Australia Limited. Newsletter [*A publication*] (APTA)

Water Res Found Aust Rep ... Water Research Foundation of Australia Limited. Report [*A publication*] (APTA)

Water Res Inst W Va Univ Inf Rep ... Water Research Institute. West Virginia University. Information Report [*A publication*]

Water Res News ... Water Research News [*A publication*]

Water Resour ... Water Resources [*A publication*]

Water Resour Bull ... Water Resources Bulletin [*A publication*]

Water Resour Bull Nev Div Water Resour ... Water Resources Bulletin. Nevada Division of Water Resources [*A publication*]

Water Resour Bull (PR) ... Water Resources Bulletin (Puerto Rico) [*A publication*]

Water Resources Res ... Water Resources Research [*A publication*]

Water Resour Circ Arkansas Geol Comm ... Water Resources Circular. Arkansas Geological Commission [*A publication*]

Water Resour (Engl Transl Vodnye Resursy) ... Water Resources (English Translation of Vodnye Resursy) [*A publication*]

Water Resour Invest ... Water Resources Investigations [*A publication*]

Water Resour Invest US Geol Surv ... Water Resources Investigations. United States Geological Survey [*A publication*]

Water Resour J Econ Soc Comm Asia Pac ... Water Resources Journal. Economic and Social Commission for Asia and the Pacific [*A publication*]

Water Resour Manag Ser ... Water Resource Management Series [*A publication*]

Water Resour Newsl ... Water Resources Newsletter [*A publication*] (APTA)

Water Resour Reconnaissance Ser Nev Div Water Resour ... Water Resources. Reconnaissance Series. Nevada Division of Water Resources [*A publication*]

Water Resour Rep Ariz State Land Dep ... Water Resources Report. Arizona State Land Department [*A publication*]

Water Resour Rep Ont Minist Environ Water Resour Branch ... Water Resources Report. Ontario Ministry of the Environment. Water Resources Branch [*A publication*]

Water Resour Res ... Water Resources Research [*A publication*]

Water Resour Res Cent VA Polytech Inst State Univ Bull ... Water Resources Research Center. Virginia Polytechnic Institute and State University. Bulletin [*A publication*]

Water Resour Rev Streamflow Ground-Water Cond ... Water Resources Review for Streamflow and Ground-Water Conditions [*United States - Canada*] [*A publication*]

Water Resour Ser Tenn Div Water Resour ... Water Resources Series. Tennessee Division of Water Resources [*A publication*]

Water Resour Symp ... Water Resources Symposium [*A publication*]

Water Res R ... Water Resources Research [*A publication*]

Water (S Afr) ... Water (South Africa) [*A publication*]

Water and San ... Water and Sanitation [*A publication*]

Water Sanit ... Water and Sanitation [*A publication*]

Water Sanit Eng ... Water and Sanitary Engineer [*A publication*]

Water Sci & Technol ... Water Science and Technology [*A publication*]

Water Serv ... Water Services [*A publication*]

Water Sewage Effl ... Water, Sewage, and Effluent [*A publication*]

Water & Sewage Works ... Water and Sewage Works [*A publication*]

Water Supply Manage ... Water Supply and Management [*England*] [*A publication*]

Water Supply Pap Geol Surv GB Hydrogeol Rep ... Water Supply Papers. Geological Survey of Great Britain. Hydrogeological Report [*A publication*]

Water Supply Pap US Geol Surv ... Water Supply Paper. United States Geological Survey [*A publication*]

Water Treat Exam ... Water Treatment and Examination [*A publication*]

Water Waste ... Water and Wastes Engineering [*A publication*]

Water & Waste Engng ... Water and Waste Engineering [*A publication*]

Water Wastes Dig ... Water and Wastes Digest [*A publication*]

Water Wastes Eng ... Water and Wastes Engineering [*A publication*]

Water Wastes Eng Ind ... Water and Wastes Engineering/Industrial [*A publication*]

Water Waste Treat ... Water and Waste Treatment [*A publication*]

Water Waste Treat J ... Water Waste Treatment Journal [*A publication*]

Water Wastewater Treat Plants Oper Newsl ... Water and Wastewater Treatment Plants Operators' Newsletter [*A publication*]

Water Water Eng ... Water and Water Engineering [*A publication*]

Water (WC and IC Staff Journal) ... Water (Water Conservation and Irrigation Commission Staff Journal) [*A publication*] (APTA)

Water Well J ... Water Well Journal [*A publication*]

Water Well Jour ... Water Well Journal [*A publication*]

Water Works Eng ... Water Works Engineering [*A publication*]

Water Works Wastes Eng ... Water Works and Wastes Engineering [*A publication*]

WATE-TV ... Knoxville, TN [*Television station call letters*]

WATF .... Waterford Wedgwood PLC [*NASDAQ symbol*] (NQ)

WATFOR ... Waterloo FORTRAN [*University of Waterloo*] [*Canada*]

WaTFS ...... Fort Steilacoom Community College, Tacoma, WA [*Library symbol*] [*Library of Congress*] (LCLS)

WaTG .... Tacoma Branch Genealogical Library, Tacoma, WA [*Library symbol*] [*Library of Congress*] (LCLS)

WaTGH ..... Tacoma General Hospital, Pierce County Medical Library, Tacoma, WA [*Library symbol*] [*Library of Congress*] (LCLS)

WaTGS ...... Church of Jesus Christ of Latter-Day Saints, Genealogical Society Library, Tacoma Branch, Tacoma, WA [*Library symbol*] [*Library of Congress*] (LCLS)

WATH .... Athens, OH [*AM radio station call letters*]

WATITC ... Western Australian Tourism Industry Training Committee

WaTJP ...... Washington State Office of Juvenile Parole Services, Tacoma, WA [*Library symbol*] [*Library of Congress*] (LCLS)

Wat Just .... Waterman's Justices' Manual [*A publication*] (DLA)

WATK .... Antigo, WI [*AM radio station call letters*]

Watk Con ... Watkins on Conveyancing [*A publication*] (DLA)

Watk Conv ... Watkins on Conveyancing [*A publication*] (DLA)

Watk Cop ... Watkins on Copyholds [*A publication*] (DLA)

Watk Copyh ... Watkins on Copyholds [*A publication*] (DLA)

Watk Des ... Watkins on Descents [*A publication*] (DLA)

WATL .... Atlanta, GA [*Television station call letters*]

WaTLG ...... Lakewood General Hospital and Convalescent Center, Tacoma, WA [*Library symbol*] [*Library of Congress*] (LCLS)

WATM-TV ... Altoona, PA [*Television station call letters*]

WATN .... Watertown, NY [*AM radio station call letters*]

WATO .... Oak Ridge, TN [*AM radio station call letters*]

WaTO .... Oakridge Group Home, Tacoma, WA [*Library symbol*] [*Library of Congress*] (LCLS)

WaTP .... Pioneer Group Home, Tacoma, WA [*Library symbol*] [*Library of Congress*] (LCLS)

WaTPC ...... Pierce County Library, Tacoma, WA [*Library symbol*] [*Library of Congress*] (LCLS)

WaTPG ...... Puget Sound General Hospital, Tacoma, WA [*Library symbol*] [*Library of Congress*] (LCLS)

WATPL ...... Wartime Traffic Priority List (NATG)

WaTPM ..... Pierce County Medical Library, Tacoma, WA [*Library symbol*] [*Library of Congress*] (LCLS)

WatPolAb ... Water Pollution Abstracts [*A publication*]

Wat Pollut Control ... Water Pollution Control [*A publication*]

Wat Pollut Res J Can ... Water Pollution Research Journal of Canada [*A publication*]

WaTPS ...... Tacoma Public Schools, Professional and Curriculum Library, Tacoma, WA [*Library symbol*] [*Library of Congress*] (LCLS)

Wat Pwr ..... Water Power [*A publication*]

WATQ-FM ... New Martinsville, WV [*FM radio station call letters*]

WATR .... American Water Resources [*NASDAQ symbol*] (NQ)

WATR .... Water Attenuation by Tritium Relaxation [*Physics*]

WATR .... Waterbury, CT [*AM radio station call letters*]

WATR .... Waterville [*AAR code*]

WATRA .... Water Research [*A publication*]

WatResAb ... Water Resources Abstracts [*A publication*]

Wat Res Fdn Aust Bull ... Water Research Foundation of Australia Limited. Bulletin [*A publication*] (APTA)

Wat Res Fdn Rep ... Water Research Foundation of Australia Limited. Report [*A publication*] (APTA)

Wat Resour Res ... Water Resources Research [*A publication*]

WATS .... Sayre, PA [*AM radio station call letters*]

WATS .... Wide-Area Military Traffic Management and Terminal Service

WATS .... Wide-Area Telecommunications [*formerly, Telephone*] Service [*American Telephone & Telegraph Co. contract billing system*]

WATS .... Women's Auxiliary Territorial Service [*British military*] (DMA)

WATS .... Women's Auxiliary Training Service

Wats Arb ... Watson on Arbitration [*A publication*] (DLA)

Wats Cler Law ... Watson's Clergyman's Law [*A publication*] (DLA)

Wats Com Man ... Watson's United States Commissioners' Manual [*A publication*] (DLA)

Wats Comp Eq ... Watson's Compendium of Equity [*A publication*] (DLA)

Wats Const Hist ... Watson's Constitutional History of Canada [*A publication*] (DLA)

Wat Serv .... Water Services [*A publication*]

Wat Set-Off ... Waterman on Set-Off [*A publication*] (DLA)

WaTSJ ...... Saint Joseph Hospital, Tacoma, WA [*Library symbol*] [*Library of Congress*] (LCLS)

Wats Med Jur ... Watson's Medical Jurisprudence [*A publication*] (DLA)

Watson....... Watson's Compendium of Equity [*2 eds.*] [*1873, 1888*] [*A publication*] (DLA)

Watson Eq ... Watson's Compendium of Equity [*A publication*] (DLA)

Watson House Bull ... Watson House Bulletin [*A publication*]

Wats Part... Watson on Partnership [*2nd ed.*] [*1807*] [*A publication*] (DLA)

Wats Sher.. Watson's Office and Duty of Sheriff [*2nd ed.*] [*1848*] [*A publication*] (DLA)

WATSTORE ... National Water Data Storage and Retrieval System [*US Geological Survey*] [*Information service or system*] (CRD)

WATT .... Cadillac, MI [*AM radio station call letters*]

WATT .... Watts Industries, Inc. [*North Andover, MA*] [*NASDAQ symbol*] (NQ)

WATTec .... Welding and Testing Technology Energy Conference [*Acronym is used as name of association*]

Wattle Res Inst Univ Natal (S Afr) Rep ... Wattle Research Institute. University of Natal (South Africa). Report [*A publication*]

Wat Tres .... Waterman on the Law of Trespass [*A publication*] (DLA)

Watts .... Watts' Pennsylvania Reports [*1832-40*] [*A publication*] (DLA)

Watts .... Watts' Reports [*16-24 West Virginia*] [*A publication*] (DLA)

Watts (PA) ... Watts' Pennsylvania Reports [*1832-40*] [*A publication*] (DLA)

Watts & S .. Watts and Sergeant's Pennsylvania Reports [*1841-45*] [*A publication*] (DLA)

Watts & Serg ... Watts and Sergeant's Pennsylvania Reports [*1841-45*] [*A publication*] (DLA)

Watts & S (PA) ... Watts and Sergeant's Pennsylvania Reports [*1841-45*] [*A publication*] (DLA)

WaTU........ University of Puget Sound, Tacoma, WA [*Library symbol*] [*Library of Congress*] (LCLS)

WATU ...... Western Approaches Tactical Unit [*Navy*]

WATV .... Birmingham, AL [*AM radio station call letters*]

Wat Vict..... Water in Victoria [*A publication*] (APTA)

WATW ...... Ashland, WI [*AM radio station call letters*]

WaTW .... Weyerhaeuser Co., Tacoma, WA [*Library symbol*] [*Library of Congress*] (LCLS)

WATW ...... Wood Awning Type Window

Wat Waste Treat ... Water and Waste Treatment [*A publication*]

Wat Wat Engng ... Water and Water Engineering [*A publication*]

WaTWH.... Western State Hospital, Staff Library, Tacoma, WA [*Library symbol*] [*Library of Congress*] (LCLS)

WaTWH-R ... Western State Hospital, Resident Library, Tacoma, WA [*Library symbol*] [*Library of Congress*] (LCLS)

WaTW-T ... Weyerhaeuser Co., Technical Center, Tacoma, WA [*Library symbol*] [*Library of Congress*] (LCLS)

WATZ .... Alpena, MI [*AM radio station call letters*]

WATZ-FM ... Alpena, MI [*FM radio station call letters*]

WAU.......... University of Washington, Seattle, WA [*OCLC symbol*] (OCLC)

WaU........... University of Washington, Seattle, WA [*Library symbol*] [*Library of Congress*] (LCLS)

wau .... Washington [*MARC country of publication code*] [*Library of Congress*] (LCCP)

WAU.......... Weapon Assignment Unit [*Military*] (CAAL)

WAUB ...... Auburn, NY [*AM radio station call letters*]

WAUC....... Wauchula, FL [*AM radio station call letters*]

WAUD....... Auburn, AL [*AM radio station call letters*]

WaU-D ...... University of Washington, Drama Library, Seattle, WA [*Library symbol*] [*Library of Congress*] (LCLS)

WaU-EA.... University of Washington, East Asia Library, Seattle, WA [*Library symbol*] [*Library of Congress*] (LCLS)

WaU-FE .... University of Washington, Far Eastern Library, Seattle, WA [*Library symbol*] [*Library of Congress*] [*Obsolete*] (LCLS)

WAUG....... New Hope, NC [*AM radio station call letters*]

WaU-HS.... University of Washington, Health Sciences Library, Seattle, WA [*Library symbol*] [*Library of Congress*] (LCLS)

WAUK....... Waukesha, WI [*AM radio station call letters*]

WaU-L....... University of Washington, Law Library, Seattle, WA [*Library symbol*] [*Library of Congress*] (LCLS)

WAU Law R ... University of Western Australia. Law Review [*A publication*] (APTA)

WAULR .... Western Australia University. Law Review [*A publication*] (APTA)

WaU-MC... University of Washington, Harborview Medical Center Library, Seattle, WA [*Library symbol*] [*Library of Congress*] (LCLS)

WAUN....... Kewaunee, WI [*FM radio station call letters*]

WA Univ Gaz ... University of Western Australia. Gazette [*A publication*] (APTA)

WA Univ Geog Lab Res Rept ... University of Western Australia. Geography Laboratory. Research Report [*A publication*] (APTA)

WAUR....... Sandwich, IL [*AM radio station call letters*]

WAUS....... Berrien Springs, MI [*FM radio station call letters*]

WAUS .... World Association of Upper Silesians (EA)

W Aust....... Western Australia

W Aust For Dep Bull ... Western Australia. Forests Department. Bulletin [*A publication*] (APTA)

W Aust Geol Surv Bull ... Western Australia. Geological Survey. Bulletin [*A publication*] (APTA)

W Aust Geol Surv 1:250000 Geol Ser ... Western Australia. Geological Survey. 1:250,000 Geological Series [*A publication*] (APTA)

W Aust Hist Soc ... Western Australian Historical Society. Journal [*A publication*]

W Austl...... Western Australian Reports [*A publication*] (DLA)

W Austl Acts ... Western Australia Acts [*A publication*] (DLA)

W Austl Ind Gaz ... Western Australian Industrial Gazette [*A publication*] (DLA)

W Austl JP ... Western Australia Justice of the Peace [*A publication*] (DLA)

W Austl LR ... Western Australian Law Reports [*A publication*] (DLA)

W Austl R .. Western Australia Law Reports [*A publication*] (DLA)

W Aust Nat ... Western Australian Naturalist [*A publication*] (APTA)

W Aust Repr Acts ... Reprinted Acts of Western Australia [*A publication*] (DLA)

WAUXCP ... West Auxiliary Airborne Command Post (MCD)

WaV.......... Fort Vancouver Regional Library, Vancouver, WA [*Library symbol*] [*Library of Congress*] (LCLS)

WAV.......... Williford Aviation, Inc. [*Atlanta, GA*] [*FAA designator*] (FAAC)

WAV.......... Wirtschaftliche Aufbau Vereinigung [*Economic Reconstruction Union*] [*Federal Republic of Germany*] [*Political party*] (PPE)

WAVA ...... Arlington, VA [*FM radio station call letters*]

WAVA ...... World Association of Veteran Athletes (EAIO)

WAVA ...... World Association of Veterinary Anatomists (EA)

WAVAW ... Women Against Violence Against Women

WAVB ...... LaJas, PR [*AM radio station call letters*]

WaVC........ Clark College, Vancouver, WA [*Library symbol*] [*Library of Congress*] (LCLS)

WAVC ...... Duluth, MN [*FM radio station call letters*]

WAVD....... Decatur, AL [*AM radio station call letters*]

WAVE ...... Louisville, KY [*Television station call letters*]

WAVE ...... Water-Augmented Vehicle

WAVE ...... Wavetech, Inc. [*NASDAQ symbol*] (NQ)

WAVE ...... Weather Altimeter Voice Equipment

Wave Electron ... Wave Electronics [*A publication*]

Wave Part Dualism ... Wave. Particle Dualism [*A publication*]

WAVES..... Weight and Value Engineering System [*Data processing*]

WAVES..... Western Australian Voluntary Euthanasia Society

WAVES..... Women Accepted for Volunteer Emergency Service [*US Navy Women's Reserve*] [*World War II and later*]

WAVES..... Women Appointed Volunteer Emergency Services [*British*] [*World War II*]

WAVF....... Hanahan, SC [*FM radio station call letters*]

WAVFH .... World Association of Veterinary Food-Hygienists [*See also AMVHA*] [*Berlin, Federal Republic of Germany*] (EAIO)

WAVH....... Mobile, AL [*FM radio station call letters*]

WaVHS.... United States Park Service, Fort Vancouver National Historical Site, Vancouver, WA [*Library symbol*] [*Library of Congress*] (LCLS)

WAVI .... Christiansted, VI [*FM radio station call letters*]

WAVK....... Marathon, FL [*FM radio station call letters*]

WAVL....... Apollo, PA [*AM radio station call letters*]

WAVLD .... World Association of Veterinary Laboratory Diagnosticians (EAIO)

WAVM....... Maynard, MA [*FM radio station call letters*]

WaVMH... Vancouver Memorial Hospital, Vancouver, WA [*Library symbol*] [*Library of Congress*] (LCLS)

WAVMI .... World Association of Veterinary Microbiologists, Immunologists, and Specialists in Infectious Diseases [*See also AMVMI*] [*Maisons-Alfort, France*] (EAIO)

WAVN....... Southaven, MS [*AM radio station call letters*]

WAVO....... Decatur, GA [*AM radio station call letters*]

WAVP ...... World Association of Veterinary Pathologists (EAIO)

WAVPM .. Women Against Violence in Pornography and Media (EA)

WAVR ...... Waverly, Inc. [*NASDAQ symbol*] (NQ)

WAVR ...... Waverly, NY [*FM radio station call letters*]

WAVS....... Davie, FL [*AM radio station call letters*]

WAVS....... Wide Angle Visual System (MCD)

WaVSB...... Washington State School for the Blind, Vancouver, WA [*Library symbol*] [*Library of Congress*] (LCLS)

WaVSD ..... Washington State School for the Deaf, Vancouver, WA [*Library symbol*] [*Library of Congress*] (LCLS)

WaVStJ ..... Saint Joseph Community Hospital, Vancouver, WA [*Library symbol*] [*Library of Congress*] (LCLS)

WAVT-FM ... Pottsville, PA [*FM radio station call letters*]

WAVU....... Albertville, AL [*AM radio station call letters*]

WAVV....... Marco, FL [*FM radio station call letters*]

WaVVA ..... United States Veterans Administration Hospital, Vancouver, WA [*Library symbol*] [*Library of Congress*] (LCLS)

WAVW...... Vero Beach, FL [*FM radio station call letters*]

WAVY-TV ... Portsmouth, VA [*Television station call letters*]

WAW........ University of Washington, School of Librarianship, Seattle, WA [*OCLC symbol*] (OCLC)

WaW......... Walla Walla Public Library, Walla Walla, WA [*Library symbol*] [*Library of Congress*] (LCLS)

WAW......... Ward's Auto World [*A publication*]

WAW......... Warsaw [*Poland*] [*Airport symbol*] (OAG)

WAW......... Waynesburg & Washington Railroad Co. [*Absorbed into Consolidated Rail Corp.*] [*AAR code*]

WAW......... Wings Airways [*Blue Bell, PA*] [*FAA designator*] (FAAC)

WAWA......	West Africa Wins Again [*A reminder that visitors to this region must exercise caution if they wish to avoid bureaucratic harrassment and overcharging*]
WAWA......	Woolens and Worsteds of America [*Defunct*] (EA)
WAWA-TV ...	Rome, GA [*Television station call letters*]
WaWC.......	Walla Walla College, College Place, WA [*Library symbol*] [*Library of Congress*] (LCLS)
WAWC......	West Africa War Council [*World War II*]
WAWD......	Fort Walton Beach, FL [*Television station call letters*]
WaWeC	Central Washington Hospital, Health Sciences Library, Wenatchee, WA [*Library symbol*] [*Library of Congress*] (LCLS)
WaWeN.....	North Central Regional Library, Wenatche, WA [*Library symbol*] [*Library of Congress*] (LCLS)
WaWeW	Wenatchee Valley College, Wenatchee, WA [*Library symbol*] [*Library of Congress*] (LCLS)
WaWeYS..	Washington State Center for Youth Services, Wenatchee, WA [*Library symbol*] [*Library of Congress*] (LCLS)
WAWF	William Allen White Foundation (EA)
WAWF	World Arm Wrestling Federation (EA)
WAWF	World Association for World Federation [*Netherlands*]
WAWG	Where Are We Going?
WaWiS	Wilbur Public Schools System, Wilbur, WA [*Library symbol*] [*Library of Congress*] (LCLS)
WAWK......	Kendallville, IN [*AM radio station call letters*]
WAWL-FM ...	Signal Mountain, TN [*FM radio station call letters*]
WaWnvGH ...	Woodenville Group Home, Woodenville, WA [*Library symbol*] [*Library of Congress*] (LCLS)
WaWP	Washington State Penitentiary, Walla Walla, WA [*Library symbol*] [*Library of Congress*] (LCLS)
WAWS	Jacksonville, FL [*Television station call letters*]
WAWV	Sylacauga, AL [*FM radio station call letters*]
WaWV	United States Veterans Administration Hospital, Walla Walla, WA [*Library symbol*] [*Library of Congress*] (LCLS)
WaWW......	Whitman College, Walla Walla, WA [*Library symbol*] [*Library of Congress*] (LCLS)
WaWWC...	Walla Walla Community College, Walla Walla, WA [*Library symbol*] [*Library of Congress*] (LCLS)
WAWZ	Zarephath, NJ [*FM radio station call letters*]
WAX.........	Waxman Industries, Inc. [*NYSE symbol*] (SPSG)
WAX.........	Weak Anion Exchanger [*Chemistry*]
WAX.........	Weapon Assignment and Target Extermination
WAXA	Anderson, SC [*Television station call letters*]
WAXD......	Wide-Angle X-Ray Diffraction
WAXE	Vero Beach, FL [*AM radio station call letters*]
WAXH......	Olyphant, PA [*FM radio station call letters*]
WAXI	Rockville, IN [*FM radio station call letters*]
WAXL	Lancaster, WI [*FM radio station call letters*]
WAXM......	Big Stone Gap, VA [*FM radio station call letters*]
WAXO	Lewisburg, TN [*AM radio station call letters*]
WAXS......	Wide-Angle X-Ray Scattering
WAXT	Alexandria, IN [*FM radio station call letters*]
WAXX	Eau Claire, WI [*FM radio station call letters*]
WAXY	Fort Lauderdale, FL [*FM radio station call letters*]
WAXZ	Georgetown, OH [*FM radio station call letters*]
WAY......	Wayne State College, Wayne, NE [*OCLC symbol*] (OCLC)
WAY.........	Waynesburg [*Pennsylvania*] [*Seismograph station code, US Geological Survey*] [*Closed*] (SEIS)
WAY.........	Waynesburg, PA [*Location identifier*] [*FAA*] (FAAL)
WAY.........	World Assembly of Youth [*Bronshoj, Denmark*] (EAIO)
WaY.........	Yakima Valley Regional Library, Yakima, WA [*Library symbol*] [*Library of Congress*] (LCLS)
WAYA	Spring City, TN [*FM radio station call letters*]
WaYacL.....	Larch Mountain Correctional Center, Staff Library, Yacolt, WA [*Library symbol*] [*Library of Congress*] (LCLS)
WaYacL-R ...	Larch Mountain Correctional Center, Resident Library, Yacolt, WA [*Library symbol*] [*Library of Congress*] (LCLS)
WAYB	Graysville, TN [*FM radio station call letters*]
WAYC	Bedford, PA [*AM radio station call letters*]
WAYC-FM ...	Bedford, PA [*FM radio station call letters*]
WAYE	Birmingham, AL [*AM radio station call letters*]
WAYED5 ..	WANATCA [*West Australian Nut and Tree Crop Association*] Yearbook [*A publication*]
WAYF.......	Mobile, AL [*FM radio station call letters*]
WaYGS......	Church of Jesus Christ of Latter-Day Saints, Genealogical Society Library, Yakima Branch, Yakima, WA [*Library symbol*] [*Library of Congress*] (LCLS)
WAYI-FM ...	Hudson Falls, NY [*FM radio station call letters*]
WAYJ.......	Fort Myers, FL [*FM radio station call letters*]
WaYJP	Washington State Office of Juvenile Parole Services, Yakima, WA [*Library symbol*] [*Library of Congress*] (LCLS)
WAYK	Melbourne, FL [*Television station call letters*]
WAYL	Richfield, MN [*AM radio station call letters*]
WaYM.......	Yakima Valley Memorial Hospital, Yakima, WA [*Library symbol*] [*Library of Congress*] (LCLS)
WAYMCA ...	World Alliance of Young Men's Christian Associations [*Geneva, Switzerland*] (EAIO)
WaYMHi...	Yakima Valley Museum and Historical Association, Yakima, WA [*Library symbol*] [*Library of Congress*] (LCLS)
WAYN......	Rockingham, NC [*AM radio station call letters*]
Wayne LR ...	Wayne Law Review [*A publication*]

Wayne L Rev ...	Wayne Law Review [*A publication*]
WAYQ.......	Daytona Beach, FL [*Television station call letters*]
WAYR.......	Orange Park, FL [*AM radio station call letters*]
WAYS.......	Macon, GA [*AM radio station call letters*]
WAYS.......	Waverley Action for Youth Services [*Australia*]
WaYSE......	Saint Elizabeth Hospital, Health Sciences Library, Yakima, WA [*Library symbol*] [*Library of Congress*] (LCLS)
Way Suppl ...	Way. Supplement [*A publication*]
WAYT	Wabash, IN [*AM radio station call letters*]
WAYV.......	Atlantic City, NJ [*FM radio station call letters*]
WAYW.......	Worcester, MA [*FM radio station call letters*]
WAYX	Waycross, GA [*AM radio station call letters*]
WAYY	Chippewa Falls, WI [*AM radio station call letters*]
WaYY	Yakima Valley College, Yakima, WA [*Library symbol*] [*Library of Congress*] (LCLS)
WaYYS......	Washington State Center for Youth Services, Yakima, WA [*Library symbol*] [*Library of Congress*] (LCLS)
WAYZ	Waynesboro, PA [*AM radio station call letters*]
WAYZ-FM ...	Waynesboro, PA [*FM radio station call letters*]
WAZE	Dawson, GA [*FM radio station call letters*]
WAZF.......	Yazoo City, MS [*AM radio station call letters*]
WAZF-FM ...	Yazoo City, MS [*FM radio station call letters*]
WAZI	Morristown, TN [*FM radio station call letters*]
WAZL........	Hazleton, PA [*AM radio station call letters*]
WAZO	Tarboro, NC [*FM radio station call letters*]
WAZQ	Orangeburg, SC [*AM radio station call letters*]
WAZR........	Woodstock, VA [*FM radio station call letters*]
WAZS.......	Summerville, SC [*AM radio station call letters*]
WAZU	Springfield, OH [*FM radio station call letters*]
WAZY-FM ...	Lafayette, IN [*FM radio station call letters*]
WB............	Wage Board [*Civil Service classification*]
WB............	Wagon Box (MSA)
W & B	Walferstan and Bristowe's Election Cases [*1859-65*] [*A publication*] (DLA)
WB............	Wall Box (ROG)
WB............	Wallboard
WB............	Warbirds of America (EA)
WB............	Warehouse Book
WB............	Wash Basin
WB............	Wash Bucket
WB............	Washable Base (ADA)
WB............	Waste Book (ROG)
WB............	Water Ballast [*Shipping*]
WB............	Water Board
W/B	Water Boiler (KSC)
WB............	Water Bottle
WB............	Water Box
WB............	Wave-Band (ADA)
WB............	Waybill [*Shipping*]
WB............	Weather Bomber [*Air Force*]
WB............	Weather Bureau [*Later, National Weather Service*] (EA)
WB............	Weatherboard (ADA)
Wb............	Weber [*Symbol*] [*SI unit of magnetic flux*]
WB............	Wechsler-Bellevue [*Psychological test*]
WB............	Wedge Biopsy [*Medicine*]
WB............	Weekly Boarding
WB............	Weekly Bulletin [*Army*] (AABC)
W/B	Weight and Balance
WB............	Weight Bearing
WB............	Weimarer Beitraege [*A publication*]
wb.............	West Berlin [*MARC country of publication code*] [*Library of Congress*] (LCCP)
WB............	Westbound
WB............	Westbridge Computer Corp. [*Toronto Stock Exchange symbol*]
WB............	Western Blot [*Blood test*]
WB............	Westminster Biographies [*A publication*]
WB............	Wet Bulb [*Thermometer, of a psychrometer*] [*Meteorology*]
WB............	Whale Boat
WB............	Wheelbarrow (MSA)
WB............	Wheelbase
WB............	Whole Blood
WB............	Whole Body [*Medicine*]
WB............	Whole Body [*Nuclear energy*] (NRCH)
WB............	Whole Bow [*Music*] (ROG)
WB............	Wideband [*Radio transmission*]
WB............	Widebeam (NATG)
WB............	Wiener Blaetter fuer die Freunde der Antike [*A publication*]
WB............	Will Be (AABC)
WB............	Winchester Word Book [*A publication*]
WB............	Wingback [*Football*]
WB............	Winner's Bitch [*Dog show term*]
W/B	Wire Bundles (MCD)
WB............	Wirebar [*Metal industry*]
WB............	Woerterbuch der Aegyptischen Sprache [*A publication*] (BJA)
WB............	Women's Bureau [*Department of Labor*]
WB............	Wood Base [*Technical drawings*]
WB............	Wood Burning [*Fireplace*] [*Classified advertising*]
WB............	Wool Back [*Knitting*]
WB............	Wool Bureau (EA)
WB............	Word Before [*Message handling*]
WB............	Work Book

WB............	Workbench (AAG)
W & B........	Works and Building Services [*British military*] (DMA)
WB............	World Bank
WB............	World Brotherhood
WB............	Worlds Beyond [*A publication*]
WB............	Worldways Canada Ltd. [*Canada*] [*ICAO designator*] (FAAC)
WB............	Wort und Brauch [*A publication*]
WB............	Write Buffer
W/B..........	Writing on Back [*Deltiology*]
WB2..........	Warramunga Array [*Australia*] [*Seismograph station code, US Geological Survey*] (SEIS)
WB3..........	Warramunga Array [*Australia*] [*Seismograph station code, US Geological Survey*] (SEIS)
WB & A	Washington, Baltimore & Annapolis Railroad [*Nickname: Wobble, Bump, and Amble*]
WBA..........	Wax Bean Agglutinin [*Biochemistry*]
WBA..........	Weekly Benefit Amount [*Unemployment insurance*]
WBA..........	Weekly of Business Aviation [*McGraw-Hill Information Services Co.*] [*Information service or system*] (CRD)
WBA..........	Western Blot Assay [*Analytical biochemistry*]
WBA..........	Wideband Amplifier
WBA..........	Wire Bundle Assembly (MCD)
WBA..........	Wollongong Buddhist Association [*Australia*]
WBA..........	Woman's Benefit Association [*Later, NABA*]
WBA..........	Works and Building, High Priority [*British*] [*World War II*]
WBA..........	World Boxing Association [*Later, WBO*] (EA)
WBA..........	World Buffalo Association Ltd. Agricultural Association (EA)
WBA..........	Worn by Astronaut [*NASA*] (KSC)
WBAA........	West Lafayette, IN [*AM radio station call letters*]
WBAB	Freeport, NY [*AM radio station call letters*]
WBAB-FM ...	Babylon, NY [*FM radio station call letters*]
WBAC	Cleveland, TN [*AM radio station call letters*]
WBAD	Leland, MS [*FM radio station call letters*]
WBAEA.....	Wholesale Beer Association Executives of America (EA)
WBAF.......	Barnesville, GA [*AM radio station call letters*]
WBAG.......	Burlington-Graham, NC [*AM radio station call letters*]
WBAI........	New York, NY [*FM radio station call letters*]
WBAI........	Wesley Bull & Associates, Incorporated [*Seattle, WA*] [*Telecommunications*] (TSSD)
WBAIS	Walworth Barbour American International School in Israel (BJA)
WBAJ.......	Blythwood, SC [*AM radio station call letters*]
WBAK	Anduki/Seria [*Brunei*] [*ICAO location identifier*] (ICLI)
WBAK-TV ...	Terre Haute, IN [*Television station call letters*]
WBAL.......	Baltimore, MD [*AM radio station call letters*]
WBAL-TV ...	Baltimore, MD [*Television station call letters*]
WBAMC ...	William Beaumont Army Medical Center (AABC)
WBAM-FM ...	Montgomery, AL [*FM radio station call letters*]
WBAN.......	Weather Bureau, Air Force, Navy [*Manuals*] [*Obsolete*]
WBANA	Wild Blueberry Association of North America (EA)
WBANK	Bank of Canada Weekly Financial Statistics [*I. P. Sharp Associates*] [*Information service or system*] (CRD)
WBAP.......	Fort Worth, TX [*AM radio station call letters*]
WBAQ	Greenville, MS [*FM radio station call letters*]
WBAR	Bartow, FL [*AM radio station call letters*]
WBAR	Wing Bar Lights [*Aviation*]
WBaraC.....	Circus World Museum, Baraboo, WI [*Library symbol*] [*Library of Congress*] (LCLS)
WBaraHi ...	Sauk County Historical Society, Baraboo, WI [*Library symbol*] [*Library of Congress*] (LCLS)
WBAS.......	Weather Bureau Airport Station [*Obsolete*]
WBAS.......	Woerterbuch der Aegyptischen Sprache [*A publication*] (BJA)
WBasR.......	Randall Consolidated School, Bassett, WI [*Library symbol*] [*Library of Congress*] (LCLS)
WBAT	Marion, IN [*AM radio station call letters*]
WBAT	Westport Bancorp, Inc. [*Westport, CT*] [*NASDAQ symbol*] (NQ)
WBAT	Wideband Adapter Transformer
WBAU.......	Garden City, NY [*FM radio station call letters*]
WBAW......	Barnwell, SC [*AM radio station call letters*]
WBAW-FM ...	Barnwell, SC [*FM radio station call letters*]
WBAWS....	Weather, Briefing, Advisory, and Warning Service (AABC)
WBAX	Wilkes-Barre, PA [*AM radio station call letters*]
WBAY-TV ...	Green Bay, WI [*Television station call letters*]
WBAZ	Southhold, NY [*FM radio station call letters*]
WBB	Beloit College, Beloit, WI [*Library symbol*] [*Library of Congress*] (LCLS)
WBB	Stebbins [*Alaska*] [*Airport symbol*] (OAG)
WBB	Stebbins, AK [*Location identifier*] [*FAA*] (FAAL)
WBB	Webb [*Del E.*] Corp. [*NYSE symbol*] (SPSG)
WBB	Wide Band Beam [*Physics*]
WBBA	Pittsfield, IL [*AM radio station call letters*]
WBBA	Western Bird Banding Association (EA)
WBBA-FM ...	Pittsfield, IL [*FM radio station call letters*]
WBBB.......	Burlington-Graham, NC [*AM radio station call letters*]
WBBC.......	Blackstone, VA [*FM radio station call letters*]
WBBC.......	[*The*] Webb Company [*NASDAQ symbol*] (NQ)
WBBD.......	Wheeling, WV [*AM radio station call letters*]
WBBE.......	Georgetown, KY [*AM radio station call letters*]
WBBF.......	Rochester, NY [*AM radio station call letters*]
WBBG.......	Youngstown, OH [*FM radio station call letters*]

WBBH-TV ...	Fort Myers, FL [*Television station call letters*]
WBBI........	Abingdon, VA [*AM radio station call letters*]
WBBJ-TV ...	Jackson, TN [*Television station call letters*]
WBBK........	Blakely, GA [*AM radio station call letters*]
WBBK-FM ...	Blakely, GA [*FM radio station call letters*]
WBBL........	Richmond, VA [*AM radio station call letters*]
WBBM	Chicago, IL [*AM radio station call letters*]
WBBM-FM ...	Chicago, IL [*FM radio station call letters*]
WBBM-TV ...	Chicago, IL [*Television station call letters*]
WBBN......	Taylorsville, MS [*FM radio station call letters*]
WBBO	Forest City, NC [*AM radio station call letters*]
WBBO-FM ...	Forest City, NC [*FM radio station call letters*]
WBBQ	Augusta, GA [*AM radio station call letters*]
WBBQ-FM ...	Augusta, GA [*FM radio station call letters*]
WBBR........	Travelers Rest, SC [*AM radio station call letters*]
WBBS.......	Great Barrington, MA [*FM radio station call letters*]
WBBT.......	Lyons, GA [*AM radio station call letters*]
WBBV.......	Vicksburg, MS [*FM radio station call letters*]
WBBW	Youngstown, OH [*AM radio station call letters*]
WBBX.......	Kingston, TN [*AM radio station call letters*]
WBBY-FM ...	Westerville, OH [*FM radio station call letters*]
WBBZ	Ponca City, OK [*AM radio station call letters*]
WBC	Bloembollencultuur [*A publication*]
WBC	Washington, DC [*Location identifier*] [*FAA*] (FAAL)
WBC	Water Binding Capacity [*Also, WHC*] [*Food industry*]
WBC	Wayland Baptist College [*Texas*]
WBC	Weather Bureau Central Office [*Obsolete*]
WBC	Weather Bureau Communications [*Obsolete*]
WBC	Welsh Books Council
WBC	Westbridge Capital Corp. [*AMEX symbol*] (SPSG)
WBC	Western Boundary Current [*Marine science*] (MSC)
WBC	Westinghouse Broadcasting Company
WBC	White Blood Cell [*or Corpuscle*] [*Medicine*]
WBC	White Blood Cell Count [*Medicine*]
WBC	Wideband Coupler
WBC	Wien Bridge Circuit [*Physics*]
WBC	Wilkes-Barre Connecting Railroad [*AAR code*]
WBC	Wilkes College Library, Wilkes-Barre, PA [*OCLC symbol*] (OCLC)
WBC	Wire Bridge Circuit
WBC	Women's Broadcasting Corporation
WBC	World Book Congress
WBC	World Boxing Council [*Information service or system*] (IID)
WBC	World Business Council [*Washington, DC*] (EA)
WBC	Wycliffe Bible Commentary [*A publication*] (BJA)
WBCA	Bay Minette, AL [*AM radio station call letters*]
WBCA	Welsh Black Cattle Association (EA)
WBCA	Women's Basketball Coaches Association (EA)
WBCA	Wyandotte Bantam Club of America (EA)
WBCB.......	Levittown-Fairless Hills, PA [*AM radio station call letters*]
WBCCI.....	Wally Byam Caravan Club International (EA)
WBCD	White Blood Cell Differential [*Hematology*]
WBCE.......	Wickliffe, KY [*AM radio station call letters*]
WBCF.......	Florence, AL [*AM radio station call letters*]
WBCG	Murfreesboro, NC [*FM radio station call letters*]
WBCH.......	Hastings, MI [*AM radio station call letters*]
WBCH-FM ...	Hastings, MI [*FM radio station call letters*]
WBCI........	Lebanon, IN [*FM radio station call letters*]
WBCK	Battle Creek, MI [*AM radio station call letters*]
WBCL........	Fort Wayne, IN [*FM radio station call letters*]
WBCM	Bay City, MI [*AM radio station call letters*]
WBCN	Boston, MA [*FM radio station call letters*]
WBCO	Bucyrus, OH [*AM radio station call letters*]
WBCO	Wallace Barnes Company
WBCO	Waveguide below Cutoff (IEEE)
WBCQ	Quakertown, PA [*AM radio station call letters*]
WBCR	Wilkes-Barre, PA [*AM radio station call letters*]
WBCR-FM ...	Beloit, WI [*FM radio station call letters*]
WBCS	Wideband Communications Subsystem
WBCT.......	Whole-Blood Clotting Time [*Hematology*]
WBCT.......	Wideband Current Transformer
WBCU	Union, SC [*AM radio station call letters*]
WBCU	Bristol, TN [*AM radio station call letters*]
WBCV	Wideband Coherent Video (IEEE)
WBCW	Jeannette, PA [*AM radio station call letters*]
WBCX	Gainesville, GA [*FM radio station call letters*]
WBD.........	Befandriana [*Madagascar*] [*Airport symbol*] (OAG)
WBD.........	Wallboard
WBD.........	Ward's Business Directory [*A publication*]
WBD.........	Washboard [*Musical instrument used in some jazz bands*]
WBD.........	Watts Bar Dam [*TVA*]
WBD.........	Wideband Data
WBD.........	Wire Bound (IEEE)
WBD.........	Worlds Beyond [*A publication*]
WBDA	Wideband Data Assembly [*Ground Communications Facility, NASA*]
WBDC	Huntingburg, IN [*FM radio station call letters*]
WBDDS.....	Weapons Bay Door Drive Subsystem [*Military*]
WBDF.......	Wideband Dicke-Fix (CET)
WBDFX.....	Wideband Dicke-Fix (MSA)
WBDG	Indianapolis, IN [*FM radio station call letters*]

WBDI .... Wideband Data Interleaver (MCD)
W & B Dig ... Walter and Bates' Ohio Digest [*A publication*] (DLA)
WBDL .... Wideband Data Line [*or Link*]
WBDNA .... Women Band Directors National Association (EA)
WBdSJ ...... Saint Joseph's Hospital, Beaver Dam, WI [*Library symbol*] [*Library of Congress*] (LCLS)
WBDX .... Trenton, GA [*FM radio station call letters*]
WBDX .... Wideband Data Switch
WBDY .... Bluefield, VA [*AM radio station call letters*]
WBDY-FM ... Bluefield, VA [*FM radio station call letters*]
WBE .... Bealanana [*Madagascar*] [*Airport symbol*] (OAG)
WBE .... Waterloo County Board of Education, Professional Education Library [*UTLAS symbol*]
WBE .... Weekblad voor Fiscaal Recht [*A publication*]
WBE .... West Bromwich [*England*] [*Seismograph station code, US Geological Survey*] [*Closed*] (SEIS)
WBE .... Whole-Body Extract [*Immunology*]
WBE .... Wideband Electronics
WBEB....... Athens, KY [*AM radio station call letters*]
WBEC....... Pittsfield, MA [*AM radio station call letters*]
WBEC-FM ... Pittsfield, MA [*FM radio station call letters*]
WBED .... Classic Corp. [*NASDAQ symbol*] (NQ)
WBEE....... Harvey, IL [*AM radio station call letters*]
WBEE-FM ... Rochester, NY [*FM radio station call letters*]
WB/EI ...... West Britain/East Ireland
WBEJ .... Elizabethton, TN [*AM radio station call letters*]
WBEL....... South Beloit, IL [*AM radio station call letters*]
WBEL....... Western Bell Communications, Inc. [*Los Angeles, CA*] [*NASDAQ symbol*] (NQ)
WBelH....... Holy Family Convent, Benet Lake, WI [*Library symbol*] [*Library of Congress*] (LCLS)
WBelSB ..... Saint Benedict's Abbey, Benet Library, Benet Lake, WI [*Library symbol*] [*Library of Congress*] (LCLS)
WBEM ...... Windber, PA [*AM radio station call letters*]
WBEN ...... Buffalo, NY [*AM radio station call letters*]
WBEP .... Wiener Beitraege zur Englischen Philologie [*A publication*]
WBer......... Berlin Public Library, Berlin, WI [*Library symbol*] [*Library of Congress*] (LCLS)
WBER....... Henrietta, NY [*FM radio station call letters*]
WBES-FM ... Dunbar, WV [*FM radio station call letters*]
WBET....... Brockton, MA [*AM radio station call letters*]
WBEU ...... Beaufort, SC [*AM radio station call letters*]
WBEV ...... Beaver Dam, WI [*AM radio station call letters*]
WBEX ...... Chillicothe, OH [*AM radio station call letters*]
WBEY....... Grasonville, MD [*FM radio station call letters*]
WBEZ....... Chicago, IL [*FM radio station call letters*]
WBF......... Wood Block Floor [*Technical drawings*]
WBF......... Workmen's Benefit Fund of the USA [*Carle Place, NY*] (EA)
WBF......... World Bridge Federation
WBFA....... Western Bohemian Fraternal Association [*Later, WFLA*] (EA)
WBFC....... Kota Kinabalu [*Malaysia*] [*ICAO location identifier*] (ICLI)
WBFC....... Stanton, KY [*AM radio station call letters*]
WBFD....... Bedford, PA [*AM radio station call letters*]
WBFF .... Baltimore, MD [*Television station call letters*]
WBFG .... Effingham, IL [*FM radio station call letters*]
WBFH ...... Bloomfield Hills, MI [*FM radio station call letters*]
WBFI .... McDaniels, KY [*FM radio station call letters*]
WBFI .... Wild Bird Feeding Institute (EA)
WBFJ .... Winston-Salem, NC [*AM radio station call letters*]
WBFL....... Bellows Falls, VT [*FM radio station call letters*]
WBFM...... Seneca, SC [*FM radio station call letters*]
WBFM...... Wideband Frequency Modulation
WBFN ...... Quitman, MS [*AM radio station call letters*]
WBFO ...... Buffalo, NY [*FM radio station call letters*]
WBFP .... Wood-Burning Fireplace [*Classified advertising*]
WBFR....... Birmingham, AL [*FM radio station call letters*]
WBFS-TV ... Miami, FL [*Television station call letters*]
WBFX....... Grand Marais, MN [*FM radio station call letters*]
WBG......... Webbing
WBGA ...... Long Atip [*Malaysia*] [*ICAO location identifier*] (ICLI)
WBGA ...... Waycross, GA [*FM radio station call letters*]
WBGB ...... Bintulu [*Malaysia*] [*ICAO location identifier*] (ICLI)
WBGB ...... Mount Dora, FL [*AM radio station call letters*]
WBGC ...... Belaga [*Malaysia*] [*ICAO location identifier*] (ICLI)
WBGC ...... Chipley, FL [*AM radio station call letters*]
WBGD....... Brick Township, NJ [*FM radio station call letters*]
WBGD....... Long Semado [*Malaysia*] [*ICAO location identifier*] (ICLI)
WBGE ...... Long Geng [*Malaysia*] [*ICAO location identifier*] (ICLI)
WBGF....... Belle Glade, FL [*FM radio station call letters*]
WBGF....... Wholesale Buyers' Gifts Fair [*British*] (ITD)
WBGG ...... Kuching [*Malaysia*] [*ICAO location identifier*] (ICLI)
WBGJ....... Limbang [*Malaysia*] [*ICAO location identifier*] (ICLI)
WBGK ...... Mukah [*Malaysia*] [*ICAO location identifier*] (ICLI)
WBGL ...... Champaign, IL [*FM radio station call letters*]
WBGL ...... Long Akah [*Indonesia*] [*ICAO location identifier*] (ICLI)
WBGM...... Marudi [*Indonesia*] [*ICAO location identifier*] (ICLI)
WBGM...... Tallahassee, FL [*AM radio station call letters*]
WBGM-FM ... Tallahassee, FL [*FM radio station call letters*]
WBGN...... Bowling Green, KY [*AM radio station call letters*]
WBGN....... Sematan [*Indonesia*] [*ICAO location identifier*] (ICLI)
WBGO....... Lio Matu [*Malaysia*] [*ICAO location identifier*] (ICLI)

WBGO....... Newark, NJ [*FM radio station call letters*]
WBGP ...... Kapit [*Indonesia*] [*ICAO location identifier*] (ICLI)
WBGP ...... Waterborne Guard Post (NVT)
WBGQ....... Bakelalan [*Malaysia*] [*ICAO location identifier*] (ICLI)
WBGR ...... Baltimore, MD [*AM radio station call letters*]
WBGR ...... Miri [*Indonesia*] [*ICAO location identifier*] (ICLI)
WBGS....... Sibu [*Malaysia*] [*ICAO location identifier*] (ICLI)
WBGT ...... Wet Bulb Globe Temperature
WBGT ...... Wet Bulb Globe Thermometer
WBGTI...... Wet Bulb Globe Temperature Index (RDA)
WBGU....... Bowling Green, OH [*FM radio station call letters*]
WBGU-TV ... Bowling Green, OH [*Television station call letters*]
WBGW...... Fort Branch, IN [*FM radio station call letters*]
WBGW...... Lawas [*Malaysia*] [*ICAO location identifier*] (ICLI)
WBGY ...... Simanggang [*Malaysia*] [*ICAO location identifier*] (ICLI)
WBGZ ...... Alton, IL [*AM radio station call letters*]
WBGZ ...... Bario [*Malaysia*] [*ICAO location identifier*] (ICLI)
WBHA....... Hot Springs, VA [*FM radio station call letters*]
WBHB...... Fitzgerald, GA [*AM radio station call letters*]
WBHC....... Hampton, SC [*AM radio station call letters*]
WBHC-FM ... Hampton, SC [*FM radio station call letters*]
WBHF....... Cartersville, GA [*AM radio station call letters*]
WBHH ...... Parris Island, SC [*FM radio station call letters*]
WBHI .... Chicago, IL [*FM radio station call letters*]
WBHL....... Florence, AL [*FM radio station call letters*]
WBHM...... Birmingham, AL [*FM radio station call letters*]
WBHN...... Bryson City, NC [*AM radio station call letters*]
WBHO ...... Weather Bureau Hurricane Forecast Office [*Obsolete*]
WBHP ...... Huntsville, AL [*AM radio station call letters*]
WBHQ....... Bloomfield, IN [*FM radio station call letters*]
WBHR....... Bellaire, OH [*FM radio station call letters*]
WBHS ...... Brunswick, ME [*FM radio station call letters*]
WBHS ...... Tampa, FL [*Television station call letters*]
WBHT ...... Brownsville, TN [*AM radio station call letters*]
WBHV ...... State College, PA [*FM radio station call letters*]
WBHY ...... Mobile, AL [*AM radio station call letters*]
WBI .... Ward Behavior Inventory [*Psychology*]
WBI .... Washington Beverage Insight [*Wells & Associates*] [*Information service or system*] (IID)
WBI .... Westburne International Industries Ltd. [*AMEX symbol*] [*Toronto Stock Exchange symbol*] (SPSG)
WBI .... Whiskey Butte [*Idaho*] [*Seismograph station code, US Geological Survey*] [*Closed*] (SEIS)
WBI .... Will Be Issued
WBI .... Wooden Box Institute [*Defunct*] (EA)
WBIB........ Centreville, AL [*AM radio station call letters*]
WBIC........ Royston, GA [*FM radio station call letters*]
WBIF........ Wideband Intermediate Frequency (MCD)
WBIG .... Gastonia, NC [*AM radio station call letters*]
WBII......... Washington Business Information, Incorporated [*Information service or system*] (IID)
WBII......... Watertown, WI [*FM radio station call letters*]
WBII......... Whirley Ball International [*NASDAQ symbol*] (NQ)
WBIL........ Tuskegee, AL [*AM radio station call letters*]
WBIL-FM ... Tuskegee, AL [*FM radio station call letters*]
WBIM-FM ... Bridgewater, MA [*FM radio station call letters*]
WBIN .... Benton, TN [*AM radio station call letters*]
WBIP........ Booneville, MS [*AM radio station call letters*]
WBIP.:...... Whitaker's Books in Print [*J. Whitaker & Sons Ltd.*] [*Information service or system*] (IID)
WBIP-FM ... Booneville, MS [*FM radio station call letters*]
WBIQ .... Birmingham, AL [*Television station call letters*]
WBIR-TV ... Knoxville, TN [*Television station call letters*]
WBIS........ Bristol, CT [*AM radio station call letters*]
WBIT........ Adel, GA [*AM radio station call letters*]
WBIU........ Denham Springs, LA [*AM radio station call letters*]
WBIV........ Natick, MA [*AM radio station call letters*]
WBIW ...... Bedford, IN [*AM radio station call letters*]
WBIZ........ Eau Claire, WI [*FM radio station call letters*]
WBJA........ Guayama, PR [*AM radio station call letters*]
WBJB-FM ... Lincroft, NJ [*FM radio station call letters*]
WBJC....... Baltimore, MD [*FM radio station call letters*]
WBJY .... Shadyside, OH [*FM radio station call letters*]
WBJZ .... Olean, NY [*FM radio station call letters*]
WBK .... Webb & Knapp (Canada) Ltd. [*Vancouver Stock Exchange symbol*]
WBK .... Western Banker [*A publication*]
WBK .... Westpac Banking ADS [*NYSE symbol*] (SPSG)
WBKA ...... Semporna [*Malaysia*] [*ICAO location identifier*] (ICLI)
WBKB-TV ... Alpena, MI [*Television station call letters*]
WBKC....... Painesville, OH [*AM radio station call letters*]
WBKD....... Lahad Datu [*Malaysia*] [*ICAO location identifier*] (ICLI)
WBKE-FM ... North Manchester, IN [*FM radio station call letters*]
WBKG ...... Keningau [*Malaysia*] [*ICAO location identifier*] (ICLI)
WBKH ...... Hattiesburg, MS [*AM radio station call letters*]
WBKI........ Bremen, GA [*AM radio station call letters*]
WBKJ .... Kosciusko, MS [*FM radio station call letters*]
WBKK ...... Kota Kinabalu [*Malaysia*] [*ICAO location identifier*] (ICLI)
WBKL....... Labuan [*Malaysia*] [*ICAO location identifier*] (ICLI)
WBKL........ Wiener Beitraege zur Kulturgeschichte und Linguistik [*A publication*]

WBKN...... Brookhaven, MS [*FM radio station call letters*]
WBKO...... Bowling Green, KY [*Television station call letters*]
WBKP....... Pamol [*Malaysia*] [*ICAO location identifier*]   (ICLI)
WBKQ...... Van Buren, ME [*FM radio station call letters*]
WBKR...... Owensboro, KY [*FM radio station call letters*]
WBKR....... Ranau [*Malaysia*] [*ICAO location identifier*]   (ICLI)
WBKS........ Sandakan [*Malaysia*] [*ICAO location identifier*]   (ICLI)
WBKT....... Brockport, NY [*FM radio station call letters*]
WBKT....... Kudat [*Malaysia*] [*ICAO location identifier*]   (ICLI)
WBKV...... West Bend, WI [*AM radio station call letters*]
WBKW...... Beckley, WV [*FM radio station call letters*]
WBKW...... Tawau [*Malaysia*] [*ICAO location identifier*]   (ICLI)
WBKZ ...... Athens, GA [*AM radio station call letters*]
W Bl.......... [*Sir William*] Blackstone's English King's Bench Reports [*1746-80*] [*A publication*]   (DLA)
WBL .... Weak Black Liquor [*Pulp and paper technology*]
WBL .... Western Biological Laboratories
WBL .... White Bluff [*Washington*] [*Seismograph station code, US Geological Survey*]   (SEIS)
WBL .... Wideband LASER
WBL .... Wideband Limiting   (IEEE)
WBL .... Women's Basketball League [*Defunct*]   (EA)
WBL .... Wood Blocking
W Bla........ [*Sir William*] Blackstone's English King's Bench Reports [*1746-80*] [*A publication*]   (DLA)
WBLA...... Elizabethtown, NC [*AM radio station call letters*]
W Black ..... [*Sir William*] Blackstone's English King's Bench Reports [*1746-80*] [*A publication*]   (ILCA)
WBLB....... Pulaski, VA [*AM radio station call letters*]
WBLC....... Lenoir City, TN [*AM radio station call letters*]
WBLC....... Water-Borne Logistics Craft
WBLD ...... Orchard Lake, MI [*AM radio station call letters*]
WBLE ...... Batesville, MS [*FM radio station call letters*]
W Bl (Eng) ... [*Sir William*] Blackstone's English King's Bench Reports [*1746-80*] [*A publication*]   (DLA)
WBLF....... Bellefonte, PA [*AM radio station call letters*]
Wbl voor Fiscaal Recht ... Weekblad voor Fiscaal Recht [*A publication*]
WBLG ...... Smiths Grove, KY [*FM radio station call letters*]
WBLI........ Patchogue, NY [*FM radio station call letters*]
WBLJ .... Dalton, GA [*AM radio station call letters*]
WBLK ...... Depew, NY [*FM radio station call letters*]
WBLL....... Bellefontaine, OH [*AM radio station call letters*]
WBLM...... Lewiston, ME [*FM radio station call letters*]
WBLO ...... Weak Black Liquor Oxidation [*Pulp and paper technology*]
WBLQ ...... Block Island, RI [*FM radio station call letters*]
WBLR....... Batesburg, SC [*AM radio station call letters*]
WBLS........ New York, NY [*AM radio station call letters*]
WBLT....... Bedford, VA [*AM radio station call letters*]
WBLV....... Twin Lake, MI [*FM radio station call letters*]
WBLW ...... Royston, GA [*AM radio station call letters*]
WBLX....... Mobile, AL [*AM radio station call letters*]
WBLX-FM ... Mobile, AL [*FM radio station call letters*]
WBLY....... Springfield, OH [*AM radio station call letters*]
WBLZ....... Hamilton, OH [*AM radio station call letters*]
WBM......... Beloit Memorial Hospital, Beloit, WI [*Library symbol*] [*Library of Congress*]   (LCLS)
WBM........ Wapenamanda [*Papua New Guinea*] [*Airport symbol*]   (OAG)
W B M .... Weber Meter
WBM........ Woerterbuch der Mythologie [*A publication*]   (BJA)
WBM........ Women's Board of Missions
WBMA...... Dedham, MA [*AM radio station call letters*]
WBMA...... Western Building Material Association   (EA)
WBMA...... Whirlpool Bath Manufacturers Association [*Glen Ellyn, IL*]   (EA)
WBMA...... Wirebound Box Manufacturers Association   (EA)
WBMB...... West Branch, MI [*AM radio station call letters*]
WBMC...... McMinnville, TN [*AM radio station call letters*]
WBMC...... Weight before Mars Capture [*NASA*]
WBMCR... Wideband Multichannel Receiver
WBMD...... Baltimore, MD [*AM radio station call letters*]
WBME...... Belfast, ME [*AM radio station call letters*]
WBMG...... Birmingham, AL [*Television station call letters*]
WBMG...... Walter Bernard and Milton Glaser [*Founders of the magazine-design firm that bears their initials*]
WBMI ...... West Branch, MI [*FM radio station call letters*]
WBMI ...... Women's Board of Missions of the Interior
WBMJ ...... San Juan, PR [*AM radio station call letters*]
WBML ...... Macon, GA [*AM radio station call letters*]
WBMO...... Weather Bureau Meteorological Observation Station [*Obsolete*]
WBMQ...... Savannah, GA [*AM radio station call letters*]
WBMR...... Telford, PA [*FM radio station call letters*]
WBMS....... Wilmington, NC [*AM radio station call letters*]
WBMS....... World Bureau of Metal Statistics [*London, England*]   (EAIO)
WBMT...... Boxford, MA [*FM radio station call letters*]
WBMW..... Wethersfield Township, NY [*FM radio station call letters*]
WBMX...... Zeeland, MI [*AM radio station call letters*]
WbMyth .... Woerterbuch der Mythologie [*A publication*]   (BJA)
WBN......... Waban, Inc. [*NYSE symbol*]   (SPSG)
WBN......... Weekly Book Newsletter [*A publication*]
WBN......... Well Behaved Net
WBN......... West by North

W Bn .... White Beacon
WBN......... Wolfenbuetteler Barock-Nachrichten [*A publication*]
WBNA...... Louisville, KY [*Television station call letters*]
WBNB-TV ... Charlotte Amalie, VI [*Television station call letters*]
WBNC....... Conway, NH [*AM radio station call letters*]
WBNC....... Washington Bancorp, Inc. [*NASDAQ symbol*]   (NQ)
WBND...... Pensacola Beach, FL [*AM radio station call letters*]
WBND...... Westbound   (FAAC)
W BNDR ... With Binder [*Freight*]
WBNE....... Benton, PA [*FM radio station call letters*]
WBNG-TV ... Binghamton, NY [*Television station call letters*]
WBNH....... Pekin, IL [*FM radio station call letters*]
WBNI .... Fort Wayne, IN [*FM radio station call letters*]
WBNJ .... Cape May Court House, NJ [*FM radio station call letters*]
WBNL ...... Boonville, IN [*AM radio station call letters*]
WBNL ...... Wideband Noise Limiting
WBNL-FM ... Boonville, IN [*FM radio station call letters*]
WBNN ...... Union City, IN [*AM radio station call letters*]
WBNO-FM ... Bryan, OH [*FM radio station call letters*]
WBNP ...... Watts Bar Nuclear Plant   (NRCH)
WBNP ...... Wood Buffalo National Park. Newsletter [*A publication*]
WBNQ ...... Bloomington, IL [*FM radio station call letters*]
WBNR ...... Beacon, NY [*AM radio station call letters*]
WBNS ..... Columbus, OH [*AM radio station call letters*]
WBNS ..... Water Boiler Neutron Source Reactor [*Nuclear energy*]
WBNS-FM ... Columbus, OH [*FM radio station call letters*]
WBNS-TV ... Columbus, OH [*Television station call letters*]
WBNT-FM ... Oneida, TN [*FM radio station call letters*]
· WBNV....... Barnesville, OH [*FM radio station call letters*]
WBNV....... Wideband Noise Voltage
WB/NWRC ... Weather Bureau/National Weather Records Center [*Obsolete*]   (KSC)
WBNX-TV ... Akron, OH [*Television station call letters*]
WBNY ...... Buffalo, NY [*FM radio station call letters*]
WBNZ...... Frankfort, MI [*FM radio station call letters*]
WBO........ Beroroha [*Madagascar*] [*Airport symbol*]   (OAG)
WBO........ Weather Bureau Office [*Later, National Weather Service*]
WBO......... Wideband Oscilloscope
WBO......... Wideband Overlap
WBO......... Wien Bridge Oscillator [*Physics*]
W/BO .... With Blowout   (MSA)
WBO......... World Boxing Organization   (EA)
WBOB ...... Galax, VA [*AM radio station call letters*]
WBOC-TV ... Salisbury, MD [*Television station call letters*]
WBOD....... Canton, IL [*FM radio station call letters*]
WBOD....... Waste Biochemical Oxygen Demand [*Oceanography*]
WBOK ...... New Orleans, LA [*AM radio station call letters*]
WBOL ...... Bolivar, TN [*AM radio station call letters*]
WBOLA .... Wasser, Boden, Luft [*A publication*]
WBOP ...... Pensacola, FL [*AM radio station call letters*]
WBOQ ...... Gloucester, MA [*FM radio station call letters*]
WBOR...... Brunswick, ME [*FM radio station call letters*]
W/BOR ..... White Border [*Deltiology*]
WBOS ...... Brookline, MA [*FM radio station call letters*]
WBOW ..... Terre Haute, IN [*AM radio station call letters*]
WBOX...... Bogalusa, LA [*AM radio station call letters*]
WBOX-FM ... Varnado, LA [*FM radio station call letters*]
WBOY-TV ... Clarksburg, WV [*Television station call letters*]
WBOZ...... Sabana Grande, PR [*AM radio station call letters*]
WBOZ-FM ... Hormigueros, PR [*FM radio station call letters*]
WBP .... Wartime Basic Plan
WBP .... Water Bank Program [*Department of Agriculture*]
WBP .... Water Binding Potential [*of protein*]
WBP .... Weather- and Boil-Proof   (IEEE)
WBP .... Woodwind World - Brass and Percussion [*A publication*]
WBPA....... Elkhorn City, KY [*AM radio station call letters*]
WBPH-TV ... Bethlehem, PA [*Television station call letters*]
WBPK....... Flemingsburg, KY [*FM radio station call letters*]
WBPM ...... Kingston, NY [*FM radio station call letters*]
WBPR....... Georgetown, SC [*FM radio station call letters*]
W v B Pr... Wetboek van Burgerlijk Procesrecht [*A publication*]
WBPS....... Winder, GA [*FM radio station call letters*]
WBPT....... Naples, FL [*FM radio station call letters*]
WBPTT .... Whole Blood Partial Thromboplastin Time [*Hematology*]
WBPV....... Charlton, MA [*FM radio station call letters*]
WBPZ....... Lock Haven, PA [*AM radio station call letters*]
WBQ......... Beaver [*Alaska*] [*Airport symbol*]   (OAG)
WBQ......... Beaver, AK [*Location identifier*] [*FAA*]   (FAAL)
WBQB ...... Fredricksburg, VA [*FM radio station call letters*]
WBQM...... Decatur, AL [*FM radio station call letters*]
WBQN...... Barceloneta, PR [*AM radio station call letters*]
WBQR ...... Attica, IN [*FM radio station call letters*]
WBR......... Water Boiler Reactor
WBR......... Westbank Resources, Inc. [*Vancouver Stock Exchange symbol*]
WBR......... Wetboek van Burgerlijke Regtsvordering [*Code of Civil Procedure*] [*Dutch*]   (ILCA)
WBR......... Whole Body Radiation
WBR......... Wideband Data Recorder
WBR......... Wideband Receiver
WBR......... Word Buffer Register   (MSA)
WBR......... Workbench Rack   (MCD)

WBRA-TV ... Roanoke, VA [*Television station call letters*]
WBRB........ Mount Clemens, MI [*AM radio station call letters*]
WBRBN .... Will Be Reported by NOTAM [*Notice to Airmen*]　(FAAC)
WBRC .... Walter Bagehot Research Council on National
　　　　　　Sovereignty　(EA)
WBRC-TV ... Birmingham, AL [*Television station call letters*]
WBRD .... Palmetto, FL [*AM radio station call letters*]
WBRD .... Wallboard
WBrE......... Elmbrook Memorial Hospital, Brookfield, WI [*Library symbol*]
　　　　　　[*Library of Congress*]　(LCLS)
WBRE-TV ... Wilkes-Barre, PA [*Television station call letters*]
WBRF........ Galax, VA [*FM radio station call letters*]
WBRG .... Lynchburg, VA [*AM radio station call letters*]
W/BRG...... Wheel Bearing [*Automotive engineering*]
WBRH........ Baton Rouge, LA [*FM radio station call letters*]
WBRH .... Weather Bureau Regional Headquarters [*Obsolete*]　(FAAC)
WBRI........ Indianapolis, IN [*AM radio station call letters*]
WBrI......... International Foundation of Employee Benefit Plans,
　　　　　　Information Center, Brookfield, WI [*Library symbol*]
　　　　　　[*Library of Congress*]　(LCLS)
WBRJ .... Marietta, OH [*AM radio station call letters*]
WBRK .... Pittsfield, MA [*AM radio station call letters*]
WBRL .... Berlin, NH [*AM radio station call letters*]
WBRM ...... Marion, NC [*AM radio station call letters*]
WBRN .... Big Rapids, MI [*AM radio station call letters*]
WBRN-FM ... Big Rapids, MI [*FM radio station call letters*]
WBro.......... Brodhead Memorial Public Library, Brodhead, WI [*Library
　　　　　　symbol*] [*Library of Congress*]　(LCLS)
WBRO....... Waynesboro, GA [*AM radio station call letters*]
WBRO .... Weather Bureau Regional Office [*Obsolete*]
W BRO ...... Worshipful Brother [*Freemasonry*]
WBRQ........ Cidra, PR [*FM radio station call letters*]
WBRR .... Bradford, PA [*FM radio station call letters*]
WBRR .... Weather Bureau RADAR Remote [*Meteorology*]
WBRS........ Waltham, MA [*FM radio station call letters*]
WBRS........ Wideband Remote Switch　(IEEE)
WBRS........ Wrought Brass　(MSA)
WBRT........ Bardstown, KY [*AM radio station call letters*]
WBRT........ Weather Bureau Radiotheolite [*Meteorology*]
WBRT........ Whole-Blood Recalcification Time [*Hematology*]
WBRU........ Providence, RI [*FM radio station call letters*]
WBRV .... Boonville, NY [*AM radio station call letters*]
WBRV-FM ... Boonville, NY [*FM radio station call letters*]
WBRW ...... Bridgewater, NJ [*AM radio station call letters*]
WBRY .... Woodbury, TN [*AM radio station call letters*]
WBRZ........ Baton Rouge, LA [*Television station call letters*]
WBS.......... Wage Board Staff
WB-S .... Wage Board, Supervisor [*Civil Service classification*]
WBS.......... Wallace Barnes Steel [*Wallace Barnes Co.*]
WBS.......... Warenbegleitschein [*Bill of Lading*] [*German*] [*Shipping*]
WBS.......... Washington Bibliographic Service [*Information service or
　　　　　　system*]　(IID)
WBS.......... Waterloo County Board of Education [*UTLAS symbol*]
WBS.......... Weight and Balance System　(MCD)
WBS.......... Welsh Bibliographical Society [*British*]
WBS.......... West by South
WBS.......... Western Base Section [*England*] [*World War II*]
WBS.......... Western Conservative Baptist Theological Seminary, Portland,
　　　　　　OR [*OCLC symbol*]　(OCLC)
WBS.......... Whole Blood Serotonin [*Biochemistry*]
WBS.......... Whole Body Shower
WBS.......... Wideband System [*Ground Communications Facility, NASA*]
WBS.......... Without Benefit of Salvage
WBS.......... Work Breakdown Sheets [*Army*]
WBS.......... Work Breakdown Structure [*Army*]
WBS.......... Work Breakdown Structure [*Data processing*]
WBSA....... Boaz, AL [*AM radio station call letters*]
WBSA........ Weather Bureau Synoptic and Aviation Reporting Station
　　　　　　[*Obsolete*]
WBSA........ Westlands Diversified Bancorp [*NASDAQ symbol*]　(NQ)
WBSB....... Baltimore, MD [*FM radio station call letters*]
WBSB........ Brunei/International [*Brunei*] [*ICAO location
　　　　　　identifier*]　(ICLI)
WBSC....... Bennettsville, SC [*AM radio station call letters*]
WBSC........ Wideband Signal Conditioner　(NASA)
WBSC........ Work Breakdown Structure Code　(MCD)
WBSCB...... Work Breakdown Structure Control Board [*Army*]　(AABC)
WBSD....... Burlington, WI [*FM radio station call letters*]
WBSF........ Melbourne, FL [*Television station call letters*]
WBSG-TV ... Brunswick, GA [*Television station call letters*]
WBSH .... Heflin, AL [*AM radio station call letters*]
WBSI........ Western Behavioral Sciences Institute　(EA)
WBSIGSTA ... Weather Bureau Signal Station [*Obsolete*]
WBSJ .... Ellisville, MS [*FM radio station call letters*]
WBSK........ Portsmouth, VA [*AM radio station call letters*]
WBSL........ Wide Beam Special LASER　(MCD)
WBSL-FM ... Sheffield, MA [*FM radio station call letters*]
WBSM........ New Bedford, MA [*AM radio station call letters*]
WBSM-FM ... Fairhaven, MA [*FM radio station call letters*]
WBSN-FM ... New Orleans, LA [*FM radio station call letters*]
WBSO .... Clinton, MA [*AM radio station call letters*]

WBSP........ Western Beet Sugar Producers [*Defunct*]
WBSR........ Pensacola, FL [*AM radio station call letters*]
WBSS-FM ... Millville, NJ [*FM radio station call letters*]
WBST........ Muncie, IN [*FM radio station call letters*]
WBST........ Webster Financial Corp. [*Waterbury, CT*] [*NASDAQ
　　　　　　symbol*]　(NQ)
WBSU .... Brockport, NY [*FM radio station call letters*]
WBSV-TV ... Venice, FL [*Television station call letters*]
WBSX........ Ann Arbor, MI [*Television station call letters*]
WBT .... Charlotte, NC [*AM radio station call letters*]
WBT .... Wet Bulb Temperature
WBT .... Wichita Board of Trade [*Defunct*]　(EA)
WBT .... Wideband Terminal　(MCD)
WBT .... Wideband Transformer [*or Transmitter*]
WBT .... Women in Broadcast Technology　(EA)
WBT .... Wycliffe Bible Translators　(EA)
WBTA .... Batavia, NY [*AM radio station call letters*]
WBTA .... Wisconsin Board of Tax Appeals Decisions [*A
　　　　　　publication*]　(DLA)
WBTA-CCH Tax Reporter ... Wisconsin Board of Tax Appeals Decisions
　　　　　　(Commerce Clearing House) [*A publication*]　(DLA)
WBTB........ Beaufort, NC [*AM radio station call letters*]
WBTC........ Uhrichsville, OH [*AM radio station call letters*]
WBTC........ Waterways Bulk Transportation Council　(EA)
WBTE........ Weapon Battery Terminal Equipment [*Air Force*]
WBTE........ Windsor, NC [*AM radio station call letters*]
WBTF........ Attica, NY [*FM radio station call letters*]
WBTF........ Wrightsville Beach Test Facility [*Department of the
　　　　　　Interior*]　(NOAA)
WBT-FM... Charlotte, NC [*FM radio station call letters*]
WBTG .... Sheffield, AL [*AM radio station call letters*]
WBTG-FM ... Sheffield, AL [*FM radio station call letters*]
WBTH........ Williamson, WV [*AM radio station call letters*]
WBTI......... Taylor, MI [*AM radio station call letters*]
WBTM ...... Danville, VA [*AM radio station call letters*]
WBTM HYDRO ... Weather Bureau Technical Memorandum: Hydrology
　　　　　　[*Office of Hydrology*] [*Washington, DC*] [*A publication*]
WBTN .... Bennington, VT [*AM radio station call letters*]
WBTO .... Linton, IN [*AM radio station call letters*]
WBTQ .... Buckhannon, WV [*FM radio station call letters*]
WBTR-FM ... Carrollton, GA [*FM radio station call letters*]
WBTS........ Bridgeport, AL [*AM radio station call letters*]
WBTS........ Waco, Beaumont, Trinity & Sabine Railway Co. [*AAR code*]
WBTS........ Whereabouts　(FAAC)
WBTS........ Wideband Transmission System　(KSC)
WBTU .... Kendallville, IN [*FM radio station call letters*]
WBTV........ Charlotte, NC [*Television station call letters*]
WBTV........ Weather Briefing Television　(AFM)
WBTW ...... Florence, SC [*Television station call letters*]
WBTX........ Broadway-Timberville, VA [*AM radio station call letters*]
WBTY .... Homerville, GA [*FM radio station call letters*]
WBU .... Boulder [*Colorado*] [*Airport symbol*]　(OAG)
WBU .... Welsh Badminton Union　(EAIO)
WBU .... Wilberforce University, Wilberforce, OH [*OCLC
　　　　　　symbol*]　(OCLC)
WBU .... World Billiards Union　(EAIO)
WBU .... World Blind Union　(EA)
WBUC ...... Buckhannon, WV [*AM radio station call letters*]
WBUC ...... Western Boundary Undercurrent [*Atlantic Ocean*]
WBUC-FM ... Buckhannon, WV [*FM radio station call letters*]
WBUD....... Trenton, NJ [*AM radio station call letters*]
WBUF .... Buffalo, NY [*FM radio station call letters*]
WBUL .... Fort Knox, KY [*AM radio station call letters*]
WBUQ ...... Bloomsburg, PA [*FM radio station call letters*]
WBUR ...... Boston, MA [*FM radio station call letters*]
WBur .... Burlington Public Library, Burlington, WI [*Library symbol*]
　　　　　　[*Library of Congress*]　(LCLS)
WBurSFC ... Saint Francis College, Burlington, WI [*Library symbol*] [*Library
　　　　　　of Congress*] [*Obsolete*]　(LCLS)
WBURY .... Westbury [*England*]
WBUS .... Kankakee, IL [*FM radio station call letters*]
WBUT .... Butler, PA [*AM radio station call letters*]
WBUU....... Indianapolis, IN [*Television station call letters*]
WBUX .... Doylestown, PA [*AM radio station call letters*]
WBUY ...... Holly Springs, MS [*Television station call letters*]
WBUZ .... Fredonia, NY [*AM radio station call letters*]
WBV .... Wideband Voltage
WBV .... Woningraad. Informatiekrant voor Woningcorporaties [*A
　　　　　　publication*]
WBVCO..... Wideband Voltage-Controlled Oscillator
WBVCXO... Wideband Voltage-Controlled Crystal Oscillator
WBVE........ Hamilton, OH [*FM radio station call letters*]
WBVI........ Fostoria, OH [*FM radio station call letters*]
WBVM ...... Tampa, FL [*FM radio station call letters*]
WBVN .... Carrier Mills, IL [*FM radio station call letters*]
WBVP....... Beaver Falls, PA [*AM radio station call letters*]
WBVR .... Russellville, KY [*FM radio station call letters*]
WBVRC..... West Bromwich Volunteer Rifle Corps [*British
　　　　　　military*]　(DMA)
WBVTR..... Wideband Video Tape Recorder
WBW .... Wilkes-Barre, PA [*Location identifier*] [*FAA*]　(FAAL)

WBW .... Wilson Butte [*Washington*] [*Seismograph station code, US Geological Survey*] (SEIS)
WBW .... World Bowling Writers (EA)
WBW .... World Business Weekly [*A publication*]
WBWA ..... Washburn, WI [*FM radio station call letters*]
WBWB ...... Bloomington, IN [*FM radio station call letters*]
WBWC ...... Berea, OH [*FM radio station call letters*]
WBWI-FM ... West Bend, WI [*FM radio station call letters*]
WBWT ...... Wright Brothers Memorial Wind Tunnel [*Massachusetts Institute of Technology*] [*Research center*] (RCD)
WBX .... Wooden Box (MSA)
WBXB .... Edenton, NC [*FM radio station call letters*]
WBXL .... Baldwinsville, NY [*FM radio station call letters*]
WBXQ .... Cresson, PA [*FM radio station call letters*]
WBXT .... Canton, OH [*AM radio station call letters*]
WBXX .... Battle Creek, MI [*FM radio station call letters*]
WBY .... Wimberly Resources [*Vancouver Stock Exchange symbol*]
WBYB........ Brewer, ME [*AM radio station call letters*]
WBYE .... Calera, AL [*AM radio station call letters*]
WBYF .... Bay City, MI [*FM radio station call letters*]
WBYQ .... Baltimore, MD [*FM radio station call letters*]
WBYR .... Van Wert, OH [*FM radio station call letters*]
WBYS .... Canton, IL [*AM radio station call letters*]
WBYS-FM ... Canton, IL [*FM radio station call letters*]
WBYU .... New Orleans, LA [*AM radio station call letters*]
WBYY .... Atlantic Beach, NC [*AM radio station call letters*]
WBYZ .... Baxley, GA [*FM radio station call letters*]
WBZ .... Boston, MA [*AM radio station call letters*]
WBZ .... Wadati-Benioff Zone [*Geology*]
WBZ .... Works and Building, Low Priority [*British*] [*World War II*]
WBZA .... Glens Falls, NY [*AM radio station call letters*]
WBZB........ Selma, NC [*AM radio station call letters*]
WBZD........ Cadiz, KY [*FM radio station call letters*]
WBZI .... Xenia, OH [*AM radio station call letters*]
WBZK .... York, SC [*AM radio station call letters*]
WBZL .... Brazil, IN [*AM radio station call letters*]
WBZM .... Chillicothe, IL [*FM radio station call letters*]
WBZN .... Racine, WI [*AM radio station call letters*]
WBZN-FM ... Racine, WI [*FM radio station call letters*]
WBZQ .... Greenville, NC [*AM radio station call letters*]
WBZR........ Destin, FL [*AM radio station call letters*]
WBZS........ Eatonville, FL [*AM radio station call letters*]
WBZ-TV..... Boston, MA [*Television station call letters*]
WBZW .... Loudonville, OH [*FM radio station call letters*]
WBZY........ New Castle, PA [*AM radio station call letters*]
WBZZ........ Pittsburgh, PA [*FM radio station call letters*]
WC............. Cudahy Public Library, Cudahy, WI [*Library symbol*] [*Library of Congress*] (LCLS)
WC............. Wage Change
WC............. Wages Council [*British*] (DCTA)
W/C .... Waiver of Coinsurance [*Fire contract clause*]
WC............. Walkways Center (EA)
WC............. Walnut Council (EA)
WC............. War Cabinet [*World War II*]
WC............. War College
WC............. War Communications
WC............. Ward Clerk [*Medicine*]
WC............. Watch Commanders
WC............. Watch Committee [*British*] (ILCA)
WC............. Water Closet [*A toilet*]
WC............. Water Cock (ROG)
WC............. Water Column [*Mechanical engineering*]
WC............. Water Content
WC............. Water-Cooled (DEN)
WC............. Waterfront Center (EA)
W/C .... Watts per Candle [*Electricity*]
W/C .... Wave Change
WC............. WCN Investment [*Vancouver Stock Exchange symbol*]
WC............. We Care (EA)
WC............. Weapon Carrier
WC............. Weapons Command [*Later, Armaments Command*] [*Army*]
WC............. Weapons Control [*or Controller*] (NVT)
WC............. Weather Condition [*Nuclear energy*] (NRCH)
W/C .... Week Commencing (ADA)
WC............. Weiman Company, Inc. [*AMEX symbol*] (SPSG)
WC............. Wesleyan Chapel (ROG)
WC............. West Central [*Refers especially to London postal district*]
WC............. West Coast Airlines, Inc.
WC............. Westbeth Corporation (EA)
WC............. Western Cedar [*Utility pole*] [*Telecommunications*] (TEL)
WC............. Western Central
WC............. Western Classification
WC............. Western Command
WC............. Westminster College [*London, England*]
WC............. Westminster Commentaries [*Oxford*] [*A publication*] (BJA)
W & C .... Westmorland and Cumberland Yeomanry [*British military*] (DMA)
WC............. Whale Center (EA)
WC............. Wheel Center (MSA)
WC............. Wheelchair
WC............. White Cell [*Medicine*]

W/C .... White Clothing [*British military*] (DMA)
W/C .... White Collar [*Worker*] (DCTA)
WC............. White Confederacy (EA)
WC............. White Count [*Hematology*]
WC............. Whooping Cough [*Medicine*]
WC............. Width Codes (AAG)
WC............. Will Call
WC............. Wills Club (EA)
WC............. Willys Club (EA)
WC............. Wilshire Club (EA)
W & C .... Wilson and Courtenay's Scotch Appeal Cases [*A publication*] (DLA)
WC............. Wing Commander [*British military*]
WC............. Wings Club (EA)
W & C .... Wire and Cable (NASA)
WC............. Wire Chief [*Test clerk*] [*Telecommunications*] (TEL)
WC............. Wisconsin Central Railroad
WC............. With Corrections [*Publishing*]
WC............. Without Charge
WC............. Woden's Coven (EAIO)
W-C........... Women-Church: an Australian Journal of Feminist Studies in Religion [*A publication*] (APTA)
WC............. Women in Communications (EA)
WC............. Women's Reserve, Communications Duties [*USNR officer designation*]
WC............. Wood Casing
WC............. Wood Covers (DS)
WC............. Woolwich College [*London, England*]
WC............. Word Count [*Data processing*]
WC............. Wordsworth Circle [*A publication*]
WC............. Work Card (AAG)
WC............. Work Center (AFM)
WC............. Work Circle (AAG)
WC............. Work Control (AAG)
WC............. Working Capital
WC............. Working Circle [*Technical drawings*]
WC............. Workmen's Circle [*New York, NY*] (EA)
WC............. Workmen's Compensation [*Department of Health and Human Services*]
WC............. World Christian [*A publication*]
WC............. World Concern (EA)
WC............. World Coordinate
WC............. World's Classics [*A publication*]
WC............. Write and Compute
WC............. Written Component [*Qualification test*] [*Military*]
WC............. Wspolczesnosc [*A publication*]
3WC........... Third Wave Civilization [*Title of record album by Ian Lloyd*]
WCA......... Warrant Claims Action [*Army*]
WCA......... Water Companies' Association [*British*]
WCA......... Weapon Control Area [*Military*] (CAAL)
WCA......... Weimaraner Club of America (EA)
WCA......... West Coast of Africa (ROG)
WCA......... West Coast Airlines, Inc.
WCA......... Westair Commuter Airlines [*Santa Rosa, CA*] [*FAA designator*] (FAAC)
WCA......... Western College Association (EA)
WCA......... Who Cares, Anyway?
WCA......... Whole Core Accident [*Nuclear energy*] (NRCH)
WCA......... Wideband Cassegrain Antenna
WCA......... Willys Club of America [*Later, WC*] (EA)
WCA......... Windmill Class Association (EA)
WCA......... Wine Conference of America (EA)
WCA......... Winston S. Churchill Association (EA)
WCA......... Wireless Cable Association (TSSD)
WCA......... Wisco of Canada Ltd. [*Vancouver Stock Exchange symbol*]
WCA......... Women's Caucus for Art (EA)
WCA......... Women's Christian Association
WCA......... Women's Cricket Association [*British*]
WCA......... Wool Council of Australia
WCA......... Workmen's Compensation Act
WCA......... World Campus Afloat [*Cruise ship educational program*] (EA)
WCA......... World Citizens Assembly [*Later, AWC*] (EA)
WCA......... World Communication Association (EA)
WCA......... Worst Case Analysis
WCAA ...... Window Coverings Association of America (EA)
WCAB ...... Rutherfordton, NC [*AM radio station call letters*]
WCAB ...... Working Committee of the Aeronautical Board
WCAC .... Sebring, FL [*FM radio station call letters*]
WCAD ...... San Juan, PR [*FM radio station call letters*]
WCAE .... Nekoosa, WI [*AM radio station call letters*]
WCAFS ..... Wideband Cassegrain Antenna Feed System
WCAG .... Oviedo, FL [*AM radio station call letters*]
WCAI .... Water Conditioning Association International [*Later, WQA*] (EA)
WCAJ........ Birmingham, AL [*Television station call letters*]
WCAL ...... Northfield, MN [*AM radio station call letters*]
WCAL-FM ... Northfield, MN [*FM radio station call letters*]
WCAM...... Camden, SC [*AM radio station call letters*]
WCAM...... Wisconsin Center for Applied Microelectronics [*University of Wisconsin - Madison*] [*Research center*] (RCD)
WCAN....... Canajoharie, NY [*FM radio station call letters*]

WCAN....... Worldwide Crisis Alerting Network (MCD)
W Can J Ant ... West Canadian Journal of Anthropology [*A publication*]
WCAO....... Baltimore, MD [*AM radio station call letters*]
WCAP ...... Lowell, MA [*AM radio station call letters*]
WCAP ...... Westinghouse Commercial Atomic Power
WCAP ...... World Climate Applications Program [*WMO*] [*ICSU*]
WCAR ...... Livonia, MI [*AM radio station call letters*]
WCAR ...... West Coast Formula Atlantic (Racing)
WCAR ...... Western Carolina Savings & Loan Association, Inc. [*NASDAQ symbol*] (NQ)
WCAS....... Western Casualty & Surety [*NASDAQ symbol*] (NQ)
WCASS ..... World Conference of Ashkenazi and Sephardi Synagogues
WCAT ...... Orange-Athol, MA [*AM radio station call letters*]
WCAT ...... Weiss Comprehensive Articulation Test [*Education*]
WCAT ...... WICAT Systems, Inc. [*NASDAQ symbol*] (NQ)
WCAT-FM ... Athol, MA [*FM radio station call letters*]
WCAU....... Philadelphia, PA [*AM radio station call letters*]
WCAU-TV ... Philadelphia, PA [*Television station call letters*]
WCAV ...... Brockton, MA [*FM radio station call letters*]
WCAW...... Charleston, WV [*AM radio station call letters*]
WCAX-TV ... Burlington, VT [*Television station call letters*]
WCAZ ...... Carthage, IL [*AM radio station call letters*]
WCAZ-FM ... Carthage, IL [*FM radio station call letters*]
WCB .... War Communications Board [*World War II*]
WCB .... Warramunga Array [*Australia*] [*Seismograph station code, US Geological Survey*] (SEIS)
WCB .... Water Control Board
WCB .... Way Control Block
WCB .... Weekly Criminal Bulletin [*Canada Law Book, Inc.*] [*Information service or system*]
WCB .... Wellington County Board of Education [*UTLAS symbol*]
WCB .... Will Call Back
WCB .... William C. Brown Publishers
WCB .... Workmen's Compensation Board
WCBA ...... Corning, NY [*AM radio station call letters*]
WCBA-FM ... Corning, NY [*FM radio station call letters*]
WCBB....... Augusta, ME [*Television station call letters*]
WCBC....... Cumberland, MD [*AM radio station call letters*]
WCBC....... West Coast Bancorp [*NASDAQ symbol*] (NQ)
WCBC....... World Candlepin Bowling Council
WCBD-TV ... Charleston, SC [*Television station call letters*]
WCBD (Vic) ... Workers Compensation Board Decisions (Victoria) [*A publication*] (APTA)
WCBD (WA) ... Workers Compensation Board Decisions (Western Australia) [*A publication*] (APTA)
WCBE....... Columbus, OH [*FM radio station call letters*]
WCBG....... Chambersburg, PA [*AM radio station call letters*]
WCBH...... Casey, IL [*FM radio station call letters*]
WCBI........ Columbus, MS [*AM radio station call letters*]
WCBI-TV ... Columbus, MS [*Television station call letters*]
WCBK ...... Workingmens Corp. [*NASDAQ symbol*] (NQ)
WCBK-FM ... Martinsville, IN [*FM radio station call letters*]
WCBL....... Benton, KY [*AM radio station call letters*]
WCBL....... World Council of Blind Lions [*Later, ACBL*] (EA)
WCBL-FM ... Benton, KY [*FM radio station call letters*]
WCBM ...... Baltimore, MD [*AM radio station call letters*]
WCBN-FM ... Ann Arbor, MI [*FM radio station call letters*]
WCBQ ...... Oxford, NC [*AM radio station call letters*]
WCBR ...... Richmond, KY [*AM radio station call letters*]
WCBR-FM ... Arlington Heights, IL [*FM radio station call letters*]
WCBS....... New York, NY [*AM radio station call letters*]
WCBS-FM ... New York, NY [*FM radio station call letters*]
WCBS-TV ... New York, NY [*Television station call letters*]
WCBSU..... West Coast Base Service Unit [*Navy*]
WCBT........ Roanoke Rapids, NC [*AM radio station call letters*]
WCBU ...... Peoria, IL [*FM radio station call letters*]
WCB (Vic) ... Workers Compensation Board Decisions (Victoria) [*A publication*] (APTA)
WCBW ...... Columbia, IL [*FM radio station call letters*]
WCBY ...... Cheboygan, MI [*AM radio station call letters*]
WCBZ........ Bowling Green, KY [*FM radio station call letters*]
WCC......... Gerard P. Weeg Computing Center [*University of Iowa*] [*Research center*] (RCD)
WCC......... Wallace Communications Consultants [*Tampa, FL*] [*Telecommunications*] (TSSD)
WCC......... War Claims Commission [*Abolished, 1954*]
WCC......... War Cover Club (EA)
WCC......... Washington's United States Circuit Court Reports [*A publication*] (DLA)
WCC......... Waste Collection Containers
WCC......... Water-Cooled Copper
WCC......... Waters Computing Center [*Rose-Hulman Institute of Technology*] [*Research center*] (RCD)
WCC......... Watson Collectors Club (EA)
WCC......... Weapon Control Computer (MCD)
WCC......... Weapon Control Console [*Military*] (CAAL)
WCC......... Weapons Control Concept (MCD)
WCC......... Welsh Consumer Council [*British*] (ILCA)
WCC......... Westchester Community College [*Valhalla, NY*]
WCC......... Westchester Community College, Technical Services, Valhalla, NY [*OCLC symbol*] (OCLC)

WCC......... Western Canada Concept [*Political party*] (PPW)
WCC .... Western Carolina College [*Later, WCU*] [*North Carolina*]
WCC .... Westminster Choir College [*Princeton, NJ*]
WCC .... Whim Creek Consolidated [*Toronto Stock Exchange symbol*]
WCC .... Whitney Communications Corporation [*New York, NY*]
WCC .... Widows Consultation Center [*Defunct*] (EA)
WCC .... Wildfire Coordinating Committee (EA)
WCC .... Wilson Cloud Chamber [*Physics*]
WCC .... Women of the Church Coalition (EA)
WCC .... Women's Classical Caucus (EA)
WCC .... Women's College Coalition (EA)
WCC .... Women's Consultative Committee [*Ministry of Labour*] [*British*] [*World War II*]
WCC .... Work Center Code
WCC .... Work Control Center (AAG)
WCC .... Workers' Compensation Cases [*A publication*] (APTA)
WCC .... Workmen's Circle Call [*A publication*]
WCC .... Workmen's Compensation Cases [*Legal*] [*British*]
WCC .... World Cheerleader Council (EA)
WCC .... World for Christ Crusade (EA)
WCC .... World Congress on Computing [*Trade show*]
WCC .... World Council of Christians (EA)
WCC .... World Council of Churches [*Geneva, Switzerland*]
WCC .... World Council of Clergy (EA)
WCC .... World Crafts Council (EA)
WCC .... Worldwide Collectors Club [*Later, ISWSC*] (EA)
WCCA ...... West Coast Crossarm Association [*Defunct*]
WCCA ...... Whiteruthenian [*Byelorussian*] Congress Committee of America [*Later, Byelorussian Congress Committee of America*] (EA)
WCCA ...... Whooping Crane Conservation Association (EA)
WCCA ...... World Court Clubs Association [*Defunct*] (EA)
WCCA ...... Worst Case Circuit Analysis
WCCB....... Charlotte, NC [*Television station call letters*]
WCCC ...... Hartford, CT [*AM radio station call letters*]
WCCC ...... Warwick China Collectors Club (EA)
WCCC ...... Wayne County Community College [*Detroit, MI*]
WCCC ...... Western Commercial [*Fresno, CA*] [*NASDAQ symbol*] (NQ)
WCCC ...... Wisconsin Clinical Cancer Center [*University of Wisconsin*] [*Research center*] (RCD)
WCCC ...... World Convention of Churches of Christ (EA)
WCCC-FM ... Hartford, CT [*FM radio station call letters*]
WCC&CRA ... World Championship Cutter and Chariot Racing Association (EA)
WCCD....... Parma, OH [*AM radio station call letters*]
WCCE....... Buie's Creek, NC [*FM radio station call letters*]
WCCE....... West Coast Commodity Exchange
WCCE....... World Conference in Computer Education [*Australia*]
WCCE....... World Council of Christian Education [*Later absorbed into Office of Education of World Council of Churches*]
WCCES ...... World Council of Comparative Education Societies (EA)
WCCESSA ... World Council of Christian Education and Sunday School Association [*Later, WCCE*] (EA)
WCCF....... Punta Gorda, FL [*AM radio station call letters*]
WCCH...... Holyoke, MA [*FM radio station call letters*]
WCCI........ Savanna, IL [*FM radio station call letters*]
WCCI........ World Council for Curriculum and Instruction (EA)
WCCJ........ Chatom, AL [*FM radio station call letters*]
WCCK ...... Erie, PA [*FM radio station call letters*]
WCCK ...... Weapons Control Check (NVT)
WCCL....... New Orleans, LA [*Television station call letters*]
WCCLS ..... Washington County Cooperative Library Services [*Library network*]
WCCM ...... Lawrence, MA [*AM radio station call letters*]
WCCMORS ... West Coast Classified Military Operations Research Symposium
WCCN ...... Neillsville, WI [*AM radio station call letters*]
WCCN-FM ... Neillsville, WI [*FM radio station call letters*]
WCC (NZ) ... Workers' Compensation Cases (New Zealand) [*A publication*] (DLA)
WCCO ...... Minneapolis, MN [*AM radio station call letters*]
WCCON.... Whether Cleared Customs or Not [*Shipping*] (DS)
W & C Conv ... Wolstenholme and Cherry's Conveyancing Statutes [*13th ed.*] [*1972*] [*A publication*] (DLA)
WCCO-TV ... Minneapolis, MN [*Television station call letters*]
WCCP....... Clemson, SC [*AM radio station call letters*]
WCCPPS... Waste Channel and Containment Pressurization and Penetration System (IEEE)
WCCQ ...... Crest Hill, IL [*FM radio station call letters*]
WCCR ...... Clarion, PA [*FM radio station call letters*]
WCCR ...... Washington's United States Circuit Court Reports [*A publication*] (DLA)
WCCRS..... Western Catholic Charismatic Renewal Services [*A publication*]
WCCS....... Homer City, PA [*AM radio station call letters*]
WCCS....... World Chamber of Commerce Service (EA)
WCCSIS.... Westchester County Community Services Information System [*Westchester Library System*] [*Information service or system*] (IID)
WCCT-FM ... Harwich, MA [*FM radio station call letters*]
WCCU ...... Urbana, IL [*Television station call letters*]
WCC/US... US Conference for the World Council of Churches (EA)

WCCV	Cartersville, GA [*FM radio station call letters*]
WCCV-TV ...	Arecibo, PR [*Television station call letters*]
WCCW	Traverse City, MI [*AM radio station call letters*]
WCCW-FM ..	Traverse City, MI [*FM radio station call letters*]
WCCX	Waukesha, WI [*FM radio station call letters*]
WCCY	Houghton, MI [*AM radio station call letters*]
WCCZ	New Smyrna Beach, FL [*AM radio station call letters*]
WCD..........	We Can Do (EA)
WCD.........	Weapons Classification Defects [*Navy*] (NG)
WCD.........	Western Canadian Mining [*Vancouver Stock Exchange symbol*]
WCD.........	Work Center Description (AFM)
WCD.........	Workshop for Cultural Democracy (EA)
WCDB	Albany, NY [*FM radio station call letters*]
WCDB	Wing Control During Boost
WCDB	Work Control Data Base (NASA)
WCDC	Adams, MA [*Television station call letters*]
WCDC	West Coast [*Naval Publications*] Distribution Center
WCDE	Elkins, WV [*FM radio station call letters*]
WCDFMA ...	Water Cooler and Drinking Fountain Manufacturers Association
WCDK	Virginia, MN [*FM radio station call letters*]
WCDL	Carbondale, PA [*AM radio station call letters*]
WCDN......	Chardon, OH [*AM radio station call letters*]
WCDO	Sidney, NY [*AM radio station call letters*]
WCDO	War Consumable Distribution Objective (AFM)
WCDO-FM ...	Sidney, NY [*FM radio station call letters*]
WCDP	Widows', Children's, and Dependents' Pension [*British*]
WCDP	World Climate Data Program [*WMO*] [*ICSU*]
WCDQ.......	Sanford, ME [*FM radio station call letters*]
W/Cdr........	Wing Commander [*British military*]
WCDR-FM ...	Cedarville, OH [*FM radio station call letters*]
WCDS	Glasgow, KY [*AM radio station call letters*]
WCDT	Winchester, TN [*AM radio station call letters*]
WCDV	Covington, IN [*FM radio station call letters*]
WCDX	Merchanicsville, VA [*FM radio station call letters*]
WCE	Weapon Control Equipment
WCE	Wessex College of English [*Australia*]
WCE	West Coast of England [*Shipping*]
WCE	Western Corporate Enterprises, Inc. [*Toronto Stock Exchange symbol*]
WCE	Wiener Canonical Expansion [*Mathematics*]
WCE	World Christian Encyclopedia [*A publication*]
WCEB	Corning, NY [*FM radio station call letters*]
WCED	Du Bois, PA [*AM radio station call letters*]
WCED	World Commission on Environment and Development (EA)
WCEE........	Mount Vernon, IL [*Television station call letters*]
WCEE........	Women's Council on Energy and the Environment (EA)
WCEF........	Ripley, WV [*FM radio station call letters*]
WCEG	Middleborough, MA [*AM radio station call letters*]
WCEH	Hawkinsville, GA [*AM radio station call letters*]
WCEH-FM ...	Hawkinsville, GA [*FM radio station call letters*]
WCEI........	Easton, MD [*AM radio station call letters*]
WCEI-FM ...	Easton, MD [*FM radio station call letters*]
WC & EL....	Workers' Compensation and Employers' Liability [*Insurance*]
WCEM	Cambridge, MD [*AM radio station call letters*]
WCEMA	West Coast Electronic Manufacturers' Association [*Later, AEA*]
WCEM-FM ...	Cambridge, MD [*FM radio station call letters*]
WCEN	Mount Pleasant, MI [*AM radio station call letters*]
WCEN-FM ...	Mount Pleasant, MI [*FM radio station call letters*]
WCEO	Wood River, IL [*AM radio station call letters*]
WCES........	Wolfson Centre for Electrochemical Science [*British*] (CB)
WCES	Women's Caucus of the Endocrine Society (EA)
WCES-TV ...	Wrens, GA [*Television station call letters*]
WCET.......	Cincinnati, OH [*Television station call letters*]
WCEU	New Smyrna Beach, FL [*Television station call letters*]
WCEU	World's Christian Endeavor Union (EA)
WCEV	Cicero, IL [*AM radio station call letters*]
WCEW	Charleston, SC [*FM radio station call letters*]
WCEZ	Columbia, SC [*FM radio station call letters*]
WCf...........	Chippewa Falls Public Library, Chippewa Falls, WI [*Library symbol*] [*Library of Congress*] (LCLS)
WCF	Waste Calcination [*or Calcining*] Facility [*Nuclear energy*]
WCF	Water Conditioning Foundation [*Later, WQA*] (EA)
WCF	White Cathode Follower
WCF	Winston Churchill Foundation (EA)
WCF	Women's Campaign Fund (EA)
WCF	Workload Control File
WCF	World Congress of Faiths - The Inter-Faith Fellowship [*London, England*] (EAIO)
WCF	World Congress of Flight
WCFA........	Wholesale Commission Florists of America [*Later, WF & FSA*]
WCFA........	Wildlife Conservation Fund of America (EA)
WCFB........	Tupelo, MS [*AM radio station call letters*]
WCFBA	World Catholic Federation for the Biblical Apostolate [*Stuttgart, Federal Republic of Germany*] (EAIO)
WCFC........	Washington Capitals Fan Club (EA)
WCFC-TV ...	Chicago, IL [*Television station call letters*]
WCFE-FM ...	Plattsburgh, NY [*FM radio station call letters*]
WCFE-TV ...	Plattsburgh, NY [*Television station call letters*]
WCFL........	Culpeper, VA [*FM radio station call letters*]
WCFM	Williamstown, MA [*FM radio station call letters*]

WCFN	Springfield, IL [*Television station call letters*]
WCfNC......	Northern Wisconsin Colony and Training School, Chippewa Falls, WI [*Library symbol*] [*Library of Congress*] (LCLS)
WCFPR	Washington Center of Foreign Policy Research (MCD)
WCFR.......	Springfield, VT [*AM radio station call letters*]
WCFR.......	Washington Citizens for Recycling (EA)
WCFRU.....	Washington Cooperative Fishery Research Unit [*University of Washington*] [*Research center*] (RCD)
WCfSJ.......	Saint Joseph's Hospital, Chippewa Falls, WI [*Library symbol*] [*Library of Congress*] (LCLS)
WCFTB	West Coast Freight Tariff Bureau
WCFT-TV ...	Tuscaloosa, AL [*Television station call letters*]
WCFW......	Chippewa Falls, WI [*FM radio station call letters*]
WCFX.......	Clare, MI [*FM radio station call letters*]
WCFY.......	Lafayette, IN [*AM radio station call letters*]
WCG.........	War Crimes Group [*British*]
WCG.........	Washington Calligraphers Guild (EA)
WCG.........	Water-Cooled Garment
WCG.........	Weapon Control Group [*Military*] (CAAL)
WCG.........	Willis Corroon ADS [*NYSE symbol*] (SPSG)
WCG.........	Women of the Church of God (EA)
WCG.........	Worldwide Church of God
WCGA......	Woodbine, GA [*AM radio station call letters*]
WCGA......	World Computer Graphics Association (EA)
WCGB......	Juana Diaz, PR [*AM radio station call letters*]
WCGC......	Belmont, NC [*AM radio station call letters*]
WCGL......	Jacksonville, FL [*AM radio station call letters*]
WCGLJO ...	World Congress of Gay and Lesbian Jewish Organizations (EA)
WCGM......	Maryville, TN [*AM radio station call letters*]
WCGM......	Writable Character Generation Module [*Data processing*] (BUR)
WCGO......	Chicago Heights, IL [*AM radio station call letters*]
WCGQ......	Columbus, GA [*FM radio station call letters*]
WCGR......	Canandaigua, NY [*AM radio station call letters*]
WCGS......	Western Collaborative Group Study [*University of California*] [*Psychology*]
WCGS......	Wolf Creek Generating Station [*Nuclear energy*] (NRCH)
WCGTC.....	World Council for Gifted and Talented Children (EA)
WCGV-TV ...	Milwaukee, WI [*Television station call letters*]
WCGW......	Nicholasville, KY [*AM radio station call letters*]
WCGY......	Lawrence, MA [*FM radio station call letters*]
WCGZ......	World Confederation of General Zionists [*Later, WCUZ*] (EA)
WCh..........	Chippewa Falls Public Library, Chippewa Falls, WI [*Library symbol*] [*Library of Congress*] [*Obsolete*] (LCLS)
WCH.........	Skyline Aviation, Inc. [*Winchester, VA*] [*FAA designator*] (FAAC)
WCH.........	Weekly Contact Hours
WCH.........	West Coast Handling
WCH.........	Working Class Hero (EA)
WCH.........	Workshop Conferences Hoechst [*Elsevier Book Series*] [*A publication*]
WCHA......	Chambersburg, PA [*AM radio station call letters*]
WCHA......	Western Collegiate Hockey Association (EA)
WCHA......	Wooden Canoe Heritage Association (EA)
WCHB......	Inkster, MI [*AM radio station call letters*]
WCHC......	Worcester, MA [*FM radio station call letters*]
WCHE......	West Chester, PA [*AM radio station call letters*]
WCHEN......	Western Council on Higher Education for Nursing
W'CHESTER ...	Winchester [*Borough in South England*] (ROG)
WCHF	Wet Crude Handling Facilities [*Petroleum engineering*]
WCHI	Chillicothe, OH [*AM radio station call letters*]
WCHI	Westworld Community Healthcare, Incorporated [*Lake Forest, CA*] [*NASDAQ symbol*] (NQ)
WCHI	Women's Council for the Histadrut in Israel (EA)
WCHJ	Brookhaven, MS [*AM radio station call letters*]
WCHK......	Canton, GA [*AM radio station call letters*]
WCHK-FM ...	Canton, GA [*FM radio station call letters*]
WCHL......	Chapel Hill, NC [*AM radio station call letters*]
WCHM......	Clarkesville, GA [*AM radio station call letters*]
WCHN	Norwich, NY [*AM radio station call letters*]
Wchnbl K K Gesellsch Aerzte Wien ...	Wochenblatt. K. K. Gesellschaft der Aerzte in Wien [*A publication*]
Wchnschr Ges Heilk ...	Wochenschrift fuer die Gesamte Heilkunde [*A publication*]
Wchnschr Tierh u Viehzucht ...	Wochenschrift fuer Tierheilkunde und Viehzucht [*A publication*]
WCHODW ...	Workshop Conferences Hoechst [*Elsevier Book Series*] [*A publication*]
WCHO-FM ...	Washington Court House, OH [*FM radio station call letters*]
WCHP.......	Champlain, NY [*AM radio station call letters*]
WCHQ	Camuy, PR [*AM radio station call letters*]
WCHQ-FM ...	Camuy, PR [*FM radio station call letters*]
WCHR......	Trenton, NJ [*AM radio station call letters*]
WCHR......	Water Chiller
WCHR......	Worldwide Creme Horse Registry (EA)
WCHS	Charleston, WV [*AM radio station call letters*]
WCHS-TV ...	Charleston, WV [*Television station call letters*]
WCHT.......	Escanaba, MI [*AM radio station call letters*]
WCHV.......	Charlottesville, VA [*AM radio station call letters*]
WCHW-FM ...	Bay City, MI [*FM radio station call letters*]
WCHX.......	Lewistown, PA [*FM radio station call letters*]

WCHY ...... Savannah, GA [*AM radio station call letters*]
WCHY-FM ... Savannah, GA [*FM radio station call letters*]
WCI .... Warner Communications, Inc. [*NYSE symbol*] (SPSG)
WCI .... Washington International College, Washington, DC [*OCLC symbol*] (OCLC)
WCI .... Weapon Control Index [*Military*] (CAAL)
WCI .... White Cast Iron
WCI .... Wildlife Conservation International (EA)
WCIA .... Champaign, IL [*Television station call letters*]
WCIA .... Welsh Centre for International Affairs [*British*] (CB)
WCIB .... Falmouth, MA [*FM radio station call letters*]
WCIC .... Pekin, IL [*FM radio station call letters*]
WCIC .... Watch Check Is Completed (FAAC)
WCID .... Friendship, NY [*FM radio station call letters*]
WCIE .... Spring Lake, NC [*AM radio station call letters*]
WCIE .... World Center for Islamic Education (EA)
WCIE-FM ... Lakeland, FL [*FM radio station call letters*]
WCIF .... Melbourne, FL [*FM radio station call letters*]
WCIG .... Mullins, SC [*FM radio station call letters*]
WCIH .... Elmira, NY [*FM radio station call letters*]
WCII .... Spencer, NY [*FM radio station call letters*]
WCIK .... Bath, NY [*FM radio station call letters*]
WCIL .... Carbondale, IL [*AM radio station call letters*]
WCIL-FM ... Carbondale, IL [*FM radio station call letters*]
WCIN .... Cincinnati, OH [*AM radio station call letters*]
WC & Ins (Eng) ... Workmen's Compensation and Insurance Reports [*1912-33*] [*England*] [*A publication*] (DLA)
WC & Ins Rep ... Workmen's Compensation and Insurance Reports [*1912-33*] [*England*] [*A publication*] (DLA)
WC Ins Rep ... Workmen's Compensation and Insurance Reports [*1912-33*] [*A publication*] (DLA)
WCIP .... Weapon Control Indicator Panel [*Military*] (CAAL)
WCIP .... World Climate Impacts Program [*WMO*] [*ICSU*]
WCIP .... World Council of Indigenous Peoples [*Ottawa, ON*] (EAIO)
WCIQ .... Mount Cheaha State Park, AL [*Television station call letters*]
WCIR .... Beckley, WV [*AM radio station call letters*]
WC & IR .... Workmen's Compensation and Insurance Reports [*1912-33*] [*England*] [*A publication*] (DLA)
WC & I Rep ... Workmen's Compensation and Insurance Reports [*1912-33*] [*A publication*] (DLA)
WCIR-FM ... Beckley, WV [*FM radio station call letters*]
WCIS .... Morganton, NC [*AM radio station call letters*]
WCIS .... Wisconsin Career Information System [*Information service or system*]
WC-ISA ..... Women's Commission of the Iranian Students Association (EA)
WCIT .... Lima, OH [*AM radio station call letters*]
WCIU .... Workshop Computer Interface Unit (MCD)
WCIU-TV ... Chicago, IL [*Television station call letters*]
WCIV .... Charleston, SC [*Television station call letters*]
WCIW .... [*The*] World Community of Al-Islam in the West
WCIX .... Miami, FL [*Television station call letters*]
WCIY .... Westmorland and Cumberland Imperial Yeomanry [*British military*] (DMA)
WCIZ .... Watertown, NY [*FM radio station call letters*]
WCJ .... White Cloud Journal of American Indian/Alaska Native Mental Health [*A publication*]
WCJA .... Western Canadian Journal of Anthropology [*A publication*]
WCJA .... World Council of Jewish Archives (EAIO)
WCJB .... Gainesville, FL [*Television station call letters*]
WCJC .... Van Buren, IN [*FM radio station call letters*]
WCJC .... Webster City Junior College [*Iowa*]
WCJC .... Wharton County Junior College [*Texas*]
WCJCC ..... World Confederation of Jewish Community Centers (EA)
WCJCS ...... World Conference of Jewish Communal Service (EA)
WCJE .... World Council on Jewish Education
WCJL .... Marinette, WI [*AM radio station call letters*]
WCJL-FM ... Menominee, MI [*FM radio station call letters*]
WCJM .... West Point, GA [*FM radio station call letters*]
WCJO .... Jackson, OH [*FM radio station call letters*]
WCJS .... World Congress of Jewish Studies [*A publication*]
WCJU .... Columbia, MS [*AM radio station call letters*]
WCJW .... Warsaw, NY [*AM radio station call letters*]
WCK .... Whiskey Creek Resources [*Vancouver Stock Exchange symbol*]
WCK .... Wilson Creek [*Kentucky*] [*Seismograph station code, US Geological Survey*] (SEIS)
WCKA ...... Sutton, WV [*FM radio station call letters*]
WCKB ...... Dunn, NC [*AM radio station call letters*]
WCKC ...... Milton, FL [*AM radio station call letters*]
WCKG ...... Elmwood Park, IL [*FM radio station call letters*]
WCKI .... Greer, SC [*FM radio station call letters*]
WCKL .... Catskill, NY [*AM radio station call letters*]
WCKN-FM ... Anderson, SC [*FM radio station call letters*]
WCKP .... Shelbyville, KY [*FM radio station call letters*]
WCKQ ...... Campbellsville, KY [*FM radio station call letters*]
WCKR ...... Hornell, NY [*FM radio station call letters*]
WCKS .... Karns, TN [*AM radio station call letters*]
WCKT .... Lehigh Acres, FL [*FM radio station call letters*]
WCKU ...... Nicholasville, KY [*FM radio station call letters*]
WCKV ...... Ceredo, WV [*FM radio station call letters*]
WCKW ...... Garyville, LA [*AM radio station call letters*]

WCKW-FM ... La Place, LA [*FM radio station call letters*]
WCKX .... London, OH [*FM radio station call letters*]
WCKY .... Cincinnati, OH [*AM radio station call letters*]
WCKZ-FM ... Gastonia, NC [*FM radio station call letters*]
WCL .... Washington College of Law, Washington, DC [*OCLC symbol*] (OCLC)
WCL .... Water Coolant Line (MCD)
WCL .... Water Coolant Loop (MCD)
WCL .... WCI Canada Limited [*Toronto Stock Exchange symbol*]
WCL .... Weekly Cost Ledger (MCD)
WCL .... Western Carolinas League [*Baseball*]
WCL .... Western Collieries Ltd. [*Australia*]
WCL .... White Clip Level [*Video technology*]
WCL .... White Cross League [*British*]
WCL .... Word Control Logic
WCL .... World Confederation of Labour [*See also CMT*] [*Brussels, Belgium*] (EAIO)
WCL .... Wright Center of Laboratories
WCLA ...... Claxton, GA [*AM radio station call letters*]
WCLA ...... West Coast Lumbermen's Association [*Later, WWPA*] (EA)
WCLA ...... Workers' Compensation Legislation in Australia [*A publication*]
WCLA-FM ... Claxton, GA [*FM radio station call letters*]
WCLB .... Camilla, GA [*AM radio station call letters*]
WCLB .... Warehouse Club, Inc. [*Skokie, IL*] [*NASDAQ symbol*] (NQ)
WCLC .... Jamestown, TN [*AM radio station call letters*]
WCLC .... Watch Check List Completed (FAAC)
WCLC-FM ... Jamestown, TN [*FM radio station call letters*]
WCLD .... Cleveland, MS [*AM radio station call letters*]
WCLD ...... Water-Cooled (AAG)
WCLD-FM ... Cleveland, MS [*FM radio station call letters*]
WCLE .... Cleveland, TN [*AM radio station call letters*]
WCLF .... Clearwater, FL [*Television station call letters*]
WCLG ...... Morgantown, WV [*AM radio station call letters*]
WCLG-FM ... Morgantown, WV [*FM radio station call letters*]
WCLH .... Wilkes-Barre, PA [*FM radio station call letters*]
WCLI .... Corning, NY [*AM radio station call letters*]
WCII .... Lakeshore Technical Institute, Educational Resource Center, Cleveland, WI [*Library symbol*] [*Library of Congress*] (LCLS)
WCLIB ...... West Coast Lumber Inspection Bureau (EA)
WCLJ .... Bloomington, IN [*Television station call letters*]
WCLJ .... Workmen's Compensation Law Journal [*A publication*] (DLA)
WCLK .... Atlanta, GA [*FM radio station call letters*]
WCLL-FM ... Wesson, MS [*FM radio station call letters*]
WCLM ...... Highland Springs, VA [*AM radio station call letters*]
WCLN .... Clinton, NC [*AM radio station call letters*]
WCLN-FM ... Clinton, NC [*FM radio station call letters*]
WCLO ...... Janesville, WI [*AM radio station call letters*]
WCLP .... Western Center on Law and Poverty (EA)
WCLP .... Women's Computer Literacy Project [*Commercial firm*] (EA)
WCLP-TV ... Chatsworth, GA [*Television station call letters*]
WCLQ ...... Wausau, WI [*FM radio station call letters*]
WCLR .... Piqua, OH [*FM radio station call letters*]
WCLR .... Workmen's Compensation Law Review [*A publication*] (DLA)
WCLS .... Oscoda, MI [*FM radio station call letters*]
WCLT .... Newark, OH [*AM radio station call letters*]
WCLT-FM ... Newark, OH [*FM radio station call letters*]
WCLU ...... Glasgow, KY [*AM radio station call letters*]
WCLV .... Cleveland, OH [*FM radio station call letters*]
WCLX .... Boyne City, MI [*FM radio station call letters*]
WCLY .... Raleigh, NC [*AM radio station call letters*]
WCLZ .... Brunswick, ME [*AM radio station call letters*]
WCLZ-FM ... Brunswick, ME [*FM radio station call letters*]
WCM .... Warland Creek [*Montana*] [*Seismograph station code, US Geological Survey*] [*Closed*] (SEIS)
WCM .... Water Control Module (KSC)
WCM .... Weapon Control Module (MCD)
WCM .... Welded Cordwood Module
WCM .... Wesleyan Calvinistic Methodists (ROG)
WCM .... Wheat Curl Mite [*Entomology*]
WCM .... Whole Cow's Milk
WCM .... Winchester City Museum [*British*]
WCM .... Winkelmann Countermeasures, Inc. [*Vancouver Stock Exchange symbol*]
WCM .... Wired-Core Matrix
WCM .... Wired-Core Memory
WCM .... Word Combine and Multiplexer
WCM .... Writable Control Memory [*Data processing*] (BUR)
W/CM² ..... Watts per Square Centimeter (CET)
WCMA ...... Corinth, MS [*AM radio station call letters*]
WCMA ...... West Coast Mineral Association (EA)
WCMA ...... Wisconsin Cheese Makers' Association (EA)
WCMA ...... Working Capital Management Account [*Merrill Lynch & Co.*]
WCMB ...... Harrisburg, PA [*AM radio station call letters*]
WCMC ...... Wildwood, NJ [*AM radio station call letters*]
WCMC ...... World Conservation Monitoring Centre [*Information service or system*] (EISS)
WCMD .... Advanced Certificate of the Welsh College of Music and Drama [*British*] (DBQ)
WCMD...... La Plata, MD [*AM radio station call letters*]

WCME ...... Boothbay Harbor, ME [*FM radio station call letters*]
WCMF ...... Rochester, NY [*FM radio station call letters*]
WCMG...... Lawrenceburg, TN [*AM radio station call letters*]
WCMH-TV ... Columbus, OH [*Television station call letters*]
WCMI .... Ashland, KY [*AM radio station call letters*]
WCMIA .... West Coast Metal Importers Association (EA)
WCMI-FM ... Catlettsburg, KY [*FM radio station call letters*]
WCMJ....... Cambridge, OH [*FM radio station call letters*]
WCML ...... Women's Caucus for the Modern Languages (EA)
WCML-FM ... Alpena, MI [*FM radio station call letters*]
WCML-TV ... Alpena, MI [*Television station call letters*]
WCMN...... Arecibo, PR [*AM radio station call letters*]
WCMN-FM ... Arecibo, PR [*FM radio station call letters*]
WCMO...... Marietta, OH [*FM radio station call letters*]
WCMP ...... Pine City, MN [*AM radio station call letters*]
WCMP-FM ... Pine City, MN [*FM radio station call letters*]
WCMQ...... Miami Springs, FL [*AM radio station call letters*]
WCMQ-FM ... Hialeah, FL [*FM radio station call letters*]
WCMR...... Elkhart, IN [*AM radio station call letters*]
WCMR...... Western Contract Management Region [*Air Force*]
WCMS....... Norfolk, VA [*AM radio station call letters*]
WCMS-FM ... Norfolk, VA [*FM radio station call letters*]
WCMT ...... Martin, TN [*AM radio station call letters*]
WCMT-FM ... Martin, TN [*FM radio station call letters*]
WCMU-FM ... Mount Pleasant, MI [*FM radio station call letters*]
WCMU-TV ... Mount Pleasant, MI [*Television station call letters*]
WCMV...... Cadillac, MI [*Television station call letters*]
WCMV...... White Clover Mosaic Virus
WCMW...... Manistee, MI [*Television station call letters*]
WCMW...... Williamsburg, VA [*FM radio station call letters*]
WCMX...... Leominster, MA [*AM radio station call letters*]
WCMY...... Ottawa, IL [*AM radio station call letters*]
WCMZ-FM ... Sault Ste. Marie, MI [*FM radio station call letters*]
WCN.......... Washoe City [*Nevada*] [*Seismograph station code, US Geological Survey*] (SEIS)
WCN.......... Wescan Energy Ltd. [*Vancouver Stock Exchange symbol*]
WCN.......... Workload Control Number (MCD)
WCN.......... World Coin News [*A publication*]
WCNA ...... Clearwater, SC [*AM radio station call letters*]
WCNB-FM ... Connersville, IN [*FM radio station call letters*]
WCNC....... Elizabeth City, NC [*AM radio station call letters*]
WCNC-TV ... Charlotte, NC [*Television station call letters*]
WCND....... Shelbyville, KY [*AM radio station call letters*]
WCNE....... Batavia, OH [*FM radio station call letters*]
WCNG....... Murphy, NC [*FM radio station call letters*]
WCNH ...... Belmont, NH [*FM radio station call letters*]
WCNI .... New London, CT [*FM radio station call letters*]
WCNJ....... Hazlet, NJ [*FM radio station call letters*]
WCNL .... Winter Cities Newsletter [*A publication*]
WCNN....... North Atlanta, GA [*AM radio station call letters*]
WCNR....... Bloomsburg, PA [*AM radio station call letters*]
WCNS ...... Latrobe, PA [*AM radio station call letters*]
WCNU....... Crestview, FL [*AM radio station call letters*]
WCNW...... Fairfield, OH [*AM radio station call letters*]
WCNX...... Middletown, CT [*AM radio station call letters*]
WCNY-FM ... Syracuse, NY [*FM radio station call letters*]
WCNY-TV ... Syracuse, NY [*Television station call letters*]
WCO.......... Columbia Helicopters, Inc. [*Lake Charles, LA*] [*FAA designator*] (FAAC)
WCO.......... War Cabinet Office [*World War II*]
WCO.......... Warrant Communication Officer [*British military*] (DMA)
WCO.......... Weapons Control Officer
WCO.......... Western Coordination Office [*Later, WOO*] [*NASA*]
WCO.......... Wrather Corporation [*AMEX symbol*] (SPSG)
WCOA....... Pensacola, FL [*AM radio station call letters*]
W Coach Clinic ... Women's Coaching Clinic [*A publication*]
W Coast Rep ... West Coast Reporter [*A publication*] (DLA)
WCOAT .... Wolfe Computer Operator Aptitude Test
WCOBL..... Wolfe Programming Language Test: COBOL
WCOC....... Women's Central Organising Committee [*Australian Labor Party, New South Wales*]
WCOD....... Western Canada Outdoors. Combining The Whooper and Defending All Outdoors [*A publication*]
WCOD-FM ... Hyannis, MA [*FM radio station call letters*]
WCOE....... La Porte, IN [*FM radio station call letters*]
WCOF....... Women's Catholic Order of Foresters [*Later, NCSF*] (EA)
WCOG....... Ridgeland, SC [*AM radio station call letters*]
WCOH ...... Newnan, GA [*AM radio station call letters*]
WCoins ...... World Coins [*A publication*]
WCOJ....... Coatesville, PA [*AM radio station call letters*]
WCOK....... Sparta, NC [*AM radio station call letters*]
WCOL....... Columbus, OH [*AM radio station call letters*]
WCOL....... Walker Color, Inc. [*NASDAQ symbol*] (NQ)
W Comm..... Wing Commander [*British military*]
WCOMMRGN ... Western Communications Region [*Air Force*]
W Comp Pres Docs ... Weekly Compilation of Presidential Documents [*A publication*]
WCOM-TV ... Mansfield, OH [*Television station call letters*]
WCON....... Cornelia, GA [*AM radio station call letters*]
WCON-FM ... Cornelia, GA [*FM radio station call letters*]
WCOO....... Immokalee, FL [*FM radio station call letters*]

WCOP .... Warner Robins, GA [*AM radio station call letters*]
WC Ops ..... Workmen's Compensation Opinions, United States Department of Commerce [*A publication*] (DLA)
WCOR....... Lebanon, TN [*AM radio station call letters*]
WCOS ...... Columbia, SC [*AM radio station call letters*]
WCOS-FM ... Columbia, SC [*FM radio station call letters*]
WCOT ...... Wall Coated Open Tubular [*Instrumentation*]
WCOTP..... World Confederation of Organizations of the Teaching Profession [*Formed by a merger of International Federation of Secondary Teachers and IFTA*] (EAIO)
WCOU...... Wheelwrights and Coachmakers Operatives' Union [*British*]
WCOV-TV ... Montgomery, AL [*Television station call letters*]
WCOW ...... Sparta, WI [*AM radio station call letters*]
WCOW-FM ... Sparta, WI [*FM radio station call letters*]
WCOX ...... Camden, AL [*AM radio station call letters*]
WCOZ....... Paris, KY [*FM radio station call letters*]
WCP .... War Control Planners (EA)
WCP .... Warner Computer Systems [*NYSE symbol*] (SPSG)
WCP .... Waste Collector Pump (IEEE)
WCP .... Wayne County Public Library, Wooster, OH [*OCLC symbol*] (OCLC)
WCP .... Weapon Control Panel [*Aviation*]
WCP .... Weapon Control Processor [*Military*] (CAAL)
WCP .... Welder Control Panel
WCP .... Western Canada Party [*Separatist political party*]
WCP .... White Combination Potentiometer
WCP .... Wing Chord Plane [*Aviation*]
WCP .... Wing Command Post (MCD)
WCP .... Woman CPA [*A publication*]
WCP .... Work Control Plan (AAG)
WCP .... World Climate Program [*WMO*] [*ICSU*]
WCP .... World Community Projects (EA)
WCP .... World Congress of Poets (EA)
WCP .... World Council of Peace (NATG)
WCPA ...... Clearfield, PA [*AM radio station call letters*]
WCPA ...... World Constitution and Parliament Association (EA)
WCPAB..... War Contracts Price Adjustment Board [*All functions dispersed, 1951*]
WCPB....... Salisbury, MD [*Television station call letters*]
WCPC....... Houston, MS [*AM radio station call letters*]
WCPC-FM ... Houston, MS [*FM radio station call letters*]
WCPD .... Waterloo Centre for Process Development [*University of Waterloo*] [*Research center*] (RCD)
WCPDD5 .. World Crops Production Utilization Description [*A publication*]
WCPE........ Raleigh, NC [*FM radio station call letters*]
WCPH .... World Congress of Professional Hypnotists (EA)
WCPM ...... Cumberland, KY [*AM radio station call letters*]
WCPMEF ... Willa Cather Pioneer Memorial and Educational Foundation (EA)
WCPN ...... Cleveland, OH [*FM radio station call letters*]
WCPO-TV ... Cincinnati, OH [*Television station call letters*]
WCPP....... Women of Color Partnership Program (EA)
WCPQ ...... Havelock, NC [*AM radio station call letters*]
WCPR....... Coamo, PR [*AM radio station call letters*]
WCPR....... Weston, Clevedon & Portishead Railway [*British*]
WCPS....... Tarboro, NC [*AM radio station call letters*]
WCPS....... Women's Caucus for Political Science (EA)
WCPS....... World Confederation of Productivity Science (EAIO)
WCPT....... Alexandria, VA [*AM radio station call letters*]
WCPT....... World Confederation for Physical Therapy [*London, England*] (EA)
WCPX-TV ... Orlando, FL [*Television station call letters*]
WCPZ....... Sandusky, OH [*FM radio station call letters*]
WCQA ...... Fredonia, NY [*FM radio station call letters*]
WCQL ...... Portsmouth, NH [*AM radio station call letters*]
WCQL-FM ... York Center, ME [*FM radio station call letters*]
WCQR ...... Waynesboro, VA [*FM radio station call letters*]
WCQS ...... Asheville, NC [*FM radio station call letters*]
WCR .... Chandalar [*Alaska*] [*Airport symbol*] (OAG)
WCR .... Chandalar Lake, AK [*Location identifier*] [*FAA*] (FAAL)
WCR .... Warm Core Ring [*Oceanography*]
WCR .... Water-Cooled Reactor
WCR .... Water-Cooled Rod
WCR .... Watercooler (AAG)
WCR .... Waterloo and City Railway (ROG)
WCR .... West Coast Review [*A publication*]
WCR .... Western Communications Region [*Air Force*] (MCD)
WCR .... Willcrest Resources Ltd. [*Vancouver Stock Exchange symbol*]
WCR .... Wire Contact Relay
WCR .... Women's Council of Realtors [*of the National Association of Realtors*] (EA)
WCR .... Word Control [*or Count*] Register
WCR .... Workers' Compensation Commission Reports of Cases [*New South Wales, Australia*] [*A publication*] (DLA)
WCR .... Workers' Compensation Reports [*New South Wales*] [*A publication*] (APTA)
WCRA .... Effingham, IL [*AM radio station call letters*]
WCRA .... Weather Control Research Association [*Later, Weather Modification Association*]
WCRA .... Western College Reading Association (EA)

WCRA .... Wet Crease Recovery Angle [*Textile technology*]
WCRB .... Waltham, MA [*FM radio station call letters*]
WCRB .... West Coast Review of Books [*A publication*]
WCRC .... Effingham, IL [*FM radio station call letters*]
WCRC .... Water Conditioning Research Council [*Later, WQRC*]   (EA)
WCRD .... Myrtle Beach, SC [*Television station call letters*]
WCRD .... War Consumables Requirements Document [*Military*]   (AFIT)
WCRE .... Cheraw, SC [*AM radio station call letters*]
WCRED .... WESCON [*Western Electronics Show and Convention*]
           Conference Record [*A publication*]
WC Rep ..... Workmen's Compensation Reports [*A publication*]   (DLA)
WCRF....... Cleveland, OH [*FM radio station call letters*]
WCRF....... Weekly Collection Report File [*IRS*]
WCRH........ Williamsport, MD [*FM radio station call letters*]
WCRI......... Eureka, IL [*FM radio station call letters*]
WCRJ-FM ... Jacksonville, FL [*FM radio station call letters*]
WCRK .... Morristown, TN [*AM radio station call letters*]
WCRL .... Oneonta, AL [*AM radio station call letters*]
WCRLA..... Western College Reading and Learning Association   (EA)
WCRM .... Fort Myers, FL [*AM radio station call letters*]
WCRN ...... Cherry Valley, MA [*AM radio station call letters*]
WCRNSW ... Workers' Compensation Commission Reports of Cases (New
           South Wales, Australia) [*A publication*]   (DLA)
WCR (NSW) ... Workers' Compensation Reports (New South Wales) [*A
           publication*]   (APTA)
WCRO .... Johnstown, PA [*AM radio station call letters*]
WCROS..... White Crossover Vote [*Political science*]
WCRP........ Guayama, PR [*FM radio station call letters*]
WCRP........ World Climate Research Programme [*WMO*] [*ICSU*]
WCRP........ World Conference on Religion and Peace   (EAIO)
WCRP/USA ... World Conference on Religion and Peace, USA Section   (EA)
WCR (Q).... Workers' Compensation Reports (Queensland) [*A
           publication*]   (APTA)
WCRQ-FM ... Arab, AL [*FM radio station call letters*]
WCR (Qld) ... Workers' Compensation Reports (Queensland) [*A
           publication*]   (APTA)
WCR (Qn) ... Workers' Compensation Reports (Queensland) [*A publication*]
WCRR .... Rural Retreat, VA [*AM radio station call letters*]
WCRS........ Greenwood, SC [*AM radio station call letters*]
WCRS........ [*The*] WCRS Group PLC [*NASDAQ symbol*]   (NQ)
WC:RS....... Women's Caucus: Religious Studies   (EA)
WCRSI ...... Western Concrete Reinforcing Steel Institute [*Later,
           CRSI*]   (EA)
WCRT .... Birmingham, AL [*AM radio station call letters*]
WCRV .... Collierville, TN [*AM radio station call letters*]
WCRW .... Chicago, IL [*AM radio station call letters*]
WCR(WA) ... Workers' Compensation Reports (Western Australia) [*A
           publication*]
WCRX .... Chicago, IL [*FM radio station call letters*]
WCRZ .... Flint, MI [*FM radio station call letters*]
WCS .... Wallace Computer Services, Inc. [*NYSE symbol*]   (SPSG)
WCS .... Wang Computer System
WCS .... Waste Collection System [*NASA*]   (MCD)
WCS .... Waste Compaction Station [*Nuclear energy*]   (NRCH)
WCS .... Weak Calf Syndrome [*Veterinary medicine*]
WCS .... Weapon Control Station [*Military*]   (CAAL)
WCS .... Weapons Control System
WCS .... Wedgwood Collectors Society [*Commercial firm*]   (EA)
WCS .... Western Cover Society   (EA)
WCS .... William Cobbett Society   (EAIO)
WCS .... Woman Citizen Series [*A publication*]
WCS .... Work Control System   (NASA)
WCS .... Work Core Storage
WCS .... World Council of Synagogues   (EA)
WCS .... Writable Control Storage [*Data processing*]
WCSA....... Ripley, MS [*AM radio station call letters*]
WCSA....... West Coast of South America
WCSB....... Cleveland, OH [*FM radio station call letters*]
WCSB....... Weapon Control Switchboard [*Military*]   (CAAL)
WCSB(G).. Weapon Control Switchboard (Gun)
WCSB(M) ... Weapon Control Switchboard (Missile)
WCSB(UB) ... Weapon Control Switchboard (Underwater Battery)
WCSC....... Weapon Control System Console
WCSC....... Weapons Control System Coordinator   (NVT)
WCSC....... West Coast Switching Center [*Jet Propulsion Laboratory,
           NASA*]
WCSC....... World Correctional Service Center   (EA)
WCSC-TV ... Charleston, SC [*Television station call letters*]
WCSF .... Joliet, IL [*FM radio station call letters*]
WCSFMA ... Wisconsin Cheese and Specialty Food Merchants
           Association   (EA)
WCSG....... Grand Rapids, MI [*FM radio station call letters*]
WCSH-TV ... Portland, ME [*Television station call letters*]
WCSI........ Columbus, IN [*AM radio station call letters*]
WCSI........ World Centre for Scientific Information
WCSI........ Worldwide Computer Services, Incorporated [*Wayne, NJ*]
           [*NASDAQ symbol*]   (NQ)
WCSICEC ... Working Committee of the Scientific Institutes for Crafts in the
           EEC Countries [*Munich, Federal Republic of
           Germany*]   (EAIO)
WCSJ .... Morris, IL [*AM radio station call letters*]

WCSK........ Kingsport, TN [*FM radio station call letters*]
WCSL........ Cherryville, NC [*AM radio station call letters*]
WCSM....... Celina, OH [*AM radio station call letters*]
WCSM....... World Congress of Sports Medicine
WCSM-FM ... Celina, OH [*FM radio station call letters*]
WCSMLL ... Western Canadian Studies in Modern Languages and Literature
           [*A publication*]
WCSP........ Crystal Springs, MS [*AM radio station call letters*]
WCSP........ Wisconsin Cheese and Sausage Promotions   (EA)
WCSPA....... West Coast Shrimp Producers Association   (EA)
WCSQ .... Central Square, NY [*FM radio station call letters*]
WCSR........ Hillsdale, MI [*AM radio station call letters*]
WCSRC..... Wild Canid Survival and Research Center - Wolf
           Sanctuary   (EA)
WCSR-FM ... Hillsdale, MI [*FM radio station call letters*]
WCSS .... Amsterdam, NY [*AM radio station call letters*]
WCSS .... Weapons Control Subsystem   (MCD)
WCSS .... Weapons Control System Simulator
WCSS .... West Coast Sound School [*Navy*]
WCST........ Berkeley Springs, WV [*AM radio station call letters*]
WCST........ Wisconsin Card Sorting Test [*Neuropsychology test*]
WCST-FM ... Berkeley Springs, WV [*FM radio station call letters*]
WCSU .... Western Connecticut State University [*Danbury*]
WCSU-FM ... Wilberforce, OH [*FM radio station call letters*]
WCSUICA ... Women's Coalition to Stop US Intervention in Central
           America [*Later, WCSUICAC*]   (EA)
WCSUICAC ... Women's Coalition to Stop US Intervention in Central
           America and the Caribbean   (EA)
WCSV .... Crossville, TN [*AM radio station call letters*]
WCSW .... Shell Lake, WI [*AM radio station call letters*]
WCSX........ Birmingham, MI [*FM radio station call letters*]
WCSX........ WCS International [*NASDAQ symbol*]   (NQ)
WCSY........ South Haven, MI [*AM radio station call letters*]
WCSY-FM ... South Haven, MI [*FM radio station call letters*]
WCT .... Trinity Memorial Hospital, Cudahy, WI [*Library symbol*]
           [*Library of Congress*]   (LCLS)
WCT .... Waukesha County Institute, Pewaukee, WI [*OCLC
           symbol*]   (OCLC)
WCT .... West Coast Travel [*Information service or system*]   (IID)
WCT .... Westek Communications, Inc. [*Vancouver Stock Exchange
           symbol*]
WCT .... World Championship Tennis, Inc.
WCT .... World Confederation of Teachers [*See also CSME*] [*Brussels,
           Belgium*]   (EAIO)
WCT .... Worthy Chief Templar
WCTA .... Alamo, TN [*AM radio station call letters*]
WCTA .... Western Coal Transportation Association   (EA)
WCTA .... World Committee for Trade Action [*See also CMAP*] [*Brussels,
           Belgium*]   (EAIO)
WCTB........ West Country Tourist Board [*British*]   (DCTA)
WCTB........ Western Carriers Tariff Bureau
WCTC........ New Brunswick, NJ [*AM radio station call letters*]
WCTD .... World Congress of Teachers of Dancing   (EA)
WCTE........ Cookeville, TN [*Television station call letters*]
WCTF........ Vernon, CT [*AM radio station call letters*]
WCTG .... Columbia, SC [*AM radio station call letters*]
WCTG .... Woodcutting   (MSA)
WCTH........ Plantation Key, FL [*FM radio station call letters*]
WCTI........ Greenville, NC [*Television station call letters*]
WCTK........ New Bedford, MA [*FM radio station call letters*]
WCTL........ Union City, PA [*FM radio station call letters*]
WCTM .... Eaton, OH [*AM radio station call letters*]
WCTN .... Potomac-Cabin John, MD [*AM radio station call letters*]
WCTO .... Smithtown, NY [*FM radio station call letters*]
WCTP........ Charleston, SC [*Television station call letters*]
WCTP........ Wire Chief Test Panel [*Telecommunications*]   (TEL)
WCTQ .... Venice, FL [*FM radio station call letters*]
WCTR .... Chestertown, MD [*AM radio station call letters*]
WCTR .... WCTU Railway Co. [*AAR code*]
WCTS....... Weapon Cost Test Site [*Military*]   (CAAL)
W Ct SA.... Union of South Africa Water Courts Decisions [*A
           publication*]   (DLA)
WCTS-FM ... Minneapolis, MN [*FM radio station call letters*]
WCTT........ Corbin, KY [*AM radio station call letters*]
WCTT........ Weapons Crew Training Test [*TCATA*]   (RDA)
WCTT-FM ... Corbin, KY [*FM radio station call letters*]
WCTU .... National Woman's Christian Temperance Union   (EA)
WCTU .... Women's Connubial Temperance Union [*Satirical*]
WCTV .... Thomasville, GA [*Television station call letters*]
WCTV .... Wometco Cable TV, Inc. [*NASDAQ symbol*]   (NQ)
WCTW ...... New Castle, IN [*AM radio station call letters*]
WCTX .... Palmyra, PA [*FM radio station call letters*]
WCTY .... Norwich, CT [*FM radio station call letters*]
WCTZ....... Clarksville, TN [*AM radio station call letters*]
WCu.......... Cumberland Public Library, Cumberland, WI [*Library symbol*]
           [*Library of Congress*]   (LCLS)
WCU......... Water Cooler Unit   (AAG)
WCU......... Weapons Control Unit   (MCD)
WCU......... West Coast University [*Los Angeles, CA*]
WCU......... Western Carolina University [*Cullowhee, NC*]
WCU......... Western Catholic Union   (EA)

WCUB....... Two Rivers, WI [*AM radio station call letters*]
WCUC-FM ... Clarion, PA [*FM radio station call letters*]
WCUE....... Cuyahoga Falls, OH [*AM radio station call letters*]
WCUG...... Cuthbert, GA [*AM radio station call letters*]
WCUH ...... Western Carolina University Herbarium
WCUK ...... West Coast of the United Kingdom
WCUL....... Culpeper, VA [*FM radio station call letters*]
WCUM...... Bridgeport, CT [*AM radio station call letters*]
WCUMBS ... Western Canadian Universities Marine Biological Society
WCUNDDP ... World Committee for the United Nations Decade of Disabled
        Persons (EA)
WCUW....... Worcester, MA [*FM radio station call letters*]
WCUZ....... Grand Rapids, MI [*AM radio station call letters*]
WCUZ....... World Confederation of United Zionists (EA)
WCUZ-FM ... Grand Rapids, MI [*FM radio station call letters*]
WCV......... Water Check Valve
WCV......... Winant and Clayton Volunteers (EA)
WCVA....... Culpeper, VA [*AM radio station call letters*]
WCVB-TV ... Boston, MA [*Television station call letters*]
WCVC....... Tallahassee, FL [*AM radio station call letters*]
WCVE ...... Richmond, VA [*FM radio station call letters*]
WCVE-TV ... Richmond, VA [*Television station call letters*]
WCVF-FM ... Fredonia, NY [*FM radio station call letters*]
WCVG...... Covington, KY [*AM radio station call letters*]
WCVH....... Flemington, NJ [*FM radio station call letters*]
WCVI....... Connellsville, PA [*AM radio station call letters*]
WCVJ....... Jefferson, OH [*FM radio station call letters*]
WCVK...... Bowling Green, KY [*FM radio station call letters*]
WCVL....... Crawfordsville, IN [*AM radio station call letters*]
WCVM...... Middlebury, VT [*FM radio station call letters*]
WCVM...... Western College of Veterinary Medicine [*Canada*]
WCVN....... Covington, KY [*Television station call letters*]
WCVO....... Gahanna, OH [*FM radio station call letters*]
WCVP....... Murphy, NC [*AM radio station call letters*]
WCVP-FM ... Robbinsville, NC [*FM radio station call letters*]
WCVQ...... Fort Campbell, KY [*FM radio station call letters*]
WCVR-FM ... Randolph, VT [*FM radio station call letters*]
WCVS....... Springfield, IL [*AM radio station call letters*]
WCVT....... Towson, MD [*FM radio station call letters*]
WCVU....... Naples, FL [*FM radio station call letters*]
WCVV ...... Belpre, OH [*FM radio station call letters*]
WCVW...... Richmond, VA [*Television station call letters*]
WCVX....... Vineyard Haven, MA [*Television station call letters*]
WCVY....... Coventry, RI [*FM radio station call letters*]
WCVZ ...... Zanesville, OH [*FM radio station call letters*]
WCW........ Western College for Women [*Ohio*]
WCW........ Western College for Women, Oxford, OH [*OCLC symbol*]
        [*Inactive*] (OCLC)
WCW........ Wood Casement Window [*Technical drawings*]
WCWA..... Toledo, OH [*AM radio station call letters*]
WCWB...... World Council for the Welfare of the Blind [*Later,
        WBU*] (EAIO)
WCWB-FM ... Trenton, FL [*FM radio station call letters*]
WCWC...... Ripon, WI [*AM radio station call letters*]
WCWE...... WCW Western Canada Water Enterprises, Inc. [*NASDAQ
        symbol*] (NQ)
WCWL ...... Stockbridge, MA [*FM radio station call letters*]
WCWN...... William Carlos Williams Newsletter [*A publication*]
WC/WO .... Working Committee on Weather Operations
WCWP ...... Brookville, NY [*FM radio station call letters*]
WCWR ...... William Carlos Williams Review [*A publication*]
WCWS....... Wooster, OH [*FM radio station call letters*]
WCWT-FM ... Centerville, OH [*FM radio station call letters*]
WCWV...... Summersville, WV [*FM radio station call letters*]
WCX......... Weak Cation Exchanger [*Chemistry*]
WCXI....... Detroit, MI [*AM radio station call letters*]
WCXJ....... Braddock, PA [*AM radio station call letters*]
WCXL....... Vero Beach, FL [*FM radio station call letters*]
WCXN....... Claremont, NC [*AM radio station call letters*]
WCXQ....... Moca, PR [*AM radio station call letters*]
WCXR-FM ... Woodbridge, VA [*FM radio station call letters*]
WCXT....... Hart, MI [*FM radio station call letters*]
WCXU....... Caribou, ME [*FM radio station call letters*]
WCXX ...... Madawaska, ME [*FM radio station call letters*]
WCY......... Viking Express, Inc. [*West Chicago, IL*] [*FAA
        designator*] (FAAC)
WCY......... World Communications Year [*1983*]
WCYB-TV ... Bristol, VA [*Television station call letters*]
WCYC ...... Chicago, IL [*FM radio station call letters*]
WCYC ...... Westmorland and Cumberland Yeomanry Cavalry [*British
        military*] (DMA)
WCYJ-FM ... Waynesburg, PA [*FM radio station call letters*]
WCYK ...... Crozet, VA [*AM radio station call letters*]
WCYK-FM ... Crozet, VA [*FM radio station call letters*]
WCYN...... Cynthiana, KY [*AM radio station call letters*]
WCYN-FM ... Cynthiana, KY [*FM radio station call letters*]
WCYS....... Worcester County Institution for Savings [*Worcester, MA*]
        [*NASDAQ symbol*] (NQ)
WCZE....... Babson Park, FL [*AM radio station call letters*]
WCZI....... Washington, NC [*FM radio station call letters*]
WCZN ...... Chester, PA [*AM radio station call letters*]

WCZX ...... Hyde Park, NY [*FM radio station call letters*]
WCZY-FM ... Mount Pleasant, MI [*FM radio station call letters*]
WD............ Decisions Won [*Boxing*]
WD............ [*Qualified for*] Deck Watch [*USNR officer classification*]
WD............ General Warranty Deed [*Real estate*]
Wd............ Seaweed [*Quality of the bottom*] [*Nautical charts*]
WD............ Two-Conductor Cables [*JETDS nomenclature*]
        [*Military*] (CET)
WD............ Wallerian Degeneration [*Medicine*]
WD............ War Damage
WD............ War Department [*Created, 1789; became Department of the
        Army, 1947*]
WD............ Ward
WD............ Wardair Canada Ltd. [*ICAO designator*] (FAAC)
WD............ Warehouse Distributor
WD............ Warranted
WD............ Washington Decisions [*A publication*] (DLA)
WD............ Waste Disposal [*Nuclear energy*] (NRCH)
WD............ Water Damage (ADA)
WD............ Water Desurger
WD............ Watt Demand Meter (MSA)
WD............ Wavelength Dispersive [*Spectrometry*]
WD............ Weapon Description (MCD)
WD............ Weapon Director [*SAGE*]
WD............ Weapons Data [*Navy*]
WD............ Weather Division [*Air Force*] (MCD)
WD............ Web Depth
WD............ [*The*] Weekly Dispatch [*A publication*]
WD............ Well Deck
W-D .... Well-Developed [*Medicine*]
WD............ Well Differentiated [*Medicine*]
WD............ Well-Drained [*Soil*]
WD............ West Division (ROG)
WD............ Westminster Dragoons [*British military*] (DMA)
WD............ Wet Dressing
WD............ Wheel Drive [*Engineering*]
WD............ When Directed
WD............ When Discovered
WD............ When Distributed [*Stock exchange term*] (SPSG)
WD............ Whole Depth
WD............ Widow
WD............ Width (MSA)
W/D .... Width-to-Diameter [*Ratio*] (KSC)
WD............ Wife's Divorce (ROG)
WD............ Will Dated [*Genealogy*] (ROG)
WD............ Wilson Dam [*TVA*]
WD............ Wilson's Disease [*Medicine*]
WD............ Wind (MSA)
WD............ Wind Deflection [*Ballistics*]
WD............ Wind Direction
WD............ Window Detector
WD............ Window Dimension [*Technical drawings*]
WD............ Winner's Dog [*Dog show term*]
WD............ Winter's Digest [*A publication*]
WD............ Wired Discrete (NASA)
WD............ With Dependents (MCD)
W/D .... Withdrawal (DLA)
WD............ Withdrawn (AFM)
WD............ Wittenberg Door [*A publication*]
W & D .... Wolferstan and Dew's English Election Cases [*1856-58*] [*A
        publication*] (DLA)
WD............ Woman's Day [*A publication*]
WD............ Wood (AAG)
WD............ Wood Door [*Technical drawings*]
WD............ Word
Wd............ Word [*A publication*]
WD............ Word Display
WD............ Work [*or Working*] Day (AFM)
WD............ Work Description (MCD)
WD............ Work Directive (MCD)
WD............ Working Distance [*Microscopy*]
WD............ Works Department
Wd............ World [*A publication*]
WD............ World Development [*A publication*]
W & D .... Wort und Dienst [*A publication*]
WD............ Would
WD............ Wrist Disarticulation [*Medicine*]
WD............ Write Data
WD............ Write Direct
WD............ Writers Digest [*A publication*]
WD............ Wrongful Detention [*British*]
WD............ Wydmar Developmental Corp. [*Vancouver Stock Exchange
        symbol*]
2WD.......... Two-Wheel Drive [*Automotive engineering*]
W 2d .... Washington State Reports, Second Series [*A
        publication*] (DLA)
4WD.......... Four-Wheel Drive [*Vehicle*]
W4D......... Worth Four-Dot Test [*Ophthalmology*]
WDA......... Aram Public Library, Delavan, WI [*Library symbol*] [*Library of
        Congress*] (LCLS)
WDA......... Wagga Diploma in Agriculture [*Australia*]

WDA......... Wallcovering Distributors Association (EA)
WDA......... Warehouse Distributors Association for Leisure and Mobile
                 Products (EA)
WDA......... Waste Disposal Authority [*British*]
WDA......... Wave Data Analyzer [*Marine science*] (MSC)
WDA......... Weapons Defended Area
WDA......... Welsh Development Agency [*United Kingdom*] (DS)
WDA......... Western District Area [*Air Force*]
WDA......... Wheel Drive Assembly
WDA......... Wholesale Distributors Association (EA)
WDA......... Wildlife Disease Association (EA)
WDA......... Wilson's Disease Association (EA)
WDA......... Withdrawal of Availability [*Military*] (AFM)
WDA......... Women's Diocesan Association [*British*]
WDA......... World Aquathemes Ltd. [*Vancouver Stock Exchange symbol*]
WDA......... World Dredging Association (MSC)
WDAC....... Lancaster, PA [*FM radio station call letters*]
WDAD....... Indiana, PA [*AM radio station call letters*]
WDAE....... Tampa, FL [*AM radio station call letters*]
WDAF....... Kansas City, MO [*AM radio station call letters*]
WDAF....... Western Desert Air Force
WDAF-TV ... Kansas City, MO [*Television station call letters*]
WDAHAC ... National Society Women Descendants of the Ancient and
                 Honorable Artillery Company (EA)
WDAK....... Alexander City, AL [*AM radio station call letters*]
WDAL....... Linden, AL [*FM radio station call letters*]
WDALMP ... Warehouse Distributors Association for Leisure and Mobile
                 Products (EA)
WDAM-TV ... Laurel, MS [*Television station call letters*]
WDAN...... Danville, IL [*AM radio station call letters*]
WDAO....... Dayton, OH [*AM radio station call letters*]
WDAP....... World Dictionary of Awards and Prizes [*A publication*]
WDAQ....... Danbury, CT [*FM radio station call letters*]
WDar......... Darien Public Library, Darien, WI [*Library symbol*] [*Library of
                 Congress*] (LCLS)
WDAR....... Darlington, SC [*AM radio station call letters*]
WDAS ...... Philadelphia, PA [*AM radio station call letters*]
WDAS-FM ... Philadelphia, PA [*FM radio station call letters*]
WDAT....... Amory, MS [*AM radio station call letters*]
WDAU....... Ozark, AL [*Television station call letters*]
WDAV....... Davidson, NC [*FM radio station call letters*]
WDAW...... Haymarket, VA [*AM radio station call letters*]
WDAX....... McRae, GA [*AM radio station call letters*]
WDAX-FM ... McRae, GA [*FM radio station call letters*]
WDAY....... Fargo, ND [*AM radio station call letters*]
WDAY-FM ... Fargo, ND [*FM radio station call letters*]
WDAY-TV ... Fargo, ND [*Television station call letters*]
WDAZ-TV ... Devils Lake, ND [*Television station call letters*]
WDB......... Suedosteuropa. Zeitschrift fuer Gegenwartsforschung [*A
                 publication*]
WdB........... Weekblad der Belastingen [*A publication*]
WDB......... Weekblad der Directe Belastingen [*A publication*]
WDB......... Westminster Dictionary of the Bible [*A publication*] (BJA)
WDB......... Wide Deadband [*NASA*]
WDB......... Wideband [*Radio*] (MCD)
WDBA....... Du Bois, PA [*FM radio station call letters*]
WDBB....... Tuscaloosa, AL [*Television station call letters*]
WDBC....... Escanaba, MI [*AM radio station call letters*]
WDBD....... Jackson, MS [*Television station call letters*]
WDBF....... Delray Beach, FL [*AM radio station call letters*]
WDBI-FM ... Tawas City, MI [*FM radio station call letters*]
WDBJ........ Roanoke, VA [*Television station call letters*]
WDBK....... Blackwood, NJ [*FM radio station call letters*]
WDBK....... Wordbook (ROG)
WDBL....... Springfield, TN [*AM radio station call letters*]
WDBL-FM ... Springfield, TN [*FM radio station call letters*]
WDBM-FM ... East Lansing, MI [*FM radio station call letters*]
WDBN...... Woodbine Petroleum, Inc. [*NASDAQ symbol*] (NQ)
WDBO....... Orlando, FL [*AM radio station call letters*]
WDBOR .... Wood Boring
WDBQ....... Dubuque, IA [*AM radio station call letters*]
WDBR ...... Springfield, IL [*FM radio station call letters*]
WDBS....... Eatonton, GA [*AM radio station call letters*]
WDBY....... Duxbury, MA [*FM radio station call letters*]
WDC......... War Damage Commission [*British*]
WDC......... War Damage Corporation [*World War II*]
WDC......... War Department Constabulary [*British military*] (DMA)
WDC......... Washington Document Center
WDC......... Waste Disposal Cask [*Nuclear energy*] (NRCH)
WDC......... Waste Disposal Code
WDC......... Water Data Center [*Department of Agriculture*] [*Information
                 service or system*] (IID)
WDC......... Weapon Delivery Computer (MCD)
WDC......... Weapon Direction Computer [*Military*] (CAAL)
WDC......... Western Defense Command [*Army*]
WDC......... Western Digital Corp. [*NYSE symbol*] (SPSG)
WDC......... Westinghouse Defense Center
WDC......... Whiskeytown Dam [*California*] [*Seismograph station code, US
                 Geological Survey*] (SEIS)
WDC......... Wideband Directional Coupler
WDC......... Women's Distance Committee (EA)

WDC......... Workers' Defence Committee [*Ghana*] [*Political party*] (PPW)
WDC......... Workers' Defense Committee [*Poland*] (PD)
WDC......... Working Direct Current (DEN)
WDC......... World Data Center [*National Academy of Sciences*] [*Data
                 collection and exchange center*]
WDC......... World Development Corporation
WDC......... World Disarmament Campaign (EAIO)
WDC......... World Disarmament Conference (NATG)
WDC......... World Druze Congress (EA)
WDC......... Write Data Check (CMD)
WDC-A..... World Data Center A [*National Academy of Sciences*]
WDCA...... World Diving Coaches Association (EA)
WDCA-TV ... Washington, DC [*Television station call letters*]
WDCB....... Glen Ellyn, IL [*FM radio station call letters*]
WDC-B..... World Data Center B [*National Academy of Sciences*]
WDCC...... Sanford, NC [*FM radio station call letters*]
WDCE ...... Richmond, VA [*FM radio station call letters*]
WDCF....... Dade City, FL [*AM radio station call letters*]
WDCG...... Durham, NC [*FM radio station call letters*]
WDCI........ Bridgeport, WV [*FM radio station call letters*]
WDCJ........ Lorton, VA [*FM radio station call letters*]
WDCL-FM ... Somerset, KY [*FM radio station call letters*]
WDCM...... Cruz Bay, VI [*FM radio station call letters*]
WDCMC ... War Department Classified Message Center [*Obsolete*] [*World
                 War II*]
WDCN...... Nashville, TN [*Television station call letters*]
WDCO....... Western Energy Development Company, Inc. [*NASDAQ
                 symbol*] (NQ)
WDCO-FM ... Cochran, GA [*FM radio station call letters*]
WDCO-TV ... Cochran, GA [*Television station call letters*]
WDCQ....... Pine Island Centre, FL [*AM radio station call letters*]
WDCR ...... Hanover, NH [*AM radio station call letters*]
WDCS ...... Weapons Data Correlation System (MCD)
WDCS ...... Women's Division of Christian Service [*of the Board of
                 Missions, The Methodist Church*]
WDCS ...... Writable Diagnostic Control Store
WDCSA.... War Department Chief of Staff, US Army [*World War II*]
WDCSM.... Walt Disney Comic Strip Maker [*Apple computer software*]
WDCT ...... Fairfax, VA [*AM radio station call letters*]
WDCT ...... Woodcut (ROG)
WDCU ...... Washington, DC [*FM radio station call letters*]
WDCV-FM ... Carlisle, PA [*FM radio station call letters*]
WDCW...... Sturgeon Bay, WI [*FM radio station call letters*]
WDCX........ Buffalo, NY [*FM radio station call letters*]
WDD......... Western Development Division [*ARDC*]
WD (2d)... Washington Decisions, Second Series [*A publication*] (DLA)
WDDC...... Portage, WI [*FM radio station call letters*]
WDDC...... Well Deck Debarkation Control [*Navy*] (CAAL)
WDDD...... Johnston City, IL [*AM radio station call letters*]
WDDD-FM ... Marion, IL [*FM radio station call letters*]
WDDJ ...... Paducah, KY [*FM radio station call letters*]
WDDO ...... Macon, GA [*AM radio station call letters*]
WDDQ ...... Adel, GA [*FM radio station call letters*]
WDDT....... Greenville, MS [*AM radio station call letters*]
WDE......... Weapons Directing Equipment (NVT)
wde............ Wood-Engraver [*MARC relator code*] [*Library of
                 Congress*] (LCCP)
WDEA ...... Ellsworth, ME [*AM radio station call letters*]
WDEB ...... Jamestown, TN [*AM radio station call letters*]
WDEB-FM ... Jamestown, TN [*FM radio station call letters*]
WDEC ...... Americus, GA [*AM radio station call letters*]
WDEC-FM ... Americus, GA [*FM radio station call letters*]
WDED...... Wounded [*Military*]
WDEE ...... Reed City, MI [*AM radio station call letters*]
WDEF...... Chattanooga, TN [*AM radio station call letters*]
WDEFA..... Welding Design and Fabrication [*A publication*]
WDEF-FM ... Chattanooga, TN [*FM radio station call letters*]
WDEF-TV ... Chattanooga, TN [*Television station call letters*]
WDEH...... Sweetwater, TN [*AM radio station call letters*]
WDEH-FM ... Sweetwater, TN [*FM radio station call letters*]
WDEK ...... De Kalb, IL [*FM radio station call letters*]
WDEL ...... Weapons Development Effectiveness Laboratory (MCD)
WDEL ...... Wilmington, DE [*AM radio station call letters*]
WDEMCO ... Walt Disney Educational Media Company
WDEN...... Macon, GA [*AM radio station call letters*]
WDEN-FM ... Macon, GA [*FM radio station call letters*]
WDEOAT ... Wolfe Data Entry Operator Aptitude Test
WDEP ...... Western Deep Levels Ltd. [*NASDAQ symbol*] (NQ)
WDEQ-FM ... De Graff, OH [*FM radio station call letters*]
WDER ...... Derry, NH [*AM radio station call letters*]
WDET-FM ... Detroit, MI [*FM radio station call letters*]
WDEV ...... Waterbury, VT [*AM radio station call letters*]
WDEX ...... Monroe, NC [*AM radio station call letters*]
WDEY ...... Lapeer, MI [*AM radio station call letters*]
WDEY-FM ... Lapeer, MI [*FM radio station call letters*]
WDEZ ...... Wausau, WI [*FM radio station call letters*]
WDF......... Wall Distribution Frame (MUGU)
WDF......... Weapon Defense Facility (AAG)
WDF......... Weather Data Facility
WDF......... Western Desert Force [*World War II*]
WDF.......... Wood Door and Frame [*Technical drawings*]

WDF	Woodruff
WDF	World Darts Federation (EAIO)
WDF	World Draughts (Checkers) Federation [*See also FMJD*] [*Dordrecht, Netherlands*] (EAIO)
WDFB	Junction City, KY [*AM radio station call letters*]
WDFC	WD-40 Company [*NASDAQ symbol*] (NQ)
WD/FE	Water Dispenser/Fire Extinguisher [*Apollo*] [*NASA*]
WDFL	Cross City, FL [*AM radio station call letters*]
WDFL-FM	Cross City, FL [*FM radio station call letters*]
WDFM	Defiance, OH [*FM radio station call letters*]
WDFP	World Day for Peace (EA)
WDFX	Detroit, MI [*FM radio station call letters*]
WDFZ	Tullahoma, TN [*AM radio station call letters*]
WDG	Enid [*Oklahoma*] [*Airport symbol*] (OAG)
WDG	Enid, OK [*Location identifier*] [*FAA*] (FAAL)
WDG	Wallace Dam [*Georgia*] [*Seismograph station code, US Geological Survey*] (SEIS)
WDG	Weapons Display Generator (MCD)
WDG	Wedgestone Financial [*NYSE symbol*] (SPSG)
WDG	Winding (MSA)
WDG	World Diplomatic Guide [*A publication*]
WDGB	Wuerzburger Diozesangeschichtsblaetter [*A publication*]
WDGC-FM	Downers Grove, IL [*FM radio station call letters*]
WDGE	Saranac Lake, NY [*FM radio station call letters*]
WDGF	War Department Ground Forces [*Obsolete*]
WDGI	Wholesale Dry Goods Institute [*Later, NATAD*]
W Dgns	Westminster Dragoons [*British military*] (DMA)
WDGO	War Department General Order [*Obsolete*]
WDGR	Dahlonega, GA [*AM radio station call letters*]
WDGS	New Albany, IN [*AM radio station call letters*]
WDGS	War Department General Staff [*Obsolete*]
WDG TBA	Wording to Be Agreed [*Insurance*] (AIA)
WDGY	Minneapolis, MN [*AM radio station call letters*]
WDH	Watery Diarrhea, Hypokalemia [*Syndrome*] [*Medicine*]
WDH	Winchell's Donut House [*NYSE symbol*] (SPSG)
WDH	Windhoek [*Namibia*] [*Airport symbol*] (OAG)
WDHA	Watery Diarrhea, Hypokalemia, Achlorhydria [*Medicine*]
WDHA-FM	Dover, NJ [*FM radio station call letters*]
WDHCB	War Department Hardship Claims Board [*Obsolete*]
WDHD	Woodhead Industries, Inc. [*NASDAQ symbol*] (NQ)
WDHH	Watery Diarrhea, Hypokalemia, Hypochlorhydria [*Syndrome*] [*Medicine*]
WDHHA	Watery Diarrhea, Hypochlorhydria, Hypokalemia, and Alkalosis [*Medicine*]
WDHN	Dothan, AL [*Television station call letters*]
WDHP	Presque Isle, ME [*FM radio station call letters*]
WDHR	Pikeville, KY [*FM radio station call letters*]
WDHS	Gaston, IN [*FM radio station call letters*]
WDHS	Worldwide Dental Health Service (EA)
WDI	War Department Intelligence [*Obsolete*]
WDI	Wardair, Inc. [*Toronto Stock Exchange symbol*]
WDI	Warfarin Dose Index
WDI	Warhead Detection Indicator (AAG)
WDI	Weapon Data Index [*Navy*] (MCD)
WDI	Weapon Delivery Impairment (NVT)
WDI	Web Depth Index
WDI	Wind Direction Indicator [*Aviation*] (FAAC)
WDI	Wood and Iron [*Freight*]
WDIA	Memphis, TN [*AM radio station call letters*]
WDIA	Weekblad der Directe Belastingen, Invoerrechten en Accijnzen [*A publication*]
WDIC	Clinchco, VA [*AM radio station call letters*]
WDICC	War Department Intelligence Collection Committee
WDIC-FM	Clincho, VA [*FM radio station call letters*]
WDICPC	War Department Intelligence Collection Planning Committee
WDIF	Marion, OH [*FM radio station call letters*]
WDIF	Women's Democratic International Federation (NATG)
W Dig	New York Weekly Digest [*A publication*] (DLA)
WDIG	Steubenville, OH [*AM radio station call letters*]
WDIH	Salisbury, MD [*FM radio station call letters*]
WDIM	With Design in Mind International [*NASDAQ symbol*] (NQ)
WDIO-TV	Duluth, MN [*Television station call letters*]
WDIQ	Dozier, AL [*Television station call letters*]
WDIR	Wind Direction
WDIRN	What Do I Read Next? [*A publication*]
WDIV	Detroit, MI [*Television station call letters*]
WDIX	Yadkinville, NC [*AM radio station call letters*]
WDIZ	Orlando, FL [*FM radio station call letters*]
WdJ	Wissenschaft des Judentums [*A publication*] (BJA)
WDJB	Windsor, NC [*FM radio station call letters*]
WDJC	Birmingham, AL [*FM radio station call letters*]
WDJK	Xenia, OH [*FM radio station call letters*]
WDJM-FM	Framingham, MA [*FM radio station call letters*]
WDJO	Cincinnati, OH [*AM radio station call letters*]
WDJQ	Alliance, OH [*FM radio station call letters*]
WDJR	Enterprise, AL [*FM radio station call letters*]
WDJS	Mount Olive, NC [*AM radio station call letters*]
WDJT-TV	Milwaukee, WI [*Television station call letters*]
WDJW	Somers, CT [*FM radio station call letters*]
WDJX	Louisville, KY [*AM radio station call letters*]
WDJX-FM	Louisville, KY [*FM radio station call letters*]

WDJY	Washington, DC [*FM radio station call letters*]
WDJZ	Bridgeport, CT [*AM radio station call letters*]
WDKA	Paducah, KY [*Television station call letters*]
WDKB	De Kalb, IL [*FM radio station call letters*]
WDKC	Fort Pierce, FL [*FM radio station call letters*]
WDKD	Kingstree, SC [*AM radio station call letters*]
WDKN	Dickson, TN [*AM radio station call letters*]
WDKT	Madison, AL [*AM radio station call letters*]
WDKX	Rochester, NY [*FM radio station call letters*]
WD KY	United States District Court for the Western District of Kentucky (DLA)
WDKY-TV	Danville, KY [*Television station call letters*]
WDL	Warren Library Association and County Division, Warren, PA [*OCLC symbol*] (OCLC)
WDL	Waveguide Directional Localizer
WDL	Weapon Data Link (MCD)
WDL	Weapons Density List (AABC)
WDL	Well-Differentiated Lymphocytic [*Lymphoma classification*]
WDL	Westdeutsche Luftwerbung [*Airline*] [*Federal Republic of Germany*]
WDL	Western Development Laboratories
WDL	Western d'Eldona Resources Ltd. [*Toronto Stock Exchange symbol*]
WDL	Wien Displacement Law [*Physics*]
WDL	Wireless Data Link
Wdl	Wirkung der Literatur [*A publication*]
WDL	Workers' Defense League (EA)
WD LA	United States District Court for the Western District of Louisiana (DLA)
WDLA	Walton, NY [*AM radio station call letters*]
WDLA-FM	Walton, NY [*FM radio station call letters*]
WDLB	Marshfield, WI [*AM radio station call letters*]
WDLC	Port Jervis, NY [*AM radio station call letters*]
WDLE-FM	Federalsburg, MD [*FM radio station call letters*]
WDLG	Lexington, MS [*FM radio station call letters*]
WDLI	Canton, OH [*Television station call letters*]
WDLK	Dadeville, AL [*AM radio station call letters*]
WDLL	Well Differentiated Lymphatic Lymphoma [*Oncology*]
WDLL	Well-Differentiated Lymphocytic Lymphoma
WDLM	East Moline, IL [*AM radio station call letters*]
WDLM-FM	East Moline, IL [*FM radio station call letters*]
WDLR	Delaware, OH [*AM radio station call letters*]
WDLS	Dallas, PA [*FM radio station call letters*]
WDLT	Chickasaw, AL [*FM radio station call letters*]
WDLX	Washington, NC [*FM radio station call letters*]
WDLY	Widely (FAAC)
WDLZ	Flint, MI [*AM radio station call letters*]
WDM	Wavelength Division Multiplex [*Telecommunications*]
WDM	Weight after Departure from Mars [*NASA*]
WDM	World Disarmament Movement [*Australia*]
WDMA	Wholesale Druggists Merchandising Association (EA)
WDMB	War Department Manpower Board [*Obsolete*]
WDMC	[*The*] Woodmoor Corp. [*NASDAQ symbol*] (NQ)
WDME	Dover-Foxcroft, ME [*AM radio station call letters*]
WDME-FM	Dover-Foxcroft, ME [*FM radio station call letters*]
WDMET	Wound Data Munitions Effectiveness Team (MCD)
WDMF	Weak Disordered Magnetic Field
WDMG	Douglas, GA [*AM radio station call letters*]
WDMG-FM	Douglas, GA [*FM radio station call letters*]
WD Mich	United States District Court for the Western District of Michigan (DLA)
WDMJ	Marquette, MI [*AM radio station call letters*]
WDML	Wiring Diagram Maintenance List
WD MO	United States District Court for the Western District of Missouri (DLA)
WDMO	Weight before Departure from Mars Orbit [*NASA*]
WDMP	Dodgeville, WI [*AM radio station call letters*]
WDMP-FM	Dodgeville, WI [*FM radio station call letters*]
WDMS	Greenville, MS [*FM radio station call letters*]
WDMV	Pocomoke City, MD [*AM radio station call letters*]
WDMX	Vienna, WV [*FM radio station call letters*]
WDN	Wooden
WDNA	Miami, FL [*FM radio station call letters*]
WDNC	Durham, NC [*AM radio station call letters*]
WDNC	United States District Court for the Western District of North Carolina (DLA)
WDND	Wilmington, IL [*FM radio station call letters*]
WDNE	Elkins, WV [*AM radio station call letters*]
WDNE-FM	Elkins, WV [*FM radio station call letters*]
WDNG	Anniston, AL [*AM radio station call letters*]
WDNH-FM	Honesdale, PA [*FM radio station call letters*]
WDNL	Danville, IL [*FM radio station call letters*]
WDNO	Laurel, DE [*FM radio station call letters*]
WDNOWRE	Wooden Ware [*Freight*]
WDNR	Chester, PA [*FM radio station call letters*]
WDNS	Bowling Green, KY [*FM radio station call letters*]
WDNT	Dayton, TN [*AM radio station call letters*]
WDNX	Olive Hill, TN [*FM radio station call letters*]
WDNY	Dansville, NY [*AM radio station call letters*]
WDNY	United States District Court for the Western District of New York (DLA)

WDO .... Web Depth Order
WdO .... Welt des Orients. Wissenschaftliche Beitraege zur Kunde des Morgenlandes [*Wuppertal/Stuttgart/Goettingen*] [*A publication*]
WDO .... Widespread Depression Orchestra
WDO .... Window   (MSA)
WDOC...... Prestonsburg, KY [*AM radio station call letters*]
WDOD ...... Chattanooga, TN [*AM radio station call letters*]
WDOD-FM ... Chattanooga, TN [*FM radio station call letters*]
WDOE....... Dunkirk, NY [*AM radio station call letters*]
WDOG ...... Allendale, SC [*AM radio station call letters*]
WDOG-FM ... Allendale, SC [*FM radio station call letters*]
WDOH...... Delphos, OH [*AM radio station call letters*]
WDOK...... Cleveland, OH [*FM radio station call letters*]
WD Okla ... United States District Court for the Western District of Oklahoma   (DLA)
WDOM ..... Providence, RI [*FM radio station call letters*]
WDON ...... Geneva, OH [*FM radio station call letters*]
WDOP....... Weighted Dilution of Precision
WDOPD.... War Department, Operations Division, General Staff [*World War II*]
WDOR....... Sturgeon Bay, WI [*AM radio station call letters*]
WDOR-FM ... Sturgeon Bay, WI [*FM radio station call letters*]
WDOS....... Oneonta, NY [*AM radio station call letters*]
WDOS .... Wooton Desk Owners Society   (EA)
WDOT....... Burlington, VT [*AM radio station call letters*]
WDOV....... Dover, DE [*AM radio station call letters*]
WDOW ..... Dowagiac, MI [*AM radio station call letters*]
WDOW-FM ... Dowagiac, MI [*FM radio station call letters*]
WDOY....... Fajardo, PR [*FM radio station call letters*]
WDP......... Weapons Direction Program
WDP.......... Wenner Difference Potentiometer
WDP.......... Women in Data Processing   (EA)
WDP.......... Wood Panel   (AAG)
WDP.......... Work Distribution Policy   (AAG)
WD PA ...... United States District Court for the Western District of Pennsylvania   (DLA)
WDPA .... Wisconsin Dairy Products Association   (EA)
WDPB .... Seaford, DE [*Television station call letters*]
WDPC .... Dallas, GA [*AM radio station call letters*]
WDPC .... Western Data Processing Center [*University of California, Los Angeles*]
WDPMG-ID ... War Department Provost Marshal General, Investigation Division [*Obsolete*]
WDPR .... Dayton, OH [*FM radio station call letters*]
WDPS....... Dayton, OH [*FM radio station call letters*]
WDPT .... Water-Drop-Penetration Time [*Agriculture*]
WDQN ...... Du Quoin, IL [*AM radio station call letters*]
WDQN-FM ... Du Quoin, IL [*FM radio station call letters*]
WDR......... Wardair International Ltd. [*Toronto Stock Exchange symbol*] [*Vancouver Stock Exchange symbol*]
Wdr.......... Wardmaster [*British military*]   (DMA)
WDR......... Westdeutscher Rundfunk [*Radio network*] [*West Germany*]
WDR......... Wide Dynamic Range
WDR......... Winder, GA [*Location identifier*] [*FAA*]   (FAAL)
WDR......... Window Definition Record [*Data processing*]
WDR......... Withdrawal
WDR......... Women's Drug Research Project   (EA)
WDR......... Write Drum
WDRAA .... Welding Research Abroad [*A publication*]
WDRB-TV ... Louisville, KY [*Television station call letters*]
WDRC .... Hartford, CT [*AM radio station call letters*]
WDRC .... Women's Defence Relief Corps [*British*] [*World War I*]
WDRC-FM ... Hartford, CT [*FM radio station call letters*]
WDRE-FM ... Garden City, NY [*FM radio station call letters*]
WDRG .... Women's Direct Response Group [*Garden City, NY*]   (EA)
WDRK .... Greenville, OH [*FM radio station call letters*]
WDRKA .... Waseda Daigaku Rikogaku Kenkyusho Hokoku [*A publication*]
Wdr L....... Wardmaster Lieutenant [*British military*]   (DMA)
WDRM-FM ... Decatur, AL [*FM radio station call letters*]
WDROP .... Water Distribution Register of Organic Pollutants [*National Institutes of Health*]
WDRP .... Windsor, NC [*FM radio station call letters*]
WDRSA..... Wood Research [*A publication*]
WDRT .... Water Detection Response Team [*DoD*]
WDRU....... Bunnell, FL [*Television station call letters*]
WDRV....... Statesville, NC [*AM radio station call letters*]
WDRZ....... Etowah, TN [*AM radio station call letters*]
WDS .... Four Winds Aviation Ltd. [*Colorado Springs, CO*] [*FAA designator*]   (FAAC)
WDS .... Washington Document Service [*Information service or system*]   (IID)
WD(S)....... Waste Disposal (System) [*Nuclear energy*]   (NRCH)
WDS .... Wavelength Dispersive Spectrometer
WDS .... Weapon Delivery System
WDS .... Weapons Directing System [*Navy*]
WDS .... Wire Data Service
WDS .... Wood Dye Stain
WDS .... Woodside [*California*] [*Seismograph station code, US Geological Survey*]   (SEIS)

WDS .... Woodward's Ltd. [*Toronto Stock Exchange symbol*] [*Vancouver Stock Exchange symbol*]
WDS .... Word Discrimination Score
WDS .... World Deist Society   (EA)
WDS .... Wounds
WDSC .... Dillon, SC [*AM radio station call letters*]
WDSD .... Dover, DE [*FM radio station call letters*]
WDSD .... Water Data Sources Directory [*US Geological Survey*] [*Information service or system*]   (CRD)
WDSD .... Wisconsin School for the Deaf, Delavan, WI [*Library symbol*] [*Library of Congress*]   (LCLS)
WDSE-TV ... Duluth, MN [*Television station call letters*]
WDSG .... Dyersburg, TN [*AM radio station call letters*]
WDSI........ Worlco Data Systems, Incorporated [*NASDAQ symbol*]   (NQ)
WDSI-TV ... Chattanooga, TN [*Television station call letters*]
WDSL........ Mocksville, NC [*AM radio station call letters*]
WdSL........ Welt der Slaven [*A publication*]
WDSM ...... Superior, WI [*AM radio station call letters*]
WDSN .... Reynoldsville, PA [*FM radio station call letters*]
WDSO .... Chesterton, IN [*FM radio station call letters*]
WDSPR..... Widespread
WDSPRD ... Widespread [*Meteorology*]   (FAAC)
WDSR .... Lake City, FL [*AM radio station call letters*]
WDSRF..... Windsor Resources, Inc. [*NASDAQ symbol*]   (NQ)
WDSS........ War Department Special Staff [*Obsolete*]
WDS SATSIM ... Weapon Direction System Satellite Simulation [*Military*]   (CAAL)
WDST........ Woodstock, NY [*FM radio station call letters*]
WDST........ Wordstar International, Inc. [*NASDAQ symbol*]   (NQ)
WD STL .... Wood or Steel [*Freight*]
WD STV.... Wood Stove [*Freight*]
WDSU-TV ... New Orleans, LA [*Television station call letters*]
WDSY....... Pittsburgh, PA [*FM radio station call letters*]
WDT......... Warmth Detection Threshold
WDT......... Watch Dog Timer
WDT......... Wear Durability Trial
WDT.......... Wedtech Corp. [*AMEX symbol*]   (SPSG)
WDT......... Weight Distribution Table
WDT.......... Width
WDT......... Wiedemann Developed Template   (MCD)
WDT......... World Cement Industries [*Vancouver Stock Exchange symbol*]
WDT......... World Development [*A publication*]
WDTC .... Western Defense Tactical Command   (AAG)
WD Tenn .. United States District Court for the Western District of Tennessee   (DLA)
WD Tex .... United States District Court for the Western District of Texas   (DLA)
WDTF....... Wetting-Drying and Temperature Fluctuation [*Geochemistry*]
WDTM...... Selmer, TN [*AM radio station call letters*]
WDTN....... Dayton, OH [*Television station call letters*]
WDTR....... Detroit, MI [*FM radio station call letters*]
WDTU....... War Dog Training Unit [*British military*]   (DMA)
WDTV ...... Weston, WV [*Television station call letters*]
WDu.......... Durand Free Library, Durand, WI [*Library symbol*] [*Library of Congress*]   (LCLS)
WdU .... Wahlpartei der Unabhaengigen [*Electoral Party of Independents*] [*Austria*] [*Political party*]   (PPE)
WDU .... Water Data Unit   (DCTA)
WDU .... Weapons Director Unit   (MCD)
WDU .... Window Deicing Unit
WDU .... Wireless Development Unit
WDU .... Workers' Defence Union [*British*]
WDUB....... Granville, OH [*FM radio station call letters*]
WDUF....... Duffield, VA [*AM radio station call letters*]
WDUK ...... Havana, IL [*FM radio station call letters*]
WDUN ...... Gainesville, GA [*AM radio station call letters*]
WDUQ ...... Pittsburgh, PA [*FM radio station call letters*]
WDUR ...... Durham, NC [*AM radio station call letters*]
WDUV....... Bradenton, FL [*FM radio station call letters*]
WDUX....... Waupaca, WI [*AM radio station call letters*]
WDUX-FM ... Waupaca, WI [*FM radio station call letters*]
WDUZ....... Green Bay, WI [*AM radio station call letters*]
WDUZ-FM .. Green Bay, WI [*FM radio station call letters*]
WDV......... War Department Vehicle [*Obsolete*]
WDV......... Western Diverging Volcanism [*Geology*]
WDV......... Written Down Value [*Accounting*]
WDVA....... Danville, VA [*AM radio station call letters*]
WD VA ..... United States District Court for the Western District of Virginia   (DLA)
WDVE....... Pittsburgh, PA [*FM radio station call letters*]
WDVH ...... Salisbury, MD [*FM radio station call letters*]
WDVI .... Dadeville, AL [*FM radio station call letters*]
WDVR....... Delaware Township, NJ [*FM radio station call letters*]
WDW........ Wholesale Dealer in Wines
WDW........ Window
WDW........ Wood and Wire [*Freight*]
WD Wash ... United States District Court for the Western District of Washington   (DLA)
WD Wis ..... United States District Court for the Western District of Wisconsin   (DLA)
WDWL ...... Bayamon, PR [*Television station call letters*]

WDWN...... Auburn, NY [*FM radio station call letters*]
WDWN...... Well Developed - Well Nourished [*Medicine*]
WDWRA... Welding in the World [*A publication*]
WDWRK.. Woodwork [*Freight*]
WDWS...... Champaign, IL [*AM radio station call letters*]
WDX......... Wavelength Dispersive X-Ray [*Spectrometer*]
WDXA...... Wave-Length Dispersive X-Ray Analysis
WDXB...... Chattanooga, TN [*AM radio station call letters*]
WDXC....... Pound, VA [*FM radio station call letters*]
WDXE....... Lawrenceburg, TN [*AM radio station call letters*]
WDXE-FM ... Lawrenceburg, TN [*FM radio station call letters*]
WDXI........ Jackson, TN [*AM radio station call letters*]
WDXL....... Lexington, TN [*AM radio station call letters*]
WDXN....... Clarksville, TN [*AM radio station call letters*]
WDXR....... Paducah, KY [*AM radio station call letters*]
WDXRF..... Wavelength-Dispersive X-Ray Fluorescence
WDXRS..... Wavelength Dispersive X-Ray Spectrometry
WDXX....... Selma, AL [*FM radio station call letters*]
WDXY...... Sumter, SC [*AM radio station call letters*]
WDXZ....... Mount Pleasant, SC [*FM radio station call letters*]
WDY......... Woody [*California*] [*Seismograph station code, US Geological Survey*] [*Closed*]   (SEIS)
WDY......... Wordy [*Used in correcting manuscripts, etc.*]
WDYL....... Chester, VA [*FM radio station call letters*]
WDYN-FM ... Chattanooga, TN [*FM radio station call letters*]
WDYT ...... What Do You Think?
WDYTYCIWSS ... Why Don't You Take Your Change In War Savings Stamps [*Cashier's sign*] [*World War II*]
WDZ......... Decatur, IL [*AM radio station call letters*]
WDZ......... Werner Dahnz Co. Ltd. [*Toronto Stock Exchange symbol*]
WDZA...... Williamsport, PA [*Television station call letters*]
WDZD....... Shallotte, NC [*FM radio station call letters*]
WDZE....... Carolina, PR [*Television station call letters*]
WDZI........ Manteo, NC [*Television station call letters*]
WDZK...... Chester, SC [*AM radio station call letters*]
WDZL....... Miami, FL [*Television station call letters*]
WDZQ....... Decatur, IL [*FM radio station call letters*]
WDZR-FM ... Etowah, TN [*FM radio station call letters*]
WDZZ-FM ... Flint, MI [*FM radio station call letters*]
WE............ Eau Claire Public Library, Eau Claire, WI [*Library symbol*] [*Library of Congress*]   (LCLS)
WE............ Staff Meteorologist [*AFSC*]
WE............ Wage Earner [*Social Security Administration*]   (OICC)
WE............ War Establishment
WE............ Watch Error [*Navigation*]
WE............ Watchman-Examiner [*A publication*]   (BJA)
WE............ Water Equivalent   (MCD)
We............ Watt Electric
WE............ WDL Flugdienst GmbH [*Federal Republic of Germany*] [*ICAO designator*]   (ICDA)
WE............ Weapons Electrical [*Navy*] [*British*]
WE............ Weapons Engineering [*Navy*] [*British*]
WE............ Weather Emergency
WE............ Webbing Equipment [*British military*]   (DMA)
We............ Weber Number [*IUPAC*]
WE............ Wednesday
W/E.......... Week Ending
WE............ Weekend   (ADA)
WE............ Wescap Enterprises Ltd. [*Vancouver Stock Exchange symbol*]
WE............ Westcoast Energy, Inc. [*NYSE symbol*]   (SPSG)
WE............ Western Electric Co.   (AAG)
We............ Western Tithe Cases [*England*] [*A publication*]   (DLA)
We............ West's English Chancery Reports [*A publication*]   (DLA)
We............ West's Reports, English House of Lords [*A publication*]   (DLA)
WE............ White Edges   (ADA)
WE............ Whole Economy [*Department of Employment*] [*British*]
W/e.......... Width-to-Length [*Ratio*]   (MDG)
WE............ Winesburg Eagle [*A publication*]
WE............ Wing Elevon   (MCD)
WE............ With Equipment   (AABC)
WE............ Withholding Exemptions [*Army*]   (AABC)
WE............ Women Educators   (EA)
WE............ Women Employed [*Chicago, IL*]   (EA)
WE............ Women in Energy   (EA)
WE............ Women Entrepreneurs [*San Francisco, CA*]   (EA)
WE............ Women Exploited   (EA)
WE............ Women's Reserve, Engineering Duties [*USNR officer designation*]
WE............ Work Experience
WE............ World Education, Inc.
WE............ World Evangelism   (EA)
WE............ Write Enable   (IEEE)
W/E.......... Writer/Editor   (MCD)
WEa.......... East Troy Public Library, East Troy, WI [*Library symbol*] [*Library of Congress*]   (LCLS)
WEA......... Eastern Washington State College, Cheney, WA [*OCLC symbol*]   (OCLC)
WEA......... Royal West of England Academy
WEA......... Wall Effect Amplifier
WEA.......... Warner-Eddison Associates, Inc. [*Information service or system*]   (IID)

WEA......... Weak Equity Axiom
WEA......... Weather   (AABC)
WEA......... Weatherford, TX [*Location identifier*] [*FAA*]   (FAAL)
WEA......... Western Economic Association International   (EA)
WEA......... Wilderness Education Association   (EA)
WEA......... Women Employed Advocates   (EA)
WEA......... Workers' Educational Association
WEAA....... Baltimore, MD [*FM radio station call letters*]
WEAAC.... Western European Airport Authorities Conference   (MCD)
WEAAP.... Western European Association for Aviation Psychology   (EA)
WEAB....... Adamsville, TN [*AM radio station call letters*]
WEA Bul ... WEA [*Workers Educational Association*] Bulletin [*A publication*]   (APTA)
WEAC....... Gaffney, SC [*AM radio station call letters*]
WEAC....... Winchester Engineering and Analytical Center [*Food and Drug Administration*] [*Winchester, MA*]   (GRD)
WEAC....... Women's Employment Action Centre [*Australia*]
WEAG....... Starke, FL [*AM radio station call letters*]
WEAG-FM ... Starke, FL [*FM radio station call letters*]
WEAI........ Lynnville, IL [*FM radio station call letters*]
WEAI........ Western Economic Association International [*Later, WEA*]   (EA)
WEAL....... Women's Equity Action League   (EA)
WEAM....... Columbus, GA [*AM radio station call letters*]
WEA-N....... Westinghouse Engineers Association National   (EA)
WEAO....... Akron, OH [*Television station call letters*]
WEAPD.... Western Air Procurement District
WEAQ....... Eau Claire, WI [*AM radio station call letters*]
WEARCON ... Weather Observation and Forecasting Control System
WEARSCHFAC ... [*Naval*] Weather Research Facility
WEAR-TV ... Pensacola, FL [*Television station call letters*]
WEAS....... Savannah, GA [*AM radio station call letters*]
WEASERVCOMM ... Weather Service Command [*Navy*]
WEAS-FM ... Savannah, GA [*FM radio station call letters*]
WEAT ...... Weathertight
WEAT ...... West Palm Beach, FL [*AM radio station call letters*]
WEAT-FM ... West Palm Beach, FL [*FM radio station call letters*]
Weather and Clim ... Weather and Climate [*A publication*]
Weather C & M ... Weather, Crops, and Markets [*A publication*]
Weather Dev Res Bull ... Weather Development and Research Bulletin [*Australia, Commonwealth Bureau of Meteorology*] [*A publication*]   (APTA)
Weather Research Bull ... Weather Research Bulletin [*A publication*]
WEAU-TV ... Eau Claire, WI [*Television station call letters*]
WEAV....... Plattsburgh, NY [*AM radio station call letters*]
WEAX ...... Angola, IN [*FM radio station call letters*]
WEAX ...... En Route Weather Forecast [*Navy*]   (NVT)
WEAY ...... Nanticoke, PA [*FM radio station call letters*]
WEAZ ...... Philadelphia, PA [*AM radio station call letters*]
WEAZ-FM ... Philadelphia, PA [*FM radio station call letters*]
WEB.......... National Westminster Bank. Quarterly Review [*A publication*]
WEB.......... Wagner Earth Bridge
WEB.......... War Engineering Board
WEB.......... Wealthbuilding [*A publication*]
WEB.......... Webbing   (AAG)
WEBA ...... Women Exploited by Abortion   (EA)
WEBA-TV ... Allendale, SC [*Television station call letters*]
WEBB....... Baltimore, MD [*AM radio station call letters*]
Webb......... Webb's Reports [*6-20 Kansas*] [*A publication*]   (DLA)
Webb......... Webb's Reports [*11-20 Texas Civil Appeals*] [*A publication*]   (DLA)
WEBB........ Writer's Electronic Bulletin Board [*Information service or system*]   (IID)
Webb A'B & W ... Webb, A'Beckett, and Williams' Reports [*A publication*]   (APTA)
Webb A'B & W Eq ... Webb, A'Beckett, and Williams' Equity Reports [*A publication*]   (APTA)
Webb A'B & W Eq ... Webb, A'Beckett, and Williams' Victorian Equity Reports [*Australia*] [*A publication*]   (DLA)
Webb A'B & W IE & M ... Webb, A'Beckett, and Williams' Insolvency, Ecclesiastical, and Matrimonial Reports [*A publication*]   (APTA)
Webb A'B & W IP & M ... Webb, A'Beckett, and Williams' Insolvency, Probate, and Matrimonial Reports [*A publication*]   (APTA)
Webb A'B & W Min ... Webb, A'Beckett, and Williams' Mining Cases [*A publication*]   (APTA)
Webb Cr Dig ... Webb's Digest of Texas Criminal Cases [*A publication*]   (DLA)
Webb & D .. Webb and Duval's Reports [*1-3 Texas*] [*A publication*]   (DLA)
Webb & Duval ... Webb and Duval's Reports [*1-3 Texas*] [*A publication*]   (DLA)
Webbia Racc Scr Bot ... Webbia; Raccolta di Scritti Botanici [*A publication*]
Webb Jud Act ... Webb on the Judicature Act [*A publication*]   (DLA)
Webb Pl & Pr ... Webb's Kansas Pleading and Practice [*A publication*]   (DLA)
Webb RR ... Webb's Railroad Laws of Maine [*A publication*]   (DLA)
Webb Supr Ct Pr ... Webb's English Supreme Court Practice [*A publication*]   (DLA)
WEBC....... Duluth, MN [*AM radio station call letters*]
WEBE....... Western European Basic Encyclopedia   (MCD)
WEBE....... Westport, CT [*FM radio station call letters*]
WEBELOS ... We'll Be Loyal Scouts [*Boy Scout slogan*]

WEBG .... Ebensburg, PA [*AM radio station call letters*]
WEBJ .... Brewton, AL [*AM radio station call letters*]
WEBN .... Cincinnati, OH [*FM radio station call letters*]
WEBO .... Owego, NY [*AM radio station call letters*]
Web Pat .... Webster's New Patent Law [*4th ed.*] [*1854*] [*A publication*] (DLA)
Web Pat Cas ... Webster's Patent Cases [*1601-1855*] [*A publication*] (DLA)
Web PC .... Webster's Patent Cases [*1601-1855*] [*A publication*] (DLA)
WEBQ .... Harrisburg, IL [*AM radio station call letters*]
WEBQ-FM ... El Dorado, IL [*AM radio station call letters*]
WEBR .... Buffalo, NY [*AM radio station call letters*]
Web R .... Webster Review [*A publication*]
WEBROCK ... Weather Buoy Rocket
WEBS .... Calhoun, GA [*AM radio station call letters*]
WEBS .... Weapons Effectiveness Buoy System
WEBS .... Webster Clothes, Inc. [*Baltimore, MD*] [*NASDAQ symbol*] (NQ)
Webs .... Webster's Patent Cases [*England*] [*A publication*] (DLA)
WEBSEC... Western Beaufort Sea Ecological Cruise [*Coast Guard*]
Webs Pat Cas ... Webster's Patent Cases [*England*] [*A publication*] (DLA)
Webst Dict ... Webster's Dictionary [*A publication*] (DLA)
Webst Dict Unab ... Webster's Unabridged Dictionary [*A publication*] (DLA)
Webster Pat Cas ... Webster's Patent Cases [*1601-1855*] [*A publication*] (DLA)
Webster Pat Cas (Eng) ... Webster's Patent Cases [*England*] [*A publication*] (DLA)
Webster in Sen Doc ... Webster in Senate Documents [*A publication*] (DLA)
Webst Int Dict ... Webster's International Dictionary [*A publication*] (DLA)
Webst New Int D ... Webster's New International Dictionary [*A publication*] (DLA)
WEBT .... Langdale, AL [*FM radio station call letters*]
Web Tr .... Trial of Professor Webster for Murder [*A publication*] (DLA)
WEBY .... Milton, FL [*AM radio station call letters*]
WEC .... District One Technical Institute, Eau Claire, Eau Claire, WI [*OCLC symbol*] (OCLC)
WEC .... Eau Claire County Hospital, Eau Claire, WI [*Library symbol*] [*Library of Congress*] (LCLS)
WEC .... Walking with Eyes Closed [*Equilibrium test*]
WEC .... Warhead Electrical Connector
WEC .... Water Export Control
WEC .... Weapon Engagement Console [*Military*] (CAAL)
WEC .... Weapon Engagement Controller [*Military*] (CAAL)
WEC .... Wescal Resources, Inc. [*Vancouver Stock Exchange symbol*]
WEC .... Westinghouse Electric Corporation
WEC .... Whole Earth Catalog [*A publication*]
WEC .... Wind Energy Conversion
WEC .... Wisconsin Energy Corporation [*NYSE symbol*] (SPSG)
WEC .... Women's Emergency Corps [*British*] [*World War I*]
WEC .... World Energy Conference [*See also CME*] [*London, England*] (EAIO)
WEC .... World Environment Center (EA)
WEC .... Worldwide Evangelization Crusade (EA)
WECA .... Western Capital Investment Corp. [*Denver, CO*] [*NASDAQ symbol*] (NQ)
WECAF.... Western Central Atlantic Fisheries Commission [*Food and Agriculture Organization of the UN*]
WECAFC .. Western Central Atlantic Fisheries Commission [*Food and Agriculture Organization of the UN*] (EAIO)
WECAF (West Cent Atl Fish Comm) Stud ... WECAF (Western Central Atlantic Fishery Commission) Studies [*A publication*]
WECB .... Weapons Evaluation and Control Bureau [*USACDA*]
WECC .... St. Mary's, GA [*AM radio station call letters*]
WECC .... White English Celtic Catholic
WECE .... Due West, SC [*FM radio station call letters*]
WECEN ..... Weather Center [*Air Force*]
WECI .... Richmond, IN [*FM radio station call letters*]
WECI .... WEC International (EA)
WECK .... Cheektowaga, NY [*AM radio station call letters*]
WECL .... Elkhorn City, KY [*FM radio station call letters*]
WECM .... Warranted Existing Class Maintained (DS)
WECN ...... Naranjito, PR [*Television station call letters*]
WECO .... Wartburg, TN [*AM radio station call letters*]
WECO .... Washington Energy Company [*NASDAQ symbol*] (NQ)
WECO .... Western Electric Company (MCD)
WECO .... Westinghouse Electric Corporation
WECOM ... Weapons Command [*Later, Armaments Command*] [*Army*]
WECON ... Weather Controlled Messages (NVT)
W Econ J ... Western Economic Journal [*A publication*]
WECPNL.. Weighted Equivalent Continuous Perceived Noise Level
WECQ-FM ... Geneva, NY [*FM radio station call letters*]
WECS .... Willimantic, CT [*FM radio station call letters*]
WECS .... Wind Energy Conversion System
WECST ..... Waste Evaporator Condensate Storage Tank [*Nuclear energy*] (NRCH)
WECT .... Wilmington, NC [*Television station call letters*]
WECU .... Peoria, IL [*FM radio station call letters*]
WECV .... Chippewa Valley Museum, Eau Claire, WI [*Library symbol*] [*Library of Congress*] (LCLS)
WECW ...... Elmira, NY [*FM radio station call letters*]
WECZ........ Punxsutawney, PA [*AM radio station call letters*]

WED .... Walter Elias Disney [*These initials also identify the theme park division of Walt Disney Enterprises*]
WED .... War Emergency Dose (DEN)
WED .... Weapons Engineering Duty [*Navy*] (NG)
WED .... Wedau [*Papua New Guinea*] [*Airport symbol*] (OAG)
WED .... Wedco Technology, Inc. [*AMEX symbol*] (SPSG)
WED .... Wednesday (EY)
WED .... West Delta Resources Ltd. [*Vancouver Stock Exchange symbol*]
WED .... Work Force Effectiveness and Development Group [*Office of Personnel Management*] (GRD)
WEDA .... Western Dredging Association (EA)
WEDA .... Women's Enterprise Development Agency [*Established in 1987*] [*British*]
WEDAC .... Westinghouse Digital Airborne Computer
WEDC ...... Chicago, IL [*AM radio station call letters*]
WEDCOM ... Weapon Effects on D-Region Communications [*Computer code*]
WEDE .... Eden, NC [*AM radio station call letters*]
WEDE .... Western Development Corp. [*NASDAQ symbol*] (NQ)
WEDGE .... Waterless Electrical Data Generating Effortless
WEDGE .... Weapon Development Glide Entry
WEDGE .... Western Education Development Group [*University of British Columbia*] [*Canada*] [*Research center*]
Wedg Gov & Laws ... Wedgwood on American Government and Laws [*A publication*] (DLA)
Wedg & Hom ... Wedgwood and Homan's Manual for Notaries and Bankers [*A publication*] (DLA)
Wedgw Dict Eng Etymology ... Wedgwood's Dictionary of English Etymology [*A publication*] (DLA)
WEDH...... Hartford, CT [*Television station call letters*]
WEDM ...... Indianapolis, IN [*FM radio station call letters*]
WEDN ...... Norwich, CT [*Television station call letters*]
WEDO ...... McKeesport, PA [*AM radio station call letters*]
WEDR ...... Miami, FL [*FM radio station call letters*]
WEDS...... Weapons Effect Display System [*AEC*]
WEDU ...... Tampa, FL [*Television station call letters*]
WEDW ...... Bridgeport, CT [*Television station call letters*]
WEDW-FM ... Stamford, CT [*FM radio station call letters*]
WEDY ...... New Haven, CT [*Television station call letters*]
WEE .... Weerberichten. Informatiebulletin over Windenergie en Zonne-Energie [*A publication*]
WEE .... Western Equine Encephalomyelitis [*Virus*]
WEEA ...... Women's Educational Equity Act [*1974*]
WEEB .... Southern Pines, NC [*AM radio station call letters*]
WEEC....... Springfield, OH [*FM radio station call letters*]
WEECN .... Women's Educational Equity Communications Network [*Defunct*]
WEED ...... Rocky Mount, NC [*AM radio station call letters*]
Weed Abstr ... Weed Abstracts [*A publication*]
Weed Res ... Weed Research [*A publication*]
Weed Sci ... Weed Science [*A publication*]
Weeds Weed Cont ... Weeds and Weed Control [*A publication*]
WEEE........ Cherry Hill, NJ [*FM radio station call letters*]
WEEF....... Highland Park, IL [*AM radio station call letters*]
WEEF....... Western Electric Educational Fund
WEEGA .... Welding Engineer [*A publication*]
WEEI........ Boston, MA [*AM radio station call letters*]
WEEJ .... Port Charlotte, FL [*FM radio station call letters*]
Week Cin LB ... Weekly Cincinnati Law Bulletin [*A publication*] (DLA)
Week Dig... New York Weekly Digest [*A publication*] (DLA)
Week Dig (NY) ... New York Weekly Digest [*A publication*] (DLA)
Week-End R ... Australian Week-End Review of Current Books, the Arts, and Entertainments [*A publication*] (APTA)
Week Jur ... Weekly Jurist [*Bloomington, IL*] [*A publication*] (DLA)
Week Law & Bk Bull ... Weekly Law and Bank Bulletin [*A publication*] (DLA)
Week Law Bull ... Weekly Law Bulletin and Ohio Law Journal [*A publication*] (DLA)
Week Law Gaz ... Weekly Law Gazette [*Ohio*] [*A publication*] (DLA)
Week L Gaz ... Weekly Law Gazette [*Ohio*] [*A publication*] (DLA)
Week L Mag ... Weekly Law Magazine [*1842-43*] [*A publication*] (DLA)
Week LR ... Weekly Law Reports [*A publication*] (DLA)
Week L Rec ... Weekly Law Record [*A publication*] (DLA)
Week L Record ... Weekly Law Record [*A publication*] (DLA)
Week LR (Eng) ... Weekly Law Reports (England) [*A publication*] (DLA)
Week L Rev ... Weekly Law Review [*San Francisco*] [*A publication*] (DLA)
Weekly Cin Law Bull ... Cincinnati Weekly Law Bulletin [*A publication*] (DLA)
Weekly Compilation Presidential Docum ... Weekly Compilation of Presidential Documents [*A publication*]
Weekly Comp of Pres Doc ... Weekly Compilation of Presidential Documents [*A publication*]
Weekly Law B ... Weekly Law Bulletin [*Ohio*] [*A publication*] (DLA)
Weekly L Bull ... Weekly Law Bulletin [*England*] [*A publication*] (DLA)
Weekly LR ... Weekly Law Reports [*England*] [*A publication*] (DLA)
Weekly NC ... Weekly Notes of Cases [*Pennsylvania*] [*A publication*] (DLA)
Weekly N L ... Weekly News Letter. United States Department of Agriculture [*A publication*]
Weekly Underw ... Weekly Underwriter [*A publication*]
Week No .... New South Wales Weekly Notes [*A publication*]
Week No .... Weekly Notes of Cases [*Pennsylvania*] [*A publication*] (DLA)

Week No	Weekly Notes of Cases (Law Reports) [*England*] [*A publication*] (DLA)
Week No Cas ...	Weekly Notes of Cases [*Pennsylvania*] [*A publication*] (DLA)
Week No Cas ...	Weekly Notes of Cases (Law Reports) [*England*] [*A publication*] (DLA)
Week Notes Cas ...	Weekly Notes of Cases (Law Reports) [*England*] [*A publication*] (DLA)
Week R	Weekly Reporter [*1853-1906*] [*A publication*] (DLA)
Week R (Eng) ...	Weekly Reporter (England) [*A publication*] (DLA)
Week Rep ..	Weekly Reporter [*England*] [*A publication*] (DLA)
Week Reptr ...	Weekly Reporter [*Bengal*] [*A publication*] (DLA)
Week Reptr ...	Weekly Reporter [*London*] [*A publication*] (DLA)
Weeks Att at Law ...	Weeks on Attorneys at Law [*A publication*] (DLA)
Weeks DA Inj ...	Weeks' Damnum Absque Injuria [*A publication*] (DLA)
Weeks Dep ...	Weeks on Depositions [*A publication*] (DLA)
Weeks Min ...	Weeks on Mines and Mineral Law [*A publication*] (DLA)
Weeks Min Leg ...	Weeks' Mining Legislation of Congress [*A publication*] (DLA)
Week Trans Rep ...	Weekly Transcript Reports [*New York*] [*A publication*] (DLA)
Week Trans Repts ...	Weekly Transcript Reports [*New York*] [*A publication*] (DLA)
WEEK-TV ...	Peoria, IL [*Television station call letters*]
WEEL-FM ...	Wheeling, WV [*FM radio station call letters*]
WEEM	Pendleton, IN [*FM radio station call letters*]
WEEN	Lafayette, TN [*AM radio station call letters*]
WEEO	Waynesboro, PA [*AM radio station call letters*]
WEEP	Pittsburgh, PA [*AM radio station call letters*]
WEEP	Women's Educational Equity Program (EA)
WEEP	Work Experience in Employer's Premises [*British*]
Weer	Weerakoon's Appeal Court Reports [*Ceylon*] [*A publication*] (DLA)
WEER	Welfare Entered Employment Rate [*Job Training and Partnership Act*] (OICC)
WEESA	Weed Science [*A publication*]
WEEU	Reading, PA [*AM radio station call letters*]
WEEV	Women, Education, and Employment in Victoria [*Australia*]
WEEX	Easton, PA [*AM radio station call letters*]
WEEZ	Heidelberg, MS [*FM radio station call letters*]
WEF	WAND [*Women's Action for Nuclear Disarmament*] Education Fund (EA)
WEF	War Emergency Formula
WEF	With Effect From
WEF	World Education Fellowship (EA)
WEF	World Evangelical Fellowship (EA)
WEFAX	Weather Facsimile Experiment [*Environmental Science Services Administration*]
WEFC	Roanoke, VA [*Television station call letters*]
WEFI	Easthampton, MA [*AM radio station call letters*]
WEFM	Michigan City, IN [*FM radio station call letters*]
WEFR	Erie, PA [*FM radio station call letters*]
WEFT	Champaign, IL [*FM radio station call letters*]
WEFT	Wings, Engines, Fuselage, Tail [*System for identifying aircraft*]
WEFX	Norwalk, CT [*FM radio station call letters*]
WEG	Wegen [*A publication*]
WEG	Wind Energy Generator
WEGA	Vega Baja, PR [*AM radio station call letters*]
Wege Soz Versicherung ...	Wege zur Sozialversicherung [*A publication*]
WEGG	Rose Hill, NC [*AM radio station call letters*]
WEGL	Auburn, AL [*FM radio station call letters*]
WEGO	Concord, NC [*AM radio station call letters*]
WEGP	Presque Isle, ME [*AM radio station call letters*]
WEGR	Memphis, TN [*FM radio station call letters*]
WEGS	Milton, FL [*FM radio station call letters*]
WEGX	Philadelphia, PA [*FM radio station call letters*]
WEH	Hungarian News Agency. Weekly Bulletin [*A publication*]
WE-H	Weapons Employment Handbook [*DASA*] (MCD)
WEHB	Grand Rapids, MI [*FM radio station call letters*]
WEHH	Elmira Heights-Horseheads, NY [*AM radio station call letters*]
Wehrmed Monatsschr ...	Wehrmedizinische Monatsschrift [*A publication*]
Wehrtech ...	Wehrtechnik [*A publication*]
Wehr und Wirt ...	Wehr und Wirtschaft [*A publication*]
WEHS	Aurora, IL [*Television station call letters*]
WEHSA	Work-Environment-Health [*A publication*]
WEHT	Evansville, IN [*Television station call letters*]
WEI	Immanuel Lutheran College, Eau Claire, WI [*Library symbol*] [*Library of Congress*] (LCLS)
WEI	Weapon Effectiveness Index (MCD)
WEI	Weipa [*Australia*] [*Airport symbol*] (OAG)
WEI	Western European Institute for Wood Preservation (EAIO)
WEI	Wherehouse Entertainment, Incorporated [*AMEX symbol*] (SPSG)
WEI	Women Employed Institute (EA)
WEI	Wood Energy Institute [*Later, WHA*] (EA)
WEI	Work Experience Instructor (OICC)
WEI	World Education (EA)
WEI	World Energy Industry [*A publication*]
WEI	World Environment Institute
Weibulls Arsb ...	Weibulls Arsbok [*A publication*]
WEIC	Charleston, IL [*AM radio station call letters*]

WEIC-FM ...	Charleston, IL [*FM radio station call letters*]
WEIF	Utica, NY [*FM radio station call letters*]
Weight Med Leg Gaz ...	Weightman's Medico-Legal Gazette [*A publication*] (DLA)
Weight M & L ...	Weightman's Marriage and Legitimacy [*1871*] [*A publication*] (DLA)
WEI/IEO ..	Western European Institute for Wood Preservation/Institut de l'Europe Occidentale pour l'Impregnation du Bois (EAIO)
WEIM	Fitchburg, MA [*AM radio station call letters*]
Weinbau Kellerwirtsch (Budapest) ...	Weinbau und Kellerwirtschaft (Budapest) [*A publication*]
Wein-Wiss ...	Wein-Wissenschaft [*A publication*]
WEIQ	Mobile, AL [*Television station call letters*]
Weir	Weir's Criminal Rulings [*India*] [*A publication*] (DLA)
WEIR	Weirton, WV [*AM radio station call letters*]
WEIR-FM ...	Cadiz, OH [*FM radio station call letters*]
WEIS	Centre, AL [*AM radio station call letters*]
WEIS	Weisfields, Inc. [*NASDAQ symbol*] (NQ)
Weiterbildungszentrum Math Kybernet Rechentech ...	Weiterbildungszentrum fuer Mathematische Kybernetik und Rechentechnik [*A publication*]
WEIU	Charleston, IL [*FM radio station call letters*]
WEIU	Women's Educational and Industrial Union (EA)
WEIU-TV ...	Charleston, IL [*Television station call letters*]
WEI/WUV ...	Weapons Effectiveness Indices/Weighted Unit Values [*Military*]
Weizmann Mem Lect ...	Weizmann Memorial Lectures [*A publication*]
WEJ	Western Economic Journal [*A publication*]
WEJC	Lexington, NC [*Television station call letters*]
WEJL	Scranton, PA [*AM radio station call letters*]
WEJT	Shelbyville, IL [*FM radio station call letters*]
WEJUA	Welding Journal [*Miami*] [*A publication*]
WEJY	Monroe, MI [*FM radio station call letters*]
WEJZ	Jacksonville, FL [*FM radio station call letters*]
WEK	Werkgever [*A publication*]
WEK	Wewak [*Papua New Guinea*] [*Seismograph station code, US Geological Survey*] (SEIS)
WEKC	Williamsburg, KY [*AM radio station call letters*]
WEKG	Jackson, KY [*AM radio station call letters*]
WEKH	Hazard, KY [*FM radio station call letters*]
WEKLA	Wiadomosci Ekologiczne [*A publication*]
WEKO	Cabo Rojo, PR [*AM radio station call letters*]
WEKR	Fayetteville, TN [*AM radio station call letters*]
WEKT	Elkton, KY [*AM radio station call letters*]
WEKU-FM ...	Richmond, KY [*FM radio station call letters*]
WEKW-TV ...	Keene, NH [*Television station call letters*]
WEKY	Richmond, KY [*AM radio station call letters*]
WEKZ	Monroe, WI [*AM radio station call letters*]
WEKZ-FM ...	Monroe, WI [*FM radio station call letters*]
WEL	Luther Hospital, Eau Claire, WI [*Library symbol*] [*Library of Congress*] (LCLS)
WEl	Matheson Memorial Library, Elkhorn, WI [*Library symbol*] [*Library of Congress*] (LCLS)
WEL	Warren Explorations Limited [*Toronto Stock Exchange symbol*]
WEL	Weapons Effects Laboratory [*Army*] (RDA)
WEL	Weapons/Equipment List
WEL	Welfare
WEL	Welkom [*South Africa*] [*Airport symbol*] (OAG)
WEL	Wellesley College, Wellesley, MA [*OCLC symbol*] (OCLC)
WEL	Wellesley Hospital, Toronto [*UTLAS symbol*]
WEL	Wellington [*New Zealand*] [*Seismograph station code, US Geological Survey*] (SEIS)
wel	Welsh [*MARC language code*] [*Library of Congress*] (LCCP)
Wel	Welsh's Irish Registry Cases [*A publication*] (DLA)
WEL	Welt-Eis-Lehre [*Cosmic Ice Theory*] [*German*]
WEL	Weltwirtschaftliches Archiv [*A publication*]
WELA	East Liverpool, OH [*FM radio station call letters*]
WELB	Elba, AL [*AM radio station call letters*]
WELB	Welbilt Corp. [*NASDAQ symbol*] (NQ)
WELC	Welch, WV [*AM radio station call letters*]
WELC-FM ...	Welch, WV [*FM radio station call letters*]
WElCL	Walworth County Law Library, Elkhorn, WI [*Library symbol*] [*Library of Congress*] (LCLS)
WELD	Fisher, WV [*AM radio station call letters*]
Weld Des and Fabr ...	Welding Design and Fabrication [*A publication*]
Weld Des Fabr ...	Welding Design and Fabrication [*A publication*]
Weld Dsgn ...	Welding Design and Fabrication [*A publication*]
Weld Eng ...	Welding Engineer [*A publication*]
Weld Fabr Des ...	Welding Fabrication and Design [*A publication*]
Weld Fabrication Design ...	Welding Fabrication and Design [*A publication*] (APTA)
Weld Fabric Design ...	Welding Fabrication and Design [*A publication*] (APTA)
WELD-FM ...	Petersburg, WV [*FM radio station call letters*]
Weld Ind	Welding Industry [*A publication*]
Welding J ..	Welding Journal [*A publication*]
Welding Rev ...	Welding Review [*A publication*]
Weld Int	Welding International [*United Kingdom*] [*A publication*]
Weld J	Welding Journal [*A publication*]
Weld J (London) ...	Welding Journal (London) [*A publication*]

Weld J (Miami) ... Welding Journal (Miami) [*A publication*]
Weld J (NY) ... Welding Journal (New York) [*A publication*]
Weld J Res Suppl ... Welding Journal Research. Supplement [*A publication*]
Weld Jrl ..... Welding Journal [*A publication*]
Weld Metal Fab ... Welding and Metal Fabrication [*A publication*]
Weld Metal Fabr ... Welding and Metal Fabrication [*A publication*]
Weld and Met Fabr ... Welding and Metal Fabrication [*A publication*]
Weld Met Fabr ... Welding and Metal Fabrication [*A publication*]
Weld News ... Welding News [*A publication*]
Weld Prod ... Welding Production [*A publication*]
Weld Prod (USSR) ... Welding Production (USSR) [*A publication*]
Weld Res Abroad ... Welding Research Abroad [*A publication*]
Weld Res C ... Welding Research Council. Bulletin [*A publication*]
Weld Res Counc Bull ... Welding Research Council. Bulletin [*A publication*]
Weld Res Counc Prog Rep ... Welding Research Council. Progress Reports [*A publication*]
Weld Res Int ... Welding Research International [*A publication*]
Weld Res (London) ... Welding Research (London) [*A publication*]
Weld Res (Miami) ... Welding Research (Miami) [*A publication*]
Weld Res (Miami Fla) ... Welding Research (Miami, Florida) [*A publication*]
Weld Res News ... Welding Research News [*A publication*]
Weld Rev .... Welding Review [*A publication*]
Weld Tech ... Welding Technique [*Japan*] [*A publication*]
Weld Wld ... Welding in the World/Le Soudage dans le Monde [*A publication*]
Weld World ... Welding in the World [*A publication*]
Weld World Soudage Monde ... Welding in the World/Le Soudage dans le Monde [*A publication*]
WELE .... Ormond Beach, FL [*AM radio station call letters*]
Weleda Korrespondenzbl Aerzte ... Weleda Korrespondenzblaetter fuer Aerzte [*A publication*]
Welfare L Bull ... Welfare Law Bulletin [*A publication*]   (DLA)
Welfare L News ... Welfare Law News [*A publication*]   (DLA)
Welf Eq ...... Welford's Equity Pleadings [*1842*] [*A publication*]   (DLA)
Welf Focus ... Welfare Focus [*A publication*]
Welf News ... Welfare News [*A publication*]
WELI .... New Haven, CT [*AM radio station call letters*]
WELK .... Elkins, WV [*FM radio station call letters*]
WELL .... Battle Creek, MI [*AM radio station call letters*]
WEIL .... Lakeland Hospital, Elkhorn, WI [*Library symbol*] [*Library of Congress*] (LCLS)
WELL .... LivingWell, Inc. [*Houston, TX*] [*NASDAQ symbol*]   (NQ)
WEILC .... Lakeland Counseling Center, Elkhorn, WI [*Library symbol*] [*Library of Congress*]   (LCLS)
WELL-FM ... Marshall, MI [*FM radio station call letters*]
Well High .. Wellbeloved on Highways [*1829*] [*A publication*]   (DLA)
Well Inventory Ser (Metric Units) Inst Geol Sci ... Well Inventory Series (Metric Units). Institute of Geological Sciences [*A publication*]
Well Serv ... Well Servicing [*A publication*]
Wells Frgo ... Wells Fargo Bank. Business Review [*A publication*]
Wells Inst Juries ... Wells on Instruction to Juries and Bills of Exception [*A publication*]   (DLA)
Wells Jur ... Wells on the Jurisdiction of Courts [*A publication*]   (DLA)
Wells L & F ... Well's Questions of Law and Facts [*A publication*]   (DLA)
Wells Mar Wom ... Wells on the Separate Property of Married Women [*A publication*]   (DLA)
Wells Rep .. Wells on Replevin [*A publication*]   (DLA)
Wells Repl ... Wells on Replevin [*A publication*]   (DLA)
Wells' Res Ad ... Wells' Res Adjudicata and Stare Decisis [*A publication*]   (DLA)
Wellw Abr ... Wellwood's Abridgment of Sea Laws [*A publication*]   (DLA)
Wellworthy Top ... Wellworthy Topics [*A publication*]
WELM ...... Elmira, NY [*AM radio station call letters*]
WELO .... Tupelo, MS [*AM radio station call letters*]
WELP .... Easley, SC [*AM radio station call letters*]
WELP .... Wisconsin Electric Power Co. [*NASDAQ symbol*]   (NQ)
WELR .... Roanoke, AL [*AM radio station call letters*]
WELR-FM ... Roanoke, AL [*FM radio station call letters*]
WELS .... Kinston, NC [*AM radio station call letters*]
WELS .... Wisconsin Evangelical Lutheran Synod
WELS .... World-Wide Engineering Logistics Support [*Military*]
Welsb H & G ... Welsby, Hurlstone, and Gordon's English Exchequer Reports [*1848-56*] [*A publication*]   (DLA)
Welsb Hurl & G ... Welsby, Hurlstone, and Gordon's English Exchequer Reports [*1848-56*] [*A publication*]   (DLA)
Welsby H & G ... Welsby, Hurlstone, and Gordon's English Exchequer Reports [*1848-56*] [*A publication*]   (DLA)
Welsby H & G (Eng) ... Welsby, Hurlstone, and Gordon's English Exchequer Reports [*1848-56*] [*A publication*]   (DLA)
Welsh .... Welsh's Irish Case of James Feighny [*1838*] [*A publication*]   (DLA)
Welsh .... Welsh's Irish Case at Siligo [*1838*] [*A publication*]   (DLA)
Welsh .... Welsh's Irish Registry Cases [*A publication*]   (DLA)
Welsh Bee J ... Welsh Bee Journal [*A publication*]
Welsh Beekprs' Ass Q Bull ... Welsh Beekeepers' Association. Quarterly Bulletin [*A publication*]
Welsh Hist ... Welsh History Review [*A publication*]
Welsh Hist Rev ... Welsh History Review [*A publication*]
Welsh H R ... Welsh History Review [*A publication*]
Welsh J Agric ... Welsh Journal of Agriculture [*A publication*]

Welsh M .... Welsh Music [*A publication*]
Welsh Plant Breed Stn (Aberystwyth) Annu Rep ... Welsh Plant Breeding Station (Aberystwyth) Annual Report [*A publication*]
Welsh Plant Breed Stn (Aberystwyth) Rep ... Welsh Plant Breeding Station (Aberystwyth). Report [*A publication*]
Welsh Plant Breed Stn (Aberystwyth) Tech Bull ... Welsh Plant Breeding Station (Aberystwyth). Technical Bulletin [*A publication*]
Welsh Plant Breed Stn Bull Ser ... Welsh Plant Breeding Station. Bulletin Series [*A publication*]
Welsh Reg Cas ... Welsh's Irish Registry Cases [*A publication*]   (DLA)
WELSTAT ... Standardisation of Social Welfare Statistics Project [*Australia*]
Welt Isl ...... Die Welt des Islam [*A publication*]
Weltlit Farbenchem ... Weltliteratur der Farbenchemie [*A publication*]
Weltraumfahrt Raketentech ... Weltraumfahrt und Raketentechnik [*A publication*]
Weltwir Arc ... Weltwirtschaftliches Archiv [*A publication*]
Weltwirt ..... Weltwirtschaft [*A publication*]
Weltwirtschaft Archiv ... Weltwirtschaftliches Archiv [*Kiel*] [*A publication*]
Weltwirtsch Archiv ... Weltwirtschaftliches Archiv [*A publication*]
WELU .... Aguadilla, PR [*Television station call letters*]
WELV .... Ellenville, NY [*AM radio station call letters*]
WELV-FM ... Ellenville, NY [*FM radio station call letters*]
WELW ...... Willoughby-Eastlake, OH [*AM radio station call letters*]
WELX .... Callahan, FL [*AM radio station call letters*]
WELY .... Ely, MN [*AM radio station call letters*]
WELZ .... Belzoni, MS [*AM radio station call letters*]
WEM .... War Eagle Mining Co. [*Vancouver Stock Exchange symbol*]
WEM .... Welfare of Enlisted Men [*Air Force*]
WEM .... West Essex Militia [*British*]
WEM .... Western European Metal Trades Employers Organization [*Cologne, Federal Republic of Germany*]   (EA)
WeM .... Western Microfilm Ltd., Edmonton, AB, Canada [*Library symbol*] [*Library of Congress*]   (LCLS)
WEM .... Western Miner [*A publication*]
WEM .... Wireless and Electrical Mechanic [*British*]   (DSUE)
WEM .... World's Epoch Makers [*A publication*]
WEM .... Woven Elastic Manufacturers Association [*Later, EFMCNTA*]   (MSA)
WEMA ..... Western Electronic Manufacturers Association [*Later, AEA*]   (EA)
WEMA ..... Woven Elastic Manufacturers Association [*Later, EFMCNTA*]   (EA)
WEMB ..... Erwin, TN [*AM radio station call letters*]
WEMC ...... Harrisonburg, VA [*FM radio station call letters*]
WEMD ...... Western Electronics Maintenance Depot
WEMG ...... Knoxville, TN [*AM radio station call letters*]
WEMI .... Neenah-Menasha, WI [*FM radio station call letters*]
WEMJ .... Laconia, NH [*AM radio station call letters*]
WEMM ..... Huntington, WV [*FM radio station call letters*]
WEMOB ... Wehrmedizinische Monatsschrift [*A publication*]
WEMOS ... International Women's Network on Pharmaceuticals [*Amsterdam, Netherlands*]   (EAIO)
WEMP ...... Milwaukee, WI [*AM radio station call letters*]
WEMR ...... Tunkhannock, PA [*AM radio station call letters*]
WEMR ...... Welding Equipment Maintenance and Repair [*UAW job classification*]
WEMR-FM ... Tunkhannock, PA [*FM radio station call letters*]
WEMSB ... Western European Military Supply Board [*NATO*]   (NATG)
WEMT ...... Greeneville, TN [*Television station call letters*]
WEMU ...... Ypsilanti, MI [*FM radio station call letters*]
WEMX ...... McConnellsburg, PA [*FM radio station call letters*]
WEN .... Waive Exchange If Necessary
Wen .... Wendell's Reports [*New York*] [*A publication*]   (DLA)
wen .... Wendic [*MARC language code*] [*Library of Congress*]   (LCCP)
WEN .... Wendy's International, Inc. [*NYSE symbol*]   (SPSG)
WEN .... Wenkite [*A zeolite*]
WEN .... Wentworth Institute of Technology, Boston, MA [*OCLC symbol*]   (OCLC)
WEN .... Wentworth Public Library [*UTLAS symbol*]
WENA ...... Penuelas, PR [*AM radio station call letters*]
WENC ...... Whiteville, NC [*AM radio station call letters*]
WEND ...... Brandon, FL [*AM radio station call letters*]
Wend .... Wendell's Reports [*1826-41*] [*New York*] [*A publication*]   (DLA)
WEND ...... Wendover [*England*]
Wend Bl .... Wendell's Blackstone [*A publication*]   (DLA)
Wendel ...... Wendell's Reports [*New York*] [*A publication*]   (DLA)
Wendell ..... Wendell's Reports [*1826-41*] [*New York*] [*A publication*]   (DLA)
Wendell Rep ... Wendell's Reports [*New York*] [*A publication*]   (DLA)
Wendell's Rep ... Wendell's Reports [*New York*] [*A publication*]   (DLA)
Wend (NY) ... Wendell's Reports [*1826-41*] [*New York*] [*A publication*]   (DLA)
Wend R ...... Wendell's Reports [*New York*] [*A publication*]   (DLA)
Wend Rep .. Wendell's Reports [*New York*] [*A publication*]   (DLA)
WENDS .... World Energy Data System [*Department of Energy*] [*Information service or system*]   (IID)
Wendt .... Wendt's Reports of Cases [*Ceylon*] [*A publication*]   (DLA)
Wendt Mar Leg ... Wendt's Maritime Legislation [*3rd ed.*] [*1888*] [*A publication*]   (DLA)
WENE .... Endicott, NY [*AM radio station call letters*]

WENELA ... Witwatersrand Native Labour Association [*Nyasaland*]
WENG....... Englewood, FL [*AM radio station call letters*]
WENH-TV ... Durham, NH [*Television station call letters*]
WENK....... Union City, TN [*AM radio station call letters*]
WENL .... Gladstone, MI [*FM radio station call letters*]
WENMD ... Water Engineering and Management [*A publication*]
Wenner-Gren Cent Int Symp Ser ... Wenner-Gren Center. International
          Symposium Series [*A publication*]
WENN-FM ... Birmingham, AL [*FM radio station call letters*]
WENO....... Nashville, TN [*AM radio station call letters*]
WENOA.... Weekly Notice to Airmen [*FAA*]
WENR....... Englewood, TN [*AM radio station call letters*]
WENS ...... Shelbyville, IN [*FM radio station call letters*]
WENS ...... World Electroless Nickel Society [*Defunct*]   (EA)
WENT ...... Gloversville, NY [*AM radio station call letters*]
W Ent........ Winch's Book of Entries [*A publication*]   (DLA)
Wentworth Mag ... Wentworth Magazine [*A publication*]   (APTA)
WENU....... Hudson Falls, NY [*FM radio station call letters*]
WENY .... Elmira, NY [*AM radio station call letters*]
WENY-TV ... Elmira, NY [*Television station call letters*]
Wenz......... Wenzell's Reports [*60 Minnesota*] [*A publication*]   (DLA)
WEO.......... War Economic Operation [*World War II*]
WEO.......... Warehouse Economy Outlet [*A & P Co.*]
WEO.......... Weaco Resources Ltd. [*Vancouver Stock Exchange symbol*]
WEO.......... Weapons Engineer Officer [*British military*]   (DMA)
WEO.......... West-Ost-Journal [*A publication*]
WEO.......... Western Europe and Others [*United Nations*]
WEO.......... Where Economy Originates [*A & P Co. marketing slogan, now
          obsolete*]
WEO.......... World Economic Outlook [*A publication*]
WEO.......... World Energy Outlook [*International Energy Agency*]
WEOA....... Beverly Hills, FL [*FM radio station call letters*]
WEOG....... Western European and Others Group [*United Nations*]
WEOK....... Poughkeepsie, NY [*AM radio station call letters*]
WEOL .... Elyria, OH [*AM radio station call letters*]
WEOS ...... Water Extraction of Orange Solids [*Citrus processing*]
WEOS-FM ... Geneva, NY [*FM radio station call letters*]
WEOW...... Key West, FL [*FM radio station call letters*]
WEOW...... Weapons Engineer Officer's Writer [*British military*]   (DMA)
WEOZ....... Saegertown, PA [*FM radio station call letters*]
WEP .... War and Emergency Plan [*DoD*]
WEP .... Waseda Economic Papers [*A publication*]
WEP .... Water Electrolysis Plenum
WEP .... Water Entry Point [*Navy*]   (CAAL)
WEP .... Water-Extended Polyester
WEP .... Weak Equivalence Principle [*Gravity*]
WEP .... Weam [*Papua New Guinea*] [*Airport symbol*]   (OAG)
WEP .... Weapon
WEP .... Weather Processor   (MCD)
WEP .... Wisconsin Experiment Package [*NASA*]   (MCD)
WEP .... Women's Equity Program   (EA)
WEP .... Work Experience Program [*Department of Labor*]
WEP .... World Employment Program [*of the International Labour
          Organization*] [*Geneva, Switzerland*] [*United Nations*]
WEP .... Writing, Editing, and Publishing
WEPA....... Eupora, MS [*AM radio station call letters*]
WEPA....... Welded Electronic Packaging Association
WEPC....... Weapons and Equipment Policy Committee [*British*]   (RDA)
WEPC....... West Chemical Products [*NASDAQ symbol*]   (NQ)
WEPCOSE ... Weapon Control Systems Engineering [*Navy*]   (NG)
WEPEX..... Weapons Exercise [*Navy*]   (NVT)
WEPG .... South Pittsburg, TN [*AM radio station call letters*]
WEPH .... Weapon Phenomenology   (RDA)
WEPM ...... Martinsburg, WV [*AM radio station call letters*]
WEPR....... Greenville, SC [*FM radio station call letters*]
WEPR....... Walker Energy Partners [*NASDAQ symbol*]   (NQ)
WEPR....... Women Executives in Public Relations [*New York, NY*]   (EA)
WEPRA..... Welding Production [*English Translation*] [*A publication*]
WEPREC... West Pakistan Research and Evaluation Center
WEPS ...... Elgin, IL [*FM radio station call letters*]
WEPS ...... Weapons System [*Navy*]
WEPSO..... Naval Weapons Services Office [*Also known as
          NAVWPNSERVO, NWSO*]
WEPTA..... War Excess Profits Tax Act [*1917*]
WEPTAC.. Weapons and Tactics Analysis Center [*Navy*]   (MCD)
WEPTRAEX ... Weapons Training Exercise   (NVT)
WEPTU..... Weapons Reserve Training Units [*Navy*]
WEPZA..... World Export Processing Zones Association [*Flagstaff,
          AZ*]   (EA)
WEQ......... Wind Erosion Equation
WEQO....... Whitley City, KY [*AM radio station call letters*]
WEQX....... Manchester, VT [*FM radio station call letters*]
WER .... Water Electrolysis Rocket
WER .... Webcor Electronics, Inc. [*AMEX symbol*]   (SPSG)
WER .... Week End Review [*A publication*]
WER .... Weight Estimating Relationship   (KSC)
WER .... Werombi [*Australia*] [*Seismograph station code, US Geological
          Survey*]   (SEIS)
WERA .... Plainfield, NJ [*AM radio station call letters*]
WERA .... Western Eastern Roadracers Association   (EA)
WERA .... Western/English Retailers of America   (EA)

WERA .... World Energy Research Authority
WERB....... Berlin, CT [*FM radio station call letters*]
WERC ...... Birmingham, AL [*AM radio station call letters*]
WERC ...... Warehousing Education and Research Council   (EA)
WERC ...... Western Energy Resources, Inc. [*NASDAQ symbol*]   (NQ)
WERC ...... Women's Education Resource Centre [*Women's Education
          Group*] [*British*]   (CB)
WERC ...... World Environment and Resources Council [*Louvain,
          Belgium*]   (EAIO)
WERE....... Cleveland, OH [*AM radio station call letters*]
WERG ...... Erie, PA [*FM radio station call letters*]
WERH....... Hamilton, AL [*AM radio station call letters*]
WERH-FM ... Hamilton, AL [*FM radio station call letters*]
WERI........ Water and Energy Research Institute of the Western Pacific
          [*University of Guam*] [*Guam*] [*Research center*]   (RCD)
WERI........ Westerly, RI [*AM radio station call letters*]
WERK ...... Muncie, IN [*AM radio station call letters*]
Werk .... Werk/Archithese [*A publication*]
WERKA.... Werkstattstechnik [*A publication*]
Werkstatt und Betr ... Werkstatt und Betrieb [*A publication*]
Werkstatt Betr ... Werkstatt und Betrieb [*A publication*]
Werkstattstech Z Ind Fertigung ... Werkstattstechnik Zeitschrift fuer
          Industrielle Fertigung [*A publication*]
Werkst Korros ... Werkstoffe und Korrosion [*A publication*]
Werkst u Korrosion ... Werkstoffe und Korrossion (Wernheim) [*A
          publication*]
WERL....... Eagle River, WI [*AM radio station call letters*]
WERL....... Water Engineering Research Laboratory [*Cincinnati, OH*]
          [*Environmental Protection Agency*]   (GRD)
WERM ...... World Encyclopedia of Recorded Music, 1925-55 [*A
          publication*]
WERN ...... Madison, WI [*FM radio station call letters*]
WERN ...... Werner Enterprises, Inc. [*Omaha, NE*] [*NASDAQ
          symbol*]   (NQ)
Wernerian N H Soc Mem ... Wernerian Natural History Society. Memoirs [*A
          publication*]
WERP....... Women's Economic Rights Project   (EA)
WERPG..... Western European Regional Planning Group [*NATO*]   (NATG)
WERR ...... Utuado Rosa, PR [*FM radio station call letters*]
WERS....... Boston, MA [*FM radio station call letters*]
WERS....... War Emergency Radio Service
WERS....... Weapons Effect Reporting Station [*Civil defense*]
WERS....... Wing Equipment Repair Squadron
WERSI ...... Committee on Women's Employment and Related Social
          Issues   (EA)
WERT....... Van Wert, OH [*AM radio station call letters*]
WERT....... Women's Economic Round Table   (EA)
WERTS..... Writers' Ever-Ready Textual Service [*Rent-A-Script*] [*Satirical*]
WERU-FM ... Blue Hill, ME [*FM radio station call letters*]
WERZ....... Exeter, NH [*FM radio station call letters*]
WES.......... Sacred Heart Hospital, Eau Claire, WI [*Library symbol*]
          [*Library of Congress*]   (LCLS)
WES.......... W. E. Schulz & Associates, Inc. [*Telecommunications
          service*]   (TSSD)
WES.......... Washington Ethical Society   (EA)
WES.......... Water Electrolysis System
WES.......... Waterways Experiment Station [*Army Corps of Engineers*]
          [*Vicksburg, MS*]
WES.......... Weapon Engineering Station   (MCD)
WES.......... Weapons Effects Systems   (MCD)
WES.......... Weather Editing Section [*FAA*]   (FAAC)
WES.......... Wes-Martin Aviation [*Red Bluff, CA*] [*FAA
          designator*]   (FAAC)
Wes .... [*Mathaeus*] Wesenbeccius [*Deceased, 1586*] [*Authority cited in
          pre-1607 legal work*]   (DSA)
WES.......... Wesleyan [*A publication*]
WES.......... Wesleyan [*Religion*]   (ROG)
WES.......... West [*or Western*]
WES.......... Westbury [*British depot code*]
WES.......... Westcorp, Inc. [*AMEX symbol*]   (SPSG)
WES.......... Westmills Carpets Ltd. [*Toronto Stock Exchange symbol*]
WES.......... Weston [*Massachusetts*] [*Seismograph station code, US
          Geological Survey*]   (SEIS)
WES.......... Weston [*Massachusetts*] [*Geomagnetic observatory code*]
WES.......... Westport Public Library, Westport, CT [*OCLC
          symbol*]   (OCLC)
WES.......... Wind Electric System [*Telecommunications*]   (TEL)
WES.......... Wisdom of the East Series [*A publication*]
WES.......... Work Environment Scale [*Test*]
WES.......... World Economic Summit
WES.......... World-Wide Education Service [*Parents' National Educational
          Union*] [*British*]
WESA....... Charleroi, PA [*AM radio station call letters*]
WESA....... White Sands National Monument [*New Mexico*]
WESA....... Wind Energy Society of America [*Inactive*]
WESA....... Wind Energy Systems Act of 1980
WESA-FM ... Charleroi, PA [*FM radio station call letters*]
Wes Aust.... West Australian [*A publication*]
WESB....... Bradford, PA [*AM radio station call letters*]
WESB....... Western Beef [*NASDAQ symbol*]   (NQ)
WESC........ Greenville, SC [*AM radio station call letters*]

WESC........ Wasatch Education Systems Corp. [*NASDAQ symbol*]   (NQ)
WESC....... Weapon Engagement Simulation Component   (MCD)
WESC....... Whole Earth Software Catalog [*A publication*]
WESCAR.. Western Carolines [*Navy*]
WESCARSUBAREA ... Western Carolines Subarea [*Navy*]
WESC-FM ... Greenville, SC [*FM radio station call letters*]
Wes CLJ ..... Westmoreland County Law Journal [*A publication*]   (DLA)
WESCO..... Walnut Export Sales Company   (EA)
WESCO..... Westinghouse Corporation
WESCOBASESERVUNIT ... West Coast Base Service Unit [*Navy*]
WESCOM ... Weapons System Cost Model
WESCOM ... Western Command [*Army*]   (AABC)
WESCON ... Western Electronics Show and Convention [*IEEE*]
WESCON Tech Pap ... WESCON [*Western Electronics Show and
          Convention*] Technical Papers [*United States*] [*A
          publication*]
WESCOSOUNDSCOL ... West Coast Sound School [*Navy*]
WESD....... Schofield, WI [*FM radio station call letters*]
WESE........ Baldwyn, MS [*FM radio station call letters*]
WESE........ Wills Eye Society of Ex-Residents   (EA)
WESED.... Weapons System Evaluation Division [*DoD*]
WESEG.... Weapons System Evaluation Group [*DoD*]
Wesen .... [*Mathaeus*] Wesenbeccius [*Deceased, 1586*] [*Authority cited in
          pre-1607 legal work*]   (DSA)
Wesenb ...... [*Mathaeus*] Wesenbeccius [*Deceased, 1586*] [*Authority cited in
          pre-1607 legal work*]   (DSA)
WESF........ Waste Encapsulation Storage Facility [*Nuclear
          energy*]   (NRCH)
WESG....... Women Executives in State Government   (EA)
WESH ...... Daytona Beach, FL [*Television station call letters*]
WESI........ Strasburg, VA [*FM radio station call letters*]
WESIAC .... Weapons Effectiveness Systems Industry Advisory
          Committee   (MCD)
Weskett Ins ... Weskett's Complete Digest of the Theory, Laws, and Practice
          of Insurance [*A publication*]   (DLA)
Wesk Ins ... Weskett's Complete Digest of the Theory, Laws, and Practice of
          Insurance [*A publication*]   (DLA)
WESL........ East St. Louis, IL [*AM radio station call letters*]
Wesley Th J ... Wesleyan Theological Journal [*A publication*]
Wesley W Spink Lect Comp Med ... Wesley W. Spink Lectures on
          Comparative Medicine [*A publication*]
WESM....... Princess Anne, MD [*FM radio station call letters*]
WESN ...... Bloomington, IL [*FM radio station call letters*]
WESO ..... Southbridge, MA [*AM radio station call letters*]
WESO ...... Weapons Engineering Service Office [*DoD*]
WESOS ..... Water-Extracted Soluble Orange Solids [*Citrus processing*]
WESP .... Dothan, AL [*FM radio station call letters*]
WESP .... War and Emergency Support Plan [*DoD*]
WESP .... Wespac Investors Trust [*NASDAQ symbol*]   (NQ)
W/E & SP ... With Equipment and Spare Parts
WESPAR .. Weapon Evaluation System Photographic Analog
          Recorder   (MCD)
WESPEX... War and Emergency Support Plan Exercise [*DoD*]
WESR....... Onley-Onancock, VA [*AM radio station call letters*]
WESRAC .. Western Research Application Center [*University of Southern
          California*]
WESREP... Weapon Engineering Station Representative   (MCD)
Wes Res Law Jo ... Western Reserve Law Journal [*A publication*]   (DLA)
Wes Res Law Jrl ... Western Reserve Law Journal [*Ohio*] [*A
          publication*]   (DLA)
WESR-FM ... Onley-Onancock, VA [*FM radio station call letters*]
WESS........ East Stroudsburg, PA [*FM radio station call letters*]
WESS .... Weapons Effect Signature Simulator
WESS .... Weapons Engagement Scoring System
WESS .... Weapons System Status
WESS .... Western European Specialists Section [*Association of College
          and Research Libraries*]
WESSEAFRON ... Western Sea Frontier [*Navy*]
WEST....... Easton, PA [*AM radio station call letters*]
WEST....... Weapons Effectiveness Simulated Threat   (MCD)
WEST....... Weapons Exhaust Study [*Military*]   (MCD)
WEST....... West One Bancorp [*NASDAQ symbol*]   (NQ)
West.......... Westbury's European Arbitration (Reilly) [*A
          publication*]   (DLA)
WEST....... Western Earth Sciences Technologies [*Research center*]   (RCD)
WEST....... Western Educational Society for Telecommunications
          [*Defunct*]   (EA)
WEST....... Western Energy Supply and Transmission Associates [*Utility
          antipollution group*]
WEST....... Western Transportation Co. [*Later, WTCO*] [*AAR code*]
West.......... Western's London Tithe Cases [*England*] [*A
          publication*]   (DLA)
West.......... Westminster [*Record label*]
West.......... Westmoreland County Law Journal [*Pennsylvania*] [*A
          publication*]   (DLA)
West.......... Weston's Reports [*11-14 Vermont*] [*A publication*]   (DLA)
West.......... West's English Chancery Reports [*A publication*]   (DLA)
West.......... West's Reports, English House of Lords [*A publication*]   (DLA)
WEST....... Women's Enlistment Screening Test [*Military*]
WESTA ..... White Sands Electromagnetic Pulse Systems Test Array [*New
          Mexico*]   (RDA)

WESTAF... Western Transport Air Force
West Afr .... West Africa [*London*] [*A publication*]
West Afr Cocoa Res Inst Tech Bull ... West African Cocoa Research Institute.
          Technical Bulletin [*A publication*]
West African J of Ed ... West African Journal of Education [*A publication*]
West Afr Inst Oil Palm Res Annu Rep ... West African Institute for Oil Palm
          Research. Annual Report [*A publication*]
West Afr J Archaeol ... West African Journal of Archaeology [*A publication*]
West Afr J Biol Appl Chem ... West African Journal of Biological and Applied
          Chemistry [*A publication*]
West Afr J Biol Chem ... West African Journal of Biological Chemistry [*A
          publication*]
West Afr J Pharmacol Drug Res ... West African Journal of Pharmacology
          and Drug Research [*A publication*]
West Afr Med J ... West African Medical Journal [*A publication*]
West Afr Med J Nigerian Pract ... West African Medical Journal and Nigerian
          Practitioner [*A publication*]
West Afr Med J Niger Med Dent Pract ... West African Medical Journal and
          Nigerian Medical and Dental Practitioner [*A publication*]
West Afr Pharm ... West African Pharmacist [*A publication*]
West Am Lit ... Western American Literature [*A publication*]
West Am Sc ... West American Scientist [*A publication*]
WESTAR .. Waterways Experiment Station Terrain Analyzer RADAR
WESTAR 6 ... [*A*] Communications satellite
West Assn Map Libs Inf Bul ... Western Association of Map Libraries.
          Information Bulletin [*A publication*]
West AULR ... Western Australia University. Law Review [*A publication*]
West Aust Clin Rep ... Western Australian Clinical Reports [*A
          publication*]   (APTA)
West Aust Conf Australas Inst Min Metall ... Western Australian Conference.
          Australasian Institute of Mining and Metallurgy [*A
          publication*]   (APTA)
West Aust Dep Agric Annu Rep ... Western Australia. Department of
          Agriculture. Annual Report [*A publication*]   (APTA)
West Aust Dep Fish Fauna Rep ... Western Australia. Department of Fisheries
          and Fauna. Report [*A publication*]
West Aust Dep Fish Wildl Rep ... Western Australia. Department of Fisheries
          and Wildlife. Report [*A publication*]
West Aust Dep Mines Annu Rep ... Western Australia. Department of Mines.
          Annual Report [*A publication*]   (APTA)
West Aust Dep Mines Miner Resour West Aust Bull ... Western Australia.
          Department of Mines. Mineral Resources of Western
          Australia. Bulletin [*A publication*]   (APTA)
West Aust Dep Mines Min Resour West Aust Bull ... Western Australia.
          Department of Mines. Mineral Resources of Western
          Australia. Bulletin [*A publication*]   (APTA)
West Aust Dep Mines Rep Gov Mineral Anal Chem ... Western Australia.
          Department of Mines. Report of the Government
          Mineralogist, Analyst, and Chemist [*A publication*]
West Aust Geol Surv Annu Prog Rep ... Western Australia. Geological Survey.
          Annual Progress Report [*A publication*]   (APTA)
West Aust Geol Surv Annu Rep ... Western Australia. Geological Survey.
          Annual Report [*A publication*]   (APTA)
West Aust Geol Surv Bull ... Western Australia. Geological Survey. Bulletin [*A
          publication*]   (APTA)
West Aust Geol Surv 1:250000 Geol Ser ... Western Australia. Geological
          Survey. 1:250,000 Geological Series [*A
          publication*]   (APTA)
West Aust Geol Surv Geol Ser Explan Notes ... Western Australia. Geological
          Survey. Geological Series. Explanatory Notes [*A
          publication*]
West Aust Geol Surv Miner Resour Bull ... Western Australia. Geological
          Survey. Mineral Resources Bulletin [*A
          publication*]   (APTA)
West Aust Geol Surv Rep ... Western Australia. Geological Survey. Report [*A
          publication*]   (APTA)
West Aust Herb Res Notes ... Western Australian Herbarium. Research Notes
          [*A publication*]
West Aust Inst Technol Gaz ... Western Australian Institute of Technology.
          Gazette [*A publication*]
West Austl ... Western Australian Reports [*A publication*]
West Aust L Rev ... University of Western Australia. Law Review [*A
          publication*]
West Aust Mar Res Lab Fish Res Bull ... Western Australian Marine Research
          Laboratories. Fisheries Research Bulletin [*A
          publication*]   (APTA)
West Aust Mus Spec Publ ... Western Australian Museum. Special
          Publication [*A publication*]   (APTA)
West Aust Nat ... Western Australian Naturalist [*A publication*]
West Aust Nat Reserve Manage Plan ... Western Australian Nature Reserve
          Management Plan [*A publication*]
West Aust Naturalist ... Western Australian Naturalist [*A
          publication*]   (APTA)
West Aust Nutgrow Soc Yearb ... Western Australian Nutgrowing Society.
          Yearbook [*A publication*]
West Aust Rep Gov Chem Lab ... Western Australia. Report. Government
          Chemical Laboratories [*A publication*]
West Austr L ... Western Australian Law Reports [*A publication*]
West Aust Sch Mines ... Western Australian School of Mines [*A publication*]
West Aust SWANS ... Western Australia SWANS [*State Wildlife Authority
          News Service*] [*A publication*]

West Aust SWANS (State Wildl Auth News Serv) ... Western Australia SWANS (State Wildlife Authority News Service) [*A publication*]
West Aust Wildl Res Cent Wildl Res Bull ... Western Australia Wildlife Research Centre. Wildlife Research Bulletin [*A publication*]
West Bird Bander ... Western Bird Bander [*A publication*]
West Birds ... Western Birds [*A publication*]
West Build ... Western Building [*United States*] [*A publication*]
West Bus.... Western Business [*A publication*]
West Canad J Anthropol ... Western Canadian Journal of Anthropology [*A publication*]
West Can Beekpr ... Western Canada Beekeeper [*A publication*]
West Can J Anthropol ... Western Canadian Journal of Anthropology [*A publication*]
West Canner Packer ... Western Canner and Packer [*A publication*]
West Can Water Sewage Conf Pap Annu Conv ... Western Canada Water and Sewage Conference. Papers Presented at the Annual Convention [*A publication*]
West Can Water and Sewage Conf Proc Annu Conv ... Western Canada Water and Sewage Conference. Proceedings of the Annual Convention [*A publication*]
West Ch ..... West's English Chancery Cases [*25 English Reprint*] [*A publication*]   (DLA)
West Chapter Int Shade Tree Conf Proc ... Western Chapter. International Shade Tree Conference. Proceedings [*A publication*]
West Chem Metall ... Western Chemist and Metallurgist [*A publication*]
West Ch (Eng) ... West's English Chancery Cases [*25 English Reprint*] [*A publication*]   (DLA)
Westchester Co Hist Soc Publ ... Westchester County Historical Society. Publications [*A publication*]
Westchester Med Bull ... Westchester Medical Bulletin [*New York*] [*A publication*]
West Chy ... West's English Chancery Cases [*25 English Reprint*] [*A publication*]   (DLA)
West City ... Western City [*A publication*]
West Coast R ... West Coast Review [*A publication*]
West Coast Rep ... West Coast Reporter [*A publication*]   (DLA)
WESTCOM ... Western Command [*Army*]
West Com .. Western's Commentaries on the Laws of England [*A publication*]   (DLA)
WESTCOMMRGN ... Western Communications Region [*Air Force*]   (AFM)
West Constr ... Western Construction [*A publication*]
West Contract ... Western Contractor [*A publication*]
West Co Rep ... West Coast Reporter [*A publication*]   (DLA)
West Crop Farm Manage N Ed ... Western Crops and Farm Management. Northern Edition [*A publication*]
West Crop Farm Manage S Ed ... Western Crops and Farm Management. Southern Edition [*A publication*]
West Dent Soc Bull ... Western Dental Society. Bulletin [*A publication*]
West Drug ... Western Druggist [*A publication*]
Westd Zeit ... Westdeutsche Zeitschrift fuer Geschichte und Kunst [*A publication*]   (OCD)
WESTE ..... Weapons Effectiveness and System Test Environment [*Air Force*]   (AFM)
WESTEC... Western Metal and Tool Exposition and Conference [*American Society for Metals*]   (TSPED)
West Econ Jour ... Western Economic Journal [*A publication*]
West Elec E ... Western Electric Engineer [*A publication*]
West Electr Eng ... Western Electric Engineer [*A publication*]
Westerm M ... Westermanns Monatshefte [*A publication*]
Westerm Monatsh ... Westermanns Monatshefte [*A publication*]
Western Am Lit ... Western American Literature [*A publication*]
Western Australia Geol Survey Rept ... Western Australia. Geological Survey. Report. Government Printer [*A publication*]
Western Australia Main Roads Dep Tech Bull ... Western Australia. Main Roads Department. Technical Bulletin [*A publication*]   (APTA)
Western Bs ... Western Business [*A publication*]
Western EE ... Western Electric Engineer [*A publication*]
Western Electric Eng ... Western Electric Engineer [*A publication*]
Western Eng ... Western Engineering [*A publication*]
Western Hist Q ... Western Historical Quarterly [*A publication*]
Western Hum R ... Western Humanities Review [*A publication*]
Western Hum Rev ... Western Humanities Review [*A publication*]
Western Law Jour ... Western Law Journal (Reprint) [*A publication*]
Western L Rev ... Western Law Review [*Canada*] [*A publication*]   (DLA)
Western Med ... Western Medicine [*A publication*]
Western Ont L Rev ... Western Ontario Law Review [*A publication*]
Western Pol Q ... Western Political Quarterly [*A publication*]
Western Res ... Western Reserve Business Review [*A publication*]
Western Reserve Hist Soc Tracts ... Western Reserve Historical Society. Tracts [*A publication*]
Western Reserve LN ... Western Reserve Law Notes [*A publication*]   (DLA)
Western Res L Rev ... Western Reserve Law Review [*A publication*]
Western Rv Sc ... Western Review of Science and Industry [*A publication*]
Western Speleol Inst Bull ... Western Speleological Institute. Bulletin [*A publication*]
Western Wash Ag Exp B ... Western Washington Agricultural Experiment Station. Monthly Bulletin [*A publication*]
West Europe Ed ... Western European Education [*A publication*]

West Eur Politics ... West European Politics [*A publication*]
West-Eur Symp Clin Chem ... West-European Symposia on Clinical Chemistry [*A publication*]
West Ext .... West on Extents [*1817*] [*A publication*]   (DLA)
Westfael Bienenztg ... Westfaelische Bienenzeitung [*A publication*]
West Farmer ... Western Farmer [*A publication*]
Westf Bienenztg ... Westfaelische Bienenzeitung [*A publication*]
West Feed .. Western Feed [*A publication*]
West Feed Seed ... Western Feed and Seed [*A publication*]
West Folk ... Western Folklore [*A publication*]
West Folkl ... Western Folklore [*A publication*]
WESTFORNET ... Western Forestry Information Network [*Forest service*] [*Library network*]
West Found Vertebr Zool Occas Pap ... Western Foundation of Vertebrate Zoology. Occasional Papers [*A publication*]
Westfriesch Jb ... Westfriesch Jaarboek [*A publication*]
West Frozen Foods ... Western Frozen Foods [*A publication*]
West Fruit Grow ... Western Fruit Grower [*A publication*]
West Gas ... Western Gas [*A publication*]
West Hist Q ... Western Historical Quarterly [*A publication*]
West HL .... West's Reports, English House of Lords [*A publication*]   (DLA)
West Horse ... Western Horseman [*A publication*]
West HR .... Western Humanities Review [*A publication*]
West Humanities Rev ... Western Humanities Review [*A publication*]
West Hum R ... Western Humanities Review [*A publication*]
West Hum Rev ... Western Humanities Review [*A publication*]
West II .... Second Statute of Westminster [*A publication*]   (DSA)
West Ind Bull ... West Indian Bulletin [*A publication*]
West Indian Med J ... West Indian Medical Journal [*A publication*]
Westinghouse Eng ... Westinghouse Engineer [*A publication*]
Westinghouse Engr ... Westinghouse Engineer [*A publication*]
West J Agric Econ ... Western Journal of Agricultural Economics [*A publication*]
West J Med ... Western Journal of Medicine [*A publication*]
West J Nurs Res ... Western Journal of Nursing Research [*A publication*]
West J Surg ... Western Journal of Surgery, Obstetrics, and Gynecology [*A publication*]
West J Surg Obstet Gynecol ... Western Journal of Surgery. Obstetrics and Gynecology [*A publication*]
West Jur .... Western Jurist [*Des Moines, Iowa*] [*A publication*]   (DLA)
Westlake Int Private Law ... Westlake's Private International Law [*A publication*]   (DLA)
WESTLANT ... Western Atlantic Area
West Law J ... Western Law Journal [*A publication*]
West Law Jour ... Western Law Journal (Reprint) [*A publication*]
West Law M ... Western Law Monthly [*Ohio*] [*A publication*]   (DLA)
West Law Mo ... Western Law Monthly (Reprint) [*Ohio*] [*A publication*]   (DLA)
West Law Month ... Western Law Monthly [*Ohio*] [*A publication*]   (DLA)
West Law Rev ... Western Law Review [*Canada*] [*A publication*]   (DLA)
WestLB...... Westdeutsche Landesbank [*West German bank*]
Westl Confl ... Westlake's Conflict of Laws [*A publication*]   (DLA)
West Legal Obser ... Western Legal Observer [*A publication*]   (DLA)
West Leg Obs ... Western Legal Observer [*A publication*]   (DLA)
West L Gaz ... Western Law Gazette [*Cincinnati, OH*] [*A publication*]   (DLA)
West Lit J .. Western Literary Journal [*A publication*]
West Livestock J ... Western Livestock Journal [*A publication*]
West LJ ..... Western Law Journal [*A publication*]
West LJ (Ohio) ... Western Law Journal (Ohio) [*A publication*]
West LM.... Western Law Monthly [*Ohio*] [*A publication*]   (DLA)
West L Mo ... Western Law Monthly [*Ohio*] [*A publication*]   (DLA)
West L Month ... Western Law Monthly [*Ohio*] [*A publication*]   (DLA)
West Locker ... Western Locker [*A publication*]
Westl Priv Int Law ... Westlake's Private International Law [*A publication*]   (DLA)
West LR..... Western Law Reporter [*Canada*] [*A publication*]   (DLA)
West LR (Can) ... Western Law Reporter [*Canada*] [*A publication*]   (DLA)
West L Rev ... Western Law Review [*A publication*]   (DLA)
West LT..... Western Law Times [*Canada*] [*A publication*]   (DLA)
Westly...... Westerly [*A publication*]
West M ...... Western Monthly Magazine [*A publication*]
WESTM.... Westminster [*London*]
Westm....... Westminster Review [*A publication*]
Westm....... Westmoreland County Law Journal [*Pennsylvania*] [*A publication*]   (DLA)
West Mach Steel World ... Western Machinery and Steel World [*A publication*]
West Malays Geol Surv Dist Mem ... West Malaysia. Geological Survey. District Memoir [*A publication*]
West Malays Geol Surv Econ Bull ... West Malaysia. Geological Survey. Economic Bulletin [*A publication*]
WESTMD ... Westmorland [*County in England*]
West Med .. Western Medicine [*A publication*]
West Med Med J West ... Western Medicine; the Medical Journal of the West [*A publication*]
West Met ... Western Metals [*A publication*]
West Metalwork ... Western Metalworking [*A publication*]
Westm Hall Chron ... Westminster Hall Chronicle and Legal Examiner [*1835-36*] [*A publication*]   (DLA)
West Miner ... Western Miner [*A publication*]
Westminster Inst Rev ... Westminster Institute Review [*A publication*]

Westminster Stud Educ ... Westminster Studies in Education [*A publication*]
Westm LJ .. Westmoreland County Law Journal [*A publication*] (DLA)
West Mo R ... Western Monthly Review [*A publication*]
Westmore Co LJ (PA) ... Westmoreland County Law Journal [*Pennsylvania*] [*A publication*] (DLA)
Westmoreland ... Westmoreland County Law Journal [*Pennsylvania*] [*A publication*] (DLA)
Westmoreland Co LJ ... Westmoreland County Law Journal [*Pennsylvania*] [*A publication*] (DLA)
Westm Th J ... Westminster Theological Journal [*A publication*]
WESTN..... Western
West Nat.... Western Naturalist [*A publication*]
WESTNAVELEX ... Naval Electronics Systems Command, Western Division, Mare Island, Vallejo, California
WESTNAVFACENGCOM ... Western Division, Naval Facilities Engineering Command
West New Engl L Rev ... Western New England Law Review [*A publication*]
West NY Mg ... Western New York Magazine [*A publication*]
West Oil Refin ... Western Oil Refining [*A publication*]
West Oil Rep ... Western Oil Reporter [*A publication*]
WESTOMP ... Western Ocean Meeting Point
Weston....... Weston's Reports [*11-14 Vermont*] [*A publication*] (DLA)
West Ont L Rev ... Western Ontario Law Review [*A publication*]
WESTPAC ... Western Pacific [*Military*]
WESTPACBACOM ... Western Pacific Base Command [*Navy*]
WEST PACK ... Western Packaging Exposition (TSPED)
WESTPACNORTH ... Western Pacific North [*Navy*] (CINC)
West PA Hist Mag ... Western Pennsylvania Historical Magazine [*A publication*]
West Paint Rev ... Western Paint Review [*A publication*]
West Pak J Agric Res ... West Pakistan Journal of Agricultural Research [*A publication*]
West Pat .... West on Patents [*A publication*] (DLA)
West Penn Hist Mag ... Western Pennsylvania Historical Magazine [*A publication*]
West Pet Refiners Assoc Tech Publ ... Western Petroleum Refiners Association. Technical Publication [*A publication*]
West Plast ... Western Plastics [*A publication*]
WESTPO ... Western Governors Policy Office
West Polit Q ... Western Political Quarterly [*A publication*]
West Polit Quart ... Western Political Quarterly [*A publication*]
West Pol Q ... Western Political Quarterly [*A publication*]
West Poult Dis Conf ... Western Poultry Disease Conference [*A publication*]
Westpr Geschichtsv Ztsch ... Westpreussischer Geschichtsverein. Zeitschrift [*A publication*]
West Pr Int Law ... Westlake's Private International Law [*7th ed.*] [*1925*] [*A publication*] (DLA)
West Pulp Pap ... Western Pulp and Paper [*A publication*]
West R .... Western Reporter [*A publication*] (DLA)
West R .... Western Review [*A publication*]
West Reg Ext Publ Co-Op Ext US Dep Ag ... Western Region Extension Publication. Cooperative Extension. United States Department of Agriculture [*A publication*]
West Reg Pub Colo St Univ Exp Stn ... Western Regional Publication. Colorado State University. Experiment Station [*A publication*]
West Rep ... Western Reporter [*A publication*] (DLA)
West Reserve Law Rev ... Western Reserve Law Review [*A publication*]
West Res Law Rev ... Western Reserve Law Review [*A publication*]
West Res L Rev ... Western Reserve Law Review [*A publication*]
West Resour Conf ... Western Resources Conference [*A publication*]
West Rev ... Westminster Review [*A publication*]
West Roads ... Western Roads [*A publication*] (APTA)
West School L Rev ... Western School Law Review [*A publication*] (DLA)
West Scot Agric Coll Res Bull ... West of Scotland Agricultural College. Research Bulletin [*A publication*]
West Scot Iron Steel Inst J ... West of Scotland Iron and Steel Institute. Journal [*A publication*]
West Scotl Agric Coll Res Bull ... West of Scotland Agricultural College. Research Bulletin [*A publication*]
WESTSEAFRON ... Western Sea Frontier [*Navy*] (MUGU)
West Shade Tree Conf Proc Annu Meet ... Western Shade Tree Conference. Proceedings of the Annual Meeting [*A publication*]
West Soc Eng J ... Western Society of Engineers. Journal [*A publication*]
West Soc Malacol Annu Rep ... Western Society of Malacologists. Annual Report [*A publication*]
West Soc Malacol Occas Pap ... Western Society of Malacologists. Occasional Paper [*A publication*]
West's Op .. West's Opinions [*City Solicitor of Philadelphia, PA*] [*A publication*] (DLA)
West's Symb ... West's Symboleographie [*Many eds.*] [*1590-1641*] [*A publication*] (DLA)
West States Jew Hist Q ... Western States Jewish Historical Quarterly [*A publication*]
West States Sect Combust Inst Pap ... Western States Section. Combustion Institute. Paper [*A publication*]
West State UL Rev ... Western State University. Law Review [*A publication*]
West St U LR ... Western State University. Law Review [*A publication*]
West St U L Rev ... Western State University. Law Review [*A publication*]
WESTT ..... Weapon System Tactical Tester
West Teach ... Western Teacher [*A publication*] (APTA)

West Tenn Hist Soc Pap ... West Tennessee Historical Society. Papers [*A publication*]
West Texas Geol Soc Pub ... West Texas Geological Society. Publication [*A publication*]
West Tex B ... West Texas Business Journal [*A publication*]
West Tex Today ... Western Texas Today [*A publication*]
West T H ... West's English Chancery Reports Tempore Hardwicke [*1736-39*] [*A publication*] (DLA)
West T Hard ... West's English Chancery Reports Tempore Hardwicke [*1736-39*] [*A publication*] (DLA)
West T Hardw ... West's English Chancery Reports Tempore Hardwicke [*1736-39*] [*A publication*] (DLA)
West Th J .. Westminster Theological Journal [*A publication*]
West Ti Cas ... Western's London Tithe Cases [*1535-1822*] [*A publication*] (DLA)
West Tithe Cas ... Western's London Tithe Cases [*England*] [*A publication*] (DLA)
WestTJ ...... Westminster Theological Journal [*Philadelphia*] [*A publication*]
West Union Tech Rev ... Western Union Technical Review [*A publication*]
West Va ... West Virginia Reports [*A publication*] (DLA)
West Va Lib ... West Virginia Libraries [*A publication*]
West Va L Rev ... Western Virginia Law Review [*A publication*] (DLA)
West Va Rep ... West Virginia Reports [*A publication*] (DLA)
West Vet ... Western Veterinarian [*A publication*]
West Virginia Geol and Econ Survey Basic Data Rept ... West Virginia. Geological and Economic Survey. Basic Data Report [*A publication*]
West Virginia Geol and Econ Survey Circ ... West Virginia. Geological and Economic Survey. Circular [*A publication*]
West Virginia L Rev ... West Virginia Law Review [*A publication*]
West Week (Can) ... Western Weekly Notes (Canada) [*A publication*] (DLA)
West Week N ... Western Weekly Notes [*Canada*] [*A publication*] (DLA)
West Week N (Can) ... Western Weekly Notes (Canada) [*A publication*] (DLA)
West Week NS ... Western Weekly, New Series [*Canada*] [*A publication*] (DLA)
West Week Rep ... Western Weekly Reports [*Canada*] [*A publication*] (DLA)
West Wildlands ... Western Wildlands [*A publication*]
West Wkly ... Western Weekly Notes (Canada) [*A publication*] (DLA)
WESU ...... Middletown, CT [*FM radio station call letters*]
WESX........ Salem, MA [*AM radio station call letters*]
WESY........ Leland, MS [*AM radio station call letters*]
WESYP .... Weapons System Plan [*Navy*] (NG)
WESZ........ Lincoln, IL [*FM radio station call letters*]
WET .... Wagethe [*Indonesia*] [*Airport symbol*] (OAG)
WET .... Waste, Environment, and Technology [*Matrix*] [*Environmental Protection Agency*]
WET .... Water Exercise Technique [*In book title "The W.E.T. Workout"*]
WET .... Weapons Effectiveness Testing
WET .... Westfort Petroleums Ltd. [*Toronto Stock Exchange symbol*]
WET .... Wet Environment Trainer [*Navy*]
WET .... Wettzell [*Federal Republic of Germany*] [*Seismograph station code, US Geological Survey*] (SEIS)
WET .... Work Experience and Training
WETA ...... War Estate Tax Act [*1917*]
WETAC .... Westinghouse Electronic Tubeless Analog Computer
WETAF .... Weather Task Force
WETA-FM ... Washington, DC [*FM radio station call letters*]
WETARFAC ... Work Element Timer and Recorder for Automatic Computing
WETA-TV ... Washington, DC [*Television station call letters*]
WETB........ Johnson City, TN [*AM radio station call letters*]
Wet Bydraes PU CHO Reeks B Natuurwet ... Wetenskaplike Bydraes van die PU [*Potchefstroomse Universiteit*] vir CHO [*Christelike Hoere Onderwys*]. Reeks B: Natuurwetenskappe [*A publication*]
WETC........ Wendell-Zebulon, NC [*AM radio station call letters*]
WETD........ Alfred, NY [*FM radio station call letters*]
Wetenskap Studiereeks ... Wetenskaplike Studiereeks [*A publication*]
WETG .... Erie, PA [*Television station call letters*]
Wet Ground Mica Assoc Inc Tech Bull ... Wet Ground Mica Association, Incorporated. Technical Bulletin [*A publication*]
WETH ...... Wetherley [*England*]
Weth .... Wethey's Reports [*Canada*] [*A publication*] (DLA)
Wethey....... Wethey's Reports, Upper Canada Queen's Bench [*A publication*] (DLA)
Weth UC.... Wethey's Reports, Upper Canada Queen's Bench [*A publication*] (DLA)
WE TIP ..... We Turn in Pushers [*Organization combating drug traffic*]
WETK........ Burlington, VT [*Television station call letters*]
WETL........ South Bend, IN [*FM radio station call letters*]
WETM .... Weather Team [*Air Force*] (AFM)
Wet Meded KNNV ... Wetenschappelijke Mededeling KNNV [*Koninklijke Nederlandse Natuurhistorische Vereniging*] [*A publication*]
WETM-TV ... Elmira, NY [*Television station call letters*]
WETN .... Wheaton, IL [*FM radio station call letters*]
WETNETNG ... Wet-Net Training [*Navy*] (NVT)
WETP........ Work Experience Training Program (OICC)
WETS........ Johnson City, TN [*FM radio station call letters*]
WETS........ Weapon Effects Training Simulator (MCD)

WETS........	Week-End Training Site [*Military*] (AABC)
Wet Samenleving ...	Wetenschap en Samenleving [*A publication*]
WETSU.....	We Eat This Stuff Up [*Army slang, bowdlerized*]
WETT........	Ocean City, MD [*AM radio station call letters*]
WETT........	Wetterau, Inc. [*NASDAQ symbol*] (NQ)
Wett	Wettstein's Novum Testamentum Graecum [*A publication*] (BJA)
Wett Gesch Bl ...	Wetterauer Geschichtsblaetter [*A publication*]
Wet Tijd.....	Wetenschappelijke Tijdingen. Vereniging voor Wetenschapp de Gent [*A publication*]
Wett Leben ...	Wetter und Leben [*A publication*]
WETV.......	Key West, FL [*Television station call letters*]
WETZ.......	New Martinsville, WV [*AM radio station call letters*]
WEU..........	University of Wisconsin-Eau Claire, Eau Claire, WI [*Library symbol*] [*Library of Congress*] (LCLS)
WEU..........	Ward's Engine Update [*A publication*]
WEU..........	Western European Union [*Also, WU*] [*See also UEO*] (EAIO)
WEUC.......	Ponce, PR [*AM radio station call letters*]
WEUC-FM ...	Ponce, PR [*FM radio station call letters*]
WEUL	Kingsford, MI [*FM radio station call letters*]
WEUP	Huntsville, AL [*AM radio station call letters*]
W Europe Educ ...	Western European Education [*A publication*]
W Eur Policies ...	West European Policies [*A publication*]
W Eur Politics ...	West European Politics [*A publication*]
WEUX.......	Chippewa Falls, WI [*Television station call letters*]
WEUZ.......	Eau Claire, WI [*AM radio station call letters*]
WEV..........	Western European Vision
WEV..........	World Economy [*A publication*]
WEVA	Emporia, VA [*AM radio station call letters*]
WEVA	World Esperantist Vegetarian Association [*See also TEVA*] [*Dublin, Republic of Ireland*] (EAIO)
WEVD	New York, NY [*AM radio station call letters*]
WEVE	Eveleth, MN [*AM radio station call letters*]
WEVE-FM ...	Eveleth, MN [*FM radio station call letters*]
WEVL.......	Memphis, TN [*FM radio station call letters*]
WEVO	Concord, NH [*FM radio station call letters*]
WEVO	Waehrungsergaenzungsverordnung [*A publication*]
WEVR	River Falls, WI [*AM radio station call letters*]
WEVR	Weaver Arms Corp. [*NASDAQ symbol*] (NQ)
WEVR-FM ...	River Falls, WI [*FM radio station call letters*]
WEVS.......	Saugatuck, MI [*FM radio station call letters*]
WEVU	Naples, FL [*Television station call letters*]
WEVV	Evansville, IN [*Television station call letters*]
WEW.........	St. Louis, MO [*AM radio station call letters*]
WEW.........	Wasser- und Energiewirtschaft [*A publication*]
WeW.........	Welt und Wort [*A publication*]
WEW.........	Western Electronic Week
WEW.........	Wewak [*Papua New Guinea*] [*Seismograph station code, US Geological Survey*] [*Closed*] (SEIS)
WEWAS....	Water Equipment Wholesalers and Suppliers [*Formerly, WEWSA*]
WEWO......	Laurinburg, NC [*AM radio station call letters*]
WEWS.......	Cleveland, OH [*Television station call letters*]
WEWSA....	Water Equipment Wholesalers and Suppliers Association [*Later, WEWAS*] (EA)
WEWV	Martinsburg, WV [*Television station call letters*]
WEWZ	Elwood, IN [*FM radio station call letters*]
WEX.........	Business Science Experts [*NOMOS Datapool*] [*Federal Republic of Germany*] [*Information service or system*] (CRD)
WEX.........	Wexford [*County in Ireland*] (ROG)
WEX.........	Win-Eldrich Mines Ltd. [*Toronto Stock Exchange symbol*]
WEX.........	Wine Exchange [*Computer network*]
WEXC	Greenville, PA [*FM radio station call letters*]
WEXC	Wolverine Exploration Co. [*NASDAQ symbol*] (NQ)
WEXF.......	Wexford [*County in Ireland*] (ROG)
WEXFD....	Wexford [*County in Ireland*]
WEXI........	Jupiter, FL [*AM radio station call letters*]
WEXITA....	Women Executives International Tourism Association (EA)
WEXL.......	Royal Oak, MI [*AM radio station call letters*]
WEXS.......	Patillas, PR [*AM radio station call letters*]
WEXT.......	Arlington, NY [*FM radio station call letters*]
WEXT.......	Wrist Extension [*Sports medicine*]
WEXY	Wilton Manors, FL [*AM radio station call letters*]
WEY	West Yellowstone, MT [*Location identifier*] [*FAA*] (FAAL)
Weyerhauser For Pap ...	Weyerhauser Forestry Paper [*A publication*]
WEYI-TV ...	Saginaw, MI [*Television station call letters*]
WEYM	Weymouth [*Municipal borough in England*]
WEYQ	Marietta, OH [*FM radio station call letters*]
WEYS.......	Key West, FL [*Television station call letters*]
WEYS.......	Weyenberg Shoe Manufacturing Co. [*NASDAQ symbol*] (NQ)
WEYY-FM ...	Talladega, AL [*FM radio station call letters*]
WEYZ.......	Erie, PA [*AM radio station call letters*]
WEZB.......	New Orleans, LA [*FM radio station call letters*]
WEZE.......	Boston, MA [*AM radio station call letters*]
WEZF.......	Burlington, VT [*FM radio station call letters*]
WEZG	North Syracuse, NY [*FM radio station call letters*]
WEZI-FM ...	Germantown, TN [*FM radio station call letters*]
WEZJ........	Williamsburg, KY [*AM radio station call letters*]
WEZL........	Charleston, SC [*FM radio station call letters*]
WEZN	Bridgeport, CT [*FM radio station call letters*]

WEZO	Rochester, NY [*AM radio station call letters*]
WEZQ	Winfield, AL [*AM radio station call letters*]
WEZR.......	Fort Wayne, IN [*AM radio station call letters*]
WEZU	Witterungseinfluesse und Zeitunterschied [*Weather factors and time difference*] [*German military - World War II*]
WEZV	Fort Wayne, IN [*FM radio station call letters*]
WEZW	Wauwatosa-Milwaukee, WI [*FM radio station call letters*]
WEZX	Scranton, PA [*FM radio station call letters*]
WEZY-FM ...	Lakeland, FL [*FM radio station call letters*]
WEZZ.......	Clanton, AL [*FM radio station call letters*]
WF............	Four-Conductor Cables [*JETDS nomenclature*] [*Military*] (CET)
WF	Waehrungsfaktura [*Foreign Exchange Invoice*] [*German*]
WF	Wake Forest University [*North Carolina*]
WF	Wallis and Futuna [*ANSI two-letter standard code*] (CNC)
wf.............	Wallis and Futuna [*MARC country of publication code*] [*Library of Congress*] (LCCP)
WF	Ward Foundation (EA)
WF	Wash Fountain (AAG)
W & F........	Water and Feed
WF	Water Filter
WF	Water Finish [*Paper*]
WF	Watershed Foundation (EA)
W + F........	Ways plus Filling [*Textile testing*]
WF	Wege der Forschung, Darmstadt, Wissenschaftliche Buchgesellschaft [*A publication*]
WF	Wehrforschung [*A publication*]
WF	Welch Fusiliers [*British military*] (DMA)
WF	Weld Fixture
WF	Welfare Appointment Full Time [*Chiropody*] [*British*]
WF	Western Folklore [*A publication*]
WF	Western Front [*World War I*]
WF	Westfaelische Forschungen [*A publication*]
WF	Westfair Foods Ltd. [*Toronto Stock Exchange symbol*]
WF	White Fathers [*Roman Catholic men's religious order*]
WF	White Female
WF	White Fir [*Botany*]
WF	Wideroe's Flyveselskap A/S [*Norway*] [*ICAO designator*] (FAAC)
WF	Wildfowl Foundation (EA)
WF	Window-Frame
WF	Windstar Foundation (EA)
WF	Wingfold
WF	Winston Furniture [*AMEX symbol*] (SPSG)
WF	Wire Foundation (EA)
WF	Wistar-Furth [*Rat strain*]
WF	Won on Foul [*Boxing*]
WF	Word Fluency [*Psychology*]
WF	Work Function [*Physics*]
W/F	Wow and Flutter
WF	Write Forward
W/F	Writing on Face [*Deltiology*]
WF	Wrong Font [*Typesetting*] [*Proofreader's mark*]
WFA	War Food Administration [*Determined military, civilian, and foreign requirements for human and animal food, and for food used industrially*] [*World War II*] [*Terminated, 1945*]
WFA	Weight-for-Age (ADA)
WFA	Weightlifting Federation of Africa (EAIO)
WFA	Western Fairs Association (EA)
WFA	Western Falconry Association [*Defunct*] (EA)
WFA	White Fish Authority [*MAFF*] [*British*]
WFA	Wide-Frequency Antenna
WFA	Wire Fabricators Association [*Naperville, IL*] (EA)
WFA	World Federalist Association (EA)
WFA	World Federation of Advertisers [*See also FMA*] [*Brussels, Belgium*] (EAIO)
WFA	World Footbag Association (EA)
WFA	World Friendship Association
WFA-TV ...	Worlds of Fantasy [*1968-*] [*A publication*]
WFAA-TV ...	Dallas, TX [*Television station call letters*]
WFAB.......	Ceiba, PR [*AM radio station call letters*]
WFAC.......	World Federal Authority Committee [*Dundas, ON*] (EAIO)
WFAD.......	Middlebury, VT [*AM radio station call letters*]
WFAE.......	Charlotte, NC [*FM radio station call letters*]
WFAFW....	World Federation of Agriculture and Food Workers (EA)
WFAH.......	Alliance, OH [*AM radio station call letters*]
WFaH.......	Hoard Historical Museum, Fort Atkinson, WI [*Library symbol*] [*Library of Congress*] (LCLS)
WFAI........	Fayetteville, NC [*AM radio station call letters*]
WFAJ........	Michigan City, IN [*FM radio station call letters*]
WFAL........	Falmouth, MA [*FM radio station call letters*]
WFALW....	Weltbund Freiheitlicher Arbeitnehmerverbande auf Liberaler Wirtschaftsgrundlage [*World Union of Liberal Trade Union Organisations - WULTUO*] [*Zurich, Switzerland*] (EAIO)
WFAM	Augusta, GA [*AM radio station call letters*]
WFAN	New York, NY [*AM radio station call letters*]
WFAOSB ..	World Food and Agricultural Outlook and Situation Board [*Department of Agriculture*]
WFAP........	Women's Funding Assistance Project (EA)

WFAPS ..... World Federation of Associations of Pediatric Surgeons [*Barcelona, Spain*] (EAIO)
WFAR....... Danbury, CT [*FM radio station call letters*]
WFAS........ White Plains, NY [*AM radio station call letters*]
WFAS-FM ... White Plains, NY [*FM radio station call letters*]
WFAU ...... Augusta, ME [*AM radio station call letters*]
WFAV....... Cordele, GA [*FM radio station call letters*]
WFAW ...... Fort Atkinson, WI [*AM radio station call letters*]
WFAW ...... World Federation of Agricultural Workers [*See also FMTA*] (EAIO)
WFAX....... Falls Church, VA [*AM radio station call letters*]
WFB.......... Waferboard Corp. Ltd. [*Toronto Stock Exchange symbol*]
WFB.......... Waterways Freight Bureau [*Inactive*] (EA)
WFB.......... Wide Flange Beam [*Metal industry*]
WFB.......... World Fellowship of Buddhists [*Bangkok, Tahiland*] (EAIO)
WFBBA ..... World Federation of Bergen-Belsen Associations (EA)
WFBC....... Greenville, SC [*AM radio station call letters*]
WFBC-FM ... Greenville, SC [*FM radio station call letters*]
WFBE....... Flint, MI [*FM radio station call letters*]
WFBF .... Buffalo, NY [*FM radio station call letters*]
WFBG....... Altoona, PA [*AM radio station call letters*]
WFBG-FM ... Altoona, PA [*FM radio station call letters*]
WFBI......... Wood Fiber Blanket Institute [*Defunct*]
WFBL........ Syracuse, NY [*AM radio station call letters*]
WFBMA.... Woven Fabric Belting Manufacturers Association (EA)
WFBN .... Lynn Haven, FL [*AM radio station call letters*]
WFBQ .... Indianapolis, IN [*FM radio station call letters*]
WFBR....... Baltimore, MD [*AM radio station call letters*]
WFBSC ..... World Federation of Building Service Contractors (EA)
WFBTMA ... World Federation of Baton Twirling and Majorette Associations (EA)
WFBY........ World Fellowship of Buddhist Youth [*Bangkok, Thailand*] (EAIO)
WFC .... Committee on the World Food Crisis [*Defunct*] (EA)
WFC .... Wake Forest College [*Later, WFU*] [*North Carolina*]
WFC .... Wall Financial Co. [*Vancouver Stock Exchange symbol*]
WFC .... Wall Financial Corp. [*Toronto Stock Exchange symbol*]
WFC .... Walleye Filter Changer
WFC .... Wallops Flight Center [*Formerly, WS*] [*NASA*]
WFC .... War Finance Committee
WFC .... Water Facts Consortium [*Defunct*] (EA)
WFC .... Weld Flange Connection
WFC .... Wells Fargo & Company [*NYSE symbol*] (SPSG)
WFC .... West Florida Coast
WFC .... Western Football Conference
WFC .... Western Forestry Center (EA)
WFC .... Wide Field Camera
WFC .... Wings Fun Club (EAIO)
WFC .... Wolf First Class [*A philanderer*] [*Slang*]
WFC .... Women's Forage Corps [*British*] [*World War I*]
WFC .... World Food Council [*United Nations*] (EAIO)
WFC .... World Forestry Center (EA)
WFC .... World Friendship Centre (EA)
WFC .... Worldwide Fiero Club (EA)
WFCA....... Ackerman, MS [*FM radio station call letters*]
WFCA....... Western Forestry and Conservation Association (EA)
WFCB........ Chillicothe, OH [*FM radio station call letters*]
WFCC....... World Federation for Cancer Care [*London, England*] (EAIO)
WFCC....... World Federation for Culture Collections (EAIO)
WFCC-FM ... Chatman, MA [*FM radio station call letters*]
WFCE........ Tarpon Springs, FL [*FM radio station call letters*]
WFCE........ World Federation of Czechoslovak Exile (EA)
WFCG .... Franklinton, LA [*AM radio station call letters*]
WFCH .... Charleston, SC [*FM radio station call letters*]
WFCI........ Franklin, IN [*FM radio station call letters*]
WFCJ .... Miamisburg, OH [*FM radio station call letters*]
WFCL........ Clintonville, WI [*AM radio station call letters*]
WFCLC ..... World Federation of Christian Life Communities [*See also FMCVC*] [*Rome, Italy*] (EAIO)
WFCM ...... Orangeburg, SC [*FM radio station call letters*]
WFCMV.... Wheeled Fuel-Consuming Motor Vehicle
WFCNLM ... World Federation of the Cossack National Liberation Movement [*Later, WFCNLMC*] (EA)
WFCNLMC ... World Federation of the Cossack National Liberation Movement of Cossackia (EA)
WFCO .... Lancaster, OH [*FM radio station call letters*]
WFCR........ Amherst, MA [*FM radio station call letters*]
WFCS........ New Britain, CT [*FM radio station call letters*]
WFCS........ Warren Five Cents Savings Bank [*Peabody, MA*] [*NASDAQ symbol*] (NQ)
WFCS........ World's Fair Collectors Society (EA)
WFCT........ Fayetteville, NC [*Television station call letters*]
WFCV........ Fort Wayne, IN [*AM radio station call letters*]
WFCY........ World Federation of Catholic Youth
WFCYWG ... World Federation of Catholic Young Women and Girls [*Later, WFCY*]
WFD .... Waveform Distortion [*Telecommunications*] (TEL)
WFD .... Westfield Minerals Ltd. [*Toronto Stock Exchange symbol*] [*Vancouver Stock Exchange symbol*]
WFD .... Wool Forward [*Knitting*]
WFD......... World Fax Directory [*Information service or system*] (IID)

WFD.......... World Federation of the Deaf [*Rome, Italy*]
WFD.......... World Food Day [*October 16*]
WFD.......... Worldwide Franchise Directory [*A publication*]
WFDA ...... World Fast-Draw Association (EA)
WFDD-FM ... Winston-Salem, NC [*FM radio station call letters*]
WFDF....... Flint, MI [*AM radio station call letters*]
WFDF....... World Flying Disc Federation (EAIO)
WFDFI ...... World Federation of Development Financing Institutions [*See also FEMIDE*] [*Madrid, Spain*] (EAIO)
WFDR ...... Manchester, GA [*AM radio station call letters*]
WFDRHL ... World Federation of Doctors Who Respect Human Life (United States Section) (EA)
WFDS........ Warm Fog Dispenser System (MCD)
WFDSA ..... World Federation of Direct Selling Associations [*Washington, DC*] (EA)
WFDSC ..... World Federation of Dark Shadows Clubs (EA)
WFDU ...... Teaneck, NJ [*FM radio station call letters*]
WFDW ...... World Federation of Democratic Women
WFDWRHL ... World Federation of Doctors Who Respect Human Life [*Ostend, Belgium*] (EAIO)
WFDY .... World Federation of Democratic Youth [*See also FMJD*] [*Budapest, Hungary*] (EAIO)
WFe .... Dwight T. Parker Public Library, Fennimore, WI [*Library symbol*] [*Library of Congress*] (LCLS)
WFE .... With Food Element
WFE .... World Federation of Europeans (By Birth or Descent) (EA)
WFEA........ Manchester, NH [*AM radio station call letters*]
WFEA........ World Federation of Educational Associations [*Later, WCOTP*] (EA)
WFEB........ Sylacauga, AL [*AM radio station call letters*]
WFEB........ Worcester Foundation for Experimental Biology
WFEC........ San Juan, PR [*Television station call letters*]
WFEF........ Terre Haute, IN [*FM radio station call letters*]
WFEL........ Towson, MD [*AM radio station call letters*]
WFEO ...... World Federation of Engineering Organizations [*Paris, France*]
WF & EQ.... Wave Filters and Equalizers (MCD)
WFET........ Marathon, FL [*Television station call letters*]
WFEWC.... World Federation of Estonian Women's Clubs (EA)
WFEX........ Western Fruit Express
WFEZ........ Williston, FL [*FM radio station call letters*]
WFF.......... Wanderer Forum Foundation (EA)
WFF.......... Well-Formed Formula [*Logic*]
WFF.......... Western Frontier Force [*British military*] (DMA)
WFF.......... Whiting Field [*Milton*] [*Florida*] [*Seismograph station code, US Geological Survey*] [*Closed*] (SEIS)
WFF.......... William Faulkner Foundation [*Defunct*] (EA)
WFF.......... Wold Farm Foods [*Commercial firm*] [*British*]
WFF.......... World Friendship Federation
WFFA........ Women's Fashion Fabrics Association (EA)
WFFC .... Ferrum, VA [*FM radio station call letters*]
WFFF .... Columbia, MS [*AM radio station call letters*]
WFFF-FM ... Columbia, MS [*FM radio station call letters*]
WFFG........ Marathon, FL [*AM radio station call letters*]
WFFL .... World Federation of Free Latvians (EA)
WFFM....... Ashburn, GA [*FM radio station call letters*]
WFFM....... World Federation of Friends of Museums [*See also FMAM*] [*Paris, France*] (EAIO)
WFFN....... Cordova, AL [*FM radio station call letters*]
WF & FSA ... Wholesale Florists and Florist Suppliers of America (EA)
WFFTH..... World Federation of Workers in Food, Tobacco, and Hotel Industries [*See also FMATH*] (EAIO)
WFFT-TV ... Fort Wayne, IN [*Television station call letters*]
WFFX........ Tuscaloosa, AL [*FM radio station call letters*]
WFG .... Water Fog
WFG .... Waveform Generator
WFGB........ Kingston, NY [*FM radio station call letters*]
WFGC .... Palm Beach, FL [*Television station call letters*]
WFGH....... Fort Gay, WV [*FM radio station call letters*]
WFGL........ Fitchburg, MA [*AM radio station call letters*]
WFGM....... Fairmont, WV [*FM radio station call letters*]
WFGN .... Gaffney, SC [*AM radio station call letters*]
WFGW ...... Black Mountain, NC [*AM radio station call letters*]
WFGX .... Fort Walton Beach, FL [*Television station call letters*]
WFH .... World Federation of Hemophilia [*Montreal, PQ*] (EA)
WFHA ...... World Federation of Hungarian Artists (EA)
WFHAAVSC ... World Federation of Health Agencies for the Advancement of Voluntary Surgical Contraception (EA)
WFHC .... Henderson, TN [*FM radio station call letters*]
WFHC .... Westside Federal Savings & Loan Association of Seattle [*NASDAQ symbol*] (NQ)
WFHFF ..... World Federation of Hungarian Freedom Fighters (EA)
WFHG....... Bristol, VA [*AM radio station call letters*]
WFHJ........ World Federation of Hungarian Jews (EA)
WFHK....... Pell City, AL [*AM radio station call letters*]
WFHL .... Decatur, IL [*Television station call letters*]
WFHM....... Vineland, NJ [*AM radio station call letters*]
WFHN...... Fairhaven, MA [*FM radio station call letters*]
WFHR....... Wisconsin Rapids, WI [*AM radio station call letters*]
WFHSLPAC ... Water-Flooded Helical Screw Low-Pressure Air Compressor [*Navy*] (CAAL)
WFI........... Fianarantsoa [*Madagascar*] [*Airport symbol*] (OAG)

WFI...........	Water for Injection [*Pharmacy*]
WFI...........	Wheat Flour Institute [*Absorbed by Miller's National Federation*] (EA)
WFI...........	Wishes and Fears Inventory [*Psychology*]
WFI...........	Wood Flooring Institute of America [*Later, WSFI*] (EA)
WFI...........	Wood Foundation Institute (EA)
WFI...........	World Faiths Insight [*A publication*]
WFI...........	World Federation of Investors (EAIO)
WFI...........	Worldwide Friendship International (EA)
WFIA........	Louisville, KY [*AM radio station call letters*]
WFIA........	Wells Fargo Investment Advisors (ECON)
WFIA........	Western Forest Industries Association (EA)
WFIC........	Collinsville, VA [*AM radio station call letters*]
WFID........	Rio Piedras, PR [*FM radio station call letters*]
WFIE-TV ..	Evansville, IN [*Television station call letters*]
WFIF........	Milford, CT [*AM radio station call letters*]
WFIG........	Sumter, SC [*AM radio station call letters*]
WFIM........	World Federation of Islamic Missions [*Karachi, Pakistan*] (EAIO)
WFIMC.....	World Federation of International Music Competitions [*See also FMCIM*] (EAIO)
WFIN	Findlay, OH [*AM radio station call letters*]
WFIN	Women and Food Information Network (EA)
WFIQ........	Florence, AL [*Television station call letters*]
WFIR........	Roanoke, VA [*AM radio station call letters*]
WFIS	Fountain Inn, SC [*AM radio station call letters*]
WFIS	World Federation of Iranian Students
WFIT........	Melbourne, FL [*FM radio station call letters*]
WFIU........	Bloomington, IN [*FM radio station call letters*]
WFIV........	Kissimmee, FL [*AM radio station call letters*]
WFIW.......	Fairfield, IL [*AM radio station call letters*]
WFIW-FM ..	Fairfield, IL [*FM radio station call letters*]
WFIX........	Huntsville, AL [*AM radio station call letters*]
WFJA	Sanford, NC [*FM radio station call letters*]
WFJJ........	World Federation of Jewish Journalists [*Tel Aviv, Israel*] (EAIO)
WFJY........	Fort Myers, FL [*FM radio station call letters*]
WFK	Frenchville [*Maine*] [*Airport symbol*] (OAG)
WFKJ	Cashtown, PA [*AM radio station call letters*]
WFKN	Franklin, KY [*AM radio station call letters*]
WFKX	Henderson, TN [*FM radio station call letters*]
WFKY.......	Frankfort, KY [*FM radio station call letters*]
WFKZ........	Plantation Key, FL [*FM radio station call letters*]
WFL...........	Windflower Mining Ltd. [*Vancouver Stock Exchange symbol*]
WFL...........	Woman's Freedom League
WFL...........	Work Flow Language [*Data processing*] (BUR)
WFL...........	World Football League [*Dissolved, 1975*]
WFL...........	Worshipful [*Freemasonry*] (ROG)
WFL...........	Wredemann-Frang Law
WFLA.......	Tampa, FL [*AM radio station call letters*]
WFLA.......	Western Fraternal Life Association (EA)
WFLA-TV ...	Tampa, FL [*Television station call letters*]
WFLB.......	Fayetteville, NC [*AM radio station call letters*]
WFLD.......	Chicago, IL [*Television station call letters*]
WFLD.......	Work/Family Life Database [*Database*]
WFLE.......	Flemingsburg, KY [*AM radio station call letters*]
WFLI........	Lookout Mountain, TN [*AM radio station call letters*]
WFLI-TV ..	Cleveland, TN [*Television station call letters*]
WFLN-FM ...	Philadelphia, PA [*FM radio station call letters*]
WFLO	Farmville, VA [*AM radio station call letters*]
WFLO-FM ...	Farmville, VA [*FM radio station call letters*]
WFLQ	French Lick, IN [*FM radio station call letters*]
WFLR.......	Dundee, NY [*AM radio station call letters*]
WFLR-FM ...	Dundee, NY [*FM radio station call letters*]
WFLRY......	World Federation of Liberal and Radical Youth [*Later, IFLRY*]
WFLS........	Fredericksburg, VA [*AM radio station call letters*]
WFLS-FM ...	Fredericksburg, VA [*FM radio station call letters*]
WFLT.......	Flint, MI [*AM radio station call letters*]
WFLU.......	Florence, SC [*AM radio station call letters*]
WFLW.......	Monticello, KY [*AM radio station call letters*]
WFLX.......	West Palm Beach, FL [*Television station call letters*]
WFLY.......	Troy, NY [*FM radio station call letters*]
WFLZ.......	Thonotosassa, FL [*AM radio station call letters*]
WFLZ-FM ...	Tampa, FL [*FM radio station call letters*]
WFM	Water Flow Meter
WFM	Waveform Monitor
WFM	Waveguide Frequency Meter
WFM	Wells Fargo Mortgage & Equity Trust [*NYSE symbol*] (SPSG)
WFM	Western Federation of Miners
WFM	Westford [*Massachusetts*] [*Seismograph station code, US Geological Survey*] (SEIS)
WFMA	Mio, MI [*FM radio station call letters*]
WFMA	World Folk Music Association (EA)
WFMB.......	Springfield, IL [*FM radio station call letters*]
WFMC	Goldsboro, NC [*AM radio station call letters*]
WFMC	Welding Filler Material Control [*Nuclear energy*] (NRCH)
WFMD	Frederick, MD [*AM radio station call letters*]
WFME.......	Newark, NJ [*FM radio station call letters*]
WFME.......	World Federation for Medical Education (EA)
WFME-TV ...	West Milford, NJ [*Television station call letters*]
WFMF.......	Baton Rouge, LA [*FM radio station call letters*]

WFMG	Richmond, IN [*FM radio station call letters*]
WFMH.......	Cullman, AL [*AM radio station call letters*]
WFMH.......	World Federation for Mental Health (EA)
WFMH-FM ...	Cullman, AL [*FM radio station call letters*]
WFMJ	Youngstown, OH [*AM radio station call letters*]
WFMJ-TV ...	Youngstown, OH [*Television station call letters*]
WFMK	East Lansing, MI [*FM radio station call letters*]
WFML.......	Vincennes, IN [*FM radio station call letters*]
WFMLTA ...	World Federation of Modern Language Teachers' Association (EA)
WFMM	Harbor Beach, MI [*FM radio station call letters*]
WFMO......	Fairmont, NC [*AM radio station call letters*]
WFMPT	Wet-Fluorescence Magnetic Particle Technique [*Corrosion crack detection*]
WFMQ	Lebanon, TN [*FM radio station call letters*]
WFMR	Menomonee Falls, WI [*FM radio station call letters*]
WFMS.......	Indianapolis, IN [*FM radio station call letters*]
WFMT.......	Chicago, IL [*FM radio station call letters*]
WFMU	East Orange, NJ [*FM radio station call letters*]
WFMU	Weather and Fixed Map Unit [*FAA*]
WFMV......	Blairstown, NJ [*FM radio station call letters*]
WFMW	Madisonville, KY [*AM radio station call letters*]
WFMW	World Federation of Methodist Women [*Seoul, Republic of Korea*] (EAIO)
WFMWNAA ...	World Federation of Methodist Women, North America Area (EA)
WFMX	Statesville, NC [*FM radio station call letters*]
WFMY-TV ...	Greensboro, NC [*Television station call letters*]
WFMZ.......	Allentown, PA [*FM radio station call letters*]
WFMZ-TV ...	Allentown, PA [*Television station call letters*]
WFN	Weapons and Facilities, Navy (NG)
WFN	Well-Formed Net
WFN	Westminster College, New Wilmington, PA [*OCLC symbol*] (OCLC)
WFN	World Federation of Neurology (EA)
WFNA	White Fuming Nitric Acid
WFNC	Fayetteville, NC [*AM radio station call letters*]
WFNM	Lancaster, PA [*FM radio station call letters*]
WFNMW ..	World Federation of Trade Unions of Non-Manual Workers [*See also FMTNM*] [*Antwerp, Belguim*] (EAIO)
WFNP.......	New Paltz, NY [*FM radio station call letters*]
WFNR	Blacksburg, VA [*AM radio station call letters*]
WFNS........	Women's Forum on National Security [*Defunct*] (EA)
WFNS........	World Federation of Neurosurgical Societies [*Nijmegen, Netherlands*] (EA)
WFNW	Naugatuck, CT [*AM radio station call letters*]
WFNX	Lynn, MA [*FM radio station call letters*]
WFNY	Syracuse, NY [*FM radio station call letters*]
WFO	Wide Field Optics
WF/O	Wife Of [*Genealogy*]
WFOB	Fostoria, OH [*AM radio station call letters*]
WFOC	Western Field Operations Center [*Bureau of Mines*] [*Spokane, WA*] (GRD)
WFOF.......	Covington, IN [*FM radio station call letters*]
WFOF.......	Wide Field Optical Filter
WFOG	Suffolk, VA [*FM radio station call letters*]
WFOM	Marietta, GA [*AM radio station call letters*]
WFon	Fond Du Lac Public Library, Fond Du Lac, WI [*Library symbol*] [*Library of Congress*] (LCLS)
WFON......	Fond Du Lac, WI [*FM radio station call letters*]
WFonM	Marian College of Fond Du Lac, Fond Du Lac, WI [*Library symbol*] [*Library of Congress*] (LCLS)
WFonMM ...	Mercury Marine, Fond Du Lac, WI [*Library symbol*] [*Library of Congress*] (LCLS)
WFonSA	Saint Agnes Hospital, Fond Du Lac, WI [*Library symbol*] [*Library of Congress*] (LCLS)
WFont........	Fontana Public Library, Fontana, WI [*Library symbol*] [*Library of Congress*] (LCLS)
WFonU	University of Wisconsin-Fond Du Lac, Fond Du Lac, WI [*Library symbol*] [*Library of Congress*] (LCLS)
WFOR	Hattiesburg, MS [*AM radio station call letters*]
WFOR	Washington Federal Savings Bank [*NASDAQ symbol*] (NQ)
WFOS........	Chesapeake, VA [*FM radio station call letters*]
WFOT.......	Huntingdon, TN [*AM radio station call letters*]
WFOT	World Federation of Occupational Therapists [*London, ON*] (EAIO)
WFOU	Margate City, NJ [*FM radio station call letters*]
WFOV	Pittsfield, ME [*FM radio station call letters*]
WFOV	Wide Field of View
WFOW	Union City, OH [*FM radio station call letters*]
WFOX	Gainesville, GA [*FM radio station call letters*]
WFOY	St. Augustine, FL [*AM radio station call letters*]
WF & P	Wabash, Frisco, and Pacific Association (EA)
WFP...........	Warm Front [*or Frontal*] Passage [*Meteorology*] (FAAC)
WFP...........	Wearout Failure Period
WFP...........	Witness for Peace (EA)
WFP...........	World Federation of Parasitologists [*Bilthoven, Netherlands*] (EAIO)
WFP...........	World Food Programme [*Rome, Italy*] [*United Nations*]
WFP...........	Worldwide Fast for Peace [*An association*] [*Defunct*] (EA)
WFPA........	Fort Payne, AL [*AM radio station call letters*]

WFPA........	Washington Forest Protection Association (EA)
WFPA........	World Federation for the Protection of Animals [*Also known as FMPA, WTB*] [*Later, WSPA*]
WFPC........	Petersburg, IN [*FM radio station call letters*]
WFPC........	Wide Field/Planetary Camera
WFPFC.....	Worldwide Wair Play for Frogs Committee (EA)
WFPG........	Atlantic City, NJ [*AM radio station call letters*]
WFPG-FM ...	Atlantic City, NJ [*FM radio station call letters*]
WFPHA	World Federation of Public Health Associations (EA)
WFPK........	Louisville, KY [*FM radio station call letters*]
WFPL........	Louisville, KY [*FM radio station call letters*]
WFPLCA....	World Federation of Pipe Line Contractors Association (EA)
WFPMA....	World Federation of Personnel Management Associations [*Alexandria, VA*] (EA)
WFPMM...	World Federation of Proprietary Medicine Manufacturers
WFPR........	Hammond, LA [*AM radio station call letters*]
WFPR........	Western Federal Savings Bank [*Mayaguez, PR*] [*NASDAQ symbol*] (NQ)
WFPS	Freeport, IL [*FM radio station call letters*]
WFPS	Wild Flower Preservation Society (EA)
WFPT	Frederick, MD [*Television station call letters*]
WFPT	Welsh Figure Preference Test [*Psychology*]
WFPT	World Federation for Physical Therapy
WFQA	Nicholson, PA [*AM radio station call letters*]
WFQS........	Franklin, NC [*FM radio station call letters*]
WFQX	Front Royal, VA [*FM radio station call letters*]
WFR	Wafer (MSA)
WFR	Weekblad voor Fiscaal Recht [*A publication*]
WFR	Wharf Resources Ltd. [*Toronto Stock Exchange symbol*]
WFR	Wheal and Flare Reaction [*Immunology*]
WFR	Wide-Finding RADAR (MCD)
WFR	Worcestershire and Sherwood Foresters Regiment [*Military unit*] [*British*]
WFRA.......	Franklin, PA [*AM radio station call letters*]
WFRA.......	Wharf Resources Ltd. [*NASDAQ symbol*] (NQ)
WFRA-FM ...	Franklin, PA [*FM radio station call letters*]
WFRB.......	Frostburg, MD [*AM radio station call letters*]
WFRBC.....	Washed, Filtered Red Blood Cells [*Hematology*]
WFRB-FM ...	Frostburg, MD [*FM radio station call letters*]
WFRC.......	Columbus, GA [*FM radio station call letters*]
WFRD.......	Hanover, NH [*FM radio station call letters*]
WFRE.......	Frederick, MD [*FM radio station call letters*]
WFRG.......	Rome, NY [*AM radio station call letters*]
WFRG-FM ...	Rome, NY [*FM radio station call letters*]
WFRJ	Johnstown, PA [*FM radio station call letters*]
WFRK.......	Coleman, FL [*AM radio station call letters*]
WFRL.......	Freeport, IL [*AM radio station call letters*]
WFRM	Coudersport, PA [*AM radio station call letters*]
WFRM-FM ...	Coudersport, PA [*FM radio station call letters*]
WFRN	Elkhart, IN [*FM radio station call letters*]
WFRO	Fremont, OH [*AM radio station call letters*]
WFRO-FM ...	Fremont, OH [*FM radio station call letters*]
WFRS........	Smithtown, NY [*FM radio station call letters*]
WFRS........	World Federation of Rose Societies [*Hurlingham, Argentina*] (EAIO)
WFRV-TV ...	Green Bay, WI [*Television station call letters*]
WFRW	Webster, NY [*FM radio station call letters*]
WFRX.......	West Frankfort, IL [*AM radio station call letters*]
WFRX-FM ...	West Frankfort, IL [*FM radio station call letters*]
WFS...........	Waterhouse-Friderichsen Syndrome [*Medicine*]
WFS...........	Weapon Fire Simulator (MCD)
WFS...........	Welfare Food Service [*British*]
WFS...........	Women for Sobriety (EA)
WFS...........	Wood Furring Strips [*Technical drawings*]
WFS...........	Work Function Surface
WFS...........	World Fertility Survey [*Program*]
WFS...........	World Food Security [*FAO program*] [*United Nations*]
WFS...........	World Future Society (EA)
WFSA........	Wash Frock Salesmen's Association (EA)
WFSA........	Western Federal Savings & Loan Association [*Marina Del Rey, CA*] [*NASDAQ symbol*] (NQ)
WFSA........	World Federation of Societies of Anaesthesiologists [*Bristol, England*] (EAIO)
WFSB	Hartford, CT [*Television station call letters*]
WFSB	Washington Federal Savings Bank [*NASDAQ symbol*] (NQ)
WFSBP.....	World Federation of the Societies of Biological Psychiatry (EA)
WFSC........	Franklin, NC [*AM radio station call letters*]
WFSE........	Edinboro, PA [*FM radio station call letters*]
WFSEC	World Fellowship of Slavic Evangelical Christians (EA)
WFSF	Ozark, AL [*AM radio station call letters*]
WFSF	World Futures Studies Federation (EA)
WFSG.......	Panama City, FL [*Television station call letters*]
WFSGI	World Federation of the Sporting Goods Industry (EAIO)
WFSH	Valparaiso-Niceville, FL [*AM radio station call letters*]
WFSI	Annapolis, MD [*FM radio station call letters*]
WFSICCM ...	World Federation of Societies of Intensive and Critical Care Medicine (EAIO)
WFSK........	Nashville, TN [*FM radio station call letters*]
WFSL	Washington Federal Savings & Loan Association [*NASDAQ symbol*] (NQ)
WFSO-FM ...	Fort Shawnee, OH [*FM radio station call letters*]

WFSP	Kingwood, WV [*AM radio station call letters*]
WFSR	Harlan, KY [*AM radio station call letters*]
WFSS	Fayetteville, NC [*FM radio station call letters*]
WFSS	Welsh Folk Song Society [*British*]
WFST	Caribou, ME [*AM radio station call letters*]
WFSt..........	Wehrmachtfuehrungsstab [*Armed Forces Operations Staff*] [*German military - World War II*]
WFSUDO ...	World Fertility Survey. Country Reports [*A publication*]
WFSU-FM ...	Tallahassee, FL [*FM radio station call letters*]
WFSU-TV ...	Tallahassee, FL [*Television station call letters*]
WFSW	World Federation of Scientific Workers [*See also FMTS*] [*ICSU*] [*London, England*] (EAIO)
WFS (World Fertil Surv) Comp Stud ...	WFS (World Fertility Survey) Comparative Studies [*A publication*]
WFSY	Panama City, FL [*FM radio station call letters*]
WFT..........	Warm Fluctuating Temperatures
WFT..........	West Fraser Timber Co. Ltd. [*Toronto Stock Exchange symbol*] [*Vancouver Stock Exchange symbol*]
WFT..........	Wildfowl Trust [*British*]
WFTA.......	Fulton, MS [*FM radio station call letters*]
WFTA.......	Winograd Fourier Transform Algorithm (MCD)
WFTA.......	World Federation of Taiwanese Associations (EA)
WFTC.......	Western Flying Training Command [*AAFWFTC*]
WFTD.......	Marietta, GA [*AM radio station call letters*]
WFTD.......	Women's Flying Training Detachment [*World War II*]
WFTF	Rutland, VT [*FM radio station call letters*]
WFTG.......	London, KY [*AM radio station call letters*]
WFTH	Richmond, VA [*AM radio station call letters*]
WFTI-FM ...	St. Petersburg, FL [*FM radio station call letters*]
WFTJW	World Federation of Travel Journalists and Writers (EA)
WFTK.......	Wake Forest, NC [*AM radio station call letters*]
WFTL........	Fort Lauderdale, FL [*AM radio station call letters*]
WFTM.......	Maysville, KY [*AM radio station call letters*]
WFTM-FM ...	Maysville, KY [*FM radio station call letters*]
WFTN	Franklin, NH [*AM radio station call letters*]
WFTN-FM ...	Franklin, NH [*FM radio station call letters*]
WFTO	Fulton, MS [*AM radio station call letters*]
WFTP........	Weapons Fly-To Point [*Military*] (CAAL)
WFTQ	Worcester, MA [*AM radio station call letters*]
WFTR........	Front Royal, VA [*AM radio station call letters*]
WFTR-FM ...	Front Royal, VA [*FM radio station call letters*]
WFTS	Tampa, FL [*Television station call letters*]
WFTS	Western Fish Toxicology Station [*Environmental Protection Agency*]
W FTTNGS ...	With Fittings [*Freight*]
WFTU	World Federation of Trade Unions [*See also FSM*] [*Prague, Czechoslovakia*] (EAIO)
WFTUNMW ...	World Federation of Trade Unions of Non-Manual Workers [*Belgium*] (EY)
WFTV	Orlando, FL [*Television station call letters*]
WFTVN	Women's Film, Television, and Video Network (EAIO)
WFTW......	Fort Walton Beach, FL [*AM radio station call letters*]
WFTX.......	Cape Coral, FL [*Television station call letters*]
WFTY	Washington, DC [*Television station call letters*]
WFU	Wake Forest University [*Winston-Salem, NC*]
WFU	War Frauds Unit
WFUCA....	World Federation of UNESCO Clubs and Associations
WFUL.......	West Florida Union List [*Library network*]
WFUM......	Flint, MI [*Television station call letters*]
WFUM-FM ...	Flint, MI [*FM radio station call letters*]
WFUN.......	Ashtabula, OH [*AM radio station call letters*]
WFUNA.....	World Federation of United Nations Associations (EA)
WFUPA.....	World Federation of Ukrainian Patriarchal Associations (EA)
WFUR	Grand Rapids, MI [*AM radio station call letters*]
WFUR-FM ...	Grand Rapids, MI [*FM radio station call letters*]
WFUV	New York, NY [*FM radio station call letters*]
WFUWO ...	World Federation of Ukrainian Women's Organizations [*Toronto, ON*] (EA)
WFVA.......	Fredericksburg, VA [*AM radio station call letters*]
WFVR.......	Valdosta, GA [*AM radio station call letters*]
WFW	Walden Forever Wild (EA)
WFWA	Fort Wayne, IN [*Television station call letters*]
WFWC......	Walden Forever Wild Committee (EA)
WFWL......	Camden, TN [*AM radio station call letters*]
WFWM......	Frostburg, MD [*FM radio station call letters*]
WFXA-FM ...	Augusta, GA [*FM radio station call letters*]
WFXB	Rocky Mount, NC [*Television station call letters*]
WFXC.......	Durham, NC [*FM radio station call letters*]
WFXD	Panama City, FL [*Television station call letters*]
WFXE.......	Columbus, GA [*FM radio station call letters*]
WFXG.......	Augusta, GA [*Television station call letters*]
WFXI........	Morehead, NC [*FM radio station call letters*]
WFXL.......	Albany, GA [*Television station call letters*]
WFXM-FM ...	Forsyth, GA [*FM radio station call letters*]
WFXN.......	Goldsboro, NC [*AM radio station call letters*]
WFXP........	Gulf Breeze, FL [*AM radio station call letters*]
WFXR.......	Harwichport, MA [*FM radio station call letters*]
WFXS........	Soddy-Daisy, TN [*FM radio station call letters*]
WFXT.......	Boston, MA [*Television station call letters*]
WFXW	Geneva, IL [*AM radio station call letters*]
WFXX........	South Williamsport, PA [*AM radio station call letters*]

WFXX-FM ... South Williamsport, PA [*FM radio station call letters*]
WFXY........ Middlesboro, KY [*AM radio station call letters*]
WFYC........ Alma, MI [*AM radio station call letters*]
WFYC-FM ... Alma, MI [*FM radio station call letters*]
WFYF........ Watertown, NY [*Television station call letters*]
WFYI........ Indianapolis, IN [*Television station call letters*]
WFYI-FM ... Indianapolis, IN [*FM radio station call letters*]
WFY/NIO ... World Federalist Youth - Youth Movement for a New
    International Order [*Amsterdam, Netherlands*]   (EAIO)
WFYR-FM ... Chicago, IL [*FM radio station call letters*]
WFY-USA ... World Federalist Youth - United States of America [*Later,
    Action for World Community: World Federalist Youth in
    the USA*]   (EA)
WFYV........ Jacksonville, FL [*AM radio station call letters*]
WFYV-FM ... Atlantic Beach, FL [*FM radio station call letters*]
WFZ .... Wirtschaftswoche [*A publication*]
WG............ Air Ecosse Ltd. [*British*] [*ICAO designator*]   (FAAC)
WG............ Riker Laboratories Ltd. [*British*] [*Research code symbol*]
WG............ Waehrungsgesetz [*A publication*]
WG............ Wage Grade [*Federal employee job classification*]
Wg............ Wandlung [*A publication*]
WG............ Wartime Guidance [*Air Force*]   (AFM)
WG............ Waste Gas [*Nuclear energy*]   (NRCH)
WG............ Water Gauge
W/G........... Water Glycol   (KSC)
WG............ Water Resources News-Clipping Service. General Issue. Water
    Management Service. Department of the Environment
    [*Ottawa*] [*A publication*]
WG............ Waveguide
WG............ Wedge   (MSA)
WG............ Wegener's Granulomatosis [*Medicine*]
WGA........... Weighing   (ROG)
WG............ Weight Guaranteed
WG............ Welsh Guards [*Military unit*] [*British*]
WG............ Welt als Geschichte Zeitschrift fuer Universalgeschichtliche
    Forschung [*A publication*]
WG............ West German
WG............ Willcox & Gibbs, Inc. [*NYSE symbol*]   (SPSG)
WG............ Window Guard   (AAG)
WG............ Wine Gallon
WG............ Wing
WG............ Wire Gauge
WG............ Wired Glass [*Technical drawings*]
W & G .... Wissen und Glauben [*A publication*]
WG............ Wissenschaft und Gegenwart [*A publication*]
WG............ With Grain
WG............ Women for Guatemala   (EA)
WG............ Working Group   (FAAC)
WG............ World Goodwill   (EA)
WG............ Wright-Giemsa [*A stain*] [*Cytology*]
WG............ Writing [*Law*]   (ROG)
4WG........... Weather Group (4th) [*Washington, DC*] [*Air Force*]
WGA........... Wagga Wagga [*Australia*] [*Airport symbol*]   (OAG)
WGA........... Waveguide Assembly
WGA........... Weekblad voor de Nederlandse Bond van
    Gemeenteambtenaren [*A publication*]
WGA........... Weekly Government Abstracts [*National Technical
    Information Service*]
WGA........... Weighted Guidelines Analysis [*Air Force*]   (MCD)
WGA........... Wells-Gardner Electronics Corp. [*AMEX symbol*]   (SPSG)
WGA........... Western Golf Association   (EA)
WGA........... Western Growers Association   (EA)
WGA........... Wheat Germ Agglutinin [*Biochemistry*]
WGA........... Wild Goose Association   (EA)
WGA........... Women Grocers of America   (EA)
WGA........... Writers Guild of America, West   (EA)
WGAA....... Cedartown, GA [*AM radio station call letters*]
WGAC....... Augusta, GA [*AM radio station call letters*]
WGAD....... Gadsden, AL [*AM radio station call letters*]
WGAE....... Girard, PA [*FM radio station call letters*]
WGAE....... Writers Guild of America, East   (EA)
WGAE-US ... World Government of the Age of Enlightenment - US   (EA)
WGAF....... West Germany Air Force
WGAI........ Elizabeth City, NC [*AM radio station call letters*]
WGAJ....... Deerfield, MA [*FM radio station call letters*]
WGAL-TV ... Lancaster, PA [*Television station call letters*]
WGAM....... Greenfield, MA [*AM radio station call letters*]
WGAN....... Portland, ME [*AM radio station call letters*]
WGAO....... Franklin, MA [*FM radio station call letters*]
WGAO....... World Guide to Abbreviations of Organizations [*A publication*]
WGAP....... Maryville, TN [*AM radio station call letters*]
WGAR....... Cleveland, OH [*AM radio station call letters*]
WGAR-FM ... Cleveland, OH [*FM radio station call letters*]
WGAS........ South Gastonia, NC [*AM radio station call letters*]
WGAT....... Gate City, VA [*AM radio station call letters*]
WGAU....... Athens, GA [*AM radio station call letters*]
WGAW....... Gardner, MA [*AM radio station call letters*]
WGAW....... Writers Guild of America, West   (EA)
WGAY-FM ... Washington, DC [*FM radio station call letters*]
WGB.......... Weekblad voor Gemeentebelangen. Orgaan van de Vereniging
    van Nederlandse Gemeenten [*A publication*]

WGB.......... Weltgewerkschaftsbund [*World Federation of Trade Unions*]
WGBA....... Green Bay, WI [*Television station call letters*]
WGBC .... Waveguide Operating below Cutoff   (IEEE)
WGBE .... Williamsport, PA [*FM radio station call letters*]
WGBF-FM ... Henderson, KY [*FM radio station call letters*]
WGBH....... Boston, MA [*AM radio station call letters*]
WGBH-TV ... Boston, MA [*Television station call letters*]
WGBI .... Scranton, PA [*AM radio station call letters*]
WGBI-FM ... Scranton, PA [*FM radio station call letters*]
WGBO-TV ... Joliet, IL [*Television station call letters*]
WGBP-FM ... Green Bay, WI [*FM radio station call letters*]
WGBQ....... Galesburg, IL [*FM radio station call letters*]
WGBR .... Goldsboro, NC [*AM radio station call letters*]
WGBS-TV ... Philadelphia, PA [*Television station call letters*]
WGBV .... Lithia Springs, GA [*AM radio station call letters*]
WGBW...... Green Bay, WI [*FM radio station call letters*]
WGBX-TV ... Boston, MA [*Television station call letters*]
WGBY-TV ... Springfield, MA [*Television station call letters*]
WGc.......... Genoa City Public Library, Genoa City, WI [*Library symbol*]
    [*Library of Congress*]   (LCLS)
WGC......... Waste Gas Compressor [*Nuclear energy*]   (NRCH)
WGC......... Waveguide Shutter
WGC......... West Georgia College [*Carollton*]
WGC......... Western Gear Corporation
WGC......... Western Governors Conference
WGC......... Winslow Gold Corp. [*Vancouver Stock Exchange symbol*]
WGC......... Wisconsin Gas Company [*NYSE symbol*]   (SPSG)
WGC......... World Games Council   (EAIO)
WGC......... World Gospel Crusades   (EA)
WGC......... Worthy Grand Chaplain [*Freemasonry*]
WGC......... Worthy Grand Conductor [*Freemasonry*]   (ROG)
WGCA........ Wisconsin Gift Cheese Association   (EA)
WGCA-FM ... Quincy, IL [*FM radio station call letters*]
WGCB .... Red Lion, PA [*AM radio station call letters*]
WGCB-FM ... Red Lion, PA [*FM radio station call letters*]
WGCB-TV ... Red Lion, PA [*Television station call letters*]
WGCC........ World Games Coordination Committee [*Karsruhe, Federal
    Republic of Germany*]   (EAIO)
WGCC-FM ... Batavia, NY [*FM radio station call letters*]
WGCD....... Chester, SC [*AM radio station call letters*]
WG/CDR .. Wing Commander [*British military*]   (NATG)
WGCDR .... Working Group for Community Development Reform   (EA)
WGCF....... Sans Souci, SC [*AM radio station call letters*]
WGCH....... Greenwich, CT [*AM radio station call letters*]
WGCI .... Chicago, IL [*AM radio station call letters*]
WGCI-FM ... Chicago, IL [*FM radio station call letters*]
WGCL .... Bloomington, IN [*AM radio station call letters*]
WGCL .... Window Glass Cutters League of America [*Later, GBBA*]   (EA)
WGCM...... Gulfport, MS [*AM radio station call letters*]
Wg Cmdr .. Wing Commander [*British military*]   (DMA)
WGCR....... Brevard, NC [*AM radio station call letters*]
WGCR....... West Georgia College. Review [*A publication*]
Wg Cr........ Wing Commander [*British military*]   (DMA)
WGCS........ Goshen, IN [*FM radio station call letters*]
WGCV .... Petersburg, VA [*AM radio station call letters*]
WGCX....... Atmore, AL [*FM radio station call letters*]
WGCY....... Gibson City, IL [*FM radio station call letters*]
WGD......... Windshield Guidance Display
WGD......... Working Group Director
WGD......... Worldwide Government Directory [*A publication*]
WGDA....... Watermelon Growers and Distributors Association
WGDC....... Waveguide Directional Coupler
WGDC....... Working Group for Democracy in Chile   (EA)
WGDHP.... Working Group on Domestic Hunger and Poverty   (EA)
WGDL....... Lares, PR [*AM radio station call letters*]
WGDL....... Waveguide Delay Line
WGDN ...... Gladwin, MI [*AM radio station call letters*]
WGDN-FM ... Gladwin, MI [*FM radio station call letters*]
WGDR....... Plainfield, VT [*FM radio station call letters*]
WGDS........ Warm Gas Distribution System
WGDS .... Waste Gas Disposal System [*Nuclear energy*]   (NRCH)
WGDT....... Waste Gas Decay Tank [*Nuclear energy*]   (NRCH)
WGE......... Walgett [*Australia*] [*Airport symbol*]   (OAG)
WGE......... World's Great Explorers [*A publication*]
WGEA .... Geneva, AL [*AM radio station call letters*]
WGEC .... Springfield, GA [*FM radio station call letters*]
WGEE .... Green Bay, WI [*AM radio station call letters*]
WGEEIA... Western Ground Electronics Engineering Installation
    Agency   (AAG)
WGEL .... Greenville, IL [*FM radio station call letters*]
WGEM ...... Quincy, IL [*AM radio station call letters*]
WGEM-FM ... Quincy, IL [*FM radio station call letters*]
WGEM-TV ... Quincy, IL [*Television station call letters*]
WGEN ...... Geneseo, IL [*AM radio station call letters*]
WGEN-FM ... Geneseo, IL [*FM radio station call letters*]
WGER .... Working Group on Extraterrestrial Resources [*Defunct*]
    [*NASA*]
WGER-FM ... Saginaw, MI [*FM radio station call letters*]
WGES....... Oswego, NY [*FM radio station call letters*]
WGET .... Gettysburg, PA [*AM radio station call letters*]
WGETS...... Wayne George Encoder Test Set

WGEV .... Beaver Falls, PA [*FM radio station call letters*]
WGEZ .... Beloit, WI [*AM radio station call letters*]
WGF .... Waveguide Filter
WGF .... Western Goals Foundation   (EA)
WGF .... Wound Glass Fiber
WGFA .... Watseka, IL [*AM radio station call letters*]
WGFA-FM ... Watseka, IL [*FM radio station call letters*]
WGFAR..... Wenner-Gren Foundation for Anthropological Research   (EA)
WGFB....... Plattsburgh, NY [*FM radio station call letters*]
WGFC .... Floyd, VA [*AM radio station call letters*]
WGFL........ High Springs, FL [*Television station call letters*]
WGFM ...... Cheboygan, MI [*FM radio station call letters*]
WGFP........ Webster, MA [*AM radio station call letters*]
WGFR .... Glens Falls, NY [*FM radio station call letters*]
WGFS........ Covington, GA [*AM radio station call letters*]
WGFT........ Youngstown, OH [*AM radio station call letters*]
WGFX .... Gallatin, TN [*FM radio station call letters*]
WGG......... Warm Gas Generator
WGG......... Worthy Grand Guardian [*Freemasonry*]
WGG......... Worthy Grand Guide [*Freemasonry*]
WGGA...... Gainesville, GA [*AM radio station call letters*]
WGGA-FM ... Cleveland, GA [*FM radio station call letters*]
WGGB .... Writers' Guild of Great Britain   (DCTA)
WGGB-TV ... Springfield, MA [*Television station call letters*]
WGGG....... Gainesville, FL [*AM radio station call letters*]
WGGG-FM ... Micanopy, FL [*FM radio station call letters*]
WGGH .... Marion, IL [*AM radio station call letters*]
WGGL-FM ... Houghton, MI [*FM radio station call letters*]
WGGM...... Chester, VA [*AM radio station call letters*]
WGGN....... Castalia, OH [*FM radio station call letters*]
WGGN-TV ... Sandusky, OH [*Television station call letters*]
WGGO .... Salamanca, NY [*AM radio station call letters*]
WGGQ....... Waupun, WI [*FM radio station call letters*]
WGGS-TV ... Greenville, SC [*Television station call letters*]
WGGT....... Greensboro, NC [*Television station call letters*]
WGGZ....... Baton Rouge, LA [*FM radio station call letters*]
WGH .... Newport News, VA [*AM radio station call letters*]
WGH .... Warren Gamaliel Harding [*US president, 1865-1923*]
WGH .... Western General Hospital [*Australia*]
WGH .... Worthy Grand Herald [*Freemasonry*]
WGHB....... Farmville, NC [*AM radio station call letters*]
WGHC....... Clayton, GA [*AM radio station call letters*]
WGH-FM ... Newport News, VA [*FM radio station call letters*]
WGHN ...... Grand Haven, MI [*AM radio station call letters*]
WGHN-FM ... Grand Haven, MI [*FM radio station call letters*]
WGHP-TV ... High Point, NC [*Television station call letters*]
WGHQ .... Kingston, NY [*AM radio station call letters*]
WGHR....... Marietta, GA [*FM radio station call letters*]
WGHS....... Glen Ellyn, IL [*FM radio station call letters*]
WGHT....... Weigh-Tronix, Inc. [*NASDAQ symbol*]   (NQ)
WGI .... Nieuwe West-Indische Gids [*A publication*]
WGI .... Waveguide Isolator
WGI .... Western Goldfields, Inc. [*Toronto Stock Exchange symbol*]
WGI .... Wirtschaftsgeographisches Institut [*A publication*]
WGI .... Within-Grade Increase
WGI .... Word of God Institute [*Later, NIWG*]   (EA)
WGI .... Work Glove Institute [*Later, WGMA*]   (EA)
WGI .... World Geophysical Interval
WGIA .... Blackshear, GA [*AM radio station call letters*]
WGIB .... Birmingham, AL [*FM radio station call letters*]
WGIC .... Wheat Gluten Industry Council   (EA)
WGIG .... Brunswick, GA [*AM radio station call letters*]
WGII .... Western Grain International, Incorporated [*NASDAQ symbol*]   (NQ)
WGII .... Working Group on Internal Instrumentation [*NASA*]
WGIL........ Galesburg, IL [*AM radio station call letters*]
WGIN........ Calhoun City, MS [*FM radio station call letters*]
WGIQ........ Louisville, AL [*Television station call letters*]
WGIR........ Manchester, NH [*AM radio station call letters*]
WGIR-FM ... Manchester, NH [*FM radio station call letters*]
WGIV........ Charlotte, NC [*AM radio station call letters*]
WGIX-FM ... Gouverneur, NY [*FM radio station call letters*]
WGJ .... Worm Gear Jack
WGJB....... World's Greatest Jazz Band
WGKA....... Atlanta, GA [*AM radio station call letters*]
WGKI .... Cadillac, MI [*Television station call letters*]
WGKT .... Buffalo, NY [*AM radio station call letters*]
WGKX....... Memphis, TN [*FM radio station call letters*]
WGKY-FM ... Greenville, KY [*FM radio station call letters*]
WGL .... Fort Wayne, IN [*AM radio station call letters*]
WGL......... Warangal [*India*] [*Seismograph station code, US Geological Survey*]   (SEIS)
WGL......... Warren, Gorham & Lamont, Inc. [*Publisher*]
WG & L .... Warren, Gorham & Lamont, Inc. [*Publisher*]
WGL......... Washington Gas Light Co. [*NYSE symbol*]   (SPSG)
WGL......... Waveguide Load
WGL......... Weapons Guidance Laboratory
WGL......... Weighted Guidelines [*DoD*]
WGL......... Westar Group Ltd. [*Toronto Stock Exchange symbol*] [*Vancouver Stock Exchange symbol*]

WGL......... Western Guidance Laboratory [*Wright Air Development Center*]   (MUGU)
WGL......... Westeuropaeische Gesellschaft fuer Luftfahrtpsychologie [*Western European Association for Aviation Psychology - WEAAP*]   (EA)
WGL......... Wire Glass   (AAG)
WGL......... Wire Grid Lens
WGL......... Wissenschaftliche Gesellschaft fuer Luftschiffahrt [*Scientific Association for Aeronautics*] [*German*]
WGL......... Wueste und Gelobtes Land [*A publication*]   (BJA)
W GLAM .. West Glamorgan [*County in Wales*]
WGLB .... Port Washington, WI [*AM radio station call letters*]
WGLB-FM ... Port Washington, WI [*FM radio station call letters*]
WGLC .... Mendota, IL [*AM radio station call letters*]
WGLC-FM ... Mendota, IL [*FM radio station call letters*]
WGLD .... Greensboro, NC [*AM radio station call letters*]
WGLE .... Lima, OH [*FM radio station call letters*]
WGLF .... Tallahassee, FL [*FM radio station call letters*]
WGLH...... Mebane, NC [*AM radio station call letters*]
WGLI .... Babylon, NY [*AM radio station call letters*]
WGLI .... Warren, Gorham & Lamont, Inc.   (DLA)
WGLL....... Mercersburg, PA [*FM radio station call letters*]
WGLO .... Pekin, IL [*FM radio station call letters*]
WGLQ .... Escanaba, MI [*FM radio station call letters*]
WGLR .... Lancaster, WI [*AM radio station call letters*]
WGLR .... Wissenschaftliche Gesellschaft fuer Luft- und Raumfahrt [*Scientific Association for Air and Space Travel*] [*German*]
WGLS-FM ... Glassboro, NJ [*FM radio station call letters*]
WGLT .... Normal, IL [*FM radio station call letters*]
WGLU .... Johnstown, PA [*FM radio station call letters*]
WGLW ...... Welsh Grand Lodge of Wales [*Freemasonry*]
WGLX .... Galion, OH [*AM radio station call letters*]
WGLY-FM ... Waterbury, VT [*FM radio station call letters*]
WGM........ Waveguide Meter
WGM........ Weighted Guidelines Method [*Navy*]
WGM........ World Gospel Mission   (EA)
WGM........ Worthy Grand Marshal [*or Master*] [*Freemasonry*]
WGMA...... Spindale, NC [*AM radio station call letters*]
WGMA...... Washington Gallery of Modern Art
WGMA...... West Gulf Maritime Association   (EA)
WGMA...... Wet Ground Mica Association [*Inactive*]   (EA)
WGMA...... Work Glove Manufacturers Association   (EA)
WGMA...... Working Group on Multilateral Assistance [*Department of the Treasury*]
WGMC...... Greece, NY [*FM radio station call letters*]
WGMC...... West Germanic [*Language, etc.*]
WGMD...... Rehoboth Beach, DE [*FM radio station call letters*]
WGME-TV ... Portland, ME [*Television station call letters*]
WGMF ..... Watkins Glen, NY [*AM radio station call letters*]
WGMK ..... Donalsonville, GA [*FM radio station call letters*]
WGML...... Hinesville, GA [*AM radio station call letters*]
WGMO ..... Shell Lake, WI [*FM radio station call letters*]
WGMR ..... Tyrone, PA [*FM radio station call letters*]
WGMS ..... Bethesda, MD [*AM radio station call letters*]
WGMS ..... World Glacier Monitoring Service [*of the International Union of Geodesy and Geophysics*]   (EA)
WGMS-FM ... Washington, DC [*FM radio station call letters*]
WGMZ-FM ... Tuscola, MI [*FM radio station call letters*]
WGN .... Chicago, IL [*AM radio station call letters*]
WGN .... Wagon
WGN .... World's Greatest Newspaper [*Sometimes used in reference to Chicago Tribune*]
WGNA...... Albany, NY [*AM radio station call letters*]
WGNB...... Indian Rocks Beach, FL [*AM radio station call letters*]
WGNE...... Panama City, FL [*AM radio station call letters*]
WGNE-FM ... Titusville, FL [*FM radio station call letters*]
WGNG...... Western Gold 'n Gas Co. [*NASDAQ symbol*]   (NQ)
WGNI...... Wilmington, NC [*AM radio station call letters*]
WGNL....... Greenwood, MS [*FM radio station call letters*]
WGNL....... Waveguide Nitrogen Load
WGNM...... Macon, GA [*Television station call letters*]
WGNN ..... Lawrenceville, GA [*AM radio station call letters*]
WGNO ..... New Orleans, LA [*Television station call letters*]
WGNP....... Albany, GA [*FM radio station call letters*]
WGNR...... Grand Rapids, MI [*FM radio station call letters*]
WGNR...... Wegener Corp. [*NASDAQ symbol*]   (NQ)
WGNRR..... Women's Global Network on Reproductive Rights [*Formerly, International Contraception, Abortion, and Sterilisation Campaign*]   (EA)
WGNS...... Murfreesboro, TN [*AM radio station call letters*]
WGNT....... Portsmouth, VA [*Television station call letters*]
WGN-TV... Chicago, IL [*Television station call letters*]
WGNU...... Granite City, IL [*AM radio station call letters*]
WGNV...... Milladore, WI [*FM radio station call letters*]
WGNX...... Atlanta, GA [*Television station call letters*]
WGNY...... Newburgh, NY [*AM radio station call letters*]
WGNY-FM ... Newburgh, NY [*FM radio station call letters*]
WGO .... Wehrmacht Graeberoffizier [*Armed forces graves registration officer*] [*German military - World War II*]
Wg O........ Wing Officer [*British military*]   (DMA)
WGO .... Winnebago Industries, Inc. [*NYSE symbol*]   (SPSG)

WGOC.......	Kingsport, TN [*AM radio station call letters*]
WGOC.......	World Government Organization Coalition (EAIO)
WGOCC....	World Government Organization Coordinating Council [*Later, WGOC*] (EA)
WGOD	Charlotte Amalie, VI [*FM radio station call letters*]
Wg Offr......	Wing Officer [*British military*] (DMA)
WGOG	Walhalla, SC [*AM radio station call letters*]
WGOH	Grayson, KY [*AM radio station call letters*]
WGOJ	Conneaut, OH [*FM radio station call letters*]
WGOK	Mobile, AL [*AM radio station call letters*]
WGOL	Lynchburg, VA [*FM radio station call letters*]
WGOM	Marion, IN [*AM radio station call letters*]
WGOS.......	High Point, NC [*AM radio station call letters*]
WGOT.......	Merrimack, NH [*Television station call letters*]
WGOT.......	Williams Grove Old Timers [*An association*] (EA)
WGOV.......	Valdosta, GA [*AM radio station call letters*]
WGOW.......	Chattanooga, TN [*AM radio station call letters*]
WGP	Waingapu [*Indonesia*] [*Airport symbol*] (OAG)
WGP	Wattle Grove Press
WGp..........	Weather Group [*Air Force*] (AFM)
WGP	Western Gas Processors [*NYSE symbol*] (SPSG)
WGP	Westgrowth Petroleums Ltd. [*Toronto Stock Exchange symbol*]
WGP	Wire Grid Polarizer
WGPA	Bethlehem, PA [*AM radio station call letters*]
WGPC	Albany, GA [*AM radio station call letters*]
WGPC-FM ...	Albany, GA [*FM radio station call letters*]
WGPH.......	Vidalia, GA [*FM radio station call letters*]
WGPMS.....	Warehousing Gross Performance Measurement System (AFM)
WGPR	Detroit, MI [*FM radio station call letters*]
WGPR-TV ...	Detroit, MI [*Television station call letters*]
WGPT	Oakland, MD [*Television station call letters*]
WGPTDR ...	Working Group for the Promotion of Tourism in the Danube Region [*Vienna, Austria*] (EAIO)
WGQR.......	Elizabethtown, NC [*FM radio station call letters*]
WGr	Brown County Library, Green Bay, WI [*Library symbol*] [*Library of Congress*] (LCLS)
WGR.........	Buffalo, NY [*AM radio station call letters*]
W Gr	Tijdschrift voor Wetenschappelijke Graphologie [*A publication*]
WGR.........	War Guidance Requirements (AFM)
WGR.........	Water Graphite Reactor Experiment [*Nuclear energy*]
WGR.........	Westbridge Resources Ltd. [*Vancouver Stock Exchange symbol*]
WGR.........	Western Gas Resources [*NYSE symbol*] (SPSG)
WGR.........	Women in Government Relations (EA)
WGR.........	Working Group Report
WGRA	Cairo, GA [*AM radio station call letters*]
WGRA	Worksheet Global Recalculation Automatic [*Data processing*]
WGrB	Bellin Memorial Hospital, Green Bay, WI [*Library symbol*] [*Library of Congress*] (LCLS)
WGRB	Campbellsville, KY [*Television station call letters*]
WGrBC......	Brown County Hospital, Green Bay, WI [*Library symbol*] [*Library of Congress*] (LCLS)
WGRC	Lewisburg, PA [*FM radio station call letters*]
WGRD-FM ...	Grand Rapids, MI [*FM radio station call letters*]
WGRE	Greencastle, IN [*FM radio station call letters*]
WGREPO ...	Western Governors Regional Energy Policy Office
WGR-FM ..	Buffalo, NY [*FM radio station call letters*]
WGRG.......	Greensboro, GA [*AM radio station call letters*]
WGRK-FM ...	Greensburg, KY [*FM radio station call letters*]
WGRL	West Gippsland Regional Library Service [*Australia*]
WGRM......	Greenwood, MS [*AM radio station call letters*]
WGRM-FM ...	Greenwood, MS [*FM radio station call letters*]
WGRN	Greenville, IL [*FM radio station call letters*]
WGrN........	Northeastern Wisconsin Technical Institute, Green Bay, WI [*Library symbol*] [*Library of Congress*] (LCLS)
WGrNM	Neville Public Museum, Green Bay, WI [*Library symbol*] [*Library of Congress*] (LCLS)
WGRO.......	Lake City, FL [*AM radio station call letters*]
WGRP	Greenville, PA [*AM radio station call letters*]
WGRQ	Colonial Beach, VA [*FM radio station call letters*]
WGRS	Florence, SC [*Television station call letters*]
WGrSM......	Saint Mary's Hospital, Green Bay, WI [*Library symbol*] [*Library of Congress*] (LCLS)
WGrSV	Saint Vincent Hospital, Green Bay, WI [*Library symbol*] [*Library of Congress*] (LCLS)
WGRT	Indianapolis, IN [*AM radio station call letters*]
WGrU	University of Wisconsin-Green Bay, Green Bay, WI [*Library symbol*] [*Library of Congress*] (LCLS)
WGRV	Greeneville, TN [*AM radio station call letters*]
WGRX	Westminster, MD [*AM radio station call letters*]
WGRY	Grayling, MI [*AM radio station call letters*]
WGRY-FM ...	Roscommon, MI [*FM radio station call letters*]
WGRZ-TV ...	Buffalo, NY [*Television station call letters*]
WG(S)........	Waste Gas (System) [*Nuclear energy*] (NRCH)
WGS	Water Gas Shift [*Chemical reaction*]
WGS	Water Glycol Service Unit (MCD)
WGS	Waterford Generating Station [*Nuclear energy*] (NRCH)
WGS	Waveguide Glide Slope
WGS	Web Guide System
WGS	World Geodetic System (MUGU)
WGS	World Government Sponsors

WGS	Worthy Grand Sentinel [*Freemasonry*]
WGSA	Ephrata, PA [*AM radio station call letters*]
WGSC.......	War Gaming and Simulation Center [*National Defense University*]
WGSE.......	Myrtle Beach, SC [*Television station call letters*]
WGSF.......	Arlington, TN [*AM radio station call letters*]
WGSI	Russell, PA [*FM radio station call letters*]
WGSIM.....	Working Group on Satellite Ionospheric Measurements [*NASA*]
WGSJ	Worm Gear Screw Jack
WGSK	South Kent, CT [*FM radio station call letters*]
WGSL.......	Loves Park, IL [*FM radio station call letters*]
WGSM	Huntington, NY [*AM radio station call letters*]
WGSN	North Myrtle Beach, SC [*AM radio station call letters*]
WGSP.......	Charlotte, NC [*AM radio station call letters*]
WGSPR	Working Group for Space Physics Research
WGSQ	Cookeville, TN [*FM radio station call letters*]
WGSR	Millen, GA [*AM radio station call letters*]
WGST	Atlanta, GA [*AM radio station call letters*]
WGST	Waste Gas Storage Tank [*Nuclear energy*] (IEEE)
WGSU	Geneseo, NY [*FM radio station call letters*]
WGSV	Guntersville, AL [*AM radio station call letters*]
WGSW	Greenwood, SC [*FM radio station call letters*]
WGSX	Bayamon, PR [*FM radio station call letters*]
WGSY	Phenix City, AL [*FM radio station call letters*]
WGT	Wayne General and Technical College, Orrville, OH [*OCLC symbol*] [*Inactive*] (OCLC)
WGT	Weight [*Shipping*] (DS)
WGTA	Summerville, GA [*AM radio station call letters*]
WGTA	Wisconsin General Test Apparatus [*Psychology*]
WGTC	New Carlisle, IN [*FM radio station call letters*]
WG-T-C....	Waveguide-to-Coaxial [*Aerospace*] (AAG)
WGTC	Working Group on Tracking and Computation [*NASA*]
WGT/COMB ...	Weighter/Combiner (MCD)
WGTD.......	Kenosha, WI [*FM radio station call letters*]
WGTE-FM ...	Toledo, OH [*FM radio station call letters*]
WGTE-TV ...	Toledo, OH [*Television station call letters*]
WGTF.......	Dothan, AL [*FM radio station call letters*]
WGTG	Wartburg, TN [*FM radio station call letters*]
WGTH.......	Richlands, VA [*FM radio station call letters*]
WGTJ........	Greenville, NC [*Television station call letters*]
WGTL	Kannapolis, NC [*AM radio station call letters*]
WGTM	Wilson, NC [*AM radio station call letters*]
WGTN	Georgetown, SC [*AM radio station call letters*]
WGTO	Cypress Gardens, FL [*AM radio station call letters*]
WGTQ	Sault Ste. Marie, MI [*Television station call letters*]
WGTR	Miami, FL [*FM radio station call letters*]
WGTS-FM ...	Takoma Park, MD [*FM radio station call letters*]
WGTT	Alabaster, AL [*AM radio station call letters*]
WGTU.......	Traverse City, MI [*Television station call letters*]
WGTV	Athens, GA [*Television station call letters*]
WGTW	Burlington, NJ [*Television station call letters*]
WGTX	De Funiak Springs, FL [*AM radio station call letters*]
WGTY	Gettysburg, PA [*FM radio station call letters*]
WGTZ	Eaton, OH [*FM radio station call letters*]
WGU.........	Working Group on Untouchables (EA)
WGUC.......	Cincinnati, OH [*FM radio station call letters*]
WGUD......	Moss Point, MS [*AM radio station call letters*]
WGUD-FM ...	Pascagoula, MS [*FM radio station call letters*]
WGUF	Marco, FL [*FM radio station call letters*]
WGUL	Dunedin, FL [*AM radio station call letters*]
WGUL-FM ...	New Port Richey, FL [*FM radio station call letters*]
WGUN	Atlanta, GA [*AM radio station call letters*]
WGUS.......	North Augusta, SC [*AM radio station call letters*]
WGUSEASA ...	Working Group of US Overseas Educational Advisers in South America (EA)
WGUS-FM ...	Augusta, GA [*FM radio station call letters*]
WGVA	Geneva, NY [*AM radio station call letters*]
WGVE	Gary, IN [*FM radio station call letters*]
WGVK	Kalamazoo, MI [*Television station call letters*]
WGVM......	Greenville, MS [*AM radio station call letters*]
WGVO.......	Greenville, OH [*FM radio station call letters*]
WGVU-FM ...	Allendale, MI [*FM radio station call letters*]
WGVU-TV ...	Grand Rapids, MI [*Television station call letters*]
WGW........	Wallila Gap [*Washington*] [*Seismograph station code, US Geological Survey*] (SEIS)
WGW........	Waveguide Window
WGW........	Wedgewood Resources [*Vancouver Stock Exchange symbol*]
WGW........	Wheat Gluten World [*A publication*] (EAAP)
WGWC......	Working Group on Weather Communications [*NATO*] (NATG)
WGWC......	World Service Authority of the World Government of World Citizens (EAIO)
WGWD......	Gretna, FL [*FM radio station call letters*]
WGWG......	Boiling Springs, NC [*FM radio station call letters*]
WGWP	Working Group on Weather Plans [*NATO*] (NATG)
WGXA	Macon, GA [*Television station call letters*]
WGXM	Dayton, OH [*FM radio station call letters*]
WGY.........	Schenectady, NY [*AM radio station call letters*]
WGY-FM ..	Schenectady, NY [*FM radio station call letters*]
WGYJ........	Atmore, AL [*AM radio station call letters*]

WGYL	Vero Beach, FL [*FM radio station call letters*]
WGYV	Greenville, AL [*AM radio station call letters*]
WGZB	Corydon, IN [*AM radio station call letters*]
WH	City-Flug GmbH [*West Germany*] [*ICAO designator*] (FAAC)
WH	Henry Wriothesley, Earl of Southampton; or Sir William Harvey; or William Hathaway; or William Herbert, Earl of Pembroke [*Possible identities of the W. H. to whom Shakespeare's sonnets were supposedly dedicated by publisher Thomas Thorpe in 1609*]
Wh	Interrogative [*Linguistics*]
WH	Wage and Hour Cases [*Bureau of National Affairs*] [*A publication*] (DLA)
W & H	Wage and Hour Division [*Department of Labor*] (OICC)
WH	Wald und Holz [*A publication*]
WH	Walking Hinge (KSC)
WH	Wall Hung [*Technical drawings*]
WH	Wall Hydrant (AAG)
W-H	Walsh-Healey Act [*Labor*]
WH	Warhead
W/H	Warheading Building (NATG)
WH	Water Heater
WH	Watt-Hour
WH	We Have, Ready with Called Party [*Telecommunications*] (TEL)
WH	Wehrmacht-Heer [*Marking on Army vehicles*] [*German military - World War II*]
WH	Welsh Horse [*British military*] (DMA)
WH	Western Hemisphere
WH	Western Hemlock [*Utility pole*] [*Telecommunications*] (TEL)
WH	Wharf
Wh	Wharton's Pennsylvania Supreme Court Reports [*1835-41*] [*A publication*] (DLA)
Wh	Wheaton's International Law [*A publication*] (DLA)
Wh	Wheaton's Reports [*14-25 United States*] [*A publication*] (DLA)
Wh	Wheeler's New York Criminal Reports [*3 vols.*] [*A publication*] (DLA)
WH	Wheelhouse (MSA)
WH	Where (AABC)
WH	Which
Wh	While (AIA)
WH	Whispered (ADA)
WH	White
WH	White [*Thoroughbred racing*]
WH	White Hornet [*Immunology*]
WH	White House
WH	Whitman Co. [*NYSE symbol*] (SPSG)
WH	Who
WH	Whore (DSUE)
WH	Wildwood House [*Publisher*] [*British*]
WH	William Heinemann [*Publisher*] [*British*]
WH	Wings of Hope [*An association*] (EA)
WH	Withholding (AFM)
WH	Work Hour (KSC)
WH	Workable Hatch [*Shipping*] (DS)
WH2	Whipple Mountains Number 2 [*California*] [*Seismograph station code, US Geological Survey*] (SEIS)
WHA	Madison, WI [*AM radio station call letters*]
WHA	W. H. Allen [*Commercial firm*] [*British*]
WHA	Wahaula [*Hawaii*] [*Seismograph station code, US Geological Survey*] (SEIS)
WHA	Walkaloosa Horse Association (EA)
WHA	Washington Headquarters Association (EA)
WHA	Weld Head Assembly
WHA	Western Hardwood Association (EA)
WHA	Western History Association (EA)
WHA	Wood Heating Alliance (EA)
WHA	World Hockey Association
WHA	Wounded by Hostile Action
WHAA	Madison, ME [*FM radio station call letters*]
WHAB	Acton, MA [*FM radio station call letters*]
WHAB	Westminster Historical Atlas to the Bible [*A publication*] (BJA)
WHAC	World Hemophilia AIDS [*Acquired Immune Deficiency Syndrome*] Center (EA)
WHACK....	Warhead Attack Cruise Killer (MCD)
WHAD	Delafield, WI [*FM radio station call letters*]
WHAG	Halfway, MD [*AM radio station call letters*]
WHAG-TV ...	Hagerstown, MD [*Television station call letters*]
WHAI	Greenfield, MA [*AM radio station call letters*]
WHAI	Walter Hinchman Associates, Incorporated [*Telecommunications*] [*Defunct*] (TSSD)
WHAI-FM ...	Greenfield, MA [*FM radio station call letters*]
WHAI-TV ...	Bridgeport, CT [*Television station call letters*]
WHAJ	Bluefield, WV [*FM radio station call letters*]
WHAK	Rogers City, MI [*AM radio station call letters*]
WHAL	Shelbyville, TN [*AM radio station call letters*]
WHAL	Wellington Hall Ltd. [*NASDAQ symbol*] (NQ)
WHAM	Rochester, NY [*AM radio station call letters*]
WHAM	Water Hammer
WHAM	Wayne Horizontal Acceleration Mechanism

WHAM	Winning the Hearts and Minds [*of the people*] [*Vietnam pacification program*]
WHAM	Work Handling and Maintenance [*Navy*] (NG)
WHAN	Sparta, GA [*FM radio station call letters*]
WHAN	Wellness and Health Activation Networks (EA)
WHAP	Hopewell, VA [*AM radio station call letters*]
WHAP	When [*or Where*] Applicable
WHAP	Women's Health and Abortion Project (EA)
WHAR	Clarksburg, WV [*AM radio station call letters*]
Whar..........	Wharton's Pennsylvania Supreme Court Reports [*1835-41*] [*A publication*] (DLA)
WHAR	Whereafter [*Legal*] [*British*] (ROG)
WHAR.......	Wild Horses of America Registry (EA)
Whar Ag ...	Wharton on Agency [*A publication*] (DLA)
Whar Am Cr L ...	Wharton's American Criminal Law [*A publication*] (DLA)
Whar Confl Law ...	Wharton's Conflict of Laws [*A publication*] (DLA)
Whar Con Law ...	Wharton's Conflict of Laws [*A publication*] (DLA)
Whar Conv ...	Wharton on Principles of Conveyancing [*1851*] [*A publication*] (DLA)
Whar Cr Ev ...	Wharton on Criminal Evidence [*A publication*] (DLA)
Whar Cri Pl ...	Wharton's Criminal Pleading and Practice [*A publication*] (DLA)
Whar Cr Law ...	Wharton's American Criminal Law [*A publication*] (DLA)
Whar Cr Pl ...	Wharton's Criminal Pleading and Practice [*A publication*] (DLA)
Whar Dig...	Wharton's Pennsylvania Digest [*A publication*] (DLA)
Whar Dom ...	Wharton on the Law of Domicile [*A publication*] (DLA)
Whar Ev....	Wharton on Evidence in Civil Issues [*A publication*] (DLA)
Whar Hom ...	Wharton's Law of Homicide [*A publication*] (DLA)
Whar Ind ...	Wharton's Precedents of Indictments and Pleas [*A publication*] (DLA)
Whar Innk ...	Wharton on Innkeepers [*1876*] [*A publication*] (DLA)
Whar Law Dic ...	Wharton's Law Lexicon [*14th ed.*] [*1938*] [*A publication*] (DLA)
Whar Leg Max ...	Wharton's Legal Maxims [*3rd ed.*] [*1903*] [*A publication*] (DLA)
Whar Neg ..	Wharton's Law of Negligence [*A publication*] (DLA)
Whar Prec Ind ...	Wharton's Precedents of Indictments and Pleas [*A publication*] (DLA)
Whar & St Med Jur ...	Wharton and Stille's Medical Jurisprudence [*A publication*] (DLA)
Whar St Tr ...	Wharton's United States State Trials [*A publication*] (DLA)
Whart.........	Legal Maxims with Observations by George Frederick Wharton [*A publication*] (DLA)
Whart.........	Wharton's Pennsylvania Supreme Court Reports [*1835-41*] [*A publication*] (DLA)
Whart Ag ...	Wharton on Agency [*A publication*] (DLA)
Whart Am Cr Law ...	Wharton's American Criminal Law [*A publication*] (DLA)
Whart Confl Laws ...	Wharton's Conflict of Laws [*A publication*] (DLA)
Whart Cr Ev ...	Wharton on Criminal Evidence [*A publication*] (DLA)
Whart Crim Law ...	Wharton's American Criminal Law [*A publication*] (DLA)
Whart Cr Law ...	Wharton's American Criminal Law [*A publication*] (DLA)
Whart Cr Pl & Prac ...	Wharton's Criminal Pleading and Practice [*A publication*] (DLA)
Whart Ev ...	Wharton on Evidence in Civil Issues [*A publication*] (DLA)
Whart Hom ...	Wharton's Law of Homicide [*A publication*] (DLA)
Whart Homicide ...	Wharton's Law of Homicide [*A publication*] (DLA)
Whart Law Dict ...	Wharton's Law Dictionary [*or Lexicon*] [*A publication*] (DLA)
Whart Law Lexicon ...	Wharton's Law Lexicon [*A publication*] (DLA)
Whart Lex ...	Wharton's Law Lexicon [*A publication*] (DLA)
Whartn Ann ...	Wharton Annual [*A publication*]
Whart Neg	Wharton on Negligence [*A publication*] (DLA)
Whartn Mag ...	Wharton Magazine [*A publication*]
Wharton.....	Wharton Magazine [*A publication*]
Wharton.....	Wharton's American Criminal Law [*A publication*] (DLA)
Wharton.....	Wharton's Law Lexicon [*A publication*] (DLA)
Wharton.....	Wharton's Pennsylvania Supreme Court Reports [*1835-41*] [*A publication*] (DLA)
Wharton Crim Evidence ...	Wharton's Criminal Evidence [*A publication*] (DLA)
Wharton Crim Proc ...	Wharton's Criminal Law and Procedure [*A publication*] (DLA)
Wharton M ...	Wharton Magazine [*A publication*]
Wharton Mag ...	Wharton Magazine [*A publication*]
Wharton Q ...	Wharton Quarterly [*A publication*]
Whart PA ..	Wharton's Pennsylvania Supreme Court Reports [*1835-41*] [*A publication*] (DLA)
Whart & S Med Jur ...	Wharton and Stille's Medical Jurisprudence [*A publication*] (DLA)
Whart State Tr ...	Wharton's United States State Trials [*A publication*] (DLA)
Whart St Tr ...	Wharton's United States State Trials [*A publication*] (DLA)
WHAS	Louisville, KY [*AM radio station call letters*]
WHAS	Whereas
WHASA	White House Army Signal Agency
WHAS-TV ...	Louisville, KY [*Television station call letters*]
WHAT	Philadelphia, PA [*AM radio station call letters*]
WHAT	What's Here and There [*Australia*] [*A publication*]

WHAT....... Winds, Heights, and Temperatures
Whats New ... What's New in Advertising and Marketing [*A publication*]
Whats New Bldg ... What's New in Building [*A publication*]
What's New Comput ... What's New in Computing [*A publication*]
Whats New in For Res ... What's New in Forest Research [*A publication*]
Whats New Home Econ ... What's New in Home Economics [*A publication*]
Whats New Plant Physiol ... What's New in Plant Physiology [*A publication*]
WHATSR ... Whatsoever
WHA-TV... Madison, WI [*Television station call letters*]
WHAV....... Haverhill, MA [*AM radio station call letters*]
WHAV....... When Available   (KSC)
WHAW ..... Weston, WV [*AM radio station call letters*]
WHAY....... Whitley City, KY [*FM radio station call letters*]
WHAZ....... Troy, NY [*AM radio station call letters*]
WHB......... Kansas City, MO [*AM radio station call letters*]
WHB.......... [*The*] Wandering Hand Brigade [*Men who are likely to take
     liberties with women*]
WHB......... Waste Heat Boiler [*Nuclear energy*]   (CAAL)
WHB......... Wheel Bumpers [*Technical drawings*]
WHB......... Which? [*A publication*]
WHB......... Wiener Humanistische Blaetter [*A publication*]
WHB......... Wire Harness Board   (MCD)
WHBB....... Selma, AL [*AM radio station call letters*]
WHBC....... Canton, OH [*AM radio station call letters*]
WHBC-FM ... Canton, OH [*FM radio station call letters*]
WHBE....... St. Andrews, SC [*AM radio station call letters*]
WHBFC..... Wayne Hann Band Fan Club   (EA)
WHBF-TV ... Rock Island, IL [*Television station call letters*]
WHBG....... Harrisonburg, VA [*AM radio station call letters*]
WHBI........ Lake Worth, FL [*Television station call letters*]
WHBK....... Marshall, NC [*AM radio station call letters*]
WHBL....... Sheboygan, WI [*AM radio station call letters*]
WH Bl....... Wiener Humanistische Blaetter [*A publication*]
WHBL....... World Home Bible League [*Later, BL*]   (EA)
WHBMA.... Wood Hat Block Manufacturers Association   (EA)
WHBM-FM ... Park Falls, WI [*FM radio station call letters*]
WHBN....... Harrodsburg, KY [*AM radio station call letters*]
WHBN-FM ... Harrodsburg, KY [*FM radio station call letters*]
WHBO ..... Pinellas Park, FL [*AM radio station call letters*]
WHBQ....... Memphis, TN [*AM radio station call letters*]
WHBQ-TV ... Memphis, TN [*Television station call letters*]
WHBR....... Pensacola, FL [*Television station call letters*]
WHBS .... Waste Heat Boiler Survey   (DS)
WHBT....... Jackson, MI [*AM radio station call letters*]
WHBU....... Anderson, IN [*AM radio station call letters*]
WHBY....... Appleton, WI [*AM radio station call letters*]
WHBY....... Whereby
WHC......... Wages for Housework Committee   (EA)
WHC......... Washington Hospital Center, Washington, DC [*OCLC
     symbol*]   (OCLC)
WHC......... Water Holding Capacity [*Also, WBC*] [*Food industry*]
WHC......... Watt-Hour Meter with Contact Device
WHC......... Westinghouse Hanford Company   (NRCH)
WHC......... White House Conference
WHC......... Whitehorse [*Yukon Territory*] [*Seismograph station code, US
     Geological Survey*]   (SEIS)
WHC......... Winchester Capital [*Vancouver Stock Exchange symbol*]
WHC......... World Hereford Council   (EAIO)
WHC......... World Heritage Committee [*See also CPM*]   (EAIO)
WHCA....... War Hazards Compensation Act
WHCA....... White House Communications Agency   (AABC)
WHCA....... White House Correspondents' Association   (EA)
WHCA....... World Hobie Class Association [*Later, IHCA*]   (EA)
WH Cas ... Wage and Hour Cases [*Bureau of National Affairs*] [*A
     publication*]   (DLA)
WHCB....... Bristol, TN [*FM radio station call letters*]
WHCC....... Waynesville, NC [*AM radio station call letters*]
WHCCY .... White House Conference on Children and Youth   (EA)
WHCDHP ... Wainwright House Center for Development of Human
     Potential [*Later, WH*]   (EA)
WHCDHR ... Wainwright House Center for Development of Human
     Resources [*Later, WH*]   (EA)
WHCE....... Highland Springs, VA [*FM radio station call letters*]
WHCF....... Bangor, ME [*FM radio station call letters*]
WHCF....... White House Conference on Families [*June 5-July 3,
     1980*]   (EGAO)
WHcGS ..... Church of Jesus Christ of Latter-Day Saints, Genealogical
     Society Library, Milwaukee Branch, Hales Corners, WI
     [*Library symbol*] [*Library of Congress*]   (LCLS)
WHCH ...... Women's Health Care House [*Australia*]
WH Chron ... Westminster Hall Chronicle and Legal Examiner [*1835-36*] [*A
     publication*]   (DLA)
WHCI........ Amherst, MA [*FM radio station call letters*]
WHCJ .... Savannah, GA [*FM radio station call letters*]
WHCL-FM ... Clinton, NY [*FM radio station call letters*]
WHCLIS... White House Conference on Library and Information Services
     [*Washington, DC, 1979*]
WHCLIST ... White House Conference on Library and Information Services
     Taskforce
WHCN ...... Hartford, CT [*FM radio station call letters*]
WHCO .... Sparta, IL [*AM radio station call letters*]

WHCO ...... Wheeled Coach Industries [*NASDAQ symbol*]   (NQ)
WHCOA.... White House Conference on Aging
WHCOLIS ... White House Conference on Library and Information Services
Wh Cr Cas ... Wheeler's New York Criminal Cases [*3 vols.*] [*A
     publication*]   (DLA)
WHCR-FM ... New York, NY [*FM radio station call letters*]
Wh Crim Cas ... Wheeler's New York Criminal Cases [*A publication*]   (DLA)
WHcS .... Sacred Heart School of Theology, Hales Corners, WI [*Library
     symbol*] [*Library of Congress*]   (LCLS)
WHCS .... Well History Control System [*Later, Historical Well Data On-
     Line*] [*Petroleum Information Corp.*] [*Information service
     or system*]   (IID)
WHCSA .... Welsh Health Common Services Authority
WHCT-TV ... Hartford, CT [*Television station call letters*]
WHCU ...... Ithaca, NY [*AM radio station call letters*]
WHCU ...... Window Heat Control Unit
WHCU-FM ... Ithaca, NY [*FM radio station call letters*]
WHD .... Wage and Hour Division [*Department of Labor*]
WHD .... Warhead
WHD .... Western Hemisphere Defense
WHD .... Wheeler Dam [*TVA*]
WHD .... Wirlwind Resources Ltd. [*Vancouver Stock Exchange symbol*]
WHDB....... Woods Hole Database, Inc. [*Information service or
     system*]   (IID)
W-HDCS... Wyeth Laboratories - Human Diploid Cell Strain [*Rabies
     vaccine*]
WHDH...... Boston, MA [*AM radio station call letters*]
WHDL...... Olean, NY [*AM radio station call letters*]
WHDM ..... McKenzie, TN [*AM radio station call letters*]
WHDM ..... Watt-Hour Demand Meter
WHDQ ..... Claremont, NH [*FM radio station call letters*]
WHDS....... Warhead Section [*Military*]   (AABC)
WHE........ Water Hammer Eliminator
WHE......... Wheaton College, Norton, MA [*OCLC symbol*]   (OCLC)
WHE......... Whole Human Embryo [*Type of cell line*]
Wheat .... Wheaton's Reports [*14-25 United States*] [*A
     publication*]   (DLA)
Wheat Board Gaz ... Wheat Board Gazette [*A publication*]
Wheat Cap ... Wheaton on Maritime Captures and Prizes [*A
     publication*]   (DLA)
Wheat El Int Law ... Wheaton's Elements of International Law [*A
     publication*]   (DLA)
WHEATH ... Wheathampstead [*England*]
Wheat Hist Law Nat ... Wheaton's History of the Law of Nations [*A
     publication*]   (DLA)
Wheat Inform Serv ... Wheat Information Service [*A publication*]
Wheat Inf Serv ... Wheat Information Service [*A publication*]
Wheat Int Law ... Wheaton's Elements of International Law [*7th ed.*] [*1944*]
     [*A publication*]   (DLA)
Wheat Int Law ... Wheaton's International Law [*A publication*]   (DLA)
Wheat Law of Nat ... Wheaton's History of the Law of Nations [*A
     publication*]   (DLA)
Wheaton .... Wheaton's Reports [*14-25 United States*] [*A
     publication*]   (DLA)
Wheat Situation Bur Agr Econ (Aust) ... Wheat Situation. Bureau of
     Agricultural Economics (Australia) [*A publication*]
Wheat Stud Food Res Inst ... Wheat Studies. Food Research Institute [*A
     publication*]
WHEB....... Portsmouth, NH [*AM radio station call letters*]
WHEB-FM ... Portsmouth, NH [*FM radio station call letters*]
WHEC....... High-Endurance Coast Guard Cutter [*Formerly,
     WAPG*]   (CINC)
WHEC....... Wildlife Habitat Enhancement Council   (EA)
WHECON ... Wheel Control   (MCD)
WHEC-TV ... Rochester, NY [*Television station call letters*]
WHED-TV ... Hanover, NH [*Television station call letters*]
WHEE....... Martinsville, VA [*AM radio station call letters*]
WHEE....... Wheel Extended [*A publication*]
Wheel....... Wheeler's New York Criminal Cases [*A publication*]   (DLA)
Wheel........ Wheelock's Reports [*32-37 Texas*] [*A publication*]   (DLA)
Wheel Abr ... Wheeler's Abridgment of American Common Law Cases [*A
     publication*]   (DLA)
Wheel Br Cas ... Wheeling Bridge Case [*A publication*]   (DLA)
Wheel Cr C ... Wheeler's New York Criminal Cases [*A publication*]   (DLA)
Wheel Cr Cas ... Wheeler's New York Criminal Cases [*A publication*]   (DLA)
Wheel Cr Ch ... Wheeler's New York Criminal Cases [*A publication*]   (DLA)
Wheel Cr Rec ... Wheeler's New York Criminal Recorder [*1 Wheeler's
     Criminal Cases*] [*A publication*]   (DLA)
Wheeler Abr ... Wheeler's Abridgment [*A publication*]   (DLA)
Wheeler Am Cr Law ... Wheeler's Abridgment of American Common Law
     Cases [*A publication*]   (DLA)
Wheeler CC ... Wheeler's New York Criminal Cases [*A publication*]   (DLA)
Wheeler Cr Cas ... Wheeler's New York Criminal Cases [*A
     publication*]   (DLA)
Wheeler Cr Cases ... Wheeler's New York Criminal Cases [*A
     publication*]   (DLA)
Wheeler Crim Cas ... Wheeler's New York Criminal Cases [*A
     publication*]   (DLA)
Wheeler's Cr Cases ... Wheeler's New York Criminal Cases [*A
     publication*]   (DLA)
Wheel Ext ... Wheel Extended [*A publication*]

Wheel Slav ... Wheeler on Slavery [*A publication*]   (DLA)
Wheel (Tex) ... Wheelock's Reports [*32-37 Texas*] [*A publication*]   (DLA)
WHEI .... Tiffin, OH [*FM radio station call letters*]
WHEL .... Roadmaster Industries, Inc. [*NASDAQ symbol*]   (NQ)
WHEN .... Syracuse, NY [*AM radio station call letters*]
WHENCESR ... Whencesoever [*Legal*] [*British*]   (ROG)
WHENR.... Whenever [*Legal*] [*British*]   (ROG)
WHENSR ... Whensoever [*Legal*] [*British*]   (ROG)
WHEO ...... Stuart, VA [*AM radio station call letters*]
WHEP .... Foley, AL [*AM radio station call letters*]
WHER .... Hattiesburg, MS [*FM radio station call letters*]
WHER .... Whether [*Legal*] [*British*]   (ROG)
Where to Find Out More about Educ ... Where to Find Out More about
          Education [*A publication*]
WHERER ... Wherever [*Legal*] [*British*]   (ROG)
WHERF .... Wood Heating Education and Research Foundation   (EA)
WHES ...... World Hunger Education Service   (EA)
Whet .... Whetstone [*A publication*]
WHETS..... Washington Higher Education Telecommunications System
          [*Washington State University*] [*Pullman*]
          [*Telecommunications service*]   (TSSD)
WHEV ...... Garner, NC [*AM radio station call letters*]
WHEW ...... Fort Myers, FL [*FM radio station call letters*]
WHEZ .... Portage, MI [*AM radio station call letters*]
WHF .... Waveguide Harmonic Filter
WHF .... Women in Housing and Finance   (EA)
WHF .... Women's Hall of Fame [*Later, NWHF*]   (EA)
WHF .... World Heritage Fund [*UNESCO*]
WHFA ...... Western Hemisphere Friendship Association   (EA)
WHFB .... Benton Harbor, MI [*AM radio station call letters*]
WHFB-FM ... Benton Harbor, MI [*FM radio station call letters*]
WHFC .... Bel Air, MD [*FM radio station call letters*]
WHFD .... Lawrenceville, VA [*AM radio station call letters*]
WHFE .... Lakeland, GA [*FM radio station call letters*]
WHFG .... Wharfage [*Shipping*]
WHFH .... Flossmoor, IL [*FM radio station call letters*]
WHFI .... Lindside, WV [*FM radio station call letters*]
WHFM ...... Southampton, NY [*FM radio station call letters*]
WHFM ...... Wherefrom [*Legal*] [*British*]   (ROG)
WHFMS..... Woman's Home and Foreign Mission Society   (EA)
WHFORE ... Wherefore [*Legal*] [*British*]   (ROG)
WHFR .... Dearborn, MI [*AM radio station call letters*]
WHFR .... Wharfinger [*Shipping*] [*British*]   (ROG)
WHFS .... Annapolis, MD [*FM radio station call letters*]
WHFT .... Miami, FL [*Television station call letters*]
WHFTB..... Waste Heat Fire Tube Boiler   (DS)
WHFTBS .. Waste Heat Fire Tube Boiler Survey   (DS)
WHF-USA ... World Health Foundation, United States of America
          [*Inactive*]   (EA)
WHFX .... Waycross, GA [*FM radio station call letters*]
WHG .... Wasserhaushaltsgesetz [*A publication*]
WH & G..... Welsby, Hurlstone, and Gordon's English Exchequer Reports
          [*1848-56*] [*A publication*]   (DLA)
WHGB...... Harrisburg, PA [*AM radio station call letters*]
WHGC....... Bennington, VT [*FM radio station call letters*]
WHGDP..... World Hunger/Global Development Program   (EA)
WHGE....... Wharfage [*Shipping*]
WHGG ...... Knoxville, TN [*FM radio station call letters*]
WHGH ...... Thomasville, GA [*AM radio station call letters*]
WHGL....... Troy, PA [*AM radio station call letters*]
WHGL-FM ... Canton, PA [*FM radio station call letters*]
WHGR....... Houghton Lake, MI [*AM radio station call letters*]
WHGS....... Haines City, FL [*FM radio station call letters*]
WHH .... Hartford Memorial Hospital, Hartford, WI [*Library symbol*]
          [*Library of Congress*]   (LCLS)
WHH .... Werthamar-Helfand-Hohenberg Theory [*Solid state physics*]
WHH .... William Henry Harrison [*US president, 1773-1841*]
WHHA ...... White House Historical Association   (EA)
WHHB ...... Holliston, MA [*FM radio station call letters*]
WHHI ...... Highland, WI [*FM radio station call letters*]
WHHL ...... Watanabe Hereditary Hyperlipidemic [*Rabbits*]
WHHM ...... Henderson, TN [*AM radio station call letters*]
WHHO ...... Hornell, NY [*AM radio station call letters*]
WHHR ...... Hilton Head Island, SC [*AM radio station call letters*]
WHHR-FM ... Hilton Head Island, SC [*FM radio station call letters*]
WHHS ...... Havertown, PA [*FM radio station call letters*]
WHHT ...... Cave City, KY [*FM radio station call letters*]
WHHV ...... Hillsville, VA [*AM radio station call letters*]
WHHY ...... Montgomery, AL [*AM radio station call letters*]
WHHY-FM ... Montgomery, AL [*FM radio station call letters*]
WHi .... State Historical Society of Wisconsin, Madison, WI [*Library
          symbol*] [*Library of Congress*]   (LCLS)
WHI .... Washington Homes, Incorporated [*NYSE symbol*]   (SPSG)
WHI .... Wave Height Indicator [*Oceanography*]
WHI .... Weekly Hospital Indemnity [*Insurance*]
WHI .... Western Highway Institute   (EA)
WHI .... Whitney [*Hawaii*] [*Seismograph station code, US Geological
          Survey*] [*Closed*]   (SEIS)
WHI .... Wild Horse Industry [*Vancouver Stock Exchange symbol*]
WHI .... Woman Health International   (EA)

WHI .... World Trade Information [*A publication*]
WHIA .... Dawson, GA [*AM radio station call letters*]
WHIA .... Woolen Hosiery Institute of America [*Defunct*]   (EA)
WHIC .... Hardinsburg, KY [*AM radio station call letters*]
WHIC .... Women's Health Information Centre [*British*]   (CB)
WHIC-FM ... Hardinsburg, KY [*FM radio station call letters*]
Which Comput ... Which Computer? [*A publication*]
Which Word Process ... Which Word Processor? [*A publication*]
Which Word Process and Off Syst ... Which Word Processor and Office
          System? [*A publication*]
WHIDDA ... Wideband High-Density Data Acquisition   (MCD)
WHIE .... Griffin, GA [*AM radio station call letters*]
WHIG .... Ward Howell International Group [*British*]
WHIJ .... Ocala, FL [*FM radio station call letters*]
WHIL .... Raeford, NC [*AM radio station call letters*]
WHIL-FM ... Mobile, AL [*FM radio station call letters*]
WHIM ...... Providence, RI [*AM radio station call letters*]
WHIM ...... Wet High-Intensity Magnet [*for mineral processing*]
WHIM ...... Women Happy in Minis [*Boise, Idaho, group opposing below-
          the-knee fashions introduced in 1970*]
WHIMSY ... Western Humor and Irony Membership. Serial Yearbook
          [*Tempe, Arizona*] [*A publication*]
WHIN .... Gallatin, TN [*AM radio station call letters*]
WHIN .... Wherein [*Legal*] [*British*]   (ROG)
WHIO .... Dayton, OH [*AM radio station call letters*]
WHIO-TV ... Dayton, OH [*Television station call letters*]
WHIP .... Mooresville, NC [*AM radio station call letters*]
WHIP .... Walks plus Hits Divided by Innings Pitched [*Baseball*]
WHIP .... Wideband High Intercept Probability
WHIPS..... Widebeam High-Density Pulsed Source   (MCD)
WHIQ....... Huntsville, AL [*Television station call letters*]
WHIR .... Danville, KY [*AM radio station call letters*]
WHIRC .... Women's Health Information Resource Collection [*Australia*]
WHIS .... Bluefield, WV [*AM radio station call letters*]
WHIS .... Whiskeytown-Shasta-Trinity National Recreation Area
WHIS .... Whistle [*Navigation*]
Whishaw.... Whishaw's Law Dictionary [*A publication*]   (DLA)
Whish LD .. Whishaw's New Law Dictionary [*1829*] [*A publication*]   (DLA)
WHISP..... Woods Hole In-Situ Pump [*Marine biology*] [*Instrumentation*]
WHIST..... Worldwide Household Goods Information System for Traffic
          Management [*Army*]   (AABC)
W Hist Q ... Western Historical Quarterly [*A publication*]
WHIT .... Madison, WI [*AM radio station call letters*]
WHIT .... Whitman Medical Corp. [*NASDAQ symbol*]   (NQ)
Whitak Liens ... Whitaker on Liens [*A publication*]   (DLA)
WHITCH .. Whitchurch [*England*]
White .... White's Justiciary Court Reports [*3 vols.*] [*Scotland*] [*A
          publication*]   (DLA)
White .... White's Reports [*31-44 Texas Appeals*] [*A publication*]   (DLA)
White .... White's Reports [*10-15 West Virginia*] [*A publication*]   (DLA)
White Char ... Whiteford on Charities [*1878*] [*A publication*]   (DLA)
White & Civ Cas Ct App ... White and Willson's Civil Cases, Texas Court of
          Appeals [*A publication*]   (DLA)
White Coll ... White's New Collection of the Laws, Etc., of Great Britain,
          France, and Spain [*A publication*]   (DLA)
White LL ... White's Land Law of California [*A publication*]   (DLA)
White Met News Lett ... White Metal News Letter [*A publication*]
White New Coll ... White's New Collection of the Laws, Etc. of Great Britain,
          France, and Spain [*A publication*]   (DLA)
Whit Eq Pr ... Whitworth. Equity Precedents [*A publication*]   (ILCA)
Whit Eq Pr ... Whitworth's Equity Precedents [*A publication*]   (DLA)
White's Ann Pen Code ... White's Annotated Penal Code [*Texas*] [*A
          publication*]   (DLA)
White's Rep ... White's Reports [*31-44 Texas Appeals*] [*A
          publication*]   (DLA)
White's Rep ... White's Reports [*10-15 West Virginia*] [*A publication*]   (DLA)
White Suppl ... White on Supplement and Revivor [*A publication*]   (DLA)
White & TL Cas ... White and Tudor's Leading Cases in Equity [*A
          publication*]   (DLA)
White & T Lead Cas Eq ... White and Tudor's Leading Cases in Equity
          [*England*] [*A publication*]   (DLA)
White & T Lead Cas in Eq (Eng) ... White and Tudor's Leading Cases in
          Equity [*England*] [*A publication*]   (DLA)
White & Tud LC ... White and Tudor's Leading Cases in Equity [*9th ed.*]
          [*1928*] [*A publication*]   (DLA)
White & Tudor ... White and Tudor's Leading Cases in Equity [*A
          publication*]   (DLA)
White & W ... White and Willson's Reports, Civil Cases, Texas Court of
          Appeals [*A publication*]   (DLA)
White & W Civ Cas Ct App ... White and Wilson's [*or Willson's*] Civil Cases,
          Texas Court of Appeals [*A publication*]   (DLA)
White & W Civil Cases Ct App ... Texas Civil Cases [*A publication*]   (DLA)
White & Willson ... Texas Civil Cases [*A publication*]   (DLA)
White W & M ... Whiteley's Weights, Measures, and Weighing Machines
          [*1879*] [*A publication*]   (DLA)
White & W (Tex) ... White and Willson's Reports, Civil Cases, Texas Court of
          Appeals [*A publication*]   (DLA)
Whit Lien... Whitaker's Rights of Lien and Stoppage in Transitu [*1812*] [*A
          publication*]   (DLA)
Whitm Adopt ... Whitemore on Adoption of Children [*A publication*]   (DLA)

Whitman Pat Cas (US) ... Whitman's Patent Cases [*United States*] [*A publication*] (DLA)
Whitm BL ... Whitmarsh's Bankrupt Law [*2nd ed.*] [*1817*] [*A publication*] (DLA)
Whitm Lib Cas ... Whitman's Massachusetts Libel Cases [*A publication*] (DLA)
Whitm Pat Cas ... Whitman's Patent Cases [*United States*] [*A publication*] (DLA)
Whitm Pat Law ... Whitman's Patent Laws of All Countries [*A publication*] (DLA)
Whitm Pat Law Rev ... Whitman's Patent Law Review [*Washington, DC*] [*A publication*] (DLA)
Whitney ..... Whitney's Land Laws [*Tennessee*] [*A publication*] (DLA)
Whit Pat .... Whitman's Patent Laws of All Countries [*A publication*] (DLA)
Whit Pat Cas ... Whitman's Patent Cases [*United States*] [*A publication*] (DLA)
WHITS..... Whitstone [*England*]
Whit Schol ... Whitgift Scholar [*British*]
Whit St Tr ... Whitaker's Rights of Lien and Stoppage in Transitu [*1812*] [*A publication*] (DLA)
Whitt.......... Whittlesey's Reports [*32-41 Missouri*] [*A publication*] (DLA)
Whittier L Rev ... Whittier Law Review [*A publication*]
WHITTL... Whittlesey [*Urban district in England*]
Whittlesey ... Whittlesey's Reports [*32-41 Missouri*] [*A publication*] (DLA)
Whitt L Rev ... Whittier Law Review [*A publication*]
WHIY....... Moulton, AL [*AM radio station call letters*]
WHIZ........ Zanesville, OH [*AM radio station call letters*]
WHIZ-FM ... Zanesville, OH [*FM radio station call letters*]
WHIZ-TV ... Zanesville, OH [*Television station call letters*]
WHJB...... Greensburg, PA [*AM radio station call letters*]
WHJC....... Matewan, WV [*AM radio station call letters*]
WHJE....... Carmel, IN [*FM radio station call letters*]
WHJJ........ Providence, RI [*AM radio station call letters*]
WHJM...... Knoxville, TN [*AM radio station call letters*]
WHJT....... Clinton, MS [*FM radio station call letters*]
WHJX....... Brunswick, GA [*FM radio station call letters*]
WHJY....... Providence, RI [*FM radio station call letters*]
WHK........ Cleveland, OH [*AM radio station call letters*]
WHKE...... Whakatane [*New Zealand*] [*Airport symbol*] (OAG)
WHKE...... Kenosha, WI [*Television station call letters*]
WHKO...... Dayton, OH [*FM radio station call letters*]
WHKP...... Hendersonville, NC [*AM radio station call letters*]
WHKQ...... Racine, WI [*FM radio station call letters*]
WHKR...... Rockledge, FL [*FM radio station call letters*]
WHKY...... Hickory, NC [*AM radio station call letters*]
WHKY-TV ... Hickory, NC [*Television station call letters*]
WHL........ Watt-Hour Meter with Loss Compensator (MSA)
WHL......... Western Hockey League
WHL......... Westland Helicopters Ltd. [*British*] (IRUK)
WHL......... Wheel (AAG)
WHL......... World Heritage List [*UNESCO*]
WHLA...... La Crosse, WI [*FM radio station call letters*]
WHLA-TV ... La Crosse, WI [*Television station call letters*]
WHLB...... Virginia, MN [*AM radio station call letters*]
WHLD...... Niagara Falls, NY [*AM radio station call letters*]
WHLD...... Wheeled
WHLDY...... Western Holdings ADR [*NASDAQ symbol*] (NQ)
WHLE...... Holly Springs, MS [*FM radio station call letters*]
WHLF....... South Boston, VA [*AM radio station call letters*]
WHLG...... Jensen Beach, FL [*FM radio station call letters*]
WHLI....... Hempstead, NY [*AM radio station call letters*]
WHLL....... Worcester, MA [*Television station call letters*]
WHLM...... Bloomsburg, PA [*FM radio station call letters*]
WHLN...... Harlan, KY [*AM radio station call letters*]
WHLO...... Akron, OH [*AM radio station call letters*]
WHLP...... Centerville, TN [*AM radio station call letters*]
WHLP-FM ... Centerville, TN [*FM radio station call letters*]
WHLQ...... Louisburg, NC [*FM radio station call letters*]
WHLS....... Port Huron, MI [*AM radio station call letters*]
WHLS....... [*The*] Wholesale Club, Inc. [*Indianapolis, IN*] [*NASDAQ symbol*] (NQ)
WHLT....... Hattiesburg, MS [*Television station call letters*]
WHLV...... Hattiesburg, MS [*AM radio station call letters*]
WHLX...... Bethlehem, WV [*FM radio station call letters*]
WHLY...... Leesburg, FL [*FM radio station call letters*]
WHLZ...... Manning, SC [*FM radio station call letters*]
WHM........ Watt-Hour Meter
WHM....... Wickham [*Australia*] [*Airport symbol*]
WHM........ Wild Horse Parks [*Montana*] [*Seismograph station code, US Geological Survey*] [*Closed*] (SEIS)
WHM........ Wonthaggi Historical Museum [*Australia*]
WHMA..... Anniston, AL [*AM radio station call letters*]
WHMA..... Women's Home Mission Association
WHMAA... Wool Hat Manufacturers Association of America (EA)
WHMA-FM ... Anniston, AL [*FM radio station call letters*]
WH Man ... Wage and Hour Reference Manual [*Bureau of National Affairs*] [*A publication*] (DLA)
WHMB-TV ... Indianapolis, IN [*Television station call letters*]
WHMC...... Conway, SC [*Television station call letters*]

WHMC...... Wilford Hall United States Air Force Medical Center [*Lackland Air Force Base, TX*] (GRD)
WHMC-FM ... Conway, SC [*FM radio station call letters*]
WHMD..... Hammond, LA [*FM radio station call letters*]
WHME...... South Bend, IN [*FM radio station call letters*]
WHME-TV ... South Bend, IN [*Television station call letters*]
WHMH-FM ... Sauk Rapids, MN [*FM radio station call letters*]
WHMI....... Howell, MI [*AM radio station call letters*]
WHMI....... Whitman Mission National Historic Site
WHMI-FM ... Howell, MI [*FM radio station call letters*]
WHMIS .... Workplace Hazardous Materials Information System [*Canada*]
WHMM .... Washington, DC [*Television station call letters*]
WHMP...... Northampton, MA [*AM radio station call letters*]
WHMP-FM ... Northampton, MA [*FM radio station call letters*]
WHMQ..... North Baltimore, OH [*FM radio station call letters*]
WHMS-FM ... Champaign, IL [*FM radio station call letters*]
WHMT...... Humboldt, TN [*AM radio station call letters*]
WHMX...... Lincoln, ME [*FM radio station call letters*]
WHN......... Wharton & Northern Railroad Co. [*Absorbed into Consolidated Rail Corp.*] [*AAR code*]
WHN........ Whonnock Industries Ltd. [*Toronto Stock Exchange symbol*] [*Vancouver Stock Exchange symbol*]
WHN........ Women's History Network (EA)
WHNC...... Henderson, NC [*AM radio station call letters*]
WHND...... Monroe, MI [*AM radio station call letters*]
WHNE...... Cumming, GA [*AM radio station call letters*]
WHNN...... Bay City, MI [*FM radio station call letters*]
WHNPA.... White House News Photographers Association (EA)
WHNR...... Whenever [*Legal*] [*British*] (ROG)
WHNRC.... Western Human Nutrition Research Center [*Department of Agriculture*] [*Research center*] (RCD)
WHNS...... Asheville, NC [*Television station call letters*]
WHNS...... Wartime Host Nation Support
WHNSR.... Whensoever [*Legal*] [*British*] (ROG)
WHNT-TV ... Huntsville, AL [*Television station call letters*]
WHNY...... McComb, MS [*AM radio station call letters*]
WHO........ Des Moines, IA [*AM radio station call letters*]
WHO......... War on Hunger Office [*Department of State*]
WHO........ Western Heraldry Organization (EA)
WHO........ Westhill Resources [*Vancouver Stock Exchange symbol*]
WHO......... [*The*] White House Office
WHO........ World Health Organization [*The pronunciation "who" is not acceptable*] [*United Nations affiliate*] [*Switzerland*] [*Databank originator*]
WHO......... World Housing Organization
WHO......... Wrist-Hand Orthosis [*Medicine*]
WHOA...... American Equine Products, Inc. [*South Norwalk, CT*] [*NASDAQ symbol*] (NQ)
WHOA...... Walking Horse Owner's Association of America (EA)
WHOA...... Why Have Overages Afterwards [*DoD*]
WHOA...... Wild Horse Organized Assistance (EA)
WHOAA ... Walking Horse Owner's Association of America (EA)
WHOA-TV ... Montgomery, AL [*Television station call letters*]
WHOB...... Nashua, NH [*FM radio station call letters*]
WHOC...... Philadelphia, MS [*AM radio station call letters*]
WHOCA.... World Health Organization. Chronicle [*A publication*]
WHO Chron ... WHO [*World Health Organization*] Chronicle [*A publication*]
WHO Chronicle ... World Health Organization. Chronicle [*A publication*]
WHOD...... Jackson, AL [*AM radio station call letters*]
WHOD-FM ... Jackson, AL [*FM radio station call letters*]
WHOE...... Avis, PA [*FM radio station call letters*]
WHO Environ Health ... WHO (World Health Organization) Environmental Health [*A publication*]
WHOER..... Whoever [*Legal*] [*British*] (ROG)
WHOF...... Whereof [*Legal*] [*British*] (ROG)
WHOF....... Wildwood, FL [*AM radio station call letters*]
WHO Food Addit Ser ... WHO [*World Health Organization*] Food Additives Series [*A publication*]
WHOG...... Fernandina Beach, FL [*AM radio station call letters*]
WHOH...... Crestline, OH [*FM radio station call letters*]
WHO Hist Int Public Health ... WHO (World Health Organization) History of International Public Health [*A publication*]
WHOI....... Peoria, IL [*Television station call letters*]
WHOI........ Woods Hole Oceanographic Institution [*Woods Hole, MA*] [*Research center*]
WHO Int Agency Res Cancer Annu Rep ... World Health Organization International Agency for Research on Cancer. Annual Report [*A publication*]
WHOI Technical Report ... Woods Hole Oceanographic Institution. Technical Report [*A publication*]
WHOK...... Lancaster, OH [*FM radio station call letters*]
WHOL....... Allentown, PA [*AM radio station call letters*]
WHO Libr Ne ... WHO [*World Health Organization*] Library News [*A publication*]
WHOM..... Mount Washington, NH [*FM radio station call letters*]
WHOMAP ... FAO [*Food and Agriculture Organization of the United Nations*] Nutritional Studies [*A publication*]
WHO Monogr Ser ... World Health Organization. Monograph Series [*A publication*]
WHON...... Centerville, IN [*AM radio station call letters*]

WHON ...... Whereon [*Legal*] [*British*]   (ROG)
WHOO ...... Orlando, FL [*AM radio station call letters*]
WHOO ...... Waterhouse Investor Services, Inc. [*NASDAQ symbol*]   (NQ)
WHO Offset Publ ... WHO [*World Health Organization*] Offset Publication
    [*A publication*]
WHOP....... Hopkinsville, KY [*AM radio station call letters*]
WHOPAY ... World Health Organization. Public Health Papers [*A*
    publication]
WHO Pestic Residues Ser ... WHO [*World Health Organization*] Pesticide
    Residues Series [*A publication*]
WHOP-FM ... Hopkinsville, KY [*FM radio station call letters*]
WHO Publ ... WHO [*World Health Organization*] Publications [*A*
    publication]
WHO Publ Hlth Pap ... WHO [*World Health Organization*] Public Health
    Papers [*A publication*]
WHO Public Health Pap ... World Health Organization. Public Health Papers
    [*A publication*]
WHO Public Health Papers ... World Health Organization. Public Health
    Papers [*A publication*]
WHOR ...... Roanoke, IN [*FM radio station call letters*]
WHOS....... Decatur, AL [*AM radio station call letters*]
WHOSOR ... Whosoever [*Legal*] [*British*]   (ROG)
WHOT ...... Campbell, OH [*AM radio station call letters*]
WHO Tech Rep Ser ... World Health Organization. Technical Report Series
    [*A publication*]
WHO Tech Rep Sers ... World Health Organization. Technical Report Series
    [*A publication*]
WHOT-FM ... Youngstown, OH [*FM radio station call letters*]
WHO-TV .. Des Moines, IA [*Television station call letters*]
WHOU ...... Houlton, ME [*AM radio station call letters*]
WHOU-FM ... Houlton, ME [*FM radio station call letters*]
Whous........ Warehouse
WHOV ...... Hampton, VA [*FM radio station call letters*]
WHOW ..... Clinton, IL [*AM radio station call letters*]
WHOW-FM ... Clinton, IL [*FM radio station call letters*]
WHOX ...... Charlestown, IN [*FM radio station call letters*]
WHOY ...... Salinas, PR [*AM radio station call letters*]
WHP.......... Harrisburg, PA [*AM radio station call letters*]
WHP.......... Los Angeles, CA [*Location identifier*] [*FAA*]   (FAAL)
WHP.......... Water Horsepower
WHP.......... West Hartford Public Library, West Hartford, CT [*OCLC*
    symbol]   (OCLC)
WHP.......... Western Health Plans, Inc. [*AMEX symbol*]   (SPSG)
WHP.......... White House Police [*Later, Executive Protective Service*]
WHPA....... Hollidaysburg, PA [*FM radio station call letters*]
WHPB....... Belton, SC [*AM radio station call letters*]
WHPC....... Garden City, NY [*FM radio station call letters*]
WHPC....... Wage and Hour and Public Contracts Division [*Obsolete*]
    [*Department of Labor*]
WHPCA .... Walsh-Healey Public Contracts Act [*1936*] [*Labor*]
WHPCD .... Wage and Hour and Public Contracts Division [*Obsolete*]
    [*Department of Labor*]
WHPE-FM ... High Point, NC [*FM radio station call letters*]
WHP-FM .. Harrisburg, PA [*FM radio station call letters*]
WHPI........ Ashland, KY [*Television station call letters*]
WHPK-FM ... Chicago, IL [*FM radio station call letters*]
whpl .... Whirlpool
WHPO....... Hoopeston, IL [*FM radio station call letters*]
WHPO....... White House Personnel Office [*Terminated, 1974*]
WHPR....... Highland Park, MI [*FM radio station call letters*]
WHP-TV ... Harrisburg, PA [*Television station call letters*]
WHPY....... Clayton, NC [*AM radio station call letters*]
WHQ......... War Headquarters   (NATG)
WHQ......... Western Historical Quarterly [*A publication*]
WHQO....... Skowhegan, ME [*FM radio station call letters*]
WHQR....... Wilmington, NC [*FM radio station call letters*]
WHQT....... Coral Gables, FL [*FM radio station call letters*]
WHR......... Vail [*Colorado*] [*Airport symbol*]   (OAG)
WHR......... Wage and Hour Reporter [*Bureau of National Affairs*] [*A*
    publication]   (DLA)
WHR......... Waste Heat Removal
W-HR....... Watt-Hour   (AAG)
WHR......... Welsh History Review [*A publication*]
WHR......... Western Hemisphere Reserve
WHR......... Western Humanities Review [*A publication*]
WHR......... Whether
WHR......... Whirlpool Corp. [*NYSE symbol*]   (SPSG)
WHR......... William H. Rorer [*Research code symbol*]
WHR......... Women and Health Roundtable   (EA)
WHR......... Working Heart Rate [*Cardiology*]
WHRA....... Western Historical Research Associates [*Defunct*]   (EA)
WHRABTS ... Whereabouts [*Legal*] [*British*]   (ROG)
WHRAC .... Wool Harvesting Research Advisory Committee [*Australia*]
WHRAS .... Whereas [*Legal*] [*British*]   (ROG)
WHRAT .... Whereat [*Legal*] [*British*]   (ROG)
WHRB....... Cambridge, MA [*FM radio station call letters*]
WHRC....... Norwell, MA [*Television station call letters*]
WHRC....... Washington Home Rule Committee [*Later, SDDC*]   (EA)
WHRC....... World Health Research Center
WHRD....... Huntington, WV [*AM radio station call letters*]
WHRF....... Bel Air, MD [*AM radio station call letters*]

WHRIN..... Wherein
WHRK....... Memphis, TN [*FM radio station call letters*]
WHRL....... Albany, NY [*FM radio station call letters*]
WHRM....... Wausau, WI [*FM radio station call letters*]
WHR Man ... Wage and Hour Reference Manual [*Bureau of National Affairs*]
    [*A publication*]   (DLA)
WHRM-TV ... Wausau, WI [*Television station call letters*]
WHRO-FM ... Norfolk, VA [*FM radio station call letters*]
WHRO-TV ... Hampton-Norfolk, VA [*Television station call letters*]
WHRS....... Winchester, KY [*AM radio station call letters*]
WHRT....... Hartselle, AL [*AM radio station call letters*]
WHRU ...... Waste Heat Recovery Unit [*Chemical engineering*]
WHRV....... Norfolk, VA [*FM radio station call letters*]
WHRW....... Binghamton, NY [*FM radio station call letters*]
WHRY....... Hurley, WI [*AM radio station call letters*]
WHRZ....... Providence, KY [*FM radio station call letters*]
WHS.......... Warehouse   (AABC)
WHS.......... Washington Headquarters Services [*Military*]
WHS.......... Water Hydraulic Section
WHS.......... Weekly Hansard - Senate [*A publication*]   (APTA)
WHS.......... Wesleyan Historical Society [*British*]
WHS.......... Western Harvest Sea [*Vancouver Stock Exchange symbol*]
WHS.......... Whalsay [*Shetland Islands*] [*Airport symbol*]   (OAG)
WHS.......... White Scale
WHS.......... William Hunter Society   (EA)
WHS.......... Wolf-Hirschorn Syndrome [*Medicine*]
WHS.......... Works. Richard Hakluyt Society [*A publication*]
WHS.......... World Health Statistics Data Base [*World Health Organization*]
    [*Information service or system*]   (IID)
WHSA ...... Brule, WI [*FM radio station call letters*]
WHSB....... Alpena, MI [*FM radio station call letters*]
WHSC....... Hartsville, SC [*AM radio station call letters*]
WHSC....... White House Science Council
WHSCH.... Whitworth Scholar [*British*]
WHSD....... Hinsdale, IL [*FM radio station call letters*]
WHSD....... W. H. Smith Distributors [*British*]
WHSE....... Newark, NJ [*Television station call letters*]
WHSE....... Warehouse   (AAG)
W/HSE....... Wheelhouse [*Automotive engineering*]
WHSG....... Monroe, GA [*Television station call letters*]
WHSH....... Marlborough, MA [*Television station call letters*]
WHSHS.... Wilbur Hot Springs Health Sanctuary   (EA)
WHSI........ Smithtown, NY [*Television station call letters*]
WHSK....... Kokomo, IN [*FM radio station call letters*]
WHSL ...... East St. Louis, IL [*Television station call letters*]
WHSLE..... Wholesale
WHSM...... Hayward, WI [*AM radio station call letters*]
WHSM-FM ... Hayward, WI [*FM radio station call letters*]
WHSMN... Warehouseman   (AABC)
WHSN....... Bangor, ME [*FM radio station call letters*]
WHSNA .... Welsh Harp Society of North America   (EA)
WHSNG.... Warehousing
WHSP ...... Vineland, NJ [*Television station call letters*]
WHSR....... White House Situation Room   (MCD)
WHSR-FM ... Winchester, MA [*FM radio station call letters*]
WHSS....... Hamilton, OH [*FM radio station call letters*]
WHSS....... White House Signal Support
WHSUPA ... Wharton School, University of Pennsylvania   (DLA)
WHSV....... Weight-Hourly Space Velocity [*Fuel technology*]
WHSV-TV ... Harrisonburg, VA [*Television station call letters*]
WHSW....... Baltimore, MD [*Television station call letters*]
WHSY....... Hattiesburg, MS [*AM radio station call letters*]
WHSY-FM ... Hattiesburg, MS [*FM radio station call letters*]
WHT.......... Watt-Hour Demand Meter, Thermal Type   (IEEE)
WHT.......... White   (AAG)
WHT.......... Whitehall Corp. [*NYSE symbol*]   (SPSG)
WHT.......... William Herschel Telescope
WHT.......... William Howard Taft [*US president, 1857-1930*]
WHT.......... Wometco Home Theatre [*Subscription television service*]
WHTA....... Calumet, MI [*Television station call letters*]
WHTA....... Walking Horse Trainers Association   (EA)
WHTB....... Fall River, MA [*AM radio station call letters*]
WHTC....... Holland, MI [*AM radio station call letters*]
WHTCA .... Wehrtechnik [*A publication*]
WHTE....... Williamston, NC [*FM radio station call letters*]
WHTF....... Starview, PA [*FM radio station call letters*]
WHTG....... Eatontown, NJ [*AM radio station call letters*]
WHTG-FM ... Eatontown, NJ [*FM radio station call letters*]
WHTH....... Heath, OH [*AM radio station call letters*]
WHTJ........ Charlottesville, VA [*Television station call letters*]
WHTK....... Port Royal, SC [*FM radio station call letters*]
Wh & TLC ... White and Tudor's Leading Cases in Equity [*9 eds.*] [*1849-
    1928*] [*A publication*]   (DLA)
WHTL-FM ... Whitehall, WI [*FM radio station call letters*]
WHTM...... Wisconsin Hydrologic Transport Model
WHTM-TV ... Harrisburg, PA [*Television station call letters*]
WHTN....... Murfreesboro, TN [*Television station call letters*]
WHTO....... Muncy, PA [*FM radio station call letters*]
WHTO ...... Whereto [*Legal*] [*British*]   (ROG)
WHTQ-FM ... Orlando, FL [*FM radio station call letters*]
WHTT....... Buffalo, NY [*AM radio station call letters*]

WHTT-FM ... Buffalo, NY [*FM radio station call letters*]
Wh & Tud .. White and Tudor's Leading Cases in Equity [*9th ed.*] [*1928*] [*A publication*]
WHTX....... Pittsburgh, PA [*FM radio station call letters*]
WHTZ....... Newark, NJ [*FM radio station call letters*]
WHU .... Well Head Unit
WHU .... Wild Horse [*Utah*] [*Seismograph station code, US Geological Survey*] (SEIS)
WHUB...... Cookeville, TN [*AM radio station call letters*]
WHUB-FM ... Cookeville, TN [*FM radio station call letters*]
WHUC ...... Hudson, NY [*AM radio station call letters*]
WHud .... Hudson Public Library, Hudson, WI [*Library symbol*] [*Library of Congress*] (LCLS)
WHUD ..... Peekskill, NY [*AM radio station call letters*]
WHudSO... Hudson Star-Observer, Hudson, WI [*Library symbol*] [*Library of Congress*] (LCLS)
WHUG ...... Jamestown, NY [*FM radio station call letters*]
WHUH ...... Houghton, MI [*FM radio station call letters*]
WHUM-FM ... Patton, PA [*FM radio station call letters*]
WHUN...... Huntingdon, PA [*AM radio station call letters*]
WHUR-FM ... Washington, DC [*FM radio station call letters*]
WHUS....... Storrs, CT [*FM radio station call letters*]
WHUT....... Anderson, IN [*AM radio station call letters*]
WHV .... Woodchuck Hepatitis Virus
WHVE....... Sarasota, FL [*FM radio station call letters*]
WHVN ...... Charlotte, NC [*AM radio station call letters*]
WHVP...... Wedged Hepatic Venous Pressure
WHVR...... Hanover, PA [*AM radio station call letters*]
WHVT....... Clyde, OH [*FM radio station call letters*]
WHVW...... Hyde Park, NY [*AM radio station call letters*]
WHVY....... Baltimore, MD [*FM radio station call letters*]
WHW .... Women Helping Women (EA)
WHWB...... Rutland, VT [*AM radio station call letters*]
WHWC...... Menomonie, WI [*FM radio station call letters*]
WHWC-TV ... Menomonie, WI [*Television station call letters*]
WHWE...... Howe, IN [*FM radio station call letters*]
WHWH ...... Princeton, NJ [*AM radio station call letters*]
WHWK..... Binghamton, NY [*FM radio station call letters*]
WHWL..... Marquette, MI [*FM radio station call letters*]
WHWPNLA ... World Health Workers for Peace and NonIntervention in Latin America (EAIO)
WHWTB ... Waste Heat Water Tube Boiler (DS)
WHWTBS ... Waste Heat Water Tube Boiler Survey (DS)
WHWTCA ... West Highland White Terrier Club of America (EA)
WHWTH .. Wherewith [*Legal*] [*British*] (ROG)
WHX......... Wheeling-Pittsburgh Steel Corp. [*NYSE symbol*] (SPSG)
WHXT....... Easton, PA [*FM radio station call letters*]
WHY......... What Have You? [*British*] (ADA)
WHY......... World Hunger Year (EA)
WHYB...... Peshtigo, WI [*FM radio station call letters*]
WHYC...... Swan Quarter, NC [*AM radio station call letters*]
WHYD...... Columbus, GA [*AM radio station call letters*]
WHYDFTFT ... What Have You Done for the Fleet Today? [*Navy*]
WHYI-FM ... Fort Lauderdale, FL [*FM radio station call letters*]
WHYL....... Carlisle, PA [*AM radio station call letters*]
WHYL-FM ... Carlisle, PA [*FM radio station call letters*]
WHYM...... Pensacola, FL [*AM radio station call letters*]
WHYN...... Springfield, MA [*AM radio station call letters*]
WHYN-FM ... Springfield, MA [*FM radio station call letters*]
WHYR....... Saco, ME [*FM radio station call letters*]
WHYT....... Detroit, MI [*FM radio station call letters*]
WHYY-FM ... Philadelphia, PA [*FM radio station call letters*]
WHYY-TV ... Wilmington, DE [*Television station call letters*]
WHYZ....... Greenville, SC [*AM radio station call letters*]
WHZI....... Hanceville, AL [*AM radio station call letters*]
WHZR....... Royal Center, IN [*FM radio station call letters*]
WHZZ-FM ... Huntingdon, TN [*FM radio station call letters*]
WI............. Oak Harbor, Whidbey Island, Washington [*Naval base*]
WI............. Walk In (ADA)
WI............. Wallops Island [*Off coast of Virginia*]
WI............. Water Injection
W & I .... Weighing and Inspection
WI............. Welding Institute [*Database originator and operator*] (EA)
WI............. Welt des Islams [*A publication*]
WI............. West Coast Airlines Ltd. [*Ghana*] [*ICAO designator*] (FAAC)
WI............. West Indies [*Formerly, BWI*]
WI............. Westerners International (EA)
WI............. Wexas International [*Commercial firm*] [*London, England*] (EAIO)
WI............. When Issued [*Stock exchange term*] (SPSG)
WI............. White Information [*Banking*] [*British*]
WI............. Wiadomosci [*A publication*]
Wi .... Wiez [*A publication*]
WI............. Wimpy International [*Commercial firm*] [*British*]
WI............. Wine Institute (EA)
WI............. Winter [*Federal Republic of Germany*] [*ICAO aircraft manufacturer identifier*] (ICAO)
WI............. Wire
WI............. Wisconsin [*Postal code*]
WI............. Wisconsin School Musician [*A publication*]
WI............. Within

WI............. Wohnungswirtschaftliche Informationen [*A publication*]
WI............. Women's Institute [*British*]
WI............. Women's Reserve, Intelligence Duties [*USNR officer designation*]
WI............. Wood Industries [*A publication*]
WI............. Woprosy Istorii [*A publication*]
WI............. Word Intelligibility
WI............. World Impact (EA)
WI............. Worldwatch Institute (EA)
WI............. Wrought Iron
WIA.......... Manitowoc Public Library, Manitowoc, WI [*OCLC symbol*] (OCLC)
WIA.......... Waking Imagined Analgesia [*Medicine*]
WIA.......... Watusi International Association (EA)
WIA.......... Western Interpreters Association [*Later, NAI*] (EA)
WIA.......... Wien-Auhof [*Austria*] [*Geomagnetic observatory code*]
WIA.......... Wirtschaftskonjunktur. Analysen, Perspektiven, Indikatoren [*A publication*]
WIA.......... Women in Aerospace (EA)
WIA.......... Women in Agribusiness [*An association*] (EA)
WIA.......... Women in the Arts Foundation (EA)
WIA.......... Wounded in Action [*Military*]
WIAA .... Interlochen, MI [*FM radio station call letters*]
WIAA .... Sabang [*Indonesia*] [*ICAO location identifier*] (ICLI)
WIAB........ Banda Aceh/Maimun Saleh [*Indonesia*] [*ICAO location identifier*] (ICLI)
WIAB........ Wilderness Alberta [*A publication*]
WIAC .... San Juan, PR [*AM radio station call letters*]
WIAC .... Women's International Art Club
WIAC-FM ... San Juan, PR [*FM radio station call letters*]
WIACLALS ... West Indian Association for Commonwealth Literature and Language Studies (EAIO)
WIACO ..... World Insulation and Acoustic Congress Organization (EA)
Wiad A....... Wiadomosci Archeologiczne. Bulletin Archeologique Polonias [*A publication*]
Wiad Bot.... Wiadomosci Botaniczne [*A publication*]
Wiad Chem ... Wiadomosci Chemiczne [*A publication*]
Wiad Ekol ... Wiadomosci Ekologiczne [*A publication*]
Wiad Elektrotech ... Wiadomosci Elektrotechniczne [*A publication*]
Wiad Gorn ... Wiadomosci Gornicze [*Poland*] [*A publication*]
Wiad Hist .. Wiadomosci Historyczne [*A publication*]
Wiad Hutn ... Wiadomosci Hutnicze [*A publication*]
Wiad Inst Melior Uzytkow Zielon (Warsaw) ... Wiadomosci. Instytut Melioracji i Uzytkow Zielonych (Warsaw) [*A publication*]
Wiad Lek ... Wiadomosci Lekarskie [*A publication*]
Wiad Mat .. Wiadomosci Matematyczne [*A publication*]
Wiad Melior Lak ... Wiadomosci Melioracyjne i Lakarskie [*A publication*]
Wiad Melior Lakarsk ... Wiadomosci Melioracyjne i Lakarskie [*A publication*]
Wiad Meteorol Gospod Wodnej ... Wiadomosci Meteorologii i Gospodarki Wodnej [*A publication*]
Wiad Naft.. Wiadomosci Naftowe [*A publication*]
Wiad Num Arch ... Wiadomosci Numizmatyczno-Archeologiczne [*Later, Wiadomosci Numizmatyczne*] [*A publication*]
Wiadom Mat ... Wiadomosci Matematyczne [*A publication*]
Wiadom Mat 2 ... Roczniki Polskiego Towarzystwa Matematycznego. Seria II. Wiadomosci Matematyczne [*A publication*]
Wiadom Statyst ... Wiadomosci Statystyczne [*A publication*]
Wiad Parazyt ... Wiadomosci Parazytologiczne [*A publication*]
Wiad Parazytol ... Wiadomosci Parazytologiczne [*A publication*]
Wiad Stat... Wiadomosci Statystyczne [*A publication*]
Wiad St Hydrol Met ... Wiadomosci Sluzby Hydrologicznej i Meteorologicznej [*A publication*]
Wiad Telekomun ... Wiadomosci Telekomunikacyjne [*A publication*]
Wiad Zielarskie ... Wiadomosci Zielarskie [*A publication*]
WIAG .... Menggala/Astrakestra [*Indonesia*] [*ICAO location identifier*] (ICLI)
WIAI.......... Danville, IL [*FM radio station call letters*]
WIAJ......... Semplak/Atang Senjaya [*Indonesia*] [*ICAO location identifier*] (ICLI)
WIAK .... Margahayu/Sulaiman [*Indonesia*] [*ICAO location identifier*] (ICLI)
WIAL........ Eau Claire, WI [*FM radio station call letters*]
WIAM........ Tasikmalaya/Cibeureum [*Indonesia*] [*ICAO location identifier*] (ICLI)
WIAM .... Williamston, NC [*AM radio station call letters*]
WIAP........ Banyumas/Wirasaba [*Indonesia*] [*ICAO location identifier*] (ICLI)
WIAP........ Wartime Individual Augmentation Program [*Military*]
WIAP........ Westinghouse Industrial Atomic Power (MCD)
WIAR .... Madiun/Iswahyudi [*Indonesia*] [*ICAO location identifier*] (ICLI)
WIAS........ Malang/Abdul Rachman Saleh [*Indonesia*] [*ICAO location identifier*] (ICLI)
WIAS........ West Indies Associated State
WIAS........ Whiteruthenian Institute of Arts and Science [*Later, BIAS*] (EA)
WIB .... Lawrence University, Appleton, WI [*OCLC symbol*] (OCLC)
WIB .... Wallcovering Information Bureau (EA)
WIB .... Wartime Information Board [*World War II*] [*Canada*]
WIB .... Weather Information Branch [*Air Force*] (MCD)

WIB .... Wetboek van de Inkomstenbelastingen [A publication]
WIB .... Wetenschapsbeleid [A publication]
WIB .... When Interrupt Block (NASA)
WIB .... When-Issued-Basis [Business term]
WIB .... Women's Information Bank (EA)
WIBA......... Madison, WI [AM radio station call letters]
WIBA-FM ... Madison, WI [FM radio station call letters]
WIBB........ Macon, GA [AM radio station call letters]
WIBB........ Pekanbaru [Indonesia] [ICAO location identifier] (ICLI)
WIBC........ Indianapolis, IN [AM radio station call letters]
WIBC........ Women's International Bowling Congress (EA)
WIBC........ World Institute of Black Communications (EA)
WIBD .... Dumai/Pinangkampai [Indonesia] [ICAO location
              identifier] (ICLI)
WIBFD...... Will Be Forwarded (NOAA)
WIBF-FM ... Jenkintown, PA [FM radio station call letters]
WIBG .... Ocean City, NJ [AM radio station call letters]
WIBI......... Carlinville, IL [FM radio station call letters]
WIBIS .... Will Be Issued (NOAA)
WI Bl .... Wirtschaftsrechtliche Informations-Blaetter [A publication]
WIBM .... Jackson, MI [AM radio station call letters]
WIBM-FM ... Jackson, MI [FM radio station call letters]
WIBN .... Earl Park, IN [FM radio station call letters]
WIBP........ Semilinang/Peranap [Indonesia] [ICAO location
              identifier] (ICLI)
WIBQ-FM ... Remsen, NY [FM radio station call letters]
WIBR........ Sipora/Rokot [Indonesia] [ICAO location identifier] (ICLI)
WIBS........ Bengkalis/Sungai Pakning [Indonesia] [ICAO location
              identifier] (ICLI)
WIBS........ Charlotte Amalie, VI [AM radio station call letters]
WIBS........ Wool Industry Bureau of Statistics [British] (CB)
WIBT........ Tanjung Balai/Sungai Bati [Indonesia] [ICAO location
              identifier] (ICLI)
WIBU .... Poynette, WI [AM radio station call letters]
WIBV........ Belleville, IL [AM radio station call letters]
WIBW .... Topeka, KS [AM radio station call letters]
WIBW-FM ... Topeka, KS [FM radio station call letters]
WIBW-TV ... Topeka, KS [Television station call letters]
WIBX........ Utica, NY [AM radio station call letters]
WIBZ........ Wedgefield, SC [FM radio station call letters]
WIC .... Medical College of Wisconsin, Milwaukee, WI [OCLC
              symbol] (OCLC)
WIC .... Warning Information Correlation (MCD)
WIC .... Washington International Center (EA)
WIC .... Wax Insulating Compound
WIC .... Wayfarer International Committee [Axminster, Devonshire,
              England] (EAIO)
WIC .... Weighted Ion Concentration [Air pollution measure]
WIC .... Welding Institute of Canada (EAIO)
WIC .... West India Committee [London, England] (EAIO)
WIC .... Wheat Industry Council (EA)
WIC .... Whitbread Investment Company [British]
WIC .... WIC Western International Communications Ltd. [Toronto
              Stock Exchange symbol] [Vancouver Stock Exchange
              symbol]
WIC .... Wick [Scotland] [Airport symbol] (OAG)
WIC .... WICOR, Inc. [NYSE symbol] (SPSG)
WIC .... Wildlife Information Center (EA)
WIC .... Windsor Institute of Complementology [Later, ICS] (EA)
WIC .... Women in Cable (EA)
WIC .... Women in Communications
WIC .... Women in Crisis (EA)
WIC .... Women, Infants, and Children [Supplemental food program]
              [Department of Agriculture]
WIC .... Women's Interart Center (EA)
WIC .... Worksheet Inspection Card
WIC .... World Institute Council (EA)
WICA .... Judgments of the West Indian Court of Appeal [A
              publication] (DLA)
WICA .... While in Control Area [Aviation] (FAAC)
WICA .... Wind Cave National Park
WICA .... Witches International Craft Association (EA)
WICB........ Ithaca, NY [FM radio station call letters]
WICB........ Women in Cell Biology (EA)
WICBC...... World Invitation Club Basketball Championships [London,
              England]
WICBE...... World Information Centre for Bilingual Education [See also
              CMIEB] [Paris, France] (EAIO)
WICC........ Bridgeport, CT [AM radio station call letters]
WICC........ Women's Inter-Church Council of Canada
WICD........ Champaign, IL [Television station call letters]
WICE........ Pawtucket, RI [AM radio station call letters]
WICF........ Women's International Cultural Federation [See also
              FICF] (EAIO)
WICH....... Norwich, CT [AM radio station call letters]
Wi Ch........ Wirtschaftspolitische Chronik [A publication]
WICHE ..... Western Interstate Commission for Higher Education
WICHE Publ ... Western Interstate Commission for Higher Education.
              Publications [A publication]
Wichita Eag ... Wichita Eagle-Beacon [A publication]
WICI.......... Elletsville, IN [AM radio station call letters]

WICI......... Women in Communications, Incorporated (EA)
WICK........ Scranton, PA [AM radio station call letters]
WICK........ Wicklow [County in Ireland] (ROG)
WICK........ Wicklund Petroleum Corp. [NASDAQ symbol] (NQ)
WICKF ..... Wickford [England]
WICKL...... Wicklow [County in Ireland]
WICL........ Work Inspection Characteristics List
WICN........ Worcester, MA [FM radio station call letters]
WICO .... Salisbury, MD [AM radio station call letters]
WICO .... W. I. Carr Sons & Co. Overseas [Stockbroker] [Hong Kong]
WICO-FM ... Salisbury, MD [FM radio station call letters]
WICR........ Indianapolis, IN [FM radio station call letters]
WICR........ Wilson's Creek Battlefield National Park
WICS........ Springfield, IL [Television station call letters]
WICS........ Women in Community Service (EA)
WICS........ Worldwide Intelligence Communications System (MCD)
WI & CTF ... Welsh Industry and Commerce Trade Fair (ITD)
WICU-TV ... Erie, PA [Television station call letters]
WICY........ Malone, NY [AM radio station call letters]
WICZ........ While in Control Zone [Aviation] (FAAC)
WICZ-TV ... Binghamton, NY [Television station call letters]
WID .... University of Wisconsin, Madison Library School, Madison, WI
              [OCLC symbol] (OCLC)
WID .... Wean, Inc. [NYSE symbol] (SPSG)
WID .... Weekly Intelligence Digest [Military] (CINC)
WID .... West India Dock
WID .... Widow [or Widower]
WID .... Width
WID .... Wind River Resources [Vancouver Stock Exchange symbol]
WID .... Window Identifier [Data processing]
WID .... Women in Development [Peace Corps]
WID .... World Institute on Disability (EA)
WIDA........ Carolina, PR [AM radio station call letters]
WIDA-FM ... Carolina, PR [FM radio station call letters]
WIDD .... Elizabethton, TN [AM radio station call letters]
WIDE .... Biddeford, ME [AM radio station call letters]
WIDE .... Wide-Angle Infinity Display Equipment
WIDE .... Widergren Communications [NASDAQ symbol] (NQ)
WIDE .... Wiring Integration Design (IEEE)
WIDETRACK ... Wideband Transmission Relay Acoustic
              Communications (MCD)
WIDF........ Women's International Democratic Federation [See also FDIF]
              [Berlin, German Democratic Republic] (EAIO)
WIDG .... St. Ignace, MI [AM radio station call letters]
Wi Di .... Wirtschaftsdienst [A publication]
WIDI .... Women in Design International [Later, DI] (EA)
WIDJET.... Waterloo Interactive Direct Job Entry Terminal System [IBM
              Corp.]
WIDL .... Caro, MI [FM radio station call letters]
WIDO........ Eutaw, AL [FM radio station call letters]
WIDOWAC ... Wing Design Optimization with Aerolastic Constraints
              [Computer program]
WIDR........ Kalamazoo, MI [FM radio station call letters]
WIDS........ Russell Springs, KY [AM radio station call letters]
WIDS........ Waterborne Intrusion Detection System (MCD)
WIDU........ Fayetteville, NC [AM radio station call letters]
WIDU........ Wireless Intelligence and Development Unit [British
              military] (DMA)
WIE .... University of Wisconsin-Superior, Jim Dan Hill Library,
              Superior, WI [OCLC symbol] (OCLC)
WIE .... With Immediate Effect (FAAC)
WIE .... Women in Engineering Centre (EAIO)
WIE .... Women in Entertainment [British]
WIE .... Women's Information Exchange (EA)
WIEB/WINB ... Western Interstate Energy Board/WINB [Western Interstate
              Nuclear Board] (EA)
WIEC........ Ponce, PR [Television station call letters]
WIEC........ World Institute of Ecology and Cancer [See also IMEC] (EAIO)
Wiederbeleb Organersatz Intensivmed ... Wiederbelebung. Organersatz.
              Intensivmedizin [A publication]
Wiederg G ... Gesetz zur Regelung der Wiedergutmachung
              Nationalsozialistischen Unrechts fuer Angehoerige des
              Oeffentlichen Dienstes [A publication]
Wiederherstellungschir Traumatol ... Wiederherstellungschirurgie und
              Traumatologie [A publication]
WIEL........ Elizabethtown, KY [AM radio station call letters]
Wien Arch Innere Med ... Wiener Archiv fuer Innere Medizin [A publication]
Wien Arch Psychol Psychiat Neurol ... Wiener Archiv fuer Psychologie,
              Psychiatrie, und Neurologie [A publication]
Wien Beitr ... Wiener Beitraege zur Englischen Philologie [A publication]
Wien Beitr Chir ... Wiener Beitraege zur Chirurgie [A publication]
Wien Beitr Gesch Med ... Wiener Beitraege zur Geschichte der Medizin [A
              publication]
Wien Chem Ztg ... Wiener Chemiker Zeitung [A publication]
Wien Entom Monatschr ... Wiener Entomologische Monatsschrift [A
              publication]
Wien Ent Rd ... Wiener Entomologische Rundschau [A publication]
Wiener Ethnohist Bl ... Wiener Ethnohistorische Blaetter [A publication]
Wiener Voelkerk Mitt ... Wiener Voelkerkundliche Mitteilungen [A
              publication]

Wiener Z Kunde Sud ... Wiener Zeitschrift fuer die Kunde Suedasiens und Archiv fuer Indische Philosophie [*Vienna*] [*A publication*]
Wien Geschichtsbl ... Wiener Geschichtsblaetter [*A publication*]
Wien Jahrb Kunstgesch ... Wiener Jahrbuch fuer Kunstgeschichte [*A publication*]
Wien Klin W ... Wiener Klinische Wochenschrift [*A publication*]
Wien Klin Wochenschr ... Wiener Klinische Wochenschrift [*A publication*]
Wien Klin Wochenschr Suppl ... Wiener Klinische Wochenschrift. Supplementum [*A publication*]
Wien Klin Ws ... Wiener Klinische Wochenschrift [*A publication*]
Wien Landwirtsch Ztg ... Wiener Landwirtschaftliche Zeitung [*A publication*]
Wien Med Presse ... Wiener Medizinische Presse [*A publication*]
Wien Med Wochenschr ... Wiener Medizinische Wochenschrift [*A publication*]
Wien Med Wochenschr (Beih) ... Wiener Medizinische Wochenschrift (Beihefte) [*A publication*]
Wien Med Wochenschr Suppl ... Wiener Medizinische Wochenschrift. Supplementum [*A publication*]
Wien Med Ws ... Wiener Medizinische Wochenschrift [*A publication*]
Wien Med Wschr ... Wiener Medizinische Wochenschrift [*A publication*]
Wien Mitt Photogr Inhalts ... Wiener Mitteilungen Photographischen Inhalts [*A publication*]
Wien Mitt Wasser Abwasser Gewaesser ... Wiener Mitteilungen. Wasser, Abwaesser, Gewaesser [*A publication*]
Wien Naturh Mus Annalen ... Wien Naturhistorischer Museum. Annalen [*A publication*]
Wien Pharm Wochenschr ... Wiener Pharmazeutische Wochenschrift [*A publication*]
Wien Praehist Z ... Wiener Praehistorische Zeitschrift [*Austria*] [*A publication*]
Wien Stud .. Wiener Studien [*A publication*] (OCD)
Wien Stud Z Klass Philol ... Wiener Studien. Zeitschrift fuer Klassische Philologie [*A publication*]
Wien Tieraerztl Monatsschr ... Wiener Tieraerztliche Monatsschrift [*A publication*]
Wien Tieraerztl Mschr ... Wiener Tieraerztliche Monatsschrift [*A publication*]
Wien Voelkerk Mitt ... Wiener Voelkerkundliche Mitteilungen [*A publication*]
Wien Z Inn Med Ihre Grenzgeb ... Wiener Zeitschrift fuer Innere Medizin und Ihre Grenzgebiete [*A publication*]
Wien Z Kunde Morgenlandes ... Wiener Zeitschrift fuer die Kunde des Morgenlandes [*A publication*]
Wien Z Kunde Sued Ostasiens ... Wiener Zeitschrift fuer die Kunde Sued- und Ostasiens und Archiv fuer Indische Philosophie [*A publication*]
Wien Z Nervenheilk Grenzgeb ... Wiener Zeitschrift fuer Nervenheilkunde und Deren Grenzgebiete [*Austria*] [*A publication*]
Wien Zs Inn Med ... Wiener Zeitschrift fuer Innere Medizin und Ihre Grenzgebiete [*A publication*]
Wien Zt ...... Wiener Zeitung [*A publication*]
WIERD ...... Wind Energy Report [*A publication*]
WIEU .... Weekly Intelligence Estimate Update [*Vietnam*]
WIEZ .... Lewistown, PA [*AM radio station call letters*]
WIF .... Mid-Wisconsin Federated Library System, Fond Du Lac, WI [*OCLC symbol*] (OCLC)
WIF .... Water Immersion Facility [*NASA*] (KSC)
WIF .... Weapons Integration Facility (MCD)
WIF .... West India Fruit & Steamship [*AAR code*]
WIF .... West Indies Federation
WIF .... Wildfire Resources Ltd. [*Vancouver Stock Exchange symbol*]
WiF .... William Faulkner [*A publication*]
WiF .... William Faulkner. Materials, Studies, and Criticism [*A publication*]
WIF .... Wilt-Inducing Factor [*Plant pathology*]
WIF .... Women in Film (EA)
WIF .... Worlds of If [*A publication*]
WIF .... Worldview International Foundation (EAIO)
WIFA .... Washington Institute of Foreign Affairs (EA)
WIFC .... Wausau, WI [*FM radio station call letters*]
WIFE .... Connersville, IN [*AM radio station call letters*]
WIFE .... Women Involved in Farm Economics (EA)
WIFE .... Women's Independent Film Exchange (EA)
WIFF .... Auburn, IN [*AM radio station call letters*]
WIFF-FM ... Auburn, IN [*FM radio station call letters*]
WIFM-FM ... Elkin, NC [*FM radio station call letters*]
WIFO .... Wildfowl [*A publication*]
WIFO-FM ... Jesup, GA [*FM radio station call letters*]
WIFP .... Women's Institute for Freedom of the Press (EA)
WIFR-TV .. Freeport, IL [*Television station call letters*]
WIFU .... Western Interprovincial Football Union [*Canada*]
WIFX .... Jenkins, KY [*AM radio station call letters*]
WIFX-FM ... Jenkins, KY [*FM radio station call letters*]
WIG .... Washington Information Group, Ltd. [*Research center*] (TSSD)
WIG .... West-Indische Gids [*A publication*]
WIG .... Wiggins Airways [*Norwood, MA*] [*FAA designator*] (FAAC)
Wig. .... Wigram on Loills [*A publication*] (DLA)
WIG .... Wing in Ground
WIG .... Wisconsin State Library, Processing Center, Madison, WI [*OCLC symbol*] (OCLC)
WIG .... Wolfram Inert Gas (MCD)

Wig Disc .... Wigram on Discovery [*2nd ed.*] [*1840*] [*A publication*] (DLA)
WIGE .... Wax-Impregnated Graphite Electrode
Wig Ev .... Wigram on Extrinsic Evidence [*A publication*] (DLA)
WIGG .... Wiggins, MS [*AM radio station call letters*]
Wight .... Wightwick's English Exchequer Reports [*145 English Reprint*] [*A publication*] (DLA)
Wight El Cas ... Wight's Scottish Election Cases [*1784-96*] [*A publication*] (DLA)
Wightw ...... Wightwick's English Exchequer Reports [*145 English Reprint*] [*A publication*] (DLA)
Wightw (Eng) ... Wightwick's English Exchequer Reports [*145 English Reprint*] [*A publication*] (DLA)
WIGL .... Orangeburg, SC [*FM radio station call letters*]
WIGM .... Medford, WI [*AM radio station call letters*]
Wigm Ev .... Wigmore on Evidence [*A publication*] (DLA)
WIGM-FM ... Medford, WI [*FM radio station call letters*]
WIGO .... Atlanta, GA [*AM radio station call letters*]
WIGO .... What Is Going On? [*Humorous definition of science*]
WIGORN .. Wigorniensis [*Signature of Bishop of Worcester*] [*British*] (ROG)
WIGS .... Gouverneur, NY [*AM radio station call letters*]
Wig Wills ... Wigmore on Wills [*A publication*] (DLA)
WIGY .... Bath, ME [*FM radio station call letters*]
WIH .... State Historical Society of Wisconsin, Madison, WI [*OCLC symbol*] (OCLC)
WIH .... Work in Hand (ILCA)
WIHN .... Normal, IL [*FM radio station call letters*]
WIHP .... Journal. Wisconsin Association for Health, Physical Education, and Recreation [*A publication*]
WIHS .... Middletown, CT [*FM radio station call letters*]
WIHS .... Western Institute for Health Studies (EA)
WII .... Beloit College Library, Beloit, WI [*OCLC symbol*] (OCLC)
WII .... Weatherford International, Incorporated [*AMEX symbol*] (SPSG)
WIIA .... Tangerang/Budiarto [*Indonesia*] [*ICAO location identifier*] (ICLI)
WIIAD .... Winrock International Institute for Agricultural Development (EA)
WIIB .... Bandung/Husein Sastranegara [*Indonesia*] [*ICAO location identifier*] (ICLI)
WIIB .... Bloomington, IN [*Television station call letters*]
WIIC .... Cirebon/Panggung [*Indonesia*] [*ICAO location identifier*] (ICLI)
WIID .... Jakarta/Kemayoran [*Indonesia*] [*ICAO location identifier*] (ICLI)
WIIG .... Jakarta/Pulau Panjang [*Indonesia*] [*ICAO location identifier*] (ICLI)
WIIH .... Jakarta/Halim Perdanakusuma [*Indonesia*] [*ICAO location identifier*] (ICLI)
WIII .... Cincinnati, OH [*Television station call letters*]
WIII .... Jakarta/Cengkareng [*Indonesia*] [*ICAO location identifier*] (ICLI)
WIIJ .... Yogyakarta/Adi Sucipto [*Indonesia*] [*ICAO location identifier*] (ICLI)
WIIK .... Kalijati [*Indonesia*] [*ICAO location identifier*] (ICLI)
WIIL .... Cilacap/Tunggul Wulung [*Indonesia*] [*ICAO location identifier*] (ICLI)
WIIM-TV ... Iron Mountain, MI [*Television station call letters*]
WIIP .... Jakarta/Pondok Cabe [*Indonesia*] [*ICAO location identifier*] (ICLI)
WIIP .... Waters Intelligent Information Processor
WIIQ .... Demopolis, AL [*Television station call letters*]
WIIR .... Pelabuhan Ratu [*Indonesia*] [*ICAO location identifier*] (ICLI)
WIIS .... Key West, FL [*FM radio station call letters*]
WIIS .... Semarang/Achmad Yani [*Indonesia*] [*ICAO location identifier*] (ICLI)
WIIS .... Wang Integrated Image System
WIIT .... Tanjung Karang/Branti [*Indonesia*] [*ICAO location identifier*] (ICLI)
WIIU .... Worker's International Industrial Union
WIIW .... Wiener Institut fuer Internationale Wirtschaftsvergleiche [*Vienna Institute for Comparative Economic Studies*] [*Information service or system*] (IID)
WIIX .... Jakarta [*Indonesia*] [*ICAO location identifier*] (ICLI)
WIIZ .... Jakarta [*Indonesia*] [*ICAO location identifier*] (ICLI)
WIJ .... Arrowhead Library System, Janesville Public Library, Janesville, WI [*OCLC symbol*] (OCLC)
WIJ .... Warburg Institute. Journal [*A publication*]
WIJK .... Evergreen, AL [*AM radio station call letters*]
WIJK-FM ... Evergreen, AL [*FM radio station call letters*]
Wijsgerig Perspect Maatsch Wet ... Wijsgerig Perspectief op Maatschappij en Wetenschap [*A publication*]
Wijsig Perspect ... Wijsgerig Perspectief op Maatschappij en Wetenschap [*A publication*]
WIJY .... Hilton Head Island, SC [*FM radio station call letters*]
WIK .... Deutsches Institut fuer Wirtschaftsforschung. Wochenbericht [*A publication*]
WIK .... Kenosha Public Library, Kenosha, WI [*OCLC symbol*] (OCLC)
WIK .... Wien-Kobenzl [*Austria*] [*Geomagnetic observatory code*]
WIKB .... Batam/Hang Nadim [*Indonesia*] [*ICAO location identifier*] (ICLI)

WIKB......... Iron River, MI [*AM radio station call letters*]
WIKB-FM ... Iron River, MI [*FM radio station call letters*]
WIKC........ Bogalusa, LA [*AM radio station call letters*]
WIKD .... Tanjung Pandan/Bulu Tumbang [*Indonesia*] [*ICAO location identifier*] (ICLI)
WIKE......... Newport, VT [*AM radio station call letters*]
WIKI......... Carrollton, KY [*FM radio station call letters*]
WIKK .... Pangkal Pinang [*Indonesia*] [*ICAO location identifier*] (ICLI)
WIKN .... Tanjung Pinang/Kijang [*Indonesia*] [*ICAO location identifier*] (ICLI)
Wiko .... Wirtschaftskonjunktur [*A publication*]
WIKQ........ Greeneville, TN [*FM radio station call letters*]
WIKS........ New Bern, NC [*FM radio station call letters*]
WIKS........ Singkep/Dabo [*Indonesia*] [*ICAO location identifier*] (ICLI)
WIKU .... Pikeville, TN [*FM radio station call letters*]
WIKX .... Leesburg, GA [*FM radio station call letters*]
WIKY .... Evansville, IN [*FM radio station call letters*]
WIKY-FM .. Evansville, IN [*FM radio station call letters*]
WIKZ......... Chambersburg, PA [*FM radio station call letters*]
WIL .... Lakeland College, Sheboygan, WI [*OCLC symbol*] (OCLC)
WIL .... Nairobi-Wilson [*Kenya*] [*Airport symbol*] (OAG)
WIL .... St. Louis, MO [*AM radio station call letters*]
WIL .... Ward Indicator Light
WIL .... White Indicating Light
WIL .... Wilco Mining Co. Ltd. [*Toronto Stock Exchange symbol*]
WIL .... Wilkes [*Antarctica*] [*Seismograph station code, US Geological Survey*] [*Closed*] (SEIS)
WIL .... Wirtschaftliche Lage in der Bundesrepublik Deutschland [*A publication*]
WIL .... Women in Leadership [*Project*]
WILA........ Danville, VA [*AM radio station call letters*]
WI Law Rev ... Wisconsin Law Review [*A publication*]
Wilberforce ... Wilberforce on Statute Law [*A publication*] (DLA)
Wilb Stat.... Wilberforce on Construction and Operation of Statutes [*1881*] [*A publication*] (DLA)
WILC......... Laurel, MD [*AM radio station call letters*]
WILC........ West Central Illinois Library Cooperative [*Library network*]
Wilc Cond .. Wilcox's Condensed Ohio Reports (Reprint) [*1-7 Ohio*] [*A publication*] (DLA)
Wilc Cond Rep ... Wilcox's Condensed Ohio Reports (Reprint) [*1-7 Ohio*] [*A publication*] (DLA)
Wilc Mun Corp ... Wilcox on Municipal Corporations [*Ohio*] [*A publication*] (DLA)
WILCO...... Western Interstate Library Coordinating Organization
WILCO...... Will Comply [*Used after "Roger"*] [*Radio term*]
Wilcox....... Wilcox's Lackawanna Reports [*Pennsylvania*] [*A publication*] (DLA)
Wilcox....... Wilcox's Reports [*10 Ohio*] [*A publication*] (DLA)
Wilcox Cond ... Wilcox's Condensed Ohio Reports [*A publication*] (DLA)
WILD .... Boston, MA [*AM radio station call letters*]
WILD .... What I Like to Do [*Psychological testing*]
WILD .... Wildey, Inc. [*NASDAQ symbol*] (NQ)
WILD .... Women's Independent Label Distribution Network (EA)
Wild Barfield Heat-Treat J ... Wild Barfield Heat-Treatment Journal [*A publication*]
Wild Barfield J ... Wild Barfield Journal [*A publication*]
Wild Camp ... Wilderness Camping [*A publication*]
Wild Cat..... Wild Cat Monthly [*A publication*] (APTA)
Wilde Conv ... Wilde's Supplement to Barton's Conveyancing [*A publication*] (DLA)
Wildenowia Beih ... Wildenowia Beiheft [*A publication*]
Wilde Sup .. Wilde's Supplement to Barton's Conveyancing [*A publication*] (DLA)
Wildfire Stat US Dep Agric For Serv ... Wildfire Statistics. United States Department of Agriculture. Forest Service [*A publication*]
Wildl A ...... Wildlife in Australia [*A publication*]
Wildl Aust ... Wildlife in Australia [*A publication*] (APTA)
Wildl Dis ... Wildlife Diseases [*A publication*]
Wildl Dis Assoc Bull ... Wildlife Disease Association. Bulletin [*A publication*]
Wildlife .... Wildlife in Australia [*A publication*] (APTA)
Wildlife A .. Wildlife in Australia [*A publication*]
Wildlife Aust ... Wildlife in Australia [*A publication*] (APTA)
Wildlife R .. Wildlife Review [*A publication*]
Wild Life Rev ... Wild Life Review [*A publication*]
Wildl Manage Bull (Ottawa) Ser 1 ... Wildlife Management Bulletin (Ottawa). Series 1 [*A publication*]
Wildl Manage Bull (Ottawa) Ser 2 ... Wildlife Management Bulletin (Ottawa). Series 2 [*A publication*]
Wildl Monogr ... Wildlife Monographs [*A publication*]
Wildl Res Q ... Wildlife Research Quarterly [*A publication*]
Wildl Rev ... Wildlife Review [*A publication*]
Wildl Rev NZ Wildl Serv ... Wildlife Review. New Zealand Wildlife Service [*A publication*]
Wildl Soc Bull ... Wildlife Society. Bulletin [*A publication*]
Wildl Wildlands Inst Monogr ... Wildlife-Wildlands Institute. Monograph [*A publication*]
Wildm Int L ... Wildman's International Law [*A publication*] (ILCA)
Wildm Int Law ... Wildman's International Law [*A publication*] (DLA)
Wildm Search ... Wildman. Search, Capture, and Prize [*A publication*] (ILCA)
WILE......... Cambridge, OH [*AM radio station call letters*]

Wiley Lib Newsl ... Wiley-Interscience Librarian's Newsletter [*A publication*]
Wiley Ser Curr Top Reprod Endocrinol ... Wiley Series on Current Topics in Reproductive Endocrinology [*A publication*]
WILF .... Wilson Foods Corp. [*NASDAQ symbol*] (NQ)
WIL-FM.... St. Louis, MO [*FM radio station call letters*]
Wilhelm-Pieck Univ Rostock Wiss Z Math Naturwiss Reihe ... Wilhelm-Pieck-Universitaet Rostock. Wissenschaftliche Zeitschrift. Mathematisch-Naturwissenschaftliche Reihe [*A publication*]
Wilhelm Roux' Arch ... Wilhelm Roux' Archiv fuer Entwicklungsmechanik der Organismen [*Later, Roux' Archives of Developmental Biology*] [*A publication*]
Wilhelm Roux' Arch Dev Biol ... Wilhelm Roux' Archives of Developmental Biology [*A publication*]
Wilhelm Roux' Arch Entwicklungsmech Org ... Wilhelm Roux' Archiv fuer Entwicklungsmechanik der Organismen [*Later, Roux' Archives of Developmental Biology*] [*A publication*]
Wilhelm Roux Arch EntwMech Org ... Wilhelm Roux' Archiv fuer Entwicklungsmechanik der Organismen [*A publication*]
WILI......... Willimantic, CT [*AM radio station call letters*]
WILI-FM... Willimantic, CT [*FM radio station call letters*]
WILJ........ West Indian Law Journal [*Jamaica*] [*A publication*] (DLA)
WILK........ Wilkes-Barre, PA [*AM radio station call letters*]
Wilk .... Wilkinson, Owen, Paterson, and Murray's New South Wales Reports [*1862-65*] [*A publication*] (DLA)
Wilk .... Wilkinson. Texas Court of Appeals and Civil Appeals [*A publication*] (DLA)
Wilk Funds ... Wilkinson on Public Funds [*1839*] [*A publication*] (DLA)
Wilk Leg Ang Sax ... Wilkins' Leges Anglo-Saxonicae Ecclesiasticae et Civiles [*A publication*] (DLA)
Wilk Lim.... Wilkinson. Limitation of Actions [*A publication*] (ILCA)
Wilk & Mur ... Wilkinson, Owen, Paterson, and Murray's New South Wales Reports [*1862-65*] [*A publication*] (DLA)
Wilk & Ow ... Wilkinson, Owen, Paterson, and Murray's New South Wales Reports [*1862-65*] [*A publication*] (DLA)
Wilk & Pat ... Wilkinson, Owen, Paterson, and Murray's New South Wales Reports [*1862-65*] [*A publication*] (DLA)
Wilk P & M ... Wilkinson, Paterson, and Murray's New South Wales Reports [*1862-65*] [*A publication*] (DLA)
Wilk Prec... Wilkinson on Precedents in Conveyancing [*4th ed.*] [*1890*] [*A publication*] (DLA)
Wilk Repl... Wilkinson on Replevin [*1825*] [*A publication*] (DLA)
Wilk Sh..... Wilkinson's Office of Sheriff [*A publication*] (DLA)
Wilk Ship... Wilkinson on Shipping [*1843*] [*A publication*] (DLA)
WILL........ Urbana, IL [*AM radio station call letters*]
WILL........ Wiley [*John*] & Sons, Inc. [*NASDAQ symbol*] (NQ)
Will .... Willes' English Common Pleas Reports [*125 English Reprint*] [*A publication*] (DLA)
Will .... William (King of England) (DLA)
Will .... Williams' Massachusetts Reports [*1 Massachusetts*] [*1804-05*] [*A publication*] (DLA)
Will .... Williams' Vermont Reports [*27-29 Vermont*] [*A publication*] (DLA)
Will .... Willson's Reports [*29-30 Texas Appeals*] [*1, 2, Texas Civil Appeals*] [*A publication*] (DLA)
WILL........ Workshop In Library Leadership [*Canada*]
WILL........ Workshop Institute for Living-Learning (EA)
Will Abr..... Williams' Abridgment of Cases [*1798-1803*] [*A publication*] (DLA)
Willamette L J ... Willamette Law Journal [*A publication*]
Willamette L Rev ... Willamette Law Review [*A publication*]
Will Ann Reg ... Williams' Annual Register [*New York*] [*A publication*] (DLA)
Will Auct.... Williams' Auctions [*5th ed.*] [*1829*] [*A publication*] (DLA)
Will Bankt ... Williams' Law and Practice of Bankruptcy [*19th ed.*] [*1977*] [*A publication*] (DLA)
Will-Bund St Tr ... Willis-Bund's Cases from State Trials [*A publication*] (DLA)
Willc Const ... Willcock's The Office of Constable [*A publication*] (DLA)
Willc Med Pr ... Willcock's Medical Profession [*1830*] [*A publication*] (DLA)
Willc Mun Corp ... Willcock's Municipal Corporation [*A publication*] (ILCA)
Willcock Mun Corp ... Willcock's Municipal Corporation [*A publication*] (DLA)
Will Com.... Williams on Rights of Common [*A publication*] (DLA)
Will Con Rep ... Texas Civil Cases [*A publication*] (DLA)
Will Cr L.... Willan's Criminal Law of Canada [*A publication*] (DLA)
Willdenowia Beih ... Willdenowia Beiheft [*A publication*]
Will Eq Jur ... Willard's Equity Jurisprudence [*A publication*] (DLA)
Will Eq Pl.. Willis on Equity Pleading [*1820*] [*A publication*] (DLA)
Willes........ Willes' English Common Pleas Reports [*125 English Reprint*] [*A publication*] (DLA)
Willes (Eng) ... Willes' English Common Pleas Reports [*125 English Reprint*] [*A publication*] (DLA)
Will Ex...... Williams on Executors [*15th ed.*] [*1970*] [*A publication*] (DLA)
WILL-FM ... Urbana, IL [*FM radio station call letters*]·
William Car ... William Carlos Williams Review [*A publication*]
William L Hutcheson Mem For Bull ... William L. Hutcheson Memorial Forest. Bulletin [*A publication*]
William and Mary Bus R ... William and Mary Business Review [*A publication*]
William and Mary Law R ... William and Mary Law Review [*A publication*]

William & Mary L Rev ... William and Mary Law Review [*A publication*]
William Mary Q ... William and Mary College Quarterly [*A publication*]
William Mitchell L Rev ... William Mitchell Law Review [*A publication*]
William M Q ... William and Mary Quarterly [*A publication*]
Williams .... Peere-Williams' English Chancery Reports [*A publication*] (DLA)
Williams .... Williams' Reports [*10-12 Utah*] [*A publication*] (DLA)
Williams .... Williams' Reports [*1 Massachusetts*] [*A publication*] (DLA)
Williams .... Williams' Vermont Reports [*27-29 Vermont*] [*A publication*] (DLA)
Williams & B Adm Jur ... Williams and Bruce's Admiralty Practice [*3 eds.*] [*1869-1902*] [*A publication*] (DLA)
Williams B Pr ... Williams' Bankruptcy Practice [*17 eds.*] [*1870-1958*] [*A publication*] (DLA)
Williams & Bruce Ad Pr ... Williams and Bruce's Admiralty Practice [*3 eds.*] [*1869-1902*] [*A publication*] (DLA)
Williams Common ... Williams on Rights of Common [*A publication*] (DLA)
Williams Ex'rs ... Williams on Executors [*A publication*] (DLA)
Williams Ex'rs R & T Ed ... Williams on Executors, Randolph and Talcott Edition [*A publication*] (DLA)
Williams P ... Peere-Williams' English Chancery Reports [*1695-1736*] [*A publication*] (DLA)
Williams Pers Prop ... Williams on Personal Property [*A publication*] (DLA)
Williams Real Prop ... Williams on Real Property [*A publication*] (DLA)
Williams Saund ... Williams' Notes to Saunders' Reports [*A publication*] (DLA)
Williams Seis ... Williams on Seisin [*A publication*] (DLA)
William W Story's Rept ... William W. Story's United States Circuit Court Reports [*A publication*] (DLA)
Willis Eq .... Willis on Equity Pleading [*1820*] [*A publication*] (DLA)
Willis Int .... Willis on Interrogatories [*A publication*] (DLA)
Williston ... Williston on Contracts [*A publication*] (DLA)
Williston ... Williston on Sales [*A publication*] (DLA)
Williston Basin Oil Rev ... Williston Basin Oil Review [*A publication*]
Willis Trust ... Willis on Trustees [*A publication*] (DLA)
Will Just .... Williams' Justice [*A publication*] (DLA)
Will LD ..... Williams' Law Dictionary [*A publication*] (DLA)
Will LJ ...... Willamette Law Journal [*A publication*]
Will LR ...... Willamette Law Review [*A publication*]
Will Mass .. Williams' Reports [*1 Massachusetts*] [*A publication*] (DLA)
Will Mass Cit ... Williams' Massachusetts Citations [*A publication*] (DLA)
Willm W & D ... Willmore, Wollaston, and Davison's English Queen's Bench Reports [*1837*] [*A publication*] (DLA)
Willm W & H ... Willmore, Wollaston, and Hodges' English Queen's Bench Reports [*1838-39*] [*A publication*] (DLA)
Will P .... Peere-Williams' English Chancery Reports [*A publication*] (DLA)
Will Per Pr ... [*J.*] Williams on Personal Property [*18th ed.*] [*1926*] [*A publication*] (DLA)
Will Pet Ch ... Williams' Petitions in Chancery [*1880*] [*A publication*] (DLA)
Will Real Ass ... Williams' Real Assets [*1861*] [*A publication*] (DLA)
Will Real Est ... Willard on Real Estate and Conveyancing [*A publication*] (DLA)
Will Real Pr ... Williams on Real Property [*A publication*] (DLA)
Will Saund ... Williams' Notes to Saunders' Reports [*A publication*] (DLA)
Wills Circ Ev ... Wills on Circumstantial Evidence [*A publication*] (DLA)
Wills Cir Ev ... Wills on Circumstantial Evidence [*A publication*] (DLA)
Will Seis .... Williams on Seisin of the Freehold [*1878*] [*A publication*] (DLA)
Wills Est Tr ... Wills, Estates, Trusts [*Prentice-Hall, Inc.*] [*A publication*] (DLA)
Wills Est & Tr (P-H) ... Wills, Estates, and Trusts (Prentice-Hall, Inc.) [*A publication*] (DLA)
Wills Est & Tr Serv P-H ... Wills, Estates, and Trust Service. Prentice-Hall [*A publication*] (DLA)
Will Sett ..... Williams on the Settlement of Real Estates [*A publication*] (DLA)
Willson .... Willson's Reports, Civil Cases [*29-30 Texas Appeals*] [*1, 2 Texas Court of Appeals*] [*A publication*] (DLA)
Willson Civ Cas Ct App ... White and Willson's Civil Cases, Texas Court of Appeals [*A publication*] (DLA)
Willson's CC ... Texas Civil Cases [*A publication*] (DLA)
Willson Tex Cr Law ... Willson's Revised Penal Code, Code of Criminal Procedure, and Penal Laws of Texas [*A publication*] (DLA)
Will St L .... Williams on the Study of the Law [*A publication*] (DLA)
WILL-TV .. Urbana, IL [*Television station call letters*]
Will VT ...... Williams' Vermont Reports [*27-29 Vermont*] [*A publication*] (DLA)
Will Woll & D ... Willmore, Wollaston, and Davison's English Queen's Bench Reports [*1837*] [*A publication*] (DLA)
Will Woll & Dav ... Willmore, Wollaston, and Davison's English Queen's Bench Reports [*1837*] [*A publication*] (DLA)
Will Woll & H ... Willmore, Wollaston, and Hodges' English Queen's Bench Reports [*1838-39*] [*A publication*] (DLA)
Will Woll & Hodg ... Willmore, Wollaston, and Hodges' English Queen's Bench Reports [*1838-39*] [*A publication*] (DLA)
WILM .... Wildlife Monographs [*A publication*]
WILM .... Wilmington, DE [*AM radio station call letters*]
WILM .... Wilmington Trust Co. [*NASDAQ symbol*] (NQ)

Wilm .... Wilmot's Notes and Opinions, King's Bench [*97 English Reprint*] [*A publication*] (DLA)
Wilm Burg ... Wilmot's Digest of the Law of Burglary [*A publication*] (DLA)
Wilm Judg ... Wilmot's Notes and Opinions, King's Bench [*97 English Reprint*] [*A publication*] (DLA)
Wilm Mort ... Wilmot on Mortgages [*A publication*] (DLA)
Wilm Op .... Wilmot's Notes and Opinions, King's Bench [*97 English Reprint*] [*A publication*] (DLA)
Wilmot's Notes ... Wilmot's Notes and Opinions, King's Bench [*97 English Reprint*] [*A publication*] (DLA)
Wilmot's Notes (Eng) ... Wilmot's Notes and Opinions, King's Bench [*97 English Reprint*] [*A publication*] (DLA)
Wilm W & D ... Willmore, Wollaston, and Davison's English Queen's Bench Reports [*A publication*] (DLA)
WILN .... Panama City, FL [*FM radio station call letters*]
WILN .... Wildlife News [*A publication*]
WILN .... Wilson [*H. J.*] Co. [*NASDAQ symbol*] (NQ)
WILO .... Frankfort, IN [*AM radio station call letters*]
WILPF .... Women's International League for Peace and Freedom [*See also LIFPL*] (EAIO)
WILPFNSW Branch Monthly Bulletin ... WILPF [*Women's International League for Peace and Freedom*]. New South Wales Branch. Monthly Bulletin [*A publication*] (APTA)
WILPF-US ... Women's International League for Peace and Freedom, US Section (EA)
WILQ .... Williamsport, PA [*FM radio station call letters*]
Wil Q .... Wilson Quarterly [*A publication*]
WI LR .... Wisconsin Law Review [*A publication*]
WILS .... Lansing, MI [*AM radio station call letters*]
WILS .... Western Illinois Library System [*Library network*]
Wils .... Wilson's English Chancery Reports [*37 English Reprint*] [*A publication*] (DLA)
Wils .... Wilson's English Common Pleas Reports, 3 [*95 English Reprint*] [*A publication*] (DLA)
Wils .... Wilson's English King's Bench Reports [*95 English Reprint*] [*1742-74*] [*A publication*] (DLA)
WILS .... Wisconsin Interlibrary Loan Service
Wils Arb .... Wilson on Arbitrations [*A publication*] (DLA)
Wils Ch ...... Wilson's English Chancery Reports [*37 English Reprint*] [*A publication*] (DLA)
Wils Ch (Eng) ... Wilson's English Chancery Reports [*37 English Reprint*] [*A publication*] (DLA)
Wils & Court ... Wilson and Courtenay's Scotch Appeal Cases [*A publication*] (DLA)
Wils CP ...... Wilson's English Common Pleas [*A publication*] (DLA)
Wils (Eng) ... Wilson's English Common Pleas Reports, 3 [*95 English Reprint*] [*A publication*] (DLA)
Wils Ent ..... Wilson's Entries and Pleading [*3 Lord Raymond's King's Bench and Common Pleas Reports*] [*England*] [*A publication*] (DLA)
Wils Ex ...... Wilson's English Exchequer Reports [*159 English Reprint*] [*1805-17*] [*A publication*] (DLA)
Wils Exch .. Wilson's English Exchequer Reports [*159 English Reprint*] [*A publication*] (DLA)
Wils Exch (Eng) ... Wilson's English Exchequer Reports [*159 English Reprint*] [*A publication*] (DLA)
Wils Fines ... Wilson on Fines and Recoveries [*A publication*] (DLA)
Wils Ind ..... Wilson's Indiana Superior Court Reports [*A publication*] (DLA)
Wils Ind Gloss ... Wilson's Glossary of Indian Terms [*A publication*] (DLA)
Wils Jud Acts ... Wilson on the Judicature Acts, Etc. [*A publication*] (DLA)
Wils KB ..... Sergeant Wilson's English King's Bench Reports [*1724-74*] [*A publication*] (DLA)
Wils Minn ... Wilson's Reports [*48-59 Minnesota*] [*A publication*] (DLA)
Wils Mod Eng Law ... Wilson's History of Modern English Law [*A publication*] (DLA)
Wilson .... Wilson Quarterly [*A publication*]
Wilson .... Wilson's English Chancery Reports [*37 English Reprint*] [*A publication*] (DLA)
Wilson .... Wilson's English King's Bench and Common Pleas Reports [*A publication*] (DLA)
Wilson .... Wilson's Exchequer in Equity Reports [*England*] [*A publication*] (DLA)
Wilson .... Wilson's Indiana Superior Court Reports [*A publication*] (DLA)
Wilson .... Wilson's Reports [*1-3 Oregon*] [*A publication*] (DLA)
Wilson .... Wilson's Reports [*48-59 Minnesota*] [*A publication*] (DLA)
Wilson B .... Wilson Bulletin [*A publication*]
Wilson Bull ... Wilson Bulletin [*A publication*]
Wilson Lib Bul ... Wilson Library Bulletin [*A publication*]
Wilson Lib Bull ... Wilson Library Bulletin [*A publication*]
Wilson Libr Bull ... Wilson Library Bulletin [*A publication*]
Wilson Q .... Wilson Quarterly [*A publication*]
Wilson & Shaw ... Wilson and Shaw's Scottish Appeal Cases [*1825-35*] [*A publication*] (DLA)
Wilson's R ... Wilson's Indiana Superior Court Reports [*A publication*] (DLA)
Wilson's Rev & Ann St ... Wilson's Revised and Annotated Statutes [*Oklahoma*] [*A publication*] (DLA)
Wilson Super Ct (Ind) ... Wilson's Indiana Superior Court Reports [*A publication*] (DLA)

Wils Oreg .. Wilson's Reports [*1-3 Oregon*] [*A publication*] (DLA)
Wils Parl L ... Wilson's Parliamentary Law [*A publication*] (DLA)
Wils PC...... Wilson's English Privy Council Reports [*A publication*] (DLA)
Wils & S... Wilson and Shaw's Scottish Appeal Cases [*1825-35*] [*A publication*] (DLA)
Wils & Sh .. Wilson and Shaw's Scottish Appeal Cases [*1825-35*] [*A publication*] (DLA)
Wils & S (Scot) ... Wilson and Shaw's Scottish Appeal Cases [*1825-35*] [*A publication*] (DLA)
Wils Super (Ind) ... Wilson's Indiana Superior Court Reports [*A publication*] (DLA)
Wils Uses... Wilson on Springing Uses [*A publication*] (DLA)
WILS/WLC ... Wisconsin Interlibrary Loan Service - Wisconsin Library Consortium [*Library network*]
Wilt A Nat Hist Mag ... Wiltshire Archaeological and Natural History Magazine [*A publication*]
WilTel....... Williams Telecommunications Co. [*Tulsa, OK*] [*Telecommunications service*] (TSSD)
WILTS ...... Wiltshire [*County in England*]
Wilts Beekprs Gaz ... Wiltshire Beekeepers' Gazette [*A publication*]
Wiltshire Archaeol Natur Hist Mag ... Wiltshire Archaeological and Natural History Magazine [*A publication*]
Wiltshire Arch Mag ... Wiltshire Archaeological Magazine [*Later, Wiltshire Archaeological and Natural History Magazine*] [*A publication*]
Wiltshire Arch Natur Hist Mag ... Wiltshire Archaeological and Natural History Magazine [*A publication*]
WILUCL.... Willamette University College of Law (DLA)
WILX-TV .. Onondaga, MI [*Television station call letters*]
WILY........ Centralia, IL [*AM radio station call letters*]
WIM .... Madison Public Library, Madison, WI [*OCLC symbol*] (OCLC)
WIM .... Waksman Institute of Microbiology [*Rutgers University*] [*Research center*] (RCD)
WIM .... Warm Ionized Medium [*Astrophysics*]
WIM .... Washington, Idaho & Montana Railway Co. [*AAR code*]
WIM .... Women in Management [*Chicago, IL*] (EA)
WIM .... Women in Mining National (EA)
WIMA ...... Labuhan Bilik/Ajamu [*Indonesia*] [*ICAO location identifier*] (ICLI)
WIMA ...... Lima, OH [*AM radio station call letters*]
WIMA ...... Women's International Motorcycle Association (EA)
WIMA ...... World International Medical Association (EA)
WIMA ...... Writing Instrument Manufacturers Association (EA)
WIMB ...... Gunung Sitoli/Binaka [*Indonesia*] [*ICAO location identifier*] (ICLI)
WIMB ...... Wimborne Minster [*Urban district in England*]
WIMC ...... Crawfordsville, IN [*FM radio station call letters*]
WIMC ...... Whom It May Concern
WIME ...... Padang Sidempuan/Aek Godang [*Indonesia*] [*ICAO location identifier*] (ICLI)
WIMEA..... Wiretap, Investigation Monitoring, and Eavesdrop Activities (MCD)
WIMG ...... Padang/Tabing [*Indonesia*] [*ICAO location identifier*] (ICLI)
WIMG ...... Trenton, NJ [*AM radio station call letters*]
WIMG ...... Women in Municipal Government (EA)
WIMI .... Ironwood, MI [*FM radio station call letters*]
WIMI .... Warburg Investment Management International
WIMI .... Warwick Insurance Managers, Inc. [*NASDAQ symbol*] (NQ)
WIMI .... Watercraft Intensively Managed Items (AABC)
WIMIS ..... Walk-In Management Information System [*Data processing*]
WIMK ...... Iron Mountain, MI [*FM radio station call letters*]
WIMK ...... Kisaran/Tanah Gambus [*Indonesia*] [*ICAO location identifier*] (ICLI)
WIML........ Kisaran/Aek Loba [*Indonesia*] [*ICAO location identifier*] (ICLI)
WIML........ Wrightsville, GA [*FM radio station call letters*]
WIMM ...... Medan/Polonia [*Indonesia*] [*ICAO location identifier*] (ICLI)
WIMM ...... Weapons Integrated Materiel Manager [*Military*]
WIMN ...... Women in Mining National (EA)
WIMO....... Winder, GA [*AM radio station call letters*]
WIMP....... Prapat/Sibisa [*Indonesia*] [*ICAO location identifier*] (ICLI)
WIMP....... WARF [*Wartime Replacement Factors*] Intermediate Materiel Processor [*Military*]
WIMP....... Weakly Interacting Massive [*or Integrated Magnetic*] Particle [*Astrophysics*]
WIMP....... Windows/Icons/Mouse/Pull-Down-Menus [*Data processing*] (BYTE)
WIMR .... Pematang Siantar/Gunung Pamela [*Indonesia*] [*ICAO location identifier*] (ICLI)
WIMS....... Sibolga/Pinang Sori [*Indonesia*] [*ICAO location identifier*] (ICLI)
WIMS....... Wartime Instruction Manual for Merchant Ships [*For deck officers of the United States Merchant Marine; popularly known as the "Convoy Bible"*] [*World War II*]
WIMS........ Waveguide Impedance Measuring Set
WIMS........ Worldwide Integrated Management of Subsistence
WIMSA..... Webster Institute for Mathematics, Science, and Arts [*Webster College*]
WIMT .... Lima, OH [*FM radio station call letters*]

WIMT .... Tebing Tingci/Pabatu [*Indonesia*] [*ICAO location identifier*] (ICLI)
WIMX ...... Harrisburg, PA [*FM radio station call letters*]
WIMZ ...... Knoxville, TN [*AM radio station call letters*]
WIMZ ...... Medan Sector [*Indonesia*] [*ICAO location identifier*] (ICLI)
WIMZ-FM ... Knoxville, TN [*FM radio station call letters*]
WIN.......... INELEC Library Project, Menomonie, WI [*OCLC symbol*] [*Inactive*] (OCLC)
WIN.......... Irwin, Australia [*Spaceflight Tracking and Data Network*] [*NASA*]
WIN.......... Water-Insoluble Nitrogen [*Analytical chemistry*]
WIN.......... Weapon Index Number [*Military*] (CAAL)
WIN.......... Weapons Interception [*Military electronics*]
WIN.......... Well Information Network [*Database*]
WIN.......... Western Information Network
WIN.......... Whip Inflation Now [*Slogan of President Gerald R. Ford's anti-inflation program, 1974*] [*Program discontinued March, 1975*]
WIN.......... White-Indian-Negro
Win .... Win Magazine [*A publication*]
Win .... Winch's English Common Pleas Reports [*124 English Reprint*] [*A publication*] (DLA)
WIN.......... Windhoek [*Namibia*] [*Seismograph station code, US Geological Survey*] (SEIS)
WIN.......... Window [*Technical drawings*]
WIN.......... Windsor Board of Education [*UTLAS symbol*]
Win .... Winer's Unreported Opinions, New York Supreme Court [*A publication*] (DLA)
WIN.......... Winn-Dixie Stores, Inc. [*NYSE symbol*] (SPSG)
Win .... Winston's North Carolina Reports [*1863-64*] [*A publication*] (DLA)
WIN.......... Winter
Win .... Winter [*A publication*]
WIN.......... Winthrop Laboratories [*Research code symbol*]
WIN.......... Winton [*Australia*] [*Airport symbol*] (OAG)
WIN.......... Wireless In-Building Network [*Motorola, Inc.*] [*Data processing*]
WIN.......... Wiswesser Line Notation [*Chemical structure*]
WIN.......... Women's International Network (EA)
WIN.......... Women's Investment Network [*Australia*]
WIN.......... Work Incentive Program [*Later, ETSC*] (EA)
WIN.......... Workshop in Nonviolence (EA)
WIN.......... World Information Network [*Information service or system*] (EISS)
WIN.......... WWMCCS [*Worldwide Military Command and Control System*] Intercomputer Network [*DoD*]
W/IN²........ Watts per Square Inch
WINA .... Charlottesville, VA [*AM radio station call letters*]
WINA .... Webb Institute of Naval Architecture [*Glen Cove, NY*]
WINA .... Witton Network Analyzer
WINB .... Western Interstate Nuclear Board (NRCH)
WINBA ...... World International Nail and Beauty Association (EA)
WINBAN .. Windward Islands' Banana Association
WINC .... Western Interstate Nuclear Compact [*Later, WIEB/WINB*]
WINC .... White Incumbent
WINC .... Winchester, VA [*AM radio station call letters*]
WINC .... Worldwide Integrated Communications [*Mohawk Data Sciences Corp.*] [*Parsippany, NJ*] [*Telecommunications*] (TSSD)
WINC-FM ... Winchester, VA [*FM radio station call letters*]
WINCH...... Winchcombe [*England*]
WINCH...... Winchester [*City in England*] (ROG)
Winch........ Winch's English Common Pleas Reports [*124 English Reprint*] [*A publication*] (DLA)
Winch (Eng) ... Winch's English Common Pleas Reports [*124 English Reprint*] [*A publication*] (DLA)
WIND........ Chicago, IL [*AM radio station call letters*]
WIND........ Weather Information Network and Display
WIND........ Windsor [*Municipal borough in England*]
WIND........ Windsor Life Insurance Co. of America [*NASDAQ symbol*] (NQ)
WIND........ Women in Distribution [*Commercial firm*]
WINDAV .. Wind Direction and Velocity Indicator [*Aviation*]
WINDEE... Wind Tunnel Data Encoding and Evaluation [*System*] [*Boeing Co.*]
Wind Energy Rep ... Wind Energy Report [*United States*] [*A publication*]
Wind Eng... Wind Engineering [*England*] [*A publication*]
Wind Engng ... Wind Engineering [*A publication*]
Wind En Rpt ... Wind Energy Report [*A publication*]
W Indian Dig ... West Indian Digest [*A publication*]
W Indian Med J ... West Indian Medical Journal [*A publication*]
W Indian World ... West Indian World [*A publication*]
WINDII..... Wind Imaging Interferometer
Wind Inst Melior Uzytkow Zielonych ... Windomosci Instytutu Melioracji i Uzytkow Zielonych [*A publication*]
W Ind Med J ... West Indian Medical Journal [*A publication*]
Wind Muz Ziemi ... Windomosci Muzeum Ziemi [*A publication*]
Wind O ... Windless Orchard [*A publication*]
Window Inds ... Window Industries [*A publication*]
Wind Power Dig ... Wind Power Digest [*A publication*]
WINDS...... Weather Information Network and Display System [*NASA*]

Windsat	Wind Satellite
Windsor	Windsor Magazine [*A publication*]
Windsor R ...	Windsor Report [*A publication*]
Windsor Yearb Access ...	Windsor Yearbook of Access to Justice [*A publication*]
Wind Technol J ...	Wind Technology Journal [*A publication*]
WINE	Brookfield, CT [*AM radio station call letters*]
WINE	Schagrins, Inc. [*NASDAQ symbol*] (NQ)
WINE	Warning and Indications in Europe (MCD)
WINE	Webb Institute of Naval Engineering
Wine Hdbk ...	Wine Marketing Handbook [*A publication*]
Win Ent......	Winch's Book of Entries [*A publication*] (DLA)
Win Eq	Winston's North Carolina Equity Reports [*A publication*] (DLA)
Wine Rev....	Wine Review [*A publication*]
Wine Vine ..	Wines and Vines Statistical Issue [*A publication*]
WINF	Winfrith [*England*]
WINF	Winnsboro, SC [*AM radio station call letters*]
Winfield Words & Phrases ...	Winfield's Adjudged Words and Phrases, with Notes [*A publication*] (DLA)
WING	Dayton, OH [*AM radio station call letters*]
Wing	Wing Newsletter [*A publication*]
Wing	Wingate's Maxims [*A publication*] (DLA)
WING	Wings West Airlines, Inc. [*Santa Monica, CA*] [*NASDAQ symbol*] (NQ)
Wing Max ...	Wingate's Maxims [*A publication*] (DLA)
Wings Afr ..	Wings over Africa [*A publication*]
WINI	Murphysboro, IL [*AM radio station call letters*]
WINJ.........	Pulaski, TN [*FM radio station call letters*]
WINK	Fort Myers, FL [*AM radio station call letters*]
WINK	Warning in Korea (MCD)
WINK	Winkleigh [*England*]
WINK-FM ...	Fort Myers, FL [*FM radio station call letters*]
WINKS......	Women in Numerous Kitchens [*World War II*]
WINK-TV ...	Fort Myers, FL [*Television station call letters*]
WINM.......	Angola, IN [*Television station call letters*]
WINN.......	Wedding Information Network, Inc. [*NASDAQ symbol*] (NQ)
Winnip Clin Q ...	Winnipeg Clinic. Quarterly [*A publication*]
WINNS	Winn Enterprises [*NASDAQ symbol*] (NQ)
WINP	Water Insoluble Nonstarchy Polysaccharide [*Food composition*]
WINQ.......	Winchendon, MA [*FM radio station call letters*]
WINR	Binghamton, NY [*AM radio station call letters*]
WINRA	Women in the National Rifle Association
WINS........	New York, NY [*AM radio station call letters*]
WINS........	Weapons and Integrated Navigation System (MCD)
WINS........	Wideband Information Network Services [*Data processing*]
WINS........	Winslow [*England*]
WINS........	Women in National Service [*Name given by Ladies' Home Journal to American housewives and their teen-age daughters, "the greatest reserve strength of America"*] [*World War II*]
WINS........	Women in Naval Service
WINS........	Women's Industrial and National Service Corps [*World War II*] [*British*]
WINSNAMS ...	Wind Indicating Systems for Navigation Aircraft in Missile Support
Winst	Winston's North Carolina Equity Reports [*A publication*] (DLA)
Winst	Winston's North Carolina Law Reports [*A publication*] (DLA)
WINST......	Winstree [*England*]
WINSTAN ...	Wings, Nonstraight-Taper Analysis (MCD)
Winst Eq	Winston's North Carolina Equity Reports [*A publication*] (DLA)
Winst Eq (NC) ...	Winston's North Carolina Equity Reports [*A publication*] (DLA)
Winst L (NC) ...	Winston's North Carolina Law Reports [*A publication*] (DLA)
WINT	Walker International Industries, Inc. [*NASDAQ symbol*] (NQ)
WINT	Winter (FAAC)
Wintertag...	Wintertagung [*A publication*]
Winter Tb ..	Winter's Naturwissenschaftliche Taschenbuecher [*A publication*]
Winterthur ...	Winterthur Portfolio [*A publication*]
Winterthur Jb ...	Winterthur Jahrbuch [*A publication*]
Winterthur Port ...	Winterthur Portfolio [*A publication*]
WINTEX...	Winter Exercise (MCD)
Winthr St M ...	Winthrop Studies on Major Modern Writers [*A publication*]
WINTON ..	[*Bishop of*] Winchester [*British*]
WINT-TV ...	Crossville, TN [*Television station call letters*]
WINU	Highland, IL [*AM radio station call letters*]
WINV	Inverness, FL [*AM radio station call letters*]
WINW.......	Canton, OH [*AM radio station call letters*]
WINX	Rockville, MD [*AM radio station call letters*]
WINY	Putnam, CT [*AM radio station call letters*]
WINZ	Miami, FL [*AM radio station call letters*]
WIO	Nashotah House, Nashotah, WI [*OCLC symbol*] (OCLC)
WIO	Wilcannia [*Australia*] [*Airport symbol*] (OAG)
WIO	Women's International ORT
WIOA	San Juan, PR [*FM radio station call letters*]
WIOB	Bengkayang [*Indonesia*] [*ICAO location identifier*] (ICLI)
WIOB	Mayaguez, PR [*FM radio station call letters*]
WIOC........	Ponce, PR [*FM radio station call letters*]
WIOD.......	Miami, FL [*AM radio station call letters*]
WIOF	Waterbury, CT [*FM radio station call letters*]
WIOG.......	Bay City, MI [*FM radio station call letters*]
WIOG.......	Nangapinoh [*Indonesia*] [*ICAO location identifier*] (ICLI)
WIOH.......	Paloh/Liku [*Indonesia*] [*ICAO location identifier*] (ICLI)
WIOI	New Boston, OH [*AM radio station call letters*]
WIOI	Singkawang II [*Indonesia*] [*ICAO location identifier*] (ICLI)
WIOI-FM ...	Brunswick, GA [*FM radio station call letters*]
WIOK	Falmouth, KY [*FM radio station call letters*]
WIOK	Ketapang/Rahadi Usman [*Indonesia*] [*ICAO location identifier*] (ICLI)
WION.......	Ionia, MI [*AM radio station call letters*]
WION.......	Natuna/Ransi [*Indonesia*] [*ICAO location identifier*] (ICLI)
WIOO........	Carlisle, PA [*AM radio station call letters*]
WIOO.......	Pontianak/Supadio [*Indonesia*] [*ICAO location identifier*] (ICLI)
WIOP	Putusibau/Pangsuma [*Indonesia*] [*ICAO location identifier*] (ICLI)
WIOQ	Philadelphia, PA [*FM radio station call letters*]
WIOS	Sintang/Susilo [*Indonesia*] [*ICAO location identifier*] (ICLI)
WIOS	Tawas City, MI [*AM radio station call letters*]
WIOT	Toledo, OH [*FM radio station call letters*]
WIOU.......	Kokomo, IN [*AM radio station call letters*]
WIOV	Ephrata, PA [*FM radio station call letters*]
WIOZ	Pontianak Sector [*Indonesia*] [*ICAO location identifier*] (ICLI)
WIOZ	Southern Pines, NC [*FM radio station call letters*]
WIP	Philadelphia, PA [*AM radio station call letters*]
WIP	Ripon College Library, Ripon, WI [*OCLC symbol*] (OCLC)
WIP	Wartime Intelligence Plan (NATG)
WIP	Weapon Indicator Panel [*Military*] (CAAL)
WIP	Weapons Installation Plan [*Navy*] (NG)
WIP	Women in Information Processing (EA)
WIP	Women in Production (EA)
WIP	Women in Publishing [*Australia*]
WIP	Work Incentive Program [*Department of Health, Education, and Welfare; Department of Labor*] (DLA)
WIP	Work in Place (AABC)
WIP	Work in Process
WIP	Work in Progress (AFM)
WIP	Work in Progress [*A publication*]
WIP	Working Group Indigenous Peoples (EAIO)
WIPA........	Jambi/Sultan Taha [*Indonesia*] [*ICAO location identifier*] (ICLI)
WIPACE ...	Wartime Intelligence Plan, Allied Command Europe (NATG)
WIPB	Muncie, IN [*Television station call letters*]
WIPC........	Rimbo Bujang [*Indonesia*] [*ICAO location identifier*] (ICLI)
WIPE.........	Tanjung Enim/Bangko [*Indonesia*] [*ICAO location identifier*] (ICLI)
WIPF	Kuala Tungkal [*Indonesia*] [*ICAO location identifier*] (ICLI)
WIPH	Sungai Penuh/Depati Parbo [*Indonesia*] [*ICAO location identifier*] (ICLI)
WIPI.........	Bungo Tebo/Pasir Mayang [*Indonesia*] [*ICAO location identifier*] (ICLI)
WIPIS........	Who Is Publishing in Science [*An Institute for Scientific Information publication*] [*Trademark*]
WIPJ	Jambi/Dusun Aro [*Indonesia*] [*ICAO location identifier*] (ICLI)
WIPL.........	Bengkulu/Padang Kemiling [*Indonesia*] [*ICAO location identifier*] (ICLI)
WIPM.......	Work in Process Measurement (MCD)
WIPM-TV ...	Mayaguez, PR [*Television station call letters*]
WIPO	World Intellectual Property Organization [*Switzerland*] (IID)
WIPP.........	Palembang/Sultan Mahmud Badaruddin II [*Indonesia*] [*ICAO location identifier*] (ICLI)
WIPP.........	Waste Isolation Pilot Plant [*Department of Energy*]
WIPP.........	Work Isolation Pilot Project [*NASA*]
WIPQ	Pendoro [*Indonesia*] [*ICAO location identifier*] (ICLI)
WIPR........	Rengat/Japura [*Indonesia*] [*ICAO location identifier*] (ICLI)
WIPR........	San Juan, PR [*AM radio station call letters*]
Wi Pr.........	Wirtschafts-Praxis [*A publication*]
WIPR-FM ...	San Juan, PR [*FM radio station call letters*]
WIPR-TV ..	San Juan, PR [*Television station call letters*]
WIPS	Ticonderoga, NY [*AM radio station call letters*]
WIPS.........	Women in Production Service [*A voluntary, semimilitary organization of women employees, primarily at the E. I. du Pont de Nemours & Co., at Richmond, Va.*] [*World War II*]
WIPS	Word Image Processing System [*Datacopy Corp.*]
WIPTC......	Women's International Professional Tennis Council (EA)
WIPU	Muko Muko [*Indonesia*] [*ICAO location identifier*] (ICLI)
WIPV.........	Keluang [*Indonesia*] [*ICAO location identifier*] (ICLI)
WIPY.........	Bentayan [*Indonesia*] [*ICAO location identifier*] (ICLI)
WIPZ........	Palembang Sector [*Indonesia*] [*ICAO location identifier*] (ICLI)
WIQ	Appleton Public Library, Appleton, WI [*OCLC symbol*] (OCLC)
WIQB	Ann Arbor, MI [*FM radio station call letters*]
WIQH........	Concord, MA [*FM radio station call letters*]
WIQI	Quincy, FL [*FM radio station call letters*]

WIQN........ Phenix City, AL [*AM radio station call letters*]
WIQO-FM ... Covington, VA [*FM radio station call letters*]
WIQQ........ Leland, MS [*FM radio station call letters*]
WIQT........ Horseheads, NY [*AM radio station call letters*]
WIQUD..... Wilson Quarterly [*A publication*]
WIR........... Racine Public Library, Racine, WI [*OCLC symbol*]   (OCLC)
WIR .... War Information Report [*British military*]   (DMA)
WIR .... Weapons Inspection Report [*Navy*]   (NG)
WIR .... Weekly Intelligence Review
WIR .... Welfare in Review [*A publication*]
WIR .... West India Regiment
WIR .... West Indian Reports [*A publication*]   (DLA)
WIR .... Western Intelligence Report [*A publication*]   (APTA)
WIR .... Western Investment Real Estate Trust SBI [*AMEX symbol*]   (SPSG)
WIR .... Wildrose Petroleum Ltd. [*Vancouver Stock Exchange symbol*]
WIR .... Wuerttemberg Israelitische Religionsgemeinschaft [*A publication*]   (BJA)
WIRA .... Fort Pierce, FL [*AM radio station call letters*]
Wirbelsacule Forsch Prax ... Wirbelsacule in Forschung und Praxis [*A publication*]
WIRC......... Hickory, NC [*AM radio station call letters*]
WIRD .... Lake Placid, NY [*AM radio station call letters*]
WIRDS...... Weather Information Remoting and Display System
WIRE......... Waseca Inter-Library Resource Exchange [*Library network*]
WIRE......... Weapons Interference Reduction Effort [*Navy*]   (NG)
WIRE......... Wildlife Review. British Columbia Ministry of Environment [*A publication*]
WIRE......... Women's International Resource Exchange   (EA)
Wire Ind..... Wire Industry [*A publication*]
Wire J .... Wire Journal [*A publication*]
Wire J Int .. Wire Journal International [*A publication*]
Wireless Eng ... Wireless Engineer [*A publication*]
Wirel Wld .. Wireless World [*A publication*]
Wirel World ... Wireless World [*A publication*]
Wire Prod .. Wire and Wire Products [*A publication*]
WIRES ...... Women in Radio and Electrical Service [*World War II*]
Wire Technol ... Wire Technology [*A publication*]
Wire and Wire Prod ... Wire and Wire Products [*A publication*]
Wire World Int ... Wire World International [*A publication*]
WIRF........ Women's International Religious Fellowship   (EA)
WIRGA ..... West Indian Royal Garrison Artillery [*British military*]   (DMA)
Wiring Install and Supplies ... Wiring Installations and Supplies [*A publication*]
WIRJ .... Humboldt, TN [*AM radio station call letters*]
Wirkerei Strickerei Tech ... Wirkerei und Strickerei Technik [*A publication*]
WIRK-FM ... West Palm Beach, FL [*FM radio station call letters*]
WIRL......... Peoria, IL [*AM radio station call letters*]
WIRMIT ... Women in RMIT [*Royal Melbourne Institute of Technology*] Group [*Australia*]
WIRO .... Ironton, OH [*AM radio station call letters*]
WIRO .... Wyoming Infrared Observatory
WIRQ .... Rochester, NY [*FM radio station call letters*]
WIRR........ Virginia-Hibbing, MN [*FM radio station call letters*]
WIRS......... Wage Information Retrieval System [*IRS*]
WIRS........ Western Illinois Regional Studies [*A publication*]
WIRS........ Workplace Industrial Relations Survey [*British*]
WIRS........ Yauco, PR [*Television station call letters*]
WIRT......... Hibbing, MN [*Television station call letters*]
Wirt.......... Wirtschaftsdienst [*A publication*]
WirtBer Lateinam Laender sowie Spanien und Port ... Wirtschaftsbericht ueber die Lateinamerikanischen Laender sowie Spanien und Portugal [*A publication*]
Wirt Futter ... Wirtschaftseigene Futter [*A publication*]
Wirt und Ges ... Wirtschaft und Gesellschaft [*A publication*]
Wirt und Investment ... Wirtschaft und Investment [*A publication*]
Wirt Pol ..... Monatsblaetter fuer Freiheitliche Wirtschaftspolitik [*A publication*]
Wirt und Recht ... Wirtschaft und Recht [*A publication*]
Wirt Reihe ... Lange Reihen zur Wirtschaftsentwicklung [*A publication*]
WIRTSCH ... Wirtschaft [*Economy, Industry*] [*German*]
Wirtschaft ... Wirtschafts-Blaetter [*A publication*]
Wirtschaftspol Chron ... Wirtschaftspolitische Chronik [*A publication*]
Wirtschaftswiss ... Wirtschaftswissenschaft [*A publication*]
Wirtsch-Dienst ... Wirtschaftsdienst [*A publication*]
Wirtsch u Recht ... Wirtschaft und Recht [*A publication*]
Wirtschseig Futter ... Wirtschaftseigene Futter [*A publication*]
Wirtsch Stat ... Wirtschaft und Statistik [*A publication*]
Wirtsch Verwalt ... Wirtschaft und Verwaltung [*German Federal Republic*] [*A publication*]
Wirtsch Wettbewerb ... Wirtschaft und Wettbewerb [*West Germany*] [*A publication*]
Wirtsch-Wiss ... Wirtschaftswissenschaft [*A publication*]
Wirt und Sozwiss Inst Mitt ... Wirtschafts- und Sozialwissenschaftliches Institut. Mitteilungen [*A publication*]
Wirt und Statis ... Wirtschaft und Statistik [*A publication*]
Wirtswoche ... Wirtschaftswoche [*A publication*]
Wirt und Wettbewerb ... Wirtschaft und Wettbewerb [*A publication*]
Wirt u Wiss ... Wirtschaft und Wissen [*A publication*]
Wirt Wiss Inst Mitt ... Wirtschaftswissenschaftliches Institut Mitteilungen [*A publication*]

Wirt in Za .. Wirtschaft in Zahlen [*A publication*]
WIRV .... Irvine, KY [*AM radio station call letters*]
WIRX......... St. Joseph, MI [*FM radio station call letters*]
WIRY......... Plattsburgh, NY [*AM radio station call letters*]
WIS........... University of Wisconsin, Stevens Point, Stevens Point, WI [*OCLC symbol*]   (OCLC)
WIS........... Washington Inventory Service
WIS........... Washington Irving Society   (EA)
WIS........... Weather Information Service [*Air Force*]   (MCD)
WIS........... Wedgwood International Seminar   (EA)
WIS........... Winchester Diversified [*Vancouver Stock Exchange symbol*]
WIS........... Wisconsin   (AAG)
Wis........... Wisconsin Reports [*A publication*]   (DLA)
Wis........... Wisdom [*Old Testament book*]
WIS........... Women in Sales Association   (EA)
WIS........... Women in Soccer   (EA)
WIS........... Women's Information Switchboard [*Australia*]
WIS........... World Impact Services   (EA)
WIS........... World of Islam [*A publication*]
WIS........... Worldwide Information System [*Navy*]
WIS........... Wright Investors' Service [*Information service or system*]   (IID)
WIS........... WWMCCS [*Worldwide Military Command and Control System*] Information Systems
WISA........ Isabela, PR [*AM radio station call letters*]
WISA........ West Indian Students Association   (EA)
WISA........ West Indies Sugar Association [*Later, SAC*]
WISA........ Wholesale Interservice Supply Agreement [*Military*]   (NG)
WISA........ Women's International Surfing Association   (EA)
Wis Acad Sci Arts Lett ... Wisconsin Academy of Sciences, Arts, and Letters [*A publication*]
Wis Acad Sciences Trans ... Wisconsin Academy of Sciences, Arts, and Letters. Transactions [*A publication*]
Wis Acad of Sci Trans ... Wisconsin Academy of Sciences, Arts, and Letters. Transactions [*A publication*]
Wis Admin Code ... Wisconsin Administrative Code [*A publication*]   (DLA)
Wis Ag Dept ... Wisconsin. Department of Agriculture. Publications [*A publication*]
Wis Ag Exp ... Wisconsin. Agricultural Experiment Station. Publications [*A publication*]
Wis Agric Exp Stn Bull ... Wisconsin. Agricultural Experiment Station. Bulletin [*A publication*]
Wis Agric Exp Stn Res Bull ... Wisconsin. Agricultural Experiment Station. Research Bulletin [*A publication*]
Wis Agric Exp Stn Res Rep ... Wisconsin. Agricultural Experiment Station. Research Report [*A publication*]
Wis Agric Exp Stn Spec Bull ... Wisconsin. Agricultural Experiment Station. Special Bulletin [*A publication*]
WISA Law Rep ... Western Indian States Agency Law Reports [*A publication*]   (DLA)
WISALR.... Western Indian States Agency Law Reports [*A publication*]   (DLA)
Wis Alum M ... Wisconsin Alumni Magazine [*A publication*]
WISAP ...... Waste Isolation Safety Assessment Program
Wis Arch... Wisconsin Archaeologist [*A publication*]
WISARD .. Wideband System for Acquiring and Recording Data
Wisb.......... Laws of Wisby [*Maritime law*] [*A publication*]   (DLA)
WISB .... Wildlife Society. Bulletin [*A publication*]
WISB .... Wisbech [*Municipal borough in England*]
WiSB .... Women in Show Business   (EA)
Wis BA Bull ... Wisconsin State Bar Association. Bulletin [*A publication*]   (DLA)
Wis Badger Bee ... Wisconsin's Badger Bee [*A publication*]
Wis Bar Bull ... Wisconsin State Bar Association. Bulletin [*A publication*]   (DLA)
Wis B Bulletin ... Wisconsin Bar Bulletin [*A publication*]
Wis Beekeep ... Wisconsin Beekeeping [*A publication*]
Wis BTA.... Wisconsin Board of Tax Appeals Reports [*A publication*]   (DLA)
WISC........ Wang Information Services Corporation [*Telecommunications service*]   (TSSD)
WISC........ Wechsler Intelligence Scale for Children [*Education*]
WISC........ Wisconsin   (AFM)
Wisc........ Wisconsin Reports [*A publication*]   (DLA)
WISC........ Wisconsin Southern Gas Co., Inc. [*NASDAQ symbol*]   (NQ)
WISC........ Women's Information and Study Centre
WISC........ Writable Instruction Set Computer [*Term coined by Phil Koopman, Jr.*]   (BYTE)
Wisc Busn ... Wisconsin Business [*A publication*]
WISCII...... Wang International Standard Code for Information Interchange [*Pronounced "whiskey"*] [*Canada*]
Wisc LB ..... Wisconsin Library Bulletin [*A publication*]
Wisc Lib Bull ... Wisconsin Library Bulletin [*A publication*]
Wisc LR..... Wisconsin Law Review [*A publication*]
Wisc Med J ... Wisconsin Medical Journal [*A publication*]
Wis Coll Agric Life Sci Res Div Res Rep ... Wisconsin College of Agricultural and Life Sciences. Research Division. Research Report [*A publication*]
Wis Coll Agric Life Sci Res Div Sci Rep Bull ... Wisconsin College of Agricultural and Life Sciences. Research Division. Science Report Bulletin [*A publication*]

WISCOM ... Wisconsin Information Science and Communications Consortium [*University of Wisconsin - Madison*] [*Research center*] (RCD)

Wis Conserv Bull ... Wisconsin Conservation Bulletin [*A publication*]

Wis Conserv Dep Tech Bull ... Wisconsin Conservation Department. Technical Bulletin [*A publication*]

Wisconsin Acad Sci Arts and Letters Trans ... Wisconsin Academy of Sciences, Arts, and Letters. Transactions [*A publication*]

Wisconsin Acad Sci Arts Lett Trans ... Wisconsin Academy of Sciences, Arts, and Letters. Transactions [*A publication*]

Wisconsin Agric Exp Stn Bull ... Wisconsin. Agricultural Experiment Station. Bulletin [*A publication*]

Wisconsin L Rev ... Wisconsin Law Review [*A publication*]

Wisconsin Med J ... Wisconsin Medical Journal [*A publication*]

Wisconsin MJ ... Wisconsin Medical Journal [*A publication*]

WISC-R ..... Wechsler Intelligence Scale for Children - Revised [*Education*]

Wisc Stud BJ ... Wisconsin Student Bar Journal [*A publication*] (DLA)

WISC-TV .. Madison, WI [*Television station call letters*]

WISD .... Wisdom [*Old Testament book*]

Wis 2d .... Wisconsin Reports, Second Series [*A publication*] (DLA)

Wis Dent Assoc J ... Wisconsin Dental Association. Journal [*A publication*]

Wis Dep Nat Resour Publ ... Wisconsin. Department of Natural Resources. Publication [*A publication*]

Wis Dep Nat Resour Tech Bull ... Wisconsin. Department of Natural Resources. Technical Bulletin [*A publication*]

Wisd of Sol ... Wisdom of Solomon [*Old Testament book*]

WISE .... Asheville, NC [*AM radio station call letters*]

WISE .... Wales, Ireland, Scotland, England [*Migrant Association of Victoria*] [*Australia*]

WISE .... Wang Intersystem Exchange

WISE .... Warning Indicators System Europe (MCD)

WISE .... Weapon Installation System Engineering

WISE .... Welsh Initiative for Specialised Employment

WISE .... Wholesalers Institutional Service Extension [*Division of National American Wholesale Grocers Association*]

WISE .... [*The*] Wiser Oil Co. [*NASDAQ symbol*] (NQ)

WISE .... Women into Science and Engineering [*1984 campaign sponsored by the Equal Opportunities Commission and the Engineering Council*] [*British*]

WISE .... Women's Information Service, Inc.

WISE .... Women's Issues, Status, and Education (EA)

WISE .... World Information Service on Energy (EA)

WISE .... World Information Synthesis and Encyclopaedia [*Project of American Association for the Advancement of Science and American Society for Information Science*]

WISE .... World Information Systems Exchange [*Defunct*] (EA)

WISE .... World-Wide Information Service [*Information service or system*] (IID)

Wis Energy Ext Serv Agric-Energy Transp Dig ... Wisconsin. Energy Extension Service. Agricultural-Energy Transportation Digest [*A publication*]

Wis Eng ..... Wisconsin Engineer [*A publication*]

Wis Eng Exp Stn Repr ... Wisconsin. Engineering Experiment Station. Reprint [*A publication*]

Wis Engineer ... Wisconsin Engineer [*A publication*]

WISER ...... Western Information System for Energy Resources [*Dataline, Inc.*] [*Canada*] [*Information service or system*]

WiseR .... Wiseman Review [*A publication*]

Wis Geol Nat Hist Surv Bull ... Wisconsin. Geological and Natural History Survey. Bulletin [*A publication*]

Wis Geol Survey Bull Inf Circ ... Wisconsin. Geological Survey. Bulletin. Information Circular [*A publication*]

Wis G S ...... Wisconsin. Geological and Natural History Survey [*A publication*]

Wis G S G Wis B ... Wisconsin. Geological Survey. Geology of Wisconsin. Bulletin [*Later, Wisconsin Geological and Natural History Survey*] [*A publication*]

WISH .... World Institute for Scientific Humanism (EA)

Wis His Col ... Wisconsin State Historical Society. Collections [*A publication*]

Wis His Proc ... Wisconsin Historical Society. Proceedings [*A publication*]

Wis His S Domesday Bk ... Wisconsin State Historical Society. Domesday Book [*A publication*]

Wis Hist Soc Proc ... Wisconsin State Historical Society. Proceedings [*A publication*]

Wis Hort .... Wisconsin Horticulture [*A publication*]

WISH-TV ... Indianapolis, IN [*Television station call letters*]

WISI .... World Index of Space Imagery [*Meteorology*]

Wis IC .... Wisconsin Industrial Commission Workmen's Compensation Reports [*A publication*] (DLA)

Wis Int'l LJ ... Wisconsin International Law Journal [*A publication*] (DLA)

Wis J Ed ... Wisconsin Journal of Education [*A publication*]

WISJMPO ... Worldwide Military Command and Control Information Systems, Joint Program Office

WISK .... Americus, GA [*AM radio station call letters*]

WISL .... Shamokin, PA [*AM radio station call letters*]

Wis Law R ... Wisconsin Law Review [*A publication*]

Wis Legis Serv ... Wisconsin Legislative Service (West) [*A publication*] (DLA)

Wis Leg N ... Wisconsin Legal News [*Milwaukee*] [*A publication*] (DLA)

Wis Lib Bul ... Wisconsin Library Bulletin [*A publication*]

Wis LN ...... Wisconsin Legal News [*Milwaukee*] [*A publication*] (DLA)

Wis LR .... Wisconsin Law Review [*A publication*]

Wis L Rev .. Wisconsin Law Review [*A publication*]

WISM .... Eau Claire, WI [*AM radio station call letters*]

Wis M .... Wisconsin Magazine of History [*A publication*]

Wis Mag Hist ... Wisconsin Magazine of History [*A publication*]

Wis Med J ... Wisconsin Medical Journal [*A publication*]

Wis M Hist ... Wisconsin Magazine of History [*A publication*]

WISN .... Milwaukee, WI [*AM radio station call letters*]

Wis Nat Resour Bull ... Wisconsin Natural Resources Bulletin [*A publication*]

Wis N H Soc B ... Wisconsin Natural History Society. Bulletin [*A publication*]

WISN-TV ... Milwaukee, WI [*Television station call letters*]

WISO .... Ponce, PR [*AM radio station call letters*]

WISP .... Kinston, NC [*AM radio station call letters*]

WISP .... Warning Improvement Study Plan (MCD)

WISP .... Wartime Information Security Program (MCD)

WISP .... Weaponization of Increased Speed Projectiles (MCD)

WISP .... Wide-Range Imaging Spectrophotometer [*Naval Oceanographic Office*]

WISP .... Women in Scholarly Publishing (EA)

Wis Paper Ind Newsl ... Wisconsin Paper Industry. Information Service Newsletter [*A publication*]

Wis Pharm ... Wisconsin Pharmacist [*A publication*]

Wis Pharm Ext Bull ... Wisconsin. Pharmacy Extension Bulletin [*A publication*]

Wi Spieg .... Wirtschaftsspiegel [*A publication*]

Wis PSC .... Wisconsin Public Service Commission Reports [*A publication*] (DLA)

Wis PSC Ops ... Wisconsin Public Service Commission Opinions and Decisions [*A publication*] (DLA)

WISR .... Butler, PA [*AM radio station call letters*]

Wis R .... Wisconsin Reports [*A publication*] (DLA)

Wis RC Ops ... Wisconsin Railroad Commission Opinions and Decisions [*A publication*] (DLA)

Wis RCR .... Wisconsin Railroad Commission Reports [*A publication*] (DLA)

Wis Rep ..... Wisconsin Reports [*A publication*] (DLA)

WISS .... Berlin, WI [*AM radio station call letters*]

WISS .... Weapon Impact Scoring System [*Navy*] (MCD)

WISS .... Weekly Induction Scheduling System [*Navy*] (NG)

WISS .... World Institute of Sephardic Studies (BJA)

WISSA ...... Wholesale Interservice Supply Support Agreements [*Military*]

Wiss Abh Dtsch Akad Landwirtschaftswiss Berlin ... Wissenschaftliche Abhandlungen der Deutschen Akademie der Landwirtschaftswissenschaften zu Berlin [*A publication*]

Wiss Abh Dtsch Materialpruefungsanst ... Wissenschaftliche Abhandlungen der Deutschen Materialpruefungsanstalten [*A publication*]

Wiss Abh Phys-Tech Bd Anst ... Wissenschaftliche Abhandlungen der Physikalisch-Technischen Bundesanstalt [*A publication*]

Wiss Abh Phys-Tech Reichsanst ... Wissenschaftliche Abhandlungen der Physikalische-Technischen Reichsanstalt [*West Germany*] [*A publication*]

Wiss Alpenvereinshefte ... Wissenschaftliche Alpenvereinshefte [*A publication*]

Wiss Ann ... Wissenschaftliche Annalen [*A publication*]

Wiss Arch Landwirtsch Abt A ... Wissenschaftliches Archiv fuer Landwirtschaft. Abteilung A. Archiv fuer Pflanzenbau [*A publication*]

Wiss Arch Landwirtsch Abt B ... Wissenschaftliches Archiv fuer Landwirtschaft. Abteilung B. Archiv fuer Tierernaehrung und Teirzucht [*A publication*]

Wis SBA Bull ... Wisconsin State Bar Association. Bulletin [*A publication*] (DLA)

Wiss Beitr Ingenieurhochsch Zwickau ... Wissenschaftliche Beitraege. Ingenieurhochschule Zwickau [*German Democratic Republic*] [*A publication*]

Wiss Beitr Martin Luther Univ (Halle Wittenberg) ... Wissenschaftliche Beitraege. Martin Luther Universitaet (Halle-Wittenberg) [*A publication*]

Wiss Beitr Martin Luther Univ (Halle Wittenberg) Reihe M ... Wissenschaftliche Beitrage. Martin Luther Universitaet (Halle-Wittenberg). Reihe M [*A publication*]

Wiss Beitr Univ (Halle) ... Wissenschaftliche Beitrage. Martin Luther Universitaet (Halle-Wittenberg) [*A publication*]

Wiss Ber AEG-Telefunken ... Wissenschaftliche Berichte AEG-Telefunken [*A publication*]

Wiss Ber EM ... Wissenschaftliche Berichte EM [*A publication*]

Wiss Ber HMFA Braunschweig ... Wissenschaftliche Berichte aus der Hochmagnetfeldanlage. Physikalische Institute. Technische Universitaet Braunschweig [*A publication*]

Wiss Dienst Ostmitteleur ... Wissenschaftlicher Dienst fuer Ostmitteleuropa [*A publication*]

Wiss Dienst Sudosteuropa ... Wissenschaftlicher Dienst Suedosteuropa [*A publication*]

Wiss Di Suedost Eur ... Wissenschaftlicher Dienst Suedosteuropa [*A publication*]

Wissenschaftstheorie- Wissenschaft Philos ... Wissenschaftstheorie- Wissenschaft und Philosophie [*A publication*]

Wissenschaftstheor Wiss Philos ... Wissenschaftstheorie- Wissenschaft und Philosophie [*A publication*]

Wissensch Inform ... Wissenschaftliche Information [*Karl-Marx-Stadt*] [*A publication*]

Wissensch Meeresuntersuch ... Wissenschaftliche Meeresuntersuchungen [*A publication*]

Wissensch Sitzungen Stochastik 80 ... Wissenschaftliche Sitzungen zur Stochastik 80 [*A publication*]

Wissensch Sitzungen Stochastik 81 ... Wissenschaftliche Sitzungen zur Stochastik 81 [*A publication*]

Wissensch Sitzungen Stochastik 82 ... Wissenschaftliche Sitzungen zur Stochastik 82 [*A publication*]

Wissensch Taschenbuecher Reihe Math Phys ... Wissenschaftliche Taschenbuecher. Reihe Mathematik/Physik [*A publication*]

Wissensch Taschenbuecher Reihe Texte Stud ... Wissenschaftliche Taschenbuecher. Reihe Texte und Studien [*A publication*]

WISS-FM ... Berlin, WI [*FM radio station call letters*]

Wiss Forschungsber Naturwiss Reihe ... Wissenschaftliche Forschungsberichte. Naturwissenschaftliche Reihe [*A publication*]

Wiss Fortschr ... Wissenschaft und Fortschritt [*A publication*]

Wiss Fortschritt ... Wissenschaft und Fortschritt [*A publication*]

Wiss Geg. ... Wissenschaft und Gegenwart [*A publication*]

Wiss Konf Ges Dtsch Naturforsch Aerzte ... Wissenschaftliche Konferenz. Gesellschaft Deutscher Naturforscher und Aerzte [*A publication*]

Wiss Kult ... Wissenschaft und Kultur [*A publication*]

WisSL .... Wisconsin Studies in Literature [*A publication*]

Wiss M Bosn ... Wissenschaftliche Mitteilungen des Bosnisch-Herzegowinischen Landesmuseums A. Archaeologie [*A publication*]

Wiss Mitt Forst Holzwirtsch ... Wissenschaftliche Mitteilungen fuer Forst und Holzwirtschaft [*A publication*]

Wiss Mitt Historiker-Ges DDR ... Wissenschaftliche Mitteilungen. Historiker-Gesellschaft der DDR [*A publication*]

Wiss Mitt Pharm Forsch Fortbild Inst Oesterr Apoth Ver ... Wissenschaftliche Mitteilungen. Pharmazeutisches Forschungs- und Fortbildungs Institut. Oesterreichischer Apotheker-Verein [*A publication*]

Wiss Mon ANT ... Wissenschaftliche Monographien zum Alten und Neuen Testament [*A publication*]

Wiss Prax Ki Ges ... Wissenschaft und Praxis in Kirche und Gesellschaft [*A publication*]

Wiss Schriftenr Tech Hochsch Karl-Marx-Stadt ... Wissenschaftliche Schriftenreihe. Technische Hochschule Karl-Marx-Stadt [*A publication*]

Wiss Taschenb ... Wissenschaftliche Taschenbuecher [*A publication*]

Wis Stat ..... Wisconsin Statutes [*A publication*] (DLA)

Wis Stat Ann (West) ... West's Wisconsin Statutes, Annotated [*A publication*] (DLA)

Wis State Cartogr Off Inf Circ ... Wisconsin State Cartographer's Office. Information Circular [*A publication*]

Wiss-Tech Fortschr Landw ... Wissenschaftlich-Technischer Fortschrift fuer die Landwirtschaft [*A publication*]

Wiss-Tech Inf VEB Kombinat Automatisierungsanlagenbau ... Wissenschaftlich-Technische Informationen des VEB Kombinat Automatisierungsanlagenbau [*A publication*]

Wis Stud Contemp Lit ... Wisconsin Studies in Contemporary Literature [*Later, Contemporary Literature*] [*A publication*]

Wiss Umwelt ISU ... Wissenschaft und Umwelt ISU [*Interdisziplinaerer Sonderbereich Umweltschutz*] [*German Federal Republic*] [*A publication*]

WissUnNT ... Wissenschaftliche Untersuchungen zum Neuen Testament [*Tuebingen*] [*A publication*] (BJA)

Wiss Unt NT ... Wissenschaftliche Untersuchungen zum Neuen Testament [*A publication*]

Wiss Veroeff DOG ... Wissenschaftliche Veroeffentlichungen der Deutschen Orient-Gesellschaft [*A publication*]

Wiss Veroeff Siemens-Werken ... Wissenschaftliche Veroeffentlichungen aus den Siemens-Werken [*A publication*]

Wiss Veroeff Tech Hochsch (Darmstadt) ... Wissenschaftliche Veroeffentlichungen. Technische Hochschule (Darmstadt) [*A publication*]

Wiss Wb .... Wissenschaft und Weltbild [*A publication*]

Wiss Weis ... Wissenschaft und Weisheit [*A publication*]

Wiss Welt .. Wissenschaft und Weltbild [*A publication*]

Wiss Weltb ... Wissenschaft und Weltbild [*A publication*]

Wiss Wirtsch Polit ... Wissenschaft, Wirtschaft, Politik [*A publication*]

Wiss Z .... Wissenschaftliche Zeitschrift [*A publication*]

WissZ .... Wissenschaftliche Zeitung. Humboldt-Universitaet [*A publication*]

Wiss Z (Berl) ... Wissenschaftliche Zeitschrift. Humboldt-Universitaet (Berlin). Gesellschafts- und Sprachwissenschaftliche Reihe [*A publication*]

Wiss Z Elektrotech ... Wissenschaftliche Zeitschrift der Elektrotechnik [*A publication*]

Wiss Z Ernst Moritz Arndt Univ (Greifswald) Math Natur Reihe ... Wissenschaftliche Zeitschrift. Ernst-Moritz-Arndt-Universitaet (Greifswald). Mathematisch-Naturwissenschaftliche Reihe [*A publication*]

Wiss Z Ernst Moritz Arndt Univ Greifswald Math Naturw Reihe ... Wissenschaftliche Zeitschrift. Ernst-Moritz-Arndt-Universitaet (Greifswald). Mathematisch-Naturwissenschaftliche Reihe [*A publication*]

Wiss Z Ernst-Moritz-Arndt-Univ Greifsw Math Naturwiss Reihe ... Wissenschaftliche Zeitschrift. Ernst-Moritz-Arndt-Universitaet (Greifswald). Mathematisch-Naturwissenschaftliche Reihe [*A publication*]

Wiss Z Friedrich-Schiller-Univ (Jena) Math Naturwiss Reihe ... Wissenschaftliche Zeitschrift. Friedrich-Schiller-Universitaet (Jena). Mathematisch-Naturwissenschaftliche Reihe [*A publication*]

Wiss Z Greifswald Ernst Moritz Arndt Univ Math Natur-Reihe ... Greifswald Ernst-Moritz-Arndt-Universitaet. Wissenschaftliche Zeitschrift. Mathematisch-Naturwissenschaftliche Reihe [*A publication*]

Wiss Z (Halle) ... Wissenschaftliche Zeitschrift. Martin-Luther-Universitaet (Halle-Wittenberg) [*A publication*]

Wiss Z Hochsch Archit Bauwes (Weimar) ... Wissenschaftliche Zeitschrift. Hochschule fuer Architektur und Bauwesen (Weimar) [*A publication*]

Wiss Z Hochsch Bauwes (Cottbus) ... Wissenschaftliche Zeitschrift. Hochschule fuer Bauwesen (Cottbus) [*A publication*]

Wiss Z Hochsch Bauwes (Leipzig) ... Wissenschaftliche Zeitschrift. Hochschule fuer Bauwesen (Leipzig) [*East Germany*] [*A publication*]

Wiss Z Hochsch Bauw (Leipzig) ... Wissenschaftliche Zeitschrift. Hochschule fuer Bauwesen (Leipzig) [*A publication*]

Wiss Z Hochsch Elektrotech (Ilmenau) ... Wissenschaftliche Zeitschrift. Hochschule fuer Elektrotechnik (Ilmenau) [*A publication*]

Wiss Z Hochsch Landwirtsch Produktionsgenoss (Meissen) ... Wissenschaftliche Zeitschrift. Hochschule fuer Landwirtschaftliche Produktionsgenossenschaften (Meissen) [*A publication*]

Wiss Z Hochsch Maschinenbau (Karl Marx-Stadt) ... Wissenschaftliche Zeitschrift. Hochschule fuer Maschinenbau (Karl Marx-Stadt) [*A publication*]

Wiss Z Hochsch Schwermaschinenbau (Magdeburg) ... Wissenschaftliche Zeitschrift. Hochschule fuer Schwermaschinenbau (Magdeburg) [*A publication*]

Wiss Z Hochschule ... Wissenschaftliche Zeitschrift. Hochschule fuer Oekonomie [*Berlin*] [*A publication*]

Wiss Z Hochsch Verkehrswesen (Dresden) ... Wissenschaftliche Zeitschrift. Hochschule fuer Verkehrswesen (Dresden) [*A publication*]

Wiss Z Hochsch Verkehrswesen Friedrich List (Dresden) ... Wissenschaftliche Zeitschrift. Hochschule fuer Verkehrswesen "Friedrich List" (Dresden). Die Anwendung Mathematischer Methoden im Transport- und Nachichtenwesen [*A publication*]

Wiss Z Humboldt-Univ (Berl) ... Wissenschaftliche Zeitschrift. Humboldt-Universitaet (Berlin) [*A publication*]

Wiss Z Humboldt-Univ (Berlin) Math-Natur Reihe ... Wissenschaftliche Zeitschrift. Humboldt-Universitaet (Berlin). Mathematisch-Naturwissenschaftliche Reihe [*A publication*]

Wiss Z Humboldt Univ (Berlin) Math Naturwiss Reihe ... Wissenschaftliche Zeitschrift. Humboldt-Universitaet (Berlin). Mathematisch-Naturwissenschaftliche Reihe [*A publication*]

Wiss Z Humboldt Univ (Berl) Math Naturwiss ... Wissenschaftliche Zeitschrift. Humboldt-Universitaet (Berlin). Mathematisch-Naturwissenschaftliche Reihe [*A publication*]

Wiss Z Humboldt-Univ (Berl) Math-Naturwiss Reihe ... Wissenschaftliche Zeitschrift. Humboldt-Universitaet (Berlin). Mathematisch-Naturwissenschaftliche Reihe [*A publication*]

Wiss Z (Jena) ... Wissenschaftliche Zeitschrift. Friedrich-Schiller-Universitaet (Jena) [*A publication*]

Wiss Z Karl-Marx Univ ... Wissenschaftliche Zeitschrift. Karl-Marx-Universitaet [*A publication*]

Wiss Z Karl-Marx-Univ (Leipzig) Math Natur Reihe ... Wissenschaftliche Zeitschrift. Karl-Marx-Universitaet (Leipzig). Mathematisch-Naturwissenschaftliche Reihe [*A publication*]

Wiss Z Karl-Marx-Univ (Leipzig) Math-Naturwiss Reihe ... Wissenschaftliche Zeitschrift. Karl-Marx-Universitaet (Leipzig). Mathematisch-Naturwissenschaftliche Reihe [*A publication*]

Wiss Z Karl-Marx-Univ (Leipz) Math-Naturwiss Reihe ... Wissenschaftliche Zeitschrift. Karl-Marx-Universitaet (Leipzig). Mathematisch-Naturwissenschaftliche Reihe [*A publication*]

Wiss Z Martin Luther Univ ... Wissenschaftliche Zeitschrift. Martin-Luther-Universitaet (Halle-Wittenberg). Mathematisch-Naturwissenschaftliche Reihe [*A publication*]

Wiss Z Martin-Luther-Univ (Halle-Wittenb) ... Wissenschaftliche Zeitschrift. Martin-Luther-Universitaet (Halle-Wittenberg) [*A publication*]

Wiss Z Martin-Luther-Univ (Halle-Wittenberg) ... Wissenschaftliche Zeitschrift. Martin-Luther-Universitaet (Halle-Wittenberg) [*A publication*]

Wiss Z Martin-Luther-Univ Halle Wittenberg Math Natur Reihe ... Wissenschaftliche Zeitschrift. Martin-Luther-Universitaet (Halle-Wittenberg). Mathematisch-Naturwissenschaftliche Reihe [*A publication*]

Wiss Z Math Naturwiss Reihe Halle Univ ... Wissenschaftliche Zeitschrift. Mathematisch-Naturwissenschaftliche Reihe. Halle Universitaet [*A publication*]

Wiss Z Paedagog Hochsch Karl Liebknecht (Potsdam) ... Wissenschaftliche Zeitschrift. Paedagogische Hochschule Karl Liebknecht (Potsdam) [*East Germany*] [*A publication*]

Wiss Z Rostock ... Wissenschaftliche Zeitschrift. Universitaet Rostock [*A publication*]

Wiss Zs TH (Dresd) ... Wissenschaftliche Zeitschrift. Technische Hochschule (Dresden) [*A publication*]

Wiss Z Tech Hochsch Chem Carl Schorlemmer (Leuna-Merseburg) ... Wissenschaftliche Zeitschrift. Technische Hochschule fuer Chemie "Carl Schorlemmer" (Leuna-Merseburg) [*A publication*]

Wiss Z Tech Hochsch Chem (Leuna-Merseburg) ... Wissenschaftliche Zeitschrift. Technische Hochschule fuer Chemie (Leuna-Merseburg) [*A publication*]

Wiss Z Tech Hochsch (Dresden) ... Wissenschaftliche Zeitschrift. Technische Hochschule (Dresden) [*East Germany*] [*A publication*]

Wiss Z Tech Hochsch (Ilmenau) ... Wissenschaftliche Zeitschrift. Technische Hochschule (Ilmenau, West Germany) [*A publication*]

Wiss Z Tech Hochsch Karl-Marx-Stadt ... Wissenschaftliche Zeitschrift. Technische Hochschule Karl-Marx-Stadt [*A publication*]

Wiss Z Tech Hochsch Karl-Marx-Stadt Sonderh ... Wissenschaftliche Zeitschrift. Technische Hochschule Karl-Marx-Stadt. Sonderheft [*A publication*]

Wiss Z Tech Hochsch (Leipzig) ... Wissenschaftliche Zeitschrift. Technische Hochschule (Leipzig) [*A publication*]

Wiss Z Tech Hochsch (Leuna-Merseburg) ... Wissenschaftliche Zeitschrift. Technische Hochschule fuer Chemie "Carl Schorlemmer" (Leuna-Merseburg) [*A publication*]

Wiss Z Tech Hochsch (Magdeburg) ... Wissenschaftliche Zeitschrift. Technische Hochschule Otto Von Guericke (Magdeburg) [*A publication*]

Wiss Z Tech Hochsch Otto von Guericke (Magdeb) ... Wissenschaftliche Zeitschrift. Technische Hochschule Otto Von Guericke (Magdeburg) [*A publication*]

Wiss Z Tech Hochsch Otto von Guericke (Magdeburg) ... Wissenschaftliche Zeitschrift. Technische Hochschule Otto Von Guericke (Magdeburg) [*A publication*]

Wiss Z Tech Hochsch Otto v Guericke (Magdeburg) ... Wissenschaftliche Zeitschrift. Technische Hochschule Otto Von Guericke (Magdeburg) [*A publication*]

Wiss Z Tech Hochsch Otto Von Guericke ... Wissenschaftliche Zeitschrift. Technische Hochschule Otto Von Guericke [*A publication*]

Wiss Z Tech Hochsch Otto Von Guericke (Magdeburg) ... Wissenschaftliche Zeitschrift. Technische Hochschule Otto Von Guericke (Magdeburg) [*A publication*]

Wiss Z Techn Hochsch Chem (Leuna-Merseburg) ... Wissenschaftliche Zeitschrift. Technische Hochschule fuer Chemie (Leuna-Merseburg) [*A publication*]

Wiss Z Techn Hochsch (Ilmenau) ... Wissenschaftliche Zeitschrift. Technische Hochschule (Ilmenau) [*A publication*]

Wiss Z Techn Hochsch Karl-Marx-Stadt ... Wissenschaftliche Zeitschrift. Technische Hochschule Karl-Marx-Stadt [*A publication*]

Wiss Z Techn Hochsch (Leuna-Merseburg) ... Wissenschaftliche Zeitschrift. Technische Hochschule (Leuna-Merseburg) [*A publication*]

Wiss Z Techn Univ (Dresden) ... Wissenschaftliche Zeitschrift. Technische Universitaet (Dresden) [*A publication*]

Wiss Z Tech Univ (Dres) ... Wissenschaftliche Zeitschrift. Technische Universitaet (Dresden) [*A publication*]

Wiss Z Tech Univ (Dresden) ... Wissenschaftliche Zeitschrift. Technische Universitaet (Dresden) [*A publication*]

Wiss Z Univ (Greifswald) ... Wissenschaftliche Zeitschrift. Ernst-Moritz-Arndt-Universitaet (Greifswald) [*A publication*]

Wiss Z Univ (Greifswald) Math-Naturwiss Reihe ... Wissenschaftliche Zeitschrift. Ernst-Moritz-Arndt-Universitaet (Greifswald). Mathematisch-Naturwissenschaftliche Reihe [*A publication*]

Wiss Z Univ (Halle) ... Wissenschaftliche Zeitschrift. Martin-Luther-Universitaet (Halle-Wittenberg) [*A publication*]

Wiss Z Univ (Halle-Wittenberg) Math-Naturwiss Reihe ... Wissenschaftliche Zeitschrift. Martin-Luther-Universitaet (Halle-Wittenberg). Mathematisch-Naturwissenschaftliche Reihe [*A publication*]

Wiss Z Univ (Jena) Math-Naturwiss Reihe ... Wissenschaftliche Zeitschrift. Friedrich-Schiller-Universitaet (Jena). Mathematisch-Naturwissenschaftliche Reihe [*A publication*]

Wiss Z Univ (Leipzig) Ges-u Sprachwiss R ... Wissenschaftliche Zeitschrift. Karl-Marx-Universitaet (Leipzig). Gesellschafts- und Sprachwissenschaftliche Reihe [*A publication*]

Wiss Z Univ (Leipzig) Math-Naturwiss Reihe ... Wissenschaftliche Zeitschrift. Karl-Marx-Universitaet (Leipzig). Mathematisch-Naturwissenschaftliche Reihe [*A publication*]

Wiss Z Univ Rostock Ges- & Sprachwiss Reihe ... Wissenschaftliche Zeitschrift. Universitaet Rostock. Gesellschafts- und Sprachwissenschaftliche Reihe [*A publication*]

Wiss Z Univ Rostock Ges Sprachwiss Reihe ... Wissenschaftliche Zeitschrift. Universitaet Rostock. Gesellschafts- und Sprachwissenschaftliche Reihe [*A publication*]

Wiss Z Univ Rostock Ges-Wiss ... Wissenschaftliche Zeitschrift. Universitaet Rostock. Gesellschafts- und Wissenschaftliche Reihe [*A publication*]

Wiss Z Univ Rostock Math-Natur Reihe ... Universitaet Rostock. Wissenschaftliche Zeitschrift. Mathematisch-Naturwissenschaftliche Reihe [*A publication*]

Wiss Z Univ Rostock Math Naturwiss Reihe ... Wissenschaftliche Zeitschrift. Universitaet Rostock. Mathematisch-Naturwissenschaftliche Reihe [*A publication*]

Wiss Z Univ Rostock Reihe Math Naturw ... Wissenschaftliche Zeitschrift. Universitaet Rostock. Reihe Mathematik und Naturwissenschaften [*A publication*]

Wiss Z Wilhelm-Pieck-Univ Rostock Naturwiss Reihe ... Wissenschaftliche Zeitschrift der Wilhelm-Pieck-Universitaet Rostock Naturwissenschaftliche Reihe [*A publication*]

WIST .... Lobelville, TN [*FM radio station call letters*]

WIST .... Whitaker Index of Schizophrenic Thinking

Wi St .... Wirtschaftswissenschaftliches Studium [*A publication*]

Wistar Inst Symp Monogr ... Wistar Institute. Symposium. Monograph [*A publication*]

Wi Stat ...... Wirtschaft und Statistik [*A publication*]

Wi u Stat .... Wirtschaft und Statistik [*A publication*]

Wis Tax App C ... Wisconsin Tax Appeals Commission Reports [*A publication*] (DLA)

Wi St G ...... Wirtschaftsstrafgesetz [*A publication*]

WIS-TV ..... Columbia, SC [*Television station call letters*]

WISU .... Federation of Westinghouse Independent Salaried Unions

WISU .... Terre Haute, IN [*FM radio station call letters*]

Wis U Bul Eng S ... Bulletin. University of Wisconsin. Engineering Series [*A publication*]

Wis Univ Coll Eng Eng Exp Stn Rep ... Wisconsin University. College of Engineering. Engineering Experiment Station. Report [*A publication*]

Wis Univ Dept Meteorology Rept Lakes and Streams Inv Comm ... Wisconsin University. Department of Meteorology. Report to the Lakes and Streams Investigations Committee [*A publication*]

Wis Univ Eng Exp Stn Bull ... Wisconsin University. Engineering Experiment Station. Bulletin [*A publication*]

Wis Univ Geol Nat Hist Surv Spec Rep ... Wisconsin University. Geological and Natural History Survey. Special Report [*A publication*]

Wis Univ Geol Natur Hist Surv Inform Circ ... Wisconsin University. Geological and Natural History Survey. Information Circular [*A publication*]

WIT .... Washington Institute of Technology [*Washington, DC*]

WIT .... Whitbread Investment Trust [*British*]

WIT .... Winnebago International Travelers (EA)

WIT .... Wiring Interface Tester (MCD)

WIT .... Wisconsin Institute of Technology

WIT .... Witco Corp. [*NYSE symbol*] (SPSG)

WIT .... Witness (AABC)

WIT .... Wittenberg University, Springfield, OH [*OCLC symbol*] (OCLC)

WIT .... Witteveen [*Netherlands*] [*Geomagnetic observatory code*]

WIT .... Witteveen [*Netherlands*] [*Seismograph station code, US Geological Survey*] (SEIS)

WIT .... Women in Telecommunications [*Defunct*] (EA)

WIT .... Women in Transition (EA)

WIT .... World Ice Theory [*Hans Horbiger*]

WITA .... Knoxville, TN [*AM radio station call letters*]

WITA .... Tapak Tuan/Teuku Cut Ali [*Indonesia*] [*ICAO location identifier*] (ICLI)

WITA .... Women in the Army (MCD)

WITA .... Women in the Arts (EA)

WITA .... Women's International Tennis Association (EA)

WITAG ...... West Indies Trade Advisory Group [*British Overseas Trade Board*] (DS)

WITAN ..... Wind-Time Analyzer

WITB-FM ... Salem, WV [*FM radio station call letters*]

WITC .... Cazenovia, NY [*FM radio station call letters*]

WITC .... Meulaboh/Cut Nyak Dien [*Indonesia*] [*ICAO location identifier*] (ICLI)

WITCH ..... Women Incensed over Traditional Coed Hoopla [*Feminist group*]

WITCH ..... Women's Independent Cinema House [*British*]

WITCH ..... Women's International Terrorist Conspiracy from Hell [*Feminist group*]

WITF .... Women's International Tennis Federation

WITF-FM ... Harrisburg, PA [*FM radio station call letters*]

WITF-TV .. Harrisburg, PA [*Television station call letters*]

WITG .... Sinabang/Lasikin [*Indonesia*] [*ICAO location identifier*] (ICLI)

WITG .... Western International Trade Group (EA)

WITH .... Baltimore, MD [*AM radio station call letters*]

WITH .... Witheridge [*England*]

With Corp Cas ... Withrow's American Corporation Cases [*A publication*] (DLA)

WITHDRL ... Withdrawal (ROG)

Withrow ..... Withrow's American Corporation Cases [*A publication*] (DLA)
Withrow ..... Withrow's Reports [*9-21 Iowa*] [*A publication*] (DLA)
WITHT ...... Without (ROG)
WITIS .... Weather Integration with Tactical Intelligence System (MCD)
WITI-TV ... Milwaukee, WI [*Television station call letters*]
Witkin Cal Summary ... Witkin's Summary of California Law [*A publication*] (DLA)
WITL......... Lansing, MI [*AM radio station call letters*]
WITL......... Lhok Sukon [*Indonesia*] [*ICAO location identifier*] (ICLI)
WITL-FM ... Lansing, MI [*FM radio station call letters*]
WITM .... Whok Seumawe/Malikus Saleh [*Indonesia*] [*ICAO location identifier*] (ICLI)
WITNED.... Witnessed
WITNESS ... Wire Installation Tester for Negating Errors by Sequencing and Standardization
WITNETH ... Witnesseth [*Legal*] [*British*] (ROG)
WITNS....... Witness [*Legal*] [*British*] (ROG)
WITN-TV ... Washington, NC [*Television station call letters*]
WITR........ Henrietta, NY [*FM radio station call letters*]
WITS .... Sebring, FL [*AM radio station call letters*]
WITS .... Seumayam [*Indonesia*] [*ICAO location identifier*] (ICLI)
WITS .... Wang Integrated Technology Show [*British*]
WITS .... Washington Interagency Telecommunications System [*GSA*]
WITS .... Weather Information Telemetry System [*Air Force*] (CET)
WITS .... West Integrated Test Stand [*NASA*]
WITS .... Women in Technical Service [*World War II*]
WITS .... Work Item Tracking System [*Nuclear energy*] (NRCH)
WITS .... Worldwide Information and Trade System
WITS .... Worldwide Interactive Trading System [*Information service or system*] (IT)
WITSEC.... Witness Security Program [*US government program for protection of witnesses whose lives are endangered by their testimony*]
WITSS....... Witnesses [*Legal*] [*British*] (ROG)
WITT........ Banda Aceh/Blangbintang [*Indonesia*] [*ICAO location identifier*] (ICLI)
WITT........ Tuscola, IL [*FM radio station call letters*]
Witthaus & Becker's Med Jur ... Witthaus and Becker's Medical Jurisprudence [*A publication*] (DLA)
Wittheit Bremen Jahrb ... Wittheit zu Bremen. Jahrbuch [*A publication*]
WITTL...... Wittlesford [*England*]
Witt Schlesw-Holst ... Witterung in Schleswig-Holstein [*A publication*]
WITV........ Charleston, SC [*Television station call letters*]
WITW........ We Interrupt This Week [*Television program*]
WITX........ Beaver Falls, PA [*FM radio station call letters*]
WITY........ Danville, IL [*AM radio station call letters*]
WITZ........ Jasper, IN [*AM radio station call letters*]
WITZ-FM ... Jasper, IN [*FM radio station call letters*]
WIU .... Warhead Interface Unit (MCD)
WIU .... Water Injection Unit
WIU .... Weather Intelligence Unit [*Army*] (MCD)
WIU .... Western Illinois University [*Macomb*]
WIU .... Western International University, Phoenix, AZ [*OCLC symbol*] (OCLC)
wiu............ Wisconsin [*MARC country of publication code*] [*Library of Congress*] (LCCP)
WIU .... Witu [*Papua New Guinea*] [*Airport symbol*] (OAG)
WIUJ......... St. Thomas, VI [*FM radio station call letters*]
WIUM....... Macomb, IL [*FM radio station call letters*]
WIUP-FM ... Indiana, PA [*FM radio station call letters*]
WIUS........ Macomb, IL [*AM radio station call letters*]
WIUV .... Castleton, VT [*FM radio station call letters*]
Wiv............ [*The*] Merry Wives of Windsor [*Shakespearean work*]
WIV .... Vakblad voor Textielreiniging [*A publication*]
WIV .... Waukesha Public Library, Waukesha, WI [*OCLC symbol*] (OCLC)
WIVA-FM ... Aguadilla, PR [*FM radio station call letters*]
WIVB-TV ... Buffalo, NY [*Television station call letters*]
Wi Verw .... Wirtschaftsverwaltung [*A publication*]
WIVI......... Charlotte Amalie, VI [*FM radio station call letters*]
WIVK .... Knoxville, TN [*AM radio station call letters*]
WIVK-FM ... Knoxville, TN [*FM radio station call letters*]
WIVV .... Vieques, PR [*AM radio station call letters*]
WIVY-FM ... Jacksonville, FL [*FM radio station call letters*]
WIW .... Marathon County Public Library, Wausau, WI [*OCLC symbol*] (OCLC)
WIW .... Wer Informiert Woruber [*Who Advises about What*] [*Gesellschaft fuer Informationsmarkt-Forschung - GIF*] [*Detmold, Federal Republic of Germany*] [*Information service or system*] (IID)
WIW? .... Who's Inventing What? [*A publication*]
WIW .... WI Wheels International [*Vancouver Stock Exchange symbol*]
WIW .... Wooded Island [*Washington*] [*Seismograph station code, US Geological Survey*] (SEIS)
WIWHA.... Western International Walking Horse Association (EA)
Wi Wi........ Wirtschaftswissenschaft [*A publication*]
Wi Wiss .... Wirtschaftswissenschaft [*A publication*]
WIWO........ Walk In, Walk Out (ADA)
WIWP....... World Institute for World Peace
WIX .... Steenbock Memorial Library, Madison, WI [*OCLC symbol*] (OCLC)

WIX .... Wait for Index (NASA)
WIX .... Wickes Companies, Inc. [*AMEX symbol*] (SPSG)
WIX .... Winex Resources, Inc. [*Vancouver Stock Exchange symbol*]
WIXAMT ... Wixamtree [*England*]
WIXC........ Hazel Green, AL [*AM radio station call letters*]
WIXE........ Monroe, NC [*AM radio station call letters*]
WIXI......... Naples Park, FL [*FM radio station call letters*]
WIXK .... New Richmond, WI [*AM radio station call letters*]
WIXK-FM ... New Richmond, WI [*FM radio station call letters*]
WIXN........ Dixon, IL [*AM radio station call letters*]
WIXN-FM ... Dixon, IL [*FM radio station call letters*]
WIXQ .... Millersville, PA [*FM radio station call letters*]
WIXT........ Syracuse, NY [*Television station call letters*]
WIXV .... Savannah, GA [*FM radio station call letters*]
WIXX........ Green Bay, WI [*FM radio station call letters*]
WIXY........ East Longmeadow, MA [*AM radio station call letters*]
WIXZ........ McKeesport, PA [*AM radio station call letters*]
WIY .... University of Wisconsin, Primate Research Center, Primate Library, Madison, WI [*OCLC symbol*] (OCLC)
WIYC........ Charlotte Amalie, VI [*FM radio station call letters*]
WIYD .... Palatka, FL [*AM radio station call letters*]
WIYN .... Deposit, NY [*FM radio station call letters*]
WIYQ .... Ebensburg, PA [*FM radio station call letters*]
WIYY........ Baltimore, MD [*FM radio station call letters*]
WiZ........... Wiedza i Zycie [*A publication*]
WiZ........... Wort in der Zeit [*A publication*]
WIZA .... Savannah, GA [*AM radio station call letters*]
WIZB........ Abbeville, AL [*FM radio station call letters*]
WIZD........ Rudolph, WI [*FM radio station call letters*]
WIZE........ Springfield, OH [*AM radio station call letters*]
WIZF........ Erlanger, KY [*FM radio station call letters*]
WIZK........ Bay Springs, MS [*AM radio station call letters*]
WIZK-FM ... Bay Springs, MS [*FM radio station call letters*]
WIZM .... La Crosse, WI [*AM radio station call letters*]
WIZM-FM ... La Crosse, WI [*FM radio station call letters*]
WIZN .... Vergennes, VT [*FM radio station call letters*]
WIZO .... Franklin, TN [*AM radio station call letters*]
WIZO .... Women's International Zionist Organization [*Tel Aviv, Israel*] (EA)
WIZR........ Johnstown, NY [*AM radio station call letters*]
WIZS........ Henderson, NC [*AM radio station call letters*]
WIZY........ East Jordan, MI [*FM radio station call letters*]
WIZZ........ Streator, IL [*AM radio station call letters*]
WJ .... Joule [*Unit of work*] (ROG)
WJ .... Nihon Kinkyori Airways [*ICAO designator*] (FAAC)
WJ .... Wars of the Jews [*of Josephus*] [*A publication*] (BJA)
WJ .... Water Jacket (MSA)
WJ .... Watkins-Johnson Co. [*NYSE symbol*] (SPSG)
wj.............. West Bank of the Jordan River [*MARC country of publication code*] [*Library of Congress*] (LCCP)
WJ .... Western Jurist [*United States*] [*A publication*] (DLA)
WJ .... Wiener Jahreshefte [*A publication*]
WJ .... Wolfram-Jahrbuch [*A publication*]
WJ .... Wood Jalousie
WJ .... World Justice [*A publication*]
WJa .... Janesville Public Library, Janesville, WI [*Library symbol*] [*Library of Congress*] (LCLS)
WJA.......... Women's Jewelry Association (EA)
WJA.......... Woolen Jobbers Association (EA)
WJA.......... World Jazz Association [*Defunct*] (EA)
WJA.......... Wuerzburger Jahrbuecher fuer die Altertumswissenschaft [*A publication*]
WJaB........ Blackhawk Technical Institute, Janesville, WI [*Library symbol*] [*Library of Congress*] (LCLS)
WJAC........ Johnstown, PA [*AM radio station call letters*]
WJAC-TV ... Johnstown, PA [*Television station call letters*]
WJAD........ Bainbridge, GA [*FM radio station call letters*]
WJAE........ Jacksonville, NC [*Television station call letters*]
WJAG........ Norfolk, NE [*AM radio station call letters*]
WJAK........ Jackson, TN [*AM radio station call letters*]
WJAL........ Hagerstown, MD [*Television station call letters*]
WJaM .... Mercy Hospital, Janesville, WI [*Library symbol*] [*Library of Congress*] (LCLS)
WJAM-FM ... Marion, AL [*FM radio station call letters*]
WJAQ .... Marianna, FL [*FM radio station call letters*]
WJAR....... Providence, RI [*Television station call letters*]
WJaRH ..... Rock County Health Care Center, Janesville, WI [*Library symbol*] [*Library of Congress*] (LCLS)
WJAS........ Pittsburgh, PA [*AM radio station call letters*]
WJAT........ Swainsboro, GA [*AM radio station call letters*]
WJAT-FM ... Swainsboro, GA [*FM radio station call letters*]
WJAX........ Jacksonville, FL [*AM radio station call letters*]
WJAY........ Mullins, SC [*AM radio station call letters*]
WJAZ........ Stamford, CT [*FM radio station call letters*]
WJB.......... Wire Jig Board (MCD)
W Jb .... Wolfram-Jahrbuch [*A publication*]
W J Barrow Res Lab Publ ... W. J. Barrow Research Laboratory. Publication [*A publication*]
WJBB........ Haleyville, AL [*AM radio station call letters*]
W Jbb Alt .. Wuerzburger Jahrbuecher fuer die Altertumswissenschaft [*A publication*]

WJBB-FM ... Haleyville, AL [*FM radio station call letters*]
WJBC .... Bloomington, IL [*AM radio station call letters*]
WJBC .... Winnipeg Jets Booster Club   (EA)
WJBD........ Salem, IL [*AM radio station call letters*]
WJBD-FM ... Salem, IL [*FM radio station call letters*]
WJBF .... Augusta, GA [*Television station call letters*]
WJBI .... Batesville, MS [*AM radio station call letters*]
WJBK-TV ... Detroit, MI [*Television station call letters*]
WJ Bl........ Wiener Juristische Blaetter [*A publication*]
WJBM........ Jerseyville, IL [*AM radio station call letters*]
WJBO .... Baton Rouge, LA [*AM radio station call letters*]
WJBR .... Wilmington, DE [*AM radio station call letters*]
WJBR-FM ... Wilmington, DE [*FM radio station call letters*]
WJBS .... Holly Hill, SC [*AM radio station call letters*]
WJBU .... Port St. Joe, FL [*AM radio station call letters*]
WJBU .... William Jennings Bryan University [*Tennessee*]
WJBY .... Rainbow City, AL [*AM radio station call letters*]
WJC.......... Washington and Jefferson College [*Pennsylvania*]
WJC.......... Washington Journalism Center   (EA)
WJC.......... William Jewell College [*Liberty, MO*]
WJC.......... Wood Junior College [*Mathison, MS*]
WJC.......... Worcester Junior College [*Massachusetts*]
WJC.......... World Jewish Congress, American Section   (EA)
WJC.......... Worthington Junior College [*Minnesota*] [*Later, Worthington Community College*]
WJCAR ..... World Jewish Congress. Annual Report [*New York*] [*A publication*]
WJCB .... Norfolk, VA [*Television station call letters*]
WJCB .... World Jersey Cattle Bureau [*Jersey, Channel Islands, England*]
WJCC .... Norfolk, MA [*AM radio station call letters*]
WJCC .... Western Joint Computer Conference
WJCC .... Women's Joint Congressional Committee   (EA)
WJCD........ Seymour, IN [*AM radio station call letters*]
WJCD-FM ... Seymour, IN [*FM radio station call letters*]
WJCF .... Nashua, NH [*FM radio station call letters*]
WJCH .... Joliet, IL [*FM radio station call letters*]
WJCIB ...... World Jewish Congress. Information Bulletin [*New York*] [*A publication*]
WJCL .... Savannah, GA [*Television station call letters*]
WJCL-FM ... Savannah, GA [*FM radio station call letters*]
WJCM........ Sebring, FL [*AM radio station call letters*]
WJCR........ Millerstown, KY [*FM radio station call letters*]
WJCS .... Bayboro, NC [*AM radio station call letters*]
WJCT .... Jacksonville, FL [*Television station call letters*]
WJCT-FM ... Jacksonville, FL [*FM radio station call letters*]
WJCV........ Jacksonville, NC [*AM radio station call letters*]
WJCW........ Johnson City, TN [*AM radio station call letters*]
WJD .... Welded Joint Design
WJDA........ Quincy, MA [*AM radio station call letters*]
WJDB........ Thomasville, AL [*AM radio station call letters*]
WJDB-FM ... Thomasville, AL [*FM radio station call letters*]
WJDJ .... Burnside, KY [*FM radio station call letters*]
WJDM ...... Elizabeth, NJ [*AM radio station call letters*]
WJDQ .... Marion, MS [*AM radio station call letters*]
WJDQ-FM ... Meridian, MS [*FM radio station call letters*]
WJDR........ Prentiss, MS [*FM radio station call letters*]
WJDW-FM ... Corydon, IN [*FM radio station call letters*]
WJDX........ Jackson, MS [*AM radio station call letters*]
WJDY........ Salisbury, MD [*AM radio station call letters*]
WJDZ........ Levittown, PR [*FM radio station call letters*]
WJE.......... Willis, Joyce, McMinnville OR [*STAC*]
WJEB-TV ... Jacksonville, FL [*Television station call letters*]
WJEC........ Vernon, AL [*FM radio station call letters*]
WJEC........ Welsh Joint Education Committee [*British*]
WJED........ Dogwood Lakes Estate, FL [*FM radio station call letters*]
WJEF .... Lafayette, IN [*FM radio station call letters*]
WJEH........ Gallipolis, OH [*AM radio station call letters*]
WJEJ........ Hagerstown, MD [*AM radio station call letters*]
WJEL........ Indianapolis, IN [*FM radio station call letters*]
WJEM........ Valdosta, GA [*AM radio station call letters*]
WJEP........ Ochlocknee, GA [*AM radio station call letters*]
WJEQ....... Macomb, IL [*FM radio station call letters*]
WJER........ Dover-New Philadelphia, OH [*AM radio station call letters*]
WJER-FM ... Dover, OH [*FM radio station call letters*]
WJES .... Johnston, SC [*AM radio station call letters*]
WJET .... Erie, PA [*FM radio station call letters*]
WJET .... Wetjet International Ltd. [*NASDAQ symbol*]   (NQ)
WJET-TV ... Erie, PA [*Television station call letters*]
WJEZ........ Pontiac, IL [*FM radio station call letters*]
WJF.......... Lancaster, CA [*Location identifier*] [*FAA*]   (FAAL)
WJF.......... Palmdale/Lancaster [*California*] Fox [*Airport symbol*]   (OAG)
WJF.......... White Jewish Female [*Classified advertising*]
WJFB .... Lebanon, TN [*Television station call letters*]
WJFC .... Jefferson City, TN [*AM radio station call letters*]
WJFC .... Waylon Jennings Fan Club   (EA)
WJFD-FM ... New Bedford, MA [*FM radio station call letters*]
WJFF........ Jeffersonville, NY [*FM radio station call letters*]
WJFFC...... Worldwide John Fogerty Fanclub   (EAIO)
WJFG........ Solvay, NY [*AM radio station call letters*]
WJFI .... Women's Jazz Festival [*Defunct*]   (EA)
WJFJ......... Women Judges' Fund for Justice   (EA)

WJFK .... Manassas, VA [*FM radio station call letters*]
WJFL .... Vicksburg, MS [*AM radio station call letters*]
WJFM........ Grand Rapids, MI [*FM radio station call letters*]
WJFR .... Jacksonville, FL [*FM radio station call letters*]
WJFW-TV ... Rhinelander, WI [*Television station call letters*]
WJFX........ New Haven, IN [*FM radio station call letters*]
WJGA-FM ... Jackson, GA [*FM radio station call letters*]
WJGC........ Jacksonville, FL [*AM radio station call letters*]
WJGF........ Romney, WV [*FM radio station call letters*]
WJGO ...... World Jewish Genealogy Organization   (EA)
WJh.......... Wiener Jahreshefte [*A publication*]
WJHB ...... Fair Bluff, NC [*AM radio station call letters*]
WJHD...... Portsmouth, RI [*FM radio station call letters*]
WJHG-TV ... Panama City, FL [*Television station call letters*]
WJHH .... Soperton, GA [*AM radio station call letters*]
WJHL-TV ... Johnson City, TN [*Television station call letters*]
WJHM..... Daytona Beach, FL [*FM radio station call letters*]
WJHO ...... Opelika, AL [*AM radio station call letters*]
WJHP...... Columbia, MS [*AM radio station call letters*]
WJHR ...... Flemington, NJ [*AM radio station call letters*]
WJHS .... Columbia City, IN [*FM radio station call letters*]
WJHU-FM ... Baltimore, MD [*FM radio station call letters*]
WJI.......... WinJak, Incorporated [*NYSE symbol*]   (SPSG)
WJI.......... Wire Journal International [*A publication*]   (EAAP)
WJIB .... Boston, MA [*FM radio station call letters*]
WJIC .... Salem, NJ [*AM radio station call letters*]
WJIE .... Okolona, KY [*FM radio station call letters*]
WJIF .... Opp, AL [*FM radio station call letters*]
WJIK .... Camp Lejeune, NC [*AM radio station call letters*]
WJIL .... Jacksonville, IL [*AM radio station call letters*]
WJIM........ Lansing, MI [*AM radio station call letters*]
WJIM-FM ... Lansing, MI [*FM radio station call letters*]
WJIR .... Key West, FL [*FM radio station call letters*]
WJIS .... Bradenton, FL [*FM radio station call letters*]
WJIT .... New York, NY [*AM radio station call letters*]
WJIV........ Cherry Valley, NY [*FM radio station call letters*]
WJIW........ Cazenovia, NY [*AM radio station call letters*]
WJIZ-FM ... Albany, GA [*FM radio station call letters*]
WJJA .... Racine, WI [*Television station call letters*]
WJJB .... Romney, WV [*FM radio station call letters*]
WJJC ...... Commerce, GA [*AM radio station call letters*]
WJJD .... Chicago, IL [*AM radio station call letters*]
WJJF .... Hope Valley, RI [*AM radio station call letters*]
WJJH .... Ashland, WI [*FM radio station call letters*]
WJJJ .... Christiansburg, VA [*AM radio station call letters*]
WJJL........ Niagara Falls, NY [*AM radio station call letters*]
WJJM .... Lewisburg, TN [*AM radio station call letters*]
WJJM-FM ... Lewisburg, TN [*FM radio station call letters*]
WJJN .... Newburgh, IN [*AM radio station call letters*]
WJJQ .... Tomahawk, WI [*AM radio station call letters*]
WJJQ-FM ... Tomahawk, WI [*FM radio station call letters*]
WJJR .... Rutland, VT [*FM radio station call letters*]
WJJS .... Lynchburg, VA [*AM radio station call letters*]
WJJT .... Jellico, TN [*AM radio station call letters*]
WJJW .... North Adams, MA [*FM radio station call letters*]
WJJY .... Baxter, MN [*AM radio station call letters*]
WJJY-FM ... Brainerd, MN [*FM radio station call letters*]
WJK......... Wiener Jahrbuch fuer Kunstgeschichte [*A publication*]
WJKA .... Wilmington, NC [*Television station call letters*]
WJKC........ Christiansted, VI [*FM radio station call letters*]
WJKG....... Wiener Jahrbuch fuer Kunstgeschichte [*A publication*]
WJ f Kg...... Wiener Jahrbuch fuer Kunstgeschichte [*A publication*]
WJKI .... Woodruff, SC [*AM radio station call letters*]
WJKL........ Elgin, IL [*FM radio station call letters*]
WJKM........ Hartsville, TN [*AM radio station call letters*]
WJKS .... Jacksonville, FL [*Television station call letters*]
WJKY .... Jamestown, KY [*AM radio station call letters*]
WJKZ .... White Bluff, TN [*AM radio station call letters*]
WJLA-TV ... Washington, DC [*Television station call letters*]
WJLB .... Detroit, MI [*FM radio station call letters*]
WJLC .... Wye Junction Latching Circulator
WJLCER... Women's Joint Legislative Committee for Equal Rights [*Defunct*]   (EA)
WJLD .... Fairfield, AL [*AM radio station call letters*]
WJLE .... Smithville, TN [*AM radio station call letters*]
WJLE-FM ... Smithville, TN [*FM radio station call letters*]
WJLF .... Gainesville, FL [*FM radio station call letters*]
WJLK .... Asbury Park, NJ [*AM radio station call letters*]
WJLK-FM ... Asbury Park, NJ [*FM radio station call letters*]
WJLM........ Salem, VA [*FM radio station call letters*]
WJLQ .... Pensacola, FL [*FM radio station call letters*]
WJLS .... Beckley, WV [*AM radio station call letters*]
WJLU........ New Smyrna Beach, FL [*FM radio station call letters*]
WJLW........ De Pere, WI [*FM radio station call letters*]
WJLY .... Ramsey, IL [*FM radio station call letters*]
WJMA...... Orange, VA [*AM radio station call letters*]
WJMB .... Brookhaven, MS [*AM radio station call letters*]
WJMC........ Rice Lake, WI [*AM radio station call letters*]
WJMC-FM ... Rice Lake, WI [*FM radio station call letters*]
WJMD ...... Hazard, KY [*FM radio station call letters*]
WJMDA.... Western Journal of Medicine [*United States*] [*A publication*]

WJMF........ Smithfield, RI [*FM radio station call letters*]
WJMG....... Hattiesburg, MS [*FM radio station call letters*]
WJMH....... Reidsville, NC [*FM radio station call letters*]
WJMI......... Jackson, MS [*FM radio station call letters*]
WJMJ........ Hartford, CT [*FM radio station call letters*]
WJMK....... Chicago, IL [*FM radio station call letters*]
WJML........ Petoskey, MI [*AM radio station call letters*]
WJML-FM ... Petoskey, MI [*FM radio station call letters*]
WJMM-FM ... Versailles, KY [*FM radio station call letters*]
WJMN-TV ... Escanaba, MI [*Television station call letters*]
WJMO....... Cleveland Heights, OH [*AM radio station call letters*]
WJMP........ Kent, OH [*AM radio station call letters*]
WJMQ....... Clintonville, WI [*FM radio station call letters*]
WJMR........ Fredericktown, OH [*FM radio station call letters*]
WJMS........ Ironwood, MI [*AM radio station call letters*]
WJMT........ Merrill, WI [*AM radio station call letters*]
WJMU....... Decatur, IL [*FM radio station call letters*]
WJMW....... Bloomsburg, PA [*AM radio station call letters*]
WJMX....... Florence, SC [*AM radio station call letters*]
WJMX-FM ... Cheraw, SC [*FM radio station call letters*]
WJMY....... Baraga, MI [*FM radio station call letters*]
WJNA........ Churchville, VA [*FM radio station call letters*]
WJNC........ Jacksonville, NC [*AM radio station call letters*]
WJNF........ Marianna, FL [*FM radio station call letters*]
WJNL........ Johnstown, PA [*AM radio station call letters*]
WJNL-FM ... Johnstown, PA [*FM radio station call letters*]
WJNO....... West Palm Beach, FL [*AM radio station call letters*]
WJNR-FM ... Iron Mountain, MI [*FM radio station call letters*]
WJNS-FM ... Yazoo City, MS [*FM radio station call letters*]
WJNT........ Pearl, MS [*AM radio station call letters*]
WJNW....... Janesville, WI [*Television station call letters*]
WJNY........ Watertown, NY [*FM radio station call letters*]
WJNZ........ Greencastle, IN [*FM radio station call letters*]
W Jo.......... [*Sir William*] Jones' English King's Bench Reports [*A publication*]   (DLA)
WJOB........ Hammond, IN [*AM radio station call letters*]
WJOD........ Galena, IL [*FM radio station call letters*]
WJOI......... Detroit, MI [*FM radio station call letters*]
WJOK....... Hobson City, AL [*AM radio station call letters*]
WJOL........ Joliet, IL [*AM radio station call letters*]
WJON....... St. Cloud, MN [*AM radio station call letters*]
W Jones ..... [*Sir William*] Jones' English King's Bench Reports [*A publication*]   (DLA)
W Jones (Eng) ... [*Sir William*] Jones' English King's Bench Reports [*A publication*]   (DLA)
WJOR .... St. Joseph, TN [*AM radio station call letters*]
WJOS........ Elkin, NC [*AM radio station call letters*]
WJOT........ Lake City, SC [*AM radio station call letters*]
WJOY .... Burlington, VT [*AM radio station call letters*]
WJP.......... Water Jet Pump
WJPA........ Washington, PA [*AM radio station call letters*]
WJPC........ Chicago, IL [*AM radio station call letters*]
WJPD........ Ishpeming, MI [*AM radio station call letters*]
WJPD-FM ... Ishpeming, MI [*FM radio station call letters*]
WJPEB...... Woodcock-Johnson Psychoeducational Battery [*Educational test*]
WJPF .... Herrin, IL [*AM radio station call letters*]
WJPH........ Monticello, FL [*FM radio station call letters*]
WJPM-TV ... Florence, SC [*Television station call letters*]
WJPR........ Lynchburg, VA [*Television station call letters*]
WJPW....... Rockford, MI [*AM radio station call letters*]
WJPZ-FM ... Syracuse, NY [*FM radio station call letters*]
WJQI......... Chesapeake, VA [*AM radio station call letters*]
WJQI-FM ... Virginia Beach, VA [*FM radio station call letters*]
WJQK........ Zeeland, MI [*FM radio station call letters*]
WJQY....... Fort Lauderdale, FL [*FM radio station call letters*]
WJQZ........ Wellsville, NY [*FM radio station call letters*]
WJR.......... Cypress Fund [*AMEX symbol*]   (SPSG)
WJR.......... Detroit, MI [*AM radio station call letters*]
WJR.......... Wajir [*Kenya*] [*Airport symbol*]   (OAG)
WJR.......... Washington Journalism Review [*A publication*]
WJR.......... World Jewish Register [*A publication*]   (BJA)
WJRA........ Priceville, AL [*AM radio station call letters*]
WJRD........ Russellville, AL [*AM radio station call letters*]
WJRE........ Kewanee, IL [*FM radio station call letters*]
WJRH .... Easton, PA [*FM radio station call letters*]
WJRI......... Lenoir, NC [*FM radio station call letters*]
WJRL........ Calhoun City, MS [*AM radio station call letters*]
WJRM....... Troy, NC [*AM radio station call letters*]
WJRO .... Glen Burnie, MD [*AM radio station call letters*]
WJRQ....... Saluda, SC [*FM radio station call letters*]
WJRS........ Jamestown, KY [*FM radio station call letters*]
WJRT-TV ... Flint, MI [*Television station call letters*]
WJRZ........ Manahawkin, NJ [*FM radio station call letters*]
WJS.......... Watchmaker, Jeweller, and Silversmith [*A publication*]
WJS.......... Wife's Judicial Separation [*Legal*] [*British*]   (ROG)
WJSA........ Jersey Shore, PA [*AM radio station call letters*]
WJSA-FM ... Jersey Shore, PA [*FM radio station call letters*]
WJSB .... Crestview, FL [*AM radio station call letters*]
WJSC-FM ... Johnson, VT [*FM radio station call letters*]
WJSK........ Lumberton, NC [*FM radio station call letters*]

WJSL .... Houghton, NY [*FM radio station call letters*]
WJSM .... Martinsburg, PA [*AM radio station call letters*]
WJSM-FM ... Martinsburg, PA [*FM radio station call letters*]
WJSN-FM ... Jackson, KY [*FM radio station call letters*]
WJSO........ Pikeville, KY [*FM radio station call letters*]
WJSP-FM ... Warm Springs, GA [*FM radio station call letters*]
WJSP-TV ... Columbus, GA [*Television station call letters*]
WJSQ .... Athens, TN [*FM radio station call letters*]
WJSR .... Birmingham, AL [*FM radio station call letters*]
WJSU........ Jackson, MS [*FM radio station call letters*]
WJSUD...... World Journal of Surgery [*A publication*]
WJSU-TV ... Anniston, AL [*Television station call letters*]
WJSV .... Morristown, NJ [*FM radio station call letters*]
WJT.......... World Journal Tribune [*Defunct New York City afternoon newspaper*]
WJTA........ Kosciusko, MS [*FM radio station call letters*]
WJTB........ North Ridgeville, OH [*AM radio station call letters*]
WJTC........ Pensacola, FL [*Television station call letters*]
WJTG........ Fort Valley, GA [*FM radio station call letters*]
WJTH .... Calhoun, GA [*AM radio station call letters*]
WJTL........ Lancaster, PA [*FM radio station call letters*]
WJTM....... Frederick, MD [*FM radio station call letters*]
WJTN....... Jamestown, NY [*AM radio station call letters*]
WJTO....... Bath, ME [*AM radio station call letters*]
WJTP........ Newland, NC [*AM radio station call letters*]
WJTT........ Red Bank, TN [*FM radio station call letters*]
WJTV .... Jackson, MS [*Television station call letters*]
WJTW....... Joliet, IL [*FM radio station call letters*]
WJTX........ Urbana, IL [*AM radio station call letters*]
WJTY........ Lancaster, WI [*FM radio station call letters*]
WJTZ........ Blountville, TN [*AM radio station call letters*]
WJu .... Juneau Public Library, Juneau, WI [*Library symbol*] [*Library of Congress*]   (LCLS)
WJUL........ Lowell, MA [*FM radio station call letters*]
WJuMe...... Dodge County Mental Health Center, Juneau, WI [*Library symbol*] [*Library of Congress*]   (LCLS)
WJUN ...... Mexico, PA [*AM radio station call letters*]
WJUN-FM ... Mexico, PA [*FM radio station call letters*]
WJURDJ .. World Journal of Urology [*A publication*]
WJVL........ Janesville, WI [*FM radio station call letters*]
WJVO .... South Jacksonville, IL [*FM radio station call letters*]
WJVS .... Cincinnati, OH [*FM radio station call letters*]
WJWF....... Columbus, MS [*AM radio station call letters*]
WJWJ-FM ... Beaufort, SC [*FM radio station call letters*]
WJWJ-TV ... Beaufort, SC [*Television station call letters*]
WJWN-TV ... San Sebastian, PR [*Television station call letters*]
WJWS .... South Hill, VA [*AM radio station call letters*]
WJWT....... Jackson, TN [*Television station call letters*]
WJW-TV... Cleveland, OH [*Television station call letters*]
WJX.......... Wajax Ltd. [*Toronto Stock Exchange symbol*]
WJXL........ Jacksonville, AL [*AM radio station call letters*]
WJXN....... Jackson, MS [*AM radio station call letters*]
WJXQ....... Jackson, MI [*FM radio station call letters*]
WJXR........ Macclenny, FL [*FM radio station call letters*]
WJXT........ Jacksonville, FL [*Television station call letters*]
WJXY........ Conway, SC [*AM radio station call letters*]
WJY.......... Westmoreland County Community College, Youngwood, PA [*OCLC symbol*]   (OCLC)
WJYA........ Buford, GA [*AM radio station call letters*]
WJYE........ Buffalo, NY [*FM radio station call letters*]
WJYF .... Nashville, GA [*FM radio station call letters*]
WJYJ .... Fredericksburg, VA [*FM radio station call letters*]
WJYM....... Bowling Green, OH [*AM radio station call letters*]
WJYO .... Mount Dora, FL [*FM radio station call letters*]
WJYP .... South Charleston, WV [*FM radio station call letters*]
WJYQ....... Moncks Corner, SC [*FM radio station call letters*]
WJYR........ Myrtle Beach, SC [*FM radio station call letters*]
WJYS .... Hammond, IN [*Television station call letters*]
WJYY .... Concord, NH [*FM radio station call letters*]
WJYZ........ Albany, GA [*AM radio station call letters*]
WJZM....... Clarksville, TN [*AM radio station call letters*]
WJZQ....... Kenosha, WI [*FM radio station call letters*]
WJZ-TV...... Baltimore, MD [*Television station call letters*]
WJZY........ Belmont, NC [*Television station call letters*]
WJZZ........ Detroit, MI [*FM radio station call letters*]
WK............ Ratioflug Luftfahrtunternehmen GmbH, Frankfurt Am Main [*West Germany*] [*ICAO designator*]   (FAAC)
wk............. Wake Island [*MARC country of publication code*] [*Library of Congress*]   (LCCP)
WK............ Warburg-Keilin System [*Cytochrome-cytochrome oxidase system*] [*Named for Otto Warburg and D. Keilin*]
WK............ Warehouse Keeper [*British*]   (ROG)
WK............ Waylands Korongo [*Tanzania*]
WK............ Weak   (FAAC)
WK............ Week   (AFM)
WK............ Well-Known
WK............ Wernicke-Korsakoff [*Syndrome*] [*Medicine*]
WK............ Western Alaska [*Airlines*]   (OAG)
WK............ Wetboek van Koophandel [*Commercial Code*] [*Dutch*]   (ILCA)
wk............. Wisselkoers [*Rate of Exchange*] [*Afrikaans*] [*Finance*]
WK............ Work

WK............ Worksheet [*Data format*]
Wk .... Wreck [*Nautical charts*]
WKa........... Kaukauna Public Library, Kaukauna, WI [*Library symbol*]
          [*Library of Congress*]   (LCLS)
WKA.......... Waffenkarren [*Weapons Cart*] [*German military - World War II*]
WKA.......... Wkay Resources [*Vancouver Stock Exchange symbol*]
WKAC...... Athens, AL [*AM radio station call letters*]
WKACC..... Work Accomplishment Code [*Navy*]   (NG)
WKAI........ Macomb, IL [*FM radio station call letters*]
WKAJ........ Saratoga Springs, NY [*AM radio station call letters*]
WKAK...... Albany, GA [*FM radio station call letters*]
WKAM...... Goshen, IN [*AM radio station call letters*]
WKAN...... Kankakee, IL [*AM radio station call letters*]
WKAP ...... Allentown, PA [*AM radio station call letters*]
WKAQ-FM ... San Juan, PR [*FM radio station call letters*]
WKAQ-TV ... San Juan, PR [*Television station call letters*]
WKAR....... East Lansing, MI [*AM radio station call letters*]
WKAR-FM ... East Lansing, MI [*FM radio station call letters*]
WKAR-TV ... East Lansing, MI [*Television station call letters*]
WKAS....... Ashland, KY [*Television station call letters*]
WKAT....... North Miami, FL [*AM radio station call letters*]
Wk Aust..... Weekend Australian [*A publication*]
WKAV ...... Charlottesville, VA [*AM radio station call letters*]
WKAX ...... Russellville, AL [*AM radio station call letters*]
WKAY ...... Kannapolis, NC [*Television station call letters*]
WKAZ ...... St. Albans, WV [*AM radio station call letters*]
WKB.......... Wentzel-Kramers-Brillouin Approximation [*Mathematics*]
WKBA....... Vinton, VA [*AM radio station call letters*]
WKBB........ West Point, MS [*FM radio station call letters*]
WKBC....... North Wilkesboro, NC [*AM radio station call letters*]
WKBC-FM ... North Wilkesboro, NC [*FM radio station call letters*]
WKBD....... Detroit, MI [*Television station call letters*]
WKBF....... Rock Island, IL [*AM radio station call letters*]
WKBH...... Holmen, WI [*AM radio station call letters*]
WKBH-FM ... Trempealeau, WI [*FM radio station call letters*]
WKBI........ St. Mary's, PA [*AM radio station call letters*]
WKBI-FM ... St. Mary's, PA [*FM radio station call letters*]
WKBJ........ Milan, TN [*AM radio station call letters*]
WKBJ........ Wentzel-Kramers-Brillouin-Jeffreys [*Approximation or Method*] [*Physics*]
WKBK ...... Keene, NH [*AM radio station call letters*]
Wkb Krb .... Weekberichten van de Kredietbank [*A publication*]
WKBL........ Covington, TN [*AM radio station call letters*]
WKBL-FM ... Covington, TN [*FM radio station call letters*]
WKBM...... Coal City, IL [*FM radio station call letters*]
WKBN....... Youngstown, OH [*AM radio station call letters*]
WKBN-FM ... Youngstown, OH [*FM radio station call letters*]
WKBN-TV ... Youngstown, OH [*Television station call letters*]
WKBO....... Harrisburg, PA [*AM radio station call letters*]
WKBQ....... Granite City, IL [*FM radio station call letters*]
WKBR....... Manchester, NH [*AM radio station call letters*]
WKBS-TV ... Altoona, PA [*Television station call letters*]
WKBT....... La Crosse, WI [*Television station call letters*]
WKBV....... Richmond, IN [*AM radio station call letters*]
WKBW-TV ... Buffalo, NY [*Television station call letters*]
WKBX ...... Kingsland, GA [*FM radio station call letters*]
WKBY ...... Chatham, VA [*AM radio station call letters*]
WKBZ ...... Muskegon, MI [*AM radio station call letters*]
WKBZ-FM ... Whitehall, MI [*FM radio station call letters*]
WKC.......... Walker Ridge [*California*] [*Seismograph station code, US Geological Survey*]   (SEIS)
WKC.......... Westminster Kennel Club   (EA)
WKCA ...... Owingsville, KY [*FM radio station call letters*]
WKCB ...... Hindman, KY [*AM radio station call letters*]
WKCB-FM ... Hindman, KY [*FM radio station call letters*]
WKCC....... Grayson, KY [*FM radio station call letters*]
WKCD....... Kittery, ME [*FM radio station call letters*]
WKCE....... Harriman, TN [*AM radio station call letters*]
WKCF....... Clermont, FL [*Television station call letters*]
WKCG....... Augusta, ME [*FM radio station call letters*]
WKCH-TV ... Knoxville, TN [*Television station call letters*]
WKCI........ Hamden, CT [*FM radio station call letters*]
WKCJ....... Lewisburg, WV [*FM radio station call letters*]
WKCK ...... Orocavis, PR [*AM radio station call letters*]
WKCL....... Ladson, SC [*FM radio station call letters*]
WKCM ...... Hawesville, KY [*AM radio station call letters*]
WKCN....... Dorchester Terrace-Brentwood, SC [*AM radio station call letters*]
WKCO....... Gambier, OH [*FM radio station call letters*]
WKCONSUPVR ... Work Control Supervisor [*Air Force*]
WKCP....... Kinston, NC [*FM radio station call letters*]
WKCQ....... Saginaw, MI [*FM radio station call letters*]
WKCR-FM ... New York, NY [*FM radio station call letters*]
WKCS....... Knoxville, TN [*FM radio station call letters*]
WKCT ...... Bowling Green, KY [*AM radio station call letters*]
WKCU....... Corinth, MS [*AM radio station call letters*]
WKCW...... Warrenton, VA [*AM radio station call letters*]
WKCX ...... Rome, GA [*FM radio station call letters*]
WKCY ...... Harrisonburg, VA [*AM radio station call letters*]
WKCY-FM ... Harrisonburg, VA [*FM radio station call letters*]

WKD......... Weekday
WKDA....... Nashville, TN [*AM radio station call letters*]
WKDAY .... Weekday
WKDB....... Asheville, NC [*FM radio station call letters*]
WKDC....... Elmhurst, IL [*AM radio station call letters*]
WKDD....... Akron, OH [*FM radio station call letters*]
WKDE....... Altavista, VA [*AM radio station call letters*]
WKDF....... Nashville, TN [*FM radio station call letters*]
WKDI........ Denton, MD [*AM radio station call letters*]
WKDJ........ Clarksdale, MS [*FM radio station call letters*]
WKDK...... Newberry, SC [*AM radio station call letters*]
WKDM...... New York, NY [*AM radio station call letters*]
WKDN-FM ... Camden, NJ [*FM radio station call letters*]
WKDO...... Liberty, KY [*AM radio station call letters*]
WKDO-FM ... Liberty, KY [*FM radio station call letters*]
WKDP....... Corbin, KY [*AM radio station call letters*]
WKDP-FM ... Corbin, KY [*FM radio station call letters*]
WKDQ....... Henderson, KY [*FM radio station call letters*]
WKDR....... Plattsburgh, NY [*AM radio station call letters*]
WKDS .... Kalamazoo, MI [*FM radio station call letters*]
WKDU...... Philadelphia, PA [*FM radio station call letters*]
WKDW...... Staunton, VA [*AM radio station call letters*]
WKDX ...... Hamlet, NC [*AM radio station call letters*]
WKDY ...... Spartanburg, SC [*AM radio station call letters*]
WKDZ ...... Cadiz, KY [*AM radio station call letters*]
WKE.......... Wake [*Wake Island*] [*Seismograph station code, US Geological Survey*] [*Closed*]   (SEIS)
WKEA-FM ... Scottsboro, AL [*FM radio station call letters*]
WKEB-TV ... Islamorada, FL [*Television station call letters*]
WKED....... Frankfort, KY [*AM radio station call letters*]
WKEE....... Huntington, WV [*AM radio station call letters*]
WKEE-FM ... Huntington, WV [*FM radio station call letters*]
WKEF....... Dayton, OH [*Television station call letters*]
WKEG....... Washington, PA [*AM radio station call letters*]
WKEI........ Kewanee, IL [*AM radio station call letters*]
W Kel........ [*William*] Kelynge's English Chancery Reports [*A publication*]   (DLA)
WKEL....... Myrtle Beach, SC [*AM radio station call letters*]
W Kelynge (Eng) ... [*William*] Kelynge's English Chancery Reports [*A publication*]   (DLA)
WKEN ...... Dover, DE [*AM radio station call letters*]
WKen........ Gilbert M. Simmons Public Library, Kenosha, WI [*Library symbol*] [*Library of Congress*]   (LCLS)
WKenA...... Armitage Academy Library, Kenosha, WI [*Library symbol*] [*Library of Congress*]   (LCLS)
WKenC ...... Carthage College, Kenosha, WI [*Library symbol*] [*Library of Congress*]   (LCLS)
WKEND.... Weekend
WKenG...... Gateway Technical Institute, Kenosha, WI [*Library symbol*] [*Library of Congress*]   (LCLS)
WKenG-E.. Gateway Technical Institute, Elkhorn Campus, Elkhorn, WI [*Library symbol*] [*Library of Congress*]   (LCLS)
WKenG-R .. Gateway Technical Institute, Racine Campus, Racine, WI [*Library symbol*] [*Library of Congress*]   (LCLS)
WKenHi..... Kenosha County Historical Association, Kenosha, WI [*Library symbol*] [*Library of Congress*]   (LCLS)
WKenM ..... Kenosha Memorial Hospital, Kenosha, WI [*Library symbol*] [*Library of Congress*]   (LCLS)
WKenOS ... Old Songs Library, Kenosha, WI [*Library symbol*] [*Library of Congress*]   (LCLS)
WKenSC.... St. Catherine's Hospital, Kenosha, WI [*Library symbol*] [*Library of Congress*]   (LCLS)
WKenSD.... Unified School District Number One, Media Center, Kenosha, WI [*Library symbol*] [*Library of Congress*]   (LCLS)
WKenSD-B ... Unified School District Number One, Mary D. Bradford High School, Kenosha, WI [*Library symbol*] [*Library of Congress*]   (LCLS)
WKenSD-R ... Unified School District Number One, Walter Reuther High School, Kenosha, WI [*Library symbol*] [*Library of Congress*]   (LCLS)
WKenSD-T ... Unified School District Number One, Tremper High School, Kenosha, WI [*Library symbol*] [*Library of Congress*]   (LCLS)
WKenU...... University of Wisconsin-Parkside, Kenosha, WI [*Library symbol*] [*Library of Congress*]   (LCLS)
WKenU-A ... University of Wisconsin-Parkside, Archives and Art Research Center, Kenosha, WI [*Library symbol*] [*Library of Congress*]   (LCLS)
WKEQ....... Burnside, KY [*AM radio station call letters*]
WKER....... Pompton Lakes, NJ [*AM radio station call letters*]
WKES........ St. Petersburg, FL [*FM radio station call letters*]
WKET....... Kettering, OH [*FM radio station call letters*]
WKEU....... Griffin, GA [*AM radio station call letters*]
WKEU-FM ... Griffin, GA [*FM radio station call letters*]
WKEW...... Greensboro, NC [*AM radio station call letters*]
WKEX ...... Blacksburg, VA [*AM radio station call letters*]
WKEY ...... Covington, VA [*AM radio station call letters*]
WKEZ-FM ... Yorktown, VA [*FM radio station call letters*]
WKF......... Well-Known Factor
WKFD .... Wickford, RI [*AM radio station call letters*]
WKFE........ Yauco, PR [*AM radio station call letters*]

WKFI........ Wilmington, OH [*AM radio station call letters*]
WKFL........ Bushnell, FL [*AM radio station call letters*]
WKFM ...... Fulton, NY [*FM radio station call letters*]
WKFN ...... Oxford, AL [*FM radio station call letters*]
WKFR-FM ... Battle Creek, MI [*FM radio station call letters*]
WKFT........ Fayetteville, NC [*Television station call letters*]
WKFX........ Kaukauna, WI [*FM radio station call letters*]
WKG......... Working (MSA)
WKGA....... Zion, IL [*AM radio station call letters*]
WKGB-FM ... Susquehanna, PA [*FM radio station call letters*]
WKGB-TV ... Bowling Green, KY [*Television station call letters*]
WKGC....... Panama City Beach, FL [*AM radio station call letters*]
WKGC-FM ... Panama City, FL [*FM radio station call letters*]
WKGG....... Cape Vincent, NY [*FM radio station call letters*]
Wkg Girls Newsl ... Working with Girls Newsletter [*A publication*]
WKGK....... Saltville, VA [*AM radio station call letters*]
WKGM...... Smithfield, VA [*AM radio station call letters*]
WKGN...... Knoxville, TN [*AM radio station call letters*]
WKGO ...... Cumberland, MD [*FM radio station call letters*]
WKGQ....... Milledgeville, GA [*AM radio station call letters*]
WKGR....... Fort Pierce, FL [*FM radio station call letters*]
WKGT ...... Century, FL [*FM radio station call letters*]
WKGV ...... Tioga, PA [*FM radio station call letters*]
WKGW ...... Utica, NY [*FM radio station call letters*]
WKGX ...... Lenoir, NC [*AM radio station call letters*]
WKHA....... Hazard, KY [*Television station call letters*]
WKHG....... Leitchfield, KY [*FM radio station call letters*]
WKHI........ Ocean City, MD [*FM radio station call letters*]
WKHJ....... Mountain Lake Park, MD [*FM radio station call letters*]
WKHK....... Colonial Heights, VA [*FM radio station call letters*]
WKHL....... York, PA [*FM radio station call letters*]
WKHL-FM ... Salladasburg, PA [*FM radio station call letters*]
WKHM...... Jackson, MI [*AM radio station call letters*]
WKHO ...... Pinehurst, NC [*AM radio station call letters*]
WKHQ-FM ... Charlevoix, MI [*FM radio station call letters*]
WKHR....... Bainbridge, OH [*FM radio station call letters*]
WKHS....... Worton, MD [*FM radio station call letters*]
WKHV....... Altavista, VA [*FM radio station call letters*]
WKHX...... Atlanta, GA [*AM radio station call letters*]
WKHX-FM ... Marietta, GA [*FM radio station call letters*]
WKHY....... Lafayette, IN [*FM radio station call letters*]
WKi.......... Kiel Public Library, Kiel, WI [*Library symbol*] [*Library of Congress*] (LCLS)
WKIC........ Hazard, KY [*AM radio station call letters*]
WKID .... Vevay, IN [*FM radio station call letters*]
WKIE......... Richmond, VA [*AM radio station call letters*]
WKIG .... Glennville, GA [*AM radio station call letters*]
WKIG-FM ... Glennville, GA [*FM radio station call letters*]
WKII......... Port Charlotte, FL [*AM radio station call letters*]
WKIJ .... Parrish, AL [*AM radio station call letters*]
WKIK .... Leonardtown, MD [*AM radio station call letters*]
WKIN .... Kingsport, TN [*AM radio station call letters*]
WKIO .... Urbana, IL [*FM radio station call letters*]
WKIP........ Poughkeepsie, NY [*AM radio station call letters*]
WKIQ .... Eustis, FL [*AM radio station call letters*]
WKIS .... Boca Raton, FL [*FM radio station call letters*]
WKIS........ Wilson Knight Interdiscipline Society (EA)
WKISF....... Wilson Knight Interdiscipline Society and Foundation (EA)
WKIT........ Brewer, ME [*AM radio station call letters*]
WKIT-FM ... Brewer, ME [*FM radio station call letters*]
WKIX .... Raleigh, NC [*AM radio station call letters*]
WKIY .... West Kent Imperial Yeomanry [*British military*] (DMA)
WKIZ .... Key West, FL [*AM radio station call letters*]
WKJ.......... Wakkanai [*Japan*] [*Airport symbol*] (OAG)
WKJA....... Belhaven, NC [*FM radio station call letters*]
WKJB....... Mayaguez, PR [*AM radio station call letters*]
WKJB-FM ... Mayaguez, PR [*FM radio station call letters*]
WKJC........ Tawas City, MI [*FM radio station call letters*]
WKJE....... Hertford, NC [*FM radio station call letters*]
WKJF....... Cadillac, MI [*AM radio station call letters*]
WKJF-FM ... Cadillac, MI [*FM radio station call letters*]
WKJG-TV ... Fort Wayne, IN [*Television station call letters*]
WKJM....... Monticello, IN [*FM radio station call letters*]
WKJN .... Baton Rouge, LA [*AM radio station call letters*]
WKJN .... Hammond, LA [*FM radio station call letters*]
WKJR....... Muskegon Heights, MI [*AM radio station call letters*]
WKJV....... Campbellsville, KY [*FM radio station call letters*]
WKJX....... Elizabeth City, NC [*FM radio station call letters*]
WKJY....... Hempstead, NY [*FM radio station call letters*]
WKJY....... Parsons, TN [*AM radio station call letters*]
WKK......... Aleknagik [*Alaska*] [*Airport symbol*] (OAG)
WKK......... Aleknagik, AK [*Location identifier*] [*FAA*] (FAAL)
WKKB....... Key Colony Beach, FL [*FM radio station call letters*]
WKKC....... Chicago, IL [*FM radio station call letters*]
WKKD....... Aurora, IL [*AM radio station call letters*]
WKKD-FM ... Aurora, IL [*FM radio station call letters*]
WKKG....... Columbus, IN [*FM radio station call letters*]
WKKI........ Celina, OH [*FM radio station call letters*]
WKKJ....... Chillicothe, OH [*FM radio station call letters*]
WKKL ...... West Barnstable, MA [*FM radio station call letters*]
WKKM...... Harrison, MI [*FM radio station call letters*]

WKKN...... Rockford, IL [*AM radio station call letters*]
WKKO...... Toledo, OH [*FM radio station call letters*]
WKKP ...... Lansing, MI [*FM radio station call letters*]
WKKQ ...... Nashwauk, MN [*AM radio station call letters*]
WKKR ...... Auburn, AL [*FM radio station call letters*]
WKKS........ Vanceburg, KY [*AM radio station call letters*]
WKKS-FM ... Vanceburg, KY [*FM radio station call letters*]
WKKT-TV ... Hopkinsville, KY [*Television station call letters*]
WKKU...... Boston, MA [*AM radio station call letters*]
WKKW-FM ... Clarksburg, WV [*FM radio station call letters*]
WKKX ...... Jerseyville, IL [*FM radio station call letters*]
WKKY ...... Moss Point, MS [*FM radio station call letters*]
WKKZ ...... Dublin, GA [*FM radio station call letters*]
WKL .... Waikoloa [*Hawaii*] [*Airport symbol*] (OAG)
WKLA ...... Canandaigua, NY [*FM radio station call letters*]
WKLA ...... Ludington, MI [*AM radio station call letters*]
WKLA-FM ... Ludington, MI [*FM radio station call letters*]
WKLB....... Manchester, KY [*AM radio station call letters*]
WKLB-FM ... Manchester, KY [*FM radio station call letters*]
WKLC-FM ... St. Albans, WV [*FM radio station call letters*]
WKLD .... Oneonta, AL [*AM radio station call letters*]
WKLE....... Lexington, KY [*Television station call letters*]
WKLEERI ... W. K. Lypynsky East European Research Institute (EA)
WKLF........ Clanton, AL [*AM radio station call letters*]
WKLG....... Rock Harbor, FL [*FM radio station call letters*]
WKLH....... Milwaukee, WI [*FM radio station call letters*]
WKLI......... Albany, NY [*FM radio station call letters*]
W Klin Wschr ... Wiener Klinische Wochenschrift [*A publication*]
WKLJ....... Oxford, MS [*FM radio station call letters*]
WKLK ...... Cloquet, MN [*AM radio station call letters*]
WKLM ...... Millersburg, OH [*FM radio station call letters*]
WKLO ...... Danville, KY [*AM radio station call letters*]
WKLP....... Keyser, WV [*AM radio station call letters*]
WKLQ ...... Holland, MI [*FM radio station call letters*]
WKLR....... Indianapolis, IN [*FM radio station call letters*]
WKLS-FM ... Atlanta, GA [*FM radio station call letters*]
WKLT....... Kalkaska, MI [*AM radio station call letters*]
WKLT-FM ... Kalkaska, MI [*FM radio station call letters*]
WKLW ...... Paintsville, KY [*AM radio station call letters*]
W Kl Ws ... Wiener Klinische Wochenschrift [*A publication*]
WKLX ...... Rochester, NY [*FM radio station call letters*]
WKLY....... Hartwell, GA [*AM radio station call letters*]
WKLY....... Weekly
Wkly Cin Law Bul ... Weekly Cincinnati Law Bulletin [*Ohio*] [*A publication*] (DLA)
Wkly Coal ... Weekly Coal Production [*A publication*]
Wkly Dig ... New York Weekly Digest [*A publication*] (DLA)
Wkly Energy Rep ... Weekly Energy Report [*United States*] [*A publication*]
Wkly Inf Bull ... Weekly Information Bulletin [*A publication*]
Wkly Law Bul ... Weekly Law Bulletin [*Ohio*] [*A publication*] (DLA)
Wkly Law Gaz ... Weekly Law Gazette [*Ohio*] [*A publication*] (DLA)
Wkly L Bul ... Weekly Law Bulletin [*Ohio*] [*A publication*] (DLA)
Wkly L Gaz ... Weekly Law Gazette [*Ohio*] [*A publication*] (DLA)
Wkly NC.... Weekly Notes of Cases [*Pennsylvania*] [*A publication*] (DLA)
Wkly Notes Cas ... Weekly Notes of Cases [*Pennsylvania*] [*A publication*] (DLA)
Wkly Notes Cas (PA) ... Weekly Notes of Cases [*Pennsylvania*] [*A publication*] (DLA)
Wkly Rec ... Weekly Record [*United States*] [*A publication*]
Wkly Rep... Weekly Reporter [*London*] [*A publication*] (DLA)
WKLZ....... Rutland, VT [*FM radio station call letters*]
WKM........ Hwange National Park [*Zimbabwe*] [*Airport symbol*] (OAG)
WKM........ State University of New York, Agricultural and Technical College, Cobleskill, Cobleskill, NY [*OCLC symbol*] (OCLC)
WKMA...... Madisonville, KY [*Television station call letters*]
WKMB ...... Stirling, NJ [*AM radio station call letters*]
WKMC...... Roaring Spring, PA [*AM radio station call letters*]
WKMD...... Loogootee, IN [*FM radio station call letters*]
WKMF ...... Flint, MI [*AM radio station call letters*]
WKMG...... Newberry, SC [*AM radio station call letters*]
WKMI ...... Kalamazoo, MI [*AM radio station call letters*]
WKMIA ...... Wakayama Igaku [*A publication*]
WKMJ....... Louisville, KY [*Television station call letters*]
WKML...... Lumberton, NC [*FM radio station call letters*]
WKMM.... Kingwood, WV [*FM radio station call letters*]
WKMO...... Hodgenville, KY [*FM radio station call letters*]
WKMP...... Rocky Mount, NC [*AM radio station call letters*]
WKMQ...... Winnebago, IL [*FM radio station call letters*]
WKMR...... Morehead, KY [*Television station call letters*]
WKMS-FM ... Murray, KY [*FM radio station call letters*]
WKMT...... Kings Mountain, NC [*AM radio station call letters*]
WKMU...... Murray, KY [*Television station call letters*]
WKMX...... Enterprise, AL [*FM radio station call letters*]
WKMY...... Princeton, WV [*FM radio station call letters*]
WKMZ...... Martinsburg, WV [*FM radio station call letters*]
WKN......... Wakunai [*Papua New Guinea*] [*Airport symbol*] (OAG)
WKN......... Weaken
Wk N .... Weekly Notes of Cases [*Pennsylvania*] [*A publication*] (DLA)
WKNC-FM ... Raleigh, NC [*FM radio station call letters*]
WKND....... Weekend

WKND.......	Windsor, CT [*AM radio station call letters*]
WKNDDH ...	Annual Report. Research Institute for Wakan-Yaku Toyama Medical and Pharmaceutical University [*A publication*]
WKNE.......	Keene, NH [*AM radio station call letters*]
WKNE-FM ...	Keene, NH [*FM radio station call letters*]
WKNF-FM ...	Oak Ridge, TN [*FM radio station call letters*]
WKNG.......	Tallapoosa, GA [*AM radio station call letters*]
WKNH	Keene, NH [*FM radio station call letters*]
WKNI.......	Lexington, AL [*AM radio station call letters*]
WKNJ.......	Lakeside, NJ [*AM radio station call letters*]
WKNJ-FM ...	Union Township, NJ [*FM radio station call letters*]
WKNL.......	Knoxville, TN [*AM radio station call letters*]
WKNL.......	Walter Kidde Nuclear Laboratories, Inc. (MCD)
WKNN.......	Moss Point, MS [*AM radio station call letters*]
WKNN-FM ...	Pascagoula, MS [*FM radio station call letters*]
WKNO-FM ...	Memphis, TN [*FM radio station call letters*]
WKNO-TV ...	Memphis, TN [*Television station call letters*]
WKNS.......	Kinston, NC [*FM radio station call letters*]
WKNU.......	Brewton, AL [*FM radio station call letters*]
WKNV.......	Dublin, VA [*AM radio station call letters*]
WKNX.......	Frankenmuth, MI [*AM radio station call letters*]
WKNY.......	Kingston, NY [*AM radio station call letters*]
WKNZ.......	Collins, MS [*FM radio station call letters*]
WKOH.......	Owensboro, KY [*Television station call letters*]
WKOI.......	Richmond, IN [*Television station call letters*]
WKOJ.......	Middletown, NY [*FM radio station call letters*]
WKOK.......	Sunbury, PA [*AM radio station call letters*]
WKOL.......	Amsterdam, NY [*AM radio station call letters*]
WKOL-FM ...	Amsterdam, NY [*FM radio station call letters*]
WKOM.......	Columbia, TN [*FM radio station call letters*]
WKON.......	Owenton, KY [*Television station call letters*]
WKOO	Jacksonville, NC [*AM radio station call letters*]
WKOR.......	Starkville, MS [*AM radio station call letters*]
WKOR-FM ...	Starkville, MS [*FM radio station call letters*]
WKOS	Rochester, NH [*AM radio station call letters*]
WKOS-FM ...	Rochester, NH [*FM radio station call letters*]
WKOV.......	Wellston, OH [*AM radio station call letters*]
WKOV-FM ...	Wellston, OH [*FM radio station call letters*]
WKOW-TV ...	Madison, WI [*Television station call letters*]
WKOX.......	Framingham, MA [*AM radio station call letters*]
WKOY.......	Bluefield, WV [*AM radio station call letters*]
WKOZ.......	Kosciusko, MS [*AM radio station call letters*]
WKP	Wochenschrift fuer Klassische Philologie [*A publication*]
WKPA.......	New Kensington, PA [*AM radio station call letters*]
WKPB.......	Henderson, KY [*FM radio station call letters*]
WKPC-TV ...	Louisville, KY [*Television station call letters*]
WKPD.......	Paducah, KY [*Television station call letters*]
WKPE.......	Orleans, MA [*AM radio station call letters*]
WKPG.......	Port Gibson, MS [*AM radio station call letters*]
WKPI.......	Pikeville, KY [*Television station call letters*]
WKPK.......	Gaylord, MI [*FM radio station call letters*]
WKPL.......	Platteville, WI [*FM radio station call letters*]
WKPO.......	Prentiss, MS [*AM radio station call letters*]
WKPQ.......	Hornell, NY [*FM radio station call letters*]
WKPR.......	Kalamazoo, MI [*AM radio station call letters*]
WKPT.......	Kingsport, TN [*AM radio station call letters*]
WKPT-TV ...	Kingsport, TN [*Television station call letters*]
WKPV.......	Ponce, PR [*Television station call letters*]
WKPX.......	Sunrise, FL [*FM radio station call letters*]
WKQB.......	St. George, SC [*FM radio station call letters*]
WKQC.......	Canaan, VT [*AM radio station call letters*]
WKQD-FM ...	Tullahoma, TN [*FM radio station call letters*]
WKQDR....	Work Queue Directory
WKQI-FM ...	Detroit, MI [*FM radio station call letters*]
WKQQ.......	Lexington, KY [*FM radio station call letters*]
WKQR.......	Citronelle, AL [*FM radio station call letters*]
WKQW.......	Oil City, PA [*AM radio station call letters*]
WKQX.......	Chicago, IL [*FM radio station call letters*]
WKQZ.......	Midland, MI [*FM radio station call letters*]
WKR	Walker's Cay [*Bahamas*] [*Airport symbol*] (OAG)
WKR	Whittaker Corp. [*NYSE symbol*] (SPSG)
WKR	Work Ranch [*California*] [*Seismograph station code, US Geological Survey*] (SEIS)
WKR	Worker
WKR	Wrecker (AAG)
WKRA.......	Holly Springs, MS [*AM radio station call letters*]
WKRA-FM ...	Holly Springs, MS [*FM radio station call letters*]
WKRB	Brooklyn, NY [*FM radio station call letters*]
WKRC	Cincinnati, OH [*AM radio station call letters*]
WKRC	World Koala Research Corp. [*Australia*]
WKRC-TV ...	Cincinnati, OH [*Television station call letters*]
WKRE-FM ...	Exmore, VA [*FM radio station call letters*]
WKRG	Mobile, AL [*AM radio station call letters*]
WKRG-FM ...	Mobile, AL [*FM radio station call letters*]
WKRG-TV ...	Mobile, AL [*Television station call letters*]
WKRI	West Warwick, RI [*AM radio station call letters*]
WKRK	Murphy, NC [*AM radio station call letters*]
WKRL	Clearwater, FL [*FM radio station call letters*]
WKRM......	Columbia, TN [*AM radio station call letters*]
WKRN-TV ...	Nashville, TN [*Television station call letters*]
WKRO.......	Cairo, IL [*AM radio station call letters*]

WKRP.......	North Vernon, IN [*AM radio station call letters*]
WKRP-TV ...	Charleston, WV [*Television station call letters*]
WKRQ.......	Cincinnati, OH [*FM radio station call letters*]
WKRR	Asheboro, NC [*FM radio station call letters*]
WKRS.......	Waukegan, IL [*AM radio station call letters*]
WKRT	Cortland, NY [*AM radio station call letters*]
WKRV	Vandalia, IL [*FM radio station call letters*]
WKRX	Roxboro, NC [*FM radio station call letters*]
WKRY	Key West, FL [*FM radio station call letters*]
WKRZ-FM ...	Wilkes-Barre, PA [*FM radio station call letters*]
WKS	Worksheet File [*Data processing*]
WKS	Workshop (AAG)
WKSA.......	Wernicke-Korsakoff Syndrome Association (EA)
WKSA-FM ...	Isabela, PR [*FM radio station call letters*]
WKSB.......	Williamsport, PA [*FM radio station call letters*]
WKSC.......	Kershaw, SC [*AM radio station call letters*]
WKSC.......	Western Kentucky State College [*Later, WKSU*]
WKSD.......	Paulding, OH [*FM radio station call letters*]
WKSE.......	Niagara Falls, NY [*FM radio station call letters*]
Wks Engng ...	Works Engineering [*A publication*]
Wks Engng Fact Serv ...	Works Engineering and Factory Services [*A publication*]
WKSF.......	Asheville, NC [*FM radio station call letters*]
WKSG.......	Mount Clemens, MI [*FM radio station call letters*]
WKSH.......	Sussex, WI [*AM radio station call letters*]
WKSI.......	Greensboro, NC [*FM radio station call letters*]
WKSJ	Prichard, AL [*AM radio station call letters*]
WKSJ-FM ...	Mobile, AL [*FM radio station call letters*]
WKSK.......	West Jefferson, NC [*AM radio station call letters*]
WKSL........	Greencastle, PA [*FM radio station call letters*]
WKSM	Fort Walton Beach, FL [*FM radio station call letters*]
Wks Mgmt ...	Works Management [*A publication*]
WKSN.......	Jamestown, NY [*AM radio station call letters*]
WKSO	Orangeburg, SC [*FM radio station call letters*]
WKSO	Somerset, KY [*Television station call letters*]
WKSP.......	Kingstree, SC [*AM radio station call letters*]
WKSP.......	Workshop
WKSQ	Ellsworth, ME [*FM radio station call letters*]
WKSR.......	Pulaski, TN [*AM radio station call letters*]
WKSS.......	Hartford-Meriden, CT [*FM radio station call letters*]
WKST.......	New Castle, PA [*AM radio station call letters*]
WKST-FM ...	Ellwood City, PA [*FM radio station call letters*]
Wk Study ...	Work Study [*A publication*]
Wk Study Mgmt Serv ...	Work Study and Management Services [*Later, Management Services*] [*A publication*]
WKSU.......	Western Kentucky State University [*Formerly, WKSC*]
WKSU-FM ...	Kent, OH [*FM radio station call letters*]
WKSV.......	Cape Charles, VA [*FM radio station call letters*]
WKSW	Urbana, OH [*FM radio station call letters*]
WKSX.......	Johnston, SC [*FM radio station call letters*]
WKSY.......	Jupiter, FL [*FM radio station call letters*]
WKSZ........	Media, PA [*FM radio station call letters*]
WKT	Wicket
WKTB.......	Richland Center, WI [*Television station call letters*]
WKTC	Goldsboro, NC [*FM radio station call letters*]
WKTD	Wilmington, NC [*AM radio station call letters*]
WKTE.......	King, NC [*AM radio station call letters*]
WKTG.......	Madisonville, KY [*FM radio station call letters*]
WKTH......	Grand Rapids, MI [*AM radio station call letters*]
WKTI........	Milwaukee, WI [*FM radio station call letters*]
WKTJ.......	Farmington, ME [*AM radio station call letters*]
WKTJ-FM ...	Farmington, ME [*FM radio station call letters*]
WKTK	Crystal River, FL [*FM radio station call letters*]
WKTL........	Struthers, OH [*FM radio station call letters*]
WKTM......	Soperton, GA [*FM radio station call letters*]
WKTN......	Kenton, OH [*FM radio station call letters*]
WKTP.......	Jonesboro, TN [*AM radio station call letters*]
WKTQ.......	South Paris, ME [*AM radio station call letters*]
WKTR.......	Earlysville, VA [*AM radio station call letters*]
WKTS.......	Sheboygan, WI [*AM radio station call letters*]
WKTT.......	Cleveland, WI [*FM radio station call letters*]
WKTU	Ocean City, NJ [*AM radio station call letters*]
WKTV.......	Utica, NY [*Television station call letters*]
WKTW	Dover Township, NJ [*FM radio station call letters*]
WKTX	Mercer, PA [*FM radio station call letters*]
WKTY	La Crosse, WI [*FM radio station call letters*]
WKTZ-FM ...	Jacksonville, FL [*FM radio station call letters*]
WKU.........	Wakaura [*Wakayama Eri*] [*Japan*] [*Seismograph station code, US Geological Survey*] (SEIS)
WKU.........	Western Kentucky University [*Formerly, WKSC*] [*Bowling Green*]
WKUB.......	Blackshear, GA [*FM radio station call letters*]
WKUBA ...	Werkstatt und Betrieb [*A publication*]
WKUL.......	Cullman, AL [*FM radio station call letters*]
WKUN.......	Monroe, GA [*AM radio station call letters*]
WKUZ.......	Wabash, IN [*FM radio station call letters*]
WKVA.......	Lewistown, PA [*AM radio station call letters*]
WKVF.......	West Kent Volunteer Force [*British military*] (DMA)
WKVI	Knox, IN [*AM radio station call letters*]
WKVI-FM ...	Knox, IN [*FM radio station call letters*]
WKVM......	San Juan, PR [*AM radio station call letters*]

WKVR-FM ... Huntingdon, PA [*FM radio station call letters*]
WKVT ...... Brattleboro, VT [*AM radio station call letters*]
WKVT-FM ... Brattleboro, VT [*FM radio station call letters*]
WKVX ...... Wooster, OH [*AM radio station call letters*]
WKWA ...... Mobile, AL [*AM radio station call letters*]
WKWC ...... Owensboro, KY [*AM radio station call letters*]
WKWF ...... Key West, FL [*AM radio station call letters*]
WKWI .... Kilmarnock, VA [*FM radio station call letters*]
WKWK ...... Wheeling, WV [*AM radio station call letters*]
WKWL ...... Florala, AL [*AM radio station call letters*]
WKWM ..... Kentwood, MI [*AM radio station call letters*]
WKWQ ...... Batesburg, SC [*FM radio station call letters*]
WKWSA.... Wiener Klinische Wochenschrift. Supplementum (Austria) [*A publication*]
WKWT ...... Union City, TN [*FM radio station call letters*]
WKWX-FM ... Savannah, TN [*FM radio station call letters*]
WKWZ ...... Syosset, NY [*FM radio station call letters*]
WKXA-FM ... Findlay, OH [*FM radio station call letters*]
WKXC .... Aiken, SC [*AM radio station call letters*]
WKXC-FM ... Aiken, SC [*FM radio station call letters*]
WKXE-FM ... White River Junction, VT [*FM radio station call letters*]
WKXF .... Eminence, KY [*AM radio station call letters*]
WKXF-FM ... Eminence, KY [*FM radio station call letters*]
WKXG .... Greenwood, MS [*AM radio station call letters*]
WKXH-FM ... Alma, GA [*FM radio station call letters*]
WKXI .... Jackson, MS [*AM radio station call letters*]
WKXJ .... South Pittsburg, TN [*FM radio station call letters*]
WKXK ...... Fort Valley, GA [*FM radio station call letters*]
WKXL ...... Concord, NH [*AM radio station call letters*]
WKXL-FM ... Concord, NH [*FM radio station call letters*]
WKXN ...... Greenville, AL [*FM radio station call letters*]
WKXO ...... Berea, KY [*AM radio station call letters*]
WKXQ ...... Rushville, IL [*FM radio station call letters*]
WKXR ...... Asheboro, NC [*AM radio station call letters*]
WKXS .... Marion, SC [*AM radio station call letters*]
WKXT ...... Sardis, MS [*AM radio station call letters*]
WKXT-TV ... Knoxville, TN [*Television station call letters*]
WKXU ...... Portage, PA [*FM radio station call letters*]
WKXV ...... Knoxville, TN [*AM radio station call letters*]
WKXW ...... Trenton, NJ [*FM radio station call letters*]
WKXX ...... Birmingham, AL [*FM radio station call letters*]
WKXY ...... Sarasota, FL [*AM radio station call letters*]
WKXZ .... Norwich, NY [*FM radio station call letters*]
WKY .... Oklahoma City, OK [*AM radio station call letters*]
WKY .... Wakayama [*Japan*] [*Seismograph station code, US Geological Survey*]   (SEIS)
WKY .... Warwickshire Yeomanry [*British military*]   (DMA)
WKY .... West Kent Yeomanry [*British military*]   (DMA)
WKY .... Wistar-Kyoto [*Rat variety*]
WKYA .... Central City, KY [*FM radio station call letters*]
WKYB .... Hemingway, SC [*AM radio station call letters*]
WKYC-TV ... Cleveland, OH [*Television station call letters*]
WKYE ...... Johnstown, PA [*FM radio station call letters*]
WKYG .... Parkersburg, WV [*AM radio station call letters*]
WKYJ .... Starkville, MS [*FM radio station call letters*]
WKYK ...... Burnsville, NC [*AM radio station call letters*]
WKYM ...... Monticello, KY [*FM radio station call letters*]
WKYN .... St. Mary's, PA [*FM radio station call letters*]
WKYO ...... Caro, MI [*AM radio station call letters*]
WKYQ .... Paducah, KY [*FM radio station call letters*]
WKYR .... Burkesville, KY [*AM radio station call letters*]
WKYR-FM ... Burkesville, KY [*FM radio station call letters*]
WKYS .... Washington, DC [*FM radio station call letters*]
WKYT-TV ... Lexington, KY [*Television station call letters*]
WKYU-FM ... Bowling Green, KY [*FM radio station call letters*]
WKYU-TV ... Bowling Green, KY [*Television station call letters*]
WKYW ...... Frankfort, KY [*FM radio station call letters*]
WKYX .... Paducah, KY [*AM radio station call letters*]
WKYY .... Lancaster, KY [*AM radio station call letters*]
WKYZ .... Gray, KY [*AM radio station call letters*]
WKZA .... Kane, PA [*AM radio station call letters*]
WKZB .... Drew, MS [*FM radio station call letters*]
WKZC .... Scottville, MI [*FM radio station call letters*]
WKZD .... Murrayville, GA [*AM radio station call letters*]
WKZE .... Sharon, CT [*AM radio station call letters*]
WKZE-FM ... Salisbury, CT [*FM radio station call letters*]
WKZG .... Keyser, WV [*FM radio station call letters*]
WKZI .... Casey, IL [*AM radio station call letters*]
WKZJ .... Lake Wales, FL [*AM radio station call letters*]
WKZK ...... North Augusta, SC [*AM radio station call letters*]
WKZL .... Winston-Salem, NC [*FM radio station call letters*]
WKZM ...... Sarasota, FL [*FM radio station call letters*]
WKZN ...... Gorham, ME [*AM radio station call letters*]
WKZO ...... Kalamazoo, MI [*AM radio station call letters*]
WKZQ .... Myrtle Beach, SC [*AM radio station call letters*]
WKZQ-FM ... Myrtle Beach, SC [*FM radio station call letters*]
WKZR .... Milledgeville, GA [*FM radio station call letters*]
WKZS .... Auburn, ME [*FM radio station call letters*]
WKZT ...... Fulton, KY [*AM radio station call letters*]
WKZT-TV ... Elizabethtown, KY [*Television station call letters*]
WKZW ...... Peoria, IL [*FM radio station call letters*]

WKZX ...... Presque Isle, ME [*AM radio station call letters*]
WKZY ...... La Belle, FL [*FM radio station call letters*]
WKZZ ...... Lynchburg, VA [*FM radio station call letters*]
WL............ Compagnie Aerienne du Languedoc [*France*] [*ICAO designator*]   (FAAC)
WL............ Lao Air Lines [*Later, LS*] [*ICAO designator*]   (FAAC)
WL............ Wagons-Lits [*Railroad Sleeping or Pullman cars in Europe*] [*French*]
WL............ Waiting List
WL............ Walther League   (EA)
WL............ War Legislation [*British*] [*World War II*]
WL............ Warner-Lambert Pharmaceutical Co.
W & L .... Washington and Lee Law Review [*A publication*]
W & L .... Washington and Lee University [*Lexington, VA*]
WL............ Water Line
WL............ Waterload Test [*Clinical chemistry*]
WL............ Wavelength [*Electronics*]
W & L .... Weapon and/or Launcher
WL............ Weapons Laboratory   (MCD)
WL............ Wehrmacht-Luftwaffe [*Marking on Air Force vehicles*] [*German military - World War II*]
W & L .... Welshpool & Llanfair Light Railway [*Wales*]
WL............ Western Larch [*Utility pole*] [*Telecommunications*]   (TEL)
WL............ Western League [*Baseball*]
WL............ Westland Helicopters Ltd. [*Great Britain*] [*ICAO aircraft manufacturer identifier*]   (ICAO)
WL............ Westminster Library [*A publication*]
WL............ Wheel Locks
WL............ Wheeler Laboratories, Inc.   (MCD)
WL............ White Laboratories, Inc. [*Research code symbol*]
WL............ White Leghorn [*Poultry*]
WL............ White Light   (MSA)
WL............ Wideband Limiter
WL............ Wiener Library [*London*]   (BJA)
WL............ Will   (FAAC)
WL............ Wind Load
WL............ Wiring List
W-L........... Wisconsin State Law Library [*Wisconsin State Library*], Madison, WI [*Library symbol*] [*Library of Congress*]   (LCLS)
WL............ With Restrictive Language   (MCD)
W & L .... Women and Literature [*A publication*]
WL............ Women's Legion [*British*] [*World War I*]
WL............ Women's Liberation   (ADA)
WL............ Women's Lobby [*Defunct*]   (EA)
WL............ Women's Reserve, Legal Specialist Duties [*USNR officer designation*]
WL............ Wool
WL............ Word in Life: Journal of Religious Education [*A publication*]   (APTA)
WL............ Word Line
WL............ Work Light
WL............ Work Line   (MSA)
WL............ Working Level
WL............ Workload   (AABC)
WL............ World of Learning [*A publication*]
WL............ World List of Future International Meetings [*A publication*]
WL............ Worldloppet   (EA)
WL............ Wydawnictwo Literackie [*A publication*]
WL............ Wydawnictwo Lodzkie [*A publication*]
WL............ Wyeth Laboratories [*Research code symbol*]
WL0 .... Water Line Zero   (KSC)
WLA .... Warner-Lambert Co. [*NYSE symbol*]   (SPSG)
WLA .... Welsh Lacrosse Association   (EAIO)
WLA .... Wescosa Lumber Association [*Defunct*]   (EA)
WLA .... Western Lacrosse Association [*Canada*]
WLA .... Western Literature Association   (EA)
WLA .... White Lung Association   (EA)
WLA .... Wire Line Adapter   (MCD)
WLA .... Wire Line Antenna
WLA .... Wissenschaftlicher Literaturanzeiger [*A publication*]
WLA .... Wittsburg Lake [*Arkansas*] [*Seismograph station code, US Geological Survey*] [*Closed*]   (SEIS)
WLA .... Women's Land Army [*Part of the United States Crop Corps*] [*World War II*]
WLA .... World Literary Academy   (EAIO)
WLAB........ Fort Wayne, IN [*FM radio station call letters*]
WLac .... La Crosse Public Library, La Crosse, WI [*Library symbol*] [*Library of Congress*]   (LCLS)
WLAC .... Nashville, TN [*AM radio station call letters*]
WLAC .... Western Labour Arbitration Cases [*A publication*]   (DLA)
WLAC-FM ... Nashville, TN [*FM radio station call letters*]
WLacFW ... United States Fish and Wildlife Service, Fish Control Laboratory, La Crosse, WI [*Library symbol*] [*Library of Congress*]   (LCLS)
WLacL....... La Crosse Lutheran Hospital, La Crosse, WI [*Library symbol*] [*Library of Congress*]   (LCLS)
WLacSF..... Saint Francis Hospital, La Crosse, WI [*Library symbol*] [*Library of Congress*]   (LCLS)
WLacU ...... University of Wisconsin-La Crosse, La Crosse, WI [*Library symbol*] [*Library of Congress*]   (LCLS)

WLacVC.... Viterbo College, La Crosse, WI [*Library symbol*] [*Library of Congress*] (LCLS)
WLAD...... Danbury, CT [*AM radio station call letters*]
WLadM..... Mount Senario College, Ladysmith, WI [*Library symbol*] [*Library of Congress*] (LCLS)
WLAE-TV ... New Orleans, LA [*Television station call letters*]
WLAF....... La Follette, TN [*AM radio station call letters*]
WLAF....... World League of American Football [*1991*]
WLAG ...... La Grange, GA [*AM radio station call letters*]
WLag .... Lake Geneva Public Library, Lake Geneva, WI [*Library symbol*] [*Library of Congress*] (LCLS)
WLagB...... Badger Union High School District, Lake Geneva, WI [*Library symbol*] [*Library of Congress*] (LCLS)
WLagF...... Franciscan Education Center, Lake Geneva, WI [*Library symbol*] [*Library of Congress*] (LCLS)
WLagSD.... Joint School District Number One, Lake Geneva, WI [*Library symbol*] [*Library of Congress*] (LCLS)
WLAJ-TV ... Lansing, MI [*Television station call letters*]
WLAK ...... Huntingdon, PA [*FM radio station call letters*]
WLAM ...... Lewiston, ME [*AM radio station call letters*]
WLAN ...... Lancaster, PA [*AM radio station call letters*]
WLAN-FM ... Lancaster, PA [*FM radio station call letters*]
WLAP....... Lexington, KY [*AM radio station call letters*]
WLAP-FM ... Lexington, KY [*FM radio station call letters*]
WLAQ ...... Rome, GA [*AM radio station call letters*]
WLAR ...... Athens, TN [*AM radio station call letters*]
WLAS....... Jacksonville, NC [*AM radio station call letters*]
WLAU ...... Laurel, MS [*AM radio station call letters*]
WLAV ...... Grand Rapids, MI [*AM radio station call letters*]
WLAV ...... Will Advise (FAAC)
WLAV-FM ... Grand Rapids, MI [*FM radio station call letters*]
WLAW ...... Fairhaven, MA [*AM radio station call letters*]
W Law Bul ... Weekly Law Bulletin [*Ohio*] [*A publication*] (DLA)
WLAX ...... La Crosse, WI [*Television station call letters*]
WLAY ...... Muscle Shoals, AL [*AM radio station call letters*]
WLAY-FM... Muscle Shoals, AL [*FM radio station call letters*]
WLAZ ...... Naples, FL [*FM radio station call letters*]
WLB .... National War Labor Board [*World War II*]
WLB .... Seagoing Buoy Tender [*Coast Guard*] (NVT)
WLB .... Wallboard (AAG)
WLB .... Weapons Logbook [*Military*] (AABC)
WLB .... Weekly Law Bulletin [*Ohio*] [*A publication*] (DLA)
WLB .... Wiener Library Bulletin [*London*] [*A publication*]
WLB .... Wilson Library Bulletin [*A publication*]
WLB .... Wisconsin Library Bulletin [*A publication*]
WLBA....... Gainesville, GA [*AM radio station call letters*]
WLBB....... Carrollton, GA [*AM radio station call letters*]
WLBC....... Muncie, IN [*AM radio station call letters*]
WLBC-FM ... Muncie, IN [*FM radio station call letters*]
WLBE....... Leesburg, FL [*AM radio station call letters*]
WLBF .... Montgomery, AL [*FM radio station call letters*]
WLBG ...... Laurens, SC [*AM radio station call letters*]
WLBH ...... Mattoon, IL [*AM radio station call letters*]
WLBH-FM... Mattoon, IL [*FM radio station call letters*]
WLBJ .... Bowling Green, KY [*AM radio station call letters*]
WLBK....... De Kalb, IL [*AM radio station call letters*]
WLBK....... [*The*] Waltham Corp. [*NASDAQ symbol*] (NQ)
WLBL....... Auburndale, WI [*AM radio station call letters*]
WLBM-TV ... Meridian, MS [*Television station call letters*]
WLBN ...... Lebanon, KY [*AM radio station call letters*]
WLBQ ...... Morgantown, KY [*AM radio station call letters*]
WLBR ...... Lebanon, PA [*AM radio station call letters*]
WLBS....... Wright Laboratories [*NASDAQ symbol*] (NQ)
WLBT....... Jackson, MS [*Television station call letters*]
WL Bull .... Weekly Law Bulletin [*Ohio*] [*A publication*] (DLA)
WL Bull (Ohio) ... Weekly Law Bulletin [*Ohio*] [*A publication*] (DLA)
WLBZ-TV ... Bangor, ME [*Television station call letters*]
WLC .... Weapon-Launching Console (MCD)
WLC .... Well Logging Console
WLC .... Wellco Enterprises, Inc. [*AMEX symbol*] (SPSG)
WLC .... West London College [*England*]
WLC .... White Light Coronagraph (KSC)
WLC .... Wildcat
WLC .... Wine Label Circle (EA)
WLC .... World Literacy of Canada (EAIO)
WLCA....... Godfrey, IL [*FM radio station call letters*]
WLCAC...... Watts Labor Community Action Committee [*Los Angeles, CA*]
WLCB-TV ... Leesburg, FL [*Television station call letters*]
WLCC....... Luray, VA [*FM radio station call letters*]
WLCC....... Walker-Lybarger Construction Company [*Colorado*]
WLCE....... White Light Coronagraph Experiment (KSC)
WLCH....... Lancaster, PA [*FM radio station call letters*]
WLCK....... Scottsville, KY [*AM radio station call letters*]
WL(CL)..... War Legislation, Civil Liabilities [*British*] [*World War II*]
WLCM....... Lancaster, SC [*AM radio station call letters*]
WLCN ...... Madisonville, KY [*Television station call letters*]
WLCO ...... Clyde, OH [*FM radio station call letters*]
WLCQ ...... Clarksville, VA [*FM radio station call letters*]
WLCR....... Lawrence Township, NJ [*FM radio station call letters*]
WLCS....... North Muskegon, MI [*FM radio station call letters*]
WLCS....... Workload and Cost Schedule [*Military*] (AABC)

WLCSS...... Weapon Launch Console Switching Section (MCD)
WLCT........ Somerset, KY [*Television station call letters*]
WLCX ...... Farmville, VA [*FM radio station call letters*]
WLCY ...... Blairsville, PA [*FM radio station call letters*]
WLD .... South African Law Reports, Witwatersrand Local Division [*A publication*] (DLA)
WLD .... Weapon Loading Director (NVT)
WLD .... Welded (MSA)
WLD .... Weldotron Corp. [*AMEX symbol*] (SPSG)
WLD .... West Longitude Date (AABC)
WLD .... Winfield/Arkansas City, KS [*Location identifier*] [*FAA*] (FAAL)
WLD .... World Technology Industry [*Vancouver Stock Exchange symbol*]
Wld Aerospace Syst ... World Aerospace System [*A publication*]
Wld Aff ...... World Affairs [*A publication*]
Wld Anim Rev ... World Animal Review [*A publication*]
Wld Cem .... World Cement [*A publication*]
Wld Cem Tech ... World Cement Technology [*Later, World Cement*] [*A publication*]
Wld Chr Ed ... World Christian Education [*A publication*]
Wld Conf Med Educ ... World Conference on Medical Education [*A publication*]
Wld Conf Psych ... World Conference of Psychiatry [*A publication*]
Wld Crops ... World Crops [*A publication*]
Wld Develop ... World Development [*A publication*]
Wld Dev Rpt ... World Development Report [*A publication*]
Wld Drink R ... World Drinks Report - World Food Report [*A publication*]
Wld En Out ... World Energy Outlook [*A publication*]
WLDF........ Women's Legal Defense Fund (EA)
Wld Fd & Drk ... World Food and Drink Report [*A publication*]
Wld Fd Probl ... World Food Problems [*A publication*]
Wld Fishg.. World Fishing [*A publication*]
Wld Food Rt ... World Food Report [*A publication*]
Wld For Congr ... World Forestry Congress. Proceedings [*A publication*]
Wld Gas Rpt ... World Gas Report [*A publication*]
Wld Gold ... World Mine Production of Gold [*A publication*]
Wld Hlth.... World's Health [*A publication*]
Wld Hlth Org Publ Hlth Pap ... World Health Organization. Public Health Papers [*A publication*]
Wld Hlth Org Techn Rep Ser ... World Health Organization. Technical Report Series [*A publication*]
W & L Dig ... Wood and Long's Digest [*Illinois*] [*A publication*] (DLA)
WLDLF ..... Wildlife
Wld Marx R ... World Marxist Review [*A publication*]
Wld Med.... World Medicine [*A publication*]
Wld Med Ass Bull ... World Medical Association. Bulletin [*A publication*]
Wld Med J ... World Medical Journal [*A publication*]
Wld Mil Ex ... World Military Expenditures and Arms Transfers [*A publication*]
Wld Mining ... World Mining Equipment [*A publication*]
Wld Money ... World Money Outlook [*A publication*]
WLDMT ... Weldment (MSA)
WLDND.... Wildland
Wld Orchid Conf ... World Orchid Conference [*A publication*]
Wld Pap Tr Rev ... World's Paper Trade Review [*A publication*]
Wld Pol...... World Politics. A Quarterly Journal of International Relations [*A publication*]
Wld Polit.... World Politics [*A publication*]
Wld Pollen Spore Flora ... World Pollen and Spore Flora [*A publication*]
Wld Poult Sci J ... World's Poultry Science Journal [*A publication*]
Wld P & PDem ... World Pulp and Paper Demand, Supply, and Trade [*A publication*]
Wld Pumps ... World Pumps [*A publication*]
WLDR ...... Traverse City, MI [*FM radio station call letters*]
WLDR ...... Welder (MSA)
WLDR ...... Wilderness Experience, Inc. [*NASDAQ symbol*] (NQ)
WLDRA .... Welder [*England*] [*A publication*]
Wld Raw Mat ... World Demand for Raw Materials in 1985 and 2000 [*A publication*]
Wld Refrig Air Condit ... World Refrigeration and Air Conditioning [*A publication*]
Wld Rev Pest Control ... World Review of Pest Control [*A publication*]
WLDS........ Jacksonville, IL [*AM radio station call letters*]
WLDS........ Weldless
Wld Sci Rev ... World Science Reviews [*A publication*]
Wld Silver ... World Production of Silver [*A publication*]
Wld's Pap Trade Rev ... World's Paper Trade Review [*A publication*]
Wld Surv.... World Survey [*A publication*]
Wld Ten...... World Tennis [*A publication*]
Wld Tobacco ... World Tobacco [*A publication*]
Wld Today ... World Today [*A publication*]
Wld Trade... World Trade. Computer Age [*A publication*]
Wld Vet Abstr J ... World Veterinary Abstracting Journal [*A publication*]
Wld Wast... Management of World Waste [*A publication*]
Wld Wide Abstr Gen Med ... World-Wide Abstracts of General Medicine [*A publication*]
Wld Work Rep ... World of Work Report [*A publication*]
WLDX ...... Fayette, AL [*AM radio station call letters*]
WLDY ...... Ladysmith, WI [*AM radio station call letters*]
WLDY-FM ... Ladysmith, WI [*FM radio station call letters*]

Wld Yrbk Educ ... World Yearbook of Education [*A publication*]
WLE .... Ward Lock Educational [*Publisher*] [*British*]
WLE .... Wellore Energy, Inc. [*Toronto Stock Exchange symbol*]
WLE .... Wheeling & Lake Erie Railway Co. [*NYSE symbol*] [*AAR code*] (SPSG)
WLEA .... Hornell, NY [*AM radio station call letters*]
WLEC .... Sandusky, OH [*AM radio station call letters*]
WLED-TV ... Littleton, NH [*Television station call letters*]
WLEE .... Richmond, VA [*AM radio station call letters*]
WLEF-TV ... Park Falls, WI [*Television station call letters*]
WLEI .... Hudson, MI [*FM radio station call letters*]
WLEL .... Leland, MI [*FM radio station call letters*]
WLEM ...... Emporium, PA [*AM radio station call letters*]
WLEN .... Adrian, MI [*FM radio station call letters*]
WLEO .... Ponce, PR [*AM radio station call letters*]
WLER-FM ... Butler, PA [*FM radio station call letters*]
WLET .... Toccoa, GA [*AM radio station call letters*]
WLEV .... Easton, PA [*FM radio station call letters*]
WLEW ...... Bad Axe, MI [*AM radio station call letters*]
WLEW-FM ... Bad Axe, MI [*FM radio station call letters*]
WLEX-TV ... Lexington, KY [*Television station call letters*]
WLEY .... Cayey, PR [*AM radio station call letters*]
WLEZ .... Elmira, NY [*FM radio station call letters*]
WLF .... Walferdange [*Belgium*] [*Seismograph station code, US Geological Survey*] (SEIS)
WLF .... Wallis and Futuna [*ANSI three-letter standard code*] (CNC)
WLF .... Washington Legal Foundation (EA)
WLF .... Welfare (AABC)
WLF .... Whole Lithosphere Failure [*Geology*]
WLF .... Williams-Landel-Ferry [*Polymer physics*]
WLF .... Wolf River Resources Ltd. [*Vancouver Stock Exchange symbol*]
W LF .... Women's Law Forum [*A publication*]
WLF .... Women's Law Fund (EA)
WLF .... Word of Life Fellowship (EA)
WLF .... Worklife [*A publication*]
WLF .... Workload Factor (AFM)
WLF .... World Law Fund (EA)
WLFA .... West Lancashire Field Artillery [*Military unit*] [*British*]
WLFA .... Wildlife Legislative Fund of America (EA)
WLFB .... Bluefield, WV [*Television station call letters*]
WLFB .... Wolfeboro Railroad Co., Inc. [*AAR code*]
WLFC .... Findlay, OH [*FM radio station call letters*]
WLFC .... Washington Library Film Circuit [*Library network*]
WLFE .... St. Albans, VT [*FM radio station call letters*]
WLFF .... St. Petersburg, FL [*AM radio station call letters*]
WLFG .... Grundy, VA [*Television station call letters*]
WLFH .... Little Falls, NY [*AM radio station call letters*]
WLFI-TV .. Lafayette, IN [*Television station call letters*]
WLFJ .... Greenville, SC [*FM radio station call letters*]
WLFL-TV ... Raleigh, NC [*Television station call letters*]
WLFM .... Appleton, WI [*FM radio station call letters*]
WLFMA .... Welding and Metal Fabrication [*A publication*]
WLFN .... La Crosse, WI [*AM radio station call letters*]
WLFQ .... Bruce, MS [*FM radio station call letters*]
WLFR .... Pomona, NJ [*FM radio station call letters*]
WLFS .... Pinconning, MI [*FM radio station call letters*]
WLFW ...... Oregon, IL [*FM radio station call letters*]
WLFX .... Welding Fixture (AAG)
WLFX .... Winchester, KY [*FM radio station call letters*]
WLG .... Waldron Ledge [*Hawaii*] [*Seismograph station code, US Geological Survey*] (SEIS)
WLG .... Washington Liaison Group (AFM)
WLG .... Weekly Law Gazette [*Ohio*] [*A publication*] (ILCA)
WLG .... Wellington [*New Zealand*] [*Airport symbol*] (OAG)
WLG .... Wiener Linguistische Gazette [*A publication*]
WL Gaz ..... Weekly Law Gazette (Reprint) [*Ohio*] [*A publication*] (DLA)
WL Gaz (Ohio) ... Weekly Law Gazette (Ohio) [*A publication*] (DLA)
WLGC .... Greenup, KY [*AM radio station call letters*]
WLGI .... Hemingway, SC [*FM radio station call letters*]
WLGN .... Logan, OH [*AM radio station call letters*]
WLGN-FM ... Logan, OH [*FM radio station call letters*]
WLGO .... Lexington, SC [*AM radio station call letters*]
WLGQ .... Gaston, NC [*FM radio station call letters*]
WLGW ...... Lancaster, NH [*AM radio station call letters*]
WLH .... Society for the Study of Women in Legal History (EA)
WLH .... Walaha [*Vanuatu*] [*Airport symbol*] (OAG)
WLH .... Wealth Resources Ltd. [*Vancouver Stock Exchange symbol*]
WLH .... Wilhelmshaven [*Federal Republic of Germany*] [*Geomagnetic observatory code*]
WLHB .... Women's League of Health and Beauty (EAIO)
WLHE .... Water LASER Heat Exchange
WLHFP .... Women's Labor History Film Project (EA)
WLHM ...... Logansport, IN [*FM radio station call letters*]
WLHN .... Anderson, IN [*FM radio station call letters*]
WLHN ...... Wolohan Lumber Co. [*NASDAQ symbol*] (NQ)
WLHPA .... Wu Li Hsueh Pao [*A publication*]
WLHQ-FM ... Enterprise, AL [*FM radio station call letters*]
WLHS .... West Chester, OH [*FM radio station call letters*]
WLHT .... Grand Rapids, MI [*FM radio station call letters*]
WLI .... Wellesley Island [*New York*] [*Seismograph station code, US Geological Survey*] [*Closed*] (SEIS)

WLI .... Wilderness Leadership International (EA)
WLI .... Women's League for Israel (EA)
WLIB .... New York, NY [*AM radio station call letters*]
WLIC .... Frostburg, MD [*FM radio station call letters*]
WLIF .... Baltimore, MD [*FM radio station call letters*]
WLIG .... Riverhead, NY [*Television station call letters*]
WLIH .... Whitneyville, PA [*FM radio station call letters*]
WLII .... Caguas, PR [*Television station call letters*]
WLIJ .... Shelbyville, TN [*AM radio station call letters*]
WLIK .... Newport, TN [*AM radio station call letters*]
WLIL .... Lenoir City, TN [*AM radio station call letters*]
WLIL-FM ... Lenoir City, TN [*FM radio station call letters*]
WLIM .... Patchogue, NY [*AM radio station call letters*]
WLIN .... Gluckstadt, MS [*FM radio station call letters*]
WLIO .... Lima, OH [*Television station call letters*]
WLIP .... Kenosha, WI [*AM radio station call letters*]
WLIR .... Spring Valley, NY [*AM radio station call letters*]
WLIR-FM ... Garden City, NY [*FM radio station call letters*]
WLIS .... Old Saybrook, CT [*AM radio station call letters*]
WLIT .... Conway, SC [*AM radio station call letters*]
W Lit .... World Literature Written in English [*A publication*]
WLIT-FM ... Chicago, IL [*FM radio station call letters*]
WLIU .... Lincoln University, PA [*FM radio station call letters*]
WLIV .... Livingston, TN [*AM radio station call letters*]
WLIW .... Garden City, NY [*Television station call letters*]
WLIX .... Islip, NY [*AM radio station call letters*]
WLIZ .... Elizabethville, PA [*FM radio station call letters*]
WLJ .... Washburn Law Journal [*A publication*]
WLJ .... Western Law Journal [*A publication*]
WLJ .... Willamette Law Journal [*A publication*] (ILCA)
WLJ .... Wyoming Law Journal [*A publication*]
WLJA .... Ellijay, GA [*AM radio station call letters*]
WLJA-FM ... Ellijay, GA [*FM radio station call letters*]
WLJC .... Beattyville, KY [*FM radio station call letters*]
WLJC-TV ... Beattyville, KY [*Television station call letters*]
WLJD .... Falmouth, VA [*AM radio station call letters*]
WLJE .... Valparaiso, IN [*FM radio station call letters*]
WLJH .... Petal, MS [*AM radio station call letters*]
WLJN .... Elmwood Township, MI [*AM radio station call letters*]
WLJN-FM ... Traverse City, MI [*FM radio station call letters*]
WL Jour ..... Washburn Law Journal [*A publication*]
WL Jour ..... Western Law Journal [*A publication*]
WL Jour ..... Willamette Law Journal [*A publication*]
WL Jour ..... Wyoming Law Journal [*A publication*]
WLJS-FM ... Jacksonville, AL [*FM radio station call letters*]
WLJT-TV ... Lexington, TN [*Television station call letters*]
WLJY .... Marshfield, WI [*FM radio station call letters*]
WLK .... Selawik [*Alaska*] [*Airport symbol*] (OAG)
WLK .... Selawik, AK [*Location identifier*] [*FAA*] (FAAL)
wlk .... Wales [*MARC country of publication code*] [*Library of Congress*] (LCCP)
WLK .... Walk
WLK .... Westlake Industry [*Vancouver Stock Exchange symbol*]
WLK .... Wiest Lake [*California*] [*Seismograph station code, US Geological Survey*] (SEIS)
WLKC .... St. Mary's, GA [*FM radio station call letters*]
WLKD .... Waupun, WI [*AM radio station call letters*]
WLKE .... Oshkosh, WI [*AM radio station call letters*]
WLKF .... Lakeland, FL [*AM radio station call letters*]
WLKI .... Angola, IN [*FM radio station call letters*]
WLKK .... Erie, PA [*AM radio station call letters*]
WLKL .... Mattoon, IL [*FM radio station call letters*]
WLKM ...... Three Rivers, MI [*AM radio station call letters*]
WLKM ...... Welkom Gold Mining Company Ltd. [*NASDAQ symbol*] (NQ)
WLKM-FM ... Three Rivers, MI [*FM radio station call letters*]
WLKO .... Fort Plain, NY [*FM radio station call letters*]
WLKQ .... Buford, GA [*FM radio station call letters*]
WLKR .... Norwalk, OH [*AM radio station call letters*]
WLKR .... Walker [*B. B.*] Co. [*NASDAQ symbol*] (NQ)
WLKR-FM ... Norwalk, OH [*FM radio station call letters*]
WLKS .... Walker-Scott Corp. [*NASDAQ symbol*] (NQ)
WLKS .... West Liberty, KY [*AM radio station call letters*]
WLKT .... Lexington, KY [*Television station call letters*]
WLKW-FM ... Providence, RI [*FM radio station call letters*]
WLKX-FM ... Forest Lake, MN [*FM radio station call letters*]
WLKY-TV ... Louisville, KY [*Television station call letters*]
WLKZ .... Wolfeboro, NH [*FM radio station call letters*]
WLL .... Williamstown [*Massachusetts*] [*Seismograph station code, US Geological Survey*] [*Closed*] (SEIS)
WLLA .... Kalamazoo, MI [*Television station call letters*]
WLLB .... Topsham, ME [*FM radio station call letters*]
WLLE .... Raleigh, NC [*AM radio station call letters*]
WLLG .... Lowville, NY [*FM radio station call letters*]
WLLH .... Lowell, MA [*AM radio station call letters*]
WLLI-FM ... Joliet, IL [*FM radio station call letters*]
WLLJ .... Cassopolis, MI [*FM radio station call letters*]
WLLK .... Somerset, KY [*FM radio station call letters*]
WLLL .... Lynchburg, VA [*AM radio station call letters*]
WLLN .... Lillington, NC [*AM radio station call letters*]
WLLR .... East Moline, IL [*FM radio station call letters*]

WLLR.......	Washington and Lee Law Review [*A publication*]
W & LLR ...	Welshpool & Llanfair Light Railway [*Wales*]
WLLS........	Hartford, KY [*AM radio station call letters*]
WLLS-FM ...	Hartford, KY [*FM radio station call letters*]
WLLT........	Polo, IL [*FM radio station call letters*]
WLLV........	Louisville, KY [*AM radio station call letters*]
WLLX........	Minor Hill, TN [*FM radio station call letters*]
WLLY........	Wilson, NC [*AM radio station call letters*]
WLLZ........	Detroit, MI [*FM radio station call letters*]
WLM.........	Warning Light Monitor
WLM.........	Wellman, Inc. [*NYSE symbol*] (CTT)
WLM.........	Western Law Monthly [*Cleveland, OH*] [*A publication*] (DLA)
WLM.........	Western Lumber Manufacturers [*An association*] [*Later, Western Timber Association*] (EA)
WLM.........	Willow Mountain [*Alaska*] [*Seismograph station code, US Geological Survey*] [*Closed*] (SEIS)
WLM.........	Wire Line MODEMS
WLM.........	Working Level Month [*Nuclear energy*]
WLMG......	New Orleans, LA [*FM radio station call letters*]
WLMH......	Morrow, OH [*FM radio station call letters*]
WLMI.......	Kane, PA [*FM radio station call letters*]
WLMJ.......	Jackson, OH [*AM radio station call letters*]
WLMO......	Worldwide Logistics Management Office [*Army*]
WLMT-TV ...	Memphis, TN [*Television station call letters*]
WLMU.......	Harrogate, TN [*FM radio station call letters*]
WLMX	Rossville, GA [*AM radio station call letters*]
WLMX-FM ...	Rossville, GA [*FM radio station call letters*]
WLN.........	Washington Library Network [*Washington State Library*] [*Olympia, WA*] [*Library network*]
WLN.........	Welcome North Mines [*Vancouver Stock Exchange symbol*]
WLN.........	Wellington [*British depot code*]
WLN.........	Western Library Network [*Formerly, Washington Library Network*] [*Library of Congress*] [*Olympia, WA*] [*Database*]
WLN.........	Wired Librarian's Newsletter [*A publication*]
WLN.........	Wiswesser Line Notation [*Chemical structure*]
WLNA.......	Peekskill, NY [*AM radio station call letters*]
WLNC.......	Laurinburg, NC [*AM radio station call letters*]
WLND.......	Cortland, OH [*AM radio station call letters*]
WLNE.......	New Bedford, MA [*Television station call letters*]
WLNED	Water Law Newsletter [*A publication*]
WLNG.......	Sag Harbor, NY [*AM radio station call letters*]
WLNG-FM ...	Sag Harbor, NY [*FM radio station call letters*]
WLNH.......	Laconia, NH [*AM radio station call letters*]
WLNH-FM ...	Laconia, NH [*FM radio station call letters*]
WLNK.......	Columbus, MS [*FM radio station call letters*]
WLNL	Horseheads, NY [*AM radio station call letters*]
WLNL	Wellness Newsletter [*A publication*]
WLNR.......	Lansing, IL [*FM radio station call letters*]
WLNS-TV ...	Lansing, MI [*Television station call letters*]
WLNX	Lincoln, IL [*FM radio station call letters*]
WLNZ-FM ...	St. Johns, MI [*FM radio station call letters*]
WLO.........	Waterloo Railroad Co. [*AAR code*]
WLO.........	Weapons Liaison Officer (NVT)
WLO.........	Wilson [*Oklahoma*] [*Seismograph station code, US Geological Survey*] (SEIS)
WLOB.......	Portland, ME [*AM radio station call letters*]
WLOC.......	Munfordville, KY [*AM radio station call letters*]
WLOC-FM ...	Munfordville, KY [*FM radio station call letters*]
WLOD.......	Loudon, TN [*AM radio station call letters*]
WLOD-FM ...	Loudon, TN [*FM radio station call letters*]
WLOE.......	Eden, NC [*AM radio station call letters*]
WLOG.......	Logan, WV [*AM radio station call letters*]
WLOH.......	Lancaster, OH [*AM radio station call letters*]
WLOI.......	La Porte, IN [*AM radio station call letters*]
WLOJ.......	New Bern, NC [*AM radio station call letters*]
WLOK.......	Memphis, TN [*AM radio station call letters*]
WLOL	Minneapolis, MN [*FM radio station call letters*]
WLON.......	Lincolnton, NC [*AM radio station call letters*]
W Lond Med J ...	West London Medical Journal [*A publication*]
WLOP	Jesup, GA [*AM radio station call letters*]
WLOQ......	Winter Park, FL [*FM radio station call letters*]
WLOR.......	Thomasville, GA [*AM radio station call letters*]
WLOR-FM ...	Thomasville, GA [*FM radio station call letters*]
WLOS.......	Asheville, NC [*Television station call letters*]
WLOT.......	Trenton, TN [*FM radio station call letters*]
WLOU.......	Louisville, KY [*AM radio station call letters*]
WLOV	Washington, GA [*AM radio station call letters*]
WLOV-FM ...	Washington, GA [*FM radio station call letters*]
WLOW......	Bluffton, SC [*FM radio station call letters*]
WLOW......	Wicklow [*County in Ireland*] (ROG)
WLOX-TV ...	Biloxi, MS [*Television station call letters*]
WLP..........	Wallops Island, NASA Center (MCD)
WLP..........	Western Legal Publications [*Database*] [*Western Legal Publications Ltd.*] [*Information service or system*] (CRD)
WLP..........	White Light Position
WLP..........	Women's Law Project (EA)
WLPA.......	Lancaster, PA [*AM radio station call letters*]
WLPB........	Woodcock Language Proficiency Battery [*Achievement test*]
WLPB-TV ...	Baton Rouge, LA [*Television station call letters*]
WL/PD......	Warner-Lambert/Parke-Davis [*Computer files of chemical and biological data*]
WLPE.......	Augusta, GA [*FM radio station call letters*]
WLPF.......	William L. Patterson Foundation (EA)
WLPH	Irondale, AL [*AM radio station call letters*]
WLPI.......	Wellington Leisure Products, Inc. [*NASDAQ symbol*] (CTT)
WLPJ-FM ...	New Port Richey, FL [*FM radio station call letters*]
WLPM......	Suffolk, VA [*AM radio station call letters*]
WLPO.......	La Salle, IL [*AM radio station call letters*]
WLPR.......	Prichard, AL [*AM radio station call letters*]
WLPS.......	Watermen and Lightermen's Protective Society [*A union*] [*British*]
WLPT.......	Jesup, GA [*FM radio station call letters*]
WLPW......	Lake Placid, NY [*FM radio station call letters*]
WLPY......	Purcellville, VA [*AM radio station call letters*]
WLQ.........	Washington University. Law Quarterly [*A publication*]
WLQH.......	Chiefland, FL [*AM radio station call letters*]
WLQI........	Rensselaer, IN [*FM radio station call letters*]
WLQM......	Franklin, VA [*AM radio station call letters*]
WLQM-FM ...	Franklin, VA [*FM radio station call letters*]
WLQR	Toledo, OH [*FM radio station call letters*]
WLQV......	Detroit, MI [*AM radio station call letters*]
WLQY......	Hollywood, FL [*AM radio station call letters*]
WLR.........	Washington Law Reporter [*District of Columbia*] [*A publication*] (DLA)
WLR.........	Washington Law Review [*A publication*]
WLR.........	Wasser, Luft, und Betrieb. Zeitschrift fuer Umwelttechnik [*A publication*]
WLR.........	Water Level Recorder
WLR.........	Weapons Locating RADAR (AABC)
WLR.........	Weekly Law Reports [*British*]
WLR.........	Weighted Linear Regression [*Mathematics*]
WLR.........	West London Railway (ROG)
WLR.........	Western Law Reporter [*Canada*] [*A publication*] (DLA)
WLR.........	Wilanour Resources Ltd. [*Toronto Stock Exchange symbol*]
WLR.........	Wisconsin Law Review [*A publication*]
WLR.........	World Law Review [*A publication*] (DLA)
WLR.........	Wrong Length Record [*Data processing*]
WLRA.......	Lockport, IL [*FM radio station call letters*]
WLRA.......	Wagner Labor Relations Act (OICC)
WLRA.......	World Leisure and Recreation Association [*Formerly, IRA*] (EA)
WLRB.......	Macomb, IL [*AM radio station call letters*]
WLRC.......	Walnut, MS [*AM radio station call letters*]
WLRD	Warning Light Relay Driver
WLRF.......	WLR Foods, Inc. [*NASDAQ symbol*] (NQ)
WLRG	Timmonsville, SC [*AM radio station call letters*]
WLRH	Huntsville, AL [*FM radio station call letters*]
WLRI........	Warner-Lambert Research Institute [*New Jersey*]
WLRM	Ridgeland, MS [*AM radio station call letters*]
WLRN-FM ...	Miami, FL [*FM radio station call letters*]
WLRN-TV ...	Miami, FL [*Television station call letters*]
WLRO	Circleville, OH [*FM radio station call letters*]
WLRP.......	San Sebastian, PR [*AM radio station call letters*]
WLRP.......	Wandsworth's Legal Resource Project [*A publication*] (DLA)
WLRQ.......	Cocoa, FL [*AM radio station call letters*]
WLRQ-FM ...	Cocoa, FL [*FM radio station call letters*]
WLRS.......	Louisville, KY [*FM radio station call letters*]
WLRT.......	Kankakee, IL [*FM radio station call letters*]
WLRV.......	Lebanon, VA [*AM radio station call letters*]
WLRW......	Champaign, IL [*FM radio station call letters*]
WLRZ........	Peru, IL [*FM radio station call letters*]
WLS.........	Chicago, IL [*AM radio station call letters*]
WLS..........	Livingston-Steuben-Wyoming BOCES [*Boards of Cooperative Educational Services*], Educational Communications Center, Geneseo, NY [*OCLC symbol*] (OCLC)
WLS..........	Wallis Island [*Wallis and Futuna Islands*] [*Airport symbol*] (OAG)
WLS..........	Water Lily Society (EA)
WLS..........	Weighted Least Squares [*Statistics*]
WLS..........	Wells
WLS..........	Welschbruch [*France*] [*Seismograph station code, US Geological Survey*] (SEIS)
WLS..........	Welsh Language Society (EA)
WLS..........	Westchester Library System [*Library network*]
WLS..........	Westchester Public Library [*UTLAS symbol*]
WLS..........	Western Launch Site [*Military*]
WLS..........	Williams Air, Inc. [*Medford Lakes, NJ*] [*FAA designator*] (FAAC)
WLS..........	Winnefox Library System [*Library network*]
WLS..........	World Listening Service (EA)
WLSA.......	Louisa, VA [*FM radio station call letters*]
WLSA.......	Wage and Labor Standards Administration (OICC)
WLSB.......	Copperhill, TN [*AM radio station call letters*]
WLSBA......	Wildlife Society. Bulletin [*A publication*]
WLSC.......	Loris, SC [*AM radio station call letters*]
WLSC.......	West Liberty State College [*West Virginia*]
WLSD.......	Big Stone Gap, VA [*AM radio station call letters*]
WLSE.......	Wallace, NC [*AM radio station call letters*]
WLSH	Lansford, PA [*AM radio station call letters*]

WLSH .... Wochenblatt der Landesbauernschaft Schleswig-Holstein [*A publication*]
WLSI .... Pikeville, KY [*AM radio station call letters*]
WLSK .... Lebanon, KY [*FM radio station call letters*]
WLSL .... Crisfield, MD [*FM radio station call letters*]
WLSL .... Walseal
WLSM .... Louisville, MS [*AM radio station call letters*]
WLSM-FM ... Louisville, MS [*FM radio station call letters*]
WLSN .... Greenville, OH [*FM radio station call letters*]
WLSP .... World List of Scientific Periodicals [*A publication*] (DIT)
WLSQ .... Dalton, GA [*AM radio station call letters*]
WLSR .... Lima, OH [*FM radio station call letters*]
WLST .... Marinette, WI [*FM radio station call letters*]
WLS-TV .... Chicago, IL [*Television station call letters*]
WLSU .... La Crosse, WI [*FM radio station call letters*]
WLSV .... Wellsville, NY [*AM radio station call letters*]
WLSW .... Scottdale, PA [*FM radio station call letters*]
WLSY .... Newburg, KY [*AM radio station call letters*]
WLSY-FM ... Jeffersontown, KY [*FM radio station call letters*]
WLSZ .... Humboldt, TN [*FM radio station call letters*]
WLT .... Weighing Less Than
WLT .... Western Law Times [*1890-95*] [*A publication*] (DLA)
WLT .... Wire Line Timing
WLT .... World Literature Today [*A publication*]
WLTA .... Clarkesville, GA [*AM radio station call letters*]
WLTAS ...... Wingfoot Lighter-Than-Air Society [*Later, Lighter-Than-Air Society*] (EA)
WLTBU ..... Watermen, Lightermen, Tugmen, and Bargemen's Union [*British*]
WLTC .... Gastonia, NC [*AM radio station call letters*]
WLTC .... Wimbledon Lawn Tennis Championship [*British*]
WLTD .... Lexington, MS [*FM radio station call letters*]
WLTE .... Minneapolis, MN [*FM radio station call letters*]
WLTE .... Warrant Loss to Enlisted Status [*Revocation of appointment*] [*Navy*]
WLTF .... Cleveland, OH [*FM radio station call letters*]
WLTG .... Panama City, FL [*AM radio station call letters*]
WLTH .... Gary, IN [*AM radio station call letters*]
WLTI .... Detroit, MI [*FM radio station call letters*]
WLTJ .... Pittsburgh, PA [*FM radio station call letters*]
WLTK .... Broadway, VA [*FM radio station call letters*]
WLTK .... Wiltek, Inc. [*NASDAQ symbol*] (NQ)
WLTL .... La Grange, IL [*FM radio station call letters*]
WLTM .... Rantoul, IL [*FM radio station call letters*]
WLTN .... Littleton, NH [*AM radio station call letters*]
WLTN .... Wilton Enterprises, Inc. [*Woodridge, IL*] [*NASDAQ symbol*] (NQ)
WLTO .... Harbor Springs, MI [*FM radio station call letters*]
WLTP .... Parkersburg, WV [*AM radio station call letters*]
WLTQ .... Milwaukee, WI [*FM radio station call letters*]
WLTR .... Columbia, SC [*FM radio station call letters*]
WLTS-FM ... Slidell, LA [*FM radio station call letters*]
WLTT .... Bethesda, MD [*FM radio station call letters*]
WLTU .... Manitowoc, WI [*FM radio station call letters*]
WLTV .... Miami, FL [*Television station call letters*]
WLTW .... New York, NY [*FM radio station call letters*]
WLTX .... Columbia, SC [*Television station call letters*]
WLTY .... Norfolk, VA [*FM radio station call letters*]
WLTZ .... Columbus, GA [*Television station call letters*]
WLU .... Washington and Lee University [*Virginia*]
WLU .... Wesleyan University, Middletown, CT [*OCLC symbol*] (OCLC)
WLU .... Wilfrid Laurier University [*Canada*]
WLub .... Wydawnictwo Lubelskie [*A publication*]
WLUC .... Women Life Underwriters Conference (EA)
WLUC-TV ... Marquette, MI [*Television station call letters*]
WLUJ .... Petersburg, IL [*FM radio station call letters*]
WLUK-TV ... Green Bay, WI [*Television station call letters*]
WLUL .... Fort Deposit, AL [*AM radio station call letters*]
WLUM-FM ... Milwaukee, WI [*FM radio station call letters*]
WLUN .... Lumberton, MS [*FM radio station call letters*]
WLUP .... Chicago, IL [*AM radio station call letters*]
WLUP-FM ... Chicago, IL [*FM radio station call letters*]
WLUR .... Lexington, VA [*FM radio station call letters*]
WLUS .... Gainesville, FL [*AM radio station call letters*]
WLUV .... Loves Park, IL [*AM radio station call letters*]
WLUV-FM ... Loves Park, IL [*FM radio station call letters*]
WLUW ...... Chicago, IL [*FM radio station call letters*]
WLUX .... Baton Rouge, LA [*AM radio station call letters*]
WLUZ .... Bayamon, PR [*AM radio station call letters*]
WLVA .... Lynchburg, VA [*AM radio station call letters*]
WLVC .... Fort Kent, ME [*AM radio station call letters*]
WLVE .... Miami Beach, FL [*FM radio station call letters*]
WLVF .... Haines City, FL [*AM radio station call letters*]
WLVG .... Cambridge, MA [*AM radio station call letters*]
WLVH .... Manchester, CT [*AM radio station call letters*]
WLVH-FM ... Hartford, CT [*FM radio station call letters*]
WLVI-TV .. Cambridge, MA [*Television station call letters*]
WLVJ .... Royal Palm Beach, FL [*AM radio station call letters*]
WLVK .... Statesville, NC [*FM radio station call letters*]
WLVL .... Lockport, NY [*AM radio station call letters*]

WLVQ .... Columbus, OH [*FM radio station call letters*]
WLVR .... Bethlehem, PA [*FM radio station call letters*]
WLVS .... Lake Worth, FL [*AM radio station call letters*]
WLVT-TV ... Allentown, PA [*Television station call letters*]
WLVU .... Dunedin, FL [*AM radio station call letters*]
WLVU-FM ... Holiday, FL [*FM radio station call letters*]
WLVW ...... Salisbury, MD [*AM radio station call letters*]
WLVX .... Bloomfield, CT [*AM radio station call letters*]
WLVY .... Elmira, NY [*FM radio station call letters*]
WLVZ .... Athens, OH [*AM radio station call letters*]
WLW .... Cincinnati, OH [*AM radio station call letters*]
WLW .... Weldwood of Canada Ltd. [*Toronto Stock Exchange symbol*]
WLW .... Willows, CA [*Location identifier*] [*FAA*] (FAAL)
WLW .... Women Library Workers (EA)
WLWE .... World Literature Written in English [*A publication*]
WLWH .... Workshop Library on World Humour (EA)
WLWI .... Montgomery, AL [*AM radio station call letters*]
WLWI-FM ... Montgomery, AL [*FM radio station call letters*]
WLWL .... Rockingham, NC [*AM radio station call letters*]
WLWR .... Brillion, WI [*FM radio station call letters*]
WLWT .... Cincinnati, OH [*Television station call letters*]
WLWZ .... Easley, SC [*FM radio station call letters*]
WLXG .... Lexington, KY [*AM radio station call letters*]
WLXI-TV .. Greensboro, NC [*Television station call letters*]
WLXN .... Lexington, NC [*AM radio station call letters*]
WLXR-FM ... La Crosse, WI [*FM radio station call letters*]
WLY .... Westerly
WLYC .... Williamsport, PA [*AM radio station call letters*]
WLYF .... Miami, FL [*FM radio station call letters*]
WLYH-TV ... Lancaster, PA [*Television station call letters*]
WLYJ .... Clarksburg, WV [*Television station call letters*]
WLYN .... Lynn, MA [*AM radio station call letters*]
WLYT .... Haverhill, MA [*FM radio station call letters*]
WLYU .... Lyons, GA [*FM radio station call letters*]
WLYX .... Memphis, TN [*FM radio station call letters*]
WLZA .... Eupora, MS [*FM radio station call letters*]
WLZQ .... South Whitley, IN [*FM radio station call letters*]
WLZR .... Milwaukee, WI [*AM radio station call letters*]
WLZR-FM ... Milwaukee, WI [*FM radio station call letters*]
WLZT .... Miami, WV [*FM radio station call letters*]
WM .... [*Qualified for*] Engineering Watch [*USNR officer classification*]
WM .... Milwaukee Public Library, Milwaukee, WI [*Library symbol*] [*Library of Congress*] (LCLS)
WM .... Multiple-Conductor Cables [*JETDS nomenclature*] [*Military*] (CET)
WM .... Waldenstrom's Macroglobulinemia [*Medicine*]
W & M .... War and Marine (DS)
WM .... War Memorial
WM .... Ward Manager [*Medicine*]
WM .... Warming
WM .... Warrant Mechanician [*British military*] (DMA)
W & M .... Washburn and Moen [*Wire gauge*]
W/M .... Washing Machine [*Classified advertising*] (ADA)
WM .... Washington Monthly [*A publication*]
WM .... Waste Management (NASA)
WM .... Water Meter
WM .... Water Monitor (DS)
WM .... Watermark
WM .... Watt Meter
WM .... Wave Meter
WM .... Ways and Means (DLA)
WM .... Weapon Mechanician [*British military*] (DMA)
WM .... Wehrmacht-Marine [*Marking on Navy vehicles*] [*German military - World War II*]
W/M .... Weight or Measurement
WM .... Welding Memorandum
WM .... Wertpapier-Mitteilungen [*A publication*]
WM .... West Midlands [*Metropolitan county in England*]
WM .... Westermanns Monatshefte [*A publication*]
WM .... Western Maryland Railway Co. [*NYSE symbol*] [*AAR code*] [*Wall Street slang name: "Wet Mary"*] (SPSG)
WM .... Wheel-Made (BJA)
WM .... White Male
WM .... White Metal
WM .... Whitten's Medium [*for cell incubation*]
Wm .... William (King of England) (DLA)
W & M .... William and Mary [*King and Queen of England*] (ROG)
W & M .... William and Mary Law Review [*A publication*]
W & M ..... Wilson & McLane, Inc. [*Information service or system*] (IID)
WM .... Windward Islands Airways International NV [*Netherlands*] [*ICAO designator*] (ICDA)
W/M .... Wing Main [*Airfield*] (NATG)
WM .... Wire Mesh
WM .... Without Margin
WM .... Women in the Mainstream (EA)
WM .... Women Marines
W & M .... Woodbury and Minot's United States Circuit Court Reports [*3 vols.*] [*A publication*] (DLA)
WM .... Word Mark (BUR)
W/M .... Words per Minute (KSC)
WM .... Work of Mary [*An association*] (EAIO)

WM............. Work Measurement [*Army*] (AABC)
WM............. Working Memory [*Psychology*]
WM............. Works Management [*A publication*]
WM............. World Markets [*British investment firm*] [*Formerly, Wood Mackenzie*]
WM............. World Meetings [*A publication*]
WM............. World Monitor [*Television program*]
WM............. World of Music [*London*] [*A publication*]
WM............. Worshipful Master [*Freemasonry*]
W/M²......... Watts per Square Meter
WMA........... Alverno College, Milwaukee, WI [*Library symbol*] [*Library of Congress*] (LCLS)
WMa........... Madison Public Library, Madison, WI [*Library symbol*] [*Library of Congress*] (LCLS)
WMA........... Mandritsara [*Madagascar*] [*Airport symbol*] (OAG)
WMA........... Wallcovering Manufacturers Association (EA)
WMA........... War Measures Act
WMA........... Washington Metropolitan Area (AFM)
WMA........... Waste Management Area [*NASA*]
WMA........... Waterbed Manufacturers Association (EA)
WMA........... Weather Modification Association (EA)
WMA........... Welding Machine Arc
WMA........... Wentworth Military Academy [*Lexington, MO*]
WMA........... West Mesa [*New Mexico*] [*Seismograph station code, US Geological Survey*] (SEIS)
WMA........... Wheelchair Motorcycle Association (EA)
WMA........... Wikalat Al-Maghreb Al-Arabi [*News agency*] [*Morocco*] (MENA)
WMA........... Wing Main Airfield (NATG)
WMA........... Women Marines Association (EA)
WMA........... Workers' Music Association [*British*]
WMA........... World Manx Association
WMA........... World Medical Association [*Ferney-Voltaire, France*]
WMA........... World Modeling Association (EA)
WMAA....... Bahau [*Malaysia*] [*ICAO location identifier*] (ICLI)
WMAA....... Warrant Master-at-Arms [*British military*] (DMA)
WMAA....... Whitney Museum of American Art [*New York, NY*]
WMAA....... World Martial Arts Association (EA)
WMAA-FM ... Jackson, MS [*FM radio station call letters*]
WMaAR....... Wisconsin Alumni Research Foundation, Madison, WI [*Library symbol*] [*Library of Congress*] (LCLS)
WMAA-TV ... Jackson, MS [*Television station call letters*]
WMAB....... Batu Pahat [*Malaysia*] [*ICAO location identifier*] (ICLI)
WMAB....... Weather Modification Advisory Board
WMAB-FM ... Mississippi State, MS [*FM radio station call letters*]
WMaBR....... Wisconsin Department of Health and Social Services, Bureau of Research, Madison, WI [*Library symbol*] [*Library of Congress*] (LCLS)
WMAB-TV ... Mississippi State, MS [*Television station call letters*]
WMAC....... Benta [*Malaysia*] [*ICAO location identifier*] (ICLI)
WMaC....... Central Wisconsin Colony, Staff Library, Madison, WI [*Library symbol*] [*Library of Congress*] (LCLS)
WMAC....... Metter, GA [*AM radio station call letters*]
WMAC....... Waste Management Advisory Council [*British*] (DCTA)
WMaCH... Wisconsin Department of Health and Social Services, Community Health Service, Madison, WI [*Library symbol*] [*Library of Congress*] (LCLS)
WMACS.... AC Spark Plug Co., Electronics Division, Milwaukee, WI [*Library symbol*] [*Library of Congress*] (LCLS)
WMaCT .... Children's Treatment Center, Madison, WI [*Library symbol*] [*Library of Congress*] (LCLS)
WMAD...... Bentong [*Malaysia*] [*ICAO location identifier*] (ICLI)
WMAD...... Sun Prairie, WI [*AM radio station call letters*]
WMAD-FM ... Sun Prairie, WI [*FM radio station call letters*]
WMAE...... Bidor [*Malaysia*] [*ICAO location identifier*] (ICLI)
WMAE-FM ... Booneville, MS [*FM radio station call letters*]
WMAE-TV ... Booneville, MS [*Television station call letters*]
WMAF...... Madison, FL [*AM radio station call letters*]
WMaF....... United States Forest Products Laboratory, Madison, WI [*Library symbol*] [*Library of Congress*] (LCLS)
WMAFPH ... World Medical Association for Perfect Health [*Also known as United States Association of Physicians*] (EA)
WMAG...... Dungun [*Malaysia*] [*ICAO location identifier*] (ICLI)
WMAG...... High Point, NC [*FM radio station call letters*]
WMaG....... Madison General Hospital, Madison, WI [*Library symbol*] [*Library of Congress*] (LCLS)
WMaG-N .. Madison General Hospital, School of Nursing, Madison, WI [*Library symbol*] [*Library of Congress*] (LCLS)
WMAH ..... Grik [*Malaysia*] [*ICAO location identifier*] (ICLI)
WMaH ...... Wisconsin Division of Health Policy and Planning Library, Madison, WI [*Library symbol*] [*Library of Congress*] (LCLS)
WMAH-FM ... Biloxi, MS [*FM radio station call letters*]
WMAH-TV ... Biloxi, MS [*Television station call letters*]
WMAI....... Gua Musang [*Malaysia*] [*ICAO location identifier*] (ICLI)
W Mail....... Western Mail [*A publication*] (APTA)
W Mail Ann ... Western Mail Annual [*A publication*] (APTA)
WMaJ .... Jackson Clinic, Madison, WI [*Library symbol*] [*Library of Congress*] (LCLS)
WMAJ....... Jendarata [*Malaysia*] [*ICAO location identifier*] (ICLI)
WMAJ........ State College, PA [*AM radio station call letters*]

WMAK...... London, KY [*AM radio station call letters*]
WMAL...... Kuala Krai [*Malaysia*] [*ICAO location identifier*] (ICLI)
WMAL...... Washington, DC [*AM radio station call letters*]
WMaLS..... Wisconsin Division for Library Services, Bureau for Reference and Local Services, Madison, WI [*Library symbol*] [*Library of Congress*] (LCLS)
WMAM...... Langkawi [*Malaysia*] [*ICAO location identifier*] (ICLI)
WMAM...... Marinette, WI [*AM radio station call letters*]
WMaM...... Methodist Hospital School of Nursing, Madison, WI [*Library symbol*] [*Library of Congress*] (LCLS)
WMaMS ... Mendota Mental Health Institute, Madison, WI [*Library symbol*] [*Library of Congress*] (LCLS)
WMan....... Manawa Public Library, Manawa, WI [*Library symbol*] [*Library of Congress*] (LCLS)
WMAN...... Mansfield, OH [*AM radio station call letters*]
WMani ...... Manitowoc Public Library, Manitowoc, WI [*Library symbol*] [*Library of Congress*] (LCLS)
WManiH ... Holy Family Hospital, Manitowoc, WI [*Library symbol*] [*Library of Congress*] (LCLS)
WManiHN ... Holy Family School of Nursing, Manitowoc, WI [*Library symbol*] [*Library of Congress*] (LCLS)
WMANT ... Wissenschaftliche Monographien zum Alten und Neuen Testament [*A publication*] (BJA)
WMAO...... Kong Kong [*Malaysia*] [*ICAO location identifier*] (ICLI)
WMAO-FM ... Greenwood, MS [*FM radio station call letters*]
WMAO-TV ... Greenwood, MS [*Television station call letters*]
WMAP ...... Kluang [*Malaysia*] [*ICAO location identifier*] (ICLI)
WMAP ...... Monroe, NC [*AM radio station call letters*]
WMAP-FM ... Pageland, SC [*FM radio station call letters*]
WMaPI...... Department of Public Instruction, Division for Library Services, Professional Library, Madison, WI [*Library symbol*] [*Library of Congress*] (LCLS)
WMaPI-CC ... Department of Public Instruction, Division for Library Services, Cooperative Children's Book Center, Madison, WI [*Library symbol*] [*Library of Congress*] (LCLS)
WMaPI-PL ... Department of Public Instruction, Division for Library Services, Public Library Services, Madison, WI [*Library symbol*] [*Library of Congress*] (LCLS)
WMaPI-RL ... Department of Public Instruction, Division for Library Services, Reference and Loan Library, Madison, WI [*Library symbol*] [*Library of Congress*] (LCLS)
WMaPR .... Wisconsin Regional Primate Research Center, Madison, WI [*Library symbol*] [*Library of Congress*] (LCLS)
WMAQ...... Chicago, IL [*AM radio station call letters*]
WMAQ...... Labis [*Malaysia*] [*ICAO location identifier*] (ICLI)
WMAQ-TV ... Chicago, IL [*Television station call letters*]
WMaR....... Raltech Scientific Services, Inc., Madison, WI [*Library symbol*] [*Library of Congress*] (LCLS)
WMAR ...... Western Marine Electronics Co. [*NASDAQ symbol*] (NQ)
WMaraS.... Saint Anthony Friary, Marathon, WI [*Library symbol*] [*Library of Congress*] (LCLS)
WMarC ..... Marshfield Clinic, Marshfield, WI [*Library symbol*] [*Library of Congress*] (LCLS)
WMARC ... World Maritime Administrative Radio Conference (DS)
WMarSJ.... Saint Joseph's Hospital, Marshfield, WI [*Library symbol*] [*Library of Congress*] (LCLS)
WMAR-TV ... Baltimore, MD [*Television station call letters*]
WMarW .... Wood County Hospital, Marshfield, WI [*Library symbol*] [*Library of Congress*] (LCLS)
WMAS ...... Springfield, MA [*AM radio station call letters*]
WMaS .... Student Association for the Study of Hallucinogens, Madison, WI [*Library symbol*] [*Library of Congress*] (LCLS)
WMAS-FM ... Springfield, MA [*FM radio station call letters*]
WMaSM ... Saint Mary's Hospital, Doctors' Library, Madison, WI [*Library symbol*] [*Library of Congress*] (LCLS)
WMaSM-N ... Saint Mary's Hospital, School of Nursing, Madison, WI [*Library symbol*] [*Library of Congress*] (LCLS)
W Mass Bus ... Western Massachusetts Business Journal [*A publication*]
WMAT ...... Lima Blas [*Malaysia*] [*ICAO location identifier*] (ICLI)
WMAT ...... Wastemate Corp. [*NASDAQ symbol*] (NQ)
WMaTC .... Madison Area Technical College, Madison, WI [*Library symbol*] [*Library of Congress*] (LCLS)
WMau........ Mauston Public Library, Mauston, WI [*Library symbol*] [*Library of Congress*] (LCLS)
WMAU...... Mersing [*Malaysia*] [*ICAO location identifier*] (ICLI)
WMAU...... Women's Martial Arts Union [*Defunct*] (EA)
WMaUCS ... University of Wisconsin-Center System, Madison, WI [*Library symbol*] [*Library of Congress*] (LCLS)
WMaUEx ... University of Wisconsin-Extension, Madison, WI [*Library symbol*] [*Library of Congress*] (LCLS)
WMAU-FM ... Bude, MS [*FM radio station call letters*]
WMAU-TV ... Bude, MS [*Television station call letters*]
WMAV...... Muar [*Malaysia*] [*ICAO location identifier*] (ICLI)
WMaVA.... United States Veterans Administration Hospital, Madison, WI [*Library symbol*] [*Library of Congress*] (LCLS)
WMAV-FM ... Oxford, MS [*FM radio station call letters*]
WMAV-TV ... Oxford, MS [*Television station call letters*]
WMaW...... Wisconsin Alumni Research Foundation Institute, Inc., Madison, WI [*Library symbol*] [*Library of Congress*] (LCLS)
WMAW-FM ... Meridian, MS [*FM radio station call letters*]

WMAW-TV ... Meridian, MS [*Television station call letters*]
WMAX...... Grand Rapids, MI [*AM radio station call letters*]
WMAY...... Springfield, IL [*AM radio station call letters*]
WMAZ...... Macon, GA [*AM radio station call letters*]
WMAZ...... Segamat [*Malaysia*] [*ICAO location identifier*]   (ICLI)
WMAZ-TV ... Macon, GA [*Television station call letters*]
WMB......... Walnut Marketing Board   (EA)
WMB......... War Mobilization Board
WMB......... Warrnambool [*Australia*] [*Airport symbol*]   (OAG)
WMB......... [*The*] Williams Companies [*NYSE symbol*]   (SPSG)
WMB......... Williamsburg Technical College, Kingstree, SC [*OCLC symbol*]   (OCLC)
WMB......... Women in Business [*A publication*]
WMBA...... Ambridge, PA [*AM radio station call letters*]
WMBA...... Sitiawan [*Malaysia*] [*ICAO location identifier*]   (ICLI)
WMBA...... Wire Machinery Builders Association [*Later, WISA*]   (EA)
WMBB...... Panama City, FL [*Television station call letters*]
WMBB...... Sungei Patani [*Malaysia*] [*ICAO location identifier*]   (ICLI)
WMBC...... Columbus, MS [*FM radio station call letters*]
WMBC...... Wisconsin Baptist State Convention, Milwaukee, WI [*Library symbol*] [*Library of Congress*]   (LCLS)
WMBD...... Peoria, IL [*AM radio station call letters*]
WMBD-TV ... Peoria, IL [*Television station call letters*]
WMBE...... Chilton, WI [*AM radio station call letters*]
WMBE...... Temerloh [*Malaysia*] [*ICAO location identifier*]   (ICLI)
WMBF...... Ulu Bernam [*Malaysia*] [*ICAO location identifier*]   (ICLI)
WMBG...... Williamsburg, VA [*AM radio station call letters*]
WMBH...... Joplin, MO [*AM radio station call letters*]
WMBH...... Kroh [*Malaysia*] [*ICAO location identifier*]   (ICLI)
WMBI...... Chicago, IL [*AM radio station call letters*]
WMBI...... Taiping [*Malaysia*] [*ICAO location identifier*]   (ICLI)
WMBI-FM ... Chicago, IL [*FM radio station call letters*]
Wm Bl........ [*Sir William*] Blackstone's English King's Bench Reports [*1746-80*] [*A publication*]   (DLA)
WMBL...... Morehead City, NC [*AM radio station call letters*]
WMBL...... Wrightsville Marine Biomedical Laboratory
WMBM..... Miami Beach, FL [*AM radio station call letters*]
WMBN-FM ... Petoskey, MI [*FM radio station call letters*]
WMBO...... Auburn, NY [*AM radio station call letters*]
WMBR...... Cambridge, MA [*FM radio station call letters*]
WMBS...... Uniontown, PA [*AM radio station call letters*]
WMBS....... West Massachusetts Bankshares, Inc. [*Greenfield, MA*] [*NASDAQ symbol*]   (NQ)
WMBT ...... Pulau Pioman [*Malaysia*] [*ICAO location identifier*]   (ICLI)
WMBT ...... Shenandoah, PA [*AM radio station call letters*]
WMBTOPCITBWTNTALI ... We May Be the Only Phone Company in Town, but We Try Not to Act Like It [*Slogan*]
WMBV ..... Dixon Mills, AL [*FM radio station call letters*]
WMBW ..... Chattanooga, TN [*FM radio station call letters*]
WMC......... Concordia College, Milwaukee, WI [*Library symbol*] [*Library of Congress*]   (LCLS)
WMC......... Memphis, TN [*AM radio station call letters*]
WMC......... War Manpower Commission [*Within the Office of Emergency Management*] [*World War II*]
WMC........ Waste Management Compartment [*NASA*]   (KSC)
WMC........ Weapons and Mobility Command [*Army*]
WMC........ Weapons Monitoring Center
WMC........ Weapons Monitoring Console
WMC........ Western Maryland College [*Westminster*]
WMC........ Western Mining Corp. Holdings ADS [*NYSE symbol*]   (SPSG)
WMC........ White Male Candidate [*Politics*]
WMC........ Wilmington College, Wilmington, OH [*OCLC symbol*]   (OCLC)
WmC......... Windsor Microfilming Company, Windsor, ON, Canada [*Library symbol*] [*Library of Congress*]   (LCLS)
WMC........ Winnemucca, NV [*Location identifier*] [*FAA*]   (FAAL)
WMC........ Wisconsin Motor Carriers Association Inc., Madison WI [*STAC*]
WMC........ Wool Manufacturers Council   (EA)
WMC........ World Meteorological Center [*World Meteorological Organization*]
WMC........ World Methodist Council   (EA)
WMC........ World Ministries Commission   (EA)
WMC........ World Missions to Children [*Later, WMF*]   (EA)
WMC........ World Muslim Congress   (BJA)
WMCA...... New York, NY [*AM radio station call letters*]
WMCB...... Martinsville, IN [*AM radio station call letters*]
WMCC...... Marion, IN [*Television station call letters*]
WMCCMEC ... Women's Missionary Council of the Christian Methodist Episcopal Church   (EA)
WMCCS.... Worldwide Military Command and Control System [*DoD*]   (MCD)
WMCCSA ... World Masters Cross-Country Ski Association   (EA)
WMCD...... Statesboro, GA [*FM radio station call letters*]
WMCE...... Erie, PA [*FM radio station call letters*]
WMC-FM ... Memphis, TN [*FM radio station call letters*]
WMCF-TV ... Montgomery, AL [*Television station call letters*]
WMCG...... Milan, GA [*FM radio station call letters*]
WMCG...... Milwaukee County General Hospital, Milwaukee, WI [*Library symbol*] [*Library of Congress*]   (LCLS)
WMCH...... Church Hill, TN [*AM radio station call letters*]

WMCH...... Columbia Hospital School of Nursing, Milwaukee, WI [*Library symbol*] [*Library of Congress*]   (LCLS)
WMCHi...... Milwaukee County Historical Society, Milwaukee, WI [*Library symbol*] [*Library of Congress*]   (LCLS)
WMCI .... World Mail Center, Incorporated [*NASDAQ symbol*]   (NQ)
WMCJ....... Moncks Corner, SC [*AM radio station call letters*]
WMcK....... William McKinley [*US president, 1843-1901*]
WMCL ...... McLeansboro, IL [*AM radio station call letters*]
WMCL ...... Wideband Communications Line
WMCL ...... William & Clarissa, Inc. [*NASDAQ symbol*]   (NQ)
WMCL ...... William Mitchell College of Law [*St. Paul, MN*]
WMCM...... Milwaukee County Institutions, Mental Health Centers Libraries, Milwaukee, WI [*Library symbol*] [*Library of Congress*]   (LCLS)
WMCM..... Rockland, ME [*FM radio station call letters*]
WMCN...... St. Paul, MN [*FM radio station call letters*]
WMCO...... New Concord, OH [*FM radio station call letters*]
WMCO...... Williams Controls, Inc. [*NASDAQ symbol*]   (NQ)
WMCP...... Columbia, TN [*AM radio station call letters*]
WMCP...... Woman's Medical College of Pennsylvania
WMCQ...... William and Mary College. Quarterly [*A publication*]
WMCQ-FM ... Richmond, KY [*FM radio station call letters*]
WMCR...... Oneida, NY [*AM radio station call letters*]
WMCR-FM ... Oneida, NY [*FM radio station call letters*]
WMCS...... Machias, ME [*AM radio station call letters*]
WMCSC.... Cardinal Stritch College, Milwaukee, WI [*Library symbol*] [*Library of Congress*]   (LCLS)
WMCT ...... Mountain City, TN [*AM radio station call letters*]
WMC-TV .. Memphis, TN [*Television station call letters*]
WMCU...... Miami, FL [*FM radio station call letters*]
WMCW..... Harvard, IL [*AM radio station call letters*]
WMCW..... World Movement of Christian Workers [*See also MMTC*] [*Brussels, Belgium*]   (EAIO)
WMCX...... West Long Branch, NJ [*FM radio station call letters*]
WMD........ Digital Equipment Corp., Westminster, Westminster, MA [*OCLC symbol*]   (OCLC)
WMD........ Doctors Hospital, Milwaukee, WI [*Library symbol*] [*Library of Congress*]   (LCLS)
WMD........ Mandabe [*Madagascar*] [*Airport symbol*]   (OAG)
WMD........ Mars Graphic Services, Inc. [*AMEX symbol*]   (SPSG)
WMD........ Water Mineral Development [*A publication*]   (APTA)
WMD........ Weapon Mounted Display
WMD........ Wind Measuring Device
WMDA...... Woodworking Machinery Distributors Association   (EA)
WMDAA... Watch Material Distributors Association of America [*Later, WMJDA*]   (EA)
W M Day Studies ... Romance Studies Presented to William Morton Day [*A publication*]
WMDB...... Nashville, TN [*AM radio station call letters*]
WMDC...... Hazlehurst, MS [*AM radio station call letters*]
WMDC-FM ... Hazlehurst, MS [*FM radio station call letters*]
WMDD...... Fajardo, PR [*AM radio station call letters*]
WMDe....... Deaconess Hospital, Milwaukee, WI [*Library symbol*] [*Library of Congress*]   (LCLS)
WMDE...... Remerton, GA [*AM radio station call letters*]
WMDH ..... New Castle, IN [*FM radio station call letters*]
WMDio...... Diocesan Library, Milwaukee, WI [*Library symbol*] [*Library of Congress*] [*Obsolete*]   (LCLS)
WMDJ ...... Martin, KY [*AM radio station call letters*]
WMDJ-FM ... Allen, KY [*FM radio station call letters*]
WMDK...... Peterborough, NH [*AM radio station call letters*]
WMDK-FM ... Peterborough, NH [*FM radio station call letters*]
WMDM-FM ... Lexington Park, MD [*FM radio station call letters*]
WMDN ..... Meridian, MS [*AM radio station call letters*]
WMDO...... Wheaton, MD [*AM radio station call letters*]
WMDR...... Alcoa, TN [*AM radio station call letters*]
WMDR...... DePaul Rehabilitation Hospital Medical Library, Milwaukee, WI [*Library symbol*] [*Library of Congress*]   (LCLS)
WMDT...... Salisbury, MD [*Television station call letters*]
WME........ Eaton Corp., Milwaukee, WI [*Library symbol*] [*Library of Congress*]   (LCLS)
WMe......... Elisha D. Smith Public Library, Menasha, WI [*Library symbol*] [*Library of Congress*]   (LCLS)
WME........ Window Meteoroid Experiment [*NASA*]   (KSC)
WME........ Women and Mathematics Education   (EA)
WME........ Worldwide Marriage Encounter   (EA)
WMEA...... Portland, ME [*FM radio station call letters*]
WMEA...... Welded Modules for Electronic Assemblies [*NASA*]
WMEA-TV ... Biddeford, ME [*Television station call letters*]
WMEB...... West Midlands Enterprise Board [*British*]   (ECON)
WMEB-FM ... Orono, ME [*FM radio station call letters*]
WMEB-TV ... Orono, ME [*Television station call letters*]
WMEC...... Medium Endurance Cutter [*Coast Guard*]   (NVT)
WMEC...... Western Military Electronics Center   (KSC)
WMECO... Western Massachusetts Electric Company
WMEC-TV ... Macomb, IL [*Television station call letters*]
WMED...... Calais, ME [*AM radio station call letters*]
WMED-TV ... Calais, ME [*Television station call letters*]
WMEE...... Fort Wayne, IN [*FM radio station call letters*]
WMEH...... Bangor, ME [*FM radio station call letters*]
WMEJ....... Proctorville, OH [*FM radio station call letters*]

WMEK......	Chase City, VA [*AM radio station call letters*]
WMEL......	Melbourne, FL [*AM radio station call letters*]
WMEM......	Presque Isle, ME [*FM radio station call letters*]
WMEM-TV ...	Presque Isle, ME [*Television station call letters*]
WMen........	Mabel Tainter Memorial Free Library, Menomonie, WI [*Library symbol*] [*Library of Congress*]　(LCLS)
WMenM....	Memorial Hospital and Nursing Home, Menomonie, WI [*Library symbol*] [*Library of Congress*]　(LCLS)
WMenofH ...	Community Memorial Hospital, Health Science Library, Menomonee Falls, WI [*Library symbol*] [*Library of Congress*]　(LCLS)
WMenU.....	University of Wisconsin-Stout, Menomonie, WI [*Library symbol*] [*Library of Congress*]　(LCLS)
WMeq........	Frank L. Weyenberg Library, Mequon, WI [*Library symbol*] [*Library of Congress*]　(LCLS)
WMEQ......	Menomonie, WI [*AM radio station call letters*]
WMEQ-FM ...	Menomonie, WI [*FM radio station call letters*]
WMeqW....	Wisconsin Lutheran Seminary, Mequon, WI [*Library symbol*] [*Library of Congress*]　(LCLS)
WMER......	Meridian, MS [*AM radio station call letters*]
WMer........	T. B. Scott Free Library, Merril, WI [*Library symbol*] [*Library of Congress*]　(LCLS)
WMET......	Gaithersburg, MD [*AM radio station call letters*]
WMET......	Valdosta, GA [*AM radio station call letters*]
WMeU.......	University of Wisconsin-Green Bay, Fox Valley Campus, Menasha, WI [*Library symbol*] [*Library of Congress*]　(LCLS)
WMEV......	Marion, VA [*AM radio station call letters*]
WMEV-FM ...	Marion, VA [*FM radio station call letters*]
WMEW.....	Waterville, ME [*FM radio station call letters*]
WMEX.....	Boston, MA [*AM radio station call letters*]
WMEY......	Seymour, TN [*FM radio station call letters*]
WMEZ......	Pensacola, FL [*FM radio station call letters*]
WMF.........	Maude Shunk Public Library, Menomonee Falls, WI [*OCLC symbol*]　(OCLC)
WMF.........	Wire Mattress Federation
WMF.........	World Mercy Fund　(EA)
WMF.........	World Missions Fellowship　(EA)
WMF.........	World Monuments Fund　(EA)
WMFC......	Kuala Lumpur [*Malaysia*] [*ICAO location identifier*]　(ICLI)
WMFC......	Monroeville, AL [*AM radio station call letters*]
WMFC-FM ...	Monroeville, AL [*FM radio station call letters*]
WMFD......	Wilmington, NC [*AM radio station call letters*]
WMFD-FM ...	Wilmington, NC [*FM radio station call letters*]
WMFE-FM ...	Orlando, FL [*FM radio station call letters*]
WMFE-TV ...	Orlando, FL [*Television station call letters*]
WMFG......	Hibbing, MN [*AM radio station call letters*]
WMFG-FM ...	Hibbing, MN [*FM radio station call letters*]
WMFJ......	Daytona Beach, FL [*AM radio station call letters*]
WMFL......	Monticello, FL [*AM radio station call letters*]
WMFM......	Petal, MS [*FM radio station call letters*]
WMFM.....	Wisconsin Scottish Rite Bodies AASR, Milwaukee, WI [*Library symbol*] [*Library of Congress*]　(LCLS)
WMFO......	Medford, MA [*FM radio station call letters*]
WMFP......	Lawrence, MA [*Television station call letters*]
WMFQ.....	Ocala, FL [*FM radio station call letters*]
WMFR.....	High Point, NC [*AM radio station call letters*]
WMFX.....	St. Andrews, SC [*FM radio station call letters*]
WMG........	Globe-Union, Inc., Milwaukee, WI [*Library symbol*] [*Library of Congress*]　(LCLS)
WMG........	Wire Measure Gauge
WMG........	Wire Metallizing Gun
WMGA......	Moultrie, GA [*AM radio station call letters*]
W & M GA ...	Washburn and Moen Gauge　(MSA)
WMGa.......	Wisconsin Gas Co., Milwaukee, WI [*Library symbol*] [*Library of Congress*]　(LCLS)
WMGC-TV ...	Binghamton, NY [*Television station call letters*]
WMGE......	Danville, KY [*FM radio station call letters*]
WMGG.....	Columbus, OH [*FM radio station call letters*]
WMGH-FM ...	Tamaqua, PA [*FM radio station call letters*]
WMGI.......	Terre Haute, IN [*FM radio station call letters*]
WMGJ......	Gadsden, AL [*AM radio station call letters*]
WMGK.....	Philadelphia, PA [*FM radio station call letters*]
WMGL.....	Ravenel, SC [*FM radio station call letters*]
WMGL.....	Wilmington Marine Geological Laboratory [*North Carolina*]　(NOAA)
WMGM.....	Atlantic City, NJ [*FM radio station call letters*]
WMGM-TV ...	Wildwood, NJ [*Television station call letters*]
WMGN......	Madison, WI [*FM radio station call letters*]
WMGO	Canton, MS [*AM radio station call letters*]
WMGP......	Parkersburg, WV [*FM radio station call letters*]
WMGQ.....	New Brunswick, NJ [*FM radio station call letters*]
WMGR.....	Bainbridge, GA [*AM radio station call letters*]
WMGR.....	Worm Gear [*Mechanical engineering*]
WMGS	Wilkes-Barre, PA [*FM radio station call letters*]
WMGT.....	Macon, GA [*Television station call letters*]
WMGU.....	Stevens Point, WI [*FM radio station call letters*]
WMGV.....	Oshkosh, WI [*FM radio station call letters*]
WMGW.....	Meadville, PA [*AM radio station call letters*]
WMGX.....	Portland, ME [*FM radio station call letters*]
WMGY.....	Montgomery, AL [*AM radio station call letters*]

WMH	Mountain Home [*Arkansas*] [*Airport symbol*]　(OAG)
WMH	Wisconsin Magazine of History [*A publication*]
WMH	WM Helijet [*Vancouver Stock Exchange symbol*]
WMHB......	Waterville, ME [*FM radio station call letters*]
WMHC......	South Hadley, MA [*FM radio station call letters*]
WMHD-FM ...	Terre Haute, IN [*FM radio station call letters*]
WMHE......	Toledo, OH [*FM radio station call letters*]
WMHE......	Women and Health [*A publication*]
WMHG-FM ...	Muskegon, MI [*FM radio station call letters*]
WMHK......	Columbia, SC [*FM radio station call letters*]
WMHN.....	Webster, NY [*FM radio station call letters*]
WMHR.....	Syracuse, NY [*FM radio station call letters*]
WMHS......	Miamisburg, OH [*FM radio station call letters*]
WMHS......	Wall-Mounted Handling System [*AEC*]
WMHS......	World Methodist Historical Society　(EA)
WMHT......	Schenectady, NY [*Television station call letters*]
WMHT-FM ...	Schenectady, NY [*FM radio station call letters*]
WMHU	Renovo, PA [*FM radio station call letters*]
WMHW-FM ...	Mount Pleasant, MI [*FM radio station call letters*]
WMHX.....	Schenectady, NY [*Television station call letters*]
WMHX-FM ...	Poughkeepsie, NY [*FM radio station call letters*]
WMHY.....	World Mental Health Year [*1960*]
WMI.........	War Materials, Incorporated
WMI.........	Washington Music Institute
WMI.........	Waveguide Moisture Indicator
WMI.........	Westmin Resources Ltd. [*Toronto Stock Exchange symbol*] [*Vancouver Stock Exchange symbol*]
WMI.........	Wildlife Management Institute　(EA)
WMI.........	Winthrop Insured Mortgage Investments II [*AMEX symbol*]　(SPSG)
WMI.........	Woodlands Mountain Institute　(EA)
WMI.........	Work Motivation Inventory [*Test*]
WMI.........	World Metal Index [*Sheffield City Libraries*] [*British*] [*Information service or system*]　(IID)
WMI.........	World Meteorological Intervals
WMIA......	Arecibo, PR [*AM radio station call letters*]
WMIA	Woodworking Machinery Importers Association of America　(EA)
WMIB	Marco Island, FL [*AM radio station call letters*]
WMIB	Waste Management Information Bureau [*Atomic Energy Authority*] [*British*] [*Information service or system*]　(IID)
WMIC......	Sandusky, MI [*AM radio station call letters*]
WMIC......	Western Microwave, Inc. [*NASDAQ symbol*]　(NQ)
WMIC/CHCC ...	Welsh Music Information Centre - Canolfan Hysbysrwydd Cerddoriaeth Cymru [*University College*]　(CB)
WMID......	Atlantic City, NJ [*AM radio station call letters*]
WMID-FM ...	Pleasantville, NJ [*FM radio station call letters*]
WMIE	Cocoa, FL [*FM radio station call letters*]
WMIH......	Gorham, NH [*FM radio station call letters*]
WMII	Hendersonville, TN [*AM radio station call letters*]
WMIK......	Middlesboro, KY [*AM radio station call letters*]
WMIK-FM ...	Middlesboro, KY [*FM radio station call letters*]
WMIL.......	Waukesha, WI [*FM radio station call letters*]
WMiltM	Milton College, Milton, WI [*Library symbol*] [*Library of Congress*]　(LCLS)
WMIM	Mount Carmel, PA [*AM radio station call letters*]
WMIN......	Maplewood, MN [*AM radio station call letters*]
WMINST ...	Westminster [*England*]
WMIO.......	Cabo Rojo, PR [*FM radio station call letters*]
WMIP........	Weapons Management Improvement Program [*Military*]　(AABC)
WMIQ......	Iron Mountain, MI [*AM radio station call letters*]
WMIR	Lake Geneva, WI [*AM radio station call letters*]
WMIS.......	Natchez, MS [*AM radio station call letters*]
WMIT	Black Mountain, NC [*FM radio station call letters*]
WMIW.....	Atlantic Beach, SC [*AM radio station call letters*]
WMIX	Mount Vernon, IL [*AM radio station call letters*]
WMIX-FM ...	Mount Vernon, IL [*FM radio station call letters*]
WMIY	Fairview, NC [*AM radio station call letters*]
WMJ	Johnson Controls, Corporate Information Center, Milwaukee, WI [*Library symbol*] [*Library of Congress*]　(LCLS)
WMJ	World of Michael Jackson　(EA)
WMJA......	Spencer, WI [*FM radio station call letters*]
WMJB......	Evansville, WI [*FM radio station call letters*]
WMJC......	Indianapolis, IN [*FM radio station call letters*]
WMJD......	Grundy, VA [*FM radio station call letters*]
WMJDA......	Watch Material and Jewelry Distributors Association [*Formerly, WMDAA*]　(EA)
WMJI.......	Cleveland, OH [*FM radio station call letters*]
WMJJ	Birmingham, AL [*FM radio station call letters*]
WMJK.......	Kissimmee, FL [*AM radio station call letters*]
WMJL.......	Marion, KY [*AM radio station call letters*]
WMJM	Cordele, GA [*AM radio station call letters*]
WMJQ......	Buffalo, NY [*FM radio station call letters*]
WMJR......	Warrenton, VA [*FM radio station call letters*]
WMJS	Prince Frederick, MD [*FM radio station call letters*]
WMJV-FM ...	Patterson, NY [*FM radio station call letters*]
WMJW.....	Magee, MS [*FM radio station call letters*]
WMJX......	Boston, MA [*FM radio station call letters*]
WMJY.......	Long Branch, NJ [*FM radio station call letters*]
WMJZ-FM ...	Gaylord, MI [*FM radio station call letters*]

WMK........ Watermark
W/(M K).... Watts per Meter Kelvin
WMK........ Weis Markets, Inc. [*NYSE symbol*]　(SPSG)
W/(M² K).. Watts per Square Meter Kelvin
WMKA...... Alor Setar/Sultan Abdul Halim [*Malaysia*] [*ICAO location identifier*]　(ICLI)
WMKB...... Butterworth [*Malaysia*] [*ICAO location identifier*]　(ICLI)
WMKB...... Ridgebury, PA [*FM radio station call letters*]
WMKC...... Kota Bahru/Sultan Ismail Petra [*Malaysia*] [*ICAO location identifier*]　(ICLI)
WMKC...... St. Ignace, MI [*FM radio station call letters*]
WMKD...... Kuantan [*Malaysia*] [*ICAO location identifier*]　(ICLI)
WMKE...... Kerteh [*Malaysia*] [*ICAO location identifier*]　(ICLI)
WMKF...... Simpang [*Malaysia*] [*ICAO location identifier*]　(ICLI)
WMKI....... Ipoh [*Malaysia*] [*ICAO location identifier*]　(ICLI)
WMKJ....... Johore Bahru [*Malaysia*] [*ICAO location identifier*]　(ICLI)
WMKJ....... Newnan, GA [*FM radio station call letters*]
WMKK...... Kuala Lumpur/International [*Malaysia*] [*ICAO location identifier*]　(ICLI)
WMKM...... Malacca [*Malaysia*] [*ICAO location identifier*]　(ICLI)
WMKN...... Kuala Trengganu/Sultan Mahmud [*Malaysia*] [*ICAO location identifier*]　(ICLI)
WMKO...... Millen, GA [*FM radio station call letters*]
WMKP...... Penang [*Malaysia*] [*ICAO location identifier*]　(ICLI)
WMKS...... Kuala Lumpur [*Malaysia*] [*ICAO location identifier*]　(ICLI)
WMKS...... Springfield, VT [*FM radio station call letters*]
WMKT...... Charlevoix, MI [*AM radio station call letters*]
WMKX...... Brookville, PA [*FM radio station call letters*]
WMKY...... Morehead, KY [*FM radio station call letters*]
WML......... Lakeside Laboratories, Milwaukee, WI [*Library symbol*] [*Library of Congress*]　(LCLS)
WML........ Malaimbandy [*Madagascar*] [*Airport symbol*]　(OAG)
WML........ Westar Mining Ltd. [*Toronto Stock Exchange symbol*] [*Vancouver Stock Exchange symbol*]
WML........ Willamette Law Journal [*A publication*]
WMLA...... Normal, IL [*AM radio station call letters*]
WMLA-FM ... Le Roy, IL [*FM radio station call letters*]
WMLB...... Glen Arbor, MI [*FM radio station call letters*]
WMLC...... Monticello, MS [*AM radio station call letters*]
WMLC...... Way of Mountain Learning Center　(EA)
WMLD...... East Point, GA [*AM radio station call letters*]
WMLH...... Lutheran Hospital of Milwaukee, Milwaukee, WI [*Library symbol*] [*Library of Congress*]　(LCLS)
WMLI....... Sauk City, WI [*FM radio station call letters*]
Wm LJ...... Willamette Law Journal [*A publication*]
WMLM...... St. Louis, MI [*AM radio station call letters*]
WMLN-FM ... Milton, MA [*FM radio station call letters*]
WMLO...... Havana, FL [*FM radio station call letters*]
WMLP...... Milton, PA [*AM radio station call letters*]
WMLQ...... Rogers City, MI [*FM radio station call letters*]
WMLR...... Hohenwald, TN [*AM radio station call letters*]
WMLR ..... William and Mary Law Review [*A publication*]
W and M LR ... William and Mary Law Review [*A publication*]
WMLR ..... William Mitchell Law Review [*A publication*]
W & M L Rev ... William and Mary Law Review [*A publication*]
WMLS...... Monroe, GA [*AM radio station call letters*]
WMLT...... Dublin, GA [*AM radio station call letters*]
WMLV...... Ironton, OH [*FM radio station call letters*]
WMLX...... Florence, KY [*AM radio station call letters*]
WMLY...... Conway, NH [*FM radio station call letters*]
WMM........ Marquette University, Milwaukee, WI [*Library symbol*] [*Library of Congress*]　(LCLS)
WMM....... Wall-Mounted Manipulator [*Nuclear energy*]　(NRCH)
Wm & M ... William and Mary (King and Queen of England)　(DLA)
WMM........ William Mitchell College of Law Library, St. Paul, MN [*OCLC symbol*]　(OCLC)
WMM....... Willow Mixed Media　(EA)
WMM....... Women Make Movies　(EA)
WMM....... World Medical Mission　(EA)
WMM........ World Movement of Mothers [*See also MMM*] [*Paris, France*]　(EAIO)
WMMA..... Wood Machinery Manufacturers of America　(EA)
Wm Mar Q ... William and Mary Quarterly [*A publication*]
Wm and Mary L Rev ... William and Mary Law Review [*A publication*]
Wm & Mary Q ... William and Mary Quarterly [*A publication*]
Wm & Mary Rev VA L ... William and Mary Review of Virginia Law [*A publication*]　(DLA)
WMMB..... Melbourne, FL [*AM radio station call letters*]
WMMB..... Milwaukee Blood Center, Inc., Milwaukee, WI [*Library symbol*] [*Library of Congress*]　(LCLS)
WMMBC .. Miller Brewing Co., Research Library, Milwaukee, WI [*Library symbol*] [*Library of Congress*]　(LCLS)
WMMC..... Marshall, IL [*FM radio station call letters*]
WMMC..... Milwaukee Children's Hospital, Milwaukee, WI [*Library symbol*] [*Library of Congress*]　(LCLS)
WMMCW ... Medical College of Wisconsin, Medical-Dental Library, Milwaukee, WI [*Library symbol*] [*Library of Congress*]　(LCLS)
WMME..... Augusta, ME [*AM radio station call letters*]
WMME-FM ... Augusta, ME [*FM radio station call letters*]
WMMG..... Brandenburg, KY [*AM radio station call letters*]

WMMG-FM ... Brandenburg, KY [*FM radio station call letters*]
WMMGIC ... MGIC Investment Corp., Milwaukee, WI [*Library symbol*] [*Library of Congress*]　(LCLS)
WMMH .... Misericordia Hospital, Milwaukee, WI [*Library symbol*] [*Library of Congress*]　(LCLS)
WMMI...... Shepherd, MI [*AM radio station call letters*]
Wm Mitchell L Rev ... William Mitchell Law Review [*A publication*]
WMMJ ..... Bethesda, MD [*FM radio station call letters*]
WMMK..... Destin, FL [*FM radio station call letters*]
WMM-L.... Marquette University, School of Law, Milwaukee, WI [*Library symbol*] [*Library of Congress*]　(LCLS)
WMML..... Mobile, AL [*AM radio station call letters*]
WMMM..... Westport, CT [*AM radio station call letters*]
WMM/MWS ... Western Material Management, Machinery, and Welding Show [*Canada*]　(ITD)
WMMN..... Fairmont, WV [*AM radio station call letters*]
WMM-N ... Marquette University, College of Nursing, Milwaukee, WI [*Library symbol*] [*Library of Congress*]　(LCLS)
WMMP..... Wood Moulding and Millwork Producers [*Later, WMMPA*]　(EA)
WMMPA .. Wood Moulding and Millwork Producers Association　(EA)
WMMQ..... Charlotte, MI [*FM radio station call letters*]
WMMR..... Philadelphia, PA [*FM radio station call letters*]
WMMRRI ... Wyoming Mining and Mineral Resource Research Institute [*University of Wyoming*] [*Research center*]　(RCD)
WMMS ..... Cleveland, OH [*FM radio station call letters*]
WMMS ..... Mount Sinai Hospital, Milwaukee, WI [*Library symbol*] [*Library of Congress*]　(LCLS)
WMMt ...... Mount Mary College, Milwaukee, WI [*Library symbol*] [*Library of Congress*]　(LCLS)
WMMT...... Whitesburg, KY [*FM radio station call letters*]
WMMTA .. World Minerals and Metals [*A publication*]
WMMus... Milwaukee Public Museum, Reference Library, Milwaukee, WI [*Library symbol*] [*Library of Congress*]　(LCLS)
WMMV..... Bay Minette, AL [*FM radio station call letters*]
WMMW..... Meriden, CT [*AM radio station call letters*]
WMMX..... Fairborn, OH [*AM radio station call letters*]
WMMY-FM ... Melbourne, FL [*FM radio station call letters*]
WMMZ...... Ocala, FL [*FM radio station call letters*]
WMN .... Maroantsetra [*Madagascar*] [*Airport symbol*]　(OAG)
WMN .... Western Morning News [*United Kingdom*] [*A publication*]
WMN .... Winnemucca [*Nevada*] [*Seismograph station code, US Geological Survey*] [*Closed*]　(SEIS)
WMNA...... Gretna, VA [*AM radio station call letters*]
WMNA-FM ... Gretna, VA [*FM radio station call letters*]
WMNB..... North Adams, MA [*AM radio station call letters*]
WMNC..... Morganton, NC [*AM radio station call letters*]
WMNF...... Tampa, FL [*FM radio station call letters*]
WMNG...... Northwest General Hospital, Milwaukee, WI [*Library symbol*] [*Library of Congress*]　(LCLS)
WMNI...... Columbus, OH [*AM radio station call letters*]
WMNI....... Wildlife Management News (Iceland) [*A publication*]
WMNJ...... Madison, NJ [*FM radio station call letters*]
WMNK..... Montawk, NY [*FM radio station call letters*]
Wmn Lib.... Women's Liberation [*A publication*]
WMNM..... Port Henry, NY [*FM radio station call letters*]
WMNR..... Monroe, CT [*FM radio station call letters*]
WMNS...... Olean, NY [*AM radio station call letters*]
WMNS...... William B. McGuire Nuclear Station　(NRCH)
WMNT...... Manati, PR [*AM radio station call letters*]
WMNY..... Elloree-Santee, SC [*AM radio station call letters*]
WMNY-FM ... Elloree-Santee, SC [*FM radio station call letters*]
WMNZ...... Montezuma, GA [*AM radio station call letters*]
WMO .... White Mountain [*Alaska*] [*Airport symbol*]　(OAG)
WMO .... White Mountain, AK [*Location identifier*] [*FAA*]　(FAAL)
WMO .... Wichita Mountains Array [*Oklahoma*] [*Seismograph station code, US Geological Survey*] [*Closed*]　(SEIS)
WMO .... Wing Maintenance Officer
WMO .... World Meteorological Organization [*See also OMM*] [*Geneva, Switzerland*] [*United Nations*]　(EAIO)
WMOA..... Marietta, OH [*AM radio station call letters*]
WMOB..... Mobile, AL [*AM radio station call letters*]
WMOBA... WMO [*World Meteorological Organization*] Bulletin [*A publication*]
WMO Bull ... WMO [*World Meteorological Organization*] Bulletin [*A publication*]
WMOC...... Chattanooga, TN [*AM radio station call letters*]
WMOD ..... Bolivar, TN [*AM radio station call letters*]
WMOG ..... Brunswick, GA [*AM radio station call letters*]
WMOH..... Hamilton, OH [*AM radio station call letters*]
WMOI...... Monmouth, IL [*FM radio station call letters*]
WMOK..... Metropolis, IL [*AM radio station call letters*]
WMoM...... Monroe Clinic, Monroe, WI [*Library symbol*] [*Library of Congress*]　(LCLS)
WMON ..... Montgomery, WV [*AM radio station call letters*]
WMOP...... Ocala, FL [*AM radio station call letters*]
WMO Publ ... WMO [*World Meteorological Organization*] Publication [*A publication*]
WMOR...... Morehead, KY [*AM radio station call letters*]
WMOR...... Westmoreland Coal Co. [*NASDAQ symbol*]　(NQ)

WMO Rep Mar Sci Aff ... World Meteorological Organization. Reports on Marine Science Affairs [*A publication*]
WMOR-FM ... Morehead, KY [*FM radio station call letters*]
WMOS ..... Bath, ME [*FM radio station call letters*]
WMoS .... Saint Clare Hospital, Monroe, WI [*Library symbol*] [*Library of Congress*] (LCLS)
WMO Spec Environ Rep ... World Meteorological Organization. Special Environmental Report [*A publication*]
WMOT ..... Murfreesboro, TN [*FM radio station call letters*]
WMO Tech Note ... World Meteorological Organization. Technical Note [*A publication*]
WMOU ..... Berlin, NH [*AM radio station call letters*]
WMOV ..... Ravenswood, WV [*AM radio station call letters*]
WMOX ..... Meridian, MS [*AM radio station call letters*]
WMP .... War and Mobilization Plan [*Air Force documents*]
WMP .... Waste Management Paper [*British*] (DCTA)
WMP .... Weapon Monitor Panel (MCD)
WMP .... Weather Modification Program [*Department of Commerce*] [*Boulder, CO*]
WMP .... Wiener Mapping Procedure
WMP .... With Much Pleasure [*Meaning, "We accept the invitation"*]
WMP .... Women and the Military Project [*An association*] (EA)
WmP .... World Microfilms Publications, London, United Kingdom [*Library symbol*] [*Library of Congress*] (LCLS)
WMPA ...... Women's Military Pilots Association (EA)
WMPB ..... Baltimore, MD [*Television station call letters*]
WMPC ...... Lapeer, MI [*AM radio station call letters*]
WMPC ...... War Materiel Procurement Capability (AFIT)
WMPCE .... World Meeting Planners Congress and Exposition [*Defunct*] (EA)
WMPCES(P) ... War Manpower Commission Employment Stabilization (Plan) [*Terminated, 1945*]
WMPG ...... Gorham, ME [*FM radio station call letters*]
WMPH ...... Wilmington, DE [*FM radio station call letters*]
WM & PHF ... Waste Management and Personal Hygiene Facility [*NASA*] (KSC)
WMPI .... Scottsburg, IN [*FM radio station call letters*]
WMPI .... Women of the Motion Picture Industry, International [*Dallas, TX*]
WMPL ...... Hancock, MI [*AM radio station call letters*]
WMPL ...... Western Maryland Public Libraries Regional Resource Center [*Library network*]
WMPL ...... World Mission Prayer League (EA)
WMPM ..... Smithfield, NC [*AM radio station call letters*]
WMPO ..... Middleport-Pomeroy, OH [*AM radio station call letters*]
WMPO ..... Weather Modification Program Office [*Marine science*] (MSC)
WMPO-FM ... Middleport-Pomeroy, OH [*FM radio station call letters*]
WMPR ...... Jackson, MS [*FM radio station call letters*]
WMPRT .... Wartime Manpower and Personnel Readiness Team [*Military*]
WMPS ...... Millington, TN [*AM radio station call letters*]
WMPT ...... Annapolis, MD [*Television station call letters*]
WMPV-TV ... Mobile, AL [*Television station call letters*]
WMPX ...... Midland, MI [*AM radio station call letters*]
WMQ .... Quarles & Brady, Law Library, Milwaukee, WI [*Library symbol*] [*Library of Congress*] (LCLS)
WMQ .... Westmount Public Library [*UTLAS symbol*]
W & M Q ... William and Mary Quarterly [*A publication*]
WMQ .... William and Mary Quarterly [*A publication*]
WMQ .... Wulumuchi [*Republic of China*] [*Seismograph station code, US Geological Survey*] (SEIS)
WMQA ...... Mexico Beach, FL [*FM radio station call letters*]
WMQC ...... Westover, WV [*FM radio station call letters*]
WMQM ..... Memphis, TN [*AM radio station call letters*]
WMQQ ..... Springfield, KY [*FM radio station call letters*]
WMQT ...... Ishpeming, MI [*FM radio station call letters*]
WMQX ...... Winston-Salem, NC [*AM radio station call letters*]
WMQX-FM ... Winston-Salem, NC [*FM radio station call letters*]
WMQZ ...... Allen, KY [*FM radio station call letters*]
WMR .... Mananara [*Madagascar*] [*Airport symbol*] (OAG)
WMR .... Reinhart, Boerner, Van Deuren, Norris and Rieselbach, Law Library, Milwaukee, WI [*Library symbol*] [*Library of Congress*] (LCLS)
WMR .... Wake Measurements RADAR [*Army*] (MCD)
WMR .... War Maintenance Reserve [*British*]
WMR .... War Materiel Requirement (AFIT)
WMR .... Water Meter
WMR .... Water-Moderated Reactor
WMR .... Wideband Multichannel Receiver
WMR .... William and Mary Review of Virginia Law [*A publication*] (DLA)
WMR .... Wonder Marine Resources [*Vancouver Stock Exchange symbol*]
WMR .... Woomera Missile Range [*Australia*]
WMR .... World Medical Relief (EA)
WMRA ...... Harrisonburg, VA [*FM radio station call letters*]
WMRC ...... Milford, MA [*AM radio station call letters*]
WMRC ...... War Minerals Relief Commission [*Department of the Interior*] [*Abolished, 1940*] (EGAO)
WMRE ...... Knoxville, TN [*FM radio station call letters*]
WMRF-FM ... Lewistown, PA [*FM radio station call letters*]
WMRI .... Marion, IN [*FM radio station call letters*]
WMRK ...... Selma, AL [*AM radio station call letters*]

WMRK ...... Westmark International, Inc. [*NASDAQ symbol*] (NQ)
WMRL ...... Water Management Research Laboratory [*Department of Agriculture*] [*Fresno, CA*] (GRD)
WMRN ...... Marion, OH [*AM radio station call letters*]
WMRN-FM ... Marion, OH [*FM radio station call letters*]
Wm Rob ..... William Robinson's English Admiralty Reports [*1838-52*] [*A publication*]
Wm Rob Adm ... William Robinson's English Admiralty Reports [*1838-52*] [*A publication*] (DLA)
WMRQ ...... Meredith, NH [*FM radio station call letters*]
WMRS ...... Monticello, IN [*FM radio station call letters*]
WMRS ...... White Mountain Research Station [*Research center*] (RCD)
WMRT ...... Marietta, OH [*FM radio station call letters*]
WMRV ...... Endicott, NY [*FM radio station call letters*]
WMRX-FM ... Beaverton, MI [*FM radio station call letters*]
WMRZ ...... Moline, IL [*AM radio station call letters*]
WMS .... Warehouse Material Stores (AAG)
WMS .... Waste Management System (MCD)
WMS .... Water Management Section [*Apollo*] [*NASA*]
WMS .... Weapons Monitoring System
WMS .... Weather Mapping System
WMS .... Wechsler Memory Scale [*Neuropsychological test*]
WMS .... Wesleyan Missionary Society
WMS .... West Middle School [*South Carolina*] [*Seismograph station code, US Geological Survey*] (SEIS)
W v M S ..... Wetboek van Militair Strafrecht [*A publication*]
WMS .... Whaling Museum Society (EA)
WMS .... Wilderness Medical Society (EA)
WMS .... Willem Mengelberg Society (EA)
WMS .... William Morris Society [*Later, WMS/AB*] (EA)
WMS .... Wind Measuring System
WMS .... WMS Industries, Inc. [*Formerly, Williams Electronics*] [*NYSE symbol*] (SPSG)
WMS .... Women for a Meaningful Summit (EA)
WMS .... Women in the Medical Service [*Army*]
WMS .... Women's Medical Specialist
WMS .... Women's Missionary Society, AME [*African Methodist Episcopal*] Church (EA)
WMS .... [*Canada's International*] Woodworking Machinery and Supply Show (ITD)
WMS .... Wool Marketing Service [*Australia*]
WMS .... Work Measurement System [*Postal Service*]
WM & S .... Work Methods and Standards
WMS .... World Magnetic Survey [*Defunct*]
WMS .... World Mariculture Society (EA)
WmS .... World Microfilms Division, Oyez Equipment Ltd., London, United Kingdom [*Library symbol*] [*Library of Congress*] (LCLS)
WMSA ...... Massena, NY [*AM radio station call letters*]
WMSA ...... Saint Anthony Hospital, Milwaukee, WI [*Library symbol*] [*Library of Congress*] (LCLS)
WMS/AB .. William Morris Society, American Branch (EA)
Wms Ann Reg ... Williams' Annual Register [*New York*] [*A publication*] (DLA)
Wms Bank ... [*R. V.*] Williams on Bankruptcy [*17 eds.*] [*1870-1958*] [*A publication*] (DLA)
Wms & Bruce ... [*R. G.*] Williams and [*Sir G.*] Bruce's Admiralty Practice [*3 eds.*] [*1865-1902*] [*A publication*] (DLA)
WMSC ...... Upper Montclair, NJ [*FM radio station call letters*]
WMSC ...... Weather Message Switching Center
WMSC ...... White Mountain Scenic Railroad [*AAR code*]
WMSC ...... Women's Medical Specialists Corps
WMSE ...... Milwaukee School of Engineering, Walter Schroeder Library, Milwaukee, WI [*Library symbol*] [*Library of Congress*] (LCLS)
WMSE ...... Milwaukee, WI [*FM radio station call letters*]
Wms Ex ..... Williams on Executors [*15th ed.*] [*1970*] [*A publication*] (DLA)
Wms Exors ... [*E. V.*] Williams on Executors [*13 eds.*] [*1832-1953*] [*A publication*] (DLA)
Wms Ex'rs ... [*E. V.*] Williams on Executors [*13 eds.*] [*1832-1953*] [*A publication*] (DLA)
Wms Exs. ... [*E. V.*] Williams on Executors [*13 eds.*] [*1832-1953*] [*A publication*] (DLA)
WMSF ...... Saint Francis Seminary, Milwaukee, WI [*Library symbol*] [*Library of Congress*] (LCLS)
WMSFH .... Saint Francis Hospital, Milwaukee, WI [*Library symbol*] [*Library of Congress*] (LCLS)
WMSFT .... Wormshaft
WMSG ...... Oakland, MD [*AM radio station call letters*]
WMSH ...... Sturgis, MI [*FM radio station call letters*]
WMSI .... Jackson, MS [*FM radio station call letters*]
WMSI .... Western Management Science Institute [*University of California*] (KSC)
WMSI .... Williams Industries, Inc. [*NASDAQ symbol*] (NQ)
WMSJ ...... Saint Joseph's Hospital, Milwaukee, WI [*Library symbol*] [*Library of Congress*] (LCLS)
WMSJ ...... William Morris Society. Journal [*A publication*]
WMSK ...... Morganfield, KY [*AM radio station call letters*]
WMSKF .... William Morris Society and Kelmscott Fellowship [*Formed by a merger of Kelmscott Fellowship and William Morris Society*] (EAIO)

WMSK-FM ... Morganfield, KY [*FM radio station call letters*]
WMSL....... Athens, GA [*FM radio station call letters*]
WMSL....... Saint Luke's Hospital, Milwaukee, WI [*Library symbol*] [*Library of Congress*] (LCLS)
WMSL....... Wet Mock Simulated Launch [*NASA*] (KSC)
WMSL....... Wichita Mountains Seismological Laboratory
WMSM ..... Saint Mary's Hospital, Milwaukee, WI [*Library symbol*] [*Library of Congress*] (LCLS)
Wms Mass ... Williams' Reports [*1 Massachusetts*] [*A publication*] (DLA)
WMSMi ..... Saint Michael Hospital, Milwaukee, WI [*Library symbol*] [*Library of Congress*] (LCLS)
WMSMN .. Saint Mary's School of Nursing, Milwaukee, WI [*Library symbol*] [*Library of Congress*] (LCLS)
Wms Notes ... Williams' Notes to Saunders' Reports [*England*] [*A publication*] (DLA)
WMSN-TV ... Madison, WI [*Television station call letters*]
WMSO ...... Wichita Mountains Seismological Observatory
WMSP ...... Elk Hills, WV [*AM radio station call letters*]
Wms P .... Peere-Williams' English Chancery Reports [*1695-1736*] [*A publication*] (DLA)
Wms Peere ... Peere-Williams' English Chancery Reports [*A publication*] (DLA)
Wms PP ... [*J.*] Williams on Personal Property [*18 eds.*] [*1848-1926*] [*A publication*] (DLA)
WMSQ ...... Havelock, NC [*FM radio station call letters*]
WMSR ...... Manchester, TN [*AM radio station call letters*]
W/(M² SR) ... Watts per Square Meter Steradian
WMSR-FM ... Manchester, TN [*FM radio station call letters*]
WMSRG.... Weather-Modification Statistical Research Groups
Wms RP..... [*J.*] Williams on Real Property [*24 eds.*] [*1824-1926*] [*A publication*] (DLA)
WMSS ...... Middletown, PA [*FM radio station call letters*]
Wms Saund ... [*Sir Edmund*] Saunders' Reports, Edited by Williams [*85 English Reprint*] [*A publication*] (DLA)
Wms Saund (Eng) ... [*Sir Edmund*] Saunders' Reports, Edited by Williams [*85 English Reprint*] [*A publication*] (DLA)
WMST...... Mount Sterling, KY [*AM radio station call letters*]
WMST-FM ... Mount Sterling, KY [*FM radio station call letters*]
Wms VT ... Williams' Vermont Reports [*27-29 Vermont*] [*A publication*] (DLA)
WMSW ..... Hatillo, PR [*AM radio station call letters*]
WMSWH .. Southeastern Wisconsin Health Systems Agency, Health Science Library, Milwaukee, WI [*Library symbol*] [*Library of Congress*] (LCLS)
WMSY-TV ... Marion, VA [*Television station call letters*]
WMT .... Auslandmerkte/Marches Etrangers [*Lausanne*] [*A publication*]
WMT .... Cedar Rapids, IA [*AM radio station call letters*]
WMT .... Wal-Mart Stores, Inc. [*NYSE symbol*] (SPSG)
WMT .... Waste Monitor Tank (IEEE)
WMT .... Weighing More Than
WMT .... West Meridian Time
WMT .... Western Motor Tariff Bureau, Los Angeles CA [*STAC*]
WMT .... Wet Metric Ton [*Waste management*]
WMTB ...... Western Motor Tariff Bureau
WMTB-FM ... Emmitsburg, MD [*FM radio station call letters*]
WMTC ...... Milwaukee Technical College, Milwaukee, WI [*Library symbol*] [*Library of Congress*] (LCLS)
WMTC ...... Vancleve, KY [*AM radio station call letters*]
WMTC ...... Waste Management Technology Center [*Oak Ridge National Laboratory*]
WMTC-N ... Milwaukee Area Technical College, North Campus Center Library, Mequon, WI [*Library symbol*] [*Library of Congress*] (LCLS)
WMTC-S... Milwaukee Area Technical College, South Campus Center Library, Oak Creek, WI [*Library symbol*] [*Library of Congress*] (LCLS)
WMTC-W ... Milwaukee Area Technical College, West Campus Center Library, West Allis, WI [*Library symbol*] [*Library of Congress*] (LCLS)
WMTD ...... Hinton, WV [*AM radio station call letters*]
WMTD-FM ... Hinton, WV [*FM radio station call letters*]
WMTE ...... Manistee, MI [*AM radio station call letters*]
WMT-FM ... Cedar Rapids, IA [*FM radio station call letters*]
WMTG ...... Dearborn, MI [*AM radio station call letters*]
WMTH ...... Park Ridge, IL [*FM radio station call letters*]
WMTH....... Westmeath [*County in Ireland*] (ROG)
WMTI .... Morovis, PR [*AM radio station call letters*]
WMTJ....... Fajardo, PR [*Television station call letters*]
WMTK ...... Littleton, NH [*FM radio station call letters*]
WMTL ...... Leitchfield, KY [*AM radio station call letters*]
WMTM ...... Moultrie, GA [*AM radio station call letters*]
WMTM-FM ... Moultrie, GA [*FM radio station call letters*]
WMTO....... Port St. Joe, FL [*FM radio station call letters*]
WMTR ...... Morristown, NJ [*AM radio station call letters*]
WMTR ...... Wheeled Mobility Test Rig [*Army*] (RDA)
WMTR-FM ... Archbold, OH [*FM radio station call letters*]
WMTS....... Murfreesboro, TN [*AM radio station call letters*]
WMTS....... Western Manufacturing Technology Show and Conference (ITD)
WMTT ...... Cookeville, TN [*Television station call letters*]
WMTT ...... Willamette Industries, Inc. [*NASDAQ symbol*] (NQ)

WMTV ...... Madison, WI [*Television station call letters*]
WMTW-TV ... Poland Spring, ME [*Television station call letters*]
WMTY ...... Greenwood, SC [*AM radio station call letters*]
WMTY-FM ... Greenwood, SC [*FM radio station call letters*]
WMTZ ...... Martinez, GA [*FM radio station call letters*]
WMU......... West Mountain [*Utah*] [*Seismograph station code, US Geological Survey*] (SEIS)
WMU......... Western Michigan University [*Kalamazoo*]
WMU......... Woman's Missionary Union (EA)
WMU......... World Maritime University [*Sweden*] (DCTA)
WMUA...... Amherst, MA [*FM radio station call letters*]
WMUB...... Oxford, OH [*FM radio station call letters*]
WMUC-FM ... College Park, MD [*FM radio station call letters*]
WMUF ...... Paris, TN [*AM radio station call letters*]
WMUF ...... Universal Foods Corp., Technical Information Services, Milwaukee, WI [*Library symbol*] [*Library of Congress*] (LCLS)
WMUH ..... Allentown, PA [*FM radio station call letters*]
WMUK ..... Kalamazoo, MI [*FM radio station call letters*]
WMUL...... Huntington, WV [*FM radio station call letters*]
WMUM...... Marathon, FL [*FM radio station call letters*]
WMUR-TV ... Manchester, NH [*Television station call letters*]
WMUS ...... Muskegon, MI [*AM radio station call letters*]
WMUSE..... World Markets for US Exports [*A publication*]
WMUS-FM ... Muskegon, MI [*FM radio station call letters*]
WMUU ..... Greenville, SC [*AM radio station call letters*]
WMUU-FM ... Greenville, SC [*FM radio station call letters*]
WMUW...... Columbus, MS [*AM radio station call letters*]
WMUW...... University of Wisconsin-Milwaukee, Milwaukee, WI [*Library symbol*] [*Library of Congress*] (LCLS)
WMUZ...... Detroit, MI [*FM radio station call letters*]
WMV......... Valuation Research Corp., Milwaukee, WI [*Library symbol*] [*Library of Congress*] (LCLS)
WMV......... War Munition Volunteers [*British*] [*World War I*]
WMV......... Watermelon Mosaic Virus
WMVA...... Martinsville, VA [*AM radio station call letters*]
WMV-E...... Watermelon Mosaic Virus E
WMVG...... Milledgeville, GA [*AM radio station call letters*]
WMVI ...... Mechanicville, NY [*AM radio station call letters*]
WMVN...... Ishpeming, MI [*AM radio station call letters*]
WMVO...... Mount Vernon, OH [*AM radio station call letters*]
WMVP...... Greenfield, WI [*AM radio station call letters*]
WMVR...... Sidney, OH [*AM radio station call letters*]
WMVR-FM ... Sidney, OH [*FM radio station call letters*]
WMVS ...... Milwaukee, WI [*Television station call letters*]
WMVT ...... Milwaukee, WI [*Television station call letters*]
WMVV...... McDonough, GA [*FM radio station call letters*]
WMVW...... Mayville, WI [*FM radio station call letters*]
WMVY...... Tisbury, MA [*FM radio station call letters*]
WMW....... Whyte & Hirschboeck, Law Library, Milwaukee, WI [*Library symbol*] [*Library of Congress*] (LCLS)
WMW....... Women's Media Workshop [*Defunct*] (EA)
WMWA...... Glenview, IL [*FM radio station call letters*]
WMWG...... Darlington, SC [*FM radio station call letters*]
WMWG.... Weichselland, Mitteilungen des Westpreussischen Geschichtsvereins [*A publication*]
WMWHL ... Wormwheel
WMWK ... Milwaukee, WI [*FM radio station call letters*]
WMWM...... Salem, MA [*FM radio station call letters*]
WMWN...... [*The*] Weatherford, Mineral Wells & Northwestern Railway Co. [*AAR code*]
WMWOA ... Wiener Medizinische Wochenschrift [*A publication*]
WMWV..... Conway, NH [*FM radio station call letters*]
WMX........ Wamena [*Indonesia*] [*Airport symbol*] (OAG)
WMX........ Waste Management, Inc. [*NYSE symbol*] [*Toronto Stock Exchange symbol*] (SPSG)
WMX........ Whirlpool, Massage, Exercise [*Medicine*]
WMXB...... Richmond, VA [*FM radio station call letters*]
WMXD...... Detroit, MI [*FM radio station call letters*]
WMXG...... Macon, MS [*FM radio station call letters*]
WMXI....... Laurel, MS [*FM radio station call letters*]
WMXJ....... Pompano Beach, FL [*FM radio station call letters*]
WMXM...... Lake Forest, IL [*FM radio station call letters*]
WMXP...... New Kensington, PA [*FM radio station call letters*]
WMXR...... Woodstock, VT [*FM radio station call letters*]
WMXW...... Vestal, NY [*FM radio station call letters*]
WMXX-FM ... Jackson, TN [*FM radio station call letters*]
WMXY...... Hogansville, GA [*AM radio station call letters*]
WMY........ Wakamiya [*Japan*] [*Seismograph station code, US Geological Survey*] [*Closed*] (SEIS)
WMY........ Weird Mystery [*A publication*]
WMYD...... Rice Lake, WI [*AM radio station call letters*]
WMYF ...... Exeter, NH [*AM radio station call letters*]
WMYG...... Braddock, PA [*FM radio station call letters*]
WMYI....... Hendersonville, NC [*FM radio station call letters*]
WMYK ...... Elizabeth City, NC [*FM radio station call letters*]
WMYM...... Minocqua, WI [*FM radio station call letters*]
WMYN...... Mayodan, NC [*AM radio station call letters*]
WMYQ...... Newton, MS [*AM radio station call letters*]
WMYQ-FM ... Newton, MS [*FM radio station call letters*]
WMYR...... Fort Myers, FL [*AM radio station call letters*]

WMYT	Carolina Beach, NC [*AM radio station call letters*]
WMYU	Sevierville, TN [*FM radio station call letters*]
WMYX	Milwaukee, WI [*FM radio station call letters*]
WMYY	Schoharie, NY [*FM radio station call letters*]
WMZK	Merrill, WI [*FM radio station call letters*]
WMZQ	Arlington, VA [*AM radio station call letters*]
WMZQ-FM ...	Washington, DC [*FM radio station call letters*]
WMZX	Owosso, MI [*FM radio station call letters*]
WN	Calcutta Weekly Notes [*A publication*] (DLA)
WN	Neenah Public Library, Neenah, WI [*Library symbol*] [*Library of Congress*] (LCLS)
WN	Nor-Fly A/S [*Norway*] [*ICAO designator*] (FAAC)
WN	Wake Newsletter [*A publication*]
WN	Washington [*Obsolete*] (ROG)
Wn	Washington Reports [*A publication*] (DLA)
WN	WAVES [*Women Accepted for Volunteer Emergency Service*] National (EA)
WN	Wawatay News [*Sioux Lookout, Ontario*] [*A publication*]
WN	Weekblad voor het Notariaat [*A publication*]
WN	Weekly Notes of English Law Reports [*A publication*] (DLA)
W & N	Weidenfeld & Nicolson [*Publisher*]
W/N...........	Weight Note [*Tea trade*] (ROG)
W-N...........	Well-Nourished [*Medicine*]
WN	Weston [*George*] Ltd. [*Toronto Stock Exchange symbol*] [*Vancouver Stock Exchange symbol*]
WN	White-Breasted Nuthatch [*Ornithology*]
WN	White Noise
WN	Wiadomosci Numizmatyczne [*A publication*]
WN	Will Not
WN	Winch (AAG)
WN	Wisconsin [*Obsolete*] (ROG)
WN	Within (ROG)
WN	Work Notice (AAG)
WN	World Neighbors (EA)
WN	Wrong Number [*Telecommunications*] (TEL)
WN	Wynn's International, Inc. [*NYSE symbol*] (SPSG)
WNA..........	Napaskiak [*Alaska*] [*Airport symbol*] (OAG)
WNA..........	Napaskiak, AK [*Location identifier*] [*FAA*] (FAAL)
WNa..........	Nashotah House, Nashotah, WI [*Library symbol*] [*Library of Congress*] (LCLS)
WNA..........	Washington [*DC*] National Airport [*FAA*]
WNA..........	Wedge Nozzle Assembly
WNA..........	Welcome to the North Atlantic [*A publication*]
WNA..........	Winter, North Atlantic [*Vessel load line mark*]
WNA..........	World Nature Association (EA)
WNAA......	Greensboro, NC [*FM radio station call letters*]
WNAAA	Women of the National Agricultural Aviation Association (EA)
WNAB	Nashville, TN [*Television station call letters*]
WNACFWB ...	Woman's National Auxiliary Convention of Free Will Baptists (EA)
WNAC-TV ...	Providence, RI [*Television station call letters*]
WNAE	Warren, PA [*AM radio station call letters*]
WNAF	Women's National Aquatic Forum (EA)
WNAH	Nashville, TN [*AM radio station call letters*]
WNAI	Word and Number Assessment Inventory [*Aptitude test*]
WNAK	Nanticoke, PA [*AM radio station call letters*]
WNAL-TV ...	Gadsden, AL [*Television station call letters*]
WNAM......	Neenah-Menasha, WI [*AM radio station call letters*]
WNAP.......	Norristown, PA [*AM radio station call letters*]
WNAP.......	Washington [*DC*] National Airport
WNAR......	Biometric Society, Western North American Region (EA)
WNAS.......	New Albany, IN [*FM radio station call letters*]
WNAT	Natchez, MS [*AM radio station call letters*]
WNAU......	New Albany, MS [*AM radio station call letters*]
WNAV	Annapolis, MD [*AM radio station call letters*]
WNAW	North Adams, MA [*AM radio station call letters*]
WNAX.......	Yankton, SD [*AM radio station call letters*]
WNAZ-FM ...	Nashville, TN [*FM radio station call letters*]
W v NB	Weekblad voor de Nederlandse Bond van Gemeenteambtenaren [*A publication*]
WNB..........	Will Not Be
WNB..........	Winter Navigation Board
WNBA	Women's National Basketball Association [*Defunct*] (EA)
WNBA	Women's National Book Association (EA)
WNBC-TV ...	New York, NY [*Television station call letters*]
WNBE	Alamo, TN [*FM radio station call letters*]
WNBF	Binghamton, NY [*AM radio station call letters*]
WNBH	New Bedford, MA [*AM radio station call letters*]
WNbH	New Berlin Memorial Hospital, New Berlin, WI [*Library symbol*] [*Library of Congress*] (LCLS)
WNBI	Park Falls, WI [*AM radio station call letters*]
WNBI-FM ...	Park Falls, WI [*FM radio station call letters*]
WNBN......	Meridian, MS [*AM radio station call letters*]
WNBR	Fuquay Varina, NC [*AM radio station call letters*]
WNBR	Wind Baron Corp. [*NASDAQ symbol*] (NQ)
WNBS	Murray, KY [*AM radio station call letters*]
WNBT	Wellsboro, PA [*AM radio station call letters*]
WNBT-FM ...	Wellsboro, PA [*FM radio station call letters*]
WNBY	Newberry, MI [*AM radio station call letters*]
WNBY-FM ...	Newberry, MI [*FM radio station call letters*]
WNBZ	Saranac Lake, NY [*AM radio station call letters*]
WNC..........	Naval War College, Newport, RI [*OCLC symbol*] (OCLC)
WNC..........	WAVES National Corporation [*An association*] (EA)
WNC..........	Weak Neutral Current [*Chemistry*]
WNC..........	Weekly Notes of Cases [*Pennsylvania*] [*A publication*] (DLA)
WNC..........	Wencarro Resources Ltd. [*Vancouver Stock Exchange symbol*]
WNC..........	Wilmington [*North Carolina*] [*Seismograph station code, US Geological Survey*] (SEIS)
WNCA	Siler City, NC [*AM radio station call letters*]
WN-CAELA ...	Women's Network of the Council for Adult Education in Latin America [*See also RM-CEAAL*] [*Quito, Ecuador*] (EAIO)
WN (Calc) ...	Calcutta Weekly Notes [*A publication*] (DLA)
WN Cas	Weekly Notes of Cases [*Pennsylvania*] [*A publication*] (DLA)
WN Cas (PA) ...	Weekly Notes of Cases [*Pennsylvania*] [*A publication*] (DLA)
WNCB	Duluth, MN [*FM radio station call letters*]
WNCC	Barnesboro, PA [*AM radio station call letters*]
WNCCC	Women's National Cancer Control Campaign [*British*]
WNCD	Niles, OH [*FM radio station call letters*]
WNCE	Lancaster, PA [*FM radio station call letters*]
WNCG	Newburyport, MA [*AM radio station call letters*]
WNCI	Columbus, OH [*FM radio station call letters*]
WNCM	Jacksonville, FL [*FM radio station call letters*]
WNCN	New York, NY [*FM radio station call letters*]
WNCO	Ashland, OH [*AM radio station call letters*]
WNCO	Winco Petroleum Corp. [*NASDAQ symbol*] (NQ)
WNCO-FM ...	Ashland, OH [*FM radio station call letters*]
WN Covers (NSW) ...	Weekly Notes Covers (New South Wales) [*A publication*] (APTA)
WNC (PA) ...	Weekly Notes of Cases [*Pennsylvania*] [*A publication*] (DLA)
WNCQ	Watertown, NY [*AM radio station call letters*]
WNCR	St. Pauls, NC [*AM radio station call letters*]
WNCS	Montpelier, VT [*FM radio station call letters*]
WNCT	Greenville, NC [*AM radio station call letters*]
WNCT-FM ...	Greenville, NC [*FM radio station call letters*]
WNCT-TV ...	Greenville, NC [*Television station call letters*]
WNCW	Spindale, NC [*FM radio station call letters*]
WNCX	Cleveland, OH [*FM radio station call letters*]
WND	Wind (KSC)
WND	Windham [*New York*] [*Seismograph station code, US Geological Survey*] (SEIS)
WND	Windmere Corp. [*NYSE symbol*] (SPSG)
WND	Wound (MSA)
Wn 2d........	Washington Reports, Second Series [*A publication*] (DLA)
WNDA	Huntsville, AL [*FM radio station call letters*]
WNDB	Daytona Beach, FL [*AM radio station call letters*]
WNDC	Baton Rouge, LA [*AM radio station call letters*]
WNDC	Woman's National Democratic Club (EA)
WNDH	Napoleon, OH [*FM radio station call letters*]
WNDI	Sullivan, IN [*AM radio station call letters*]
WNDI-FM ...	Sullivan, IN [*FM radio station call letters*]
WNDLS......	Windlass
WNDN-FM ...	Salisbury, NC [*FM radio station call letters*]
WNDO	Weather Network Duty Officer [*Air Force*] (AFM)
WNDR.......	Syracuse, NY [*AM radio station call letters*]
WNDR.......	Winder
WNDS	Derry, NH [*Television station call letters*]
WNDS	Windsor Industries [*NASDAQ symbol*] (NQ)
WNDT.......	Danville, VA [*AM radio station call letters*]
WNDT.......	[*The*] Wendt-Bristol Co. [*Columbus, OH*] [*NASDAQ symbol*] (NQ)
WNDU	South Bend, IN [*AM radio station call letters*]
WNDU-FM ...	South Bend, IN [*FM radio station call letters*]
WNDU-TV ...	South Bend, IN [*Television station call letters*]
WNDY	Crawfordsville, IN [*FM radio station call letters*]
WNDZ	Portage, IN [*AM radio station call letters*]
WNE	Welsh National Eisteddfod (DAS)
WNE..........	Western New England College, Springfield, MA [*OCLC symbol*] (OCLC)
WNEA	Newnan, GA [*AM radio station call letters*]
WNEB	Worcester, MA [*AM radio station call letters*]
WNEC	Western New England College [*Springfield, MA*]
WNEC-FM ...	Henniker, NH [*FM radio station call letters*]
WNED-FM ...	Buffalo, NY [*FM radio station call letters*]
WNED-TV ...	Buffalo, NY [*Television station call letters*]
WNEG	Toccoa, GA [*AM radio station call letters*]
WNEG-TV ...	Toccoa, GA [*Television station call letters*]
WNEH	Greenwood, SC [*Television station call letters*]
WNEK-FM ...	Springfield, MA [*FM radio station call letters*]
WNEL	Caguas, PR [*AM radio station call letters*]
WNelH	New London Community Hospital, Health Science Library, New London, WI [*Library symbol*] [*Library of Congress*] (LCLS)
WNEM-TV ...	Bay City, MI [*Television station call letters*]
WN (Eng) ...	Weekly Notes of English Law Reports [*A publication*] (DLA)
W N Eng LR ...	Western New England Law Review [*A publication*]
WNEO-TV ...	Alliance, OH [*Television station call letters*]
WNEP-TV ...	Scranton, PA [*Television station call letters*]
WNEQ-TV ...	Buffalo, NY [*Television station call letters*]
WNER	Ozark, AL [*FM radio station call letters*]
WNES	Central City, KY [*AM radio station call letters*]

WNET .... Newark, NJ [*Television station call letters*]
WNEV-TV ... Boston, MA [*Television station call letters*]
WNEW ...... New York, NY [*AM radio station call letters*]
W New Eng L Rev ... Western New England Law Review [*A publication*]
WNEW-FM ... New York, NY [*FM radio station call letters*]
WNEX ...... Macon, GA [*AM radio station call letters*]
WNEZ .... New Britain, CT [*AM radio station call letters*]
WNF .... Well-Nourished Female [*Medicine*]
WNF .... [*The*] Winfield Railroad Co. [*AAR code*]
WNFA ...... Port Huron, MI [*FM radio station call letters*]
WNFB .... Lake City, FL [*FM radio station call letters*]
WNFC .... Willie Nelson Fan Club   (EA)
WNFGA ..... Woman's National Farm and Garden Association   (EA)
WNFI .... Palatka, FL [*AM radio station call letters*]
WNFK .... Perry, FL [*FM radio station call letters*]
WNFL .... Green Bay, WI [*AM radio station call letters*]
WNFM ...... Reedsburg, WI [*FM radio station call letters*]
WNFM ...... World Nuclear Fuel Market   (NRCH)
WNFR .... Winifrede Railroad Co. [*AAR code*]
WNFT .... Jacksonville, FL [*Television station call letters*]
WNG .... Wang Laboratories, Inc., Lowell, MA [*OCLC symbol*]   (OCLC)
WNG .... Warning   (AFM)
WNG .... Weighing
WNG .... West New Guinea
WNG .... Williams Natural Gas Co. [*NYSE symbol*]   (SPSG)
WNG .... Wing [*of a ship*]   (DS)
WNG .... Wingst [*Federal Republic of Germany*] [*Geomagnetic observatory code*]
WNGA .... Nashville, GA [*AM radio station call letters*]
WNGA .... Wholesale Nursery Growers of America   (EA)
WNGC .... Athens, GA [*FM radio station call letters*]
WNGC .... Western Natural Gas Company [*NASDAQ symbol*]   (NQ)
WNGGA ..... Welsh National Gymanfa Ganu Association   (EA)
WNGM-TV ... Athens, GA [*Television station call letters*]
WNGO ...... Mayfield, KY [*AM radio station call letters*]
WNGS ...... West Palm Beach, FL [*FM radio station call letters*]
WNGZ .... Montour Falls, NY [*FM radio station call letters*]
WNH .... Whiteface [*New Hampshire*] [*Seismograph station code, US Geological Survey*]   (SEIS)
WNHA .... Concord, NH [*AM radio station call letters*]
WNHC .... New Haven, CT [*AM radio station call letters*]
WNHP .... Washington Natural Heritage Program [*Washington State Department of Natural Resources*] [*Olympia*] [*Information service or system*]   (IID)
WNHP .... Wyoming Natural Heritage Program [*Wyoming State Department of Environmental Quality*] [*Cheyenne*] [*Information service or system*]   (IID)
WNHS ...... Chesapeake, VA [*FM radio station call letters*]
WNHU ...... West Haven, CT [*FM radio station call letters*]
WNHV ...... White River Junction, VT [*AM radio station call letters*]
WNI .... Wang Institute of Graduate Studies, Tyngsboro, MA [*OCLC symbol*]   (OCLC)
WNI .... Windkracht Nederland Information Centre [*Netherlands Wind Energy Information Centre*] [*Nethergy Ltd.*] [*Database producer*]   (IID)
WNI .... Women's National Institute [*Defunct*]   (EA)
WNIB .... Chicago, IL [*FM radio station call letters*]
WNIC .... Detroit, MI [*FM radio station call letters*]
WNIK .... Arecibo, PR [*AM radio station call letters*]
WNIK-FM ... Arecibo, PR [*FM radio station call letters*]
WNIL .... Niles, MI [*AM radio station call letters*]
WNIM .... Wide-Area-Network Module [*Telecommunications*]
WNIN .... Evansville, IN [*Television station call letters*]
WNIN-FM ... Evansville, IN [*FM radio station call letters*]
WNINTEL ... Warning Notice: Sensitive Intelligence Sources and Methods Involved   (MCD)
WNIO .... Niles, OH [*AM radio station call letters*]
WNIR .... Kent, OH [*FM radio station call letters*]
WNIS .... Norfolk, VA [*AM radio station call letters*]
WNIT-TV ... South Bend, IN [*Television station call letters*]
WNIU .... De Kalb, IL [*FM radio station call letters*]
WNIV .... Atlanta, GA [*AM radio station call letters*]
WNIX .... Greenville, MS [*AM radio station call letters*]
WNIZ-FM ... Zion, IL [*FM radio station call letters*]
WNJ .... Whitman Numismatic Journal [*A publication*]
WNJB .... New Brunswick, NJ [*Television station call letters*]
WNJC-FM ... Senatobia, MS [*FM radio station call letters*]
WNJM .... Montclair, NJ [*Television station call letters*]
WNJO .... Seaside Park, NJ [*AM radio station call letters*]
WNJR .... Newark, NJ [*AM radio station call letters*]
WNJS .... Camden, NJ [*Television station call letters*]
WNJT .... Trenton, NJ [*Television station call letters*]
WNJU .... Linden, NJ [*Television station call letters*]
WNJX-TV ... Mayaguez, PR [*Television station call letters*]
WNJY .... Delphi, IN [*FM radio station call letters*]
WNKC .... Kimberly-Clark Corp., Research and Engineering Library, Neenah, WI [*Library symbol*] [*Library of Congress*]   (LCLS)
WNKJ .... Hopkinsville, KY [*FM radio station call letters*]
WNKO .... Newark, OH [*FM radio station call letters*]
WNKU .... Highland Heights, KY [*FM radio station call letters*]

WNKV ...... St. Johnsbury, VT [*FM radio station call letters*]
WNKY ...... Neon, KY [*AM radio station call letters*]
WNL .... Nicolet College, Learning Resources Center, Rhinelander, WI [*OCLC symbol*]   (OCLC)
WNL .... Waveguide Nitrogen Load
Wn L .... Wayne Law Review [*A publication*]
WNL .... Within Normal Limits [*Medicine*]
WNLA .... Indianola, MS [*AM radio station call letters*]
WNLA ...... Witwatersrand Native Labour Association [*Nyasaland*]
WNLA-FM ... Indianola, MS [*FM radio station call letters*]
WNLB .... Rocky Mount, VA [*AM radio station call letters*]
WNLC .... New London, CT [*AM radio station call letters*]
WNLE .... Fernadina Beach, FL [*FM radio station call letters*]
WNLF .... Charlotte, NC [*AM radio station call letters*]
WNLK .... Norwalk, CT [*AM radio station call letters*]
WNLN .... Western Nigeria Legal Notice [*A publication*]   (DLA)
WNLR .... Churchville, VA [*AM radio station call letters*]
Wn LR ...... Washington Law Review [*A publication*]
Wn LR ...... Wayne Law Review [*A publication*]
WNLR ...... Weighted Nonlinear Regression [*Mathematics*]
WNLR ...... Western Nigeria Law Reports [*A publication*]   (DLA)
WNLSC ...... Women's National Land Service Corps [*British*] [*World War I*]
WNLT .... Clearwater, FL [*FM radio station call letters*]
WNM .... Warm Neutral Medium [*Astrophysics*]
WNM .... Washington National Monument
WNM .... Well-Nourished Male [*Medicine*]
WNM .... White Noise Making [*Psychology*]
WNMA ..... Washington National Monument Association   (EA)
WNMB ...... North Myrtle Beach, SC [*FM radio station call letters*]
WNMC ...... Weather Network Management Center [*Air Force*]   (AFM)
WNMC ...... Wincom Corporation [*NASDAQ symbol*]   (NQ)
WNMC-FM ... Traverse City, MI [*FM radio station call letters*]
WNMH ...... Northfield, MA [*FM radio station call letters*]
WN Misc ... Weekly Notes, Miscellaneous [*A publication*]   (DLA)
WNMT ...... Garden City, GA [*AM radio station call letters*]
WNMU-FM ... Marquette, MI [*FM radio station call letters*]
WNMU-TV ... Marquette, MI [*Television station call letters*]
WNMX ...... Newberry, SC [*FM radio station call letters*]
WNN .... World News Network [*In Muriel Dobbin's novel "Going Live"*]
WNNC .... Newton, NC [*AM radio station call letters*]
WNND .... Fuquay Varina, NC [*FM radio station call letters*]
WNNE-TV ... Hartford, VT [*Television station call letters*]
WNNH ...... Henniker, NH [*FM radio station call letters*]
WNNJ .... Newton, NJ [*AM radio station call letters*]
WNNJ-FM ... Newton, NJ [*FM radio station call letters*]
WNNK ...... Harrisburg, PA [*FM radio station call letters*]
WNNN ...... Canton, NJ [*AM radio station call letters*]
WNNO ...... Wisconsin Dells, WI [*AM radio station call letters*]
WNNO-FM ... Wisconsin Dells, WI [*FM radio station call letters*]
WNNQ ...... Ashburn, GA [*AM radio station call letters*]
WNNR-FM ... Sodus, NY [*FM radio station call letters*]
WNNR Spes Versl ... WNNR [*Suid-Afrikaanse Wetenskaplike en Nywerheidnavorsingsraad*] Spesiale Verslag [*A publication*]
WNNS ...... Springfield, IL [*FM radio station call letters*]
WN (NSW) ... Weekly Notes (New South Wales) [*A publication*]   (APTA)
WNNT .... Warsaw, VA [*AM radio station call letters*]
WNNT-FM ... Warsaw, VA [*FM radio station call letters*]
WNNW ...... Salem, NH [*AM radio station call letters*]
WNNZ ...... Springfield, MA [*AM radio station call letters*]
WNO .... Welsh National Opera
WNO .... Wharton & Northern Railroad Co. [*Later, WHN*] [*AAR code*]
WNO .... Wrong Number [*Telecommunications*]   (TEL)
WNOC ...... Wake Forest, NC [*AM radio station call letters*]
WNOE ...... New Orleans, LA [*AM radio station call letters*]
WNOE-FM ... New Orleans, LA [*FM radio station call letters*]
WNOG ...... Naples, FL [*AM radio station call letters*]
WNOI .... Flora, IL [*FM radio station call letters*]
WNOK-FM ... Columbia, SC [*FM radio station call letters*]
WNOL-TV ... New Orleans, LA [*Television station call letters*]
WNOO ...... Chattanooga, TN [*AM radio station call letters*]
WNOP ...... Newport, KY [*AM radio station call letters*]
WNOR ...... Norfolk, VA [*AM radio station call letters*]
WNOR-FM ... Norfolk, VA [*FM radio station call letters*]
WNOS ...... New Bern, NC [*AM radio station call letters*]
WNOV ...... Milwaukee, WI [*AM radio station call letters*]
WNOW ...... Mint Hill, NC [*AM radio station call letters*]
WNOX ...... Jefferson City, TN [*FM radio station call letters*]
WNOZ ...... Aguadilla, PR [*AM radio station call letters*]
WNP .... Naga [*Phillipines*] [*Airport symbol*]   (OAG)
WNP .... Washington Nuclear Plant   (NRCH)
WNP .... Welsh Nationalist Party   (DAS)
WNP .... Will Not Proceed
WNP .... Will Not Process
WNP .... Wire Nonpayment
WNPB-TV ... Morgantown, WV [*Television station call letters*]
WNPC .... Newport, TN [*AM radio station call letters*]
WNPC .... Women's National Press Club [*Later, WPC*]   (EA)
WNPE-TV ... Watertown, NY [*Television station call letters*]
WNPI-TV ... Norwood, NY [*Television station call letters*]
WNPL-TV ... Naples, FL [*Television station call letters*]

WNPQ....... New Philadelphia, OH [*FM radio station call letters*]
WNPR....... Norwich, CT [*FM radio station call letters*]
WNPT....... Tuscaloosa, AL [*AM radio station call letters*]
WNPT-FM ... Linden, AL [*FM radio station call letters*]
WNPV....... Lansdale, PA [*AM radio station call letters*]
WNPW...... Wide, Notched P Wave [*Cardiology*]
WNQM...... Nashville, TN [*AM radio station call letters*]
WNR......... Weapons Neutron Research Facility [*Los Alamos*]
WNR......... Weekblad voor Notaris-Ambt en Registratie [*A publication*]
WNR......... Western NORAD Region
WNR......... Windorah [*Australia*] [*Airport symbol*]   (OAG)
WNR......... Winners Corp. [*NYSE symbol*] [*Later, VCC*]   (SPSG)
WNR......... World New Religion [*An association*]   (EA)
WNRC....... Washington National Records Center [*GSA*]   (AABC)
WNRC....... Women's National Republican Club   (EA)
WNRCEN ... Washington National Records Center [*GSA*]
WNRE....... Circleville, OH [*AM radio station call letters*]
WNRE....... Whiteshell Nuclear Research Establishment [*Atomic Energy of Canada Ltd.*] [*Research center*]
WNRG...... Grundy, VA [*AM radio station call letters*]
WNRG...... WEPCo Energy Co. [*Cleveland, OH*] [*NASDAQ symbol*]   (NQ)
WNRI....... Woonsocket, RI [*AM radio station call letters*]
WNRJ........ Pittsburgh, PA [*FM radio station call letters*]
WNRK....... Newark, DE [*AM radio station call letters*]
WNRR....... Bellevue, OH [*FM radio station call letters*]
WNRS....... Saline, MI [*AM radio station call letters*]
WNRT....... Manati, PR [*FM radio station call letters*]
WNRV....... Narrows-Pearisburg, VA [*AM radio station call letters*]
WNRV-FM ... Narrows, VA [*FM radio station call letters*]
WNRW...... Winston-Salem, NC [*Television station call letters*]
WNS......... Nawab Shah [*Pakistan*] [*Airport symbol*]   (OAG)
WNS......... Technieuws Washington. Korte Berichten op Technisch Wetenschappelijk Gebied [*A publication*]
WNS......... Women's News Service
WNS......... Worldwide News Service. Jewish Telegraphic Agency   (BJA)
WNS......... Wren Resources Ltd. [*Vancouver Stock Exchange symbol*]
WNSA....... Woman's National Sabbath Alliance [*Defunct*]
WNSB....... Norfolk, VA [*FM radio station call letters*]
WNSB....... West Newton Savings Bank [*West Newton, MA*] [*NASDAQ symbol*]   (NQ)
WNSC-FM ... Rock Hill, SC [*FM radio station call letters*]
WNSC-TV ... Rock Hill, SC [*Television station call letters*]
WNSEA..... Wood Naval Stores Export Association
WNSH...... Beverly, MA [*AM radio station call letters*]
WNSI........ Sanford, FL [*AM radio station call letters*]
WNSI........ WNS, Incorporated [*Houston, TX*] [*NASDAQ symbol*]   (NQ)
WNSL........ A. W. Wright Nuclear Structure Laboratory [*Yale University*] [*Research center*]   (RCD)
WNSL....... Laurel, MS [*FM radio station call letters*]
WNSN....... South Bend, IN [*AM radio station call letters*]
WNSR....... New York, NY [*FM radio station call letters*]
WNSR....... West Nova Scotia Regiment   (DMA)
WNST....... Milton, WV [*AM radio station call letters*]
WNST....... Winston Mills, Inc. [*NASDAQ symbol*]   (NQ)
WNSY...... Port Allegany, PA [*FM radio station call letters*]
WNT......... Foreign Trade [*A publication*]
WNT......... Washington National Corp. [*NYSE symbol*]   (SPSG)
Wn T......... Washington Territory Reports [*1854-88*] [*A publication*]   (ILCA)
WNT......... Waste Neutralization Tank [*Nuclear energy*]   (NRCH)
WNT......... What's New in Travel [*CompuServe Information Service*] [*Information service or system*]   (CRD)
WNT......... World News Tonight [*Television program*]
WNTA...... Augusta, GA [*AM radio station call letters*]
WNTC....... Theda Clark Memorial Hospital, Neenah, WI [*Library symbol*] [*Library of Congress*]   (LCLS)
WNTE....... Mansfield, PA [*FM radio station call letters*]
WNTF....... Western Naval Task Force [*Navy*]
WNTH...... Winnetka, IL [*FM radio station call letters*]
WNTI........ Hackettstown, NJ [*FM radio station call letters*]
WNTK....... Newport, NH [*AM radio station call letters*]
WNTL....... Indian Head, MD [*AM radio station call letters*]
WNTL....... Winterhalter, Inc. [*NASDAQ symbol*]   (NQ)
WNTN....... Morristown, TN [*AM radio station call letters*]
WNTN....... Newton, MA [*AM radio station call letters*]
WNTQ....... Syracuse, NY [*FM radio station call letters*]
WNTR....... Silver Spring, MD [*AM radio station call letters*]
Wntr Sldr... Winter Soldier [*A publication*]
WNTS....... Indianapolis, IN [*AM radio station call letters*]
WNTT....... Tazewell, TN [*AM radio station call letters*]
WNTV....... Greenville, SC [*Television station call letters*]
WNTX....... Nantucket, MA [*FM radio station call letters*]
WNTXD..... Wentex International, Inc. [*NASDAQ symbol*]   (NQ)
WNTY...... Southington, CT [*AM radio station call letters*]
WNTZ....... Natchez, MS [*Television station call letters*]
WNU .... Western Newspaper Union
WNUA...... Chicago, IL [*FM radio station call letters*]
WNUB-FM ... Northfield, VT [*FM radio station call letters*]
WNUE....... Fort Walton Beach, FL [*AM radio station call letters*]
WNUR-FM ... Evanston, IL [*FM radio station call letters*]
WNUS....... Belpre, OH [*FM radio station call letters*]

WNUV-TV ... Baltimore, MD [*Television station call letters*]
WNUY....... Bluffton, IN [*FM radio station call letters*]
WNUZ....... Talladega, AL [*AM radio station call letters*]
WNV......... Wehrmachtnachrichtenverbindungen [*Armed Forces Signal Communications*] [*German military - World War II*]
WNV......... West Nile Virus
WNVA...... Norton, VA [*AM radio station call letters*]
WNVA-FM ... Norton, VA [*FM radio station call letters*]
WNVC....... Fairfax, VA [*Television station call letters*]
WNVL....... Nicholasville, KY [*AM radio station call letters*]
WNVR....... Vernon Hills, IL [*AM radio station call letters*]
WNVT....... Goldvein, VA [*Television station call letters*]
WNVZ....... Norfolk, VA [*FM radio station call letters*]
WNW........ Superior Public Library, Superior, WI [*OCLC symbol*]   (OCLC)
WNW........ Wenatchee [*Washington*] [*Seismograph station code, US Geological Survey*]   (SEIS)
WNW........ West-Northwest
WNWC...... Madison, WI [*FM radio station call letters*]
WNWI....... Valparaiso, IN [*AM radio station call letters*]
WNWK...... Newark, NJ [*FM radio station call letters*]
WNWN .... Coldwater, MI [*FM radio station call letters*]
WNWO-TV ... Toledo, OH [*Television station call letters*]
WNWRN.. West-Northwestern [*Meteorology*]   (FAAC)
WNWS...... South Miami, FL [*AM radio station call letters*]
WNWV...... Elyria, OH [*FM radio station call letters*]
WNWWD ... West-Northwestward [*Meteorology*]   (FAAC)
WNWY...... Norway, MI [*FM radio station call letters*]
WNWZ...... Germantown, TN [*AM radio station call letters*]
WNXT....... Portsmouth, OH [*AM radio station call letters*]
WNXT-FM ... Portsmouth, OH [*FM radio station call letters*]
WNY......... Washington [*DC*] Naval Yard
WNY......... Wilmington [*New York*] [*Seismograph station code, US Geological Survey*]   (SEIS)
WNY......... Wynyard [*Australia*] [*Airport symbol*]   (OAG)
WNYB-TV ... Buffalo, NY [*Television station call letters*]
WNYC....... New York, NY [*AM radio station call letters*]
WNYC-FM ... New York, NY [*FM radio station call letters*]
WNYC-TV ... New York, NY [*Television station call letters*]
WNYE....... New York, NY [*FM radio station call letters*]
WNYE-TV ... New York, NY [*Television station call letters*]
WNYG....... Babylon, NY [*AM radio station call letters*]
WNYHSL ... Western New York Health Science Librarians [*Library network*]
WNYK....... Nyack, NY [*FM radio station call letters*]
WNYLRC ... Western New York Library Resources Council [*Buffalo, NY*] [*Library network*]
WNYNRC ... Western New York Nuclear Research Center Reactor   (NRCH)
WNYP-FM ... Cortland, NY [*FM radio station call letters*]
WNYR-FM ... Waterloo, NY [*FM radio station call letters*]
WNYS .... Canton, NY [*AM radio station call letters*]
WNYT....... Albany, NY [*Television station call letters*]
WNYU-FM ... New York, NY [*FM radio station call letters*]
WNYV....... Whitehall, NY [*FM radio station call letters*]
WNYW...... New York, NY [*Television station call letters*]
WNYZ....... Utica, NY [*AM radio station call letters*]
WNZ......... Wairakei [*New Zealand*] [*Seismograph station code, US Geological Survey*]   (SEIS)
WNZE....... Plymouth, IN [*FM radio station call letters*]
WNZK....... Westland, MI [*FM radio station call letters*]
WNZQ....... St. Cloud, FL [*AM radio station call letters*]
WNZR....... Mount Vernon, OH [*FM radio station call letters*]
WNZT....... Columbia, PA [*AM radio station call letters*]
WO .... Wait Order
WO .... Walkover
WO .... War Office [*British*]
WO .... War Orientation [*Navy*]
WO .... Warning Order
WO .... Warrant Officer [*Usually in combination with numbers to denote serviceman's grade*] [*Military*]
WO .... Wash Out [*Medicine*]
WO .... Washington Office [*FAA*]   (FAAC)
W/O........... Water-in-Oil
WO .... Water Outlet Gasket [*Automotive engineering*]
WO .... Wechselordnung [*Law Regarding Bills of Exchange*] [*German*]
WO .... Welfare Officer [*British military*]   (DMA)
WO .... Welsh Office   (DCTA)
WO .... Welt des Orients [*A publication*]
WO .... Western Operation
WO .... White Oval [*on Jupiter*]
WO .... Wind Offset
WO .... Wipe Out   (MSA)
WO .... Wireless Operator
WO .... Without   (AFM)
wo............ Wollastonite [*CIPW classification*] [*Geology*]
WO .... Women
WO .... Women Outdoors   (EA)
WO .... Women's Reserve, Ordnance Duties [*USNR officer designation*]
WO .... Work Order
WO .... Working Overseer   (ADA)
WO .... World Airways, Inc. [*ICAO designator*]   (FAAC)
WO .... World of Opera [*A publication*]

W/O.........	Write-Off [*Accounting*]
WO	Write Only
WO	Write Out
WO	Writer Officer [*British military*] (DMA)
W/O.........	Written Order [*Medicine*]
WO1	Warrant Officer One [*Army*]
WOA.........	Warrant Officers Association of the United States of America [*Defunct*] (EA)
WOA.........	Washington Office on Africa (EA)
WOA.........	Weapons Orientation Advanced (AFM)
WOA.........	Web Offset Association (EA)
WOA.........	Work Order Authorization (MCD)
WOA.........	WorldCorp., Inc. [*NYSE symbol*] (SPSG)
WOAB......	Ozark, AL [*FM radio station call letters*]
WOAC......	Canton, OH [*Television station call letters*]
WOAD......	Jackson, MS [*AM radio station call letters*]
WOAI.......	San Antonio, TX [*AM radio station call letters*]
WOAK ...	La Grange, GA [*FM radio station call letters*]
WOAL-FM ..	Pippa Passes, KY [*FM radio station call letters*]
WOAP......	Owosso, MI [*AM radio station call letters*]
WOAR......	Women Organized Against Rape
WOAS......	Ontonagon, MI [*FM radio station call letters*]
WOAS......	Wave-Off Advisory System [*Aircraft carrier*] [*Navy*]
WOAY......	Oak Hill, WV [*AM radio station call letters*]
WOAY-TV ...	Oak Hill, WV [*Television station call letters*]
WOB.........	Washed Overboard [*Shipping*]
WOB.........	Weight on Bit [*Drilling technology*]
WOB.........	Woburn [*Parish in England*]
WOB.........	Work Order Bin (MCD)
WOB.........	World of Banking [*A publication*]
WOBC-FM ...	Oberlin, OH [*FM radio station call letters*]
WOBG......	Clarksburg, WV [*AM radio station call letters*]
WOBL......	Oberlin, OH [*AM radio station call letters*]
WOBM......	Lakewood, NJ [*AM radio station call letters*]
WOBM-FM ...	Toms River, NJ [*FM radio station call letters*]
WOBN......	Westerville, OH [*FM radio station call letters*]
W O BNDR ...	Without Binder [*Freight*]
WOBO......	Batavia, OH [*FM radio station call letters*]
W/OBO.....	Without Blowout (MSA)
WOBO......	World Organization of Building Officials (EA)
WOBR......	Wanchese, NC [*AM radio station call letters*]
WOBR-FM ...	Wanchese, NC [*FM radio station call letters*]
WOBS	First Woburn Bancorp, Inc. [*NASDAQ symbol*] (NQ)
WOBS	New Albany, IN [*AM radio station call letters*]
WOBT	Rhinelander, WI [*AM radio station call letters*]
WOC.........	Davenport, IA [*AM radio station call letters*]
WOC.........	Waiting on Cement
WOC.........	Water-Oil Contact
WOC.........	Wilshire Oil Company of Texas [*NYSE symbol*] (SPSG)
WOC.........	Win Over Communism [*A fund-raising subsidiary of the Unification Church*]
WOC.........	Wing Operations Center (CINC)
WOC.........	Without Compensation (ADA)
WOC.........	Women's Ordination Conference (EA)
WOC.........	Wood's Oriental Cases [*Malaya*] [*A publication*] (DLA)
WOC.........	Work and Occupations [*A publication*]
WOC.........	Work Order Control (MCD)
WOC.........	World Coal [*A publication*]
WOC.........	World Oceanographic Center (MSC)
WOCA......	Ocala, FL [*AM radio station call letters*]
WOCA......	World Outside Communist Areas
WOCAR......	Aviation Warrant Officer Career Course [*Army*]
WOCB......	West Yarmouth, MA [*AM radio station call letters*]
WOCB-FM ...	West Yarmouth, MA [*FM radio station call letters*]
WOCCI......	War Office Central Card Index [*British military*] (DMA)
WOccM......	Memorial Hospital at Oconomowoc, Oconomowoc, WI [*Library symbol*] [*Library of Congress*] (LCLS)
WOccR	Redemptionist Seminary, Oconomowoc, WI [*Library symbol*] [*Library of Congress*] (LCLS)
WOCCU	World Council of Credit Unions [*Madison, WI*] (EA)
WOCD......	Amsterdam, NY [*Television station call letters*]
WOCE......	World Ocean Circulation Experiment [*World Climate Research Programme*]
WOCG......	Huntsville, AL [*FM radio station call letters*]
Wochbl Papierfabr ...	Wochenblatt fuer Papierfabrikation [*A publication*]
Wochenschr Brau ...	Wochenschrift fuer Brauerei [*A publication*]
Woch Pap Fab ...	Wochenblatt fuer Papierfabrikation [*A publication*]
WOCIT......	We Oppose Computers in Tournaments [*A chess players' group, formed in 1983*]
WOCL......	De Land, FL [*FM radio station call letters*]
WOCL......	War Office Casualty List [*British military*] (DMA)
WOCLS.....	World Ocean and Cruise Liner Society (EA)
WOCMDC ...	Warrant Officer Candidate Military Development Course
WOCN......	Miami, FL [*AM radio station call letters*]
WOCO......	Oconto, WI [*AM radio station call letters*]
WOCO......	World of Computers [*NASDAQ symbol*] (NQ)
WOCO......	World Council of Young Men's Service Clubs (EA)
WOCOD......	World Coal [*A publication*]
WOCO-FM ...	Oconto, WI [*FM radio station call letters*]
WOCP......	World Organization of China Painters (EA)
WOCQ.......	Berlin, MD [*FM radio station call letters*]
WOCR......	Olivet, MI [*FM radio station call letters*]
WOCS......	Work Order Control System (MCD)
WOCT......	Albany, GA [*Television station call letters*]
WOCT......	WAC [*Women's Army Corps*] Officer Candidate Test (AABC)
WOCU......	War on Community Ugliness [*Program*] [*Defunct*] (EA)
WOCV......	Oneida, TN [*AM radio station call letters*]
WOD........	Washington & Old Dominion R. R. [*AAR code*]
WOD........	Wind over Deck (MCD)
WOD........	Without Dependents [*Military*] (AFM)
WOD........	Woodstream Corp. [*AMEX symbol*] (SPSG)
WODA......	World Organization of Dredging Associations (EA)
WODADIBOF ...	Workshop on the Determination of Anti-Epileptic Drugs in Body Fluids
WODC......	Virginia Beach, VA [*FM radio station call letters*]
WODC......	Women's Olympic Distance Committee [*Later, WDC*] (EA)
WODCON ...	World Dredging Conference
WODCON ...	World Organization of Dredging Associations Proceedings of World Dredging Congress [*A publication*] (EAAP)
WODD......	Wave-Off Decision Device (MCD)
WODD......	World Oceanographic Data Display
WODDIN ...	Worldwide On-Line Data and Document Intelligence System
WODECO ...	Western Offshore Drilling & Exploration Company
WODED....	World Development [*A publication*]
WODI......	Brookneal, VA [*AM radio station call letters*]
WODJ......	Greenville, MI [*AM radio station call letters*]
WODS......	Boston, MA [*FM radio station call letters*]
WODY......	Bassett, VA [*AM radio station call letters*]
WODZ......	Memphis, TN [*AM radio station call letters*]
WOE.........	Warhead Output Evaluation (MCD)
WOE.........	Watchdogs on Environment
WOE.........	Withdrawal of Enthusiasm [*Airline pilots objection to "Welcome aboard" talks*]
WOE.........	Without Enclosure (MCD)
WOE.........	Without Equipment
WOE.........	World Economy [*A publication*]
WOE.........	Wound of Entry [*Medicine*]
WOEC......	Warrant Officer Entry Course [*Military*] (INF)
WOEC-RC ...	Warrant Office Entry Course, Reserve Component [*Army*] (INF)
WOEL-FM ...	Elkton, MD [*FM radio station call letters*]
Woelm Publ ...	Woelm Publication [*A publication*]
WOEQ......	Royal Palm Beach, FL [*FM radio station call letters*]
Woerner Adm'n ...	Woerner's Treatise on the American Law of Administration [*A publication*] (DLA)
Woert Sach ...	Woerter und Sachen [*A publication*]
WOES	Ovid-Elsie, MI [*FM radio station call letters*]
WOES	Warrant Officer Education System
W/OE & SP ...	Without Equipment and Spare Parts
WOEZ-FM ...	Milton, PA [*FM radio station call letters*]
WOF.........	Walk on Floor [*Ataxia*]
WOF.........	Warmed-Over Flavor [*Food technology*]
WOF.........	Work of Fracture [*Ceramic property*]
WOF.........	Worlds of Fantasy [*1950-1954*] [*A publication*]
WOFA......	Westinghouse Optimized Fuel Assembly [*Nuclear energy*] (NRCH)
WOFC	Western Ohio Film Circuit [*Library network*]
WOFE	Rockwood, TN [*AM radio station call letters*]
WOFF.......	Camilla, GA [*FM radio station call letters*]
WOFF.......	Weight of Fuel Flow (MCD)
WOFG......	Wolf Financial Group, Inc. [*New York, NY*] [*NASDAQ symbol*] (NQ)
WOFI	Wood Office Furniture Institute (EA)
WOFIWU ...	World Federation of Industrial Workers' Unions
WOFL	Orlando, FL [*Television station call letters*]
WOFM......	Moycock, NC [*FM radio station call letters*]
WOFP	Wearout Failure Period
WOFR......	Washington Court House, OH [*AM radio station call letters*]
WOFS.......	Weather Observing and Forecasting System [*Air Force*] (MCD)
W O FTTNGS ...	Without Fittings [*Freight*]
WOFX	Fairfield, OH [*FM radio station call letters*]
WOG	Water-Oil-Gas (AAG)
WOG	Weapon Order Generation [*Military*] (CAAL)
WOG	Werner Oil & Gas Co. [*Vancouver Stock Exchange symbol*]
WOG	Westernized Oriental Gentleman [*Singapore term for native following Western fashions*] [*Other translations include "Wily Oriental Gentleman" and "Wonderful Oriental Gentleman"*]
WOG	With Other Goods [*Business term*]
WOG	Work Order Generator [*Military*]
WOG	World Organization of Gastroenterology [*See also OMGE*] [*Edinburgh, Scotland*] (EAIO)
WOG	Wrath of God [*Israeli counterterrorist group*]
WOGA......	Western Oil and Gas Association (EA)
WOGL......	Philadelphia, PA [*FM radio station call letters*]
WOGO	Hallie, WI [*AM radio station call letters*]
WOGR......	Charlotte, NC [*AM radio station call letters*]
WOGS......	Wrath of God Syndrome
WOGSC	World Organisation of General Systems and Cybernetics [*Lytham St. Annes, Lancashire, England*] (EAIO)
WOGX......	Ocala, FL [*Television station call letters*]
WOH.........	War on Hunger [*Program*] (EA)

WOH	Washington Office on Haiti (EA)
WOH	Western Oklahoma Herbarium [*Southwest Oklahoma State University*]
WOH	Wings of Hope [*An association*] (EA)
WOH	Work on Hand [*Insurance*]
WOHC	Warrant Officer Hospital Corps
WOHE	World Health [*A publication*]
WOHELO ...	Work, Health, Love [*Camp Fire Girls slogan*]
WOHH	Women's Organization of Hapoel Hamizrachi [*Later, EWA*] (EA)
WOHI	East Liverpool, OH [*AM radio station call letters*]
WOHMA ..	Waste Oil Heating Manufacturers Association (EA)
WOHO	Toledo, OH [*AM radio station call letters*]
WOHP	World Organization for Human Potential (EA)
WO & HPS ...	Wall Oven and Hot Plates [*Classified advertising*] (ADA)
WOHRC	Women's Occupational Health Resource Center (EA)
WOHS	Shelby, NC [*AM radio station call letters*]
WOHT	Jackson, MS [*AM radio station call letters*]
WOI	Ames, IA [*AM radio station call letters*]
WOI	Wealth of India [*A publication*]
WOI	World Income Fund, Inc. [*AMEX symbol*] (CTT)
WOI	World Opportunities International (EA)
WOIC	Columbia, SC [*AM radio station call letters*]
WOI-FM ...	Ames, IA [*FM radio station call letters*]
WOIL	Wright Brothers Energy, Inc. [*San Antonio, TX*] [*NASDAQ symbol*] (NQ)
WOIO	Shaker Heights, OH [*Television station call letters*]
WOIR	Homestead, FL [*AM radio station call letters*]
WOIS	Worn Out in Service [*Military*]
WOI-TV ...	Ames, IA [*Television station call letters*]
WOIZ	Guayanilla, PR [*AM radio station call letters*]
WOJAC	World Organization for Jews from Arab Countries (EA)
WOJB	Reserve, WI [*FM radio station call letters*]
WOJC	Willys Overland Jeepster Club (EA)
WOJD	World Organization of Jewish Deaf [*Tel Aviv, Israel*] (EAIO)
WOJG	Warrant Officer Junior Grade
WOJO	Evanston, IL [*FM radio station call letters*]
Wojsk Przegl Tech ...	Wojskowy Przeglad Techniczny [*Poland*] [*A publication*]
WOJY	Farrell, PA [*AM radio station call letters*]
WOJY-FM ...	Sharpsville, PA [*FM radio station call letters*]
WOK	Wiener Oeffentlicher Kueche [*Viennese Open Kitchen*] [*Nonprofit temperance restaurant chain*] [*Austria*]
WOK	Wokingham [*Municipal borough in England*]
WOK	Wonken [*Venezuela*] [*Airport symbol*] (OAG)
WOKA	Douglas, GA [*AM radio station call letters*]
WOKA-FM ...	Douglas, GA [*FM radio station call letters*]
WOKC	Okeechobee, FL [*AM radio station call letters*]
WOKC-FM ...	Okeechobee, FL [*FM radio station call letters*]
WOKD	Arcadia, FL [*FM radio station call letters*]
WOKE	Charleston, SC [*AM radio station call letters*]
WOKF	Folkston, GA [*FM radio station call letters*]
WOKG	Warren, OH [*AM radio station call letters*]
WOKH	Bardstown, KY [*FM radio station call letters*]
WOKI-FM ...	Oak Ridge, TN [*FM radio station call letters*]
WOKJ	Jackson, MS [*AM radio station call letters*]
WOKK	Meridian, MS [*FM radio station call letters*]
WOKN-FM ...	Goldsboro, NC [*FM radio station call letters*]
WOKQ	Dover, NH [*FM radio station call letters*]
WOKR	Rochester, NY [*Television station call letters*]
WOKR	Willys-Overland-Knight Registry (EA)
WOKS	Columbus, GA [*AM radio station call letters*]
WOKT	Cannonsburg, KY [*AM radio station call letters*]
WOKV	Jacksonville, FL [*AM radio station call letters*]
WOKW	Curwensville, PA [*FM radio station call letters*]
WOKX	High Point, NC [*AM radio station call letters*]
WOKY	Milwaukee, WI [*AM radio station call letters*]
WOKZ	Muncie, IN [*FM radio station call letters*]
WOL	Wainoco Oil Co. [*NYSE symbol*] (SPSG)
WOL	War-Office Letter [*An order or an instruction*] [*British*]
WOL	Washington, DC [*AM radio station call letters*]
WOL	Wedge Opening Load
WOL	Weird and Occult Library [*A publication*]
WOL	Wharf Owner's Liability [*Insurance*]
Wol	Wolcott's Chancery Reports [*7 Delaware*] [*A publication*] (DLA)
Wol	Wollaston's English Bail Court Reports [*A publication*] (DLA)
WOL	Wollongong [*Australia*] [*Airport symbol*]
wol	Wolof [*MARC language code*] [*Library of Congress*] (LCCP)
WOL	Wolverton [*England*] [*Seismograph station code, US Geological Survey*] (SEIS)
WOL	Worklife [*Canada*] [*A publication*]
WOLA	Barranquitas, PR [*AM radio station call letters*]
WOLA	Washington Office on Latin America (EA)
WOLC	Princess Anne, MD [*FM radio station call letters*]
WOLD	Marion, VA [*AM radio station call letters*]
WOLD-FM ...	Marion, VA [*FM radio station call letters*]
WOLE-TV ...	Aguadilla, PR [*Television station call letters*]
WOLF	Committee for Wildlife on the Last Frontier
WOLF	Syracuse, NY [*AM radio station call letters*]
WOLF	Wayne Oakland Library Federation [*Library network*]

WOLF	Work Order Load Forecast (MCD)
Wolf & B	Wolferstan and Bristow's English Election Cases [*1859-65*] [*A publication*] (DLA)
Wolf & D	Wolferstan and Dew's English Election Cases [*1856-58*] [*A publication*] (DLA)
Wolf Dr de la Nat ...	Wolffius. Droit de la Nature [*A publication*] (DLA)
Wolfen-Buetteler B ...	Wolfenbuetteler Beitraege [*A publication*]
Wolfenbuetteler Forsch ...	Wolfenbuetteler Forschungen [*A publication*]
Wolff Inst ...	Wolffius. Institutiones Juris Naturae et Gentium [*A publication*] (DLA)
Wolff Inst Nat ...	Wolffius. Institutiones Juris Naturae et Gentium [*A publication*] (DLA)
Wolffius	Wolffius. Institutiones Juris Naturae et Gentium [*A publication*] (DLA)
Wolffius Inst ...	Wolffius. Institutiones Juris Naturae et Gentium [*A publication*] (DLA)
WOLF-TV ...	Scranton, PA [*Television station call letters*]
WOLL	Riviera Beach, FL [*FM radio station call letters*]
Woll	Wollaston's English Bail Court Reports, Practice Cases [*1840-41*] [*A publication*] (DLA)
Woll BC ...	Wollaston's English Bail Court Reports [*A publication*] (DLA)
Wollen- Leinen-Ind ...	Wollen- und Leinen-Industrie [*A publication*]
WOLM	Lake Mary, FL [*AM radio station call letters*]
WOLM	Wainoco Oil Corp. [*NASDAQ symbol*] (NQ)
WOLO-TV ...	Columbia, SC [*Television station call letters*]
WOLR	Branford, FL [*FM radio station call letters*]
WOLS	Florence, SC [*AM radio station call letters*]
WOLV	Wolverton [*Urban district in England*]
WOLW	Cadillac, MI [*FM radio station call letters*]
WOLX-FM ...	Baraboo, WI [*FM radio station call letters*]
WOLY	Battle Creek, MI [*AM radio station call letters*]
WOM	Weapons Output Makeup
WOM	Wideband Optical Modulation
WOM	Wireless Operator Mechanic [*British*] (DSUE)
WOM	Wise Old Men [*Term used to refer to group of US statesmen including Dean Acheson, Charles Bohlen, Averell Harriman, George Kennan, Robert Lovett, and John McCloy*]
WOM	Write-Only Memory [*Data processing*]
WOM	Write Optional Memory (IEEE)
WOMA ...	Algoma, WI [*FM radio station call letters*]
WOMAA...	Works Management [*A publication*]
WOMAN ..	World Organization of Mothers of All Nations
Woman Art J ...	Woman's Art Journal [*A publication*]
Woman Cit ...	Woman Citizen [*A publication*]
Woman Home C ...	Woman's Home Companion [*A publication*]
Woman Offend Rep ...	Woman Offender Report [*A publication*] (DLA)
Woman's H C ...	Woman's Home Companion [*A publication*]
Woman's J ...	Woman's Journal [*A publication*]
WOMBAT ...	Waves on Magnetized Beams and Turbulence [*Physics*] (ADA)
WOMC	Detroit, MI [*FM radio station call letters*]
Women	Women/Poems [*A publication*]
Women Coach Clin ...	Women's Coaching Clinic [*A publication*]
Women of Eur ...	Women of Europe [*A publication*]
Women and Hist ...	Women and History [*A publication*]
Women and L ...	Women and Law [*A publication*]
Women Labour Conf Pap ...	Women and Labour Conference. Papers [*A publication*]
Women Law J ...	Women Lawyers Journal [*A publication*]
Women Lawyers J ...	Women Lawyers Journal [*A publication*]
Women & Lit ...	Women and Literature [*A publication*]
Women Lit ...	Women and Literature [*A publication*]
Women L Jour ...	Women Lawyers Journal [*A publication*]
Women L Jour ...	Women's Law Journal [*A publication*] (DLA)
Women Rev ...	Women and Revolution [*A publication*]
Women Rights L Rep ...	Women's Rights Law Reporter [*A publication*]
Women's Bur Bull ...	Women's Bureau Bulletin [*A publication*]
Women's LJ ...	Women's Law Journal [*A publication*] (DLA)
Women's L Rptr ...	Women's Law Reporter [*A publication*] (DLA)
Women's Review ...	Women's Review of Books [*A publication*]
Women's Rights L Rep ...	Women's Rights Law Reporter [*A publication*]
Women's Rights L Reptr ...	Women's Rights Law Reporter [*A publication*] (ILCA)
Women's Rights L Rptr ...	Women's Rights Law Reporter [*A publication*]
Women's Rts L Rep Rutgers Univ ...	Women's Rights Law Reporter. Rutgers University [*A publication*]
Women's Stud Assoc Conf Pap ...	Women's Studies Association. Conference Papers [*New Zealand*] [*A publication*]
Women's Studies ...	Women's Studies: An Interdisciplinary Journal [*A publication*]
Womens Studs Newsl ...	Women's Studies Newsletter [*A publication*]
Women Stud ...	Women's Studies: An Interdisciplinary Journal [*A publication*]
Women Stud Abstracts ...	Women Studies Abstracts [*A publication*]
Women & Ther ...	Women and Therapy [*A publication*]
Women Wear ...	Women's Wear Daily [*A publication*]
Women Wkrs Bull ...	Women Workers Bulletin [*A publication*]
WOMG	Columbia, SC [*AM radio station call letters*]
WOMG-FM ...	Columbia, SC [*FM radio station call letters*]
WomHealth ...	Women and Health [*A publication*]
WOMI	Owensboro, KY [*AM radio station call letters*]

Wom March ... Women on the March [*New Delhi*] [*A publication*]
WOMN ..... Women's Health Centers of America, Inc. [*San Diego, CA*] [*NASDAQ symbol*]　(NQ)
Womn Prss ... Women's Press [*A publication*]
Womn Rgts ... Women's Rights Law Reporter [*A publication*]
Womn Sprt ... Womanspirit [*A publication*]
WOMP ..... Bellaire, OH [*AM radio station call letters*]
WOMP ..... Western Ocean Meeting Point　(DMA)
WOMP ..... World Order Models Project
WOMP-FM ... Bellaire, OH [*FM radio station call letters*]
WOMPI .... Women of the Motion Picture Industry, International　(EA)
WOMR ..... Provincetown, MA [*FM radio station call letters*]
Womspk ..... Womanspeak [*A publication*]
WOMT ...... Manitowoc, WI [*AM radio station call letters*]
WOMUA .... World of Music [*A publication*]
WOMX ...... Orlando, FL [*AM radio station call letters*]
WOMX-FM ... Orlando, FL [*FM radio station call letters*]
WON .... Wool over Needle [*Knitting*]
WON .... Work Order Number　(MCD)
WONA ...... Winona, MS [*AM radio station call letters*]
WONAAC ... Women's National Abortion Action Coalition [*Defunct*]
WONA-FM ... Winona, MS [*FM radio station call letters*]
WONARD ... Woman's Organization of the National Association of Retail Druggists　(EA)
WONC .... Naperville, IL [*FM radio station call letters*]
WONCA .... World Organization of National Colleges, Academies, and Academic Associations of General Practitioners/Family Physicians [*Australia*]　(EAIO)
WOND ...... Pleasantville, NJ [*AM radio station call letters*]
WONE ...... Dayton, OH [*AM radio station call letters*]
WONE .... Westwood One, Inc. [*Culver City, CA*] [*NASDAQ symbol*]　(NQ)
WONE-FM ... Akron, OH [*FM radio station call letters*]
WONF .... With Other Natural Flavors [*Food science*]
WONF .... Wonford [*England*]
WONG ...... Canton, MS [*AM radio station call letters*]
WONG ...... Weight on Nose Gear [*Aviation*]　(MCD)
WONN ...... Lakeland, FL [*AM radio station call letters*]
WONO ...... Black Mountain, NC [*AM radio station call letters*]
WONQ ...... Orlando, FL [*AM radio station call letters*]
WONS .... Pleasure Ridge Park, KY [*AM radio station call letters*]
Wont Land Reg ... Wontner's Land Registry Practice [*12th ed.*] [*1975*] [*A publication*]　(DLA)
W Ont L Rev ... Western Ontario Law Review [*A publication*]
WONU ...... Kankakee, IL [*FM radio station call letters*]
WONW ..... Defiance, OH [*AM radio station call letters*]
WONX .... Evanston, IL [*AM radio station call letters*]
WONY .... Oneonta, NY [*FM radio station call letters*]
WOO .... College of Wooster, Wooster, OH [*OCLC symbol*]　(OCLC)
WOO .... Waiting on Orders
WOO .... Warrant Ordnance Officer [*Navy*] [*British*]
WOO .... Werke ohne Opuszahl [*Works without Opus Number*] [*Music*]
WOO .... Western Operations Office [*Later, WSO*] [*NASA*]
WOO .... Woodchopper, AK [*Location identifier*] [*FAA*]　(FAAL)
WOO .... Woodstock [*Maryland*] [*Seismograph station code, US Geological Survey*] [*Closed*]　(SEIS)
WOO .... World Oceanographic Organization
WOOD ...... Grand Rapids, MI [*AM radio station call letters*]
Wood .... Wood on Mercantile Agreements [*A publication*]　(DLA)
Wood .... Wood's English Tithe Cases, Exchequer [*4 vols.*] [*A publication*]　(DLA)
Wood .... Woods' United States Circuit Court Reports [*A publication*]　(DLA)
WOOD ...... Woodward & Lothrop [*NASDAQ symbol*]　(NQ)
Woodb & M ... Woodbury and Minot's United States Circuit Court Reports [*A publication*]　(DLA)
Woodb & Min (CC) ... Woodbury and Minot's United States Circuit Court Reports, First Circuit [*A publication*]　(DLA)
Wood Brass Perc ... Woodwind, Brass, and Percussion [*A publication*]
Wood Civ L ... Wood's Institutes of the Civil Law of England [*A publication*]　(DLA)
Wood Com L ... Wood's Institutes of the Common Law [*A publication*]　(DLA)
Wood Conv ... Wood on Conveyancing [*A publication*]　(DLA)
Wood Decr ... Wood's Tithe Cases [*England*] [*A publication*]　(DLA)
Wooddesson Lect ... Wooddesson's Lecture [*A publication*]　(DLA)
Woodd Lect ... Wooddesson's Lectures on the Laws of England [*A publication*]　(DLA)
Wood El Jur ... Wooddeson's Elements of Jurisprudence [*A publication*]　(DLA)
Woodf .... Woodfall on Landlord and Tenant [*25 eds.*] [*1802-1958*] [*A publication*]　(DLA)
WOODF .... Woodford [*England*]
Woodf Cel Tr ... Woodfall's Celebrated Trials [*A publication*]　(DLA)
Woodf Landl & T ... Woodfall on Landlord and Tenant [*25 eds.*] [*1802-1958*] [*A publication*]　(DLA)
Woodf Landl & Ten ... Woodfall on Landlord and Tenant [*25 eds.*] [*1802-1958*] [*A publication*]　(DLA)
Woodf L & T ... Woodfall on Landlord and Tenant [*28th ed.*] [*1978*] [*A publication*]　(DLA)
WOOD-FM ... Grand Rapids, MI [*FM radio station call letters*]

Woodf Parl Deb ... Woodfall's Parliamentary Debates [*A publication*]　(DLA)
Wood H ...... Hutton Wood's Decrees in Tithe Cases [*England*] [*A publication*]　(DLA)
Wood Ind ... Wood Industry [*A publication*]
Wood Inst .. Wood's Institutes of English Law [*A publication*]　(DLA)
Wood Inst Com Law ... Wood's Institutes of the Common Law [*A publication*]　(DLA)
Wood Inst Eng L ... Wood's Institutes of English Law [*A publication*]　(DLA)
WOODL .... Woodleigh [*England*]
Wood Landl & Ten ... Wood on Landlord and Tenant [*A publication*]　(DLA)
Wood Land & T ... Wood on Landlord and Tenant [*A publication*]　(DLA)
Woodlds Res Index ... Woodlands Research Index. Pulp and Paper Research Institute of Canada [*A publication*]
Wood Lect ... Wooddesson's Lectures on the Laws of England [*A publication*]　(DLA)
Wood Lim .. Wood on Limitation of Actions [*A publication*]　(DLA)
Woodl Pap Pulp Pap Res Inst Can ... Woodlands Papers. Pulp and Paper Research Institute of Canada [*A publication*]
Woodl Res Note Union Camp Corp ... Woodland Research Notes. Union Camp Corporation [*A publication*]
Woodl Sect Index Canad Pulp Pap Ass ... Woodlands Section Index. Canadian Pulp and Paper Association [*A publication*]
Wood & M ... Woodbury and Minot's United States Circuit Court Reports [*A publication*]　(DLA)
Wood Mag ... Woodwind Magazine [*A publication*]
Wood Man ... Wood on Mandamus [*A publication*]　(DLA)
Woodman Cr Cas ... Woodman's Reports of Thacher's Criminal Cases [*Massachusetts*] [*A publication*]　(DLA)
Wood Mast & Serv ... Wood on Master and Servant [*A publication*]　(DLA)
Wood Mayne Dam ... Wood's Mayne on Damages [*A publication*]　(DLA)
WOODMEM ... Leonard Wood Memorial [*Later, LWM*] [*Also known as American Leprosy Foundation*]　(EA)
Wood & Minot ... Woodbury and Minot's United States Circuit Court Reports [*A publication*]　(DLA)
Woodm & T For Med ... Woodman and Tidy on Forensic Medicine [*A publication*]　(DLA)
Wood Nuis ... Wood on Nuisances [*A publication*]　(DLA)
Wood Preserv ... Wood Preserving [*A publication*]
Wood Preserv (Chicago) ... Wood Preserving (Chicago) [*A publication*]
Wood Preserv N ... Wood Preserving News [*A publication*]
Wood Preserv News ... Wood Preserving News [*A publication*]
Wood Pres Rep For Prod Res Ind Developm Comm (Philippines) ... Wood Preservation Report. Forest Products Research and Industries Development Commission College (Laguna, Philippines) [*A publication*]
Wood Prod ... Wood and Wood Products [*A publication*]
Wood Res ... Wood Research [*A publication*]
Wood Ry Law ... Wood's Law of Railroads [*A publication*]　(DLA)
Woods .... Woods' United States Circuit Court Reports [*A publication*]　(DLA)
Woods CC ... Woods' United States Circuit Court Reports [*A publication*]　(DLA)
Wood Sci .... Wood Science [*A publication*]
Wood Sci Te ... Wood Science and Technology [*A publication*]
Wood Sci Technol ... Wood Science and Technology [*A publication*]
Wood's Civ Law ... Wood's Institutes of the Civil Law of England [*A publication*]　(DLA)
Wood's Dig ... Wood's Digest of Laws [*California*] [*A publication*]　(DLA)
Woods Hole Oceanogr Inst Annu Rep ... Woods Hole Oceanographic Institution. Annual Report [*A publication*]
Woods Hole Oceanogr Inst Annu Sea Grant Rep ... Woods Hole Oceanographic Institution. Annual Sea Grant Report [*A publication*]
Woods Hole Oceanogr Inst Collect Reprints ... Woods Hole Oceanographic Institution. Collected Reprints [*A publication*]
Woods Hole Oceanogr Inst Tech Rep ... Woods Hole Oceanographic Institution. Technical Report [*A publication*]
Woods Ins ... Wood on Fire Insurance [*A publication*]　(DLA)
Woods Ins ... Wood's Institutes of English Law [*A publication*]　(DLA)
Wood's Inst Civ L ... Wood's Institutes of the Civil Law of England [*A publication*]　(DLA)
Wood's Inst Com L ... Wood's Institutes of the Common Law [*A publication*]　(DLA)
Wood South Afr ... Wood Southern Africa [*A publication*]
Wood's R ... Wood's Manitoba Reports [*1875-83*] [*A publication*]　(DLA)
Woods St Frauds ... Wood's Treatise on the Statutes of Frauds [*A publication*]　(DLA)
WOODST ... Wood Strength [*Botany*]
WOODSTEIN ... [*Bob*] Woodward and [*Carl*] Bernstein [*Washington Post reporters who uncovered the Watergate story*]
Wood Sthn Afr ... Wood Southern Africa [*A publication*]
Wood Tech ... Wood Technic [*A publication*]
Wood Ti Cas ... Wood's Tithe Cases [*1650-1798*] [*A publication*]　(DLA)
Wood Tit Cas ... Wood's Tithe Cases [*1650-1798*] [*A publication*]　(DLA)
Wood Tr M ... Wood on Trade Marks [*1876*] [*A publication*]　(DLA)
Woodw .... Woodward's Decisions [*Pennsylvania*] [*A publication*]　(DLA)
Woodw Dec ... Woodward's Decisions [*1861-74*] [*Pennsylvania*] [*A publication*]　(DLA)
Woodw Dec PA ... Woodward's Decisions [*1861-74*] [*Pennsylvania*] [*A publication*]　(DLA)
Woodwind B ... Woodwind, Brass, and Percussion [*A publication*]

Woodwkg Ind ... Woodworking Industry [*A publication*]
Wood Wood Prod ... Wood and Wood Products [*A publication*]
Wood & Wood Prod ... Wood and Wood Products [*A publication*]
Wood World ... Woodwind World [*Later, Woodwind World - Brass and Percussion*] [*A publication*]
Wood World-Brass ... Woodwind World - Brass and Percussion [*A publication*]
WOODWT ... Wood Weight [*Botany*]
WOOF ...... Dothan, AL [*AM radio station call letters*]
Woof ...... Well-Off, Older Folks [*Lifestyle classification*]
Woof .... Well-Off, Over Fifty [*Lifestyle classification*]
WOOF-FM ... Dothan, AL [*FM radio station call letters*]
WOOG ...... Kissimmee, FL [*FM radio station call letters*]
Wool .... Woolworth's United States Circuit Court Reports [*A publication*] (DLA)
Wool CC .... Woolworth's United States Circuit Court Reports (Miller's Decisions) [*A publication*] (DLA)
Woolf Adult ... Woolf on Adulterations [*1874*] [*A publication*] (DLA)
Wool Int ..... Woolsey's Introduction to Study of International Law [*6th ed.*] [*1888*] [*A publication*] (DLA)
Woolr Cert ... Woolrych's Certificates [*1826*] [*A publication*] (DLA)
Woolr Com ... Woolrych's Rights of Common [*2nd ed.*] [*1850*] [*A publication*] (DLA)
Woolr Cr L ... Woolrych's Criminal Law [*1862*] [*A publication*] (DLA)
Wool Rec.... Wool Record [*A publication*]
Wool Rec.... Wool Record and Textile World [*A publication*]
Wool Rec Text World ... Wool Record and Textile World [*A publication*]
Woolr LW ... Woolrych's Law of Waters [*2nd ed.*] [*1851*] [*A publication*]
Woolr PW ... Woolrych's Party Walls [*1845*] [*A publication*] (DLA)
Woolr Sew ... Woolrych's Sewert [*3rd ed.*] [*1864*] [*A publication*] (DLA)
Woolr Waters ... Woolrych's Law of Waters [*A publication*] (DLA)
Woolr Ways ... Woolrych's Law of Ways [*2nd ed.*] [*1847*] [*A publication*] (DLA)
Woolr Wind L ... Woolrych's Window Lights [*2nd ed.*] [*1864*] [*A publication*] (DLA)
Wool Sci Rev ... Wool Science Review [*A publication*]
Woolsey Polit Science ... Woolsey's Political Science [*A publication*] (DLA)
Wools Int L ... Woolsey's Introduction to Study of International Law [*6th ed.*] [*1888*] [*A publication*] (DLA)
Wools Pol Science ... Woolsey's Political Science [*A publication*] (DLA)
Wool Tech ... Wool Technology [*A publication*]
Wool Tech ... Wool Technology and Sheep Breeding [*A publication*] (APTA)
Wool Technol ... Wool Technology [*A publication*] (APTA)
Wool Technol ... Wool Technology and Sheep Breeding [*A publication*] (APTA)
Wool Technol Sheep Breed ... Wool Technology and Sheep Breeding [*A publication*]
Wool Technol (Syd) ... Wool Technology (Sydney) [*A publication*] (APTA)
Wool Tech & Sheep ... Wool Technology and Sheep Breeding [*A publication*] (APTA)
Wool Tech & Sheep Breeding ... Wool Technology and Sheep Breeding [*A publication*] (APTA)
Woolw .... Woolworth's Reports [*1 Nebraska*] [*A publication*] (DLA)
Woolw .... Woolworth's United States Circuit Court Reports [*A publication*] (DLA)
Woolwld ..... Woolworld [*New Zealand*] [*A publication*]
Woolworth ... Woolworth's United States Circuit Court Reports [*A publication*] (DLA)
Woolworth's Cir Ct R ... Woolworth's United States Circuit Court Reports [*A publication*] (DLA)
Woolw Rep ... Woolworth's Reports [*1 Nebraska*] [*A publication*] (DLA)
Woolw Rep ... Woolworth's United States Circuit Court Reports [*A publication*] (DLA)
WOOMB... World Organization of the Ovulation Method - Billings, USA [*Later, Families of the Americas Foundation*]
Woopie...... Well-Off Older Person [*Lifestyle classification*]
Woo Sok Univ Med J ... Woo Sok University. Medical Journal [*A publication*]
WOOW ..... Greenville, NC [*AM radio station call letters*]
WOOZ-FM ... Harrisburg, IL [*FM radio station call letters*]
WOP .... War on Poverty (OICC)
WOP .... Wing Outer Panel [*Aviation*]
WOP .... Wireless Operator [*RAF slang*] [*World War II*]
WOP .... Without Passport [*Stamped on papers of turn-of-the-century immigrants who were arriving to work in specific factories or on railroad gangs. A high percentage of these immigrants were Italian, and the designation eventually became a derogatory term for members of that nationality. Alternate theories hold that the term means "Works on Pavement" or that it derived from the Spanish "guapo" through the Sicilian "guappo," a tough, brave man*]
WOP .... Without Payment
W/O/P....... Without Penalty
WOP......... Without Personnel
WOP......... Without Preference [*Rating*]
WOP......... Without Priorities
WOP......... World Oil Project [*National Science Foundation*] [*Massachusetts Institute of Technology*] (IID)
WOPA ...... Chicago, IL [*AM radio station call letters*]
WOPA .... War Overtime Pay Act of 1943

W O PAR... Without Partition [*Freight*]
WOPC .... World Oceanographic Data Processing and Services Center (MSC)
WOPD...... Warrant Officer Professional Development [*Military*] (MCD)
WOPE ...... Without Personnel and Equipment
Wo Peo...... Work and People [*A publication*]
WOPHA.... Woman Physician [*A publication*]
WOPOP .... WOPOP: Working Papers on Photography [*A publication*] (APTA)
WOPP .... Opp, AL [*AM radio station call letters*]
WOPR ...... Oak Park, MI [*FM radio station call letters*]
WOPR .... War Operation Plan Response [*Pronounced "whopper"*] [*Name of NORAD computer in film "WarGames"*]
WOQ .... Wave Officers' Quarters
WOQI........ Ponce, PR [*FM radio station call letters*]
WOQT...... Warrant Officer Qualification Test [*Military*]
WOR......... New York, NY [*AM radio station call letters*]
WOR......... Water-Oil Ratio
WOR......... White and Orange [*Buoy*]
WOR......... White Owners Register (EA)
WOR......... Wool Record and Textile World [*A publication*]
WOR......... Worcester [*Massachusetts*] [*Seismograph station code, US Geological Survey*] [*Closed*] (SEIS)
WOR......... Work Order Register (MCD)
WOR......... Work Order Release (MCD)
WOR......... Work Order Request
WOR......... Work Outline Retrieval (MCD)
WoR......... World Review [*A publication*]
Wor......... Worldview [*A publication*]
WOR......... Worshipful
WOR......... Worthen Banking Corp. [*AMEX symbol*] (SPSG)
WORA...... Mayaguez, PR [*AM radio station call letters*]
WORAM... Word-Oriented Random Access Memory [*Data processing*] (MCD)
WORA-TV ... Mayaguez, PR [*Television station call letters*]
WORB...... Farmington Hills, MI [*FM radio station call letters*]
WORBAT ... Wartime Order of Battle (NATG)
Wor Bib Leg ... Worrall's Bibliotheca Legum [*A publication*] (DLA)
WORC...... Washington Operations Research Council (MCD)
WORC...... Worcester, MA [*AM radio station call letters*]
WORC...... Worcestershire [*County in England*]
Worcest Dict ... Worcester's Dictionary [*A publication*] (DLA)
Worcester... Worcester's Dictionary of the English Language [*A publication*] (DLA)
Worcester Med News ... Worcester Medical News [*Massachusetts*] [*A publication*]
Worcester Mus Ann ... Worcester, Massachusetts. Worcester Art Museum. Annual [*A publication*]
Worcester Mus N Bul ... Worcester, Massachusetts. Worcester Art Museum. News Bulletin and Calendar [*A publication*]
Worc M...... Worcester Magazine [*A publication*]
WORCS..... Worcestershire [*County in England*]
WORCS..... Work Ordering and Reporting Communication System [*Army*]
WORD....... Spartanburg, SC [*AM radio station call letters*]
Wor Dict ... Worcester's Dictionary [*A publication*] (DLA)
Word and Inf Process ... Word and Information Processing [*A publication*]
Word Proc ... Word Processing and Information Systems [*A publication*]
Word Process Comput Inf Systems ... Word Processing Computer Information Systems [*A publication*]
Word Process and Inf Syst ... Word Processing and Information Systems [*A publication*]
Word Process Now ... Word Processing Now [*A publication*]
Word Process Syst ... Word Processing Systems [*A publication*]
Word Process World ... Word Processing World [*A publication*]
WordsC...... Wordsworth Circle [*A publication*]
Words Elect ... Wordsworth's Law of Elections [*6th ed.*] [*1868*] [*A publication*] (DLA)
Words Elect Cas ... Wordsworth's Election Cases [*England*] [*A publication*] (DLA)
Words JS... Wordsworth's Law of Joint-Stock Companies [*A publication*] (DLA)
Words Min ... Wordsworth's Law of Mining [*A publication*] (DLA)
Words Pat ... Wordsworth's Law of Patents [*A publication*] (DLA)
Words Ry & C ... Wordsworth's Railway and Canal Companies [*A publication*] (DLA)
Wordsworth ... Wordsworth Circle [*A publication*]
Word W ..... Word Watching [*A publication*]
WORG....... Orangeburg, SC [*AM radio station call letters*]
WORI .... Oak Ridge, TN [*AM radio station call letters*]
WORI .... World Order Research Institute
WORK...... Barre, VT [*FM radio station call letters*]
WORK...... WORKLIT Database [*Australia*]
WORKD.... Worklife [*A publication*]
Work-Environ-Health ... Work-Environment-Health [*A publication*]
WORKHO ... Workhouse [*British*] (ROG)
Working Papers ... Working Papers for a New Society [*A publication*]
Workmen's Comp L Rep ... Workmen's Compensation Law Reporter [*Commerce Clearing House*] [*A publication*] (DLA)
Workmen's Comp L Rep CCH ... Workmen's Compensation Law Reports. Commerce Clearing House [*A publication*]

Workmen's Comp L Rev ... Workmen's Compensation Law Review [*A publication*] (DLA)
Work Pap Aust Arid Zone Res Conf ... Working Papers. Australian Arid Zone Research Conference [*A publication*] (APTA)
Work Pap Aust Cereal Pasture Plant Breed Conf ... Working Papers. Australian Cereal and Pasture Plant Breeding Conference [*A publication*] (APTA)
Work Pap Bur Meteorol ... Working Paper. Bureau of Meteorology [*A publication*] (APTA)
Work Papers ... Working Papers Magazine [*A publication*]
Work Pap Giannini Found Agric Econ Calif Agric Exp Stn ... Working Paper. Giannini Foundation of Agricultural Economics. California Agricultural Experiment Station [*A publication*]
Work Pap Lang Linguist ... Working Papers in Language and Linguistics [*A publication*] (APTA)
Work Pap Ling (H) ... Working Papers in Linguistics (Honolulu) [*A publication*]
Work Pap New Soc ... Working Papers for a New Society [*A publication*]
Work Plant Maint ... Work and Plant Maintenance [*A publication*]
Work Prog ... Work in Progress [*A publication*]
Work Rel Abstr ... Work Related Abstracts [*A publication*]
Works Courts ... Works on Courts and Their Jurisdiction [*A publication*] (DLA)
Works Eng ... Works Engineering [*England*] [*A publication*]
Works Eng Fact Serv ... Works Engineering and Factory Services [*A publication*]
Workshop Conf Hoechst ... Workshop Conferences Hoechst [*A publication*]
Workshop Ser Pharmacol Sect Nat Inst Ment Health ... Workshop Series. Pharmacology Section. National Institute of Mental Health [*A publication*]
Works Inst Higher Nerv Act Acad Sci USSR Pathophysiol Ser ... Works. Institute of Higher Nervous Activity. Academy of Sciences of the USSR. Pathophysiological Series [*A publication*]
Works Inst Higher Nerv Act Acad Sci USSR Physiol Ser ... Works. Institute of Higher Nervous Activity. Academy of Sciences of the USSR. Physiological Series [*A publication*]
Works Inst Higher Nerv Act Pathophysiol Ser ... Works. Institute of Higher Nervous Activity. Pathophysiological Series [*A publication*]
Works Inst Higher Nerv Act Physiol Ser ... Works. Institute of Higher Nervous Activity. Physiological Series [*A publication*]
Works Pavlov Inst Physiol Acad Sci USSR ... Works. Pavlov Institute of Physiology. Academy of Sciences of the USSR [*A publication*]
Works and Plant Maint ... Works and Plant Maintenance [*A publication*]
Works Pr ... Works' Practice, Pleading, and Forms [*A publication*] (DLA)
Work Study and Manage Serv ... Work Study and Management Services [*Later, Management Services*] [*A publication*]
Work Vang ... Workers Vanguard [*A publication*]
Work Wom ... Working Woman [*A publication*]
WORL .... Christmas, FL [*AM radio station call letters*]
WORL .... Worlco, Inc. [*NASDAQ symbol*] (NQ)
World .... National Geographic World [*A publication*]
World .... World Magazine [*A publication*]
World A ..... World Archaeology [*A publication*]
World Aff... World Affairs [*A publication*]
World Affairs J ... World Affairs. Journal [*A publication*]
World Aff Q ... World Affairs. Quarterly [*A publication*]
World Ag ... World Agriculture [*A publication*]
World Agr ... World Agriculture [*A publication*]
World Agric ... World Agriculture [*A publication*]
World Agri Econ & Rural Sociol Abstr ... World Agricultural Economics and Rural Sociology Abstracts [*A publication*]
World Alum Abstr ... World Aluminum Abstracts [*A publication*]
World Anim Rev ... World Animal Review [*A publication*]
World Anthropol ... World Anthropology [*A publication*]
World Archa ... World Archaeology [*A publication*]
World Archaeol ... World Archaeology [*A publication*]
World Assn for Adult Ed B ... World Association for Adult Education. Bulletin [*A publication*]
World Bibl Social Security ... World Bibliography of Social Security [*A publication*]
World Bus W ... World Business Weekly [*A publication*]
World Cem ... World Cement [*London*] [*A publication*]
World Cem Technol ... World Cement Technology [*Later, World Cement*] [*A publication*]
World Commod Rep Met Ed ... World Commodity Report. Metals Edition [*A publication*]
World Conf Earthquake Eng Proc ... World Conference on Earthquake Engineering. Proceedings [*A publication*]
World Constr ... World Construction [*A publication*]
World Crops Prod Util Descr ... World Crops Production Utilization Description [*A publication*]
World Dev ... World Development [*Oxford*] [*A publication*]
World Devel ... World Development [*A publication*]
WORLDDIDAC ... World Association of Manufacturers and Distributors of Educational Materials (EAIO)
World Dist ... World Distribution [*A publication*]
World Dredging & Mar Const ... World Dredging and Marine Construction [*A publication*]

World Dredging Mar Constr ... World Dredging and Marine Construction [*A publication*]
World Econ ... World Economy [*England*] [*A publication*]
World Eco S ... World Economic Survey. Supplement [*A publication*]
World Educ Rep ... World Education Reports [*A publication*]
World Energy Conf Trans ... World Energy Conference. Transactions [*A publication*]
World Farm ... World Farming [*A publication*]
World Fertil Surv Ctry Rep ... World Fertility Survey. Country Reports [*A publication*]
World Fertil Surv Sci Rep ... World Fertility Survey. Scientific Reports [*A publication*]
World Fish Abstr ... World Fisheries Abstracts [*A publication*]
World For Ser Bull ... World Forestry Series. Bulletin [*A publication*]
World Health Organ Chron ... World Health Organization. Chronicle [*A publication*]
World Health Organ Tech Rep Ser ... World Health Organization. Technical Report Series [*A publication*]
World Health Stat Q ... World Health Statistics. Quarterly [*A publication*]
World Health Stat Rep ... World Health Statistics. Report [*A publication*]
World Highw ... World Highways [*A publication*]
World Hosp ... World Hospitals [*A publication*]
World Ir Nurs ... World of Irish Nursing [*A publication*]
World Jnl Trib ... World Journal Tribune [*Defunct New York City afternoon newspaper*] [*A publication*]
World J Surg ... World Journal of Surgery [*A publication*]
World J Urol ... World Journal of Urology [*A publication*]
World Jus .. World Justice [*A publication*]
World List Pub Stds ... Worldwide List of Published Standards [*A publication*]
World Lit T ... World Literature Today [*A publication*]
World Lit Today ... World Literature Today [*A publication*]
World L Rev ... World Law Review [*A publication*] (DLA)
World M .... World of Music [*A publication*]
World Marxist R ... World Marxist Review [*A publication*]
World Marx R ... World Marxist Review [*A publication*]
World Med ... World Medicine [*A publication*]
World Med Electron ... World Medical Electronics [*England*] [*A publication*]
World Med Instrum ... World Medical Instrumentation [*England*] [*A publication*]
World Med J ... World Medical Journal [*A publication*]
World Meet Outside US Can ... World Meetings: Outside United States and Canada [*A publication*]
World Meet Outs US Can ... World Meetings: Outside United States and Canada [*A publication*]
World Meet US Can ... World Meetings: United States and Canada [*A publication*]
World Metal Statis ... World Metal Statistics [*A publication*]
World Meteorol Organ Bull ... World Meteorological Organization. Bulletin [*A publication*]
World Meteorol Organ Publ ... World Meteorological Organization. Publications [*A publication*]
World Min ... World Mining [*A publication*]
World Min Equip ... World Mining Equipment [*A publication*]
World Miner Met ... World Minerals and Metals [*A publication*]
World Miner Stat ... World Mineral Statistics [*A publication*]
World Min US Ed ... World Mining. United States Edition [*A publication*]
World Mus ... World of Music [*A publication*]
World Neurol ... World Neurology [*A publication*]
World O ..... World Order [*A publication*]
World Obstet Gynecol ... World of Obstetrics and Gynecology [*Japan*] [*A publication*]
World Oil... World Oil Forecast. Review Issue [*A publication*]
World Outl ... World Outlook [*A publication*]
World Patent Inf ... World Patent Information [*A publication*]
World Pet... World Petroleum [*A publication*]
World Pet Cong Prepr ... World Petroleum Congress. Preprints [*A publication*]
World Pet Congr Proc ... World Petroleum Congress. Proceedings [*A publication*]
World Petrol ... World Petroleum [*A publication*]
World Pol... World Policy [*A publication*]
World Pol... World Politics [*A publication*]
World Poult ... World's Poultry Science Journal [*A publication*]
World Poultry Sci J ... World's Poultry Science Journal [*A publication*]
World Press R ... World Press Review [*A publication*]
World R ..... World Review [*A publication*]
World Refrig ... World Refrigeration [*England*] [*A publication*]
World Rep ... World Report [*A publication*]
World Resour ... World Resources [*A publication*]
World Rev ... World Review [*A publication*]
World Rev Anim Prod ... World Review of Animal Production [*A publication*]
World Rev Nutr Diet ... World Review of Nutrition and Dietetics [*A publication*]
World Rev Pest Contr ... World Review of Pest Control [*A publication*]
World Rev Pest Control ... World Review of Pest Control [*A publication*]
World R Pest Control ... World Review of Pest Control [*A publication*]
WORLDS ... Western Ohio Regional Library Development System [*Library network*]
World's Butter Rev ... World's Butter Review [*A publication*]
World Sci News ... World Science News [*India*] [*A publication*]

World's Pap Trade Rev ... World's Paper Trade Review [*A publication*]
World's Poultry Cong Conf Papers Sect C ... World's Poultry Congress. Conference Papers. Section C [*A publication*]
World's Poultry Sci J ... World's Poultry Science Journal [*A publication*]
World's Poult Sci J ... World's Poultry Science Journal [*A publication*]
World Steel (Jpn) ... World of Steel (Japan) [*A publication*]
World Steel Metalwork Export Man ... World Steel and Metalworking Export Manual [*A publication*]
World Surface Coat Abs ... World Surface Coatings Abstracts [*A publication*]
World Surf Coat ... World Surface Coatings Abstracts [*A publication*]
World Surv ... World Survey [*A publication*]
World Text Abstr ... World Textile Abstracts [*A publication*]
World Textile Abs ... World Textile Abstracts [*A publication*]
World Textile Abstr ... World Textile Abstracts [*A publication*]
World Trade LJ ... World Trade Law Journal [*A publication*]   (DLA)
Worldwatch Pap ... Worldwatch Paper [*A publication*]
WorldWIDE ... World Women in the Environment [*Formerly, World Women in Defense of the Environment*]   (EA)
Worldwide Abstr ... Worldwide Abstracts [*A publication*]
Worldwide List Published Stand ... Worldwide List of Published Standards [*A publication*]
World-Wide MinAbs ... World-Wide Mining Abstracts [*A publication*]
Worldwide Nucl Power ... Worldwide Nuclear Power [*A publication*]
World Yr Bk Ed ... World Yearbook of Education [*A publication*]
WORM...... Earthworm, Inc. [*NASDAQ symbol*]   (NQ)
WORM...... Savannah, TN [*AM radio station call letters*]
Worm........ White, Older Rich Man [*Lifestyle classification*]
WORM...... Write Once, Read Mainly [*or Many Times, or Mostly*] [*Data processing*]
WORM-FM ... Savannah, TN [*FM radio station call letters*]
Worm R ..... Wormwood Review [*A publication*]
Worm Runner's Dig ... Worm Runner's Digest [*A publication*]
WORMS ...... World Organization to Restore Male Supremacy   (EA)
WORN....... Write Once, Read Never [*Data processing*]
WORO........ Corozal, PR [*FM radio station call letters*]
WOROM... Write-Only Read-Only Memory [*Data processing*]   (MDG)
WORP....... Word Processing [*Data processing*]   (DCTA)
Wor Pol...... World Politics [*A publication*]
WORR........ Quebradillas, PR [*AM radio station call letters*]
Wor R.......... World Review [*A publication*]   (APTA)
WORSAMS ... Worldwide Organizational Structure for Army Medical Support   (AABC)
WORSE9... World Resources [*A publication*]
WORT....... Madison, WI [*FM radio station call letters*]
WORTAC ... Westinghouse Overall RADAR Tester and Calibrator
Worth Jur .. Worthington's Power of Juries [*1825*] [*A publication*]   (DLA)
Worth Prec Wills ... Worthington's General Precedent for Wills [*5th ed.*] [*1852*] [*A publication*]   (DLA)
Worth Star T ... Fort Worth Star-Telegram [*A publication*]
Wort Wahr ... Wort und Wahrheit [*A publication*]
WORV....... Hattiesburg, MS [*AM radio station call letters*]
WORW...... Port Huron, MI [*FM radio station call letters*]
WORX....... Madison, IN [*AM radio station call letters*]
WORX-FM ... Madison, IN [*FM radio station call letters*]
WOS.......... Web Offset Section [*Later, WOA*]   (EA)
WOS.......... Wilson Ornithological Society   (EA)
WOS.......... Winchester Financial [*Vancouver Stock Exchange symbol*]
WOS.......... Wonders of the Spaceways [*A publication*]
WOS.......... Worcester [*British depot code*]
WOSAC .... Worldwide Synchronization of Atomic Clocks
WOSB....... War Office Selection Board [*British*]
WOSB ...... Weather Observation Site Building   (AABC)
WOSC....... Western Oregon State College
WOSC ...... World Organisation of Systems and Cybernetics   (EAIO)
WOSD....... Weapons Operational Systems Development [*NORAD*]
WOSE....... Port Clinton, OH [*FM radio station call letters*]
WOSF....... Work Order Status File   (MCD)
WOsh........ Oshkosh Public Library, Oshkosh, WI [*Library symbol*] [*Library of Congress*]   (LCLS)
WOSH....... Oshkosh, WI [*AM radio station call letters*]
WOshM..... Mercy Hospital, Nursing Library, Oshkosh, WI [*Library symbol*] [*Library of Congress*]   (LCLS)
WOshM-M ... Mercy Medical Center, Medical Library, Oshkosh, WI [*Library symbol*] [*Library of Congress*]   (LCLS)
WOshU ..... University of Wisconsin-Oshkosh, Oshkosh, WI [*Library symbol*] [*Library of Congress*]   (LCLS)
WOSIC...... Watchmakers of Switzerland Information Center   (EA)
WOSL........ Women's Overseas Service League   (EA)
WOSM...... Ocean Springs, MS [*FM radio station call letters*]
WOSO........ San Juan, PR [*AM radio station call letters*]
WOSS........ Ossining, NY [*FM radio station call letters*]
WOSSU..... Women on Stamps Study Unit [*American Topical Association*]   (EA)
WOST .... World's Oldest Socketed Tool [*A copper implement made around 2500BC and possibly used for digging or chopping. It was discovered in 1966 at Non Nok Tha, Thailand, by archeologist Donn Bayard*]
WOST-TV ... Block Island, RI [*Television station call letters*]
WOSU....... Columbus, OH [*AM radio station call letters*]
WOSUS..... Wang Office Systems User Society   (CSR)
WOSU-TV ... Columbus, OH [*Television station call letters*]

WOSV....... Mansfield, OH [*FM radio station call letters*]
WOT.......... Wide-Open Throttle
WOT.......... Worlds of Tomorrow [*A publication*]
WOTB ...... Middletown, RI [*FM radio station call letters*]
WOTB ...... Welfare of the Blind   (EA)
WOTCU .... Wave-Off and Transition Control Unit
WOTD....... Winamac, IN [*FM radio station call letters*]
WOTF .... Writers of the Future [*Science fiction writing award*]
WOTH ...... Surgoinsville, TN [*FM radio station call letters*]
WOTHDJ ... Women and Therapy [*A publication*]
WOTJ....... Morehead City, NC [*FM radio station call letters*]
WOTK....... World-Wide Technology, Inc. [*NASDAQ symbol*]   (NQ)
WOTL....... Toledo, OH [*FM radio station call letters*]
WOTO....... Women on Their Own [*An association*]   (EA)
WOTR....... Statesboro, GA [*FM radio station call letters*]
WOTR....... Wolf Trap Farm Park [*National Park Service designation*]
WOTRAC ... Woods Hole Oceanographic Institution. Technical Report [*A publication*]
WOTS....... Mitchell, IN [*FM radio station call letters*]
WOTS....... Warrant Officer Training System [*Military*]   (INF)
WOTT....... Wolves on the Track [*A group of philanderers looking for girls*] [*Slang*]
WOTTCS.. Warrant Officer Technical and Tactical Certification System [*Army*]
Wott Leg Wal ... Wotton. Leges Wallicae [*A publication*]   (DLA)
WOTV....... Grand Rapids, MI [*Television station call letters*]
WOU .... Work Opportunities Unlimited
WOUB....... Athens, OH [*AM radio station call letters*]
WOUB-FM ... Athens, OH [*FM radio station call letters*]
WOUB-TV ... Athens, OH [*Television station call letters*]
WOUC-FM ... Cambridge, OH [*FM radio station call letters*]
WOUC-TV ... Cambridge, OH [*Television station call letters*]
WOUI........ Chicago, IL [*FM radio station call letters*]
WOUL....... Ironton, OH [*FM radio station call letters*]
WOUR....... Utica, NY [*FM radio station call letters*]
WOV.......... Warren & Ouachita Valley Railway Co. [*AAR code*]
WOV.......... Wolverine Technologies, Inc. [*NYSE symbol*]   (SPSG)
WOVI....... Novi, MI [*FM radio station call letters*]
WOVK....... Wheeling, WV [*FM radio station call letters*]
WOVO....... Glasgow, KY [*FM radio station call letters*]
WOVR-FM ... Versailles, IN [*FM radio station call letters*]
WOVV....... Fort Pierce, FL [*FM radio station call letters*]
WOW .... Omaha, NE [*AM radio station call letters*]
WOW .... Waiting on Weather [*Ocean storms*]
WOW .... War on Want [*An association*]   (EAIO)
WOW .... War on Waste [*Navy*]
WOW .... War on Words
WOW .... Washington Opportunities for Women
WOW .... Weight-on-Wheels   (NASA)
WOW .... Wereld in Ontwikkeling. Veertiendaags Overzicht van Tijdschriftartikelen en Rapporten over Problemen van de Ontwikkelingsgebieden [*A publication*]
WOW .... Wider Opportunities for Women   (EA)
WOW .... Woman Ordnance Worker
WOW .... Women Our Wonders [*Antifeminist men's group*]
WOW .... Women on Wheels   (EA)
WOW .... Women on Wine   (EA)
WOW .... Woodmen of the World   (EA)
WOW .... Word on the Way
WOW .... World of Winners [*A publication*]
WOW .... World of Work [*Career-oriented course of study*]
WOW .... Worlds of Wonder [*Electronic toy manufacturer*]
WOW .... Worldwide Equities Ltd. [*Toronto Stock Exchange symbol*]
WOW .... Worn-Out Wolf [*An aging philanderer*] [*Slang*]
WOW .... Worst-on-Worst
Wow .... Wort und Wahrheit [*A publication*]
WOW .... Written Order of Withdrawal [*Banking*]
WoWa........ Wort und Wahrheit [*A publication*]
WOWAR... Work Order and Work Accomplishment Record
WOWATE ... World War II Equivalent [*Three-year and eight-month unit of time measurement proposed by former Under Secretary of the Navy R. James Woolsey*]
WOWB...... Little Falls, NY [*FM radio station call letters*]
WOWBDG ... Instytut Zootechniki w Polsce Wyniki Oceny Wartosci Hodowlanej Buhajow [*A publication*]
WOWE....... Vassar, MI [*FM radio station call letters*]
WOW-FM ... Omaha, NE [*FM radio station call letters*]
WOWI....... Norfolk, VA [*FM radio station call letters*]
WOWI....... Women on Words and Images   (EA)
WOWI....... Worlds of Wonder, Incorporated [*Fremont, CA*] [*NASDAQ symbol*]   (NQ)
W & O Wills ... Wilgram and O'Hara on Wills [*A publication*]   (DLA)
WOWK-TV ... Huntington, WV [*Television station call letters*]
WOWLON ... Weight-on-Wheels Lock-On [*NASA*]   (NASA)
WOWL-TV ... Florence, AL [*Television station call letters*]
WOWN ..... Shawano, WI [*FM radio station call letters*]
WOWN ..... Without Winch
WOWO ..... Fort Wayne, IN [*AM radio station call letters*]
WOWO-FM ... Huntington, IN [*FM radio station call letters*]
WOWQ ..... DuBois, PA [*FM radio station call letters*]
WOWS .... Wire Obstacle Warning System   (IEEE)

WOWS...... Women Ordnance Workers [*A national voluntary organization*] [*World War II*]
WOWSER ... We Only Want Social Evils Righted [*Said to be the translation for an Australian acronym describing a prudish reformer*]
WOWT...... Omaha, NE [*Television station call letters*]
WOWW...... Pensacola, FL [*FM radio station call letters*]
WOXD...... Oxford, MS [*FM radio station call letters*]
WOXO-FM ... Norway, ME [*FM radio station call letters*]
WOXR...... Oxford, AL [*AM radio station call letters*]
WOXY...... Oxford, OH [*FM radio station call letters*]
WOYE-FM ... Mayaguez, PR [*FM radio station call letters*]
WOYK...... York, PA [*AM radio station call letters*]
WOYL...... Oil City, PA [*AM radio station call letters*]
WOYS...... Apalachicola, FL [*FM radio station call letters*]
WOZI...... Presque Isle, ME [*FM radio station call letters*]
WOZK...... Ozark, AL [*AM radio station call letters*]
WOZN...... Key West, FL [*FM radio station call letters*]
WOZQ...... Northampton, MA [*FM radio station call letters*]
WOZZ...... New London, WI [*FM radio station call letters*]
WP............ Empresa de Aviacion Aeronaves del Peru [*ICAO designator*] (FAAC)
WP............ Pakistan Law Reports, West Pakistan Series [*A publication*] (DLA)
WP............ Portage Free Public Library, Portage, WI [*Library symbol*] [*Library of Congress*] (LCLS)
WP............ Waiting Period (OICC)
WP............ Waiver of Premium [*Insurance*]
WP............ Waman Puma [*A publication*]
WP............ War and Peace Foundation (EA)
WP............ War Plans
WP............ Warm Pipe [*Nuclear energy*] (NRCH)
WP............ Warming Pan [*Refers to a clergyman holding a job under a bond of resignation*] [*Obsolete*] [*Slang*] [*British*] (DSUE)
WP............ Warsaw Pact (NATG)
WP............ Washington Post [*A publication*]
WP............ Waste Pipe [*Technical drawings*]
WP............ Wastepaper
WP............ Water Packed
WP............ Water Plane (MSA)
WP............ Water Point
WP............ Water Propeller (AAG)
WP............ Water Pump (AAG)
WP............ Waterproof
WP............ Way-Point
WP............ We the People [*Later, WPU*] (EA)
WP............ Weapons Power
WP............ Weather Permitting
WP............ Weatherproof
WP............ Weekly Premium [*Insurance*]
WP............ Weight Penalty
WP............ Welding Procedure [*Nuclear energy*] (NRCH)
WP............ Wespercorp [*AMEX symbol*] (SPSG)
WP............ West Point
WP............ [*The*] Western Pacific Railroad Co. [*AAR code*]
WP............ Western Pine [*Utility pole*] [*Telecommunications*] (TEL)
WP............ Wet Process (MSA)
WP............ Wettable Powder
WP............ Wheel of Progress (EA)
WP............ Whirlpool [*Medicine*]
WP............ White Painted (BJA)
WP............ White Paper (ADA)
WP............ White Phosphorus [*Military*]
WP............ Wide Pore [*Chromatography*]
WP............ Wiedza Powszechna [*A publication*]
WP............ Wild Pitch [*Baseball*]
WP............ Will Proceed To
WP............ Will Proved [*Legal*] [*British*] (ROG)
WP............ Windfall Profit
WP............ Winning Pitcher [*Baseball*]
WP............ Wire Payment
WP............ Without Prejudice
WP............ Wolfe Pack (EA)
WP............ Wolseley Pattern [*British military*] (DMA)
W and P ..... Women and Performance [*A publication*]
WP............ Wood Pattern (MSA)
WP............ Woodstock Papers [*A publication*]
WP............ Word Processing [*Movement to improve secretarial/clerical function through a managed system of people, procedures, and modern office equipment*]
WP............ Word Processor (ADA)
WP............ Word Punch
WP............ Work Package (NASA)
W/P............ Work Picture [*or Print*] [*Cinematography*]
WP............ Work Procedure [*Nuclear energy*] (NRCH)
WP............ Work Program (NATG)
WP............ Work in Progress [*A publication*]
WP............ Working Paper
WP............ Working Party
WP............ Working Point
WP............ Working Pressure
WP............ World Peacemakers (EA)

WP............ World Petroleum [*A publication*]
WP............ World Politics [*A publication*]
WP............ World Priorities (EA)
WP............ Worship
WP............ Worthy Patriarch
WP............ Wrist Pitch (MCD)
WP............ Write Protect
WP............ Writers for Peace (EA)
WP3........... Working Party Three [*Economic Policy Committee of the Organization for Economic Cooperation and Development*]
WPA.......... Wagner-Peyser Act [*1933*] (OICC)
WPA.......... Water Pump Assembly
WPA.......... Webb-Pomerene Act [*1918*]
WPA.......... Western Pine Association [*Later, WWPA*] (EA)
WPA.......... Western Pistachio Association (EA)
WPA.......... Western Psychological Association (MCD)
WPA.......... Wet-Process Phosphoric Acid [*Fertilizer*]
WPA.......... Wheelchair Pilots Association (EA)
WPA.......... Whiskey Painters of America (EA)
WPA.......... William Penn Association [*Pittsburgh, PA*] (EA)
WPA.......... With Particular Average
WPA.......... Women's Prison Association (EA)
WPA.......... Woody Point [*Australia*] [*Seismograph station code, US Geological Survey*] [*Closed*] (SEIS)
WPA.......... Work Package Action (MCD)
WPA.......... Work Package Address (MCD)
WPA.......... Working People's Alliance [*Guyana*] (PD)
WPA.......... Works Progress Administration [*Created, 1935, to operate public works projects for unemployed persons; name changed to Work Projects Administration, 1939; later, absorbed by Federal Works Agency, which was terminated in 1942*]
WPA.......... Workshop of the Players Art [*New York City*]
WPA.......... World Parliament Association
WPA.......... World Pheasant Association [*Reading, Berkshire, England*] (EAIO)
WPA.......... World Presbyterian Alliance
WPA.......... World Press Archives [*A publication*]
WPA.......... World Psychiatric Association [*Copenhagen, Denmark*] (EAIO)
WPA.......... Worst Possible Accident [*Nuclear safety*]
WPAA....... Andover, MA [*FM radio station call letters*]
WPAB....... Ponce, PR [*AM radio station call letters*]
WPAB....... Word Processing Aptitude Battery [*Test*]
WPAB....... Word Processor Assessment Battery [*Selection and placement test*]
WPAC....... Ogdensburg, NY [*FM radio station call letters*]
WPAC....... Walden Pond Advisory Committee (EA)
WPAC....... Working Program Advisory Committee [*DoD*]
WPAD....... Paducah, KY [*AM radio station call letters*]
WPAFB..... Wright-Patterson Air Force Base [*Ohio*]
W PA Hist Mag ... Western Pennsylvania Historical Magazine [*A publication*]
WPAJ....... Danville, VA [*Television station call letters*]
WPAK....... Farmville, VA [*AM radio station call letters*]
W Pakistan J Agr Res ... West Pakistan Journal of Agricultural Research [*A publication*]
WPAL....... Charleston, SC [*AM radio station call letters*]
WPAM...... Pottsville, PA [*AM radio station call letters*]
WPAN...... Fort Walton Beach, FL [*Television station call letters*]
WPAP-FM ... Panama City, FL [*FM radio station call letters*]
WPAQ....... Mount Airy, NC [*AM radio station call letters*]
WPAQ....... Westra Preschool Assessment Questionnaire
WPAR....... Claremont, NC [*FM radio station call letters*]
W PAR...... With Partition [*Freight*]
WP/AS...... Word Processing/Administrative Support [*Extension of Word Processing*]
WPAS....... Zephyrhills, FL [*AM radio station call letters*]
WPAT....... Atauro [*East Timor*] [*ICAO location identifier*] (ICLI)
WPAT....... Paterson, NJ [*AM radio station call letters*]
WPAT....... Wolfe Programming Aptitude Test
WPATC.... Western Pennsylvania Advanced Technology Center [*Research center*] (RCD)
WPAT-FM ... Paterson, NJ [*FM radio station call letters*]
WPA-USA ... World Pheasant Association of the USA (EA)
WPAWA ... World Professional Armwrestling Association (EA)
WPAX....... Thomasville, GA [*AM radio station call letters*]
WPAY...... Portsmouth, OH [*AM radio station call letters*]
WPAY-FM ... Portsmouth, OH [*FM radio station call letters*]
WPAZ....... Pottstown, PA [*AM radio station call letters*]
WPB......... Gunboat [*Coast Guard*] (NVT)
WPB......... Port Berge [*Madagascar*] [*Airport symbol*] (OAG)
WPB......... Wall Plate Box
WPB......... War Production Board [*World War II*]
WPB......... Waste Processing Building [*Nuclear energy*] (NRCH)
WPB......... Wastepaper Basket [*or Bin*]
WPB......... Whirlpool Bath [*Medicine*]
WPB......... Wide Pulse Blanking (MCD)
WPB......... Wiener Enterprises, Inc. [*AMEX symbol*] (SPSG)
WPB......... World Peace Brigade (EA)

WPB	Write Printer Binary
WPBA.......	Atlanta, GA [*Television station call letters*]
WPBA.......	Women Professional Bowlers Association (EA)
WPBA.......	Women's Professional Billiard Alliance (EA)
WPBC.......	Bangor, ME [*FM radio station call letters*]
WPBC.......	Western Pacific Base Command [*Marianas*] [*World War II*]
WPBCWS ...	Waste Processing Building Chilled Water System [*Nuclear energy*] (NRCH)
WPBE.......	Conyers, GA [*AM radio station call letters*]
WPBEF	West Pakistan Bank Employees' Federation
WPBF.......	Tequesta, FL [*Television station call letters*]
WPBG	West Palm Beach, FL [*AM radio station call letters*]
WPBIC.....	Walker Problem Behavior Identification Checklist [*Education*]
WPBK.......	Whitehall, MI [*AM radio station call letters*]
WPBL.......	Women's Professional Basketball League [*Defunct*] (EA)
WPBN-TV ...	Traverse City, MI [*Television station call letters*]
WPBO-TV ...	Portsmouth, OH [*Television station call letters*]
WPBR.......	Palm Beach, FL [*AM radio station call letters*]
WPBRL.....	Warsaw Pact/Ballistic Research Laboratory (MCD)
WPBT.......	Miami, FL [*Television station call letters*]
WPBX.......	Southampton, NY [*FM radio station call letters*]
WPBY-TV ...	Huntington, WV [*Television station call letters*]
WPC	Walter P. Chrysler Club (EA)
WPC	War Pensions Committee [*British military*] (DMA)
WPC	Warrior Preparation Center [*Kaiserslautern, Federal Republic of Germany*] [*USAREUR*]
WPC	Warsaw Pact Countries (MCD)
WPC	Washington Press Club [*Formerly, WNPC*]
WPC	Waste Product Costs [*Solid waste management*]
WPC	Water Pollution Control
WPC	Watts per Candle [*Electricity*]
WPC	Webster's Patent Cases [*1601-1855*] [*A publication*] (DLA)
WPC	Wedge Power Clamp
WPC	Weldable Printed Circuit
WPC	Wheat Protein Concentrate [*Food technology*]
WPC	Whey Protein Concentrate [*Food technology*]
WPC	William Penn College [*Oskaloosa, IA*]
WPC	William Peterson College of New Jersey
WPC	Wired Program Computer
WPC	Wisconsin Electric Power Company [*NYSE symbol*] (SPSG)
WPC	Wollaston's English Bail Court Reports, Practice Cases [*A publication*] (DLA)
WPC	Woman Police Constable [*Scotland Yard*]
WPC	Women's Political Caucus
WPC	Wood-Plastic Combination [*or Composite*]
WPC	Word Processing Center
WPC	Work Package Concept (MCD)
WP + C.....	Work Planning and Control [*Data processing*]
WPC	Workers Party of Canada
WPC	World Peace Congress
WPC	World Peace Council [*See also CMP*] (EAIO)
WPC	World Petroleum Congresses - a Forum for Petroleum Science, Technology, Economics, and Management (EAIO)
WPC	World Philatelic Congress of Holy Land, Israel, and Judaica Societies (EA)
WPC	World Planning Chart [*Aviation*]
WPC	World Pooling Committee (MCD)
WPC	World Power Conference [*Later, WEC*]
WPC	World Print Council (EA)
WPC	World Pumpkin Confederation (EA)
WPCA	Water Pollution Control Administration [*Department of the Interior*]
WPCA	Wool Pullers Council of America (EA)
WPCAA.....	White Park Cattle Association of America (EA)
WP Cas.....	Webster's Patent Cases [*1601-1855*] [*A publication*] (DLA)
WP Cas......	Wollaston's English Bail Court Reports, Practice Cases [*A publication*] (DLA)
WPCB.......	Western Pennsylvania Christian Broadcasting Co. [*A cable TV station*]
WPCB-TV ...	Greensburg, PA [*Television station call letters*]
WPCC.......	Clinton, SC [*AM radio station call letters*]
WPCC.......	Wilson Pharmaceutical & Chemical Corporation
WPCC.......	World Paper Currency Collectors (EA)
WPCC.......	WPC [*Walter P. Chrysler*] Club (EA)
WPCD	Champaign, IL [*FM radio station call letters*]
WPCE.......	Portsmouth, VA [*AM radio station call letters*]
WPCF.......	Panama City Beach, FL [*AM radio station call letters*]
WPCF.......	Water Pollution Control Federation (EA)
WPCF.......	Water Pollution Control Federation. Journal [*A publication*]
WPCF-FM ...	Panama City Beach, FL [*FM radio station call letters*]
WPCF Highlights ...	Water Pollution Control Federation. Highlights [*A publication*]
WPCFJ......	Water Pollution Control Federation. Journal [*A publication*]
WPCH.......	Atlanta, GA [*AM radio station call letters*]
WPCHLIJS ...	World Philatelic Congress of Holy Land, Israel, and Judaica Societies (EA)
WPCI.......	Greenville, SC [*AM radio station call letters*]
WPCJ.......	Pittsford, MI [*FM radio station call letters*]
WPCM	Burlington-Graham, NC [*FM radio station call letters*]
WPCN	Mount Pocono, PA [*AM radio station call letters*]
WPCND	Women's Patriotic Conference on National Defense (EA)

WPCO	Mount Vernon, IN [*AM radio station call letters*]
WPCO	Whiting Petroleum Corporation [*Denver, CO*] [*NASDAQ symbol*] (NQ)
WPCR.......	Water Pollution Control Research [*Environmental Protection Agency*]
WPCR-FM ...	Plymouth, NH [*FM radio station call letters*]
WPCS........	Pensacola, FL [*FM radio station call letters*]
WPCSA	Welsh Pony and Cob Society of America (EA)
WPCV.......	Winter Haven, FL [*FM radio station call letters*]
WPCX.......	Auburn, NY [*FM radio station call letters*]
WPD	War Plan Division [*World War II*]
WPD	Western Procurement Division [*Marine Corps*]
WPD	Work Package Description [*NASA*] (NASA)
WPD	World Pharmaceuticals Directory [*A publication*]
WPD	Write Printer Decimal
WPDA	Writing Pushdown Acceptor
WPDB	Suai [*East Timor*] [*ICAO location identifier*] (ICLI)
WPDC	Elizabethtown, PA [*AM radio station call letters*]
W/PDC.....	Workers'/People's Defence Committee [*Political party*] [*Ghana*]
WPDES.....	Waste Pollution Discharge Elimination System (IEEE)
WPDE-TV ...	Florence, SC [*Television station call letters*]
WPDH.......	Poughkeepsie, NY [*FM radio station call letters*]
WPDJ.......	Huntington, IN [*AM radio station call letters*]
WPDL.......	Dili [*East Timor*] [*ICAO location identifier*] (ICLI)
WPDM......	Potsdam, NY [*AM radio station call letters*]
WPDQ.......	Jacksonville, FL [*AM radio station call letters*]
WPDR.......	Portage, WI [*AM radio station call letters*]
WPDX.......	Clarksburg, WV [*AM radio station call letters*]
WPDX.......	Word Processing Document Exchange Program
WPDX-FM ...	Clarksburg, WV [*FM radio station call letters*]
WPE	West Pittston-Exeter Railroad Co. [*AAR code*]
WPE	Western Pacific Energy [*Vancouver Stock Exchange symbol*]
WPE	Western Plastics Exposition [*HBJ Expositions and Conferences*] (TSPED)
WPE	Work and People [*A publication*]
WPEA.......	Exeter, NH [*FM radio station call letters*]
WPEB.......	Philadelphia, PA [*FM radio station call letters*]
WPEC.......	Baucau [*East Timor*] [*ICAO location identifier*] (ICLI)
WPEC.......	Weapons Production Engineering Center [*Navy*]
WPEC.......	West Palm Beach, FL [*Television station call letters*]
WPEC.......	World Plan Executive Council [*Later, WGAE-US*] (EA)
WPEG.......	Concord, NC [*FM radio station call letters*]
WPEH	Louisville, GA [*AM radio station call letters*]
WPEH-FM ...	Louisville, GA [*FM radio station call letters*]
WPEL.......	Montrose, PA [*AM radio station call letters*]
WPEL-FM ...	Montrose, PA [*FM radio station call letters*]
WPEN	Philadelphia, PA [*AM radio station call letters*]
WPEO	Peoria, IL [*AM radio station call letters*]
WPEP.......	Taunton, MA [*AM radio station call letters*]
WPES.......	Ashland, VA [*AM radio station call letters*]
WPET.......	Greensboro, NC [*AM radio station call letters*]
WPET.......	Western Petroleum Corp. [*NASDAQ symbol*] (NQ)
W Petro 2000 ...	World Petroleum Availability 1980-2000 [*A publication*]
WPeW	Waukesha County Technical Institute, Pewaukee, WI [*Library symbol*] [*Library of Congress*] (LCLS)
WPEX.......	Hampton, VA [*AM radio station call letters*]
WPEZ.......	Macon, GA [*FM radio station call letters*]
WPF..........	War and Peace Foundation (EA)
WPF..........	Watcor Purification Systems, Inc. [*Vancouver Stock Exchange symbol*]
WPF..........	Weather Profile Facility
WPF..........	Weight, Power, Fulcrum
WPF..........	Whale Protection Fund (EA)
WPF..........	Wirtschaftspruefung [*A publication*]
WPF..........	Work Process Flow [*NASA*] (NASA)
WPF..........	World Peace Foundation (EA)
WPF..........	World Prohibition Federation
WPF..........	Worldwide Pen Friends (EA)
WPFA.......	Pensacola, FL [*AM radio station call letters*]
WPFA.......	William Penn Fraternal Association [*Later, WPA*] (EA)
WPFB	Middletown, OH [*AM radio station call letters*]
WPFB-FM ...	Middletown, OH [*FM radio station call letters*]
WPFC.......	Commission for Fisheries Research in the West Pacific
WPFC.......	Waterproof Fan Cooled (MSA)
WPFC.......	Westbeth Playwrights Feminist Collective [*Defunct*] (EA)
WPFC.......	William Perry Fan Club (EA)
WPFC.......	World Press Freedom Committee (EA)
WPFD.......	Fairview, TN [*AM radio station call letters*]
WPFDM......	Working Papers. Fondazione Dalle Molle [*A publication*]
WPFILD....	West Point Fellowship in Leader Development [*US Military Academy*] (INF)
WPFL.......	Fuiloro [*East Timor*] [*ICAO location identifier*] (ICLI)
WPFL.......	West Pakistan Federation of Labor
WPFL.......	Winter Park, FL [*FM radio station call letters*]
WPFL.......	Worshipful (ROG)
WPFM.......	Panama City, FL [*FM radio station call letters*]
WPFM.......	Wiping Form (AAG)
WPFR-FM ...	Terre Haute, IN [*FM radio station call letters*]
WPFT........	Baton Rouge, LA [*Television station call letters*]
WPFTA	White Plate Flat Trackers Association (EA)

WPFUL.....	Worshipful
WPFW.......	Washington, DC [*FM radio station call letters*]
WPG..........	Waterproofing (AAG)
WPG..........	Weighted Pair Group
WPG..........	West Point Graduate
WPG........	Wiping (MSA)
WPG..........	Worcester Polytechnic Institute, Worcester, MA [*OCLC symbol*] (OCLC)
WPG..........	Work Package Grouping [*NASA*] (NASA)
WPGA.......	Perry, GA [*AM radio station call letters*]
WPGA-FM ...	Perry, GA [*FM radio station call letters*]
WPGC.......	Morningside, MD [*AM radio station call letters*]
WPGC-FM ...	Morningside, MD [*FM radio station call letters*]
WPGD.......	Hendersonville, TN [*Television station call letters*]
WPGH-TV ..	Pittsburgh, PA [*Television station call letters*]
WPGI........	Western Publishing Group, Incorporated [*New York, NY*] [*NASDAQ symbol*] (NQ)
WPGM......	Danville, PA [*AM radio station call letters*]
WPGM-FM ...	Danville, PA [*FM radio station call letters*]
WPGO.......	Shallotte, NC [*FM radio station call letters*]
WPGP.......	Pendleton, SC [*AM radio station call letters*]
WPGR.......	Philadelphia, PA [*AM radio station call letters*]
WPGS.......	Mims, FL [*AM radio station call letters*]
WPGT	Group Fore - Women's Pro Golf Tour (EA)
WPGT	Roanoke Rapids, NC [*FM radio station call letters*]
WPGU	Urbana, IL [*FM radio station call letters*]
WPGW......	Portland, IN [*AM radio station call letters*]
WPGW-FM ...	Portland, IN [*FM radio station call letters*]
W & PH	Wage and Purchase Hire
WPH..........	West Pit [*Hawaii*] [*Seismograph station code, US Geological Survey*] [*Closed*] (SEIS)
WPH..........	William Penn House (EA)
WPH..........	WPL Holdings [*NYSE symbol*] (SPSG)
WPHB......	Philipsburg, PA [*AM radio station call letters*]
WPHB-FM ...	Philipsburg, PA [*FM radio station call letters*]
WPHC.......	Waverly, TN [*AM radio station call letters*]
WPHE.......	Phoenixville, PA [*AM radio station call letters*]
WPHI.......	Western Pennsylvania Horological Institute
WPHK.......	Blountstown, FL [*AM radio station call letters*]
WPHL-TV ...	Philadelphia, PA [*Television station call letters*]
WPHM......	Port Huron, MI [*AM radio station call letters*]
WPHM......	Western Pennsylvania Historical Magazine [*A publication*]
WPHN.......	Gaylord, MI [*FM radio station call letters*]
WPHOA.....	Women Public Health Officer's Association [*British*]
WPHP	Wheeling, WV [*FM radio station call letters*]
WPHR.......	Cleveland, OH [*FM radio station call letters*]
WPHS	Warren, MI [*FM radio station call letters*]
WPHUJ	Working Papers. Hebrew University of Jerusalem [*A publication*]
WPI	Wall Paper Institute [*Later, Wallcovering Manufacturers Association*] (EA)
WPI	Waxed Paper Institute [*Later, FPA*] (EA)
WPI	Wedding Photographers International (EA)
WPI	West Pride Industry [*Vancouver Stock Exchange symbol*]
WPI	Western Personality Inventory [*Psychology*]
WPI	Whey Products Institute [*Later, ADPI*] (EA)
WPI	Wholesale Price Index [*Economics*]
WPI	Women and Priests Involved (EA)
WPI	Women's Peace Initiative (EA)
WPI	Worcester Polytechnic Institute [*Massachusetts*]
WPI	Work Process Indicator (NASA)
WPI	Work Progress Indicator [*NASA*] (NASA)
WPI	World Patents Index [*Derwent Publications Ltd.*] [*Database*]
WPI	World Peace One [*An association*] (EA)
WPI	World Policy Institute (EA)
WPI	World Press Institute (EA)
WPIC.......	Sharon, PA [*AM radio station call letters*]
WPIC........	Western Psychiatric Institute and Clinic [*University of Pittsburgh*] [*Research center*] (RCD)
WPID	Piedmont, AL [*AM radio station call letters*]
WPIE........	Trumansburg, NY [*AM radio station call letters*]
WPIG........	Olean, NY [*FM radio station call letters*]
WPIO	Titusville, FL [*FM radio station call letters*]
WPIQ	Brunswick, GA [*AM radio station call letters*]
WP/IS	Word Processing and Information Systems [*A publication*]
WPIT........	Pittsburgh, PA [*AM radio station call letters*]
WPIT-FM ...	Pittsburgh, PA [*FM radio station call letters*]
WPIX........	New York, NY [*Television station call letters*]
WPJ..........	Weakened Plane Joint
WPJB	Narragansett Pier, RI [*FM radio station call letters*]
WPJC	Adjuntas, PR [*AM radio station call letters*]
WPJK	Orangeburg, SC [*AM radio station call letters*]
WPJL	Raleigh, NC [*AM radio station call letters*]
WPJM.......	Greer, SC [*AM radio station call letters*]
WPK.........	Air-Lift Associates, Inc. [*Morrisville, NC*] [*FAA designator*] (FAAC)
WPK	Winpak Ltd. [*Toronto Stock Exchange symbol*]
WPKE........	Pikeville, KY [*AM radio station call letters*]
WPKM	Scarborough, ME [*FM radio station call letters*]
WPKN	Bridgeport, CT [*FM radio station call letters*]
WPKO-FM ...	Bellefontaine, OH [*FM radio station call letters*]
WPKT........	Middlefield, CT [*FM radio station call letters*]
WPKY.......	Princeton, KY [*AM radio station call letters*]
WPKY-FM ..	Princeton, KY [*FM radio station call letters*]
WPKZ.......	Elkton, VA [*FM radio station call letters*]
WPL..........	War Plan, Long-Range (CINC)
WPL..........	Warren Public Library, Warren, OH [*OCLC symbol*] (OCLC)
WPL..........	Waste Pickle Liquor [*Industrial waste*]
WPL..........	Wave Propagation Laboratory [*Boulder, CO*] [*National Oceanic and Atmospheric Administration*]
WPL..........	Winnipeg Public Library [*UTLAS symbol*]
WPL..........	Working Papers in Linguistics [*A publication*]
WPL..........	Worshipful
WPL..........	Worst Path Loss
WPLA........	Plant City, FL [*AM radio station call letters*]
WPlaU......	University of Wisconsin-Platteville, Platteville, WI [*Library symbol*] [*Library of Congress*] (LCLS)
WPLB-FM ...	Greenville, MI [*FM radio station call letters*]
WPLC........	Spotsylvania, VA [*FM radio station call letters*]
WPLG........	Miami, FL [*Television station call letters*]
WPLH	Tifton, GA [*FM radio station call letters*]
WPLJ	New York, NY [*FM radio station call letters*]
WPLJ	White Port and Lemon Juice [*Title of both song and drink*]
WPLM.......	Plymouth, MA [*AM radio station call letters*]
WPLM-FM ...	Plymouth, MA [*FM radio station call letters*]
WPLN	Nashville, TN [*FM radio station call letters*]
WPLO	Water Port Liaison Office [*or Officer*] [*Air Force*] (AFM)
WPLR.......	New Haven, CT [*FM radio station call letters*]
WPLS	Western Plains Library System [*Library network*]
WPLS-FM ...	Greenville, SC [*FM radio station call letters*]
WPLT........	Plattsburgh, NY [*FM radio station call letters*]
WPLTO.....	Western Plateau [*FAA*] (FAAC)
WPLU	Working Papers. Lund University. Department of Linguistics [*A publication*]
WPLUH	Working Papers in Linguistics (University of Hawaii) [*A publication*]
WPLV.......	West Point, GA [*AM radio station call letters*]
WPLW.......	Carnegie, PA [*AM radio station call letters*]
WPLX........	Germantown, TN [*AM radio station call letters*]
WPLY	Plymouth, WI [*AM radio station call letters*]
WPlyM	Mission House Theological Seminary, Plymouth, WI [*Library symbol*] [*Library of Congress*] (LCLS)
WPLZ-FM ...	Petersburg, VA [*FM radio station call letters*]
WPM.........	War Plan, Mid-Range
WPM.........	War Planning Memorandum (NATG)
WPM.........	Waterproof Membrane
WPM.........	West Point-Pepperell, Inc. [*NYSE symbol*] (SPSG)
WPM.........	Western Premium [*Vancouver Stock Exchange symbol*]
WPM.........	White Pine [*Michigan*] [*Seismograph station code, US Geological Survey*] (SEIS)
WPM.........	Wipim [*Papua New Guinea*] [*Airport symbol*] (OAG)
WPM.........	Wire-Wound Porous Material
WPM........	Wood Plastic Material
WPM........	Words per Minute
WPM........	Work Package Management (MCD)
WPM.........	World Presbyterian Missions (EA)
WPM.........	Write Program Memory [*Data processing*]
WPM.........	Write Protect Memory
WPMA	Waterproof Paper Manufacturers Association [*Later, API*]
WPMA	Windows/Presentation Manager Association (EA)
WPMA	Wood Products Manufacturers Association (EA)
WPMA	Writing Paper Manufacturers Association [*Later, API*] (EA)
WPMB	Vandalia, IL [*AM radio station call letters*]
WPMC	Jellico, TN [*Television station call letters*]
WPMC	Waxed Paper Merchandising Council [*Defunct*]
WPMCP.....	Work Package Manpower and Cost Plan [*NASA*] (NASA)
WPME	Women for Peace in the Middle East (EA)
WPMH......	Portsmouth, VA [*AM radio station call letters*]
WPMI.......	Mobile, AL [*Television station call letters*]
WPMN.......	Maliana [*East Timor*] [*ICAO location identifier*] (ICLI)
WPMRR......	Work Package Milestone Progress Report (MCD)
WPMT	York, PA [*Television station call letters*]
WPMW.....	Mullens, WV [*FM radio station call letters*]
WPN.........	Weapon (AAG)
WPN.........	Weapons Procurement, Navy (NVT)
WPN.........	Wolverhampton [*British depot code*]
WPN.........	Write Punch [*Data processing*] (MCD)
WPNA	Oak Park, IL [*AM radio station call letters*]
WPNA	World Proof Numismatic Association (EA)
WPNC	Plymouth, NC [*AM radio station call letters*]
WPNC-FM ...	Plymouth, NC [*FM radio station call letters*]
WPNE	Green Bay, WI [*Television station call letters*]
WPNE-FM ...	Green Bay, WI [*FM radio station call letters*]
WPNF.......	Brevard, NC [*AM radio station call letters*]
WPNFPT ..	Weapon Fly-to-Point (NVT)
WPNGL	Workpapers in Papua New Guinea Languages [*A publication*]
WPNH.......	Plymouth, NH [*AM radio station call letters*]
WPNH-FM ...	Plymouth, NH [*FM radio station call letters*]
WPNI	Kentland, IN [*FM radio station call letters*]
WPNL	Clinton, IN [*FM radio station call letters*]
WPNR	Weekblad voor Privaatrecht, Notariaat, en Registratie [*A publication*]

WPNR-FM ... Utica, NY [*FM radio station call letters*]
WPNSTA .. Weapons Station
WPNTS..... War Plan Naval Transportation Service
WPO......... War Plan Orange [*World War II*]
WPO......... Warsaw Pact Organization   (MCD)
WPO......... Washington Post Co. Class B [*NYSE symbol*]   (SPSG)
WPO......... Water for Peace Office [*Department of State*]
WPO......... Water Programs Office [*Environmental Protection Agency*]
WPO......... World Packaging Organization [*See also OME*] [*Paris, France*]   (EAIO)
WPO......... World Ploughing Organisation [*Carlisle, Cumbria, England*]   (EAIO)
WPOA....... Western Pacific Orthopaedic Association   (EA)
WPOB-FM ... Plainview, NY [*FM radio station call letters*]
WPOC....... Baltimore, MD [*FM radio station call letters*]
WPOC....... Oecussi [*East Timor*] [*ICAO location identifier*]   (ICLI)
WPOC....... Water and Pollution Control [*A publication*]
WPOCA .... Water Pollution Control [*Maidstone, England*] [*A publication*]
WPoCC...... ICA [*International Co-Operative Alliance*] Working Party on Co-Operative Communications   (EAIO)
WPoCP..... ICA [*International Co-Operative Alliance*] Working Party on Co-Operative Press [*Later, WPoCC*]   (EAIO)
WPOD....... Water Port of Debarkation   (AFM)
WPOE....... Water Port of Embarkation   (AFM)
WPOG....... Willard Pease Oil & Gas Co. [*NASDAQ symbol*]   (NQ)
WPOK....... Pontiac, IL [*AM radio station call letters*]
W Pol Q ..... Western Political Quarterly [*A publication*]
WPOM....... Riviera Beach, FL [*AM radio station call letters*]
WPON....... Pontiac, MI [*AM radio station call letters*]
WPOP .... Hartford, CT [*AM radio station call letters*]
WPOR .... Portland, ME [*AM radio station call letters*]
WPOR-FM ... Portland, ME [*FM radio station call letters*]
WPOS-FM ... Holland, OH [*FM radio station call letters*]
WPOW...... Miami, FL [*FM radio station call letters*]
WPP.......... UCLA [*University of California at Los Angeles*] Working Papers in Phonetics [*A publication*]
WPP.......... Wage Pause Program [*Business term*]   (ADA)
WPP.......... Washington Promotion Plan [*FAA*]   (FAAC)
WPP.......... Water Pump Package [*NASA*]
WPP.......... Waterproof Paper Packing
WPP.......... Weapon Position Preparation   (MCD)
WPP.......... Weapons Production Program
WPP.......... Web Printing Press
WPP.......... Weibull Probability Paper [*Statistics*]
WPP.......... Windward Passage Patrol [*Navy*]   (NVT)
WPP.......... Work Package Plan [*NASA*]   (NASA)
WPP.......... World Pen Pals   (EA)
WPP.......... Writing Proficiency Program [*Educational test*]
WPPA....... Pottsville, PA [*AM radio station call letters*]
WPPB-TV .. Boca Raton, FL [*Television station call letters*]
WPPC....... Penuelas, PR [*AM radio station call letters*]
WPPC....... Warning Point Photocell
WPPC....... West Penn Power Company
WPPC....... West Point Parents Club   (EA)
WPPD....... Whole-Powder-Pattern Decomposition [*Crystallography*]
WPPDA..... Welfare and Pension Plans Disclosure Act [*1958*] [*Department of Labor*]
WPPG....... WPP Group PLC [*NASDAQ symbol*]   (NQ)
WPPI........ Carrollton, GA [*AM radio station call letters*]
WPP/IS..... Writing Proficiency Program/Intermediate System [*Educational test*]
WPPL........ Blue Ridge, GA [*FM radio station call letters*]
WPPM....... Weight Part per Million
WPPO .... Wood Products Purchasing Office [*Defense Construction Supply Center*] [*Defense Supply Agency*]
WPPS....... Work Package Planning Sheet [*NASA*]   (NASA)
WPPSI....... Wechsler Preschool and Primary Scale of Intelligence [*Education*]
WPPSS...... Washington Public Power Supply System [*Nicknamed "Whoops"*]
WPPW....... Association of Western Pulp and Paper Workers
WPQ........ Western Political Quarterly [*A publication*]
WPQR .... Welding Procedure Qualification Record [*Nuclear energy*]   (NRCH)
WPQR-FM ... Uniontown, PA [*FM radio station call letters*]
WPR .... Ward Pound Ridge [*New York*] [*Seismograph station code, US Geological Survey*]   (SEIS)
WPR .... Wartime Personnel Requirements   (NATG)
WPR .... Webster's Patent Reports [*England*] [*A publication*]   (DLA)
WPR .... Weekblad voor Privaatrecht, Notariaat, en Registratie [*A publication*]
WPR .... Weekly Pharmacy Reports: The Green Sheet [*A publication*]
WPR .... White Puerto Rican
WPR .... Widescope Resources Ltd. [*Vancouver Stock Exchange symbol*]
WPR .... Witness Protection and Relocation [*Government agency in film "F/X"*]
WPR .... Woodpecker Repellent [*In company name, WPR Co.*]
WPR .... Working Party on Rationing [*Allied German Occupation Forces*]
WPR .... Working Pressure
WPRA .... Mayaguez, PR [*AM radio station call letters*]

WPRA .... Women's Professional Racquetball Association   (EA)
WPRA .... Women's Professional Rodeo Association   (EA)
WPRB....... Princeton, NJ [*FM radio station call letters*]
WPRC........ Lincoln, IL [*AM radio station call letters*]
WPRCDZ ... International Conference on Water Pollution Research. Proceedings [*A publication*]
WPRD .... Winter Park, FL [*AM radio station call letters*]
WPRE........ Prairie du Chien, WI [*AM radio station call letters*]
WPRE-FM .. Prairie du Chien, WI [*FM radio station call letters*]
WPRI........ Wartime Pacific Routing Instructions [*Navy*]
WPRI-TV .. Providence, RI [*Television station call letters*]
WPRJ .... Mount Pleasant, MI [*AM radio station call letters*]
WPRK........ Winter Park, FL [*FM radio station call letters*]
WPRL........ Lorman, MS [*FM radio station call letters*]
WPRL........ Water Pollution Research Laboratory [*British*]
WPRM-FM ... San Juan, PR [*FM radio station call letters*]
WPRN .... Butler, AL [*AM radio station call letters*]
WPRO .... Providence, RI [*AM radio station call letters*]
WPRO-FM ... Providence, RI [*FM radio station call letters*]
WPRP........ Ponce, PR [*AM radio station call letters*]
WPRQ........ Colonial Heights, TN [*AM radio station call letters*]
WPRR........ Altoona, PA [*FM radio station call letters*]
WPRS........ Paris, IL [*AM radio station call letters*]
WPRS........ Water and Power Resources Service [*Formerly, Bureau of Reclamation*] [*Department of the Interior*] [*Name changed back to Bureau of Reclamation, 1981*]
WPRS........ Wittenborn Psychiatric Rating Scale
WPRT........ Prestonsburg, KY [*AM radio station call letters*]
WPRV-TV ... Fajardo, PR [*Television station call letters*]
WPRW ...... Manassas, VA [*AM radio station call letters*]
WPRX........ Glasgow, KY [*FM radio station call letters*]
WPRY........ Perry, FL [*AM radio station call letters*]
WPRZ........ Warrenton, VA [*AM radio station call letters*]
WPS........... International Association of Word Processing Specialists [*Formerly, NAWPS*]   (EA)
WPS........... War Plan, Short-Range
WPS........... War Planning Slate   (CINC)
WPS........... Warner Publishing Services
WPS........... Waste Processing System [*Nuclear energy*]   (NRCH)
WPS........... Water Phase Salt [*of smoked food*]
WPS........... Water Pressure Switch
WPS........... Water Purification System
WPS........... Watermen's Protective Society [*A union*] [*British*]
WPS........... Waterproof Shroud
WPS........... Watts per Steradian
WPS........... Wave Power Source
WPS........... Waveform Processing System
WPS........... Weapons Program Section
WPS........... Welding Procedure Specification [*Nuclear energy*]   (NRCH)
WPS........... White Power Structure
WPS........... Widowed Persons Service   (EA)
WPS........... Wind Power System
WPS........... Wireless Preservation Society [*British*]
WPS........... Wisconsin Public Service Corp. [*NYSE symbol*]   (SPSG)
WPS........... With Prior Service
WPS........... Women in Public Service   (EA)
WPS........... Women's Peace Army [*Australia*]
WPS........... Word Processing System   (BUR)
WPS........... Words per Second
WPS........... Workstation Publishing Software
WPS........... World Photography Society   (EA)
WPS........... World Politics Simulation
WPS........... World Population Society   (EA)
WPS........... Worldwide Plug and Socket [*Proposed standard electrical plug for international use*] [*Pronounced "whoops"*]
WPSA........ Paul Smith's, NY [*FM radio station call letters*]
WPSA........ Welsh Pony Society of America [*Later, WPCSA*]   (EA)
WPSA........ World Professional Squash Association   (EA)
WPSA........ World's Poultry Science Association [*See also AVI*] [*Celle, Federal Republic of Germany*]   (EAIO)
WPSA........ World's Poultry Science Association, USA Branch   (EA)
WPSC....... Pageland, SC [*AM radio station call letters*]
WPSC....... Shipping Control War Plan [*Navy*]
WPSC-FM ... Wayne, NJ [*FM radio station call letters*]
WPSD-TV ... Paducah, KY [*Television station call letters*]
WPSI........ Word Processing Society, Incorporated   (EA)
WPSI........ World Poetry Society Intercontinental   (EA)
WPSK-FM ... Pulaski, VA [*FM radio station call letters*]
WPSL........ Port St. Lucie, FL [*AM radio station call letters*]
WPSL........ Western Primary Standard Laboratory
WPSM....... Fort Walton Beach, FL [*FM radio station call letters*]
WPSM....... Same [*East Timor*] [*ICAO location identifier*]   (ICLI)
WPSO....... New Port Richey, FL [*AM radio station call letters*]
WPSR........ Evansville, IN [*FM radio station call letters*]
WPSR........ Weekly Performance Status Report   (MCD)
WPS-RA.... World Pro Skiing-Racers Association [*Defunct*]   (EA)
WPST....... Trenton, NJ [*AM radio station call letters*]
WPSU....... State College, PA [*FM radio station call letters*]
WPSX-TV ... Clearfield, PA [*Television station call letters*]
WPT .... Paper. European Journal for the Pulp, Paper, and Board Industries [*A publication*]

WP & T......	War Plans and Training
WPT	Waypoint (FAAC)
WPT	Western Personnel Tests [*General intelligence test*]
WPT	Windfall Profit Tax
WPT	With Promotion To (NOAA)
WPT	Wolfe Screening Test for Programming Aptitude
WPT	Word Processing Test
WPT	Workers' Party of Turkey
WPT	Working Point [*Technical drawings*]
WPTA.......	Fort Wayne, IN [*Television station call letters*]
WPTA.......	Wooden Pail and Tub Association
WPTB.......	Statesboro, GA [*AM radio station call letters*]
WPTB.......	Wartime Prices and Trade Board
WPTD	Kettering, OH [*Television station call letters*]
WPTF	National Council for a World Peace Tax Fund (EA)
WPTF	Raleigh, NC [*AM radio station call letters*]
WPTF-TV ...	Durham, NC [*Television station call letters*]
WPTG	West Point, VA [*FM radio station call letters*]
WPTI........	Wildlife Preservation Trust International (EA)
WPTJ	Johnstown, PA [*Television station call letters*]
WPTL	Canton, NC [*Television station call letters*]
WPTLC	World Peace through Law Center (EA)
WPTM	Roanoke Rapids, NC [*FM radio station call letters*]
WPTN	Cookeville, TN [*AM radio station call letters*]
WPTNG	Weapons Training (NVT)
WPTO	Oxford, OH [*Television station call letters*]
WPTR.......	Albany, NY [*AM radio station call letters*]
WPTR.......	Wespac Investors Trust II [*NASDAQ symbol*] (NQ)
WPTS-FM ...	Pittsburgh, PA [*FM radio station call letters*]
WPTT-TV ...	Pittsburgh, PA [*Television station call letters*]
WPTV.......	West Palm Beach, FL [*Television station call letters*]
WPTW	Piqua, OH [*AM radio station call letters*]
WPTX.......	Lexington Park, MD [*AM radio station call letters*]
WPTY-TV ...	Memphis, TN [*Television station call letters*]
WPTZ.......	North Pole, NY [*Television station call letters*]
WPU	We the People, United (EA)
WPU	With Power Unit (NATG)
WPU	Women's Protestant Union [*British*]
WPU	Write Punch [*Data processing*]
WPUB-FM ...	Camden, SC [*FM radio station call letters*]
WPUC	Waste-Paper Utilization Council [*Defunct*]
W/PUG	Word Processing Users' Group
WPUL	South Daytona, FL [*AM radio station call letters*]
WPUM	Rensselaer, IN [*FM radio station call letters*]
WPUR	Americus, GA [*FM radio station call letters*]
WPUT	Brewster, NY [*AM radio station call letters*]
WPUV	Pulaski, VA [*AM radio station call letters*]
WPVG	Boonsboro, MD [*AM radio station call letters*]
WPVI-TV ..	Philadelphia, PA [*Television station call letters*]
WPVM	Howland, ME [*FM radio station call letters*]
WPVQ	Vieques [*East Timor*] [*ICAO location identifier*] (ICLI)
WPVR.......	Roanoke, VA [*FM radio station call letters*]
WPW	Wolff-Parkinson-White [*Syndrome*] [*Cardiology*]
WPWB	Byron, GA [*AM radio station call letters*]
WPWC	Dumfries-Triangle, VA [*AM radio station call letters*]
WPWM	Wide Pulse Width Modulation
WPWOD...	Will Proceed Without Delay
WPWR	World-Wide Plantation Walker Registry (EA)
WPWR-TV ...	Gary, IN [*Television station call letters*]
WPWS......	Milledgeville, GA [*FM radio station call letters*]
WPWT	Philadelphia, PA [*FM radio station call letters*]
WPXC.......	Hyannis, MA [*FM radio station call letters*]
WPXI........	Pittsburgh, PA [*Television station call letters*]
WPXN	Paxton, IL [*FM radio station call letters*]
WPXR-FM ...	Rock Island, IL [*FM radio station call letters*]
WPXT.......	Portland, ME [*Television station call letters*]
WPXY.......	Rochester, NY [*AM radio station call letters*]
WPXY-FM ...	Rochester, NY [*FM radio station call letters*]
WPXZ-FM ...	Punxsutawney, PA [*FM radio station call letters*]
WPY	White Pass & Yukon Corp. Ltd. [*Toronto Stock Exchange symbol*] [*Vancouver Stock Exchange symbol*] [*AAR code*]
WPY	World Population Year [*1974*] [*United Nations*]
WPYB.......	Benson, NC [*AM radio station call letters*]
WPYEEJS ...	Working Papers in Yiddish and East European Jewish Studies [*A publication*]
WPYK.......	Dora, AL [*AM radio station call letters*]
WP&YR.....	White Pass & Yukon Railway [*Nickname: Wait Patiently and You'll Ride*]
WPYX.......	Albany, NY [*FM radio station call letters*]
WPZ	Waipapa Point [*New Zealand*] [*Seismograph station code, US Geological Survey*] [*Closed*] (SEIS)
WPZ	Wiener Praehistorische Zeitschrift [*A publication*]
WPZA.......	Ann Arbor, MI [*AM radio station call letters*]
WPZX.......	Oswego, NY [*FM radio station call letters*]
WPZZ.......	Franklin, IN [*FM radio station call letters*]
WQ	Bahamas World Airlines Ltd. [*ICAO designator*] (FAAC)
WQ	Science Wonder Quarterly [*A publication*]
WQ	Wilson Quarterly [*A publication*]
WQ	Wind Quarterly [*A publication*]
WQ	Wonder Stories Quarterly [*A publication*]
WQ	Wool Quarterly [*A publication*]

WQA.........	Water Quality Association (EA)
WQA.........	Weld Quality Assurance
WQAB.......	Philippi, WV [*FM radio station call letters*]
WQAD-TV ...	Moline, IL [*Television station call letters*]
WQAL.......	Cleveland, OH [*FM radio station call letters*]
WQAM.....	Miami, FL [*AM radio station call letters*]
WQAQ.......	Hamden, CT [*FM radio station call letters*]
WQAZ.......	Cleveland, MS [*FM radio station call letters*]
WQB.........	Water-Quality Biological [*Survey*] [*Army*] (RDA)
WQBA......	Miami, FL [*AM radio station call letters*]
WQBA-FM ...	Miami, FL [*FM radio station call letters*]
WQBB	Powell, TN [*AM radio station call letters*]
WQBC......	Vicksburg, MS [*AM radio station call letters*]
WQBE......	Charleston, WV [*AM radio station call letters*]
WQBE-FM ...	Charleston, WV [*FM radio station call letters*]
WQBH......	Detroit, MI [*AM radio station call letters*]
WQBK......	Rensselaer, NY [*AM radio station call letters*]
WQBK-FM ...	Rensselaer, NY [*FM radio station call letters*]
WQBN......	Temple Terrace, FL [*AM radio station call letters*]
WQBQ......	Leesburg, FL [*AM radio station call letters*]
WQBR......	Atlantic Beach, FL [*AM radio station call letters*]
WQBS	San Juan, PR [*AM radio station call letters*]
WQBZ.......	Fort Valley, GA [*FM radio station call letters*]
WQC.........	Quinsigamond Community College, Worcester, MA [*OCLC symbol*] (OCLC)
WQC.........	Water Quality Certification [*Nuclear energy*] (NRCH)
WQC..........	Wheat Quality Council (EA)
WQCB......	Brewer, ME [*FM radio station call letters*]
WQCD......	New York, NY [*FM radio station call letters*]
WQCH	La Fayette, GA [*AM radio station call letters*]
WQCK......	Clinton, LA [*FM radio station call letters*]
WQCM.....	Halfway, MD [*FM radio station call letters*]
WQCR.......	Burlington, VT [*FM radio station call letters*]
WQCS	Fort Pierce, FL [*FM radio station call letters*]
WQCT	Bryan, OH [*AM radio station call letters*]
WQCY.......	Quincy, IL [*FM radio station call letters*]
WQDK......	Ahoskie, NC [*FM radio station call letters*]
WQDR.......	Raleigh, NC [*FM radio station call letters*]
WQDY......	Calais, ME [*AM radio station call letters*]
WQDY-FM ...	Calais, ME [*FM radio station call letters*]
WQEC.......	Quincy, IL [*Television station call letters*]
WQEC/C...	Weapons Quality Engineering Center, Crane [*Indiana*]
WQED.......	Pittsburgh, PA [*Television station call letters*]
WQED-FM ...	Pittsburgh, PA [*FM radio station call letters*]
WQEL	Bucyrus, OH [*FM radio station call letters*]
WQEN......	Gadsden, AL [*FM radio station call letters*]
WQEQ......	Freeland, PA [*FM radio station call letters*]
WQEX.......	Pittsburgh, PA [*Television station call letters*]
WQEZ	Fort Myers Beach, FL [*FM radio station call letters*]
WQF.........	Wider Quaker Fellowship (EA)
WQFL........	Rockford, IL [*FM radio station call letters*]
WQFM......	Milwaukee, WI [*FM radio station call letters*]
WQFS........	Greensboro, NC [*FM radio station call letters*]
WQFX.......	Gulfport, MS [*AM radio station call letters*]
WQFX-FM ...	Gulfport, MS [*FM radio station call letters*]
WQGL.......	Butler, AL [*FM radio station call letters*]
WQGN-FM ...	Groton, CT [*FM radio station call letters*]
WQHI........	Lafayette, IN [*FM radio station call letters*]
WQHK......	Fort Wayne, IN [*AM radio station call letters*]
WQHL.......	Live Oak, FL [*AM radio station call letters*]
WQHL-FM ...	Live Oak, FL [*FM radio station call letters*]
WQHQ......	Ocean City-Salisbury, MD [*FM radio station call letters*]
WQHS......	Cleveland, OH [*Television station call letters*]
WQHT......	New York, NY [*FM radio station call letters*]
WQHY	Prestonsburg, KY [*FM radio station call letters*]
WQI..........	Water Quality Index
WQI..........	Water Quality Instrument
WQIC-FM ...	Marion, MS [*FM radio station call letters*]
WQID........	Biloxi, MS [*FM radio station call letters*]
WQII........	San Juan, PR [*AM radio station call letters*]
WQIK........	Jacksonville, FL [*AM radio station call letters*]
WQIK-FM ...	Jacksonville, FL [*FM radio station call letters*]
WQIN.......	Lykens, PA [*AM radio station call letters*]
WQIO.......	Mount Vernon, OH [*FM radio station call letters*]
WQIS........	Laurel, MS [*AM radio station call letters*]
WQIS........	Water Quality Insurance Syndicate (EA)
WQIX	Horseheads, NY [*FM radio station call letters*]
WQIZ	St. George, SC [*AM radio station call letters*]
WQJU	Mifflintown, PA [*FM radio station call letters*]
WQJY.......	West Salem, WI [*FM radio station call letters*]
WQKI	St. Matthews, SC [*AM radio station call letters*]
WQKK......	Metter, GA [*FM radio station call letters*]
WQKR.......	Portland, TN [*AM radio station call letters*]
WQKS	Hopkinsville, KY [*AM radio station call letters*]
WQKT	Wooster, OH [*FM radio station call letters*]
WQKX......	Sunbury, PA [*FM radio station call letters*]
WQKY	Emporium, PA [*FM radio station call letters*]
WQLA.......	La Follette, TN [*FM radio station call letters*]
WQLC.......	Watertown, FL [*FM radio station call letters*]
WQLK.......	Richmond, IN [*FM radio station call letters*]
WQLL	Sarasota, FL [*AM radio station call letters*]

WQLM-FM ... Punta Gorda, FL [*FM radio station call letters*]
WQLN....... Erie, PA [*Television station call letters*]
WQLN-FM ... Erie, PA [*FM radio station call letters*]
WQLR....... Kalamazoo, MI [*FM radio station call letters*]
WQLT....... Florence, AL [*FM radio station call letters*]
WQLX....... Galion, OH [*FM radio station call letters*]
WQM........ University of Massachusetts, Medical Center, Worcester, MA [*OCLC symbol*]   (OCLC)
WQM........ Water Quality Management
WQMA....... Marks, MS [*AM radio station call letters*]
WQMD..... Water Quantity Measuring Device
WQMF...... Jeffersonville, IN [*FM radio station call letters*]
WQMG...... Greensboro, NC [*AM radio station call letters*]
WQMG-FM ... Greensboro, NC [*FM radio station call letters*]
WQMP...... Water Quality Management Project
WQMR...... Mechanicsville, MD [*FM radio station call letters*]
WQMT...... Chatsworth, GA [*FM radio station call letters*]
WQMU ..... Indiana, PA [*FM radio station call letters*]
WQMX...... Medina, OH [*FM radio station call letters*]
WQMZ...... Charlottesville, VA [*FM radio station call letters*]
WQNA...... Springfield, IL [*FM radio station call letters*]
WQNS...... Waynesville, NC [*FM radio station call letters*]
WQNX...... Aberdeen, NC [*AM radio station call letters*]
WQNY...... Ithaca, NY [*FM radio station call letters*]
WQNZ...... Natchez, MS [*FM radio station call letters*]
WQO .... Water Quality Office [*Later, OWP*] [*Environmental Protection Agency*]
WQOK...... South Boston, VA [*FM radio station call letters*]
WQON ...... Grayling, MI [*FM radio station call letters*]
WQOW-TV ... Eau Claire, WI [*Television station call letters*]
WQOX...... Memphis, TN [*FM radio station call letters*]
WQPM...... Princeton, MN [*AM radio station call letters*]
WQPM-FM ... Princeton, MN [*FM radio station call letters*]
WQPN...... Moundsville, WV [*AM radio station call letters*]
WQPO...... Harrisonburg, VA [*FM radio station call letters*]
WQPR...... Muscle Shoals, AL [*FM radio station call letters*]
WQPT-TV ... Moline, IL [*Television station call letters*]
WQPW...... Valdosta, GA [*FM radio station call letters*]
WQQB....... Bowling Green, KY [*Television station call letters*]
WQQK...... Hendersonville, TN [*FM radio station call letters*]
WQQW ..... Waterbury, CT [*AM radio station call letters*]
WQQY...... Saratoga Springs, NY [*FM radio station call letters*]
WQRA...... Warrenton, VA [*FM radio station call letters*]
WQRC...... Barnstable, MA [*FM radio station call letters*]
WQRC....... Water Quality Research Council   (EA)
WQRF-TV ... Rockford, IL [*Television station call letters*]
WQRI .... Bristol, RI [*FM radio station call letters*]
WQRK...... Bedford, IN [*FM radio station call letters*]
WQRL...... Benton, IL [*FM radio station call letters*]
WQRM...... Smethport, PA [*FM radio station call letters*]
WQRP...... West Carollton, OH [*FM radio station call letters*]
WQRS .... Detroit, MI [*FM radio station call letters*]
WQRT...... Salamanca, NY [*FM radio station call letters*]
WQRX...... Valley Head, AL [*AM radio station call letters*]
WQSA...... Sarasota, FL [*AM radio station call letters*]
WQSB .... Albertville, AL [*FM radio station call letters*]
WQSC....... Andrews, SC [*AM radio station call letters*]
WQSF-FM ... Williamsburg, VA [*FM radio station call letters*]
WQSI........ Frederick, MD [*AM radio station call letters*]
WQSM...... Fayetteville, NC [*FM radio station call letters*]
WQSN....... Kalamazoo, MI [*AM radio station call letters*]
WQSR...... Catonsville, MD [*FM radio station call letters*]
WQSS........ Camden, ME [*FM radio station call letters*]
WQST ...... Forest, MS [*AM radio station call letters*]
WQST-FM ... Forest, MS [*FM radio station call letters*]
WQSU...... Selinsgrove, PA [*FM radio station call letters*]
WQT .... Water Quench Test
WQTC-FM ... Manitowoc, WI [*FM radio station call letters*]
WQTE ...... Adrian, MI [*FM radio station call letters*]
WQTI .... Marion, SC [*FM radio station call letters*]
WQTL....... Ottawa, OH [*FM radio station call letters*]
WQTO...... Ponce, PR [*Television station call letters*]
WQTQ...... Hartford, CT [*FM radio station call letters*]
WQTR...... Lake City, SC [*FM radio station call letters*]
WQTU...... Rome, GA [*FM radio station call letters*]
WQTV...... Boston, MA [*Television station call letters*]
WQTW...... Latrobe, PA [*AM radio station call letters*]
WQTY....... Linton, IN [*FM radio station call letters*]
WQTZ....... Decatur, IN [*FM radio station call letters*]
WQUE....... New Orleans, LA [*AM radio station call letters*]
WQUE-FM ... New Orleans, LA [*FM radio station call letters*]
WQUH...... De Funiak Springs, FL [*FM radio station call letters*]
WQUIS ..... Water Quality Indicator System [*Marine science*]   (MSC)
WQUT....... Johnson City, TN [*FM radio station call letters*]
WQVR...... Southbridge, MA [*FM radio station call letters*]
WQWK...... State College, PA [*FM radio station call letters*]
WQWM...... Kaukauna, WI [*AM radio station call letters*]
WQWQ ..... Muskegon Heights, MI [*FM radio station call letters*]
WQXB....... Grenada, MS [*FM radio station call letters*]
WQXC....... Otsego, MI [*AM radio station call letters*]
WQXC-FM ... Otsego, MI [*FM radio station call letters*]

WQXE....... Elizabethtown, KY [*FM radio station call letters*]
WQXI........ Atlanta, GA [*AM radio station call letters*]
WQXJ........ Clayton, GA [*FM radio station call letters*]
WQXK........ Salem, OH [*FM radio station call letters*]
WQXL ...... Columbia, SC [*AM radio station call letters*]
WQXM....... Gordon, GA [*AM radio station call letters*]
WQXM-FM ... Gordon, GA [*FM radio station call letters*]
WQXO....... Munising, MI [*AM radio station call letters*]
WQXO-FM ... Munising, MI [*FM radio station call letters*]
WQXR........ New York, NY [*AM radio station call letters*]
WQXR-FM ... New York, NY [*FM radio station call letters*]
WQXT .... Owego, NY [*FM radio station call letters*]
WQXX....... Morganton, NC [*FM radio station call letters*]
WQXY....... New Orleans, LA [*FM radio station call letters*]
WQXZ....... Taylorsville, NC [*AM radio station call letters*]
WQYK...... Seffner, FL [*AM radio station call letters*]
WQYK-FM ... St. Petersburg, FL [*FM radio station call letters*]
WQYX....... Clearfield, PA [*FM radio station call letters*]
WQZK-FM ... Keyser, WV [*FM radio station call letters*]
WQZQ........ Dickson, TN [*FM radio station call letters*]
WQZX....... Greenville, AL [*FM radio station call letters*]
WQZY....... Dublin, GA [*FM radio station call letters*]
WQZZ .... Sturgeon Bay, WI [*FM radio station call letters*]
WR............ Journal of Water Resources Planning and Management [*A publication*]
WR............ Sutherland's Weekly Report [*India*] [*A publication*]   (DLA)
WR............ Wagons-Restaurants [*Railroad dining cars in Europe*] [*French*]
WR............ Wall Receptacle   (MUGU)
WR............ War Reserve   (AABC)
WR............ War Risk
WR............ War Risk Insurance Decisions [*United States*] [*A publication*]   (DLA)
WR............ Wardrobe
WR............ Wardroom [*Navy*]
WR............ Warehouse Receipt [*Often negotiable*]
WR............ Warner-Lambert Pharmaceutical Co. [*Research code symbol*]
WR............ Wartime Report   (MCD)
WR............ Wartime Requirements [*Air Force document*]   (AFM)
W/R........... Was Received
WR............ Washington Report. News and World Report Newsletter [*A publication*]
WR............ Washout Rate
WR............ Washroom
WR............ Wassermann Reaction [*Test for syphilis*] [*Medicine*]
WR............ Water and Rail [*Transportation*]
W & R .... Water and Rail [*Transportation*]
WR............ Water Repellant [*Technical drawings*]
W/R........... Water/Rock [*Ratio*] [*Geochemistry*]
WR............ Wave Retardation   (DEN)
WR............ Waveguide, Rectangular
WR............ Weapon Radius   (NVT)
WR............ Weapon Range   (NATG)
WR............ Weapons Requirement [*DoD*]
WR............ Wear Resistant
WR............ Weather Reconnaissance
WR............ Weather Resistant   (MSA)
WR............ Weekly Record [*A publication*]
WR............ Weekly Reporter [*England*] [*A publication*]   (DLA)
WR............ Weekly Reporter [*Bengal*] [*A publication*]   (DLA)
WR............ Weekly Reporter, Cape Provincial Division [*South Africa*] [*A publication*]   (DLA)
WR............ Weekly Review [*A publication*]
WR............ Welfare Recipient   (OICC)
W & R .... Welfare and Recreation [*Navy*]
WR............ Wendell's Reports [*1826-41*] [*New York*] [*A publication*]   (DLA)
WR............ Western Review [*A publication*]
WR............ West's English Chancery Reports Tempore Hardwicke [*1736-39*] [*A publication*]   (DLA)
WR............ Wet Runway [*Aviation*]   (FAAC)
W/R........... White Room [*NASA*]   (KSC)
WR............ Whiteshell Reactor [*Canada*]
WR............ Whole Rock [*Geology*]
WR............ Wide Range [*Nuclear energy*]   (NRCH)
WR............ Wide Receiver [*Football*]
WR............ Wild Rose Resources [*Vancouver Stock Exchange symbol*]
WR............ Willelmus Rex [*King William*]
WR............ Wilson Repeater   (IEEE)
WR............ Wiping Reflex [*Physiology*]
WR............ Wire Recorder   (DEN)
WR............ Wire Rope   (AAG)
WR............ Wirral Railway [*British*]   (ROG)
WR............ Wisconsin Reports [*A publication*]   (DLA)
WR............ Wiseman Review [*A publication*]
WR............ Wissenschaftsrat [*Science Council*] [*Germany*]
WR............ With Rights [*Securities*]
WR............ Wolf-Raye [*Star classification*]
WR............ Wolseley Register   (EA)
WR............ Women's Reserve [*Navy*]
WR............ Women's Review [*A publication*]
WR............ Women's Roundtable   (EA)

WR.............. Woodmen Rangers   (EA)
WR.............. Word Restoration
WR.............. Work Request   (MCD)
WR.............. Work Requirement   (CAAL)
WR.............. Working Register
WR.............. World Reporter [*World Council of Credit Unions*] [*A publication*]
WR.............. World River [*Geology*]
WR.............. Worthington Register   (EA)
WR.............. Wrap
WR.............. Wrench   (MSA)
Wr.............. Wright [*Blood group*]
Wr.............. Wright's Reports [*37-50 Pennsylvania*] [*A publication*]   (DLA)
WR.............. Wrist [*Medicine*]
WR.............. Wrist Roll   (NASA)
WR.............. Write
WR.............. Writer   (MSA)
wr.............. Wrong
WR2.......... Warramunga Array [*Australia*] [*Seismograph station code, US Geological Survey*]   (SEIS)
WRA.......... Walter Reed Army Medical Center, Washington, DC [*OCLC symbol*]   (OCLC)
WRA.......... War Relocation Authority [*Within Office of Emergency Management*] [*To provide for the relocation of persons whose removal seemed necessary for national security, and for their maintenance and supervision*] [*World War II*]
WRA.......... War Reserve Allowance   (CINC)
WRA.......... Ward Room Attendant [*British military*]   (DMA)
WRA.......... Warramunga Array [*Australia*] [*Seismograph station code, US Geological Survey*]   (SEIS)
WRA.......... Waste Regulation Authority [*United Kingdom*]
WRA.......... Water Research Association [*British*]   (DCTA)
WRA.......... Water Resources Abstracts [*Database*] [*A publication*]
WRA.......... Weapons Replaceable [*or Replacement*] Assembly
WRA.......... Western Railroad Association   (EA)
WRA.......... Western Range Association   (EA)
WRA.......... Whiteware Research Association [*Defunct*]   (EA)
WRA.......... Windarra Minerals Ltd. [*Vancouver Stock Exchange symbol*] [*Toronto Stock Exchange symbol*]
WRA.......... With the Rule Astigmatism [*Ophthalmology*]
WRA.......... Women's Rabbinic Alliance [*Later, WSA*]   (EA)
WRA.......... Work Related Abstracts [*A publication*]
WRAA........ Luray, VA [*AM radio station call letters*]
WRAANC ... Women's Royal Australian Army Nursing Corps
WRAB....... Arab, AL [*AM radio station call letters*]
WRABD .... Wilhelm Roux' Archives of Developmental Biology [*A publication*]
WRABDT ... Roux's Archives of Developmental Biology [*A publication*]
WR/ABPR ... Weekly Record/American Book Publishing Record [*A publication*]
WRac......... Racine Public Library, Racine, WI [*Library symbol*] [*Library of Congress*]   (LCLS)
WRAC....... Water and Resources Advisory Committee [*Australian Environment Council*]
WRAC....... West Union, OH [*FM radio station call letters*]
WRAC....... Willow Run Aeronautical Center [*Michigan*]   (MCD)
WRAC....... Women's Royal Army Corps [*British*]
WRacC....... Racine County Institutions Medical Library, Racine, WI [*Library symbol*] [*Library of Congress*]   (LCLS)
WRacCL... Racine County Law Library, Racine, WI [*Library symbol*] [*Library of Congress*]   (LCLS)
WRacD ...... DeKoven Foundation for Church Work, Racine, WI [*Library symbol*] [*Library of Congress*]   (LCLS)
WRACELD ... Wounds Received in Action [*Incurred in*] Combat with the Enemy or in Line of Duty [*Army*]   (AABC)
WRacGS.... Girl Scouts of Racine County, Racine, WI [*Library symbol*] [*Library of Congress*]   (LCLS)
WRacJ .... S. C. Johnson & Son, Inc., Racine, WI [*Library symbol*] [*Library of Congress*]   (LCLS)
WRacSD.... Racine Unified School District Number One, Racine, WI [*Library symbol*] [*Library of Congress*]   (LCLS)
WRacSL .... Saint Luke's Memorial Hospital, School of Nursing, Racine, WI [*Library symbol*] [*Library of Congress*]   (LCLS)
WRacSM... Saint Mary's Hospital, Racine, WI [*Library symbol*] [*Library of Congress*]   (LCLS)
WRacWa .. Walker Manufacturing Co., Racine, WI [*Library symbol*] [*Library of Congress*]   (LCLS)
WRacWM ... Wustum Museum of Fine Arts, Racine, WI [*Library symbol*] [*Library of Congress*]   (LCLS)
WRacWP... Western Publishing Co., Inc., Racine, WI [*Library symbol*] [*Library of Congress*]   (LCLS)
WRacY ...... Young Radiator Co., Racine, WI [*Library symbol*] [*Library of Congress*]   (LCLS)
WRAD....... Radford, VA [*AM radio station call letters*]
WRAF....... Toccoa Falls, GA [*FM radio station call letters*]
WRAF....... Women's Royal Air Force [*British*]
WRAFVR.. Women's Royal Air Force Volunteer Reserve [*British military*]   (DMA)
WRAG....... Carrollton, AL [*AM radio station call letters*]
WRAI .... San Juan, PR [*AM radio station call letters*]
WRAIN ..... Walter Reed Army Institute of Nursing   (AABC)

WRAIR...... Walter Reed Army Institute of Research [*Washington, DC*]   (MCD)
WRAIS..... Wide Range Analog Input Subsystem
WRAJ....... Anna, IL [*AM radio station call letters*]
WRAJ-FM ... Anna, IL [*FM radio station call letters*]
WRAK....... Williamsport, PA [*AM radio station call letters*]
WRAL .... Raleigh, NC [*FM radio station call letters*]
WRALC.... Warner Robins Air Logistics Center [*Formerly, WRAMA*]   (MCD)
WRAL-TV ... Raleigh, NC [*Television station call letters*]
WRAM...... Monmouth, IL [*AM radio station call letters*]
WRAM...... Water Resources Assessment Methodology [*Army Corps of Engineers*]
WRAM..... Wide-Range Recording and Monitoring [*System*] [*Radiation*]
WRAMA .. Warner Robins Air Materiel Area [*Later, WRALC*]
WRAMC .. Walter Reed Army Medical Center
WRAMC Prog Notes ... WRAMC [*Walter Reed Army Medical Center*] Progress Notes [*A publication*]
WRANG.... Wrangler   (ROG)
WRANS .... Women's Royal Australian Naval Service
WRAP .... Waste Reduction Assessments Program [*Environmental Protection Agency*]
WRAP .... Water Reactor Analysis Program [*Nuclear energy*]   (NRCH)
WRAP .... Weapons Readiness Achievement Program   (MUGU)
WRAP .... Weapons Readiness Analysis Program [*Navy*]
WRAP .... Women's Radical Action Project [*Feminist group*]
WRAP .... Woodland Resource Analysis Program [*Tennessee Valley Authority*]
WRAP .... Worker Readjustment Program [*Department of Labor*]
WRAP .... World Risk Analysis Package [*S. J. Rundt & Associates*] [*Information service or system*]   (IID)
WRAR ...... Tappahannock, VA [*AM radio station call letters*]
WRAR-FM ... Tappahannock, VA [*FM radio station call letters*]
WRAS........ Atlanta, GA [*FM radio station call letters*]
WRAS........ Women's Reserve Ambulance Society [*British*] [*World War I*]
WRASPD .. World Rehabilitation Association for the Psycho-Socially Disabled   (EA)
WRAT .... Wide-Range Achievement Test
Wrat-R..... Wide Range Achievement Test-Revised
WRAV ...... Ravena, NY [*FM radio station call letters*]
WRAW...... Reading, PA [*AM radio station call letters*]
WRAX ...... Bedford, PA [*FM radio station call letters*]
WRAY ...... Princeton, IN [*AM radio station call letters*]
WRAY-FM ... Princeton, IN [*FM radio station call letters*]
WRB.......... Macon/Warner Robins, GA [*Location identifier*] [*FAA*]   (FAAL)
WRB.......... Walter Reed Army Medical Center, Post/Patient Library, Washington, DC [*OCLC symbol*]   (OCLC)
WRB.......... War Refugee Board [*Terminated, 1945*]
WRB.......... Wardrobe   (MSA)
WRB.......... Warramunga Array [*Australia*] [*Seismograph station code, US Geological Survey*]   (SEIS)
WRB.......... Water Resources Board [*British*]   (DCTA)
WRBA .... Springfield, FL [*FM radio station call letters*]
WRBA .... World Robotic Boxing Association   (EA)
WRBB........ Banjarmasin/Syamsuddin Noor [*Indonesia*] [*ICAO location identifier*]   (ICLI)
WRBB........ Boston, MA [*FM radio station call letters*]
WRBC .... Batu Licin [*Indonesia*] [*ICAO location identifier*]   (ICLI)
WRBC .... Lewiston, ME [*FM radio station call letters*]
WRBC .... Weather Relay Broadcast Center
WRBD .... Pompano Beach, FL [*AM radio station call letters*]
WRBE........ Lucedale, MS [*AM radio station call letters*]
WRBH...... New Orleans, LA [*FM radio station call letters*]
WRBI........ Batesville, IN [*FM radio station call letters*]
WRBI........ Pangkalan Bun/Iskandar [*Indonesia*] [*ICAO location identifier*]   (ICLI)
WRBK ...... Flomaton, AL [*AM radio station call letters*]
WRBK .... Kotabaru/Setagen [*Indonesia*] [*ICAO location identifier*]   (ICLI)
WRBL........ Columbus, GA [*Television station call letters*]
WRBM ...... Muaratewe/Beringin [*Indonesia*] [*ICAO location identifier*]   (ICLI)
WRBN .... Tanjung/Warukin [*Indonesia*] [*ICAO location identifier*]   (ICLI)
WRBND .... Wire Bound
WRBP........ Palangkaraya/Panarung [*Indonesia*] [*ICAO location identifier*]   (ICLI)
WRBQ .... St. Petersburg, FL [*AM radio station call letters*]
WRBQ-FM ... Tampa, FL [*FM radio station call letters*]
WRBR........ Richland, MS [*AM radio station call letters*]
WRBR .... Wright Brothers National Memorial
WRBS........ Baltimore, MD [*FM radio station call letters*]
WRBS........ Sampit/H. Hasan [*Indonesia*] [*ICAO location identifier*]   (ICLI)
WRBT........ Mt. Carmel, IL [*FM radio station call letters*]
WRBT........ Teluk Kepayang [*Indonesia*] [*ICAO location identifier*]   (ICLI)
WRBU .... Buntok/Sanggau [*Indonesia*] [*ICAO location identifier*]   (ICLI)
WRBZ........ Banjarmasin Sector [*Indonesia*] [*ICAO location identifier*]   (ICLI)
WRBZ........ Milford, OH [*FM radio station call letters*]

WRC.........	W. R. Carpenter Airlines [*Australia*]
WRC.........	War Resources Council [*Terminated*]
WRC.........	Washed Red Cells [*Medicine*]
WRC.........	Washington Research Council [*Research center*]　(RCD)
WRC.........	Water Research Centre [*Research center*] [*British*]　(IRC)
WRC.........	Water Resources Center [*University of Illinois*]
WRC.........	Water Resources Congress　(EA)
WRC.........	Water Resources Council [*Inactive*]
WRC.........	Water-Retention Coefficient
WRC.........	Weapons Release Computer [*or Controller*]
WRC.........	Weather Relay Center
WRC.........	Weekly Readiness Check
WRC.........	Welding Research Council　(EA)
WRC.........	Well to Right of Course [*Aviation*]　(FAAC)
WRC.........	Werewolf Research Center　(EA)
WRC.........	Wildland Resources Center [*University of California*] [*Research center*]　(RCD)
WRC.........	Wildlife Rehabilitation Council　(EA)
WRC.........	Williams Ranch [*California*] [*Seismograph station code, US Geological Survey*] [*Closed*]　(SEIS)
WRC.........	Wollongong Workers Research Centre [*Australia*]
WRC.........	Women's Relief Corps
WRC.........	Women's Rights Committee　(EA)
WRC.........	World Relief Canada
WRC.........	World Relief Corporation　(EA)
WRC.........	World Romani Congress
WRCA......	W. R. Carpenter Airlines [*Australia*]
WRCA......	Waltham, MA [*AM radio station call letters*]
WRCA......	Western Red Cedar Association　(EA)
WR Calc.....	Sutherland's Weekly Reporter, Calcutta [*India*] [*A publication*]　(DLA)
WRCB......	War Relief Control Board [*President's*]
WRCB-TV ...	Chattanooga, TN [*Television station call letters*]
WRCC......	Cape Coral, FL [*FM radio station call letters*]
WRCCC.....	Wheeler AFB Range Communications Control Center　(MCD)
WRCCHE ...	Western Regional Consortium, Librarians' Networking Committee [*Library network*]
WRCD......	Clyde, NY [*FM radio station call letters*]
WRCF.......	Whale Research and Conservation Fund　(EA)
WRCG......	Columbus, GA [*AM radio station call letters*]
WRCGR	Women's Reserve of the Coast Guard Reserve
Wr Ch	Wright's Ohio Reports [*1831-34*] [*A publication*]　(DLA)
WRCH-FM ...	New Britain, CT [*FM radio station call letters*]
WRCI.......	Hillsboro, NH [*FM radio station call letters*]
WRC Inf	WRC [*Water Research Centre*] Information [*A publication*]
WRCK......	Utica, NY [*FM radio station call letters*]
WRCLA.....	Western Red Cedar Lumber Association　(EA)
WRCN-FM ...	Riverhead, NY [*FM radio station call letters*]
WRCNS.....	Women's Royal Canadian Naval Service [*World War II*]
WRCO......	Richland Center, WI [*AM radio station call letters*]
WRCO-FM ...	Richland Center, WI [*FM radio station call letters*]
WRCP.......	Providence, RI [*AM radio station call letters*]
WRCPATT ...	World Rabbinic Committee for the Preservation of Ancient Tombs in Tiberias　(EA)
WRCQ-FM ...	Dunn, NC [*FM radio station call letters*]
WRCR......	Rushville, IN [*FM radio station call letters*]
WRCR.......	Wife's Restitution of Conjugal Rights [*Law suit*] [*British*]　(ROG)
WRCR.......	Wisconsin Railroad Commission Reports [*A publication*]　(DLA)
WRCR.......	Wyoming Resources Corporation [*NASDAQ symbol*]　(NQ)
WRC Research Report ...	Water Resources Center. Research Report [*A publication*]
WRCS.......	Ahoskie, NC [*AM radio station call letters*]
WRCS.......	Weapons Release Computer Set [*or System*]　(MCD)
WRCT.......	Pittsburgh, PA [*FM radio station call letters*]
WRC-TV ...	Washington, DC [*Television station call letters*]
WRCU-FM ...	Hamilton, NY [*FM radio station call letters*]
WRCW.......	Canton, OH [*AM radio station call letters*]
WRCZ.......	Pittsfield, MA [*FM radio station call letters*]
WRD.........	Warden [*Washington*] [*Seismograph station code, US Geological Survey*]　(SEIS)
WRD.........	Water Resources Division [*US Geological Survey*]
WRD.........	Words [*A publication*]
WRD.........	World's Fair [*A publication*]
WRD.........	Worm Runner's Digest [*A satirical publication*]
WRDB......	Reedsburg, WI [*AM radio station call letters*]
WRDB.......	Worldwide Water Resources Database
WRDC.......	Boyle, MS [*AM radio station call letters*]
WRDC.......	Western Rural Development Center [*Oregon State University*] [*Research center*]　(RCD)
WRDC.......	Westinghouse Research and Development Center　(MCD)
WRDC.......	Wool Research and Development Council [*Australia*]
WR & DC...	Wool Research and Development Council [*Australia*]
WRDC.......	Wright Research and Development Center [*Wright-Patterson Air Force Base*]　(GRD)
WRDG......	Burlington, NC [*Television station call letters*]
WRDI	We Remember Dean International　(EA)
WRDIR......	Wrong Direction
WRDJ........	Daleville, AL [*AM radio station call letters*]
WRDJ-FM ...	Bridgewater, VA [*FM radio station call letters*]

WRDL	Ashland, OH [*FM radio station call letters*]
WRDN.......	Durand, WI [*AM radio station call letters*]
WRDN-FM ...	Durand, WI [*FM radio station call letters*]
WRDR.......	Egg Harbor, NJ [*FM radio station call letters*]
WRDU.......	Wilson, NC [*FM radio station call letters*]
WRDV.......	Warminster, PA [*FM radio station call letters*]
WRDW......	Augusta, GA [*AM radio station call letters*]
WRDW-FM ...	Wrens, GA [*FM radio station call letters*]
WRDW-TV ...	Augusta, GA [*Television station call letters*]
WRDX.......	Salisbury, NC [*FM radio station call letters*]
WRDZ.......	Cleveland, OH [*AM radio station call letters*]
WRE	Tokyo Financial Review [*A publication*]
WRE	Washington Real Estate Investment Trust [*AMEX symbol*]　(SPSG)
WRE	Weapon Research Establishment
WRE	Whangarei [*New Zealand*] [*Airport symbol*]　(OAG)
WRE	Winston Resources Ltd. [*Vancouver Stock Exchange symbol*]
WREA	Dayton, TN [*AM radio station call letters*]
WREAFS...	Waste Reduction Evaluation at Federal Sites [*Environmental Protection Agency*]
WREB......	Holyoke, MA [*AM radio station call letters*]
WREC	Memphis, TN [*AM radio station call letters*]
WRECISS ...	Weapons Research Establishment Camera Interception Single Shot
WRECS......	Weapon Radiation Effects on Communications Systems　(MCD)
WRED	Gibsonville, OH [*FM radio station call letters*]
WREDAC ...	Weapons Research Establishment Digital Automatic Computer
WREE.......	Women for Racial and Economic Equality　(EA)
WREF........	Ridgefield, CT [*AM radio station call letters*]
WREFC.....	We Remember Elvis Fan Club　(EA)
WREF-FM ...	Sharon, CT [*FM radio station call letters*]
W/REG......	Window Regulator [*Automotive engineering*]
W Reg R.....	Wetboek van Registratierechten [*A publication*]
WREG-TV ...	Memphis, TN [*Television station call letters*]
WREH.......	Reston, VA [*AM radio station call letters*]
WREI........	Quebradillas, PR [*FM radio station call letters*]
WREI........	Wisconsin Real Estate Investment Trust [*NASDAQ symbol*]　(NQ)
WREI........	Women's Research and Education Institute　(EA)
WREK	Atlanta, GA [*FM radio station call letters*]
WREL.......	Lexington, VA [*AM radio station call letters*]
WREM	Monticello, ME [*AM radio station call letters*]
WREN.......	Topeka, KS [*AM radio station call letters*]
WRENACK ...	WREN [*Women's Royal Naval Service*] Assistant Cook [*British military*]　(DMA)
WRENAM ...	WREN [*Women's Royal Naval Service*] Air Mechanic [*British military*]　(DMA)
WRENCINE(AB) ...	WREN [*Women's Royal Naval Service*] Cinema Operator (Able) [*British military*]　(DMA)
WRENCINE(ORD) ...	WREN [*Women's Royal Naval Service*] Cinema Operator (Ordinary) [*British military*]　(DMA)
WRENCK ...	WREN [*Women's Royal Naval Service*] Cook [*British military*]　(DMA)
WRENDHYG ...	WREN [*Women's Royal Naval Service*] Dental Hygienist [*British military*]　(DMA)
WRENDSA ...	WREN [*Women's Royal Naval Service*] Dental Surgery Assistant [*British military*]　(DMA)
WRENEDUC ...	WREN [*Women's Royal Naval Service*] Education Assistant [*British military*]　(DMA)
WRENMET ...	WREN [*Women's Royal Naval Service*] Meteorological Observer [*British military*]　(DMA)
WRENMT ...	WREN [*Women's Royal Naval Service*] Motor Transport Driver [*British military*]　(DMA)
WRENPHOT ...	WREN [*Women's Royal Naval Service*] Photographer [*British military*]　(DMA)
WRENQA ...	WREN [*Women's Royal Naval Service*] Quarters Assistant [*British military*]　(DMA)
WREN(R) ...	WREN [*Women's Royal Naval Service*] (RADAR) [*British military*]　(DMA)
WRENREG ...	WREN [*Women's Royal Naval Service*] Regulating [*British military*]　(DMA)
WRENREM ...	WREN [*Women's Royal Naval Service*] Radio Electrical Mechanic [*British military*]　(DMA)
WRENRO(M)1 ...	WREN [*Women's Royal Naval Service*] Radio Operator (Morse) 1st Class [*British military*]　(DMA)
WRENRO(M)2 ...	WREN [*Women's Royal Naval Service*] Radio Operator (Morse) 2nd Class [*British military*]　(DMA)
WRENS.....	Women's Royal Naval Service [*Acronym is a phonetic reference to members of this British service branch*] [*Also, WRNS*]
WRENSA ...	WREN [*Women's Royal Naval Service*] Stores Accountant [*British military*]　(DMA)
WRENS(C) ...	WREN [*Women's Royal Naval Service*] Stores Assistant (Clothes) [*British military*]　(DMA)
WRENS(S) ...	WREN [*Women's Royal Naval Service*] Stores Assistant (Stores) [*British military*]　(DMA)
WRENSTD ...	WREN [*Women's Royal Naval Service*] Steward [*British military*]　(DMA)
WRENS(V) ...	WREN [*Women's Royal Naval Service*] Stores Assistant (Victualling) [*British military*]　(DMA)

WRENTEL ... WREN [*Women's Royal Naval Service*] Telephonist [*British military*]   (DMA)
WRENTSA ... WREN [*Women's Royal Naval Service*] Training Support Assistant [*British military*]   (DMA)
WRENWA ... WREN [*Women's Royal Naval Service*] Weapon Analyst [*British military*]   (DMA)
WRENWTR(G) ... WREN [*Women's Royal Naval Service*] Writer (General) [*British military*]   (DMA)
WRENWTR(P) ... WREN [*Women's Royal Naval Service*] Writer (Pay) [*British military*]   (DMA)
WRENWTR(S) ... WREN [*Women's Royal Naval Service*] Writer (Shorthand) [*British military*]   (DMA)
WREO-FM ... Ashtabula, OH [*FM radio station call letters*]
W Rep .... West's English Chancery Reports Tempore Hardwicke [*1736-39*] [*A publication*]   (DLA)
WRERA..... Water Resources Research [*A publication*]
WRES........ Cocoa, FL [*Television station call letters*]
WRESAT .. Weapons Research Establishment Satellite [*Australia*]
W Res L Rev ... Western Reserve Law Review [*A publication*]
WREST .... Washington Regional Engineers, Scientists, and Technicians
WREST .... Wide Range Employability Sample Test
Wrest .... Wrestling USA [*A publication*]
WRET....... Wespac Investors Trust III [*NASDAQ symbol*]   (NQ)
WRET-TV .. Spartanburg, SC [*Television station call letters*]
WREU .... Western Railway Employees' Union [*India*]
WREV .... Reidsville, NC [*AM radio station call letters*]
WREX ...... Wrexham [*City in Wales*]
WREX-TV ... Rockford, IL [*Television station call letters*]
WREY .... Millville, NJ [*AM radio station call letters*]
WREZ........ Metropolis, IL [*FM radio station call letters*]
WRF .... University of Wisconsin, River Falls, River Falls, WI [*OCLC symbol*]   (OCLC)
WRF .... Weak Radial Field
WRF .... Weibull Reliability Function [*Statistics*]
WRF .... Wheat Ridge Foundation   (EA)
WRF .... World Rehabilitation Fund   (EA)
WRF .... World Research Foundation   (EA)
WRFA........ Largo, FL [*AM radio station call letters*]
W R Far East ... Weekly Review of the Far East [*A publication*]
WRFB........ Stowe, VT [*FM radio station call letters*]
WRFC........ Athens, GA [*AM radio station call letters*]
WRFD ...... Columbus-Worthington, OH [*AM radio station call letters*]
WRFE........ Aguada, PR [*FM radio station call letters*]
WRFG .... Atlanta, GA [*FM radio station call letters*]
WRFL........ Lexington, KY [*FM radio station call letters*]
WRFM ...... Hialeah, FL [*AM radio station call letters*]
WRFR....... Franklin, NC [*FM radio station call letters*]
WRFS .... Garrisonville, VA [*AM radio station call letters*]
WRFT....... Indianapolis, IN [*FM radio station call letters*]
WRfU .... University of Wisconsin-River Falls, River Falls, WI [*Library symbol*] [*Library of Congress*]   (LCLS)
WRFW ...... River Falls, WI [*FM radio station call letters*]
WRFX........ Kannapolis, NC [*FM radio station call letters*]
WRFY-FM ... Reading, PA [*FM radio station call letters*]
WRG .... Wearing   (MSA)
WRG .... Westport Research Group [*Information service or system*]   (EISS)
WRG .... White River [*Alaska*] [*Seismograph station code, US Geological Survey*]   (SEIS)
WRG .... Wire Routing Guide   (MCD)
WRG .... Wiring
WRG .... Wrangell [*Alaska*] [*Airport symbol*]   (OAG)
WRG .... Wrangell, AK [*Location identifier*] [*FAA*]   (FAAL)
WRG .... Wrong [*Telecommunications*]   (TEL)
WRGA .... Rome, GA [*AM radio station call letters*]
WRGA .... Western River Guides Association   (EA)
WRGB .... Schenectady, NY [*Television station call letters*]
WRGC....... Sylva, NC [*AM radio station call letters*]
WRGH....... Walter Reed General Hospital   (MCD)
WRGM...... Ontario, OH [*AM radio station call letters*]
WRGN....... Sweet Valley, PA [*FM radio station call letters*]
WRGR .... Tupper Lake, NY [*FM radio station call letters*]
WRGR .... Wringer
WRGS .... Rogersville, TN [*AM radio station call letters*]
WRGT-TV ... Dayton, OH [*Television station call letters*]
WRh........... Rhinelander Public Library, Rhinelander, WI [*Library symbol*] [*Library of Congress*]   (LCLS)
WRH......... Warnkenhagen [*German Democratic Republic*] [*Geomagnetic observatory code*]
WRH......... William Randolph Hearst [*American newspaper publisher, 1863-1951*]
WRH......... World Radio Handbook
WRHB....... Barnesboro, PA [*FM radio station call letters*]
WRHC....... Coral Gables, FL [*AM radio station call letters*]
WRHD....... Riverhead, NY [*AM radio station call letters*]
WRHI....... Rock Hill, SC [*AM radio station call letters*]
WRHL....... Rochelle, IL [*AM radio station call letters*]
WRHL-FM ... Rochelle, IL [*FM radio station call letters*]
WRHM...... Lancaster, SC [*FM radio station call letters*]
WRHN ...... Rhinelander, WI [*FM radio station call letters*]
WRHO ...... Oneonta, NY [*FM radio station call letters*]

WRHP....... Syracuse, NY [*FM radio station call letters*]
WRHS...... Park Forest, IL [*FM radio station call letters*]
WRHT...... Morehead, NC [*FM radio station call letters*]
WRHU ...... Hempstead, NY [*FM radio station call letters*]
WRHX...... Herndon, VA [*AM radio station call letters*]
WRI .... International Water Resources Institute [*George Washington University*] [*Research center*]   (RCD)
WRI .... War Resisters International [*London, England*]
WRI .... War Risks Insurance [*British*]
WRI .... Water Research Institute [*West Virginia University*] [*Research center*]   (RCD)
WRI .... Water-Resources Investigation [*A publication*]
WRI .... Waterloo Research Institute [*University of Waterloo*] [*Research center*]   (RCD)
WRI .... Weatherstrip Research Institute
WRI .... Weingarten Realty, Incorporated [*NYSE symbol*]   (SPSG)
WRI .... Welfare Research, Incorporated   (EA)
WRI .... Western Research Institute [*Laramie, WY*] [*Department of Energy*]   (GRD)
WRI .... Wire Reinforcement Institute   (EA)
WRI .... Wire Rope Institute
WRI .... World Research, Incorporated [*San Diego, CA*]   (EA)
WRI .... World Resources Institute   (EA)
WRI .... Wrightstown, NJ [*Location identifier*] [*FAA*]   (FAAL)
WRIB....... Providence, RI [*AM radio station call letters*]
WRIC........ Richlands, VA [*AM radio station call letters*]
WRIE....... Erie, PA [*AM radio station call letters*]
WRIF........ Detroit, MI [*FM radio station call letters*]
WRIF........ Water Resources Information File [*Terrain Analysis Center*] [*Army*]
WRIG........ Schofield, WI [*AM radio station call letters*]
Wright........ Wright's Ohio Reports [*1831-34*] [*A publication*]   (DLA)
Wright........ Wright's Reports [*37-50 Pennsylvania*] [*A publication*]   (DLA)
Wright Ch ... Wright's Ohio Reports [*1831-34*] [*A publication*]   (DLA)
Wright Cr Cons ... Wright's Criminal Conspiracies [*1873*] [*A publication*]   (DLA)
Wright NP ... Wright's Ohio Nisi Prius Reports [*A publication*]   (DLA)
Wright (Ohio C) ... Wright's Ohio Reports [*A publication*]   (DLA)
Wright R .... Wright's Ohio Reports [*A publication*]   (DLA)
Wright's Rep ... Wright's Ohio Reports [*A publication*]   (DLA)
Wright St L ... Wright's Advice on the Study of the Law [*A publication*]   (DLA)
Wright Ten ... Wright on Tenures [*A publication*]   (DLA)
WRII.......... Waste Recovery, Incorporated [*Dallas, TX*] [*NASDAQ symbol*]   (NQ)
WRIJ .... Masontown, PA [*FM radio station call letters*]
WRIK .... Brookport, IL [*AM radio station call letters*]
WRIK-FM ... Metropolis, IL [*FM radio station call letters*]
WRIN .... Rensselaer, IN [*AM radio station call letters*]
WRINS...... Women's Royal Indian Naval Service [*British military*]   (DMA)
WRIO .... Ponce, PR [*FM radio station call letters*]
WRIOT ..... Wide Range Interest and Opinion Test
WRipC....... Ripon College, Ripon, WI [*Library symbol*] [*Library of Congress*]   (LCLS)
WRIPT ...... Wide Range Intelligence-Personality Test [*Personality development test*] [*Psychology*]
WRIQ .... Radford, VA [*FM radio station call letters*]
WRI Rep.... WRI [*Wattle Research Institute*] Report [*A publication*]
WRIS........ Roanoke, VA [*AM radio station call letters*]
WRIS........ Water Resources Information System   (NOAA)
WRISC ...... Western Regional Information Service Center [*University of California*] [*Information service or system*] [*Defunct*]   (IID)
WRISE ...... Waste Reduction Institute for Scientists and Engineers [*Environmental Protection Agency*]
WRIST ...... Women's Repetition Injury Support Team [*Australia*]
WRIS Technical Bulletin ... Water Resources Information System. Technical Bulletin [*A publication*]
WRIT........ Wright [*William E.*] Co. [*NASDAQ symbol*]   (NQ)
Writ Cent S ... Writers of the 21st Century. Series [*A publication*]
WRITE...... Waste Reduction Innovative Technology Evaluation [*Environmental Protection Agency*]
WRITG..... Writing   (ROG)
Writ Ring... Writers' Ring [*A publication*]
WRIU .... Kingston, RI [*FM radio station call letters*]
WRIU .... Write Interface Unit
WRIV .... Riverhead, NY [*AM radio station call letters*]
WRIX........ Homeland Park, SC [*AM radio station call letters*]
WRIX-FM ... Honea Path, SC [*FM radio station call letters*]
WRIZ-FM ... Lakeview, MI [*FM radio station call letters*]
WRJ.......... Wallraf-Richartz-Jahrbuch [*A publication*]
WRJA-FM ... Sumter, SC [*FM radio station call letters*]
WRJA-TV ... Sumter, SC [*Television station call letters*]
WRJB .... Camden, TN [*AM radio station call letters*]
WRJC........ Mauston, WI [*AM radio station call letters*]
WRJCD9... Water Pollution Research Journal of Canada [*A publication*]
WRJC-FM ... Mauston, WI [*FM radio station call letters*]
WRJH .... Brandon, MS [*FM radio station call letters*]
WRJI .... Crooksville, OH [*FM radio station call letters*]
WRJM-FM ... Geneva, AL [*FM radio station call letters*]
WRJM-TV ... Troy, AL [*Television station call letters*]

WRJN........ Racine, WI [*AM radio station call letters*]
WRJO .... Eagle River, WI [*FM radio station call letters*]
WRJQ........ Appleton, WI [*AM radio station call letters*]
WRJS .... Oil City, PA [*FM radio station call letters*]
WRJT .... Monterey, TN [*FM radio station call letters*]
WRJW....... Picayune, MS [*AM radio station call letters*]
WRJZ........ Knoxville, TN [*AM radio station call letters*]
WRK......... Wall & Redekop Corp. [*Toronto Stock Exchange symbol*]
            [*Vancouver Stock Exchange symbol*]
WRK......... Westdeutsche Rektorenkonferenz [*West German Standing
            Committee of University Heads*]
WRK......... Work (FAAC)
WRK......... Wrecker
WRKA...... Atambua/Haliwen [*Indonesia*] [*ICAO location
            identifier*] (ICLI)
WRKA...... St. Matthews, KY [*FM radio station call letters*]
WRKB ...... Bajawa/Padhameleda [*Indonesia*] [*ICAO location
            identifier*] (ICLI)
WRKB ...... Kannapolis, NC [*AM radio station call letters*]
WRKC ...... Maumere/Wai Oti [*Indonesia*] [*ICAO location
            identifier*] (ICLI)
WRKC ...... Wilkes-Barre, PA [*FM radio station call letters*]
WRKD...... Rockland, ME [*AM radio station call letters*]
WRKE ...... Ende/Ipi [*Indonesia*] [*ICAO location identifier*] (ICLI)
WRKE ...... Ocean View, DE [*FM radio station call letters*]
WRKF....... Baton Rouge, LA [*FM radio station call letters*]
WRKF....... Maskolen [*Indonesia*] [*ICAO location identifier*] (ICLI)
WRKG ...... Lorain, OH [*AM radio station call letters*]
WRKG ...... Ruteng/Satartacik [*Indonesia*] [*ICAO location
            identifier*] (ICLI)
WRKI .... Brookfield, CT [*FM radio station call letters*]
WRKI .... Mbai [*Indonesia*] [*ICAO location identifier*] (ICLI)
WRKJ ...... Mena [*Indonesia*] [*ICAO location identifier*] (ICLI)
WRKK ...... Kupang/Eltari [*Indonesia*] [*ICAO location identifier*] (ICLI)
WRKL........ Larantuka/Gewayentana [*Indonesia*] [*ICAO location
            identifier*] (ICLI)
WRKL........ New City, NY [*AM radio station call letters*]
WRKM ..... Carthage, TN [*AM radio station call letters*]
WRKM ..... Kalabahi/Mali [*Indonesia*] [*ICAO location identifier*] (ICLI)
WRKM-FM ... Carthage, TN [*FM radio station call letters*]
WRKN...... Brandon, MS [*AM radio station call letters*]
WRKN...... Naikliu [*Indonesia*] [*ICAO location identifier*] (ICLI)
WRKO....... Boston, MA [*AM radio station call letters*]
WRKO....... Labuhan Bajo/Mutiara II [*Indonesia*] [*ICAO location
            identifier*] (ICLI)
WRKP........ Moundsville, WV [*FM radio station call letters*]
Wrk Paper ... Working Papers for a New Society [*A publication*]
Wrk Power ... Workers Power [*A publication*]
WRKQ....... Madisonville, TN [*AM radio station call letters*]
WRKR ...... Portage, MI [*FM radio station call letters*]
WRKR ...... Rote/Lekunik [*Indonesia*] [*ICAO location identifier*] (ICLI)
WRKS........ Sabu/Tardanu [*Indonesia*] [*ICAO location identifier*] (ICLI)
WRKS-FM ... New York, NY [*FM radio station call letters*]
WRKT ...... North East, PA [*AM radio station call letters*]
WRKT-FM ... North East, PA [*FM radio station call letters*]
WRKU-FM ... Grove City, PA [*FM radio station call letters*]
Wrk World ... Workers' World [*A publication*]
WRKX ...... Ottawa, IL [*FM radio station call letters*]
WRKY ...... Steubenville, OH [*FM radio station call letters*]
WRKZ ...... Hershey, PA [*FM radio station call letters*]
WRKZ ...... Kupang Sector [*Indonesia*] [*ICAO location identifier*] (ICLI)
WRl........... Rice Lake Public Library, Rice Lake, WI [*Library symbol*]
            [*Library of Congress*] (LCLS)
WRL .... War Resisters League (EA)
WRL .... Wellcome Research Laboratories [*Research center*]
            [*British*] (IRC)
WRL .... Western Reserve Law Review [*A publication*] (ILCA)
WRL .... Westinghouse Research Laboratories (KSC)
WRL .... Wien Radiation Law [*Physics*]
WRL .... Willow Run Laboratory [*NASA*] (KSC)
WRL .... Wing Reference Line [*Aviation*]
WRL .... Worland [*Wyoming*] [*Airport symbol*] (OAG)
WRL .... Worland, WY [*Location identifier*] [*FAA*] (FAAL)
WRLA ...... Sangata [*Indonesia*] [*ICAO location identifier*] (ICLI)
WRLB....... Florence, NJ [*AM radio station call letters*]
WRLB....... Long Bawan/Juvai Semaring [*Indonesia*] [*ICAO location
            identifier*] (ICLI)
WRLC....... Bontang [*Indonesia*] [*ICAO location identifier*] (ICLI)
WRLC....... Williamsport, PA [*FM radio station call letters*]
WRLD ...... Batu Putih/Talisayam [*Indonesia*] [*ICAO location
            identifier*] (ICLI)
WRLD ...... Lanett, AL [*AM radio station call letters*]
WRLD ...... World Container Corp. [*Burnsville, MN*] [*NASDAQ
            symbol*] (NQ)
WRLF........ Fairmont, WV [*FM radio station call letters*]
WRLG ...... Tanjung Selor/Tanjung Harapan [*Indonesia*] [*ICAO location
            identifier*] (ICLI)
WRLH....... Tanah Grogot [*Indonesia*] [*ICAO location identifier*] (ICLI)
WRLH-TV ... Richmond, VA [*Television station call letters*]
WRLI........ Tiong Chong [*Indonesia*] [*ICAO location identifier*] (ICLI)

WRLK........ Tanjung Redep/Kalimarau [*Indonesia*] [*ICAO location
            identifier*] (ICLI)
WRLK-TV ... Columbia, SC [*Television station call letters*]
WRLL........ Balikpapan/Sepinggan [*Indonesia*] [*ICAO location
            identifier*] (ICLI)
WRLM ...... Malinau [*Indonesia*] [*ICAO location identifier*] (ICLI)
WRLN ...... Long Mawang [*Indonesia*] [*ICAO location identifier*] (ICLI)
WRLO ...... Ongko Asa [*Indonesia*] [*ICAO location identifier*] (ICLI)
WRLO-FM ... Antigo, WI [*FM radio station call letters*]
WRLR........ Taraken [*Indonesia*] [*ICAO location identifier*] (ICLI)
W R LR..... Women's Rights Law Reporter [*A publication*]
WRLRAR ... University of Wisconsin. Water Resources Center.
            Eutrophication Information Program. Literature Review [*A
            publication*]
WRLS........ Samarinda/Temindung [*Indonesia*] [*ICAO location
            identifier*] (ICLI)
WRLS........ Working Reference of Livestock Regulatory Establishments,
            Stations, and Officials [*A publication*]
WRLS-FM ... Hayward, WI [*FM radio station call letters*]
WRLT........ Madison, TN [*AM radio station call letters*]
WRLT........ Tanjung Santan [*Indonesia*] [*ICAO location identifier*] (ICLI)
WRLT-FM ... Franklin, TN [*FM radio station call letters*]
WRLU ...... Sangkulirang [*Indonesia*] [*ICAO location identifier*] (ICLI)
WRLU ...... Watermen and Riverside Labourers' Union [*British*]
WRLV....... Salyersville, KY [*AM radio station call letters*]
WRLV-FM ... Salyersville, KY [*FM radio station call letters*]
WRLW ...... Muara Wahau [*Indonesia*] [*ICAO location identifier*] (ICLI)
WRLX........ Tuscaloosa, AL [*AM radio station call letters*]
WRLX........ World Airways, Inc. [*Air carrier designation symbol*]
WRM......... War Readiness Materiel [*Air Force*]
WRM......... War Reserve Mobilization (CINC)
WRM......... War Reserve Munitions
WRM......... Warm (FAAC)
WRM......... Warmifontaine [*Belgium*] [*Seismograph station code, US
            Geological Survey*] (SEIS)
WRM......... Water Removal Mechanism
WRM......... West Rim Resources, Inc. [*Vancouver Stock Exchange symbol*]
WRM......... What Really Matters
WR(M)...... Wide Range (Monitor) [*Nuclear energy*] (NRCH)
WRM......... Worcester State College, Worcester, MA [*OCLC
            symbol*] (OCLC)
WRM......... Working Reference Material [*Nuclear energy*] (NRCH)
WRM......... World Rainforest Movement [*Penang, Malaysia*] (EAIO)
WRMA ..... Mount Morris, IL [*FM radio station call letters*]
WRMA ..... Welded Ring Manufacturers Association [*Defunct*]
WRMB ...... Boynton Beach, FL [*FM radio station call letters*]
WRMC-FM ... Middlebury, VT [*FM radio station call letters*]
WRMF....... Palm Beach, FL [*FM radio station call letters*]
WRMF....... World Radio Missionary Fellowship (EA)
WRMFNT ... Warm Front [*Meteorology*] (FAAC)
WRMG...... Red Bay, AL [*AM radio station call letters*]
WRMJ....... Aledo, IL [*FM radio station call letters*]
WRMM...... Rochester, NY [*FM radio station call letters*]
WRMN...... Elgin, IL [*AM radio station call letters*]
WRMN...... Wireman (AABC)
WRMR...... Cleveland, OH [*AM radio station call letters*]
WRMR ...... War Reserve Materiel Requirement (AFIT)
WRMRATE ... War Readiness Materiel Rating [*Air Force*]
WRMRB .... War Reserve Materiel Requirement Balance (AFIT)
WRMRP.... War Reserve Materiel Requirement Protectable (AFIT)
WRMRS.... War Reserve Materiel Rating System
WRMS ...... Beardstown, IL [*AM radio station call letters*]
WRMS ...... War Reserve Materiel Stocks
WRMS ...... Watts Root-Mean-Square
WRMS-FM ... Beardstown, IL [*FM radio station call letters*]
WRMSTAT ... War Readiness Materiel Status [*Air Force*]
WRMT ...... Rocky Mount, NC [*AM radio station call letters*]
WRMT ...... Woodcock Reading Mastery Tests [*Educational test*]
WRMU...... Alliance, OH [*FM radio station call letters*]
WRMX...... Murfreesboro, TN [*FM radio station call letters*]
WRN......... Blue Bell, Inc. [*Greensboro, NC*] [*FAA designator*] (FAAC)
WRN......... War Relief for Nicaraguans (EA)
WRN......... Warnaco of Canada Ltd. [*Toronto Stock Exchange symbol*]
WRN......... Warning (MSA)
WRN......... Western
WRN......... Wool Round Needle [*Knitting*]
WRNA ...... China Grove, NC [*AM radio station call letters*]
WRNB ...... Warren Bancorp, Inc. [*NASDAQ symbol*] (NQ)
WRNC ...... Reidsville, NC [*AM radio station call letters*]
WRNG...... Warning (FAAC)
WRNI ...... Wide-Range Neutron Indicator (IEEE)
WRNI ...... Wide-Range Nuclear Instrument (IEEE)
WRNJ........ Hackettstown, NJ [*AM radio station call letters*]
WRNL........ Richmond, VA [*AM radio station call letters*]
WRNLR ..... Western Region of Nigeria Law Reports [*A publication*] (DLA)
WRNOA ... Washington Reef Net Owners Association (EA)
WRNO-FM ... New Orleans, LA [*FM radio station call letters*]
WRNQ....... Poughkeepsie, NY [*FM radio station call letters*]
WRNR....... Martinsburg, WV [*AM radio station call letters*]
WRNR ...... West Riding National Reserve [*British military*] (DMA)
WRNR .... Women's Royal Naval Reserve [*British military*] (DMA)

WRNS ...... Kinston, NC [*AM radio station call letters*]
WRNS ...... Women's Royal Naval Service [*Also, WRENS*] [*A member is familiarly called a "Wren"*] [*British*]
WRNS-FM ... Kinston, NC [*FM radio station call letters*]
WRNSR..... Women's Royal Naval Service Reserve [*British military*] (DMA)
WRNT ...... Warrant (AABC)
WRNT ...... Warrenton Railroad Co. [*Later, WAR*] [*AAR code*]
WRNVR ... Women's Royal Naval Volunteer Reserve [*British military*] (DMA)
WRNWCA ... Western Red and Northern White Cedar Association [*Later, WRCA*] (EA)
WRNY ...... Rome, NY [*AM radio station call letters*]
WRNZ ...... Lancaster, KY [*FM radio station call letters*]
WRO .... ARC [*Agricultural Research Council*] Weed Research Organization [*Research center*] [*British*] (IRC)
WRO .... Rotor-Aids, Inc. [*Abbeville, LA*] [*FAA designator*] (FAAC)
WRO .... War Records Office
WRO .... War Risks Only
WRO .... Water Rights Office [*Bureau of Indian Affairs*]
WRO .... Western Regional Office
WRO .... Wichita River Oil [*AMEX symbol*] (SPSG)
WRO .... Work Release Order (MCD)
WRO .... Worship Resources Office [*An association*] (EA)
WRO .... Wroclaw [*Poland*] [*Airport symbol*] (OAG)
WROA ...... Gulfport, MS [*AM radio station call letters*]
W Rob .... [*W.*] Robinson's English Admiralty Reports [*166 English Reprint*] [*A publication*] (DLA)
WROB ...... West Point, MS [*AM radio station call letters*]
W Rob Adm ... [*W.*] Robinson's English Admiralty Reports [*166 English Reprint*] [*A publication*] (DLA)
W Rob Adm (Eng) ... [*W.*] Robinson's English Admiralty Reports [*166 English Reprint*] [*A publication*] (DLA)
Wrocl Zap Num ... Wroclawskie Zapiski Numizmatyczne [*A publication*]
WROC-TV ... Rochester, NY [*Television station call letters*]
WROD ...... Daytona Beach, FL [*AM radio station call letters*]
WROE ...... Neenah-Menasha, WI [*FM radio station call letters*]
WROG ...... Cumberland, MD [*FM radio station call letters*]
Wr Ohio ..... Wright's Ohio Reports [*A publication*] (DLA)
WROI .... Rochester, IN [*FM radio station call letters*]
WROK ...... Rockford, IL [*AM radio station call letters*]
WROL ...... Boston, MA [*AM radio station call letters*]
WROM ...... Rome, GA [*AM radio station call letters*]
WRON ...... Ronceverte, WV [*AM radio station call letters*]
WRON-FM ... Ronceverte, WV [*FM radio station call letters*]
WROPA2 .. University of Wisconsin. Water Resources Center. Eutrophication Information Program. Occasional Paper [*A publication*]
WROQ-FM ... Charlotte, NC [*FM radio station call letters*]
WROR ...... Boston, MA [*FM radio station call letters*]
WROS ...... Jacksonville, FL [*AM radio station call letters*]
W Roux A DB ... Wilhelm Roux' Archives of Developmental Biology [*A publication*]
WROV ...... Roanoke, VA [*AM radio station call letters*]
WROV-FM ... Martinsville, VA [*FM radio station call letters*]
WROW ...... Albany, NY [*AM radio station call letters*]
WROW-FM ... Albany, NY [*FM radio station call letters*]
WROX ...... Clarksdale, MS [*AM radio station call letters*]
WROY ...... Carmi, IL [*AM radio station call letters*]
WROZ ...... Owensboro, KY [*Television station call letters*]
WRP .... United States News and World Report [*A publication*]
WRP .... Water Resource Planning
WRP .... Water Resources Publications
WRP .... Weapons Release Programmer
WRP .... Weather Research Program [*Boulder, CO*] [*Department of Commerce*] (GRD)
WRP .... Wiener Random Process [*Mathematics*]
WRP .... Wildlife Research Project
WRP .... Wing Reference Plan [*Aviation*]
WRP .... Women's Rights Project (EA)
WRP .... Workers' Revolutionary Party [*British*] (PPW)
WRPA ...... Water Resources Planning Act [*1965*]
Wr PA .... Wright's Reports [*37-50 Pennsylvania*] [*A publication*] (DLA)
WRPC ...... San German, PR [*AM radio station call letters*]
WRPC ...... Weather Records Processing Centers
WRPG ...... Warping
WRPI .... Troy, NY [*FM radio station call letters*]
WRPL ...... Wadesboro, NC [*FM radio station call letters*]
WRPLS .... Western Regional Public Library System [*Library network*]
WRPM ...... Poplarville, MS [*AM radio station call letters*]
WRPN-FM ... Ripon, WI [*FM radio station call letters*]
WRPPD..... Wrapped
WRPQ ...... Baraboo, WI [*AM radio station call letters*]
WRPR ...... Mahwah, NJ [*FM radio station call letters*]
WRPR ...... Wrapper
WRPS ...... Rockland, MA [*FM radio station call letters*]
WRPS ...... WearEver-Proctor Silex, Inc. [*Chillicothe, OH*] [*NASDAQ symbol*] (NQ)
WRPSM ..... War Reserve Publication Shipment Memorandum
WRPX ...... Hudson, WI [*AM radio station call letters*]
WRPZ ...... Paris, KY [*AM radio station call letters*]

WRQ .... Westinghouse Resolver/Quantizer (IEEE)
WRQC ...... Cleveland Heights, OH [*FM radio station call letters*]
WRQK ...... Canton, OH [*FM radio station call letters*]
WRQL ...... Rupert, VT [*FM radio station call letters*]
WRQN ...... Bowling Green, OH [*FM radio station call letters*]
WRQR ...... Farmville, NC [*FM radio station call letters*]
WRQT ...... Bear Lake, MI [*FM radio station call letters*]
WRQX ...... Washington, DC [*FM radio station call letters*]
WRR .... Dallas, TX [*FM radio station call letters*]
WRR .... Warm Run Record
WRR .... Warrington, Inc. [*Toronto Stock Exchange symbol*]
WRR .... Water Resource Region [*Water Resources Council*]
WRR .... Water Resources Research [*A publication*] (NOAA)
WRR .... Woodmen Rangers and Rangerettes (EA)
WRRA ...... Frederiksted, VI [*AM radio station call letters*]
WRRA ...... Mataram/Selaparang [*Indonesia*] [*ICAO location identifier*] (ICLI)
WRRA ...... Water Resources Research Act [*1964*]
WRRB ...... Bima/Palibelo [*Indonesia*] [*ICAO location identifier*] (ICLI)
WRRC ...... Lawrenceville, NJ [*FM radio station call letters*]
WRRC ...... Massachusetts Water Resources Research Center [*University of Massachusetts*] [*Research center*] (RCD)
WRRC ...... Water Resources Research Center [*University of Arizona*] [*Research center*] (RCD)
WRRC ...... Water Resources Research Center [*Purdue University*] [*Research center*] (RCD)
WRRC ...... Water Resources Research Center [*Indiana University*] [*Research center*] (RCD)
WRRC ...... Water Resources Research Center [*University of Hawaii*] [*Research center*] (RCD)
WRRC ...... Water Resources Research Center [*University of Minnesota of Minneapolis Saint Paul*] [*Research center*] (RCD)
WRRC ...... Western Rail Road Company [*AAR code*]
WRRC ...... Western Regional Research Center [*Department of Agriculture*] [*Albany, CA*] (GRD)
WRRC ...... Western Regional Resource Center [*University of Oregon*] [*Research center*] (RCD)
WRRC ...... Willow Run Research Center [*Air Force*]
WRRC ...... Women's Research and Resources Centre (EAIO)
WRRC ...... Women's Research and Resources Centre Newsletter [*A publication*]
WRRC Report (Washington) ... Water Resources Research Center. Report (Washington) [*A publication*]
WRRC Spec Rep Univ MD ... WRRC [*Water Resources Research Center*] Special Report. University of Maryland [*A publication*]
WRRD ...... Blennerhassett, WV [*AM radio station call letters*]
WRRE ...... Juncos, PR [*AM radio station call letters*]
WRRF .... Washington, NC [*AM radio station call letters*]
WRRG ...... River Grove, IL [*FM radio station call letters*]
WRRH ...... Franklin Lakes, NJ [*FM radio station call letters*]
WRRI .... Alabama Water Resources Research Institute [*Auburn, AL*] [*Department of the Interior*] (GRD)
WRRI .... Water Resources Research Institute [*Oregon State University*] [*Research center*] (RCD)
WRRI .... Water Resources Research Institute [*Clemson University*] [*Research center*]
WRRI .... Water Resources Research Institute [*New Mexico State University*] [*Research center*] (RCD)
WRRI Auburn Univ Bull ... WRRI [*Water Resources Research Institute*]. Auburn University. Bulletin [*A publication*]
WRRK ...... Manistee, MI [*FM radio station call letters*]
WRRL .... Rainelle, WV [*AM radio station call letters*]
WRRL-FM ... Rainelle, WV [*FM radio station call letters*]
WRRM ...... Cincinnati, OH [*FM radio station call letters*]
WRRN ...... Warren, PA [*FM radio station call letters*]
WRRO ...... Warren, OH [*AM radio station call letters*]
WRRR ...... Bali International/Ngurah Rai [*Indonesia*] [*ICAO location identifier*] (ICLI)
WRRR ...... Rockford, IL [*AM radio station call letters*]
WRRR ...... Walter Reed Research Reactor [*Military*]
WRRR-FM ... St. Mary's, WV [*FM radio station call letters*]
WRRS .... Sumbawa/Sumbawa Besar [*Indonesia*] [*ICAO location identifier*] (ICLI)
WRRS .... Wire Relay Radio System
WRRT ...... Waikabubak/Tambolaka [*Indonesia*] [*ICAO location identifier*] (ICLI)
WRRW ...... Waingapu/Mau Hau [*Indonesia*] [*ICAO location identifier*] (ICLI)
WRRZ ...... Bali [*Indonesia*] [*ICAO location identifier*] (ICLI)
WRRZ ...... Clinton, NC [*AM radio station call letters*]
WRS .... Walter Reed Society (EA)
WRS .... War Reserve Stocks (AABC)
WRS .... Warning and Report System (CET)
WRS .... Warsak [*Pakistan*] [*Seismograph station code, US Geological Survey*] (SEIS)
WRS .... Wasabi Resources Ltd. [*Toronto Stock Exchange symbol*] [*Vancouver Stock Exchange symbol*]
WRS .... Washington Representative Services, Inc. [*Information service or system*] (IID)
WRS .... Water Recirculation System
WRS .... Water Recovery Subsystem [*NASA*] (KSC)

WRS .... Wave Radiometer System
WRS .... Weapons Recommendation Sheet (MCD)
WRS .... Weather RADAR Set [*or System*]
WRS .... Weather Reconnaissance Squadron [*Air Force*] (CINC)
WRS .... Western Massachusetts Regional Library System, Springfield, MA [*OCLC symbol*] (OCLC)
WRS .... Wide-Range Sensor
WRS .... Winston Resources Ltd. [*AMEX symbol*] (SPSG)
WRS .... Word Recognition System
WRS .... Working Transmission Reference System [*Telecommunications*] (TEL)
WRS .... Worse (FAAC)
WRS .... Write Strobe
WRSA........ Decatur, AL [*FM radio station call letters*]
WRSA........ War Reserve Stocks for Allies (MCD)
WRSA........ World Rabbit Science Association [*Cheltenham, Gloucestershire, England*] (EAIO)
WRSC........ Cepu/Ngloram [*Indonesia*] [*ICAO location identifier*] (ICLI)
WRSC........ State College, PA [*AM radio station call letters*]
WRSD .... Folsom, PA [*FM radio station call letters*]
WRSE-FM ... Elmhurst, IL [*FM radio station call letters*]
WRSF .... Columbia, NC [*FM radio station call letters*]
WRSFA ..... Western Reinforcing Steel Fabricators Association
WRSG .... Binghamton, NY [*AM radio station call letters*]
WRSH .... Rockingham, NC [*FM radio station call letters*]
WRSI .... Greenfield, MA [*FM radio station call letters*]
WRSIC ...... Water Resources Scientific Information Center [*US Geological Survey*] [*Reston, VA*] [*Database originator*]
WRSJ .... Bayamon, PR [*AM radio station call letters*]
WRSJ .... Surabaya/Juanda [*Indonesia*] [*ICAO location identifier*] (ICLI)
WRSK........ War Readiness Spares Kit [*Air Force*] (AFM)
WRSL........ Stanford, KY [*AM radio station call letters*]
WRSL-FM ... Stanford, KY [*FM radio station call letters*]
WRSM ...... Sumiton, AL [*AM radio station call letters*]
WRSP .... Surabaya/Perak [*Indonesia*] [*ICAO location identifier*] (ICLI)
WRSP .... World Register of Scientific Periodicals
WRSP-TV ... Springfield, IL [*Television station call letters*]
WRSQ .... Solo/Adi Sumarmo Wiryokusumo [*Indonesia*] [*ICAO location identifier*] (ICLI)
WRSq .... Weather Reconnaissance Squadron [*Air Force*] (AFM)
WRSR....... Two Harbors, MN [*FM radio station call letters*]
WRSR........ Water Reactor Safety Research [*Nuclear energy*] (NRCH)
WRSS .... San Sebastian, PR [*AM radio station call letters*]
WRSS .... Surabaya/Gedangan [*Indonesia*] [*ICAO location identifier*] (ICLI)
WRST........ Sumenep/Trunojoyo [*Indonesia*] [*ICAO location identifier*] (ICLI)
WRST-FM ... Oshkosh, WI [*FM radio station call letters*]
WRSU-FM ... New Brunswick, NJ [*FM radio station call letters*]
WRSV........ Rocky Mount, NC [*FM radio station call letters*]
WRSW....... Warsaw, IN [*AM radio station call letters*]
WRSW-FM ... Warsaw, IN [*FM radio station call letters*]
WRT .... Warrior River Terminal Co. [*AAR code*]
WRT .... Water Round Torpedo (MSA)
WRT .... Westerra Resources Ltd. [*Vancouver Stock Exchange symbol*]
WRT .... With Reference To
WRT .... With Respect To (KSC)
WRT .... Wright Air Lines, Inc. [*Cleveland, OH*] [*FAA designator*] (FAAC)
WRT .... Wright-Hargreaves Mines Ltd. [*Toronto Stock Exchange symbol*] (SPSG)
WRT .... Wrought
WRTA .... Altoona, PA [*AM radio station call letters*]
WRTA .... Western Railroad Traffic Association (EA)
WRTB....... Washington, IN [*FM radio station call letters*]
WRTB....... Wire Rope Technical Board (EA)
WRTC .... Working Reference Telephone Circuit [*Telecommunications*] (TEL)
WRTC .... [*The*] Writer Corporation [*NASDAQ symbol*] (NQ)
WRTC-FM ... Hartford, CT [*FM radio station call letters*]
WRTE........ Cahokia, IL [*FM radio station call letters*]
WRTH....... World Radio TV Handbook [*A publication*]
WRTHG.... Worthing [*City in England*]
WRTI .... Philadelphia, PA [*FM radio station call letters*]
WRTL........ Rantoul, IL [*AM radio station call letters*]
WRTN ...... New Rochelle, NY [*FM radio station call letters*]
WRTP........ Chapel Hill, NC [*AM radio station call letters*]
WRTU .... San Juan, PR [*FM radio station call letters*]
WRTV .... Indianapolis, IN [*Television station call letters*]
WRU........ Watershed Research Unit [*Department of Agriculture*] [*Columbia, MO*] (GRD)
WRU......... Wave Run-Up
WRU......... Western Reserve University [*Later, Case Western Reserve University*]
WRU......... Western Reserve University. Bulletin [*A publication*]
WRU......... Wheat Research Unit [*Australia*]
WRU......... Who Are You? [*Communication*]
WRUC....... Schenectady, NY [*FM radio station call letters*]
WRUF ...... Gainesville, FL [*AM radio station call letters*]
WRUF-FM ... Gainesville, FL [*FM radio station call letters*]
WRUL........ Carmi, IL [*FM radio station call letters*]

WRUM...... Rumford, ME [*AM radio station call letters*]
WRUN...... Utica, NY [*AM radio station call letters*]
WRUP .... Marquette, MI [*FM radio station call letters*]
WRUR-FM ... Rochester, NY [*FM radio station call letters*]
WRUS .... Russellville, KY [*AM radio station call letters*]
WRUV....... Burlington, VT [*FM radio station call letters*]
WRUW-FM ... Cleveland, OH [*FM radio station call letters*]
WRV .... Water Relief Valve
WRV .... Water-Retention Value
WRV .... West Riding Volunteers [*British military*] (DMA)
WRVA .... Richmond, VA [*AM radio station call letters*]
WRVC .... Huntington, WV [*AM radio station call letters*]
WRVC-FM ... Ashland, KY [*FM radio station call letters*]
WRVE .... Watertown, NY [*FM radio station call letters*]
WRVG .... Georgetown, KY [*FM radio station call letters*]
WRVI .... Virden, IL [*FM radio station call letters*]
WRVK .... Mount Vernon, KY [*AM radio station call letters*]
WRVL........ Lynchburg, VA [*FM radio station call letters*]
WRVM....... Suring, WI [*FM radio station call letters*]
WRVN....... Utica, NY [*FM radio station call letters*]
WRVO .... Oswego, NY [*FM radio station call letters*]
WRVQ .... Richmond, VA [*FM radio station call letters*]
WRVR-FM ... Memphis, TN [*FM radio station call letters*]
WRVS....... Women's Royal Voluntary Service [*Formerly, WVS*] [*British*]
WRVS-FM ... Elizabeth City, NC [*FM radio station call letters*]
WRVT .... Rutland, VT [*FM radio station call letters*]
WRVU .... Nashville, TN [*FM radio station call letters*]
WRVW ...... Hudson, NY [*FM radio station call letters*]
WRVX .... Mt. Carmel, TN [*AM radio station call letters*]
WRVY-FM ... Henry, IL [*FM radio station call letters*]
WR(W)...... War Reserve (Weapon)
WRW........ Will's Air [*Barnstable, MA*] [*FAA designator*] (FAAC)
WRWA ...... Dothan, AL [*FM radio station call letters*]
WRWC ...... Rockton, IL [*FM radio station call letters*]
WRWD...... Highland, NY [*FM radio station call letters*]
WRWg...... Weather Reconnaissance Wing [*Air Force*] (AFM)
WRWH...... Cleveland, GA [*AM radio station call letters*]
WRWK ...... Warwick Railway Co. [*AAR code*]
WRWR-TV ... San Juan, PR [*Television station call letters*]
WRWX ...... Sanibel, FL [*FM radio station call letters*]
WRX .... Western Refrigerator Line Co. [*AAR code*]
WRXB .... St. Petersburg Beach, FL [*AM radio station call letters*]
WRXC .... Shelton, CT [*FM radio station call letters*]
WRXJ .... Jacksonville, FL [*AM radio station call letters*]
WRXK .... Bonita Springs, FL [*FM radio station call letters*]
WRXL........ Richmond, VA [*FM radio station call letters*]
WRXO .... Roxboro, NC [*AM radio station call letters*]
WRXR .... Aiken, SC [*AM radio station call letters*]
WRXR-FM ... Aiken, SC [*FM radio station call letters*]
WRXX .... Centralia, IL [*FM radio station call letters*]
WRXY-TV ... Tice, FL [*Television station call letters*]
WRY .... Westray [*Scotland*] [*Airport symbol*] (OAG)
WRY .... Wheeling Railway
WRY .... World Refugee Year
WRYM ...... New Britain, CT [*AM radio station call letters*]
WRYT .... Edwardsville, IL [*AM radio station call letters*]
WRZ......... Western Rift Zone [*Geology*]
WRZAA ..... Weltraumfahrt und Raketentechnik [*A publication*]
WRZI .... Buffalo, KY [*FM radio station call letters*]
WRZN .... Hernando, FL [*AM radio station call letters*]
WRZQ-FM ... Greenburg, IN [*FM radio station call letters*]
WRZZ .... Ravenswood, WV [*FM radio station call letters*]
WS .... Single Conductor Cable [*JETDS nomenclature*] [*Military*] (CET)
WS .... Superior Public Library, Superior, WI [*Library symbol*] [*Library of Congress*] (LCLS)
WS .... Wagner's Missouri Statutes [*A publication*] (DLA)
WS .... Wall Street
WS .... Wallops Station [*Later, WFC*] [*NASA*]
WS .... War Scale (ADA)
WS .... War Service
WS .... War Substantive [*British military*] (DMA)
WS .... Ware Shoals Railroad Co. [*AAR code*]
WS .... Warm Shop [*Nuclear energy*] (NRCH)
WS .... Warthin-Starry [*Silver impregnation stain*]
WS .... Washine Chemical Corp. [*Research code symbol*]
WS .... Waste Stack [*Technical drawings*]
WS .... Waste System
WS .... Water Safety
WS .... Water Servicer (NASA)
WS .... Water Soluble
WS .... Water-Storage Cell [*Botany*]
WS .... Water Supply
WS .... Water Surface [*Elevation*]
WS .... Water System
WS .... Watered Stock
WS .... Watt Second
W/s........... Watt-Seconds
W & S........ Watts and Sergeant's Pennsylvania Reports [*1841-1845*] [*A publication*] (DLA)
W/S........... Watts per Steradian (NG)

WS	Wave Soldering
WS	Weak Signals [*Radio*]
WS	Weapon System
WS	Weapons Specifications (NG)
W/S	Weapons System
WS	Weather Service
W/S	Weather Ship (NATG)
WS	Weather Squadron (MCD)
WS	Weather Station
WS	Weatherstripping (AAG)
WS	Wedgwood Society (EA)
WS	Wee Scots (EA)
WS	Weirton Steel Corp. [*NYSE symbol*] (SPSG)
WS	Welsh Society (EA)
WS	Welt der Slaven [*A publication*]
WS	West Saxon [*Dialect of Old English*] [*Language, etc.*]
WS	West Semitic (BJA)
WS	Western Samoa [*ANSI two-letter standard code*] (CNC)
ws	Western Samoa [*MARC country of publication code*] [*Library of Congress*] (LCCP)
WS	Western Speech [*A publication*]
WS	Wet Smoothed (BJA)
W v S	Wetboek van Strafrecht [*A publication*]
WS	Wetted Surface
WS	Wheat Straw
W & S	Whiskey and Soda
WS	White Sisters [*Missionary Sisters of Our Lady of Africa*] [*Roman Catholic religious order*]
WS	White Sucker [*Ichthyology*]
WS	White-Throated Sparrow [*Ornithology*]
WS	Wide Shot [*Photography*]
WSI	Wiener Studien [*A publication*]
W-S	Wigner-Seitz [*Construction cell*] [*Solid state physics*]
WS	Wilderness Society (EA)
WS	[*The*] Wildlife Society
WS	Will Ship (MCD)
WS	Williams Syndrome [*Medicine*]
WS	Willow Society (EA)
W & S	Wilson and Shaw's Scotch Appeal Cases, English House of Lords [*A publication*] (DLA)
WS	Wind Shield (NASA)
WS	Wind Speed
WSP	Windsonde (KSC)
WS	Windspeaker [*A publication*]
WS	Wing Station [*Aviation*]
WS	Wire Send [*Telecommunications*] (TEL)
WS	Wireless Set (MCD)
WS	Wirtschaft und Statistik [*Germany*]
WS	Wirtschaftsflug Rhein Main GmbH & Co. KG [*West Germany*] [*ICAO designator*] (FAAC)
Ws	Wisdom [*Old Testament Book*] (BJA)
W/S	With Stock [*Business term*]
WS	Withholding Statement (AAG)
W & S	Woerter und Sachen [*A publication*]
WS	Woerter und Sachen [*A publication*]
WS	Women's Services [*Military*] [*British*]
WS	Women's Size
WS	Women's Studies: An Interdisciplinary Journal [*A publication*]
WS	Women's Suffrage (ROG)
WS	Wonder Stories [*A publication*]
WS	Wood-Sheathed Deck [*of a ship*] (DS)
WS	Woomera Space Centre [*Australia*]
WS	Word Study [*A publication*]
WS	Word Sync
WS	WordStar [*Computer program*]
WS	Work Stand (MCD)
WS	Work Statement (AAG)
W/S	Work Station [*NASA*] (NASA)
WS	Work Stoppage (AAG)
WS	Working Space
WS	Working Storage [*Data processing*] (MDG)
WS	Worksheet (AAG)
WS	Worldscale
WS	Worldwide Searches (EA)
WS	Wort und Sinn [*A publication*]
WS	Worthy Sister (BJA)
WS	Writer to the Signet [*British*]
WS	Wrought Steel (MSA)
4WS	Four-Wheel Steering [*Automotive engineering*]
WSA	Intereconomics. Monthly Review of International Trade and Development [*A publication*]
WSA	Wagner Society of America (EA)
WSA	War Shipping Administration [*Within Office of Emergency Management*] [*World War II*]
WSA	War Supplies Agency (NATG)
WSA	Water-Soluble Adjuvant [*Immunology*]
WSA	Waveguide Slot Array
WSA	Weapons Systems Analysis [*Army*] (AABC)
WSA	Web Sling Association [*Later, WSTDA*] (EA)
WSA	Weed Society of America [*Later, WSSA*] (EA)
WSA	West Sea Development [*Vancouver Stock Exchange symbol*]

WSA	Western Slavonic Association [*Later, WSA Fraternal Life*] (EA)
WSA	Western Surfing Association (EA)
WSA	Western Surgical Association (EA)
WSA	Wholesale Stationers' Association (EA)
WSA	Wilderness Study Area [*Department of the Interior*]
WSA	Williams Syndrome Association (EA)
WSA	Winter Soldier Archive (EA)
WSA	Wisconsin Statutes Annotated [*A publication*] (DLA)
WSA	Wolfenbuetteler Studien zur Aufklarung [*A publication*]
WSA	Wolverine Society of America (EA)
WSA	Women Studies Abstracts [*A publication*]
WSA	Women's Sports Association [*Australia*]
WSA	Women's Student Association (EA)
WSA	Wonder Story Annual [*A publication*]
WSA	Workplace Standards Administration [*Department of Labor*]
WSA	World Sign Associates (EA)
WSA	Writers' Sodality of America [*Defunct*]
WSAA	Waveguide Slot Array Antenna
WSAA	Western States Angus Association (EA)
WSAAA	Western States Advertising Agencies Association (EA)
WSAC	Washington State Apple Commission (EA)
WSAC	Water Space Amenity Commission [*British*] (DCTA)
WSAC	West of Scotland Agricultural College [*United Kingdom*] (IRUK)
WSAD	Weapon System Analysis Division [*Navy*]
WSAE	Spring Arbor, MI [*FM radio station call letters*]
WSAF	Trion, GA [*AM radio station call letters*]
WSAG	Sembawang [*Singapore*] [*ICAO location identifier*] (ICLI)
WSAG	Washington Special Action Group [*National Security Council*]
WSAH	World Smoking and Health [*A publication*]
WSAI	Cincinnati, OH [*AM radio station call letters*]
WSAI	[*The*] Wine Society of America, Inc. [*NASDAQ symbol*] (NQ)
WSAJ	Grove City, PA [*AM radio station call letters*]
WSAJ-FM ...	Grove City, PA [*FM radio station call letters*]
WSAK	Sullivan, IL [*FM radio station call letters*]
WSAL	Logansport, IN [*AM radio station call letters*]
WSAM	Saginaw, MI [*AM radio station call letters*]
WSAM	Weapon Systems Acquisition Management [*Navy*] (MCD)
WSAN	Vieques, PR [*FM radio station call letters*]
WSAO	Senatobia, MS [*AM radio station call letters*]
WSAO	Weapon System Analysis Office [*Navy*] (MCD)
WSAP	Paya Lebar [*Singapore*] [*ICAO location identifier*] (ICLI)
WSAP	Weapon Status and Approval Panel [*Military*] (CAAL)
WSAP	Weapon System Acquisition Process (MCD)
WSAP	Weighted Sensitivity Analysis Program [*Environmental Protection Agency*]
W & S App ...	Wilson and Shaw's Scotch Appeal Cases, English House of Lords [*A publication*] (DLA)
WSAQ	Port Huron, MI [*FM radio station call letters*]
WSAR	Fall River, MA [*AM radio station call letters*]
WSAR	Singapore [*Singapore*] [*ICAO location identifier*] (ICLI)
WSAR	Weekly Significant Action Report (AFIT)
WSAS	Weapon System Acceptance Schedule (AAG)
WSASSA ...	Wholesale School, Art, and Stationery Supplies Association [*Later, WSA*] (EA)
WSAT	Salisbury, NC [*AM radio station call letters*]
WSAT	Tengah [*Singapore*] [*ICAO location identifier*] (ICLI)
WSAT	Weapon Systems Accuracy [*formerly, Acceptance*] Trials [*Navy*] (NG)
WSATO	War Shipping Administration Training Organization [*Terminated*]
WSAU	Wausau Paper Mills Co. [*NASDAQ symbol*] (NQ)
WSAU	Wausau, WI [*AM radio station call letters*]
WSAVA	World Small Animal Veterinary Association [*See also AMVPA*] [*Hatfield, Hertfordshire, England*] (EAIO)
WSAV-TV ...	Savannah, GA [*Television station call letters*]
WSAWD ...	White Sands Air Weather Detachment [*New Mexico*]
WSA-WGWC ...	World Service Authority of the World Government of World Citizens (EA)
WSAW-TV ...	Wausau, WI [*Television station call letters*]
WSAX	West Saxon [*Dialect of Old English*] [*Language, etc.*]
WSAY	Salem, VA [*AM radio station call letters*]
WSAZ-TV ...	Huntington, WV [*Television station call letters*]
WSB	Atlanta, GA [*AM radio station call letters*]
WSB	Steamboat Bay, AK [*Location identifier*] [*FAA*] (FAAL)
WSB	Wage Stabilization Board [*Terminated, 1953*]
Wsb	Washburn Law Journal [*A publication*]
WSB	Water-Soluble Base
WSB	Water Spray Boiler (NASA)
WSB	Weekly Statistical Bulletin [*Database*] [*American Petroleum Institute*] [*Information service or system*] (CRD)
WSB	Wheat-Soya Blend (EA)
WSB	Will Send Boat
WSB	World Scout Bureau [*Geneva, Switzerland*] (EA)
WSBA	York, PA [*AM radio station call letters*]
WSBB	New Smyrna Beach, FL [*AM radio station call letters*]
WSBC	Chicago, IL [*AM radio station call letters*]
WSBC	Wesbanco, Inc. [*NASDAQ symbol*] (NQ)
WSbD	Door County Library, Sturgeon Bay, WI [*Library symbol*] [*Library of Congress*] (LCLS)

WSBE-TV ... Providence, RI [*Television station call letters*]
WSBF-FM ... Clemson, SC [*FM radio station call letters*]
WSB-FM... Atlanta, GA [*FM radio station call letters*]
WSBG........ Stroudsburg, PA [*FM radio station call letters*]
WSBH .... Warren, VT [*FM radio station call letters*]
WSBI .... Static, TN [*AM radio station call letters*]
WSBK........ Western Bank [*Coos Bay, OR*] [*NASDAQ symbol*]   (NQ)
WSBK-TV ... Boston, MA [*Television station call letters*]
WSBM...... Florence, AL [*AM radio station call letters*]
WSBM...... Wheat Soilborne Mosaic Virus
WSBMV ... Wheat Soilborne Mosaic Virus
WSBN-TV ... Norton, VA [*Television station call letters*]
WSBP........ Western Society of Business Publications [*Defunct*]   (EA)
WSBR........ Boca Raton, FL [*AM radio station call letters*]
WSBS .... Great Barrington, MA [*AM radio station call letters*]
WSBSA ...... Weapon System Base Supply Account [*Military*]   (AFIT)
WSBT........ South Bend, IN [*AM radio station call letters*]
WSBT-TV ... South Bend, IN [*Television station call letters*]
WSB-TV ... Atlanta, GA [*Television station call letters*]
WSBU .... St. Bonaventure, NY [*FM radio station call letters*]
WSBU ...... Wahlenbergia. Scripta Botanica Umensia [*A publication*]
WSBV........ South Boston, VA [*AM radio station call letters*]
WSBW ...... Weddell Sea Bottom Water [*Oceanography*]
WSBX........ [*The*] Washington Savings Bank FSB [*NASDAQ symbol*]   (NQ)
WSBY-FM ... Salisbury, MD [*FM radio station call letters*]
WSC .... Ebareport. Weekly Special Survey of Turkish Business, Industrial Investment, and Contracts Markets [*A publication*]
WSC .... Wall Street Computer Review [*A publication*]
WSC .... Washington Science Center [*Maryland*] [*Seismograph station code, US Geological Survey*] [*Closed*]   (SEIS)
WSC .... Water Systems Council   (EA)
WSC .... Weapon System Computer   (MCD)
WSC .... Weapon System Console [*Military*]   (CAAL)
WSC .... Weapon System Contractor
WSC .... Weapon System Costing [*Navy*]
WSC .... Weber State College [*Ogden, UT*]
WSC .... Wesco Financial Corp. [*AMEX symbol*]   (SPSG)
WSC .... Westair Commuter Airlines [*Santa Rosa, CA*] [*FAA designator*]   (FAAC)
WSC .... Westech Resources Ltd. [*Vancouver Stock Exchange symbol*]
WSC .... Western Sahara Campaign for Human Rights and Humanitarian Relief   (EA)
WSC .... Western Simulation Council
WSC .... Western Snow Conference   (EA)
WSC .... Western Snow Conference. Proceedings [*A publication*]
WSC .... White Sisters of Charity of St. Vincent de Paul [*Roman Catholic religious order*]
WSC .... Wideband Signal Conditioner   (MCD)
WSC .... Wildcat Service Corporation   (EA)
WSC .... Wilkinson Sword Company [*British military*]   (DMA)
WSC .... Willetton Sports Club [*Australia*]
WSC .... Wind Sounding Capability
WSC .... Wing Security Control [*Air Force*]   (AFM)
WSC .... Winona State College [*Later, Winona State University*] [*Minnesota*]
WSC .... Winston Spencer Churchill [*1874-1965*] [*British statesman and prime minister*]
WSC .... Wisconsin State College [*Later, University of Wisconsin*]
WSC .... Working Security Committee [*Navy*]
WSC .... World Series Cricket
WSC .... World Spanish Congress   (EA)
WSC .... World Spiritual Council   (EA)
WSC .... World Straw Conference
WSC .... World Survey of Climatology [*Elsevier Book Series*] [*A publication*]
WSC .... Wrap-Spring Clutch
WSC .... Wright State, Celina Branch, Celina, OH [*OCLC symbol*]   (OCLC)
WSC .... Writing Services Center
WSCA........ Weather Service Cooperating Agencies [*National Weather Service*]   (NOAA)
WSCA........ World Surface Coatings Abstracts [*Paint Research Association*] [*Information service or system*] [*A publication*]
WSCB........ Springfield, MA [*FM radio station call letters*]
WSCC........ Somerset, KY [*FM radio station call letters*]
WSCC........ Weapon System Configuration Control [*Navy*]   (AAG)
WSCC........ Weather Service Communications Center [*National Weather Service*]   (NOAA)
WSCC........ Western State College of Colorado [*Gunnison*]
WSCC........ Western Systems Coordinating Council [*Regional power council*]
WSCC........ Work Station Control Center [*NASA*]   (NASA)
WSCCM...... Weapon System Configuration Control Manual [*Navy*]   (NG)
WSCD .... Welfare and Service Conditions Department [*British military*]   (DMA)
WSCD-FM ... Duluth, MN [*FM radio station call letters*]
WSCF........ World Student Christian Federation   (EA)
WSCF Books ... World Student Christian Federation Books [*A publication*]
WSCG........ Corinth, NY [*FM radio station call letters*]

WSCH ...... Aurora-Rising Sun, IN [*FM radio station call letters*]
WSCH .... Weather Service Communications Handbook [*National Weather Service*]   (NOAA)
WSCHP....... Wen Shih Che Hsueh-Pao [*Taiwan University*] [*A publication*]
WSCI........ Charleston, SC [*FM radio station call letters*]
WSCI......... Washington Scientific Industries, Inc. [*NASDAQ symbol*]   (NQ)
WSCL........ Salisbury, MD [*FM radio station call letters*]
WSCL........ Wisconsin Studies in Contemporary Literature [*Later, Contemporary Literature*] [*A publication*]
WSCM...... Cobleskill, NY [*AM radio station call letters*]
WSCM...... Weapon System Compatible Munition [*Military*]
WSCMB... Weapon System Configuration Management Board   (MCD)
WSCN ...... Cloquet, MN [*FM radio station call letters*]
WSCO ...... Suring, WI [*Television station call letters*]
WSCO ...... Weber State College [*Odgen, UT*]
WSCOC..... Wills Sainte Claire Owners Club   (EA)
WSCP........ Sandy Creek-Pulaski, NY [*AM radio station call letters*]
WSCP........ Weapons System Control Point
WSCPA .... Western States Section. Combustion Institute. Paper [*United States*] [*A publication*]
WSCP-FM ... Pulaski, NY [*FM radio station call letters*]
WSCQ .... West Columbia, SC [*FM radio station call letters*]
WSCR .... Scranton, PA [*AM radio station call letters*]
WSCS .... Washington State College. Studies [*A publication*]
WSCS .... Waste Solidification and Compaction Station [*Nuclear energy*]   (NRCH)
WSCS .... Weapon System Communications System   (AAG)
WSCS .... Wide Sense Cyclo-Stationary [*Communication*]
WSCSR ..... Weapons System Contract Status Report [*Navy*]   (NG)
WSCT........ Wainscot [*Technical drawings*]
WSCV....... Fort Lauderdale, FL [*Television station call letters*]
WSCW....... South Charleston, WV [*AM radio station call letters*]
WSCZ........ Greenwood, SC [*FM radio station call letters*]
WSD .... Sheboygan County Federated Library System, Mead Public Library, Sheboygan, WI [*OCLC symbol*]   (OCLC)
WSD .... Warfare Systems Directorate   (MCD)
WSD .... Weapon Support Detachment   (MCD)
WSD .... Weapon System Designator
WSD .... Weapon System Development [*Military*]   (CAAL)
WSD .... Weapon System Director
WSD .... Weapons System Demonstration   (MCD)
WSD .... White Sands, NM [*Location identifier*] [*FAA*]   (FAAL)
WSD .... Wind Speed Detector
WSD .... Wirtschaftsdienst. Wirtschaftspolitische Monatsschrift [*A publication*]
WSD .... Working Stress Design [*Nuclear energy*]   (NRCH)
WSD .... World Space Directory [*A publication*]
WSD .... World Systems Division [*of Communications Satellite Corp.*] [*Telecommunications*]   (TEL)
WSDA ...... Nashville, TN [*Television station call letters*]
WSDA ...... Water and Sewer Distributors of America   (EA)
WSDB...... World Studies Data Bank   (IID)
WSDC ...... Weapon System Design Criteria   (AAG)
WSDC ...... Weapons System Designator Code   (NVT)
WSDC ...... Wisconsin State Data Center [*Wisconsin State Department of Administration*] [*Madison*] [*Information service or system*]   (IID)
WSDD ...... Weapon Status Digital Display
WSDH...... Sandwich, MA [*FM radio station call letters*]
WSDL........ Weapons System Development Laboratory
WSDL........ Weapons Systems Data Link   (MCD)
WSDM ...... Weapon System Data Module
WSDM-FM ... Brazil, IN [*FM radio station call letters*]
WSDP........ Plymouth, MI [*FM radio station call letters*]
WSDP....... Weapons System Development Plan
WSDQ ...... Dunlap, TN [*AM radio station call letters*]
WSDR ...... Sterling, IL [*AM radio station call letters*]
WSDS....... Ypsilanti, MI [*AM radio station call letters*]
WSDT....... Soddy-Daisy, TN [*AM radio station call letters*]
WSD/TD... Weapon System Demonstration Test Directive   (AAG)
WSE.......... National Weather Service Employees Organization
WSE.......... Weapon Support Equipment [*Navy*]   (NG)
WSE.......... Weapon System Engineering [*Navy*]   (NG)
WSE.......... Weapons System Evaluator   (MCD)
WSE.......... Weapons Systems Effectiveness
WSE.......... West-Southeast   (ROG)
WSE.......... Western Allenbee Oil & Gas Co. Ltd. [*Vancouver Stock Exchange symbol*]
WSE.......... Western Society of Engineers
WSE.......... Wound, Skin, Enteric [*Isolation*] [*Medicine*]
WSEA .... Georgetown, DE [*AM radio station call letters*]
WSEB........ Englewood, FL [*FM radio station call letters*]
WSEC........ Jacksonville, IL [*Television station call letters*]
WSEC........ Washington State Electronics Council
WSEC........ Watt-Second   (AAG)
WSECL ..... Weapon System Equipment Component List
WSED........ Weapon System Electrical Diagrams
WSEES...... Weapon System Electromagnetic Environment Simulator   (MCD)
WSEE-TV ... Erie, PA [*Television station call letters*]

WSEF.......	Weapons System Evaluation Facility (MCD)
WSEF.......	Weapons Systems Effectiveness Factors
WSEFGT...	Weapons System Evaluation Facility Group Test (MCD)
WSEG........	Weapon System Evaluation Group [*DoD and Air Force*] (MCD)
WSEI........	Olney, IL [*FM radio station call letters*]
WSEIAC ...	Weapon System Effectiveness Industry Advisory Committee
WSEK.......	Somerset, KY [*FM radio station call letters*]
WSEL.......	Pontotoc, MS [*AM radio station call letters*]
WSEL.......	Weapon System Engineering Laboratory
WSEL-FM ..	Pontotoc, MS [*FM radio station call letters*]
WSEM......	Donalsonville, GA [*AM radio station call letters*]
WSEM......	Weapon System Evaluation Missile [*Air Force*] (AFM)
WSem	West Semitic (BJA)
WSEN	Baldwinsville, NY [*AM radio station call letters*]
WSEN-FM ...	Baldwinsville, NY [*FM radio station call letters*]
WSEO	Weather Service Evaluation Officer [*National Weather Service*]
WSEP........	Waste Solidification Engineering Prototype Plant [*Nuclear energy*]
WSEP.......	Weapon System Evaluation Program [*Air Force*]
WSER.......	Elkton, MD [*AM radio station call letters*]
WSES	Waterford Steam Electric Station [*Nuclear energy*] (NRCH)
WSESA	Weapon System and Equipment Support Analysis
WSET.......	Weapon System Evaluation Test [*Navy*] (NG)
WSET.......	Writers and Scholars Educational Trust [*London, England*] (EAIO)
WSET-TV ...	Lynchburg, VA [*Television station call letters*]
WSEV.......	Sevierville, TN [*AM radio station call letters*]
WSEV-FM ...	Gatlinburg, TN [*FM radio station call letters*]
WSEZ........	Paoli, IN [*AM radio station call letters*]
WSF.........	Waste Shipping Facility [*Nuclear energy*] (NRCH)
WSF..........	Water/Sand Fillable
WSF..........	Water-Soluble Fraction
WSF..........	Water Supply Forecast (NOAA)
WSF..........	Weapon System File (MCD)
WSF..........	Weather Support Force [*Military*] (AFM)
WSF..........	Week Second Feet
WSF..........	Well Spouse Foundation (EA)
WSF..........	Well-Springs Foundation (EA)
WSFA.......	Western Sea Frontier [*Navy*]
WSF..........	William Shatner Fellowship (EA)
WSF..........	Women for a Secure Future (EA)
WSF..........	Women's Sports Foundation (EA)
WSF..........	Work Station Facility
WSF..........	World Salt Foundation (EA)
WSF..........	World Scout Foundation [*Geneva, Switzerland*] (EAIO)
WSF..........	World Sephardi Federation [*See also FSM*] [*Geneva, Switzerland*] (EAIO)
WSF..........	World SF [*Science Fiction*] (EA)
WSFA.......	Montgomery, AL [*Television station call letters*]
WSFB	Quitman, GA [*AM radio station call letters*]
WSFC.......	Somerset, KY [*AM radio station call letters*]
WSFC.......	Wall Street Financial Corp. [*NASDAQ symbol*] (NQ)
WSFC.......	White Sands Field Center [*New Mexico*]
WSFI........	Wood and Synthetic Flooring Institute (EA)
WSFJ.......	Newark, OH [*Television station call letters*]
WSFL.......	New Bern, NC [*AM radio station call letters*]
WSFL-FM ..	New Bern, NC [*FM radio station call letters*]
WSFM......	Southport, NC [*AM radio station call letters*]
WSFO	Weather Service Forecast Office [*National Weather Service*]
WSFP	World Showcase Fellowship Program [*Walt Disney World*]
WSFPF......	Westfort Petroleums Ltd. [*NASDAQ symbol*] (NQ)
WSFP-FM ...	Fort Myers, FL [*FM radio station call letters*]
WSFP-TV ...	Fort Myers, FL [*Television station call letters*]
WSFS	Wilmington Savings Fund Society FSB [*Wilmington, DE*] [*NASDAQ symbol*] (NQ)
WSFS	World Science Fiction Society (EA)
WSFT	Thomaston, GA [*AM radio station call letters*]
WSFU-FM ...	Union Springs, AL [*FM radio station call letters*]
WSFW......	Seneca Falls, NY [*AM radio station call letters*]
WSFW-FM ...	Seneca Falls, NY [*FM radio station call letters*]
WSFX.......	Nanticoke, PA [*FM radio station call letters*]
WSG	International Wool Study Group
WSG	Washington [*Pennsylvania*] [*Airport symbol*] (OAG)
WSG	Wells Gold Ltd. [*Vancouver Stock Exchange symbol*]
WSG	Wesleyan Service Guild [*Defunct*] (EA)
WSG	Winter Study Group
WSG	Wire Strain Gauge
WSG	Wired Shelf Group [*Telecommunications*] (TEL)
WSG	Worthiest Soldier in the Group
WSGA	Savannah, GA [*AM radio station call letters*]
WSGA	Water Soluble Gum Association (EA)
WSGA	Wine and Spirits Guild of America (EA)
WSGB.......	Sutton, WV [*AM radio station call letters*]
WSGC.......	Williams-Sonoma, Inc. [*NASDAQ symbol*] (NQ)
WSGD-FM ...	Carbondale, PA [*FM radio station call letters*]
WSGE........	Dallas, NC [*FM radio station call letters*]
WSGE........	Western Society of Gear Engineers (MCD)
WSGG	Scottsboro, AL [*AM radio station call letters*]
WSGH.......	Lewisville, NC [*AM radio station call letters*]
WSGI........	Springfield, TN [*AM radio station call letters*]

WSGL.......	Naples, FL [*FM radio station call letters*]
WSGM	Staunton, VA [*FM radio station call letters*]
WSGN	Gadsden, AL [*FM radio station call letters*]
WSGO	Oswego, NY [*AM radio station call letters*]
WSGR-FM ...	Port Huron, MI [*FM radio station call letters*]
WSGS.......	Hazard, KY [*FM radio station call letters*]
WSGT.......	White Sands Ground Terminal [*NASA*] (MCD)
WSGU	Window Sash Glaziers' Union [*British*]
WSGW	Saginaw, MI [*AM radio station call letters*]
WSGX	Sarasota, FL [*AM radio station call letters*]
WSGY	Tifton, GA [*FM radio station call letters*]
Wsh..........	Washington State Reports [*A publication*] (DLA)
WSH.........	Weather Service Headquarters (NOAA)
WsH.........	William S. Hein & Co., Inc., Buffalo, NY [*Library symbol*] [*Library of Congress*] (LCLS)
WSH.........	Wilshire Energy Resources, Inc. [*Toronto Stock Exchange symbol*]
WS and H ..	World Smoking and Health [*A publication*]
WSha	Bringham Memorial Library, Sharon, WI [*Library symbol*] [*Library of Congress*] (LCLS)
WSHA	Raleigh, NC [*FM radio station call letters*]
WShawGS ...	Church of Jesus Christ of Latter-Day Saints, Genealogical Society Library, Wisconsin East District Branch, Shawano, WI [*Library symbol*] [*Library of Congress*] (LCLS)
WSHC	Shepherdstown, WV [*FM radio station call letters*]
WSHE	Fort Lauderdale, FL [*FM radio station call letters*]
WShe	Mead Public Library, Sheboygan, WI [*Library symbol*] [*Library of Congress*] (LCLS)
WSheL.......	Lakeland College, Sheboygan, WI [*Library symbol*] [*Library of Congress*] (LCLS)
WSheM	Sheboygan Memorial Hospital, Sheboygan, WI [*Library symbol*] [*Library of Congress*] (LCLS)
WSheSN...	Saint Nicholas Hospital, Sheboygan, WI [*Library symbol*] [*Library of Congress*] (LCLS)
WSheU	University of Wisconsin Center-Sheboygan, Sheboygan, WI [*Library symbol*] [*Library of Congress*] (LCLS)
WSHF	Wives Self-Help Foundation (EA)
WSHFT....	Wind Shift (FAAC)
WSHG.......	Washing (MSA)
WSHGA.....	Washington State Holly Growers Association [*Defunct*] (EA)
WSHH.......	Pittsburgh, PA [*FM radio station call letters*]
WSHI	Washington Homes, Inc. [*NASDAQ symbol*] (NQ)
WSHJ.......	Southfield, MI [*FM radio station call letters*]
WSHLD	Windshield (AAG)
WSHL-FM ...	Easton, MA [*FM radio station call letters*]
WSHN.......	Fremont, MI [*AM radio station call letters*]
WSHN-FM...	Fremont, MI [*FM radio station call letters*]
WSHO	New Orleans, LA [*AM radio station call letters*]
WSHP	Shippensburg, PA [*AM radio station call letters*]
WSHPA8...	Acta Microbiologica Sinica [*A publication*]
WSHQ.......	Cobleskill, NY [*FM radio station call letters*]
WSHR	Lake Ronkonkoma, NY [*FM radio station call letters*]
WSHR	Washer (MSA)
WSHS.......	Sheboygan, WI [*FM radio station call letters*]
WSHU	Fairfield, CT [*FM radio station call letters*]
WSHV	South Hill, VA [*FM radio station call letters*]
WSHW......	Frankfort, IN [*FM radio station call letters*]
WSHX	Danville, VT [*FM radio station call letters*]
WSHY	Shelbyville, IL [*AM radio station call letters*]
WSHZ	Rotterdam, NY [*FM radio station call letters*]
WSI..........	Wafer-Scale Integration [*Microelectronics*]
WSI..........	WaferScale Integration, Inc.
WSI..........	Waingapu [*Sumba Island*] [*Seismograph station code, US Geological Survey*] (SEIS)
WSI..........	War Service Indefinite
WSI..........	Water Safety Instructor [*Red Cross*]
WSI..........	Water Ski Industry Association (EA)
WSI..........	Water Solubility Index [*Analytical chemistry*]
WSI..........	Water Stability Index [*Agronomy*]
WSI..........	Weapon System Integration (MCD)
WSI..........	Weather Services International Corp. [*Information service or system*] (IID)
WSI..........	Wind Speed Indicator
WSI..........	World Synoptic Interval
WSI..........	Writers and Scholars International [*London, England*] (EAIO)
WSIA.......	Staten Island, NY [*FM radio station call letters*]
WSIA.......	Water Ski Industry Association (EA)
WSIA.......	Water Supply Improvement Association [*Later, IDA*] (EA)
WSIA.......	Weapons Systems Integration Agent (MCD)
WSIA J.....	WSIA [*Water Supply Improvement Association*] Journal [*United States*] [*A publication*]
WSIA Journal ...	Water Supply Improvement Association. Journal [*A publication*]
WSIB........	Selmer, TN [*FM radio station call letters*]
WSIC........	Statesville, NC [*AM radio station call letters*]
WSIC........	Watchmakers of Switzerland Information Center (EA)
WSIE........	Edwardsville, IL [*FM radio station call letters*]
WSIF	Wilkesboro, NC [*FM radio station call letters*]
WSIG........	Mount Jackson, VA [*FM radio station call letters*]
WSI/L.......	War Supporting Industries and Logistics (MCD)
WSIL-TV ..	Harrisburg, IL [*Television station call letters*]

WSIM........	Water Separation Index, Modified
WSI Mitt ...	WSI [*Wirtschafts- und Sozialwissenschaftliches Institut*] Mitteilungen [*German Federal Republic*] [*A publication*]
WSIP.........	Paintsville, KY [*AM radio station call letters*]
WSIP-FM ...	Paintsville, KY [*FM radio station call letters*]
WSIR........	White Sands Integrated Range [*New Mexico*] (AAG)
WSIR.........	Winter Haven, FL [*AM radio station call letters*]
WSIT.........	Washington State Institute of Technology (KSC)
WSIT	Water Safety Instructor Trainer [*Red Cross*]
WSITS........	Weapon System Interface Trade Study [*Military*]
WSIU.........	Carbondale, IL [*FM radio station call letters*]
WSIU-TV ...	Carbondale, IL [*Television station call letters*]
WSIV.........	East Syracuse, NY [*AM radio station call letters*]
WSIX.........	Nashville, TN [*AM radio station call letters*]
WSIX-FM ...	Nashville, TN [*FM radio station call letters*]
WSIY.........	West Somerset Imperial Yeomanry [*British military*] (DMA)
WSIZ........	Ocilla, GA [*AM radio station call letters*]
WSJ	San Juan, AK [*Location identifier*] [*FAA*] (FAAL)
WSJ	Wall Street Journal [*A publication*]
WSJ	Wiener Slawistisches Jahrbuch [*A publication*]
WSJ	Worm Screw Jack
WSJ	WSFA [*Washington Science Fiction Association*] Journal [*A publication*]
WSJB-FM ...	Standish, ME [*FM radio station call letters*]
WSJC........	Magee, MS [*AM radio station call letters*]
WSJC........	Singapore [*Singapore*] [*ICAO location identifier*] (ICLI)
WSJE	San Juan, PR [*FM radio station call letters*]
WSJ Europe ...	Wall Street Journal. European Edition [*A publication*]
WSJHQ........	Western States Jewish Historical Quarterly [*A publication*]
WSJK-TV ...	Sneedville, TN [*Television station call letters*]
WSJL	Cape May, NJ [*FM radio station call letters*]
WSJM........	St. Joseph, MI [*AM radio station call letters*]
WSJ NJ.....	Wall Street Journal 3 Star. Eastern (Princeton, NJ) Edition [*A publication*]
W S Jour....	Wallace Stevens Journal [*A publication*]
WSJP	Murray, KY [*AM radio station call letters*]
WSJR	Madawaska, ME [*AM radio station call letters*]
WSJS........	Winston-Salem, NC [*AM radio station call letters*]
WSJU	San Juan, PR [*Television station call letters*]
WSJV	Elkhart, IN [*Television station call letters*]
WSJY	Fort Atkinson, WI [*FM radio station call letters*]
WSK	Waste Age [*A publication*]
WSKA........	Port Huron, MI [*Television station call letters*]
WSKB........	Westfield, MA [*FM radio station call letters*]
WSKE........	Everett, PA [*AM radio station call letters*]
WSKE-FM ...	Everett, PA [*FM radio station call letters*]
WSKG	Binghamton, NY [*Television station call letters*]
WSKG-FM ...	Binghamton, NY [*FM radio station call letters*]
WSKI........	Montpelier, VT [*AM radio station call letters*]
WSKN	Prattville, AL [*AM radio station call letters*]
WSKO	Buffalo Gap, VA [*FM radio station call letters*]
WSKQ	Newark, NJ [*AM radio station call letters*]
WSKQ-FM ...	New York, NY [*FM radio station call letters*]
WSKS........	Sparta, GA [*FM radio station call letters*]
WSKT........	Spencer, IN [*FM radio station call letters*]
WSKV.......	Stanton, KY [*FM radio station call letters*]
WSKW	Skowhegan, ME [*AM radio station call letters*]
WSKY	Asheville, NC [*AM radio station call letters*]
WSKZ........	Chattanooga, TN [*FM radio station call letters*]
WSL..........	War Substantive Lieutenant [*British*]
WSL..........	Warren Spring Laboratory [*British*] (DCTA)
Ws L..........	Washington Law Review [*A publication*]
WSL..........	Weather Seal (AAG)
WSL..........	Welt der Slaven [*A publication*]
WSL..........	Western Savings & Loan Association [*NYSE symbol*] (SPSG)
WSL..........	Windscale
WSLA.......	Slidell, LA [*AM radio station call letters*]
W Sl A	Wiener Slawistischer Almanach [*A publication*]
WSlav	Welt der Slaven [*A publication*]
WSLB........	Ogdensburg, NY [*AM radio station call letters*]
WSLBA	Wasser, Luft, und Betrieb [*A publication*]
WSLC.......	Roanoke, VA [*AM radio station call letters*]
WSLC	World Shortwave Listeners Club (EA)
WSLF	Western Somali Liberation Front
WSLG.......	Gonzales, LA [*AM radio station call letters*]
WSLI	Jackson, MS [*AM radio station call letters*]
WSLI-FM ...	Jackson, MS [*FM radio station call letters*]
WSL-INT ..	Weltbund zum Schutze des Lebens [*World Union for the Protection of Life - WUPL-INT*] (EAIO)
WSLJb	Wiener Slawistisches Jahrbuch [*A publication*]
WSLK	Hyden, KY [*AM radio station call letters*]
WSLL	Saranac Lake, NY [*FM radio station call letters*]
WSLM.......	Salem, IN [*AM radio station call letters*]
WSLM-FM ...	Salem, IN [*FM radio station call letters*]
WSLN.......	Delaware, OH [*FM radio station call letters*]
WSLO.......	Malone, NY [*FM radio station call letters*]
WSLO.......	Weapon System Logistics Officer [*Air Force*] (AFM)
WSLQ.......	Roanoke, VA [*FM radio station call letters*]
WSLR........	Akron, OH [*AM radio station call letters*]
WSLR........	Weapon System Logistic Reviews [*Navy*] (NG)

WSLS	War Service Land Settlement Scheme [*Australia*]
WSLS-TV ...	Roanoke, VA [*Television station call letters*]
WSLT........	Ocean City, NJ [*FM radio station call letters*]
WSLU........	Canton, NY [*FM radio station call letters*]
WSLV........	Ardmore, TN [*AM radio station call letters*]
WSLW......	White Sulphur Springs, WV [*AM radio station call letters*]
WSLX......	New Canaan, CT [*FM radio station call letters*]
WSLY.......	York, AL [*FM radio station call letters*]
WSM	Nashville, TN [*AM radio station call letters*]
WSM	Weapon Support Manager [*Air Force*]
WSM	Weapon System Manager [*Air Force*] (AFM)
WSM	Weapon System Manual
WSM	West-Mar Resources Ltd. [*Vancouver Stock Exchange symbol*]
WSM	Western Samoa [*ANSI three-letter standard code*] (CNC)
WSM	Western Society of Malacologists (EA)
WSM	Wheat Streak Mosaic [*Plant pathology*]
WSM	White Single Male [*Classified advertising*]
WSM	Wigner-Seitz Method [*Solid state physics*]
WSM	Wiseman [*Alaska*] [*Airport symbol*] (OAG)
WSM	Wiseman, AK [*Location identifier*] [*FAA*] (FAAL)
WSM	Women's Suffrage Movement (ROG)
WSM	World Solar Markets [*A publication*]
WSM	Wright State University, Health Sciences Library, Dayton, OH [*OCLC symbol*] (OCLC)
WSMA	Marine City, MI [*AM radio station call letters*]
WSMA	Western States Meat Association (EA)
WSMA	Window Shade Manufacturers Association (EA)
WSMAC...	Weapon System Maintenance Action Center
WSMaT....	Weapon System Management Team [*Army*] (RDA)
WSMB......	New Orleans, LA [*AM radio station call letters*]
WSMC......	Weapons System Management Codes [*Navy*]
WSMC......	Western Space and Missile Center [*Air Force*] [*Vandenberg Air Force Base, CA*]
WSMC......	Western States Movers Conference
WSMC......	WestMarc Communications, Inc. [*NASDAQ symbol*] (NQ)
WSMC-FM ...	Collegedale, TN [*FM radio station call letters*]
WSMD	St. Mary's City, MD [*FM radio station call letters*]
WSME.......	Sanford, ME [*AM radio station call letters*]
WSM-FM ...	Nashville, TN [*FM radio station call letters*]
WSMG	Greeneville, TN [*AM radio station call letters*]
WSMH......	Flint, MI [*Television station call letters*]
WSMI........	Litchfield, IL [*AM radio station call letters*]
WSMI-FM ...	Litchfield, IL [*FM radio station call letters*]
WSMJ	Cave City, KY [*AM radio station call letters*]
WSML.......	Graham, NC [*AM radio station call letters*]
WSML......	Saltfree Meal [*Airline notation*]
WSMN	Nashua, NH [*AM radio station call letters*]
WSMO	Weapon System Materiel Officer [*Air Force*] (AFM)
WSMO	Weather Service Meteorological Observatory [*or Observations*] [*National Weather Service*] (NOAA)
WSMP.......	WSMP, Inc. [*Formerly, Western Steer Mom 'n' Pop's, Inc.*] [*NASDAQ symbol*] (SPSG)
WSMPA....	Western States Meat Association (EA)
WSMQ	Bessemer, AL [*AM radio station call letters*]
WSMR	White Sands Missile Range [*Army*] [*New Mexico*]
WSMR-FM ...	Dayton, OH [*FM radio station call letters*]
WSMS.......	Memphis, TN [*FM radio station call letters*]
WSMT.......	Sparta, TN [*AM radio station call letters*]
WSMT.......	Weapons System Maintenance Test (MCD)
WSMTC....	White Sands Missile Test Center [*New Mexico*]
WSMT-FM ...	Sparta, TN [*FM radio station call letters*]
WSMTT	White Star Mobile Training Teams [*Military*] (CINC)
WSMU-FM ...	North Dartmouth, MA [*FM radio station call letters*]
WSMV	Nashville, TN [*Television station call letters*]
WSMV	Wheat Streak Mosaic Virus
WSMX	Winston-Salem, NC [*AM radio station call letters*]
WSMY	Weldon, NC [*AM radio station call letters*]
WSMYA....	Washington Monthly [*A publication*]
WSMZ.......	Coleman, MI [*FM radio station call letters*]
WSN	South Naknek [*Alaska*] [*Airport symbol*] (OAG)
WSN	South Naknek, AK [*Location identifier*] [*FAA*] (FAAL)
WSN	Spokane County Library, Spokane, WA [*OCLC symbol*] [*Inactive*] (OCLC)
WSN	Wallace Stevens Newsletter [*A publication*]
WSN	Warm Springs [*Nevada*] [*Seismograph station code, US Geological Survey*] [*Closed*] (SEIS)
WSN	Water-Soluble Nitrogen [*Analytical chemistry*]
WSN	Western Co. of North America [*NYSE symbol*] (SPSG)
WSN	Western Resources Technology [*Vancouver Stock Exchange symbol*]
WSN	Western Society of Naturalists (EA)
WSNA Mini J ...	Washington State Nurses Association. Mini Journal [*A publication*]
WSNC	Winston-Salem, NC [*FM radio station call letters*]
WSND-FM ...	Notre Dame, IN [*FM radio station call letters*]
WSNE	Taunton, MA [*FM radio station call letters*]
WSNG	Torrington, CT [*AM radio station call letters*]
WSNGT	White Sands NASA Ground Terminal (MCD)
WSNI........	Philadelphia, PA [*FM radio station call letters*]
WSNJ........	Bridgeton, NJ [*AM radio station call letters*]
WSNJ-FM ...	Bridgeton, NJ [*FM radio station call letters*]

WSNL........ East St. Louis, IL [*FM radio station call letters*]
WSNN........ Potsdam, NY [*FM radio station call letters*]
WSNO........ Barre, VT [*AM radio station call letters*]
WSNP........ Water-Soluble Nonstarchy Polysaccharide [*Food composition*]
WSNQ........ Gaylord, MI [*AM radio station call letters*]
WSNR-TV ... Syracuse, NY [*Television station call letters*]
WSNS......... Chicago, IL [*Television station call letters*]
WSNSCA.. Washable Suits, Novelties, and Sportswear Contractors Association (EA)
WSNT .... Sandersville, GA [*AM radio station call letters*]
WSNT-FM ... Sandersville, GA [*FM radio station call letters*]
WSNV........ Nelsonville, OH [*FM radio station call letters*]
WSNW........ Seneca, SC [*AM radio station call letters*]
WSNX-FM ... Muskegon, MI [*FM radio station call letters*]
WSNY........ Columbus, OH [*FM radio station call letters*]
WSNY........ Wagner Society of New York (EA)
WSNZ........ Muskegon, MI [*AM radio station call letters*]
WSO........... Warrant Stores Officer [*Navy*] [*British*]
WSO........... Washabo [*Suriname*] [*Airport symbol*] (OAG)
WSO........... Washington Standardization Officers
WSO........... Water Service Operator (MCD)
WSO........... Watsco, Inc. [*AMEX symbol*] (SPSG)
WSO........... Weapon System Officer [*or Operator*] [*Air Force*] (AFM)
WSO........... Weapon System Operator
WSO........... Weather Service Office [*National Weather Service*] (NOAA)
WSO........... Western Support Office [*Formerly, WOO*] [*NASA*]
WSO........... White Sands Operations [*New Mexico*] [*Formerly, White Sands Missile Operations*] [*NASA*]
WSO........... Wilcox Solar Observatory
WSO........... World Simulation Organization
WSO........... WRAF [*Women's Royal Naval Air Force*] Staff Officer [*British military*] (DMA)
WSO(AG) ... Weather Service Office for Agriculture [*National Weather Service*] (NOAA)
WSO(AV) ... Weather Service Office for Aviation [*National Weather Service*] (NOAA)
WSOC .... Charlotte, NC [*AM radio station call letters*]
WSOC .... Weapon System Operational Concept (AAG)
W Soc E J .. Western Society of Engineers. Journal [*A publication*]
WSOC-FM ... Charlotte, NC [*FM radio station call letters*]
WSOC-TV ... Charlotte, NC [*Television station call letters*]
WSOE .... Elon College, NC [*FM radio station call letters*]
WSOEA..... Wholesale Stationery and Office Equipment Association [*Later, WSA*] (EA)
WSOF-FM ... Madisonville, KY [*FM radio station call letters*]
WSO(FW) ... Weather Service Office for Fire-Weather [*National Weather Service*] (NOAA)
WSOK .... Savannah, GA [*AM radio station call letters*]
WSOL........ San German, PR [*AM radio station call letters*]
WSOM...... Weather Service Operations Manual [*National Weather Service*] (FAAC)
WSON...... Henderson, KY [*AM radio station call letters*]
WSON...... Worldwide Satellite Observing Network (MCD)
WSOO...... Sault Ste. Marie, MI [*AM radio station call letters*]
WSOP........ White Supercalendered Offset Paper [*Publishing*]
WSOR ...... Naples, FL [*FM radio station call letters*]
WSOS........ St. Augustine, FL [*FM radio station call letters*]
WSOT .... Weapon System Operability Test [*Military*] (CAAL)
WSOU ...... South Orange, NJ [*FM radio station call letters*]
WSOY .... Decatur, IL [*AM radio station call letters*]
WSOY .... Werner Soederstroem Osakeyhtio [*Book printer*] [*Finland*]
WSOY-FM ... Decatur, IL [*FM radio station call letters*]
W/SP......... Warheads and Special Projects Laboratory [*Picatinny Arsenal*]
WSP.......... Washington School of Psychiatry
WSP.......... Washington Square Press [*Publisher's imprint*]
WSP.......... Water Spray Protection [*Shipping*] (DS)
WSP.......... Water Supply Papers
WSP.......... Water Supply Point
WSP.......... Weapon Support Processor [*Military*] (CAAL)
WSP.......... Weapon Systems Pouch (AFM)
WSP.......... Weibull Shape Parameter [*Statistics*]
WSP.......... West Penn Power Co. [*NYSE symbol*] (SPSG)
WSP.......... Wideband Signal Processor
WSP.......... Winspear Resources [*Vancouver Stock Exchange symbol*]
WSP.......... Women Strike for Peace (EA)
WSP.......... Work Simplification Program [*Military*]
WSP.......... Work Study Program (OICC)
WSP.......... Working Steam Pressure
WSP.......... Workshop (NATG)
WSP.......... Wright State University, Piqua Branch Campus, Piqua, OH [*OCLC symbol*] (OCLC)
Wsp........... Wspolczesnosc [*Warsaw*] [*A publication*]
WSpa .... Sparta Free Library, Sparta, WI [*Library symbol*] [*Library of Congress*] (LCLS)
WSPA........ Spartanburg, SC [*AM radio station call letters*]
WSPA........ World Society for the Protection of Animals [*Formed by a merger of WFPA and ISPA*] (EA)
WSPACS... Weapon Systems Planning [*or Programming*] and Control System
WSPA-FM ... Spartanburg, SC [*FM radio station call letters*]
WSPAT ..... Wolfe-Spence Programming Aptitude Test

WSPA-TV ... Spartanburg, SC [*Television station call letters*]
WSPC........ St. Paul, VA [*AM radio station call letters*]
WSPC........ Weapons System Partnerships Committee [*NATO*] (NATG)
WSPC........ Weapons System Program Code [*Defense Supply Agency*]
WSPC........ Women's Social and Political Coalition [*Australia*]
WSPD....... Toledo, OH [*AM radio station call letters*]
WSPD....... Weapon System Planning Document (NVT)
WSPD....... Weapons System Planning Data [*Navy*]
WSPF........ Watergate Special Prosecution Force [*Terminated, 1977*] [*Department of Justice*]
WSPG....... Wall Street Planning Group (EA)
WSPG....... Weapon System Phasing Group
WSPG....... Weapon System Purchasing Group
WSPG....... White Sands Proving Ground [*New Mexico*] [*Obsolete*]
WSPGL...... Weapon System Program Guide List
WSPH .... Murray, KY [*Television station call letters*]
WSPI .... Shamokin, PA [*FM radio station call letters*]
WSPL .... La Crosse, WI [*FM radio station call letters*]
WSPN....... Saratoga Springs, NY [*FM radio station call letters*]
WSPO....... Stevens Point, WI [*AM radio station call letters*]
WSPO....... Weapon System Project Office [*Air Force*]
WSPOP...... Weapon System Phase-Out Procedure [*Air Force*] (AFM)
W Sports .... Women's Sports [*A publication*]
WSPPD..... Weapons Systems Personnel Planning Data (MCD)
WSPQ....... Springville, NY [*AM radio station call letters*]
WSPR....... Springfield, MA [*AM radio station call letters*]
WSPRD..... Weapons Systems Progress Reporting Data
WSPS .... Concord, NH [*FM radio station call letters*]
WSpS......... Saint Michael's Hospital, Stevens Point, WI [*Library symbol*] [*Library of Congress*] (LCLS)
WSPS .... Wire Strike Protection System (MCD)
WSPT .... Stevens Point, WI [*FM radio station call letters*]
WSpU .... University of Wisconsin-Stevens Point, Stevens Point, WI [*Library symbol*] [*Library of Congress*] (LCLS)
WSPU....... Women's Social and Political Union [*British*]
WSPUS ..... World Socialist Party of the United States (EA)
WSPY....... Plano, IL [*FM radio station call letters*]
WSPZ........ Douglasville, GA [*AM radio station call letters*]
WSQ .... Wake Seeding and Quenching
WSq .... Weather Squadron [*Air Force*] (AFM)
WSQ .... Wonder Stories Quarterly [*A publication*]
WSQG-FM ... Ithaca, NY [*FM radio station call letters*]
WSQR .... Sycamore, IL [*AM radio station call letters*]
WSQV .... Berwick, PA [*AM radio station call letters*]
WSR .... War Service Regulation
WSR .... Warm Springs Repeater [*Nevada*] [*Seismograph station code, US Geological Survey*] [*Closed*] (SEIS)
WSR .... Warren & Saline River Railroad Co. [*AAR code*]
WSR .... Waterschapsbelangen [*A publication*]
W/sr........... Watts per Steradian
WSR .... Weak Signal Reception
WSR .... Weapon System Reliability [*Air Force*] (AFM)
WSR .... Weapon Systems Requirement (MCD)
WSR .... Weapons Spares Report [*Navy*]
WSR .... Weapons Status Report [*Navy*] (NG)
WSR .... Weapons System Review (NVT)
WSR .... Weather Surveillance RADAR
WSR .... Weekly Summary Report
WSR .... Wet Snow on Runway [*Aviation*] (FAAC)
WSR .... Wild and Scenic Rivers Act
WSR .... Windsor Resources, Inc. [*Vancouver Stock Exchange symbol*]
WSR .... Wire Shift Register
WSR .... Wood-Shingle Roof [*Technical drawings*]
WSR .... World Students Relief
WSRA........ Guayama, PR [*FM radio station call letters*]
WSRA........ Wild and Scenic Rivers Act
WSRB........ Wall Street Review of Books [*A publication*]
WSRB........ Walpole, MA [*FM radio station call letters*]
WSRC........ Durham, NC [*AM radio station call letters*]
WSRCC..... War, Strikes, Riots, and Civil Commotions [*Insurance*] (AIA)
WSRD ...... Johnstown, NY [*FM radio station call letters*]
WSRE........ Pensacola, FL [*Television station call letters*]
WSRF........ Fort Lauderdale, FL [*AM radio station call letters*]
WSRG........ Edmonton, KY [*FM radio station call letters*]
WSRH .... Weather Service Regional Headquarters [*National Weather Service*] (NOAA)
WSRI........ World Safety Research Institute
WSRK........ Oneonta, NY [*FM radio station call letters*]
WSRL........ Water Supply Research Laboratory [*National Environmental Research Center*]
WSRL........ Weapons Systems Research Laboratory [*Australia*]
WSRL........ Wisconsin Survey Research Laboratory [*University of Wisconsin*] [*Research center*] (RCD)
WSRM ...... Weather Surveillance RADAR Manual (NOAA)
WSRN-FM ... Swarthmore, PA [*FM radio station call letters*]
WSRO .... Marlboro, MA [*AM radio station call letters*]
WSRO .... Weapon System Replacement Operations (MCD)
WSRO .... World Sugar Research Organisation (EAIO)
WSRP........ Weapons System Requisitioning Procedure [*Military*] (AABC)
WSRQ .... Bushnell, KY [*FM radio station call letters*]
WSRR........ West Shore Railroad

WSRS........	Wildlife Sound Recording Society [*British*]
WSRS........	Worcester, MA [*FM radio station call letters*]
WSRT........	Weapon System Readiness Test
WSRT........	Weapons System Reliability Test (CINC)
WSRT........	Westerbork Synthesis Radio Telescope
WSRU........	Slippery Rock, PA [*FM radio station call letters*]
WSRW.......	Hillsboro, OH [*AM radio station call letters*]
WSRW-FM ...	Hillsboro, OH [*FM radio station call letters*]
WSRX........	Fort Meyers, FL [*FM radio station call letters*]
WSRZ........	Sarasota, FL [*FM radio station call letters*]
WSS...........	War Savings Staff
WSS...........	Warfare Systems School [*Air Force*] (AFM)
WSS...........	Weapon Support Systems
WSS...........	Weapon System Specification (AAG)
WSS...........	Weather Service Specialist [*National Weather Service*]
WSS...........	Weekend Stress Syndrome [*Psychiatry*]
WSS...........	Wheelwrights' and Smiths' Society [*A union*] [*British*]
WSS...........	Winston-Salem Southbound Railway Co. [*AAR code*]
WSS...........	Women's Social Services [*Salvation Army*]
WSS...........	Women's Studies Section [*Association of College and Research Libraries*]
WSS...........	Work Summarization System (MCD)
WSS...........	Workpack Scheduling System [*Industrial engineering*]
WSS...........	World Ship Society [*Haywards Heath, West Sussex, England*]
WSSA........	Morrow, GA [*AM radio station call letters*]
WSSA........	Weapon System Support Activities (AAG)
WSSA........	Weed Science Society of America (EA)
WSSA........	Welsh Secondary Schools Association [*British*]
WSSA........	Western Social Science Association (EA)
WSSA........	White Sands Signal Agency [*New Mexico*] [*Military*] (MCD)
WSSA........	Wine and Spirits Shippers Association (EA)
WSSA........	World Secret Service Association [*Later, WAD*] (EA)
WSSAB.....	Weller-Strawser Scales of Adaptive Behavior [*Educational test*]
WSSBA	Western Single Side Band Association (EA)
WSSB-FM ...	Orangeburg, SC [*FM radio station call letters*]
WSSC........	Sumter, SC [*AM radio station call letters*]
WSSC........	Weapon System Support Center (AAG)
WSSC........	Weapon System Support Code [*Navy*] (NG)
WSSCA	Welsh Springer Spaniel Club of America (EA)
WSSCA	White Sands Signal Corps Agency [*New Mexico*] [*Military*] (AAG)
WSSCL.....	Weapon System Stock Control List (AAG)
WSSD........	Chicago, IL [*FM radio station call letters*]
WSSD........	Weapon System Support Development (MCD)
WSSF	Weather Service Support Facility [*National Weather Service*] (FAAC)
WSSFN	World Society for Stereotactic and Functional Neurosurgery (EA)
WSSG........	Weapon System Support Group (MCD)
WSSH-FM ...	Lowell, MA [*FM radio station call letters*]
WSSI	Carthage, MS [*AM radio station call letters*]
WSSI	Women's Social Service for Israel (EA)
WSSIB.......	WWMCCS [*Worldwide Military Command and Control System*] Standard System Information Base (MCD)
WSSI-FM ...	Carthage, MS [*FM radio station call letters*]
WSSJ.........	Camden, NJ [*AM radio station call letters*]
WSSL........	Greenville, SC [*AM radio station call letters*]
WSSL........	Seletar [*Singapore*] [*ICAO location identifier*] (ICLI)
WSSL........	Weapon System Stock/Support List [*Air Force*] (AFIT)
WSSL........	Western Secondary Standards Laboratory
WSSL-FM ...	Gray Court, SC [*FM radio station call letters*]
WSSM.......	Weapon System Staff Manager [*Army*] (RDA)
WSSM.......	Weapon System Support Manager (AAG)
WSSMV.....	Wheat Spindle Streak Mosaic Virus
WSSN........	Weston, WV [*FM radio station call letters*]
WSSO........	Starkville, MS [*AM radio station call letters*]
WSSO........	Weapon System Support Officer [*Army*] (RDA)
WSSP	Cocoa Beach, FL [*FM radio station call letters*]
WSSP	Weapon Systems Support Program [*Defense Supply Agency*]
WSSPM......	Weapons System Support Program Manager (AFIT)
WSSQ........	Sterling, IL [*FM radio station call letters*]
WSSRS.....	Waksman Social Skills Rating Scale
WSSS	Singapore Changi [*Singapore*] [*ICAO location identifier*] (ICLI)
WSSS	Weapon System Storage Site
WSSSFAF ...	Wartime Standard Support System for Foreign Armed Forces (MCD)
WSSSP......	Western States Small School Project
WSST-TV ...	Cordele, GA [*Television station call letters*]
WSSU........	Springfield, IL [*FM radio station call letters*]
WSSU........	Weather Service Support Unit [*National Weather Service*] (FAAC)
WSSV........	Stillwater, NY [*AM radio station call letters*]
WSSW.......	Mackinaw City, MI [*FM radio station call letters*]
WSSX........	Wessex Corp. [*Franklin, TN*] [*NASDAQ symbol*] (NQ)
WSSX-FM ...	Charleston, SC [*FM radio station call letters*]
WSSY........	Evanston, IL [*AM radio station call letters*]
WSSZ........	Greensburg, PA [*FM radio station call letters*]
WSt...........	D. R. Moon Memorial Library, Stanley, WI [*Library symbol*] [*Library of Congress*] (LCLS)
WST..........	Water Supply Tank

WST..........	Weapon Safety Trainer
WST..........	Weapon System Test
WST..........	Weapon System Trainer [*Navy*]
WST..........	Weightlessness Simulation Test
WST..........	West Co., Inc. [*NYSE symbol*] (SPSG)
WST..........	Westerly [*Rhode Island*] [*Airport symbol*] (OAG)
WST..........	Westerly, RI [*Location identifier*] [*FAA*] (FAAL)
WST..........	Western Air Express [*Houston, TX*] [*FAA designator*] (FAAC)
WST..........	Western Standard Time [*Australia*]
W St...........	Wiener Studien [*A publication*]
WST..........	Wine and Spirit [*A publication*]
WSt...........	Word Study [*A publication*]
WST..........	World Ship Trust [*Cambridge, England*]
WST..........	Write Symbol Table
WSTA........	Charlotte Amalie, VI [*AM radio station call letters*]
WSTA........	Weapon System Task Analysis (AAG)
WSTA........	White Slave Traffic Act
WSTB........	Streetsboro, OH [*FM radio station call letters*]
WSTC........	Stamford, CT [*AM radio station call letters*]
WSTC........	Weapon System Total Complex
WSTC........	Weapons System Test Card (MCD)
WSTC........	Willimantic State Teachers College [*Connecticut*]
WSTCH.....	Wasatch Range [*National Weather Service*] (FAAC)
WSTD........	Standish, MI [*FM radio station call letters*]
WSTDA	Web Sling and Tiedown Association (EA)
WSTE........	Ponce, PR [*Television station call letters*]
WSTEA	Weapon System Training Effectiveness Analysis
WSTED	Water Science and Technology [*A publication*]
WSTE MAT ...	Waste Material [*Freight*]
WSTF	Cocoa Beach, FL [*FM radio station call letters*]
WSTF	Western Financial Corp. [*NASDAQ symbol*] (NQ)
WSTF	White Sands Test Facility [*New Mexico*] [*Military*]
WStG........	Wehrstrafgesetz [*Military Criminal Law*] [*German*] (ILCA)
WSTH	Columbus, GA [*AM radio station call letters*]
WSTH	Weapon System Tactical Handbook (MCD)
WSTH-FM ...	Alexander City, AL [*FM radio station call letters*]
WSTI	Welded Steel Tube Institute [*Later, STINA*] (EA)
WSTI-FM ...	Quitman, GA [*FM radio station call letters*]
WSTJ	St. Johnsbury, VT [*AM radio station call letters*]
WSTK........	Colonial Heights, VA [*AM radio station call letters*]
WSTL........	South Glens Falls, NY [*AM radio station call letters*]
WSTL........	Weapon System Test Laboratory
WSTL........	Whistle (MSA)
WStL & P ..	Wabash, St. Louis & Pacific Railway
WSTM.......	Western Micro Technology, Inc. [*NASDAQ symbol*] (NQ)
WSTM.......	White Sands Missile Range Transverse Mercator [*Army*] (AABC)
WSTM-TV ...	Syracuse, NY [*Television station call letters*]
WSTN	Somerville, TN [*AM radio station call letters*]
WSTN	Western
WSTN	Weston [*Roy F.*], Inc. [*West Chester, PA*] [*NASDAQ symbol*] (NQ)
WSTO	Owensboro, KY [*FM radio station call letters*]
WSTP	Salisbury, NC [*AM radio station call letters*]
WSTP	Weapon System Test Program
W & StP....	Winona & St. Peter Railroad
WSTPN.....	Wrist Pin
WSTQ	Streator, IL [*FM radio station call letters*]
WSTR........	Sturgis, MI [*AM radio station call letters*]
WSTR........	Westar Corp. [*Las Vegas, NV*] [*NASDAQ symbol*] (NQ)
W v Str.......	Wetboek van Strafrecht [*A publication*]
WSTR-FM ...	Smyrna, GA [*FM radio station call letters*]
WSTS	Laurinburg, NC [*FM radio station call letters*]
WSTS	Weapon System Training Set (AFM)
WSTS	Western States Life Insurance [*NASDAQ symbol*] (NQ)
WSTS	World Semiconductor Trade Statistics [*Semiconductor Industry Association*] [*Information service or system*] (IID)
WSTSA	Wall Street Transcript [*A publication*]
WSTSHD ...	Watershed
WSTU	Stuart, FL [*AM radio station call letters*]
W St UL Rev ...	Western State University. Law Review [*A publication*]
WSTV.......	Steubenville, OH [*AM radio station call letters*]
WSTW	Westworld Resources, Inc. [*NASDAQ symbol*] (NQ)
WSTW	Wilmington, DE [*FM radio station call letters*]
WSTX........	Christiansted, VI [*AM radio station call letters*]
WSTX........	Westronix, Inc. [*Midvale, UT*] [*NASDAQ symbol*] (NQ)
WSTX-FM ...	Christiansted, VI [*FM radio station call letters*]
WSTZ-FM ...	Vicksburg, MS [*FM radio station call letters*]
WSU	University of Wisconsin-Superior, Superior, WI [*Library symbol*] [*Library of Congress*] (LCLS)
WSU	Washington State University
WSU	Wasu [*Papua New Guinea*] [*Airport symbol*] (OAG)
WSU	Water Servicing Unit (NASA)
WSU	Wayne State University [*Michigan*]
WSU	Windmill Study Unit [*American Topical Association*] (EA)
WSU	Women on Stamps Unit [*American Topical Association*] (EA)
WSU	Work Station Utility
WSU	Wright State University, Dayton, OH [*OCLC symbol*] (OCLC)
WSUA	Miami, FL [*AM radio station call letters*]
WSUB	Groton, CT [*AM radio station call letters*]
W Succ R ...	Wetboek van Successierechten [*A publication*]

WSUC-FM ... Cortland, NY [*FM radio station call letters*]
WSUE .... Sault Ste. Marie, MI [*FM radio station call letters*]
WSUH...... Oxford, MS [*AM radio station call letters*]
WSU/HB... Human Biology. Official Publication. Human Biology Council. Wayne State University. School of Medicine [*A publication*]
WSUI........ Iowa City, IA [*AM radio station call letters*]
WSUL-FM ... Monticello, NY [*FM radio station call letters*]
WSUN...... St. Petersburg, FL [*AM radio station call letters*]
WSUOPR ... Washington State University, Open Pool Reactor
WSUP...... Platteville, WI [*FM radio station call letters*]
WSUR-TV ... Ponce, PR [*Television station call letters*]
WSUS....... Franklin, NJ [*FM radio station call letters*]
WSUV ...... Fort Myers Villas, FL [*FM radio station call letters*]
WSUW ...... Whitewater, WI [*FM radio station call letters*]
WSUX ...... Seaford, DE [*AM radio station call letters*]
WSUX-FM ... Seaford, DE [*FM radio station call letters*]
WSUZ ...... Palatka, FL [*AM radio station call letters*]
WSV .... Wall Street Ventures [*Vancouver Stock Exchange symbol*]
WSV .... Water Solenoid Valve
WSV .... Water-Soluble Vitamin
WSVA...... Harrisonburg, VA [*AM radio station call letters*]
WSVA...... Wang Software Vendors' Association [*Defunct*]   (EA)
WSVE....... Jacksonville, FL [*AM radio station call letters*]
WSVG ...... Mount Jackson, VA [*AM radio station call letters*]
WSVH .... Savannah, GA [*FM radio station call letters*]
WSVI .... Christiansted, VI [*Television station call letters*]
WSVL........ Shelbyville, IN [*AM radio station call letters*]
WSVM ...... Valdese, NC [*AM radio station call letters*]
WSVN ...... Miami, FL [*Television station call letters*]
WSVQ ...... Harrogate, TN [*AM radio station call letters*]
WSVS .... Crewe, VA [*AM radio station call letters*]
WSVS .... Wiland Services, Inc. [*Boulder, CO*] [*NASDAQ symbol*]   (NQ)
WSVS-FM ... Crewe, VA [*FM radio station call letters*]
WSVT....... Smyrna, TN [*AM radio station call letters*]
WSW .... Southwest Wisconsin Library System, Fennimore, WI [*OCLC symbol*]   (OCLC)
WSW .... Wall Street Week [*Television program*]
WSW .... West-Southwest
WSW .... Western Shelf Water [*Oceanography*]
WSW .... White Sidewall [*Tires*]
WSW .... Wirtschaftswissenschaft [*A publication*]
WSWA ...... Wine and Spirits Wholesalers of America   (EA)
WSWB-TV ... Scranton, PA [*Television station call letters*]
WSWI .... Evansville, IN [*AM radio station call letters*]
WSWL........ Warheads and Special Weapons Laboratory   (MCD)
WSWMA .. Water and Sewage Works Manufacturers Association [*Later, WWEMA*]   (EA)
WSWMA .. Western States Weights and Measures Association
WSWN ...... Belle Glade, FL [*AM radio station call letters*]
WSWO ...... Wilmington, OH [*FM radio station call letters*]
WSWOA ... Water and Sewage Works [*A publication*]
WSWP-TV ... Grandview, WV [*Television station call letters*]
WSWR...... Shelby, OH [*FM radio station call letters*]
WSWRN ...... West-Southwestern [*Meteorology*]   (FAAC)
WSWSA .... Wasserwirtschaft-Wassertechnik [*A publication*]
WSWT...... Peoria, IL [*FM radio station call letters*]
WSWTA.... Wasserwirtschaft [*A publication*]
WSWV ...... Pennington Gap, VA [*AM radio station call letters*]
WSWV-FM ... Pennington Gap, VA [*FM radio station call letters*]
WSWWD .. West-Southwestward [*Meteorology*]   (FAAC)
WSWZ...... Lancaster, OH [*FM radio station call letters*]
WSX .... Western Air Lines, Inc. [*Later, WAL*] [*NYSE symbol*]   (SPSG)
WSY .... Airlie Beach [*Australia*] [*Airport symbol*]
WSY .... West Somerset Yeomanry [*British military*]   (DMA)
WSYA....... Montgomery, AL [*AM radio station call letters*]
WSYA-FM ... Montgomery, AL [*FM radio station call letters*]
WSYB....... Rutland, VT [*AM radio station call letters*]
WSYC....... West Somerset Yeomanry Cavalry [*British military*]   (DMA)
WSYC-FM ... Shippensburg, PA [*FM radio station call letters*]
WSYD ...... Mount Airy, NC [*AM radio station call letters*]
WSYI....... Irwinton, GA [*FM radio station call letters*]
WSYL....... Sylvania, GA [*AM radio station call letters*]
WSYM-TV ... Lansing, MI [*Television station call letters*]
WSYN ...... Georgetown, SC [*FM radio station call letters*]
WSYP...... White Sulphur Springs & Yellowstone Park Railway Co. [*AAR code*]
WSYR....... Syracuse, NY [*AM radio station call letters*]
WSYT....... Syracuse, NY [*Television station call letters*]
WSYW-FM ... Danville, IN [*FM radio station call letters*]
WSYX....... Columbus, OH [*Television station call letters*]
WSYY....... Millinocket, ME [*AM radio station call letters*]
WSYY-FM ... Millinocket, ME [*FM radio station call letters*]
WSZ........... Vereniging Surinaams Bedrijfsleven. Weekbericht [*A publication*]
WSZ........... Westport [*New Zealand*] [*Airport symbol*]   (OAG)
WSZ........... Wheat-Sheep Zone [*Agriculture*]
WSZE-TV ... Saipan, CM [*Television station call letters*]
WT............ Three-Conductor Cables [*JETDS nomenclature*] [*Military*]   (CET)

WT............ WAAC Ltd. - Nigeria Airways [*Nigeria*] [*ICAO designator*]   (ICDA)
WT............ Waist Tether [*NASA*]   (KSC)
WT............ Wait Time [*Computer order entry*]
W/T.......... Walkie-Talkie
WT............ Wall Thickness [*Nuclear energy*]   (NRCH)
WT............ War Tax
WT............ War Transport [*British military*]   (DMA)
WT............ Warm Tone [*Photography*]
WT............ Warning Tag   (AAG)
WT............ Warrant
WT............ Warrant Telegraphist [*British military*]   (DMA)
WT............ Wartime
WT............ Wash Trough
WT............ Washington Territory [*Prior to statehood*]
WT............ Washington Territory Reports [*1854-88*] [*A publication*]   (DLA)
WT............ Waste Tank
WT............ Watch Time
WT............ Watchdog Timer   (MCD)
WT............ Watchdogs of the Treasury   (EA)
WT............ Water Tank
WT............ Water Tanker [*British*]
WT............ Water Tender [*Navy*]
WT............ Water Thermometer
WT............ Water-Tube Boiler [*Naval*]
WT............ Watertight
WT............ Waveguide Transmission
WT............ Weapon Test
WT............ Weapon Training   (MCD)
WT............ Weapons Technician [*Air Force*]   (AFM)
WT............ Weapons Tight [*Weapons will engage only objects identified as hostile*]
WT............ Weight   (AAG)
WT............ Weird Tales [*A publication*]
WT............ Weldwood Transportation Ltd. [*AAR code*]
WT............ Wellhead Tax [*Oil industry*]
WT............ Wetenschappelijke Tijdingen [*A publication*]
WT............ Whiffle Tree [*Structural test*]   (AAG)
WT............ White Pennant [*Navy*] [*British*]
WT............ Wieczory Teatralne [*A publication*]
WT............ Wild Track [*Cinematography*]
WT............ Wild Type [*of a species*] [*Genetics*]
WT............ Will Talk [*Telecommunications*]   (TEL)
WT............ William Tell Gunnery Mate
WT............ Wilms' Tumor [*Oncology*]
WT............ Wind Tunnel
WT............ Winterization Test   (AAG)
WT............ [*The*] Winter's Tale [*Shakespearean work*]
WT............ Wire Ticket [*NASA*]   (NASA)
WT............ Wire Transfer [*Banking*]
WT............ Wireless Telegraphy [*or Telephony*]
WT............ Wireless Transmitter
WT............ Wireless Truck [*British*]
WT............ With Tape
WT............ With Title [*Bibliography*]
WT............ Withholding Tax [*IRS*]
WT............ Without
WT............ Wood Threshold   (MSA)
WT............ Word Target [*Psychology*]
WT............ Word Terminal
WT............ Word Type
W/T.......... Work Track [*Cinematography*]
WT............ Workshop Trains [*British*]
WT............ World Tobacco [*A publication*]
WT............ Worldteam   (EA)
WT............ Written Testimony   (BJA)
WT............ Wyoming Territory
WT's.......... Working Tools [*Freemasonry*]
WTA.......... Tambohorano [*Madagascar*] [*Airport symbol*]   (OAG)
WTA.......... Washington Technological Association   (MCD)
WTA.......... Water Transport Association   (EA)
WTA.......... Welded Tube Co. of America [*AMEX symbol*]   (SPSG)
WTA.......... Western Timber Association   (EA)
WTA.......... Window Test Apparatus
WTA.......... Wire Traceability and Accountability [*NASA*]   (NASA)
WTA.......... Wissenschaftlich-Technischer Arbeitskreis fuer Denkmalpflege und Bauwerksanierung [*International Association for the Protection of Monuments and Restoration of Buildings*]   (EAIO)
WTA.......... Women's Tennis Association [*Later, WITA*]   (EA)
WTA.......... World Tax Report [*London*] [*A publication*]
WTA.......... World Teleport Association [*New York, NY*] [*Telecommunications*]   (TSSD)
WTA.......... World Textile Abstracts [*Information service or system*] [*A publication*]
WTA.......... Wyoming Trucking Association, Casper WY [*STAC*]
WTAB...... Tabor City, NC [*AM radio station call letters*]
WTAC...... Flint, MI [*AM radio station call letters*]
WTAD....... Quincy, IL [*AM radio station call letters*]
WTAE ...... Pittsburgh, PA [*AM radio station call letters*]

WTAE-TV ... Pittsburgh, PA [*Television station call letters*]
WTAG ...... Worcester, MA [*AM radio station call letters*]
WTAI........ Melbourne, FL [*AM radio station call letters*]
WTAJ-TV ... Altoona, PA [*Television station call letters*]
WTAK ...... Huntsville, AL [*AM radio station call letters*]
WTAL .... Tallahassee, FL [*AM radio station call letters*]
WTAN ...... Clearwater, FL [*AM radio station call letters*]
WTAO .... Murphysboro, IL [*FM radio station call letters*]
WTAP-TV ... Parkersburg, WV [*Television station call letters*]
WTAQ .... La Grange, IL [*AM radio station call letters*]
WTAR .... Norfolk, VA [*AM radio station call letters*]
WTAS....... Crete, IL [*FM radio station call letters*]
WTAT-TV ... Charleston, SC [*Television station call letters*]
WTAU .... Albany, GA [*Television station call letters*]
WT Aux B ... Water-Tube Auxiliary Boiler   (DS)
WTAW ...... College Station, TX [*AM radio station call letters*]
WTAX .... Springfield, IL [*AM radio station call letters*]
W/TAX...... Withholding Tax [*IRS*]   (AAG)
WTAY .... Robinson, IL [*AM radio station call letters*]
WTAY-FM ... Robinson, IL [*FM radio station call letters*]
WTAZ .... Morton, IL [*FM radio station call letters*]
WTB .... Wales Tourist Board   (DCTA)
WTB .... War Transportation Board [*World War II*]
WTB .... Water-Tube Boiler [*Naval*]
WTB .... Welttierschutzbund [*Also known as WFPA, FMPA*] [*World Federation for the Protection of Animals*]
WTB .... Where's the Beef? [*Slogan created by the Dancer Fitzgerald Sample advertising agency for Wendy's International, Inc.*]
WTB .... Wilderness Trail Bike
WTB .... Willamette Tariff Bureau Inc., Portland OR [*STAC*]
WTB .... Woerterbuch [*Dictionary*] [*German*]   (ROG)
WTBB........ Bonifay, FL [*FM radio station call letters*]
WTBC-FM ... Williston, VT [*FM radio station call letters*]
WTBD .... Work to Be Done   (ADA)
WTBF........ Troy, AL [*AM radio station call letters*]
WTBG .... Brownsville, TN [*FM radio station call letters*]
WTBH .... Chiefland, FL [*FM radio station call letters*]
WTBI........ Pickens, SC [*AM radio station call letters*]
WTBI-FM ... Greenville, SC [*FM radio station call letters*]
WTBK........ Manchester, KY [*FM radio station call letters*]
WTBK........ Westerbeke Corp. [*Avon, MA*] [*NASDAQ symbol*]   (NQ)
WTBL........ Central City, KY [*AM radio station call letters*]
WTBL........ McConnelsville, OH [*FM radio station call letters*]
WTBM .... Mexico, ME [*FM radio station call letters*]
WTBO .... Cumberland, MD [*AM radio station call letters*]
WTBQ ...... Warwick, NY [*AM radio station call letters*]
WTBR........ War Trade Board Rulings [*United States*] [*A publication*]   (DLA)
WTBR-FM ... Pittsfield, MA [*FM radio station call letters*]
WTBS........ Atlanta, GA [*Television station call letters*]
WTBS........ Water-Tube Boiler Survey   (DS)
WTB & TS ... Watch Tower Bible and Tract Society
WTBU .... Bar Harbor, ME [*FM radio station call letters*]
WTBX .... Hibbing, MN [*FM radio station call letters*]
WTBY .... Poughkeepsie, NY [*Television station call letters*]
WTBZ........ Grafton, WV [*AM radio station call letters*]
WTBZ-FM ... Grafton, WV [*FM radio station call letters*]
WTC .... New York [*New York*] Battery Park [*Airport symbol*]   (OAG)
WTC .... Wangaratta Technical College [*Australia*]
WTC .... War Transport Council [*Later, ITWC*] [*World War II*]
WTC .... Waste Water Technology Centre [*Canada*]   (ECON)
WTC .... Water Thermal and Chemical Technology Center [*University of California*] [*Research center*]   (RCD)
WTC .... Waterton [*Colorado*] [*Seismograph station code, US Geological Survey*] [*Closed*]   (SEIS)
WTC .... Well-Tempered Clavier [*Compositions of J. S. Bach*]
WTC .... Western Telecommunications Consulting Co. [*Los Angeles, CA*] [*Telecommunications*]   (TSSD)
WTC .... Wind Temperature Correction
WTC .... Wire Test Chamber
WTC .... Women's Talent Corps [*Later, CHS*]   (EA)
WTC .... Women's Theater Council
WTC .... Workload Transaction Code [*Navy*]   (NG)
WTC .... World Trade Center [*New York City*]
WTC .... World Trade Center of New Orleans [*New Orleans, LA*]   (EA)
WTCA .... Plymouth, IN [*AM radio station call letters*]
WTCA .... Water Terminal Clearance Authority [*Army*]   (AABC)
WTCA .... Welsh Terrier Club of America   (EA)
WTCA .... Wood Truss Council of America   (EA)
WTCA .... World Tasar Class Association   (EAIO)
WTCA .... World Trade Centers Association   (EA)
WTCARES ... Welsh Terrier Club of America Rescue Service   (EA)
WTCB....... Orangeburg, SC [*FM radio station call letters*]
WTCB....... Water Tender Construction Battalion [*Navy*]
WTCC....... Springfield, MA [*FM radio station call letters*]
WTCC........ Water Turbine Closed Coupled   (MSA)
WTCE....... Fort Pierce, FL [*Television station call letters*]
WTCG ...... Andalusia, AL [*AM radio station call letters*]
WTCH....... Shawano, WI [*AM radio station call letters*]
WTCI........ Chattanooga, TN [*Television station call letters*]

WTCI........ Western Telecommunications, Incorporated [*Englewood, CO*] [*Telecommunications*]
WTCIB...... Women's Travelers Center and Information Bank [*Later, WIB*]   (EA)
WTCJ .... Tell City, IN [*AM radio station call letters*]
WTCK ...... World Trade Center Korea
WTCL .... Chattahoochee, FL [*AM radio station call letters*]
WTCM ...... Traverse City, MI [*AM radio station call letters*]
WTCM ...... Weld Timer Control Module
WTCM-FM ... Traverse City, MI [*FM radio station call letters*]
WTCN .... Stillwater, MN [*AM radio station call letters*]
WTCO .... Campbellsville, KY [*AM radio station call letters*]
WTCO .... Western Transportation Company [*AAR code*]
WTCQ ...... Vidalia, GA [*FM radio station call letters*]
WTCR ...... Kenova, WV [*AM radio station call letters*]
WTCR-FM ... Huntington, WV [*FM radio station call letters*]
WTCS....... Fairmont, WV [*AM radio station call letters*]
WTCS....... Windshield Temperature Control Systems
WTCT........ Marion, IL [*Television station call letters*]
WTCV .... Greenup, KY [*AM radio station call letters*]
WTCV .... Weapon and Tracked Combat Vehicle   (MCD)
WTCW ...... Whitesburg, KY [*AM radio station call letters*]
WTCX .... Dayton, TN [*FM radio station call letters*]
WTD......... War Trade Department [*British*] [*World War II*]
WTD......... Water Turbine Direct   (MSA)
WTD......... Watertight Door
WTD......... Weapons Training Detachment [*Military*]
WTD......... Weighted Total Demerits [*Lubricating oil test*]
WTD......... Whitland [*British depot code*]
WTD......... Wind Tunnel Data
WTD......... World Today [*London*] [*A publication*]
WTD......... World Trade Directory [*A publication*] [*Department of Commerce*]
wtdb........... Water-Tube Domestic Boiler   (DS)
WTDI .... WTD Industries, Inc. [*Portland, OR*] [*NASDAQ symbol*]   (NQ)
WTDR ...... World Trade Directory Reports [*A publication*] [*Department of Commerce*]
WTDY ...... Madison, WI [*AM radio station call letters*]
WTE .... Waste-to-Energy [*Resource recycling*]
WTE .... Wattle Tannin Equivalent [*Chemistry*]
WTE .... Westate Resources, Inc. [*Vancouver Stock Exchange symbol*]
WTE .... World Tapes for Education [*Defunct*]
WTE .... Worse than Expected [*Politics*]
WTE .... Wotje [*Marshall Islands*] [*Airport symbol*]   (OAG)
W Teach..... Western Teacher [*A publication*]
WTEB........ New Bern, NC [*FM radio station call letters*]
WTEC........ Warrantech Corp. [*New York, NY*] [*NASDAQ symbol*]   (NQ)
WTEK........ Waste Technology Corp. [*New York, NY*] [*NASDAQ symbol*]   (NQ)
WTEL........ Philadelphia, PA [*AM radio station call letters*]
WTEL........ Walker Telecommunications Corp. [*NASDAQ symbol*]   (NQ)
W Tel .... Warrant Telegraphist [*British military*]
WTEN .... Albany, NY [*Television station call letters*]
W Ten .... Wright's Introduction to the Law of Tenures [*A publication*]   (DLA)
W & T Eq Ca ... White and Tudor's Leading Cases in Equity [*9 eds.*] [*1849-1928*] [*A publication*]   (DLA)
W TER ...... Washington Territory
WTES........ West Tennessee Experiment Station [*University of Tennessee at Knoxville*] [*Research center*]   (RCD)
WTF........... Waste Treatment Facility [*Nuclear energy*]   (IEEE)
WTF........... Waste Water Treatment Facility [*Nuclear energy*]   (NRCH)
WTF........... Welcome to Finland [*A publication*]
WTF........... Western Task Force [*Navy*]
WTF........... Will to Fire
WTF........... Wisconsin Test Facility [*Navy*]
WTF........... World Taekwondo Federation [*Seoul, Republic of Korea*]   (EAIO)
WTF........... World Timecapsule Fund   (EA)
WTFAA..... Washington Task Force on African Affairs [*Defunct*]   (EA)
WTFDA..... Worldwide Television-FM DX Association   (EA)
WTFM....... Kingsport, TN [*FM radio station call letters*]
WTFPA...... Wolf Trap Foundation for the Performing Arts   (EA)
WTG .... Waiting   (MSA)
WTG .... Weighting   (MSA)
WTG .... Williams Telecommunications Group [*Telecommunications service*]   (TSSD)
WTG .... Wind Tape Generation
WTG .... Wind Turbine Generator
WTG .... Worker Trait Group
WTGA .... Thomaston, GA [*AM radio station call letters*]
WTGA-FM ... Thomaston, GA [*FM radio station call letters*]
WTGC ...... Lewisburg, PA [*AM radio station call letters*]
WTGE-FM ... Baton Rouge, LA [*FM radio station call letters*]
WTGH....... Cayce, SC [*AM radio station call letters*]
WTGI-TV ... Wilmington, DE [*Television station call letters*]
WTGL-TV ... Cocoa, FL [*Television station call letters*]
WTGN...... Lima, OH [*FM radio station call letters*]
WTGP .... Greenville, PA [*FM radio station call letters*]
WTGQ........ Cairo, GA [*FM radio station call letters*]

WTGR .... Point Pleasant, WV [*AM radio station call letters*]
WTGR ...... Welcome to Greenland [*A publication*]
WTGS .... Hardeeville, SC [*Television station call letters*]
WTGV-FM ... Sandusky, MI [*FM radio station call letters*]
WTGY .... Charleston, MS [*FM radio station call letters*]
WTHE .... Mineola, NY [*AM radio station call letters*]
WTHE .... Workshop Test and Handling Equipment [*Military*] (CAAL)
WTHG .... Worthington Industries, Inc. [*NASDAQ symbol*] (NQ)
WTHI .... Terre Haute, IN [*AM radio station call letters*]
WTHI-FM ... Terre Haute, IN [*FM radio station call letters*]
WTHI-TV ... Terre Haute, IN [*Television station call letters*]
W Th J ...... Westminster Theological Journal [*A publication*]
WTHL .... Somerset, KY [*AM radio station call letters*]
WTHM .... Glen Arbor, MI [*FM radio station call letters*]
WTHO-FM ... Thomson, GA [*FM radio station call letters*]
WTHP .... Thomasville, NC [*FM radio station call letters*]
WTHPRF ... Weatherproof (MSA)
WTHR .... Indianapolis, IN [*Television station call letters*]
WTHR .... Weather
WTHR .... Weatherford [*R. V.*] Co. [*NASDAQ symbol*] (NQ)
WTHRA ...... Weather [*London*] [*A publication*]
WTHS .... Holland, MI [*FM radio station call letters*]
WTHT .... Portland, ME [*FM radio station call letters*]
WTHU .... Thurmont, MD [*AM radio station call letters*]
WTHV .... Hancock, MI [*FM radio station call letters*]
WTHWA ... Weatherwise [*A publication*]
WTHX-TV ... Manitowoc, WI [*Television station call letters*]
WTHZ .... Tallahassee, FL [*FM radio station call letters*]
WTI .... Weapons Training Instruction (MCD)
WTI .... Welcome to Iceland [*A publication*]
WTI .... West Texas Intermediate [*Crude oil*] (ECON)
WTI .... Wheelabrator Technologies, Inc. [*NYSE symbol*] (SPSG)
WTI .... Work Training in Industry
WTI .... World Trade Institute
WTI .... World Translations Index [*International Translations Centre*] [*Information service or system*]
WTIB .... Iuka, MS [*FM radio station call letters*]
WTIC .... Hartford, CT [*AM radio station call letters*]
WTICB .... Worldwide Travel Information Contact Book [*A publication*]
WTIC-FM ... Hartford, CT [*FM radio station call letters*]
WTIC-TV ... Hartford, CT [*Television station call letters*]
WTID .... Reform, AL [*FM radio station call letters*]
WTID .... World Travel Information Directory [*A publication*]
WTIE .... Wastewater Treatment Information Exchange [*National Small Flows Clearinghouse*]
WTIF .... Tifton, GA [*AM radio station call letters*]
WTIG .... Massillon, OH [*AM radio station call letters*]
WTIJ .... Roxbury, NH [*AM radio station call letters*]
WTIK .... Durham, NC [*AM radio station call letters*]
WTIL .... Mayaguez, PR [*AM radio station call letters*]
WTIM .... Taylorville, IL [*AM radio station call letters*]
WTIN .... Ponce, PR [*Television station call letters*]
WTIQ .... Manistique, MI [*AM radio station call letters*]
WTIQ-FM ... Gulliver, MI [*FM radio station call letters*]
WTIS .... Tampa, FL [*AM radio station call letters*]
WTIU .... Bloomington, IN [*Television station call letters*]
WTIV .... Titusville, PA [*AM radio station call letters*]
WTIX .... New Orleans, LA [*AM radio station call letters*]
WTJ .... Wedge Type Jack
WTJ .... Westminster Theological Journal [*A publication*]
WTJ .... Wrin, T. J., San Francisco CA [*STAC*]
WTJA .... Jamestown, NY [*Television station call letters*]
WTJB .... Columbus, GA [*FM radio station call letters*]
WTJC .... Springfield, OH [*Television station call letters*]
WTJH .... East Point, GA [*AM radio station call letters*]
WTJP .... Gadsden, AL [*Television station call letters*]
WTJR .... Quincy, IL [*Television station call letters*]
WTJS .... Jackson, TN [*AM radio station call letters*]
WTJT .... Crestview, FL [*FM radio station call letters*]
WTJU .... Charlottesville, VA [*FM radio station call letters*]
WTJX-TV ... Charlotte Amalie, VI [*Television station call letters*]
WTJY .... Taylorville, IL [*FM radio station call letters*]
WTJZ .... Newport News, VA [*AM radio station call letters*]
WTK .... Noatak [*Alaska*] [*Airport symbol*] (OAG)
WTK .... Noatak, AK [*Location identifier*] [*FAA*] (FAAL)
WTKI-FM ... Gulfport, MS [*FM radio station call letters*]
WTKK .... Manassas, VA [*Television station call letters*]
WTKK .... Wen-Tzu Kai-Ko [*A publication*]
WTKL .... Baton Rouge, LA [*AM radio station call letters*]
WTKM .... Hartford, WI [*AM radio station call letters*]
WTKM-FM ... Hartford, WI [*FM radio station call letters*]
WTKN .... Pinellas Park, FL [*AM radio station call letters*]
WTKO .... Ithaca, NY [*AM radio station call letters*]
WTKR-TV ... Norfolk, VA [*Television station call letters*]
WTKS .... Burnettown, SC [*AM radio station call letters*]
WTKT .... Georgetown, KY [*FM radio station call letters*]
WTKX .... Pensacola, FL [*FM radio station call letters*]
WTKY .... Tompkinsville, KY [*AM radio station call letters*]
WTKY-FM ... Tompkinsville, KY [*FM radio station call letters*]
WTL .... Tuntatuliak [*Alaska*] [*Airport symbol*] (OAG)
WTL .... Western Canadian Land [*Vancouver Stock Exchange symbol*]

WTL .... Western Trunk Line Committee, Chicago IL [*STAC*]
WTL .... Wyle Test Laboratories
WTLB .... Utica, NY [*AM radio station call letters*]
WTLC .... Indianapolis, IN [*FM radio station call letters*]
WTLC .... Western Tele-Communications, Inc. [*Englewood, CO*] [*NASDAQ symbol*] (NQ)
WTLC .... Western Trunk Line Committee
W & TLC ... White and Tudor's Leading Cases in Equity [*9 eds.*] [*1849-1928*] [*A publication*] (DLA)
WTLG .... Starke, FL [*FM radio station call letters*]
WTLH .... Bainbridge, GA [*Television station call letters*]
WTLJ .... Muskegon, MI [*Television station call letters*]
WTLK .... Taylorsville, NC [*AM radio station call letters*]
WTLL .... Live Oak, FL [*Television station call letters*]
WTLN .... Apopka, FL [*AM radio station call letters*]
WTLN-FM ... Apopka, FL [*FM radio station call letters*]
WTLO .... Somerset, KY [*AM radio station call letters*]
WTLR .... State College, PA [*FM radio station call letters*]
WTLS .... Tallassee, AL [*AM radio station call letters*]
WTLS .... West Texas Library System [*Library network*]
WTLV .... Jacksonville, FL [*Television station call letters*]
WTLW ...... Lima, OH [*Television station call letters*]
WTLZ .... Saginaw, MI [*FM radio station call letters*]
WTM .... Western Mail [*United Kingdom*] [*A publication*]
WTM .... Wind Tunnel Memorandum
WTM .... Wind Tunnel Model
WTM .... World Travel Market [*Trade show*] [*British*] (ITD)
WTMA ...... Charleston, SC [*AM radio station call letters*]
WTMA ...... Wood Tank Manufacturers Association (EA)
WTMB ...... Tomah, WI [*AM radio station call letters*]
WTMC ...... Ocala, FL [*AM radio station call letters*]
WTME ...... Auburn, ME [*AM radio station call letters*]
WTMG ...... Tallahassee, FL [*FM radio station call letters*]
WTMI .... Miami, FL [*FM radio station call letters*]
WTMJ ...... Milwaukee, WI [*AM radio station call letters*]
WTMJ-TV ... Milwaukee, WI [*Television station call letters*]
WTMP ...... Temple Terrace, FL [*AM radio station call letters*]
WTMR ...... Camden, NJ [*AM radio station call letters*]
WTMRF ..... Westmount Resources Ltd. [*NASDAQ symbol*] (NQ)
WTMS .... Presque Isle, ME [*FM radio station call letters*]
WTMS .... World Trade in Minerals Data Base System [*Data processing*]
WTMT .... Louisville, KY [*AM radio station call letters*]
WTMV .... Lakeland, FL [*Television station call letters*]
WTMW .... Arlington, VA [*Television station call letters*]
WTMX ...... Skokie, IL [*FM radio station call letters*]
WTMX ...... Wang Telephone Message Exchange [*Wang Laboratories, Inc.*] [*Telecommunications service*] (TSSD)
WTN .... Journal of World Trade Law [*A publication*]
WTN .... Western Technical Net [*Air Force*]
WTN .... Wind Tunnel Note
WTN .... Witness
WTN .... Wroclawskie Towarzystwo Naukowe [*A publication*]
WTNC .... Thomasville, NC [*AM radio station call letters*]
WTNE .... Trenton, TN [*AM radio station call letters*]
WTNH-TV ... New Haven, CT [*Television station call letters*]
WTNI .... Hartsville, SC [*AM radio station call letters*]
WTNJ .... Mount Hope, WV [*FM radio station call letters*]
WTNK .... Destin, FL [*Television station call letters*]
WTNL .... Reidsville, GA [*AM radio station call letters*]
WTNN .... Farragut, TN [*AM radio station call letters*]
WTNR .... Waynesboro, TN [*AM radio station call letters*]
WTNS .... Coshocton, OH [*AM radio station call letters*]
WTNS-FM ... Coshocton, OH [*FM radio station call letters*]
WTNSTH ... Witnesseth [*Legal*] [*British*] (ROG)
WTNT .... Tallahassee, FL [*FM radio station call letters*]
WTNV .... Jackson, TN [*FM radio station call letters*]
WTNX .... Lynchburg, TN [*AM radio station call letters*]
WTNY .... Watertown, NY [*AM radio station call letters*]
WTNY-FM ... Watertown, NY [*FM radio station call letters*]
WTO .... Warsaw Treaty Organization
WTO .... Westam Oil Ltd. [*Vancouver Stock Exchange symbol*]
WTO .... WESTPAC [*Western Pacific*] Transportation Office (CINC)
WTO .... Wireless Telegraphy Officer [*British military*] (DMA)
WTO .... World Tourism Organization [*Madrid, Spain*]
WTO .... Wotho [*Marshall Islands*] [*Airport symbol*] (OAG)
WTO .... Write-to-Operator [*Data processing*] (IBMDP)
WTOB .... Winston-Salem, NC [*AM radio station call letters*]
WTOC-TV ... Savannah, GA [*Television station call letters*]
WTOD .... Toledo, OH [*AM radio station call letters*]
WTOE .... Spruce Pine, NC [*AM radio station call letters*]
WTOEW ... Welcome to Our Elvis World (EA)
WTOF-FM ... Canton, OH [*FM radio station call letters*]
WTOG .... St. Petersburg, FL [*Television station call letters*]
WTOH ...... Mobile, AL [*FM radio station call letters*]
WTOH ...... Western Ohio Railroad Co. [*AAR code*]
WTOJ .... Carthage, NY [*FM radio station call letters*]
WTOK-TV ... Meridian, MS [*Television station call letters*]
WTOL-TV ... Toledo, OH [*Television station call letters*]
WTOM-TV ... Cheboygan, MI [*Television station call letters*]
WTON .... Staunton, VA [*AM radio station call letters*]
WTON-FM ... Staunton, VA [*FM radio station call letters*]

WTOO.......	Asheville, NC [*AM radio station call letters*]
WTOP.......	Washington, DC [*AM radio station call letters*]
WTOQ.......	Platteville, WI [*AM radio station call letters*]
WTOR.......	Write-to-Operator with Reply [*Data processing*] (IBMDP)
WTOS	Western Test Range Office of Safety [*Air Force*] (MCD)
WTOS-FM ...	Skowhegan, ME [*FM radio station call letters*]
WTOT	Marianna, FL [*AM radio station call letters*]
WToVA	United States Veterans Administration Hospital, Tomah, WI [*Library symbol*] [*Library of Congress*] (LCLS)
WTOV-TV ...	Steubenville, OH [*Television station call letters*]
WTOW.......	Washington, NC [*AM radio station call letters*]
WTOX.......	Lincoln, ME [*AM radio station call letters*]
WTOY.......	Roanoke, VA [*AM radio station call letters*]
WTP	Warrant to Pollute
WTP	Waste Water Treatment Plant [*Also, WWTP*]
WTP	Water Treatment Plant [*Nuclear energy*] (NRCH)
WTP	Weapons Testing Program (AAG)
WTP	Wiggins Teape Paper [*Commercial firm*] [*British*]
WTP	Woitape [*Papua New Guinea*] [*Airport symbol*] (OAG)
WTP	World Tape Pals (EA)
WTPA.......	Mechanicsburg, PA [*FM radio station call letters*]
WTPA.......	Wheelchair Tennis Players Association (EA)
WTPBC.....	Wool Textiles Production Board of Control [*British*] [*World War I*]
WTPC.......	Elsah, IL [*FM radio station call letters*]
WTPI........	Indianapolis, IN [*FM radio station call letters*]
WTPM	Aguadilla, PR [*FM radio station call letters*]
WTPR.......	Paris, TN [*AM radio station call letters*]
WTPR.......	Wetterau Properties, Inc. [*NASDAQ symbol*] (NQ)
WTQR.......	Winston-Salem, NC [*FM radio station call letters*]
WTQX	Selma, AL [*AM radio station call letters*]
WTR	Sierra Spring Water Co. [*AMEX symbol*] (SPSG)
WTR	Waiter
WTR	War Tax Resistance [*An association*] [*Defunct*] (EA)
WTR	Warstar Resources, Inc. [*Vancouver Stock Exchange symbol*]
WTR	Water
WTR	Water Turnover Rate [*Physiology*]
WTR	Waterford and Tranmore Railway [*British*] (ROG)
WTR	Waters Associates, Milford, MA [*OCLC symbol*] (OCLC)
WTR	Waterville [*Colby College*] [*Maine*] [*Seismograph station code, US Geological Survey*] (SEIS)
WTR	Weekly Transcript Reports [*New York*] [*A publication*] (DLA)
WTR	Well to Right [*Aviation*] (FAAC)
WTR	Western Test Range [*Formerly, Pacific Missile Range*] [*Air Force*]
WTR	Westinghouse Test Reactor
WTR	Winter
WTR	Work Transfer Record (KSC)
WTR	Work Transfer Request
WTR	World Travel [*A publication*]
WTR	Wrightsville & Tennille R. R. [*AAR code*]
WTR	Writer
WTRA	Mayaguez, PR [*Television station call letters*]
WTRB.......	Ripley, TN [*AM radio station call letters*]
WTRC.......	Elkhart, IN [*AM radio station call letters*]
WTRC	Weapon Test Reports Committee [*AEC-DoD*]
WTRC	Women's Training and Resources Corporation
WTRE.......	Greensburg, IN [*AM radio station call letters*]
WTRF-TV ...	Wheeling, WV [*Television station call letters*]
WTRG	Rocky Mount, NC [*FM radio station call letters*]
WTRH.......	Charlotte Amalie, VI [*FM radio station call letters*]
WTRI........	Brunswick, MD [*AM radio station call letters*]
WTRJ........	Troy, OH [*FM radio station call letters*]
WTRM	Western Test Range Manual [*Air Force*] (MCD)
WTRM	Winchester, VA [*FM radio station call letters*]
WTRN	Tyrone, PA [*AM radio station call letters*]
WTRO.......	Dyersburg, TN [*AM radio station call letters*]
WTRP.......	La Grange, GA [*AM radio station call letters*]
WTRPP.....	Water Pump Propeller [*on a ship*] (DS)
WTRPRF...	Waterproof (MSA)
WTRPRFG ...	Waterproofing
WTRQ	Warsaw, NC [*AM radio station call letters*]
WTRS........	Dunnellon, FL [*AM radio station call letters*]
WTRS........	Waters Instruments, Inc. [*NASDAQ symbol*] (NQ)
WTRS-FM ...	Dunellon, FL [*FM radio station call letters*]
WTRSYS...	Water System (MCD)
WTRT........	Florence, AL [*Television station call letters*]
WTRTT.....	Watertight (MSA)
WTRW	Two Rivers, WI [*AM radio station call letters*]
WTRY.......	Troy, NY [*AM radio station call letters*]
WTRZ........	Winterize (AAG)
WTRZ-FM ...	McMinnville, TN [*FM radio station call letters*]
WTRZN	Winterization (AAG)
WTS..........	Tsiroanomandidy [*Madagascar*] [*Airport symbol*] (OAG)
WTS..........	War Training Service [*of the Civil Aeronautics Administration*] [*Formerly Civilian Pilot Training*] [*World War II*]
WTS..........	Watermen's Trade Society [*A union*] [*British*]
WTS..........	Watersport. Maandblad voor de Zeilsport. Motorbootsport [*A publication*]
WTS..........	Weapons Training Site [*Military*]
WTS..........	Western Tariff Service Inc., Oakland CA [*STAC*]
WTS..........	Westminster Theological Seminary, Philadelphia, PA [*OCLC symbol*] (OCLC)
WTS..........	Whale Tumor Story [*Urban folklore term coined by Rodney Dale*]
WTS..........	Wind Tunnel Study
WTS..........	Wing Tank Structure
WTS..........	Winterswijk [*Netherlands*] [*Seismograph station code, US Geological Survey*] (SEIS)
WTS..........	Women's Transport Service [*British*]
WTS..........	Women's Transportation Seminar [*Later, WTSN*] (EA)
WTS..........	Word Terminal Synchronous
4WTS........	Four-Wire Terminating Set [*Telecommunications*] (TEL)
WTSA........	Brattleboro, VT [*AM radio station call letters*]
WTSA........	Wood Turners and Shapers Association [*Later, WPMA*] (EA)
WTSA-FM ...	Brattleboro, VT [*FM radio station call letters*]
WTSB.......	Lumberton, NC [*AM radio station call letters*]
WTSB.......	Wood Turners Service Bureau [*Later, WPMA*]
WTSC.......	West Texas State College [*Later, WTSU*]
WTSC.......	Wet Tantalum Slug Capacitor (NASA)
WTSC-FM ...	Potsdam, NY [*FM radio station call letters*]
WTSF.......	Ashland, KY [*Television station call letters*]
WTSFLW ...	Women's Trade Society of Fancy Leather Workers [*A union*] [*British*]
WTSH.......	Rome, GA [*AM radio station call letters*]
WTSH-FM ...	Rockmart, GA [*FM radio station call letters*]
WTSI........	Western Tar Sands, Inc. [*NASDAQ symbol*] (NQ)
WTSJ........	Cincinnati, OH [*AM radio station call letters*]
WTSK.......	Tuscaloosa, AL [*AM radio station call letters*]
WTSL.......	Hanover, NH [*AM radio station call letters*]
WTSL-FM ...	Hanover, NH [*FM radio station call letters*]
WTSN	Dover, NH [*AM radio station call letters*]
WTSN	Women's Transportation Seminar-National (EA)
WTSNG	Witnessing [*Legal*] [*British*] (ROG)
WTSO	Madison, WI [*AM radio station call letters*]
WTSPT	Waterspout
WTSP-TV ...	St. Petersburg, FL [*Television station call letters*]
WTSR.......	Trenton, NJ [*FM radio station call letters*]
WTSU	Troy, AL [*FM radio station call letters*]
WTSU	West Texas State University [*Formerly, WTSC*]
WTSU-TV ...	Montgomery, AL [*Television station call letters*]
WTSV	Claremont, NH [*AM radio station call letters*]
WTSX.......	Port Jervis, NY [*FM radio station call letters*]
WTT	Weapon Tactics Trainer (MCD)
WTT	Weird Terror Tales [*A publication*]
WTT	Western Tank Truck Carriers' Conference Inc., Denver CO [*STAC*]
WTT	Westmount Resources Ltd. [*Toronto Stock Exchange symbol*]
WTT	Wind Tunnel Test
WTT	Working Timetable (DCTA)
WTT	World Team Tennis [*League*]
WTTA	St. Petersburg, FL [*Television station call letters*]
WTTB.......	Vero Beach, FL [*AM radio station call letters*]
WTTC.......	Towanda, PA [*AM radio station call letters*]
WTTC.......	Western Technical Training Command [*AAFWTTC*]
WTTC.......	World Technology & Trading [*NASDAQ symbol*] (NQ)
WTTC-FM ...	Towanda, PA [*FM radio station call letters*]
WTTE.......	Columbus, OH [*Television station call letters*]
WTTF.......	Tiffin, OH [*AM radio station call letters*]
WTTF.......	Welcome to the Faeroes [*A publication*]
WTTF-FM ...	Tiffin, OH [*FM radio station call letters*]
WTTG	Washington, DC [*Television station call letters*]
WTTI........	Dalton, GA [*AM radio station call letters*]
WTTK.......	Kokomo, IN [*Television station call letters*]
WTTL.......	Madisonville, KY [*AM radio station call letters*]
WTTM	Trenton, NJ [*AM radio station call letters*]
WTTN	Watertown, WI [*AM radio station call letters*]
WTTO	Birmingham, AL [*Television station call letters*]
WTTR.......	Westminster, MD [*AM radio station call letters*]
WTTS.......	Bloomington, IN [*FM radio station call letters*]
WTTT.......	Amherst, MA [*AM radio station call letters*]
WTTU	Cookeville, TN [*FM radio station call letters*]
WTTV.......	Bloomington, IN [*Television station call letters*]
WTTW	Chicago, IL [*Television station call letters*] [*Letters stand for "Windows to the World"*]
WTTX.......	Appomattox, VA [*AM radio station call letters*]
WTTX-FM ...	Appomattox, VA [*FM radio station call letters*]
WTU	Washington University, St. Louis, MO [*OCLC symbol*] (OCLC)
WTU	Weekly TIF [*Taxpayer Information File*] Update [*IRS*]
WTU	Whitetails Unlimited (EA)
WTUA	St. Stephen, SC [*FM radio station call letters*]
WTUB.......	Georgetown, SC [*FM radio station call letters*]
WTUE.......	Dayton, OH [*FM radio station call letters*]
WTUF.......	Boston, GA [*FM radio station call letters*]
WTUG	Tuscaloosa, AL [*FM radio station call letters*]
WTUJ........	Ridgeland, MS [*AM radio station call letters*]
WTUK.......	Harlan, KY [*AM radio station call letters*]
WTUL.......	New Orleans, LA [*FM radio station call letters*]
WTUN	Pocatilico, WV [*FM radio station call letters*]
WTUP	Tupelo, MS [*AM radio station call letters*]
WTUR........	Truro, MA [*FM radio station call letters*]

WTURB	Water Turbine (MSA)
WTURN	White Turnout [*Political science*]
WTUS	Mannington, WV [*FM radio station call letters*]
WTUV	Utica, NY [*Television station call letters*]
WTUX	Indianapolis, IN [*AM radio station call letters*]
WTV	Water Tank Vessel [*Navy*]
WTVA	Tupelo, MS [*Television station call letters*]
WTVA	Wider Television Access [*British*]
WTVB	Coldwater, MI [*AM radio station call letters*]
WTVC	Chattanooga, TN [*Television station call letters*]
WTVD	Durham, NC [*Television station call letters*]
WTVE	Reading, PA [*Television station call letters*]
WTVF	Nashville, TN [*Television station call letters*]
WTVG	Toledo, OH [*Television station call letters*]
WTVH	Syracuse, NY [*Television station call letters*]
WTVI	Charlotte, NC [*Television station call letters*]
WTVJ	Miami, FL [*Television station call letters*]
WTVL	Waterville, ME [*AM radio station call letters*]
WTVL-FM ...	Waterville, ME [*FM radio station call letters*]
WTVM	Columbus, GA [*Television station call letters*]
WTVN	Columbus, OH [*AM radio station call letters*]
WTVO	Rockford, IL [*Television station call letters*]
WTVP	Peoria, IL [*Television station call letters*]
WTVQ-TV ...	Lexington, KY [*Television station call letters*]
WTVR	Richmond, VA [*AM radio station call letters*]
WTVR-FM ...	Richmond, VA [*FM radio station call letters*]
WTVR-TV ...	Richmond, VA [*Television station call letters*]
WTVS	Detroit, MI [*Television station call letters*]
WTVT	Tampa, FL [*Television station call letters*]
WTVU	New Haven, CT [*Television station call letters*]
WTVW	Evansville, IN [*Television station call letters*]
WTVX	Fort Pierce, FL [*Television station call letters*]
WTVY	Dothan, AL [*Television station call letters*]
WTVY-FM ...	Dothan, AL [*FM radio station call letters*]
WTVZ	Norfolk, VA [*Television station call letters*]
WTw	Joseph Mann Library, Two Rivers, WI [*Library symbol*] [*Library of Congress*] (LCLS)
WTW	Materials Reclamation Weekly [*A publication*]
WTW	Wall to Wall [*Technical drawings*]
WTW	West Thumb [*Wyoming*] [*Seismograph station code, US Geological Survey*] (SEIS)
WTW	Writers and Their Work [*A publication*]
WTW	Wroclawskie Towarzystwo Naukowe [*A publication*]
WTWA	Thomson, GA [*AM radio station call letters*]
WTWA	World Trade Writers Association [*New York, NY*] (EA)
WTWB	Auburndale, FL [*AM radio station call letters*]
WTWC	Tallahassee, FL [*Television station call letters*]
WT (Werkstattstech) Z Ind Fertigung ...	WT (Werkstattstechnik). Zeitschrift fuer Industrielle Fertigung [*A publication*]
WTWF	Woodville, FL [*AM radio station call letters*]
WTWO	Terre Haute, IN [*Television station call letters*]
WTWR-FM ...	Monroe, MI [*FM radio station call letters*]
WTWS	New London, CT [*Television station call letters*]
WTWS	Wall to Wall Sound & Video, Inc. [*Cinnaminson, NJ*] [*NASDAQ symbol*] (NQ)
WTWX-FM ...	Guntersville, AL [*FM radio station call letters*]
WTWZ	Clinton, MS [*AM radio station call letters*]
WTX	West Texas Utilities Co. [*AMEX symbol*] (SPSG)
WTXF-TV ...	Philadelphia, PA [*Television station call letters*]
WTXI	Ripley, MS [*FM radio station call letters*]
WTXL-TV ...	Tallahassee, FL [*Television station call letters*]
WTXN	Lafayette, AL [*AM radio station call letters*]
WTXT	Fayette, AL [*FM radio station call letters*]
WTXX	Waterbury, CT [*Television station call letters*]
WTXY	Whiteville, NC [*AM radio station call letters*]
WTY	Westley Mines Ltd. [*Toronto Stock Exchange symbol*] [*Vancouver Stock Exchange symbol*]
WTYD	New London, CT [*FM radio station call letters*]
WTYF	World Theosophical Youth Federation [*Porto Alegre, Brazil*] (EAIO)
WTYJ	Fayette, MS [*FM radio station call letters*]
WTYL	Tylertown, MS [*AM radio station call letters*]
WTYL-FM ...	Tylertown, MS [*FM radio station call letters*]
WTYN	Tryon, NC [*AM radio station call letters*]
WTYN	Youngstown, OH [*FM radio station call letters*]
WTYO	Hammonton, NJ [*AM radio station call letters*]
WTYR	Soddy-Daisy, TN [*AM radio station call letters*]
W Ty R	Washington Territory Reports [*1854-88*] [*A publication*] (DLA)
WTYS	Marianna, FL [*AM radio station call letters*]
WTYX	Jackson, MS [*FM radio station call letters*]
WTZ	Weird Tales [*1973-*] [*A publication*]
WTZ	Western Trinity Resource [*Vancouver Stock Exchange symbol*]
WTZ	Whakatane [*New Zealand*] [*Seismograph station code, US Geological Survey*] (SEIS)
WTZA	Kingston, NY [*Television station call letters*]
WTZE	Tazewell, VA [*AM radio station call letters*]
WTZE-FM ...	Tazewell, VA [*FM radio station call letters*]
WTZH	Meridian, MS [*Television station call letters*]
WTZIA	WT [*Werkstattstechnik*]. Zeitschrift fuer Industrielle Fertigung [*A publication*]

Wt Z Ind Fe ...	Werkstattstechnik Zeitschrift fuer Industrielle Fertigung [*A publication*]
WT Z Ind Fertigung ...	WT [*Werkstattstechnik*]. Zeitschrift fuer Industrielle Fertigung [*A publication*]
WTZQ	Hendersonville, NC [*AM radio station call letters*]
WTZX	Sparta, TN [*AM radio station call letters*]
WU	University of Wisconsin, Madison, WI [*Library symbol*] [*Library of Congress*] (LCLS)
WU	Weather Underground (EA)
WU	Weekly Underwriter [*A publication*]
WU	Wesleyan University
WU	Western European Union [*Also, WEU*] (NATG)
WU	Western Union Corp. [*NYSE symbol*] (SPSG)
WU	Western Union Telegraph Co. (TSSD)
WU	Whitetails Unlimited (EA)
WU	Window Unit (MSA)
WU	Work Unit [*Air Force*] (AFM)
w/u	Work-Up
WU	Workshop Unit (MSA)
WU	World Union [*Pondicherry, India*] (EA)
WU-A	University of Wisconsin, Agricultural Library, Madison, WI [*Library symbol*] [*Library of Congress*] (LCLS)
WUA	Weapon Utility Analysis
WUA	Western Underwriters Association [*Later, ISO*]
WUA	Work Unit Assignment [*Navy*] (NG)
WUAA	Marquette, MI [*Television station call letters*]
WUAA	Wartime Unit Aircraft Activity (AFM)
WUAB	Lorain, OH [*Television station call letters*]
WUAG	Greensboro, NC [*FM radio station call letters*]
WUAL-FM ...	Tuscaloosa, AL [*FM radio station call letters*]
WUAR	Women United Against Rape
WUAT	Pikeville, TN [*AM radio station call letters*]
WUAW	Erwin, NC [*FM radio station call letters*]
WUBE	Cincinnati, OH [*FM radio station call letters*]
WUBOA	Wasser und Boden [*A publication*]
WUBU	Portage, MI [*FM radio station call letters*]
WUBW	World Union of Black Writers [*See also UEMN*] (EAIO)
WUC	Western Union Corporation
WUC	Work Unit Code
WUC	Writers Union of Canada
WUC	Wu-han [*Republic of China*] [*Seismograph station code, US Geological Survey*] (SEIS)
WUCDU	World Union of Christian Democratic Women [*Venezuela*] [*Political party*] (EAIO)
WUCF	Work Unit Code File (NASA)
WUCF-FM ...	Orlando, FL [*FM radio station call letters*]
WUCI-FM ...	Binghamton, NY [*FM radio station call letters*]
WUCM	Work Unit Code Manual
WUCM-TV ...	University Center, MI [*Television station call letters*]
WUCO	Marysville, OH [*AM radio station call letters*]
WUCOS	Western European Union Chiefs of Staff (NATG)
WUCP	Summerdale, PA [*FM radio station call letters*]
WUCPS	World Union of Catholic Philosophical Societies (EA)
WUCT	World Union of Catholic Teachers
WUCWO ...	World Union of Catholic Women's Organizations [*Rosemere, PQ*] (EAIO)
WUCX-FM ...	Bay City, MI [*FM radio station call letters*]
WUCX-TV ...	Bad Axe, MI [*Television station call letters*]
WuD	Wort und Dienst. Jahrbuch der Theologischen Schule Bethel [*Bethel Bei Bielefeld*] [*A publication*]
WUDB	Work Unit Data Bank
WU-DE	University of Wisconsin, Center for Demography and Ecology, Madison, WI [*Library symbol*] [*Library of Congress*] (LCLS)
WUDO	Western European Union Defense Organization (NATG)
WUDZ	Sweet Briar, VA [*FM radio station call letters*]
WU-E	University of Wisconsin, Engineering Library, Madison, WI [*Library symbol*] [*Library of Congress*] (LCLS)
WUE	Water-Use Efficiency [*Agriculture*]
WUE	Work Unit Engineer
WUEC	Eau Claire, WI [*FM radio station call letters*]
WUEMI	Western Union Electronic Mail, Incorporated [*McLean, VA*] [*Telecommunications*] (TSSD)
Wuerttemb Aerztebl ...	Wuerttembergisches Aerzteblatt [*A publication*]
Wuerttemberg Blaetter Km ...	Wuerttembergische Blaetter fuer Kirchenmusik [*A publication*]
Wuerttemb Wochenbl Landwirt ...	Wuerttembergisches Wochenblatt fuer Landwirtschaft [*A publication*]
Wuerzb Jb Alt Wiss ...	Wuerzburger Jahrbuecher fuer die Altertumswissenschaft [*A publication*]
Wuerzburg Geogr Arb ...	Wuerzburger Geographische Arbeiten [*A publication*]
Wuerz Jb....	Wuerzburger Jahrbuecher fuer die Altertumswissenschaft [*A publication*]
WUEV	Evansville, IN [*FM radio station call letters*]
WUEZ-FM ...	Morris, IL [*FM radio station call letters*]
WUF	Wattle-Urea-Formaldehyde [*Adhesive component*]
WUF	Western United Front [*Fiji*] [*Political party*] (PPW)
WUF	World Underwater Federation (ASF)
WUF	World Union of Free Thinkers

WUF.........	World University, Miami Learning Resource Center, Miami, FL [*OCLC symbol*] (OCLC)
WUFE.......	Baxley, GA [*AM radio station call letters*]
WUFEC.....	Western European Union Finance and Economic Committee (NATG)
WUFF.......	Eastman, GA [*AM radio station call letters*]
WUFF-FM ...	Eastman, GA [*FM radio station call letters*]
WUFK	Fort Kent, ME [*FM radio station call letters*]
WUFL........	Sterling Heights, MI [*AM radio station call letters*]
WUFM.......	Lebanon, PA [*FM radio station call letters*]
WUFN........	Albion, MI [*FM radio station call letters*]
WUFO........	Amherst, NY [*AM radio station call letters*]
WUFR........	World Union of Free Romanians [*See also UMRL*] [*Creteil, France*] (EAIO)
WUFS........	World Union of French-Speakers [*See also UMVF*] (EAIO)
WUFT	Gainesville, FL [*Television station call letters*]
WUFT-FM ...	Gainesville, FL [*FM radio station call letters*]
WUFTU	World Union of Free Trade Unions
WUFX-FM ...	Buffalo, NY [*FM radio station call letters*]
WUg..........	Graham Public Library, Union Grove, WI [*Library symbol*] [*Library of Congress*] (LCLS)
WUG........	Wau [*Papua New Guinea*] [*Airport symbol*] (OAG)
WuG.........	Wissenschaft und Gegenwart [*A publication*]
WUGA.......	Athens, GA [*FM radio station call letters*]
WUGGAO ...	Contributions to Geology. University of Wyoming [*A publication*]
WUGN	Midland, MI [*FM radio station call letters*]
WUGO	Grayson, KY [*FM radio station call letters*]
WUgSC	Southern Wisconsin Colony and Training School, Medical Library, Union Grove, WI [*Library symbol*] [*Library of Congress*] (LCLS)
WUH	Wu-han [*Republic of China*] [*Seismograph station code, US Geological Survey*] (SEIS)
WUH	Wuhan [*China*] [*Airport symbol*] (OAG)
Wuhan Univ J Nat Sci ...	Wuhan University Journal. Natural Sciences [*People's Republic of China*] [*A publication*]
WUHF	Rochester, NY [*Television station call letters*]
WUHN......	Pittsfield, MA [*AM radio station call letters*]
WUHQ-TV ...	Battle Creek, MI [*Television station call letters*]
WUHS........	Urbana, OH [*AM radio station call letters*]
WUI.........	Western Union International [*Division of WUI, Inc.*]
WUIS........	Water Use Information System [*Westinghouse Hanford Co.*] (IID)
WUIS........	Work Unit Information System [*Database*] [*DTIC*]
WUIV	Icard Township, NC [*AM radio station call letters*]
WUJA	Caguas, PR [*Television station call letters*]
WUJC.......	University Heights, OH [*FM radio station call letters*]
WUJS........	World Union of Jewish Students [*Jerusalem, Israel*]
WUKEE8 ..	Wuyi Science Journal [*A publication*]
WUKO.......	World Union of Karatedo Organizations [*Solna, Sweden*] (EAIO)
WUKY	Lexington, KY [*FM radio station call letters*]
WU-L.........	University of Wisconsin, Law Library, Madison, WI [*Library symbol*] [*Library of Congress*] (LCLS)
WUL..........	Washington University, Law Library, St. Louis, MO [*OCLC symbol*] (OCLC)
WUL..........	Workers Unity League [*Canada*]
WULA	Eufaula, AL [*AM radio station call letters*]
WULA-FM ...	Eufaula, AL [*FM radio station call letters*]
WULC	West Virginia Union Catalog Interlibrary Loan Network [*Library network*]
WULDS.....	Western Union Long Distance Service [*Western Union Telegraph Co.*] [*Upper Saddle River, NJ*] [*Telecommunications*] (TSSD)
WULF........	Alma, GA [*AM radio station call letters*]
WULF........	Wulf Oil Corp. [*NASDAQ symbol*] (NQ)
WU-LT......	University of Wisconsin, Land Tenure Center, Madison, WI [*Library symbol*] [*Library of Congress*] (LCLS)
WULTUO ...	World Union of Liberal Trade Union Organisations [*See also WFALW*] [*Zurich, Switzerland*] (EAIO)
WU-M	University of Wisconsin, School of Medicine, Madison, WI [*Library symbol*] [*Library of Congress*] (LCLS)
WUM........	Washington University, School of Medicine, St. Louis, MO [*OCLC symbol*] (OCLC)
WUM........	Women's Universal Movement [*Defunct*] (EA)
WUM........	Work Unit Manager
WUM........	World Union of Mapam [*See also UMM*] (EAIO)
WUMB-FM ...	Boston, MA [*FM radio station call letters*]
WUME-FM ...	Paoli, IN [*FM radio station call letters*]
WUMF-FM ...	Farmington, ME [*FM radio station call letters*]
WUMP......	White, Urban, Middle Class, Protestant
WUMPS.....	Women Umpires [*World War II*]
WUMS	University, MS [*FM radio station call letters*]
WUMS	Woman's Union Missionary Society of America [*Later, UFCS*] (EA)
WUMTPT ...	World Union of Martyred Towns, Peace Towns (EAIO)
WUN	Wiluna [*Australia*] [*Airport symbol*] (OAG)
WUNC.......	Chapel Hill, NC [*FM radio station call letters*]
WUNC-TV ...	Chapel Hill, NC [*Television station call letters*]
W Underw ...	Weekly Underwriter [*A publication*]
WUND-TV ...	Columbia, NC [*Television station call letters*]

WUNE-TV ...	Linville, NC [*Television station call letters*]
WUNF-TV ...	Asheville, NC [*Television station call letters*]
WUNG-TV ...	Concord, NC [*Television station call letters*]
WUNH	Durham, NH [*FM radio station call letters*]
WUNJ-TV ...	Wilmington, NC [*Television station call letters*]
Wunk	WASP Funk [*1960's pop music*]
WUNK-TV ...	Greenville, NC [*Television station call letters*]
WUNL-TV ...	Winston-Salem, NC [*Television station call letters*]
WUNM-TV ...	Jacksonville, NC [*Television station call letters*]
WUNN	Mason, MI [*AM radio station call letters*]
WUNO	San Juan, PR [*AM radio station call letters*]
WUNP-TV ...	Roanoke Rapids, NC [*Television station call letters*]
WUNR.......	Brookline, MA [*AM radio station call letters*]
WUNS	World Union of National Socialists (EA)
WUNT.......	Wissenschaftliche Untersuchungen zum Neuen Testament [*Tuebingen*] [*A publication*] (BJA)
WUNV.......	Albany, GA [*FM radio station call letters*]
WUNY.......	Utica, NY [*FM radio station call letters*]
WUOG	Athens, GA [*FM radio station call letters*]
WUOL.......	Louisville, KY [*FM radio station call letters*]
WUOM	Ann Arbor, MI [*FM radio station call letters*]
WUOSY	World Union of Organizations for the Safeguard of Youth [*Later, UMOSEA*]
WUOT......	Knoxville, TN [*FM radio station call letters*]
WUP........	Work Unit Plan [*Navy*] (NG)
WUPA	Wupatki National Monument
WUPE	Pittsfield, MA [*FM radio station call letters*]
WUPI	Presque Isle, ME [*FM radio station call letters*]
WUPJ	World Union for Progressive Judaism (EA)
WUPL-INT ...	World Union for the Protection of Life [*See also WSL-INT*] (EAIO)
WUPM......	Ironwood, MI [*FM radio station call letters*]
WUPO.......	World Union of Pythagorean Organizations [*Ivybridge, Devonshire, England*] (EAIO)
WUPPE.....	Wisconsin Ultraviolet Photo-Polarimeter Experiment
WUPQ......	Newberry, MI [*FM radio station call letters*]
WUPR.......	Utuado-Rosa, PR [*AM radio station call letters*]
WUPS.......	Houghton Lake, MI [*FM radio station call letters*]
WUPS.......	World Union of Process Servers
WUPW	Toledo, OH [*Television station call letters*]
WUPY	Ontonagon, MI [*FM radio station call letters*]
WUR.........	Wirtschaft und Recht. Zeitschrift fuer Wirtschaftspolitik und Wirtschaftsrecht mit Einschluss des Sozialrechtes und Arbeidsrechtes [*A publication*]
WUR.........	World University Roundtable
WUR.........	Wurltech Industries [*NYSE symbol*] (SPSG)
WURB	Western Utilization Research Branch (MCD)
WURC.......	Holly Springs, MS [*FM radio station call letters*]
WURD.......	Philadelphia, PA [*AM radio station call letters*]
WURG......	Orlando, FL [*FM radio station call letters*]
WURL	Moody, AL [*AM radio station call letters*]
Wurmser	[*Bernhardus*] Wurmserus [*Flourished, 16th century*] [*Authority cited in pre-1607 legal work*] (DSA)
WUS.........	Washington University. Studies [*A publication*]
WUS.........	Wirtschaft und Statistik [*A publication*]
WUS.........	Woerterbuch der Ugaritischen Sprache [*A publication*] (BJA)
WUS.........	Word Underscore Character [*Data processing*]
WUS.........	World University Service [*See also EUM*] [*Geneva, Switzerland*] (EAIO)
WUSA.......	Washington, DC [*Television station call letters*]
WUSA	Waterfowl USA (EA)
WUSA-FM ...	Tampa, FL [*FM radio station call letters*]
WUSB	Stony Brook, NY [*FM radio station call letters*]
WUSC	Weather of US Cities [*A publication*]
WUSC	World University Service of Canada [*See also EUMC*]
WUSC-FM ...	Columbia, SC [*FM radio station call letters*]
WUSCI......	Western Union Space Communications, Incorporated (MCD)
WUSF.......	Tampa, FL [*FM radio station call letters*]
WUSF-TV ...	Tampa, FL [*Television station call letters*]
WUSG	World Union Saint Gabriel [*Esher, Surrey, England*] (EAIO)
WUSI-TV ...	Olney, IL [*Television station call letters*]
WUSJ-FM ...	Elizabethton, TN [*FM radio station call letters*]
WUSL.......	Philadelphia, PA [*FM radio station call letters*]
WUSL.......	Washburn University School of Law (DLA)
WUSL.......	Women's United Service League [*British*]
WUSM-FM ...	Hattiesburg, MS [*FM radio station call letters*]
WUSN	Chicago, IL [*FM radio station call letters*]
WUSO	Springfield, OH [*FM radio station call letters*]
WUSP.......	World Union of Stockholm Pioneers (EAIO)
WUSQ......	Winchester, VA [*AM radio station call letters*]
WUSQ-FM ...	Winchester, VA [*FM radio station call letters*]
WUSS.......	Atlantic City, NJ [*AM radio station call letters*]
WUSt........	Warenumsatzsteuer [*Purchase Tax*] [*German*]
WUST.......	Washington, DC [*AM radio station call letters*]
WUS-US ...	World University Service/USA (EA)
WUSW	Oshkosh, WI [*FM radio station call letters*]
WUSY	Cleveland, TN [*FM radio station call letters*]
WUSY	World Union for the Safeguard of Youth
WUT.........	Warm Up Time
WUT.........	Washburn University of Topeka [*Kansas*]

WUT......... Western Union Telegraph Co. [*Upper Saddle River, NJ*] [*NYSE symbol*] (SPSG)
WUTA....... Washington University Technology Associates
WUTC....... Chattanooga, TN [*FM radio station call letters*]
WUTC....... Western Union Telegraph Co.
WUTELCO ... Western Union Telegraph Co.
WUTHH ... World Union of Tnuat Haherut Hatzorar [*Tel Aviv, Israel*] (EAIO)
WUTK....... Knoxville, TN [*AM radio station call letters*]
WUTK-FM ... Knoxville, TN [*FM radio station call letters*]
WUTM....... Martin, TN [*FM radio station call letters*]
WUTQ....... Utica, NY [*AM radio station call letters*]
WUTR....... Utica, NY [*Television station call letters*]
WUTS....... Sewanee, TN [*FM radio station call letters*]
WUTS....... Work Unit Time Standard [*Air Force*] (AFM)
WUTS....... Work Unit Tracking Subsystem (MCD)
WUTV....... Buffalo, NY [*Television station call letters*]
WUTZ....... Summertown, TN [*FM radio station call letters*]
WUU .... Wau [*Sudan*] [*Airport symbol*] (OAG)
WUUA....... World Union for a Universal Alphabet (EA)
WUUC....... West Ulster Unionist Council [*Northern Ireland*]
WUUF....... Statesboro, GA [*FM radio station call letters*]
WUUN...... Women United for United Nations (EA)
WUUU ..... Rome, NY [*FM radio station call letters*]
WUV......... Weighted Unit Value (MCD)
WUV......... Wuvulu Island [*Papua New Guinea*] [*Airport symbol*] (OAG)
WUVA....... Charlottesville, VA [*FM radio station call letters*]
WUVCI ..... Western Union VideoConferencing, Incorporated [*Defunct*] (TSSD)
WUVT-FM ... Blacksburg, VA [*FM radio station call letters*]
WUVU....... St. Augustine, FL [*FM radio station call letters*]
WUVX....... Knox, IN [*FM radio station call letters*]
WuW......... Welt und Wort [*A publication*]
WUW......... Wu-wei [*Republic of China*] [*Seismograph station code, US Geological Survey*] (SEIS)
WU-WA .... University of Wisconsin, Woodman Astronomical Library, Madison, WI [*Library symbol*] [*Library of Congress*] (LCLS)
WuWahr .... Wort und Wahrheit [*A publication*]
WuWelt ..... Wissenschaft und Weltbild [*A publication*]
WUWF...... Pensacola, FL [*FM radio station call letters*]
WUWM..... Milwaukee, WI [*FM radio station call letters*]
WUX......... Western Union Exchange [*Teleprinter*]
WUXA....... Portsmouth, OH [*Television station call letters*]
Wuyi Sci J ... Wuyi Science Journal [*A publication*]
WV............ Avair Ltd. [*Ireland*] [*ICAO designator*] (FAAC)
WV............ Diwag [*Germany*] [*Research code symbol*]
WV............ Wall Vent [*Technical drawings*]
WV............ Water Valve (ROG)
WV............ Wave (FAAC)
W/V .... Weight/Volume [*Concentration*] [*Chemistry*]
WV............ West Virginia [*Postal code*]
Wv............. West Virginia Library Commission, Charleston, WV [*Library symbol*] [*Library of Congress*] (LCLS)
WV............ West Virginia Reports [*A publication*] (DLA)
WV............ Westminster Version of the Bible [*A publication*] (BJA)
WV............ Whispered Voice
W/V .... Wind Vector [*or Velocity*] [*Navigation*]
WV............ Wireless Van [*British*]
WV............ Working Voltage (MSA)
WV............ World Vision [*A publication*]
WV............ World Vision [*An association*] (EA)
WVA.......... Alderson-Broaddus College, Philippi, WV [*OCLC symbol*] (OCLC)
WVA.......... War Veterans Administration [*Canada*]
WVA.......... Watervliet Arsenal [*New York*] [*Army*]
W VA .... West Virginia (AAG)
W Va......... West Virginia Supreme Court Reports [*A publication*] (DLA)
WVA.......... West Vlaanderen Werkt [*A publication*]
WVA.......... World Veterinary Association [*See also AMV*] [*Madrid, Spain*] (EAIO)
W Va Acad Sci Proc ... West Virginia Academy of Sciences. Proceedings [*A publication*]
W Va Acts ... Acts of the Legislature of West Virginia [*A publication*] (DLA)
W Va Ag Dept ... West Virginia. Department of Agriculture. Publications [*A publication*]
W Va Ag Exp ... West Virginia. Agricultural Experiment Station. Publications [*A publication*]
W Va Agric Exp Stn Bull ... West Virginia. Agricultural Experiment Station. Bulletin [*A publication*]
W Va Agric Exp Stn Cir ... West Virginia. Agricultural Experiment Station. Circular [*A publication*]
W Va Agric Exp Stn Circ ... West Virginia. Agricultural Experiment Station. Circular [*A publication*]
W Va Agric Exp Stn Curr Rep ... West Virginia. Agricultural Experiment Station. Current Report [*A publication*]
W Va Agric Exp Stn Misc Publ ... West Virginia. Agricultural Experiment Station. Miscellaneous Publication [*A publication*]
W Va Agric For ... West Virginia Agriculture and Forestry [*A publication*]
W Va Agric For Exp Stn Bull ... West Virginia. Agricultural and Forestry Experiment Station. Bulletin [*A publication*]

WVAB .... Virginia Beach, VA [*AM radio station call letters*]
WVAB .... War Veterans Allowance Board [*Canada*]
WVAC .... Adrian, MI [*FM radio station call letters*]
WvAC .... Concord College, Athens, WV [*Library symbol*] [*Library of Congress*] (LCLS)
WVAC .... Working Voltage, Alternating Current (DEN)
W Va Coal Min Inst Proc ... West Virginia Coal Mining Institute. Proceedings [*A publication*]
W Va Code ... West Virginia Code [*A publication*] (DLA)
W Va Const ... West Virginia Constitution [*A publication*] (DLA)
W Va Crim Just Rev ... West Virginia Criminal Justice Review [*A publication*] (DLA)
W Va Dent J ... West Virginia Dental Journal [*A publication*]
W Va Dep Mines Annu Rep ... West Virginia. Department of Mines. Annual Report [*A publication*]
WVAF........ Charleston, WV [*FM radio station call letters*]
W Va For Notes ... West Virginia Forestry Notes [*A publication*]
W Va Geol Econ Surv Basic Data Rep ... West Virginia. Geological and Economic Survey. Basic Data Report [*A publication*]
W Va Geol Econ Surv Bull ... West Virginia. Geological and Economic Survey. Bulletin [*A publication*]
W Va Geol Econ Surv Circ Ser ... West Virginia. Geological and Economic Survey. Circular Series [*A publication*]
W Va Geol Econ Surv Cir Ser ... West Virginia. Geological and Economic Survey. Circular Series [*A publication*]
W Va Geol Econ Surv Coal Geol Bull ... West Virginia. Geological and Economic Survey. Coal Geology Bulletin [*A publication*]
W Va Geol Econ Surv Environ Geol Bull ... West Virginia. Geological and Economic Survey. Environmental Geology Bulletin [*A publication*]
W Va Geol Econ Surv Miner Resour Ser ... West Virginia. Geological and Economic Survey. Mineral Resources Series [*A publication*]
W Va Geol Econ Surv Newsl ... West Virginia. Geological and Economic Survey. Newsletter [*A publication*]
W Va Geol Econ Surv Rep Archeol Invest ... West Virginia. Geological and Economic Survey. Report of Archeological Investigations [*A publication*]
W Va Geol Econ Surv Rep Invest ... West Virginia. Geological and Economic Survey. Report of Investigations [*A publication*]
W Va Geol Econ Surv River Basin Bull ... West Virginia. Geological and Economic Survey. River Basin Bulletin [*A publication*]
W Va Geol Surv Rep ... West Virginia. Geological Survey. Reports [*A publication*]
W Va Geol Surv Rep Invest ... West Virginia. Geological Survey. Report of Investigations [*A publication*]
W Va G S... West Virginia. Geological Survey [*A publication*]
WVaH........ West Virginia History [*A publication*]
W Va His ... West Virginia History [*A publication*]
W Va Hist ... West Virginia History. A Quarterly Magazine [*A publication*]
WVAH-TV ... Charleston, WV [*Television station call letters*]
WVAL .... Sauk Rapids, MN [*AM radio station call letters*]
W Va Law Q ... West Virginia Law Quarterly and the Bar [*A publication*]
W Va Law R ... West Virginia Law Review [*A publication*]
W Va Law Reports ... West Virginia Reports [*A publication*] (DLA)
W Va Lib ... West Virginia Libraries [*A publication*]
W Va Libr ... West Virginia Libraries [*A publication*]
W Va LQ... West Virginia Law Quarterly [*A publication*] (DLA)
W Va LR... West Virginia Law Review [*A publication*]
W Va L Rev ... West Virginia Law Review [*A publication*]
WVALSA .. Whitewater Valley Area Library Services Authority [*Library network*]
WVAM...... Altoona, PA [*AM radio station call letters*]
W Va Med J ... West Virginia Medical Journal [*A publication*]
WVAN-TV ... Savannah, GA [*Television station call letters*]
W Va PSCR ... West Virginia Public Service Commission Report [*A publication*] (DLA)
W Va PUR ... West Virginia Public Utility Commission Reports [*A publication*] (DLA)
WVAQ....... Morgantown, WV [*FM radio station call letters*]
WVAR .... Richwood, WV [*AM radio station call letters*]
Wv-Ar .... West Virginia Department of Archives and History, Charleston, WV [*Library symbol*] [*Library of Congress*] (LCLS)
WVARAY ... West Virginia University. Agricultural Experiment Station. Current Report [*A publication*]
W Va Rep... West Virginia Reports [*A publication*] (DLA)
W Var Sports ... Women's Varsity Sports [*A publication*]
WVAS....... Montgomery, AL [*FM radio station call letters*]
WVAS....... Wake Vortex Avoidance System [*FAA*]
WVAST...... Washer Visual Acuity Screening Technique [*Visual ability test*]
W Va Univ Agric Exp Stn Curr Rep ... West Virginia University. Agricultural Experiment Station. Current Report [*A publication*]
W Va Univ Agric For Exp Stn Curr Rep ... West Virginia University. Agricultural and Forestry Experiment Station. Current Report [*A publication*]
W Va Univ Agri Exp Stn Bull ... West Virginia University. Agricultural Experiment Station. Bulletin [*A publication*]
W Va Univ Bull Proc Annu Appalachian Gas Meas Short Course ... West Virginia University. Bulletin. Proceedings. Annual Appalachian Gas Measurement Short Course [*A publication*]

W Va Univ Coal Res Bur Sch Mines Tech Rep ... West Virginia University. Coal Research Bureau. School of Mines. Technical Report [*Morgantown, West Virginia*] [*A publication*]

W Va Univ Coal Res Bur Tech Rep ... West Virginia University. Coal Research Bureau. Technical Report [*A publication*]

W Va Univ Eng Exp Sta Tech Bull ... West Virginia University. Engineering Experiment Station. Technical Bulletin [*A publication*]

W Va Univ Eng Exp Stn Bull ... West Virginia University. Engineering Experiment Station. Bulletin [*A publication*]

W Va Univ Eng Exp Stn Res Bull ... West Virginia University. Engineering Experiment Station. Research Bulletin [*A publication*]

W Va Univ Eng Exp Stn Tech Bull ... West Virginia University. Engineering Experiment Station. Technical Bulletin [*A publication*]

W Va Univ Rp Bd Reg ... West Virginia University. Report of the Board of Regents [*A publication*]

W Va U Phil ... West Virginia University. Philological Papers [*A publication*]

WVAY .... Wilmington, VT [*FM radio station call letters*]

WVAZ .... Oak Park, IL [*FM radio station call letters*]

WvB .... Beckley-Raleigh County Library, Beckley, WV [*Library symbol*] [*Library of Congress*] (LCLS)

WVB .... Bethany College, Bethany, WV [*OCLC symbol*] (OCLC)

WVB .... Walvis Bay [*Namibia*] [*Airport symbol*] (OAG)

Wv-B .... West Virginia Library Commission, Book Express Unit, Charleston, WV [*Library symbol*] [*Library of Congress*] (LCLS)

WVBA .... Frankfort, KY [*FM radio station call letters*]

WVBA .... Wholesale Variety Bakers Association (EA)

WvBC .... Beckley College, Beckley, WV [*Library symbol*] [*Library of Congress*] (LCLS)

WVBC .... Bethany, WV [*FM radio station call letters*]

WvBeC....... Bethany College, Bethany, WV [*Library symbol*] [*Library of Congress*] (LCLS)

WVBF....... Framingham, MA [*FM radio station call letters*]

WvBl.......... Bluefield Public Library, Bluefield, WV [*Library symbol*] [*Library of Congress*] (LCLS)

WvBlS....... Bluefield State College, Bluefield, WV [*Library symbol*] [*Library of Congress*] (LCLS)

WvBrA....... Appalachian Bible Institute, Bradley, WV [*Library symbol*] [*Library of Congress*] (LCLS)

WVBR-FM ... Ithaca, NY [*FM radio station call letters*]

WvBri......... Benedum Civic Center Public Library, Bridgeport, WV [*Library symbol*] [*Library of Congress*] (LCLS)

WVBS-FM ... Burgaw, NC [*FM radio station call letters*]

WVBT........ Virginia Beach, VA [*Television station call letters*]

WvBu........ Stonewall Jackson Regional Library, Buckhannon, WV [*Library symbol*] [*Library of Congress*] (LCLS)

WVBU-FM ... Lewisburg, PA [*FM radio station call letters*]

WvBuW ..... West Virginia Wesleyan College, Buckhannon, WV [*Library symbol*] [*Library of Congress*] (LCLS)

WvBV .... United States Veterans Administration Hospital, Beckley, WV [*Library symbol*] [*Library of Congress*] (LCLS)

WVBX .... Georgetown, SC [*AM radio station call letters*]

WvC........... Kanawha County Public Library, Charleston, WV [*Library symbol*] [*Library of Congress*] (LCLS)

WVC.......... West Virginia Code [*1899*] [*A publication*] (DLA)

WVC.......... Western Veterinary Conference (EA)

WVCA .... Selma, AL [*FM radio station call letters*]

WvCA .... West Virginia Department of Agriculture, Charleston, WV [*Library symbol*] [*Library of Congress*] (LCLS)

WvCAE...... Appalachian Educational Laboratory, Inc., Charleston, WV [*Library symbol*] [*Library of Congress*] (LCLS)

WvCAP...... West Virginia Air Pollution Control Commission, Charleston, WV [*Library symbol*] [*Library of Congress*] (LCLS)

WVCB .... Shallotte, NC [*AM radio station call letters*]

WvCBHi.... West Virginia Baptist Historical Society Deposit, Department of Archives and History, Charleston, WV [*Library symbol*] [*Library of Congress*] (LCLS)

WVCC .... Linesville, PA [*FM radio station call letters*]

WvCCD ..... West Virginia Department of Civil and Defense Mobilization, Charleston, WV [*Library symbol*] [*Library of Congress*] (LCLS)

WVCF........ Ocoee, FL [*AM radio station call letters*]

WVCF........ Welsh Venture Capital Funds

WvCFM..... West Virginia State Fire Marshal's Department, Charleston, WV [*Library symbol*] [*Library of Congress*] (LCLS)

WVCG .... Coral Gables, FL [*AM radio station call letters*]

WvCGH.... Charleston General Hospital, Charleston, WV [*Library symbol*] [*Library of Congress*] (LCLS)

WvCH....... Chester, PA [*AM radio station call letters*]

WvCH........ West Virginia Department of Health, Charleston, WV [*Library symbol*] [*Library of Congress*] (LCLS)

WvCheC ... Consolidated Gas Supply Corp., Chelyan, WV [*Library symbol*] [*Library of Congress*] (LCLS)

WvCHi....... West Virginia Department of Highways, Charleston, WV [*Library symbol*] [*Library of Congress*] (LCLS)

WvCl.......... Clarksburg Public Library, Clarksburg, WV [*Library symbol*] [*Library of Congress*] (LCLS)

WvClC....... Consolidated Gas Supply Corp., Clarksburg, WV [*Library symbol*] [*Library of Congress*] (LCLS)

WvCM .... Morris Harvey College, Charleston, WV [*Library symbol*] [*Library of Congress*] (LCLS)

WvCMH.... West Virginia Department of Mental Health, Charleston, WV [*Library symbol*] [*Library of Congress*] (LCLS)

WvCMi...... West Virginia Department of Mines, Charleston, WV [*Library symbol*] [*Library of Congress*] (LCLS)

WvCNR ..... West Virginia Department of Natural Resources, Charleston, WV [*Library symbol*] [*Library of Congress*] (LCLS)

WVCP....... Gallatin, TN [*FM radio station call letters*]

WvCPS ...... West Virginia Department of Public Safety, Charleston, WV [*Library symbol*] [*Library of Congress*] (LCLS)

WVCR-FM ... Loudonville, NY [*FM radio station call letters*]

WVCS .... California, PA [*FM radio station call letters*]

WVCT .... Keavy, KY [*FM radio station call letters*]

WvCTS...... West Virginia State Technical Services, Charleston, WV [*Library symbol*] [*Library of Congress*] (LCLS)

WvCVR..... West Virginia Division of Vocational Rehabilitation, Charleston, WV [*Library symbol*] [*Library of Congress*] (LCLS)

WVCX .... Tomah, WI [*FM radio station call letters*]

WVCY .... Milwaukee, WI [*FM radio station call letters*]

WVCY-TV ... Milwaukee, WI [*Television station call letters*]

WVD......... Dane County Hospital, Verona, WI [*Library symbol*] [*Library of Congress*] (LCLS)

WVD......... Davis and Elkins College, Elkins, WV [*OCLC symbol*] (OCLC)

WVD......... Waived (AABC)

WVDC....... Working Voltage, Direct Current

WVDF....... Wolverhampton Volunteer Defence Force [*British military*] (DMA)

WVDOG.... Wissenschaftliche Veroeffentlichungen der Deutschen Orient-Gesellschaft [*A publication*]

WVE......... Water Vapor Electrolysis [*Cell*]

WVE.......... Wind Velocity East (MCD)

WVEC-TV ... Hampton, VA [*Television station call letters*]

WvED .... Davis and Elkins College, Elkins, WV [*Library symbol*] [*Library of Congress*] (LCLS)

WVEE....... Atlanta, GA [*FM radio station call letters*]

WVEE....... Wheeled Vehicle Experimental Establishment [*British*]

WVEF....... Camden, SC [*AM radio station call letters*]

WVEH....... East Hampton, NY [*FM radio station call letters*]

WVEH....... Wheel Vehicle (AABC)

WVEL....... Pekin, IL [*AM radio station call letters*]

WVEM ...... Springfield, IL [*FM radio station call letters*]

WVEM ...... Water Vapor Electrolysis Module [*NASA*]

WVEO ...... Aguadilla, PR [*Television station call letters*]

WVEP ...... Martinsburg, WV [*FM radio station call letters*]

WVER ...... Rutland, VT [*Television station call letters*]

WVEU .... Atlanta, GA [*Television station call letters*]

WVEZ-FM ... Louisville, KY [*FM radio station call letters*]

WVF .... Fairmont State College, Fairmont, WV [*OCLC symbol*] (OCLC)

WvF .... Marion County Public Library, Fairmont, WV [*Library symbol*] [*Library of Congress*] (LCLS)

WVF .... United States Council, World Veterans Federation (EA)

WVF .... Wave Vector Filter

WVF .... West Virginia Folklore [*A publication*]

WVF .... World Veterans Federation [*See also FMAC*] [*Paris, France*] (EAIO)

WVF .... World Veterans Fund (EA)

WvFa .... Fayette County Public Library, Fayetteville, WV [*Library symbol*] [*Library of Congress*] (LCLS)

WVFC........ McConnellsburg, PA [*AM radio station call letters*]

WVFJ-FM ... Manchester, GA [*FM radio station call letters*]

WVFM ...... Campton, NH [*FM radio station call letters*]

WvFMHi... Marion County Historical Society, Fairmont, WV [*Library symbol*] [*Library of Congress*] (LCLS)

WvFS......... Fairmont State College, Fairmont, WV [*Library symbol*] [*Library of Congress*] (LCLS)

WVFS........ Tallahassee, FL [*FM radio station call letters*]

WVFT........ Roanoke, VA [*Television station call letters*]

WVG......... West Virginia State College/College of Graduate Studies, Institute, WV [*OCLC symbol*] (OCLC)

WVGA .... Valdosta, GA [*Television station call letters*]

WVGB .... Beaufort, SC [*AM radio station call letters*]

WvGbN..... National Radio Astronomy Observatory, Green Bank, WV [*Library symbol*] [*Library of Congress*] (LCLS)

WvGlS ...... Glenville State College, Glenville, WV [*Library symbol*] [*Library of Congress*] (LCLS)

WVGN....... Charlotte Amalie, VI [*FM radio station call letters*]

WVGO....... Richmond, VA [*FM radio station call letters*]

WVGR....... Grand Rapids, MI [*FM radio station call letters*]

WVGS .... Statesboro, GA [*FM radio station call letters*]

WVH........ Marshall University, Huntington, WV [*OCLC symbol*] (OCLC)

WVH .... West Virginia History [*A publication*]

WVHA....... Wirtschaftsverwaltungshauptamt (BJA)

WvHB....... Pearl S. Buck Birthplace Museum, Hillsboro, WV [*Library symbol*] [*Library of Congress*] (LCLS)

WVHF-FM ... Clarksburg, WV [*FM radio station call letters*]

WvHfP....... United States Park Service, Harpers Ferry National Historical Park, Harpers Ferry, WV [*Library symbol*] [*Library of Congress*] (LCLS)

WVHI........ Evansville, IN [*AM radio station call letters*]

WVHM...... Benton, KY [*FM radio station call letters*]
WVHP....... West Virginia Association for Health, Physical Education, Recreation, and Dance. Journal [*A publication*]
WVHP-FM ... Highland Park, NJ [*FM radio station call letters*]
WvHu .... Cabell-Huntington Public Library [*Western Counties Regional Library*], Huntington, WV [*Library symbol*] [*Library of Congress*] (LCLS)
WvHuB..... Basic Systems, Inc., Huntington, WV [*Library symbol*] [*Library of Congress*] (LCLS)
WvHuE...... United States Army, Corps of Engineers, Huntington, WV [*Library symbol*] [*Library of Congress*] (LCLS)
WvHuG...... Huntington Galleries, Huntington, WV [*Library symbol*] [*Library of Congress*] (LCLS)
WvHuH ..... Holland-Suco Color Co., Huntington, WV [*Library symbol*] [*Library of Congress*] (LCLS)
WvHuM..... Marshall University, Huntington, WV [*Library symbol*] [*Library of Congress*] (LCLS)
WvHuV...... United States Veterans Administration Hospital, Huntington, WV [*Library symbol*] [*Library of Congress*] (LCLS)
WVi........... Viroqua Public Library, Viroqua, WI [*Library symbol*] [*Library of Congress*] (LCLS)
WVI .... Watsonville, CA [*Location identifier*] [*FAA*] (FAAL)
WVI .... Work Values Inventory [*Psychometrics*]
WVI .... World Vision International
WVIA-FM ... Scranton, PA [*FM radio station call letters*]
WVIA-TV ... Scranton, PA [*Television station call letters*]
WvIC.......... West Virginia State College, Institute, WV [*Library symbol*] [*Library of Congress*] (LCLS)
WVIC-FM ... East Lansing, MI [*FM radio station call letters*]
WvICG....... West Virginia College of Graduate Studies, Institute, WV [*Library symbol*] [*Library of Congress*] (LCLS)
WVID .... Anasco, PR [*FM radio station call letters*]
WVII-TV... Bangor, ME [*Television station call letters*]
WVIJ .... Port Charlotte, FL [*FM radio station call letters*]
WVIK .... Rock Island, IL [*FM radio station call letters*]
WVIL........ Villas, NJ [*FM radio station call letters*]
WVIM-FM ... Coldwater, MS [*FM radio station call letters*]
WVIN .... Bath, NY [*AM radio station call letters*]
WVIN-FM ... Bath, NY [*FM radio station call letters*]
WVIO .... Blowing Rock, NC [*AM radio station call letters*]
WVIP .... Mount Kisco, NY [*AM radio station call letters*]
WVIP-FM ... Mount Kisco, NY [*FM radio station call letters*]
WVIQ .... Christiansted, VI [*FM radio station call letters*]
WVIR-TV ... Charlottesville, VA [*Television station call letters*]
WVIS .... Christiansted, VI [*FM radio station call letters*]
WVIT........ New Britain, CT [*Television station call letters*]
WVIT........ West Virginia Institute of Technology
WVIZ-TV ... Cleveland, OH [*Television station call letters*]
WVJC........ Mount Carmel, IL [*FM radio station call letters*]
WVJP....... Caguas, PR [*AM radio station call letters*]
WVJP-FM ... Caguas, PR [*FM radio station call letters*]
WVJS .... Owensboro, KY [*AM radio station call letters*]
WVJZ........ Orange, VA [*FM radio station call letters*]
WVK .... Kanawha County Public Library, Charleston, WV [*OCLC symbol*] (OCLC)
WvK .... Keyser-Mineral County Public and Potomac Valley Regional Library, Keyser, WV [*Library symbol*] [*Library of Congress*] (LCLS)
WVK .... Manakara [*Madagascar*] [*Airport symbol*] (OAG)
WVKC .... Galesburg, IL [*FM radio station call letters*]
WvKeFW ... Bureau of Sport Fisheries and Wildlife, Eastern Fish Disease Laboratory, Kearneysville, WV [*Library symbol*] [*Library of Congress*] (LCLS)
WVKG .... Pentwater, MI [*FM radio station call letters*]
WVKM ...... Matewan, WV [*FM radio station call letters*]
WVKO .... Columbus, OH [*AM radio station call letters*]
WvKP .... Potomac State College, Keyser, WV [*Library symbol*] [*Library of Congress*] (LCLS)
WVKR-FM ... Poughkeepsie, NY [*FM radio station call letters*]
WVKV .... Hurricane, WV [*AM radio station call letters*]
WVKY .... Louisa, KY [*AM radio station call letters*]
WVKZ .... Schenectady, NY [*AM radio station call letters*]
WVKZ-FM ... Clifton Park, NY [*FM radio station call letters*]
WVL .... Warfare Vision Laboratory [*Army*]
WVL .... Waterville [*Maine*] [*Airport symbol*] (OAG)
WVL .... Waterville, ME [*Location identifier*] [*FAA*] (FAAL)
WVL .... West Virginia Law Review [*A publication*]
Wv-L......... West Virginia State Law Library, Charleston, WV [*Library symbol*] [*Library of Congress*] (LCLS)
WVLA ...... Baton Rouge, LA [*Television station call letters*]
WVLA ...... Woodville, MS [*FM radio station call letters*]
WVLB....... Wheeled Vehicle Launched Bridge (MCD)
WVLD .... Valdosta, GA [*AM radio station call letters*]
WvLe.......... Greenbrier County Public Library, Lewisburg, WV [*Library symbol*] [*Library of Congress*] (LCLS)
WVLE....... Scottsville, KY [*FM radio station call letters*]
WvLeG....... Greenbrier College, Lewisburg, WV [*Library symbol*] [*Library of Congress*] (LCLS)
WVLG .... Wuerttembergische Vierteljahresschrift fuer Landesgeschichte [*A publication*]
WVLI........ Buena Vista, VA [*FM radio station call letters*]

WVLJ .... Monticello, IL [*FM radio station call letters*]
WVLK ...... Lexington, KY [*AM radio station call letters*]
WVLK-FM ... Lexington, KY [*FM radio station call letters*]
WVLN .... Olney, IL [*AM radio station call letters*]
WVLQ .... West Virginia Law Quarterly [*A publication*] (DLA)
WVLR........ West Virginia Law Review [*A publication*]
Wv-LS........ West Virginia Library Commission, Library Science Department, Charleston, WV [*Library symbol*] [*Library of Congress*] (LCLS)
WVLT....... Vineland, NJ [*FM radio station call letters*]
WVLY....... Water Valley, MS [*AM radio station call letters*]
WvM......... Morgantown Public Library, Morgantown, WV [*Library symbol*] [*Library of Congress*] (LCLS)
WVM........ West Virginia Medical Center, Morgantown, WV [*OCLC symbol*] [*Inactive*] (OCLC)
WVM........ Wiener Voelkerkundliche Mitteilungen [*A publication*]
WvMa....... Martinsburg-Berkeley County Public Library, Martinsburg, WV [*Library symbol*] [*Library of Congress*] (LCLS)
WVMA ...... Oak Hill, WV [*FM radio station call letters*]
WVMA ...... Women's Veterinary Medical Association [*Later, AWV*]
WvMaV ..... United States Veterans Administration Center, Martinsburg, WV [*Library symbol*] [*Library of Congress*] (LCLS)
WvMBM ... United States Bureau of Mines, Morgantown, WV [*Library symbol*] [*Library of Congress*] (LCLS)
WVMC....... Mansfield, OH [*FM radio station call letters*]
WvMc........ McMechen Public Library, McMechen, WV [*Library symbol*] [*Library of Congress*] (LCLS)
WVMG...... Cochran, GA [*AM radio station call letters*]
WVMG-FM ... Cochran, GA [*FM radio station call letters*]
WVMH-FM ... Mars Hill, NC [*FM radio station call letters*]
WVMI .... Biloxi, MS [*AM radio station call letters*]
WvMIL...... Institute for Labor Studies, Appalachian Center, Morgantown, WV [*Library symbol*] [*Library of Congress*] (LCLS)
WVMM ..... Grantham, PA [*FM radio station call letters*]
WvMNIO .. United States Public Health Service, National Institute for Occupational Safety and Health, Appalachian Laboratory for Occupational Safety and Health Library, Morgantown, WV (LCLS)
WvMo........ City-County Public Library, Moundsville, WV [*Library symbol*] [*Library of Congress*] (LCLS)
WvMonI .... West Virginia Institute of Technology, Montgomery, WV [*Library symbol*] [*Library of Congress*] (LCLS)
WVMR....... Frost, WV [*AM radio station call letters*]
WVMT ...... Burlington, VT [*AM radio station call letters*]
WVMT ...... Wavemat, Inc. [*NASDAQ symbol*] (NQ)
WVMV ...... Wisteria Vein Mosaic Virus
WVMW-FM ... Scranton, PA [*FM radio station call letters*]
WVN......... Water Vapor Nitrogen [*Nuclear energy*] (NRCH)
WVN......... West Virginia Northern Railroad Co. [*AAR code*]
WVN......... Wind Velocity North (MCD)
WVN......... Woven
WVNA ...... Tuscumbia, AL [*AM radio station call letters*]
WVNA-FM ... Tuscumbia, AL [*FM radio station call letters*]
WVNC....... Canton, NY [*FM radio station call letters*]
WVNE....... Leicester, MA [*AM radio station call letters*]
WVNET .... West Virginia Network for Educational Telecomputing [*Research center*] (RCD)
WVNH .... West Rutland, VT [*FM radio station call letters*]
WvNiK....... West Virginia University, Kanawha Valley Graduate Center, Nitro, WV [*Library symbol*] [*Library of Congress*] (LCLS)
WVNJ .... Oakland, NJ [*AM radio station call letters*]
WvNmM....... Mobay Chemical Corp., Research Library, New Martinsville, WV [*Library symbol*] [*Library of Congress*] (LCLS)
WVNN....... Athens, AL [*AM radio station call letters*]
WVNO-FM ... Mansfield, OH [*FM radio station call letters*]
WVNP....... Wheeling, WV [*FM radio station call letters*]
WVNR....... Poultney, VT [*AM radio station call letters*]
WVNS .... Charleston, WV [*FM radio station call letters*]
WVNY .... Burlington, VT [*Television station call letters*]
WVOA....... DeRuyter, NY [*FM radio station call letters*]
WVOB....... Dothan, AL [*FM radio station call letters*]
WVOC....... Columbia, SC [*AM radio station call letters*]
WVOD....... Manteo, NC [*FM radio station call letters*]
WVOE....... Chadbourn, NC [*AM radio station call letters*]
WVOF .... Fairfield, CT [*FM radio station call letters*]
WVOG....... New Orleans, LA [*AM radio station call letters*]
WVOH ...... Hazlehurst, GA [*AM radio station call letters*]
WVOH-FM ... Hazlehurst, GA [*FM radio station call letters*]
WVOI........ Toledo, OH [*AM radio station call letters*]
WVOJ .... Jacksonville, FL [*AM radio station call letters*]
WVOK....... Birmingham, AL [*AM radio station call letters*]
WVOL....... Berry Hill, TN [*AM radio station call letters*]
WVOM...... Iuka, MS [*AM radio station call letters*]
WVON....... Cicero, IL [*AM radio station call letters*]
WVOP....... Vidalia, GA [*AM radio station call letters*]
WVOR-FM ... Rochester, NY [*FM radio station call letters*]
WVOS ...... Liberty, NY [*AM radio station call letters*]
WVOS-FM ... Liberty, NY [*FM radio station call letters*]
WVOT....... Wilson, NC [*AM radio station call letters*]
WVOV....... Danville, VA [*AM radio station call letters*]
WVOW...... Logan, WV [*AM radio station call letters*]

WVOW-FM ... Logan, WV [*FM radio station call letters*]
WVOX....... New Rochelle, NY [*AM radio station call letters*]
WVOZ....... San Juan, PR [*AM radio station call letters*]
WVOZ-FM ... Carolina, PR [*FM radio station call letters*]
WvP........... Carnegie Library of Parkersburg and Wood County, Parkersburg, WV [*Library symbol*] [*Library of Congress*]   (LCLS)
WVP.......... Water Vapor Permeability [*Physical chemistry*]
WVP.......... Women's Vote Project   (EA)
WVPA .... World Veterinary Poultry Association [*See also AMVA*] [*Huntingdon, Cambridgeshire, England*]   (EAIO)
WVPB....... Beckley, WV [*FM radio station call letters*]
WvPC........ Parkersburg Community College, Parkersburg, WV [*Library symbol*] [*Library of Congress*]   (LCLS)
WVPE....... Elkhart, IN [*FM radio station call letters*]
WVPG ...... Parkersburg, WV [*FM radio station call letters*]
WVPH....... Piscataway, NJ [*FM radio station call letters*]
WvPhA ...... Alderson-Broaddus College, Philippi, WV [*Library symbol*] [*Library of Congress*]   (LCLS)
WVPM ...... Morgantown, WV [*FM radio station call letters*]
WVPN ...... Charleston, WV [*FM radio station call letters*]
WvPO .... Ohio Valley College, Parkersburg, WV [*Library symbol*] [*Library of Congress*]   (LCLS)
WVPO ...... Stroudsburg, PA [*AM radio station call letters*]
WVPR....... Windsor, VT [*FM radio station call letters*]
WVPS....... Burlington, VT [*FM radio station call letters*]
WVPT....... Staunton, VA [*Television station call letters*]
WVPV ...... Beaver Dam, KY [*FM radio station call letters*]
WVPW ...... Buckhannon, WV [*FM radio station call letters*]
WVR........ Wakefield Volunteer Rifles [*British military*]   (DMA)
WVR......... Wellington Volunteer Rifles [*British military*]   (DMA)
Wv-R........ West Virginia Library Commission, Reference Department, WV [*Library symbol*] [*Library of Congress*]   (LCLS)
WVR......... West Virginia Reports [*A publication*]   (DLA)
WVR......... Within Visual Range [*Missile*]   (MCD)
WVR......... Women's Volunteer Reserve [*British*] [*World War I*]
WVRAAM ... Within Visual Range Air-to-Air Missile
WVRC ...... Spencer, WV [*AM radio station call letters*]
WVRC ...... Wabash Valley Railroad Company [*AAR code*]
WVRC .... Wolverhampton Volunteer Rifle Corps [*British military*]   (DMA)
WVRD...... Belzoni, MS [*FM radio station call letters*]
WV Rep ..... West Virginia Reports [*A publication*]   (DLA)
WVRK ...... Columbus, GA [*FM radio station call letters*]
WVRQ ...... Viroqua, WI [*AM radio station call letters*]
WVRQ-FM ... Viroqua, WI [*FM radio station call letters*]
WVRRTC ... West Virginia Rehabilitation Research and Training Center [*West Virginia University*] [*Research center*]   (RCD)
WVRS....... Warrenton, NC [*FM radio station call letters*]
WVRU....... Radford, VA [*FM radio station call letters*]
WVRY .... Waverly, TN [*FM radio station call letters*]
WVS .... Water Vapor Sensor
W-V(S)....... Women's Reserve, Emergency Duties [*USNR commissioned officer designation*]
WVS .... Women's Voluntary Services [*Coordinated work of women for national service*] [*Later, WRVS*] [*British*] [*World War II*]
WVSA....... Vernon, AL [*AM radio station call letters*]
WVSA....... Weidingsvereniging van Suidelike Afrika [*Grassland Society of Southern Africa - GSSA*] [*Howick, South Africa*]   (EAIO)
WvSaC....... Salem College, Salem, WV [*Library symbol*] [*Library of Congress*]   (LCLS)
WVSB-TV ... West Point, MS [*Television station call letters*]
WVSC....... Somerset, PA [*AM radio station call letters*]
WVSC....... West Virginia State College
W-V(S) (CEC) ... Women's Reserve, Civil Engineering Corps Duties [*USNR commissioned officer designation*]
WVSC-FM ... Somerset, PA [*FM radio station call letters*]
WvScU....... Union Carbide Corp., South Charleston, WV [*Library symbol*] [*Library of Congress*]   (LCLS)
WVSD ...... Itta Bena, MS [*FM radio station call letters*]
W-V(S) (DC) ... Women's Reserve, Dental Corps Duties [*USNR commissioned officer designation*]
WVSG ...... Cornwall, NY [*AM radio station call letters*]
WVSH ...... Huntington, IN [*FM radio station call letters*]
WvSh .... Shepherdstown Public Library, Shepherdstown, WV [*Library symbol*] [*Library of Congress*]   (LCLS)
W-V(S) (H) ... Women's Reserve, Hospital Corps Duties [*USNR commissioned officer designation*]
WvShS....... Shepherd College, Shepherdstown, WV [*Library symbol*] [*Library of Congress*]   (LCLS)
WVSM ...... Rainsville, AL [*AM radio station call letters*]
W-V(S) (MC) ... Women's Reserve, Medical Corps Duties [*USNR commissioned officer designation*]
WVSN .... Humacao, PR [*Television station call letters*]
WVSR....... Charleston, WV [*AM radio station call letters*]
WVSR-FM ... Charleston, WV [*FM radio station call letters*]
WVSS .... Menomonie, WI [*FM radio station call letters*]
W-V(S) (SC) ... Women's Reserve, Supply Corps Duties [*USNR commissioned officer designation*]
WVST........ Petersburg, VA [*FM radio station call letters*]
WVSU-FM ... Birmingham, AL [*FM radio station call letters*]

WVSV........ Stevenson, AL [*FM radio station call letters*]
WVT.......... Water Vapor Transmission
WVT .... Watervliet Arsenal [*New York*] [*Army*]
WVT .... West Virginia Institute of Technology, Montgomery, WV [*OCLC symbol*]   (OCLC)
WVTA ...... Windsor, VT [*Television station call letters*]
WVTB....... St. Johnsbury, VT [*Television station call letters*]
WVTC .... Randolph, VT [*FM radio station call letters*]
WVTF....... Roanoke, VA [*FM radio station call letters*]
WVTF....... Western Visayan Task Force [*World War II*]
WVTH....... Goodman, MS [*FM radio station call letters*]
WVTK ...... Wavetek Corp. [*NASDAQ symbol*]   (NQ)
WVTM-TV ... Birmingham, AL [*Television station call letters*]
WVTR .... Water Vapor Transmission Rate
WVTU ...... Charlottesville, VA [*FM radio station call letters*]
WVTV ...... Milwaukee, WI [*Television station call letters*]
wvu .... West Virginia [*MARC country of publication code*] [*Library of Congress*]   (LCCP)
WVU......... West Virginia University
WVU......... West Virginia University Library, Morgantown, WV [*OCLC symbol*]   (OCLC)
WvU......... West Virginia University, Morgantown, WV [*Library symbol*] [*Library of Congress*]   (LCLS)
WvU-AE.... West Virginia University, Agricultural Engineering Library, Morgantown, WV [*Library symbol*] [*Library of Congress*]   (LCLS)
WVUA-FM ... Tuscaloosa, AL [*FM radio station call letters*]
WVUB....... Vincennes, IN [*FM radio station call letters*]
WVUBPL.. West Virginia University. Bulletin. Philological Studies [*A publication*]
WVUD-FM ... Kettering, OH [*FM radio station call letters*]
WVUE....... New Orleans, LA [*Television station call letters*]
WvU-J .... West Virginia University, School of Journalism, Morgantown, WV [*Library symbol*] [*Library of Congress*]   (LCLS)
WvU-L....... West Virginia University, College of Law, Morgantown, WV [*Library symbol*] [*Library of Congress*]   (LCLS)
WVUM...... Coral Gables, FL [*FM radio station call letters*]
WvU-M ..... West Virginia University, Medical Center, Morgantown, WV [*Library symbol*] [*Library of Congress*]   (LCLS)
WvU-Mu ... West Virginia University, Music Library, Morgantown, WV [*Library symbol*] [*Library of Congress*]   (LCLS)
WV Univ Agric For Exp Stn Misc Publ ... West Virginia University. Agriculture and Forestry Experiment Station. Miscellaneous Publication [*A publication*]
WvU-P....... West Virginia University, Physical Sciences Library, Morgantown, WV [*Library symbol*] [*Library of Congress*]   (LCLS)
WVUPP..... West Virginia University. Philological Papers [*A publication*]
WVUR-FM ... Valparaiso, IN [*FM radio station call letters*]
WVUT....... Vincennes, IN [*Television station call letters*]
WVUV....... Leone, AS [*AM radio station call letters*]
WVUV-FM ... Leone, AS [*FM radio station call letters*]
WVV......... Whole Virus Vaccine [*Immunology*]
WVVA ...... Bluefield, WV [*Television station call letters*]
WVVE .... Stonington, CT [*FM radio station call letters*]
WVVS........ Valdosta, GA [*FM radio station call letters*]
WVVV ...... Blacksburg, VA [*FM radio station call letters*]
WVVW...... St. Marys, WV [*AM radio station call letters*]
WVVX ...... Highland Park, IL [*FM radio station call letters*]
WVVY .... Grifton, NC [*FM radio station call letters*]
WvW......... Ohio County Public Library, Wheeling, WV [*Library symbol*] [*Library of Congress*]   (LCLS)
WVW......... Westview Resources [*Vancouver Stock Exchange symbol*]
WvWaB ..... Borg-Warner Corp., Borg-Warner Chemicals Technical Center, Washington, WV [*Library symbol*] [*Library of Congress*]   (LCLS)
WVWC...... Buckhannon, WV [*FM radio station call letters*]
WVWC...... West Virginia Wesleyan College
WvWC....... Wheeling College, Wheeling, WV [*Library symbol*] [*Library of Congress*]   (LCLS)
WvWelW... West Liberty State College, West Liberty, WV [*Library symbol*] [*Library of Congress*]   (LCLS)
WvWEPA ... United States Environmental Protection Agency, Wheeling Field Office, Wheeling, WV [*Library symbol*] [*Library of Congress*]   (LCLS)
WvWH....... Wheeling Hospital, Medical Library, Wheeling, WV [*Library symbol*] [*Library of Congress*]   (LCLS)
WVWI .... Charlotte Amalie, VI [*AM radio station call letters*]
WvWO....... Oglebay Institute, Wheeling, WV [*Library symbol*] [*Library of Congress*]   (LCLS)
WVWV ...... Huntington, WV [*FM radio station call letters*]
WVXC .... Chillicothe, OH [*FM radio station call letters*]
WVXM...... West Union, OH [*FM radio station call letters*]
WVXR .... Richmond, IN [*FM radio station call letters*]
WVXU....... Cincinnati, OH [*FM radio station call letters*]
WVYC .... York, PA [*FM radio station call letters*]
WVZN .... Lynchburg, VA [*AM radio station call letters*]
WW.......... Australian Women's Weekly [*A publication*]   (APTA)
W & W .... De Witt and Weeresinghe's Appeal Court Reports [*Ceylon*] [*A publication*]   (DLA)

WW............ Israel Aircraft Industries Ltd. [*ICAO aircraft manufacturer identifier*]   (ICAO)
WW............ Journal of Waterway, Port, Coastal, and Ocean Engineering [*A publication*]
W & W .... Wahlstrom & Widstrand [*Publisher*] [*Sweden*]
WW............ Walking Wounded   (ADA)
WW............ Wall-to-Wall [*Carpeting*] [*Classified advertising*]
WW............ Wardroom Window [*Aerospace*]   (KSC)
WW............ Warehouse Warrant
WW............ Warrant Writer [*Navy*] [*British*]
WW............ Waste Watch   (EA)
WW............ Water Waste   (NASA)
WW............ Water-White
WG............ Waterwall   (MSA)
WW............ Waterworks
WW............ Weather Wing   (MCD)
WW............ Weather Working
WW............ Weight Watchers [*An association*]
W/W.......... Weight/Weight
WW............ Welfare Worker [*British military*]   (DMA)
WW............ Well Water [*Nuclear energy*]   (NRCH)
WW............ Westwater Industries Ltd. [*Toronto Stock Exchange symbol*]
W/W.......... Wheel Well   (MCD)
W & W .... White and Wilson's [*or Willson's*] Civil Cases, Texas Court of Appeals [*A publication*]   (DLA)
WW............ White Wyandotte [*Poultry*]
WW............ Wholesale Wine [*License*]
WW............ Who's Who [*A publication*]
WW............ Widow [*Genealogy*]
W/W.......... Wild Weasel [*Aerospace*]
WW............ Wilderness Watch   (EA)
W & W .... Williams & Wilkins [*Publishing company*]
WW............ Winchester & Western Railroad Co. [*AAR code*]
W/W.......... Winding to Winding   (MSA)
WW............ Wines of Westhorpe [*Commercial firm*] [*British*]
WW............ Winged Warriors/National B-Body Owners Association   (EA)
WW............ Wire Way [*Technical drawings*]
WW............ Wire-Wound
WW............ Wire Wrap   (NASA)
WW............ Wirkendes Wort [*A publication*]
W u W .... Wirtschaft und Wettbewerb [*German*] [*A publication*]
WW............ Wirtschaftswoche-Datenbank [*Economic Week Data Bank*] [*Society for Public Economics*] [*Federal Republic of Germany*] [*Information service or system*]   (IID)
WW............ Wissenschaft und Weisheit [*A publication*]
WW............ With Warrants [*Stock exchange term*]   (SPSG)
WW............ Woman's World [*A publication*]
WW............ Women in the Wind [*An association*]   (EA)
WW............ [*Thomas*] Woodrow Wilson [*US president, 1856-1924*]
WW............ Woodwind [*Instrument*] [*Music*]
WW............ Working Woman [*A publication*]
WW............ Working Women, National Association of Officeworkers   (EA)
WW............ World War
WW............ Worldwide
WW............ Worldwide Equities Ltd. [*Toronto Stock Exchange symbol*]
WW............ Wound Width [*Forestry*]
WW............ Writers and Their Work [*British Council*]
Ww............ Wroclaw [*A publication*]
WW............ Wyatt and Webb's Reports [*A publication*]   (DLA)
W & W .... Wyatt and Webb's Victorian Reports [*A publication*]   (APTA)
WW............ Zas Airlines of Egypt [*Egypt*] [*ICAO designator*]   (FAAC)
1WW.......... Weather Wing (1st) [*California*] [*Air Force*]
2WW.......... Weather Wing (2nd) [*New York*] [*Air Force*]
3WW.......... Weather Wing (3rd) [*Nebraska*] [*Air Force*]
4WW.......... Weather Wing (4th) [*Colorado*] [*Air Force*]
6WW.......... Weather Wing (6th) [*Washington, DC*] [*Air Force*]
7WW.......... Weather Wing (7th) [*Illinois*] [*Air Force*]
WWA......... Wallcovering Wholesalers Association [*Later, WDA*]   (EA)
WWa.......... Wauwatosa Public Library, Wauwatosa, WI [*Library symbol*] [*Library of Congress*]   (LCLS)
WWA......... Welsh Water Authority   (DCTA)
WWA......... Western Writers of America   (EA)
WWA......... Who's Who in America [*A publication*]
WWA......... Who's Who in Art [*A publication*]
WWA......... Who's Who in Australia [*A publication*]
WWA......... With the Will Annexed
WWA......... Woolens and Worsteds of America [*Defunct*]
WWA......... World Warning Agency   (MCD)
WWA......... World Water [*A publication*]
WWA......... World Waterpark Association   (EA)
WWA......... World Watusi Association   (EA)
WWA......... World Wide Airlines, Inc.
WWAA....... Westfalen Warmblood Association of America   (EA)
WWAB....... Lakeland, FL [*AM radio station call letters*]
W & W & A'B ... Wyatt, Webb, and A'Beckett's Reports [*A publication*]   (APTA)
WW & A'B ... Wyatt, Webb, and A'Beckett's Victorian Reports [*A publication*]   (APTA)
WWABCC ... World Wide Avon Bottle Collectors Club   (EA)
WW & A'B (E) ... Wyatt, Webb, and A'Beckett's Reports (Equity) [*A publication*]   (APTA)

W & W & A'B (Eq) ... Wyatt, Webb, and A'Beckett's Reports (Equity) [*A publication*]   (APTA)
WW & A'B (IE & M) ... Wyatt, Webb, and A'Beckett's Reports (Insolvency, Ecclesiastical, and Matrimonial) [*A publication*]   (APTA)
WW & A'B (M) ... Wyatt, Webb, and A'Beckett's Reports (Mining) [*A publication*]   (APTA)
W & W & A'B (Min) ... Wyatt, Webb, and A'Beckett's Reports (Mining) [*A publication*]   (APTA)
WWABNCP ... Worldwide Airborne Command Post [*Air Force*]   (AFM)
WWAC...... Western World Avon Club   (EA)
WWAC-TV ... Atlantic City, NJ [*Television station call letters*]
WWAEA ... Water and Wastes Engineering [*A publication*]
WWAG...... McKee, KY [*FM radio station call letters*]
WWAK...... Redwater Lake, FL [*AM radio station call letters*]
WWal........ Walworth Memorial Library, Walworth, WI [*Library symbol*] [*Library of Congress*]   (LCLS)
WWalPS.... Walworth Public Schools, Walworth, WI [*Library symbol*] [*Library of Congress*]   (LCLS)
WWalSD ... North Walworth School District Number Five, Walworth, WI [*Library symbol*] [*Library of Congress*]   (LCLS)
WWAM.... Columbus, WI [*FM radio station call letters*]
WWaMP ... Milwaukee Psychiatric Hospital, Wauwatosa, WI [*Library symbol*] [*Library of Congress*]   (LCLS)
WWAP...... Worldwide Asset Position [*Military*]   (AABC)
WWARA ... Weltwirtschaftliches Archiv [*A publication*]
WWAS ...... Williamsport, PA [*FM radio station call letters*]
WWAS ...... World-Wide Academy of Scholars [*Defunct*]   (EA)
WWAS ...... World Wide Air Services [*Australia*]
WWaSC..... Saint Camillus Hospital, Wauwatosa, WI [*Library symbol*] [*Library of Congress*]   (LCLS)
WWAT ...... Chillicothe, OH [*Television station call letters*]
WWat .... Watertown Free Public Library, Watertown, WI [*Library symbol*] [*Library of Congress*]   (LCLS)
WWATA ... Water and Waste Treatment [*A publication*]
WWatf....... Waterford Public Library, Waterford, WI [*Library symbol*] [*Library of Congress*]   (LCLS)
WWatfH.... Holy Redeemer College, Waterford, WI [*Library symbol*] [*Library of Congress*]   (LCLS)
WWatN ..... Northwestern College, Watertown, WI [*Library symbol*] [*Library of Congress*]   (LCLS)
WWau........ Waukesha Public Library, Waukesha, WI [*Library symbol*] [*Library of Congress*]   (LCLS)
WWauC ..... Carroll College, Waukesha, WI [*Library symbol*] [*Library of Congress*]   (LCLS)
WWauH .... Waukesha Memorial Hospital, Waukesha, WI [*Library symbol*] [*Library of Congress*]   (LCLS)
WWauHi ... Waukesha County Historical Society, Waukesha, WI [*Library symbol*] [*Library of Congress*]   (LCLS)
WWauI ...... Waukesha County Institution, Waukesha, WI [*Library symbol*] [*Library of Congress*]   (LCLS)
WWaupa.... Waupaca Free Public Library, Waupaca, WI [*Library symbol*] [*Library of Congress*]   (LCLS)
WWauU..... University of Wisconsin Center-Waukesha County, Waukesha, WI [*Library symbol*] [*Library of Congress*]   (LCLS)
WWAV ..... Santa Rosa Beach, FL [*FM radio station call letters*]
WWAX...... Olyphant, PA [*AM radio station call letters*]
WWAY ...... Wilmington, NC [*Television station call letters*]
W Ways .... Word Ways [*A publication*]
WWAZ...... Providence, RI [*AM radio station call letters*]
WWB........ Waterways Freight Bureau, Washington DC [*STAC*]
WWb........ West Bend Public Library, West Bend, WI [*Library symbol*] [*Library of Congress*]   (LCLS)
WWB........ Women's World Banking [*Financial organization*]
WWB........ Writers War Board
WWBA...... Madison, FL [*FM radio station call letters*]
WWBA...... Walt Whitman Birthplace Association   (EA)
WWBA...... Western Wooden Box Association   (EA)
WWBA...... Who's Who among Black Americans [*A publication*]
WWBC...... Cocoa, FL [*AM radio station call letters*]
WWBC...... Washington Bancorporation [*NASDAQ symbol*]   (NQ)
WWBD..... Bamberg-Denmark, SC [*AM radio station call letters*]
WWBE..... Mifflinburg, PA [*FM radio station call letters*]
WWBF...... Bartow, FL [*AM radio station call letters*]
WWBF...... Woodrow Wilson Birthplace Foundation   (EA)
WWBPU ... World Wide Baraca-Philathea Union   (EA)
WWBR ...... Harriman, TN [*AM radio station call letters*]
WWBR-FM ... Harriman, TN [*FM radio station call letters*]
WWBT ...... Richmond, VA [*Television station call letters*]
WWbU....... University of Wisconsin Center-Washington County, West Bend, WI [*Library symbol*] [*Library of Congress*]   (LCLS)
WWBZ ...... Vineland, NJ [*AM radio station call letters*]
WWC........ Citizen's Library, Washington, PA [*OCLC symbol*]   (OCLC)
WWC........ Walla Walla College [*Washington*]
WWC........ Warren Wilson College [*Swannan, NC*]
WWC........ Wavy Walled Cylinder
WWC........ Who's Who in Consulting [*A publication*]
WWC........ William Woods College [*Fulton, MO*]
WWC........ World's Wristwrestling Championship   (EA)
WWC........ Woven Wire Cloth
WWCA...... Gary, IN [*AM radio station call letters*]
WWCA...... Women's Welsh Clubs of America   (EA)

WWCB ...... Corry, PA [*AM radio station call letters*]
WW & CB ... Weekly Weather and Crop Bulletin [*A publication*]
WWCC ...... Honesdale, PA [*AM radio station call letters*]
WWCC ...... Western Wisconsin Communications Cooperative
       [*Independence, WI*] [*Telecommunications*] (TSSD)
W & WCC ... White and Wilson's [*or Willson's*] Civil Cases, Texas Court of
       Appeals [*A publication*] (DLA)
WWCCIS .. World-Wide Command and Control Information
       System (MCD)
WWCD ...... Grove City, OH [*FM radio station call letters*]
WWCH ...... Clarion, PA [*AM radio station call letters*]
WWCICS .. Wolfe-Winrow CICS/VS Command Level Proficiency Test
       [*Data processing*]
W & W Civ Cases Court of Appeals ... White and Wilson's [*or Willson's*] Civil
       Cases, Texas Court of Appeals [*A publication*] (DLA)
WWCJ ...... Jackson, MS [*FM radio station call letters*]
WWCK ...... Flint, MI [*AM radio station call letters*]
WWCK-FM ... Flint, MI [*FM radio station call letters*]
WWCL ...... Lehigh Acres, FL [*AM radio station call letters*]
WWCM ...... Ypsilanti, MI [*AM radio station call letters*]
WWCO ...... Waterbury, CT [*AM radio station call letters*]
W & W Con Cases ... White and Wilson's [*or Willson's*] Civil Cases, Texas
       Court of Appeals [*A publication*] (DLA)
W & W Con Rep ... White and Wilson's [*or Willson's*] Civil Cases, Texas
       Court of Appeals [*A publication*] (DLA)
WWCP ...... Walking Wounded Collecting Post [*Military*]
WWCP-TV ... Johnstown, PA [*Television station call letters*]
WWCS ...... Canonsburg, PA [*AM radio station call letters*]
WWCT ...... Peoria, IL [*FM radio station call letters*]
WWCT Regt ... Wellington, West Coast, and Taranaki Regiment [*British
       military*] (DMA)
WWCTU ... World's Woman's Christian Temperance Union
       [*Australia*] (EAIO)
WWCU ...... Cullowhee, NC [*FM radio station call letters*]
WWD .... Cape May [*New Jersey*] [*Airport symbol*] (OAG)
WWd .... Kilbourn Public Library, Wisconsin Dells, WI [*Library symbol*]
       [*Library of Congress*] (LCLS)
WWD .... Weather Working Days [*Construction*]
WWD .... Weird World [*A publication*]
WWD .... Wildwood, NJ [*Location identifier*] [*FAA*] (FAAL)
WW & D .... Willmore, Wollaston, and Davison's English Queen's Bench
       Reports [*1837*] [*A publication*] (DLA)
WWD .... Windward (KSC)
WWD .... Women's Wear Daily [*A publication*]
WWDB ...... Philadelphia, PA [*FM radio station call letters*]
WWDC ...... Washington, DC [*AM radio station call letters*]
WWDCFC ... World-Wide Dave Clark Fan Club [*Defunct*] (EAIO)
WWDC-FM ... Washington, DC [*FM radio station call letters*]
WWDE-FM ... Hampton, VA [*FM radio station call letters*]
WWdepSN ... Saint Norbert College, West De Pere, WI [*Library symbol*]
       [*Library of Congress*] (LCLS)
wwdFHEx ... Weather Working Days, Fridays, and Holidays Excluded
       [*Shipping*] (DS)
WWDJ ...... Hackensack, NJ [*AM radio station call letters*]
WWDL-FM ... Scranton, PA [*FM radio station call letters*]
WWDM ..... Sumter, SC [*FM radio station call letters*]
WWDMS .. Worldwide Standard Data Management System (MCD)
WWDR ...... Hardeeville, SC [*FM radio station call letters*]
W Wdr ...... Warrant Wardmaster [*British military*] (DMA)
WWDS ...... Muncie, IN [*FM radio station call letters*]
WWDSA .... Worldwide Digital System Architecture
WWDSHEX ... Weather Working Days, Sundays, and Holidays
       Excluded (DS)
WWE .... Wide World of Entertainment [*TV program*]
WWe .... Wissenschaft und Weisheit [*A publication*]
WWE .... Worldwide Energy Corp. [*Toronto Stock Exchange
       symbol*] (SPSG)
W & W (E) ... Wyatt and Webb's Reports (Equity) [*A publication*] (APTA)
WWea .... West Allis Public Library, West Allis, WI [*Library symbol*]
       [*Library of Congress*] (LCLS)
WWeaJ ...... Janlen Enterprises, West Allis, WI [*Library symbol*] [*Library of
       Congress*] (LCLS)
WWeaM .... West Allis Memorial Hospital, West Allis, WI [*Library symbol*]
       [*Library of Congress*] (LCLS)
WWEB ...... Wallingford, CT [*FM radio station call letters*]
WWEF .... Working Women Education Fund (EA)
WWEL ...... London, KY [*FM radio station call letters*]
WWEMA .. Water and Wastewater Equipment Manufacturers
       Association (EA)
WWENA ... Water and Water Engineering [*A publication*]
W & W (Eq) ... Wyatt and Webb's Reports (Equity) [*A publication*] (APTA)
WWER ...... Dryden, NY [*FM radio station call letters*]
WWES ...... Hot Springs, VA [*AM radio station call letters*]
WWEV ...... Cumming, GA [*FM radio station call letters*]
WWEZ ...... Cincinnati, OH [*FM radio station call letters*]
WWF .... War/Watch Foundation (EA)
WWF .... Washington Workshops Foundation (EA)
WWF .... Waterside Workers' Federation of Australia
WWF .... Welded Wire Fabric [*Technical drawings*]
WWF .... Wire Wrap Fixture
WWF .... Wonder Woman Foundation (EA)

WWF .... World Wildlife Fund (EA)
WWF .... WorldWide Fund for Nature (EA)
WWFC ...... Worldwide Fair Play for Frogs Committee
WWFE...... Miami, FL [*AM radio station call letters*]
WWFF ...... Marathon, FL [*FM radio station call letters*]
WWFI .... World Wildlife Fund International [*Later, Worldwide Fund for
       Nature*] (EAIO)
WWFL ...... Clermont, FL [*AM radio station call letters*]
WWFM ..... Trenton, NJ [*FM radio station call letters*]
WWFR ...... Okeechobee, FL [*FM radio station call letters*]
WWFS ...... West Wales Field Society [*British*]
WWF-US .. World Wildlife Fund - United States (EA)
WWFX ..... Belfast, ME [*FM radio station call letters*]
WWG .... HSIA [*Halogenated Solvent Industry Alliance*] Water Work
       Group [*Defunct*] (EA)
WWg .... Weather Wing [*Air Force*] (AFM)
WWG .... Wiederwerbgesetz (BJA)
WWGC ...... Carrollton, GA [*FM radio station call letters*]
WWGL ...... Lexington, NC [*FM radio station call letters*]
WWGM ..... Nashville, TN [*AM radio station call letters*]
WWGN ...... Wildlife Working Group. Newsletter [*A publication*]
WWGP ...... Sanford, NC [*AM radio station call letters*]
WWGP ...... Ward White Group PLC [*NASDAQ symbol*] (NQ)
WWGR ...... La Follette, TN [*AM radio station call letters*]
WWGS ...... Tifton, GA [*AM radio station call letters*]
WWGT ...... Westbrook, ME [*AM radio station call letters*]
WWGT-FM ... Portland, ME [*FM radio station call letters*]
WWH .... W. W. Harrington's Reports [*31-39 Delaware*] [*A
       publication*] (DLA)
WW & H.... Willmore, Wollaston, and Hodges' English Queen's Bench
       Reports [*1838-39*] [*A publication*] (DLA)
W/WH .... With/Warhead [*Nuclear*]
WWH .... Women Working Home [*A publication*]
WWHA ..... Who's Who among Hispanic Americans [*A publication*]
W W Harr ... [*W. W.*] Harrington's Reports [*31-39 Delaware*] [*A
       publication*] (DLA)
W W Harr Del ... [*W. W.*] Harrington's Reports [*31-39 Delaware*] [*A
       publication*] (DLA)
WWHB ...... Hampton Bays, NY [*FM radio station call letters*]
WWHE ...... Woman Who Has Everything
WW & H (Eng) ... Willmore, Wollaston, and Hodges' English Queen's Bench
       Reports [*1838-39*] [*A publication*] (DLA)
WWHI .... Muncie, IN [*FM radio station call letters*]
WWhiwSD ... Whitewater Unified School District, Joint Number One,
       Whitewater, WI [*Library symbol*] [*Library of
       Congress*] (LCLS)
WWhiwU... University of Wisconsin-Whitewater, Whitewater, WI [*Library
       symbol*] [*Library of Congress*] (LCLS)
WWHL ...... Waterwheel
WWHN ..... Joliet, IL [*AM radio station call letters*]
WWHR ...... Bowling Green, KY [*FM radio station call letters*]
WWHRAWAC ... World Wide Horse Registry for the American White and
       the American Creme (EA)
WWHS ...... Western World Haiku Society (EA)
WWHS-FM ... Hampden-Sydney, VA [*FM radio station call letters*]
WWHT-FM ... Goose Creek, SC [*FM radio station call letters*]
WWHY ...... Milan, TN [*AM radio station call letters*]
WWI .... Weight Watchers International [*Commercial firm*] (EA)
WWI .... Whirlwind I
WWI .... Who's Who in Israel [*A publication*]
WWI .... Working Women's Institute (EA)
WWI .... World War I
WWI AERO ... World War I Aeroplanes (EA)
WWIB ...... Ladysmith, WI [*FM radio station call letters*]
WW & IB... Western Weighing and Inspection Bureau
WWIC ...... Scottsboro, AL [*AM radio station call letters*]
WWiC........ Winnebago County Hospital, Winnebago, WI [*Library symbol*]
       [*Library of Congress*] (LCLS)
WWICC.... Women's Welfare Issues Consultative Committee [*Australia*]
WWICS ..... Woodrow Wilson International Center for Scholars (EA)
W & W (IE & M) ... Wyatt and Webb's Reports (Insolvency, Ecclesiastical,
       and Matrimonial) [*A publication*] (APTA)
WWIH .... High Point, NC [*FM radio station call letters*]
WWII .... Shiremanstown, PA [*AM radio station call letters*]
WWII .... World War II
WWIIHSLB ... World War II Honorable Service Lapel Button (AFM)
WWIII .... World War III
WWIIVM ... World War II Victory Medal [*Military decoration*]
WWil .... Barrett Memorial Library, Williams Bay, WI [*Library symbol*]
       [*Library of Congress*] (LCLS)
WWIL .... Wilmington, NC [*AM radio station call letters*]
WWIMS.... Worldwide Integrated Management of Subsistence
       [*Military*] (NVT)
WWIN ...... Baltimore, MD [*AM radio station call letters*]
WWIN .... Western Waste Industries [*NASDAQ symbol*] (NQ)
WWIN-FM ... Glen Burnie, MD [*FM radio station call letters*]
WWIO ...... Worldwide Inventory Objective (AABC)
WWiP........ Park View Health Center, Winnebago, WI [*Library symbol*]
       [*Library of Congress*] (LCLS)
WWIS........ Black River Falls, WI [*AM radio station call letters*]

WWiS .... Winnebago State Hospital, Winnebago, WI [*Library symbol*] [*Library of Congress*] (LCLS)
WWIS .... Worldwide Information Services
WWIS-FM ... Black River Falls, WI [*FM radio station call letters*]
WWIT .... Canton, NC [*AM radio station call letters*]
WWIT .... Who's Who in the Theatre [*A publication*]
WWITC .... Worldwide Improved Technical Control (MCD)
WWIVM ... World War I Victory Medal [*Military decoration*]
WWIZ .... Mercer, PA [*FM radio station call letters*]
WWJ .... Detroit, MI [*AM radio station call letters*]
WWJ .... Who's Who in Japan [*A publication*]
WWJB ...... Brooksville, FL [*AM radio station call letters*]
WWJC ...... Duluth, MN [*AM radio station call letters*]
WWJCC .... Worldwide Joint Coordinator Center [*NATO*] (NATG)
WWJM ..... New Lexington, OH [*FM radio station call letters*]
WWJO ...... St. Cloud, MN [*FM radio station call letters*]
WWJOA ... Water Well Journal [*A publication*]
WWJQ ...... Holland, MI [*AM radio station call letters*]
WWJR .... Sheboygan, WI [*FM radio station call letters*]
WWJY .... Crown Point, IN [*FM radio station call letters*]
WWJZ .... Mount Holly, NJ [*AM radio station call letters*]
WWK .... Continental Iron and Steel Trade Reports. Iron and Steel Trade Market Reports and Special Information [*A publication*]
WWK .... Wewak [*Papua New Guinea*] [*Airport symbol*] (OAG)
WWKA ...... Orlando, FL [*FM radio station call letters*]
WWKB ...... Buffalo, NY [*AM radio station call letters*]
WWKC ...... Caldwell, OH [*FM radio station call letters*]
WWKC ...... White Wolf-Kern Canyon [*Geological fault*]
WWKF ...... Fulton, KY [*FM radio station call letters*]
WWKI .... Kokomo, IN [*FM radio station call letters*]
WWKL ...... Harrisburg, PA [*FM radio station call letters*]
WWKM ..... Harrison, MI [*AM radio station call letters*]
WWKO ...... Cocoa, FL [*AM radio station call letters*]
WWKS ...... Beaver Falls, PA [*FM radio station call letters*]
WWKT ...... Kingstree, SC [*FM radio station call letters*]
WWKX ...... Woonsocket, RI [*FM radio station call letters*]
WWKY ...... Louisville, KY [*AM radio station call letters*]
WWKZ ...... New Albany, MS [*FM radio station call letters*]
WWL .... New Orleans, LA [*AM radio station call letters*]
W & W (L) ... Wyatt and Webb's Reports (Law) [*A publication*] (APTA)
WWLA ...... Lewiston, ME [*Television station call letters*]
WWLF-TV ... Hazleton, PA [*Television station call letters*]
WWLI .... Providence, RI [*FM radio station call letters*]
WWLIS ..... Woodmen of the World Life Insurance Society (EA)
WWLK ...... Eddyville, KY [*AM radio station call letters*]
WWL2M .. Women Who Love Too Much [*Bestselling book by Robin Norwood*]
WWLO ...... Gainesville, FL [*AM radio station call letters*]
WWLODS ... Wire and Wire-Like Object Detection System [*Helicopter*] (MCD)
WWLP ...... Springfield, MA [*Television station call letters*]
WWLR ...... Lyndonville, VT [*FM radio station call letters*]
WWLS .... Moore, OK [*AM radio station call letters*]
WWLT ...... Bamberg, SC [*FM radio station call letters*]
WWLTM... Women Who Love Too Much [*Title of book by Robin Norwood*]
WWL-TV .. New Orleans, LA [*Television station call letters*]
WWLV ...... Daytona Beach, FL [*FM radio station call letters*]
WWLX ...... Lawrenceburg, TN [*AM radio station call letters*]
WWLZ ...... Cadillac, MI [*FM radio station call letters*]
WWM .... Ons Nuis Vakblad voor de Meubelhandel, Meubelmakerij, Meubelindustrie, Interieurarchitecteur, Behangerij, Stoffeerderij, en Detailhandel in Woningtextiel [*A publication*]
WWM .... Weekly Women's Magazine [*Manila*] [*A publication*]
WWM .... Weizsaecker-Williams Method [*Physics*]
WWM .... Welded Wire Matrix
WWM .... Wings West, Inc. [*Santa Monica, CA*] [*FAA designator*] (FAAC)
WWM .... Wire Wrap Machine
WWM .... Working Woman [*A publication*]
WWM .... World-Wide Missions (EA)
WWM .... Worldwide Monitor [*Vancouver Stock Exchange symbol*]
WWMCCS ... Worldwide Military Command and Control System [*DoD*]
WWMD..... Hagerstown, MD [*FM radio station call letters*]
WWME ...... Worldwide Marriage Encounter (EA)
WWMG ..... Shelby, NC [*FM radio station call letters*]
WWMH .... Minocqua, WI [*FM radio station call letters*]
WWMJ ...... Ellsworth, ME [*FM radio station call letters*]
WWML ..... Wood, Wire, and Metal Lathers' International Union [*Later, UBC*] (EA)
WWMMP ... Western Wood Moulding and Millwork Producers [*Later, WMMPA*] (EA)
WWMP ..... Western Wood Moulding Producers [*Later, WMMPA*] (EA)
WWMR..... Rumford, ME [*FM radio station call letters*]
WWMS ..... Oxford, MS [*FM radio station call letters*]
WWMS ..... Water and Waste Management Subsystem [*NASA*] (KSC)
WWMS ..... Who's Who in Malaysia and Singapore [*A publication*]
WWMT..... Kalamazoo, MI [*Television station call letters*]
WWMX..... Baltimore, MD [*FM radio station call letters*]
WWMY...... Eden, NC [*FM radio station call letters*]

WWN......... Walt Whitman Newsletter [*A publication*]
WWN......... Washington Women's Network (EA)
WWN......... With Winch
WWNC...... Asheville, NC [*AM radio station call letters*]
WWNFF..... Woodrow Wilson National Fellowship Foundation (EA)
WWNH ..... Madbury, NH [*AM radio station call letters*]
WWNH ..... War Will Never Happen [*Philosophy attributed to the Defense Department by former Deputy Assistant Secretary of Defense John F. Ahearne*] [*1987*]
WWNK-FM ... Cincinnati, OH [*FM radio station call letters*]
WWNN ..... Pompano Beach, FL [*AM radio station call letters*]
WWNO ..... New Orleans, LA [*FM radio station call letters*]
WWNR..... Beckley, WV [*AM radio station call letters*]
WWNS ..... Statesboro, GA [*AM radio station call letters*]
WWNS ..... World Wide News Service (BJA)
WWNSS..... Worldwide Network of Standard Seismograph [*Stations*]
WWNT..... Dothan, AL [*AM radio station call letters*]
WWNW..... New Wilmington, PA [*FM radio station call letters*]
WWNY-TV .. Carthage, NY [*Television station call letters*]
WWNZ..... Orlando, FL [*AM radio station call letters*]
WWO .... Warrant Writer Officer [*British military*] (DMA)
WW/O...... Widow Of [*Genealogy*]
WWO .... Wing Warrant Officer [*RAF*] [*British*]
WWOC...... Avalon, NJ [*FM radio station call letters*]
WWOD ..... Lynchburg, VA [*AM radio station call letters*]
WWOJ ...... Avon Park, FL [*FM radio station call letters*]
WWOK...... Evansville, IN [*AM radio station call letters*]
WWON ...... Woonsocket, RI [*AM radio station call letters*]
WWooH..... Howard Young Medical Center, Woodruff, WI [*Library symbol*] [*Library of Congress*] (LCLS)
W Work (Lond) ... World's Work (London) [*A publication*]
WWOR-TV ... Secaucus, NJ [*Television station call letters*]
WWoVA .... United States Veterans Administration Hospital, Wood, WI [*Library symbol*] [*Library of Congress*] (LCLS)
WWOW..... Conneaut, OH [*AM radio station call letters*]
WWOZ..... New Orleans, LA [*FM radio station call letters*]
WWP......... Walden Woods Project [*An association*] (EA)
WWP......... Washington Water Power Co. [*NYSE symbol*] (SPSG)
WWP......... Water Wall (Peripheral Jet) (AAG)
WWP......... Weather Wing Pamphlet [*Air Force*] (MCD)
WWP......... Wire Wrap Panels (MCD)
WWP......... Workers World Party [*Political party*] (EA)
WWP......... Working Water Pressure
WWP......... World Weather Program [*National Science Foundation*]
WWPA ...... Western Wood Products Association (EA)
WWPA ...... Williamsport, PA [*AM radio station call letters*]
WWPA ...... Woven Wire Products Association (EA)
WWPB ...... Hagerstown, MD [*Television station call letters*]
WWPB ...... Worldwide Women Professional Bowlers (EA)
WWpC....... Central State Hospital, Waupun, WI [*Library symbol*] [*Library of Congress*] (LCLS)
WWPD ..... Marion, SC [*FM radio station call letters*]
WWPG ..... Widows' War Pensions and Gratuities [*British*]
WWPH ..... Princeton Junction, NJ [*FM radio station call letters*]
WWPLS .... World Wide Pet Lovers Society [*Defunct*] (EA)
WWPMU .. World-Wide Prayer and Missionary Union (EA)
WWPN ..... Westernport, MD [*FM radio station call letters*]
WWPR ..... Sharon, CT [*FM radio station call letters*]
W/WPR..... Windshield Wiper [*Automotive engineering*]
WWPSA .... Western World Pet Supply Association (EA)
WWPT ..... Westport, CT [*FM radio station call letters*]
WWPV-FM ... Colchester, VT [*FM radio station call letters*]
WWPZ ...... Petoskey, MI [*AM radio station call letters*]
WWQC...... Quincy, IL [*FM radio station call letters*]
WWQM-FM ... Middleton, WI [*FM radio station call letters*]
WWQQ-FM ... Wilmington, NC [*FM radio station call letters*]
WWr.......... McMillan Memorial Library, Wisconsin Rapids, WI [*Library symbol*] [*Library of Congress*] (LCLS)
WWR......... Walt Whitman Review [*A publication*]
WWR......... Washington Weekly Report [*Independent Bankers Association of America*] [*A publication*]
WWR......... Washington Western [*AAR code*]
WWR......... Western Warner Oils [*Vancouver Stock Exchange symbol*]
WWR......... Western Weekly Reports [*Carswell Co. Ltd.*] [*Canada*] [*Information service or system*] (CRD)
WWR......... Widower [*Genealogy*]
WWR......... Wire-Wound Resistor
WWR......... Wisconsin Rapids, McMillan Library, Wisconsin Rapids, WI [*OCLC symbol*] (OCLC)
WWR......... Woodill Wildfire Registry (EA)
WWR......... Woodward, OK [*Location identifier*] [*FAA*] (FAAL)
WWRB ...... Pittston, PA [*FM radio station call letters*]
WWRC...... Washington, DC [*AM radio station call letters*]
WWRC...... Wyoming Water Research Center [*University of Wyoming*] [*Research center*] (RCD)
WWRD...... Wilson, NC [*Television station call letters*]
WWREC.... Western Washington Research and Extension Center [*Washington State University*] [*Research center*] (RCD)
WWRF ...... Who's Who Resource File [*Minority Business Development Agency*] [*Database*]
WWRJ........ Hollywood, SC [*AM radio station call letters*]

WWRK......	Elberton, GA [*AM radio station call letters*]
WWRK-FM ...	Elberton, GA [*FM radio station call letters*]
WWRL	New York, NY [*AM radio station call letters*]
WWRM......	St. Petersburg, FL [*FM radio station call letters*]
WWR (NS) ...	Western Weekly Reports, New Series [*Canada*] [*A publication*]　(DLA)
WWRS......	Mayville, WI [*Television station call letters*]
WWRS......	Wash-Water Recovery System [*in a spacecraft*] [*NASA*]
WWRT	Algood, TN [*AM radio station call letters*]
WWRV	New York, NY [*AM radio station call letters*]
WWRW	Wisconsin Rapids, WI [*FM radio station call letters*]
WWRX	Westerly, RI [*FM radio station call letters*]
WWS	Walker Wingsail Systems [*Shipbuilding*] [*British*]
WWS	Water Wall (Side Skegs)　(AAG)
WWS	Water and Waste Subsystem [*Aerospace*]　(MCD)
WWs..........	Wausau Public Library, Wausau, WI [*Library symbol*] [*Library of Congress*]　(LCLS)
WW(S)......	Well Water (System) [*Nuclear energy*]　(NRCH)
WWS	Western Writers Series [*A publication*]
WWS	Wind and Watermill Section [*of the Society for the Protection of Ancient Buildings*]　(EA)
WWS	Woman's Workshop　(EA)
WWS	Women's Welfare Service [*Defunct*]　(EA)
WWS	World Weather System
WWS	World Wide Minerals Ltd. [*Toronto Stock Exchange symbol*] [*Vancouver Stock Exchange symbol*]
WWSA	Walt Whitman Society of America [*Defunct*]　(EA)
WWSA	Who's Who in Saudi Arabia [*A publication*]
WWSA	Women's War Service Auxiliary [*British military*]　(DMA)
WWSB......	Sarasota, FL [*Television station call letters*]
WWSC......	Glens Falls, NY [*AM radio station call letters*]
WWSCA......	Wirtschaft und Wissenschaft [*A publication*]
WWSD	Quincy, FL [*AM radio station call letters*]
WWSD	Women's War Savings Division
WWSE......	Jamestown, NY [*FM radio station call letters*]
WWSF......	Andalusia, AL [*AM radio station call letters*]
WWSF......	World-Wide Stroke Foundation　(EA)
WWSF-FM ...	Andalusia, AL [*FM radio station call letters*]
WWSH	Hazleton, PA [*AM radio station call letters*]
WWSJ	St. Johns, MI [*AM radio station call letters*]
WWSL......	Philadelphia, MS [*FM radio station call letters*]
WWsMC ...	Marathon Health Care Center, Wausau, WI [*Library symbol*] [*Library of Congress*]　(LCLS)
WWSN	Dayton, OH [*FM radio station call letters*]
WWSN	Worldwide Seismology Net [*National Bureau of Standards*]
WWSP......	Stevens Point, WI [*FM radio station call letters*]
WWSP......	Worldwide Surveillance Program [*Military*]　(NG)
WWSR	St. Albans, VT [*AM radio station call letters*]
WWSRA....	Western Winter Sports Representatives Association　(EA)
WWSSB	World-Wide Software Support Branch　(MCD)
WWSSN....	World-Wide Standard Seismograph Network [*Earthquake detection*]
WWSSN....	Worldwide Standardized Seismograph Network [*US Geological Survey*]
WWSU	Dayton, OH [*FM radio station call letters*]
WWSU	World Water Ski Union [*See also UMSN*] [*Montreux, Switzerland*]　(EAIO)
WWSVA....	Worldwide Secure Voice Architecture　(MCD)
WWSVCS ...	World-Wide Secure Voice Communications System　(MCD)
WWSVCS ...	World-Wide Secure Voice Conference System　(MCD)
WWSW	Pittsburgh, PA [*AM radio station call letters*]
WWsW	Wausau Hospitals, Inc., Wausau, WI [*Library symbol*] [*Library of Congress*]　(LCLS)
WWSW-FM ...	Pittsburgh, PA [*FM radio station call letters*]
WWsWV ...	Wisconsin Valley Library Service, Wausau, WI [*Library symbol*] [*Library of Congress*]　(LCLS)
WWT	Newtok [*Alaska*] [*Airport symbol*]　(OAG)
WWT	Newtok, AK [*Location identifier*] [*FAA*]　(FAAL)
WWT	Who's Who in Technology [*A publication*]
WWTC	Minneapolis, MN [*AM radio station call letters*]
WWTC	Wagga Wagga Teachers College [*Australia*]
WWTCA	World War Tank Corps Association　(EA)
WWTCIP ..	Worldwide Technical Control Improvement Program　(MCD)
WWTG......	Stanwood, MI [*AM radio station call letters*]
WWTK	Lake Placid, FL [*AM radio station call letters*]
WWTK	Weitek Corp. [*NASDAQ symbol*]　(CTT)
WWTO-TV ...	La Salle, IL [*Television station call letters*]
WWTP	Waste Water Treatment Plant [*Also, WTP*]
WWTR-FM ...	Bethany Beach, DE [*FM radio station call letters*]
WWTS	Waste Water Treatment System
WWTT	Worldwide Tapetalk [*An association*]　(EA)
WWTV	Cadillac, MI [*Television station call letters*]
WWTV	Western World-Samuel Communications, Inc. [*Formerly, Western-World TV*] [*NASDAQ symbol*]　(NQ)
WWU........	Western Washington University
WWUF......	Waycross, GA [*FM radio station call letters*]
WWUH	West Hartford, CT [*FM radio station call letters*]
WWUI	Working Women's United Institute [*Later, WWI*]　(EA)
WWUN-FM ...	Clarksdale, MS [*FM radio station call letters*]
WWUP-TV ...	Sault Ste. Marie, MI [*Television station call letters*]
WWUS......	Big Pine Key, FL [*FM radio station call letters*]

WWV........	Walla Walla Valley Railway Co. [*AAR code*]
WWV........	Wheeling College, Wheeling, WV [*OCLC symbol*]　(OCLC)
WWV........	World Wide Time [*National Bureau of Standards call letters*]　(MUGU)
WWV........	World Wide Vermiculture [*An association*]　(EA)
WWVA......	Wheeling, WV [*AM radio station call letters*]
WWVH......	World Wide Time Hawaii [*National Bureau of Standards call letters*]　(MUGU)
W & W Vict ...	Wyatt and Webb's Victorian Reports [*1864-69*] [*Australia*] [*A publication*]　(DLA)
WWVR	West Terre Haute, IN [*FM radio station call letters*]
WWVR	Wire-Wound Variable Resistor
WWVU-FM ...	Morgantown, WV [*FM radio station call letters*]
WWW........	Who Was Who [*A publication*]
WWW........	[*The*] Who, What, or Where Game [*Also, 3W's*] [*Television show*]
WWW........	Wirtschaft und Wettbewerb. Zeitschrift fuer Kartellrecht, Wettbewerbsrecht, Marktorganisation [*A publication*]
WWW........	Wolverine World Wide, Inc. [*NYSE symbol*]　(SPSG)
WWW........	World Weather Watch [*World Meteorological Organization*] [*Databank*]　(IID)
WWW........	Worldwide Warranty [*Canon USA, Inc.*]
WWWB.....	High Point, NC [*FM radio station call letters*]
WWWC.....	Wilkesboro, NC [*AM radio station call letters*]
WWWC.....	World without War Council　(EA)
WWWCR ..	World Wide White and Creme Horse Registry　(EA)
WWWE.....	Cleveland, OH [*AM radio station call letters*]
WWWF.....	Worldwide Wrestling Federation [*Later, WWF*]
WWWFC...	[*Kitty*] Wells-[*Johnny*] Wright-[*Bobby*] Wright International Fan Club　(EA)
WWWG.....	Rochester, NY [*AM radio station call letters*]
WWWI.....	Widows of World War I　(EA)
WWWJ.....	Who's Who in World Jewry [*A publication*]　(BJA)
WWWM...	Sylvania, OH [*FM radio station call letters*]
WWWM...	[*The*] W. W. Williams Co. [*NASDAQ symbol*]　(NQ)
WWWN...	Vienna, GA [*AM radio station call letters*]
WWWO.....	Hartford City, IN [*FM radio station call letters*]
WWWP.....	Franklin, VA [*FM radio station call letters*]
WWWT.....	Randolph, VT [*AM radio station call letters*]
WWWTTUTWTU ...	We Won't Write to Them until They Write to Us [*A servicemen's club*]
WWWU.....	Winchester, VA [*FM radio station call letters*]
WWWV.....	Charlottesville, VA [*FM radio station call letters*]
WWWV.....	Women World War Veterans　(EA)
WWWW...	Detroit, MI [*FM radio station call letters*]
WWWW...	Who's Who in the World of Women [*Australia*] [*A publication*]
WWWX.....	Albemarle, NC [*AM radio station call letters*]
WWWY.....	Columbus, IN [*FM radio station call letters*]
WWWZ.....	Summerville, SC [*FM radio station call letters*]
WWX........	World Wide Exchange [*Commercial firm*]　(EA)
WWXL......	Manchester, KY [*AM radio station call letters*]
WWXL-FM ...	Manchester, KY [*FM radio station call letters*]
WWXX......	Alpharetta, GA [*AM radio station call letters*]
WWY........	Warwickshire and Worcestershire Yeomanry [*British military*]　(DMA)
WWY........	West Wyalong [*Australia*] [*Airport symbol*]　(OAG)
WWY........	Wrigley [*Wm.*] Jr. Co. [*NYSE symbol*]　(SPSG)
WWYN.....	McKenzie, TN [*FM radio station call letters*]
WWYO.....	Pineville, WV [*AM radio station call letters*]
WWYZ......	Waterbury, CT [*FM radio station call letters*]
WWZ........	Willow Resources Ltd. [*Vancouver Stock Exchange symbol*]
WWZD......	New Albany, MS [*FM radio station call letters*]
WWZQ......	Aberdeen, MS [*AM radio station call letters*]
WWZQ-FM ...	Aberdeen, MS [*FM radio station call letters*]
WWZR	Port St. Joe, FL [*FM radio station call letters*]
WWZU......	Lock Haven, PA [*FM radio station call letters*]
WX............	Air NSW [*New South Wales*] [*Airline code*] [*Australia*]
WX............	American Eagle Airlines, Inc. [*ICAO designator*]　(FAAC)
WX............	Wawatay News Extra. Special Issues [*A publication*]
WX............	Wax
WX............	Weather
WX............	Westinghouse Electric Corp. [*NYSE symbol*] [*Wall Street slang name: "Wex"*]　(SPSG)
WX............	Wireless [*Communications*]
WX............	Women's Extra [*Size*]
WXAC......	Reading, PA [*FM radio station call letters*]
WXAG	Athens, GA [*AM radio station call letters*]
WXAL	Demopolis, AL [*AM radio station call letters*]
WXAM......	Buffalo, KY [*AM radio station call letters*]
WXAN......	Ava, IL [*FM radio station call letters*]
WxB........	Wax Bite [*Dentistry*]
WXBA	Brentwood, NY [*FM radio station call letters*]
WXBG	Burgaw, NC [*FM radio station call letters*]
WXBK	Albertville, AL [*AM radio station call letters*]
WXBM-FM ...	Milton, FL [*FM radio station call letters*]
WXBQ-FM ...	Bristol, TN [*FM radio station call letters*]
WXC........	Westinghouse Canada, Inc. [*Toronto Stock Exchange symbol*]
WXCC......	Williamson, WV [*FM radio station call letters*]
WXCE	Amery, WI [*AM radio station call letters*]
WXCF.......	Clifton Forge, VA [*AM radio station call letters*]
WXCF-FM ...	Clifton Forge, VA [*FM radio station call letters*]

WXCH....... Charleston, SC [*AM radio station call letters*]
WXCI........ Danbury, CT [*FM radio station call letters*]
WXCL....... Peoria, IL [*AM radio station call letters*]
WXCL-FM ... Perkin, IL [*FM radio station call letters*]
WXCO....... Wausau, WI [*AM radio station call letters*]
WXCON...... Pilot Reports by Qualified Weather Personnel on Weather
     Reconnaissance Flights [*Aviation code*] (FAAC)
WXCR ...... Safety Harbor, FL [*FM radio station call letters*]
WXCT ...... Hamden, CT [*AM radio station call letters*]
WXCV ...... Homosassa Springs, FL [*FM radio station call letters*]
WXCY ...... Havre de Grace, MD [*FM radio station call letters*]
WXD......... Meteorological RADAR Station [*ITU designation*] (CET)
WXD......... Waxed
WXD......... Westrex Development Corp. [*Vancouver Stock Exchange
     symbol*]
WXDJ....... Homestead, FL [*FM radio station call letters*]
WXDR....... Newark, DE [*FM radio station call letters*]
WXDU....... Durham, NC [*FM radio station call letters*]
WXDZ....... Callaway, FL [*FM radio station call letters*]
WXEE....... Welch, WV [*AM radio station call letters*]
WXEL....... West Palm Beach, FL [*FM radio station call letters*]
WXEL-TV ... West Palm Beach, FL [*Television station call letters*]
WXEW ...... Yabucoa, PR [*AM radio station call letters*]
WXEX-TV ... Petersburg, VA [*Television station call letters*]
WXEZ........ Chicago, IL [*AM radio station call letters*]
WXEZ-FM ... Chicago, IL [*FM radio station call letters*]
WXFM ...... Decatur, IL [*FM radio station call letters*]
WXFX....... Prattville, AL [*FM radio station call letters*]
WXG......... Warning (MUGU)
WXGA-TV ... Waycross, GA [*Television station call letters*]
WXGC....... Milledgeville, GA [*FM radio station call letters*]
WXGI .... Richmond, VA [*AM radio station call letters*]
WXGL .... Lewiston, ME [*AM radio station call letters*]
WXGL-FM ... Lewiston, ME [*FM radio station call letters*]
WXGM...... Gloucester, VA [*AM radio station call letters*]
WXGR ...... Bay St. Louis, MS [*AM radio station call letters*]
WXGT ...... Columbus, OH [*FM radio station call letters*]
WXGZ-TV ... Appleton, WI [*Television station call letters*]
WXIA-TV ... Atlanta, GA [*Television station call letters*]
WXIC....... Waverly, OH [*AM radio station call letters*]
WXID ...... Mayfield, KY [*FM radio station call letters*]
WXIE........ Oakland, MD [*FM radio station call letters*]
WXII........ Winston-Salem, NC [*Television station call letters*]
WXIK .... Brownville, NY [*AM radio station call letters*]
WXIL........ Parkersburg, WV [*FM radio station call letters*]
WXIN ...... Indianapolis, IN [*Television station call letters*]
WXIR........ Plainfield, OH [*FM radio station call letters*]
WXIS .... Erwin, TN [*FM radio station call letters*]
WXIT........ Charleston, WV [*AM radio station call letters*]
WXIX-TV ... Newport, KY [*Television station call letters*]
WXIZ........ Waverly, OH [*FM radio station call letters*]
WXJM-FM ... Washington, PA [*FM radio station call letters*]
WXKC ...... Erie, PA [*FM radio station call letters*]
WXKE ...... Fort Wayne, IN [*FM radio station call letters*]
WXKG ...... Livingston, TN [*FM radio station call letters*]
WXKI .... Salem, WV [*FM radio station call letters*]
WXKL....... Sanford, NC [*AM radio station call letters*]
WXKO ...... Fort Valley, GA [*AM radio station call letters*]
WXKO-FM ... Pana, IL [*FM radio station call letters*]
WXKQ ...... Whitesburg, KY [*FM radio station call letters*]
WXKS........ Medford, MA [*AM radio station call letters*]
WXKS-FM ... Medford, MA [*FM radio station call letters*]
WXKU ...... York, PA [*AM radio station call letters*]
WXKW ...... Allentown, PA [*AM radio station call letters*]
WXKX ...... Parkersburg, WV [*FM radio station call letters*]
WXKZ-FM ... Prestonsburg, KY [*FM radio station call letters*]
WXL......... Wix, Inc. [*Toronto Stock Exchange symbol*]
WXLA ...... Dimondale, MI [*AM radio station call letters*]
WXLC ...... Waukegan, IL [*FM radio station call letters*]
WXLE ...... Johnstown, OH [*FM radio station call letters*]
WXLF....... Rock Hill, SC [*AM radio station call letters*]
WXLI........ Dublin, GA [*AM radio station call letters*]
WXLK....... Roanoke, VA [*FM radio station call letters*]
WXLL....... Decatur, GA [*AM radio station call letters*]
WXLN....... Louisville, KY [*FM radio station call letters*]
WXLO ...... Fitchburg, MA [*FM radio station call letters*]
WXLP....... Moline, IL [*FM radio station call letters*]
WXLQ ...... Hinesville, GA [*FM radio station call letters*]
WXLR....... Hahira, GA [*AM radio station call letters*]
WXLS........ Biloxi, MS [*AM radio station call letters*]
WXLS-FM ... Gulfport, MS [*FM radio station call letters*]
WXLT....... McComb, MS [*FM radio station call letters*]
WXLV....... Schnecksville, PA [*FM radio station call letters*]
WXLW ...... Indianapolis, IN [*AM radio station call letters*]
WXLY........ North Charleston, SC [*FM radio station call letters*]
WXM........ Worcester Art Museum, Worcester, MA [*OCLC
     symbol*] (OCLC)
WXMB ...... Surfside Beach-Garden City, SC [*AM radio station call letters*]
WXMC...... Parsippany-Troy Hills, NJ [*AM radio station call letters*]
WXMI .... Grand Rapids, MI [*Television station call letters*]
WXMJ-FM ... Mount Union, PA [*FM radio station call letters*]

WXMT-TV ... Nashville, TN [*Television station call letters*]
WXMX....... Upper Arlington, OH [*FM radio station call letters*]
WXOK....... Baton Rouge, LA [*AM radio station call letters*]
WXON....... Detroit, MI [*Television station call letters*]
WXOQ...... Selmer, TN [*FM radio station call letters*]
WXOW-TV ... La Crosse, WI [*Television station call letters*]
WXOX....... Bay City, MI [*AM radio station call letters*]
WxP........... Wax Pattern [*Dentistry*]
WXPL....... Fitchburg, MA [*FM radio station call letters*]
WXPN....... Philadelphia, PA [*FM radio station call letters*]
WXPR....... Rhinelander, WI [*FM radio station call letters*]
WXPX....... West Hazleton, PA [*AM radio station call letters*]
WXQK....... Spring City, TN [*AM radio station call letters*]
WXQR....... Jacksonville, NC [*FM radio station call letters*]
WXR......... Radiosonde Station [*ITU designation*] (CET)
WXR......... Weather RADAR
WXRA ...... North Syracuse, NY [*AM radio station call letters*]
WXRC ...... Hickory, NC [*FM radio station call letters*]
WXRCNSq ... Weather Reconnaissance Squadron [*Air Force*]
WXRECCO ... Weather Reconnaissance Flight [*Navy*] (NVT)
WXRF....... Guayama, PR [*AM radio station call letters*]
WXRI....... Windsor, VA [*FM radio station call letters*]
WXRK ...... New York, NY [*FM radio station call letters*]
WXRL ...... Lancaster, NY [*AM radio station call letters*]
WXRO ...... Beaver Dam, WI [*FM radio station call letters*]
WXRQ ...... Mount Pleasant, TN [*AM radio station call letters*]
WXRS....... Swainsboro, GA [*AM radio station call letters*]
WXRS-FM ... Swainsboro, GA [*FM radio station call letters*]
WXRT ...... Chicago, IL [*FM radio station call letters*]
WXRZ ...... Corinth, MS [*FM radio station call letters*]
WXTA ...... Edinboro, PA [*FM radio station call letters*]
WXTC-FM ... Charleston, SC [*FM radio station call letters*]
WXTL....... Jacksonville Beach, FL [*AM radio station call letters*]
WXTN ...... Lexington, MS [*AM radio station call letters*]
WXTQ ...... Athens, OH [*FM radio station call letters*]
WXTR-FM ... Waldorf, MD [*FM radio station call letters*]
WXTRN .... Weak External Reference [*Data processing*] (BUR)
WXTS-FM ... Toledo, OH [*FM radio station call letters*]
WXTU ...... Philadelphia, PA [*FM radio station call letters*]
WXTV ...... Paterson, NJ [*Television station call letters*]
WXTX ...... Columbus, GA [*Television station call letters*]
WXTY ...... Ticonderoga, NY [*FM radio station call letters*]
WXTZ........ Indianapolis, IN [*FM radio station call letters*]
WXVA ...... Charles Town, WV [*AM radio station call letters*]
WXVA-FM ... Charles Town, WV [*FM radio station call letters*]
WXVI .... Montgomery, AL [*AM radio station call letters*]
WXVK ...... Coal Grove, OH [*FM radio station call letters*]
WXVL....... Crossville, TN [*FM radio station call letters*]
WXVO ...... Oliver Springs, TN [*FM radio station call letters*]
WXVQ ...... De Land, FL [*AM radio station call letters*]
WXVS....... Waycross, GA [*FM radio station call letters*]
WXVT ...... Greenville, MS [*Television station call letters*]
WXVW ...... Jeffersonville, IN [*AM radio station call letters*]
WXVX ...... Monroeville, PA [*AM radio station call letters*]
WXWY ...... Robertsdale, AL [*AM radio station call letters*]
WXXA-TV ... Albany, NY [*Television station call letters*]
WXXI........ Rochester, NY [*AM radio station call letters*]
WXXI-FM ... Rochester, NY [*FM radio station call letters*]
WXXI-TV ... Rochester, NY [*Television station call letters*]
WXXK-FM ... Newport, NH [*FM radio station call letters*]
WXXO....... Winter Garden, FL [*AM radio station call letters*]
WXXQ....... Freeport, IL [*FM radio station call letters*]
WXXR....... Cullman, AL [*AM radio station call letters*]
WXXU....... Cocoa Beach, FL [*AM radio station call letters*]
WXXV-TV ... Gulfport, MS [*Television station call letters*]
WXXX ...... South Burlington, VT [*FM radio station call letters*]
WXYB ...... Zeeland, MI [*FM radio station call letters*]
WXYC ...... Chapel Hill, NC [*FM radio station call letters*]
WXYT ...... Detroit, MI [*AM radio station call letters*]
WXYU ...... Lynchburg, VA [*FM radio station call letters*]
WXYV ...... Baltimore, MD [*FM radio station call letters*]
WXYX ...... Bayamon, PR [*FM radio station call letters*]
WXYZ-TV ... Detroit, MI [*Television station call letters*]
WXZY ...... Ruckersville, VA [*FM radio station call letters*]
WY........... Oman Aviation Services Co. Ltd. [*Oman*] [*ICAO
     designator*] (FAAC)
WY............ Warwickshire Yeomanry [*British military*] (DMA)
WY............ Washington Yards [*Navy*]
WY............ Way (ADA)
WY............ Western Yiddish (BJA)
WY............ Wey [*Unit of weight*]
WY............ Weyerhaeuser Co. [*NYSE symbol*] (SPSG)
WY............ Wherry (ROG)
WY............ Woman's Year
WY............ Wrist Yaw (MCD)
WY............ Wyeth Laboratories [*Research code symbol*]
WY............ Wyoming [*Postal code*]
WY............ Wyoming Music Educator News-Letter [*A publication*]
WY............ Wyoming Reports [*A publication*] (DLA)
Wy............. Wyoming State Library, Cheyenne, WY [*Library symbol*]
     [*Library of Congress*] (LCLS)

Wy.............. Wythe's Virginia Chancery Reports [*1788-99*] [*A publication*] (DLA)
WyA........... Lincoln County Library, Afton Branch, Afton, WY [*Library symbol*] [*Library of Congress*] (LCLS)
WYA.......... Whyalla [*Australia*] [*Airport symbol*] (OAG)
WYA.......... Writers for Young Adults [*A publication*]
WYA.......... Wyangala [*Australia*] [*Seismograph station code, US Geological Survey*] [*Closed*] (SEIS)
WyAGS...... Church of Jesus Christ of Latter-Day Saints, Genealogical Society Library, Afton Branch, Afton, WY [*Library symbol*] [*Library of Congress*] (LCLS)
WYAI........ La Grange, GA [*FM radio station call letters*]
WYAIO....... Will You Accept, If Offered [*the position of*] (FAAC)
WYAJ........ Sudbury, MA [*FM radio station call letters*]
WYAK-FM ... Surfside Beach-Garden City, SC [*FM radio station call letters*]
WYAL....... Scotland Neck, NC [*AM radio station call letters*]
Wy-Ar........ Wyoming State Archives and Historical Department, Cheyenne, WY [*Library symbol*] [*Library of Congress*] (LCLS)
WYAT....... New Orleans, LA [*AM radio station call letters*]
Wyatt Prac Reg ... Wyatt's Practical Register in Chancery [*1800*] [*A publication*] (DLA)
Wyatt Pr R ... Wyatt's Practical Register in Chancery [*1800*] [*A publication*] (DLA)
Wyatt & W ... Wyatt and Webb's Reports [*A publication*] (APTA)
Wyatt W & A'B ... Wyatt, Webb, and A'Beckett's Reports [*A publication*] (DLA)
Wyatt W & A'B (Eq) ... Wyatt, Webb, and A'Beckett's Reports (Equity) [*A publication*] (APTA)
Wyatt W & A'B IE & M ... Wyatt, Webb, and A'Beckett's Reports (Insolvency, Ecclesiastical, and Matrimonial) [*A publication*] (APTA)
Wyatt W & A'B IP & M ... Wyatt, Webb, and A'Beckett's Victorian Insolvency, Probate, and Matrimonial Reports [*A publication*] (APTA)
Wyatt W & A'B Min ... Wyatt, Webb, and A'Beckett's Reports (Mining) [*A publication*] (APTA)
Wyatt & Webb ... Wyatt and Webb's Reports [*A publication*] (APTA)
Wyatt & W (Eq) ... Wyatt and Webb's Reports (Equity) [*A publication*] (APTA)
Wyatt & W (IE & M) ... Wyatt and Webb's Reports (Insolvency, Ecclesiastical, and Matrimonial) [*A publication*] (APTA)
Wyatt & W (IP & M) ... Wyatt and Webb's Reports (Insolvency, Probate, and Matrimonial) [*A publication*] (APTA)
Wyatt & W Min ... Wyatt and Webb's Victorian Mining Cases [*Australia*] [*A publication*] (DLA)
Wyat & W Eq ... Wyatt and Webb's Victorian Equity Reports [*Australia*] [*A publication*] (DLA)
WYAV .... Conway, SC [*FM radio station call letters*]
WYAY .... Gainesville, GA [*FM radio station call letters*]
WYBB....... Folly Beach, SC [*FM radio station call letters*]
WYBC-FM ... New Haven, CT [*FM radio station call letters*]
WYBE........ Philadelphia, PA [*Television station call letters*]
WYBG ...... Massena, NY [*AM radio station call letters*]
WYBL....... Western Young Buddhist League (EA)
WYBR-FM ... Belvidere, IL [*FM radio station call letters*]
WYBT........ Blountstown, FL [*AM radio station call letters*]
WyBu........ Johnson County Library, Buffalo, WY [*Library symbol*] [*Library of Congress*] (LCLS)
WyC........... Laramie County Library System, Cheyenne, WY [*Library symbol*] [*Library of Congress*] (LCLS)
WYC .... Warwickshire Yeomanry Cavalry [*British military*] (DMA)
WYC .... Wiley College, Marshall, TX [*OCLC symbol*] [*Inactive*] (OCLC)
WYC .... Wycombe [*England*]
WYCA .... Hammond, IN [*FM radio station call letters*]
WyCa .... Natrona County Public Library, Casper, WY [*Library symbol*] [*Library of Congress*] (LCLS)
WyCaC ...... Casper College, Casper, WY [*Library symbol*] [*Library of Congress*] (LCLS)
WyCaCH ... Wyoming State Children's Home, Casper, WY [*Library symbol*] [*Library of Congress*] (LCLS)
WyCaD ...... Wyoming School for the Deaf, Casper, WY [*Library symbol*] [*Library of Congress*] (LCLS)
WyCaGS.... Church of Jesus Christ of Latter-Day Saints, Genealogical Society Library, Casper Branch, Casper, WY [*Library symbol*] [*Library of Congress*] (LCLS)
WYCB .... Washington, DC [*AM radio station call letters*]
WYCC .... Chicago, IL [*Television station call letters*]
WyCC .... Laramie County Community College, Cheyenne, WY [*Library symbol*] [*Library of Congress*] (LCLS)
WYCC .... Write Your Congressman Club (EA)
WyCDA ..... Wyoming Department of Agriculture, Cheyenne, WY [*Library symbol*] [*Library of Congress*] (LCLS)
WyCDE ..... Wyoming Department of Education, Cheyenne, WY [*Library symbol*] [*Library of Congress*] (LCLS)
WYCE .... Wyoming, MI [*FM radio station call letters*]
WYCF .... World Youth Crusade for Freedom (EA)
WYCFD...... World Youth Congress on Food and Development (EAIO)
WyCGF...... Wyoming Game and Fish Commission, Cheyenne, WY [*Library symbol*] [*Library of Congress*] (LCLS)

WyCGS...... Church of Jesus Christ of Latter-Day Saints, Genealogical Society Library, Cheyenne Branch, Cheyenne, WY [*Library symbol*] [*Library of Congress*] (LCLS)
WYCH .... Utica, MS [*FM radio station call letters*]
WyCHD.... Wyoming Highway Department, Cheyenne, WY [*Library symbol*] [*Library of Congress*] (LCLS)
Wychowanie M Szkole ... Wychowanie Muzyczne w Szkole [*A publication*]
WyCHS ..... Wyoming Department of Health and Social Services, Cheyenne, WY [*Library symbol*] [*Library of Congress*] (LCLS)
WYCL........ Boyertown, PA [*FM radio station call letters*]
WYCM ...... Murfreesboro, NC [*AM radio station call letters*]
WyCMS..... Laramie County Medical Society, Cheyenne, WY [*Library symbol*] [*Library of Congress*] (LCLS)
WYCO .... Wausau, WI [*FM radio station call letters*]
WyCoB ...... Buffalo Bill Museum, Cody, WY [*Library symbol*] [*Library of Congress*] (LCLS)
WyCoGS.... Church of Jesus Christ of Latter-Day Saints, Genealogical Society Library, Cody Branch, Cody, WY [*Library symbol*] [*Library of Congress*] (LCLS)
WYCQ ...... Shelbyville, TN [*FM radio station call letters*]
WYCR .... York-Hanover, PA [*FM radio station call letters*]
WYCS .... Yorktown, VA [*FM radio station call letters*]
WyCSE...... State Engineer's Office, Cheyenne, WY [*Library symbol*] [*Library of Congress*] (LCLS)
WYCV ...... Granite Falls, NC [*AM radio station call letters*]
WyCV .... United States Veterans Administration Center, Cheyenne, WY [*Library symbol*] [*Library of Congress*] (LCLS)
Wy-D .... Wyoming State Documents, Cheyenne, WY [*Library symbol*] [*Library of Congress*] (LCLS)
WYDC .... Corning, NY [*Television station call letters*]
WYDD...... Blacksburg, VA [*Television station call letters*]
WYDE .... Birmingham, AL [*AM radio station call letters*]
WYDI .... Fond Du Lac, WI [*Television station call letters*]
Wy Dic....... Wyatt's Dickens' Chancery Reports [*A publication*] (DLA)
Wy Dick..... Dickens' English Chancery Reports, by Wyatt [*A publication*] (DLA)
WYDIWYG ... What You Digitize Is What You Get
WYDJ....... Dalton, GA [*Television station call letters*]
WYDL .... Union City, TN [*Television station call letters*]
WYDM...... Batavia, NY [*Television station call letters*]
WYDN...... Worcester, MA [*Television station call letters*]
WyDo......... Converse County Library, Douglas, WY [*Library symbol*] [*Library of Congress*] (LCLS)
WYDO...... Greenville, NC [*Television station call letters*]
WYDP .... Orange Park, FL [*Television station call letters*]
Wydz Mat Fiz Chem Uniw Poznan Ser Fiz ... Wydzial Matematyki Fizyki i Chemii Uniwersytet Imeni Adama Mickiewicza w Poznaniu Seria Fizyaka [*A publication*]
WYE .... Yengema [*Sierra Leone*] [*Airport symbol*] (OAG)
WYEA .... Sylacauga, AL [*FM radio station call letters*]
Wye Coll Dep Hop Res Annu Rep ... Wye College. Department of Hop Research. Annual Report [*A publication*]
WYED .... Goldsboro, NC [*Television station call letters*]
WYEF....... Yorkshire, NY [*FM radio station call letters*]
WY Energy Ext Serv Update ... Wyoming. Energy Extension Service. Update [*A publication*]
WYEP-FM ... Pittsburgh, PA [*FM radio station call letters*]
WYER .... Mount Carmel, IL [*AM radio station call letters*]
WYES-TV ... New Orleans, LA [*Television station call letters*]
WyEvGS.... Church of Jesus Christ of Latter-Day Saints, Genealogical Society Library, Evanston Branch, Evanston, WY [*Library symbol*] [*Library of Congress*] (LCLS)
WyEvSH.... Wyoming State Hospital, Evanston, WY [*Library symbol*] [*Library of Congress*] (LCLS)
WYEZ........ Elkhart, IN [*FM radio station call letters*]
WYF .... World Youth Forum [*Defunct*] (EA)
WYFA....... Waynesboro, GA [*FM radio station call letters*]
WYFB....... Gainesville, FL [*FM radio station call letters*]
WYFC....... Clinton, TN [*FM radio station call letters*]
WyFEW..... United States Air Force, Francis E. Warren Air Force Base, Cheyenne, WY [*Library symbol*] [*Library of Congress*] (LCLS)
WyFEW-I ... United States Air Force Institute of Technology, Detachment 9, Francis E. Warren Air Force Base, Cheyenne, WY [*Library symbol*] [*Library of Congress*] (LCLS)
WYFF-TV ... Greenville, SC [*Television station call letters*]
WYFG ...... Gaffney, SC [*FM radio station call letters*]
WYFH .... North Charleston, SC [*FM radio station call letters*]
WYFI........ Norfolk, VA [*FM radio station call letters*]
WYFJ .... Ashland, VA [*FM radio station call letters*]
WYFK....... Columbus, GA [*FM radio station call letters*]
WYFL........ Henderson, NC [*FM radio station call letters*]
WyFlL........ Fort Laramie Historic Site, Fort Laramie, WY [*Library symbol*] [*Library of Congress*] (LCLS)
WYFM ...... Sharon, PA [*FM radio station call letters*]
WYFO ...... Lakeland, FL [*FM radio station call letters*]
WYFS....... Savannah, GA [*FM radio station call letters*]
WYFT........ Luray, VA [*FM radio station call letters*]
WYFX....... Boynton Beach, FL [*AM radio station call letters*]
WYG......... Wyoming Airlines Ltd. [*Denver, CO*] [*FAA designator*] (FAAC)

WYGC .... Gainesville, FL [*FM radio station call letters*]
WYGINS... What You Get Is No Surprise [*Pronounced "wiggins"*] [*Coined by Dave Tarrant, president of Lotus Development Corp.'s graphics products group*]
WYGL .... Selinsgrove, PA [*AM radio station call letters*]
WYGR .... Wyoming, MI [*AM radio station call letters*]
WYHS .... Hollywood, FL [*Television station call letters*]
WYHT .... Mansfield, OH [*FM radio station call letters*]
WYHY .... Lebanon, TN [*FM radio station call letters*]
WYIC .... Noblesville, IN [*AM radio station call letters*]
WYII .... Williamsport, MD [*FM radio station call letters*]
WYIM .... Ocala, FL [*Television station call letters*]
WYIN .... Gary, IN [*Television station call letters*]
WYJCA ..... Wool Yarn Jobbers Credit Association [*Defunct*]   (EA)
WYJD .... Brewton, AL [*FM radio station call letters*]
WYJY .... Biddeford, ME [*FM radio station call letters*]
WYKC .... Grenada, MS [*AM radio station call letters*]
WyKc .... Johnson County Library, Kaycee Branch, Kaycee, WY [*Library symbol*] [*Library of Congress*]   (LCLS)
WyKe .... Lincoln County Library, Kemmerer, WY [*Library symbol*] [*Library of Congress*]   (LCLS)
Wykeham Eng Technol Ser ... Wykeham Engineering and Technology Series [*A publication*]
Wykeham Sci Ser ... Wykeham Science Series [*A publication*]
WYKK .... Quitman, MS [*FM radio station call letters*]
WYKM ...... Rupert, WV [*AM radio station call letters*]
WYKR .... Wells River, VT [*AM radio station call letters*]
WYKR-FM ... Haverhill, NH [*FM radio station call letters*]
WYKS .... Gainesville, FL [*FM radio station call letters*]
WYKX .... Escanaba, MI [*FM radio station call letters*]
WYKZ .... Beaufort, SC [*FM radio station call letters*]
WYL .... Laramie County Library System, Cheyenne, WY [*OCLC symbol*]   (OCLC)
WYL .... Wyle Laboratories [*NYSE symbol*]   (SPSG)
WyLan .... Fremont County Library, Lander, WY [*Library symbol*] [*Library of Congress*]   (LCLS)
WyLanT .... Wyoming State Training School, Lander, WY [*Library symbol*] [*Library of Congress*]   (LCLS)
WyLar........ Albany County Public Library, Laramie, WY [*Library symbol*] [*Library of Congress*]   (LCLS)
WyLarBM ... United States Bureau of Mines, Laramie Petroleum Research Center, Laramie, WY [*Library symbol*] [*Library of Congress*]   (LCLS)
WyLarHN ... Wyoming Health Science Network, University of Wyoming, Laramie, WY [*Library symbol*] [*Library of Congress*]   (LCLS)
WyLarSh ... Sherwood Hall, Laramie, WY [*Library symbol*] [*Library of Congress*]   (LCLS)
WyLarSM ... Saint Matthew's Cathedral, Laramie, WY [*Library symbol*] [*Library of Congress*]   (LCLS)
WYLD .... New Orleans, LA [*AM radio station call letters*]
WYLD-FM ... New Orleans, LA [*FM radio station call letters*]
WYLF .... Penn Yan, NY [*AM radio station call letters*]
WYLIWYS ... Where You Look Is What You Select
WY LJ .... Wyoming Law Journal [*A publication*]
WYLL........ Des Plaines, IL [*FM radio station call letters*]
WYLO .... Jackson, WI [*AM radio station call letters*]
WyLoGS.... Church of Jesus Christ of Latter-Day Saints, Genealogical Society Library, Lovell Branch, Lovell, WY [*Library symbol*] [*Library of Congress*]   (LCLS)
WYLR-FM ... Glens Falls, NY [*FM radio station call letters*]
WYLS........ York, AL [*AM radio station call letters*]
WYLT........ Raleigh, NC [*FM radio station call letters*]
WyLu .... Niobrara County Library, Lusk, WY [*Library symbol*] [*Library of Congress*]   (LCLS)
WYLV........ Alcoa, TN [*FM radio station call letters*]
WYM......... Wyoming Health Science Network, Laramie, WY [*OCLC symbol*]   (OCLC)
Wyman....... Wyman's Reports [*India*] [*A publication*]   (DLA)
WYMB ...... Manning, SC [*AM radio station call letters*]
WYMC ...... Mayfield, KY [*AM radio station call letters*]
WYMC-FM ... Wickliffe, KY [*FM radio station call letters*]
WYMG ...... Jacksonville, IL [*FM radio station call letters*]
WYMJ-FM ... Beavercreek, OH [*FM radio station call letters*]
WYMN...... Wyman-Gordon Co. [*NASDAQ symbol*]   (NQ)
WYMS ...... Milwaukee, WI [*FM radio station call letters*]
WYMT-TV ... Hazard, KY [*Television station call letters*]
WYMX ...... Greenwood, MS [*FM radio station call letters*]
WYN......... Walwyn, Inc. [*Toronto Stock Exchange symbol*]
WYN .... Wyndham [*Australia*] [*Airport symbol*]
WYNA .... Tabor City, NC [*FM radio station call letters*]
WYNB ...... Wyoming National Bancorporation [*NASDAQ symbol*]   (NQ)
WYNC...... Yanceyville, NC [*AM radio station call letters*]
WYND...... De Land, FL [*AM radio station call letters*]
WYND-FM ... Hatteras, NC [*FM radio station call letters*]
WYNE .... Kimberly, WI [*AM radio station call letters*]
WyNe......... Weston County Public Library, Newcastle, WY [*Library symbol*] [*Library of Congress*]   (LCLS)
WYNF .... Tampa, FL [*FM radio station call letters*]
WYNG-FM ... Evansville, IN [*FM radio station call letters*]
WYNI .... Monroeville, AL [*AM radio station call letters*]

WYNK....... Baton Rouge, LA [*AM radio station call letters*]
WYNK-FM ... Baton Rouge, LA [*FM radio station call letters*]
WYNN...... Florence, SC [*AM radio station call letters*]
Wynne Bov ... Wynne's Bovill's Patent Cases [*A publication*]   (DLA)
Wynne Eun ... Wynne's Eunomus [*A publication*]   (DLA)
WYNN-FM ... Florence, SC [*FM radio station call letters*]
WYNO...... Nelsonville, OH [*AM radio station call letters*]
WYNQ-FM ... Maryville, TN [*FM radio station call letters*]
WYNS ...... Lehighton, PA [*AM radio station call letters*]
WYNT ...... Upper Sandusky, OH [*FM radio station call letters*]
WYNU...... Milan, TN [*FM radio station call letters*]
WYNX ...... Smyrna, GA [*AM radio station call letters*]
WYNY ...... Lake Success, NY [*FM radio station call letters*]
WYNZ ...... Portland, ME [*AM radio station call letters*]
WYNZ-FM ... Westbrook, ME [*FM radio station call letters*]
WYO......... US Aviation [*Riverton, WY*] [*FAA designator*]   (FAAC)
WYO .... Wyoming   (AAG)
WYO......... Wyoming Array [*Wyoming*] [*Seismograph station code, US Geological Survey*]   (SEIS)
Wyo........... Wyoming Reports [*A publication*]   (DLA)
Wyo Ag Exp ... Wyoming. Agricultural Experiment Station. Publications [*A publication*]
Wyo Agric Exp Stn Bull ... Wyoming. Agricultural Experiment Station. Bulletin [*A publication*]
Wyo Agric Exp Stn Cir ... Wyoming. Agricultural Experiment Station. Circular [*A publication*]
Wyo Agric Exp Stn Res J ... Wyoming. Agricultural Experiment Station. Research Journal [*A publication*]
Wyo Agric Exp Stn Sci Monogr ... Wyoming. Agricultural Experiment Station. Science Monograph [*A publication*]
Wyo Agric Ext Serv Bull ... Wyoming. Agricultural Extension Service. Bulletin [*A publication*]
WYOC....... High Springs, FL [*FM radio station call letters*]
Wyo Game Fish Comm Bull ... Wyoming. Game and Fish Commission. Bulletin [*A publication*]
Wyo Geol Assoc Earth Sci Bull ... Wyoming Geological Association. Earth Science Bulletin [*A publication*]
Wyo Geol Assoc Guideb Ann Field Conf ... Wyoming Geological Association. Guidebook. Annual Field Conference [*A publication*]
Wyo Geol Survey Bull Rept Inv ... Wyoming. Geological Survey. Bulletin. Report of Investigations [*A publication*]
Wyo Geol Surv Prelim Rep ... Wyoming. Geological Survey. Preliminary Report [*A publication*]
Wyo Geol Surv Rep Invest ... Wyoming. Geological Survey. Report of Investigations [*A publication*]
Wyo G Off B Wyo St G ... Wyoming. Geologist's Office. Bulletin. Wyoming State Geologist [*A publication*]
Wyo His Col ... Wyoming State Historical Department. Proceedings and Collections [*A publication*]
Wyo Issues ... Wyoming Issues [*A publication*]
Wyo Lib Roundup ... Wyoming Library Roundup [*A publication*]
Wyo L J ..... Wyoming Law Journal [*A publication*]
WYOM..... Wyoming   (ROG)
Wyom......... Wyoming Reports [*A publication*]   (DLA)
Wyoming Geol Survey Prelim Rept ... Wyoming. Geological Survey. Preliminary Report [*A publication*]
Wyoming Hist G Soc Pr Pub ... Wyoming Historical and Geological Society. Proceedings and Collections. Publications [*A publication*]
Wyo Nurse ... Wyoming Nurse [*Formerly, Wyoming Nurses Newsletter*] [*A publication*]
Wyo Nurses News ... Wyoming Nurses Newsletter [*Later, Wyoming Nurse*] [*A publication*]
WYOO....... Springfield, FL [*FM radio station call letters*]
WYOR...... Brentwood, TN [*AM radio station call letters*]
Wyo Range Manage ... Wyoming Range Management [*A publication*]
Wyo Roundup ... Wyoming Roundup [*A publication*]
Wyo Sess Laws ... Session Laws of Wyoming [*A publication*]   (DLA)
Wyo Stat ... Wyoming Statutes [*A publication*]   (ILCA)
Wyo St G ... Wyoming State Geologist [*A publication*]
WYOU....... Scranton, PA [*Television station call letters*]
WYOU-FM ... Bangor, ME [*FM radio station call letters*]
Wyo Univ Dep Geol Contrib Geol ... Wyoming University. Department of Geology. Contributions to Geology [*A publication*]
Wyo Univ Nat Resour Res Inst Bull ... Wyoming University. Natural Resources Research Institute. Bulletin [*A publication*]
Wyo Univ Nat Resour Res Inst Inf Cir ... Wyoming University. Natural Resources Research Institute. Information Circular [*A publication*]
Wyo Univ Natur Resour Inst Inform Circ ... Wyoming University. Natural Resources Institute. Information Circular [*A publication*]
Wyo Univ Sch Mines B ... Wyoming University. School of Mines. Bulletin [*A publication*]
Wyo Univ Water Resour Res Inst Water Resour Ser ... Wyoming University. Water Resources Research Institute. Water Resources Series [*A publication*]
Wyo Wild Life ... Wyoming Wild Life [*A publication*]
WYPC....... Gallipolis, OH [*FM radio station call letters*]
WyPdS....... Sublette County Library, Pinedale, WY [*Library symbol*] [*Library of Congress*]   (LCLS)
WyPN........ Northwest Community College, Powell, WY [*Library symbol*] [*Library of Congress*]   (LCLS)

Wy Pr R..... Wyatt's Practical Register in Chancery [*England*] [*A publication*]   (DLA)
WYR.......... Waybo Resources Ltd. [*Vancouver Stock Exchange symbol*]
WYR.......... [*The*] West Yorkshire Regiment [*Army*] [*British*]
WYRE........ Annapolis, MD [*AM radio station call letters*]
WyRi.......... Fremont County Library, Riverton Branch, Riverton, WY [*Library symbol*] [*Library of Congress*]   (LCLS)
WyRiC....... Central Wyoming Community College, Riverton, WY [*Library symbol*] [*Library of Congress*]   (LCLS)
WYRK....... Buffalo, NY [*FM radio station call letters*]
WYRN....... Louisburg, NC [*AM radio station call letters*]
WYRQ....... Little Falls, MN [*FM radio station call letters*]
WYRS........ Jersey Shore, PA [*FM radio station call letters*]
WyRsW..... Western Wyoming College, Rock Springs, WY [*Library symbol*] [*Library of Congress*]   (LCLS)
WYRU....... Red Springs, NC [*AM radio station call letters*]
WYRV....... Cedar Bluff, VA [*AM radio station call letters*]
WYRY....... Hinsdale, NH [*FM radio station call letters*]
WYS.......... West Yellowstone, MT [*Location identifier*] [*FAA*]   (FAAL)
WYS.......... Wyandotte Southern Railroad Co. [*AAR code*]
WYS.......... Wyse Technology [*NYSE symbol*]   (SPSG)
WYSE........ Bainbridge, GA [*AM radio station call letters*]
WYSE........ Wyse Technology [*San Jose, CA*] [*NASDAQ symbol*]   (NQ)
WYSH........ Clinton, TN [*AM radio station call letters*]
WyShCD ... Wheden Cancer Detection Foundation, Sheridan, WY [*Library symbol*] [*Library of Congress*]   (LCLS)
WyShF....... Sheridan County Fulmer Public Library, Sheridan, WY [*Library symbol*] [*Library of Congress*]   (LCLS)
WyShGS.... Wyoming Girls' School, Sheridan, WY [*Library symbol*] [*Library of Congress*]   (LCLS)
WyShMH ... Northern Wyoming Mental Health Center, Sheridan, WY [*Library symbol*] [*Library of Congress*]   (LCLS)
WyShS....... Sheridan College, Sheridan, WY [*Library symbol*] [*Library of Congress*]   (LCLS)
WyShV ...... United States Veterans Administration Hospital, Sheridan, WY [*Library symbol*] [*Library of Congress*]   (LCLS)
WYSIAYG ... What You See Is All You Get
WYSIMOLWYG ... What You See Is More or Less What You Get [*Pronounced "wizzi-mole-wig"*]
WYSIWYG ... What You See Is What You Get [*Pronounced "wizziwig"*] [*Indicates that video display on word processor bears a high-quality resemblance to printed page that will result*]
WYSL........ Avon, NY [*AM radio station call letters*]
WYSN .... Central City, PA [*FM radio station call letters*]
WYSO .... Yellow Springs, OH [*FM radio station call letters*]
WYSP....... Philadelphia, PA [*FM radio station call letters*]
WYSS........ Sault Ste. Marie, MI [*FM radio station call letters*]
WYST .... Baltimore, MD [*AM radio station call letters*]
WYST-FM ... Baltimore, MD [*FM radio station call letters*]
WYSU .... Youngstown, OH [*FM radio station call letters*]
WYSY........ Aurora, IL [*AM radio station call letters*]
WYSY-FM ... Aurora, IL [*FM radio station call letters*]
WYT .... Wyandotte Terminal Railroad Co. [*AAR code*]
WYTE....... Whiting, WI [*FM radio station call letters*]
WYTH...... Madison, GA [*AM radio station call letters*]
Wythe .... Wythe's Virginia Chancery Reports [*1788-99*] [*A publication*]   (DLA)
Wythe Ch (VA) ... Wythe's Virginia Chancery Reports [*1788-99*] [*A publication*]   (DLA)
Wythe Cty Hist Rev ... Wythe County Historical Review [*A publication*]
Wythes CC ... Wythe's Virginia Chancery Reports [*1788-99*] [*A publication*]   (DLA)
Wythe's R .. Wythe's Virginia Chancery Reports [*1788-99*] [*A publication*]   (DLA)
Wythe's Rep ... Wythe's Virginia Chancery Reports [*1788-99*] [*A publication*]   (DLA)
Wythe (VA) ... Wythe's Virginia Chancery Reports [*1788-99*] [*A publication*]   (DLA)
WyThP ...... Wyoming Pioneer Home, Thermopolis, WY [*Library symbol*] [*Library of Congress*]   (LCLS)
WYTI........ Rocky Mount, VA [*AM radio station call letters*]
WyTJ........ Wesleyan Theological Journal [*A publication*]
WYTK....... Washington, PA [*FM radio station call letters*]
WYTL....... Terre Haute, IN [*AM radio station call letters*]
WYTM-FM ... Fayetteville, TN [*FM radio station call letters*]
WyToE ...... Eastern Wyoming College, Torrington, WY [*Library symbol*] [*Library of Congress*]   (LCLS)
WyTs .... Washakie County Library, Ten Sleep Branch, Ten Sleep, WY [*Library symbol*] [*Library of Congress*]   (LCLS)
WYTV .... Youngstown, OH [*Television station call letters*]
WYTW ...... Cadillac, MI [*FM radio station call letters*]
WYTZ........ Chicago, IL [*FM radio station call letters*]
WyU.......... University of Wyoming, Laramie, WY [*Library symbol*] [*Library of Congress*]   (LCLS)
WYU.......... University of Wyoming, Library, Laramie, WY [*OCLC symbol*]   (OCLC)
wyu............ Wyoming [*MARC country of publication code*] [*Library of Congress*]   (LCCP)
WyU-Ar..... University of Wyoming, Archive of Contemporary History, Laramie, WY [*Library symbol*] [*Library of Congress*]   (LCLS)

WyUp .... Weston County Public Library, Upton Branch, Upton, WY [*Library symbol*] [*Library of Congress*]   (LCLS)
WYUR-FM ... Ripon, WI [*FM radio station call letters*]
WYUS .... Milford, DE [*AM radio station call letters*]
WYUT .... Herkimer, NY [*AM radio station call letters*]
WYUT-FM ... Herkimer, NY [*FM radio station call letters*]
WYVC .... Camden, AL [*FM radio station call letters*]
WYVE .... Wytheville, VA [*AM radio station call letters*]
WYW......... Weltwirtschaft [*A publication*]
Wy & W ..... Wyatt and Webb's Victorian Equity Reports [*Australia*] [*A publication*]   (DLA)
WyWo........ Washakie County Library, Worland, WY [*Library symbol*] [*Library of Congress*]   (LCLS)
WyWoI ...... Wyoming Industrial Institute, Worland, WY [*Library symbol*] [*Library of Congress*]   (LCLS)
WYWY ...... Barbourville, KY [*AM radio station call letters*]
WYWY-FM ... Barbourville, KY [*FM radio station call letters*]
WYXC .... Cartersville, GA [*AM radio station call letters*]
WYXI........ Athens, TN [*AM radio station call letters*]
WYXX ...... Holland, MI [*FM radio station call letters*]
WYXY .... Cypress Gardens, FL [*AM radio station call letters*]
WYYC .... West Yorkshire Yeomanry Cavalry [*British military*]   (DMA)
WYYD .... Amherst, VA [*FM radio station call letters*]
WYYN .... Tallahassee, FL [*AM radio station call letters*]
WYYS .... Cayce, SC [*FM radio station call letters*]
WYYY .... Syracuse, NY [*FM radio station call letters*]
WYYZ .... Jasper, GA [*AM radio station call letters*]
WYZ.......... Wyoming State Library, Cheyenne, WY [*OCLC symbol*]   (OCLC)
WYZB....... Mary Esther, FL [*FM radio station call letters*]
WYZD....... Dobson, NC [*AM radio station call letters*]
WYZE....... Atlanta, GA [*AM radio station call letters*]
WYZQ .... Hazard, KY [*AM radio station call letters*]
Wyz Szkol Ped Krakow Rocznik Nauk-Dydakt Prace Dydakt Mat ... Wyzsza Szkola Pedagogiczna w Krakowie. Rocznik Naukowo-Dydaktyczny. Prace z Dydaktyki Matematyki [*A publication*]
Wyz Szkol Ped Krakow Rocznik Nauk-Dydakt Prace Mat ... Wyzsza Szkola Pedagogiczna w Krakowie. Rocznik Naukowo-Dydaktyczny. Prace Matematyczne [*A publication*]
WYZZ-TV ... Bloomington, IL [*Television station call letters*]
WZ............. Royal Swazi National Airways Corp. [*Swaziland*] [*ICAO designator*]   (FAAC)
WZ............. War Zone
Wz............. Warenzeichen [*Trademark*] [*German*]
WZ............. Westfaelische Zeitschrift [*A publication*]
WZ............. Wiedza i Zycie [*A publication*]
WZ............. Wissenschaftliche Zeitschrift [*A publication*]
W i d Z....... Wort in der Zeit [*A publication*]
WZ............. Wort in der Zeit [*A publication*]
WZAC .... Madison, WV [*AM radio station call letters*]
WZAC-FM ... Danville, WV [*FM radio station call letters*]
WZAD....... Wurtsboro, NY [*FM radio station call letters*]
WZAK....... Cleveland, OH [*FM radio station call letters*]
WZAL....... McDonough, GA [*AM radio station call letters*]
WZAM...... Norfolk, VA [*AM radio station call letters*]
WZAP....... Bristol, VA [*AM radio station call letters*]
WZAR .... Ponce, PR [*FM radio station call letters*]
WZAT .... Savannah, GA [*FM radio station call letters*]
WZAZ .... Jacksonville, FL [*AM radio station call letters*]
WZAZ-FM ... Green Cove Springs, FL [*FM radio station call letters*]
WZB .... Wissenschaftszentrum Berlin fuer Sozialforschung [*Social Science Research Center Berlin*] [*Research center*] [*German*]   (ECON)
WZBC....... Newton, MA [*FM radio station call letters*]
WZ (Berlin) ... Wissenschaftliche Zeitschrift. Humboldt-Universitaet (Berlin) [*A publication*]
WZBH....... Georgetown, DE [*FM radio station call letters*]
WZBO....... Edenton, NC [*AM radio station call letters*]
WZBO-FM ... Edenton, NC [*FM radio station call letters*]
WZBQ .... Tuscaloosa, AL [*AM radio station call letters*]
WZBQ-FM ... Jasper, AL [*FM radio station call letters*]
WZBS....... Ponce, PR [*AM radio station call letters*]
WZBT....... Gettysburg, PA [*FM radio station call letters*]
WZBZ....... Ridgeland, SC [*FM radio station call letters*]
WZCL....... Norfolk, VA [*FM radio station call letters*]
WzD........... Wege zur Dichtung [*A publication*]
WZDM....... Vincennes, IN [*FM radio station call letters*]
WZDQ .... Humboldt, TN [*FM radio station call letters*]
WZDX....... Huntsville, AL [*Television station call letters*]
WZEE....... Madison, WI [*FM radio station call letters*]
W Zegel ..... Wetboek der Zegelrechten [*A publication*]
WZEL....... Young Harris, GA [*AM radio station call letters*]
WZEMAUG ... Wissenschaftliche Zeitschrift. Ernst-Moritz-Arndt-Universitaet (Greifswald). Gesellschafts- und Sprachwissenschaftliche Reihe [*A publication*]
WZEP....... De Funiak Springs, FL [*AM radio station call letters*]
WZEW....... Fairhope, AL [*FM radio station call letters*]
WZE Wiss Z Elektrotech ... WZE. Wissenschaftliche Zeitschrift der Elektrotechnik [*East Germany*] [*A publication*]
WZEZ........ Nashville, TN [*FM radio station call letters*]

WZFL........ Centreville, MS [*AM radio station call letters*]
WZFL-FM ... Centreville, MS [*FM radio station call letters*]
WZFM....... Briarcliff Manor, NY [*FM radio station call letters*]
WZFMA.... Wissenschaftliche Zeitschrift. Friedrich-Schiller-Universitaet
        (Jena). Mathematisch-Naturwissenschaftliche Reihe [*A
        publication*]
WZFR........ Tomah, WI [*FM radio station call letters*]
WZFSU ..... Wissenschaftliche Zeitschrift. Friedrich-Schiller-Universitaet
        (Jena). Gesellschafts- und Sprachwissenschaftliche Reihe
        [*A publication*]
WZFSUJ ... Wissenschaftliche Zeitschrift. Friedrich-Schiller-Universitaet
        (Jena). Gesellschafts- und Sprachwissenschaftliche Reihe
        [*A publication*]
WZFSUJ GSR ... Wissenschaftliche Zeitschrift. Friedrich-Schiller-
        Universitaet (Jena). Gesellschafts- und
        Sprachwissenschaftliche Reihe [*A publication*]
WZFX........ Whiteville, NC [*FM radio station call letters*]
WZG......... Wissenschaftliche Zeitschrift fuer Juedische Geschichte [*A
        publication*] (BJA)
WZGC .... Atlanta, GA [*FM radio station call letters*]
WZGK .... Westdeutsche Zeitschrift fuer Geschichte und Kunst [*A
        publication*]
WZGO....... Portage, PA [*AM radio station call letters*]
WZ (Griefswald) ... Wissenschaftliche Zeitschrift. Ernst-Moritz-Arndt-
        Universitaet (Greifswald) [*A publication*]
WZ (Halle) ... Wissenschaftliche Zeitschrift. Martin-Luther-Universitaet
        (Halle-Wittenberg) [*A publication*]
WZHMA... Wissenschaftliche Zeitschrift. Humboldt-Universitaet (Berlin).
        Mathematisch-Naturwissenschaftliche Reihe [*A
        publication*]
WZHT .... Troy, AL [*FM radio station call letters*]
WZHU....... Wissenschaftliche Zeitschrift. Humboldt-Universitaet (Berlin).
        Gesellschafts- und Sprachwissenschaftliche Reihe [*A
        publication*]
WZHUB.... Wissenschaftliche Zeitschrift. Humboldt-Universitaet (Berlin).
        Gesellschafts- und Sprachwissenschaftliche Reihe [*A
        publication*]
WZI .... Winzen International, Inc. [*Vancouver Stock Exchange symbol*]
WZID .... Manchester, NH [*FM radio station call letters*]
WZIP .... Akron, OH [*FM radio station call letters*]
WZIX......... Artesia, MS [*FM radio station call letters*]
WZJ.......... Wissenschaftliche Zeitschrift. Friedrich-Schiller-Universitaet
        (Jena) [*A publication*]
WZ (Jena) ... Wissenschaftliche Zeitschrift. Friedrich-Schiller-Universitaet
        (Jena) [*A publication*]
WZJM....... Harrisonburg, VA [*FM radio station call letters*]
WZJS .... Banner Elk, NC [*FM radio station call letters*]
WZJT .... Wissenschaftliche Zeitschrift fuer Juedische Theologie [*A
        publication*] (BJA)
WZJTh...... Wissenschaftliche Zeitschrift fuer Juedische Theologie [*A
        publication*] (BJA)
WZJY .... Mt. Pleasant, SC [*AM radio station call letters*]
WZKB .... Wallace, NC [*FM radio station call letters*]
WZKG .... Charleston, SC [*AM radio station call letters*]
WZKM ...... Wiener Zeitschrift fuer die Kunde des Morgenlandes [*A
        publication*]
WZKMU ... Wissenschaftliche Zeitschrift. Karl-Marx-Universitaet [*Leipzig*]
        [*A publication*]
WZKMUL ... Wissenschaftliche Zeitschrift. Karl-Marx-Universitaet
        (Leipzig). Gesellschafts- und Sprachwissenschaftliche Reihe
        [*A publication*]
WZKO....... Pineville, KY [*FM radio station call letters*]
WZKS........ Jesup, GA [*FM radio station call letters*]
WZKS........ Wiener Zeitschrift fuer die Kunde Suedasiens und Archiv fuer
        Indische Philosophie [*A publication*]
WZKSO..... Wiener Zeitschrift fuer die Kunde Sued- und Ostasiens und
        Archiv fuer Indische Philosophie [*A publication*]
WZKT .... Waynesboro, VA [*AM radio station call letters*]
WZKX .... Poplarville, MS [*FM radio station call letters*]
WZKY .... Albemarle, NC [*AM radio station call letters*]
WZKZ .... Corning, NY [*FM radio station call letters*]
WZL .... Wissenschaftliche Zeitschrift. Karl-Marx-Universitaet (Leipzig)
        [*A publication*]
WZLA-FM ... Abbeville, SC [*FM radio station call letters*]
WZLE........ Lorain, OH [*FM radio station call letters*]
WZ (Leipzig) ... Wissenschaftliche Zeitschrift. Karl-Marx-Universitaet
        (Leipzig) [*A publication*]
WZLI......... Toccoa, GA [*FM radio station call letters*]
WZLM ...... Dadeville, AL [*FM radio station call letters*]
WZLQ .... Tupelo, MS [*FM radio station call letters*]
WZLS........ Valdosta, GA [*FM radio station call letters*]
WZLT........ Lexington, TN [*FM radio station call letters*]
WZLX........ Boston, MA [*FM radio station call letters*]
WZLY........ Wellesley, MA [*FM radio station call letters*]
WZLZ........ Quincy, IL [*FM radio station call letters*]
WZMB ...... Greenville, NC [*FM radio station call letters*]
WZMG ...... Opelika, AL [*AM radio station call letters*]
WZMLU ... Wissenschaftliche Zeitschrift. Martin-Luther-Universitaet [*A
        publication*]

WZMLUH ... Wissenschaftliche Zeitschrift. Martin-Luther-Universitaet
        (Halle-Wittenberg). Gesellschafts- und
        Sprachwissenschaftliche Reihe [*A publication*]
WZMM-FM ... Wheeling, WV [*FM radio station call letters*]
WZMQ...... Key Largo, FL [*FM radio station call letters*]
WZMU ...... Wissenschaftliche Zeitschrift. Karl-Marx-Universitaet
        [*Leipzig*]. Gesellschafts- und Sprachwissenschaftliche
        Reihe [*A publication*]
WZMX ...... Russellville, AL [*FM radio station call letters*]
WZNDA .... Wiener Zeitschrift fuer Nervenheilkunde und Deren
        Grenzgebiete [*A publication*]
WZNF .... Rantoul, IL [*FM radio station call letters*]
WZNJ........ Demopolis, AL [*FM radio station call letters*]
WZNPS..... William H. Zimmer Nuclear Power Station [*Also,
        ZPS*] (NRCH)
WZNS .... Dillon, SC [*FM radio station call letters*]
WZNT .... San Juan, PR [*FM radio station call letters*]
WZNY .... Augusta, GA [*FM radio station call letters*]
WZO......... Wein Zollordnung [*Wine Duty Order*] [*German*]
WZOA .... Women's Zionist Organization of America
WZOB .... Fort Payne, AL [*AM radio station call letters*]
WZOE .... Princeton, IL [*AM radio station call letters*]
WZOE-FM ... Princeton, IL [*FM radio station call letters*]
WZOK .... Rockford, IL [*FM radio station call letters*]
WZOL .... Luquillo, PR [*FM radio station call letters*]
WZOM...... Defiance, OH [*FM radio station call letters*]
WZON ...... Bangor, ME [*AM radio station call letters*]
WZOO .... Asheboro, NC [*AM radio station call letters*]
WZOO-FM ... Edgewood, OH [*FM radio station call letters*]
WZOQ....... Wapakoneta, OH [*FM radio station call letters*]
WZOR .... Immokalee, FL [*AM radio station call letters*]
WZOT .... Rockmart, GA [*AM radio station call letters*]
WZOU....... Boston, MA [*FM radio station call letters*]
WZOW...... Goshen, IN [*FM radio station call letters*]
WZOZ........ Oneonta, NY [*FM radio station call letters*]
WZPHP..... Wissenschaftliche Zeitschrift. Paedagogische Hochschule
        (Potsdam). Gesellschafts- und Sprachwissenschaftliche
        Reihe [*A publication*]
WZPK....... Berlin, NH [*FM radio station call letters*]
WZPL....... Greenfield, IN [*FM radio station call letters*]
WZPQ .... Jasper, AL [*AM radio station call letters*]
WZPR....... Meadville, PA [*FM radio station call letters*]
WZQB .... Warner Robins, GA [*AM radio station call letters*]
WZQK .... Coeburn, VA [*FM radio station call letters*]
WZQQ....... Hyden, KY [*FM radio station call letters*]
WZRD .... Chicago, IL [*FM radio station call letters*]
WZRH .... Picayune, MS [*FM radio station call letters*]
WZRI........ Cleveland, MS [*FM radio station call letters*]
WZRK ...... Hancock, MI [*FM radio station call letters*]
WZRO .... Farmer City, IL [*FM radio station call letters*]
WZ Rostock ... Wissenschaftliche Zeitschrift. Universitaet Rostock [*A
        publication*]
WZRQ .... Columbia City, IN [*FM radio station call letters*]
WZRR .... Birmingham, AL [*FM radio station call letters*]
WZRT .... Rutland, VT [*FM radio station call letters*]
WZRX .... Jackson, MS [*AM radio station call letters*]
WZRZ .... North Fort Myers, FL [*AM radio station call letters*]
WZSH .... South Bristol Township, NY [*FM radio station call letters*]
WZsl .... Wissenschaftliche Zeitschrift. Karl-Marx-Universitaet.
        Gesellschafts- und Sprachwissenschaftliche Reihe [*Leipzig*]
        [*A publication*]
WZST........ Appomattox, VA [*FM radio station call letters*]
WZT .... Wartegg-Zeichentest [*Wartegg Symbol Test*] [*German*]
        [*Psychology*]
WZTA .... Miami Beach, FL [*FM radio station call letters*]
WZTDA..... Wissenschaftliche Zeitschrift. Technische Hochschule (Dresden)
        [*A publication*]
WZTKA..... Wissenschaftliche Zeitschrift. Technische Hochschule Karl-
        Marx-Stadt [*A publication*]
WZTN ...... Montgomery, AL [*AM radio station call letters*]
WZTR........ Milwaukee, WI [*FM radio station call letters*]
WZTT....... Rhinelander, WI [*FM radio station call letters*]
WZTV .... Nashville, TN [*Television station call letters*]
WZTZ........ Elba, AL [*FM radio station call letters*]
WZUB .... Wissenschaftliche Zeitschrift. Humboldt-Universitaet (Berlin).
        Gesellschafts- und Sprachwissenschaftliche Reihe [*A
        publication*]
WZUG....... Wissenschaftliche Zeitschrift. Ernst-Moritz-Arndt-Universitaet
        (Greifswald) [*A publication*]
WZUH....... Wissenschaftliche Zeitschrift. Martin-Luther-Universitaet
        (Halle-Wittenberg). Gesellschafts- und
        Sprachwissenschaftliche Reihe [*A publication*]
WZUHW..... Wissenschaftliche Zeitschrift. Martin-Luther-Universitaet
        (Halle-Wittenberg). Gesellschafts- und
        Sprachwissenschaftliche Reihe [*A publication*]
WZUJ........ Wissenschaftliche Zeitschrift. Friedrich-Schiller-Universitaet
        (Jena) [*A publication*]
WZUL....... Wissenschaftliche Zeitschrift. Karl-Marx-Universitaet (Leipzig)
        [*A publication*]

WZUL .... Wissenschaftliche Zeitschrift. Universitaet Leipzig. Gesellschafts- und Sprachwissenschaftliche Reihe [*A publication*]
WZULeipzig ... Wissenschaftliche Zeitschrift. Karl-Marx Universitaet. Gesellschafts- und Sprachwissenschaftliche Reihe (Leipzig) [*A publication*]
WZUR .... Wissenschaftliche Zeitschrift. Universitaet Rostock [*A publication*]
WZUU .... Galva, IL [*FM radio station call letters*]
WZUW ...... Wissenschaftliche Zeitschrift. Universitaet Wien [*A publication*]
WZV .... Wiener Zeitschrift fuer Volkskunde [*A publication*]
WZVN ...... Lowell, IN [*FM radio station call letters*]
WZW .... Worcester Public Library, Worcester, MA [*OCLC symbol*] (OCLC)
WZWW ..... Bellefonte, PA [*FM radio station call letters*]
WZWZ ...... Kokomo, IN [*FM radio station call letters*]
WZXK .... Ashland, VA [*Television station call letters*]
WZXL........ Wildwood, NJ [*FM radio station call letters*]
WZXR .... Indianola, MS [*FM radio station call letters*]
WZXY ...... Kingsport, TN [*FM radio station call letters*]
WZY .... Nassau [*Bahamas*] [*Airport symbol*] (OAG)
WZYC-FM ... Newport, NC [*FM radio station call letters*]
WZYP........ Athens, AL [*FM radio station call letters*]
WZYQ .... Braddock Heights, MD [*FM radio station call letters*]
WZYX .... Cowan, TN [*AM radio station call letters*]
WZYZ .... Fairmont, NC [*FM radio station call letters*]
WZZA ...... Tuscumbia, AL [*AM radio station call letters*]
WZZD .... Philadelphia, PA [*AM radio station call letters*]
WZZE........ Glen Mills, PA [*FM radio station call letters*]
WZZF-FM ... Hopkinsville, KY [*FM radio station call letters*]
WZZI........ Manteo, NC [*FM radio station call letters*]
WZZK ...... Birmingham, AL [*AM radio station call letters*]
WZZK-FM ... Birmingham, AL [*FM radio station call letters*]
WZZM-TV ... Grand Rapids, MI [*Television station call letters*]
WZZO ...... Bethlehem, PA [*FM radio station call letters*]
WZZP........ South Bend, IN [*FM radio station call letters*]
WZZQ .... Terre Haute, IN [*FM radio station call letters*]
WZZR ...... Stuart, FL [*FM radio station call letters*]
WZZT........ Morrison, IL [*FM radio station call letters*]
WZZU ...... Burlington-Graham, NC [*FM radio station call letters*]
WZZX ...... Lineville, AL [*AM radio station call letters*]
WZZY ...... Winchester, IN [*FM radio station call letters*]
WZZZ........ Fulton, NY [*AM radio station call letters*]

X

X................ Amino Acid, Unknown or Other [*Symbol*] [*Biochemistry*]
X................ Any Point on a Great Circle
X................ Arithmetic Mean [*Statistics*]
X................ By [*As in 9 x 12*]
X................ Central Drug Research Institute [*India*] [*Research code symbol*]
X................ Chile [*IYRU nationality code*] (IYR)
X................ Christus [*Christ*] [*Latin*]
X................ Closed at All Times (Except When in Actual Use) [*Ship's fittings classification*]
X................ Cross [*As in X-roads*]
X................ Crystal Cut [*Symbol*] (DEN)
X................ Drill Sergeant [*Army skill qualification identifier*] (INF)
X................ Ethnikon Agrotikon Komma Xiton [*National Agrarian Party "X"*] [*Political party*] (PPE)
X................ Ex-Husband [*or Ex-Wife*] [*Slang*]
X................ Ex-Interest [*Without the right to interest*] [*Finance*]
X................ Examination [*Slang*]
X................ Exchange
X................ Exclusive [*Concession in a circus or carnival*]
X................ Exercise [*British military*] (DMA)
X................ Exhibitions [*Trade fairs, etc.*] [*Public-performance tariff class*] [*British*]
X................ Exophoria Distance [*Ophthalmology*]
X................ Experimental [*Military*] (AABC)
X................ Explosion [*Military*] (CAAL)
X................ Export [*Economics*]
X................ Extension (AAG)
X................ Extra
X................ Female Chromosome
X................ Frost
X................ Horizontal Deflection [*Symbol*] (DEN)
X................ Index [*Data processing*]
X................ Intersect (FAAC)
X................ Kiss [*Correspondence*]
X................ Komma Xiton Ethnikis Antistasseos [*"X" National Resistance Party*] [*Political party*] (PPE)
X................ Lateral [*RADAR*]
X................ Midweek Travel [*Airline fare code*]
X................ Mistake [*or Error*] [*Symbol*]
X................ No Protest [*Banking*]
X................ No-Wind Distance between Pressure Pattern Observations
X................ Parallactic Angle
X................ Persons under Eighteen [*Sixteen in some localities*] Not Admitted [*Movie rating*]
X................ Psychological Problem [*Classification system used by doctors on Ellis Island to detain, re-examine, and possibly deny entry to certain immigrants*]
X................ Raw Score [*Psychology*]
X................ Reactance [*Symbol*] [*IUPAC*] (AAG)
X................ Research [*or Experimental*] [*Designation for all US military aircraft*]
X................ St. Andrew's Cross
X................ Simes [*Italy*] [*Research code symbol*]
X................ Strike [*Bowling symbol*]
X................ Submersible Craft [*Self-propelled*] [*Navy ship symbol*]
x................ Takes [*As in K x B - King Takes Bishop*] [*Chess*]
X................ Ten [*Roman numeral*]
X................ Times [*Multiplication sign*] [*Mathematics*]
X................ Toilet [*Slang*]
X................ Transistor [*Symbol*] (DEN)
X................ Transmit
X................ [*The First*] Unknown Quantity [*Mathematics*] (ROG)
X................ USX Corp. [*Formerly, US Steel Corp.*] [*NYSE symbol*] [*Wall Street slang name: "Steel"*] (SPSG)
X................ X-Axis
X................ X-Ray [*Phonetic alphabet*] [*Pre-World War II*] [*World War II*] [*International*] (DSUE)
X................ X-Ray (KSC)
X................ X-Ray Assistant [*British military*]
X................ X Records [*Division of RCA-Victor*] [*Record label*]
X................ Xanthosine [*One-letter symbol; see Xao*]

X................ Xerxes [*Phonetic alphabet*] [*Royal Navy*] [*World War I*] (DSUE)
X................ Xylem [*Botany*]
x................ Xylose [*As substituent on nucleoside*] [*Biochemistry*]
x................ Xylose [*One-letter symbol; see Xyl*]
3X............ Guinea [*Aircraft nationality and registration mark*] (FAAC)
4X............ Israel [*Aircraft nationality and registration mark*] (FAAC)
5X............ Uganda [*Aircraft nationality and registration mark*] (FAAC)
X (Cars) ..... Designation for General Motors front-wheel-drive cars [*Citation, Omega, Phoenix, Skylark*]
X (Hour).... Hour at which shipping evacuation is ordered from major ports [*NATO exercises*] (NATG)
X (Mode).... Extraordinary Mode (MCD)
XA............ Aeronautical Radio, Inc. [*ICAO designator*] (FAAC)
XA............ Auxiliary Amplifier (AAG)
xa............ Christmas Island [*Indian Ocean*] [*MARC country of publication code*] [*Library of Congress*] (LCCP)
XA............ Experimental (Air Force)
XA............ Extended Architecture [*Data processing*]
XA............ Mexico [*Aircraft nationality and registration mark*] (FAAC)
XA............ Transmission Adapter (MDG)
Xa............ Xanadu [*A publication*]
Xa............ Xanthine [*Biochemistry*]
XA............ Xanthurenic Acid [*Clinical chemistry*]
XAAM...... Experimental Air-to-Air Missile [*Air Force, NASA*]
XAARAY... US Department of Agriculture. Agricultural Research Service. ARS [*A publication*]
XACIAH ... US Department of Agriculture. Plant Inventory [*A publication*]
XACIC...... X-Ray Attenuation Coefficient Information Center [*National Institute of Standards and Technology*]
XACT........ X Automatic Code Translation (IEEE)
XAD.......... Experimental and Development
XADMAY ... US Air Force. Technical Documentary Report. SAM-TDR [*A publication*]
XADRAF... US Army. Diamond Ordnance Fuze Laboratories. Technical Report [*A publication*]
XAFH .... X-Band Antenna Feed Horn
XAID .... ADI Electronics [*NASDAQ symbol*] (NQ)
XAK .... Cargo Ship, Merchant Marine Manned
XAL .... Xenon Arc Lamp
XALNA ..... Research Note FPL. Forest Products Laboratory [*United States*] [*A publication*]
XAM......... Merchant Ship Converted to a Minesweeper [*Navy symbol*] [*Obsolete*]
Xan............ Xanthine [*Biochemistry*]
XANES...... X-Ray Absorption Near-Edge Structure [*Spectroscopy*]
XANST...... Xanthium strumarium [*Cocklebur*]
xanth.......... Xanthomatosis
Xao............ Xanthosine [*Also, X*] [*A nucleoside*]
XAP .... Chapeco [*Brazil*] [*Airport symbol*] (OAG)
XAP .... Merchant Transport [*Ship symbol*]
XAPC......... Merchant Coastal Transport, Small [*Ship symbol*]
XARM ...... Cross Arm (AAG)
XART......... Artagraph Reproduction Technology, Inc. [*NASDAQ symbol*] (NQ)
XAS........... Experimental Air Specification Weapons [*Navy*] (NG)
XAS........... X-Band Antenna System
XAS........... X-Ray Absorption Spectroscopy
XASM....... Experimental Air-to-Surface Missile [*Air Force, NASA*]
XAT .... X-Ray Analysis Trial
XAV .... Auxiliary Seaplane Tender [*Ship symbol*]
XAV .... Xavier University, Cincinnati, OH [*OCLC symbol*] (OCLC)
XAY .... Camp Atterbury, IN [*Location identifier*] [*FAA*] (FAAL)
xb............. Cocos [*Keeling*] Islands [*MARC country of publication code*] [*Library of Congress*] (LCCP)
XB............ Crossbar [*Bell System*]
XB............ Experimental Bomber (MCD)
XB............ Exploding Bridge-Wire
XB............ International Air Transport Association (IATA) [*ICAO designator*] (ICDA)
XB............ Mexico [*Aircraft nationality and registration mark*] (FAAC)

XBAR.........	Crossbar
XBASIC.....	Extension of BASIC [*Data processing*]
XBB	Berne Public Library, Berne, IN [*OCLC symbol*] (OCLC)
XBC	"B" Corp. [*Toronto Stock Exchange symbol*]
XBC	External Block Controller
XBE	Shasta Air, Inc. [*Yreka, CA*] [*FAA designator*] (FAAC)
XBF...........	Bird Leasing, Inc. [*North Andover, MA*] [*FAA designator*] (FAAC)
XBF...........	Fort Wayne, IN [*Location identifier*] [*FAA*] (FAAL)
XBG	Bogande [*Upper Volta*] [*Airport symbol*] (OAG)
XBG	National Jet Corp. [*West Mifflin, PA*] [*FAA designator*] (FAAC)
XBH	Northern Airlines [*Vineyard Haven, MA*] [*FAA designator*] (FAAC)
XBIOS.......	Extended BIOS [*Basic Input/Output System*] [*Operating system*]
XBJ	Valley Airlines [*Frenchville, ME*] [*FAA designator*] (FAAC)
XBK	Bellair Airways [*Houston, TX*] [*FAA designator*] (FAAC)
XBK	Xebeck [*Type of ship*] (ROG)
XBL...........	Extension Bell [*Telecommunications*] (TEL)
XBL...........	Northstar Aviation [*Redding, CA*] [*FAA designator*] (FAAC)
XBLD........	Extrabold [*Typography*]
XBM	Extended BASIC Mode [*International Computers Ltd.*]
XBM	State University of New York, College at Brockport, Brockport, NY [*OCLC symbol*] (OCLC)
XBMIA......	Report of Investigations. United States Bureau of Mines [*A publication*]
XBN	Biniguni [*Papua New Guinea*] [*Airport symbol*] (OAG)
XBO	Sajen Air, Inc. [*Manchester, NH*] [*FAA designator*] (FAAC)
x bon..........	Ex-Bonification [*Ex-Bonus*] [*Stock exchange*] [*French*]
XBP	Bancshare Portfolio Corp. [*Toronto Stock Exchange symbol*]
XBQ	Denver Charters, Inc. [*Englewood, CO*] [*FAA designator*] (FAAC)
XBR	Aero Coach Aviation International, Inc. [*Ft. Lauderdale, FL*] [*FAA designator*] (FAAC)
XBR	Brockville [*Canada*] [*Airport symbol*] (OAG)
XBR	Experimental Breeder Reactor
XBR	Ozark, AL [*Location identifier*] [*FAA*] (FAAL)
XBRA........	Cross Bracing [*MSA*]
XBS...........	Ace Air Cargo Express, Inc. [*Brook Park, OH*] [*FAA designator*] (FAAC)
XBT	Crossbar Tandem [*Telecommunications*] (TEL)
XBT	Desert Sun Airlines [*Long Beach, CA*] [*FAA designator*] (FAAC)
XBT	Expendable Bathythermograph [*Oceanography*]
XBU	Arcata Flying Service [*McKinleyville, CA*] [*FAA designator*] (FAAC)
XBV	Western Pacific Express, Inc. [*Van Nuys, CA*] [*FAA designator*] (FAAC)
XBW	Waring Aviation, Inc. [*Charlottesville, VA*] [*FAA designator*] (FAAC)
XBX	Air Cargo America, Inc. [*Miami, FL*] [*FAA designator*] (FAAC)
XBY	Cosmopolitan Airlines, Inc. [*Farmingdale, NY*] [*FAA designator*] (FAAC)
XBZ	Chesapeake Transport, Inc. [*Arlington, VA*] [*FAA designator*] (FAAC)
XC	Air Routing International Corp. [*ICAO designator*] (FAAC)
Xc	Capacitive Reactance
XC	Cross-Clamp [*of carotid artery*]
XC	Cross Country [*Also, XCY*]
X-C	Ex-Coupon [*Without the right to coupons, as of a bond*] [*Finance*]
XC	Expendable Case (MCD)
XC	Experimental Cargo Aircraft
xc	Maldives [*MARC country of publication code*] [*Library of Congress*] (LCCP)
XC	Mexico [*Aircraft nationality and registration mark*] (FAAC)
XC	X-Chromosome
XC	Xanthomonus Campestris [*Bacteriology*]
XC	Xerox Copy
XCA	Air East of Delaware, Inc. [*Wilmington, DE*] [*FAA designator*] (FAAC)
XCB	Aero Trends, Inc. [*San Jose, CA*] [*FAA designator*] (FAAC)
XCB	Extended Core Barrel [*Drilling technology*]
XCC	Air Vectors Airways, Inc. [*Newburg, NY*] [*FAA designator*] (FAAC)
XCD	Air Associates Ltd. [*Kansas City, MO*] [*FAA designator*] (FAAC)
XCD	Canadian Dollar [*Vancouver Stock Exchange symbol*]
XCE	Aerotransit [*Danvers, MA*] [*FAA designator*] (FAAC)
XCE	X-Band Cassegrain Experimental
XCEL........	Excel Bancorp, Inc. [*Quincy, MA*] [*NASDAQ symbol*] (NQ)
XCF...........	Air Niagara, Inc. [*Niagara Falls, NY*] [*FAA designator*] (FAAC)
XCG	Atlantic Express, Inc. [*East Farmingdale, NY*] [*FAA designator*] (FAAC)
XCG	Experimental Cargo Glider
X-CGD......	X-Linked Chronic Granulomatous Disease [*Medicine*]
XCH..........	Exchange (AAG)
XCH..........	Flight East [*North Hollywood, CA*] [*FAA designator*] (FAAC)
XCI	X-Chromosome Inactivation [*Genetics*]
XCIT.........	Excitation (AAG)
XCJ............	Eastman Airways [*Farmingdale, NJ*] [*FAA designator*] (FAAC)
XCK	Richland Aviation [*Sidney, MT*] [*FAA designator*] (FAAC)
XCL..........	Armed Merchant Cruiser [*Navy symbol*]
XCL..........	Excess Current Liabilities [*Insurance*]
XCL..........	Excluded from General Declassification Schedule (MCD)
XCL..........	Exploration Co. of Louisiana, Inc. [*AMEX symbol*] (SPSG)
XCL..........	Green Aero, Inc. [*Flint, MI*] [*FAA designator*] (FAAC)
XCL..........	X-Cal Resources Ltd. [*Toronto Stock Exchange symbol*]
XCMD........	External Command [*Data processing*]
XCN..........	Northern Airways, Inc. [*Grand Forks, ND*] [*FAA designator*] (FAAC)
XCNGR	Exchanger (AAG)
XCO..........	Cross Connection
XCOM......	Exterior Communications [*Military*] (CAAL)
XCONN......	Cross Connection
XCORA	Xcor International, Inc. Cl A [*NASDAQ symbol*] (NQ)
xcoup........	Ex-Coupon [*Ex-Coupon*] [*Stock exchange*] [*French*]
XCP...........	Ex-Coupon [*Without the right to coupons, as of a bond*] [*Finance*]
XCP...........	Except (FAAC)
XCP...........	Expendable Current Profiler [*Instrumentation, oceanography*]
XCPT.........	Except (KSC)
XCR	Little Falls, MN [*Location identifier*] [*FAA*] (FAAL)
XCRDA	Research and Development Report. United States Office of Coal Research [*A publication*]
XCS	Cape Seppings, AK [*Location identifier*] [*FAA*] (FAAL)
XCS	Cross-Country Skiing
XCS	Ten Call Seconds [*Telecommunications*] (TEL)
XCS	Xerox Computer Services [*Xerox Corp.*]
XCT	X-Band Communications Transponder
X Ctry Skier ...	X-Country Skier [*A publication*]
XCU	Explosion Collapse, Underground Operations
XC & UC....	Exclusive of Covering and Uncovering
XCVR........	Transceiver (AAG)
XCY	Cross Country [*Also, XC*]
XD.............	Bureau Veritas SA [*France*] [*ICAO designator*] (ICDA)
XD.............	Crossed [*Telecommunications*] (TEL)
XD.............	Ex-Directory [*Telecommunications*] (TEL)
X-D	Ex-Dividend [*Without the right to dividend*] [*Finance*] (SPSG)
xd	Ex-Dividende [*Ex-Dividend*] [*French*] [*Finance*]
X/D............	Ex Dividendum [*Without (or Exclusive) of Dividend*] [*Finance*] (ROG)
XD.............	Examined (ROG)
XD.............	Executed (ROG)
XD.............	Executive Development [*Civil Service Commission*]
X & D	Experiment and Development [*Flotilla*] [*Landing Craft*]
XD.............	Exploratory Development [*Military*] (MCD)
XD.............	Extra Dense
XD.............	Xylem Disease [*Plant pathology*]
XDA..........	X-Band Drive Amplifier
XDC..........	Xylene-Dioxane-Cellosolve [*Scintillation solvent*]
XDCR........	Transducer (AAG)
XDE..........	Xylene-Dioxane-Ethanol [*Scintillation solvent*]
XDER........	Transducer
XDH	Xanthine Dehydrogenase [*An enzyme*]
XDI	Xylene Diisocyanate [*Organic chemistry*]
XDIGA	US Geological Survey. Bulletin [*A publication*]
X-Dis.........	Ex-Distribution
X-Div.........	Ex-Dividend [*Without the right to dividend*] [*Finance*]
XDIVU	Naval Experimental Diving Unit
XDM..........	State University of New York, Agricultural and Technical College at Delhi, Delhi, NY [*OCLC symbol*] (OCLC)
XDM..........	X-Ray Density Measurement
XDP	X-Ray Density Probe
XDP	X-Ray Diffraction Powder
XDP	Xanthosine Diphosphate [*Biochemistry*]
XDP	Xeroderma Pigmentosum [*Inherited, disfiguring syndrome*]
XDPC.........	X-Ray Diffraction Powder Camera
XDPS.........	X-Band Diode Phase Shifter
XDR	Crusader (ROG)
x dr	Ex-Droits [*Ex-Rights*] [*French*] [*Finance*]
XDR...........	External Data Representation [*Data processing*]
XDR...........	Transducer (AAG)
XDS	X-Ray Diffraction System
XDS	Xerox Data Systems [*Formerly, SDS*]
XDT	Xenon Discharge Tube
XDUCER...	Transducer
XDUP	Extended Disk Utilities Program [*Data processing*]
XDY	Valdosta Moody Air Force Base, GA [*Location identifier*] [*FAA*] (FAAL)
XE	Canadian Express Ltd. [*Toronto Stock Exchange symbol*] [*Vancouver Stock Exchange symbol*]
XE	Euro Control [*Belgium*] [*ICAO designator*] (FAAC)
XE	Experimental Engine [*NASA*]
Xe	Xenon [*Chemical element*]
XEBC........	Xebec [*NASDAQ symbol*] (NQ)
XEC	Execute
XECF........	Experimental Engine - Cold Flow Configuration [*NERVA*]
XED	Medford, OK [*Location identifier*] [*FAA*] (FAAL)

XEDS.........	X-Ray Energy Dispersive System [*Microparticle analysis*]
XEF...........	Xenon Fluoride (MCD)
XEG...........	X-Ray Emission Gauge
XEG	Xerox Education Group
XEL...........	Excelsior Life Insurance Co. [*Toronto Stock Exchange symbol*]
XELEDOP ...	Transmitting Elementary Dipole with Optional Polarity (MCD)
Xen.............	De Xenophane [*of Aristotle*] [*Classical studies*] (OCD)
XEN...........	Xenia, OH [*Location identifier*] [*FAA*] (FAAL)
Xen.............	Xenophon [*428-354BC*] [*Classical studies*] (OCD)
XEPPDW ..	US Environmental Protection Agency. Office of Pesticide Programs. Substitute Chemical Program. EPA-540 [*A publication*]
XEQ...........	Execute
XER	Xerox Corp., Xerox Library Services, Webster, NY [*OCLC symbol*] (OCLC)
XER	Xerox Reproduction (AAG)
XERB.........	Experimental Environmental Research Buoy [*Marine science*] (MSC)
XERG	Xonics Electron Radiography [*Medical x-ray imaging equipment*]
XES...........	X-Ray Emission Spectra
XES...........	X-Ray Energy Spectrometry
XETA.........	Xeta Corp. [*NASDAQ symbol*] (NQ)
XF	Experimental Fighter
XF	Extended Family [*Unitarian Universalist program*]
XF	Extra Fine
xf	Extremely Fine [*Philately*]
xf	Midway Islands [*MARC country of publication code*] [*Library of Congress*] (LCCP)
XF	Xudozestvennyj Fol'klor [*A publication*]
X15-F	Model number used by Eastman Kodak Co. [*Name is said to have been derived from symbol on magicube (X), product's place in sales line (15), and flip-flash unit that replaced magicube (F)*]
XFA	Cross-Field Acceleration
XFA	X-Ray Fluorescence Absorption
XFC...........	Extended Function Code
XFC...........	Transfer Charge [*Telecommunications*] (TEL)
XFC...........	X-Band Frequency Converter
XFD	Crossfeed (NASA)
XFD	X-Ray Flow Detection
XFER.........	Transfer (AAG)
XFES.........	Xerox Family Education Services
XFH...........	X-Band Feed Horn
XfL.............	Cross in Front of Left Foot [*Dance terminology*]
XFLT	Expanded Flight Line Tester
XFM	Expeditionary Force Message [*Usually, EFM*] [*Low-rate cable or radio message selected from a list of standard wordings*]
XFM	State University of New York, College at Fredonia, Fredonia, NY [*OCLC symbol*] (OCLC)
XFM	X-Band Ferrite Modulator
XFMR........	Transformer (AAG)
XFN	Victoria, TX [*Location identifier*] [*FAA*] (FAAL)
XFQH	Xenon-Filled Quartz Helix
XFR...........	Transfer
XFRMR......	Transformer
XFS...........	Fort Sill, OK [*Location identifier*] [*FAA*] (FAAL)
XFS...........	X-Ray Fluorescence Spectroscopy
XFS...........	Xenogenic Fetal Skin [*Medicine*]
XFT...........	Xenon Flash Tube
XFWFA7.....	US Fish and Wildlife Service. Fishery Bulletin [*A publication*]
XFWLAP....	US Fish and Wildlife Service. Wildlife Leaflet [*A publication*]
XG	Crossing
XG.............	IMP Group Ltd. Aviation Services [*Canada*] [*ICAO designator*] (FAAC)
XGAM.......	Experimental Guided Air Missiles
XGDS	Exempt from General Declassification Schedule (MCD)
Xge............	Exchange [*Business term*]
XGG..........	Gorom-Gorom [*Upper Volta*] [*Airport symbol*] (OAG)
X-Gluc......	X-Glucuronide
XGP	Xanthogranulomatous Pyelonephritis [*Medicine*]
XGP	Xerox Graphic Printer [*Xerox Corp.*]
XGPRT......	Xanthine-Guanine Phosphoribosyltransferase [*An enzyme*]
XGRAPHY ...	Xylography [*Wood engraving*] (ROG)
XH	Experimental Helicopter
xh	Niue [*MARC country of publication code*] [*Library of Congress*] (LCCP)
XH	Sign-Filled Half-Word Designator [*Data processing*]
XH	Special Handling Service for Aircraft [*ICAO designator*] (ICDA)
XH	Xerogrammata Hochschulschriften [*A publication*]
XHAIR........	Cross Hair [IEEE]
XHE	Hawaii Express [*Los Angeles, CA*] [*FAA designator*] (FAAC)
XHF	Extra-High Frequency (NVT)
XHM	X-Ray Hazard Meter
XHMO.......	Extended Hueckel Molecular Orbit [*Atomic physics*] (IEEE)
xho.............	Xhosa [*MARC language code*] [*Library of Congress*] (LCCP)
XHR...........	Extra-High Reliability
XHS	Indiana Historical Society, Indianapolis, IN [*OCLC symbol*] (OCLC)

XHST	Exhaust (AAG)
XHV...........	Extreme High Vacuum
XHVY	Extra Heavy
X-I.............	Ex-Interest [*Without the right to interest*] [*Finance*]
XI	International Aeradio Ltd. [*United Kingdom*] [*ICAO designator*] (ICDA)
xi	St. Christopher-Nevis-Anguilla [*MARC country of publication code*] [*Library of Congress*] (LCCP)
XIA	X-Band Inteferometer Antenna
XIB	IBM Corp., Library Processing Center, White Plains, NY [*OCLC symbol*] (OCLC)
XIC	Convent of Immaculate Conception Sisters of St. Benedict, Ferdinand, IN [*OCLC symbol*] (OCLC)
XIC	Transmission Interface Converter
XIC	Xichang [*China*] [*Airport symbol*] (OAG)
XICO	Xicor, Inc. [*NASDAQ symbol*] (NQ)
XICS........	Xerox Integrated Composition System [*Xerox Corp.*] [*Computer typesetting system*]
XICTMD...	Xerox International Center for Training and Management Development [*Leesburg, VA*]
XID	Exchange Identification
XIDX	Xidex Corp. [*NASDAQ symbol*] (NQ)
XII.............	Washington, DC [*Location identifier*] [*FAA*] (FAAL)
XII P	Testaments of the Twelve Patriarchs [*Pseudepigrapha*]
XIM	Ithaca College, Ithaca, NY [*OCLC symbol*] (OCLC)
XIM	X-Ray Intensity Meter
XIMIA.......	Information Circular. United States Bureau of Mines [*A publication*]
XIN	Ex-Interest [*Without the right to interest*] [*Finance*]
XING	Crossing (MCD)
XINT	Ex-Interest [*Without the right to interest*] [*Finance*]
XI/O	Execute Input/Output (DEN)
XIOX.........	XIOX Corp. [*Burlingame, CA*] [*NASDAQ symbol*] (NQ)
XIP...........	Execute-in-Place [*Data processing*]
XIP...........	Xerox Individualized Publishing
XIPC.........	Extended Interprocess Communications Facilities
Xi Psi Phi Q ...	Xi Psi Phi Quarterly [*A publication*]
XIRS.........	Xenon Infrared Searchlight
XIS...........	Xenon Infrared Searchlight
XIS...........	XPRESS Information Services (IID)
XIT...........	Extra Input Terminal
XIWSA	US Geological Survey. Water-Supply Paper [*A publication*]
XJ.............	Assistance Aeroportuaire de l'Aeroport de Paris [*France*] [*ICAO designator*] (ICDA)
xj	St. Helena [*MARC country of publication code*] [*Library of Congress*] (LCCP)
XJM...........	Schenectady County Community College, Schenectady, NY [*OCLC symbol*] (OCLC)
XJN	Milwaukee, WI [*Location identifier*] [*FAA*] (FAAL)
XJP...........	Jasper Public Library, Jasper, IN [*OCLC symbol*] (OCLC)
XK	Agence pour la Securite de la Navigation Aerienne en Afrique et a Madagascar (ASECNA) [*ICAO designator*] (ICDA)
xk	St. Lucia [*MARC country of publication code*] [*Library of Congress*] (LCCP)
XK	X-Band Klystron
XL	Cross-Reference List
XL	Crystal
XL	Excess Lactate
XL	Execution Language [*Data processing*]
XL	Extra Large [*or Long*] [*Size*]
xl	St. Pierre and Miquelon [*MARC country of publication code*] [*Library of Congress*] (LCCP)
XL	Telecomunicacoes Aeronauticas Sociedada Anonima (TASA) [*Brazil*] [*ICAO designator*] (ICDA)
XL	Unmarried Lady [*Citizens band radio slang*]
XL	X-Axis of Spacelab [*NASA*] (NASA)
XL	Xudozestvennaja Literatura [*A publication*]
XL	Xylose-Lysine [*Agar base*] [*Microbiology*]
XLA	X-Band Limiter Attenuator
XLATION ...	Translation
XLB...........	Xylem-Limited Bacteria [*Plant pathology*]
XLC...........	Extra Large Capacity
XLC...........	Extra Luxurious Chaparral
XLC...........	Indiana University, School of Medicine, Medical Education Resources Program, Indianapolis, IN [*OCLC symbol*] (OCLC)
XLC...........	Xenon Lamp Collimator
XLD	Experimental LASER Device (MCD)
XLD	Xylose-Lysine-Deoxycholate [*Growth medium*]
XLDC.........	XL/Datacomp, Inc. [*Hinsdale, IL*] [*NASDAQ symbol*] (NQ)
XLDT.........	Xenon LASER Discharge Tube
XLE...........	Columbus, GA [*Location identifier*] [*FAA*] (FAAL)
XLF...........	XL Food Systems Ltd. [*Toronto Stock Exchange symbol*]
XLGX.........	Xylogics, Inc. [*NASDAQ symbol*] (NQ)
xlh	Extra Large Hinge [*Philately*]
XLI.............	Extra-Low Interstitial [*Alloy*]
XLISP........	Extension of LISP [*List Processor*] 1.5 [*Programming language*] (CSR)
XLIST........	Execution List (MCD)
XLM	St. Lawrence University, Canton, NY [*OCLC symbol*] (OCLC)
XLMR........	X-Linked Mental Retardation [*Genetics*]

XLP...........	Extended-Life Protection [*Automotive engineering*]
XLP...........	X-Linked Lymphoproliferative Syndrome [*Medicine*]
XLPE.........	Cross-Linked Polyethylene [*Organic chemistry*] (NRCH)
XLPS.........	X-Linked Lymphoproliferative Syndrome [*Medicine*]
XLPS.........	Xenon Lamp Power Supply
XLR...........	Experimental Liquid Rocket [*Air Force, NASA*]
XLR...........	X-Linked, Lymphocyte-Regulated [*Genetics*]
XLS...........	St. Louis [*Senegal*] [*Airport symbol*] (OAG)
XLS...........	Xenon Light Source
XLS...........	Xerox Learning Systems
XLSS.........	Xenon Light Source System
XLT...........	Xenon LASER Tube
XLTN........	Translation (NASA)
XLTR........	Translator (MSA)
XL & UL....	Exclusive of Loading and Unloading
XLWB.......	Extra-Long Wheelbase
XM............	Christmas
XM............	Excitation Monochromator
XM............	Expanded Memory
XM............	Experimental Missile [*Air Force, NASA*]
XM............	Experimental Model
XM............	Research Missile [*NATO*]
xm	St. Vincent [*MARC country of publication code*] [*Library of Congress*] (LCCP)
XM............	Servicios a la Navegacion en el Espacio Aereo Mexicano (SENEAM) [*Mexico*] [*ICAO designator*] (ICDA)
XMAP	Sweeper Device [*Navy symbol*]
XMAS........	Christmas
XMAS........	Extended Mission Apollo Simulation [*NASA*] (IEEE)
X/MBR......	Cross Member [*Automotive engineering*]
XMC.........	Borough of Manhattan Community College, New York, NY [*OCLC symbol*] (OCLC)
XmC.........	Standard Microfilm Reproductions Ltd., Scarborough, ON, Canada [*Library symbol*] [*Library of Congress*] (LCLS)
XMD.........	Ozark, AL [*Location identifier*] [*FAA*] (FAAL)
XME.........	Medgar Evers College of the City University of New York, Brooklyn, NY [*OCLC symbol*] (OCLC)
XMED.......	Xtramedics, Inc. [*NASDAQ symbol*] (NQ)
XMFR.......	Transformer (AAG)
XMG........	Mahendranagar [*Nepal*] [*Airport symbol*] (OAG)
XMH	Manihi [*French Polynesia*] [*Airport symbol*] (OAG)
XMI	Christmas Island [*Seismograph station code, US Geological Survey*] (SEIS)
XMI	Masasi [*Tanzania*] [*Airport symbol*] (OAG)
XMI	Seymour-Moss International Ltd. [*Vancouver Stock Exchange symbol*]
XMIT........	Transmit [*or Transmitter*]
XML	Miles Laboratories, Inc., Miles Pharmaceutical Division, West Haven, CT [*OCLC symbol*] (OCLC)
XML	Minlaton [*Australia*] [*Airport symbol*] [*Obsolete*] (OAG)
XMM........	State University of New York, Agricultural and Technical College at Morrisville, Morrisville, NY [*OCLC symbol*] (OCLC)
XMOFA	Bureau of Mines. Open File Report [*United States*] [*A publication*]
XMP.........	Marion Public Library, Marion, IN [*OCLC symbol*] (OCLC)
XMP.........	Xanthosine Monophosphate [*Biochemistry*]
XMR.........	Cape Canaveral, FL [*Location identifier*] [*FAA*] (FAAL)
XMS.........	Experimental Development Specification [*Military*] (CAAL)
XMS.........	X-Band Microwave Source
XMS	Xavier Mission Sisters [*Catholic Mission Sisters of St. Francis Xavier*] [*Roman Catholic religious order*]
XMS	Xerox Memory System
XMSN	Transmission (AAG)
XMT.........	Exempt (NVT)
XMT.........	Transmit (MSA)
XMT.........	X-Band Microwave Transmitter
XMTD.......	Transmitted (MCD)
XMTG.......	Transmitting
XMTL........	Transmittal (IEEE)
XMTPB.....	Technical Progress Report. United States Bureau of Mines [*A publication*]
XMTR	Transmitter
XMT-REC ...	Transmit-Receive (AAG)
XMTR-REC ...	Transmitter-Receiver
XN.............	Canadian National Telecommunications [*Canada*] [*ICAO designator*] (ICDA)
XN.............	Christian
XN.............	Ex-New [*Without the right to new stocks or shares*] [*Stock exchange term*] (SPSG)
XN.............	Experimental (Navy)
XNA.........	Xinhua News Agency [*China*]
XNB.........	X-Band Navigation Beacon
XNBSA......	National Bureau of Standards. Special Publication [*United States*] [*A publication*]
XNC.........	Nazareth College of Rochester, Rochester, NY [*OCLC symbol*] (OCLC)
XNEW	Ex New Issue [*Without the right to new stocks or shares*] [*Stock exchange term*]
XNIPA.......	United States. Naval Institute. Proceedings [*A publication*]

XNL	NELINET [*New England Library Information Network*], Newton, MA [*OCLC symbol*] (OCLC)
XNN..........	Xining [*China*] [*Airport symbol*] (OAG)
XNO	North, SC [*Location identifier*] [*FAA*] (FAAL)
XNOS........	Experimental Network Operating System
XNRX	Xenerex Corp. [*NASDAQ symbol*] (NQ)
XNS	Xerox Network Systems [*Telecommunications*]
XNTY	Christianity
XNWRA	US News and World Report [*A publication*]
XNX	Xenex Industries & Resources Ltd. [*Vancouver Stock Exchange symbol*]
XO............	Crystal Oscillator (IEEE)
XO............	Executive Officer [*Military*]
XO............	Expenditure Order [*Military*] (AABC)
XO............	Experimental Officer [*Also, EO, ExO*] [*Ministry of Agriculture, Fisheries, and Food*] [*British*]
XO............	Extra Old [*Designation on brandy labels*]
XO............	X-Axis of Orbiter [*NASA*] (NASA)
XO............	Xanthine Oxidase [*Also, XOD*] [*An enzyme*]
XO............	Xylenol Orange [*An indicator*] [*Chemistry*]
XOB..........	Xenon Optical Beacon
XOC..........	Experimental On-Line Capabilities [*Data processing*]
XOD..........	Xanthine Oxidase [*Also, XO*] [*An enzyme*]
XOFF........	Transmitter Off (BUR)
XOID........	Xyloid [*Woody*] (ROG)
XOMA.......	XOMA Corp. [*Berkeley, CA*] [*NASDAQ symbol*] (NQ)
XON..........	Cross-Office Highway [*Telecommunications*] (TEL)
XON	Exxon Corp. [*NYSE symbol*] (SPSG)
XON	Transmitter On (BUR)
XOP..........	Extended Operation
XOR..........	Exclusive Or [*Gates*] [*Data processing*]
XOS..........	Cross-Office Slot [*Telecommunications*] (TEL)
XOS..........	Extra Outsize [*Clothing*]
XOS	Xerox Operating System
XOVR........	Exovir, Inc. [*NASDAQ symbol*] (NQ)
XOW.........	Express Order Wire [*Telecommunications*] (TEL)
XOXIA	Xonics, Inc. Cl A [*NASDAQ symbol*] (NQ)
XP	Expansionist Party of the United States [*Political party*] (EA)
XP	Expres Paye [*Express Paid*] [*French*]
XP	Express Paid
XP	Express Parcel Systems [*Europe*]
XP	Fire Resistive Protected [*Insurance classification*]
XP	Radio Aeronautica Paraguaya Sociedad Anonima (RAPSA) [*Paraguay*] [*ICAO designator*] (ICDA)
xp	Spratly Islands [*MARC country of publication code*] [*Library of Congress*] (LCCP)
XP	Sun Exploration & Production Co. [*NYSE symbol*] [*Later, ORX*] (CTT)
XP	X-Axis of Payload [*NASA*] (NASA)
XP	Xeroderma Pigmentosum [*Inherited, disfiguring syndrome*]
XPA	Pama [*Upper Volta*] [*Airport symbol*] (OAG)
XPA	X-Band Parametric Amplifier
XPA	X-Band Passive Array
XPA	X-Band Planar Array
XPA	X-Band Power Amplifier
XPAA........	X-Band Planar Array Antenna
XPARD6....	EPA [*Environmental Protection Agency*] Environmental Protection Technology Series [*A publication*]
XPARD6....	US Environmental Protection Agency. Office of Research and Development. Research Reports. Ecological Research Series [*A publication*]
XPARS	External Research Publication and Retrieval System [*Department of State*]
XPC..........	Christus [*Christ*] [*Latin*]
XPC..........	Expect (FAAC)
XPD..........	Cross-Polarization Discrimination [*Telecommunications*]
XPD..........	Expedient Demise [*Used as title of novel by Len Deighton*]
XPD..........	Expedite (MUGU)
XPDR	Transponder (MUGU)
XPG..........	Converted merchant ships, assigned to antisubmarine patrol or convoy escort [*Navy symbol*]
XPH..........	Port Heiden, AK [*Location identifier*] [*FAA*] (FAAL)
XPHS........	Xylan Polyhydrogensulfate [*Antineoplastic drug*]
XPI...........	Cross-Polarization Interference [*in radio transmission*]
XPL..........	Explosive (AAG)
XPLOR.....	Xerox 9700 Users' Association (EA)
XPLOS......	Explosive (FAAC)
XPLR.........	Xplor Corp. [*NASDAQ symbol*] (NQ)
XPLT........	Exploit (MUGU)
XPM.........	Expanded Metal [*Heavy gauge*]
XPM	Xerox Planning Model [*A computerized representation of the Xerox Corp.'s operations*]
XPN..........	Expansion (AAG)
XPNDR	Transponder (AAG)
XPONDER ...	Transponder
X-POP	X-Body Axis Perpendicular to Orbit Plane [*Aerospace*]
XPP..........	Express Paid Letter (ROG)
XPP..........	Xi Psi Phi [*Fraternity*]
XPP...........	Xylem Pressure Potential [*Botany*]
XPPA........	X-Band Pseudopassive Array
XPPA.........	X-Band Pulsed Power Amplifier

XPR	Ex-Privileges [*Without the right to privileges*] [*Finance*]
x pri	Ex-Privileges [*Without the right to privileges*] [*Finance*] (DS)
XPS	X-Band Phase Shifter
XPS	X-Ray Photoemission Spectroscopy
XPSW	External Processor Status Word
XPT	Crosspoint [*Switching element*] (MSA)
XPT	Export
XPT	Express Paid Telegraph
XPT	Express Passenger Train [*Australia*]
XPT	External Page Table [*Data processing*] (BUR)
XPT	X-Band Pulse Transmitter
XPU	West Kuparuk, AK [*Location identifier*] [*FAA*] (FAAL)
XPW	American Ex-Prisoners of War (EA)
XQ	Cross-Question [*Transcripts*]
XQ	Experimental Target Drone [*Air Force, NASA*]
X/Q	Relative Concentration [*Symbol*] (NRCH)
XQA	Greenville, ME [*Location identifier*] [*FAA*] (FAAL)
XQH	Xenon Quartz Helix
XQM	Queens College, Flushing, NY [*OCLC symbol*] (OCLC)
XQP	Quepos [*Costa Rica*] [*Airport symbol*] (OAG)
XR	Cross Reference (MCD)
XR	Empresa de Servicios Aeronauticos [*Cuba*] [*ICAO designator*] (ICDA)
XR	Ex-Rights [*Without Rights*] [*Investment term*]
XR	Examiner (ROG)
XR	Export Reactor [*Nuclear energy*] (NRCH)
XR	Extended Range [*Film*] [*Briteline Corp.*]
XR	External Reset
XR	Index Register
XR	No Returns Permitted [*Business term*]
XR	RY II Financial Corp. [*Toronto Stock Exchange symbol*]
XR	X: A Quarterly Review [*A publication*]
XR	X-Ray
9XR	Rwanda [*Aircraft nationality and registration mark*] (FAAC)
XRA	X-Ray Assistant [*British military*] (DMA)
XRAY	GENDEX Corp. [*NASDAQ symbol*] (NQ)
X-Ray Spect ...	X-Ray Spectrometry [*A publication*]
X-Ray Spectrom ...	X-Ray Spectrometry [*A publication*]
XRB	X-Band RADAR Beacon
XRC	Xerox Research Centre of Canada Library [*UTLAS symbol*]
XRCD	X-Ray Crystal Density
XRD	X-Ray Diffraction [*or Diffractometer*]
XRDF	X-Ray Radial Distance Function [*Surface chemistry analysis*]
XRDS	Crossroads
X-REA	X-Ray Events Analyzer (KSC)
X-REF	Cross Reference (NG)
XREP	Auxiliary Report (FAAC)
XRF	Experimental Reproduction Film (DIT)
XRF	Explosion Release Factor [*Nuclear energy*] (NRCH)
XRF	Rockefeller Foundation, Library, New York, NY [*OCLC symbol*] (OCLC)
XRF	X-Ray Fluorescence [*Spectrometry*]
XRFS	X-Ray Fluorescence Spectrometer
XRG	X-Ray Generator [*Instrumentation*]
XRGP	Extended Range Guided Projectiles (MCD)
XRI	Xenium Resources, Inc. [*Vancouver Stock Exchange symbol*]
XRII	X-Ray Image Intensifier
XRIT	X-Rite, Inc. [*NASDAQ symbol*] (NQ)
XRL	Extended-Range Lance [*Missile*]
XRL	X-Ray LASER
XRM	External Relational Memory
XRM	Extra Range Multigrade [*Automotive engineering*]
XRM	X-Ray Microanalyzer [*or Microscopy*] (IEEE)
XRN	RY NT Financial Corp. [*Toronto Stock Exchange symbol*]
XROI	X-Ray Optical Interferometer
XRP	X-Ray and Photofluorography Technician [*Navy*]
XRP	X-Ray Polychromator
XRPM	X-Ray Projection Microscope (IEEE)
XRRAAH ..	US Forest Service. Rocky Mountain Forest and Range Experiment Station. Research Highlights. Annual Report [*A publication*]
XRS	X-Ray Spectrometry
XRT	Ex-Rights [*Without Rights*] [*Investment term*] (SPSG)
XRT	Extended-Range TOW
XRT	X-Ray Technician [*Navy*]
X-RT	X-Ray Telescope (MCD)
XRT	X-Ray Therapy [*or Treatment*]
XRTOW	Extended-Range TOW [*Tube-Launched, Optically Tracked, Wire-Guided*] [*Weapon*] (MCD)
X-RTS	Ex-Rights [*Without Rights*] [*Investment term*]
XRW	Fort Campbell, KY [*Location identifier*] [*FAA*] (FAAL)
XRX	Xerox Corp. [*NYSE symbol*] (SPSG)
XRY	Jerez De La Frontera [*Spain*] [*Airport symbol*] (OAG)
XRY	RY Financial Corp. [*Toronto Stock Exchange symbol*]
XRY	Yakima, WA [*Location identifier*] [*FAA*] (FAAL)
XS	Atmospherics (FAAC)
XS	Christus [*Christ*] [*Latin*]
XS	Cross Section
XS	Excess
XS	Expenses
XS	Extra Small

XS	Extra Strong
XS	Extremely Severe [*Rock climbing*]
XS	Societe Internationale de Telecommunications Aeronautiques, Societe Cooperative (SITA) [*ICAO designator*] (ICDA)
XS	X-Axis of Solid Rocket Booster [*NASA*] (NASA)
XS	Xerces Society (EA)
XS3	Excess Three [*Code*]
XS-11	Excess Eleven [*1967 group of scientist-astronauts selected by NASA*]
XSA	Cross-Sectional Area [*Cardiology*]
XSA	X-Band Satellite Antenna
XSAL	Xenon Short Arc Lamp
XSB	Xavier Society for the Blind (EA)
XSC	South Caicos [*British West Indies*] [*Airport symbol*] (OAG)
XSC	Southampton Center of Long Island University, Southampton, NY [*OCLC symbol*] (OCLC)
XSCI	Xsirius Superconductivity, Inc. [*NASDAQ symbol*] (NQ)
XSCR	Xscribe Corp. [*NASDAQ symbol*] (NQ)
XSD	Southeast Dubois County, School Corp. Library, Ferdinand, IN [*OCLC symbol*] (OCLC)
XSD	Tonopah, NV [*Location identifier*] [*FAA*] (FAAL)
XSE	Sebba [*Upper Volta*] [*Airport symbol*] (OAG)
XSECT	Cross Section
XSF	Springfield, OH [*Location identifier*] [*FAA*] (FAAL)
XSF	X-Ray Scattering Facility
XSIR	Xsirius Scientific, Inc. [*Marina Del Ray, CA*] [*NASDAQ symbol*] (NQ)
XSL	Experimental Space Laboratory
XSM	Experimental Strategic Missile
XSM	Experimental Surface Missile
XSM	X-Ray Stress Measurement
XSOA	Excess Speed of Advance Authorized [*Navy*] (NVT)
X-SONAD ...	Experimental Sonic Azimuth Detector (MCD)
XSP	Singapore-Seletar [*Singapore*] [*Airport symbol*] (OAG)
XSP	Xi Sigma Pi [*Fraternity*]
XSP	Xylem Sap Potential [*Botany*]
XSPV	Experimental Solid Propellant Vehicle
XSR	X-Band Scatterometer RADAR
XSS	Experimental Space Station [*NASA*]
XSS	Xenon Solar Simulator
XST	Experimental Stealth Tactical Demonstrator [*Air Force*]
XST	Xylem Sap Tension [*Botany*]
XSTA	X-Band Satellite Tracking Antenna
XSTD	Expendable Salinity/Temperature/Depth Probe [*Oceanography*] (MSC)
XSTD	X-Band Stripline Tunnel Diode
XSTDA	X-Band Stripline Tunnel Diode Amplifier
XSTR	Extra Strong (MSA)
XSTR	Transistor (AAG)
XSTT	Excess Transit Time
XSV	Expendable Sound Velocimeter [*Oceanography*] (MSC)
XT	Christ
XT	Cross Talk (IEEE)
XT	Exotropia Near [*Ophthalmology*]
XT	Servicos Auxiliares de Transportes Aereos (SATA) [*Brazil*] [*ICAO designator*] (ICDA)
XT	Upper Volta [*Aircraft nationality and registration mark*] (FAAC)
XT	X-Axis of External Tank [*NASA*] (NASA)
XT	X-Ray Tube
XTA	X-Band Tracking Antenna
XTAL	Crystal
XTAL	XTAL Corp. [*Burnsville, MN*] [*NASDAQ symbol*] (NQ)
XTALK	Crosstalk [*Telecommunications*] (MSA)
XTASI	Exchange of Technical Apollo Simulation Information [*NASA*] (IEEE)
XTC	Exco Technologies Ltd. [*Toronto Stock Exchange symbol*]
XTC	External Transmit Clock
XTE	X-Ray Timing Explorer
XTEL	Cross Tell (IEEE)
XTEL	Executive Telecommunications, Inc. [*Tulsa, OK*] [*NASDAQ symbol*] (NQ)
XTEN	Xerox Telecommunications Network [*Proposed*] (TSSD)
XTGX	TGX Corp. [*NASDAQ symbol*] (NQ)
XTIAN	Christian
XTLK	Cross Talk [*Aviation*] (FAAC)
XTLO	Crystal Oscillator
XTM	Experimental Test Model
XTN	Christian (ROG)
XTND	Extend [*or Extended*]
XTO	X-Band Triode Oscillator
XTON	EXECUTONE Information Systems, Inc. [*NASDAQ symbol*] (SPSG)
XTP	Xanthosine Triphosphate [*Biochemistry*]
XTPA	X-Band Tunable Parametric Amplifier
XTR	X-Ray Transition Radiation
XTR	XTRA Corp. [*NYSE symbol*] (SPSG)
XTRA	Extra (ROG)
XTRM	Extreme
XTRY	Extraordinary (ROG)
XTS	Cross-Tell Simulator (IEEE)

XTV .... Xerox Team Vision [*Xerox Business Products and Systems Group*] [*El Segundo, CA*] (TSSD)
XTWA .... X-Band Traveling Wave Amplifier
XTWM ...... X-Band Traveling Wave MASER
XTX .... New York Tax Exempt Income [*AMEX symbol*] (SPSG)
XTX .... X-Band Transmitter
XTY .... Christianity
XU .... Aerorepresentaciones Tupac Amaru [*Peru*] [*ICAO designator*] (ICDA)
XU .... Cambodia [*Aircraft nationality and registration mark*] (FAAC)
XU .... Excretory Urogram [*Medicine*]
XU .... Fire Resistive Unprotected [*Insurance classification*]
XU .... X Unit [*A unit of wavelength*]
XU .... Xavier University [*Louisiana; Ohio*]
XUB .... Circleville, OH [*Location identifier*] [*FAA*] (FAAL)
XUG .... Xyvision Users Group (EA)
XUM .... Xenium [*Gift*] (ROG)
XUS .... Xavier University. Studies [*A publication*]
XUV .... Extreme Ultraviolet
XV .... Administration de Aeropuertos y Servicios Auxiliares a la Nauegacion Aerea [*AASANA*] [*Bolivia*] [*ICAO designator*] (FAAC)
XV .... Vietnam [*Aircraft nationality and registration mark*] (FAAC)
XV .... X-Ray Vision
XVA .... X-Ray Vidicon Analysis
XVERS ...... Transverse (AAG)
XVII S....... XVIIe Siecle [*A publication*]
xVit .... Xenopus Vitellogenin
XVN .... Venice, FL [*Location identifier*] [*FAA*] (FAAL)
XVP .... Executive Vice President
XVR .... Exchange Voltage Regulator [*Telecommunications*] (TEL)
XVT .... Extensible Virtual Toolkit [*Data processing*]
XVT .... Rome, NY [*Location identifier*] [*FAA*] (FAAL)
XVTR .... Transverter (AAG)
XW .... Ex-Warrants [*Without Warrants*] [*Finance*] (SPSG)
XW .... Experimental Warhead
XW .... Extra Wide [*Size*]
XW .... Laos [*Aircraft nationality and registration mark*] (FAAC)
X-WARR ... Ex-Warrants [*Without Warrants*] [*Finance*]
XWAVE..... Extraordinary Wave (IEEE)
X-WAY ...... Expressway
XWB .... Ozark, Fort Rucker, AL [*Location identifier*] [*FAA*] (FAAL)
XWC .... Wabash-Carnegie Public Library, Wabash, IN [*OCLC symbol*] (OCLC)
XWCC .... Expanded Water Column Characterization [*Oceanography*] (MSC)
XWS .... Experimental Weapon Specification
XWS .... Experimental Weapon System
XWY .... West Union, IA [*Location identifier*] [*FAA*] (FAAL)
XX .... Dos Equis [*Beer*] [*Standard Brands, Inc.*]
XX .... Double Excellent
XX .... Doublecross Committee [*British military*] (DMA)
XX .... Feminine Chromosome Pair
XX .... Heavy [*Used to qualify weather phenomena such as rain, e.g., heavy rain equals XXRA*] [*Aviation code*] (FAAC)
xx .... No Place [*or Unknown*] [*MARC country of publication code*] [*Library of Congress*] (LCCP)
X-X............. Pitch Axis [*Aerospace*] (AAG)
XX .... Twenty Committee [*British espionage unit named after a "double-cross" operation it conducted during World War II*]
XX .... Without Securities or Warrants [*Business term*]
XXC .... University of South Dakota, Card Reproduction Project, Vermillion, SD [*OCLC symbol*] (OCLC)
XXC .... Xerox Canada, Inc. [*Toronto Stock Exchange symbol*]
XXL .... Extra-Extra Large [*Size*]
XXS .... Extra-Extra Strong
XXSTR ...... Double Extra Strong
XXUS........ Maxxus, Inc. [*NASDAQ symbol*] (NQ)
XXX .... International Urgency Signal
XXX .... Peru, IN [*Location identifier*] [*FAA*] (FAAL)
XXX .... Test Flight Plan [*Aviation code*] (FAAC)
XXX .... Triple Excellent
XY .... Burma [*Aircraft nationality and registration mark*] (FAAC)
XY .... Masculine Chromosome Pair
XY .... Spouse [*Citizens band radio slang*]
XY .... Xylography [*Wood engraving*] (ROG)
XYA .... X-Y Axis
XYA .... Yandina [*Solomon Islands*] [*Airport symbol*] (OAG)
XYAT........ X-Y Axis Table
XYC .... Irvine, KY [*Location identifier*] [*FAA*] (FAAL)
XYD......... Daughter [*Citizens band radio slang*]
XYL .... Ex-Young-Lady [*Wife*] [*Amateur radio slang*]
XYL .... Xylocaine [*Topical anesthetic*] [*Astra trademark for lidocaine*]
XYL .... Xylophone [*Music*]
Xyl.......... Xylose [*Also, x*] [*A sugar*]
XYLO .... Xylophone [*Music*] (ADA)
XYM .... Husband [*Citizens band radio slang*]
XYO........... Mayotte [*ANSI three-letter standard code*] (CNC)
XYP .... X-Y Plotter
XYR .... X-Y Recorder

XYrDev...... Ten-Year Device [*Military decoration*]
XYVI.......... Xyvision, Inc. [*Wakefield, MA*] [*NASDAQ symbol*] (NQ)
XYX .... Xytronyx, Inc. [*AMEX symbol*] (SPSG)
XYXXU ..... High Plains Genetics Uts [*NASDAQ symbol*] (NQ)
XYZ .... Examine Your Zipper
XYZ .... Extra Years of Zest [*Gerontology*]
XZ .... Burma [*Aircraft nationality and registration mark*] (FAAC)
XZY .... Philadelphia, PA [*Location identifier*] [*FAA*] (FAAL)

Y

Y................ Admittance [*Symbol*] [*IUPAC*]
Y................ Alleghany Corp. [*NYSE symbol*] (SPSG)
Y................ Closed at Sea (for High Degree of Emergency Readiness) [*Ship's fittings classification*]
Y................ Coach [*Airline fare code*]
Y................ Doublecross [*i.e., to betray*] [*Criminal slang*]
Y................ Except Sixth Form [*For the wearing of schoolgirls' uniforms*] [*British*]
Y................ Late Operating Contact [*Symbol*] (DEN)
Y................ Luminance
Y................ Male Chromosome
Y................ Nominal Gross National Product
Y................ Pathfinder [*Army skill qualification identifier*] (INF)
Y................ Planck Function [*Symbol*] [*IUPAC*]
Y................ Prototype [*Designation for all US military aircraft*]
Y................ [*A*] Pyrimidine Nucleoside [*One-letter symbol; see Pyd*]
Y................ Symbol for Upsilon
Y................ Tanker [*Army symbol*]
Y................ Three-Phase Star Connection [*Symbol*] (DEN)
Y................ Transitional Testing [*Aircraft*]
Y................ Tyrosine [*One-letter symbol; see Tyr*]
Y................ [*The Second*] Unknown Quantity [*Mathematics*] (ROG)
Y................ Vertical Deflection [*Symbol*] (DEN)
Y................ Y-Axis
Y................ Yacht (ADA)
Y................ Yankee [*Phonetic alphabet*] [*International*] (DSUE)
Y................ Yard [*Measure*]
Y................ Yaw
Y................ Yea [*Vote*]
Y................ Year
Y................ Yeates' Pennsylvania Reports [*1791-1808*] [*A publication*] (DLA)
Y................ Yellow [*Horticulture*]
Y................ Yellow [*Phonetic alphabet*] [*Royal Navy*] [*World War I*] (DSUE)
Y................ Yen [*Monetary unit in Japan*]
Y................ Yeoman
Y................ Yersinea [*A genus of bacteria*]
Y................ Yerushalmi [*Palestinian Talmud*] (BJA)
Y................ Yield [*Stock exchange term*] [*Agriculture*]
Y................ Yoke [*Phonetic alphabet*] [*World War II*] (DSUE)
Y................ Yorker [*Phonetic alphabet*] [*Pre-World War II*] (DSUE)
Y................ Yoshitomi Pharmaceutical Ind. Co. Ltd. [*Japan*] [*Research code symbol*]
Y................ You
Y................ Young Men's [*or Women's*] Christian Association [*Short form of reference, especially to the group's building or specific facility, as "the Y swimming pool"*]
Y................ Young Vic [*British theatrical company*]
Y................ Younger [*or Youngest*]
Y................ Young's Modulus of Elasticity [*Symbol*] [*See also E, YME*]
Y................ Your
Y................ Yttrium [*Preferred form, but see also Yt*] [*Chemical element*]
Y................ Yugoslavia [*IYRU nationality code*] (IYR)
Y................ Yukon News [*A publication*]
Y................ Yukon Standard Time [*Aviation*] (FAAC)
Y................ Yuppie [*As in Y-people*]
4Y................ Selective Service classification suggested by comedian Bob Hope for himself during World War II [*Y stood for "yellow"*]
5Y................ Kenya [*Aircraft nationality and registration mark*] (FAAC)
6Y................ Jamaica [*Aircraft nationality and registration mark*] (FAAC)
9Y................ Trinidad and Tobago [*Aircraft nationality and registration mark*] (FAAC)
Y (Day) ...... June 1, 1944, the deadline for all preparations for the Normandy invasion [*World War II*]
YA.............. Afghanistan [*Aircraft nationality and registration mark*] (FAAC)
YA.............. Ash Lighter [*Navy symbol*]
YA.............. Government Civil Aviation Authority [*ICAO designator*] (ICDA)

YA............. Yachting Association [*Australia*]
YA............. Yaw Axis
YA............. Yeda-'am. Journal. Hebrew Folklore Society [*Tel-Aviv*] [*A publication*]
YA............. YIVO Annual [*A publication*]
Y/A............. York-Antwerp Rules [*Marine insurance*]
YA............. Yosemite Association (EA)
YA............. Young Adult [*Refers to books published for this market*]
YA............. Young Anglican [*Australia*]
YA............. Young Audiences (EA)
YAA........... Yachtsmen's Association of America (EA)
YAA........... Youth Ambassadors of America [*Later, YAI*] (EA)
YAA........... Yugoslav Survey [*A publication*]
YAAR......... Yacimientos Arqueologicos [*Database*] [*Ministerio de Cultura*] [*Spanish*] [*Information service or system*] (CRD)
YAASC...... Youth Affairs Advisory Sub-Committee [*Australia*]
YABA......... Yacht Architects and Brokers Association (EA)
YABA......... Young American Bowling Alliance (EA)
YABC........ Yesterday's Authors of Books for Children [*A publication*]
YABRI....... Young Adult Book Review Index [*A publication*]
YAC........... Yeast Artificial Chromosome [*Genetics*] [*Biochemistry*]
YAC........... Young Adult Council of National Social Welfare Assembly (EA)
YAC........... Young Astronaut Council (EA)
YACC......... Young Adult Conservation Corps
YACC......... Young America's Campaign Committee [*Later, FCM*] (EA)
YACE........ Yukon Alpine Centennial Expedition
Yacht......... Yachting [*A publication*]
YACTOFF ... Yaw Actuator Offset (KSC)
Yad........... Yadaim (BJA)
YAD........... Young's Nova Scotia Admiralty Decisions [*A publication*] (DLA)
Yad Energ.. Yadrena Energiya [*A publication*]
Yadernaya Fiz ... Akademiya Nauk SSSR. Yadernaya Fizika [*A publication*]
Yad Fiz....... Yadernaya Fizika [*A publication*]
Yad Geofiz ... Yadernaya Geofizika [*A publication*]
Yad-Geofiz Issled Geofiz Sb ... Yaderno-Geofizicheskie Issledovaniya, Geofizicheskii Sbornik [*USSR*] [*A publication*]
YADH........ Yeast Alcohol Dehydrogenase [*An enzyme*]
Ya Div Q .... Yale Divinity Quarterly [*New Haven, CT*] [*A publication*]
Yad Konstanty ... Yadernye Konstanty [*A publication*]
Yad Magn Rezon ... Yadernyi Magnitnyi Rezonans [*A publication*]
Yad Magn Rezon Org Khim ... Yadernyi Magnitnyi Rezonans v Organicheskoi Khimii [*A publication*]
Yad Priborostr ... Yadernoe Priborostroenie [*USSR*] [*A publication*]
Yad Vashem Stud Eur Jew Catastrophe Resist ... Yad Vashem Studies on the European Jewish Catastrophe and Resistance [*A publication*]
YAEC........ Yankee Atomic Electric Company
YAF .... Asbestos Hill [*Canada*] [*Airport symbol*] [*Obsolete*] (OAG)
YAF .... Yidishe Arbeter Froyen (BJA)
YAF .... Young Americans for Freedom (EA)
YAF .... Young America's Foundation (EA)
YAF .... Yugoslavian Air Force
YAG........... Fort Frances [*Canada*] [*Airport symbol*] (OAG)
YAG........... Miscellaneous Auxiliary [*Self-propelled*] [*Navy ship symbol*]
YAG........... Yagi [*Kashiwara*] [*Japan*] [*Seismograph station code, US Geological Survey*] [*Closed*] (SEIS)
YAG........... Young Actors Guild (EA)
YAG........... Yttrium-Aluminum Garnet [*LASER technology*]
YAGL .... Yttrium Aluminum Garnet LASER
YAGR........ Ocean RADAR Station Ship [*Navy symbol*] [*Obsolete*]
YAH.......... Alfred University, Alfred, NY [*OCLC symbol*] (OCLC)
YAH.......... Yahtse [*Alaska*] [*Seismograph station code, US Geological Survey*] (SEIS)
YAI .... Young Adult Institute and Workshop (EA)
YAI .... Youth Ambassadors International (EA)
YAIC......... Young American Indian Council
YAJ........... Yeda-'am. Journal. Hebrew Folklore Society [*Tel-Aviv*] [*A publication*]
YAJ........... Yorkshire Archaeological Journal [*A publication*]

YAK .... Yakovlev [*Russian aircraft symbol; initialism taken from name of aircraft's designer*]
YAK .... Yakutat [*Alaska*] [*Airport symbol*] (OAG)
YAK .... Yakutsk [*USSR*] [*Seismograph station code, US Geological Survey*] (SEIS)
YAK .... Yakutsk [*USSR*] [*Geomagnetic observatory code*]
YAKUA ..... Yakuzaigaku [*A publication*]
YAKUA2 ... Archives of Practical Pharmacy [*A publication*]
Yakugaku Zasshi J Pharmaceut Soc Jap ... Yakugaku Zasshi/Journal of the Pharmaceutical Society of Japan [*A publication*]
Yal .... Yalkut Shim'oni (BJA)
YAL .... Yalta [*USSR*] [*Seismograph station code, US Geological Survey*] [*Closed*] (SEIS)
YAL .... Yosemite Airlines [*Columbia, CA*] [*FAA designator*] (FAAC)
YAL .... Yttrium Aluminum LASER
Yale Art Gal Bul ... Yale University. Art Gallery. Bulletin [*A publication*]
Yale Associates Bul ... Yale University. Associates in Fine Arts. Bulletin [*A publication*]
Yale Bicen Pub Contr Miner ... Yale Bicentennial Publications. Contributions to Mineralogy and Petrography [*A publication*]
Yale ClSt .... Yale Classical Studies [*A publication*]
Yale Div Q ... Yale Divinity Quarterly [*A publication*]
Yale Forestry Bull ... Yale University. School of Forestry. Bulletin [*A publication*]
Yale French Stud ... Yale French Studies [*A publication*]
Yale Fr St... Yale French Studies [*A publication*]
Yale Fr Stud ... Yale French Studies [*A publication*]
Yale Ital S ... Yale Italian Studies [*A publication*]
Yale J Biol ... Yale Journal of Biology and Medicine [*A publication*]
Yale J Biol Med ... Yale Journal of Biology and Medicine [*A publication*]
Yale J World Pub Ord ... Yale Journal of World Public Order [*A publication*]
Yale Law J ... Yale Law Journal [*A publication*]
Yale Lit Mag ... Yale Literary Magazine [*A publication*]
Yale L J ..... Yale Law Journal [*A publication*]
Yale L & Pol'y Rev ... Yale Law and Policy Review [*A publication*] (DLA)
Yale Math Monographs ... Yale Mathematical Monographs [*A publication*]
Yale R .... Yale Review [*A publication*]
Yale Rev ..... Yale Review [*A publication*]
Yale Rev Law & Soc Act'n ... Yale Review of Law and Social Action [*A publication*] (DLA)
Yale Rev of L and Soc Action ... Yale Review of Law and Social Action [*A publication*] (DLA)
Yale Sci ...... Yale Scientific [*A publication*]
Yale Scient Mag ... Yale Scientific Magazine [*A publication*]
Yale Sci Mag ... Yale Scientific Magazine [*A publication*]
Yale Sc Mo ... Yale Scientific Monthly [*A publication*]
Yale Stud World PO ... Yale Studies in World Public Order [*A publication*]
Yale Stud World Pub Ord ... Yale Studies in World Public Order [*A publication*]
Yale St Wld Pub Ord ... Yale Studies in World Public Order [*A publication*]
Yale U Lib Gaz ... Yale University. Library. Gazette [*A publication*]
Yale U Libr ... Yale University. Library. Gazette [*A publication*]
Yale Univ Art Gal Bull ... Yale University. Art Gallery. Bulletin [*A publication*]
Yale Univ B ... Yale University. Art Gallery. Bulletin [*A publication*]
Yale Univ Lib Gaz ... Yale University. Library. Gazette [*A publication*]
Yale Univ Peabody Mus Nat Hist Annu Rep ... Yale University. Peabody Museum of Natural History. Annual Report [*A publication*]
Yale Univ Peabody Mus Nat Hist Bull ... Yale University. Peabody Museum of Natural History. Bulletin [*A publication*]
Yale Univ Peabody Mus Nat History Bull ... Yale University. Peabody Museum of Natural History. Bulletin [*A publication*]
Yale Univ Sch For Bull ... Yale University. School of Forestry. Bulletin [*A publication*]
Yale Univ Sch For Environ Stud Bull ... Yale University. School of Forestry and Environmental Studies. Bulletin [*A publication*]
Yalkut Le-Sivim Tekhnol U-Minhal Shel Tekst ... Yalkut Le-sivim Tekhnologyah U-Minhal Shel Tekstil [*A publication*]
Y Alm .... Yurosholayimer Almanakh [*A publication*]
YalMakh ... Yalkut Makhiri (BJA)
YAM .... American Museum of Natural History, New York, NY [*OCLC symbol*] (OCLC)
YAM .... Sault Ste. Marie [*Canada*] [*Airport symbol*] (OAG)
YAM .... Yamagata [*Japan*] [*Seismograph station code, US Geological Survey*] (SEIS)
YAM .... Yet Another MODEM [*Modulator-Demodulator*] [*Communications program*]
YAM .... Young Australian Male [*Lifestyle classification*]
Yamaguchi Med ... Yamaguchi Medicine [*Japan*] [*A publication*]
YAN .... Yancey Railroad Co. [*AAR code*]
YAN .... Yangoru [*Papua New Guinea*] [*Seismograph station code, US Geological Survey*] (SEIS)
YANCON ... Yankee Conference [*College sports*]
YANGPAT ... Yangtze Patrol, Asiatic Fleet [*Navy*]
YANK .... Yankee (ROG)
YANK .... Youth of America Needs to Know
yao .... Yao (Bantu) [*MARC language code*] [*Library of Congress*] (LCCP)
YAO .... Yaounde [*Cameroon*] [*Airport symbol*] (OAG)
YAP .... Yap [*Caroline Islands*] [*Airport symbol*] (OAG)

YAP .... Yaw and Pitch
YAP .... Yield Analysis Pattern [*Data processing*]
Yap .... Young Aspiring Professional [*Lifestyle classification*] [*In book title "YAP; the Official Young Aspiring Professional's Fast-Track Handbook"*]
YAP .... Younger American Playwright [*Slang*]
YAPD .... Young Americans of Polish Descent (EA)
YAPLO .... Yorkshire Association of Power Loom Overlookers [*A union*] [*British*] (DCTA)
Yappie .... Young Artist Professional [*Lifestyle classification*]
YAPRA .... Yadernoe Priborostroenie [*A publication*]
YAR .... Yemen Arab Republic
YAR .... York-Antwerp Rules [*Marine insurance*]
YARA .... Young Americans for Responsible Action
Y-ARD .... Yarrow Admiralty Research Department [*Navy*] [*British*]
Yard R .... Yardbird Reader [*A publication*]
Yarosl Gos Univ Mezhvuz Temat Sb ... Yaroslavskii Gosudarstvennyi Universitet. Mezhvuzovskii Tematicheskii Sbornik [*A publication*]
YARU .... Yale Arbovirus Research Unit [*Yale University*] [*Research center*] (RCD)
YAS .... Yasodhara Ashram Society (EA)
YAS .... Yaw Attitude Sensor
YASD .... Young Adult Services Division - of ALA [*American Library Association*] (EA)
YASIG .... Young Adult Special Interest Group [*Canadian Library Association*]
YASOQB ... Ye Anciente and Secret Order of Quiet Birdmen (EA)
YAT .... Attawapiskat [*Canada*] [*Airport symbol*] (OAG)
YAT .... Yaldymych [*USSR*] [*Seismograph station code, US Geological Survey*] [*Closed*] (SEIS)
Yate-Lee ..... Yates-Lee on Bankruptcy [*3rd ed.*] [*1887*] [*A publication*] (DLA)
Yates Sel Cas ... Yates' Select Cases [*1809*] [*New York*] [*A publication*] (DLA)
Yates Sel Cas (NY) ... Yates' Select Cases [*1809*] [*New York*] [*A publication*] (DLA)
YATS .... Youth Attitude Tracking Survey [*Navy*]
YAUI .... Yet Another User Interface [*Data processing*]
YAVIS .... Young, Attractive, Verbal, Intelligent, and Successful
Yawata Tech Rep ... Yawata Technical Report [*A publication*]
YAWF .... Youth Against War and Fascism (EA)
Yawnie .... Youngish Anglophone of Westmount and Notre-Dame-De-Grace [*Lifestyle classification*] [*Canadian Yuppie identified in Keith Harrison's novel "After Six Days"*]
YAWP .... Yet Another Word Processor (BYTE)
YB .... Meteorological Operational Telecommunications Network Europe [*ICAO designator*] (ICDA)
YB .... Yard Bird [*Confined to camp*] [*Military slang*]
YB .... Year Book of Reports of Cases [*A publication*]
YB .... Year Books [*Law*] [*United Kingdom*] [*A publication*]
YB .... Yearbook
Yb .... Yearbook of Comparative and General Literature [*A publication*]
YB .... Yellowknife Bear Resources, Inc. [*Toronto Stock Exchange symbol*]
YB .... Yeshiva Benarroch. Tetuan (BJA)
YB .... YIVO Bleter [*Vilna/New York*] [*A publication*]
YB .... Yorkshire Bulletin of Economic and Social Research [*A publication*]
YB .... Your Business [*A publication*] (ADA)
YB .... Ysgrifau Beirniadol [*A publication*]
Yb .... Ytterbium [*Chemical element*]
YBA .... Youth Basketball Association [*Joint program of NBA Players' Association and YMCA*]
YBAAA ...... Yearbook. Association of Attenders of Alumni of the Hague Academy of International Law [*A publication*] (DLA)
Yb Agric Coop ... Yearbook of Agricultural Cooperation [*A publication*]
Yb Agric US Dep Agric ... Yearbook of Agriculture. US Department of Agriculture [*A publication*]
YB Air & Space L ... Yearbook of Air and Space Law [*A publication*] (DLA)
YB Ames .... Year Book. Ames Foundation [*A publication*] (DLA)
YBASL .... Yearbook of Air and Space Law [*A publication*] (DLA)
YBBFC .... Younger Brothers Band Fan Club (EA)
YBC .... Baie Comeau [*Canada*] [*Airport symbol*] (OAG)
YBC .... Yale Babylonian Collection (BJA)
YBCA .... Yearbook of Commercial Arbitration [*A publication*] (DLA)
Yb Calif Avocado Soc ... Yearbook. California Avocado Society [*A publication*]
YBCO .... Yttrium Barium Copper Oxide [*Inorganic chemistry*]
YBD .... Bowdock [*Navy symbol*]
YBD .... Yellow Band Resources [*Vancouver Stock Exchange symbol*]
YBD .... Young British Designers
YBDRE3 ... Year Book of Diagnostic Radiology [*A publication*]
YBDSA .... Yacht Designers and Surveyors Association (EAIO)
YBE .... Stewart Aviation Services, Inc. [*FAA designator*] (FAAC)
YBE .... Uranium City [*Canada*] [*Airport symbol*] (OAG)
YBE .... York Borough Board of Education, Professional Education Library [*UTLAS symbol*]
YB Ed I ...... Year Books of Edward I [*A publication*] (DLA)
Yb Educ ...... Yearbook of Education [*A publication*]

YB Eur Conv on Human Rights ... Year Book. European Convention on Human Rights [*A publication*]   (DLA)
Yb of the Eur Conv on Human Rights ... Yearbook. European Convention on Human Rights [*The Hague, Netherlands*] [*A publication*]   (DLA)
YB Europ Conv HR ... Yearbook. European Convention on Human Rights [*The Hague, Netherlands*] [*A publication*]   (DLA)
YBG .... Saguenay [*Canada*] [*Airport symbol*]   (OAG)
Yb Gen Med ... Yearbook of General Medicine [*A publication*]
Yb Gen Surg ... Yearbook of General Surgery [*A publication*]
Yb Gloucester Beekprs Ass ... Yearbook. Gloucestershire Bee-Keepers Association [*A publication*]
YBHSEQ... Year Book of Hand Surgery [*A publication*]
YB Human Rights ... Yearbook on Human Rights [*A publication*]   (DLA)
YB Hum Rts ... Yearbook on Human Rights [*A publication*]   (DLA)
YBI............ Youth Business Initiative [*Australia*]
YBICJ........ Yearbook. International Court of Justice [*A publication*]   (DLA)
YBICSU .... Yearbook. International Council of Scientific Unions [*A publication*]
YBIEC ...... Yugoslav Bank for International Economic Cooperation
Yb Ind Orthop Surg ... Yearbook of Industrial and Orthopedic Surgery [*A publication*]
Yb Inter Amer M Research ... Yearbook for Inter-American Musical Research [*A publication*]
Yb Int Folk M Council ... Yearbook. International Folk Music Council [*A publication*]
YB Int L Comm ... Yearbook. International Law Community [*A publication*]   (DLA)
YB Int'l L Comm'n ... Yearbook. International Law Commission [*A publication*]   (DLA)
YB Int'l Org ... Yearbook of International Organizations [*A publication*]   (DLA)
YBJ............ Baie Johan Beetz [*Canada*] [*Airport symbol*]   (OAG)
YBK .... Baker Lake [*Canada*] [*Airport symbol*]   (OAG)
YBL............ Campbell River [*Canada*] [*Airport symbol*]   (OAG)
YB League ... Yearbook. League of Nations [*A publication*]   (DLA)
Yb of Leg Stud ... Year Book of Legal Studies [*Madras, India*] [*A publication*]   (DLA)
YbLitgSt .... Yearbook of Liturgical Studies [*Notre Dame, IN*] [*A publication*]
YBM .... State University of New York, College at Buffalo, Buffalo, NY [*OCLC symbol*]   (OCLC)
Yb Med ...... Yearbook of Medicine [*A publication*]
Yb Med Ass Great Cy NY ... Yearbook. Medical Association of the Greater City of New York [*A publication*]
Yb Neurol Psychiat Endocr ... Yearbook of Neurology, Psychiatry, Endocrinology, and Neurosurgery [*A publication*]
Yb Ophthal ... Yearbook of Ophthalmology [*A publication*]
YBP............ Years before Present
YBPC......... Young Black Programmers Coalition   (EA)
Yb Pediat ... Yearbook of Pediatrics [*A publication*]
YB P1 Edw II ... Year Books, Part 1, Edward II [*A publication*]   (DLA)
Yb Phys Med Rehabil ... Yearbook of Physical Medicine and Rehabilitation [*A publication*]
Yb Phys Soc ... Yearbook. Physical Society [*A publication*]
YBPS......... Yearbook. British Pirandello Society [*A publication*]
YBR .... Brandon [*Canada*] [*Airport symbol*]   (OAG)
YBR .... Sludge Removal Barge [*Navy*]
YBR .... Yellow Brick Road [*Intelligence test*]
YBRA......... Yellowstone-Bighorn Research Association   (EA)
Yb R Hort Soc ... Yearbook. Royal Horticulture Society [*A publication*]
YB Rich II ... Bellewe's Les Ans du Roy Richard le Second [*1378-1400*] [*A publication*]   (DLA)
YBRIF ...... Yellowknife Bear Resources, Inc. [*NASDAQ symbol*]   (NQ)
YB (Rolls Ser) ... Year Books, Rolls Series [*1292-1546*] [*A publication*]   (DLA)
YB (RS)..... Year Books, Rolls Series [*1292-1546*] [*A publication*]   (DLA)
YB (RS)..... Year Books, Rolls Series, Edited by Horwood [*1292-1307*] [*A publication*]   (DLA)
YB (RS)..... Year Books, Rolls Series, Edited by Horwood and Pike [*1337-46*] [*A publication*]   (DLA)
Yb R Vet Agric Coll ... Yearbook. Royal Veterinary and Agricultural College [*A publication*]
YBSC........ Year Books, Selected Cases [*A publication*]   (DLA)
YB Sch L.... Year Books of School Law [*A publication*]   (DLA)
YB (Sel Soc) ... Year Books, Selden Society [*1307-19*] [*A publication*]   (DLA)
Yb Soc........ Yearbook. Royal Society of London [*A publication*]
Yb Soc Pol Britain ... Yearbook of Social Policy in Britain [*A publication*]
YB (SS)...... Year Books, Selden Society [*1307-19*] [*A publication*]   (DLA)
YBT .... Yale Oriental Series. Babylonian Texts [*New Haven, CT*] [*A publication*]   (BJA)
YBT .... Youssef Ben Tachfine [*Morocco*] [*Seismograph station code, US Geological Survey*]   (SEIS)
YBUN....... Yearbook of the United Nations [*A publication*]   (DLA)
Yb US Dep Agric ... Yearbook. United States Department of Agriculture [*A publication*]
YBV .... Berens River [*Canada*] [*Airport symbol*]   (OAG)
Yb Wld Aff ... Yearbook of World Affairs [*A publication*]
Yb World Aff ... Yearbook of World Affairs [*A publication*]
YB World Pol ... Yearbook of World Polity [*A publication*]   (DLA)

YBX .... Blanc Sablon [*Canada*] [*Airport symbol*]   (OAG)
Yb Yorks Beekprs Ass ... Yearbook. Yorkshire Beekeepers Association [*A publication*]
Y/C .... Luminance, Color
YC............. Open Lighter [*Non-self-propelled*] [*Navy symbol*]
YC............. Rescue Coordination Center [*ICAO designator*]   (ICDA)
YC............. Y-Chromosome
YC............. Yacht Club
YC............. Yale College   (ROG)
YC............. Yankee Conference [*College sports*]
YC............. Yard Craft [*Navy symbol*]
YC............. Yaw Channel
YC............. Yaw Coupling
YC............. Yeomanry Cavalry [*Military*] [*British*]
YC............. Yesterday's Children   (EA)
YC............. Yola Clay Loam [*A soil type*]
Y & C .... Younge and Collyer's English Chancery Reports [*1841-43*] [*A publication*]   (DLA)
Y & C .... Younge and Collyer's English Exchequer Equity Reports [*1834-42*] [*A publication*]   (DLA)
y/c .... Your Cable   (DS)
YC............. Youth Clubs [*Public-performance tariff class*] [*British*]
YC............. Youth Conservative [*Political party*] [*British*]
YCA .... Yachting Club of America   (EA)
YCA .... Yale-China Association   (EA)
YCA .... Yield Component Analysis [*Botany*]
YCA .... Young Concert Artists   (EA)
YCA .... Young Conservative Alliance of America [*Later, Campus Action Network*]   (EA)
YCAP........ Youth Committee Against Poverty
YCB .... Cambridge Bay [*Canada*] [*Airport symbol*]   (OAG)
YCB .... Yeast Carbon Base
YCB .... Yellow Creek Bluff [*Alaska*] [*Seismograph station code, US Geological Survey*]   (SEIS)
YCC .... Computer Center [*Yale University*] [*Research center*]   (RCD)
YCC .... Yearbook of Comparative Criticism [*A publication*]
YCC .... York Centre [*Vancouver Stock Exchange symbol*]
YCC .... Youth Civic Center
YCC .... Youth Conservation Corps   (EA)
YCC .... Yuma City-County Public Library, Yuma, AZ [*OCLC symbol*]   (OCLC)
YCCA .... National Youth Council on Civic Affairs [*Superseded by CCNYA*]   (EA)
YCCA .... Yorkshire Canary Club of America   (EA)
Y & CCC.... Younge and Collyer's English Chancery Cases [*62-63 English Reprint*] [*1841-43*] [*A publication*]   (DLA)
Y & C Ch ... Younge and Collyer's English Chancery Reports [*1841-43*] [*A publication*]   (DLA)
Y & C Ch Cas ... Younge and Collyer's English Chancery Cases [*62-63 English Reprint*] [*1841-43*] [*A publication*]   (DLA)
YCCIP ...... Youth Community Conservation and Improvement Projects [*Department of Labor*]
YCD .... Fueling Barge [*Navy symbol*] [*Obsolete*]
YCD .... Nanaimo [*Canada*] [*Airport symbol*]   (OAG)
YCD .... Youth Correction Division [*Department of Justice*]
YCEE........ Youth Cost per Entered Employment [*Job Training and Partnership Act*]   (OICC)
Y & C Ex.... Younge and Collyer's English Exchequer Equity Reports [*1834-42*] [*A publication*]   (DLA)
Y & C Exch ... Younge and Collyer's English Exchequer Equity Reports [*1834-42*] [*A publication*]   (DLA)
YCF........... Car Float [*Non-self-propelled*] [*Navy symbol*]
YCF........... Yankee Critical Facility [*Nuclear energy*]
YCF........... Young Calvinist Federation   (EA)
YCF........... Young Conservative Foundation [*Later, CAF*]   (EA)
YCF........... Youth Citizenship Fund   (EA)
YCG .... Castlegar [*Canada*] [*Airport symbol*]   (OAG)
YCGL........ Yearbook of Comparative and General Literature [*A publication*]
YCH..........: Chatham [*Canada*] [*Airport symbol*]   (OAG)
YCHP .... Yenching Journal of Chinese Studies [*A publication*]
YCI .... Year-Class Strength Index [*Pisciculture*]
YCI .... Young Communist International [*Dissolved, 1943*]
YCJCYAQFTJB ... Your Curiosity Just Cost You a Quarter for the Jukebox [*Tavern sign*]
YCK .... Open Cargo Lighter [*Navy ship symbol*] [*Obsolete*]
YCKKAK... Acta Gerontologica Japonica [*A publication*]
YCL........... Charlo [*Canada*] [*Airport symbol*]   (OAG)
YCL........... Yolk Cytoplasmic Layer [*Embryology*]
YCL........... Young Communist League of the United States of America   (EA)
YCL........... Youth Counseling League   (EA)
YCLA......... Young Circle League of America [*Later, Workmen's Circle*]   (EA)
YCLS .... Yale Classical Studies [*A publication*]
YCM .... State University of New York, College at Cortland, Cortland, NY [*OCLC symbol*]   (OCLC)
YCM .... YMCA Camp [*Montana*] [*Seismograph station code, US Geological Survey*] [*Closed*]   (SEIS)
YCM .... Young Christian Movement [*Formerly, YCW*] [*Defunct*]
YCMD .... Yaw Gimbal Command   (KSC)

YCN........... Cochrane [*Canada*] [*Airport symbol*]   (OAG)
YCNP .... Yellow Creek Nuclear Plant   (NRCH)
YCO........... Coppermine [*Canada*] [*Airport symbol*]   (OAG)
Y & Coll ..... Younge and Collyer's English Chancery Reports [*1841-43*] [*A publication*]   (DLA)
Y & Coll ..... Younge and Collyer's English Exchequer Equity Reports [*1834-42*] [*A publication*]   (DLA)
YCOMA .... Yearbook. Coke Oven Managers' Association [*A publication*]
YCP........... Yaw Coupling Parameter
YCp........... Yeast Centromere Plasmid [*Genetics*]
YCP........... York College of Pennsylvania, York, PA [*OCLC symbol*]   (OCLC)
YCP........... Youth Challenge Program
YCR .... Cross Lake [*Canada*] [*Airport symbol*]   (OAG)
YCS........... High School Young Christian Students   (EA)
YCS........... Yale Classical Studies [*A publication*]
YCS........... Yorkshire Celtic Studies [*A publication*]
YCS........... Young Collector Series [*A publication*]
YCS........... Youth Community Service [*ACTION project*]
YCSL......... Yorkridge-Calvert Savings & Loan Association [*NASDAQ symbol*]   (NQ)
YCSM........ Young Christian Student Movement
YCSN......... Yukon Conservation Society. Newsletter [*A publication*]
Y C T......... Young Cinema and Theatre [*A publication*]
YCTF .... Younger Chemists Task Force [*American Chemical Society*]
YCTSD ...... Yugoslav Center for Technical and Scientific Documentation [*Information service or system*]   (IID)
YCU .... Youth Clubs United
YCV .... Aircraft Transportation Lighter [*Non-self-propelled*] [*Navy symbol*]
YCV .... Young Citizens Volunteers [*14th (Service) Battalion, Royal Irish Rifles*] [*British military*]   (DMA)
YCW .... Young Christian Workers [*Later, YCM*]   (EA)
YCWCDP ... Acta Botanica Yunnanica [*A publication*]
YCY .... Clyde River [*Canada*] [*Airport symbol*]   (OAG)
YCZ .... Yellow Caution Zone [*Runway lighting*] [*Aviation*]
YD............. Authority Supervising the Aerodrome [*ICAO designator*]   (ICDA)
Y & D .... Bureau of Yards and Docks [*Later, NFEC*] [*Navy*]
YD............. Floating Crane [*Non-self-propelled*] [*Navy symbol*]
YD............. People's Democratic Republic of Yemen [*ANSI two-letter standard code*]   (CNC)
YD............. Yard [*Navy*]
YD............. Yard [*Measure*]
YD............. Yaw Deviation
YD............. Yoreh De'ah. Shulhan 'Arukh   (BJA)
YD............. Yorkshire Dragoons [*British military*]   (DMA)
YD³............ Cubic Yard
YDA.......... Yesterday   (FAAC)
YDA.......... Young Democrats of America   (EA)
YDAW .... Dawson Public Library, Yukon [*Library symbol*] [*National Library of Canada*]   (NLC)
YDAY .... Yesterday [*Business term*]
YDB........... Yield Diffusion Bonding
YDB........... Youth Development Bureau [*Department of Health and Human Services*]
YDC........... Yaw Damper Computer
YDC........... Yeast Extract - Dextrose Calcium Carbonate Agar [*Microbiology*]
YDC........... Yiddish Dictionary Committee   (EA)
YDC........... Youth for Development and Cooperation   (EAIO)
YDCA........ Young Democratic Clubs of America [*Later, YDA*]   (EA)
YDDPA ..... Youth Development and Delinquency Prevention Administration [*Later, Youth Development Bureau*] [*HEW*]
YDF .... Deer Lake [*Canada*] [*Airport symbol*]   (OAG)
YDG.......... District Degaussing Vessel [*Navy symbol*]
YDI .... Youth Development, Incorporated   (EA)
YDKGA ..... Yamaguchi Daigaku Kogakubu Kenkyu Hokoku [*A publication*]
YDLA .... Young Democratic Labor Association [*Australia*]
YDM.......... State University of New York, College of Ceramics at Alfred University, Alfred, NY [*OCLC symbol*]   (OCLC)
YDN.......... Dauphin [*Canada*] [*Airport symbol*]   (OAG)
YDNGAU ... Bulletin. Faculty of Agriculture. Yamaguchi University [*A publication*]
YDPCK...... Klondike National Historic Site, Parks Canada [*Lieu Historique National Klondike, Parcs Canada*] Dawson City, Yukon [*Library symbol*] [*National Library of Canada*]   (NLC)
YDQ........... Dawson Creek [*Canada*] [*Airport symbol*]   (OAG)
YDQ........... Yale Divinity Quarterly [*A publication*]
YDS .... Yards   (MCD)
YDS .... Yorkshire Dialect Society. Transactions [*A publication*]
YDSD .... Yards and Docks Supply Depot [*Obsolete*] [*Navy*]
YDSO .... Yards and Docks Supply Office [*Navy*]
YDT .... Diving Tender [*Non-self-propelled*] [*Navy symbol*]
YE............. Lighter, Ammunition [*Navy symbol*]
YE............. Year End
YE............. Yeast Enolase [*An enzyme*]
YE ... Yellow Edges
YE............. Yellow Enzyme [*Biochemistry*]

ye............... Yemen Arab Republic [*MARC country of publication code*] [*Library of Congress*]   (LCCP)
YE .... Yemen Arab Republic [*ANSI two-letter standard code*]   (CNC)
YE .... Yevreyskaya Entsiklopediya [*A publication*]   (BJA)
YE .... Youth Entry [*British military*]   (DMA)
YEA .... Yaw Error Amplifier
YEA .... Year of Energy Action
YEA .... Yeast Extract Agar [*Microbiology*]
Yea .... Yeates' Pennsylvania Reports [*1791-1808*] [*A publication*]   (DLA)
YEA .... Young Engineers Australia
YEA .... Youth Emotions Anonymous   (EA)
YEA .... Youth Evangelism Association   (EA)
Yearb Agr Co-Op ... Yearbook of Agricultural Co-Operation [*A publication*]
Yearb Agric US Dep Agric ... Yearbook of Agriculture. US Department of Agriculture [*A publication*]
Yearb Agr USDA ... Yearbook of Agriculture. US Department of Agriculture [*A publication*]
Yearb Am Iron Steel Inst ... Yearbook. American Iron and Steel Institute [*A publication*]
Yearb Am Pulp Pap Mil Supt Assoc ... Yearbook. American Pulp and Paper Mill Superintendents Association [*A publication*]
Yearb Anesth ... Yearbook of Anesthesia [*A publication*]
Yearb Bharat Krishak Samaj ... Yearbook. Bharat Krishak Samaj [*A publication*]
Yearb Bur Miner Resour Geol Geophys ... Yearbook. Bureau of Mineral Resources. Geology and Geophysics [*A publication*]
Yearb Bur Miner Resour Geol Geo-Phys (Aus) ... Yearbook. Bureau of Mineral Resources. Geology and Geophysics (Australia) [*A publication*]
Yearb Calif Avocado Soc ... Yearbook. California Avocado Society [*A publication*]
Yearb Calif Macad Soc ... Yearbook. California Macadamia Society [*A publication*]
Yearb Carnegie Inst Wash ... Yearbook. Carnegie Institute of Washington [*A publication*]
Yearb Child Lit Assoc ... Yearbook. Children's Literature Association [*A publication*]
Yearb Coke Oven Managers' Assoc ... Yearbook. Coke Oven Managers' Association [*England*] [*A publication*]
Yearb Dermatol Syphilol ... Yearbook of Dermatology and Syphilology [*A publication*]
Yearb Drug Ther ... Yearbook of Drug Therapy [*A publication*]
Yearb Endocrinol ... Yearbook of Endocrinology [*A publication*]
Yearb Engl Stud ... Yearbook of English Studies [*A publication*]
Yearb Est Learned Soc Am ... Yearbook. Estonian Learned Society in America [*A publication*]
Yearb Fac Agr Univ Ankara ... Yearbook. Faculty of Agriculture. University of Ankara [*A publication*]
Yearb Gen Surg ... Yearbook of General Surgery [*A publication*]
Yearb Inst Geochem Sib Div Acad Sci (USSR) ... Yearbook. Institute of Geochemistry. Siberian Division. Academy of Sciences (USSR) [*A publication*]
Yearb Leo Baeck Inst ... Yearbook. Leo Baeck Institute [*A publication*]
Yearb Med ... Yearbook of Medicine [*A publication*]
Yearb Nat Farmers' Ass ... Yearbook. National Farmers' Association [*A publication*]
Yearb Natl Inst Sci India ... Yearbook. National Institute of Sciences of India [*A publication*]
Year Book Aust ... Year Book Australia [*A publication*]
Year Book Carnegie Inst Wash ... Year Book. Carnegie Institution of Washington [*A publication*]
Year Book Diagn Radiol ... Year Book of Diagnostic Radiology [*A publication*]
Yearbook East-Eur Econ ... Yearbook of East-European Economics [*A publication*]
Year Book Hand Surg ... Year Book of Hand Surgery [*A publication*]
Year Book Indian Natl Sci Acad ... Year Book. Indian National Science Academy [*A publication*]
Year Book Indian Nat Sci Acad ... Year Book. Indian National Science Academy [*A publication*]
Year Book Natl Auricula Primula Soc North Sec ... Year Book. National Auricula and Primula Society. Northern Section [*A publication*]
Year Book Nucl Med ... Year Book of Nuclear Medicine [*United States*] [*A publication*]
Year Book Obstet Gynecol ... Year Book of Obstetrics and Gynecology [*A publication*]
Yearb Pap Ind Manage Assoc ... Yearbook. Paper Industry Management Association [*A publication*]
Yearb Pathol Clin Pathol ... Yearbook of Pathology and Clinical Pathology [*A publication*]
Yearb Pediatr ... Yearbook of Pediatrics [*A publication*]
Yearb Pharm ... Yearbook of Pharmacy [*A publication*]
Yearb P7 Hen VI ... Year Books, Part 7, Henry VI [*A publication*]   (DLA)
Yearb Phys Anthropol ... Yearbook of Physical Anthropology [*A publication*]
Yearb R Asiat Soc Bengal ... Yearbook. Royal Asiatic Society of Bengal [*A publication*]
Year Endocrinol ... Year in Endocrinology [*A publication*]
Year Immunol ... Year in Immunology [*A publication*]
Year Metab ... Year in Metabolism [*A publication*]

Yeates .... Yeates' Pennsylvania Reports [*1791-1808*] [*A publication*] (DLA)
Yeates (PA) ... Yeates' Pennsylvania Reports [*1791-1808*] [*A publication*] (DLA)
Yeats Eliot ... Yeats Eliot Review [*A publication*]
Yeb .... Yebamoth (BJA)
YEC .... Youngest Empty Cell
YEC .... Youth Employment Competency (OICC)
YEC .... Youth Exchange Centre [*Seymour Mews House*] [*British*] (CB)
YEC .... Yugoslav Economic Community (ECON)
YECL .... Young Evangelical Churchmen's League [*Australia*]
YedNum ..... Yedi'ot Numismatiyot be-Yisrael. Jerusalem (BJA)
YEDPA ...... Youth Employment and Demonstration Projects Act of 1977
YEDTA ...... Youth Employment and Demonstration Training Act [*Department of the Interior*]
YEE .... Yale Economic Essays [*A publication*]
Yeepie .... Youthful Energetic Elderly Person Involved in Everything [*Aging yuppie*] [*Lifestyle classification*]
YEER .... Youth Entered Employment Rate [*Job Training and Partnership Act*] (OICC)
Ye Et Rg Rt ... Yorkshire East Riding Regiment [*British military*] (DMA)
YEF .... Young Executives Forum [*Automotive Service Industry Association*]
YEG .... Edmonton [*Canada*] [*Airport symbol*] (OAG)
YEG .... Yeast Extract - Glucose [*Medium*]
YEH .... Yellow Enzyme, Reduced [*Biochemistry*]
YEIMEY ... Year in Immunology [*A publication*]
YEIS .... Yamaha Energy Induction System
YEK .... Eskimo Point [*Canada*] [*Airport symbol*] (OAG)
YEL .... Elliot Lake [*Canada*] [*Airport symbol*] (OAG)
YEL .... Equitable Life Assurance Society of the United States, General Library, New York, NY [*OCLC symbol*] (OCLC)
YEL .... Yellow (AAG)
Yel .... Yelverton's English King's Bench Reports [*1603-13*] [*A publication*] (DLA)
YEL .... Young England Library [*A publication*]
YEL .... Youth Employment Lobby [*Canada*]
YELD .... Yeldham [*England*]
YELL .... Yellow Freight System, Inc. of Delaware [*NASDAQ symbol*] (NQ)
YELL .... Yellowstone National Park
Yellow B R ... Yellow Brick Road [*A publication*]
Yellowstone-Bighorn Research Proj Contr ... Yellowstone-Bighorn Research Project. Contribution [*A publication*]
Yellowstone Libr and Mus Assoc Yellowstone Interpretive Ser ... Yellowstone Library and Museum Association. Yellowstone Interpretive Series [*A publication*]
yelsh .... Yellowish [*Philately*]
Yelv .... Yelverton's English King's Bench Reports [*1603-13*] [*A publication*] (DLA)
Yelv (Eng) ... Yelverton's English King's Bench Reports [*1603-13*] [*A publication*] (DLA)
YEM .... Empire State College, Saratoga Springs, NY [*OCLC symbol*] [*Inactive*] (OCLC)
YEM .... Yemen (Sanaa) [*ANSI three-letter standard code*] (CNC)
YEMI .... Youngwood Electronic Metals, Incorporated [*NASDAQ symbol*] (NQ)
YEO .... Yeomanry
YEO .... Yeovil [*British depot code*]
YEO .... Young Entrepreneurs Organization [*Wichita, KS*] (EA)
YEO .... Youth Employment Officer [*British*]
Yeomy .... Yeomanry [*British military*] (DMA)
YEp .... Yeast Episomal Plasmid [*Genetics*]
YEPD .... Yeast Extract - Peptone Dextrose [*Medium*]
YER .... Yeats Eliot Review [*A publication*]
Yer .... Yerger's Tennessee Supreme Court Reports [*A publication*] (DLA)
YER .... Yerkesik [*Turkey*] [*Seismograph station code, US Geological Survey*] (SEIS)
Yer .... Yerushalmi [*Palestinian Talmud*] (BJA)
Yerg .... Yerger's Tennessee Reports [*9-18 Tennessee*] [*A publication*] (DLA)
Yerg (Tenn) ... Yerger's Tennessee Reports [*9-18 Tennessee*] [*A publication*] (DLA)
YES .... Yearbook of English Studies [*A publication*]
YES .... Years of Extra Savings
YES .... Yeast Extract Sucrose [*Cell growth medium*]
YES .... Yogurt Extra Smooth [*Trademark of the Dannon Co., Inc.*]
YES .... Young Entomologists' Society (EA)
YES .... Young Executive Society [*Automotive Warehouse Distributors Association*]
YES .... Youth Education Services [*Summer program*]
YES .... Youth Emergency Service
YES .... Youth Employment Service [*Department of Employment*] [*British*] (EA)
YES .... Youth Employment Support Volunteers Program [*ACTION*]
YES .... Youth Entering Service to America [*In YES Foundation, a volunteer organization proposed by the Bush administration*]
YES .... Youth Exhibiting Stamps [*US Postal Service*]
YESS .... Yankee Energy System, Inc. [*NASDAQ symbol*] (NQ)

Yessis Rev ... Yessis Review of Soviet Physical Education and Sports [*A publication*]
YEST .... Yesterday (DSUE)
YESTU ...... Yellowstone Reserves Uts [*NASDAQ symbol*] (NQ)
YESTY ...... Yesterday
YET .... Youth Effectiveness Training [*A course of study*]
YETM .... Yetminster [*England*]
YETP .... Youth Employment and Training Programs [*Department of Labor*]
Yeung Nam Univ Inst Ind Technol Rep ... Yeung Nam University. Institute of Industrial Technology. Report [*A publication*]
YEV .... Inuvik [*Canada*] [*Airport symbol*] (OAG)
Yev .... Yevamot (BJA)
YF .... Aeronautical Fixed Station [*ICAO designator*] (ICDA)
YF .... Covered Lighter [*Self-propelled*] [*Navy symbol*]
YF .... Wife [*Citizens band radio slang*]
YF .... Yawmiyyaet Filastiniyya (BJA)
YF .... Yerushalmi Fragments [*A publication*] (BJA)
YF .... Young Filmakers Foundation (EA)
YFA .... Fort Albany [*Canada*] [*Airport symbol*] (OAG)
YFB .... Ferryboat or Launch [*Self-propelled*] [*Navy symbol*]
YFB .... First Boston Corp., New York, NY [*OCLC symbol*] (OCLC)
YFB .... Frobisher Bay [*Canada*] [*Airport symbol*] (OAG)
YFC .... Fredericton [*Canada*] [*Airport symbol*] (OAG)
YFC .... Yakima Firing Center (MCD)
YFC .... Young Farmers' Club [*British*]
YFCI .... Youth for Christ International [*See also JPC*] [*Singapore, Singapore*] (EAIO)
YFC/USA ... Youth for Christ/USA (EA)
YFD .... Yard Floating Dry Dock [*Non-self-propelled*] [*Navy symbol*]
YFDC .... Youth Film Distribution Center (EA)
YFE .... Forestville [*Canada*] [*Airport symbol*] (OAG)
YFEC .... Youth Forum of the European Communities [*See also FJCE*] (EAIO)
YFED .... York Financial Corp. [*York, PA*] [*NASDAQ symbol*] (NQ)
YFF .... Waltham, MA [*Location identifier*] [*FAA*] (FAAL)
YFM .... State University of New York, Agricultural and Technical College at Farmingdale, Farmingdale, NY [*OCLC symbol*] (OCLC)
YFN .... Covered Lighter [*Non-self-propelled*] [*Navy symbol*]
YFNA .... Young Friends of North America (EA)
YFNB .... Large Covered Lighter [*Non-self-propelled*] [*Navy symbol*]
YFND .... Dry Dock Companion Craft [*Non-self-propelled*] [*Navy symbol*]
YFNG .... Covered Lighter (Special Purpose) [*Later, YFNX*] [*Navy symbol*]
YFNX .... Lighter (Special Purpose) [*Non-self-propelled*] [*Navy symbol*]
YFO .... Flin Flon [*Manitoba*] [*Airport symbol*] (OAG)
Y-FOS .... Y-Force Operations Staff [*Army*] [*World War II*]
YFP .... Floating Power Barge [*Non-self-propelled*] [*Navy symbol*]
YFR .... Refrigerated Covered Lighter [*Self-propelled*] [*Navy symbol*]
YFRN .... Refrigerated Covered Lighter [*Non-self-propelled*] [*Navy symbol*]
YFRT .... Covered Lighter (Range Tender) [*Self-propelled*] [*Navy symbol*]
YFS .... Fort Simpson [*Canada*] [*Airport symbol*] (OAG)
YFS .... Yale French Studies [*A publication*]
YFS .... Young Flying Service [*Harlingen, TX*] [*FAA designator*] (FAAC)
YFT .... Torpedo Transportation Lighter [*Navy symbol*] [*Obsolete*]
YFTU .... Yugoslavia Federation of Trade Unions
YFU .... Harbor Utility Craft [*Self-propelled*] [*Navy symbol*]
YFU .... Why Have You Forsaken Us? Letter [*Fundraising*]
YFU .... Yard Freight Unit
YFU .... Youth for Understanding (EA)
YF/VA .... Young Filmakers/Video Arts [*Also known as Young Filmakers Foundation*] (EA)
YF(XYL) .... Wife (Ex-Young-Lady) [*Amateur radio slang*]
YG .... Garbage Lighter [*Self-propelled*] [*Navy symbol*]
YG .... Yankee Group [*Boston, MA*] [*Information service or system*] [*Telecommunications*] (TSSD)
YG .... Yard Gully
YG .... Year Group
YG .... Yellow-Green
YG .... Yellow-Green Beacon [*Aviation*]
YGA .... Gagnon [*Canada*] [*Airport symbol*] (OAG)
YGB .... Gillies Bay [*Canada*] [*Airport symbol*] (OAG)
YGC .... Yahweh and the Gods of Canaan [*A publication*] (BJA)
YGF .... General Foods Technical Center, White Plains, NY [*OCLC symbol*] (OCLC)
YGIS .... Youth Guarantee Information Services [*Australia*]
YGJ .... Yonago [*Japan*] [*Airport symbol*] (OAG)
YGK .... Kingston [*Canada*] [*Airport symbol*] (OAG)
YGKKA ..... Yuki Gosei Kagaku Kyokaishi [*A publication*]
YGKSA ...... Yogyo Kyokai Shi [*A publication*]
YGL .... La Grande [*Canada*] [*Airport symbol*] (OAG)
YGL .... Yttrium Garnet LASER
YGM .... State University of New York, College at Geneseo, Geneseo, NY [*OCLC symbol*] (OCLC)
YGM .... Young Grandmother
YGN .... Garbage Lighter [*Non-self-propelled*] [*Navy symbol*]

YGNR........ Yukon Government News Release [*A publication*]
YGO.......... Gods Narrows [*Canada*] [*Airport symbol*]   (OAG)
YGP........... Gaspe [*Canada*] [*Airport symbol*]   (OAG)
YGQ.......... Geraldton [*Canada*] [*Airport symbol*]   (OAG)
YGR........... Iles De La Madeleine [*Canada*] [*Airport symbol*]   (OAG)
YGRP........ Y & A Goup, Inc. [*NASDAQ symbol*]   (NQ)
YGS .... Yale Germanic Studies [*A publication*]
YGS .... Year of Grace Survey   (DS)
YGS .... Young Guard Society [*Later, GS*]   (EA)
YGV.......... Havre Saint Pierre [*Canada*] [*Airport symbol*]   (OAG)
YGW.......... Great Whale [*Canada*] [*Airport symbol*]   (OAG)
YGX.......... Gillam [*Canada*] [*Airport symbol*]   (OAG)
YH .... Lighter, Ambulance [*Navy symbol*] [*Obsolete*]
YH .... RADAR Beacon [*Maps and charts*]
YH .... Yorkshire Hussars [*British military*]   (DMA)
YH .... Youth Hostel
YHA........... Youth Homeless Allowance [*Australia*]
YHA........... Youth Hostels Association
YHB........... House Boat [*Navy symbol*]
YHD .... Dryden [*Canada*] [*Airport symbol*]   (OAG)
YHHPAL..... Acta Pharmaceutica Sinica [*A publication*]
YHI........... Holman Island [*Canada*] [*Airport symbol*]   (OAG)
YHIY .... Yorkshire Hussars Imperial Yeomanry [*British military*]   (DMA)
YHJPCK ... Kluane National Park, Parks Canada [*Parc National Kluane, Parcs Canada*] Haines Junction, Yukon [*Library symbol*] [*National Library of Canada*]   (NLC)
YHK........... Gjoa Haven [*Canada*] [*Airport symbol*]   (OAG)
YHLC .... Salvage Lift Craft, Heavy [*Non-self-propelled*] [*Navy ship symbol*]
YHM .... Hamilton [*Canada*] [*Airport symbol*]   (OAG)
YHM .... Hamilton College, Clinton, NY [*OCLC symbol*]   (OCLC)
YHMA....... Yukon Historical and Museums Association. Newsletter [*A publication*]
YHMAN.... Yukon Historical and Museums Association. Newsletter [*A publication*]
YHN .... Hornepayne [*Canada*] [*Airport symbol*]   (OAG)
YHP.......... Yokogawa Hewlett Packard Ltd. [*Japan*]
YHPA .... Your Heritage Protection Association   (EA)
YHR........... Harrington Harbour [*Canada*] [*Airport symbol*]   (OAG)
YHS .... Yukuharu Haiku Society [*Superseded by Yuki Teikei Haiku Society*]   (EA)
YHT.......... Heating Scow [*Navy symbol*]
YHT.......... Young-Helmholtz Theory [*Physics*]
YHWH ...... Yahweh [*Old Testament term for God*]
YHY.......... Hay River [*Canada*] [*Airport symbol*]   (OAG)
YHZ.......... Halifax [*Canada*] [*Airport symbol*]   (OAG)
YI .... Iraq [*Aircraft nationality and registration mark*]   (FAAC)
YI .... Young, Intact Animals [*Endocrinology*]
YI .... Yukon Indian News [*A publication*]
YIB............. Atikokan [*Canada*] [*Airport symbol*]   (OAG)
yid............. Yiddish [*MARC language code*] [*Library of Congress*]   (LCCP)
YIE............. Young Interference Experiment [*Physics*]
YIEPP....... Youth Incentive Entitlement Pilot Projects [*Department of Labor*]
YIF............ St. Augustin [*Canada*] [*Airport symbol*]   (OAG)
YIFMC ...... Yearbook. International Folk Music Council [*A publication*]
YIG .... Yttrium Iron Garnet
YIGIB .... Your Improved Group Insurance Benefits
YIH .... Yichang [*China*] [*Airport symbol*]   (OAG)
YIIJS......... Young Israel Institute for Jewish Studies [*Defunct*]   (EA)
YIK .... Ivugivik [*Canada*] [*Airport symbol*]   (OAG)
YIL........... Yellow Indicating Light   (IEEE)
YILAG....... Yidishe Landvirtshaftlekhe Gezelshaft [*A publication*]   (BJA)
YIN .... Niagara County Community College, Sanborn, NY [*OCLC symbol*]   (OCLC)
YIN .... Yingkow [*Republic of China*] [*Seismograph station code, US Geological Survey*]   (SEIS)
YIN .... Yining [*China*] [*Airport symbol*]   (OAG)
YIO .... Pond Inlet [*Canada*] [*Airport symbol*]   (OAG)
YIP............ Willow Run Airport, Detroit, Michigan [*Airport symbol*]
YIp............ Yeast Integrating Plasmid [*Genetics*]
YIP............ Youth International Party [*Members known as "yippies"*]
YIPL.......... Youth International Party Line [*Superseded by Technological American Party*]
YIPME ...... Youth Institute for Peace in the Middle East   (EA)
Yippie....... Young Indicted Professional [*Lifestyle classification*]
Yiptime ..... Yipster Times [*A publication*]
YIR .... Yearly Infrastructure Report   (NATG)
YIS............ Yearbook of Italian Studies [*A publication*]
YIT........... Your Income Tax [*Computerized version of J. K. Lasser's book by the same name*]
YITB......... Yours in the Bond [*Motto of fraternity Tau Kappa Epsilon*]
Y It S........ Yale Italian Studies [*A publication*]
YIV .... Island Lake [*Canada*] [*Airport symbol*]   (OAG)
YIVO .... Yidisher Visnshaftlekher Institut [*Yiddish Scientific Institute*]
YIVO .... YIVO Annual of Jewish Social Science [*A publication*]
YJ............. RADAR Homing Beacon [*Maps and charts*]
YJ............. Yellow Jacket [*Immunology*]
Y & J .... Younge and Jervis' English Exchequer Reports [*1826-30*] [*A publication*]   (DLA)

YJ.............. Youth Journal [*A publication*]
YJ.............. Yuppie Jeep
YJCS .... Yenching Journal of Chinese Studies [*A publication*]
YJF........... Fort Liard [*Canada*] [*Airport symbol*]   (OAG)
YJK........... Yellowjack Resources [*Vancouver Stock Exchange symbol*]
YJM........... Fulton-Montgomery Community College, Johnstown, NY [*OCLC symbol*]   (OCLC)
YJS .... Yale Judaica Series [*A publication*]   (BJA)
YJT........... Stephenville [*Canada*] [*Airport symbol*]   (OAG)
YJV........... Yellow Jacket Venom [*Immunology*]
YK .... RADAR Beacon [*Maps and charts*]
YK .... Syria [*Aircraft nationality and registration mark*]   (FAAC)
YK .... Yakovlev [*USSR*] [*ICAO aircraft manufacturer identifier*]   (ICAO)
YK .... Yapi-Kredi Bank [*Turkey*]   (ECON)
YK .... Yiddishe Kultur [*A publication*]
YK .... Yom Kippur   (BJA)
YK .... York Antibodies [*Immunology*]
YKA........... Kamloops [*Canada*] [*Airport symbol*]   (OAG)
YKA........... Yellowknife Array [*Northwest Territories*] [*Seismograph station code, US Geological Survey*]   (SEIS)
YKB .... Yapi-Kredi Bank [*Turkey*]
YKB .... Yukon Bibliography [*Boreal Institute for Northern Studies*] [*Canada*] [*Information service or system*] [*Information service or system*]   (CRD)
YKC .... Kingsborough Community College of the City University of New York, Brooklyn, NY [*OCLC symbol*]   (OCLC)
YKC .... Yellowknife [*Northwest Territories*] [*Geomagnetic observatory code*]
YKC .... Yellowknife [*Northwest Territories*] [*Seismograph station code, US Geological Survey*]   (SEIS)
ykc............. Yukon Territory [*MARC country of publication code*] [*Library of Congress*]   (LCCP)
YKE .... Yankee Power, Inc. [*Vancouver Stock Exchange symbol*]
YKIGA...... Yokohama Igaku [*A publication*]
YKK .... Yoshido Kogyo Kabushiki-Kaishi [*Yoshida Industries Ltd.*] [*Japan*]
YKKKA...... Yakugaku Kenkyu [*A publication*]
YKKKA8... Japanese Journal of Pharmacy and Chemistry [*A publication*]
YKKZA...... Yakugaku Zasshi [*Journal of the Pharmaceutical Society of Japan*] [*A publication*]
YKL .... Schefferville [*Canada*] [*Airport symbol*]   (OAG)
YKM .... Corning Museum of Glass, Corning, NY [*OCLC symbol*]   (OCLC)
YKM .... Yaak [*Montana*] [*Seismograph station code, US Geological Survey*]   (SEIS)
YKM .... Yakima [*Washington*] [*Airport symbol*]   (OAG)
YKM .... Young Kibbutz Movement   (EA)
YKN........... Yankton [*South Dakota*] [*Airport symbol*]   (OAG)
YKN........... Yukon [*FAA*]   (FAAC)
YKQ........... Rupert House [*Canada*] [*Airport symbol*]   (OAG)
YKR........... Yukon Revenue Mines [*Vancouver Stock Exchange symbol*]
YKS........... Yakushima [*Japan*] [*Seismograph station code, US Geological Survey*] [*Closed*]   (SEIS)
YKS........... Yorkshire [*County in England*]
YKT .... Yakutat [*Alaska*] [*Seismograph station code, US Geological Survey*] [*Closed*]   (SEIS)
YKU .... Fort George [*Canada*] [*Airport symbol*]   (OAG)
YKU .... Yakutat [*Alaska*] [*Seismograph station code, US Geological Survey*]   (SEIS)
YKUF........ Yiddisher Kultur Farband   (EA)
YKW.......... Yom Kippur War   (BJA)
YKX.......... Kirkland Lake [*Canada*] [*Airport symbol*]   (OAG)
YKYRA...... Yakubutsu Ryoho [*A publication*]
YKZ........... Toronto [*Canada*] Buttonville Airport [*Airport symbol*]   (OAG)
YL .... Aircraft Accident Authority [*ICAO designator*]   (ICDA)
YL .... Approach Light Lane [*Aviation code*]   (FAAC)
YL .... Y-Axis of Spacelab [*NASA*]   (NASA)
YL .... Yad La-Kore. La-Safran ule-Pe'ile Tarbut   (BJA)
YL .... Yawl   (ROG)
YL .... Yellow [*Maps and charts*]
Y & L........ York and Lancaster Regiment [*Military unit*] [*British*]   (DMA)
YL .... Young Lady [*Amateur radio slang*]
YL .... Young Life   (EA)
YL .... Youth Liberation Press   (EA)
YLA........... Open Landing Lighter [*Navy symbol*]
YLB........... Lac La Biche [*Canada*] [*Airport symbol*]
YLC........... Clinton Community College, Plattsburgh, NY [*OCLC symbol*]   (OCLC)
YLC........... Young Life Campaign   (EA)
YLD .... Chapleau [*Canada*] [*Airport symbol*]   (OAG)
YLD .... High Income Advantage Trust [*NYSE symbol*]   (SPSG)
YLD .... Yield [*Investment term*]
YLDG .... Yielding   (ROG)
YLG .... Yale University. Library. Gazette [*A publication*]
YLG News ... Library Association. Youth Libraries Group News [*A publication*]
YLH........... High-Income Advantage Trust III [*NYSE symbol*]   (SPSG)
YLI............ [*The*] Yorkshire Light Infantry [*Military unit*] [*British*]
YLI............ Young Ladies Institute   (EA)
YLJ .... Meadow Lake [*Canada*] [*Airport symbol*] [*Obsolete*]   (OAG)

YLJ............	Yale Law Journal [*A publication*]
YLL............	Lederle Laboratories, Pearl River, NY [*OCLC symbol*] (OCLC)
YLL............	Lloydminster [*Canada*] [*Airport symbol*] (OAG)
YLLC........	Salvage Lift Craft, Light [*Self-propelled*] [*Navy ship symbol*]
YLM..........	Yale Literary Magazine [*A publication*]
YLP...........	Mingan [*Canada*] [*Airport symbol*] [*Obsolete*] (OAG)
YLR	YAG [*Yttrium Aluminum Garnet*] LASER Range-Finder
Y & LR	York and Lancaster Regiment [*Military unit*] [*British*]
YLR	York Legal Record [*Pennsylvania*] [*A publication*] (DLA)
YLRL........	Young Ladies Radio League
YLS	Young Lawyers Section [*Law Society of New South Wales*] [*Australia*]
YLSN........	Young Lawyers Section Newsletter [*Australia*] [*A publication*]
YLSTN......	Yellowstone [*FAA*] (FAAC)
YLT...........	High Income Advantage Trust II [*NYSE symbol*] (CTT)
YLT...........	Yellow Light (MSA)
YLT...........	Yu-Yen-Hsueh Lun-Ts'ung [*Essays in Linguistics*] [*A publication*]
YLW	Kelowna [*Canada*] [*Airport symbol*] (OAG)
YLW	Yellow (ADA)
YM............	Dredge [*Self-propelled*] [*Navy symbol*]
YM.........	Meteorological Office [*ICAO designator*] (ICDA)
YM..........	Prototype Missile (NATG)
YM..........	Yacht Measurement
YM............	Yawing Moment (KSC)
YM..........	Yearly Meetings [*Quakers*]
YM............	Yeast Extract - Malt Extract [*Medium*]
YM............	Yellow Man
YM............	Yellow Metal
YM............	Young Man [*A publication*]
YM............	Young Men's [*Christian Association*]
YM............	Young Miss Magazine [*A publication*]
YM............	[*Reference*] Your Message
YMA..........	Mayo [*Canada*] [*Airport symbol*] (OAG)
YMA..........	Yarn Merchants Association [*Defunct*] (EA)
YMA..........	Young Menswear Association (EA)
YMB	Yeast Malt Broth
YMC.........	Moore-Cottrell Subscription Agencies, Inc., North Cohocton, NY [*OCLC symbol*] (OCLC)
YMC.........	Your Marketing Consultant [*An electronic publication*]
YMC.........	Youth and Music Canada
YMCA	Young Men's Christian Association
YMCAIPS ...	YMCA [*Young Men's Christian Association*] International Program Services (EA)
YMCA-USA ...	Young Men's Christian Associations of the United States of America (EA)
YMCU.......	Young Men's Christian Union
YMD..........	People's Democratic Republic of Yemen [*ANSI three-letter standard code*] (CNC)
YMD..........	[*Reference*] Your Message Date
YME	Matane [*Canada*] [*Airport symbol*] (OAG)
YME	Young's Modulus of Elasticity [*See also E, Y*]
YMF	Young Musicians Foundation (EA)
YMFS........	Young Men's Friendly Society [*British*]
YMHA.......	Young Men's Hebrew Association [*Later, YM-YWHA*]
YMHSI......	Yedi'ot ha-Makhon le-Heker ha-Shirah ha-'Ivrit. Jerusalem (BJA)
YMI	Young Men's Institute (EA)
YMISIG	Young Mensa International Special Interest Group [*Defunct*] (EA)
YMJODW ...	Bulletin. Yamagata University. Medical Science [*A publication*]
YML	Young Men's Lyceum
YMLC........	Salvage Lift Craft, Medium [*Non-self-propelled*] [*Navy ship symbol*]
YMM........	Fort McMurray [*Canada*] [*Airport symbol*] (OAG)
YMM.........	Yeast Minimal Medium [*Microorganism growth medium*]
YMM........	Youngstown and Mahoning County Public Library, Youngstown, OH [*OCLC symbol*] (OCLC)
YMML......	Young Methodist Missionary League [*Australia*]
YMMY......	Yedi'ot ha-Makhon le-Mada'ei ha-Yahadut. Jerusalem (BJA)
YMO.........	Moosonee [*Canada*] [*Airport symbol*] (OAG)
YMO.........	Yellow Magic Orchestra [*Musical group*] [*Japan*]
YMP	Motor Mine Planter [*Navy symbol*]
YMP	Yacht Materially Prejudiced [*Yacht racing*] (IYR)
YMP	Young Managing Printers [*British Printing Industries Federation*]
YMP	Youth Mobility Program (OICC)
YMPE........	Year's Maximum Pensionable Earnings
YMS	Auxiliary Motor Minesweeper [*Navy symbol*]
YMS	Yaw Microwave Sensor
YMS	Yield Measurement System
YMS	Yurimaguas [*Peru*] [*Airport symbol*] (OAG)
YMT	Chibougamau [*Canada*] [*Airport symbol*] (OAG)
YMT	Motor Tug [*Navy symbol*]
YMTM	Yikal Maya Than (Mexico) [*A publication*]
Y & MV	Yazoo & Mississippi Valley Railroad Co.
YMX..........	Montreal [*Canada*] Mirabel International Airport [*Airport symbol*] (OAG)
YM-YWHA ...	Young Men's and Young Women's Hebrew Association (EA)
YN............	International NOTAM Office [*ICAO designator*] (ICDA)

YN..............	Net Tender [*Navy symbol*] [*Obsolete*]
YN..............	Night Coach [*Airline fare code*]
YN..............	Yellowknifer [*A publication*]
YN..............	Yeoman [*Navy rating*]
YN..............	Yes-No [*Response prompt*]
YN..............	Young Numismatist [*A publication*]
YN..............	[*The*] Youngstown & Northern Railroad Co. [*AAR code*]
YN1............	Yeoman, First Class [*Navy rating*]
YN2............	Yeoman, Second Class [*Navy rating*]
YN3............	Yeoman, Third Class [*Navy rating*]
YNA	Naiashquan [*Canada*] [*Airport symbol*] (OAG)
YNB	Yanbu [*Saudi Arabia*] [*Airport symbol*] (OAG)
YNB	Yeast Nitrogen Base
YNC...........	Paint Hills [*Canada*] [*Airport symbol*] (OAG)
YNC...........	Yeoman, Chief [*Navy rating*]
YNC...........	Yinchuan [*Republic of China*] [*Seismograph station code, US Geological Survey*] (SEIS)
YNCM........	Yeoman, Master Chief [*Navy rating*]
YNCS........	Yeoman, Senior Chief [*Navy rating*]
YND..........	Gatineau/Hull [*Canada*] [*Airport symbol*] (OAG)
YNE	Nor East Commuter Airlines [*East Boston, MA*] [*FAA designator*] (FAAC)
YNE	Norway House [*Canada*] [*Airport symbol*] (OAG)
YNER	Yale Near Eastern Researches [*New Haven/London*] [*A publication*]
YNG...........	Gate Craft [*Non-self-propelled*] [*Navy symbol*]
YNG...........	Youngstown [*Ohio*] [*Airport symbol*] (OAG)
YNG...........	Youngstown State University, Youngstown, OH [*OCLC symbol*] (OCLC)
YNHA	Yosemite Natural History Association (EA)
YNHH.......	Yale-New Haven Hospital
YNK...........	Yankee Companies, Inc. [*AMEX symbol*] [*Later, NEG*] (SPSG)
YNM..........	Matagami [*Canada*] [*Airport symbol*] (OAG)
YNP...........	Young National Party [*Australia*] [*Political party*] (ADA)
YNPA.........	Young National Party of Australia [*Political party*] (ADA)
YNPS.........	Yankee Nuclear Power Station (NRCH)
YNR...........	Yorkshire, North Riding [*County in England*] (ROG)
YNSA	Seaman Apprentice, Yeoman, Striker [*Navy rating*]
YNSN........	Seaman, Yeoman, Striker [*Navy rating*]
YNT	Net Tender [*Tug Class*] [*Navy symbol*] [*Obsolete*]
YNT	Yellowstone National Travelers (EA)
YNTO........	Yugoslav National Tourist Office (EA)
YNV	Yanov [*USSR*] [*Later, LVV*] [*Geomagnetic observatory code*]
YO.............	Aeronautical Information Service Unit [*ICAO designator*] (ICDA)
YO.............	Airline ticket that can be used on any airline
YO.............	Fuel Oil Barge [*Self-propelled*] [*Navy symbol*]
YO.............	Mayotte [*ANSI two-letter standard code*] (CNC)
YO.............	Y-Axis of Orbiter [*NASA*] (NASA)
YO.............	Yarn Over [*Knitting*]
YO.............	Year-Old
YO.............	Yes [*Citizens band radio slang*]
Yo.............	Yoma (BJA)
YO.............	Young Officer [*British military*] (DMA)
Yo.............	Younge's English Exchequer Equity Reports [*159 English Reprint*] [*A publication*] (DLA)
YOAN........	Youth of All Nations (EA)
YOB...........	Year of Birth
YOB...........	Youth Opportunities Board
YoB	Yushodo Booksellers Ltd., Tokyo, Japan [*Library symbol*] [*Library of Congress*] (LCLS)
YOBGAD ..	Year Book of Obstetrics and Gynecology [*A publication*]
YOC...........	Old Crow [*Canada*] [*Airport symbol*] (OAG)
YOC...........	Youth Opportunity Campaign [*Civil Service Commission*]
YOC...........	Youth Opportunity Centers
YOC...........	Youth Opportunity Corps
YOCHINPROJ ...	Younger Chemists International Project [*American Chemical Society*]
YOCM........	International Yogurt Co. [*NASDAQ symbol*] (NQ)
YOD..........	Cold Lake [*Canada*] [*Airport symbol*] (OAG)
YOD..........	Year of Death
YOG...........	Central Aviation, Inc. [*Chicago, IL*] [*FAA designator*] (FAAC)
YOG...........	Gasoline Barge [*Self-propelled*] [*Navy symbol*]
Yoga Jnl....	Yoga Journal [*A publication*]
YOGN........	Gasoline Barge [*Non-self-propelled*] [*Navy symbol*]
YOH	Oxford House [*Canada*] [*Airport symbol*] (OAG)
YOJ	High Level [*Canada*] [*Airport symbol*] (OAG)
YOJ	Yonagunijima [*Ryukyu Islands*] [*Seismograph station code, US Geological Survey*] (SEIS)
YOK...........	Yokohama [*Japan*] [*Seismograph station code, US Geological Survey*] (SEIS)
Yokogawa Tech Rep ...	Yokogawa Technical Report [*Japan*] [*A publication*]
Yokohama Math J ...	Yokohama Mathematical Journal [*A publication*]
Yokohama Med Bull ...	Yokohama Medical Bulletin [*A publication*]
Yokohama Med J ...	Yokohama Medical Journal [*Japan*] [*A publication*]
Yoko Iga....	Yokohama Igaku [*A publication*]
Yoko Med Bull ...	Yokohama Medical Bulletin [*A publication*]
Yokufukai Geriatr J ...	Yokufukai Geriatric Journal [*A publication*]
YOL...........	Yola [*Nigeria*] [*Airport symbol*] (OAG)

YOM.......... State University of New York, College at Oswego, Oswego, NY [*OCLC symbol*]   (OCLC)
YOM.......... Year of Marriage
Yom........... Yoma   (BJA)
YON .... Fuel Oil Barge [*Non-self-propelled*] [*Navy symbol*]
YON .... Yonago [*Japan*] [*Seismograph station code, US Geological Survey*]   (SEIS)
YON .... Yonkers School System, Yonkers, NY [*OCLC symbol*]   (OCLC)
Yona Acta Med ... Yonago Acta Medica [*A publication*]
Yon Act Med ... Yonago Acta Medica [*A publication*]
Yonago Acta Med ... Yonago Acta Medica [*A publication*]
Yona Iga Zass ... Yonago Igaku Zasshi [*A publication*]
Yonsei Eng Rep ... Yonsei Engineering Report [*A publication*]
Yonsei Eng Rev ... Yonsei Engineering Review [*South Korea*] [*A publication*]
Yonsei J Med Sci ... Yonsei Journal of Medical Science [*A publication*]
Yonsei Med J ... Yonsei Medical Journal [*A publication*]
Yonsei Rep Trop Med ... Yonsei Reports on Tropical Medicine [*A publication*]
Yool Waste ... Yool on Waste, Nuisance, and Trespass [*1863*] [*A publication*]   (DLA)
YOP .... Rainbow Lake [*Canada*] [*Airport symbol*]   (OAG)
YOP .... Youth Opportunities Programme [*British*]   (DCTA)
YOR .... Bulletin of Economic Research [*A publication*]
YOR .... Yale Oriental Research [*A publication*]   (BJA)
yor .... Yoruba [*MARC language code*] [*Library of Congress*]   (LCCP)
York .... York Legal Record [*Pennsylvania*] [*A publication*]   (DLA)
YORK .... York Research Corp. [*NASDAQ symbol*]   (NQ)
York Ass .... Clayton's English Reports, York Assizes [*A publication*]   (DLA)
YorkCoHS ... York County Historical Society. Papers [*A publication*]
York Leg Rec ... York Legal Record [*Pennsylvania*] [*A publication*]   (DLA)
York Leg Record ... York Legal Record [*Pennsylvania*] [*A publication*]   (DLA)
York Leg Rec (PA) ... York Legal Record [*Pennsylvania*] [*A publication*]   (DLA)
York Papers Ling ... York Papers in Linguistics [*A publication*]
YORKS...... Yorkshire [*County in England*]
Yorks Beekpr ... Yorkshire Beekeeper [*A publication*]
Yorks Bull Econ Soc Res ... Yorkshire Bulletin of Economic and Social Research [*A publication*]
Yorks Geol Soc Occas Publ ... Yorkshire Geological Society. Occasional Publication [*A publication*]
Yorkshire A J ... Yorkshire Archaeological Journal [*A publication*]
Yorkshire Archaeol J ... Yorkshire Archaeological Journal [*A publication*]
Yorkshire Arch J ... Yorkshire Archaeological Journal [*A publication*]
Yorkshire Archt ... Yorkshire Architect [*A publication*]
Yorkshire Geol Soc Proc ... Yorkshire Geological Society. Proceedings [*A publication*]
Yorkshire G Polyt Soc Pr ... Yorkshire Geological and Polytechnic Society. Proceedings [*A publication*]
YOS .... Oil Storage Barge [*Non-self-propelled*] [*Navy symbol*]
YOS .... Yale Oriental Series [*A publication*]
YOS .... Years of Service [*Army*]   (INF)
YOS .... Yosiwara [*Japan*] [*Seismograph station code, US Geological Survey*] [*Closed*]   (SEIS)
YOSE........ Yosemite National Park
YoShiR ...... Yokohama Shiritsu Daigaku Ronso [*Bulletin. Yokohama Municipal University Society*] [*A publication*]
YOSR .... Yale Oriental Series. Researches [*A publication*]
YOT .... Yale Oriental Texts [*A publication*]   (BJA)
YOTS........ Youth Ocean Training Scheme [*Australia*]
YOU........... Young [*Australia*] [*Seismograph station code, US Geological Survey*]   (SEIS)
You........... Younge's English Exchequer Equity Reports [*159 English Reprint*] [*A publication*]   (DLA)
YOU.......... Youngman Oil & Gas [*Vancouver Stock Exchange symbol*]
YOU.......... Youth Opportunities Unlimited [*Project*]   (EA)
YOU.......... Youth Organizations United
You & Coll Ch ... Younge and Collyer's English Chancery Reports [*1841-43*] [*A publication*]   (DLA)
You & Coll Ex ... Younge and Collyer's English Exchequer Equity Reports [*1834-42*] [*A publication*]   (DLA)
You & Jerv ... Younge and Jervis' English Exchequer Reports [*A publication*]   (DLA)
Young........ Young's Reports [*21-47 Minnesota*] [*A publication*]   (DLA)
Young Adm ... Young's Nova Scotia Admiralty Cases [*A publication*]   (DLA)
Young Adm Dec ... Young's Nova Scotia Vice-Admiralty Decisions [*A publication*]   (DLA)
Young Adm Dec (Nov Sc) ... Young's Nova Scotia Vice-Admiralty Decisions [*A publication*]   (DLA)
Young Athl ... Young Athlete [*A publication*]
Young Child ... Young Children [*A publication*]
Young Cinema ... Young Cinema and Theatre [*A publication*]
Younge .... Younge's English Exchequer Equity Reports [*159 English Reprint*] [*A publication*]   (DLA)
Younge & C Ch ... Younge and Collyer's English Chancery Reports [*62-63 English Reprint*] [*A publication*]   (DLA)
Younge & C Ch Cas (Eng) ... Younge and Collyer's English Chancery Cases [*62-63 English Reprint*] [*A publication*]   (DLA)
Younge & C Exch ... Younge and Collyer's English Exchequer Equity Reports [*160 English Reprint*] [*A publication*]   (DLA)

Younge & C Exch (Eng) ... Younge and Collyer's English Exchequer Equity Reports [*160 English Reprint*] [*A publication*]   (DLA)
Younge & Ch Cas ... Younge and Collyer's English Chancery Cases [*62-63 English Reprint*] [*1841-43*] [*A publication*]   (DLA)
Younge & Coll Ch ... Younge and Collyer's English Chancery Reports [*62-63 English Reprint*] [*A publication*]   (DLA)
Younge & Coll Ex ... Younge and Collyer's English Exchequer Equity Reports [*160 English Reprint*] [*A publication*]   (DLA)
Younge Exch ... Younge's English Exchequer Equity Reports [*159 English Reprint*] [*1830-32*] [*A publication*]   (DLA)
Younge Exch (Eng) ... Younge's English Exchequer Equity Reports [*159 English Reprint*] [*A publication*]   (DLA)
Younge & J ... Younge and Jervis' English Exchequer Reports [*148 English Reprint*] [*A publication*]   (DLA)
Younge & Je ... Younge and Jervis' English Exchequer Reports [*148 English Reprint*] [*A publication*]   (DLA)
Younge & J (Eng) ... Younge and Jervis' English Exchequer Reports [*148 English Reprint*] [*A publication*]   (DLA)
Younge & Jerv ... Younge and Jervis' English Exchequer Reports [*148 English Reprint*] [*A publication*]   (DLA)
Younge ML Cas ... Younge's English Maritime Law Cases [*A publication*]   (DLA)
Young Lib .. Young Liberal [*A publication*]   (APTA)
Young ML Cas ... Young's English Maritime Law Cases [*A publication*]   (DLA)
Young Naut Dict ... Young's Nautical Dictionary [*A publication*]   (DLA)
Young VA Dec ... Young's Nova Scotia Vice-Admiralty Decisions [*A publication*]   (DLA)
YOUR........ Your Own United Resources, Inc.   (OICC)
Your Comput ... Your Computer [*A publication*]
Your Mus Cue ... Your Musical Cue [*A publication*]
Your Okla Dent Assoc J ... Your Oklahoma Dental Association Journal [*A publication*]
Your Radiol ... Your Radiologist [*A publication*]
YOUSA ..... Youth Organizations USA   (EA)
Youth Aid Bull ... Youth Aid Bulletin [*A publication*]
YOUTHS ... Youth Order United Toward Highway Safety   (EA)
Youth Soc... Youth and Society [*A publication*]
Youth in Soc ... Youth in Society [*A publication*]
Youth and Soc ... Youth and Society [*A publication*]
Youth Train News ... Youth Training News [*A publication*]
YOW.......... Ottawa [*Canada*] [*Airport symbol*]   (OAG)
YOYUA ..... Yoyuen [*A publication*]
YP .... Patrol Craft [*Self-propelled*] [*Navy symbol*]
YP .... Robex Collection Center [*ICAO designator*]   (FAAC)
YP .... Y-Axis of Payload [*NASA*]   (NASA)
YP .... Yard Patrol
YP .... Yellow Pine
YP .... Yield Point [*Ordinarily expressed in PSI*]
YP .... Yorkshire Post [*A publication*]
YP .... Young People
YP .... Your Problem
3YP .... Three Year Plan [*From George Orwell's novel, "1984"*]
YPA .... Port Authority of New York and New Jersey Library, New York, NY [*OCLC symbol*]   (OCLC)
YPA .... Prince Albert [*Canada*] [*Airport symbol*]   (OAG)
YPA .... Yaw Precession Amplifier
YPA .... Yearbook Printers Association   (EA)
YPB........... Yeast Peptone Broth [*Microbiology*]
YPBF .... Yellow Sheet Price of Beef [*Business term*]
YPD .... Floating Pile Driver [*Non-self-propelled*] [*Navy symbol*]
YPD .... Parry Sound [*Canada*] [*Airport symbol*]   (OAG)
YPD .... Yaw Phase Detector
YPD .... Yeast Extract-Peptones, Dextrose Medium [*Microbiology*]
YPD .... Yellow Pages Datasystem [*National Planning Data Corp.*] [*Database*]
YPE........... Peace River [*Canada*] [*Airport symbol*]   (OAG)
YPE........... Yoho Pitch Extractor
YPEC........ Young Printing Executives Club of New York   (EA)
Yperm .... Yperman. Bulletin de la Societe Belge d'Histoire de la Medecine [*A publication*]
YPG .... Yuma Proving Ground [*Arizona*] [*Army*]   (AABC)
YPH .... Port Harrison [*Canada*] [*Airport symbol*]   (OAG)
YPHJA ...... Yo-Up Hoeji [*A publication*]
YPI............ Youth Policy Institute   (EA)
YPI............ Youth Pride, Incorporated   (EA)
YPK .... Pontoon Stowage Barge [*Navy symbol*] [*Obsolete*]
YPL........... Pickle Lake [*Canada*] [*Airport symbol*]   (OAG)
YPL........... White Plains Public Library, White Plains, NY [*OCLC symbol*]   (OCLC)
YPL........... York Papers in Linguistics [*A publication*]
YPL........... York Public Library [*UTLAS symbol*]
YPL........... Young People's Literature [*A publication*]
YPLA .... Young People's LOGO Association   (EA)
YPLA .... Your Public Lands. US Department of the Interior. Bureau of Land Mangement [*A publication*]
YPLB .... Yellow Sheet Price of Lamb [*Business term*]
YPLL .... Years of Potential Life Lost [*Epidemiology*]
YPM .... Saint Pierre [*Saint Pierre and Miquelon*] [*Airport symbol*]   (OAG)

YPM .... State University of New York, College at Plattsburgh, Plattsburgh, NY [*OCLC symbol*]   (OCLC)
YPM .... Yale Peabody Museum
YPM .... Yokefellowship Prison Ministry   (EA)
YPN .... Port Menier [*Canada*] [*Airport symbol*]   (OAG)
YPND .... Young People for Nuclear Disarmament [*Australia*]
YPO .... Young Presidents' Organization   (EA)
YPO .... Youth Programs Office [*Bureau of Indian Affairs*]
Y-POP .... Y-Body Axis Perpendicular to Orbit Plane [*Aerospace*]
YPPK .... Yellow Sheet Price of Pork [*Business term*]
YPQ .... Peterborough [*Canada*] [*Airport symbol*]   (OAG)
YPR .... Prince Rupert [*Canada*] [*Airport symbol*]   (OAG)
YPR .... Yale Poetry Review [*A publication*]
YPR .... Yanks Peak Resources [*Vancouver Stock Exchange symbol*]
YPR .... Youth Population Ratio   (OICC)
YPS .... Yards per Second
YPS .... Yellow Pages Service [*Telecommunications*]   (TEL)
YPSCE .... Young People's Society of Christian Endeavor
YPSL .... Young Peoples Socialist League [*Later, YSD*]   (EA)
YPSSRB .... Yukon Public Service Staff Relations Board [*Canada*]
YPVS .... Yamaha Power Valve System
YPW .... Powell River [*Canada*] [*Airport symbol*]   (OAG)
YPW .... Putnam-Northern Westchester BOCES [*Boards of Cooperative Educational Services*], Yorktown Heights, NY [*OCLC symbol*]   (OCLC)
YPX .... Povungnituk [*Canada*] [*Airport symbol*]   (OAG)
YPY .... Fort Chipewyan [*Canada*] [*Airport symbol*]   (OAG)
YPZ .... Young Poalei Zion   (BJA)
YQ .... Youth Quarterly [*A publication*]
YQB .... Quebec [*Canada*] [*Airport symbol*]   (OAG)
YQD .... [*The*] Pas [*Canada*] [*Airport symbol*]   (OAG)
YQF .... Red Deer [*Canada*] [*Airport symbol*] [*Obsolete*]   (OAG)
YQG .... Windsor [*Canada*] [*Airport symbol*]   (OAG)
YQH .... Watson Lake [*Canada*] [*Airport symbol*]   (OAG)
YQI .... Yarmouth [*Canada*] [*Airport symbol*]   (OAG)
YQK .... Kenora [*Canada*] [*Airport symbol*]   (OAG)
YQL .... Lethbridge [*Canada*] [*Airport symbol*]   (OAG)
YQM .... Moncton [*Canada*] [*Airport symbol*]   (OAG)
YQQ .... Comox [*Canada*] [*Airport symbol*]   (OAG)
YQR .... Regina [*Canada*] [*Airport symbol*]   (OAG)
YQR .... Rochester Public Library, Rochester, NY [*OCLC symbol*]   (OCLC)
YQT .... Thunder Bay [*Canada*] [*Airport symbol*]   (OAG)
YQU .... Grande Prairie [*Canada*] [*Airport symbol*]   (OAG)
YQV .... Yorkton [*Canada*] [*Airport symbol*]   (OAG)
YQX .... Gander [*Canada*] [*Airport symbol*]   (OAG)
YQY .... Sydney [*Canada*] [*Airport symbol*]   (OAG)
YQZ .... Quesnel [*Canada*] [*Airport symbol*]   (OAG)
YR .... Airline ticket that can be used only on airline issuing it
YR .... Floating Workshop [*Non-self-propelled*] [*Navy symbol*]
YR .... Romania [*Aircraft nationality and registration mark*]   (FAAC)
YR .... Yale Review [*A publication*]
YR .... Yaw Ring
Y-R .... Yaw-Roll   (AAG)
YR .... Year [*Online database field identifier*]   (EY)
Yr .... Yearbook   (BJA)
YR .... Yemeni Riyal   (BJA)
YR .... Young Republican
Y & R .... Young & Rubicam International [*Advertising agency*]
YR .... Younger
YR .... Your   (AAG)
YR .... Youth Resources   (EA)
YR .... Yukon Reports [*Maritime Law Book Co. Ltd.*] [*Canada*] [*Information service or system*]   (CRD)
YRA .... Yacht Racing Association [*British*]
YRAA .... Youth Refuge and Accommodation Association [*Australia*]
YRAC .... Yacht Racing Associations Council   (EA)
YRAP........ Yellow Page Rate Base Analysis Plan [*Bell System*]
YRB .... Resolute [*Canada*] [*Airport symbol*]   (OAG)
YRB .... Submarine Repair and Berthing Barge [*Non-self-propelled*] [*Navy symbol*]
YRB .... Yorbeau Resources, Inc. [*Toronto Stock Exchange symbol*]
YRBK........ Yearbook
Yrbk Agric ... Yearbook of Agriculture. Using Our Natural Resources [*A publication*]
Yrbk Austl ... Yearbook Australia [*A publication*]
Yr Bk (Charleston SC) ... Year Book (Charleston, South Carolina) [*A publication*]
Yrbk Compar & Gen Lit ... Yearbook of Comparative and General Literature [*A publication*]
Yrbk Comp & Gen Lit ... Yearbook of Comparative and General Literature [*A publication*]
Yrbk Sch Law ... Yearbook of School Law [*A publication*]
Yrbk Sp Educ ... Yearbook of Special Education [*A publication*]
Yrbk World Aff ... Yearbook of World Affairs [*London*] [*A publication*]
YRBM .... Submarine Repair, Berthing, and Messing Barge [*Non-self-propelled*] [*Navy symbol*]
YRBM(L) .. Submarine Repair, Berthing, and Messing Barge (Large) [*Navy symbol*]
YRC .... Submarine Rescue Chamber [*Navy symbol*]
YRC .... Yaw Ratio Controller   (MCD)

YRDH .... Floating Dry Dock Workshop (Hull) [*Non-self-propelled*] [*Navy symbol*]
YRDM .... Floating Dry Dock Workshop (Machine) [*Non-self-propelled*] [*Navy symbol*]
YRDST ...... Year-Round Daylight Saving Time
YRF.......... Yoga Research Foundation   (EA)
YRFC......... [*The*] Young and the Restless Fan Club   (EA)
YRFLN ...... Year Flown   (MCD)
YRI .... Riviere-Du-Loup [*Canada*] [*Airport symbol*] [*Obsolete*]   (OAG)
YRI .... Yri-York Ltd. [*Toronto Stock Exchange symbol*]
YRINY....... Youth Research Institute of New York   (EA)
YRJ........... Roberval [*Canada*] [*Airport symbol*] [*Obsolete*]   (OAG)
YRK .... York International Corp. [*NYSE symbol*]   (SPSG)
YRK .... York, KY [*Location identifier*] [*FAA*]   (FAAL)
YRK .... York University Library [*UTLAS symbol*]
YRL .... Covered Lighter (Repair) [*Navy symbol*] [*Obsolete*]
YRL .... Red Lake [*Canada*] [*Airport symbol*]   (OAG)
YRL .... York University Law Library [*UTLAS symbol*]
YRLY........ Yearly   (ROG)
YRM .... Rensselaer Polytechnic Institute, Troy, NY [*OCLC symbol*]   (OCLC)
YRNF .... Young Republican National Federation   (EA)
YRR .... Radiological Repair Barge [*Non-self-propelled*] [*Navy symbol*]
YRR .... Scenic Airlines [*Las Vegas, NV*] [*FAA designator*]   (FAAC)
YRS .... Red Sucker Lake [*Canada*] [*Airport symbol*]   (OAG)
YRS .... Yale Romanic Studies [*A publication*]
YRS .... Yearbook of Romanian Studies [*A publication*]
YRS........... Yours
YRS .... Yugoslav Relief Society
YRST .... Salvage Craft Tender [*Non-self-propelled*] [*Navy ship symbol*]
YRT .... Rankin Inlet [*Canada*] [*Airport symbol*]   (OAG)
YRT .... Yearly Renewable Term [*Insurance*]
YRT .... Yellowroot Tea [*Folk remedy, extract of buttercup root*]
YRTMA.... Yonsei Reports on Tropical Medicine [*A publication*]
YS .... Aeronautical Station [*ICAO designator*]   (ICDA)
YS .... El Salvador [*Aircraft nationality and registration mark*]   (FAAC)
YS .... Nihon Aeroplane Manufacturing Co. Ltd. [*Japan*] [*ICAO aircraft manufacturer identifier*]   (ICAO)
ys............. Southern Yemen (Aden) [*MARC country of publication code*] [*Library of Congress*]   (LCCP)
YS .... Stevedoring Barge [*Navy symbol*] [*Obsolete*]
YS .... Y-Axis of Solid Rocket Booster [*NASA*]   (NASA)
YS .... Yacht Service [*British military*]   (DMA)
YS .... Yard Superintendent
YS .... Yardstick
YS .... Yellow-Bellied Sapsucker [*Ornithology*]
YS .... Yellow Spot
YS .... Yeoman of Signals [*Australia*]
YS .... Yidishe Shprakh [*A publication*]
YS .... Yield Spread [*Investment term*]
YS .... Yield Strength [*Ordinarily expressed in PSI*]
YS .... Yield Stress
YS .... Yoshida Sarcoma [*Medicine*]
YS .... Young Soldier
YS .... Younger Son   (ROG)
YS .... Youngstown & Southern Railway Co. [*AAR code*]
YSA........... Young Socialist Alliance   (EA)
YSA........... Youth Service America   (EA)
YSAAP ...... Youth Supported Accommodation Assistance Program [*Australia*]
YSAF........ Young Scientists of America Foundation   (EA)
YSB........... Salomon Brothers Library, New York, NY [*OCLC symbol*]   (OCLC)
YSB........... Sudbury [*Canada*] [*Airport symbol*]   (OAG)
YSB........... Yacht Safety Bureau   (EA)
YSB........... Yield Stress Bonding
YSC........... South Central Research Library Council, Ithaca, NY [*OCLC symbol*]   (OCLC)
YSC........... Yearly Spares Cost   (MCD)
YSCECP Reports ... Yugoslav-Serbo-Croatian-English Contrastive Project. Reports [*A publication*]
YSCECP Studies ... Yugoslav-Serbo-Croatian-English Contrastive Project. Studies [*A publication*]
YSCO........ Yes Clothing Co. [*NASDAQ symbol*]   (NQ)
YSD .... Seaplane Wrecking Derrick [*Self-propelled*] [*Navy symbol*]
YSD .... Young Social Democrats   (EA)
YSDB........ Yield Stress Diffusion Bonding
YSE........... Yale Studies in English [*A publication*]
YSE........... Yaw Steering Error
YS/E .... Yield Strength to Elastic Modulus Ratio [*Dentistry*]
YSF........... Stoney Rapids [*Canada*] [*Airport symbol*]   (OAG)
YSF........... Yield Safety Factor [*IEEE*]
YSG .... Young Solicitors' Group [*British*]
YSh .... Yidishe Shprakh [*A publication*]
YSHBDP... Bulletin. Vegetable and Ornamental Crops Research Station. Series B [*Morioka*] [*A publication*]
YSI........... Sans Souci [*Canada*] [*Airport symbol*]   (OAG)
YSI............ Yellow Springs Instrument Co.

YSICSA ..... Yellow Springs Institute for Contemporary Studies and the Arts (EA)
YSJ .... Saint John [*Canada*] [*Airport symbol*] (OAG)
YSK .... Sanikiluaq [*Canada*] [*Airport symbol*] (OAG)
YSK .... Yokosuka [*Japan*] [*Seismograph station code, US Geological Survey*] [*Closed*] (SEIS)
YSKOD8 ... Japanese Journal of Psychopharmacology [*A publication*]
YSL .... Saint Leonard [*Canada*] [*Airport symbol*] (OAG)
YSL .... Yolk Syncytial Layer [*Embryology*]
YSL .... Young Sowers' League [*British*]
YSL .... Yves Saint Laurent [*French couturier*]
Y-SLAV ..... Yugoslavia
YSLF .... Yield Strength Load Factor (IEEE)
YSM .... Fort Smith [*Canada*] [*Airport symbol*] (OAG)
YSM .... State University of New York at Stony Brook, Stony Brook, NY [*OCLC symbol*] (OCLC)
YSM .... Yangtze Service Medal
YSM .... Young Socialist Movement
YSNC .... Youth Suicide National Center (EA)
YSO .... Young Stellar Object
YSP .... Pontoon Salvage Vessel [*Navy symbol*]
YSP .... Years Service for Severance Pay Purposes [*Military*]
YSP .... Yemen Socialist Party [*South Yemen*] [*Political party*] (PD)
YSR .... Nanisivik [*Canada*] [*Airport symbol*] (OAG)
YSR .... Sludge Removal Barge [*Non-self-propelled*] [*Navy symbol*]
YSR .... Years of Service Required
YSS .... Youth Services Scheme [*Australia*]
YSS .... Yuzhno-Sakhalinsk [*USSR*] [*Seismograph station code, US Geological Survey*] (SEIS)
YSS .... Yuzhno-Sakhalinsk [*USSR*] [*Geomagnetic observatory code*]
YST .... Saint Therese Point [*Canada*] [*Airport symbol*] (OAG)
YST .... Yolk Sac Tumor [*Oncology*]
YST .... Youngest
YSTC .... Yorkshire Society of Textile Craftsmen [*A union*] [*British*] (DCTA)
YSY .... Sachs Harbour [*Canada*] [*Airport symbol*] (OAG)
YT .... Harbor Tug [*Navy symbol*]
YT .... Telecommunication Authority [*ICAO designator*] (ICDA)
YT .... Y-Axis of External Tank [*NASA*] (NASA)
YT .... Yacht (ROG)
YT .... Yankee Team [*Phase of the Indochina bombing operation during US military involvement in Vietnam*]
YT .... Yaw Trim (MCD)
YT .... Yom Tov (BJA)
Yt .... Yttrium [*See also Y*] [*Chemical element*]
YT .... Yukon Territory [*Canada*] [*Postal code*]
YTA .... Pembroke [*Canada*] [*Airport symbol*] (OAG)
YTA .... Yaw Trim Angle
YTA .... Yiddish Theatrical Alliance (EA)
YTB .... Large Harbor Tug [*Self-propelled*] [*Navy symbol*]
YTB .... Yard Tug Big [*Navy*]
YTB .... Yarn to Back [*Knitting*] (ADA)
YTB .... Yield to Broker [*Investment term*]
YTB .... Yuma Test Branch [*Army*] [*Yuma, AZ*]
YTC .... Yield to Call [*Investment term*]
YTC .... Yorkshire Trust Co. [*Toronto Stock Exchange symbol*] [*Vancouver Stock Exchange symbol*]
YTC .... Youth Training Centre [*Australia*]
YTCA .... Yorkshire Terrier Club of America (EA)
YTD .... Year to Date (MCD)
YTD .... Young Tree Decline [*Plant pathology*]
YTE .... Cape Dorset [*Canada*] [*Airport symbol*] (OAG)
YTEC .... Yarsley Technical Centre Ltd. [*Research center*] [*British*] (IRC)
YTELSA ..... Yearbook. Estonian Learned Society in America [*A publication*]
YTEP .... Youth Training and Employment Project
YTF .... Yad Tikvah Foundation (EA)
YTF .... Yarn to Front [*Knitting*] (ADA)
YTH .... Thompson [*Canada*] [*Airport symbol*] (OAG)
YTHJ .... Yeshivath Torah Hayim in Jerusalem (EA)
YTI .... Yeshiba Toledot Isaac. Tetuan (BJA)
YTJ .... Terrace Bay [*Canada*] [*Airport symbol*] (OAG)
YTL .... Big Trout Lake [*Canada*] [*Airport symbol*] (OAG)
YTL .... Small Harbor Tug [*Self-propelled*] [*Navy symbol*]
YTL .... Youth Tennis League (EA)
YTM .... Medium Harbor Tug [*Self-propelled*] [*Navy symbol*]
YTM .... State University of New York, College at Utica-Rome, Utica, NY [*OCLC symbol*] (OCLC)
YTM .... Yearbook for Traditional Music [*A publication*]
YTM .... Yield to Maturity [*Investment term*]
YTRES ...... Yankee Tractor Rocket Escape System (MCD)
YTS .... Timmins [*Canada*] [*Airport symbol*] (OAG)
YTS .... Youth Training Scheme [*British*]
YTS .... Yuma Test Station [*Missiles*]
YTT .... Torpedo Testing Barge [*Navy symbol*] [*Obsolete*]
YTTBT ...... Yield Threshold Test Ban Treaty [*1976*]
YTU .... Yarra Theological Union [*Australia*]
YTV .... Yaw Thrust Vector
YTV .... Yorkshire Television [*British*]
YTX .... Planned District Craft [*Navy symbol*]
YTZ .... Toronto [*Canada*] [*Airport symbol*] (OAG)

YU .... Yale Divinity School, New Haven, CT [*OCLC symbol*] [*Inactive*] (OCLC)
YU .... Yale University
YU .... Yeshiva University [*New York*]
YU .... Yugoslavia [*Aircraft nationality and registration mark*] (FAAC)
YU .... Yugoslavia [*ANSI two-letter standard code*] (CNC)
yu .... Yugoslavia [*MARC country of publication code*] [*Library of Congress*] (LCCP)
YU .... Yukon News [*A publication*]
Yu .... Yunost' [*Moscow*] [*A publication*]
Yuasa Tech Inf ... Yuasa Technical Information [*Japan*] [*A publication*]
YUB .... Tuktoyaktuk [*Canada*] [*Airport symbol*] (OAG)
YUBA .... Yuba Natural Resources, Inc. [*NASDAQ symbol*] (NQ)
Yubbie .... Young Urban Baby [*Lifestyle classification*]
Yubbie .... Young Urban Breadwinner [*Lifestyle classification*]
YuBN .... Narodna Biblioteka Socijalisticke Republike Srbije, Beograd, Yugoslavia [*Library symbol*] [*Library of Congress*] (LCLS)
YUBO .... Yucca House National Monument
YUC .... Yucana Resources, Inc. [*Vancouver Stock Exchange symbol*]
YUC .... Yucatan
Yuca .... Young Upwardly Mobile Cuban-American [*Lifestyle classification*]
Yucca .... Young Up-and-Coming Cuban American [*Lifestyle classification*]
YUCI .... Yeshiva University Cumulative Index of Films of Jewish Interest [*A publication*] (BJA)
Yuckie .... Young Ultimate Creative Kitscher [*Lifestyle classification*]
Yuckie .... Young Urban Catholic [*Lifestyle classification*]
YUEN .... Yukon Economic News [*A publication*]
YUF .... Pelly Bay [*Canada*] [*Airport symbol*] (OAG)
Yuffie .... Young Urban Failure [*Lifestyle classification*]
YUG .... Yugawaralite [*A zeolite*]
YUG .... Yugoslavia [*ANSI three-letter standard code*] (CNC)
Yugo Exprt ... Yugoslavia Export [*A publication*]
Yugo L .... Yugoslav Law [*A publication*] (DLA)
Yugos .... Yugoslavia
Yugoslav L ... Yugoslav Law [*A publication*]
Yugosl Chem Pap ... Yugoslav Chemical Papers [*A publication*]
Yugosl Hop Symp Proc ... Yugoslav Hop Symposium. Proceedings [*A publication*]
Yugosl Law ... Yugoslav Law [*A publication*]
Yugosl Surv ... Yugoslav Survey [*A publication*]
Yugosl Zavod Geol Geofiz Istrazivanja Raspr ... Yugoslavia Zavod za Geoloska i Geofizicka Istrazivanja. Rasprave [*A publication*]
Yugosl Zavod Geol Geofiz Istrazivanja Vesn Geol ... Yugoslavia Zavod za Geoloska i Geofizicka Istrazivanja. Vesnik. Geologija. Serija A [*Belgrade*] [*A publication*]
Yug Soc Soil Sci Publ ... Yugoslav Society of Soil Science. Publication [*A publication*]
Yug Surv .... Yugoslav Survey [*A publication*]
YUHPAA .. Acta Horticulturalia [*Peking*] [*A publication*]
YU/IJCS ... International Journal of Comparative Sociology. York University. Department of Sociology and Anthropology [*Toronto, Canada*] [*A publication*]
YUIN .... Yukon Indian News [*A publication*]
YUK .... Youth Uncovering Krud [*Antipollution organization in Schenectady, New York*]
YUK .... Yuzhno-Kurilsk [*USSR*] [*Seismograph station code, US Geological Survey*] (SEIS)
YUKN .... Yukon Energy Corp. [*St. Paul, MN*] [*NASDAQ symbol*] (NQ)
Yuk Ord ..... Yukon Ordinances [*Canada*] [*A publication*] (DLA)
Yuk Rev Ord ... Yukon Revised Ordinances [*Canada*] [*A publication*] (DLA)
Yuk Stat ..... Statutes of the Yukon Territory [*A publication*]
YUL .... Montreal [*Canada*] [*Airport symbol*] (OAG)
YUL .... Yale University Library
YULG .... Yale University. Library. Gazette [*A publication*]
Yullie .... Young Urban Laborer [*Lifestyle classification*]
YUM .... Yale Medical School, New Haven, CT [*OCLC symbol*] [*Inactive*] (OCLC)
YUM .... Yuma [*Arizona*] [*Airport symbol*] (OAG)
YUM .... Yuma Gold Mines Ltd. [*Vancouver Stock Exchange symbol*]
YUM .... Yumen [*Republic of China*] [*Seismograph station code, US Geological Survey*] (SEIS)
Yummie ...... Young Upwardly Mobile Marxist [*Lifestyle classification*]
Yummie ...... Young Upwardly Mobile Mountains [*Rocky Mountains*] [*Geological take-off on the abbreviation, Yuppie*] [*Canada*]
Yummie ...... Young Urban Minister [*Lifestyle classification*]
Yummy ...... Young Upwardly Mobile Mommy [*Lifestyle classification*]
Yumpie .... Young Upwardly Mobile Professional [*Lifestyle classification*]
Yumpy .... Young Upwardly Mobile Papa [*Lifestyle classification*]
YUMY .... Tofruzen, Inc. [*NASDAQ symbol*] (NQ)
YUN .... Yearbook of the United Nations [*A publication*] (DLA)
YUO .... Yuojima [*Bonin Islands*] [*Seismograph station code, US Geological Survey*] [*Closed*] (SEIS)
Yuplis .... Young Urban Professional Library Information Specialist [*Lifestyle classification*]
Yuppie .... Young Urban Professional [*Lifestyle classification*] [*In book title "The Yuppie Handbook"*]

YUR.......... Yuriko Resources [*Vancouver Stock Exchange symbol*]
Yurpie .... Young, Urban Republican Professional [*Lifestyle classification*]
YUS .... Yale University, New Haven, CT [*OCLC symbol*] (OCLC)
YUS .... Yushan [*Mount Morrison*] [*Republic of China*] [*Seismograph station code, US Geological Survey*] (SEIS)
YuSaN .... Narodne Biblioteka Bosne i Hercegovine [*National Library of Bosnia and Herzegovina*], Sarajevo, Yugoslavia [*Library symbol*] [*Library of Congress*] (LCLS)
YuSkN .... Nacionalna Biblioteka na Makedonija "Kliment Ohridaki", Skopje, Yugoslavia [*Library symbol*] [*Library of Congress*] (LCLS)
Yussie........ Young Unescorted Single [*Lifestyle classification*]
YUTR .... Yukon Teacher [*A publication*]
YUUD........ Yukon Update [*A publication*]
YUWM...... Yukon Water Management Bulletin. Westwater Research Centre [*A publication*]
YUX.......... Hall Beach [*Canada*] [*Airport symbol*] (OAG)
YUY.......... Rouyn-Noranda [*Canada*] [*Airport symbol*] (OAG)
YuZU .... Nacionalna i Sveucilisna Biblioteka [*National and University Library of Croatia*], Zagreb, Yugoslavia [*Library symbol*] [*Library of Congress*] (LCLS)
YV .... Drone Aircraft Catapult Control Craft [*Navy symbol*] [*Obsolete*]
YV .... Venezuela [*Aircraft nationality and registration mark*] (FAAC)
YV .... Yad Vashem (EAIO)
YVA .... Moroni [*Comoro Islands*] [*Airport symbol*] (OAG)
YVA .... Yad Vashem Archives (BJA)
YVA .... Young Volunteers in ACTION
YVB .... Bonaventure [*Canada*] [*Airport symbol*] (OAG)
YVC .... Catapult Lighter [*Navy symbol*]
YVC .... Lac La Ronge [*Canada*] [*Airport symbol*] (OAG)
YVC .... Yellow Varnish Cambric
Y Viewers... Young Viewers [*A publication*]
YVM .... Broughton [*Canada*] [*Airport symbol*] (OAG)
YVO.......... Onondaga Library System, Syracuse, NY [*OCLC symbol*] (OCLC)
YVO.......... Val D'Or [*Canada*] [*Airport symbol*] (OAG)
YVP .... Fort Chimo [*Canada*] [*Airport symbol*] (OAG)
YVQ.......... Norman Wells [*Canada*] [*Airport symbol*] (OAG)
YVR .... Vancouver [*Canada*] [*Airport symbol*] (OAG)
YVS .... Yad Vashem Studies [*A publication*]
YVT .... Buffalo Narrows [*Canada*] [*Airport symbol*] [*Obsolete*] (OAG)
YVT .... Yakima Valley Transportation Co. [*AAR code*]
YVT .... Youth Visiting Team [*British military*] (DMA)
YW .... Military Flight Operational Control Center [*ICAO designator*] (ICDA)
YW .... Water Barge [*Self-propelled*] [*Navy symbol*]
YW .... Whitehorse Public Library, Yukon [*Library symbol*] [*National Library of Canada*] (NLC)
YW .... Year's Work in English Studies [*A publication*]
YW .... Yellow-White
YW .... Young Woman [*A publication*]
YW .... Young Women of the Church of Jesus Christ of Latter-Day Saints (EA)
YW .... Young Women's [*Christian Association*]
YW .... Yreka Western Railroad Co. [*AAR code*]
YWA .... Year's Work in Archaeology [*A publication*]
YWA .... Yukon Archives, Whitehorse, Yukon [*Library symbol*] [*National Library of Canada*] (NLC)
YWAM...... Youth with a Mission (EA)
YWC .... Year's Work in Classical Studies [*A publication*]
YWC .... Yukon College, Whitehorse, Yukon [*Library symbol*] [*National Library of Canada*] (NLC)
YWCA ...... World Young Women's Christian Association (EAIO)
YWCA ...... Young Women Committed to Action [*Feminist group*]
YWCA-USA ... Young Women's Christian Association of the United States of America (EA)
YWCJCLS ... Young Women of the Church of Jesus Christ of Latter-Day Saints [*Later, YW*] (EA)
YWCS....... Year's Work in Classical Studies [*A publication*]
YWCTU .... Young Women's Christian Temperance Union
YWDN...... Water Distilling Barge [*Non-self-propelled*] [*Navy symbol*]
YWE .... Year's Work in English Studies [*A publication*]
YWED .... Department of Economic Development: Mines and Small Business, Government of the Yukon, Whitehorse, Yukon [*Library symbol*] [*National Library of Canada*] (NLC)
YWEEP..... Environmental Protection Service, Environment Canada [*Service de la Protection de l'Environnement, Environnement Canada*] Whitehorse, Yukon [*Library symbol*] [*National Library of Canada*] (NLC)
YWES....... Year's Work in English Studies [*A publication*]
YWF .... Young World Federalists [*Later, World Federalist Youth*]
YWFD .... Young World Food and Development [*UN Food and Agriculture Organization*]
YWG.......... Winnipeg [*Canada*] [*Airport symbol*] (OAG)
YWGASOYA ... You Won't Get Ahead Sitting on Your Afterdeck [*Slang*] [*Bowdlerized version*]
YWH.......... Victoria [*Canada*] [*Airport symbol*] (OAG)
YWHA....... Young Women's Hebrew Association [*Later, YM-YWHA*]

YWHHR ... Department of Health and Human Resources, Government of the Yukon, Whitehorse, Yukon [*Library symbol*] [*National Library of Canada*] (NLC)
YWHS ...... Whitehorse Historical Society, Yukon [*Library symbol*] [*National Library of Canada*] (NLC)
YWHS ...... Young Women's Help Society [*British*]
YWIN .... Northern Program, Indian and Northern Affairs Canada [*Programme du Nord, Affaires Indiennes et du Nord Canada*] [*Library symbol*] [*National Library of Canada*] (BIB)
YWK.......... Wabush [*Canada*] [*Airport symbol*] (OAG)
YWL .... Williams Lake [*Canada*] [*Airport symbol*] (OAG)
YWL .... Yawl
YWL .... Yukon Law Library, Whitehorse, Yukon [*Library symbol*] [*National Library of Canada*] (NLC)
YWLL........ Young Workers Liberation League
YWLS .... Library Services Branch, Government of the Yukon, Whitehorse, Yukon [*Library symbol*] [*National Library of Canada*] (NLC)
YWM .... United States Military Academy, West Point, NY [*OCLC symbol*] (OCLC)
YWML ..... Year's Work in Modern Language Studies [*A publication*]
YWMLS... Year's Work in Modern Language Studies [*A publication*]
YWN.......... Water Barge [*Non-self-propelled*] [*Navy symbol*]
YWN.......... Winisk [*Canada*] [*Airport symbol*] (OAG)
YWOM ..... [*The*] Old Log Church Museum, Whitehorse, Yukon [*Library symbol*] [*National Library of Canada*] (NLC)
YWP .... Sir Hugh Young's Working Party for Estimation of Civilian Relief Requirements [*World War II*]
YWPCN .... National Historic Sites, Parks Canada [*Lieux Historiques Nationaux, Parcs Canada*] Whitehorse, Yukon [*Library symbol*] [*National Library of Canada*] (NLC)
YWPG .... Young World Promotion Group [*UN Food and Agriculture Organization*]
YWR .... Yorkshire, West Riding [*County in England*] (ROG)
YWRR ...... Department of Renewable Resources, Government of the Yukon, Whitehorse, Yukon [*Library symbol*] [*National Library of Canada*] (NLC)
YWS .... Young Wales Society
YWS .... Young Workers Scheme [*British*]
YWT .... Yard-Walk-Throughs [*Navy*] (NG)
YWTA .... Department of Territorial Affairs, Government of the Yukon, Whitehorse, Yukon [*Library symbol*] [*Obsolete*] [*National Library of Canada*] (NLC)
YWU.......... Yiddish Writers Union (EA)
YWY .... Wrigley [*Canada*] [*Airport symbol*] (OAG)
YX .... Military Service or Organization [*ICAO designator*] (ICDA)
YXC .... Cranbrook [*Canada*] [*Airport symbol*] (OAG)
YXD.......... Edmonton [*Canada*] Municipal Airport [*Airport symbol*] (OAG)
YXE .... Saskatoon [*Canada*] [*Airport symbol*] (OAG)
YXF .... Four County Library System, Binghamton, NY [*OCLC symbol*] (OCLC)
YXH.......... Medicine Hat [*Canada*] [*Airport symbol*] (OAG)
YXJ............ Fort St. John [*Canada*] [*Airport symbol*] (OAG)
YXK .... Rimouski [*Canada*] [*Airport symbol*] (OAG)
YXL .... Sioux Lookout [*Canada*] [*Airport symbol*] (OAG)
YXO .... Houghton College, Buffalo Campus, West Seneca, NY [*OCLC symbol*] (OCLC)
YXP .... Pangnirtung [*Canada*] [*Airport symbol*] (OAG)
YXR .... Earlton [*Canada*] [*Airport symbol*] (OAG)
YXS .... Prince George [*Canada*] [*Airport symbol*] (OAG)
YXT .... Terrace [*Canada*] [*Airport symbol*] (OAG)
YXU .... London [*Canada*] [*Airport symbol*] (OAG)
YXX .... Abbotsford [*Canada*] [*Airport symbol*]
YXY .... Whitehorse [*Canada*] [*Airport symbol*] (OAG)
YXZ .... Wawa [*Canada*] [*Airport symbol*] (OAG)
YY............. Organization not allocated a 2-letter designator on an exclusive basis [*ICAO designator*] (ICDA)
YY .... Robert Lynd [*American author, 1892-1970*] [*Pseudonym*]
Y-Y............ Yaw Axis (AAG)
YY .... Yedi'ot Yanai (BJA)
YYB .... North Bay [*Canada*] [*Airport symbol*] (OAG)
YYC .... Calgary [*Canada*] [*Airport symbol*] (OAG)
YYCI......... Youth-to-Youth Committee International (EA)
YYD.......... Smithers [*Canada*] [*Airport symbol*] (OAG)
YYE .... Fort Nelson [*Canada*] [*Airport symbol*] (OAG)
YYF .... Penticton [*Canada*] [*Airport symbol*] (OAG)
YYG .... Charlottetown [*Canada*] [*Airport symbol*] (OAG)
YYH.......... Spence Bay [*Canada*] [*Airport symbol*] (OAG)
YYJ........... Victoria [*Canada*] [*Airport symbol*] (OAG)
YYL .... Lynn Lake [*Canada*] [*Airport symbol*] [*Obsolete*] (OAG)
YYP .... Yarns of Yesteryear Project (EA)
YYP .... Yeshiva University, New York, NY [*OCLC symbol*] (OCLC)
YYQ.......... Churchill [*Canada*] [*Airport symbol*] (OAG)
YYR .... Goose Bay [*Canada*] [*Airport symbol*] (OAG)
YYR .... Year of the Young Reader [*1989*] [*Library of Congress campaign*]
YYS........... Yo-Yo Stock [*Investment term*]
YYSCI .... Youth-to-Youth Sports Committee International (EA)
YYT .... St. Johns [*Canada*] [*Airport symbol*] (OAG)

YYU .... Kapuskasing [*Canada*] [*Airport symbol*]   (OAG)
YYY .... Mont-Joli [*Canada*] [*Airport symbol*]   (OAG)
YYY .... Yugntruf - Youth for Yiddish   (EA)
YYYC .... Yu-Yen Yen-Chiu [*Linguistic Researches*] [*A publication*]
YYZ .... Toronto [*Canada*] [*Airport symbol*]   (OAG)
YZ .... MET Databank [*ICAO designator*]   (ICDA)
YZA .... Albany Law School, Albany, NY [*OCLC symbol*]   (OCLC)
YZF .... Yellowknife [*Canada*] [*Airport symbol*]   (OAG)
YZG .... Sugluk [*Canada*] [*Airport symbol*]   (OAG)
YZP .... Sandspit [*Canada*] [*Airport symbol*]   (OAG)
YZR .... Sarnia [*Canada*] [*Airport symbol*]   (OAG)
YZS .... Coral Harbour [*Canada*] [*Airport symbol*]   (OAG)
YZSZ .... Yarlung Zangbo Suture Zone [*Geophysics*]
YZT .... Port Hardy [*Canada*] [*Airport symbol*]   (OAG)
YZV .... Sept-Iles [*Canada*] [*Airport symbol*]   (OAG)

Z

Z............... Administrative Aircraft [*When a suffix to Navy plane designation*]
Z............... Atomic Number [*Symbol*]
z............... Aza [*As substituent on nucleoside*] [*Biochemistry*]
Z............... Azimuth Angle
z............... Charge Number of a Cell Reaction [*Symbol*] [*Electrochemistry*]
Z............... Collision Number [*Symbol*] [*IUPAC*]
Z............... Compression Factor [*Symbol*] [*Thermodynamics*]
Z............... Contraction [*Medicine*]
Z............... Coriolis Correction
Z............... Figure of Merit [*Symbol*]   (DEN)
Z............... Glutamic Acid [*or Glutamine*] [*Also, Glx*] [*Symbol*] [*An amino acid*]
Z............... Greenwich Mean Time   (FAAC)
Z............... Impedance [*Symbol*] [*IUPAC*]
Z............... Jet Terminal Area [*Aviation symbol*]   (FAAC)
Z............... Normally Open [*Ship's fittings classification*]
z............... Partition Function, Particle [*Symbol*] [*IUPAC*]
Z............... Partition Function, System [*Symbol*] [*IUPAC*]
Z............... Planning [*Aircraft classification letter*]
Z............... Stadia [*Speedways, race tracks, etc.*] [*Public-performance tariff class*] [*British*]
Z............... Standard Score [*Psychology*]
Z............... Switzerland [*IYRU nationality code*]   (IYR)
Z............... Symbol for Magnetic Reluctance   (ROG)
Z............... Tower Control [*Aviation symbol*]   (FAAC)
Z............... [*The Third*] Unknown Quantity [*Mathematics*]   (ROG)
Z............... Vertical component of the earth's magnetic field
Z............... Weekend Travel [*Also, W*] [*Airline fare code*]
Z............... Woolworth Corp. [*NYSE symbol*] [*Wall Street slang name: "Five & Dime"*] [*Toronto Stock Exchange symbol*]   (SPSG)
Z............... Z-Axis
Z............... [*Franciscus*] Zabarella [*Deceased, 1417*] [*Authority cited in pre-1607 legal work*]   (DSA)
Z............... Zagreb [*A publication*]
Z............... Zaire [*Monetary unit in Zaire*]
Z............... Zambon [*Italy*] [*Research code symbol*]
Z............... Zebra [*Phonetic alphabet*] [*Royal Navy*] [*World War I*] [*Pre-World War II*] [*World War II*]   (DSUE)
Z............... Zeitschrift [*Review*] [*German*]   (ILCA)
Z............... Zeitschrift fuer Romanische Philologie [*A publication*]
Z............... Zeitung [*Newspaper, Review*] [*German*]   (ILCA)
Z............... Zenith
Z............... Zenith Distance [*Navigation*]
Z............... Zentralblatt [*Official Gazette*] [*German*]   (ILCA)
Z............... Zentrumspartei [*Center Party*] [*German*] [*Political party*]   (PPE)
Z............... Zero
Z............... Zero Rate [*Valued added tax*]
Z............... Zerubbabel [*Freemasonry*]   (ROG)
Z............... Zinc [*Chemical symbol is Zn*]
Z............... Zionist
Z............... Zircon [*CIPW classification*] [*Geology*]
Z............... Zirconium [*Chemical element*] [*Symbol is Zr*]   (ROG)
Z............... Zivot [*A publication*]
Z............... Zloty [*Monetary unit*] [*Poland*]
Z............... Zoen Tencararius [*Flourished, 13th century*] [*Authority cited in pre-1607 legal work*]   (DSA)
Z............... Zoll [*Customs Duty*] [*German*]
Z............... Zone
Z............... Zone Marker
Z............... Zone Meridian [*Lower or upper branch*]
Z............... Zora [*A publication*]
Z............... Zuender [*Fuze*] [*German military*]
Z............... Zuercher Bibel   (BJA)
Z............... Zulu [*Phonetic alphabet*] [*International*]   (DSUE)
Z............... Zulu Time [*Greenwich Mean Time*]   (AFM)
(Z)............... Zusammen [*Together*] [*Chemistry*]
Z............... Zven'ya [*A publication*]
Z............... Zwingliana [*A publication*]

Z............... Zycie [*A publication*]
Z............... Zyma AG [*Switzerland*] [*Research code symbol*]
Z (Day)....... Zero Day [*The date fixed for any important military operation*] [*British*]
ZA............. Approach Control Office [*ICAO designator*]   (ICDA)
ZA............. South Africa [*ANSI two-letter standard code*]   (CNC)
Za............. Zabriskie's Reports [*21-24 New Jersey*] [*A publication*]   (DLA)
Z-A............ Zaire-Afrique [*A publication*]
za............... Zambia [*MARC country of publication code*] [*Library of Congress*]   (LCCP)
Z f A .... Zeitschrift fuer Agrargeschichte und Agrarsoziologie [*A publication*]
Z f A .... Zeitschrift fuer Anatomie und Entwicklungsgeschichte [*A publication*]
ZA............. Zeitschrift fuer Assyriologie und Verwandte Gebiete [*A publication*]
ZA............. Zeitschrift fuer Assyriologie und Vorderasiatische Archaeologie [*Berlin*] [*A publication*]
ZA............. Zeitschrift fuer Astrophysik [*A publication*]
Z f A .... Zeitschrift fuer Astrophysik [*A publication*]
ZA............. Zeitschrift fuer Deutsches Altertum und Deutsche Literatur [*A publication*]
ZA............. Zenith Angle [*Geophysics*]
ZA............. Zentralarchiv fuer Empirische Sozialforschung [*Central Archives for Empirical Social Research*] [*University of Cologne*] [*Information service or system*]   (IID)
ZA............. Zero and Add
ZA............. Zero Adjuster   (MSA)
ZA............. Zinc-Aluminum [*An alloy*]
ZA............. Zionist Archives [*A publication*]
ZA............. Ziva Antika [*A publication*]
ZA............. Zone of Action
ZA............. Zoologischer Anzeiger [*A publication*]
ZA............. Zunz Archive. Jewish National and University Library [*Jerusalem*] [*A publication*]
ZAA .... Alice Arm/Kitsault [*Canada*] [*Airport symbol*]   (OAG)
ZAA .... Zartman Association of America   (EA)
ZAA .... Zeeman-Effect Atomic Absorption [*Spectrometry*]
ZAA .... Zeitschrift fuer Anglistik und Amerikanistik [*A publication*]
ZAA .... Zero Angle of Attack
Z Aachener Geschichtsver ... Zeitschrift. Aachener Geschichtsverein [*A publication*]
Z Aach Gesch Ver ... Zeitschrift. Aachener Geschichtsverein [*A publication*]
ZAAK .... Zeitschrift fuer Aesthetik und Allgemeine Kunstwissenschaft [*A publication*]
ZAAP........ Zero Antiaircraft Potential [*Missile*]
ZAB .... Albuquerque, NM [*Location identifier*] [*FAA*]   (FAAL)
Zab............ [*Franciscus*] Zabarella [*Deceased, 1417*] [*Authority cited in pre-1607 legal work*]   (DSA)
Zab............ Zabim   (BJA)
ZAB .... Zabrze [*Poland*] [*Seismograph station code, US Geological Survey*]   (SEIS)
ZAB .... Zinc-Air Battery
Zaba.......... [*Franciscus*] Zabarella [*Deceased, 1417*] [*Authority cited in pre-1607 legal work*]   (DSA)
ZABIA....... Zastita Bilja [*A publication*]
Zab Land Laws ... Zabriskie on the Public Land Laws of the United States [*A publication*]   (DLA)
Zab (NJ).... Zabriskie's Reports [*21-24 New Jersey*] [*A publication*]   (DLA)
ZABS......... Zab's Backyard Hots, Inc. [*Pittsford, NY*] [*NASDAQ symbol*]   (NQ)
Zaby Przyr Nieozyw ... Zabytki Przyrody Nieozywionej Ziem Rzeczpospolitej Polskiej [*A publication*]
ZACFA ...... Fresenius' Zeitschrift fuer Analytische Chemie [*A publication*]
ZACH .... Zacharias [*Old Testament book*] [*Douay version*]
ZA Ch .... Zeitschrift fuer Angewandte Chemie [*A publication*]
ZA Ch .... Zeitschrift fuer Anorganische Chemie [*A publication*]
ZA Ch .... Zurnal Analiticeskoj Chimii [*A publication*]
Z Acker-Pflanzenb ... Zeitschrift fuer Acker- und Pflanzenbau [*A publication*]
Z Acker Pflanzenbau ... Zeitschrift fuer Acker- und Pflanzenbau [*A publication*]

Z Acker u Pflbau ... Zeitschrift fuer Acker- und Pflanzenbau [*A publication*]
ZACMA .... Zeitschrift fuer Anorganische Chemie [*A publication*]
ZAD .... Zadar [*Yugoslavia*] [*Airport symbol*] (OAG)
ZAD .... Zenith Angle Distribution
ZADCC ...... Zone Air Defense Control Center (NATG)
ZADI .... Zentralstelle fuer Agrardokumentation und -Information
[*Center for Agricultural Documentation and Information*]
[*Databank originator*] [*Information service or system*]
[*Federal Republic of Germany*] (IID)
Zad Rev ...... Zadarska Revija [*A publication*]
ZADS .... Zeitschrift. Allgemeiner Deutsche Sprachverein [*A publication*]
ZAED .... Zentralstelle fuer Atomkernenergie-Dokumentation beim
Gmelin-Institut [*Central Agency for Atomic Energy
Documentation of the Gmelin Institute*] [*Germany*]
[*Database originator*] [*Also, AED*]
ZAED Phys Daten ... ZAED [*Zentralstelle fuer Atomkernenergie-
Dokumentation*] Physik Daten [*A publication*]
ZAeg .... Zeitschrift fuer Aegyptische Sprache und Altertumskunde [*A
publication*]
ZAEG .... Zeitschrift fuer Anatomie und Entwicklungsgeschichte [*A
publication*]
Z Aeg Spr... Zeitschrift fuer Aegyptische Sprache und Altertumskunde [*A
publication*]
Z Aegypt Sprache ... Zeitschrift fuer Aegyptische Sprache und
Altertumskunde [*A publication*]
Z Aegypt Sprache Altertumskd ... Zeitschrift fuer Aegyptische Sprache und
Altertumskunde [*A publication*]
ZAEKD ...... Zeszyty Naukowe. Akademia Ekonomiczna w Krakowie [*A
publication*]
Za Ekon Mater ... Za Ekonomiyu Materialov [*A publication*]
Za Ekon Topl ... Za Ekonomiyu Topliva [*A publication*]
Z Aerosol Forsch Ther ... Zeitschrift fuer Aerosol Forschung und Therapie [*A
publication*]
Z Aerztl Fortbild ... Zeitschrift fuer Aerztliche Fortbildung [*A publication*]
Z Aerztl Fortbild (Jena) ... Zeitschrift fuer Aerztliche Fortbildung (Jena) [*A
publication*]
Z Ae S .... Zeitschrift fuer Aegyptische Sprache und Altertumskunde [*A
publication*]
Z Aes Allg Kunst ... Zeitschrift fuer Aesthetik und Allgemeine
Kunstwissenschaft [*A publication*]
ZAF........... South Africa [*ANSI three-letter standard code*] (CNC)
ZAF........... Zero Alignment Fixture
ZAFBA ...... Zeitschrift fuer Aerztliche Fortbildung [*A publication*]
ZAG .... Zagreb [*Agram*] [*Yugoslavia*] [*Seismograph station code, US
Geological Survey*] (SEIS)
ZAG .... Zagreb [*Yugoslavia*] [*Airport symbol*] (OAG)
Zagad Ekon Roln ... Zagadnienia Ekonomiki Rolnej [*A publication*]
Zagadn Ekon Roln ... Zagadnienia Ekonomiki Rolnej [*A publication*]
Zagadn Eksploatacji Masz ... Zagadnienia Eksploatacji Maszyn [*Poland*] [*A
publication*]
Zagadnienia Drgan Nieliniowych ... Zagadnienia Drgan Nieliniowych
[*Nonlinear Vibration Problems*] [*A publication*]
Zagadnienie Dyn Rozwoju Czlowieka Zesz Probl Kosmosu ... Zagadnienie
Dynamiki Rozwoju Czlowieka Zeszyty Problemowe
Kosmosu [*A publication*]
Zagad Tech Fal Ultradziek ... Zagadnienia Techniki Fal Ultradzwiekowych [*A
publication*]
ZAGGD ..... Zeszyty Naukowe Akademii Gorniczo-Hutniczej Imienia
Stanislawa Staszica. Gornictwo [*A publication*]
Z Agrargesch Agrarsoziol ... Zeitschrift fuer Agrargeschichte und
Agrarsoziologie [*A publication*]
Z Agrargesch u -Soziol ... Zeitschrift fuer Agrargeschichte und Agrarsoziologie
[*A publication*]
Zagreber Studien ... Zagreber Germanistische Studien [*A publication*]
ZAGV .... Zeitschrift. Aachener Geschichtsverein [*A publication*]
ZAH........... Zahedan [*Iran*] [*Airport symbol*] (OAG)
ZAHAL ..... Z'va Hagana Le'Israel [*Israel Defense Forces*] [*Hebrew*]
Zahnaerztebl (Baden-Wuerttemb) ... Zahnaerzteblatt (Baden-Wuerttemberg)
[*A publication*]
Zahnaerztl Gesundheitsdienst ... Zahnaerztlicher Gesundheitsdienst [*A
publication*]
Zahnaerztl Mitt ... Zahnaerztliche Mitteilungen [*A publication*]
Zahnaerztl Prax ... Zahnaerztliche Praxis [*A publication*]
Zahnaerztl Praxisfuehr ... Zahnaerztliche Praxisfuehrung [*A publication*]
Zahnaerztl Rundsch ... Zahnaerztliche Rundschau [*A publication*]
Zahnaerztl Welt ... Zahnaerztliche Welt [*A publication*]
Zahnaerztl Welt Zahnaerztl Reform ... Zahnaerztliche Welt und
Zahnaerztliche Reform [*A publication*]
Zahnaerztl Welt Zahnaerztl Rundsch ... Zahnaerztliche Welt, Zahnaerztliche
Rundschau [*A publication*]
Zahnerh Kd ... Zahnerhaltungskunde [*A publication*]
Zahn Inf Die ... Zahnaerztlicher Informationsdienst [*A publication*]
Zahn-Mund-Kieferheilkd ... Zahn-, Mund-, und Kieferheilkunde [*A
publication*]
Zahn- Mund- Kieferheilkd Zentralbl ... Zahn-, Mund-, und Kieferheilkunde
mit Zentralblatt [*German Democratic Republic*] [*A
publication*]
Zahn Prax ... Zahnaerztliche Praxis [*A publication*]
Zahn Rd ..... Zahnaerztliche Rundschau [*A publication*]
Zahntechn ... Zahntechnik [*A publication*]
Zahntechn ... Zahntechniker [*A publication*]

Zahntechn Nachr ... Zahntechnische Nachrichten [*A publication*]
ZAI .... Zeirei Agudath Israel (EA)
ZAI .... Zero Address Instruction
ZAICEL ..... Zeitschrift fuer Angewandte Ichthyologie [*A publication*]
Zaire-Afr .... Zaire-Afrique [*A publication*]
ZAK .... Zakamensk [*USSR*] [*Seismograph station code, US Geological
Survey*] (SEIS)
ZAK .... Zeitschrift fuer Aesthetik und Kunstwissenschaft [*A
publication*]
ZAK .... Zeitschrift fuer Schweizerische Archaeologie und
Kunstgeschichte [*A publication*]
Zakhist Rosl ... Zakhist Roslin [*A publication*]
Za Khlopk Nezavisimost ... Za Khlopkovuyu Nezavisimost [*A publication*]
Zakhyst Rosl Resp Mizhvid Temat Nauk Zb ... Zakhyst Roslyn Respublikans
'Kyi Mizhvidomchyi Tematychnyi Naukovyi Zbirnyk [*A
publication*]
Zakonomern Raspred Promesnykh Tsentrov Ionnykh Krist ...
Zakonomernosti Raspredeleniya Promesnykh Tsentrov v
Ionnykh Kristallakh [*A publication*]
Zakonomern Razmeshcheniya Polezn Iskop ... Zakonomernosti
Razmeshcheniya Poleznykh Iskopaemykh [*A publication*]
Zakupki Sel'skokhoz Prod ... Zakupki Sel'skokhozyaistvennykh Produktov [*A
publication*]
ZAL .... State University of New York, Albany Library School, Albany,
NY [*OCLC symbol*] (OCLC)
ZAL .... Zeitschrift fuer Arabische Linguistik [*A publication*]
ZAL .... Zeitschrift fuer Auslaendische Landwirtschaft [*A publication*]
ZAL .... Zionist Archives and Library (BJA)
ZALIS .... Zinc and Lead International Service
Z Allgemeine Wissenschaftstheorie ... Zeitschrift fuer Allgemeine
Wissenschaftstheorie [*A publication*]
Z Allgemeinmed ... Zeitschrift fuer Allgemeinmedizin [*A publication*]
Z f Allg Med ... Zeitschrift fuer Allgemeinmedizin [*A publication*]
Z Allg Med ... Zeitschrift fuer Allgemeinmedizin der Landaerzt [*A
publication*]
Z Allg Mikr ... Zeitschrift fuer Allgemeine Mikrobiologie [*A publication*]
Z Allg Mikrobiol ... Zeitschrift fuer Allgemeine Mikrobiologie. Morphologie,
Physiologie, Genetik, und Oekologie der Mikrorganismen
[*A publication*]
Z Allg Oesterr Apoth Ver ... Zeitschrift. Allgemeiner Oesterreichische
Apotheker-Verein [*A publication*]
Z Allg Physiol ... Zeitschrift fuer Allgemeine Physiologie [*A publication*]
Z Allg Wiss ... Zeitschrift fuer Allgemeine Wissenschaftstheorie [*A
publication*]
Z Allg Wissenschaftstheor ... Zeitschrift fuer Allgemeine Wissenschaftstheorie
[*A publication*]
Z Alternsforsch ... Zeitschrift fuer Alternsforschung [*A publication*]
Z Altt W ..... Zeitschrift fuer die Alttestamentliche Wissenschaft [*A
publication*]
Z Alt Wiss ... Zeitschrift fuer die Alttestamentliche Wissenschaft [*A
publication*]
ZAM .... State University of New York, Agricultural and Technical
College at Alfred, Alfred, NY [*OCLC symbol*] (OCLC)
ZAM .... Z-Axis Modulation
ZAM .... Zamboanga [*Philippines*] [*Airport symbol*] (OAG)
ZAM .... Zeitschrift fuer Askese und Mystik [*A publication*]
Zambia Dep Game Fish Fish Res Bull ... Zambia. Department of Game and
Fisheries. Fisheries Research Bulletin [*A publication*]
Zambia Dep Wildl Fish Natl Parks Annu Rep ... Zambia. Department of
Wildlife, Fisheries, and National Parks. Annual Report [*A
publication*]
Zambia Div For Res Annu Rep ... Zambia. Division of Forest Research.
Annual Report [*A publication*]
Zambia Div For Res Res Pam ... Zambia. Division of Forest Research.
Research Pamphlet [*A publication*]
Zambia For Res Bull ... Zambia Forest Research Bulletin [*A publication*]
Zambia Geogr Assoc Mag ... Zambia Geographical Association. Magazine [*A
publication*]
Zambia Geol Surv Annu Rep ... Zambia. Geological Survey. Annual Report [*A
publication*]
Zambia Geol Surv Dep Annu Rep ... Zambia. Geological Survey. Department
Annual Report [*A publication*]
Zambia Geol Surv Dep Econ Rep ... Zambia. Ministry of Lands and Mines.
Geological Survey Department. Economic Report [*A
publication*]
Zambia Geol Surv Econ Rep ... Zambia. Geological Survey. Economic Report
[*A publication*]
Zambia Geol Surv Rec ... Zambia. Geological Survey. Records [*A publication*]
Zambia Geol Surv Tech Rep ... Zambia. Geological Survey. Technical Report
[*A publication*]
Zambia J Sci Technol ... Zambia Journal of Science and Technology [*A
publication*]
Zambia LJ ... Zambia Law Journal [*A publication*] (DLA)
Zambia Minist Lands Nat Resour For Res Bull ... Zambia. Ministry of Lands
and Natural Resources. Forest Research Bulletin [*A
publication*]
Zambia Minist Rural Dev For Res Bull ... Zambia. Ministry of Rural
Development. Forest Research Bulletin [*A publication*]
Zambia Nurse J ... Zambia Nurse Journal [*A publication*]
Zambia Rep Geol Surv ... Zambia. Ministry of Lands and Mines. Report of the
Geological Survey [*A publication*]

ZA Mech.... Zeitschrift fuer Angewandte Mechanik [*A publication*]

Zam LJ...... Zambia Law Journal [*A publication*]   (DLA)

ZAMM...... Zeitschrift fuer Angewandte Mathematik und Mechanik [*A publication*]

ZAMM...... Zen and the Art of Motorcycle Maintenance [*A novel*]

ZAMNA.... ZFA (Zeitschrift fuer Allgemeinmedizin) [*A publication*]

ZAMP .... Zeitschrift fuer Angewandte Mathematik und Physik [*A publication*]

ZAMS........ Zero-Age Main Sequence [*Astronomy*]

ZAN.......... Anchorage, AK [*Location identifier*] [*FAA*]   (FAAL)

ZAN.......... Zante [*Greece*] [*Seismograph station code, US Geological Survey*]   (SEIS)

ZAN.......... Zantop International Airlines, Inc. [*Ypsilanti, MI*] [*FAA designator*]   (FAAC)

ZANA........ Zambia News Agency

Z Anal Chem ... Fresenius' Zeitschrift fuer Analytische Chemie [*A publication*]

Z Analit Chim ... Zurnal Analiticeskoj Chimii [*A publication*]

Z Analyt Chem ... Zeitschrift fuer Analytische Chemie [*A publication*]

Z Anat Entwicklungsgesch ... Zeitschrift fuer Anatomie und Entwicklungsgeschichte [*A publication*]

ZANC........ Zambia National Congress - Southern Rhodesia

ZANCA ..... Zeitschrift fuer Analytische Chemie [*A publication*]

Z An Ch ..... Zeitschrift fuer Anorganische Chemie [*A publication*]

Z An Chim ... Zurnal Analiticeskoj Chimii [*A publication*]

ZANCO Ser A ... ZANCO. Scientific Journal of Sulaimaniyah University. Series A. Pure and Applied Sciences [*A publication*]

ZANCO Ser A Pure Appl Sci ... ZANCO. Series A. Pure and Applied Sciences [*A publication*]

Zane.......... Zane's Reports [*4-9 Utah*] [*A publication*]   (DLA)

ZANF .... Zeitschrift fuer Assyriologie und Vorderasiatische Altertumskunde. Neue Folge [*A publication*]

Z Ang & Amerik ... Zeitschrift fuer Anglistik und Amerikanistik [*A publication*]

Z Angew Baeder Klimaheilkd ... Zeitschrift fuer Angewandte Baeder und Klimaheilkunde [*A publication*]

Z Angew Chem ... Zeitschrift fuer Angewandte Chemie und Zentralblatt fuer Technische Chemie [*A publication*]

Z Angew Entomol ... Zeitschrift fuer Angewandte Entomologie [*A publication*]

Z Angew Geol ... Zeitschrift fuer Angewandte Geologie [*A publication*]

Z Angew Ichthyol ... Zeitschrift fuer Angewandte Ichthyologie [*A publication*]

Z Angew Math Mech ... Zeitschrift fuer Angewandte Mathematik und Mechanik [*A publication*]

Z Angew Math und Mech ... Zeitschrift fuer Angewandte Mathematik und Mechanik [*A publication*]

Z Angew Math Phys ... Zeitschrift fuer Angewandte Mathematik und Physik [*A publication*]

Z Angew Met ... Zeitschrift fuer Angewandte Meteorologie [*A publication*]

Z Angew Mikrosk Klin Chem ... Zeitschrift fuer Angewandte Mikroskopic und Klinische Chemie [*A publication*]

Z Angew Photogr Wiss Tech ... Zeitschrift fuer Angewandte Photographie in Wissenschaft und Technik [*A publication*]

Z Angew Phys ... Zeitschrift fuer Angewandte Physik [*A publication*]

Z Angew Psychol ... Zeitschrift fuer Angewandte Psychologie und Psychologische Forschung [*A publication*]

Z Angew Zool ... Zeitschrift fuer Angewandte Zoologie [*A publication*]

Z Ang Geol ... Zeitschrift fuer Angewandte Geologie [*A publication*]

Z Anglis Am ... Zeitschrift fuer Anglistik und Amerikanistik [*A publication*]

Z Ang Ma Me ... Zeitschrift fuer Angewandte Mathematik und Mechanik [*A publication*]

Z Ang Math ... Zeitschrift fuer Angewandte Mathematik und Physik [*A publication*]

Z Ang Math Mech ... Zeitschrift fuer Angewandte Mathematik und Mechanik [*A publication*]

Z Ang Math Phys ... Zeitschrift fuer Angewandte Mathematik und Physik [*A publication*]

Z Ang Ph.... Zeitschrift fuer Angewandte Physik [*A publication*]

ZANLA ..... Zimbabwe African National Liberation Army   (PD)

Z Anorg A C ... Zeitschrift fuer Anorganische und Allgemeine Chemie [*A publication*]

Z Anorg Allg Chem ... Zeitschrift fuer Anorganische und Allgemeine Chemie [*A publication*]

Z Anorg Chem ... Zeitschrift fuer Anorganische und Allgemeine Chemie [*A publication*]

ZANPA ..... Zeitschrift fuer Experimentelle und Angewandte Psychologie [*A publication*]

ZAnt.......... Ziva Antika [*A publication*]

Z Antimikrob Antineoplast Chemother ... Zeitschrift fuer Antimikrobielle und Antineoplastische Chemotherapie [*A publication*]

ZANU....... Zimbabwe African National Union [*Political party*]   (PPW)

ZANU-PF ... Zimbabwe African National Union - Patriotic Front [*Political party*]   (PD)

ZANZ .... Zanzibar

Zanzibar Protect Ann Rep Med Dept ... Zanzibar Protectorate. Annual Report on the Medical Department [*A publication*]

Zanzib Prot LR ... Zanzibar Protectorate Law Reports [*Africa*] [*A publication*]   (DLA)

Z Ao Ch ..... Zeitschrift fuer Anorganische Chemie [*A publication*]

ZA Oe R..... Zeitschrift fuer Auslaendisches Oeffentliches Recht und Voelkerrecht [*A publication*]

ZA Oe RV ... Zeitschrift fuer Auslaendisches Oeffentliches Recht und Voelkerrecht [*A publication*]

ZAO RV .... Zeitschrift fuer Auslaendisches Oeffentliches Recht und Voelkerrecht [*A publication*]

Za Ovladenie Tekh Kamenougol'n Promsti ... Za Ovladenie Tekhnikoi v Kamenougol'noi Promyshlennosti [*A publication*]

ZAP .... Helionetics, Inc. [*AMEX symbol*]   (SPSG)

zap............. Zapotec [*MARC language code*] [*Library of Congress*]   (LCCP)

ZAP .... Zero Ability to Pay [*Real estate*]

ZAP .... Zero and Add Packed

ZAP .... Zero Antiaircraft Potential [*Missile*]   (MCD)

ZAP .... Znamenity Amerikansky Pisatel [*Famous American Writer*] [*Russian*]

ZAP .... Zoological Action Program [*Defunct*]   (EA)

Zapadne Karpaty Ser Geol ... Zapadne Karpaty. Seria Geologia [*A publication*]

Zapadn Karpaty Ser Paleontol ... Zapadne Karpaty. Seria Paleontologia [*A publication*]

Zap Arm Otd Vses Mineral Ova ... Zapiski Armyanskogo Otdeleniya Vsesoyuznogo Mineralogicheskogo Obshchestva [*A publication*]

ZAPB........ Zinc-Air Primary Battery

Zap Beloruss Gos Inst Sel'sk Lesn Khoz ... Zapiski Belorusskogo Gosudarstvennogo Instituta Sel'skogo i Lesnogo Khozyaistva [*A publication*]

Zap Cukotsk Kraeved Muz ... Zapiski Cukotskogo Kraevedceskogo Muzeja [*A publication*]

Zap GO...... Zapiski Geograficeskogo Obscestva [*A publication*]

Zap Inst Jaz Lit Ist ... Zapiski Gosudarstvennogo Instituta Jazyka, Literatury, i Istorii [*A publication*]

Zap Inst Khim Akad Nauk Ukr RSR ... Zapiski Institutu Khimii Akademiya Nauk Ukrains'koi RSR [*A publication*]

Zapisnici Srp Geol Drus ... Zapisnici Srpskog Geoloskog Drustva [*A publication*]

Zap Kalm Nauc Issl Inst Jaz Lit Ist ... Zapiski. Kalmyckij Naucno-Issledovatel'skij Institut Jazyka, Literatury, i Istorii [*A publication*]

Zap Khar'k S-Kh Inst ... Zapiski Khar'kovskogo Sel'skokhozyaistvennogo Instituta [*A publication*]

Zap Kiiv Tov Prirodozn ... Zapiski Kiivs'kogo Tovaristva Prirodoznavtsiv [*A publication*]

Zap Kirg Otd Vses Mineral Ova ... Zapiski Kirgizskogo Otdeleniya Vsesoyuznogo Mineralogicheskogo Obshchestva [*A publication*]

Zap KORGO ... Zapiski Kavkazskogo Otdela Russkogo Geograficeskogo Obscestva [*A publication*]

Zap Leningrad Sel'skokhoz Inst ... Zapiski Leningradskogo Sel'skokhozyaistvennogo Instituta [*A publication*]

Zap Leningr Gorn Inst ... Zapiski Leningradskogo Gornogo Instituta [*USSR*] [*A publication*]

Zap Leningr Sel'-Khoz Inst ... Zapiski Leningradskogo Sel'skokhozyaistvennogo Instituta [*A publication*]

Zap Leningr S-Kh Inst ... Zapiski Leningradskogo Sel'skokhozyaistvennogo Instituta [*A publication*]

Zap Nauchn Semin ... Zapiski Nauchnykh Seminarov [*A publication*]

Zap Nauchn Semin Leningr Otd Mat Inst Akad Nauk SSSR ... Zapiski Nauchnykh Seminarov Leningradskoe Otdelenie Matematicheskii Institut Akademia Nauk SSSR [*USSR*] [*A publication*]

Zap Nauchn Sem Leningrad Otdel Mat Inst Steklov (LOMI) ... Zapiski Nauchnykh Seminarov Leningradskogo Otdeleniya Matematicheskogo Instituta Imeni V. A. Steklova Akademii Nauk SSSR (LOMI) [*A publication*]

Zap Naucn Sem Leningrad Otdel Mat Inst Steklov ... Zapiski Naucnyh Seminarov Leningradskogo Otdelenija Matematiceskogo Instituta Imeni V. A. Steklova Akademii Nauk SSSR [*A publication*]

Zap Odess Ark Obshch ... Zapiski Odesskoe Arkheologicheskoe Obshchestvo [*Odessa, USSR*] [*A publication*]

ZAPPA ...... Zentralblatt fuer Allgemeine Pathologie und Pathologische Anatomie [*A publication*]

Za Prog Proizvod ... Za Progress Proizvodstva [*A publication*]

Zap Ross Mineral Ova ... Zapiski Rossiiskogo Mineralogicheskogo Obshchestva [*A publication*]

ZAPS........ Cooper Life Sciences, Inc. [*NASDAQ symbol*]   (NQ)

Zap SKK Gor NII ... Zapiski Severo-Kavkazskogo Kraevogo Gorskogo Naucno-Issledovatel'skogo Instituta [*A publication*]

Zap Sverdl Otd Vses Bot Ova ... Zapiski Sverdlovskogo Otdeleniya Vsesoyuznogo Botanicheskogo Obshchestva [*A publication*]

Zap Sverdlov Otd Vsesoyuz Bot Obshch ... Zapiski Sverdlovskogo Otdeleniya Vsesoyuznogo Botanicheskogo Obshchestva [*A publication*]

Zap Tadzh Otd Vses Mineral Ova ... Zapiski Tadzhikskogo Otdeleniya Vsesoyuznogo Mineralogicheskogo Obshchestva [*A publication*]

Zap Tsentr Kavk Otd Vses Bot Ova ... Zapiski Tsentral'no-Kavkazskogo Otdeleniya Vsesoyuznogo Botanicheskogo Obshchestva [*A publication*]

ZAPU .... Zimbabwe African People's Union

Zap Ukr Otd Vses Mineral Ova ... Zapiski Ukrainskogo Otdeleniya Vsesoyuznogo Mineralogicheskogo Obshchestva [*A publication*]

Zap Uzb Otd Vses Mineral Ova ... Zapiski Uzbekistanskogo Otdeleniya Vsesoyuznogo Mineralogicheskogo Obshchestva [*A publication*]

Zap Voronezh Sel'-Khoz Inst ... Zapiski Voronezhskogo Sel'skokhozyaistvennogo Instituta [*A publication*]

Zap Voronezh S-Kh Inst ... Zapiski Voronezhskogo Sel'skokhozyaistvennogo Instituta [*A publication*]

Zap Vost Sib Otd Vses Mineral Ova ... Zapiski Vostochno-Sibirskogo Otdeleniya Vsesoyuznogo Mineralogicheskogo Obshchestva [*A publication*]

Zap Vses Mineral Obshchest ... Zapiski Vsesoyuznogo Mineralogicheskogo Obshchestva [*A publication*]

Zap Vses Mineral O-Va ... Zapiski Vsesoyuznogo Mineralogicheskogo Obshchestva [*A publication*]

Zap Zabaik Fil Geogr Ova SSSR ... Zapiski Zabaikal'skogo Filiala Geograficheskogo Obshchestva SSSR [*A publication*]

Zap Zabaik Otd Vses Geogr O-Va ... Zapiski Zabaikal'skogo Otdela Vsesoyuznogo Geograficheskogo Obshchestva [*A publication*]

ZAR .... Zaire [*ANSI three-letter standard code*]   (CNC)

ZAR .... Zaria [*Nigeria*] [*Geomagnetic observatory code*]

ZAR .... Zeus Acquisition RADAR [*Missile defense*]

Z Arbeitsgem Oesterr Entomol ... Zeitschrift. Arbeitsgemeinschaft Oesterreichischer Entomologen [*A publication*]

Z Arbeitswiss N F ... Zeitschrift fuer Arbeitswissenschaft. Neue Folge [*A publication*]

Z Archaeol ... Zeitschrift fuer Archaeologie [*A publication*]

Za Rekonstr Tekst Promsti ... Za Rekonstruktsiyu Tekstil'noi Promyshlennosti [*A publication*]

ZARP .... Zuid Afrikaansche Republick Politie [*South African Republic Police*]   (DSUE)

ZARSA ...... Zeszyty Naukowe. Akademia Rolnicza w Szczecinie [*A publication*]

ZarSl .... Zaranie Slaskie [*A publication*]

Zas .... [*Udalricus*] Zasius [*Deceased, 1535*] [*Authority cited in pre-1607 legal work*]   (DSA)

ZAS .... Zeitschrift fuer Aegyptische Sprache und Altertumskunde [*A publication*]

ZAS .... Zero Access Storage

ZAS .... Zymosan-Activated Serum [*Immunology*]

ZASA .... Zeitschrift fuer Aegyptische Sprache und Altertumskunde [*A publication*]

Zashch Korroz Khim Promsti ... Zashchita ot Korrozii v Khimicheskoi Promyshlennosti [*A publication*]

Zashch Met ... Zashchita Metallov [*A publication*]

Zashch Pokrytiya Met ... Zashchitnye Pokrytiya na Metallakh [*A publication*]

Zashch Rast (Kiev) ... Zashchita Rastenii (Kiev) [*A publication*]

Zashch Rast (Leningrad) ... Zashchita Rastenii (Leningrad) [*A publication*]

Zashch Rast (Mosc) ... Zashchita Rastenii (Moscow) [*A publication*]

Zashch Rast (Moscow) ... Zashchita Rastenii (Moscow) [*A publication*]

Zashch Rast Vred Bolez ... Zashchita Rastenii ot Vreditelei i Boleznei [*A publication*]

Zashch Rast Vred Bolezn ... Zashchita Rastenii ot Vreditelei i Boleznei [*A publication*]

Zashch Rast Vredit Bolez ... Zashchita Rastenii ot Vreditelei i Boleznei [*A publication*]

Zashch Truboprovodov Korroz ... Zashchita Truboprovodov ot Korrozii [*A publication*]

Zasi .... [*Udalricus*] Zasius [*Deceased, 1535*] [*Authority cited in pre-1607 legal work*]   (DSA)

Z Asiat Studien ... Zentralasiatische Studien [*Bonn*] [*A publication*]

Za Soc Zemed ... Za Socialisticke Zemedelstvi [*A publication*]

Za Sots Sel' -Khoz Nauku ... Za Sotsialisticheskuyu Sel'skokhozyaistvennuyu Nauku [*A publication*]

Za Sots Sel'skokhoz Nauku Ser A ... Za Sotsialisticheskuyu Sel'skokhozyaistvennuyu Nauku. Seriya A [*A publication*]

Z Assyr ...... Zeitschrift fuer Assyriologie [*A publication*]

Zast Bilja ... Zastita Bilja [*A publication*]

Z Asthet Al ... Zeitschrift fuer Asthetik und Allgemeine Kunstwissenschaft [*A publication*]

ZastMat ..... Zastosowania Matematyki [*A publication*]

Zast Mater ... Zastita Materijala [*A publication*]

Zastos Mat ... Polska Akademia Nauk. Instytut Matematyczny. Zastosowania Matematyki [*A publication*]

Zastosow Mat ... Zastosowania Matematyki [*A publication*]

Z Astrophys ... Zeitschrift fuer Astrophysik [*West Germany*] [*A publication*]

ZAT .... Zantop Airways, Inc.

ZAT .... Zhaotong [*China*] [*Airport symbol*]   (OAG)

ZAT .... Zinc Atmospheric Tracer

ZAT .... Zydowska Agencja Telegraficzna   (BJA)

ZATB .... Zeitschrift fuer die Alttestamentliche Wissenschaft. Beihefte [*A publication*]

Za Tekh Prog (Baku) ... Za Tekhnicheskii Progress (Baku) [*A publication*]

Za Tekh Prog (Gorkly) ... Za Tekhnicheskii Progress (Gorkly) [*A publication*]

ZATPA ...... Za Tekhnicheskii Progress [*A publication*]

Za Turf Ind ... Za Turfyanuyu Industriyu [*A publication*]

ZATW .... Zeitschrift fuer die Alttestamentliche Wissenschaft [*A publication*]

ZAU .... Chicago, IL [*Location identifier*] [*FAA*]   (FAAL)

Z Augenheilkd ... Zeitschrift fuer Augenheilkunde [*A publication*]

Z Auslaend Landwirtsch ... Zeitschrift fuer Auslaendische Landwirtschaft [*A publication*]

Z Auslaend Oeff Voelkerrecht ... Zeitschrift fuer Auslaendisches Oeffentliches Recht und Voelkerrecht [*A publication*]

Z Ausland Landwirt ... Zeitschrift fuer Auslaendische Landwirtschaft [*A publication*]

Z Ausl Oeff R ... Zeitschrift fuer Auslaendisches Oeffentliches Recht und Voelkerrecht [*A publication*]

Z Ausl Oeff Recht Voelkerrecht ... Zeitschrift fuer Auslaendisches Oeffentliches Recht und Voelkerrecht [*A publication*]

Z Ausl Oeff RVR ... Zeitschrift fuer Auslaendisches Oeffentliches Recht und Voelkerrecht [*A publication*]

ZAV .... Zavalla [*Texas*] [*Seismograph station code, US Geological Survey*] [*Closed*]   (SEIS)

Zav .... Zavim   (BJA)

ZAVA .... Zeitschrift fuer Assyriologie und Vorderasiatische Archaeologie [*A publication*]

Zav Lab ...... Zavodskaya Laboratoriya [*A publication*]

Zavod Lab ... Zavodskaya Laboratoriya [*A publication*]

ZAW .... Zeitschrift fuer die Alttestamentliche Wissenschaft [*A publication*]

ZAWEA ..... Zahnaerztliche Welt [*A publication*]

ZAZ .... Zaragoza [*Spain*] [*Airport symbol*]   (OAG)

ZB .... Repetitive Flight Plan Office [*ICAO designator*]   (ICDA)

ZB .... Zeitschrift fuer Balkanologie [*A publication*]

ZB .... Zeitschrift fuer Betriebswirtschaft [*A publication*]

ZB .... Zeitschrift fuer Botanik [*A publication*]

ZB .... Zentralblatt fuer Bibliothekswesen [*A publication*]

ZB .... Zero Beat [*Radio*]

ZB .... Zimbabwe [*IYRU nationality code*]   (IYR)

ZB .... Zimbabwe Banking Corporation Ltd.

ZB .... Zinc Borate [*Trademark for a flame retardant compound*] [*Humphrey Chemical Co.*]

ZB .... Zuercher Bibel   (BJA)

ZB .... Zum Beispiel [*For Example*] [*German*]

ZBA .... Zeitschrift fuer Arbeitswissenschaft [*A publication*]

ZBA .... Zero-Based Analysis   (ADA)

ZBA .... Zero Bias Anomaly

ZBA .... Zero Bracket Amount [*IRS*]

ZBAA .... Beijing/Capital [*China*] [*ICAO location identifier*]   (ICLI)

ZBalk .... Zeitschrift fuer Balkanologie [*A publication*]

Z Bayer Kg ... Zeitschrift fuer Bayerische Kirchengeschichte [*A publication*]

Z Bayer Ldg ... Zeitschrift fuer Bayerische Landesgeschichte [*A publication*]

Z Bayer Revisions Ver ... Zeitschrift. Bayerischer Revisions Verein [*A publication*]

Z Bay Land Gesch ... Zeitschrift fuer Bayerische Landesgeschichte [*A publication*]

ZBB .... Zeitschrift fuer Bibliothekswesen und Bibliographie [*A publication*]

ZBB .... Zentralblatt fuer Bibliothekswesen [*A publication*]

ZBB .... Zero-Base Budgeting

ZBBB .... Beijing City [*China*] [*ICAO location identifier*]   (ICLI)

Zb f Bibl ...... Zentralblatt fuer Bibliothekswesen [*A publication*]

Zb Bioteh Fak Univ Edvarda Kardelja Ljublj Kmetijstvo ... Zbornik Biotehniske Fakultete Univerze Edvarda Kardelja v Ljubljani. Kmetijstvo [*A publication*]

Zb Bioteh Fak Univ Ljubljani ... Zbornik Biotehniske Fakultete Univerze v Ljubljani [*A publication*]

Zb Bioteh Fak Univ Ljublj Kmetijstvo ... Zbornik Biotehniske Fakultete Univerze v Ljubljani. Kmetijstvo [*A publication*]

Zb Bioteh Fak Univ Ljublj Vet ... Zbornik Biotehniske Fakultete Univerze v Ljubljani. Veterinarstvo [*A publication*]

Zb Bioteh Fak Univ Ljublj Vet Supl ... Zbornik Biotehniske Fakultete Univerze v Ljubljani. Veterinarstvo. Suplement [*A publication*]

Zb Biotehn Fak Univ Ljublj ... Zbornik Biotehniske Fakultete Univerze v Ljubljani [*A publication*]

ZBBW .... Zentralblatt fuer Bibliothekswesen [*A publication*]

ZBC .... Zebec Resources [*Vancouver Stock Exchange symbol*]

ZBCSA ...... Zentralblatt fuer Chirurgie. Supplement [*A publication*]

ZBDC .... Zinc Dibutyldithiocarbamate [*Organic chemistry*]

ZBDLG ...... Zuercher Beitraege zur Deutschen Literatur und Geistesgeschichte [*A publication*]

ZBDSS ...... Zuercher Beitraege zur Deutschen Sprach- und Stilgeschichte [*A publication*]

ZBE .... Zinc Battery Electrode

Z Beih .... Beihefte. Zeitschrift fuer Romanische Philologie [*A publication*]

Z Beleuchtungswes Heizungs- Lueftungstech ... Zeitschrift fuer Beleuchtungswesen Heizungs- und Lueftungstechnik [*A publication*]

Z Berg Gesch V ... Zeitschrift. Bergischer Geschichtsverein [*A publication*]

Z Berg Huetten Salinenwes Dtsch Reich ... Zeitschrift fuer das Berg-, Huetten-, und Salinenwesen im Deutschen Reich [*A publication*]

Z Bergrecht ... Zeitschrift fuer Bergrecht [*West Germany*] [*A publication*]

Z Betriebsw ... Zeitschrift fuer Betriebswirtschaft [*A publication*]

Z Betriebswirtsch ... Zeitschrift fuer Betriebswirtschaft [*A publication*]

Z Bevoelkerungswiss ... Zeitschrift fuer die Bevoelkerungswissenschaft [*A publication*]

Z Bewasserungswirtsch ... Zeitschrift fuer Bewasserungswirtschaft [*A publication*]

ZBF........... Zeitschrift fuer Betriebswirtschaftliche Forschung [*A publication*]

ZBF........... Zeitschrift fuer Buecherfreunde [*A publication*]

ZbFL......... Zbornik za Filologiju i Lingvistiku [*A publication*]

ZBG......... Zeitschrift. Bergischer Geschichtsverein [*A publication*]

Zb Geol Vied Zapadne Karpaty ... Zbornik Geologichych Vied Zapadne Karpaty [*A publication*]

ZBGR .... Schweizerische Zeitschrift fuer Beurkundungs- und Grundbuchrecht [*A publication*]

ZBGV .... Zeitschrift. Bergischer Geschichtsverein [*A publication*]

ZBHH........ Huhhot [*China*] [*ICAO location identifier*] (ICLI)

Z Bibl und Bibliog ... Zeitschrift fuer Bibliothekswesen und Bibliographie [*A publication*]

Z Bibliot u Bibliog ... Zeitschrift fuer Bibliothekswesen und Bibliographie [*A publication*]

Z Bibliothekswes Bibliogr ... Zeitschrift fuer Bibliothekswesen und Bibliographie [*A publication*]

Z Bibliothekswesen und Bibl ... Zeitschrift fuer Bibliothekswesen und Bibliographie [*A publication*]

Z Bienenforsch ... Zeitschrift fuer Bienenforschung [*A publication*]

Z Binnenfisch DDR ... Zeitschrift fuer die Binnenfischerei der DDR [*A publication*]

Zb Inst Khim Tekhnol Akad Nauk Ukr RSR ... Zbirnik Institutu Khimichnoi Tekhnologii Akademiya Nauk Ukrains'koi RSR [*A publication*]

Z Biochem ... Zeitschrift fuer Biochemie [*A publication*]

Z Biol .... Zeitschrift fuer Biologie [*A publication*]

Z Biol Tech Method ... Zeitschrift fuer Biologische Technik und Methodik [*A publication*]

Zbirka Izbran Poglav Fiz ... Zbirka Izbranih Poglavij iz Fizike [*A publication*]

Zbirka Izbran Poglav Mat ... Zbirka Izbranih Poglavij iz Matematike [*A publication*]

ZbirP......... Zbirnyk Prac' Naukovoji Sevcenkivs'koji Konferenciji [*A publication*]

ZBJV .... Zeitschrift. Bernischer Juristen-Verein [*A publication*]

ZBK .... Zeitschrift fuer Bildende Kunst [*A publication*]

ZBK .... Zeitschrift fuer Buchkunde [*A publication*]

ZBKG .... Zeitschrift fuer Bayerische Kirchengeschichte [*A publication*]

ZBL........... Brooklyn Law School, Brooklyn, NY [*OCLC symbol*] (OCLC)

ZBL........... Zeitschrift fuer Bayerische Landesgeschichte [*A publication*]

Zbl............. Zentralblatt fuer Mathematik und Ihre Grenzgebiete [*A publication*]

ZBL........... Zero-Based Linearity

Zbl Allg Path ... Zentralblatt fuer Allgemeine Pathologie und Pathologische Anatomie [*A publication*]

Zbl A Med ... Zentralblatt fuer Arbeitsmedizin und Arbeitsschutz [*Later, Zentralblatt fuer Arbeitsmedizin, Arbeitsschutz, und Prophylaxe*] [*A publication*]

ZBLAN...... Zirconium, Barium, Lanthanum, Aluminum, Sodium Fluoride [*Molar composition of glass*] [*Chemistry*]

Zbl Bakt A ... Zentralblatt fuer Bakteriologie. Reihe A [*A publication*]

Zbl Bakt B ... Zentralblatt fuer Bakteriologie. Reihe B [*A publication*]

Zbl f Bibl.... Zentralblatt fuer Bibliothekswesen [*A publication*]

Zbl DDR.... Zentralblatt der Deutschen Demokratischen Republik [*A publication*] (DLA)

Zb Lek Fak (Kosice) ... Zbornik Lekarskej Fakulty (Kosice) [*A publication*]

ZBLG........ Zeitschrift fuer Bayerische Landesgeschichte [*A publication*]

Zbl Math ... Zentralblatt fuer Mathematik und Ihre Grenzgebiete [*A publication*]

Zbl Soz Vers ... Zentralblatt fuer Sozialversicherung und Versorgung [*German*] [*A publication*] (DLA)

Zbl Vet A ... Zentralblatt fuer Veterinaermedizin. Reihe A [*A publication*]

Zbl Vet B ... Zentralblatt fuer Veterinaermedizin. Reihe B [*A publication*]

ZBM .... State University of New York, College at Oneonta, Oneonta, NY [*OCLC symbol*] (OCLC)

Zb Meteorol Hidrol Rad ... Zbornik Meteoroloskih i Hidroloskih Radova [*Yugoslavia*] [*A publication*]

ZBMP........ Zero-Base Media Planning

ZbMS .... Zbornik Matice Srpske [*A publication*]

ZBN.......... Brookhaven National Laboratory, Upton, NY [*OCLC symbol*] (OCLC)

Zb Nauk Pr Aspir Kiiv Inzh Budiv Inst ... Zbirnik Naukovikh Prats Aspirantiv Kiivs'kii Inzhenerno-Budivel'nii Institut [*A publication*]

Zb Nauk Pr Aspir Kyyiv Univ Pryr Nauky ... Zbirnyk Naukovykh Prats' Aspirantiv Kyyivski Universytet Pryrodni Nauky [*A publication*]

Zb Nauk Pr Bilotserk Dos Sel Statsiya ... Zbirnyk Naukovykh Prats' Bilotserkiv'sta Doslidno-Selektivonna Statsiya [*A publication*]

Zb Nauk Pr Khim Sil'sk Hospod Ukr Sil'skohospod Akad ... Zbirnyk Naukovykh Prats' Khimicheskoho Sil'skoho Hospodarstva Ukrayinskoyi Sil'skohospodarskoyi Akademiyi [*A publication*]

Zb Nauk Pr Kiiv Budiv Inst ... Zbirnik Naukovikh Prats Kiivs'kii Budivel'nii Institut [*A publication*]

Zb Nauk Pr L'viv Med Inst ... Zbirnyk Naukovykh Prats' L'viv'kyi Medychyni Instytut [*A publication*]

Zb Nauk Pr Umans'kyi Sil'skohospod Inst ... Zbirnyk Naukovykh Prats' Umans'kyi Sil'skohospodarskyi Instytut [*A publication*]

Zb Nauk Rob Khark Derzh Med Inst ... Zbirnik Naukovikh Robit Kharkivs'kogo Derzhavnogo Medichnogo Institutu [*A publication*]

ZbNPAF ..... Zbirnyk Naukovych Prac' Aspirantiv z Filolohiji [*A publication*]

ZBO .... Bowen [*Australia*] [*Airport symbol*] [*Obsolete*] (OAG)

ZBO .... Zone of British Occupation [*Military*]

Zbor Arheol Muz ... Zbornik na Arheoloskiot Muzej [*A publication*]

Zbor Muz Primenjene Umet ... Zbornik Muzej Primenjene Umetnosti [*A publication*]

Zbor Narod Muz Beogradu ... Zbornik Narodnog Muzeja u Beogradu [*A publication*]

Zborn Biotehn Fak Univ Ljublj Kmet ... Zbornik Biotehniske Fakultete Univerze v Ljubljani. Kmetijstvo [*A publication*]

Zbornik Rad Mat Inst (Beograd) ... Zbornik Radova. Matematicki Institut (Beograd) [*A publication*]

Zborn Rad ... Zbornik Radova [*A publication*]

Zborn Rad Poljopriv Fak Univ Beogr ... Zbornik Radova. Poljoprivrednog Fakulteta. Universitet u Beogradu [*A publication*]

Zborn Slov Nar Muz Prir Vedy ... Zbornik Slovenskeho Narodneho Muzea Prirodne Vedy [*A publication*]

Zbor Slov Narod Muz ... Zbornik Slovenskeho Narodneho Muzea [*A publication*]

Z Bot .... Zeitschrift fuer Botanik [*A publication*]

ZBOW .... Baotou [*China*] [*ICAO location identifier*] (ICLI)

ZBP........... Zero-Base Programming [*Military*]

ZBPE......... Beijing [*China*] [*ICAO location identifier*] (ICLI)

ZBPHA...... Zentralblatt fuer Bakteriologie, Parasitenkunde, Infektionskrankheiten, und Hygiene. Abteilung 1. Medizinisch-Hygienische Bakteriologie, Virusforschung, und Parasitologie. Originale [*A publication*]

Zb Prac Chem Fak SVST (Bratislava) ... Zbornik Prac Chemickotechnologickej Fakulty SVST (Bratislava) [*A publication*]

Zb Prav Fak Zagrebu ... Zbornik Pravnog Fakulteta u Zagrebu [*A publication*]

Zb Pr Belarus Dzyarzh Med Inst ... Zbornik Prats. Belaruski Dzyarzhauny Medychny Instytut [*A publication*]

Zb Pr Chemickotechnol Fak SVST ... Zbornik Prac Chemickotechnologickej Fakulty SVST [*A publication*]

Zb Pr Chem-Technol Fak SVST ... Zbornik Prac Chemickotechnologickej Fakulty SVST [*A publication*]

Zb Pr Inst Teploenerg Akad Nauk Ukr RSR ... Zbirnik Prats' Institut Teploenergetiki Akademiya Nauk Ukrains'koi RSR [*A publication*]

Zb Prir Nauke Matica Srp ... Zbornik za Prirodne Nauke Matica Srpska [*A publication*]

Zb Pr Nauk Inst Fiziol Kyyiv Univ ... Zbirnyk Prats' Naukovodoslidnyts'koho Instyta Fiziolohiyi Kyyivs'koho Universytetu [*A publication*]

Zb Pr Naukovodosl Inst Fiziol Kyyiv Univ ... Zbirnyk Prats' Naukovodoslidnyts'koho Instytuta Fiziolohiyi Kyyivs'koho Universytetu [*A publication*]

Zb Pr Ukr Derzh Inst Nauk Prakt Vet ... Zbirnik Prats' Ukrains'kii Derzhavnii Institut Naukovoi ta Praktichnoi Veterin arii [*A publication*]

Zb Pr Ukr Inst Eksp Vet ... Zbirnik Prats' Ukrains'kogo Institutu Eksperimental'noi Veterinarii [*A publication*]

Zb Pr Zool Muz Akad Nauk Ukr RSR ... Zbirnyk Prats' Zoolohichnoho Muzeyu Akademiyi Nauk Ukrayinskoyi RSR [*A publication*]

ZBR .... Chah-Bahar [*Iran*] [*Airport symbol*] (OAG)

ZbR .... Zbirnyk Robit Aspirantiv Romano-Germans'koji i Klazycnoji Filolohiji [*A publication*]

ZBR .... Zero-Base Review

ZBR .... Zero Beat Reception [*Radio*]

ZBR .... Zero Bend Radius

Zb Rab Belarus Sel'Ska-Gaspad Inst ... Zbornik Rabot Belaruskaga Sel'ska-Gaspadarchaga Instytuta [*A publication*]

Zb Rad Biol Inst (Beograd) ... Zbornik Radova. Bioloski Institut (Beograd) [*A publication*]

Zb Rad Biol Inst NR Srbye Beogr ... Zbornik Radova. Bioloski Institut NR Srbye Beograd [*A publication*]

Zb Rad Math Inst Beograd NS ... Beograd Matematicki Institut. Zbornik Radova. Nouvelle Serie [*A publication*]

Zb Rad Mat Inst (Beograd) ... Zbornik Radova. Nova Serija. Matematicki Institut (Beograd). Zbornik Radova. Nova Serija [*A publication*]

Zb Rad Poljopr Fak Univ Beogradu ... Zbornik Radova. Poljoprivrednog Fakulteta. Universitet u Beogradu [*A publication*]

Zb Rad Poljopr Inst ... Zbornik Radova. Poljoprivredni Institut [*A publication*]

Zb Rad Poljopr Inst (Osijek) ... Zbornik Radova. Poljoprivredni Institut (Osijek) [*A publication*]

Zb Rad Poljopriv Fak Univ Beogradu ... Zbornik Radova. Poljoprivrednog Fakulteta. Universitet u Beogradu [*A publication*]

Zb Rad Prir Mat Fak ... Zbornik Radova. Prirodno-Matematickog Fakulteta [*Yugoslavia*] [*A publication*]

Zb Rad Prir-Mat Fak Ser Fiz ... Zbornik Radova. Prirodno-Matematickog Fakulteta. Serija za Fiziku [*A publication*]

Zb Rad Prir-Mat Fak Univ Novom Sadu ... Zbornik Radova. Prirodno-Matematickog Fakulteta Univerzitet u Novom Sadu [*A publication*]
Zb Rad Rud Geol Fak ... Zbornik Radova. Rudarsko-Geoloskog Fakulteta [*A publication*]
Zb Rad Srp Akad Nauka Geol Inst ... Zbornik Radova. Srpska Akademija Nauka Geoloski Institut [*A publication*]
Zb Rad Zavod Ratarstvo (Sarajevo) ... Zbornik Radova. Zavod za Ratarstvo (Sarajevo) [*A publication*]
Zbraslav Res Inst Land Reclam Improv Sci Monogr ... Zbraslav Research Institute for Land Reclamation and Improvement. Scientific Monograph [*A publication*]
ZbRFFZ ..... Zbornik Radova. Filozofskog Fakulteta. Svencilista u Zagrebu [*A publication*]
ZbRL .... Zbirnyk Robit Aspirantiv L'Vivskij Derzavnyj Universitet [*A publication*]
Zb Robit Aspir L'Viv Univ Pryr Nauk ... Zbirnyk Robit Aspirantiv L'Vivs'kyi Universytet Pryrodnykh Nauk [*A publication*]
ZBRS .... Z's Briefs. CPSU [*Cooperative Park Studies Unit, University of Alaska*] Newsletter [*A publication*]
ZbS .... Zbornik za Slavistiku [*A publication*]
ZBS .... Zeitschrift. Deutscher Verein fuer Buchwesen und Schrifttum [*A publication*]
ZBS .... Zivena Beneficial Society (EA)
ZbSAN ...... Zbornik Radova. Srpske Akademije Nauke [*A publication*]
ZBSB .... Zeitschriftenkatalog der Bayerischen Staatsbibliothek, Munchen [*Serials Catalogue of the Bavarian State Library, Munich*] [*Deutsches Bibliotheksinstitut*] [*Federal Republic of Germany*] [*Information service or system*] (CRD)
Zb Slov Nar Muzea Prir Vedy ... Zbornik Slovenskeho Narodneho Muzea Prirodne Vedy [*A publication*]
Zb Slov Nar Muz Prir Vedy ... Zbornik Slovenskeho Narodneho Muzea Prirodne Vedy [*A publication*]
ZBST .... ZZZZ Best Co., Inc. [*Reseda, CA*] [*NASDAQ symbol*] (NQ)
ZBT .... Zeta Beta Tau [*Fraternity*]
ZBT .... Zion Bemishpat Tipadeh (Isaiah 1:27) (BJA)
ZBTJ .... Tianjin/Zhangguizhuang [*China*] [*ICAO location identifier*] (ICLI)
Zb Ved Prac Lesn Fak Vys Sk Lesn Drev Zvolene ... Zbornik Vedeckych Prac Lesnickej Fakulty Vysokej Skoly Lesnickej a Drevarskej vo Zvolene [*Czechoslovakia*] [*A publication*]
Zb Ved Pr Vys Sk Tech Kosiciach ... Zbornik Vedeckych Prac. Vysokej Skoly Technickej v Kosiciach [*A publication*]
Zb Vojnomed Akad ... Zbornik Vojnomedicinske Akademije [*A publication*]
Zb Vychodoslovenskeho Muzea Ser AB Prir Vedy ... Zbornik Vychodoslovenskeho Muzea. Seria AB. Prirodne Vedy [*Kosice*] [*A publication*]
Zb Vysk Pr Vysk Ustav Zvaracskeho Bratislave ... Zbornik Vyskumnych Prac Vyskumneho Ustavu Zvaracskeho v Bratislave [*A publication*]
Zb Vyzk Pr Odboru Pap Celulozy ... Zbornik Vyzkumnych Prac z Odboru Papiera a Celulozy [*A publication*]
ZBW .... Boston, MA [*Location identifier*] [*FAA*] (FAAL)
ZBW .... Zeitschrift fuer Betriebswirtschaft [*A publication*]
ZBW .... Zentralblatt fuer Bibliothekswesen [*A publication*]
ZBYN .... Taiyuan/Wusu [*China*] [*ICAO location identifier*] (ICLI)
Zb Zgodovino Naravoslovja Tek ... Zbornik za Zgodovino Naravoslovja in Teknike [*A publication*]
Z-C .... Zapalote-Chico [*Race of maize*]
Zc .... Zechariah (BJA)
ZC .... Ziegfeld Club (EA)
ZC .... Zinfandel Club [*London, England*] (EAIO)
ZC .... Zone Capacity
Z of C .... Zones of Communications [*Military*]
ZCA .... Z Club of America (EA)
ZCAD .... Zycad Corp. [*NASDAQ symbol*] (NQ)
Z/CAL .... Zero Calibration (MCD)
ZCB .... Chase Manhattan Bank, New York, NY [*OCLC symbol*] (OCLC)
ZCB .... Zinc-Coated Bolt
ZCC .... Zeppelin Collectors Club (EA)
ZCC .... Zirconia-Coated Crucible
ZCCI .... Zippy Collectors Club (EA)
ZCCM .... Zambian Consolidated Copper Mines
ZCD .... Zero Crossing Detector
ZCG .... Impedance Cardiogram (NASA)
Z Chem ...... Zeitschrift fuer Chemie [*A publication*]
Z Chem Apparatenkd ... Zeitschrift fuer Chemische Apparatenkunde [*A publication*]
Z Chemie (Lpz) ... Zeitschrift fuer Chemie (Leipzig) [*A publication*]
Z Chem Ind Kolloide ... Zeitschrift fuer Chemie und Industrie der Kolloide [*A publication*]
Z Chemother Verw Geb Teil 1 ... Zeitschrift fuer Chemotherapie und Verwandte Gebiete. Teil 1. Originale [*A publication*]
Z Chemother Verw Geb Teil 2 ... Zeitschrift fuer Chemotherapie und Verwandte Gebiete. Teil 2. Referate [*A publication*]
ZChK .... Zeitschrift fuer Christliche Kunst [*A publication*]
ZChrK .... Zeitschrift fuer Christliche Kunst [*A publication*]
ZCIC .... Zirconia-Coated Iridium Crucible
ZCK .... Zeitschrift fuer Christliche Kunst [*A publication*]
ZCL .... Zacatecas [*Mexico*] [*Airport symbol*] (OAG)

ZCM .... CM Preference Corp. [*Toronto Stock Exchange symbol*]
ZCM .... State University of New York, Agricultural and Technical College at Canton, Canton, NY [*OCLC symbol*] (OCLC)
ZCMI .... Zion's Cooperative Mercantile Institution [*Department store in Salt Lake City, UT*]
ZCN .... Zinc-Coated Nut
ZCP .... Zeitschrift fuer Celtische Philologie [*A publication*]
ZCP .... Zinc Chromate Primer
ZCPh .... Zeitschrift fuer Celtische Philologie [*A publication*]
ZCR .... Zero Crossing Rate
ZCR .... Zero-Temperature Coefficient Resistor
ZCS .... Zinc-Coated Screw
ZCW .... Zinc-Coated Washer
ZCZ .... Cazenovia College, Witherill Learning Center, Cazenovia, NY [*OCLC symbol*] (OCLC)
ZCzest .... Ziemia Czestochowska [*A publication*]
ZD .... Air Traffic Flow Control Unit [*ICAO designator*] (ICDA)
ZD .... Zeitschrift fuer Deutschkunde [*A publication*]
ZD .... Zener Diode
ZD .... Zenith Distance [*Navigation*]
ZD .... Zero Defects
ZD .... Zielsprache Deutsch [*A publication*]
ZD .... ZIP Code Distribution
ZD .... Zone Description
ZDA .... Zeitschrift fuer Deutsches Altertum und Deutsche Literatur [*A publication*]
ZDA .... Zinc Development Association [*London, England*] (EAIO)
ZDADL ..... Zeitschrift fuer Deutsches Altertum und Deutsche Literatur [*A publication*]
ZDA/LDA/CA ... Zinc Development Association/Lead Development Association/Cadmium Association [*Information service or system*] (IID)
Z f D Altert ... Zeitschrift fuer Deutsches Altertum und Deutsche Literatur [*A publication*]
Z Dampfkessel Maschinenbetr ... Zeitschrift fuer Dampfkessel und Maschinenbetrieb [*A publication*]
Z Dampfkesselunters Versicher Ges ... Zeitschrift. Dampfkesseluntersuchungs- und Versicherungs-Gesellschaft [*A publication*]
ZDB .... Zeitschrift fuer Deutsche Bildung [*A publication*]
ZDB .... Zeitschriftendatenbank [*German Union Catalog of Serials*] [*Deutsches Bibliotheksinstitut*] [*Federal Republic of Germany*] [*Information service or system*] (CRD)
ZDC .... Philip Crosby Association [*AMEX symbol*] (SPSG)
ZDC .... Washington, DC [*Location identifier*] [*FAA*] (FAAL)
ZDC .... Zero Defects Council
ZDC .... Zeus Defense Center [*Missile defense*]
ZDC .... Zinc Dibenzyldithiocarbamate [*Rubber accelerator*]
ZDC .... Zinc Die Casting
ZDCTBS ..... Zeus Defense Center Tape and Buffer System [*Missiles*] (IEEE)
ZDD .... Zero Delay Device
ZDDB .... Zip Code Demographic Data Base [*Demographic Research Co., Inc.*] [*Information service or system*] (CRD)
ZDDP .... Zinc Dialkyldithiophosphate [*Organic chemistry*]
ZDE .... Zagreb Dance Ensemble [*Yugoslavia*]
ZDE .... Zentralstelle Dokumentation Elektrotechnik [*Electrical Engineering Documentation Center*] [*Federal Republic of Germany*] [*Originator and database*] [*Information service or system*] (IID)
ZDemogr .... Zeitschrift fuer Demographie und Statistik der Juden [*A publication*]
Z Desinfekt Gesundheitswes ... Zeitschrift fuer Desinfektions- und Gesundheitswesen [*A publication*]
Z Deut Alt ... Zeitschrift fuer Deutsches Altertum und Deutsche Literatur [*A publication*]
Z Deut Geol Ges ... Zeitschrift. Deutsche Geologische Gesellschaft [*A publication*]
Z Deut Phil ... Zeitschrift fuer Deutsche Philologie [*A publication*]
Z Deuts Morgen G ... Zeitschrift. Deutsche Morgenlaendische Gesellschaft [*Wiesbaden*] [*A publication*]
Z Deut Ver ... Zeitschrift. Deutschen Verein fuer Kunstwissenschaft [*A publication*]
ZDF .... Zweites Deutsches Fernsehen [*Television network*] [*West Germany*]
ZDFALP .... Z Dziejow Form Artystycznych Literaturze Polskiej [*A publication*]
ZDG .... Corning Community College, Corning, NY [*OCLC symbol*] (OCLC)
ZDG .... Zeitschrift fuer Deutsche Geistesgeschichte [*A publication*]
ZDG .... Zeitschrift fuer Deutsche Geisteswissenschaft [*A publication*]
ZDG .... Zinc-Doped Germanium
ZDGG .... Zeitschrift fuer Deutsche Geistesgeschichte [*A publication*]
ZDK .... Zeitschrift fuer Deutsche Kunst [*A publication*]
ZDK .... Zen-Do Kai Martial Arts Association, International (EA)
ZDKAA ...... Zdravookhranenie Kazakhstana [*A publication*]
ZDKP .... Zeitschrift fuer Deutsche Kulturphilosophie [*A publication*]
ZDL .... Zeitschrift fuer Dialektologie und Linguistik [*A publication*]
ZDM .... Zeitschrift fuer Deutsche Mundarten [*A publication*]
ZDM .... Zentralblatt fuer Didaktik der Mathematik [*A publication*]
ZDMG .... Zeitschrift. Deutsche Morgenlaendische Gesellschaft [*A publication*]

ZD Musik.. Zeitschriftendienst Musik [*A publication*]
Z DNA....... Deoxyribonucleic Acid, Zigzag [*DNA with left-handed helix*] [*Biochemistry, genetics*]
Z Dnipr INO ... Zapiski Dnipropetrovs'kogo Institutu Narodnoi Osviti [*A publication*]
Zdorov'e Nauch Pop Gig Zhurnal ... Zdorov'e Nauchno Populiarnyi Gigienicheskii Zhurnal [*A publication*]
ZDP .... Zeitschrift fuer Deutsche Philologie [*A publication*]
ZDP .... Zero Defects Program
ZDP .... Zero Defects Proposal
ZDP .... Zero Delivery Pressure   (IEEE)
ZDP .... Zimbabwe Democratic Party [*Political party*]   (PPW)
ZDPA .... Zero Defects Program Audit
ZDPG .... Zero Defects Program Guideline
ZDPh .... Zeitschrift fuer Deutsche Philologie [*A publication*]
Z f D Phil.. Zeitschrift fuer Deutsche Philologie [*A publication*]
ZDPO .... Zero Defects Program Objective
ZDPR........ Zero Defects Program Responsibility
ZDPV......... Zeitschrift. Deutscher Palaestinaverein [*A publication*]
ZDR .... Zentraldeutsche Rundfunk [*Central German Radio*]
ZDR .... Zeus Discrimination RADAR [*Missile defense*]
Zdrav Aktual ... Zdravotnicke Aktuality [*A publication*]
Zdrav Delo ... Zdravno Delo [*A publication*]
Zdravookhr Beloruss ... Zdravookhranenie Belorussii [*A publication*]
Zdravookhr Belorussii ... Zdravookhranenie Belorussii [*A publication*]
Zdravookhr Kaz ... Zdravookhranenie Kazakhstana [*A publication*]
Zdravookhr Kirg ... Zdravookhranenie Kirgizii [*A publication*]
Zdravookhr Ross Fed ... Zdravookhranenie Rossiiskoi Federatsii [*A publication*]
Zdravookhr Sov Est Sb ... Zdravookhranenie Sovetskoi Estonii Sbornik [*A publication*]
Zdravookhr Tadzh ... Zdravookhranenie Tadzhikistana [*A publication*]
Zdravookhr Turkm ... Zdravookhranenie Turkmenistana [*A publication*]
Zdrav Prac ... Zdravotnicka Pracovnice [*A publication*]
Zdravst Vest ... Zdravstveni Vestnik [*A publication*]
Zdrav Techn Vzduchotech ... Zdravotni Technika a Vzduchotechnika [*A publication*]
Zdrav Tech Vzduchotech ... Zdravotni Technika a Vzduchotechnika [*A publication*]
Zdrav Vestn ... Zdravstveni Vestnik [*A publication*]
Zdrow Publiczne ... Zdrowie Publiczne [*A publication*]
ZDS .... Zeitschrift fuer Deutsche Sprache [*A publication*]
ZDS .... Zinc Detection System
ZDSJ .... Zeitschrift fuer Demographie und Statistik der Juden [*A publication*]
ZDStJ .... Zeitschrift fuer Demographie und Statistik der Juden [*A publication*]
Zdt.............. Die Zoologie des Talmuds [*L. Lewysohn*] [*A publication*]   (BJA)
ZDT .... Zero-Ductility Transition   (IEEE)
Z Dt Geol Ges ... Zeitschrift. Deutsche Geologische Gesellschaft [*A publication*]
Z Dt Phil... Zeitschrift fuer Deutsche Philologie [*A publication*]
Z Dtschen Morgenlaend Ges ... Zeitschrift. Deutsche Morgenlaendische Gesellschaft [*A publication*]
Z Dtsch Gemmol Ges ... Zeitschrift der Deutschen Gemmologischen Gesellschaft (Idar-Oberstein) [*A publication*]
Z Dtsch Geol Ges ... Zeitschrift. Deutsche Geologische Gesellschaft [*A publication*]
Z Dtschl Druckgewerbe ... Zeitschrift fuer Deutschlands Drueckgewerbe [*A publication*]
Z Dtsch Morgenl Ges ... Zeitschrift. Deutsche Morganlaendische Gesellschaft [*A publication*]
Z Dtsch Oel Fett Ind ... Zeitschrift der Deutschen Oel- und Fett-Industrie [*A publication*]
Z Dtsch Philol ... Zeitschrift fuer Deutsche Philologie [*A publication*]
Z Dt Spr..... Zeitschrift fuer Deutsche Sprache [*A publication*]
ZDV .... Denver, CO [*Location identifier*] [*FAA*]   (FAAL)
ZDV .... Zero Dead Volume [*Chromatography*]
ZDV .... Zidovudine [*Antiviral*]
ZDVGMS ... Zeitschrift. Deutscher Verein fuer die Geschichte Maehrens und Schlesiens [*A publication*]
ZDV f Kw... Zeitschrift. Deutscher Verein fuer Kunstwissenschaft [*A publication*]
ZDV Kw..... Zeitschrift. Deutscher Verein fuer Kunstwissenschaft [*A publication*]
ZDW.......... Zeitschrift fuer Deutsche Wortforschung [*A publication*]
ZDWDSU ... Zeitschrift fuer Deutschwissenschaft und Deutschunterricht [*A publication*]
ZDWF .... Zeitschrift fuer Deutsche Wortforschung [*A publication*]
ZE .... Flight Information Database [*ICAO designator*]   (ICDA)
ZE .... Zeitschrift fuer Ethnologie [*A publication*]
ZE .... Zenith Electronics Corp. [*NYSE symbol*]   (SPSG)
ZE .... Zero Balance Entry [*Banking*]
ZE .... Zero Effusion
ZE .... Zollinger-Ellison [*Syndrome*] [*Medicine*]
ZE .... Zone Effect
ZE .... Zone Electrophoresis [*Analytical biochemistry*]
ZEA .... Zero Energy Assembly [*Nuclear energy*]
ZEA .... Zero Entropy Automorphism
ZEASA ...... Zeitschrift fuer Astrophysik [*A publication*]

Zeb............. Zebahim (BJA)
ZEB............ Zebra (ROG)
ZEBED ...... Zeitschrift fuer Bergrecht [*A publication*]
ZEBFA ...... Zhurnal Evolyutsionnoi Biokhimii i Fiziologii [*A publication*]
ZEBLA ...... Zeitschrift fuer Biologie [*A publication*]
ZEBRA ...... Zero Balance, Reimbursable Account [*Year-end reclassification of taxable income*]
ZEBRA ...... Zero Energy Breeder Reactor Assembly [*British*]
Zec .... Zechariah [*Old Testament book*]
ZEC .... Zero Energy Coefficient
ZEC .... Zinc-Electrochemical Cell
ZEC .... Zurich Energy Corporation [*Vancouver Stock Exchange symbol*]
ZECC......... Zinc-Electrochemical Cell
ZECC......... Zonal Electric Comfort Council [*Defunct*]   (EA)
Zech .... Zechariah [*Old Testament book*]
ZECM........ Zonal Elementary Circulative Mechanism
ZECODK... Zeitschrift fuer Experimentelle Chirurgie. Transplantation und Kunstliche Organe [*A publication*]
ZED .... Zero Energy Deuterium [*Type of nuclear reactor*]
ZED .... Zero Express Dialing
ZED .... Zimbabwe Environment and Design [*A publication*]
ZED .... Zur Erkenntnis der Dichtung [*A publication*]
ZEDRON .. Blimp Squadron [*Later separated into BLIMPRON and Blimp-HEDRON*] [*Navy*]
ZEE............ Zeitschrift fuer Evangelische Ethik [*A publication*]
Z EEG-EMG ... Zeitschrift fuer EEG-EMG [*Elektroenzephalographie, Elektromyographie, und Verwandte Gebiete*] [*German Federal Republic*] [*A publication*]
ZEELA ...... Zeitschrift fuer Elektrochemie [*A publication*]
ZEEP......... Zero End Expiratory Pressure [*Medicine*]
ZEEP........ Zero Energy Experimental Pile [*Nuclear reactor*] [*Canada*]
Zeews Fruittelersbl ... Zeeuws Fruittelersblad [*A publication*]
ZEF............ Elkin, NC [*Location identifier*] [*FAA*]   (FAAL)
ZEF............ Zeitschrift fuer Erziehungswissenschaftliche Forschung [*A publication*]
ZEG .... Senggo [*Indonesia*] [*Airport symbol*]   (OAG)
ZEG .... Zero Economic Growth
ZEG .... Zero Energy Growth
ZEGL........ [*The*] Ziegler Co., Inc. [*NASDAQ symbol*]   (NQ)
ZEH .... Zeit. Wochenzeitung [*A publication*]
Zei............. Das Zeichen [*A publication*]
ZEI............ Zero Environmental Impact
Zeich Zeit .. Zeichen der Zeit [*A publication*]
ZEINA....... Zeitschrift fuer Instrumentenkunde [*A publication*]
Z Eisenbahnwes und Verkehrstech Glasers ... Zeitschrift fuer Eisenbahnwesen und Verkehrstechnik. Glasers. Annalen [*A publication*]
Z Eisenbahnwes Verkehrstech Glasers Ann ... Zeitschrift fuer Eisenbahnwesen und Verkehrstechnik. Glasers. Annalen [*A publication*]
Z Eis Kaelte Ind ... Zeitschrift fuer Eis-und Kaelte-Industrie [*A publication*]
Zeiss Inf..... Zeiss Information [*A publication*]
Zeiss Mitt .. Zeiss Mitteilungen [*A publication*]
Zeiss-Mitt Fortschr Tech Opt ... Zeiss-Mitteilungen ueber Fortschritte der Technischen Optik [*A publication*]
Zeiss-Mitt Fortsch Tech Optik ... Zeiss-Mitteilungen ueber Fortschritte der Technischen Optik [*A publication*]
Zeit Angewandte Phot ... Zeitschrift Angewandte Photographie [*A publication*]
Zeit f Deutk ... Zeitschrift fuer Deutschkunde [*A publication*]
Zeit f Deut Phil ... Zeitschrift fuer Deutsche Philologie [*A publication*]
Zeitgeschic ... Zeitgeschichte [*A publication*]
Zeit Physik ... Zeitschrift fuer Physik [*A publication*]
Zeit f Rom Phil ... Zeitschrift fuer Romanische Philologie [*A publication*]
Zeitschr Angew Geologie ... Zeitschrift fuer Angewandte Geologie [*A publication*]
Zeitschr Anorg u Allg Chemie ... Zeitschrift fuer Anorganische und Allgemeine Chemie [*A publication*]
Zeitschr Geomorphologie ... Zeitschrift fuer Geomorphologie [*A publication*]
Zeitschr Geomorphologie Neue Folge ... Zeitschrift fuer Geomorphologie. Neue Folge [*A publication*]
Zeitschr Geophysik ... Zeitschrift fuer Geophysik [*A publication*]
Zeitschr Gletscherkunde u Glazialgeologie ... Zeitschrift fuer Gletscherkunde und Glazialgeologie [*A publication*]
Zeitschr Kristallographie ... Zeitschrift fuer Kristallographie [*A publication*]
Zeitschr Physikal Chemie ... Zeitschrift fuer Physikalische Chemie [*A publication*]
Zeit f Volk ... Zeitschrift fuer Volkskunde [*A publication*]
Zeitw.......... Zeitwende [*A publication*]
Zeitwahr .... Zeitschrift fuer Wahrscheinlichkeitstheorie [*A publication*]
ZEIZA .... Zeitschrift fuer Elektrische Informations- und Energietechnik [*A publication*]
ZEK .... Zeitschrift fuer Evangelisches Kirchenrecht [*A publication*]
ZEKIA .... Zeitschrift fuer Kinderheilkunde [*A publication*]
ZEKID8..... Zeitschrift fuer Kinderchirurgie [*A publication*]
Z Eks Klin Med ... Zurnal Eksperimental'noj i Kliniceskoj Mediciny [*A publication*]
Z Eksper Teoret Fiz ... Zurnal Eksperimental'noi i Teoreticeskoi Fiziki [*A publication*]
ZEL............ Bella Bella [*Canada*] [*Airport symbol*]   (OAG)

ZEL............ Equitable Life Assurance Society of the United States, Medical Library, New York, NY [*OCLC symbol*]   (OCLC)
ZEL............ Zelovo [*Enthusiastically*] [*Music*]   (ROG)
ZEL............ Zero-Length Launch [*Missiles*]
ZELAD........ Zeitschrift fuer Laermbekaempfung [*A publication*]
Z El Ch ...... Zeitschrift fuer Elektrochemie und Angewandte Physikalische Chemie [*A publication*]
Z Elek Informations- und Energietech ... Zeitschrift fuer Elektrische Informations- und Energietechnik [*A publication*]
Z Elektr Inf & Energietech ... Zeitschrift fuer Elektrische Informations- und Energietechnik [*IET*] [*A publication*]
Z Elektr Inf Energietech ... Zeitschrift fuer Elektrische Informations- und Energietechnik [*A publication*]
Z Elektr Informationstech Energietech ... Zeitschrift fuer Elektrische Informations- und Energietechnik [*IET*] [*A publication*]
Z Elektr Inform Energietech ... Zeitschrift fuer Elektrische Informations- und Energietechnik [*A publication*]
Z Elektrochem ... Zeitschrift fuer Elektrochemie [*A publication*]
Z Elektrochem Angew Phy Chem ... Zeitschrift fuer Elektrochemie und Angewandte Physikalische Chemie [*A publication*]
Z Elektrotech ... Zeitschrift fuer Elektrotechnik [*West Germany*] [*A publication*]
Zelezarski Zb ... Zelezarski Zbornik [*A publication*]
ZELL......... Zero-Length Launch [*Missiles*]   (MCD)
Zell Papier ... Zellstoff und Papier [*A publication*]
Zellstoffchem Abh ... Zellstoffchemische Abhandlungen [*A publication*]
Zellst Pap ... Zellstoff und Papier [*A publication*]
Zellst Pap (Berlin) ... Zellstoff und Papier (Berlin) [*A publication*]
Zellst Pap (Leipzig) ... Zellstoff und Papier (Leipzig) [*A publication*]
Zellwolle Dtsch Kunstseiden Ztg ... Zellwolle und Deutsche Kunstseiden-Zeitung [*A publication*]
ZELMAL .. Zero-Length Launch and Mat Landing [*Missiles*]   (MCD)
ZELTB ...... Zeitschrift fuer Elektrotechnik [*A publication*]
Z El Techn ... Zeitschrift fuer Elektrotechnik [*A publication*]
ZEM .... East Main [*Canada*] [*Airport symbol*]   (OAG)
ZEM .... Hobart and William Smith Colleges, Geneva, NY [*OCLC symbol*]   (OCLC)
ZEM .... Zero Electrophoretic Mobility [*Analytical chemistry*]
Zem Beton ... Zement und Beton [*A publication*]
Zemed Arch ... Zemedelsky Archiv [*A publication*]
Zemed Ekon ... Zemedelska Ekonomika [*A publication*]
Zemed Tech ... Zemedelska Technika [*Czechoslovakia*] [*A publication*]
Zemed Tech Cesk Akad Zemed Ustav Vedeckotech Inf Zemed ... Zemedelska Technika. Ceskoslovenska Akademii Zemedelska Ustav Vedeckotechnickych Informaci Pro Zemedelstvi [*A publication*]
Zemed Zahr ... Zemedeistvi v Zahranici [*A publication*]
Zemep Sb ... Zemepisny Sbornik [*A publication*]
ZEMGA .... Zeszyty Naukowe Akademii Gorniczo-Hutniczej. Elektryfikacja i Mechanizacja Gornictwa i Hutnictwa [*A publication*]
ZEMHA .... Zeitschrift fuer Erzbergbau und Metallhuettenwesen [*A publication*]
ZEMIDI .... Zentralblatt fuer Mikrobiologie [*A publication*]
Zem-Kalk-Gips ... Zement-Kalk-Gips [*A publication*]
Zemled .... Zemledelie [*A publication*]
Zemled Mekh ... Zemledel'cheskaya Mekhanika [*A publication*]
Zemled Zhivotnovod Mold ... Zemledelie i Zhivotnovodstvo Moldavii [*A publication*]
Zemlerob Resp Mizhvid Temat Nauk Zb ... Zemlerobstvo Respublikans'kyi Mizhvidomchyi Tematychnyi Naukovyi Zbirnyk [*A publication*]
Zemleustroistvo Plan Sel'sk Naselennykh Punktov Geod ... Zemleustroistvo. Planirovka Sel'skikh Naselennykh Punktov i Geodeziya [*A publication*]
Zemlj Biljka ... Zemljiste i Biljka [*A publication*]
Zemlya Sib Dal'nevost ... Zemlya Sibirskaya Dal'nevostochnaya [*A publication*]
Zeml Zhivot Moldav ... Zemledelie i Zhivotnovodstvo Moldavii [*A publication*]
Zem ve Sk .. Zemepis ve Skole [*A publication*]
ZEMTR ..... Zeus Early Missile Test RADAR [*Missile defense*]   (AABC)
ZEN .... Zeitgeist, Enhancement, and Nonglare [*Camera lens finish developed by Sigma*]
zen .... Zenaga [*MARC language code*] [*Library of Congress*]   (LCCP)
ZEN .... Zenith Laboratories, Inc. [*NYSE symbol*]   (SPSG)
Zen .... Zenzelinus de Cassanis [*Deceased, 1334*] [*Authority cited in pre-1607 legal work*]   (DSA)
Z Energiewirtsch ... Zeitschrift fuer Energiewirtschaft [*German Federal Republic*] [*A publication*]
ZENITH .... Zero Energy Nitrogen-Heated Thermal Reactor [*British*]   (MCD)
ZENO .... Zenox, Inc. [*NASDAQ symbol*]   (NQ)
ZENT .... Zentec Corp. [*NASDAQ symbol*]   (NQ)
Zentbl Bakt ParasitKde ... Zentralblatt fuer Bakteriologie, Parasitenkunde, Infektionskrankheiten, und Hygiene [*A publication*]
Zentbl Bakt ParasitKed Abt 1 or 2 ... Zentralblatt fuer Bakteriologie, Parasitenkunde, Infektionskrankheiten, und Hygiene. Abteilung 1 or 2 [*A publication*]
Zentbl Biblioth ... Zentralblatt fuer Bibliothekswesen [*A publication*]
Zentbl Vet Med B ... Zentralblatt fuer Veterinaermedizin. Reihe B [*A publication*]

Zent Eur Giesserei Ztg ... Zentral-Europaeische Giesserei-Zeitung [*A publication*]
Zent Math ... Zentralblatt fuer Mathematik und Ihre Grenzgebiete [*A publication*]
Zentralb Bakteriol Parasitenkd Infektionskr ... Zentralblatt fuer Bakteriologie, Parasitenkunde, und Infektionskrankheiten [*A publication*]
Zentralbl Allg Pathol ... Zentralblatt fuer Allgemeine Pathologie und Pathologische Anatomie [*A publication*]
Zentralbl Allg Pathol Pathol Anat ... Zentralblatt fuer Allgemeine Pathologie und Pathologische Anatomie [*A publication*]
Zentralbl Arbeitsmed ... Zentralblatt fuer Arbeitsmedizin und Arbeitsschutz [*Later, Zentralblatt fuer Arbeitsmedizin, Arbeitsschutz, und Prophylaxe*] [*A publication*]
Zentralbl Arbeitsmed Arbeitsschutz ... Zentralblatt fuer Arbeitsmedizin und Arbeitsschutz [*Later, Zentralblatt fuer Arbeitsmedizin, Arbeitsschutz, und Prophylaxe*] [*A publication*]
Zentralbl Arbeitsmed Arbeitsschutz Prophyl ... Zentralblatt fuer Arbeitsmedizin, Arbeitsschutz, und Prophylaxe [*West Germany*] [*A publication*]
Zentralbl Arbeitsmed Arbeitsschutz Prophylaxe ... Zentralblatt fuer Arbeitsmedizin, Arbeitsschutz, und Prophylaxe [*A publication*]
Zentralbl Arbeitsmed Arbeitsschutz Prophyl Ergon ... Zentralblatt fuer Arbeitsmedizin, Arbeitsschutz, Prophylaxe, und Ergonomie [*German Federal Republic*] [*A publication*]
Zentralbl Bakteriol ... Zentralblatt fuer Bakteriologie [*A publication*]
Zentralbl Bakteriol (B) ... Zentralblatt fuer Bakteriologie, Parasitenkunde, Infektionskrankheiten, und Hygiene. Erste Abteilung. Originale Reihe B. Hygiene, Betriebshygiene, Praeventive Medizin [*A publication*]
Zentralbl Bakteriol Mikrobiol Hyg Abt 1 Orig A ... Zentralblatt fuer Bakteriologie, Mikrobiologie, und Hygiene. Abteilung 1. Originale A. Medizinische Mikrobiologie, Infektionskrankheiten, und Parasitologie [*A publication*]
Zentralbl Bakteriol Mikrobiol Hyg I Abt Orig C ... Zentralblatt fuer Bakteriologie, Mikrobiologie, und Hygiene. I Abteilung. Originale C [*A publication*]
Zentralbl Bakteriol Mikrobiol Hyg Ser A ... Zentralblatt fuer Bakteriologie, Mikrobiologie, und Hygiene. Series A. Medical Microbiology, Infectious Diseases, Virology, Parasitology [*A publication*]
Zentralbl Bakteriol Mikrobiol Hyg Ser B ... Zentralblatt fuer Bakteriologie, Mikrobiologie, und Hygiene. Serie B. Umwelthygiene, Krankenhaushygiene, Arbeitshygiene, Praeventive Medizin [*A publication*]
Zentralbl Bakteriol Naturwiss ... Zentralblatt fuer Bakteriologie, Parasitenkunde, Infektionskrankheiten, und Hygiene. Zweite Naturwissenschaftliche Abteilung. Mikrobiologie der Landwirtschaft der Technologie und des Umweltschutzes [*A publication*]
Zentralbl Bakteriol Orig A ... Zentralblatt fuer Bakteriologie, Parasitenkunde, Infektionskrankheiten, und Hygiene. Erste Abteilung. Originale Reihe A. Medizinische Mikrobiologie und Parasitologie [*A publication*]
Zentralbl Bakteriol (Orig B) ... Zentralblatt fuer Bakteriologie, Parasitenkunde, Infektionskrankheiten, und Hygiene. Erste Abteilung. Originale Reihe B. Hygiene, Betriebshygiene, Praeventive Medizin [*A publication*]
Zentralbl Bakteriol Parasitenkd Infektionskr Abt 1 ... Zentralblatt fuer Bakteriologie, Parasitenkunde, und Infektionskrankheiten. Abteilung 1. Medizinische-Hygienische Bakteriologie Virusforschung und Tierische Parasitologie [*A publication*]
Zentralbl Bakteriol Parasitenkd Infektionskrankheiten Hyg II ... Zentralblatt fuer Bakteriologie, Parasitenkunde, Infektionskrankheiten, und Hygiene. Naturwissenschaftliche Abteilung [*A publication*]
Zentralbl Bakteriol Parasitenkd Infektionskr Hyg Abt 1 Orig ... Zentralblatt fuer Bakteriologie, Parasitenkunde, Infektionskrankheiten, und Hygiene. Abteilung 1 Originale [*A publication*]
Zentralbl Bakteriol Parasitenkd Infektionskr Hyg Abt 1 Ref ... Zentralblatt fuer Bakteriologie, Parasitenkunde, Infektionskrankheiten, und Hygiene. Abteilung 1. Medizinisch-Hygienische Bakteriologie, Virusforschung, und Parasitologie. Referate [*A publication*]
Zentralbl Bakteriol Parasitenkd Infektionskr Hyge Abt 1 Suppl ... Zentralblatt fuer Bakteriologie, Parasitenkunde, Infektionskrankheiten, und Hygiene. Abteilung 1. Supplementheft [*A publication*]
Zentralbl Bakteriol Parasitenkd Infektionskr Hyg Abt 2 ... Zentralblatt fuer Bakteriologie, Parasitenkunde, Infektionskrankheiten, und Hygiene. Abteilung 2. Allgemeine Landwirtschaftliche und Technische Mikrobiologie [*A publication*]
Zentralbl Bakteriol Parasitenk Infektionskr Hyg ... Zentralblatt fuer Bakteriologie, Parasitenkunde, Infektionskrankheiten, und Hygiene [*A publication*]
Zentralbl Bauverwaltung ... Zentralblatt der Bauverwaltung [*A publication*]
Zentralbl Bibliothekswesen ... Zentralblatt fuer Bibliothekswesen [*A publication*]
Zentralbl Biochem Biophys ... Zentralblatt fuer Biochemie und Biophysik [*A publication*]
Zentralbl Biol Aerosol-Forsch ... Zentralblatt fuer Biologische Aerosol-Forschung [*A publication*]

Zentralbl Chir ... Zentralblatt fuer Chirurgie [*A publication*]
Zentralbl Chir Suppl ... Zentralblatt fuer Chirurgie. Supplement [*A publication*]
Zentralbl Exp Med ... Zentralblatt der Experimentellen Medizin [*A publication*]
Zentralbl Geol Palaeontol Teil 1 ... Zentralblatt fuer Geologie und Palaeontologie. Teil 1. Allgemeine, Angewandte, Regionale, und Historische Geologie [*A publication*]
Zentralbl Geol Palaeontol Teil 2 ... Zentralblatt fuer Geologie und Palaeontologie. Teil 2. Palaeontologie [*A publication*]
Zentralbl Gesamte Forstwes ... Zentralblatt fuer das Gesamte Forstwesen [*A publication*]
Zentralbl Gesamte Hyg Einschluss Bakteriol Immunitaetsl ... Zentralblatt fuer die Gesamte Hygiene mit Einschluss der Bakteriologie und Immunitaetslehre [*A publication*]
Zentralbl Gesamte Hyg Ihre Grenzgeb ... Zentralblatt fuer die Gesamte Hygiene und Ihre Grenzgebiete [*A publication*]
Zentralbl Gesamte Physiol Pathol Stoffwechsels ... Zentralblatt fuer die Gesamte Physiologie und Pathologie des Stoffwechsels [*A publication*]
Zentralbl Gesamte Radiol ... Zentralblatt fuer die Gesamte Radiologie [*A publication*]
Zentralbl Gesamte Rechtsmed ... Zentralblatt fuer die Gesamte Rechtsmedizin und Ihre Grenzgebiete [*A publication*]
Zentralbl Ges Hyg ... Zentralblatt fuer die Gesamte Hygiene und Ihre Grenzgebiete [*A publication*]
Zentralbl Gewerbehyg Unfallverhuet ... Zentralblatt fuer Gewerbehygiene und Unfallverhuetung [*A publication*]
Zentralbl Gynaekol ... Zentralblatt fuer Gynaekologie [*A publication*]
Zentralbl Huetten Walzwerke ... Zentralblatt der Huetten- und Walzwerke [*A publication*]
Zentralbl Hyg Umweltmed ... Zentralblatt fuer Hygiene und Umweltmedizin [*A publication*]
Zentralbl Industriebau ... Zentralblatt fuer Industriebau [*A publication*]
Zentralbl Inn Med ... Zentralblatt fuer Innere Medizin [*A publication*]
Zentralbl Mineral Geol Palaeontol ... Zentralblatt fuer Mineralogie, Geologie, und Palaeontologie [*A publication*]
Zentralbl Mineral Geol Palaeontol Teil 1 ... Zentralblatt fuer Mineralogie, Geologie, und Palaeontologie. Teil 1. Kristallographie und Mineralogie [*A publication*]
Zentralbl Mineral Geol Palaeontol Teil 2 ... Zentralblatt fuer Mineralogie, Geologie, und Palaeontologie. Teil 2. Gesteinskunde, Lagerstaettenkunde, Allgemeine, und Angewandte Geologie [*A publication*]
Zentralbl Mineral Geol Palaeontol Teil 3 ... Zentralblatt fuer Mineralogie, Geologie, und Palaeontologie. Teil 3. Historische und Regionale Geologie, Palaeontologie [*A publication*]
Zentralbl Mineral Teil 1 ... Zentralblatt fuer Mineralogie. Teil 1. Kristallographie und Mineralogie [*A publication*]
Zentralbl Mineral Teil 2 ... Zentralblatt fuer Mineralogie. Teil 2. Petrographie, Technische Mineralogie, Geochemie, und Lagerstaettenkunde [*A publication*]
Zentralbl Neurochir ... Zentralblatt fuer Neurochirurgie [*A publication*]
Zentralbl Papierind ... Zentralblatt fuer die Papierindustrie [*A publication*]
Zentralbl Pharm ... Zentralblatt fuer Pharmazie [*A publication*]
Zentralbl Pharm Pharmakother Laboratoriumsdiagn ... Zentralblatt fuer Pharmazie, Pharmakotherapie, und Laboratoriumsdiagnostik [*A publication*]
Zentralbl Phlebol ... Zentralblatt fuer Phlebologie [*A publication*]
Zentralbl Physiol ... Zentralblatt fuer Physiologie [*A publication*]
Zentralbl Verkehrs-Med Verkehrs-Psychol Luft- Raumfahrt-Med ... Zentralblatt fuer Verkehrs-Medizin, Verkehrs-Psychologie Luft-, und Raumfahrt-Medizin [*A publication*]
Zentralbl Veterinaermed ... Zentralblatt fuer Veterinaermedizin [*A publication*]
Zentralbl Veterinaermed Beih ... Zentralblatt fuer Veterinaermedizin. Beiheft [*A publication*]
Zentralbl Veterinaermed Reihe A ... Zentralblatt fuer Veterinaermedizin. Reihe A [*A publication*]
Zentralbl Veterinaermed Reihe B ... Zentralblatt fuer Veterinaermedizin. Reihe B [*A publication*]
Zentralbl Veterinaermed Reihe C ... Zentralblatt fuer Veterinaermedizin. Reihe C [*A publication*]
Zentralinst Kernforsch Rossendorf Dresden (Ber) ... Zentralinstitut fuer Kernforschung Rossendorf bei Dresden (Bericht) [*A publication*]
Zentralinst Versuchstierzucht Annu Rep ... Zentralinstitut fuer Versuchstierzucht. Annual Report [*A publication*]
Zentr Bibl .. Zentralblatt fuer Bibliothekswesen [*A publication*]
Zentr Org Ges Chir ... Zentralorgan fuer die Gesamte Chirurgie und Ihre Grenzgebiete [*A publication*]
Z Entwick P ... Zeitschrift fuer Entwicklungspsychologie und Paedagogische Psychologie [*A publication*]
Zent Ztg Opt Mech ... Zentral-Zeitung fuer Optik und Mechanik [*A publication*]
ZENXC...... Zenex Synthetic Lubricants, Inc. [*NASDAQ symbol*] (NQ)
Zenz .... Zenzelinus de Cassanis [*Deceased, 1334*] [*Authority cited in pre-1607 legal work*] (DSA)
ZEOS........ Zeos International Ltd. [*NASDAQ symbol*] (NQ)
Zep .... Zephaniah [*Old Testament book*]
ZEP........... Zeppelin (DSUE)

ZEPAD...... Zeitschrift fuer Parlamentsfragen [*A publication*]
Zeph........... Zephaniah [*Old Testament book*]
ZEPHYR... Zero Energy Plutonium-Fueled Fast Reactor [*British*] (DEN)
ZEPL........ Zero Excess Propellants Line
ZER .... Pottsville, PA [*Location identifier*] [*FAA*] (FAAL)
Zer.............. Zera'im (BJA)
ZER .... Zero Energy Reflection
ZERA........ Zero Energy Critical Assemblies Reactor [*British*] (DEN)
ZERC........ Zero Energy Reflection Coefficient
Z Erdkundeunterricht ... Zeitschrift fuer den Erdkundeunterricht [*A publication*]
Z Erdk Unt ... Zeitschrift fuer den Erdkundeunterricht [*A publication*]
ZERED...... Zeitschrift fuer Rechtspolitik [*A publication*]
Z Erkr Atmungsorgane ... Zeitschrift fuer Erkrankungen der Atmungsorgane [*A publication*]
ZERLINA ... Zero Energy Reactor for Lattice Investigation and New Assemblies [*India*]
Z Ernaehrung ... Zeitschrift fuer Ernaehrungswissenschaft [*A publication*]
Z Ernaehrungsw ... Zeitschrift fuer Ernaehrungswissenschaft [*A publication*]
Z Ernaehrungswiss ... Zeitschrift fuer Ernaehrungswissenschaft [*A publication*]
Z Ernaehrungswiss Suppl ... Zeitschrift fuer Ernaehrungswissenschaft. Supplementa [*A publication*]
Z Ernaehr Wiss ... Zeitschrift fuer Ernaehrungwissenschaft [*A publication*]
Zernovoe Khoz ... Zernovoe Khozyaistvo [*A publication*]
Zernovye Maslichn Kul't ... Zernovye i Maslichnye Kul'tury [*A publication*]
Zero Popul Growth Natl Rep ... Zero Population Growth. National Reporter [*A publication*]
Zero Un...... Zero Un Hebdo [*A publication*]
ZERT........ Zero Reaction Tool
Z Erzbergbau Metallhuettenwes ... Zeitschrift fuer Erzbergbau und Metallhuettenwesen [*German Federal Republic*] [*A publication*]
ZES........... Zeitschrift fuer Eingeborenen-Sprachen [*A publication*]
ZES........... Zero Energy System [*Nuclear energy*]
ZES........... Zil Elwannyen Sesel [*Formerly, Zil Eliogne Sesel, then Zil Elwagne Sesel*]
ZES........... Zollinger-Ellison Syndrome [*Medicine*]
ZES........ Zone Electrophoresis System
ZESIA .... Zeitschrift fuer Sinnephysiologie [*A publication*]
ZE Spr .... Zeitschrift fuer Eingeborenen-Sprachen [*A publication*]
ZEST .... Zinc, E-Vitamin, Siberian Ginseng, Turnera [*Health product*] [*British*]
ZESTA ...... Zeitschrift fuer Schweisstechnik [*A publication*]
Zesz Muz Etnogr Wrocl ... Zeszyty Muzeum Etnograficznego Wroclawie [*A publication*]
Zesz Nauk Akad Ekon ... Zeszyty Naukowe Akademii Ekonomicznej w Katowicach [*A publication*]
Zesz Nauk Akad Ekon Krakow ... Zeszyty Naukowe Akademii Ekonomicznej w Krakowie [*A publication*]
Zesz Nauk Akad Ekon Poznan ... Zeszyty Naukowe Akademii Ekonomicznej w Poznaniu [*A publication*]
Zesz Nauk Akad Ekon Poznaniu Ser 2 ... Zeszyty Naukowe. Akademia Ekonomiczna w Poznaniu. Seria 2. Prace Habilitacyjne i Doktorskie [*A publication*]
Zesz Nauk Akad Ekon Wroclaw ... Zeszyty Naukowe Akademii Ekonomicznej w Wroclawiu [*A publication*]
Zesz Nauk Akad Gorn Hutn (Cracow) Eletryf Mech Gorn Hutn ... Zeszyty Naukowe Akademii Gorniczo-Hutniczej (Cracow). Elektryfikacja i Mechanizacja Gornictwa i Hutnictwa [*A publication*]
Zesz Nauk Akad Gorn Hutn (Cracow) Geol ... Zeszyty Naukowe Akademii Gorniczo-Hutniczej (Cracow). Geologia [*A publication*]
Zesz Nauk Akad Gorn-Hutn (Cracow) Mat Fiz Chem ... Zeszyty Naukowe Akademii Gorniczo-Hutniczej (Cracow). Matematyka, Fizyka, Chemia [*A publication*]
Zesz Nauk Akad Gorn-Hutn (Cracow) Metal Odlew ... Zeszyty Naukowe Akademii Gorniczo-Hutniczej (Cracow). Metalurgia i Odlewnictwo [*A publication*]
Zesz Nauk Akad Gorn Hutn (Cracow) Rozpr ... Zeszyty Naukowe Akademii Gorniczo-Hutniczej (Cracow). Rozprawy [*A publication*]
Zesz Nauk Akad Gorn-Hutn Im Stanislawa Staszica Ceram ... Zeszyty Naukowe Akademii Gorniczo-Hutniczej Imienia Stanislawa Staszica. Ceramica [*A publication*]
Zesz Nauk Akad Gorn-Hutn Im Stanislawa Staszica Geol ... Zeszyty Naukowe Akademii Gorniczo-Hutniczej Imienia Stanislawa Staszica. Geologia [*A publication*]
Zesz Nauk Akad Gorn-Hutn Im Stanislawa Staszica Gorn ... Zeszyty Naukowe Akademii Gorniczo-Hutniczej Imienia Stanislawa Staszica. Gornictwo [*A publication*]
Zesz Nauk Akad Gorn-Hutn Im Stanislawa Staszica Mat Fiz Chem ... Zeszyty Naukowe Akademii Gorniczo-Hutniczej Imienia Stanislawa Staszica. Matematyka, Fizyka, Chemia [*A publication*]
Zesz Nauk Akad Gorn-Hutn Im Stanislawa Staszica Metal Odlew ... Zeszyty Naukowe Akademii Gorniczo-Hutniczej Imienia Stanislawa Staszica. Metalurgia i Odlewnictwo [*A publication*]

Zesz Nauk Akad Gorn-Hutn Im Stanislawa Staszica Ser Autom ... Zeszyty Naukowe Akademii Gorniczo-Hutniczej Imienia Stanislawa Staszica. Seria Automatyka [*Poland*] [*A publication*]

Zesz Nauk Akad Gorn-Hutn Im Stanislawa Staszica Zesz Spec ... Zeszyty Naukowe Akademii Gorniczo-Hutniczej Imienia Stanislawa Staszica. Zeszyt Specjalny [*A publication*]

Zesz Nauk Akad Gorn-Hutn Im Staszica Gorn ... Zeszyty Naukowe Akademii Gorniczo-Hutniczej Imienia Stanislawa Staszica. Gornictwo [*A publication*]

Zesz Nauk Akad Gorn-Hutn Im Staszica Mat Fiz Chem ... Zeszyty Naukowe Akademii Gorniczo-Hutniczej Imienia Stanislawa Staszica. Matematyka, Fizyka, Chemia [*A publication*]

Zesz Nauk Akad Gorn-Hutn Im Staszica Zesz Spec ... Zeszyty Naukowe Akademii Gorniczo-Hutniczej Imienia Stanislawa Staszica. Zeszyt Specjalny [*A publication*]

Zesz Nauk Akad Gorn-Hutn (Krakow) Ceram ... Zeszyty Naukowe Akademii Gorniczo-Hutniczej (Krakow). Ceramika [*A publication*]

Zesz Nauk Akad Gorn-Hutn (Krakow) Elektryf Mech Gorn Hutn ... Zeszyty Naukowe Akademii Gorniczo-Hutniczej (Krakow). Elektryfikacja i Mechanizacja Gornictwa i Hutnictwa [*A publication*]

Zesz Nauk Akad Gorn-Hutn (Krakow) Geol ... Zeszyty Naukowe Akademii Gorniczo-Hutniczej (Krakow). Geologia [*A publication*]

Zesz Nauk Akad Gorn-Hutn (Krakow) Gorn ... Zeszyty Naukowe Akademii Gorniczo-Hutniczej (Krakow). Gornictwo [*A publication*]

Zesz Nauk Akad Gorn-Hutn Krakowie Rozpr ... Zeszyty Naukowe Akademii Gorniczo-Hutniczej w Krakowie. Rozprawy [*Poland*] [*A publication*]

Zesz Nauk Akad Gorn-Hutn (Krakow) Mat Fiz Chem ... Zeszyty Naukowe Akademii Gorniczo-Hutniczej (Krakow). Matematyka, Fizyka, Chemia [*A publication*]

Zesz Nauk Akad Gorn-Hutn (Krakow) Metal Odlew ... Zeszyty Naukowe Akademii Gorniczo-Hutniczej (Krakow). Metalurgia i Odlewnictwo [*A publication*]

Zesz Nauk Akad Gorn-Hutn (Krakow) Ses Nauk ... Zeszyty Naukowe Akademii Gorniczo-Hutniczej (Krakow). Sesja Naukowa [*A publication*]

Zesz Nauk Akad Gorn-Hutn (Krakow) Sozologia Sozotechnika ... Zeszyty Naukowe Akademii Gorniczo-Hutniczej (Krakow). Sozologia i Sozotechnika [*Poland*] [*A publication*]

Zesz Nauk Akad Gorn-Hutn (Krakow) Zesz Spec ... Zeszyty Naukowe Akademii Gorniczo-Hutniczej (Krakow). Zeszyty Specjalny [*A publication*]

Zesz Nauk Akad Gorn-Hutn Stanislawa Staszica Geol ... Zeszyty Naukowe Akademii Gorniczo-Hutniczej Imienia Stanislawa Staszica. Geologia [*A publication*]

Zesz Nauk Akad Gorn-Hutn Stanisl Staszica ... Zeszyty Naukowe Akademii Gorniczo-Hutniczej Imienia Stanislawa Staszica. Metalurgia i Odlewnictwo [*A publication*]

Zesz Nauk Akad Gorn-Hutn Stanisl Staszica Autom ... Zeszyty Naukowe Akademii Gorniczo-Hutniczej Imienia Stanislawa Staszica. Automatyka [*A publication*]

Zesz Nauk Akad Gorn-Hutn Stanisl Staszica Geol ... Zeszyty Naukowe Akademii Gorniczo-Hutniczej Imienia Stanislawa Staszica. Geologia [*Poland*] [*A publication*]

Zesz Nauk Akad Gorn-Hutn Stanisl Staszica Mat Fiz Chem ... Zeszyty Naukowe Akademii Gorniczo-Hutniczej Imienia Stanislawa Staszica. Matematyka, Fizyka, Chemia [*A publication*]

Zesz Nauk Akad Roln Szczecinie ... Zeszyty Naukowe. Akademia Rolnicza w Szczecinie [*Poland*] [*A publication*]

Zesz Nauk Akad Roln Szczecinie Ser Rybactwo Morsk ... Zeszyty Naukowe Akademii Rolniczej w Szczecinie. Seria Rybactwo Morskie [*Poland*] [*A publication*]

Zesz Nauk Akad Roln Tech Olsztynie ... Zeszyty Naukowe Akademii Rolniczo-Technicznej w Olsztynie [*A publication*]

Zesz Nauk Akad Roln Tech Olsztynie Roln ... Zeszyty Naukowe Akademii Rolniczo-Technicznej w Olsztynie. Rolnictwo [*A publication*]

Zesz Nauk Akad Roln Tech Olsztynie Technol Zywn ... Zeszyty Naukowe Akademii Rolniczo-Technicznej w Olsztynie. Technologia Zywnosci [*A publication*]

Zesz Nauk Akad Roln Tech Olsztynie Zootech ... Zeszyty Naukowe Akademii Rolniczo-Technicznej w Olsztynie. Zootechnika [*A publication*]

Zesz Nauk Akad Roln Warszawie Melior Rolne ... Zeszyty Naukowe Akademii Rolniczej w Warszawie. Melioracje Rolne [*A publication*]

Zesz Nauk Akad Roln Warszawie Ogrod ... Zeszyty Naukowe Akademii Rolniczej w Warszawie. Ogrodnictwo [*A publication*]

Zesz Nauk Akad Roln Warszawie Technol Drewna ... Zeszyty Naukowe Akademii Rolniczej w Warszawie. Technologia Drewna [*A publication*]

Zesz Nauk Akad Roln Warszawie Technol Rolno Spozyw ... Zeszyty Naukowe Akademii Rolniczej w Warszawie. Technologia Rolno-Spozyweza [*A publication*]

Zesz Nauk Akad Roln Warszawie Zootech ... Zeszyty Naukowe Akademii Rolniczej w Warszawie. Zootechnika [*A publication*]

Zesz Nauk Akad Roln Wroclawiu Melior ... Zeszyty Naukowe Akademii Rolniczej we Wroclawiu. Melioracja [*A publication*]

Zesz Nauk Akad Roln Wroclawiu Roln ... Zeszyty Naukowe Akademii Rolniczej we Wroclawiu. Rolnictwo [*A publication*]

Zesz Nauk Akad Roln Wroclawiu Weter ... Zeszyty Naukowe Akademii Rolniczej we Wroclawiu. Weterynaria [*A publication*]

Zesz Nauk Akad Roln Wroclawiu Zootech ... Zeszyty Naukowe Akademii Rolniczej we Wroclawiu. Zootechnika [*A publication*]

Zesz Nauk Akad Roln Wrocl Wet ... Zeszyty Naukowe Akademii Rolniczej we Wroclawiu. Weterynaria [*A publication*]

Zesz Nauk Gorn ... Zeszyty Naukowe Gornictwo [*A publication*]

Zesz Nauk Inst Ciezkiej Synt Org Blachowni Slask ... Zeszyty Naukowe Instytut Ciezkiej Syntezy Organicznej w Blachowni Slaskiej [*A publication*]

Zesz Nauk Lesn Akad Roln Warsz ... Zeszyty Naukowe. Lesnictwo-Akademia Rolnicza w Warszawie [*A publication*]

Zesz Nauk Mat Fiz Chem ... Zeszyty Naukowe. Matematyka, Fizyka, Chemia [*Poland*] [*A publication*]

Zesz Nauk Mechan Budownictwo Akad Roln-Tech Olsztyn ... Zeszyty Naukowe. Mechanika i Budownictwo-Akademia Rolniczo-Techniczna w Olsztynie [*A publication*]

Zesz Nauk Melior Rolne Akad Roln Warsz ... Zeszyty Naukowe. Melioracje Rolne-Akademia Rolnicza w Warszawie [*A publication*]

Zesz Nauk Ochr Wod Rybactwo Srodladowe ... Zeszyty Naukowe. Ochrona Wod i Rybactwo Srodladowe [*A publication*]

Zesz Nauk Politech Czestochow ... Zeszyty Naukowe Politechniki Czestochowskiej [*A publication*]

Zesz Nauk Politech Czestochow Metal ... Zeszyty Naukowe Politechniki Czestochowskiej. Metalurgia [*A publication*]

Zesz Nauk Politech Czestochow Nauki Tech Hutn ... Zeszyty Naukowe Politechniki Czestochowskiej. Nauki Techniczne. Hutnictwo [*Poland*] [*A publication*]

Zesz Nauk Politech Gdansk Chem ... Zeszyty Naukowe Politechniki Gdanskiej. Chemia [*A publication*]

Zesz Nauk Politech Gdansk Elektr ... Zeszyty Naukowe Politechniki Gdanskiej. Elektryka [*A publication*]

Zesz Nauk Politech Gdansk Fiz ... Zeszyty Naukowe Politechniki Gdanskiej. Fizyka [*A publication*]

Zesz Nauk Politech Gdansk Mat ... Zeszyty Naukowe Politechniki Gdanskiej. Matematyka [*A publication*]

Zesz Nauk Politech Gdansk Mech ... Zeszyty Naukowe Politechniki Gdanskiej. Mechanika [*A publication*]

Zesz Nauk Politech Krakow Chem ... Zeszyty Naukowe Politechniki Krakowskiej. Chemia [*A publication*]

Zesz Nauk Politech Krakow Mech ... Zeszyty Naukowe Politechniki Krakowskiej. Mechanika [*A publication*]

Zesz Nauk Politech Lod Budow ... Zeszyty Naukowe Politechniki Lodzkiej. Budownictwo [*A publication*]

Zesz Nauk Politech Lodz Chem ... Zeszyty Naukowe Politechniki Lodzkiej. Chemia [*A publication*]

Zesz Nauk Politech Lodz Chem Spozyw ... Zeszyty Naukowe Politechniki Lodzkiej. Chemia Spozywcza [*A publication*]

Zesz Nauk Politech Lodz Elek ... Zeszyty Naukowe Politechniki Lodzkiej. Elektryka [*A publication*]

Zesz Nauk Politech Lodz Elektr ... Zeszyty Naukowe Politechniki Lodzkiej. Elektryka [*A publication*]

Zesz Nauk Politech Lodz Fiz ... Zeszyty Naukowe Politechnika Lodzka. Fizyka [*A publication*]

Zesz Nauk Politech Lodz Inz Chem ... Zeszyty Naukowe Politechniki Lodzkiej. Inzynieria Chemiczna [*A publication*]

Zesz Nauk Politech Lodz Mech ... Zeszyty Naukowe Politechniki Lodzkiej. Mechanika [*A publication*]

Zesz Nauk Politech Lodz Wlok ... Zeszyty Naukowe Politechniki Lodzkiej. Wlokiennictwo [*A publication*]

Zesz Nauk Politech Poznan Chem Inz Chem ... Zeszyty Naukowe Politechniki Poznanskiej. Chemia i Inzynieria Chemiczna [*A publication*]

Zesz Nauk Politech Poznan Elektr ... Zeszyty Naukowe Politechniki Poznanskiej. Elektryka [*A publication*]

Zesz Nauk Politech Rzeszowskiej ... Zeszyty Naukowe Politechniki Rzeszowskiej [*A publication*]

Zesz Nauk Politech Slask ... Zeszyty Naukowe Politechniki Slaskiej [*A publication*]

Zesz Nauk Politech Slaska Energ ... Zeszyty Naukowe Politechnika Slaska. Energetyka [*A publication*]

Zesz Nauk Politech Slask Chem ... Zeszyty Naukowe Politechniki Slaskiej. Chemia [*A publication*]

Zesz Nauk Politech Slask Energ ... Zeszyty Naukowe Politechniki Slaskiej. Energetyka [*A publication*]

Zesz Nauk Politech Slask Gorn ... Zeszyty Naukowe Politechniki Slaskiej. Gornictwo [*A publication*]

Zesz Nauk Politech Slask Hutn ... Zeszyty Naukowe Politechniki Slaskiej. Hutnictwo [*A publication*]

Zesz Nauk Politech Slask Inz Sanit ... Zeszyty Naukowe Politechniki Slaskiej. Inzynieria Sanitarna [*A publication*]

Zesz Nauk Politech Slask Ser Elektr ... Zeszyty Naukowe Politechniki Slaskiej. Seria Elektryka [*A publication*]

Zesz Nauk Politech Slask Ser Mat-Fiz ... Zeszyty Naukowe Politechniki Slaskiej. Seria Matematyka-Fizyka [*A publication*]

Zesz Nauk Politech Swietokrz Probl Nauk Podst ... Zeszyty Naukowe Politechniki Swietokrzyska. Problemy Nauk Podstawowych [*A publication*]

Zesz Nauk Politech Szezecin Chem ... Zeszyty Naukowe Politechniki Szezecinskiej. Chemia [*A publication*]

Zesz Nauk Politech Szezecin Pr Monogr ... Zeszyty Naukowe Politechniki Szezecinskiej. Prace Monografiezne [*A publication*]

Zesz Nauk Politech Warsz Chem ... Zeszyty Naukowe Politechniki Warszawskiej. Chemia [*A publication*]

Zesz Nauk Politech Wroclaw Chem ... Zeszyty Naukowe Politechniki Wroclawskiej. Chemia [*A publication*]

Zesz Nauk Roln Akad Roln Warsz ... Zeszyty Naukowe. Rolnictwo Akademia Rolnicza w Warszawie [*A publication*]

Zesz Nauk Szk Gl Gospod Wiejsk Akad Roln Warszawie Ogrod ... Zeszyty Naukowe Szkoly Glownej Gospodarstwa Wiejskiego. Akademii Rolniczej w Warszawie. Ogrodnictwo [*A publication*]

Zesz Nauk Szk Gl Gospod Wiejsk Akad Roln Warszawie Wter ... Zeszyty Naukowe Szkoly Glownej Gospodarstwa Wiejskiego. Akademii Rolniczej w Warszawie. Weterynaria [*A publication*]

Zesz Nauk Szk Gl Gospod Wiejsk Akad Roln Warszawie Zootech ... Zeszyty Naukowe Szkoly Glownej Gospodarstwa Wiejskiego. Akademii Rolniczej w Warszawie. Zootechnika [*A publication*]

Zesz Nauk Szk Gl Gospod Wiejsk Akad Roln Warsz Ogrodn ... Zeszyty Naukowe Szkoly Glownej Gospodarstwa Wiejskiego Akademii Rolniczej w Warszawie Ogrodnictwo [*A publication*]

Zesz Nauk Szk Gl Gospod Wiejsk Warszawie Melior Rolne ... Zeszyty Naukowe Szkoly Glownej Gospodarstwa Wiejskiego w Warszawie. Melioracje Rolne [*A publication*]

Zesz Nauk Szk Gl Gospod Wiejsk Warszawie Ogrod ... Zeszyty Naukowe Szkoly Glownej Gospodarstwa Wiejskiego w Warszawie. Ogrodnictwo [*A publication*]

Zesz Nauk Szk Gl Gospod Wiejsk Warszawie Roln ... Zeszyty Naukowe Szkoly Glownej Gospodarstwa Wiejskiego w Warszawie. Rolnictwo [*Poland*] [*A publication*]

Zesz Nauk Szk Gl Gospod Wiejsk Warszawie Technol Drewna ... Zeszyty Naukowe Szkoly Glownej Gospodarstwa Wiejskiego w Warszawie. Technologia Drewna [*A publication*]

Zesz Nauk Szk Gl Gospod Wiejsk Warszawie Zootech ... Zeszyty Naukowe Szkoly Glownej Gospodarstwa Wiejskiego w Warszawie. Zootechnika [*A publication*]

Zesz Nauk Szk Glo Gospod Wiejsk Warszawie Lesn ... Zeszyty Naukowe Szkoly Glownej Gospodarstwa Wiejskiego w Warszawie. Lesnictwo [*A publication*]

Zesz Nauk Szk Glow Gospod Wiejsk Warszawie ... Zeszyty Naukowe Szkoly Glownej Gospodarstwa Wiejskiego w Warszawie [*A publication*]

Zesz Nauk Szk Glown Plan Statystyki ... Zeszyty Naukowe Szkoly Glownej Planowania i Statystyki [*A publication*]

Zesz Nauk Szkol Gospod Wiejsk Warsz (Lesn) ... Zeszyty Naukowe Szkola Glowna Gospodarstwa Wiejskiego w Warszawie (Lesnictwo) [*A publication*]

Zesz Nauk Szkol Gospod Wiejsk Warsz Technol Drewna ... Zeszyty Naukowe Szkola Glowna Gospodarstwa Wiejskiego w Warszawie. Technologia Drewna [*A publication*]

Zesz Nauk Technol Drewna Akad Roln Warsz ... Zeszyty Naukowe. Technologia Drewna-Akademia Rolnicza w Warszawie [*A publication*]

Zesz Nauk Technol Zywn Akad Roln-Tech Olsztynie ... Zeszyty Naukowe. Technologia Zywnosci-Akademia Rolniczo-Techniczna w Olsztynie [*A publication*]

Zesz Nauk Tech Wyzsza Szk Inz Lublinie ... Zeszyty Naukowo-Techniczny Wyzsza Szkola Inzynierska w Lublinie [*A publication*]

ZeszNauKUL ... Zeszyty Naukowe Katolickiego Uniwersytetu Lubelskiego [*Lublin*] [*A publication*]

Zesz Nauk Uniw Jagiellon Acta Cosmol ... Zeszyty Naukowe Uniwersytetu Jagiellonskiego. Acta Cosmologica [*A publication*]

Zesz Nauk Uniw Jagiellon Pr Biol Mol ... Zeszyty Naukowe Uniwersytetu Jagiellonskiego. Prace Biologii Molekularnej [*Poland*] [*A publication*]

Zesz Nauk Uniw Jagiellon Pr Chem ... Zeszyty Naukowe Uniwersytetu Jagiellonskiego. Prace Chemiczne [*Poland*] [*A publication*]

Zesz Nauk Uniw Jagiellon Pr Etnogr ... Zeszyty Naukowe Uniwersytetu Jagiellonskiego. Prace Etnograficzne [*A publication*]

Zesz Nauk Uniw Jagiellon Pr Fiz ... Zeszyty Naukowe Uniwersytetu Jagiellonskiego. Prace Fizyczne [*A publication*]

Zesz Nauk Uniw Jagiellon Pr Zool ... Zeszyty Naukowe Uniwersytetu Jagiellonskiego. Prace Zoologiczne [*A publication*]

Zesz Nauk Uniw Jagiellon Ser Nauk Mat Przy ... Zeszyty Naukowe Uniwersytetu Jagiellonskiego. Seria Nauk Matematyezno-Przyrodniczych. Matematyka, Fizyka, Chemia [*A publication*]

Zesz Nauk Uniw Jagiellonsk Pr Bot ... Zeszyty Naukowe Uniwersytetu Jagiellonskiego. Prace Botaniczne [*A publication*]

Zesz Nauk Uniw Jagiellonsk Zool ... Zeszyty Naukowe Uniwersytetu Jagiellonskiego. Prace Zoologiczne [*A publication*]

Zesz Nauk Uniw Lodz ... Zeszyty Naukowe Uniwersytetu Lodzkiego [*A publication*]

Zesz Nauk Uniw Lodz Fiz ... Zeszyty Naukowe Uniwersytetu Lodzkiego. Fizyka [*A publication*]

Zesz Nauk Uniw Lodz Nauki Humanist-Spolecz ... Zeszyty Naukowe Uniwersytetu Lodzkiego. Nauki Humanistyczno-Spoleczne [*A publication*]

Zesz Nauk Uniw Lodz Nauki Mat Przyr ... Zeszyty Naukowe Uniwersytetu Lodzkiego. Nauki Matematyczno-Przyrodnicze [*A publication*]

Zesz Nauk Uniw Lodz Ser II ... Zeszyty Naukowe Uniwersytetu Lodzkiego. Seria II. Nauki Matematyczno-Przyrodnicze [*Poland*] [*A publication*]

Zesz Nauk Uniw Lodz Ser III ... Zeszyty Naukowe Uniwersytetu Lodzkiego. Seria III [*A publication*]

Zesz Nauk Uniw Mikolja Kopernika Torun ... Zeszyty Naukowe Uniwersytetu Imienia Mikolaja Kopernika w Toruniu [*A publication*]

Zesz Nauk Uniw Poznaniu Mat Fiz Chem ... Zeszyty Naukowe Uniwersytetu Imienia Adama Mickiewicza w Poznaniu. Matematyka, Fizyka, Chemia [*A publication*]

Zesz Nauk Uniw Slaski Katowicach Seke Chem ... Zeszyty Naukowe Uniwersytet Slaski w Katowicach Sekeja Chemii [*A publication*]

Zesz Nauk Weter Akad Roln Warsz ... Zeszyty Naukowe. Weterynaria-Akademia Rolnicza w Warszawie [*A publication*]

Zesz Nauk Wydz Mat Fiz Chem Uniw Gdanski Chem ... Zeszyty Naukowe Wydzialu Matematyki, Fizyki, Chemii. Uniwersytet Gdanski. Seria Chemia [*A publication*]

Zesz Nauk Wyzs Szk Ekon Poznaniu ... Zeszyty Naukowe Wyzszej Szkoly Ekonomicznej w Poznaniu [*A publication*]

Zesz Nauk Wyzs Szk Roln Krakowie ... Zeszyty Naukowe Wyzszej Szkoly Rolniczej w Krakowie [*A publication*]

Zesz Nauk Wyzs Szk Roln Krakowie Zootech ... Zeszyty Naukowe Wyzszej Szkoly Rolniczej w Krakowie. Zootechnika [*A publication*]

Zesz Nauk Wyzs Szk Roln Olsztynie ... Zeszyty Naukowe Wyzszej Szkoly Rolniczej w Olsztynie [*A publication*]

Zesz Nauk Wyzs Szk Roln Szczecinie ... Zeszyty Naukowe Wyzsza Szkola Rolnicza w Szczecinie [*A publication*]

Zesz Nauk Wyzs Szk Roln Wroclawiu ... Zeszyty Naukowe Wyzszej Szkoly Rolniczej we Wroclawiu [*A publication*]

Zesz Nauk Wyzs Szk Roln Wroclawiu Wet ... Zeszyty Naukowe Wyzszej Szkoly Rolniczej we Wroclawiu. Weterynaria [*A publication*]

Zesz Nauk Wyzsza Szk Ekon Poznaniu Ser 2 ... Zeszyty Naukowe Wyzsza Szkola Ekonomiczna w Poznaniu. Seria 2. Prace Habilitacyjne i Doktorskie [*A publication*]

Zesz Nauk Wyz Szkol Ekon ... Zeszyty Naukowe Wyzszej Szkoly Ekonomicznej w Katowicach [*A publication*]

Zesz Nauk Wyzsz Szk Inz Bialymstoku Mat Fiz Chem ... Zeszyty Naukowe Wyzszej Szkoly Inzynierskiej w Bialymstoku Matematyka, Fizyka, Chemia [*A publication*]

Zesz Nauk Wyzsz Szkoly Ekon Katowic ... Zeszyty Naukowe Wyzszej Szkoly Ekonomicznej w Katowicach [*A publication*]

Zesz Nauk Wyzsz Szkoly Ekon Poznan ... Zeszyty Naukowe Wyzszej Szkoly Ekonomicznej w Poznaniu [*A publication*]

Zesz Nauk Wyzsz Szk Pedagog Gdansku Mat Fiz Chem ... Zeszyty Naukowe Wyzszej Szkoly Pedagogicznej w Gdansku. Matematyka, Fizyka, Chemia [*A publication*]

Zesz Nauk Wyzsz Szk Pedagog Katowicach Sekc Fiz ... Zeszyty Naukowe Wyzszej Szkoly Pedagogicznej w Katowicach. Sekcja Fizyki [*A publication*]

Zesz Nauk Wyzsz Szk Roln Olsztynie ... Zeszyty Naukowe Wyzszej Szkoly Rolniczej w Olsztynie [*A publication*]

Zesz Nauk Wyzsz Szk Roln Szczecinie ... Zeszyty Naukowe Wyzszej Szkoly Rolniczej w Szczecinie [*A publication*]

Zesz Nauk Wyzsz Szk Roln Wroclawiu Melior ... Zeszyty Naukowe Wyzszej Szkoly Rolniczej we Wroclawiu. Melioracja [*A publication*]

Zesz Nauk Wyzsz Szk Roln Wroclawiu Roln ... Zeszyty Naukowe Wyzszej Szkoly Rolniczej we Wroclawiu. Rolnictwo [*A publication*]

Zesz Nauk Wyzsz Szk Roln Wroclawiu Weter ... Zeszyty Naukowe Wyzszej Szkoly Rolniczej we Wroclawiu. Weterynaria [*A publication*]

Zesz Nauk Wyzsz Szk Roln Wroclawiu Zootech ... Zeszyty Naukowe Wyzszej Szkoly Rolniczej we Wroclawiu. Zootechnika [*A publication*]

Zesz Nauk Wyzsz Szk Roln Wrocl Melior ... Zeszyty Naukowe Wyzszej Szkoly Rolniczej we Wroclawiu. Melioracja [*A publication*]

Zesz Nauk Wyzsz Szk Roln Wrocl Roln ... Zeszyty Naukowe Wyzszej Szkoly Rolniczej we Wroclawiu. Rolnictwo [*A publication*]

Zesz Nauk Zootech Akad Roln-Tech Olsztyn ... Zeszyty Naukowe. Zootechnika-Akademia Rolniczo-Techniczna w Olsztynie [*A publication*]

Zesz Nauk Zootech Akad Roln Warsz ... Zeszyty Naukowe. Zootechnika-Akademia Rolnicza w Warszawie [*A publication*]

Zesz NWSP ... Zeszyty Naukowe Wyzsza Szkola Pedagogiczna w Katowicach [*A publication*]

Zesz Probl Gorn ... Zeszyty Problemowe Gornictwa [*A publication*]

Zesz Probl Kosmosu ... Zeszyty Problemowe Kosmosu [*A publication*]

Zesz Probl Nauki Pol ... Zeszyty Problemowe Nauki Polskiej [*A publication*]

Zesz Probl Postep Nauk Roln ... Zeszyty Problemowe Postepow Nauk Rolniczych [*A publication*]

Zesz Probl Postepow Nauk Roln ... Zeszyty Problemowe Postepow Nauk Rolniczych [*A publication*]

Zesz Prob Postepow Nauk Roln ... Zeszyty Problemowe Postepow Nauk Rolniczych [*A publication*]

Zeszty Nauk Uniw Jagiellon Prace Mat ... Zeszyty Naukowe Uniwersytetu Jagiellonskiego. Prace Matematyczne [*A publication*]
Zesz Wrocl ... Zeszyty Wroclawskie [*A publication*]
Zeszyty Nauk Akad Gorn-Hutniczej Mat Fiz Chem ... Zeszyty Naukowe Akademii Gorniczo-Hutniczej Imienia Stanislawa Staszica. Matematyka, Fizyka, Chemia [*A publication*]
Zeszyty Nauk Politech Lodz Mat ... Zeszyty Naukowe Politechniki Lodzkiej. Matematyka [*A publication*]
Zeszyty Nauk Politech Slask Automat ... Zeszyty Naukowe Politechniki Slaskiej. Automatyka [*A publication*]
Zeszyty Nauk Politech Slask Mat-Fiz ... Zeszyty Naukowe Politechniki Slaskiej. Seria Matematyka-Fizyka [*A publication*]
Zeszyty Nauk Politech Szczecin ... Zeszyty Naukowe Politechniki Szezecinskiej [*A publication*]
Zeszyty Nauk Szkoly Glown Planowania i Statyst ... Zeszyty Naukowe Szkoly Glownej Planowania i Statystyki [*A publication*]
Zeszyty Nauk Uniw Jagiellon Prace Fiz ... Zeszyty Naukowe Uniwersytetu Jagiellonskiego. Prace Fizyczne [*A publication*]
Zeszyty Nauk Wyz Szkoly Ped w Opolu Fiz ... Zeszyty Naukowe Wyzszej Szkoly Pedagogicznej w Opolu. Fizyka [*A publication*]
Zeszyty Nauk Wyz Szkoly Ped w Opolu Mat ... Zeszyty Naukowe Wyzszej Szkoly Pedagogicznej w Opolu. Matematyka [*A publication*]
ZET........... Zero-Gravity Expulsion Technique
ZETA......... Zero Energy Thermonuclear Apparatus [*or Assembly*] [*AEC*]
ZETF......... Zurnal Eksperimental'noi i Teoreticeskoi Fiziki [*A publication*]
ZETFA...... Zhurnal Eksperimentalnoi i Teoreticheskoi Fiziki [*A publication*]
ZEthn........ Zeitschrift fuer Ethnologie [*A publication*]
Z Ethnolog ... Zeitschrift fuer Ethnologie [*A publication*]
ZETK........ Zetek, Inc. [*NASDAQ symbol*]   (NQ)
ZETR......... Zero Energy Thermal Reactor [*British*]
ZETUA...... Zeitschrift fuer Tuberkulose und Erkrankungen der Thoraxorgane [*A publication*]
ZEUMD.... Zeitschrift fuer Umweltpolitik [*A publication*]
Zeumer's Q St ... Zeumer's Quellen und Studien zur Verfassungsgeschichte des Deutschen Reichs in Mittelalter und Neuzeit [*A publication*]
ZEURA...... Zeitschrift fuer Urologie [*A publication*]
ZEUS........ Zero Energy Uranium System [*British*]
ZEUS........ Zeus Components, Inc. [*Port Chester, NY*] [*NASDAQ symbol*]   (NQ)
Zev............ Zevahim   (BJA)
Z Evan Eth ... Zeitschrift fuer Evangelische Ethik [*A publication*]
ZEVBA...... Zeitschrift fuer Vererbungslehre [*A publication*]
ZevE......... Zeitschrift fuer Evangelische Ethik. Gutersloh [*A publication*]   (BJA)
Z Ev Ethik ... Zeitschrift fuer Evangelische Ethik [*A publication*]
ZEV Glasers Ann ... ZEV [*Zeitschrift fuer Eisenbahnwesen und Verkehrstechnik*] Glasers. Annalen [*A publication*]
Z Ev K....... Zeitschrift fuer Evangelisches Kirchenrecht [*A publication*]
Z Ev Kr ... Zeitschrift fuer Evangelisches Kirchenrecht [*A publication*]
ZEvR......... Zeitschrift fuer die Evangelischen Religionsunterricht [*A publication*]   (BJA)
Z Exp Angew Psychol ... Zeitschrift fuer Experimentelle und Angewandte Psychologie [*A publication*]
Z Exp A Psy ... Zeitschrift fuer Experimentelle und Angewandte Psychologie [*A publication*]
Z Exp Chir ... Zeitschrift fuer Experimentelle Chirurgie [*A publication*]
Z Exp Chir Chir Forsch ... Zeitschrift fuer Experimentelle Chirurgie und Chirurgische Forschung [*A publication*]
Z Exper & Angew Psychol ... Zeitschrift fuer Experimentelle und Angewandte Psychologie [*A publication*]
Z Exp Pathol Ther ... Zeitschrift fuer Experimentelle Pathologie und Therapie [*A publication*]
ZF .... Center in charge of a Flight Information Region or an Upper Flight Information Region when the message is relevant to a VFR [*Visual Flight Rules*] Flight [*See also ZQ*] [*ICAO designator*]   (ICDA)
ZF .... Free Balloon [*Navy symbol*]
ZF .... Zahnradfabrik Friedrichshafen AG [*West Germany*]
ZF .... Zentralblatt fuer das Gesamte Forstwesen [*A publication*]
ZF .... Zermelo-Fraenkel [*Set theory*] [*Mathematics*]
ZF .... Zero Frequency
ZF .... Ziegfeld Follies
ZF .... Zona Fasciculata [*Of adrenal cortex*] [*Anatomy*]
ZF .... Zona Franca [*A publication*]
ZF .... Zone of Fire [*Military*]   (AAG)
ZF .... Zweig Fund [*NYSE symbol*]   (SPSG)
ZfA........... Zeitschrift fuer Archaeologie [*A publication*]
ZFA (Dresden) ... Zeitschrift fuer Alternsforschung (Dresden) [*A publication*]
ZFAL........ Zacherley Fans at Large   (EA)
Z Farben Ind ... Zeitschrift fuer Farben Industrie [*A publication*]
Z Farben Text Chem ... Zeitschrift fuer Farben- und Textil-Chemie [*A publication*]
ZFA (Stuttgart) ... Zeitschrift fuer Allgemeinmedizin (Stuttgart) [*A publication*]
ZFAX........ ZFAX Image Corp. [*NASDAQ symbol*]   (NQ)
ZFB........... Signals Fading Badly
ZfB........... Zeitschrift fuer Buecherfreunde [*A publication*]
ZFC........... Zero Failure Criteria   (IEEE)

ZFC........... Zipp-Forming Cells [*Immunology*]
ZFC........... Zirconia Fuel Cell
ZFDF........ Zeitschrift fuer Freie Deutsche Forschung [*A publication*]
ZFDG .... Zeitschrift fuer Deutsche Geistesgeschichte [*A publication*]
ZFDNMR ... Zero-Field Deuterium Nuclear Magnetic Resonance
ZfDPh........ Zeitschrift fuer Deutsche Philologie [*A publication*]
ZfDSdJ...... Zeitschrift fuer Demographie und Statistik der Juden [*A publication*]
ZfE............ Zeitschrift fuer Ethnologie [*A publication*]
ZFE........... Zone of Flow Establishment
ZFEU........ Zeitschrift fuer Franzoesischen und Englischen Unterricht [*A publication*]
ZFFB .... Zbornik Filozofskog Fakulteta (Belgrade) [*A publication*]
ZfG .... Zeitschrift fuer Geschichtswissenschaft [*A publication*]
ZFGV........ Zeitschrift. Freiburger Geschichtsvereine [*A publication*]
ZfHb .... Zeitschrift fuer Hebraeische Bibliographie [*A publication*]
ZFI-Mitt.... ZFI [*Zentralinstitut fuer Isotopen- und Strahlenforschung*]- Mitteilungen [*East Germany*] [*A publication*]
Z Fisch Hilfswiss ... Zeitschrift fuer Fischerei und Deren Hilfswissenschaften [*A publication*]
ZfK............ Zeitschrift fuer Kunstgeschichte [*A publication*]
ZFKPhil..... Zbornik Filozofickej Fakulty Univerzity Komenskeho-Philologica [*A publication*]
ZFL........... Zbornik za Filologiju i Lingvistiku [*A publication*]
ZFL........... Zeitschrift fuer Luftrecht- und Weltraumrechtsfragen [*German*] [*A publication*]   (DLA)
Z Fleisch Milchhyg ... Zeitschrift fuer Fleisch- und Milchhygiene [*A publication*]
Z Flugwiss ... Zeitschrift fuer Flugwissenschaften [*A publication*]
Z Flugwiss und Weltraumforsch ... Zeitschrift fuer Flugwissenschaften und Weltraumforschung [*A publication*]
Z Flugwiss Weltraumforsch ... Zeitschrift fuer Flugwissenschaften und Weltraumforschung [*A publication*]
ZFM .... Community College of the Finger Lakes, Canandaigua, NY [*OCLC symbol*]   (OCLC)
ZFM .... Fort McPherson [*Canada*] [*Airport symbol*]   (OAG)
ZFM .... Zeitschrift fuer Musik [*A publication*]
Zf Mus Theorie ... Zeitschrift fuer Musiktheorie [*A publication*]
ZfMw........ Zeitschrift fuer Musikwissenschaft [*A publication*]
ZfN........... Zeitschrift fuer Numismatik [*A publication*]
ZFNMR...... Zero-Field Nuclear Magnetic Resonance
ZFNU .... Zeitschrift fuer Neusprachlichen Unterricht [*A publication*]
ZFO .... ZFO. Zeitschrift fuer Fuehrung und Organisation [*A publication*]
Z Forst Jagdwes ... Zeitschrift fuer Forst- und Jagdwesen [*A publication*]
ZfP .... Dokumentation Zerstorungsfreie Pruefung [*Nondestructive Testing Documentation*] [*Federal Institute for Materials Testing*] [*Information service or system*]   (IID)
ZFP........... Zyglo-Fluorescent Penetrant
ZfPhF .... Zeitschrift fuer Philosophische Forschung [*A publication*]
ZFPT......... Zyglo-Fluorescent Penetrant Testing
Z Franzoesische Spr Lit ... Zeitschrift fuer Franzoesische Sprache und Literatur [*A publication*]
ZfRG .... Zeitschrift fuer Religions- und Geistesgeschichte [*A publication*]
ZfRP .... Zeitschrift fuer Romanische Philologie [*A publication*]
ZFRPH .... Zeitschrift fuer Romanische Philologie [*A publication*]
ZFrSL........ Zeitschrift fuer Franzoesische Sprache und Literatur [*A publication*]
ZfRuGg...... Zeitschrift fuer Religions- und Geistesgeschichte [*A publication*]
ZfS .... Zeitschrift fuer Semitistik und Verwandte Gebiete [*Leipzig*] [*A publication*]
ZFS........... Zero Field Splitting
ZFSC......... Zero-Field Splitting Constant [*Physics*]
ZfSchKg..... Zeitschrift fuer Schweizerische Kirchengeschichte [*A publication*]
ZFSH......... Z & Z Fashions Ltd. [*NASDAQ symbol*]   (NQ)
ZFSL.......... Zeitschrift fuer Franzoesische Sprache und Literatur [*A publication*]
Zft f Celt Phil ... Zeitschrift fuer Celtische Philologie [*A publication*]
Zft f D Alt .. Zeitschrift fuer Deutsches Altertum und Deutsche Literatur [*A publication*]
Zft f Fr Sp u Lit ... Zeitschrift fuer Franzoesische Sprache und Literatur [*A publication*]
Zft f Rom Phil ... Zeitschrift fuer Romanische Philologie [*A publication*]
ZFV........... Fort Severn [*Canada*] [*Airport symbol*]   (OAG)
ZfV............ Zeitschrift fuer Versicherungswesen [*German*] [*A publication*]   (DLA)
ZFV........... Zeitschrift fuer Volkskunde [*A publication*]
ZFW.......... Fort Worth, TX [*Location identifier*] [*FAA*]   (FAAL)
ZFW .... Zero Fuel Weight [*Aviation*]
ZFYZD....... Zhonghua Fangshe Yixue Yu Fanghu Zazhi [*A publication*]
ZfZ............ Zeitschrift fuer Assyriologie [*Leipzig/Berlin*] [*A publication*]
ZG............. Air Traffic Control [*ICAO designator*]   (ICDA)
ZG............. Zap Gun
Z-G............ Zapalote-Grande [*Race of maize*]
ZG............. Zeitschrift fuer Geomorphologie. Gebrueder Borntraeger [*A publication*]
ZG............. Zeitschrift fuer Germanistik [*A publication*]
ZG............. Zero Gravity   (IEEE)

ZG.............. Zerstoerergeschwader [*Twin-engine fighter wing*] [*German military - World War II*]
ZG.............. Zinc Gluconate [*Organic chemistry*]
ZG.............. Zollgesetz [*Tariff Law*] [*German*]
ZG.............. Zona Glomerulosa [*Of adrenal cortex*] [*Anatomy*]
ZG.............. Zoological Gardens
ZG.............. Zymbal Gland [*Anatomy*]
Z Gaerungsphysiol ... Zeitschrift fuer Gaerungsphysiologie [*A publication*]
ZGAKE...... Zeitschrift fuer Geschichte und Altertumskunde der Ermlands [*A publication*]
Z Gastroent ... Zeitschrift fuer Gastroenterologie [*A publication*]
Z Gastroenterol ... Zeitschrift fuer Gastroenterologie [*A publication*]
Z Gastroenterol Verh ... Zeitschrift fuer Gastroenterologie. Verhandlungsband [*A publication*]
ZGCS......... Changsha/Datuopu [*China*] [*ICAO location identifier*] (ICLI)
ZGDJ........ Zeitschrift zur Geschichte des Deutschen Judentums [*A publication*]
ZGE.......... Zero-Gravity Effect
ZGE.......... Zero-Gravity Environment
ZGE.......... Zero-Gravity Expulsion
Z Geburtshilfe Gynaekol ... Zeitschrift fuer Geburtshilfe und Gynaekologie [*Later, Zeitschrift fuer Geburtshilfe und Perinatologie*] [*A publication*]
Z Geburtshilfe Perinatol ... Zeitschrift fuer Geburtshilfe und Perinatologie [*A publication*]
ZGEIA....... Zhurnal Gigieny, Epidemiologii, Mikrobiologii, i Immunologii [*A publication*]
ZGEMA .... Zeitschrift fuer die Gesamte Experimentelle Medizin [*A publication*]
ZGEN........ ZG Energy Corp. [*NASDAQ symbol*] (NQ)
Z Geol Wiss ... Zeitschrift fuer Geologische Wissenschaften [*A publication*]
Z Geomorph ... Zeitschrift fuer Geomorphologie [*A publication*]
Z Geomorphol ... Zeitschrift fuer Geomorphologie [*A publication*]
Z Geomorphol Suppl ... Zeitschrift fuer Geomorphologie. Supplementband [*A publication*]
Z Geophys ... Zeitschrift fuer Geophysik [*German Federal Republic*] [*A publication*]
Z Ger Ling ... Zeitschrift fuer Germanistische Linguistik [*A publication*]
Z Gerontol ... Zeitschrift fuer Gerontologie [*A publication*]
Z Gesamte Brauwes ... Zeitschrift fuer das Gesamte Brauwesen [*A publication*]
Z Gesamte Exp Med ... Zeitschrift fuer die Gesamte Experimentelle Medizin [*A publication*]
Z Gesamte Exp Med Einschl Exp Chir ... Zeitschrift fuer die Gesamte Experimentelle Medizin. Einschliesslich Experimenteller Chirurgie [*A publication*]
Z Gesamte Forstwes ... Zeitschrift fuer das Gesamte Forstwesen [*A publication*]
Z Gesamte Genossenschaftswes ... Zeitschrift fuer das Gesamte Genossenschaftswesen [*A publication*]
Z Gesamte Genossenschaftswesen ... Zeitschrift fuer das Gesamte Genossenschaftswesen [*A publication*]
Z Gesamte Getreide Muehlen Baeckereiwes ... Zeitschrift fuer das Gesamte Getreide Muehlen- und Baeckereiwesen [*A publication*]
Z Gesamte Getreidewes ... Zeitschrift fuer das Gesamte Getreidewesen [*A publication*]
Z Gesamte Giessereiprax ... Zeitschrift fuer die Gesamte Giessereipraxis [*A publication*]
Z Gesamte Hyg ... Zeitschrift fuer die Gesamte Hygiene und Ihre Grenzgebiete [*A publication*]
Z Gesamte Hyg Grenzgeb ... Zeitschrift fuer die Gesamte Hygiene und Ihre Grenzgebiete [*A publication*]
Z Gesamte Hyg Ihre Grenzgeb ... Zeitschrift fuer die Gesamte Hygiene und Ihre Grenzgebiete [*A publication*]
Z Gesamte Inn Med ... Zeitschrift fuer die Gesamte Innere Medizin und Ihre Grenzgebiete [*A publication*]
Z Gesamte Inn Med Grenzgeb ... Zeitschrift fuer die Gesamte Innere Medizin und Ihre Grenzgebiete [*A publication*]
Z Gesamte Inn Med Grenzgeb Klin Pathol Exp ... Zeitschrift fuer die Gesamte Innere Medizin und Ihre Grenzgebiete. Klinik, Pathologie, Experiment [*A publication*]
Z Gesamte Inn Med Ihre Grenzgeb ... Zeitschrift fuer die Gesamte Innere Medizin und Ihre Grenzgebiete [*A publication*]
Z Gesamte Inn Med Ihre Grenzgeb Suppl ... Zeitschrift fuer die Gesamte Innere Medizin und Ihre Grenzgebiete. Supplementum [*East Germany*] [*A publication*]
Z Gesamte Kaelte Ind ... Zeitschrift fuer die Gesamte Kaelte-Industrie [*A publication*]
Z Gesamte Kaelte Ind Beih Ser 1 ... Zeitschrift fuer die Gesamte Kaelte-Industrie. Beihefte. Serie 1 [*A publication*]
Z Gesamte Kaelte Ind Beih Ser 2 ... Zeitschrift fuer die Gesamte Kaelte-Industrie. Beihefte. Serie 2 [*A publication*]
Z Gesamte Kaelte-Ind Beih Ser 3 ... Zeitschrift fuer die Gesamte Kaelte-Industrie. Beihefte. Serie 3 [*A publication*]
Z Gesamte Kreditwesen ... Zeitschrift fuer das Gesamte Kreditwesen [*A publication*]
Z Gesamte Muehlenwes ... Zeitschrift fuer das Gesamte Muehlenwesen [*A publication*]
Z Gesamte Naturwiss ... Zeitschrift fuer die Gesamte Naturwissenschaft [*A publication*]

Z Gesamte Nervenheilkd Psychother ... Zeitschrift fuer die Gesamte Nervenheilkunde und Psychotherapie [*German Democratic Republic*] [*A publication*]
Z Gesamte Neurol Psychiatr ... Zeitschrift fuer die Gesamte Neurologie und Psychiatrie [*A publication*]
Z Gesamte Phys Ther ... Zeitschrift fuer die Gesamte Physikalische Therapie [*A publication*]
Z Gesamte Schiess-Sprengstoffw ... Zeitschrift fuer das Gesamte Schiess- und Sprengstoffwesen mit der Sonderabteilung Gasschutz [*West Germany*] [*A publication*]
Z Gesamte Schiess Sprengstoffwes ... Zeitschrift fuer das Gesamte Schiess- und Sprengstoffwesen [*A publication*]
Z Gesamte Staatswiss ... Zeitschrift fuer die Gesamte Staatswissenschaft [*A publication*]
Z Gesamte Textilind ... Zeitschrift fuer die Gesamte Textilindustrie [*A publication*]
Z Gesamte Text-Ind ... Zeitschrift fuer die Gesamte Textil-Industrie [*A publication*]
Z Gesamte Versicherungswiss ... Zeitschrift fuer die Gesamte Versicherungswissenschaft [*A publication*]
Z Gesch Erzieh u Unterr ... Zeitschrift fuer Geschichte der Erziehung und des Unterrichts [*A publication*]
Z Geschichtsw ... Zeitschrift fuer Geschichtswissenschaft [*A publication*]
ZGeschJud ... Zeitschrift fuer die Geschichte der Juden [*A publication*]
Z Gesch Oberrhein ... Zeitschrift fuer die Geschichte des Oberrheins [*A publication*]
Z Gesch Saar ... Zeitschrift fuer die Geschichte der Saargegend [*A publication*]
Z Geschv (Muelheim) ... Zeitschrift. Geschichtsverein Muelheim an der Ruhr (Muelheim, West Germany) [*A publication*]
Z Gesch-Wiss ... Zeitschrift fuer Geschichtswissenschaft [*A publication*]
Z Ges Exp Med ... Zeitschrift fuer die Gesamte Experimentelle Medizin [*A publication*]
Z Ges Inn Med ... Zeitschrift fuer die Gesamte Innere Medizin und Ihre Grenzgebiete [*A publication*]
Z Ges Staatswiss ... Zeitschrift fuer die Gesamte Staatswissenschaft [*A publication*]
Z Gesundheitstech Staedtehyg ... Zeitschrift fuer Gesundheitstechnik und Staedtehygiene [*A publication*]
ZGET........ Zero-Gravity Expulsion Technique
ZGEU .... Zeitschrift fuer Geschichte der Erziehung und des Unterrichts [*A publication*]
ZGF .... Grand Forks [*Canada*] [*Airport symbol*] [*Obsolete*] (OAG)
ZGF .... Zero Gravity Facility [*NASA*]
ZGG.......... Zeitschrift fuer das Gesamte Genossenschaftswesen [*A publication*]
ZGG.......... Zero-Gravity Generator
ZGGG........ Guangzhou/Baiyun [*China*] [*ICAO location identifier*] (ICLI)
ZGGJT ...... Zeitschrift. Gesellschaft fuer die Geschichte der Juden in der Tschechoslowakei [*A publication*]
ZGGYA ..... Zeitschrift fuer Geburtshilfe und Gynaekologie [*Later, Zeitschrift fuer Geburtshilfe und Perinatologie*] [*A publication*]
ZGH.......... Zonal Gravity Harmonic
ZGHK........ Haikou [*China*] [*ICAO location identifier*] (ICLI)
ZGI .... Gods River [*Canada*] [*Airport symbol*] (OAG)
ZGJ........... Zeitschrift fuer die Geschichte der Juden [*A publication*]
ZGJD........ Zeitschrift fuer die Geschichte der Juden in Deutschland [*Braunschwig/Berlin*] [*A publication*]
ZGJT .... Zeitschrift. Gesellschaft fuer die Geschichte der Juden in der Tschechoslowakei [*A publication*]
ZGKL........ Guilin [*China*] [*ICAO location identifier*] (ICLI)
ZGL .... Zeitschrift fuer Germanistische Linguistik [*A publication*]
Z Gletscherk Glazialgeol ... Zeitschrift fuer Gletscherkunde und Glazialgeologie [*A publication*]
ZGM.......... City University of New York, Graduate School, New York, NY [*OCLC symbol*] (OCLC)
ZGM.......... Zinc Glycinate Marker [*Immunochemistry*]
ZGMFA..... Zeszyty Naukowe Akademii Gorniczo-Hutniczej (Cracow). Matematyka, Fizyka, Chemia [*A publication*]
ZGMPA..... Zeitschrift fuer Geomorphologie [*A publication*]
ZGMT .... Zu Gott Mein Trost [*In God My Comfort*] [*German*] [*Motto of Ernst, Duke of Braunschweig-Luneburg (1564-1611)*]
ZGN.......... Zaghouan [*Tunisia*] [*Seismograph station code, US Geological Survey*] (SEIS)
ZGNN....... Nanning/Wuxu [*China*] [*ICAO location identifier*] (ICLI)
ZGO........ Zeitschrift fuer die Geschichte des Oberrheins [*A publication*]
Z Godschmiede Juwelerie Graveure ... Zeitschrift fuer Goldschmiede Juwelerie und Graveure [*A publication*]
ZGOR........ Zeitschrift fuer die Geschichte des Oberrheins [*A publication*]
ZGOrh....... Zeitschrift fuer die Geschichte des Oberrheins [*A publication*]
ZGOW....... Shantou [*China*] [*ICAO location identifier*] (ICLI)
ZGR .... Little Grand Rapids [*Canada*] [*Airport symbol*] (OAG)
ZGS .... Gethsemani [*Canada*] [*Airport symbol*] (OAG)
ZGS .... Zeitschrift fuer die Gesamte Staatswissenschaft [*A publication*]
ZGS .... Zero Gradient Synchrotron [*AEC*]
ZGS .... Zero-Gravity Shower
ZGS .... Zero-Gravity Simulator
ZGS .... Zirconia Grain Stabilized [*Metal alloys*]
ZGS .... Zone Gradient Synchrotron [*Nickname: Ziggy*]
ZGSHG ..... Zeitschrift. Gesellschaft fuer Schleswig-Holsteinische Geschichte [*A publication*]

ZGSSA ...... Zeitschrift fuer das Gesamte Schiess- und Sprengstoffwesen mit der Sonderabteilung Gasschutz [*A publication*]
ZGT .... Zero-Gravity Trainer [*NASA*]   (NASA)
ZGUA .... Guangzhou City [*China*] [*ICAO location identifier*]   (ICLI)
ZGW .... Zeitschrift fuer Geschichtswissenschaft [*A publication*]
ZGWBS ...... Zero-Gravity Whole Body Shower
ZGWS .... Zane Grey's West Society   (EA)
ZGZAE6 ..... Chinese Journal of Orthopedics [*A publication*]
ZGZJ .... Zhanjiang [*China*] [*ICAO location identifier*]   (ICLI)
ZGZU .... Guangzhou [*China*] [*ICAO location identifier*]   (ICLI)
ZH............. Helicopter Air Traffic Control [*ICAO designator*]   (ICDA)
ZH............. Zinc Heads [*Freight*]
ZH............. Zonal Harmonic
ZH............. Zone Heater
zH.............. Zu Haenden [*Attention Of, Care Of, To Be Delivered To*] [*German*]   (GPO)
ZHA........... Zhangjiang [*China*] [*Airport symbol*]   (OAG)
Z Hals Nasen Ohrenheilkd ... Zeitschrift fuer Hals Nasen- und Ohrenheilkunde [*A publication*]
Zh Analit Khim ... Zhurnal Analitcheskoi Khimii [*A publication*]
Zh Anal Khim ... Zhurnal Analiticheskoi Khimii [*A publication*]
Z Haut-Geschlechtskr ... Zeitschrift fuer Haut- und Geschlechtskrankheiten [*A publication*]
Z Hautkr.... Zeitschrift fuer Hautkrankheiten [*A publication*]
ZHB.......... Zeitschrift fuer Hebraeische Bibliographie [*A publication*]
ZHCC .... Zhengzhou [*China*] [*ICAO location identifier*]   (ICLI)
zHd .... Zu Haenden [*Attention Of, Care Of, To Be Delivered To*] [*German*]
Zh Ehksp Teor Fiz Pis'ma Red ... Zhurnal Ehksperimental'noj i Teoreticheskoj Fiziki Pis'ma - Redaktsiyu [*USSR*] [*A publication*]
Zh Eksp Biol Med ... Zhurnal Eksperimental'noi Biologii i Meditsiny [*A publication*]
Zh Eksp Klin Med ... Zhurnal Eksperimentalnoi i Klinicheskoi Meditsiny [*A publication*]
Zh Eksp Teo ... Zhurnal Eksperimentalnoi i Teoreticheskoi Fiziki [*A publication*]
Zh Eksp i Teor Fiz ... Zhurnal Eksperimentalnoi i Teoreticheskoi Fiziki [*A publication*]
Zh Eksp Teor Fiz ... Zhurnal Eksperimentalnoi i Teoreticheskoi Fiziki [*A publication*]
Zh Eksp Teor Fiz Pis ... Zhurnal Eksperimentalnoi i Teoreticheskoi Fiziki. Pis'ma [*A publication*]
Zh Eksp Teor Fiz Pis'ma ... Zhurnal Eksperimental'noi i Teoreticheskoi Fiziki. Pis'ma [*A publication*]
Zh Eksp and Teor Fiz Pis'ma v Red ... Zhurnal Eksperimental'noi i Teoreticheskoi Fiziki. Pis'ma v Redaktsiyu [*A publication*]
Zheleznodorozhn Transp ... Zheleznodorozhnyi Transport [*USSR*] [*A publication*]
Zhelezn Splavy ... Zhelezeye Splavy [*A publication*]
Zhelezobeton Konstr Chelyabinsk ... Zhelezobetonnye Konstruktsii Chelyabinsk [*A publication*]
Zh Evol Biokhim Fiziol ... Zhurnal Evolyutsionnoi Biokhimii i Fiziologii [*A publication*]
ZHF .... Schmalenbachs Zeitschrift fuer Betriebswirtschaftliche Forschung [*A publication*]
ZHF .... Zone Heat Flux
Zh Fiz Khem Tsiklu Vseukr Akad Nauk ... Zhurnal Fizichno-Khemichnogo Tsiklu Vseukrains'ka Akademiya Nauk [*A publication*]
Zh Fiz Khim ... Zhurnal Fizicheskoi Khimii [*A publication*]
Zh Geofiz ... Zhurnal Geofiziki [*A publication*]
Zh Gig Epidemiol Mikrobiol Immunol ... Zhurnal Gigieny, Epidemiologii, Mikrobiologii, i Immunologii [*A publication*]
ZHHH....... Wuhan/Nanhu [*China*] [*ICAO location identifier*]   (ICLI)
Zhidkofazn Okislenie Nepredel'nykh Org Soedin ... Zhidkofaznoe Okislenie Nepredel'nykh Organicheskikh Soedinenii [*A publication*]
Zhilishchnoe Kommunal'n Khoz ... Zhilishchnoe i Kommunal'noe Khozyaistvo [*A publication*]
Z Hist Fors ... Zeitschrift fuer Historische Forschung [*A publication*]
Zhivot Nauki ... Zhivotnovudni Nauki [*A publication*]
Zhivotnov'd Nauki ... Zhivotnov'dni Nauki [*A publication*]
Zhivotnovod ... Zhivotnovodstvo [*A publication*]
Zhivotnovod Vet ... Zhivotnovodstvo i Veterinariya [*A publication*]
Zhivotnovud ... Zhivotnovudstvo [*A publication*]
Zhivotnovud Nauki ... Zhivotnovudni Nauki [*A publication*]
ZHJID....... Zhongguo Jiguang [*A publication*]
Zh Khim Promsti ... Zhurnal Khimicheskoi Promyshlennosti [*A publication*]
ZHKPA ..... Zhurnal Khimicheskoi Promyshlennosti [*A publication*]
ZHL.......... Hofstra University, Law School, Library, Hempstead, NY [*OCLC symbol*]   (OCLC)
ZHM.......... Hunter College of the City University of New York, New York, NY [*OCLC symbol*]   (OCLC)
Zh Mikrob E ... Zhurnal Mikrobiologii, Epidemiologii, i Immunobiologii [*A publication*]
Zh Mikrobiol Epidemiol Immunobiol ... Zhurnal Mikrobiologii, Epidemiologii, i Immunobiologii [*A publication*]
Zh Mikrobiol Immunobiol ... Zhurnal Mikrobiologii i Immunobiologii [*A publication*]
ZHN .... Honolulu, HI [*Location identifier*] [*FAA*]   (FAAL)
Zh Nauchnoi i Prikl Fotogr i Kinematogr ... Zhurnal Nauchnoi i Prikladnoi Fotografii i Kinematografii [*A publication*]

Zh Nauchn Prikl Fotogr Kinematogr ... Zhurnal Nauchnoi i Prikladnoi Fotografii i Kinematografii [*A publication*]
Zh Nauch Prik Foto Kinematog ... Zhurnal Nauchnoi i Prikladnoi Fotografii i Kinematografii [*A publication*]
Zh Neorg Kh ... Zhurnal Neorganicheskoi Khimii [*A publication*]
Zh Neorg Khim ... Zhurnal Neorganicheskoi Khimii [*A publication*]
Zh Nevropatol Psikhiatr ... Zhurnal Nevropatologii i Psikhiatrii Imeni S. S. Korsakova [*A publication*]
Zh Nevropatol Psikhiatr Im S S Korsakova ... Zhurnal Nevropatologii i Psikhiatrii Imeni S. S. Korsakova [*A publication*]
ZHNID...... Zhongguo Niangzao [*A publication*]
Zh NP Fotog ... Zhurnal Nauchnoi i Prikladnoi Fotografii i Kinematografii [*A publication*]
Zh Obs Biol ... Zhurnal Obshchei Biologii [*A publication*]
Zh Obshch Biol ... Zhurnal Obshchei Biologii [*A publication*]
Zh Obshchei Khim ... Zhurnal Obshchei Khimii [*A publication*]
Zh Obshch Khim ... Zhurnal Obshchei Khimii [*A publication*]
Zh Obs Kh ... Zhurnal Obshchei Khimii [*A publication*]
Zh Opytn Agron ... Zhurnal Opytnoi Agronomii [*A publication*]
Zh Org Kh ... Zhurnal Organicheskoi Khimii [*A publication*]
Zh Org Khim ... Zhurnal Organicheskoi Khimii [*A publication*]
ZHPMA .... Zentralblatt fuer Bakteriologie, Parasitenkunde, Infektionskrankheiten, und Hygiene. Erste Abteilung. Originale Reihe B. Hygiene, Betriebshygiene, Praeventive Medizin [*A publication*]
ZHPMAT ... Zentralblatt fuer Bakteriologie, Parasitenkunde, Infektionskrankheiten, und Hygiene. Erste Abteilung. Originale Reihe B. Hygiene, Betriebshygiene, Praeventive Medizin [*A publication*]
Zh Priki Mekhan Tekh Fiz ... Zhurnal Prikladnoi Mekhaniki i Tekhnicheskoi Fiziki [*A publication*]
Zh Prikl Fiz ... Zhurnal Prikladnoi Fiziki [*A publication*]
Zh Prikl Khim ... Zhurnal Prikladnoi Khimii [*A publication*]
Zh Prikl Mekh Tekh Fiz ... Zhurnal Prikladnoi Mekhaniki i Tekhnicheskoi Fiziki [*A publication*]
Zh Prikl Spektrosk ... Zhurnal Prikladnoi Spektroskopii [*A publication*]
ZHR.......... Zirconium Hydride Reactor
Zh Rezin Promsti ... Zhurnal Rezinovoi Promyshlennosti [*A publication*]
Zh Russ Fiz-Khim Ova ... Zhurnal Russkago Fiziko-Khimicheskago Obshchestva [*A publication*]
Zh Russ Fiz-Khim Ova Chast Fiz ... Zhurnal Russkogo Fiziko-Khimicheskogo Obshchestva Chast Fizicheskaya [*A publication*]
Zh Russ Fiz Khim Ova Chast Khim ... Zhurnal Russkogo Fiziko-Khimicheskogo Ovshchestva Chast Khimicheskaya [*A publication*]
Zh Russ Khim Ova ... Zhurnal Russkago Khimicheskago Obshchestva [*A publication*]
Zh Russ Khim Ova Fiz Ova ... Zhurnal Russkago Khimicheskago Obshchestva i Fizicheskago Obshchestva [*A publication*]
Zh Russ Metall Ova ... Zhurnal Russkogo Metallurgicheskogo Obshchestva [*A publication*]
ZHSA .... Zeiss Historica Society of America   (EA)
Zh Sakh Promsti ... Zhurnal Sakharnoi Promyshlennosti [*A publication*]
Zh Strukt Khim ... Zhurnal Strukturnoi Khimii [*A publication*]
ZHT.......... Zeitschrift fuer Historische Theologie [*A publication*]
Zh Tekh Fiz ... Zhurnal Tekhnicheskoi Fiziki [*A publication*]
ZHU .... Houston, TX [*Location identifier*] [*FAA*]   (FAAL)
ZHUCA ..... Zpravy Hornickeho Ustavu CSAV [*Ceskoslovenska Akademie Ved*] [*A publication*]
Zhurnal Mikrobiol ... Zhurnal Mikrobiologii [*A publication*]
Zh Ushn Nos Gorl Bolezn ... Zhurnal Ushnykh Nosovykh i Gorlovykh Boleznei [*A publication*]
Zh Ushn Nosov Gorlov Bolez ... Zhurnal Ushnykh Nosovykh i Gorlovykh Boleznei [*A publication*]
Zhu Us Nos i Gorl Bol ... Zhurnal Ushnykh Nosovykh i Gorlovykh Boleznei [*A publication*]
ZHVNAS .. Animal Science [*Sofia*] [*A publication*]
ZHVNS ..... Zeitschrift. Historischer Verein fuer Niedersachsen [*A publication*]
Zh Vopr Neirokhir ... Zhurnal Voprosy Neirokhirurgii Imeni N. N. Burdenko [*A publication*]
ZHVS .... Zeitschrift. Historischer Verein fuer Steiermark [*A publication*]
Zh Vses Khi ... Zhurnal Vsesoyuznogo Khimicheskogo Obshchestva Imeni D. I. Mendeleeva [*A publication*]
Zh Vses Khim Obshch ... Zhurnal Vsesoyuznogo Khimicheskogo Obshchestva [*A publication*]
Zh Vses Khim Ova ... Zhurnal Vsesoyuznogo Khimicheskogo Obshchestva Imeni D. I. Mendeleeva [*A publication*]
Zh Vses Khim O-Va Im D I Mendeleeva ... Zhurnal Vsesoyuznogo Khimicheskogo Obshchestva Imeni D. I. Mendeleeva [*A publication*]
Zh Vychisl Mat i Mat Fiz ... Zhurnal Vychislitel'noi Matematiki i Matematicheske Fiziki [*A publication*]
Zh Vychisl Mat Mat Fiz ... Zhurnal Vychislitel'noi Matematiki i Matematicheske Fiziki [*A publication*]
Zh Vyssh Nerv Deyat ... Zhurnal Vysshei Nervnoi Deyatel'nosti [*A publication*]
Zh Vyssh Nervn Deyat Im I P Pavlova ... Zhurnal Vysshei Nervnoi Deyatel'nosti Imeni I. P. Pavlova [*A publication*]
Zh Vyss Ner ... Zhurnal Vysshei Nervnoi Deyatel'nosti Imeni I. P. Pavlova [*A publication*]

ZHW.......... Ziekenhuis [*A publication*]
ZHWH ...... Wuhan [*China*] [*ICAO location identifier*]   (ICLI)
Z Hyg.......... Zeitschrift fuer Hygiene [*A publication*]
ZHYGA ..... Zeitschrift fuer die Gesamte Hygiene und Ihre Grenzgebiete [*A publication*]
Z Hyg Infektionskr ... Zeitschrift fuer Hygiene und Infektionskrankheiten [*A publication*]
Z Hyg Infekt Kr ... Zeitschrift fuer Hygiene und Infektionskrankheiten [*A publication*]
Z Hyg InfektKrankh ... Zeitschrift fuer Hygiene und Infektionskrankheiten [*A publication*]
Z Hyg Zool Schaedlingsbekaempf ... Zeitschrift fuer Hygienische Zoologie und Schaedlingsbekaempfung [*A publication*]
ZI .... Flight Information Center [*ICAO designator*]   (ICDA)
Z I .... Zeitschrift fuer Instrumentenbau [*A publication*]
ZI .... Zero Input
ZI .... Zinc Institute [*Defunct*]   (EA)
ZI .... Zonal Index
Z of I .... Zone of Interior [*Military*]
ZI .... Zone of Interior [*Military*]
ZI .... Zonta International   (EA)
Z/I............. Zoom In [*Cinematography and Video*]
ZIA .... ZIA Airlines [*Las Cruces, NM*] [*FAA designator*]   (FAAC)
ZIA .... Zone of Interior Armies
ZIAD .... Ziyad, Inc. [*NASDAQ symbol*]   (NQ)
ZIALA .... Zeitschrift fuer Immunitaets- und Allergieforschung [*A publication*]
ZIAVA .... Zeitschrift fuer Induktive Abstammungs- und Vererbungslehre [*A publication*]
ZIAX.......... Zantop International Airlines, Inc. [*Air carrier designation symbol*]
ZIC............ Zirconia-Iridium Crucible
Zi de Cmo... Ziliolus de Cremona [*Authority cited in pre-1607 legal work*]   (DSA)
ZICON ...... Zone of the Interior Consumers Network   (MCD)
ZID .... Indianapolis, IN [*Location identifier*] [*FAA*]   (FAAL)
ZID .... Zentralinstitut fuer Information und Dokumentation [*Central Institute for Information and Documentation*] [*Information service or system*]   (EISS)
ZIE............ Zone Immunoelectrophoresis [*Analytical biochemistry*]
ZIF............ Zenix Income Fund [*NYSE symbol*]   (SPSG)
ZIF............ Zero Insertion Force [*Electronics*]
ZIFT .... Zygote Intrafallopian Transfer [*Obstetrics*]
ZIG .... Ziguinchor [*Senegal*] [*Airport symbol*]   (OAG)
ZIG .... Zoster Immune Globulin [*Immunology*]
ZIGO .... Zygo Corp. [*NASDAQ symbol*]   (NQ)
ZIH .... Hofstra University, Hempstead, NY [*OCLC symbol*]   (OCLC)
ZIH .... Zihuatanejo [*Mexico*] [*Airport symbol*]   (OAG)
ZII............. Zeitschrift fuer Indologie und Iranistik [*Leipzig*] [*A publication*]
ZIID........... Zentralinstitut fuer Information und Dokumentation [*Central Institute for Information and Documentation*] [*German Democratic Republic*] [*Information service or system*]   (IID)
ZI Int.......... ZI [*Ziegelindustrie*] International [*West Germany*] [*A publication*]
ZIK .... Zbornik Istorije Knijizevnosti [*A publication*]
ZIL............ Zork Interactive Language [*Computer science*]
ZILA.......... Zila, Inc. [*NASDAQ symbol*]   (NQ)
Zilla CD ..... Zilla Court Decisions, Bengal, Madras, Northwest Provinces [*India*] [*A publication*]   (DLA)
ZiM........... Ziemia i Morze [*A publication*]
Zim............ Zimbabwe
ZIM .... Zimchurud [*USSR*] [*Seismograph station code, US Geological Survey*] [*Closed*]   (SEIS)
ZIM .... Zimmer Corp. [*AMEX symbol*]   (SPSG)
ZIM .... Zonal Interdiction Missile   (NVT)
Zimbabwe Agric J ... Zimbabwe Agricultural Journal [*A publication*]
Zimbabwe Div Livest Pastures Annu Rep ... Zimbabwe. Division of Livestock and Pastures. Annual Report [*A publication*]
Zimbabwe Eng ... Zimbabwe Engineer [*A publication*]
Zimbabwe J Agric Res ... Zimbabwe Journal of Agricultural Research [*A publication*]
Zimbabwe J Econ ... Zimbabwe Journal of Economics [*A publication*]
Zimbabwe Rhod Nurse ... Zimbabwe Rhodesia Nurse [*A publication*]
Zimbabwe Rhod Sci News ... Zimbabwe-Rhodesia Science News [*A publication*]
Zimbabwe Sci News ... Zimbabwe Science News [*A publication*]
Zimbabwe Vet J ... Zimbabwe Veterinary Journal [*A publication*]
Zimb Agric J ... Zimbabwe Agricultural Journal [*A publication*]
ZIMBANK ... Zimbabwe Banking Corporation Ltd.
Zimb Eng ... Zimbabwe Engineer [*A publication*]
Zimb J Agric Res ... Zimbabwe Journal of Agricultural Research [*A publication*]
Zimb Law J ... Zimbabwe Law Journal [*A publication*]
Zimb Libr... Zimbabwe Librarian [*A publication*]
Zimb Sci News ... Zimbabwe Science News [*A publication*]
ZIMG .... Zeitschrift. Internationale Musik Gesellschaft [*A publication*]
Z Immun -Allergie-Forsch ... Zeitschrift fuer Immunitaets- und Allergieforschung [*A publication*]
Z Immun Exp ... Zeitschrift fuer Immunitaetsforschung. Experimentelle und Klinische Immunologie [*A publication*]

Z ImmunForsch Exp Ther ... Zeitschrift fuer Immunitaetsforschung und Experimentelle Therapie [*A publication*]
Z Immunitaets-Allergieforsch ... Zeitschrift fuer Immunitaets- und Allergieforschung [*A publication*]
Z Immunitaetsforsch ... Zeitschrift fuer Immunitaetsforschung [*A publication*]
Z Immunitaetsforsch Allerg Klin Immunol ... Zeitschrift fuer Immunitaetsforschung. Allergie und Klinische Immunologie [*A publication*]
Z Immunitaetsforsch Exp Klin Immunol ... Zeitschrift fuer Immunitaetsforschung. Experimentelle und Klinische Immunologie [*A publication*]
Z Immunitaetsforsch Exp Klin Immunol Suppl ... Zeitschrift fuer Immunitaetsforschung. Experimentelle und Klinische Immunologie. Supplemente [*A publication*]
Z Immunitaetsforsch Exp Ther ... Zeitschrift fuer Immunitaetsforschung und Experimentelle Therapie [*A publication*]
Z Immunitaetsforsch Exp Ther 1 ... Zeitschrift fuer Immunitaetsforschung und Experimentelle Therapie. 1. Originale [*A publication*]
Z Immunitaetsforsch Exp Ther 2 ... Zeitschrift fuer Immunitaetsforschung und Experimentelle Therapie. 2. Referate [*A publication*]
Z Immunitaetsforsch Exp Ther 1 Abt Orig ... Zeitschrift fuer Immunitaetsforschung und Experimentelle Therapie. 1. Abteilung Originale [*A publication*]
Z Immunitaetsforsch Immunobiol ... Zeitschrift fuer Immunitaetsforschung. Immunobiology [*A publication*]
Z Immunitaetsforsch Immunobiol Suppl ... Zeitschrift fuer Immunitaetsforschung. Immunobiology. Supplemente [*A publication*]
Z Immunitaetsforsch Suppl ... Zeitschrift fuer Immunitaetsforschung. Supplemente [*A publication*]
ZIMordASSR ... Zapiski Naucno-Issledovatel'nogo Instituta pri Sovete Ministrov Mordovskoj ASSR [*A publication*]
ZIMR.......... ZIM Energy Corp. [*Houston, TX*] [*NASDAQ symbol*]   (NQ)
ZIN .... Mount Zion Church [*South Carolina*] [*Seismograph station code, US Geological Survey*] [*Closed*]   (SEIS)
Zinat Raksti Rigas Politeh Inst ... Zinatniskie Raksti. Rigas Politehniskais Instituts [*A publication*]
Zinc Abstr ... Zinc Abstracts [*A publication*]
Zinc/Cadmium Res Dig ... Zinc/Cadmium Research Digest [*A publication*]
Zinc Res Dig ... Zinc Research Digest [*A publication*]
Z Indukt Abstammungs-Vererbungsl ... Zeitschrift fuer Induktive Abstammungs- und Vererbungslehre [*A publication*]
Z Indukt Abstamm u Vererblehre ... Zeitschrift fuer Induktive Abstammungs- und Vererbungslehre [*A publication*]
ZinEB .... Zinc Ethylenebis(dithiocarbamate) [*Agricultural fungicide*]
Zink .... Zero Income, No Kids [*Lifestyle classification*]
Zinn Ca Tr ... Zinn's Select Cases in the Law of Trusts [*A publication*]   (DLA)
Zinn Verwend ... Zinn und Seine Verwendung [*A publication*]
Z Instrum... Zeitschrift fuer Instrumentenkunde [*West Germany*] [*A publication*]
Z Instrumentenk ... Zeitschrift fuer Instrumentenkunde [*A publication*]
Z Instrumentenkd ... Zeitschrift fuer Instrumentenkunde [*A publication*]
Z Int Inst Zuckerruebenforsch ... Zeitschrift. Internationales Institut fuer Zuckerforschung [*A publication*]
Z Int Ver Bohring Bohrtech ... Zeitschrift. Internationaler Verein der Bohringenieure und Bohrtechniker [*A publication*]
ZIO .... Zinc Iodide-Osmium [*Biological staining procedure*]
Zion........... Zionism   (BJA)
ZION .... Zions Bancorporation [*NASDAQ symbol*]   (NQ)
ZiP .... Za i Przeciw [*A publication*]
ZIP............ Zero Interest Payment [*Banking*]
ZIP............ Zigzag In-Line Package [*Wells American*] [*Data processing*]
ZIP............ Zinc Impurity Photodetector
ZIP............ ZIP Target Marketing [*A publication*]
ZIP............ Zone Improvement Plan [*Postal Service code*]
ZIP............ Zone Information Protocol   (BYTE)
ZIP............ Zoster Immune Plasma [*Immunology*]
ZIPA .... Zimbabwe People's Army
ZIPE .... Zentralinstitut Physik der Erde [*Potsdam*]
ZIPP .... National Reference Publishing, Inc. [*Dallas, TX*] [*NASDAQ symbol*]   (NQ)
Zipp........... Zone of Inhibited Phage Plaques [*Immunology*]
ZIPRA .... Zimbabwe Independent People's Revolutionary Army   (PD)
ZIR............ Zero Internal Resistance
Ziraat Derg ... Ziraat Dergisi [*A publication*]
Ziraat Fak Derg Ege Univ ... Ziraat Fakultesi Dergisi Ege Universitesi [*A publication*]
Zisin J Seismol Soc Jpn ... Zisin/Journal of the Seismological Society of Japan [*A publication*]
Zisin Seismol Soc Jap J ... Zisin/Seismological Society of Japan. Journal [*A publication*]
ZIS Mitt .... ZIS [*Zentralinstitut fuer Schweisstechnik*] Mitteilungen [*A publication*]
ZISS.......... Zebulun Israel Seafaring Society   (EA)
ZIS (Zentralinst Schweisstech DDR) Mitt ... ZIS (Zentralinstitut fuer Schweisstechnik der Deutschen Demokratischen Republik) Mitteilungen [*A publication*]
ZIT............ Zeitschrift Interne Revision [*Germany*] [*A publication*]
ZITI.......... Sidari Corp. [*NASDAQ symbol*]   (NQ)
ZITL.......... Zitel Corp. [*NASDAQ symbol*]   (NQ)
Ziv A .... Archiv fuer die Zivilistische Praxis [*A publication*]

Ziva .... Ziva. Casopis pro Biologickou Praci [*A publication*]
ZIVAN .... Zapiski Instituta Vostokoveden'ia Akademii Nauk SSSR [*A publication*]
Zivocisna Vyroba Cesk Akad Zemed Ustav Vedeckotech Inf Zemed ... Zivocisna Vyroba-Ceskoslovenska Akademie Zemedelska. Ustav Vedeckotechnickych Informaci pro Zemedelstvi [*A publication*]
Zivoc Vyroba ... Zivocisna Vyroba [*A publication*]
Zivotn Prostr ... Zivotne Prostredie [*A publication*]
ZIVP .... Zivotne Prostredie [*Czechoslovakia*] [*A publication*]
Ziv Pr .... Archiv fuer die Zivilistische Praxis [*A publication*]
Ziz .... Zizit (BJA)
ZJ .... Zeszyty Jezykoznawcze [*A publication*]
ZJ .... Zipper Jacket
ZJ .... Zivi Jezici [*A publication*]
Z Jagdwiss ... Zeitschrift fuer Jagdwissenschaft [*A publication*]
ZJARDK ... Zimbabwe Journal of Agricultural Research [*A publication*]
ZJC .... State University of New York, Central Administration, Albany, NY [*OCLC symbol*] (OCLC)
ZJKF .... Zpravy Jednoty Klasickych Filologu [*A publication*]
Z Journ ...... Zeitschrift fuer Journalistik [*A publication*]
ZJSTD .... Zambia Journal of Science and Technology [*A publication*]
ZJX .... Jacksonville, FL [*Location identifier*] [*FAA*] (FAAL)
ZK .... Barrage Balloon [*Navy symbol*]
ZK .... New Zealand [*Aircraft nationality and registration mark*] (FAAC)
ZK .... Schering AG [*Germany*] [*Research code symbol*]
ZK .... Zachary Kurintner Books Ltd. [*British*]
ZK .... Zeitschrift fuer Keilschriftforschung und Verwandte Gebiete [*A publication*]
ZK .... Zeitschrift fuer Kirchengeschichte [*A publication*]
ZK .... Zeitschrift fuer Kunstgeschichte [*A publication*]
ZK .... Zeitschrift fuer Kunstwissenschaft [*A publication*]
ZK .... Zentralkommittee [*Central Committee*] [*of the Socialist Union Party of the German Democratic Republic*]
ZK .... Zera' Kodesh (BJA)
ZKA .... Zeitschrift fuer Kulturaustausch [*A publication*]
ZKA .... Zentralkatalog der Auslaendischen Literatur [*A publication*]
Z Kardiol .... Zeitschrift fuer Kardiologie [*A publication*]
Z Kardiol Suppl ... Zeitschrift fuer Kardiologie. Supplementum [*A publication*]
ZKB .... Bomber [*Russian aircraft symbol*]
ZKB .... Kasaba Bay [*Zambia*] [*Airport symbol*] (OAG)
ZKC .... Kansas City, MO [*Location identifier*] [*FAA*] (FAAL)
ZKC .... Keuka College, Lightner Library, Keuka Park, NY [*OCLC symbol*] (OCLC)
ZK Ch .... Zeitschrift fuer Kinderchirurgie und Grenzgebiete [*A publication*]
ZKE .... Kaschechewan [*Canada*] [*Airport symbol*] (OAG)
ZKG .... Kegaska [*Canada*] [*Airport symbol*] (OAG)
ZKG .... Zeitschrift fuer Kirchengeschichte [*A publication*]
ZKG .... Zeitschrift fuer Kunstgeschichte [*A publication*]
ZKHH .... Hamhung [*Democratic People's Republic of Korea*] [*ICAO location identifier*] (ICLI)
ZKIA .... Pyongyang [*Democratic People's Republic of Korea*] [*ICAO location identifier*] (ICLI)
Z Kindch G ... Zeitschrift fuer Kinderchirurgie und Grenzgebiete [*A publication*]
Z Kinderchir Grenzgeb ... Zeitschrift fuer Kinderchirurgie und Grenzgebiete [*A publication*]
Z Kinderheilkd ... Zeitschrift fuer Kinderheilkunde [*A publication*]
Z Kinder-Jugendpsychiatr ... Zeitschrift fuer Kinder- und Jugendpsychiatrie [*A publication*]
Z Kinderpsychiatr ... Zeitschrift fuer Kinderpsychiatrie [*A publication*]
Z Kind Jug ... Zeitschrift fuer Kinder- und Jugendpsychiatrie [*A publication*]
Z Kirch G ... Zeitschrift fuer Kirchengeschichte [*A publication*]
ZKJ .... Zbornik za Knjizevnost i Jezik [*A publication*]
ZKKC .... Kimchaek [*Democratic People's Republic of Korea*] [*ICAO location identifier*] (ICLI)
ZKKK .... Pyongyang [*Democratic People's Republic of Korea*] [*ICAO location identifier*] (ICLI)
ZKKOBW ... Cancer Research and Clinical Oncology [*A publication*]
ZKKODY .. Gerontology Extension Lectures [*A publication*]
ZKLCA ...... Zeitschrift fuer Klinische Chemie [*A publication*]
Z Klin Chem ... Zeitschrift fuer Klinische Chemie und Klinische Biochemie [*A publication*]
Z Klin Chemie ... Zeitschrift fuer Klinische Chemie [*A publication*]
Z Klin Chem Klin Biochem ... Zeitschrift fuer Klinische Chemie und Klinische Biochemie [*A publication*]
Z Klin Med ... Zeitschrift fuer Klinische Medizin [*A publication*]
Z Klin Psychol Psychopathol Psychother ... Zeitschrift fuer Klinische Psychologie, Psychopathologie, und Psychotherapie [*A publication*]
Z Klin Psychol Psychother ... Zeitschrift fuer Klinische Psychologie und Psychotherapie [*A publication*]
Z Kl M .... Zeitschrift fuer Klinische Medizin [*A publication*]
ZKM .... Zeitschrift fuer die Kunde des Morgenlandes [*A publication*]
ZKN .... Training Balloon [*Navy symbol*]
ZKO .... Observation Balloon [*Navy symbol*]
Z Koeln Zoo ... Zeitschrift des Koelner Zoo [*A publication*]

Z Kompr Fluess Gase Pressluft-Ind ... Zeitschrift fuer Komprimierte und Fluessige Gase Sowie fuer die Pressluft-Industrie [*A publication*]
ZK Ph .... Zeitschrift fuer Keltische Philologie [*A publication*]
ZKPVF ...... Zeitschrift fuer Keltische Philologie und Volksforschung [*A publication*]
ZKPY .... Pyongyang/Sunan [*Democratic People's Republic of Korea*] [*ICAO location identifier*] (ICLI)
ZKR .... Zeitschrift fuer das Gesamte Kreditwesen [*A publication*]
ZKR .... Zeitschrift fuer Kirchenrecht [*A publication*]
Z Kr .... Zeitschrift fuer Kristallographie, Kristallgeometrie, Kristallphysik, Kristallchemie [*A publication*]
Z Krankenpfl ... Zeitschrift fuer Krankenpflege [*A publication*]
Z Krebsf Kl ... Zeitschrift fuer Krebsforschung und Klinische Onkologie [*A publication*]
Z Krebsforsch ... Zeitschrift fuer Krebsforschung [*A publication*]
Z Krebsforsch Klin Onkol ... Zeitschrift fuer Krebsforschung und Klinische Onkologie [*A publication*]
Z Kreislaufforsch ... Zeitschrift fuer Kreislaufforschung [*A publication*]
Z Kreisl Forsch ... Zeitschrift fuer Kreislaufforschung [*A publication*]
Z Kr F .... Zeitschrift fuer Krebsforschung [*A publication*]
Z Krist .... Zeitschrift fuer Kristallographie, Kristallgeometrie, Kristallphysik, Kristallchemie [*A publication*]
Z Kristall ... Zeitschrift fuer Kristallographie, Kristallgeometrie, Kristallphysik, Kristallchemie [*A publication*]
Z Kristallogr ... Zeitschrift fuer Kristallographie [*A publication*]
Z Kristallogr Kristallgeom Kristallphys Kristallchem ... Zeitschrift fuer Kristallographie, Kristallgeometrie, Kristallphysik, Kristallchemie [*A publication*]
Z Kristallogr Mineral ... Zeitschrift fuer Kristallographie und Mineralogie [*A publication*]
ZKRU .... Zeitschrift fuer Katholischen Religionsunterricht [*A publication*]
ZKRVD ...... Zmiesana Komisia o Rybolove vo Vodach Dunaja [*Joint Danube Fishery Commission - JDFC*] [*Zilina, Czechoslovakia*] (EAIO)
ZKSC .... Sunchon [*Democratic People's Republic of Korea*] [*ICAO location identifier*] (ICLI)
ZKSR .... Sesura [*Democratic People's Republic of Korea*] [*ICAO location identifier*] (ICLI)
ZKT .... Zeitschrift fuer Katholische Theologie [*A publication*]
ZKTh .... Zeitschrift fuer Katholische Theologie [*A publication*]
ZKUFAK ... Journal of Rural Engineering and Development [*A publication*]
ZKuG .... Zeitschrift fuer Kunstgeschichte [*A publication*]
ZKUJ .... Uiju [*Democratic People's Republic of Korea*] [*ICAO location identifier*] (ICLI)
Z Kult G ..... Zeitschrift fuer Kulturgeschichte [*A publication*]
Z Kult-Tech Flurberein ... Zeitschrift fuer Kulturtechnik und Flurbereinigung [*A publication*]
Z Kulturaustausch ... Zeitschrift fuer Kulturaustausch [*A publication*]
Z Kulturtech ... Zeitschrift fuer Kulturtechnik [*A publication*]
Z Kulturtech Flurbereinig ... Zeitschrift fuer Kulturtechnik und Flurbereinigung [*A publication*]
Z Kulturtech Landentwicklung ... Zeitschrift fuer Kulturtechnik und Landentwicklung [*A publication*]
ZKunstG .... Zeitschrift fuer Kunstgeschichte [*A publication*]
Z Kunstges ... Zeitschrift fuer Kunstgeschichte [*A publication*]
Z Kunstgesc ... Zeitschrift fuer Kunstgeschichte [*A publication*]
Z Kunstgesch ... Zeitschrift fuer Kunstgeschichte [*A publication*]
Z Kunstwis ... Zeitschrift fuer Kunstwissenschaft [*A publication*]
ZKW .... Zeitschrift fuer Kunstwissenschaft [*A publication*]
zkW .... Zero Kilowatt (IEEE)
ZKW .... Zi-ka-wei [*Republic of China*] [*Seismograph station code, US Geological Survey*] (SEIS)
ZKWL .... Zeitschrift fuer Kirchliche Wissenschaft und Kirchliches Leben [*Leipzig*] [*A publication*]
ZL .... Freezing Drizzle [*Meteorology*] (FAAC)
ZL .... New Zealand [*Aircraft nationality and registration mark*] (FAAC)
ZL .... Z-Axis of Spacelab [*NASA*] (NASA)
ZL .... Zavodskaja Laboratorija [*A publication*]
ZL .... Zero Lift
ZL .... Zloty [*Monetary unit*] [*Poland*] (EY)
ZL .... Zycie Literackie [*A publication*]
ZLA .... Los Angeles, CA [*Location identifier*] [*FAA*] (FAAL)
Z Laboratoriumsdiagn ... Zeitschrift fuer Laboratoriumsdiagnostik [*A publication*]
ZLAN .... Lanzhou City [*China*] [*ICAO location identifier*] (ICLI)
Z Landeskult ... Zeitschrift fuer Landeskultur [*A publication*]
Z Landwirsch Versuchswes Dtsch Oesterr ... Zeitschrift fuer das Landwirtschaftliche Versuchswesen im Deutsch-Oesterreich [*A publication*]
Z Landwirtsch Vers Untersuchungswes ... Zeitschrift fuer Landwirtschaftliches Versuchs- und Untersuchungswesen [*A publication*]
Z Landwirt Vers Untersuchungsw ... Zeitschrift fuer Landwirtschaftliches Versuchs- und Untersuchungswesen [*A publication*]
Z Landw Ver u Unters Wes ... Zeitschrift fuer Landwirtschaftliches Versuchs- und Untersuchungswesen [*A publication*]
Z Lar Rhinol Otol ... Zeitschrift fuer Laryngologie, Rhinologie, Otologie, und Ihre Grenzgebiete [*A publication*]

Z Laryngol Rhinol Otol ... Zeitschrift fuer Laryngologie, Rhinologie, Otologie, und Ihre Grenzgebiete [*A publication*]
Z Laryngol Rhinol Otol Grenzgeb ... Zeitschrift fuer Laryngologie, Rhinologie, Otologie, und Ihre Grenzgebiete [*A publication*]
Z Laryngol Rhinol Otol Ihre Grenzgeb ... Zeitschrift fuer Laryngologie, Rhinologie, Otologie, und Ihre Grenzgebiete [*A publication*]
ZLB........... Balboa, Canal Zone [*Location identifier*] [*FAA*]   (FAAL)
ZLC........... Salt Lake City, UT [*Location identifier*] [*FAA*]   (FAAL)
ZLC........... Zero Lift Cord
ZLC........... Zinc, Lead, and Cadmium Abstracts [*Zinc Development Association/Lead Development Association/Codmium Association*] [*Great Britain*] [*Defunct*] [*Information service or system*]   (CRD)
ZLD .... Zero Level Drift
ZLD .... Zero Lift Drag
ZLD .... Zodiacal Light Device
ZLDI......... Zentralstelle fuer Luft- Raumfahrtdokumentation und Information [*Center for Documentation and Information in Aeronautics and Astronautics*] [*Information service or system*] [*West Germany*]
ZLE........... Zaba Lee Enterprises [*Vancouver Stock Exchange symbol*]
Z Lebensmit ... Zeitschrift fuer Lebensmittel- Untersuchung und Forschung [*A publication*]
Z Lebensmittelunters u Forsch ... Zeitschrift fuer Lebensmittel- Untersuchung und Forschung [*A publication*]
Z Lebensmittel Untersuch Forsch ... Zeitschrift fuer Lebensmittel- Untersuchung und Forschung [*A publication*]
Z Lebensmitt Untersuch ... Zeitschrift fuer Lebensmittel- Untersuchung und Forschung [*A publication*]
Z Lebensm-Technol-Verfahrenstech ... Zeitschrift fuer Lebensmittel- Technologie und Verfahrenstechnik [*German Federal Republic*] [*A publication*]
Z Lebensm-Unters Forsch ... Zeitschrift fuer Lebensmittel- Untersuchung und Forschung [*A publication*]
Z Leder Gerberei Chem ... Zeitschrift fuer Leder- und Gerberei-Chemie [*A publication*]
ZLG .... Zero Line Gap
ZLGIA....... Zapiski Leningradskogo Gornogo Instituta [*A publication*]
ZLH........... Lincoln Hospital, Bronx, NY [*OCLC symbol*]   (OCLC)
ZLH........... [*F.*] Zorell. Lexicon Hebraicum [*A publication*]   (BJA)
ZLHW....... Lanzhou [*China*] [*ICAO location identifier*]   (ICLI)
ZLIC......... Yinchuan [*China*] [*ICAO location identifier*]   (ICLI)
ZLISP........ Zilog List Processor [*Programming language*] [*1979*]   (CSR)
ZLit........... Zycie Literackie [*Krakow*] [*A publication*]
Z Lit Wiss ... Zeitschrift fuer Literaturwissenschaft [*A publication*]
ZLJ............ Zambia Law Journal [*A publication*]   (DLA)
ZLJM........ Zusters van Liefe Jezus en Maria [*Sisters of Charity of Jesus and Mary - SCJM*] [*Brussels, Belgium*]   (EAIO)
ZLJQ......... Jiuquan [*China*] [*ICAO location identifier*]   (ICLI)
ZLK........... Zaleski, OH [*Location identifier*] [*FAA*]   (FAAL)
ZLL........... Zero-Length Launch [*Missiles*]
ZLL........... Zero Lot Line [*Real estate*]
ZLLL .... Lanzhou/Zhongchuan [*China*] [*ICAO location identifier*]   (ICLI)
ZLM .... State University of New York, College at New Paltz, New Paltz, NY [*OCLC symbol*]   (OCLC)
ZLN .... Zwiazek Ludowo-Narodowy [*Populist-Nationalist Alliance*] [*Poland*] [*Political party*]   (PPE)
ZLO .... Manzanillo [*Mexico*] [*Airport symbol*]   (OAG)
ZLP........... Zongo [*La Paz*] [*Bolivia*] [*Seismograph station code, US Geological Survey*]   (SEIS)
ZLR........... Zanzibar Law Reports [*1919-50*] [*A publication*]   (DLA)
ZLR........... Zanzibar Protectorate Law Reports [*1868-1950*] [*A publication*]   (DLA)
ZLROA...... Zeitschrift fuer Laryngologie, Rhinologie, Otologie [*A publication*]
ZLSIA........ Zapiski Leningradskogo Sel'skokhozyaistvennogo Instituta [*A publication*]
ZLSM........ Zeiss Light Section Microscope
ZLSN........ Xian [*China*] [*ICAO location identifier*]   (ICLI)
ZLT........... La Tabatiere [*Canada*] [*Airport symbol*]   (OAG)
ZLThK....... Zeitschrift fuer die Gesamte Lutherische Theologie und Kirche [*Leipzig*] [*A publication*]
ZLTO........ Zero-Length Takeoff   (MCD)
Z Luft-Weltraumrecht ... Zeitschrift fuer Luft- und Weltraumrecht [*A publication*]
Z-LV .... Z-Axis along Local Vertical   (MCD)
ZLV........... Zero-Length Vector
ZLW .... Zeitschrift fuer Luftrecht und Weltraum-Rechtsfragen [*A publication*]
ZLXN .... Xining [*China*] [*ICAO location identifier*]   (ICLI)
ZLYA........ Yanan [*China*] [*ICAO location identifier*]   (ICLI)
Z Lymphol ... Zeitschrift fuer Lymphologie [*A publication*]
ZM............ Impedance Measuring Devices [*JETDS nomenclature*] [*Military*]   (CET)
ZM............ New Zealand [*Aircraft nationality and registration mark*]   (FAAC)
ZM............ Zahnaerztliche Mitteilungen [*A publication*]
ZM............ Zambia [*ANSI two-letter standard code*]   (CNC)
ZM............ Zeitschrift fuer Militaergeschichte [*A publication*]

ZM............ Zeitschrift fuer Missionskunde [*A publication*]
ZM............ Zeitschrift fuer Mundartforschung [*A publication*]
ZM............ Zeitschrift fuer Musik [*A publication*]
ZM............ Zero Marker   (MCD)
ZM............ Zoom/MODEM [*ZOOM Telephonics, Inc.*]
Z-M........... Zuckerman-Moloff [*Sewage treatment method*]
ZM............ Zycie i Mysl [*A publication*]
ZMA .... Miami, FL [*Location identifier*] [*FAA*]   (FAAL)
ZMA .... Zinc Metaarsenite [*Insecticide, wood preservative*]
ZM-AF ...... Zeitschrift fuer Mikroskopische-Anatomische Forschung [*A publication*]
ZMaF........ Zeitschrift fuer Mundartforschung [*A publication*]
ZMag........ Z Magazine [*Zambia*] [*A publication*]
ZMAR .... Zeus Multifunction Array RADAR [*Missile defense*]
Z Markt Meinungs und Zukunftsforsch ... Zeitschrift fuer Marktforschung, Meinungsforschung, und Zukunftsforschung [*A publication*]
Z Math Log ... Zeitschrift fuer Mathematische Logik und Grundlagen der Mathematik [*A publication*]
Z Math Logik Grundlagen Math ... Zeitschrift fuer Mathematische Logik und Grundlagen der Mathematik [*A publication*]
Z Math Logik Grundlag Math ... Zeitschrift fuer Mathematische Logik und Grundlagen der Mathematik [*A publication*]
Z Mat Phys ... Zeitschrift fuer Mathematik und Physik [*East Germany*] [*A publication*]
ZMB .... Zambia [*ANSI three-letter standard code*]   (CNC)
ZMB .... Zero Moisture Basis [*Chemical analysis*]
ZMBT........ Zinc Mercaptobenzimidazole [*Organic chemistry*]
ZMBT........ Zinc Mercaptobenzothiazole [*Organic chemistry*]
ZMBTA...... Zement und Beton [*A publication*]
ZMC .... Manhattan College, Library, Bronx, NY [*OCLC symbol*]   (OCLC)
ZMD......... Zung Measurement of Depression [*Scale*]
ZMDC...... Zinc Dimethyldithiocarbamate [*Organic chemistry*]
ZME .... Memphis, TN [*Location identifier*] [*FAA*]   (FAAL)
Z Med Chem ... Zeitschrift fuer Medizinische Chemie [*A publication*]
Z Med Isotopenforsch Deren Grenzgeb ... Zeitschrift fuer Medizinische Isotopenforschung und Deren Grenzgebiete [*A publication*]
Z Med Lab Diagn ... Zeitschrift fuer Medizinische Laboratoriumsdiagnostik [*A publication*]
Z Med Laboratoriumsdiagn ... Zeitschrift fuer Medizinische Laboratoriumsdiagnostik [*A publication*]
Z Med Labortech ... Zeitschrift fuer Medizinische Labortechnik [*A publication*]
Z Med Mikrobiol Immunol ... Zeitschrift fuer Medizinische Mikrobiologie und Immunologie [*A publication*]
Z Med Mikrosk ... Zeitschrift fuer Medizinische Mikroskopie [*A publication*]
ZMEIA...... Zhurnal Mikrobiologii, Epidemiologii, i Immunobiologii [*A publication*]
Z Menschl Vererb-Konstitutionsl ... Zeitschrift fuer Menschliche Vererbungs- und Konstitutionslehre [*A publication*]
Z Metallk... Zeitschrift fuer Metallkunde [*A publication*]
Z Metallkd ... Zeitschrift fuer Metallkunde [*A publication*]
Z Metallkun ... Zeitschrift fuer Metallkunde [*A publication*]
Z Meteorol ... Zeitschrift fuer Meteorologie [*A publication*]
Z Met Schmuckwaren Fabr Verchrom ... Zeitschrift fuer Metall- und Schmuckwaren. Fabrikation sowie Verchromung [*A publication*]
ZMF......... Zeitschrift fuer Mundartforschung [*A publication*]
ZMFWA.... Zeszyty Naukowe. Matematyka, Fizyka, Chemia [*A publication*]
ZMG .... Zentralblatt fuer Mathematik und Ihre Grenzgebiete [*A publication*]
ZMH.......... Zeitschrift. Museum Hildesheim [*A publication*]
Z Mikrosk Anat Forsch ... Zeitschrift fuer Mikroskopische-Anatomische Forschung [*A publication*]
Z Mikrosk-Anat Forsch (Leipz) ... Zeitschrift fuer Mikroskopische-Anatomische Forschung (Leipzig) [*A publication*]
Z Militaermed ... Zeitschrift fuer Militaermedizin [*East Germany*] [*A publication*]
Z Miss....... Zeitschrift fuer Missionswissenschaft und Religionswissenschaft [*A publication*]
Z Miss-u Relig Wiss ... Zeitschrift fuer Missionswissenschaft und Religionswissenschaft [*A publication*]
Z Miss W... Zeitschrift fuer Missionswissenschaft und Religionswissenschaft [*A publication*]
ZMK .... Zeitschrift fuer Missionskunde und Religionswissenschaft [*A publication*]
ZMK .... Zpravodaj Mistopisne Komise CSAV [*Ceskoslovenske Akademie Ved*] [*A publication*]
ZMKBA6... Zeszyty Naukowe Uniwersytetu Mikolaja Kopernika w Toruniu. Nauki Matematyczno-Przyrodnicze Biologia [*A publication*]
ZMKR .... Zone Marker
ZML .... Medical Library Center of New York, Standardized Cataloging Service, New York, NY [*OCLC symbol*]   (OCLC)
ZMM......... State University of New York, Maritime College, Bronx, NY [*OCLC symbol*]   (OCLC)
ZMM......... Zeitschrift fuer Marktforschung, Meinungsforschung, und Zukunftsforschung [*A publication*]
ZMM......... Zone Melting Model

ZMMAS.... Zodiacal Microparticle Multiparameter Analysis System [*NASA*]

ZMMD...... Zurich, Mainz, Munich, Darmstadt [*A joint European university effort on ALGOL processors*]

ZMMPAO ... Zentralblatt fuer Bakteriologie, Parasitenkunde, Infektionskrankheiten, und Hygiene. Erste Abteilung. Originale Reihe A. Medizinische Mikrobiologie und Parasitologie [*A publication*]

ZMNP....... Zurnal Ministerstva Narodnogo Prosvescenija [*A publication*]

Z Morph Okol Tiere ... Zeitschrift fuer Morphologie und Oekologie der Tiere [*A publication*]

Z Morphol Anthropol ... Zeitschrift fuer Morphologie und Anthropologie [*A publication*]

Z Morphol Oekol Tiere ... Zeitschrift fuer Morphologie und Oekologie der Tiere [*A publication*]

Z Morphol Tiere ... Zeitschrift fuer Morphologie der Tiere [*A publication*]

Z Morph Tie ... Zeitschrift fuer Morphologie der Tiere [*A publication*]

ZMOTA .... Zeitschrift fuer Morphologie und Oekologie der Tiere [*A publication*]

ZMP.......... Minneapolis, MN [*Location identifier*] [*FAA*] (FAAL)

ZMP.......... Zeitschrift fuer Musikpaedagogik [*A publication*]

ZMP.......... Zurnal Moskovskoi Patriarkhii [*Moscow*] [*A publication*]

ZMPHA .... Zeitschrift fuer Mathematik und Physik [*A publication*]

ZMR.......... Zeitschrift fuer Missionswissenschaft und Religionswissenschaft [*A publication*]

ZMR.......... Zone-Melting Recrystallization [*Crystallography*]

ZMRI........ Zinc Metals Research Institute

ZMRW...... Zeitschrift fuer Missionswissenschaft und Religionswissenschaft [*A publication*]

ZMS.......... Zbornik Matice Srpske [*A publication*]

ZMT.......... Masset [*Canada*] [*Airport symbol*] (OAG)

ZMT.......... ZIP [*Zone Improvement Plan*] Mail Translator [*Postal Service*]

ZMT.......... Zoom Telephonics [*Vancouver Stock Exchange symbol*]

Z Mth........ Zeitschrift fuer Musiktheorie [*A publication*]

ZMtheorie ... Zeitschrift fuer Musiktheorie [*A publication*]

ZMUC....... Zoologisk Museum, University of Copenhagen [*Denmark*]

ZMVKA .... Zeitschrift fuer Menschliche Vererbungs- und Konstitutionslehre [*A publication*]

ZMW........ Zeitschrift fuer Missionswissenschaft [*A publication*]

Z Mw .... Zeitschrift fuer Musikwissenschaft [*A publication*]

ZMX........ Zemex Corp. [*NYSE symbol*] (SPSG)

Z Mykol..... Zeitschrift fuer Mykologie [*A publication*]

ZN.............. Airship (Nonrigid) [*Navy symbol*]

Zn.............. True Azimuth [*Symbol*] (MUGU)

ZN.............. Zeitschrift fuer Namenforschung [*A publication*]

ZN.............. Zeitschrift fuer Nationaloekonomie [*A publication*]

ZN.............. Zeitschrift fuer Numismatik [*A publication*]

ZN.............. Zenith

ZN.............. Zeszyty Naukowe [*A publication*]

ZN.............. Ziehl-Neelsen [*A biological stain*]

Zn.............. Zinc [*Chemical element*]

Zn.............. Znamya [*Moscow*] [*A publication*]

ZN.............. Zone

ZN.............. Zycie Nauki [*A publication*]

ZNA.......... Nanaimo [*Canada*] Harbour Airport [*Airport symbol*] (OAG)

ZNa........... Zycie Nauki [*A publication*]

ZNACD..... Zeszyty Naukowe Akademii Gorniczo-Hutniczej Imienia Stanislawa Staszica. Matematyka, Fizyka, Chemia [*A publication*]

ZNAGA..... Zeszyty Naukowe Akademii Gorniczo-Hutniczej w Krakowie. Rozprawy [*A publication*]

ZNAGB .... Zeszyty Naukowe Akademii Gorniczo-Hutniczej (Krakow). Gornictwo [*A publication*]

ZNAGD..... Zeszyty Naukowe Akademii Gorniczo-Hutniczej Imienia Stanislawa Staszica. Geologia [*A publication*]

ZNAGDF .. Akademia Gorniczo-Hutnicza Imienia Stanislawa Staszica w Krakowie Zeszyty Naukowe Geologia [*A publication*]

ZNAHD..... Zeszyty Naukowe Akademii Gorniczo-Hutniczej Imienia Stanislawa Staszica. Elektryfikacja i Mechanizacja Gornictwa i Hutnictwa [*A publication*]

Z Nahrungsm Unters Hyg Warenkd ... Zeitschrift fuer Nahrungsmittel- Untersuchung Hygiene und Warenkunde [*A publication*]

ZNAND..... Zootecnica e Nutrizione Animale [*A publication*]

Z Nat F ..... Zeitschrift fuer Naturforschung [*A publication*]

Z Natforsch ... Zeitschrift fuer Naturforschung [*A publication*]

Z Nationalo ... Zeitschrift fuer Nationaloekonomie [*A publication*]

Z Nationaloekon ... Zeitschrift fuer Nationaloekonomie [*A publication*]

Z Nationaloekonom ... Zeitschrift fuer Nationaloekonomie [*A publication*]

Z Nat-Oekon ... Zeitschrift fuer Nationaloekonomie [*A publication*]

Z Naturf B ... Zeitschrift fuer Naturforschung. Teil B [*A publication*]

Z Naturf C ... Zeitschrift fuer Naturforschung. Teil C. Biochemie, Biophysik, Biologie, Virologie [*A publication*]

Z Naturfo A ... Zeitschrift fuer Naturforschung. A [*A publication*]

Z Naturfo B ... Zeitschrift fuer Naturforschung. B [*A publication*]

Z Naturfo C ... Zeitschrift fuer Naturforschung. C [*A publication*]

Z Naturforsch ... Zeitschrift fuer Naturforschung [*A publication*]

Z Naturforsch A ... Zeitschrift fuer Naturforschung. Teil A. Astrophysik, Physik, und Physikalische Chemie [*A publication*]

Z Naturforsch B ... Zeitschrift fuer Naturforschung. Teil B [*A publication*]

Z Naturforsch B Anorg Chem Org Chem ... Zeitschrift fuer Naturforschung. Teil B. Anorganische Chemie, Organische Chemie [*A publication*]

Z Naturforsch B Anorg Chem Org Chem Biochem Biophys Biol ... Zeitschrift fuer Naturforschung. Teil B. Anorganische Chemie, Organische Chemie, Biochemie, Biophysik, Biologie [*West Germany*] [*A publication*]

Z Naturforsch C Biochem Biophys Biol Virol ... Zeitschrift fuer Naturforschung. Teil C. Biochemie, Biophysik, Biologie, Virologie [*West Germany*] [*A publication*]

Z Naturforsch C Biosci ... Zeitschrift fuer Naturforschung. Teil C. Biosciences [*West Germany*] [*A publication*]

Z Naturforsch Sect B ... Zeitschrift fuer Naturforschung. Section B. Inorganic Chemistry, Organic Chemistry [*A publication*]

Z Naturforsch Sect C Biosci ... Zeitschrift fuer Naturforschung. Section C. Biosciences [*A publication*]

Z Naturforsch Teil A ... Zeitschrift fuer Naturforschung. Teil A [*A publication*]

Z Naturforsch Teil C ... Zeitschrift fuer Naturforschung. Teil C. Biosciences [*A publication*]

Z Naturforsch Teil C Biochem Biophys Biol Virol ... Zeitschrift fuer Naturforschung. Teil C. Biochemie, Biophysik, Biologie, Virologie [*A publication*]

Z Naturheilk ... Zeitschrift fuer Naturheilkunde [*A publication*]

Z Naturwiss-Med Grundlagenforsch ... Zeitschrift fuer Naturwissenschaftlich- Medizinische Grundlagenforschung [*A publication*]

Z Naurforsch Teil B ... Zeitschrift fuer Naturforschung. Teil B. Anorganische Chemie, Organische Chemie [*A publication*]

ZNC.......... New York City Technical College, Library, Brooklyn, NY [*OCLC symbol*] (OCLC)

ZNC.......... Nyack, AK [*Location identifier*] [*FAA*] (FAAL)

ZNC.......... Zone of Nonproliferating Cells [*Cytology*]

ZNCAV ..... Zdenku Nejedlemu Ceskoslovenska Akademie Ved [*A publication*]

ZN Ch........ Zurnal Neorganiceskoj Chimii [*A publication*]

ZND.......... Zinder [*Niger*] [*Airport symbol*] (OAG)

ZNE.......... Newman [*Australia*] [*Airport symbol*] (OAG)

Z Neorg Chim ... Zurnal Neorganiceskoj Chimii [*A publication*]

Z Neurol..... Zeitschrift fuer Neurologie [*A publication*]

Z Neutral ... Zeitschrift Neutralitaet [*A publication*]

Z Neut W ... Zeitschrift fuer die Neutestamentliche Wissenschaft [*A publication*]

Z Neut Wiss ... Zeitschrift fuer die Neutestamentliche Wissenschaft und die Kunde der Aelteren Kirche [*A publication*]

ZNF .... Zeitschrift fuer Namenforschung [*A publication*]

ZNG........... Negginan [*Canada*] [*Airport symbol*] (OAG)

ZNG........... Zeszyty Naukowe Wydzialu Humanistycznego, Wyzsza Szkola Pedagogiczna w Gdansku [*A publication*]

ZnG........... Zinc Gluconate [*Organic chemistry*]

ZNGGA ..... Zeszyty Naukowe Akademii Gorniczo-Hutniczej (Krakow). Geologia [*A publication*]

ZNGI .... Zero Net Growth Isocline [*Ecological graph*]

ZNH .... Airship, Air-Sea Rescue [*Navy symbol*]

ZNIC .... Zonic Corp. [*NASDAQ symbol*] (NQ)

ZNIO .... Zaklad Narodowy Imeni Ossolinskich [*A publication*]

ZNJ........... Airship, Utility [*Navy symbol*]

ZNK.......... Zeszyty Naukowe, Sekcja Jezykoznawcza, Wyzsza Szkola Pedagogiczna w Katowicach [*A publication*]

ZNKUL ..... Zeszyty Naukowe Katolickiego Uniwersytetu Lubelskiego [*A publication*]

ZNLSA ...... Zeszyty Naukowe Politechniki Lodzkiej. Chemia Spozywcza [*A publication*]

ZNM.......... Nioga Library System, Niagara Falls, NY [*OCLC symbol*] (OCLC)

ZNN........... Nonrigid Training Airship [*Navy symbol*]

ZNO........... Nonrigid Observation Airship [*Navy symbol*]

ZNO........... North Country Community College, Saranac Lake, NY [*OCLC symbol*] (OCLC)

ZNO........... Zeitschrift fuer Nationaloekonomie [*A publication*]

ZNO........... Zenco Resources, Inc. [*Vancouver Stock Exchange symbol*]

ZNP .... Nonrigid Patrol Airship [*Navy symbol*]

ZNP .... Zanzibar Nationalist Party

ZnP .... Zinc Protoporphyrin [*Biochemistry*]

ZNP .... Zinc Pyrithione [*Antibacterial*]

ZNP .... Zion Nuclear Plant (NRCH)

ZNPEA ...... Zeszyty Naukowe Politechniki Lodzkiej. Elektryka [*A publication*]

ZNPED ...... Zeszyty Naukowe Politechniki Poznanskiej. Elektryka [*A publication*]

ZNPIA....... Zhurnal Nevropatologii i Psikhiatrii Imeni S. S. Korsakova [*A publication*]

ZNPPD...... Zeszyty Naukowe Politechniki Swietokrzyskiej. Seria P. Problemy Nauk Podstawowych [*A publication*]

ZNR .... Zinc Resistor

ZNS .... Nonrigid Scouting Airship [*Navy symbol*]

ZNS .... Zeitschrift fuer Neuere Sprachen [*A publication*]

ZnS .... Zinc Sulfide (BYTE)

ZNSCA...... Zeszyty Naukowe Politechniki Slaskiej. Chemia [*A publication*]

ZNSGA...... Zeszyty Naukowe Politechniki Slaskiej. Gornictwo [*A publication*]

ZNSL......... Zeitschrift fuer Neufranzoesische Sprache und Literatur [*A publication*]
ZNSPK...... Zeszyty Naukowe Wyzszej Szkoly Pedagogicznej (Katowice) [*A publication*]
ZNSPO...... Zeszyty Naukowe Wyzszej Szkoly Pedagogicznej (Opole) [*A publication*]
ZNSSA...... Zeszyty Naukowe Akademii Gorniczo-Hutniczej (Krakow). Sozologia i Sozotechnika [*A publication*]
ZNT .... Zenith National Insurance Corp. [*NYSE symbol*] (SPSG)
ZNTFA...... Zeitschrift fuer Naturforschung [*A publication*]
ZNTHA..... Zeszyty Naukowe Politechniki Czestochowskiej. Nauki Techniczne. Hutnictwo [*A publication*]
ZNTL......... Zehntel, Inc. [*Walnut Creek, CA*] [*NASDAQ symbol*] (NQ)
Z Ntl W...... Zeitschrift fuer die Neutestamentliche Wissenschaft [*A publication*]
ZNTS......... Zapysky Naukovoho Tovarystva Imeny Svecenka [*A publication*]
ZNTSL...... Zapysky Naukovoho Tovarystva Imeny Svecenka (Literature Series) [*A publication*]
ZNTW....... Zeitschrift fuer die Neutestamentliche Wissenschaft [*A publication*]
ZNTZA...... Zeszyty Naukowe Akademii Rolniczo-Technicznej w Olsztynie. Technologia Zywnosci [*A publication*]
ZNU.......... Namu [*Canada*] [*Airport symbol*] [*Obsolete*] (OAG)
ZNU.......... Zeitschrift fuer Neusprachlichen Unterricht [*A publication*]
ZNUFA ..... Zeszyty Naukowe Uniwersytetu Jagiellonskiego. Prace Fizyczne [*A publication*]
ZNUG........ Zeszyty Naukowe Uniwersytetu Gdanskiego [*A publication*]
ZNUIA ...... Zeszyty Naukowe Uniwersytetu Imienia Adama Mickiewicza w Poznaniu. Matematyka, Fizyka, Chemia [*A publication*]
ZNUJ .... Zeszyty Naukowe Uniwersytetu Jagiellonskiego [*A publication*]
ZNUL .... Zeszyty Naukowe Uniwersytetu Lodzkiego [*A publication*]
ZNULHist ... Zeszyty Naukowe Uniwersytetu Lodzkiego. Nauki Humanistyczno-Spoleczne. Historia [*A publication*]
ZNum........ Zeitschrift fuer Numismatik [*A publication*]
ZNUMD..... Zeszyty Naukowe Uniwersytetu Jagiellonskiego. Prace Biologii Molekularnej [*A publication*]
ZNUMK.... Zeszyty Naukowe Uniwersytetu Mikolaja Kopernika [*A publication*]
ZNUnWr ... Zeszyty Naukowe Uniwersytetu Wroclawskiego [*A publication*]
ZNUP .... Zeszyty Naukowe Uniwersytetu Imienia Adama Mickiewicza w Poznaniu [*A publication*]
ZNUPHSzt ... Zeszyty Naukowe Uniwersytetu Imienia Adama Mickiewicza w Poznaniu. Historia Sztuki [*A publication*]
ZNUT .... Zeszyty Naukowe Uniwersytetu Mikolaja Kopernika w Toruniu. Nauki Humanistyczno-Spoleczne [*A publication*]
ZNUW....... Zeszyty Naukowe Uniwersytetu Wroclawskiego Imienia B. Bieruta [*A publication*]
ZNUZA ..... Zeszyty Naukowe Uniwersytetu Jagiellonskiego. Prace Zoologiczne [*A publication*]
ZNW.......... Zeitschrift fuer die Neutestamentliche Wissenschaft [*A publication*]
ZNWFA..... Zeszyty Naukowe Wyzszej Szkoly Pedagogicznej w Katowicach. Sekcja Fizyki [*A publication*]
ZNWKAK ... Zeitschrift fuer die Neutestamentliche Wissenschaft und die Kunde der Aelteren Kirche [*A publication*]
ZNWKU.... Zeitschrift fuer die Neutestamentliche Wissenschaft und die Kunde des Urchristentums [*A publication*]
ZNWSPK.. Zeszyty Naukowe Wyzszej Szkoly Pedagogicznej (Katowice) [*A publication*]
ZNWSPO ... Zeszyty Naukowe Wyzszej Szkoly Pedagogicznej (Opole) [*A publication*]
ZNWSPOp ... Zeszyty Naukowe, Jezykoznawstwo, Wyzsza Szkola Pedagogiczna w Opolu [*A publication*]
ZNXPO ...... Zeus-Nike X Program Office [*Missiles*] (MCD)
ZNY .... New York, NY [*Location identifier*] [*FAA*] (FAAL)
ZNZ.......... Zanzibar [*Tanzania*] [*Airport symbol*] (OAG)
ZNZSA...... Zeszyty Naukowe Akademii Gorniczo-Hutniczej (Cracow). Zeszyt Specjalny [*A publication*]
ZO............. Oceanic Air Traffic Control [*ICAO designator*] (ICDA)
ZO............. Z-Axis of Orbiter [*NASA*] (NASA)
ZO............. Zeitschrift fuer Organisation [*A publication*]
ZO............. Zeitschrift fuer Ortsnamenforschung [*A publication*]
ZO............. Zeitschrift fuer Ostforschung [*A publication*]
ZO............. Zero Output
Zo............. Zoen Tencararius [*Flourished, 13th century*] [*Authority cited in pre-1607 legal work*] (DSA)
ZO............. Zoological Origin
Z/O .... Zoom Out [*Cinematography*]
ZOA.......... Oakland, CA [*Location identifier*] [*FAA*] (FAAL)
ZOA.......... Zionist Organization of America (EA)
Zo A .... Zoologischer Anzeiger [*A publication*]
Zoannet...... [*Franciscus*] Zoannettus [*Deceased, 1586*] [*Authority cited in pre-1607 legal work*] (DSA)
ZOB.......... Cleveland, OH [*Location identifier*] [*FAA*] (FAAL)
Z Oberschles Berg-Huettenmaenn Ver Kat ... Zeitschrift des Oberschlesischen Berg- und Huettenmaennischen Vereins zu Katowiee [*A publication*]
ZOBIDX.... Zoo Biology [*A publication*]
ZOBO........ Zongo [*La Paz*] [*Bolivia*] [*Seismograph station code, US Geological Survey*] (SEIS)

Zobozdrav Vestn ... Zobozdravstveni Vestnik [*A publication*]
Z Obsc Biol ... Zurnal Obscej Biologii [*A publication*]
Z Obsc Chim ... Zurnal Obscej Chimii [*A publication*]
ZOBW .... Zeitschrift fuer Oesterreichisches Bibliothekswesen [*A publication*]
ZOC.......... Zone of Convenience (ADA)
ZOD.......... Zero Order Detector (MCD)
ZOD.......... Zodiac (ROG)
Zod........... Zodiac Records [*Record label*]
ZODIAC.... Zone Defense Integrated Active Capability (IEEE)
ZOE.......... Zero Energy
ZOE.......... Zinc Oxide-Eugenol [*Dental cement*]
ZOE.......... Zone of Entry [*Military*] (AABC)
ZOE.......... Zone of Exclusion (MCD)
Z Oeff Chem ... Zeitschrift fuer Oeffentliche Chemie [*A publication*]
Z Oeff Gem Wirtsch Unterneh ... Zeitschrift fuer Oeffentliche und Gemeinwirtschaftliche Unternehmen [*A publication*]
ZOEG........ Zeitschrift fuer die Oesterreichischen Gymnasien [*A publication*]
ZOEG........ Zeitschrift fuer Osteuropaeische Geschichte [*A publication*]
Z Oe IAV ... Zeitschrift des Oesterreichischen Ingenieur und Architekten Vereins [*A publication*]
ZOEMS..... Zeitschrift fuer die Oesterreichischen Mittelschulen [*A publication*]
ZOEP........ Zoe Products, Inc. [*NASDAQ symbol*] (NQ)
Z Oesterr Entomol Ver ... Zeitschrift. Oesterreichischer Entomologe-Verein [*A publication*]
Z Oesterr Ing Archit Ver ... Zeitschrift des Oesterreichischen Ingenieur und Architekten Vereins [*A publication*]
Z Oesterr Ver Gas Wasserfachmaennern ... Zeitschrift. Oesterreichischer Verein von Gas- und Wasserfachmaennern [*A publication*]
ZOest G ..... Zeitschrift fuer die Oesterreichischen Gymnasien [*A publication*]
ZOF .... Ocean Falls [*Canada*] [*Airport symbol*] [*Obsolete*] (OAG)
ZOf .... Zeitschrift fuer Ostforschung [*A publication*]
ZOF .... Zone of Fire [*Military*]
ZOfo.......... Zeitschrift fuer Ostforschung [*A publication*]
ZOG.......... Paramaribo [*Suriname*] [*Airport symbol*]
ZOG.......... Zeitschrift fuer Osteuropaeische Geschichte [*A publication*]
ZOG.......... Zionist Occupational Government
ZOGAAV .. Zoologische Gaerten [*A publication*]
ZOH .... Zero Order Hold [*Telescope*]
ZOLD .... Zeroth Order Logarithmic Distribution
ZOLGA ...... Zoologica [*A publication*]
Zolnierz Pol ... Zolnierz Polski [*Poland*] [*A publication*]
Zolotaya Promst ... Zolotaya Promyslennost [*A publication*]
ZOMO....... Zmotoryzowane Oddzialy Milicji Obywatelskiej [*Motorized Units of People's Militia*] [*Poland's riot police*]
ZON.......... Zeitschrift fuer Ortsnamenforschung [*A publication*]
ZON.......... Zonda [*Argentina*] [*Seismograph station code, US Geological Survey*] (SEIS)
ZON.......... Zone Petroleum Corp. [*Vancouver Stock Exchange symbol*]
Zonar .... Zonaras [*Twelfth century AD*] [*Classical studies*] (OCD)
ZOND........ [*The*] Zondervan Corp. [*NASDAQ symbol*] (NQ)
ZONEF...... Zone Petroleum Corp. [*NASDAQ symbol*] (NQ)
Zoning and Plan L Rep ... Zoning and Planning Law Report [*A publication*]
ZOO.......... Minnesota Zoological Garden, Apple Valley, MN [*OCLC symbol*] (OCLC)
ZOOACT .. Zoological Action Committee (EA)
Zoo Biol ..... Zoo Biology [*A publication*]
ZOOCHEM ... Zoochemistry (ROG)
ZOOGEOG ... Zoogeography (ROG)
Zooiatr Rev Med Vet Prod Pecu ... Zooiatria Revista de Medicina Veterinaria y Produccion Pecuaria [*A publication*]
ZOOL .... Zoological [*or Zoology*]
Zool Abh (Dres) ... Zoologische Abhandlungen (Dresden) [*A publication*]
Zool Afr .... Zoologica Africana [*A publication*]
Zool Ann .... Zoologische Annalen [*A publication*]
Zool Anz .... Zoologischer Anzeiger [*A publication*]
Zool Anzeiger ... Zoologischer Anzeiger [*A publication*]
Zool Anz (Leipzig) ... Zoologischer Anzeiger (Leipzig) [*A publication*]
Zool Anz Suppl ... Zoologische Anzeiger. Supplement [*A publication*]
Zool B .... Zoological Bulletin [*A publication*]
Zool Beitr... Zoologische Beitraege [*A publication*]
Zool Ber ..... Zoologischer Bericht [*A publication*]
Zool Bidr Upps ... Zoologiska Bidrag fran Uppsala [*A publication*]
Zool Bidr Uppsala ... Zoologiska Bidrag fran Uppsala [*A publication*]
Zool Bijdr.. Zoologische Bijdragen [*A publication*]
Zool Biol Mar ... Zoologia e Biologia Marinha [*A publication*]
Zool Biol Mar (Nova Ser) ... Zoologia e Biologia Marinha (Sao Paulo) (Nova Serie) [*A publication*]
Zool Entomol Listy ... Zoologicke a Entomologicke Listy [*A publication*]
Zool Gaert ... Zoologische Gaerten [*A publication*]
Zool Gart (Lpz) ... Zoologische Gaerten (Leipzig) [*A publication*]
Zool Inst Fac Sci Univ Tokyo Annu Rep ... Zoological Institute. Faculty of Science. University of Tokyo. Annual Report [*A publication*]
Zool Jahrb ... Zoologische Jahrbuecher-Abteilung Allgemeine Zoologie und Physiologie der Tiere [*A publication*]

Zool Jahrb Abt Allg Zool Physiol Tiere ... Zoologische Jahrbuecher. Abteilung fuer Allgemeine Zoologie und Physiologie der Tiere [*A publication*]
Zool Jahrb Abt Anat Ontog Tiere ... Zoologische Jahrbuecher. Abteilung fuer Anatomie und Ontogenie der Tiere [*A publication*]
Zool Jahrb Abt Syst (Jena) ... Zoologische Jahrbuecher. Abteilung fuer Systematik Oekologie und Geographie der Tiere (Jena) [*A publication*]
Zool Jahrb Abt Syst Oekol Geogr Tiere ... Zoologische Jahrbuecher. Abteilung fuer Systematik Oekologie und Geographie der Tiere [*A publication*]
Zool Jb....... Zoologische Jahrbuecher [*A publication*]
Zool Jb Abt Allg Zool Physiol Tiere ... Zoologische Jahrbuecher. Abteilung fuer Allgemeine Zoologie und Physiologie der Tiere [*A publication*]
Zool Jb Abt Syst Okol Geog Tiere ... Zoologische Jahrbuecher. Abteilung fuer Systematik Oekologie und Geographie der Tiere [*A publication*]
Zool Jhrb Abt Allg Zool Physiol Tiere ... Zoologische Jahrbuecher. Abteilung fuer Allgemeine Zoologie und Physiologie der Tiere [*A publication*]
Zool J Linn ... Zoological Journal. Linnean Society [*A publication*]
Zool J Linn Soc ... Zoological Journal. Linnean Society [*A publication*]
Zool Listy... Zoologicke Listy [*A publication*]
Zool Mag... Zoological Magazine [*A publication*]
Zool Mag (Tokyo) ... Zoological Magazine (Tokyo) [*A publication*]
Zool Meded (Leiden) ... Zoologische Mededelingen (Leiden) [*A publication*]
Zool Meded Rijks Mus Nat Hist Leiden ... Zoologische Mededelingen. Rijks Museum van Natuurlijke Historie te Leiden [*A publication*]
Zool Muz Raksti Invertebrata ... Zoologijas Muzeja Raksti. Invertebrata [*A publication*]
Zoologica Pol ... Zoologica Poloniae [*A publication*]
Zoologica Scr ... Zoologica Scripta [*A publication*]
Zool Orient ... Zoologica Orientalis [*A publication*]
Zool Pol ..... Zoologica Poloniae [*A publication*]
Zool Publ Victoria Univ Wellington ... Zoology Publications. Victoria University of Wellington [*A publication*]
Zool Rec ...... Zoological Record [*A publication*]
Zool Res ...... Zoological Research [*A publication*]
Zool Revy... Zoologisk Revy [*A publication*]
Zool Sci..... Zoological Science [*A publication*]
Zool Sci (Tokyo) ... Zoological Science (Tokyo) [*A publication*]
Zool Scr ..... Zoologica Scripta [*A publication*]
Zool Soc Egypt Bull ... Zoological Society of Egypt. Bulletin [*A publication*]
Zool Soc London Pr ... Zoological Society of London. Proceedings [*A publication*]
Zool Soc London Proc ... Zoological Society of London. Proceedings [*A publication*]
Zool Verh... Zoologische Verhandelingen [*A publication*]
Zool Verh (Leiden) ... Zoologische Verhandelingen (Leiden) [*A publication*]
Zool Verh Rijksmus Nat Hist (Leiden) ... Zoologische Verhandelingen. Rijksmuseum van Natuurlijke Historie (Leiden) [*A publication*]
Zool Z .... Zoologicheskii Zhurnal [*A publication*]
Zool Zentralbl ... Zoologisches Zentralblatt [*A publication*]
Zool Zh ...... Zoologicheskii Zhurnal [*A publication*]
Zoonoses Res ... Zoonoses Research [*A publication*]
ZOOPH..... Zoophytology (ROG)
Zoophysiol Ecol ... Zoophysiology and Ecology [*A publication*]
Zoo Rec...... Zoological Record [*A publication*]
ZOOREO.. Zoologica Orientalis [*A publication*]
Zoo Rev Parque Zool Barc ... Zoo Revista del Parque Zoologico de Barcelona [*A publication*]
Zootech Experiment Stn Res Bull ... Zootechnical Experiment Station. Research Bulletin [*A publication*]
Zootec Nutr Anim ... Zootecnica e Nutrizione Animale [*A publication*]
Zootec Vet ... Zootecnica e Veterinaria [*A publication*]
Zootec Vet Agric ... Zootecnica. Veterinaria e Agricoltura [*A publication*]
Zootec Vita ... Zootecnia e Vita [*A publication*]
ZOP .... Zero Order Predictor
ZOP .... Zinc Oxide Pigment
ZOPA .... Zinc Oxide Producers' Association [*European Council of Chemical Manufacturers Federations*] [*Brussels, Belgium*]   (EAIO)
Z Operations Res Ser A-B ... Zeitschrift fuer Operations Research. Serie A. Serie B [*A publication*]
Z Oper Res B ... Zeitschrift fuer Operations Research. Serie B. Praxis [*A publication*]
Z Oper Res Ser A ... Zeitschrift fuer Operations Research. Serie A. Theorie [*A publication*]
Z Oper Res Ser A-B ... Zeitschrift fuer Operations Research. Serie A. Serie B [*A publication*]
Z Oper Res Ser B ... Zeitschrift fuer Operations Research. Serie B. Praxis [*A publication*]
ZOPI.......... Zero Order Polynomial Interpolator
ZOPP.......... Zero Order Polynomial Predictor
ZOR............. Zeitschrift fuer Operations Research [*A publication*]
ZOR.......... Zinc Oxide Resistor
ZOR........... Zone of Reconnaissance
ZOR........... Zorah Media Corp. [*Vancouver Stock Exchange symbol*]

Z Organ ..... Zeitschrift fuer Organisation [*A publication*]
ZORPB........ Zeitschrift fuer Operations Research. Serie B. Praxis [*A publication*]
ZORRO..... Zero Offset Rapid Reaction Ordnance
Z Orthop .... Zeitschrift fuer Orthopaedie und Ihre Grenzgebiete [*A publication*]
Z Orthop Grenzgeb ... Zeitschrift fuer Orthopaedie und Ihre Grenzgebiete [*A publication*]
Z Orthop Ihre Grenzgeb ... Zeitschrift fuer Orthopaedie und Ihre Grenzgebiete [*A publication*]
ZOS .... Zapata Corp. [*NYSE symbol*] [*Toronto Stock Exchange symbol*]
ZOS .... Zoom Optical System
ZOSC........ Zoologica Scripta [*A publication*]
Z Ostforsch ... Zeitschrift fuer Ostforschung [*A publication*]
Z fur die Ost Gym ... Zeitschrift fuer die Oesterreichischen Gymnasien [*A publication*]   (OCD)
Zouch Adm ... Zouche's Admiralty Jurisdiction [*A publication*]   (DLA)
ZOVBW .... Zeitschrift. Oesterreichischer Verein fuer Bibliothekswesen [*A publication*]
ZOW.......... State University of New York, College at Old Westbury, Old Westbury, NY [*OCLC symbol*]   (OCLC)
ZOX........... Ground Zero [*Nevada*] [*Seismograph station code, US Geological Survey*] [*Closed*]   (SEIS)
ZP .... Air Traffic Services Reporting Office [*ICAO designator*]   (ICDA)
ZP .... Paraguay [*Aircraft nationality and registration mark*]   (FAAC)
ZP .... Patrol and Escort Aircraft [*Lighter-than-Air*] [*Navy symbol*]   (MUGU)
ZP .... Revlon, Inc. [*Research code symbol*]
ZP .... Z-Axis of Payload [*NASA*]   (NASA)
ZP .... Zadok Perspectives [*A publication*]   (APTA)
ZP .... Zeitschrift fuer Phonetik [*A publication*]
ZP .... Zeitschrift fuer Politik [*A publication*]
ZP .... Zep Energy [*Vancouver Stock Exchange symbol*]
Zp............. Zephaniah   (BJA)
Zp............. Zona Pellucida [*Embryology*]
ZP .... Zweeppartij [*Whipping Party*] [*Political party*] [*Belgium*]
ZPA .... Zero Period Acceleration [*Nuclear energy*]   (NRCH)
ZPA .... Zeus Program Analysis [*Missiles*]
ZPA .... Zone of Polarizing Activity [*Embryology, genetics*]
ZPAAD...... Zeitschrift fuer Physik. Sektion A. Atoms and Nuclei [*A publication*]
ZPalV .... Zeitschrift. Deutscher Palaestinaverein [*A publication*]
ZPapEpigr ... Zeitschrift fuer Papyrologie und Epigraphik [*A publication*]   (BJA)
Z Pap Pappe Zellul Holzst ... Zeitschrift fuer Papier. Pappe, Zellulose, und Holzstoff [*A publication*]
Z Papyrologie Epigraphik ... Zeitschrift fuer Papyrologie und Epigraphik [*A publication*]
ZPAR........ Zeus Phased Array RADAR [*Missile defense*]
Z Parapsych ... Zeitschrift fuer Parapsychologie und Grenzgebiete der Psychologie [*A publication*]
Z Parasiten ... Zeitschrift fuer Parasitenkunde [*A publication*]
Z Parasitenkd ... Zeitschrift fuer Parasitenkunde [*A publication*]
Z ParasitKde ... Zeitschrift fuer Parasitenkunde [*A publication*]
Z Parlamentsfr ... Zeitschrift fuer Parlamentsfragen [*German Federal Republic*] [*A publication*]
Z Parlamentsfragen ... Zeitschrift fuer Parlamentsfragen [*A publication*]
ZPAS .... Zeitschrift fuer Phonetik und Allgemeine Sprachwissenschaft [*A publication*]
ZPB............ Zinc Primary Battery
ZPBBD...... Zeitschrift fuer Physik. Sektion B. Condensed Matter and Quanta [*A publication*]
ZPC............ Zero Point of Charge
ZPC............ Zinc-Phosphate Coating
ZPCA......... Zugzwang Postal Chess Association   (EA)
ZPCAA...... Zeitschrift fuer Physikalische Chemie. Abteilung A. Chemische Thermodynamik, Kinetik, Elektrochemie, Eigenschaftslehre [*A publication*]
ZPCBA...... Zeitschrift fuer Physikalische Chemie. Abteilung B. Chemie der Elementarprozesse, Aufbau der Materie [*A publication*]
ZPCHA ..... Zeitschrift fuer Physiologische Chemie [*A publication*]
ZPCLA ..... Zeitschrift fuer Physikalische Chemie (Leipzig) [*A publication*]
ZPD .... Zero Path Difference
ZPDBA...... Zeitschrift fuer Pflanzenernaehrung, Duengung, und Bodenkunde [*A publication*]
ZPE........... Zeitschrift fuer Papyrologie und Epigraphik [*A publication*]
ZPE........... Zero Point Energy
ZPE........... Zeta Phi Eta
ZPED........ Zeus Production Evaluation Program [*Missiles*]   (MCD)
ZPEN........ Zeus Project Engineer Network [*Missiles*]
ZPF............ Zeitschrift fuer Philosophische Forschung [*A publication*]
ZPFL......... Zanzibar and Pemba Federation of Labour
Z Pflanzenernaehr Bodenkd ... Zeitschrift fuer Pflanzenernaehrung und Bodenkunde [*A publication*]
Z Pflanzenernaehr Dueng ... Zeitschrift fuer Pflanzenernaehrung und Duengung [*A publication*]
Z Pflanzenernaehr Dueng Bodenkd ... Zeitschrift fuer Pflanzenernaehrung, Duengung, und Bodenkunde [*Later, Zeitschrift fuer Pflanzenernaehrung und Bodenkunde*] [*A publication*]

Z Pflanzenernahr Dung Bodenkd ... Zeitschrift fuer Pflanzenernaehrung, Duengung, und Bodenkunde [*A publication*]
Z Pflanzenkr ... Zeitschrift fuer Pflanzenkrankheiten [*A publication*]
Z Pflanzenkr Gallenkd ... Zeitschrift fuer Pflanzenkrankheiten und Gallenkunde [*A publication*]
Z Pflanzenkr Pflanzenschutz ... Zeitschrift fuer Pflanzenkrankheiten, Pflanzenpathologie, und Pflanzenschutz [*A publication*]
Z Pflanzenkr Pflanzenpathol Pflanzenschutz Sonderh ... Zeitschrift fuer Pflanzenkrankheiten, Pflanzenpathologie, und Pflanzenschutz. Sonderheft [*A publication*]
Z Pflanzenkr Pflanzenschutz ... Zeitschrift fuer Pflanzenkrankheiten und Pflanzenschutz [*A publication*]
Z Pflanzenp ... Zeitschrift fuer Pflanzenphysiologie [*A publication*]
Z Pflanzenphysiol ... Zeitschrift fuer Pflanzenphysiologie [*A publication*]
Z Pflanzenz ... Zeitschrift fuer Pflanzenzuechtung [*A publication*]
Z Pflanzenzuecht ... Zeitschrift fuer Pflanzenzuechtung [*A publication*]
Z PflErnahr Bodenk ... Zeitschrift fuer Pflanzenernaehrung und Bodenkunde [*A publication*]
Z PflErnahr Dung Bodenk ... Zeitschrift fuer Pflanzenernaehrung, Duengung, und Bodenkunde [*Later, Zeitschrift fuer Pflanzenernaehrung und Bodenkunde*] [*A publication*]
Z PflKrankh ... Zeitschrift fuer Pflanzenkrankheiten, Pflanzenpathologie, und Pflanzenschutz [*A publication*]
Z PflKrankh PflSchutz ... Zeitschrift fuer Pflanzenkrankheiten und Pflanzenschutz [*A publication*]
Z PflPhysiol ... Zeitschrift fuer Pflanzenphysiologie [*A publication*]
Z Pflzuecht ... Zeitschrift fuer Pflanzenzuechtung [*A publication*]
ZPG .... Airship Group [*Navy symbol*]
ZPG .... Zero Population Growth (EA)
ZPh .... Zeitschrift fuer Psychologie [*A publication*]
ZPH .... Zephyrhills, FL [*Location identifier*] [*FAA*] (FAAL)
ZPhF .... Zeitschrift fuer Philosophische Forschung [*A publication*]
Z Phil Forsch ... Zeitschrift fuer Philosophische Forschung [*A publication*]
Z Philos F .. Zeitschrift fuer Philosophische Forschung [*A publication*]
Z Philos Forsch ... Zeitschrift fuer Philosophische Forschung [*A publication*]
ZPhon .... Zeitschrift fuer Phonetik und Allgemeine Sprachwissenschaft [*A publication*]
Z Phonetik Sprachwiss Komm Forsch ... Zeitschrift fuer Phonetik, Sprachwissenschaft, und Kommunikationsforschung [*A publication*]
Z Phon Sprachwiss Kommunikationsforsch ... Zeitschrift fuer Phonetik, Sprachwissenschaft, und Kommunikationsforschung [*A publication*]
Z Phys .... Zeitschrift fuer Physik [*A publication*]
Z Phys A .... Zeitschrift fuer Physik. Sektion A. Atoms and Nuclei [*A publication*]
Z Phys B .... Zeitschrift fuer Physik. Sektion B. Condensed Matter and Quanta [*A publication*]
Z Phys C .... Zeitschrift fuer Physik. Sektion C. Particles and Fields [*German Federal Republic*] [*A publication*]
Z Phys Chem Abt A ... Zeitschrift fuer Physikalische Chemie. Abteilung A. Chemische Thermodynamik, Kinetik, Elektrochemie, Eigenschaftslehre [*A publication*]
Z Phys Chem Abt B ... Zeitschrift fuer Physikalische Chemie. Abteilung B. Chemie der Elementarprozesse, Aufbau der Materie [*A publication*]
Z Phys Chem Frankf Ausg Neue Folge ... Zeitschrift fuer Physikalische Chemie. Frankfurter Ausgabe. Neue Folge [*West Germany*] [*A publication*]
Z Phys Chem (Frankfurt/Main) ... Zeitschrift fuer Physikalische Chemie (Frankfurt/Main) [*A publication*]
Z Phys Chemie Stoechiom Verwandschaftsl ... Zeitschrift fuer Physikalische Chemie, Stoechiometrie, und Verwandtschaftslehre [*A publication*]
Z Phys Chem (Leipzig) ... Zeitschrift fuer Physikalische Chemie (Leipzig) [*A publication*]
Z Phys Chem Materialforsch ... Zeitschrift fuer Physikalisch-Chemische Materialforschung [*A publication*]
Z Phys Chem Neue Folge ... Zeitschrift fuer Physikalische Chemie. Neue Folge [*A publication*]
Z Phys Chem Neue Fo (Wiesbaden) ... Zeitschrift fuer Physikalische Chemie. Neue Folge (Wiesbaden) [*A publication*]
Z Phys Chem (Wiesbaden) ... Zeitschrift fuer Physikalische Chemie (Wiesbaden) [*A publication*]
Z Phys Ch (F) ... Zeitschrift fuer Physikalische Chemie (Frankfurt) [*A publication*]
Z Phys Ch (L) ... Zeitschrift fuer Physikalische Chemie (Leipzig) [*A publication*]
Z Phys Diaet Ther ... Zeitschrift fuer Physikalische und Diaetetische Therapie [*A publication*]
Z Physik .... Zeitschrift fuer Physik [*A publication*]
Z Physiol Chem ... Zeitschrift fuer Physiologische Chemie [*A publication*]
Z Physiol Chem Hoppe-Seylers ... Zeitschrift fuer Physiologische Chemie. Hoppe-Seylers [*German Federal Republic*] [*A publication*]
Z Physiother ... Zeitschrift fuer Physiotherapie [*A publication*]
ZPI .... New York State Psychiatric Institute, Medical Library Center of New York, New York, NY [*OCLC symbol*] (OCLC)

ZPID .... Zentralstelle fuer Psychologische Information und Dokumentation [*Center for Psychological Information and Documentation*] [*Federal Republic of Germany*] [*Database operator*] [*Information service or system*] (IID)
Z Pilzkd ..... Zeitschrift fuer Pilzkunde [*A publication*]
ZPJIAK ..... Zbirnyk Prat Jewrejskiej Istorychno-Arkheologichnoj Komisji [*Kiev*] [*A publication*]
ZPKM .... Kunming [*China*] [*ICAO location identifier*] (ICLI)
ZPL .... Zero-Phonon Line [*Physics*]
Z Plast Chir ... Zeitschrift fuer Plastische Chirurgie [*A publication*]
ZPM .... State University of New York, College at Purchase, Purchase, NY [*OCLC symbol*] (OCLC)
ZPMPA ..... Zeitschrift fuer Psychotherapie und Medizinische Psychologie [*A publication*]
ZPN .... Impedance Pneumograph [*Apollo*] [*NASA*]
ZPO .... Zeus Project Office [*Missiles*]
ZPO .... Zinc Peroxide [*Pharmacology*]
ZPO .... Zivilprozessordnung [*German Code of Civil Procedure*] (DLA)
Z Polit .... Zeitschrift fuer Politik [*A publication*]
Z Politik .... Zeitschrift fuer Politik [*A publication*]
Z Pol N F ... Zeitschrift fuer Politik. Neue Folge [*A publication*]
ZPP .... Zimbabwe Progressive Party [*Political party*] (PPW)
ZPP .... Zinc Protophorphyrin [*Biochemistry*]
ZPPA .... Zeitschrift fuer Wissenschaftliche Photographie, Photophysik, und Photochemie [*A publication*]
ZPPP .... Kunming/Wujiaba [*China*] [*ICAO location identifier*] (ICLI)
ZPPP .... Zanzibar and Pemba People's Party
ZPPR .... Zero Power Plutonium Reactor [*Nuclear energy*]
ZPR .... Zero Power Reactor [*Nuclear energy*]
Z Praeklin Geriatr ... Zeitschrift fuer Praeklinische Geriatrie [*A publication*]
Z Praeklin Klin Geriatr ... Zeitschrift fuer Praeklinische und Klinische Geriatrie [*A publication*]
Z Praeventivmed ... Zeitschrift fuer Praeventivmedizin [*A publication*]
Z Prakt Anaesth ... Zeitschrift fuer Praktische Anaesthesie, Wiederbelebung, und- Intensivtherapie [*A publication*]
Z Prakt Geol ... Zeitschrift fuer Praktische Geologie [*A publication*]
Z Praventivmed ... Zeitschrift fuer Praeventivmedizin [*A publication*]
Zpravy .... Zpravy pro Cestinare [*A publication*]
Zpr Cesk Keram Sklarske Spol ... Zpravy Ceskoslovenske Keramicke a Sklarske Spolecnosti [*A publication*]
ZPRF .... Zero Power Reactor Facility [*AEC*]
Z Prikl Meh i Tehn Fiz ... Zurnal Prikladnoi Mehaniki i Tehniceskoi Fiziki [*A publication*]
ZprMK .... Zpravodaj Mistopisne Komise CSAV [*Ceskoslovenske Akademie Ved*] [*A publication*]
ZPRON ..... Patrol [*Lighter-than-Air*] Squadron [*Navy symbol*]
ZPRSN ...... Zurich Provisional Relative Sunspot Number [*NASA*]
ZPs .... Zeitschrift fuer Psychologie [*A publication*]
ZPS .... [*William H.*] Zimmer Nuclear Power Station [*Also, WZNPS*] (NRCH)
ZPSEA ...... Zeszyty Naukowe Politechnika Slaska. Energetyka [*A publication*]
ZPSIA .... Zeitschrift fuer Psychologie und Physiologie der Sinnesorgane [*A publication*]
ZPSK .... Zeitschrift fuer Phonetik, Sprachwissenschaft, und Kommunikationsforschung [*A publication*]
ZPSMA ..... Zeitschrift fuer Psychosomatische Medizin [*Later, Zeitschrift fuer Psychosomatische Medizin und Psychoanalyse*] [*A publication*]
ZPSS .... Z Polskich Studiow Slawistycznych [*A publication*]
ZPSS .... Zion Probabilistic Safety Study [*Nuclear energy*] (NRCH)
Z Psych Hyg ... Zeitschrift fuer Psychische Hygiene [*A publication*]
Z Psychol ... Zeitschrift fuer Psychologie [*A publication*]
Z Psycholog ... Zeitschrift fuer Psychologie [*A publication*]
Z Psychol Physiol Sinnesorg ... Zeitschrift fuer Psychologie und Physiologie der Sinnesorgane [*East Germany*] [*A publication*]
Z Psychol Z Angew Psychol ... Zeitschrift fuer Psychologie mit Zeitschrift fuer Angewandte Psychologie [*A publication*]
Z Psychol Z Angew Psychol Charakterkd ... Zeitschrift fuer Psychologie mit Zeitschrift fuer Angewandte Psychologie und Charakterkunde [*A publication*]
Z Psychos M ... Zeitschrift fuer Psychosomatische Medizin und Psychoanalyse [*A publication*]
Z Psychosom Med ... Zeitschrift fuer Psychosomatische Medizin [*Later, Zeitschrift fuer Psychosomatische Medizin und Psychoanalyse*] [*A publication*]
Z Psychosom Med Psychoanal ... Zeitschrift fuer Psychosomatische Medizin und Psychoanalyse [*A publication*]
Z Psychother Med Psychol ... Zeitschrift fuer Psychotherapie und Medizinische Psychologie [*A publication*]
Z Psychot M ... Zeitschrift fuer Psychotherapie und Medizinische Psychologie [*A publication*]
ZPT .... Zero Power Test
ZPT .... Zoxazolamine Paralysis Time [*In experimental animals*]
ZPWCA ..... Zeszyty Naukowe Politechniki Wroclawskiej. Chemia [*A publication*]
ZPYFA ...... Zeitschrift fuer Physikalische Chemie. Frankfurter Ausgabe. Neue Folge [*A publication*]

ZQ.............. Center in charge of a flight information region or an upper flight information region when the message is relevant to an IFR [*Instrument Flight Rules*] flight [*See also ZF*] [*ICAO designator*] (ICDA)

ZQC........... Queensborough Community College of the City University of New York, Library, Bayside, NY [*OCLC symbol*] (OCLC)

ZQM.......... State University of New York, College at Potsdam, Potsdam, NY [*OCLC symbol*] (OCLC)

ZQN........... Queenstown [*New Zealand*] [*Airport symbol*] (OAG)

ZQT........... Zero Quantum Transition [*Physics*]

ZR.............. Area Control Center [*ICAO designator*] (ICDA)

ZR.............. Freezing Rain [*Meteorology*] (FAAC)

ZR.............. Rigid Airship [*Navy symbol*]

ZR.............. Zadarska Revija [*A publication*]

ZR.............. Zaire [*ANSI two-letter standard code*] (CNC)

ZR.............. Zentralrat [*Central Board*] [*German*]

ZR.............. Zero Coupon Issue (Security) [*In bond listings of newspapers*]

ZR.............. Zionist Record [*A publication*]

ZR.............. Zionist Review [*A publication*]

Zr .... Zirconium [*Chemical element*]

ZR.............. Zona Reticularis [*Of adrenal cortex*] [*Anatomy*]

ZR.............. Zone Refined

ZR.............. Zone of Responsibility

ZR.............. Zoological Record [*A publication*]

ZR.............. Zoological Record Online [*Bio Sciences Information Service*] [*Information service or system*] (IID)

ZRA .... Zero Resistance Ammeter [*Instrumentation*]

ZRC .... Zenith Radio Corporation

ZRDI......... Zionic Research and Development Institute (EA)

ZRE .... Zero Rate Error (MCD)

ZREC........ Zoological Records [*BioSciences Information Service*]

Z Rechtsmed ... Zeitschrift fuer Rechtsmedizin [*Journal of Legal Medicine*] [*A publication*]

Z Rechtspolit ... Zeitschrift fuer Rechtspolitik [*A publication*]

Z Reich Geschmackstoffe ... Zeitschrift fuer Reich- und Geschmackstoffe [*A publication*]

Z Rel Geistesges ... Zeitschrift fuer Religions- und Geistesgeschichte [*Koeln*] [*A publication*]

Z Rel Gg..... Zeitschrift fuer Religions- und Geistesgeschichte [*A publication*]

Z Relig- u Geistesgesch ... Zeitschrift fuer Religions- und Geistesgeschichte [*A publication*]

Z Relig Geistesgesch ... Zeitschrift fuer Religions- und Geistesgeschichte [*A publication*]

Z Reproduktionstech ... Zeitschrift fuer Reproduktionstechnik [*A publication*]

ZRG .... Zeitschrift fuer Religions- und Geistesgeschichte [*A publication*]

ZRG .... Zeitschrift der Savigny-Stiftung fuer Rechtsgeschichte [*A publication*]

ZRGA .... Zeitschrift. Savigny-Stiftung fuer Rechtsgeschichte. Germanistische Abteilung [*A publication*]

ZRGG .... Zeitschrift fuer Religions- und Geistesgeschichte [*A publication*]

ZRG (GA) ... Zeitschrift. Savigny-Stiftung fuer Rechtsgeschichte. Germanistische Abteilung [*A publication*]

ZRGGB...... Zeitschrift fuer Religions- und Geistesgeschichte. Beihefte [*A publication*]

ZRGGS...... Zeitschrift fuer Religions- und Geistesgeschichte. Sonderhefte [*A publication*]

ZRH.......... Zurich [*Switzerland*] [*Airport symbol*] (OAG)

Z Rheumaforsch ... Zeitschrift fuer Rheumaforschung [*A publication*]

Z Rheumatol ... Zeitschrift fuer Rheumatologie [*A publication*]

Z Rheumatol Suppl ... Zeitschrift fuer Rheumatologie. Supplement [*A publication*]

ZRHMB .... Zeitschrift fuer Rheumatologie [*A publication*]

ZRI............ Serui [*Indonesia*] [*Airport symbol*] (OAG)

ZRI............ Zeitschrift fuer die Religioesen Interessen des Judentums [*Berlin*] [*A publication*]

ZRI............ Zosen [*A publication*]

ZRIO .... Zimbabwe Rhodesian Information Office [*An association*] (EA)

ZRL........... Zagadnienia Rodzajow Literackich [*A publication*]

ZRM .... Sarmi [*Indonesia*] [*Airport symbol*] (OAG)

ZRN .... Rigid Training Airship [*Navy symbol*]

ZRN .... Zurn Industries, Inc. [*NYSE symbol*] (SPSG)

ZRNI .... Zapiski Russkogo Naucnogo Instituta [*A publication*]

ZRO........... Zero Corp. [*NYSE symbol*] (SPSG)

ZRO........... Zoological Record Online [*A publication*]

ZRO........... Zoological Record Outline

Z Roman Ph ... Zeitschrift fuer Romanische Philologie [*A publication*]

Zroshuvane Zemlerob ... Zroshuvane Zemlerobstvo [*A publication*]

Zrosh Zemlerob ... Zroshuvane Zemlerobstvo [*A publication*]

ZRP........... Rigid Patrol Airship [*Navy symbol*]

ZRP........... Zeitschrift fuer Romanische Philologie [*A publication*]

ZRP........... Zero Radial Play

ZRPBA ...... Zbornik Radova. Poljoprivrednog Fakulteta. Universitet u Beogradu [*A publication*]

ZRPH .... Zeitschrift fuer Romanische Philologie [*A publication*]

ZRS........... Rigid Scouting Airship [*Navy symbol*]

ZRS........... Russell Sage College, Troy, NY [*OCLC symbol*] (OCLC)

ZRSAN...... Zbornik Radova. Srpske Akademije Nauke [*A publication*]

ZRSG......... Zoological Record Search Guide [*A publication*]

ZRSNDI .... Zimbabwe Science News [*A publication*]

ZRT .... Zero Reaction Tool

ZRTLS...... Zwolse Reeks van Taal- en Letterkundige Studies [*A publication*]

ZRU .... Zeitschrift fuer den Russisch-Unterricht [*A publication*]

ZRV .... Zero-Relative Velocity

ZRZ .... Zbornik Radova. Svenciliste u Zagrebu [*A publication*]

Z/S............ Operational Display System

ZS .... SARSAT Centre [*France*] [*ICAO designator*] (FAAC)

ZS .... Union of South Africa [*Aircraft nationality and registration mark*] (FAAC)

ZS .... Z-Axis of Solid Rocket Booster [*NASA*] (NASA)

ZS .... Zeitschrift [*Review*] [*German*] (ILCA)

ZS .... Zeitschrift fuer die Gesamte Staatswissenschaft [*A publication*]

ZS .... Zeitschrift fuer Semitistik und Verwandte Gebiete [*Leipzig*] [*A publication*]

ZS .... Zeitschrift fuer Slawistik [*Berlin*] [*A publication*]

ZS .... Zero Shift

ZS .... Zero and Subtract

ZS .... Zero Sum [*Genetics*]

ZS .... Zero Suppress

ZS .... Zoological Society [*British*]

ZS .... Zoosporangia [*Botany*]

ZSA........... San Salvador [*Bahamas*] [*Airport symbol*] (OAG)

ZSA........... Southern Tier Library System, Corning, NY [*OCLC symbol*] (OCLC)

ZSA........... Zero-Set Amplifier (MSA)

Z Saeugetierkd ... Zeitschrift fuer Saeugetierkunde [*A publication*]

ZSAK........ Zeitschrift fuer Schweizerische Archaeologie und Kunstgeschichte [*A publication*]

ZSAKG...... Zeitschrift fuer Schweizerische Archaeologie und Kunstgeschichte [*A publication*]

Zs Allg Erdk ... Zeitschrift fuer Allgemeine Erdkunde [*A publication*]

ZSAM........ Xiamen [*China*] [*ICAO location identifier*] (ICLI)

Zs Anorg Chem ... Zeitschrift fuer Anorganische Chemie [*A publication*]

ZSAT......... Zinc Sulfide Atmospheric Tracer

ZSav.......... Zeitschrift. Savigny-Stiftung fuer Rechtsgeschichte. Romanistische Abteilung [*A publication*]

Z Savigny-Stift Rechtsgesch Kanon Abt ... Zeitschrift. Savigny-Stiftung fuer Rechtsgeschichte. Kanonistische Abteilung [*A publication*]

ZSavRG ..... Zeitschrift. Savigny-Stiftung fuer Rechtsgeschichte. Romanistische Abteilung [*Weimar*] [*A publication*]

ZSB........... Zinc Storage Battery

Zs Berg- Huetten- u Salinen-Wesen ... Zeitschrift fuer das Berg-, Huetten-, und Salinenwesen [*A publication*]

ZSC........... Stauffer Chemical Co., Information Services, Dobbs Ferry, NY [*OCLC symbol*] (OCLC)

ZSC........... Zero Subcarrier Chromaticity

ZSC........... Zinc Silicate Coat

ZSC........... Zose [*Shanghai Seh-Shan*] [*Republic of China*] [*Seismograph station code, US Geological Survey*] (SEIS)

ZSC........... Zose [*Republic of China*] [*Geomagnetic observatory code*]

ZS Ch......... Zurnal Strukturnoj Chimii [*A publication*]

Zschft f Ausl u Intl Privatr ... Zeitschrift fuer Auslaendisches und Internationales Privatrecht [*Berlin and Tubingen, Germany*] [*A publication*] (DLA)

Zschft Luft- u Weltr-Recht ... Zeitschrift fuer Luftrecht- und Weltraumrechtsfragen [*A publication*] (DLA)

Zschft Rechtsvergl ... Zeitschrift fuer Rechtsvergleichung [*Vienna, Austria*] [*A publication*] (DLA)

Zschft Savigny-Germ ... Zeitschrift. Savigny-Stiftung fuer Rechtsgeschichte. Germanistische Abteilung [*A publication*]

Zschft Savigny-Kanon ... Zeitschrift. Savigny-Stiftung fuer Rechtsgeschichte. Kanonistische Abteilung [*A publication*]

Zschft Savigny-Rom ... Zeitschrift. Savigny-Stiftung fuer Rechtsgeschichte. Romanistische Abteilung

Zschft f Vergl Rechtswissenschaft ... Zeitschrift fuer Vergleichende Rechtswissenschaft [*A publication*]

Z Sch G...... Zeitschrift fuer Schweizerische Geschichte [*A publication*]

Zschift f Ausl Offentl Recht ... Zeitschrift fuer Auslaendisches Oeffentliches Recht und Voelkerrecht [*A publication*]

Z Sch Kg .... Zeitschrift fuer Schweizerische Kirchengeschichte [*A publication*]

Z Schles Holst Gesch ... Zeitschrift. Gesellschaft fuer Schleswig-Holsteinische Geschichte [*Kiel, West Germany*] [*A publication*]

Z Sch R ...... Zeitschrift fuer Schweizerisches Recht [*A publication*]

Z Schw AKg ... Zeitschrift fuer Schweizerische Archaeologie und Kunstgeschichte [*A publication*]

Z Schweisstech ... Zeitschrift fuer Schweisstechnik [*A publication*]

Z Schweiz Archaeol Kunstgesch ... Zeitschrift fuer Schweizerische Archaeologie und Kunstgeschichte [*A publication*]

Z Schweiz Arch Kunstgesch ... Zeitschrift fuer Schweizerische Archaeologie und Kunstgeschichte [*A publication*]

Z f Schweiz Recht ... Zeitschrift fuer Schweizerisches Recht/Revue de Droit Suisse/Revista di Diritto Svizzero [*Basel, Switzerland*] [*A publication*] (DLA)

ZSchwG ..... Zeitschrift fuer Schweizerische Geschichte [*A publication*]

Z Schw KG ... Zeitschrift fuer Schweizerische Kirchengeschichte [*A publication*]

ZSCN......... Nanchang [*China*] [*ICAO location identifier*] (ICLI)

ZSD .... Zebra Stripe Display
ZSD .... Zinc Sulfide Detector
ZSDG .... Zeitschrift fuer Sudetendeutsche Geschichte [*A publication*]
Zs D Morg Ges ... Zeitschrift der Deutschen Morgenlaendischen Gesellschaft [*A publication*]
ZSDS .... Zinc Sulfide Detection System
ZSE........... Seattle, WA [*Location identifier*] [*FAA*] (FAAL)
ZSE .... Zimbabwe Stock Exchange
ZSEM .... Zeitschrift fuer Semitistik und Verwandte Gebiete [*Leipzig*] [*A publication*]
Z Semiotik ... Zeitschrift fuer Semiotik [*A publication*]
ZSEV .... Z-Seven Fund, Inc. [*NASDAQ symbol*] (NQ)
Z Sev-Dvin OIMK ... Zapiski Severo-Dvinskogo Obscestva Izucenija Mestnogo Kraja [*A publication*]
ZSF .... Zeitschrift fuer Sozialforschung [*A publication*]
ZSFZ .... Fuzhou [*China*] [*ICAO location identifier*] (ICLI)
ZSG .... Zeitschrift fuer Schweizerische Geschichte [*A publication*]
ZSG .... Zero-Speed Generator
Zs Ges Naturw ... Zeitschrift fuer die Gesamten Naturwissenschaften [*A publication*]
Zs Gletscherk ... Zeitschrift fuer Gletscherkunde [*A publication*]
ZSGZ......... Ganzhou [*China*] [*ICAO location identifier*] (ICLI)
ZSHA .... Shanghai [*China*] [*ICAO location identifier*] (ICLI)
ZSHC .... Hangzhou/Jianqiao [*China*] [*ICAO location identifier*] (ICLI)
ZSHG .... Zeitschrift der Gesellschaft fuer Schleswig-Holsteinische Geschichte [*A publication*]
ZSI............ Z Solar Inertial (MCD)
ZSI............ Zero Size Image
ZSI............ Zytec Systems, Inc. [*Toronto Stock Exchange symbol*] [*Vancouver Stock Exchange symbol*]
ZSIL .... Zytec Systems, Inc. [*NASDAQ symbol*] (NQ)
Z Sinnephysiol ... Zeitschrift fuer Sinnephysiologie [*East Germany*] [*A publication*]
ZSISA........ Zeszyty Naukowe Politechniki Slaskiej. Inzynieria Sanitarna [*A publication*]
ZSJ .... St. John's University Library, Jamaica, NY [*OCLC symbol*] (OCLC)
ZSJ .... Zangri, S. J., Chicago IL [*STAC*]
ZSJA .... Jian [*China*] [*ICAO location identifier*] (ICLI)
ZSK........... Ze Skarbca Kultury [*A publication*]
ZSK........... Zeitschrift fuer Schweizerische Kirchengeschichte [*A publication*]
ZSKG........ Zeitschrift fuer Schweizerische Kirchengeschichte [*A publication*]
ZSKHA..... Zeitschrift fuer Kinderheilkunde. Referate [*A publication*]
Zs Kryst ..... Zeitschrift fuer Krystallographie und Mineralogie [*A publication*]
ZSL........... Zeitschrift fuer Slawistik [*A publication*]
ZSL........... ZEROSLOTLAN [*Avatar Technologies, Inc.*] [*In Alliance ZSL, a PC network*]
ZSL........... Zjednoczone Stronnictwo Ludowe [*United Peasants' Party*] [*Poland*] [*Political party*] (PPW)
Z Slav Ph ... Zeitschrift fuer Slavische Philologie [*A publication*]
Z Slav Phil ... Zeitschrift fuer Slavische Philologie [*A publication*]
Z Slav Philol ... Zeitschrift fuer Slavische Philolog [*A publication*]
Z Slawistik ... Zeitschrift fuer Slawistik [*A publication*]
ZSLPh .... Zeitschrift fuer Slavische Philologie [*A publication*]
Zs Miner (Leonhard) ... Zeitschrift fuer Mineralogie (Leonhard) [*A publication*]
ZSN .... Zoological Station of Naples
ZSN .... Zurich Sunspot Number [*Astrophysics*]
ZSNED7..... Zimbabwe Science News [*A publication*]
ZSNJ .... Nanjing [*China*] [*ICAO location identifier*] (ICLI)
ZSNMAS .. Acta Rerum Naturalium. Musei Nationalis Slovaci Bratislava [*A publication*]
ZSNUA ..... Zeitschrift fuer Neurologie [*A publication*]
ZSOB........ Zinc-Silver-Oxide Battery (RDA)
ZSOF .... Hefei/Luogang [*China*] [*ICAO location identifier*] (ICLI)
Z Soz .... Zeitschrift fuer Sozialpsychologie [*A publication*]
Z Sozialpsy ... Zeitschrift fuer Sozialpsychologie [*A publication*]
Z Sozialreform ... Zeitschrift fuer Sozialreform [*German Federal Republic*] [*A publication*]
Z Soziol ..... Zeitschrift fuer Soziologie [*A publication*]
Z Soziolog .. Zeitschrift fuer Soziologie [*A publication*]
Z Soz Psych ... Zeitschrift fuer Sozialpsychologie [*A publication*]
Z Soz Psychol ... Zeitschrift fuer Sozialpsychologie [*A publication*]
Z Soz Ref ... Zeitschrift fuer Sozialreform [*A publication*]
Z Sozreform ... Zeitschrift fuer Sozialreform [*A publication*]
ZSP........... Zeitschrift fuer Slavische Philologie [*A publication*]
ZSPG........ Zero-Speed Pulse Generator
ZS Ph .... Zeitschrift fuer Slavische Philologie [*A publication*]
Z Spiritusind ... Zeitschrift fuer Spiritusindustrie [*A publication*]
Zs Prak G .. Zeitschrift fuer Praktische Geologie [*A publication*]
ZSQD .... Qingdao [*China*] [*ICAO location identifier*] (ICLI)
ZSR........... Zeitschrift der Savigny-Stiftung fuer Rechtsgeschichte [*A publication*]
ZSR........... Zeitschrift fuer Schweizerisches Recht [*A publication*]
ZSR........... Zeitschrift fuer Sozialreform [*A publication*]
ZS-RDS ..... Zung Self-Rating Depression Scale [*Psychology*]
ZSRG......... Zeitschrift der Savigny-Stiftung fuer Rechtsgeschichte [*A publication*]

ZSRK........ Zeitschrift. Savigny-Stiftung fuer Rechtsgeschichte. Kanonistische Abteilung [*A publication*]
ZSRS .... Zung Self-Rating Scale [*For depression*]
ZSS .... Sassandra [*Ivory Coast*] [*Airport symbol*] (OAG)
ZSS .... Zeitschrift der Savigny-Stiftung fuer Rechtsgeschichte [*A publication*]
ZSS .... Zen Studies Society (EA)
ZSS .... Zinc Sulfide System
ZSSA .... Shanghai City [*China*] [*ICAO location identifier*] (ICLI)
ZSSA .... Zoological Society of Southern Africa [*See also DUSA*] [*Port Elizabeth, South Africa*] (EAIO)
ZSSGerm... Zeitschrift. Savigny-Stiftung fuer Rechtsgeschichte. Germanistische Abteilung [*A publication*]
ZSSKanon ... Zeitschrift. Savigny-Stiftung fuer Rechtsgeschichte. Kanonistische Abteilung [*Weimar*] [*A publication*]
ZSSL......... Shanghai/Longhua [*China*] [*ICAO location identifier*] (ICLI)
ZSS f R ...... Zeitschrift der Savigny-Stiftung fuer Rechtsgeschichte [*A publication*]
ZSSR .... Zeitschrift der Savigny-Stiftung fuer Rechtsgeschichte [*A publication*]
ZSSRGGerm ... Zeitschrift. Savigny-Stiftung fuer Rechtsgeschichte. Germanistische Abteilung [*A publication*]
ZSSRGKan ... Zeitschrift. Savigny-Stiftung fuer Rechtsgeschichte. Kanonistische Abteilung [*A publication*]
ZSSRGRom ... Zeitschrift. Savigny-Stiftung fuer Rechtsgeschichte. Romanistische Abteilung [*A publication*]
zssro .... Zapsana Spolecnost s Rucenim Omezenym [*Incorporated Limited Liability Company*] [*Czechoslovakian*]
ZSSRom .... Zeitschrift. Savigny-Stiftung fuer Rechtsgeschichte. Romanistische Abteilung [*A publication*]
ZSSS......... Shanghai/Hongqiao [*China*] [*ICAO location identifier*] (ICLI)
ZST........... Bratislava [*Czechoslovakia*] [*Seismograph station code, US Geological Survey*] (SEIS)
ZST........... Stewart [*Canada*] [*Airport symbol*] (OAG)
ZST........... Zeitschrift fuer Systematische Theologie [*A publication*]
ZST........... Zentralabteilung Strahlenschutz [*Central Department for Radiation Protection*] [*Federal Republic of Germany*]
ZST........... Zinc Sulfide Tracer
ZST........... Zona Slobodne Trgovine [*European Free Trade Zone*]
ZST........... Zone Standard Time
Z Staatsw ... Zeitschrift fuer die Gesamte Staatswissenschaft [*A publication*]
ZSTh......... Zeitschrift fuer Systematische Theologie [*Guetersloh/Berlin*] [*A publication*]
ZSTN........ Jinan [*China*] [*ICAO location identifier*] (ICLI)
Z Stomatol ... Zeitschrift fuer Stomatologie [*A publication*]
Z Str R ...... Schweizerische Zeitschrift fuer Strafrecht [*A publication*]
Z Strukturn Him ... Zurnal Strukturnoi Himii. Akademija Nauk SSR. Sibirskoe Otdelenie [*A publication*]
Z Str W ...... Zeitschrift fuer die Gesamte Strafrechtswissenschaft [*A publication*]
Z St W........ Zeitschrift fuer die Gesamte Staatswissenschaft [*A publication*]
Z St W........ Zeitschrift fuer die Gesamte Strafrechtswissenschaft [*A publication*]
ZSU .... San Juan, PR [*Location identifier*] [*FAA*] (FAAL)
ZSV........... Schweizerische Zeitschrift fuer Volkswirtschaft und Statistik [*A publication*]
Zs Vulkan .. Zeitschrift fuer Vulkanologie [*A publication*]
ZSW......... Prince Rupert [*Canada*] [*Airport symbol*] [*Obsolete*] (OAG)
Z Sw.......... Zeitschrift fuer die Gesamte Staatswissenschaft [*A publication*]
ZSW......... Zeitschrift fuer Sozialwissenschaft [*A publication*]
ZSWODE ... Zeszyty Naukowe Szkoly Glownej Gospodarstwa Wiejskiego. Akademii Rolniczej w Warszawie. Ogrodnictwo [*A publication*]
ZSWRA ..... Zeszyty Naukowe Szkoly Glownej Gospodarstwa Wiejskiego w Warszawie. Rolnictwo [*A publication*]
ZSysTh ...... Zeitschrift fuer Systematische Theologie [*Guetersloh/Berlin*] [*A publication*]
ZT .... Aerodrome Control Tower [*ICAO designator*] (ICDA)
ZT .... Training Aircraft [*Lighter-than-Air*] [*Navy symbol*] (MUGU)
ZT .... Union of South Africa [*Aircraft nationality and registration mark*] (FAAC)
ZT .... Z-Axis of External Tank [*NASA*] (NASA)
ZT .... Zachary Taylor [*US president, 1784-1850*]
ZT .... Zeitschrift fuer Tierpsychologie [*A publication*]
ZT .... Zipper Tubing
ZT .... Zone Time [*Navigation*]
ZT .... Zuercher Taschenbuch [*A publication*]
ZTA .... Zeta Tau Alpha [*Sorority*]
ZTAT........ Zero Turn-Around Time [*Microcomputer*] [*Hitachi Ltd.*]
ZTB.......... Tete A La Baleine [*Canada*] [*Airport symbol*] (OAG)
ZTB.......... Zuercher Taschenbuch [*A publication*]
Ztbl .... Zentralblatt [*Official Gazette*] [*German*]
ZTC .... Zero-Temperature Coefficient (MSA)
ZTCL........ Zytec Computers Limited [*Dallas, TX*] [*NASDAQ symbol*] (NQ)
Z Tech Biol ... Zeitschrift fuer Technische Biologie [*A publication*]
Z Techn Fiz ... Zurnal Techniceskoj Fiziki [*A publication*]
Z Tech Phys ... Zeitschrift fuer Technische Physik [*A publication*]
Z Tech Ueberwach ... Zeitschrift fuer die Technische Ueberwachung [*A publication*]

Z Tech Univ (Berlin) ... Zeitschrift. Technische Universitaet (Berlin) [*A publication*]
Z Tech Univ (Hannover) ... Zeitschrift. Technische Universitaet (Hannover) [*German Federal Republic*] [*A publication*]
Ztg .... Zeitung [*Newspaper, Review*] [*German*] (ILCA)
ZTG .... Zolltarifgesetz [*A publication*]
ZTGAK ...... Zeitschrift fuer Thueringische Geschichte und Altertumskunde [*A publication*]
Ztg Gesunde ... Zeitung fuer Gesunde [*A publication*]
ZTH .... Zakinthos [*Greece*] [*Airport symbol*] (OAG)
Z Theol Kir ... Zeitschrift fuer Theologie und Kirche [*A publication*]
Z Th K ...... Zeitschrift fuer Theologie und Kirche [*A publication*]
Z Th Kirche ... Zeitschrift fuer Theologie und Kirche [*A publication*]
Z Tierernaehr Futtermittelkd ... Zeitschrift fuer Tierernaehrung und Futtermittelkunde [*A publication*]
Z Tierphysiol ... Zeitschrift fuer Tierphysiologie, Tierernaehrung, und Futtermittelkunde [*A publication*]
Z Tierphysiol Tierernaehr Futtermittelk ... Zeitschrift fuer Tierphysiologie, Tierernaehrung, und Futtermittelkunde [*A publication*]
Z Tierphysiol Tiernaehr Futtermittelkd ... Zeitschrift fuer Tierphysiologie, Tierernaehrung, und Futtermittelkunde [*A publication*]
Z Tierpsychol ... Zeitschrift fuer Tierpsychologie [*A publication*]
Z Tierpsychol Beih ... Zeitschrift fuer Tierpsychologie. Beiheft [*A publication*]
Z Tierz Zuechtungsbiol ... Zeitschrift fuer Tierzuechtung und Zuechtungsbiologie [*A publication*]
ZTJWG ..... Zeus Target Joint Working Group [*Missiles*] (AAG)
ZTK .... Zeitschrift fuer Theologie und Kirche [*A publication*]
ZTL .... Atlanta, GA [*Location identifier*] [*FAA*] (FAAL)
ZTL .... Touro Law Library, New York, NY [*OCLC symbol*] (OCLC)
ZTM .... Mid-York Library System, Utica, NY [*OCLC symbol*] (OCLC)
ZTN .... Zinc Tannate of Naloxone [*Opiate antagonist*]
ZTO .... Zero Time Outage [*Nuclear energy*] (NRCH)
ZTO .... Zone Transportation Officer [*Military*]
ZTOS .... Zydowskie Towarzystwo Ochrony Sierot [*A publication*]
ZTOS .... Zydowskie Towarzystwo Opieki Spolecznej [*A publication*]
ZTP .... Zero-Temperature Plasma
ZTP .... Zydowskie Towarzystwo Przeciwgruzliczego [*A publication*]
ZTPHA ...... Zeitschrift fuer Technische Physik [*A publication*]
ZTPSA ...... Zeitschrift fuer Psychologie [*A publication*]
ZTR .... Zweig Total Return Fund, Inc. [*NYSE symbol*] (CTT)
Ztrbl .... Zentralblatt [*Official Gazette*] [*German*]
Z Tropenmed Parasitol ... Zeitschrift fuer Tropenmedizin und Parasitologie [*A publication*]
Z Trop Med ... Zeitschrift fuer Tropenmedizin und Parasitologie [*A publication*]
ZTRX .... Zytrex Corp. [*NASDAQ symbol*] (NQ)
Ztsch f Angew Psychol ... Zeitschrift fuer Angewandte Psychologie und Psychologische Forschung [*A publication*]
Ztsch f Angew Psychol Sammelforsch ... Zeitschrift fuer Angewandte Psychologie und Psychologische Sammelforschung [*A publication*]
Ztsch Gesch Erzieh u Unterr ... Zeitschrift fuer Geschichte der Erziehung und des Unterrichts [*A publication*]
Ztsch Mikr Fleischschau ... Zeitschrift fuer Mikroskopische Fleischschau und Populaere Mikroskopie [*A publication*]
Ztsch Militaeraerzte (Tokyo) ... Zeitschrift fuer Militaeraerzte (Tokyo) [*A publication*]
ZTSCHR ... Zeitschrift [*Review*] [*German*]
Ztschr Aerztli Fortbild ... Zeitschrift fuer Aerztliche Fortbildung [*A publication*]
Ztschr Augenh ... Zeitschrift fuer Augenheilkunde [*A publication*]
Ztschr Fleisch u Milchhyg ... Zeitschrift fuer Fleisch- und Milchhygiene [*A publication*]
Ztschr Genossensch Tierversich ... Zeitschrift fuer Genossenschaftlichen Tierversicherung [*A publication*]
Ztschr Gewerbe Hyg ... Zeitschrift fuer Gewerbe Hygiene [*A publication*]
Ztschr Hyg ... Zeitschrift fuer Hygiene [*A publication*]
Ztschr Hyg u Infektionskr ... Zeitschrift fuer Hygiene und Infektionskrankheiten [*A publication*]
Ztschr Immunitaetsforsch u Exper Therap ... Zeitschrift fuer Immunitaetsforschung und Experimentelle Therapie [*A publication*]
Ztschr Infektionskr Haustiere ... Zeitschrift fuer Infektionskrankheiten, Parasitaere Krankheiten, und Hygiene der Haustiere [*A publication*]
Ztschr Klin Med (Berlin) ... Zeitschrift fuer Klinische Medizin (Berlin) [*A publication*]
Ztschr Krebsforsch ... Zeitschrift fuer Krebsforschung [*A publication*]
Ztschr Morphol u Oekol Tiere ... Zeitschrift fuer Morphologie und Oekologie der Tiere [*A publication*]
Ztschr Ophth ... Zeitschrift fuer die Ophthalmologie [*A publication*]
Ztschr Parasitenk (Berlin) ... Zeitschrift fuer Parasitenkunde (Berlin) [*A publication*]
Ztschr Parasitenk (Jena) ... Zeitschrift fuer Parasitenkunde (Jena) [*A publication*]
Ztschr Physiol Chem ... Zeitschrift fuer Physiologische Chemie [*A publication*]
Ztschr Tokio Med Gesellsch ... Zeitschrift. Tokio Medizinische Gesellschaft [*A publication*]
Ztschr Vergleich Physiol ... Zeitschrift fuer Vergleichende Physiologie [*A publication*]

Ztschr Veterinaerk ... Zeitschrift fuer Veterinaerkunde [*A publication*]
Ztschr Wissensch Mikr ... Zeitschrift fuer Wissenschaftliche Mikroskopie [*A publication*]
Ztschr Wissensch Zool ... Zeitschrift fuer Wissenschaftliche Zoologie [*A publication*]
Z Tuberk .... Zeitschrift fuer Tuberkulose [*A publication*]
Z Tuberk Erkr Thoraxorgane ... Zeitschrift fuer Tuberkulose und Erkrankungen der Thoraxorgane [*A publication*]
Z Tuberkulose Erkr Thoraxogane ... Zeitschrift fuer Tuberkulose und Erkrankungen der Thoraxorgane [*A publication*]
ZTUWA .... Zeitschrift Technische Ueberwachung [*A publication*]
ZT Zue .... Zeitschrift fuer Tierzuechtung und Zuechtungsbiologie [*A publication*]
ZU .... Union of South Africa [*Aircraft nationality and registration mark*] (FAAC)
ZU .... Upper Area Control Center [*ICAO designator*] (ICDA)
ZU .... Utility Aircraft [*Lighter-than-Air*] [*Navy symbol*] (MUGU)
ZU .... Zeitlich Untauglich [*Temporarily Unfit*] [*German military - World War II*]
ZUA .... Agana, GU [*Location identifier*] [*FAA*] (FAAL)
ZUA .... Central New York Union List of Serials, Syracuse, NY [*OCLC symbol*] (OCLC)
ZUB .... Allied Chemical Corp., Library, Solvay, NY [*OCLC symbol*] (OCLC)
ZuB .... Zuercher Bibelkommentare [*A publication*]
ZUBEAQ ... Revue de Medecine des Accidents et des Maladies Professionnelles [*A publication*]
Zubolek Pregl ... Zubolekarski Pregled [*A publication*]
ZUC .... American Foundation for Management Research, Library, Hamilton, NY [*OCLC symbol*] (OCLC)
ZU Ch .... Zeitschrift fuer Urologische Chirurgie [*A publication*]
ZUCK .... Chongqing [*China*] [*ICAO location identifier*] (ICLI)
Zucker Beih ... Zucker Beihefte [*A publication*]
Zucker Frucht Gemueseverwert ... Zucker- Frucht- und Gemueseverwertung [*A publication*]
Zucker Sonderbeil ... Zucker Sonderbeilage [*A publication*]
Zucker Suesswaren Wirtsch ... Zucker- und Suesswaren Wirtschaft [*A publication*]
Zuck u SuesswarWirt ... Zucker- und Suesswaren Wirtschaft [*A publication*]
ZUD .... Bristol Laboratories, Library, Syracuse, NY [*OCLC symbol*] (OCLC)
ZUE .... Carrier Corp., Library, Syracuse, NY [*OCLC symbol*] (OCLC)
ZUE .... Zuni Energy [*Vancouver Stock Exchange symbol*]
Zuercher Beitraege ... Zuercher Beitraege zur Geschichtswissenschaft [*A publication*]
Zuercher Beitraege ... Zuercher Beitraege zur Rechtswissenschaft [*A publication*]
Zuer Univ Geol Inst-Eidgenoss Tech Hochsch Geol Inst Mitt ... Zuerich Universitaet. Geologisches Institut - Eidgenoessische Technische Hochschule. Geologisches Institut. Mitteilungen [*A publication*]
ZUG .... Community-General Hospital, Staff Library, Syracuse, NY [*OCLC symbol*] (OCLC)
ZUG .... Zugdidi [*USSR*] [*Seismograph station code, US Geological Survey*] [*Closed*] (SEIS)
ZugerNjb ... Zuger Neujahrsblatt [*A publication*]
ZUGY .... Guiyang [*China*] [*ICAO location identifier*] (ICLI)
ZUH .... Education Opportunity Center of the State University of New York, Syracuse, NY [*OCLC symbol*] (OCLC)
ZUI .... General Electric Co., Electronics Park Library, Syracuse, NY [*OCLC symbol*] (OCLC)
ZUJ .... General Electric Co., Information Resources Library, Utica, NY [*OCLC symbol*] (OCLC)
ZUJCA ...... Zeszyty Naukowe Uniwersytetu Jagiellonskiego. Prace Chemiczne [*A publication*]
ZUK .... United States Veterans Administration, Hospital Library, Syracuse, NY [*OCLC symbol*] (OCLC)
ZUL .... Agway, Inc., Library, Syracuse, NY [*OCLC symbol*] (OCLC)
zul .... Zulu [*MARC language code*] [*Library of Congress*] (LCCP)
ZUL .... Zurich-Lageren [*Switzerland*] [*Seismograph station code, US Geological Survey*] (SEIS)
ZULS .... Lhasa [*China*] [*ICAO location identifier*] (ICLI)
ZUM .... Churchill Falls [*Canada*] [*Airport symbol*] (OAG)
ZUM .... Supreme Court, Fifth Judicial District, Law Library, Utica, NY [*OCLC symbol*] (OCLC)
ZUM .... Zeitschrift fuer Urheber und Medienrecht [*Journal for Copyright and Communication*] [*NOMOS Datapool*] [*Database producer*]
ZUM .... Zimbabwe Unity Movement [*Political party*] (ECON)
Z Umweltpolit ... Zeitschrift fuer Umweltpolitik [*A publication*]
ZUN .... Saint Joseph's Hospital, Health Center Library, Syracuse, NY [*OCLC symbol*] (OCLC)
zun .... Zuni [*MARC language code*] [*Library of Congress*] (LCCP)
ZUN .... Zuni Pueblo, NM [*Location identifier*] [*FAA*] (FAAL)
ZUNBA ...... Zhurnal Ushnykh Nosovykh i Gorlovykh Boleznei [*A publication*]
Z Unfallmed Berufskr ... Zeitschrift fuer Unfallmedizin und Berufskrankheiten [*A publication*]
Z Unter Lebensm ... Zeitschrift fuer Untersuchung der Lebensmittel [*A publication*]

Z Unters Lebensmittel ... Zeitschrift fuer Untersuchung der Lebensmittel [*A publication*]
Z Unters Nahr Genussm Gebrauchsgegenstaende ... Zeitschrift fuer Untersuchung der Nahrungs- und Genussmittel Sowie der Gebrauchsgegenstaende [*A publication*]
Z Unters Nahr-u Genussmittel ... Zeitschrift fuer Untersuchung der Nahrungs- und Genussmittel [*A publication*]
ZUO.......... Utica Mutual Insurance Co., Library, New Hartford, NY [*OCLC symbol*] (OCLC)
ZUP .... Utica/Marcy Psychiatric Center, Utica Campus Library, Utica, NY [*OCLC symbol*] (OCLC)
ZuP .... Zellstoff und Papier [*A publication*]
ZUP .... Zone a Urbaniser en Priorite [*Priority Urbanization Zone*] [*French*]
ZUPO .... Zimbabwe United People's Organization [*Political party*] (PPW)
ZUQ .... Saint Luke's Memorial Hospital Center, Medical Library, Utica, NY [*OCLC symbol*] (OCLC)
ZUR .... Hancock Airbase Library, Hancock Field, NY [*OCLC symbol*] (OCLC)
ZUR .... Zurfund International Ltd. [*Vancouver Stock Exchange symbol*]
ZUR .... Zurich [*Switzerland*] [*Seismograph station code, US Geological Survey*] (SEIS)
Zur Didak Phys Chem ... Zur Didaktik der Physik und Chemie [*A publication*]
ZURF........ Zeus Up-Range Facility [*Missiles*] (AAG)
Z Urol .... Zeitschrift fuer Urologie [*German Democratic Republic*] [*A publication*]
Z Urol Chir ... Zeitschrift fuer Urologische Chirurgie [*A publication*]
Z Urol Nephrol ... Zeitschrift fuer Urologie und Nephrologie [*A publication*]
ZUS .... Utica/Marcy Psychiatric Center, Marcy Campus Library, Utica, NY [*OCLC symbol*] (OCLC)
ZUS .... Zusammen [*Together*] [*Music*]
Zuschl .... Zuschlag [*Extra Charge*] [*German*]
ZUT .... Maria Regina College, Library, Syracuse, NY [*OCLC symbol*] (OCLC)
ZUTRON .. Airship Utility Squadron [*Navy symbol*]
ZUU.......... Masonic Medical Research Laboratory, Library, Utica, NY [*OCLC symbol*] (OCLC)
ZUUU........ Chengdu [*China*] [*ICAO location identifier*] (ICLI)
ZUW .... Munson-Williams-Proctor Institute, Library, Utica, NY [*OCLC symbol*] (OCLC)
ZUX .... Mohawk Valley Learning Resource Center, Utica Library, Utica, NY [*OCLC symbol*] (OCLC)
ZUY .... Special Metals Corp., Library, New Hartford, NY [*OCLC symbol*] (OCLC)
ZUZ.......... Crouse-Irving Hospital, School of Nursing, Library, Syracuse, NY [*OCLC symbol*] (OCLC)
ZUZZ .... Zug und Zerschneidezuender [*Pull-and-Cut Igniter*] [*German military - World War II*]
Z & V .... Zeiten und Voelker [*A publication*]
ZV .... Zeitschrift fuer Versicherung [*A publication*]
ZV .... Zeitschrift fuer Volkskunde [*A publication*]
ZV .... Zu Verfuegung [*At Disposal*] [*Business term*] [*German*]
Zv .... Zvezda [*A publication*]
ZVA .... Jervis Public Library, Rome, NY [*OCLC symbol*] (OCLC)
ZVA .... Miandrivazo [*Madagascar*] [*Airport symbol*] (OAG)
Zvaracsky Sb ... Zvaracsky Sbornik [*A publication*]
ZVB .... Syracuse Research Corp., Library, Syracuse, NY [*OCLC symbol*] (OCLC)
ZVC .... Utica Public Library, Utica, NY [*OCLC symbol*] (OCLC)
ZVD .... Supreme Court of New York, Library, Syracuse, NY [*OCLC symbol*] (OCLC)
ZVEI .... Zentralverband der Elektrotechnischen Industrie [*Electrical Equipment Industry Association*] [*Federal Republic of Germany*] (EY)
Z Verbraucherpol ... Zeitschrift fuer Verbraucherpolitik [*A publication*]
Z Verbungsl ... Zeitschrift fuer Vererbungslehre [*A publication*]
Z Ver Dtsch Ing ... Zeitschrift. Verein Deutscher Ingenieure [*A publication*]
Z Ver Dtsch Zucker Ind ... Zeitschrift. Verein der Deutschen Zucker-Industrie [*A publication*]
Z Ver Dtsch Zucker Ind Allg Teil ... Zeitschrift. Verein der Deutschen Zucker-Industrie. Allgemeiner Teil [*A publication*]
Z Ver Dtsch Zucker Ind Tech Teil ... Zeitschrift. Verein der Deutschen Zucker-Industrie. Technischer Teil [*A publication*]
Z Vererbungsl ... Zeitschrift fuer Vererbungslehre [*A publication*]
Z Vergl Physiol ... Zeitschrift fuer Vergleichende Physiologie [*A publication*]
Z Ver Hess Gesch Landesk ... Zeitschrift. Verein fuer Hessische Geschichte und Landeskunde [*A publication*]
Z Ver Hessische Gesch ... Zeitschrift. Verein fuer Hessische Geschichte und Landeskunde [*A publication*]
Z Verkehrssicherheit ... Zeitschrift fuer Verkehrssicherheit [*A publication*]
Z Verkehrswiss ... Zeitschrift fuer Verkehrswissenschaft [*A publication*]
Z Vermessungswes ... Zeitschrift fuer Vermessungswesen [*A publication*]
Zverolek Obz ... Zverolekarsky Obzor [*A publication*]
Z Vers Kund ... Zeitschrift fuer Versuchstierkunde [*A publication*]
Z Versuchstierkd ... Zeitschrift fuer Versuchstierkunde [*A publication*]
ZVF........... Zero-Velocity Fading [*Aviation*] (AIA)
ZVfD.......... Zionistische Vereinigung fuer Deutschaland [*Zionist Federation of Germany*]

ZVGAK ..... Zeitschrift fuer Vaterlaendische Geschichte und Altertumskunde [*A publication*]
Z Vgl Physiol ... Zeitschrift fuer Vergleichende Physiologie [*A publication*]
ZVGMS..... Zeitschrift. Deutscher Verein fuer die Geschichte Maehrens und Schlesiens [*A publication*]
ZVHFA ..... Zeitschrift fuer Vitamin-, Hormon-, und Fermentforschung [*A publication*]
ZVHG....... Zeitschrift. Verein fuer Hamburgische Geschichte [*A publication*]
ZVHGLK .. Zeitschrift. Verein fuer Hessische Geschichte und Landeskunde [*A publication*]
Z VitamForsch ... Zeitschrift fuer Vitaminforschung [*A publication*]
Z Vitam-Horm- u Fermentforsch ... Zeitschrift fuer Vitamin-, Hormon-, und Fermentforschung [*A publication*]
Z Vitam-Horm-Fermentforsch ... Zeitschrift fuer Vitamin-, Hormon-, und Fermentforschung [*A publication*]
Z Vitaminforsch ... Zeitschrift fuer Vitaminforschung [*A publication*]
ZVK .... Zeitschrift fuer Volkskunde [*A publication*]
ZVKOA ..... Zhurnal Vsesoyuznogo Khimicheskogo Obshchestva Imeni D. I. Mendeleeva [*A publication*]
ZVKPS ...... Zeitschrift. Verein fuer Kirchengeschichte in der Provinz Sachsen und Anhalt [*A publication*]
ZVL........... Zeitschrift fuer Vergleichende Literaturgeschichte [*A publication*]
ZVM .... Mohawk Valley Community College, Utica, NY [*OCLC symbol*] (OCLC)
ZVNDA ..... Zhurnal Vysshei Nervnoi Deyatel'nosti Imeni I. P. Pavlova [*A publication*]
ZVO .... Zapiski Vostochnovo Otdeleniia [*A publication*]
Z Volksernaehr ... Zeitschrift fuer Volksernaehrung [*A publication*]
Z Volkskund ... Zeitschrift fuer Volkskunde [*A publication*]
Z Volkskunde ... Zeitschrift fuer Volkskunde [*A publication*]
ZVORAO .. Zapiski Vostochnovo Otdeleniia Imperatorskovo Ruskavo Arkheologicheskavo Obshchestva [*A publication*]
ZVR .... Zener Voltage Regulator
ZVRD .... Zener Voltage Regulator Diode
ZVRW .... Zeitschrift fuer Vergleichende Rechtswissenschaft [*A publication*]
ZVS........... Zeitschrift fuer Vergleichende Sprachforschung [*A publication*]
ZVS........... Zero Voltage Switch
ZVT .... Zeitschrift fuer Verkehrswissenschaft [*A publication*]
ZVTGA..... Zeitschrift. Verein fuer Thueringische Geschichte und Altertumskunde [*A publication*]
ZVTGAK... Zeitschrift. Verein fuer Thueringische Geschichte und Altertumskunde [*A publication*]
ZVV .... Zeitschrift. Verein fuer Volkskunde [*A publication*]
ZvV .... Zvezda Vostoka [*A publication*]
Z Vycisl Mat i Mat Fiz ... Zurnal Vycislitel'noi Matematiki i Matematiceskoi Fiziki [*A publication*]
ZVZ .... Zavitz Technology, Inc. [*Toronto Stock Exchange symbol*]
ZW .... Air Wisconsin [*Airline code*]
ZW .... Zeitwende Monatsschrift [*A publication*]
ZW .... Zero Wait [*Industrial engineering*]
ZW .... Zero Wear
ZW .... Zimbabwe [*ANSI two-letter standard code*] (CNC)
Zw .... Zwischensatz [*Interpolation*] [*Music*]
ZWA .... Andapa [*Madagascar*] [*Airport symbol*] (OAG)
Z Wahrscheinlichkeitstheorie und Verw Gebiete ... Zeitschrift fuer Wahrscheinlichkeitstheorie und Verwandte Gebiete [*A publication*]
Z Wahrsch V ... Zeitschrift fuer Wahrscheinlichkeitstheorie und Verwandte Gebiete [*A publication*]
Z Wahrsch Verw Gebiete ... Zeitschrift fuer Wahrscheinlichkeitstheorie und Verwandte Gebiete [*A publication*]
ZWAK .... Aksu [*China*] [*ICAO location identifier*] (ICLI)
Z Wasser Abwasser Forsch ... Zeitschrift fuer Wasser- und Abwasserforschung [*A publication*]
Z Wasser u Abwasserforsch ... Zeitschrift fuer Wasser- und Abwasserforschung [*A publication*]
Z Wasserrecht ... Zeitschrift fuer Wasserrecht [*A publication*]
Z Wasser Versorg Abwasserkunde ... Zeitschrift fuer Wasser-Versorgung und Abwasserkunde [*A publication*]
ZWBAA..... Zeitschrift fuer Wissenschaftliche Biologie. Abteilung A [*A publication*]
ZWC .... Zero Word Count
ZWC .... Zone Wind Computer
ZWE .... Zimbabwe [*ANSI three-letter standard code*] (CNC)
Z Weltforstwirtsch ... Zeitschrift fuer Weltforstwirtschaft [*A publication*]
Z Werkstofftech ... Zeitschrift fuer Werkstofftechnik [*A publication*]
Z Werkstofftech J Mater Technol ... Zeitschrift fuer Werkstofftechnik/Journal of Materials Technology [*A publication*]
ZWF Z Wirtsch Fertigung ... ZWF. Zeitschrift fuer Wirtschaftliche Fertigung [*A publication*]
ZWG .... Sudhoffs Archiv. Zeitschrift fuer Wissenschaftsgeschichte [*A publication*]
ZWHM...... Hami [*China*] [*ICAO location identifier*] (ICLI)
ZWIBA...... Zeitschrift fuer Wissenschaftliche Insektenbiologie [*A publication*]
Z Wien Ent Ges ... Zeitschrift. Wiener Entomologische Gesellschaft [*A publication*]

Z Wien Entomol Ges ... Zeitschrift. Wiener Entomologische Gesellschaft [*A publication*]

Z Wien Entomol Ver ... Zeitschrift. Wiener Entomologe-Verein [*A publication*]

Zwierzeta Lab ... Zwierzeta Laboratoryjne [*A publication*]

Z Wirtschaftsgeog ... Zeitschrift fuer Wirtschaftsgeographie [*A publication*]

Z Wirtschaftsgeographie ... Zeitschrift fuer Wirtschaftsgeographie [*West Germany*] [*A publication*]

Z Wirtschaftsgruppe Zuckerind ... Zeitschrift. Wirtschaftsgruppe Zuckerindustrie [*A publication*]

Z Wirtschaftsgruppe Zuckerind Allg Teil ... Zeitschrift. Wirtschaftsgruppe Zuckerindustrie. Allgemeiner Teil [*A publication*]

Z Wirtschaftsgruppe Zuckerind Tech Teil ... Zeitschrift. Wirtschaftsgruppe Zuckerindustrie. Technischer Teil [*A publication*]

Z Wirtschaftspol ... Zeitschrift fuer Wirtschaftspolitik [*A publication*]

Z Wirtsch Fertigung ... Zeitschrift fuer Wirtschaftliche Fertigung [*A publication*]

Z Wirtsch -u Soz -Wiss ... Zeitschrift fuer Wirtschafts- und Sozialwissenschaften [*A publication*]

Z Wirt- und Sozialwiss ... Zeitschrift fuer Wirtschafts- und Sozialwissenschaften [*A publication*]

Z Wiss Biol Abt A ... Zeitschrift fuer Wissenschaftliche Biologie. Abteilung A [*West Germany*] [*A publication*]

Z Wiss InsektBiol ... Zeitschrift fuer Wissenschaftliche Insektenbiologie [*A publication*]

Z Wiss Insektenbiol ... Zeitschrift fuer Wissenschaftliche Insektenbiologie [*West Germany*] [*A publication*]

Z Wiss Mikrosk ... Zeitschrift fuer Wissenschaftliche Mikroskopie und fuer Mikroskopische Technik [*A publication*]

Z Wiss Mikrosk Mikrosk Tech ... Zeitschrift fuer Wissenschaftliche Mikroskopie und fuer Mikroskopische Technik [*A publication*]

Z Wiss Phot ... Zeitschrift fuer Wissenschaftliche Photographie, Photophysik, und Photochemie [*A publication*]

Z Wiss Photogr Photophys Photchem ... Zeitschrift fuer Wissenschaftliche Photographie, Photophysik, und Photochemie [*A publication*]

Z Wiss Photogr Photophys Photochem ... Zeitschrift fuer Wissenschaftliche Photographie, Photophysik, und Photochemie [*East Germany*] [*A publication*]

Z Wiss Zool ... Zeitschrift fuer Wissenschaftliche Zoologie [*A publication*]

Z Wiss Zool Abt A ... Zeitschrift fuer Wissenschaftliche Zoologie. Abteilung A [*A publication*]

ZWKC .... Kuqa [*China*] [*ICAO location identifier*] (ICLI)

ZWL .... Wollaston Lake [*Canada*] [*Airport symbol*] (OAG)

ZWL .... Zeitschrift fuer Wuerttembergische Landesgeschichte [*A publication*]

ZWL .... Zero Wavelength

ZWLG .... Zeitschrift fuer Wuerttembergische Landesgeschichte [*A publication*]

ZWMIA ..... Zeitschrift fuer Wissenschaftliche Mikroskopie und fuer Mikroskopische Technik [*A publication*]

ZWMZDP ... Chinese Journal of Microbiology and Immunology [*Beijing*] [*A publication*]

ZWO .... Zuiver Wentenschappelijk Orderzock [*Netherlands*]

ZWOK .... Zirconium-Water Oxidation Kinetics (NRCH)

ZWP .... Zeitschrift fuer Wissenschaftliche Photographie, Photophysik, und Photochemie [*A publication*]

ZWP .... Zone Wind Plotter

ZWPGV ..... Zeitschrift. Westpreussischer Geschichtsverein [*A publication*]

ZWR .... ZWR. Zahnaerztliche Welt, Zahnaerztliche Rundschau, Zahnaerztliche Reform [*A publication*]

ZWS .... Zentralwohlfahrtsstelle der Juden in Deutschland [*A publication*] (BJA)

ZWS .... Zonal Wind Stress [*Meteorology*]

ZWSH .... Kashi [*China*] [*ICAO location identifier*] (ICLI)

ZWSt .... Zentralwohlfahrtsstelle der Juden in Deutschland [*A publication*] (BJA)

ZWT .... Zeitschrift fuer Wissenschaftliche Theologie [*A publication*]

ZWTh .... Zeitschrift fuer Wissenschaftliche Theologie [*A publication*]

ZWTN .... Hotan [*China*] [*ICAO location identifier*] (ICLI)

ZWU .... Union College, Schenectady, NY [*OCLC symbol*] (OCLC)

ZWUQ .... Urumqi [*China*] [*ICAO location identifier*] (ICLI)

ZWV .... Zero Wave Velocity

ZWW .... Zonal Westerly Wind [*Climatology*]

ZWWW ...... Urumqi/Diwopu [*China*] [*ICAO location identifier*] (ICLI)

ZWYN .... Yining [*China*] [*ICAO location identifier*] (ICLI)

ZXC .... City College of New York, New York, NY [*OCLC symbol*] (OCLC)

ZXCFAR ... Zero Crossing Constant False Alarm Rate (MSA)

ZXMP .... Zero Transmission Power

ZXX .... Exxon Corp., Information Center, Technical Service Coordinator, New York, NY [*OCLC symbol*] (OCLC)

ZY .... Aerodrome Security Services [*ICAO designator*] (FAAC)

ZY .... Zayre Corp. [*NYSE symbol*] [*Later, TJX*] (SPSG)

Zy .... Zygon [*A publication*]

ZYB .... Zionist Year Book [*A publication*] (BJA)

ZYCC .... Changchun [*China*] [*ICAO location identifier*] (ICLI)

Zycie Weteryn ... Zycie Weterynaryjne [*A publication*]

ZYDXDM ... Journal. Zhejiang Medical University [*A publication*]

ZYG .... Zygote Resources [*Vancouver Stock Exchange symbol*]

ZYHB .... Harbin/Yanjiagang [*China*] [*ICAO location identifier*] (ICLI)

ZYL .... Sylhet [*Bangladesh*] [*Airport symbol*] (OAG)

ZYLA .... Hailar [*China*] [*ICAO location identifier*] (ICLI)

Zymol Chem Colloidi ... Zymologica e Chemica dei Colloidi [*A publication*]

ZYMV .... Zucchini Yellow Mosaic Virus

ZYP .... Zefkrome Yarn Program [*Dow Chemical Co.*]

ZYQQ .... Qiqihar [*China*] [*ICAO location identifier*] (ICLI)

ZYSH .... Shenyang [*China*] [*ICAO location identifier*] (ICLI)

ZYTL .... Dalian [*China*] [*ICAO location identifier*] (ICLI)

ZYU .... New York University, New York, NY [*OCLC symbol*] (OCLC)

ZYWE .... Zeszyty Wroclawskie [*A publication*]

Zywienie Czlowieka Metab ... Zywienie Czlowieka i Metabolizm [*A publication*]

ZYYY .... Shenyang/Dongta [*China*] [*ICAO location identifier*] (ICLI)

ZZ .... Aircraft in Flight [*ICAO designator*] (ICDA)

ZZ .... Datum Position [*Arbitrary*] [*Navy*] [*British*]

ZZ .... Lighter-than-Air [*Aircraft*] [*Navy symbol*] (MUGU)

Z-Z .... Roll Axis [*Aerospace*] (AAG)

Z d Z .... Zeichen der Zeit [*A publication*]

ZZ .... Zeitschrift fuer die Wissenschaft des Judentums [*Leopold Zunz*] [*A publication*] (BJA)

ZZ .... Zig-Zag

Zz .... Zinszahl [*Tax Figure*] [*German*]

ZZ .... Zinziber [*Ginger*] [*Pharmacology*] (ROG)

ZZ .... Zu [*or Zur*] Zeit [*At This Time*] [*German*]

ZZ .... Zugzuender [*Pull Igniter*] [*German military - World War II*]

ZZA .... Zamak Zinc Alloy

ZZACA ...... Zeitschrift fuer Zellforschung und Mikroskopische Anatomie [*A publication*]

ZZC .... Zero-Zero Condition

ZZD .... Zig-Zag Diagram

Z Zellforsch Mikrosk Anat ... Zeitschrift fuer Zellforschung und Mikroskopische Anatomie [*A publication*]

Z Zellforsch Mikrosk Anat Abt Histochem ... Zeitschrift fuer Zellforschung und Mikroskopische Anatomie. Abteilung Histochemie [*A publication*]

Z Zool Syst Evolutionsforsch ... Zeitschrift fuer Zoologische Systematik und Evolutionsforschung [*A publication*]

ZZR .... Zig-Zag Rectifier

ZZR .... Zigzag Riveting (MSA)

ZzS .... Zbornik za Slavistiku [*A publication*]

ZZT .... Zu Zu [*Tennessee*] [*Seismograph station code, US Geological Survey*] [*Closed*] (SEIS)

ZZTFC ...... ZZ Top Fan Club (EA)

Z Zuckerind ... Zeitschrift fuer die Zuckerindustrie [*A publication*]

Z Zuckerind Boehm ... Zeitschrift fuer die Zuckerindustrie in Boehmen [*A publication*]

Z Zuckerind Boehm Machren ... Zeitschrift fuer die Zuckerindustrie in Boehmen-Machren [*A publication*]

Z Zuckerind Cech Repub ... Zeitschrift fuer die Zuckerindustrie der Cechoslovakoschen Republik [*A publication*]

Z Zuckind .. Zeitschrift fuer die Zuckerindustrie [*A publication*]

Z Zuecht A ... Zeitschrift fuer Zuechtung. A [*A publication*]

Z Zuecht B ... Zeitschrift fuer Zuechtung. B [*A publication*]

ZZV .... Zanesville, OH [*Location identifier*] [*FAA*] (FAAL)

ZZV .... Zero-Zero Visibility

ZZW .... Zero-Zero Weather

ZZZZ .... Unknown Elements in Formatted Flight Plan [*Aviation code*] (FAAC)